The New York Times

CROSSWORD PUZZLE
DICTIONARY

The New York Times

CROSSWORD PUZZLE DICTIONARY

• Second Edition •

By

Tom Pulliam and Clare Grundman

A HUDSON GROUP BOOK

WARNER BOOKS

A Warner Communications Company

Warner Books Edition

Copyright © 1974, 1977, 1984 by Thomas Pulliam and Clare Grundman

This Warner Books edition is published by arrangement with
Times Books, a division of Random House, Inc.,
201 East 50th Street, New York, NY 10022

Produced in association with Morningside Editorial Associates, Inc.
Designed by Martin Connell

Warner Books, Inc., 666 Fifth Avenue, New York, NY 10103
A Warner Communications Company

Printed in the United States of America

First Warner Books Printing: April 1986

10 9 8 7 6 5 4 3 2

Library of Congress Cataloging-in-Publication Data

Pulliam, Tom.
    The New York times crossword puzzle dictionary.

    "A Hudson Group book."
    Reprint. Originally published: 2nd ed. New York,
N.Y. : Times Books.
    1. Crossword puzzles—Glossaries, vocabularies, etc.
I. Grundman, Clare, 1913-   . II. New York times.
III. Title.
[GV1507.C7P83 1986]   793.73′2′0321   86-1693
ISBN 0-446-38250-7 (U.S.A.) (pbk.)
        0-446-38251-5 (Canada) (pbk.)

PREFACE to the First Edition

THE NEW YORK TIMES CROSSWORD PUZZLE DICTIONARY exceeds in completeness and scope all other puzzle dictionaries. No useful word has been omitted. Not only have puzzles themselves been combed for synonyms that are used over and over, but also a word-for-word reading of major unabridged dictionaries, both current and old, has produced a thoroughly complete and extensive checklist.

Each of us has been solving and compiling puzzles for many years, and our chief purpose has been to design a practical and easy-to-use dictionary, in the belief that your needs and requirements for such a volume closely reflect our own. For example, the synonyms are arranged by the number of letters, and then alphabetized so you can quickly find the very word that fills the spaces in the puzzle. Another feature, one that seems obvious for a crossword puzzle dictionary but is not found in most of them, is that all words are printed in easy-to-read capital letters. The type has been chosen with great care for its legibility, and the three-column format not only provides a short line of type to scan but also enables us to get a very large number of words on each page.

Synonyms of great length have been omitted to give room for the shorter, more useful words. The puzzler can always "fill in" the very long words provided he has a good supply of short common synonyms. We have placed, therefore, an arbitrary ceiling of eight-letter word-lenghts, knowing this will satisfy almost all needs. Here and there, however, you will find occasional exceptions to this rule. These are synonyms of such frequent, interesting, and normal usage that their omission might handicap the puzzler.

The "shaded boxes" scattered through the book are a notable and unique feature of THE NEW YORK TIMES CROSSWORD PUZZLE DICTIONARY. They collect under one heading a variety of categories and synonyms that you would have a hard time finding in other dictionaries. For example, when you are confronted by the clue "Brazilian river" merely turn to the shaded area marked BRAZIL, where you will find several excellent possibilities. Similarly, look for a "Philippine native" under PHILIPPINES, or a "Scottish measure" under SCOTLAND.

Another useful feature is the lavish listing of phrases. For instance, instead of being confronted by the simple clue "Sword," you may run up against "Double-edged sword." Under the entry word SWORD in this dictionary you will find ample phrases that qualify the entry word or more sharply specify its meaning. Also, given the definition "Turn aside," simply look under TURN and find that phrase, along with many others.

THE NEW YORK TIMES CROSSWORD PUZZLE DICTIONARY is a versatile reference book that you will want to keep on your desk or next to your chair for help, not only with crossword puzzles, but also for a large variety of other puzzles and contests. In addition, it will be invaluable for writers, speakers, and the like, for (with more than one-half million words) it is one of the largest books of synonyms ever published. Its simple arrangement makes it far easier to use than the standard thesauri.

Our hope is that you will come to use this new word book as we might. Get to know it and be adventuresome! If the first entry you consult does not corner the exact word you are seeking, let any listing at that spot lead you to a cross-reference. Follow this track until you have the right word "treed."

A project of this scope may well have been beyond the ability of only two to accomplish. We have required and welcomed top-flight support during our work. Although many might be named, special note must be given to the efforts of Richard Martz and David House of Dartmouth College, who were responsible for much of the computerization; also, to Gorton Carruth and Robert O'Brien of Morningside Associates. Each made his individual contributions, which we gratefully acknowledge.

Happy word hunting!

Tom Pulliam
Clare Grundman

1974

PREFACE to the Second Edition

This Second Edition of THE NEW YORK TIMES CROSSWORD PUZZLE DIC-TIONARY greatly augments the First Edition. We have added approximately 100,000 new entry words and synonyms into a new four-column format, which maintains the same easy-to-read features and the large numbers of words per page, including many new longer words. An outstanding innovation of this Second Edition is the inclusion of the titles of major works of literature and music, as well as their authors and composers, and the names of characters in books, plays, operas, etc. Another very important addition is the listing of famous people from various walks of life—painters, physicians, playwrights, botanists, etc.—as well as those men and women who have won Nobel Prizes and who have been inducted into the Hall of Fame. We have also assembled what we believe to be the most comprehensive listing of prefixes, suffixes, and combining forms, which are *listed by meaning*, and the largest list of biblical, mythological, and literary relationships ever to appear in a crossword puzzle dictionary. And, of course, we have retained from the First Edition the unique "shaded boxes" that feature pertinent facts about geographical locations.

We would like to acknowledge once more the excellent assistance of Gorton Carruth and Robert O'Brien of Morningside Editorial Associates and to thank the many puzzlers who have sent us their compliments and suggestions.

Again, we wish you happy word hunting!

T. P.
C. G.

1984

The New York Times

CROSSWORD PUZZLE

DICTIONARY

A

A AY HA AIR ARY PER ALFA EACH ALPHA
(EVER —) ARROW
AA LAVA
AAL AL MULBERRY
AARDVARK ANTEATER EDENTATE
AARDWOLF HYAENID
AARON (BROTHER OF —) MOSES
(BURIAL PLACE OF —) HOR
(FATHER OF —) AMRAM
(MOTHER OF —) JOCHEBED
(SISTER OF —) MIRIAM
(SON OF —) ABIHU NADAB ELEAZAR ITHAMAR
(WIFE OF —) ELISHEBA
AARONIC LEVITIC LEVITICAL
AB HATI
ABA ABAYAH
ABACA HEMP FIBER LUPIS LINAGA MANILA
ABACK SHORT
ABACUS SOROBAN SHWANPAN
ABADDON PIT HELL ABYSS SATAN APOLLYON
ABAFT AFT BACK BAFT ABAFF ASTERN BEHIND REARWARD
(— THE BEAM) LARGE
ABALONE EAR PAUA AWABI NACRE ORMER UHLLO ASSEIR MOLLUSK
ABANDON EGO CAST DROP FLEE JUNK QUIT SINK ABAND ALLAY CHUCK DITCH EXPEL LEAVE PLANT REMIT SCRAP WAIVE YIELD ABJURE BANISH BETRAY DESERT DEVEST DISUSE DIVEST EXPOSE FOREGO FORHOO FORLET MAROON RECANT REFUSE REJECT RELENT RESIGN SLOUGH VACATE DEPLORE DISCARD FORFEIT FORSAKE SCUTTLE ABDICATE FORHOOIE FORSWEAR JETTISON RASHNESS RENOUNCE SURCEASE RELINQUISH
(WITH —) DESPERATELY
ABANDONED BAD LEFT LORN LOST VACANT WICKED CORRUPT FORLORN PROJECT DEPRAVED DERELICT DESERTED DESOLATE FLAGRANT FORSAKEN
ABANDONING
(PREF.) LIPO
ABANDONMENT BURIAL APOSTASY ABATEMENT
(— OF RESTRAINT) LETUP
ABANGA ADY
ABAS (FATHER OF —) CELEUS LYNCEUS
(MOTHER OF —) METANIRA HYPERMNESTRA
(SON OF —) PROETUS ACRISIUS
ABASE SINK VAIL AVALE AVILE BLAME DEMIT DIMIT LOWER

SHAME ABJECT BEMEAN DEBASE DEFAME DEJECT DEMEAN DEPOSE GROVEL HUMBLE LESSEN MEEKEN REDUCE DEGRADE DEPRESS MORTIFY DIMINISH DISGRACE DISHONOR
ABASED ABAISSE DEJECTED
ABASH AWE COW BASH BAZE DASH AVALE ESBAY SHAME HUMBLE AFFRONT CONFUSE MORTIFY BEWILDER BROWBEAT CONFOUND
ABASHED BLANK CHEAP SHAMED ASHAMED FOOLISH SHEEPISH
ABASHMENT VERGOYNE
ABATE EBB END LOW CALM CURB FAIK FALL MEND OMIT SLOW SOFT VAIL VOID WANE ALLAY ALLOW ANNUL APPAL BREAK CHECK LOWER QUASH RELAX REMIT SLAKE SWAGE ASLAKE DEDUCT LESSEN PACIFY REBATE REDUCE RELENT ABOLISH ASSUAGE CASSARE CHANCER NULLIFY QUALIFY SLACKEN SUBSIDE DECREASE DIMINISH MITIGATE MODERATE OVERBLOW PALLIATE
ABATEMENT DELF FALL ALLAY DELFT DELPH LETUP GUSSET MIOSIS RABATE DECREASE DISCOUNT PROSTRATION
(— OF DISEASE) LYSIS
ABATIS OBSTACLE SLASHING
ABAXIAL DORSAL
ABBA FATHER
ABBAY ABBACY
ABBE MONK CLERIC CURATE PRIEST
ABBESS AMMA VICARESS
ABBEY ABADIA ABBAYE PRIORY CONVENT NUNNERY CLOISTER
ABBOT ABBAS COARB ARCHIMANDRITE
(— OF MISRULE) BISHOP
ABBREVIATE CUT CLIP DOCK PRUNE DIGEST ABRIDGE BOBTAIL CURTAIL SHORTEN CONDENSE CONTRACT TRUNCATE
ABBREVIATED SHORT BOBTAIL CRYPTIC MUTILATE
ABBREVIATION LAPSE SIGLUM SYMBOL
(PL.) SIGLA
ABC ALPHABET
ABDA (FATHER OF —) SHAMMUA
(SON OF) ADONIRAM
ABDEEL (SON OF —) SHELEMIAH
ABDERITE FOOL SCOFFER SIMPLETON
ABDI (SON OF —) KISHI
ABDICATE CEDE QUIT DEMIT EXPEL LEAVE REMIT DEPOSE

DISOWN FOREGO RESIGN RETIRE VACATE ABANDON DISCLAIM RENOUNCE
ABDICATION DRIFT
ABDIEL (FATHER OF —) GUNI
(SON OF —) AHI
ABDOMEN BOUK WOMB ALVUS APRON BELLY MELON MIRAC PLEON THARM PAUNCH VENTER STOMACH
(PREF.) CELI COELI VENTR(I)(O)
ABDOMINAL BELLY HEMAL CELIAC COELIAC VENTRAL VISCERAL
ABDON (FATHER OF —) MICAH HILLEL JEHIEL SHASHAK
ABDUCT LURE TAKE STEAL ABDUCE KIDNAP RAVISH SPIRIT CAPTURE
ABDUCTION APAGOGE RAPTURE
ABDUCTION FROM THE SERAGLIO (CHARACTER IN —) OSMIN PASHA BLONDE BELMONTE PEDRILLO CONSTANZE
(COMPOSER OF —) MOZART
ABDUCTOR SPIRIT
ABEAM ABREAST
ABECEDARIAN TYRO NOVICE LEARNER BEGINNER
ABECEDARIUS ABC
ABED SICK RESTING RETIRED SLEEPING
ABEL (BROTHER OF —) CAIN SETH
(FATHER OF —) ADAM
(MOTHER OF —) EVE
(PARENT OF —) ADAM
ABE LINCOLN IN ILLINOIS
(AUTHOR OF —) SHERWOOD
(CHARACTER IN —) ABE ANN GALE MARY SETH TODD GREEN SPEED GRAHAM JIMMIE MENTOR NINIAN BOWLING DOUGLAS EDWARDS HERNDON RUTLEDGE
ABELMOSK MUSK MALLOW
ABENCERAGES (CHARACTER IN —) ALMANSOR
(COMPOSER OF —) CHERUBINI
ABENCERRAJE (AUTHOR OF —) VILLEGAS
(CHARACTER IN —) JARIFA NARVAEZ RODRIGO ABINDARRAEZ
ABERDEEN ANGUS BLACK DODDY DODDIE
ABERRANT WILD CLAMMY DEVIANT ABNORMAL STRAYING VARIABLE
ABERRATION SLIP WARP ERROR FAULT LAPSE MANIA DELIRIUM DELUSION INSANITY
ABESSIVE CARITIVE
ABET AID EGG BACK HELP BOOST COACH ASSIST FOMENT INCITE SECOND SUCCOR UPHOLD COMFORT CONNIVE ESPOUSE

FORWARD FURTHER SUPPORT SUSTAIN ADVOCATE BEFRIEND
ABETO ACXOYATL
ABETTING CONFEDERATE
ABETTOR FAUTOR ADVOCATE PROMOTER
ABEYANCE ABEYANCY DORMANCY
ABEYANT LATENT
ABHIMANYU (FATHER OF —) ARJUNA
(VICTIM OF —) LAKSHMANA
ABHOR UG IRK HATE SHUN AGRISE DETEST LOATHE DESPISE DISLIKE EXECRATE ABOMINATE
ABHORRENCE HATE ODIUM HATRED HORROR DISGUST DISLIKE SCUNNER AVERSION LOATHING
ABHORRENT ODIOUS UGSOME HATEFUL ABSONANT INFAMOUS REPUGNANT
ABI (SON OF —) HEZEKIAH
ABIA (FATHER OF —) BECHER SAMUEL JEROBOAM REHOBOAM
(HUSBAND OF —) HEZRON
ABIATHAR (FATHER OF —) AHIMELECH
ABIDA (FATHER OF —) MIDIAN
ABIDE BE WIN WON BEAR BIDE KEEP LAST LEND LIVE REST STAY WAIT ABEAR AWAIT DELAY EXIST HABIT PAUSE STAND SWELL TARRY ENDURE HARBOR LINGER REMAIN RESIDE SUBMIT INHABIT SOJOURN SUBSIST SUSTAIN CONTINUE TOLERATE
(— BY) HOLD
ABIDING ABY FAST STABLE LASTING
ABIDINGNESS PERMANENCE
ABIEL (SON OF —) KISH
ABIES FIRS CONIFERS
ABIETATE SYLVATE
ABIEZER (FATHER OF —) GILEAD
ABIGAIL MAID
(HUSBAND OF —) DAVID NABAL JETHER
(SON OF —) AMASA DANIEL CHILEAB
ABIGEUS ABACTOR
ABIHAIL (DAUGHTER OF —) ESTHER
(FATHER OF —) HURI ELIAB
(HUSBAND OF —) ABISHUR REHOBOAM
(SON OF —) ZURIEL
ABIHU (BROTHER OF —) NADAB
(FATHER OF —) AARON
(MOTHER OF —) ELISHEBA
ABIHUD (FATHER OF —) BELA
ABIJAH (FATHER OF —) DAVID SAMUEL JEROBOAM REHOBOAM
(SON OF —) ASA HEZEKIAH
ABILITY G CAN MAY CLAY EASE

FORM HAND CLASS FLAIR FORCE MIGHT POWER SKILL STUFF VERVE ENERGY ENGINE INGINE MAUGHT STROKE TALENT CALIBER CUNNING FACULTY POTENCY APTITUDE CAPACITY STRENGTH
(— TO ENTER) ACCESS
(— TO THROW) ARM
(BATTING —) STICKWORK
(CREATIVE —) IMAGINATION
(INVENTIVE —) CONTRIVANCE
(MENTAL —) INGENY BRAINPOWER
ABIMELECH (BROTHER OF —) JOTHAM
(FATHER OF —) GIDEON ABIATHA
ABINADAB (FATHER OF —) SAUL JESSE
ABINOAM (SON OF —) BARAK
ABIPON CORONADO
ABIRAM (FATHER OF —) HIEL ELIAB
ABISHAI (BROTHER OF —) JOAB ASAHEL
(MOTHER OF —) ZERUIAH
ABISHALOM (DAUGHTER OF —) MAACHAH
ABISHUA (FATHER OF —) BELA PHINEHAS
(SON OF —) BUKKI
ABISHUR (FATHER OF —) SHAMMAI
ABITAL (HUSBAND OF —) DAVID
ABITUB (FATHER OF —) SHAHARAIM
(MOTHER OF —) HUSHIM
ABJECT LOW BASE MEAN POOR SUNK VILE HELOT PRONE SORRY CRAVEN MENIAL PALTRY SORDID SUPINE FAWNING FORLORN IGNOBLE SERVILE SLAVISH BEGGARLY CRINGING DEGRADED DOWNCAST LISTLESS WRETCHED
ABJOINT ABSTRICT
ABJURE DENY NITTE SPURN ESCHEW RECALL RECANT REJECT RESIGN REVOKE ABANDON DISAVOW EJURATE RETRACT ABNEGATE DISCLAIM FORSWEAR RENOUNCE
ABLAUT APOPHONY
ABLAZE ALOW AFIRE ALOWE ABLEEZE BURNING GLOWING RADIANT GLEAMING INFLAMED
ABLE APT BIG CAN FIT FERE ADEPT HABIL SMART THERE CLEVER EXPERT FACILE FITTED HABILE POTENT STRONG BASTANT CAPABLE DOUGHTY DEXTROUS POSSIBLE POWERFUL SKILLFUL SUITABLE TALENTED VIGOROUS
(— TO WALK) FEERIE FEIRIE
(SUFF.) (— TO) FUL
ABLE-BODIED YAL YALD YAULD
ABLENESS
(SUFF.) ABILITY IBILITY
ABLUTION BATH WIDU WUDU WUZU LOTION BAPTISM BATHING WASHING
ABNAKI WABANAKI
ABNEGATE DENY ABJURE FOREGO REFUSE REJECT DISAVOW DISCLAIM FORSWEAR IMMOLATE RENOUNCE
ABNER (BROTHER OF —) KISH
(FATHER OF —) NER

(SLAYER OF —) JOAB
(SON OF —) JAASIEL
(WIFE OF —) RIZPAH
ABNORMAL ENORM QUEER UTTER ERRATIC UNUSUAL VICIOUS ABERRANT ATYPICAL FREAKISH TERATOID ANOMALOUS MONSTROUS
(PREF.) ANOM(O) DYS MAL PARA POLY PSEUD(O)
ABNORMALITY ATAXY ATAXIA LETHAL ANOMALY BROWNING DEMENTIA ENORMITY
(CATTLE —) SAWDUST
ABOARD ON ONTO ACROSS ATHWART
ABODE COT DAR HUT INN WON BODE CELL FLAT HALL HOME NEST OMEN REST SEAT TENT WOON BEING BOWER DELAY HAUNT HOUSE MANOR PITCH RESET SIEGE SUITE ABIDAL BIDING ESTATE ADDRESS COTTAGE HABITAT LODGING MANSION SITTING CUNABULA DOMICILE DWELLING RESIANCE TENEMENT
(— OF DEAD) DAR AARU HELL ARALU HADES ORCUS SHEOL HEAVEN SHADES XIBALBA
(— OF DELIGHT) ELYSIUM
(— OF EVIL POWERS) ABYSS
(— OF GIANTS) UTGARD
(— OF GODS) MERU ASGARD OLYMPUS
(— OF LOST SOULS) ABADDON
(— OF SOULS) LIMBO
(ANIMAL —) ZOO MENAGERIE
(CELESTIAL —) HEAVEN
(FILTHY —) STY STYE
(MISERABLE —) DOGHOLE
(SHELTERED —) SHADE
ABOLISH END BLOT KILL ABATE ANNUL ERASE FORDO QUASH CANCEL EFFACE FOREDO RECALL REPEAL REVOKE VACATE DESTROY NULLIFY RESCIND REVERSE ABROGATE
ABOLITION EXTINCTION
ABOMA BOA BOM BOMA
ABOMASUM READ REED
ABOMINABLE VILE RUSTY CURSED ODIOUS ROTTEN BEASTLY HATEFUL HEINOUS MALEDICT NEFANDOUS
ABOMINABLY BEASTLY
ABOMINATE HATE ABHOR DETEST LOATHE EXECRATE
ABOMINATION EVIL CRIME CURSE HORROR PLAGUE DISGUST AVERSION
ABONGO BABONGO
ABORAL DORSAL ABACTINAL
ABORIGINAL ABO YAO FIRST NATAL BINGHI NATIVE SAVAGE NATURAL PRIMARY ORIGINAL
(— WOMAN) GIN
ABORIGINE KA KHA TODA ALFUR BAIGA BLACK BOONG DASYU MAORI MYALL ALFURO ARANDA ARANTA ARUNTA BINGHI INDIAN KIPPER KODAGA NATIVE SAVAGE

ADIBASI CHINHWAN WARRAGAL WARRIGAL
ABORT SLIP
ABORTION ABORT FAILURE CASTLING FETICIDE MISBIRTH
ABORTIVE IDLE VAIN BLIND FUTILE BOOTLESS
ABOUND SNY FLOW SNEE TEEM COVER FLEET SWARM REDOUND OVERFLOW
(SUFF.) ULENT
ABOUNDING RIFE FLUSH ROUTH COPIOUS REPLETE TEEMING UBEROUS ABUNDANT AFFLUENT PROLIFIC
(SUFF.) IOUS OSE OUS
ABOUT BY IN OF ON RE SAY AWAY NEAR SOME UMBE UPON ANENT ASTIR CIRCA ABROAD ACTIVE ALMOST ANENST AROUND CIRCUM TOWARD ENVIRON CIRCITER
(PREF.) AMB(I) AMPH(I)(O) CIRCUM HYPER PERI
ABOUT-FACE FLOP
ABOVE ON UP OER SUP ATOP OVER PAST UPON ABEEN ABOON ABUNE ALOFT SUPRA BEFORE BEYOND HIGHER THEREUP OVERHEAD SUPERIOR
(— GENERAL LEVEL) APART
(PREF.) EP EPH EPI HYPER OVER SUPER SUPRA SUR
ABRADE RAW RUB BARK FILE FRET GALL RASP SAND WEAR CHAFE ERASE GRATE GRAZE GRIND SCORE SCUFF TOUCH SCOTCH SCRAPE IRRITATE
ABRADER FILE RASP EMERY SANDER ABRASER GRINDER SCRAPER
ABRAHAM (BIRTHPLACE OF —) UR
(BROTHER OF —) HARAN NAHOR
(CONCUBINE OF —) HAGAR
(FATHER OF —) TERAH
(GRANDFATHER OF —) NAHOR
(GRANDSON OF —) ESAU
(NEPHEW OF —) LOT
(SON OF —) ISAAC MEDAN SHUAH MIDIAN ZIMRAN ISHMAEL JOKSHAN
(WIFE OF —) SARAH KETURAH
ABRASION BURN GALL OUCH SCAR SORE GRAZE BRUISE BLASTING
ABRASIVE SAND EMERY PUMICE QUARTZ SILICA ALUNDUM ERODENT ABRADANT CORUNDUM PUMICITE SCRUBBER
ABRAXAS GEM STONE AMULET ABRASAX
ABREAST EVEN AFRONT BESIDE HANGING
ABRET BREAD WAFER
ABRI SHED COVER DUGOUT SHELTER
ABRIDGE CUT DOCK LASK BRIEF ELIDE LIMIT RASEE RAZEE BRIDGE REDUCE SHRINK CURTAIL DEPRIVE REWRITE SHORTEN ABSTRACT BREVIATE COMPRESS CONDENSE CONTRACT DIMINISH RETRENCH SIMPLIFY ABBREVIATE

ABRIDGED TAIL
ABRIDGEMENT BRIEF ABREGE DIGEST PRECIS RESUME SKETCH COMPEND EPITOME PANDECT SUMMARY SUMMULA ABSTRACT BOILDOWN BREVIARY SYNOPSIS ABBREVIATION ABBREVIATURE
ABROAD OFF ASEA AWAY ABOUT ASTIR FORTH ABREED AFIELD ASTRAY WIDELY DISTANT OUTWARD OVERSEA OFFSHORE
ABROGATE ANNUL QUASH REMIT CANCEL REPEAL REVOKE VACATE ABOLISH NULLIFY RESCIND DISSOLVE OVERRULE
ABRUPT BOLD CURT DEAD FAST RUDE BLUFF BLUNT BRIEF BRUSK HASTY ICTIC PLUMP QUICK ROUGH SHARP SHEER SHORT STEEP STUNT SURLY TERSE TOTAL CHOPPY CRAGGY CRUSTY PROMPT RUGGED SUDDEN ANGULAR BRUSQUE PRERUPT VIOLENT HEADLONG VERTICAL PRECIPITATE
(NOT —) SOFT
ABRUPTLY BANG SHARP SHORT STEEPLY SUDDENLY
ABSALOM (FATHER OF —) DAVID
(MOTHER OF —) MAACHAH
(SISTER OF —) TAMAR
(SLAYER OF —) JOAB
ABSALOM, ABSALOM (AUTHOR OF —) FAULKNER
(CHARACTER IN —) BON ROSA ELLEN HENRY JUDITH SHREVE SUTPEN THOMAS CHARLES COMPSON GOODHUE QUENTIN MCCANNON COLDFIELD
ABSAROKA CROW
ABSCESS BOIL MORO SORE ULCER FESTER INCOME LESION QUINSY VOMICA EXITURE GUMBOIL PARULIS APOSTEME SQUINACY
ABSCISIC ACID DORMIN
ABSCISSA X COSINE
ABSCISSION APOCOPE
ABSCOND GO FLY RUN BOLT FLEE HIDE QUIT ELOPE SCRAM SMOKE DECAMP DEPART DESERT ELOINE ESCAPE LEVANT WITHDRAW
ABSENCE CUT LACK VOID WANT BLANK LEAVE DEFECT REMOVE VACUUM DEFAULT FAILURE VACANCY FURLOUGH
(— FROM DUTY) LIBERTY
(— FROM ONE'S COUNTRY) EXILE
(— OF AN ORGAN) AGENESIA AGENESIS
(— OF BIAS) DETACHMENT
(— OF CEREMONY) FAMILIARITY
(— OF FAMILIARITY) DISTANCE
(— OF FEELING) APATHY
(— OF FEVER) APYREXY APYREXIA
(— OF FORM) ENTROPY
(— OF GOVERNMENT) ANARCHY
(— OF INHIBITIONS) ANIMALITY
(— OF LIGHT) BLACK DARKNESS
(— OF MARRIAGE) AGAMY
(— OF MIND) ABSTRACTION
(— OF NAILS) ANONYCHIA
(— OF PAIN) ANODYNIA

(— OF PIGMENTATION) ACHROMA
ACHROMIA
(— OF SKULL) ACRANIA
(— OF TAIL) ANURY
(— OF TASTE) AGEUSIA
(— OF TRUMPS) CHICANE
(— OF TRUTH) FALSEHOOD
(PREF.) DYS ECTRO NON
ABSENT CUT OFF OUT AWAY
AWOL GONE LOST WANE DESERT
MUSING LACKING MISSING
WANTING ABSORBED DREAMING
(— IN MIND) ABSTRACT
(PREF.) ECTRO
ABSENTMINDED MUSED MUSING
DISTRAIT DREAMING
ABSTRACTED
ABSENTMINDEDNESS
STARGAZING
ABSINTHE AJENJO GENIPI
ABSOLUTE GOD ONE TAO TAT
DEAD DOWN FAIR FINE FREE
MEAR MEER MERE PLAT PLUM
PURE RANK REAL SELF TRUE
VERY BLANK CLEAR FIXED PLUMB
SHEER STARK TOTAL UTTER
WHOLE ENTIRE PROPER SEVERE
SIMPLE SQUARE BRAHMAN
CERTAIN PERFECT PLENARY
ABSTRACT COMPLETE DESPOTIC
EVENDOWN EXPLICIT IMPLICIT
POSITIVE
(— TEMPERATURE) T
(NOT —) NISI FINITE CONDITIONAL
ABSOLUTELY YEA YES AMEN
DONE GOLD DEAD FAIR JUOT
PLAT SLAP PLAIN PLUMB STARK
BARELY FAIRLY FLATLY SIMPLY
WHOLLY SHEERLY ENTIRELY
EVENDOWN
ABSOLUTION EXCUSE PARDON
SHRIFT LOOSING SHRIVING
ABSOLUTISM CAESARISM
DESPOTISM
ABSOLVE FREE QUIT CLEAR LOOSE
REMIT ACQUIT ASSOIL EXCUSE
EXEMPT FINISH PARDON SHRIVE
UNBIND CLEANSE FORGIVE
JUSTIFY RELEASE DISPENSE
LIBERATE OVERLOOK
ABSORB EAT FIX SOP SUP BLOT
SOAK SUCK TAKE AMUSE DRINK
MERGE RIVET UNITE DEVOUR
ENGAGE ENGULF ENWRAP IMBIBE
INGEST INSORB INWRAP OCCUPY
SPONGE STIFLE COMBINE
CONSUME ENGROSS IMMERSE
INVOLVE OCCLUDE SWALLOW
ABSORBED DEEP GONE LOST
RAPT SUNK FIXED ABSENT
BURIED ENRAPT HIPPED INTENT
PLUNGED RIVETED WRAPPED
IMMERSED ABSTRACTED
(— BY) ALL
ABSORBENT BASE DOPE FOMES
BARYTA SPONGY ANTACID
SORBENT ANTIACID BIBULOUS
DRINKING
ABSORBER SNUBBER
(— OF MONEY) LICKPENNY
(SHOCK —) BUFFER DAMPER
ABSORPTION AUTISM
PREOCCUPATION

(— UNIT) SABIN
ABSQUATULATE DECAMP
ABSCOND
ABSTAIN DENY FAST KEEP STAY
AVOID CEASE SPARE SPURN
WAIVE DESIST DISUSE ESCHEW
FOREGO REFUSE REJECT
FORBEAR REFRAIN RESTRAIN
TEETOTAL WITHHOLD
(— FROM) FAST FORGO LEAVE
ABJURE ESCHEW FOREGO
REFRAIN
ABSTAINER TOTE RECHABITE
ABSTEMIOUS SOBER ACETIC
SLENDER MODERATE
ABSTENTION CELIBACY CHASTITY
ABSTERGE WIPE BATHE CLEAN
PURGE RINSE
ABSTINENCE ENCRATY
ABSTINENT SOBER ABSTEMIOUS
ABSTRACT CULL DEED DRAW
NOTE PART PURE TAKE BRIEF
IDEAL STEAL ABSORB DEDUCT
DETACH DIGEST DIVERT DOCKET
NOETIC PRECIS REMOVE ABRIDGE
COMPEND EXCERPT ISOLATE
PURLOIN SECRETE SUMMARY
VIDIMUS ABSTRUSE ACADEMIC
ARGUMENT BREVIATE DISCRETE
PRESCIND SEPARATE SYLLABUS
SYNOPSIS TABLEITY WITHDRAW
METAPHYSICAL
(NOT —) CONCRETE
(PL.) PARATITLA PARATITLES
ABSTRACTED REMOTE
ABSTRACTION STUDY ENTITY
ABSENCE REVERIE ABSTRACT
QUODDITY
ABSTRUSE DARK DEEP HIGH
HIDDEN MYSTIC REMOTE SECRET
SUBTLE CURIOUS OBSCURE
RETIRED ABSTRACT ACROATIC
ESOTERIC PROFOUND
METAPHYSICAL
ABSURD HOT RICH WILD DOTTY
DROLL FALSE INANE INEPT SILLY
SCREWY STUPID ASININE
FATUOUS FOOLISH LAPUTAN
ABSONANT DOGGEREL FABULOUS
COCKAMAMY MONSTROUS
RIDICULOUS PREPOSTEROUS
ABSURDITY BETISE FATUITY
FOOLERY FOPPERY WALTROT
MAGGOTRY NONSENSE
UNREASON
ABUNA METRAN
ABUNDANCE WON COPY FLOW
MORT SONS WONE CHEAP DEPTH
FLUSH FOUTH POWER RIVER
ROUTH ROWTH SCADS SONSE
STORE WRECK BOUNTY FOISON
GALORE LAVISH OODLES PLENTY
POWDER RICHES TALENT UBERTY
WEALTH FLUENCY LASHINS
PLEROMA SATIETY BELLYFUL
FULLNESS LASHINGS OPULENCE
PLEURISY RIMPTION PLENITUDE
REDUNDANCY
(IN —) APLENTY
ABUNDANT FAT OLD FREE LUSH
MUCH RANK RICH RIFE AMPLE
FLUSH HEFTY LARGE OPIME
ROUTH ROWTH STORE DEMOID

GALORE HEARTY ROUTHY
APLENTY COPIOUS FERTILE
FULSOME LIBERAL OPULENT
PROFUSE REPLETE TEEMING
UBERANT UBEROUS WEALTHY
AFFLUENT FRUITFUL GENEROUS
NUMEROUS PLENTIFUL
(NOT —) LIGHT SPARE
(PREF.) HADR(O) LARGI
ABUNDANTLY RIFE WELL FREELY
PLENTY LARGELY HEARTILY
ABUSE MAR MOB TAX BUSE CALL
DRUB FLAY GAFF HARM HURT
LACK MAUL RAIL RUIN SLAM
TEEN VAIN BASTE BLAST CRIME
CURSE FAULT GRIEF SCOLD
SLANG SNASH SPOIL BERATE
DEFILE INJURE INSULT MALIGN
MISSAY MISUSE MUMBLE PUNISH
RAVISH REVILE TANCEL TANSEL
VILIFY YATTER AFFRONT
BACKJAW BEDEVIL DECEIVE
DESPITE FALSIFY MISBEDE
MISCALL MISNAME OBLOQUY
OUTRAGE PERVERT PROFANE
SLANDER TRADUCE UPBRAID
VIOLATE BALLARAG BUSINESS
DISHONOR FRUMPERY LANGUAGE
MALTREAT MISAPPLY MISTREAT
REPROACH SLAPDASH
ABUSED DOWNTROD
DOWNTRODDEN
ABUSIVE FOUL DIRTY SHREWD
CORRUPT SATIRIC CHEATING
INSOLENT LIBELOUS
ABUT BUTT JOIN REST TOUCH
ADJOIN BORDER BUTTAL
PROJECT
ABUTILON MALLOW
ABUTMENT CRIB PIER ALETTE
BUTTRESS
ABUTTING FLUSH ADJACENT
ABY ABIDING
ABYSM ABIME BISME DOWNFALL
ABYSMAL DEEP DREARY
PROFOUND UNENDING
WRETCHED
ABYSS PIT POT DEEP GULF HELL
VOID ABYSM CHAOS CHASM
DEPTH GORGE ABRUPT BOTTOM
VORAGO ABADDON AVERNUS
GEHENNA SWALLOW DOWNFALL
INTERVAL
ABYSSAL ABYSMAL BASSALIAN
ABYSSINIA (SEE ETHIOPIA)
ABYSSINIAN SIDI ABASSIN
(— BANANA) ENSETE
ACACALLIS (FATHER OF) MINOS
(MOTHER OF —) PASIPHAE
(SON OF —) GARAMAS
AMPHITHEMIS
ACACIA GUM JAM KOA WELD
WOLD BABUL GIDYA MULGA
MYALL SIRIS THORN TIMBE VEREK
WOALD WOULD ARABIC BABLAH
BINDER GIDGEA GIDGEE GIDYEA
HASHAB LEGUME LOCUST
MIMOSA SALLEE WATTLE YARRAN
BLUEBUSH BRIGALOW CHAPARRO
IRONWOOD ROSEWOOD
ACADEMIC IVY RIGID FORMAL
ACADEME CLASSIC DONNISH
ERUDITE LEARNED POMPIER

PEDANTIC PLATONIC
ACADEMY LYCEE CRUSCA LYCEUM
MANEGE SCHOOL ACADEME
COLLEGE SOCIETY YESHIVA
SEMINARY
(RIDING —) MANAGE MANEGE
ACADIAN CAJUN
ACAJOU CAJU CAJOO CAJOU
ACALEPH MEDUSA MEDUSAN
ACAMAS (BROTHER OF —)
ARCHELOCHUS
(FATHER OF —) ANTENOR THESEUS
EUSSORUS
(MOTHER OF —) THEANO PHAEDRA
(SLAYER OF —) AJAX MERIONES
(SON OF —) MUNITUS
ACANA ALMIQUE
ACANTHA FIN SPINE THORN
PRICKLE ACANTHON
ACAPU WALNUT WACAPOU
CHAPERNO
ACARID MITE NYMPH NYMPHA
OCTOPOD DIBRANCH
PROTONYMPH
ACARNAN (BROTHER OF —)
AMPHOTERUS
(FATHER OF —) ALCMAEON
(MOTHER OF —) CALLIRRHOE
ACASTUS (FATHER OF —) PELIAS
(SLAYER OF —) PELEUS
(WIFE OF —) HIPPOLYTE
ACAUDAL BOBBED ANUROUS
ECAUDATE TAILLESS
ACAULESCENT STEMLESS
ACCEDE LET AGREE ALLOW ENTER
GRANT YIELD ACCORD ASSENT
ATTAIN COMPLY CONCUR
CONCEDE CONFORM CONSENT
ACCELERATE GUN REV RUN HYPO
JAZZ RACE URGE DRIVE FAVOR
FORCE HURRY SPEED HASTEN
ADVANCE FORWARD FURTHER
QUICKEN ANTEDATE DISPATCH
EXPEDITE INCREASE THROTTLE
ACCELERATING
(PREF.) AUXO
ACCELERATION PICKUP SPEEDUP
(— OF REACTION) CATALYSIS
(— UNIT) STAPP
ACCELERATOR GAS GUN SPEEDER
BETATRON BEVATRON THROTTLE
(LINEAR —) LINAC
ACCENT BEAT BIRR BLAS BURR
MARK TONE ACUTE GRAVE ICTUS
PITCH PULSE SOUND THROB
VERGE BROGUE LENGTH RHYTHM
STRESS THESIS EMPHASIS
(DORIC —) PLATEASM
(IRISH —) BROGUE
(MUSICAL —) BEAT
(WITHOUT AN —) ATONIC
ACCENTED FZ SFZ TONIC STRONG
MARCATO MARCANDO SFORZATO
ACCENTUATE ACCENT
ACCENTUATION DECLAMATION
ENHANCEMENT
ACCEPT BUY EAT BEAR FANG
HAVE HOLD JUMP TAKE ADMIT
ADOPT AGREE ALLOW HONOR
INFER MARRY ASSENT ASSUME
AVOUCH POCKET APPROVE
BELIEVE CONCEDE EMBRACE
ESPOUSE RECEIVE

(— AS ONE'S OWN) NOSTRIFICATE
(— AS TRUE) ACCREDIT
(— AT RANDOM) DRAW
(— BETS) BOOK
(— EAGERLY) LEAP
(— INHERITANCE) ADIATE
(— READILY) SWALLOW
(— WITHOUT QUESTION) ABIDE

ACCEPTABLE LIEF VALID SIGHTLY
WELCOME GRACIOUS PASSABLE
PLEASANT

ACCEPTANCE PASS SNAFF ADITIO
TAQLID PASSAGE CREDENCE
CURRENCY
(— OF INHERITANCE) CERNITURE
(— OF ORDER) ALLOTMENT

ACCEPTATION MEANING
ACCEPTANCE

ACCEPTED GOING VULGAR
POPULAR APPROVED CREDITED
ORTHODOX STANDARD
(NOT —) OUT
(WIDELY —) INVETERATE

ACCEPTOR BASE

ACCESS FIT WAY ADIT DOOR GATE
PATH ROAD ENTRY GOING ROUTE
ACCOST AVENUE COMING
ENTREE PORTAL STREET
ADVANCE APPROACH ENTRANCE
PAROXYSM RECOURSE
(— OF DISEASE) ATTACK

ACCESSIBILITY EXPOSURE

ACCESSIBLE NEAR OPEN HANDY
PATENT AFFABLE PRESENT
FAMILIAR PERVIOUS SOCIABLE

ACCESSION ENTER ACCESS
AFFLUX ALLUVIO ILLAPSE
ADDITION ALLUVION ENTRANCE
INCREASE

ACCESSORY HAT AIDE ALLY
DOME TOOL EXTRA SCARF
HELPER ABETTOR ADAPTER
ADAPTOR ADJUNCT ANCILLA
ENCLAVE FITTING FIXTURE
ADDITIVE HATSTAND ORNAMENT
(PL.) ADDENDA FIXINGS
STAFFAGE

ACCIACCATURA MORDENT

ACCIDENT HAP CASE LUCK EVENT
GRIEF PRANG SHUNT CHANCE
HAZARD INJURY MISHAP
FORTUNE QUALITY CALAMITY
CASUALTY DISASTER FORTUITY
INCIDENT
(— IN CAR RACING) SHUNT
(AUTOMOBILE —) FATAL
(EUCHARISTIC —S) SPECIES

ACCIDENTAL ODD CASUAL
CHANCE RANDOM EXTERNAL

ACCIPITER HAWK

ACCLAIM CRY CLAP FAME HAIL
LAUD ROOT CHEER CLAIM ECLAT
EXTOL SHOUT PRAISE APPLAUD
HOSANNA OVATION PLAUDIT
RECLAME WELCOME APPLAUSE
(NOISY —) RIOT

ACCLAMATION CRY VOTE CHEER
SHOUT ACCLAIM HOSANNA
PLAUDIT APPLAUSE

ACCLIMATE ENURE INURE
HARDEN SEASON ACCUSTOM

ACCLIMATIZE SALT ADAPT
HARDEN SEASON

ACCLIVITY BANK BROW HILL RISE
GRADE PITCH SLANT SLOPE
TALUS ASCENT HEIGHT INCLINE

ACCOLADE EMMY KISS RITE SIGN
AWARD HONOR KUDOS MEDAL
OSCAR TOKEN SYMBOL EMBRACE
GARLAND CEREMONY

ACCOMMODATE AID BED BOW
FIT CAMP GIVE HELP HOLD LEND
SORT SUIT ADAPT BOARD DEFER
FAVOR HOUSE LODGE SERVE
YIELD ADJUST COMPLY FAVOUR
OBLIGE SETTLE CONFORM
CONTAIN FASHION ATTEMPER
GARRISON

ACCOMMODATING OBLIGING

ACCOMMODATION LOAN BERTH
CLASS BERTHAGE GIFFGAFF
(— BILL) KITE
(PL.) PASSAGE

ACCOMPANIED FRAUGHT

ACCOMPANIMENT SON ALBA
BURDEN ESCORT OOMPAH
ADJUNCT DESCANT SUPPORT
OBLIGATO
(PLAY JAZZ —) COMP
(PL.) FIXINGS

ACCOMPANIST JONGLEUR

ACCOMPANY SEE FARE FERE JOIN
LEAD TEND WAIT BRING PILOT
ASSIST ATTEND CONCUR CONVEY
CONVOY ESCORT FOLLOW
SECOND SQUIRE COEXIST
CONDUCT CONSORT SUPPORT
CHAPERON

ACCOMPANYING FELLOW
ADJUNCT
(PREF.) SYMPHORI

ACCOMPLICE PAL AIDE ALLY
CHUM BUDDY CRONY LOUKE
SHILL TILER BONNET COHORT
FELLOW HELPER ABETTOR
FEODARY FEUDARY HUSTLER
PARTNER STEERER

ACCOMPLISH DO GO END WIN
CHAR FILL WORK ENACT EQUIP
FETCH FORTH SWING AFFORD
ATTAIN EFFECT FINISH FULFIL
MANAGE VIRTUE ABSOLVE
ACHIEVE CHEVISE COMPASS
EXECUTE EXPLETE FULFILL
FURNISH OPERATE PERFECT
PERFORM REALIZE SUCCEED
COMPLETE CONTRIVE DISPATCH
ENGINEER OUTCARRY NEGOTIATE

ACCOMPLISHED APT ABLE ARCH
DONE ADEPT ENDED GREAT
TERSE BESEEN EXPERT
HANDSOME TALENTED

ACCOMPLISHMENT ART END
DEED FEAT PASS CRAFT SKILL
EFFECT TALENT EARNING
QUALITY FRUITION LEARNING
(PRIOR —) ANTICIPATION

ACCORD GIVE JIBE JUMP SUIT
UNIT AGREE ALLOW ATONE
AWARD BEFIT CHIME CHORD
CORDE GRANT LEVEL STAND
TALLY UNITY ACCEDE ADJUST
ASSENT BESTOW BETEEM
COMPLY CONCUR SETTLE UNISON
COMPORT COMPOSE CONCEDE
CONCERT CONCORD CONGREE

CONSENT CONSORT HARMONY
RAPPORT RESPOND UNANIME
DIAPASON SYMPATHY
(— WITH) SUIT
(IN —) ALONG

ACCORDANCE CONCERT
CONSENT
(IN —) ALONG

ACCORDANT EVEN ATTUNED
AGREEING COHERENT SUITABLE

ACCORDING (— TO) AD BY AUX
SEC EMFORTH ENFORTH
PURSUANT SECUNDUM
(— TO ART) SA
(— TO LAW) SL

ACCORDINGLY SO THEN THUS
HENCE IGITUR

ACCORDION LANTUM FLUTINA
FLAUTINO

ACCOST BAIL HAIL MASH MEET
ABORD ASSAY BOARD GREET
SPEAK ACCESS BROACH HALLOO
SALUTE ACCOAST ADDRESS
SOLICIT APPROACH GREETING

ACCOUCHEUR OBSTETRICIAN

ACCOUCHEUSE MIDWIFE

ACCOUNT TAB BILL BOOK DEEM
DRAW ITEM NICK NOTE RATE
REDE SAKE TAIL TALE TELL TEXT
WORD AUDIT BLAME CHALK
COUNT JUDGE SAKE STATE
STORY VALUE WORTH BATTEL
CREDIT DETAIL ESTEEM HORARY
LEGEND NOTICE PROFIT REASON
RECKON RECORD REGARD RELATE
RENDER REPORT REPUTE TREATY
ACCOMPT COMPOST COMPUTE
EXPLAIN JOURNAL LEXICON
NARRATE PROCESS RECITAL
TAILZIE BREVIARY CONSIDER
ESTIMATE RELATION TREATISE
BORDEREAU MONOGRAPH
RECKONING PRESENTATION
(— FOR) SAVE EXPLAIN
(ACCURATE —) GRIFF GRIFFIN
(CREDIT —) TICK
(LONG —) ILIAD MEGILLAH
(LONG, INVOLVED —) MEGILLA
MEGILLAH
(TRAVEL —) ITINERARY
(PL.) BATTELS

ACCOUNTABILITY DETAIL
LIABILITY

ACCOUNTABLE LIABLE AMENABLE

ACCOUNTANT CLERK SIRCAR
SIRKAR AUDITOR PESHKAR
PUTWARI KULKARNI MUTSUDDY
RECKONER

ACCOUNTANT-GENERAL
DAFTARDAR DEFTERDAR

ACCOUNTING TASK REASON
COSTING

ACCOUTER ARM RIG GIRD ARRAY
DRESS EQUIP ATTIRE CLOTHE
OUTFIT BEDIGHT FURNISH
HARNESS PROVIDE

ACCOUTERMENTS GEAR TIRE
DRESS ATTIRE GRAITH

ACCREDIT ALLOT VOUCH CREDIT
DEPUTE APPOINT APPROVE
ASCRIBE BELIEVE CERTIFY
CONFIRM ENDORSE LICENSE
SANCTION

ACCRETION SUM GAIN GROWTH
DEPOSIT EXUDATE ADDITION
ADHESION INCREASE
(INJURIOUS —) RUST

ACCRUAL ACCRUE DEMERIT

ACCRUE ADD WIN EARN GAIN
GROW PILE ARISE ENSUE ENURE
INCUR INURE ISSUE MATURE
RESULT SPRING ACQUIRE
COLLECT REDOUND ACCRESCE
CUMULATE INCREASE

ACCUMULATE DRAW FUND GROW
HEAP HIVE MASS PILE SAVE
AMASS DRIFT HOARD STACK
STORE TOTAL ACCRUE GARNER
GATHER MUSTER SCRAPE
COLLECT CONGEST HARVEST
INCREASE

ACCUMULATION DRIP DUMP
FUND GAIN HEAP MASS PILE
LODGE STACK STORE ANLAGE
BACKUP BUDGET COLUMN
DEBRIS GARNER BACKLOG
CUMULUS DEPOSIT DOSSIER
MORAINE DIVIDEND INTEREST
(— OF FLUID) EDEMA OEDEMA
ASCITES
(— OF FORCE) CHARGE
(— OF SNOW) ALIMENTATION
(— OF TRIFLES) FLOTSAM
(— ON CONCRETE) LAITANCE

ACCURACY NICETY FIDELITY
JUSTNESS PRECISION
(— OF ADJUSTMENT) TRAM
(HISTORICAL —) SYNCHRONISM

ACCURATE JUST LEAL NICE TRUE
CLOSE EXACT FLUSH RIGHT
NARROW PROPER SEVERE STRICT
CAREFUL CORRECT CURIOUS
PRECISE FAITHFUL PERQUEER
PUNCTUAL RIGOROUS TRUTHFUL
(NOT —) IMPURE
(UNPLEASANTLY —) BRUTAL

ACCURATELY JUST FAIRLY
JUSTLY CLOSELY EXACTLY
INSOOTH

ACCURSED FEY CURSED DAMNED
DOOMED FORBID SACRED
WARIED BLASTED MALEDICT

ACCUSATION BEEF WITE BLAME
CAUSE CRIME POINT WHITE
APPEAL ATTACK CHARGE THREAP
THREEP ACCUSAL SCANDAL
DELATION
(FALSE —) SUGGESTION

ACCUSATORY WRAYFUL

ACCUSE TAX WRY CALL FILE NOTE
SHOW SLUR TASK WITE WRAY
ACOUP ARGUE BLAME PEACH
TAINT TOUCH WHITE APPEAL
ATTACH ATTACK BECALL BEWRAY
CHARGE DEFAME DELATE DETECT
INDICT INTENT MURMUR
APPEACH ARRAIGN ATTAINT
CENSURE IMPEACH IMPLEAD
TRADUCE CHASTISE COMPLAIN
DENOUNCE QUESTION REDARGUE
REPROACH
(— UNJUSTLY) SLANDER

ACCUSER CHARGER DELATOR
LIBELANT

ACCUSING CULPATORY
DENUNCIATORY

ACCUSTOM URE USE WIN WON HAFT WONT ADAPT BREAK DRILL ENURE FLESH HABIT HAUNT INURE TRAIN ADDICT ADJUST CUSTOM INDUCE SEASON CONSORT EDUCATE TOUGHEN ACQUAINT
(— HORSE TO BIT) MOUTH
(— TO PASTURE) HAFT
ACCUSTOMED TAME USED WONE WONT USUAL USANT INURED CHRONIC CURRENT HABITED CONSUETE
ACE AS ALS JOT ONE PIP TIB ATOM CARD HERO MARK TOPS UNIT ADEPT BASTO FLYER POINT BULLET EXPERT AVIATOR BRISQUE PARTICLE
(— OF CLUBS) BASTA BASTO
(— OF SPADES) SPADILLE SPADILLO
(— OF TRUMPS) TIB HONOR PUNTO
(THREE —S) GLEEK
ACEDIA SLOTH ACCIDIA ACCIDIE
ACEPHALOUS HEADLESS
ACER NEGUNDO
ACERB ACID HARD SOUR TART ACRID HARSH SHARP BITTER SEVERE
ACERBAS (WIFE OF —) ELISSA
ACERBATE EMBITTER IRRITATE
ACERBITY ACRIMONY ASPERITY SEVERITY TARTNESS
ACESTES (FATHER OF —) CRIMISUS
(MOTHER OF —) EGESTA
(WIFE OF —) ENTELLA
ACETABULUM PAN PYXIS CUPULE ACETABLE HOLDFAST
ACETAL KETAL FORMAL KETATE BUTYRAL
ACETALDEHYDE ETHYL ETHANAL ALDEHYDE
ACETIC SOUR SHARP ZOONIC
ACETOPHENETIDIN PHENACETIN
ACETYLENE TOLAN ALKINE ALKYNE ETHINE ETHYNE TOLANE
ACHAEMENES (BROTHER OF —) XERXES
(FATHER OF —) DARIUS
(SLAYER OF —) INARUS
ACHAEUS (FATHER OF —) XUTHUS
(MOTHER OF —) CREUSA
ACHBOR (FATHER OF —) MICHAIAH
(SON OF —) BAALHANAN
ACHE AKE NAG NIP ECHE GELL HURT LONG PAIN PANG PINE RACK WARK WERK HACHE SMART STANG STOUN THROB THROE WARCH YEARN DESIRE MISERY STITCH STOUND TWINGE TWITCH ANGUISH EARACHE SORENESS
ACHENE CYPSELA UTRICLE
ACHIEVE DO END GET WIN EARN GAIN HACK HAVE MAKE FETCH FORCE NOTCH REACH SCORE AFFORD ARRIVE ATTAIN EFFECT FINISH OBTAIN CHEVISE COMPASS EXPLOIT FULFILL PERFORM PROCURE PRODUCE REALIZE SUCCEED TRIUMPH COMPLETE CONCLUDE CONTRIVE ACCOMPLISH

(— HARMONY) AGREE
(— ORIENTATION) ADJUST
ACHIEVEMENT ACT JOB DEED FEAT WORK ACTION CAREER RESULT EXPLOIT HARVEST PROWESS FELICITY
ACHILLEA PTARMICA
ACHILLES PELIDES
(COMPANION OF —) PATROCLUS
(FATHER OF —) PELEUS
(FRIEND OF —) PATROCLUS
(HORSE OF —) XANTHUS
(MOTHER OF —) THETIS
(SLAYER OF —) PARIS
ACHIM (FATHER OF —) SADOC
(SON OF —) ELIUD
ACHIOTE OLEANA ACHUETE ANNATTO ARNATTA ARNATTO
ACHRAS SAPOTA
ACHROMACYTE SHADOW
ACHROMATIC GRAY GREY NEUTRAL
ACHSAH (FATHER OF —) CALEB
(HUSBAND OF —) OTHNIEL
ACICULAR SPLINTERY
ACID DRY YAR DIAL DOPA KEEN PABA SOUR TART ACERB ACRID ALGIN AMINO CERIN EAGER HARSH LYSIN MALIC OLEUM RHEIN SHARP ULMIC ABRINE ALLIIN BITING BITTER GLYCIN LYSINE NIACIN PROLIN SERINE TWEAKY VALINE ACERBIC ACETOSE CERASIN FILICIN GLYCINE PROLINE STEARIN VINEGAR ORNITHINE PENICILLIN
(NITRIC) AQUAFORTIS
(PREF.) ACETO OXY
(SUFF.) (— RADICAL) OYL
ACID HYDROGEN
(SUFF.) HYDRIC
ACIDITY ACOR VERDURE ACERBITY SOURNESS VERJUICE
ACIS (FATHER OF —) FAUNUS
(LOVER OF —) GALATEA
(MOTHER OF —) SYMAETHIS
(SLAYER OF —) POLYPHEMUS
ACIS & GALATEA (CHARACTER IN —) ACIS GALATEA POLYPHEMUS
(COMPOSER OF —) HANDEL
ACKNOWLEDGE NOD OWN AVER AVOW SIGN ADMIT ADOPT ALLOW GRANT KITHE KYTHE THANK YIELD ACCEDE ACCEPT AGNIZE ANSWER ASSENT AVOUCH BEKNOW COUTHE FATHER REWARD CONCEDE CONFESS DECLARE OBSERVE PROFESS DISCLOSE RECOGNIZE
ACKNOWLEDGEMENT GRANT THANK AVOWAL CREDIT SHRIFT APOLOGY AGNITION COGNOVIT COGNISANCE COGNIZANCE RECOGNITION
(— OF MISTAKE) JEOFAIL
(— OF SIN) PECCAVI
ACLE AKLE IRUL JAMBA IRONWOOD PYENGADU
ACLYS HURLBAT
ACME IT ACE CAP TOP APEX CULM HIGH PEAK CREST PITCH POINT STATE APOGEE CLIMAX COMBLE CRISIS CULMEN HEIGHT HEYDAY

SUMMIT ZENITH CUMULUS SUBLIME CAPSHEAF CAPSTONE PINNACLE
ACNE WHELK ROSACEA
ACOLYTE BOY HELPER NOVICE SERVER LEARNER PATENER THURIFER
ACOMIA BALDNESS
ACONITE BIKH ACONITUM NAPELLUS
ACORN NUT MAST GLAND OVEST BALANUS BELLOTA BELLOTE
(— CUPS) VALONIA
(PL.) MAST CAMATA PANNAGE CAMATINA
(PREF.) BALAN(I)(O) GLANDI GLANDULI
ACORN-SHAPED BALANOID
ACOUSTICS SONICS PHONICS
ACQUAINT KNOW TELL TEACH VERSE ADVISE INFORM NOTIFY SCHOOL APPRISE APPRIZE POSSESS RESOLVE
ACQUAINTANCE KITH HABIT COUSIN FRIEND GOSSIP PICKUP AFFINITY FAMILIAR INTIMATE
(CLOSE —) HABIT INWARDNESS
(PRACTICAL —) PRACTICE PRACTISE
(PL.) KITH SOCIETY
ACQUAINTED ACQUENT VERSANT
ACQUIESCE BOW ABIDE AGREE CHIME YIELD ACCEDE ACCEPT ASSENT COMPLY CONCUR SUBMIT CONCEDE CONFIRM CONFORM CONSENT
ACQUIRABLE
(PREF.) CTETO
ACQUIRE ADD BAG BUY GET WIN EARN FORM GAIN GRAB HAVE MAKE REAP ADOPT AMASS ANNEX BEGET CHEVY CHIVY GLEAN LEARN REACH SEIZE STEAL ATTAIN CHIVEY CHIVVY DERIVE EFFECT GARNER OBTAIN SECURE SNATCH COLLECT CONQUER DEVELOP PROCURE RECEIVE CONTRACT
(— DESIRABLE QUALITY) AGE
(— KNOWLEDGE) LERE
ACQUISITION WIN GAIN LUCRE ACQUEST ACQUIST GETTING CONQUEST ACCESSION
(DISHONEST —) GRAFT
ACQUIT PAY FREE QUIT CLEAR QUIET ASSOIL BEHAVE BESTOW EXCUSE PARDON ABSOLVE COMPORT CONDUCT RELEASE REQUITE LIBERATE OVERLOOK UNCHARGE ASSOILZIE
ACQUITTAL EXCUSE ABSOLUTION
ACQUITTANCE QUIETUS RELEASE
ACRE AKER LAND ACKER FIELD STANG ARPENT COLLOP FARMHOLD
(QUARTER —) ROOD
(120 —S) HIDE
(2-3RDS —) COVER
(PL.) ACREAGE
ACREMAN CARUCARIUS
ACRID HOT ACID BASK KEEN SOUR HARSH ROUGH SHARP SURLY BITING BITTER CAUSTIC PUNGENT

REEKING UNSAVORY VIRULENT
ACRIMONIOUS MAD ACID KEEN ACRID ANGRY GRUFF HARSH IRATE SHARP SNELL SURLY BITTER CAUSTIC STINGING VIRULENT
ACRIMONY VIRUS ACERBITY ASPERITY PUNGENCY SOURNESS ANIMOSITY
ACRISIUS (BROTHER OF —) PROETUS
(DAUGHTER OF —) DANAE
(FATHER OF —) ABAS
(MOTHER OF —) AGLAIA
(SLAYER OF —) PERSEUS
(WIFE OF —) AGANIPPE EURYDICE
ACROBAT ZANY KINKER GYMNAST TOPPLER TUMBLER BALANCER AERIALIST ROPEWALKER
ACROPOLIS FORT HILL POLIS CADMEA CITADEL LARISSA
ACROSOME IDIOSOME IDIOZOME
ACROSS OVER SPAN YOND CROSS ABOARD THWART ATHWART OPPOSITE TRAVERSE
(CLEAN —) SHORT
(PREF.) DIA OVER TRANS
ACROSTIC ABC AGLA DORA GAME POEM TANAK PHRASE PUZZLE TANACH
ACRYLIC PROPENOIC
ACT BE DO GO APE LAW LET ACTU AUTO BILL COME DEAL DEED DORA FACT FEAT HOCK JEST MAKE MOVE PART PASS PLAY SKIT SLIM TAKE TURN WORK ACTUS DRAMA EDICT EMOTE ENTRY EXERT FEIGN GRACE KARMA MODEL SCENE SHIFT STUNT ACTION BEHAVE BESTIR DECREE DEMEAN FACTUM MANAGE RAGMAN COMPORT EXECUTE EXPLOIT PERFORM PORTRAY PRETEND STATUTE FUNCTION PRETENSE SIMULATE
(— AFFECTEDLY) MIMP
(— AS WANTON) RIG
(— AWKWARDLY) HOCKER
(— BEFORE) ANTICIPATE
(— BLUNDERINGLY) BULL
(— DECEITFULLY) DOUBLE
(— DISHONESTLY) FUDGE
(— FOOLISHLY) FON FONNE FOLEYE FOOTER FOOTLE
(— FRIVOLOUSLY) FRIVOL FRIBBLE
(— IN THEATER) GAFF
(— INDECISIVELY) DITHER
(— INDEPENDENTLY) SEVER
(— OF APPROVAL) EUGE
(— OF BEGGING) CADGE
(— OF CIVILITY) CURTSY DEVOIR CURTSEY
(— OF KINDNESS) CARESS BENEFIT
(— OF LABOR) DILIGENCE
(— OF PRAYER) DEVOTION
(— OF STUPIDITY) BETISE
(— OF TRICKERY) COG
(— OUT) ENACT DRAMATIZE
(— PLAYFULLY) DALLY BANTER
(— QUICKLY) GIRD
(— RASHLY) RACKLE
(— SPORTIVELY) DAFF
(— SUDDENLY) FLASH

(— TIMIDLY) NESH
(— TOGETHER) AGREE COACT CONCUR CONCORD
(— TRIFLINGLY) JANK
(— UP TO) EVEN
(— UPON) TOUCH AFFECT HANDLE
(— VIGOROUSLY) TWIG
(COMICAL —) JIG
(CONVENTIONAL —) AMENITY
(CORRUPT —) DEPRAVITY
(CRIMINAL —) INFAMY
(DARING —) ESCAPADE
(DECEITFUL —) ABUSE
(DECEPTIVE —) FEINT
(ECCENTRIC —) CANTRIP
(EVIL —) MALEFICENCE
(FAULTY —) PARAPRAXIS
(FOOLISH —) DIDO IDIOTISM
(FORBIDDEN —) CRIME
(FORMAL —) CEREMONY
(HABITUAL —) EXERCISE
(HASTY —) FLING
(HOSTILE —) BLOW
(INJURIOUS —) SPOIL
(LAUDATORY —) COUP
(LITURGICAL —) LAVABO
(LIVELY —) JIG
(MERITORIOUS —) MITZVAH
(MISCHIEVOUS —) DIDO CANTRAP CANTRIP
(OFFENSIVE —) AFFRONT
(OFFICIAL —S) ACTA
(PLAYFUL —) RALLERY RAILLERY
(PRAISEWORTHY —) DEMERIT
(RUDE —) INCIVILITY
(SUDDEN VIOLENT —) BENSEL BENSIL
(THOUGHTLESS —) FOLLY
(UNMANNERLY —) SOLECISM
(UNUSUAL —) STUNT
(VALOROUS —) WORSHIP
(VARIETY —) SKETCH
(WRONG —) DERELICT DERELICTUM
(PL.) DOINGS
(SUFF.) ADE ATE CY ICE ION ISM TH
ACTAEON (FATHER OF —) ARISTAEUS
(MOTHER OF —) AUTONOE
ACTINAL ORAL
ACTING AGENT SERVING
(— AGAINST) ADVERSE
(— BY TURN) ALTERN
(— ODDLY) HAYWIRE
(— RAPIDLY) DRASTIC
(UNSKILLFUL —) BUNGLING
ACTINIAN OPELET VESTLET
ACTINOST RADIAL RADIALE
ACTINOZOAN SEAFLOWER
ACTION ACT AIR DAP JOB PAS ACTO CASE DEED FACT FRAY GEST PLAY PLOY PUSH SHOW STEP SUIT WORK ACTIO DOING EDICT FIGHT FLING GESTE ISSUE THING TREAD VENUE AFFAIR AGENCY BATTLE BEFOOT COMBAT PRAXIS CONDUCT FACTION GESTURE PROCESS TANQUAM ACTIVITY BEHAVIOR BUSINESS CONFLICT FUNCTION PRACTICE PRACTISE

(— BETWEEN HORSE AND RIDER) APPUI
(— OF DRAMA) EPITASIS
(— OF WIND) EOLATION
(— PAINTING) TACHISM
(ABSURD —S) BOSH
(ANTAGONISTIC —) ATOMISM
(BLAMEWORTHY —) WITE
(CAPRICIOUS —) FREAK
(CHEMICAL —) ACTINISM
(COARSE —) HARLOTRY
(COOPERATIVE —) SYNERGISM
(COURT —) LAW SUIT ASSIZE LAWSUIT QUERELA QUERELE
(CRUEL —) RUTH
(CUSTOMARY —) COURSE
(EXAGGERATED —) PRODUCTION
(EXTEMPORE —) SCHEDIASM
(FANTASTIC —) ABTIC
(FINAL —) CATASTROPHE
(FOOLISH —) FOPPERY INEPTITUDE
(FRISKY —) FRISKIN
(FRIVOLOUS —) DALLIANCE
(HOSTILE —) OPPOSITION
(IMPULSIVE —) STAMPEDE
(INDIRECT —) WINDLASS
(INITIAL —) LEADOFF INDUCTION
(JOINT —) COACTION
(LEGAL —) DEBT SUIT ACCOUNT DETINET DETINUE PROCEEDING
(MEAN —S) DOGGERY
(MILITARY —) SWEEP OPERATION
(ODD —S) JIMJAMS
(PLAYFUL —) FUN FROLIC
(RASH —) HASTE
(REPEATED —) DRUM DOUBLE
(SUDDEN —) FLISK
(SYMBOLIC —) CHARADE
(TACTLESS —) GAUCHERIE
(UNAVOIDABLE —) FORCEPUT
(UNINTERMITTED —) HEAT
(VIOLENT —) AFFRAY
(WHIMSICAL —S) HUMORS HUMOURS
(WILY —) WRINKLE
(PREF.) CIN(O) CINET(O) KIN(O) KINESI KINET(O)
(SUFF.) ADE AL ANCE ANT ARD ATION CY ENCE ESIS ING ISATION IVE IZATION MENT OSIS PRACTIC PRAXIA PRAXIS SIS
(CHARACTERIZED BY —) SOME
(SMALL —) LE LING
ACTIS (FATHER OF —) RHODE
(MOTHER OF —) HELIUS
ACTIVATE SPARK ACTIFY ELICIT
ACTIVATION
(SUFF.) KINESIS
ACTIVATOR GOAD
ACTIVE UP YAL YAP YEP BUSY GAIN LISH LIST PERT RASH SPRY TRIG WHAT YALD YARE YEPE YERN ABOUT AGILE ALERT ALIVE ASTIR BRISK DEEDY FRESH LIGHT LINGY LUSTY NIPPY PEART QUICK READY SMART SNELL SPICY SPRIG STOUT SWANK VIVID WIGHT YAULD YERNE ACTUAL BOUNCY CLEVER DIRECT FEERIE FEIRIE FIERCE HEARTY LIVELY LIVING MOVING NIMBLE PROMPT QUIVER SEMMIT SPEEDY SPRACK SPROIL SPRUCE SPRUNT SWANKY

WIMBLE DASHING DEEDFUL DELIVER DYNAMIC HOPPING HUMMING KINETIC STHENIC THRODDY YANKING ANIMATED ATHLETIC BRAWLING DILIGENT SPIRITED VIGOROUS
(NORMALLY —) ABOUT
ACTIVELY DOWN BUSILY DEEDILY HEARTILY
ACTIVITY ACT ADO GOG VIR FIZZ LIFE PLAY PUSH STIR BLAST CAPER EVENT HEART RAJAS RALLY TRADE VIGOR ACTION AGENCY BUSTLE ENERGY HUSTLE SATTVA SPROIL AGILITY CALLING BUSINESS EXERCISE FUNCTION MOVEMENT PARERGON STIRRING OCCUPATION
(— OF INTELLECT) NOESIS
(CHOICE OF —) THING
(FUNCTIONAL —) SHOP
(GAY —) MERRYMAKING
(MENTAL —) CONCEIT BRAINWORK MENTATION
(SHARED —) COMMUNITY
(SPHERE OF —) SCENE
(TROUBLESOME —) COIL
(SUFF.) OR
(OUTBURST OF —) FEST
ACTON HOGTON HAQUETON
ACTOR HAM DOER HERO LEAD MIME STAR AGENT BUFFO COMIC DROLL EXTRA HEAVY MIMIC PLANT SERIO SUPER ARTIST BUSKER COWBOY DISEUR FEEDER FIDDLE MUMMER PLAYER PUPPET STAGER TOMMER ARTISTE CABOTIN DISEUSE HISTRIO PRIMOMO ROSCIUS STORMER TROUPER AISTEOIR COMEDIAN HISTRION JUVENILE STROLLER THESPIAN
(BROTHER OF —) AUGEAS
(DAUGHTER OF —) POLYMELA
(FATHER OF —) DIOMEDES MYRMIDON
(INDIFFERENT —) JAY
(INEPT —) HAM
(INFERIOR —) SHINE
(MOTHER OF —) DEION PASIDICE
(SON OF —) CTEATUS EURYTUS MENOETIUS
(PREF.) HISTRIO
ACTRESS DIVA STAR INGENUE STARLET FARCEUSE PREMIERE THESPIAN
ACTUAL GOOD HARD REAL TRUE VERY POSIT RIGHT BODILY FACTUAL GENUINE CONCRETE DEFINITE EXISTING MATERIAL POSITIVE TANGIBLE
ACTUALITY ACT FACT BEING VERITY REALITY ENERGEIA REALNESS
ACTUALLY BUT DONE TRULY FAIRLY ITSELF REALLY
(NOT —) NOMINALLY
ACTUATE ACT EGG RUN DRAW MOVE URGE ENACT IMPEL ROUSE START AROUSE COMPEL EXCITE INCITE INDUCE AGITATE ANIMATE ENLIVEN INSPIRE POINTED SHARPEN MOTIVATE PERSUADE

ACUITY FINENESS
ACUMEN WIT INSIGHT CAPACITY KEENNESS SAGACITY
ACUTE ACID FINE HIGH KEEN TART HEAVY QUICK SHARP SMART SNACK SNELL ARGUTE ASTUTE CRYING SHREWD SHRILL SUBTLE TREBLE URGENT CRUCIAL FEELING INTENSE POINTED VIOLENT CRITICAL INCISIVE POIGNANT ACUMINATE PENETRATING PENETRATIVE
(MOST —) DIRE
(NOT —) SLOW GRAVE CHRONIC
(PREF.) OXY
ACUTENESS DEPTH SENSE ACUITY ACUMEN NOSTRIL INCISION SAGACITY SUBTLETY
(— OF SMELL) HYPEROSMIA
ACYCLIC SPIRAL ALIPHATIC
ACYLOIN
(SUFF.) OIN
ADA (BROTHER OF —) PIXODARUS
(HUSBAND & BROTHER OF —) IDRIEUS
ADAD RAMMAN
ADAGE SAW DICT REDE TEXT WORD AXIOM MAXIM MOTTO HOMILY SAYING TRUISM WHEEZE BROMIDE PRECEPT PROVERB APHORISM APOTHEGM PAROEMIA
ADAGIO ADAGE ADAGIETTO
ADAH (HUSBAND OF —) ESAU LAMECH
(SON OF —) JABAL JUBAL ELIPHAZ
ADAIAH (FATHER OF —) SHIMHI JEROHAM
ADALIA (FATHER OF —) HAMAN
ADAM ADE EDIE ADKIN
(GRANDSON OF —) ENOS ENOCH
(SON OF —) ABEL CAIN SETH
(TEACHER OF —) RAISEL
(WIFE OF —) EVE LILITH
ADAM-AND-EVE CRAWFOOT
ADAMANT FIRM GRIM HARD SOLID STONY ADAMAS DIAMOND UNMOVED OBDURATE SOLIDITY STUBBORN
ADAMANTINE FIRM BORON STONE VAJRA ADAMANT
ADAM BEDE (AUTHOR OF —) ELIOT
(CHARACTER IN —) ADAM SETH DINAH HETTY ARTHUR BARTLE IRVINE MARTIN MASSEY MORRIS POYSER SORREL DONNITHORNE
ADAMITE PICARD
ADAM'S APPLE GUZZLE THROATBOLL
ADAM'S NEEDLE YUCCA
ADAPT APT FIT PLY PUT EDIT MOLD SORT SUIT AGREE HUMOR INURE SHAPE TALLY ADJUST CHANGE COMPLY DERIVE DOCTOR HUMOUR TEMPER ARRANGE CONFORM CONVERT FASHION PREPARE QUALIFY ATTEMPER CONTRIVE EQUALIZE MODULATE REGULATE ACCOMMODATE
ADAPTABILITY FLUIDITY ELASTICITY
ADAPTABLE LABILE ELASTIC PLASTIC PLIABLE FLEXUOUS

ADAPTATION CONSERTION
ADAPTED FIT FOR FITTED SUITED CONGENIAL
ADAPTER KIT ARRANGER
ADAXIAL SUPERIOR POSTERIOR
ADBEEL (FATHER OF —) ISHMAEL
ADD AD EIK EKE SAY SUM TOT CAST FOOT GAIN JOIN LEND PLUS TOTE AFFIX ANNEX GIVEN TOTAL UNITE ACCRUE ADJECT APPEND ATTACH CONFER FIGURE RECKON SUPPLY ACCRETE AUGMENT COMBINE COMPILE COMPUTE ENLARGE SUBJOIN SUMMATE INCREASE
(— ALCOHOL) SPIKE
(— FUEL) BEET
(— IN WRITING) ASCRIBE
(— TO) ADORN ENRICH AUGMENT
(— UP) SUM TOT COUNT TOTAL AMOUNT
(— WORT TO BEER) KRAUSEN
ADDA SCINK SKINK LIZARD
ADDAR (FATHER OF —) BELA
ADDAX PYGARG PYGARGUS
ADDED AND EKE PLUS ADJUNCT
(— SOMETHING) TILLY
ADDEND SUMMAND
ADDER ATHER KRAIT VIPER ELAPID NADDER NEDDER ELAPOID HAGWORM HYPNALE
ADDER'S-TONGUE LILY LILIUM COXCOMB ROOSTERS
ADDERWORT BISTORT
ADDI (FATHER OF —) COSAM
(SON OF —) MELCHI
ADDICT FAN BUFF DOPE DOPY HYPE USER COKEY COKIE FIEND HOPPY HOUND JUNKY SLAVE BOTARY DEVOTE JUNKER JUNKIE DELIVER DEVOTEE HABITUE HOPHEAD SNIFTER ACCUSTOM DOPEHEAD SNOWBIRD
ADDICTED GIVEN PRONE HOOKED BIBULOUS
ADDICTION HABIT MONKEY BIBACITY
ADDITION AND EIK EKE ELL TAB TOO ALSO ELSE GAIN PLUS AFFIX RIDER ACCESS ACCRUE AUGEND ENCORE GANSEL INCOME PREFIX ADJUNCT ADVANCE AUCTARY CODICIL JOINING PENDANT UNITING ADDENDUM INCREASE MANTISSA ACCESSION
(— TO ARTICLE) SHIRTTAIL
(— TO BEEHIVE) IMP
(— TO MASS) FARCE FARSE
(— TO PRICE) ADVANCE
(— TO WORD) PARAGOGE
(EXTRANEOUS —) ACCRETION
(TRIVIAL —) FILIP FILLIP
(PREF.) (IN —) SUPER
ADDITIONAL NEW ELSE MORE ADDED EXTRA FRESH OTHER TIDDER TOTHER ANOTHER BESIDES FURTHER ACCESSORY
ADDITIVE CUMOL CUMENE PRESERVATIVE
ADDLE EARN HOME IDLE MIRE AMAZE FILTH RIPEN SPOIL CURDLE MUDDLE THRIVE AGITATE CONFUSE BEFUDDLE BEWILDER
ADDLED ASEA EMPTY PUTRID MUDDLED UNSOUND
ADDRA DAMA NANGER
ADDRESS AIM SUE WOO BACK CALL EASE HAIL HOME MINT PRAY TACT TALK TULK TURN ABODE APPLY BOARD COURT DRESS ELOGE GREET POISE SKILL SPEAK TREAT ACCOST ADJUST APPEAL BOUNCE CHARGE DEVOTE DIRECT EULOGY MANNER PARLEY SALUTE SERMON SPEECH BEHIGHT CONDUCT CONSIGN ENTRUST LECTURE ORATION TUTOYER APPROACH DEDICATE DELIVERY DISPATCH FACILITY HARANGUE INSCRIBE PETITION
(— FAMILIARLY) TOM TUTOYER
(— SAUCILY) CHYAK CHYACK
(METHOD OF —) TONE
(PULPIT —) KHUTBA KHUTBAH
ADDUCE BEAR CITE GIVE NAME ALLAY ARGUE BRING INFER OFFER QUOTE ALLEGE ASSIGN OBJECT ADVANCE COUNTER MENTION PRESENT
ADE SQUASH
ADEPS FAT LARD
ADEPT ACE APT DON ABLE HANDY ADROIT ARTIST CRAFTY DEACON EXPERT MASTER VERSED ANCIENT ARTISTE CAPABLE DABSTER MAHATMA DEXTROUS SKILLFUL PROFICIENT
ADEQUATE DUE FIT ABLE FAIR FULL GOOD MEET WELL AMPLE DIGNE EQUAL COMMON DECENT ENOUGH PROPER CONDIGN SUITABLE COMMENSURATE SATISFACTORY
ADER (FATHER OF —) BERIAH
ADHERE HEW HUG CLAG CLAM CLOG GLUE HOLD JOIN KEEP LINK ABIDE AFFIX APPLY CLEAM CLING STICK UNITE ATTACH CEMENT CLEAVE COHERE FREEZE ACCRETE ANNERRE PERSIST
ADHERENCE CLING ABIDANCE ADHESION ARIANISM FIDELITY
ADHERENT IST ITE AIDE ALLY JAIN SIKH ADEPT BAHAI BLACK BONPA DEIST JAINA SIDER SPIKE STOOP FACTOR KIRKER VOTARY APRISTA BAHAIST CHANIST FASCIST FLACIAN GNOSTIC NICAEAN OWENIAN SECTARY SEQUELA THOMIST AGATHIST BELIEVER BUDDHIST CABALIST DISCIPLE FAITHFUL FATALIST FOLLOWER HUMANIST HYLICIST IMPERIAL PARTISAN RETAINER SERVITOR SOCINIAN UPHOLDER MONTANIST
(PL.) FOLD FOLLOWING
(SUFF.) ITE
ADHERING PERTINACIOUS
ADHESION BLOCKING STICKAGE SYNECHIA
ADHESIVE GUM WAX BOND CLAM GLUE SIZE TAPE DABBY DAUBY PASTE TACKY BINDER CEMENT CLINGY GLUTEN MASTIC PLUCKY SMEARY STICKY HOTMELT MOUNTANT MUCILAGE TENACIOUS
(PREF.) GLUT
ADHIBIT USE ADMIT AFFIX APPLY ATTACH
ADIANTUM MAIDENHAIR
ADIEL (SON OF —) AZMAVETH
ADIEU ADEW ADDIO ADIOS LEAVE FAREWELL
ADIPOSE FAT HARD SUET FATTY OBESE PURSY SQUAT TALLOW
ADIT DOOK DOOR ENTRY SOUGH STULM ACCESS TUNNEL PASSAGE APPROACH ENTRANCE
ADJACENT NEAR NIGH CLOSE FLUSH HANDY BESIDE NEARBY MEETING VICINAL ABUTTING TOUCHING CONTIGUOUS
(PREF.) (— TO) AC AD AF AG AL AP AS AT
ADJECTIVE ADNOUN DIPTOTE EPITHET NOMINAL MODIFIER
ADJOIN ADD ABUT BUTT JOIN LINE TACK COAST MARCH TOUCH UNITE ACCOST APPEND ATTACH BORDER CONTACT NEIGHBOR
ADJOINING VICINAL
ADJOURN END MOVE RISE STAY ARISE CLOSE DEFER DELAY RECESS SUSPEND DISSOLVE POSTPONE PROROGUE
ADJUDGE TRY ARET DEEM FIND GIVE HOLD RATE ALLOT AREAD AREED ARETT AWARD GRANT JUDGE ORDER ADDEEM ADDICT ADDOOM ASSIGN DECERN DECIDE DECREE ORDAIN REGARD BEHIGHT CONDEMN SENTENCE
(— GUILTY) DAMN
(— NOT GUILTY) ABSOLVE
ADJUDICATE ACT TRY HEAR PASS RULE JUDGE DECIDE ESTEEM RECKON REGARD SETTLE ADJUDGE CONSIDER SENTENCE
ADJUNCT AID HELP PART WORD ANNEX DEVICE PHRASE ADJOINT ANCILLA EPITHET FITTING GARNISH PERTAIN TEACHER ADDITION ADDITIVE APPANAGE APPENDIX ORNAMENT
ADJURATION OATH APPEAL SWEARING
ADJURE ASK BEG BID BIND ETHE PRAY CRAVE PLEAD SWEAR APPEAL CHARGE OBTEST BESEECH COMMAND CONJURE CONTEST ENTREAT REQUEST UNSWEAR
ADJUST FIT FIX SET CAST EASE FORM FREE GEAR JUST LINE PARE RATE SIZE SORT SUIT TRAM TRIM TRUE ADAPT ADMIT ALIGN ALINE ANGLE COAPT EQUAL FRAME PATCH RANGE RIGHT SHAPE ACCORD ATTUNE HAMMER JUSTEN ORIENT SETTLE SQUARE TEMPER WANGLE ADDRESS ARRANGE BALANCE CHANCER COMPOSE CONCERT CONFORM CORRECT DISPOSE JUSTIFY PREPARE RECTIFY COMPOUND REGULATE ACCOMMODATE
(— A LOOM) GATE
(— DULY) CONCENT
(— SAIL) FLATTEN
(PREF.) CO
ADJUSTED KEYED
ADJUSTER FIXER FITTER ASSESSOR
ADJUSTMENT FIT GEAR MISE TRIM FITNESS FITTING CHANCERY
ADJUTANT AIDE ALLY STORK ARGALA HELPER HURGILA MARABOU OFFICER
ADJUVANT AIDE HELPER ADJUNCT HELPFUL
ADLAI (SON OF —) SHAPHAT
AD-LIB FAKE
ADMAN HUCKSTER
ADMEASURE METE
ADMETUS (FATHER OF —) PHERES
(WIFE OF —) ALCESTIS
ADMINISTER DO RUN DEAL DEEM DOSE GIVE MOVE RULE APPLY SERVE TREAT DIRECT GOVERN MANAGE SETTLE SUPPLY TENDER ADHIBIT CONDUCE CONDUCT CONTROL EXECUTE EXHIBIT FURNISH HUSBAND DISPENSE MINISTER
(— FORCIBLY) HAND
(— SACRAMENT) BISHOP HOUSEL
ADMINISTRATION HELM RULE SWAY POLICY TAHSIL CONDUCT DIOCESE ECONOMY RECTORY REGIMEN CARRIAGE DISPOSAL MINISTRY
(— OF OATH) JURATION
(CORRUPT —) MALVERSATION
(REVENUE —) HACIENDA
ADMINISTRATOR CAID HELM QAID GABBAI MANAGER TRUSTEE DIRECTOR EXECUTOR MINISTER PROVICAR PROCONSUL
(INCA —) CURACA
(MORMON —) APOSTLE
ADMIRABLE FINE GOOD HIGH GRAND GREAT LUMMY PROUD DIVINE AMIABLE CAPITAL ELEGANT MIRANDA RIPPING
ADMIRAL (ALSO SEE NAVAL OFFICER) FLAG AMREL AMRELLE CAPITAN FLAGMAN GENERAL NAVARCH
ADMIRATION CULT FUROR GLORY ESTEEM LIKING WONDER CONCEIT WORSHIP
(— FOR BIGNESS) JUMBOISM
ADMIRE DIG LIKE LOVE ADORE EXTOL HONOR PRIZE VALUE ESTEEM MARVEL REGARD REVERE WONDER ADULATE APPROVE DELIGHT IDOLIZE RESPECT VENERATE
ADMIRER FAN BEAU LOVER SWAIN AMATEUR DEVOTEE FOLLOWER IDOLATER
(PL.) FOLLOWING
ADMISSION FEE ADIT CALL ENTRY ACCESS CHARGE ENTREE TICKET APOLOGY CONSENT INGRESS ENTRANCE RECEPTION CONCESSION

(— TO BAR) CALL

ADMIT KEN LET OWN AVER AVOW BEAR TAKE AGREE ALLOW ENTER GRANT IMMIT INLET ACCEDE ACCEPT ADJUST ASSENT AVOUCH ENROLL INDUCT PERMIT SUFFER ADHIBIT CONCEDE CONFESS INCLUDE PROFESS RECEIVE SUFFICE INITIATE
(— AS MEMBER) INDUCT
(— AS VALID) SUSTAIN

ADMITTANCE ACCESS ADMITTY ENTRANCE

ADMITTING THOUGH

ADMIX DALLOP DOLLOP

ADMIXTURE DASH ALLOY BLEND SHADE SPICE TINGE DALLOP DOLLOP FLAVOR LEAVEN STREAK MIXTURE SOUPCON COMPOUND INFUSION

ADMONISH WARN CHIDE SCOLD ADVISE ENJOIN EXHORT NOTIFY REBUKE REMIND SCHOOL CAUTION COUNSEL MONITOR REPROVE

ADMONITION ITEM ADVICE CAVEAT HOMILY CAUTION LECTURE REPROOF WARNING DOCUMENT REMINDER

ADNATE ADHERENT EPIGYNOUS
(— TO CALYX) INFERIOR

ADO DO COIL DEED FUSS ROUT STIR WORK HURRY TOUSE TOWSE BOTHER BUSTLE EFFORT FLURRY HUBBUB POTHER RUCKUS BLATHER BLETHER SPUTTER TROUBLE TURMOIL BUSINESS

ADOBE MUD CLAY DOBE DOBY SILT BRICK DOBIE TAPIA MUDCAP

ADOLESCENCE TEENS YOUTH NONAGE PUBERTY MINORITY

ADOLESCENT LAD TEEN YOUNG YOUTH TEENER IMMATURE TEENAGER

ADONIJAH (BROTHER OF —) AMNON ABSALOM CHILEAB
(FATHER OF —) DAVID
(MOTHER OF —) HAGGITH
(SLAYER OF —) BENAIAH

ADONIS ADON
(FATHER OF —) CINYRAS
(MOTHER OF —) MYRRH MYRRHA

ADOPT TAKE STEAL ACCEPT ASSUME ATTACH BORROW CHOOSE FATHER FOLLOW FOSTER MOTHER ACQUIRE EMBRACE ESPOUSE RECEIVE WELCOME ADVOCATE ARROGATE MAINTAIN

ADOPTION ESPOUSAL
(— OF DEBTS) ASSUMPTION

ADORABLE LOVELY LOVABLE CHARMING

ADORATION HOMAGE WORSHIP DEVOTION
(— OF GOD) LOVE

ADORE DOTE LAUD LOVE EXALT EXTOL HONOR WURTH ADMIRE ESTEEM PRAISE REVERE GLORIFY IDOLIZE WORSHIP VENERATE

ADORN DUB FIG GEM ORN SET BEAD BUSK DECK DILL DINK FOIL GAUD GILD LACE OUCH PICK PINK POSH STUD SWAG TRIM ADORE

ANORN ARRAY BEDUB BEGEM BELAY BESEE BRAVE CROWN DIGHT DRAPE DRESS FRONT GRACE HIGHT INLAY JEWEL MENSK PRANK PRICK PRIDE PRIMP PRINK ROUGE SPLAY SPRIG TRICK AGUISE ATTIRE ATTRAP BECOME BEDECK BETRIM BLAZON BROOCH CLOTHE COLLAR DAMASK DIADEM EMBOSS ENAMEL ENRICH ENROBE FIGURE FINIFY FRIEZE FRINGE GRAITH INSTAL INVEST ORNIFY POUNCE PURFLE QUAINT STATUE SUBORN TASSEL ADONISE APPAREL BEDIGHT BEDIZEN COMMEND CORONET DEPAINT DIGNIFY EMPEARL FEATHER FOLIAGE FURNISH GARNISH GLORIFY GRATIFY IMPLUME SPANGLE VARNISH BEAUTIFY DECORATE EMBLAZON FLOURISH ORNAMENT SPLENDOR

ADORNED CLAD BESEEN DAEDAL ORNATE PICKED BRAIDED CLOTHED COLORED DAISIED FIGURED
(SHOWILY —) BEPRANKED

ADORNMENT TIRE ADORN DRESS PRIDE BEAUTY DECORE TAHALI TINSEL DECKING OUNDING PRANKING TIREMENT

ADRAMMELECH (BROTHER OF —) SHAREZER
(FATHER OF —) SENNACHERIB

ADRASTUS (BROTHER OF —) MECISTEUS
(DAUGHTER OF —) AEGIA DEIPYLE
(FATHER OF —) TALAUS GORDIUS
(MOTHER OF —) LYSIMACHE
(SISTER OF —) ERIPHYLE

ADRESTUS (BROTHER OF —) AMPHIUS
(FATHER OF —) MENOPS
(SLAYER OF —) DIOMEDES

ADRIANA LECOUVREUR
(CHARACTER IN —) ADRIANA MAURICE BOUILLON MICHONNET
(COMPOSER OF —)CILEA

ADRIEL (FATHER OF —) BARZILLAI
(WIFE OF —) MERAB

ADRIFT ASEA LOST AWAFT LIGAN LOOSE AFLOAT DERELICT FLOATING UNMOORED

ADROIT DEFT EASY FEAT GOOD NEAT SLIM ADEPT HANDY READY SMART SNACK TIGHT TRICK ARTFUL CLEVER EXPERT HABILE NIMBLE CUNNING DEXTROUS HANDSOME SKILLFUL

ADROITNESS ART EASE TACT KNACK SKILL ADDRESS FACILITY

ADSORBENT BASE EARTH SILICA

ADULATE FAWN LAUD GLOSS GLOZE PRAISE FLATTER

ADULATION GLOSE GLOZE PRAISE INCENSE FLATTERY

ADULT MAN FULL MANLY MATURE EPHEBIC GROWNUP THRIVEN

ADULTERANT DOPE MULTUM ALMEIDINA

ADULTERATE CUT MIX CARD DASH LOAD ABUSE ALLOY HOCUS

TAINT DEACON DEBASE DEFILE DILUTE EXTEND MANAGE WEAKEN BASTARD CORRUPT FALSIFY VITIATE DENATURE IMPURIFY SPURIOUS

ADULTERATED CUT SHAM IMPURE CORRUPT SPURIOUS

ADULTEROUS ERRING

ADULTERY AVOUTRY CUCKOLDOM CUCKOLDRY MISCONDUCT

ADUMBRATE IMAGE SHADE VAGUE OBSCURE SUGGEST INTIMATE

ADUMBRATION SHADE SHADOW PHANTASM

ADUNCOUS BENT HOOKED

ADUST BURNT FIERY GLOOMY SALLOW PARCHED SCORCHED SUNBURNT

ADVANCE GO AID PAY SOP WAY BULL CITE COME DASH GAIN HELP INCH LAUD LEND LIFT LOAN MARK MOVE NEAR NOSE PASS PUSH RISE SHOW STEP WORM AVANT BOOST BRING CREEP ENTER EXALT EXTOL FAVOR FORGE MARCH OFFER PLACE PREST RAISE SERVE SPEED STAIR STAKE THROW ADDUCE ADMOVE ALLEGE AMOUNT ASSIGN ASSIST AVAUNT BETTER DEGREE EXTEND FAVOUR GROWTH HASTEN INCEDE INROAD PREFER PREPAY SCHOOL STRIDE STRIKE THRIVE TRAVEL VAUNCE BENEFIT DEVELOP ELEVATE ENHANCE FORTHGO FORWARD FURTHER HEADWAY IMPREST IMPROVE PROCEED PROCESS PROMOTE PROMOVE PROPOSE PROSPER PROVECT SUCCEED ADDITION DEVELOPE HEIGHTEN INCREASE PROGRESS PROGRESSION
(— BY CUTTING) DRIVE
(— BY LEAPS) SALTATION
(— IN LIFE) WAY
(— LABORIOUSLY) STRIVE
(— OBLIQUELY) SIDLE
(— ONE'S POINT) TAKE
(— SLOWLY) INCH WORM CRAWL CREEP
(— WAVERINGLY) HOBBLE
(— WITH EFFORT) DRAG
(DIFFICULT —) SLOG
(GRADUAL —) ILLAPSE
(STEADY —) SWING
(SUDDEN —) SHOOT
(VIGOROUS —) SWING
(PL.) APPROACHES

ADVANCED FAR DEEP GONE HIGH LATE AHEAD OUTER FORWARD IMPREST LIBERAL VANWARD FOREMOST
(— IN AGE) DEEP ANTIQUATED
(— IN YEARS) SENIOR AGEABLE ELDERLY
(MOST —) EXTREME FARTHEST FOREMOST HEADMOST
(WELL —) AGED

ADVANCEMENT UP GOOD ASCENT INCREASE

ADVANTAGE AD BOT USE VAN BEST BOOT BOTE DRAW DROP

EDGE GAIN GOOD HANK JUMP MEND NOTE ODDS PULL SAKE VAIL AVAIL BULGE BUNCE FAVOR FRAME FRUIT KINCH LAUGH POINT SPEED START STEAD USAGE BEHALF BEHOOF BETTER CARROT EFFECT PROFIT ACCOUNT BENEFIT CAPITAL EXPLOIT FORDEAL FURTHER PROMOTE PURPOSE UTILITY VANTAGE HANDICAP INTEREST LEVERAGE OVERHAND OVERPLUS PERCENTAGE
(ACCIDENTAL —) FLUKE
(UNDUE —) ABUSE

ADVANTAGEOUS GOOD JOLI WELL JOLIE GOLDEN PLUMMY SPEEDY USEFUL ELIGIBLE BEHOVEFUL PROPITIOUS
(PREF.) EU

ADVENT COMING INCOME ARRIVAL APPROACH PAROUSIA

ADVENTITIOUS CASUAL FOREIGN STRANGE ACQUIRED EPISODIC ACCESSORY

ADVENTURE GEST LARK RISK SEEK WAGE EVENT GESTE PERIL QUEST AUNTER AUNTRE CHANCE DANGER HAZARD EMPRISE EMPRIZE FORTUNE VENTURE ESCAPADE JEOPARDY

ADVENTURER ROUTIER ARGONAUT PICAROON

ADVENTURESS DEMIREP DEMIMONDAINE

ADVENTUROUS BOLD RASH DARING ERRANT AUNTROUS RECKLESS

ADVERSARY FOE ENEMY RIVAL SATAN FOEMAN OPPONENT
(— OF GOD) DEVIL
(PREF.) ENSTATO

ADVERSE FOE ILL EVIL CROSS LOATH THRAW AVERSE INFEST WITHER AWKWARD COUNTER DIVERSE FROWARD HOSTILE OPPOSED CONTRARY INIMICAL OPPOSING OPPOSITE OVERWART THRAWART
(PREF.) COUNTER

ADVERSITY ILL WOE CROSS DECAY NIGHT MISERY SORROW WITHER ILLNESS TROUBLE CALAMITY DISTRESS MISFORTUNE

ADVERT HEED AVERT RECUR REFER ALLUDE ATTEND RETURN REVERT OBSERVE CONSIDER

ADVERTISE CRY BARK BILL CALL PLUG PUFF STAR WARN BLURB INFORM NOTIFY PARADE DECLARE DISPLAY OBSERVE PLACARD PUBLISH ANNOUNCE PROCLAIM

ADVERTISED AFFICHE

ADVERTISEMENT AD BILL SIGN BLURB CHANT PITCH PROMO ADVERT CACHET DODGER NOTICE POSTER TEASER AFFICHE PLACARD STUFFER CIRCULAR HANDBILL

ADVERTISING BUSH BILLING PUFFERY
(EXTRAVAGANT —) HYPE

ADVICE AVIS AVYS LORE NEWS REDE AVYSE STEER ADVISO DEVICE NOTICE CAUTION CONSEIL COUNSEL OPINION TIDINGS GUIDANCE MONITION (PL.) INFORMATION

ADVISABLE BOOK PROPER PRUDENT

ADVISE SAY READ REDE TELL VISE WARN WISE AREAD AREED COACH GUIDE WEISE WEIZE ADJURE ADVISO BEREDE CONFER DEVISE EXHORT INFORM PONDER REVEAL APPRISE APPRIZE COUNSEL ACQUAINT ADMONISH CONSIDER RECOMMEND (— AGAINST) DISSUADE

ADVISED DELIBERATE

ADVISER AIDE TOUT COACH COMES TUTOR DOCTOR EGERIA LAWYER NESTOR ADVISOR MONITOR STARETS TEACHER ATTORNEY CROUPIER DIRECTOR FIELDMAN PREACHER

ADVISORY URGING PRUDENT

ADVOCACY BOOM FAVOR AVOWRY FAVOUR ARIANISM

ADVOCATE PRO ABET BACK PUSH URGE VOGT ACTOR ADOPT FAVOR PLEAD ASSERT AVOWRY BACKER DEFEND IDEIST LAWYER PATRON SYNDIC ABETTOR APOSTLE DECLAIM ENDORSE ESPOUSE EXPOUND FASCIST GOLDBUG PATRIOT PLEADER PROCTOR PROMOTE SCHOLAR SUPPORT ATTORNEY CHAMPION CLUBBIST DEFENSOR HUMANIST PARTISAN PREACHER PARACLETE PROPONENT (— FAVORED BY JUDGE) PEAT (— OF REVOLT) ANARCH (SUFF.) ARIAN CRAT

ADVOWSON ADVOCACY TENEMENT PATRONAGE

ADZ AX AXE ADZE EDGE ADDIS ADDICE EATCHE THIXLE HATCHET

AEACUS (FATHER OF —) ZEUS JUPITER (MOTHER OF —) AEGINA (SON OF —) PELEUS PHOCUS TELAMON (WIFE OF —) ENDEIS

AECHMAGORAS (FATHER OF —) HERCULES (MOTHER OF —) PHIALO

AECIUM CAEOMA

AEDON (BROTHER OF —) AMPHION (FATHER OF —) PANDAREUS (HUSBAND OF —) ZETHUS POLYTECHNUS (MOTHER OF —) HARMOTHOE (SON OF —) ITYLUS

AEETES (DAUGHTER OF —) MEDEA (FATHER OF —) HELIOS (MOTHER OF —) PERSA PERSEIS (SON OF —) APSYRTUS

AEGAEON (BROTHER OF —) GYGES COTTUS (FATHER OF —) URANUS (MOTHER OF —) GE GAEA (WIFE OF —) AEMILIA

AEGEAN SEA (ANCIENT PEOPLE

OF —) PSARA PSYRA SAMIAN LELEGES SAMIOTE (GULF OF —) SAROS (ISLAND OF —) COS IOS KEOS NIOS RODI SCIO CHIOS LEROS MELOS NAXOS PAROS PATMO SAMOS SIROS TENOS THERA ANDROS IKARIA IMBROS LEMNOS LESBOS RHODES SKYROS (RIVER INTO —) STRUMA VARDAR MARISTA (TOWN ON —) CHIOS VATHY MYTILENE

AEGEON (WIFE OF —) AEMILIA

AEGEUS (BROTHER OF —) LYCUS NISUS PALLAS (FATHER OF —) PANDION (SON OF —) THESEUS (WIFE OF —) PYLIA

AEGIA (FATHER OF —) ADRASTUS (HUSBAND OF —) POLYNICES (SON OF —) THERSANDER

AEGINA (FATHER OF —) ASOPUS (MOTHER OF —) METOPE (SON OF —) AEACUS

AEGIR HLER GYMIR (WIFE OF —) RAN

AEGIRITE ACMITE

AEGIS EGIS SHIELD AUSPICE DEFENCE DEFENSE

AEGISTHUS (FATHER OF —) THYESTES (MOTHER OF —) PELOPIA (SLAYER OF —) ORESTES

AEGLE (BROTHER OF —) PHAETHON (FATHER OF —) HELIUS (MOTHER OF —) CLYMENE

AEGYPTUS (BROTHER OF —) DANAUS (FATHER OF —) BELUS (MOTHER OF —) ANCHINOE (SON OF —) LYNCEUS

AENEAS (COMPANION OF —) ACHATES (FATHER OF —) ANCHISES (GREAT-GRANDSON OF —) BRUT (MOTHER OF —) VENUS APHRODITE (SON OF —) IULUS ASCANIUS (WIFE OF —) CREUSA LAVINIA

AENEID (AUTHOR OF —) VIRGIL (CHARACTER IN —) ANNA DIDO JUNO VENUS AENEAS PALLAS TURNUS EVANDER LATINUS LAVINIA ANCHISES ASCANIUS

AENGUS (MOTHER OF —) BOANN

AEOLUS (BROTHER OF —) DORUS XUTHUS (DAUGHTER OF —) ARNE CANACE ALCYONE HALCYONE (FATHER OF —) HELLEN HIPPOTES (MOTHER OF —) ORSEIS (SON OF —) ATHAMAS CRETHEUS SISYPHUS SALMONEUS

AEON AGE EON ERA AION AEVUM CYCLE KALPA PERIOD (PAIR OF —S) SYZYGY

AEPYTUS (FATHER OF —) CRESPHONTES (MOTHER OF —) MEROPE

AERATE AERIFY CHARGE INFLATE

AERIAL AERY AIRY TWIN AFRIF LOFTY DIPOLE UNREAL AEOLIAN

ANTENNA ETHEREAL

AERIALIST FLIER FLYER

AERIE AERY AIRE AYRE EYRY NEST AIERY BROOD EYRIE

AERIFORM UNREAL GASEOUS

AEROBE BACTERIUM

AERODROME AIRPORT AIRFIELD

AEROEMBOLISM BENDS

AEROFOIL SLAT ROTOR

AEROLITE AEROLITH

AERONAUT PILOT SKYMAN

AERONAUTICS AVIATION

AEROPE (DAUGHTER OF —) ANAXIBIA (FATHER OF —) CATREUS CERHEUS (HUSBAND OF —) ATREUS PLISTHENES (LOVER OF —) THYRESTES (SISTER OF —) CLYMENE (SON OF —) MENELAUS AGAMEMNON

AEROPLANE (SEE AIRPLANE)

AEROSE BRASSY

AEROSTAT AIRSHIP BALLOON AIRCRAFT

AERUGO RUST PATINA

AESACUS (FATHER OF —) PRIAM (LOVER OF —) HESPERIA (MOTHER OF —) ARISBE ALEXIRRHOE

AESEPUS (BROTHER OF —) PEDASUS (FATHER OF —) BUCOLION (MOTHER OF —) ABARBAREA (SLAYER OF —) EURYALUS

AESON (BROTHER OF —) PELIAS (FATHER OF —) CRETHEUS (MOTHER OF —) TYRO (SON OF —) JASON (WIFE OF —) ALCIMEDA

AESTHETIC ARTISTIC ESTHETIC TASTEFUL

AETA ITA

AETHALIDES (FATHER OF —) HERMES MERCURY (MOTHER OF —) EUPOLEMIA

AETHRA (FATHER OF —) OCEANUS PITTHEUS (MOTHER OF —) TETHYS (SON OF —) HYAS THESEUS

AETOLUS (FATHER OF —) ENDYMION (SON OF —) CALYDON PLEURON (WIFE OF —) PRONOE

AFAR OFF AWAY SAHO FERNE FERREN REMOTE YFERRE DANAKIL DANKALI DISTANT

AFARA LIMBA

AFFABLE FAIR OPEN BLAND CIVIL FRANK SUAVE BENIGN FACILE FORTHY GENIAL SOCIAL URBANE AMIABLE CORDIAL GENERAL LIKABLE CHARMING FAMILIAR FRIENDLY GRACIOUS PLEASANT SOCIABLE TOWARDLY CONVERSABLE

AFFAIR DO JOB PIE BLOW CASE DUEL GEAR PLOY BRAWL CAUSE EVENT FIGHT LEVEE PARTY THING ACTION BATTLE BEHALF DOMENT EFFEIR MATTER SETOUT SHAURI BLOWOUT CONCERN FUNERAL HOEDOWN JOURNEY

LIAISON PALAVER SHEBANG BUSINESS COMETHER ENDEAVOR HYPOTHEC INTRIGUE OCCASION PROCEEDING (CONFUSED —) SCHEMOZZLE (CRITICAL —) KANKEDORT (LOVE —) LOVE AMOUR INTRIGUE (SOCIAL —) FORMAL JUNKET SUPPER (STATE —S) ESTATE (PL.) SQUARES OCCASIONS

AFFECT AIL AIR HIT BEAR MELT MOVE POSE RINE SHAM STIR SWAY ALLOT ALTER ANNOY ASSAY COLOR DRIVE FANCY FEIGN HAUNT IMPEL MINCE SHOCK TOUCH ASPIRE ASSIGN ASSUME CHANGE DESIRE MOLEST SOFTEN STRIKE THRILL ATTAINT ATTINGE BEWITCH CONCERN EMOTION FEELING IMPRESS OPERATE PASSION PRETEND PROFESS ALLOCATE DISPOSED FREQUENT INTEREST SIMULATE (— BY HANDLING) TOUCH (— FAVORABLY) LIKE (— INJURIOUSLY) INTERESS (— STRONGLY) HIT HOLD SURPRISE (— WITH EXCITEMENT) BLOW

AFFECTATION AIR AIRS POSE SHAM FRILL GRACE MINCE CHICHI CONCEIT DISPLAY FOPPERY FROUNCE GRIMACE PIETISM FONDNESS PRETENSE PUPPYISM (PL.) LUGS

AFFECTED MOY AIRY CAMP FEAT AILED APISH MOVED POSEY CHICHI FALLAL FEISTY FORMAL PRETTY QUAINT SEIZED FEIGNED MINIKIN MISSISH REACHED SMITTEN STILTED TAFFETA TAFFETY TOUCHED INVOLVED PRECIEUX PRECIOUS RECHERCHE (— BY DECAY) DOTY (— WITH RABIES) MAD (SOMETHING —) CAMP (SUFF.) IC ICAL PATH(IA)(IC)(Y)

AFFECTING AIRIFIED FRAPPANT POIGNANT TOUCHING

AFFECTION LOVE WAFF ALOHA AMOUR BOTCH FLAME HEART CHERTE DOTAGE ESTEEM HYDROA MALADY REGARD THRUSH AILMENT CHARITY EMOTION FEELING PASSION SYMPTOM CHLOASMA DEARNESS DEVOTION FONDNESS KINDNESS MELICERA TENDENCY (PARENTAL —) STORGE (PL.) HEART HEARTSTRINGS (SUFF.) OMA PATHY

AFFECTIONATE DEAR FOND WARM ARDENT DOTING LOVING TENDER AMOROUS CORDIAL DEVOTED EARNEST ZEALOUS ATTACHED PARENTAL SISTERLY

AFFECTIVE SENSIBLE

AFFERENT BEAR ESODIC SENSORY ADVEHENT INFERENT

AFFIANCE AFFY FAITH TRUST ASSURE ENGAGE ENSURE FIANCE PLEDGE PLIGHT SPOUSE BETROTH

PROMISE CONTRACT RELIANCE

AFFIANCED INTENDED

AFFIANT DEPONENT AFFIDAVIT

AFFIDAVIT DAVY OATH AFFIANT AFFIDAVY AFFYDAVY

AFFILIATE ALLY UNIT ADOPT MERGE UNITE ATTACH BRANCH RELATE ASCRIBE CHAPTER CONNECT FILIATE

AFFINITY KIN TELE FAMILY LIKING AVIDITY CHEMISM KINDRED KINSHIP RAPPORT ALLIANCE GOSSIPRY HOMOLOGY RELATION SYMPATHY COGNATION
(PREF.) (— FOR) TROP(IDO)(O)
(SUFF.) (— FOR) PHIL(A)(AE)(E) (IA)(ISM)(IST)(OUS)(US)(Y) TROPE TROPISM

AFFIRM PUT AFFY AVER AVOW TAKE POSIT STATE SWEAR TRUTH VOUCH ADHERE ALLEGE ASSERT ATTEST AVOUCH DEPOSE RATIFY SUBMIT THREAP THREEP VERIFY ASSEVER CONFIRM DECLARE PROFESS PROTEST TESTIFY MAINTAIN PREDICATE

AFFIRMATION SAY VOW YES AMEN OATH WORD DIXIT PONENT THESIS AVERRAL AVERMENT

AFFIRMATIVE AY AYE NOD YAH YEA YEP YES AMEN ATEN YEAH PONENT DOGMATIC POSITIVE

AFFIX ADD FIX PEN PIN SET CASE CLIP FAST JOIN NAIL SEAL SIGN ANNEX INFIX STAMP UNITE ANCHOR APPEND ATTACH FASTEN SETTLE STAPLE ADHIBIT CONNECT ENTITLE FORMANT IMPRESS PLASTER SUBJOIN

AFFLATUS FURY FUROR FRENZY VISION IMPULSE

AFFLICT AIL RUE TRY VEX COMB FIRE HOLD HURT PAIN PINE RACK TUKE ARRAY ASSAY BESET CURSE GRILL GRIPE HARRY PINCH PRESS SEIZE SMITE TRYST VISIT WOUND WRING BURDEN GRIEVE HARASS HUMBLE INFECT MOLEST PESTER REMORD SCORCH STRAIN STRESS STRIKE CHASTEN INFLICT OPPRESS SCOURGE TORMENT TROUBLE DISTRESS LACERATE STRAITEN

AFFLICTED JOB SAD SORRY AILING WOEFUL GRIEVED HAUNTED SMITTEN IMPAIRED STRICKEN TROUBLED

AFFLICTION WOE EVIL LOSS PAIN SORE TEEN TINE TRAY ASSAY CROSS GRIEF PRESS SMART STOUR BUFFET DURESS MISERY PATHOS PLAGUE SORROW STRESS THRONG AILMENT DISEASE ILLNESS PASSION PURSUIT SCOURGE TORTURE TROUBLE CALAMITY DISTRESS HARDSHIP SEVERITY SICKNESS VEXATION MARTYRDOM
(PL.) CUP
(SUFF.) (— WITH) ITIS

AFFLICTIVE SAD DIRE SORE SOUR HEAVY SEVERE

AFFLUENCE EASE AFFLUX INFLUX PLENTY RICHES WEALTH FORTUNE OPULENCE

AFFLUENT FAT RICH FLUSH RIVER STEAM BRANCH SPRUIT COPIOUS FLOWING HALCYON OPULENT WEALTHY ABUNDANT INFLUENT

AFFORD GO BEAR GIVE LEND GRANT INCUR OFFER STAND THOLE YIELD CONFER ENDURE MANAGE SUPPLY ACHIEVE FORWARD FURNISH FURTHER PRODUCE PROVIDE MINISTER

AFFRAY FEUD FRAY RIOT ALARM BRAWL BROIL CLASH FIGHT MELEE SCARE SPURN ATTACK BATTLE COMBAT EFFRAY ENFRAI FRIGHT STRIFE TERROR TUMULT ASSAULT CONTEST QUARREL SCUFFLE STARTLE FRIGHTEN STRUGGLE

AFFRIGHT COW FEAR AGAST ALARM DAUNT DOUBT DREAD SCARE AGRISE APPALL DISMAY CONFUSE STARTLE TERRIFY FRIGHTEN

AFFRONT CUT DEFY SLAP ABUSE BEARD PEEVE HARASS INJURE INSULT NETTLE OFFEND SLIGHT STRUNT ASSAULT OFFENCE OFFENSE OUTRAGE PROVOKE CONFRONT DISGRACE ILLTREAT IRRITATE CONTUMELY

AFFUSION POURING INFUSION

AFGHAN RUG GHAN COVER DURANI HASARA HAZARA PATHAN BLANKET PAKHTUN PUKHTUN ACHAKZAI COVERLET

AFGHAN FOX CORSAC CORSAK

AFICIONADO FAN AMATEUR DEVOTEE FOLLOWER

AFIELD ABROAD ASTRAY

AFIRE ALOW ALOWE EAGER ABLAZE AFLAME ARDENT BURNING FLAMING

A-FLAT AS AIS

AFLOAT ASEA ASWIM AWAFT AWASH ADRIFT BUOYED NATANT ABROACH FLOODED UNFIXED FLOATING

AFOOT ABOUT AGATE ASTIR ABROAD TOWARD WALKING

AFOREMENTIONED SAID SUCH

AFORESAID SAME DITTO NAMED PRIOR PREVIOUS

AFORETIME ERE FORMER FORMERLY

AFRAID RAD REDE ADRAD FRAID PAVID REDDE TIMID AGHAST CRAVEN FEARED SCARED WROTHE AFEARED ALARMED ANXIOUS ASCARED CHICKEN FEARFUL GASTFUL COWARDLY GHASTFUL TIMOROUS

AFREET JINN AFRIT DEMON GIANT IFRIT JINNI AFRITE EFREET

AFRESH ANEW ANON OVER AGAIN NEWLY DENOVO ENCORE REPEATED

AFRICAINE, L' (CHARACTER IN —) INEZ DAGAMA SELIKA NELUSKO
(COMPOSER OF —) MEYERBEER

AFRICAN BOER AFRIC

AFRICAN MARIGOLD KHAKIBOS

AFRIKAANS TAAL DUTCH

AFRO NATURAL

AFT BACK REAR ABAFT AFTER ASTERN BEHIND
(FARTHEST —) AFTERMOST

AFTER A AB BY TO AFT EFT FOR SIN ANON NEXT PAST POST SYNE ABAFT APRES ARTER EFTER INFRA LATER SINCE ASTERN BEHIND BEYOND FOLLOW HINDER
(— MEALS) PC
(PREF.) EPH EPI INFRA META POST

AFTERBIRTH HEAM SECUNDINE SOOTERKIN

AFTERBODY TONNEAU

AFTERBURNER AUGMENTER

AFTEREFFECT SEQUEL SEQUELA
(PL.) HANGOVER

AFTERGRASS FOG AFTERFEED

AFTERIMAGE SPECTRUM PHOTOGENE SENSATION
(KIND OF —) PURKINJE

AFTERMATH FOG ETCH LOSS ISSUE ROWEN ROWET TRAIL TRAIN ARRISH EDDISH EDGREW EDGROW EFFECT PROFIT RESULT SEQUEL UPSHOT EAGRASS STUBBLE BACKWASH

AFTERMOST LAST HINDMOST

AFTERNOON AFTER TARDE UNDERN EVENING TEATIME

AFTERPIECE JIG EPODE EXODE EXODIUM POSTLUDE

AFTERSONG EPODE

AFTERSWARM CAST SPEW SPUE CASTLING

AFTERTASTE TWANG FAREWELL

AFTERTHOUGHT FOOTNOTE

AFTERWARD EFT POST SITH THEN APRES LATER EFTSOON EFTSOONS

AGA AGHA LORD CHIEF
(WIFE OF —) BEGUM

AGAIN OR TO BIS EFT YET AGIN ANEW ANON AYEN AYIN BACK MORE OVER NEWLY AFRESH DENOVO ENCORE ITERUM EFTSOON FRESHLY FURTHER EFTSOONS MOREOVER
(— AND AGAIN) AND
(PREF.) ANA OVER PALI RE

AGAINST BY IN UP CON GIN NON AGIN ANTI GAIN INTO WITH AGAIN ANENT AYENS UNTIL ANENST AVERSE AYENST CONTRA GAINST UPTILL VERSUS FERNENT FORNENT OPPOSED ADVERSUS CONTRAIR FORENENT FORNENST FORINST
(— HOPE) AGLEE AGLEY
(PREF.) ANTH ANTI CAT(A) CATH CONTRA ENANTIO GAIN OB

AGAL HEADROPE

AGALLOCH AGGUR ALOES GAROO GARROO GARROW TAMBAC LINALOE AGALWOOD CALAMBAC

AGAMA AGA AGHA GUANA

AGAMID IGUANA LIZARD AGAMIAN

AGAMEDE (FATHER OF —) AUGEAS (HUSBAND OF —) MULIUS

AGAMEMNON (BROTHER OF —) MENELAUS (DAUGHTER OF —) ELECTRA IPHIGENIA (FATHER OF —) PLISTHENES (GRANDFATHER OF —) ATREUS (SON OF —) ORESTES (WIFE OF —) CLYTEMNESTRA

AGAMID AGA AGHA BALETE BALITI

AGAPANTHUS TULBAGHIA LOVEFLOWER

AGAPE LOVE OPEN FEAST GAPING YAWNING

AGAR MOSS GELOSE KANTEN GELOSIN GELOSINE

AGARIC BLEWITS BLUSHER FLYBANE LEPIOTA

AGASP EAGER GASPING

AGATE TAW ONYX RUBY SARD ACHATE GAGATE MARBLE PEBBLE QUARTZ

AGATI SESBANIA

AGAVE ALOE LILY AGAUE AMOLE DATIL SISAL LILIUM MAGUEY MESCAL PULQUE ZAPUPE CANTALA KARATTO KERATTO TEQUILA HENEQUEN HENIQUEN JINIQUEN SOAPWEED (BROTHER OF —) POLYDORUS (FATHER OF —) CADMUS (HUSBAND OF —) ECHION (MOTHER OF —) HARMONIA (SISTER OF —) INO SEMELE AUTONOE (SON OF —) PENTHEUS

AGE ALD BIN DAY ELD EON ERA AEON EDGE OLAM TIME YUGA AETAT CYCLE EPOCH OLDEN RIPEN SECLE WORLD YEARS MATURE MELLOW PERIOD SIECLE WITHER CENTURY DEVELOP GLACIAL OLDNESS SECULUM SENESCE VORHAND ANCIENTY DURATION ETERNITY LIFETIME MAJORITY MATURITY (— OF MOON) EPACT (— OF 100 YEARS) CENTENARY (ADVANCED —) DOTAGE (BEING UNDER 13 YEARS OF —) PRETEEN (EARLY MIDDLE —) SUMMER (GREAT —) ANTIQUITY GRANDEVITY (OLD —) CRUTCH SENIUM VETUSTY SENILITY (PREF.) (OLD —) GERONT(O) PRESBY(O) (SUFF.) AEVAL EVAL (HAVING APPROXIMATE — OF) ISH ISTIC

AGED AE AET AGY OLD RIPE ANILE HOARY OLDEN PASSE FEEBLE INFIRM MATURE SENILE WINTRY YEARED ANCIENT ELDERLY OGYGIAN WINTERED (NOT —) GREEN (WELL —) STALE

AGEE AJEE AWRY AGLEY ASKEW (SON OF —) SHAMMAH

AGELESS ETERNAL TIMELESS

AGELONG SECULAR SAECULAR

AGENCY DINT HAND CHECK FORCE LEVER MEANS MOYEN ORGAN PROXY ACTION BUREAU MEDIUM OFFICE ARBITER BENEFIT BROKERY FACULTY LIBRARY MACHINE ACTIVITY COMPTOIR COURTESY MINISTRY (PUBLIC —) AUTHORITY (RESTORATIVE —) BALM (SUPPOSITITIOUS —) ENTELECHY (THERAPEUTIC —) MODALITY

AGENDUM SLATE DOCKET RECORD RITUAL PROGRAM

AGENOR (BROTHER OF —) BELUS (DAUGHTER OF —) EUROPA (FATHER OF —) ANTENOR NEPTUNE (MOTHER OF —) LIBYA (SON OF —) CILIX CADMUS PHOENIX (WIFE OF —) TELEPHASSA

AGENT SPY AMIN DOER ETCH GENE ACTOR AMEEN BUYER CAUSE ENVOY MEANS ORGAN PROXY REEVE RIDER VAKIL WALLA ADUROL ASSIGN ATOPEN BROKER BURSAR COMMIS DEALER DEPUTY ENGINE FACTOR FITTER KEHAYA LEDGER MEDIUM MINION MUKTAR PESKAR SELLER SYNDIC VAKEEL WALLAH BAILIFF BLISTER CHANNEL COUCHER DRASTIC FACIENT FEDERAL HUSBAND LEAGUER MOOKTAR MOONTAR MUKTEAR MUTAGEN OFFICER PESHKAR PROCTOR SCALPER APPROVER ATTORNEY AUMILDAR CATALYST EMISSARY EXECUTOR GOMASHTA GOMASTAH IMPROVER INCITANT INSTITOR MINISTER MOOKHTAR OPERATOR PROMOTER QUAESTOR RESIDENT SALESMAN VIRUCIDE MIDDLEMAN OPERATIVE SATELLITE SENESCHAL MAINSPRING PROCURATOR PLENIPOTENTIARY (— AGAINST LEPROSY) DAPSONE (— INVESTIGATING DRUG VIOLATIONS) NARC NARK (— OF CROMWELL) AGITATOR (ANTIKNOCK —) ADDITIVE ALKYLATE (CLEANSING —) SOAP (CONFIDENTIAL —) AMIN AMEEN (DESTRUCTIVE —) DEVOURER (EMPLOYMENT —) PADRONE (ENFORCEMENT —) LAW (ESPIONAGE —) COURIER (FISCAL —) STEWARD (HEALING —) BALSAM (MEDICINAL —) DRASTIC (NARCOTIC —) NARC NARK GAZER (OXIDIZING —) NINHYDRIN (PRESS —) FLACK (PUBLICITY —) BEATER (PURCHASING —) CIRCAR SIRCAR SIRKAR (SECRET —) SBIRRO (STIMULATING —) FILIP FILLIP (SUBVERSIVE —) STOOGE (SWEETENING —) DULCIN

(UNDERCOVER —) SPOOK (VOLATILE —) SPIRIT (WETTING —) SPREADER (SUFF.) ANT FIER STAT(IC)(ICS)

AGESILAUS (BROTHER OF —) AGIS (FATHER OF —) ARCHIDAMUS (MOTHER OF —) EUPOLIA

AGGLOMERATE HEAP LUMP MASS PILE SELF SLAG WIND CHAOS GATHER CLUSTER COLLECT

AGGLOMERATION HORDE CONGERY FAVELLA CONGERIE

AGGRANDIZE LIFT BOOST EXALT RAISE ADVANCE AUGMENT DIGNIFY ELEVATE ENLARGE MAGNIFY PROMOTE INCREASE

AGGRAVATE IRK NAG VEX FEED LOAD TWIT ANGER ANNOY TAUNT TEASE BURDEN PESTER WORSEN AGGREGE BEDEVIL ENHANCE ENLARGE MAGNIFY PROVOKE AGGRIEVE HEIGHTEN INCREASE IRRITATE

AGGRAVATED ACUTE

AGGREEABLE ACCEPTABLE

AGGREGATE ADD ALL SET SUM AUGE BAND BULK CLON CLUB COMB DEME FLOC GOUT LATH MASS BLOCK BUNCH CLASS CLONE COVER CROWD FIELD GROSS SHOOT TOTAL UNITE WHOLE AMOUNT BALLAS DOMAIN PLUREL VOLUME ASBOLAN COLLECT ARCULITE ASBOLANE ASBOLITE AXIOLITE COMPOUND COVERAGE CUMULITE ENSEMBLE MANIFOLD MULTEITY TOTALITY (— OF MICA) BOOK (— OF MINERALS) EYE (— OF ORE) KIDNEY (— OF POINTS) CELL (— OF RELATED THINGS) SHMEAR SCHMEAR (— OF STATEMENTS) AUTHORITY (— OF TISSUES) BODY (MATHEMATICAL —) FIELD SEQUENCE (MOLECULAR —) MICELLE (SOIL —) PED (SUFF.) ERY

AGGREGATION HEAD HERD NEST CLUMP CUTIN FLOCK GORGE GROUP LURRY SWARM COLONY FAMILY NATION SYSTEM CLUSTER CONGERY GALLERY SORITES CONGERIE EUMERISM

AGGRESSION WAR RAID ATTACK INJURY ASSAULT OFFENSE INVASION

AGGRESSIVE BUTCH PUSHY PUSHING AGONISTIC

AGGRESSIVENESS CRUST DEFIANCE BELLICOSITY

AGGRIEVE TRY HARM HURT PAIN HARRY WRONG INJURE AFFLICT OPPRESS TROUBLE DISTRESS

AGGRIEVED SORE OFFENDED

AGHAST AGAST AFRAID

AGHRERATH (FATHER OF —) PESHENG (SLAYER OF —) AFRASIAB

AGILAWOOD AGALLOCH AGALLOCHUM

AGILE DEFT FAST LISH SPRY WIRY ADEPT ALERT BRISK CATTY ELFIN FLEET LITHE NIFTY NIPPY QUICK WANLE WITHY ACTIVE ADROIT FEERIE FEIRIE LIMBER LISSOM LITHER LIVELY LUTHER NIMBLE QUIVER SUPPLE WANDLE LISSOME SALIENT SPRINGE SPRINGY ATHLETIC

AGILITY LEVITY SPROIL SLEIGHT ACTIVITY LEGERITY SALIENCE

AGING BINNING (PREMATURE —) GERODERMA GERODERMIA

AGIO BATTA DISAGIO PREMIUM DISCOUNT EXCHANGE

AGIST TAX FEED RATE GRAZE PASTURE

AGITATE FAN IRK JAR VEX WEY FRET FUSS MOVE PLOT RILE ROCK SEEK STIR TEEM ALARM ALTER BREAK BROIL CHURN DRIVE HARRY IMPEL QUAKE ROUSE SHAKE AROUSE BETOSS BUSKLE DEBATE DEVISE EXCITE FOMENT HARASS INCITE JABBLE JOSTLE JUMBLE JUSTLE LATHER MANAGE RATTLE RUFFLE SEETHE ACTUATE CANVASS COMMOVE CONCUSS DISCUSS DISTURB PERTURB REVOLVE TEMPEST TORMENT TROUBLE ACTIVATE CONTRIVE CONVULSE DISQUIET DISTRACT TRANSACT (— A LIQUID) SPARGE

AGITATED WILD HECTIC STEWED STORMY YEASTY AGITATO ESTUOUS UNQUIET AESTUOUS FEVERISH FLURRIED SEETHING OVERWROUGHT

AGITATION GOG JAR JOG BOIL FEAR FLAP FRET FURY GUST HEAT ITCH JERK JOLT SNIT ALARM DANCE HURRY QUAKE SHAKE STORM STOUR TWEAK YEAST BREEZE BUSTLE DITHER ENERGY FIZZLE FLIGHT FLURRY FRENZY JABBLE MOTION PUCKER QUIVER RIPPLE SHAKES TAKING TREMOR TUMULT WELTER EMOTION FERMENT FLUSTER FLUTTER MADNESS RAMPAGE STICKLE SWITHER TEMPEST TURMOIL DISQUIET PAROXYSM UPHEAVAL COMMOTION (— AND PROPAGANDA) AGITPROP

AGITATOR HOG TREATER

AGLAIA (FATHER OF —) JUPITER (MOTHER OF —) EURYNOME (SISTER OF —) THALIA EUPHROSYNE

AGLET TAB TAG LACE STUD PLATE AIGLET PENDANT SPANGLE HAWTHORN STAYLACE

AGLEY AWRY AGLEE ASIDE ASKEW WRONG

AGLYCON GENIN NONSUGAR SAPOGENIN

AGNATE AKIN ALLIED COGNATE KINDRED

AGNEL MOUTON

AGNOETE THEMISTIAN
AGNOMEN NAME ALIAS EPITHET
SURNAME COGNOMEN
NICKNAME
AGNOSTIC ATHEIST DOUBTER
SKEPTIC NESCIENT
AGO BY SIN BACK ERST GONE PAST
SENS SYNE YGOE YORE ABACK
AGONE SINCE YGONE SINSYNE
BACKWARD
(LONG —) ANCIENTLY
AGOG AVID KEEN ASTIR EAGER
LIVELY EXCITED VIGILANT
AGONIZE BEAR RACK STRAIN
WRITHE
AGONIZING GRINDING
HARROWING
AGONY ACHE PAIN PANG DOLOR
GRIEF GRIPE PANIC STOUR
THRAW THROE TRIAL ACHING
ANGUISH ANXIETY EMOTION
TORMENT TORTURE TRAVAIL
DISTRESS PAROXYSM
AGOUTI CAPA CAVY PACA ACUCHI
AGOUTY ACOUCHI ACOUCHY
AGRARIAN RURAL PASTORAL
PRAEDIAL
AGRAULOS (DAUGHTER OF —)
HERSE PANDROSOS
(FATHER OF —) ACTAEUS
(HUSBAND OF —) CECROPS
AGREE FAY FIT GEE HIT PAN YES
GIBE GREE JIBE JUMP MEET SIDE
SORT SUIT ADMIT ALLOW ATONE
BLEND CHECK CLICK CLOSE
FADGE GRANT HITCH JUTTY
LEVEL MATCH PIECE STAND
TALLY UNITE YIELD ACCEDE
ACCEPT ACCORD ADHERE ASSENT
ASSORT COMPLY CONCUR
CONDOG COTTON ENGAGE
REWARD SETTLE SQUARE SUBMIT
ARRANGE BARGAIN COMPORT
CONCEDE CONFORM CONGREE
CONGRUE CONSENT CONSIGN
DARESAY PACTION PROMISE
COINCIDE COMPOUND
CONTRACT COVENANT
QUADRATE
(— MUTUALLY) STIPULATE
(— TO) ACCEPT
(— TO JOIN) ADHERE
(— UPON) TAILYE TAILZEE TAILZIE
(— WITH) SIT LIKE SIDE TAIL
ANSWER
AGREEABLE AMEN EASY FAIR FINE
GOOD KIND LIEF NICE SOFT
WEME AMENE CANNY DULCE
GRATE JOLIE JOLLY LITHE LUSTY
QUEME READY SAPID SMIRK
SUANT SUAVE SUENT SWEET
COMELY COWDIE DAINTY DULCET
KINDLY LIKELY MELLOW SAVORY
SMOOTH SUITED ADAPTED
AMABLE AMIABLE COUTHIE
DOUCEUR TUNABLE WELCOME
WILLING WINSOME AMENABLE
CHARMING DELICATE GRATEFUL
LIKESOME LOVESOME OBLIGING
PLACABLE PLAUSIVE PLEASANT
PLEASING PURSUANT SOCIABLE
SUITABLE THANKFUL CONGENIAL
PALATABLE

(NOT —) ABHORRENT
(UNPLEASANTLY —) SACCHARINE
AGREEING CONNATE CONTENT
ACCORDANT ACCORDING
AGREEMENT GO FIT NOD AXIS
BOND DEAL FINE LINE MISE PACT
TACK TAIL TRUE ATONE COVIN
LEASE MATCH TERMS TOUCH
TRUTH TRYST UNITY ACCORD
ACTION ASSENT CARTEL CAUTIO
COMART COMITY COVINE DICKER
LEAGUE PACTUM PLEDGE TREATY
UNISON ANALOGY BARGAIN
CLOSING CLOSURE COMPACT
CONCERT CONSENT CONSORT
CONSULT ENTENTE HARMONY
ONENESS PACTION RAPPORT
CONTRACT DIAPASON SANCTION
SORTANCE SYMPATHY
ACCEPTANCE ACCORDANCE
(— TO JOIN) ADHESION
(GRAMMATICAL —) ATTRACTION
(SECRET —) CAHOOT CAHOOTS
COLLUSION
AGRICANE (SLAYER OF —)
ORLANDO
AGRICULTURAL ARABLE
GEOPONIC GEOPONICAL
AGRICULTURE FARMING GAINAGE
TILLAGE AGRONOMY
(— SYSTEM) KOLKHOZ
(PREF.) AGRO
AGRICULTURIST THO FARMER
GROWER SANTAL PLANTER
RANCHER
AMERICAN REID MORTON RUFFIN
TAYLOR THOMAS WATSON
BORLAUG
CANADIAN MACKAY SAUNDERS
ENGLISH TULL YOUNG
GERMAN NAUMANN
SWISS SAUSSURE
AGRIMONY CLIVE BONESET
BORWORT HEMPWEED
AGRITO AGARITA MAHONIA
ALGERITO ASHBERRY
AGRIUS (BROTHER OF —) LATINUS
TELEGONUS
(FATHER OF —) ULYSSES
ODYSSEUS PORTHAON
(MOTHER OF —) GAEA CIRCE
EURYTE
(SON OF —) THERSITES
AGRONOMIST (ALSO SEE
AGRICULTURIST)
AGROUND SEWED ASHORE
BEACHED STRANDED
AGRYPHA LOGION
AGRYPNIA INSOMNIA
SLEEPLESSNESS
AGUACATE AHUACA AVOCADO
AGUAMAS PINGUIN
AGUE CHILL EXIES FEVER MALARIA
QUARTAN SHAKING SHIVERS
AGUE TREE SASSAFRAS
AGUEWEED BONESET
AGUR (FATHER OF —) JAKEH
AH AY ACH
AHAB (FATHER OF —) OMRI
(NEIGHBOR OF —) NABOTH
(WIFE OF —) JEZEBEL
AHAR AGEE AJEE

AHARAH (FATHER OF —) BENJAMIN
AHARTALAV YARROW MILFOIL
AHASBAI (SON OF —) ELIPHELET
AHAZ (FATHER OF —) MICAH
JOTHAM
AHAZIAH (FATHER OF —) AHAB
JEHORAM
(MOTHER OF —) JEZEBEL
ATHALIAH
AHBAN (FATHER OF —) ABISUR
(MOTHER OF —) ABIHAIL
AHEAD ON UP ALEE FORE AFORE
ALONG DORMY BEFORE DORMIE
ONWARD ALREADY ENDWAYS
ENDWISE FORWARD LEADING
ADELANTE ADVANCED ANTERIOR
(— OF TIME) FAST
(STRAIGHT —) FORERIGHT
AHEM HUM
AHIAH (FATHER OF —) AHITUB
JERAHMEEL
(SON OF —) BAASHA
AHIAM (FATHER OF —) SHARAR
AHIEZER (FATHER OF —)
AMMISHADDAI
AHIHUD (FATHER OF —) SHELOMI
AHIKAM (FATHER OF —) SHAPHAN
(SON OF —) GEDALIAH
AHILUD (SON OF —) BAANA
JEHOSHAPHAT
AHIMAAZ (DAUGHTER OF —)
AHINOAM
(FATHER OF —) ZADOK
AHIMELECH (FATHER OF —) AHITUB
AHINADAB (FATHER OF —) IDDO
AHINOAM (FATHER OF —) AHIMAAZ
(HUSBAND OF —) SAUL DAVID
(SON OF —) AMNON
AHIO (FATHER OF —) BERIAH JEHIEL
ABINADAB
AHIRAM (FATHER OF —) BENJAMIN
AHISAMACH (SON OF —) AHOLIAB
AHISHAHAR (FATHER OF —) BILHAN
AHITUB (FATHER OF —) AMARIAH
PHINEHAS
(SON OF —) ZADOK AHIJAH
AHIMELECH
AHLAI (FATHER OF —) SHESHAN
(HUSBAND OF —) JARHA
(SON OF —) ZABAD
AHOAH (FATHER OF —) BENJAMIN
AHOLIBAMAH (FATHER OF —)
ANAH
(HUSBAND OF —) ESAU
AHOY AVAST
AHUEHUETE CEDAR SABINO
CYPRESS
AHURA MAZDA ORMAZD
AHUZAM (FATHER OF —) ASHUR
(MOTHER OF —) NAARAH
AH WILDERNESS (AUTHOR OF —)
ONEILL
(CHARACTER IN —) BELLE DAVID
MILLER MURIEL RICHARD
MCCOMBER
AIAH (BROTHER OF —) ANAH
(DAUGHTER OF —) RIZPAH
(FATHER OF —) ZIBEON
AID KEY ABET BACK BEET HAND
HELP PONY REDE ALLAY BOOST
COACH FAVOR GRANT SERVE
SPEED TREAT ASSIST CRUTCH
FAVOUR FRIEND PROFIT RELIEF

REMEDY RESCUE SECOND
SUCCOR SUPPLY UPHOLD
ADVANCE AIDANCE ANCILLA
BACKING BENEFIT COMFORT
ENDORSE FORWARD FURTHER
INDORSE RELIEVE SECOURS
SERVICE SUBSIDY SUPPORT
ADJUVATE AUXILIUM BEFRIEND
SUFFRAGE
(— A VESSEL) HOVEL
(— SECRETLY) SUBAID
(COMPLEXION —) FUCUS
(MORMON —) COUNSELOR
COUNSELLOR
AIDA (CHARACTER IN —) AIDA
AMNERIS RADAMES AMONASRO
(COMPOSER OF —) VERDI
AIDAN (FATHER OF —) GABRAN
AIDE AID BEAGLE DEPUTY SECOND
OFFICER ORDERLY ADJUTANT
GALLOPER PARAPROFESSIONAL
(BULLFIGHTER'S —) CAPEADOR
AIGRETTE EGRET HERON PLUME
SPRAY AIGRET FEATHERS
AIL ILE AILD EILE EYLE FAIL PAIN
PINE AFFECT BOTHER FALTER
SUFFER AFFLICT DECLINE
TROUBLE COMPLAIN DISTRESS
AILANTHUS SUMAC SUMACH
AILING SICK CRAZY CRONK DONCY
DONSY SOBER DONSIE SICKLY
UNWELL CRAICHY CREACHY
AILMENT AIL ILL PIP COUGH
MALADY DISEASE ILLNESS
DISORDER SICKNESS WEAKNESS
(SUDDEN —) WAFF
AIM END LAY TRY BEAD BEAM
BEND BENT BUTT FINE GLEE
GOAL HEAD HOLD LEAD MARK
MINT PLAN SAKE SEEK TEMP
VIEW VIZY WINK ACIES BLANK
DRIVE ESSAY ETTLE GUESS LEVEL
POINT PRICK SCOPE SIGHT TRAIN
VISIE VIZZY ASPIRE DESIGN
DIRECT ESTEEM INTEND INTENT
OBJECT SCHEME STRIVE ADDRESS
ATTEMPT CHIMERA MEANING
PRETEND PURPOSE RESPECT
STAGGER CHIMAERA CONSIDER
ENDEAVOR ESTIMATE
PRETENSE STEERING
TENTAMEN
(— A KICK) FLING
(— AT) EYE AFFECT
(— FURTIVELY) STEAL
(— INDIRECTLY) GLANCE
AIMED FAST
(— AT) AFFECTED
AIMING LEVEL GUNLAYING
AIMLESS IDLE BLIND CHANCE
RANDOM DRIFTING
AIMLESSNESS FLANERIE
AIR AER PEW SKY AERE ARIA AURA
AYRE BROW DIRT FEEL LILT LOFT
MIEN PORT POSE SONG TELL
TUNE VENT WIND ETHER FRILL
OZONE UTTER VOICE AERATE
AETHER ALLURE ASPECT BROACH
CACHET MANNER MELODY
OSTENT PIAFFE REGARD REGION
STRAIN VANITY WELKIN WITHER
BEARING DISPLAY EXHIBIT
EXPRESS FANFARE MALARIA

NEPHELE PIAFFER ATTITUDE
BEHAVIOR CARRIAGE PRESENCE
(— COOLED) WATERLESS
(— EXHALED) BLAST
(— IN MOTION) BREATH
(— PLANT) LIFELEAF
(BOASTFUL —) PARADO
(CONFIDENT —) BRAVURA
(COOL —) FRESCO
(COQUETTISH —) MINAUDERIE
(FETID —) REEK
(FOUL —) DIRT
(HAUGHTY —S) AI TITUDES
(MUSICAL —) ARIA SOLO TUNE
BRAWL MELODY ARIETTA
ARIETTE BRAVURA CANZONE
MUSETTE CAVATINE
(POMPOUS —) SWELL
(PUT ON —S) PROSS
(STALE —) STEAM
(STIFLING —) SMORE
(THE —) GATE
(WARM —) OAM
(PL.) LUGS FRONT
(PREF.) AER(O) ATM(O) PNEO
PNEUM(A)(ATA)(O)(ON)(ONO)
PNEUSTA

AIRCRAFT KITE ABORT BLIMP
CRAFT FLYER PLANE GLIDER
AEROBUS AERONEF AIRSHIP
BALLOON AEROBOAT AERODYNE
AEROSTAT AIRLINER AIRPLANE
AUTOGIRO AUTOGYRO GYRODYNE
ROTORCRAFT ORNITHOPTER
(UNIDENTIFIED —) UFO BOGY
BOGEY BOGIE
AIRCRAFTSMAN ERK
AIRCREWMAN KICKER AIREDALE
AIRFIELD AERODROME SATELLITE
AIRFOIL FIN FLAP SLAT BLADE
SURFACE AEROFOIL ELEVATOR
AIRILY JAUNTILY
AIRLESS STUFFY STIFLING
AIRLINE FEEDER SKYWAY
NONSKED
AIRMAN ACE FLIER FLYER
BIRDMAN WARBIRD AERONAUT
WASTEMAN
AIRPLANE BUS CUB JET MIG SST
BAKA GYRO KILL KITE SHIP ZERO
AVION CAMEL CRATE FLIER FLYER
FRITZ GOTHA HEINE JENNY LINER
PLANE SCOUT SNOOP BOMBER
CANARD CHASER COPTER FERRET
FESSEL FOKKER GLIDER JENNIE
PUSHER SMOKER TANDEM
VESSEL VIMANA AERONEF
AVIATIK AVIETTE BIPLANE
CLIPPER FIGHTER FLIVVER
FLYAWAY HOTSHOT PENGUIN
SNOOPER SPOTTER TRACTOR
WARBIRD AEROSTAT ALBATROS
KAMIKAZE SEAPLANE SKYCOACH
SKYCRAFT SOCIABLE STRUTTER
TRIPLANE TURBOJET WARPLANE
AEROPLANE MONOPLANE
(PART OF —) FIN POD TAB FLAP
WING BLADE CABIN PYLON
RADAR ENGINE RUDDER AILERON
COCKPIT COWLING SPOILER
ELEVATOR REVERSER STABILIZER
SUPPRESSOR

(REMOTE-CONTROLLED —) DRONE
(TYPE OF —) TRIJET
AIR PLANT LIFELEAF LIVELEAF
AIRPORT DROME AIRPARK
JETPORT SCUTTLE AIRDROME
AIRFIELD
AIRSHIP (SEE ALSO AIRPLANE AND
AIRCRAFT) SHIP BLIMP GASBAG
AERONAT AEROSTAT PARSEVAL
ZEPPELIN
AIRSTREAM PEW DOWNWASH
AIRSTRIP LILY
AIRTIGHT SEALED AIRPROOF
HERMETIC
AIRWAY MONKEY RETURN
SKYWAY AIRWAVE WINDWAY
WINDROAD
AIRY GAY COOL RARE THIN EMPTY
HUFFY LIGHT MERRY WINDY
AERIAL BLITHE BREEZY FLUFFY
JAUNTY JOCUND LIVELY STARRY
AIRLIKE AIRSOME HAUGHTY
JOCULAR SFOGATO AFFECTED
ANIMATED DEBONAIR DELICATE
ETHEREAL FLIPPANT GRACEFUL
SPARKISH TRIFLING VOLATILE
AISLE WAY YLE AILE LANE NAVE
WALK ALLEE ALLEY FEEDWAY
GANGWAY PASSAGE CORRIDOR
AIT OAT EYOT HOLM ILOT ISLE
EIGHT ISLET ISLOT
AITCHBONE ICEBONE EDGEBONE
AJA (FATHER OF —) RAGHU DILIPA
AJAR OPEN DISCORDANT
AJAX AIAS
(FATHER OF —) OILEUS TELAMON
(MOTHER OF —) ERIBOEA
PERIBOEA
AJIGARTA (SON OF —) SUNAHSEPA
AJONJOLI SESAME
AJOWAN AJAVA AIWAIN
AKALI SHAHIDI
AKAN (FATHER OF —) EZER
AKEAKE AKE HOPBUSH
IRONWOOD
AKHA KAW
AKIMBO ANGLED AKEMBOLL
AKENBOLD
AKIN SIB LIKE NEAR NIGH ALIKE
CLOSE AGNATE ALLIED COUSIN
SIBBED TENDER COGNATE
CONNATE GERMANE RELATED
SIMILAR
(— ON MALE SIDE) AGNATIC
(NOT —) UNSIB
AKKUB (FATHER OF —) ELIOENAI
AKRA ACCRA INKRA
AKU VICTORFISH
AL AAL AWL MULBERRY
ALA AXIL DRUM WING AXILLA
RECESS NOSEWING

LAKE: MARTIN
MOUNTAIN: CHEAHA LOOKOUT
RACCOON
NATIVE: LIZARD
RIVER: PEA COOSA CAHABA
MOBILE SIPSEY TENSAW
CONECUH PERDIDO SEPULGA
WARRIOR TOMBIGBEE
TALLAPOOSA
STATE BIRD: YELLOWHAMMER
STATE FISH: TARPON
STATE FLOWER: CAMELLIA
STATE TREE: PINE LONGLEAF
TOWN: OPP PIPER SELMA ATHENS
CORONA HEFLIN JASPER
LANETT LINDEN MARION
MOBILE SAMSON BREWTON
FLORALA GADSDEN ANNISTON
SYLACAUGA TUSCALOOSA

ALABASTER GYPSUM TECALI
ONYCHITE
ALACK ALAS ALAKE
ALACRITY HASTE SPEED CELERITY
RAPIDITY
ALAMEDA MALL WALK
ALAMETH (FATHER OF —) BECHER
ALAN ALAND ALANT ALAUNT
ALANG-ALANG COGON KOGON
ALANS GHUZ OGHUZ
ALANTIN INULIN
ALAR PTERIC WINGED AXILLARY
WINGLIKE
ALARBUS (MOTHER OF —) TAMORA
ALARDO (BROTHER OF —)
BRADAMANT
ALARM COW DIN BELL FEAR FRAY
GAST LARM ALERT BROIL CLOCK
DAUNT FEEZE LARUM NOISE
PANIC ROUSE SCARE SIREN
START STILL UPSET AFFRAY
ALARUM APPALL AROUSE
ATTACK BUZZER DISMAY EXCITE
FRIGHT OUTCRY SIGNAL TERROR
TOCSIN DISTURB GLOPPEN
GLOPPEN MOUNTEE STARTLE
TERRIFY TORPEDO WARNING
AFFRIGHT DISQUIET FRIGHTEN
SURPRISE CONSTERNATION
(FIRE —) STILL FIREBOX
ALARMED SCARY SCAREY
FEARFUL GASTFUL AFFRAYED
GHASTFUL SCAREFUL STREAKED
ALARMER HUER
ALARMING SCARY SCAREY
FEARFUL SCAREFUL
ALAS AY ACH HEU LAS OCH VAE
WOE EHEU HECH OIME WALY
ALACK HALAS HELAS OIMEE
HARROW OCHONE OTOTOI
WAESUCK ULLAGONE WAESUCKS
WELLADAY WELLAWAY

ALABAMA
CAPITAL: MONTGOMERY
COUNTY: LEE BIBB CLAY DALE
PIKE COOSA HENRY LAMAR
MACON PERRY BLOUNT BUTLER
COFFEE DALLAS ELMORE
ETOWAH GENEVA GREENE
MARION MONROE MORGAN
SHELBY SUMTER WILCOX
CHILTON

ALASKA
CAPITAL: JUNEAU
ISLAND: ADAK ATKA ATTU UMNAK
KODIAK UNIMAK AFOGNAK
DIOMEDE NUNIVAK
ISLAND GROUP: RAT ALEUTIAN
PRIBILOF ANDREANOF
LAKE: NAKNEK ILIAMNA
MOUNTAIN: BONA VETA
SPURR KATMAI PAVLOF

FORAKER MCKINLEY
MOUNTAIN RANGE: CRAZY BROOKS
KAIYUH CHUGACH
KILBUCK WRANGELL
NATIVE: ALEUT AHTENA ESKIMO
INGALIK KOYUKON TLINGIT
PENINSULA: KENAI SEWARD
RIVER: CHENA KOBUK YUKON
COPPER NOATAK TANANA
KOYUKUK SUSITNA CHULITNA
COLVILLE KUSKOKWIM
PORCUPINE
STATE BIRD: PTARMIGAN
STATE FLOWER: FORGETMENOT
STATE TREE: SPRUCE
TOWN: EEK NOME RUBY KENAI
SITKA BARROW JUNEAU
KODIAK NENANA SKAGWAY
KOTZEBUE ANCHORAGE
FAIRBANKS KETCHIKAN
VOLCANO: KUKAK SPURR GRIGGS
KATMAI MAGEIK MARTIN
PAVLOF DOUGLAS ILIAMNA
REDOUBT TORBERT TRIDENT
WRANGELL

ALASTRIM AMAAS
ALB ALBE AUBE CAMISIA CHRISOM
VESTMENT
ALBACORE TUNA TUNNY GERMAN
GERMON LONGFIN ALALONGA
ALALUNGA MACKEREL SCOMBRID

ALBANIA
ANCIENT PEOPLE: ILLYRIAN
CAPITAL: TIRANA TIRANE
COIN: LEK FRANC GUINTAR
KING: ZOG
LAKE: ULZE OHRID PRESPA
SCUTARI OHRIDSKO
MOUNTAIN: KORAB SHALA PINDUS
KORITNIK
REGION: EPIRUS
RIVER: MAT DRIN OSUM SEMAN
BOJANA ERZENI SEMENI VIJOSE
SHKUMBI
TOWN: LIN FIER KLOS LESH BERAT
CROIA DUKAT KORCE KRUJE
PECIN PEQIN QUKES RUBIC
SPASH VLONE VLORE AVLONA
BERATI BITSAN DARDHE
DURRES KORRCE PERMET
PRESHE TIRANA VALONA
ALESSIO DURAZZO KORITZA
SCUTARI SHKODER
TRIBE: GEG CHAM GHEG TOSK

ALBANIAN GEG GHEG GUEG
ARNAUT SKIPETAR
ALBATROSS GONY GOON GONEY
GOONY NELLY FABRIC GOONEY
GOONIE QUAKER SEABIRD
ALCATRAS BLUEBIRD
STINKPOT
ALBEIT ALL ALBE ALBEE ALLBE
THOUGH HOWBEIT
ALBERIC (WIFE OF —) MAROZIA
ALBERTA (CAPITAL OF —)
EDMONTON
(LAKE OF —) BANFF JASPER
WATERTON
(RIVER OF —) BOW OLDMAN
WAPITI ATHABASCA

(TOWN OF —) CALGARY REDDEER LETHBRIDGE MEDICINEHAT
ALBIGENSIANS CATHARI
ALBINISM ALPHOSIS
ALBINO LEUCAETHIOP
ALBITE PERICLINE
ALBIZZIA SIRIS
ALBOIN (FATHER OF —) ALDUIN
(SLAYER OF —) HELMICHIS
(WIFE OF —) ROSAMUNDA
ALBUM ALBE BOOK RECORD VOLUME REGISTER
ALBUMEN WHITE
ALBUMIN ALBUMEN PHASELIN SYNTONIN
ALBUMINOID ELASTIN FIBROIN KERATIN PROTEIN SERICIN COLLAGEN GORGONIN
ALBURNUM SAP BLEA SPLINT SAPWOOD
ALBUS BLANCO
ALCAEUS (DAUGHTER OF —) ANAXO
(FATHER OF —) PERSEUS ANDROGEUS
(MOTHER OF —) ANDROMEDA
(SON OF —) AMPHITRYON
ALCAIDE CADE CAID QAID JUDGE ALCADE
ALCATHOUS (FATHER OF —) PELOPS
(MOTHER OF —) HIPPODAMIA
(SLAYER OF —) OENOMAUS IDOMENEUS
(WIFE OF —) EUACHME
ALCESTIS (AUTHOR OF —) EURIPIDES
(CHARACTER IN —) APOLLO ADMETUS ALCESTIS HERCULES THANATOS
(FATHER OF —) PELIAS
(HUSBAND OF —) ADMETUS
ALCHEMIST ADEPT ARTIST CHEMIC CHEMICK CHEMIST HERMETIC
(AUTHOR OF —) JONSON
(CHARACTER IN —) DOL ABEL FACE SURLY COMMON DAPPER MAMMON PLIANT SUBTLE ANANIAS DRUGGER EPICURE KASTRIL LOVEWIT WHOLESOME TRIBULATION
ALCHEMY ART MAGIC ALCUMY CHYMIA SPAGYRIC
(GOD OF —) HERMES
ALCHFRITH (FATHER OF —) OSWIU
(MOTHER OF —) EANFLAED
(WIFE OF —) CYNEBURH
ALCHORNEA DOVEWOOD
ALCIBIADES (FATHER OF —) CLINIAS
(MOTHER OF —) DINOMACHE
ALCIMEDE (FATHER OF —) PHYLACUS
(HUSBAND OF —) AESON
(MOTHER OF —) CLYMENE
(SON OF —) JASON
ALCIMEDES (BROTHER OF —) ARGUS MEDEUS PHERES MERMERUS TISANDER THESSALUS
(FATHER OF —) JASON
(MOTHER OF —) MEDEA

ALCINA (SISTER OF —) MORGANA LOGISTILLA
(VICTIM OF —) RUGGIERO
ALCINOUS (DAUGHTER OF —) NAUSICAA
(FATHER OF —) NAUSITHOUS
(MOTHER OF —) PERIBOEA
(WIFE OF —) ARETE
ALCIPPE (DAUGHTER OF —) MARPESSA
(HUSBAND OF —) EVENUS METION
(SON OF —) DAEDALUS
ALCIS (FATHER OF —) ANTIPOENUS
(SISTER OF —) ANDROCLEA
ALCITHOE (FATHER OF —) MINYAS
(SISTER OF —) ARSIPPE LEUCIPPE
ALCMAEON (FATHER OF —) AMPHIARAUS
(MOTHER OF —) ERIPHYLE
(WIFE OF —) CALLIRRHOE ALPHESIBOEA
ALCMENE (FATHER OF —) ELECTRYON
(HUSBAND OF —) AMPHITRYON
(SON OF —) HERCULES IPHICLES
ALCOHOL ALKY ETHAL ETHYL IDITE LEDOL NEROL VINYL AMYROL ANDROL CEDROL ELEMOL GLYCOL GUAIOL HYDROL IDITOL LUPEOL LUTEIN METHYL PHYTOL SPIRIT STERIN STERNO STEROL TALITE ACRITOL ADONITE ALDITOL ALKANOL ANISOIN BORNEOL BUTANOL CAROTOL DECANOL ETHANOL FENCHOL HEPTITE HEXITOL INOSITE MANNITE MENTHOL PULEGOL QUINITE SCOPINE SORBITE STETHAL STYRONE TAGETOL TALITOL TROPINE XYLITOL CATECHOL LINALOOL MANNITOL METHANOL GLYCERINE PYRIDOXINE
(ETHYL —) METHS
ALCOHOLATE SPIRIT ESSENCE
ALCOHOLIC ALKY
(NOT —) SOFT
ALCOHOLOMETER GENOMETER VINOMETER
ALCOVE BAY NOOK BOWER NICHE ORIEL STALL CARREL RECESS CARRELL CUBICLE DINETTE RETREAT SERVERY ALHACENA SNUGGERY TABLINUM
ALCYONE (BROTHER OF —) EURYSTHEUS
(FATHER OF —) ATLAS AEOLUS
(HUSBAND OF —) CEYX
(MOTHER OF —) ENARETE PLEIONE
(SON OF —) ANTHAS HYRIEUS
ALDABELLA (BROTHER OF —) OLIVIERO BRANDIMARTE
(FATHER OF —) MONODANTES
(HUSBAND OF —) ORLANDO
ALDEHYDE ALDOL CITRAL ALKANAL CHLORAL COGENER DECANAL GLYOXAL HEXANAL RETINAL ACROLEIN CONGENER FURFURAL PIPERONAL PYRIDOXINE
ALDER ARN OLER ALNUS ELDER OWLER SAGEROSE

(PREF.) ALNI
ALDERMAN BAILIE SENIOR HEADMAN
ALDFRITH (BROTHER OF —) ECGFRITH
(FATHER OF —) OSWIU
ALE MUM NOG BASS BEER BOCK BREW FLIP MILD NOGG PURL SCUD YELL AUDIT CLINK DARBY JOUGH LAGER NAPPY STOUT ALEGAR PORTER STINGO SWANKY BITTERS MOROCCO OCTOBER PHARAOH HUGMATEE
(— BREWED WITH BRACKISH WATER) TIPPER
(— MIXED WITH SWEETENER) BRAGGET
(INFERIOR —) SWANKY SWANKEY
(NEW —) SWATS
(SOUR —) ALEGAR
(SPICED —) SWIG
(STRONG —) MUM HUFF BURTON STINGO HUFFCAP
(WEAK —) TWOPENNY
ALEATORY HAZARDOUS
ALEBION (BROTHER OF —) BERGION DERCYNUS
(FATHER OF —) NEPTUNE POSEIDON
(SLAYER OF —) HERCULES
ALECOST COSTMARY
ALECTRYON TITOKI
ALEE AHEAD LEEWARD
ALEHOUSE PUB TAVERN BARROOM MUGHOUSE POTHOUSE
ALEKO (CHARACTER IN —) ALEKO ARENSKY ZEMFIRA
(COMPOSER OF —) RACHMANINOFF
ALEMBIC LIMBEC LIMBECK CUCURBIT
(PART OF —) HEAD LAMP CUCURBIT RECEIVER
ALERT APT GAY HEP HIP YAL YEP FOXY GLEG KEEN LIVE PERT SNAP TRIG WAKE WARN WARY YALD YEPE ACUTE AGILE ALARM ALIVE AWAKE AWARE BREME BRISK EAGER ERECT LEERY MERRY NIPPY PEART PEERT QUICK READY SHACK SHARP SIREN SLICK SWIFT TIGHT WAKER YAULD ACTIVE ALARUM ARRECT BRIGHT DAPPER LIVELY NIMBLE PROMPT SLIPPY SPRACK SUDDEN TIPTOE TOCSIN WACKER CAREFUL KNOWING WAKEFUL WORKING PREPARED THOUGHTY VIGILANT WAKERIFE WATCHFUL
ALERTNESS NOUS SNAP APTNESS APTITUDE
(MENTAL —) WIT
ALETES (FATHER OF —) HIPPOTES AEGISTHUS
(MOTHER OF —) CLYTEMNESTRA
(SLAYER OF —) ORESTES
ALETTE WING ABUTMENT
ALEUT ATKA ORARIAN UNALASKA
ALEUTIANS (ISLANDS AND ISLAND GROUPS OF —) FOX RAT ADAK ATKA ATTU NEAR KISKA UMNAK KODIAK
(TOWN OF —) UNALASKA

(VOLCANO ON —) SHISHALDIN
ALEWIFE BANG ALLICE ALOOFE BUCKIE ALEWHAP HERRING OLDWIFE POMPANO WALLEYE GRAYBACK GREYBACK SAWBELLY SKIPJACK
ALEXANDER ALEX PARIS SAWNY ELLICK SAWNEY SAWNIE ISKANDER
(BIRTHPLACE OF —) PELLA
(FATHER OF —) SIMON
(HORSE OF —) BUCEPHALUS
ALEXIARES (FATHER OF —) HERCULES
(MOTHER OF —) HEBE
ALFA HALFA ESPARTO
ALFALFA HAY MEDIC FODDER LEGUME LUCERN LUCERNE
ALFILARIA ERODIUM FILAREE FILARIA PINWEED PINGRASS
ALFORJA BAG POUCH WALLET ALFARGA ALFORGE
ALGA NORI ALGAL BROWN FUCUS JELLY SLAKE SLOAK SLOKE DESMID DIATOM FUNORI NOSTOC AMANORI GULAMAN HAITSAI OARWEED SEAWEED ANABAENA FERNLEAF GELIDIUM HAIRWEED ROCKWEED SEABEARD SILKWEED SPOROGEN WHIPCORD ZOOGLOEA
ALGAE (PREF.) PHYC(O)
(SUFF.) PHYCEAE
ALGARROBA CAROB CALDEN
ALGEBRA LOGISTIC
ALGEBRAIC COSSIC
ALGENIB MIRFAK

DJELFA DZIOUA FRENDA
GUELMA SKIKDA BOGHARI
MASCARA MILIANA NEGRINE
NEMOURS OUARGLA TEBESSA
TLEMCEN
WEIGHT: ROTL

ALGERINE COOLOOLY KOOLOOLY
ALGID COLD COOL CHILLY CLAMMY
ALGOLOGY VERATRIN PHYCOLOGY
ALGONKIAN CREE EOZOIC
(— **ROCKS**) UNKAR
ALIAS ELSE OTHER AYLESS
ASSUMED EPITHET
ALIBI PLEA EXCUSE APOLOGY
PRETEXT
ALIDADE INDEX DIOPTER
ALIEN GER DEED FREMD METIC
ALAUNT ALLTUD AUBAIN CONVEY
EXOTIC INMATE REMOTE
ADVERSE DENIZEN FOREIGN
FRAMMIT INVADER OUTLAND
STRANGE DETAINEE STRANGER
TRANSFER
ALIENATE PART WEAN ALIEN
AVERT ANNALY CONVEY DEMISE
DEVEST FREEZE FORFEIT
SUBVERT AMORTIZE DISUNITE
ESTRANGE MORTMAIN SEPARATE
STRANGER TRANSFER WITHDRAW
ALIENATION GIFT DISTASTE
DISUNION DISUNITY DIVISION
DONATION INSANITY
ALIENIST PSYCHOPATH
PSYCHIATRIST
ALIGHT DROP LAND LEND REST
STOP AVALE LATCH LIGHT LODGE
PERCH ROOST STOOP SWOOP
ARRIVE SETTLE BURNING
DESCEND
ALIGN LINE TRAM TRUE ALINE
ARRAY DRESS RANGE ADJUST
ARRANGE MARSHAL
(— **PAPER**) JOG
ALIGNED FAIR COLORED
COLLINEAR
ALIGNMENT KELTER KILTER
GROUPING ORIENTATION
ALII ARIKI
ALIKE AKIN BOTH LIKE SAME
EQUAL INLIKE SQUARE YLICHE
EQUALLY SIMILAR UNIFORM
(PREF.) HOM(O) ISO
ALIMENT PAP FOOD FUEL BROMA
MANNA VIANDS ALIMONY
PABULUM RATIONS
ALIMONY ALIMENT
ALINDA (**FATHER OF** —) ALPHONSO
ALIPHATIC FATTY ACYCLIC
ALIVE VIF BUSY KEEN SPRY VIVE
AGILE ALERT ALIFE ASTIR AWARE
BEING BRISK FRESH GREEN QUICK
VITAL AROUND EXTANT LIVING
SLIPPY ANIMATE VIBRANT
ANIMATED EXISTENT SENSIBLE
SWARMING
(PREF.) VIVI
ALKALI LYE REH BASE BRAK KALI
SALT SODA USAR BRACK CAUSTIC
(PREF.) KALI
ALKALOID BASE ERGOT ESERE
ARICIN BRUCIN CEVINE CODEIN
CONINE CURINE ESERIN QUINIA

QUININ ACONINE ARABINE
ARICINE ATROPIA BOGAINE
BOLDINE BRUCINE CAFFEIN
COCAINE CODEINE CONIINE
EMETINE HARMINE HYGRINE
JERVINE KAIRINE NARCEIN
NEOPINE OUABAIN PTOMAIN
QUININE SCOPINE SINAPIN
SOLANIN SOPHORA VIOLINE
CURARINE CYTISINE PIPERINE
MESCALINE QUINIDINE
YOHIMBINE PAPAVERINE
PILOCARPINE
ALKANE PARAFFIN
ALKANET BUGLOSS PUCCOON
REDROOT
ALKANNIN ORCANET ANCHUSIN
ORCHANET
ALKENE OLEFIN
ALKYD GLYPTAL
ALL A AL ANY SUM EACH FULL
TOTE AUGHT EVERY GROSS
OMNES OUGHT QUITE TOTAL
TOTUM TUTTA TUTTO WHOLE
ENTIRE SOLELY WHOLLY PLENARY
ENTIRELY EVERYONE TOTALITY
(— **BUT ABSOLUTELY**) ALMOST
(— **IN**) ALTOGETHER
(— **TOGETHER**) COLLECTEDLY
(**AND** —) ANA
(**AT** —) AVA ANYWISE ANYTHING
ANYWHERE
(**OF** —) AVA
(PREF.) CUNCTI OMN(I) PAM PAN
PANT(A)(O) PASI
ALLANITE CERINE CERITE ORTHITE
ALLAY AID LAY CALM CITE COOL
EASE HELP HUSH STAY ABATE
AGATE ALLOY CHARM CHECK
DELAY QUELL QUIET SALVE SLAKE
STILL ADDUCE LESSEN PACIFY
QUENCH REDUCE SOFTEN
SOLACE SOOTHE STANCH
SUBDUE TEMPER APPEASE
ASSUAGE COMFORT COMPOSE
LIGHTEN MOLLIFY RELIEVE
REPRESS STAUNCH MITIGATE
PALLIATE
ALLAYED DEFERRED
ALLEGATION PLEA COUNT VOUCH
CHARGE ESSOIN AVERRAL
FICTION PROFERT SCANDAL
SURMISE AVERMENT SCIENTER
PRETENSION
ALLEGE LAY SAY AVER AVOW CITE
SHOW URGE ALLAY CLAIM FEIGN
INFER LEDGE OFFER PLEAD
QUOTE STATE SWEAR TRUMP
VOUCH ADDUCE AFFIRM ASSERT
ASSIGN CHARGE DEPOSE ESSOIN
OBTEND RECITE ADVANCE
ASCRIBE DECLARE LIGHTEN
PRESENT PROFESS PROPOSE
MAINTAIN
ALLEGED SUPPOSED SURMISED
ALLEGIANCE FOY TIE DUTY FAITH
HONOR FEALTY HOMAGE LYANCE
LOYALTY SERVAGE SERVICE
TRIBUTE CIVILITY DEVOTION
FIDELITY LIGEANCE
ALLEGORICAL PARABOLIC
SYMBOLICAL
ALLEGORICALLY SECRETLY

ALLEGORIZE TALMUDIZE
ALLEGORY MYTH TALE FABLE
STORY EMBLEM PARABLE
APOLOGUE METAPHOR
ALLELUIA AEVIA LAUDS
ALL-EMBRACING INFINITE
SWEEPING
ALLERGEN INHALANT
ALLERGY ATOPY IDIOBLAPSIS
ALLEVIATE AID BALM CALM CURE
EASE HELP ABATE ALLAY QUIET
ALIGHT ALLEGE LENIFY LESSEN
PACIFY SOFTEN SOLACE SOOTHE
SUCCOR SUPPLE TEMPER
ASSUAGE COMPOSE CONSOLE
CORRECT LENIATE LIGHTEN
MOLLIFY RELEASE RELIEVE
DIMINISH MITIGATE MODERATE
PALLIATE
ALLEVIATION ALAY SOLACE
ALLEY MIG ROW WAY CHAR LANE
LEAD MALL MEWS PASS PATH
VENT WALK WENT WIND WYND
AISLE ALLEE BLIND BYWAY
CHARE ENTRY TEWER WEENT
ALLEGE PEEWEE SMOOTH
TRANCE VENNEL PASSAGE
(**BLIND** —) LOKE STOP CLOSE
POCKET IMPASSE
ALL FOR LOVE (**AUTHOR OF** —)
DRYDEN
(**CHARACTER IN** —) ANTONY
OCTAVIA OCTAVIUS CLEOPATRA
DOLABELLA VENTIDIUS
ALLHALLOWTIDE HOLLANTIDE
ALLHEAL PANACEA VALERIAN
WOUNDWORT
ALLIANCE AXIS PACT UNION
ACCORD FUSION LEAGUE LYANCE
TREATY COMPACT ENTENTE
SOCIETY AFFINITY AGNATION
CACTALES COVENANT DREIBUND
FEDERACY FUNGALES LILIALES
TRIPLICE CONSOCIATION
(— **IN WAR**) SYMMACHY
ALLICE SHAD ALEWIFE POMPANO
ALLIED SIB AKIN AGNATE COUSIN
JOINED LINKED UNITED COGNATE
CONNATE FEDERAL GERMANE
KINDRED RELATED SIMILAR
RELATIVE
ALLIGATOR GATOR NIGER CAIMAN
CAYMAN CROTCH JACARE LIZARD
TRAVOY YACARE CRAWLER
CREEPER LAGARTO TRAVOIS
ALAGARTO LORICATE
(— **PEAR**) ZABACA AVOCADO
AGUACATE
(— **TURTLE**) LOGGERHEAD
(**MALE** —) BULL
ALLIGATORING WEBBING
ALL-INCLUSIVE GLOBAL
ALLITERATION RHYME LETTER
ALLITERATIVE LITERAL
ALLIUM LILY ONION GARLIC
ALLNESS OMNEITY OMNITUDE
ALLOCATE DEAL DOLE METE RATE
ALLOT AWARD SHARE AFFECT
ASSIGN OUTPLACE
ALLOCATION DRAW DESIGNATION
ALLODIAL UDAL
ALLOT FIX SET ARET BILL CAST
DEAL DOLE GIVE MARK METE

PART RATE SORT ALLOW ARETT
AWARD CAVEL GRANT SHARE
ACCORD AFFECT ASSIGN BESTOW
DEPUTE DESIGN DIRECT INTEND
ORDAIN RATION ACCOUNT
APPOINT DESTINE PRORATE
QUARTER SPECIFY TRIBUTE
ALLOCATE PROPORTION
(— **QUARTERS**) CANTON
ALLOTMENT CUT LOT DOLE CAVEL
SHARE RATION SIZING LOTMENT
LOTTERY PORTION DIVISION
PITTANCE
ALLOW LET LOW BEAR GIVE HAVE
LEND LOAN ADMIT DEFER GRANT
LEAVE STAND THOLE YIELD
ACCEPT ACCORD ASSIGN BESTOW
BETEEM ENABLE ENDURE PERMIT
SUFFER APPROVE CONCEDE
CONFESS LICENCE LICENSE
SUFFICE SUPPOSE SUSTAIN
CONSIDER DISPENSE SANCTION
TOLERATE
ALLOWABLE FREE LICIT LAWFUL
PERMISSIBLE
ALLOWANCE BOT FEE ICE AGIO
BOTE DOLE EASE EDGE GIFT HIRE
ODDS RATE SALT SIZE ARRAS
BATTA CLOFF GRANT LEAVE
RATIO SHARE STENT STINT
BOUCHE BOUNTY CORODY
FODDER MARGIN RATING REGAIN
SALARY SEQUEL TANTUM
ALIMENT ALIMONY CORRODY
DIETARY DIOBELY LEAKAGE
LOWANCE PENSION PORTION
PREBEND SCALAGE STIPEND
TEARAGE APPENAGE APPROVAL
BREAKAGE DISCOUNT DRAFTAGE
ORDINARY QUANTITY SANCTION
SOLATIUM VIATICUM
(— **FOR EXPENSES**) DIET
(— **FOR MAINTENANCE**) ALIMENT
(— **FOR THICKNESS**) BOXING
(— **FOR WASTE**) TRET
(— **FOR WEIGHT**) BUG TARE DRAFT
DRAUGHT
(— **OF ARROWS**) SHEAF
(— **OF FOOD**) DIET BOUCHE
DIETARY
(— **OF TIME OR DISTANCE**) LAW
(— **TO COMPETITOR**)
(**CLOTHING** —) INLAY
(**CORRECTIVE** —) SALT
(**EXTRA** —) BUCKSHEE
(**NEGATIVE** —) INTERFERENCE
ALLOWED VENIAL LICENTIATE
(**NOT** —) ILLICIT FORBIDDEN
ALLOWING THOUGH
ALLOY LAY LOY MIX AICH ASEM
ALPAX BIDRI BIDRY BRASS CALIN
DURAL FLINT INVAR MOKUM
MONEL TERNE ALBATA ALNICO
ALUMEL BIDREE BILLON BRONZE
CERMET GARBLE ILLIUM LATTEN
LEAVEN NEOGEN NIELLO OCCAMY
OREIDE OROIDE PEWTER SOLDER
TAMBAC TOMBAC TOMBAK
ACIERAL ALCHEMY AMALGAM
BABBITT BIDDERY ELINVAR
INCONEL MIXTURE PAKTONG
PERLITE RHEOTAN RHODITE

SEMILOR SIMILOR TAENITE
TUTANIA TUTENAG ALFENIDE
ARGENTON ARSEDINE AWARUITE
CALAMINE CARACOLI CARACOLY
DORALIUM ELECTRUM EUTECTIC
GUNMETAL HARDENER KAMACITE
METALINE NICHROME ORICHALC
ROMANIUM STELLITE PINCHBECK
PORPORINO
ALL-PERVADING UNIVERSAL
ALL QUIET ON WESTERN FRONT
(AUTHOR OF —) REMARQUE
(CHARACTER IN —) PAUL KROPP
ALBERT BAUMER MULLER
TJADENS KEMMERICH STANILAUS
KATCYINSKY
ALL RIGHT OK YES OKAY AGREED
OKEYDOKE
ALLSEED FLAXSEED BURSTWORT
ALL SOULS' DAY SOULMASS
ALLSPICE BUBBY PIMENTO
ALL'S WELL THAT ENDS WELL
(AUTHOR OF —) SHAKESPEARE
(CHARACTER IN —) DIANA LAFEU
HELENA BERTRAM LAVACHE
MARIANA PAROLLES VIOLENTA
ALLTHORN JUNCO
ALLUDE HINT IMPLY POINT REFER
ADVERT GLANCE RELATE
CONNOTE MENTION SUGGEST
INDICATE INTIMATE
ALLURE IT AIR COY WIN WOO BAIT
DRAW LEAD LURE MOVE SWAY
WILE ANGLE BRIBE CHARM
COURT DECOY SNARE TEMPT
ALLECT ENTICE ENTRAP ILLURE
INDUCE INVITE SEDUCE ATTRACT
BEGUILE ENSNARE BLANDISH
INESCATE INVEIGLE PERSUADE
SIRENING
ALLUREMENT BAIT CORD LURE
ALLURE GLAMOR GUDGEON
AGACERIE SOLICITATION
ALLURING GREEN TAKING
AGACANT SIRENIC SUGARED
TAKEFUL CATCHING CHARMING
ENTICING FETCHING TEMPTING
ALLUSION HINT TWIT TOUCH
GLANCE REFLEX INKLING
MENTION INNUENDO INSTANCE
REFERENCE
ALLUSIVE CANTING
ALLUVIUM WASH
ALLY PAL AIDE JOIN RANGE UNION
UNITE BACKER COXCOX FRIEND
HELPER LEAGUE ALLIANT
CONNECT PARTNER ADHERENT
CONFEDER FEDERATE
(PL.) FOEDERATI
ALMANAC ORDO PADDY
CALENDAR
ALMEMAR BEMA BIMA BIMAH
ALMIGHTY GOD GREAT CREATOR
EXTREME JEHOVAH INFINITE
POWERFUL PUISSANT
OMNIPOTENT
ALMOND DOE PILI BADAM CHUFA
JORDAN KAMANI KANARI
AMYGDAL BISCUIT TALISAY
ALMANDER ALMENDRO
AMYGDALA ROSACEAN VALENCIA
(— BROWN) WOOD

(— SHAPED OBJECT) MANDORLA
(PREF.) AMYGDAL(O) MANDEL(O)
ALMONRY AMBRY
ALMOST JUST LIKE MOST MUCH
NEAR NIGH ABOUT ANEAR CLOSE
AMAIST FECKLY MOSTLY NEARLY
NIGHLY MUCHWHAT WELLMOST
WELLNEAR PRACTICALLY
(PREF.) PARA PEN(E)
ALMS DOLE GIFT ALMOIN AUMOUS
AWMOUS BOUNTY CORBAN
MAUNDY RELIEF ALMOIGN
CHARITY HANDOUT PASSADE
DEVOTION DONATION GRATUITY
OFFERING PITTANCE
BENEFACTION
ALMSHOUSE POORHOUSE
WORKHOUSE
ALMSMAN BLUECOAT
ALMUCE HOOD AMICE VAGAS
TIPPET VAKASS VARKAS
ALODIUM ODAL ODEL ODHAL
ESTATE PROPERTY
ALOE PITA AGAVE
ALOEUS (FATHER OF —) NEPTUNE
POSEIDON
(MOTHER OF —) CANACE
(SON OF —) OTUS EPHIALTES
(WIFE OF —) IPHIMEDIA
ALOFT UP HIGH ABOVE AHIGH
UPWARD AHEIGHT SKYWARD
OVERHEAD
(PREF.) HYPS(I)(O)
ALONE ALL ONE BARE LANE LORN
ONLY SOLE SOLO ALOOF APART
SOLUS SIMPLY SINGLE SOLEIN
SOLELY SULLEN UNIQUE ALONELY
FORLORN UNAIDED DESOLATE
DETACHED ISOLATED SEPARATE
SOLITARY
(ALL —) LEELANE LEELONE
(PREF.) MANI MON(O) SOLI
(SUFF.) MONAS
ALONG ON UP VIA AWAY LANG
WITH YOND AHEAD LONGS
BESIDE FORBYE FOREBY ONWARD
ALONGST ENDLONG FORWARD
PARALLEL TOGETHER
(— THE MARGIN) DOWN
(— WITH) AND
(WELL —) ENDWAYS ENDWISE
(PREF.) (— WITH) SYM
ALONGSIDE AT BY ASIDE CLOSE
ABOARD BESIDE ABREAST
FORNENT SIDLINS FORNENST
PARALLEL
(PREF.) PAR(A)
ALOOF DRY ICY SHY COLD COOL
ABACK ALONE APART PROUD
ABEIGH FROSTY OTIOSE REMOTE
SILENT SKEIGH DISTANT
REMOVED RESERVED
ALOPECIA PELADE ATRICHIA
BALDNESS
ALOPECURUS FOXTAIL
ALOUD OUT
ALPACA PACO
ALPENGLOW AFTERGLOW
ALPENSTOCK STOCK BERGSTOCK
ALPHABET ABC ABCEE ABSEY
CUFIC KUFIC LATIN ONMUN
ORDER BISAYA BRAHMI CIPHER

GLAGOL HANGUL HANKUL KAITHI
NAGARI PRIMER ROMAJI SARADA
SCRIPT TAGALA VISAYA ALJAMIA
FUTHARK KALEKAH LETTERS
PESHITO ALJAMIAH CROSSROW
GUJARATI GURMUKHI
(— SQUARE) TABLEAU
(ARABIC —) BA FA HA RA TA YA
ZA AYN DAD DAL JIM KAF KHA
LAM MIM NUN QAF SAD SIN THA
WAW ZAY ALIF DHAL SHIN
GHAYN
(GREEK —) MU NU PI XI CHI ETA
PHI PSI RHO TAU BETA IOTA ZETA
ALPHA DELTA GAMMA KAPPA
OMEGA SIGMA THETA LAMBDA
EPSILON OMICRON UPSILON
(HEBREW —) HE PE MEM NUN SIN
TAW WAW AYIN BETH HETH
KAPH QOPH RESH SHIN TETH
YODH ALEPH GIMEL SADHE ZAYIN
DALETH LAMEDH SAMEKH
ALPHAEUS (SON OF —) JAMES
MATTHEW
ALPHESIBOEA (FATHER OF —) BIAS
PHEGEUS
(HUSBAND OF —) ALCMAEON
(SON OF —) ADONIS
ALPS (LAKE IN —) ZUG COMO ISEO
THUN GARDA BRIENZ GENEVA
ZURICH LUCERNE MAGGIORE
CONSTANCE
(PASS IN —) SPLUGA ARLBERG
BRENNER SIMPLON SPLUGEN
SEMPIONE
(PEAK IN —) ROSA VISO BLANC
LEONE TRIGLAV VOLJNAC
EISENHUT PARADISO HOCHSTUHL
MARMOLADA MONTBLANC
KELLERWAND SACCARELLO
(VALLEY IN —) ZERMATT
CHAMONIX ENGADINE
INTERLAKEN GRINDELWALD
LAUTERBRUNNEN
ALREADY EEN NOW DONE EVEN
SINCE BEFORE
ALSACE-LORRAINE REICHSLAND
ALSINE ALLBONE
ALSO SO ALS AND EKE TOO YET
ERST ITEM MORE PLUS ALONG
DITTO BESIDES FURTHER
THERETO LIKEWISE MOREOVER
(— KNOWN AS) AKA
ALTAMONT (WIFE OF —) CALISTA
ALTAR ARA BEMA BOMOS TABLE
WEVED ACERRA AUTERE HAIKAL
SHRINE TRIPOD VEDIKA CHANCEL
CHANTRY ESCHARA SCROBIS
THYMELE OMPHALOS REPOSOIR
REPOSITORY
(— BACK) TABLE
(— TOP) MENSA
ALTARPIECE ANCONA DIPTYCH
TRIPTYCH
ALTAZIMUTH ABA
ALTER COOK DRAW EDIT GELD
MOVE RASE TURN VARY VEER
WEND ADAPT AMEND BREAK
ELIDE EMEND FORGE RESET
SHAPE SHIFT ADJUST BUSHEL
CENSOR CHANGE DEFORM
IMMUTE JIGGER MODIFY MUTATE
NEUTER REVISE TEMPER UNSAME

CHAFFER COMMUTE CONVERT
CORRECT CORRUPT DISTORT
FASHION QUALIFY STRANGE
ACTIVATE EXCHANGE
(— APPEARANCE) WRY
(— BOUNDARIES) DEACON
(— BRANDS) DUFF
(— DIRECTION) BREAK
(— STANCE) CLOSE
ALTERATION DOWN CROSS
ACTION CHANGE JANGLE DISEASE
HEMIOLA MUTATION UPHEAVAL
(— OF BOUNDARY) ERUB ERUV
ALTERATIVE LAPPA FUMARIA
ALTERCATE JANGLE STICKLE
WRANGLE
ALTERCATION SPAT TIFF TILT
BRAWL BROIL CROSS FIGHT
BARNEY BICKER FRACAS JANGLE
STRIFE BRABBLE CONTEST
DISPUTE PASSAGE QUARREL
WRANGLE SQUABBLE
ALTERED BURNT BROKEN VARIED
ANOTHER FEIGNED ADJUSTED
(PREF.) EPH EPI
ALTERNATE ELSE SWAY VARY
OTHER RECUR SHIFT ALTERN
CHANGE RINGER ROTATE SECOND
SEESAW SPIRAL EXCHANGE
INTERMIT TRAVERSE
(— LEAPS AND DIVES) GREYHOUND
(PREF.) CO COUNTER
ALTERNATELY ABOUT
RECIPROCALLY
ALTERNATION ADDITION
(— OF GENERATIONS)
METAGENESIS
ALTERNATIVE OR FORK HORN
BACKUP CHOICE EITHER OPTION
DISJUNCT ELECTION
(PREF.) ALLELO
ALTERNATOR MAGNETO
ALTHAEA MALLOW
(FATHER OF —) THESTIUS
(HUSBAND OF —) OENEUS
(SON OF —) MELEAGER
ALTHAEMENES (FATHER OF —)
CATREUS
(SISTER OF —) AEROPE CLYMENE
APEMOSYNE
ALTHORN SAX ALTO ALTUS
SAXHORN
ALTHOUGH ALL EEN SET ALBE
ALIF EVEN THAT WHEN WHILE
ALBEIT THOUGH WHENAS
DESPITE HOWBEIT WHEREAS
ALTITUDE APEX PEAK HIGHT
LEVEL PITCH HEIGHT STATURE
ALTO MEAN ALTUS ALTHORN
SAXHORN
ALTOGETHER ALL NUDE QUITE
SHEER STICK AGREAT ALGATE
BODILY FREELY WHOLLY EXACTLY
TOTALLY UTTERLY ALLTHING
ENTIRELY
ALTRUISM OTHERISM
ALTRUISTIC HEROIC HEROICAL
ALUDEL POT LUDEL UDELL
ALULA LOBE WING ALULET
SQUAMA TEGULA LOBULUS
WINGLET CALYPTER
ALULIM ALOROS
ALUM AUM ALME ALUMEN MIGITE

TSCHER STYPTIC HARDENER KALINITE

(FEATHER —) ALUNOGEN

ALUMINA ARGIL ALOXITE

ALUMNUS GRAD PUPIL GRADUATE

ALUMROOT HEUCHERA

ALUR LUR LURI

ALVAN (FATHER OF —) SHOBAL

ALVEARY HIVE BEEHIVE

ALVEOLA FAVEOLUS

ALVEOLAR SPUMOID GINGIVAL

ALVEOLATE FAVOSE FAVOUS PITTED

ALWAYS O AY AYE EEN EER EVER SIMLE STILL ALWISE SEMPRE ALGATES FOREVER EVERMORE

ALYSSUM ALISON MADWORT

ALZIRA (CHARACTER IN —) ALZIRA GUSMAN ZAMORO

(COMPOSER OF —) VERDI

AM M AME HAM

(— NOT) NAM AINT AMNT

(I —) CHAM CHYM

AMA CUP AMULA CRUET DIVER VESSEL CHALICE

AMABILE GENTLE TENDER

AMACRATIC AMASTHENIC

AMADAVAT WAXBILL TIGERBIRD

AMADIS (COMPOSER OF —) LULLY

AMADOU PUNK TINDER

AMAH NURSE SERVANT

AMAHL AND THE NIGHT VISITORS (COMPOSER OF —) MENOTTI

AMAIN GREATLY FORCIBLY

AMAL (FATHER OF —) HELEM

AMALA AMLAH

AMALASONTHA (FATHER OF —) THEODORIC

AMALEK (FATHER OF —) ELIPHAZ

(MOTHER OF —) TIMNAH

AMALGAM ALLOY MAGNESIA ARQUERITE

AMALGAMATE MIX FUSE JOIN ALLOY BLEND MARRY MERGE UNITE BLUNGE MINGLE COMBINE COALESCE COMPOUND

AMALGAMATION MERGER ADDITION

AMALGAMATOR PLATEMAN

AMANORI NORI LAVER

AMANUENSIS PENMAN SCRIBE TYPIST RECORDER

AMARANTA (HUSBAND OF —) BARTOLUS

AMARANTH JATACO PIGWEED FLORAMOR

(PL.) LIGHTHOUSES

AMARIAH (FATHER OF —) BANI MERAIOTH

(SON OF —) AHITUB

AMARILLO FUSTIC

AMARYLLIS LILY AGAVE CRINUM SNOWFLAKE

AMASA (FATHER OF —) ITHRA HADLAI JETHER

(MOTHER OF —) ABIGAIL

AMASAI (SON OF —) MAHATH

AMASHAI (FATHER OF —) AZAREEL

AMASIAH (FATHER OF —) ZICHRI

AMASS HEAP HILL MASS PILE SAVE GROSS HOARD STACK STORE GATHER COLLECT

COMPILE CONGEST ENGROSS ASSEMBLE OVERHEAP ACCUMULATE

AMATA (DAUGHTER OF —) LAVINIA

(HUSBAND OF —) LATINUS

AMATEUR HAM TIRO TYRO NOVICE SUNDAY VOTARY ADMIRER DABBLER DEVOTEE FANCIER JACKLEG PATRIOT VARMENT VARMINT BEGINNER

AMATEURISH BUSH TYRONIC

AMATORY EROTIC LOVING TENDER AMOROUS GALLANT ANACREONTIC

AMAZE AWE MAZE STAM STUN ALARM FERLY ASTONY AWHAPE WONDER ASTOUND CONFUSE IMPRESS PERPLEX STAGGER STUPEFY ASTONISH BEWILDER CONFOUND DUMFOUND FRIGHTEN SURPRISE

AMAZED AGAZED BUSHED ASTONIED

AMAZEMENT STAM AMAZE FERLY GHAST FERLIE FRENZY WONDER MADNESS SURPRISE CONSTERNATION

AMAZIAH (FATHER OF —) JOASH

AMAZON VIRAGO

AMBARI KANAF KENAF KANAFF

AMBASSADOR AGENT ELCHI ENVOY VAKIL DEPUTY ELCHEE LEDGER LEGATE NUNCIO VAKEEL EMBASSY LEAGUER CAPUCIUS DIPLOMAT MINISTER

AMBASSADORIAL PETIAL

AMBASSADORS (AUTHOR OF —) JAMES

(CHARACTER IN —) JIM MAMIE MARIA SARAH JEANNE POCOCK GOSTREY LAMBERT NEWSOME CHADWICK STRETHER WAYMARSH

AMBER GRIS LIME AWMER RESIN FUSTIC LAMMER SUCCIN YELLOW BURMITE AMBEROID ELECTRUM SUNSTONE

(PREF.) ELECTRO SUCCIN(I)(O)

AMBERFISH JUREL CARANX KAHALA RUNNER CARANGID CARANGIN KINGFISH MACKEREL MEDREGAL

AMBERGRIS AMBER AMBRACAN

AMBERJACK ALMICORE CORONADO

AMBIENCE MILIEU AMBIANCE

AMBIGUITY AMBAGE PARADOX

AMBIGUOUS DARK VAGUE DOUBLE FORKED LOUCHE CRYPTIC DUBIOUS DOUBTFUL SLIPPERY SPURIOUS

(NOT —) EXPRESS

AMBIT LIMIT SCOPE SPACE BOUNDS EXTENT SPHERE CIRCUIT COMPASS BOUNDARY PRECINCT

AMBITION ATE GOAL HOPE WISH GLORY DESIRE PURPOSE PRETENSION

AMBITIONLESS DRIFTING

AMBITIOUS AVID BOLD HIGH KEEN EAGER ETTLE SHOWY EMULOUS ASPIRANT ASPIRING

AMBITUS TENOR

AMBIVALENCE BIPOLARITY

AMBIVALENT EQUIVOCAL

AMBLE FOOL GAIT MOOCH PADNAG MEANDER SAUNTER TRIPPLE

AMBLING TOLUTATION

AMBO DESK PULPIT

AMBOCEPTOR COPULA MEDIATOR

AMBOYNA LINGOA KIABOOCA

AMBROSIA AMRITA AMBROSE KINGWEED

AMBROSIAL DIVINE FRAGRANT

AMBRY SAFE CHEST NICHE AUMRIE CLOSET PANTRY RECESS ALMONRY ARMOIRE ARMARIUM CUPBOARD

AMBULANCE PANNIER AUXILIUM BRANCARD

AMBULATE GAD HIKE MOVE WALK

AMBULATORY ALURE GALLERY PORTICO CLOISTER PERAMBLE

AMBUSCADE WATCH WAYLAY BUSHMENT

AMBUSH NAB LURE LURK TRAP WAIT AWAIT BLIND BUSSE CATCH COVER LURCH SHOMA SNARE STALE TRAIN WATCH INBUSH THREAT WAYLAY FORELAY SCUPPER DISGUISE ENBUSSHE

(SUFF.) (ONE IN —) DOLOPS

AMCHOOR AMHAR

AMELIA (AUTHOR OF —) FIELDING

(CHARACTER IN —) BOOTH JAMES TRENT AMELIA HARRIS ATKINSON HARRISON MATTHEWS ELIZABETH

AMELIORATE EASE HELP MEND AMEND EMEND BETTER REFORM IMPROVE PROMOTE

AMEN YEA TRULY ASSENT SOBEIT VERILY APPROVAL SANCTION

AMENABLE OPEN LIABLE PLIANT SUBJECT OBEDIENT MALLEABLE

AMEND END BEET HEAL MEND ALTER ATONE BEETE EMEND REDUB BETTER CHANGE DOCTOR REFORM REMEDY REPAIR REPEAL REVISE CONVERT CORRECT ENLARGE IMPROVE RECOVER RECTIFY REDRESS RESTORE CHASTISE

AMENDING COMPENSATION

AMENDMENT RIDER AMENDS REFORM SLEEPER

AMENDS BOOT MEND ASSETH ASSYTH REWARD APOLOGY REDRESS

AMENITY JOY COMITY FEATURE SUAVITY CIVILITY COURTESY MILDNESS

(PL.) AGREMENS FROUFROU NICETIES

AMENT JUL CHAT IDIOT IULUS MORON CATKIN CACHRYS CATTAIL GOSLING IMBECILE NUCAMENT

AMERCE FINE MERCE MULCT TREAT AFFEER PUNISH SCONCE CONDEMN FORFEIT

AMERCEMENT MULCT UNLAW BLOODWIT

AMERICA INDIA

AMERICAN YANK GRINGO YANKEE YANQUI AMERICA WESTERN

JONATHAN COLUMBIAN

(— OF EUROPEAN STOCK) WASP

(AUTHOR OF —) JAMES

(CHARACTER IN —) BREAD CINTRE CLAIRE NEWMAN NIOCHE TRISTRAM VALENTIN BELLEGARDE CHRISTOPHER

AMERICAN GRAY JAKO

AMERICANISM HECKERISM

AMERICAN TRAGEDY (AUTHOR OF —) DREISER

(CHARACTER IN —) ALDEN CLYDE SAMUEL SONDRA ROBERTA FINCHLEY GRIFFITHS

AMESTRIS (FATHER OF —) OTANES ONOPHAS

(WIFE OF —) XERXES

AMETHYST ONEGITE CORUNDUM

AMIABILITY DOUCEUR

AMIABLE GOOD KIND WARM SWEET CLEVER GENIAL GENTLE LOVING MELLOW SMOOTH TENDER AFFABLE LOVABLE WINSOME CHARMING ENGAGING FRIENDLY OBLIGING PLEASING

AMICABLE KIND FRIENDLY NEIGHBORLY

AMICE AMIT AMYS CAPE COWL HOOD EPHOD ALMUCE DOMINO TIPPET VAKASS AMICTUS VESTMENT

AMID IN OMEL AMELL AMONG AMIDST DURING IMELLE AMONGST BETWEEN

AMIDAS (BROTHER OF —) BRACIDAS

AMIDE LACTAM SULTAM ANILIDE ARYLIDE PEPTIDE

AMILDAR AUMIL

AMINE ANILIN ANILINE

AMISS ILL MIS AWRY BIAS AGATE AGLEY ASKEW WONKY WRONG ACROSS AGRIEF ASTRAY FAULTY MISTAKE IMPROPER

(PREF.) MIS PAR(A)

AMITTAI (SON OF —) JONAH

AMITY PEACE ACCORD CONCORD HARMONY

AMMA ABBESS MOTHER

AMMIEL (DAUGHTER OF —) BATHSHEBA

(FATHER OF —) OBEDEDOM

(SON OF —) MACHIR

AMMIHUD (FATHER OF —) TALMAI PEDAHEL SHEMUEL ELISHAMA

AMMINADAB (FATHER OF —) RAM ARAM KOHATH UZZIEL

(SON OF —) NAASSON

AMMISHADDAI (SON OF —) AHIEZER

AMMIZABAD (FATHER OF —) BENAIAH

AMMONIA HARTSHORN

AMMONITE POLYPOD AMMONOID BACULITE CACULOID CERATITE SALIGRAM

AMMONIUM CARBONATE HARTSHORN

AMMUNITION AMMO AMMU ARMS SHOT BOMBS FODDER POWDER SHELLS BULLETS GRENADES MATERIAL MATERIEL ORDNANCE SHRAPNEL

AMNESIA LAPSE FORGETFULNESS

AMNESTY COWLE PARDON OBLIVION

AMNION SAC CAUL SEROSA INDUSIUM MEMBRANE

AMNON (FATHER OF —) DAVID (HALF-SISTER OF —) TAMAR

AMOBARBITAL AMYTAL

AMOEBA AMEBA AMEBULA PROTEUS AMOEBULA RHIZOPOD

AMOK MAD AMUCK CRAZY CRAZED VIOLENT FRENZIED

AMOLE EMOL AMOULI AMOLILLA MANFREDA

AMON (FATHER OF —) MANASSEH (SON OF —) JOSIAH

AMONG IN MID AMID INTO MANG MONG OMEL WITH AMANG AMELL MIDST AMIDST BIMONG IMELLE WITHIN BETWEEN (— OTHER THINGS) IA (PREF.) EPH EPI INTER

AMOR EROS LOVE CUPID AMOROSO

AMORAL NEUTRAL NONMORAL

AMORET (HUSBAND OF —) SCUDAMORE (SISTER OF —) BELPHOEBE

AMORITE CANAANITE

AMOROUS FOND GAMY SOFT WARM CADGY JOLLY MUSHY NUTTY ARDENT COQUET EROTIC LOVELY LOVING SPOONY TENDER WANTON AMATIVE AMATORY AMIABLE FERVENT GALLANT JEALOUS SMICKER LOVESOME VENEREAN

AMORPHOUS VAGUE ATELENE HYALINE DEFORMED FORMLESS RESINOUS

AMORT ALAMORT DEJECTED LIFELESS

AMORTIZE DESTROY MORTISE ALIENATE

AMOUNT GO GOB LOT SUM SUP TOT ANTE BODY COME DOSE DRAW FECK KIND LEVY MESS REAM RISE SOUD SOWD TALE UNIT WARE CHUNK COUNT GROSS MOUNT PRICE REACH STACK STORE STUFF TOTAL WHOLE BUDGET DEGREE DOSAGE EFFECT EXTENT FIGURE MATTER NUMBER SUPPLY ADVANCE FOOTING QUANTUM SCRUPLE SIGNIFY SLATHER TODDICK INCREASE QUANTITY SPOONFUL SURMOUNT VALLIDOM (— BORNE BY BEAST) SEAM (— CARRIED AT ONE TIME) GANG (— DUE) BILL SCORE (— HELD) CAPACITY (— OF BASS) BOOMINESS (— OF CONCRETE) LIFT (— OF DYE) STRIKE (— OF FLOW) STRENGTH (— OF FREIGHT) CARLOAD (— OF GAS) BREATH (— OF HERRINGS) CRANNAGE (— OF LEAKAGE) SLIP (— OF LIQUOR) SLUG (— OF MEDICINE) DOSAGE (— OF MONEY) BEAN BOND CASH SCOT

(— OF OIL) ALLOWABLE (— OF PAYMENT) FOOTAGE (— OF POWDER) INCREMENT (— OF SOIL) INTHROW (— OF WATER) CATCHMENT (— OF WORK) ASSIGNMENT (— OWED) LIABILITY OBLIGATION (— PAID) COST (— TURNED BY SPADE) GRAFT (APPRECIABLE —) BEANS (COMPLETE —) FULL (CONSIDERABLE —) MIGHT HANTLE HATFUL (EXACT —) NICK (EXTRA —) BONUS (GREAT —) MICKLE INFINITY MOUNTAIN (GROSS —) SLUMP (INADEQUATE —) DEFICIENCY (INDEFINITE —) BAIT SNAG SOME (INFINITESIMAL —) IOTA (INSIGNIFICANT —) SCRAT PEANUTS (LARGE —) GOB LOB JUNT LUMP MINT RAFT SNAG SWAG SIEGE SLASH SPATE BOODLE SOMDEL BONANZA SOMDIEL CARTLOAD MUCHNESS SOMEDEAL (LAVISH —) SLATHER (LEAST POSSIBLE —) GRAIN AMBSACE (LIMITED —) SPRINKLING (MINUTE —) HAIR FLEABITE (RENT —) GALE (SIZABLE —) CHUNK SMART (SLIGHT —) ADDED SNACK TILLY TINGE (SMALL —) ACE BIT DAB TAD DITE DOIT DRAM DRIB FLOW HINT HOOT INCH LICK MITE SNAP SONG SPOT SPECK SPURT TRACE DRAPPY PICKLE SMIDGE TICKET CAPSULE DRAPPIE GLIMMER KENNING SMIDGEN SMIDGIN THOUGHT (SMALLEST —) JOT STIVER STEEVER STUIVER (TENFOLD —) DECUPLE (USUAL —) GRIST (WHOLE —) ALL SUBSTANCE (YEARLY —) ANNUITY (SUFF.) ANCE ANT ENCE

AMOUR DRURY DRUERY AMOURET INTRIGUE PARAMOUR

AMOZ (SON OF —) ISAIAH

AMPERSAND AND ALSO PLUS AMPASSY IPSEAND

AMPHETAMINE UPPER BENZEDRINE

AMPHIALUS (MOTHER OF —) CECROPIA

AMPHIARAUS (DAUGHTER OF —) EURYDICE DEMONASSA (FATHER OF —) OICLES (MOTHER OF —) HYPERMNESTRA (SON OF —) ALCMAEON AMPHILOCHUS (WIFE OF —) ERIPHYLE

AMPHIBIA BATRACHIA

AMPHIBIAN EFT OLM FROG HYLA NEWT RANA TOAD ANURA SIREN SNAKE AMPHIB AXOLOTL CAUDATE ERYOPID PROTEUS

TADPOLE AISTOPOD SALAMANDER

AMPHIBOLE EDENITE ORALITE URALITE ASBESTOS CROSSITE TREMOLITE SMARAGDITE

AMPHICARPA FALCATA

AMPHICTYON (FATHER OF —) DEUCALION (MOTHER OF —) PYRRHA

AMPHIGASTRIUM UNDERLEAF

AMPHILOCHUS (FATHER OF —) AMPHIARAUS (MOTHER OF —) ERIPHYLE

AMPHION (BROTHER OF —) ZETHUS (FATHER OF —) ZEUS IASUS JUPITER (MOTHER OF —) ANTIOPE (WIFE OF —) NIOBE

AMPHIOXUS LANCELET

AMPHIPOD SHRIMP

AMPHISSA (FATHER OF —) ECHETUS MACAREUS (MOTHER OF —) CANACHE

AMPHISSUS (FATHER OF —) APOLLO (MOTHER OF —) DRYOPE

AMPHITHEA (DAUGHTER OF —) ANTICLEA (HUSBAND OF —) AUTOLYCUS

AMPHITHEATER BOWL OVAL ARENA CAVEA CIRCUS CIRQUE STADIUM THEATER

AMPHITRITE (FATHER OF —) NEREUS OCEANUS (HUSBAND OF —) NEPTUNE POSEIDON (MOTHER OF —) TETHYS (SON OF —) TRITON

AMPHITRYON (AUTHOR OF —) PLAUTUS (CHARACTER IN —) SOSIA ALCMENA JUPITER MERCURY AMPHITRYON (DOG OF —) LAELAPS (FATHER OF —) ALCAEUS (MOTHER OF —) HIPPONOME (WIFE OF —) ALCMENE

AMPHORA JUG URN VASE CADUS DIOTA PELIKE

AMPHOTERUS (BROTHER OF —) ACARNAN (FATHER OF —) ALCMAEON (MOTHER OF —) CALLIRRHOE

AMPLE BIG FAIR FULL GOOD MUCH RICH SIDE WIDE BROAD GREAT LARGE LUCKY PLUMP ROOMY ROUND SONSY WALLY ENOUGH HEARTY PLENTY PROLIX COPIOUS LIBERAL OPULENT WEALTHY ABUNDANT ADEQUATE BARONIAL GENEROUS HANDSOME SPACIOUS PLENTIFUL

AMPLIFICATION GAIN

AMPLIFIED EXTENDED

AMPLIFIER BOOSTER REPEATER

AMPLIFY PAD FARCE FARSE SWELL WIDEN DILATE EXPAND EXTEND STRESS AUGMENT ENLARGE STRETCH AMPLIATE HEIGHTEN INCREASE LENGTHEN MULTIPLY

AMPLITUDE BULK

LATITUDE OPULENCE

AMPLY LARGE

AMPUTATE CUT LOP PRUNE SEVER CURTAIL

AMPUTATION APOCOPE ABLATION

AMPYCUS (FATHER OF —) PELIAS (MOTHER OF —) CHLORIS (SON OF —) MOPSUS

AMRAM (FATHER OF —) BANI DISHON (SON OF —) MOSES

AMRITA RASA

AMULA AMA VESSEL

AMULET GEM MET HAND JUJU MOJO PLUM CHARM IMAGE MENAT SAFFI SAFIE TOKEN FETISH GRIGRI MASCOT SAPHIE SCROLL TABLET ABRAXAS AMALETT ICHTHUS ICHTHYS PERIAPT CHURINGA GREEGREE HAGSTONE LIGATURE ORNAMENT TALISMAN PHYLACTERY

AMULIUS (BROTHER OF —) NUMITOR (FATHER OF —) PROCAS (NEPHEW OF —) LAUSUS

AMURRU MARTU

AMUSE GAME LAKE ENJOY MIRTH SHORT SPORT ABSORB DELUDE DIVERT ENGAGE FROLIC PLEASE POPJOY SOLACE TICKLE BEGUILE DISPORT GRATIFY PASTIME BEWILDER DISTRACT RECREATE

AMUSEMENT FAD FUN JEU GAME JEST LAKE PLAY MIRTH SPORT LAKING MUSERY PASTIME COTTABUS LAUGHTER PLEASURE (PL.) MIDWAY

AMUSING RICH COMIC DROLL FUNNY MERRY WITTY COMICAL FOOLISH KILLING RISIBLE FARCICAL HUMOROUS PLEASANT SPORTFUL

AMYCLAS (FATHER OF —) LACEDAEMON (MOTHER OF —) SPARTE (SON OF —) HYACINTHUS

AMYCUS (FATHER OF —) NEPTUNE POSEIDON (MOTHER OF —) MELIA (SLAYER OF —) POLLUX

AMYGDALA TONSIL

AMYL AMYDON PENTYL ISOAMYL

AMYLASE PTYALIN DIASTASE

AMYMONE (FATHER OF —) DANAUS (HUSBAND OF —) ENCELADUS (SON OF —) NAUPLIUS

AMYNTOR (FATHER OF —) ORMENUS (SON OF —) PHOENIX (WIFE OF —) CLEOBULE

AMYTHAON (BROTHER OF —) AESON PHERES (FATHER OF —) CRETHEUS (MOTHER OF —) TYRO (SON OF —) BIAS MELAMPUS (WIFE OF —) IDOMENE

AN ONE ARTICLE

ANA EVENTS OMNIANA SAYINGS

ANABAPTIST DIPPER ABECEDARIAN

ANABAS MARTINICO

ANABATIC DESCENDING

ANABO NABO ANABONG
ANABRANCH BRANCH
TALLYWALKA
ANACAONA (BROTHER OF —)
BEHECHIO
(HUSBAND OF —) CAONABO
ANACHARSIS (BROTHER OF —)
SAULIUS
ANACHRONISM SOLECISM
ANACONDA BOA ABOLLA SUCURI
SUCURY CAMOUDIE SUCURUJU
ANACREONTIC TEIAN
ANACRUSIS UPBEAT
ANADEM CROWN DIADEM FILLET
WREATH CHAPLET CORONET
GARLAND
ANAGNOST LECTOR READER
ANAGOGICAL MYSTICAL
ANAGRAM REBUS PUZZLE
METAGRAM LOGOGRIPH
(PL.) VERBARIUM
ANAGUA KNACKAWAY
KNOCKAWAY
ANAH (DAUGHTER OF —)
AHOLIBAMAH
(FATHER OF —) ZIBEON
ANAL PODICAL
ANALABOS CLOAK
ANALGESIC ANODYNE CODEINE
ANTIPYRIN PHENALGIN
ANALOGICAL NORMAL
ANALOGOUS LIKE SIMILAR
ANALOGUE DFDT ANALOG
ANALOGY QIYAS PARALLEL
PREDISONE
(CLOSE —) PARITY
ANALYSIS TEST INDEX STUDY
ANATOMY AUTOPSY SCANSION
SOLUTION
(BLOWPIPE —) PYROLOGY
(CHARACTER —) PSYCHOGRAPH
(ECONOMIC —) DYNAMICS
(LOGICAL —) SYLLOGISM
ANALYTIC SUBTLE REGULAR
(NOT —) SYNTHETIC SYNTHETICAL
ANALYTICAL CLINICAL DIVISIVE
ANALYZE RUN PART SIFT ASSAY
BREAK PARSE SENSE STUDY
WEIGH ASSESS DIVIDE REDUCE
DISSECT EXAMINE ITEMIZE
RESOLVE TITRATE UNPIECE
APPRAISE CONSTRUE DIAGNOSE
SEPARATE
(— ACCOUNT) AGE
(— VERSE) SCAN
ANAMITE TWINE
ANANAS ANANA PINGUIN
ANANI (FATHER OF —) ELIOENAI
ANANIAS LIAR SIDRACH
(FATHER OF —) NEDEBAEUS
(WIFE OF —) SAPPHIRA
ANANSI NANCY
ANAPEST ANTIDACTYL
ANARCHIST RED PROVO REBEL
ANARCH NIHILIST REDSHIRT
ANARCHY RIOT CHAOS REVOLT
LICENSE MISRULE
DISORDER
ANASARCA DROPSY
ANASAZI PUEBLO PLATEAU
ANASCHISTIC EUMITOTIC
ANASTOMOSIS GLOMUS
ANASTROPHE INVERSION

ANATASE OCTAHEDRITE
ANATH (SON OF —) SHAMGAR
ANATHEMA WO BAN MUD WOE
OATH CURSE CENSURE
ANATHEMATIZE BAN CURSE
ACCURSE EXECRATE
ANATHOTH (FATHER OF —) BECHER
ANATOMIST AMERICAN TODD
ALLEN EVANS SABIN WYMAN
DWIGHT KNOWER
COGHILL HERRICK
STOCKARD
AUSTRIAN HYRTL
BELGIAN VESALIUS
DANISH STENO
DUTCH TULP GRAAF CAMPER
COITER DUBOIS
ENGLISH GRAY OWEN JONES
QUAIN COWPER HARVEY HAVERS
HILTON HUNTER WILLIS
FRENCH ROBIN DUVERNEY
DUPUYTREN POISEUILLE
CRUVEILHIER
GERMAN HIS FICK ROUX HENLE
MEYER BRAUNE EBERTH KRAUSE
MECKEL MULLER RATHKE
WAGNER FRORIEP SIEBOLD
ANDERSCH BISCHOFF HARTMANN
MEISSNER SCHULTZE SCHWALBE
WRISBERG GEGENBAUR
HELMHOLTZ LIEBERKUHN
SOEMMERRING WEIDENREICH
GREEK RUFUS HEROPHILUS
ERASISTRATUS
ITALIAN CORTI ASELLI PACINI
SCARPA VAROLI CALDANI
COLOMBO COTUGNO ROLANDO
MALPIGHI EUSTACHIO FALLOPIUS
PACCHIONI
SCOTTISH BELL MONRO FERRIER
GOODSIR PETTIGREW
MACALISTER
SWEDISH KEY
SWISS BAUHIN HALLER HARDER
BRUNNER
ANATOMIZE ANALYZE DISSECT
ANATOMY TOPOLOGY
(— OF HORSE) HIPPOTOMY
(MICROSCOPIC —) HISTOLOGY
(VEGETABLE —) PHYTOTOMY
ANAX (FATHER OF —) URANUS
(MOTHER OF —) GE GAEA
(SON OF —) ASTERIUS
ANAXARETE (LOVER OF —) IPHIS
ANAXIBIA (DAUGHTER OF —)
PELOPEA ALCESTIS PISIDICE
(FATHER OF —) BIAS
(HUSBAND OF —) PELIAS
(SON OF —) ACASTUS
ANAXO (BROTHER OF —)
AMPHITRYON
(DAUGHTER OF —) ALCMENE
(FATHER OF —) ALCAEUS
(HUSBAND OF —) ELECTRYON
ANCAEUS (FATHER OF —) ALEUS
NEPTUNE LYCURGUS POSEIDON
(MOTHER OF —) ASTYPALAEA
(SON OF —) AGAPENOR
ANCESTOR ION MIL ADAM EBER
HETH ROOT SIRE DORUS ELDER
STOCK APETUS ATAVUS AUTHOR
BELDAM EPONYM FATHER
MANNUS MILEDH PARENT STIPES

ANCIENT BELDAME BELSIRE
EPAPHUS FLEANCE FORBEAR
IAPETUS ISHMAEL KACHINA
SAKULYA DARDANUS FOREBEAR
FOREGOER MILESIUS MYRMIDON
RELATIVE PREDECESSOR
PRIMOGENITOR
(— CULT) MANISM
(—S OF GOTLANDERS) GEAT
(MAORI —) TIKI TUPUNA
(PL.) OLDERS ANCESTRY
ANCESTRAL AVAL AVITAL AVITIC
LINEAL FAMILIAL
ANCESTRY KIN RACE SEED ATHEL
FAMILY ORIGIN PEOPLE SOURCE
STRAIN DESCENT KINDRED
LINEAGE BREEDING PEDIGREE
ANCHINOE (FATHER OF —) NILUS
(HUSBAND OF —) BELUS
(SON OF —) DANAUS AEGYPTUS
ANCHISES (FATHER OF —) CAPYS
(MOTHER OF —) THEMIS
(SON OF —) AENEAS
ANCHOR FIX BIND DRAG DRUG
HOOK MOOR REST SLUG SPUD
STOP AFFIX BERTH BOWER
KEDGE RIVET SHEET STOCK
ATTACH DROGUE FASTEN HERMIT
KEDGER KELLEG SECURE STREAM
CHAPLET CONNECT DEADMAN
GRAPNEL GROUSER
KILLICK MUDHOOK
SUPPORT COCKBILL
(— IN PLACE) ACOCKBILL
(— RING) TORUS
(AT —) ASTAY
(BEAM —) WALL
(PART OF —) ARM EYE KEY PEE
PIN BALL BILL HEAD HOOP PALM
RING CROWN FLUKE STOCK
TREND THROAT
ANCHORAGE DOCK STAY HARBOR
REFUGE RIDING MOORAGE
ABUTMENT BERTHAGE
ROOTHOLD
ANCHORITE MONK HERMIT
ACHORET ASCETIC EREMITE
RECLUSE STYLITE
ANCHOVY NEHU BOCON SPRAT
HERRING SARDINE
(PL.) ALICI
ANCHUSA OXTONGUE
ANCHUSIN ALKANET
ANCIENT ELD OLD AGED AULD
FERN HIGH HOAR IAGO YORE
EARLY ELDER HOARY OLDEN
BYGONE ENSIGN FORMER NOETIC
PISTOL PRIMAL VETUST ANTIENT
ANTIQUE ARCHAIC ARCHEAN
CLASSIC OGYGEAN OGYGIAN
HISTORIC NOACHIAN OBSOLETE
PRIMEVAL PRISTINE
(MOST —) ELDEST
(PREF.) ARCHAE PALAE(O)
PALE(O)
(— ORIGIN) PALE
ANCIENTLY OLD HIGH
ANCILLA HELPER ADJUNCT
SERVANT
ANCON ELBOW CORBEL CONSOLE
AND N U AN ET SO ANT TOO ALSO
PLUS BESIDES FURTHER
MOREOVER

(— SO FORTH) ETC USW
ANDAMAN MINCOPI MINKOPI
MINCOPIE
ANDESITE BONINITE TIMAZITE
PROPYLITE
ANDHAKA (FATHER OF —) KASYAPA
(MOTHER OF —) DITI
(SLAYER OF —) SHIVA
ANDIRON DOG CHENET COBIRON
FIREDOG HESSIAN HANDIRON
LANDIRON
ANDORRA (LANGUAGE OF —)
CATALAN
(NATIVE OF —) ANDOSIAN
(RIVER OF —) VALIRA
ANDRADITE APLOME GARNET
ANDRAEMON (FATHER OF —)
OXYLUS
(MOTHER OF —) GORGE DRYOPE
(SON OF —) THOAS
**ANDREA CHENIER (CHARACTER IN
—)** ANDREA COIGNY GERARD
CHENIER MADELEINE
(COMPOSER OF —) GIORDANO
ANDROCLES AND THE LION
(AUTHOR OF —) SHAW
(CHARACTER IN —) LAVINIA
MEGAERA ANDROCLES
FERROVIUS
ANDROCONIUM STIGMA PLUMULE
ANDROGEUS (FATHER OF —) MINOS
(MOTHER OF —) PASIPHAE
ANDROID ROBOT AUTOMATON
ANDROMACHE (AUTHOR OF —)
EURIPIDES
(CHARACTER IN —) PELEUS THETIS
ORESTES PYRRHUS HERMIONE
MENELAUS MOLOSSUS
ANDROMACHE NEOPTOLEMUS
(FATHER OF —) EETION
(HUSBAND OF —) HECTOR
HELENUS NEOPTOLEMUS
(SON OF —) PIELUS ASTYANAX
MOLOSSUS PERGAMUS
ANDROMEDA (FATHER OF —)
CEPHEUS
(MOTHER OF —) CASSIOPEA
(RESCUER OF —) PERSEUS
ANDROMEDE BIELID
ANDRON (FATHER OF —) ANIUS
(SISTER OF —) OENO ELAIS
SPERMO
ANECDOTAL LITERARY
ANECDOTE GAG TOY JOKE TALE
YARN EVENT STORY SKETCH
HAGGADA EXEMPLUM
HAGGADAH
ANECHOIC DEAD
ANEMIA SURRA SURRAH ANAEMIA
HYPAEMA HYPHEMA HYPHEMIA
ISCHEMIA SPANEMIA CHLOROSIS
ANEMIC LOW PALE WEAK MEALY
WATERY LIFELESS
(PREF.) CHLOR(O)
ANEMONE LILY CRASS EMONY
POLYP OPELET BOWBELLS
SNOWDROP
ANENT ON RE ABOUT ANENST
BESIDE TOWARD AGAINST
OPPOSITE
ANESTHESIA BLOCK CORYL
SPINAL

ANESTHETIC GAS ETHER ACOINE EVIPAN OBTUSE OPIATE COCAINE DULLING MENTHOL METOPRYL PARAFORM PROCAINE SEDATIVE PHENOCAIN METHOXYFLURANE **(SUFF.)** CAINE

ANESTHETIZE FREEZE ETHERIZE

ANEW OVER AGAIN NEWLY AFRESH ITERUM NEWLINS NEWLINGS RECENTLY **(PREF.)** RE

ANFRACTUOUS SPIRAL BENDING SINUOUS WINDING TORTUOUS

ANGEL MAH DEVA EBUS ANGLE ARDOR ARIEL DAEVA DULIA NAKIR YAKSA ABDIEL ARIOCH BACKER BELIAL CHERUB MONKIR MUNKAR NEKKAR SERAPH SPIRIT THRONE UZZIEL YAKSHA ANGELET EGREGOR ISRAFEL RAPHAEL SPONSOR WATCHER ZADKIEL ZOPHIEL APOLLYON GUARDIAN ITHURIEL SUPERNAL **(— OF DEATH)** AZRAEL SAMMAEL **(DESTROYING —)** ABADDON **(FALLEN —S)** HELL **(GUARDIAN —)** YAKSA YAKSHA YAKSHI **(RECORDING —)** SIJIL SIJILL **(PL.)** HOST FRAVASHI SERAPHIM

ANGELFISH MONK MUNK ANGEL QUOTT RHINA SQUAT MONACH CICHLID FLATFISH KINGSTON MONKFISH SQUATINA

ANGELIC SAINTLY BEATIFIC CHERUBIC HEAVENLY SERAPHIC

ANGELICA JELLICA ARCHANGEL **(FATHER OF —)** GALAPHRON **(LOVER OF —)** ORLANDO

ANGELIN PACAY ANGELEEN

ANGELIQUE (CHARACTER IN —) CHARLOT BONIFACE ANGELIQUE **(COMPOSER OF —)** IBERT

ANGER ARR IRE IRK MAD VEX BATE BILE BURN CRAB FELL FUME FURY GALL GRIM HUFF MOOD RAGE RILE ROIL RUFF TEEN TIFF ANNOY BIRSE GRAME GRIPE HATEL IRISH PIQUE SPONK SPUNK STURT THRAW WRATH BOTHER CHOLER DANDER ENRAGE EXCITE GRIEVE MONKEY NETTLE OFFEND RANCOR SPLEEN TALENT TEMPER WARMTH BURNING DESPITE DUDGEON EMOTION INCENSE INFLAME PASSION PROVOKE STOMACH ACRIMONY DISTRESS EBENEZER IRRITATE VEXATION

ANGERED SORE AGRAMED PELTISH INCENSED

ANGICO CURUPAY

ANGINA PRUNELLA

ANGIOSPERM HARDWOOD METASPERM

ANGLE IN BOB DIP ELL OUT TEE WRO CANT COIN COOK DRAW FISH FORK HADE KEEN KNEE LEAD NOOK PEAK SITE WICK ANCON ARRIS AXIAL BEVEL BIGHT CHOIL COIGN DRAFT DRIFT ELBOW FLEAM GROIN GUISE INGLE PHASE POINT QUOIN SLANT SLOPE ALLURE ANGULE ASPECT CANTON CORNEL CORNER DIRECT ENGHLE EPAULE HADING LAGGEN LAGGIN OCTANT SCHEME SQUARE TORNUS ANGLIAN ANGULUS ANOMALY AZIMUTH BASTION DRAUGHT GIMMICK KNUCKLE PERIGON RAVELIN SALIENT ARGUMENT DECALAGE DIHEDRAL FISHHOOK INTRIGUE SHOULDER OBLIQUITY **(— OF BEVEL)** FLEAM FLEEM **(— OF BOWSPRIT)** STEEVE STEEVING **(— OF CLUB HEAD)** LIE **(— OF EYELIDS)** CANTHUS **(— OF HAT BRIM)** BREAK **(— OF HIPBONE)** HOOK **(— OF LEAF)** AXIL **(— OF RAFTER)** HEEL **(— OF TIMBER KNEE)** BREECH **(DRIFT —)** LEEWAY **(OBTUSE —)** HEEL BULLNOSE **(ROCK —)** DIEDRE **(ROOF —)** HIP FASTIGIUM **(ROUND —)** PERIGON **(SALIENT —)** ARIS ARRIS PIEND **(PREF.)** ANGULO GON(I)(IO)(Y)(YO) **(SUFF.)** GON

ANGLED CANTED NOOKED ANGULATE **(PREF.)** ACUTI

ANGLER MONK FRIAR THIEF SLIMER LOPHIID RODSTER SPINNER WIDEGAB WIDEGAP ALLMOUTH FROGFISH MONKFISH PISCATOR TOADFISH WALTONIAN

ANGLESMITH SLABMAN

ANGLEWORM ESS WORM FISHWORM

ANGLICAN EPISCOPAL

ANGLO CAUCASIAN

ANGOLA

CAPITAL: LUANDA
COIN: MACUTA MACUTE
DISTRICT: CABINDA
KINGDOM: BAKONGO
LANGUAGE: BANTU KIMBUNDU
MOUNTAIN: LOVITI
PLATEAU: PLANALTO
PORT: LOBITO LUANDA
RIVER: CONGO CUITO KASAI CUANDO CUANZA CUNENE KUNENE KWANDO KWANZA CUBANGO
TOWN: LOBITO LUANDA LUBANGO BENGUELA MOSSAMEDES NOVALISBOA
TRIBE: BANTU KIKONGO
WATERFALL: RUACANA

ANGORA CAT GOAT ANGOLA RABBIT

ANGRILY ANGERLY IRATELY FUMINGLY

ANGRY MAD ASHY EVIL GRIM GRUM HIGH RILY ROID ROSY SORE WARM WAXY WILD WRAW CROOK CROSS GRAME HUFFY IRATE IROUS MOODY RATTY RILEY SNAKY STUNT VEXED WEMOD WROTH BIRSIT CHAFED CROUSE FRENZY FUMING FUMOUS HEATED IREFUL LOADED SHIRTY SNAKEY STUFFY FRETFUL FURIOUS HOPPING IRACUND PAINFUL ROPABLE SNAKISH SPLEENY UPTIGHT CHOLERIC INFLAMED RIGOROUS SPITFIRE TEMPERED VEHEMENT WREAKFUL PASSIONATE **(BE —)** STEAM

ANGRY-LOOKING THUNDERY

ANGUISH WOE ACHE HARM HURT PAIN PANG RACK TRAY AGONY ANGST ANGUS DOLOR GRIEF THROE MISERY REGRET SORROW ANGOISE ANGWICH REMORSE TORMENT TORTURE TRAVAIL DISTRESS

ANGUISHED GRIEFFUL

ANGULAR BONE BONY EDGY LEAN SLIM THIN GAUNT SHARP ABRUPT POINTED SCRAWNY CORNERED **(NOT —)** SOFT **(PREF.)** ANG

ANGULARITY EDGINESS

ANGUS FORFAR FORFARSHIRE

ANHYDRIDE LACTAM SULTAM FULGIDE LACTIDE SULTONE GLUCOSAN MANNITAN SORBITAN

ANHYDRITE VULPINITE

ANHYDROUS DRY DESICCATED

ANI WITCH CUCKOO JEWBIRD KEELBILL KEELBIRD TICKBIRD

ANIAM (FATHER OF —) SHEMIDAH

ANIARA (COMPOSER OF —) BLOMDAHL

ANIMADVERSION BLAME REMARK CENSURE COMMENT REPROOF WARNING MONITION REPROACH REFLECTION

ANIMAL (ALSO SEE UNDER SPECIFIC HEADINGS) DEER BEAST BIPED BLACK BRUTE GRADE GROSS LUSTY STORE STRAY BRUTAL CARNAL DAPPLE DESPOT FLESHY KICKER MAMMAL RODENT SILVAN SORREL SPONGE SYLVAN BEASTIE BREEDER CARRION CRITTER SENSUAL BURROWER CREATURE EMIGRANT ORGANISM PREDATOR **(— COLLECTION)** LARDER **(— FOR MARKET)** STOCKER **(— INHABITED BY SPIRIT)** GUACA HUACA **(— LIVING IN CAVES)** TROGLOBITE **(— OF LITTLE VALUE)** SCALAWAG SKALAWAG **(— RESEMBLING MAN)** HOMINOID **(— SHOT)** KILL **(— WITH BLACK COAT AND MARKINGS)** PARSON **(— WITH DOCKED TAIL)** CURTAL **(—S AS RENT)** CAIN **(BEEF —)** BONER GRASSER **(BOVINE —)** BOSS BRUTE **(BROKEN-DOWN —)** CROCK **(CARNIVOROUS —)** SARCOPHILE **(CASTRATED —)** SEG SEGG SPAY SPADO GELDING **(COLD-BLOODED —)** ECTOTHERM **(CREATED —)** BARAMIN **(DECOY —)** COACH **(DOMESTIC —)** DOER SCRUB BESTIAL FOLLOWER SCRUBBER **(DRAFT —)** AVER AIVER **(EMACIATED —)** FRAME SKELETON **(FABULOUS —)** KYLIN BUNYIP DRAGON ACEPHAL GRIFFIN GRIFFON GRYPHON UNICORN SEMITAUR TRAGELAPH **(FEMALE —)** HEN SHE LADY JENNY SHEDER **(FERAL —)** CIMAROON CIMARRON CIMMARON **(FLEA-RIDDEN —)** FLEABAG **(FOOTLESS —)** APOD APODE **(FOSSIL —)** ZOOLITE **(FREAKISH —)** FERLY FERLIE **(GRASSHOPPER-EATING —)** WHANGAM **(GRAY —)** GRIZZLE **(GRAZING —)** HERBAGER **(GREEDY —)** GORB **(HORNED —)** HORN REEM **(HYPOTHETICAL —)** PROAVIS **(IMAGINARY —)** WHANGAM CATAWAMPUS **(LOWER —)** BEAST CREATURE **(LUSTY OR PLUMP —)** BILCH BILSH **(MALE —)** HE TOM BUCK BULL JACK STAG JOHNNY BACHELOR **(MARINE —)** LANCELET **(MATURE —)** SENIOR **(MEAT —)** CHOPPER **(MISCHIEVOUS —)** ELF **(MYTHICAL —)** HODAG KYLIN MOONACK **(ODD —)** SPLACKNUCK **(PACK —)** HUNIA SUMPTER **(PET —)** CADE **(PURSUED —S)** GAME **(ROASTED —)** BARBECUE BARBEQUE **(SADDLE —)** LOPER **(SCRAWNY —)** SCRAG **(SHORN —)** SHEAR **(SKINNY —)** SCRAE **(SLUGGISH —)** DRUMBLE **(SOLID-HOOFED —)** SOLIPED **(SPOTTED —)** CALICO **(STOCKY —)** BLOCK **(STUNTED —)** SHARGAR SHARGER **(THICKSET —)** NUGGET **(TOTEM —)** EPONYM **(UNBRANDED —)** SLICK **(UNCASTRATED —)** ENTIRE **(UNDERSIZED —)** DURGAN DURGEN **(UNHOUSED —)** OUTLER OUTLIER **(UNWEANED —)** SUCKER **(WANDERING —)** STRAY ESTRAY **(WARM-BLOODED —)** ENDOTHERM HAEMATHERM **(WATER —)** AQUATIC AQUATILE **(WEAK —)** DRAG DOWNER **(WILD —)** SAVAGE WILDLING **(WING-FOOTED —)** ALIPED **(WORNOUT —)** KANCKER **(WORTHLESS —)** CARRION **(YOUNG —)** HOG BIRD HOGG JOEY SHOT TOTO STORE JUNIOR PULLUS FATLING LITTLIN KINDLING LITTLING SUCKLING YOUNGLET

(2-HORNED —) BICORN BICORNE
(PL.) ZOA FAUNA NECTON
NEKTON
(PREF.) ZO(E)(IDIO)(IDO)(O)
ZOOLOGICO
(RUMINATING —) MERYC(O)
(SUFF.) ACEA AD THERE THERIA
THERIUM ZOA ZOIC ZOON
ANIMALCULISM SPERMISM
ANIMALITY HOGGERY
ANIMALS
(SUFF.) ATA IDA IDEA INI
ANIMA MUNDI WELTGEIST
ANIMATE ACT PEP FIRE MOVE
PERK STIR URGE ALIVE BRISK
CHEER DRIVE FLUSH IMBUE
IMPEL LIGHT LIVEN QUICK ROUSE
VITAL AROUSE BRIGHT ENSOUL
EXCITE INCITE INDUCE INFORM
KINDLE LIVING PROMPT SPIRIT
VIVIFY ACTUATE COMFORT
ENLIVEN INSPIRE QUICKEN
ACTIVATE ENERGIZE INSPIRIT
VITALIZE
(NOT —) BRUTE
ANIMATED UP GAY VIF GLAD VIVE
ALIVE ANIME BRISK QUICK VITAL
VIVID ACTIVE ARDENT BLITHE
BOUNCY BRISKY LIVELY LIVING
SPARKY SPUNKY BUOYANT
JOCULAR STHENIC BOUNCING
INSTINCT LIFESOME SPIRITED
VIGOROUS
ANIMATION BRIO VERVE
ANIME COPAL ELEMI RESIN ROSIN
ANIMATO
ANIMIKEAN LAWSON
ANIMISM NATURISM
ANIMOSITY HATE PIQUE SPITE
ANIMUS ENMITY HATRED MALICE
RANCOR DISLIKE ACRIMONY
ANIMUS MIND ONDE WILL EFFORT
ENMITY SPIRIT TEMPER ATTITUDE
ANIRUDDHA (FATHER OF —)
PRADYUMNA
ANISE ANET DILL CUMEN UMBEL
FENNEL SIKIMI SHIKIMI
ANIUS (DAUGHTER OF —) OENO
ELAIS SPERMO
(FATHER OF —) APOLLO
(MOTHER OF —) RHOEO CREUSA
(SON OF —) ANDRON
(WIFE OF —) DORIPPE
ANKH TAU
ANKLE COOT CUIT HOCK QUIT
ANCLE QUEET TALUS WRIST
TARSUS SHACKLE
(COCKED —S) KNUCKLING
(PREF.) TAL(I)(O) TARS(I)(O)
ANKLEBONE TALUS ASTRAGAL
ANKLET SHOE SOCK BANGLE
FETTER SHACKLE
ANLAGE INCEPT PROTON INITIAL
BLASTEMA
ANNA (FATHER OF —) BELUS
(SISTER OF —) DIDO
ANNA BOLENA (CHARACTER IN —)
ANNE JANE HENRY PERCY
BOLEYN SEYMOUR
(COMPOSER OF —) DONIZETTI
ANNA KARENINA (AUTHOR OF —)
TOLSTOY

(CHARACTER IN —) ANNA KITTY
LEVIN ALEXEI STEPAN KARENIN
VRONSKY OBLONSKY
KONSTANTINE SHTCHERBATSKY
ANNALIST WRITER RECORDER
ANNALS FASTI NIHONGI REGISTER
ANNAM (ALSO SEE VIETNAM)
VIETNAM
(BOAT OF —) GAYYOU GAYDIANG
(MEASURE OF —) LY GON NGU
QUO SAO TAT PHAN THAT SHITA
THUOC TRUONG
(TOWN OF —) HUE VINH TOURANE
QUANGTRI
(WEIGHT OF —) CAN BINH DONG
ANNAS (FATHER OF —) SETHI
ANNATTO OTTER URUCU ORLEAN
ROUCOU SALMON ACHIOTE
ACHUETE ANNOTTO ARNATTO
ORLEANS
ANNEAL BAKE FUSE HEAT SMELT
TEMPER INFLAME TOUGHEN
GRAPHITE
ANNEALER TUBER HEATER
ANNEALING LIGHTING
ANNELID NAID WORM LUGWORM
SERPULA ANNULATE SANDWORM
SERPULAN OLIGOCHAETE
ANNEX ADD ELL LAY JOIN AFFIX
SEIZE UNITE ADJECT ANNECT
APPEND ATTACH FASTEN
ACQUIRE CONNECT FIXTURE
POSTFIX SUBJOIN ADDITION
ANNEXURE DOCUMENT
PENTHOUSE
ANNIHILATE END OUT KILL RAZE
RUIN SLAY ABATE ANNUL ERASE
WRECK DELETE DEVOUR NOUGHT
QUENCH REDUCE ABOLISH
DESTROY EXPUNGE DECIMATE
UNCREATE DISCREATE PULVERIZE
ANNIHILATION FANA NEGATION
ANNIVERSARY FETE MASS EMBER
FEAST ANNUAL JUBILEE YEARDAY
BIRTHDAY FESTIVAL YAHRZEIT
(100TH —) CENTENNIAL
(1000TH —) MILLENIUM
(150TH —) SESQUICENTENNIAL
(200TH —) BIMILLENARY
BIMILLENIUM
(25TH —) SEMIJUBILEE
(50TH —) SEMICENTENNIAL
ANNONA ATIS ATTA ATEES
ANNOTATE EDIT NOTE STET
GLOSS BENOTE NOTIFY POSTIL
REMARK APOSTIL COMMENT
EXPLAIN FOOTNOTE
ANNOTATION APOSTIL COMMENT
SCHOLION SCHOLIUM
ANNOTATOR NOTIST SCHOLIAST
ANNOUNCE BID CRY BODE CALL
DEEM MAKE SCRY SHOW SING
TELL BRUIT CLAIM KNELL STATE
VOICE ASSERT BLAZON BROACH
DENOTE HERALD INFORM
PREACH REPORT REVEAL SIGNAL
SPRING STEVEN DECLARE
DIVULGE FORERUN GAZETTE
PUBLISH SIGNIFY DENOUNCE
FORETELL INTIMATE PROCLAIM
RENOUNCE SENTENCE
ANNOUNCEMENT BID CRY HAT
BILL CALL LEAD ALARM BANCO

BANNS BLURB EDICT ALARUM
DECREE DICTUM NOTICE
GAZETTE SENSING BULLETIN
CIRCULAR DECISION RESCRIPT
PROCLAMATION
(— OF DAWN) AUBADE
ANNOUNCER NEBO PAGE CRIER
EMCEE CALLER HERALD NUNCIO
GONGMAN GRINDER SPIELER
NUNCIATE SPRUIKER
ANNOY ARR BUG DUN EAT EGG
GET GIG HOX IRE IRK NAG NOY
NYE TRY VEX BAIT BORE BURN
FASH FRET FUSS GALL GRIG HALE
HARM HAZE HUFF HUMP NARK
PAIN RILE ROIL CHAFE CHASE
CHEVY CHIVY DEVIL GRAMY
GRATE HARRY PEEVE PIQUE
SPITE STURT TEASE THORN
UPSET WEARY WORRY BADGER
BOTHER CADDLE CHIVEY CHIVVY
EARWIG ENRAGE GRAVEL
HAGGLE HARASS HATTER HECKLE
HECTOR INFEST INJURE MADDEN
MOLEST NEEDLE NETTLE OFFEND
PESTER POTTER RATTLE REHETE
RUFFLE TICKLE BEDEVIL DISTURB
HOTFOOT JACKSON TERRIFY
TROUBLE ACERBATE CONTRARY
DISTRESS IRRITATE PERSECUTE
ANNOYANCE VEX FASH PEST
WEED CROSS GRIEF LOATH SPITE
STALL THORN INSECT PESTER
DISGUST FASHERY NOYANCE
TROUBLE UMBRAGE FASHERIE
FLEABITE NOISANCE NUISANCE
PINPRICK
ANNOYED SORE INSULTED
ANNOYING TARE PESKY NOYOUS
DISEASY HATEFUL IRKSOME
NOISOME PAINFUL TARSOME
FASHIOUS FRETSOME NIGGLING
SPITEFUL TIRESOME PROVOKING
PESTIFEROUS
ANNOYINGLY CONFOUNDED
CONFOUNDEDLY
ANNUAL BOOK BUGLE PLANT
FLOWER YEARLY ANNUARY
BUGSEED BUGWEED ETESIAN
GIFTBOOK PERIODIC YEARBOOK
(OLD WORLD —) WELD
ANNUITY CENSO CONSOL INCOME
PENSION TONTINE PERPETUITY
ANNUL TOL CASS NULL TOLL
UNDO VOID ADNUL AVOID BLANK
ELIDE ERASE QUASH REMIT
RETEX UNLAW CANCEL FRIVOL
NEGATE RECALL REPEAL REVERT
REVOKE UNLIVE VACATE ABOLISH
CASHIER CASSARE CASSATE
DESTROY NULLIFY RESCIND
RETRACT REVERSE VACUATE
ABROGATE ARROGATE DEROGATE
DISANNUL DISSOLVE IMBECILE
OVERRIDE OVERRULE
ANNULAR BANDED CYCLIC RINGED
ANNULATE CINGULAR CIRCULAR
ANNULARLY RINGWISE
ANNULET RING RIDGE FILLET
ANNULUS MOLDING
ANNULMENT UNDOING
ABATEMENT
ANNULUS RING ANNULE

COLLAR GYROMA
INDUSIUM
ANNUNCIATION MARYMASS
ANNUNCIATOR TELLER
INDICATOR
ANOA BUFFALO SAPIUTAN
ANODE PLATE ZINCOID
ANODIC ASCENDING
ANODYNE BALM ACOPON BROMAL
OPIATE REMEDY EUGENOL
SOOTHER NARCOTIC SEDATIVE
CHLORODYNE
ANOINT FAT OIL RUB BALM BEAT
CERE NARD ANELE ANOIL CREAM
CROWN ENOIL LATCH NUNCT
PRUNE SALVE SMARM SMEAR
SMERL CHRISM GREASE INUNCT
SPREAD THRASH MOISTEN
UNGUENT
ANOINTMENT CHRISMATORY
ANOMALOUS ODD DIFFORM
STRANGE UNUSUAL ABERRANT
ABNORMAL ATYPICAL PECULIAR
ANOMALY CREEPER CYCLOPY
EPILOIA PARADOX CYCLOPIA
ANON NAN ANEW ONCE SOON
AGAIN LATER AFRESH BEDEEN
BEDENE THENCE SHORTLY
ANONYMITY NOBODYNESS
ANONYMOUS UNKNOWN
NAMELESS UNAVOWED
UNSIGNED
ANOPLURA PARASITA PEDICULINA
ANOTHER NEW THAT ALIAS FRESH
SECOND TIDDER TOTHER
ANITHER FURTHER
(PREF.) ALTERO
(ONE —) ALLELO
ANOXIA ASPHYXIA
ANSHUMANT (FATHER OF —)
ASAMANJAS
(GRANDFATHER OF —) SAGARA
ANSWER DO IT SAY SIT ECHO
MEET PLEA REIN SUIT ATONE
AVAIL COMES COVER JAWAB
REACT REPLY SERVE LETTER
REJOIN RESULT RETORT RETURN
RIPOST ACCOUNT COUNTER
DEFENCE DEFENSE FULFILL
RESPOND SATISFY ANTIPHON
COMEBACK PLEADING REBUTTAL
REPARTEE RESPONSE SOLUTION
(— BACK) CHOP
(— FOR) FORM VANG
(— IN FUGUE) COMES
(— THE PURPOSE) DO FIT SUIT
AVAIL SERVE
(DECISIVE —) SOCKDOLAGER
SOCKDOLOGER
(LEGAL —) DUPLY
ANSWERABLE EQUAL LIABLE
FITTING ADEQUATE AMENABLE
ANSWERER USHABTI
ANSWERING
(PREF.) COUNTER
ANT ANAI ANAY ANER ATTA GYNE
MIRE AMPTE EMMET KELEP
MAXIM MINIM NURSE SAUBA
SIAFU SLAVE AMAZON DRIVER
ERGATE NASUTE NEUTER
WORKER BULLDOG FORAGER
FORMICE OUVRIER PISMIRE
PISSANT PONERID REPLETE

SOLDIER TERMITE ACULEATA
DORYLINE FORMICID GYNECOID
HONEYPOT MACRANER
MICRANER MYRMICID TAPINOMA
(— LION) DOODLEBUG
(— SHRIKE) BATARA
(— STUDY) MYRMECOLOGY
(— THRUSH) PITTA
(— TREE) WORMIGO
(PART OF —) EYE WAIST GASTER
ANTENNA MANDIBLE
(WORKER —) ERGATE
(PREF.) FORMI(CI) MYRMECO
MYRMO TERMITO
(SUFF.) MYRMEX
ANTA PIER PARASTAS PEDESTAL
PILASTER
ANTACID SATURANT
ANTAEUS (FATHER OF —) NEPTUNE
POSEIDON
(MOTHER OF —) GE GAEA
ANTAGONISM WAR ANIMUS
ENMITY QUARREL AVERSION
CONFLICT
(IN —) COUNTER
ANTAGONIST FOE ENEMY PARTY
RIVAL FOEMAN BATTLER
WARRIOR COPEMATE OPPONENT
OPPOSITE WRANGLER
(— OF DRUGS) NALAXONE
NALOXONE
ANTAGONISTIC ADVERSE
COUNTER HOSTILE ANTERGIC
CONTRARY INIMICAL OPPONENT
OPPOSITE
(— TO GROWTH) ANTIBLASTIC
(NOT —) SYMPATHETIC
(PREF.) ENANTIO
ANTAGONIZE OPPOSE CONTEST
ANTARCTICA (MOUNTAIN ON —)
TYREE GARDNER KIRKPATRICK
(VOLCANO ON —) EREBUS
MELBOURNE
ANT BEAR BEAR ERDVARK
AARDVARK ANTEATER EDENTATE
TAMANOIR
ANTE PAY STAKE
ANTEATER TAPIR NUMBAT
ECHIDNA TAMANDU AARDVARK
AARDWOLF DASYURID EDENTATE
PANGOLIN TAMANDUA
TAMANOIR
ANTEBRACHIUM CUBIT CUBITAL
CUBITUS FOREARM
ANTECEDENT FORE CAUSE PRIOR
FORMER REASON WHENCE
PREMISE ANTERIOR PREVIOUS
PRECEDING PRECEDENCE
PREVENIENT
(— OF CANON) GUIDA
ANTECHAMBER LIWAN
ANTEDATE PRECEDE PREDATE
FOREDATE PREEXIST
ANTEDATED FORETIMED
ANTELOPE GNU KID KOB RAM SUS
ASTE BISA BUCK DODA DUST
GUIB IBEX KOBA KUDU ORYX
PUKU ROAN SUNI TOPI TORA
ADDAX BAIRA BEIRA BEISA BEKRA
BOHOR BONGO BOVID BUBAL
CHIRU ELAND GORAL GUIBA
IPETE LICHI NAGOR NYALA ORIBI
PEELE PERON SABLE SAIGA SASIN

SEROW TAKIN YAKIN BAGWYN
BHOKRA BUBALE CABREE CABRET
CABRIE CABRIT CHOUKA DIKDIK
DUIKER DUYKER DZEREN DZERIN
DZERON GOORAL GRIMME
HEROLA IMPALA INYALA KOODOO
LECHWE LELWEL NAKONG NILGAI
NILGAU PALLAH POOKOO
PYGARG RHEBOK ALGAZEL
BLAUBOK BLESBOK BUBALIS
CHAMOIS CHIKARA DEFASSA
GAZELLE GEMSBOK GERENUK
GREENUK GRYSBOK MADOQUA
REDBUCK RHEEBOK SASSABY
STEMBOK AGACELLA BLEEKBOK
BLESBUCK BONTEBOK BOSCHBOK
BUSHBUCK KORRIGUM LEUCORYX
REEDBUCK STEENBOK
PRONGHORN
(YOUNG —) KID LAMB
ANTENNA DISH HORN LOOP PALP
TIER YAGI AERIAL DIPOLE FEELER
TACTOR DOUBLET WHISKER
MONOPOLE PARABOLA RADIATOR
ANTENNATA INSECTA
ANTENOR (FATHER OF —) AESYETES
(MOTHER OF —) CLEOMESTRA
(WIFE OF —) THEANO
ANTERIOR FORNE FRONT PRIOR
ATLOID BEFORE FORMER
ANTICUS PRORSAL VENTRAL
ATLANTAL INFERIOR PREVIOUS
PRECEDING
(PREF.) ANTER(O) EPH EPI PRE
PRO
ANTEROOM HALL FOYER LOBBY
ENTRANCE
ANTEROS (BROTHER OF —) EROS
(FATHER OF —) ARES MARS
(MOTHER OF —) APHRODITE
ANTEWAR PREBELLUM
ANTHAS (FATHER OF —) NEPTUNE
POSEIDON
(MOTHER OF —) ALCYONE
ANTHELION HALO NIMBUS
ANTISUN AUREOLE
ANTHELMINTIC CUNIC BRAYERA
EMBELIN PINKROOT SCAMMONY
SANTONICA PIPERAZINE
PHENOTHIAZINE
ANTHEM HYMN SONG AGNUS
MOTET PSALM INTROIT RESPOND
ASPERGES ISODICON
(JAPANESE —) KIMIGAYO
ANTHEMIUS (FATHER OF —)
PROCOPIUS
ANTHER TIP AGLET CHIVE THECA
ANTHESIS BLOOM BLOSSOM
ANTHILL BANK TUMP
ANTHOCYANIN ENIN OENIN
BETANIN PUNICIN VIOLANIN
ANTHOLOGIST RHAPSODE
RHAPSODIST
ANTHOLOGY ANA POSY ALBUM
SYLVA CORPUS READER
GARLAND SYNTAGMA
CHRESTOMATHY
ANTHOZOAN CORAL POLYP
ANEMONE GULINULA
ANTHRACITE CULM
ANTHRACONITE STINKSTONE
SWINESTONE
ANTHRAX SANG

CHARBON BLACKLEG
ANTHROPOLOGIST TOTEMIST
CULTURALIST
AMERICAN BOAS MEAD DIXON
HOUGH JENKS SAPIR STARR
BUTLER DORSEY HOLMES
HOOTON LAUFER PUTNAM
BRINTON FOLKMAR KROEBER
SPINDEN WISSLER BENEDICT
HRDLICKA MACCURDY
MACDONALD HERSKOVITS
GOLDENWEISER
AUSTRIAN LUSCHAN
ENGLISH KEITH PERRY SMITH
TYLOR BEDDOE HADDON HOWITT
LEAKEY MARETT RIVERS
FINNISH WESTERMARCK
FRENCH HAMY BROCA DENIKER
LAPOUGE TOPINARD MORTILLET
HOVELACQUE MANOUVRIER
GERMAN WAITZ GUNTHER
HARTMANN SCHWALBE
BLUMENBACH WEIDENREICH
SCHOETENSACK
ITALIAN SERGI MANTEGAZZA
SCOTTISH FRAZER MONBODDO
ANTHROPOPHAGITE CANNIBAL
ANTIA (BELOVED OF —)
BELLEROPHON
(FATHER OF —) IOBATES
(HUSBAND OF —) PROETUS
ANTIAIRCRAFT ARCHIE
ANTIANEIRA (FATHER OF —)
MENETES
(SON OF —) ECHION ERYTUS
ANTIBALLOONER SEPARATOR
ANTIBIOTIC BIOTIC ABIOTIC
HUMULON TYLOSIN CIRCULIN
CITRININ CLAVACIN CLAVATIN
COLISTIN FRADICIN HUMULONE
NEOMYCIN NYSTATIN SUBTILIN
POLYMYCIN PUROMYCIN
OLIGOMYCIN PENICILLIN
RIFAMPICIN
ANTIBODY LYSIN REAGIN BLOCKER
GLUTININ PRECIPITIN
ANTIC TOY DIDO FOOL WILD
CAPER CLOWN COMIC DROLL
MERRY PRANK STUNT GAMBOL
BUFFOON CAPRICE GAMBADE
GAMBADO
ANTICIPATE BALK BEAT HOPE
JUMP WISH ALLOT AUGUR AWAIT
DREAD PSYCH SENSE STALL
DIVINE EXPECT PSYCHE THWART
DEVANCE FORERUN FORESEE
OBVIATE PORTEND PREPARE
PREVENE PREVENT PROPOSE
RESPECT SUPPOSE ANTEDATE
FORECAST FOREFEEL FORETAKE
PROSPECT
ANTICIPATION TYPE ODIUM
AUGURY OPINION THOUGHT
PROSPECT PROLEPSIS
PRESCIENCE PREMONITION
ANTICIPATORY PREVENIENT
ANTICLEA (FATHER OF —)
AUTOLYCUS
(HUSBAND OF —) LAERTES
(SON OF —) ULYSSES ODYSSEUS
ANTICLIMAX BATHOS
ANTICLINE ARCH DOME NAPPE
ISOCLINE OVERFOLD

ANTICYCLONE HIGH
ANTIDEPRESSANT PARGYLINE
NORTRIPTYLINE
ANTIDOTE GUACO BEZOAR EMETIC
GALENA REMEDY THERIAC
DELETERY THERIACA BEZOARDIC
MITHRIDATE BLEXIPHARMIC
ANTIGEN N LYSOGEN BIOLOGIC
PRECIPITINOGEN
ANTIGERMANISM
VANSITTARTISM
ANTIGONE (AUTHOR OF —)
SOPHOCLES
(BROTHER OF —) POLYNICES
(CHARACTER IN —) CREON
HAEMON ISMENE ANTIGONE
TIRESIAS
(FATHER OF —) OEDIPUS
(MOTHER OF —) JOCASTA
ANTIGORITE SERPENTINE
ANTILOCHUS (FATHER OF —)
NESTOR
(MOTHER OF —) ANAXIBIA
(SLAYER OF —) MEMNON
ANTIMALARIAL PENTAQUIN
PENTAQUINE
ANTIMASK ANTIC ANTICK
ANTIMONIAL STIBIAL
ANTIMONY SB KOHL REGULUS
STIBIUM
(PREF.) STIB(IO)
ANTIMONY SULFIDE SURMA
SOORMA
ANTINOMIAN FIDUCIARY
ANTINOMY PARADOX
ANTIOPE (FATHER OF —) NYCTEUS
(HUSBAND OF —) LYCUS THESEUS
(SISTER OF —) HIPPOLYTE
(SON OF —) ZETHUS AMPHION
HIPPOLYTUS
ANTIOXIDANT SESAMOL
ANTIPATHY HATE ODIUM ENMITY
NAUSEA RANCOR ALLERGY
DISGUST DISLIKE AVERSION
DISTASTE DYSPATHY LOATHING
ANTIPHON SALVE GRADUAL
PLACEBO GRADUALE
ANTIPHONALLY CHOIRWISE
ANTHEMWISE
ANTIPHONARY LEDGER
ANTIPHUS (BROTHER OF —)
MESTHLES
(FATHER OF —) PRIAM
TALAEMENES
(HALF-BROTHER OF —) ISUS
(MOTHER OF —) HECUBA
ANTIPODAL ANTARCTIC
ANTIPYRETIC SALOL MALARIN
THALLIN THALLINE
ANTIQUARY ARCHAIST
ANTIQUARIAN
ANTIQUATED OLD AGED FUSTY
MOSSY PASSE FOGRAM FOSSIL
VOIDED ANCIENT ARCHAIC
FOGYISH NOACHIAN OBSOLETE
OUTDATED OUTMODED
TIMEWORN
ANTIQUE ANTIC RELIC SIRUP
SYRUP VIRTU ANTICK NOETIC
ANCIENT ARCHAIC NOACHIC
NOACHIAN OUTMODED
ARCHAICAL
ANTIQUITY ELD OLD PAST YORE

RELIC OLDNESS ANCIENCE
ANCIENCY
(PL.) ARCHEOLOGY
ARCHAEOLOGY
ANTIRED WHITE
ANTI-SEMITISM JUDOPHOBIA
ANTISEPTIC CAVA EGOL KAVA
SALT AMIDO AMINE EUPAD
EUSOL IODOL SALOL AMADOL
IATROL IODINE KRELOS PHENOL
PICROL ALCOHOL ALUMNOL
ARBUTIN ASEPTIC COLYTIC
LORETIN STERILE TACHIOL
TEUCRIN THALLIN CREOSOTE
ICHTHYOL KAVAKAVA METAPHEN
TEREBENE THALLINE MERBROMIN
ACRIFLAVINE
ANTISOCIAL HOSTILE ANARCHIST
ANTISPASMODIC KELLIN SAMBUL
SUMBAL SUMBUL KHELLIN
PAPAVERINE STRAMONIUM
PENTOBARBITAL
ANTISTROPHE REVERT
COUNTERTURN
ANTITHESIS AND CONTRAST
ANTITHETICAL OPPOSITE
ANTITOXIN SERUM BIOLOGIC
ANTIVIVISECTIONIST BESTIARIAN
ANTLER DAG HORN KNOB RIAL
TRAY DAGUE RIGHT ROYAL
SHOOT SPIKE BOSSET SHOVEL
TROCHE SPELLER DEERHORN
SURROYAL TROCHING
(— POINT) TROCHING
(PL.) HEAD ATTIRE
ANT LION DOODLEBUG
NEUROPTERAN
ANTONINA (HUSBAND OF —)
BELISARIUS
ANTONY AND CLEOPATRA
(AUTHOR OF —) SHAKESPEARE
(CHARACTER IN —) EROS IRAS
MENAS PHILO ALEXAS ANTONY
GALLUS SCARUS SEXTUS SILIUS
TAURUS AGRIPPA LEPIDUS
MARDIAN OCTAVIA THYREUS
VARRIUS CANIDIUS CHARMIAN
DERCETAS DIOMEDES DOMITIUS
MECAENAS OCTAVIUS SELEUCUS
CLEOPATRA DEMETRIUS
DOLABELLA VENTIDIUS
EUPHRONIUS MENECRATES
PROCULEIUS
ANTONYM OPPOSITE
ANTOTHIJAH (FATHER OF —)
JEROHAM
ANTSHRIKE BATARA
ANT THRUSH PITTA
ANT TREE HORMIGO
ANUB (FATHER OF —) COZ
ANUS ASS ARSE BUNG VENT SIEGE
TEWEL
(PREF.) ANO PROCT(O)
(SUFF.) PROCTA
ANVIL BLOCK INCUS SNARL STAKE
STITH TEEST STETHY STITHY
ANDVILE ANFEELD BICKERN
BEAKIRON
(— SUPPORT) STOCK
(MINIATURE —) STAKE STUMP
(PREF.) INCUD(O)
ANXIETY HOW CARE CARK FEAR
FRAY PAIN ALARM ANGOR ANGST

DOUBT DREAD PANIC WORRY
KIAUGH PUCKER ANGUISH
CAUTION CHAGRIN CONCERN
SCRUPLE TENSION THOUGHT
TROUBLE DISQUIET SUSPENSE
SOLICITUDE
ANXIOUS AGOG BUSY FOND TOEY
EAGER FIRST UPSET AFRAID
UNEASY ANGUISH CAREFUL
CARKING EARNFUL FORWARD
TIDIOSE UNQUIET DESIROUS
RESTLESS THOUGHTY WATCHFUL
CONCERNED
ANY A AN AY AIR ALL ARY ONI
ONY AIRY EVER PART SOME
WHAT
(— WHATEVER) ALL
ANYBODY ANY ONE ANYONE
SOMEONE
ANYHOW HOW NOHOW NOWAY
ALWAYS ANYWAY
ANYONE HE MAN ANYBODY
ANYTHING THAT AUGHT OUGHT
ANYWAY NOHOW ALWAYS
ANYWHERE EIHWER OWHERE
UBIQUE ANYPLACE
ANYWISE ANYHOW ANYWAY
ANYWAYS
AOUDAD ARUI UDAD AUDAD
SHEEP CHAMOIS
APACE FAST QUICK QUICKLY
RAPIDLY SPEEDILY
APACHE YUMA PADUCA CIBECUE
VAQUERO QUERECHO
MESCALERO
APAGOGE ABDUCTION
APAP EPIPHI
APAR APARA BOLITA MATACO
APART BY OFF AWAY BOUT ELSE
ALONE ALOOF AROOM ASIDE
RIVEN SOLUS SPLIT YTWYN
ABREID ATWAIN LONELY SUNDRY
ASUNDER ENISLED REMOVED
SEVERAL SEVERED SEPARATE
PIECEMEAL
(— FROM) BARRING
(WIDE —) ASPAR
(WIDELY —) ABROAD
(PREF.) CHORI DI DICH
APARTMENT BUT PAD WON DIGS
FLAT HALL ROOM STEW WENE
WONE WOON ABODE BOWER
OECUS ORIEL ROOMS SALON
SOLAR SUITE ANDRON CLOSET
DECKER DINGLE DUPLEX GROTTO
LYCEUM SALOON SINGLE SOLLAR
SPENCE STANZA BUTTERY
CHAMBER COCKPIT GALLERY
MANSION PRIVACY BUILDING
EPHEBEUM SHOWROOM
SOLARIUM TENEMENT THALAMUS
MAISONETTE
(— FOR IDOL) TING
(— IN CASTLE) BOWER
(— IN CHURCH) SACRISTY
(— OF WARSHIP) COCKPIT
(BACHELOR —) GARCONNIERE
(OUTER —) BUT
(PRIVATE —) MAHAL PARADISE
(RENTED —) LET
(PL.) GYNAECEUM
APATHETIC CALM COLD COOL
DEAD DOWF DULL BLASE DOWFF

INERT STOIC GLASSY SUPINE
TORPID ADENOID PASSIVE
UNMOVED LISTLESS SLUGGISH
LETHARGIC PERFUNCTORY
APATHY SLOTH ACEDIA CAFARD
PHLEGM TORPOR LANGUOR
DOLDRUMS DULLNESS LETHARGY
OMISSION STOICISM STOLIDITY
APATITE IJOLITE MOROXITE
PHOSPHORITE
APAYAO ISNEG
APE KRA LAR PAN BOOR COPY
DUPE FOOL MAHA MIME MOCK
SHAM BEROK CLOWN MAGOT
MIMIC ORANG PONGO PYGMY
APELET BABOON GELADA GIBBON
LANGUR MARTEN MARTIN
MONKEY OURANG PARROT
PONGID SIMIAN SIMIID BUFFOON
COPYCAT EMULATE GORILLA
IMITATE PORTRAY PRIMATE
SATYRUS SIAMANG DURUKULI
IMITATOR MANTEGAR SIMULATE
ORANGUTAN
(— STUDY) PITHECOLOGY
(PREF.) PITHEC(O)
(SUFF.) PITHECUS
APEAK VERTICAL
APEIRON MATTER
APER BOAR MIME SNOB CLOWN
MOCKER BUFFOON COPYCAT
APERCU DIGEST GLANCE PRECIS
SKETCH INSIGHT OUTLINE
APERIENT LAX OPENER CASCARA
APERIODIC DEADBEAT
APERITIF WHET CINZANO
DUBONNET
APERTURE F EYE GAP OPE VUE
BOLE BORE HOLE LEAK PASS
PORE RIMA SLIT SLOT VENT
BREAK CHASM CLEFT CRACK
LIGHT MOUTH PUPIL STOMA
CUTOUT HIATUS KEYWAY
LOUVER WINDOW FISSURE
KEYHOLE OPENING ORIFICE
OSTIOLE PINHOLE PUNCTUM
SWALLOW TROMPIL APERTION
FENESTRA LOOPHOLE OVERTURE
SPIRACLE
APEX EPI PIN TIP TOP ACME AUGE
CONE CUSP NOON PEAK RUFF
CREST HIGHT PITCH POINT SPIRE
APOGEE CLIMAX CRISIS CUPULA
GENION HEIGHT SUMMIT TITTLE
VERTEX ZENITH CACUMEN
EVEREST PAPILLA PUNCTUM
PINNACLE
(— OF HELMET) CREST
(PREF.) APIC(O)
(SUFF.) ACE
APHAREUS (BROTHER OF —)
LEUCIPPUS
(FATHER OF —) PERIERES
(MOTHER OF —) GORGOPHONE
(SON OF —) IDAS LYNCEUS
(WIFE OF —) ARENE
APHASIA ALALIA ALEXIA JARGON
APHEMIA ASYMBOLIA
APHID APHIS LOUSE APTERA
BLIGHT COLLIER DIMERAN
MIGRANS PUCERON BLACKFLY
GREENFLY GYNOPARA HOMOPTER
APHIDAS (DAUGHTER OF —) ANTIA

(FATHER OF —) ARCAS
(MOTHER OF —) ERATO MEGANIRA
CHRYSOPELIA
(SON OF —) ALEUS
APHORISM SAW ADAGE AXIOM
GNOME MAXIM MOTTO SUTRA
SUTTA DICTUM SAYING WISDOM
EPIGRAM PRECEPT PROVERB
APOTHEGM PISHOGUE
APHORISTIC GNOMIC
APHRODISIAC DEWTRY DAMIANA
VENEREAL VENEREOUS
APHRODITE VENUS CYPRIS
URANIA ANTHEIA MYLITTA
CYTHEREA PANDEMOS
(FATHER OF —) ZEUS JUPITER
(HUSBAND OF —) VULCAN
(MOTHER OF —) DIONE
(SON OF —) EROS CUPID AENEAS
APIARIST SKEPPIST
APIARY HIVE SKEP BEEYARD
BEEHOUSE
APICULTURE BEEKEEPING
APIECE UP ALL PER EACH
SERIATIM
APIKORES BECORESH
APIO ARRACACH ARRACACHA
APIOS SOIA SOJA GLYCINE
APIS HAPI
(FATHER OF —) APOLLO
PHORONEUS
(MOTHER OF —) LAODICE
APISH SILLY FOPPISH AFFECTED
APITONG BAGAC HAPITON
KERUING
APIUM UMBEL
APLITE HAPLITE
APLOMB TACT NERVE POISE
SURETY COOLNESS
APOCALYPSE SHOWING
REVELATION
APOCHRYPHA PSEUDEPIGRAPHA
APOCRISIARY RESPONSAL
APOCRYPHAL SHAM FALSE
UNREAL DOUBTFUL FABULOUS
FICTIOUS
APODAL FOOTLESS
APOGEE ACME APEX AUGE PEAK
CLIMAX ZENITH
APOGON AMIA CARDINAL
APOLLO SUN PAEAN DELIUS
AGYIEUS APOLLON LYKEIOS
PATROUS PHOEBUS PYTHIUS
CYNTHIUS PYTHAEUS
(FATHER OF —) ZEUS JUPITER
(MOTHER OF —) LETO LATONA
(SISTER OF —) DIANA ARTEMIS
APOLLYON DEVIL SATAN
ABADDON
APOLOGETIC SORRY
APOLOGUE MYTH FABLE STORY
APOLOGY PARABLE ALLEGORY
APOLOGY PLEA ALIBI AMENDS
EXCUSE PARDON REGRET
PRETEXT SCRUPLE APOLOGIA
APOPHYGE SCAPE ESCAPE
APOPLEXY ESCA SHOCK STROKE
POPLESIE
APOSTASY FALL LAPSE
APOSTATE RAT LAPSED CONVERT
HERETIC PERVERT SECEDER
DESERTER DISLOYAL RECREANT
RENEGADE TURNCOAT

APOSTLE ESCAPE TEACHER DISCIPLE FOLLOWER PREACHER **(BIBLICAL —)** JOHN JUDE LEVI PAUL DENIS JAMES JUDAS PETER SIMON ANDREW PHILIP THOMAS DIDYMUS MATTHEW BARNABAS MATTHIAS

APOSTLE BIRD CATBIRD

APOSTROPHE TUISM TURNWAY TURNTALE

APOTHECARY CHEMIC SPICER CHEMICK DRUGGIST

APOTHECIUM CUP PELTA TRICA SHIELD ARDELLA LIRELLA PATELLA

APOTHEGM SAW DICT ADAGE AXIOM GNOME MAXIM SUTRA DICTUM SAYING SUTTAH PROVERB APHORISM SENTENCE

APOTHEOSIS DEIFICATION CONSECRATION

APOTHEOSIZE DEIFY EXALT ELEVATE GLORIFY CANONIZE

APPAIM (FATHER OF —) NADAB

APPALL STUN APPAL DAUNT SHOCK DISMAY REDUCE REVOLT WEAKEN ASTOUND DEPRESS DISGUST DISMISS HORRIFY TERRIFY AFFRIGHT ASTONISH ENFEEBLE FRIGHTEN OVERCOME

APPALLING AWFUL AWESOME FEARFUL TERRIBLE TERRIFIC

APPANAGE GRANT ADJUNCT APANAGE

APPARATUS AID BOX GUN LOG SET ADON DRAG ETNA FAKE GEAR GRIP HECK HELM LAMP LIFT STOW TIRE TOOL BURET GANCH HOIST HORSE LEECH RELAY SCUBA SHEAR SIREN SONAR STILL STOVE SWING BUDDLE BUFFER COILER COOKER DEVICE DINGUS ENGINE FEEDER FILTER FOGGER GADGET GEYSER GRAITH LADDER LIFTER MILKER ORRERY OUTFIT REFLUX SEESAW SHEARS SMOKER SMUDGE TACKLE TIPPLE TREMIE TROMPE AERATOR ALEMBIC APPAREL AUTOMAT BAGGAGE BALANCE BASCULE BURETTE DERRICK ECHELON FURNACE GASOGEN GRILLER HOISTER INHALER ISOTRON MACHINE MEGAFOG PINCERS PRESSER SOXHLET SPRAYER STIRRER TELEPIX TREMOLO TRIMMER UTENSIL AGITATOR AQUALUNG BLOWDOWN CALUTRON CONVEYER CONVEYOR CRYOSTAT DIALYZER DIAPHOTE DIGESTER DRENCHER DUMBBELL EOLIPILE EQUIPAGE ERGOSTAT GASIFIER GAZOGENE INJECTOR ISOSCOPE JACQUARD OSMOGENE OZONIZER PULMOTOR PURIFIER RECORDER REDUCTOR REHEATER SCRUBBER SOFTENER STRIPPER ABSORPTIOMETER **(— IN STOMACH OF LOBSTER)** LADY **(SEGMENTAL —)** BRAINSTEM **(SUFF.)** STAT(IC)(ICS)

APPAREL DECK FARE GARB GEAR ROBE SECT TIRE WEAR WEDE ADORN ARRAY BESEE CLOTH DRESS EQUIP HABIT TUNIC ATTIRE CLOTHE GRAITH OUTFIT PARURE ROBING CLOBBER COSTUME FURNISH GARMENT HARNESS PREPARE RAIMENT VESTURE CLOTHING FOOTWEAR HEADWEAR WARDROBE **(HEAD —)** MILLINERY **(MILITARY —)** WARENTMENT **(RICH —)** ARRAY

APPARENT OPEN BREEM BREME CLEAR OVERT PLAIN FORMAL PARENT PATENT PHANIC CERTAIN EVIDENT GLARING OBVIOUS SEEMING SHALLOW VISIBLE DISTINCT ILLUSORY MANIFEST PALPABLE PROBABLE SEMBLANT SEMBLABLE OSTENSIBLE

APPARENTLY (PREF.) QUASI

APPARITION HUE HANT SHOW DREAM FANCY FETCH GHOST HAUNT IMAGE LARVA PHASM SHADE SHAPE SPOOK ASPECT DOUBLE IDOLUM SOWLTH SPIRIT SPRITE STOUND SWARTH TAISCH THURSE VISION WRAITH DISPLAY EIDOLON FANTASY FEATURE PHANTOM SPECTER SPECTRE EPIPHANY ILLUSION PHANTASM PRESENCE REVENANT SPECTRUM SEMBLANCE

APPARITOR BEADLE PARURE PARITOR SUMMONER

APPEAL ASK BEG BID CRY CALL CASE PLEA SEEK SUIT APPLY CHARM CLEPE REFER SPEAK ACCUSE ADJURE AVOUCH INVOKE PRAYER SUMMON ADDRESS CONJURE ENTREAT IMPLORE REQUEST SOLICIT APPROACH ENTREATY PETITION ADJURATION **(— TO)** APPLY AVOUCH INVOKE ARRAIGN **(SEX —)** IT OOMPH

APPEALING CUTE NICE CATCHY CLEVER CUNNING SUGARED PLEASANT **(STRIKINGLY —)** ZINGY

APPEAR BID CAR EYE GET COME DAWN FARE LOOK LOOM MAKE MEET PEER REAR RISE SEEM WALK ARISE ENTER ISSUE KITHE KYTHE OCCUR SOUND THINK ARRIVE BESEEM EMERGE INFORM REGARD SPRING BLOSSOM COMPEAR DEVELOP OUTCROP RESEMBLE **(— AND DISAPPEAR)** COOK **(— BRIEFLY)** GLINT **(— DIRECTLY BEFORE)** AFFRONT **(— SUDDENLY)** BURST **(— UNEXPECTEDLY)** BLOOM IRRUPT (PREF.) PHANER(O) PHANTA PHANTO

APPEARANCE AIR CUT HUE CAST FARE FORM GARB IDEA LATE LEEN LOOK MIEN SHOW VIEW BLUSH COLOR EIDOS FAVOR FRONT GUISE HABIT PHASE PHASM SHAPE SIGHT SOUND SPICE ASPECT EFFECT FACIES FAVOUR MANNER OBJECT OSTENT REGARD VISAGE ARRIVAL DISPLAY FARRAND FASHION FEATURE GLIMPSE OUTSIDE RESPECT SHOWING SPECIES ARTEFACT ARTIFACT EPIPHANY ILLUSION LIKENESS PRESENCE PRETENSE SEMBLANCE **(— OF LIGHT ON HAIR)** HAG **(CLOUDED —)** HAZE CHILL **(CONSPICUOUS —)** FIGURE **(DISTINCTIVE —)** AURA **(FIRST —)** DAWN DEBUT SPRING **(IMPOVERISHED —)** BEGGARY **(MERE —)** INTENTIONAL **(MOCK —)** SIMULACRUM **(MOTTLED —)** ROE DAPPLE **(MOTTLED SKY —)** BLINK **(OUTWARD —)** FACE SEEM SHOW FACADE APPAREL BALLOON SEEMING SURFACE **(PERSONAL —)** PRESENCE **(STRIPED —)** ROE **(SUPERNATURAL —)** APPARITION **(SURFACE —)** TOUR BLOOM **(UNGAINLY —)** ANGULARITY **(VAGUE —)** BLUR (PREF.) SPECTRO (SUFF.) OPSIA OPSIO OPSIS OPSY PHANE PHANOUS PHANT PHANY

APPEASE LAY PAY CALM EASE HUSH SATE ALLAY ALONE ATONE MEASE PEACE PEASE QUIET SLAKE STILL DEFRAY GENTLE MEEKEN MODIFY PACIFY PLEASE SOFTEN SOOTHE ASSUAGE CONTENT DULCIFY GRATIFY MOLLIFY PLACATE SATISFY STICKLE SUFFICE SWEETEN MITIGATE PROPITIATE **(— APPETITE)** STAY

APPEASEMENT MUNICHISM

APPELLATION NAME TERM GODDY STYLE TITLE APPEAL CALLING EPITHET GOODMAN SURNAME COGNOMEN METRONYM NICKNAME

APPEND ADD PIN TAG CLIP HANG JOIN TACK AFFIX ANNEX ADJOIN ATTACH FASTEN AUGMENT SUBJOIN

APPENDAGE ARM AWN FIN LEG TAB TAG ARIL BARB CAUD FLAP HOOK HORN LIMB LOBE SPUR TAIL AFFIX BEARD CAUDA CERAS EXITE RIDER SCALE TROLL WHISK CERCUS CIRRUS CORONA ELATER ENDITE LAGENA LIGULE PALPUS PAPPUS STIPEL STYLET SUFFIX UROPOD ADJUNCT ANTENNA AURICLE CODICIL EARLOBE EMBLAST FIXTURE FURCULA GONOPOD HOUSING MALELLA PENDANT STIPULE SWIMMER THIMBLE TRAILER WINGLET ADDITION ADHERENT ASCIDIUM BRACHIUM EMPODIUM FILAMENT GNATHITE PEDIPALP PENDICLE PHYLLOID PREDELLA RHABDITE SYNTROPE MAXILLIPED

(— ON MOCCASIN) TRAILER **(EAR-SHAPED —)** AURICLE (PL.) ADNEXA ANNEXA FORCEPS

APPENDIX EKE ANNEX LABEL APPEND VERMIX AURICLE CODICIL PENDANT ADDENDUM AURICULA EPILOGUE

APPERCEPTION RECOGNITION

APPERTAIN LIE FALL REFER BELONG EFFEIR RELATE CONCERN PERTAIN

APPETITE MAW YEN LUST PICA TUCK URGE WILL ZEST BELLY BLOOD GORGE GREED GUSTO TASTE TWIST BULIMY DESIRE FAMINE GENIUS GODOWN HUNGER LIKING OREXIS RELISH STROKE TALENT BULIMIA CRAVING EDACITY LONGING PASSION STOMACH SWALLOW WANTING CUPIDITY FONDNESS GULOSITY TENDENCY **(— LOSS)** ANOREXIA **(ANIMAL —)** BLOOD **(CANINE —)** PHAGEDENA **(EXCESSIVE —)** LIMOSIS GULOSITY POLYPHAGIA **(PERVERTED —)** MALACIA (SUFF.) OREXIA **(— FOR)** PHIL(A)(AE)(E)(IA)(ISM) (IST)(OUS)(US)(Y)

APPETIZER WET WHET SAUCE CANAPE RELISH SAVORY CEVICHE SASHIMI APERITIF COCKTAIL DUBONNET

APPETIZING NICE GUSTY SAVORY GUSTFUL GUSTABLE PALATABLE

APPLAUD HUM CLAP LAUD RISE ROOT RUFF CHEER EXTOL HUZZA PRAISE ACCLAIM APPROVE COMMENT ENDORSE HOSANNA PLAUDIT

APPLAUSE CLAP HAND BRAVO CHEER ECLAT HUZZA SALVO HURRAH PRAISE ACCLAIM OVATION CLAPPING

APPLE PIP CRAB OHIA POME COPEI JAMBO BEEFIN BIFFIN CODLIN DOUCIN ESOPUS GOLDIN KARELA KAVIKA MACUPA MAKOPA PIPPIN PUFFIN RENNET RUSSET BALDWIN BEAUFIN CODLING COSTARD FAMEUSE GOLDING PEELING POMEROY RAMBURE RIBSTON RUDDOCK WAGENER WEALTHY WINESAP AMPALAYA COCCAGEE CORTLAND GREENING JONATHAN MCINTOSH NONESUCH PARADISE PEARMAIN POMANDER POROPORO QUEENING REINETTE ROSACEAN SWEETING WHITSOUR QUARENDEN **(— OF PERU)** JIMSON JIMPSON SHOOFLY **(BITTER —)** COLOCYNTH **(CRAB —)** CRAB SCRAB WHARRE POWITCH **(EMU —)** COLANE **(GOLDEN —)** BEL BAEL **(LIKE AN —)** POMACEOUS **(PEELED —)** DUMPLING **(SHRIVELED —)** CRUMPLING

(SLICED DRIED —S) SNITS SNITZ SCHNITZ

(SMALL —) CODLIN CODLING

(SMALL —S) GRIGGLES

(THORN —) MAD METEL

(PREF.) POMI POMO

APPLEBERRY DUMPLING

APPLEJOHN DEUSAN DEUZAN

APPLE-POLISH BROWNNOSE

APPLIANCE GEAR GRAB IRON TOOL BRACE CLAMP DEVIL FLIER FLYER GLODE SHADE BONNET BREWER DEVICE ENGINE FABRIC GADGET GAITER JUICER SPLINT WINDLE CHARGER MACHINE SCRAPER STOPPER UTENSIL BALANCER DEVIATOR

APPLICABLE APT FIT MEET PROPER USEFUL FITTING PLIABLE APPOSITE RELATIVE RELEVANT SUITABLE

(UNIVERSALLY —) CATHOLIC

(WIDELY —) BROAD

APPLICANT PROSPECT

APPLICATION USE DAUB FORM BLANK TOPIC APPEAL EFFORT ADDRESS EPITHEM REQUEST EPITHEME LENITIVE PETITION PRACTICE SEDULITY

(— OF KNOWLEDGE) PRACTICE PRACTISE

(— TO WRONG PURPOSE) ABUSE

(MEDICINAL —) PLASTER DRESSING FRONTING LENITIVE

(MENTAL —) INTENTION

APPLICATOR COLPOSTAT

APPLIED (CLOSELY —) ACCUMBENT

(PREF.) TECHNO

APPLIQUE DAG DAGGE ATTACH DESIGN ORNAMENT

APPLY ASK LAY PLY PUT RUB SET USE BEAR BEND CLAP DAUB GIVE HOLD MOVE SEEK TOIL TURN WORK ADAPT GRIND IMPLY LABOR LIKEN REFER SMEAR ADDICT APPEAL APPOSE BESTOW BETAKE BUCKLE COMPLY DEVOTE DIRECT EMPLOY EXTEND RESORT ADHIBIT COMPARE CONFORM IMPRESS OVERLAY PERTAIN REQUEST SOLICIT UTILIZE DEDICATE DISPENSE MINISTER PETITION

(— BRAKE) BUR

(— COSMETICS) DO POP

(— GRAPHITE) BLACKLEAD

(— GREASE) ARM

(— HOT CLOTHS) FOMENT

(— IMPROPERLY) ABUSE

(— ONESELF) ATTEND INTEND MUCKLE ADDRESS

(— PIGMENT) DRAG

(— TO) CONSULT CONTACT

APPOGGIATURA BACKFALL ACCIACCATURA

(DOUBLE —) FALL

APPOINT ARM FIX SET CALL DECK GIVE MAKE NAME ALLOT ARRAY AWARD COOPT CREST DIGHT ELECT ENACT EQUIP INSET PITCH PLACE POINT SHAPE SLATE ASSIGN ASSIZE ATTACH CREATE DECREE DEPUTE DETAIL DEVISE

DIRECT ENTAIL ORDAIN OUTFIT SETTLE STEVEN TAILYE ARRAIGN CONFIRM DESTINE DISPOSE FURNISH GAZETTE RESOLVE TAILZIE DELEGATE DEPUTIZE INDICATE NOMINATE ORDINATE

(— A CLERIC) COLLATE

(— BEFOREHAND) STALL

APPOINTEE PLACEMAN

APPOINTMENT SET DATE BERTH ORDER TRYST BILLET OFFICE STEVEN COMMAND STATION CREATION DELEGACY POSITION

(— OF HEIR) INSTITUTION

APPORTION LOT DEAL DOLE MARK METE PART RATE ALLOT AWARD CAVEL GRANT PARAL SHARE SHIFT WEIGH APPLOT ASSESS ASSIGN DIVIDE PARCEL RATION TAVERN ARRANGE BALANCE QUARTER ALLOCATE DESCRIBE ADMEASURE PROPORTION

APPORTIONMENT DIVISION

APPOSITE APT PAT COGENT TIMELY GERMANE INCIDENT RELATIVE RELEVANT SUITABLE

APPRAISAL APPRIZAL

APPRAISE GAGE LOVE METE RATE ASSAY GAUGE JUDGE PRICE PRIZE VALUE ASSESS ESTEEM EVALUE PONDER PRAISE SURVEY ADJUDGE ANALYZE COMMEND ESTIMATE EVALUATE

APPRECIABLE ANY SENSIBLE PERCEPTIBLE

APPRECIATE DIG FEEL LOVE JUDGE PRIZE RAISE SAVOR TASTE VALUE ADMIRE ESTEEM SAVOUR ADVANCE APPRIZE APPROVE CHERISH REALIZE INCREASE TREASURE

APPRECIATION EYE GUSTO SENSE CONCEIT PERCEPTION

APPRECIATIVE AWAKE GRATEFUL

(— OF BEAUTY) ESTHETIC AESTHETIC

APPREHEND COP GET LAG NAB SEE FEAR HEAR KNOW NOTE SCAN TAKE VIEW CATCH DREAD GRASP GRIPE INTUE SEIZE ARREST BEHOLD DETAIN INTEND INTUIT BELIEVE CAPTURE CONCEIT ENDOUTE FORESEE IMAGINE REALIZE RECEIVE SENSATE SUPPOSE CONCEIVE DISCOVER OVERTAKE PERCEIVE

APPREHENDED GRIPPIT

APPREHENSIBLE NOETIC SENSATE SENSIBLE

APPREHENSION FEAR FRAY PAIN PANG SCAN WERE ALARM DOUBT DREAD FANCY WORRY ARREST DISMAY NOESIS ANXIETY CAPTURE CONCERN PRESAGE SUSPECT DISTRUST MISTRUST SUSPENSE COGNITION PREHENSION

APPREHENSIVE APT JUMPY FEARED MORBID ANXIOUS FEARFUL JEALOUS NERVOUS STREAKY UPTIGHT DOUBTFUL SOLICITOUS

APPRENTICE CUB BIND BOOT

SNOB TYRO CADET DEVIL BURSCH HELPER JOCKEY NOVICE BANKMAN GROMMET LEARNER TRAINEE WAISTER APRENDIZ BEGINNER JACKAROO PRENTICE SERVITOR TURNOVER

APPRENTICESHIP SERVITUDE

APPRISE WARN LEARN TEACH ADVISE INFORM NOTIFY REVEAL APPRIZE ACQUAINT DISCLOSE INSTRUCT

APPROACH TRY ADIT BUMP BURN CHAT COME COST DRAW NEAR NERE NIGH ROAD ABORD BOARD CLOSE COAST ESSAY STALK VERGE ACCEDE ACCESS ACCOST ADVENT ANIMUS APPEAL BORDER BREAST BROACH COMING GATHER IMPEND PROACH TRENCH ADVANCE AGGRESS APPULSE CONTACT PREFACE SEAGATE SUCCEED CONVERGE NEIGHBOR ONCOMING

(— FROM WINDWARD) BEAR

(— GAME) DRAW

(— HOSTILELY) SWAY

(— NEAR) TOUCH

(— OF NIGHT) FALL

(— TENDENCY) ADIENCE

(INVITING —) PASS

APPROACHABLE COMMON AFFABLE ACCESSIBLE

APPROACHING LIKE COMING TOWARD ONCOMING

APPROBATION TEST FAVOR PROOF TRIAL ASSENT FAVOUR LOANGE PRAISE REGARD REPUTE PLAUDIT APPLAUSE APPROVAL SANCTION

APPROPRIATE ADD APT DUE FIT LAY PAT AKIN CRIB FEAT GOOD GRAB GRIP HELP JUST MEET SINK SUIT TAKE ALLOT ANNEX FITTY HAPPY RIGHT STEAL USURP ASSELF ASSIGN ASSUME BORROW DECENT DEVOTE DEVOUR DIGEST GATHER GENTIL KINDLY PILFER PIRATE PROPER TIMELY WORTHY APPROVE APROPOS CABBAGE CONDIGN CONVERT FITTING GERMANE GRABBLE GRADELY IMPOUND PREEMPT PURLOIN RELATED SECRETE SWALLOW ACCROACH APPOSITE ARROGATE BECOMING DESERVED EMBEZZLE GRACEFUL HANDSOME IDONEOUS PECULIAR PROPERTY RELEVANT RIGHTFUL SUITABLE

(— UNLAWFULLY) HEIST STEAL

(MOST —) CHOICE

APPROPRIATENESS APTNESS DECENCY FITNESS APTITUDE

(NICE —) ELEGANCE

APPROPRIATION FUND VOTE DEVOTION

(FRAUDULENT —) CON EMBEZZLEMENT

APPROVAL AMEN ECLAT ASSENT ESTEEM APPROOF CONSENT PLAUDIT SUPPORT APPLAUSE BLESSING SANCTION SUFFRAGE AGREEMENT

APPROVE DO OK BUY DIG TRY

AMEN HAVE LIKE OKAY OKEH PASS TEST VOTE ALLOW BLESS CLEAR FAVOR PROVE VALUE ACCEPT ADMIRE BISHOP CONCUR RATIFY APPLAUD CERTIFY COMMEND CONFIRM CONSENT ENDORSE EXHIBIT INDORSE SUPPORT ACCREDIT MANIFEST SANCTION

APPROVED TRYE EXPERT PROBAL ACCEPTED ORTHODOX

(NOT —) OUT

APPROVING HEARTY

APPROXIMATE NEAR ABOUT CIRCA CLOSE COAST ROUGH COARSE GENERAL NOMINAL APPROACH ESTIMATE

APPROXIMATELY SAY AWAY GAIN MUCH NIGH SOME ABOUT CIRCA ALMOST AROUND NEARLY TOWARD CRUDELY ROUGHLY

APPROXIMATING COMPARATIVE

APPROXIMATION CIRCA COUNTERFEIT

APPURTENANCE GEAR ANNEX ASSIGN EFFEIR ADJUNCT COMFORT APPANAGE PENDICLE

(PL.) ADDENDA

APRICOT COT UME ANSU MUME ABRICOCK BLENHEIM

(DRIED —S) MEBOS MEEBOS

A PRIORI PURE

APRON BIB CAP BASE BOOT BRAT DICK RAMP SLOP TAYO TIER COVER EPHOD BARVEL BISHOP CANVAS DAIDLE DICKEY NAPRON RUNWAY SHIELD TARMAC TOUSER BRATTLE CANVASS DAIDLIE GREMIAL TABLIER LAMBSKIN PINAFORE PRASKEEN

(— OF FURNITURE) PETTICOAT

(— OF SEAT) FALL

(CHILD'S —) TIER BISWOP SLIPPER

(LEATHER —) DICK DICKY BARVEL DICKEY BARMFEL BARVELL BARMSKIN

(MASON'S —) LAMBSKIN

(SILKEN —) GREMIAL

(PL.) ARMITAS

APROPOS APT FIT PAT MEET TIMELY RELEVANT SUITABLE

APSE BEMA APSIS NICHE CONCHA EXEDRA RECESS

APSIS APSE AUGE

APSYRTUS (FATHER OF —) AEETES

(MOTHER OF —) IDYIA ASTERODIA

(SISTER OF —) MEDEA

APT FIT PAT YAP ABLE DEFT FAIN FEAT GLEG KEEN VAIN WONT ADEPT ALERT HAPPY PRONE QUICK READY ASPERT CLEVER DOCILE KITTLE LIABLE LIKELY PRETTY SUITED TOWARD APROPOS CAPABLE FITTING IDONEAL WILLING APPOSITE DEXTROUS DISPOSED HANDSOME IDONEOUS INCLINED POIGNANT PRACTIVE PREPARED SKILLFUL SUITABLE

(— TO TURN) WALT

APTERYX KIWI RATITE KIVIKIVI KIWIKIWI

APTITUDE ART BENT GIFT HEAD

TURN CRAFT FLAIR HABIT KNACK
SKILL VERVE GENIUS TALENT
ABILITY CONDUCT FACULTY
FITNESS LEANING CAPACITY
INSTINCT TENDENCY
APTLY PAT
APTNESS GIFT KNACK SKILL
APTITUDE FELICITY
APUS CYPSELUS MICROPUS
AQUARIUS SKINKER
AQUEDUCT AQUA DUCT CANAL
AQUAGE SPECUS CHANNEL
CONDUIT PASSAGE
(— OF SILVIUS) ITER
AQUEOUS HYDATOID WATERISH
AQUILA (WIFE OF —) PRISCILLA
AQUILANT (BROTHER OF —)
GRYPHON
ARA MACAW
(FATHER OF —) JETHER
ARAB AHL AUS IBAD OMAN SLEB
WAIF ARABY GAMIN NOMAD
SAUDI TATAR SEMITE SLUBBI
URCHIN ARABIAN BEDOUIN
SARACEN SOLUBBI AZZAZAME
KABABISH LARRIKIN SLOUBBIE
YEMENITE
ARABELLA (CHARACTER IN —)
MATTEO ZDENKA WALDNER
ARABELLA MANDRYKA
(COMPOSER OF —) STRAUSS
ARABESQUE ORNATE

ARABIA

COIN: LARI CARAT DINAR KABIK
RIYAL
DESERT: NYD ANKAF DEHNA
NAFUD NEFUD
GARMENT: ABA HAIK CABAAN
BURNOUS
GODDESS: ALLAT
HOLY CITY: MECCA MEDINA
HOLY LAND: HEJAZ
ISLAND: SOCOTRA
JUDGE: CADI
KINGDOM: NEJD
MEASURE: DEN SAA FERK KIST
ACHIR BARID CABDA CAFIZ
COVID CUDDY MAKUK QASAB
TEMAN WOIBE ZUDDA ARTABA
ASSBAA COVIDO FEDDAN
GARIBA GHALVA CAPHITE
FARSAKH FARSANG KILADJA
MARHALE NUSFIAH
MOUNTAIN: NEBO HOREB SINAI
PORT: ADEN
RULER: AMIR EMIR AMEER EMEER
STATE: ASIR OMAN YEMEN
KUWAIT
TOWN: ABHA ADEN BEDA BERA
HAIL RIAD SANA TAIF DUBAI
HAUTA HOFUF JIDDA MECCA
MOCHA QATIF TAIZZ YENBO
ANAIZA MANAMA MATRAH
MEDINA RIYADH SALALA
SHAQRA BURAIDA HODEIDA
MUKALLA ONEIZAH SHARJAH
TRIBE: AUS ASIR IRAD TEMA
KEDAR DIENDEL SHUKRIA
WEIGHT: ROTL BAHAR CHEKI
KELLA MAUND NASCH NEVAT
OCQUE OUKIA RATEL TOMAN
VAKIA BOKARD DIRHEM

MISKAL FARSALAH

ARABIC CARSHUNI GARSHUNI
KARSHUNI THAMUDIC
(— ALPHABET) BA FA HA RA TA YA
ZA AYN DAD DAL JIM KAF KHA
LAM MIM NUN QAF SAD SIN THA
WAW ZAY ALIF DHAL SHIN
GHAYN
ARABLE FERTILE PLOWABLE
TILLABLE
ARACHNID CRAB MITE TICK TAINT
ACARID ACARUS CARTER SPIDER
CARTARE OCTOPOD PEDIPALP
SCORPION SOLPUGID
PSEUDOSCORPION
ARAD (FATHER OF —) BERIAH
ARAGONITE ALABASTER
ARAIN ARRAND
ARAKANESE MAGHI
ARAM (FATHER OF —) ESROM
HEZRON KEMUEL SHAMER
ARAMAIC SYRIAC MANDAEAN
(— TRANSLATION) TARGUM
ARAN (BROTHER OF —) UZ
(FATHER OF —) DISHAN
ARANEA EPEIRA
ARAPAIMA PIRARUCU
ARAPONGA BELLBIRD
ARAROBA ZEBRAWOOD
ARAROS (FATHER OF —)
ARISTOPHANES
ARAUCANIAN AUCA PAMPA
MAPOCHE MOLUCHE PAMPERO
PICUNCHE
ARAWA AOTEA MATATUA
ARAWAK ARUA BARE URAN
ARAUA BAURE CAMPA CHANE
GUANA INERI SIUSI BAINOA
BANIVA GUINAU IGNERI GOAJIRO
IPURINA CAQUETIO CUSTENAU
ARBALEST BALISTER CROSSBOW
ARBITER JUDGE CRITIC ODDMAN
UMPIRE ADVISER DAYSMAN
ODDSMAN OVERMAN REFEREE
DICTATOR STICKLER
ARBITRAGE SHUNTING
ARBITRARY SEVERE THETIC
WILLFUL ABSOLUTE DESPOTIC
MASTERLY
(NOT —) FREE
ARBITRATE DECIDE MEDIATE
ARBITRATION DAYMENT
ARBITRATOR REF JUDGE UMPIRE
ARBITER MUNSIFF REFEREE
MEDIATOR
ARBOR BAR AXLE BEAM ABODE
BOWER SHAFT STAFF STALK
TRAIL ARBOUR BOWERY GARDEN
HERBER PANDAL RAMADA
VOIDER BERCEAU HARBOUR
MANDREL MANDRIL ORCHARD
PERGOLA RETREAT SPINDLE
TRELLIS FRESCADE TONNELLE
ARBORVITAE AKEKI ALERCE
ARBUTUS IVY MAYFLOWER
ARC BOW ARCH BEND FOIL HALO
CURVE HANCE ORBIT SPARK
SWING FOGBOW FOLIUM OCTANT
RADIAN COMPASS RAINBOW
FROSTBOW
(— OF HORIZON) AZIMUTH
AMPLITUDE

(ELECTRIC —) SPARK
ARCA BOX CHEST PATEN ARCULA
ARCADE ORB AVENUE LOGGIA
STREET GALLERY PORTICO
ARCATURE CLOISTER
ARCANE RUNIC HIDDEN SECRET
MYSTERIOUS
ARCAS (FATHER OF —) ZEUS
JUPITER
(MOTHER OF —) CALLISTO
ARCESIUS (FATHER OF —) ZEUS
JUPITER CEPHALUS
(MOTHER OF —) PROCRIS
EURYODIA
(SON OF —) LAERTES
ARCH ARC BOW COY SET SLY BACK
BEND COPE COVE DOME HARP
HOOP IRIS LEER OGEE PASS PEND
PERT SPAN ARCUS CHIEF CURVE
FAULD GREAT HANCE HUNCH
INBOW JOWEL OGIVE PAUKY
PAWKY POKEY PRIME ROACH
SAUCY SWEEP VAULT ARCADE
BRIDGE CALCAR CAMBER CLEVER
DIADEM FOGBOW FORNIX GIRDLE
IMPISH INVERT LANCET MANTEL
SPRING SUNBOW WICKET
ZYGOMA ARCHWAY CONCAVE
CUNNING EMINENT GATEWAY
ROGUISH SEGMENT SQUINCH
SUPPORT TESTUDO TRIUMPH
WAGGISH ALVEOLAR ESPIEGLE
FOGEATER OVERCAST
SCUNCHEON
(— OF SKY) FIRMAMENT
(DENTAL —) ARCADE
(LOGGING —) SULKY
(PART OF —) PIER CHORD IMPOST
PILLAR ABUTMENT EXTRADOS
INTRADOS KEYSTONE SKEWBACK
SPANDREL SPRINGER VOUSSOIR
(PL.) SUBARCUATION
ARCHAEOCYTE SORITE
ARCHAEOLOGIST POTHUNTER
PREHISTORIAN
AMERICAN CLAY DAVIS SHEAR
BARBER BUTLER GORDON
HAYNES HEWETT HOLMES
MORELY PARKER PORTER SNYDER
SQUIER MERRIAM NUTTALL
SAVILLE SPEISER BREASTED
CUMMINGS ROBINSON STERRETT
THOMPSON CARPENTER
MOOREHEAD RICHARDSON
FROTHINGHAM
AUSTRIAN ARNETH STUDNICZKA
CANADIAN CURRELLY
CZECH HROZNY
DANISH ZOEGA MULLER POULSEN
WORSAAE BRONDSTED
MATHIASSEN STEENSTRUP
DUTCH GRUYTERE
ENGLISH BELL COOK GANN GELL
HALL BUDGE EVANS RYMER
STEIN CARTER CHILDE LAYARD
MURRAY NEWTON WARREN
BEAZLEY BRAYLEY BURROWS
DAWKINS DODWELL FELLOWS
GARDNER HOGARTH PENROSE
WOOLLEY GARSTANG HAMILTON
LAWRENCE RIDGEWAY STEPHENS
THOMPSON BABINGTON
FRENCH LEBAS MAURY PUGIN

VOGUE BREUIL CAGNAT CHOISY
CLARAC COCHET FORBIN GAIDOZ
LARTET MORGAN PERROT
SAULCY BABELON CHANTRE
CHARNAY DELATRE HOMOLLE
LEBLANT POTTIER BERTRAND
DIEULAFOY LENORMANT
DECHELETTE QUATREMERE
WADDINGTON LECHEVALIER
GERMAN MAU ROSS TREU ADLER
BRAUN BRUNN CONZE SARRE
ANDRAE BECKER HELBIG HILLER
MULLER NISSEN SCHOLL CURTIUS
GERHARD LASAULX WELCKER
WIEGAND BENNDORF BOTTIGER
ESSENWEIN KOLDEWEY
KOSSINNA PETERSEN LOESCHCKE
MICHAELIS SCHLIEMANN
FURTWANGLER WINCKELMANN
GREEK TSOUNTAS
ICELANDIC MAGNUSSON
IRISH STOKES ODONOVAN
MACALISTER
ITALIAN BONI LANZI ROSSI
CANINA FIORELLI LANCIANI
MARUCCHI VISCONTI
RUSSIAN KOPPEN POGODIN
CHWOLSON
SCOTTISH RAMSAY BURGESS
SWEDISH BRENNER MONTELIUS
SWISS KELLER
ARCHAIC OLD ANCIENT ANTIQUE
HISTORIC OBSOLETE
(PREF.) PALE
ARCHANGEL SATAN URIEL
GABRIEL MICHAEL RAPHAEL
HIERARCH
ARCHBISHOP HATTO PRELATE
PRIMATE ORDINARY
ARCHDEMON BELFAGOR
BELFAZOR
ARCHDIOCESE EPARCHY
ARCHDUKE ERZHERZOG
ARCHEAN EOZOIC
ARCHED ARCHY CONVEX ARCUATE
EMBOWED VAULTED HOOPLIKE
CAMERATED
(— IN) CONCAVE
(PREF.) TOX(I)(O) TOXIC(O)
ARCHEGONIUM CALYPTRA
OOANGIUM
ARCHELAUS (BROTHER OF —)
PHILIP ANTIPAS
(FATHER OF —) HEROD
(MOTHER OF —) MALTHAKE
ARCHEMORUS (FATHER OF —)
LYCURGUS
(MOTHER OF —) EURYDICE
(NURSE OF —) HYPSIPYLE
ARCHER BOW CLIM CLYM BOWER
BUTTY CUPID ROVER BOWBOY
BOWMAN BOWYER SHOOTER
PANDARUS
(EQUIPMENT OF —) TACKLE
ARCHERY TOXOLOGY ARTILLERY
(— SPACE) PETTICOAT
(PREF.) TOX(I)(O) TOXIC(O)
ARCHETYPE IDEA MODEL FIGURE
SAMPLE ESSENCE EXAMPLE
PARAGON PATTERN EXEMPLAR
FRAVASHI ORIGINAL PROTOTYPE
ARCHIL CORKE CORCIR CORKER
PERSIS CUDBEAR LECANORA

ORCHILLA ORSEILLE
ARCHING CAMBER
ARCHITECT MAKER ARTIST
ARTISAN BUILDER CREATOR
PLANNER BEZALEEL DESIGNER
SURVEYOR
AMERICAN DAY COBB COPE CRAM
CRET HOOD HOWE HUNT KAHN
PELZ POPE POST TOWN WARE
ALLEN BACON CASEY DAVIS
FLAGG GOULD HEINS HOBAN
MCKIM MILLS PRICE WAUGH
WHITE BARBER GEDDES GILMAN
GRAHAM HAIGHT HOWARD
JENNEY ROGERS WALKER
WALTER WARREN WRIGHT
BRAGDON BRUNNER BURNHAM
CARRERE CORBETT EIDLITZ
GILBERT GOODHUE GRIFFIN
HOWELLS KENDALL KIESLER
KIMBALL LAFARGE LESCAZE
PARSONS PEABODY PLOWMAN
RAYMOND STURGIS TUTHILL
BENJAMIN BOSWORTH BULFINCH
COOLIDGE HARRISON HASTINGS
HOLABIRD MCINTIRE SULLIVAN
THOMPSON THORNTON
VANBRUNT MAGONIGLE
RICHARDSON STEWARDSON
STRICKLAND HARDENBERGH
WHEELWRIGHT
AUSTRIAN NULL WAGNER
FERSTEL HASENAUER
HOLZMEISTER
BELGIAN VELDE POELAERT
CZECH ZITEK
DANISH NYROP HANSEN
DUTCH OUD KEYSER BERLAGE
CUYPERS LOMBARD MOREELSE
EGYPTIAN CALLINICUS
ENGLISH KENT NASH SHAW TITE
WEBB WREN ADAMS BAKER
BARRY BLORE DANCE GLOAG
GOTCH GWILT JONES SCOTT
SOANE STONE WYATT BODLEY
CLARKE COOPER HANSOM
PAXTON STREET STUART
BECKETT BENTLEY JACKSON
KNOWLES LUTYENS PEARSON
PENROSE RICKMAN ATKINSON
CHAMBERS COCKERAM FLETCHER
NESFIELD VANBRUGH
CHAMPNEYS HAWKSMOOR
NICHOLSON WILKINSON
LANCHESTER WATERHOUSE
ABERCROMBIE BUTTERFIELD
PENNETHORNE
FINNISH AALTO SAARINEN
GESELLIUS
FRENCH DUC ETEX COTTE DUBAN
LEVAU MAROT PUGET BENARD
BERAIN BROSSE LEFUEL LESCOT
NEPVEU ANTOINE BALTARD
BLONDEL BULLANT DAVIOUD
DELORME FORMIGE GABRIEL
GARNIER MANSART PERCIER
ANDROUET CHALGRIN CUVILLES
FELIBIEN FONTAINE HITTORFF
LEPAUTRE SOUFFLOT LEMERCIER
LECORBUSIER
GERMAN HOLL LENZ ADLER
ERWIN GEDON LENNE KLENZE
MESSEL MOLLER SEMPER STULER

BEHRENS FRIESEN GROPIUS
NEUMANN OLBRICH POELZIG
HEGEMANN LANGHANS SCHINKEL
SCHLUTER ESSENWEIN
POPPELMANN KNOBELSDORFF
GREEK ICTINUS DOXIADIS
MNESICLES SOSTRATUS
DINOCRATES HIPPODAMUS
POLYCLITUS CALLICRATES
HUNGARIAN STEINDL
ITALIAN BONI DANTI GENGA
NERVI PORTA POZZO VINCI
AGNOLO ALESSI BONOMI CIGOLI
GIOTTO IUVARA ROMANO SERING
SOLARI SUARDI VASARI ALBERTI
ALGARDI BERNINI BIBIENA
CAGNOLA CONTINO CORTONA
FONTANA GUARINI LAURANA
MADERNA PERUZZI TIBALDI
TRIBOLO VIGNOLA AGOSTINO
AMMANATI BRAMANTE CIVITALI
GIOCONDO LOMBARDO PALLADIO
PIRANESI SCAMOZZI BORROMINI
PIERMARINI SANMICHELI
SERVANDONI VANVITELLI
PRIMATICCIO BRUNELLESCHI
MICHELANGELO
ROMAN COSMATI COSSUTIUS
RUSSIAN BRYULOV
SCOTTISH ADAM MACKINTOSH
SPANISH CANO HERRERA
VILLANUEVA
SWEDISH TESSIN OSTBERG
TENGBOM
TURKISH SINAN
ARCHITECTURAL TECTONIC
OECODOMIC
ARCHITECTURE DRAVIDA
ARCHITRAVE EPISTYLE PLATBAND
ARCHIVES TABULARY
TABULARIUM
ARCHIVOLT RING ARCHBAND
HEADBAND
ARCHLUTE THEORBO
ARCHON RULER DIRECTOR
OFFICIAL THESMOTHETE
ARCHWAY ARCH PEND ARCUS
PAILOO PAILOU
ARC LAMP MONOPHOTE
ARCOGRAPH BOW
ARCO SALTANDO SPICCATO
ARCTIC ICY COLD COOL GELID
POLAR BOREAL CHILLY FRIGID
GALOSH NORTHERN OVERSHOE
ARCTIUM LAPPA
ARCTOID URSINE
ARD (FATHER OF —) BELA
ARDENT HOT AVID FOND KEEN
LIVE WARM EAGER FIERY GLEDY
RETHE SHARP ABLAZE FERVID
FIERCE IGNITE STRONG TORRID
AMOROUS BURNING CORDIAL
DEVOTED EARNEST FEELING
FERVENT FLAMING FORWARD
GLOWING INTENSE SHINING
ZEALOUS DESIROUS EMPRESSE
FEVERISH FLAGRANT ROMANTIC
SANGUINE SCALDING SPORTIVE
VEHEMENT PERFERVID
ARDON (FATHER OF —) CALEB
(MOTHER OF —) AZUBAH
ARDOR DASH EDGE ELAN FIRE
GLOW HEAT LOVE ZEST ESTRO

FLAME GUSTO HEART TAPAS
VERVE WRATH DESIRE FERVOR
FOUGUE METTLE SPIRIT SPLEEN
WARMTH ARDENCY EARNEST
ENTRAIN PASSION DEVOTION
FEROCITY VIOLENCE VIVACITY
ARDUOUS HARD LOFTY STEEP
STIFF SEVERE TRYING ONEROUS
EXACTING TIRESOME TOILSOME
ARDYS (FATHER OF —) GYGES
ARE MU RE AIR ARN ARUN HARE
AREA BELT PALE SIZE TREF ZONE
BASIN COAST COURT FIELD
PLACE RANGE REALM SCENE
SCOPE SPACE TRACT ACCENT
AREOLA EXTENT GROUND
LOCALE MOARIA REGION SECTOR
SPHERE SPREAD VOLUME
ACREAGE AMENITY AREAWAY
CIRCUIT COMPASS CONTENT
COUNTRY ENVIRON EXPANSE
KINGDOM PURLIEU SURFACE
CAPACITY DISTRICT
ENCEINTE PLOTTAGE
PROVINCE
(— AT INTERSECTION) CIRCUS
(— BETWEEN FILLETS) CANALIS
(— IN BACTERIAL CULTURE)
PLAQUE
(— IN CARTOON) BALLOON
(— IN HOSTILE TERRITORY)
AIRHEAD
(— OF ACTIVITY) METIER
(— OF EXPERIENCE) BOOK
(— OF FLAG) CANTON
(— OF OLDER LAND) KIPUKA
(— OF OPEN WATER AMID ICE)
POLYNYA
(— OF RIDGES) BILO
(— OF TIMBERLAND) CHENA
(— ON MOON) MARE WANE TERRA
(— UNIT) TAN YOKE LABOR
VIRGATE PLETHRON PLOWGANG
PLOWGATE
(BLANK —) BITE HOLE
(COMBAT —) GLACIS
(CONTINENTAL —) MOARIA
(CULTURAL —) HORIZON
(CURLING —) PARISH
(DARK — OF MOON) MARE MARIA
(DENUDED —) BURN
(DIKED —) SLUSHPIT
(ELONGATED —) BELT
(ENCLOSED —) FOLD SEPT
(EXTRAMURAL —) BANLIEUE
(FENCED —) CAGE COMPOUND
(FERTILE —) HAMMOCK
(FLOORING —) SQUARE
(FORTIFIED —) BASTION ENCEINTE
(GATHERING —) MANDAPA
(HUNTING —) SURROUND
(INFESTED —) FLYBELT
(LOW-LYING —) GLADE SWALE
COULEE COULIE GUTTER
(LUMINOUS —) AUREOLA AUREOLE
(MINE —) SQUEEZE
(NUCLEAR —) HEARTH ECUMENE
(OPEN —) COURT LAUND CAMPUS
SQUARE HAGGARD
(OVERGROWN —) COGONAL
(PASTURE —) SOUM
(PAVED —) CAUSEY
(PLOWED —) BREAK

(RESIDENTIAL —) BANLIEU
BANLIEUE
(SHOPPING —) MALL
(SLUM —) STEW
(SMALL —) AREOLA
(SMOKING —) BULLPEN
(STERN —) AFTERPART
(SUBURBAN —) ADDITION
FAUBOURG
(SUNKEN —) SAG
(SWAMPY —) SLASH
(TEST —) MILACRE
(TIDAL —) CLAMFLAT
(TRANSITION —) ECOTONE
(TREELESS —) SLICK
(TUMID —) CERE
(UNCLEARED —) BUSH
(UPLAND —) COTEAU
(VOLCANIC —) SOLFATARA
(WASTE —) FOREST
(WOODED —) HAG BOSK BOSQUE
(SUFF.) (GEOGRAPHIC —) GAEA
GEA
ARECA ARAK ARCHA BETEL
ARELI (FATHER OF —) GAD
ARENA AREA LIST OVAL RING RINK
COURT FIELD SCENE SCOPE
SPACE STAGE CIRCUS CIRQUE
REGION SPHERE COCKPIT
STADIUM TERRAIN THEATER
BULLRING
ARENACEOUS SANDY GRITTY
SABULOUS
AREOLA PIT AREA RING SPOT
SPACE
ARES MARS ENYALIUS GRADIVUS
QUIRINUS
(FATHER OF —) ZEUS JUPITER
(MOTHER OF —) ENYO HERA JUNO
(SON OF —) REMUS CYCNUS
ROMULUS
ARETE (FATHER OF —) DIONYSIUS
(HUSBAND OF —) DION ALCINOUS
(MOTHER OF —) ARISTOMACHE
AREUS (BROTHER OF —) TALAUS
LEODOCUS
(FATHER OF —) BIAS
(MOTHER OF —) PERO
ARGALA STORK MARABOU
ARGALI AMMON ARKAR AOUDAD
ARGAN IRONWOOD
ARGANTE (DAUGHTER OF —)
OCTAVIA ZERBINETTE
ARGENT LUNA MOON PEARL
WHITE BLANCH SILVER CRYSTAL
SHINING SILVERY

ARGENTINA
CAPITAL: BUENOSAIRES
COIN: PESO CENTAVO ARGENTINO
DANCE: TANGO CUANDO GAUCHO
FALLS: GRANDE IGUAZU
INDIAN: LULE GUARANI
LAKE: VIEDMA CARDIEL FAGNANO
MUSTERS
MEASURE: SINO VARA LEGUA
CUADRA FANEGA LASTRE
MANZANA
MOUNTAIN: TORO ANDES CHATO
LAUDO MAIPU POTRO CONICO
PISSIS RINCON FAMATINA
MURALLON OLIVARES
TRONADOR ZAPALERI

ACONCAGUA INCAHUASI TUPUNGATO MERCEDARIO LLULLAILLACO
PLAIN: PAMPA PAMPAS
PORT: ROSARIO
PROVINCE: CHACO JUJUY SALTA CHUBUT CORDOBA FORMOSA LARIOJA MENDOZA NEUQUEN TUCUMAN MISIONES PATAGONIA
REGION: CHACO PATAGONIA
RIVER: SALI ATUEL CHICO COYLE DULCE LIMAY NEGRO PLATA TEUCO BLANCO CHUBUT CUARTO FLORES GRANDE PARANA QUINTO SALADO BERMEJO DESEADO MENDOZA TERCERO TUNUYAN SENGUERR

TOWN: AZUL GOYA ORAN PUAN BAHIA JUNIN LANUS LUJAN METAN SALTA PARANA RAWSON RUFINO VIEDMA ZARATE BOLIVAR CORDOBA DOLORES FORMOSA LABANDA MENDOZA NEUQUEN POSADAS RAFAELA ROSARIO TUCUMAN USHUAIA GALLEGOS CATAMARCA
VOLCANO: LANIN MAIPU DOMUYO PETEROA TUPUNGATO
WATERFALL: IGUAZU
WEIGHT: LAST GRANO LIBRA QUINTAL TONELADA

ARGES (BROTHER OF —) BRONTES STEROPES
(FATHER OF —) URANUS
(MOTHER OF —) GE GAEA
ARGIA (FATHER OF —) OCEANUS ADRASTUS
(HUSBAND OF —) INACHUS POLYBUS POLYNICES ARISTODEMUS
(MOTHER OF —) TETHYS AMPHITHEA
(SON OF —) ARGUS PROCLES EURYSTHENES
ARGIL CLAY ALUMINA
ARGIOPE (DAUGHTER OF —) EUROPA
(HUSBAND OF —) AGENOR
(SON OF —) CILIX CADMUS THASUS CERCYON PHINEUS PHOENIX
ARGOL TARTAR
ARGOSY SHIP FLEET GALLEON RAGUSYE
ARGOT CANT FLASH LINGO SLANG JARGON PATOIS DIALECT
ARGUE JAW ARGY CHOP FUSS MEAN MOOT MOVE SPAR WORD ARGIE CAVIL ORATE PLEAD PROVE TREAT ACCUSE ADDUCE CAFFLE DEBATE EVINCE HASSLE REASON ARRAIGN CONTEND CONTEST COUNTER DISCUSS DISPUTE WRANGLE ERGOTIZE INDICATE MAINTAIN PERSUADE QUESTION TRAVERSE
(— DEDUCTIVELY) SYLLOGIZE
(— SUBTLY) DISTINGUISH

ARGUER JAW
ARGUMENT ROW AGON BEEF BLUE CASE FUSS MOOT PLEA SPAR TEXT CLASH DEBAT INDEX KNIFE LEMMA PROOF THEME TOPIC BARNEY COMBAT CORKER DEBATE DUSTUP ELENCH HASSLE MATTER TUSSLE APAGOGE CLAMPER DEFENCE DEFENSE DILEMMA DISPUTE ESSENCE FLUBDUB POLEMIC RHUBARB SOPHISM SORITES SUMMARY ABSTRACT CLINCHER COURSING EVIDENCE SPARRING TRILEMMA REASONING PARALOGISM PERSUASION
(INVALID —) SOPHISM
(THEORETICAL —) ACADEMICS
ARGUMENTATION DEBATE DISPUTE ERGOTISM
ARGUMENTATIVE ERISTIC FRATCHY FORENSIC
ARGUS (FATHER OF —) ZEUS JUPITER PHRIXUS
(MOTHER OF —) ARGIA NIOBE CHALCIOPE
(SLAYER OF —) HERMES MERCURY
ARGUSFISH SCAT
ARHAT MONK LOHAN RAKAN SAINT ARAHANT
ARIA AIR SOLO SONG TUNE MELODY SORTIE ARIETTA ARIETTE SORTITA
ARIADNE (FATHER OF —) MINOS
(HUSBAND OF —) THESEUS
(MOTHER OF —) PASIPHAE
ARIADNE AUF NAXOS
(CHARACTER IN —) ARIADNE BACCHUS ZERBINETTA
(COMPOSER OF —) STRAUSS
ARIAN AGNOETE AGNOITE HOMOEAN ANOMOIAN EUSEBIAN
ARID DRY BALD BARE DULL LEAN BARREN DESERT JEJUNE MEAGER DROUTHY PARCHED STERILE THIRSTY DROUGHTY WITHERED
ARIDAI (FATHER OF —) HAMAN
ARIDATHA (FATHER OF —) HAMAN
ARIDITY DROUTH DROUGHT SICCITY
ARIKARA REE
ARIL POD ARILLUS COATING ARILLODE
ARIODANTE (COMPOSER OF —) HANDEL
ARIODANTES (LOVER OF —) GENEURA
ARISAI (FATHER OF —) HAMAN
ARISBE (FATHER OF —) MEROPS
(HUSBAND OF —) PRIAM DARDANUS HYRTACUS
(SON OF —) ASIUS NISUS AESACUS
ARISE WAX COME FLOW FORM GROW LIFT REAR RISE SOAR STEM AWAKE BEGIN BUILD EXIST ISSUE MOUNT RAISE SPRAY STAND START SURGE TOWER WAKEN ACCRUE AMOUNT APPEAR ASCEND ATTAIN DERIVE EMERGE HAPPEN KITTLE SPRING DEVELOP EMANATE EXSURGE PROCEED REDOUND SOURDRE

ARISING LEVEE EMERGENT
(PREF.) **(— WITHIN)** IDIO
ARISTAEUS (DAUGHTER OF —) MACRIS
(FATHER OF —) APOLLO
(MOTHER OF —) CYRENE
(SON OF —) ACTAEON
(WIFE OF —) AUTONOE
ARISTE (BROTHER OF —) CHRYSALE
ARISTO (BROTHER OF —) SGANARELLE
ARISTOCRACY CLASS ELITE GENTRY ARISTOI SAMURAI NOBILITY OPTIMACY
ARISTOCRAT LORD NOBLE ARISTO JUNKER GRANDEE PARVENU EUPATRID OPTIMATE PATRICIAN
(RUSSIAN —) BOIAR BOYAR BOYARD
(PL.) ARISTOI
ARISTOCRATIC HIGH TONY NOBLE QUALITY CAVALIER BELGRAVIAN
ARISTODEMUS (BROTHER OF —) TEMENUS CRESPHONTES
(FATHER OF —) ARISTOMACHUS
(SON OF —) PROCLES EURYSTHENES
(WIFE OF —) ARGEIA
ARISTOTELIAN PERIPATETIC
ARITHMETIC SUM AUGRIM ALGORISM
ARITHMOMETER MULTIPLIER

ARIZONA
CAPITAL: PHOENIX
COUNTY: GILA PIMA YUMA PINAL APACHE MOHAVE NAVAJO COCHISE YAVAPAI COCONINO GREENLEE MARICOPA SANTACRUZ
INDIAN: HOPI PIMA YUMA NAVAHO NAVAJO PAPAGO HUALAPAI
MOUNTAIN: BANGS GROOM LEMMON TURRET HUALPAI PASTORA MERIDIAN
MOUNTAIN RANGE: GILA KOFA MOHAWK GALIURO HUALPAI AQUARIUS BUCKSKIN
PEAK: HUMPHREYS
RIVER: GILA SALT ZUNI VERDE PUERCO COLORADO
STATE BIRD: CACTUSWREN
STATE FLOWER: SAGUARO
STATE NICKNAME: OCOTILLO
STATE TREE: PALOVERDE
TOWN: AJO ELOY MESA NACO YUMA GLOBE LEUPP TEMPE BISBEE JEROME MCNARY SALOME TOLTEC TUCSON CLIFTON CORTARO KINGMAN MORENCI NOGALES PHOENIX SAFFORD FREDONIA PRESCOTT FLAGSTAFF TOMBSTONE

ARJUN KUMBUK
ARJUNA (FATHER OF —) PANDU
(SON OF —) ABHIMANYU
ARK BIN BOX BOAT SHIP BARGE CHEST HUTCH BASKET COFFER REFUGE WANGAN RETREAT SHELTER WANIGAN FLATBOAT
ARKANSAN ARKANSAWYER

ARKANSAS
CAPITAL: LITTLEROCK
COUNTY: LEE CLAY DREW PIKE POLK POPE YELL BOONE CROSS DESHA IZARD LOGAN SHARP STONE BAXTER CHICOT LONOKE SEARCY CALHOUN PRAIRIE PULASKI OUACHITA
INDIAN: CADDO OSAGE QUAPAW CHOCTAW CHEROKEE
LAKE: CONWAY NIMROD GREESON NORFORK OUACHITA
MOUNTAIN: RICH GAYLOR MAGAZINE
MOUNTAIN RANGE: OZARK OUACHITA
NATIVE: TOOTHPICK
NICKNAME: WONDER
RIVER: RED WHITE SALINE BUFFALO CURRENT COSSATOT OUACHITA
STATE BIRD: MOCKINGBIRD
STATE FLOWER: APPLE BLOSSOM
STATE TREE: SHORTLEAFPINE
TOWN: COY CUY KEO OLA ROE ULM ALMA BONO CASA DELL DIAZ MORO ENOLA PERLA RISON RONDO WYNNE ALICIA JASPER PIGGOTT

ARKOSE ARENITE SANDSTONE
ARLECCHINO (CHARACTER IN —) LEANDRO BOMBASTO COLUMBINE HARLEQUIN
(COMPOSER OF —) BUSONI
ARLESIANA, L' (CHARACTER IN —) ROSA MAMMAI METIFIO VIVETTE FEDERICO
(COMPOSER OF —) CILEA
ARM FIN OAR TOE BOOM HEEL LIMB WING BLADE BOUGH CRANE EQUIP FENCE FIORD FIRTH FJORD FORCE GARDY INLET MIGHT OXTER POWER RIFLE SNORD STOCK BRANCH CRUTCH ENERGY FRETUM GIBBET MEMBER OUTFIT PINION RADIAL SLEEVE TAPPET WEAPON CATCHER DERRICK DRAWARM FLIPPER FOREARM FORTIFY FURNISH GARNISH HARNESS OCKSTER PREPARE PROTECT PROVIDE QUILLON SUPPORT ARMORIAL CROSSARM FOLLOWER FORELIMB PULLDOWN SOUPBONE STRENGTH TRANSEPT
(— HOLDING FLINT) HAMMER
(— OF BARNACLE) CIRRUS CIRRHUS
(— OF CHAIR) ELBOW
(— OF CRANE) JIB GIBBET RAMHEAD
(— OF GIN) START
(— OF PROPELLER) BLADE
(— OF RECORD PLAYER) PICKUP
(— OF SEA) COVE FLOW MEER MERE BRACE CANAL FIRTH FRITH GRAIN FRETUM ESTUARY EURIPUS
(— OF SPINNING MULE) SICKLE
(— OF WINDMILL) VANE WHIP
(— WITH GAFF) HEEL
(INDEX —) DIOPTER
(IRON —) CRANE

(LEVER —) SWEEP NIGGER
(PITCHING —) SOUPBONE
(PL.) ARMORY ARMAMENT
(PREF.) BRACHI
ARMADA NAVY FLEET FLOTILLA
ARMADILLO APAR PEBA TATU
APARA POYOU TATOU BOLITA
MATACO MATICO MULITA
PELUDO DASYPOD TATOUAY
TATUASU EDENTATE KABASSOU
LORICATE PANGOLIN
ARMAMENT ARMADA BATTERY
ARMATURE ARMING KEEPER
LIFTER
ARMBAND BRASSARD
ARMCHAIR BERGERE FAUTEUIL
ARMED FLUTE HEELED DAGGERED
WEAPONED

▶ **ARMENIA** ◀
ANCIENT CAPITAL: ANI ARTASHAT
ARTAXATA
ANCIENT NAME: MINNI
CAPITAL: ERIVAN
FORTRESS: EREBUNI
HERO: ARA ARAM HAIK ARAME
VARTAN
KING: ASHOT GAGIK TRDAT ZAREH
DIKRAN ARTAKIAS ARTASHES
TIGRANES ZARIADES
KINGDOM: URARTU VANNIC
CILICIA SOPHENE ARDSRUNI
LAKE: VAN SEVAN URMIA
MOUNTAIN: ARA ALAGEZ ARARAT
TAUNUS ALADAGH ARAGATS
KARABAKH
NATIVE: ARMEN GOMER
RIVER: KUR ARAS KURA ARAKS
CYRUS HALYS ZANGA ARAXES
RAZDAN TIGRIS EUPHRATES
SAINT: SAHAK MESROP
TOWN: VAN SIVAS BITLIS EREVAN
ERIVAN ERZURUM TRABZON
YEREVAN

ARMENIAN ERMYN HADJI HAIKH
ARMFUL LOCK YAFFLE
ARMHOLE MAIL SCYE OXTER
ARMSCYE ARMSEYE ARMSIZE
ARMIDE (CHARACTER IN —) ARMIDA
RINALDO
(COMPOSER OF —) GLUCK
ARMINIO (COMPOSER OF —)
HANDEL
ARMISTICE LULL PEACE TRUCE
INDUCIAE
ARMLET BANGLE TABLET TORQUE
ARMHOOP
ARMONI (FATHER OF —) SAUL
(MOTHER OF —) RIZPAH
ARMOR (AND SPECIFIC PIECES
THEREOF) ARMS BACK BOOT
EGIS JAMB MAIL TACE WEED
ACTON AMURE BARDS BRACE
CUISH CULET DORON GUARD
GUIGE JAMBE PIECE PLATE
PROOF SCALE STEEL TAPUL
TASSE TRUSS ARMLET ARMOUR
BEAVER BRINIE BRUNIE BYRNIE
CAMAIL CORIUM COUTER CRANET
CUISSE GORGET GRAITH GREAVE
JAMBER POLEYN RONDEL SECRET
SHIELD TASSET THORAX TONLET

TUILLE VOIDER AILETTE
ARMHOOP BESAGNE BROIGNE
CORSLET CUIRASS DEFENSE
EPAULET HARNESS HAUBERK
JAZERAN KNEELET LAMBOYS
PALETTE PANOPLY PLACATE
POITREL REREDOS ROUNDEL
SABATON VENTAIL BRASSARD
PAULDRON RAMENTUM
VAMBRACE BAINBERGS
RONDACHEPALLETTE
(— ON TREE) TROPHY
(— PLATE) TUILLE
(ELBOW —) CUBITIERE
(FOOT —) SABATON SABBATON
SOLLERET
(HEAD —) CASQUE HELMET
PALLET SCONCE
(HORSE —) BARB BARD BARDE
CRINET CHAMFRON CRINIERE
CHAMFRAIN
(LEATHER —) CORIUM
(LEG —) BOOT JAMB CUISH JAMBE
CUISSE GREAVE JAMBER TUILLE
JAMBEAU CHAUSSES
(NECK —) COLLAR GORGET
(PADDED —) GAMBESON
(SUIT OF —) CAST STAND
(PREF.) HOPL(O)
ARMOR-BEARER SQUIRE ARMIGER
CUSTREL
ARMORED PANZER
ARMORER GUNSMITH ARTIFICER
ARMORICAN BRETON
ARMORY ARSENAL HERALDRY
ARMPIT ALA OXTER AXILLA
ARMHOLE
ARMS TACKLE
(PREF.) HOPL(O)
**ARMS AND THE MAN (AUTHOR OF
—)** SHAW
(CHARACTER IN —) LOUKA RAINA
NICOLA PETKOFF SERGIUS
CATHERINE BLUNTSCHLI
ARMY FERD HERE HOST IMPI LEVY
MAIN ARRAY CROWD FORCE
HERSE HORDE POWER RANKS
ZOMBI COHORT HONVED LEGION
NUMBER THRONG TROOPS
MILITIA BATTALIA CHIVALRY
MILITARY
(HOSTILE —) FOE
(VOLUNTEER —) VOLAR
(PL.) SABAOTH
(PREF.) STRATO
ARMY OFFICER (ALSO SEE
SOLDIER)
ARMYWORM GRASSWORM
ARNE (FATHER OF —) AEOLUS
(HUSBAND OF —) METAPONTUS
(MOTHER OF —) THEA
(SON OF —) AELOUS BOEOTUS
ARNOTTO ROUCOU
AROD (FATHER OF —) GAD
AROID APII ARAD TARO APIUM
KRUBI TANIA KONJAK TANIER
YAUTIA PINUELA CALADIUM
CUNJEVOI MOCOMOCO
AROMA NOSE ODOR NIDOR SAVOR
SCENT SMELL SNUFF SPICE
FLAVOR BOUQUET PERFUME
REDOLENCE
(— OF WINE) BLOOM

AROMATIC BALMY SPICY SWEET
MASTIC ODOROUS PIQUANT
PUNGENT FRAGRANT REDOLENT
SPICEFUL
AROUND NEAR UMBE ABOUT
CIRCA CIRCUM ENVIRON
(PREF.) AMBI AMPHI CIRCUM
PERI
AROUSAL INDUCTION
AROUSE SOW CALL CITE FIRE GAIN
HEAT MOVE REAR SPUR STIR
WAKE WHET ADAWE ALARM
ALERT AWAKE EVOKE FLESH
PIQUE RAISE RALLY ROUSE
ROUST SHAKE STEER WAKEN
ABRAID AWAKEN ELICIT EXCITE
FOMENT INCITE INDUCE KINDLE
REVIVE SUMMON THRILL
ACTUATE AGITATE CONNOTE
INCENSE INFLAME INSPIRE
PROVOKE SUGGEST INSPIRIT
(— DISPLEASURE) AGGRAVATE
(— ENMITY) ESTRANGE
(— WRATH) SPLEEN
ARPEGGIATE BREAK
ARPEGGIO SWEEP ROULADE
FLOURISH
(— EFFECT) RASGADO
ARPHAXAD (FATHER OF —) SHEM
ARRACACHA APIO ARRA
ARRACK ARAK RACK ARAKI
RACKAPEE
ARRAIGN TRY CITE ARGUE PEACH
ACCUSE CHARGE IMPUTE INDICT
INDITE SUMMON APPOINT
IMPEACH DENOUNCE
ARRANGE DO FIX LAY RAY SET
CAST COMB EDIT FILE FORM
PLAN PLAT RAIL RULE SIDE SIZE
SORT TIER TIFT WORK ADAPT
AGREE ALIGN ALINE ARRAY BESEE
CURRY DRAPE DRESS ETTLE
FANCY FRAME GRADE ORDER
PITCH RANGE SCORE SHAPE
SHIFT SPACE STALL TRICK
ADJUST BRANCH CODIFY DAIKER
DESIGN DEVISE FETTLE INFORM
ORDAIN SETTLE SOLUTE TAILYE
ADDRESS APPOINT BESPEAK
CATALOG COLLATE COMPONE
COMPOSE CONCERT DISPOSE
ENRANGE GRADATE MARSHAL
PERMUTE PREPARE REDRESS
SERIATE TAILZEE TAILZIE
ALPHABET CLASSIFY CONCLUDE
ORGANIZE REGULATE TABULATE
COLLOCATE CONJOBBLE
NEGOTIATE STIPULATE
ORCHESTRATE
(— BEFOREHAND) FORLAY
FORELAY
(— FANTASTICALLY) HARLEQUINIZE
(— FASTIDIOUSLY) PREEN
(— HAIR) SET TED COIF TRUSS
COIFFE
(— HARMONIOUSLY) GRADATE
(— IN FLOCKS) HIRSEL HIRSLE
(— IN FOLDS) DRAPE
(— IN LAYERS) DESS TIER
(— IN ROW) RACE
(— STRAW) HAULM
(— SYSTEMATICALLY) DIGEST
(— WITH BEST AT TOP) DEACON

ARRANGEMENT FIX FLY LAY RAY
DEAL FLOW PLAT RANK TIFF
ARRAY BUILD DRAPE INDEX
ORDER SETUP BORDER DESIGN
HOOKUP LAYOUT SCHEME
SETOUT SYNTAX SYSTEM TREATY
BLEEDER INTERIM POSTURE
TONTINE ATTITUDE CONTRACT
DISPOSAL GROUPING POSITURE
SEQUENCE ORDONNANCE
ORIENTATION BANDSTRATION
ORCHESTRATION
(— IN LOCK) DETECTOR
(— OF BRISTLES) CHAETOTAXY
(— OF CHESS PAWNS) CHAIN
(— OF COMPUTER ELEMENTS)
ARRAY
(— OF DRAPERIES) CAST
(— OF FLOWERS) CASCADE
CORSAGE IKEBANA PARTERRE
(— OF GRADES) CURVE
(— OF GUNS) ARMADA
(— OF HAIRDO) FORETOP
(— OF HAIRS) SCOPA
(— OF HOOKS) GIG
(— OF LOOM BARS) GRIFF GRIFFE
(— OF ROCKS) BEDDING
(— OF TACKLE) BURTON
(— OF TIMBER) ANCHOR
(— OF TROOPS) ECHELON
(CIRCULAR —) CYCLE
(DISHONEST —) CROSS
(GEOMETRICAL —) LATTICE
(ORDERED —) PERMUTATION
(SECRET —) PACK
(TRADITIONAL —) AKOLUTHIA
AKOLOUTHIA
(PREF.) TAX(EO)(I)(O)
(LACK OF —) ATAXO
(SUFF.) OSIS TACTIC TAXIS TAXY
ARRANGING ORDONNANT
(JAPANESE ART OF FLOWER —)
IKEBANA
ARRANT BAD THIEF OUTLAW
ROBBER VAGRANT OUTRIGHT
PRECIOUS RASCALLY
ARRAS ORRIS ARISTE DRAPERY
TAPESTRY
ARRASTRA TAHONA
ARRAU JURARA
ARRAY DON DUB FIG ARMY BUSK
DECK DOLL FYRD GALA GARB
HOST POMP RAIL RANK ROBE
VEST ADORN ALIGN ALINE ATOUR
DRESS EQUIP HABIT HARKA
HEDGE ORDER ADIGHT AGUISE
ATTIRE ATTRAP BEDECK CLOTHE
DEVISE FETTLE FINERY GRAITH
INVEST MUSTER PLIGHT SERIES
SETOUT SHROUD ADDRESS
AFFAITE AFFLICT APPAREL
ARRANGE BATTERY BEDIGHT
COMPANY DISPLAY DISPOSE
ENVELOP FURNISH FYRDUNG
MARSHAL PANOPLY REPAREL
ACCOUTER
(— OF CHEMICALS) ARA
(— OF GUNS) BROADSIDE
(— OF TROOPS) PAREL
(— OF WEAPONS) ARMORY
(— TASTELESSLY) DAUB
(BATTLE —) ACIES HERSE
BATTALIA

ARRAYED HABITED ABULYEIT
ARREAR DEBT BEHIND UNPAID
ARRIERE
(IN —S) BACK BEHIND
ARREST CAP COP FIX FOB LAG
NAB NIP VAG BALK CURB FALL
GLOM GRAB HALT HOLD JAIL
KEEP NAIL NICK PULL REST SHOP
SIST STAY STOP ARRET CATCH
CHECK DELAY PINCH REEST SEIZE
STILL STUNT ATTACH BRIDLE
COLLAR DECREE DETAIN ENGAGE
FINGER HINDER PLEDGE RETARD
SLOUGH SNEEZE THWART
CAPTION CAPTURE CUSTODY
SUSPEND IMPRISON OBSTRUCT
RESTRAIN
(— OF BLEEDING) HEMOSTASIS
(— OF DEVELOPMENT) ABORTION
(PUT UNDER —) BUST
ARRESTER (SPARK —) BONNET
ARRESTING BOLD SEIZING
MAGNETIC PLEASING STRIKING
ARRET EDICT ARREST DECREE
DECISION JUDGMENT
ARRHA HANDGELD
ARRIS PIEN ANGLE PIEND ARRIDGE
ARRIVAL COMER IKBAL VENUE
ADVENT COMING INCOMING
REACHING
(— TIME RECORD) OS
(NEW —) ROOINEK
ARRIVE GO SEY COME FALL FLOW
GAIN LAND LEND RIVE LIGHT
OCCUR REACH WORTH ACCEDE
APPEAR ATTAIN HAPPEN OBTAIN
UPCOME COMPASS
(— AT) GET HIT FIND GAIN HENT
MAKE BRING EDUCE FETCH
GUESS SEIZE ATTAIN DERIVE
ESTIMATE
ARRIVED-IN DONE
ARROBA ROVE
ARROGANCE PRIDE SWANK
TUMOR BOWWOW HUBRIS
BOBANCE CONCEIT DISDAIN
EGOTISM HAUTEUR STOMACH
BOLDNESS SUCCUDRY SURQUIDY
ARROGANT BOLD COXY HIGH
MOOD COBBY COCKY GREAT
HUFFY JOLLY LOFTY PROUD
STOUT SURLY WLONK ASSUME
CHESTY FIERCE LORDLY UPPISH
UPPITY WANTON FORWARD
FROSTED HAUGHTY HAUTAIN
HUFFISH POMPOUS STATELY
TOPPING AFFECTED ASSUMING
CAVALIER FASTUOUS IMPUDENT
SNUFFING SUPERIOR TUMOROUS
OVERBEARING OVERWEENING
ARROGATE GRAB TAKE CLAIM
SEIZE USURP ASSUME ADROGATE
ARROW FLO PIN ROD SEL BOLT
DART REED SELF SELL SHOT VIRE
BLUNT DEATH FLANE ROVER
SHAFT ARCHER FLIGHT GANYIE
GARROT QUARRY SPRITE TACKLE
WEAPON BOBTAIL DOGBOLT
MISSILE POINTER PROJECT
QUARREL SAGITTA SPINNER
FISHTAIL FORKHEAD
(— ARUM) TUCKAHOE
(— IN GRASS) GREEN SNAKE

(— IN LEG OF STAND) FOOT
(FIRE —) MALLEOLUS
(PART OF —) TIP BUTT HEAD NOCK
PILE POINT SHAFT FEATHER
FLETCHING
(POISONED —) DERRID SUMPIT
(WOBBLING —) FISHTAIL
(PREF.) BELO(NO) HASTATO
SAGITTI SAGITTO TOX(I)(ICO)(O)
ARROWHEAD BUNT FORK HEAD
PILE FLUKE POINT NEOLITH
ARTIFACT CROWBILL FORKHEAD
SPICULUM
ARROWROOT PIA ARUM MUSA
SAGU ARARU CANNA TACCA
TIKOR ARARAO CURCUMA
ARROWSMITH (AUTHOR OF —)
LEWIS
(CHARACTER IN —) MAX ALMUS
JOYCE LEORA SILVA TERRY
LANYON MARTIN GUSTAVE
WICKETT GOTTLIEB SONDELIUS
ARROWSMITH PICKERBAUGH
ARROWWORM SAGITTA
CHAETOGNATH
ARROYO DRAW BROOK CREEK
GULCH GULLY HONDO ZANJA
RAVINE STREAM CHANNEL
BARRANCA BARRANCO
ARSENAL ARMORY SUPPLY
MAGAZINE
ARSENOPYRITE MISPICKEL
ARSHIN ARCHIN ALTSCHIN
(ONE-24TH OF —) PARMAK
PARMACK
ARSINOE (DAUGHTER OF —) ERIOPIS
(FATHER OF —) PHEGEUS
LEUCIPPUS
(HUSBAND OF —) ALCMAEON
(MOTHER OF —) PHILODICE
(SISTER OF —) PHOEBE HILAIRA
ARSIS BEAT ICTUS SOUND
RHYTHM UPBEAT DOWNBEAT
ARSON FIRE CRIME FELONY
BURNING
ARSONIST ARSONITE
ARSPHENAMINE SIX SALVARSAN
ART WILE CRAFT KNACK KUNST
MAGIC SKILL TRADE MISTER
TECHNE ARTWORK CALLING
CUNNING DESCANT DISCANT
FACULTY FINESSE MYSTERY
SCIENCE APTITUDE ARTIFICE
BUSINESS LEARNING PRACTICE
PRACTISE
(— OF APPLYING TESTS) DOCIMASY
(— OF BLAZONING) ARMORY
(— OF CALCULATING) ALGORISM
ALGORITHM
(— OF DEFENSE) SKIRMISH
(— OF FLOWER ARRANGEMENT)
IKEBANA
(— OF HEALING) LEECHCRAFT
(— OF HORSEMANSHIP) MANEGE
(— OF PREPARING COLORS)
GUMPTION
(— OF SPEECH) RHETORIC
(— OF TYING KNOTS IN PATTERN)
MACRAME
(DIABOLIC —) DEVILRY DEVILTRY
(DRAMATIC —) STAGE
(JAPANESE — MOVEMENT) YAMATO
YAMATOE

(JUNK —) NEODADA
(LEG —) CHEESECAKE
(MAGIC —) WITHERCRAFT
(MYSTERIOUS —) CABALA KABALA
CABBALA KABBALA QABBALA
CABBALAH KABBALAH QABBALAH
(OCCULT —) THEURGY
(SHODDY —) BONDIEUSERIE
(TYPE OF —) STREETSCAPE
(PREF.) TECHNI TECHNO TYP(I)(O)
(SUFF.) ERY SHIP TECHNICS
TECHNY TYPAL TYPE TYPIC TYPY
(RELATING TO —) METRIC
ARTAXERXES (COMPOSER OF —)
ARNE
ARTEMIS UPIS DELIA DIANA
PHOEBE CYNTHIA AMARYSIA
ARTERY WAY PATH ROAD AORTA
PULSE ROUTE COURSE DENTAL
FACIAL RADIAL STREET VESSEL
ANONYMA CAROTID COELIAC
CONDUIT HIGHWAY SCIATIC
VAGINAL CEREBRAL CERVICAL
CORONARY DORSALIS EMULGENT
PROFUNDA
ARTFUL APT FLY SLY FOXY WILY
AGILE DOWNY PAWKY SUAVE
ADROIT CLEVER CRAFTY FACILE
PRETTY QUAINT SCHEMY
SHREWD SMOOTH TRICKY
CROOKED CUNNING KNOWING
PLAITED POLITIC PRACTIC
SUBTILE VULPINE
DEXTROUS SCHEMING
STEALTHY
ARTFULNESS CUNNING ARTIFICE
SUBTLETY
ART GRAY QUAKER SEAMIST
ARTHRITIS GOUT CARPITIS
ARTHROPOD GOLACH GOLOCH
SPIDER CHILOPOD DIPLOPOD
PERIPATUS
ARTICHOKE BUR CANADA CYNARA
CARDOON CHOROGI CROSNES
KNOTROOT
ARTICLE A AN YE LOT ONE THE
BOOK ITEM TERM BRIEF CHEAT
ESSAY GEANE PAPER PIECE
PLANK POINT STORY THEME
THING CLAUSE DETAIL LEADER
NOTICE OBJECT REPORT FEATURE
BROCHURE CAUSERIE DOCTRINE
PARTICLE POSTFACE TREATISE
(— OF CLOTHING) DUD DIDO
APRON CLOUT DICKY FANCY
THING CASUAL DICKEY GARMENT
COINTISE CREATION
(— OF FOOD) CATE KNACK
(— OF FURNITURE) STICK
(— OF LITTLE WORTH) DIDO
(— OF SILK) SQUEEZE
(— OF TRADE) PADNAG
(— OF UNUSUAL SIZE) IMPERIAL
(—S OF FAITH) CREDENDA
(—S OF MERCHANDISE) CHAFFER
(CAST-IRON —S) KENTLEDGE
(CHEAP —) CAMELOT
(DECORATIVE —) LACKER LACQUER
(FANCY —) CONCEIT
(FIVE —S) HAND
(GENUINE —) GOODS
(HANDICRAFT —) BOONDOGGLE
(INFERIOR —S) SHODDY

(METAL —S) BATTERY
(MISCELLANEOUS —S) SUNDRIES
(NONDESCRIPT —) DODAD
DOODAB DOODAD WHATNOT
(SECONDHAND —) JUNK
(SHOWY —) FRIPPERY
(VALUABLE —S) SWAG
(WORTHLESS —) TRANGAM
ARTICULATE BACK JOIN CLEAR
FRAME JOINT SPEAK UNITE
UTTER VOCAL ACCENT FLUENT
VERBAL EXPRESS JOINTED
PHONATE DISTINCT SYLLABLE
ARTICULATED BACK BLADE
DENTAL DORSAL LABIAL JOINTED
ALVEOLAR CEREBRAL
VERTEBRATE
ARTICULATION NODE JOINT
VOICE SUTURE ARTHRON
JUNCTURE SYNTAXIS
(DEFECTIVE —) LALLATION
LAMBDACISM
ARTIFACT CELT DISC DISK BATON
GUACA HUACA AMGARN BRONZE
EOLITH FABRIC GORGET REJECT
RONDEL SAGAIE SKEWER
ABRADER ARTEFAC DISCOID
RACLOIR SCRAPER ARTEFACT
DATEMARK RONDELLE TRANCHET
(PL.) CACHE CERAUNIA
ARTIFICE ART GIN JET GAUD
HOAX JOUK PLAN PLOT RUSE
TURN WILE BLIND CHEAT COVIN
CRAFT CROCK CROOK DODGE
DRAFT FEINT FETCH FRAUD
GUILE SHIFT SKILL STALL TRAIN
TRICK CAUTEL DECEIT DEVICE
DOUBLE ENGINE CHICANE
COMPASS CUNNING DODGERY
DRAUGHT EVASION FINESSE
SHUFFLE SLEIGHT COZENAGE
DISGUISE DOUBLING INTRIGUE
MANAGERY MANEUVER PRACTICE
PRACTISE PRETENSE STRATEGY
TRICKERY WINDLASS
(PL.) CABAL CRANS
ARTIFICER WRIGHT ARTIFEX
WORKMAN DAEDALUS LAPIDARY
MECHANIC OPIFICER TVASHTAR
TVASHTRI
ARTIFICIAL CUTE SHAM BOGUS
DUMMY FAKED FALSE ARTFUL
ERSATZ FORCED FORGED UNREAL
ASSUMED BASTARD FEIGNED
PLASTIC AFFECTED FABULOUS
FALSETTO POSTICHE POSTIQUE
SPURIOUS
(NOT —) REAL NATURAL
(OVERLY —) ALEXANDRIAN
(SOMETHING —) CAMP
ARTIFICIALITY MANNERISM
ARTILLERY (OR PIECE THEREOF)
ARMS GUNS DRAKE SAKER
CANNON MINION HEAVIES
LANTACA LANTAKA CANNONRY
ORDNANCE
(— FIRE) STONK RAFALE
ARTILLERYMAN GUN GUNNER
LASCAR REDLEG LASHKAR
ENGINEER TOPECHEE
ARTISAN FEVER SMITH ARTIST
COOPER ARTIFEX TARKHAN
WORKMAN KAMMALAN LETTERER

MECHANIC OPIFICER OPERATIVE SILVERSMITH
ARTISANSHIP FOLKCRAFT
ARTIST (ALSO SEE PAINTER) DAB NABI POET ACTOR ADEPT BRUSH HILDA RAPIN DANCER ETCHER EXPERT FICTOR MASTER SINGER WIZARD ARTISAN ARTISTE ARTSMAN FAUVIST OPERANT PAINTER PONTIST SCHEMER ANIMATOR COLORIST FUSINIST IDEALIST LADISLAW LETTERER MAGICIAN MUSICIAN SCULPTOR SKETCHER STIPPLER PASTELIST PRIMITIVE MINIMALIST PASTELLIST
(— **SCHOOL**) LUMINISM
(**SIDEWALK** —) SCREEVER
(PL.) SCHOOL
ARTISTIC ARTLY DAEDAL EXPERT ESTHETIC PAINTERLY
(— **MATERIAL**) KITSCH
(— **QUALITY**) VERTU VIRTU
ARTISTRY FOLKCRAFT
ARTLESS NAIF OPEN FRANK NAIVE PLAIN SEELY CANDID RUSTIC SIMPLE GIRLISH NATURAL INNOCENT
ARTS TRIVIUM
ARTY CHICHI
ARUM ARAD TARO AROID CALALU DRAGON TAWKEE WAMPEE MANDRAKE TUCKAHOE
ARVIRAGUS CADWAL
(**FATHER OF** —) CYMBELINE
(**WIFE OF** —) DORIGEN
ARYAN MEDE SLAV OSSET NORDIC OSSETE
(**NOT** —) ANARYA
ARZA (**SLAYER OF** —) ZIMRI
AS S SO ALS FOR HOW QUA ALSO INTO LIKE SOME THAT THUS TILL WHEN EQUAL QUOAD SINCE WHILE BRONZE WHENAS BECAUSE EQUALLY SIMILAR QUATENUS
(— **FAR AS**) TO INTO QUATENUS
(— **IT WERE**) FAIRLY
(— **LONG AS**) SOBEIT
(— **MUCH**) ALSMEKILL
(— **SOON**) ALSOON ASTITE ALSWITH DIRECTLY
(— **TO**) QUOAD
(— **WELL**) EVEN
(— **WELL AS**) FORBY FORBYE
(— **YET**) HITHERTO
ASA (**FATHER OF** —) ABIJAH
ASAFETIDA HING LASER FERULA
ASAHEL (**BROTHER OF** —) JOAB
(**MOTHER OF** —) ZERUIAH
(**SLAYER OF** —) ABNER
(**SON OF** —) JONATHAN
(**UNCLE OF** —) DAVID
ASANDER (**BROTHER OF** —) PARMENION
(**FATHER OF** —) PHILOTAS
ASAPH (**FATHER OF** —) BECHERIAH
(**SON OF** —) JOAH ASARELAH
ASARABACCA HAZEL FOALFOOT
ASAREEL (**FATHER OF** —) JEHALELEEL
ASARELAH (**FATHER OF** —) ASAPH

ASBESTOS ABBEST XYLITE AMIANTH ABSISTOS ALBESTON AMIANTUS WOODROCK
(**BLUE** —) CROCIDOLITE
ASCALAPHUS (**BROTHER OF** —) IALMENUS
(**FATHER OF** —) ARES MARS ACHERON
(**MOTHER OF** —) ORPHNE GORGYRA ASTYOCHE
(**SLAYER OF** —) DEIPHOBUS
ASCEND UP STY RISE SOAR STYE UPGO ARISE CLIMB MOUNT SCALE STAIR TOWER AMOUNT ASPIRE BREAST CLIMAX UPRISE CLAMBER UPCLIMB ESCALATE PROGRESS
ASCENDANCY SWAY POWER CONTROL MASTERY SUCCESS DOMINION OWERANCE PRESTIGE
ASCENDANT MOUNTANT ASSURGENT
ASCENDING ANODAL ANODIC ORIENT UPHILL UPWARD ANABATIC ASPIRANT SUBERECT
(— **WITHOUT A TURN**) FLYING
ASCENSION APOTHEOSIS
ASCENT STY HILL RAMP RISE RIST UPGO CLIMB GLORY GRADE MOUNT RAISE SCEND SLOPE STEEP STEPS STILL UPWAY SOURCE STAIRS UPCOME UPGANG UPHILL UPRISE UPWITH INCLINE GOALING UPGRADE UPSWING EMINENCE GRADIENT
ASCERTAIN GET SEE SET TRY FEEL FIND TELL COUNT GLEAN LEARN PITCH PROVE ASSURE ATTAIN FIGURE ANALYSE ANALYZE APPRISE APPRIZE COMPUTE MEASURE UNEARTH DISCOVER
ASCETIC NUN MONK SOFI SUFI YATI YOGI DANDY FAKIR FRIAR SADHU SOFEE STOIC YOGIN CHASTE ESSENE HERMIT SADDHU SEVERE SOOFEE STRICT ADAMITE AUSTERE BHIKSHU DEVOTEE EREMITE RECLUSE SRAMANA STYLITE TAPASVI AVADHUTA MARABOUT NAZARITE SANNYASI
(PL.) THERAPEUTAE
ASCIDIAN POLYP CUNGEBOI CUNGEVOI TETHYDAN TUNICATE
ASCIDIUM PITCHER VASCULUM
ASCOCARP ASCOMA
ASCOGONIUM ARCHICARP
ASCOMA CUPULE
ASCRIBABLE DUE
ASCRIBE LAY ARET EVEN GIVE APPLY BLAME COUNT GUESS IMPLY INFER PLACE REFER TITLE ACCUSE ALLEGE ARETTE ASSIGN ATTACH CHARGE CREDIT IMPUTE PREFER RECKON RELATE ASCRIVE ENTITLE ACCREDIT ARROGATE DEDICATE INSCRIBE INTITULE
ASCRIPTION LAUD CREDIT ADDITION
ASCUS BAG SAC THECA ASCELLUS
ASEA LOST ADDLED ADRIFT

PUZZLED SAILING CONFUSED
ASEMIA ASYMBOLIA
ASENATH (**FATHER OF** —) POTIPHERAH
(**HUSBAND OF** —) JOSEPH
(**SON OF** —) EPHRAIM MANASSEH
ASEXUAL AGAMIC AGAMOUS
(PREF.) AGAM(O)
ASH AS ALS ASE ASS FIG RON COKE SORB ARTAR ASHEN EMBER FRAIN ROWAN CINDER CORPSE DOTTEL DOTTLE WICKEN CLINKER RESIDUE DOGBERRY FRAXINUS HOOPWOOD WINETREE
(**SILKY** —) CEDAR
(PL.) ASE AXAN KELP SOIL ASHEN VAREC WASTE BREEZE CINDERS PULVERIN
ASHAMED MEAN NACE NAIS ABASHED HANGDOG HONTOUS SHAMEFACED
ASHBEL (**FATHER OF** —) BENJAMIN
ASH-BLOND CENDRE
ASH-COLORED CINEREAL CINEREOUS
ASHEN WAN GRAY GREY PALE WAXEN WHITE PALLID GHASTLY BLANCHED CINEREAL
ASHER (**FATHER OF** —) JACOB
(**MOTHER OF** —) ZILPAH
ASHES (— **OF CREMATED BODY**) CREMAINS
(PREF.) CINE SPODO TEPHRA TEPHRO
ASHKENAZ (**FATHER OF** —) GOMER
ASHKUKU CONY DAMAN HYRAX
ASHLAR ASELAR RANGEWORK
ASHORE ACOST ALAND AGROUND BEACHED STRANDED
ASHTAVAKRA (**FATHER OF** —) KAHODA
ASHTRAY SPITKID SPITKIT
ASHUR FEROHER
(**FATHER OF** —) HEZRON
(**MOTHER OF** —) ABIAH
(**WIFE OF** —) HELAH
ASHVATH (**FATHER OF** —) JAPHLET
ASHWEED GOUTWEED
ASIA (**FATHER OF** —) OCEANUS
(**HUSBAND OF** —) IAPETUS
(**MOTHER OF** —) TETHYS
(**SON OF** —) ATLAS EPIMETHEUS PROMETHEUS

ASIA
(ALSO SEE SPECIFIC COUNTRIES)
DESERT: GOBI TAKLAMAKAN
LAKE: ARAL URMIA BAYKAL CASPIAN BALKHASH
MOUNTAIN: FUJI DJAJA JANNU KAMET PAMIR ARARAT KUNGUR KUNLUN LHOTSE MAKALU MUZTAG NOSHAQ NUPTSE SEMERU TRIVOR EVEREST RATHONG ANNAPURNA
NATION: IRAN IRAQ LAOS BURMA CHINA INDIA JAPAN NEPAL QATAR SYRIA YEMEN BHUTAN ISRAEL JORDAN RUSSIA TAIWAN TURKEY BAHRAIN LEBANON SENEGAL VIETNAM CAMBODIA MALAYSIA

MONGOLIA PAKISTAN THAILAND INDONESIA KAMPUCHEA SINGAPORE BANGLADESH NORTHKOREA SOUTHKOREA AFGHANISTAN SAUDIARABIA SOVIETUNION UNITEDARABEMIRATES
RANGE: ALTAI KOLYMA HIMALAYA
RIVER: OB SI AMUR LENA URAL INDUS GANGES MEKONG TIGRIS HWANGHO SALWEEN TANGTZE YENISEI EUPHRATES IRRAWADDY
VOLCANO: APO USU FUGI GEDE TAAL AGUNG ALAID DEMPO MAYON RAUNG MARAPI MERAPI SEMERU SINILA SLAMET ULAWUN BULOSAN

SUNDORO TAMBORA TJAREME GAMALAMA KERINTJE RINDJANI TOLBACHIK
WATERFALL: JOG GOKAK KEGON MEKONG CAUVERY

ASIDE BY BYE OFF AGEE AWAY GONE NEAR PAST AGLEY ALOOF APART ASKEW FORBY ASLANT ASTRAY BESIDE BEYOND BYHAND FORBYE FORTHBY LATERAL PRIVATE WHISPER OVERHAND RESERVED SECRETLY SEPARATE SIDEWISE OVERBOARD
ASININE DULL CRASS DENSE INEPT SILLY ABSURD ASSISH OBTUSE SIMPLE STUPID DOLTISH FATUOUS FOOLISH IDIOTIC
ASIUS (**FATHER OF** —) DYMAS HYRTACUS
(**SISTER OF** —) HECUBA
(**SLAYER OF** —) AJAX IDOMENUS
ASK BEG SPY SUE FAND PRAY QUIZ CLAIM CRAVE EXACT FRAYN PLEAD QUERY SPEAK SPEER SPEIR SPELL SPERE ADJURE DEMAND DESIRE EXAMIN EXPECT FRAIST FRAYNE INVITE BESEECH BESPEAK CONSULT ENTREAT IMPLORE INQUIRE REQUEST REQUIRE SOLICIT PETITION QUESTION
(— **ALMS**) CANT THIG
(— **FOR**) BEG BID CRY DUN LAIT SEEK BESPEAK INQUIRE REQUEST
(— **PAYMENT**) CHARGE
ASKANCE AWRY ASKEW ASKILE CROOKED SIDEWAYS
ASKEW CAM AGEE ALOP AWRY AZEW AGLEE AGLEY AMISS ATILT CRAZY GLEED TIPSY ASKANT ASLANT ATWIST FLOOEY SKEWED SKIVIE ASQUINT CROOKED OBLIQUE BIASWISE COCKEYED SIDELING
ASKING ROGATION
ASLANT ASIDE SLOPE
(PREF.) PLAGI(O)
ASLEEP DEAD FAST IDLE LATENT NUMBED DORMANT NAPPING
ASOCIAL EGREGIOUS
ASOKA (**FATHER OF** —) BINDUSARA
ASOPUS (**DAUGHTER OF** —) ORNIA

THEBE AEGINA ASOPIS CLEONE PIRENE SINOPE CHALCIS CORCYRA SALAMIS TANAGRA THESPEIA
(SON OF —) ISMENUS PELASGUS
(WIFE OF —) METOPE
ASP ESP ASPIC ASPIDE URAEUS
ASPAR (FATHER OF —) ARDABURIUS
ASPARAGUS LILY GRASS SPRUE ASPERGE SPARAGE SPERAGE
(— GARNISH) PRINCESS
ASPATHA (FATHER OF —) HAMAN
ASPECT AIR HUE WAY AURA BROW FACE HAND KIND LEER LOOK MIEN SIDE VIEW VULT ANGLE COLOR DECIL FACET GUISE IMAGE NORMA PHASE SIGHT STAGE TRINE VISOR VIZOR DECILE FACIES FIGURE GLANCE MANNER PHASIS REGARD VISAGE APPAREL BEARING ESSENCE FEATURE MALEFIC OUTLOOK RESPECT RETRAIT SEXTILE SHOWING SPECIES CARRIAGE CONSPECT FOREHEAD OUTSIGHT PROSPECT QUINTILE CHARACTER SEMBLANCE
(— OF CURVE) INSIDE
(— OF EMOTION) AFFECT
(— OF MOON) CRESCENT
(— OF MUSICAL NUANCES) AGOGICS
(BALEFUL —) DISASTER
(CULTURAL —) EMANATION
(DETERMINING —) HEART
(EXTERNAL —) PHYSIOGNOMY
(FACIAL —) EXPRESSION
(LANGUAGE —) DURATIVE
(PRIMARY —) HIGHWAY
(QUARTILE —) SQUARE
(SECONDARY —) BYWAY
ASPEN APS ASP ALAMO NITHER POPLAR POPPLE QUAKER QUAKING TREMBLE
ASPER AKCHA AKCHEH OTHMANY
ASPERGILLUM HYSSOP SPRINKLE STRINKLE
ASPERITY IRE RIGOR ACERBITY ACRIMONY TARTNESS ANIMOSITY
ASPERSE SKIT SLUR SPOT ABUSE DECRY LIBEL SPRAY DEFAME DEFILE MALIGN REVILE SHOWER VILIFY APPEACH BLACKEN DETRACT LAMPOON SLANDER TARNISH TRADUCE BESMIRCH FORSPEAK SPRINKLE
ASPERSION SLUR BAPTISM CALUMNY INNUENDO
ASPHALT BREA PITCH SLIME FILLER MANJAK BITUMEN CUTBACK MANJACK BYERLITE UINTAITE
ASPHALTUM CONGO
ASPHODEL KNAVERY AFFODILL
ASPHYXIA APNEA APNOEA ACROTISM
ASPIC JELLY GELATIN GELATINE LAVENDER
ASPIRATE ROUGH SPIRITUS
ASPIRATION GOAL IDEAL DESIRE RECOIL SIGHTS AMBITION PRETENSION
ASPIRE AIM STY HOPE LONG MINT

RISE SEEK SOAR WISH ETTLE MOUNT TOWER YEARN ASCEND ATTAIN DESIRE PRETEND
ASPIRIN FEBRIFUGE
ASPIRING ASPIRANT
ASRIEL (FATHER OF —) GILEAD
ASS DOLT FOOL JADE KHUR MOKE BURRO CHUMP CUDDY DICKY DUNCE EQUID GUDDA HINNY CUDDIE DAPPLE DICKEY DONKEY ONAGER ASINEGO ASSHEAD JACKASS LONGEAR MALTESE SOLIPED IMBECILE
(FEMALE —) JENNY JENNET
(MALE —S) JACKSTOCK
(WILD —) KIANG KULAN KYANG KIYANG KOULAN ONAGER HEMIPPE CHIGETAI GHORKHAR HEMIONUS
(PL.) JACKSTOCK
(PREF.) ONISCI ONO
ASSAI MANICOLE
ASSAIL WOO BEAT FRAY HOOT JUMP PELT SAIL ASSAY BESET PRESS SHOCK STONE WHACK WHANG ACCUSE ATTACK BATTER BICKER BULLET HURTLE IMPUGN INFEST INSULT INVADE MALIGN MOLEST OFFEND OPPUGN RATTLE SAILYE SCATHE STRIKE ASSAULT ATTEMPT BELABOR BESEIGE BOMBARD CATCALL ENFORCE ASSEMBLE BLUDGEON TOMAHAWK
ASSAILANT ONSETTER
ASSAM (MOUNTAIN OF —) JAPVO
(STATE OF —) KHASI MANIPUR
(TOWN OF —) IMPHAL SADIYA GAUHATI SHILLONG
(TRIBE OF —) AO AKA AOR AHOM GARO NAGA
ASSARACUS (BROTHER OF —) ILUS GANYMEDE
(FATHER OF —) TROS
(MOTHER OF —) CALLIRRHOE
(SISTER OF —) CLEOPATRA
(SON OF —) CAPYS
ASSART SART THWAITE
ASSASSIN THAG THUG BRAVE BRAVO FEDAI FIDAI CUTTLE FIDAWI KILLER SLAYER RUFFIAN STABBER TORPEDO HACKSTER MURDERER SICARIUS
ASSASSINATE KILL SLAY MURDER REMOVE
ASSASSINATION THUGGEE
ASSAULT MUG BEAT BLOW COSH FRAY RAID SLUG ABUSE ALARM ASSAY BRUNT HARRY ONSET POISE POUND SHOCK SMITE STORM STOUR VENUE AFFRAY ALARUM ASSAIL ATTACK BREACH BUFFET CHARGE ENGINE EXTENT HOLDUP INSULT INVADE NAPALM ONFALL STOUND STOUSH THRUST YOKING ATTEMPT BOMBARD DESCENT LAMBAST PURSUIT RUNNING VIOLATE INVASION OUTBURST
ASSAY RUN SAY TRY TEST ESSAY PROOF PROVE TOUCH TRIAL ASSAIL ATTACK EFFORT ANALYZE ATTEMPT EXAMINE TASTING

ANALYSIS APPRAISE ENDEAVOR ESTIMATE HARDSHIP
ASSAYER POTDAR TESTER
ASSAYING DOCIMASY
ASSEMBLAGE ARMY BODY CAMP CLOT COMA CREW HERD HOST MASS PACK RUCK BUNCH CHOIR COURT CROWD DRIFT DROVE FLOCK GROUP LEVEE POSSE QUIRE SALON SHOCK SWARM CONVOY GALAXY HOOKUP RESORT SPREAD SYSTEM THRONG CIRCUIT CLUSTER COLLEGE COMPANY COMPLEX CONVENT CULTURE SOCIETY STATION STATUTE TABAGIE ASSEMBLY AUDITORY CONGRESS MULTIPLE PARLIAMENT
(— OF FOSSILS) COLONY
(— OF INTEGERS) IDEAL
(CONFUSED —) FARRAGO
ASSEMBLE FIT LAY POD SAM BULK CALL HERD HOST KNOT MASS MEET ROUT SAMM AMASS ASAME FLOCK PIECE RALLY TROOP UNITE COUPLE GATHER HUDDLE MUSTER SUMMON COLLATE COLLECT COMPILE CONDUCE CONVENE CONVOKE RECRUIT CONGRESS CONGREGATE
(— CARDS) BUNCH
ASSEMBLED ACCOYLD
ASSEMBLER BONDER
ASSEMBLY HUI SUM BAUD BEVY BOGY DIET DRUM DUMA FEIS HOEY MALL MOOT RAAD ROUT SEJM SEYM TING AGORA BOGEY BOULE COURT COVEN CURIA DOUMA FORUM GROUP JUNTA LEVEE PARTY PRESS SABHA SETUP SOBOR SYNOD THING TROOP AENACH AONACH ASSIZE BOBBIN BUSING CHAPEL COETUS COVINE GEMOTE MAJLIS PARADE PLENUM POWWOW SEIMAS SENATE STEVEN CHAMBER CHAPTER COLLEGE COMITIA COMMAND COMPANY CONCION CONSORT CONVENT COUNCIL DIETINE EOTATES FOLKMOT HUSTING LANDTAG MEETING PENSION SERVICE SESSION SOCIETY SYNAGOG SYNAXIS TEMPEST TYNWALD ZEMSTVO AUDIENCE CONCLAVE CONGRESS ECCLESIA FOLKMOOT PLACITUM PORTMOTE PRESENCE SEDERUNT SOBRANJE TINEWALD TRIBUNAL VOLKSTAG WARDMOTE CONCOURSE
(— HOUSE) KASHIM
(— OF BLESSED) HEAVEN
(— OF CONDUCTORS) BUS
(— OF DEPUTIES) AMPHICTYONA
(— OF ELDERS) KGOTLA
(— OF WITCHES) COVEN SABBAT SABBATH
(AFTERNOON —) LEVEE
(BOY SCOUT —) JAMBOREE
(CLOSED —) CONCLAVE
(FASTENER —) SEMS
(GRENADE —) BOUCHON
(PL.) COMITIA

ASSENT AYE BOW NOD YEA YES AMEN SEAL SENT ADMIT AGREE GRANT YIELD ACCEDE ACCEPT ACCORD BELIEF CHORUS COMPLY CONCUR SUBMIT UNISON APPROVE CONCEDE CONFESS CONFORM CONSENT ADHESION CONSTATE OKEYDOKE SANCTION SUFFRAGE ACCESSION OKEYDOKEY
ASSERT LAY BRAG SHOW VOICE AFFIRM ALLEGE ASSURE AVOUCH DEFEND DEPONE DEPOSE INTEND INTENT THREAP UPHOLD ADVANCE BETOKEN CONFIRM CONTEND DECLARE PROTEST SUPPORT ADVOCATE CHAMPION CONSTATE MAINTAIN OUTSTAND POSITIVE PREDICATE
ASSERTION VOW FACT HOTI CLAIM VOUCH AVERMENT
(— OF MASCULINITY) MACHISMO
(BOASTFUL —) JACTATION
(DUBIOUS —) PLINYISM
ASSERTIVE BRASH DOGMATIC POSITIVE
ASSESS LAY TAX CESS DOOM LEVY MISE RATE SCOT TOLL AGIST CENSE PRICE STENT TEIND VALUE AFFEER ASSIZE CHARGE EXTEND IMPOSE SAMPLE MEASURE APPRAISE ESTIMATE
ASSESSMENT FEE LUG TAX CESS DUTY LEVY SCOT TOLL CULET JUMMA PRICE RATAL STENT TITHE WORTH EXTENT IMPOST PURVEY SURTAX TARIFF SCUTAGE BRIGBOTE TAXATION
ASSESSOR JUDGE MUFTI RATER CESSOR LISTER TASKER AUDITOR STENTOR TAXATOR
(PL.) FINTADORES
ASSET PLUS HONOR GETPENNY PROPERTY RESOURCE STRENGTH
ASSETS GOODS MEANS MONEY STOCK CREDIT WEALTH CAPITAL EFFECTS ACCOUNTS PROPERTY RESOURCE
ASSEVERATE SAY VOW AVER AVOW STATE SWEAR AFFIRM ALLEGE ASSERT ASSURE DECLARE PROTEST
ASSEVERATION VOW OATH
ASSHUR (FATHER OF —) SHEM
ASSIDUOUS BUSY GREAT ACTIVE DEVOTED PENIBLE STUDIED DILIGENT FREQUENT SEDULOUS STUDIOUS
ASSIGN FIX LET PUT SET ARET CAST CEDE DEAL DOLE DRAW GIVE METE RATE SEAL SHOW SIGN ALLOT ALLOW APPLY ARETT AWARD DIGHT ENDOW REFER SHIFT TITLE ADDUCE AFFECT ALLEGE ATTACH CHARGE CONVEY DESIGN DIRECT ENTAIL ORDAIN ACCOUNT ADJUDGE APPOINT ASCRIBE CONSIGN DISPOSE ENTITLE SPECIFY STATION TRIBUTE ALLOCATE ANTEDATE ARROGATE DELEGATE INSCRIBE TRANSFER
(— QUARTERS) BILLET

(— TASK) STINT
ASSIGNATION DATE MEET TRYST
MEETING
ASSIGNMENT DECK DUTY TASK
CHORE GRIND STENT STINT
TUNCA CESSIO LESSON CESSION
BUSINESS HOMEWORK
PLACEMENT
ASSIGNOR CEDOR CEDENS
CEDENT
ASSIMILATE MIX ONE FUSE
ADAPT ALTER BLEND LEARN
MERGE ABSORB DIGEST IMBIBE
COMPARE CONCOCT RESEMBLE
ASSIMILATION ECHOISM
HOMEOSIS RECOGNITION
(— OF FOOD) CONCOCTION
ASSINIBOIN HOHE
ASSIR (FATHER OF —) KORAH
EBIASAPH JECONIAH
ASSIST AID ABET BACK HELP JOIN
AVAIL BOOST COACH FAVOR
NURSE SERVE SPEED STEAD
ATTEND ESCORT PROMPT
SECOND SQUIRE SUCCOR BENEFIT
COMFORT FURTHER RELIEVE
SUPPORT SUSTAIN ADJUVATE
BEFRIEND
(— A READER) FESCUE
(— AT) STAY
ASSISTANCE AID ALMS CAST GIFT
HAND HELP LIFT BOOST FAVOR
HEEZE RELIEF REMEDY SUCCOR
SUPPLY ADJUTOR COMFORT
SECOURS SUBSIDY SUPPORT
AUXILIUM EASEMENT GIFFGAFF
LARGESSE
ASSISTANT CAD AIDE ALLY HAND
HELP MAID MATE PUNK SOUS
ZANY CLERK GROOM USHER
VALET AIDANT BUMPER COMMIS
CURATE DEPUTY FLUNKY HELPER
LEGATE NIPPER SECOND TULTUL
YEOMAN ABETTOR ACOLYTE
ADJOINT ADJUNCT DOORMAN
DRESSER HOGGLER PADRINO
PARTNER PROVOST RUBBLER
SHIFTER STRIKER SWAMPER
ADJUTANT ADJUVANT FELDSHER
GOMASHTA LECTURER MINISTER
OFFSIDER PARASITE SERVITOR
SIDESMAN SUBPRIOR
(— TO ANIMAL SHOW JUDGE)
STEWARD
(AUCTIONEER'S —) SPOTTER
(DYEING —) CARRIER
(GUNNER'S —) MATROSS
(MASON'S —) GOUJAT
(MATADOR'S —) CHULO
(POLICE —) CORPORAL
(SURVEYOR'S —) CHAINMAN
(WAITER'S —) BUSBOY OMNIBUS
ASSOCIATE MIX PAL AIDE ALLY
BAND CHUM HERD JOIN LINK
MATE MOOP MOUP PEER WALK
WIFE YOKE BLEND BUDDY CRONY
HABER MATCH TRAIN TROOP
ASSORT ATTACH ATTEND
CHABER COHORT COUSIN FASTEN
FELLOW FRIEND HELPER HOBNOB
MARROW MEDDLE MEMBER
MINGLE PUISNE PUISNY RELATE
SOCIUS SPOUSE TRAVEL

ADJUNCT ASSOCIE BRACKET
COALITE COMMUNE COMPANY
COMPEER COMRADE CONNECT
CONSORT HUSBAND PARTNER
PEWMATE SOCIATE COMPLICE
CONFRERE CONJOINT CONVERSE
COPEMATE FAMILIAR FEDERATE
FOLLOWER FREQUENT GADSHILL
IDENTIFY INTIMATE PARTAKER
ACCOMPANY ACCOMPLICE
(— WITH) FRAT MOOP MOUP
(DEMON —) FLY
(PL.) ENTOURAGE
ASSOCIATED
(PREF.) SYM
(SUFF.) IC(AL)
ASSOCIATION HUI BODY BOND
BUND CLUB GILD HONG HUNT
TONG ARTEL BOARD GUILD
HANSA HANSE SANGH TRUCK
UNION CARTEL CERCLE CHAPEL
COMITY CONGER GRANGE
LEAGUE LEGION LYCEUM PLEDGE
SANGHA SCHOLA VEREIN CIRCUIT
COMBINE COMPANY CONSORT
CONTACT CONVENT COUNCIL
SOCIETY SOROSIS SYNOECY
AFFINITY ALLIANCE ASSEMBLY
ATHENEUM CONVERSE HABITUDE
INTIMACY SODALITY SYNOMOSY
TAALBOND ORGANIZATION
(— OF FOSSILS) FAUNULA
FAUNULE
(ANTAGONISTIC —) ANTIBIOSIS
(BOOK-SELLERS' —) CONGER
(CLOSE —) HARNESS INTIMACY
(EMPLOYERS' —) GREMIO
(FARMERS' —) GRANGE
(IN —) ALONG
(LABOR —) ARTEL UNION
(RELIGIOUS —) SAMAJ
(SECRET —) CABAL
(STUDENTS' —) CORPS
(SYMBIOTIC —) ACAROPHILY
ASSOIL RID SOIL ATONE CLEAR
SOLVE ACQUIT PARDON REFUTE
ABSOLVE DELIVER EXPIATE
FORGIVE RELEASE RESOLVE
ASSONANCE PUN RHYME
PARAGRAM
ASSORT BOLT CULL SUIT WINNOW
(— COINS) SHROFF
ASSORTED CHOW CHOWCHOW
ASSORTER FEEDER LOOKER
ASSORTMENT BAG LOT SET OLIO
BATCH BUNCH GROUP SUITE
RAGBAG MIXTURE
(— OF TYPE) BILL FONT
(COMPLETE —) STANDARD
ASSUAGE BEET CALM EASE LIOS
LISS ABATE ALLAY CHARM DELAY
LISSE MEASE SALVE SLAKE STILL
SWAGE LENIFY LESSEN MODIFY
PACIFY QUENCH REDUCE SOFTEN
SOLACE SOOTHE TEMPER
APPEASE COMFORT MOLLIFY
QUALIFY RELIEVE SATISFY
DIMINISH MITIGATE MODERATE
ASSUASIVE MILD LENIENT
LENITIVE SOOTHING
ASSUME DON PUT SAY SET BEAR
DARE FANG GIVE MASK PULL
SHAM SHIP TAKE ADOPT ANNEX

CLOAK ELECT FEIGN GUESS
INDUE INFER RAISE USURP
ACCEPT AFFECT BETAKE CLOTHE
FIGURE ASSUMPT BELIEVE
PREMISE PRESUME PRETEND
RECEIVE SUBSUME SUPPOSE
SURMISE ACCROACH ARROGATE
SIMULATE PERSONATE
POSTULATE
(— CHARACTER) ACT AFFECT
(— FORM) ENGENDER
(— OFFICE) ACCEDE
(— PAINTING STANCE) BACK
ASSUMED ALIAS FALSE GIVEN
FEIGNED AFFECTED BORROWED
ASSUMING LOFTY UPPISH UPPITY
AFFECTED ARROGANT SUPERIOR
ASSUMPTION DONNEE THESIS
BALLOON FICTION SURMISE
HOMEOSIS MARYMASS PRETENCE
PRETENSE PRESUMPTION
(BASIC —) BEGINNING
(EMPTY —) IMAGINATION
ASSURANCE FACE GALL SEAL
BRASS CHEEK FAITH NERVE
TRUST APLOMB AVOUCH BELIEF
CAUTIO CREDIT PLEVIN PLIGHT
SAFETY COURAGE PROMISE
WARRANT AUDACITY BOLDNESS
COOLNESS FIRMANCE FOREHEAD
SECURITY SUREMENT
ASSURE AFFY AVER SURE TELL
CINCH HIGHT VOUCH AFFEER
ASSERT AVOUCH ENSURE INSURE
PLEDGE SECURE SEKERE SICCAR
SICKER WITTER BETROTH CERTIFY
CONFIRM DECLARE HEARTEN
PROMISE PROTEST RESOLVE
WARRANT AFFIANCE CONVINCE
EMBOLDEN PERSUADE
ASSURED BOLD CALM COLD FIRM
PERT SURE BOUND SIKER SLUSH
FACILE PROBAL SECURE SICCAR
SICKER CERTAIN POSITIVE
(— OF SUCCESS) MADE
(BLUNTLY —) KNOCKDOWN
ASSUREDLY AMEN SOON INDEED
PERDIE REDELY SICCAR SICKER
SURELY VERILY HARDILY
WITTERLY
ASSYRIA ASHUR ASSUR ASSHUR
(CAPITAL OF —) CALAH NINEVEH
ASSYRIAN NESTORIAN
(— PLUM) SEBESTEN
ASTER ARNICA COCASH AMELLUS
BEEWEED BONESET EUASTER
ASTROFEL COMPOSIT CYTASTER
MONASTER STARWORT STOKESIA
ASTERIA (DAUGHTER OF —) HECATE
(FATHER OF —) COEUS
(HUSBAND OF —) PERSES
(MOTHER OF —) PHOEBE
(SISTER OF —) LETO LATONA
ASTERISK MARK STAR ASTER
ASTERISM WINDMILL
(THREE —S) ASTERISM
ASTERIUS (BROTHER OF —)
AMPHION
(FATHER OF —) ANAX HYPERASIUS
(SLAYER OF —) MILETUS
ASTERN AFT BAFT HIND REAR
ABAFT APOOP BEHIND

OCCIPUT BACKWARD
ASTEROID EROS HEBE IRIS JUNO
CERES DIONE FLORA IRENE METIS
VESTA ASTREA EGERIA EUROPA
HYGEIA PALLAS PLANET PSYCHE
THALIA THEMIS THETIS ELECTRA
EUNOMIA FORTUNA LUTETIA
CALLIOPE MASSALIA PLANTOID
STARFISH STARLIKE VICTORIA
ASTHMA PHTHISIC
ASTHMATIC POUCY PURSY
POUCEY WHEEZY PANTING
PUFFING
ASTIR UP AGOG ABOUT AFOOT
AGATE ALERT GOING ACTIVE
AROUND ASTEER MOVING
ROUSED ABROACH EXCITED
STIRRING VIGILANT
ASTONISH AWE DAZE STAM
AMAZE KNOCK SHOCK DAMMER
MARVEL STOUND ASTOUND
GLOPPEN IMPRESS STARTLE
AMERVEIL BEWILDER CONFOUND
SURPRISE
ASTONISHING AMAZING
FABULOUS MARVELOUS
MARVELLOUS
ASTONISHMENT MUSE FERLY
DISMAY FARLEY MARVEL STOUND
WONDER SURPRISE
ASTOUND BEAT STUN ABASH
AMAZE APPAL SHOCK STOUN
APPALL STOUND STAGGER
STUPEFY STUPEND TERRIFY
ASTONISH CONFOUND SURPRISE
ASTOUNDING STUNNING
ASTRAEA (FATHER OF —) ZEUS
JUPITER
(MOTHER OF —) THEMIS
(SISTER OF —) PUDICITIA
ASTRAEUS (BROTHER OF —) PALLAS
PERSES
(FATHER OF —) CRIUS
(MOTHER OF —) EURYBIA
ASTRAGAL TALUS CHAPLET
CORNICE BAGUETTE
ASTRAGALAR
(PREF.) TALO
ASTRAGALUS TALUS VETCH
ASTRAKHAN BOKHARA
ASTRAL REMOTE STARRY STELLAR
ASTRAEAN SIDEREAL STARLIKE
ASTRAY AWRY LOST WILL ABORD
AGATE AGLEE AGLEY AMISS
ASIDE GLEED WRONG ABROAD
AFIELD ERRANT ERRING FAULTY
DEPAYSE DEVIOUS FORLORN
SINNING WILSOME MISTAKEN
STRAYING
ASTRIDE ATOP ABOARD ACHEVAL
SPANNING
ASTRINGENCY ACERBITY
ACRIMONY
ASTRINGENT ACID ALUM COTO
SOUR TART ACERB HARSH
ROUGH SAPAN STERN CORNUS
MASTIC PONTIC SEVERE TANNIN
ALUMNOL AUSTERE BINDING
CATECHU PUCKERY RHATANY
STYPTIC GERANIUM TRILLIUM
(NOT —) SOFT
ASTROLOGER JOTI JOSHI ARTIST
JOTISI MERLIN ZADKIEL SCHEMIST

ASTROLOGY STARCRAFT MATHEMATICALS

ASTRONOMER JOTI JOSHI JOTISI
AMERICAN SEE BOND BOSS HALE HALL HILL POOR REES TODD VERY ADAMS BAADE BAUER BOWEN CHASE ELKIN FROST HOUGH PEASE SWIFT YOUNG AITKEN BAILEY CANNON DRAPER HOLDEN HUBBLE HUSSEY JACOBY KEELER LOOMIS LOWELL PETERS PORTER ROGERS SEARES WALKER WATSON WILSON BARNARD BURNHAM EASTMAN FLEMING GILLIES LANGLEY LITTELL MERRILL MITCHEL MOULTON NEWCOMB PERRINE RITCHEY RUSSELL SAFFORD SHAPLEY SLIPHER WHITNEY BOWDITCH CAMPBELL CHANDLER COMSTOCK DOUGLASS HARKNESS STEBBINS TOMBAUGH WINTHROP WOODWARD ALEXANDER DOOLITTLE LEUSCHNER MOREHOUSE PRITCHETT HARRINGTON RUTHERFURD SCHAEBERLE RITTENHOUSE SCHLESINGER EICHELBERGER
AUSTRIAN FALB HAGEN LITTROW PURBACH
BELGIAN QUETELET
CANADIAN KLOTZ PLASKETT
DANISH BRAHE DREYER HANSEN ROEMER SCHUMACHER LONGOMONTANUS
DUTCH BLAEU SITTER HUYGENS KAPTEYN
EGYPTIAN PTOLEMY
ENGLISH AIRY HIND POND RYLE TODD WARD ADAMS BAILY DYSON INNES JEANS JONES MASON MAIN MURIS WALES CLERKE DARWIN HALLEY LOVELL BRADLEY CHALLIS CLAXTON GREGORY HUGGINS LOCKYER LUBBOCK MICHELL PARSONS PENROSE PROCTOR BRISBANE COPELAND EDDINTON GLAISHER GOMPERTZ HERSCHEL HORROCKS FLAMSTEED MASKELYNE PRITCHARD CARRINGTON GELLIBRAND GROOMBRIDGE SHEEPSHANKS
FINNISH STONE
FRENCH BIOT FAYE LYOT PONS WOLF HENRY LOEWY RAYET FERNEL MOREUX PICARD VALLOT BORELLY BOUVARD CASSINI DELISLE JANSSEN LALANDE LAPLACE MARALDI MESSIER MOUCHEZ PUISEUX DELAMBRE DELAUNAY LACAILLE LAGRANGE BIGOURDAN CHACORNAC LEMONNIER LEVERRIER TISSERAND BURCKHARDT FLAMMARION MAUPERTUIS
GERMAN BEER BODE WOLF ZACH BAYER BIELA ENCKE GALLE GAUSS GRAFF KEMPF KNOPF MAYER ARNOLD ARREST AUWERS BRUHNS HARZER IDELER KEPLER LAMONT MADLER MARIUS MOBIUS MULLER OLBERS PETERS

RUMKER SPORER STRUYE TEMPEL AMBRONN APIANUS BRENDEL BRUNNOW LAMBERT SCHONER SCHWABE FOERSTER GUTHNICK HARTMANN LINDENAU MERCATOR RHATICUS SCHEINER WINNECKE FABRICIUS PALITZSCH SCHONFELD
GREEK CONON METON AUTOLYCUS CALLIPPUS CLEOMEDES OENOPIDES SOSIGENES HIPPARCHUS THEODOSIUS ANAXIMANDER ARISTARCHUS CLEOSTRATUS ERATOSTHENES
INDIAN ARYABHATA BRAHMAGUPTA
IRISH BALL MOLYNEUX
ITALIAN AMICI FRISI DONATI ORIANI PIAZZI SECCHI BORELLI GALILEI RICCIOLI TACCHINI BIANCHINI BOSCOVICH FRACASTORO SCHIAPARELLI
NORWEGIAN HANSTEEN
POLISH COPERNICUS
RUSSIAN BREDICHIN
SCOTTISH GILL NICHOL WILSON GREGORY ANDERSON FERGUSON HENDERSON
SWEDISH DUNER BOHLIN GYLDEN CELSIUS ANGSTROM BACKLUND STROMGREN

ASTRONOMICAL FAR HUGE GREAT URANIC DISTANT IMMENSE URANIAN COLOSSAL INFINITE
(— INSTRUMENT) ARMILL

ASTRONOMY WAGON WAGONER WAGGONER

ASTUTE SLY FOXY KEEN WILY ACUTE CANNY QUICK SHARP SMART CLEVER CRAFTY NASUTE SHREWD CUNNING KNOWING SKILLED

ASTYAGES (FATHER OF —) CYAXARES
ASTYANAX (FATHER OF —) HECTOR
(MOTHER OF —) ANDROMACHE
ASTYDAMIA (FATHER OF —) PELOPS
(MOTHER OF —) HIPPODAMIA
(SON OF —) AMPHITRYON
ASTYOCHE (DAUGHTER OF —) PHYLEUS
(LOVER OF —) HERCULES
(SON OF —) TLEPOLEMUS
ASUNDER ATWO APART SPLIT ATWAIN SUNDER SUNDRY DIVIDED DIVORCED YSOWNDIR
(PREF.) AP(H) DI DICH(O)
ASURA VARUNA
ASVATTHAMAN (FATHER OF —) DRONA
(MOTHER OF —) KRIPA
ASYLUM ARK HOME JAIL ALTAR COVER GRITH HAVEN BEDLAM HARBOR REFUGE ALSATIA COLLEGE HOSPICE RETREAT SHELTER BUGHOUSE MADHOUSE NUTHOUSE
ASYMMETRIC PEDIAL
AS YOU LIKE IT (AUTHOR OF —) SHAKESPEARE

(CHARACTER IN —) ADAM CELIA CORIN PHEBE AMIENS AUDREY DENNIS JAQUES LEBEAU OLIVER CHARLES MARTEXT ORLANDO SILVIUS WILLIAM ROSALIND FREDERICK TOUCHSTONE
AT A AL AU BY IN TO ALS TIL TILL UNTO ATTEN THERE HEREAT
(— ALL) ANY AVA EER EVER HALF OUGHT SOEVER HOWEVER
ATABAL DRUM TABOR ATTABAL
ATALANTA (CHARACTER IN —) MERCURY ATALANTA MELEAGER
(COMPOSER OF —) HANDEL
(FATHER OF —) IASUS
(HUSBAND OF —) MELANION HIPPOMENES
(MOTHER OF —) CLYMENE
ATAMAN CHIEF JUDGE HETMAN HEADMAN
ATARAH (HUSBAND OF —) JERAHMEEL
(SON OF —) ONAM
ATAVISM REVERSION
ATELIER SHOP STUDIO BOTTEGA WORKSHOP
ATEO WAKEA
ATES SWEETSOP
ATHALARIC (FATHER OF —) EUTHELRIC
(MOTHER OF —) AMALASUINTHA
ATHALIAH (FATHER OF —) AHAB
(HUSBAND OF —) JEHORAM
(MOTHER OF —) JEZEBEL
ATHAMAS (DAUGHTER OF —) HELLE
(FATHER OF —) AEOLUS
(MOTHER OF —) ENARETE
(SON OF —) PHRIXUS LEARCHUS PALAEMON
(WIFE OF —) INO NEPHELE
ATHANAGILD (DAUGHTER OF —) BRUNEHILDE GALESWINTHA
ATHANOR OVEN ATHENOR FURNACE
ATHAPASKAN HAW HARE HUPA KATO KASKA AHTENA BEAVER CHETCO GILENO LASSIK SARCEE SEKANI CARRIER CHILULA KOYUKON KUTCHIN
ATHEIST ZENDIK DOUBTER INFIDEL NASTIKA AGNOSTIC APIKOROS NETHEIST
ATHENA ALEA AUGE NIKE ALERA AREIA ERGANE HIPPIA HYGEIA ITONIA PALLAS POLIAS AIANTIS MINERVA APATURIA
ATHENIAN ATTIC CHORAGUS CHOREGUS
ATHLAI (FATHER OF —) BEBAI
ATHLETE PRO BLUE JOCK KEMP STAR BOXER COLOR CRACK CUTEY CUTIE TURNER ACROBAT AMATEUR GYMNAST STICKER TUMBLER VARMINT GAMESTER REPEATER WRESTLER PENTATHLETE
(COLLEGE —) REDSHIRT
ATHLETIC AGILE BURLY LUSTY VITAL BRAWNY GYMNIC ROBUST SINEWY STRONG BOARDLY BOORDLY MUSCULAR POWERFUL VIGOROUS
ATHLETICS GAMES

SPORT EXERCISE
AT-HOME ASSEMBLY
ATHWART CROSS ABOARD ACROSS ASLANT OBLIQUE SIDEWISE TRAVERSE
ATLAS BOOK LIST MAPS TOME TITAN TELAMON MAINSTAY
(DAUGHTERS OF —) ATLANTIDES
(FATHER OF —) IAPETUS
(MOTHER OF —) CLYMENE
(WIFE OF —) PLEIONE
ATLE ETHEL
ATMAN ATMA ATTA SELF
ATMOSPHERE AIR SKY AURA FEEL LIFT MOOD TONE AROMA CLIME DECOR ETHER PLACE SMELL FROWST MIASMA NIMBUS SPHERE WELKIN FEELING HYALINE QUALIFY AMBIANCE AMBIENCE
(— OF DISCOURAGEMENT) CHILL
(CHARACTERISTIC —) VIBE
(NOXIOUS —) MIASMA
(SECTION OF —) SOLENOID
(SENSED —) KARMA
(STALE —) FROUST FROWST
(STUFFY —) FUG
(SUFFOCATING —) STIFLE
ATMOSPHERIC AERIAL
ATMOSPHERICS STATIC STRAYS SFERICS SPHERICS
ATOM ACE BIT ION JOT DIAD DYAD HAET HATE IOTA MITE MOTE WHIT ATOMY HENAD LABEL MONAD SHADE SPECK TINGE ADATOM BRIDGE CARBYL HEPTAD ISOBAR TETRAD ATOMIZE BODIKIN IONOGEN ISOTOPE NUCLIDE RADICAL SPECIES FUNCTION ISOSTERE MOLECULE PARTICLE PERISSAD QUANTITY CORPUSCLE SCINTILLA
(— TOTALITY) MATTER
(COMBINING —) ACCEPTOR
(TAGGED —) TRACER
(PL.) SMITHERS SMITHEREENS
ATOMIC TINY MINUTE NUCLEAR
ATOMIZE PULVERIZE
ATOMIZER SPRAY SPARGE SCENTER SPRAYER AIRBRUSH ODORATOR PERFUMER
ATOMS
(PREF.) (CONTAINING 20 —) EICOS
(CONTAINING 4 CARBON —) BUT
(HAVING ARRANGEMENT OF —) GALA GALACTO
(PRESENCE OF 2 NITROGEN —) DIAZ
ATONE AGREE AMEND ACCORD ANSWER ASSOIL RANSOM REDEEM REPENT APPEASE EXPIATE RESTORE SATISFY
(— FOR) ABY BYE ABYE MEND ABIDE ABEGGE
ATONEMENT MEND RANSOM MICHTAM PENANCE SATISFACTION ACCEPTILATION
ATOP ACOR
ATORAI DAURI
ATOSSA (FATHER OF —) CYRUS
(HUSBAND OF —) DARIUS SMERDIS CAMBYSES
ATRABILIOUS GLUM ADUST GLOOMY MOROSE SULLEN

ATRAMENTOUS INKY
ATRAX (DAUGHTER OF —) CAENIS
HIPPODAMIA
(FATHER OF —) PENEUS
(MOTHER OF —) BURA
ATREUS (BROTHER OF —) THYESTES
(FATHER OF —) PELOPS
(HALF-BROTHER OF —) THYESTES
(MOTHER OF —) HIPPODAMIA
(SON OF —) MENELAUS
(WIFE OF —) AEROPE
ATRIP AWEIGH
ATRIUM HALL ATRIO COURT
CAVITY AURICLE CHAMBER
PASSAGE
ATROCIOUS BAD DARK RANK VILE
AWFUL BLACK CRUEL GROSS
ATROCE BRUTAL ODIOUS SAVAGE
WICKED HEINOUS UNGODLY
VIOLENT FLAGRANT GRIEVOUS
HORRIBLE TERRIBLE MONSTROUS
ATROPHIC AUANTIC
ATROPHY RUST STUNT TABES
MACIES MOLDER SHRINK STARVE
SWEENY WITHER SWINNEY
WASTING STULTIFY
(PREF.) NECR(O)
ATROPINE DATURINE
ATTACH ADD FIX PUT SET SEW
TAG TIE BIND BOLT GLUE HANG
JOIN LINK SPAN TAKE VEST WELD
ADOPT AFFIX ANNEX BEWED
CLING FOUND HINGE HITCH
LATCH PASTE SCREW SEIZE
SPEND STICK TACHE TATCH
UNITE ACCUSE ADDICT ADHERE
ADJOIN APPEND ARREST CEMENT
DEVOTE ENGAGE ENTAIL ENTIRE
FASTEN FATHER INDICT SPLINE
ADHIBIT APPOINT ASCRIBE
CONNECT ESPOUSE SUBJOIN
(— TEMPORARILY) SECOND
ATTACHED FAST FOND ADNATE
DOTING ADJUNCT BIGOTED
SESSILE ADSCRIPT INSERTED
ATTACHING INCIDENT ALLIGATION
ATTACHMENT ARM GAG BAIL
BALE DRUM FLAY HEAD HECK
LOVE MOTE SHIM SHOE AMOUR
CHUCK CRUSH DOBBY DODAD
FENCE GUARD STRIG AFFAIR
BEATER BINDER BUMPER DAMSEL
DOBBIE DOCTOR DOODAD
DREDGE FELLER FETICH FETISH
HEMMER HILLER LAPPET LAYBOY
MARKER PACKER PICKUP SECTOR
SHIELD SIDING ADAPTOR AFFAIRE
BIGOTRY BRAIDER CREASER
DROPPER FAGOTER FITTING
GIGBACK HEADSET HOLDING
JOINTER KNOCKUP LEVELER
SPANNER SPRAYER DEVOTION
DINGDONG FASTNESS FIXATION
FONDNESS GOVERNOR HEADREST
ATTACK FIT HIT HOP MUG SIC
BAIT BOMB BOUT CLAW COSH
DINT FAKE FANG FORK FRAY
GANG GIVE HOOK JUMP PAIL
PANG RAID RISE RUSH SAIL SICK
SLOW TACK TURN WADE YOKE
ABUSE ALARM ASSAY BEGIN
BESET BLAST BLITZ BOARD
BRASH BRUNT CATCH CHECK

DRIVE FIGHT FLUSH FORAY
FORCE GLIDE HARRY ICTUS
ONSET POISE PULSE SALLY SCUFF
SMITE SOUSE SPASM SPELL
STORM ACCESS ACCUSE ACTION
AFFRAY AFFRET ASSAIL ATTAME
BATTLE BICKER BODRAG CHARGE
CRISIS DOUBLE ENVAYE EXPUGN
EXTENT GRUDGE INDICT INFEST
INSULT INVADE OFFEND ONFALL
ONRUSH POUNCE RUFFLE
SAVAGE SHOWER SORTIE
STOUND STRIKE STROKE TACKLE
TAKING THRUST AGGRESS
ASPERSE ASSAULT ATTEMPT
BARRAGE BELABOR BELIBEL
BESEIGE BOMBARD CENSURE
CRUSADE DESCENT OFFENSE
PICKOUT POTSHOT RUNNING
SCALING SEIZURE STACKER
CAMISADE CAMISADO ENDEAVOR
ESCALADE PAROXYSM SKIRMISH
SURPRISE TOMAHAWK OFFENSIVE
ONSLAUGHT PENETRATION
(— IN COCKFIGHT) SHUFFLE
(— OF ILLNESS) GO DWAM DWALM
ACCESS
(— OF SICKNESS) WHIP SEIZURE
(— TO ROB) THUG
(— WITH SHOUTS) HUE
(— WITH WORDS) STOUSH
(— ZEALOUSLY) CRUSADE
(BOMBING —) PRANG
(CHESS —) FORK
(CRITICAL —) SLATING
(FENCING —) GLIDE
(LIGHT —) TOUCH
(NIGHT —) CAMISADO
(SLIGHT —) WAFF
(SUDDEN —) ICTUS RAPTUS
SURPRISE
(SUICIDAL —) KAMIKAZE
(SURPRISE —) ALARM ALARUM
(VERBAL —) FIRE BLUDGEON
(SUFF.) LEPSIA LEPSIS LEPSY
LEPT(IC)
ATTACKER AGGRESSOR
OFFENDANT
(SUFF.) MASTIX
ATTACK ON THE MILL
(CHARACTER IN —) MERLIER
DOMINIQUE FRANCOISE
MARCELLINE
(COMPOSER OF —) BRUNEAU
ATTAI (FATHER OF —) REHOBOAM
(MOTHER OF —) AHLAI MAACHAH
ATTAIN GO GET HIT WIN BUMP
COME EARN GAIN RISE SORT
ARISE CATCH COVER CROSS
FETCH PROVE REACH TOUCH
ACCEDE AMOUNT ARRIVE ASPIRE
EFFECT OBTAIN SECURE STRIKE
ACHIEVE ACQUIRE COMPASS
PROCURE SUCCEED OVERTAKE
(— TO ACCOMPLISH) FIND FORCE
ATTAINMENT ARRIVAL ADEPTION
ENERGEIA PURCHASE
(— OF NIRVANA) MOKSHA
(SCHOLARLY —) LETTERS
ATTAR ITR OIL ATAR OTTO ATHAK
OTTAR ESSENCE PERFUME
ATTEMPT GO PUT SAY SHY TRY
BOUT BURL DARE DASH FAND

FIST FOND HACK JUMP MIND
MINT MIRD OSSE SEEK SHOT
SLAP STAB WAGE WORK ASSAY
BEGIN ESSAY ETTLE FLING FRAME
OFFER ONSET PRESS PROOF
PROVE START TEMPT TRIAL
WHACK ASSAIL ATTACK EFFORT
FRAIST STRIVE ENFORCE IMITATE
PRETEND PROFFER STAGGER
VENTURE CONATION ENDEAVOR
EXERTION PURCHASE TENTAMEN
(— TO AROUSE) AGITATE
(— TO BRIBE) APPROACH
(— TO INFLUENCE) AGITATION
(ABORTIVE —) FUTILITY
(PREF.) PEIRA
ATTEND GO HO HOA HOO SEE
FAND HEAR HEED LIST MIND
OYES OYEZ STAY TEND WAIT
WALK APPLY AUDIT AWAIT
GUARD LAKEY NURSE SERVE
TREAT VISIT WATCH ASSIST
CONVEY ESCORT FOLLOW
HARKEN INTEND LISTEN SECOND
SHADOW SQUIRE CONDUCT
CONSORT ESQUIRE HEARKEN
LACQUEY PERPEND RETINUE
ACCOMPANY
(— A LADY) WAIT
(— FUNERAL) FOLLOW
(— REGULARLY) KEEP
(— TO) MIND TREAT FETTLE
INTEND
(— UPON) TENT CHASE CHAPERON
ATTENDANCE GATE SUIT CHAPEL
NUMBER OFFICE REGARD
SERVICE PRESENCE
ATTENDANT BOY FLY LAD JACK
MAID MUTE PAGE PEON SYCE
ZANY CADDY COMES GILLY
GROOM GUIDE JAGER USHER
VALET ALEXAS CADDIE DACTYL
DAMSEL EMILIA ESCORT FRIEND
GESITH GILLIE HAIDUK HOGMAN
JAEGER KAVASS MINION PORTER
SQUIRE STOCAH TUBMAN VARLET
VERGER WAITER YEOMAN
ALIPTES ARMORER BULLDOG
CHOBDAR COURIER CROSSER
DAMOSEL FAMULUS FENELLA
FOOTBOY GHILLIE HALLMAN
HOSTESS JACKMAN LINKMAN
ORDERLY PAGEBOY PIQUEUR
PRESSER SEQUENT SERVANT
SHIPBOY SPOUTER TRABANT
TRESSEL ATTENDEE BEACHBOY
CHASSEUR CORYBANT CRUTCHER
FEWTERER FOLLOWER GATHERER
HANDMAID HENCHBOY
HENCHMAN HOUSEMAN
MINISTER MYRMIDON OBSERVER
OUTRIDER ROSALINE SERGEANT
SERJEANT STAFFIER TIPSTAFF
WATERMAN OBSERVANT
PURSUIVANT
(— OF CYBELE) CORYBANT
(CROSSING —) GATEMAN
(KNIGHT'S —) SWAIN CUSTREL
ESQUIRE
(PALACE —S) BOSTANGI
(PROCTOR'S —) BULLDOG
(YOUNG —) BOY LAD JACK PAGE
KNIGHT

(PL.) MEINY STAFF CORTEGE
RETINUE
ATTENDED FRAUGHT
ATTENTION EAR CARE GAUM
HEED HIST MARK MIND NOTE
RUSH SHUN TENT COURT FLOOR
GUARD STUDY TASTE DETAIL
FAVORS NOTICE REGARD
ACCOUNT ACHTUNG ADDRESS
EARNEST HEARING RESPECT
THOUGHT AUDIENCE
(— FROM SUPERIOR) TASHRIF
TASHRFFF
(— TO PETTY ITEMS) MICROLOGY
(AMOROUS —) GALLANTRY
(FIXED —) DHARANA
(FLATTERING —) HOMAGE
(PLEASING —) INCENSE
(SPECIAL —) ACCENT
ATTENTIVE WARY ALERT AWAKE
CIVIL CLOSE SHARP TENTY
ARRECT INTENT POLITE CAREFUL
GALLANT HEEDFUL LISTFUL
MINDFUL PRESENT DILIGENT
OBEDIENT STUDIOUS THOUGHTY
VIGILANT WATCHFUL
(— TO) IMMINENT
ATTENUATE SAP DRAW FINE THIN
WATER DILUTE LESSEN RAREFY
REDUCE WEAKEN SLENDER
AVIANIZE DECREASE DIMINISH
EMACIATE ENFEEBLE TAPERING
ATTENUATED GAUNT AERIAL
DILUTED SPINDLY FINESPUN
SMORZATO
ATTENUATION LOGO
ATTENUATOR PAD
ATTEST CHOP SEAL SIGN PROVE
STATE SWEAR VOUCH ADJURE
AFFIRM INVOKE RECORD WITTEN
CERTIFY CONFESS CONFIRM
CONSIGN TESTIFY WARRANT
WITNESS EVIDENCE INDICATE
MANIFEST
ATTESTATION VOUCH DOCKET
RECORD
ATTESTED SWORN CERTIFIED
ATTIC LOFT CELER SOLAR SOLER
GARRET TALLET GRENIER
COCKLOFT
(— SIDE) SKEELING
ATTILA (BROTHER OF —) BLEDA
(CHARACTER IN —) LEO EZIO
ATTILA FORESTO ODABELLA
(COMPOSER OF —) VERDI
(FATHER OF —) MUNDZUK
(WIFE OF —) HILDA ILDICO
ATTIRE (ALSO SEE DRESS) BEGO
BUSK SUIT TIRE ADORN ARRAY
BIGAN DRESS HABIT AGUISE
ENROBE PLIGHT REVEST TOILET
ADDRESS APPAREL DUBBING
PANOPLY ACCOUTER CLEADING
EQUIPAGE FEATHERS
(EPISCOPAL —) PONTIFICAL
(FORMAL —) BALLDRESS
(SHINING —) SHEEN
ATTIRED TRICKSY
ATTITUDE AIR CUE SET BIAS MIEN
MOOD POSE SIDE ANGLE FRAME
HEART PHASE SHAPE SHELL
SIGHT SLANT STAND ACTION
ANIMUS ASPECT MANNER SPIRIT

STANCE BEARING FEELING GESTURE POSTURE STATION STOMACH BEHAVIOR CARAPACE CROTCHET HABITUDE POSITION PREPOSSESSION
(— OF HUNTING DOG) POINT
(PREVAILING —) STREAM
ATTORNEY DOER AGENT AVOUE PROXY VAKIL DEPUTY FACTOR FISCAL LAWYER LEGIST MUKTAR SYNDIC VAKEEL PROCTOR ADVOCATE PROSECUTOR
ATTRACT BAIT CALL DRAW LURE PULL TILL WIND BRING CATCH CHARM COURT FETCH TEMPT ALLURE ATTACH ENGAGE ENLIST ENTICE GATHER INVITE SEDUCE STRIKE BEWITCH PROCURE INTEREST MAGNETIZE
(— FISH) CHUM
ATTRACTANT (MOTH SEX —) GYPLURE
ATTRACTION BAIT CALL CARD CLOU DRAW PULL CHARM DRAFT FAVOR SPELL TRACT APPEAL DESIRE FAVOUR MAGNET BLOWOFF COITION DRAUGHT GRAVITY INDRAFT ADHESION AFFINITY COHESION CONTRACT PENCHANT SIDESHOW WITCHERY
ATTRACTIVE BRAW CHIC CUTE FAIR FOXY GOOD NICE BONNY DISHY FATAL JOLLY NIFTY QUEME SWEET COMELY FLASHY FRUITY HEPPEN LOVELY PRETTY SAVORY SNAZZY TAKING TRICKY AMIABLE CIRCEAN CUNNING EYEABLE EYESOME GRADELY LIKABLE WINNING WINSOME ALLURING CHARMING ENGAGING ENTICING FEATURED FETCHING GRACEFUL GRACIOUS HANDSOME INVITING SPECIOUS TEMPTING VENEREAN PERSONABLE PREPOSSESSING
(— TO OPPOSITE SEX) EPIGAMIC
(FALSELY —) MERETRICIOUS
(NOT —) FOUL INCURIOUS
(STRIKINGLY —) ZINGY
ATTRACTIVENESS CHARM GRACE LOOKS BEAUTY GLAMOR AMENITY GLITTER AFFINITY HARLOTRY
ATTRIBUTABLE DUE
ATTRIBUTE FOX OWE PUT GIVE MARK SIGN TYPE ALLOT BADGE BLAME CHARM PLACE POWER REFER ALLEGE ALLUDE ARRECT ASSERT ASSIGN BESTOW CHARGE CREDIT IMPUTE PREFER REPUTE SYMBOL ADJUNCT APANAGE ASCRIBE COUNTER ESSENCE PERTAIN QUALITY ACCREDIT APPANAGE ARROGATE GRANDITY INTITULE PROPERTY PROPRIUM STRENGTH
(— WRONGFULLY) FOIST
(—S OF ROCKS) GEOLOGY
(PL.) SARIRA SHARIRA
ATTRIBUTION ACCENT THEORY ANIMISM ETIOLOGY
ATTRITION WEAR GRIEF REGRET SORROW ANGUISH ABRASION BLASTING FRICTION

ATTUNE KEY TUNE ADAPT AGREE ACCORD ADJUST TEMPER PREPARE
ATUA AKUA DEMON SPIRIT
ATYPICAL BIZARRE ABERRANT GROTESQUE
AUBADE ALBA
AUBERGE INN ALBERGO
AUBERGINE EGGPLANT
AUBURN ABRAM BLOND CACHA CUTCH BLONDE CACHOU CATECHU GOREVAN TULIPWOOD
AU COURANT CONTEMPORARY
AUCTION CANT ROUP SALE SELL VEND COKER TRADE BARTER BRIDGE HAMMER OUTCRY TROVER VENDUE OUTROOP UNCTION DISPOSAL KNOCKOUT PORTSALE
AUCTIONEER CRIER CRYER OUTCRIER
AUDACIOUS BOLD BRASH BRAVE FRACK HARDY SAUCY AUDACE BRAZEN CHEEKY DARING FORWARD ARROGANT FEARLESS IMPUDENT INSOLENT INTREPID SPIRITED BAREFACED
(NOT —) CIVIL
AUDACITY CHEEK NERVE COURAGE BOLDNESS TEMERITY PRESUMPTION
AUDIBLE RIFE ALOUD CLEAR HEARD AUTOMATIC
AUDIENCE EAR PIT FANS AUDIT COURT FLOOR HOUSE PUBLIC GALLERY HEARING ASSEMBLY AUDITORY TRIBUNAL
AUDIT SCAN CHECK PROBE APPOSE RECKON VERIFY ACCOUNT EXAMINE INQUIRE INSPECT ESTIMATE
AUDITION HEARING
AUDITOR CENSOR HEARER APPOSER AUDIENT PITTITE COUNTOUR DISCIPLE LISTENER
AUDITORIUM HALL ROOM CAVEA FRONT ODEUM THEATER AUDITORY
AUDITORY ORAL OTIC AURAL AUDILE ACOUSTIC AUDITIVE
AUGE (FATHER OF —) ALEUS
(HUSBAND OF —) TEUTHRAS
(MOTHER OF —) NAERA
(SON OF —) TELEPHUS
AUGER BIT POD BORE BORAL BORER GRILL BORING GIMLET NAUGER WIMBLE PIERCER TEREBRA
(PREF.) TRYPAN(O)
AUGHT ACHT EAWT AUCHT OWNED CIPHER NAUGHT WORTHY NOTHING VALIANT ANYTHING
AUGMENT ADD EKE FEED GROW HELP URGE BOOST EXALT SWELL APPEND DILATE EXPAND EXTEND AMPLIFY BALLOON ENHANCE ENLARGE IMPROVE INFLAME MAGNIFY COMPOUND HEIGHTEN INCREASE MAJORATE MULTIPLY
(— IN STRENGTH) INGROSS
AUGMENTATION RISE EKING SWELL GROWTH

AUCTARY ADDITION
AUGMENTED SHARP EXTREME
AUGUR BODE OMEN SEER SPEAK AUSPEX DIVINE BETOKEN CONJECT FORESEE OMINATE PORTEND PREDICT PRESAGE PROMISE PROPHET SIGNIFY DENOUNCE FOREBODE FORESHOW FORETELL FOREWARN INDICATE PROPHESY
AUGURY ORE OMEN RITE SIGN SOOTH TOKEN HANSEL RITUAL AUSPICE HANDSEL PRESAGE CEREMONY
AUGUST AWFUL GRAND NOBLE KINGLY SERENE SOLEMN EXALTED STATELY IMPOSING MAJESTIC
(FIRST DAY OF —) LAMMAS LUGNAS LUGHNAS LUGNASAD
(PREF.) SEBASTO
AUGUSTINIAN AUSTIN ASSUMPTIONIST
AUHUHU HOLA
AUK FALK LOOM ARRIE DIVER LEMOT MURRE NODDY SCOOT SCOUT SKOUT MARROT PUFFIN ROTCHE STARIK TINKER DOVEKEY DOVEKIE PENGUIN PYGOPOD SEAFOWL WILLOCK GAIRFOWL GAREFOWL ROCKBIRD RAZORBILL
AULA HALL COURT EMBLIC
AUNT TIA BAWD AUNTY NAUNT TANTA TANTE AUNTIE GOSSIP
(— SALLY) STICKS
AURA AIR HALO ODOR PUFF AROMA SAVOR SMELL BREEZE BUZZARD ESSENCE FEELING
(CHARACTERISTIC —) VIBE
(SENSED —) KARMA
AURAL OTIC
AUREATE GOLDEN ORNATE ROCOCO YELLOW
AUREOLE HALO CROWN GLORY LIGHT AREOLA CORONA GLORIA NIMBUS VESICA GLORIOLE MANDORLA
AUREUS (HALF —) SEMIS
AURICLE EAR PINNA ATRIUM EARLET TRUMPET PAVILION
AURICULATE EARED
AURIGA WAGONER WAGGONER
AURIST OTOLOGIST
AUROCHS TUR UROX URUS BISON WISENT BONASUS
AURORA EOS DAWN DRAPERY MORNING
AURORA BOREALIS DANCERS STREAMERS
AUSPICE CARE OMEN SIGN AUGURY PORTENT GUIDANCE
(PL.) EGIS AEGIS
AUSPICIOUS FAIR GOOD TWINE WHITE BRIGHT CHANCY DEXTER CHANCEY FAVORING PROPITIOUS PROSPEROUS
AUSTERE BARE COLD HARD SOUR BLEAK BUDGE GRAVE GRUFF HARSH RIGID ROUGH SHARP STERN STIFF STOUR BITTER

CHASTE FORMAL RUGGED SEVERE SIMPLE SOMBER STRICT SULLEN TETRIC ASCETIC CRABBED DANTEAN EARNEST SERIOUS GRANITIC RIGOROUS TETRICAL ASTRINGENT PURITANICAL
AUSTERITY RIGOR CATOISM RIGORISM SIMPLICITY
AUSTRAL SOUTHERN

AUSTRALIA	
ABORIGINE:	MYALL
CAPE:	HOWE
CAPITAL:	CANBERRA
COIN:	DUMP POUND SHILLING
DESERT:	STURT GIBSON TANAMI SIMPSON
HARBOR:	DARWIN BRISBANE FREMANTLE MELBOURNE NEWCASTLE
ISLAND:	CATO COCOS FRASER KOOLAN CORINGA KANGAROO LACEPEDE MELVILLE ROTTNEST TASMANIA
LAKE:	EYRE COWAN FROME BARLEE BULLOO LEFROY AMADEUS BLANCHE EVERARD GREGORY TORRENS GAIRDNER NABBEROO DISAPPOINTMENT
LANGUAGE:	YABBER
MEASURE:	SAUM
MOUNTAIN:	OLGA BRUCE LEGGE CRADLE GARNET GAWLER MAGNET STUART BONGONG GREGORY WILHELM CUTHBERT JUSGRAVE MULLIGAN KOSCIUSKO
MOUNTAIN RANGE:	DARLING FLINDERS
NATIVE:	ABO MARA BINGE AUSSIE DIGGER BILLIJIM KANGAROO WARRAGAL WARRIGAL JINDYWOROBAK
PENINSULA:	EYRE
RIVER:	DALY SWAN BULLO COMET FINKE ISAAC PAROO ROPER SNOWY YARRA BARCOO BARWON CULGOA DAWSON DEGREY DARLING FITZROY LACHLAN STAATEN WARREGO BURDEKIN FLINDERS GEORGINA VICTORIA
SEA:	CORAL TIMOR TASMAN ARAFURA
SOLDIER:	DIGGER SWADDY BILLIJIM
STATE:	TASMANIA VICTORIA QUEENSLAND
STRAIT:	TORRES
TOWN:	AYR YASS DUBBO PERTH WAGGA ALBURY AUBURN CAIRNS CASINO COBURG DARWIN HOBART MACKAY SYDNEY BENDIGO GEELONG KOGARAH MILDURA MITCHAM ADELAIDE BRISBANE ESSENDON RANDWICK RINGWOOD MELBOURNE TOOWOOMBA
VALLEY:	GROSE JAMIESON MEGALONG
WATER HOLE:	BILLABONG
WATERFALL:	TULLY COOMERA

WALLAMAN WENTWORTH
WOLLOMOMBI
WOMAN: LUBRA

AUSTRALIAN ANZAC AUSSIE
DIGGER AUSTRAL CURRENCY
KANGAROO WARRAGAL
WARRIGAL
(— GIRL) LUBRA

AUSTRIA
ANCIENT PEOPLE: HUNS AVARS
RAETIANS SLOVENES
BAVARIANS
CAPITAL: WIEN VIENNA
CELTIC KINGDOM: NORICUM
COIN: DUCAT KRONE FLORIN
HELLER ZEHNER GROSCHEN
SCHILLING
DUCHY: STYRIA CARNIOLA
CARINTHIA
EMPEROR: CHARLES FRANCIS
FERDINAND
LAKE: ALMSEE FERTOTO
MONDSEE BODENSEE
TRAUNSEE CONSTANCE
NEUSIEDLER
MEASURE: FASS FUSS JOCH MASS
MUTH YOKE HALBE LINIE MEILE
METZE PFIFF PUNKT ACHTEL
BECHER SEIDEL DLAFTER
VIERTEL DREILING
MOUNTAIN: STUBAI EISENERZ
RHATIKON KITZBUHEL
NATIVE: STYRIAN TYROLEAN
NOBILITY: RITTER
PASS: LOIBL ARLBERG BRENNER
PLOCKEN
PROVINCE: TIROL TYROL STYRIA
VIENNA SALZBURG CARINTHIA
VORARLBERG
RIVER: INN MUR DRAU ENNS
KAMP LECH MURZ RAAB
DONAU MARCH SALZA
THAYA TRAUN
DANUBE SALZACH
RIVER PORT: LINZ KREMS VIENNA
ROMAN PROVINCE: RAETIA
NORICUM PANNONIA
TOWN: ENNS GRAZ LECH LINZ
RIED WELS WIEN GMUND LIENZ
STEYR TRAUN LEOBEN VIENNA
BREGENZ MODLING SPITTAL
VILLACH DORNBIRN SALZBURG
INNSBRUCK
WATERFALL: KRIMML GASTEIN
GOLLING
WEIGHT: MARC SAUM UNZE
DENAT KARCH PFUND STEIN
CENTNER PFENNIG VIERLING

AUTACOID HORMONE INCRETION
AUTARCHIC FREE
AUTHENTIC ECHT PURE REAL
SURE TRUE EXACT PUCCA PUCKA
PUKKA RIGHT VALID ACTUAL
DINKUM PROPER CORRECT
CURRENT GENUINE SINCERE
CREDIBLE OFFICIAL ORIGINAL
RELIABLE
AUTHENTICATE SEAL PROVE
VOUCH ATTEST SIGNET VERIFY
APPROVE CONFIRM LEGALIZE

AUTHOR DOER JUDE SIRE JUDAS
MAKER RULER AUCTOR FACTOR
FORGER LOKMAN PARENT
PENMAN SCRIBE SOURCE WRITER
ANCIENT CLASSIC CREATOR
ELOHIST FOUNDER LOLLIUS
ANCESTOR BEGETTER COMPILER
COMPOSER IDEALIST IMMORTAL
INVENTOR JEHOVIST ORIGINAL
PAYYETAN PRODUCER
(BAD —) BLOTTER
(PL.) SS
AMERICAN LEA LEE POE AGEE
BAUM BEER BELL BOYD BUCK
COOK DANA GALE GREY HALL
HUME HUNT KEMP KREY KYNE
LANE LONG LOOS MACY MAYO
NASH PAUL POST RAND SHAW
WARD WOOD ADAMS ADLER
AIKEN ALGER ALSOP BACON
BASSO BATES BEACH BENET
BINNS BOYLE BROWN BRUSH
CABLE CAHAN CANBY CHILD
COOKE CRANE DAVIS DIETZ
DODGE EARLE EATON ELLIS
EVANS FOOTE GATES GREEN
HECHT HURST KELLY KEYES
LEWIS LODGE MAJOR MARCH
MASON OGDEN OHARA PAINE
POOLE QUEEN REESE REEVE
RIVES SIMMS SMITH STEIN STONE
STONG STOUT STOWE THANE
TRINE TWAIN TUDOR TULLY
VANCE VORSE WALSH WATTS
WEEMS WELLS WHITE WILEY
WOLFE WYLIE ADAMIC ALCOTT
ARTHUR AUSTIN BAILEY BARNES
BECKER BELLOW BESSIE BISHOP
BRALEY BRINIG BROWNE
BURMAN BURNET CABELL
CAPOTE CARMER CARSON
CATHER CATLIN CATTON CLARKE
COLTON COOPER CORBIN CORLEY
CROUSE DARGAN DAVIES
DELAND DEVOTO DILLON
DOWNEY EVARTS FARSON
FERBER FIELDS FINLEY FISHER
FLEBBE FORBES FULLER GILMAN
GORMAN GUNTER HALPER
HARRIS HERBST HOBART HOLMES
HOOKER HORGAN HOSMER
HOWARD HUGHES IRVING
JEWETT KELLER KESTER KUMMER
LARCOM LIBBEY LONDON LOVETT
LUMMIS MAILER MARTIN MCEVOY
MILLAY MILLER MORLEY MORROW
NATHAN NORRIS PARKER PITKIN
PORTER POWELL PROUTY
RHODES ROURKE RUNYON
SALTUS STEELE STREET STRONG
SUCKOW TAYLOR THAYER
THOMAS TUTTLE UPDIKE VEBLEN
WARNER WATKIN WERNER
WILDER WILLIS WILSON WINTER
WISTER WRIGHT YERKES ALDRICH
ANDREWS BANNING BELLAMY
BENNETT BIGELOW BOYESEN
BOYNTON BURGESS BURNETT
CALKINS CARROLL CHILTON
CLEMENS COMFORT COURNOS
COZZENS CUMMINS CURWOOD
DERLETH DREISER EDMONDS
ELLIOTT ELLISON ERSKINE

FARRELL FAWCETT FERNALD
FINEMAN FOLLETT FRANKEN
FREEMAN GARLAND GIFFORD
GLASGOW GRATTAN HAMMETT
HEYWARD HOLDING HOPKINS
JOHNSON KELLAND KILVERT
KOMROFF LAFARGE LARDNER
LINCOLN MASTERS MULFORD
MUMFORD MURFREE NABOKOV
OSTENSO PARROTT PEATTIE
PRESTON PRUETTE ROBERTS
ROLVAAG SAMPSON SAROYAN
TARBELL TERHUNE THOREAU
THURBER TRAUBEL VANDYKE
VANLOON VOLLMER WEBSTER
WESCOTT WHARTON WHITNEY
WOOLSON YOUMANS ATHERTON
ATKINSON AYSCOUGH BAKELESS
BARRETTO BILLINGS BRADFORD
BURDETTE CALDWELL CANTWELL
CHAMBERS CLEGHORN COLLISON
CONNOLLY CONVERSE
CRAWFORD DONNELLY
FAULKNER FERGUSON FREDERIC
GELLHORN GLASPELL GOODRICH
HAGEDORN HARRISON JOHNSTON
KIRKLAND LATHBURY MACAULAY
MACGRATH MARQUAND
MELVILLE MICHENER MITCHELL
NORDHOFF PERELMAN PETERKIN
PHILLIPS PROKOSCH RAWLINGS
REPPLIER RICHARDS RINEHART
SALINGER SEDGWICK SPINGARN
SPOFFORD STANFORD STARRETT
STEPHENS STOCKTON STODDARD
TIETJENS TORRENCE TURNBULL
VANDOREN WESTCOTT
WIDDEMER WILLIAMS ALTSHELER
BACHELLER BERCOVICI
BODENHEIM BROMFIELD
BURROUGHS DOSPASSOS
CARPENTER CHURCHILL
EGGLESTON GRANBERRY
HAWTHORNE HEMINGWAY
KORZYBSKI LANCASTER
MCCULLERS NICHOLSON
OSULLIVAN SIGOURNEY
STALLINGS STEINBECK
STEVENSON STRIBLING
CLENDENING FITZGERALD
MCCUTCHEON SOUTHWORTH
TARKINGTON TROWBRIDGE
UNTERMEYER VANVECHTEN
CANTACUZENE CHAMBERLAIN
GERSTENBERG MINNIGERODE
STRATEMEYER HERGESHEIMER
ARGENTINIAN GALVEZ MARMOL
CANDIOTI CAPDEVILA
AUSTRALIAN BECKE WHITE
BROWNE CLARKE LAWSON
CALVERT COLLINS EGERTON
TRAVERS PRICHARD VILLIERS
CAMBRIDGE RICHARDSON
AUSTRIAN BAYER KAFKA PRAED
ZWEIG WERFEL BARTSCH
COLERUS NEUMANN PICHLER
ROSEGGER SCHREKER ALTENBERG
BURCKHARD SCHNITZLER
BELGIAN COSTER HYMANS PICARD
EEKHOUD LEMONNIER
BRAZILIAN TAUNAY GUIMARAES
VERISSIMO
BULGARIAN VAZOV

CANADIAN SETON SULTE PARKER
MCLUHAN SERVICE CHAMBERS
MCDOWELL STRINGER SULLIVAN
CALLAGHAN MACDONALD
MACLENNAN PICKTHALL
CHILEAN CORTES
COLOMBIAN CARO REYES CUERVO
CARRASQUILLA
CZECH LANGER HOLECEK JIRASEK
VANCURRA
DANISH BANG NEXO HERTZ KIDDE
SKRAM LARSEN RORDAM
BAUDITZ CLAUSEN DINESEN
TANDRUP ANDERSEN INGEMANN
BUCHHOLTZ DRACHMANN
JORGENSEN MICHAELIS
BREGENDAHL
DUTCH LOOY BEKKER CREMER
EMANTS LENNEP MAARTENS
ENGLISH DAY LEE BECK BEHN
BELL BRAY COLE DANE ERTZ
FENN FORD GLYN HULL HUME
LAMB LEVY LONG LYLY MORE
MUIR PAUL PAYN REED REID RICE
SHAW WARD WEBB WEST WOOD
WREN ADAMS AMORY AYRES
BARRY BATES BAYLY BERRY
BLOOM CRABB BURKE CAINE
CRAIK CROWE DEFOE DIGBY
DIXON DOYLE ELIOT ELLIS GIBBS
HARDY HEARD HEVER JEANS
KEOWN LEVER LEWIS LOCKE
LUCAS MASON MAYNE MCFEE
MOORE MUNRO MURRY ORCZY
POWYS RAMEE READE ROPES
SCOTT SHARP SHIEL SHUTE
SMITH STEEL STERN SWIFT
WELLS WYLIE YONGE YOUNG
ANGELL ASCHAM ASHTON ASTELL
AUSTEN AUSTIN BELLOC BENSON
BESANT BORROW BRIDGE
BRONTE BROPHY BULLEN BURGIN
BURTON CANNAN CASTLE
CHURCH CONRAD CRONIN
FARNOL FELKIN FOSTER GODWIN
GOUDGE GRAVES GREENE HILTON
HOLTBY HORLER HOWELL
HUDSON HUGHES HUXLEY
LANDON LANDOR LYTTON
MACHEN MORGAN MORTON
MURRAY NESBIT NORTON
ONIONS ORMSBY PALMER
PORTER POWELL REEVES SANDYS
SAYERS SEWELL SHANKS SOUTAR
SPRING STERNE TAYLOR WALTON
WARNER WARREN WATSON
WEYMAN AGUILAR ASHFORD
BAGNOLD BALDWIN BARCLAY
BENNETT BENTLEY BERNERS
BOLITHO BOTTOME BULLETT
BUNBURY CHAMIER COCKTON
COLLINS CORELLI DEEPING
DICKENS DODGSON DOUGLAS
DUDENEY EDWARDS FARJEON
FIRBANK FORSTER FREEMAN
GARNETT GASKELL GISSING
GOLDING GUTHRIE HAGGARD
HASSALL HAWKINS HEWLETT
HICHENS HORNUNG JACKSON
JOHNSON KENNEDY KIPLING
LAMBURN LEHMANN MARRYAT
MAUGHAM MAXWELL MCKENNA
MITFORD MONTAGU MORISON

NICHOLS OXENHAM PEACOCK
PERTWEE RANSOME RITCHIE
ROBERTS SASSOON SHELLEY
SITWELL SMEDLEY SOWERBY
SPENDER TOLKIEN VACHELL
WADDELL WALLACE WALPOLE
ZIMMERN BARBAULD BARTLETT
CHRISTIE DASHWOOD FIELDING
FLETCHER FORESTER HAMILTON
HARRADEN KERNAHAN KINGSLEY
KNOBLOCK KOESTLER LAWRENCE
MACAULAY MARRIOTT MEREDITH
MORDAUNT OLLIVANT PATTISON
SINCLAIR SMOLLETT STANNARD
STRETTON THIRKELL TROLLOPE
WALMSLEY ZANGWILL
AINSWORTH ALDINGTON
BERESFORD BLACKMORE
BLACKWOOD BROUGHTON
CARPENTER CHURCHILL
DEQUINCEY DUMAURIER
GERHARDIE GOLDSMITH
GREENWELL GREENWOOD
HENRIQUES KINGSMILL
LINKLATER LLEWELLYN
MANSFIELD MITCHISON
MONKHOUSE OPPENHEIM
PEMBERTON PHILLPOTS
PICKTHALL PRIESTLEY RADCLIFFE
ROBERTSON SCHREINER
SOUTHWOLD STACPOOLE
THACKERAY TREVELYAN
WHITEHEAD WILKINSON
WILLCOCKS WODEHOUSE
FOTHERGILL GALSWORTHY
HUTCHINSON MEYERSTEIN
RICHARDSON SHORTHOUSE
SWINNERTON WILLIAMSON
YOUNGHUSBAND
ESTONIAN TAMMSAARE
FINNISH AHO KIVI CANTH KALLAS
CYGNAUS SALMINEN SILLANPAA
TAVASTSTJERNA
FRENCH FOA GAY NAU SUE AIDE
HUGO KARR KOCKLOTI MAEL
SAND UZES ZOLA BAZIN BEDEL
BLOCH BOVET CAMUS CARCO
CEARD COLET DUMAS FABRE
HEMON LOUYS OHNET PEYRE
ROSNY VERNE ACHARD AGOULT
ARAGON ARGENS ARLAND
AULNOY AVENEL BALZAC BEDIER
BENOIT BERAUD BISSON BLOUET
BRUEYS CLADEL CRAVEN DAUDET
DONIOL EPINAY FAYARD FRANCE
HUZARD IMBERT LESAGE MOULIE
PROUST REBOUX SARTRE SCHURE
TROYAT VERCEL ANCELOT
ARNAULT BAUMANN BEHAINE
BERNARD BERQUIN BONNARD
BOURGET BOUVIER CAZOTTE
COCTEAU COLETTE DEBERLY
DELTEIL DURTAIN FEYDEAU
FONTANE HERMANT HERVIEU
HOFFMAN LAVEDAN LEBLANC
LERMINA MALRAUX MAURIAC
MERIMEE MONNIER PREVOST
REGNIER ROLLAND ROMAINS
SANDEAU SIMENON TENDRON
ASSOLANT BANVILLE BARBUSSE
BEAUVOIR BENJAMIN BERENGER
BERNANOS BERTRAND BONVALOT
BORDEAUX BOYLESVE BRUNHOFF

CENDRARS CHARTIER CLARETIE
DORGELES DUFRESNY ESTAUNIE
FEUILLET FLAUBERT GENEVOIX
GONCOURT GREVILLE HOUSSAYE
HUYSMANS LATAILLE MALHERBE
MARIETON MARIVAUX MONTEPIN
MONTFORT ROUSSEAU SAVIGNON
SCHOPFER SOUPAULT STENDHAL
VALLETTE VOLTAIRE BEAUCHAMP
BOUHELIER CHERVILLE
COULEVAIN DESCHANEL
FONTAINAS MARMONTEL
MIOMANDRE POURTALES
SENANCOUR BAZANCOURT
DESJARDINS FAUCONNIER
MAUPASSANT MARGUERITTE
GERMAN APEL BALL BAUM BOLL
BURG HOLZ KURZ MANN ARNDT
BULOW BUSSE GRASS GROTH
HAGEN HALBE HAUFF HESSE
HUBER KUHNE LANGE LAUBE
MUGGE MUNDT RAABE UNRUH
ZESEN ZWEIG BECKER BEREND
BINZER BLUNCK BUICKE CONRAD
DAUMER DREYER HAUSER
HEYDEN JENSEN JOHNST KNIGGE
LEWALD LUDWIG MILLER MORIKE
MUSAUS REUTER VIEBIG WERNER
BERTUCH BRONNEN CONRADI
DAUBLER FALLADA FREYTAG
GLAESER GUTZKOW HEIBERG
KRETZER LAROCHE NEUMANN
OSTWALD REDWITZ SEGHERS
VULPIUS AUERBACH BORKENAU
BRENTANO ECKSTEIN HAUSMANN
HOFFMANN KOTZEBUE LIENHARD
MEISSNER REMARQUE ROQUETTE
WOLZOGEN ZSCHOKKE BEYERLEIN
GANGHOFER IMMERMANN
SCHUCKING SUDERMANN
UECHTRITZ WILBRANDT
WITZLEBEN ZERKAULEN
ZOBELTITZ FLAISCHLEN
GERSTACKER KELLERMANN
SPIELHAGEN WASSERMANN
WILDERMUTH HASENCLEVER
FEUCHTWANGER
GREEK IOPHON PLUTARCH
ONOSANDER
GUATEMALAN ASTRUIAS
HUNGARIAN FAY BIRO JOKAI
FOLDES JOSIKA KARMAN SALTEN
HEGEDUS VAMBERY HARSANYI
KORMENDI
ICELANDIC KAMBAN ARNASON
LAXNESS SAEMUND
GUNNARSSON THORODDSEN
GUDMUNDSSON
INDIAN ANAND SORABJI
CHATTERJI SHRIDHARANI
IRISH BEHAN BOWEN COYLE
CROLY DOYLE GWYNN JOYCE
LETTS LOVER MOORE TYNAN
BARLOW BROOKE ERVINE GRAVES
LESLIE MARTIN OGRADY OKELLY
PEARSE BECKETT CARLETON
CORKERY LAWLESS MACGILL
MATURIN MAXWELL KAVANAGH
OFAOLAIN ORIORDAN STEPHENS
OFLAHERTY TODHUNTER
WARBURTON BARRINGTON
MCALLISTER SOMERVILLE
ISRAELI AGNON

ITALIAN VARE SERAO FARINA
MAFFEI PAPINI BARRILI CARCANO
DELEDDA GIACOMO MANZONI
ALBRIZZI BERSEZIO BOCCACCIO
CHIARELLI CORRADINI
DANNUNZIO FOGAZZARO
GUERRAZZI BELGIOIOSO
BERTINELLI PREZZOLINI
CASTELNUOVO
JAPANESE BAKIN TAMAI
FUKUZAWA KAWABATA
LATVIAN RAINIS
MEXICAN GAMBOA
NEW ZEALAND ADAMS MARSH
LYTTLETON
NORWEGIAN LIE BULL FONHUS
HAMSUN UNDSET COLLETT
GARBORG ELVESTAD KIELLAND
ASBJORNSEN
PERUVIAN PALMA URETA ALEGRIA
CACERES
POLISH REJ PRUS STRUG ANCZYC
BERENT GOETEL BALUCKI
REYMONT WITTLIN ZAPOLSKA
ZELENSKI ZEROMSKI ZULAWSKI
MILKOWSKI NALKOWSKA
DANILOWSKI KONOPNICKA
KRASZEWSKI CHMIELOWSKI
OSSENDOWSKI SIENKIEWICZ
KORZENIOWSKI
PORTUGUESE LOBO BRAGA SOUSA
DANTAS MORAES
ROMAN VELLEIUS
RUMANIAN GOGA NEGRUZZI
CARAGIALE RADULESCU
RUSSIAN BUNIN FEDIN GOGOL
GORKI FADEEV GLINKA LEONOV
LESKOV AKSAKOV ALDANOV
ANDREEV GARSHIN GLADKOV
PILNYAK ROMANOV TOLSTOI
KARAMZIN BULGAKOV POTEKHIN
TURGENEV USPENSKI VERESAEV
BESTUZHEV EHRENBURG
GONCHAROV KOROLENKO
LERMONTOV PASTERNAK
SHOLOKHOV SUMAROKOV
DOSTOEVSKI YUSHKEVICH
ZOSHCHENKO AMFITEATROV
ARTSYBASHEV GRIGOROVICH
LAZHECHNIKOV SOLZHENITSYN
SCOTTISH GUNN BEITH BROWN
JACOB MUNRO SCOTT BARRIE
BUCHAN SHAIRP WATSON
BALFOUR FERRIER MACLEOD
BUCHANAN CRAUFURD
CROCKETT LOCKHART MAITLAND
MARSHALL OLIPHANT URQUHART
FINDLATER MACDONALD
MACKENZIE MOLESWORTH
SOUTH AFRICA CLOETE PLOMER
MILLIN
SPANISH ALAS RIVAS ROJAS
TRIGO ALEMAN BAROJA PEREDA
ESPINEL CABALLERO CERVANTES
SWEDISH CARLEN EDGREN
MOBERG AHLGREN ALMQVIST
LAGERLOF SCHWARTZ
BACKSTROM LUNDEGARD
LAGERKVIST STREINDBERG
WETTERBERGH
SWISS ROD FREY HEER SPYRI
KAISER BITZIUS FEDERER
OLIVIER

WELSH MAP EVANS PRYCE
WYNNE DAVIES
AUTHORITATIVE GRAVE CLASSIC
OFFICIAL ORACULAR POSITIVE
TEXTUARY MAGISTERIAL
(PREF.) CURIO
AUTHORITY LAW ROD SEE BALL
RULE SWAY ADEPT BOARD FAITH
POWER RICHE RIGHT STAMP
SWING TITLE ARTIST AUTHOR
CREDIT DANGER EMPERY EXPERT
FASCES PUNDIT REGENT REGIME
SWINGE WEIGHT AMITATE
COMMAND CONTROL DYNASTY
FACULTY LEADING LICENCE
LICENSE POTENCY SCEPTER
WARRANT DISPOSAL DOMINION
DOMINIUM HEGEMONY LORDSHIP
PRESTIGE SANCTION STRENGTH
PROCURATION
(— OF SWITZERLAND) BUNDESRAT
(ARBITRARY —) ABOVE
(MORAL —) MANA
(ONE HIGHEST IN —) SUPREMO
(ROYAL —) SCEPTRE SOVRANTY
(SPIRITUAL —) KEYS KHILAFAT
(SUPREME —) SAY SIRCAR SIRKAR
(TEACHING —) MAGISTERIUM
(UNLIMITED —) AUTOCRACY
(PL.) ISNAD SIRCAR
(SUFF.) CRACY CRAT(IC)
AUTHORIZATION FIAT BARAT
BERAT PASSPORT SANCTION
WARRANTY PERMISSION
AUTHORIZE LET LEAL VEST ALLOW
CLEAR CLOTHE PERMIT RATIFY
APPROVE EMPOWER ENDORSE
ENTITLE INDORSE JUSTIFY
LICENSE WARRANT ACCREDIT
DELEGATE LEGALIZE SANCTION
AUTHORIZED LEGAL OFFICIAL
AUTHORSHIP PENCRAFT
PATERNITY
AUTO (ALSO SEE AUTOMOBILE)
CRATE CHUMMY LIZZIE
AUTOBIOGRAPHY VITA MEMOIR
AUTOCHTHONOUS NATIVE
EDAPHIC ENDEMIC
AUTOCLAVE DIGESTER DIGESTOR
AUTOCRACY MONARCHY
AUTOCRAT CHAM CZAR TSAR
TZAR MOGUL CAESAR DESPOT
AUTARCH MONARCH DICTATOR
MONOCRAT
AUTOCRATIC ABSOLUTE
AUTO-DA-FE AUTO SERMO
AUTOGRAPH NAME SIGN MANUAL
INSCRIBE
AUTOLYCUS (DAUGHTER OF —)
ANTICLEA
(FATHER OF —) HERMES MERCURY
(HALF-BROTHER OF —) PHILAMMON
(MOTHER OF —) CHIONE
AUTOMATIC REFLEX MACHINE
MECHANICAL
(PREF.) SELF
AUTOMATON GOLEM ROBOT
AUTOMA ANDROID MACHINE
AUTOMOBILE BUG BUS CAR SIX
AUTO FOUR HEAP JEEP PONY
TRAP BUGGY COACH COUPE
CRATE EIGHT PONEY RACER
SEDAN BUCKET CHUMMY

CUSTOM JALOPY JUNKER
SALOON WHEELS AUTOCAR
COMPACT FLIVVER HACKNEY
HARDTOP MACHINE MINICAR
PHAETON STEAMER TORPEDO
VOITURE CARRYALL DRAGSTER
ELECTRIC ROADSTER SQUADROL
SUBURBAN VICTORIA HATCHBACK
NOTCHBACK
(CONVERTIBLE —) DROPHEAD
(DEMONSTRATOR —) DEMO
(MIDGET —) DOODLEBUG
(NOISY —) BANGER
(SMALL —) MINI
AUTONOE (FATHER OF —) CADMUS
  (HUSBAND OF —) ARISTAEUS
  (MOTHER OF —) HARMONIA
  (SISTER OF —) AGAVE
  (SON OF —) ACTAEON
AUTONOMOUS FREE SEPARATE
AUTONOMY SOVEREIGNTY
  SEPARATENESS
  (— OF GOD) ASEITY ASEITAS
AUTOPSY NECROPSY
AUTUMN FALL KHARIF AUTOMPNE
  FALLTIME MATURITY
AUXILIARY AID SUB AIDE ALLY
  ANSAR AIDING BRANCH DONKEY
  HELPER ABETTER ABETTOR
  ADJUNCT HELPING PARTNER
  ADJUTANT ANCILLARY
  PERIPHERAL
  (PL.) FOEDERATI
AVAIL DO AID DOW USE BOOT
  HELP FADGE SERVE SKILL STEAD
  VALUE MOMENT PROFIT BENEFIT
  BESTEAD PREVAIL SERVICE
  SUCCEED SUFFICE UTILIZE
  SUBSERVE
  (— ONESELF) EMBRACE IMPROVE
  SUBSERVE
AVAILABLE FIT FREE OPEN FLUSH
  HANDY LOOSE READY PATENT
  USABLE PRESENT VISIBLE
AVALANCHE SLIDE LAWINE
  VOLLENGE
AVANT-COURIER HERALD
  SCURRIER
AVANT-GARDE LITERATI
AVARICE GREED MAMMON MISERY
  AVIDITY CUPIDITY RAPACITY
AVARICIOUS CLOSE SLOAN
  GREEDY HAVING HUNGRY SORDID
  STINGY GRIPING GRIPPLE ITCHING
  MISERLY COVETOUS GRASPING
AVATAR BALARAMA EPIPHANY
AVELLANEOUS HAZEL
AVENGE REPAY RIGHT VISIT
  WRACK WREAK AWREAK PUNISH
  BEWREAK REQUITE REVENGE
  SATISFY CHASTISE
AVENGER KANAIMA NEMESIS
  WREAKER
AVENS GEUM BENNET BAREFOOT
AVENTURINE SUNSTONE
  GOLDSTONE
AVENUE RUE WAY GATE MALL
  PIKE ROAD ALLEE ALLEY DRIVE
  ENTRY ACCESS ARCADE ARTERY
  DROMOS RIDING STREET
  AVENIDA OPENING PASSAGE
AVER SAY AIVER CLAIM PROVE
  STATE SWEAR AFFIRM ALLEGE

ASSERT ASSURE AVOUCH DEPOSE
  VERIFY DECLARE JUSTIFY
  PROFESS PROTEST
AVERAGE PAR SUM DUTY FAIR
  MEAN NORM RULE SOSO RATIO
  USUAL VALUE CHARGE MEDIAL
  MEDIAN MEDIUM MIDDLE
  NORMAL TARIFF ARRIAGE
  ESTIMATE MEDIOCRE MIDDLING
  MODERATE ORDINARY OVERHEAD
  QUANTITY STANDARD
  (NOT —) BORDERLINE
AVERSE LOTH BALKY LOATH
  AFRAID ADVERSE AGAINST
  OPPOSED BACKWARD INIMICAL
  OPPOSITE PERVERSE RELUCTANT
  (— TO) ABOVE
AVERSION TOY HATE DERRY
  ODIUM ENMITY HATRED HORROR
  PHOBIA REGRET DESPITE DISDAIN
  DISGUST DISLIKE MISLIKE
  DISTASTE ABOMINATION
  (— TO FOOD) APOSITIA
  (— TO WORK) ERGOPHOBIA
AVERT WRY BEND FEND MOVE
  SHUN TURN WARD AVOID DETER
  DODGE EVADE PARRY SHEER
  TWIST DEFRAY DIVERT RETARD
  SHIELD DECLINE DEFLECT
  EXPIATE PREVENT ALIENATE
  ESTRANGE FOREFEND WITHTURN
AVIARY CAGE HOUSE VOLARY
  ORNITHON
AVIATOR ACE FLIER FLYER PILOT
  AIRMAN FLYING ICARUS BIRDMAN
  LOOPIST LUFBERY MANBIRD
  SOLOIST
AVID AGOG KEEN WARM EAGER
  ARDENT GREEDY HUNGRY
  JEJUNE ANXIOUS ATHIRST
  CRAVING LONGING THIRSTY
  DESIROUS GRASPING
AVIDITY AVARICE CUPIDITY
AVIFAUNA BIRDS ORNIS BIRDLIFE
AVIKOM JACKS
AVOCADO COYO PEAR PALTA
  AHUACA CHININ MARROW
  PERSEA ZABOCA ABACATE
  ABBOGADA AGUACATE ALLIGATO
AVOCET BARKER TILTER YELPER
  SCOOPER
AVOID FLY SHY BALK FLEE HELP
  MISS PASS QUIT SAVE SHUN VOID
  WARE ABHOR ANNUL AVERT
  BURKE DITCH DODGE ELUDE
  EVADE EVITE FEIGN HEDGE
  PARRY SHIFT SHIRK SKIRT SKULK
  SLACK SPAIR SPARE START
  WANDE WONDE ABJURE BLENCH
  BYPASS DETOUR ESCAPE ESCHEW
  REFUTE REMOVE VACATE
  ABSTAIN DECLINE EVITATE
  FORBEAR FORSAKE REFRAIN
  (— A PUNCH) SLIP
  (— COMMITMENT) FUDGE
  (— EXPENSE) HELP MISS SKIVE
  (— OVERWORKING) FAVOR
  (— RESPONSIBILITY) BLUDGE
  (— SUPERHIGHWAY) SHUNPIKE
  (PREF.) PHYGO
AVOIDANCE DODGE OUTLET
  EVASION ESCHEWAL
  (— OF RISK) CAUTION

(PREF.) PHOB(O)
AVOUCH AVER ASSERT
AVOW OWN BIND WARE ADMIT
  STATE AFFIRM ASSERT AVOUCH
  DEPONE DEPOSE DEVOTE
  CONFESS DECLARE JUSTIFY
  PROFESS MAINTAIN
AVOWAL OATH WORD AVOURE
  PROTEST
AVOWED FRANK SWORN STATED
  DECLARED
AWAIT BIDE HEED KEEP PEND
  STAY TEND WAIT ABIDE TARRY
  WATCH ATTEND EXPECT IMPEND
  REMAIN WAYLAY
  (— PAYMENT) CARRY
AWAITING BEFORE BIDING
AWAKE DAW STIR WAKE ADAWE
  ALERT ALIVE AWARE ROUSE
  ABRADE ABRAID ACTIVE AROUSE
  AWAKEN EXCITE CAREFUL
  HEEDFUL STARTLE VIGILANT
AWAKEN DAW STIR ALERT
  AROUSE BESTIR EXCITE KINDLE
AWAKENING REVIVAL WAKEFUL
AWARD LAW ARET GIVE KUDO
  MARK MEED METE WARD ALLOT
  ARETT GRANT MEDAL PRICE
  PRIZE ACCORD ACTION ADDEEM
  ADDOOM ADWARD ASSIGN
  BESTOW BOUNTY CONFER
  DECIDE MODIFY ADJUDGE
  APPOINT CONSIGN CUSTODY
  KEEPING ACCOLADE SENTENCE
  (MOVIE —) OSCAR
  (RADIO OR TELEVISION —) CLIO
  (RECORDING —) GRAMMIE
  (STATUETTE —) GRAMMY
  (THEATER —) OBIE
  (THEATRICAL —) TONY
  (WRITING —) HUGO
  (PL.) DESERTS
AWARE HEP RECK SURE WARE
  WARY WISE ALERT ALIVE AWAKE
  JERRY BEWARE KNOWING
  MINDFUL APPRISED INFORMED
  SENSIBLE SENTIENT VIGILANT
  WATCHFUL
AWARENESS EAR FEEL SENSE
  FEELING INSIGHT COGNITION
  SENSATION PERCEPTION
  (— OF WORTH) APPRECIATION
AWAY BY TO AWA FRO OFF OUT
  VIA WAY AFAR GONE PAST SCAT
  YOND ALONG APART ASIDE
  FORTH HENCE ABROAD ABSENT
  BEGONE ONWARD THENCE
  DISTANT FROWARD FAREWELL
  (— FROM) DOWN WITH ALONE
  ALOOF APART BESIDE
  (— FROM HOME) AFIELD OUTLAND
  (— FROM PORT) AFLOAT
  (FARTHER —) BEYOND
  (PREF.) DE E
  (— FROM) APH APO
AWE COW FEAR AMAZE DAUNT
  DREAD SCARE FRIGHT HORROR
  REGARD TERROR WONDER
  BUFFALO RESPECT ASTONISH
  BEWILDER OVERCOME RELIGION
AWE-INSPIRING GODFUL SOLEMN
  AWESOME RELIGIO FEARSOME
  OLYMPIAN

AWESOME EERY FELL HOLY
  AWFUL EERIE WEIRD SOLEMN
  DREADED GHOSTLY
AWESTRUCK SILENT
AWETO WERI
AWFUL DIRE FINE UGLY DREAD
  GHAST AUGUST HORRID
  AWESOME FEARFUL HIDEOUS
  SATANIC DREADFUL SHOCKING
  TERRIBLE
AWFULLY AWFUL FIERCE
AWKWARD AWK CAR GAUM
  UNCO BLATE CRANK FALSE
  FUDGY GAUMY GAWKY GOATY
  INAPT INEPT SPLAY STIFF
  UNCOW LINKED UNKID CLUMSY
  GAUCHE RUSTIC STICKY THUMBY
  UNEASY WOODEN ADVERSE
  BOORISH CUBBISH FROWARD
  HALTING LOUTISH LUMPISH
  STILTED UNCANNY UNCOUTH
  UNHANDY UNREADY BUNGLING
  CLOWNISH FECKLESS LUBBERLY
  PERVERSE UNGAINLY UNTOWARD
  UNWIELDY CLOUTERLY
  MALADROIT
  (— PERSON) TAWPY TUMFIE
  (NOT —) FACILE
AWL BROD BROG NAIL NALL PROD
  PROG BRODE ELSEN NALLE
  BROACH DRIVER ELSHIN FIBULA
  GIMLET BRADAWL SCRIBER
  STABBER
AWN AIL EAR JAG BARB BEAK
  JAGG PILE ARISTA BRISTLE
  (— OF BARLEY) HORN
  (— OF OATS) JAG JAGG
  (PL.) BEARD
AWNED BARBATE
AWNING TILT BLIND SHADE
  VELUM CANOPY SEMIAN SHADER
  TIENDA TENTORY SEMIANNA
  SUNBLIND SUNSHADE VELARIUM
AWNLESS NOT NOTT HUMBLE
  HUMMEL POLLARD MUTICOUS
AWRY CAM WRY AGEE BIAS SKEW
  AGLEY AMISS ASKEW GLEED
  GLEYD SNAFU WONKY WRONG
  ACROSS ASIDEN BLOOEY BLOOIE
  CAMMED FLOOEY SKIVIE THRAWN
  ASKANCE ASQUINT ATHWART
  CROOKED OBLIQUE PERVERSE
AX ADZ AXE ADZE EAWT HACHE
  MATAX BIFACE PICKEL PIOLET
  POLEAX THIXLE TWIBIL BESAGUE
  BOUCHER BROADAX CHOPPER
  CLEAVER HATCHET JEDDING
  PULASKI TWIBILL FRANCISC
  PALSTAVE SUNDERER
  TOMAHAWK
  (DOUBLE —) LABRYS
  (HEADSMAN'S —) MANNAIA
  (MASON'S —) CAVEL
  (PART OF —) EAR EYE BUTT FACE
  HAFT HEAD POLL BLADE HELVE
  HANDLE
  (WOODEN —) MACANA
  (PREF.) SECURI
AXHAMMER CAVEL CAVIL KEVEL
  KNAPPER
AXIAL VENTRAL
AXIL ALA
AXILLA AXIS ARMPIT SHOULDER

AXIOM SAW ADAGE MAXIM MOTTO BYWORD DICTUM SAYING TRUISM DIGNITY PRECEPT PROVERB APHORISM APOTHEGM DIGNITAS PETITION SENTENCE POSTULATE

AXIOMATIC PRIMITIVE

AXIS AXE NUT AXLE STEM ARBOR HINGE STALK ARBOUR CAUDEX CENTER CHITRA RACHIS CAULOME CORNCOB DENTATA POLAXIS SPINDLE SUCCULA SYMPODE TENDRIL AXLETREE MONOPODE
(— OF COCHLEA) MODIOLUS
(PREF.) AX(I)(IO)(O)(ONO)

AXLE EX BAR COD PIN AXIS BOGY ARBOR BOGEY BOGIE EXTRE SHAFT AXTREE SLEEVE MANDREL SPINDLE SUCCULA

AXOLOTL SIREDON

AXON PROCESS

AYAH IYA CHAY EYAH MAID NURSE

AYE I AY EY EYE PRO YEA YES EVER ALWAYS ASSENT FOREVER

AYESHA (HUSBAND OF —) MOHAMMED

AYU AI SWEETFISH

AZALEA ERICA MINERVA CARDINAL

AZALIAH (SON OF —) SHAPHAN

AZANIAH (SON OF —) JESHUA

AZAREEL (FATHER OF —) BANI JEROHAM
(SON OF —) AMASHAI MAASIAI

AZARIAH (FATHER OF —) JEHU ODED ETHAN NATHAN AHIMAAZ JEROHAM JOHANAN MAASEIAH JEHALELEL ZEPHANIAH JEHOSHAPHAT
(SON OF —) JOEL

AZAZ (SON OF —) BELA

AZAZEL EBLIS

AZAZIAH (SON OF —) HOSHEA

AZIMUTH ZN ARC BEARING

AZMAVETH (SON OF —) PELET JEZIEL

AZOLE PYRROLE

AZOR (FATHER OF —) ELIAKIM

AZRIEL (SON OF —) SERAIAH

AZRIKAM (FATHER OF —) AZEL NEARIAH
(SLAYER OF —) ZICHRI

AZTEC AZTECA MEXICA MEXICAN TENOCHCA

AZUBAH (HUSBAND OF —) CALEB
(SON OF —) JEHOSHAPHAT

AZUR (SON OF —) HANANIAH JAAZANIAH

AZURE BICE BLUE HURT JOVE COBALT JOVIAL JUPITER CERULEAN SAPPHIRE

AZZAN (SON OF —) PALTIEL

B

B SI BEE BAKER BRAVO
(— FLAT) ZA BEMOL
BA TRIPOS
BAA MAA MAE BLEAT
BAANA (FATHER OF —) AHILUD
(SON OF —) ZADOK
BAANAH (BROTHER OF —) RECHAB
(FATHER OF —) HUSHAI RIMMON
(SLAYER OF —) DAVID
(SON OF —) HELEB HELED
BAARA (HUSBAND OF —)
SHAHARAIM
BAASHA (FATHER OF —) AHIJAH
BABBAR UTU UTUO
BABBITT PHILISTINE
(AUTHOR OF —) LEWIS
(CHARACTER IN —) TED MYRA
PAUL TANIS ZILLA GEORGE
VERONA BABBITT JUDIQUE
REISLING
BABBLE CHAT GASH KNAP PURL
TOVE BABIL BLATE CLACK CLYDE
GLOCK HAVER PRATE TAVER
WLAFF CACKLE DITHER GABBLE
GAGGLE GLAVER GOSSIP JANGLE
MURMUR PALTER PIFFLE RABBLE
TAIVER TUMULT BLABBER
BLATHER BLETHER BLUSTER
BRABBLE CHATTER CHIPPER
CLATTER PRATTLE SMATTER
TWADDLE TWATTLE GLAISTER
BABBLER CACKLER BLATEROON
STIPITURE
BABBLING LALLATION
(PREF.) LALO
BABEL DIN MEDLEY TUMULT
CHARIVARI CONFUSION
BABESIA APIOSOMA NUTTALIA
PIROPLASMA
BABOON APE PAP PAPA DRILL
ADONIS BAVIAN CHACMA GIRRIT
PAPION SPHINX BABUINA
MANDRILL HAMADRYAD
BABUL SANT SUNT ACACIA
BABOOT GARRAT GONAKE
NEBNEB ATTALEH GONAKIE
BABUSHKA SCARF KERCHIEF
BABY MOP BABA BABE CHAP DOLL
JOEY TOTO WEAN BAIRN CHILD
HUMOR SPOIL WAYNE CHRISM
CODDLE FONDLE INFANT MOPPET
PAMPER PUPPET SQUALL WEANIE
BAMBINO CHRISOM INDULGE
PAPOOSE PREEMIE WADDLER
BABY CARRIAGE PRAM BUGGY
WAGON GOCART STROLLER
PERAMBULATOR
BABYISH TIDDY PULING SIMPLE
PUERILE CHILDISH
BABYLONIA CHALDEA
BABYLONIAN (— CYCLE) SAROS
BABY'S BREATH GYP GYPSOPHILA
BACALAO MURRE SCAMP

ABADEJO CODFISH GROUPER
GUILLEMOT
BACCATE BERRIED
BACCHANAL DEVOTEE REVELER
CAROUSER
BACCHANTE FROW MAENAD
BACCHUS LIBER LYAEUS BROMIUS
DIONYSUS
(AUNT OF —) INO
(FATHER OF —) ZEUS JUPITER
(MOTHER OF —) SEMELE
BACHELOR BACH SEAL BATCH
GARCON WANTER BACULERE
BENEDICT CELIBATE
BACILLUS GERM VIRUS MICROBE
BACK AID FRO TUB VAT ABET
BAKE BECK FULL HIND HINT NAPE
NATA REAR TAIL ABACK AGAIN
ANGEL BROAD CHINE DORSE
NOTUM SPINE SPLAT STERN
VOUCH ASSIST DORSUM HINDER
RETRAL SECOND SOOTHE
TERGUM TROUGH UPHOLD
VERIFY CISTERN ENDORSE
FINANCE POSTERN RIGGING
SPONSOR SUPPORT SUSTAIN
BACKWARD FULLBACK HALFBACK
MAINTAIN
(— A ROWBOAT) STERN
(— OF ANIMAL) RIG TERGUM
(— OF ARCHERY TARGET) BOSS
(— OF AWNING) RIDGEROPE
(— OF BOOK) DORSE SPINE
(— OF BULL) ROOF
(— OF HAND) OPISTHENAR
(— OF HEAD) NODDLE NIDDICK
OCCIPUT
(— OF INSECT) NOTUM
(— OF NECK) NAPE NUQUE
SCRUFF
(— OF PAGE) FV
(— OUT) BEG JIB DUCK FLUNK
CRAWFISH
(— TO BACK) ADDORSED
(— UP) ABET VERIFY
(— WATER) STERN SHEAVE
(SHOWING —) TERGANT
(PREF.) ANA DORSI DORSO
NOT(O) OPISTH(O) POST RE RETRO
TERGI TERGO
(AT THE — OF) OPISTH(O) POSTERO
(BENT —) RECURVI RECURVO
(SUFF.) NOTUS
BACKACHE NOTALGIA
BACKBITING CATTY DETRACTION
BACKBOARD BANK MONITOR
BACKBONE BACK GRIT GUTS
CHINE NERVE PLUCK RIDGE
SPINA SPINE LADDER METTLE
SPIRIT GRISTLE RIGBANE SPINULE
STAMINA VERTEBRA
(— OF FISH) GRATE
BACKCOUNTRY BUSH STICKS

BOONIES BACKLAND BACKVELD
BOONDOCKS
BACKDROP OLEO
BACKER ANGEL
BACKFIELD SECONDARY
BACKFIRE BOOMERANG
BACKFLASH GUTTER
BACKGAMMON IRISH LURCH
TABLE FAYLES GAMMON TABLES
BACKGAME TICKTACK VERQUERE
(— MAN) BLOT TABLEMAN
BACKGROUND FOND REAR
GROUND OFFING LINEAGE
SETTING BACKDROP DISTANCE
EXTERIOR OFFSCAPE TRAINING
EDUCATION
(— OF FLOWERS) BOCAGE
(MUSICAL —) SUPPORT
BACKHANDED AWKWARD
BACKHOE PULLSHOVEL
BACKHOUSE PRIVY OUTHOUSE
BACKING AID EGIS AEGIS BACKUP
BEHIND LINING MUSLIN REFUSE
SUPPORT HEARTING FINANCING
(LEGAL —) TEETH
BACKLASH LASH SHAKE SLACK
BACKLOG RESERVE SURPLUS
BACKBRAND
BACKPACK GEAR LOAD
BACKPIECE DOSSIERE
BACKPLATE REREDOS
BACKREST LAZYBACK
BACKROPE GOBLINE
BACKSEY SEY SIRLOIN
BACKSLIDE FALL LAPSE DESERT
REVERT RELAPSE
BACKSPIN DRAG UNDERCUT
UNDERSPIN
BACKSTITCH PURL PEARL
BACKSTOP BUTT
BACK TALK LIP SASS
BACKWARD FRO JAY LAX YON
BACK CRAB DARK DULL LOTH
ABACK AREAR BLATE INAPT
LOATH THRAW UNAPT ARREAR
ASTERN AVERSE BYGONE POSTIC
RETRAD RETRAL STUPID ARRIERE
BASHFUL LAGGARD LAGGING
REVERSE UPSTAGE DILATORY
IGNORANT LATEWARD PERVERSE
REARWARD RINKYDINK TAILFIRST
(PREF.) OPISTH(O) RE RETRO
BACKWARDNESS DARKNESS
BARBARISM
BACKWARDS YON ABACK
AROUND
(PREF.) OPISO PALI(M)(N)
BACKWATER EBB COVE SLEW
SLUE BAYOU BOGAN SHEAVE
SLOUGH RETRACT RETREAT
BACKWASH BILLABONG
BACKWOODSMAN HICK WOODSY
BUCKSKIN HILLBILLY

BACKWORT COMFREY
BACON PIG BARD MEAT PORK
BARDE JAMON PRIZE SPECK
FLITCH GAMMON RUSTIC
SAWNEY GAMBONE SOWBELLY
BACOPA BRAMIA
BACTERIOLOGIST AMERICAN GAY
KAHN NOVY PARK BURKE CRAIG
ERNST MOORE PLOTZ BERGEY
ENDERS JORDAN FRANCIS
KENDALL NOGUCHI THEILER
ZINSSER
BELGIAN BORDET
BRAZILIAN CHAGAS
CANADIAN WESBROOK
CUBAN AGRAMONTE
ENGLISH TWORT FLEMING
FRENCH ROUX RAMON MARTIN
LAVERAN NICOLLE
CHAMBERLAND
GERMAN KOCH FLUGGE GAFFKY
GRUBER HUEPPE BEHRING
EHRLICH GARTNER LOFFLER
FRAENKEL PFEIFFER UHLENHUTH
WASSERMANN
JAPANESE HATA SHIGA KITAZATO
RUMANIAN BABES
RUSSIAN METCHNIKOFF
SPANISH FERRAN
SWISS YERSIN
BACTERIUM ROD COLI GERM
AEROBE COCCUS CYTODE
ANTHRAX CHOLERA MICROBE
PROTEUS SARCINA VIBRION
BACILLUS LISTERIA PATHOGEN
BOTULINUS CYTOPHAGA
HEMOPHILE INFECTANT
INFECTION SPIRILLUM
MICROCOCCUS PNEUMOCOCCUS
SCHIZOMYCETE
PNEUMOBACILLUS
BAD BIG DUD ILL SAD EVIL FULL
HARD LEWD POOR PUNK QUED
SICK SOUR VILE WICK ADDLE
GAMMY LOUSY NASTY SORRY
WEARY WORST WRONG ARRANT
FAULTY LITHER LUTHER NOUGHT
ROTTEN SEVERE SHREWD SINFUL
UNGOOD UNKIND WICKED
BALEFUL BANEFUL CHRONIC
CORRUPT FEARFUL HARMFUL
HEINOUS HURTFUL IMMORAL
INUTILE NAUGHTY SPOILED
TAINTED UNLUCKY UNMORAL
UNSOUND VICIOUS ANNOYING
CRIMINAL DEPRAVED DOGGEREL
FIENDISH FLAGRANT INFERIOR
PRECIOUS SINISTER UNSUITED
(— MANNERS) TROLLOPE
(OUTRAGEOUSLY —) GRIEVOUS
(OUTSTANDINGLY —) ARRANT
PIACULAR
(RATHER —) INDIFFERENT

(VERY —) ALMIGHTY EXECRABLE
(PREF.) CAC(O) CACH DYS KAK(O)
MAL(E) MIS
(SUFF.) CACE
BADDERLOCKS MURLIN PURSES
HENWARE SEAWEED
HONEYWARE
BADEBEC (HUSBAND OF —)
GARGANTUA
(SON OF —) PANTAGRUEL
BADGE PIN BLUE MARK SIGN STAR
COLOR CREST CROSS FAVOR
HONOR ORDER PATCH TOKEN
WINGS BUTTON BUZZER COLLAR
EMBLEM ENSIGN FASCES GARTER
GIGLIO PLAQUE SHIELD SYMBOL
TIPONI WEEPER CHEVRON
EPAULET FEATHER BRASSARD
EPISEMON INSIGNIA SCAPULAR
VERNICLE EPAULETTE
COGNISANCE
(JAPANESE —) MON KIRIMON
(RUSSIAN —) ZNAK
BADGER NAG PAT BAIT GRAY
GREY GRIS MELE PATE ANNOY
BRACE BROCK BRUSH CHEVY
CHIVY HURON MELES PAHMI
RATED RATEL TAXEL TAXUS
TEASE WORRY BAUSON BAWSON
BOTHER BRAROW CHIVVY
HAGGLE HARASS HAWKER
HECKLE KIDDER MELINE PESTER
TELEDU WOMBAT BAUSOND
GRISARD TORMENT BRAIREAU
BULLYRAG CARCAJOU HUCKSTER
IRRITATE STINKARD MISTONUSK
(— STATE) WISCONSIN
(AUSTRALIAN —) WOMBAT
(COMPANY OF —S) CETE
(LIKE A —) MELINE
BADINAGE FOOL CHAFF JOKER
BANTER RAILLERY TRIFLING
BADLANDS MALPAIS
BADLY BAD ILL EVIL HARD ILLY
SICK SADLY EVILLY HARDLY
POORLY UNWELL FAULTILY
WICKEDLY VICIOUSLY
(PREF.) MAL
BADMINTON POONA
BADNESS MALICE PRAVITY
UNVALUE EVILNESS
(SUFF.) CACE
**BADROULBOUDOUR (HUSBAND OF
—)** ALADDIN
BAD-TEMPERED FOUL ANGRY
STINGY CRABBED GROUCHY
BAFFLE FOX GET BALK BEAT FOIL
LICK MATE POSE STOP UNDO
CHEAT CHECK ELUDE EVADE
FLING STICK STUMP BLENCH
BOGGLE DEFEAT DELUDE FICKLE
INFAMY OUTWIT PUZZLE RESIST
THWART BUFFALO CONFUSE
DECEIVE QUIBBLE STONKER
BEWILDER CONFOUND DISGRACE
JUGGLING
BAFFLED BEATEN
BAFFLING SHREWD ELUSIVE
BAG COD KIT MAT NET PAD POD
POT SAC CELL DRAG GRIP LOBE
MAIL POCK POKE SACK TOOT
TRAP WOMB BELLY BOUGE BULSE
CATCH DILLI DILLY EMERY FLOAT

HUSSY PETER POUCH PURSE
SCRIP SEIZE SNARE STEAL
BLOUSE BUDGET CAVITY ENTRAP
FOLLIS GASBAG MATAPI PAGGLE
POCKET POUNCE SACHET SEABAG
VALISE WALLET ALFORJA
BALLOON BEANBAG BLISTER
BUCKRAM CANTINA CAPCASE
CAPTURE CUSHION GAMEBAG
GOMUKHI HANDBAG HOLDALL
RETICLE SANDBAG SARPLER
SATCHEL TRAVOIS BALLONET
CARRYALL CORNSACK ENTRAILS
ENVELOPE FOLLICLE KNAPSACK
MONEYBAG OVERSLIP POCHETTE
RETICULE RUCKSACK SUITCASE
WINESKIN MULTIWALL
WEEKENDER PORTMANTEAU
(— BULGING) SWAG
(— FOR LETTERS) MAIL POUCH
KAREETA MAILBAG POSTBAG
(— FOR TOOLS) WALLET
(— OF ANISEED) DRAG
(— WITH POCKETS) TIDE TIDY
(AUSTRALIAN —) SWAG DILLI
SHIRT SHAMMY
(GAS —) CELL
(GRAB —) FISHPOND
(HAWSE —) JACKASS
(LEATHER —) JAG JAGG ASKOS
BUDGE BOUGET MUSSUK
(NET —) SNOOD GARLAND
(SEWING —) HUSSY
(SLEEPING —) FUMBA FLEABAG
SLEEPER
(WATER —) CHAGAL CHAGEN
CHAGUL
(PREF.) UTRI
(SUFF.) SACCATE SACCI SACCO
BAGASSE BEGASS LINAGA MEGASS
BAGATELLE CANON TRUNK VERSE
CANNON TRIFLE NOTHING
BAGEL ROLL BIALY
BAGGAGE ARMS GEAR MINX
SWAG CUTTY HUZZY NASTY
SAMAN STUFF TENTS TRASH
WENCH HARLOT REFUSE TRASHY
TRUNKS CLOTHES DUNNAGE
EFFECTS FARDAGE PLUNDER
RUBBISH SALMARY SUMPTER
VALISES CARRIAGE HARLOTRY
RUBBISHY UTENSILS
BAGGAGE CAR WAGON FOURGON
BAGGER SACKER BATCHER
BAGGING SOUTAGE
BAGGY LOOSE POCKY PURSY
FLABBY PUFFED PURSIVE
SACCATE
BAGNIO BAIN BATH BAGNE
PRISON BROTHEL HOTHOUSE
BAGPIPE MUSE PIPE PIVA DRONE
TITTY BIGNOU BINIOU CHORUS
GEWGAW MUSETTE PIFFERO
SAMBUKE DULCIMER SYMPHONY
ZAMPOGNA CORNAMUTE
CORNEMUSE SYMPHONIA
(PART OF —) BAG CORD PIPE
DRONE MOUNT STOCK TASSEL
CHANTER WINDBAG BLOWPIPE
BAGUETTE CHAPLET
BAH PO FOH PAH POH ROT RATS
FAUGH PSHAW NONSENSE
BAHAMAS (CAPITAL OF —) NASSAU

(ISLAND OF —) ABACO EXUMA
ANDROS BIMINI
(TOWN IN —) FREEPORT
BAHRAIN (CAPITAL OF —) MANAMA
(MONEY OF —) FILS DINAR
(TOWN OF —) RIFAA JIDHAFS
BAIL BOW DIP ANDI BALE BOND
HOOP LADE LAVE RING RYND
YOKE LADLE SCOOP THROW
VOUCH BUCKET HANDLE PLEDGE
SECURE SURETY VADIUM
CAUTION CUSTODY DELIVER
RELEASE REPLEVY BAILSMAN
BULWARKS SECURITY
GUARANTEE
(— OUT) ABANDON
BAILEE LESSEE POSITOR
CONDUCTOR
BAILER SPOUCHER
BAILIFF FOUD GRAB HIND AGENT
REEVE SAFFO SCULT STAFF
BAILIE BAILLI BEADLE BEAGLE
DEPUTY FACTOR GRIEVE LOOKER
OFFICE PORTER PREVOT SCHOUT
VARLET BUMTRAP GRIPPER
PROVOST PUTTOCK SHERIFF
STEWARD APPROVER HUISSIER
OVERSEER TIPSTAFF CATCHPOLE
CATCHPOLL CONSTABLE
HUNDREDER PORTREEVE
SENESCHAL WAPENTAKE
BAILIWICK AREA FIELD DOMAIN
OFFICE PROVINCE
BAILMENT MUTUUM
BAILOR LESSOR
BAIN NEAR LITHE READY SHORT
DIRECT LIMBER SUPPLE
FORWARD WILLING
BAIT BAD BOB COG DAP LUG BITE
CAST CHUM FEED HALT HANK
LURE PLUG TAIL DECOY HOUND
LEGER SHACK SLATE SQUID
STALE TEMPT TRAIN WORRY
ALLURE APPAST ATTACK BADGER
BERLEY ENTICE HARASS HECKLE
HECTOR KILLER LEDGER REPAST
SHRAPE SLIVER FULCRUM
GUDGEON PROVOKE TAGTAIL
TOLLING TORMENT BRANLING
CUNGEBOI BRANDLING
(— FOR BIRDS) SHRAP SHRAPE
(— FOR COD) CAPELIN
(GREASY —) ROGUE
(GROUND —) BERLEY
(MAGGOT —) GENTLE
(SCENTED —) DRAG
BAITING HANK
BAIZE BAY BAYES BAYETA DOMETT
BOCKING
BAKE DRY BURN COCT COOK FIRE
BATCH BROIL GRILL PARCH
ROAST ANNEAL HARDEN BISCUIT
PISTATE SCALLOP CLAMBAKE
ESCALLOP
(— EGGS) SHIRR
(— THOROUGHLY) SOAK
BAKED COCTILE
(— IN EARTH OVEN) KALUA
(— PRODUCT) KICHEL
BAKER OVEN FIRER BAXTER
BURNER FURNER PISTOR
FURNACE OVENMAN ROASTER
BAKER BIRD HORNERO

BAKING CUIT BATCH COCTION
FURNAGE ASSATION
BAKONGO FIOT
BALAAM (FATHER OF —) BEOR
BALACHONG NGAPI
BALAK (FATHER OF —) ZIPPOR
BALANCE BEAM EVEN PEIS REST
SWAY TRIM COVER PEISE PEISE
POISE SCALE TRONE WEIGH
WEIHE ADJUST AUNCEL CANCEL
EMBLEM EQUATE KELTER KELVIN
KILTER LAUNCE OFFSET SANITY
SQUARE STRIKE DESEMER
LIBRATE OVERRUN RESIDUE
TRABUCH TRUTINE EQUALITY
EQUALIZE EQUATION SERENITY
WESTPHAL TREBUCHET
PROPORTION
(— DUE) ARREAR
(— IN ACCOUNT) CREDIT
(— OF SAILS) ATRY
(MENTAL —) HEAD
(PREF.) STATO
BALANCED EVEN EQUAL LEVEL
APOISE KITTLE WEIGHED
COMPLETE QUADRATE TOGETHER
(PREF.) SYM
BALANCER HALTER ACROBAT
GYMNAST HALTERE
BALATA ICICA BULLACE
BEEFWOOD BORRACHA
BALCONY POY ORIEL PORCH
STOOP CIRCLE GAZEBO PIAZZA
PODIUM SOLLAR BALAGAN
GALLERY MIRADOR PERGOLA
TERRACE BRATTICE CANTORIA
VERANDAH MEZZANINE
BALD RAW BARE BASE BOLD
CRUDE DODDY NAKED PLAIN
CALLOW PALTRY PEELED PILLED
SIMPLE CALVOUS EPILOSE
LITERAL POLLARD GLABROUS
HAIRLESS TONSURED
(— HEAD) PILGARLIC
(— SPOT) TONSURE
(PREF.) PHALACRO
BALDACHIN CANOPY CIBORIUM
BALDER BALDR BALDUR
BAELDAEG
(CHILD OF —) FORSETE FORSETI
(FATHER OF —) ODIN
(SLAYER OF —) HOTH LOKE LOKI
HOTHR
(WIFE OF —) NANNA
BALDERDASH ROT GUFF PUNK
TRASH TRIPE DRIVEL JARGON
FLUBDUB NONSENSE
BALDUCTUM RIGMAROLE
BALDMONEY MEU
BALDNESS ACOMIA CALVITY
ALOPECIA ATRICHIA OPHIASIS
CALVITIES
BALDPATE ZUISIN POACHER
BALDRIC BELT LACE GIRDLE
ZODIAC BALTEUS SUPPORT
NECKLACE
BALE NO GIB NOT WOE EVIL FIRE
HARM LAVE PACK PYRE BLOCK
CRATE DEATH FARDO SERON
BALLOT BUNDLE EMBALE SEROON
SORROW PACKAGE SARPLER
BALEARIC ISLANDS (ISLAND OF —)
IBIZA CABRERA MAJORCA

MINORCA CONEJERA
(MEASURE OF —) PALMO MISURA
QUARTA QUARTIN BARCELLA
(TOWN OF —) IBIZA MAHON
PALMA
(WEIGHT OF —) CARGO CORTA
QUARTANO
BALEEN WHALEBONE
BALEFUL BAD EVIL DEADLY
MALIGN SACRED SULLEN MALEFIC
NOXIOUS RUINOUS SIDERAL
SINISTER WRETCHED
MALEFICENT
BALI (CAPITAL OF —) DENPASAR
(DANCE OF —) ARDJA BARIS KRISS
BARONG KETJAK MONKEY
DJANGER
(MOUNTAIN OF —) AGOENG
(MUSICAL INSTRUMENT OF —)
GAMELAN
(RICE FIELD OF —) SAWAII
(STRAIT OF —) LOMBOK
(TOWN OF —) SINGARADJA
BALIN (BROTHER OF —) SUGRIVA
(SLAYER OF —) RAMA
BALINGHASAY ANAM ANAN
BALK GAG HEN HUE JIB JUB SHY
BEAM BILK BUCK BULL COND FOIL
GORM HADE HEAP LICK LOFT
MISS OMIT PROP SHUN SKIP SLIP
STAY STOP AVOID BAULK BLOCK
CHECK CLAMP DEMUR HUNCH
MOUND REBEL REEST RIDGE
STAKE STICK WAVER BAFFLE
DEFEAT FALTER HINDER IMPEDE
OUTWIT RAFTER REFUSE STRAIN
THWART BLUNDER CODLING
GALLOWS ISTHMUS MISTAKE
(— IN FISHING) HUE COND
(HALF —) FLITCH
(PL.) MIDDLES
BALKAN (— COIN) NOVCIC
(— COUNTRY) GREECE SERBIA
ALBANIA RUMANIA BULGARIA
(— INSTRUMENT) GUSLA
(— RIVER) JIU OLT IBAR JIUL SAVA
TISA OLTUL DANUBE MORAVA
(— SEA) BLACK AEGEAN IONIAN
ADRIATIC
BALKER HUER CONNER
BALKY NAPPY STICK MULISH
REESTY RESTIVE CONTRARY
STUBBORN OBSTINATE
BALL IN BAL BOB FLY HOP NOB
ORB PEA TOY BEAD BOWL CLEW
CLUE KNOB KNOP KNUR PICK PILL
POME PROM TRAP DANCE EDGER
FAULT FLOAT GLOBE GLOME
HURLY ORBIT PEARL PUPPY
SHAPE SNACK SPORT TRUCK
BULLET BUTTON HOOKER HURLEY
MOONIE MUDDLE PEELEE PELLET
PELOTA POMMEL POMPON
RONDEL RUNDLE SPHERE
SQUASH BALLOON CONFUSE
FLOATER GLOBULE INCURVE
INSHOOT KNAPPAN LEATHER
MANDREL PELOTON RIDOTTO
SLITTER ASSEMBLY BASEBALL
BISCAYEN FANDANGO FOOTBALL
GROUNDER HANDBALL QUENELLE
SOFTBALL SPHEROID TRAPBALL
(— AS SHIP'S SIGNAL) SHAPE

(— FOR MUSKET) GOLI SLUG
(— OF CLAY) KNICKER
(— OF RICE OR MEAT) PINDA
(— OF THREAD) COP CLEW CLUE
GOME BOTTOM COPPIN
WHARROW
(— OF THUMB) THENAR CUSHION
(— OF WASTE IRON) COBBLE
(— USED IN SHINTY) PEG
(—S OF MEDICI FAMILY) PALLE
(BILLIARD —) SPOT IVORY
SNOOKER
(BOWLED —) TICE CURVE SKYER
BAILER BUMPER FIZZER GOOGLY
KICKER POODLE SEAMER YORKER
CREEPER SNORTER SPINNER
BREAKBACK CROSSOVER
INSWINGER
(BOWLING —) DODO JACK
(CORK —) PLUMBER
(CRICKET —) SNICK SHOOTER
(DECORATIVE —) DRAGEE
(FIVES —) SNACK
(GOLF —) PUTTY
(HARD —) SNUG
(HOCKEY —) NUN NUR ORR
(INK —) PUMPET
(MEAT —S) CECILS
(SKITTLE —) CHEESE
(TENNIS —) PALM
(WOODEN —) KNUR
(PREF.) GLOBI GLOBO SPHAER(O)
SPHER(O)
(SUFF.) SPHAERA SPHERE
SPHERIC(AL)
DALLAD JIG LAI LAY LILT MELE
POEM SONG CAROL DERRY
FANCY BALLET BYLINA CARVAL
SONNET BALLANT CANZONE
CORRIDO GWERZIOU SINGSONG
BALLAST BED CRIB LOAD TRIM
METAL POISE STONE BOTTOM
BURDEN GRAVEL WEIGHT
BALANCE LASTAGE SANDBAG
DRAGROPE KENTLEDGE
SABURRATE
BALLET BALLAD MASQUE BOURREE
PANTOMIME
(— MOVEMENT) VOLE TEMPS
APLOMB OUVERT POINTE RELEVE
RETIRE ALLONGE ARRONDI
ASSEMBLE ATTITUDE ARABESQUE
BALLHOOTER BRUTTER
BALLISTA SWEEP MANGONEL
BALLOON BAG BALL BLIMP
EXPAND GASBAG AIRSHIP
DISTEND DRACHEN INFLATE
SAUSAGE SKYHOOK AEROSTAT
ENVELOPE DIRIGIBLE
(TRIAL —) KITE
BALLOONING BOSOMY
BALLOONIST AERONAUT
BALLOON VINE FAROLITO
HEARTPEA HEARTSEED
BALLOT BALE POLL PROX VOTE
ELECT PROXY VOICE BILLET
CHOICE POLICY TICKET SUFFRAGE
BALLROOM SALOON
BALLYHOO BALLY HOOPLA
BALM OIL BEEB BITO DAUB SALVE
ANOINT BALSAM EMBALM LOTION
RELIEF SOLACE SOOTHE
ANODYNE BESMEAR COMFORT

PERFUME UNGUENT OINTMENT
(— OF GILEAD) CANADA
OPOBALSAM
BALMORAL CAP BOOT SHOE
BALMY MILD SOFT BLAND DAFFY
MOONY SPICY SUNNY SWEET
GENTLE INSANE SERENE HEALING
LENIENT AROMATIC BALSAMIC
DRESSING FRAGRANT SOOTHING
BALONEY BUNK HOOEY BUSHWA
BUSHWAH
BALSA RAFT FLOAT GUANO POLAK
POLACK BOBWOOD CORKWOOD
BALSAM BALM RIGA TOLU UMIRI
COPALM GURJAN GURJUN
STORAX AMPALEA COPAIBA
CREEPER AMPALAYA BDELLIUM
BENJAMIN OINTMENT
BALSAM APPLE KARELA
AMARGOSA AMPALAYA
BALSAMINE
BALSAM FIR SAPIN BAUMIER
BALSAM POPLAR TACAMAHAC
BALSAMROOT SUNFLOWER
BALSAMWEED MOONSHINE
FEATHERWEED
BALT YOD ESTH LETT ESTONIAN
BALTIC (— GULF) RIGA DANZIG
BOTHNIA FINLAND
(— ISLAND) AERO DAGO FARO
OSEL ALAND ALSEN OESEL
OLAND GOTLAND HIIUMAA
BORNHOLM
(— PORT) KIEL RIGA MEMEL REVAL
DANZIG GDANSK TALINN LEIPAJA
(— RIVER) ODER ODRA DVINA
VIADUA
(— TOWN) MEMEL DANZIG
GDANSK LEIPAJA
BALUCHISTAN (— CULTURE)
QUETTA
BALUSTER SPOKE COLUMEL
BANISTER COLUMELLA
BALUSTRADE BARRER PARAPET
RAILING BALCONET BANISTER
BAMBOO DHA CANE REED BATAK
GLUMAL GUADUA TONKIN
BATAKAN WANGHEE WHANGEE
(SACRED —) NANDIN
(WOVEN —) SAWALI
BAMBOOZLE DUPE HAVE CHEAT
COZEN GRILL CAJOLE HUMBUG
BUFFALO BUNBAZE DECEIVE
DEFRAUD MYSTIFY PERPLEX
BAN BAR WOE TABU VETO BANAL
BANUS BLOCK CURSE EDICT
ORDER TABOO BANISH CENSOR
ENJOIN FORBID HINDER INVOKE
NOTICE OUTLAW CONDEMN
EXCLUDE ANATHEMA DENOUNCE
EXECRATE PROHIBIT
(— ON NEWS) BLACKOUT
BANA (DAUGHTER OF —) USHA
BANAK UCUUBA
BANAL FLAT CORNY INANE SILLY
STALE TRITE VAPID JEJUNE
INSIPID MUNDANE TRIVIAL
BANANA FEI FIG MUSA SABA
BERRY ENSETE FINGER SAGING
LACATAN PLATANO SAGUING
SUNBEAM PLANTAIN
BAND BAR GAD HUB TIE TUB ZON
BEAD BELT BEND BOND CAME

CASH CORD CREW CUFF FALL
FERD FESS GANG GATE GIRT
HOOD HOOP KNOT LACE LIST
RING SASH SHOE TAPE WISP
ZONA ZONE AMPYX BANDY BRAID
CHOIR CLAMP CORSE COVEY
COVIN CRAPE CROWN FEMUR
FLOCK FRAME GIRTH GORGE
GUARD JATHA LABEL MEINY
NOISE PANEL PATTE PRIDE QUIRE
SABOT SNOOD STRAP STRIP
STROP TAPIS TORSE TRACK TRIBE
UNITE WERED WITHE ARMLET
BENDEL BINDER BORDER BOYANG
BRIDGE BUNDLE CIMBIA CLAVUS
COHORT COLLAR COLLET COPULA
COVINE CHANCE CRAVAT DECKLE
FASCIA FETTER FILLET FRIEZE
FRINGE FUNNEL GAMMON
GARTER GASKET GIRDLE HYPHEN
LEGLET MATRIX NIPPER NORSEL
PLEDGE RADULA REGULA ROLLER
SCREED STRAKE STRING STRIPE
SWATHE TAENIA TETHER TISSUE
WEEPER BINDING BLANKET
CHAMBUL CIRCLET COMPANY
ENOMOTY FERRULE FRONTAL
GARLAND HATBAND HEADING
NECKTIE ORPHREY PALLIUM
PIGTAIL PROMISE SEQUELA
SHACKLE SHOEING SWADDLE
VINCULUM
(— ACROSS SUNSPOT) BRIDGE
(— AROUND MAST) PARREL
(— FOR HEAD) VITTA
(— IN BRAIN) LIGULA FRENULUM
FUNICULUS
(— IN ROCKS) FAHLBAND
(— OF CLAY) COTTLE
(— OF COLOR) SOCK SLASH STRIA
LACING FASCIOLE
(— OF CRAPE) WEED SCARF
(— OF INDIANS) SHIVWITS
(— OF PILLAGERS) SKINNERS
(— OF PIPERS) POVERTY
(— OF PURPLE) CLAVUS
(— OF STRAW) GAD SIMMON
(— OF TISSUE) TISSUE
(— OF 13 WITCHES) COVEN
(— ON SHIELD) ENDORSE
(— TO COMPRESS CHEEKS)
CAPISTRUM
(— TOGETHER) BANDY
(ARMED —) JATHA POSSE
(ARMOR —) TONLET
(CIRCULAR —) HOOP RING ANNULE
WREATH
(DANCE —) CHORO COMBO
(DECORATIVE —) PATTE LEGLET
CORNICE ARCHIVOLT
(DIVIDING —) CLOISON
(EUCHARISTIC —) MANIPLE
(FOREHEAD —) INFULA
(IRON —) FRET GATE TRUSS
FUNNEL STRAKE
(LACE —) SCALLOP
(MUSICIANS —) CONCERT
(RADIO —) CHANNEL
(RESONANCE —) FORMANT
(STREET —) MARIACHI
(TRIBAL —) AIMAK
(PL.) GRIPES INTERLACERY
(PREF.) TAENI(A)(O) ZON(I)(O)

(SUFF.) (CILIATED —)
TROCH(A)(AL)(OUS)(US)
BANDAGE BAND BELT BIND TAPE
BLIND BRACE CLOUT DRESS
GALEA LINEN SLING SPICA SWARF
SWATH TRUSS BINDER COLLAR
CRAVAT FASCIA FETTLE FILLET
LIGATE NIPPER ROLLER SWARTH
SWATHE SWEATH REVERSE
ROLLING SWADDLE TRUSSER
ACCIPTER CAPELINE CINCTURE
GAUNTLET LIGAMENT LIGATURE
SCAPULAR STOCKING CAPISTRUM
(— FOR NOSE) ACCIPTER
(EYE —) MUFFLER
(FINGER —) HOVEL
(JAW —) FUNDA
(PL.) SWADDLING
BANDALORE QUIZ
BANDANNA WEB TURBAN
BANDANA PULICAT PULICATE
PULLICAT
BANDEAU BAND STRIP FILLET
BRASSIERE
BANDICOOT RAT MARL BILBI
BILBY BADGER BIELBY PINKIE
QUENDA
BANDIT CACA TORY BRAVO THIEF
BANISH HAIDUK HEYDUK
OUTLAW ROBBER BANDIDO
BRIGAND LADRONE TULISAN
BUSHWACK MARAUDER
MIQUELET PICAROON RAPPAREE
BANDOLERO
(PL.) MANZAS
BANDLEADER MASTER MAESTRO
CHORAGUS CONDUCTOR
BANDORE PANDORA PANDURA
(PREF.) PANDURI
BANDSMAN WINDJAMMER
BANDSTAND KIOSK STAND
BANDY VIE BAND CART CHOP
SWAP TRADE LEAGUE RACKET
STRIVE CHAFFER CONTEND
DISCUSS CARRIAGE EXCHANGE
SHUTTLECOCK
(— WORDS) REVIE GIFFGAFF
BANE BAN WOE BONE EVIL HARM
KILL PEST RUIN CURSE DEATH
VENOM INJURY MURDER POISON
SLAYER NEMESIS SCOURGE
MISCHIEF MURDERER NUISANCE
BANEBERRY COHOSH REDBERRY
TOADROOT GRAPEWORT
BANEFUL BAD ILL EVIL VILE
SWART HARMFUL HURTFUL
NOXIOUS RUINOUS VENOMOUS
SINISTRAL PERNICIOUS
BANG POM RAP BAFF BEAT BLOW
BOOT DASH DOCK DRUB POUF
SCAT SLAM SWAP SWOP TANK
BLAFF CLASH CRACK DRIVE
EXCEL FORCE IMPEL POUND
SLAKE SLUMP SOUND SPANG
STRAM THUMP WHACK WHANG
WHUMP BOUNCE CUDGEL
ENERGY FRINGE STRIKE THRASH
THUNGE THWACK SARDINE
SURPASS THUNDER FORELOCK
(— ON HEAD) BRAIN
BANGLADESH (CAPITAL OF —)
DACCA
(COIN OF —TH) TAKA

(MONEY OF —) TAKA
(NATIVE OF —) BENGALI
(RIVER OF —) GANGES
(TOWN IN —) KHULNA
CHITTAGONG
BANGLE ORNAMENT
BANG-UP SLAP CRACK TIPTOP
BANISH BAN FREE ABAND EJECT
EXILE EXPEL FLEME WAIVE
WREAK BANDIT DEPORT DISPEL
DISTER FORSAY OUTLAW
ABANDON CONDEMN CONFINE
DISMISS DIVORCE EXCLUDE
DISPLACE RELEGATE
BANISHED FUGITIVE
BANISHMENT EXILE BANNIMUS
OUTLAWRY XENELASY
OSTRACISM XENELASIA
BANISTER RAILING BALUSTER
BANJO BOX BANJORE BANJORINE
BANK BAR BAY COP JUG RIM ROW
BINK BRAE BREW BUTT CAJA
DIKE DUNE DYKE EDGE HEAD
HILL LINK MASS PILE RAKE RAMP
RIPA RIVE SAND SCAR SEAT SIDE
TIER WEIR BANCO BENCH BLUFF
BRINK COAST DITCH EARTH
FENCE HOVER HURST LEVEE
MARGE MOUND MOUNT RIDGE
SAVER SHARE SHELF SHOAL
SHORE SLOPE STACK STAGE
TRUST BANQUE BORROW CAISSE
CAUSEY CRADGE DEGREE
DEPEND DOUBLE MARGIN
RANDOM RECKON RIVAGE
STRAND ANTHILL BANKING
CUSHION DEPOSIT LOMBARD
POTTERY SANDBAG SHALLOW
WINDROW BARRANCA PLATFORM
TRAVERSE
(— A FIRE) REST
(— FOR DRYING BRICKS) HACK
(— OF CANAL) BERM BERME
HEELPATH
(— OF EARTH) COP DAM DITCH
(— OF RIVER) RIPA WHARF
STRAND
(— OF SAND OR MUD) BAR SCALP
(— OF SNOW) WREATH
SNOWDRIFT
(— OF TURF) SUNK
(OVERHANGING —) BREW HOVER
(RUSSIAN —) CRAPETTE
(STEEP —) HEUCH HEUGH WOUGH
BARRANCA BARRANCO
(PREF.) RIPI
BANKER BOOK SETH SETT FACTOR
FINDER SAHKAR SHROFF SOUCAR
SOWCAR LOMBARD MARWARI
MONEYER SPONSOR TAILLEUR
BANQUETER FINANCIER
BANKNOTE CRISP FLIMSY SCREEN
(FORGED —) STUMER
BANKRUPT SAP BONG BUNG BUST
DUCK RUMP BREAK BROKE DRAIN
SMASH STRIP BROKEN BUSTED
DYVOUR QUISBY CRACKED
DEPLETE
BANKRUPTCY SMASH FAILURE
SMASHUP
BANKSMAN LANDER HILLMAN
BANLIEUE LOWY ENVIRONS
BANNER FANE FLAG JACK SIGN

COLOR ENSIGN FANNON PENNON
LABARUM LEADING PENNANT
SALIENT BANDEROL BRATTACH
FOREMOST GONFALON ORIFLAMB
STANDARD STREAMER VEXILLUM
BEAUSEANT ORIFLAMME
(— ON TRUMPET) TABARD
(FUNERAL —) BANNEROL
GUMPHEON GUMPHION
(PL.) ENSIGNRY
BANNOCK PANAK DIGGER
JANNOCK
BANNS CRY BANS CRIES NOTICE
SIBRET SIBRIT SIBREDE
SPURRINGS
BANQUET FETE MEAL DIFFA FEAST
DINNER JUNKET MANGER REGALE
REGALO REPAST SEUDAH SPREAD
AHAAINA CONVITO CONVIVE
NAMGERY REGALIO CAROUSAL
FESTIVAL SYMPOSIUM SYSSITION
BANQUETER CONVIVE
SYMPOSIAST
BANQUETING EPULATION
TRENCHERING
BANSHEE BOW SIDHE
BANTAM COCK GRIG BANTY
DANDY SAUCY CHICKEN
SEBRIGHT COMBATIVE
BANTENG OX TSINE BANTIN
TEMADAU
BANTER COD KID RAG ROT CHIP
FOOL JEST JOKE JOSH MOCK
QUIZ RAIL RAZZ BORAK CHAFF
DRAPE JOLLY QUEER RALLY
ROAST TAUNT TRICK DELUDE
DERIDE HAGGLE SATIRE BADINER
STASHIE BADINAGE CHAFFING
GIFFGAFF RAILLERY RIDICULE
BANTU ILA BULU GOGO GUHA
HEHE YAKA ZULU DUALA KAFIR
KAMBA KIOKO KONDE KONGO
LAMBA SHONA SWAZI BANYAI
BASUTO DAMARA HERERO KAFFIR
NATIVE THONGA WAGUHA
YAKALA CABINDA MASHONA
SWAHILI WACHAGA
(— LANGUAGE) ILA RONGA
NYANJA THONGA NYAMWEZI
BANYAN BUR BURR BANIYA
BUNNIA JAGUEY
BAOBAB MOWANA IMBONDO
TEBELDI CALABASH ADANSONIA
BAPTISM CLEANSING IMMERSION
PALINGENY PERFUSION
BAPTISMAL FONTAL
BAPTIST DIPPER DOPPER
DIDAPPER SEPARATE TRASKITE
BAPTIZE DIP DEPE FULL NAME
HEAVE VOLOW PLUNGE PURIFY
ASPERSE CLEANSE IMMERSE
CHRISTEN SPRINKLE
BAPTIZED ILLUMINATE
BAR BAN DAM FID FOX GAD LAW
LEG RIB ROD TAP AXLE BALK
BAND BANK BAUR BEAM BOLT
BOOM BULL CAKE CHAR CORE
CROW DRAG FLAT GATE HIDE
JOKE LOCK MAKE OUST POLE
RACK RAIL REEF SAVE SETT SHUT
SKID SLAB SLAT SLIP SLOT SNIB
STOP TREE YARD ARBOR BAULK
BENCH BETTY BILBO BLOCK

BLOOM BRACE CATCH CLASP
CLOSE COURT CRAMP CREEL
DEBAR DETER DOLLY EASER
EMBAR ESTOP FENCE FORCE
GEMEL HEDGE HORSE HUMET
LEVER PERCH PILOT PINCH PITCH
RANCE RATCH SHADE SHAFT
SHAPE SIGHT SLOTE SNEAK SPELL
SPOON SPRAG STAFF STANG
STAVE STEEK STRAP STRIP STRUT
SWIPE TRACE YAIRD ANCONY
BARRET BATTEN BILLET BISTRO
BODEGA BROOCH BUMPER
CRUTCH DOFFER DOLLEY DOLLIE
EVENER EXCEPT EYEBAR FASTEN
FORBAR FORBID FORCER FORSET
GRILLE HEAVER HINDER LADDER
MEAGRE NORMAN PEELER
RABBLE RADIAL RETURN RIFFLE
SALOON SHADES SHANTY
STOWER STRIPE TABLET TANGLE
TILLER TOGGLE BARRACE
BARRAGE BARRIER BOBSTAY
BOLSTER BUVETTE CHANNEL
CHARIOT CONFINE COUNTER
DRAWBAR EXCLUDE GALLOWS
MANDREL MANDRIL OVERARM
PREVENT SCRATCH SIDEBAR
SNIBBLE SPINDLE STEMMER
TOMBOLO TOPRAIL TRUNDLE
WIREBAR ASTRAGAL KNIFEWAY
MURDERER PESSULUS
(— FOR TAPPING FURNACE) LANCET
(— IN FABRIC) BARRE
(— IN RIVER) CHAR SANDBAR
(— IN SEA) SWASH
(— OF CULTIVATOR) ARCH
(— OF DOOR) SLOT STANG
(— OF ELECTRIC SWITCH) BLADE
(— OF GATE) SPAR LEDGE
(— OF HARROW) BULL
(— OF LOOM) EASER SWORD
BATTEN BACKSTAY
(— OF RAYS) SHOOT
(— OF STEEL) BLOOM BILLET
STIRRUP
(— OF WAGON) SHETH
(— ON SIDE OF BOWSPRIT)
WHISKER
(— ON WINDMILL) UPLONG
(— SUPPORTING MILLSTONE)
MOLINE
(— WITH SHACKLES) BILBOES
(— WITH SPIKES) HERISSON
(CAST IRON —) SOW
(CONNECTING —) ZYGON
(HERALDIC —) FESS FESSE HUMET
LABEL
(JOINTED —) CHILL
(MINING —) MOIL
(NOTCHED —) RISP SKEY
(PAIR OF —S) GEMEL GEMMEL
(REFRESHMENT —) BUFFET
CANTEEN
(SOAP FRAME —) SESS
(STIRRING —) CRUTCH
(TAMPING —) STEMMER
(TYPEWRITER —) BAIL BALE
SPACER SHUTTLE
(WEAVING —) TEMPLE
(WHEEL —) AXLE SPOKE
BARACHEL (SON OF —) ELIHU
BARAK (FATHER OF —) ABINOAM

BARANI BRANDY
BARB AWN BUR JAG MOW BURR
CLIP FILE FLUE HAIR HERL HOOK
JAGG BEARD HORSE POINT RIDGE
SHAFT SPEAR PIGEON STRAIN
TIPPET WITTER BARBARY
BARBULE BRISTLE FILAMENT
KINGFISH
(— OF ARROW) HOOK WING BEARD
WITTER
(— OF FEATHER) HARL HERL
RAMUS PINNULA FILAMENT
(— OF HARPOON) FLUE FLUKE
(PREF.) ONC(O)
BARBADOS (CAPITAL OF —)
BRIDGETOWN
(MOUNTAIN OF —) HILLARY
(NATIVE OF —) BIM
BARBADOS CHERRY ACEROLA
BARBAREA CAMPE
BARBARIAN HUN BOOR GOTH
RUDE WILD ALIEN BRUTE SAVAGE
VANDAL RUFFIAN FOREIGNER
UNTUTORED TRAMONTANE
BARBARIC GROSS ATROCIOUS
BARBARISM CANT DATISM
SAVAGISM SOLECISM
BARBARITY FERITY CRUELTY
FELLNESS FEROCITY RUDENESS
SAVAGERY BRUTALITY
BARBAROUS FELL RUDE WILD
CRUEL BRUTAL FIERCE GOTHIC
BESTIAL FOREIGN HUNNISH
INHUMAN SLAVISH UNCIVIL
IGNORANT CUTTHROAT
FEROCIOUS PRIMITIVE
BARBARY MAGOT MAGHRIB
MOGHRIB
(— STATE) TUNIS ALGIERS
MOROCCO TRIPOLI
BARBASCO CUBE JOEWOOD
BARBECUE ASADO BOCAN
BUCCAN
BARBEL BEARD CIRRUS WATTLE
BARBLET CYPRINID
BARBER NAI FIGARO POLLER
SHAVER TONSOR SCRAPER
TONSURE
(— FISH) TANG
BARBER OF BAGDAD (CHARACTER
IN —) ABUL BEKAR CALIPH
MARGIANA NUREDDIN
(COMPOSER OF —) CORNELIUS
BARBER OF SEVILLE (CHARACTER
IN —) BERTHA FIGARO ROSINA
BARTOLO LINDORO ALMAVIVA
(COMPOSER OF —) ROSSINI
BARBERRY MAHONIA
BARBET BARBION BARMKIN
DREAMER BARBICAN PUFFBIRD
WATERRUG IRONSMITH
PEARLBIRD THICKHEAD
TIGERBIRD
BARBITAL VERONAL
BARBITURATE DOWNER SECONAL
PENTOBARBITAL PHENOBARBITAL
BARBULE RADIUS RADIOLUS
BARCHESTER TOWERS (AUTHOR
OF —) TROLLOPE
(CHARACTER IN —) BOLD SLOPE
ARABIN BERTIE NERONI ELEANOR
GRANTLY HARDING OBADIAH
PROUDIE SEPTIMUS STANHOPE

CHARLOTTE ETHELBERT
QUIVERFUL
BARD BHAT MUSE POET SCOP
SWAN DRUID OVATE RUNER
SCALD SKALD OSSIAN SHAPER
SINGER BARDING PENBARD
MINSTREL MUSICIAN TALIESEN
DEMODOCUS SEANNACHIE
BARE DRY BALD LEAN MERE NUDE
POOR THIN ALONE BLEAK CRUDE
EMPTY NAKED PLAIN PLUME
SCANT STARK STRIP WASTE
BARISH BARREN CALLOW
DENUDE DIVERT DIVEST EXPOSE
HISTIE MARGIN MEAGER MEAGRE
PALTRY PILLED REVEAL SCARRY
SIMPLE DIVULGE EXPOSED
UNARMED UNCOVER DENUDATE
DESOLATE DISCLOSE STRIPPED
DESTITUTE
(— TEETH) TUCK
(NOT —) COOL
(PREF.) GYMN NUDI PSIL(O)
BAREFACED GLARING IMPUDENT
AUDACIOUS SHAMELESS
BARELY JIMP JUST ONLY FANIT
HARDLY MERELY POORLY SIMPLY
UNEATH UNNETH NAKEDLY
UNNETHE EDGEWAYS SCANTILY
SCARCELY SLIGHTLY
BARER NAVVY DELVER FEIGHER
MUCKMAN CALLOWER
BARFISH DORAB
BARGAIN GO BUY RUG WOD COPE
DEAL HUCK KOOP MART MISE
PACT PICK RUGG SALE SELL SNIP
SONG TROG WHIZ CHEAP FIGHT
PRICE STEAL TROKE TRUCK
WHACK WHIZZ BARTER DICKER
HAGGLE HIGGLE INDENT NIFFER
PALTER CHAFFER CHEAPEN
COMPACT CONTEND CONTEST
DISPOSE PACTION TRAFFIC
CONTRACT COVENANT
PENNORTH PURCHASE STRUGGLE
WANWORTH PENNYWORTH
(— HARD) PRIG
(— IN MINING) STURT
BARGAINER NIP KITE COPER
COWPER CHAFFERER
(SHARP —) SCREW
BARGAINING MART ACHATE
CHAFFER CHEAPING HUCKSTERY
BARGE ARK BOX BOY HOY TOW
TUB BARK BOAT FUST LUMP
PRAM RAFT SCOW TROW BARCA
CASCO DUMMY FOIST LUNGE
LURCH PRAAM SCOLD SHREW
VIXEN BARQUE BERATE BUGERO
DREDGE GALLEY GYASSA
PRAHAM REBUKE STUMPY
TENDER THRUST WHERRY
BALLOON BIRLING BIRLINN
CHALANA DROGHER GABBARD
GABBART GONDOLA LIGHTER
OMNIBUS TOWBOAT TUMBLER
TUMBRIL BILLYBOY BUDGEROW
CARRIAGE BUCENTAUR
MOORPUNKY
(COAL —) KEEL
(TOWED —) BUTTY
BARGEMAN PUG BARGEE BARGER
HOYMAN HUFFLER

BARGHEST PADFOOT
BARITE CAUK CAWK TIFF CAULK
BARYTES BARYTINE HEPATITE
BARK AGO BAG BAY OUF RUB TAN
WAP YAP YIP BAFF BOAT BOOF
COAT COTO DITA HOWL HUSK
OPEN PEEL PELT PILL REND RIND
ROSS SKIN SNAP TAPA WAFF
YAFF YAWP YELP YIPE AABEC
BALAT BARCA BARGE COUGH
MOCHA NIEPA SHELL SHOUT
SPEAK STRIP TIMBE YAMPH
YOUFF ABRADE AGAMID AVARAM
BARKEY BOWWOW CASSIA
CORNUS CORTEX GIRDLE MASSOY
SINTOC TRANKY WAFFLE YAFFLE
CASCARA MALAMBO MESENNA
PEREIRA PHLOEUM SOLICIT
TANBARK DOUNDAKE EUONYMUS
FRANGULA GRANATUM
MEZEREUM WOODSKIN
RHYTIDOME QUERCITEON
(AROMATIC —) CANELLA
CULILAWAN
(EXTERIOR OF —) ROSS
(INNER —) BAST
(LAYER OF —) HAT
(PREF.) CORTICI CORTICO PHELLO
PHLO(E)(EO) QUIN(O)
BARKER BUFFER DOORMAN
GRINDER SPIELER SPUDDER
SPRUIKER CHARLATAN
BARKING BAY SPUD QUEST
LATRANT LATRATION
BARLEY BIG BEAR BENT BERE BIGG
GRAIN SPRAT LICORN HORDEUM
WHITECORN
(AWN OF —) HORN
(GROUND —) TSAMBA
(HULLED —) PTISAN
(REFUSE —) SHAG FLINTS
(PREF.) ALPHITO CRITHO
BARLEY CAKE
(PREF.) MAZO
BARN BYRE AMBAR LATHE STALL
GRANGE STABLE SKIPPER
COWHOUSE
(— OWL) LULU MADGE
(COW —) SAUR SHIPPON
(PART OF —) BAY HIP DOOR EAVE
APRON GABLE RIDGE VERGE
AWNING CUPOLA DORMER
PENTHOUSE VENTILATOR
WEATHERVANE
BARNACLE BRAY BREY ACORN
LEPAS CYPRIS ANATIFA BALANID
LEPADID CIRRIPED GNATHOPOD
SACCULINA
BARNBURNER SOFT
BARNSTORM TOUR
BARNYARD PIGHTLE BACKSIDE
FARMYARD STRAWYARD
BAROMETER GLASS ANEROID
OROMETER STATOSCOPE
BARON THANE DAIMIO BARONET
FREEMAN FREIHERR
(COURT —) HALLMOOT
BARONY HAN DOMAIN
BAROQUE GOTHIC ORNATE
ROCOCO GROTESQUE IRREGULAR
BAROTO VINTA
BARRACK CAMP BOTHY CASERN
CANNABA CUARTEL

BARRACKS HOOCH HOOTCH
BARRACUDA CUDA KAKU SPET
BARRY PELON SNAKE SNOEK
SNOOK BECUNA PICUDA SCOOTS
SENNET VICUDA KATONKEL
SCOOTERS
BARRAGE BAR ATTACK VOLLEY
BARRIER DRUMFIRE UMBRELLA
CANNONADE FUSILLADE
BARRAMUNDA SALMON CYCLOID
DIPNOAN FLATHEAD CERATODUS
BARRED CUCKOO RIBBED STRIPED
BARREL FAT HUB KEG TUN VAT
BUTT CADE CASK DRUM KANG
TREE WOOD BOWIE QUILL SHELL
STAND UNION FESSEL GIRNAL
GIRNEL HOGGET RUMBLE RUNLET
TIERCE TUMBLE VESSEL CALAMUS
CISTERN PACKAGE RATTLER
RUNDLET TUMBLER CYLINDER
HOGSHEAD KILDERKIN
(— OF FEATHER) CALAMUS
(— OF REVOLVER) CHAMBER
(— ROW) LONGER
(— WITH CRANKS) VANGEE
(CAPSTAN —) SPOOL
(CORE —) LANTERN
(HERRING —) CADE CRAN
(PART OF —) HEAD HOOP CHIME
STAVE BOTTOM
(SMALL —) KEG KIT CADE KNAG
RUNLET BARRICO RUNDLET
(TAR —) CLAVIE
BARRELHOUSE GUTBUCKET
BARREN DRY ARID BARE BOWY
DEAD DEAF DOUR DULL FILD
GAST GELD LEAN NUDE POOR
SALT SECK YELD YELL ADDLE
BLEAK BLUNT BOWEY DRAPE
DUSTY EMPTY GAUNT GHAST
GUESS NAKED STARK STERN
WASTE YEILD DESERT EFFETE
FALLOW HISTIE HUNGRY JEJUNE
MEAGER STUPID SAPLESS
STERILE DESOLATE IMPOTENT
TEEMLESS TREELESS
(NOT —) FACILE FECUND
(PL.) LANDES
(PREF.) STEIRO
BARREN GROUND (AUTHOR OF —)
GLASGOW
(CHARACTER IN —) JASON RUFUS
GENEVA JOSIAH NATHAN OAKLEY
PEDLAR DORINDA ELLGOOD
GREYLOCK
BARRENNESS DEARTH VACANCY
EMPTINESS
BARRICADE BAR STOP BLOCK
CLOSE FENCE ABATIS PRISON
BARRAGE BARRIER DEFENSE
FORTIFY OBSTRUCT RAMFORCE
REVETMENT ROADBLOCK
(— OF TREES) ABATIS
BARRIER ALP BAR DAM BALK
BOMA CRIB CROY DIKE DOOR
DYKE FOSS GATE LINE LOCK PALE
STOP WALL WEIR BAULK BOUND
CHAIN FENCE FOSSE GRILL
HEDGE LIMIT STILE STUMP
CORDON GLACIS GRILLE HURDLE
SCREEN TREBLE BARRAGE
CEILING CHICANE CURTAIN
GALLERY PARAPET RAILING

RAMPART BOUNDARY FORTRESS FRONTIER STOCKADE STRENGTH TRAVERSE
(**— ACROSS RIVER**) STILL KIDDLE
(**— IN TRUCK**) HEADER
(**— OF TREES**) SHELTERBELT
(**ARTIFICIAL —**) FOSS FOSSE
(**PROTECTIVE —**) REDOUBT
(**TRAFFIC —**) SEPARATOR
(**PL.**) BAIL
(**PREF.**) HERCO
BARRING BUT SAVE CLOSED
BARRISTER COLT BARMAN JUNIOR LAWYER TUBMAN COUNSEL POSTMAN TEMPLAR ADVOCATE ATTORNEY SERJEANT
(**PL.**) BAR
BARROOM PUB CAFE HOUSE SALOON CANTINA DOGGERY GROCERY TAPROOM DRAMSHOP DRINKERY EXCHANGE GROGGERY GROGSHOP
BARROW HOD HOG BANK BIER DUNE GALT HILL MOTE TUMP CARRY GRAVE GURRY HURLY MOUND SEDAN TRUCK BURROW GALGAL KURGAN NAVETA HILLOCK TROLLEY TUMULUS MOUNTAIN PUSHCART
BARRULET VIVRE
BARTENDER MIXER BARMAN BARMAID SKINKER TAPSTER
BARTER CHAP CHOP COPE COUP HAWK MANG MONG SELL SWAP TROG VEND CORSE TRADE TROKE TRUCK DICKER NIFFER SCORSE BARGAIN CAMBIUM CHAFFER PERMUTE TRAFFIC TRUCKLE COMMERCE EXCHANGE TRUCKAGE
BARTERED BRIDE (**CHARACTER IN —**) JASEK JENIK KECAL MICHA TOBIAS MARENKA ESMERALDA
(**COMPOSER OF —**) SMETANA
BARTERER COPER COWPER TRUCKER
BARUCH (**FATHER OF —**) NERIAH ZABBAI COLHOZEH
BARYTES CAUK CAWK HEPATITE
BARZILLAI (**SON OF —**) ADRIEL
BASAL BASIC BASILAR RADICAL
BASALT MARBLE NAVITE DIABASE GHIZITE KULAITE POTTERY AUGANITE BANDAITE BASANITE DOLERITE ANAMESITE ARAPAHITE MELAPHYRE SUDBURITE VARIOLITE
(**DECOMPOSED —**) WACKE
BASE BED DEN HUB LOW TUT ANIL CLAM EVIL FOOT FOUL HUBB HUNK LEWD MEAN POOR RELY REST ROOT SACK STAY STEM STEP VILE BASIS BLOCK CHEAP DIRTY FIRST FLOOR FOUND LACHE MUDDY PETTY SNIDE SOCLE STAND STOOL WORSE ABJECT BOTTOM BRASSY COARSE COMMON DEMISS GROUND GRUBBY HARLOT HUMBLE MENIAL NOUGHT PALTRY PATAND PATTEN PERRON PODIUM RASCAL SECOND SHABBY SORDID VULGAR BASTARD

CAITIFF COMICAL CURRISH DEBASED FOOTING HANGDOG HILDING HOUSING IGNOBLE OUTPOST PEASANT ROINISH SERVILE SLAVISH STADDLE STANDER SUBBASE SUPPORT CHURLISH COISTREL COISTRIL DEGRADED DRAWHEAD HARLOTRY HOLDFAST INFAMOUS INFERIOR MECHANIC MESCHANT PEDESTAL PEDIMENT RASCALLY SCULLION SHAMEFUL STANDARD STEPPING SUBSTRAT UNWORTHY WRETCHED NIDDERING
(**— IN QUALITY**) LEADEN
(**— OF CANNON**) SOUL
(**— OF OPERATIONS**) BOOK HOME
(**— OF OVULE**) CHALAZA
(**— OF PETAL**) CLAW
(**— OF PLANT**) CAUDEX
(**— OF POLLINIUM**) DISC DISK
(**— OF ROCK**) MAGMA
(**— OF TUBER**) HEEL
(**CHEMICAL —**) ACRIDAN ADENINE ANSERIN CHOLINE GUANINE ACRIDANE ACTININE AGMATINE ALDIMINE ALKALOID ANSERINE CONYRINE GALEGINE KETIMINE LEPIDINE SEMIDINE
(**HIDDEN —**) LAIR
(**HOME —**) DEN
(**LEAF —**) FOVEA
(**LOGARITHM —**) E RADIX
(**SECOND —**) KEYSTONE
(**STALKLIKE —**) CNIDOPOD
(**PREF.**) BASI TAPIN(O)
(**SUFF.**) HEDRAL
BASEBALL PILL APPLE DUSTER FLOATER INSHOOT LEATHER BEANBALL HARDBALL HORSEHIDE STICKBALL
(**— PLAYER**) YANNIGAN
BASEBOARD GRIN SKIRT PLINTH EASEMENT MOPBOARD SKIRTING WASHBOARD
BASE-DEALING BROKING
BASELESS IDLE UNFOUNDED
BASEMAN SACKER
BASEMENT BASE CELLAR TAHKHANA
BASENESS FELONY VILITY BEGGARY SQUALOR TURPITUDE
BASH BAT LAM BEAT BLOW DENT MASH SWAT WHAM WHOP ABASH SLOSH SMASH BRUISE STRIKE
BASHEMATH (**FATHER OF —**) ISHMAEL
(**HUSBAND OF —**) ESAU
BASHFUL COY SHY HELO SHAN BLATE HELOE TIMID MODEST PUDENT ASHAMED DAUNTED BACKWARD BLUSHING DAPHNEAN DISMAYED LOATHFUL PUDIBUND RETIRING SACKLESS SHAMEFUL SHEEPISH SKITTISH VERECUND SHAMEFACED
BASHFULNESS PUDOR SHYNESS
BASIC NET BASE BASAL VITAL BOTTOM BEDROCK CANONIC CENTRAL CLASSIC PRIMARY ZINCOUS CARDINAL ULTIMATE

ELEMENTAL ESSENTIAL SUBSTRATE
BASIL TULASI
BASILICA (**PART OF —**) APSE BEMA NAVE AISLE ALTAR NARTHEX TRANSEPT
BASIN DOP PAN BOWL COMB COVE DISH DOCK EWER FLOW FONT GULF LAKE PARK SINK SLAD TALA TANK COMBE LAVER SLAKE STOUP BASSON BULLAN CHAFER CIRQUE HOLLOW LAVABO LEKANE LOUTER MARINA VALLEY VESSEL CUVETTE PISCINA RECEIPT URCEOLE BIRDBATH CESSPOOL LAVATORY RECEPTOR VANITORY WASHBOWL GEMELLION
(**DESERT —**) PLAYA
(**GEOLOGICAL —**) BOLSON
(**MOUNTAIN —**) HOYA PUNA
(**ROCK —**) KEEVE KIEVE
(**PREF.**) LECAN(O)
BASIS BASE FOND FOOT FORM FUND ROOT SILL AXIOM RADIX STOCK ANLAGE BOTTOM GROUND ACCOUNT BEDROCK FOOTING PREMISE SUPPORT GRAVAMEN STRENGTH AUTHORITY CRITERION FUNDAMENT GROUNDSEL SUBSTANCE
BASK SUN BEEK LAZE WARM ACRID BATHE ENJOY REVEL BITTER REJOICE APRICATE
BASKET IE ARK COB FAN HOT KIT LUG PAD PED PEG POT RIP TAP TOP BUCK CAUL COBB COOP CORB CORF CRIB FLAT GOAL HOTT IEIE KIPE KISH KIST KITT LEAP MAND MAUN SKEP TAPE TILL TOUR TRUG WEEL CABAS CASSY CESTA CHEST CRAIL CRASH CRATE CREEL DEVIL DILLI DILLY FRAIL GRATE MAUND MOLLY NATTE RUSKY SCULL SWILL WILLY BEACON BOKARK CASSIE CLEAVE COFFIN COURGE CRADLE DORSEL DORSER DOSSER FANNER FASCET GABION HAMPER HOBBET HOBBIT HOPPET JICARA JUNKET KIBSEY KIPSEY MOCOCK MOLLIE MURLIN PEGALL PETARA POTTLE PUNNET SEQUIN SERPET TAPPET TEANAL TOPNET VOIDER WINDEL WINDLE WISKET ZEQUIN CANASTA CORBEIL CRESSET FLASKET HANAPER MURLAIN PANNIER PATTARA PITARAH PRICKLE SCUTTLE SEEDLIP SHALLOW SKEOUGH SKIPPET WATTAPE WHISKET CALATHUS CANISTER CHEQUEEN ZECCHINO
(**— BOTTOM**) SLATH
(**— FOR CRUMBS**) VOIDER
(**— FOR EELS**) BUCK COURGE
(**— FOR FIGS**) TAP CABAS FRAIL TAPNET
(**— FOR FRUIT**) CALA MOLLY CALATHOS
(**FISH —**) CRAN HASK
(**PART OF —**) RIB RIM FOOT JOIN RAND SLEW WALE FITCH STAKE

UPSET BORDER HANDLE
BASKET MAKER ANASAZI
BASKETRY UPSET
BASKETWORK TEE SLEW WALE SLATH STAKE SLATHE STROKE SLEWING
BASMATH (**FATHER OF —**) SOLOMON
(**HUSBAND OF —**) AHIMAAZ
BASQUE VASCON EUSCARA EUSCARO IBERIAN BISCAYAN
(**— DIALECT**) LABOURDIN
(**PL.**) VASCONA VASCONES
BAS-RELIEF PLAQUETTE
BASS LOW PES CHUB DEEP DRUM FOOT ROCK BASSO DRONE HURON ROCHE SWEGO VOICE BORDUN BRASSE BURDEN CHERNA GROUND JUMPER REDEYE SINGER STRIPE ACHIGAN BARFISH BOURDON BROWNIE GROWLER JEWFISH STRIPER BACHELOR BIGMOUTH BLUEFISH CABRILLA CONTINUO ROCKFISH SPOTTAIL STREAKER TALLYWAG WELSHMAN LINESIDES
(**— DRUM**) TAMBURONE
(**— PART**) ALBERTI
(**GROUND —**) OSTINATO
(**LEADING —**) SUCCENTOR
(**THOROUGH —**) BC
BASSOON CURTAL FAGOTT BOMBARD FAGOTTE FAGOTTO
(**PART OF —**) BELL BOOT BUTT WING CROOK JOINT
BASSWOOD LIN BASS WAHOO LINDEN WICOPY DADDYNUT WHITEWOOD
BAST LIBER RAMIE PHLOEM NOSEBURN
BASTARD GET SOB BASE FALSE CANNON COWSON GALLEY HYBRID IMPURE MAMZER BYSPELL GETLING LOWBRED MONGREL WOSBIRD BANTLING BASEBORN MISBEGET NAMELESS SPURIOUS WHORESON
(**PREF.**) NOTH(O)
BASTE SEW BEAT CANE COOK DRUB LARD TACK FLAMB SAUCE CUDGEL JIPPER PUNISH STITCH THRASH
BASTION JETTY BULWARK LUNETTE MOINEAU
(**PART OF —**) FACE RAMP ANGLE FLANK GORGE CURTAIN BANQUETTE
BAT CAT HIT WAD BACK BAKE BATE BEAT CLUB FOWL GAIT JACK LUMP MASS SWAT TRAP WINK BANDY BATON BRICK CHUCK FUNGO HARPY PIECE SPREE STICK ALIPED BACKIE BASTON BEETLE CUDGEL DRIVER KALONG PADDLE POMMEL RACKET STRIKE STROKE WILLOW BAUCKIE FLUTTER JAVELIN MORMOPS NOCTULE VAMPIRE BLUDGEON ROUSETTE SEROTINE BARBASTEL REREMOUSE CHEIROPTER
(**PART OF —**) KNOB MEAT LABEL BARREL HANDLE SIGNATURE

(PREF.) NYCTERI
(SUFF.) NYCTERIS
BATAK (— DIALECT) TOBA
BATCH LOT BAKE BREW CAST CROP FINE MASS MESS SORT BUNCH FLOOR GROUP BAKING CHEESE MAKING BOILING BREWING FORMULA MIXTURE RAISING QUANTITY
(— OF EGGS) SETTING
(— OF GRAIN) GRIST
(— OF MAIL) SEPARATION
BATCHER BAGGER
BATE BAIT BEET PUER PURE GRAIN
BATELEUR BERGHAAN
BATEMAN DRENCHER
BATFISH ANGLER DIABLO MALTHE DEVILFISH
BATH DIP TUB BAIN BATE PERT TOSH BATHE LAVER STEEP THERM BAGNIO DOUCHE LIQUOR MIKVAH PICKLE PLUNGE SHOWER SPONGE BALNEUM LAVACRE ABLUTION BALNEARY
(FOOT —) PEDILUVIUM
(HOT —) STEW SCALD STUFE THERM STUPHE THERME
(MUD —) ILLUTATION
(PHOTOGRAPHIC —) FIXER
(SITZ —) BIDET SITZBAD SEMICUPE INSESSION
(SPINNING —) DOPE
(STEAM —) SAUNA
(TANNING —) BATE SOAK
(TURKISH —) HAMMAM HUMMUM HOTHOUSE
(PREF.) BALNE(O)
BATHE BAY TUB BAIN BASK DOOK LAVE STEW WASH CLEAN DOUSE DOWSE EMBAY SOUSE STEEP ENWRAP FOMENT SHOWER SPLASH EMBATHE IMMERSE PERVADE SUFFUSE PERMEATE
BATHHOUSE SEW STEW SAUNA STUFE BAGNIO CABANA HAMMAM STUPHE BALNEARY
BATHING LAVACRE LAVEMENT
(— SUIT) SLIP TOGS MAILLOT
(SAND —) SABURRATION
BATHROBE PEIGNOIR
BATHROOM BIFFY BALNEARY
BATHSHEBA (FATHER OF —) ELIAM AMMIEL
(HUSBAND OF —) DAVID URIAH
(SON OF —) NATHAN SHIMEA SHOBAB SOLOMON
BATHTUB TUB TOSH LAVACRE
BATIA (FATHER OF —) TEUCER
(HUSBAND OF —) DARDANUS
(SON OF —) HIPPOCOON ERICHTHONIUS
BATON ROD BEND BURN WAND STAFF STICK BAGUET BASTON CUDGEL BOURDON SCEPTER SCEPTRE BAGUETTE CROSSBAR TRUNCHEON
BATSMAN BAT BATTER HITTER SLOGGER SLUGGER STRIKER
BATTALION WARD CONREY
BATTEN END LAY RIB SLEY CLEAT LEDGE BATTON BEATER ENRICH FATTEN REEPER THRIVE FERTILIZE

(PL.) SPARRING
BATTER RAM BEAT DENT MAIM MAUL CLOUR DINGE FRUSH PASTE POUND SMASH BALLER BRUISE BUFFET HAMMER HATTER HITTER PUMMEL THRING TUMBLE BATSMAN BOMBARD CRIPPLE DESTROY FRITTER SHATTER SLUGGER STRIKER DEMOLISH
BATTERCAKE WAFFLE CRUMPET
BATTERING BLAST LACING
BATTERY PILE SINK TIRE TROOP RADEAU EXCITER SINKBOX SINKBOAT ACCUMULATOR
(GUN —) SWINGER
BATTLE WAR CAMP DUEL FEUD FRAY MART MEET TILT TOIL UNDO BRUSH FIELD FIGHT JOUST STOUR ACTION AFFAIR AFFRAY CAMLAN COMBAT SHOWER STRIVE CONTEND CONTEST HOSTING JOURNAL JOURNEY WARFARE CONFLICT SKIRMISH STRUGGLE ENCOUNTER NAUMACHIA THEOMACHY
(PREF.) MACHO
(SUFF.) MACHIA MACHY
BATTLE-AX WIFLE POLEAX SPARTH TWIBIL BROADAX HALBERD TWIBIL WHIFFLE FAUCHARD FRANCISC
BATTLE CRY CRY BANZAI ENSIGN GERONIMO SLUGHORN BEAUSEANT
BATTLEFIELD ARENA BLAIR CHAMP TAHUA CHAMPAIGN
BATTLEGROUND COCKPIT TERRAIN
BATTLEMENT KERNEL MERION PINION BARMKIN CORNELLE MURDRESS
(PART OF —) CRENEL MERLON MACHIOLATION
BATTLE OF LEGNANO
(CHARACTER IN —) LIDA ARRIGO ROLANDO FREDERICK BARBAROSSA
(COMPOSER OF —) VERDI
BATTLESHIP MAINE CARRIER
BATTUS (FATHER OF —) POLYMNESTUS
(MOTHER OF —) PHRONIMA
BATTY BATS BUGGY CRAZY SILLY BATLIKE FOOLISH
BAUBLE BOW TOY BEAD GAUD BUTTON GEWGAW TRIFLE MAROTTE TRINKET GIMCRACK PLAYTHING
BAWD AUNT HARE DIRTY MADAM DEFILE MADAME PANDER COMMODE MACKEREL PROCURER PURVEYOR
BAWDINESS RAUNCH
BAWDRY SCULDUDDERY
BAWDY LEWD DIRTY SCARLET
BAWL CRY HOWL ROAR ROUT YAUP YAWP BLORE GOLLY SHOUT BELLOW BOOHOO GOLLAR OUTCRY GLAISTER
(— OUT) JUMP CRACK SCOLD
BAY ARM COD DAM RIA VOE BANK BARK CHOP COVE GULF HOLE HOPE HOWL LOCH ROAN TREE

WICK YAUP YAWP BAHIA BASIN BAYOU BERRY BIGHT COLOR CREEK FIORD FJORD FLEET HAVEN HORSE INLET LOUGH MOUTH ORIEL QUEST SINUS SPEAK TRAVE BABBLE HARBOR LAUREL RECESS SEVERY TONGUE WINDOW BADIOUS BAYGALL ENCLOSE ESTUARY MALABAR SILANGA ULULATE BREWSTER CHESTNUT
(— OF BARN) GOAF SKEELING SKILLING SKILLION
(— OF LIBRARY) CLASSIS
(— STATE) MASSACHUSETTS
(SWEET —) BREWSTER BEAVERWOOD
BAYBERRY AUSU PIMIENTA WAXBERRY
BAYOU SLEW SLOO SLUE BROOK CREEK INLET RIVER OUTLET SLOUGH STREAM RIVULET BACKWATER
BAY WINDOW ORIEL MIRADOR
BAZAAR FAIR FETE SALE AGORA BURSE CHAWK CHOWK MARKET ALCAZAR CANTEEN BOOKFAIR EMPORIUM BEZESTEEN
BDELLIUM GUGAL GUGUL GOOGUL
BE ABE AER BES BEEN BETH BIST LIVE ABIDE EXIST OCCUR WORTH REMAIN BREATHE CONSIST SUBSIST CONTINUE
BEACH AIR BANK CHIP MOOR NARD RIPA SAND SLIP COAST PLAGE PLAYA PRAYA SHORE GROUND SHILLA STRAND HARDWAY SEASIDE SHINGLE LAKESHORE
(— RIDGE) FULL
(PROJECTING —) CUSP
(SANDY —) MACHAIR
(PREF.) THIN(O)
BEACH APPLE CANAJONG
BEACHCOMBER SEASONER STRANDLOOPER
BEACHED AGROUND
BEACH FLEA SCUD SCREW SANDBOY
BEACH GRASS STAR SPIRE MARRAM BENTSTAR
BEACON MARK PIKE SIGN BAKEN FANAL GUIDE PHARE RACON ENSIGN PHAROS RAMARK SIGNAL CRESSET SEAMARK WARNING BALEFIRE NEEDFIRE SIGNPOST STANDARD
BEAD NIB POT DROP FOAM GAUD AGGRI AGGRY BUGLE FILET GRAIN KNURL PEARL QUIRK SIGHT STAFF ARANGO BAGUET BAUBLE BICONE BUBBLE CORNET FILLET PELLET PIPPER POPPET PRAYER RONDEL WAMPUM CABLING DEWDROP GLOBULE MOLDING SPARKLE TRINKET AVEMARIA CABOCHON
(ROSARY —) GAUD PATERNOSTER
(SHELL —S) SEWAN
BEADING VEINING
(PL.) TASBIH
BEADLE CRIER MACER POKER USHER BEDRAL BUMBLE HARMAN

HERALD BAILIFF NUTHOOK OFFICER SERVITOR SUMMONER APPARITOR MESSENGER
BEADSMAN BEGGAR HERMIT BLUEGOWN GOWNSMAN
BEAK NEB NIB BECK BILL CLAP NOSE PIKE PROW LORUM SNOUT SWORD TUTEL MASTER NOZZLE SPERON WEAPON EMBOLON EMBOLUM FOREBOW MOLDING ROSTRUM BEAKHEAD MANDIBLE CAPITULUM
(— OF SHELL) UMBO
(— OF SHIP) SPERON
(— OF SWORDFISH) SWORD
(PREF.) RHAMPH(O) RHYNCH(O) ROSTR(I)(O)
(SUFF.) RHYNCHUS RHYNCUS ROSTRAL
BEAKED NASUTE
BEAKER CUP HORN TASS BIKER BOCAL BOUSE GLASS BARECA
BEAM BAR LEG RAY TIE BALK BEAK BOOM EMIT GLOW PLAT SILE SILL SKID SPAR STUD ARBOR BAULK CABER FLASH GLEAM GLEED JOIST LIGHT RAYON SHAPE SHINE SHOOT SMILE SPEAR STANG STOCK TRAVE BINDER BULKER CAMBER CHEESE CULVER FLITCH GIRDER GLANCE HEADER MANTEL NEEDLE RAFTER SUMMER TIMBER TRABES TREVIS WALKER BALANCE BUMPKIN CATHEAD CHANNEL CHEVRON DORMANT DRAWBAR FRIJOLE MADRIER PINRAIL RADIATE SLEEPER SUPPORT TRANSOM TRIMMER TYNDALL AXLETREE BROWPOST HERISSON PADSTONE PLOWHEAD ROOFTREE STENTREL TEMPLATE BRESSUMMER
(— OF LIGHT) CHINK GLEED RAYON SHAFT PENCIL SIGNAL STREAM SUNBEAM STRICTURE
(HIGH —) BRIGHTS
(LARGE —) BALK LACE BAULK SUMMER
(LOW —) DIM
(SANIO'S —) CRASSULA
(WEAVER'S —) TRAM TAVIL
(PL.) CRANEWAY
(PREF.) DOCO
BEAMER SCUDDER
BEAMING GAY ROSY BRIGHT LUCENT MASSIVE RADIANT SHINING
BEAMY BROAD BRIGHT JOYOUS LUCENT MASSIVE RADIANT MIRTHFUL
BEAN BON NIB URD CHAP FABA FAVA GRAM HABA HEAD LIMA POLE SNAP TEKE TICK BRAIN CARAT PULSE SIEVA SKULL CACOON CASTER COLLAR FELLOW KIDNEY LABLAB LENTIL NIPPLE NOGGIN RUNNER RUTTEE SEEWEE STRIKE TEPARY THRASH TRIFLE CALABAR FRIJOLE MAZAGAN PHASEMY SNAPPER WINDSOR BONAVIST BONNYVIS RAMBUTAN TICKBEAN TORNILLO
(— CURD) TOFU

(LOCUST —) CAROB
(MESCAL —) SOPHORA
(PL.) NIBS FASELS FESELS
PODDER PODWARE
(PREF.) FABI
BEANIE DINK
BEAN-SHAPED FABIFORM
BEANSHOOTER TRUNK
PEASHOOTER
BEAN TREE BOGUM
BEAN TREFOIL LABURNUM
BEAR GO CUB LUG BALU BERN
BORN CAST DREE DUBB FURE
GEST GIVE HAVE HOLD LIFT TEEM
TOTE URSA WEAR ABEAR ABIDE
ALLOW BALOO BEGET BHALU
BREED BRING BROOK BROWN
BRUIN CARRY DREIE DRIVE GESTE
ISSUE KOALA POLAR PRESS
SPARE STAND STICK THOLE
THROW WEIGH WIELD YIELD
AFFORD BEHAVE BRUANG
CONVEY ENDURE IMPORT INFANT
KADIAK KINDLE KODIAK PIERCE
RENDER SUFFER THRUST UPHOLD
URSULA WOMBAT WOOBUT
ABROOKE ARCTOID BROWNIE
COMPORT CONDUCT EPHRAIM
FORBEAR GRIZZLY MUSQUAW
PRODUCE STOMACH SUPPORT
SUSTAIN UNDERGO FISSIPED
SILVERTIP
(— EXPENSES) DEFRAY
(— FLOWERS) FLOURISH
(— FRUIT) FRUCTIFY
(— INVESTIGATION) WASH
(— ON) CONCERN
(— OUT) PROPORT
(— PATIENTLY) DIGEST
(— UP) CAPE ENDURE SUSTAIN
(— WITH CREDIT) BROOK
(— WITNESS) TEEM SPEAK ATTEST
DEPOSE
(— YOUNG) FIND CALVE CHILD
(MALE —) BOAR
(SLOTH —) ASWAIL
(PREF.) ARCT(O) URSI
(SUFF.) FER(ENCE)(ENT)(OUS)
GEN(E)(ESIA)(ESIS)(ETIC)(IC)
(IN)(OUS)(Y) GER(ENCE)(ENT)(OUS)
BEARBERRY LARB WHORTLE
BILBERRY DOGBERRY FOXBERRY
CREASHAKS
BEARD ANE AWN AVEL BARB DEFY
FACE FUZZ NECK NOSE PEAK
TUFT ZIFFS ARISTA BEAVER
GOATEE TASSEL AFFRONT
BARBULE CHARLEY CHARLIE
VANDYKE IMPERIAL STILETTO
WHISKERS BILLYGOAT
(— OF GRAIN) AIL AWN
(— TREATISE) POGONOLOGY
(SMALL —) BARBET
(PREF.) ATHERO POGON(O)
(SUFF.) POGON
BEARDED AWNIE HAIRY BARBED
BARBATE HIRSUTE POGONIATE
WHISKERED
BEARDLESS NOT NOTT IMBERBE
POLLARD
BEARDTONGUE PENSTEMON
BEARER NEWS HAMAL MACER
BEADLE HAMMAL HOLDER

PACKER PORTER ANCIENT
CARRIER JAMPANI PINCERN
CHAPRASI ESCUDERO PORTATOR
STANDARD MESSENGER
SUPPORTER
(— OF GREAT BURDEN) ATLAS
(ARMOR —) ESQUIRE
(BURDEN —) HAMAL HAMMAL
(CROZIER —) CROCIARY
(CUP —) SAKI COPPER
(PALANQUIN —) BOY SIRDAR
MUSAHAR
(SHIELD —) SQUIRE ESCUDERO
(STANDARD —) ANCIENT
(STRETCHER —) BRANCARDIER
(SWORD —) PORTGLAVE
PORTGLAIVE
(PREF.) PORTE
BEARING AIM AIR COD BALL DUCT
GEST MIEN ORLE PORT RUBY
BIRTH FRONT GESTE HABIT
JEWEL POISE SETUP TENUE
TREND ALLURE APPORT ASPECT
BILLET CHARGE COURSE DEPORT
GERENT GIGLIO MANNER ORIENT
SADDLE THRUST VOIDER
ADDRESS AZIMUTH CONDUCT
FASHION GESTURE MEANING
POSTURE PURPORT RHODING
SUPPORT AMENANCE ATTITUDE
BEHAVIOR BIRTHING CARRIAGE
DELIVERY DEMEANOR FOOTSTEP
PEDESTAL PRESENCE PRESSURE
RELATION STANDARD TENDENCY
TOURNURE YIELDING REFERENCE
(— FRUIT) FRUCTED
(— OUTWARD) EFFERENT
(ARROGANT —) HUFF
(HERALDIC —) GAD DELF ENTE
GORE MARK ORLE PALL WEEL
CROWN DELFT DELPH FUSIL
LAVER PHEON BILLET DEVICE
ENSIGN GOUTTE CHAPLET
CLARION DEMIVOL PLASQUE
QUARTER ORDINARY QUENTISE
TRESSURE
(PERSONAL —) GARB
(PREF.) PHOR(O)
(SUFF.) GEROUS IGEROUS PARA
PAROUS PHORA PHORE(SIS)
PHORIA PHOROUS PHORUS
BEARLIKE URSINE
BEAR'S-EAR AURICULA
BEAR'S-FOOT OXHEAL PEGROOTS
BEARSKIN BUSBY
BEAR STATE ARKANSAS
BEAST BETE HOOF BRUTE VACHE
ANIMAL JUMENT MONSTER
MUSIMON VENISON BEHEMOTH
BLIGHTER OPINICUS
(— OF BURDEN) JUMENT SUMPTER
(CASTRATED —) SPADO
(DEAD —) MORKIN
(FABULOUS —) YALE THRIS
BAGWYN TRICORN DINGMAUL
EPIMACUS OPINICUS GYASCUTUS
(HORNED —) RETHER ROTHER
(STURDY —) NUGGET
(WILD —) FERIN FERINE OUTLAW
UNBEAST
(WILD —S) ZIIM
(3-HORNED —) TRICORN
(PREF.) THER(A)(IO)(O)

(SUFF.) THERE THERIA THERIUM
BEASTLY GROSS PRONE ANIMAL
BRUTAL WICKED BESTIAL
BRUTISH INHUMAN SWINISH
OFFENSIVE
BEAT BAT BUM COB DAD FAN FIB
LAM PIP PLY PUG PUN RUN TAN
TAP TAW TEW TIE WAX BAFF
BAIT BANG BASH BATE BELT BEST
BLOW BOLT BRAY BUFF CANE
CAST CHAP CLAP CLUB COIL
COLT COMB CRAB DAUD DING
DINT DRUB DUMP DUNT FELL
FIRK FLAP FLAX FLOG FRAM FRAP
FRAT GROW HAZE JOWL KILL
LACE LAMP LASH LICK LOUK
LUMP LUSH MAUL MELL MEND
MILL PAIK PALE PANT PELT POLT
POSS PRAT ROUT SCAT SLAM
SLAT SLOG SOCK SOLE SOWL
STUB SWAP SWOP TACK TAKD
TICK TRIM TUCK TUND TWIG
WALK WARP WELT WHIP WHOP
WIPE BANDY BASTE BATON
BEPAT BERRY BIRCH BLESS
CHURN CLINK CREAM CURRY
DOUSE DRASH DRESS DRIVE
FEEZE FIGHT FILCH FLAIL FLANK
FORGE ICTUS INLAY KNOCK
LABOR NEVEL NOINT POUND
PULSE PUNCH ROUGH ROUND
SCATT SCOOP SCOUR SKELP   ·
STAMP STRAP SWACK SWING
TARGE THREP THROB THUMP
TREAD TRUMP UPEND WADDY
WHACK WHANG WORST ACCENT
ANOINT BAMBOO BATTER BENSEL
BETTLE BOUNCE BUFFET COTTON
CUDGEL DEFEAT DOWSEL
FEAGUE FETTLE HAMMER
HAMPER JACKET KNEVEL LARRUP
LATHER NEAVIL NODDLE OUTRUN
PUMMEL RADDLE REBUKE REESLE
RHYTHM SCUTCH SQUASH
STOUND STOUSH STRIKE STRIPE
STROKE SUGGIL SWINGE SWITCH
TANSEL TEWTAW TEWTER
THRASH THREAP THREIP THREPE
THRESH TICKLE WAGGLE WALLOP
WATTLE WUTHER ASSAULT
BATTUTA BELABOR BLATTER
BLISTER CADENCE CANVASS
CONQUER CONTUSE EXHAUST
FATIGUE FLYFLAP KNUCKLE
LAMBACK LAMBAST LOBTAIL
LOUNDER PULSATE REESHIE
SHELLAC SURPASS SWABBLE
SWADDLE TROLLOP TROUNCE
VIBRATE MALLEATE PALPITATE
SPIFLICATE
(— ABOUT) BUSK BANGLE
(— AGAINST) BLAD
(— AGAINST THE WIND) LAVEER
(— BACK) REBUFF
(— BARLEY) PAIL WARM
(— CLOTHES) BATTLE
(— COVERT) TUFT
(— DOWN) LAY FELL FULL ABATE
FLASH
(— EGGS) CAST
(— FIBERS) BRUSH
(— HIGH) LEAP
(— IT) LAM

(— OF DRUM) RUFF RAPPEL
RATTAN
(— OF HEART) DUNT STROKE
(— ON BUTTOCKS) COB
(— SEVERELY) DRUB LUMP SOAK
BASTE SOUSE LATHER
(— SMALL) CHAP
(— TO AND FRO) BANDY
(— TO WINDWARD) LAVEER
(— WINGS) BATE FLAP
(— WITH HAMMER) DOLLY
(— WITH WHIP) SJAMBOK
(— WOODS) TUSK
(MUSICAL —) BOUNCE BATTUTA
(WEAK —) ARSIS
(PREF.) TYPTO
BEATEN BEAT BETE BATTU PARTY
TRITE TRADED
BEATER RAB MAUL SEAL CANER
LACER STOCK DASHER DRIVER
MALLET TRIMMER SCUTCHER
THRESHER
BEATIFIC DEIFIC ELYSIAN
BEATIFY SAINT HALLOW HEAVEN
ENCHANT GLORIFY SANCTIFY
BEATING COB COBB LICK TUND
BEANS DOUSE JESSE PULSE STICK
HAZING HIDING ROPAND TATTOO
BASHING BATTERY BELTING
CLANKER DASHING DUSTING
LICKING SKELPIN WELTING
WHALING BIRCHING DRESSING
DRUBBING RIBROAST SLOSHING
WHIPPING JACKETING
STRAPPADO PERCUSSION
BEATITUDE JOY BLISS BENISON
MACARISM HAPPINESS
**BEATRICE DI TENDA (CHARACTER
IN —)** AGNESE FILIPPO BEATRICE
VISCONTI OROMBELLO
(COMPOSER OF —) BELLINI
**BEATRICE ET BENEDICT
(CHARACTER IN —)** HERO CLAUDIO
BEATRICE BENEDICT SOMARONE
(COMPOSER OF —) BERLIOZ
BEAU BEW BOY CHAP BLADE
DANDY FLAME LOVER SPARK
SWELL ADONIS ESCORT FELLOW
GARCON STEADY SUITOR TATTLE
ADMIRER AIMWELL BRAVERY
COURTER COXCOMB CUPIDON
GALLANT SPARKER FOLLOWER
BEAU GREGORY COCKEYE
BEAUTIFUL FAIR FINE GLAD GOOD
MEAR MEER MERE WALY BELLE
BONNY KALON LUSTY SHEEN
WLITY WLONK BLITHE BONNIE
COMELY DECORE FREELY LOVELY
POETIC PRETTY VENUST ANGELIC
ELEGANT FORMOSE FORMOUS
TEMPEAN TOKALON CHARMING
DELICATE ESTHETIC FAIRSOME
GORGEOUS GRACEFUL
HANDSOME LUCULENT SPECIOUS
MAGNIFICENT
(PREF.) CALI CALLI CALLO CALO
PULCHRI
BEAUTIFY FAIR GILD ADORN
GRACE HIGHT PREEN PRIMP
PRUNE BEAUTY BEDECK DECORE
ENAMEL QUAINT ADONIZE
ENHANCE GARNISH GLORIFY
DECORATE FAIRHEAD

EMBELLISH PULCHRIFY
BEAUTY FACE FAIR FORM GLEE
BEAUT BELLE CHARM FAVOR
GLORY GRACE PRIDE WLITE
FINERY LOOKER LOVELY POLISH
DECORUM FEATURE TOKALON
SPLENDOR FORMOSITY
(— OF FORM) SYMMETRY
(— OF STYLE) ELEGANCE
(PREF.) CALI CALLI CALLO CALO
PULCHRI
BEAVER BOOMER CASTOR RODENT
PRALINE MUSHROOM SEWELLEL
STARLING
(— SKIN) PLEW
(— STATE) OREGON
(DARK —) NUTMEG
BEBAI (SON OF —) ZECHARIAH
BEBEERINE CURINE
BEBEERU SWEETWOOD
GREENHEART
BECAUSE AS SO FOR THAT BEING
CAUSE SINCE THERE FORWHY
THROUGH INASMUCH
BECCAFICO FIGEATER FIGPECKER
BECHE-DE-MER PIDGIN TREPANG
BECHER (FATHER OF —) EPHRAIM
BENJAMIN
BECHORATH (FATHER OF —)
APHIAH
BECK RUN VAT BECON BROOK
(— AND CALL) DEVOTION
BECKEN CYMBALS
BECKET SQUILGEE SQUILLGEE
BECKON BOW NOD WAG BECK
WAFT WAVE CURTSY SUMMON
BIDDING COMMAND CURTSEY
GESTURE
BECKONING WAFTURE
BECLOUD HIDE MASK BEDIM
DARKEN MUDDLE MYSTIFY
OBSCURE OBNUBILATE
BECLOUDED FOGGY
BECOME GO FIT GET RAX SET SIT
WAX COME FALL GROW LIKE
PASS SUIT TAKE TILL WEAR
ADORN BEFIT GRACE PROVE
WORTH ACCORD BEFALL BESEEM
BETIDE CHANGE IWORTH
BEHOOVE FLATTER PROCEED
(— A PARTY) ACCEDE
(— AUDIBLE) ARISE
(— DAMP) EVE
(— DAZED) DWAM DWALM
(— DIM) DASWEN
(— DROWSY) DOW
(— FAT) GRAZE
(— FLUID) FLOW FLUX LEACH
(— KNOWN) GO KITHE KYTHE
SPUNK
(— MOLDY) FUST MOUL FINEW
(— MOROSE) SOUR
(— ROUND) GLOBE
(— SOUR) FOX BLINK CARVE
(SUFF.) IZE
BECOMING FIT FEAT GOOD BHAVA
FITTY RIGHT COMELY DUEFUL
GAINLY PROPER DECORUM
FARRAND FARRANT DECOROUS
HANDSOME SUITABLE WISELIKE
(SUFF.) ESCENT
(PROCESS OF —) ESCENCE
(STATE OF —) ESCENCE

BECOMINGLY TALLY
BED COT HAY KIP PAD PAN TYE
BAND BASE BODY BUNK DOSS
DOWN FLOP FORM LAIR PLOT
SACK VEIN WADI WADY BERTH
BOIST COUCH FLASK FLOCK
GRATE GROVE LAYER ROOST
THORE BORDER BOTTOM COUCHE
CRADLE GIRDLE HOTBED LIBKEN
LIBKIN LITTER MATRIX OSIERY
PALLET STRATA CHANNEL
CHARPOY FLEABAG HAMMOCK
LODGING QUARTER REPOSAL
SEEDBED SETTING STRATUM
SUBSOIL TRUCKLE TRUNDLE
BASSINET CAPSTONE LENTICLE
PLANCHER SHAKEDOWN
(— DOWN) DOSS
(— IN WAGON) KATEL
(— OF ANIMAL) LAIR KENNEL
(— OF CLAY) CLOD
(— OF COAL) BRAT DELF SEAM
(— OF EMBERS) GRIESHOCH
(— OF FIRE CLAY) THILL
(— OF FURNACE) HEARTH
(— OF GUN-CARRIAGE) FLASK
(— OF HAND PRESS) COFFIN
(— OF OYSTERS) PLANT
(— OF REFUSE) NITRIARY
(— OF ROCK) CAP PLUM
(— OF ROSES) ROSARY
(— OF SEDIMENT) WARP
(— OF SHELLFISH) BANK
(— OF STONES) SHINGLE
(— OF STREAM) DRAW WASH
NULLAH BILLABONG STREAMWAY
(CREEK —) COULEE COULIE
(DRIED LAKE —) CHOTT SEBKA
SHOTT
(FEATHER —) TIE TYE
(FOLDING —) SLAWBANK
(LOW —) LOWBOY
(OYSTER —) STEW LAYER SCALP
CLAIRE LAYING OYSTERAGE
(RUBBLE —) CALLOW
(SEED —) SEMINARY
(WATER-BEARING —) AQUAFER
AQUIFER
(WOODEN —) RUSTBANK
(PREF.) CLIN(O) STRATI STROMATI
STROMATO
(SUFF.) STROMA
BEDAD (SON OF —) HADAD
BEDAN (FATHER OF —) GILEAD
BEDAUB CLAG CLAT DAUB MOIL
SOIL SLAKE SMEAR PARGET
SLUBBER SLAISTER BEPLASTER
BEDBUG BUG CHINK CIMEX
CHINCH CHINTZ COREID PUNESE
VERMIN CIMICID PUNAISE
REDCOAT CONENOSE HEMIPTER
HOUSEBUG
BEDCHAMBER RUELLE BEDROOM
CUBICLE
BEDCLOTHES COVER BEDDING
CLOTHES
BEDCOVER COMFORTER
PALAMPORE
BEDDING BEDROLL DOMESTICS
BEDECK GEM BEDO LARD TRAP
ADORN ARRAY DIGHT GRACE
PRINK ORNAMENT EMBELLISH
BEDECKED PRINKY

BEDEIAH (FATHER OF —) BANI
BEDEVIL ABUSE ANNOY BESET
WORRY HARASS MUDDLE PESTER
BEWITCH CONFUSE TORMENT
BEDEW DEW SHOWER EMBATHE
IRRORATE
BEDIZEN DAUB ADORN ARRAY
DIZEN BEDAUB
BEDLAM RIOT NOISE RUDAS
ASYLUM TUMULT UPROAR
MADNESS MADHOUSE
BETHLEHEM
BEDOUIN ABSI ARAB BEDU MOOR
NOMAD BADAWI BEDAWEE
SHAMMAR HOWEITAT
BEDQUILT POURPOINT
BEDRAGGLE DAG TRACHLE
BEDRAGGLED FORLORN
SHOPWORN
BEDRAIL RAVE RATHE
BEDRIDDEN ILL AILING BEDFAST
(NOT —) AFOOT
BEDROCK LEDGE NADIR SHELF
BOTTOM HARDPAN STONEHEAD
BEDROLL BINDLE
BEDROOM FLAT BERTH CABIN
BEDDER DORMER BOUDOIR
CHAMBER CUBICULO WARDROBE
GARDEROBE
BEDSORE ANACLISIS DECUBITUS
BEDSPREAD ALEZE STRAIL
BEDCOVER COVERLET COVERLID
BEDSTEAD BED COT CRIB HATCH
STEAD STAPLE ANGAREP
CHARPOY
BEDSTRAW CRUDWORT
CURDWORT FLEAWEED
BEDFLOWER CROSSWORT
SCRAMBLER
BED TESTER SPARVER
BEDWARMER CURATE
BEE DOR FLY APIS BEVY KING RING
KARBI MASON NOMIA NURSE
PARTY DINGAR DRONEL DRONER
FROLIC INSECT NOTION TORQUE
TSETSE WORKER ANDRENA
DEBORAH KOOTCHA MELISSA
RAISING SERPENT STINGER
SWERVER TRIGONA ANDRENID
ANGELITO HONEYBEE QUILTING
SCOPIED SHUCKING WAXMAKER
GATHERING
(QUEEN —) KING
(PL.) BEEN BONE HIVE SPEW
SOCIALES
(PREF.) API
BEEBREAD CERAGO AMBROSIA
BEECH BUCK BIRCH MYRTLE
FLINDOSA FLINDOSY
(PREF.) FAGI FAGO
BEECHNUT SPLITNUT
(PL.) BUCK MAST PANNAGE
BEEF JERK BEEVE BULLY GRIPE
JERKY VIFDA VIVDA CASSON
CUTTER CHARQUI TOPSIDE
COMPLAIN COMPOUND PASTRAMI
PIPIKAULA
(— FOR SLAUGHTER) MART
(BOILED —) BOUILLI
(BROILED —) CHURRASCO
(CORN —) BULLY
(CUT OF —) SEY LOIN RUMP SIDE
BARON CHINE CHUCK FLANK

ROAST ROUND SHANK STEAK
ALOYAU CUTLET SADDLE BRISKET
KNUCKLE QUARTER SIRLOIN
EDGEBONE SHOULDER
AITCHBONE NINEHOLES
RATTLERAN
(GROUND —) HAMBURGER
(INFERIOR —) COMPOUND
(JERKED —) TASAJO BILTONG
CHARQUE CHARQUI
(LEAN —) LIRE
(SALTED —) JUNK VIFDA
BEEF BREAD SWEETBREAD
BEEFEATER OXBIRD BUPHAGA
OXBITER OXPECKER TICKBIRD
BEEFWOOD TOA BELAH BELAR
FILAO
BEEFY HEAVY HEFTY SOLID
BRAWNY FLESHY
BEE GLUE PROPOLIS
BEEHIVE GUM BUTT GUME HIVE
SKEP PYCHE STAND STATE STOCK
SWARM APIARY HOPPET
ALVEARY SWARMER BEEHOUSE
PRAESEPE
(— STATE) UTAH
(— TOMB) TREASURY
BEEKEEPER HIVER BEEMAN
BEEHERD APIARIST SKEPPIST
BEELIADA (FATHER OF —) DAVID
BEELZEBUB DEVIL
BEEN BE BON SEE BONE
BEE PLANT GUACO STINKWEED
BEER ALE MUM BIER BOCK BREW
FARO GAIL GROG GYLE HOPS
KVAS MALT MILD QUAS SCUD
SUDS BELCH CHANG CHICA
GROUT KVASS LAGER POMBE
QUASS SCUDS STOUT WEISS
CHICHA DOUBLE GATTER LIQUOR
PORTER SPRUCE STINGO SWANKY
SWIPES WALLOP ZYTHUM
CERVEZA PANGASI PHARAOH
PILSNER TANKARD TAPLASH
TAPWORT CERVISIA PILSENER
(ADD TO —) KRAUSEN
(BAD —) TACK TAPLASH
(HOT — AND GIN) PURL
(INFERIOR —) BELCH SWANKY
(SMALL —) TIFF GROUT
(SOUR —) BEEREGAR
(STRONG —) HUFF NAPPY DOUBLE
STINGO
(THIN —) PRITCH SWIPES
(TIBETAN —) CHANG
(WARM — AND OATMEAL) STORRY
(WEAK —) BEVERAGE
BEERA (FATHER OF —) ZOPHAH
BEERHOUSE KNEIPE TIDDLYWINK
BEERI (DAUGHTER OF —) JUDITH
(SON OF —) HOSEA
BEESWAX CAPPING
BEET CHARD MANGEL MANGOLD
STECHLING
(SUGAR —) BOLTER
BEETLE BAT BOB BUG JUT RAM
BEAT BUZZ FLEA FOWL GOGA
GOGO IPID MAUL MELL STAG
TROX TURK UANG AMARA ATLAS
BORER BULGE CAROB CHUCK
CLOCK DRIVE FIDIA GOGGA HISPA
LYCID MELOE SAGRA TIGER
BATLET CHAFER CLERID COCUYO

CUCUYO ELATER GOLACH
GOLOCH HISTER JUTOUT KHAPRA
LICTUS MALLET MELOID PESTLE
PRUNER PTINID SAWYER SCARAB
WEAVER WEEVIL ADELOPS
BRUCHID BUZZARD CADELLE
CARABID CARABUS CLOCKER
CUCUJID FIDDLER FIREFLY
GIRDLER GOLDBUG HORNBUG
LADYBUG LUCANID PAUSSID
PRIONID PROJECT SILPHID
SKIPPER SNAPPER SOLDIER
TANBARK TICKLER ATEUCHUS
CALOSOMA CETONIAN COCKTAIL
CURCULIO DYTISCID ENGRAVER
EROTYLID FIGEATER GLOWWORM
HARDBACK LADYBIRD LAMPYRID
LOWERING RUTELIAN RUTELIAN
SCOLYTID SEARCHER SHARNBUD
SHARNBUG SKIPJACK SPHINDID
SQUASHER SQUEAKER SYMPHILE
TOKTOKJE WHIRLWIG
DEDEMERID LONGICORN
OSTOMATID TUMBLEBUG
TWIRLIGIG WHIRLIGIG
SCAPHIDIUM RHYNCHOPHORAN
(PL.) XYLOPHAGA
BEEWEED TONGUE
BEFALL HAP COME LIMP SORT
TIDE TIME CHEFE CHIVE OCCUR
SHAPE ASTART BECOME BETIDE
HAPPEN PERTAIN
BEFIT DOW SIT COME LONG SEEM
SORT SUIT BESET SERVE BECOME
BEHOVE BESEEM BETIDE
BEHOOVE
BEFITTING FIT AFTER DECENT
PROPER WORTHY SEEMING
THRIFTY BECOMING DECOROUS
SORTABLE
(**PROFESSIONALLY —**) ETHICAL
(SUFF.) LY
BEFOG GAUM CLOUD OBSANE
CONFUSE MYSTIFY
BEFOOL BOB FON SOT BURN COLT
CRAP DOLT DUPE FODE JADE
POOP ASSOT ELUDE FONNE
BEFLUM DIDDLE TRIFLE FOOLIFY
BEFORE OR TO AIR BUT ERE FOR
GIN TIL ANTE FORE SAID TILL
YORE AFORE AHEAD ANENT
AVANT CORAM FIRST FORBY
FORNE FRONT PRIOR SOPRA
UNTIL FORBYE FORMER RATHER
SOONER TOFORE WITHIN
AGAINST ALREADY EARLIER
FORTHBY FORWARD
(**— LONG**) SOON ERELONG
(**JUST —**) TOWARD FORMERLY
(PREF.) FORE OB PRAE PRE PRO
PROTER(O)
BEFOREHAND AFORE
BEFOUL FILE SLUT SOIL BERAY
DIRTY GRUFT BEMIRE DAGGLE
DARKEN DEFILE DRABBLE
FEWMAND POLLUTE SLUTTER
BESQUIRT ENTANGLE
BEFOULED SHARNY
BEFRIEND AID ABET HELP FAVOR
ASSIST BENFIT FOSTER FRIEND
SUCCOR SUPPORT SUSTAIN
BEFUDDLE BOX GAS ADDLE BESOT
MUDDLE BECLOUD CONFUSE

FLUSTER MYSTIFY STUPEFY
BEFUDDLED REE MUSED
BEG ASK BID CRY SUE WOO CANT
COAX KICK MOVE MUMP PRAY
PRIG SEEK SORN SUIT THIG TRAM
CADGE CRAVE MAUND MOOCH
PLEAD SCAFF SHOOL TEASE
YEARN ADJURE FLEECH BESEECH
ENTREAT IMPLORE MAUNDER
REQUEST SKELDER SOLICIT
PETITION OBSECRATE
PANHANDLE
BEGET GET WIN BEAR HAVE KIND
SIRE BREED YIELD BIGATE
CREATE FATHER ACQUIRE
ENGRAFF CONCEIVE ENGENDER
GENERATE PROCREATE
(PREF.) GON(O) GONIDIO GONIMO
GONIO
BEGETTER SIRE AUTHOR FATHER
MOTHER PARENT
BEGETTING
(SUFF.)
GON(E)(IDIUM)(IMO)(IUM)(Y)
BEGGAR BLOB PROG RUIN ASKER
HALFY LAZAR RANDY ROGUE
THRUM TRAMP ARMINE BACACH
BIDDER CADGER CANTER
DYVOUR MUMPER PARIAH
PAUPER SORNER WRETCH
ABRAHAM ALMSMAN BAIRAGI
BEGSTER JARKMAN LAZARUS
MAUNDER PARDHAN PROCTOR
RUFFLER SCAFFER SORNARI
STEMMER THIGGER ABRAMMAN
BADGEMAN BEADSMAN
BESOGNIO BEZONIAN BLUEGOWN
DUMMERER GLASSMAN PALLIARD
STROLLER WHIPJACK MENDICANT
SCHNORRER
(**— DESCRIPTION**) PASS
(PL.) GUEUX
BEGGARED PEELED
BEGGARLY MEAN POOR CHEAP
PETTY SORRY ABJECT PALTRY
PILLED PEGRALL BANKRUPT
INDIGENT HUNGARIAN
BEGGAR'S-LICE STICKWEED
BEGGARS' OPERA (**AUTHOR OF —**)
GAY
(**CHARACTER IN —**) LUCY POLLY
LOCKIT PEACHUM MACHEATH
BEGGAR-TICK CUCKOLD
(PL.) BOOTJACKS
BEGGARY THIG WANT INDIGENCE
PAUPERISM
BEGGING MAUND CRAVING
OPENERS MENDICANT
THOMASING
(**— FOR FOOD**) SCRANNING
(**FRAUDULENT —**) TRUANDISE
BEGHARD PICARD
BEGIN GIN GYN HIT FALL FANG
HEAD JUMP LEAD OPEN RISE
TAME YOKE ARISE ENTER FRONT
START ATTACK ATTAME INCEPT
SPRING STREAK COMMENCE
INCHOATE INITIATE
BEGINNER BOOT PUNK TIRO TYRO
ROOKY SOFTA GINNER NOVICE
ROOKIE SOPHTA AMATEUR
ENTRANT RECRUIT RUBBLER
STUDENT TRAINEE FRESHMAN

INCEPTOR NEOPHYTE NEWCOMER
NOVELIST ABECEDARIAN
BEGINNING EGG ORD DAWN EDGE
GERM HEAD RISE ROOT SEED
ALPHA BIRTH DEBUT ENTRY
FIRST FRONT ONSET START
VAUNT AURORA INCOME INSTIL
ONCOME ORIGIN OUTSET SETOUT
SOURCE SPRING CALENDS
DAWNING GENESIS HANDSEL
INCIPIT INFANCY INITIAL INITION
KALENDS NASCENT OPENING
SUNRISE ENTRANCE EXORDIUM
INCHOATE OUTSTART RUDIMENT
(**NEW —**) EPOCH
(PL.) INCUNABULA
(PREF.) ACR(O)
(SUFF.) ARCH ARCHIC ARCHY
ESCENT
BEGONE OFF OUT VIA AWAY SCAT
SHOO SCOOT SCRAM AROINT
AVAUNT DEPART SKIDOO
SKIDDOO VAMOOSE
BEGONIA GAIETY GAYETY
BEGRIME COOM SOIL COLLY DITCH
GRIME BECOOM SMIRCH SMUDGE
BRUCKLE
BEGRIMED DIRTY GRIMY SMUDGY
CINDERY SMIRCHY
BEGRUDGE ENVY GRUDGE MALIGN
JALOUSE
BEGTI NAIR COCKUP
BEGUILE FOX COAX FODE FOIL
FOND GULL LURE VAMP WILE
WISE AMUSE CHARM CHEAT
COZEN ELUDE EVADE GUILE
TEMPT TRICK TROLL TRYST WEIZE
BRIGUE BUTTER DELUDE DIVERT
ENTRAP JUGGLE VAMPEY
DECEIVE ENSNARE FLATTER
FLUMMER MISLEAD
MOUNTEBANK
BEHALF HALF PART SAKE SIDE
FAVOR SCORE STEAD AFFAIR
MATTER PROFIT BENEFIT
DEFENCE SUPPORT INTEREST
BEHAVE DO ACT LET BEAR FARE
HAVE KEEP MAKE PLAY WALK
WORK ABEAR CARRY REACT
TREAT ACQUIT DEMEAN DEPORT
HANDLE COMPORT CONDUCT
CONTAIN DISPORT GESTURE
MANAGER FUNCTION REGULATE
RESTRAIN
(**— AFFECTEDLY**) MOP
(**— AWKWARDLY**) GAUM HOCKER
(**— BOLDLY**) GAUSTER
(**— BRASHLY**) HOOK
(**— CHURLISHLY**) CARL
(**— EVASIVELY**) DODGE
(**— FOOLISHLY**) DOLT
(**— MISCHIEVOUSLY**) LARK
(**— NOISILY**) HELL REHAYTE
(**— OSTENTATIOUSLY**) SWANK
(**— VULGARLY**) RAMP
BEHAVING
(SUFF.) ANT ENT
BEHAVIOR AIR MIEN PORT RULE
THEW WALK FRONT GUISE HABIT
LATES USAGE ACTION COURSE
GOINGS MANNER ACTIONS
BEARING BIGOTRY COMPORT
CONDUCT DECORUM ERGASIA

FACTION FASHION HAVANCE
HAVINGS AMENANCE ATTITUDE
BLINDISM BREEDING BYRONICS
CARRIAGE FUNCTION MAINTAIN
PERFORMANCE
(**ARROGANT —**) SIDE SWAGGER
(**COURTEOUS —**) COMITY
COURTESY
(**DECENT —**) CIVILITY
(**FOOLISH —**) SIMPLES SOTTISE
(**GOAL-DIRECTED —**) HORME
(**IMPROPER —**) MISCONDUCT
(**LIVELY —**) TITTUP
(**LOUTISH —**) BUFFOONERY
(**RIOTOUS —**) RAMPAGE
(**SILLY —**) SPOONISM
(**STUDIED —**) ART
(**UNDERHANDED —**)
SKULLDUGGERY
BEHEAD NECK
BEHEST BID LAW HEST RULE
ORDER DEMAND BIDDING
COMMAND MANDATE
BEHIND AFT HINT PAST RUMP
ABACK ABAFF ABAFT AFTER
AHIND AREAR LATER PASSE
TARDY ARREAR ASTERN DERERE
BACKWARD DILATORY
(PREF.) META POST POSTERO
RETRO
BEHINDHAND TARDY LAGGARD
DILATORY HINDERLY
BEHOLD LA LO EYE SEE SPY ECCE
ESPY GAZE HOLD KEEP LOOK
SCAN STOP TOOT VIEW VISE
WAIT HOLDE OCULE SIGHT VOILA
WATCH ASPECT DESCRY MIRROR
REGARD RETAIN DISCERN
OBSERVE SURVISE WITNESS
BEHOLDEN OWING AFFINED
BOUNDEN OBLIGED INDEBTED
BEHOOVE DOW FIT NEED SUIT
THAR BEFIT OUGHT THARF
BELONG PROPER REQUIRE
BEIGE HOP TAN ECRU HOPI GREGE
DORADO GREIGE STRING
SUNBURN
BEING ENS ESSE FEAL SELF ENTIA
GNOME HUMAN SHAPE TROLL
ANIMAL ENTITY EXTANT LIVING
MORTAL PERSON SYSTEM
ESSENCE PRESENT REALITY
VIVENCY CREATURE EXISTENT
ONTOLOGY PRESENCE STANDING
(**ANIMATE —**) LIFE JAGAT
(**CELESTIAL —**) ANGEL CHERUB
SERAPH WATCHER DIVINITY
(**DIMINUTIVE —**) ELF GNOME
(**DIVINE —**) DEV DEVA DEMIGOD
(**ESSENCE OF —**) SAT
(**ETERNAL —**) EON AEON
(**EVIL —**) DEVIL GHOUL
(**FABULOUS —**) TENGU TORNIT
(**HUMAN —**) BODY BUCK JACK
SOUL BLADE HUMAN SLIME
ANIMAL ADAMITE CREATURE
RATIONAL CHRISTIAN
(**IDEAL —**) IMMORTAL
(**ILL-FAVORED —**) BLASTIE
(**IMAGINARY —**) SYLPH
TERMAGANT
(**INNER —**) INWARD SPRITE
INBEING

(INNERMOST —) HEART
(INTRINSIC —) ESSENCE
(LEGENDARY —) GIANT
(LIVING —) BLOOD WIGHT
(MATERIAL —) HYLIC
(PERFECT —) GOD
(PHYSICAL —) FLESH
(SEMIDIVINE —) SHEDU LAMASSU
(SMALL —) INCHLING
(SO —) SAEBEINS
(SUPERNATURAL —) DEV MAN
AKUA ATUA DEVA IANN ZEMI
ADARO BALAM DAEVA DEMON
FAIRY TROLL WIGHT DAEMON
GARUDA GODKIN SPIRIT GODLING
FOLLETTO HAMINGJA
(SUPREME —) DEITY MONAD
NYAMBE NZAMBI CREATOR
(TRUE —) OUSIA
(PREF.) ONT(O) ZO(E)(IDIO)(IDO)(O)
ZOOLOGICO
(HUMAN —) ANTHROP(O)
(SUFF.) IC(AL) ZOA ZOIC ZOON
BELA (FATHER OF —) AZAZ BEOR
BENJAMIN
BELABOR PLY BEAT DRUB LASH
WORK ASSAIL BOUNCE CUDGEL
HAMMER HAMPER THRASH
THWACK
BELAY BESET BELAGE INVEST
WAYLAY BESEIGE
BELCH YEX BOCK BOKE BOLK BURP
GALP RASP RIFT ERUCT FRUCT
REBOKE ERUCTATE
BELCHING DRAGII
BELDAM HAG FURY TROT CRONE
RUDAS ALECTO ERINYS RUDOUS
VIRAGO BELDAME JEZEBEL
TISIPHONE
BELEAGUER BELAY BESET INVEST
ASSAULT BESEIGE LEAGUER
BLOCKADE SURROUND
BELEM PARA
BELEMNITE ARTIFACT KERAUNION
BELFRY SHED TOWER BEFFROY
CLOCHER CLOGHEAD BELLHOUSE
BELGIAN CONGO (CAPITAL OF —)
LEOPOLDVILLE
(LAKE IN —) KIVU MWERU ALBERT
(PROVINCE OF —) KIVA KASAI
EQUATOR KATANGA ORIENTAL
(RIVER IN —) RUKI KASAI LINDI
LOMAMI LUKUGA UBANGI
ARUWIMI LULONGA
(TOWN IN —) BOMA LULUABOURG

BELGIUM
CANAL: YSER UNION ALBERT
CAMPINE
CAPITAL: BRUSSELS BRUXELLES
GAUL TRIBE: REMI BELGAE NERVII
MEASURE: VAT AUNE LAST PIED
CARAT PERCHE BOISSEAU
MOUNTAIN: BOTRANGE
NAME: BELGIE BELGIQUE
PLATEAU: ARDENNES HOHEVENN
PORT: OSTEND ANTWERP
PROVINCE: LIEGE NAMUR
ANTWERP BRABANT
HAINAUT LIMBURG
FLANDERS HAINAULT
RIVER: LYS DYLE LEIE MAAS MARK
YSER BOUCO DEMER LESSE

MEUSE NETHE RUPEL SENNE
DENDER ESCAUT MANJEL
OURTHE SAMBRE SEMOIS
VESDRE WARCHE AMBLEVE
SCHELDT
TOWN: AS AAT ANS ATH HAL HUY
MOL SPA AATH AMAY ASSE
BOOM BREE DOEL GAND GEEL
GENK GENT HOEI LIER LOOZ
MONS VISE WAHA ZELE AALST
ALOST ARLON CINEY EEKLO
ESSEN EUPEN EVERE GENCK
GHENT HEIST IEPER JETTE
JUMET LIEGE NAMUR RONSE
TIELT UCCLE VORST WEZET
YNOIR YPRES AARLEN ANVERS
BERGEN BILZEN BRUGES
DEURNE ELSENE IZEGEM
LEUVEN LIERRE MERXEM
OPWIJK OSTEND ANTWERP
ARDOOIE BERCHEM DOORWIK
HERSTAL HOBOKEN IXELLES
LOUVAIN MECHLIN ROULERS
SERAING TONGRES TOURNAI
BRUSSELS COURTRAI KORTRIJK
MECHELEN MOUSCRON
TONGEREN TURNHOUT
VERVIERS WATERLOO
WEIGHT: LAST CARAT LIVRE
POUND CHARGE CHARIOT
ESTERLIN

BELIE BELONG DEFAME BESEIGE
FALSIFY PERTAIN SLANDER
TRADUCE DISGUISE STRUMPET
SURROUND MISREPRESENT
BELIEF CRY FAY ISM LEVE MIND
SECT TAKE TROW VIEW VOTE
WEEN CAUSE CREDO CREED
DOGMA FAITH OBEAH TENET
TROTH TRUST CREDIT GROUND
CRIANCE FEELING HOLDING
OPINION TROWING ARYANISM
BITHEISM CREDENCE
DOCTRINE FINALISM
HUMANISM RELIANCE
PREPOSSESSION
(— IN DEVILS) DIABOLISM
(— IN GHOSTS) EIDOLISM
(CONVENTIONAL —) PIETY
(FALSE —) DELUSION
(GROUNDLESS —) CANARD
(MORTAL —) HALL
(READY —) ACCEPTATION
(SHALLOW —) BALLOON
(SUPERSTITIOUS —) FREET
(TRADITIONAL —) ICON IKON
EIKON
(UNFOUNDED —) FICTON
BELIEVABLE PLAUSIBLE
BELIEVE BUY WIS DEEM FEEL
HOLD TAKE TREW TROW WEEN
CREED FAITH FANCY GUESS
JUDGE SEPAD THINK TRUST
ACCEPT CREDIT ESTEEM EXPECT
DARESAY SUPPOSE ACCREDIT
CONSIDER CREDENCE
(— ERRONEOUSLY) FEIGN
(— NAIVELY) SWALLOW
(— UNCRITICALLY) EAT
BELIEVER IST LEVER BOTARY
KITABI CREDENS
ADHERENT ARMINIAN

(SUFF.) ARIAN
BELISARIO (CHARACTER IN —)
ANTONIA EUTRIPIO BELISARIUS
(COMPOSER OF —) DONIZETTI
BELISE (BROTHER OF —)
PHILAMINTE
BELITTLE DECRY DWARF SNEER
BEMEAN MINISH SLIGHT DETRACT
DIMINUE LIGHTLY MINIMIZE
VILIPEND DENIGRATE DISCREDIT
DISPARAGE
BELITTLER ZOILUS
BELIZE (CAPITAL OF —) BELMOPAN
BELL HUB TOM CALL FAIR GONG
HUBB RING ROAR CHIME CLOAK
CLOCK CODON FLARE KNELL
SWELL TENOR BASKET BELLOW
BUBBLE CLOCHE CROTAL
CURFEW PHONIC SOCKET TAPPER
TOCSIN TOLLER TREBLE TRIPLE
VESPER ANGELUS BLOSSOM
CAMPANA CAMPANE COROLLA
COWBELL JANGLER JINGLER
LOWBELL SKELLAT SKILLET
TAMBOUR TANTONY TINKLER
CASCABEL COCKBELL DINGDONG
DOORBELL HANDBELL HAWKBELL
MORTBELL PAVILLON STARTLER
TINGTANG
(ALARM —) TOCSIN
(CLOSED —) CROTAL
(EVENING —) CURFEW
(FUNERAL —) TELLER
(HAND —) CLAG
(LARGE —) SIGNUM
(LOWEST —) BORDON BOURDON
(PART OF —) BOW LIP HEAD
CROWN MOUTH WAIST CLAPPER
SHOULDER
(PASSING —) KNELL
(SACRING —) SQUILLA
(SLEIGH —) GRELOT CROTALUM
(PREF.) CAMPANI CAMPANO
BELLABELLA HAELTZUK HEILTSUK
BELLADONNA DWALE MANICON
BANEWORT DAFTBERRY
DWAYBERRY MYDRIATIC
NIGHTSHADE
BELLARIA (HUSBAND OF —)
PANDOSTO
BELLARMINE GRAYBEARD
GREYBEARD LONGBEARD
BELLBIRD MAKO SHRIKE COTINGA
ARAPUNGA KORIMAKO
MAKOMAKO CAMPANERO
BELLBOY BUTTONS
BELLE SPARK TOAST
(SPANISH —) MAJA
BELLEEK POTTERY CHAMPAGNE
**BELLE HELENE, LE (COMPOSER OF
—)** OFFENBACH
BELLEROPHON (FATHER OF —)
GLAUCUS
(MOTHER OF —) EURYMEDE
BELLFLOWER RAMPION
BELLWORT HASKWORT IVYBELLS
MILKWORT
BELLHOP BELLBOY HALLBOY
CHASSEUR
BELLICOSE MAD IRATE WARFUL
HOSTILE WARLIKE MILITANT
BELLIGERENT BRISTLY HOSTILE
WARLIKE CHOLERIC FIGHTING

JINGOIST COMBATIVE IRASCIBLE
LITIGIOUS WRANGLING
PUGNACIOUS
BELLISANT (HUSBAND OF —)
ALEXANDER
(SON OF —) ORSON VALENTINE
BELLOW CRY LOW MOO YAP BAWL
BEAL BELL GAPE ROAR ROME
ROUT YAUP YAWP BELVE BLART
BLORE CROON ROUST SHOUT
TROAT BULLER CLAMOR
RUMMES BLUSTER
RUMMISH ULULATE
BELLOWING ROUT ROUST BELLING
BLATANT BOATION MUGIENT
BELLOWS BELY LUNGS BULIES
FEEDER SANDER WINKER
SYLPHON WINDBAG
EXPELLER
(SMALL —) PLUFF
(STORAGE —) RESERVOIR
(PREF.) PHYSA PHYSALLO PHYSO
BELLOWS FISH BUGLER SNIPEFISH
BELL RINGER TOLL YOUTH TOLLER
CLINKUM
BELLWETHER MASTER
BELLY BAG COD GIE GUT MAW
POD BOUK BUNT FILL KYTE MARY
WAME WEAM WOMB BINGY
BOSOM BULGE FRONT GORGE
PLEON TABLE THARM THERM
TRIPE BAGGIE BINGEE HUNGER
PAUNCH VENTER ABDOMEN
BALLOON STOMACH TUMBREL
APPETITE
(PREF.) CELI COELI(O) GASTER(O)
GASTR(I)(O) VENTRI VENTRO
(SUFF.) GASTER GASTRIA
BELLYACHE COMPLAIN
COLLYWOBBLES
BELLYBAND WANTY
BELLYING BUNTING PREGNANT
BELONG BE GO FIT LIE BEAR FALL
RELY APPLY BELIE GROUP AFFEIR
INHERE RELATE RETAIN
BEHOOVE PERTAIN
APPERTAIN SUBSCRIBE
BELONGING
(SUFF.) EAE
(— TO) AR ARY EAN INE ISE
ORIUM
BELONGINGS ALLS DUDS FARE
GEAR GOODS TRAPS ASSETS
DUFFEL DUFFLE ESTATE USINGS
BAGGAGE EFFECTS CHATTELS
PROPERTY PURPRISE FURNITURE
HOUSEHOLD PARAPHERNALIA
BELOVED DEAR IDOL LIEF AIMEE
BOSOM CHERI SWEET ADORED
CHERIE MINION DARLING
PRECIOUS
(MOST —) ADERLIEFEST
BELOW ALOW BAJO DOWN ABLOW
AFTER INFRA NEATH SOTTO
UNDER BEHIND BENEATH
(PREF.) INFERO INFRA SUB
BELT LAS AREA BAND BEAT BLOW
CEST FELT GIRD LACE LIST MARK
RING SASH SLUG ZONE GIRTH
MITER MITRE PATTE STRAP STRIP
SWATH TRACT WAIST WHACK
ZONAR ZONIC BODICE CENTER
CESTUS CINGLE FETTLE GIRDLE

INVEST LUNGER REGION STRAIT
STRIPE SWATHE ZONNAR ZONULE
BALDRIC BALTEUS CIRCUIT
PASSAGE BALTHEUS CEINTURE
CINCTURE CINGULUM ELEVATOR
ENCIRCLE MECHANIC SURROUND
(— OF FOG) BLANKET
(ASTROLOGICAL —) CLIMATE
(CONVEYOR —) HAUL
(ENDLESS —) APRON CREEPER
(GREEK —) ZOSTER
(HINDU SWAMP —) TERAI
(MACHINE —) SWIFTER
(MINERAL —) RANGE
(PART OF —) TIP HOLE FRAME
PANEL PRONG BUCKLE FILLER
KEEPER LINING PIPING TONGUE
STITCHING
(TREE —) BERM BERME
(PL.) BALTEI
(PREF.) ZON(O)
BELTED ZONATE GIRDLED
CINCTURED
(— WITH WHITE) SHEETED
BELUGA HUSE HUSO HAUSEN
MARSOON WHITEFISH
BELUS (BROTHER OF —) AGENOR
(FATHER OF —) NEPTUNE
POSEIDON
(MOTHER OF —) LIBYA EURYNOME
(SON OF —) DANAUS CEPHEUS
AEGYPTUS
BELVEDERE GAZEBO LOOKOUT
BELVIDERA (FATHER OF —) PRIULI
(HUSBAND OF —) JAFFIER
BELVIDERE MIRADOR
BEMIRE DAG SOIL JARBLE
BEMOAN RUE MEAN MOAN SIGH
MOURN PLAIN BEWAIL LAMENT
DEPLORE
BEMUSE SOT BULL DAZE AMUSE
BEMUSED DOPY DOPEY PIXILATED
MOONSTRUCK
BENAIAH (FATHER OF —) JEHOIADA
(SON OF —) PELATIAH
BENCH PEW BANC BANK BENK
BERM BINK DAIS DEAS FORM
MESA SEAT SILL STEP TRAM
BASIN BASON BERME BREAK
CABIN CHAIR FORME JUDGE
PLANK STALL STOOL BANCUS
BANKER SCONCE SEDILE SETTEE
SETTLE SITTER COUNTER
DRESSER REPOSAL SHAMBLE
SITTING TRESTLE TRIBUNE
ALEBENCH
(— FOR DAIRY TUBS) TRAM
(— FOR KNEADING DOUGH) BREAK
(OUTDOOR —) EXEDRA EXHEDRA
(PLAYER'S —) WOOD
(ROWER'S —) BANK THOFT ZYGON
THWART
(SHOEMAKER'S —) FORME
(WORKMAN'S —) SIEGE
BEND BOW NID NIP PLY SAG SET
WIN WRY ABOW ARCH BENT
BOOL BUCK COPE CURB DOME
FAUD FLEX FOLD GENU HOOK
KINK LEAN LOUT PLOY RUMP
TURN VERT WEEP ANGLE BATON
BIGHT BREAK COUCH COUDE
COURB CRANK CRIMP CRINK
CROOK CULGE CURVE DROOP

FLECT FRESE HINGE HUNCH
INBOW KNEEL PLASH PLICA
QUIRL ROUND SCRAG SKELP
SLANT STOOP TREND TWINE
TWIST BOUGHT BUCKLE CAMBER
CONVEX COTICE CROUCH
COMPASS
(SUFF.) FLECT(ION) FLEX(ION)
BENDER BUM JAG LEG BUST
DRUNK SPREE BRIDGE WHOPPER
GUZZLING SIXPENCE BRANNIGAN
INFLECTOR
BENDING BOW SAG KNEE KNOT
PLIE CROOK CURVE LITHE TWIST
PLIANT SUPPLE TWISTY ANFRACT
FLEXION HOGGING SINUOUS
BUCKLING FLECTION
(— OF ROCK) DRAG
(BALLET —) PLIE
(PREF.) SPHINGO
BENDY TREE MIRO MAHOE
BENEATH ALOW ANETH BELOW
LOWER UNDER ANEATH
(PREF.) HYPO INFRA SUB
BENEDICITE BENISON CANTICLE
BENEDICT NEOGAMIST
BENEDICTINE CLUNIAC
CAMALDOLESE TIRONENSIAN
BENEDICTION ABOT AMEN ABOTH
NANDI AMIDAH BROCHO PRAYER
BENISON BERAKAH BLESSING
BENEFACTION ALMS BOON GIFT
PRESENT DONATION GRATUITY
BENEFACTOR AGENT ANGEL
DONOR FRIEND HELPER PATRON
SAVIOR MAECENAS PROMOTER
BENEFICE FEE FEU FEUD FIEF
FAVOR SCARF CURACY LIVING
BENEFIT CANONRY PRELACY
RECTORY TOTQUOT DONATIVE
KINDNESS SINECURE VICARAGE
PLURALITY
BENEFICENCE BOON GIFT GRACE
BOUNTY CHARITY GOODNESS
KINDNESS
BENEFICENT KINDLY AMIABLE
BENEFIC GRACIOUS
BENEFICIAL GOOD USEFUL
HEALTHY HELPFUL BONITARY
SALUTARY SANATIVE SINGULAR
AVAILABLE BENIGNANT
DESIRABLE ENJOYABLE
HEALTHFUL LUCRATIVE
REWARDING WHOLESOME
PROFITABLE
BENEFICIARY HEIR USER DONEE
CESTUI CESTUY USUARY VASSAL
LEGATEE FEUDATORY
(SUFF.) EE
BENEFIT AID USE BOON BOOT
GAIN GIFT GOOD HELP PROW
SAKE AVAIL BOOST FRUIT SELTH
STEAD VISIT ASSIST BEHALF
BEHOOF BETTER FRINGE PROFIT
SALUTE USANCE ADVANCE
BESPEAK CONCERT DESERVE
IMPROVE SERVICE UTILITY
BEFRIEND INTEREST
BENEVOLENCE JEN BOUNTY
GOODNESS GOODWILL HUMANITY
BENEVOLENT GOOD KING BENIGN
KINDLY LOVING AMIABLE LIBERAL
GENEROUS AVUNCULAR

BENIGNANT ALTRUISTIC
PROPITIOUS
BENHANAN (FATHER OF —) SHIMON
BEN HUR (AUTHOR OF —) WALLACE
(CHARACTER IN —) HUR IRAS
JUDAH ESTHER TIRZAH MESSALA
BALTHASAR SIMONIDES
BENIGN BOON GOOD KIND MILD
BLAND SWEET TRINE GENIAL
GENTLE AFFABLE BENEFIC
BENEDICT GRACIOUS INNOCENT
SALUTARY FAVORABLE
WHOLESOME
BENIGNANT KIND BLAND GENIAL
LIBERAL GRACIOUS MERCIFUL
BENIN (CAPITAL OF —) PORTONOVO
(TOWN IN —) COTONOU
BENISON BENEDICTION
BENJAMIN (FATHER OF —) HARIM
JACOB BILHAN
(MOTHER OF —) RACHEL
(SON OF —) ARD EHI BELA GERA
ROSH ASHBEL BECHER HUPPIM
MUPPIM NAAMAN
BENNET CLOVEWORT
BENNISEED SESAME
BENO TUBA
BENT AIM BOW SET BIAS CAST
CURB GIFT TURN BANDY BOUND
BOWED BOWLY COUDE COURB
CRANK CRUMP FLAIR HUMOR
KNACK LURCH PRONE SQUAT
SWING TASTE TREND AKIMBO
ANLAGE BENNET BIASED BRACED
COURBE COURSE CURVED
DOGLEG ENERGH GENIUS
HOOKED INTENT LIKING NECKED
SQUINT SWAYED TALENT
ADUNCAL ARCUATE BUCKLED
CROOKED CURVANT EMBOWED
FLEXION FLEXURE IMPETUS
INTENSE LEANING LEVELED
PRONATE STOOPED STOOPED
TENSION ADUNCUS APTITUDE
ARCUATED CRUMPLED DECLINED
FLECTION IMMINENT INFLEXED
PENCHANT REFLEXED TENDENCY
(— AT THE END) HAMATE HOGGED
GRYPANIAN
(— DOWNWARD) BOWED
DECURVED INCUMBENT
RECLINATE
(— IN) INCAVATE
(— INWARD) ADUNC
(— OF MIND) GEME AFFECTION
(EASILY —) LITHY
(NATURAL —) SWING
(SPECIAL —) VERVE
(PREF.) ANKYL(O) CAMPTO CURVI
CYPH(O) CYRT(O) SCOLIO
BEN-TEAK NANDI NANAWOOD
BENUMB NIP DAZE DUNT NUMB
STUN CHILL DAVER DOZEN
SCRAM SHRAM CUMBER DEADEN
PERISH STOUND BINOMEN
FRETISH FRETIZE STIFFEN
STUPEFY TORPEDO TORPEFY
BENUMBED CHILL SCRAM ASLEEP
CLUMSE CLUMSY FROZEN TORPID
CLUMPST SHRAMMED
BENUMBING LEADEN
**BENVENUTO CELLINI (CHARACTER
IN —)** POMPEO TERESA ASCANIO

CELLINI BALDUCCI SALVIATA
BENVENUTO FIERAMOSCA
(COMPOSER OF —) BERLIOZ
BENZAYDA (LOVER OF —) OZWY
BENZENE PHENE BENZIN BENZOL
PHENENE
(SUFF.) PHEN(E)
BENZINE
(PREF.) PHEN(O)
BENZOIN BENJOIN LINDERA
BENJAMIN FIXATIVE
(SUFF.) OIN
BEOR (SON OF —) BELA BALAAM
BEOWULF (AUTHOR OF —)
UNKNOWN
(CHARACTER IN —) WIGLAF
BEOWULF GRENDEL HIGELAC
UNFERTH AESCHERE HONDSCIO
HROTHGAR
BEQUEATH GIVE WILL ENDOW
LEAVE OFFER BESTOW COMMIT
DEMISE DEVISE LEGATE QUETHE
BEQUEST COMMEND TRANSMIT
BEQUEST GIFT WILL LEGACY
BEQUEATH HERITAGE PITTANCE
ENDOWMENT BENEFACTION
BERACHIAH (SON OF —) ASAPH
BERAIAH (FATHER OF —) SHIMHI
BERATE JAW NAG DRUB LASH
RAIL ABUSE BASTE CHIDE SCOLD
SCORE SLATE REVILE CENSURE
REPROVE UPBRAID CHASTISE
BERBER RIF RIFF KABYL SHLUH
KABYLE SHILHA HARATIN
MZABITE SHILLUH HARRATIN
MOZABITE
(— CHIEF) CAID
BERCEUSE CRADLESONG
WIEGENLIED
BEREAVE ROB STRIP WIDOW
DIVEST SADDEN DEPRIVE
DESPOIL
BEREAVED ORB BEREFT VIDUOUS
WIDOWED DESOLATE
BEREAVEMENT ORBITY ORBITUDE
VIDUATION
BERECHIAH (SON OF —) ASAPH
MESHULLAM ZECHARIAH
BEREFT ORB LORN LOST POOR
QUIT WIDOW ORBATE FORLORN
FORFAIRN DESTITUTE
BERG FLOE BARROW ICEBERG
FLOEBERG
BERGAMOT BOSE BERGAMA
BURGAMOT
BERI (FATHER OF —) ZOPHAH
BERIAH (FATHER OF —) ASHER
EPHRAIM
BERIBERI KAKKE
BERITH BRIS BRISS BRITH
BERM BERME LISIERE HEELPATH
BERNICE (FATHER OF —) HEROD
BERRY BAY DEW HAW ALEY BEAT
CRAN POHA RASP BACCA BLACK
CUBEB FRUIT GRAIN GRAPE
LANSA MOUND SALAL SAVIN
BURROW LANSAT LANSEH
SABINE THRESH CURRANT
ETAERIO HILLOCK ACROSARC
ALLSPICE COWBERRY
DEWBERRY HAWEBAKE
PERSIMMON POKEBERRY
SASKATOON PEPPERCORN

SHEEPBERRY POMEGRANATE
(ACID —) CURRANT
(COFFEE —) CHERRY
(DRIED —) PASA
(JUMPER —) ABHAL
(LAUREL —) BAY
(POISONOUS —) BANEBERRY
(PREF.) BACCI COCC(I)(O)
BERTH BED JOB BUNK DOCK SLIP
SOPT CABIN PLACE UPPER BILLET
OFFICE SECURE LODGING
MOORING SLIPWAY POSITION
ANCHORAGE
BERTHA (FATHER OF —) CARIBERT
(HUSBAND OF —) PEPIN
HEREWARD
(SON OF —) CHARLES
BERYL EMERALD AERODIES
HELIODOR GOSHENITE
MORGANITE AQUAMARINE
BERYLLIA GLUCINA GLUCINE
BERYLLIUM GLUCINUM
BESEECH ASK BEG BID CRY SUE
WOO PRAY CRAVE HALSE PLEAD
PRESS ADJURE APPEAL OBTEST
CONJURE ENTREAT IMPLORE
SOLICIT IMPETRATE OBSECRATE
BESET PLY SET SIT BEGO SAIL
STUD ALLOT BELAY BIGAN HARRY
PRESS SIEGE SPEND STEAD
ASSAIL ATTACK HARASS INFEST
OBSESS WAYLAY ARRANGE
BESIEGE OVERSET PERPLEX
BLOCKADE ENCUMBER
ENTHRONG OBSTRUCT
SURROUND BELEAGUER
BESHOW SKIL CUDDY CUDDEN
CUDDIE BADDOCK COALFISH
SKILFISH
BESIDE BY HEAR INBY ALONG
ANENT ASIDE FORBY ABREAST
AGAINST FORNENT ADJACENT
FORNENST
(— ONE ANOTHER) ABREAST
(— ONESELF) FEY
(PREF.) EPH EPI PAR(A)
BESIDES BY TO AND BUT TOO YET
ALSO ELSE MORE OVER THEN
UNTO WITH ABOVE AGAIN FORBY
SUPRA BESIDE BEYOND EXCEPT
FORBYE WITHAL THERETO
WITHOUT LIKEWISE MOREOVER
(PREF.) EPH EPI PROS
BESIEGE GIRD GIRT BELAY BELIE
BESET SIEGE STORM ATTACK
OBSESS OBSIDE PESTER PLAGUE
COMPASS SOLICIT SURROUND
BELEAGUER
BESMEAR RAY BALM DAUB SOIL
APPLY COVER GRIME GRUFT
MUDDY SLAKE SMEAR SULLY
TAINT BEDAUB PLATCH BESLIME
SMOTHER BESMIRCH BESLUBBER
BESMIRCH TAR DASH SLUR SOIL
SMEAR SULLY SLURRY SMIRCH
ASPERSE BLACKEN DRAGGLE
TURPIFY DISCOLOR
BESMIRCHED MACULATE
MACULATED
BESMUT CROCK
BESOM COW MAP DRAB BISME
BROOM SWEEP SLOVEN HEATHER
BESOT DULL ASOTE ASSOT

MUDDLE STUPID STUPEFY
BEFUDDLE
BESPANGLE DOT STAR STUD
ADORN JEWEL INVENT SPRINKLE
BESPATTER BLOT DASH JAUP SOIL
SPOT MUDDY PLASH STAIN SULLY
BEGARY SPARGE ASPERSE
SCATTER SMOTTER REPROACH
SPRINKLE
BESPEAK CITE HINT SHOW ARGUE
IMPLY ORDER SPEAK TRYST
ACCOST ATTEST ENGAGE STEVEN
ADDRESS ARRANGE BENEFIT
BETOKEN DISCUSS EXCLAIM
RESERVE FORETELL INDICATE
BESPECKLE DASH
BESPRINKLE DROP SHED POWDER
ASPERSE BESTREW BESPRING
SPRINKLE BEQUIRTLE
BEST O ACE BEAT GOOD LACE
MOST PICK TOPS WALE ELITE
EXCEL WORST CHOICE DEFEAT
FINEST FLOWER OUTWIT SUNDAY
TIPTOP UTMOST ARISTOS
CONQUER GARLAND LARGEST
OPTIMUM PALMARY DAMNDEST
GREATEST KOHINOOR OUTMATCH
OUTSTRIP POSSIBLE TOPNOTCH
VANQUISH
(SUNDAY —) BRAWS
(PREF.) ARIST(O)
BESTIAL LOW VILE WILD BRUTE
FERAL PRONE BRUTAL FILTHY
BEASTLY BRUTISH INHUMAN
SENSUAL BELLUINE DEPRAVED
BESTIR STIR AWAKE SHIFT STEER
AROUSE HUSTLE
(— ONESELF) LEG
BEST MAN PARANYMPH
BESTOW ADD PUT USE CAST DEAL
DOTE GIVE SEND STOW TAKE
WARE ALLOT ALLOW APPLY
AWARD BESET GRANT INFER
LODGE PLACE SPEND THOLE
WREAK ACCORD BETEEM CONFER
DEMISE DEVOTE DIVIDE DONATE
DOTATE EMPLOY ENTAIL ESTATE
EXTEND IMPART IMPOSE RENDER
SHOWER COLLATE COMMEND
DISPOSE ENLARGE EROGATE
INDULGE INSTATE PARTAKE
PRESENT QUARTER TRIBUTE
BEQUEATH
(— LAVISHLY) HEAP
(— UPON) GIFT
BESTOWAL DOLE DISPOSAL
COLLATION LARGITION
(— OF PRAISE) ACCOLADE
BESTRIDE HORSE STRIDE
STRADDLE OVERSTRIDE
BET GO UP BAS BOX LAY PUT SET
VIE WAD ANTE BACK BRAG CHIP
GAGE HOLD JACK NOIR PAIR
PLAY PLOT PUNT RISK WAGE
BOUND CARRE HEDGE ROUGE
SAVER SPORT STAKE WAGER
GAMBLE HAZARD IMPAIR
MANQUE MILIEU PLEDGE
DERNIER PREMIER
ACCUMULATOR
(— AGAINST) MILK COPPER
(— AT LONG ODDS) SKINNER
(— BOLDLY) BLUFF

(— CHIP) CHECK
(FARO —) SLEEPER
(HEDGING —) SAVER
(POKER —) BLIND
BETA AND GAMMA GUARDS
BETAKE GO GET HIE MOVE TAKE
APPLY CATCH GRANT ASSUME
COMMIT REMOVE REPAIR RESORT
COMMEND JOURNEY WITHDRAW
(— ONESELF) BUN HIT BOUN MARK
PIKE TEEM AVOID FOUND HAUNT
REFER TRUSS YIELD
(— ONESELF TO MILL) SUE
BETEL PAN IKMO ITMO SERI SIRI
SIRIH PINANG PUPULO
BETEL LEAF PAN BUYO PAUN
PAWNE
BETEL NUT BONGA BONYA BUNGA
SUPARI
BETHABARA NOIBWOOD
GREENHEART
BETHEL BETHESDA
BETHINK TAKE THINK ADVISE
DEVISE RECALL REFLECT
CONSIDER REMEMBER RECOLLECT
(— ONE'S SELF) MIN MINE
UMBETHINK
BETHLEHEM BEDLAM
BETHROOT TRILLIUM
BETHUEL (DAUGHTER OF —)
REBEKAH
(FATHER OF —) NAHOR
(MOTHER OF —) MILCAH
(UNCLE OF —) ABRAHAM
BETIDE HAP TIDE BEFIT OCCUR
TRITE WORTH BECOME BEFALL
CHANCE HAPPEN BETOKEN
PRESAGE
BETIMES ANON RATH SOON EARLY
RATHE TIMEOUS SPEEDILY
FORTHWITH
BETOKEN MARK NOTE SHOW SIGN
AUGUR TOKEN ASSERT BETIDE
DENOTE EVINCE IMPORT
SHADOW BESPEAK EXPRESS
OBLIQUE PORTEND PRESAGE
SIGNIFY FOREBODE FORESHOW
INDICATE
BETONY BROOMWORT
BETRAY BLAB BLOW BOIL GULL
SELL SHOP SILE SING SPOT TELL
TRAY UNDO WRAY ABUSE CROSS
FALSE PEACH ROUND SPILL SPLIT
SWICK SWIKE ACCUSE BEWRAY
DELUDE DESCRY DESERT QUATCH
REVEAL SEDUCE SNITCH SQUEAL
BEGUILE DECEIVE FALSIFY
MISLEAD PROMOTE TRAITOR
DISCLOSE DISCOVER
(— CONFIDENCES) SPILL
BETRAYAL RAP ABUSE ACCUSE
TREASON GIVEAWAY PRODITION
BETRAYER RAT JUDAS SKUNK
SEDUCER TRAITOR DERELICT
RECREANT SQUEALER
BETRAYING TELLTALE
BETROTH AFFY EARL TOKEN
TROTH TRUTH ASSURE ENGAGE
ENSURE PLEDGE PLIGHT ESPOUSE
PROMISE AFFIANCE CONTRACT
DESPOUSE HANDFAST
BETROTHED SURE VOWED
ASSURED ENGAGED HANDFAST

INTENDED COMBINATE
(AUTHOR OF —) MANZONI
(CHARACTER IN —) LUCIA RENZO
RODRIGO ABBONDIO BORROMEO
CRISTOFORO
BETTA PLAKAT
BETTER AID TOP BEET MEND
AMEND EMEND EXCEL SAFER
WISER BIGGER EXCEED REFORM
ADVANCE CHOICER CORRECT
GREATER IMPROVE PROMOTE
RECTIFY RELIEVE SUPPORT
SURPASS EMINENCE INCREASE
SUPERIOR
(— A SCORE) BREAK
(— THAN ORDINARY) EXTRA
BETTING ACTION GAMBLING
(— SYSTEM) PAROLI ALEMBERT
BETTOR ORALER
BETTY JENNY COTBETTY JOCRISSE
MOLLYCOT WIFECARL
BETWEEN AMID EMEL AMELL
AMONG ENTRE TWEEN YTWYN
ATWEEN ATWIXT TWEESH
AVERAGE BETWIXT
(PREF.) DI INTER INTRA
BEUDANITE CORKITE
BEVEL BLOW CANT CONE EDGE
PUSH REAM ANGLE BEARD BEZEL
MITER MITRE SLANT SLOPE
SNAPE SPLAY ASLANT CIPHER
RHYMER CHAMFER INCLINE
OBLIQUE
(— EDGES) BEARD
(WITHOUT —) FLAT
BEVERAGE ADE ALE AVA CUP NOG
POP RUM SAP TEA BEER BREW
CHIA GROG MABI MATE MEAD
MILK NIPA SODA WHIG WINE
CHOCA CIDER CLARY COCOA
DRAFT DRINK JULEP LAGER
LEBAN MORAT MULSE NEGUS
PUNCH SHRUB SMASH TREAT
TWIST WATER BISHOP COFFEE
EGGNOG LIQUID LIQUOR NECTAR
PORTER SPRUCE TISWIN
BUNNELL CASSINA CORDIAL
LIMEADE OENOMEL POTABLE
STEPONY TULAPAI ALEBERRY
COCKTAIL LEMONADE PIQUETTE
POTATION SANGAREE SWITCHEL
BADMINTON CALIBOGUS
CHOCOLATE GINGERADE
ORANGEADE POMPERKIN
SOMETHING
(— FROM COW'S MILK) KEFIR
KEPHIR
(— FROM PEPPERS) KAVA
KAVAKAVA
(— FROM SAP) TUBA
(— OF BUTTERMILK AND WATER)
BLAND
(— OF CHAMPAGNE) POPE
(— OF HONEY AND WATER)
METHEGLIN
(— OF HOT MILK) POSSET
(— OF PORT WINE) BISHOP
(— OF VINEGAR AND WATER)
POSCA
(ALCOHOLIC —) DEW ARAK SAKE
SAKI ARRAK BASIG SHRUB
SNAPS STUFF ARRACK

FIREWATER STIMULANT
(COLA —) DOPE
(EFFERVESCENT —) FIZZ
(FERMENTED —) BASI KAVA KUMYS
KUMISS
(FRUIT —) BEVERAGE
(INSIPID —) WASH
(MEXICAN —) TEPACHE
(POLYNESIAN —) AVA KAVA
(WEAK —) LAP
(PL.) WAIPIRO
BEVY HERD PACK COVEY DROVE
FLOCK GROUP SWARM FLIGHT
SCHOOL COMPANY
BEWAIL CRY RUE WEY KEEN
MOAN RAME SIGH WAIL WEEP
MOURN PLAIN BEMOAN GRIEVE
LAMENT PLAINT SORROW
THROPE DEPLORE COMPLAIN
BEWARE WAR CAVE GARE HEED
SHUN TENT WARD AVOID SPEND
ESCHEW WARNING
BEWILDER FOG FOX MAR BEAT
DAZE FOIL GAUM MAZE STUN
ABASH ADDLE AMAZE AMUSE
DEAVE DIZZY BAFFLE BEMIST
BEMUSE BOTHER DAZZLE
DUDDER MOIDER MOMBLE
MUDDLE PUZZLE WANDER
WILDER BUFFALO BUMBAZE
CONFUSE FLASKER MYSTIFY
NONPLUS PERPLEX STAGGER
STUPEFY ASTONISH CONFOUND
DISTRACT ENTANGLE OVERMUSE
SQUATTER SURPRISE
(PREF.) PLAZO
BEWILDERED MAR ASEA LOST
MANG WILL AGAPE DAZED
MAZED MUZZY BUSHED MAPPED
BEMAZED STUPENT WILSOME
CONFUSED HELPLESS WILLYARD
PERPLEXED
BEWILDERMENT AWE FOG DAZE
MISMAZE STICKLE AMAZEMENT
CONFUSION PERPLEXITY
BEWITCH HEX WISH BLINK CHARM
MAGIC OBEAH SPELL WITCH
ENAMOR ENTICE GLAMOR GRIGRI
HOODOO STRIKE THRILL ATTRACT
BEDEVIL DELIGHT ENCHANT
GLAMOUR ENSORCEL FORSPEAK
GREEGREE OVERLOOK
BEWITCHED HAGGED
BEWITCHING SIREN
BEYOND BY FREE OVER YOND
ABOVE ASIDE AYOND FORBY
ULTRA BEHIND BEYANT YONDER
BENEATH BESIDES FORTHBY
FURTHER OUTGATE PASSING
WITHOUT OVERMORE SUPERIOR
HEREAFTER
(— DOUBT) ASSURED
(— ORDINARY METHODS) AFIELD
(— THE MARK) GONE
(— THE SEA) ULTRAMARINE
(— THIS) STILL
(GO —) OVERSHOOT
(PREF.) EXTRA HYPER META
OVER PARA PERI PRETER SUPER
TRANS ULTRA
BEYOND HUMAN POWER
(AUTHOR OF —) BJORNSON
(CHARACTER IN —) SANG CLARA

ELIAS HANNA ADOLPH RACHAEL
ROBERTS
BEZALEEL (FATHER OF —) URI
BEZEL RIM TOP EDGE OUCH SEAL
BEVIL BEZIL CROWN FACET
CHATON FLANGE MARQUISE
TEMPLATE
BEZER (FATHER OF —) ZOPHAH
BEZIQUE PENCHANT
BEZOAR GOATSTONE HIPPOLITH
B-GIRL SITTER
BHAKTA BHAGAVATA
BHANG BANG BENG BENJ HEMP
HASHISH
BHARAL TUR HALL NAHOOR
BURRHEL
BHARTRIHARI (BROTHER OF —)
VIKRAMADITYA
BHIKSHU GELONG
BHIMA (FATHER OF —) VAYU
PANDU
(MOTHER OF —) KUNTI PRITHA
BHUTAN (ASSEMBLY OF —)
TSONGDU
(CAPITAL OF —) THIMPHU
(CURRENCY OF —) PAISA RUPEE
(LANGUAGE OF —) DZONGKHA
(RIVER OF —) MACHU MANAS
AMOCHU
BHUTAN PINE KAIL
BIANCA (HUSBAND OF —) FAZIO
LEONTIO
(SISTER OF —) KATHERINE
BIANNUAL BIYEARLY
BIANOR (FATHER OF —) TIBERIS
(MOTHER OF —) MANTO
BIAS PLY WRY AWRY BENT CANT
SWAY WARP AMISS COLOR
FAVOR POISE SLANT SLOPE
SWING TWIST BIGOTRY INCLINE
OBLIQUE SUGGEST CLINAMEN
COLORING DIAGONAL TENDENCY
PREJUDICE PROCEDURE
SPECTACLE
(— IN NEWS REPORTING) PLUGOLA
(BROTHER OF —) MELAMPUS
(FATHER OF —) AMYTHAON
(MOTHER OF —) IDOMENE
(WIFE OF —) PERO IPHIANASSA
BIASED SLANT ANGLED COLORED
PARTIAL
BIB SIP BRAT POUT APRON BLAIN
DRINK BRASSY FEEDER TIPPLE
TUCKER BAVETTE
(CHILD'S —) BISHOP
(LEATHER —) DICK
BIBLE BOOK VULGATE SCRIPTURE
(— TEXT) MIKRA MIQRA
(BOOK OF —) EX CHR COL COR
DAN EPH GAL GEN HAB HAG HEB
HOS JER JOB KIN LAM LEV MAL
MIC NAH NEH NUM PET REV ROM
SAM TIM ACTS AMOS CANT DEUT
EZEK EZRA JOEL JOHN JUDE
JUDG LUKE MARK MATT OBAD
PHIL PROV RUTH SONG ZECH
ZEPH HOSEA JAMES JONAH
KINGS MICAH NAHUM PETER
THESS TITUS DANIEL ECCLES
ESTHER EXODUS HAGGAI ISAIAH
JOSHUA JUDGES PHILEM PSALMS
ROMANS SAMUEL EZEKIEL
GENESIS HEBREWS MALACHI

MATTHEW NUMBERS OBADIAH
TIMOTHY JEREMIAH NEHEMIAH
PHILEMON PROVERBS CANTICLES
EPHESIANS GALATIANS LEVITICUS
ZECHARIAH ZEPHANIAH
CHRONICLES COLOSSIANS
REVELATION CORINTHIANS
DEUTERONOMY PHILIPPIANS
ECCLESIASTES LAMENTATIONS
THESSALONIANS
(SYRIAC VERSION OF —) PESHITO
BIBLE LEAF COSTMARY
BIBULOUS DRINKING BIBACIOUS
BICKER JAR WAR BOWL SPAR TIFF
ARGUE BRAWL CAVIL FIGHT
ASSAIL ATTACK BATTLE
CONTEND DISPUTE PICKEER
QUARREL QUIBBLE WRANGLE
PETTIFOG SKIRMISH SQUABBLE
BICKERN ANVIL BEAKIRON
BICUSPID PREMOLAR
BICYCLE BIKE QUAD CORGI CORGY
CYCLE HOBBY MOUNT STEED
WHEEL JIGGER ORNARY SAFETY
TANDEM ORDINAR TRIPLET
ORDINARY ROADSTER
(PART OF —) ARM LUG RIM CLIP
FORK POST RACK RING SEAT
STAY STEM TIRE CHAIN GUARD
PEDAL SHIFT SPOKE FENDER
HANGER SADDLE DOWNTUBE
SPROCKET CHAINWHEEL
DERAILLEUR
(PLACE WHERE —S ARE SERVICED)
CYCLERY
BID GO BEG NAP BEDE BODE CALL
GIVE HEST HIST PRAY TELL WISH
CHEAP CLEPE FRAGE OFFER
ORDER ADJURE CHARGE DIRECT
ENJOIN INVITE REVEAL SIMPLE
SUMMON TENDER BALANCE
CHEAPEN COMMAND DECLARE
DROPVIE ENTREAT PROFFER
ANNOUNCE PROCLAIM PROPOSAL
(— ADIEU) TEACH
(— AT AUCTION) CRY
(— IN CARDS) CUE FROG JUMP
PASS SKIP SOLO FRAGE GRAND
NULLO SHIFT BOSTON DEFEND
DEMAND DENIAL DOUBLE
SMUDGE BLUCHER COMMAND
SHUTOUT SUPPORT CONTRACT
REDOUBLE SCHMEISS
(SEALED —) TICKET
BIDDING BEHEST AUCTION
BIDDANCE DIRECTIVE
BIDE FACE STAY WAIT ABIDE
AWAIT DWELL TARRY WATCH
ENDURE REMAIN SUFFER
SOJOURN CONTINUE TOLERATE
BIDENS CUCKOLD MANZANILLA
BIDET SITZBAD INSESSION
BIDRI VIDRY BIDDERY TUTENAG
BIENNIAL TRIETERIC
BIER BEAR PYRE FRAME GRAVE
HANDY HORSE TABUT COFFIN
HEARSE LITTER SUPPORT
FERETORY FERETRUM
BIFURCATION WYE FORK SPLIT
BRANCH CROTCH CRUTCH
FORKING DIVISION DICHOTOMY
BIG FAT BARO BOLD HUGE MUCH
VAST BULKY CHIEF GAUCY

GRAND GREAT GROSS HUSKY
LARGE GAUCIE MIGHTY BIGGISH
BUMPING EMINENT HUMMING
LEADING MASSIVE POMPOUS
UPRIGHT VIOLENT BOASTFUL
BOUNCING ENORMOUS
GENEROUS GIGANTIC IMPOSING
PLUMPING PREGNANT SLAPPING
SWANKING SWAPPING THUMPING
(— WITH YOUNG) FULL GRAVID
(MARVELOUSLY —) TREMENDOUS
(PREF.) MAGNI
BIGFOOT SASQUATCH
BIGHORN ARGAL AOUDAD ARGALI
CIMARRON
BIGHT BAY BEND BITE COIL GULF
LOOP ROVE ANGLE CURVE INLET
NOOSE BOUGHT CORNER
HOLLOW POCKET
BIGNESS BULK
BIGOT CAFARD ZEALOT FANATIC
MUMPSIMUS
BIGOTED BIASED NARROW
HIDEBOUND ILLIBERAL
SECTARIAN
BIGOTRY INTOLERANCE
BIGROOT MANROOT BITTERROOT
BIG SHOT HEAVY MUCKAMUCK
BIG SKY COUNTRY MONTANA
BIKINI (TOPLESS —) MONOKINI
BILE BOIL GALL HUMP VENOM
CHOLER GROWTH ATRABILE
MELANCHOLY
(PREF.) BILI CHOL(E)(O)
(SUFF.) CHOLIA CHOLY
BILGE PUMP SCUM BOUGE BULGE
BILLAGE THURROCK
BILHAH (SON OF —) DAN NAPHTALI
BILHAN (FATHER OF —) JEDIAEL
BILIMBI CAMIAS KAMIAS
CUCUMBER
BILINGUAL DIGLOT
BILIOUS GALLISH LIVERISH
BILIOUSNESS LIVER CHOLER
BILK DO GYP BALK HOAX CHEAT
COZEN TRICK DELUDE FLEECE
SWEDGE DECEIVE DEFRAUD
SWINDLE
BILL ACT DUN GET LAW NEB NIB
TAB BEAK CHIT CLAP GETT KITE
NOTE PECK SHOT CHECK ENTRY
LIBEL SCORE CARESS CHARGE
DOCKET INDICT LAWING PECKER
PICKAX POSTER STRIKE DERTRUM
INVOICE LAMPOON MATTOCK
PLACARD PROGRAM REMANET
STATUTE BILLHOOK DOCUMENT
HEADLAND INNOCENT PETITION
TREASURY RECKONING
ACCEPTANCE
(— OF ANCHOR) PEE PEAK
(— OF COMPLAINT) QUERELA
(— OF CREDIT) ANGEL
(— OF DIVORCE) GET GETT
(— OF EXCHANGE) SOLA HUNDI
DEVISE
(— OF FARE) MENU CARTE
(— OF PARCELS) FACTURE
(COUNTERFEIT —S) STIFF
(DOLLAR —) BUCK SPOT SINGLE
FROGSKIN
(REVOLUTIONARY —) ASSIGNAT
(10-DOLLAR —) TEN

TENNER SAWBUCK
(100-DOLLAR —) CENTURY
(2-DOLLAR —) DEUCE
(5-DOLLAR —) FIN VEE FIVE FIVER
BILLET BAR GAD HUT LAY LOG
LOOP NOTE PASS POST SPOT
BERTH ENROL HOUSE LODGE
ORDER SHIDE SPRAG STICK
STRAP BALLOT BULLET COUPON
ENROLL HARBOR LETTER LIBBET
NOTICE TICKET BEARING EPISTLE
MISSIVE POLLACK COALFISH
DOCUMENT FIREWOOD
ORNAMENT POSITION QUARTERS
(— SOLDIERS) CESS
BILLET-DOUX CAPON
BILLETING LIVERY
BILLFISH GAR LONGJAWS SAILFISH
SPEARFISH
BILLFOLD WALLET NOTECASE
BILLHOOK BILL DHAW HOOK
PAWPAW SLASHER SNAGGER
SCIMITAR
BILLIARD BALL IVORY
BILLIARD CUE MACE MAST
(TIP OF —) LEATHER
BILLIARDS PILLS TRUCKS
(LAWN —) TROCO
BILLINGSGATE ABUSE SLAPDASH
BILLION MILLIARD
(PREF.) GIGA
BILLIONTH
(PREF.) BICRO NANO
**BILL OF MARRIAGE (CHARACTER
IN —)** MILL FANNY SLOOK TOBIAS
EDOARDO
(COMPOSER OF —) ROSSINI
BILLON BAIOC VELLON BAJOCCO
BILLOW SEA BLOW WAVE BULGE
CLOUD FLOAT SURGE SWELL
RESACA RIPPLE ROLLER WALLOW
BREAKER UNDULATE
BILLY CAW CHAP CLUB GOAT
MACE MATE BATON FANNY
NEDDY CUDGEL FANNIE FELLOW
BROTHER COMRADE BILLIKIN
BILLYCAN BLUDGEON JACKSHAY
BLACKJACK TRUNCHEON
BILLY BUDD (CHARACTER IN —)
BUDD VERE BILLY CLAGGART
(COMPOSER OF —) BRITTEN
BILSHAN (COMPANION OF —)
ZERUBBABEL
BIMAH ALMEMAR ALMEMOR
BIMHAL (FATHER OF —) JAPHLET
BIN ARK BOX CUB GUM BING BONE
CART CRIB VINA FRAME HUTCH
KENCH PUNGI STALL STORE
WAGON BASKET BUNKER GARNER
HAMPER MANGER POCKET
TROUGH WITHIN BLEACHER
(— FOR CEMENT) SILO
(— FOR FISH) KENCH
(— FOR GRAIN) ARK
BINARY HYDRIDE
BINATE DUAL DOUBLE PAIRED
COUPLED TWOFOLD GEMINATE
BINAURAL DIOTIC
BIND JAM LAP TIE WAP EARL FAST
FRAP GIRD GYVE HOLD HOOP
KNIT KNOT LASH MAIL NAIL TAPE
YERK BRACE CADGE CHAIN CINCH
EDDER GIRTH SNAKE STICK

STRAP TRUSS ATTACH BUNDLE
COMMIT EMBIND ENGAGE FETTER
FREEZE GARTER GIRDLE LIGATE
OBLIGE STRAIN SWATHE TETHER
WRITHE ARTICLE ASTRAIN
BANDAGE CONFINE EMBOUND
ENCHAIN GRAPPLE SHACKLE
SWADDLE ASTRINGE CONCLUDE
FLIGHTER HANDFAST INNODATE
LIGATURE OBLIGATE RESTRAIN
(— A FALCON) MAIL
(— BY LEASE) THIRL
(— BY PLEDGE) GAGE SWEAR
(— IN BUNDLE) KID BAVIN
(— INTO SHEAVES) GAVEL THRAVE
(— ONESELF) ADHERE
(— TO SECRECY) TILE
(— TOGETHER) LIME FAGOT SEIZE
CEMENT FAGGOT ASTRINGE
RELIGATE COLLIGATE
(— UP) KILT BAVIN TRUSS
UPBAND ASTRICT REVOLVE
(— WINGS) PINION
(— WITH THREAD) OOP
(PREF.) SPHINGO
(SUFF.) SPHINX
BINDER BAND BEAM BOND CORD
ROPE BALER COVER FRAME
LEVER FILLET FOLDER GIRDER
HEADER LIGNIN TARMAC
HAYBAND BONDSTONE
BOOKMAKER
BINDING TAG BAND CORD GARD
HARD LEAR ROPE TAPE YAPP
COVER VALID CADDIS EDGING
RIBBON BOUNDEN CADDICE
GALLOON LAPPING MOUSING
WEBBING FAITHFUL LIGATIVE
LIGATORY STRINGENT
OBLIGATORY
(— FAST) IRON
(— OF BOOK) BOCK FACE YAPP
(— OF GOLD) BISSET
(— ON DRESS) FENT
(SUFF.) DESIS
BINDLESTIFF BUM
BINDWEED BINE WIRE CREEPER
TIEVINE BEARBIND BEARBINE
BELLBINE BINEWEED CORNBIND
HELLWEED MILKMAID WOODBINE
WITHYWIND
BINE WIRE
BINGE BAT BOW HIT BLOW BUST
SOAK TEAR TOOT BEANO PARTY
SOUSE SPRAY SPREE CRINGE
BLOWOFF CAROUSAL
BINGO KENO BEANO LOTTO
BRANDY SCREENO TOMBOLA
BINNACLE PYX BITTACLE
BINNUI (FATHER OF —) HENADAD
(SON OF —) NOADIAH
BINOCULARS GLASS
BINOMIAL DIONYM BINOMEN
BIOCHEMIST AMERICAN CORI
BLOCH MOORE OCHOA ALSBERG
AXELROD LIPMANN OSBORNE
SHAFFER KORNBERG NIRENBERG
ARGENTINIAN LELOIR
CANADIAN COLLIP
ENGLISH KREBS PERUTZ PORTER
SANGER MITCHELL
FRENCH MONOD DUCLAUX
GERMAN LYNEN

BIODEGRADABLE SOFT
BIOGEOGRAPHY CHOROLOGY
BIOGRAPHER PLUTARCH
SCOTTISH BOSWELL
BIOGRAPHY BIO LIFE VITA
MEMOIR ACCOUNT HISTORY
RECOUNT PSYCHOGRAPH
(— OF SAINTS) HAGIOGRAPHA
HAGIOGRAPHY
BIOLOGIST NATURALIST
AMERICAN EAST JUST LUTZ WALD
CHILD CLARK LURIA MINOT
PEARL SHULL TYLER WOODS
BAILEY BEADLE BUMPUS FISHER
JORDAN LITTLE OSBORN PALADE
WELLER CONKLIN HERRICK
HERSHEY WETMORE CHAMBERS
DELBRUCK HARRISON SEDGWICK
STOCKARD
AUSTRIAN STEINACH
BELGIAN CLAUDE
CUBAN FINLAY
ENGLISH CRICK HUXLEY MIVART
BATESON COBBOLD KENDREW
MEDAWAR ROMANES CUMMINGS
NICHOLSON
FRENCH GIARD CARREL NOCARD
BOUCHARD LEDANTEC
GERMAN WOLFF DRIESCH
HAECKEL UEXKULL WEISMANN
MUCKERMANN
IRISH ALLMAN
NORWEGIAN MJOEN
RUSSIAN GURVICH LYSENKO
SCOTTISH GEDDES THOMSON
BIOPHORE BIOGEN PLASOME
BIOPLAST MICELLA MICELLE
BIOTITE MICA ANOMITE
MEROXENE RUBELLAN
BIOTOPE STATION
BIPARTITE
(PREF.) DIPHY
BIPED DIPODE HINDQUARTERS
BIRCH COW BIRK CANE FLOG WHIP
ALDER ALNUS CANOE SWISH
BETULA BIRKEN TAWHAI HICKORY
BIRD ANI DAW DOG JAY NUN PIE
TIT TUI CHAT COOT CROW DOVE
FOWL IBIS JACK KAGU KITE KNOT
LARK QUIT RUFF TERN TODY
WING WREN BAKER BRANT
CHUCK CLEAR COVEY EGRET
FINCH FLIER FLYER GOOSE HOBBY
JUNCO LARID LIVER PEWEE
PEWIT RAVEN ROBIN SNIPE STILT
SWIFT TEREK TURCO TWITE
VIREO BULBUL DICKEY DIPPER
DRIVER DRONGO DUCKER DUNLIN
FALCON FINGER GROUSE GUINEA
HOOPOE HOOTER JACANA
JAEGER LINNET MARTEN MOCKER
NESTER ORIOLE OSCINE PHOEBE
PLOVER SHRIKE SILVAN SINGER
SITTER SYLVAN THRUSH TROGON
TURNIX VERDIN YAWPER
ANTBIRD BABBLER BLUEJAY
BUNTING BUSTARD BUZZARD
CATBIRD CHIRPER COTINGA
COURLAN FEATHER FLAPPER
FLICKER FLIGGER FLOPPER
GRACKLE HALCYON HORNERO
HURGILA INCOMER IRRISOR
JACAMAR JACKDAW KINGLET

MINIVET MOULTER ORTOLAN
PEACOCK PERCHER QUILLER
REDWING SCRAPER SKINNER
SKYLARK SPARROW SUNBIRD
SWALLOW TANAGER TINAMOU
TITLARK TOMFOOL WARBLER
WAXWING WAYBUNG ACCENTOR
AIRPLANE AMADAVAT ANNOTINE
BLACKCAP BLACKNEB BLUEBIRD
BOATBILL BOBOLINK BOBWHITE
BUBBLING CAGELING CARINATE
COCKBIRD COCORICO DREPANID
FERNBIRD FIREBIRD FIRETAIL
GROSBEAK GRUIFORM IBISBILL
JUVENILE KILLDEER KINGBIRD
LOBEFOOT LONGSPUR OXPECKER
PALMIPED PHEASANT PLUMIPED
POORWILL PREACHER REDSTART
SALTATOR SONGBIRD STARLING
SURFBIRD SWAMPHEN TAPACOLO
THRASHER THROSTLE TITMOUSE
TREMBLER UMBRETTE WHINCHAT
WOODCHAT WOODCOCK
YEARBIRD COCKYOLLY CROSSBILL
ROADRUNNER MOCKINGBIRD
(— OF BRILLIANT PLUMAGE) TODY
JALAP BARBET ORIOLE TROGON
JACAMAR KIROMBO MINIVET
TANAGER
(— OF INDIA) BAYA KALA SHAMA
(— OF OMEN) WAYBIRD
(— OF PREY) OWL HAWK KITE
EAGLE ELANT GLEAD GLEDE
STOOP EAGLET ELANET BUZZARD
GOSHAWK STOOPER VULTURE
ACCIPITER
(AFRICAN —) TAHA QUELEA
TOURACO UMBRETTE NAPECREST
(AUSTRALIAN —) EMU ROA LORY
ARARA LEIPOA BOOBOOK
BUSTARD FIGBIRD WAYBUNG
BELLBIRD LORIKEET LYREBIRD
MANUCODE
(BIG-BEAKED —) BECARD HORNBILL
(CRESTED —) KAGU COPPY
HOATZIN TOPKNOT
(CROCODILE —) TROCHIL
(DECOY —) CALL STOOL
(DIVING —) AUK LOON GREBE
DARTER DOPPER DUCKER
GRAYLING PLUNGEON
(EUROPEAN —) ANI DAW MEW
QUA CIRL DARR KITE MALL MORO
QUIS ROOK STAG WHIM YITE
AMSEL BOONK GLEDE MAVIS
MERLE OUSEL OUZEL SACER
SAKER SERIN TARIN TEREK TERIN
WHAUP AVOCET CUCKOO
CUSHAT GAYLAG GODWIT
MARTEN MERLIN MISSEL REDCAP
WHEWER WINDLE WINNEL
WRANNY BITTERN BUSTARD
HAYBIRD KESTREL MOTACIL
ORTOLAN SAKERET STARNEL
WHISKEY WINNARD WITWALL
BARGOOSE CHEPSTER DOTTEREL
GARGANEY REDSTART
WHEATEAR WHEYBIRD
WHIMBREL WRANNOCK
YOLDRING
(EXTINCT —) MOA DODO JIBI KIWI
MAMO RUKH OFFBIRD
(FABULOUS —) FUM ROC FUNG

HALCYON OOFBIRD WHISTLER
(FEMALE —) HEN JENNY
(FICTITIOUS —) JAYHAWK PHOENIX
(FISH-CATCHING —) OSPREY
CRABIER
(FLEDGLING —) SQUAB
(FLIGHTLESS —) EMU GOR MOA
DODO EYAS GORB GULL KAGU
KIWI CALLOW GORLIN APTERYX
GORLING NESTLER OSTRICH
PENGUIN BUBBLING NESTLING
(FRIGATE —) IOA IWA
(FRUIT-EATING —) COLY
(GALLOWS —) HEMPY HEMPIE
(GAME —) QUAIL SNIPE COLIMA
GROUSE INCOME FLAPPER
INCOMER
(GREEN —) SIRGANG
(HAWAIIAN —) IO OO AVA IOA IWA
OOA IIWI JIBI KOAE MAMO MOHO
OMAO OOAA KAMAO PALILA
(HORN-HEADED —) KAMICHI
(INJURED —) CRIPPLE
(LARGEST —) LAMMERGEIER
(LIMICOLINE —) PRATINCOLE
(MADAGASCAR —) KIROMBO
(MECHANICAL —) ORTHOPTER
(MYTHICAL —) FUM ROC GANZA
SIMURG SIMURGH
(NEW ZEALAND —) KEA MOA OII
ROA HUIA KAKA KIWI KOKO KUKU
KULU PEHO RURU TITI WEKA
POAKA KAKAPO KOKAKO KUKUPA
APTERYX KORIMAKO MOREPORK
NOTORNIS
(PASSERINE —) QUIT FINCH
SPARROW STARNEL SWALLOW
SYLVIID DREPANID FALCONET
FERNBIRD GRALLINA JACKBIRD
OVENBIRD
(PERTAINING TO —S) OSCINE
(RAPACIOUS —) SKUA JAEGER
(RASORIAL —) SCRATCHER
(RUNNING —) COURSER
(SAMOAN —) IAO
(SEA —) AUK ERN ERNE GONY
GULL PINK SMEW TERN EIDER
SOLAN FULMAR GANNET
HAGDON OSPREY PETREL PUFFIN
PELICAN SEAFOWL MURRELET
MALLEMUCK
(SHORE —) REE RAIL SORA SNIPE
STILT WADER AVOCET CURLEW
PLOVER WILLET WRYBILL
SHEATHBILL
(SHORT-TAILED —) BREVE
(SINGING —) LARK WREN PIPIT
ROBIN VEERY VIREO CANARY
LINNET MOCKER ORIOLE OSCINE
SINGER THRUSH WARBLER
FAUVETTE REDSTART
NIGHTINGALE
(SMALL —) TIT TODY WREN DICKY
PEGGY PIPIT TYDIE VIREO DICKEY
LINNET SISKIN TOMTIT CREEPER
SPARROW TITLARK COCORICO
GNATSNAP PERCOLIN STARLING
WHEATEAR
(SOUTH AMERICAN —) GUAN MINA
MITU MYNA RARA TOCA BAKER
CHAJA JOPIM TURCO BARBET
BECARD CHUNGA TOUCAN
CARIAMA OILBIRD BELLBIRD

BOATBILL CARACARA GUACHARO
HOACTZIN PUFFBIRD SCREAMER
TAPACOLO TAPACULO TERUTERO
(STYLIZED —) DISTELFINK
(TROPICAL —) ANI GUAN KOAE
TODY BOS'N BOSUN JALAP
BARBET BECARD MOTMOT
TROGON JACAMAR MANAKIN
WIGTAIL LONGTAIL SALTATOR
(WADING —) HERN IBIS RAIL SORA
CRANE HERON SNIPE STILT
STORK ARGALA AVOCET GODWIT
JACANA LIMPKIN BOATBILL
FLAMINGO SHOEBILL SHOEBIRD
SANDERLING
(WILD —S) GALLINAE
(YEAR-OLD —) ANNOTINE
(YOUNG —) EYA GULL PIPER
CHEEPER FLAPPER NESTLER
BIRDIKIN NESTLING
(PL.) AVIFAUNA POLYMYODI
PRAECOCES
(PREF.) AVI ORNIS ORNITH(I)(O)
(SUFF.) ORNIS ORNITHES
BIRD BOLT BURBOLT QUARREL
BIRD CAGE AVIARY PINJRA
VOLARY VOLERY PADDOCK
BIRDCATCHER FOWLER
BIRD CHERRY DOGWOOD
EGGBERRY HACKWOOD
HAGBERRY
BIRDLIFE ORNIS
BIRDLIME GLUE LIME BELIME
VISCUM BIRDGLUE
BIRD OF PARADISE APUS
MANUCODE RIFLEBIRD
BIRDS (AUTHOR OF —)
ARISTOPHANES
(CHARACTER IN —) EPOPS TEREUS
BASILEIA EUELPIDES
PISTHETAERUS
BIRD'S-FOOT FOWLFOOT
SERRADELLA
BIRD'S KNEE SUFFRAGO
BIRD'S MANTLE STRAGULUM
BIRENO (WIFE OF —) OLIMPIA
BIRI BIDI
BIRTH KIN BEAR FALL BLOOD
BURDEN GENTRY ORIGIN
BEARING BORNING DESCENT
GENESIS LINEAGE DELIVERY
GENITURE NASCENCY NATALITY
NATIVITY
(FALSE —) SOOTERKIN
(GENTLE —) GENTILITY
(HIGH —) PARAGE
(HONORABLE —) BLOOD
(OF LOW —) CRESTLESS
(OF NOBLE —) CORONETED
(PREF.) NATI
(SUFF.) (GIVING —) PARA PAROUS
BIRTHMARK MOLE IMAGE NAEVE
NEVUS BLEMISH SPILOMA
SIGNATURE
BIRTHRATE NATALITY FERTILITY
BIRTHRIGHT KIND BIRTHDOM
HERITAGE
BIRTHROOT BATHROOT
BATHWORT DEATHROOT
DISHCLOTH SQUAWROOT
BIRTHWORT GUACO ASARUM
BATHROOT
BISAYAN AKLAN CEBUAN

AKLANON CEBUANO
BISCUIT BUN NUT BAKE ROLL
RUSK SNAP WOOD BREAD COOKY
SCONE WAFER BISQUE COOKIE
DODGER MALLOW MUFFIN
PARKIN SIMNEL CRACKER
GALETTE PENTILE PRETZEL
RATAFIA RATIFIA CRACKNEL
HARDTACK ZWIEBACK
(BROKEN —S) DUNDERFUNK
(COLOR —) DOE PAWNEE
BISECT FORK CROSS HALVE SPLIT
CLEAVE DIVIDE MIDDLE
SEPARATE
BISECTION MEDIATION
BISEXUAL ACDC
BISHOP EP ABBA EPUS LAWN
PAPA POPE ANGEL COARB DENIS
ARCHER BUSTLE DESPOT EPARCH
EXARCH MAGPIE PRESUL PRIEST
PRIMUS ROCHET ROCKAT
PONTIFF PRELATE PRIMATE
TULCHAN ANTISTES DIOCESAN
DIRECTOR ORDINARY OVERSEER
PONTIFEX PATRIARCH
(— AND MARTYR) EM
(CHESS —) ALFIN ALPHYN ARCHER
BISHOP'S-WEED AMMI AMMEOS
KHELLA WILLIAM BOLEWORT
BULLWORT GOUTWEED
TOOTHPICK
BISKOP BRUSHER STEENBRAS
BISMARK KRAPFE KRAPFEN
BISMUTH WISMUTH TINGLASS
BISON BUGLE BOVINE MITHAN
WISENT AUROCHS BONASUS
BUFFALO
BISTORT PATIENCE ADDERWORT
ASTROLOGE SNAKEWEED
SNAKEWORT
BISTRO BAR CAFE TAVERN
WINESHOP ESTAMINET
NIGHTCLUB
BIT ACE FID FIP GAG JOT NIP ORT
PIP TAD WEE ATOM BITE BITT
CHIP CROP CURB DITE DOIT DRIB
FLAW FOOD GRUE HAET HATE
HOOT IOTA ITEM LEVY MITE
MOTE PART SLUT SNAP SNIP
SPOT TOOL WHIT AUGER BLADE
CHECK CRUMB DRILL GROAT
PATCH PEZZO PIECE POINT
SCRAP SHRED SMACK SNACK
SPECK STEEK TASTE THRUM
WIGHT BITTIE BRIDLE CANNON
EATING MORSEL PELHAM PICKLE
SCATCH SHTICK SIPPET SMIDGE
SPLICE STITCH STIVER THOGHT
TITTLE TRIFLE BRADOON
BRIDOON CHILENO GLIMMER
MORCEAU PALLION PORTION
SMIDGEN SMIDGIN SNAFFLE
TRANEEN FISHTAIL FRACTION
FRAGMENT QUANTITY SMIDGEON
SMITCHIN TWOPENNY
(— OF GOSSIP) HEARING
(— OF INFORMATION) GRIFF
GRIFFIN WRINKLE
(— OF KEY) WEB
(— OF LAND) CROOK
(— OF METAL) FLITTER
(— OF TOAST) SNIPPET
(— TO EAT) MUNGEY

(—S AND PIECES) GUBBINS
GUBBINGS
(—S OF COKE) BREEZE
(—S OF WRITING) EXCERPTA
(CUTTING —) CHASER
(DRILL —) CROWN
(FANCIFUL —) FLAM
(FIPPENY —) SIXPENCE
(FLORID —) FLOURISH
(HORSE'S —) KEVEL SNODE
CANNON PELHAM SCATCH
SNAFFLE BASTONET
(LEAST —) FIG JOT RAP HANG LICK
GHOST GROAT RIZZOM STITCH
(LITTLE —) PICK TOUCH BITTOCK
REMNANT SOUPCON
(ONE — PER SECOND) BAUD
(ONE BILLION —S) GIGABIT
(ONE-QUARTER —) GILL
(SEQUENCE OF —S) BYTE
(SMALL —) BLEB GLIM SPUNK
(SMALL —S) SMATTER
(THEATRICAL —) SHTICK SCHTICK
(TINY —) SPECK DRIBBLE SCRINCH
TODDICK
(PL.) SMITHERS SMITHEREENS
BITCH DO GYP BICK LAMP SLUT
BRACH BROOD CHEAT GROUSE
COMPLAIN
BITE BIT CUT EAT JAW NIP BAIT
CHAM CHEW ETCH FOOD GASH
GNAP GNAW HOLD KNAP MEAL
RIVE SNAP TAKE CHACK CHAMM
CHAMP CHEAT GNASH PINCH
SEIZE SMART SNACK STING
TOOTH TRICK CRUNCH MORSEL
NIBBLE PIERCE SAVAGE BUGBITE
CHEATER CORRODE FORBITE
IMPRESS MORSURE MUNCHET
PARTAKE SHARPER SLANDER
(— AT) HIT
(— GREEDILY) HANCH
(— REPEATEDLY) CHAMP
BITER
(SUFF.) DECTES
BITHIAH (HUSBAND OF —) MERED
BITING BIT HOT ACID HOAR KEEN
ACRID NIPPY QUICK SHARP SNELL
BITTER RODENT SEVERE SHREWD
STINGY TEETHY TWEAKY CAUSTIC
CUTTING MORDANT MORSURE
NIPPING PUNGENT SUBACID
DRILLING INCISIVE PIERCING
POIGNANT SCALDING SCATHING
STINGING ACIDULOUS
MORDACIOUS
BITIS ECHIDNA
BITO BALM HAJILIJ
BITON (BROTHER OF —) CLEOBIS
(MOTHER OF —) CYDIPPE
BITT BLOCK KNIGHT BOLLARD
(PL.) RANGEHEADS
BITTER AWA GAL ACID ACRE ASIM
BASK KEEN MARA RUDE SALT
SORE SOUR TART ACERB ACRID
AMARA ASPER BLEAK EAGER
HARSH IRATE SHARP SNELL
BITING PICRIC SEVERE AUSTERE
CAUSTIC CRABBED CUTTING
FERVENT GALLING GALLISH
PAINFUL PUNGENT SATIRIC
POIGNANT SARDONIC
STINGING SUBAMARE

VIRULENT ACRIMONIOUS
(PREF.) PICR(O)
(SUFF.) PICRIN
BITTER APPLE COLOCYNTH
BITTER BIT SMALLPOX
BITTERBUSH SNAKEROOT
BITTER CLOVER YELLOWTOP
BITTERLY SOUR FELLY BITTER
ROUNDLY CURSEDLY
BITTERN BUMP SOCO BOONK
BUTOR HERON BITORE BUMBLE
BUMMLE BUTTAL KAKKAK
BLITTER BUMMLER ERICIUS
DUNKADOO GRUIFORM
LONGNECK
(FLOCK OF —) SEDGE SIEGE
BITTERNESS RUE ACOR BILE FELL
GALL ATTER MARAH ENMITY
MALICE RANCOR AMARITY
ACERBITY ACRIDITY ACRIMONY
ASPERITY FERVENCY SEVERITY
WORMWOOD
(EXTREME —) VIRULENCE
(WITH —) AMAREVOLE
BITTER PIT STIPPEN
BITTERROOT LEWISIA
TOBACCOROOT
BITTERS AMER
BITTER SPAR DOLOMITE
BITTERSWEET FELLEN DOGWOOD
LOBSTER SOLANUM WAXWORK
DULCAMARA FELONWOOD
FELONWORT FEVERTWIG
WITHYWIND WOLFBERRY
BITTER VETCH ERS
BITTERWEED RAGWEED
HORSEWEED
BITTERWORT FELWORT
DANDELION
BITUMEN TAR CONGO PITCH SLIME
MALTHA ASPHALT CARBENE
ALKITRAN ALCHITRAN ELATERITE
BIVALENT DIATOMIC
BIVALVE HEN CLAM SPAT PINNA
COCKLE DIATOM MUSSEL OYSTER
MOLLUSK NUCULID PANDORA
SCALLOP TOHEROA
BIVOUAC CAMP ETAPE WATCH
ENCAMP SHELTER
BIZARRE ODD ANTIC DEDAL
OUTRE QUEER QUAINT ANTICAL
BAROQUE CURIOUS FANCIFUL
ECCENTRIC FANTASTIC
GROTESQUE OUTLANDISH
BLAB LAB CHAT BLART BLATE
CHEEP CLACK PEACH BABBLE
BETRAY GOSSIP REVEAL SQUEAL
TATTLE BLABBER CHATTER
CLATTER
BLACK DHU JET WAN CALO CROW
DARK EBON FOUL INKY NOIR PIKY
SOOT BUGLE COLLY DUSKY
DWALE MURKY NEGRO NOIRE
RAVEN SABLE SOOTY TARRY
THICK ATROUS BRUNET DISMAL
ETHIOP GLOOMY MURREY PITCHY
SULLEN ABAISER AFRICAN
BLACKEN DIAMOND MELANIC
NEGRITO NIGRINE NIGROUS
PICEOUS SWARTHY UNCLEAN
MOURNFUL
(— AND BLUE) LIVID
(— OUT) CONK

(BONE —) SPODIUM
(BROWNISH —) LAVA
(GREENISH —) CORBEAU
(IVORY —) ABAISER
(LIGHT-SKINNED —) BROWN
(RATHER —) DUSKISH
(VIOLET —) CROW
(PREF.) ATRO MAVRO MEL(A)
MELAN(O) NIGRI
(SUFF.) MELANE
BLACKAMOOR BLECK NEGRO
MORIAN NEGRESS ETHIOPIAN
BLACK ARROW (AUTHOR OF —)
STEVENSON
(CHARACTER IN —) DICK ELLIS
OATES DANIEL JOANNA OLIVER
SEDLEY LAWLESS RICHARD
SHELTON BRACKLEY DUCKWORTH
BLACK ASH HOOPWOOD
BLACKBALL PIP PILL BALLOT
EXCLUDE HEEBALL OSTRACIZE
BLACK BASS HURON TROUT
ACHIGAN GROWLER OCHIGAN
BLACKBERRY AGAWAM LAWTON
BRAMBLE DEWBERRY MULBERRY
ROSACEAN
(— BUSH) MORE
BLACKBIRD ANI DAW PIE CROW
MERL AMSEL COLLY MERLE
OUSEL OUZEL RAVEN BLACKY
COLLEY MAIZER BLACKIE
COWBIRD GRACKLE JACKDAW
REDWING WOOFELL TROOPIAL
BLACKBOARD CHALKBOARD
GREENBOARD
BLACKBREAM TARWHINE
BLACK-BROWED GLOOMY
BLACK BRYONY LILY LILIUM
OXBERRY BINDWEED MANDRAKE
BLACK BUCK SASIN
BLACKCAP GULL JACK PEGGY
HAYBIRD WARBLER MOCKBIRD
TITMOUSE JACKSTRAW
RASPBERRY
BLACKDAMP STYTH STYTHE
CHOKEDAMP
BLACKDRINK YAPON YAUPON
BLACKEN INK TAR CHAR CORK
SMUT SOIL SOOT BLECK CLOUD
COLLY JAPAN SMOKE SULLY
BEFOUL BLATCH DARKEN
DEFAME MALIGN SMEETH SMIRCH
SMUTCH VILIFY ASPERSE
BENEGRO NIGRIFY SLANDER
SMOLDER TRADUCE BESMIRCH
BLACKENED REECHY
BLACKEYE COWPEA
BLACKFELLOW BLACKBOY
YAMMADJI
BLACKFIN CISCO SESIS
BLACKFISH GRIND TAUTOG
BORLASE DOGFISH GRAMPUS
POTHEAD HARDHEAD
BLACKFLY GNAT SIMULIID
BLACKFOOT BLOOD KAINAH
PIEGAN SIKSIKA SIHASAPA
BLACK GROUPER MERO AGUAJI
WARSAW GARRUPA
BLACKGUARD SHAG BLECK CATSO
GAMIN GUARD SNUFF SWEEP
ROTTER LADRONE SKELLUM
VAGRANT BLAGGARD CRIMINAL
LARRIKIN VAGABOND SCOUNDREL

BLACK GUILLEMOT CUTTY TYSTE
SCRABE DOVEKEY DOVEKIE
SCRABER PUFFINET
BLACK GUM TUPELO HORNPIPE
STINKWOOD
BLACK HAW SLOE BOOTS ALISIER
STAGBUSH VIBURNUM
BLACKHEAD COMEDO
BLACK HOLE COLLAPSAR
BLACK HOREHOUND HENBIT
ARCHANGEL
BLACK HORSE SUCKER SUCKEREL
BLACKING LINK BLECK BLATCH
BLEACH ATRAMENT
BLACK IRONWOOD AXMASTER
AXEMASTER
BLACKISH DUSKY MOREL SWART
BLACKY
BLACKJACK OAK SAP CLUB COSH
DUCK FLAG JACK BETLE BILLY
BLENDE JERKIN BOMBARD
NATURAL BLUDGEON
BLACKLEG LEG FIRE SCAB SNOB
ANTHRAX GAMBLER JACKLEG
APOSTATE BLACKNEB BLACKNOB
SWINDLER KNOBSTICK
BLACK LETTER GOTHIC
BLACKLY SABLY
BLACK MAGIC DIABLERIE
BLACKMAIL BRIBE CHOUT COERCE
EXTORT RANSOM TRIBUTE
CHANTAGE
BLACKMAILER GHOUL BRIBER
LEECHER
BLACK MANGROVE COURIDA
BLACK MEDIC HOP TREFOIL
NONESUCH SHAMROCK
BLACKNESS GRIME DARKNESS
NIGRITUDE
BLACK NIGHTSHADE MOREL
DUSCLE SOLANUM BLUEBERRY
MOONSHADE TROMPILLO
BLACK OLIVE OXHORN
BLACK PEPPER PIMENTA
BLACK PINE MATAI
BLACK POISON WALNUT
BLACK RHINOCEROS BORELE
KEITLOA UPEYGAN
BLACK SALLY SALLEE
MUZZLEWOOD
BLACK SANICLE LUNGWORT
MASTERWORT
BLACK SHANK LANAS
BLACK SKIMMER CUTWATER
SHEARBILL
BLACKSMITH GOW SMUG LOHAR
SHOER SMITH PLOVER SMITHY
VULCAN BROOKIE FARRIER
STRIKER BURNEWIN IRONSMITH
BLACKSNAKE WHIP QUIRT RACER
ELAPID RUNNER COLUBRID
BLACK SPECK DARTROSE
BLACK SPURGE FLUXWEED
BLACKTAIL DASSY DASSIE
BLACK TERN DARR STARN
BLACKTHORN HAW SLOE SNAG
SCROG GRIBBLE SLOEBUSH
SLOETREE SNAGBUSH
BLACK-VARNISH TREE THEETSEE
BLACK VULTURE URUBU CORBIE
ZOPILOTE
BLACK WALNUT NOGAL
BLACKWATER STATE NEBRASKA

BLACK WIDOW POKOMOO
BLACK WOLF KARAKURT
BLACKWOOD BITI LIGHTWOOD
BLACKWORT COMFREY
BLADDER SAC VES VESICA
AMPULLA BLATHER BLISTER
INFLATE UROCYST UTRICLE
VESICLE
(AIR —) POKE SWIM SOUND
SINGALLY
(PREF.) ASC(I)(IDI)(IDIO)(O)
CYST(I)(O) PHYSO VESICO
(SUFF.) CYST(IS)
BLADDER-AND-STRING BUMBASS
BLADDER CAMPION BEHN BEHEN
SILENE COWBELL SNAPPER
RATTLEBOX
BLADDER KETMIE MODESTY
BLADDERNUT BAGNUT
BLADDERWORT POPWEED
BLADDER WRACK CUTWEED
KELPWARE
BLADE BIT FIN FOP OAR SAW WEB
BLOW BONE BOWL EDGE FLAG
HEAD LEAF LIMB TANG WEAK
BLOOD BRAND DANDY FLUKE
GRAIN GUIDE HEALD KNIFE
LANCE SHEAR SPARK SPEAR
SPIRE SWORD BLUNGE BUCKET
BUSTER CUTTER DOCTOR FOIBLE
HEDDLE LAMINA PAGINA RIPPER
ROARER SCYTHE SICKLE TOLEDO
BAYONET CHIPPER GALLANT
POLESAW SCALPEL SCAPULA
SCRAPER SPINNER MOLDBOARD
PROPELLER
(— OF FAN) VANE
(— OF GRASS) PILE CHIRE SPEAR
SPIRE STRAP TRANEEN
(— OF KNIFE) TANG GRAIN
(— OF LEAF) LIMB LAMINA
(— OF MORION) COMB
(— OF OAR) PALM PEEL PELL
WASH
(— OF SCISSORS) BILL
(— OF YOUNG GRAIN) SORAGE
(CULTIVATOR —) SWEEP
DUCKFOOT
(SKATE —) RUNNER
(SURGICAL —) LEUCOTOME
(SUFF.) SPATH
BLAES CAM
BLAFFERT PLAPPERT
BLAIN RUBY SORE BULLA BLISTER
INFLAME PUSTULE
BLAKE MCKAY
BLAMABLE FAULTY CULPABLE
BLAME CALL CHOP HURT LACK
ONUS SAKE SPOT TWIT WITE
CHIDE FAULT GUILT ODIUM
PINCH SHEND SNAPE SWICK
SWIKE THANK TOUCH WHITE
ACCUSE ATTASK BUMBLE
BURDEN CHARGE DIRDUM PLIGHT
REBUKE REVILE SCANCE APPOINT
ASCRIBE CENSURE CONDEMN
CULPATE OBLOQUY REPROOF
REPROVE SLANDER UPBRAID
WITHNIM REPROACH
BLAMED BLINDING BLISTERING
BLAMELESS PURE ENTIRE
PERFECT INNOCENT SACKLESS
SPOTLESS WITELESS RIGHTEOUS

BLAMEWORTHY GUILTY CRIMINAL CULPABLE REPROBATE

BLANCH FADE PALE BLENK CHALK SCALD WHITE APPALL ARGENT BIANCA BLEACH BLENCH FALLOW WHITEN ETIOLATE

BLANCHED ASHEN MEALY ETIOLATE BLOODLESS COLORLESS

BLANCMANGE FLUMMERY

BLAND COLD KIND MILD OILY OPEN SOFT SLEEK SUAVE BENIGN BREEZY GENIAL GENTLE SMOOTH URBANE AFFABLE AMIABLE LENIENT VANILLA FAVONIAN GRACIOUS UNCTUOUS

BLANDISH COAX CHARM ALLURE BLANCH CAJOLE FONDLE SMOOTH FLATTER WHEEDLE HONEYFUGLE

BLANDLY CREAMILY

BLANK BARE BURR FLAN FORM SHOT VOID ANNUL BLIND BREAK CHASM CLEAN EMPTY FALSE RANGE SPACE WASTE WHITE COUPON VACANT ANTIQUE BRINDLE NONPLUS UNMIXED VACUOUS UNFILLED

BLANKED BLIND

BLANKET RUG BROT MAUD WRAP BLUEY COTTA COVER CUMLY LAYER MANTA PATTU QUILT SHEET SUGAN THROW AFGHAN COOLER CUMBLY GLOBAL KAMBAL MANTLE PALLET PONCHO PUTTOO SERAPE SOOGAN STIFLE STROUD TILPAH CHIRIPA DOUBLER SMOTHER WHITTLE COVERLET MACKINAW
(**— A VESSEL**) WRONG
(**— OF SKINS**) KAROSS
(**— WITH BOMBS**) SATURATE
(**BUSHMAN'S —**) BLUEY
(**QUILTED —**) BROT
(**SADDLE —**) CORONA
(**PREF.**) REGO

BLANKETING DUFFEL DUFFLE

BLANKNESS VACUITY NEGATION

BLARE PEAL BLART BLAST BLEAR NOISE BLAZON SCREAM FANFARE TANTARA TRUMPET

BLARNEY CON TAFFY BUTTER CAJOLE SAWDER FLATTER WHEEDLE

BLAS GIL RUY

BLASPHEME ABUSE CURSE DEFAME REVILE PROFANE

BLASPHEMOUS BAD RIBALD IMPIOUS PROFANE

BLASPHEMY CALUMNY CURSING IMPIETY ANATHEMA SWEARING

BLAST BUB NIP WAP BANG BLOW FRAP GALE GUST RUIN RUST SHOT TOOT WAFF WIND BLAME BLIST BLORE SPLIT STUNT TRUMP ATTACK BLIGHT BUGGER FORBID NIDDER NITHER REBUFF VOLLEY WITHER BLUSTER DESPOIL EXPLODE SHATTER SHRIVEL DYNAMITE OUTBURST PROCLAIM WHIRLPUFF
(**— OF WIND**) GUST RISE PERRY PIRRIE VENTOSITY
(**— ON HORN**) TOOT PRYSE

(**— WITH COLD**) SNEAP
(**FURIOUS —**) SNIFTER
(**RAINY —**) BLATTER

BLASTED BLAME BLAMED BLIGHTED BLINDING BLINKING

BLASTER FROSTER SHOOTER SHOTMAN

BLASTING SCATHING SHOOTING STELLATION
(**— METHOD**) MUDCAP

BLASTOMERE MESOMERE MACROMERE MICROMERE

BLASTULA PLACULA PLANULA PLANULAN

BLATANT GLIB LOUD BRASH GROSS NOISY SILLY VOCAL COARSE GARISH TONANT VULGAR BRAWLING STRIDENT

BLATHER STIR BLEAT BABBLE WAFFLE BLITHER PRATTLE NONSENSE

BLAUBOK ETAAC BLUEBUCK

BLAZE LOW BURN FIRE GLOW HACK LEAM LOWE LUNT MARK SHOT SPOT FLAME FLARE FLASH GLARE GLEAM GLORY INGLE RATCH SHINE STARE STEAM TORCH BLAZON BLEEZE BONFIRE PIONEER SPLENDOR
(**— OUT**) FLAP

BLAZING AFIRE FIERY FLAMY LIGHT FLAMING FLARING

BLAZING STAR LIATRIS GRUBROOT SNAKEROOT

BLAZON DECK SHOW ADORN BLARE BLAZE BOAST DEPICT SHIELD DECLARE DISPLAY EXHIBIT PUBLISH EMBLAZON INSCRIBE

BLAZONED ARMED BANNERED

BLEACH SUN WASH BLEAK CHALK CROFT POACH BLANCH BLENCH CHLORE PURIFY WHITEN DECOLOR LIGHTEN BLONDINE ETIOLATE PEROXIDE
(**— PULP**) POTCH

BLEACHER WHITSTER

BLEACHERS SCAFFOLD

BLEAK DIM RAW BLAE BLAY COLD DOUR GRAY PALE ABLET OURIE SPRAT STARK SWALE ALBURN BITTER BLEACH DISMAL DREARY FRIGID PALLID CUTTING DESOLATE CHEERLESS

BLEAK HOUSE (**AUTHOR OF —**) DICKENS
(**CHARACTER IN —**) JO ADA JOHN ALLAN CLARE FLITE GUPPY KROOK BUCKET ESTHER RAWDON DEDLOCK JELLYBY RICHARD WILLIAM CARSTONE CHADBAND JARNDYCE SKIMPOLE LEICESTER SUMMERSON WOODCOURT TULKINGHORN

BLEAT BAA BLAT BLEA YARM BLART BLATE BLATHER BLUSTER WHICKER

BLEATING BALANT

BLEB BLOB BULLA BUBBLE BLISTER PUSTULE VESICLE SWELLING

BLEED FLUX MILK WEEP BLOOD LEECH MULCT SWEAT SWINDLE

TEICHER PHLEBOTOMIZE

BLEEDER STICKER

BLEEDING BLOODY SANGLANT

BLEEDING HEART EARDROP DICENTRA

BLEMISH MAR BLOT BLUR DENT FLAW GALL LACK MAIM MARK MOIL MOLE RIFT SAKE SCAR SLUR SPOT TASH VICE WANT AMPER BLAME BOTCH BRECK CLOUD CRACK FAULT FLECK MULCT NAEVE SPECK STAIN SULLY TACHE TAINT TOUCH BLOTCH BREACH DEFAME DEFECT IMPAIR INJURE MACULA MACULE MAYHEM SMIRCH STIGMA BUBUKLE CATFACE DEFAULT FAILING FISSURE SUNSPOT MACULATION
(**— IN CLOTH**) AMPER SULLY
(**— IN PAPER**) FISHEYE
(**PRINTING —**) MACKLE

BLEMISHED BAD WEMMY

BLENCH FOIL SHUN WILE AVOID ELUDE EVADE QUAIL SHAKE SHIRK TRICK BAFFLE BLANCH BLEACH FLINCH RECOIL SHRINK DECEIVE

BLEND MIX RUN BLOT FADE FUSE JOIN MELT MENG MOLD ADMIX BLIND CREAM GRADE MERGE MOULD PUREE SHADE SMEAR SPOIL STAIN TINGE UNITE BLUNGE COMMIX CRASIS DAZZLE MINGLE TEMPER COMBINE CONFUSE CORRUPT DECEIVE GRADATE MIXTURE POLLUTE COALESCE CONCRETE IMMINGLE TINCTURE CONTEMPER
(**— OF NOISES**) CHARM
(**— OF SHERRY**) SOLERA
(**— OF WINES**) CUVEE

BLENDE JACK SPHALERITE

BLENDED FONDU FUSED MIXED MERGED MINGLED CONFLATE CONFLUENT

BLENDING FUSION HOTCHPOT

BLENNY GUNNEL SHANNY EELPOUT JUGULAR KELPFISH SENORITA WOLFFISH WRYMOUTH QUILLFISH ROCKSKIPPER

BLESBOK NUNNI BLESBUCK

BLESS KEEP SAIN WAVE ADORE ANELE BENSH CROSS EXTOL FAVOR GUARD THANK VISIT WOUND CROUCH FAVOUR HALLOW PRAISE THRASH APPROVE BEATIFY EMBLISS GLORIFY PROTECT MACARIZE PRESERVE SANCTIFY

BLESSED HOLY BLEST HAPPY SEELY DIVINE JOYFUL SACRED SEELFUL BENEDICT BHAGAVAT BLISSFUL BLOOMING HALLOWED HEAVENLY CELESTIAL

BLESSEDNESS BLISS FELICITY BEATITUDE HAPPINESS

BLESSING BOON GIFT SAIN BLISS DUKAN GRACE SORRA BARAKA DUCHAN PRAISE BENISON DARSHAN WORSHIP BERACHAH FELICITY MACARISM BEATITUDE
(**PL.**) CUP

BLEU DE ROI SEVRES

BLIGHT NIP FIRE RUIN RUST SMUT SOKA BLAST BRANT FROST SNEAP MILDEW NITHER TAKING WITHER DESTROY
(**PREF.**) UREDO

BLIND BET POT ANTE BOMA DARK DEAD DULL HIDE HOOD SEEL BISME BLANK BLEND CHICK CLOAK DUNCH SHADE STAKE STALL WAGER AMBUSH BISSON BLENDE DARKEN DAZZLE SCREEN SECRET AIMLESS ANTIQUE BANDAGE BATTERY BENIGHT ECLIPSE EYELESS OBSCURE PRETEXT RAYLESS SHUTTER ABORTIVE ARTIFICE BAYARDLY BLINDING EXCECATE HOODWINK IGNORANT INVOLVED JALOUSIE OUTSHINE PURBLIND UMBRELLA VENETIAN
(**— IN ONE EYE**) PEED GLEED GLEYD
(**— MAN**) MOLE
(**HALF —**) STARBLIND
(**PL.**) PERSIENNES
(**PREF.**) CECO TYPHL(O)

BLIND ALLEY LOKE STOP POCKET IMPASSE

BLINDER FLAP HOOD BLIND BLUFF LUNET WINKER BLINKER EYEFLAP LUNETTE HOODWINK BLINDFOLD

BLINDFOLD MOP DARK BLINK BLUFF SCARF MUFFLE BANDAGE BLINDER OBSCURE ENCLOSER HEEDLESS HOODWINK RECKLESS CONCEALED

BLINDING BISME BISSON

BLINDMAN'S BLUFF POST HOODWINK

BLINDNESS BISSON CECITY MYOPSY ABLEPSY ANOPSIA MEROPIA ABLEPSIA DARKNESS IGNORANCE
(**— TO TRUTH**) AVIDYA AVIJJA
(**COLOR —**) ACHROBIA MONOCHROMATISM
(**DAY —**) HEMERALOPIA
(**NIGHT —**) NYCTALOPIA
(**PARTIAL —**) MEROPIA HEMIOPSIA
(**RED-GREEN —**) DALTONISM
(**SNOW —**) CHIONABLEPSIA
(**STUDY OF —**) TYPHLOLOGY
(**TEMPORARY —**) MOONBLINK

BLINDSTITCH FELL

BLINDWORM SLOW ORVET ANGUID HAGWORM SLOWWORM

BLIND-YOUR-EYES GANGWA ALIPATA

BLINK BAT PINK SHUN WINK BLUSH CHEAT FLASH GLEAM SHINE TRICK GLANCE IGNORE OBTUSE WAPPER BLINTER CONDONE GLIMMER GLIMPSE NEGLECT NICTATE SPARKLE TWINKLE

BLINKER EYE BLINK BLUFF LIGHT SIGNAL WAPPER WINKER BLINDER FLASHER GOGGLES COQUETTE HOODWINK MACKEREL

BLINTZE BLIN BLINTZ PANCAKE

BLIP PIP ECHO

BLISS JOY EDEN KAIF SEEL SEIL BLESS GLORY ANANDA HEAVEN DELIGHT ECSTASY GLADDEN NIRVANA RAPTURE FELICITY GLADNESS PARADISE PLEASURE

BLISSFUL HOLY SEELY BLITHE BLESSED ELYSIAN UTOPIAN BEATIFIED GLORIFIED

BLISTER BEAT BLAB BLEB BLOB BLOW BOIL BURN LASH QUAT APTHA BLAIN BLIBE BULGE BULLA TOPIC VESIC APHTHA BUBBLE CUPOLA SCORCH SOTTER TETTER BLADDER BLUSTER SCALDER SKELLER VESICLE VESICATE (PREF.) PUSTULI VESICUL(O)

BLISTERED BULLATE

BLITHE GAY GLAD BONNY BUXOM HAPPY JOLLY MERRY BONNIE JOVIAL JOYOUS LIVELY GAYSOME JOCULAR WINSOME CHEERFUL GLADSOME SPRIGHTLY

BLIZZARD BLOW GALE WIND BURAN PURGA RETORT SNIFTER SQUELCHER (— STATE) SD SDAK

BLOAT BLOW BLAST BLOWN FLOAT HOOVE HOVEN PUFFY SWELL BOWDEN EXPAND TUMEFY DISTEND FERMENT INFLATE

BLOATED FOZY BLOAT BROSY CURED FOGGY HOVEN PUFFY TUMID GOTCHY SODDEN TURGID POMPOUS REPLETE

BLOATER MOONEYE

BLOB LIP WEN BEAD BLEB BLOT BOIL CLOT DAUB DROP GLOB GOUT LUMP MARK MASS BUBBLE DALLOP DOLLOP PIMPLE SPLASH BLEMISH BLISTER BLOSSOM GLOBULE PUSTULE SPLOTCH

BLOC RING BLOCK CABAL PARTY UNION CLIQUE BENELUX FACTION

BLOCK AME BAR COB COG DAM DIE DIT DOG FID HOB HUB JAM KEY NOG ROW TOP VOL BALK BASE BEAR BILK BLOC BUCK BUNT CAKE CLOG CUBE DRUM FOIL FOUL FROG GLUT HEAD JAMB LEAD MASK MASS MOCK QUAR STAY STEP STOP TRIG BAULK BRICK CHAIR CHECK CHEEK CHUMP CLAMP CLEAT CLOSE COVER DETER DOLLY DUMMY EMBAR FLOAT HEART HORST JUMBO NUDGE PARRY PATCH SHAPE SLUMP SPIKE SPOKE STOCK STUFF STUMP ASSIZE DENTIL DOLLEY DOMINO FIPPLE FORMER HAMPER HINDER IMPEDE KIBOSH MONKEY MUFFLE MUTULE OPPOSE OUTWIT QUERRE RIPPER SADDLE SCOTCH SNATCH SQUARE STREET STYMIE TAPLET THWART TROLLY WAYLAY BOLLOCK BOLSTER BUCKLER CONDEMN DEADEYE ERRATIC INHIBIT OUTLINE PREVENT QUADREL RAMHEAD STONKER TRIGGER TROLLEY BLOCKADE DEADHEAD ELECTRET FOLLOWER KEYSTONE MONOLITH

OBSTACLE OBSTRUCT STOPPAGE WITHSPAR BRIQUETTE
(— A WHEEL) SCOTE
(— AT SPAR END) STEEVE
(— FOR SKIDDING LOGS) BICYCLE
(— FOR SLAVE SALES) CATASTA
(— IN SPEAKING) STAMMER
(— OF BUILDINGS) INSULA
(— OF COAL) JUD JUDD
(— OF EARTH'S CRUST) HORST
(— OF GRANITE) SET
(— OF ICE) SERAC
(— OF LAND) FORTY
(— OF SEATS) CUNEUS
(— OF TIMBER) BOLT JUGGLE
(— SUPPORTING MAST) STEP
(— THE WAY) SCOAT
(— UP) BAR DAM CLOY QUIRT CONDEMN OPPILATE FORECLOSE
(— WITH HOLE IN IT) WAPP EUPHROE
(— WITH PROJECTING CORE) SETTLE
(—S OF STONE) DIMENSION
(ARCHITECTURAL —) DRUM STONE DENTIL IMPOST MUTULE PLINTH DOSSERET
(CHOPPING —) HACKLOG
(CLAY —) DRAWBAR
(FAULT —) MASSIF
(FELTED —) DAMPER
(FOOTBALL —) CRACKBACK
(FULCRUM —) GLUT
(FUSE —) CUTOUT
(HOSPITAL —) PAVILION
(IRON —) USE VOL BITT ANVIL CHAIR
(LOGGING —) LEAD JUMBO
(NAUTICAL —) CHOCK HEART STOCK SADDLE DEADEYE FAIRLEAD
(ORNAMENTAL —) BOSS MODILLION
(PAVING —) SET CUBE SETT STONE WHEELER
(PLASTER —) BATTER
(POLISHING —) BUFF FLOAT RABOT
(PRINTING —) CUT QUAD RISER QUADRAT
(PULLEY —) CRAWL
(SANDSTONE —) SARSEN
(SQUARED —) MITCHEL
(STUMBLING —) HURTING
(TACKLE —) CALO TONGUE
(VAULTING —) BUCK HORSE

BLOCKADE DAM FERM BESET BLOCK EMBAR SIEGE WHISKY BESIEGE EMBARGO BLOCKAGE OBSTRUCT BARRICADE BELEAGUER

BLOCKAGE LOGJAM

BLOCKER CASER BRACER

BLOCKHEAD ASS LUG OAF BUST CLOT COOF COOT DAFF DOLT FOOL MOME NOWT STUB BLOCK BOOBY CHUMP CUDDY GOLEM GOOSY IDIOT NINNY SNIPE SUMPH DIMWIT DISARD NITWIT NOODLE TUMPHY TURNIP ASSHEAD BUZZARD DIZZARD DULBERT JACKASS LACKWIT MUDHEAD NOGHEAD TOMFOOL REEFHEAD BONEHEAD CLODPATE

CLODPOLL CODSHEAD DULLHEAD DULLPATE DUMBHEAD DUMMKOPF GAMPHREL HARDHEAD JOLTHEAD LUNKHEAD

BLOCKHOUSE SPUR PUNTAL GARRISON

BLOCKING JAM JAMB DUNNAGE BLOCKADE CROSSING

BLOKE MAN CHAP COVE TOFF BLOAK JOKER FELLOW

BLOLLY BEEFWOOD CORKWOOD PORKWOOD

BLOND BAN FAIR LIGHT BLONDE FLAXEN GOLDEN YELLOW LEUCOUS BLONDINE (AUTUMN —) FAWN

BLOOD KIN SAP GORE LIFE MASS MOOD RACE SANG SANK BLADE BLUDE BLUID CRUOR FLESH FLUID SERUM STOCK CLARET INDRED KAINAH SLUDGE GALLANT KINSHIP KINSMAN LINEAGE RELATION TROPHEMA (CORRUPT —) YOUSTIR (HALF —) DEMISANG (PREF.) HAEM(A)(O) HAEMAT(O) HEM(A)(O) HEMAT(O) SANGUI SANGUINO SANO (SUFF.) AEMIA EMIA HAEMIA HEMIA

BLOOD CLOT (PREF.) THROMB(O)

BLOODCURDLING GORY HORROR

BLOODFLOWER HIPPO REDHEAD BLOODWEED

BLOODHOUND LYM LYAM LYME HOUND LIMER SLOTH BANDOG LEAMER SLEUTH TIEDOG LYAMHOUND SLEUTHHOUND

BLOODIED BEBLED

BLOODLESS DEAD ANEMIC ANAEMIC INHUMAN TURNIPY LIFELESS UNFEELING

BLOODLETTER BLEEDER

BLOOD PHEASANT ITHAGINE

BLOODROOT PUCCOON REDROOT BOLOROOT COONROOT CORNROOT TURMERIC SANGUINARIA

BLOODSHED DEATH CARNAGE VIOLENCE SLAUGHTER

BLOODSHOT RED INFLAMED

BLOODSTAINED GORY

BLOODSTONE SANGUINE HEMACHATE

BLOODSUCKER LEECH SPONGER VAMPIRE

BLOODTHIRSTINESS ACHARNEMENT

BLOODTHIRSTY BLOODY CARNAL SANGUINE TIGERISH FEROCIOUS MURDEROUS SANGUINARY

BLOOD VESSEL VEIN COMES HEMAD ARTERY CAPILLARY (PREF.) ANGIO

BLOODWOOD AJHAR JAROOL

BLOODY GORY RUDE BALLY BLODE CRUEL RUDDY BLUGGY CRUENT PLUCKY CRIMSON BLEEDING DEATHFUL HEMATOSE INFAMOUS SANGLANT BUTCHERLY CRUENTOUS FEROCIOUS

MERCILESS MURDEROUS SANGUINARY

BLOODY BARK LANCEPOD

BLOOM DEW BLOW CAST HAZE KNOT BLURT BLUSH CHILL BLOOTH BLOWTH BLOSSOM BLOWING ANTHESIS BLOOMING FLOREATE FLOURISH (— OF WILLOW) GULL (— ON INSECT) POLLEN (— ON SHELL) CUTICLE (— ON TREE) GOSLING (METAL —S) HEAT (POWDERY —) PRUINA

BLOOMER ERROR BLOWER BLUNDER FAILURE

BLOOMERS KNICKERS PANTALETS

BLOOMERY FORGE HEARTH FURNACE

BLOOMING PERT ROSY FLUSH FRESH GREEN PRIME ABLOOM FLORID BLOWING FLAMING ROSEATE BLINKING

BLOOPER BLOOMER

BLOSSOM BUD BELL BLOB BLOW CHIP SILK BLOOM LEHUA FLOWER BLOWING BURGEON PROSPER BOURGEON FLOURISH (BLIGHTED —) BLAST (HERALDIC —) FRASE FRAISE (PL.) SET BLOSSOMRY

BLOSSOMING BLOWTH FLORAISON FLORULENT (— AFTER NOON) POMERIDIAN

BLOT MAR BLOB BLUR DAUB SOIL SPOT BLACK BLANK BLEND BLOTE ERASE SMEAR SPECK STAIN SULLY BLOTCH CANCEL DAMAGE EFFACE IMPAIR MACULA SHADOW SMIRCH SMOUCH SMUDGE SMUTCH STIGMA BLEMISH ECLIPSE EXPUNGE INKBLOT OBSCURE SPLOTCH TARNISH DISGRACE REPROACH (— OUT) OUT BURY ANNUL ERASE CANCEL DELETE EXPUNGE

BLOTCH DAB BLOT DASH GOUT MONK SPOT AMPER PATCH SMEAR SPLAT STAIN MACULA MOTTLE PLOTCH PURPLE SMIRCH SPLASH STIGMA BLEMISH PUSTULE SPLOTCH ERUPTION MACULATE (PL.) BLIBE (PREF.) MACUL(I)(O)

BLOTCHED SCABBY PIEBALD MACULATE SCABROUS SPLASHED MACULATED (SUFF.) MACULATE

BLOTCHY SCOVY

BLOTTER BLAD

BLOUSE CHOLI MIDDY SHIRT SMOCK TUNIC CAMISA GUIMPE JUMPER CASAQUE VAREUSE CAMISOLE CASAQUIN JIRKINET (BUSHMAN'S —) BLUEY

BLOW BOB COB COP CUT DAB DAD DUB FAN FIB HIT JAB JAR NAP ONE PAT PEG POP RAP TAP TIP TIT WAP ANDE BAFF BANG BASH BEAT BELT BIFF BIRR BLAD BLAW BRAG BUFF BULL BUMP BUTT CHAP CHOP CONK COUP CRIG

CUFF DASH DAUD DENT DING
DINT DIRD DOLE DRAW DRUB
DUNT DUSH FLAP FLEG FLIG
FUFF FUNK GALE GOWF GUST
HACK HUFF HURT JOLT KNAP
KNEE LASH LEAD LEFT LICK LOUK
LUSH MINT ONER PAIK PALT
PANT PASS PICK PIRR PLUG POLT
PUCK PUFF PUSH SCAT SCUD
SLAM SLAP SLAT SLUG SOCK
SPAT STOP SWAP SWAT SWOP
SWOT THUD WELT WHAP WHOP
WIND WIPE YANK BINGE BLADE
BLAST BLIZZ BLOOM BOAST
BRUNT BURST CLAUT CLINK
CLOUR CLOUT CLUMP CLUNK
CRUMP CRUNT CURSE DEVEL
DOUSE DOWSE DUNCH FACER
FILIP FLACK FLICK FLIRT GOWFF
ICTUS IMPEL KNOCK OUTER
PALMY PANDY PASTE PEISE
PLUMP PLUNK PUNCH RIGHT
SHAKE SHOCK SKELP SKIRL SKITE
SLASH SLIPE SLOSH SMACK
SMASH SMITE SNICK SOUND
SOUSE SPANK SPEND STORM
STRIP SURGE SWACK SWEEP
SWIPE THROW THUMP TOUCH
TRICE WHACK WHANG WHIFF
WHOOF WHUFF BELTER BENSEL
BENSIL BETRAY BOUNCE BUFFET
CONKER DEPART DIRDUM
DUNDER EXPAND FILLIP FISTER
FLOWER FROLIC HANDER HUFFLE
LARRUP REBUKE SIFFLE STOUSH
STRIPE STROKE SWITCH THUNGE
THWACK WALLOP WINDER
AFFLATE ASSAULT ATTAINT
BELLOWS BENSAIL BLOSSOM
BLOWOUT BLUSTER BOASTER
COUNTER CRUSHER DESTROY
INFLATE KNOCKER LAMBACK
LOUNDER MOUTHER PUBLISH
SHATTER SMACKER SPANKER
SQUELCH WHAMPLE WHIFFLE
WHIRRET WHITHER CALAMITY
DISASTER KNOCKOUT PASHWAFF
SASARARA SICKENER
SIDEWINDER
(— ABRASIVES) BLAST
(— CEMENT) KIBOSH
(— GUSTILY) FLAW TUCK WINNOW
(— IN PUFFS) FAFF
(— NOSE) SNITE
(— OFF STEAM) SNIFT
(— ON CHEEK) ALAPA
(— ON HEAD) NOB CONK CLOUR
CONKER NOBBER TOPPER
NOBBLER
(— ON NOSE) NOSER CANKER
NOZZLER SMELLER
(— SMOKE) NOSE
(— SOFTLY) BREATHE
(— UP) BOMB BLAST DYNAMITE
SUFFLATE
(— VIOLENTLY) STORM
(— WITH CUDGEL) DUB DRUB
CRUNT
(— WITH FIST) BOP BOX PEG BELT
HOOK CLOUT BUFFET
ROUNDHOUSE
(— WITH FOOT) BOOT KICK SPURN

(DECISIVE —) SOCKDOLAGER
SOCKDOLOGER
(FENCING —) MONTANT
(GENTLE —) CHUCK
(GLANCING —) SCUFF
(HARD —) SLOG STOT YANK BEVEL
SWACK TWITCHER
(HEAVY —) DAD DONG DRUB
DUNT ONER SLAM SLUG CLOUT
KNOCK POISE SOUSE SQUAT
STAVE SWASH STOUND PLUMPER
REEMISH
(MOCK —) FEINT
(NOISY —) DUNDER DUNNER
(RESOUNDING —) CLAP CRACK
(SHARP —) BAT NAP CLIP KNAP
SLAP SPAT CLICK FLICK FLEWIT
STINGER
(SLIGHT —) SCLAFF
(SMART —) CLIP FLIP SKELP SKITE
YANKER
BLOWCASE EGG
BLOWER PAN DRIER DRYER
WHALE FANNER PUFFER
BELLOWS BLOOMER BOOSTER
MUMBLER BRAGGART OUTBURST
(GLASS —) GAFFER
BLOWGUN SUMPIT SUMPITAN
SARBACANE PEASHOOTER
BLOWHOLE BLOW GLOUP SPOUT
SPIRACLE
(— IN STEEL) ROAK
BLOWING ABLOW BLAST BLORE
GUSTY BLUSTER BLUSTERY
(— AT LOW SPEED) SLACK
(— AT RIGHT ANGLES) SIDE
(— OF WHALE) SPOUT
BLOWN STALE TIRED OPENED
WINDED BLOSSOM SWOLLEN
TAINTED BETRAYED FLYBLOWN
INFLATED
BLOWOUT BLOW FEED MEAL
BURST VALLEY FLAMEOUT
BLOWPIPE HOD
BLOWSY DOWDY BLOUSY BLOWZY
FROWZY
BLOWY DUSTY
BLUBBER CRY FAT SOB BLUB
FOAM WAIL WEEP BIBLE MELON
PIECE SPECK SPICK SWELL THICK
WHINE BUBBLE FLITCH LIPPER
LUBBER MEDUSA NETTLE SEETHE
BLABBER BLUSTER SLOBBER
SWOLLEN WHIMPER
(— AT WHALE'S NECK) CANT
(CUT WHALE —) FLENSE
(REFUSE —) FENKS FOOTING
FRITTERS
BLUDGEON BAT HIT SAP CLUB
COSH MACE BILLY STICK TOWEL
COERCE COURSE BLACKJACK
TRUNCHEON
BLUE (ALSO SEE COLOR) HAW LOW
SAD SKY AQUA BICE BLAE GLUM
SAXE TEAL WOAD AZURE BERYL
LIVID NIKKO PERSE SMALL
WAGET COBALT GLOOMY INDIGO
LUPINE ORIENT PEWTER SEVERE
TRYPAN CELESTE CYANINE
GENTIAN GOBELIN HYPPISH
LEARNED LIBERTY LOBELIA
MATELOT MISTBLU MURILLO
NATTIER PEACOCK QUIMPER

REGATTA WATCHET CERULEAN
DEJECTED LABRADOR LARKSPUR
LITERARY MAZARINE MIDNIGHT
NATIONAL SAPPHIRE
WEDGWOOD POMPADOUR
(BLACKISH —) BLO BLOO
(DULL —) HAW
(ROYAL —) HATHOR
(SHADE OF —) INDE
(PREF.) CYAN(O) IND(I)(O) INDICO
(SUFF.) (— PIGMENT) CYAN(IC)
BLUEBELL CROWBELL HAREBELL
BLUEBERRY OHELO STONER
PALBERRY RABBITEYE VACCINIUM
BLUEBIRD (— GUIDE) LEADER
BLUE-BLACK BLO
BLUEBLOSSOM LILAC
BLUEBONNET CAP SCOT BLUECAP
BLUEBOTTLE BLUET BLAVER
BARBEAU BLAWORT BLOWFLY
BLUECAP BLUECUP BRUSHES
HARDOCK BLUEBLAW HYACINTH
CORNBINKS
BLUE CREEPER LOVE
BLUE CURLS FLEASEED FLEAWEED
BLUE-EYED GRASS PIGROOT
SATINFLOWER
BLUEFIN TUNNY
BLUEFISH ELF BASS ELFT SHAD
TUNA HORSE SAURY DARZEE
TAILER TAILOR FATBACK
SKIPJACK WEAKFISH
(YOUNG OF —) SNAPPER
WHITEFISH
BLUEGILL BREAM SUNFISH
PONDFISH PUMPKINSEED
BLUE GOOSE BALDHEAD
BLUEGRASS STATE KENTUCKY
BLUE GREEN VENICE
BLUE GUM FEVERGUM
EUCALYPTUS
BLUE HEN STATE DELAWARE
BLUE HERON CRANE NAILROD
BLUEJACKET SAILOR DRAGMAN
BLUEJOINT REDTOP BLUETOPS
BLUENESS (— OF SKIN) CYANOSIS
BLUE PETER ASK
BLUE PINE LIM
BLUE POINTER MAKO
BLUEPRINT MAP PLAN PLOT
DRAFT TRACE SKETCH DIAGRAM
PROJECT CYANOTYPE
BLUE RUNNER JUREL
BLUES MARE DUMPS CAFARD
DISMAL GLOOMS DISMALS
HORRORS HUMDRUM MEGRIMS
SADNESS DOLDRUMS DOLEFULS
MULLIGRUBS
BLUE SHEEP BURHEL
BLUE SLATE SKAILLIE
BLUESTOCKING BASBLEU
BLUE SUCCORY CATNACHE
CUPIDONE
BLUET PISSABED EYEBRIGHT
INNOCENCE
BLUE TIT NUN STONECHAT
BLUE TITMOUSE YAUP TYDIE
TIDIFE BLUECAP
BLUETONGUE THICKHEAD
BLUE VERVAIN IRONWEED
BLUE VINNY DORSET
BLUEWEED ECHIUM IRONWEED
ADDERWORT

BLUFF ALTO BANK BRAG CURT
FOOL RUDE BLUNT BRAVE BURLY
CLIFF FRANK GRUFF SHORT
SURLY SWANK WINDY ABRUPT
BOUNCE CRUSTY BLINDER
BLINKER BLUFTER BRUSQUE
DECEIVE UNCIVIL BARRANCA
BARRANCO CHURLISH HOODWINK
IMPOLITE
BLUISH-GRAY MERLE
BLUMEA PLACUS
BLUNDER ERR MIX BALK BONE
BOOB BUBU BULL DOLT FLUB
GAFF ROIL SKEW SLIP STIR TRIP
BEVUE BONER BOTCH BREAK
ERROR FAULT FLUFF GAFFE
LAPSE MISDO BOGGLE BOOBOO
BUMBLE BUMMLE BUNGLE
ESCAPE FUMBLE GAZEBO
HOWLER MAFFLE MINGLE
MUDDLE BLOOMER BLOOPER
CLANGER CONFUSE DERANGE
FAILURE FLOATER MISTAKE
OVERSEE SOTTISE STUMBLE
PRATFALL SOLECISM
(— IN LANGUAGE) BULL
(— IN SPEECH) SOLECISM
(VERBAL —) SLIPSLAP SLIPSLOP
BLUNDERBUSS TRABU TRABUCO
TRABUCHO TROMBONE
ESPINGOLE
BLUNDERER BUMBLER BUMMLER
KNOTHEAD LUMBERER
BLUNDERING AWKWARD
BUMBLING
BLUNT BALD BATE BULL CURT
DAMP DULL FLAT MULL SNUB
ABATE BLATE BLUFF BRUSK
DUBBY INERT MORNE PLAIN
PLUMP STUNT CANDID CLUMSY
DEADEN DIRECT OBTUND OBTUSE
REBATE RETUND SHEATH STUBBY
STUPID BRUSQUE DISEDGE
HACKNEY SHEATHE SNUBBED
SPADISH STUBBED STUPEFY
HEBETATE
BLUNTED
(PREF.) OBTUSI
BLUNTLY PLAT PLUMP FLATLY
CRUDELY FRANKLY
BLUR DIM FOG HUM BLOB BLOT
FADE FUZZ MIST SLUR SOIL SPOT
BLEAR CLOUD FUDGE SHAKE
SMEAR STAIN SULLY MACKLE
MACULE SMUDGE STIGMA
BLEMISH CONFUSE FEATHER
OBSCURE TAILING
BLURB AD BOLT PUFF RAVE BRIEF
NOTICE
BLURRED FAINT FUZZY MUZZY
VAGUE WOOZY BLEARY BLURRY
CLOUDY SMEARY SMUDGY
SWIMMY WOOLLY CLOUDED
COMATIC EDGELESS FLANNELLY
BLURT BLAT BOLT PLUMP
BLUNDER EXCLAIM
BLUSH BLUE GLOW BLINK COLOR
FLUSH GLEAM PAINT ROUGE
TINGE CHANGE GLANCE MANTLE
REDDEN CRIMSON FLICKER
SCARLET LIKENESS JOSEPHINE
BLUSHING RED ROSY ABLUSH
ROSEATE FLUSHING ROSACEOUS

BLUSTER BEEF BLOW DING HUFF RAGE RAIL RANT BLAST BLEAT BLORE BOAST BRACE BULLY NOISE STORM SWANK BABBLE BELLOW BOUNCE FRAPLE HECTOR HUFFLE TUMULT WUTHER BLUBBER BRAVADO FLUSTER GAUSTER ROISTER SWAGGER WHITHER BOASTING BULLYING THREATEN RODOMONTADE

BLUSTERER SWAG FLASH HECTOR HUFFER FRAPLER HUFFCAP TEARCAT CACAFOGO FANFARON

BLUSTERING BOG LOUD BLUFF BRASH BULLY VAPORS HUFFCAP VAPOURS ARROGANT BULLYING

BOA BOM BOID BOMA ABOMA JIBOA SCARF THROW ABOLLA ADJIGA GIBOIA JOBOYA PYTHON ADJIGER CAMOODI EMPEROR PEROPOD ANACONDA CORALLUS

BOADICEA (HUSBAND OF —) PRASUTAGUS

BOAR HOG APER SUID BRAWN SWINE BARROW HOGGET TUSKER BRAWNER SOUNDER SUIDIAN VENISON WILRONE BRISTLER SANGLIER HOGGASTER
(— CRY) FREAM
(— HEAD) HURE
(— IN 2ND YEAR) HOGGET
(— IN 3RD YEAR) HOGSTEER HOGGASTER
(STY) FRANK
(YOUNG —) GRISE SOUNDER
(PREF.) SUI

BOARD EAT LAG PAX TOE DAIL DEAL DECK DIET EATS FARE FLIP HACK JOIN KEEP LATH MEAT SHIP SIGN SLAT TRAY TRIP ASTEL BUIRD CHESE CLEAR COARD COUCH COURT ENTER FOUND HOUSE LODGE MEALS PANEL PLANK RATCH SHIDE STAGE STALL SWALE TABLE THEAL ABACUS ACCOST ASTYLL COMMON PALLET PLANCH RANDOM RIBBON SHIELD SIDING TUCKER CABINET CHAMBER COUNCIL CRIMPER DUOVIRI ENPLANE ENTRAIN KNEELER PALETTE PENSION PLANCHE SCRAPER TABLING TRANSOM WHATMAN APPROACH ASSEMBLY BOXBOARD CUPBOARD EXCLUDER FETIALES KEYBOARD LAPBOARD PEGBOARD TRIBUNAL PRESSBOARD MORTARBOARD
(— FOR FALCON'S MEAT) HACK
(— OF BRIDGE) CHESS
(— OF LOOM) CARD
(— OF MILL WHEEL) AWE
(— ON CALF'S NOSE) BLAB
(— OVER) BERTH
(— WITH GROOVE) COULISSE
(— WITH HANDLE) CLAPPER
(— WITH NUMBER) SLATE
(— WITH PINS) RIDDLE
(— WITH TEETH) HACKLE RUFFER
(BLOCKHEAD —) DOLL
(CHANNEL —) PAN
(CHESS —) TABLER

(DRAWING —) COQUILLE
(EXHIBITION —) FRAME
(FLOOR —) KEY
(GAME —) HALMA
(HEART-SHAPED —) PLANCHET
(MORTAR —) HAWK
(NOTCHED —) HORSE
(OTTER —) DOOR
(POLING —) RUNNER
(PRESSED —S) FELT
(PULP-PRESSING —) COUCH
(RABBETED —S) SHIPLAP
(SHEATHING —S) SARKING
(STRIKE —) SCREED
(TANNING —) BEAM
(TIIIN —) SHIDE SARKING
(THIN —S) SLITWORK
(WARPING —) BARTREE

BOARDER MEALER TABLER GRAINER PENSIONER SOJOURNER TRANSIENT

BOARDING LIVERY

BOARDINGHOUSE FONDA HOUSE PENSION

BOARDWALK MARINA DUCKBOARD

BOARWOOD CHEWSTICK

BOAST BOG GAB JET BEEF BLAW BLOW BRAG CROW POMP PUFF RAVE VANT WIND WOST YELP BLAST BRAVE CRACK CRAKE EXTOL EXULT GLORY PRATE QUACK ROOSE SCOLD SKITE VAPOR VAUNT VOUST YOLPE AMOUNT BLAZON BLEEZE BOUNCE CLAMOR FLAUNT INSULT MENACE OUTCRY SPLORE BLUSTER BRAVING CLAMOUR DEVAUNT DISPLAY GLORIFY SWAGGER FLOURISH THREATEN VANTERIE VAUNTERY

BOASTER BLOW HUFF GALAH SKITE BLOWER CROWER GASCON PEDANT PRATER SHAKER BLOWOFF BOUNCER BRAGGER BRAVADO CRACKER RUFFLER BLOWHARD BRAGGART CACAFUGO FANFARON GLORIOSO JINGOIST RODOMONT TARTARIN WOUSTOUR

BOASTFUL BIG BRAG HIGH COCKY LARGE BRAGGY PARADO BOBADIL JACTANT VAUNTIE FANFARON GLORIOUS GASCONADE THRASONIC

BOASTFULLY SIDE LARGE

BOASTFULNESS GLORY EGOTISM WINDINESS

BOASTING BLOW HUFF YELP BOAST CRACK PRATE ROOSE QUACKY BOBANCE GASSING JACTANCE JACTANCY QUACKISH VAPORING VAUNTAGE VENTOSITY RODOMONTADE
(EMPTY —) GAS

BOAT ARK BUM BUN CAT COG COT DOW GIG MON TUB ACON BAIT BARK BOOT BRIG CARV CHOP COCK DHOW DINK DORY DUMP FLAT FOUZ JUNK PAIR PLAT PRAM PUNT RAFT SCOW SHIP SKAG TACK TODE TOPO TROW WAKA YAWL YOLE ACCON AVISO

BANCA BARCA BARGE BARIS BATEL BIDAR BOLIA BOYER BULLY BUYER CANOE COBLE CRAFT DHONI DINGY FERRY FOIST FORTY FUNNY JOLLY KETCH LAKER LINER NADIR OOLAK PIECE PILOT PRAAM RACER SHELL SHOUT SIKAR SKIFF SKIFT SMACK TOPPO UMIAK WAAPA WHIFF XEBEC ZEBEC BAIDAK BANGKA BATEAU BAWLEY BELLUM BILALO BORLEY BOTTOM BOUTRE CAIQUE CARVEL CAYUCO CHEBEC COCKLE CRUISE CUTTER DINGHY DREDGE DRIVER DROVER DUGOUT FLATTY GALLEY GARVEY GAYYOU GLIDER HOOKER JAGGER JIGGER KEELER KICKER KUPHAR LERRET MAILER NAGGAR NUGGAR PACKET PEAPOD PEDULE PICARD PINKIE PLAYTE PULWAR RANDAN ROCKER SANDAL SCAPHE SCHOUW SCHUYT SETTEE SINGLE SKERRY STRUSE TANKER TENDER TIMBER TOGGER TORPID TRANKY TROUGH VESSEL WAFTER WHERRY ZEBECK AIRBOAT ALMADIA ANGEYOK BALLOEN BALLOON BAULEAH BUMBOAT CAISSON CARRIER CATCHER CORACLE COROLAN CRUISER CURRACH DOGBODY DRIFTER DROGHER FLATTIE FLEETER FLYBOAT FOYBOAT FRIGATE GALIASSA GASBOAT GEORDIE GONDOLA HOVELER HUFFLER KELLECK LIGHTER MACHINE MASOOLA NACELLE PEARLER PEDIWAK PINNACE PIRAGUA POOKAWN PUTELEE SCOOTER SCULLER SHALLOP SHARPIE SHIKARA SIKHARA SKAFFIE SKIPPET SPONGER SPYBOAT STEAMER TRAWLER TUCKNER TUMBREL TUMBRIL VEDETTE WHIRREY BALANGAY BARANGAY BILLYBOY BOOMBOAT BULLBOAT BUMBARGE CANALLER CHALOUPE CHEBACCO CHELINGA CHELINGO COCKBOAT COROCORE DAHABEAH DUCKBOAT FIREBOAT FLAGBOAT KEELBOAT LIFEBOAT MACKINAW MONOXYLE NEWSBOAT OYSTERER PALANDER PANCHWAY PESSONER PESSULUS PULLBOAT SAILBOAT SCHOKKER SCHOONER SURFBOAT TONGKANG TRANSFER OUTRIGGER
(— OF MALTA) DGHAISA
(— WITH SAILS AND OARS) LYMPHIAD
(ABANDONED —) DERELICT
(CHEMICAL —) CAPSULE
(CHINESE —) JUNK SAMPAN
(CLUMSY —) HOOKER DROGHER
(COLLEGE —) TORPID
(DISPATCH —) AVISO PACKET
(ESKIMO —) KAMIK UMIAK OOMIAC UMIACK
(FERRY —) BAC CUTT
(FISHING —) COG BOVO BUSS DONI CANOA COBLE DHONI NOBBY

PYKAR SMACK VINTA BALDIE BAWLEY BORLEY DOGGER DROVER FISHER KUPHAR NICKEY SANDAL SCAFFY SEINER SEXERN TOSHER VOLYER CARAVEL CRABBER DRAGGER FOLLYER POOKAUN SHARPIE SKAFFIE TRAWLER DRAGBOAT GAROOKUH SHRIMPER
(FLAT-BOTTOM —) ARK BAC BUN DORY FLAT PLAT PRAM PUNT SCOW BARGE COBLE DOREY FLOAT MOSES PRAAM SHOUT BATEAU BUGEYE GAYYOU PUTELI GONDOLA LIGHTER FLATBOAT GUNDELOW JOHNBOAT
(FLY —) BUSS FLUTE FLIGHT
(GANGES —) PUTELI
(HIGHLAND —) BIRLINN
(INCENSE —) NEF SHIP NAVICULA
(MALAY —) COROCORE GALLIVAT
(MORTAR —) PALANDER
(OPEN —) WHIFF LERRET SHALLOP
(PATROL —) SPITKID SPITKIT
(RACING —) SIX FOUR EIGHT SCULL SHELL SINGLE TORPID SCULLER
(SHIP'S —) GIG MOSES DINGEY DINGHY LAUNCH TENDER PINNACE
(SKIN —) BIDAR BAIDAR ANGEYOK BIDARKA BULLBOAT
(SMALL —) CARTOPPER
(WICKER —) KUFA GOOFA GOOFAH CURACLE
(3-OAR —) RANDAN
(6-OAR —) SEXERN
(8-OAR —) SHIP
(PL.) LIGHTERAGE
(PREF.) CYMBI CYMBO
(SUFF.) SCAPH

BOATBUILDING SETWORK
BOATHOOK STOWER HITCHER
BOATMAN DANDI DANDY PHAON BARGER BOWMAN CHARON YAWLER HOBBLER HOVELER HUFFLER COBLEMAN VOYAGEUR WATERMAN GONDOLIER
BOAT SEAT TAFT
BOAT-SHAPED
(PREF.) SCAPH(O)
BOAT SHELL YET SWEETMEAT
BOATSWAIN BOSN BOSUN SERANG TINDAL
BOAZ (FATHER OF —) SALMA SALMON
(SON OF —) OBED
(WIFE OF —) RUTH
BOB BAB BOW CUT DAB DIP HOD JOG POP RAP TAP BALL BLOW BUFF CALF CLIP CLOD COIN CORK DUCK GRUB JEER JERK JEST KNOB MOCK WORM BUNCH CHEAT DANCE FILCH FLOAT FLOUT SHAKE TAUNT TRICK BINGLE BOBBER BOBBLE BUFFET CURTSY DELUDE HOBBLE POMMEL POPPLE STRIKE WEIGHT BOBSLED BOBTAIL CLUSTER HAIRCUT PAGEBOY PENDANT PLUMMET REFRAIN SHINGLE SHILLING
(— UP) LOLLOP

BOBAC PAHMI TARBAGAN
BOBBER CORK DUCK FLOAT
BOBFLY
BOBBIN PIN CONE CORD PIRN
REEL BRAID QUILL SPOOL
BROCHE HANGER SKREEL TAVELL
WORKER RATCHET SPINDLE
TARELLE TORCHON
(PL.) BONES
BOBBINET ILLUSION
BOBBLE ERROR
BOBOLINK DEER REED SUCKER
BUNTING MAYBIRD ORTOLAN
REEDBIRD RICEBIRD
BOBSLED BOB DRAY BOBLET
RIPPER TRAVERSE
BOBWHITE COLIN QUAIL
PARTRIDGE
BOCACCIO JACK TOMCOD
BOCCACCIO TRECENTIST
BOCCARELLA NOSEHOLE
BOCCARO YIHSING
BOCE BOGUE OXEYE
BOCHERU (FATHER OF —) AZEL
BODE OMEN SIGN STOP AUGUR
OFFER HERALD MESSAGE
PORTEND PRESAGE FOREBODE
FORECAST FORESHOW FORETELL
INDICATE
BODHISATTVA KWANNON
MAITREYA AVALOKITA
PADMAPANI
BODICE JUPE CHOLI GILET JUMPS
WAIST BASQUE BOLERO CORSET
JELICK LYFKIE CORSAGE
OVERBODY SLIPBODY
BODIERON BOREGAT
BODILY SOLID SOMAL ACTUAL
CARNAL FLESHLY SOMATIC
CORPORAL ENTIRELY EXTERNAL
MATERIAL PERSONAL PHYSICAL
SARKICAL VISCERAL CORPOREAL
(NOT —) INTERIOR
BODKIN AWL PIN POINT BROACH
DAGGER NEEDLE POPPER
HAIRPIN PONIARD STILETTO
EYELETEER
BODLE TURNER
BODO CACHARI
BODY BAND BELL BOLE BOOK
BOUK BUCK BULK CREW DEHA
FORM HEAD LICH MASS MOLD
NAVE RIND RUPA SOMA STEM
ATOMY FLESH FRAME HABIT
MOULD SHANK STIFF TORSO
TRUNK CORMUS CORPSE CORPUS
CUERPO EXTENT FUSEAU LICHAM
PERSON SARIRA AIRFOIL
ANATOMY CADAVER CARCASS
COMPANY ECONOMY QUANTUM
SKINFUL SUPTION TEXTURE
CORSAINT DEMARCHY EXTENSUM
MAJORITY QUARROME TENEMENT
PERSONNEL
(— OF ARROW) SHAFT STELE
(— OF BELIEVERS) FAITH
(— OF CANONS) CHAPTER
(— OF CARDINALS) CONCLAVE
(— OF CHILDREN) INFANTRY
(— OF CHRISTIANS) KOINONIA
COMMUNION
(— OF DOCTRINES) DOGMA

(— OF ECHINODERM) DISC DISK
(— OF EVIDENCE) CASE CORPUS
(— OF FIBERS) FORNIX
(— OF HELMET) BELL
(— OF ISLAMIC CUSTOM) SUNNA
SUNNAH
(— OF KNOWLEDGE) STUFF
(— OF LAW) CODE SHAR HALAKA
SHARIA PANDECT SHARIAT
HALACHAH
(— OF MANKIND) HERD
(— OF MUSCLE) BELLY
(— OF NOTIONS) FOLKLORE
(— OF OFFICERS) BUREAU
(— OF ORE) BUNCH MANTO
(— OF PIGMENT) EYESPOT
IMPASTO
(— OF POETRY) EPOS
(— OF PRINCIPLES) ORGANON
(— OF ROCK) DIKE DYKE HORSE
STOCK BIOHERM MUDFLOW
INTRUSION
(— OF SINGERS) CHORUS
(— OF STUDENTS) CLASS
(— OF TEN) DECURY
(— OF TENANTS) GAVEL HOMAGE
(— OF THIEVES) SCHOOL
(— OF TRADITIONS) HADIT HADITH
(— OF TROOPS) FORCE TAXIS
AMBUSH BATTLE CONREY
SCREEN SQUARE BRIGADE
LASHKAR SUPPORT BATTALIA
GARRISON
(— OF TYPE) SHANK
(— OF VASSALS) BAN MANRED
(— OF WARRIORS) IMPI
(— OF WATER) BAY RIP SEA BAHR
FORD HEAD LAKE LAVE POND
POOL WAVE ABYSS BAYOU DRINK
FLOOD OCEAN SHARD SHERD
SWASH LAGOON NYANZA
STREAM FLOWAGE SWALLOW
(— OF WELLBORN MEN)
COMITATUS
(— OF WRITINGS) SMRTI SMRITI
(— OF 12 MEN) DOUZAINE
(— POLITIC) ESTATE
(— RIDDLED BY BULLETS) SIEVE
(CAROTID —) GLOMUS
(CART —) SIRPEA
(CELESTIAL —) SUN BALL COMET
PLANET SPHERE ELEMENT
ASTEROID PLANETOID SATELLITE
PLANETESIMAL
(COMPACT —) GLOBE
(CONDUCTING —) GROUND
(CORPORATE —) SOCIETY
(DEAD —) LICH MORT CADAVER
CARCASS CARRION SUBJECT
(ECCLESIASTICAL —) CLASSIS
(ELASTIC —) CUSHION
(EXTENDED —) LENGTH
(FAT —) EPIPLOON
(FRUITING —) CONK CLAVA
ASCOCARP MAZAEDIUM
(GLOBULAR —) NOB KNOB
(GOVERNING —) KAHAL SYNOD
DURBAR SENATE DECARCHY
DIRECTORY
(HAT —) HOOD
(HEAVENLY —) SUN LAMP STAR
COMET LIGHT CANDLE
(HYALINE —) DRUSE

(IMMUNE —) DESMON
(JUDICIAL —) FORUM
(LEGISLATIVE —) CHAMBER
ASSEMBLY CONGRESS LAGTHING
PARLIAMENT
(MAIN — OF ARMY) BATTLE
(MATHEMATICAL —) FILAMENT
(MORMON —) BISHOPRIC
(MORTAL —) KHET
(POROUS —) MADREPORITE
(PRESBYTERIAN —) SESSION
JUDICATORY
(RELIGIOUS —) SECT CONVENT
(REPRODUCTIVE —) EGG GEMMA
SPORE GEMMULA
(SONOROUS —) PHONIC
(SPIRITUAL —) SAHU
(SWELLING —) BOSS
(WAGON —) BED BUCK PUNT
(PREF.) CORPORI SOMAT(O)
SOMATICO SOMO
(SUFF.) CY DEMA
SOMA(TO)(TOUS) SOME SOMIA
SOMIC SOMOUS SOMUS
(— OF A KIND) ID
BODYGUARD THANE ESCORT
INWARD HUSCARL RETINUE
TRABANT THINGMAN WARDCORS
BOER TAKHAAR AFRIKANER
BOG BUG CAR DUB FEN GOG HAG
BOLD CARR CESS FLOW MIRE
MOOR MOSS OOZE QUAG SINK
SLEW SLUE SPEW STOG SUDS
SYRT WASH LETCH MARSH MIZZY
SAUCY SLADE SLOCK SWAMP
MORASS MUSKEG POLDER
SLOUGH CRIPPLE FORWARD
PEATERY TURBARY QUAGMIRE
(PEAT —) CESS MOSS PETARY
YARPHA
(PREF.) HELO
BOG ASPHODEL KNAVERY
BOGEY BUG COW HAG BOGIE
BOGLE DEVIL GNOME TRUCK
BOGGLE BOOGER GOBLIN
BOGGARD BOGGART BUGABOO
BUGBEAR SPECTER SPECTRE
BOGGLE JIB SHY BALK FOIL STOP
ALARM BOTCH DEMUR SCARE
START STICK BAFFLE BUNGLE
GOBLIN SHRINK BAUCHLE
BLUNDER PERPLEX SCRUPLE
STUMBLE FRIGHTEN HESITATE
BOGGY WET DEEP MIRY SOFT
FENNY FOGGY GOUTY HAGGY
MOSSY SNAPY SPEWY MARISH
MARSHY QUAGGY SLOBBY
SWAMPY WAUGHY BOGGISH
QUEACHY SQUASHY
BOGIER RIDER GEARMAN
BOGLAND SLADE
BOG MANGANESE WAD
LAMPADITE
BOGO ABILO ABILAO
BOGOMILE PATARIN PATARINE
BOGUS FAKE SHAM FALSE PHONY
SPURIOUS
BOHEME, LA (CHARACTER IN —)
MIMI COLLINE MUSETTA
RODOLFO MARCELLO
SCHAUNARD
(COMPOSER OF —) PUCCINI
BOHEMIAN ARTY PICARA PICARD

PICARO ARTISTIC
(— RIVER) ELBE VLTAVA LUZNICE
BEROUNKA
(— TOWN) PISEK PLZEN PRAHA
TABOR PILSEN PRAGUE
BOHEMIAN GIRL (COMPOSER OF —)
BALFE
BOHOR REEDBUCK
BOIL FRY PET STY BILE BLOB BOLL
BRAN BUCK BUMP COCT COOK
COWL LEEP PLAY PUSH QUAT
RAGE SEED SORE STEW STYE
TEEM WALL WALM WELL BLAIN
BOTCH BREDE STEAM BETRAY
BUBBLE BULDER BULLER BURBLE
DECOCT GALLOP PIMPLE RISING
SEETHE SIMMER TOTTLE WABBLE
WOBBLE ANTHRAX BEALING
BREEDER CATHAIR ELIXATE
ESTUATE INFLAME AESTUATE
EBULLATE FURUNCLE PHLEGMON
CARBUNCLE
(— IN LYE) BUCK
(— SYRUP) PEARL
(SAND —) BLOWOUT
(PREF.) COCTO DOTHI(EN)(O) ZEO
BOILED SOD SODDEN
(— WITHOUT SAUCE) ANGLAISE
BOILER YET REEF STILL COPPER
KETTLE RETORT TEACHE ALEMBIC
CALDRON FURNACE
(SALT —) WELLER
BOILING WALM ABOIL FERVID
COCTION FERVENT SCALDING
SEETHING ELIXATION
BOILING POINT
(PREF.) COCTO
BOISTERER (MASTER OF —)
FORTUNIO
BOISTEROUS GURL HIGH LOUD
RUDE WILD BURLY GURLY NOISY
RANDY ROARY ROUGH WINDY
COARSE RUGGED SHANDY
STOCKY STORMY STRONG
UNRULY FURIOUS MASSIVE
ROARING VIOLENT BIGMOUTH
CUMBROUS LARRIKIN STRIDENT
VEHEMENT ROBUSTIOUS
BOLD BIG BOG MOD YEP DERF
HARD KEEN PERT RASH RUDE
TALL WHAT YEPE APERT BARDY
BIELD BRASH BRAVE BRENT
FRACK FREAK FRECK GALLY
HARDY JOLLY LARGE MANLY
NERVY PAWKY PEART POKEY
RUDAS SAUCY STEEP STOUT
WLONK ABRUPT AUDACE BRASSY
BRAZEN CROUSE DARING FIERCE
HEROIC PLUCKY PRETTY STRONG
ASSURED DASHING DEFIANT
FORWARD GRIVOIS HAUGHTY
MASSIVE VALIANT ARROGANT
FAMILIAR FEARLESS IMMODEST
IMPUDENT INTREPID MALAPERT
POWERFUL RESOLUTE TEMEROUS
(NOT —) GENTEEL
BOLDFACE BOLD BLACK FULLFACE
BOLDLY CRANK BARELY CROUSE
HARDLY HARDILY ROUNDLY
STRONGLY
BOLDNESS BROW DARE FACE
GALL BIELD CHEEK NERVE PLUCK
VIGOR DARING BRAVERY

COURAGE FREEDOM AUDACITY TEMERITY
(— OF SPEECH) PARRHESIA
BOLDO NUTMEG
BOLE CLAY DOSE STEM BOLUS CRYPT TRUNK RUDDLE TIMBER
BOLETUS CEPE
BOLIDE FIREBALL
BOLIVIA PILE

BOLIVIA
CAPITAL: LAPAZ SUCRE
COIN: TOMIN CENTAVO
DEPARTMENT: LAPAZ ORURO PANDO ELBENI POTOSI TARIJA
INDIAN: URO INCA ITEN MOXO URAN ARAWAK AYMARA CHARCA CHICHA IXIAMA TACANA PUQUINA QUECHUA SIRIONE TUMUPASA
LAKE: POOPO COIPASA ROGAGUA AULLAGAS TITICACA
MEASURE: LEAGUE CELEMIN
MOUNTAIN: JARA CUSCO CUZCO PUPUYA SAJAMA SORATA ILLAMPU ANCOHUMA ILLIMANI ZAPALERI
MOUNTAINS: ANDES SUNSAS SANSIMON SANTIAGO
PANPIPE: SICU SIKU
PLATEAU: ALTIPLANO
RIVER: BENI YATA ABUNA APERE BOOPI LAUCA ORTON BAURES GRANDE ICHILO ITENEZ MADIDI MAMORE MIZQUE TARIJA YACUMA GUAPORE ITONAMA MACHUPO BENECITO INAMBARI PARAGUAY PARAPETI
SALT DEPOSIT: UYUNI EMPEXA
SWAMP: IZOZOG
TOWN: IVO ICLA ITAU MOJO POJO SAYA YACO YATA YURA CLIZA LAPAZ LLICA ORURO QUIME SUCRE UNCIA UYUNI ZONGO GUAQUI POTOSI TARIJA
VOLCANO: OLLAGUE
WEIGHT: LIBRA MARCO

BOLL BOW POD BULB KNOB SNAP ONION BUBBLE CAPSULE
BOLLARD BITT KEVEL DOLPHIN DEADHEAD
(—S AND BITTS) APOSTLES
BOLLER STRIPPER
BOLL WEEVIL PICUDO
BOLO MACHETE SUNDANG
BOLSHEVISM COMMUNISM SOVIETISM
BOLSHEVIST BOLO
BOLSTER AID PAD JACK PILLOW CUSHION HEADING STIFFEN SUPPORT BACKSTOP BALUSTER COMPRESS MAINTAIN
BOLT BAR JAG KEY LUE PEN PIN ROD RUN BEAT BURR CRAM DART DUMP FLEE GULP LOCK PAWL SHUT SIFT SLOT SNIB SPAR STUD ARROW BILBO CLOSE ELOPE FLASH FLOUR GORGE LATCH RIVET SETUP SHAFT STOCK ASSORT DECAMP DESERT FASTEN FLIGHT GANYIE GARBLE MOOTER PINTLE PURIFY QUARRY

REFINE SAFETY SEARCE SECURE SNIBEL STREAK STRONG TOGGLE WINNOW BAYBOLT QUARREL EYEBOLT MISSILE QUARREL SETBOLT SHACKLE SLABBER THUNDER DRAWBOLT FASTENER FISHBOLT FLATHEAD KINGBOLT RINGBOLT SEPARATE SLUMMOCK STAMPEDE
(— FOOD) SKOFF
(DOOR —) DRAWBOLT
(FIERY —) RESHEPH
(LIGHTNING —) SHAFT
(THUNDER —) FULMEN
(PREF.) GOMPHO
BOLTER BOLT DRESSER MUGWUMP
BOLTHEAD MATRASS
BOMB DUD EGG ROC AZON BOOM FRAG BLARE CRUMP PRANG RAZON SHELL SQUIB ASHCAN SALUTE AEROSOL BALLOON BOMBARD GRENADE MARMITE AEROBOMB FIREBALL WHIZBANG PINEAPPLE
(— RELEASE) TOGGLE
(TRENCH —) MINNIE
(PL.) STICK
BOMBARD BOMB CRUMP SHELL ATTACK BATTER BOTTLE STRAFE
BOMBARDMENT BLITZ SIEGE ATTACK RAFALE STRAFE BATTERY SHELLING
BOMBARDON TUBA NICOLO POMMER BRUMMER
BOMBAST GAS PAD PUFF RAGE RANT RAVE STUFF TUMOR BLUSTER FUSTIAN TYMPANY BALLYHOO BOASTING RHAPSODY TURGIDITY
BOMBASTIC PUFFY TUMID VOCAL WINDY FLUENT HEROIC MOUTHY TURGID BLOATED BOMBAST FLOWERY FUSTIAN OROTUND POMPOUS RANTING STILTED SWOLLEN INFLATED SWELLING
(— STYLE) TYMPANY
BOMBAY DUCK BUMMALO
BONACE TREE NOSEBURN
BONACI AGUAJI
BONA FIDE LEVEL GENUINE AUTHENTIC
BONANZA BUNCH
BONANZA STATE MONTANA
BONBON CANDY CREAM GOODY DAINTY CARAMEL COSAQUE SNAPPER CONFETTO
(PL.) CONFETTI
BOND BON DOG TIE VOW ANDI BAIL BAND DUTY FIVE FOUR GLUE GYVE HOLD KNOT LINK NOTE YOKE BOUND CHAIN NEXUS SWATH BINDER CEDULA CEMENT CONNEX COPULA COUPLE ENGAGE ESCROW FETTER LEAGUE PLEDGE SOLDER SWATHE FOREIGN HUSBAND LIAISON LIBERTY LINKAGE MANACLE SHACKLE STATUTE ADHESIVE CONTRACT COVENANT LIGAMENT LIGATION LIGATURE MORTGAGE SECURITY VADIMONY VINCULUM
(EMOTIONAL —) RAPPORT

(PL.) IRON KHAKIS SHORTS
(PREF.) DESM(A)(IDI)(IDIO)(O)
ETHMO OSSE(O) OSSI OST(E)(EO)
(SUFF.) **(CONTAINING TRIPLE —)** OLIC
BONDAGE YOKE THRALL HELOTRY SERFDOM SLAVERY BONDSHIP THIRLING CAPTIVITY SERVITUDE
BONDED CATTED ENGAGED
BONDMAN CARL ESNE PEON SERF CHURL HELOT SLAVE STOOGE SURETY THRALL VASSAL CHATTEL PEASANT SERVANT VILLEIN BONDSMAN
BONDSTONE BINDER BONDER KEYSTONE
BONE OS DIB HIP LUZ RIB TOT BANE ULNA BLADE FEMUR HYOID ILIUM INCUS JUGAL SLATE STONE TALUS TIBIA UNION VOMER CANNON COCCYX CONCHA COPULA CUBOID EPURAL FIBULA FILLET HAMATE NUCHAL PECTEN RADIAL SPLINT STAPES TRIPOD UNGUIS ZYGOMA DENTARY PALATAL PROOTIC CORACOID PALATINE PERIOTIC PISIFORM QUADRATE NAVICULAR OPERCULAR METACARPAL
(ANKLE —) TALUS
(HIP —) HUGGIN
(PUBIC —) PECTEN
(SHIN —) CNEMIS
(THIGH —) FEMUR
(PREF.) ETHO OSSE(O) OSSI OST(E)(EO)
(SUFF.) OST(EON)(EUS)(OSIS)
BONED
(SUFF.) OSTEUS
BONEFISH OIO MACABI GRUBBER BONYFISH LADYFISH
BONER BUBU FLUB ROCK ERROR BRODIE STAYER STUMER BLOOMER BLOOPER BLUNDER MISTAKE STEELER STUMOUR
BONES
(PREF.) **(— OF HAND OR FOOT)** PHALANGI(A)
BONESET COMFREY AGUEWEED EUPATORY HEMPWEEK
BONEYARD STOCK
BONFIRE BLAZE TANDLE TAWNIE BALEFIRE BURNFIRE NEEDFIRE
BONGO DOR
BONING SAP
BONITO AKU ATU NICE COBIA SARDA BONITA ROBALO ALBACORE KATONKEL MACKEREL SCOMBRID SKIPJACK
BONNET CAP HAT COWL HOOD POKE POXY SCON COVER DECOY SCONE SHAPE TOQUE CAPOTE MOBCAP SLOUCH CHAPEAU COMMODE CORONET LEGHORN SOWBACK VOLUPER BALMORAL BONGRACE HEADGEAR
BONNET MONKEY ZATI MUNGA TOQUE MACACO RILAWA MACAQUE
BONNY GAY FINE MERRY PLUMP BLITHE BONNIE PRETTY STRONG HEALTHY BUDGEREE HANDSOME BEAUTIFUL

BONTOK IGOROT
BONUS GIN TIP GIFT MEED AWARD BRIBE BUNCE BUNTS PILON PRIZE SPIFF REGALO REWARD CUMSHAW DOUCEUR PREMIUM SUBSIDY BOUNTITH DIVIDEND TANTIEME LAGNIAPPE
BON VIVANT SPORT EPICURE
BON VIVEUR FLANEUR
BONY HARD LANK THIN LANKY STIFF TOUGH OSTEAL SKINNY ANGULAR OSSEOUS SCRAGGY SKELETAL
BONYFISH MENHADEN
BOOB ASS OAF FOOL GOON GOOP DUNCE GOONY NEDDY NITWIT
BOOBOOK OWL PEHO RURU CUCKOO MOPOKE MOPEHAWK MOREPORK
BOOB TUBE BOX
BOOBY GAWK GONY SULA DUNCE IDIOT LOSER PATCH PRIZE SILLY SLEIGH STUPID CAMANAY PIQUERO GOOSECAP
BOOBYALLA DOGWOOD WATERBUSH
BOODLE LOOT SWAG CROWD GRAFT BUDDLE NOODLE PLUNDER CABOODLE
BOOGEYMAN PADFOOT TANKERABOGUS
BOOJUM SNARK
BOOK MO LIL LOG CHAP CODE FORM HEFT OPUS PAGE TEXT TOME ALBUM ALDUS BIBLE CANON CANTO CODEX DETUR DIARY DIVAN ENTER FLETA FOLIO FROST GUIDE KITAB LIBEL LIBER QUAIR QUIRE RAZEE ZOHAR ALDINE ANONYM BODONI CURSUS DOCKET HERBAL LEDGER MAHZOR MANUAL MISSAL NUMBER REBIND RECORD RITUAL SCHOOL TICKET TROPER VOLUME BLOTTER CATALOG COUCHER DIETARY DISCARD FEODARY GARLAND GRAMMAR JOURNAL LAWBOOK LEXICON MANDALA OCTAPLA OMNIBUS ORDINAL OUTBOOK PEERAGE RECITER SAMHITA SERVICE SLEEPER SPEAKER SPELLER SYNAXAR TERRIER TICKLER TRAVAIL TRIGLOT TYPICON TYPICUM WRITING BANKBOOK BROCHURE CALCULUS CASEBOOK CASHBOOK CHAPBOOK COOKBOOK COPYBOOK DECRETAL DOCUMENT FESTIVAL GIFTBOOK GOSPELER HANDBOOK HARDBACK HERDBOOK JESTBOOK JUVENILE LIBRETTO PASTORAL POMANDER POSTBOOK REGISTER SONGBOOK STUDBOOK SYNAXARY TALEBOOK TRIODION TWENTYMO VESPERAL PAPERBACK PONTIFICAL NOMENCLATOR PROCESSIONAL PHARMACOPOEIA
(— BACK) DORSE
(— FOR HARVARD GRADUATE) DETUR

(— OF CHARTS) WAGONER PORTOLAN
(— OF HERALDRY) ARMORY ARMORIAL
(— OF MAPS) ATLAS
(— OF PSALMS) PSALTER TEHILLIM
(— OF RULES) HOYLE
(— OF SERVICES) PIE
(— OF SOLUTIONS) KEY
(— OF THE MASS) ORDO
(—S KEPT IN PRINT) BACKLIST
(CHEAP —) BLOOD
(CHINESE —) CHING
(COMMONPLACE —) ADVERSARIA
(ELEMENTARY —) PRIMER
(FOLDED —) ORIHON
(JOKE —) JOE JESTBOOK
(MEMORANDUM —) AGENDA JOTTER TICKLER
(MINIATURE —) BIBELOT
(PART OF —) CASE FLAP COVER HINGE JOINT SPINE TITLE JACKET LINING ENDLEAF BACKBONE ENDPAPER HEADBAND BACKSTRIP SHELFBACK
(PRAYER —) PORTAS SIDDUR PORTASS PORTHORS
(READING —) ABC ABCEE ABSEY
(RECORD —) LIBER TICKLER
(RELIGIOUS —) KITAB KORAN QURAN GOSPEL HORARY KYRIAL PROSAR GRADUAL KYRIALE BREVIARY MEGILLAH ORDINARY SYNAXARY
(SERVICE —) COMES GRAIL TEXTUS
(SLOW-SELLING —) PLUG
(STRANGE —S) CURIOSA
(UNBOUND —) CAHIER
(PL.) LIBRI SHELF STUDY EROTICA SCRIPTURE
(PREF.) BIBLIO LIBRI
BOOKBINDING STUB YAPP STRING
BOOKCASE DESK STAGE STALL SCRINE PLUTEUS CREDENZA
BOOK COVER LID SIDE FOREL RECTO VERSO FORREL REVERSE REVERSO
BOOKISH BOOKY ERUDITE INKHORN PEDANTIC STUDIOUS
BOOKLET FOLDER NOVELET BROCHURE
BOOK LOUSE PSOCID
BOOKMAKER LAYER BOOKER BOOKIE
BOOKMARK MARKER TASSEL REGISTER
BOOK PALM TARA TALIERA
BOOKSHELF DESK PLUTEUS (PL.) CLASSIS
BOOKWORM GOME GRUB NERD TOOL WONK CEREB GNURD GRIND SQUID SPIDER WEENIE
BOOM JIB BEAM BOMB BUMP CRIB POLE ROAR SPAR BRAIL CHAIN CRANE CROON PROBE BUMPKIN CATHEAD CURTAIN RESOUND SUPPORT BOWSPRIT FLOURISH
(CRANE —) ARM GIB JIB
BOOMERANG KALIE KILEY KYLIE WANGO ATLATL BOUNCE RECOIL LEEWILL REBOUND WOMERAH WOOMERA BACKFIRE HORNERAH

LEEANGLE RICOCHET TROMBASH
BOOMING HUMMING ROARING
BOOM IRON WITHE CRANCE
BOON GAY BENE GIFT GOOD KIND BOUND FAVOR GRANT MERRY ORDER BENIGN BOUNTY GOODLY JOVIAL PRAYER BENEFIT COMMAND PRESENT BLESSING INTIMATE PETITION BENEFACTION
BOOR CAD OAF BOER BORE CARL HICK JACK KERN LOUT PILL RUNT SLOB CHUFF CHURL CLOWN KERNE SLAVE BUMKIN CARLOT CLUNCH HOBLOB JOBSON JOSKIN LUBBER LUMMOX RUSTIC BUMPKIN CAUBOGE GROBIAN PEASANT VILLAIN BOEOTIAN BOSTHOON CLODHOPPER
BOORISH ILL RUDE GAWKY ROUGH RUNTY SURLY CLUMSY RUSTIC SAVAGE SULLEN VULGAR WOOLEN AWKWARD CRABBED HIRSUTE HOBLIKE KERNISH LOUTISH PEAKISH ROISTER UNCOUTH VILLAIN WOOLLEN BOEOTIAN CARTERLY CHURLISH CLODDISH CLOWNISH LUBBERLY SWAINISH UNGAINLY
BOORISHNESS VILLAINY GROBIANISM
BOOST AID LEG ABET BACK BOOM HELP LIFT PLUG PUSH COACH EXALT HOIST HOOSH RAISE ASSIST ADVANCE COMMEND ELEVATE ENDORSE PROMOTE INCREASE
BOOT PAC PAD USE CURE GAIN HALF HELP HOOF KICK PUNT SHOE SOCK AVAIL BOOTY DERBY EJECT JEMMY KAMIK PEWEE SPOIL BOOTEE BUDGET BUSKIN CASING CHUKKA CRAKOW ENRICH FUMBLE GAITER GALOSH INSHOE JEMIMA JOCKEY MUKLUK PEDULE SHEATH BENEFIT BOTTINE COTHURN COWHIDE CRUISER HESSIAN HIGHLOW SEABOOT SHOEPAC VANTAGE BALMORAL BOTTEKIN CHASSURE COVERING FINNESKO JACKBOOT LARRIGAN NAPOLEON COTHURNUS
(— OF CARRIAGE) FOREBOOT
(— ON SADDLE) GAMBADE GAMBADO
(HALF —) PAC BUSKIN COCKER SKILTY BRODEKIN
(HOB-NAILED —) BAT
(HORSE'S —) SCALPER
(LUMBERMAN'S —) CRUISER
(MARINE —) SKINHEAD
(RIDING —) JEMMY JIMMY JODHPUR
(SEALSKIN —) KAMIK
(STOUT —) STOGA STOGY
(TORTURE —) SQUEEZER
(PL.) OVERS FINNESKO HESSIANS
BOOTBLACK SHINER BLACKER SHOEBOY
BOOTED OCREATE
BOOTES WAINMAN HERDSMAN
BOOTH BOX BULK COOP DESK

LOGE SHED SHOP SOOK BOTHY CABIN CRAME HOUSE KIOSK LIWAN LODGE PITCH SLANG STALL STAND BOTHAN PAGODA PANDAL PAYBOX SUCCAH SUKKAH TIENDA BALAGAN COCKSHY TABERNA
BOOTLACE LACET THONG
BOOTLEG SHY SLY ILLEGAL ILLICIT
BOOTY BOOT FANG GAIN LOOT PELF PREY SACK SWAG BUTIN CHEAT FORAY GRAFT PRIZE CREAGH FLEECE SPOILS DESPOIL PILLAGE PLUNDER SPREAGH SPREATH STEALTH PURCHASE SPUILZIE STEALAGE
BOOZE BOLL BOUT BUDGE DRINK HOOCH SPREE FUDDLE LIQUOR
BOOZY TIPPLE LIQUORY
BOPHUTHATSWANA (CAPITAL OF —) MMABATHO
(TOWN OF —) TEMBA MABOPANE GARANKUWA
BORAGE ANCHUSA
BORAX FLUX TINCAL
(— SOURCE) KERNITE
BORDER CUT HEM RIM TAB ABUT BABK BRIM CURB DADO EAVE EDGE LIMB LINE LIST LOVE MARK NARK ORLE RAND ROON RUND SIDE TRIM WELL WELT BOARD BOUND BRAID BRINK CHEEK COAST COSTA DRAFT FILET FLANK FOREL FRAME FRILL GUARD LIMIT MARCH MARGE MARLI PLAIT SHORE SKIRT STRIP SWAGE TOUCH VERGE ACCOST ADJOIN COTISE EDGING FILLET FORREL FRINGE IMPALE LACING LIMBUS LISERE MARGIN ORFRAY PURFLE QUADRA SCREED STRIPE TANIKO WEEPER CONFINE DRAUGHT FIMBRIA FLOROON MARGENT SELVAGE VALANCE BOUNDARY DOUBLING FRONTIER MARCHESE NEIGHBOR OUTSKIRT PLATBAND SKIRTING SURROUND TERMINUS TRESSOUR TRESSURE
(— OF EXTERNAL EAR) HELIX
(— OF LACE) PICOT
(— OF ROCK) SALBAND
(— OF SAIL) DOUBLING
(— OF SHIELD) BORDURE
(— OF STREAM) ROND
(— ON) ABUT ACCOST AFFRONT NEIGHBOR
(FLOWERED —) FLOROON
(ORNAMENTAL —) PURL WAGE FRAME FRINGE MATTING DENTELLE TRESSURE
(RIBBON —) FRILAL
(PL.) CONFINE PURLIEU CONFINES
(PREF.) CRASPEDO LIMBI
BORDERED ORLE LIMBATE
BORDERING MARGENT FRONTIER
BORE BIT CUT EAT IRK JET TAP DRAG FLAT HOLE JUMP PALL PILL POKE REAM RUSH SINK SIZE TIDE TIRE TOOL ANNOY CHINK DRILL EAGRE ENNUI GAUGE GOUGE OUGHT PLONK PRICK PUNCH SUGUR TEWEL THIRL TRICK

VAPOR WEARY BEFOOL CANNON GIMLET PIERCE THRILL THRUST TUNNEL WIMBLE BROMIDE CALIBER CALIBRE CONCAVE CREVICE HUMDRUM NUDNICK OPENING AIGUILLE CAPILLUS DIAMETER DRAWBORE GRATIANO POROROCA
(— OF CANNON) SOUL CHASE
(PREF.) FORAMINI
BOREAL NORTHERN
BOREAS AQUILO AQUILON
(BROTHER OF —) NOTUS HESPERUS ZEPHYRUS
(DAUGHTER OF —) CLEOPATRA
(FATHER OF —) ASTRAEUS
(MOTHER OF —) EOS AURORA
(SON OF —) ZETES CALAIS
BORED BLASE WEARY ENNUYEE TEDIOUS SATIATED
BOREDOM YAWN ENNUI ACEDIA TEDIUM
(FEELING OF —) BLAHS
BORELE KEITLOA UPEYGAN
BORER MOLE BARDEE WIMBLE HAGFISH TANBARK TERMITE TERRIER FLATHEAD SHIPWORM WOODWORM
(PREF.) TRYPAN(O)
BORING DIM DRY FLAT SLOW BROACH STODGY STUPID TIRING LUMPISH TEDIOUS PIERCING TIRESOME TEREBRANT
(— TOOL) AIGUILLE
(SOMETHING —) DRAG
BORIS GODUNOV (CHARACTER IN —) BORIS PIMEN DMITRY GRIGORY MISSAIL RANGONI SHUISKY VARLAAM
(COMPOSER OF —) MUSSORGSKY
BORN N NEE NATE INNATE NASCENT NATURAL UTERINE ORIGINAL
(PREMATURELY —) SLINK ABORTIVE
(WELL —) FREE EUGENIC
(SUFF.) GEN(E)(ESIA)(ESIS)(ETIC) (IC)(IN)(OUS)(Y)
BORNE RODE NARROW CARRIED ENDURED
(— AFFRONTEE) CABOCHED
(— LOWER THAN USUAL) ABASED
(— ON WATER) AFLOAT

WEIGHT: PARA CHAPAH

BORO MARIANA
BORON BORAX ULEXITE
BORORO COROADO
BOROUGH BURG CITY PORT TOWN
WICK BORGO BRUSH BURGH
CASTLE COUNTY CITADEL
FORTESS VILLAGE TOWNSHIP
(SUFF.) BURG
BORROW BOT BITE COPY HIRE
KICK LOAN SHIN TAKE THIG
ADOPT STEAL TOUCH DESUME
DUPLEX PLEDGE STRIKE SURETY
CHEVISE HOSTAGE MUTUATE
TITHING
BORROWED SECONDHAND
BORROWER BOT CRIB MUTUARY
BORS (BROTHER OF —) BAN
(UNCLE OF —) LANCELOT
BOS OX NEAT TAURUS
BOSH END ROT JOKE SHOW TALK
TOSH FUDGE TRASH BUSHWA
FIGURE FLAUNT HUMBUG TRIVIA
TOSHERY GALBANUM NONSENSE
POPPYCOCK
BOSKY BUSHY TIPSY WOODY
FUDDLED
BOSNIA-HERZEGOVINA (RIVER OF
—) BOSNA DRINA NERETVA
(TOWN OF —) TUZLA MAGLAJ
MOSTAR VISOKO SARAJEVO
BOSOM LAP BARM BUST CLOSE
DICKY HEART SINUS BREAST
CAVITY DESIRE DICKEY RECESS
BELOVED EMBRACE GREMIAL
INCLOSE INTIMATE POITRINE
(— OF DRESS) SQUARE
(FALSE —) PLUMPER
BOSS BUR HUB MOP NOB ORB PAD
POP BAAS BEAD BOCE BUHR
BURR COCK CZAR KNOB KNOP
KNOT NAIL NAVE NULL STUD
TSAR BULLA BULLY BWANA CHIEF
EMPTY JEWEL KNOSP ORDER
OWNER PEARL ANCHOR BROOCH
BUCKRA BUTTON CHEESE DIRECT
HOLLOW HONCHO MANAGE
MASTER OCULUS PATERA PELLET
SHIELD BULLION CACIQUE
CAPATAZ CAPTAIN CUSHION
FOREMAN HASSOCK HEADMAN
HOBNAIL MANAGER PADRONE
PHALERA SPANGLE SPONSON
DIRECTOR DOMINEER MISERERE
OMPHALOS OVERSEER UMBILICUS
(— OF LOGGING CAMP) BULLY
(— OF SHIELD) UMBO
(FIRE —) GASMAN
(LEATHER —) BUTTON
(MINE —) SHIFTER SHIFTMAN
(POLITICAL —) CACIQUE CAUDILLO
(STRAW —) BULL LEADER
(PREF.) UMBO
BOSSY PUSHY
BOSTONIAN HUBBITE
BOTANIST AMERICAN AMES BEAL
COOK GRAY HOWE ROSE BROWN
CLUTE GAGER HEALD JAMES
JONES LOGAN MOORE PURSH
SEARS SHULL SMALL VASEY
BAILEY BESSEY CANNON CARVER

CUTLER DUDLEY DUGGAR
FARLOW HARRIS HOWELL JEPSON
LEMMON PEIRCE SHANTZ TAYLOR
TORREY WATSON BARTRAM
BIGELOW BRITTON COULTER
CROCKER ELLIOTT FERNALD
GOODALE HOLLICK JOHNSON
MERRILL PEATTIE POLLARD
RYDBERG SWINGLE THURBER
CALDWELL CAMPBELL COPELAND
KNOWLTON MARSHALL TRELEASE
BLAKESLEE FAIRCHILD
LONGWORTH NIEUWLAND
OSTERHOUT SULLIVANT
UNDERWOOD CHAMBERLAIN
AUSTRIAN UNGER KERNER
MENDEL JACQUIN HABERLANDT
BELGIAN LINDEN
CANADIAN SAUNDERS
DANISH HANSEN WARMING
JOHANNSEN RAUNKIAER
DUTCH TREUB DODOENS
ENGLISH WARD BOWER BUDDLE
CLARKE DARWIN GERARD
HOOKER HUDSON MARTYN
PAXTON TURNER BENNETT
FORSYTH HAWORTH HENSLOW
JACKSON LINDLEY DRYANDER
SIBTHORP BABINGTON
FRENCH BORNET MAGNOL MIRBEL
THURET TRECUL BONNIER
JUSSIEU LECLUSE MICHAUX
TULASNE DECAISNE MILLARDET
JACQUEMONT TOURNEFORT
VANTIEGHEM DESFONTAINES
GERMAN BOCK COHN KOCH LINK
MOHL ZINN BLUME DRUDE
FUCHS KUNTH SACHS ENGLER
GLOXIN GMELIN GOEBEL HEDWIG
KUNTZE MIGULA REINKE
CORRENS EICHLER FITTING
GARTNER JUNGIUS KARSTEN
KUTZING MOLISCH PFEFFER
RIVINUS WARBURG BRUNFELS
LEDEBOUR LONITZER SPRENGEL
DILLENIUS GRISEBACH
KOLREUTER CAMERARIUS
HOFMEISTER PRINGSHEIM
REICHENBACH STRASBURGER
HUNGARIAN ENDLICHER
IRISH HARVEY
ITALIAN TONI CORTI ALPINI
BECCARI CESALPINO
JAPANESE IKENO
NORWEGIAN GUNNERUS
RUSSIAN BUNGE FAMINTSYN
SCOTTISH AITON BROWN
DOUGLAS FORTUNE MORISON
FALCONER
SPANISH CAVANILLES
SWEDISH DAHL KALM FRIES
RETZIUS ACHARIUS AFZELIUS
LINNAEUS THUNBERG
ANDERSSON BROMELIUS
SWISS BAUHIN VAUCHER
CANDOLLE
BOTANY HERBARISM PHYTOLOGY
BOTCH MAR MUX BOIL BOSS FLUB
MEND MESS MULL SORE BITCH
BODGE BUTCH FLUFF FUDGE
SPOIL STICK BOGGLE BOLLIX
BUMBLE BUNGLE COBBLE JUMBLE

MUCKER REPAIR TINKER
BLUNDER BUTCHER CLAMPER
SCAMBLE SCLATCH SLUBBER
SWELLING
BOTCHER GRILSE SALMON TINKER
BUNGLER BUTCHER CLOUTER
COBBLER
BOTCHERY PATCHERY
BOTE KINBOT MAGBOTE CARTBOTE
FRITHBOT PLOWBOTE WAINBOTE
BOTFLY BOTT BREEZE GADBEE
GADFLY NITTER CANOPID
OESTRID TORSALO DIPTERAN
OESTRIAN
BOTH BO ALL TWO BAITH EQUALLY
(PREF.) AMBI AMBO AMPH(I)(O)
BIS
(— SIDES) AMPHI
BOTHER ADO AIL BUG IRK NAG
VEX FASH FAZE FUSS JADE WORK
ANNOY DEAVE KNOCK PHASE
TEASE TRADE WORRY BADGER
BUSTLE CUMBER DITHER FLURRY
GRAVEL HARASS MEDDLE MITHER
MOIDER MOLEST MUCKLE PESTER
PLAGUE POTHER POTTER PUTTER
PUZZLE TAMPER CONFUSE
DISTURB FASHERY GRIZZLE
PERPLEX TERRIFY TRACHLE
TROUBLE BEWILDER DISTRESS
IRRITATE NUISANCE
BOTOCUDO BORUN AIMORE
AYMORO
BOTONEE TREFLEE FLEURONE
BO TREE PIPAL

BOTTLE JUG BOSS SKIN VIAL VIOL
AMPUL ASKOS BETTY BOCAL
BUIRE BURET CADUS COOJA
CROFT CRUET CRUSE FIFTH
FLASK GIRBA GLASS GOURD
HOUSE PHIAL SPLIT VERRE
ALUDEL BACBUC BUNDLE CARAFE
CARBOY CASTER CASTOR CHAGUL
CHATTY CREWET DORUCK
DUBBER FESSEL FIASCO FLACON
FLAGON GOGLET GUTTUS
JORDAN LAGENA MAGNUM
MARINE MATARA NURSER
PACKER SIPHON VESSEL WOULFF
BALLOON BIBERON BOMBARD
BOMBOLA BURETTE CANTEEN
CARAFON COSTREL DEADMAN

FLACKET FLOATER GRENADE
INKHORN BOMBONNE BORACHIO
BUILDING CALABASH DECANTER
DEMIJOHN GARDEVIN JEROBOAM
MARIOTTE PRESERVE REHOBOAM
PEPPERBOX
(— IN WICKER) CARBOY DEMIJOHN
(EGYPTIAN —) DORUCK
(EMPTY —) MARINE
(HOT-WATER —) PIG
(LARGE —) KIT JEROBOAM
(LEATHER —) BOOT JACK DUBBA
BUDGET DUBBER DUPPER
MATARA BOMBARD BORACHIO
WHINNOCK WINESKIN
(OVERSIZED —) BALTHAZAR
(PAIR OF —S) GEMEL GEMMEL
(PART OF —) LIP CORK KICK NECK
PUNT MOUTH MUZZLE CAPSULE
SHOULDER
(PILGRIM'S —) AMPULLA
(SMALL —) VIAL AMPUL PHIAL
SPLIT FLACON AMPOULE TICKLER
CRUISKEN CRUISKEEN
(18 —S OF WINE) RIDDLE
(40 —S) KEMPLE
(PREF.) UTRI
BOTTLE CAP CAPSULE
BOTTLE CARRIER FASCET
BOTTLE CASE CELLAR
BOTTLEHEAD DOEGLING
BOTTLER COOPER
BOTTOM ASS BED ARSE BASE
DALE DOUP FLAT FOND FOOT
FUND HOLM LEES REAR ROOT
ABYSS BASIS DREGS FLOOR LAIGH
NADIR BATHOS FOUNCE FUNDUS
GROUND GUTTER LAAGTE LEEGTE
BEDROCK LOWLAND SUPPORT
SURFACE BUTTOCKS INTERVAL
SEDIMENT TETRAPOD
(— OF BENCH) TOE
(— OF CUPOLA) HEARTH
(— OF FURROW) SOLE
(— OF PAGE) TAIL
(— OF PISTOL GRIP) BUTT
(— OF POT) POTSTONE
(— OF PRINTER'S GALLEY) SLICE
(— OF PULLEY BLOCK) BREECH
(— OF SEA) GROUND BENTHOS
(— OF SOLE) NAUMK NAUMKEAG
(MARSHY —) SIKE
(ROCK —) HARDPAN
(PL.) HOLM HOLME
BOTTOM-DWELLING DEMERSAL
BOTTOMER FOOTMAN
STATIONMAN
BOTTOMLAND STRATH
BOTTOMLESS ABYSMAL
BOTULISM LAMSIEKTE LAMZIEKTE
BOUDOIR ROOM BOWER CABIN
BEDROOM CABINET
BOUGH ARM LEG LIMB TWIG
CHUCK SHOOT SPRAY SPRIG
BRANCH RAMAGE SHROUD
GALLOWS PHYLLIS OFFSHOOT
SHOULDER
(— ON TAVERN) BUSH
(— USED AS TORCH) ROUGHIE
(PL.) RAMAGE DUNNAGE
RAMMAGE
BOUGHT KEFT

STORE ZEBINA
BOUGIE CANDLE COLLYRIE
FILIFORM
BOULDER NOB KELK KNOB ROCK
STONE GIBBER BOOTHER
DORNICK ERRATIC GRAYBACK
HARDHEAD MEGALITH POTSTONE
BOULE BIRNE
BOULEVARD DRIVE PRADO
AVENUE STREET ALAMEDA
HIGHWAY TERRACE CORNICHE
BOULTER TRAWL SPILLER SPILLET
BOUNCE DAP HOP BANG BLOW
BRAG BUMP DING DIRD FIRE
GATE JUMP LEAP SACK STOT
BOAST BOUND BULLY CAROM
CHUCK EJECT KNOCK SCOLD
THUMP VERVE BLAGUE MORGAY
SPIRIT SPRING STRIKE ADDRESS
BLUSTER CHOUNCE DISMISS
REBOUND SWAGGER PROCLAIM
RICOCHET
BOUNCER CHUCKER SCROUGER
BOUNCING BIG BUXOM LUSTY
STOUT BOUNCY HEALTHY
WALLOPING
(— OF TONGUE) FLAP
BOUNCING BET SOAPWORT
BOUND DAP END HOP LOP BENT
BIND BOND BONE BROW BUTT
DART GIRT JUMP LEAP LIST MERE
RAMP RISE SCUD SKIP STEM STOT
SURE TERM WALL AMBIT BORNE
BOURN FIXED GOING LIMIT
READY SALLY SCOUP SKELP
START STEND STING TILED VAULT
VERGE BORDER BOUNCE BOURNE
BUTTAL CAVORT CURVET DEFINE
DOMAIN FINISH GAMBOL GIRDED
HURDLE JETTED LIABLE LOLLOP
OBLIGE PRANCE SPRING AFFINED
BARRIER CERTAIN CHAINED
CLOSURE CONFINE CONTAIN
COSTIVE DELIMIT DRESSED
GAMBADO INCLUDE REBOUND
SALTATE SECURED SUBSULT
TERMINE TRUSSED BOUNDARY
CONFINED DESTINED ENCLOSED
FASCIATE FRONTIER HANDFAST
LANDMARK LIMITATE OBLIGATE
PINIONED PRECINCT PREPARED
RESTRICT SHACKLED
(— BY OATH) SWORN
(— BY OBLIGATION) AFFINED
(NOT —) SOLUTE
(RIGIDLY —) STATIC STATICAL
(PL.) PALE AMBIT MOUND
CLOSURE COMPASS CONFINE
PURLIEUS PERIPHERY
BOUNDARY AHU END RIM DOLE
DOOL EDGE FINE FORM LINE LIST
MARK MEAR MEER MERE META
METE PALE SURF TERM TRIG
WALL AMBIT BOURN CLOSE
FENCE FRAME FRONT HEDGE
LIMES LIMIT MARCH MEITH
MOUND SHORE VERGE BORDER
COLLET DEFINE OCTROI OCTROY
TROPIC BARRIER BOUNDER
BUTTING COMPASS FURLONG
OUTLINE CURBLINE FRONTIER
LANDLINE LIMITARY PRECINCT
TERMINUS UMSTROKE PERIMETER

PERIPHERY MAGNETOPAUSE
(PL.) ABUTTALS ENVIRONS
(PREF.) HORO LIMI ORI TERMINO
(— OF AIR MASS) FRONTO
BOUNDER ROUE
BOUNDLESS VAST UNTOLD
ENDLESS ETERNAL INFINITE
UNLIMITED
BOUNTEOUS BOON CROWNED
LIBERAL PLENTEOUS
BOUNTIFUL GOOD LUSH RICH
AMPLE FREELY LAVISH LIBERAL
PROFUSE ABUNDANT GENEROUS
BOUNTY BOON GIFT MEED AWARD
BONUS GRANT LARGE VALOR
WORTH BONTEE REWARD VIRTUE
LARGESS PREMIUM PRESENT
PROWESS SUBSIDY DONATIVE
GOODNESS GRATUITY KINDNESS
BOUQUET BOB AURA ODOR POSY
AROMA BLOOM CIGAR POSEY
SHEAF SPRAY BOWPOT BUSKET
SHOWER CORSAGE NOSEGAY
BOUGHPOT
(— GARNI) FAGOT FAGGOT
BOURGEOIS ORGON COMMON
POOTER STUPID BOORISH
BURGHER
BOURGEOIS GENTILHOMME
(AUTHOR OF —) MOLIERE
(CHARACTER IN —) CLEANTE
LUCILLE COVIELLE JOURDAIN
BOURSE BOLSA BORSE CAMBIO
BOURTREE ELDER
BOUT GO JOB BOOT FALL PULL
TURN BOOZE BRASH CRASH
ESSAY FIGHT MATCH PLUCK
ROUND TRIAL VENNY VENUE
ATTACK COURSE FRACAS YOKING
ASSAULT ATTEMPT CAROUSE
CIRCUIT CONTEST DEBAUCH
OUTSIDE WITHOUT CONFLICT
(DRINKING —) BAT BEND BUST
TIRL BOOZE SPRAY SPREE
RANDAN SCREED SPLORE
CAROUSE GAEDOWN WASSAIL
POTATION
BOUTONNIERE BOUQUET
BUTTONHOLE
BOUW BAHU BAHOE
BOVATE OSKEN OXGANG OXGATE
OXLAND
(TWO —S) HUSBANDLAND
BOVINE OX BOS COW BOSS BULL
CALF DULL NEAT SLOW ZEBU
BEAST BISON STEER ANIMAL
COWISH HUMLIE HUMMEL OXLIKE
ROTHER BULLOCK TAURINE
BANGTAIL LEPTOBOS
BOW ARC LEG LUG NOD SAW TIE
YEW ARCH BAIL BEAK BECK BEND
BENT CURB DUCK FOLD FORE
GORA JOUK KNEE KNOT LATH
LOUT MOVE PROW SELF STEM
SWIM TRUE TURN WEND BINGE
CLINE CONGE COQUE COUCH
CROOK CRUSH CURVE DEFER
GOURA HONOR KNEEL NOEUD
SHIKO STICK STOOP VENIE YIELD
ARCHER ASSENT BAUBLE BUCKLE
CONGEE CRINGE CROUCH CURTSY
FIDDLE FOGBOW RIBBON SALAAM
SALUTE SCRAPE SUBMIT SWERVE

TOURTE WEAPON DEPRESS
FOREBOW FORMBOW HANDBOW
INCLINE INFLECT LONGBOW
NECKTIE RAINBOW ARBALEST
COURTESY CRESCENT ENTRANCE
FOGEATER GREETING
STONEBOW TRUELOVE
OBEISANCE
(— DOWN) ALOUT HUMBLE
(— IN ONE PIECE) SELF
(— LOW) BINGE
(— OF PLOW) DRAIL
(— OF VESSEL) HEAD PROW STEM
ENTRANCE
(— ON SCRAPER) BAIL BALE
(— ON SEA) ATRY
(— OUTWARD) CONVEX
(— SLIGHTLY) ADDRESS
(OVERHANGING —) SWIM
(PART OF —) DIP TIP BACK FACE
GRIP LIMB LOOP NOCK BELLY
BRIDGE HANDLE RECURVE
SERVING BOWSTRING
(PART OF VIOLIN —) NUT TIP FROG
HAIR HEAD POINT SCREW STICK
(PREF.) ARCI ARCO TOX(I)(ICO)(O)
BOWED ARCO BENT BANDY KNEED
ARCATE ARCATO CURVED
BULGING CURVANT SHAMBLE
DOWNBENT
(PREF.) TOX(I)(O)
BOWELS GUT GUTS WOMB BELLY
COLON ROPES VISCERA ENTRAILS
(PREF.) VISCER(I)(O)
BOWER RUN BOOR JACK NOOK
SALE ABODE ARBOR JOKER
KNAVE ANCHOR BOWERY LEFSEL
PANDAL BERCEAU CABINET
CHAMBER COTTAGE EMBOWER
ENCLOSE LEVESEL PERGOLA
RETREAT SHELTER TRELLIS
THALAMUS
(— FOR SNAKES) KISI
(GARDEN —) ALCOVE
BOWERBIRD CATBIRD
COLLARBIRD
BOWFIN AMIA GANOID LAWYER
MORGAY SAWYER CHOUPIC
DOGFISH GRINDAL GRINDLE
GRINNEL MUDFISH
BOWIE STATE ARKANSAS
BOWING CERNUOUS FEATHERING
BOWL CAP CUP PAN TUN COUP
ROLL TASS TRAY WOOD ARENA
BASIN BOWIE DEPAS GUARD
JORUM KITTY LAVER MAZER
PHIAL PITCH ROGAN SCALE
TANOA TAZZA TREEN TROLL
BEAKER BICKER CHAWAN CLOSET
COOTIE CRATER FESSEL JICARA
KETTLE LEKANE MAZARD
MORTAR PIGGIN TROUGH
TUREEN VESSEL BRIMMER
DITCHER DOUBLER DUGGLER
SCYPHUS SKYPHOS SPILLER
STADIUM TOUCHER TRINDLE
TRUNDLE WHISKIN AQUARIUM
BRIDECUP FISHBOWL JEROBOAM
LAVATORY MONTEITH REHOBOAM
PORRINGER
(— ILLEGALLY) JERK
(— OF PIPE) CHILLUM STUMMEL
(— ON PEDESTAL) TAZZA SALVER

(— OUT) YORK
(— THAT TOUCHED JACK) TOUCHER
(— WITH TWO HANDLES) CAP
DEPAS
(DRINKING —) TUN TASS
(MARBLE CUTTER'S —) SEBILLA
(OBLONG —) PITCHI
(PUNCH —) SNEAKER
(SHALLOW —) CAP COUPE
WHISKIN
(SMALL —) JACK
(SOUP —) ECUELLE
(SUGAR —) SUGAR SUCRIER
(TOILET —) HOPPER
(WOODEN —) CAP BOWIE COGIE
KITTY ROGAN BASSIE BICKER
COGGIE COOTIE
BOWLEG OUTKNEE
BOWLEGGED BANDY VALGUS
BOWLER HAT POT DERBY KEGLER
PINMAN SPINNER TRUNDLER
(CRICKET —S) ATTACK
BOWLINE BOWLIN FARGOOD
BOWLING BOWLS ATTACK
KEGLING TENPINS
BOWLS RINK BOCCE BOCCIE
BOWMAN ARCHER
BOW-SHAPED ARCATE
BOWSTRING SERVING
BOWYER BOWER ARTILLER
BOX BED BIN CAR EAR FUR GIG KIT
LOB LUG PIX PYX TYE ARCA BARK
BODY BOOT CAGE CAJA CASE
CIST CRIB CUFF CYST DRAB FLAT
HEAD LOGE MILL PACK PUNG
SCOB SEAT SLAP SLUG SPAR
STOW TILL TRAY ARBOR BARGE
BIJOU BOIST BUIST BUXUS
CADDY CAPSA CHEST CLOUT
CRATE FIGHT FRAME HUTCH
LADLE POUCH PUNCH SHRUB
STALL TRUNK ASCHAM BRUISE
BUFFET BUNKER CARTON CASKET
COFFER COFFIN DRAWER GRILLE
HAMPER HATBOX HAYBOX
HOPPER ICEBOX MAROON
MOCUCK PATRON PETARA PILLAR
SAGGER SHRINE STRIKE TARBOX
VANITY ARCANUM BANDBOX
BATTERY BOXTREE BOXWOOD
CABINET CAISSON CARRIER
CASHBOX CASQUET CASSONE
COFFRET CONFINE COREBOX
DICEBOX DREDGER DUSTBOX
ENCLOSE EXHAUST FOSTELL
FREEZER HANAPER JACKBOX
PACKAGE PILLBOX PITARAH
PRINTER SANDBOX SCATULA
SHELTER TRUMMEL WHERRET
BOXTHORN DOVECOTE DRAGEOIR
JUNCTION LAVARIUM MATCHBOX
POMANDER SHOWCASE SLIPCASE
SOLANDER SWEATBOX
PEPPERBOX PHYLACTERY
(— FOR CARRYING COAL) DAN
(— FOR CUTLERY) CANTEEN
(— FOR FIRE) CHAUFFER
(— FOR FISH) CAR NID
(— FOR MONEY OFFERING) ARCA
LADLE
(— FOR SALT) DRAB
(— FOR SEAL) SKIPPET
(— FOR SEED) LEAP

(— FOR TOBACCO) BUTT DOSS
CADDY SARATOGA
(— IN TIMEPIECE) BARREL
(— IN WHEEL HUB) FUR
(— OF BIRCHBARK) MOCUCK
(— OF CYLINDER) BUSH
(— OF FIRE CLAY) SAGGAR SAGGER
(— OF ORGAN) BOOT SWELL
(— TO SHELTER BELL) SCONCE
(— USED AS DARKROOM) TENT
(BERRY —) HALLOCK
(BREAD —) BARGE
(CANDLE —) BARK
(CIRCULAR —) THIMBLE
(COLLECTION —) BROD
(COMPASS —) KETTLE BINNACLE
(FANCY —) ETUI ETWEE
(FLOATING —) CAISSON
(FOUNDRY —) FRAME
(IRON —) HANGER
(JUGGLER'S —) TRANKA
(MONEY —) CASH SAFE PIRLIE
(PERFUME —) CASSOLETTE
(PIVOTING —) TOUR
(PRINTING —) TURTLE
(REFRIGERATOR —) COOLER
(SHALLOW —) FLAT BACKET
HARBOR
(SNUFF —) MILL MULL
(TEA —) CADDY
(TIN —) TRUMMEL VASCULUM
(PREF.) CAPSULI CAPSULO CISTO
PYXID(O)
BOX BRIER INDIGO INKBERRY
BOXCAR LOWRY STOCKCAR
BOX ELDER MAPLE NEGUNDO
BOXER PUG CHAMP DARES
BANTAM MILLER NOBBER TANKER
WELTER BRUISER CRUISER
FIGHTER SLUGGER SPARRER
BUFFETER PUGILIST SOUTHPAW
BOXFISH CHAPIN COWFISH
SHELLFISH TRUNKFISH
BOXING PLUG RING SAVATE
PARINGS SCIENCE SPARRING
(— GLOVE) MUFFLE
BOX TORTOISE COOTER
BOXWOOD KNYSNA DUDGEON
BOXY BLOCKY
BOY BO BUB FAG GUY HIM LAD
PUR TAD BOYO CHAP LOON NINO
PAGE PUER BILLY BUBBY BUDDY
CHABO CHILD CRACK GAMIN
GILPY GROOM KNAVE PUTTO
ROGUE SWAIN VALET YOUTH
BIRKIE BUTTON CALLAN CHOKRA
GAFFER GARCON MANNIE
MASTER NIPPER RASCAL SHAVER
STIRRA UMFAAN URCHIN
BOUCHAL CALLANT DRAWBOY
GLEANER GOSSOON GRUMMET
JACKBOY RUBBLER SERVANT
SPADGER TRAPPER CLERGION
HENCHBOY MUCHACHO
SPALPEEN
(— DRESSED AS WOMAN)
MALINCHE
(— OF FREE BIRTH) CAMILLUS
(ALTAR —) ACOLYTE THURIFER
(AWKWARD —) CUB CALF
GRUMMET
(BOLD —) SPALPEEN
(CHIMNEY SWEEPER'S —) CHUMMY

(CHOIR —) CHILD
(CLEANING —) BUSBOY
(COLLIER'S —) HODDER
(EFFEMINATE —) SISSY
MOLLYCODDLE
(ERRAND —) GALOPIN
(FIRST-YEAR —) GYTE
(HEAD —) SENIOR CAPTAIN
(ILL-MANNERED —) CUB
(MISCHIEVOUS —) NICKUM
(MY —) AVICK
(NATIVE —) MOWGLI
(NON-JEWISH —) SHEGETZ
(OFFICE —) DUFTRY DUFTERY
(PERT —) CRACK
(POOR —) HERO
(ROGUISH —) CRACK GAMIN
URCHIN
(SAUCY —) NACKET
(SERVING —) KNAVE PEDEE
CHOKRA MOUSSE FOOTBOY
GOSSOON
(SILLY —) CALF
(SMALL —) BO BUDDY UMFAAN
SPADGER
(SPRIGHTLY —) CRACK
(STABLE —) MAFU MAFOO
MEHTAR
(TOWN —) CAD
(YOUNG —) LAD SONNY YOUTH
NIPPER
(PL.) BOYHOOD
(PREF.) PAED(O) PAID(O) PED(O)
BOYCOTT MITE SHUN AVOID
DEBAR BLACKBALL
BOYFRIEND BEAU STEADY
BRABANTIO (DAUGHTER OF —)
DESDEMONA
BRACE LEG MAN TIE TWO BEND
BIND CASE FRAP GIRD JACK KNEE
LACE MARK PAIR PROP SPUR
STAY STEM STUD CLAMP CRANK
DWANG GIRTH HOUND NERVE
POISE RIDER SHORE STOCK
STRUT ANKLET BINDER BRACHE
CLENCH COLLAR COUPLE CRUTCH
FASTEN FATHOM HURTER SPLINT
STRING WIMBLE BOTTINE
BRACKET EMBRACE REFRESH
SPANNER STIFFEN SUPPORT
ACCOLADE BITBRACE BITSTALK
BITSTOCK BUTTRESS CROSSBAR
ENCIRCLE
(— A YARD) TRAVERSE
(— ACROSS CABLE) STUD
(— AND HALF) LEASH
(— BETWEEN FRAMES) TOM
(— FOR POST) SPUR
(— UP) ACCINGE SHARPEN
(PART OF —) BOW HEAD JAWS
PAWL RING CHUCK CRANK QUILL
SHELL HANDLE RATCHET
(PL.) BRIDGING
BRACED BENT
(— ABACK) ABOX
BRACELET BAND RING ARMIL
CHAIN ARMLET BANGLE GRIVNA
ARMILLA CIRCLET MANACLE
POIGNET RACETTE WRISTER
BARRULET HANDCUFF MUFFETEE
WRISTLET
(— USED AS MONEY) MANILLA
(SHELL —) SANKHA

BRACER TONIC SHORER BLOCKER
ARMGUARD STIFFENER
STIMULANT
BRACHIAL HUMERAL
BRACHIOPOD ATREMATE
ATRYPOID SPIRIFER
BRACHIUM ARM
BRACHYCEPHALIC
ROUNDHEADED
BRACING CRISP QUICK TONIC
DUNNAGE
BRACKEN FERN TARA BRAKE
PLAID
BRACKET BIBB COCK CONK FORK
GATE PUNK ANCON BELOW
BRACE CLASS CONCH COUCH
CRANE CRANK CROOK LEVEL
SHELF STRUT TRUSS ANCONE
BECKET BRIDGE CORBEL COUPLE
GUSSET HANGER LADDER
MUTULE SADDLE SCONCE
BECKETT CONSOLE DERRICK
FEATHER FIXTURE GATELEG
LOOKOUT POTENCE SPONSON
SPOTTED BRAGWORT CATEGORY
CROTCHET MISERERE SPECKLED
STRADDLE MODILLION
CANTILEVER
(PL.) HOOKS CROOKS
BRACKISH YAR FOIST SALTY
BRACKY SALINE BREACHY
SALTISH NAUSEOUS
BRACT HUSK LEAF GLUME LEMMA
PALEA PALET SCALE SPADIX
SPATHE BRACTLET PHYLLARY
BRACTEOLE PROPHILL
BRAD PIN NAIL PRIG RIVET SPRIG
BRADAMANT (BROTHER OF —)
RINALDO
(HUSBAND OF —) ROGERO
BRAE BANK BRAY BROW HILL
CLEVE SLOPE WOUGH CLEEVE
VALLEY
BRAG GAB JET BLAH BLAW BLOW
CROW DEFY FACE HUFF PUFF
WIND WOST YELP BLUFF BOAST
CRACK FLIRD PREEN SKITE STRUT
VAUNT BLEEZE BOUNCE INSULT
SPLORE SPROSE SQUIRT DISPLAY
GAUSTER ROISTER SWAGGER
BRAGGART FLOURISH PRETENSE
THREATEN
BRAGGART BRAG PUFF BOAST
FACER BLOWER CROWER GASCON
HECTOR POTGUN SKITER THRASO
BLOWOFF BOASTER BOBADIL
BOUNCER CRACKER RUFFLER
SHALLOW VAPORER BANGSTER
BLOWHARD CACAFUGO
FANFARON PAROLLES PUCKFIST
RENOWNER RODOMONT
SKIPJACK
BRAGGARTISM COCKALORUM
BRAGGING ROOSE JACTANCE
RODOMONT THRASONIC
BRAHMA KA SELF BRAMAH
BRAHMAN ARYAN HINDU PUNDIT
SMARTA BRAHMIN
BRAID CUE BRAY GIMP JERK LACE
PLAT TAIL TRIM BREDE FANCY
FREAK JIFFY LACET MILAN ONSET
ORRIS PLAIT PLEAT QUEUE START
TAGAL TRACE TRADE TRESS

TRICK TWINE VOMIT WEAVE
BOBBIN BORDER CORDON EDGING
GALLON LACING MOMENT PLIGHT
RIBBON RICRAC SENNET SNATCH
STRING BANDING BULLION
CAPRICE ENTWINE UPBRAID
BRANDISH ORNAMENT REPROACH
RICKRACK SOUTACHE TRIMMING
(— FOR HATS) SENNET SINNET
(— OF WIG) SNAKE
(LINEN —) INKLE
BRAIDER RATCHER
BRAIDING FROG BREDE
BRAIN MAD BEAN HARN MIND
PATE UTAC WITS AXION HAIRN
HAURN SKULL NODDLE PSYCHE
FURIOUS SENSORY THINKER
CEREBRUM
(PL.) HARN PATE SCONCE
HEADPIECE
(PREF.) CEREBELLI CEREBELLO
CEREBR(I)(O) ENCEPHAL(O)
(SUFF.) ENCEPHALIA
ENCEPHALUS ENCEPHALY
BRAINLESS SILLY STUPID FOOLISH
WITLESS
BRAINPAN PAN HARNPAN
PANNICLE
BRAIN SAND SABULUM
BRAIZE BECKER
BRAKE COW BULL BURR CAGE
CLOG CURB DRAG FERN LOCK
RACK SKID SLOW STAY TARA
TRAP TRIG BLOCK CHECK COPSE
DELAY DETER GRIPE SNARE
SPOKE SPRAG VOMIT BRIDLE
CONVOY HARROW HINDER
REMORA RETARD STAYER
WARABI BRACKEN DEADMAN
DILEMMA SLIPPER STOPPER
THICKET TRIGGER DRAGROPE
RETARDER
BRAKEMAN GUARD SHACK SHAKE
BRAKIE NIPPER DILLIER SNAPPER
SWAMPER DILLYMAN INCLINER
TRAINMAN
BRAKES ANCHORS
BRAMBLE WHIN BRIER RHAMN
THIEF THORN BUMBLE JAGGER
LAWYER STICKER DEWBERRY
MAYBERRY NESSBERRY
(PREF.) BATO
BRAMBLE BUSH TUTU GRANJENO
BRAMBLING KATE SNOWHAMMER
BRAMBLY DUMAL SPINY THORNY
PRICKLY
BRAN GRIT SEED DARAK TREAT
CEREAL CHESIL CHISEL POLLARD
TOPPING BEESWING
(— AND MEAL) SHORTS
(CORNMEAL —) HUSK
(FINE —) POLLEN
(UNSORTED —) RUBBLES
(PREF.) PITYRO
BRANCH ARM BOW COW KOW LAP
LEG LOP RAY RUN BARB BROG
BUSH CHAT FANG FORK LIMB
PALM PART RAME RICE RISE
SNAG SNUG SPUR STEM STUD
TANG TWIG YARD AXITE BAYOU
BOUGH BREAK BRIAR BRIER
CREEK DRUPA GRAIN LAYER
LULOV PLASH PRONG RAMUS

REISE SCROG SHOOT SHRAG SPRAY SPRIG STICK TWIST VIMEN WITHE BUREAU CLADUS DIVIDE DRUKPA EXOPOD GERMEN GREAVE GROWTH LEADER MEMBER OFFSET OUTLET PHYLUM PORTIO RADDLE RAMAGE RAMIFY RUNNER SHROUD SPRANG STOLON STREAM TAPOUN CHAPTER CLADODE DIALECT DIVERGE ENDOPOD FURCATE LATERAL PHYLLIS RAMULUS TENDRIL TORRENT ANAPHYTE BRONCHUS DISTRICT EFFLUENT OFFSHOOT PEASTICK SCAFFOLD SPRANGLE TRAILING PHYLLOCLADE RAMIFICATION
(— OF ANTLER) SPELLER ADVANCER
(— OF COLONY) STIPE
(— OF CRAFT) INDUSTRY
(— OF FAMILY) SEPT
(— OF FEATHER) BARB
(— OF HORN) RIAL ANTLER
(— OF IVY) BUSH
(— OF LEARNING) ART STUDY FACULTY KNOWLEDGE
(— OF MATHEMATICS) ALGEBRA CALCULUS
(— OF THALLUS) STICHID
(— OF TREASURY) FISCUS
(DEAD —) FLAG
(EVERGREEN —S) GREENS
(LANGUAGE —) INDIC
(LOCAL —) COURT
(MINE —) LEADER
(PALM —) LULAB
(RAILWAY —) LYE
(SMALL —) RICE
(YOUNGER —) CADET
(PL.) LOFT RAMI SKIRT SPRAY RAMAGE CYPRESS DEADWOOD
(PREF.) CLON(O) FRONDI RAMI RAMOSO RAMULI
(SUFF.) RAMOSE
BRANCHED FORKY FORKED RAMATE RAMOSE CLADOSE TROCHED RAMIFORM
(SUFF.) CLADOUS
BRANCHES
(SUFF.) (HAVING —) CLEMA
BRANCHIA GILL
BRANCHING ARMY RAMOSE FURCATE DICHOTOMY
BRANCHIOPOD SHRIMP
BRANCHLET RAMULUS SPILLER
BRAND BIRN BLOT BURN CHOP FLAW KIND MARK NOTE SEAR SMIT SMOT SORT VENT WIPE BUIST INURE LABEL SCEAR STAIN STAMP SWORD TAINT TORCH BARREL MARQUE STIGMA FLAMBEAU NAMEPLATE
BRANDIMART (SLAYER OF —) GRADASSO
(WIFE OF —) FLORDELIS
BRANDING IRON BRAND CAUTER SEARER CAUTERY
BRANDISH WAG DART STIR WAVE WIND BLESS BRAID SHAKE SWING WIELD FLAUNT HURTLE QUAVER RUFFLE STRAIN WINNOW

FLUTTER GLITTER SWAGGER VIBRATE WAMPISH FLOURISH VAMBRASH
BRANDY DOP VSO BOOF FINE JACK MARC VSOP BINGO MOBBY NANTS NANTZ PEACH RAKIA VVSOP CINDER COGNAC GRAPPA KIRSCH PUPELO RAKIJA VISNEY ANISADO AQUAVIT QUETSCH ARMAGNAC CALVADOS SLIVOVIC SLIVOVITZ AGUARDIENTE
BRANK MUMPS BRIDLE PILLORY
BRANLE BRAWL
BRANT ROUT ERECT PROUD QUINK SHEER STEEP ROUGHT
BRASH GAY BOLD FACY RASH HASTY NERVY SAUCY STORM ATTACK RUBBLE BRITTLE FORWARD IMPUDENT TACTLESS BALDFACED
BRASQUE STEEP
BRASS CASH ALLOY MONEY NERVE BRAZEN BRONZE MASLIN ORMOLU OFFICER ORICHALC
(— PLAYER) WINDJAMMER
(PREF.) CHALC(O) CHALK(O)
BRASSARD ARMBAND
BRASSEY BIB
BRASSIERE BANDEAU
BRASSY LOUD RUDE BRAZEN COARSE SHRILL IMPUDENT STRIDENT OVERBLOWN
BRAT BIB GET IMP BROT FILM SCUM APRON BAIRN BILSH BROLL CHILD CLOAK GAITT INFANT MANTLE TERROR URCHIN GARMENT BANTLING
BRATTICER AIRMAN CANVASMAN
BRAVADO POMP BRAW PRIDE STORM HECTOR BLUSTER BOMBAST BRAVERY SWAGGER VAUNTERY GASCONISM
BRAVE BOLD BRAW DARE DEFY FACE FINE GAME GOOD PROW TALL WILD ADORN BOAST BRAVO BULLY FELON HARDY JOLLY MANLY MOODY ORPED ROMAN STIFF STOUT VAUNT WIGHT BRAWLY BREAST DARING HEROIC MANFUL PLUCKY SANNUP STURDY BRAVADO DOUGHTY GALLANT HAUTAIN SOLDIER SWAGGER VALIANT VENTURE WARRIOR CAVALIER DEFIANCE EMBOLDEN FEARLESS INTREPID LIONLIKE STALWART SUPERIOR VALOROUS VIRTUOUS
BRAVELY BIG FINELY
BRAVE NEW WORLD (AUTHOR OF —) HUXLEY
(CHARACTER IN —) JOHN MARX MOND CROWNE LENINA WATSON BERNARD MUSTAPHA HELMHOLTZ
BRAVERY GRIT VALOR SPIRIT VIRTUE BRAVADO BRAVURA COURAGE HEROISM JOLLITY MANHEAD MANHOOD PROWESS BOLDNESS CHIVALRY
BRAVO OLE RAH EUGE THUG BRAVE BULLY BANDIT CUTTER BRAVADO SHABASH VILLAIN APPLAUSE ASSASSIN

BRAWL DIN ROW BEEF CLEM DUST FRAY RIOT BLIND BROIL CHIDE CLASH FIGHT FLYTE MELEE REVEL SCOLD SCRAP AFFRAY BICKER FRACAS FRATCH HABBLE REVILE RUFFLE RUMPUS SHINDY STOUSH STRIFE TUMULT UPROAR YATTER BAGARRE BOBBERY BRABBLE BRANGLE DISCORD DISPUTE QUARREL SCUFFLE TUILYIE WRANGLE COMPLAIN RIXATION SQUABBLE STRAMASH
BRAWLER FRATCH NICKER SQUARER FRAMPLER NIGHTCAP OUTCRIER
BRAWLING NOISY BLATANT FLITING SCAMBLING SHEMOZZLE
BRAWN BEEF BOAR LIRE PORK FLESH SINEW FATTEN MUSCLE MANPOWER STRENGTH
(MOCK —) HEADCHEESE
BRAWNY BEEFY FLESHY ROBUST SINEWY SQUARE STRONG STURDY CALLOUS MUSCULAR POWERFUL STALWART
BRAXY BRADSOT
BRAY CRY MIX RUB BEAT ROUT TOOL CRUSH GRIND NOISE POUND STAMP BRUISE HEEHAW OUTCRY PESTLE THRASH WHINNY
BRAYERA KOSO CUSSO KOSSO
BRAZEN BOLD CALM HARD PERT BRASS HARDY HARSH SASSY AENEAN BRASSY BLATANT CALLOUS FORWARD IMMODEST IMPUDENT INSOLENT METALLIC
BRAZENFACED CHEEKY
BRAZIER HEARTH MANGAL BRASERO HIBACHI REREDOS SCALDINO
BRAZIL ROSET

BRAZIL
BAY: MARAJO IGRANDE SEPETIBA GUANABARA
BIRD: MITU MITUA
CAPE: FRIO BLANCO BUZIOS GURUPY ORANGE SAOTOME SAOROQUE
CAPITAL: BRASILIA
COIN: JOE REIS CONTO DOBRA HALFJOE MILREIS CRUZEIRO
DAM: FURNAS ITAIPU PEIXOTO
DANCE: SAMBA MAXIXE
ESTUARY: PARA
FALLS: IGUACU IGUASSU
INDIAN: ANTA ACROA ARARA ARAUA BRAVO CARIB GUANA ARAWAK CARAJA CARAYAN JAVAHAI TARIANA BOTOCUDO CHAMBIOA
ISLAND: MARACA MARAJO BANANAL CARDOSO CAVIANA MEXIANA COMPRIDA
LAKE: AIMA FEIA MIRIM
MEASURE: PE MOIO PIPA SACK VARA BRACA FANGA LEGOA MILHA PALMO PASSO TONEL CANADA COVADO CUARTA LEAGUE QUARTO TAREFA ALQUIER GARRAFA ALQUEIRE
MOUNTAIN: URUCUM BANDEIRA ITATIAIA

MOUNTAINS: MAR GERAL ORGAN PIAUI ACARAI GURUPI ORGAOS PARIMA AMAMBAI CARAJAS GRADAUS RONCADOR TOMBADOR
NATIVE: CABOCLO CURIBOCA MAMELUCO PAULISTA
PORT: RIO PARA BAHIA BELEM NATAL SANTOS PELOTAS SALVADOR
PRESIDENT: BRAS DUTRA FILHO VARGAS
RIVER: APA ICA DOCE GEIO IVAI JARI PARA PARU SONO TEFE ABUNA ANAUA APORE CAPIM CLARO CORUA ICANA IRIRI ITAPI JURUA JUTAI MANSO NEGRO PARDO PIAUI PRETO TIETE TURVO URUBU VERDE XINGU AJUANA AMAZON ARINOS BALSAS BRANCO CANUMA CONTAS CUIABA DEMINI GRAJAU GRANDE GURUPI IBICUI IGUACU JAPURA JAVARI MEARIM MORTES MUCURI PARANA PURPUS RONURO SANGUE TACUTU TIBAGI UATUMA UAUPES VELHAS CORUMBA IGUASSU MADEIRA PARAIBA SUCURIU TAPAJOS TAQUARI TEODORO URUGUAI ARAGUAIA PADAUIRI PARACATU PARAGUAI PARNAIBA SOLIMOES TARAUACA
STATE: ACRE PARA AMAPA BAHIA CEARA GOIAS GOYAZ PIAUI PARANA PIAUHY ALAGOAS GUAPORE PARAIBA RORAIMA SERGIPE AMAZONAS MARANHAO PARAHIBA PARAHYBA RONDONIA SAOPAULO
TOWN: ACU EXU ICO IPU ITU JAU LUZ RIO UBA BAGE FARO IBIA IJUI ITAI LAPA LINS PARA PIUI TUPA UNAI BAHIA BAIAO BAURU BELEM CEARA NATAL NEVES CAMPOS CUIABA ILHEUS MACEIO MANAOS MANAUS OLINDA RECIFE SANTOS ARACAJU CARUARU CITORIA GOIANIA ITABUNA JUNDIAI NITEROI PELOTAS TAUBATE UBERABA ANAPOLIS BRASILIA CAMPINAS CURITIBA LONDRINA SALVADOR SOROCABA TERESINA
TREE: APA ICICA UCUUBA ARARIBA WALLABA
WATERFALL: GLASS IGUAZU
WEIGHT: BAG ONCA LIBRA ARROBA OITAVA ARRATEL QUILATE QUINTAL TONELADA

BRAZIL NUT JUVIA CASTANA
BRAZILWOOD SAPPAN VERZINO HYPERNIC PEACHWOOD SAPPANWOOD
BREACH GAP CHAP FLAW GOOL RENT RIFT SLAP BRACK BRECK BURST CHASM CLEFT CRACK PAUSE SPLIT WOUND BRUISE

HARBOR HERNIA HIATUS INROAD
SCHISM SCREED SLUICE ASSAULT
BLEMISH DISPUTE FISSURE
OPENING QUARREL RUPTURE
BREAKING CREVASSE FRACTION
FRACTURE INTERVAL OUTBREAK
SOLUTION TRESPASS
(— IN DIKE) GOOL
(— IN SEAWAY)
(— OF CONTINUITY) SALTUS
(— OF DUTY) BARRATRY
(— OF ETIQUETTE) SOLECISM
(— OF FAITH) TREASON
(— OF GRAMMAR) SOLECISM
(— OF MORALITY) SCAPE VAGARY
(— OF PEACE) AFFRAY FRACTION
(— OF UNITY) SCHISM
BREAD BAP BUN PAN BODY BRAD
DIET FARE FOOD LOAF PAIN
PONE RIMA ROLL RUSH RUSK
TOKE AZYME BATCH BATON
BOXTY CAPER CHEAT KISRA
LIMPA MICHE ROOTY TOMMY
CHAPON COCKET DAMPER
DODGER ENZYME HALLAH KANKIE
MASLIN MATZOS PANNAM
SIMNEL TAMMIE WASTEL
YANNAM ALIMENT BANNOCK
EULOGIA MANCHET POPOVER
STOLLEN TOASTER CORNCAKE
HARDTACK SOFTTACK TORTILLA
ZWIEBACK PUMPERNICKEL
(— AND MILK) POBS PANADA
POBBIES
(— BOX) PANETIERE
(— QUALITY) PANETTY
(BATCH OF —) CAST
(BUTTERED —) CAPER
(DRY —) TOKE
(EUCHARISTIC —) BODY HOST
AZYME
(FANCY —) BRAID
(MAIZE —) PIKI
(OATMEAL —) ANACK JANNOCK
(POTATO —) FADGE
(QUICK —) SCONE
(S. AFRICAN —) DIKA
(SLICE OF —) TARTINE TRENCHER
(SMALL LOAF OF —) COB
(SMALL PIECE OF —) SIPPET
MEALOCK
(SOPPED —) MISER BREWIS
BROWIS
(SWEET —) BUN BROWNIE
STOLLEN
(TOASTED —) SIPPET
(UNLEAVENED —) AZYM AZYME
BANNOCK CHAPATTI
(WHEAT —) CHEAT HOVIS COCKET
MANCHET
(PREF.) ARTO PANI
BREADBOARD PANEL
BREADED ANGLAISE
BREADFRUIT MASI RIMA RIMAS
DUGDUG NANGCA CAMANSI
CASTANA ANTIPOLO BREADNUT
CHESTNUT
BREADNUT RAM
BREADROOT PSORALEA
BREADTH BEAM
BREADWINNING GAP BOON BUST
DASH HINT KNAP PICK PLOW
REND RENT RIFT RIVE

BREAK GO CUT JAR LOP TEN ABRA
BUST CHIP DRAG FALL FLAW
KNAP PART RUIN RUSH SLIP
SNAP STEP STOP TEAR TURN
UNDO WASH WORK ALTER BLANK
BRACK BURST CHECK CHINK
CLEFT COMMA CRACK CRAZE
DAUNT FALSE FRACT FRUSH
LAPSE PAUSE PLUCK ROUGH
SEVER SMASH SOLVE SPAWN
SPELT STAVE SWING WOUND
BRUISE CABBLE CHANGE CLEAVE
CRANNY CUTOUT DEFEAT HIATUS
IMPAIR LACUNA PIERCE SALTUS
SHREND SPRING TEWTAW
TEWTER BLUNDER CAESURA
CRACKLE CRANKLE CREVICE
CRUMBLE DESTROY DISABLE
DISPART DISRUPT EXHAUST
FISSURE GRITTLE INFRACT
INTERIM OPENING RESPITE
RUPTURE SHATTER TAILING
VARIATE BREATHER CREVASSE
DIERESIS DIFFRACT FRACTION
FRACTURE FRAGMENT INFRINGE
INTERVAL SEPARATE SOLUTION
STRAMASH
(— APART) SUNDER DISRUPT
SHATTER
(— AWAY) BOLT ESCAPE
(— BOULDERS) BULLDOZE
(— DOWN) CONK FAIL GIVE CRAZE
CROCK PLASH TRAIK BRUISE
TUMBLE ANALYZE FOUNDER
REFRACT COLLAPSE INFRINGE
(— FORCE) BAFFLE
(— FORTH) BOIL ERUPT EVENT
FLASH EXPLODE
(— FROM ICE MASS) CALVE
(— GLASS) SHREND DRAGADE
(— IN) ENTER
(— IN PIECES) CHAP DICE KNAP
CRASH CRAZE SMASH SMOKE
SHIVER CRUMBLE FRITTER
SMATTER DEMOLISH DIFFRACT
DISJOINT SPLINTER STRAMASH
(— IN WAVES) JABBLE
(— IN YARN) SMASH
(— INTO) BROACH IRRUPT
(— INTO FOAM) COMB
(— INWARD) STAVE
(— LANCE) TAINT
(— OF CONTINUITY) SALTUS
(— OFF) NUB DROP SNAP CEASE
LEAVE ABRUPT DIREMPT
PRETERMIT
(— OFF END) SNUB
(— OPEN) BUST CHOP FORCE
(— ORE) COB SPALL SPAWL
(— OUT) ERUPT START ASSURD
STRIKE
(— RANKS) DISMISS
(— SHARPLY) KNACK
(— SILENCE) QUATCH QUETCH
(— SKIN) GALL
(— SLATE) SCULP
(— STONE) CAVIL KEVEL
(— THE BACK) CHINE
(— THROUGH) BEAT FORCE
BREACH
(— THROUGH SHELL) PIP
(— UP) BUCK FALL MELT FLOUR

SEVER SPALE SPLIT STASH INCIDE
DEGRADE DISTURB REFRACT
DISSECT DISTURB REFRACT
SCARIFY SCATTER CROSSCUT
DISJOINT DISPERSE DISSOLVE
DISUNIFY FRAGMENT
(— UP EARTH) HACK FALLOW
(— UP SIEGE) LEVY
(— WATER) FIN
(— WINDOWS) NICK
(STEM —) BROWNING
(SUFF.) CLASE CLASIA CLAST(IC)
BREAKABLE BRITTLE BRUCKLE
FRIABLE DELICATE FRANGIBLE
BREAKAGE GRIEF
BREAKAX IRONWOOD
BREAKDOWN JUBA EDGER
BURNOUT DEBACLE HOEDOWN
COLLAPSE DILUTION
(— OF RIND) ADUSTIOSIS
(ELECTRIC —) AVALANCHE
BREAKER JUMP SURF WAVE
BARECA BEAKER BILLOW COMBER
ROLLER CRACKER SLEDGER
LEDGEMAN SCRAPPER
(— OF WORD) WARLOCK
(CIRCUIT —) CUTOUT
(ROCK —) ALLIGATOR
(PL.) BREACH
(SUFF.) CLASTIC
BREAKFAST BRUNCH DEJEUNE
DISJUNE DEJEUNER DISJEUNE
BREAKING BREACH BREAKUP
FRACTION FRACTURE SOLUTION
(— FORTH) ERUPTIVE
(— OFF) CHIPPING ABRUPTION
(— UP) DEBACLE ANALYSIS
(SUFF.) CLASE CLASIA CLAST(IC)
(— INTO SMALL PIECES) THRIPSIS
BREAKSTONE SAXIFRAGE
BREAKWATER COB DAM COBB
CROY DIKE MOLE PIER PILE QUAY
JETTY GROYNE REFUGE
BULWARK STOCKADE
BREAM TAI BRIM CARP CHAD
SCUP SHAD ZOPE BROOM ROMAN
BALEEN BARWIN BRAISE SARGUS
OLDWIFE SUNFISH WAREHOU
CYPRINID FLATFISH TARWHINE
STEENTJIE
BREAST DUG BUMP CROP FACE
BOOBY BOSOM BRAVE BUBBY
CHEST HEART MAMMA PETTO
STALL PECTUS POMMEL THORAX
BRISKET COUNTER KNOCKER
FOREBOWS
(— OF HORSE) COUNTER
(PHOTOGRAPH OF —S)
MAMMOGRAM
(PL.) BUST
(PREF.) MAMM(I)(ILLI) MAST(O)
MAZ(O) PECTORI STERN(O)
STETH(O)
BREASTBAND HORSE
BREASTBONE BREAST STERNUM
XIPHOID
BREASTHOOK CRUTCH FOREHOOK
BREASTPIECE RABAT RABBI
BREASTPLATE EGIS URIM AEGIS
BREAST BYRNIE GORGET LORICA
ORACLE SHIELD THORAX CUIRASS
PALETTE POITREL PECTORAL
PLASTRON RATIONAL

BREASTS
(SUFF.) MASTIA
BREASTWORK FORT REDAN
SANGAR SCHANZ SCHERM
SCONCE SUNGAR BRATTLE
PARAPET PLUTEUS RAMPART
BARBETTE BRATTICE
BREATH AIR ANDE GASP HUFF
LIFE ONDE PANT PECH PUFF SIGH
WAFT WIND BLAST PAUSE SCENT
SMELL VAPOR WHIFF WHIFT
BREEZE FLATUS PNEUMA
HALITUS INSTANT RESPITE
SUSPIRE SPIRACLE
(— OF WIND) SPIRIT
(BAD —) OZOSTOMIA
(DIVINE —) NEPHESH
(LIFE —) PRANA SPIRIT
(STINKING —) FUMOSITY
(PREF.) PNEO PNEUM(A)(O)
PNEUMATO PNEUMON(O)
RESPIRO SPIRACULI SPIRO
(SUFF.) PNEA PNEUSTA PNOEA
BREATHE ANDE LIVE ONDE PANT
PECH PUFF SIGH VENT EXIST
EXUDE SPEAK SPIRE UTTER
ASPIRE EXHALE INHALE WHEEZE
AFFLATE EMANATE RESPIRE
SUSPIRE
(— HEAVILY) FOB PECH FNESE
SOUGH THROTTLE
(— LABORIOUSLY) GASP
(— NOISILY) SOUGH SNOTTER
(— UPON) FAN
BREATHER PAUSE
BREATHING AIR ALIVE PNEUMA
SPIRIT GASPING AFFLATUS
SPIRITUS SPIRATION
(— HEAVILY) SUSPIRIOUS
(LABORED —) ASTHMA
(ROUGH —) ASPER
(SMOOTH —) LENE LENIS
BREATHLESSNESS TIFT
BREATHY HOLLOW ADENOID
BRECCIA BROCKRAM
BRED (WELL —) FREE
BREECH BORE BUTT DOUP BLOCK
BRICK CULOTTE DRODDUM
BUTTOCKS CYLINDER DERRIERE
BREECHBLOCK BLOCK VENTPIECE
BREECHCLOTH HIPPEN HIPPING
BREECHES HOSE CHAPS JEANS
LEVIS SLOPS STOCK TREWS
BRACAE BRAGAS BREEKS GASKIN
SMALLS TIGHTS TROUSE
BOMBARDS BREEKUMS
JODHPURS KICKSIES KNICKERS
LEATHERS TROUSERS
PANTALOON SMALLCLOTHES
BREED GET ILK BEAR KIND RACE
REAR SORT BEGET BROOD CASTE
CAUSE CLASS FANCY HATCH
ISSUE RAISE STOCK STORE TRAIN
CREATE GENDER STRAIN
EDUCATE NOURISH PRODUCE
PROGENY SPECIES VARIETY
ENGENDER GENERATE INSTRUCT
MULTIPLY PULLULATE
(DWARF —) TOY
BREEDER RANCHER AURELIAN
HERDSMAN HORSEMAN
(FISH —) MILTER
BREEDING ORIGIN DESCENT

NURTURE TUPPING BEHAVIOR
CIVILITY PREGNANT TRAINING
(GOOD —) GENTRY
BREEZE AIR AURA BLOW FLAW
GALE GUST PIRR STIR WIND
BLAST RUMOR SLANT WALTZ
BREATH DOCTOR REPORT SLATCH
SPIRIT ZEPHYR FRESHEN
MUZZLER QUARREL VIRASON
WHISPER
(COOL —) DOCTOR
(GENTLE —) AIR AURA ZEPHYR
(LAND —) TERRAL
(STIFF —) STOUR TIFTER
BREEZE FLY WHAME
BREEZY AIRY BRISK FRESH WINDY
AIRISH
BRETHREN IKHWAN
BRETON ARMORICAN
BREVE NOTE WRIT BRIEF MINIM
ORDER SHORT PRECEPT
BREVIARY ORDO CURSUS DIGEST
LEDGER PORTAS COUCHER
EPITOME SUMMARY ABSTRACT
PORTESSE PORTHORS
BREVITY SYNTOMY LACONISM
UNLENGTH BRIEFNESS
SHORTNESS TERSENESS
BRACHYLOGY
BREW ALE MIX BEER BOIL MAKE
PLOT POUR DRINK HATCH STOUT
BROWST DEVISE DILUTE FOMENT
GATHER LIQUOR SEETHE
CONCOCT INCLINE PREPARE
CONTRIVE
(HOME —) SAMOGON
BREWER TUNNER
BREWERY BRASSERIE
BREWING GAIL GYLE BROWST
BUMMOCK
BRIBE BUD BUY FEE FIX OIL ROB
SOP TIP BAIT DASH GIFT HAVE
HIRE MEED MOIL PALM VAIL
WAGE BONUS CUDDY GRAFT
OFFER STEAL SUGAR TEMPT
TOUCH EXTORT GREASE HAMPER
NOBBLE PAYOLA SQUARE
SUBORN CORRUPT DOUCEUR
SWEETEN TICKLER GRATUITY
VENALIZE
(— TO POLICEMAN) NUT
BRIBERY MEED
BRIC-A-BRAC CURIO VERTU VIRTU
BIBELOT TROCKERY TRUMPERY
BRICK BAT BUR BURR GLUT MARL
PAVE TILE BLOCK GAULT QUARL
SLOPE SPLIT STOCK STONE
TOOTH CUTTER FELLOW HEADER
PAMENT PAVIOR BACKING
CLINKER FLETTON GRIZZLE
PERPEND SOLDIER BURNOVER
(— WALL) NECK
(CRACKED —) CHUFF SHUFF
(FINAL HALF —) JACK
(IMPERFECT —) SHIPPER
BURNOVER
(PILE OF —S) HACK CLAMP
(PULVERIZED —) SOORKY SOORKEE
(SECOND QUALITY —S) BRINDLES
(SECOND-RATE —) GRIZZLE
(SOFT —) CUTTER RUBBER
PICKING
(SQUARE —) QUADREL

(STACK OF —) LIFT
(SUN-DRIED —) BAT ADOBE
(UNBURNT —) ADOBE
(WOODEN —) DOOK
(PL.) CLAYWARE
(PREF.) PLINTHI
BRICKLAYER BRICKY MASONER
BRICKMAKER MOLDER
BRICKWORK HOB BRICKING
BRIDAL NUPTIAL BRIDALTY
BRIDE KALLAH SPOUSE SHULAMITE
BRIDE OF LAMMERMOOR
(AUTHOR OF —) SCOTT
(CHARACTER IN —) LUCY CALEB
EDGAR FRANK ASHTON HAYSTON
WILLIAM RAVENSWOOD
BALDERSTONE
BRIDE-PRICE LOBOLD LOBOLO
BRIDESHEAD REVISITED (AUTHOR
OF —) WAUGH
(CHARACTER IN —) BOY REX CARA
KURT BERYL CELIA JULIA RYDER
BRIDEY ANTHONY BLANCHE
CHARLES MOTTRAM CORDELIA
MUSPRATT SAMGRASS
MARCHMAIN MULCASTER
SEBASTIAN BRIDESHEAD
BRIDESMAID PARANYMPH
BRIDEWELL MILLDOLL
BRIDGE WAY BRIG LINK NOSE
PONS PONT REST SPAN WIEN
CROSS SIRAT TOWIE GANTRY
ISLAND JIGGER RUNWAY SANGAR
AUCTION BASCULE BIFROST
CONNECT CULVERT EXOSTRA
PASSAGE PASSING PINNOCK
PONCEAU PONTOON PROPONS
TRAJECT TRESTLE VIADUCT
CONTRACT TRAVERSE DUPLICATE
(— OF MUSICAL INSTRUMENT)
MAGAS CHEVALET CHEVILLE
(— TO PARADISE) ALSIRAT
(ARCADED —) RIALTO
(CONTRACT —) CHICAGO GHOULIE
PLAFOND
(FLUE —) ALTAR
(GATEWAY —) GOUT
(HOSE —) JUMPER
(IMPEDANCE —) DIPLEXER
(NATURAL —) ARCH
(PLANK —) LIGGER
(ROPE SUSPENSION —) JOOLA
(RUDE —) CLAPPER
(PREF.) GEPHYR(O) PONTI PONTO
BRIDGEMAKER PONTIFEX
BRIDGEMAN EBBMAN
BRIDGE OF SAN LUIS REY
(AUTHOR OF —) WILDER
(CHARACTER IN —) PIO JAIME
PILAR MANUEL PEPITA ESTEBAN
JUNIPER PERICHOLE
MONTEMAYOR
BRIDGING ASTRIDE STRUTTING
BRIDLE BIT CURB REIN RULE
BRAKE BRANK BRIDE CHECK
GUARD GUIDE STRUT DIRECT
GOVERN HALTER MASTER SIMPER
SUBDUE BLINDER CONTROL
LORMERY REPRESS SNAFFLE
SWAGGER CAVESSON RESTRAIN
SUPPRESS
BRIDLE PATH SPURWAY
BRIEF FEW CURT LIST RIFE WRIT

BLURB BREVE CHARM PITHY
QUICK SHORT TERSE ABRUPT
COMMON CURTAL FLYING
HOURLY LETTER LITTLE SNIPPY
SUDDEN ABRIDGE CAPSULE
COMPACT COMPOSE CONCISE
CRYPTIC INVOICE LACONIC
MANDATE OUTLINE PRECEPT
SUMMARY BREVIATE CONDENSE
FLEETING FLITTING SNATCHED
SNIPPETY SUCCINCT SYLLABUS
(PREF.) BREVI
BRIEF CASE FOLIO TASHIE
BRIEFLY BRIEF ENFIN SHORTLY
BRIER BARB PIPE BRIAR THORN
SMILAX BRUYERE PRICKER
INKBERRY
BRIER TREE PIPER
BRIG RIG JAIL PRISON GEORDIE
BRIGADE TERZO CAMPOO
BRIGAND THIEF USKOK BANDIT
KLEPHT LATRON PIRATE ROBBER
CATERAN KETTRIN LADRONE
ROUTIER SOLDIER PICAROON
(PL.) TCHETNITSI
BRIGANDINE PLACCATE
BRIGHT APT GAY NET FINE GILD
GLAD GLEG HIGH LIVE ROSY
ACUTE AGLOW ALERT ANIME
BEAMY BRAVE CLEAR CRISP
EAGLE FLARY FRESH GEMMY
JOLLY LIGHT LUCID NITID PRINT
QUICK RIANT SHARP SHEEN
SHEER SHINY SMART SMOLT
STEEP SUNNY TINNY VIVID WHITE
WITTY BERTHA CHEERY CLEVER
FLASHY FLORID GARISH LIMPID
LIVELY LUCENT ORIENT SERENE
SHRILL SILVER BEAMISH
DIAMOND DILUCID FORWARD
FULGENT LAMBENT RADIANT
RINGING SHINING ANIMATED
CHEERFUL FLASHING GLEAMING
LIGHTFUL LUMINOUS LUSTROUS
SPLENDID SPLENDOR STARLIKE
SUNSHINY
(BLINDINGLY —) GLARING
(NOT —) SOFT
(OFFENSIVELY —) GARISH
(SOFTLY —) LAMBENT
(PREF.) AETHIO AGLAO LAMPR(O)
BRIGHTEN GILD LAMP BLOOM
CHEER CLEAR FLAME GLOZE
LIGHT LIVEN SHINE SNUFF
CANTLE ENGILD POLISH ANIMATE
BURNISH EMBRAVE ENLIVEN
FURBISH LIGHTEN REFRESH
SMARTEN ILLUMINE
BRIGHTENER FLUOROL
BRIGHTLY GAY CLEAR LIGHT
SHEEN BRIGHT FRESHLY SHEENLY
BRIGHTNESS SUN BLAZE BLOOM
ECLAT FLAME GLARE GLEAM
GLINT GLORY GLOSS LIGHT NITOR
SHEEN SHINE ACUMEN BRIGHT
CANDOR FULGOR LUSTER
CLARITY GLISTEN GLITTER
LAMBERT NITENCY SPARKLE
RADIANCE SPLENDOR BRILLIANCE
(— OF TOBACCO) FLASH
(— UNIT) STILB
(UNIT OF —) NIT
(PREF.) GANO

BRIGUE BLAT
BRILLIANCE FAME BLARE BLAZE
ECLAT FLAME GLARE GLORY
SHINE VALUE KEENNESS
RADIANCE SPLENDOR VIVACITY
REFULGENCE
BRILLIANCY FIRE BLARE ECLAT
GLORY REFLET CLARITY GLITTER
ORIENCY RADIANCE SPLENDOR
BRILLIANT GAY GOOD KEEN SAGE
WISE BREME QUICK VIVID BRIGHT
CLEVER GIFTED LIVELY PURPLE
SIGNAL BRAVURA BRITTLE
EMINENT FLAMING GLARING
LAMBENT LAMPING LOZENGE
PRISMAL RADIANT SHINING
BLINDING DAZZLING DIZZYING
GLORIOUS INSPIRED LUCULENT
LUMINOUS SLASHING SPLENDID
PRISMATIC
(TRANSIENTLY —) METEORIC
BRIM LIP RIM RUT SEA EDGE TURF
BLUFF BRINK MARGE OCEAN
VERGE WATER BORDER MARGIN
TURNUP COPULATE STRUMPET
(— OF HAT) FLAP LEAF POKE
BRINK TARFE SLOUCH
BRIMFUL TIPFUL TOPFUL
CROWNED
BRIMMING BIG FULL ABRIM
BRIMSTONE SULFUR VIRAGO
SULPHUR BRINSTON SPITFIRE
(PREF.) THI(O)
BRIMSTONY LURID
BRINDLED TABBY TAWNY
BRANDED FLECKED STREAKED
BRINE SEA MAIN SALT BRACK
LEACH OCEAN TEARS PICKLE
MARINADE
BRINER COBBERER
BRING DO LAY TEE WIN BEAR
BUCK CALL FIRK LEAD STOP TAKE
TEEM CARRY DRIVE ENDUE
FETCH INCUR APPORT ARRIVE
CONVEY DEDUCE CONDUCE
CONDUCT EXHIBIT PROCURE
PRODUCE
(— ABOUT) DO SEE BREW MAKE
STAY TEEM CAUSE DIGHT FRAME
INFER MOYEN SHAPE SWING
CREATE EFFECT INVOKE SECURE
SPIRIT COMPASS CONDUCE
INSPIRE OPERATE PROCURE
PRODUCE CATALYZE OCCASION
TRANSACT PERPETRATE
(— ABOUT CAPTURE) ACCOUNT
(— BACK) REFER EFFECT RECALL
REDUCE REDUCT RELATE RETURN
REVIVE REVOKE PRODUCE
RESTORE OCCASION RETRIEVE
TRANSACT
(— BEFORE) HAUL
(— CHARGE) APPEACH
(— DOWN) LAY DROP FALL FELL
STOP ABATE COUCH EMBASE
SOFTEN DECLINE DESCEND
DISMOUNT OVERTHROW
(— DOWN STEER) HOOLIHAN
(— FORTH) CAST FOAL GIVE MAKE
TEEM EDUCE HATCH ISSUE
SPAWN THROW PROFER DELIVER
TRADUCE ENGENDER PROCREATE
(— FORTH YOUNG) EAN KID YEAN

(— **FORWARD**) CITE LEAD INFER ADDUCE ALLEGE ADJUST ADVANCE PROPOSE
(— **IN**) EARN INFER USHER IMPORT INDUCE INVECT REPORT RETURN ADHIBIT
(— **INTO BATTLE**) COMMIT
(— **INTO COURT**) SIST
(— **INTO DISGRACE**) FOUL
(— **LOW**) AVALE DEGRADE SUPPLANT
(— **ON**) INFER INDUCE
(— **ONESELF**) GET
(— **OUT**) DRAW ACCENT ELICIT DISINTER HEIGHTEN
(— **OVER**) CONVERT
(— **SHIP INTO POSITION**) EASE
(— **TO A HALT**) STICK
(— **TO AN END**) DO END FIT DOCK DRAW REDD CEASE FORDO DECIDE EXPIRE FINISH FOREDO FULFIL DISJOIN INCLUDE COMPLETE CONCLUDE DISSOLVE SURCEASE
(— **TO BAY**) CORNER
(— **TO BEAR**) EXERT
(— **TO HEEL**) FACE
(— **TO LIFE**) EVOKE ANIMATE
(— **TO LIGHT**) GRUB REAP DREDGE ELICIT EXPOSE REVEAL UNEARTH DISCLOSE DISCOVER
(— **TO NAUGHT**) DASH FOIL UNDO NEGATE CONFUTE DESTROY
(— **TO PERFECTION**) RIPEN
(— **TO STOP**) CURB HALT ARREST
(— **TO THE GROUND**) GRASS
(— **TOGETHER**) JOIN AMASS RAISE UNITE ADDUCT CONFER CORRAL ENGAGE ENLINK GATHER SUMMON COLLATE COLLECT COMPILE COMPORT ASSEMBLE CONFLATE ENSEMBLE
(— **UP**) REAR BREED NURSE RAISE TRAIN NURSLE NUZZLE UPREAR EDUCATE NOURISH
(SUFF.) FER(ENCE)(ENT)(OUS)
(— **ABOUT**) FIC(AL)(ATE)(ATION) (ATIVE)(ATOR)(ATORY)(E)(ENCE) (ENT)(IAL)(IARY)(IENT) FIQUE
BRINGING-UP BREEDING EDUCATION
BRINJAL EGGPLANT
BRINK END EVE LIP RIM SEA BANK BRIM EDGE FOSS MARGE SHORE VERGE BORDER MARGIN MARGENT PRECIPICE
BRINY BRACK SALTY SALINE BRACKISH MURIATED
BRIOCHE ROLL STICH SAVARIN
BRISE-SOLEIL BLIND SUNBREAK SUNSHADE
BRISK GAY BRAG BUSY CANT FAST KEEN PERK PERT RACY RASH SPRY TRIG VIVE YARE YERN AGILE ALERT ALIVE BUDGE BUXOM CANTY COBBY CRANK CRISP FRESH FRISK KEDGE NIPPY PEART PEPPY PERKY QUICK ROUND ZIPPY ACTIVE BREEZY COCKET CROUSE DAPPER FLICKY LIVELY NIMBLE SNAPPY SPRACK SPRUNT TROTTY VIVACE ALLEGRO CHIPPER HUMMING ROUSING

ANIMATED BRUSHING FRISKFUL GALLIARD RATTLING SMACKING SPANKING SPIRITED
BRISKLY YERN SHARP YERNE BUSILY CROUSE ALLEGRO ROUNDLY
BRISKNESS ALACRITY VIRITOOT
BRISTLE AWN JAG RIB BARB HAIR JAGG SETA TELA BIRSE BRUSH PARCH PREEN STARE STRUT STYLE TOAST CHAETA PALPUS RUFFLE SETULA STIVER STRIGA STYLET GLOCHIS SMELLER STUBBLE WHISKER ACICULUM FRENULUM SPICULUM VIBRISSA VIBRACULUM
(PREF.) CHAET(I)(O) CHETO HIRSUTO HORRI SETI SETULI
(SUFF.) CHAETA CHAETES CHAETUS
BRISTLED HERISSE HORRENT
BRISTLE-SHAPED STYLOID
BRISTLING ROUGH HISPID HORRID SETOSE THORNY HORRENT SCRUBBY SPINOUS
BRISTLY BIRSY PENNY SETOSE STUBBY SCRUBBY STICKLE
BRITAIN (PREF.) BRITO
BRITISH ENGLISH BRITANNIC WHITEHALL
BRITISH COLUMBIA (CAPITAL OF —) VICTORIA
(**MOUNTAINS OF —**) COAST CARIBOO CASCADE PURCELL SELKIRK MUNASHEE
(**RIVER OF —**) NASS LIARD PEACE FRASER SKEENA STIKINE
(**TOWN OF —**) KELOWNA KAMLOOPS VANCOUVER
BRITISH HONDURAS (**BAY OF —**) CHETUMAL
(**CAPITAL OF —**) BELMOPAN
(**FORMER CAPITAL OF —**) BELIZE
(**MOUNTAIN RANGE OF —**) MAYA
(**TOWN OF —**) CAYO STANN COROZAL
BRITOMARTIS (**FATHER OF —**) ZEUS JUPITER
(**MOTHER OF —**) CARME
BRITON CELT SCOT BRYTHON
BRITTANY ARMORICA
(**NATIVE OF —**) BRETON
BRITTLE DRY FROW WEAK BRASH CANDY CRIMP CRISP CRUMP EAGER FRAIL FROWY FRUSH SHORT SPALT CRISPY CRUMPY FEEBLE FROUGH GINGER IMFIRM SLIGHT BRICKLE BRUCKLE CRACKLY FRAGILE FRIABLE REDSEAR SHIVERY SMOPPLE BRITCHEL DELICATE SNAPPISH
BRITTLEBUSH ENCELIA
BRITTLE STAR OPHIUROID
BROACH AIR AWL CUT PIN ROD TAP OPEN OUCH SHED SPIT SPUR STAB TAME VEER VENT BEGIN DRESS DRIFT PRICK RIMER SPOOL START VOICE ATTAME BORING BROOCH DRIVER FIBULA LAUNCH PIERCE REAMER RHYMER STRIKE ENLARGE EXPRESS PUBLISH SPINDLE SQUARER VIOLATE

WIDENER APPROACH DEFLOWER DRIFTPIN INCISION PORPOISE
BROAD DEEP FREE VAST WIDE AMPLE BEAMY BRAID DORIC GROSS LARGE LARGO PLAIN ROOMY SPLAY SQUAB STOUT THICK WOMAN COARSE GLOBAL BELCHER EVIDENT GENERAL GRIVOIS LIBERAL OBVIOUS PLATOID BARNYARD SPACIOUS TOLERANT
(— **AND FLAT**) PLATOID
(**NOT —**) STRAIT
(PREF.) EURY LATI PLAT(Y)
BROADBILL GAYA RAYA GAPER SCAUP BOATBILL SHOVELER SWORDFISH
BROADCAST AIR SOW SEED SEND CARRY RADIO STREW AIRING SPREAD DECLARE DIFFUSE PUBLISH SCATTER ANNOUNCE TELEVISE TRANSMIT
BROADCLOTH CASTOR SUCLAT TAUNTON
BROADEN BREDE WIDEN DILATE EXPAND EXTEND SPREAD ENNOBLE
BROADHORN ARK
BROADNESS BIGNESS LIBERALITY
BROADSIDE TIRE BROAD GARLAND
BROADSWORD BILL KRIS GLAIVE HANGER SPATHA CUTLASS FERRARA CLAYMORE MONTANTO SCIMITAR
BROBDINGNAGIAN HUGE
BROCADE ACCA BROCHE KINCOB KINKHAB NISHIKI BAUDEKIN DAMASSIN
BROCADED BROCHE
BROCCOLI ASPARAGUS
BROCCOLI BROWN GOAT LOAM PLOVER RABBIT
BROCHURE TRACT BOOKLET PAMPHLET TREATISE
BROCKET PITA STAG BROCK SPITTER
BRODIAEA GRASSNUT
BROGAN STOGA STOGY BROGUE STOGIE
BROGUE STOGY STOGIE
BROIL ROW BURN CHAR FEUD FRAY GRID HEAT TOIL ALARM BRAWL GRILL MELEE SCRAP SWELT AFFRAY BIRSLE BRAISE GRILLY SPLORE SQUEAL TUMULT BRANDER BRULYIE CARBONE CONTEST DISCORD DISPUTE EMBROIL FRIZZLE GARBOIL QUARREL SIMULTY BARBECUE BLOODWIT CONFLICT GRILLADE STRAMASH
BROILER GRILL SEARER CHICKEN POUSSIN
BROKE HOG LOW BUST STONY STONEY CHICANE UPTIGHT BANKRUPT
BROKEN DOWN DUFF RENT RUDE TORN BLOWN BROKE BURST FRACT GAPPY HAIRY KAPUT ROMPU ROUGH TAMED BRASHY HACKLY RUINED SHAKEN CRACKED CRUSHED FRACTED

REDUCED SUBDUED VICIOUS WHIPPED BANKRUPT CONTRITE OUTLAWED RUPTURED TATTERED WEAKENED
(— **BUT NOT TRAINED**) GREEN
(— **IN**) STOVEN
(— **IN HEALTH**) CRAZY
(— **OFF**) ABRUPT
(**EASILY —**) GINGER
(PREF.) FRACTO
BROKEN-DOWN HAYWIRE DISJASKED DISJASKIT
BROKER AGENT CRIMP BANIAN BANYAN CORSER DEALER FACTOR JOBBER BROGGER CHANGER COURSER MONEYER PEDDLER REALTOR SCALPER HUCKSTER INSTITOR MERCHANT
BROKERAGE AGIOTAGE
BROMATIUM KOHLRABI
BROME CHEAT
BROMEGRASS CHESS
BROMIA (**HUSBAND OF —**) SOSIA
BROMO ACID EOSIN EOSINE
BROMUS DRAWK
BRONCHITIS HUSK HOOSE HOOZE
BRONCO PONY PONEY CAYUSE BRONCHO MUSTANG
BRONCOBUSTER BUSTER GINETE BUCKAROO
BRONZE AES TAN BUST ALLOY BROWN COWBOY ORMOLU STATUE ASIATIC GUNMETAL
(— **AGE CULTURE**) UBAID
(**ANTIQUE —**) CACAO
(**GILDED —**) VERMEIL
(**MEDAL —**) CALABASH
(PREF.) CHALC(O) CHALK(O)
BRONZEWING SQUATTER
BROOCH BAR PIN BOSS LACE OUCH PRIN PROP CAMEO CLASP MORSE PREEN SLIDE SPRAY SPRIG FIBULA NOUCHE PLAQUE SHIELD FERMAIL PETALON CROTCHET ORNAMENT SUNBURST
BROOD EYE FRY NYE SET SIT MOPE NEST NIDE RACE TEAM TRIP WEEP AERIE BREED CLOCK COVER COVEY FLOCK GLOOM GROUP HATCH HOVER ISSUE SEDGE STOCK WORRY YOUNG CLETCH CLUTCH FAMILY KINDLE LITTER PONDER PROGENY SPECIES CLECKING COGITATE INCUBATE KINDLING MEDITATE
(— **OF BIRDS**) AERY AERIE COVEY EYRIE SEDGE SIEGE
(— **OF PHEASANTS**) EYE NID NYE NIDE
BROODER HOVER MOTHER NURSERY
BROOK RUN BEAR BECK BURN GHYL GILL LAKE RILL RUSH SIKE ABIDE BAYOU BOURN CREEK FLEET GLIDE STAND STELL TCHAI ARROYO BRANCH CANADA DIGEST ENDURE GUTTER RINDLE RIVOSE RUNLET RUNNEL SICKET STREAM SUFFER ABROOKE COMPORT CONCOCT STOMACH QUEBRADA TOLERATE
(**RIPPLING —**) PURL

(SALT —) LICK
BROOKLET BECK DOKE RILL RILLET RUNNEL RILLOCK RIVULET
BROOM COW MOP FRAY SWAB WISP BESOM BISME BREAM BRUSH SCRUB SPART SWEEP UALIS WHISK GENISTA HAGWEED WHISKER HACKWEED SPLINTER
(DYER'S —) GENET DYEWOOD
(NATIVE —) DOGWOOD
(TOPS OF —) SCOPARIUS
(PREF.) SCOPI SCOPULI
BROOMCORN HURL
BROOMCORN MILLET HIRSE PANIC PANICLE KADIKANE
BROOMRAPE HELLROOT HERBBANE
BROOMROOT SACATON ZACATON
BROSE ATHOLE CROWDIE
BROTH SEW BREE BROO FOND KAIL KALE SOUP GLAZE STOCK BREWIS CULLIS JUSSAL JUSSEL LIQUOR SKILLY CALDERA POTTAGE SOUCHIE SUPPING BOUILLON CONSOMME PISHPASH POSSODIE POWSOWDY
BROTHEL KIP CRIB STEW BAGNE HOUSE BAGNIO BORDEL CORINTH LUPANAR SHEBANG BORDELLO CATHOUSE HOOKSHOP HOTHOUSE JOYHOUSE SERAGLIO
BROTHER FR BUB FRA KIN PAL SIB BHAI BRER EGIL FRAY MATE MONK PEER BILLY BUBBY BUDDY CADET FRERE FRIAR FELLOW FRAILE FRATER GERMAN COMRADE SIBLING FOSTERER
(HUSBAND'S —) LEVIR
(LAY —) SCOLOG
(WIFE'S —) AFFINE
(YOUNGER —) CADET
(PL.) FF ADELPHI BRETHREN CURIATII HARLUNGEN
(PREF.) ADELPHO FRATRI
(SUFF.) ADELPHIA ADELPHOUS
BROTHERHOOD GILD GUILD LODGE ORDER PAPEY FRIARY BRATSVO CHISHTI THIASOS THIASUS BRODHULL SODALITY
(— OF FREEMASONS) CRAFT
(LITERARY —) FELIBRIGE
BROTHER-IN-LAW MAUGH
BROTHERS KARAMAZOV
(AUTHOR OF —) DOSTOEVSKI
(CHARACTER IN —) IVAN ALEXEY DMITRI FYODOR ALYOSHA KATRINA ZOSSIMA GRUSHENKA SMERDYAKOV
BROUGHAM PILLBOX CARRIAGE
BROUGHT BROCHT
(— FROM ELSEWHERE) DERIVED
(— TO BAY) CORNERED
(— TOGETHER) CONFLATE
(— UP BY HAND) CADE
BROW TOP BRAE EDGE MIEN SNAB BOUND BRINK CREST EAVES FRONT RIDGE SLOPE BOLDNESS FOREHEAD
BROWBEAT BOSS FACE ABASH BULLY BOUNCE HECTOR DEPRESS DUMBCOW OUTFACE SWAGGER
BROWBEATEN HACKED
BROWN (ALSO SEE COLOR) ART

DUN TAN ARAB COIN COOK DARK GOAT LION SEAR ABRAM ACORN ARGUS BRUNO DUSKY HAZEL KAFFA MOSUL PABLO PENNY QUAIL SEDGE SEPIA TAWNY TENNE TOAST UMBER APACHE BEAVER BRUNET BURNET GLOOMY MALAGA MANILA MASTIC MOHAWK PALOMA PLOVER PONGEE RABBIT RUSSET SENNET TANNED TURTLE WIGWAM ASPHALT FUSCOUS HARVEST LIBERIA MUSCADE OAKWOOD OXBLOOD POMPEII PRAIRIE REDWOOD TANBARK TOBACCO VESUVIN BRUNETTE MOCCASIN MUSHROOM PHEASANT PERSIMMON PYGMALION
(CONDOR —) TIFFIN
(DARK —) BURNET
(GRAYISH —) DUN
(HAIR —) ARGALI
(LIGHT —) ALOMA ALESAN STRING
(OLIVE —) BARK AUTUMN
(REDDISH —) BAY SORE SEPIA AUBURN CROTAL GINGER RUSSET SORREL AMBROSIA
(YELLOWISH —) AZTEC ALMOND BAMBOO BLONDE BEESWAX ALDERNEY
(PREF.) AITHO
BROWNBACK DOWITCH DOWITCHER
BROWNED ADUST
BROWN HEART RAAN
BROWNIE ELK NIS COOKY DOBBY NISSE URISK DOBBIE GOBLIN URUISG
BROWNING SCALD SCORCH SUNTAN
BROWNISH UMBER BURNET
(— BLACK) LAVA
BROWNSTONE CHESTNUT
BROWSE BRUT CROP FEED GRAZE FORAGE NIBBLE PASTURE
BRUCITE NEMALITE
BRUISE JAM BASH BRAY BUBU DENT DUNT HURT JAMB MAIM MAUL SORE STUN TUND BLACK BREAK BRIZZ CRUSH CURRY DELVE DINGE FRUSH POUND PUNCH SQUAT BATTER BREACH HATTER INJURY INTUSE MANGLE POUNCE SHINER STOUND SUGGIL BATTERY CONTUND CROWNER DAMMISH DISABLE
(— FLAX) BRAKE
BRUISED HURT LIVID FROISSE
BRUIT DIN FAME RALE ROAR TELL NOISE RUMOR SOUND BLAZON CLAMOR REPORT DECLARE HEARSAY
BRUNEI (— WEIGHT) PARA CHAPAH
(COIN OF —) SEN
(TOWN OF —) SERIA
BRUNET DARK BLACK BROWN GIPSY GYPSY MORENA SWARTHY BRUNETTE MORENITA
BRUNHILD (HUSBAND OF —) GUNTHER
BRUNT JAR BLOW JOLT CLASH FORCE ONSET SHOCK ATTACK

EFFORT IMPACT STRAIN STRESS ASSAULT OUTBURST VIOLENCE
BRUSH DIP DUB PIG TIP BOSH CARD COMB DUST FLAP FLAT FRAY KIYI SKIM SWAB BROOM CHAPE CLEAN COPSE FIGHT FITCH GRAZE LINER SABLE SCOPA SCRUB SCUFF SWEEP SWOOP WHISK BADGER BATTLE BRIGHT BROSSE DABBER DAUBER DUSTER MOGOTE PALLET PENCIL PICKUP PUTOIS RIGGER RUBBER SPONGE STROKE TEASEL CLEANSE FOXTAIL GRAINER GROOMER MOTTLER STIPPLE STRIPER THICKET SCRUBBER SKIRMISH SOFTENER STIPPLER TARBRUSH NAILBRUSH PAINTBRUSH
(— ASIDE) SCUFF
(— IN DANCING) SCUFFLE
(— OF HAIR) PENICIL
(— OF TWIGS) COW
(— TO CLEAN SHIP BOTTOM) HOG
(BLUNT —) BLENDER
(DENSE —) BUNDOCKS BOONDOCKS
(ELECTRIC —) DOCTOR
(EMPHASIZED —) SLAP
(FLESH —) SCRAPER STRIGIL
(GROWTH OF —) SYLVAGE
(POLLEN —) SCOPA SAROTHRUM
(SMALL —) TOOL FITCH FITCHEW
(PREF.) MUSCARI SCOPI
BRUSHER LIMBER LIPPER
BRUSH MAKER FLIRTY FLICKER
BRUSH SHUNT PIGTAIL
BRUSHWOOD HAG RICE RONE RUSH BAVIN BRAKE BRUSH COPSE FRITH REISE SCROG SCRUB SPRAY COPPET GARSIL MALLEE RAMMEL SCRAWL SCRUNT SHROGS TINNET TINSEL COPPICE ROUGHIE TEENAGE THICKET WOODRIS BUSHWOOD OVENWOOD
BRUSQUE CURT RUDE BLUFF BLUNT GRUFF HASTY ROUGH SHORT ABRUPT VIOLENT CAVALIER IMPOLITE
BRUTAL CRUEL FERAL GROSS CARNAL COARSE SAVAGE BEASTLY BESTIAL BRUTISH CADDISH DOGGISH INHUMAN BELLUINE INHUMANE INSOLENT RUTHLESS
BRUTE BETE BEAST GROSS YAHOO ANIMAL BRUTAL SAVAGE BEASTLY BESTIAL BRUTISH GORILLA RUFFIAN
BRUTISH FELL CRUEL BRUTAL CARNAL FIERCE SAVAGE STUPID BESTIAL INHUMAN SENSUAL GADARENE
BRYONY HOP NEP ALRAUN COWBIND MANDRAKE
(— FRUIT) OXBERRY
BRYOPHYTE ANOPHYTE LIVERWORT
BRYOZOAN POLYZOAN
BRYTHONIC CYMRIC KYMRIC BRITTONIC
BUBBLE AIR BUB BEAD BELL BLEB BLOB BOIL BOLL DUPE FOAM

GLOB SCUM SEED CAPER CHEAT EMPTY VAPOR BURBLE DELUDE HOTTER POPPLE SEETHE SOTTER TRIFLE BLISTER BLUBBER DECEIVE GLOBULE DELUSIVE
(— IN GLASS) BOIL REAM SEED BLISTER
(PL.) SUDS
(PREF.) BULLI
BUBBLING GAY BULLER BURBLY BOILING GASSING EFFUSIVE
BUBINGA KEVAZINGO
BUBO EMEROD
BUCCANEER PIRATE RIFLER ROBBER VIKING CORSAIR MARINER SPOILER MAROONER PICAROON
BUCHMANITE GROUPER
BUCHU BUKA DIOSMA
BUCK FOB RAM BOIL BUTT DEER DUDE MALE PRIG REAR SOAK STAG TOFF WASH BLOOD DANDY PITCH SASIN STEEP BASKET DOLLAR OPPOSE RESIST STRIVE SAWBUCK BUCKJUMP BUCKWASH
(— IN 1ST YEAR) FAWN
(— IN 2ND YEAR) PRICKET
(— IN 3RD YEAR) SORREL
(— IN 4TH YEAR) SORE
(— STEADILY) SUNFISH
(— UP) BRACE
BUCKBEAN BOGBEAN THREEFOLD
BUCKER DOLLYMAN
BUCKET SAY TUB BAIL BOOT BOWK CAGE GRAB MEAL PAIL SKIP BOWIE CHEAT SCOOP SKEEL STOOP STOUP BAILER DIPPER DRENCH HOPPET KIBBLE SITULA SUCKER VESSEL FERMAIL GRAPPLE SNAPPER SWINDLE CANNIKIN HEDGEHOG PAINTPOT
(— ON MILL WHEEL) AW AWE EIE
(— ON WHEELS) SKIP
(GLASS-MAKING —) CUVETTE
(GRAVEL —) GRAB
(HOISTING —) HUDGE
(PART OF —) EAR RIM BAIL BODY CURL HANDLE
(TWO —S OF WATER) GAIT
BUCKEYE STATE OHIO
BUCKLAW HAYSTON
BUCKLE BOW BEND CURL KINK OUCH TACH TACK WARP BRACE CLASP MARRY STRAP TACHE TWIST FIBULA CONTEND FERMAIL GRAPPLE FASTENER STRUGGLE
BUCKLER CRAB BLOCK PELTA SCUTE TARGE SHIELD TAIRGE TARGET BUCKLUM BUCKRAM ROTELLA ROUNDEL SHUTTER RONDACHE
BUCKLING KINK UPSET
BUCK RAKE SWEEP
BUCKRAM STIFFENER
BUCKTHORN COMA RHAMN SCROG WAHOO ALATERN CASCARA BEARWOOD FRANGULA LOTEBUSH WAYTHORN STINKWOOD
BUCKTHORN BROWN SUMAC SUMACH
BUCKWHEAT BUCK CRAP BRANK WRIGHT KNOTWEED SARRAZIN

POLYGONUM
(PL.) FAGOPYRUM
BUCOLIC IDYL LOCAL NAIVE
RURAL FARMER RUSTIC SIMPLE
COWHERD ECLOGUE AGRESTIC
HERDSMAN PASTORAL
BUCOLION (FATHER OF —)
LAOMEDON
(SON OF —) AESEPUS PEDASUS
(WIFE OF —) ABARBAREA
BUD BUR EYE GEM IMP PIP BULB
BURR CION FORM GERM GIRL
GROW KNOP KNOT WORK CAPOT
CHILD CLOVE GEMMA GRAFT
SCION SHOOT SPRIT SPURT
YOUTH BUDLET BULBIL BUTTON
FLOWER GERMIN OCULUS OILLET
SPROUT BLOSSOM BROTHER
CABBAGE GEMMULE PLUMULE
ROSEBUD TENDRON BOURGEON
BULBILLA
(BLIGHTED —) BLAST
(BROOD —) SOREDIUM
(UNDEVELOPED —) EYE
(UNOPENED —) KNOSP
(PL.) CAPERS
(PREF.) BLAST(O) GEMMI GEMMO
BUDDENBROOKS (AUTHOR OF —)
MANN
(CHARACTER IN —) TOM JEAN
TONI ERICA GERDA HANNO
JOHANN THOMAS ANTONIE
GRUNLICH CHRISTIAN
PERMANEDER
BUDDHA FO FOH BUTSU JATAKA
GAUTAMA GNANANA DAIDUTOU
(— STORY) JATAKA
(FATHER OF —) SUDDHODANA
(SON OF —) KAHULA
BUDDHISM DAIJO FOISM KEGON
CHANISM LAMAISM HINAYANA
(— CODE) VINAYA
(BRANCH OF —) MAHAYANA
BUDDHIST (— DOCTRINE) ANATTA
TRIKAYA
(— FESTIVAL) WESAK
(— PATH) VEHICLE
(— SCHOOL) RITSU
(— SECT) SHIN TENDAI
BUDDLE TYE FRAME BODDLE
SLIMER STRIPE TROUGH
BUDDY BO BOY BUD PAL JACK
MATE COBBER DIGGER BROTHER
COMRADE COMPADRE TENTMATE
BUDGE FUR JEE BOGY MOVE STIR
BOOZE BRISK MUDGE STIFF THIEF
JOCUND LIQUOR SOLEMN
AUSTERE POMPOUS MOVEMENT
BUDGET BAG BOGY BOOT PACK
PLAN ROLL BATCH BOGEY BOGIE
BUNCH STOCK STORE BOTTLE
BUNDLE PARCEL SOCKET WALLET
PROGRAM
BUFF ASH BOB FAN TAN BLOW
COAT CURT FIRM SHINE SNUFF
SPARK BUFFET POLISH STURDY
STAMMER STUTTER NAUMKEAG
(TILLEUL —) ALABASTER
BUFFALO OX ANOA ARNA ARNI
BUFF STAG ARNEE BISON BUGLE
BUFFLE HAMPER KERBAU
MURRAH WUNTEE CARABAO
CARIBOU GAZELLE OVERAWE

TIMARAU ZAMOUSE BEWILDER
SAPIUTAN SELADANG
BUFFALO CHIPS BODEWASH
BUFFALO FISH SUCKER BUFFALO
BIGMOUTH GOURDHEAD
BUFFER DOG PAD FROG RACK
BUMPER FENDER HURTER PISTOL
CUSHION
BUFFET BAR BOB BOX BEAT BLAD
BLOW BUFF CUFF GOWF PLAT
SCAT SLAP TOSS YANK FILIP
KNOCK SCUFF SCUFT SMITE
STOOL ABACUS BATTER FILLIP
FLEWIT SERVER SETOUT STRIKE
STRIVE THRASH COLPHEG
CONTEND COUNTER HASSOCK
SMACKER SQUELCH CREDENCE
CREDENZA CUPBOARD
SPANGHEW
BUFFETING DIRD SKITE DUSTING
BUFFLEHEAD DUCK FOOL CLOWN
BUFFLE DIPPER DOPPER
MARIONET WOOLHEAD
MERRYWING
BUFFOON DOR WAG WIT APER
FOOL JAPE MIME MOME VICE
ZANY ACTOR ANTIC BUFFO
CLOWN COMIC DROLE DROLL
HARLOT JESTER MUMMER
STOOGE ANTIQUE BOUFFON
FARCEUR JUGGLER PIERROT
PLAYBOY SCOGGIN TOMFOOL
BALATRON GRACIOSO HUMORIST
MACAROON MERRYMAN
OWLGLASS PLEASANT RIDICULE
PANTALOON OGANAMOUOII
PUNCHINELLO
BUFFOONERY JAPERY ZANYISM
CLOWNERY TOMFOOLERY
BUG (ALSO SEE INSECT) DOR FLAW
GERM IDEA MITE BOGEY BULGE
FIEND LYGUS ROACH ARADID
BEDBUG BEETLE BUGGER CAPSID
CHINCH COREID CORUCO ELATER
INSECT SALDID SCHEME TINGID
BELLIED BOATMAN BUGBEAR
CIMICID CORSAIR FORWARD
POMPOUS STRIDER BARBEIRO
CONENOSE HEMIPTER HOBBYIST
NAUCORID VINCHUCA
(RED —) CHIGGA CHIGGER
(SOW —) SLATER
(PREF.) CIMI(CI)
(SUFF.) CORIS
BUGABOO BOGY FEAR GOGA
GOGO OGRE TURK ALARM BOGEY
BOGIE GOGGA BODACH GOBLIN
BUGBEAR SPECTER SPECTRE
WORRICOW
BUGANDA (— KING) KABAKA
BUGBANE COHOSH BUGWORT
RICHWEED HELLEBORE
BUGBEAR BUG COW BOGY OGRE
BOGEY BOGIE CADDY MORMO
POKER BOGGLE BOGGART
BUGABOO FEARBABE SCAREBUG
BUGGER SOD CHAP BOOGER
FELLOW PERSON RASCAL
HERETIC
BUGGY CART SHAY TRAP NUTTY
CALESA CABOOSE CALESIN
FOOLISH VEHICLE DEMENTED
INFESTED ROADSTER STANHOPE

BUGLE BEAD HORN BLACK
BUFFALO BULLOCK CLARION
HUTCHET TRUMPET KEYBUGLE
(— CALL) WARISON
(PART OF —) CUP RIM BELL BITE
EDGE
(YELLOW —) IVA
BUGLER WINDJAMMER
BUGLOSS ALKANET ANCHUSA
BLUEWEED OXTONGUE
BUILD BIG SET FORM LEVY MAKE
REAR TELD CREAT DRIVE EDIFY
ERECT FOUND FRAME HOUSE
RAISE SHAPE THROW FABRIC
GRAITH TAILLE TIMBER COMPILE
EXTRUCT FASHION ASSEMBLE
PHYSIQUE
(— FIRE) CHUNK
(— HASTILY) CLAP
(— NEST) AERIE NIDIFY
(— UP) AGGRADE
(BODY —) HABITUS
BUILDER EPEUS MAKER BIGGAR
EPEIUS HANGER ERECTOR
ENGINEER TECTONIC
(DAM —) DAMMER
(PREF.) TECTO
(SUFF.) TECT
BUILDING GIN CASA CRIB DOME
FLAT HALL IGLU JAIL LAND PILE
SHED SHOP SLAB SPOT TELD
ABBEY AEDES ARENA BLOCK
COURT FOLLY FRAME HOTEL
HOUSE IGLOO JAWAB STORE
STUDY ARMORY BIGGIN BOTTLE
CASINO CHAPEL FABRIC GARAGE
HAMMAM INSULA LYCEUM
PALACE SCHOOL SUCCOR
BREWERY BROODER CARBARN
COLLEGE DIORAMA EDIFICE
FACTORY FLATTOP FOUNDRY
KURHAUS MANSION PALAZZO
SALTERN STATION SYNAGOG
ATHENEUM BAGHOUSE BASILICA
BROLETTO CHANCERY DIPTEROS
DRYHOUSE DWELLING DYEHOUSE
ELEVATOR EPHEBEUM FIRETRAP
GASHOUSE GINHOUSE HOTHOUSE
ICEHOUSE MAGAZINE NYMPHEUM
PANORAMA SERAPEUM
STEMMERY TAXPAYER TENEMENT
VELODROME OBSERVATORY
OUTBUILDING PLANETARIUM
MEETINGHOUSE
(— FOR AIRCRAFT) DOCK
(— GROUPS) HAM
(— OF STONE) KAABA CASHEL
TRUDDO TRULLO
(— ON POSTS) PATAKA
(— WITH TRIANGULAR FRONT)
AFRAME
(BUDDHIST —) TOPE
(CIRCULAR —) THOLE THOLOS
ROTUNDA
(CRUDE —) SHANTY
(DILAPIDATED —) ROOKERY
FIRETRAP
(EXHIBITION —) MUSEUM
(FARM —) BARN STABLE
HACIENDA
(FORTIFIED —) CASTLE
(GLOOMY —) MAUSOLEUM
(GRAIN —) GARNER

(GROUP OF —S) CLUSTER
(JAI ALAI —) FRONTON
(MOVABLE —) TURRET
(ORNAMENTAL —) ALCOVE
(PUBLIC —) CASINO THEATER
THEATRE COLISEUM
(QUADRANGULAR —) TETRAGON
(QUARANTINE —) LAZARET
(ROUND —) THOLUS
(SACRED —) CHURCH MOSQUE
TEMPLE SACRARY PANTHEON
SARAPEUM
(SERIES OF —S) SWEEP
(SLIGHT —) SHED
(SMALL —) HUT COOP HOCK
EDICULE
(SPORTS —) CAGE
(STATELY —) DOME
(STORAGE —) BARN HORREUM
(SUBSIDIARY —) ANNEX
(TALL —) SKYSCRAPER
(TRADE —) HALL
(UNCOMFORTABLE —) ARK
(PL.) FUNDUS
BUILT SET BOUKIT STACKED
TIMBERED
(COMPACTLY —) CORKY
(HEAVILY —) BLOCKY
(LOOSELY —) GANGLING
(STRONGLY —) BURLY GROSS
QUARRY
(WELL —) BUIRDLY
BUKIDNON MONTES BINOKID
BUKKI (FATHER OF —) JOGLI
ABISHUA
(SON OF —) UZZI
BULB BUD SET BLUB CORM IXIA
KNOB LAMP ROOT SEED SEGO
CAMAS CHIVE CLOVE FLOAT
GLOBE ONION SWELL TUBER
BULBIL BULBUS CAMASS CROCUS
GARLIC OFFSET SCILLA BABIANA
GALTONIA SPARAXIS TRITONIA
PHOTOFLASH
(— OF PERCUSSION) CONCHOID
(LIGHT —) HELION
(ONION —) BUTTON
(PL.) SQUILL
(PREF.) BULBI BULBO
BULBIL CHIVE BULBLET
(PL.) SPAWN
BULBLET CHIVE CORMEL BULBULE
NUCLEUS PROPAGO
BULBUL KALA BUHLBUHL
GREENBUL LEAFBIRD

BULGARIA
ASSEMBLY: SOBRANJE SOBRANYE
CAPE: EMINE SABLA KURATAN
CAPITAL: SOFIA
COIN: LEV LEW STOTINKA
COMMUNE: SLIVEN SLIVNO
SISTOVA
GULF: BURGAS
MEASURE: OKA OKE KRINE LEKHE
MOUNTAIN: BOTEV SAPKA
MUSALA VIKHREN
MOUNTAINS: PIRIN BALKAN
RHODOPE
PEOPLE: SLAV TATAR BULGAR
SLAVIC
RIVER: LOM VIT ARDA OSMA ISKER
MESTA DANUBE MARICA

OGOSTA STRUMA YANTRA
MARITSA STRYAMA TUNDZHA
TOWN: RILA RUSE AYTOS BUTAN
BYCLU ELENA ISKRA STARA
VARNA BLEVEN BURGAS
DULOVO LEVSKY PLEVNA
SHUMEN SHUMLA SLIVEN
SLIVNO WIDDIN YAMBOL
ZAGORA GABROVO KARLOVO
PLOVDIV SISTOVA TIRNOVO
RUSTCHUK
WEIGHT: OKA OKE TOVAR

BULGARIAN POMAK
BULGE BAG BUG JUT SAG BIAS
BULB BUMP CASK HUMP KNOB
LUMP PANT BILGE BLOAT BOUGE
FLASK POUCH START STRUT
SWELL BEETLE BILLOW COCKLE
EXTEND PUCKER WALLET BLISTER
PROJECT OVERHANG PROTRUDE
SWELLING PROJECTION
(— OUT) TUT BELLY BOWDEN
STRUNT
(OFFENSIVE —) SALIENT
BULGING FULL BOMBE BOWED
BUGGY GOUTY PUDGY TUMID
BAGGED BUNCHY CONVEX
GOOGLY TOROSE GAMPISH
GIBBOUS GOUTISH SWOLLEN
BOUFFANT PROPTOSIS
BULK BODY BOUK FECK HEAP HEFT
HOLD HULK HULL LUMP MASS
MOLE PILE SIZE BURLY CARGO
GROSS MIGHT POWER SLUMP
STALL SWELL CORPSE EXPAND
EXTENT FIGURE VOLUME BIGNESS
MAJORITY QUANTITY
(PREF.) ONCO
BULKHEAD CHECK BATTERY
PARTITION
BULKY BIG MAIN BURLY GROSS
LARGE LUSTY PUDGY STOUT
CLUMSY STODGY HULKING
LUMPING MASSIVE VOLUMED
WEIGHTY CUMBROUS UNWIELDY
(PREF.) PYCN(O)
BULL COP SEG APIS BEEF BILL JEST
MALE ROAN SEAL SEGG SLIP
STOT TORO ZEBU BACIS BEEVE
BOBBY BONER BOVID BRUTE
CROCK DRINK EDICT ERROR
ANIMAL BOVINE BUSHWA LETTER
PEELER TAURUS BULLOCK
BUSHWAH CRITTER CRUSADE
NOVILLO TAURINE CAJOLERY
DOCUMENT FLATTERY IRISHISM
(— AREA) QUERENCIA
(— KILLING) VOLAPIE
(HORNLESS —) DODDY DODDIE
(HUMAN-HEADED —) SHEDU
CAMASSU
(YOUNG —) STOT BUGLE MICKY
STIRK STOTT BULLOCK
(PL.) BATTERY
(PREF.) TAUR(I)(O)
BULLA BLEB BULL SEAL BLAIN
BLISTER VESICLE
BULL CELL TORIL
BULLDOG BULL BULLER BULLDOZE
BULLDOZE COW RAM BULLY
FORCE SCOOP COERCE
BROWBEAT BULLYRAG RESTRAIN

BULLDOZER (PART OF —) ARM EYE
SHOE TANK BLADE FRAME IDLER
LEVER LIGHT STRUT TRACK
CANOPY FENDER GRILLE ROLLER
CLEANER HOUSING MUFFLER
CYLINDER
BULLET GUN BALL LEAD PILL SHOT
SLUG TOWEL CONOID DUMDUM
PELLET PICKET SINKER TRACER
DINGBAT MISSILE PELLOCK
PROJECT SPITZER BISCAYAN
MUSHROOM WADCUTTER
(PL.) BALL LEAD STUFF
BULLETIN ITEM MEMO NOTICE
POSTER REPORT SERIAL
PROGRAM NEWSBILL
BULLFIGHT CORRIDA NOVILLADA
BULLFIGHTER TORERO MATADOR
PICADOR CAPEADOR TOREADOR
NOVILLERO
BULLFIGHTING REJONEO
TAUROMACHY
BULLFINCH ALP OLP HOOP MAWP
MONK NOPE OLPH POPE HEDGE
TANNY TAWNY MONACH
REDBIRD REDHOOP SHIRLEY
BLOODALP TONYHOOP
BULLHEAD CUR POUT POGGE
COTTOID
BULLHORN HAILER
BULLIMONG FARRAGE
BULLION BILLOT
BULLISH STIFF
BULLOCK HOG HOGG NEAT NOWT
STOT BUGLE COACH KNOUT
STEER STIRK BOVINE
(AUSTRALIAN —) SNAIL
(BAD-TEMPERED —) RAGER
(DECOY —) COACH
BULL-ROARER BUZZ BUMMER
BUZZER ROARER TUNDUN
HUMBUZZ TURNDUN WHIZZER
BULL'S-EYE EYE BULL DUMP GOLD
BLANK OXEYE WHITE TARGET
ROUNDEL
BULL SNAKE GOPHER
BULL TROUT TRUFF
BULLY COW NUT BOAT BOSS FACE
FINE GOOD HAZE HUFF MATE
BRAVE BRAVO GREAT JOLLY
SNOOL TIGER VAPOR BOUNCE
CUTTER CUTTLE HARASS HECTOR
HUFFER JOVIAL RUFFLE TYRANT
BLUSTER BOUNCER BULLOCK
DARLING DASHING GALLANT
GAUSTER HUFFCAP ROISTER
RUFFIAN RUFFLER SLASHER
SOLDIER SWAGGER BANGSTER
BARRATER BLUDGEON
BROWBEAT BULLDOZE DOMINEER
FRAMPLER NIGHTCAP RABIATOR
(MASTIC —) ACOMA
BULLY TREE BALATA BULLACE
GAUSTER BEEFWOOD
BULRUSH REED RISP RUSH TULE
SEDGE BUMBLE GLUMAL AKAAKAI
CATTAIL PAPYRUS SCIRPUS
TUSSOCK
BULWARK BAIL FORT WALL FENCE
JETTY MANTA MOUND TOWER
SCONCE WARDER BASTION
DEFENCE DEFENSE PARAPET
PROTECT RAMPART WEREWALL

BUM BEG DIN BOMB BOOM HOBO
DRINK DRONE IDLER MOOCH
SHACK STIFF TRAMP FROLIC
GUZZLE SPONGE SQUEEF
GUZZLER LAYABOUT VAGABOND
BINDLESTIFF
BUMBLE ERR
BUMBLEBEE DOR CLOCK BUMBEE
BUMBLE CARDER BUMBLER
BUMMER SKIDDER
BUMP CRY HIP HIT NOB BANG
BLOW BOOM BUNK DIRD JOLT
JOWL KNOB LUMP WHAP WHOP
BARGE BULGE CLASH CLOUR
CLOUT DUNCH KNOCK ORGAN
THUMP BOUNCE CANNON
IMPACT JOUNCE NODULE STRIKE
BITTERN COLLIDE CONFLICT
SWELLING
(— IN SKI RUN) MOGUL
(— ON WHALE'S HEAD) HOVEL
BUMPER BOWL FINE GOOD FACER
GLASS ROUSE BUFFER CASABE
FENDER GOBLET HURFER KELTIE
BRIMMER DINGMAN CARANGID
(— GUARD) OVERRIDER
BUMPKIN JAY YAP BEAM BOOM
BOOR CHAW CLOD GAWK HICK
LOUT PUTT RUBE SWAB SWAD
TIKE TYKE CHURL CLOWN ROBIN
YAHOO YOKEL FARMER JOSKIN
LUMMOX RUSTIC BUCOLIC
CAUBOGE HAWBUCK
BUMPTIOUS COXY BRASH COCKSY
BUN PUG CHOU BRICK COOKIE
BUNAH (FATHER OF —) JERAHMEEL
BUNCH BOB SET BALE BOSS CHOU
CLEW CLUB CLUE COMA KICK
KNOB KNOT PACK SWAD TUFT
WISP BREAK CLUMP FAGOT
FLOCK KNOLL PAHIL THUMP
CLUTCH GAGGLE HUDDLE
(— OF BANANAS) HAND STEM
(— OF FLAX) HEAD STRICK
(— OF FLOWERS) BOWPOT
BOUQUET BOUGHPOT
(— OF FRUIT) HOG STRAP
(— OF GRAIN) RIP
(— OF GRAPES) RAISIN
(— OF GRASS) WHISK
(— OF HAIR) COB
(— OF HERBS) BOUQUET
(— OF IVY) BUSH
(— OF TOBACCO LEAVES) HAND
BREAK
(— OF TWIGS) COW KOW
(— UP) SHRUG
(SMALL —) WISP
BUNCHER BINDER
BUNCHY TRUSS
BUNCOMBE HOOEY BUNKUM
BUND BAND QUAY PRAYA LEAGUE
SOCIETY
BUNDLE KID LOT PAD TOD WAD
WAP BALE BAND BEAT BOLT
BOOK BUNG DRUG DRUM GARB
HANK HAUL HEAD KNOT LOCK
PACK ROLL SWAG BLUEY BULTO
BUNCH FADGE FAGOT GAVEL
GLEAN GROUP LITCH NICKY
PETER SHEAF SKEIN TARRY
TRACE TRUSS TURSE WADGE
BARSOM BATTEN BINDLE BOTTLE

BUDGET DRIVER DUFTER FAGGOT
FARDEL FASCES FUMBLE GATHER
KNITCH LOGGIN NUMBER PACKET
PARCEL SCROLL THRAVE
DORLACH FASCINE GARBAGE
MATILDA PACKAGE FASCICLE
TROUSSEAU
(— OF BOARDS) BOLT
(— OF CELLULOSE) MICROFIBRIL
(— OF FASCINES) ROULEAU
(— OF FIBRILS) AXONEME
(— OF FILAMENTS) BYSSUS
(— OF FLAX) BEET HEAD
(— OF HAIR) LEECH
(— OF HAY, STRAW, ETC.) WAP
WASE WISP GAVEL SHEAF
BATTEN BOLTIN BOTTLE TIPPLE
WINDLING
(— OF HEATH) KID
(— OF HIDES) KIP
(— OF NERVE FIBERS) TRACT
COLUMN
(— OF PAPERS) SPUR DUFTER
(— OF RODS) FASCES
(— OF SACKS) BADGER
(— OF SACRED TWIGS) BARSOM
(— OF THONGS) KNOUT
(— OF TOBACCO) CARROT
(— OF TWIGS) BIRCH BROOM
FAGGOT
(— OF WOOD) PIMP BAVIN FAGOT
(— OF YARN) HAUL SLIP
(— OF 60 SKINS) TURN
(BUSHMAN'S —) DRUM BLUEY
BUNG CORK DOOK PLUG SHIVE
SPILE STOPPER
BUNGEY KIT
BUNGI-BUNGI STAVEWOOD
BUNGLE ERR BOOB DUFF FLUB
GOOF MESS MUCK MUFF MULL
BLUNK BOTCH FAULT FLUFF
FUDGE MISDO SPOIL STICK
BOGGLE BOLLIX BUMBLE FOOZLE
FUMBLE MANGLE MOMBLE
MUCKER MUDDLE TAILOR
TOGGLE BAUCHLE BLUNDER
BUTCHERY SHAMMOCK
BUNGLER MUFF LUMMOX PUDDLE
TINKER BLUNKER BUMBLER
BUMMLER FOOZLER DAUBSTER
SCHLEMIEL
BUNGLING FLUFF FUDGY INERT
CLUMSY AWKWARD TINKERLY
MUDDLEHEADED
BUNG START FLOGGER
BUNION ONION WYROCK
CARBUNCLE
BUNJI-BUNJI CUDGERIE
BUNK BED CAR BLAA BLAH CASE
JUNK SACK ABIDE BERTH BUNKO
FRAME HOKUM HOOEY LEAVE
LODGE SLEEP TRUCK BUNKUM
TIMBER BALONEY BOLSTER
CHICORY HEMLOCK TWADDLE
BUNCOMBE COBBLERS MALARKEY
NONSENSE
BUNKHOUSE BULLPEN
BUNKUM BLAH BUNK FUDGE
HOKUM HOOPLA BALONEY
BUNCOMBE MALARKEY
BUNTAL BURI BANGKOK
BUNTING EBB POP CIRL FLAG PAPE
POPE CHINK DUMPY FINCH

PLUMP COTTON STOCKY TOWHEE
UNTIDY COWBIRD ETAMINE
GARMENT OATFOWL ORTOLAN
ROUNDED BELLYING BOBOLINK
PRUSIANO RICEBIRD RINGBIRD
SLOVENLY NONPAREIL
BUNTON DIVIDER
BUNUS (FATHER OF —) HERMES
(MOTHER OF —) ALCIDAMEA
BUOY DAN WAFT BAKEN ELATE
FLOAT LAGAN RAISE BEACON
MARKER DOLPHIN SUSTAIN
DEADHEAD LEVITATE MAKEFAST
SONOBUOY
BUOYANCY BALON BALLON
LEVITY SPRING ELATION
BUOYANT GAY CORKY HAPPY
LIGHT BLITHE BOUNCY FLOATY
LIVELY ELASTIC HOPEFUL
JOCULAR LILTING SPRINGY
ANIMATED CHEERFUL SANGUINE
SPIRITED VOLATILE
BUPHAGUS (FATHER OF —)
IAPETUS
(MOTHER OF —) THORNAX
(SLAYER OF —) ARTEMIS
BUR BUZZ TEAZEL STICKER
BURBARK AKONGE BOXBUSH
BURRBARK
BURBOT COD CONY CUSK LING
LOTA CONEY LOCHE LAWYER
MORGAY DOGFISH EELPOUT
GUDGEON BIRDBOLT
BURBUNG BORA
BURDEN TAX VEX BIRN CARE CARK
CLAG CLUG DRAG DUTY FARE
FOOT GANG LADE LOAD MUCK
ONUS PORT SEAM TACK TASK
BIRTH CARGO CROWD CRUSH
DRONE HEAVY LABOR MIDST
CHARGE CUMBER ENTAIL FARDEL
HAMPER IMPOSE LADING SADDLE
THRACK WEIGHT BALLAST
BURTHEN CONVETH FRAUGHT
FREIGHT HAGRIDE ONERATE
OPPRESS REFRAIN REPRISE
SUMPTER TROUBLE CAPACITY
CARRIAGE ENCUMBER ENGREGGE
HANDICAP OVERCOME PRESSURE
QUANTITY RUMBELOW
MILLSTONE RESPONSIBILITY
(— OF SONG) WHEEL FADING
HOLDING OVERTURN OVERWORD
(FINANCIAL —) EXPENSE
BURDENED HEAVY LADEN GRAVID
FRAUGHT HARASSED
BURDENER INCUBUS
BURDENSOME HEAVY IRKSOME
ONEROUS WEIGHTY CUMBROUS
GRIEVOUS GRINDING LOADSOME
BURDOCK DOCK GOBO CLITE
CLOTE CLOTS DRAIN LAPPA
BARDANE BURWEED BUZZIES
CADILLO CLOTBUR HARDOCK
HAREBUR CLEAVERS HAULBACK
BUREAU DESK CHEST AGENCY
EXCISE OFFICE CENTRAL DRESSER
AGITPROP
BUREAUCRAT MANDARIN
BURFISH ATINGA
BURGEON BUD GROW ERUPT
SHOOT SPROUT
BURGESS CITIZEN FREEMAN

PORTMAN COMMONER GORGIBUS
(PL.) BURGWARE
BURG GRASS SANDBUR
COCKSPUR SANDSPUR
BURGLAR YEGG CRACK THIEF
GOPHER ROBBER RAFFLES
YEGGMAN PETERMAN PICKLOCK
BURGLARY BREAK CRACK THEFT
LARCENY ROBBERY STEALAGE
BURGUNDY MACON POMMARD
VOUGEOT TONNERRE
BURIAL FUNERARY INTERMENT
(— MOUND) TOLA HUACA
BURIAL PLACE AHU TOMB GRAVE
BURIAL GIGUNU LAYSTOW
PYRAMID CATACOMB CEMETERY
GOLGOTHA LAYSTALL
BURIED HIDDEN HUMATE SEPULT
ABSORBED IMBEDDED
(NOT —) UNRESTED
(RECENTLY —) GREEN
BURIN GRAVER PLASTIC
BURL BURR KNAR KNOT LUMP
KNAUR PIMPLE PUSTULE
BURLAP GUNNY CROCUS BAGGING
HESSIAN SACKING WRAPPING
BURLER LECKER SPILER
BURLESQUE APE ODD COPY JEST
MIME SKIT BURLY DROLL FARCE
REVUE COMEDY OVERDO PARODY
BUFFOON JOCULAR MIMICRY
MOCKERY OVERACT DOGGEREL
RIDICULE TRAVESTY
BURLY BIG FAT BLUFF BULKY
GROSS HEAVY HUSKY LARGE
LUSTY NOBLE OBESE STOUT
THICK TRAMP BOWERLY BUIRDLY
MASTIFF STATELY IMPOSING

BURMA

BAY: BENGAL HUNTER HEANZAY
CAPITAL: RANGOON
DIVISION: PEGU MAGWE ARAKAN
KARENNI SAGAING MANDALAY
IRRAWADDY TENASSERIM
GULF: MARTABAN
MEASURE: LY DHA GON LAN MAU
NGU SAO TAO TAT BYEE DAIN
PHAN SEIT TAUN TENG THAT
SALAY SHITA THUOC LAMANY
PALGAT TRUONG CHAIVAI
OKTHABAH
MONEY: KYAT
MOUNTAIN: POPA NATTAUNG
SARAMATI VICTORIA
MOUNTAINS: CHIN NAGA DAWNA
KACHIN KARENNI PEGUYOMA
NATIVE: AO VU WA LAI LAO MON
PYU TAI CHIN KADU KUKI LOLO
MIAO NAGA SEMA SGAU SGAW
SHAN THAI KAREN KHMER
LHOTA BIRMAN BURMAN
KACHIN RENGMA PALAUNG
ARAKANESE
PLATEAU: SHAN
PORT: AKYAB BASSEIN HENZADA
MOULMEIN
RIVER: HKA NMAI PEGU MEKONG
SALWIN SHWELI KALADAN
MALIKHA MYITNGE SALWEEN
SITTANG CHINDWIN INDAWGYI
IRRAWADDY
SEA: ANDAMAN

TOWN: YE AVA PEGU AKYAB
BHAMO KARBE KATHA MINBU
PAPUN PROME TAVOY HSENWI
HSIPAW LASHIO MAYMYO
MONYWA SHWEBO BASSEIN
HENZADA PAKOKKU RANGOON
MANDALAY MOULMEIN
WEIGHT: TA CAN MAT MOO PAI
VIS BINH DONG KYAT RUAY
VISS BAHAR BEHAR CANDY
TICAL TICUL ABUCCO PEIKTHA

BUR MARIGOLD BACLIN CUCKOLD
BURMESE KADU BIRMAN
ARAKANESE
BURN BREN BREW CHAR FIRE
GLOW PLOT RAZE RILL SEAR SERE
TEND TIND ADUST BLAZE BROIL
BROOK CENSE CHARK CLAMP
FLAME FLARE PARCH PLOUT
QUICK ROAST SCALD SCAUM
SINGE SWEAL WASTE WATER
CLOZLE IGNIFY NIGGER SCORCH
SIZZLE STREAM CHARPIT
COMBURE COMBUST CONSUME
CREMATE CROZZLE FLICKER
FRIZZLE INCENSE OXIDIZE
RIVULET SCOWDER SMOLDER
FLAGRATE SQUANDER
AMBUSTION
(— FEEBLY) GUTTER
(— FITFULLY) FLICKER
(— IN) INURE
(— MIDNIGHT OIL) LUCUBRATE
(— OUT) GUT
(— UP) ADUST EXUST
(— WITH LITTLE FLAME) SMUDGE
(LET —) BISHOP
(PREF.) COMBURI
BURNED ADUST COMBUST
(PREF.) AITHO
BURNER BEAK KORO BAKER PILOT
ARGAND BUNSEN CENSER
BATSWING CALCINER GASLIGHT
THURIBLE WELSBACH
BURNET SELFHEAL BLOODWORT
BURNING HOT FIRE LIVE ADUST
AFIRE ANGRY BLAZE CALID
EAGER FIERY FLAME GLEDY
QUICK SCALD URENT ABLAZE
ARDENT FERVID FIRING LIVING
TORRID USTION ADURENT
CAUSTIC CAUTERY FERVENT
FLAMING GLARING GLOWING
INTENSE MORDANT SCOWDER
SHINING ARDUROUS EXCITING
FLAGRANT INUSTION MUIRBURN
PARCHING SCOUTHER
(— BRIGHTLY) LIGHT
(— OF FORESTS IN INDIA) JHOOM
(MALICIOUS —) ARSON
(NO LONGER —) EXTINCT
(PREF.) IGNI
BURNING BUSH WAHOO
BURNISH RUB GLAZE GLOSS INLAY
POLISH FURBISH
BURNISHER AGATE BUFFER
GLAZER FROTTON POLISHER
BURP BOKE BELCH BUBBLE
BURR NUT PAD RIB BARB BIRR
BOSS BUZZ HALO KNOB PILE RING
ROVE SLUG WHIR BRIAR BURGH
CROUP WHARL WHIRR BANYAN

CIRCLE CORONA TEASEL TUNNEL
WASHER CORONET STICKER
PARASITE
(— IN WOOD) GNAR KNAR
(— OF ANTLER) CORONET
(— ON TYPE) RAG
BURRO ASS DONKEY
BURROW BED DEN DIG SET BURY
HEAP HOLE HOWK MINE MOLE
PIPE ROOT TUBE BERRY COUCH
EARTH MOUND FURROW ROOTLE
TUNNEL CLAPPER GALLERY
PASSAGE SHELTER EXCAVATE
WORMHOLE
(— AS EEL) MUD
(— IN) MOIL
(— OF BADGER) SET
(— OF OTTER) COUCH
(FOSSIL —) SCOLITE
BURROWS TOWN
BURSA SAC SACK POUCH CAVITY
BURSULA
BURSAR BOWSER PURSER TERRAR
BOUCHER CASHIER
BURSE CASE SHOP FOREL BAZAAR
BOURSE POCKET
BURST FIT FLY POP BLOW BUST
DASH GUSH GUST LOSS LOUP
REND SCAT TILT BLAST BLOUT
BREAK CRACK ERUPT FLAFF
FLASH GRAZE REAVE SALVO
SCATT SHOUT SPASM SPLIT
START STAVE BROKEN DAMAGE
INJURY SPROUT EXPLODE
IMPLODE RUPTURE SHATTER
AIRBURST OUTBREAK SUNDERED
(— ASUNDER) OUTRIVE
(— FORTH) ERUPT SALLY EXPIRE
BALLOON
(— IN) IRRUPT IMPLODE
(— INTO FRAGMENTS) FLITTER
(— INTO LAUGHTER) BUFF
(— OF ACTIVITY) BRASH SPURT
SPRINT SPLURGE
(— OF ARTILLERY) GRAZE RAFALE
(— OF CHEERS) SALVO
(— OF ENERGY) BANG
(— OF FIRING) COUGH
(— OF HARMONIOUS SOUND)
DIAPASON
(— OF LIGHT) FLASH GLORY
(— OF SPEED) KICK FLUTTER
(— OF TEARS) BLURT
(— OF TEMPER) FUFF BOUTADE
(— OF WIND) FLAW
(— OPEN) DEHISCE UPBRAST
(— OUT) BUFF PRORUMP
(— THE HEART) RIVE
(SUFF.) RRHAGE RRHAGIA
RRHAGY
BURSTER GALE LUGGER CRACKER
BURSTING TUMID ABURST
BLOWOUT RUPTION ERUPTING

BURUNDI

CAPITAL: BUJUMBURA
COIN: FRANC
LAKE: RUGWERO TSHOHOHA
NATIVE: TWA HUTU BANTU
PYGMY TUTSI WATUSI
RIVER: KAGERA RUVUBU RUZIZI
AKANYARU MALAGARAZI
TOWN: NGOZI BURURI KITEGA

BURY URN CAMP HIDE MOOL RAKE TURF VEIL CLOAK COVER EARTH GRAVE INTER INURN PLANT VAULT WHELM ENTOMB ENWOMB HEARSE INHUME SEPULT SHROUD BEDELVE CONCEAL ENGROSS IMMERSE PITHOLE REPRESS SECRETE FUNERATE INHEARSE SUBMERGE SEPULCHER
BUS CAMION JITNEY JEEPNEY MINIBUS
BUSBOY OMNIBUS PICCOLO
BUSH TOD BUTT BOSCH BURSE CLUMP GROVE PLASH SCRAY SHRUB BOUCHE BRANCH BUSKET MAQUIS TAVERN BOSCAGE BOUCHON CLUSTER OUTBACK THICKET BUSHLAND
(— OF HAIR) GLIB
(— SICKNESS) TAURANGA
(BLACKBERRY —) BRAMBLE
(STUNTED —) SCROG
(PL.) RUFFMANS
(PREF.) THAMN(O)
BUSHBUCK BONGO
BUSH CLOVER HAGI
BUSH COW ZAMOUSE
BUSHEL FOO FOU GOB LOT MET EPHA EPHI EPHAH BUCKET MODIUS STRICK
(1-HALF —) TOVET
(1-HALF TO 3-4THS —) CABOT
(1-4TH —) PECK
(1.6 —) FANEGA
(3 TO 5 —S) SACK
(3-4THS —) SKIPPLE
(4 —S) COMB COOMB
(41.28 —) WEY
(8 —S) SEAM
BUSHER SWAMPER
BUSHGRASS WOODREED
BUSHING BUSH COAK DRILL LINER BOUCHE COLLET LINING SLEEVE BOUCHON FERRULE GROMMET PADDING
(HALF —) STEP
BUSHMAN GUNG BUSHY KHUAI ABATOA ABATWA WHALER BUSHBOY SWAGMAN NEGRILLO
(PL.) SAN SAAN
BUSHMASTER CURUCUCU SURUCUCU
BUSHWHACKER PAPAW PAWPAW
BUSHY BOSKY SHOCK DUMOSE DUMOUS BUSHMAN QUEACHY
BUSIED VERSANT
BUSILY THRANG
BUSINESS ADO ART BIZ FAT JOB PIE CARE FEAT FIRM FUSS GAME GEAR LINE NOTE TASK WORK CAUSE CRAFT ERGON TRADE TRUCK AFFAIR CUSTOM EMPLOY ERRAND MATTER METIER NEGOCE OFFICE PIDGIN PIGEON RACKET TURKEY ACCOUNT CALLING CONCERN JOURNEY PALAVER TRADING TRAFFIC ACTIVITY AGIOTAGE BESOIGNE COMMERCE FOLLOWER INDUSTRY INTEREST VOCATION

OCCASIONS OCCUPATION
(COMIC —) LAZZO
(MONKEY —) JOUKERY PAWKERY
(STAGE —) BYPLAY
BUSINESSMAN TYCOON POACHER BOURGEOIS CONVERTER
BUSKIN BOOT SHOE CALIGA BOTTINE COTHURN BRODEKIN COTHURNUS
BUSSU UBUSSU TROOLIE
BUST BUMP FAIL RUIN TAME BOSOM BREAK BURST BUSTO CHEST EDGAR FLUNK SPREE BRONZE DEMOTE REDUCE STATUE TURKEY DEGRADE DISMISS FAILURE PROTOME PORTRAIT
(— SHAPE) TAILLE
BUSTARD KORI OTIS WATO PAAUW TURKEY BEBILYA HOUBARA KORHAAN FLORICAN GOMPAAUW
(PREF.) OTIDI
BUSTIC AUSUBO CASSADA
BUSTLE ADO TEW BUZZ FIKE FRAY FUSS JUMP STIR WHEW WHIR FRISK HASTE HYPER KNOCK PAVIE STEER WHIRL WHIRR BISHOP BUMBLE ENERGY FISSLE FISTLE FLURRY FUSTLE HUDDLE HUSTLE POTHER PUDDER RACKET ROMAGE RUFFLE TATTER THRONG TUMULT UNREST UPROAR CLATTER CLUTTER CONTEND LOUSTER SCOWDER SCUFFLE SCUFTER SPUFFLE ACTIVITY IMPROVER SPLUTTER STRUGGLE TOURNURE CRINOLETTE
BUSTLING ADO BUSY FUSSY SPOFFISH STIRRING
BUSY FAST FELL APPLY BRISK QUICK ACTIVE EIDENT EMPLOY INTENT LIVELY OCCUPY STEERY THRONG UNIDLE ENGAGED HOPPING HUMMING OPEROSE TROUBLE WORKING DILIGENT EMPLOYED EXERCISE OCCUPIED SEDULOUS TIRELESS UNTIRING PRAGMATIC PRAGMATICAL
(— ONESELF) STRAP
(NOT —) SLACK
BUSYBODY BUSY SNOOP EARWIG SPOFFY ARDELIO MARPLOT MEDDLER SNOOPER FACTOTUM QUIDNUNC PRAGMATIC
BUT AC LO MA BIT SED YEA YET MERE ONLY SAVE ARRAH STILL ALWAYS EXCEPT UNLESS BESIDES HOWBEIT HOWEVER
BUTCHER KILL SLAY BUTCH SPOIL BUNGLE KIDDER LEGGER LEMMER MURDER VENDOR BOTCHER BRAINER BRITTEN FLESHER MEATMAN PORKMAN KILLCALF PIGSTICK SLAUGHTER
BUTCHERBIRD SHRIKE MATAGASSE
BUTCHER'S-BROOM RUSCUS BRUSCUS
BUTCHERY MURDER CARNAGE MASSACRE SHAMBLES SLAUGHTER

BUTEA DHAK
BUTEO BUZZARD
BUTES (BROTHER OF —) ERECHTHEUS
(FATHER OF —) NEPTUNE PANDION POSEIDON
(SISTER OF —) PROCNE PHILOMELA
(WIFE OF —) CHTHONIA
BUTLER SOMLER YEOMAN BOTELER SERVANT SPENCER STEWARD CELLARER CONSUMAH KHANSAMA STEPHANO MAJORDOMO
BUTT JUR JUT MOT PIT PUT RAM RUN TOY TUP BUCK BUNT BURT BUSH CART CASK DISH DOSS FOOL GOAD GOAL GOAT HORN JOLT JURR PIPE POLL PUCK PUSH STUB TANG TOPE TURR BOUND DUNCH HINGE JOINT MOUND ROACH SCOPE STOCK STUMP BREECH TARGET THRUST BEEHIVE BUTTOCK PARAPET PROJECT REVERSE STUMMEL ARIETATE FLATFISH FLOUNDER RIDICULE SACKBUTT
(— FOR RIDICULE) GAME SPORT STALE COCKSHY
(— OF CIGAR) DOCK SNIPE
(— OF HORSEHIDE) SHELL
(— OF JOKE) JEST SCOGGIN JESTWORD
(CIGARETTE —) BUMPER
(HALF —) BEND
BUTTE HILL PICACHO
BUTTER SHEA CLART COCUM BAMBUK BEURRE CAJOLE SPREAD BLARNEY FLATTER
(— MEASURE) SPAN
(ARTIFICIAL —) BOSH OLEO BOSCH MARGARINE
(BROWNED IN —) NOISETTE
(PRUNE —) LEKVAR
(SEMIFLUID —) GHI GHEE
BUTTER-AND-EGGS RANSTEAD TOADFLAX
BUTTERBUR CLEAT CLOTE ELDIN GALON GALLON OXWORT GILTCUP FLEADOCK
BUTTERCUP BOLT CYME CRAZY ANEMONE CRAISEY CROWTOE GILTCUP GOLDCUP KINGCOB KINGCUP CRAWFOOT CROWFOOT FROGWORT PASQUEFLOWER
BUTTERFISH GUNNEL POMPANO WHITING PALOMETA SKIPJACK
BUTTERFLY IO BLUE ARGUS ELFIN GHOST NYMPH QUEEN SATYR SWIFT WHITE ZEBRA ADONIS ALPINE APOLLO CALIGO COPPER DANAID HOPPER IDALIA JUGATE MORPHO PIERID PROGNE PSYCHE SULFUR THECLA URSULA VIOLET YELLOW ADMIRAL BUCKEYE DIURNAL DOLPHIN EMPEROR FRENATE MONARCH PIERINE SATYRID SKIPPER SULPHUR TROILUS TUSSOCK VANESSA VICEROY ARTHEMIS CECROPIA CRESCENT GRAYLING HESPERID ITHOMIID WANDERER METALMARK
(— BREEDER) AURELIAN

BUTTERFLY FISH MOJARRA FLATFISH
BUTTERFLY WEED FLUXROOT MILKWEED WINDROOT
BUTTERMILK WHIG JOCOQUE SOURDOOK
(— AND WATER) BLAND
BUTTERSCOTCH TOFFY
BUTTERTREE MAHWA
BUTTERWORT BEANWEED ROTGRASS SHEEPWEED
BUTTERY BOTRY LARDER SPENCE BUTLERY SPICERY
BUTTOCKS ASS BUM CAN FUD HAM ARSE BUNS BUTT CULE DOCK DOUP DUFF LEND POOP PRAT SEAT TAIL TOBY CROUP FANNY NATES SLATS STERN TOUTE BEHIND BOTTOM BREECH CURPIN HEINIE HINDER CROUPON CRUPPER DRODDUM HURDIES KEISTER BACKSIDE DERRIERE NATIFORM POSTERIOR
(PRACTICE OF EXPOSING —) MOONING
(PREF.) NATI PYG(O)
(SUFF.) PROCTA PYGAL PYGE PYGIA(N) PYGOUS PYGUS
BUTTON BUD ZIP BOSS CHIN DOME HOOK KNOB KNOP SPUR TUFT BADGE CATCH GLIDE OLIVE PEARL PRILL BARREL BAUBLE BOUTON BUCKLE GLIDER SHINER TOGGLE TROCHE DEWDROP HORNTIP KNICKER NETSUKE PRESSEL REGULUS DOORBELL FASTENER OLIVETTE
BUTTONBUSH BUCKBRUSH SWAMPWOOD
BUTTONHOLE EYE LOOP SLIT
BUTTON SNAKEROOT LIATRIS SAWWORT
BUTTONWOOD COTONIER
BUTTRESS NOSE PIER PILE PROP SPUR STAY BRACE BRICK ALLETTE OUTCAST OUTSHOT SUPPORT TAMBOUR ABUTMENT
(— MEMBER) TIRE
BUTYL TETRYL
BUXOM MILD AMPLE JOLLY PLUMP PRONE SONSY BLITHE CRUMBY CRUMMY FLORID FODGEL HUMBLE PLIANT SONSIE BOWERLY BOUNCING FLEXIBLE OBEDIENT OBLIGING YIELDING JUNOESQUE
BUY CHAP COFF COUP GAIN HAVE SHOP SNIP TAKE BRIBE CLAIM TRADE ABEGGE MARKET RANSOM REDEEM SECURE ACQUIRE CHAFFER PURCHASE
(— BACK) REPRISE
(— OFF) APPEASE
(— UP STOCKS) COVER
BUYER CHAP AGENT CATER BEGGER EMPTOR PATRON VENDEE CHAPMAN SHOPPER ACHATOUR CUSTOMER PROSPECT
(— OF CLOTH) REDUBBER
BUYING ACATE ACHATE EMPTION
(— MANIA) ONIOMANIA
BUZ (FATHER OF —) NAHOR
(MOTHER OF —) MILCAH

BUZI
(SON OF —) EZEKIEL
BUZZ HUM BURR CALL DASH HISS
HUSS HUZZ RING WHIR FANCY
FLING PHONE RUMOR BUMBLE
NOTION WHISPER
BUZZARD AURA FOOL HAWK PERN
BUTEO GLADE GLEDE HARPY
STOOP BEETLE CURLEW PREYER
STUPID PUDDOCK PUTTOCK
VULTURE BROMVOEL
BUZZER BEE BELL ALARM HOWLER
SIGNAL WHIZZER
BY A P X AB AI OF TO AGO BYE
GIN PAR PER TIL ABUT ANON
INTO NEAR PAST TILL APART

ASIDE CLOSE FORBY BESIDE
TOWARD BESIDES THROUGH
(— AND BY) BELIVE BIMEBY
(— FAR) EASILY
(— HEART) PERQUEIR
(— HOOK OR CROOK) HABNAB
(— MEANS OF) PER MOYENANT
(— NO MEANS) NA
(— REASON OF THIS) HEREAT
(— STEALTH) STOWLINS
(— SURPRISE) ABACK
(— THE DAY) PD
(— THE ORDER OF) O
(— THE WAY) APROPOS
(— THIS TIME) ALREADY
(— WAY OF) VIA

(GONE —) AGO PAST
(NEAR —) GIN
(PREF.) PRETER
BY-BIDDER FUNK CAPPER PUFFER
BYBLIS (BROTHER OF —) CAUNUS
(FATHER OF —) MILETUS
(MOTHER OF —) IDOTHEA
BY-CHANNEL BAYOU BRANCH
BYCOKET ABACOT ABOCOCKET
BYGONE PAST YORE OLDEN
BYPAST FORMER ANCIENT
ELAPSED BACKWARD DEPARTED
FOREPAST PRETERIT
BYPASS JUMP SHUN AVOID
BURKE EVADE SHUNT CUTOFF
DETOUR CIRCUIT OUTFLANK

BYPATH LANE BYWAY
UNDERWALK
BY-PRODUCT SCRAP SHORTS
EFFLUVIUM MIDDLINGS
OUTGROWTH
BYRE SHIPPEN COWHOUSE
BYROAD BOREEN
BYWAY LANE PATH ALLEY BYPATH
BYWALK OUTWAY SIDEWAY
BYWORD ADAGE AXIOM MOTTO
BYNAME DIVERB PHRASE SAYING
NAYWORD PROVERB NICKNAME
REPROACH
BY-WORK PARERGON

C

C DO CEE DOH COCA CHARLIE HUNDRED

CAAMA FOX ASSE SILVER

CAB FLY KAB TAXI ARABA ARANA CABIN NODDY GHARRI CRAWLER HACKNEY SHOWFUL TAXICAB VETTURA COUPELET MOTORCAB
(HINDU —) JUDKA
(LOW-HUNG —) HERDIC
(2-PONY —) KOSONG
(4-WHEELED —) BOUNDE BOUNDER DROSHKY GROWLER

CABAL PLOT RING JUNTA PARTY BRIGUE CLIQUE SCHEME SECRET CHATTER CONSULT COUNCIL DISPUTE FACTION TALKING INTRIGUE CAMARILLA

CABALISTIC MYSTIC

CABARET CAFE TAVERN

CABASSOU XENURUS

CABBAGE CAB CHOU CRIB KALE WORT CROUT FILCH SAVOY STEAL STOCK PECHAY PILFER TAILOR BOWKAIL OXHEART PAKCHOI PALMITO PURLOIN BORECOLE COLEWORT CRUCIFER CULTIGEN DRUMHEAD KOHLRABI KERGUELEN
(STUFFED —) HOLISHKES
(PL.) WORTS

CABBAGE BARK ANGELIM ANGELIN

CABBAGE SOUP SHCHI STCHI SHTCHEE

CABBAGE STALK CASTOCK

CABDRIVER HACK MUSH CABBY CABMAN COCHER MUSHER COCHERO HACKMAN

CABIN BOX CAB COT DEN HUT CAVE CELL CREW CRIB SHED TILT BOOTH CHOZA COACH CUDDY FELZE HOVEL LODGE SHACK BOHAWN CABANA CASITA LITTER REFUGE SALOON SHANTY SHELTY WIGWAM BEDROOM BOUDOIR COTTAGE HUDDOCK MUDSILL
(— ON SHIP'S DECK) TEXAS ROUNDHOUSE
(DOUBLE —) SADDLEBAG
(RUSSIAN LOG —) IZBA

CABINET BOX BUHL CASE FILE SINK AMBRY BAHUT BOARD CABIN CHEST BAFFLE BUREAU CLOSET ICEBOX ALMIRAH BOUDOIR COMMODE CONSOLE COUNCIL ETAGERE FREEZER JUKEBOX WHATNOT CELLARET CUPBOARD MINISTRY SHOWCASE VARGUENO MONOCLEID
(FILING —) MORGUE

CABINETMAKER EBENISTE

CABLE GUY TOW BOOM COAX CORD FAST JUNK LINK ROPE STAY WIRE CABLET GANGER STRAND TETHER COAXIAL GUNLINE SKYLINE CATENARY HIGHLINE TELEGRAM UMBILICAL
(— WITH EYE AT EACH END) STRAP
(— WOUND) KECKLING
(CHAIN —) BOOM
(DERRICK —) BACKSTAY
(SPLICED —) SHOT
(SUSPENDED —) ROPEWAY

CABLE CAR TELFER TELPHER

CABLED RUDENTED

CABMAN IZVOZCHIK

CABOCHON CAB SHELL CARBUNCLE

CABOODLE KIT LOT CALABASH

CABOOSE CAB CAR VAN CRIB HACK BUGGY CRUMMY GALLEY PALACE BOUNCER COOKROOM DOGHOUSE

CABRILLA CONY GAPER GROUPER

CABSTAND HASARD HAZARD

CABUYA PITEIRA

CACAO BROMA COCOA ARRIBA COCKER CRIOLLO FORASTERO

CACHARI BODA

CACHE BURY HIDE DEPOT STASH STORE SCREEN CONCEAL DEPOSIT TREASURE

CACHET SEAL STAMP WAFER ESSENCE KONSEAL

CACIQUE BUNYAH CASSICAN HANGNEST

CACKEREL MENDOLE

CACKLE CANK CONK CLACK LAUGH BABBLE GABBLE GAGGLE GIGGLE GOSSIP KECKLE TITTER CHACKLE CHATTER SNICKER TWADDLE LAUGHTER

CACKLING GOOSE GREASER

CACOMISTLE CIVET ARCTOID RINGTAIL BASSARISK

CACOON SEGRA SEQUA

CACOPHONOUS HARSH RAUCOUS JANGLING STRIDENT

CACTUS BLEO DILDO NOPAL BAVOSO CARDON CEREUS CHAUTE CHENDE CHINOA CHOLLA COCHAL MESCAL PEYOTE PEYOTL TASAJO AIRAMPO BISAGRE BISNAGA SAGUARO ALICOCHE CHICHIPE PITAHAYA XEROPHIL
(— FRUIT) MUYUSA

CAD CUR BOOR CHUM HEEL CHURL SWEEP BRAKJE MUCKER RASCAL ROTTER BOUNDER DASTARD BLIGHTER ASSISTANT

CADASTRAL UNIT YOKE

CADAVER BODY STIFF CORPSE CARCASS SUBJECT SKELETON

CADAVEROUS PALE GAUNT LIVID PALLID GHASTLY HAGGARD

CADDIE NACKET

CADDIS FLY DUN CADEW SEDGE CADBIT

CADDISWORM PIPER

CADDO ADAI TEXAS EYEISH HAINAI KICHAI HASINAI

CADE LAMB SOCK

CADENAS NEF

CADENCE BEAT FALL IAMB LILT PACE TONE CLOSE METER METRE SOUND SWING THROB DACTYL IAMBUS JINGLE RHYTHM BACCHIC ANAPAEST CLAUSULA MOVEMENT MEDIATION

CADENZA MELISMA BARIOLAGE

CADET SON DODO GOAT PLEBE YOUTH EMBRYO JUNIOR SERGEANT

CADGE BEG BOT BUM TIE BIND HAWK CARRY MOOCH PEDDLE SPONGE SCROUNGE

CADGER BOT BUM DEALER HAWKER CARRIER PACKMAN SPONGER HUCKSTER SCAMBLER

CADGY KEDGY MERRY WANTON AMOROUS LUSTFUL CHEERFUL MIRTHFUL

CADMUS (DAUGHTER OF —) INO AGAVE SEMELE AUTONOE
(FATHER OF —) AGENOR
(MOTHER OF —) TELEPHASSA
(SISTER OF —) EUROPA
(SON OF —) POLYDORUS
(WIFE OF —) HARMONIA

CADRE CORE FRAME

CADUCEUS WAND STAFF SCEPTER SCEPTRE KERYKEION

CAECUM TYPHLON
(PREF.) ILEO TYPHL(O)

CAESURA REST STOP BREAK PAUSE INTERVAL DIAERESIS

CAFE BARROOM CABARET ESTAMINET
(— AU LAIT) ALESAN
(ROADSIDE —) BUVETTE

CAFE CREME SUEDE

CAFETERIA AUTOMAT

CAFFEINE THEIN THEINE

CAGAYAN IBANAG

CAGE BOX CAR GIG MEW PEN COOP CORF CRIB GOAL BRAKE CAVEA GRATE HUTCH AVIARY BASKET BUCKET CHAPEL ENCAGE FLIGHT PRISON CHANTRY CONFINE ENCLOSE LANTERN SHELTER TUMBREL TUMBRIL CARRIAGE ELEVATOR IMPRISON LAVARIUM RETAINER SCAFFOLD STRAINER
(— FOR HAWKS) MEW
(— FOR HENS) CAVEY CAVIE
(— OF MINE SHAFT) GIG
(— OF TRAM) CABIN
(BIRD —) AVIARY PINJRA VOLARY BIRDCAGE
(FIRE —) CRESSET
(LOBSTER —) CORF CREEL

CAGED PENT CAPTIVE

CAGER ONSETTER

CAGEY CAGY WARY COONY

CAGMAG KEGMEG

CAGOT AGOTE

CAHITA YAQUI

CAHOT PITCHHOLE

CAIMAN CAYMAN JACARE ALLIGATOR

CAIN (BROTHER OF —) ABEL SETH
(FATHER OF —) ADAM
(MOTHER OF —) EVE
(SON OF —) ENOCH

CAINAN (FATHER OF —) ENOS ARPHAXAD
(SON OF —) SALA MAHALALEEL

CAINGANG COROADO AWEIKOMA CORONADO

CAIRN MAN PIKE MOUND RAISE GALGAL CATSTONE STONEMAN

CAIRNGORM MORION SMOKESTONE

CAISSON BOX PONT CAMEL CHEST WAGON COFFER PONTON SAUCER CAMAILE CHAMBER LACUNAR PONTOON
(— DISEASE) BENDS

CAITIFF BASE MEAN VILE COWARD WICKED CAPTIVE COWARDLY PRISONER WRETCHED

CAJOLE COG CON JIG COAX FLAM FLUM PALP WORD CARNY CHEAT CURRY DECOY FRAIK INGLE JOLLY TEASE BEFLUM CARNEY DELUDE DIDDLE ENTICE FRAISE HUMBUG WHILLY BEGUILE BEHONEY CUITTLE FLATTER PALAVER SOOTHER TWEEDLE WHEEDLE BLANDISH

CAJOLERY FRAIK SOOTH TAFFY WILES BUTTER FRAISE WHILLY BLARNEY DAUBERY FLATTERY

CAKE BAR BUN NUT WIG BAKE BALL FLAE FOOL LUMP MASS MOLE PUFF TART ARVAL BATTY BLOCK BOXTY COOKY CRUST CUPID FADGE KYAAK SCONE SHIVE TORTE WAFER WEDGE BARKLE CIMBAL COOKIE DAMPER ECLAIR GATEAU HALLAH HARDEN KICHEL KUCHEN NACKET PARKIN PASTRY POPLIN SIMNEL TABLET WASTEL ASHCAKE BANBURY BANNOCK BRIOCHE BROWNIE CAKETTE CARAWAY CROZZLE CRUMPET CUPCAKE FAIRING GALETTE HOECAKE MANCHET NUTCAKE OATCAKE PANCAKE PLASTER POPADAM CHRIMSEL

CLAPCAKE KUGELHOF MADELINE MARZIPAN SEEDCAKE SOLIDIFY SOULCAKE TORTILLA TURNPIKE
(— OF CLAY) PLATTEN
(— OF COCONUT PULP) POONAC
(— OF MEAL) DODGER
(— OF RUBBER) BISCUIT
(ALMOND —) RATAFIA
(CREOLE RICE —) CALA
(FANCY —) SUNKET
(FLAT —) PLATE BUNUELO GALETTE PLACENT CHRIMSEL
(FOURTH PART OF —) FARL FARLE
(FRIED —) WONDER CRULLER DOUGHNUT
(GINGER —) BOLIVAR
(GRIDDLE —) LATKE FLIPPER FRITTER FLAPJACK
(HOLIDAY —) SIMNEL
(HONEY —) LEKACH
(LAMB AND WHEAT —) KIBBE KIBBEH
(LEAVENED —) BAP
(NEW YEAR'S —) HAGMENA HOGMANAY
(OATEN —) BANNOCK
(OIL —) GRIT POONAC
(PLUM —) SIMNEL
(POTATO —) FADGE
(PRESS —) CACHAZA
(RUM —) BABA
(SEED —) WIG SEEDCAKE
(TEA —) LUNN SCONE PIKELET
(THIN —) WAFER JUMBLE BANNOCK TORTILLA
(UNLEAVENED —) CHAPATI CHAPATTI
(YEAST —) KOJI
(PL.) AMSATH COLYBA
CAKED CLIT
CAKE PULLER KNOCKER
CAKES AND ALE (AUTHOR OF —) MAUGHAM
(CHARACTER IN —) AMY KEAR KEMP ALROY ROSIE EDWARD GEORGE ASHENDEN TRAFFORD DRIFFIELD
CALABA BIRMA GALBA
CALABASH GOURD CURUBA JICARA
CALABASH TREE HIGUERO
CALABOOSE JUG BRIG JAIL STIR POKEY PRISON CABOOSE BASTILLE HOOSEGOW
CALABUR TREE CAPULI CAPULIN SILKWOOD
CALAIS (BROTHER OF —) ZETES
(FATHER OF —) BOREAS
(MOTHER OF —) ORITHYIA
CALAMANCO MANKIE
CALAMINE CADMIA
CALAMITOUS BAD SAD DIRE EVIL BLACK FATAL BITTER DISMAL TRAGIC WOEFUL ADVERSE BALEFUL DIREFUL HAPLESS RUINOUS UNHAPPY UNLUCKY GRIEVOUS TRAGICAL WRETCHED
CALAMITY ILL WOE BLOW DOOM EVIL RUIN RUTH SLAP HYDRA STORM WRACK MISERY ONCOME PLAGUE SORROW EXTREME SCOURGE ACCIDENT DISASTER DISTRESS FATALITY

JUDGMENT MISCHIEF
CALAMONDIN ORANGE CALAMANSI
CALAMUS PEN CANE REED QUILL ACORUS RATTAN ROTANG
CALANGAY ABACAY COCKATOO
CALANTHA (FATHER OF —) AMYCLAS
CALASH CALESA GALECHE
CALCANEUM FIBULARE HYPOTARSUS
CALCAR OVEN SPUR FURNACE CALCARIUM PREHALLUX
CALCEOLARIA FAGELIA IONIDIUM
CALCIFY CRETIFY
CALCINING BURNING
CALCINO MUSCADINE
CALCITE APHRITE CALCSPAR ALABASTER ARAGONITE ARGENTINE HISLOPITE
CALCIUM LIME
CALCIUM CARBONATE WHITING DRIPSTONE
CALCULATE AIM SUM CALK CAST PLAN RATE TELL COUNT FRAME THINK CIPHER DESIGN EXPECT FIGURE NUMBER RECKON ACCOUNT AVERAGE CALLATE COMPUTE PREPARE CONSIDER ESTIMATE FORECAST
(— BY ASTROLOGY) ERECT
CALCULATED COLD MEASURED
CALCULATING COLD WISE BRITTLE CAUTIOUS
CALCULATION CARE SHARE CALCUL ACCOUNT CAUTION WORKING CALCULUS FORECAST HINDCAST PRUDENCE
(PL.) FIGURES
CALCULATOR TABLE ABACUS ABACIST SOROBAN CALCULER COMPUTER ISOGRAPH
CALCULUS STONE UROLITH ANALYSIS
(PREF.) LITH(O)
(SUFF.) LITE LITH(IC) LITIC
CALDRON POT RED VAT LEAD ALFET BOILER KELDER KETTLE TRIPOD VESSEL CALDERA CAULDRON
CALEB (DAUGHTER OF —) ACHSAH
(FATHER OF —) HEZRON JEPHUNNEH
(SON OF —) HUR
CALENDAR ORDO DIARY FASTI ALMANAC CALENDS JOURNAL KALENDS REGISTER SCHEDULE
(— OF MARTYRS) MENOLOGY
(PL.) FASTI
CALENDER TABBY SCHREINER
CALENDERER CANROYER SMOOTHER
CALENDS K KAL
CALF CA BOB BOX BOY LEG BOSS BUSS DOLT VEAL VEAU BOBBY BOSSY BUNCH DOGIE MOGGY PODDY RANNY SOOKY YOUTH MUSCLE VEALER WEANER BULCHIN FATLING SLEEPER CALFLING
(LIKE A —) VITULINE
(PREMATURE —) SLINK

(UNBRANDED —) LONGEAR SLEEPER
(YEARLING —) BUD DAIRT
(YOUNG —) DEACON
(PL.) CAURE
CALF'S-FOOT JELLY SULZE FISNOGA
CALFSKIN OOZE COROVA VELLUM GRASSER TULCHAN VEALSKIN
CALIBER BORE RANK DEGREE TALENT ABILITY BREADTH COMPASS QUALITY CAPACITY DIAMETER MAGNITUDE
(HIGH —) STATURE
CALIBRATED BRIX BEAUME BALLING
CALICHE CALCRETE TEPETATE NITRATINE
CALICO BLAY PINTO SALLO CHINTZ SALLOO CROYDON SPOTTED DUNGAREE GOLDFISH
CALICO ASTER WISEWEED
CALICOBACK STINKBUG
CALICO BASS CRAPPIE BACHELOR
CALICUT KOZHIKODE

CALIFORNIA

CAPITAL: SACRAMENTO
COLLEGE: MILLS POMONA WHITTIER
COUNTY: INYO KERN MONO NAPA YOLO YUBA MARIN MODOC COLUSA LASSEN MERCED PLACER PLUMAS SHASTA SOLANO SONOMA SUTTER TEHAMA TULARE ALAMEDA VENTURA SISKIYOU CALAVERAS
DESERT: MOJAVE COLORADO
INDIAN: HUPA POMO YANA YUKI KAROK MAIDU MIWOK WAPPO WIYOT YUROK PATWIN SHASTA TOLOWA YOKUTS CHUMASH LUISENO SALINAN SERRANO DIEGUENO
LAKE: MONO SODA EAGLE OWENS TAHOE SALTON TULARE ALMANOR BERRYESSA
MOUNTAIN: MUIR LASSEN SHASTA WHITNEY
NAME: ELDORADO
PARK: LASSEN SEQUOIA YOSEMITE
PRESIDENT: NIXON
PRISON: ALCATRAZ
RIVER: EEL MAD PIT KERN OWENS PUTAH STONY FEATHER KLAMATH RUBICON TRINITY SACRAMENTO
STATE BIRD: QUAIL
STATE FLOWER: POPPY
STATE NICKNAME: GOLDEN
STATE TREE: REDWOOD
TOWN: LODI AZUSA CHICO CHINO INDIO BLYTHE CARMEL COVINA EUREKA FRESNO LOMPOC MERCED OXNARD POMONA SONOMA TULARE ALAMEDA BURBANK GARDENA NEEDLES SALINAS VALLEJO VISALIA ALTADENA BERKELEY PASADENA REDLANDS CUCAMONGA

UNIVERSITY: USC UCLA CALTECH STANFORD

CALIPER JENNY ODDLEGS CALIPERS
CALIPH ABU ALI BEKR IMAM OMAR CALIF OTHMAN ABBASID UMAYYAD
CALISTA (HUSBAND OF —) ALTAMONT CLEANDER
(LOVER OF —) LOTHARIO LYSANDER
CALISTO, LA (CHARACTER IN —) PAN JOVE JUNO DIANA LYCAON CALISTO MERCURY ENDYMION
(COMPOSER OF —) CAVALLI
CALIXTINE UTRAQUIST
CALK (ALSO SEE CAULK) JAG NAP PAY COPY CORK FILL STOP CAULK CLOSE HORSE ROUGH CAREEN CALTROP CHINTZE OCCLUDE SILENCE
CALKING OAKUM
CALL HO KA BAN BID CRY CUP DUB HOY SAY SEE CITE COOP HAIL JERK NAME NOTE PAGE PIST ROUP STOP TERM TOOT YELL BEDUB CHUCK CLAIM CLEPE CLOCK ELECT HALLO HIGHT HOLLA PHONE ROUSE SHOUT SPEAK STYLE UTTER VISIT VOUCH WAKEN YODEL ACCUSE APPEAL AROUSE BECALL CHANGE DEMAND HALLOA HALLOO INVITE INVOKE MUSTER QUETHE SUMMON TEKIAH TERUAH YELPER ACCLAIM ADDRESS APPOINT BEHIGHT BETITLE COLLECT COMMAND CONVENE CONVOKE DECLARE ENTITLE IMPEACH INQUIRE INSTYLE MOUNTEE WHISTLE ANNOUNCE APPELATE ASSEMBLE NOMINATE PROCLAIM VOCATION
(— A BET) STAY
(— ALOUD) COUNT
(— BACK) RECALL REVOKE
(— COARSELY) ROUP ROUP
(— DOWN) BRAWL DEVOCATE IMPRECATE
(— FOR) CRY TAKE CLAIM EXACT DEMAND DESIRE COLLECT SOLICIT
(— FOR HELP) SOS
(— FOR HOGS) SOOK SOOEY
(— FOR PARLEY) CHAMADE
(— FORTH) STIR EVOKE ELICIT INDUCE INVOKE ATTRACT PROVOKE SUGGEST
(— HOUNDS) LIFT
(— IN ANGER) GREET
(— IN CHILDRENS' GAMES) FAN FEN FIN VENTS
(— IN MARBLES) DUBS
(— IN WHIST) ABUNDANCE
(— INTO QUESTION) IMPUGN OPPUGN
(— LOUDLY) CRY HAIL ACCLAIM
(— MAN BY MAN) ARRAY
(— ON TELEPHONE) BUZZ
(— OUT) HAIL LURE ASCRY EVOKE

HALLO GOLLAR GOLLER HOLLER HULLOO
(— TO ACCOUNT) AREASON CONTROL
(— TO ARMS) ALARM ALARUM RAPPEL
(— TO BELLBOY) FRONT
(— TO CAT) CHEET
(— TO COURT) ARRAIGN
(— TO COWS) PROO SOOK COBOSS SOOKIE
(— TO FOOD) SOSS
(— TO HORSE) HIE HUP WAY PROO
(— TO MIND) CITE MING RECORD BETHINK RECOLLECT
(— TO PRAYER) ADAN AZAN
(— TO READINESS) ALERT
(— TO SPARROW) PHIP PHIPPE
(— TO WITNESS) APPEAL
(— UPON) ASK SEE CITE GREDE HALSE BECALL DEPOSE ENGAGE SUMMON ADDRESS BESEECH IMPLORE
(BIRD'S —) WEET
(BOATSWAIN'S —) WINDING
(BRIDGE —) DOUBLE
(BUGLE —) POST HALLALI STABLES
(CLOSE —) TOUCH
(DUCK —) SQUAWKER
(FRIENDLY —) CEILIDH
(HUNTING —) MOT RECHATE RECHEAT
(MORNING —) MATIN
(NAUTICAL —) AHOY
(SHEPHERD'S —) OVEY
(SPORTSMAN'S —) HOICKS YOICKS HALLALI
(SQUARE DANCE —) GEE HAW
(STAGE TRUMPET —) SENNET SINNET
(TRUMPET —) BERLOQUE

CALLA ARUM LILY DRAGON MAYFLOWER
CALLBOY FRONT CALLER HALLBOY
CALLED NEMPT
CALLER FLOORMAN
CALLIGRAPHER PENMAN WRITER COPYIST ENGROSSER
CALLIGRAPHY LETTERING CHIROGRAPHY
CALLING ART JOB WAY CALL HAIL RANK TRADE CAREER METIER NAMING OUTCRY MISSION MYSTERY PURSUIT STATION SUMMONS WARNING BUSINESS FUNCTION POSITION SHOUTING VOCATION
CALLIOPE (FATHER OF —) ZEUS JUPITER
(MOTHER OF —) MNEMOSYNE
(SON OF —) ORPHEUS
CALLIRRHOE (FATHER OF —) OCEANUS
(HUSBAND OF —) TROS ALCMAEON
(SON OF —) ILUS GANYMEDE ASSARACUS
CALLISTO (FATHER OF —) LYCAON
(SON OF —) ARCAS
CALLITHRIX HAPALE JACCHUS
CALLOP YELLOWBELLY
CALLOSAL TRABAL
CALLOSITY SEG CALLUS SITFAST TYLOSIS CHESTNUT

CALLOUS HARD HORNY TOUGH BRAWNY OBTUSE SEARED TORPID WAUKIT DEDOLENT OBDURATE
CALLOUSED BRAWNY
CALLOW BALD BARE CRUDE GREEN SQUAB JEJUNE MARSHY IMMATURE UNFORMED YOUTHFUL
CALLUS SEG POROMA TYLOMA CALLOUS
(PREF.) PORA PORO
CALM LAY LEE COOL DILL EASY EVEN FAIR FLAT HUSH LOWN LULL MEES MILD REST SOFT STAY ABATE ALLAY CHARM LEVEL LITHE LOUND MEASE PEACE QUELL QUIET SLEEK SMOLT SOBER STILL STOIC STREW APLOMB DEFUSE DOCILE GENTLE GLASSY IRENIC PACIFY PLACID SEDATE SERENE SETTLE SILENT SLATCH SLIGHT SMOOTH SOOTHE STEADY APPEASE ASSUAGE CALMATO COMPOSE GLACIAL HALCYON MOLLIFY PACIFIC PATIENT PLACATE QUALIFY QUIETEN RESTFUL UNMOVED CALMNESS COMPOSED DECOROUS MODERATE PEACEFUL PLACABLE RESTRAIN SERENITY TRANQUIL UNRUFFLE POSSESSED PHILOSOPHIC
(INTERNAL —) HARMONY
(NOT —) BOISTEROUS
CALMLY COOLY COOLLY STILLY
CALMNESS CALM LULL POISE PHLEGM REPOSE SERENE TEMPER ATARAXY COOLNESS SERENITY SOBRIETY STILLNESS
CALNO KULLANI
CALOMEL TURPETH
CALORIC THERMOGEN
CALORIE THERM THERME
CALQUE LOANSHIFT
CALTROP CROWTOE GALTRAP BULLHEAD CROWFOOT
CALUMNIATE BLOT SLUR TEEN BELIE LIBEL ACCUSE ATTACK BEFOUL DEFAME MALIGN REVILE VILIFY ASPERSE BLACKEN SLANDER TRADUCE
CALUMNIATION SATIRE ASPERSION
CALUMNY SLUR DEPRAVE OBLOQUY ASPERSION
CALVA CALOTTE SINCIPUT
CALVARIA SKULLCAP
CALVARY GOLGOTHA
CALVE FRESHEN
CALVINIST GENEVAN GOMARIAN
CALYCE (FATHER OF —) AEOLUS
(MOTHER OF —) ENARETE
(SON OF —) ENDYMION
CALYCULUS CELL CALYX
CALYPTER ALULA SQUAMA
CALYPTRA CAP VEIL EPIGONIUM
CALYX CUP POP HULL HUSK LEAF CULOT SEPAL SHUCK
(PREF.) CALYC(I)(O)
CAM COG AWRY LOBE TRIG ASKEW CATCH SNAIL WIPER LIFTER TAPPET CROOKED TRIPPET KNOCKOFF PERVERSE ROLLBACK

CAMACHILE INGA HUAMUCHIL
CAMAGON MABOLO
CAMAS LOBELIA
CAMBER SET ARCH SWEEP ROUNDUP CROSSFALL

CAMBODIA
CAPE: SAMIT
CAPITAL: PNOMPENH PHNOMPENH
COIN: RIEL PUTTAN PIASTER
GULF: SIAM
LAKE: TONLESAP
MOUNTAIN: PAN AURAL
MOUNTAINS: DANGREK CARDAMOM ELEPHANT
NAME: CAMBOJA CAMBODGE KAMPUCHEA
NATIVE: CHAM KHMER
RIVER: SAN SEN BASSAC MEKONG PORONG SREPOK SEKHONG TONLESAP
RUINS: ANGKORWAT
TOWN: REAM TAKEO KAMPOT KRATIE PURSAT KOHNIEH KRACHEH ROVIENG SAMRONG PNOMPENH SISOPHON
WEIGHT: MACE TAEL

CAMBRIC BATISTE PERCALE
CAMBUSCAN (SON OF —) CANACE CAMBALLO ALGARSIFE
CAME BAND CALM
CAMEL COLT OONT DELOUL DROMED FENDER HAGEEN MEHARI CAISSON TYLOPOD BACTRIAN RUMINANT DROMEDARY
CAMEL GRASS SCHOENANTH
CAMELLIA JAPONICA
CAMEL LIP CHILOMA
CAMELOPARD GIRAFFE
CAMEO GEM GAMAHE CAMAIEU CARVING PHALERA RELIEVO ANAGLYPH
CAMERA KINO KODAK CHAMBER MINICAM PANORAM ENLARGER MINIATURE VERASCOPE
(— TUBE) VIDICON
(PART OF —) LUG BODY DOOR KNOB LENS LOCK CRANK DRIVE FOCUS LATCH SCALE STRAP TIMER BUTTON SENSOR SOCKET WINDOW ADVANCE BELLOWS LANYARD RELEASE SHUTTER PHOTOCELL TRANSDUCER VIEWFINDER
CAMERAMAN LENSMAN
CAMEROON (CAPITAL OF —) YAOUNDE
(RIVER OF —) DJA NYONG SANAGA
(TOWN OF —) EDEA POLI YOKO BAFIA KRIBI DOUALA
CAMILLA (FATHER OF —) METABUS
(SLAYER OF —) ARUNS
CAMILLE (AUTHOR OF —) DUMAS
(CHARACTER IN —) DUVAL ARMAND NANINE CAMILLE GAUTIER PRUDENCE VARVILLE
CAMIRUS (FATHER OF —) CERCAPHUS
(MOTHER OF —) CYDIPPE
CAMISOLE WAISTCOAT

CAMLET MOHAIR PARAGON BARRACAN
CAMOMILE OXEYE MORGAN MAYWEED
CAMOUFLAGE FAKE HIDE DAZZLE MUFFLE SCREEN CONCEAL DISGUISE
CAMOUFLET STIFLER
CAMP TAN PEST TENT DOUAR ETAPE HORDE SIEGE TABOR CASTLE LAAGER SUGARY BIVOUAC HUTMENT LASHKAR LODGING MAHALLA PALANKA ZAREEBA QUARTERS
(— OUT) MAROON OUTLIE
(HOBO —) JUNGLE
(LUMBER —) CHANTIER
(PREF.) CASTRA
(SUFF.) CASTER CESTER CHESTER
CAMPA ANDA ANDI ANTI
CAMPAIGN BLITZ DRIVE PLAIN WHOOP CANVASS CRUSADE JOURNEY SERVICE SOLICIT WARFARE
(STUNT —) JIHAD
CAMPANA GUTTA
CAMPANERO COTINGA ARAPUNGA BELLBIRD COTINGID
CAMPANILE TOWER BELFRY CLOCHER STEEPLE CARILLON
CAMPANULA BELLWORT
CAMPESTRAL AGRARIAN
CAMPHOL BORNEOL
CAMPHOR ASARONE BORNEOL MENTHOL
(ANISE —) ANETHOLE
CAMPHOR TREE KADUR KAPOR
CAMPING BIVOUAC
CAMPION ROBIN COWBELL
CAMPUS GATE QUAD YARD FIELD
CAN CUP JUG MAY MOW POT TIN ABLE FIRE JAIL BILLY CADDY COULD ESHIN OILER SHALL SKILL BOTTLE VESSEL ABILITY BOMBARD CANIKIN CAPABLE CREAMER DISMISS GROWLER PIPETTE BILLYCAN CONSERVE PRESERVE
(— FOR LIQUOR) JACK
(— ON WHEELS) DANDY
(BULGED —) SWELL FLIPPER
(DEFECTIVE —) SPRINGER
(LEAKY —) LEAKER
(MILK —) CHURN
(TIN —) DESTROYER
(TRASH —) DUSTBIN
(PREF.) SCYPH(I)(O)
CANAAN (FATHER OF —) HAM
CANAANITE ARKITE HIVITE AMORITE HIVVITE JEBUSITE
CANACE (BROTHER OF —) MACAREUS
(FATHER OF —) AEOLUS
(MOTHER OF —) ENARETE
(SON OF —) TRIOPAS

CANADA
(ALSO SEE SPECIFIC PROVINCES)
BAY: JAMES HUDSON UNGAVA GEORGIAN
CAPITAL: OTTAWA
INDIAN: CREE COMOX HAIDA NISKA SARSI STALO MICMAC

NAHANE NOOTKA SARCEE
SEKANE CARRIER NANAIMO
SHUSWAP SONGISH TAHLTAN
ALGONKIN COWICHAN
LILLOOET MALECITE SQUAMISH
TSATTINE
ISLAND: READ BANKS BYLOT
COATS DEVON SABLE BAFFIN
MANSEL VICTORIA ANTICOSTI
VANCOUVER
ISLANDS: PARRY BELCHER
BATHURST MAGDALEN
LAKE: BEAR CREE GARRY RAINY
SLAVE LOUISE SIMCOE ABITIBI
DUBAWNT NIPIGON KOOTENAY
OKANAGAN NIPISSING
MEASURE: MINOT PERCH ARPENT
CHAINON
MOUNTAIN: LOGAN ROYAL
ROBSON TREMBLANT
MOUNTAIN RANGE: SKEENA
CARIBOO PEMBINA STELIAS
COLUMBIA LAURENTIAN
NATIVE: CANUCK
PARK: YOHO BANFF ACADIA
JASPER
PENINSULA: GASPE BOOTHIA
MELVILLE
PROVINCE: BC NB NS MAN ONT
PEI QUE ALTA SASK QUEBEC
ALBERTA ONTARIO MANITOBA
NOVASCOTIA NEWBRUNSWICK
NEWFOUNDLAND
SASKATCHEWAN
PROVINCIAL CAPITAL: QUEBEC
REGINA STJOHN HALIFAX
TORONTO EDMONTON
VICTORIA WINNIPEG
CHARLOTTETOWN
RIVER: HAY RED BACK PEEL PEACE
SLAVE YUKON FRASER NELSON
OTTAWA SKEENA THELON
KOKOSAK PEMBINA PETAWAWA
SAGUENAY MACKENZIE
RICHELIEU
STRAIT: CABOT DEASE HECATE
HUDSON GEORGIA
SYMBOL: MAPLELEAF
TERRITORY: YUKON
TOWN: HULL BANFF LAVAL
GUELPH OSHAWA REGINA
SARNIA CALGARY HALIFAX
MONCTON NANAIMO SUDBURY
TORONTO WELLAND WINDSOR
KINGSTON MONTREAL
VICTORIA WINNIPEG
SASKATOON VANCOUVER
UNIVERSITY: MCGILL DALHOUSIE
WATERFALL: DELLA PANTHER
TAKAKKAW

CANADA BLUEBERRY SOURTOP
CANADA GOOSE HONKER
BUSTARD OUTARDE
CANADA JAY MEATBIRD
MOOSEBIRD
CANADA LYNX PISHU LUCIVEE
CANADA PLUM CHENEY
CANADA VIOLET JUNEFLOWER
CANADIAN CANUCK
CANAILLE MOB FLOUR RABBLE
DOGGERY RIFFRAFF
CANAL CUT CANO DUCT LODE

PIPE SHAT TUBE BAYOU DITCH
DRAIN FOSSA GRAFF KLONG
SCALA ZANJA ESTERO GROOVE
KENNEL STRAIT TRENCH VAGINA
ACEQUIA APHODUS CHANNEL
CONDUIT FOREBAY RACEWAY
SHIPWAY TOWPATH AQUEDUCT
EMISSARY IRRIGANT MILLRACE
PROSODUS VOLKMANN
(— LABORER) NAVIGATOR
(ALIMENTARY —) GUT ENTERON
INTESTINE
(ANATOMICAL —) SCALA MEATUS
(CARINAL —) LACUNA
(PREF.) MEATO
CANARD DUCK HOAX RUMOR
GRAPEVINE
CANARY DICKY FRILL SERIN
LIZARD ROLLER CAYENNE
CHOPPER JONQUIL SQUEALER
(— HYBRID) MULE

CANARY ISLAND
CAPITAL: SANTACRUZ
ISLAND: ROCA CLARA FERRO
LOBOS PALMA ROCCA GOMERA
HIERRO INFERNO GRACIOSA
TENERIFE LANZAROTE
MEASURE: FANEGADA
MOUNTAIN: TEYDE LACRUZ
ELCUMBRE TENERIFE
PROVINCE: LASPALMAS
TOWN: LAGUNA ARRECIFE
VALVERDE
VOLCANO: TENEGUIA

CANARY MOSS CORKIR
CANASTA SAMBA BOLIVIA
CANCEL BLOT DASH DELE OMIT
UNDO VENT WIPE ABORT ADEEM
ANNUL BELAY CROSS ERASE
QUASH REMIT SCORE SCRUB
DELETE EFFACE KILLER RECALL
REMOVE REVOKE STROKE
ABOLISH DESTROY EXPUNGE
NULLIFY RESCIND RETRACT
SCRATCH SUBLATE UNWRITE
ABROGATE OVERRIDE
OBLITERATE
CANCELED OFF
CANCELER BUMPER STAMPER
CANCELLATION GRID CANCEL
REVOKE RECISION SURRENDER
CANCER WOLF KASHYAPA
SCIRRHUS
(PREF.) CARCIN(O)
CANCERWORT FLUELLIN
CANDAREEN FAN FEN
CANDELABRUM PHAROS
MENORAH GIRANDOLE
CANDID FAIR JUST OPEN PURE
BLUNT CLEAR FRANK NAIVE
PLAIN HONEST ARTLESS
JANNOCK SINCERE EVENDOWN
INNOCENT SPLENDID STRAIGHT
PLAINSPOKEN
CANDIDA (AUTHOR OF —) SHAW
(CHARACTER IN —) MORELL
CANDIDA MARCHBANKS
CANDIDATE AGREGE LEGACY
ESQUIRE NOMINEE ASPIRANT
GRADUAND ORDINAND
PROSPECT

(DOCTORAL —) ABD
CANDIDE (AUTHOR OF —) VOLTAIRE
(CHARACTER IN —) CACAMBO
CANDIDE PANGLOSS PAQUETTE
CUNEGONDE
CANDIDIASIS MONILIASIS
CANDIED GLACE
CANDLE DIP WAX GLIM SIZE SLUT
LIGHT SPERM TAPER TOLLY
TORCH BOUGIE CIERGE MORTAR
PLANET SHAMUS SLUSHY
TALLOW TORTIS CANDELA
PERCHER PRICKET SHAMMES
AMANDINE
(IMITATION —) JUDAS
(SQUARE —) QUARRIER
CANDLEFISH SKIL EULACHON
HOOLAKIN OOLACHAN SKILFISH
SABLEFISH
CANDLEHOLDER SPIDER
CANDLEMAKER CHANDLER
TALLOWER
CANDLEMAS TERM MARYMASS
CANDLENUT AMA LAMA BIABO
KUKUI IGUAPE KEMIRI LUMBANG
ABURAGIRI
CANDLESNUFFER DOUTER
CANDLESTAND TORCHERE
CANDLESTICK BUGIA DYKER
JESSE STICK CRUSIE LAMPAD
MORTAR SCONCE PASCHAL
PRICKET CHANDLER DICERION
FLAMBEAU STANDARD TORCHERE
TRIKERION
CANDLEWICK MATCH SNAST
SHROUD
(CHARRED PART OF —) SNOT
SNUFF SNOTTING
CANDLEWOOD CIRIO OCOTILLO
TABANUCO
CANDOR PURITY FAIRNESS
KINDNESS INTEGRITY SIMPLICITY
CANDY DROP DUMP KISS PIPE
ROCK CREAM CRISP DULCE
FUDGE GLACE GUNDY LOLLY
NABIT SPICE SQUIB SWEET TAFFY
BONBON COMFIT HUMBUG
NOGADA NOUGAT PATTIE PENIDE
BRITTLE CANDIEL CARAMEL
CONGEAL FLATTER FONDATE
GUMDROP SWEETEN SWEETIE
TORRONE ALPHENIC LOLLIPOP
STICKJAW PEPPERMINT
(PL.) CUTS CONFETTI
CANDYTUFT CRUCIFER
(PL.) IBERIS
CANE ROD BEAT CRAB DART FLOG
PIPE REED STEM TUBE WAND
WHIP BIRCH GIBBY GUNDY LANCE
STAFF STICK SWISH TOLLY
WADDY BAMBOO JAMBEE KEBBIE
PUNISH RATTAN CALAMUS
HICKORY KIPPEEN MALACCA
SCOURGE STADDLE TICKLER
WHANGEE GIBSTAFF
(BLACK —) JAPAN
(END OF —) FRAZE
(SPLIT —) CANEWORK
CANELLA CINNAMON WHITEWOOD
CANELO CIXO
CANESCENT HOARY
CANE TREE BEJUCO
CANFIELD KLONDIKE

CANICULA SIRIUS
CANINE CUR DOG FOX PUP FISC
TUSH WOLF DOGLY DOGLIKE
LANIARY EYETOOTH
CANING RATTAN BIRCHING
CANISTEL TIES EGGFRUIT
CANNA ACHIRA GOLDBIRD
CANNABIS BHANG GANJA GUAZA
GUNJA HEMPWORT
(— TOPS) TAKROURI
CANNEL BONE FURCULE
CANNEL COAL AMPELITE
CANNER CANMAN TINNER
CANNIBAL WINDIGO LESTRIGON
THYESTEAN
CANNON BIT EAR GUN BASE SHOT
TUBE ASPIC CAROM CRACK
MOYEN PIECE SACRE SACRI
SAKER SHANK SLING THIEF
BARKER BICORN CURTAL FALCON
FOWLER JINGAL LICORN MORTAR
POTGUN BASTARD BOMBARD
BULLDOG CHAMBER HANDGUN
LOMBARD MOYENNE ROBINET
SERPENT STINGER GUNLOCK
BASILISK CULVERIN HOWITZER
MURDERER OERLIKON ORDNANCE
SPITFIRE CARAMBOLE
CARRONADE ZUMBOORUK
(— OF BELL) EAR
(CARRIAGE OF —) NADRIER
(DISCHARGE OF —) TIRE
(DUMMY —) QUAKER
(PART OF —) BASE BORE FACE
KNOR NECK OGEE RING VENT
CHASE FILET SWELL BREECH
BUTTON FILLET MUZZLE
CHAMBER DOLPHIN GUNLOCK
RIMBASE ASTRAGAL CASCABEL
TRUNNION REINFORCE
CANNONBALL GUN PILL BULLET
GUNSTONE
CANNON BOSS TRUNNION
CANNON PLUG TAMPION
CANNOT CANT CANNA DONNA
DOWNA UNABLE
CANNULA TROCAR
CANNY SLY COZY SNUG WARY
WILY WISE COONY LUCKY PAWKY
QUIET CLEVER FRUGAL GENTLE
SHREWD STEADY CAREFUL
CUNNING KNOWING PRUDENT
QUIETLY THRIFTY CAUTIOUS
SKILLFUL WATCHFUL
CANOE AMA KIAK LISI PAHI PROA
WAKA AOTEA ARAWA BANCA
BIRCH BONGO BUNGO CANKA
KAYAK KOLEK PRAHU SKIFF
TONEE UMIAK VINTA WAAPA
BAIDAR BALLAM BAROTO CORIAL
CUNNER DUGOUT OOMIAK
PAOPAO PITPAN PUNGEY TAINUI
TROUGH ALMADIA BIDARKA
BUCKEYE CANADER CASCARA
CORACLE CURIARA CURRANE
HOROUTA LAKATOI PIRAGUA
PIROGUE BALANGAY BARANGAY
FALTBOAT FOLDBOAT MONOXYLE
MONTARIA TAKITUMU
THAMAKAU TSUKUPIN
WOODSKIN
CANON FEN LAW CODE FUGA
HYMN LAUD LIST ROTA RULE

SONG AXIOM GORGE GULCH
MODEL NODUS ROUND TABLE
TENET ACTION DECREE GNOMON
BROCARD LIBRARY PRECEPT
STATUTE DECISION MATHURIN
STAGIARY STANDARD SACRISTAN
PREBENDARY
PREMONSTRATENSIAN
(BODY OF —S) CHAPTER
CANONICAL CANONIC ACCEPTED
ORTHODOX
(NOT —) APOCHRYPHAL
CANOODLE PET CARESS FONDLE
CAN OPENER CHURCHKEY
CANOPY SKY CEIL COPE DAIS
HOOD TILT CHUPA CROWN
HOVEL SHADE STATE VAULT
AWNING BUBBLE CELURE ESTATE
FINIAL GABLET HUPPAH PELMET
SHADOW TESTER CEILING
HEAVENS MARQUEE SHELTER
SPARVER BASILICA CIBORIUM
COVERING OVERWOOD PAVILION
SEMIANNA SHAMIANA
TABENACLE
(— ABOVE THRONE) STATE
(— FOR LIVESTOCK) HOVEL
(— OF ALTAR) DAIS CIBORIUM
(— OF HEAVEN) VAULT
(— OVER BROODER) HOVER
(BED —) TESTER SPARVER
(HEARSE —) MAJESTY
CANT TIP COAX HEEL LEAN LIST
NOOK SING TILT TURN ARGOT
BEVEL CHANT DRIFT FLASH HIELD
LINGO LUSTY MERRY NICHE
PITCH SHARE SLANG SLANT
SLOPE WHINE CAREEN CASTER
CORNER INTONE JARGON LIVELY
PATOIS PATTER SNIVEL AUCTION
DIALECT INCLINE PORTION
SINGING WHEEDLE CHEERFUL
PRETENSE VIGOROUS
CANTABRIGIAN CANTAB
CAMBRIDGE
CANTALA MAGUEY
CANTALOUPE MELON
MUSKMELON
CANTANKEROUS ILL CURSED
CUSSED ORNERY KICKISH PIGGISH
CANKERED CONTRARY PERVERSE
CANTATA MOTET SERENATA
VILLANCICO
CANTEEN BAR FLASK BAZAAR
CANTINA
CANTER JOG RUN GAIT LOPE PACE
RACK AUBIN ROGUE BEGGAR
WHINER TRIPPLE SNUFFLER
VAGABOND
CANTERBURY BELL MILKWORT
CAMPANULA
**CANTERBURY TALES (AUTHOR OF
—)** CHAUCER
(CHARACTER IN —) NUN COOK
DYER HOST MONK WIFE CLERK
FRIAR REEVE DOCTOR KNIGHT
MILLER PARSON PRIEST SQUIRE
WEAVER YEOMAN CHAUCER
PLOWMAN SHIPMAN FRANKLIN
MANCIPLE MERCHANT PARDONER
PRIORESS SERGEANT SUMMONER
CARPENTER HABERDASHER
CANTICLE ODE HYMN LAUD SONG

CANTO ANTHEM CANTIC HIRMOS
BRAVURA MAGNIFICAT
CANTILEVER LOOKOUT SEMIBEAM
CARTOUCHE
CANTING CANT PIOUS SNUFFLING
CANTO AIR FIT BOOK DUAN PACE
RUNE SONG VERSE MELODY
PASSUS CANTICLE
CANTON ANGLE UNION CORNER
VOLOST PORTION QUARTER
SECTION DISTRICT DIVISION
(HALF —) ESQUIRE
CANTOR HAZAN HAZZAN SINGER
CHANTER CHAZZAN SOLOIST
PSALMIST
CANVAS FLY PAT DUCK GLUT
PATA SAIL TARP TENT TEWK
CLOTH COAST SCRIM TOILE VITRY
BALINE BURLAP CATGUT LINING
MUSLIN PICTURE POLDAVY
SACKING SCUTAGE DRABBLER
PAINTING VANDELAS SAILCLOTH
(— FOR CONVEYING GRAIN) APRON
(OLD CONDEMNED —)
RUMBOWLINE
(RUBBERIZED —) TOSH
(STUFFED —) BOLSTER
(TARRED —) COAT
CANVASBACK CAN DIVER CHEVAL
DUCKER POCHARD BULLNECK
CANVASS BEAT CASE DRUM
HAWK POLL SIFT RANDY STUDY
DEBATE PEDDLE SEARCH
AGITATE DISCUSS EXAMINE
SOLICIT TROUNCE CAMPAIGN
CONSIDER
CANVASSER AGENT POLLER
ROADMAN
CANYON CAJON CHASM COULE
GORGE GULCH ARROYO CANADA
RAVINE
CAOUTCHOUC RUBBER ELATERITE
CAP CUP FEZ HAT LID PAD POT
TAJ TAM TIP TOP ACME CALL
COIF CORK COWL DINK DOME
DOWD ETON GAGE HOOD HURE
JOAN KEEP KEPI MATE SHOE
SHOW TOPI BERET BOINA BUSBY
CHIEF COVER CROWN EXCEL
FANON GALEA HOUVE KULAH
MATCH MUTCH OUTDO PHANO
PUNCH SEIZE SHAKO TOPEE
TRUMP ARREST BARRAD BARRET
BEANIE BIGGIN BIRRUS BONNET
CALPAC CLIMAX COCKUP CORNET
GALERA HELMET HUBCAP JINNAH
MOBCAP PILEUS PINNER PRIMER
PUZZLE SUMMIT TABARD
TURBAN ALOPEKE BIRETTA
CALOTTE CAMAURO CAPITAL
CEREVIS CHAPEAU CHECHIA
CLOSURE COMMODE FERRULE
FLATCAP FORAGER HEADCAP
OVERLIE OVERTOP PERPLEX
PETASOS PILLBOX PILLION
SOWBACK SURPASS THIMBLE
TURNCAP ACROSOME BALMORAL
BEARSKIN BYCOCKET CAPELINE
CHAPERON COONSKIN ELECTRIC
FOLLOWER HEADGEAR PHRYGIUM
SKEWBACK SKULLCAP SURPRISE
TARBOOSH
(— FOR PILEDRIVER) PUNCH

(— OF FLAGSTAFF) TRUCK
(— OF FOAM) HOOD
(— OF PIER) CUSHION
(— OF PYXIDIUM) LID
(— OF WATCH) DOME CROWN
(— ON MAST) TRUCK
(ACADEMIC —) MORTARBOARD
(BISHOP'S —) HURA HURE
(CANADIAN —) TUQUE
(CHIMNEY —) GRANNY
(HORSEMAN'S —) MONTERO
(HUNTER'S —) MONTERA
MONTERO
(ICE —) BRAE CALOTTE
(JESTER'S —) COXCOMB FOOLSCAP
(MILITARY —) KEPI BUSBY SHAKO
(MOUNTAIN —) SCALP
(PERCUSSION —) AMORCE
CAPSULE
(PERUVIAN —) CHULLO
(POPE'S —) CAMAURO
(ROOT —) CALYPTRA
(TRIANGULAR —) KALPAK
(WOMAN'S —) TOY CAUL DOWD
JOAN KELL MUTCH COMMODE
VOLUPER BIGGONET
(WOOLEN —) BOINA TOQUE
TUQUE
(PREF.) PILEI PILEO PILO
CAPABILITY POWER STROIL
ABILITY CONDUCT FACULTY
POTENCY CAPACITY
CAPABLE APT CAN FIT ABLE GOOD
ADEPT CAPAX FENDY TIGHT
EXPERT SKILLED POWERFUL
(— OF BEING DEFENDED) TENABLE
(— OF BEING DRAWN OUT) DUCTILE
(— OF BEING SEVERED) SEVTILE
(— OF BEING THROWN) MISSILE
(— OF BEING UTTERED) EFFABLE
(— OF FLYING) VOLANT
(— OF SUBMISSION) AMENABLE
(NORMALLY —) ABOUT
(SUFF.) ABLE IBLE
(— OF) ILE
CAPACIOUS FULL SIDE WIDE
AMPLE BROAD LARGE ROOMY
WOMBY GOODLY ROOMFUL
CAPTIOUS ROOMSOME SPACIOUS
CAPACITOR CONDENSER
CAPACITY BACK BENT BIND DISH
GIFT GIVE SIZE TURN BLAST
FLAIR FORCE KNACK MODEL
POWER SKILL SPACE AGENCY
BOTTOM BURDEN ENERGY
ENGINE EXTENT GENIUS MODULE
SPREAD TALENT VOLUME ABILITY
CALIBER CALIBRE CONTENT
FACULTY FITNESS QUALITY
APTITUDE INSTINCT STRENGTH
INFLUENCE
(— FOR EATING) STROKE
(— FOR ENDURANCE) STAY
(— FOR HIGHER KNOWLEDGE)
INTELLECT
(— OF LATHE) SWING
(— OF SHIP) BURDEN
(CIVIL —) CAPUT
(INNATE —S) STAMINA
(INTELLECTUAL —) BROW
(LOAD-PULLING —) DRAFT
DRAUGHT
(MENTAL —S) BELFRY

(SPECIAL —) KNACK
(UNIT OF —) MUD MUID LAGEN
KISHEN MEDIMNUS KILDERKIN
(UNLIMITED —) INFINITY
CAPANEUS (FATHER OF —)
HIPPONOUS BELLEROPHON
(SLAYER OF —) JUPITER
(SON OF —) STHENELUS
(WIFE OF —) EVADNE
CAPARISON DECK TRAP HOUSE
COVERING TRAPPING
CAPE RAS COPE GAPE HEAD HOOK
LOOK NAZE NECK NESS SKAW
TANG WRIT AMICE CAPPA CLOAK
FICHU ORALE POINT SAGUM
STARE STOLE TALMA BERTHA
BYRRUS CABAAN CHAPEL
DOLMAN MANTLE SONTAG
TABARD TIPPET CHLAMYS
LEATHER MANTEEL MOZETTA
SALIENT TANJONG VANDYKE
CIRCULAR COLLARET HEADLAND
LAMBSKIN MANTILLA MOZZETTA
PALATINE PELERINE SEALSKIN
RAINPROOF
(— OF SKINS) KAROSS
(— OF STRAW) MINO
(BULLFIGHTER'S —) CAPA
(CLERGICAL —) ALMUCE
(DRESSING —) TOILET
(FEATHER —) AHUULA
(HOODED —) HUKE DOMINO
(LACE OR SILK —) VISITE
(LOW —) TANG
(PAPAL —) FANO FANON FANUM
ORALE PHANO
(RAIN —) CAPOTE
CAPE ANTEATER AARDVARK
CAPE ARMADILLO PANGOLIN
CAPE GOOSEBERRY POHA
CAPE HEN STINKER STINKPOT
CAPELIN SMELT ICEFISH
CAPE PIGEON PINTADO
CAPE POLECAT ZORIL MUISHOND
CAPER HOP JET DIDO HOIT JUMP
LEAP ROMP SKIP SKIT ANTIC
BRANK DANCE FLING FLISK FRISK
PRANK SAUCE SCOUP SHRUB
CAVORT CURVET FRISCO FROLIC
GAMBOL GAMOND PRANCE
SPRING TITTUP VAGARY CORSAIR
COURANT FRISCAL GAMBADO
PRANKLE CAPRIOLE MARIGOLD
(— ABOUT) FLING CAVORT
(SILLY —) SHINE
CAPER SPURGE CATEPUCE
CAPE TOWN BOVENLAND
**CAPE VERDE ISLANDS (CAPITAL
OF —)** PRAIA
(TOWN OF —) MINDELO
(VOLCANO ON —) FOGO
CAPHITE KIST
CAPITAL CAP CASH CITY FUND
GOOD LIMA MAIN RARE SEAT
BASIC CHIEF FATAL GREAT
MAJOR MONEY MUANG STOCK
VITAL DEADLY HEADLY IMPOST
LETTER LISBON MORTAL PRIMAL
UNCIAL WEALTH CENTRAL
CHATTEL DRESDEN LEADING
RADICAL SERIOUS WEIGHTY
CABECERA CATALLUM CHAPTER
CHAPTREL DOSSERET SWINGING

(— OF HEAVEN) AMARAVATI
(— OF HELL) PANDEMONIUM
(DIVISION OF —) ABACUS
(GAMBLER'S —) STAKE
(INADEQUATE —) SHOESTRING
CAPITATUM MAGNUM
CAPITELLUM KNOP
CAPITOL STATEHOUSE
CAPITOLINE SATURNIAN
CAPITULATION MUNICH TREATY
CAPITULUM HEAD KNOP
ANTHODIUM
CAPOTE HOOD CAPPO CLOAK
BONNET MANTLE TOPPER
CAPPER CORKER SEALER STEERER
CAPPY TALLOWY
CAPRICCIO (CHARACTER IN —)
FLAMAND OLIVIER MADELEINE
(COMPOSER OF —) STRAUSS
CAPRICE FAD TOY KINK MOOD
WHIM ANTIC BRAID CRANK
FANCY FREAK HUMOR QUIRK
CHANGE MAGGOT NOTION
SPLEEN TEMPER VAGARY
WHIMSY BOUTADE CONCEIT
CROCHET IMPULSE TANTRUM
WHIMSEY
CAPRICIOUS DIZZY DODDY FLUKY
MOODY CHANCY FICKLE FITFUL
KITTLE PLATTY WANTON
COMICAL ERRATIC FLIGHTY
MAGGOTY MOONISH PEEVISH
VAGRANT WAYWARD EPISODAL
FANCIFUL FREAKISH HUMOROUS
PERVERSE SKITTISH UNSTEADY
VARIABLE VOLATILE CROTCHETY
FANTASTIC VAGARIOUS
CAPRICIOUSNESS FREAK
CAPRICORN GOAT
CAPRIPEDE SATYR
CAPRYL RUTYL DECANOYL
CAPSHEAF CAP HOOD
CAPSICUM AJI PEPPER
(— SAUCE) TABASCO
CAPSID MIRID
CAPSIZE COUP KEEL PURL UPSET
WRONG WHEMMLE OVERTURN
CAPSTAN CRAB DRUM DANDY
HOIST LEVER NIGGER CYLINDER
WINDLASS
CAPSTONE LECH TOPSTONE
CAPSULE CAP POD URN BOLL
CASE CYST PILL SEED PEARL
PERLE SHELL THECA WAFER
AMPULE BARROW CACHET
COCOON OOCYST SHEATH
AMPOULE EYEBALL OTOCYST
SEEDBOX SILIQUE VANILLA
PERICARP PYXIDIUM
(SPACE —) TERRELLA
(PREF.) THEC(A)(I)(O)
CAPTAIN BO BOH CID BAAS HEAD
JOAB RAIS REIS BARAK CHIEF
LEADER MASTER NAAMAN
SOTNIK CAPITAN FOREMAN
HEADMAN MANAGER PATROON
SKIPPER FLUELLEN GOVERNOR
SUBAHDAR
(— OF ARAB VESSEL) NACODAR
(— OF CAVALRY) RESSALDAR
RITMASTER
(— OF CRICKET TEAM) SKIPPER
(— OF CURLING TEAM) SKIP

(— OF PRIVATEER) CAPER
(— OF SHIP) WAFTER
(STRICT —) SUNDOWNER
CAPTAINS COURAGEOUS
(AUTHOR OF —) KIPLING
(CHARACTER IN —) DAN JACK
DISKO TROOP CHEYNE HARVEY
MANUEL SALTERS
**CAPTAIN'S DAUGHTER (AUTHOR
OF —)** PUSHKIN
(CHARACTER IN —) MARIA PETER
ALEXEI ZOURIN EMELYAN
GRINEFF GRINYEV EGOROVNA
IVANOVNA MIRONOFF PUGACHEV
SHVABRIN VASILISA SAVELITCH
POUGATCHEFF
CAPTION TITLE LEADER LEGEND
CUTLINE HEADING SUBHEAD
CITATION HEADLINE SUBTITLE
CAPTIOUS CRAFY TESTY CRAFTY
SEVERE CARPING CYNICAL
FRETFUL PEEVISH TETTISH
ALLURING CATCHING CAVILING
CONTRARY CRITICAL
CAPTIOUSLY TUTLY
CAPTIVATE WIN TAKE CATCH
CHARM ALLURE ENAMOR PLEASE
RAVISH SUBDUE ATTRACT
BEWITCH CAPTIVE CAPTURE
ENCHANT ENTHRALL OVERTAKE
SURPRISE
CAPTIVATED EPRIS EPRISE
CAPTIVE
CAPTIVATING TAKING KILLING
WINNING WINSOME CATCHING
CAPTIVE SLAVE DANIEL ENAMOR
THRALL BRISEIS CAITIFF CAITIVE
PRISONER
(— OF HERCULES) IOLE
CAPTIVITY BOND IRON BONDS
CHAINS DURESS BONDAGE
SERFDOM SLAVERY
CAPTOR TAKER VICTOR CATCHER
CAPTURE BAG COP FIX GET NAB
NET WIN FALL FANG GRAB HOOK
LAND PREY SNIB TAKE TRAP TREE
CARRY CATCH FORCE PINCH
PRIZE PURSE RAVEN SEIZE
SWOOP ARREST COLLAR CORRAL
ENTRAP GOBBLE OBTAIN PIRACY
REDUCE TAKING CAPTIVE
LOWBELL SEIZURE WINNING
EXCHANGE SURPRISE UNDERNIM
(— BACKGAMMON PIECE) HIT
(— BIRDS) TOODLE
(— GAME) SATCHEL
(— OF ALL PRIZES) SWEEP
(— TROUT) TICKLE
CAPUCHIN MONKEY CAY SAI
CEPID SAJOU WEEPER SAPAJOU
RINGTAIL
CAPULIN CEREZA
CAPYBARA CAVY CARPINCHO
CAPYS (FATHER OF —) ASSARACUS
(SON OF —) ANCHISES
(WIFE OF —) THEMISTE
CAR BOX BUS PIG AUTO BOGY
BUNK DOLL DRAG DUMP GRIP
JEEP RATH TRAM ZULU BOGEY
COACH CRATE DINER DUMMY
GURRY HUTCH JIMMY RATHA
SEDAN STOCK TRAIN TRUCK
WRONG BASKET BOXCAR BUFFET

CHIPPY DINGEY DINGHY DUPLEX
HOPPER JIGGER JINGLE SALOON
SETOFF SMOKER TOURER
AWKWARD CARROCH CHARIOT
COMBINE FLATCAR FREEZER
GIRAFFE GONDOLA HANDCAR
SIDECAR TELPHER TRAILER
TROLLEY VEHICLE VETTURA
AMPHICAR DRAGSTER HORSECAR
OUTSIDER QUADRIGA ROADSTER
SINISTER
(— FOR TRAIN CREW) CABOOSE
(— ON RAIL) TROLLEY
(BAGGAGE —) BLIND
(CABLE —) GONDOLA
(COAL —) HUTCH JIMMY WAGON
WAGGON
(ELECTRIC —) TELFER TELPHER
(ELEVATOR —) CAB CAGE
(EMPTY —) EMPTY IDLER
(JAUNTING —) SIDECAR
(LOG —) BUNK
(LOW-WHEELED —) HUTCH
TRUCKLE
(MINE —) SKIP LARRY BARNEY
GIRAFFE GUNBOAT
(MONORAIL —) GYROCAR
(OBSERVATION —) BUGGY
(OLD —) JUNKER
(POLICE —) CRUISER
(SMALL —) MINICAB
(TROLLEY —) SHORT
(USED —) DOG
CARABAO BUFF BUFFALO
CARACAL GORKUN STAGUSH
CARACARA HAWK CARANCHA
CHIMANGO
CARACOLE FRISK CAREER
CARADOC BALA CRADOCK
CARAFE CROFT BOTTLE
CARAGUATA CHAGUAR
CARAJURA CHICA
CARAMBOLA BLIMBING
BALIMBING
CARAMEL BLACKJACK
CARAPA CRAB CRAPPO
CRABWOOD
CARAPACE CRUST SHELL LORICA
SHIELD CALAPASH
(SUFF.) STEGE STEGITE
CARATE PINTA
CARATHIS (SON OF —) VATHEK
CARAVAN VAN TREK TRIP FLEET
TRAIN CAFILA COFFLE CONVOY
SAFARI TRAVEL JOURNEY
VEHICLE CONDUCTA
CARAVANSARY INN CHAN KHAN
HOTEL SERAI ZAYAT HOSTEL
IMARET CHOULTRY HOSTELRY
SERAGLIO
CARAWAY CARVY UMBEL
CARBAMATE MEPROBAMATE
CARBINE STEN DRAGON MUSKET
DRAGOON ESCOPET
CARBOHYDRATE SUGAR AMYLAN
GELOSE INULIN STARCH
FUCOSAN GLUCIDE CELLULIN
DEXTRINE DEXTROSE GLYCOGEN
GRAMININ PENTOSAN TRITICIN
CELLULOSE PARAMYLUM
POLYSACCHARIDE
CARBON COAL COKE COPY SOOT
NORIT CRAYON DIAMOND

REPLICA CHARCOAL
GRAPHITE SCHUNGITE
(PREF.) ANTHRAC(O)
(SUFF.) ANE
CARBONADO BORT BOART BOORT
CARBON
CARBONATE BURN CHAR FIZZ
AERATE ALKALI ENLIVEN
ENERGIZER
CARBONATOR GASMAN
CARBON DIOXIDE
(SUFF.) CAPNIA
CARBONIZER PICKLER
CARBORUNDUM EMERY ABRASIVE
SILUNDUM
CARBOXYL
(SUFF.) (CONTAINING —) OIC ONIC
CARBUNCLE RUBY PYROPE
ANTHRAX CHARBOCLE
(PREF.) ANTHRAC(O)
CARBURETOR CARB DIFFUSER
VAPORIZER
CARCASS BEEF BODY BOUK CASE
CULL BLOCK MUMMY CORPSE
CARRION
(— OF WHALE) CRANG KRANG
KRENG
CARCERULE SARCOBASIS
CARD ACE MAP PAM WAG CLUB
COMB DRAW FACE FIVE FOUR
JACK KING MENU PLAN ROVE
STOP BALOP BLANK CARTE
CHART CHECK DEUCE DUMMY
EIGHT ENTRY EQUAL FICHE FLATS
GREEN HEART HONOR JOKER
LOSER PIECE QUEEN SPADE
STAMP STIFF TAROT TEASE
BENDER CARTEL CONVEX FILLER
KICKER KNIGHT PIGEON READER
SECOND TICKET TOWSER
BRAGGER BRISQUE DIAMOND
PROGRAM RELEASE STARTER
STOPPER TAROCCO TRIUMPH
BOOKMARK COMOQUER
DECKHEAD DRAWCARD
SCHEDULE SCRIBBLE SQUEEZER
STRIPPER TIMECARD
(— IN OMBRE) MANILLE
(— LAST IN BOX) HOCK HOCKELTY
(— WOOL) TUM ROVE
(ACE OF CLUBS —) BASTA BASTO
MATADOR PUPPYFOOT
(ACE OF SPADES —) MATADOR
SPADILLE
(ACE OF TRUMPS —) TIB
(AVIATOR'S —) CARNET
(CLUB —) OAK
(COMPASS —) FLY ROSE
(CRIBBAGE —S) CRIB
(DEAD —) SLEEPER
(DIAMOND —) PICK CARREAU
(DISCARDED —S) CRIB
(DRAWING —) BLOWOFF
(FARO —) SODA
(FOUR —) CATER QUATRE
(FOURTH —) CASE
(HIGHEST UNPLAYED —) COMMAND
(JOKER —) BRAGGER MISTIGRIS
(KING, QUEEN OR KNAVE —) COST
FACE
(KNAVE —) PAM TOM JACK
BOWER EQUES MAKER NODDY
COQUIN KNIGHT PICARO VARLET

WENZEL CUSTREL PEASANT
VILLAIN VARLETTO
(LAYOUT OF —S) TABLEAU
(LOW —) GUARD
(MARKED —) STAMP
(POSTAL —) COVER
(PULLING —S) TIRE
(QUEEN AND KNAVE —S) INTRIGO
INTRIGUE
(RUN OF —S) SEQUENCE
(SPADE —) PICK DIGGER
(STOCK —) TALON
(THIRD HIGHEST TRUMP —) BASTA
(THREE —) TREY THREE
(WILD —) FREAK
(3 ACE —S) CORONA
(3 FACE —S) GLEEK
(3 —S IN SEQUENCE) TIERCE
FOURCHETTE
(3 —S OF KIND) TRIO TRICON
PAIRIAL TRIPLET
(4 OF TRUMPS —) TIDDY
(5 FACE —S) BLAZE
(7, 8 AND 9 —S) VOIDS
CARDAMOM KNOBWOOD
CARDBOARD CARD PALL BLANK
BOGUS CARTON BRISTOL
TAGBOARD PAPERBOARD
(TWO —S) SPHEROGRAPH
CARDER TOZER TEASER TUMMER
CARDIALGIA HEARTBURN
CARDIGAN CORGI WAMUS FABRIC
JACKET WAMPUS SWEATER
CARDINAL MAIN BASIC CHIEF
CLOAK VITAL ALEPHA CLERIC
DATARY PRINCE RADICAL
ALEFNULL ALEFZERO CAMPEIUS
PENITENTIARY
CARDINALATE PURPLE
CARDINAL BIRD CARNAL REDBIRD
REDLEGS GROSBEAK REDSHANK
CARDINAL FISH FUCINITA
ALFONCINO
CARDSHARP TRAMPOSO
CARDSHARPER GREEK SHARPER
SPIELER
CARE DO DOW HOW CARK CURE
DUTY FASH FRET HEED KEEP
KEPE MIND PASS RECK SOIN
TEND TENT WISH YEME COUNT
GRIEF GUARD NURSE PAINS
SORGE TRUST WORRY BURDEN
CARIEN CHARGE CUMBER DESIRE
GRIEVE KIAUGH LAMENT REGARD
SORROW ANXIETY AUSPICE
CAUTION CHERISH CONCERN
CULTURE CUSTODY KEEPING
RESPECT RUNNING SCRUPLE
THOUGHT TUITION BUSINESS
PERIERGY TENDMENT
NURTURANCE PRECAUTION
SOLICITUDE
(— FOR) KNOW MIND RECK TEND
WARD FORCE NURSE SAVOR
FATHER MATTER REGARD
CHERISH PROCURE
(— FOR ONESELF) BACH
(— OF HOUSEHOLD) HUSBANDRY
(— OF LIVESTOCK) CHORE
(JUDICIOUS —) LEISURE
(WATCHFUL —) TENDANCE
OVERSIGHT
CAREEN GIP CANT HEEL KEEL LIST

TILT VEER LURCH SLOPE
SWIFT INCLINE
CAREER RUN WAY LIFE ROAD
RUSH TRADE CHARGE COURSE
GALLOP CALLING CARIERE
PURSUIT
(MILITARY —) ARMS SERVICE
CAREFREE EASY FRANK HAPPY
BREEZY DEGAGE HOLIDAY
DEBONAIR
CAREFUL BUSY WARY CANNY
CHARY CLOSE EXACT HOOLY
TENTY CHOICE DAINTY EIDENT
EYEFUL FRUGAL NARROW
TENDER ANXIOUS CURIOUS
ENVIOUS GUARDED HEEDFUL
PAINFUL PRUDENT THRIFTY
ACCURATE CAUTIOUS CRITICAL
DILIGENT DISCREET DREADFUL
GINGERLY MOURNFUL PUNCTUAL
TROUBLED VIGILANT WATCHFUL
OBSERVANT METICULOUS
SOLICITOUS PUNCTILIOUS
CAREFULLY HOOLY NARROW
CANNILY CHARILY TENTILY
CHOICELY GINGERLY
CAREFULNESS CAUTION
CARELESS LAX COOL EASY LASH
RASH MESSY SLACK CASUAL
OVERLY RAKISH REMISS SECURE
SLOPPY SUPINE UNTIDY UNWARY
CURSORY LANGUID SLIGHTY
UNCANNY HEEDLESS LISTLESS
MINDLESS RECKLESS SLATTERN
SLIPSHOD SLOVENLY YEMELESS
NEGLECTFUL SLATTERNLY
CARELESSLY SLACK OVERLY
SLACKLY SLIGHTLY
CARELESSNESS LACHES LAXITY
INCAUTION
CARESS COY HUG PAT PET BILL
CLAP DAUT DAWT KISS MUCH
NECK INGLE NURSE CODDLE
COSSET CUDDLE FONDLE PAMPER
STROKE CHERISH EMBRACE
FLATTER BLANDISH CANOODLE
LALLYGAG
CARETAKER KEEPER WARDER
JANITOR
CARGO BULK LAST LOAD BURDEN
LADING FREIGHT PACKAGE
PORTAGE CARGASON PROPERTY
SHIPLOAD SHIPMENT TRAFFICS
CARIAMA CHUNGA SERIEMA
CARIB GALIBI CALINAGO
CARIBBEAN (— GULF) DARIEN
HONDURAS
(— ISLAND) CUBA SABA ARUBA
HAITI NEVIS BEQUIA NASSAU
TOBAGO ANTIGUA BARBUDA
BONAIRE CURACAO GRENADA
JAMAICA TORTOLA ANGUILLA
BARBADOS DOMINICA TRINIDAD
GUADELOUPE MONTSERRAT
(— ISLAND GROUP) TURKS CAICOS
CAYMAN LEEWARD ANTILLES
WINDWARD
CARIBE PIRAI PIRANHA
CHARACINE
CARIBOU STAG RANGIFER
REINDEER
CARICATURE APE COPY MOCK
SKIT FARCE LIBEL MIMIC SQUIB

OVERDO PARODY SATIRE
CARTOON TRAVESTY BURLESQUE
CARILLONNEUR CAMPANIST
BELLMASTER
CARINA KEEL
CARIOUS ROTTEN
CARMELITE EXTERN TERESIAN
CARMEN (CHARACTER IN —) JOSE
CARMEN ZUNIGA MICAELA
ESCAMILLO
(COMPOSER OF —) BIZET
CARMI (FATHER OF —) REUBEN
(SON OF —) ACHAN
CARMINATIVE GINGER CALAMUS
CAMPHOR ANETHOLE VALERIAN
CARMINE RED LAKE CRIMSON
SCARLET
CARNAGE WAL MURDER POGROM
STRAGE BUTCHERY MASSACRE
BLOODSHED SLAUGHTER
CARNAL CROW LEWD GROSS
ANIMAL BODILY SEXUAL BESTIAL
BRUTISH EARTHLY FLESHLY
SECULAR SENSUAL WORLDLY
MATERILA PANDEMIC PHYSICAL
TEMPORAL
CARNATION JACK PINK FLAKE
BIZARRE PICOTEE DAYBREAK
DIANTHUS GRENADINE
MALMAISON
CARNELIAN SARD COPPER
(BEAD OF —) ARANGO
CARNIVAL FETE SHOW CARNY
CANVAS APOKREA CANVASS
REVELRY FASCHING FESTIVAL
CARNIVORE CAT DOG FOX BEAR
COON LION LYNX MINK PUMA
SEAL WOLF CIVET GENET HYENA
OTTER PANDA PEKAN RATEL
SABLE STOAT TIGER BADGER
COUGAR ERMINE FELINE FERRET
FISHER FOUSSA JACKAL JAGUAR
MARTEN OCELOT POSSUM
SERVAL WEASEL DASYURE
GLUTTON LEOPARD MEERKAT
POLECAT RACCOON TIGRESS
AARDWOLF MONGOOSE
OPPOSSUM PREDACEAN
ZOOPHAGAN
(FOSSIL —) CREODONT
CARNIVOROUS SARCOPHAGOUS
CAROB HUSK LOCUST ALGAROBA
CAROL LAY NOEL SING SONG
DITTY YODEL WARBLE WASSAIL
MADRIGAL AGUINALDO
CAROLINA ALLSPICE SHRUB
**CAROLINE ISLANDS (— ISLAND
GROUP)** PALAU
(ISLAND OF —) YAP HALL PALU
TRUK PELEW PULAP OROLUK
PONAPE WOLEAI PELELIU
(TOWN OF —) LOT NIF RUNU
KOROR MUTOK TOMIL PONAPE
MALAKAL GARUSUUN
CAROLINGIAN KARLING
CAROM SHOT BOUNCE CANNON
GLANCE STRIKE REBOUND
BILLIARD CARAMBOLE
CAROUSAL BAT GELL LARK ORGY
RIOT ROMP TOOT BINGE FEAST
RANDY REVEL ROUSE SPRAY
SPREE FROLIC SHINDY SPLORE
BANQUET CAROUSE REVELRY

WASSAIL DRINKING
FESTIVAL JAMBOREE
CAROUSE JET BOUT HELL RANT
TEAR TOOT BINGE BIRLE BOUSE
DRINK QUAFF RANDY REVEL
ROUSE SPREE TOAST COURANT
JOLLIFY WASSAIL CAROUSAL
CAROUSER BACCHANT
BACCHANAL
CAROUSING REVEL RAFFING
CARP KOI NAG BITE DRUM SING
SNAG TALK YERK CAVIL PINCH
PRATE SCOLD SPEAK CENSOR
NIBBLE RECITE TWITCH CENSURE
CHATTER CRUCIAN QUIBBLE
COMPLAIN CYPRINID GOLDFISH
(CRUCIAN —) GIBEL
(LAKE —) DRUM LAKER
(PREF.) CYPRIN(O)
CARPAL ACTINOST
CARPEL ACHENE CARPID COCCUS
MERICARP CARPOPHYL
(PL.) CORE
CARPENTER ANT LOHAR FITTER
FRAMER HOUSER JOINER PINNER
WRIGHT BUILDER HOWSOUR
WOODMAN INDENTER TECTONIC
TIMBERER PITWRIGHT
SHIPWRIGHT
(SHIP'S —) CHIPS
(PREF.) TECTO
CARPENTRY WOODWORK
WRIGHTRY
CARPER MOME CRITIC
CARPET MAT RUG AGRA KALI
KUBA HERAT KILIM SARUK SCOLD
SUMAK TAPET TAPIS TEKKE
USHAK AFGHAN FLOSSA FRIEZE
KASHAN KIDDER KIRMAN LAVEHR
NAMMAD RUNNER SAROUK
SAXONY SELJUK SMYRNA TABRIZ
VELVET WILTON DHURRIE
GIORDES HAMADAN INGRAIN
ISFAHAN ISPAHAN SHEMAKA
TEHERAN AKHISSAR AMRITSAR
BRUSSELS COVERING FOOTPACE
KARABAGH MOQUETTE TAPESTRY
TURCOMAN VENETIAN
AXMINSTER SITRINGEE
(HOLY —) KISWA
(PILELESS —) KILIM GELEEM
CARPETING FILLING
CARPET SHARK WOBBEGONG
CARPET SHELL EEROCK PULLET
CARPETWEED FICOID FICOIDAL
MESEMBRYANTHEMUM
CARPING CRAB CAPTIOUS
CAVILING CRITICAL
CARPSUCKER QUILLBACK
CARPUS WRIST CARPOPODITE
CARRAGEEN KILLEEN
CARREL STALL CUBICLE
CARRIAGE AIR CAB CAR FLY GIG
RIG RUT SET VIS ARBA BIGA CART
CHAR DRAG DUKE EKKA GAIT
GARB HACK LOAD MIEN PORT
RUTH SHAY TEAM TRAP WYNN
ARABA BANDY BRAKE BREAK
BRETT BUGGY CHAIR COACH
COUPE ESSED FRONT JUTKA
MIDGE NODDY PANEL POISE
SADOO SETUP SULKY TENUE
TONGA TRUCK WAGON BURDEN

CALASH CHAISE CHARET CISIUM
CONVOY DENNET FIACRE GHARRY
GOCART HANSOM HERDIC
KOSONG LANDAU MANNER
MOTION PORTER REMISE SADDLE
SPIDER SURREY TANDEM TELEGA
TROIKA BAGGAGE BEARING
BERLINE BOUNDER BRITSKA
CALECHE CALESIN CARAVAN
CARIOLE CAROCHE CHARIOT
COACHEE CONDUCT CROYDON
DOGCART DOSADOS DROSHKY
FORECAR GESTURE HACKMAN
HACKNEY MINIBUS PHAETON
POSCHAY SHANDRY SKYHOOK
TALLYHO TARTANA TILBURY
TRANSIT TROLLEY UNICORN
VECTURE VEHICLE VETTURA
VOITURE VOLANTE WAFTAGE
BAROUCHE BEHAVIOR
BROUGHAM CARRIOLE CARRYALL
CLARENCE CURRICLE DEARBORN
DEMEANOR DORMEUSE
EQUIPAGE PORTANCE PRESENCE
ROCKAWAY SOCIABLE STANHOPE
TARANTAS TOURNURE VICTORIA
(— OF HANDPRESS) COFFIN
(— OF HORSE) AIR
(AMMUNITION —) CAISSON
(CEREMONIAL —) RATH
(ELEVATED —) LIFT
(GUN —) CHASSIS
(INDIAN —) RUT EKKA BANDY
GHARRI GHARRY
(JAVANESE —) SADO SADOO
(LIVERY —) REMISE
(LOG —) DRAG
(PUBLIC —) FLY OMNIBUS
CARRIAGE HOUSE REMISE
CARRIER HOD BASE JEEP SHIP
TRAM BUGGY HAMAL KAHAR
MACER PLANE SABOT TAMEN
TIGER BARKIS BEARER CADGER
COOLIE HAMMAL HODMAN
JAGGER PACKER PORTER
RUNNER TAILER WEASEL
DRAYMAN DROGHER FLATTOP
POSTMAN REMOVER TACULLI
TROTTER VEHICLE CARGADOR
CARRYALL PORTATOR RAILROAD
TEAMSTER SUBSTRATE
(COAL —) FLATIRON
(COLOR —) LURRIER
(ENDLESS —) TAILER
(FIRE —) PORTFIRE
(MAIL —) COURIER POSTMAN
(WATER —) BHISTI BHEESTY
(PREF.) PORTE
CARRION KET VILE OFFAL CORPSE
HOODIE REFUSE ROTTEN
CARCASS CORRUPT DOGMEAT
CROWBAIT
CARRION BIRD SCAVENGER
CARRION CROW DOWP HOODY
URUBU CORBIE HOODIE
GERCROW
CARROT UMBEL CONIUM DAUCUS
CACHRYS SECRETE BUPLEVER
HILLTROT
(DEADLY —) DRIAS
(PERUVIAN —) ARRACACH
(PREPARED WITH —S) CRECY
CARROTING SECRETAGE

CARROUSEL RIDE
WHIRLGIG QUADRILLE
CARRY CAR HUG JAG LUG BEAR
BUCK CART DRAY FARE GEST
HAVE HOLD HUMP LEAD PACK
PORT SHOW TAKE TOTE TUMP
BRING BROOK CADGE CROSS
FERRY GESTE GUIDE POISE
WALTZ WEIGH BEHAVE CONVEY
CONVOY DELATE DEPORT DERIVE
EXTEND COMPORT CONDUCT
CONTAIN ENTRAIN PORTAGE
PRODUCE SUPPORT SUSTAIN
UNDERGO BAJULATE CONTINUE
TRANSFER TRANSMIT
(— AWAY) FIRK DRAIN REAVE
SWEEP TRUSS ABLATE ASPORT
(— EFFIGY) GUY
(— FORWARD) EXTEND
(— IN OXCART) KURVEY
(— LIQUOR) BOOTLEG
(— OFF) RAP HENT LIFE SACK
FETCH HEAVE RIFLE SCOUR
SWOOP ABDUCT ASPORT BRAZEN
KIDNAP SPIRIT
(— ON) DO RUN WAR HAVE LEAD
LEVY WAGE APPLY DRIVE ENSUE
FIGHT TRAIN CREATE DEMEAN
FOLLOW MANAGE OCCUPY
CONDUCT EXERCISE MAINTAIN
TRANSACT
(— ONESELF) HOLD
(— ONWARD) CONTINUE
(— OUT) DO ACT END GIVE LAST
HONOR AFFORD EFFECT ACHIEVE
EXECUTE FULFILL PERFORM
SATISFY PERPETRATE
(— UPWARD) RAP ESCALATE
(SUFF.) GER(ENCE)(ENT)(OUS)
PHER PHORA PHORE(SIS) PHORIA
PHOROUS PHORUS
(— ON) IZE
CARRYALL BUS CASE WAGON
CARRIAGE
CARRYING BURDEN GERENT
FRAUGHT
(— AWAY) REVEHENT
(— ON) GESTION
(— WEIGHT) EFFECTIVE
(PREF.) **(— ON)** PHORO
CART CAR JAG POT RUT BUTT
CHAR COOP COUP DRAY HAUL
JANG LEAD LOAD PLOW PUTT
RUTH TOTE WAIN ARABA BANDY
BOGEY BOGIE CADDY CARRY
DANDY DILLY DOLLY SULKY
TONGA TRUCK WAGON BARROW
CADDIE CHAISE CHARET CISIUM
CONVEY DOLLIE DUMPER GHARRI
GHARRY JIGGER JINKER KURUMA
LIMBER PLOUGH SPIDER CARIOLE
CARRETA CHARIOT DOGCART
GUJERAT HACKERY MORFREY
SHALLOW SHANDRY TROLLEY
TRUNDLE TUMBLER TUMBREL
TUMBRIL VEHICLE BUCKCART
DUMPCART HANDCART
PUSHCART
(— WITH TANK) TUMBLER
(BULLOCK —) BANDY HACKERY
(COSTER'S —) TROLL
(COVERED —) JINGLE CARIOLE
(FARMER'S —) PUTT

GAMBO MORPHREY
(FREIGHT —) CARRETON
(LOG —) TUG BUNK
(LUMBER —) GILL BUMMER
(MILKMAN'S —) PRAM
(OX —) RECKLA
(PARCELS —) FLY
(TIMBER —) CUTS
(TIP —) COOP COUP COUPE
(UNDERSLUNG —) FLOAT
(2-PONY —) KOSONG
(2-WHEELED —) BANDY BUGGY
SULKY CARRETA TUMBREL
(3-WHEELED —) PORTER
CARTE MAP CARD LIST MENU
CHART CHARTER DIAGRAM
CARTE BLANCHE BLANK
CARTEL CARD DEFY PACT POOL
SHIP PAPER TRUST CORNER
LETTER TREATY CONTRACT
SYNDICATE
CARTER CARMAN JAGGER LEADER
DRAYMAN LADEMAN TRUCKER
HORSEMAN TEAMSTER
CARTILAGE COPULA TISSUE
CRICOID EPIURAL GRISTLE
RADIALE STERNUM TARSALE
THYROID CHONDRUS EPIPUBIS
HYPOHYAL SESAMOID TURBINAL
(— UNDER DOG'S TONGUE) LYTTA
(PREF.) CHONDR(I)(IO)(O) CRICO
(SUFF.) CHONDRIA CHONDRY
CRINUS
CARTILAGINOUS CHONDRIC
CARTLOAD SEAM
CARTOGRAPH MAP PLAT CHART
CARTOGRAPHER CHARTIST
MAPMAKER
AMERICAN GANNETT HUTCHINS
SOUTHACK STEVENSON
ENGLISH SPEED
GERMAN KIEPERT STIELER
PETERMANN WALDSEEMULLER
RUSSIAN KAULBARS
SWISS SIEGFRIED
CARTON BOX CASE SHELL
CARTOON EPURE ANIMATION
CARTOONIST **AMERICAN** NAST
BLOCK DUFFY KIRBY OPPER
SEGAR YOUNG BRIGGS DORGAN
KEMBLE NEWELL POWERS
DARLING GRUELLE KEPPLER
MCMANUS GOLDBERG OUTCAULT
SCHULTZE WILLIAMS NANKIVELL
FITZPATRICK
AUSTRALIAN LINDSAY
DUTCH RAEMAEKERS
ENGLISH LOW DYSON TENNIEL
ROBINSON
CARTOUCHE MESA OVAL
DURANGO CARTRIDGE
CARTRIDGE BAG CASE HULL
BLANK SHELL SHORT BULLET
MAGNUM PATRON CAPSULE
TORPEDO HANDLOAD SHOTSHELL
(PART OF —) RIM CASE HEAD
NOSE SLUG CRIMP BULLET
JACKET PRIMER
(TAPE —) CASSETTE
CARTULARY COUCHER
CARTWHEEL CLOGWHEEL
CARUCATE CARVE PLOWLAND
CARUNCLE ARIL

COMB STROPHIOLE
CARVE CUT ALAY SIDE BEHEW
BREAK GRAVE KIRVE MINCE
SHEAR SPLAY SPOIL THIGH INCISE
QUINSE SCULPT THWITE TRENCH
UNLACE ENCHASE ENGRAIL
ENGRAVE DISJOINT MALAHACK
SCULLION
(— A BIRD) WING
(— CHICKEN) FRUSH
(— GOOSE) REAR
(— HEN) SPOIL
(— PEACOCK) DISFIGURE
(— PLOVER) MINCE
(— SWAN) LIFT
(PREF.) GLYPHO GLYPT(O)
SCULPTO
(SUFF.) GLYPH
CARVED CARVEN GLYPHIC INCISED
(PREF.) GLYPT(O)
CARVER BODGER KIRVER CROPPER
FROSTER IVORIST CISELEUR
TRENCHER
CARVING CAMEO GLYPH IVORY
ENTAIL SCRIVE GLYPTIC MASKOID
NICKING APLUSTRE INTAGLIO
TRIPTYCH PETROGLYPH
(CIRCULAR —) TONDO
CARYA HICORIA
CARYATID TELAMON CANEPHORA
(PART OF —) GAINE
CARYOCAR SOUARI
CARYOPHYLLUS JAMBOSA
CARYOPSIS SEED
CASCABEL POMMEL POMMELION
CASCADE LIN FALL LINN FORCE
SPOUT CATARACT
CASCARA BUCKTHORN WAHOO
SHITTIM
CASCARILLA CROTON GOATWEED
SWEETWOOD
CASE BAG BOX CUP HAP LEG POD
POT PYX BIND BOOT BUNK BURR
CASK COPE DEED DESK DOCK
DOME FILE PACK PAIR ROLL SUIT
TICK BRACE BRIEF BULLA BURSE
CADDY CASUS CAUSE CHAPE
COVER CRATE EVENT FOLIO
FOREL HUSSY HUTCH PRESS
PYXIS SHELL STATE THECA THING
TRIAL ACTION AFFAIR APPEAL
BARREL BINDER BOXING CARTON
CASING CELLAR CHANCE CHRISM
COFFIN COUPLE LOCKET LORICA
MATTER PATRON PENNER
PETARD POPPET QUIVER RIDDLE
SHEATH SHRINE STATOR SURVEY
TASHIE TWEEZE VALISE VANITY
CABINET CAMISIA CAPCASE
CAPSULE COUNTER CUSHION
DIECASE ENCLOSE ENVELOP
EXAMPLE GEARBOX HOLDALL
HOLSTER HOUSING HUMIDOR
INCLOSE LAWSUIT LUNETTE
PACKAGE REMANET SATCHEL
SHIPPER WARDIAN ACCIDENT
ARGUMENT BOOKCASE CARRYALL
CUPBOARD ENVELOPE EQUIPAGE
EXEMPLAR GARDEVIN INSTANCE
KNAPSACK PACKSACK PORTFIRE
SHOWCASE SITUATED
SOLANDER TANTALUS
PORTFOLIO

(— CONTAINING ELEVATOR BELT) LEG
(— ENCLOSING CLOCK DIAL) HOOD
(— FOR BOTTLES) CELLARET
(— FOR CARDS) SHOE
(— FOR COMPASS) BINNACLE
(— FOR EXPLOSIVES) TRUNK
(— FOR JEWELS) TYE
(— FOR MAINSPRING) BARILLET
(— FOR MOLD) COPE CHAPE
(— FOR MUMMY) SLEDGE
(— FOR PISTOL) HOLSTER
(— FOR PULLEY) BLOCK
(— FOR RIFLE) BOOT
(— FOR SEWING ITEMS) HUSSY
(— FOR TOOLS) TROUSSE
(— FOR TWEEZERS) BUBBLEBOW
(— FOR WRITING MATERIALS) STANDISH
(— IN WATCH) DOME BARREL
(— OF) A
(— OF FLOUR BOLTER) HUTCH
(— OF VENETIAN BLIND) HEADBOX
(— WITH COMPARTMENTS) RIDDLE
(BONY —) CARAPACE
(CARTRIDGE —) DOP CARTOUCHE
(COSMETIC —) COMPACT
(COURT —) LAWSUIT
(EGG —) OVISAC OOTHECA
(FIREWORKS —) LANCE
(GRAMMATICAL —) DATIVE ESSIVE LATIVE ELATIVE FACTIVE ABLATIVE EQUATIVE ERGATIVE GENITIVE ILLATIVE LOCATIVE VOCATIVE ACCUSATIVE
(HOPELESS —) GONER
(LARVA —) INDUSIUM
(LUGGAGE —) IMPERIAL
(ORNAMENTAL —) ETUI
(PAPER —) COFFIN
(PILLOW —) SLIP
(WICKER —) HASK BARROW HANAPER
(WING —) SHARD
(WRITING —) KALAMDAN
(PREF.) THEC(A)(I)(O)
(EGG —) OOTHEC(O)
(SUFF.) THECA THECIUM
CASED BOUND
CASEMENT SASH LUKET WINDOW
CASE OF SERGEANT GRISCHA
(AUTHOR OF —) ZWEIG
(CHARACTER IN —) BABKA LYCHOW GRISCHA WILHELMI WINFRIED BJUSCHEFF PAPROTKIN PONSANSKI SCHIEFFENZAHN
CASHEW ACAJOU ANACARD
CASHIER CASS CAST BREAK DEALER POTDAR PURSER CHECKER DISMISS
CASHIERED BROKEN DEGOMME
CASHMERE KASHMIR PRUNELL
CASH REGISTER DAMPER REGEST GREFFIER RECORDER REGISTER
CASING BODY BOOT BUNG CASE CURB HULL SHOE SKIN TIRE APRON BELLY DERMA EPHOD GAINE LINER ROUND STOCK TRUNK BOXING COFFIN COLLET JACKET KISHKE LINING SCROLL SHEATH VOLUTE COWLING FEEDBOX HOUSING MANHEAD

OUTCASE STAVING THIMBLE CACHEPOT COVERING PLOWSHOE SHIRTING WHEELBOX
(— FOR BRAIN) HARNPAN
CASK KEG PIN TUB TUN VAT BOSS BUTT CADE COWL DRUM KNAG PIPE RAPE RIER SLIP TREE WOOD ANKER BOWIE BULGE FOIST STAND UNION BARECA BARREL CARDEL CASQUE DOLIUM FIRKIN FOODER LONGER OCTAVE TIERCE WINGER BARRICO BREAKER FOSTELL LEAGUER RUNDLET SACKBUT CASSETTE HOGSHEAD PUNCHEON QUARDEEL ROUNDLET KILDERKIN
(BREWING —) UNION
(LOCKED —) TANTALUS
(PERFORATED —) POT
(SMALL —) KEG TUB KNAG STOOP STOUP
(WINE —) FAT TUN BOSS BUTT PIPE TIERCE HOGSHEAD
(PL.) COOPERAGE
CASKET BOX PIX TYE CASE CASK CIST TILL TOMB BUIST CHEST ACERRA CHASSE COFFER COFFIN SHRINE CADENAS FOSTELL CASSETTE
CASQUE CASK HORN GALEA HELMET BRASSET
CASSABANANA CURUBA
CASSANDRA (BROTHER OF —) HELENUS
(FATHER OF —) PRIAM
(HUSBAND OF —) AGAMEMNON
(MOTHER OF —) HECUBA
(SLAYER OF —) CLYTEMNESTRA
CASSAREEP CAXIRI
CASSAVA AIPI YUCA AIPIM YUCCA CASIRI CAZIBI MANIOC TAPIOCA
CASSEROLE TUREEN COCOTTE MARMITE TERRINE TZIMMES
CASSIA KEZIA SENNA SICKLEPOD
CASSIA FISTULA AMALTAS
CASSIMERE ZEPHYR
CASSINI OLEG
CASSITERITE TINSTONE
CASSITES KUSHSHU
CASSOCK GOWN SLOP VEST APRON GIPPO PRIEST PELISSE SOUTANE ZIMARRA
CASSOWARY EMU MURUP MOORUP RATITE
CAST MEW PUT SET BILL DART HURL MOLD MOLT PICK SHED SLAT SLIP SPEW SWAK TINT TOSS TREE TURN WHAP WHOP WURP BLOCK BRAID CHUCK COOST DEUCE DRIVE EJECT ERECT FLING FLIRT FOUND FUSIL HEAVE IMAGE KEIST PITCH SHADE SHAPE SHOOT SLING STAMP THROW TINGE COLLAR INJECT NOSING STRIKE STRIND THRILL AGARWAL CASHIER DEPOSIT DISCARD MOULAGE VIBRATE CASTLING CONSPECT OUTSLING POLYTYPE TINCTURE
(— A SPELL) TAKE HOODOO BESPELL BEWITCH FORSPEAK
(— ASIDE) DICE FLING
(— ASPERSIONS) SLUR

SKLENT APPEACH
(— AWAY) DUMP SHOVE DEJECT REJECT
(— DICE) WHIRL
(— DISCREDIT) GLANCE
(— DOWN) DASH DUMP HURL SINK ABASE AMATE AMORT AWARP STREW ABATTU ABJECT DECAST DEJECT DEMISS THRING ECLIPSE RUINATE DEJECTED
(— FORTH) SPEW SPUE WARP BELCH BRAID LAUNCH
(— GLOOM) DUSK CLOUD DARKEN DEPRESS
(— IN A MOLD) STRIKE
(— LOTS) CAVEL
(— METAL) YET
(— OF DICE) COUP DEUCE
(— OF HERRINGS) WARP
(— OF LANGUAGE) IDIOM
(— OF NET) SHOT SHOOT
(— OFF) DAFF JILT MOLT SHED DITCH LOSSE SHAKE SLIRT SLUFF WAIVE CASTEN DEVEST REFUSE REJECT SLOUGH ABDICATE RENOUNCE
(— ON GROUND) TERRE
(— OUT) EGEST EJECT EXPEL BANISH ABANDON EXTRUDE OSTRACIZE
(— SHADOW) ADUMBRATE
(— UP) SUM LEVY UPBRAID
(FRESHLY —) GREEN
(PLASTER —) CUIRASS
(SUFF.) JECT
CASTANET KNACKER KNOCKER SNAPPER TCHAPAN CROTALUM
CASTAWAY WAIF WEFT TRAMP CRUSOE REJECT OUTCAST DERELICT STRANDED
CASTE (OR CASTE MEMBER) DOM MEO AHIR BHAR BHAT GOLA JATI KOLI KORI MALI MINA PASI TELI BAGDI BANIA DHOBY GOALA IRAVA KAHAR KUMNI KUNBI KURMI LADHA LOHAR MAHAR PALLI PUGGI SAMAR SANSI SINGH SONAR SUDRA TANTI VARNA ARORAS BAIDYA BALIJA BANIAN BHANGI CHAMAR CHETTY CHUHRA DHANUK DHOBIE DOSADH DURZEE HOLEYA HOLIYA ILAVAN JAJMAN KALWAR KAMBOH KHATRI KUMHAR KURUBA LOHANA MADIGA NATION PALLAR PRABHU PULAYA PULIAN PURVOE RAJPUT VAISYA AGARWAL BRAHMAN BRAHMIN DHANGAR GADARIA HARIJAN KAYASTH KOMATI KURUMBA NISHADA VELLALA KAMMALAN KHANDAIT PARAIYAN POVINDAH RAJBANSI VAKKALIGA
(LOWER —S) PANCHAMA
CASTER VIAL CRUET CRUSE PHIAL CASTOR HORRAL HURLER MASTER ROLLER FOUNDER PITCHER TRUCKLE TRUNDLE
(SURF —) SQUIDDER
CASTIGATE LASH EMEND SCARE SCORE BERATE PUNISH REVISE STRAFE SUBDUE CANVASS CENSURE CHASTEN CORRECT

LEATHER REPROVE CHASTISE KEELHAUL LAMBASTE FUSTIGATE OBJURGATE
CASTIGATION HELL LASHING DRESSING
CASTILIAN BROWN TANAGRA
CASTING DIE PIG CAST FONT KEEP MOLD TYMP BLOCK CHOCK CHUCK FOUND MOULD BILLET BUMPER MATRIX MISRUN SPIDER COULAGE DARTING SEGMENT SEPARATOR SORTILEGE
(— LOTS) SORTITION
(— OF HOROSCOPE) APOTELESM
(— OVERBOARD) JETTISON
(PL.) SPRAY FOUNDRY
CAST IRON YETLING
CASTLE BURY FORT HALL KEEP ROCK ROOK ABODE BROCH COURT MORRO PIECE CASBAH BASTILE BOROUGH CHATEAU CITADEL SCHLOSS UDOLPHO BASTILE CASTELET CASTILLO FASTNESS FORTRESS STAROSTY TINTAGEL
(— IN CHESS) JUEZ ROOK TOUR JUDGE TOWER
(PART OF —) KEEP MOAT WARD MOUNT TOWER WHARF BAILEY BRIDGE DONJON TURRET BASTION BULWARK DUNGEON OUTWORK RAMPART BARBICAN CASEMATE GATEHOUSE BATTLEMENT DRAWBRIDGE PORTCULLIS
(SMALL —) PEEL TOWER CASTLET CHATELET
CASTLE OF OTRANTO (AUTHOR OF —) WALPOLE
(CHARACTER IN —) CONRAD JEROME MANFRED MATILDA ISABELLA THEODORE
CASTOR BEAVER LEATHER TRUCKLE TRUNDLE BARKSTONE
(— AND POLLUX) TWINS GEMINI DIOSCURI
CASTOR AND POLLUX
(CHARACTER IN —) CASTOR PHOEBE POLLUX JUPITER MERCURY TELAIRA
(COMPOSER OF —) RAMEAU
CASTOR-OIL
(PREF.) RICIN(I)
CASTOR-OIL PLANT KIKI MAMONA PALMCRIST
CASTRATE CUT FIX GIB LIB GELD GLIB SPAY SWIG THIN ALTER CAPON DESEX PRUNE STEER CHANGE EUNUCH NEUTER EVIRATE CAPONIZE MUTILATE SATURNIZE
CASTRATED CUT GIBBED NEUTER UNPAVED
CASTRATO EUNUCH EVIRATO TENORINO
CASUAL GLIB ORRA STRAY BLITHE BYHAND CHANCE FOLKSY RANDOM CASALTY CURSORY LEISURE NATURAL OFFHAND RUNNING GLANCING INFORMAL PROMISCUOUS
CASUALTY LOSS DEATH CADUAC CHANCE HAZARD INJURY MISHAP

ACCIDENT DISASTER
CASUARINA BEEFWOOD
CASUIST JESUIT
CAT GIB RAT SOW TAB CHAT EYRA
FLOG LION LYNX MISS PARD
PUMA PUSS CHAUS CIVET FELID
GATOL KITTY MANUL MEWER
MOGGY OUNCE PUSSY SMOKE
TABBY TIGER TILER WHITE ZIBET
ANGORA COUGAR FELINE
JAGUAR KITTEN KODKOD MALKIN
MARGAY MAWKIN MIAUER
MOUSER MUSION NEUTER
OCELOT PAJERO PURRER SERVAL
TIBERT TORTIE BURMESE
CARACAL CATHEAD CATLING
CHEETAH KITLING KUICHUA
LEOPARD LINSANG PANTHER
PERSIAN SIAMESE TIGRESS
WILDCAT WRAWLER BAUDRONS
DASYURID FISSIPED PUSSYCAT
RINGTAIL
(**— CRY**) WAW
(**— GROUP**) CLOWDER
(**FEMALE —**) QUEEN WHEENCAT
(**MALE —**) GIB TOM TOMCAT
(**PART OF —**) EAR EYE PAW TOE
HEEL KNEE LIPS LOIN NAPE NECK
RUMP TAIL BELLY BREAK ELBOW
FLANK SHANK THIGH WRIST
FEELER DEWCLAW LEATHER
WHISKER FOREHEAD SHOULDER
VIBRISSA METATARSUS
(**ROOF-PROWLING —**) TILER
(**TAILLESS —**) RUMPY
(**PREF.**) AELUR(O) AILUR(O)
FELIN(O)
CATACHRESIS ABUSION
CATACHRESTICAL ABUSIVE
CATACLYSM FLOOD DELUGE
DEBACLE DISASTER UPHEAVAL
CATACOMB TOMB CRYPT VAULT
CEMETERY HYPOGEUM
(PL.) ARENARIAE
CATADROMOUS SEAGOING
CATALECTIC HEMIAMB
TRUNCATED
CATALEPSY TRANCE SEIZURE
CATATONY
CATALOG PIE PYE BILL BOOK LIST
ROLL ROTA BRIEF CANON FLIER
FLYER INDEX PINAX AUTHOR
RAGGER RAGMAN RECORD
ROSTER ARRANGE BEADROW
DIPTYCH NOTITIA BEADROLL
BULLETIN CALENDAR CLASSIFY
REGISTER SCHEDULE SYLLABUS
CATALOGUE DIDASCALY
INVENTORY
CATALUFA SCAD TORO BIGEYE
CATALYST CARRIER SAUSAGE
ZIEGLER CATALYTE HOPCALITE
(**NEGATIVE —**) INHIBITER
CATAMARAN RAFT TROW BALSA
FLOAT GUNBOAT JANGADA
MONITOR AUNTSARY
CATAMITE INGLE GUNSEL NINGLE
PATHIC BARDASH GANYMEDE
CATAMOUNT LYNX PUMA
COUGAR
CATAPLASM PELOID POULTICE
CATAPULT GUN BIBLE SLING
SWEEP THROW HURTLE LAUNCH

ONAGER TREPAN ALACRAN
BRICOLE PEDRERO TORMENT
TRABUCH WARWOLF BALLISTA
CROSSBOW DONDAINE
LAUNCHER MANGONEL
MARTINET SCORPION SPRINGAL
STONEBOW
CATARACT LIN FALL LINN FALLS
FLOOD PEARL DELUGE CASCADE
NIAGARA CATADUPE OVERFALL
VICTORIA
CATARRH MUR COLD MURR POSE
RHEUM CORYZA NASITIS
CATASTROPHE ACCIDENT
CALAMITY DISASTER CATACLYSM
CATCH BAG COB COG COP GET GIN
KEP NAB NET NIP DRAW FANG
GLOM HASP HAUL HAWK HENT
HOLD HOOK LAND MAKE MEET
MESS NAIL NICK PAWL SAVE
SEAR SNAG SNAP SNIB STOP
TAKE TRAP TREE VANG BENET
CHAPE CLASP CLEEK CREEL
FETCH GLOVE GRASP HITCH
KETCH KNACK LASSO LATCH
PLANT SEIZE SNARE SNICK
SWOOP TRICK TROLL ARREST
ATTAIN BUTTON CLUTCH CORNER
CORRAL DETECT DETENT ENGAGE
ENMESH ENTRAP IMMESH
LOCKET NOBBLE NOODLE SNATCH
SPRENT TAIGLE TAKING TURNEL
ATTRACT CAPTURE ENSNARE
GIMMICK GRAPNEL RELEASE
SNIGGLE SPRINGE TRIGGER
CONTRACT CRANNAGE ENTANGLE
FASTNESS HOLDBACK HOLDFAST
OVERTAKE SNAPHAAN SURPRISE
(**— AT PROPER TIME**) NICK
(**— ATTENTION**) FLAG
(**— BIRDS**) BATFOWL BIRDLIME
(**— EELS**) SNIGGLE
(**— FIRE**) SPUNK IGNITE KINDLE
(**— FISH**) JAB JIG GILL HANG
GILLNET
(**— FISH WITH HANDS**) GUDDLE
GRABBLE HANDFAST
(**— IN VOICE**) FETCH
(**— OF DOOR**) LATCH SNECK SNICK
(**— OF FISH**) FARE HAUL SHOT
TACK TRIP SHACK
(**— ONE'S BREATH**) GASP CHINK
(**— SIGHT OF**) SPY ESPY SPOT
DESCRY
(**CRICKET —**) DOLLY
(**RATCHET —**) CLICK
(**SAFETY —**) CLEVIS
CATCHER TAKER BIRDER FANGER
LARKER RECEIVER
CATCHFLY SILENE FLYBANE
CATCHING CATCHY TAKING
ALLURING ARRESTING
CATCHPOLE BAILIFF PUTTOCK
CATCHWEED CLEAVERS
CATCHWORD CUE TAG MOTTO
BYWORD PHRASE SLOGAN
STARTER CATCHCRY SHIBBOLETH
CATCHY CATCHING APPEALING
CATECHISM QUIZ GUIDE MANUAL
CARRITCH QUESTIONS
CATECHU COTCH CUTCH KHAIR
GAMBIER
CATECHUMEN PUPIL AUDIENT

AUDITOR CONVERT BEGINNER
NEOPHYTE COMPETENT
CATEGORICAL DIRECT ABSOLUTE
EXPLICIT KNOCKDOWN
CATEGORIZE CODE HAVE
CATEGORY WAY KING RANK TALE
CLASS FIELD GENRE GENUS
ORDER STYLE FAMILY LEAGUE
NUMBER RUBRIC SERIES SPECIES
DIVISION PIGEONHOLE
PREDICAMENT
(**— OF TENSES**) INFECTUM
(**HIGHEST —**) IDEA
(**PRIMARY —**) SUBSTANCE
(**TAXONOMIC —**) FORM FORMA
GENUS TAXON COHORT LEGION
SUBCLASS SUBGENUS SUBFAMILY
CATER CUT FEED HUMOR SERVE
TREAT PANDER PURVEY SUPPLY
PROVIDE
(PREF.) OPSONI OPSONO
CATERER ACATER MANCIPLE
CATERINA CORNARO (**CHARACTER
IN —**) ANDREAS GERARDO
CATERINA MOCENIGO LUSIGNANO
(**COMPOSER OF —**) DONIZETTI
CATERPILLAR CAT MUGA AWETO
ERUCA CANKER LOOPER PALMER
PORINA RISPER TAILOR WOUBIT
CUTWORM TRACTOR WEBWORM
HANGWORM HORNWORM
SILKWORM SKINWORM
WORTWORM PALMERWORM
(PREF.) CAMPO ERUCI
(SUFF.) CAMPA
CATERWAUL CRY HOWL WAIL
MIAUL WRAWL
CATFACE ARR SCAR
CATFISH MUD CUSK ELOD POUT
RAAD SHAL WOOF BAGRE DORAD
RAASH BARBER DOCMAC GLANIS
GOONCH GOUJON HASSAR
MADTOM MUDCAT BARBUDO
CANDIRU COBBLER FIDDLER
PYGIDID SILURID WALLAGO
BULLHEAD BULLPOUT CORYDORA
FLATHEAD MATHEMEG PLOTOSID
SQUEAKER STONECAT
CATGUT THARM THAIRM CATLING
WHIPCORD
CATHARI BULGARI PATARINE
CATHARTIC ALOIN BRYONY
PHYSIC CALOMEL RHUBARB
SCOURER EUONYMUS EVACUANT
HYDRAGOG KALADANA LAPACTIC
LAXATIVE SCAMMONY SOLUTIVE
SOLUTORY PURGATIVE
PODOPHYLLIN
CATHAYAN KITAN
CATHEDRA SEE
CATHEDRAL DOM SEE DUOMO
SOBOR MARTYRY MEMORIA
MINSTER BASILICA
(**PART OF —**) ARCH ROOF CROSS
GABLE IMAGE LABEL SPIRE
TOWER BELFRY FINIAL LINTEL
LOUVER PORTAL WINDOW
CROCKET GALLERY LOZENGE
MOLDING MULLION TRACERY
TREFOIL PINNACLE TYMPANUM
DRIPSTONE THROATING
TRIFORIUM CINQUEFOIL
CLERESTORY QUATREFOIL

CATHEXIS CHARGE
CATHODE K KA FILAMENT
ELECTRODE HYDROGODE
CATHOLIC BROAD GENERAL
LIBERAL TOLERANT
CATHOLICISM PAPISM POPERY
CATHOLICON PANACEA
CATKIN RAG TAG CHAT GULL
AGLET AMENT IULUS PUSSY
CACHRYS CATTAIL GOSLING
(PREF.) AMENTI
CATMINT NEP
CATNAP NAP DOZE
CATNIP NEP CATARIA CATMINT
CATWORT
CATREUS (**DAUGHTER OF —**)
AEROPE CLYMENE APEMOSYNE
(**FATHER OF —**) MINOS
(**MOTHER OF —**) PASIPHAE
(**SON OF —**) ALTHAEMENES
CAT'S-CLAW LONGPOD
ESCAMBRON
CAT'S CRADLE HEI
CAT'S-EAR GOSMORE CAPEWEED
FLATWEED
CAT'S EYE CHATOYANT
CAT'S-FOOT PUSSYTOE
CATTAIL DOD DODD FLAG MUSK
RUSH TULE AMENT BAYON BLECK
CLOUD RAUPO REREE WONGA
CATKIN GLADEN TOTORA
BULRUSH GLADDON MATREED
BLACKCAP CARBUNGI FLAXTAIL
CAT THYME HULWORT
CATTLE ZO BOW FEE GIR AVER
DHAN GAUR KINE NEAT NOWT
OXEN ZEBU ZOBO DEVON STOCK
ANKOLI DURHAM GALYAK
ONGOLE ROTHER SINDHI SUSSEX
BESTIAL NELLORE REDPOLL
COMPOUND OUTSIGHT TUBICORN
(**— CARRIED OFF**) SPREATH
(**BREED OF —**) ANGUS BORAN
DEVON FJALL KERRY KYLOE
SANGA SANGU ANGONI ANKOLE
ANKOLI DEXTER DURHAM FULANI
JERSEY SUSSEX BAROTSE
BRAFORD BRAHMAN COASTER
CRIOLLA GUZERAT HARIANA
SAHIWAL ALDERNEY AYRSHIRE
CHARBRAY FRIBOURG FRIESIAN
GALLOWAY GUERNSEY HEREFORD
HOLSTEIN KANGAYAM LONGHORN
(**DWARF —**) NATA NIATA
(**WILD YOUNG —**) KANGAROO
(PREF.) BOVI
CATTLE-BREEDER AHIR ALUR
CATTLE DEALER DROVER
CATTLEHIDE BUFF CROUPON
CATTLEMAN FAZENDEIRO
CATTLE MARKET SALEYARD
CATTLE PEN KRAAL
CATTLE RAID SPRAITH SPREAGH
CATTLE RUN STATION
CATTLE STEALER ABACTOR
ABIGEUS
CATTLE YARD CANCHA
CATTY KIN KATI
CAUCASIAN WHITE IRANIAN
EUROPEAN JAPHETIC PALEFACE
(**— LANGUAGE**) UDI UDIC UDIN
(PL.) MELANOI
CAUCHO ULE RUBBER

CAUCUS PRIMARY
CAUDAL POSTERIOR
(PREF.) UR(O)
CAUDATA URODELA
CAUDEX STIPE
CAUGHT GRIPPIT ENTANGLED
CAUL HOW WEB KEEL KELL TRUG
VEIL GALEA HOUVE DORLOT
CREPINE KERCHER NETWORK
OMENTUM MEMBRANE SILLYHOW
TRESSOUR TRESSURE
(PREF.) AMNIO OMENT(O)
CAULDRON KOHUA CALDRON
CAULICLE SCAPEL ROSTELLUM
CAULIFLOWER BROCCOLI
SNOWBALL CHOUFLEUR
CAULK CALK CORK FILL FLAG
CHINSE
CAUNUS (FATHER OF —) MILETUS
(MOTHER OF —) CYANEE
(SISTER OF —) BYBLIS
CAUSAL GENETIC
CAUSE DO AIM GAR ISM KEY LET
WAY CASE CHAT FATE HOTI LEAD
MAKE MOVE ROOT SAKE SPUR
SUIT AGENT ARCHE BASIS BREED
CAUSA FRAME PARTY SKILL
SLAKE WREAK YIELD ADDICT
CREATE EFFECT ELICIT GOSSIP
GROUND INDUCE INVOKE
MALADY MANNER MATTER
MOTIVE OBJECT ORIGIN PARENT
REASON RESORT SOURCE SPEECH
SPRING CHESOUN CONCERN
DISEASE LAWSUIT PROCURE
PRODUCE PROVOKE QUARREL
SUBJECT BUSINESS ENGENDER
GENERATE INSTANCE MOVEMENT
OCCASION WHEREFORE
MAINSPRING
(— A SORE) RANKLE
(— DAMAGE) DAMNIFY
(— FOR COMPLAINT) COMEBACK
(— OF RUIN) BANE
(— OF TERROR) AFFRIGHT
(— OF TROUBLE) TRACHLE
(— PAIN) URN
(— TO ARCH) ROACH
(— TO CONTRACT) PUCKER
(— TO CROUCH) COUCH
(— TO DESERT) DEFECT
(— TO END) ACHIEVE
(— TO MOVE RAPIDLY) GIG
(— TO PROJECT) JET
(— TO RESULT) ISSUE
(— TO STICK) MIRE
(— TO SWELL) BINGE EMBOSS
(— TO THICKEN) CURD
(FINAL —) END
(FORM-GIVING —) IDEA
(IMMEDIATE —) SIGNAL
(PRIMAL —) URGRUND
(PREF.) AETIO AITIO CAUSI ETIO
(SUFF.) FIC(AL)(ATE)(ATION)(ATIVE)
(ATOR)(ATORY)(E)(ENCE)(ENT)(IAL)
(IARY)(IENT) FIQUE
CAUSED
(SUFF.) **(— BY)** IC(AL)
CAUSEWAY WAY DIKE ROAD
HIGHWAY CHAUSSEE
CAUSING
(SUFF.) ABLE FACIENT
FACT(ION)(IVE)(ORY) IBLE

CAUSTIC LYE ACID TART ACRID
QUICK SALTY SHARP SNELL
ACIDIC BITING BITTER SEVERE
BURNING CAUTERY CUTTING
ERODENT MORDANT NIPPING
PUNGENT PYROTIC SATIRIC
ALKALINE DIERETIC SCATHING
SNAPPISH STINGING ACIDULOUS
SARCASTIC MORDACIOUS
CAUSTICITY ACRIMONY
CAUTERIZATION USTION
INUSTION
CAUTERIZE BURN CHAR FIRE SEAR
BRAND INUST SINGE
CAUTERY MOXA
CAUTION CARE FEAR HEED WARN
GUARD ADVICE CAUTEL CAVEAT
EXHORT ANXIETY COUNSEL
PRECEPT PROVISO WARNING
ADMONISH FORECAST
FOREWARN MONITION PRUDENCE
WARINESS
CAUTIOUS SHY SAFE WARE WARY
ALERT CANNY CHARY SIKER
FABIAN HOOLIE SICKER TENDER
TIPTOE CAREFUL CURIOUS
ENVIOUS FEARFUL FERDFUL
GUARDED PRUDENT DISCREET
SUSPENSE VIGILANT CAUTELOUS
CAUTIOUSLY CANNY CANNILY
CHARILY EASYLIKE GINGERLY
TENDERLY
CAVAL
(PREF.) VEN(I)(O)
CAVALCADE RAID RIDE MARCH
TRAIN PARADE SAFARI COMPANY
JOURNEY PAGEANT
CAVALIER GAY CAVY CURT EASY
FINE BRAVE FRANK MOUNT
RIDER ESCORT KNIGHT BRUSQUE
GALLANT HAUGHTY OFFHAND
SOLDIER CAVALERO ROYALIST
CHAMBERER CHEVALIER
COMMANDER
CAVALLA CERO JACK TORO ULUA
JUREL CARANX CARANGID
CREVALLE SCOMBRID
CAVALLERIA RUSTICANA
(CHARACTER IN —) LOLA ALFIO
TURIDDU SANTUZZA
(COMPOSER OF —) MASCAGNI
CAVALRY HORSE HEAVIES
CHIVALRY HORSEMEN YEOMANRY
CAVALRYMAN SOWAR SPAHI
SUWAR HUSSAR JINETE LANCER
REITER ARGOLET COURIER
DRAGOON PLUNGER SABREUR
TROOPER GENDARME HORSEMAN
SILLADAR STRADIOT
(PL.) FORAGERS
CAVE DEN TIP COVE HOLE LAIR
MINE REAR SINK TOSS WEEM
ANTAR ANTRE CABIN CACHE
CALVE CAVEA CRYPT DELVE
FOGOU SLADE SPEOS STORE
UPSET BEWARE CAVERN CAVITY
CELLAR DUGOUT GROTTO
HOLLOW LARDER LUSTER
PANTRY PLUNGE SHROUD
MANSION RESERVE SPELUNK
CASTILLO COLLAPSE OVERTURN
MITHRAEUM
(— IN) COLT

(ANIMAL LIVING IN —)
TROGLODYTE
(PREF.) SPELEO
CAVEAT BEWARE NOTICE
CAUTION WARNING
CAVE-DWELLER HORITE
TROGLODYTE
CAVE-DWELLING NATUFIAN
(PREF.) TROGLO
CAVEMAN NEANDERTHAL
CAVER SPELUNKER
CAVERN DEN CAVE COVE GROT
HOLE LAIR WEEM CROFT VAULT
ANTRUM CAVITY GROTTO
HOLLOW SPELUNK
(PREF.) ANTR(O)
CAVERNOUS ERECTILE
CAVESSON CHAIN
CAVETTO GULA GORGE
CAVIAR OVA ROE IKRA GARUM
IKARY
CAVIL CARK CARP HAFT HAGGLE
CAPTION CHICANE QUARREL
QUIBBLE PETTIFOG QUIDDITY
FORMALIZE
CAVILER CRITIC GIRDER HAFTER
ZOILUS
CAVILING CAPTIOUS CRITICAL
PICAYUNE
CAVITIED
(SUFF.) COELOUS COELUS
CAVITY BAG CUP PIT SAC ABRI
AXIL CASE CAVE CELL DALK DENT
DUCT HOLE MIND MINE VEIN
VOID WELL WOMB ABYSS BOSOM
BURSA CRYPT DRUSE FOSSA
GEODE GOUGE LUMEN MOUTH
ORBIT SCOOP SINUS ANTRUM
AREOLE ATRIUM AXILLA BORING
CAECUM CAMERA CAVERN
COELIA COELOM COTYLE CRATER
DEBLAI GROTTO HOLLOW
LACUNA POCKET RECESS SCAPHA
SOCKET VACUUM VOMICA
ABDOMEN CHAMBER CISTERN
CYATHUS DIOCOEL KYATHOS
LOCULUS MORTISE VACUITY
VACUOLE VESICLE ALVEOLUS
BROODSAC EPICOELE FOLLICLE
WELLHOLE VESTIBULE
(— IN BONE) LACUNA
(— IN CASTING) PIPE
(— IN HEAD OF WHALE) CASE
(— IN HILLSIDE) ABRI
(— IN LAVA) AMYGDALE
AMYGDULE
(— IN MINE) BAG
(— IN ROCK) KETTLE
(— MADE BY SEALS) IGLOO
(— OF SEA-SHELL) FLUE
(ALTAR —) TOMB
(BODY —) GUT BELLY CLOACA
THORAX ABDOMEN STOMACH
PSEUDOCOEL PERICARDIUM
(CHEST —) THORAX
(CRYSTAL-LINED —) VUGG DRUSE
GEODE
(GUN —) BORE
(NASAL —) CAVUM
(SUBTERRANEAN —) SLUGGA
(PREF.) ALVEOL(I)(O) ANTR(O)
CAEC(I)(O) CEC(I)(O) CEL(I)(O)
COEL(I)(O)

(SUFF.) CELE COELE COELUS
CAVORT PLAY BOUND CAPER
CURVET GAMBOL PRANCE
CAVY PACA PONY AGOUTI APEREA
CAYUSE CAPYBARA
(FEMALE —) SOW
CAW KA CRY CALL CROAK QUARK
QUAWK
CAYMAN JACARE
CAYSTER (DAUGHTER OF —)
SEMIRAMIS
(FATHER OF —) ACHILLES
(MOTHER OF —) PENTHESILEA
CAYUSE CAVY PONY BRONCO
MUSTANG
CEASE HO BOW CUT DIE END LIN
BALK BLIN DROP FINE HALT HOLD
LIFT LISS QUIT REST SACE SHUT
STAY STOP STOW AVAST CLOSE
DOWSE LEAVE PAUSE PETER
STINT SWICK WAIVE DESIST
DEVALL EXPIRE FINISH FORGET
ABSTAIN OUTGIVE REFRAIN
SUSPEND INTERMIT OVERGIVE
SURCEASE
(— MILKING COW) SINE
(— TEMPORARILY) LIFT
(— TO ASSERT) ABANDON
CEASELESS EVER ENDLESS
ETERNAL IMMORTAL UNENDING
CEASING CESSER CESSATION
CEBUS SAI
CECILIA SIS SISSU
CECROPS (DAUGHTER OF —) HERSE
AGLAUROS PANDROSOS
(WIFE OF —) AGLAURUS
CECUM
(PREF.) TYPHL(O)
CEDAR SUGI TOON SAVIN AROLLA
DEODAR SABINA TUMION
CYPRESS JUNIPER WAXWING
CALANTAS PAHAUTEA
CEDAR SWAMP GREENING
CEDAR WAXWING RECOLLET
CEDE CESS GIVE AWARD GRANT
LEAVE WAIVE YIELD ASSIGN
RESIGN SUBMIT CONCEDE
RENOUNCE TRANSFER
CEDILLA TITTLE
CEIBA KAPOK BENTANG POCHOTE
CEIL LINE SYLE OVERLAY
WAINSCOT
CEILING TOP DOME LACE LOFT
CHUTT CUPOLA LINING SCREEN
SOFFIT SYLING CURTAIN
LACUNAR PLAFOND TESTUDO
COVERING DECKHAND OVERHEAD
PANELING PLANCHER SEMIDOME
CELAENO (FATHER OF —) ATLAS
(MOTHER OF —) PLEIONE
(SON OF —) LYCUS NYCTEUS
CELANDINE FICARY KILLWORT
PILEWORT WARTWEED
WARTWORT FELONWORT
JEWELWEED
CELEBES (GULF OF —) BONE TOLO
TOMINI
(ISLAND OF —) MUNA BUTUNG
PELENG SULAWESI
(PEOPLE OF —) TORAJA
(TOWN OF —) BUOL LUWUK
MANADO MAKASAR
CELEBRATE FETE KEEP SING

CHANT DITTY EXTOL HONOR
REVEL SACRE SPEAK BESING
CHAUNT EXTOLL PRAISE ELEGIZE
EXECUTE GLORIFY MAFFICK
OBSERVE EMBLAZON EULOGIZE
PROCLAIM
(— 2 MASSES) BINATE DUPLICATE

CELEBRATED KEPT FAMED NOTED
FAMOUS EMINENT FEASTED
RENOMME STORIED FABULOUS
GLORIOUS NOTIFIED OBSERVED
RENOWNED

CELEBRATION FED FETE GALA
POPE RITE FESTA REVEL COOLIN
CUSTOM DOMENT EASTER FIESTA
POWWOW RENOWN SIMHAH
BLOWOUT HAGMENA HOLIDAY
JUBILEE PASCHAL SHINDIG
SIMCHAH BINATION BIRTHDAY
HOGMANAY MAKAHIKI OCCASION
OLYMPIAD POTLATCH SHIVAREE
FESTIVITY HOOLAULEA
JUNKETING MERRIMENT
MILLENIUM

CELEBRATOR JUBILIST
CELEBRITY FAME LION NAME
STAR CELEB ECLAT RENOWN
REPUTE

CELERITY HASTE HURRY SPEED
DISPATCH RAPIDITY VELOCITY
SWIFTNESS

CELERY SIT ACHE STICK UMBEL
KARPAS SALARY CELERIAC
SMALLAGE

CELESTIAL HOLY DIVINE HEAVEN
URANIO ANGELIO OLIINEOE
ETHERED EMPYREAL ETHEREAL
HEAVENLY OLYMPIAN

CELESTITE APOTOME
CELEUS (SON OF —) DEMOPHON
TRIPTOLEMUS
(WIFE OF —) METANIRA

CELIBACY CHASTITY VIRGINITY
CELIBATE CLERK CHASTE SINGLE
BACHELOR SPINSTER

CELL BOX EGG BAND BOOT CAGE
CYTE DISC DISK GERM GONE
HOLE JAIL KILL ASCUS CABIN
CAROL CLINK CRYPT CYTON
FIBER FIBRE GHOST GLAND
GROUP OOTID TMEMA TORIL
VAULT ZOOID ANAXON CEPTOR
COCCUS COOLER CYTODE
GAMETE GONIUM INAXON
NEURON PRISON SHIELD SIPHON
SYPHON WESTON ZYGOTE
AGAMETE AMEBULA APOCYTE
CELLULE CHAMBER CLOCHAN
CLOSTER COCCOID CUBICLE
DIPLOID DUNGEON ELEMENT
EPICYTE EUPLOID HAPLOID
HEMATID INITIAL LOCULUS
MYOCYTE NEURONE OOBLAST
PAPILLA PLASTID RENETTE
SEGMENT SPORONT STEREID
TRISOME UTRICLE VESICLE
AMACRINE BASOCYTE BASOPHIL
BIFORINE BIOPLAST CLOGHAUN
DIKARYON FAVEOLUS GLIOCYTE
GONIDIUM GONOCYTE HEMOCYTE
HOLDOVER IDIOSOME LOCELLUS
MYOBLAST ORGANULE PROSORUS
RECEPTOR SCLEREID SPERMULE

SYNERGID TRACHEID TRIPLOID
ZOOBLAST MACROCYTE
MICROCYTE MYELOCYTE
OSTEOCYTE PHAGOCYTE
PROGAMETE MELANOCYTE
MOTONEURON NEUTROPHIL
OSTEOCLAST MELANOBLAST
MELANOPHORE ODONTOBLAST
(— CONTAINING LATEX) LATICIFER
(— OF LEADERS) CADRE
(BEE —) PIPE
(CLUSTER OF —S) MORULA
(DETENTION —) BULLPEN
(PART OF —) SAP NUCLEUS
PLASTID VACUOLE MEMBRANE
CENTRIOLE ECTOPLASM
ENDOPLASM NUCLEOLUS
RETICULUM CENTROSOME
CHONDRIOSOME
(PHOTOELECTRIC —) EYE PEC
PHOTOCELL
(PRISON —) BING HOLE CABIN
CLINK COOLER JIGGER
(STAB —) BAND
(THIN-WALLED —S) STOMIUM
(VOLTAIC —) BATTERY
(PL.) LAURA POTLINE SWEATBOX
(PREF.) CYT(IO)(O) GAMET(O)
GONIDI ONT(O) THYRE(O) THYRO
(SUFF.) BLAST(IC)(Y) CYTE
PHAG(A)(E)(O)(OUS)(US)(Y) PLASIA
PLASIS PLASM(A)(IA)(IC)
PLATI(IC)(Y) SPONGIA(E)(N)
SPONGIUM THYRIS

CELLA NAOS
CELLAR CAVE VAULT BODEGA
PALACE FAVISSA HYPOGEE
BASEMENT HYPOGEUM
MATAMORO VAULTAGE

CELLARET TANTALUS
CELLARMAN SOMMELIER
CELLULAR
(SUFF.) ENCHYMA ENCHYMATA
CELLULOID XYLONITE
CELLULOSE CRUMB AMYLOID
LIGNOSE TAMIDINE

CELT GAEL GAUL KELT MANX IRISH
WELSH BRETON BRITON EOLITH
GADHEL GOIDEL BRYTHON
CORNISH PALSTAFF PALSTAVE
(PL.) CYMRY KYMRY

CELTIC ERSE GAEL SCOTCH
CEMBALO DULCIMER ZIMBALON
CEMENT FIX KIT TIE GLUE HEAL
JOIN KNIT LIME LUTE SLIP BETON
GROUT IMBED PASTE PUTTY
SIMON STICK TABBY UNITE
BINDER CHUNAM COHERE
FASTEN FILLER GULGUL KIBOSH
MALTHA MASTIC MORTAR
OOGLEA SOLDER ASPHALT
MIXTION ADHESIVE ALBOLITE
ALBOLITH CEMENTUM HADIGEON
SOLIDIFY SOLUTION
(BEES' —) PROPOLIS
(SUFF.) LITE LITH(IC) LITIC

CEMENTER GLUER GLUEMAN
SMEARER

CEMENT MIXER TEMPERER
CEMETERY HOWF KILL LAIR
LITTEN CHARNEL BONEYARD
CATACOMB GOLGOTHA URNFIELD
NECROPOLIS

CENCHRIAS (FATHER OF —)
POSEIDON
(MOTHER OF —) PIRENE
(SLAYER OF —) ARTEMIS

CENCI (AUTHOR OF —) SHELLEY
(CHARACTER IN —) CENCI MARZIO
ORSINO CAMILLO GIACOMO
OLIMPIO SAVELLA BEATRICE
BERNARDO LUCRETIA

CENERENTOLA, LA (CHARACTER IN
—) TISBE RAMIRO ALIDORO
DANDINI ANGELINA CLORINDA
MAGNIFICO CINDERELLA
(COMPOSER OF —) ROSSINI

CENOBITE NUN MONK FRIAR
ESSENE RECLUSE MONASTIC
SYNODITE

CENOTAPH TOMB
CENSE THURIFY
CENSER INCENSER THURIBLE
CASSOLETTE

CENSOR CRITIC SCREEN SYNDIC
LAUNDER RESTRICT SUPPRESS

CENSORIOUS SEVERE BLAMING
CARPING BLAMEFUL CAPTIOUS
CRITICAL CULPABLE SLASHING

CENSORSHIP WRAPS ASSIZE
CENSURE

CENSURABLE TAXABLE BLAMABLE
CULPABLE

CENSURE BAN HIT NIP RAP TAP
TAX WIG CALL CARP DEEM DRUB
FLAY HELL LASH RATE SLAP TASK
WITE BEANS BLAME CHIDE CURSE
DECRY FAULT HOKER JUDGE
FINCH SCOLD SLANG SLASH
SLATE TAUNT TOUCH WHITE
ACCUSE ATTACK BERATE CHARGE
REBUFF REBUKE REFORM
REMORD STRAFE TARGUE TIRADE
APPEACH BLISTER CHASTEN
CONDEMN CONTROL DECRIAL
DYSLOGY IMPEACH IMPROVE
INVEIGH REPROOF REPROVE
SCARIFY TRADUCE TROUNCE
UPBRAID BACKBITE CHASTISE
DISALLOW JUDGMENT LANGUAGE
REPROACH SATIRIZE SENTENCE
STRICTURE ADMONITION

CENSUS LIST POLL CENSE COUNT
LUSTER LUSTRUM CAPITATION

CENT RED DUIT SANT BROWNIE
CENTAVO STUIVER
(ODD —S) BREAKAGE
(12 1-2 —S) LEVY

CENTAUR CHIRON NESSUS
HORSEMAN BUCENTAUR
SAGITTARY

CENTAURUS (FATHER OF —) IXION
(MOTHER OF —) NEPHELE

CENTAURY BEHN BEHEN
SABBATIA EARTHGALL

CENTENNIAL STATE COLORADO
CENTER COR EYE GIG HUB MID
AXIS CORE NAVE SEAT SNAP
YOLK FOCUS FOYER GLOME
HEART MIDST PIVOT SPINE
BOTTOM CENTRE MIDDLE PIPPER
STAPLE TEMPLE CENTRUM
ESSENCE LINEMAN NUCLEUS
UMBILIC INCENTER OMPHALOS
SNAPBACK
(— FOR SPINDLE) GIG

(— FOR TARGET) EYE PIN PINHOLE
(— OF ACTIVITY) HUB HIVE
(— OF ARCH) COOM
(— OF ASSURANCE) FORTRESS
(— OF ATTRACTION) FOCUS STAGE
CYNOSURE POLESTAR
(— OF BASKET) SLATHER
(— OF CITY) DOWNTOWN
(— OF CULTIVATION) HOME
(— OF CULTURE) ATHENS
(— OF DIAMOND) WELL
(— OF ESCUTCHEON) NOMBRIL
(OF FIGURE) CENTROID
(— OF FISHING NET) BUNT
(— OF FLOWER) EYE
(— OF HURRICANE) EYE
(— OF OPERATIONS) SHOP
(— OF POPULATION) CITY
(— OF POWER) SEE SIEGE
(— OF STAGE) LIMELIGHT
(— OF STRENGTH) GANGLION
(BASKETBALL —) PIVOTMAN
(COLLECTION —) ENTREPOT
(COMMERCIAL —) MACHI
EMPORIUM
(HARD —) KNOT
(INTIMATE —) BOSOM
(LATHE —) PIKE
(NERVOUS —) BRAIN NIDUS
(NEURAL —) APPESTAT
(PROPAGANDA —) AGITPUNKT
(REHABILITATION —) HOSTEL
(TRADING —) BEACH EXCHANGE
(VITAL —) HEARTH HEARTBEAT
(PREF.) CENTR(I)(O)
(SUFF.) CENTRIC

CENTERING COOM COOMB
CENTRY FANTAIL

CENTERPIECE ROSACE
DORMANT EPERGNE
DUCHESSE

CENTETES TENREC
CENTIARE LI
CENTIGRADE CELSIUS
CENTIME RAPPEN
CENTIMETER GAL
CENTIPEDE VEI VERI EARWIG
GOLACH GOLOCH POLYPOD
CHILOPOD MULTIPED MYRIAPOD
SANTAPEE SCUTIGER
SCOLOPENDRA

CENTRAL MID AXIAL BASIC CHIEF
FOCAL MIXED PRIME MEDIAN
MIDDLE CAPITAL CENTRIC
LEADING NUCLEAR PIVOTAL
PRIMARY CARDINAL
DOMINANT
(PREF.) CENTR(I)(O)

GRIMARI ZEMONGO
BERBERATI BOSSANGOA

CENTRAL AMERICAN LADINO
NATION: RICA COSTA BELIZE
HONDURAS GUATEMALA
ELSALVADOR
(— TREE) TUNO TUNU
CENTRANTH SPURFLOWER
CENTRIFUGAL EFFERENT
RADIATING
CENTRIFUGE CYCLONE
SEPARATOR
CENTRIPETAL AFFERENT
CENTROSOME CENTRUM
CENTRIOLE
CENTRUM CORE
CENTURIED SECULAR
CENTURY AGE TON SECLE SIECLE
(14TH —) TRECENTO
CENTURY PLANT ALOE PITA
AGAVE MAGUEY CANTALA
TEQUILA MONOCARP
CENWALH (FATHER OF —)
CYNEGILS
CEPHALALGIA SODA HEADACHE
CEPHALIC CRANIAL ATLANTAL
CEREBRAL
CEPHALOPOD SQUID CUTTLE
INKFISH OCTOPUS SPIRULA
DIBRANCH SCAPHITE
CEPHALOTHORAX PROSOMA
CEPHALUS (FATHER OF —) DEION
(MOTHER OF —) DIOMEDE
(WIFE OF —) PROCRIS
CEPHEUS (BROTHER OF —) DANAUS
AEGYPTUS AMPHIDAMAS
(DAUGHTER OF —) ANDROMEDA
(FATHER OF —) ALEUS BELUS
(MOTHER OF —) ANCHINOE
(WIFE OF —) CASSIOPEA
CERAMICS TILES POTTERY
CERAMUS (FATHER OF —) BACCHUS
DIONYSUS
(MOTHER OF —) ARIADNE
CERATE WAX LARD SALVE
UNGUENT OINTMENT
CERATOBRANCHIAL APOHYAL
CERCYON (DAUGHTER OF —) ALOPE
(FATHER OF —) NEPTUNE
POSEIDON HEPHAESTUS
(SLAYER OF —) THESEUS
CEREAL RYE BEAN BRAN CORN
MUSH OATS RICE SAMP TEFF
ARZUN GRAIN MAIZE SPELT
WHEAT BARLEY BINDER FARINA
HOMINY PABLUM OATMEAL
SOYBEAN PORRIDGE
CEREAL LEAF FLAG
CEREBRAL CEPHALIC INVERTED
(PREF.) PSYCH(O)
CEREBRATION THOUGHT
CEREBROSIDE KERASIN
CEREMENT SHROUD
CEREMONIAL FORM PRIM RITE
STIFF FORMAL RIALTY RITUAL
SOLEMN PRECISE STUDIED
TRIUMPH UPANAYA AVERSION
SPLENDOR
CEREMONIOUS GRAND LOFTY
STIFF FORMAL PROPER SOLEMN
PRECISE STATELY STUDIED
CEREMONY BRIS FETE FORM

GAUD HAKO ORGY POMP RITE
SEAL SHOW SIGN SING BERIT
DANCE DOSEH STATE ACTION
AUGURY BERITH BRIDAL BURIAL
EXEQUY GOMBAY HOMAGE
KERIAH MALKAH MAUNDY NIPTER
OFFICE PARADE POWWOW
REVIEW RITUAL SALUTE BAPTISM
DISPLAY KIDDUSH MELAVEH
OVATION PAGEANT PANAGIA
PORTENT PRODIGY TAHARAH
ACCOLADE APOLUSIS ASPERGES
COEMPTIO CRIOBOLY ENCAENIA
EXERCISE FUNCTION HABDALAH
HAKAFOTH HERALDRY MARRIAGE
OCCASION SKEYTING INAUGURAL
INDUCTION ORDINANCE
OBSERVANCE
(GRADUATION —) CAPPING
(HAZING —) CREELING
(MARRIAGE —) ESPOUSAL
(TEA —) CHANOYU
(PL.) DEGREE HOLIES AGENDUM
FERALIA JUSTMENTS
CERES DEMETER
(DAUGHTER OF —) PROSERPINE
PHERREPHATTA
(FATHER OF —) SATURN
(MOTHER OF —) VESTA
CERINTHE HONEYWORT
CERO SEARER SIERRA CAVALLA
PINTADO KINGFISH
CERTAIN COLD COOL DEAD FAST
FIRM FREE REAL SEAL SURE TRUE
BOUND CLEAR EXACT FIXED
PLAIN SIKER ACTUAL MEMORY
SECURE SICKER STATED WITTER
ASSURED PERFECT PRECISE
SETTLED SRADDHA ABSOLUTE
APPARENT CONSTANT OFFICIAL
PALPABLE POSITIVE RELIABLE
RESOLVED UNERRING CONFIDENT
CERTAINLY AY AYE WIS AMEN
IWIS SOON SURE WHAT YWIS
TRULY CERTES INDEED PERDIE
SICCAR SICKER SURELY VERILY
HARDILY EVERMORE FORSOOTH
SECURELY NATURALLY
(MOST —) SO
CERTAINTY YEA CERT PIPE SNIP
CINCH POLICY SURETY SURENESS
CONSTANCY
(LACK OF —) SCRUPLE
CERTIFICATE BOND CHIT CHECK
DEMIT JURAT LIBEL SCRIP TALON
TITLE AMPARO ATTEST CEDULA
COUPON INDENT PATENT
POTTAH RETURN TICKET VERIFY
CERTIFY CONSTAT DIPLOMA
VOUCHER WARRANT WAYBILL
AEGROTAT JUDGMENT KABBALAH
NAVICERT REGISTER REGISTRY
SECURITY TESCARIA TESTAMUR
TEZKIRAH NOTARIZATION
(CUSTOMHOUSE —) COCKET
(MARRIAGE —) LINES
(MINER'S —) LICENCE LICENSE
(PILOT'S —) BRANCH
(SERVANT'S —) CHIT
CERTIFICATION PASS STAMP
APPROVAL HECHSHER
CLEARANCE DISCHARGE
CERTIFIED SWORN

CERTIFY AVOW VISE SWEAR
AFFIRM ASSURE ATTEST DEPOSE
EVINCE VERIFY WITTER APPROVE
ENDORSE LICENSE TESTIFY
ACCREDIT
CERTITUDE CERTAIN CONFIDENCE
CERULEAN BLUE AZURE COELIN
CYANEAN CYANEOUS
CERUMEN WAX EARWAX
CERVIX NECK
CESS BOG TAX CEDE DUTY LEVY
LUCK RATE ABWAB SLOPE YIELD
IMPOST MEASURE SURRENDER
(BAD —) SORRA
CESSATION HO END HOO BLIN
HALT HUSH LISS LULL REST STAY
STOP BREAK CEASE CLOSE DEVAL
LETUP LISSE PAUSE SLACK STINT
TRUCE CUTOFF DEMISE DISUSE
OFFSET PERIOD RECESS CEASING
CLOSURE RESPITE ABEYANCE
BLACKOUT DESITION INTERVAL
SHUTDOWN STOPPAGE
SURCEASE SUSPENSE
(— OF HOSTILITIES) TRUCE
INDUCIAE ARMISTICE
(— OF LIFE) DEATH
(— OF RESPIRATION) APNEA
APNOEA
(— OF WORK) HARTAL
CESSPOOL SINK SUMP SINKER
CISTERN JAWHOLE SINKHOLE
SUSPIRAL
CESTODE POLYZOAN
CESTRUM POISONBERRY
CESTUS CEST CESTON HURLBAT
GAUNTLET WHIRLBAT
CETACEAN ORC CETE ORCA SUSU
WHALE BELUGA COWFISH
DOLPHIN GRAMPUS NARWHAL
MUTILATE PORPOISE
CETO (BROTHER OF —) PHORCYS
(DAUGHTERS OF —) GRAEAE
GORGONS HESPERIDES
(FATHER OF —) PONTUS
(MOTHER OF —) GAEA
CEYLON (SEE SRI LANKA)
SERENDIP TAPROBANE
CEYLONESE CEYLON BURGHER
CEYLON MOSS GULAMAN
CGS UNIT STILB STOKE
CHA TSIA CHAIS
CHACMA BAVIAN BOBBEJAAN

CHAD
CAPITAL: NDJAMENA
COIN: FRANC FRANCCFA
LAKE: CHAD
NATIVE: ARAB SARA KREDA
MASSA TOUBOU KAMADJA
MOUNDAN
PLATEAU: ENNEDI
RIVER: CHARI SHARI LOGONE
BAHRAOUK
TOWN: ATI BOL LAI MAO FADA
FAYA MONGO ABECHE BOKORO
BONGOR LARGEAU MOUNDOU
FORTLAMY MOUSSORO

CHADOR PHULKARI
CHAETA UNCINUS
CHAETOCHLOA SETARIA
CHAETOPOD SCALEBACK

CHAETURA DRAB BEAR
CHAFE IRK RUB VEX FRET FRIG
FROT FUME GALD GALL HEAT
JOSH RAGE WARM WEAR ANGER
ANNOY CHAFF GRIND SCOLD
SNUFF WORRY WRING ABRADE
BANTER EXCITE FRIDGE HARASS
INJURY NETTLE RANKLE INCENSE
INFLAME SNUFFLE FRICTION
IRRITATE RAILLERY
CHAFER CRESSET
CHAFF GUY HAY PUG RAG ROT
BRAN CAFF CHIP GRIT GUFF JOSH
PULU QUIZ RAZZ BORAK CHIAK
CHYAK DROSS GLUME HULLS
HUSKS JOLLY RALLY SLACK
STOUR STRAW TEASE TRASH
BANTER BHOOSA REFUSE
CAVINGS TAILING RAILLERY
RIDICULE SHELLING
CHAFFER BANDY SIEVE WARES
BUYING DICKER HAGGLE HIGGLE
MARKET PALTER BARGAIN
CHATTER SELLING TRAFFIC
EXCHANGE
CHAFFINCH PINK CHINK SPINK
TWINK ROBERD SCOBBY SHILFA
SKELLY ROBINET SNABBIE
WETBIRD
CHAFFY SCALY ACEROSE ACEROUS
PALEATE
CHAFING GALLING IMPATIENCE
CHAGRIN ENVY SPITE VEXATION
CHAGRINED SICK ASHAMED
CHAIN FOB GUY NET ROW SET
TEW TIE TOE TOW TUG TYE BIND
BOND CURB FALL FAST FILE GYVE
JOIN LINE LINK SEAL SOAM TEAM
BRAIL CABLE GROUP GUARD
LEASH SHANK SHEET SLANG
SLING SUITE TRACE TRAIN
WRASE CARCAN CATENA COLLAR
CORDON FASTEN FETTER
GANGER HANGER HOBBLE
JACKER JIGGER LINKER RACKAN
SECURE SERIES STRING TETHER
TOGGLE BOBSTAY CATFALL
CHIGNON CONNECT EMBRACE
ENSLAVE LASHING MANACLE
NETWORK PAINTER PENDANT
SAUTOIR SHACKLE TACKLER
BACKROPE BRACELET CARCANET
GLEIPNIR LINKWORK NECKLACE
RECEPTOR RESTRAIN RIGWIDDY
STROBILA WOOLDING
(— FOR ANCHOR) CATFALL
PAINTER
(— FOR BINDING) JACKER TACKLER
(— FOR WRAPPING MAST)
WOOLDING
(— OF AUTHORITIES) ISNAD
(— OF DUNES) SAIF SEIF
(— OF MOUNTAINS) RANGE
(— OF ROCKS) REEF
(— ON CONVICT'S LEG) SLANG
(— TO BIND CATTLE) SEAL
(DECORATIVE —) FESTOON
(ENDLESS —) CREEPER
(MAGIC —) GLEIPNIR
(SHORT —) SHANK
(SUSPENDED —) CATENARY
(WATCH —) FOB ALBERT
(PL.) IRONS CONVEYOR

(PREF.) HORMO STREPHO
STREPSI STREPT(O)
CHAIN LINK SHUT COPULA
SWIVEL
CHAINMAN CLASHY CLASHEE
LINEMAN TAPEMAN
CHAIN-SHAPED CATENOID
CHAIR KEEP SEAT SHOP HORSE
SEDAN STOOL ESTATE OFFICE
PULPIT ROCKER SADDLE SITTER
TONJON CACOLET COMMODE
FANBACK GONDOLA SITTING
VOYEUSE WINDSOR ARMCHAIR
CARRIAGE CATHEDRA FAUTEUIL
KANGAROO SGABELLO VOLTAIRE
(— OF STATE) THRONE
(— SLUNG FROM POLE) KACO
TALABON
(— WITH CANOPY) STATE
(BISHOP'S —) CATHEDRA
FALDSTOOL
(EASY —) COGSWELL
(GREEK —) KLISMOS
(MINING —) DOG
(PART OF —) ARM EAR LEG BACK
POST RUNG SEAT SLAT CREST
STILE STUMP ROCKER ARMREST
SPINDLE BACKRAIL HEADPIECE
(PORTABLE —) SEDAN
(SEDAN —) NORIMONO
(SPRING —) PERCH
(THRONE —) SHINZA
CHAIRMAN HEAD CHAIR EMCEE
PRESES SPEAKER CONVENER
DIRECTOR MODERATOR
PROLOCUTOR
(PREF.) SYMPOSI
CHAISE GIG SHAY CHAIR CALESIN
CARRIAGE CURRICLE
SHANDRYDAN
CHAISE LONGUE DAYBED
DUCHESSE
CHALAZA TREAD TREADLE
GALLATURE
CHALCEDONY ONYX OPAL SARD
AGATE CHERT PRASE CATEYE
JASPER PLASMA QUARTZ
CARNEOL ENHYROS OPALINE
SARDINE SARDIUS CORNELIAN
CHALCIOPE (FATHER OF —) AEETES
(HUSBAND OF —) PHRIXUS
(MOTHER OF —) ASTERODIA
(SISTER OF —) MEDEA
(SON OF —) ARGUS MELAS
PHRONTIS CYTISSORUS
CHALCIS (CHILDREN OF —)
CURETES CORYBANTES
(FATHER OF —) ASOPUS
(MOTHER OF —) METOPE
CHALCOPYRITE RUN
CHALDEAN KALDANI BABYLONIAN
(— MEASURE) CANE FOOT MAKUK
QASAB ARTABA GARIBA GHALVA
MANSION
(— RIVER) TIGRIS EUPHRATES
(— TOWN) UR
CHALICE AMA CUP BOWL CALIX
GRAIL REGAL GOBLET KRASIS
CHALK CAUK CORK PALE SCAR
TALC TICK CRETA FLOUR SCORE
BLANCH BLEACH CRAYON CREDIT
RUBBLE WHITEN ACCOUNT
WHITING

(GREEN —) PRASINE
(HARD —) HURLOCK
(RED —) RUBRIC
(SURVEYOR'S —) KEEL
(PREF.) CALC(I)(IO)(O) CALCAREO
CHALKBOARD GREENBOARD
CHALKSTONE TOPHUS
CHALKY CRETACIC CRETACEOUS
CHALLENGE HEN VIE BRAG CALL
DARE DEFY FACE GAGE ASSAY
BANCO BLAME BRAVE CLAIM
QUERY STUMP ACCUSE APPEAL
BANTER CARTEL CHARGE DACKER
DAIKER DEMAND DESCRY FORBID
IMPUGN INFIRM INVITE RECUSE
SERDAB ARRAIGN CENSURE
IMPEACH PROVOKE REPROVE
SOLICIT SUMMONS CHAMPION
DARRAIGN DEFIANCE GAUNTLET
QUESTION REPROACH
(— A BULL) CITE
CHALLENGING PIQUANT
BLOODSHOT
CHALONE AUTACOID
CHALYBEATE MARTIAL
CHALYBITE SIDERITE
CHAMBER ODA AGER CELL CIST
DOME FLAT FOLD HALL IWAN
KIVA ROOM SALE TOMB BOWER
CAVUM COURT GOMER HOUSE
SENAT SHAFT SOLAR SOLER
STOVE ATRIUM CAMARA CAMERA
COFFER HEADER HOLLOW
MIHRAB SENADO SENATE SOLLAR
SPRING STANZA WILSON
BEDROOM ONIOOON OHALMEN
CHANNEL CHAUMER CONCAVE
CUBICLE FAVISSA FIREBOX
GALLERY GEHENNA MANSION
RECEIPT CASEMATE CYLINDER
DIFFUSER FOUNTAIN GROSSRAT
SMOKEBOX SNEMOVNA
THALAMUS
(— FOR MOLTEN GLASS) FONT
(— IN FURNACE) SHAFT DOGHOUSE
(— OF EAR) SACCULE UTRICLE
(— POT) JORDAN JEROBOAM
(AIR —) SPONSON
(AUDIENCE —) DURBAR
(BOMBPROOF —) CASEMATE
(CLIMATE CONTROL —) BIOTRON
(FIRE —) ARCH STOVE COCKLE
FIREBOX
(FORTIFICATION —) BUNKER
(OPEN —) LANTERN
(ORGAN —) SWELL
(PISTON —) BARREL
(PRIVATE —) CLOSET CONCLAVE
(PUEBLO —) KIVA ESTUFA
(SLEEPING —) BEDROOM
WARDROBE
(SMALL —) LOCULUS
(SUPPLY —) MAGAZINE
(UNDERGROUND —) CAVE CRYPT
CAVERN SERDAB HYPOGEE
(WATERTIGHT —) CAISSON
(PREF.) THALAM(I)(O)
(SUFF.) CELE COELE COELUS
CHAMBERLAIN EUNUCH FACTOR
SERVANT STEWARD PALATINE
POLONIUS
CHAMELEON ANOLE ANOLI
LACERT SAURIAN

CHAMFER BEVEL CHIMB CHIME
CHINE FLUTE CIPHER
FURROW GROOVE
CHAMOIS GEMS IZARD AOUDAD
SHAMMY
CHAMOMILE MAYWEED
MARGUERITE
CHAMONT (SISTER OF —) MONIMIA
CHAMP BITE CHAW FIRM HARD
MASH CHANK CHOMP FIELD
GNASH TRAMPLE
CHAMPAGNE AY BUBBLY SIMKIN
BELLEEK SILLERY
CHAMPION ACE AID FAN ABET
BACK BOSS DEFY HERO KEMP
GHAZI ASSERT ATTEND DEFEND
KNIGHT PATRON SQUIRE VICTOR
APOSTLE ESPOUSE FIGHTER
PALADIN PROTECT ADVOCATE
DEFENDER PALMERIN
PROTAGONIST
CHAMPIONING
(PREF.) PRO
CHAMPIONSHIP TITLE LAURELS
ADVOCACY
CHAMPLEVE INLAID
CHANCE DIE HAP LOT CASE CAST
DINT DRAW FATE LINE LUCK
ODDS RISK SHOT SHOW TIDE
BREAK ETTLE STAKE WHACK
BETIDE CASUAL GAMBLE HAPPEN
HAZARD MISHAP RANDOM
SQUEAK TUMBLE AIMLESS
FORTUNE OPENING STUMBLE
VANTAGE VENTURE ACCIDENT
CASUALTY EVENTUAL FORTUITY
QUESTION ALEATORIC
OPPORTUNITY PERADVENTURE
(ADVERSE —) HAZARD
(EVEN —) TOSSUP
(SLIGHT —) PRAYER
(PL.) PROSPECTS
(PREF.) TYCH(O)
CHANCEL BEMA CHOIR ADYTUM
CHANCELLOR LOGOTHETE
CHANDELIER CORONA LUSTER
PHAROS PENDANT CHANDLER
GASELIER
CHANDLER TALLOWER
CHANE OREJON
CHANGE MEW CHOP FLOP MOLT
MOVE ODDS PEAL TURN VARY
VEER WARP WEND ADAPT ALTER
AMEND BREAK COINS EMEND
MOULT SHIFT THROW ADJUST
BECOME DIFFER DIGEST IMMUTE
MODIFY MUANCE MUTATE
REMOVE REVAMP REVISE SWITCH
WISSEL WRIXLE COMMUTE
CONVERT CUTOVER DEVIATE
FLUXION MORTIFY BECOMING
DENATURE EXCHANGE INNOVATE
LENITION MUTATION REVISION
TRANSFER TRANSUME VARIANCE
PERMUTATION METAMORPHISM
MODIFICATION METAMORPHOSIS
(— APPEARANCE) DISGUISE
(— COLOR) TURN
(— COURSE) GYBE JIBE
(— DIRECTION) CUT CANT CHOP
HAUL KNEE VEER ANGLE BREAK
SHIFT
(— FOR BETTER) HELP

(— FOR WORSE) BEDEVIL
(— FORM) DEVELOP
(— GAIT) BREAK
(— GRADUALLY) PASS GRADUATE
(— IN COURSE) SHEER
(— IN DIRECTION) JOG KNEE STEP
(— IN ELEVATION) FORK
(— IN LAKE LEVEL) SEICHE
(— IN SIZE) ASTOGENY
(— INTO VAPOR) FLASH
(— MONEY) WISSEL
(— OF FORM) SET
(— OF GEAR) KICKDOWN
(— OF MIND) CAPRICE
(— OF MOOD) VARY
(— OF PITCH) MOTION INFLECT
(— OF SEA LEVEL) EUSTACY
(— OF SOUND) BREAKING
(— OF WORD) ANAGRAM
(— ONE'S HEART) REPENT
(— PACE) BREAK
(— POSITION) STIR FLEET HOTCH
(— QUICKLY) FLY
(— RESIDENCE) FLIT
(— SHAPE) DRAW CREEP DEFORM
(ABNORMAL —) LESION
(ABRUPT —) DOGLEG SALTATION
(GEAR —) KICKDOWN
(GRADUAL —) DRIFT
(PRESSURE —) ALLOBAR
(SHORT —) FLUFF
(SMALL —) GROCERY
(UNEXPECTED —) SWITCH
(PL.) DOUBLES PLASTIQUE
(PREF.) ALLAGO ALLASSO AMOEBI
AMOEBO MUTA MUTO
(SUFF.) MUTE
CHANGEABLE EEMIS GIDDY IMMIS
LIGHT WINDY CHOPPY FICKLE
FITFUL GERFUL KETCHY LABILE
MOBILE MOTLEY MUABLE SHIFTY
WANKLE BRUCKLE ERRATIC
MUTABLE PROTEAN UNSTAID
VARIANT VARIOUS VOLUBLE
AMENABLE CATCHING GLIBBERY
MOVEABLE SKITTISH TICKLISH
UNSTABLE VARIABLE VEERABLE
VOLATILE WEATHERY
CHAMELEON VERSATILE
CHANGEABLENESS LEVITY
CAPRICE VIBRATION
CHANGED VARIED ANOTHER
CHANGEFUL FICKLE SHIFTY
MUTABLE RESTLESS
CHANGELESS CONSISTENT
CHANGELING AUF AWF OAF DOLT
FOOL CHILD DUNCE IDIOT
WAVERER IMBECILE KILLCROP
RENEGADE TURNCOAT
CHANGING FLUXIBLE ALTERNATE
(— MONEY) AGIO
(CONTINUALLY —) FLOATING
CHANK SANK CONCH
CHANNEL CUT GAT POD REE RUT
SOW CANO CAVA DEEP DIKE
DUCT DYKE FLUE GATE GOOL
GOTE GOUT GURT KILL KYLE LAKE
LANE PACE PIPE RACE SLEW
SLOO VALE VEIN WADI WADY
BAYOU CANAL CARRY CHASE
COWAL DITCH DRAIN DRILL
FLUME FLUTE GLYPH GUIDE
INSET LATCH QUIRK RIVER SINUS

SLIDE SOUND STOOL STOVE STRIA SWASH AIRWAY ALVEUS ARROYO ARTERY BRANCH COURSE CUTOFF ESTERO FURROW GROOVE GULLET GUTTER HOLLOW KENNEL KEYWAY LAGOON MEDIUM OFFLET OILWAY RABBET RESACA RIVOSE RUNWAY SLOUGH SLUICE SPECUS STRAIT STRAND STREAM THROAT TROUGH CHAMFER CONDUCT CONDUIT CULVERT CUNETTE EURIPUS OFFTAKE PASSAGE RACEWAY RIVULET SHIPWAY SILANGA STRIGIL THALWEG TIDEWAY WASHOUT AQUEDUCT FLOODWAY GUIDEWAY GUNKHOLE RACELINE SCOURWAY SPILLWAY CANNELURE
(— FOR MOLTEN METAL) SOW GATE RUNNER
(— IN CLOTH) FLUTE
(— IN ICE FIELD) LEAD
(— IN MOLD) SPRAY
(— OF AQUEDUCT) SPECUS
(— ON A DECK) CHIMB CHIME
(— ON WHALE) SCARF
(ARTIFICIAL —) GAT GOUT
(DRAINAGE —) GAW
(ENGLISH —) SLEEVE
(INCLINED —) SHOOT
(INFORMATION —) PIPELINE
(IRRIGATION —) AUWAI DROVE
(LYMPH —) CISTERNA
(SECONDARY —) BINNACLE
(SLOPING —) CHUTE SHUTE
(PREF.) CANALI RHYN(O) SOLEN(O) VAS(I)(O)
CHANNELBILL RAINFOWL
CHANNELED FLUTED
CHANT CANT MELE SING SONG TONE CAROL PSALM SOUGH ANTHEM CANTUS INTONE LITANY WARBLE CHORTLE INTROIT PROSODE REQUIEM WORSHIP ALLELUIA ANTIPHON CANTICLE SINGSONG PLAINSONG CANTILLATE
CHANTER STICK CANTOR SINGER BAGPIPE SONGSTER CHALUMEAU
(— OF BAGPIPE) OBOE
CHANTERELLE CANTINO
CHANTING CHARM HAZANUT ANTIPHONY CHAZZANUT
CHANTLATE SPROCKET
CHANTRY CAGE
CHAOS NU NUN PIE APSU GULF HYLE MESS VOID ABYSS BABEL CHASM JUMBLE MATTER TOPHET ANARCHY MIXTURE DISORDER SHAMBLES TAILSPIN TOHUBOHU
CHAOTIC MUDDLED CONFUSED FORMLESS TUMULTUARY
CHAP BOY BUY DOG LAD MAN RAP WAG BEAN BEAT BIRD BLOW CHIP CHOP COVE DICK DUCK HIND JOHN KIBE MASH MATE NABS SNAP BILLY BLOKE BUCKO BULLY BUYER CHAFT CHINK CLEFT CRACK FRUIT KNOCK LOVER RUMMY SCOUT SPLIT SPORT SPRAY SWIPE TRADE

YOUTH BARTER BOHUNK BREACH BUGGER CALLAN CHOOSE CODGER CUFFIN FELLOW FOUTER FOUTRA GAFFER GEEZER JOSSER KIPPER SHAVER STRIKE STROKE TURNIP BASTARD BROTHER CALLANT FISSURE HUSBAND ROUGHEN BLIGHTER CUSTOMER DIVISION MERCHANT
(— HANDS) RACK SPRAY
(— IN SKIN) KIN KIBE
(FINE —) BULLY
(OLD —) BO GEEZER
(PLUCKY —) COCK
(QUEER —) GALOOT
(S.AFRICAN —) KEREL
(YOUNG —) GAFFER
(PL.) CHOPS
CHAPARRAL MONTE CHAMISAL BUCKTHORN
CHAPARRO YAYA
CHAPBOOK CHAP GARLAND
CHAPE CRAMPET MORDANT
CHAPEL CAGE CAPE COPE COWL HOOD CLOAK CRYPT PORCH SALEM BETHEL BEULAH CHARRE CHURCH HAIKAL MORADA SHRINE CAPELLA CHANTRY CHAPLET CHARNEL CHHATRI GALILEE MARTYRY MEETING MEMORIA ORATORY SACRARY SERVICE BETHESDA DEACONRY DIACONIA FERETORY FERETRUM PARABEMA SACELLUM SODALITY
(UNDERGROUND —) SHROUDS
CHAPERON HOOD ATTEND DUENNA ESCORT MATRON GRIFFIN PROTECT GUARDIAN TRAPPING
CHAPLAIN PADRE LEVITE ALMONER CONDUCT ALTARIST ORDINARY
CHAPLET BEAD ORLE STUD CROWN ANADEM ANCHOR CIRCLE FILLET JAMBER JAMMER ROSARY STAPLE TROPHY WREATH CORONAL CORONET GARLAND MOULDING NECKLACE ORNAMENT
(PREF.) STEMMATI
CHAPMAN CHAP BUYER DEALER HAWKER TRADER COPEMAN PEDDLER CUSTOMER MERCHANT
CHAPPIE JOCKEY
CHAPS FLEWS BREECHES LEGGINGS OVERALLS
CHAPTER BODY CELL PACE POST CAPUT COURT LODGE BRANCH CABILDO CAPITAL CORRECT COUNCIL MEETING SECTION ASSEMBLY
(— OF BOOK) CAPITAL
(— OF KORAN) SURA SURAH
(— OF SOCIETY) CAMP CIRCLE
CHAR BURN CART COAL SEAR BROIL CHARK CHORE SHARD SINGE TROUT SCORCH BLACKEN CHARIOT TORGOCH REDBELLY SAIBLING SALMONID SANDBANK
(PL.) SALVELINI
CHARA MUSKGRASS
CHARACIN DORADO DOURADE BLOODFIN

CHARACTER AURA BALL BENT CARD CASE CLAY CLEF DASH ECAD FLAT FOND FORM HAIR KIND MAKE MARK MOLD NOTE PART ROLE RUNE SIGN SORT TONE TRIM TYPE BRAND COLOR ETHIC ETHOS FIBER HABIT HEART HUMOR INDEX SAVOR STAMP TENOR TOKEN TRAIT WRITE CARACT CIPHER COCKUP DAGGER DIRECT EMBLEM FIGURE GENIUS HANGER LETTER MANNER METTLE NATURE REPUTE SIGLUM SPIRIT STRIPE SYMBOL CALIBER CLOTHES EDITION ENGRAVE ESSENCE IMPRESS QUALITY CAPACITY FRACTION IDENTITY INFERIOR INSCRIBE LIGATURE SELFHOOD SYLLABIC DESCENDER PARAGRAPH PERSONAGE
(— IN DRAMA) CHORUS
(— IN PLAY) DAME BESSY
(— OF SOIL) LAIR
(ASSUMED —) ROLE FIGURE INCOGNITO
(BAD —) DROLE BUDMASH
(BASIC —) BOTTOM
(CHIEF —) AGONIST
(CHINESE —) SHOU RADICAL
(COMMON —) COMMUNITY
(ESSENTIAL —) ALLOY
(FIRM —) BACKBONE
(GIVE — TO) TONE
(GREEK —) SAMPI
(JAPANESE —S) HIBUNCI
(MENDELIAN —) ALLEL ALLELE
(PHYSICAL —) ARMENOID
(PRIME —) ESSENCE
(SHIFTLESS —) BEAT
(STOCK —) BESSY MACCUS
(TESTED —) ASSAY
(TRIED —) TOUCH
(VULGAR —S) ONMUN
(PL.) MANA
(SUFF.) ERY
(HAVING — OF) IC(AL)
CHARACTERISTIC CAST COST MARK MIEN ANGLE AROMA GRACE POINT TACHE TOKEN TRAIT TRICK ACCENT BEAUTY NATURE STIGMA STROKE ADJUNCT AMENITY FEATURE IMPRESS QUALITY SPECIES TYPICAL ACTIVITY HEADMARK PECULIAR PROPERTY SYMBOLIC PARAMETER PROPRIETY PECULIARITY PARTICULARITY QUALIFICATION
(— OF ANTIBODIES) AVIDITY
(ADVENTITIOUS —) ACCIDENT
(DISTINGUISHING —) SPECIES HALLMARK BIRTHMARK
(PECULIAR —) IDIOPATHY
(PL.) CORNERS FACULTY
(SUFF.) IC(AL)
(— OF) ISH ISTIC LY
CHARACTERIZATION ELOGY ELOGIUM
CHARACTERIZE MARK STYLE DEFINE DEPICT TITULE ENGRAVE ENTITLE IMPRINT PORTRAY DESCRIBE INDICATE INSCRIBE

CHARACTERIZED
(SUFF.) **(— BY)** AL FUL IAL IC(AL) LEW
CHARACTERLESS INANE
CHARADES GAME
CHARCOAL COAL CARBO CHARK CARBON FUSAIN PENCIL BLACKEN SPODIUM SCRIBBET
CHARGE FEE LAP LAY RAP TAX BEEF BILL BUCK CALL CARE CARK CAST COST CURE DUES DUTY FILL GIBE KEEP LADE LIEN LOAD NICK NOTE ONUS RACK RATE REST RUSH SHOT SIZE SOAK SPAR TASK TOLL WARD WIKE AGIST BLAME CAUSE CHALK COUNT CRIME DEBIT EXTRA GYRON ONSET ORDER PRICE REFER SCORE SHOCK STICK STING THING TRUST ACCUSE ADJURE ALLEGE APPEAL ASSESS ATTACK BEHEST BURDEN CAREER CENSUS COURSE CREDIT DAMAGE DEFAME DEMAND DITTAY ENJOIN ENURNY EXCESS IMPOSE IMPUTE METAGE OBJECT OFFICE PIPAGE REATUS SURMIT SURTAX TARIFF TOWAGE WEIGHT ACIDIZE ANNULET ARRAIGN ARTICLE ASCRIBE ASSAULT AVERAGE BOATAGE CARTAGE CENSURE CHEVRON CLAMPER COMMAND CONCERN CONJURE CORKAGE CORNAGE CUSTODY DOCKAGE DRAYAGE EMBASSY EXPENSE FLOTAGE HAULAGE IGNITER IMPEACH KEEPING MANDATE MILEAGE MISSION MIXTURE MOORAGE PANNAGE QUAYAGE REPRISE SIDEAGE SLANDER SLIDAGE SURMISE WARPAGE BILLBACK BRASSAGE CASUALTY CHASTISE CRESCENT DELAYAGE DENOUNCE LEGATION ORDINARY OVERLOAD PLANKAGE POUNDAGE PROVINCE QUESTION SLINGING SPENDING STANDAGE TUTORAGE VIGORISH COMPLAINT ACCUSATION ACCUSEMENT
(— AGAINST) TILT
(— BATTERY) SOAK BOOST
(— EXCESSIVELY) FLEECE
(— FALSELY) SURMISE
(— OF FIREARM) LOAD AMORCE
(— OF MENTAL ENERGY) CATHEXIS
(— OF METAL) HEAT
(— OF ORE) POST
(— TO BE PAID) LAW
(— UPON PROPERTY) LIEN
(— WITH CRIME) ACCUSE DELATE INDICT ARTICLE ATTAINT IMPEACH
(— WITH GAS) AERATE
(AGGREGATE —S) BOOK
(CANNON —) GRAPE
(COVER —) COUVERT
(DEPTH —) CAN
(EXPLOSIVE —) CAP BLAST SNAKE SQUIB TULIP BOOSTER BURSTER IGNITER
(FALSE —) CALUMNY
(HERALDIC —) DELF DROP GIRON GYRON LABEL BEZANT BILLET

DRAGON GURGES
BEARING ESQUIRE
(MAILING —) FRANKAGE
(POWDER —) GRAIN
(SHAPED —) BEEHIVE
(SPIRITUAL —) CURE
(TEMPORARY —) CARE
(WINE —) CORKAGE
CHARGED UP HOT LADEN BELAST
BILLETY BILLETTE ELECTRIC
INSTINCT
(— WITH EMOTION) SWOLLEN
CHARGEHAND CLICKER
CHARGEMAN BLASTER
CHARGER DISH HORSE MOUNT
STEED ACCUSER COURSER
PLATTER TROOPER
CHARILY FRUGALLY GINGERLY
CHARIOT CAR BIGA CART CHAR
RATH WAIN BUGGY CHAIR ESSED
RATHA TRIGA WAGON CHARET
QUADRIGA
CHARIOTEER AURIGA CARTER
DRIVER IOLAUS LEADER CARTARE
WAGONER MYRTILUS
AUTOMEDON
CHARITABLE KIND BENIGN
HUMANE LENIENT LIBERAL
GENEROUS
CHARITY ALMS DOLE GIFT LOVE
PITY RUTH MERCY BASKET
BOUNTY CARITAS HANDOUT
LARGESS LENIENCE TZEDAKAH
CHARIVARI BABEL SHALLAL
SERENADE SHIVAREE
CHARLATAN FAKE CHEAT FAKER
FRAUD QUACK CABOTIN EMPIRIC
IMPOSTER MAGICIAN SYCOPHANT
MOUNTEBANK QUACKSALVER
CHARLES II DAVID
CHARLIE MCCARTHY STOOGE
CHARLOCK KRAUT RUNCH
HARLOCK KEDLOCK KERLOCK
MUSTARD SINAPIS YELLOWS
CHARDOCK CHEDLOCK SKEDLOCK
SKELLOCH
CHARM IT GBO KEY OBI CALM
CHIC HAND JINX JUJU JYNX
LUCK MOJO PLAY RUNE SNOW
SONG TAKE TILL ZOGO ALLAY
AROMA BRIEF CATCH FAVOR
FREET FREIT GRACE LAMIN
MAGIC OBEAH OOMPH SAFFI
SAFIE SPELL VENUS WANGA
WEIRD ALLURE AMULET BEAUTY
CARACT DEASIL ENAMOR ENGAGE
ENTICE FETISH GLAMOR GRIGRI
INCANT MANTRA MELODY
PLEASE SAPHIE SCARAB SOOTHE
SUBDUE SUMMON VOODOO
ABRAXAS ASSUAGE ATTRACT
BEGUILE BEWITCH CANTION
CANTRIP CONJURE CONTROL
DELIGHT ENCHANT ENTHRAL
FLATTER HEITIKI PERIAPT
PHILTER PHILTRE SINGING
SORCERY BLESSING BRELOQUE
COMETHER COQUETRY ENTHRALL
ENTRANCE GLAUMRIE GREEGREE
PISHOGUE PRACTICE TALISMAN
CAPTIVATE MAGNETIZE
PATERNOSTER
CHARMED CAPTIVE

CHARMER SIREN EXORCIST
MAGICIAN SORCERER
ENCHANTER
CHARMING LEPID SWEET GOLDEN
WIZARD AMIABLE DARLING
EYESOME TEMPEAN WINNING
WINSOME ADORABLE DELICATE
GRACEFUL LOVESOME
PICTURESQUE
CHARNEL GHASTLY CEMETERY
GOLGOTHA
CHARON (FATHER OF —) EREBUS
(MOTHER OF —) NOX
CHARPOY COT
CHARQUI JERKY XARQUE
CHART MAP BILL CARD MARK
PLAN PLAT PLOT ROSE CARTE
GRAPH STILL RECORD SCHEME
DIAGRAM EMAGRAM EXPLORE
ISOTYPE OUTLINE PROJECT
DOCUMENT DOPEBOOK
MERCATOR PLATFORM
(— BOOK) WAGONER
(— FROM AIR) AEROVIEW
(— MARK) VIGIA
(— OF A COURSE) RUTTER
(MARINER'S —) ROSE RUTTER
(WEATHER —) ANALOGUE
NEPHANALYSIS
CHARTER FIX LET BOND BOOK
DEED HIRE RENT CARTE CHART
FUERO GRANT LEASE SANAD
CHARTA PERMIT SUNNUD
DIPLOMA CONTRACT GRUNDLOV
HEIRLOOM LANDBOOK
MONOPOLY PANCHART
CHARTERHOUSE OF PARMA
(AUTHOR OF —) STENDHAL
(CHARACTER IN —) GINA CONTI
DONGO MOSCA CLELIA FAUSTA
GILETTI FABRIZIO FERRANTE
MARIETTA PIETRANERA
CHARWOMAN CHARER CHARLADY
PORTRESS JANITRESS
CHARY SHY DEAR WARY CHERE
SCANT SPARE DAINTY FRUGAL
PRIZED SKIMPY CAREFUL
CURIOUS SPARING CAUTIOUS
HESITANT PRECIOUS RESERVED
SPAREFUL VIGILANT
CHASE FOG SIC SUE FALL HUNT
JERL SHAG SHOO SICK ANNOY
CATCH CHEVY CHIVY DRIVE
HARRY HOUND SCORE SHACK
CACCIA CHIVVY CHOUSE EMBOSS
FOLLOW FRIEZE FURROW GALLOP
GROOVE HALLOO HARASS
HOLLOW INDENT PURSUE
QUARRY SCORSE TRENCH
CHANNEL ENGRAVE HUNTING
PURSUIT ORNAMENT PURCHASE
(— GAME) COURSE
(— HARD) RATTLE
CHASER RAM DRINK HOUND
FROGGER
(WOMAN —) SHEEPBITER
CHASING CISELURE
CHASM GAP KIN PIT GULF RIFT
YAWN ABYSS BLANK CANON
CHAOS CLEFT GORGE BREACH
CANYON HIATUS FISSURE
MEGARON SWALLOW VACANCY
APERTURE CREVASSE

INTERVAL VACATION
CHASSE SLIP GLIDE SASHAY
CHASSEUR HUNTER BELLBOY
DOORMAN FOOTMAN HUNTSMAN
CHASSIS SASH FRAME FIGURE
CHASTE CAST PURE ATTIC CLEAN
ZONED DECENT HONEST MODEST
PROPER SEVERE VESTAL VIRGIN
CLEANLY PUDICAL REFINED
CELIBATE INNOCENT VIRGINLY
VIRTUOUS CONTINENT
CHASTEN RATE ABASE SMITE
SMOTE SNEAP SOBER HUMBLE
PUNISH REBUKE REFINE SUBDUE
TEMPER AFFLICT CENSURE
CORRECT NURTURE CHASTISE
MODERATE RESTRAIN
CHASTISE BEAT FIRK FLOG LASH
SLAP TRIM WHIP AMEND BLAME
FEEZE SCOLD SPANK SPILL STRAP
TAUNT ACCUSE ANOINT BERATE
CHARGE DISPLE PUNISH PURIFY
REBUKE REFINE STRAFE SWINGE
TEMPER THRASH TICKLE
CHASTEN CORRECT REPROVE
SCOURGE SHINGLE SUSPECT
CASTIGATE
CHASTISEMENT ROD HELL TOCO
TOKO CENSURE PAYMENT
FLOGGING
(DIVINE —) WRATH
CHASTITY HONOR PURITY VIRTUE
HONESTY MODESTY PEDENCY
CELIBACY GOODNESS PUDICITY
INNOCENCE
CHASUBLE CASULA DEACON
INFULA PLANET PAENULA
PIANETA VESTMENT
CHAT GAS JAW MAG RAP BIRD
CHIN CONE COZE DISH GIST TALK
TELL TOVE TWIG YARN AMENT
CAUSE COOSE CRACK DALLY
PITCH POINT PRATE PROSE
PROSS SPEAK SPIKE VISIT BABBLE
BRANCH CATKIN CONFAB COURSE
DEVICE GABBLE GIBBER GOSSIP
GOSTER HOBNOB JABBER NATTER
POTATO POTTER SAMARA
CHAFFER CHATTER CAUSERIE
CHATTERY CONVERSE SPIKELET
STROBILE
CHATEAU HOUSE TOWER CASTLE
MANSION SCHLOSS CHATELET
FORTRESS
CHATON BASIL BEZEL BEZIL STONE
COATING SETTING
CHATTEL CATTLE PLEDGE
DEODAND FIXTURE CATALLUM
PERSONAL
(DISTRAINT OF —S) NAAM
(PL.) STUFF FARLEU FARLEY
COMODATO HOUSEHOLD
CHATTER GAB JAW MAG YAP
BLAB CARP CHAT CHIN CLAP
CLAT DISH GASH HACK KNAP
RICK TALK TEAR YIRR CABAL
CLACK CLASH GARRE HAVER
PRATE SHAKE BABBLE BRUDGE
CACKLE CLAVER GABBLE GIBBER
GOSSIP JABBER JANGLE JARGON
PALTER RATTLE SHIVER TATTER
TATTLE TINKLE YAMMER YATTER
BLABBER BRABBLE CHACKLE

CHAFFER CHIPPER CHITTER
CLACKET CLATTER CLITTER
GABNASH NASHGOB PALAVER
PRABBLE PRATING PRATTLE
SHATTER SMATTER TRATTLE
TWATTLE TWITTER TWITTLE
WHITTER BABBLING LOLLYGAG
SCHMOOSE VERBIAGE
(SUFF.) LALIA
CHATTERBOX JAY MAG PIET
BUCCO CLACK CRYSTE GOSSIP
MAGPIE
CHATTERER JAY MAG PIE BLAB
CHUET CHEWET GABBER MAGPIE
RATTLE HAVERER
CHATTERING PIET BABBLY
CHAVISH POPPING TWITTER
BABBLING
CHATTY CHIRRUPY GARRULOUS
CHAUFFEUR DRIVER SHOVER
TESTER
CHAUVINISM JINGOISM
CHAUVINIST JINGO JINGOIST
CHAW JAW VEX CHEW ENVY MULL
GRIND PONDER
CHAYOTE CHOCHO TALLOTE
HUISQUIL MIRLITON
CHEAP LOW BASE GAIN POOR VILE
BORAX CLOSE FLASH GAUDY
GROSS KITCH LIGHT MUCKY
NASTY PRICE SNIDE TATTY TIGHT
TINNY VALUE ABJECT BRUMMY
CHEESY COMMON CRUMBY
CRUMMY JITNEY LEADEN PLENTY
SHODDY SORDID STINGY TAWDRY
TRASHY UNDEAR BARGAIN
CHINTZY POPULAR TINHORN
INFERIOR PENNORTH SIXPENNY
TWOPENNY BRUMMAGEM
PINCHBECK
(— ITEM) TWOFER
(PREF.) VILI
CHEAPEN DOCK STALE VILIFY
SMALLEN
CHEAP SKATE STIFF PIKER
CHEAT DO BAM BOB COG CON FOB
FOP FUB GIP GUM GYP JEW JIG
NIP TOP BEAT BILK BITE BULL
BURN CLIP COLT CRIB DISH DUFF
DUPE FAKE FIRK FLAM FLUM
GECK GULL HAVE HOAX JILT JINK
JOUK KNAP LIAR MACE MUMP
NAIL NICK NOSE POOP PULL
REAM ROOK SELL SHAM SILE SKIN
SLUR SNAP SWAP SWOP TRIM
WEED WIPE BITCH BLINK BOOTY
BUNCO BUNKO COZEN CROOK
CULLY DODGE FAKER FLING FOIST
FOURB FRAUD FUDGE GLEEK
GOUGE GREEK GUILE HOCUS
KNAVE LURCH MULCT PINCH
PLOAT ROGUE SCAMP SCREW
SHARP SHORT SLANG SPOIL STICK
STIFF STING SWICK SWIKE TOUCH
TRICK VERSE WRINK BAFFLE
BLANCH BUBBLE BUCKET CHIAUS
CHISEL CHOUSE CLOYNE COGGER
DADDLE DECEIT DELUDE DERIDE
DIDDLE DOODLE DUFFER
EMUNGE EUCHRE FIDDLE FLEECE
GAZUMP GREASE HUMBUG
HUMMER HUSTLE ILLUDE INTAKE
JOCKEY NIGGLE NOBBLE NUZZLE

OUTWIT RADDLE RENEGE RIPOFF SHAVER SHICER SNUDGE SUCKER TWICER ABUSION BEGUILE BUBBLER CHICANE CULLION DECEIVE DEFRAUD ESCHEAT FAITOUR FINAGLE FINESSE FOISTER GUDGEON JUGGLER MISLEAD PLUNDER QUIBBLE SHARPER SHIFTER SKELDER SLICKER SWINDLE VERNEUK ARTIFICE BEJUGGLE CHALDESE CHISELER DELUSION HOODWINK IMPOSTOR INTRIGUE OUTREACH OVERTAKE PICAROON SHAMMOCK SWINDLER BAMBOOZLE CIRCUMVENT SHORTCHANGE

CHEATED SOLD

CHEATER BITE GULL KNAVE BILKER INTAKE TOPPER SHARPER FINAGLER TREACHER

CHEATING HOCUS BARRAT ODLING ABUSIVE FUBBERY MICHERY ROGUERY CHEATERY JUGGLING TRICKERY

CHECK BIT DAM HAP LID NAB NIP SAY SET TAB BAIL BALK BEAT BILK BILL CHIP CHIT COOK CRIB CURB DAMP FACE FOIL GAGE HURT ITEM KITE PAWL REIN SKID SNEB SNIB SNIP SNUB STAY STEM STOP STUB TAKE TEST TICK TRIG TURN TWIT WERE ABORT ALLAY ANNUL BAULK BLOCK BRAKE CATCH CHIDE CHILL CHING CHOKE CRACK CROOK DAUNT DELAY DETER DRAFT EMBAR FACER FAULT GAUGE LIMIT MODER PAUSE QUELL REPEL SNAPE SPOKE STALL STILL STUNT TALLY TAUNT THROW TOKEN TRASH WAVER ARAYNE ARREST ATTACK BAFFLE BOTTLE BRIDLE CHEQUE COUPON DAMPEN DEFEAT DETAIN DETENT DURESS GRAVEL HAFFET HAFFIT HINDER IMPEDE OPPOSE OUTWIT QUENCH RABBET REBATE REBUFF REBUKE RETURN SCOTCH STANCH STAYER STIFLE STYMIE TICKET VERIFY ANSTOSS AWEBAND BACKSET BECLOUD COMMAND CONTAIN CONTROL COUNTER CURTAIN DRAUGHT INHIBIT MONITOR REFRAIN REPRESS REPROOF REPROVE REPULSE REVERSE SETBACK SNAFFLE STAUNCH STOPPER TRAMMEL TROUBLE BULKHEAD ENCUMBER HOLDBACK OBSTRUCT PULLBACK RESTRAIN WITHHOLD **(— ENTHUSIASM)** DISMAY **(— GRADUALLY)** CUSHION **(— GROWTH)** BLAST STINT STUNT **(— IN GLASS)** SPLIT **(— IN TIMBER)** STARSHAKE **(— MOTION)** SPRAG **(— OF HORSE)** SACCADE **(— PASSER)** PAPERHANGER **(— PROGRESS)** DEFEAT **(FORGED —)** STIFF STUMER **(HOLD IN —)** COMPESCE **(RESTAURANT —)** LAWING

(WORTHLESS —) DUD STUMER **(PREF.)** ISCH(O)

CHECKED CHECK BEATEN CLOSED CAPTIVE STOPPED

CHECKER DAM DICE FRET KING CHECK FREAK FRECK PIECE WHITE DAMPER DRAUGHT

CHECKERBERRY JINKS DRUNKARD TEABERRY

CHECKERBOARD TABLE DAMBROD DAMBOARD

CHECKERED PIED VAIR DICED PLAID CHECKY MOTLEY

CHECKERS DRAFTS CHEQUERS DRAUGHTS

CHECKERWORK TESSEL CHECKER TESSERA

CHECKING REST BLOCK SETBACK EBRILLADE **(SUFF.)** SCHESIS SCHETIC

CHECKMATE LICK MATE STOP UNDO BAFFLE CORNER DEFEAT OUTWIT STYMIE THWART SUIMATE

CHECKSTONE CHUCK

CHEDDAR CHEESE

CHEEK CHAP CHOP GALL GENA JAMB JOLE JOWL LEER SASS WANG WANK BUCCA CHOKE CHYAK CRUST NERVE SAUCE SHICK CHYACK HAFFET HAFFIT OXCHEEK AUDACITY TEMERITY **(— OF SPUR)** SHANK **(— OF VISE)** CHAP **(PREF.)** BUCCO MEL PAREI(A)

CHEEKBONE MALAR ZYGOMA

CHEEKY BOLD

CHEEP PIP YAP YIP CHIP HINT PEEP PULE CHIRP CREAK TWEET SQUEAK TATTLE

CHEER OLE RAH FARE FOOD MIND ROOT VIVA YELL BRAVO BRISK CHIRK ELATE ERECT FEAST HEART HUZZA JOLLY MIRTH SHOUT SPORT TIGER WHOOP CANTLE CHERRY GAIETY HOORAY HURRAH HUZZAH REHETE SOLACE VIANDS ACCLAIM ANIMATE APPLAUD CHERISH COMFORT CONSOLE ENCHEER GLADDEN HEARTEN JOLLITY LIGHTEN REFRESH REJOICE SUPPORT UPRAISE APPLAUSE BRIGHTEN HILARITY INSPIRIT RECREATE VIVACITY **(BURST OF —S)** SALVO **(GOOD —)** WELFARE **(JAPANESE —)** BANZAI **(SORRY —)** PENANCE

CHEERFUL GAY CANT GLAD GLEG GOOD HIGH ROSY BONNY CADGY CANTY CHIRK DOUCE HAPPY JOLLY LIGHT MERRY PEART READY SAPPY SUNNY VAUDY BLITHE BRIGHT CHEERY CHIRPY CROUSE GAWSIE GENIAL HEARTY HILARY JOCUND LIVELY BUOYANT CHERRLY CHIPPER HOLIDAY JOCULAR SMILING WINSOME CHEERING CHIRRUPY EUPEPTIC FRIENDLY GLADSOME HOMELIKE SANGUINE SUNBEAMY SUNSHINE **(PREF.)** HILARO

CHEERFULLY GLADLY CANTILY CHEERLY JOLLILY LIGHTLY CHEERILY GENIALLY

CHEERFULNESS JOY GLEE TAIT CHEER CHERTE GAIETY GAYETY LEVITY SPIRIT JOLLITY BUOYANCY FESTIVAL GLADNESS HILARITY

CHEERING GLAD CORDIAL CHEERFUL CHIRPING

CHEERLESS SAD BLAE COLD DIRE DRAB GLUM GRAY BLEAK DREAR ELYNG WASTE DISMAL DREARY GLOOMY WINTRY DOLEFUL FORLORN JOYLESS SUNLESS DEJECTED DESOLATE LITHLESS

CHEER PINE CHIL

CHEERY BUXOM BRIGHT BOBBISH GAYSOME

CHEESE OKA BLUE BRIE EDAM FETA HAND JACK TRIP APPLE BRICK COLBY CREAM DAISY DERBY GOUDA GRANA KENNO MAHON QUESO SWISS WHEEL ZIEGA ZIGER ASIAGO BARRIE BONDON BRYNZA BURGOS CANTAL CASSAN DUNLOP GLARUS JUNKET MYSOST ROMANO RONCAL SAANEN SBRINZ TILSIT ZAMORA ZIEGER ANGELOT CHEDDAR CHEVRET COTTAGE CROWDIE FONTINA FROMAGE GJEDOST GRUYERE KEBBUCK LASELVA PRIMOST PROVOLA RICOTTA SAPSAGO SERRANO STILTON TETILLA TRUCKLE AMERICAN CABRALES CHESHIRE EMMENTAL LONGHORN MUENSTER PARMESAN PECORINO RACLETTE SANSIMON SLIPCOAT TRONCHON LEICESTER MOUSETRAP PROVOLONE ROQUEFORT WILTSHIRE MOZZARELLA NEUFCHATEL SERVILLETA **(— FANCIER)** TUROPHILE **(— IN OATMEAL)** CABOC **(INFERIOR —)** DICK **(LARGE —)** KEBBOC **(WELSH —)** CAERPHILLY **(PREF.)** TURO CASE(O) TYR(O)

CHEESEPARING STINGY

CHEESE VAT CHESSEL CHESSART

CHEESEWOOD BONEWOOD WHITEWOOD

CHEETAH CAT OUNCE YOUSE YOUZE GUEPARD

CHEF COOK COMMIS SAUCIER CUISINIER

CHEFOO YENTAI

CHELA HAND MANUS NIPPER PINCER

CHELATE COMPLEX

CHELICERA FALX FANG FALCER MANDIBLE

CHELLIAN ABBEVILLIAN

CHELUBAI (FATHER OF —) HEZRON

CHEMICAL (ALSO SEE SPECIFIC HEADINGS) ACID BASE SALT ALKALI BLEACH CHEMIC DODGER SAFENER ADDITIVE ALGICIDE CATALYST DEHORNER **(PREF.)** ACETO ALCO ALDO AMIDO AMYL(I)(O) AZ(O) BENZ(O)

BOR(O) BROM(O) BUT(YR)(YRO) CADM(I)(O) CAPRO CARB(O) CHAVI(O) CUMO DIAZO DIOL DUPLO EKA ESTERI FORM(O) GLY(O) IDO IMIDO IMINO KER(O) KET(O) LAUR LIP LYSO LYXO MAL(O) MENTH(O) MERCUR(O) METH MOLYBD MURIO NAPHTH NITRATO NITRILO NITROSO NOR OLEO ORTHO OSMIO OX OXAL(O) OXIDI OXIDO OXIMIDO OXO OXY OZO PENT(A) PERI PHLOR(O) PHTHAL(O) PIPTO PLUMB(I)(O) POLY PROP PROS PROTE(O) PYRROL(O) SYN TOL(U) **(SUFF.)** AMIN(E)(O) ANE ASE ATE ENE ID(E) ILE INE INOL INONE ION ITE ITOL IUM OIC OIN OL OLE OLIC OLID(E) ON(E) ONIC ONIUM OSAN OSE OSIDE OUS OYL PHORE RETIN THIN(E) YL YNE ZYME

CHEMIN-DE-FER SHIMMY

CHEMISE SARK SHIFT SHIRT SIMAR SMOCK CAMISA SHIMMY LINGERIE

CHEMISETTE SHAM GUIMPE TUCKER PARTLET

CHEMIST ANALYST ASSAYER CHEMICK BENCHMAN COLORIST DRUGGIST **AMERICAN** DOW ABEL CADY DANA HALE HALL HARE HART HUNT KING LAMB LIND LOEB LONG REID UREY CLARK COOKE CROSS DROWN DUMEZ FLORY GOOCH HAMOR HERTY KRAUS LEWIS LIBBY MOORE NOYES POWER SEMON SMITH SNELL STINE WILEY BROWNE BUCHER BURTON CALVIN CLARKE CRAFTS DORSET DUDLEY EGLOFF HOLMES HOOVER LEVENE MENDEL MORGAN MUNROE PALMER ROBLIN ROGERS SHIMER TORREY WARREN ALDRICH ANDREWS ATWATER CASTNER CUSHMAN DUSHMAN GIAUQUE GODLOVE GOMBERG GUTHRIE HARKINS KHORANA MIDGLEY ONSAGER PAULING SEABORG SHERMAN SLOSSON WHITNEY BANCROFT BENEDICT CHANDLER COOLIDGE COTTRELL FRANKLIN HORSFORD LANGMUIR LIPSCOMB MCCOLLUM MCMILLAN MULLIKEN RICHARDS SILLIMAN SPRINGER STODDARD WILLIAMS WOODWARD ALEXANDER CAROTHERS HENDERSON NIEUWLAND PATTERSON CHITTENDEN HILLEBRAND **AUSTRIAN** KUHN EMICH PREGL PRECHTL **BELGIAN** STAS SOLVAY BAEKELAND PRIGOGINE **CZECH** BRAUNER HEYROVSKY **DANISH** THOMSEN BRONSTED KJELDAHL SORENSEN **DUTCH** COHEN MULDER HOMBERG **ENGLISH** ABEL BELL DAVY POPE SWAN TODD ABNEY BOYLE CROSS DAKIN HENRY MARSH PROUT SODDY YOUNG BARTON BRANDE DALTON DONNAN

GREGOR HARDEN MARTIN MILLER PERKIN PORTER RAMSAY THORPE TILDEN WATSON ANDREWS CROOKES DANIELL FARADAY HAWORTH HODGKIN NORRISH TENNANT TRAVERS HATCHETT PLAYFAIR ROBINSON WILLIAMS ARMSTRONG CORNFORTH FRANKLAND GLADSTONE PRIESTLEY WILKINSON HINSHELWOOD

FRENCH BAUME BEHAL CONTE CURIE DUFAY DUMAS FREMY LEBEL LEBON WURTZ BALARD CLAUDE DARCET GERNEZ GUIMET LEMERY NAQUET ORFILA PERRIN PROUST RAOULT CHAPTAL DAUBENY FRIEDEL GLENARD LAURENT LEBLANC LUMIERE MACQUER MOISSAN PASTEUR PELOUZE THENARD BERTRAND CAVENTOU CHEVREUL COURTOIS DEBIERNE DEMARCAY FOURCROY FOURNEAU GERHARDT GRIGNARD KUHLMANN REGNAULT SABATIER BERTHELOT LAVOISIER LECLANCHE LENORMAND PELLETIER VAUQUELIN BERTHOLLET CHARDONNET DUBRUNFAUT LECHATELIER BOUSSINGAULT SCHUTZENBERGER

GERMAN CARO HAHN KOPP MOND ALDER BOSCH DIELS EIGEN FRANK HABER KNORR KOLBE LONGE MEYER STAHL ACHARD BAEYER BECHER BREDIG BUNSEN DOMAGK FITTIG GIESEL GRAEBE KOSSEL LIEBIG MAGNUS NERNST TRAUBE WOHLER BERGIUS BISCHOF BUCHNER CASSIUS CURTIUS ERDMANN FEHLING FISCHER GLAUBER HOFMANN OSTWALD TIEMANN WALLACH WIELAND WINDAUS ZIEGLER KLAPROTH MARGGRAF SPRENGEL BEILSTEIN BUTENANDT FRESENIUS LADENBURG LAMPADIUS SCHEIBLER SCHONBEIN STRASSMAN WIEDEMANN ZSIGMONDY BODENSTEIN DOBEREINER ERLENMEYER LIEBERMANN STAUDINGER STROHMEYER GOLDSCHMIDT UNVERDORBEN WILLSTATTER MITSCHERLICH

HUNGARIAN HEVESY
IRISH KIRWAN STEWART
ITALIAN NATTA COVELLI FABRONI SOBRERO AVOGADRO CIAMICIAN CANNIZZARO BRUGNATELLI
JAPANESE TAKAMINE
NORWEGIAN WAAGE HASSEL GULDBERG
POLISH MOSCICKI
RUSSIAN BACH WALDEN SEMENOV BUTLEROV MENDELEV ZELINSKI
SCOTTISH URE BELL BLACK BROWN DEWAR YOUNG BEILBY GRAHAM THOMSON
SPANISH RODRIGUEZ
SWEDISH CLEVE BERGMAN

SCHEELE MOSANDER SEFSTROM SVEDBERG ARRHENIUS BERZELIUS CRONSTEDT BLOMSTRAND ABDERHALDEN
SWISS NEF GLASER KARRER MULLER PRELOG WERNER MARIGNAC SAUSSURE REICHSTEIN
CHEMOSTERILANT METEPA
CHENAANAH (FATHER OF —) BILHAN
CHENDE CHINOA
CHENFISH KINGFISH
CHENILLE SNAIL
CHEQUEEN BASKET SEQUIN ZEQUIN CECCHINE ZECCHINO
CHERAN (FATHER OF —) DISHON
CHERAW SARA
CHEREMIS MARI
CHERISH AID HUG PET BEAR DOTE HAVE HOPE LIKE LOVE SAVE ADORE BOSOM BROOD CHEER CLING COWER ENJOY NURSE PRIZE VALUE CARESS ESTEEM FADDLE FONDLE FOSTER GRUDGE HARBOR MOTHER NESTLE NUZZLE PAMPER PETTLE REVERE COMFORT EMBOSOM EMBRACE INDULGE NOURISH NURTURE PROTECT SUPPORT SUSTAIN ENSHRINE INSPIRIT PRESERVE TREASURE
CHERISHED PET DEAR BOSOM DANDILY AFFECTED PRECIOUS
CHEROOT MANILA TRICHI TRICHY
CHERRY BING CHUP DUKE FUJI GEAN MERRY MOREL CORNEL MAZARD BURBANK CAPULIN CHAPMAN LAMBERT MAHALEB MARASCA MAYDUKE MORELLO OXHEART PITANGA WINDSOR AMARELLE DURACINE EGGBERRY LUKEWARD NAPOLEON ROSACEAN BIGARREAU MARASCHINO MONTMORENCY
CHERRY BLOSSOM HEBE
CHERRY-COLORED CERISE
CHERRY ORCHARD (AUTHOR OF —) CHEKHOV
(CHARACTER IN —) ANYA GAYEV VARYA YASHA DUNYASHA LOPAKHIN RANEVSKY TROFIMOV CHARLOTTE
CHERRY PLUM MYROBALAN
CHERRY STONE PAIP
CHERT BOONE WHINSTONE
CHERUB AMOR EROS ANGEL CUPID SERAPH SPIRIT AMORINO AMORETTO CHERUBIM
CHERVIL BUN KECK ARFOIL CERFOIL COWWEED HONEWORT MILKWEED RATSBANE
CHESED (FATHER OF —) NAHOR
CHESS CHEAT SHOGI CHECKER SKITTLES
(— MOVE) ZUGZWANG
CHESSBOARD CHESS TABLE CHECKER
CHESSMAN PIN KING PIECE CHECKER CHEQUER
(— SET) MEINY MEINIE
(ANY — BUT PAWN) OFFICER
(BISHOP —) ALFIN ALPHIN ARCHER

(CASTLE —) JUEZ ROOK TOUR UDGE JUDGE LEDGE TOWER
(KNIGHT —) HORSE CHEVALIER
(PAWN —) PON POUNE
(QUEEN —) FERS FIERS PHEARSE
CHEST ARK BOX CUB FIX KIT PIX PYX ARCA BUST CAJA CASH CIST CYST FUND KIST SAFE SCOB AMBRY BAHUT BUIST CADDY FRONT HOARD HUTCH RAZEE SISTA TRUNK ALMOIN BASKET BREAST BUNKER BUREAU CAISSE CAJETA CASKET COFFER COFFIN FORCER GIRNAL GIRNEL HAMPER JORDAN LARNAX LOCKER LOWBOY SCRINE SHRINE SPRUCE STRIPE THORAX WANGAN BRAZIER BRISKET CAISSON CAPCASE CASSONE COMMODE DEPOSIT DRAWERS DRESSER ENCLOSE HIGHBOY TOOLBOX WANIGAN WINDBAG CISTVAEN CUPBOARD FORCELET MANIFOLD STANDARD TREASURE TREASURY
(— FOR CUTLERY) CANTEEN
(— FOR FISH) CAUF
(— OF ORES) CAXON
(FRONT OF —) BREAST
(MEDICINE —) INRO
(PREF.) STERN(O) STETH(O) THORAC(I)(O)
CHESTNUT JOKE LING RATA BROWN HORSE CASTOR MARRON SATIVA CRENATA DENTATA
(HORSE —) CONKER
(POLYNESIAN —) RATA
(WATER —) LING
(PREF.) CASTANO
CHESTNUT-COLORED BAY ROAN BADIOUS
CHEVAL-DE-FRISE TURNPIKE
CHEVAL GLASS PSYCHE
CHEVALIER CADET NOBLE KNIGHT GALLANT CAVALIER HORSEMAN
CHEVIN CHUB CHEVESNE
CHEVRON BEAM MARK WOUND RAFTER STRIPE ZIGZAG
CHEVROTAIN MUSK NAPU DEERLET KANCHIL MEMINNA PLANDOK TRAGULE BOOMORAH PEESOREH RUMINANT
CHEW CUD EAT GUM TAW BITE CHAM CHAW GNAW NOSH QUID CHAMP CHONK GRIND MUNCH RUMEN CRUNCH MUMBLE CHUMBLE MEDITATE RUMINATE MANDUCATE
(— UP NOISILY) CHANK GROUZE
CHEWINK FINCH JOREE TOWHEE GRASSET
CHEYENNE DOG
CHIAN SCIAN
CHIANTI FLORENCE
CHIASTOLITE MACLE ANDALUSITE
CHIBCHA MUISCA
CHIC PERT POSH TRIG TRIM KIPPY NATTY NIFTY SMART CHICHI DAPPER GIGOLO MODISH ELEGANT STYLISH
CHICAGO PORKOPOLIS
CHICANE DECEPTION
CHICANERY DIRT RUSE WILE FEINT TRICK ARTIFICE

INTRIGUE TRICKERY DECEPTION PETTIFOGGERY
CHICHI TONY
CHICK BIRD GIRL PEEP TICK CHILD NATTY POULET SCREEN SEQUIN SPROUT CHICKEN CHUCKIE
CHICKADEE TOMTIT BLACKCAP TITMOUSE
CHICKAREE BOOMER
CHICKEN HEN KIP COCK FOWL BIDDY CAPON CHICK CHILD CHOOK CHUCK DEEDY FRYER LAYER MANOC POULT SILKY TIMID AFRAID CHICKY PULLET SULTAN SUSSEX TURKEN ANCOBAR BOARDER BROILER DIBBLER POUSSIN ROASTER ROOSTER SCRATCH ARAUCANA COCKEREL PHASANID SPRINGER
(— SHELTER) MOTHER
CHICKEN COOP CAVY CAVIE
CHICKEN POX SOREHEAD VARICELLA
CHICK-PEA CHIT GRAM CHICH CICER COWGRAM SOWGRAM GARBANZO GARVANCE
(PL.) FASELS
CHICKWEED BLINK BLINKS SPURRY ALLBONE STARWORT
CHICO SAPODILLA
CHICORY BUNK CREPIS ENDIVE SUCCORY WITLOOF BLUEWEED COMPOSIT
CHIDE BAN FUSS RAIL RATE BLAME CHECK FLITE FLYTE SCOLD SNEAP BERATE REBUFF REBUKE SCHOOL THREAP THREAT THREEP TONGUE CENSURE REPROVE UPBRAID WRANGLE ADMONISH BETONGUE LAMBASTE REPROACH
CHIEF (ALSO SEE CHIEFTAIN) BO AGA BIG BOH CAP CID COB DUX MIR MOI TOP AGHA ALII ARCH ARII BOSS CAID CHEF COCK DATO DEAN DOEG DUCE DUKE HEAD HIER HIGH INCA JARL JEFE KAID KHAN KING MAIN MICO MOST NAIK ONLY QAID RAIS RAJA REIS TYEE ALDER ALPHA ARIKI DATTO ELDER FIRST GREAT MAJOR MATAI NAYAK PRIMA PRIME PRIMO RAJAH RULER THANE TITAN VITAL ZAQUE ZIPPA ADALID CABEZA DEPUTY FLAITH HEADLY INKOSI KEHAYA KUBERA KUVERA LEADER LULUAI MASTER MIRDHA NAIQUE PENLOP PRABHU PRIMAL RECTOR SACHEM SAYYID SHAYKH SHEIKH SHERIF STAPLE SUDDER TOPMAN TURNUS CAPITAL CAPTAIN CENTRAL EMINENT FOREMAN GENERAL HEADMAN INGOMAR LEADING LEMPIRA MUGWUMP OVERMAN PADRONE PALMARY POLYGAR PRELATE PREMIER PRIMARY SHEREEF STELLAR SUPREME TOPSMAN TRIBUNE CABOCEER CAPITANO CARDINAL DECURION DIRECTOR DOMINANT ELDORADO ESPECIAL FOREMOST GOVERNOR HEADSMAN HIERARCH INTIMATE MOKADDAM

PREMIERE SAGAMORE STAROSTA SUBCHIEF PENDRAGON
(— IN INDIA) PRABHU SIRDAR
(— OF ADVOCATES) BATONNIER
(— OF RELIGIOUS ORDER) GENERAL
(— OF TITHING) BORSHOLDING
(— OF 10 MEN) DEAN
(CHINOOK —) TYEE
(CLAN —) TOISECH
(INDIAN —) SUNCK SACHEM SUNCKE CACIQUE MOCUDDUM SAGAMORE
(MOHAMMEDAN —) DATO DATTO SAYID SAYYID
(SCHOOL —) DUX
(SCOTTISH —) MAORMOR
(TIBETAN —) POMBO
(TURKISH —) AGA AGHA
(PREF.) ARCH(I) PROT(O)
CHIEFLY MAINLY LARGELY
CHIEFTAIN BEG CHAM EMIR HEAD JARL KHAN ASTUR CHIEF EMEER LEADER SIRDAR CAUDILLO HIAWATHA
CHIEFTAINCY STOOL CHIEFRY
CHIEFTAINESS QUEEN
CHIFFCHAFF PEGGY CHIPCHAP CHIPCHOP
CHIFFON SHEER
CHIFFONIER BUREAU CABINET COMMODE
CHIGGER BICHO PIQUE CHIGGA CHIGOE GIGGER JIGGER LEPTUS WHEELWORM
CHIGNON COB KNOT COBBE TWIST
CHIGOE SIKA BICHO NIGUA PIQUE SCREW CHIGGA ENIGUA JIGGER SANDBOY SANDWORM
CHIH FU PREFECT
CHILBLAIN KIBE MULE BLAIN MOOLS MOULS PERNIO
CHILD BEN BOY BUD ELF GET IMP KID LAD SON SOT TAD TOT WAY BABA BABE BABY BATA BIRD BRAT CHIT CION FOOD GIRL GYTE PAGE PUSS TIKE TINY TOTO TROT TYKE WEAN BAIRN BIRTH BROLL BROWL CHICK CHIEL COOKY ELFIN GAMIN ISSUE KEIKI OLIVE POULT SCION TIDDY TRICK WAYNE WENCH WHELP CHERUB COLLOP COOKIE ENFANT FILIUS FOSTER INFANT MOPPET NIPPER PLEDGE PROLES STUMPY TACKER TODDLE URCHIN BAMBINO CHOOKIE CHOPPER CHRISOM COCKNEY DICKENS GANGREL GYTLING KINCHIN KITLING LAMBKIN PAPOOSE PRETEEN PROGENY STICHEL SUBTEEN TIDDLER TODDLER TROTTIE WRAWLER YOUNKER BANTLING CHISELER DAUGHTER EPIGONUS JUVENILE LITTLING NURSLING PRATTLER RUNABOUT WEANLING WHIMLING PRESCHOOLER
(— OF THE WORLD) WELTKIND
(— UNDER 7 YEARS) INFANS
(BAD-MANNERED —) GOOP
(BAPTISMAL —) CHRISOM
(CHUBBY —) CHUNK
(ELF'S —) AUF OAF CHANGELING
(FAVORITE —) BENJAMIN

(FOSTER —) DAULT NORRY NURRY FOSTER REARLING
(ILLEGITIMATE —) MISHAP BASTARD
(INNOCENT —) CHRISOM
(LAST-BORN —) DILLING
(LOVED —) JOY
(MERRY —) SUNBEAM
(MISCHIEVOUS —) IMP LIMB TIKE DICKENS
(NAKED —) SCUDDY
(NEWBORN —) NEONATE STRANGER
(PAUPER —) MINDER
(PLAYFUL —) ELF WANTON
(PLUMP —) FOB FUB
(PRECOCIOUS —) PRODIGY
(PURE —) DOVE
(ROWDY —) HOODLUM
(SMALL —) TAD TOT MITE SPUD GAITT KIDDY TIDDY TOTUM KIDLET PEEWEE TACKER BAIRNIE
(SPOILED —) CADE COSSET WANTON COCKNEY
(STUNTED —) URF
(TROUBLESOME —) PICKLE STICHEL
(UNMANNERLY —) SMATCHET
(YOUNG —) BABY JOEY INFANT SQUIRT GANGREL NESTLER TODDLER BANTLING INNOCENT LITTLING SUCKLING
(YOUNGEST —) WRIG DILLING
(PREF.) INFANTI PAED(O) PAID(O) PED(O) TECHNO TECNO TEKNO
CHILDBED JIZZEN
CHILDBIRTH LABOR CRYING INLYING TRAVAIL OXYTOCIA
(— WOMAN) PUERPERA
(PREF.) LOCHIO LOCHO TOCO TOKO
(SUFF.) TOCIA TOCO(US) TOKIA TOKO(US)
CHILDHOOD INFANCY CHILDAGE
(2ND —) DOTAGE TWICHILD
CHILDISH TID WEAK DANSY NAIVE PETTY SILLY YOUNG CHITTY PULING SIMPLE WEANLY ASININE BABYISH CHILDLY FOOLISH KIDDISH PEEVISH PROGENY PUERILE UNMANLY BAIRNISH BRATTISH IMMATURE TOOTLING
CHILDLESS ORBATE
CHILDREN ISSUE PROLES STRAIN PROGENY OFFSPRING
(NUMBER OF —) PARITY
(SUFF.) PAEDES
CHILE SOCOMPA
(— INDIAN) FUEGIAN

CHILE

BAY: COOK EYRE NENA TARN LOMAS OTWAY SARCO DARWIN INUTIL MORENO STOKES TONGOY DYNELEY INGLESA SKYRING DESOLATE
CAPE: DYER HORN CHOROS HORNOS QUILAN TABLAS DESEADO BASCUNAN CARRANZA
CAPITAL: SANTIAGO
CHANNEL: ANCHO CHEAP BEAGLE COCKBURN MORALEDA
COIN: PESO LIBRA

CONDOR ESCUDO
DESERT: ATACAMA
GULF: ANCUD GUAFO PENAS ARAUCO
INDIAN: ONA AUCA INCA ONAN ARAUCA CHANGO YAHGAN FUEGIAN MAPUCHE MOLUCHE PAMPEAN PATAGON RANQUEL ALIKULUF PICUNCHE TSONECAN
ISLAND: LUZ PRAT BYRON GUAFO HOSTE MOCHA NUEVA NUNEZ VIDAL CHILOE DAWSON EASTER LENNOX PIAZZI PICTON QUILAN RIESCO STOSCH TALCAN ANGAMOS CAMPANA HANOVER REFUGIO TRANQUI CLARENCE HUAMBLIN NALCAYEC NAVARINO TRAIGUEN
ISLANDS: CHONOS HERMITE PAJAROS CHAUQUES
ISTHMUS: OFQUI
LAKE: TORO RANCO YELCHO PUYEHUE RUPANCO
MEASURE: VARA LEGUA LINEA CUADRA FANEGA
MOUNTAIN: MACA TORO CHATO MAIPO PAINE POTRO PULAR TORRE YOGAN APIWAN BURNEY CONICO JERVIS POQUIS RINCON CHALTEL COPIAPO FITZROY PALPANA VELLUDA COCHRANE TRONADOR YANTELES
MOUNTAINS: ANDES DARWIN ALMEIDA DOMEYKO
NATIVE: PATAGONIAN
PENINSULA: HARDY LACUY TAITAO TUMBES
POINT: TORO GALLO LILES LOBOS LOROS MORRO TALCA TETAS VIEJA CACHOS GALERA MOLLES ANGAMOS LAVAPIE
PORT: LOTA TOME ARICA COQUIMBO
PROVINCE: AISEN ARICA AYSEN MAULE NUBLE TALCA ARAUCO BIOBIO CAUTIN CHILOE CURICO OSORNO ATACAMA LINARES MALLECO COQUIMBO OHIGGINS SANTIAGO TARAPACA VALDIVIA
RIVER: LOA LAJA YALI ALHUE AZAPA BRAVO BUENO ELQUI ITATA LAUCA LLUTA MAIPO MAULE PUELO RAHUE RAPEL VITOR BIOBIO CAMINA CHOAPA CHOROS CISNES COLINA HUASCO LIMARI MORADO PALENA POSCUA TOLTEN COPIAPO VALDIVIA
SHRUB: LITRE
STRAIT: NELSON MAGELLAN
TOWN: BOCO CUYA LEBU LOTA OCOA TOCO TOME ARICA TALCA ARAUCO CURICO GATICO OSORNO SERENA TEMUCO VICUNA YUMBEL YUNGAY CALDERA CHILLAN COPIAPO COQUIMBO RANCAGUA SANTIAGO VALDIVIA
TREE: RAULI
VOLCANO: LANIN MAIPO ANTUCO

LASCAR LLAIMA OSORNO OYAHUE TACORA LAUTARO PETEROA SOCOMAP VILLARICA GUALLATIRI
WEIGHT: GRANO LIBRA QUINTAL
WIND: SURES

CHILEAB (FATHER OF —) DAVID
(MOTHER OF —) ABIGAIL
CHILE-BELLS COPIHUE LAPAGERIA
CHI-LIN KYLIN UNICORN
CHILION (DAUGHTER OF —) ORPAH
(MOTHER OF —) NAOMI
CHILL ICE RAW AGUE COLD COOL DAZY ALGID ALGOR DAVER GELID OURIE RIGOR SCHEL SHAKE FRAPPE FREEZE FRIGID FROSTY SHIVER SNELLY DEPRESS FRETISH FRISSON MALARIA COLDNESS
CHILLED ACOLD CHILL FROZEN STARVEN
CHILLING ICY COLD EERY BLEAK EERIE NIPPY CHILLY WINTRY GLACIAL NIPPING SHIVERY
CHILLY RAW COLD COOL LASH ALGID BLEAK HUNCH NIPPY PARKY AGUISH AIRISH ARCTIC CRIMMY FROSTY FROZEN LEEPIT CAULDRIFE
CHIMAERA BELUE DRAGON CATFISH PLACOID RATFISH RATTAIL DOODSKOP
CHIME DIN RIM BELL EDGE PEAL RING SUIT TING TINK AGREE CHIMB CHINE PRATE ACCORD CLOCHE CYMBAL JINGLE MELODY CONCORD HARMONY SINGSONG
(PL.) BELL
CHIMER CYMAR SIMAR CHIMAR TABARD
CHIMERA FANCY MIRAGE MOSAIC POMATO ILLUSION
CHIMERICAL VAIN WILD INSANE UTOPIAN DELUSIVE FANCIFUL ROMANTIC IMAGINARY
CHIMNEY BAG LUM TUN FLUE LUMM PIPE TUBE VENT GULLY STACK STALK TEWEL CHIMLA FUNNEL LOUVER SMOKER TUNNEL FISSURE OPENING ORIFICE FUMIDUCT SMOKESTACK
CHIMNEY CAP TURNCAP
CHIMNEY CORNER FIRESIDE INGLENOOK
CHIMNEY COWL COW
CHIMNEY HOOD JACK
CHIMNEY PIECE PAREL
CHIMNEY PIPE TALLBOY
CHIMNEY POST SPEER
CHIMNEY SEAT SCONCE
CHIMNEY SWEEP SWEEP CHUMMY FLUEMAN RAMONEUR
CHIMPANZEE APE CHIMP JACKO JOCKO PIGMY PYGMY NCHEGA PIGMEW PYGMEAN
CHIN JAW CHAT TSIN MENTUM CHOLLER
(— POINT) MENTON POGONION
(DOUBLE —) BUCCULA CHOLLER
(PREF.) GENIO MENTI MENTO
CHINA WARE JAPAN LENOX SPODE CATHAY PARIAN SEVRES CERAMIC CHEENEY DRESDEN

LIMOGES MEISSEN POTTERY CINCHONA CROCKERY EGGSHELL

CHINA
ABORIGINE: YAO MANS MIAO MANTZU YAOMIN MIAOTSE
AREA UNIT: MU MOU MOW
BASIN: TARIM
BAY: LAICHOW HANGCHOW
BUDDHA: FO
CAPE: OLWANPI
CAPITAL: PEKING TAIPEI PEIPING
CHANNEL: BASHI
COIN: PU CASH CENT MACE TAEL TIAO YUAN CHIAO SYCEE DOLLAR
DEPRESSION: TURFAN
DESERT: GOBI ORDOS SHAMO ALASHAN TAKLAMAKAN
DIALECT: WU MIN AMOY HAKKA CANTON HSIANG SWATOW FOOCHOW WENCHOW KANHAKKA MANDARIN
DRY LAKE: LOPNOR
DYNASTY: WU HAN SHU SUI WEI YIN CHIN CHOU HSIA HSIN MING SUNG TANG YUAN CHING SHANG
GULF: POHAI CHIHLI TONKIN PECHILI LIAOTUNG
ISLAND: AMOY FLAT MACAO MATSU NAMKI CHUSAN HAINAN PRATAS QUEMOY TAIWAN YUHWAN FORMOSA HUNGTOW TUNGSHA CHOUCHAN KULANGSU STAUNTON
ISLANDS: PENGHU TACHEN CHUSHAN MIAOTAO
LAKE: TAI CHAO KAOYU OLING TELLI BAMTSO BORNOR EBINOR ERHHAI KHANKA LOPNOR NAMTSO POYANG CHALING HUNGTSE KARANOR KOKONOR HULUNNOR MONTCALM TAROKTSO TELLINOR TIENCHIH TSINGHAI TUNGTING
MEASURE: HO HU KO LI MU PU TO TU FAN FEN PAU TOU TUN YIN CHIH FANG KISH PARA QUEI SHIH TSUN CHANG CHING SHENG SHING CHUPAK KUNGHO KUNGLI KUNGMU KUNGFEN KUNGYIN KUNGCHIH
MOUNTAIN: OMI OMEI SUNG KAILAS POBEDA EVEREST MUZTABH SUNGSHAN
MOUNTAINS: ALTAY KUNLUN ALASHAN KUENLUN MEILING MINSHAN NANLING NANSHAN TANGLHA BOGDOULA HIMALAYA TAPASHAN TAYULING TIENSHAN WUYLISHAN
NAME: CATHAY
NATIVE: PAT
PENINSULA: LEICHU LUICHOW LIAOTUNG
PORT: AMOY WUHU AIGUN SHASI ANTUNG CANTON CHEFOO DAIREN ICHANG NINGPO PAKHOI SWATOW SZEMAO WUCHOW YOCHOW FOOCHOW

HUNCHUN MENGTSZ NANKING SAMSHUI SANTUAO SOOCHOW WENCHOW CHANGSHA HANGCHOW KIUKIANG KONGMOON LUNGCHOW SHANGHAI TENGYUEH TIENTSIN TSINGTAO WANHSIEN
PROVINCE: HONAN HOPEI HUNAN HUPEI HUPEN JEHOL KANSU KIRIN TIBET ANHWEI FUKIEN SHANSI SHENSI TAIWAN YUNNAN KIANGSI KWANGSI NGANHUI CHEKIANG KWEICHOW LIAONING MONGOLIA SHANTUNG SZECHWAN TSINGHAI MANCHURIA
RELIGION: JU SHINTO TAOISM BUDDHISM
RESERVOIR: SUNGARI
RIVER: SI HAN ILI MIN NEN PEI WEI AMUR HUAI LOHO TUNG YALU YUAN YUEN ARGUN FENHO MACHU PEIHO TARIM TUMEN WEIHO CHUMAR DRECHU DZACHU KHOTAN KUMARA LIAOHO MANASS MEKONG OCHINA URUNGU YELLOW HOANGHO HWANGHO KERULEN KIALING SALWEEN SIKIANG SUNGARI TSANGPO WUKIANG YANGTZE YARKAND YUKIANG CHERCHEN HANKIANG HUNGSHUI MINKIANG
RULER: WANG
SEA: ECHINA SCHINA YELLOW
STRAIT: HAINAN TAIWAN FORMOSA
TOWN: BAI NOH AHPA AMOY ANSI ANTA AQSU FUYU GUMA HAMI HUMA IPIN KIAN KISI LINI LOHO LUTA MOHO MOYU MULI NIYA NOHO NURA OMIN OWPU RIMA SAKA SIAN TALI TAYU WUHU WUSU WUTU YAAN CHIAI FUSIN HOFEI ICHUN JEHOL KIRIN KOKLU LHASA MACAO PENKI SHASI TAIAN TALAI TUTZE TUYUN TZEPO WUHAN WUSIH YENKI YULIN YUMEN ANSHAN ANTUNG CANTON CHENDU DAIREN FUCHAU FUSHUN HANKOW HANTAN HARBIN HOIHOW KALGAN LOYANG LUSHUN MUKDEN NINGPO PAOTOW PEKING PENGPU SUCHOW SWATOW TAINAN TAIPEI TALIEN TSINAN YUNNAN CHUNGTU FATSHAN FOOCHOW HANYANG HUHEHOT KAIFENG KUNMING KWEISUI LANCHOW NANKING PAOTING PEIPING SOOCHOW TAIYUAN TIANJIN TZEKUNG URUMCHI WUCHANG YENPING CHANGSHA CHAOCHOW CHENGTEH CHINCHOW HANGCHOW KIAOCHOW KWEIYANG NANCHANG QARAQASH SHANGHAI SHENYANG SIANGTAN TANGSHAN TENGCHOW TIENTSIN TSINGTAO

TUNGCHOW CHUNGKING
WEIGHT: LI TA FAN FEN HAO KIN SSU TAN YIN CHEE CHIN DONG MACE SHIH TAEL CATTY CHIEN LIANG PICUL TCHIN HAIKWAN KUNGFEN KUNGSSU KUNGCHIN

CHINABERRY LILAC AZEDARACH CHINABALL SOAPBERRY
CHINA BLUE NIKKO
CHINA HAT HAELTZUK HEILTSUK
CHINAMAN CHOW JOHN JOHNNY CELESTIAL (PL.) TANKA
CHINA ROSE MANETTI HIBISCUS
CHINA STONE PETUNSE
CHINA TREE LILAC HAGBUSH
CHINCHILLA ABROCOME VIZCACHA
CHINE BACK IKAT CHINK CRACK CREST GORGE RIDGE SPINE CLEAVE RAVINE SPROUT CREVICE
CHINESE PAT BABA CHOW CERAI CHINK SERES SERIC SINIC MANZAS MONGOL ASIATIC CATAIAN CHINOIS PIGTAIL SANGLEY (PREF.) CHINO SINICO SINO
CHINESE ARTICHOKE CROSNE CHOROGI CROSNES STACHYS KNOTROOT
CHINESE CABBAGE PECHAY PAKCHOI
CHINESE DATE BER JUJUBE
CHINESE GELATIN AGAR
CHING TSING
CHINGPAW KACHIN SINGPHO YAWYINS
CHINIOFON YATREN
CHINK GAP BORE CASH CHAP COIN JINK KINK RENT RIFT RIME SCAR BOORE CHECK CHINE CHUNK CLEFT CRACK GRIKE KNACK MONEY CRANNY RICTUS SPRAIN CHINKLE CREVICE FISSURE APERTURE
CHINPIECE BARBEL
CHINQUAPIN OAK BONNET BONNETS CANDOCK CHESTNUT WANKAPIN YOCKERNUT
CHINTZ PINTADO SALAMPORE
CHIONE (FATHER OF —) BOREAS DAEDALION
(**HUSBAND OF —**) NEPTUNE
(**MOTHER OF —**) ORITHYIA DAEDALION
(**SLAYER OF —**) DIANA
(**SON OF —**) EUMOLPUS AUTOLYCUS PHILAMMON
CHIOT SCIOT
CHIP BIT CPU CUT DIB GAG HEW NIG BONE CHAP CLIP HACK KNAP KNOP NICK PARE SAND SKIN SNIP SNUB BEACH CHECK CRACK FLAKE PIECE SCRAP SKELF SLICE SPALE SPALL SPALT SPAWL SPELL SPOON WASTE BORING CHISEL GALLET MARKER NOODLE COUNTER SHAVING CHIPPING COSSETTE FRAGMENT SPLINTER WHITLING
(**— OF SOLDER**) LINK
(**— OF WOOD**) SPOON

(**— OUT**) DESEAM
(**BUFFALO —S**) BODEWASH
(**CORN —S**) FRITOS
(**POTATO —**) CRISP
(**SUPPLY OF —S**) STACK
CHIPMAN SCRAPMAN
CHIPMUNK CHIPPY GOPHER GRINNY HACKEE GRINNIE SQUIRREL
CHIPPENDALE AFGHAN
CHIPPER GAY SPRY CHIRP PERKY BABBLE COCKEY FIERCE HACKER KIPPER LIVELY CHATTER CHIRRUP TWITTER CHEERFUL
CHIPPINGS SWARF
CHIRO BONYFISH FRANCESCA
CHIROGRAPHY WRITING
CHIRON (— AS CONSTELLATION) SAGITTARIUS
(**FATHER OF —**) SATURN
(**MOTHER OF —**) PHILYRA
CHIROPODIST PEDICURE CORNCUTTER
CHIRP PEW PIP PEEK PEEP PIPE PULE TWIT WEAK CHEEP CHELP CHIRK CHIRL CHIRM CHIRT TWEET TWINK CHIPPER CHIRRUP CHITTER REJOICE SHATTER TWEEDLE TWITTER WHEETLE WHITTER
CHIRR PITTER
CHIRU SUS
CHISEL BUR CUT GAD CHIP ETCH FORM MOIL PARE SEAT SETT TANG TOOL BRUZZ BURIN CARVE CHEAT DROVE GOUGE HARDY POINT SCOOP SLICK STIFF BROACH CHESIL FIRMER FORMER GRAVEL HAGGLE POMMEL QUARRY REAMER TOOLER BARGAIN BOASTER BOLSTER CHIPPER ENGRAVE GRADINE GRUBBER POINTER QUARREL SCOOPER SCORPER SHINGLE CROSSCUT SPLITTER
(**BLACKSMITH'S —**) HARDY HARDIE
(**FLINT —**) TRANCHET
(**ICE —**) SPUD
(**JEWELER'S —**) SCAUPER SCORPER
(**PREHISTORIC —**) CELT
(**STONEMASON'S —**) TOOL DROVE POMMEL TOOLER SPLITTER
(**TOOTHED —**) GRADINE
(**TRIANGULAR —**) BUR BURR
(**WHEELWRIGHT'S —**) BRUZZ
(PREF.) CELTI
CHISELER CHEAT CROOK COYOTE GOUGER
CHISLON (SON OF —) ELIDAD
CHIT DAB TAB BILL NOTE DRAFT LETTER VOUCHER
CHITARRONE ARCHLUTE
CHITCHAT GAB GASH GUFF TALK BANTER GOSSIP GOSSIPRY BAVARDAGE
CHITINOUS SHELLY
CHITON EXOMIS DIPLOIS EXOMION
CHITTAMWOOD IRONWOOD
CHIVALROUS BRAVE CIVIL NOBLE PREUX GENTLE POLITE GALLANT GENTEEL VALIANT WARLIKE KNIGHTLY
CHIVE CIVE SIVE CIVET

SITHE ALLIUM
CHIVY RUN VEX BAIT HUNT RACE
CHASE CHEVY TEASE BADGER
CHIVVY FLIGHT HARASS PURSUE
PURSUIT SCAMPER TORMENT
MANEUVER
CHLOASMA MOTH
CHLOR LEMON
CHLORDIAZEPOXIDE LIBRIUM
CHLORIDE BUTTER CALOMEL
MURIATE ALEMBROTH
CHLORINE OXYGEN
CHLORION SPHEX
CHLORIS (BROTHER OF —) AMYCLAS
(FATHER OF —) AMPHION
(HUSBAND OF —) NELEUS
ZEPHYRUS
(MOTHER OF —) NIOBE
(SON OF —) NESTOR
CHLORITE AMESITE
CHOANA COLLAR
CHOBDAR USHER CHOPDAR
CHOCK COG PAD BLOCK BRACE
CHUCK CLEAT SPOKE SPRAG
WEDGE SCOTCH
(PL.) STOWWOOD
CHOCOLATE BUD CANDY COCOA
NORFOLK JACOLATT
CHOGAK SHOQ
CHOICE BET ODD TRY BEST FINE
FORE GOOD MIND PICK RARE
WALE WEAL WILL CREAM ELITE
PRIME VOICE CHOSEN DAINTY
DESIRE FLOWER OPTION PICKED
PLUMMY SELECT DILEMMA
ELEGANT EXCERPT PERMISS
DELICATE ELECTION EXIMIOUS
UNCOMMON VOLITION
RECHERCHE PREFERENCE
(FAVORITE —) STANDBY
(FREE —) SWING DRUTHERS
CHOICEST PRIMROSE
CHOIR KERE QUIRE CHAPEL
CHORUS CHORALE CONCERT
KAPELLE PSALMODY
CHOIRBOY CLERGEON CHORISTER
CHOIR LEADER CANTOR
CHORAGUS CHORISTER
PRECENTOR
CHOIRMASTER CHORAGUS
CHOKE DAM GAG GOB CLOG DAMP
PLUG QUAR STOP WARP CHECK
CHOCK CLOSE GRAIN GRANE
SCRAG WORRY ACCLOY HINDER
IMPEDE STIFLE SWARVE CONGEST
QUACKLE QUEAZEN QUERKEN
REPRESS SILENCE SMOLDER
SMOTHER OBSTRUCT QUEASOME
SCUMFISH STOPPAGE STRANGLE
SUPPRESS THROTTLE
(— OFF) BESET
(— UP) CLOY GORGE STUFF
CHOKEBERRY DOGBERRY
SOAPBERRY
CHOKED FOUL WOOLY WOOLLY
CLOTTED
CHOKEDAMP STYTHE BLACKDAMP
CHOKERMAN CHAINER CHAINMAN
CHOKWE KIOKO
CHOLER IRE BILE FURY RAGE
ANGER WRATH SPLEEN TEMPER
DISTEMPER
CHOLERIC MAD ANGRY CROSS

FIERY HUFFY TESTY FUMISH
IREFUL TOUCHY BILIOUS
ENRAGED IRACUND PEEVISH
PEPPERY WASPISH WRATHFUL
IMPATIENT
CHOLIAMB SCAZON
CHONDRIOME CYTOME
CHOOSE OPT TRY CHAP CULL LIKE
LIST LOVE LUST PICK TAKE VOTE
WALE WEAL ADOPT ELECT PRICK
ANOINT DECIDE PLEASE PREFER
SELECT EMBRACE ESPOUSE
EXTRACT SEPARATE
CHOOSY PICKY CHOICY FINICAL
CHOP AX AXE CUT HAG HEW JAW
LOP CHAP CHIP DICE GASH HACK
HASH HOWL RIVE SLIT CARVE
CLEFT CRACK KNOCK MINCE
NOTCH SLASH STAMP TRADE
TRUCK WHANG BARTER CHANGE
CLEAVE INCISE EXCHANGE
(— OFF) SNIG
(— SMALL) DEVIL MINCE
(— UP) HACKLE
(— WITH DULL AX) BUTTE
(DOG'S —) FLEW
(PORK —) GRISKIN
CHOPINE CIOPPINO PANTOFLE
CHOPPED CUT CHAPPED
CHOPPER SAX MINCER CLEAVER
SLASHER TRANCHET
CHOPPINESS CHOP JABBLE
CHOPPING BLOCK HACKLOG
CHOPPING TOOL (— CULTURE)
SOAN SOHAN
CHOPPY BUMPY LOPPY LUMPY
PECKY ROUGH SHORT POPPLY
CHORAL (— SOCIETY) ORPHEON
CHORD CORD DYAD ROLL TONE
CORDE NERVE TRIAD TRINE
ACCORD STRING TENDON
TETRAD CADENCE CONCORD
HARMONY ARPEGGIO DIAMETER
FILAMENT SFORZANDO
CHORDATA VERTEBRA
CHORE JOB JOT CHAR DUTY TASK
CHARE KNACK STINT ERRAND
BUSINESS
CHOREA JUMP JERKS
CHOREOGRAPHY TERPSICHORE
CHORION SEROSA
CHORISTER SINGER CHANTER
CHOIRBOY
CHORUS SONG CHOIR DRONE
QUIRE ACCORD ASSENT BURDEN
UNISON CHORALE HOLDING
REFRAIN RESPONSE THYMELICI
(— IN PLAY) GREX
CHOSEN ELECT ELITE SORTED
ELECTED FANCIED AFFECTED
SELECTED
(PREF.) LECTO
CHOUGH COW CHANK CHEWET
CORBIE CHOCARD
CHOWRY COWTAIL
CHRISM CREAM CREME MURON
MYRON
CHRIST X KING LORD TRUE JUDGE
RANSOM VERITY MESSIAH
SAVIOUR DRIGHTEN PARAMOUR
(INFANT —) BAMBINO
CHRISTEN NAME KIRSEN BAPTIZE
CHRISTENING GOSSIPING

CHRISTIAN XN XT XTIAN UNIATE
GENTILE THOMEAN CHRISTEN
EBIONITE GALILEAN MELCHITE
NAZARENE ORIENTAL STONEITE
TRADITOR COLOSSIAN
(JEWISH —) JUDAIZER
(PL.) FLOCK LAPSED ACEPHALI
FAITHFUL
CHRISTIANIA CRISTY
CHRISTIANITY WAY XTY XNTY
CHRISTMAS NOEL YULE HOLIDAY
NATIVITY YULETIDE MIDWINTER
CHRISTMAS ROSE BEARFOOT
LUNGWORT MELAMPOD
PEDELION
CHRISTOPHE COLOMB
(COMPOSER OF —) MILHAUD
CHRIST'S-THORN NABK JUJUBE
ZIZYPHUS
CHROMA COLOR QUALITY
CHROMATIC HUEFUL FLAMING
SEMITONAL
CHROMATOPHORE ALLOPHORE
LIPOPHORE UNIVALENT
RHODOPLAST
CHROMOLITHOGRAPH
OLEOGRAPH
CHROMOSOME DIAD DYAD IDANT
HOMOLOG ALLOSOME AUTOSOME
IDIOSOME MONOSOME
KARYOMERE LEPTONEMA
PLANOSOME
(PL.) GEMINI
(SUFF.) (HAVING — NUMBER) PLOID
CHROMOSPHERE SIERRA
CHRONIC FIXED SEVERE INTENSE
CONSTANT STUBBORN
CHRONICLE BRUT ANNAL DIARY
ENACT RECORD ACCOUNT
HISTORY RECITAL CORNICLE
REGISTER
(PL.) ANNALS ARCHIVE
PARALIPOMENON
CHRONICLER WRITER CHRONIST
COMPILER RECORDER HISTORIAN
SEANNACHIE
CHRONOLOGICAL TEMPORAL
CHRONOMETER DIAL HACK CLOCK
TIMER WATCH
CHRYSAL FRET
CHRYSALIS KELL PUPA AURELIA
CHRYSANTHEMUM MUM KIKU
OXEYE SPOON BRUTUS POMPON
KIKUMON KIRIMON AZALEAMUM
PYRETHRUM MARGUERITE
CHRYSEIS (FATHER OF —) CHRYSES
CHRYSIN FLAVONE
CHRYSIPPUS (FATHER OF —)
PELOPS
(MOTHER OF —) ASTYOCHE
(SLAYER OF —) HIPPODAMIA
CHRYSOBERYL CATEYE
CHRYSOPAL CYMOPHANE
CHRYSOLITE OLIVINE PERIDOT
CHRYSOPAL
CHRYSOPHANIC RHEUMIC (SEE
CRYSOPHANIC)
CHRYSOTILE ASBESTOS
CHTHONIAN INFERNAL
CHUB DACE DOLT FOOL KIYI LOUT
POLL CHOPA CHEVIN SHINER
CYPRINID FALLFISH MACKEREL
CHAVENDER HORNYHEAD

CHUBBY FAT CHUFF FUBSY PLUMP
PUDGY CHOATY CHUFFY PLUMPY
ROTUND ROLYPOLY
CHUB MACKEREL TINK TINKER
HARDHEAD SCOMBRID
CHUCK HEN LOG PIG CHUG GRUB
HURL JERK LUMP TOSS CHOCK
CLUCK PITCH THROW BOUNCE
CHUCKY COLLET CHUCKLE
DISCARD
CHUCK-A-LUCK SWEAT HAZARD
BIRDCAGE
CHUCKER CROZER
CHUCK-FARTHING CHUCK
KNICKER
CHUCKHOLE CAHOT CHUGHOLE
CHUCKLE CHUCK CLUCK EXULT
LAUGH GIGGLE GIZZEN KECKLE
SMUDGE TITTER CHORTLE
CHUD VEPS VEPSE
CHUDDAR PHULKARI
CHUFA SEDGE GLUMAL CYPRESS
EARTHNUT GALANGAL TIGERNUT
GROUNDNUT
CHUM CAD PAL BAIT MATE PARD
TOLE TOLL BUDDY BUTTY CRONY
SPROG AIKANE CHUMMY COBBER
COPAIN FRIEND PARDNER
ROOMMATE
(— AROUND) HOBNOB
CHUMMY GREAT MATEY PALLY
FAMILIAR
CHUMP ASS DOLT HEAD BLOCK
PUMPKIN ENDPIECE SCHLEMIEL
CHUNCHO CHAMA
CHUNK DAB DAD FID GOB PAT
WAD JUNK JUNT SLUG CHOCK
CHUCK CLAUT PIECE THROW
WHANG WHANK GOBBET
DORNICK KNUCKLE LUNCHEON
CHUNKY LUMPY PLUMP SQUAT
STOUT THICK TRUSS BLOCKY
CHUBBY STOCKY CHUNKED
CHURCH DOM SEE DOME FANE
FOLD HIGH KILL KIRK KURK TERA
ABBEY AUTEM FAITH FLOCK
KOVIL SAMAJ TITLE BETHEL
CHAPEL CHARGE HIERON SPOUSE
TEMPLE EDIFICE FANACLE
IGLESIA LATERAN MEMORIA
MINSTER ORATORY RECTORY
STATION TEMPLET BASILICA
EBENEZER ECCLESIA PECULIAR
PROCATHEDRAL
(— BOOK) TRIODION
(CHRISTIAN —) BODY ISRAEL
HERITAGE
(PREF.) ECCLESI(O)
ECCLESIASTICO
CHURCHMAN KIRKMAN
(HIGH —) PUSEYITE PRELATIST
(LOW —) SIM LOWBOY SIMEONITE
CHURCH SERVICE HEARING
TENEBRAE
CHURCHWARDEN STRAW
WARDEN WARNER
CHURCHYARD HAW LITTEN
CEMETERY KIRKYARD
CHURL CAD MAN BOOR CARL
GNOF HIND LOUT SERF CARLE
CEORL CHUFF GNOFF KNAVE
MISER BODACH CARLOT HARLOT
LUBBER RUSTIC VASSAL YEOMAN

BONDMAN FREEMAN HASKARD
HUSBAND NIGGARD PEASANT
VILLAIN VILLEIN
CURMUDGEON

CHURLISH MEAN BLUFF GRUFF
ROUGH RUNTY SURLY URSAL
CRABBY RUSTIC SORDID SULLEN
VULGAR BOORISH CARLAGE
CARLISH CRABBED CURRISH
DOGGISH INCIVIL PEEVISH
VIOLENT

CHURN BEAT BOIL KIRN MOIL STIR
DRILL SHAKE BUBBLE SEETHE
AGITATE BARATTE TRUNDLE

CHUTE RUSH SLIP TUBE FLUME
HURRY RAPID SHOOT SLIDE
HOPPER TROUGH DECLINE
DESCENT DOWNFALL STAMPEDE
TELEGRAPH
(MINING —) PASS TELEGRAPH

CHUZA (WIFE OF —) JOANNA

CIBOL SYBO ONION SYBOW
SHALLOT

CIBORIUM PIX PYX CANOPY
CIVORY COFFER CIMBORIO

CICADA CAD CIGALE JARFLY
LOCUST TETTIX LYREMAN
HOMOPTER

CICATRICE FESTER

CICATRICLE TREAD GALLATURE

CICATRIX EYE MARK SCAB SCAR
SEAM

CICATRIZE FESTER SCARIFY

CICELY MYRRH

CICERO TULLY

CICERONE GUIDE PILOT MENTOR
ORATOR COURIER SIGHTSMAN

CICERONIAN TULLIAN

CID HERO CAMPEADOR
(AUTHOR OF —) CORNEILLE
(CHARACTER IN —) GOMES DIEGUE
SANCHE CHIMENE FERNAND
URRAQUE RODRIGUE

CID, EL (COMPOSER OF —)
MASSENET

CIDER PERRY PERKIN SWANKY
SYDDIR POMMAGE SCRUMPY
BEVERAGE COCCAGEE
(HARD —) APPLEJACK
(INFERIOR —) SWANKY

CIGAR PURO TOBY WEED BREVA
CLARO SEGAR SHUCK SMOKE
CONCHA CORONA HAVANA
MADURA MADURO MANILA
STOGIE TWOFER BOUQUET
CHEROOT CULEBRA LONDRES
REGALIA TRABUCO COLORADO
LOCOFOCO PANATELA PERFECTO
PICKWICK PURITANO
(PART OF —) BAND FOOT HEAD
TUCK FILLER WRAPPER

CIGARETTE CIG FAG BIRI BUTT
KING PILL SKAG CUBEB JOINT
SHUCK SMOKE GASPER REEFER
CIGARITO
(— BUTT) ROACH
(MARIHUANA —) JOINT STICK
(PART OF —) BAND FOOT PAPER
FILTER

CIGARFISH SCAD QUIAQUIA

CILIATION
(SUFF.) TRICHA TRICHI(A)
TRICHOUS TRICHY

CILIUM HAIR LASH EYELASH
UNCINUS BARBICEL CILIOLUM
(PREF.) BLEPHAR(O)

CILIX (BROTHER OF —) CADMUS
THANUS PHINEUS PHOENIX
(FATHER OF —) AGENOR
(MOTHER OF —) TELEPHASSA
(SISTER OF —) EUROPA

CILLOSIS LIFEBLOOD

CIMBALOM CEMBALON DULCIMER

CIMEX BEDBUG ACANTHIA

CIMON (FATHER OF —) MILTIADES
(MOTHER OF —) HEGESIPYLE

CINCH BELT GIRD GRIP PIPE SNAP
GIRTH GRAVY BREEZE CINCHA
FASTEN PIANOLA SINECURE

CINCHONA CHINA QUINA

CINCHONA BARK
(PREF.) QUIN(O)

CINCINNATI PORKOPOLIS

CINCTURE BAND BELT GIRD HALO
LIST RING ZONE GIRTH CENTER
CESTUS COLLAR FILLET GIRDLE
BALDRIC COMPASS ENCIRCLE
SURCINGLE

CINDER ASH TAP COAL GRAY SCAR
SLAG CHARK DROSS EMBER
DANDER SCORIA CLINKER
FOXTAIL RESIDUE
(REFUSE —) BREEZE
(VOLCANIC —) LAPILLUS
(PL.) GLEEDS

CINEMATIZE FILMIZE

CINEMATOGRAPH KINO
VERISCOPE VITAGRAPH

CINERARIA SENECIO

CINGULUM BAND RIDGE GIRDLE

CINNABAR MINIUM

CINNAMON CANEL SPICE CASSIA
SANELA STACTE CANELLA
BARBASCO
(WILD —) BAYBERRY

CINNAMONROOT FLYBANE
FLEAWORT

CINNAMON STONE GARNET
ESSONITE

CINQUEFOIL FRASIER COWBERRY
HARDHACK ROSACEAN
QUINTFOIL SILVERWEED

CINYRAS (DAUGHTER OF —)
MYRRHA
(FATHER OF —) APOLLO
(SON OF —) ADONIS

CION BUD IMP SECT SLIP GRAFT
SCION SHOOT UVULA SARMENT
GRAFTING

CIPHER KEY NIL CODE NULL ZERO
ALBAM AUGHT OUGHT DECODE
DEVICE FIGURE LETTER NAUGHT
NOUGHT NUMBER SYMBOL
ATHBASH NULLITY MONOGRAM
VIGENERE NOTHINGLY

CIRCASSIAN ADIGHE KABARD
CHERKESS KABARDIN

CIRCE SIREN TEMPTER
(BROTHER OF —) AEETES
(FATHER OF —) SOL
(LOVER OF —) ULYSSES ODYSSEUS
(MOTHER OF —) PERSE
(SON OF —) TELEGONUS

CIRCINATE SCORPIOID

CIRCLE DOT LAP ORB RED SET
CLUE CULT DISK GYRE HALO

HOOP IRIS LOOP MARU ORBE
RING RINK ROLL TOUR TURN
ZONE BLACK CAROL CLASS
CROWN CYCLE FETCH FRAME
GROUP KREIS MONDE ORBIT
PEARL REALM RHOMB RIGOL
ROUND ROWEL SWIRL TWIRL
BEZANT BROUGH CIRCUS CIRQUE
CLIQUE COLLET COLURE CORDON
CORONA DIADEM EQUANT
GIRDLE RONDEL ROTATE RUNDLE
SPIRAL SYSTEM TROPIC AZIMUTH
CHUKKAR CHUKKER CIRCLET
CIRCUIT COMPANY COMPASS
CORONET COTERIE ENCLOSE
HORIZON MONTHON REVOLVE
RINGLET DEFERENT ECLIPTIC
FROSTBOW ROUNDURE
SURROUND
(— AROUND ORGAN) ANNULET
(— IN BULL'S-EYE) CARTON
(— OF FRIED DOUGH) POPADUM
(— OF HELL) MALEBOLGE
(— OF MONOLITHS) CROMLECH
(— TRACED BY HORSE) VOLT
(ASTRONOMICAL —) EQUANT
EPICYCLE
(DANCE —) GALLEY
(FAIRY —) RINGLET
(GREAT —) EQUATOR ECLIPTIC
MERIDIAN
(IMAGINARY —) CYCLE DEFERENT
(INNER —) BOSOM
(MYSTIC —) MANDALA
(PARHELIC —) FROSTBOW
(QUARTER —) ARC
(STONE —) CAROL HURLER
GORSEDD CROMLECH
(TRAVERSE —) RACER
(TWO —S) CACHET
(PREF.) CYCL(O) GYRO

CIRCLET BAND HALO HOOP RING
CROWN RIGOL VERGE BANGLE
CIRQUE CORONA WREATH
CIRCUIT CORONET VALLARY
BRACELET HEADBAND
(PREF.) STEPHAN(O)

CIRCUIT LAP AREA BOUT EYRE
ITER LOOP TOUR WEND ZONE
AMBIT CHAIN CYCLE ORBIT
ROUND ROUTE VIRON AMBAGE
BUFFER CIRCLE DETOUR DOUBLE
SPHERE UMGANG ZODIAC
ADAPTER ADDRESS COMARCA
COMPASS COUNTER DIOCESE
ACCEPTER DIPLEXER
DISTRICT PERIPLUS
PROGRESS
(BRANCH —) LEG
(COMPUTER —) NOR NAND
(ELECTRIC —) LEG LOOP DOUBLER
SQUELCH SECONDARY
(ELECTRONIC —) GATE
(INTEGRATED —) CHIP

CIRCUITOUS MAZY CURVED
CROOKED DEVIOUS OBLIQUE
SINUOUS TWISTED VAGRANT
WINDING FLEXUOUS INDIRECT
RAMBLING TORTUOUS
AMBAGIOUS DECEITFUL
DEVIATING WANDERING
ROUNDABOUT
(— METHOD) WINDLASS

CIRCULAR O BILL FLIER FLYER
LIBEL ORBAL ORBED ROUND
DODGER FOLDER RINGED
WHEELY ANNULAR COMPASS
CYCLOID DISCOID DISLIKE
HANDOUT PERFECT RUNDLED
COMPLETE DOPEBOOK ENCYCLIC
GLOBULAR INFINITE
NUMMULAR PAMPHLET
DOPESHEET ORBICULAR

CIRCULAR-KNIT SEAMLESS

CIRCULATE GO AIR MIX MOVE
PASS RISE TURN WALK WIND
BANDY TROLL CANARD PURVEY
ROTATE SCURRY SPHERE SPREAD
WANDER CANVASS
CONVECT DIFFUSE
PUBLISH CONVOLVE

CIRCULATING WAIF AFLOAT
AMBIENT CURRENT

CIRCULATION ISSUE COURSE
COVERAGE CURRENCY

CIRCUMCISER MOHEL

CIRCUMCISION BRITH PERITOMY

CIRCUMFERENCE ARC AUGE
AMBIT APSIS GIRTH VERGE
BORDER BOUNDS CIRCLE LIMITS
COMPASS BOUNDARY
SURROUND
(— OF SHELL) LIMBUS

CIRCUMFERENTOR PLANCHETTE

CIRCUMFLEX DOGHOUSE
(INVERTED —) HACEK

CIRCUMLOCUTION AMBAGE
CIRCUIT WINDING VERBIAGE

CIRCUMNAVIGATION PERIPLUS

CIRCUMSCRIBE BOUND FENCE
LIMIT DEFINE CAPTURE CONFINE
ENCLOSE ENVIRON ENCIRCLE
RESTRAIN RESTRICT SURROUND
CONSCRIBE

CIRCUMSCRIBED NARROW
INSULAR LIMITED
(PREF.) CIRCUM

CIRCUMSPECT SHY WARY WISE
ALERT CHARY CAREFUL GUARDED
PRUDENT CAUTIOUS DISCREET
VIGILANT WATCHFUL

CIRCUMSPECTION RESPECT
PRUDENCE WARINESS

CIRCUMSTANCE GO FIX CASE
FACT ITEM NOTE EVENT PHASE
POINT START STATE THING
AFFAIR DETAIL FACTOR PICKLE
CALLING ELEMENT EPISODE
INCIDENT INSTANCE POSITION
OCCURRENCE PARTICULAR
(CRITICAL —S) EXTREMES
(EXECRABLE —) ATROCITY
(LUDICROUS —) JEST
(PL.) CIRCS STATE TERMS ESTATE
FORTUNE

CIRCUMSTANCED OFF

CIRCUMSTANTIAL EXACT
FORMAL MINUTE PRECISE
DETAILED ITEMIZED PARTICULAR

CIRCUMSTANTIATE SUPPORT
EVIDENCE

CIRCUMVENT BALK BEAT DISH
DUPE FOIL CHEAT CHECK COZEN
EVADE OUTGO TRICK BAFFLE
DELUDE ENTRAP NOBBLE
OUTWIT THWART CAPTURE

DECEIVE DEFRAUD ENSNARE PREVENT OUTFLANK SURROUND UNDERFONG

CIRCUS RING SHOW ARENA CANVAS CIRCLE CIRQUE CARNIVAL
(— LOT) TOBER
(— RING) TAN

CIRQUE CWM CIRC BASIN CIRCLE CIRCUS CORRIE RECESS CIRCLET EROSION

CIS SYN NERAL NORMAL

CISCO KIYI BLOAT BLOATER BLUEFIN LONGJAW MOONEYE BLACKFIN GRAYBACK TULLIBEE WHITEFIN

CISKEI (CAPITAL OF —) BISHO
(TOWN OF —) ALICE ZWELITSHA

CISSA SIRGANG

CISSEUS (BROTHER OF —) GYAS
(COMPANION OF —) HERCULES
(FATHER OF —) MELAMPUS
(SLAYER OF —) AENEAS

CISSUS TREEBINE

CIST BOX KIST TOMB CHEST CISTA QUOIT CASKET CHAMBER KISTVAEN

CISTERCIAN TRAPPIST

CISTERN BAC FAT SAC TUB URN VAT BACK PANT SUMP TANK URNA WELL LAVER CAVITY CAISSON CHULTUN CUVETTE STEEPER FEEDHEAD

CITADEL ARX FORT HALL ALAMO BURSA BYRSA TOWER CASTLE BOROUGH CHESTER KREMLIN ALHAMBRA FASTNESS FORTRESS TOOTHILL ACROPOLIS

CITATION CITAL NOTICE MENTION SUMMONS EPIGRAPH MONITION AUTHORITY EVOCATION

CITE CALL NAME SIST TELL ALLAY EVOKE QUOTE REFER ACCITE ACCUSE ADDUCE ALLEGE AROUSE AVOUCH EXCITE INVOKE NOTIFY RECITE REPEAT SUMMON ADVANCE ARRAIGN BESPEAK CONVENT EXCERPT EXTRACT IMPEACH MENTION INDICATE INSTANCE REHEARSE

CITHARA CITHER CITOLE PHORMINX

CITHERN ZITTERN LANGSPEL

CITIZEN CIT ALLY VOTER NATIVE BURGESS BURGHER CITOYEN CLERUCH DENIZEN ELECTOR FLATCAP FREEMAN OPPIDAN SUBJECT TOWNMAN AMERICAN CIVILIAN COMMONER CONSCIVE DOMESTIC NATIONAL OCCUPANT RESIDENT
(— OF SECOND CLASS) KNIGHT HIPPEUS
(—S OF MEDINA) ANSAR
(FOREIGN-BORN —) ALIEN
(PL.) SUBJECT PERIOECI CITIZENRY

CITIZENRY COUNTRY SUBJECT

CITRAL GERANIAL

CITRON LIME CEDRA LEMON CEDRAT ETHROG YELLOW BERGAMOT

CITTERN LAUD CITHERN PENORCON

CITY FU WON BURG DORP TOWN URBS WOON ZION BURGH CALNO EKRON JEBUS LILLE MANOA PIECE PLACE POLIS SETTE STEAD VILLE CALNEH CENTER CIUDAD CUTHAH GILEAD JAMNIA JEBUSI LAGADO NAGARA PITHOM STAPLE BABYLON CAMBALU CHESTER ELLASAR FREEDOM JABNEEL MECHLIN CABECERA ELDORADO MAGAZINE PALENQUE
(— LIFE) ASHCAN
(ANCIENT —) PERGAMUM
(CAPITAL —) SEAT
(CHIEF —) CAPITAL CABECERA MEGAPOLIS
(RICH —) MAGAZINE
(TREASURE —) RAAMSES
(WICKED —) BABYLON
(PREF.) URBI
(SUFF.) GRAD POLE POLIS POLITAN POLITE

CITY-STATE POLIS CIVITAS

CIVET CAT CIT GENET RASSE ZIBET BONDAR FOUSSA MUSANG PAGUMA ZIBETH CIVETTA FOSSANE LINSANG NANDINE POLECAT ZIBETUM ZINSANG FANALOKA MONGOOSE TANGALUNG

CIVIC LAY CIVIL SUAVE URBAN POLITE URBANE CIVICAL SECULAR

CIVIL FAIR HEND HENDE SUAVE POLITE URBANE AFFABLE AMIABLE COURTLY ELEGANT GALLANT POLITIC REFINED SECULAR DISCREET GRACIOUS OBLIGING POLISHED WELLBRED

CIVILIAN CIT CIVIE CIVIL CIVVY PEKIN MOHAIR CITIZEN TEACHER CIVILIST GOWNSMAN NONCOMBATANT
(— ENTERTAINING SOLDIER) PYKE

CIVILITY BONTE COURT COMITY NOTICE AMENITY COURTESY URBANITY GENTILITY
(PL.) HONORS HONOURS

CIVILIZATION ISLAM KULTUR POLICE CULTURE ECUMENE CIVILITY
(GREEK —) HELLENISM

CIVILIZE TAME TEACH TRAIN POLISH REFINE EDUCATE HUMANIZE URBANIZE

CIVILIZED CHRISTIAN

CLABBER LOP MUD MIRE CURDLE LOPPER CLAUBER

CLACKDISH CLICKET

CLAD DREST ROBED BESEEN CLEDDE DECKED ADORNED ARRAYED ATTIRED CLOTHED COVERED DRESSED SHEATHED
(— IN PURPLE) PORPORATE
(SCANTILY —) SINGLY

CLADOSE RAMOSE CLADINE BRANCHED

CLAIM ASK DUE AVER AVOW CALL CASE DIBS LIEN MINE NAME PLEA COLOR DRAFT EXACT PLEAD RIGHT SHOUT TITLE ASSERT DEMAND DESIRE ELICIT EQUITY

INTEND RECKON ACCLAIM COLLECT DERECHO DRAUGHT PRETEND PRETEXT PROFESS RECLAIM REQUIRE SOLICIT ARROGATE DARRAIGN INTEREST MAINTAIN PRETENCE PRETENSE PROCLAIM SUBCLAIM CHALLENGE POSTULATE PRETENSION PRESCRIPTION
(— IN BUSINESS) CAPITAL
(— TO BE BELIEVED) AUTHORITY
(FALSE —) JACTATION
(FORESTER'S —) PUTURE
(INDIAN LEGAL —) HAK HAKH
(MINING —) SHICER

CLAIMANT CLAIMER USURPER PRETENDER

CLAIRE PARK

CLAIRVOYANCE INSIGHT VOYANCE LUCIDITY SAGACITY TELOPSIS PRECOGNITION

CLAIRVOYANT FEY SEER OMENER PROPHET SEERESS

CLAM MYA BASE CLOG DAUB GLAM HUSH MEAN BLUNT CLAMP CRASH GAPER GLAUM GRASP GROPE PAHUA RAZOR SHELL SMEAR SOLEN SPOUT STICK VENUS ADHERE CLUTCH GWEDUC QUAHOG STICKY BIVALVE CLANGOR COQUINA MOLLUSK STEAMER ADHESIVE BULLNOSE SHIPWORM NANNINOSE
(PART OF —) BEAK FOOT SHELL VALVE MANTLE SIPHON UMBONE ORIFICE

CLAMBAKE BAKE RALLY CLAMAROO SQUANTUM

CLAMBER CLIMB SCALE CLAVER SCRAWM SPRAWL RAMMACK SCRABBLE SCRAMBLE SPRACHLE STRUGGLE

CLAMMY DAMP DANK SOFT WACK MOIST SAMMY STICKY WAUGHY FLACCID SQUIDGY CLAMMISH

CLAMOR CRY DIN HUE BARK BERE BUNK GAFF RANE RERD ROAR ROUP ROUT SONG UTAS WAIL BLARE BOAST BRUIT CHIDE CHIRM NOISE OUTAS RERDE RUMOR SHOUT BELLOW BOWWOW HUBBUB OUTCRY QUETHE RACKET TUMULT UPROAR YATTER CLAMOUR EXCLAIM ORATION STASHIE NORATION PILILLOO PULLALUE SHOUTING
(— AGAINST) DECRY

CLAMOROUS NIP LOUD NOISY VOCAL BLATANT CLAMANT DINSOME YELLING BRAWLING DECRYING OPENMOUTHED OBSTREPEROUS

CLAMP DOG HOG LUG NIP PIN SET BAIL BALE BEND BOLT BURY CLAM GLAM GRIP JACK MUTE NAIL VISE YOKE BLOCK BRACE CLASP CRAMP GLAND GLAUM HORSE CLINCH FASTEN MOPHEAD STIRRUP FASTENER HOLDFAST
(— FOR BASS DRUM) SPUR
(— FOR CORK) AGRAFE AGRAFFE
(— FOR FLASK) GLAND

(— ON TUBE) PINCHCOCK
(STORAGE —) GRAVE

CLAMSHELL CLAM GRAB SHUCK

CLAN ATI HAN KIN SET SIB CULT GENS HAPU NAME RACE SECT SEPT SIOL UNIT AIMAK AYLLU CLASS GENOS GROUP HORDE PARTY TRIBE ABUSUA CLIQUE FAMILY SENAAH ABIEZER KINDRED PHRATRY SATSUMA SOCIETY ZADRUGA CALPULLI DIVISION
(— SUBDIVISION) OBE

CLANDESTINE BYE SLY FOXY HEDGE PRIVY QUIET SNEAK COVERT HIDDEN SECRET BOOTLEG FURTIVE ILLICIT BACKDOOR HIDLINGS STEALTHY

CLANG DIN DING PEAL RING TONK CLANK CLASH NOISE JANGLE TIMBRE

CLANGOR DIN CLAM ROAR CLANG HUBBUB UPROAR

CLANGOROUS BRAZEN PLANGENT

CLANGULA HARELDA

CLANK RING RACKLE

CLAP BANG CHOP FLAP PEAL SLAP SPAT TACK CHEER CLINK CRACK SMITE POSTER STRIKE STROKE APPLAUD CHATTER CLAPPER PLAUDIT HANDCLAP
(— OF THUNDER) DINT
(— ON) CRACK

CLAPBOARD KNAPPLE CLAPHOLT

CLAPNET DAYNET

CLAPPER CLAP CLACK RATTLE TONGUE JINGLET KNACKER KNOCKER CROTALUM
(— OF BELL) TONGUE
(PL.) BONES

CLAPTRAP HOKUM TRASH TRIPE BLAGUE BUNKUM DEVICE EYEWASH FUSTIAN BUNCOMBE NONSENSE TRICKERY

CLARE MINORESS

CLARENCE GROWLER

CLARET TERSE PONTAC LAFITTE BORDEAUX BADMINTON

CLARIAS HARMOOT KARMOUTH

CLARIBEL (HUSBAND OF —) PHAON

CLARICE (BROTHER OF —) HUON
(HUSBAND OF —) RINALDO

CLARIFIED PURED LAUTER

CLARIFY CLAY FINE CLEAN CLEAR PURGE SNUFF PURIFY REFINE RENDER SERENE SETTLE CLEANSE DESPUME EXPLAIN GLORIFY DEFECATE DEPURATE ELIQUATE SIMPLIFY

CLARIN ACOCOTL

CLARINET BEN BIN BON BEEN BONE REED AULOS CLARY PUNGI CLARONE LAUNEDDAS
(PART OF —) KEY PAD BELL CORK REED CLAMP COVER BARREL LIGATURE MOUTHPIECE FINGERPLATE

CLARION REST CLARE CLARY CLEAR CLARINO SUFFLUE TRUMPET

CLARISSA HARLOWE (AUTHOR OF —) RICHARDSON
(CHARACTER IN —) HOWE JOHN

JAMES MORDEN ROBERT SOLMES
BELFORD HARLOWE WILLIAM
ARABELLA CLARISSA LOVELACE
SINCLAIR
CLARITY GLORY SPLENDOR
STRENGTH CLEARNESS
SIMPLICITY
CLARY ORVAL CLARRE SALVIA
CLASH JAR BANG BOLT BUMP
DASH FRAY NEWS SLAM BRAWL
BRUNT CHECK CRASH CROSS
FIGHT FRUSH KNOCK OCCUR
PRATE SHOCK AFFRAY DIFFER
GOSSIP HURTLE IMPACT JOSTLE
STRIFE STRIKE TATTLE THRUST
THWART COLLIDE DISCORD
SCANDAL ARGUMENT CONFLICT
(— OF WORDS) BARGE
CLASHING HARSH CONFLICT
FRICTION COLLISION
CLASP HUG PIN CLIP DOME FOLD
GRAB GRIP HASP HOLD HOOK
HOOP KEEP OUCH STAY TACH
BRACE CATCH CLING GRASP
MORSE PREEN SEIZE SLIDE SPANG
TACHE ACCOLL AGRAFE AMPLEX
BECLIP BROOCH BUCKLE CLENCH
CLUTCH ENFOLD ENWRAP
FASTEN FIBULA GIMMER GIMMOR
INCLIP INFOLD JIMMER STRAIN
TASSEL AGRAFFE AMPLECT
EMBRACE ENTWINE FERMAIL
HOLDING MOUSING TENDRIL
BARRETTE CORSELET FASTENER
SURROUND
(— HANDS) SHAKE WRING
CLASPING AMPLECTANT
CLASS ILK BRAN CHOP FORM KIND
RACE RANK RATE SECT SORT
SUIT TYPE YEAR BREED CASTE
GENRE GENUS GRADE GROUP
ORDER RANGE TRIBE VARNA
VERGE ASSORT CIRCLE CLINIC
DECURY FAMILY GENDER LEAGUE
MISTER NATION PHYLUM RATING
RECKON REMOVE RUBRIC STRAIN
STRIPE CATALOG FACTION
LECTURE REGIMEN SEMINAR
SPECIES VARIETY CATEGORY
DESCRIBE DIVISION GENOTYPE
GEOMOROI
(— OF BARDS) THULIR
(— OF GOODS) BRAND
(— OF OUTCASTS) BRAND
(— OF PEOPLE) FOLK SALARIAT
(— OF SECURITIES) LEGAL
(— OF SHASTRAS) SRUTI SHRUTI
(— OF SOUNDS) ENDING
(— OF TEASELS) KINGS
(ARISTOCRATIC —) ARISTOI
(CHOICEST —) ROBUR
(DEPRESSED —) PANCHAMA
(FIRST —) GAY
(HEREDITARY —) CASTE
(JAPANESE —) HEIMIN KWAZOKU
(LABORING —) PARAIYAN
PROLETARIAT
(LEARNED —) VATES CLERISY
(LOWER —) BELOW GENTE
(LOWEST —) LAG SCUM
(PEASANT —) JACQUERIE
(SLAVEHOLDING —) CHIVALRY
(SOCIAL —) ESTATE SHIZOKU

(WORKING —) TOIL
(PREF.) CRATO
(SUFF.) CY OIDA OIDEA OIDEI
CLASSIC VINTAGE AUGUSTAN
CLASSICAL PURE ATTIC GREEK
LATIN ROMAN CHASTE CLASSIC
ACADEMIC HELLENIC MASTERLY
(NOT —) BASE
CLASSICALLY IDEALLY
CLASSIFICATION FILE RANK RATE
SORT CODEN GENRE GENUS
GRADE ORDER TAXIS RATING
SYSTEM ANALYSIS CATEGORY
DIVISION TAXONOMY
BREAKDOWN
CLASSIFIED SECRET
CLASSIFIER COUNTER SEPARATOR
CLASSIFY CODE LIST RANK RATE
SIZE SORT SUIT TAPE TYPE BREAK
CLASS DRAFT GRADE GROUP
LABEL RANGE TRIBE ASSORT
CODIFY DIGEST DIVIDE IMPOST
TICKET ACCOUNT ARRANGE
BRACKET BRIGADE CATALOG
DISPOSE DRAUGHT GRAMMAR
MARSHAL SUBSUME REGISTER
PIGEONHOLE
(— TOGETHER) SLUMP
CLASSIS CONFERENCE
CLATHRATE LATTICED
CLATTER DIN JAR CLACK NOISE
RUMOR BABBLE GABBLE GOSSIP
HOTTER HURTLE RACKLE RATTLE
TATTLE BLATTER CHATTER
CLUNTER CLUTTER PRATTLE
REESHLE SHATTER SLAMBANG
CLATTERING CLATTERY
SLITHERING
CLAUSE ITEM PART CLOSE COMMA
JOKER PLANK RIDER SALVO
TROPE MEMBER PHRASE
ADJUNCT ARTICLE COMMATA
PASSAGE PROVISO SLEEPER
APODOSIS CLAUSULA PARTICLE
PETITION REDDENDO SENTENCE
TENENDAS TENENDUM
NOVODAMUS
(— IN CREED) FILIOQUE
(— IN WRIT) TESTE
(— OF WILL) DEVISE
(ADDITIONAL —) RIDER
(SUBORDINATE —) PROTASIS
CLAVACIN PATULIN
CLAVER PRATE CLOVER GOSSIP
CHATTER CLABBER CLAIVER
CLAMBER
CLAVICHORD CLAVIER MANICORD
UNICHORD CLARIGOLD
MONOCHORD
CLAVICLE FURCULE COLLARBONE
CLAVIER MANUAL KLAVIER
CLAVUS CORN BUNION HELOMA
CLAW DIG PEG CLEE CRAB FANG
FAWN HAND HOOK NAIL PULL
SERE TEAR UNCE CHELA CLAUT
CLOOF CLUFE COURT GRASP
GRIFF ONGLE SCLAW SEIZE
TALON UNCUS CLUNCH CLUTCH
CRATCH NIPPER POUNCE SCRAPE
SINGLE UNGUAL UNGUIS UNGULA
WEAPON CRUBEEN FALCULA
FLATTER SCRATCH SHUTTLE
WHEEDLE SCRABBLE

(PL.) CLUTCH
(PREF.) CHEL(I)(O) ONYCH(O)
UNGUI
(SUFF.) ONYCHA ONYCHES
ONYCHIA ONYCHUS ONYX
CLAY BAT COB PUG WAD WAX
BASS BEND BODY BOLE BOTT
GALT GLEY LOAM LUTE MARL
MIRE PAPA SMIT TILL ARGIL
BRICK CLOAM EARTH GAULT
LOESS OCHRE PASTE RABAT
TASCO BINDER CLEDGE CLUNCH
KAOLIN PUDDLE SAGGER
DAUBING MOULDER RASHING
CAMSTANE CAMSTONE CIMOLITE
FIRECLAY GUMBOTIL LATERITE
LIFELESS SINOPITE SMECTITE
(— FOR MELTING POTS) TASCO
(— IN GLASS) TEAR
(— IRON) BULL
(— LAYER) VARVE
(— USED MEDICALLY) FANGO
(COVERED WITH —) LUTOSE
(HARD —) BEND
(HARDENED —) METAL
(INDURATED —) BASS CLUNCH
(PIECE OF FIRED —) TILE
(PIPE —) CAMSTANE CAMSTONE
(POTTER'S —) SLIP ARGIL
PETUNTSE
(REMOVE —) UNLUTE
(SURPLUS —) SPARE
(TOUGH —) LECK
(3-ARMED, HARD-FIRED —) STILT
(PREF.) ARGILL(O) ARGILLACEO
PEL(O)
CLAYEY BOLAR HEAVY MALMY
MARLY CLEDGY LUTOSE ARGILLIC
CLAYMORE FERRARA MORGLAY
CLAY PIGEON BIRD CLAY
CLAYSTONE LECK
CLAYWARE GLOST
CLEADING CLOTHING
CLEAN DO FAY FEY HOE MOP NET
DRUM DUST FAIR NEAT PURE
REDD RIPE SIDE SMUG SWAB
TRIM WASH WIPE CLEAR CURRY
EMPTY FEIGH GRAVE SCOUR
SCRUB SMART SWEEP TERSE
TOSHY BARREL CHASTE CLEVER
KOSHER PURIFY SPANDY APINOID
BANDBOX CHAMOIS CLEANLY
CLEANSE CLEARLY FURBISH
PERFECT SWINGLE ABSTERGE
BACKWASH BRIGHTLY DEXTROUS
ENTIRELY RENOVATE SCAVENGE
SPOTLESS UNSOILED
(— A FUR) DRUM
(— A QUILL) DUTCH
(— BOAT) CAREEN
(— BY SCRAPING) GRAVE
(— BY SMOKE) SMEEK
(— CANNON) SCALE
(— FIREARM) WORM
(— FLAX) SWINGLE
(— IN ACID) BLANCH
(— OUT) USH SPEAR
(— SHIP'S BOTTOM) HOG BREAM
GRAVE
(— UP) DISPATCH
(RITUALLY —) KOSHER
CLEAN-CUT CRISP
CLEANED BRIGHT

CLEANER SOAP BORAX PURER
FOLDER GUMMER RAMROD
FLUEMAN SPOTTER CLEANSER
(AIR —) CAN
(GRAIN —) KICKER
CLEAN-LIMBED CLEVER
CLEAN-LINED SPRUCE
CLEANLY PURE CLEAN ADROIT
ARTFUL CHASTE FAIRLY SPANDY
CORRECT ELEGANT INNOCENT
SKILLFUL
CLEANNESS PURITY
CLEANSE FAY BRAN CARD COMB
FARM HEAL PICK SOAP WASH
BROOM BRUSH CLEAN CLEAR
DIGHT DRESS FEIGH FLAME
FLUSH PURGE RINSE SCOUR
SCRUB SNUFF BOTTOM CAREEN
EMUNGE PICKLE PURIFY REFINE
SPONGE WILLOW BAPTIZE
CLARIFY DEBRIDE DETERGE
EXPIATE LAUNDER MUNDIFY
SWEETEN ABSTERGE DEPURATE
OFFSCOUR RENOVATE SCAVENGE
SPRINKLE
CLEANSER LYE SOAP CLEANER
PURIFIER DETERGENT DETERSIVE
CLEANSING BATH FLUSH ABLUENT
CLYSMIC WASHING ABLUTION
CLEANING LAVATION DETERGENT
MENDATORY ABSTERGENT
(CEREMONIAL —) LAVABO
PURGATION
CLEANTE (FATHER OF —)
HARPAGON
(LOVER OF —) ANGÉLIQUE
(SISTER OF —) ELMIRE
CLEANTHE (BROTHER OF —) SIPHAX
CLEANTHIS (HUSBAND OF —) SOSIA
CLEANUP KILLING SWEEPUP
CLEAR HOT JAM NET RID WAY
CAST EASY FAIR FINE FLAT FREE
GAIN GRUB JUMP NEAT OPEN
OVER PURE PUTE QUIT REDD
RIFE SHUT SLAM VOID ACUTE
ATRIP AZURE BREAK BREME
BRENT BROAD CHUCK CLEAN
CRISP DRIVE LIGHT LUCID NAKED
PLAIN PRINT PRUNE SCOUR
SHARP SMOLT SUNNY SUTEL
SWEEP UNTIE VIVID ACQUIT
AERIAL ASSOIL BRIGHT CANDID
CLEVER EXCUSE EXEMPT FLUTED
LAUTER LIMPID LIQUID LUCENT
PATENT PURIFY REMBLE SERENE
SETTLE SHRILL SMOOTH UNSTOP
ABSOLVE CAPITAL CLARIFY
CLARION CRYSTAL DELIVER
DILUCID EVIDENT EXPLAIN
EXPRESS GLARING GRAPHIC
LIGHTEN OBVIOUS PERVIAL
RELEASE SILVERY THROUGH
ACCREDIT APPARENT BRIGHTEN
BULLDOZE DEFINITE DISTINCT
EXPLICIT LUCULENT LUMINOUS
MANIFEST PELLUCID REVELANT
PERSPICUOUS
(— AWAY) FAY FEY FEIGH BANISH
DISPEL DISCUSS
(— FROM) ALOOF
(— LAND) CURE BRUSH SLASH
DEADEN
(— OF GROUND) ATRIP AWEIGH

(— OF MUD) SLUTCH
(— OF SCUM) SKIM
(— OF TUFTS) HOB
(— OUT) BLOW HOOK SWAMP
SKIDDOO HIGHTAIL DISCHARGE
(— PATH) FRAY HACK BUSHWACK
(— THROAT) HOICK HOUGH
(— UP) SOLVE ASSOIL RESOLVE
DISSOLVE UNSHADOW
(NOT —) DULL DUSKY FOGGY
INEVIDENT
CLEARANCE CHOP ROOM RUNBY
BACKLASH ALLOWANCE
(— FOR SHIP) PRATIQUE
CLEAR-CUT LUCID SHARP DIRECT
CONCISE DECIDED CHISELED
DEFINITE DISTINCT INCISIVE
TRENCHANT
CLEARHEADED LUCID
CLEARING SART FIELD FRITH
GLADE SHADE TRACT ALCOVE
ASSART RIDING RIDDING
SLASHING
CLEARLY FAIR CLEAR LIGHT REDLY
FAIRLY FRANKLY PATENTLY
WITTERLY
CLEAR-MINDEDNESS LUCIDITY
CLEARNESS CLARITY FINESSE
EVIDENCE FINENESS
CLEARWEED RICHWEED
CLEAT BITT STUD BLOCK CHOCK
KEVEL LEDGE RANGE WEDGE
BATTEN RIFFLE BOLLARD
COXCOMB GROUSER SIRMARK
SUPPORT SURMARK
CLEAVAGE RIFT CLEFT WASSIE
FISSION FISSURE WEDGING
DIVISION SCISSION
(PREF.) SCHISTO SCHIZ(O)
(SUFF.) CLASE SCHISIS SCHIST
CLEAVE CUT RIP CHOP HANG
HOLD JOIN LINK PART RELY REND
RIFT RIVE SLIT TEAR BREAK
CARVE CHAWN CHINE CLAVE
CLEFT CLING CLOVE CRACK
SEVER SHALE SHARE SHEAR SLIVE
SPLAT STICK ADHERE BISECT
COHERE DIVIDE FURROW PIERCE
SLEAVE SUNDER DISPART
FISSURE SEPARATE
(— OFF) SCIND
CLEAVER CLIVE CLEAVE FROWER
PARANG CHOPPER PARANGI
CLEAVERS GRIP CLOTE CLOTS
CLITHE HAIRIF HAIRUP BURHEAD
LOVEMAN PIGTAIL BIRDLIME
CLEAVING DYSTOME FISSION
DYSTOMIC
(— READILY) EUTOMOUS
CLECHE URDE URDY URDEE
CLEF KEY CLIVE CHIAVETTA
CLEFT CUT GAP JAG CHAP CHOP
FENT FLAW GASH NOCK REFT
RIFT RILL RIMA RIVE SLIT BIFID
BREAK CHASM CHAWN CHINK
CLOFF CLOVE CRACK CREEK
CRENA GULCH KLOOF RILLE
RIVEN SINUS SPLIT BREACH
CHAPPY CLEAVE CLOUGH CLOVEN
CRANNY CROTCH DIVIDE LISSOM
PARTED RECESS RICTUS STIGMA
BLASTED CHIMNEY CREVICE
DIVIDED FISSURE OPENING

SLIFTER APERTURE CREVASSE
FRACTURE INCISION INCISURA
MULTIFID SCISSURA SCISSURE
PALMATIFID
(— BETWEEN HILLS) SLACK RAVINE
(— IN HOOF) SEAM
(— IN THE POSTERIORS) NOCK
(— OF BUTTOCKS) CREASE
(PREF.) FISSI SCHISTO SCHIZ(O)
(SUFF.) FID FIDATE
CLEMATIS PIPESTEM CURLYHEAD
CLEMENCY ORE PITY GRACE
MERCY LENITY QUARTER
KINDNESS LENIENCY MILDNESS
CLEMENT MILD SOFT WARM
GENTLE LENIENT MERCIFUL
**CLEMENZA DI TITO (CHARACTER
IN —)** TITUS ANNIUS SEXTUS
BERENICE SERVILIA VITELLIA
(COMPOSER OF —) MOZART
CLENCH FIST GRIP GRIT HOLD
NAIL BRACE CLASP CLENK CLINT
CLOSE GRASP CLINCH CLUTCH
DOUBLE
(— FIST) GRIPE
CLEONTE (LOVER OF —) LUCILLE
CLEOPATRA (BROTHER OF —) ILUS
ZETES CALAIS GANYMEDE
ASSARACUS
(FATHER OF —) IDAS TROS BOREAS
PTOLEMY
(HUSBAND OF —) PHILIP PHINEUS
PTOLEMY MELEAGER
(MOTHER OF —) MARPESSA
ORITHYIA CALLIRRHOE
CLEPE CLUPIEN
CLEPSYDRA GURRY GHURRY
CLERGY CLOTH CRAPE CHURCH
CLERISY MINISTRY
(BODY OF —) PULPIT
CLERGYMAN ABBA ABBE DEAN
PAPA CANON CLERK FROCK
PADRE PILOT PRIOR RABBI VICAR
BISHOP CLERIC CURATE DEACON
DIVINE DOMINE PAROCH PARSON
PASTOR PRIEST RECTOR SUPPLY
CASSOCK PRELATE CARDINAL
CHAPLAIN CLERICAL DIOCESAN
EMERITUS LECTURER MINISTER
ORDINARY PREACHER REVEREND
SQUARSON PRESBYTER
PREBENDARY REVIVALIST
CLERIC ABBE CLERK FROCK
DEACON GALLAH LEVITE PRIEST
ACOLYTE GOLIARD ANAGNOST
CLERICAL BLACK CLERIC CLERKISH
PARSONIC PARSONLY
CLERIMOND (BROTHER OF —)
FERRAGUS
(HUSBAND OF —) VALENTINE
CLERIMONT (LOVER OF —)
CLARINDA
CLERK NUN BABU MONK AGENT
AWARD BABOO CLARK FILER
RALPH WRITE BILLER CHASER
CLERIC COMMIS GRADER HERMIT
KITMAN LAYMAN MAPPER
MASTER MUNSHI PANDIT
PENMAN PRIEST PUNDIT RALPHO
SCRIBE SIRCAR TELLER WRITER
YEOMAN ACOLYTE ACTUARY
BOOKMAN CARCOON COMPOSE
DOPSTER GOMASTA PIARIST

SCHOLAR SHIPPER SHOPMAN
STUFFER CLERGEON CLERGION
CLERKESS CURSITOR EMPLOYEE
GREFFIER MUTSUDDY PENCLERK
RECORDER SALESMAN
(— OF ST PAUL) BARNABITE
(CHIEF —) PROTHONOTARY
(HOTEL —) DESKMAN
CLERKLY LEARNED SCRIBAL
CLERGIAL SCHOLARLY
CLEVE BRAE CLIFF CLEEVE
HILLSIDE
CLEVER APT SLY ABLE CUTE DEFT
FEAT FELL FINE FOXY GLEG GNIB
GOOD HEND KEEN NEAT SLIM
SPRY AGILE ALERT CANNY CLEAN
CLEAR CUNNY FALSE FEATY
FENDY HANDY HEADY HENDE
LITHE QUICK SHARP SLICK SMART
SNACK WITTY ACTIVE ADROIT
ARTFUL ASTUTE BRIGHT CRAFTY
EXPERT HABILE HEPPEN KITTLE
KNACKY NEATLY NIMBLE PRETTY
SHREWD SPIFFY STALKY SUBTLE
AMIABLE CUNNING GNOSTIC
PARLISH PARLOUS VARMENT
VARMINT DEXTROUS HANDSOME
OBLIGING SKILLFUL TALENTED
CLEVERLY SLICK FEATLY TIDELY
SMARTLY ASTUTELY
CLEVERNESS CAN CHIC NOUS
TACT KNACK SKILL ESPRIT
INDUSTRY DEXTERITY
CLEVIS COP DEE HAKE CLEVY
COPSE BRIDGE BRIDLE MUZZLE
SHACKLE PLOWHEAD
CLEW BALL CLUE HINT GLOBE
GLOME SKEIN BOTTOM HURDLE
THREAD
CLICHE COMMONPLACE
CLICK DOG DOT DASH PAWL SLAP
TICK AGREE CATCH FORGE SNECK
SNICK DETENT PALLET RATCHET
(HEEL —S) BELLS
(TELEGRAPH —) DASH
CLICK BEETLE ELATER
CLIENT CEILE JAJMAN PATRON
PATIENT CUSTOMER HENCHMAN
RETAINER
CLIENTELE PUBLIC CLIENTRY
CLIFF HOE NIP CRAG HILL KLIP
ROCK SCAR BLUFF CLEVE CLINT
HEUCH HEUGH KRANS SCARP
SHORE SLOPE STEEP CLEEVE
HEIGHT KRANTZ PISKUN
CLOGWYN HILLSIDE PALISADE
TRAVERSE
(BROKEN —) CRAG
(ICE —) ICEBLINK
(LINE OF —S) PALISADE
(PREF.) CREMNO
CLIFFY SCARRY
CLIMATE SKY SUN MOOD CLIME
HEAVEN REGION TEMPER
ATTITUDE
(SCIENCE OF —) PHENOLOGY
(PREF.) METEOR(O)
CLIMAX CAP TOP ACME APEX
HEAD NEAR PEAK SHUT CREST
CROWN MOUNT SCALE TIGHT
APOGEE ASCEND FINISH HEIGHT
PAYOFF SHINNY SUMMIT ZENITH
BLOWOFF EVEREST CAPSHEAF

CAPSTONE EPIPLOCE
CULMINATION
CLIMB GAD STY COON RAMP RISE
SHIN SKIN SOAR STYE CREEP
GRIMP MOUNT SCALE SKLIM
SPEED SPEEL SWARM TWINE
ASCEND ASCENT BREAST SCLIMB
SCRAWM SHINNY SWARVE
SWERVE CLAMBER SCRAMBLE
TRAVERSE
(— ABOARD) HOP
(— DOWN) LIGHT UNSCALE
(— IN MOUNTAINEERING) CHIMNEY
(— OVER) SURMOUNT
CLIMBER CUBE AKALA AKELA
KAIWI TIMBO RIGGER SCALER
COWHAGE CRAMPON CREEPER
(MOUNTAIN —) ALPINIST
CLIMBING RAMPANT SCANDENT
(MOUNTAIN —) ALPINISM
CLIMBING FERN NITO AGSAM
CLIMBING IRON SPUR PRICK
CRAMPET CRAMPIT CRAMPON
CREEPER PRICKER CRAMPBIT
CLIMBING PALM RATTAN
CLIMBING PEPPER BETEL
CLIMBING ROSE SCRAMBLE
CLINCH FIX GET HUG TOE BIND
GRIP LOCK NAIL SEAL CLAMP
CLING CLINK CLINT GRASP RIVET
SEIZE CLENCH CLUTCH FASTEN
SECURE SNATCH CONFIRM
EMBRACE GRAPPLE SCUFFLE
COMPLETE CONCLUDE HOLDFAST
CLING HUG BANK HANG HOLD
RELY CLASP HITCH STICK TRUST
ADHERE CLEAVE CLINCH COHERE
DEPEND FASTEN SHRINK WITHER
CHERISH EMBRACE SHRIVEL
CONTRACT
CLINGER LIMPET
CLINGFISH SUCKER TESTAR
TETARD SUCKFISH
CLINGING CLUNG HUGGING
ADHAMANT ADHERENT
OSCULANT
CLINK ALE JUG PUT RAP BEAT
BLOW BRIG CASH CLAP COIN JAIL
MOVE RING SLAP CHINK KLINK
LATCH MONEY RHYME SEIZE
CLINCH JINGLE LOCKUP MOMENT
PRISON STRIKE TINKLE INSTANT
JINGLING
CLINKER BUR BUHR BURR SCAR
SLAG WASTE HOLLANDER
(PL.) BREEZE
CLINKER-BUILT SHINGLED
LAPSTRAKE
CLINOMETER TRIMMER
CLINTONIA BLUEBEAD DOGBERRY
COWTONGUE
CLIP BAT BOB CUT DOD HUG LIP
LOP MOW NIG NIP BARB BEAK
CHIP COLL CROP DOCK DODD
FLAG HOLD PACE PARE POLL
SNIP TRIM BRUSH CLASP DRESS
FORCE LUNET MINCE PRUNE
SHAVE SHEAR SHRIP SNICK STEEK
CLUPPE CLUTCH CRUTCH FASTEN
GADGET HINDER HOLDER LACING
CALIPER CURTAIL CURTAIN
EMBRACE HICKORY LUNETTE
SCISSOR SHORTEN DIMINISH

ENCIRCLE RETAINER
(— A COIN) SHORTEN
(— OF LEAD) TINGLE
(— WOOL) CRUTCH
(CARTRIDGE —) CHARGER
(HAIR —) BARRETTE
(SPRING —) JACK
CLIPPED TONSURED
CLIPPER BOAT SHIP DOCKER
SLICER CHAINER CLAMMER
CLEANER GRABMAN GRIPPER
SHEARER SNAPPER
CLIPPING BOB SCROW CUTTING
SNIPPING
(—S OF METAL) SCISSEL
(PL.) BRASH SHORTS EXCERPTA
CLIQUE COT MOB SET BLOC CLAN
CLUB GANG KNOT PUSH RING
CABAL CROWD GROUP JUNTO
WRITE CIRCLE CLETCH SCHISM
COTERIE FACTION CONCLAVE
SODALITY CAMARILLA
CLISTHENES (FATHER OF —)
MEGACLES
(MOTHER OF —) AGARISTA
CLITANDRE (LOVER OF —) LUCINDE
CELIMENE ANGELIQUE
CLITELLUM GIRDLE SADDLE
CINGULUM
CLOAK ABA HAP BRAT CAPA CAPE
COPE HIDE HUKE IZAR MANT
MASK PALL RAIL ROBE VEIL
WRAP AMICE BURKA CAPOT
CHOGA COVER GREGO GUISE
JELAB MANTA MANTO PILCH
SAGUM SHUBA TALAR TALMA
TILMA ABOLLA AHUULA ASSUME
BAUTTA CAMAIL CAPOTE CASTER
CHAMMA CHAPEL CHIMER
DOLMAN JOSEPH MANTLE
MANTUA PHAROS PONCHO
RHASON SCREEN SERAPE SHIELD
SHROUD TABARD VISITE ALICULA
BAVAROY CASSOCK CHLAMYS
CHUDDAR CONCEAL COURTBY
GARMENT MANTEAU PAENULA
PALLIUM PELISSE PELLARD
PRETEXT ROKELAY SHELTER
SURCOAT ZIMARRA ALBORNOZ
BURNOOSE CAPUCHIN CARDINAL
DISGUISE INTRIGUE MANTILLA
PALLIATE ROQUELAURE
(— OF FEATHERS) MAMO AHUULA
(— WITH CROSSES) ANALABOS
(CORONATION —) SACCOS
(HOODED —) HUKE CAPOT BAUTTA
BIRRUS BAVAROY CARDINAL
DJELLABA
(INQUISITION —) SANBENITO
(RED —) CAPE
(RUSSIAN —) SARAFAN
(SOLDIER'S —) SAGUM MANTEEL
(WATERPROOF —) GOSSAMER
(PREF.) PALLIO
CLOAKED PALLIATE
CLOAKROOM VESTRY VESTIARY
CLOAM DAUB CLOMB CROCKERY
CLOCHE BELL
CLOCK NEF BELL CALL DIAL GOER
GONG TIME WRAP BUNDY CLUCK
GURRY HATCH HURRY KNOCK
METER QUIRK STYLE VERGE
WATCH BEETLE CROUCH CHURRY

ORLAGE TICKER SKELPER STRIKER
TATTLER HOROLOGE INCUBATE
ORNAMENT RECORDER SOLARIUM
TELLTALE
(— IN FORM OF SHIP) NEF
(— ON STOCKING) QUIRK GUSHET
GUSSET
(— WITH PENDULUM) PENDULE
(PART OF —) BOB ROD BASE DIAL
DOOR FACE FOOT HAND HOOD
RING ROPE CHAIN CREST PLATE
TRUCK FINIAL PLINTH WEIGHT
CHAPTER NUMERAL PENDULUM
SPANDREL
(TIME —) BUNDY
(WATER —) GURRY GHURRY
SOLARIUM CLEPSYDRA
CLOCKER SIZER TIMER RAILBIRD
CLOCKWISE DEASIL DESSIL
SUNWISE POSITIVE
CLOD SOD CLAT CLOT DOLT DULL
LOUT LUMP SLOB TURF CLOUT
CLOWN DIVOT EARTH GLEBE
GROSS KNOLL YOKEL CLATCH
GROUND STUPID BUMPKIN
CLODDISH GROSS STUPID
BOORISH
CLODHOPPER BOOR CLOD SHOE
RUSTIC HOBNAIL PLOWMAN
CLODIA LESBIA
CLODPATE CLOT DOLT FOOL
RAMHEAD CLODPOLE CLODPOLL
IMBECILE
CLODPOLE BOOR BUMPKIN
CLOG FUR GUM JAM LOG BALL
CLAG CLAM CLOY CURB DRAG
GAUM GLUB LEAD LOAD LUMP
SHOE SKID STOP BLIND BLOCK
CHECK CHOKE DANCE SABOT
SPOKE TRASH ACCLOY ADHERE
BURDEN CHOPIN COBCAB
DAGGLE ENCLOG FETTER FREEZE
GALOSH HAMPER HOBBLE
IMPEDE PATINE PATTEN REMORA
SANDAL SECQUE WEIGHT
CONGEST CREEPER ENGLEIM
FETLOCK PERPLEX SHACKLE
SPANCEL TRAMMEL TRIGGER
BEDAGGLE COALESCE ENCUMBER
OBSTRUCT OVERSHOE RESTRAIN
(— A FILE) PIN
(WOODEN —S) GETA GETAS
CLOG ALMANAC STAFF
CLOGGED FOUL FURRY PINNY
FROZEN CLOTTED BEGUMMED
CLOGGING CLOGGY FOULING
CUMBROUS
CLOGGY DULL HEAVY LUMPY
STICKY
CLOISONNE SHIPPO
CLOISTER HALL STOA ABBEY AISLE
ARCADE FRIARY IMMURE PIAZZA
PRIORY CLOSTER CONVENT
NUNNERY MONASTERY
CLOISTER AND THE HEARTH
(AUTHOR OF —) READE
(CHARACTER IN —) KATE DENYS
ELIAS GILES MARIE PETER
BRANDT GERARD MARTIN PIETRO
ELIASON MARGARET
GHYSBRECHT
CLOISTERED RECLUSE

CLONE DESMA SPICULE
CLORINDA (SLAYER OF —)
TANCRED
CLOSE BY IN CAP END GUM HAW
HOT TYE AKIN BUNG CHOP CLAP
CLIT DAUB FAST FILL FINE FIRM
GRIP HARD HIDE LOUK MEET
NEAR NIGH QUIT SEAL SHUT
SLAM SNUG SPAR STOP TINE
WINK WYND ZERO ANEAR BLOCK
BREAK CEASE CHEAP CHIEF
COAPT DENSE FENCE FINIS FLIRT
GARTH GROSS ISSUE MUGGY
SNECK SOLID STEEK STICK STIVY
THICK TIGHT BUCKLE BUTTON
CLAUSE CLENCH CLUTCH DOUBLE
EFFECT EXPIRY FINALE FINISH
INSTOP INWARD NARROW
NEARBY PERIOD SECRET SETTLE
SILENT STANCH STINGY STITCH
STRAIT STRICT STUFFY THRONG
ADJOURN BOROUGH CLOSING
CLOSISH COMPACT CONDEMN
CONTEXT COSTIVE EXTREME
GRAPPLE MISERLY OCCLUDE
POCKETY PUTHERY RAMPIRE
RECLUDE SHUTTER SIMILAR
STAUNCH STOPPER ACCURATE
ADJACENT BLOCKADE CLAUSULA
COMPLETE COMPRESS CONCLUDE
ENCEINTE ESPECIAL FAMILIAR
FINALIZE HAIRLINE IMMINENT
INTIMATE OBTURATE PARCLOSE
PRECLUDE STIFLING PROXIMATE
(— BY) FORBY AROUND BESIDE
FOREBY HEREBY FORTHBY
SISTERING
(— EYES OF HAWK) SEEL
(— IN) BESET ENCLOSE INCLOSE
(— IN ON) TAKE
(— THE MOUTH) STOPPLE
(— TO) BY INBY NEAR NIGH
ANEAR INBYE ALMOST AGAINST
(— TO BATSMAN) SILLY
(— TO COMMUNICATION) CORDON
(— TO QUARRY) HOT
(— TO THE HEART) DEAR
(— TO THE WIND) SHARP
(— TOGETHER) COLLAPSE
(— UP) DIT CORK DITT FILL FOLD
STOP SERRY UPCLOSE
(— WITH) BIND
(— WITH A CLICK) SNECK
(PARTIALLY —) HOOD
(VERY —) CHIEF STINGY
(PREF.) PLESI(O) PYCN(O) STEN(O)
(SUFF.) STENOSIS
CLOSE-COUPLED COMPACT
CLOSED DARK DOWN SHUT CLOSE
LUCKEN UNOPEN BLOCKED
COVERED
(— AT ONE END) BLIND
(PREF.) CLEIST CLIST OCCLUSO
CLOSEFISTED MEAN NEAR FISTY
TIGHT SNIPPY STINGY MISERLY
HANDFAST
CLOSE-FITTING FIT HARD MEET
SNUG THEAT THEET TIGHT
THIGHT PRINCESS SUCCINCT
PRINCESSE
CLOSE-IN SILLY
CLOSE-KNIT TRUSSED
CLOSE-LIPPED SILENT

CLOSELY FAST JUST NEAR WELL
SADLY ALMOST BARELY HARDLY
NARROW NEARLY JUNCTLY
STRICTLY
CLOSEMOUTHED SECRET SILENT
TACITURN
(NOT —) LEAKY
CLOSENESS DENSITY SECRECY
FIDELITY INTIMACY NEARNESS
PARSIMONY
CLOSER VAMPER CLOSURE
CLOSEST NEXT NEAREST
CLOSESTOOL STOLE
CLOSET ARK EWRY ROOM SAFE
ZETA AMBRY CUBBY CUDDY
PRESS LOCKER PANTRY SECRET
CABINET CONCEAL PRIVATE
CONCLAVE CUPBOARD GARDEVIN
WARDROBE
CLOSING FLY SLAM SNAP CLINCH
CLOSURE CLOTURE CLAUDENT
PHASEOUT BUTTONING
(— DOWN OF OPERATIONS)
PHASEOUT
CLOSURE END GAG BOLT SEAL
BOUND LIMIT ATRESIA CLOTURE
FERRULE TENSION CLAUSURE
FINALITY KANGAROO
(SUFF.) CLEISIS CLISIS
CLOT DOT GEL CLAG CLAT GOUT
JELL LUMP MASS MOLE SHED
CLART CLUMP GRUME BALTER
COTTER LAPPER LOPPER
CLODDER EMBOLUS THICKEN
CLODPATE COAGULUM
CONCRETE SOLIDIFY THROMBUS
(PREF.) THROMB(O)
CLOTH DAB RAG BLUE COAT DRAB
DRAP ECRU FELT FILE PALL SEAM
WARE WOOF BEIGE BLUET CABAN
CLOUT DITTO FOULE GOODS
GREEN LODEN LUNGI MOORY
PRINT STUPE TAMMY TAWNY
TIBET TOILE TWEED TWILL
WIGAN ALPACA AWNING BENGAL
BYSSUS CANAMO CANVAS
CHADOR CLAITH CLERGY COVERT
DOMETT DORSEL DOSSAL DOSSER
DRAPET DUSTER FABRIC LIVERY
LONGYI LOWELL MELLAY MULETA
NAPKIN RENGUE REXINE SARONG
SURNAP TILLOT WITNEY ACETATE
BAGGING BOULTEL CHADDAR
CHRISOM COATING CRIMSON
DRAPERY DUSTRAG FALDING
GARMENT JACONET ORLEANS
PANUELO RAIMENT SACKING
SURNAPE TEXTILE WATCHET
WORSTED BATSWING CHRISMAL
COMPRESS CORPORAL CRAMOISY
DWELLING FROCKING HOMESPUN
LAMBSKIN MATERIAL PHULKARI
RADEVORE SHAATNEZ SHEETING
THICKSET TOILINET
(— FOR BELT) SHROUD
(— FOR WIPING TABLE) FILE
(— FOR WRAPPING FABRICS) TILLET
(— FOR WRAPPING THE DEAD)
CEREMENT
(— HANGING FROM WAISTBAND)
LANGOOTY
(— OF GOLD) CICLATON

CHECKLATON
(— OF SINGLE WIDTH) STRAITS
(— REMAINING AFTER CUTTING)
CABBAGE
(— WORN LIKE KILT) LAVALAVA
(— OF GOLD) SONERI
(ALTAR —) TOWEL PENDLE
PALLIUM VESPERAL CATASARKA
(ARABIAN —) HAIK CABAN
CABAAN
(BAPTISMAL —) CHRISOM
(BARK —) TAPA TAPPA
(BED —) COVER SPREAD
(BLACK —) KISWA KISWAH
(BLUE —) PERSE
(COARSE —) KELT DOZEN DUROY
RUDGE BURREL CANGAN
DOWLAS DOZENS FORFAR FRIEZE
HODDEN KERSEY KHARVA
KHARWA STAMIN STROUD
TAPALO WADMAL CAMBAYE
COTONIA DRUGGET FORFARS
RAPLOCH RUGGING SARPLER
SOUTAGE FLUSHING RADEVORE
SARCILIS
(COMMUNION —) FANON SINDON
ANIMETTA CORPORAL
PURIFICATOR
(COTTON —) BAFT JEAN TOBE
ADATI BLUET CAFFA CRASH
DURRY JEANS KHADI KHAKI
SURAT BEAVER CALICO CANGAN
DOWLAS DURRIE GANZIE
HUMHUM KALMUK NANKIN
PENANG CAMBAYE FUSTIAN
GALATEA GINGHAM JACONET
KHADDAR LASTING NANKEEN
REGATTA BOGOTANA CRETONNE
DOMESTIC MUSLINET
(CRIMSON —) CRAMASIE
CRAMOISY
(DECORATIVE —) SCARF
(EMBROIDERED —) SAMPLER
BAUDEKIN
(FINE —) SINDON
(GLASS —) DORON
(GOAT-WOOL —) ABA ABBA ABAYA
SLING
(GREEN —) KENDAL
(GUNNY —) TAT
(HAIR —) ABA ABBA CILICE
(HEMP —) PINAYUSA
(HOMESPUN —) KELT KHADI
PATTU PUTTOO HEADING
KHADDAR
(INFERIOR —) MOCKADO
(LAP —) GREMIAL
(LINEN —) BRIN LINE GULIX
DOWLAS FORFAR BRABANT
LOCKRAM SILESIA BLANCARD
CORPORAL DRILLING GAMBROON
GHENTING LINCLOTH
(LONG —) LUNGI WHITE LUNGEE
(ORNAMENTAL —) TRAP DOSSAL
DOSSEL
(PACK —) MANTA
(PACKING —) SOUTAGE
(PIECE OF —) APRON CLOUT
GODET LANGOOTY
(PURLOINED —) CABBAGE
(RICH —) SCARLET
(SADDLE —) PANEL NUMNAH
SHABRACK

(SILK —) CAFFA BENGAL PATOLA
LUSTRING
(SOAKED —) BUCK
(SOFT —) RUGINE
(STAGE —) BACKDROP
(STARCHED —) GUIMPE
(STRIPED —) RAY
(STRONG —) CANVAS DURANCE
BARRACAN
(TWILLED —) JANE JEAN
BARATHEA GAMBROON
(UNDYED —) HODDEN
(WASHING —) SHAMMY CHAMOIS
(WAX —) MUMJUMA
(WET —) DAB
(WOOL —) SAY DRAB PUKE BEIGE
BUREL DOZEN DUROY LAINE
STARA TAMIS TAMMY BURNET
DOZENS DUFFEL HODDEN
KENDAL KERSEY MEDLEY MELTON
MUSTER SATARA SAXONY
STAMIN TAMINY TARTAN
BASTARD BLANKET DUNSTER
FLANNEL RAPLOCH ROPLOCH
RUGGING BEARSKIN BOMBAZET
BUCKSKIN FLORENCE SARCILIS
VENETIAN PETERSHAM
BOMBAZETTE
(WORSTED —) RASH SHAG
BOTANY BOMBAZET
(PREF.) HISTI(O)
CLOTHE DON DUB HAP LAP RIG
TOG BUSK COAT DECK GARB GIRD
GOWN ROBE VEST ADORN ARRAY
CLEAD CLEED DRESS ENDOW
ENDUE FLESH FROCK HABIT
INDUE ATTIRE BEWRAP SHRIDE
SHROUD SWATHE ADDRESS
APPAREL FEATHER RAIMENT
VESTURE ACCOUTER ACCOUTRE
CLOTHED CLAD BECLAD HABITED
CLOTHES CASE DUDS GARB GEAR
GORE KAPA SUIT TACK TOGS
WEAR BRAWS CLAES DUCKS
HABIT ATTIRE FARDEL SHROUD
TROGGS APPAREL BAGGAGE
COSTUME IRONING RAIMENT
REGALIA THREADS TOGGERY
VESTURE WEARING CLOTHING
FEATHERS FRIPPERY GARMENTS
INDUMENT
(CASTOFF —) FRIPPERY
(DAINTY —) PRETTIES
(DRESS —) WAMPUM
(FINE —) BRAWS
(HANDSOME —) BRAVERY
(MOURNING —) DOLE
(SHOWY —) LUGS
(SOAKED —) BUCK
CLOTHES DRYER AIRER TUMBLER
CLOTHESPIN PEG
CLOTHESPRESS ARMOIRE
TALLBOY WARDROBE
CLOTH FOLDER CUTTLER
CLOTHING (ALSO SEE CLOTHES)
BACK BLUE BRAT COAT GARB
GEAR SEAM WEAR ARRAY BUREL
CLOTH DRESS GREEN HABIT
JABOT STUFF ATTIRE FARDEL
ROBING VESTRY APPAREL
CLOBBER CLOTHES CRIMSON
DRAPERY OUTWALL RAIMENT
VESTURE WEEDERY INDUMENT

KNITWEAR MENSWEAR
ORNAMENT SLOPWORK VESTIARY
VESTMENT
(BLACK —) SABLE
(COARSE —) BUREL
(INFORMAL —) PLAYWEAR
(LOWER —) LAP
(MUSLIM —) IHRAM
(NAUTICAL —) SLOPS
(SHEER —) FLIMSIES
(SHOWY —) SHEEN FINERY
(WOMEN'S —) FRILLIES
(WORK —) FATIGUES
(SUFF.) ESTHES
CLOTHING DEALER HOSIER
CLOTHWORKER FULLER
CLOTILDA (FATHER OF —)
CHILPERIC
(HUSBAND OF —) CLOVIS
AMALARIC
(UNCLE OF —) GUNDEBALD
CLOTTED GORY CLOTTY CLOUTED
GARGETY GRUMOUS LIVERED
CLOTURE GAG CLOSURE
CLOUD DOG FOG NUE SKY BLUR
DAMP DARK DUST FOOL HAZE
HELM HIDE MIST PUFF REEK
SMUR ARCUS BEDIM BEFOG
BLOOM DRIFT GLOOM MUDDY
NUBIA OXEYE SHADE STAIN
SULLY SWARM TAINT VAPOR
CIRRUS DAMAGE DARKEN
DEEPEN DEFAME FUNNEL
MUDDLE NEBULA NIMBUS PILEUS
POTHER SCREEN SHADOW
STIGMA BLACKEN CONFUSE
CUMULUS ECLIPSE FUMULUS
GRANULE OBSCURE POOTHER
STRATUS SUNSPOT TARNISH
CLOUDCAP CLOUDLET COCKTAIL
NIGHTCAP NUBILATE OVERCAST
WOOLPACK
(— OF DUST OR VAPOR) STEW
SMOTHER
(— OF MIST) SOP
(— OVER MOUNTAIN) HELM
(FLYING —) RACK
(HIGH —) CIRRUS
(HORIZONTAL —) STRATUS
(MASS OF HIGH —S) RACK
(MASSY —) CUMULUS
(NUCLEAR —) FIREBALL
(RAIN —) NIMBUS
(PL.) SCUD SOUP CARRY GASHES
(PREF.) CIRR(I)(O) CIRRH(I)(O)
NEBULI NEPHEL(I)(O) NEPHO
NIMBI NIMBU
CLOUDBERRY AKPEK MOLKA
AVERIN
(FRUIT OF —) NOOP
CLOUDED HAZY DIRTY DUSTY
FILMY JASPE MUCKY SHADY
ACLOUD GLOOMY TURBID
INFUMATE NEBULOUS
CLOUDINESS FAIR HAZE GLOOM
MUDDLE NUBECULA
CLOUDING DAPPLE
(— OF EYE) CATARACT
CLOUDLESS AZURE CLEAR BRIGHT
CLOUDY DIM DARK DULL HAZY
BLEAR FILMY FOGGY MISTY
MUDDY MURKY SHADY GLOOMY
LOWERY OPAQUE SMURRY

VEILED BLURRED CLOUDED
NEBULAR OBSCURE CONFUSED
NUBILOUS OVERCAST VAPOROUS
CLOUGH CLUF CLEFT CLOES
CLEUCH CLEUGH RAVINE VALLEY
CLOUT BAT BOX DAB HIT LAP
BEAT BLOW BUMP CLOD CLUB
CUFF JOIN MEND NAIL SLAP
SLUG SWAT PATCH SMITE
WHACK KLOWET STRIKE TACKET
TARGET THRASH WASHER
BANDAGE BOSTHOON
CLOVE GAP NAIL CHIVE CLEFT
GILLY BUTTON CLEAVE RAVINE
SHERRY GILLIVER
CLOVE BROWN EAGLE
CLOVEN CLEFT SPLIT DIVIDED
BISULCATE
CLOVEN-FOOTED SLIT FISSIPED
CLOVE PINK GELOFER GRENAD'N
CLOVER RED HAGI SEED HUBAM
LOTUS MEDIC NARDU PUSSY
ALSIKE BERSIM LADINO LEGUME
LUXURY NARDOO ALFALFA
BERSEEM BERSINE CLAIVER
COMFORT LUCERNE MELILOT
SAPLING TREFOIL TRIFOLY
COWGRASS HAREFOOT
NAPOLEON PUSSYCAT SHAMROCK
SUCKLING YELLOWTOP
CLOVER DODDER AILWEED
EPITHYME HAILWEED HAIRWEED
HALEWEED
CLOWN HOB OAF PUT APER BOOR
FOOL GAUM GOFF JOEY LOUT
MIME MOME SWAD ZANY ANTIC
BUFFO CHUFF CHURL COMIC
FESTE IDIOT MIMER PATCH
PUNCH WAMBA ZANNI AUGUST
BODACH CHOUGH HOBBIL JESTER
JOSKIN LUBBER RUSTIC STOOGE
AUGUSTE BODDAGH BUFFOON
BUMPKIN CHARLEY COSTARD
KOSHARE LAVACHE LOBSTER
MUDHEAD PEASANT PIERROT
PLAYBOY SCOFFER TOMFOOL
COVIELLO KOYEMSHI MERRYMAN
WHITEFACE PUNCHINELLO
CLOWNISH RAW RUDE ZANY
GAWKY ROUGH BORREL CLUMSY
COARSE RUSTIC AWKWARD
BOORISH BORRELL HOBLIKE
KERNISH LOBBISH LOUTISH
UNCIVIL VILLAIN BOEOTIAN
CLUBBISH SWADDISH UNGAINLY
CLOY CLOG GLUT NAIL PALL SATE
GORGE PRICK ACCLOY PIERCE
SATIATE SATISFY SURFEIT
SATURATE
CLOYED BLASE
CLOYER SNAP
CLOYING GOOEY SWEET VANILLA
CLOYSOME LUSCIOUS
SACCHARINE
CLUB BAT DOG HIT HUI SET BEAT
CANE JOIN MACE MALL MAUL
MERE POLT TEAM BAFFY BANDY
BATON BILLY BUNCH CLOUT
HURLY KEBBY LODGE MASHY
ORDER STAFF STICK TOWEL
UNITE YOKEL ZONTA BULGER
CERCLE CIRCLE CLIQUE CUDGEL
HURLEY KEBBIE LIBBET MACANA

MASHIE MENAGE MUCKLE
NULLAH PRIEST STRIKE TAIAHA
VEREIN WEAPON WHITES
BOURDON CAMBUCA COLLEGE
COUNCIL HETAERY HETAIRY
SOROSIS ATHENEUM BLUDGEON
CATSTICK SODALITY SORORITY
SPONTOON TERTULIA
KNOBKERRY
(— IN PLAYING CARDS) OAK
(— OF ANTENNA) CLAVUS
(BASEBALL —) FARM
(GOLF —) IRON WOOD BAFFY
CLEEK MASHY SPOON STICK
BRASSY BULGER DRIVER JIGGER
LOFTER MASHIE PUTTER BLASTER
MIDIRON NIBLICK PITCHER
(MAORI —) MERE MERAI MARREE
(POLICEMAN'S —) SAP BILLY
PANTOON SPONTON SPONTOON
NIGHTSTICK
(POLITICAL —) ROTA FASCIO
HETAERY HETAIRY
(SPIKED —) ALLIDE
(WAR —) WADDY
(WOMEN'S —) SOROSIS SORORITY
(PREF.) CLAVI CORDYL(O)
RHOPAL(O)
(SUFF.) CORYNUS
CLUB CARRIER CLAVIGER
CLUBFOOT TALUS VARUS VALGUS
TALIPES CYLLOSIS POLTFOOT
CLUB, GOLF (PART OF —) TOE FACE
GRIP HEAD HEEL NECK NOSE
SOLE HOSEL SHAFT
CLUB MOSS MOSS FOFEET
LYCOPOD PILIGAN CROWFOOT
FERNWORT
CLUBROOT CLUB ANBURY
ANBERRY HANBURY CLUBBING
CLUBFOOT
CLUB RUSH RUSH SEDGE GLUMAL
DEERHAIR
CLUCK HEN FUSS CHUCK CLACK
CLICK CLOCK CLOOK
CLUE KEY TIP BALL CLEW HINT
IDEA LEAD GUIDE TWINE
BOTTOM CLAVIS THREAD
INNUENDO
CLUMP SOP TOD BLOW BUSH
CLOT HEAP KNOT LUMP MASS
MOSS MOTT TOPE TUFT TUMP
TURB BLUFF BUNCH CLAMP
GROUP GROVE HOUSE PATCH
PLUMP STUMP TREAD WUDGE
CLUNCH DOLLOP LUMPER
BOSCAGE CLUMPER CLUSTER
THICKET
(— OF BRIERS OR ROSES) ROAN
RONE
(— OF CELLS) SLUDGE
(— OF SHRUBS) BUSH
(— OF SPORANGIA) SORUS
(— OF TREES) BLUFF HOUSE
HURST HYRST BOSQUE
CLUMSILY SOUSE GREENLY
GAUCHELY
CLUMSY AWK FLOB LEWD NUMB
RUDE BLUNT BULKY GAUMY
GAWKY HOGGY HULKY INAPT
INEPT SCRAM SPLAY STIFF STOGY
CLUMPY GAUCHE LUBBER
NOGGEN THUMBY WOODEN

AWKWARD BOORISH CHUCKLE
LOUTISH LUMPISH UNHANDY
UNREADY BENUMBED BUNGLING
CLOWNISH FOOTLESS GAUMLESS
HANDLESS LUMBERLY TACTLESS
UNGAINLY UNWIELDY CLOUTERLY
PONDEROUS
(NOT —) FINE
CLUSTER BOB BOG BUSH CLOT
COMA CONE CYME KNOT LUMP
TUFT BUNCH CLUMP DRUSE
GROUP PLUMP SHEAF SORUS
CENTER COLONY GATHER
MORULA PLEIAD REGIME
BOUROCK CLUTHER DOLPHIN
ENVIRON FOLIAGE FASCICLE
NUCLEATE SURROUND
(— AS BEES) BALL KNIT
(— OF BANANAS) HAND
(— OF BRANCHES) SPRAY
(— OF CRYSTALS) DRUSE
(— OF FEATHERS) MUFF
(— OF FIBERS) NEP
(— OF FLOWERS) CYME TRUSS
CORYMB ANTHEMY PANICLE
(— OF HAIRS) MYSTAX
(— OF METAL BALLS) GRAPE
(— OF NODULES) GRAPES
(— OF PILES) DOLPHIN
(— OF PLANTS) BED
(— OF RAYS) AIGRETTE
(— OF SPORES) SORUS
(— OF STARS) PRAESEPE
(— OF TINES) TROCHE
(— OF WOOL) NEP
(CONFUSED —) SPLATTER
(GERM CELL —) MORULA
(SUSPENDED —) SWAG
(PREF.) CORYMBI CYM(I)(O)
KYM(I)(O) RACEMI RACEMO
CLUSTER BEAN GUAR
CLUSTERED TUFTED RACEMOSE
AGGREGATE CONGLOMERATE
CLUTCH HUG NAB SET CLAM
CLAW CLEM CLIP FIST GLAM
GRAB GRIP NEST BROOD CATCH
CLASP CLAUT CLEEK CLICK
GLAUM GRASP GRIPE GRISP
HATCH LEVER POWER SEIZE
TALON CLEACH CLENCH CLETCH
CLINCH CUTOUT FASTEN RETAIN
SNATCH CLAUGHT CONTROL
CRAMPON COUPLING
(— OF EGGS) SET LAWTER LAYING
SETTING SITTING LAUGHTER
CLUTCHING GRIP GRIPING
CLUTTER MESS STUFF BUSTLE
CUMBER LITTER CLATTER
DISORDER CONFUSION
CLUTTERED CLATTY CLOTTED
CLYMENE (DAUGHTER OF —)
ALCIMEDE
(FATHER OF —) MINYAS CATREUS
OCEANUS
(HUSBAND OF —) IAPETUS
NAUPLIUS PHYLACUS
(MOTHER OF —) TETHYS
(SON OF —) OEAX ATLAS IPHICLUS
PHAETHON MENOETIUS
PALAMEDES
CLYPEUS NASUS EPISTOME
PRELABRUM

CLYSTER LAVEMENT INJECTION
CLYTEMNESTRA (BROTHER OF —)
CASTOR POLLUX POLYDEUCES
(DAUGHTER OF —) ELECTRA
LAODICE IPHIGENIA IPHINASSA
CHRYSOTHEMIS
(FATHER OF —) TYNDAREUS
(HUSBAND OF —) TANTALUS
AGAMEMNON
(LOVER OF —) AEGISTHUS
(MOTHER OF —) LEDA
(SISTER OF —) HELENA
(SON OF —) ORESTES
CLYTIUS (BROTHER OF —) PRIAM
(FATHER OF —) EURYTUS
LAOMEDON
(MOTHER OF —) GAEA
(SLAYER OF —) HERCULES
(SON OF —) CALETOR
COACH BUS CAR FLY DRAG HACK
HELP ARABA BOGEY BOGIE BRIEF
CABIN FLIER FLYER PILOT PRIME
STAGE TEACH TRAIN TUTOR
ADVISE DIRECT FIACRE JARVEY
SALOON ADVISER CHARIOT
COACHER CONCORD GONDOLA
PREPARE RATTLER TALLYHO
CARRIAGE DORMEUSE PUPILIZE
(FAST —) FLIER FLYER
(HACKNEY —) FIACRE JARVEY
(HEAVY —) DRAG
(SLOW —) SLOWPOKE
(3-WHEELED —) TRICYCLE
COACHMAN FLY FISH JEHU WHIP
PILOT COACHY DRIVER COACHEE
COACHER YAMSHIK YEMSCHIK
COACTION EXPLOITATION
COADJUTOR PRIOR
COAGULANT CURD RENNET
STYPTIC COAGULUM GELATINE
COAGULATE GEL SET CAKE CLOD
CLOT CURD JELL QUAIL YEARN
COTTER CURDLE LAPPER LOBBER
LOPPER POSSET CLABBER
CLOTTER CONGEAL PECTIZE
THICKEN COAGULUM CONCRETE
SOLIDIFY
COAGULATED CRUDY CURDY
LIVERED
COAGULATION GOUT CLOTTER
COAGULUM CLOT THROMBUS
COAL RIB BASS DUFF FUEL SWAD
BLOCK CHARK EMBER GHOST
GLEED STOKE BARING BRAZIL
BURGEE CANNEL CARBON CINDER
FIRING SPLINT BACKING
BOGHEAD BRIGHTS BYERITE
COBBLES LIGNITE RATTLER
VITRAIN AMPELITE LANDSALE
(— IN PLACE) SOLID
(— PILLAR) STOOK
(— SLAB) SKIP
(BAD —) SMUT
(BED OF —) SEAM
(DIRTY —) RASH
(FINE —) DUFF SCREENINGS
(IMPURE —) SWAD
(LARGE BLOCK OF —) JUD JUDD
(LIVE OR GLOWING —) GLEED
GLEYD
(REFUSE —) BREEZE
(SIZE OF —) EGG NUT PEA LUMP

RICE SLACK STOVE BARLEY
BROKEN CHESTNUT WALLSEND
BUCKWHEAT
(SLATY —) BASS BONE BONY
(SMALL LUMP OF —) NUBBLING
(SMALL PORTION OF UNCUT —)
PANEL
(PREF.) ANTHRAC(O) CARBONI
COAL BED SEAM
COALBIN BUNKER
COAL BROKER CRIMP
COAL CAR JIMMY
COAL CHUTE DOCK
COAL DUST COOM CULM SMUT
COOMB
COALESCE MIX CLOG FUSE JOIN
BLEND MERGE UNITE COHERE
EMBODY MINGLE SINTER
COMBINE
COALESCENCE UNION FUSION
LEAGUE CAPTURE SYNANTHY
COALFISH SEY PARR COLEY
CUDDY SEITH BESHOW BILLET
CUDDEN PODLER SAITHE SILLOC
BADDOCK GLASHAN GLASSIN
PILTOCK POLLACK
(YOUNG —) PODLER PODLEY
COMAMIE POODLER SILLOCK
GRAYFISH
COALITION FRONT TRUST UNION
FUSION LEAGUE MERGER
ENTENTE ALLIANCE
COAL OIL KEROSENE
COALRAKE HOE FREGGIN
FRUGGAN SCRAPPLE
COAL WORKER GEORDIE HURRIER
COAL YARD REE
COAMING CURB LEDGE COMBING
COARSE FAT LOW RAW BASE BULL
DANK FOUL HARD HASK LEWD
LOUD RANK RUDE SOUR VILE
BAWDY BRASH BROAD CRASS
CRUDE DIRTY GREAT GROFF
GROSS HARSH HASKY HEAVY
LARGE LOOSE PLAIN RANDY
ROUGH ROUTH ROWTY RUDAS
STOGY STOUR THICK UNORN
BLOWSY BRAZEN BRUTAL
CALLOW CHUFFY COMMON
DUDGEN EARTHY IMPURE INCULT
RANDIE RIBALD ROUDAS RUDOUS
RUGGED RUSSET RUSTIC SULTRY
UNFELE VULGAR BLATANT
CARLAGE CARLISH CRIBBLE
FULSOME GOATISH LOUTISH
LOWBRED OBSCENE PROFANE
RAPLOCH RAUCOUS ROINISH
SENSUAL BARBARIC CLOWNISH
HOMESPUN IMMODEST INDECENT
PLEBEIAN STUBBORN UNCHASTE
COARSE-FIBERED STRONG
COARSE-GRAINED DRY GRUFF
COARSELY BROADLY HARSHLY
COARSEN HACKNEY
COAST BANK LAND RIPA BEACH
BOARD CLIFF SHORE SLIDE
WARTH ADJOIN BORDER RIVAGE
STRAND BOBSLED SEASIDE
APPROACH SEABOARD SEASHORE
COASTAL ORARIAN
COASTER MAT SLED TILE DOLLY
TROUT BARCON CRADLE CREEPER
MISTICO TOBOGGAN

COASTLAND MAREMMA
COAT FUR LAY PEE SAC TOG BARK
BLUE BUFF CONY DAUB FOIL
FOLD HIDE HUSK JACK JAMA
JUPE MIDI PINK RIND SACK SCAB
SEAL TOGE ZINC BENNY CLOTH
CONEY COVER CRUST FLASH
FROCK GLACE GLAZE HABIT
JAMAH JEMMY LAYER OILER
PAINT PLATE QUYTE SAQUE
SHELL TERVE ALPACA BYRNIE
COATEE DUSTER ENAMEL EXTIMA
GROUND HACKLE INTIMA INVEST
JACKET JOSEPH KIRTLE LACKER
MANTLE MELOTE PARGET PELAGE
RABBIT REEFER SEALER SILVER
SLOUGH STUCCO TABARD
VENEER BEESWAX BOBTAIL
CASSOCK COATING COURTBY
CRISPIN CUTAWAY GARMENT
GROGRAM INCRUST KARAKUL
LACQUER OILCOAT OVERLAY
PALETOT PELISSE PLASTER
SHELLAC SHOOTER SPENCER
STRATUM SUBCOAT SURCOAT
SURTOUT SWAGGER TOGEMAN
TOPCOAT VESTURE BENJAMIN
COURTEPY GRAPHITE INTONACO
MACKINAW MEMBRANE
OVERCOAT ROCKELAY SEALSKIN
SHERWANI SILICATE TEGUMENT
TRENCHER OUTERCOAT
PETERSHAM REDINGOTE
(— **FOOD**) DREDGE
(— **LENS**) BLOOM
(— **OF ARMS**) CREST BLAZON
BEARINGS
(— **OF BIRD SKINS**) TEMIAK
(— **OF BLOOD VESSEL**) MEDIA
(— **OF CARIBOU SKINS**) KOOLETAH
(— **OF DEFENSE**) JACK
(— **OF EYE**) CHOROID
(— **OF EYEBALL**) SCLERA
(— **OF GRAVEL**) BLOTTER
(— **OF INDIA**) ACHKAN
(— **OF MAIL**) FROCK BRINIE BYRNIE
SECRET HAUBERK CATAPHRACT
(— **OF ORGAN**) INTIMA
(— **OF OVULE**) PRIMINE
(— **OF PLASTER**) SET ARRICCIO
BROWNING INTONACO
(— **OF SEED**) ARIL BRAN EPISPERM
(— **OF WOOL**) FLEECE
(— **WITH ALLOY**) TERNE
(— **WITH PITCH**) PAY
(— **WORN UNDER ARMOR**)
GAMBESON
(**DEER'S WINTER** —) BLUE
(**FIRST** — **OF TIN**) LIST
(**FUR** —) ANARAK ANORAK
(**HAIR** —) MELOTE
(**HOODED** —) GREGO CAPOTE
(**LONG** —) MAXI JIBBA JIBBAH
KAPOTE DJIBBAH MAXICOAT
NEWMARKET
(**LOOSE** —) CASSOCK PALETOT
INVERNESS
(**MILITARY** —) TUNIC BLOUSE
BUFFCOAT
(**OLD** —) MUMMOCK
(**RIDING** —) JOSEPH
(**SACKCLOTH** —) SANBENITO
(**SEALSKIN** —) NETCHA

(**SHEEPSKIN** —) ZAMARRA
ZAMARRO
(**SHORT** —) PEA JUMP MIDI SACK
TERNE JERKIN REEFER PEACOAT
(**THREE-QUARTER LENGTH** —)
ACHKAN
(**WATERPROOF** —) BURSATI
SLICKER
(**WOMAN'S** —) CARACO DOLMAN
(**WOOLLY** —) LANUGO
COATED GLACE BACKED FURRED
LOADED CANDIED
COAT HANGER SHOULDER
COATI NASUA TEJON NARICA
PISOTE ARCTOID
COATING (ALSO SEE COAT) FUR
GUM ARIL DOPE DRAB FILM FLOR
HAIR HOAR SKIN BLOOM FLASH
GLACE GLAZE ICING SCALE
BEAVER CHATON COVERT
CRUSTA FINISH JACKET PATINA
VENEER BACKING DIPCOAT
FURRING GILDING LACQUER
OVERLAY PLATING TINNING
ACIERAGE CAMBOUIS CLADDING
EMULSION FLOODING MUCILAGE
OVERCOAT PERIDIUM
PLASTERING
(— **OF BACTERIA**) SLIME
(— **OF GLASS**) MOILES FOLIATION
(— **OF GLUE**) ENAMEL
(— **OF ICE**) GLAZE
(— **OF SEED**) TESTA
(— **OF TONGUE**) ATTER
(**CORROSION** —) RUST
(**POWDERY** —) DOWN
(**PRUINOUS** —) FARINA
(**WALL** —) GROUT
COATLICUE (**HUSBAND OF** —)
MIXCOATL
(**SON OF** —) HUITZILOPOCHTLI
COATTAIL LABIE LAPPET
COAX BEG COY PET CANT DUPE
FAGE FAWN LURE URGE WILE
JOLLY TEASE BANTER CAJOLE
CUITLE CUTTER ENTICE FLEECH
SEDUCE BEGUILE CROODLE
CROWDLE CRUDDLE FLATTER
IMPLORE SOOTHER WHEEDLE
BLANDISH COLLOGUE INVEIGLE
PERSUADE
COAXIAL CONCENTRIC
COB EAR LOB MEW COBB
COBBERER ROARER ROUSER
COBBLE DARN MEND PAVE BOTCH
PATCH BUNGLE COGGLE REPAIR
COBBLER PIE SNOB SHEEP SOLER
SUTOR ARTIST COZIER SOUTER
BOTCHER CATFISH CRISPIN
POMPANO SADDLER CHUCKLER
SCORPION SNOBSCAT
COBBLERFISH COBBLER SUNFISH
SHOEMAKER
COBBY STOUT HEARTY LIVELY
STOCKY COMPACT
COBLE MULE KOBIL
COBNUT COB OUABE HOGNUT
PIGNUT
COBRA ASP NAG HAJE NAGA NAJA
KRAIT VIPER ELAPID URAEUS
COBWEB NET TRAP SNARE WEVET
GOSSAMER
COCA CUCA KHOKA TRUXILLO

COCAINE COKE SNOW
(— **MIXED WITH HEROIN**)
SPEEDBALL
COCASH ASTER SWANWEED
COCCOID BERRYLIKE
COCCULUS CEBATHA FISHBERRY
COCCYX
(**PREF.**) COCCYG(O) COCCYGEO
COCHE MOCOA
COCHINEAL GRAIN BLANCO
COCCUS GRANILLA
COCHINEAL FIG NOPAL
COCHINEAL INSECT VERMIL
VERMEIL VERMILION
COCK COX TAP BANK BOOT COIL
FOWL HEAP KORA PILE RICK
SPAN COCKY COQUE FIGHT FUGIE
GALLO SHOCK STACK STRUT
VALVE YOWLE CRAVEN FAUCET
HAMMER HEELER LEADER
CONTEND GORCOCK PETCOCK
ROOSTER SWAGGER ASTROLOG
COCKBIRD COCKEREL COXBONES
GAMECOCK JERMONAL
STOPCOCK
(— **GUNLOCK**) NAB
(— **OF HAY**) HIPPLE
(— **OF THE WALK**) KINGFISH
(— **WITHOUT COURAGE**) CRAVEN
(— **WITHOUT SPURS**) MUCKNA
(**FIGHTING** —) FUGIE HEELER
TURNPOKE
(**TURKEY** —) STAG
(**WATER** —) KORA
(**WEATHER** —) FANE VANE
(**PREF.**) ALECTORO ALECTRYO
GALLI
COCKADE KNOT BADGE COCKARD
ROSETTE TRICOLOR
COCKATIEL QUARRION
COCKATOO ARA ARARA COCKY
GALAH MACAW ABACAY COCKIE
PARROT CORELLA JACATOO
CALANGAY GANGGANG
COCKATOO BUSH BLUEBERRY
COCKBOAT COG COCK SCULL
COGBOAT
COCKCHAFER OAKWEB BUZZARD
HUMBUZZ
COCKED HAT SCRAPER RAMILLIE
COCKER CODDLE COGGER CUITER
QUIVER SPANIEL
COCKEREL COCK SLIP BANTAM
COCKFIGHT MAIN
COCKINESS SWAGGER
COCKLE COCK GALL GITH KILN
OAST BULGE KAKEL SHELL STOVE
DARNEL NUCULA PALOUR
PUCKER RIPPLE WABBLE ZIZANY
CUCKOLD WRINKLE HARDHEAD
(**PREF.**) CONCH(O)
COCKLEBUR COTS CLOTE COCKLE
BURDOCK BURWEED CADILLO
CLOTBUR CUCKOLD CLOTWEED
DITCHBUR
COCKNEY ARRY ORTHERIS
LONDONESE
COCKPIT PIT RING RINK WELL
ARENA CABIN FIELD GALLERA
COCKROACH BUG DRUM ROACH
BEETLE BLATTID DRUMMER
KNOCKER
COCKSCOMB CREST COXCOMB

COCKSPUR FINGRIGO GARABATO
COCKTAIL SOUR ZOOM BRONX
CRUSTA GIBSON MAITAI COBBLER
MARTINI NEGRONI SAZERAC
SIDECAR STINGER SWIZZLE
APERITIF DAIQUIRI MARGARITA
COCKY PERK PERT CRANK PERKY
CROUSE FARMER JAUNTY
COCKING ARROGANT
COCO KOKO BROMA COCOA COKER
YUNTIA
COCOA MAHAL TURTLE PATASHTE
COCOA BROWN PUEBLO
COCONUT COCO COCKER NARGIL
COCOANUT
COCONUT FIBER COIR KAIR KYAR
CAYAR
COCONUT MEAT COPRA
COCONUT PALM KOKO NIOG
COCOON POD CLEW CLUE KELL
SCAB SHED SHELL BOTTOM
DOUPION FOLLICLE
COCO PLUM ICACO HICACO
COCOWOOD KOKRA
COCUSWOOD KOKRA
COD BAG BIB COR KID POD AXLE
BANK CUSK FOOL GADE HOAX
HUSK POOR ROCK BELLY DORSE
DROUD GADID POUCH SCROD
SHALE SHAUP TORSK BURBOT
CODGER CULTUS ESCROD
FELLOW MULVEL PILLOW POCKET
TOMCOD WACHNA BACALAO
CODFISH CODLING CUSHION
KEELING KILLING MILWELL
MORRHUA SCROTUM CABELIAU
DOLEFISH KABBELOW KLIPFISH
ROCKLING
(**BUFFALO** —) LING
(**CURED** —) DUNFISH
(**DRIED** —) STOCK
(**PILE OF DRIED** —) YAFFLE
(**SALTED** —) COR KLIPFISH
HABERDINE
(**YOUNG** —) SPRAG
CODA CAUDA RONDO EPILOG
FINALE CODETTA EPILOGUE
POSTLUDE
CODDLE PET BABY CADE COOK
MUCH HUMOR NURSE SMALM
SPOIL CARESS COCKER COSSET
COTTON FONDLE PAMPER PTISAN
QUADLE PARBOIL
CODE BCD LAW FLAG CANON
CODEX DOGMA FUERO CIPHER
DIGEST SECRET SIGNAL MULTEKA
PRECEPT DOOMBOOK
MICROCODE
(— **OF CHIVALRY**) BUSHIDO
(— **OF LAWS**) ADA ADAT PANDECT
SHERIAT DOOMBOOK
(— **OF RULES**) VINAYA
(— **OF WHAT IS FITTING**) DECORUM
PROTOCOL
(**COMPUTER** —) ASCII
(**PUNCHCARD** —) HOLLERITH
CODETTA CONDUIT
CODEX ALEF CODE ALEPH ANNAL
CODFISH POOR SPRAG TORSK
KEELING
CODGER COD CUFF CHURL CRANK
MISER FELLOW NIGGARD

CODICIL ANNEX LABEL SCRIPT
CODIFY INDEX DIGEST CLASSIFY
CODLING HAKE
CODOL RETINOL
COEFFICIENT CUMULANT
  AUSTAUSCH
COELENTERATE POLYP MEDUSA
  ACALEPH RADIATE ACALEPHE
COENOBIUM COLONY
COENOCYTE SYMPLASM
  SYMPLAST SYNCYTIUM
COENZYME NAD NADP COFACTOR
COERCE COW CURB MAKE BULLY
  CHECK DRIVE FORCE ORDER
  COHERT COMPEL HIJACK
  CONGUSS ENFORCE REPRESS
  SANDBAG BLUDGEON BULLDOZE
  DISTRAIN RESTRAIN RESTRICT
  BLACKJACK
COERCION HEAT FORCE DURESS
  COMMAND
COEUR D'ALENE SKITSWISH
COEUS (BROTHER OF —)
  ENCELADUS
  (DAUGHTER OF —) LETO LATONA
  ASTERIA
  (FATHER OF —) URANUS
  (MOTHER OF —) GAEA
  (SISTER OF —) FAMA RUMOR
  (WIFE OF —) PHOEBE
COFFEE JO JOE RIO CAFE COHO
  COHU JAVA MILD MOCHA
  BOGOTA BRAZIL CAUFLE CHAOUA
  JAMOKE SANTOS TRIAGE
  ARABICA BOURBON MELANGE
  SUMATRA ESPRESSO MAZAGRAN
  MEDELLIN TRILLADO
COFFEE BEAN QUAKER
COFFEEBERRY JOJOBA CASCARA
  SOYBEAN PEABERRY
COFFEE CAKE KUCHEN
COFFEEHOUSE INN CAFE
  CAFENEH CAFENER CAFENET
COFFEEMAKER SILEX
COFFEEPOT PERCOLATOR
COFFEE TREE BONDUC CHICOT
  VIRGILIA
COFFER ARK BOX DAM PYX CHEST
  HUTCH TRUNK CASKET FORCER
  FORCET SPRUCE TRENCH
  CAISSON CASHBOX CASSOON
  COFFRET LACUNAR LAQUEAR
  CIBORIUM STANDARD
COFFIN BIER CASE CIST KIST MOLD
  PALL SHELL BASKET CASING
  CASKET COFFER HEARSE TROUGH
  THROUGH
  (LEADEN —) COPE
COG CAM LIE NOG CAUK COCK
  GEAR JEST CATCH CHEAT CHOCK
  CHUCK COGUE COZEN TENON
  TOOTH TRICK WEDGE WHEEL
  CAJOLE COGGING DECEIVE
  PRODUCE QUIBBLE WHEEDLE
COGENT GOOD PITHY VALID
  POTENT STRONG TELLING
  FORCIBLE POWERFUL PREGNANT
COGITATE MULL MUSE PLAN
  THINK PONDER CONNATE
  MEDIATE REFLECT CONSIDER
COGNATE KIN AKIN ALIKE ALLIED
  COGENER KINDRED RELATED

  SIMILAR BANDHAVA RELATIVE
  APOPHONIC
COGNITION GNOSIS NOESIS
  KENNING KNOWLEDGE
  PERCEPTION
  (SUFF.) GNOSIA GNOSIS GNOSTIC
  GNOSY
COGNITIVE KNOWING EPISTEMIC
COGNIZANCE KEN WIT HEED
  MARK BADGE CREST EMBLEM
  NOTICE BEARING COCKADE
  KNOWING PRIVITY WITTING
COGNIZANT WARE WISE AWAKE
  AWARE GUILTY KNOWING
  WITTING ACKNOWNE SENSIBLE
  (BE —) DEEM
COGNOMEN NAME BYNAME
  AGNOMEN SURNAME NICKNAME
  PATRONYM
COGON ILLUK KUNAI LALANG
COGWOOD CERILLO
COHABIT BED LIVE DWELL
  ADHERE OCCUPY COMPANY
  ACCUSTOM
CO-HEIR PARCENER
COHERE FIT BOND GLUE SUIT
  AGREE CLING SEIZE STICK UNITE
  ADHERE CEMENT CLEAVE
  CONNECT COINCIDE
COHERENCE UNION CONSENT
  CONTEXT COHESION STRENGTH
COHERENT SERRIED
COHESION BOND ADHESION
  HARDNESS STRENGTH
COHESIVE FATTY TENACIOUS
COHESIVENESS TENACITY
COHOBA PARICA
COHOSH SQUAWROOT
  PAPOOSEROOT
COHUNE COROJO COROZO
COIF CAP HOW HOOD HOUVE
  BEGGIN BIGGIN BURLET HAIRDO
  QUAIFE ARRANGE CALOTTE
  BIGGONET COIFFURE SKULLCAP
COIFFURE COIF HEAD HAIRDO
  TUTULUS TRESSURE
COIL ADO WIN WIP ANSA CLEW
  CURL FAKE FANK FURL FUSS
  HANK LINK LOOP ROLL TUFT
  WIND ENROL FLAKE HELIX QUERL
  QUILE ROUND SPIRE TENSE
  TESLA TWINE TWIRL TWIST
  WHORL WRING BOBBIN BOTTOM
  BOUGHT DIMMER ENROLL
  GLOMUS HEATER RENDER
  RUNDLE SPIRAL TEASER TOROID
  TUMULT UPWIND VOLUME
  WINDUP WREATH ENTRAIL
  HAYCOCK INVOLVE PRIMARY
  RINGLET ROULEAU SNAKING
  TICKLER TROUBLE WREATHE
  COFUSION CONVOLVE ENCIRCLE
  INDUCTOR OVERCOIL
  (— IN STILL) SCROLL
  (— INTO BALL) WIRE
  (— OF CAPILLARIES) TUFT
  (— OF HAIR) BUN PUG
  (— OF SNAKE) FOLD
  (— OF WIRE) BOBBIN SOLENOID
  (INDUCTION —) JIGGER
  (PREF.) SPIR(I)(O) SPIRILLO
COILED GYRATE TORTILE WRITHEN

COILER FLARER
COILING SPIRY
COIN AS BU PU AVO BAN BIT BOO
  COB DAM DIE DUB ECU FIL JOE
  KIP LAT LEK LEU LEV LEY ORI PUL
  SEN SOL TRA WEN WON ZUZ
  ABAS ANNA ATTE BAHT BATZ
  BESA CASH CENT CHIP CHON
  DEMY DIME DOIT DONG DOTT
  DUMP DURO FELS FILS GILL GROS
  GROT HARP HOON HWAN JACK
  JANE KRAN KYAT LEVY LION MAIL
  MAKE MERK MILL MINT MITE
  MULE OBAN ONZA OORD PARA
  PAUL PESA PESO PICE POND
  POUL QUAN RAND RIAL ROCK
  RYAL SCAD SENT SINK SIZE SLUG
  TAEL TARA TARE TARI TARO TIAO
  TREY TYPE UNIT ACKEY AGNEL
  AGORA AKCHA ALBUS ALTIN
  ALTUN AMANI ANGEL ANGLE
  ASPER BAIOC BAIZA BATTE BEKAR
  BELGA BETSO BEZZO BISTI BLANC
  BLANK BODLE BROAD BROWN
  CHINK CLINK COIGN CONTO
  COROA CROSS CROWN CUNYE
  DARIC DINAR DISME DOBLA
  DUCAT EAGLE EYRIR FANAM
  FANON FODDA FRANC GAZET
  GRANO GROAT GROSZ HALER
  HECTE JACOB JULIO JUSTO
  KOBAN KRONA KRONE KROON
  LIARD LIBRA LITRA LIVRE LOUIS
  MEDAL MEDIN MEDIO MILAN
  MOHUR MOPUS NOBLE NOMOS
  OBANG ORKEY ORKYN PAISA
  PAOLO PARDO PENNY PERAU
  PESSA PIECE PLACK PLATE POALI
  POALO PROOF PRUTA QUART
  QUINE RAPPE REBIA RIDER RIYAL
  ROYAL RUBLE RUPIA SAIGA
  SAPEK SCEAT SCUDO SCUTE
  SEMIS SHAHI SICCA SMASH
  SOLDO STAMP STYCA SUCRE
  TALER TANGA TANKA TEMPO
  THRIP TICAL TRIME UNCIA UNITE
  WHITE ABASSI ABBASI AFGHAN
  AHMADI ARGENT ASSARY
  AUREUS AZTECA BALBOA BAUBEE
  BAWBEE BEAVER BEZANT BIANCO
  BLANCO BOGACH BRONZE CARLIN
  CENTAS CHAISE COBANG
  CONDOR COPPER CORONA
  CUARTO CUNZIE DECIME DENARY
  DENIER DERHAM DINDER DIOBOL
  DIRHAM DIXAIN DIZAIN DOBLON
  DODKIN DOLLAR DOPPIA DOUBLE
  ESCUDO FILLER FLORIN FOLLIS
  FORINT GEORGE GIULIO GOURDE
  GRIVNA GROSSO GUINEA GULDEN
  HARPER HELLER ICHIBU ITZEBU
  JUSLIK KLIPPE KOPECK KORONA
  KORUNA LAUREL LEPTON
  MACUTA MAHBUB MAIDEN
  MANCUS MEDINO MISKAL NICKEL
  NORKYN OCHAVO OCTAVE
  ONGARO PADUAN PAGODA
  PARDAO PATACA PATART PHILIP
  PRUTAH QUEZAL ROSARY
  SALUNG SALUTE SATANG SEQUIN
  SESKIN SHEKEL SHIELD SIGLOS
  SINKER SIXAIN SOMALO SOVRAN

  STATER STELLA STIVER TALENT
  TARGET TESTAO TESTER TESTON
  THALER THOMAN TOSTON TRIENS
  TUMAIN TUNGAH TURNER
  TURNEY TURTLE UNGARO
  VINTEM XERIFF YUZLIK ZECHIN
  ZEHNER ZEQUIN ALFONSO
  ALTILIK ANGELET ANGELOT
  ANGOLAR ANGSTER BAIOCCO
  BAJOCCO BARBONE BOLIVAR
  CARDECU CARLINE CARLINO
  CAROLIN CAROLUS CENTAVO
  CHALCUS CHALKOS CORDOBA
  COUNTER CRUSADO DAMPANG
  DRACHMA DUCATON DUPLONE
  ESCALAN FANTASY JACOBUS
  JOANNES KASBEKE KREUZER
  LEMPIRA LEONINE LEOPARD
  LUIGINO MANGOUR MARENGO
  MOIDORE MONARCH MUZOONA
  NOUMMOS ONCETTA PAHLAVI
  PARISIS PATACAO PATAGON
  PATAQUE PENNING PFENNIG
  PISTOLE QUADRIN QUARTER
  QUATTIE QUETZAL QUINYIE
  REDDOCK RUDDOCK RUSPONE
  SANTIMS SCRUPLE SEXTANS
  SILIQUA SIZEINE SOLIDUS SPECIES
  STAMPEE STOOTER STUIVER
  SULTANE TALLERO TEECALL
  THRYMSA TORNESE TRIOBOL
  UNICORN XERAFIN ALBERTIN
  AMBROSIN AQUILINO AUGUSTAL
  AUKSINAS BAETZNER BAGATINE
  BECHTLER BLAFFERT BLANKEEL
  BLANKILO BROCKAGE CAVALIER
  CHINKERS CHUCKRAM COLONIAL
  COURONNE CROCKARD CRUZEIRO
  DECUSSIS DENARIUS DIDRACHM
  DIOBOLON DOUBLOON EQUIPAGA
  FARTHING FILIPPIC FREDERIK
  GAZZETTA GENOVINO GIGLIATO
  GIUSTINA GROSCHEN HARDHEAD
  HYPERPER IMPERIAL ISABELLA
  JOHANNES KREUTZER LUSHBURG
  MACARONI MAJIDIEH MARAVEDI
  MARCELLO METALLIK MILESIMA
  PATACOON PAVILION PICAYUNE
  PIEDFORT PISTOLET PLAPPERT
  PORTAGUE QUADRANS
  QUADRINE QUARTINE QUINCUNX
  RESTRIKE RIGMAREE RISDALER
  RIXDALER SCUDDICK SEMUNCIA
  SESTERCE SHILLING SIXPENCE
  SKILLING SLEEPING SOLIDARE
  STERLING STOTINKA SULTANIN
  TENPENNY TETROBOL THIRTEEN
  TWOPENCE ZECCHINO
  BRACTEATE
  (— AROUND NECK) TALI
  (— HAVING MINTING ERROR) FIDO
  (— IMPERFECTLY MINTED)
  BROCKAGE
  (— OF TRIFLING VALUE) RAP
  (BASE —) SHAND SHEEN SINKER
  (COUNTERFEIT —) RAP GRAY GREY
  SLIP SHEEN SHOFUL STUMER
  STUMOR
  (PLUGGED —) PLUG
  (SMALL THICK —) DUMP
  (PL.) AGOROT CHANGE CHINKS
  SERIES COINAGE

(PREF.) NUMISMATO NUMMI
COINAGE FICTION GALUMPH
MINTAGE
COINCIDE FIT GEE JIBE JUMP
AGREE TALLY CONCUR
COINCIDENT EVEN TOGETHER
COINCIDING CONGRUENT
CONSILIENT
COINER MONIER MONEYER
SMASHER
COITION SOIL VENERY MEETING
CONGRESS
COKE ASK COAL COLK CORE DOPE
CHARK COCAINE
(BROKEN —) BREEZE
COL GAP NEK HALS JOCH PASS
HALSE SWIRE SADDLE
COLANDER SIEVE STRAINER
COLAXAIS (BROTHER OF —)
ARPOXAIS LIPOXAIS
(FATHER OF —) TARGITAUS
COLCOTHAR SAFFRON TUSCANY
COLD FLU ICY MUR NIP COOL
DEAD DULL HARD HASK HOAR
MURR ROUP SOUR ACALE ACOLD
AGUED ALGID BLEAK CHILL CRISP
FISHY FRORE GELID GLACE GLARE
OORIE OURIE PARKY POOSE
RHEUM SHARP SNELL STONY
VIRUS ARCTIC BITTER BOREAL
CHILLY CLAMMY CRIMMY FREDDO
FRIGID FRIGOR FROSTY GLASSY
MARBLY STECKY WAIRCH WINTRY
BRITTLE CATARRH CHILLED
COLDISH COSTIVE DISTANT
FROSTED GLACIAL INHUMAN
MORFOND SHIVERY STRANGE
FREEZING MORFOUND PIERCING
RESERVED RHIGOSIS STANDOFF
UNHEATED REPULSIVE
(— IN HEAD) POSE POOSE CORYZA
CATARRH GRAVEDO SNIVELS
SNIFFLES SNIFTERS
(BITTER —) ARCTIC
(VERY —) FRIGID PEEVISH
(PREF.) CRY(O) FRIGO FRIGORI
KRY(O) PSYCHRO
COLD-BLOODED BRUTAL LEEPIT
COLD CUTS ASSIETTE
COLD-HEARTED COLD FROZEN
BLOODLESS
COLDLY DRILY DRYLY
COLDNESS COLD FROST STEEL
PHLEGM ALGIDITY ASPERITY
DISTANCE FROIDEUR
COLDONG FRIARBIRD
COLE CALE KAIL KALE COLZA
FRIGOR COLEWORT
COLESEED NAVEW
COLEUS KOORKA
COLEWORT COLE KALE RIBE
STOCK CABBAGE
(SPROUT OF —) STOVEN
COLIC BATS FRET BATTS GUTTIE
BELLYACHE
COLICROOT UNICORN ALOEROOT
HUSKROOT HUSKWORT
STARWORT
COLIMA TAPA IRONWOOD
COLISEUM HALL STADIUM
THEATER COLOSSEUM
COLL HUG CLIP CULL POLL PRUNE
EMBRACE

COLLABORATE AID ASSIST
COOPERATE
COLLAGEN OSSEIN
COLLAPSE CAVE FALL FLOP FOLD
GIVE SINK CRASH SLUMP WRECK
BUCKLE SHRINK TUMBLE CAPSIZE
CROPPER CRUMBLE CRUMPLE
DEBACLE DEFLATE FAILURE
FLUMMOX FOUNDER SMASHUP
CONTRACT DOWNFALL TAILSPIN
PROSTRATION
COLLAPSED QUAT CLUNG
COLLAPSIBLE FOLDING
COLLAPSING FAILURE COLLABENT
COLLAR CAP FUR NAB BAND BOSS
ETON FALL FANO GILL GRAB
POKE RING RUFF CHAIN DICKY
FANON FANUM FICHU PHANO
RUCHE SEIZE STOCK TRASH
WHISK BERTHA CARCAN CHOKER
COLLET COLLUM DICKEY GORGET
PARRAL PARREL RABATO REBATO
SADDLE SLEEVE TACKLE TORQUE
TUCKER TURNUP BOBACHE
BOBECHE CAPTURE CHIGNON
CIRCLET PANUELO PARTLET
POTHOOK REBATER SHACKLE
STICKUP VANDYKE CARCANET
CINCTURE NECKBAND NECKLACE
RABATINE STARCHER TURNDOWN
(— FOR HORSE) BARGHAM
BRECHAM
(HIGH —) GILLS JAMPOT
(HORSE —) BRECHAM
(IRON —) JOUG JOUGS CARCAN
POTHOOKS
(LACE —) SCALLOP
(MAGISTRATE'S —) GOLILLA
(ROMAN —) RABAT
(WHEEL-SHAPED —) RUFF
(WOODEN —) CANG CANGUE
COLLAR BEAM SPANNER
SPANPIECE
COLLARBONE CLAVICLE
COLL'ARCO ARCATO
COLLARED ACCOLLE ACCOLLEE
TORQUATE
COLLAR PAD AFTERWALE
COLLATE BESTOW CONFER VERIFY
COMPARE
COLLATERAL SIDE MARGIN
OBLIQUE INDIRECT PARALLEL
SECURITY
COLLATION TEA MEAL BEVER
LUNCH REPAST SERMON
ADDRESS READING DEJEUNER
HOTCHPOT TREATISE
COLLEAGUE AIDE ALLY UNITE
DEPUTY SOCIUS ADJUNCT
COLLEGE COMPEER CONSORT
PARTNER CONFRERE CONSPIRE
COLLECT JUG SAM TAX CALL
CARD CULL DRAW HEAP LEVY
LIFT PICK PILE POOL REAR SAMM
SAVE AMASS CROWD GLEAN
GROUP HOARD RAISE STORE
SWEEP ACCOIL ACCRUE CENTER
CONFER GARNER GATHER
MUSTER PRAYER SEMBLE SHEAVE
UPTAKE ARCHIVE CLUSTER
COMPILE CONGEST ENGROSS
IMPOUND RAMMASS RECUEIL
SCAMBLE SYNAPTE ASSEMBLE

CONFLATE CONTRACT CUPBOARD
INGATHER RESEMBLE SCRAMBLE
SCROUNGE
(— AND DRIVE INTO ENCLOSURE)
WEAR
(— FOOD) FORAGE
(— GRAIN) GAVEL
(— INTO COVEY) JUG
(— MONEY) NOB
(— WAGES) UPLIFT
COLLECTED CALM COOL SOBER
SERENE PRESENT COMPOSED
(PREF.) ATHRO
COLLECTION ANA BAG KIT SET
BAND BEVY BOOK CLAN CROP
FILE HEAD HEAP KNOT LEVY OLIO
RAFT SORT ALBUM ANNEX BATCH
BUDGE BUNCH DEPOT FLOCK
GLEAN GROUP HOARD KITTY
SHEAF STORE SUITE SWATH
AFFLUX BUDGET BUNDLE
CONGER CORPUS FARDEL
MISHNA PARCEL RAGBAG RECULE
SORITE SPRING SWATHE TUMBLE
ACCOUNT BOILING BULLARY
CLUSTER COLLECT CONGERY
EXHIBIT FERNERY FISTFUL
FLUTTER GALLERY QUOTITY
RECUEIL SAMHITA SMATTER
SMYTRIE SYLLOGE TERRIER
ASSEMBLY CABOODLE CONGERIE
CUSTOMAL FASCICLE GATHERUM
GLOSSARY JINGBANG ROMESCOT
ROMESHOT SYNTAGMA
(— AT FOX HUNT) CAP
(— OF ANIMALS) ZOO HEAD
(— OF BOOKCASES) STACK
(— OF BOOKS) SET BIBLE CANON
LIBRARY
(— OF CONIFERS) PINETUM
(— OF DATA) GROUND
(— OF FORMULAS) CODEX
(— OF FOUR) TETRAD
(— OF HUTS) BUSTEE
(— OF LAWS) CODE
(— OF MAPS) ATLAS
(— OF OBJECTS) AFFAIR
(— OF OPINIONS) SYMPOSIUM
(— OF PERSONS) BOODLE
(— OF PLANTS) SERTULE
(— OF POEMS) DIVAN DIWAN
SYLVA ANTHOLOGY
(— OF PUS) ABSCESS HYPOPYON
(— OF REVENUES) TAHSIL TEHSIL
(— OF ROCKS) SUITE
(— OF RULES) SUTRA SUTTA
(— OF SAMPLES) SWATCH
(— OF SAYINGS) ANA
(— OF SPECIMENS) CABINET
(— OF STAFFS) SYSTEM
(— OF STORIES) LEGEND
(— OF TIPS) TRONC
(— OF TOOLS) LAYOUT
(— OF TREES) SERINGAL
(— OF UNWANTED ANIMALS)
LARDER
(— OF WRITINGS) CORPUS
(— OF 24 SHEETS) QUIRE
(CONFUSED —) CLUTTER
(MISCELLANEOUS —) OLIO FARDEL
SMYTRIE
(VAST —) CLOUD
(SUFF.) ERY

COLLECTIVE GROUP AGGREGATE
COLLECTIVIST COMMUNIST
SOCIALIST
COLLECTOR COMB CAMEIST
CURIOSO DUSTMAN FURIOSO
UPTAKER ANTIQUER COUNTOUR
GATHERER OOLOGIST STAMPMAN
VIRTUOSO ZAMINDAR
(— ITEMS) RARIORA
(— OF BUTTERFLIES) AURELIAN
(— OF HERBS) SIMPLER
(— OF REVENUE) AUMIL AUMILDAR
TALUKDAR ZAMINDAR
(CUSTOMS —) HOPPO CUSTOMER
(TAX —) CAID QAID GABBAI
PUBLICAN TAHSILDAR
COLLECTORATE TALUK
COLLEEN GIRL LASS MISS BELLE
CAILIN DAMSEL
COLLEGE TOL HALL AGGIE HOUSE
LYCEE CAMPUS COLAGE SCHOOL
SIWASH ACADEMY MADRASA
SEMINARY
COLLEGER TUG
COLLET BAND NECK RING CHUCK
CULET CASING CIRCLE COLLAR
COLLUM FLANGE BUSHING
COLLIDE HIT RAM BUMP DASH
FRAY HURT BARGE CLASH CRASH
KNOCK SHOCK SMITE WRECK
CANNON HURTLE STRIKE THRUST
(— WITH) PRANG
(— WITH) IMPINGE
COLLIE KELPIE BEARDIE
COLLIER MINER PLOVER GEORDIE
COILYEAR FLATIRON SCUTCHER
COLLIQUATION SYNTEXIS
COLLISION HIT FOUL CLASH
CRASH PRANG SHOCK HURTLE
IMPACT JOSTLE PILEUP SMASHUP
CLASHING CONFLICT
COLLOCATE SET PLACE ARRANGE
COLLOID GEL
COLLOQUIAL FAMILIAR INFORMAL
COLLOQUIUM INDUCEMENT
COLLOQUY CHAT TALK PARLEY
DIALOGUE
COLLOTYPE ARTOTYPE HELIOTYPE
COLLUDE PLOT SCHEME CONNIVE
COLLOGUE CONSPIRE
COLLUM NECK
COLLUSION DECEIT CAHOOTS
SECRECY PRACTICE PRACTISE
COLLUSIVE COVINOUS COLLUSORY

COLOMBIA

CAPE: VELA AGUJA MARZO
AUGUSTA
CAPITAL: BOGOTA
CAY: VELA VIGIA RONCADOR
COIN: PESO REAL CONDOR
PESETA CENTAVO
FORMER NAME: DARIEN
NEWGRANADA
GULF: URABA CUPICA DARIEN
TIBUGA TORTUGAS
INDIAN: BORO CUNA HOKA MACU
MUZO PAEZ CARIB CATIO
CHOCO COFAN COGUI CUBEO
GUANE PIJAO SEONA ARAWAK
BETOYA CALIMA INGANO
SALIVA TAHAMI TUCANO
TUNEBO YAHUNA ACHAGUA

ANDAQUI CHIBCHA CHIMILA
GUAHIBO GUAJIRO PANCHES
PUINAVE PUITOTO QUECHUA
TAIRONA GUARAUNO
MOTILONE
INLET: TUMACO
ISLAND: BARU NAIPO FUERTE
GORGONA CUSACHON
MEASURE: VARA AZUMBRE
CELEMIN
MOUNTAIN: CHITA HUILA PURACE
TOLIMA
MOUNTAINS: ABIBE ANDES BAUDO
COCUY AYAPEL PERIJA TUNAHI
CHAMUSA ORIENGAL
PLAINS: LLANOS
POINT: CRUCES LACRUZ SOLANO
CARIBANA GALLINAS
PORT: LORICA CARTAGENA
PROVINCE: META CAUCA CHOCO
HUILA VALLE ARAUCA BOYACA
CALDAS NARINO TOLIMA
VAUPES BOLIVAR CAQUETA
GUAJIRE VICHADA AMAZONAS
PUTUMAYO
RIVER: UVA BITA META MUCO
SINU TOMO UPIA YARI BAUDO
CAUCA CESAR ISANA MESAI
NECHI PATIA PAUTO SUCIO
AMAZON ARAUCA ARIARI
ATRATO CAGUAN VAUPES
YAPURA CAQUETA GUAINIA
INIRIDA TRUANDO VICHADA
APAPORIS CASANARE
GUAVIARE PUTUMAYO
MAGDALENA
TOWN: TEN ANZA BUGA CALI
MITU MUZO PAEZ SIPI TADO
TOLU YARI BELLO CHINU GUAPI
NEIVA PASTO TUNJA BOGOTA
CUCUTA IBAGUE QUIBDO
SANGIL CARTAGO LETICIA
PALMIRA PEREIRA POPAYAN
GIRARDOT MEDELLIN
MONTERIA CARTAGENA
TREE: ARBOLOCO
VOLCANO: PURACE
WEIGHT: BAG SACO CARGA LIBRA
QUILATE QUINTAL

COLON CROWN POINT HEMISTICH
MESYMNION
COLONIAL OVERSEA OVERSEAS
COLONIST BOOR COLON FATHER
CUTHEAN PIONEER PLANTER
SETTLER EMIGRANT
(— IN SICILY) SIKELIOT
(AUSTRALIAN —) STERLING
(PL.) DEHAITES DEHAVITES
COLONIZE ECIZE FOUND PLANT
GATHER SETTLE MIGRATE
COLONIZER OECIST OEKIST
COLONNADE ROW STOA PORCH
PARVIS PIAZZA XYSTUS EUSTYLE
GALLERY PARVISE PERGOLA
PORTICO TERRACE CHOULTRY
DIASTYLE PERISTYLE
COLONNETTE COLUMELLA
COLONY STATE STOCK SWARM
CENOBE CORMUS APOIKIA
COLONIA CENOBIUM GANNETRY
PLANTATION POLYZOARIUM
(— OF BEES) HIVE SKEP SWARM

(BRYOZOAN —) ESCHARA
COLOR (ALSO SEE SPECIFIC COLOR)
DIP DYE HUE BLEE CAST FAKE
FLAG PUKE SUIT TINT TONE
BADGE BLUSH GLAZE GLOSS
GRAIN PAINT SHADE STAIN TAINT
TASTE TENNE TINCT TINGE
TOUCH BANNER BLEACH BOTTOM
BRIDGE CHROMA ENSIGN INFECT
LOCKET MANTLE RADDLE
REDDEN STREAK TEMPER
COULEUR DEPAINT DISTORT
ENGRAIN PENNANT PIGMENT
SPECKLE COLORING STANDARD
TERTIARY TINCTURE
(— IMPARTED TO HERRINGS)
GILDING
(— LOSS) POLIOSIS
(— OF BIRD) SMUT
(— OF BODY) HEAT
(— OF EYES OF FOWLS) DAW
(— OF HUMAN FLESH) CARNATION
(— OF REFLECTED LIGHT)
OVERTONE
(— OF ROCK) STONE
(BLUE —) FOG JAY SKY WAD AQUA
BICE CIEL CYAN DELF DUSK IRIS
NAVY PAON SAXE WADE WOAD
ZINC AZURE BERYL BLUET CADET
CAPRI CHING COPEN DELFT
DELPH DIANA DRAKE EMAIL
GRAPE METAL NIKKO ORION
PEARL ROYAL SLATE SMALT
SMOKE VANDA CANTON CENDRE
COELIN ENSIGN GROTTO HATHOR
INDIGO LUPINE MARINE MASCOT
MIGNON ORIENT PENSEE
ROMANY SEVRES VENICE ZENITH
CELESTE CERAMIC CHICORY
DUSTBLU GOBELIN HORIZON
LIBERTY LOBELIA LOGWOOD
MATELOT PEACOCK PETUNIA
RAMESES SISTINE SIXTINE
ABSINTHE BLUEBIRD BLUEWOOD
BRITTANY CAESIOUS CATTLEYA
CERULEAN CERULEUM DUCKLING
ELECTRIC GENDARME HYACINTH
INFANTRY LABRADOR LARKSPUR
MASCOTTE MAZARINE MIDNIGHT
MOONBEAM NATIONAL SAPPHIRE
TWILIGHT WEDGWOOD
(BROWN —) BAY ELK FOX OAK
TAN ARAB BARK BOLE BRAN
BURE CAIN CLAY CORK CUBA
DATE DEER DRAB DUST ECRU
FAON FAWN GOAT GOLD HOPI
IRON LAMA LION MAST MESA
MUSK SEAL SIAM TEAK ACORN
ADUST ALOMA AZTEC BEIGE
BISON BLOND BLUSH BOLUS
BRIAR BRICK BRIER BROWN
BUNNY CACAO CAMEL CANNA
CLOVE COCOA CONGO EAGLE
FRIAR FUDGE GIPSY GRAIN GYPSY
HAZEL HENNA KAFFA KHAKI
LIVER MAHAL MALAY MECCA
MINIM MUMMY NEGRO OTTER
PABLO QUAIL SABEL SEDGE SEPIA
SIENA SIRUP SNUFF SUDAN
SUEDE SUMAC SYRUP TABAC
TAFFY TENNE TOAST TOPAZ
AFGHAN ALESAN ALMOND
APACHE ARGALI AUBURN

BAMBOO BEAVER BISQUE BISTER
BISTRE BLONDE BRONCO BRONZE
BURNET COCHIN COFFEE
CONDOR COOKIE COWBOY
CROTAL DORADO ESKIMO
FALLOW GINGER GRAVEL GROUSE
HAVANA ISABEL LOUTRE
MAROON MERIDA MOHAWK
MUFFIN NUTMEG ORIOLE
PAWNEE PLOVER PUEBLO RABBIT
RACKET RUDDLE RUSSET SAHARA
SANTOS SHERRY SORREL SPHINX
SPONGE STRING STUCCO
SUMACH SUNTAN THRUSH TIFFIN
TURTLE ASPHALT BADIOUS
BEESWAX BITUMEN BRACKEN
BRONCHO CALDRON CATTAIL
CIGARET COCONUT COTRINE
CRACKER DOGWOOD DURANGO
FEUILLE FILBERT GAZELLE
GOREVAN HARVEST LEATHER
LIBERIA MALABAR MIRADOR
MORDORE MOROCCO MUSCADE
MUSTANG NORFOLK OAKWOOD
PERIQUE PRALINE RACQUET
ROSARIO SABELLA SUNBURN
SUNDOWN TALLYHO TANBARK
TOBACCO TUSCANY ALDERNEY
ALGERIAN AMBROSIA BISMARCK
BOBOLINK CALABASH CARTOUCH
CAULDRON CINNAMON
CLAYBANK CORDOVAN
DOUBLOON ETRUSCAN
EUCHROME HAZELNUT ISABELLA
KOLINSKY LEAFMOLD MANDALAY
MOCCASIN MOLESKIN MOROCCAN
MUSHROOM NOISETTE PHEASANT
SAUTERNE SHAGBARK STARLING
TAMARACK TEAKWOOD
TERRAPIN TORTOISE WOODBARK
(DEAD-LEAF —) FILEMOT
(DEEP —) DARK
(FAST —) GRAIN
(GREEN —) BOA FIR IVY ALOE BICE
FERN JADE LEEK MOSS NILE SAGE
ALOES CEDRE CHLOR DRAKE
FAIRY HOLLY KELLY LOVAT OLIVE
SPRAY CANNON EMPIRE HUNTER
JASPER LAUREL LIERRE LIZARD
MEADOW MOUSSE MYRTLE
SPRUCE VERDET CELADON
CITRINE CORBEAU CRESSON
CYPRESS EMERALD INGENUE
JADEITE JUNIPER MESANGE
NEPTUNE OLIVINE PERIDOT
SEAFOAM SERPENT TILLEUL
VERDURE BAYBERRY CHASSEUR
COPPERAS EMERAUDE GLAUCOUS
GLOWWORM PARAKEET
PERRUCHE PISTACHE POPINJAY
SHAMROCK TARRAGON VIRIDIAN
WOODLAND
(GRIZZLED —) AGOUTI AGOUTY
(LACK OF —) PALLOR
(OF A DARKISH —) SUBFUSE
(OTHER —S) OR ASH BAT DOE DUN
JET TEA CHIP CORN CROW DAWN
DOVE GRAY GREY GULL HEMP
LAVA LEAD MODE MOLE NICE
NUDE PLUM PORT PUKE ROAN
RUST SAND SOOT WOOD AMBER
BEACH BLACK CAMEO CERES
CHILE CHILI COPRA CRANE CRASH

CREAM DWALE EBONY FLESH
GRAPE GREBE GREGE MAUVE
MOUSE PANSY PHLOX PLOMB
PRAWN PRUNE PUTTY RIFLE
SABLE SPICE STEEL THYME TWINE
ANATTO AURORA AUTUMN
CASTOR CINDER COLLIE CORCIR
DAHLIA DAMSON DENVER
EVEQUE FIESTA FUSTIC GAMBIA
GRIEGE KASPER MALLOW
MODENA NAVAHO NAVAJO
NIMBUS NUTRIA ONDINE ORCHID
OXFORD OYSTER PEANUT PEBBLE
PIGEON QUAKER RAISIN RESEDA
ROUCOU SEASAN SILVER TUSCAN
VANITY VESTAL VIOLET WALNUT
ADMIRAL ANNATTO ARBUTUS
ARDOISE ARNATTA BEGONIA
BERMUDA BLOSSOM BRINDLE
CARAIBE CARAMEL CORBEAU
COTRINE COWSLIP CRACKER
CRUISER MORELLO MURILLO
NATURAL OPHELIA PELICAN
PONTIFF POPCORN PRELATE
PUMPKIN QUIMPER REGATTA
ROSEBUD SAKKARA SANDUST
SPARROW SUNBEAM THISTLE
TUSSORE VERVAIN VIOLINE
WEIGELA WHEATEN ALUMINUM
AMARANTH AMETHYST BLONDINE
CARMETTA CHARCOAL CLEMATIS
COCOBOLO COQUETTE CREVETTE
CYCLAMEN EGGPLANT EMINENCE
FELDGRAU FLAMINGO GILLIVER
GRAPHITE GUNMETAL
HONEYDEW IMPERIAL JACINTHE
LAVENDER MARATHON MORILLON
MULBERRY PALMETTO
ROSEWOOD SAUTERNE SQUIRREL
SUNBURST WIRELESS WISTARIA
WISTERIA CARNELIAN
(RED —) DAWN FLEA GOLF GOYA
HEBE LAKE MIST PUCE RUBY
TULY WINE AGATE BRASS BRICK
CANNA CANON CEDAR CORAL
CUTCH EMBER FLAME FLASH
GULES LILAC MELON NYMPH
PEACH PEONY POPPY ROSET
SIENA SPARK TOTEM ACAJOU
ARCHIL AURORE AUTUMN
AZALEA BRAZIL CANYON CARROT
CATSUP CERISE CHERRY CHERUB
CLARET COGNAC DAMASK FRAISE
GAIETY GARNET GAYETY GRANET
JOCKEY KERMES MADDER
MALAGA MIKADO MURREY
NECTAR ORCHIL PATISE SALMON
SANDIX SHRIMP SIERRA SULTAN
TITIAN TOMATO AFRICAN
ANAMITE ANEMONE BEGONIA
BISCUIT BOKHARA CARMINE
CASTORY CATAWBA CATCHUP
CATECHU CRIMSON CURRANT
FIREFLY FUCHSIA FUCHSIN
GRANATE GRANITE HEATHER
INDIANA KETCHUP LACQUER
LOBSTER MAGENTA MASCARA
NACARAT OXBLOOD PAPRIKA
POMPEII PONCEAU REDWOOD
ROSETAN ROSETTE RUBELLE
SAFFLOR SARAVAN SCARLET
SINOPLE STAMMEL SULTANA
VERMEIL ALKERMES AMARANTH

ARCHILLA BISMARCK BORDEAUX BURGUNDY CAMELLIA CARDINAL CHAUDRON CHEROKEE CHERUBIM CHESTNUT COCOANUT CONFETTI DAMONICO DIANTHUS DUBONNET EVENGLOW GERANIUM GRENADIN GRIDELIN MAHOGANY MANDARIN MAROCAIN NACARINE TOREADOR
(SOLID —) SOLID
(TONE —) TIMBRE
(YELLOW —) HAY RAT WAX BEAR BUFF CLAY CORN CUIR ECRU FLAX GOLD LIME LIME MOTH WELD WOLD ACIER ALOMA AZTEC BEIGE BLAKE BRASS CRASH CREAM GRAIN HONEY IVORY LEMON MAIZE MAPLE SHELL STRAW TAUPE WOULD ACACIA ALMOND BANANA CANARY CATHAY CHROME CITRON CITRUS CROCUS DORADO FALLOW MANILA MASTIC MIMOSA NANKIN NUGGET OXGALL SULFUR SUNRAY SUNSET ANTIQUE APRICOT BISCUIT CAVALRY CHAMOIS GAMBOGE JASMINE JONQUIL LEGHORN MEXICAN NANKEEN PRAIRIE RHUBARB SAFFRON SULPHUR SUNGLOW ANTELOPE CALABASH CAPUCINE COCKATOO DAFFODIL EGGSHELL GENERALL GOLDMIST MARIGOLD ORPIMENT PRIMROSE SNOWSHOE
(PL.) FLAG
(PREF.) CHROM(AT)(ATO)(I)(IDIO)(O)
(HAVING DARK —) FUSCO
(SUFF.) CHROIA CHROIC CHROID CHROMASIA CHROME CHROMIA CHROMY CHROOUS
COLORABLE SPECIOUS PLAUSIBLE

COLORADO
CAPITAL: DENVER
COLLEGE: REGIS
COUNTY: BACA MESA YUMA OTERO OURAY ROUTT GILPIN CHAFFEE
MOUNTAIN: OSO LONGS PIKES ELBERT
MOUNTAIN RANGE: ROCKY
NATIVE: ROVER
PARK: ESTES
RIVER: YAMPA DOLORES APISHAPA ARIKAREE GUNNISON PURGATOIRE
STATE FLOWER: COLUMBINE
STATE NICKNAME: CENTENNIAL
STATE TREE: SPRUCE
TOWN: ASPEN DELTA LAMAR GOLDEN PUEBLO SALIDA ALAMOSA BOULDER DURANGO GREELEY GUNNISON LOVELAND TRINIDAD

COLORATION BLEE PILE FLASH CLOUDING COLORISM SCHILLER PIGMENTATION
COLORATURA GORGIA SOPRANO
COLOR-BLINDNESS DALTONISM
COLORED FAW HUED MALE BIASED DEPAINT STAINED

(— IN RED) RUBRIC
(— LIKE PIPE BOWL) TROUSERED
(BRILLIANTLY —) SUPERB FLAMING PSYCHEDELIC
(HIGHLY —) CHROMATIC PRISMATIC
(PARTI —) PIED PIEBALD
(UNIFORMLY —) HARD
(PREF.) CHROM(AT)(ATO)(I)(IDIO)(O)
(SUFF.) CHROME CHROOUS
COLORFUL GAY BRAVE JUICY VIVID COLORY GOLDEN FREAKED GORGEOUS
COLORING DYE BLEE TINT PAINT TINGE TINGENT BRONZING PAINTING TINCTURE
(— MATTER) TINCTION
(SUFF.) CHROMY
COLORING MATTER
(SUFF.) PHYLL(A)(OUS)(UM)(Y)
COLORLESS WAN DRAB DULL PALE ASHEN BLAKE BLANK PLAIN MOUSEY PALLID HUELESS NEUTRAL ACHROMIC ACHROOUS BLANCHED ETIOLATE LIFELESS
(PREF.) LEUC(O)
COLOSSAL BIG HUGE VAST GREAT JUMBO LARGE IMMENSE TITANIC ENORMOUS GIGANTIC MONSTROUS
COLOSSUS GIANT TITAN STATUE COLOSSO MONOLITH
COLOSTRUM FOREMILK AFTERINGS
COLT FOAL STAG FILLY POTRO STAIG HOGGET POLEYN STAGGIE EQUULEUS
COLTER LAVER COOTER COULTER FOREIRON
COLTSFOOT DOCK CLOTE HOOFS CLEATS FARFARA LAGWORT SOWFOOT BULLFOOT CLAYWEED FOALFOOT
COLUGO COBEGO
COLUMBATE NIOBATE
COLUMBIA SINKIUSE
COLUMBINE AQUILEGE BLUEBELL CHUCKIES ROCKBELL
COLUMBITE DIANITE NIOBITE
COLUMELLA STALACE
COLUMN COG LAT ROW FILE FUST GOAL LINE POLE POST PROP STUB BAGUE SHAFT STELA STELE TORSO TRUNK WURTZ ASOKAN CORNER GNOMON PILLAR SCAPUS STAPLE STRING TSWETT COLUMEL SUPPORT VIGREUX CYLINDER PILASTER
(— IN EAR) MODIOLUS
(— OF FIGURES) SUM
(— OF FILAMENTS) SYNEMA
(— OF MOLTEN ROCK) PLUME
(BUDDHIST —) LAT
(FIGURE USED AS —) ATLAS TELAMON
(PART OF —) BASE DADO NECK OVOLO SHAFT TORUS ABACUS PLINTH REGLET SCOTIA CAPITAL ECHINUS FLUTING ASTRAGAL CINCTURE COLARENO PEDESTAL
(ROCK —) HOODOO
(ROULETTE —) DERNIER

(SPINAL —) HORN SPINE BACKBONE
(STRUCTURAL —) LALLY
(TWISTED —) TORSO
COLUMNAR TERETE STELENE COLUMNAL VERTICAL
COLUMNIST WRITER ANALYST
COLY MOUSEBIRD
COLZA SARSON
COMA TUFT BUNCH CARUS SLEEP SOPOR STUPOR SUBETH TORPOR TRANCE SEMICOMA CHEVELURE
COMATOSE OUT DROWSY LETHARGIC
COMB CARD GILL KAME LASH RACK RAKE REDD REED SEEK TOZE BREAK BRUSH CAMBE CLEAN CREST CTENE CURRY FLISK RAVEL TEASE HACKLE SMOOTH CUSHION HATCHEL WRAITHE BEATILLE CARUNCLE TORTOISE
(WEAVING —) RADDLE
(PREF.) CTEN(O) LOPH(I)(IO)(O) PECTINATO
COMBAT WAR BLOW BOUT COPE DUEL FRAY MEEK MEET RUSH TILT CLASH FIGHT JOUST REPEL STOUR ACTION AFFRAY BATTLE MEDLEY OPPOSE RESIST SHOWER STRIFE CONTEND CONTEST COUNTER DERAIGN DISPUTE EXPLOIT SCUFFLE SERVICE ARGUMENT CONFLICT STRUGGLE
(— BETWEEN KNIGHTS) JOUST
(FUTILE —) SCIAMACHY
(SHAM —) SCIOMACHY
(SINGLE —) DUOMACHY
COMBATANT DUELER BATTLER FIGHTER CHAMPION GLADIATOR
COMBATIVE BANTAM MILITANT AGONISTIC BELLICOSE DEPENDENT PUGNACIOUS AGONISTICAL
COMBE HOPE
COMBED CRESTED
COMBER WAVE HANDER BREAKER KEMPSTER
COMBINATION KEY BLOC CLUB GANG PACT POOL RING CABAL COMBO GROUP JUNTO PARTY TRUST UNION CARTEL CLIQUE CORNER CRASIS FUSION LEAGUE MEDLEY MERGER AMALGAM BATTERY COMBINE CONSORT COTERIE FACTION HARMONY JOINING MIXTURE ADDITION ALLIANCE ENSEMBLE MONOPOLY GOODLIBET
(— OF CARDS) SET BUILD FLUSH SPREAD STRAIGHT
(— OF CIRCUMSTANCES) ACTION
(— OF COLORS) HARLEQUIN
(— OF FACES) FORM
(— OF FIRMS) TRUST
(— OF INTAGLIO FORMS) GRYLLI
(— OF NUMBERS) GIG SADDLE
(— OF TACKLES) JEERS
(— OF TONES) CHORD
(— OF 10) DECUPLET
(DANCE —) SEQUENCE
(HARMONIOUS —) CONCORD
(NOSE-JAW —) LAYBACK

(SCORING —) IMPERIAL
(PREF.) HAPT(O)
COMBINE ADD FIX MIX WED BIND BLOC CLUB JOIN NICK POOL BLEND GROUP JOINT MARRY MERGE TOTAL UNITE ABSORB CONCUR LEAGUE MEDDLE MERGER MINGLE SPLICE ACCRETE AMALGAM COMPACT CONJOIN CONJURE MACHINE COALESCE COMPOUND CONCRETE CONDENSE CONFLATE CONSTRUE CONTRACT CUMULATE FEDERATE ORCHESTRATE
(— AGAINST) BOYCOTT
(— WITH GAS) AERATE
(— WITH WATER) AQUATE
COMBINED GUM BOUND FIXED JOINT UNITED CONJOINT
COMBUSTIBLE FUEL FIERY ARDENT CINDER PICEOUS BURNABLE
COMBUSTION FIRE HEAT FLAME THERM TUMULT BURNING BACKFIRE
COME BE GET LAY COOP DRAW FALL GROW HAUL PASS WHEN ARISE CHIVE FETCH ISSUE LIGHT OCCUR REACH ACCRUE ADVENE APPEAR ARRIVE BECOME BEFALL EMERGE HAPPEN OBTAIN SPRING ADVANCE DEVELOP EMANATE PROCEED APPROACH PRACTICE
(— ABOUT) ARISE CHANCE
(— AFTER) SUE FOLLOW
(— APART) FRAY SHED BREAK STAVE
(— BACK) REVERSE
(— BEFORE) FORERUN PREVENE ANTECEDE ANTEDATE
(— DOWN) AVALE SWOOP ALIGHT DESCEND SUCCEED DISMOUNT
(— FORTH) EMIT BREAK ISSUE ACCEDE FORTHGO FURNACE
(— FORWARD) ACCEDE
(— IN CONTACT) ATTINGE
(— IN SECOND) PLACE
(— IN THIRD) SHOW
(— INTO BLOOM) BURST BLOSSOM
(— INTO COLLISION) MEET CLASH COLLIDE
(— INTO EXISTENCE) FORM BEGIN ACCRUE HAPPEN SPRING
(— INTO POSSESSION) ACQUIRE INHERIT
(— OF AGE) MAJORIZE
(— OFF) HARL PEEL
(— OUT) ISSUE APPEAR EMERGE EMANATE
(— SUDDENLY) CLAP
(— THROUGH) DELIVER
(— TO) TOUCH ADVENE STRIKE RECOVER REVERSE
(— TO BELIEVE IN) ADOPT
(— TO CONCLUSION) DECIDE
(— TO DIE) DO DIE SET DROP EXPIRE FINISH SURCEASE
(— TO GRIEF) FOUNDER
(— TO HAND) OFFER
(— TO LIGHT) SPUNK DEVELOP
(— TO MIND) OCCUR STRIKE
(— TO NOTHING) ABORT
(— TO PASS) SORT BREAK LIGHT

BEFALL BETIDE HAPPEN
(— TO PERFECTION) RIPEN
(— TO TERMS) AGREE TRYST
ACCORD BARGAIN COMPOSE
COMPOUND ACCOMMODATE
(— TOGETHER) ADD HERD JOIN
MEET AMASS CONCUR COUPLE
GATHER COLLECT COMBINE
CONVENE ASSEMBLE
(— UNDER) SUBVENE
(— UPON) FIND CROSS INVENT
STRIKE OVERTAKE
(FULLY —) EXPIATE
COMEBACK RALLY ANSWER
RETORT RETURN REBOUND
HAULBACK RECOVERY REPARTEE
COMECRUDO CARRIZO
COMEDIAN WAG WIT CARD
ACTOR ANTIC CLOWN COMIC
GAGMAN JESTER BUFFOON
FUNSTER COMOEDUS FUNMAKER
FUNNYMAN PATTERER
COMEDO BLACKHEAD
COMEDOWN BATHOS DESCENT
LETDOWN
COMEDY SOCK DRAMA FARCE
LAZZO REVUE SITCOM COMEDIA
TEMACHA COMOEDIA TRAVESTY
BACCHIDES SLAPSTICK
(HEROIC —) NATAKA
(PREF.) COMICO
**COMEDY OF ERRORS (AUTHOR OF
—)** SHAKESPEARE
(CHARACTER IN —) LUCE PINCH
AEGEON ANGELO DROMIO
ADRIANA AEMILIA EPHESUS
LUCIANA SOLINUS BALTHAZAR
ANTIPHOLUS
COMELINESS GRACE DECORUM
FEATURE VENUSTY PULCHRITUDE
COMELY FAIR GOOD HEND PERT
TALL TIDY WEME BONNY BUXOM
HENDE QUEME SONCY SONSY
TIGHT DECENT FORMAL GOODLY
LIKELY LIKING LOVELY PRETTY
PROPER SEEMLY SONSIE VENUST
FARRANT FORMFUL SIGHTLY
BECOMING DECOROUS FEATURED
GRACEFUL HANDSOME PLEASING
SUITABLE
COMET STAR METEOR XIPHIAS
(— HEAD) COMA
COMEUPPANCE REBUKE DESERTS
BUSINESS
COMFIT CANDY SUCKLE CONFECT
PRALINE CONSERVE PRESERVE
COMFORT AID EASE REST STAY
BIELD CHEER LIGHT SOOTH VISIT
ENDURE RELIEF REPOSE SOLACE
SOOTHE SUCCOR ANIMATE
ASSUAGE CHERISH CONFIRM
CONSOLE ENLIVEN GLADDEN
REFRESH RELIEVE SUPPORT
SUSTAIN INSPIRIT NEPENTHE
PLEASURE REASSURE
COMFORTABLE RUG BEIN BIEN
COSH COSY COZY EASY FEEL FEIL
LIKE SNUG TOSH TRIG CANNY
COMFY COUTH CUSHY LITHE
QUEME QUILT SCARF SONCY
COUTHY HEPPEN PENTIT SONSIE
RELAXED RESTFUL CHEERFUL
DELICATE EUPHORIC HOMELIKE

WRISTLET GEMUTLICH
COMFORTABLY SWEETLY
COMFORTED CONSOLATE
COMFORTER PUFF COVER EIDER
NAHUM QUILT SCARF TIPPET
CHEERER PACIFIER
COMFORTING TOSY TOSIE
FRIENDLY
COMFORTLESS DREARY FORLORN
UNCOUTH DESOLATE EITHLESS
COMFREY DAISY BONESET
BACKWORT KNITBACK
BRUISEWORT
COMIC DROLL FUNNY STRIP
BUFFONE COMIQUE THALIAN
COMEDIAN FARCICAL
COMICAL LOW BASE BUFFO
DROLL FUNNY MERRY QUEER
STRIP WITTY BOUFFE AMUSING
CARTOON JOCULAR RISIBLE
STRANGE TRIVIAL HUMOROUS
TICKLISH BURLESQUE SPLITTING
COMING DUE ANON COME NEXT
VENUE ADVENT FUTURE
TOWARD ARRIVAL FOOTING
FORWARD BECOMING DESERVED
NAISSANT PAROUSIA
(— AFTER) LATTER
(— AND GOING) FITFUL
(— INTO BEING) BIRTH GENESIS
(— NEAR) ACCESSION
(— OUT) ISSUE EGRESS
(— TO) ADIT
(— TO OFFICE) ACCESS ACCESSION
(— TOGETHER) SEANCE CONGRESS
COUPLING GATHERING
(SECOND —) PAROUSIA
COMMA POINT VIRGULE
(SCRATCH —) DIAGONAL
COMMAND DO BID SAW SOH
BECK BODE BOON CALL COME
EASY FIAT HEST HETE MAND
RATE RULE SWAY WARN WILL
WISH WORD BEKEN CHECK
COVER EDICT EXACT FORCE
HIGHT ORDER POWER SWEEP
UKASE ADJURE BEHEST CHARGE
COMPEL DEGREE DEMAND
DEVICE DIRECT ENJOIN GOVERN
HOOKUM IMPOSE MASTER
ORACLE ORDAIN STEVEN
SUMMON APPOINT BEHIGHT
BIDDING CONCERN CONTROL
DICTATE JUSSION JUSSIVE
LEADING MANDATE OFFICER
PRECEPT REQUIRE SKIPPER
WARRANT BIDDANCE DOMINEER
IMPERATE INSTRUCT MANDAMUS
RESTRAIN
(— OF ARMY) CONDUCT
(— TO HORSE) GEE HAW HUP
HUPP WHOA GIDDAP HUDDUP
(— TO TURN LEFT) HAW
(— TO TURN RIGHT) GEE HUP HUPP
(MAGICIAN'S —) PRESTO
COMMANDANT GOVERNOR
KILLADAR
COMMANDED IMPERATE
COMMANDEER PRESS
(— AN AIRPLANE) SKYJACK
COMMANDER CID CIO DUX DUKE
EMIR HEAD JEFE BLOKE CHIEF
EMEER ADALID LEADER MASTER

RAMMER TARTAN ALCALDE
CAPTAIN CROWNER DECARCH
DEKARCH DRUNGAR EMPEROR
GENERAL KHALIFA MARSHAL
NAVARCH OFFICER VAIVODE
HERETOGA HIPPARCH LOCHAGER
LOCHAGUS MYRIARCH PHYLARCH
RISALDAR SERASKER TAXIARCH
TETRARCH VINTENER
PROCONSUL
(— IN CHIEF) SIRDAR TARTAN
TURTAN ADMIRAL GENERAL
COMMANDERY PRECEPTORY
COMMANDING DOMINANT
IMPERANT IMPERIAL IMPOSING
COMMANDMENT LAW RULE
ORDER COMMAND MITZVAH
PRECEPT BODEWORD
(DIVINE —) LAW
(TEN —S) DECALOG DECALOGUE
COMMANDO RAIDER RANGER
CHINDIT FEDAYEE
COMMELINA DEWFLOWER
COMMEMORATE FETE KEEP
FEAST REMENE EPITAPH
MEMORATE MONUMENT
REMEMBER MEMORIALIZE
COMMEMORATION AWARD
MEDAL COMMEM PLAQUE
JUBILEE MEMORIA MENTION
SERVICE EBENEZER ENCAENIA
MEMORIAL REMEMBRANCE
COMMEMORATIVE HONORARY
MEMORIAL
COMMENCE FALL FANG FILE
MOVE OPEN ARISE BEGIN FOUND
START ARRAME EMBARK INCEPT
LAUNCH SPRING STREAK STREEK
INITIATE
COMMENCEMENT ONSET ORIGIN
OUTSET KICKOFF OPENING
ENTRANCE
COMMENCING INITIAL NASCENT
INCIPIENT
COMMEND KEN PAT GIVE LAUD
ADORN ALOSE BEKEN BOOST
EXTOL GRACE OFFER BESTOW
BETAKE COMMIT PRAISE RESIGN
APPLAUD APPROVE BESPEAK
BETEACH DELIVER ENTRUST
INTRUST BEQUEATH
COMMENDABLE GOOD WORTHY
LOVABLE LOWABLE LAUDABLE
COMMENDATION LAUD PRAISE
CITATION
(EFFUSIVE —) SLAVER
(MARKED —) APPLAUSE
COMMENSAL EPIZOON MESSMATE
COMMENSALISM SYNOECY
SYMPHILY COMMUNISM
COMMENSURATE EVEN EQUAL
ENOUGH ADEQUATE RELEVANT
COMMENT BARB BRAG GIBE JIBE
NOTE TALK WORD ASIDE BREAK
DUNCE GLOSS GLOZE CUTTER
DILATE GAMBIT NOTATE POSTIL
REMARK SCANCE CAPTION
DESCANT DISCUSS EXPLAIN
EXPOUND ADDENDUM SCHOLION
SCHOLIUM DISPRAISE
(— DISAPPROVINGLY) HARRUMPH
(CAUSTIC —) SATIRE
(ILL-TIMED —) CLANGER

(MARGINAL —) APOSTIL
COMMENTARY GLOSS GEMARA
MEMOIR SATIRE ACCOUNT
COMMENT MEKILTA POSTILS
FOOTNOTE GLOSSARY TREATISE
COMMENTATOR HAKAM CRITIC
GLOZER ANALYST GLOSSIST
SCHOLIAST
COMMERCE TRADE BARTER
CHANGE TRAFFIC BUSINESS
EXCHANGE MERCATURE
NAVIGATION
COMMERCIAL STORE TRADY
TRADAL MERCHANT TRADEFUL
(— ESTABLISHMENT) HONG
COMMERCIALISM HUCKSTERISM
COMMERCIALISM
COMMINGLE MIX FUSE JOIN
BLEND IMMIX MERGE UNITE
MINGLE COMBINE COMINGE
EMBROIL COMMEDDLE
COMMINUTE MILL CRUSH GRIND
POUND POUNCE POWDER
COMMINUTED FINE
COMMISERATE PITY
COMMISERATION EMPATHY
SYMPATHY
COMMISSION PLAT SEND TASK
BOARD PRESS TRUST BRANCH
BREVET CHARGE DEMAND
DEPUTE ERRAND LEGACY OFFICE
ORDAIN PERMIT COMMAND
CONSIGN DUOVIRI EMPOWER
FITTAGE GOSPLAN MANDATE
MISSION SQUEEZE WARRANT
CORNETCY DELEGATE ENCHARGE
INTERPOL OVERRIDE POUNDAGE
(— AS CAPTAIN) POST
COMMISSIONAIRE CADDY CADDIE
DUBASH
COMMISSIONER ENVOY TRIER
LEDGER ARRAYER OFFICER
PRISTAW DELEGATE
COMMISSURE VINCULUM
COMMIT DO GIVE PULL STOW
TAKE ALLOT ARRET HIGHT LEAVE
REFER TEACH ARETTE ASSIGN
BETAKE ENGAGE PERMIT
REMAND BEHIGHT BETEACH
COMMAND COMMEND COMMISE
CONFIDE CONSIGN DELIVER
DEPOSIT ENTRUST INTRUSE
INTRUST BEQUEATH DEDICATE
DELEGATE IMPRISON RELEGATE
RECOMMEND PERPETRATE
(— ERROR) SNAPPER
(— MONEY) INVEST
(— TO BATTLE) LAUNCH
(— TO JAIL) JUG
(— TO MEMORY) CON LEARN
MEMORIZE
(— VIOLENCE) TOUCH
COMMITMENT OBLIGATION
COMMITTAL COMPROMISE
COMMITTED (— TO) ENGAGE
COMMITTEE BODY JURY RUMP
BOARD GROUP JUNTA TABLE
BUREAU SOVIET COUNCIL
DELEGACY POLITBURO
PRESIDIUM SYNDICATE
COMMIXTURE MIXTURE
HOTCHPOT CONFUSION
IMMISSION

COMMODE CAP CHEST STOOL TOPKNOT CUPBOARD FONTANGE
COMMODIOUS FIT AMPLE ROOMY PROPER USEFUL SPACIOUS SUITABLE CAVERNOUS
COMMODITY ITEM WARE GOODS STUFF EXPORT FUTURE STAPLE ARTICLE SHIPMENT
(**— SOLD SHORT**) BEAR
(**UNSALABLE —**) DRUG
(**PL.**) KIND SPOTS CHANDLERY
COMMON LAY LOW NOA TYE BASE MEAN RIFE TOWN VILE BANAL BRIEF CHEAP EJIDO EXIDO GREEN GRIMY GROSS JOINT LEASE OFTEN SLACK STALE TACKY TRITE USUAL COARSE DEMOID FAMOUS MODERN MUTUAL ORNERY PROPIO PUBLIC SIMPLE VULGAR AVERAGE CURRENT DEMOTIC GENERAL GENERIC IGNOBLE NATURAL POPULAR PROFANE RAFFISH REGULAR TRIVIAL UNNOBLE VILLAIN BANAUSIC EPIDEMIC FAMILIAR FREQUENT HABITUAL MECHANIC MEDIOCRE ORDINARY PANDEMIC PLEBEIAN TRIFLING TRITICAL RECIPROCAL
(**— OF ESTOVERS**) BOT BOTE
(**IN —**) ALIKE
(**NOT —**) UNTRADED
(**PL.**) COMMUNE
(**PREF.**) CAEN(O) CEN(O) COEN(O) HOM(O)
COMMONER SNOB CEORL PLEBE SIMPLE BURGESS CITIZEN STUDENT ROTURIER
COMMONLY OFTEN VULGO FAMILIARLY
COMMONNESS IDIOTISM COMMUNITY VULGARITY
COMMON PEOPLE VULGUS
COMMONPLACE DULL FADE WORN BANAL DAILY PLAIN PROSE PROSY STALE TOPIC TRIPY TRITE USUAL COMMON GARDEN HOMELY MODERN TRUISM VULGAR FADAISE HUMDRUM INSIPID PROSAIC TEDIOUS TRIVIAL BANALITY BROMIDIC COPYBOOK EVERYDAY ORDINARY RUMTYTOO PEDESTRIAN
COMMONPLACENESS BATHOS HUMDRUM
COMMON SENSE WIT NOUS SALT GUMPTION
COMMONWEAL WEAL REPUBLIC
COMMONWEALTH POLIS STATE ESTATE PUBLIC WEALTH COMONTE COUNTRY COMMONTY
(**IDEAL —**) UTOPIA
COMMOTION DO ADO DIN BREE DUST FLAP FRAY FUSS HEAT HELL RIOT STIR TOSS WHIR ALARM FLARE FUROR HURLY HURRY STORM STOUR WHIRL BUSTLE CATHRO FISSLE FISTLE FLURRY FRACAS FRAISE FURORE GARRAY HOOPLA HOTTER MOTION NYMPH PHRASE POTHER RUFFLE SHINDY SPLORE SQUALL STEERY TUMULT UNREST UPSTIR WELTER BLATHER

BLUSTER CATOUSE CLATTER KIPPAGE SHINDIG TAMASHA TEMPEST TURMOIL DISORDER ERUPTION REMOTION STIRRAGE STRAMASH TIRRIVEE UPHEAVAL UPRISING
COMMUNAL EJIDAL
COMMUNE MIR AREA DEME TALK ARGUE REALM SHARE TREAT ADVISE CONFER DEBATE IMPORT PARLEY REVEAL CONSULT DISCUSS DIVULGE COMMERCE CONVERSE DISTRICT STANITZA TOWNSHIP
COMMUNICABLE OPEN FRANK CATCHING SOCIABLE
COMMUNICATE SAY GIVE SHOW SIGN TELL BREAK DRILL SPEAK YIELD BESTOW COMMON CONVEY IMPART INFECT INFORM REVEAL SIGNAL ADDRESS BREATHE DECLARE DICTATE DIVULGE CONVERSE DESCRIBE INTIMATE
(**— BY ALLUSION**) IMPLY
COMMUNICATION CALL NOTE WORD CABLE FAVOR LETTER SPEECH ADDRESS DIVULGE GALLERY MESSAGE COMETHER LANGUAGE TELEGRAM MEMORANDUM
(**— SERVICE**) TELEX
COMMUNICATIVE FREE SOCIABLE EXPANSIVE
COMMUNION CULT HOST MASS SECT TALK CREED FAITH SHARE UNITY CHURCH HOMILY COMMUNE CONCORD NAGMAAL SYNAGOG ANTIPHON COMMERCE CONVERSE KOINONIA VIATICUM
(**— SERVICE**) ACTION
COMMUNISM LENINISM SOVIETISM
COMMUNIST RED COMMIE SOVIET COMRADE
COMMUNITY MIR BODY BURG CITY CLAN DESA MARK MURA DESSA FIRCA STATE THORP CENOBY CLIMAX COLONY FAMILY HAMLET MILLET NATION POLITY PUBLIC SOCIES ANTHILL BOHEMIA COMMUNE COMONTE CONVENT HERONRY KINGDOM PHALANX SOCIETY VILLAGE ZADRUGA AUTONOMY COMMONTY DISTRICT LIKENESS PRIORATE PROVINCE SODALITY SWEEPDOM TOWNSHIP
(**— OF ANCHORITES**) LAURA
(**— OF INTERESTS**) KINSHIP
(**— OF KNIGHTS TEMPLARS**) PRECEPTORY
(**— OF NATURE**) RACE
(**— OF ORGANISMS**) GAMODEME
(**— OF TURKS**) KIZILBASH
(**COOPERATIVE —**) PHALANSTERY
(**ECOLOGICAL —**) PROCLIMAX
(**JEWISH —**) JEWRY KOLEL ALJAMA SHTETL JUDAISM SHTETEL SYNAGOG KEHILLAH
(**MAORI —**) KAIK KAIKA
(**PERUVIAN —**) AYLLU COMUNIDAD
(**PLANT —**) HEATH FOREST ALTERNE ENCLAVE
(**RELIGIOUS —**) CENOBY SAMGHA

SANGHA CONVENT CENOBIUM
(**RUSSIAN —**) MIR
(**UTOPIAN —**) PANTISOCRACY
(**VILLAGE —**) IKHWAN
COMMUTATE COMMUTE UNDIRECT
COMMUTATIVE ABELIAN
COMMUTATOR BREAK BREAKER RHEOTROPE
COMMUTE ALTER CHANGE TRAVEL CONVERT EXCHANGE
COMOROS (**CAPITAL OF —**) MORONI
(**ISLAND OF —**) MWALI MOHELI NZWANI ANJOUAN NJAZIDJA
(**VOLCANO OF —**) KARTHALA
COMPACT SAD BALL BOND CASE FAST FIRM HARD KNIT PACK PACT PLOT SNUG TRIM TRUE BRIEF CLOSE COVIN CROWD DENSE GROSS HARDY HORNY MATCH PITHY SOLID SPISS TERSE THICK TIGHT BEETLE COMART HARDEN LEAGUE SHRINK SPISSY STOCKY VANITY BARGAIN CONCISE CONCORD CROWDED NUGGETY PACTION SERRIED TABLOID ALLIANCE CONDENSE CONTRACT COVENANT FLAPJACK HEAVYSET SOLIDIFY SUCCINCT PELLETIZE
(**PREF.**) GLOMERO GLOMERULO PYCN(O) PYKN(O)
COMPACTED SAD CROWDED
(**PREF.**) PECTO
COMPACTNESS BODY DENSITY FASTNESS SOLIDITY INTENSITY
COMPANION PAL SOC CHUM FERE MAKE MATE PEER TWIN WIFE BILLY BUDDY BULLY BUTTY CHINA COMES CRONY CULLY DARES GREEK MATCH MATEY MAUGH RIVAL SPORT ATTEND BELAMY BILLIE BROLGA COBBER COHORT COMATE CUMMER CUPMAN DUENNA EGERIA ESCORT FELLOW FRIEND GESITH GOSSIP KIMMER MARROW PANION SHADOW SPOUSE STEADY TROJAN ACHATES COMPANY COMPEER COMRADE CONSORT ELPENOR FRANION HUSBAND PARTNER SOCIATE SOCIETY SPECIAL BARNACLE BEAUPERE COMPADRE CORRIVAL EPHESIAN EPHESINE FAITHFUL FAMILIAR HELPMATE PARALLEL PLAYFERE SYNODITE
(**ARCHER'S —**) BUTTY
(**DRINKING —**) CUPMATE
(**POT —**) ALEKNIGHT
(**READING —**) LECTRICE
(**TABLE —**) CONVICTOR
(**PL.**) SOCIETY
(**PREF.**) HETAERO
COMPANIONABLE FERE MATEY SOCIAL CORDIAL FELLOWLY GRACIOUS SOCIABLE
COMPANIONSHIP FERE SHIP HAUNT COMPANY SOCIETY AFFINITY
COMPANY CRY MOB SET BAND BEVY BODY CORE CREW CRUE FARE FERE FIRM GANG GEST

GING HERD HOST MANY PUSH ROUT SORT TEAM TURM AERIE COVEN COVEY CROWD FLOCK FLOTE GESTE GROUP GUEST HORDE JATHA MEINY PARTY SQUAD SUITE TROOP TURMA CIRCLE CLIQUE COHORT COVINE CURNEY DECURY LOCHUS OUTFIT RESORT THRAVE THRONG TROUPE TWENTY VOLLEY BATTERY COLLEGE CONDUCT CONSORT HOLDING JIMBANG MANIPLE SOCIETE SOCIETY THIASOS THIASUS VISITOR ASSEMBLY FAISCEAU FOLKMOOT JINGBANG PRESENCE
(**— OF BADGERS**) CETE
(**— OF BIRDS**) BANK
(**— OF BOOKSELLERS**) CONGER
(**— OF DANCERS**) COMPARSA
(**— OF HERDSMEN**) BOOLY BOOLEY
(**— OF HORSEMEN**) TROOP
(**— OF MARTENS**) RICHESSE
(**— OF SINGERS**) CHOIR QUIRE CHORUS
(**— OF THE FAITHFUL**) FOLD
(**— OF TRAVELERS**) CAFILA CAVALCADE
(**— OF WOMEN**) GAGGLE
(**— OF WORSHIPPERS**) THIASUS
(**EXCLUSIVE —**) CROWD
(**FINANCIAL —**) FACTOR
(**FIRE —**) SQUAD
(**MILITARY —**) WATCH DECURY VENLIN PELOTON VEXILLUM
(**RECORDING —**) LABEL
(**SUITABLE —**) BESORT
COMPARABLE LIKE SAME SIMILAR
COMPARATIVE
(**SUFF.**) ER IOR
COMPARE VIE EVEN LIKE SIZE APPLY EQUAL LIKEN MATCH SCALE TALLY ALLUDE CONFER PARIFY RELATE SEMBLE BALANCE BRACKET COLLATE EXAMINE SENIBLE SIGNIFY ASSEMBLE CONFRONT CONTRAST ESTIMATE PARALLEL RESEMBLE SIMILIZE
(**— WITH**) TO
COMPARISON SIMILE ANALOGY BALANCE COMPARE PARABLE PARAGON DISIMILE LIKENESS LIKENING METAPHOR PARALLEL
COMPARTMENT BAY BIN BOX CAB POD CELL DECK FLUE PANE PART SLOT WELL ABODE CABIN HATCH HUTCH PANEL STALL VOLET ABACUS ALCOVE BUNKER GARAGE HOPPER MUFFLE REGION SEVERY SMOKER ALVEOLE CABINET CAPSULE CELLULE CHAMBER FIREBOX HOUSING KITCHEN LOCULUS MANSION ROTONDE SECTION ALVEOLUS COALHOLE DIVISION FOREPEAK GRINTERN LOCELLUS STEERAGE TRAVERSE PIGEONHOLE
(**— FOR COAL**) BUNKER
(**— FOR TREATING ORE**) KITCHEN
(**— IN BARN**) BAY
(**— IN CAR**) BOOT
(**— IN STOVE**) BROILER
(**— OF COACH**) IMPERIAL

(— OF ROOF) SEVERY
(— OF WINDOW) LIGHT
(— ON GAMEBOARD) STORE
(— ON ROULETTE WHEEL) EAGLE
(— ON TRAIN) COUCHETTE
(CARGO —) HOLD
(DETACHABLE —) POD
(GAS-TIGHT —) BALLONET
(GUNNER'S —) BLISTER
(REFRIGERATOR —) CHILLER
(SLEEPING —) CUBICLE
(STAGECOACH —) COUPE
(STORAGE—) BOOT
COMPASS BOW AREA DIAL GAIN
ROOM ROSE SIZE TOUR AMBIT
FIELD GAMUT RANGE REACH
SCOPE SWEEP TENOR WHEEL
ARRIVE ATTAIN BOUNDS CIRCLE
DEGREE DEVICE DIACLE EFFECT
EXTENT MERIST MODULE SPHERE
SPREAD VOLUME ACHIEVE
AZIMUTH CALIBER CIRCUIT
CONFINE DIVIDER EMBRACE
ENCLOSE ENVIRON HORIZON
IMAGINE PELORUS PURVIEW
TRAMMEL BOUNDARY CINCTURE
CIRCUITY DIAPASON PRACTICE
PRACTISE SURROUND
(— IN SHIP'S CABIN) TELLTALE
(— NEEDLE END) LILY
(— OF MELODY) AMBITUS
(— OF TONES) DIAPASON
(— OF VOICE) GAMUT SCALE
(— POINT) RHUMB
(BELL-MAKING —) CROOK
(PART OF —) PIN CARD DOME
HOOD PIVOT HOUSING BINNACLE
COMPASS BOX KETTLE
COMPASS CARD ROSE PEDRERO
PERRIER
COMPASSION RUE PITY RUTH
GRACE HEART MERCY PIETY
SORRY KARUNA LENITY REMORSE
STOMACH CLEMENCY HUMANITY
KINDNESS SYMPATHY
COMPASSIONATE MEEK RUTH
SOFT HUMAN GENTLE TENDER
CLEMENT PIETOSO PITEOUS
PITIFUL GRACIOUS MERCIFUL
COMPASS PLANT PILOTWEED
ROSINWEED
COMPASS QUARTER PLAGE
COMPASS SIGHT VANE
COMPATIBLE AKIN CIVIL ARTISTIC
SUITABLE
COMPATRIOT NATIVE PATRIOT
SYNETHNIC
COMPEL GAR MAKE MOVE URGE
BRING CAUSE COACT DRIVE
EXACT FORCE IMPEL PRESS
SHOVE COERCE ENJOIN EXTORT
INCITE OBLIGE THREAT ACTUATE
AFFORCE ATTRACT COMMAND
DRAGOON ENFORCE NECESSE
REQUIRE VIOLENCE NECESSITATE
(— TO GO) HALE
(— TO PAY) STICK
COMPELLED HAS FAIN MUST
BOUND FORCED ENFORCED
COMPELLING COGENT STRONG
TELLING BRUISING FORCEFUL
COMPELLINGLY BADLY
COMPENDIOUS BRIEF SHORT

DIRECT COMPACT CONCISE
SUMMARY SUCCINCT
COMPENDIUM LIST BRIEF APERCU
DIGEST PRECIS SKETCH SURVEY
CATALOG COMPEND EPITOME
LEXICON MEDULLA OUTLINE
PANDECT SUMMARY SYLLOGE
ABSTRACT BREVIARY BREVIATE
LANDSKIP SYLLABUS SYNOPSIS
ABRIDGEMENT
COMPENSATE PAY JIBE AGREE
ATONE COVER REPAY TALLY
OFFSET RECOUP REDEEM
REWARD SQUARE COMMUTE
CORRECT PLASTER REDRESS
REPRISE REQUITE RESTORE
SATISFY COMPENSE DISPENSE
EQUALIZE
COMPENSATION BOT FEE PAY
UTU BOOT BOTE HIRE MEND
TOLL BONUS LOWER WAGES
AMENDS ANGILD GERSUM
OFFSET REWARD SALARY SETOFF
DAMAGES FREIGHT PAYMENT
REDRESS SALVAGE STIPEND
BREAKAGE DONATIVE EARNINGS
INTEREST OCTOGILD PILOTAGE
PITTANCE REQUITAL SOLATIUM
(— FOR INJURY) SATISFACTION
(— FOR KILLING MAN) MANBOT
MANBOTE
(MEAGER —) PITTANCE
(WORKER'S —) COMPO
COMPENSATORILY EVEN
COMPETE PIT VIE COPE KEMP
TEND CLASH MATCH RIVAL
STRIVE CONTEND CONTEST
EMULATE CORRIVAL
(— WITH) BUCK
COMPETENCE SKILL ABILITY
FACULTY CAPACITY
COMPETENCY MAY CAPACITY
COMPETENT UP APT CAN FIT
ABLE GOOD HOME MEET SANE
ADEPT CAPAX SMART SWEET
TIGHT INTACT LAWFUL WORTHY
CAPABLE ENDOWED SKILLED
ADEQUATE SUITABLE QUALIFIED
COMPETITION VIE DRAW GAME
HEAT JUMP MATCH PRIZE TRIAL
WAGER CONTEST PARAGON
RIVALRY BIATHLON CONCOURS
CONFLICT
(— AMONG REAPERS) KEMP
(VERSE —) TENSON
COMPETITOR FOE ENEMY MATCH
RIVAL WAGER COUSIN PLAYER
AGONIST ENTRANT CORRIVAL
FAVORITE GAMESTER OPPONENT
COMPILATION ANA BOOK CODE
CENTO DIGEST CASEBOOK
DIRECTORY GATHERING
COMPILE ADD EDIT AMASS
GATHER SELECT ARRANGE
COLLECT COMPOSE PREPARE
COMPILER AUTHOR EDITOR
GATHERER GLOSSIST SCISSORER
COMPLACENT CALM SMUG
PLACID FATUOUS PRIGGISH
COMPLACENTLY FATLY
COMPLAIN AIL YIP BEEF CARP
CRIB FRET FUSS GREX KEEN KICK
KREX MEAN MOAN MOOT MUTE

RULE WAIL YELP YIRN BITCH
BLEAT BRAWL CRAKE CROAK
CROON GRIPE GROWL GRUMP
GRUNT PINGE PLAIN WHINE
BEWAIL CHARGE COTTER CREATE
GRIEVE GROUSE GRUTCH HOLLER
KVETCH MURMUR PEENGE
REPINE SQUAWK THREAP
THROPE WHINGE YAMMER
CHUNNER DEPLORE GRIZZLE
GRUMBLE INVEIGH PROTEST
BELLYACHE
COMPLAINANT ACTOR ASKER
ORATOR ACCUSER PLAINER
QUERENT RELATOR
COMPLAINING BRAY PULY
LATRANT QUERENT DOLEANCE
QUERULOUS
COMPLAINT RAP BEEF FUSS
HOWL MEAN MOAN WAIL BITCH
GRIPE GROWL WHINE CHESON
GROUCH GROUSE GRUDGE
GRUTCH HOLLER LAMENT
MALADY PLAINT REPINE SQUAWK
AILMENT DISEASE GRUMBLE
ILLNESS PROTEST QUARREL
QUERELE RECLAMA TRAGEDY
COMPLAIN DISORDER DOLEANCE
GRAVAMEN JEREMIAD
COMPLAISANCE AMENITY
SUAVITY FACILITY URBANITY
COMPLAISANT BON ABLE EASY
KIND BUXOM CIVIL SUAVE
BONAIR POLITE SMOOTH SUPPLE
URBANE AFFABLE AMIABLE
BOWABLE LENIENT GRACIOUS
OBLIGING PLEASING
COMPLEMENT CREW GANG FORCE
TALLY ALEXIN AMOUNT COUSIN
ADJUNCT OBVERSE PENDANT
(MILITARY —) STRENGTH
COMPLEMENTARY OPPOSITE
(PREF.) COUNTER
COMPLETE DO ALL CAP END BLUE
DASH DEAD DEEP FAIR FILL FINE
FULL JUST PASS PURE RANK
VERY CLEAN CLOSE CROWN
EVERY GROSS LARGE PLAIN
PLUMB POINT PUCCA PUKKA
QUITE RIPEN ROUND SOLID
SOUND STARK TOTAL UTTER
WHOLE CHOATE DAMPEN
DEADLY EFFECT ENTIRE FINISH
GLOBAL HOLLOW INTACT
MATURE PROPER SINGLE STRICT
VESTED ACHIEVE CONFIRM
EXECUTE EXPLETE FULFILL
GERMANE OUTWORK PERFECT
PLENARY REALIZE REPLETE
SPHERAL ABSOLUTE BLINKING
CIRCULAR CONCLUDE FINALIZE
IMPLICIT INTEGRAL OUTRIGHT
OVERCOME PRECIOUS PROFOUND
THOROUGH BODACIOUS
NEGOTIATE ACCOMPLISH
(— CARELESSLY) HUDDLE
(— IN SYLLABLES) ACATHLECTIC
(REMARKABLY —) SPLENDID
(PREF.) HOL(O) TEL(E)(EO)
COMPLETED PAU OVER CLOSED
SUMMED COMPLETE FINISHED
(NOT —) DURATIVE
COMPLETELY ALL JAM BARE BUCK

FAIR FLAT GOOD SLAM SLAP
SPAN BLACK CLEAN CLOSE FULLY
PLUMB QUITE SHEER SMACK
SPANG STARK STICK STOCK
UTTER BODILY ENTIRE GAINLY
HOLLOW PURELY SPANDY
WHOLLY ALGATES BLANKLY
THROUGH CLEVERLY DIRECTLY
ENTIRELY HEARTILY OUTRIGHT
(PREF.) DE DIS OB PAN
COMPLETENESS DEPTH ALLNESS
FULLNESS RIPENESS INTEGRITY
PLENITUDE
COMPLETION END CROWN FINISH
(PREF.) TELEUT(O)
COMPLEX HARD MAZY BEING
ETHOS FIELD HYOID MIXED
ADDUCT DESERT KNOTTY SYSTEM
CULTURE NETWORK SAMKARA
SINUOUS TANGLED TWISTED
ABSTRUSE COMPOUND
EQUATION EXCHANGE INVOLVED
MANIFOLD SAMSKARA
SYNDROME MACROCOSM
(— OF CHARACTERISTICS)
PERSONALITY
(— OF DIALECTS) HINDI
(— OF HORMONES) CALINE
(— OF IDEAS) EGO SYSTEM
(— OF SHOPS) MALL
(BASEMENT —) FLOOR
(NOT —) SIMPLE
COMPLEXION HUE RUD BLEE
CAST LEER LOOK RUDD TINT
COLOR HUMOR STATE TENOR
TINGE ASPECT TEMPER
COLORING
(BAD —) DYSCHROA
COMPLEXITY NODUS SCHEME
TANGLE INTRIGUE
COMPLIANCE TRUE ASSENT
MUNICH CESSION CONSENT
HARMONY OBSEQUY ABIDANCE
CIVILITY FACILITY FORMALITY
COMPLIANT EASY MEEK OILY
SOFT BUXOM FACILE PLIANT
SUPPLE COMMODE DUCTILE
DUTIFUL WILLING OBEDIENT
TOWARDLY YIELDING
COMPLICATE INTORT PUZZLE
TANGLE EMBROIL INVOLVE
PERPLEX BEWILDER INTRIGUE
INTRICATE
COMPLICATED HARD KNOTTY
PROLIX COMPLEX GORDIAN
SNARLED TANGLED INVOLVED
PLEXIFORM
COMPLICATION KNOT NODE PLOT
NODUS SNARL TANGLE INTRIGUE
COMPLIMENT GIFT KUDO LAUD
EXTOL EULOGY PRAISE SALAAM
SALUTE ADULATE APPLAUD
BOUQUET COMMEND DOUCEUR
FLATTER TRIBUTE ENCOMIUM
FLUMMERY GRATUITY GREETING
COMPLY PLY CEDE OBEY ABIDE
ADAPT AGREE APPLY YIELD
ACCEDE ACCORD ASSENT ENFOLD
SUBMIT CONFORM EMBRACE
OBSERVE
(— WITH) OBEY SERVE OBSERVE
SATISFY

COMPONE GOBONE GOBONY
COMPONENT KEY DRAG FORM
ITEM PART UNIT GIVEN FACTOR
MEMBER SIMPLE ELEMENT
FORMANT PARTIAL CONJUNCT
INTEGRAL
(— OF ARMY) CAVALRY
(— OF CELL WALLS) CALLOSE
(ELECTRIC —S) CIRCUITRY
(PHYSICAL —S) HARDWARE
(PRINCIPAL —) BASIS
COMPORT ACT BEAR HAVE HOLD
JIBE KEEP SUIT ABEAR AGREE
BROOK CARRY TALLY ACCORD
ACQUIT BEHAVE DEMEAN
ENDURE SQUARE CONDUCT
COMPORTMENT DEALING
BEHAVIOR DEMEANOR
COMPOSE BAT PEN SET CALM
COMP DITE FORM LULL MAKE
ALLAY BREVE BRIEF CLERK CLINK
COUCH DIGHT DRAFT FRAME
ORDER PATCH PIECE SPELL STICK
WRITE ACCORD ADJUST CREATE
DESIGN GRAITH INDITE RECITE
REDACT SETTLE SOOTHE STEADY
ARRANGE COMPACT COMPILE
COMPONE CONCOCT CONFORM
DICTATE DISPOSE DRAUGHT
FASHION PATIENT PRODUCE
TYPESET COMPOUND COMPRISE
REGULATE
(— POETRY) MAKE SING
COMPOSED SET CALM COOL
QUIET SOBER WROTE DEMURE
DIGEST PLACID SEDATE SERENE
COMPACT WRITTEN COMPOUND
DECOROUS TOGETHER TRANQUIL
(— IN METER) FOOTED
(ILL —) LAME
COMPOSEDNESS SOSSIEGO
COMPOSER BARD POET LYRIC
ODIST AUTHOR LYRIST PENMAN
WRITER CONTEUR ELEGIST
FANTAST MAESTRO COLORIST
ELEGIAST IDYLLIST ILIADIST
MELODIST MONODIST MUSICIAN
PHANTAST TUNESMITH
AMERICAN FRY BIRD BOND CAGE
COLE IVES KERN ROOT BEACH
BLOCH DANKS FOOTE HANDY
HAYDN HOMER NEVIN OHARA
PRATT SCOTT SOUSA WEILL
BARBER CADMAN HARRIS KRENEK
LOOMIS PALMER PARKER PISTON
PORTER SEEGER SPEAKS SUESSE
TAYLOR WINNER ANTHEIL
BRISTOW CHASINS COPLAND
DEKOVEN GILBERT GOLDMAN
HAESCHE HERBERT MENOTTI
PARROTT RODGERS SCHUMAN
THOMSON YOUMANS BARTLETT
BROCKWAY BURLEIGH CHADWICK
CONVERSE GERSHWIN GOODRICH
GRAINGER KREISLER SESSIONS
THOMPSON ARMSTRONG
BERNSTEIN CARPENTER
ELLINGTON MACDOWELL
ARGENTINIAN CASTRO
AUSTRIAN FUX GAL BERG WOLF
BRULL DRDLA MOTTL ZAYTZ
BLEYLE CZERNY EYBLER LANNER
MOZART BITTNER NEUKOMM

STRAUSS BRUCKNER DIABELLI
GYROWETZ KORNGOLD REZNICEK
SCHUBERT HEUBERGER
MILLOCKER SCHONBERG
GANSBACHER ALBRECHTSBERGER
BELGIAN FETIS LEKEU BENOIT
BERIOT BLOCKX BRASIN DUMONT
FRANCK GRISAR JONGEN
GEVAERT HUBERTI LEMMENS
MATHIEU CAMPENHOUT
BRAZILIAN GOMES VILLALOBOS
CANADIAN BRANSCOMB
CZECH BENDL NOVAK DVORAK
FIBICH FORSTER JANACEK
KUBELIK SMETANA DESPAUER
NESWADBA KALLIWODA
KOVAROVIC MYSLIVECEK
DANISH ENNA GADE HAMERIK
NIELSEN HARTMANN
DUTCH FODOR OBRECHT
ARCADELT WAGENAAR
SWEELINCK
ENGLISH BAX TYE ARNE BLOW
BYRD CARR CLAY HOOK MONK
BACHE BLISS BOYCE CAREY
COOKE COWEN CROFT ELGAR
ELVEY FIELD HOLST LAWES
LOCKE PARRY SCOTT TOVEY
ARNOLD ASHTON AUSTIN AVISON
BARNBY BISHOP BRIDGE COATES
COWARD CRAMER CROTCH
CROUCH CUSINS DAVIES DELIUS
DIBDIN GERMAN GLOVER GREENE
HANDEL LAMOND LINLEY
MCEWEN ONEILL PARKER TALLIS
THOMAS WALTON WILSON
ATTWOOD BANTOCK BARNETT
BENNETT CELLIER COLEMAN
DUNHILL FARRANT GIBBONS
HORSLEY IRELAND JACKSON
LATROBE NOVELLO PURCELL
STAINER STORACE BENJAMIN
BOUGHTON SULLIVAN TYRWHITT
ARMSTRONG CALDICOTT
HESELTINE MACFARRNE
MACKENZIE SOMERVELL
GOLDSCHMIDT RAVENSCROFT
FINNISH PACIUS KAJANUS
MADETOJA MELARTIN PALMGREN
SIBELIUS WEGELIUS JARNEFELT
MERIKANTO
FRENCH ERB HUE ADAM INDY
LALO ALARD ALKAN AUBER
AURIC BAZIN BIZET COHEN DAVID
DUKAS FAURE GOUVY HERVE
IBERT LULLY MASSE MEHUL
RAVEL REBER REYER SATIE
WIDOR AUBERT AUDRAN
CAMPRA CHOPIN DANCLA
DAQUIN DUBOIS DUPARC
GODARD GOSSEC GOUNOD
HALEVY HEROLD LECOCQ LEROUX
PIERNE STRAUS THOMAS BERLIOZ
BERTINI BOESSET BRUNEAU
CAMBERT CHELARD COQUARD
DEBUSSY DELIBES DUCASSE
GUIRAUD LACOMBE LAPARRA
LECLAIR LESUEUR MARTINI
MILHAUD POULENC SCHMITT
CHABRIER CHAUSSON COUPERIN
DALAYRAC ERLANGER GOUDIMEL
GUILMANT HONEGGER LEFEBVRE
MAILLART MASSENET MESSAGER

MONSIGNY BOELLMANN
BOIELDIEU CHAMINADE
OFFENBACH WECKERLIN
BURGMULLER DESAUGIERS
DESTOUCHES PLANQUETTE
WALDTEUFEL CHARPENTIER
GERMAN ABT ETT AHLE BACH
BOHM BOTT DORN GOTZ HAAS
KAUN LOBE ORFF RAFF ABERT
BIBER BLECH BOEHE BRUCH
DANZI EBERS FASCH FESCA FINCK
FRANK GENEE GLUCK GRAUN
GRELL KLEIN LOEWE NEEFE
WEBER ALBERT AMBROS BECKER
BERGER BOHNER BRAHMS
COMMER CRUGER ECKERT EITNER
FLOTOW HILLER JENSEN KOHLER
KUCKEN KUHLAU KUHNAU
LINCKE MAHLER WAGNER
WINTER BARGIEL CONRADI
EBERLIN HASSLER JARNACH
MOLIQUE NAUMANN RICHTER
SILCHER STRAUSS WULLNER
ZOLLNER AGRICOLA BENEDICT
BRAMBACH DIETRICH DRAESEKE
EBERWEIN HOFFMANN HOLSTEIN
KAMINSKI KEUSSLER KIRCHNER
KREUTZER PFITZNER REINECKE
SCHUMANN VOLKMANN
AIBLINGER AMBROSIUS
BEETHOVEN BRAUNFELS
BUXTEHUDE CANNABICH
DELLINGER HINDEMITH
KLUGHARDT MARSCHNER
MATTHESON MEYERBEER
NEITHARDT REICHARDT
BELLERMANN BLUMENTHAL
DESTOUCHES PRAETORIUS
SCHARWENKA HUMPERDINCK
MENDELSSOHN FRANCKENSTEIN
LEICHTENTRITT
HUNGARIAN ERKEL HUBAY LEHAR
LISZT BARTOK KODALY KUSSER
JOACHIM ROMBERG DOHNANYI
GOLDMARK
IRISH BALFE OSBORNE WALLACE
ITALIAN LOTI PAER PERI ARAIA
BAINI BOITO BRAGA CESTI CLARI
COSTA VERDI ALFANO ANERIO
ARDITI ARTUSI BUSONI CIAMPI
COCCIA MERULO NANINI PACINI
PEROSI VECCHI ALBERTI ALLEGRI
ANFOSSI ARIOSTI BASSANI
BAZZINI BELLINI BERTONI
BIANCHI CACCINI CALDARA
CAMBINI CASELLA CAVALLI
COLONNA CONCONE CORELLI
DURANTE FERRARI FLORIMO
PICCINI PORPORA PUCCINI
ROSSINI SALIERI TARTINI TOSELLI
VIADANA VIVALDI ZACCONI
ZARLINO AGOSTINI ALBINONI
BERNABEI CLEMENTI FIORILLO
GABRIELI GAGLIANO GIORDANI
GIORDANO JOMMELLI LEGRENZI
MARCELLO MASCAGNI PRATELLA
RAIMONDI RESPIGHI SPONTINI
ANIMUCCIA BANCHIERI
BONONCINI BOTTESINI
BRAMBILLA CARISSIMI CAVALIERI
CHERUBINI DONIZETTI GUGLIELMI
LOCATELLI MALIPIERO
MARCHETTI MORLACCHI

PAISIELLO PERGOLESI SCARLATTI
TOMMASINI VICENTINO
BOCCHERINI CAMPAGNOLI
MERCADANTE MONTEVERDI
PALESTRINA PONCHIELLI
ZINGARELLI LEONCAVALLO
MEXICAN CHAVEZ CARRILLO
NORWEGIAN GRIEG KJERULF
NORDRAAK SVENDSEN
SCHJELDERUP
POLISH KOLBERG FITELBERG
KAMIENSKI KARLOWICZ
MONIUSZKO NOSKOWSKI
SZYMANOWSKI
PORTUGUESE ARNEIRO MACHADO
BOMTEMPO PORTOGALLO
RUMANIAN ENESCO OTESCUA
RUSSIAN LVOV SEROV GLINKA
LIADOV ONEGIN TANEEV ARENSKI
BORODIN REBIKOV GODOWSKY
LIPAUNOV SCRIABIN BALAKIREV
CHEREPNIN GLAZOUNOV
KASHPEROV KASTALSKI
MUSORGSKI PROKOFIEV
KALINNIKOV MOUSORGSKY
STRAVINSKY AZANCHEVSKI
BORTNYANSKI TCHAIKOVSKY
KHACHATURIAN RACHMANINOFF
SHOSTAKOVICH
SCOTTISH GOW SPOTTISWOODE
SPANISH ARBOS FALLA CASALS
ALBENIZ MARTINI PEDRELL
BARBIERI GÜERRERO VICTORIA
SWEDISH ALFVEN HALLEN
ATTERBERG HALLSTROM
WENNERBERG
SWISS EGLI HEGAR HUBER
VENEZUELAN CARRENO
WELSH EVANS PARRY
COMPOSITE HYBRID ITALIC
MOTLEY COMPLEX COMPOSED
CONCRETE INTEGRAL
COMPOSITION ANA DITE MASS
OPUS WORK CENTO DITTY
DRAMA FUGUE GETUP MURKY
PIECE POESY STUCK THEME
ACCORD EULOGY FILLER HAIKAI
LESSON MAGGOT MONODY
THESIS THREAD VULGUS ARTICLE
COMPOST CONSIST DISPLAY
EBURINE EPISTLE MIXTURE
PICTURE STOPPER WRITING
ACROSTIC CAUSERIE COMPOUND
DIALOGUE DIAPENTE EXERCISE
FANTASIA FROTTAGE HEELBALL
(— FOR BILLIARD BALLS) COMPO
(— TO BE ACTED) PLAY DRAMA
(— TO FILL LEATHER) STUFF
(AMOROUS —) EROTIC
(ARTISTIC —) COLLAGE
(BAGPIPE —) PORT
(BANKRUPT'S —) COMPO
(BUILDING —) STAFF
(CHORAL —) MOTET CANTATA
ORATORIO
(GUMMY —) GROUND
(HAND —) CASEWORK
(HUMOROUS —) BURLA
(IMPERFECT —) SOOTERKIN
(INSTRUMENTAL —) AIR GATO
FANCY RONDO GROUND SKETCH
SONATA TIENTO BOURREE
CANZONE BERCEUSE CONCERTO

FANTASIA RHAPSODY SYMPHONY
PASSACAGLIA
(LITERARY —) BOOK CENTO DEBAT
ESSAY PIECE COMEDY SATIRE
SKETCH THESIS TREATISE
(MAGIC —) HELLBROTH
(MUSICAL —) DUET GLEE IDYL
OPUS SOLO SONG TRIO BURLA
CANON DANCE ELEGY ETUDE
GAZEL FUGUE IDYLL MOTET
NONET SCORE STUDY ADAGIO
ARIOSO AZIONE ENTREE GHAZEL
HOCKET HOQUET SEPTET SEXTET
BALLADE BOURREE BOUTADE
BRAVURA ORGANUM QUARTET
SCHERZO TOCCATA CAVATINA
CHACONNE CLAUSULA
CONCERTO INNOMINE SERENADE
SINFONIA STANDARD SYMPHONY
ANTIPHONY OFFERTORY
PROCESSIONAL
(NARRATIVE —) BALLAD
(PLASTIC —) CEMENT
(POETIC —) GLOSS KAVYA
(RAMBLING —) SATIRE RHAPSODY
(RELIGIOUS —) MOTET ANTHEM
HYMNIC CANTATA ORATORIO
(RUBBER —) GUM
(VEDIC —) GAYATRI
(VITREOUS —) ENAMEL
(VOCAL —) ARIA SOLO SONG
CANON ANTHEM ELEVATIO
CONDUCTUS
(PL.) JUVENILIA LITERATURE
COMPOSITOR COMP TYPO ADMAN
SETTER BANKMAN CASEMAN
CLICKER PRINTER STONEMAN
COMPOST PELF SOIL MINGLE
COMPOTE MIXTURE COMPOUND
DRESSING
COMPOSURE BOND MIEN POISE
QUIET UNION REPOSE TEMPER
BALANCE POSTURE CALMNESS
SERENITY
(LOSE —) CHOKE
COMPOTATION SYMPOSIUM
COMPOTE BOWL COMPORT
COMPOST
COMPOUND MIX BASE FILL JOIN
MIXT SOUR TEPA ALKYL ALLOY
AMIDE AMINE BLEND ESTER
FURIL UNION ACETAL ADJUST
ALKIDE BORANE COMMIX COPULA
IODIDE JUMBLE KETONE MEDLEY
PHENOL POLYOL PTERIN PYRONE
SETTLE TEMPER URACIL URAMIL
AGATHIN ALCOHOL ALLICIN
ALLOXAN AMALGAM AMIDATE
AMIDINE AMINATE AMMONIA
COMBINE COMPLEX COMPONE
COMPOSE COMPOST DVANDVA
KAMPONG KHELLIN PHORBIN
PREPARE SPIRANE STEROID
AGLUCONE AGLYCONE ALIZARIN
ALKOXIDE AMMONATE ANTIPODE
APIGENIN BRAZILIN CEROMIDE
COMPOSED FUCHSONE GARDENIN
GENTISIN GOSSYPOL IODOFORM
ISOLOGUE STYRACIN
(ADHESIVE —) SALVE
(COMBINING —) ACCEPTOR
(POISONOUS —) KETENE CACODYL
GLYCINE HELENIN STIBINE

(SYNTHETIC —) ANDROGEN
SORBITAN
(PREF.) (PARENT —) NOR
(SUFF.) GENIN
(CARBON —) ENE
COMPOUNDED CONCRETE
COMPOSITE
COMPOUNDER TANKER
COMPOUNDING INTIMACY
COMPREHEND GET SEE KNOW
TAKE TWIG COVER GRASP IMPLY
LATCH REACH SAVVY SEIZE
SENSE SKILL SMOKE SPELL
ATTAIN BOTTOM DIGEST EMBODY
FATHOM FOLLOW PIERCE UPTAKE
COMPASS CONTAIN DISCERN
EMBRACE ENCLOSE IMAGINE
INCLUDE INVOLVE REALIZE
RECEIVE SWALLOW COMPRISE
CONCEIVE CONCLUDE PERCEIVE
COMPREHENSIBLE EXOTERIC
INCLUDED SENSABLE SCRUTABLE
COMPREHENSION HOLD SABE
GRASP SAVVY SENSE ESPRIT
FATHOM NOESIS UPTAKE
EPITOME INSIGHT KNOWING
SUMMARY BEARINGS
PREHENSION
COMPREHENSIVE BIG FULL WIDE
BROAD GRAND LARGE GLOBAL
SCOPIC CAPABLE CONCISE
GENERAL GENERIC CATHOLIC
ENCYCLIC SPACIOUS
COMPREHENSIVENESS POWER
SCOPE EXTENT BREADTH
WIDENESS LARGENESS
COMPRESS NIP TIE BALE BIND
FIRM LACE WRAP CLING CRAMP
CROWD CRUSH PINCH PRESS
SMASH BUNDLE DEFORM DIGEST
GATHER SHRINK STRAIN THRONG
ABRIDGE ASTRICT BOLSTER
CABBAGE COMPACT CURTAIL
DEFLATE EMBRACE FLATTEN
PLEDGET REPRESS SQUEEZE
SQUINCH ASTRINGE CONDENSE
CONTRACT LAMINATE PEMMICAN
RESTRAIN SUPPRESS
(— WOOL) DUMP
(MEDICAL —) BOLSTER PLEDGET
COMPRESSED STRICT CROWDED
SUCCINCT ANGUSTATE
COARCTATE
COMPRESSION CRUSH SQUEEZE
PRESSURE THLIPSIS
(PREF.) SYMPIESO SYMPIEZO
COMPRESSOR PUMP ROTARY
CONDENSER
COMPRISE HOLD COVER IMPLY
SEIZE ATTACH CONFER EMBODY
EMPLOY MUSTER COMPOSE
CONTAIN EMBRACE ENCLOSE
INCLUDE INVOLVE CONCEIVE
PERCEIVE
COMPROMISE FINE TRIM COMMIT
INTERIM COMPOUND ENDANGER
PALLIATE
COMPROMISING FALSE
COMPULSION NEED URGE FORCE
PRESS DURESS STRESS IMPULSE
COACTION COERCION DISTRESS
EXACTION PERFORCE NECESSITY
COMPULSORY COERCIVE

FORCIBLE NECESSARY
COMPUNCTION QUALM REGRET
SORROW REMORSE SCRUPLE
PENITENCE
COMPURGATOR COJUROR
COSWEARER
COMPUTATION COMPOT
ACCOUNT COMPUTE CALCULUS
COMPUTUS ESTIMATE
RECKONING
COMPUTE ADD SUM CAST ITEM
RATE COUNT TALLY VALUE
ASSESS CIPHER FIGURE NUMBER
RECKON ACCOUNT BALANCE
SUPPUTE ESTIMATE CALCULATE
COMPUTER ADDER ENIAC MANIAC
MAINFRAME PROCESSOR
MINICOMPUTER
(— LANGUAGE) FORTRAN
(PARTS OF — SYSTEM) HARDWARE
COMRADE PAL ALLY CHUM MATE
PEER BILLY BUDDY BUTTY CRONY
HABER HAVER TOWNY BURSCH
CHABER CHAVER COPAIN COUSIN
DIGGER ENGIDU FELLOE FRATER
FRIEND GOSSIP HEARTY BROTHER
COMPEER CONVIVE BEAUPERE
CAMARADA CAMARADE
COMORADO CONFRERE
COPEMATE TOVARICH
SKAINSMATE
(— AT TABLE) CONVIVE
(PL.) SOCE
COMRADESHIP CAMARADERIE
CON DO RAP ANTI KNOW LEAD
LOOK PORE QUIN READ SCAN
CHEAT CUNNE GUIDE KNOCK
LEARN STEER STUDY DIRECT
PERUSE REGARD VERSUS
AGAINST DECEIVE EXAMINE
INSPECT OPPOSED SWINDLE
CONCAVE CAVE VOID CAMUS
MINUS ARCHED DISHED HOLLOW
SIMOUS VAULTY VAULTED
CRESCENT INCURVED
(SUFF.) COELOUS COELUS
CONCAVITY COVE DISH CONCHA
HOLLOW VENTER KNEEPAN
CONCEAL MEW WRY BURY DERN
FEAL HIDE KEEP LENE MASK
SCUG SILE VEIL VEST WRAP
BLIND BOSOM CACHE CLOAK
COUCH COVER FEIGN LAYNE
PLANT SHADE BURROW CLOSET
DOCTOR ELOIGN EMBOSS
HUDDLE HUGGER IMBOSK
OCCULT POCKET SCREEN
SHADOW SHIELD SHROUD STIFLE
VIZARD ABSCOND ENVELOP
OPPRESS PLASTER SECRETE
SMOTHER BESCREEN DISGUISE
ENSCONCE PALLIATE PRETENCE
PRETENSE WITHHOLD
(— A FUGITIVE) HARBOR
(— A TRAIL) TRASH
(— INFORMATION) LAYNE
(— TO AVOID TAX) SKIM
CONCEALED DERN SCUG SNUG
BLIND PRIVY BURROW COVERT
HIDDEN LATENT OCCULT PERDUE
SECRET VEILED COVERED
LARVATE WRAPPED
ABSTRUSE CRYPTOUS

HIDEAWAY RECONDITE
(— BY) BENEATH
(PREF.) ADEL(O)
CONCEALING DESIGNING
OBVELATION
CONCEALMENT MEW LAIN COVER
FRAUD NIGHT STALE SECRECY
CELATION VELATION SECRETION
(— OF TREASURE) MISPRISION
(IN —) DOGGO
CONCEDE OWN CEDE GIVE ADMIT
AGREE ALLOW GRANT WAIVE
YETTE YIELD ACCORD ASSENT
BETEEM CONFESS OTTROYE
BEGRUDGE ACKNOWLEDGE
(— AS ADVANTAGE) SPOT
CONCEIT EGO TOY IDEA SIDE
WIND CRANK FANCY KNACK
POESY PRIDE QUIRK BABERY
DEVICE NOTION VAGARY VANITY
BIGHEAD CAPRICE EGOTISM
OUTRAGE TYMPANY CONCETTO
FLIMFLAM
CONCEITED BUG BRAG COXY FESS
VAIN CHUFF COCKY FLORY HUFFY
PENSY PROUD SAUCY CLEVER
BIGGETY BIGGITY ARROGANT
DOGMATIC NOSEWISE PENSEFUL
PRIGGISH SNOBBISH
CONCEIVABLE EARTHLY POSSIBLE
CONCEIVE FORM HOLD MAKE
PLAN TEEM WEEN BEGIN BRAIN
CATCH DREAM FANCY FRAME
GUESS IMAGE THINK DESIGN
DEVISE IDEATE INTEND PONDER
SETTLE GESTATE IMAGINE
REALIZE SUPPOSE SUSPECT
COMPRISE CONTRIVE ENVISAGE
CONCENTRATE AIM FIX MASS PILE
BUNCH COACT EXALT FOCUS
PURSE UNIFY ARREST ATTEND
CENTER CITRIN DECOCT DISTIL
FIXATE GATHER SINGLE COMPACT
CONGEST DISTILL ENGROSS
ESSENCE EXTRACT THICKEN
ABSOLUTE APPROACH ASSEMBLE
CONDENSE CONTRACT FOCALIZE
GRADUATE
(— ORE) STRAKE
CONCENTRATED HARD DENSE
FIXED INTENT STRONG EXALTED
INTENSE
(NOT —) DIFFUSE
CONCENTRATION BRIX TITER
CENTER BALLING SAMADHI
ACTIVITY FIXATION PELMANISM
(— OF ARTILLERY FIRE) STONK
(— OF ENERGY) EXCITON
(— OF GRAPE JUICE) BESHMET
(— OF PLANTS) BED
(EXCESS —) MONOMANIA
CONCEPT GUT GUTS IDEA FANCY
IMAGE BEGRIFF CONCEIT OPINION
THOUGHT ABSOLUTE CATEGORY
PLURALISM PERCEPTION
CONCEPTION ENS IDEA VIEW
EIDOS FANCY FETUS IMAGE
BELIEF DESIGN EMBRYO ENTITY
NOTION CONCEIT CONCEPT
PROJECT PURPOSE
CATEGORY ESTHETIC
NOTATION RATIONAL
(— OF IDEA) HENT

(— OF ONESELF) BOVARISM BOVARYSM
(ABSTRACT —) ARCHETYPE
(FALSE —) IDOL DELUSION
(QUICKNESS OF —) PREGNANCY
CONCEPTUAL IDEAL NOTIONAL
CONCEPTUALISM SERMONISM
CONCERN BUG BEAR CARE FEAR
FIRM GEAR HAND PART RECK
SAKE APPLY CAUSE CERNE DRIVE
EVENT GRIEF HEART SORGE
STAND TOUCH WORRY AFFAIR
AFFECT BEHOLD CHARGE DIRECT
EMPLOY FINGER IMPORT MATTER
REGARD ANXIETY ARTICLE
BOTTLER COMPANY DISTURB
FUNERAL INVOLVE PERTAIN
RESPECT SHEBANG SOLICIT
TROUBLE BUSINESS HYPOTHEC
INTEREST JEALOUSY
(— ONESELF) DEAL PASS TOUCH
INTERMIT
(INDUSTRIAL —) COLOSSUS
(PRUDISH —) COMSTOCKERY
(SOMETHING CAUSING —)
ALBATROSS
(SPECIAL —) ACCENT
(WORLDLY —S) EARTH
(SUFF.) (— FOR) ITIS
CONCERNED INTENT ANXIOUS
VERSANT WORRIED ATWITTER
BOTHERED
CONCERNING BY OF ON RE TO
FOR TIL TILL ABOUT ANENT
ANENST APROPOS TOUCHING
CONCERT POP PLAN RECK UNITE
ACCORD DEVISE SMOKER
ARRANGE BENEFIT CONCENT
CONCORD CONSORT CONSULT
HARMONY POPULAR RECITAL
NEGOTIATE
CONCERTINA ORGAN LANTUM
SQUIFFER BANDONION
MELOPHONE
CONCESSION BOON FAVOR
GRANT LEASE STOOP ASSENT
GAMBIT OCTROY CESSION
EPITROPE MYNPACHT ADMISSION
ALLOWANCE PRIVILEGE
CONCESSIONAIRE GRIFTER
CONCH CONK PUNK SHELL COCKLE
MUSSEL STROMB STROMBUS
CONCIERGE PORTER SUISSE
WARDEN DVORNIK JANITOR
CONCILIATE GET CALM EASE GAIN
ATONE HONEY THING ADJUST
PACIFY SOFTEN ACQUIRE
APPEASE CONCILE MOLLIFY
PLACATE SATISFY PROPITIATE
CONCILIATOR ARBITRATOR
CONCILIATORY MILD SOFT
GENTLE GIVING IRENIC LENIENT
PACIFIC WINNING IRENICAL
LENITIVE TREATABLE
CONCISE CURT NEAT TRIG BRIEF
CRISP PITHY SHORT TERSE
COGENT CUTTED COMPACT
LACONIC POINTED PRECISE
SERRIED SUMMARY TABLOID
MUTILATE PREGNANT SUCCINCT
CONCISELY PRESSLY ELLIPTICALLY
CONCISENESS BREVITY ECONOMY
SYNTOMY FASTNESS

SYNTOMIA BRACHYOLOGY
CONCLAMATION SHOUT
CONCLAVE SOBOR CLOSET
CHAMBER MEETING AREOPAGY
ASSEMBLY
CONCLUDE BAR END AMEN FINE
REST TAKE CLOSE DRIVE ESTOP
INFER JUDGE LIMIT CLINCH
DECIDE DEDUCE EXPIRE FIGURE
FINISH GATHER INDUCE PERIOD
REASON RECKON SETTLE
ACHIEVE ARRANGE COLLECT
CONFINE EMBRACE ENCLOSE
RESOLVE SUPPOSE COMPLETE
DISPATCH ESTIMATE GRADUATE
PARCLOSE RESTRAIN
CONCLUDED OVER COMPLETE
CONCLUDING LAST DESITIVE
CONCLUSION END AMEN CODA
ERGO FINE LAST TERM CLOSE
ENVOY EVENT FINIS ISSUE LOOSE
POINT ENDING FINALE FINISH
PERIOD RESULT SEQUEL THIRTY
UPSHOT CLOSURE CURTAIN
FINDING OUTCOME SEQUELA
VERDICT APODOSIS DECISION
EPILOGUE FINALITY FRUITION
GODSPEED ILLATION ILLATIVE
JUDGMENT PARCLOSE SENTENCE
(— OF ARIA) CABALETTA
(FINAL —) ISSUE
(RANDOM —) SURMISE
(PL.) COLLATION
CONCLUSIVE LAST FINAL VALID
COGENT CERTAIN EVIDENT
EXTREME TELLING DECISIVE
DEFINITE ULTIMATE
CONCOCT MIX BREW COOK FAKE
PLAN PLOT VAMP FRAME HATCH
THINK DECOCT DEVISE DIGEST
INVENT MINGLE REFINE SCHEME
COMPOSE CONFECT PERFECT
PREPARE COMPOUND INTRIGUE
CONCOCTION PLAN PLOT MUMMY
DEVICE MUMMIA BREWING
MIXTURE SNEEZER BUSINESS
COMPOUND
CONCOMITANT SEQUELA
INCIDENT ACCESSORY ASSOCIATE
ATTENDANT ATTENDING
COMPANION CONJOINED
COOPERANT SATELLITE
CONCORD PART AGREE AMITY
PEACE TERMS UNION UNITY
TREATY UNISON COMPACT
CONCENT CONCERT HARMONY
ONENESS QUARTER COVENANT
SYMPATHY COMMUNITY
(— OF SOUNDS) SYMPHONIA
CONCORDANT UNISON TUNABLE
TUNEFUL HARMONIC UNISONAL
UNISONOUS
CONCOURSE CROWD HAUNT
PLACE POINT REPAIR RESORT
THRONG COMPANY ASSEMBLY
FREQUENCE
(INFERNAL —) HELL
CONCRESCENCE ADHESION
CONCRETE CLOT FIRM HARD REAL
BETON GROUT SOLID UNITE
ACTUAL CEMENT GUNITE
COMBINE CONGEAL SPECIAL
COALESCE COMPOUND POSITIVE

TANGIBLE AEROCRETE
CONCRETION CLOT KNOT MESS
FLINT FUSIL PEARL STONE
BEZOAR DOGGER NODULE
TOPHUS LITHITE OTOLITH
CALCULUS POTSTONE SEBOLITH
(— IN BAMBOO) TABASHIR
TABASHEER
CONCUBINAGE KARAO KAREWA
HETAERISM
CONCUBINE DASI MOLL HAGAR
RIZPAH BEDMATE HETAIRA
ODALISK MISTRESS ODALISQUE
CONCUPISCENCE DESIRE
CONCUPISCENT ANTSY
CONCUR HAND JIBE JOIN AGREE
CHECK CHIME UNITE ACCEDE
ACCORD ASSENT CONDOG
APPROVE COMBINE CONSENT
CONVENT COINCIDE CONSPIRE
CONVERGE
(— IN) SUBSCRIBE
CONCURRENCE UNION ASSENT
BESTOW CONSENT CONSORT
MEETING ADHESION SYNDROME
ADMISSION
CONCURRENT COEVAL UNITED
MEETING COPUNCTAL
CONCUSSION BUMP SHOCK
IMPACT ICEQUAKE COMMOTION
CONDEMN BAN CAST DAMN DEEM
DOOM FILE FINE HISS BLAME
BLESS DECRY JUDGE AMERCE
ATTAIN AWREAK BANISH DETEST
ADJUDGE CENSURE CONVICT
DENOUNCE FORJUDGE
REPROACH SENTENCE PROSCRIBE
CONDEMNATION BAN DOOM
BLAME CENSURE DECRIAL
BRICKBAT
CONDEMNATORY SEVERE
ADVERSE
CONDEMNED FATAL DAMNED
CONDENSATION BAN STORY
DIGEST CAPSULE BOILDOWN
CONDENSE CUT JIG BRIEF UNITE
DECOCT DIGEST HARDEN LESSEN
NARROW REDUCE SHRINK
ABRIDGE CAPSULE COMBINE
COMPACT DEFLATE DENSATE
DISTILL SHORTEN SQUEEZE
THICKEN COMPRESS CONTRACT
DIMINISH PEMMICAN SOLIDIFY
CONDENSED CURT BRIEF CAPSULE
COMPACT CONCISE SUMMARY
TABLOID ABSORBED
CONDENSER ALUDEL REFLUX
BALANCER CAPACITOR
CONDER HUER
CONDESCEND DEIGN FAVOR
GRANT STOOP ASSENT OBLIGE
SUBMIT CONCEDE DESCEND
CONDESCENDING AVUNCULAR
CONDESCENSION STOOP DISDAIN
COURTESY DIGNATION
CONDIGN DUE FIT FAIR JUST
SEVERE WORTHY ADEQUATE
SUITABLE
CONDIMENT SOY HERB KARI MACE
SAGE SALT CAPER CURRY DULCE
DULSE SAUCE SPICE THYME
AIWAIN AJOWAN CATSUP
CLOVES GARLIC PEPPER RELISH

SAMBAL TAMARA BADIANE
CANELLA CHUTNEY KETCHUP
MUSTARD OREGANO PAPRIKA
VINEGAR ALLSPICE BALACHAN
BLATJANG DRESSING SEASONER
TURMERIC
CONDITION IF AND FIG PLY WAY
CASE FORM HOOD MODE PASS
RANK ROTE TERM TIFF TRIM
ANGLE BIRTH CAUSE CENSE
CLASS COLOR COVIN ESTRE
FACET JOKER PLACE POINT
SHAPE STAGE STATE THEAT
WHACK AGENCY DEGREE
DONNEE ESTATE FETTLE GENTRY
MORALE MUSCLE PLIGHT STATUS
STRING ARTICLE CALLING
FEATHER FOOTING PLISKIE
PREMISE PREPARE PROVISO
STATION SUSPEND COVENANT
OCCASION POSITION PROTASIS
STANDING PREDICAMENT
REQUIREMENT
(— OF ANXIETY) CARK
(—,OF BODY) HEAT AFFECTION
(— OF FATIGUE) FRAZZLE
(— OF FLUCTUATION) EURIPUS
(— STATED BEFOREHAND) PREMISE
(BEING IN DIRTY —) GRUNGY
(CHANCE —) ACCIDENT
(DEBASED —) CACHEXY CACHEXIA
(DEPRESSED —) DOWNBEAT
(DETERMINING —) GROUND
(DIRTY —) CLAT
(DISEASED —) DIEBACK
(DISGRACEFUL —) IGNOMINY
(DRUNKEN —) BUN
(FLOURISHING —) HEALTH
(GENERAL —) VOGUE
(HABITUAL —) TENOR
(MEAN —) DUST
(MISERABLE —) SQUALOR
(MORBID —) HOLDOVER
(MOST APPROPRIATE —) CHECKER
(NECESSARY —) MEAN
(NEUROTIC —) LATAH
(ORDERLY —) DECENCY
(PAINFUL —) CRICK
(PERMANENT —) HEXIS
(PROPER —) KILTER
(PROTECTIVE —) CALLUS CALLOUS
(SCURFY —) BUCKSKIN
(STATIONARY —) JIB
(SUBLIME —) HEAVEN
(SURROUNDING —) AIR
(TRUE —) SIZE
(UNEQUAL —) ODDS
(UNPROSPEROUS —) ILLTH
(UNWHOLESOME —) MALADY
(WEATHER —S) ELEMENTS
(PL.) HAND TERMS STRINGS
(SUFF.) ACITY ATION DOM ERY
ICE ICITY ILITY ION ISM MENT
NESS OR OSIS SHIP TH TY
(MORBID —) IASIS
CONDITIONAL EVENTUAL
CONNEXIVE PROVISORY
QUALIFIED
CONDITIONED FINITE LIMITED
CONDITIONER DEGGER
CONDITIONING EDUCATION
HYPOTHESIS
CONDOLENCE PITY RUTH

EMPATHY SYMPATHY
CONDONE BLINK REMIT ACQUIT
EXCUSE FORGET IGNORE PARDON
ABSOLVE FORGIVE OVERLOOK
CONDOR TIFFIN BUZZARD
VULTURE
CONDUCE GO AID HELP HIRE LEAD
TEND BRING GUIDE CONFER
EFFECT ENGAGE ADVANCE
CONDUCT FURTHER REDOUND
CONDUCT ACT CON RUN USE WIN
BEAR CALL COND CONN DEED
FACT FARE FIRK FORM GARB
GEST HAND KEEP LEAD MIEN
PLAY QUIT RULE SHOW TAKE
WAGE WALK BATON CARRY
CHAIR DRESS DRIVE FETCH GESTE
GUARD GUIDE HABIT MAYNE
SITHE TRADE TRAIN USAGE
USHER ACTION ATTEND BEHAVE
COLORS CONVEY CONVOY
COURSE DEDUCE DEMEAN
DEPORT DIRECT ESCORT GOVERN
INDUCT MANAGE MANNER
SQUIRE ACTIONS BEARING
CHANNEL COMPERE COMPORT
CONDITE CONDUCE CONDUIT
CONTAIN CONTROL EXECUTE
GALLANT GESTION OFFICER
OPERATE WIREWAY ARRIVISM
BEHAVIOR CARRIAGE CHAPLAIN
COURTESY DEMEANOR GUIDANCE
REGULATE SHEPHERD TRANSACT
(— ONESELF) DO ACT ACQUIT
BEHAVE BESTOW DEMEAN
DEPORT COMFORT CONTAIN
DISPORT ENTREAT MAINTAIN
(APPROPRIATE —) DHARMA
(BRASH —) FACE
(CONVENTIONAL —) PRAXIS
(DISORDERLY —) RANDAN
(DORMANT —) LATENCY
(ETHICAL —) HONOR
(PROPER —) CRICKET
(RECKLESS —) DEVILRY DEVILTRY
(RIGHT —) TE TAO
(RIOTOUS —) RANDAN
(SAFE —) KOWL COWLE
(SEDITIOUS —) MISPRISION
(SHOWY —) BRAVADO
(SLOPPY —) SWASH
(VAINGLORIOUS —) HEROICS
(WANTON —) RUFF
(WEAK —) FOLLY
CONDUCTANCE G
(UNIT OF —) MHO SIEMENS
CONDUCTION COURSING
CONDUCTOR CON BOND CADE
LEAD MAIN BRUSH GUARD
SHUNT SPOUT TRUNK BRIDGE
BUSMAN CARMAN CONVOY
COPPER ESCORT FEEDER LEADER
OFFSET RETURN CAPTAIN
CATHODE MAESTRO MANAGER
AQUEDUCT BATONIST CICERONE
CONVEYOR DIRECTOR EMPLOYEE
FILAMENT STICKMAN ANELECTRIC
(— OF FESTIVAL) SKUDLER
(ELECTRIC —) FILAMENT
(LIGHTNING —) ROD
(OMNIBUS —) CAD
(WOMAN —) CLIPPIE
(PL.) SERVICE

(SUFF.) EER
CONDUIT BOSS DUCT GOUT MAIN
PIPE SINK TUBE WIRE CABLE
CANAL CUNDY SEWER STACK
HEADER SLUICE TROUGH
CARRIER CHANNEL CHIMNEY
CONDITE CONDUCT CULVERT
CUNDITE EXHAUST FOGGARA
LATERAL LAUNDER PASSAGE
WIREWAY AQUEDUCT OLEODUCT
PENSTOCK WASTEWAY
(PL.) LIMBERS
CONDYLOMA SYCOMA
CONE CAP YOW CHAT KING MOXA
PINA TOOT CONUS CRACK SCREW
SHAPE SPIRE YOWIE BOBBIN
CONOID MONTRE PASTIL
CLUSTER CONELET CONIOLE
FISSURE FRUSTUM PROLONG
PYRAMID STROBIL THIMBLE
CANNELON DUMPLING GALBULUS
PASTILLE PINECONE STROBILE
STROBILUS
(— OF CLOTH) VANE
(— OF FIR) YOW YOWIE STROBIL
STROBILE STROBILUS
(— OF GUNPOWDER) PEEOY
(— OF HOP PLANT) BUR BURR
(— OF SILVER AMALGAM) PINA
(— ON LOG END) CAP
(— ON SHOE) CLEAT
(— STRUCTURE) NURAGHE
(HALF —) FORME NAPPE
(ICE CREAM —) ICE CORNET
(INVERTED —) HOPPER
(PAPER —) SPILL CUFFIN
(ROPE-MAKING —) TOP
(TOP CUT FROM —) UNGULA
(VOLCANIC —) PUY MONTICULE
(PL.) HOPS
(PREF.) CON(I)(ICO)(O) STROBILI
CONENOSE BEDBUG BARBEIRO
CONESTOGA WAGON CARAVAN
CONEY CONY HYRAX HYRACID
GUATIBERO
CONFAB CHAT TALK POWWOW
CONFLAB PRATTLE
CONFECTION CHOW MOSS CANDY
DULCE MEBOS SWEET BONBON
COCKLE COMFIT DAINTY DRAGEE
HALVAH JUNKET MAJOON
NOUGAT SWEETY TABLET
CARAMEL CONFECT FONDANT
MIXTURE POMFRET PRALINE
SEATRON SUCCADE ANGELICA
CHOWCHOW CODINIAC
COMPOUND CONSERVE DELICACY
MARZIPAN PRESERVE QUIDDANY
SUBTLETY MARSHMALLOW
CONFECTIONERY CIMBAL
CONFISERIE
CONFEDERACY BUND COVIN
CREEK JUNTA KEDAR UNION
COVINE LEAGUE COMPLOT
ALLIANCE COVENANT FEDERACY
ILLINOIS BLACKFOOT
CONFEDERATE AID PAL REB ALLY
BAND PUFF COVER REBEL STALL
UNITE LEAGUE SANTAR ABETTER
ABETTOR CONJURE FEDARIE
FEDERAL FEODARY PARTNER
STEERER CONSPIRE FEDERARY
FEDERATE

(— SOLDIER) CONFED JOHNNY
GRAYBACK GRAYCOAT GREYBACK
(PICKPOCKET'S —) STALL
CONFEDERATION BODY BUND
ZUPA GUEUX UNION LEAGUE
COMPACT HASINAI SOCIETY
ALLIANCE COVENANT
CONFER DUB GIVE MEET TALK
AWARD ENDOW FEOFF GRANT
INFER PARLE SPEND TREAT
ADVISE BESTOW COMMON
CONFAB DONATE ENTAIL HUDDLE
IMPARL IMPART INVEST PARLEY
POWWOW COLLATE COMMUNE
COMPARE CONDUCE CONSULT
CONTACT COUNSEL DISCUSS
INSTATE PRESENT COLLOGUE
COMPRISE CONVERGE NEGOTIATE
(— DEGREE UPON) CAP
(— KNIGHTHOOD UPON) DUB
CONFERENCE DIET TALK SYNOD
TREAT TRUST CAUCUS CONFAB
HUDDLE INDABA KORERO PARLEY
PARVIS POWWOW SUMMIT
CIRCUIT COUNCIL MEETING
PALAVER PARLING SEMINAR
COLLOQUE COLLOQUY CONCLAVE
CONGRESS PRACTICE PRACTISE
TUTORIAL PARLIAMENT
(SCIENCE —) PUGWASH
CONFERRING GRANT DATION
CONFESS OWN AVOW FESS KNOW
SING ADMIT GRANT KITHE
ACKNOW AGNISE ATTEST
AVOUCH BEKNOW COUTHE
RENDER REVEAL SHRIFT SHRIVE
SQUEAK CONCEDE DIVULGE
PROFESS WHITTLE DISBOSOM
DISCLOSE DISCOVER MANIFEST
ACKNOWLEDGE
CONFESSION ALHET CREDO
CREED GRANT AVOWAL SHRIFT
SHRIVE VIDDUI ASHAMNU
FORMULA PECCAVI COGNOVIT
(MUTUAL —) SHARING
CONFESSIONAL SHRIFT MALCHUS
CONFESSOR FATHER SHRIFT
SHRIVER
CONFIDANT PRIVY FRIEND
INWARD PRIVADO INTIMATE
CONFIDE AFFY RELY TELL TRUST
COMMIT DEPEND LIPPEN BELIEVE
CONSIGN ENTRUST INTRUST
(— IN) VENTURE
CONFIDENCE FACE HARK HOPE
BIELD CHEEK FAITH STOCK TRUST
APLOMB BELIEF CREDIT FIANCE
FIDUCE METTLE MORALE SECRET
SPIRIT SURETY COUNSEL
COURAGE PRIVITY AFFIANCE
BOLDNESS CREDENCE RELIANCE
SECURITY SURENESS
CONFIDENT BOLD SMUG SURE
COCKY CRANK HARDY SIKER
CROUSE SECURE SICKER TRAIST
ASSURED CERTAIN HOPEFUL
RELIANT CONSTANT FEARLESS
FIDUCIAL IMPUDENT POSITIVE
SANGUINE TRUSTFUL
CONFIDENTIAL PACK BOSOM
PRIVY CLOSET COVERT HUSHED
INWARD SECRET PRIVATE
ESOTERIC FAMILIAR INTIMATE

CONFIDING TRUSTY CREDENT
RELIANT TRUSTFUL CONFIDENT
CONFIGURATION FORM SHAPE
FIGURE BANDING CONTOUR
DIAMOND GESTALT OUTLINE
GEOMETRY POSITURE
OPPOSITION PERSPECTIVE
(CELESTIAL —) SYZYGY
CONFINE BAR BOX CUB DAM HEM
MEW NUN PEN PIN STY TIE BAIL
BIND BOOM CAGE COOP CRIB
FOLD HASP JAIL KEEP LACE LOCK
PEND SEAL SHUT SPAN STEW
STOP STOW BOUND CABIN CHAIN
COART CRAMP CROWD DELAY
FENCE HOUSE LIMIT MARCH
PINCH POUND STICK STINT THIRL
BORDER BOTTLE COARCT CORRAL
EMBANK FETTER FORBAR
HAMPER HURDLE IMMURE
IMPALE IMPARK INTERN KENNEL
PINION POCKET PRISON STRAIN
TETHER ASTRICT CHAMBER
COMPASS CONTAIN IMPOUND
INCLUDE MANACLE PINFOLD
POISTER RECLOSE SECLUDE
SHACKLE TRAMMEL BASTILLE
BOUNDARY CLOISTER CONCLUDE
DISTRAIN FOCALIZE
IMPRISON RESTRAIN
STRAITEN
(PL.) AMBIT PURLIEU PERIPHERY
CONFINED ILL FAST PENT BOUND
CAGED CLOSE CRAMP BEDRID
IMPALE IMPENT PENTIT SEALED
CAPTIVE CRAMPED CRIBBED
LIMITED SQUEEZY IMPENDED
IMPLICIT INTERNED
PAROCHIAL
(— TO CERTAIN AREA) ENDEMIC
(— TO SELECT GROUP) ESOTERIC
CONFINEMENT MEW BOND HOLD
JAIL WARD CRYING GATING
DURANCE INLYING JANKERS
WARDING CLAUSURE
FIRMANCE GROANING
SOLITARY
CONFINING NARROW
CONFIRM FIX SET FIRM SEAL
PROVE VOUCH AFFEER AFFIRM
ASSENT ASSURE ATTEST AVOUCH
BISHOP CLINCH FASTEN HARDEN
RATIFY REABLE SECOND SETTLE
STABLE VERIFY APPROVE
COMFORT COMPACT CONSIGN
ENDORSE FORTIFY JUSTIFY
PROPORT SUPPORT SUSTAIN
THICKEN ACCREDIT CONVINCE
CORROBER ENTRENCH INSTRUCT
SANCTION STRENGTH
VALIDATE CORROBORATE
REDETERMINE
CONFIRMATION PROOF CHRISM
SANCTION
CONFIRMED SET FIXED SWORN
ARRANT STABLE CERTAIN
CHRONIC AFFEERED HABITUAL
HARDENED RATIFIED
CONFISCATE GRAB SEIZE USURP
CONDEMN CONFISK ESCHEAT
PUBLISH DISTRAIN
CONFISCATION ESCHEAT
INCENSION

CONFLAGRATION FIRE BLAZE FEVER BURNING INFERNO

CONFLICT JAR WAR AGON BATE BOUT BUMP CAMP DUEL FRAY MEET MUSS RIFT AGONY BROIL BRUSH CLASH FIGHT GRIPS STOUR ACTION BATTLE COMBAT MUTINY OPPOSE SCRAPE SHOWER STRIFE CONTEND CONTEST DISCORD SCUFFLE WARFARE ANTIMONY CLASHING DISAGREE MILITATE SKIRMISH STRIVING STRUGGLE COLLISION COLLUCTATION
(DRAMATIC —) AGON
(FINAL —) ARMAGEDDON

CONFLICTING ADVERSE ABHORRENT

CONFLUENCE FORK CROWD INFALL CONFLUX MEETING JUNCTION

CONFORM DO GO FIT HEW BEND LEAN OBEY SORT SUIT ABIDE ADAPT AGREE APPLY SHAPE YIELD ACCEDE ADJUST ASSENT COMPLY CONFER SETTLE SQUARE SUBMIT COMPOSE CONFIRM
(— TO) KEEP MEET ANSWER BEHAVE SATISFY

CONFORMABLE DONE SUING SUITED CONFORM PURSUANT QUADRANT

CONFORMATION FORM BUILD
(MENTAL —) SAMSKARA

CONFORMING FAIR SAME COMELY DECENT CORRECT CONGRUOUS

CONFORMIST BOY COMPLIER

CONFORMITY FIT ACCORD DHARMA EQUITY HARMONY JUSTICE KEEPING ACCURACY AFFINITY JUSTNESS LIKENESS SYMMETRY CONGRUITY FORMALITY ACCORDANCE CONSERTION
(— TO LAW) DECENCY LEGALITY

CONFOUND MIX BLOW DASH MATE MAZE ROUT STAM STUN WHIP ABASH ADDLE AMAZE APPAL BLAST FOUND SHEND SPOIL STUMP WASTE AWHAPE BAFFLE BUNKER COMMIT DISMAY DUDDER MINGLE MUDDLE RABBIT RATTLE ASTOUND BUMBAZE CONFUSE CONFUTE CORRUPT DESTROY FLUMMOX FORLESE MISTAKE NONPLUS PERPLEX PETRIFY STUMBLE STUPEFY ASTONISH BABELIZE BEWILDER DISTRACT DUMFOUND SURPRISE SPIFLICATE

CONFOUNDED MATE BALLY BLAME RUDDY BLAMED DEUCED POCKED BLASTED BLESSED MURRAIN PEEVISH DUMMERED JIGGERED SWITCHED CONSARNED
(BE —) ABAVE ABAWE

CONFRATERNITY BODY UNION SOCIETY CONFRAIRY

CONFRONT DARE DEFY FACE MEET NOSE BEARD BRACE BRAVE CROSS FRONT STAND ACCOST ASSAIL BREAST OPPOSE RESIST VISAGE AFFRONT COMPARE OUTFACE PROPOSE ENVISAGE THREATEN

CONFRONTING BEFORE ADVERSE ABUTTING CONFRONT

CONFUSE BOX FOX MIX BALL DASH DAZE DOIT DOZE DUST GAUM HARL MAZE MUSS ROIL ROUT ABASH ADDLE AMAZE BEFOG BITCH BLEND CLOUD DEAVE DIZZY MUDDY SHEND SHENT SNARL STEER TWIST UPSET BAFFLE BEDAZE BEMUSE BOTHER BURBLE CADDLE COMMIT CORPSE DUDDER DUDDLE FLURRY FUDDLE GRAVEL JUMBLE MADDLE MAFFLE MAMMER MASKER MIZZLE MOIDER MOMBLE MUDDLE PUZZLE RAFFLE RATTLE TWITCH WIMPLE BECLOUD BEDEVIL BLUNDER BUMBAZE DERANGE DIFFUSE EMBROIL FLUSTER GARBOIL GIDDIFY MISTAKE MYSTIFY NONPLUS PERPLEX PERTURB SCATTER SHUFFLE STUPEFY UNRAVEL BEFUDDLE BEWILDER CONFLATE CONFOUND DISORDER DISTRACT DUMFOUND ENTANGLE MISORDER SQUATTER OBFUSCATE
(— AN ACTOR) CORPSE
(— BY NOISE) DUDDER

CONFUSED ASEA LOST ADDLE DIZZY FOGGY FUZZY HEAVY MISTY MUDDY MUZZY VAGUE WESTY WOOLY BLOTTO CLOUDY DOILED DOITED DRUMLY JUMBLY MEDLEY MOPISH MUSHED SHAGGY TAVERT WOOLLY BEMUSED BLURRED CHAOTIC CLOUDED CONFUSE DIFFUSE MIFFLED OBSCURE RATTLED STUPENT COCKEYED DERANGED FLURRIED INVOLVED MUDDLEHEADED

CONFUSING DIZZY MAZEFUL BAFFLING BLINDING DIZZYING

CONFUSION PI DIN PIE COIL DUST FLAP FUSS HARL MESS MOIL RIOT AMAZE ATAXY BABEL CHAOS CHEVY CHIVY DERAY FRASE HAVOC HURLY LARRY LURRY SNAFU SNARL STROW ATAXIA BABBLE BAFFLE BALLUP BEDLAM BUMBLE CHIVVY DUDDER FRAISE HABBLE HOBBLE HUBBUB HUDDLE JABBLE JUMBLE MASTIC MUCKER MUDDLE POTHER PUCKER RABBLE RUFFLE RUMPUS THRONG TOPHET TUMULT UPROAR WELTER ANARCHY BLUNDER BLUSTER CLUTTER COBWEBS FARRAGE FLUTTER GARBOIL HURLING KIPPAGE LOUSTER MISMAZE MISRULE ROOKERY RUMMAGE SCADDLE SCOWDER TOPHETH TURMOIL WHEMMEL WIDDRIM BABELISM DISARRAY DISORDER EQUIVOKE HOOROOSH SCOUTHER SHAMBLES SPLUTTER STRAMASH TOHUBOHU

CONFUTATION DISPROOF

CONFUTE DENY EVICT REBUT EVINCE EXPOSE REFUTE FALSIFY IMPROVE SILENCE SUBVERT CONCLUDE CONFOUND CONVINCE DISPROVE INFRINGE OVERCOME REDARGUE

CONGEAL GEL ICE SET GEAL JELL CANDY COTTER CURDLE FREEZE HARDEN STIFFEN STORKEN THICKEN CONCRETE SOLIDIFY
(— INTO HOARFROST) RIME

CONGEALED FROZEN

CONGELATION FROST

CONGENER BEAVER DOTTREL DOTTEREL

CONGENIAL SIB BOON HAPPY NATAL NATIVE AMIABLE CONNATE KINDRED

CONGENITAL INNATE CONNATE CONNATAL GENETOUS

CONGERIES CALCULARY COLLECTION

CONGEST STUFF IMPACT

CONGESTED INJECTED

CONGESTION JAM HEAP LAMPAS LAMPERS CROWDING STOPPAGE

CONGLOMERATE HEAP MASS PILE ROCK STACK BANKET PSEPHITE NAGELFLUH
(-S OF JAPAN) ZAIBATSU

CONGLOMERATION HUDDLE GLOMMOX IMBROGLIO

CONGO MUMMY ASPHALTUM

CONGO

CAPITAL: BRAZZAVILLE
COIN: FRANC FRANCCFA
LAKE: MWERU TUMBA UPEMBA LEOPOLD
NATIVE: SUSA VILI MANTU PYGMY BATEKE MBOCHI WABUMA BAKONGO BANGALA
PLATEAU: BATEKE
RIVER: UELE CONGO KWILU LULUA NGOKO NIARI SANGA WAMBA KWENGE LOANGE SANGHA UBANGI KOUILOU LUBILASH
TOWN: EWO EPENA HOLLE JACOB OKOYO SEMBE MAKOUA OUESSO ZANAGA DOLISIE ENYELLE LOUBOMO SOUANKE DJAMBALA BRAZZAVILLE
TRIBUTARY: LOMAMI UBANGI ARUWIMA LUALABA LUAPULA ITIMBIRI

CONGOU KEEMUN

CONGRATULATE HUG JOY LAUD GREET SALUTE FLATTER MACARIZE

CONGRATULATION PARABIEN
(PL.) GRATTERS

CONGREGATE HERD MASS MEET PACK TEEM GROUP SWARM TROOP GATHER MUSTER COLLECT CONVENE ASSEMBLE

CONGREGATION PEW BODY FOLD HERD HOST MASS FLOCK SAMAJ SWARM CHURCH PARISH COMPANY MEETING ORATORY SYNAXIS ASSEMBLY

BRETHREN CHAPELRY
(— OF WITCHES) COVEN
(JEWISH —) KOLEL ALJAMA SYNAGOG
(PL.) CHARGE

CONGRESS MOD DAIL DIET SYNOD UYEZD OBLAST OUYEZD POWWOW COUNCIL GORSEDD MEETING ASSEMBLY CONCLAVE

CONGRESSMAN SENATOR DOUGHFACE

CONGRUITY ACCORD CONCORD FITNESS HARMONY KEEPING SYMMETRY COHERENCE

CONGRUOUS CONGRUE HARMONIC SUITABLE ACCORDING

CONICAL CONIC TAPER COPPED MITRAL COPPLED TAPERING
(PREF.) TURBIN(I)(O) TURBINATO

CONICALLY
(PREF.) TURBINATO

CONIDIUM CIDIUM ARTHROSPORE

CONIFER FIR YEW PINE CEDAR LARCH SPRUCE SOFTWOOD EVERGREEN

CONIFERAE PINALES

CONIUM HEMLOCK

CONJECTURE AIM CAST PLOT ROVE SHOT VIEW AUGUR ETTLE FANCY GUESS OPINE THINK BELIEF DIVINE THEORY CONJECT IMAGINE OPINION PRESUME SUPPOSE SURMISE SUSPECT HINDCAST SUPPOSAL

CONJOIN JOIN KNIT ATTEND EMPALE IMPALE ALLIGATE

CONJOINED JOINED JUGATE LINKED JUGATED CONJUNCT TOUCHING

CONJOINTLY JUNCTLY TOGETHER

CONJUGAL SPOUSAL CONNUBIAL

CONJUGATE YOKED JOINED UNITED COUPLED INFLECT PARONYMOUS

CONJUGATION SYNGAMY ZYGOSIS CYTOGAMY ENDOGAMY SYNOPSIS

CONJUNCTION AS ET IF OR AND BUT NOR TIE THAN JOINT SINCE SYNOD UNION UNITY THOUGH COITION CONSORT JOINDER CONJUNCT RATIONAL
(PREF.) (IN —) CO

CONJUNCTURE SEASON

CONJURATION ART CHARM MAGIC SPELL VOODOO EXORCISM

CONJURE PRAY WISH CHARM HALSE ADJURE ENJOIN INVENT INVOKE SUMMON BESEECH COMBINE ENTREAT IMAGINE CONSPIRE CONTRIVE EXORCIZE
(— UP) RAISE

CONJURE MAN CUNJAH CUNJER GOOFER GUFFER

CONJURER MAGE PELLAR POWWOW SHAMAN WIZARD JUGGLER WARLOCK WIELARE ANGEKKOK JONGLEUR MAGICIAN PYTHONIC SORCERER

CONJURING JADU JADOO CONJURY VOODOOISM

CONK FAIL HEAD KONK NOSE FAINT KNOCK STALL BRACKET

CONNECT COG PUT TIE ALLY BIND

BOND GEAR GLUE JOIN KNIT KNOT LINK AFFIX CHAIN MARRY NITCH UNITE ATTACH BRIDGE CEMENT COHERE COMMIT CONNEX COUPLE ENLINK FASTEN RELATE SPLICE COMBINE ENCHAIN INVOLVE APPARENT CATENATE CONTINUE DOVETAIL INTERTIE
(— TREADLE) CORD
CONNECTED ALLIED CONNEX AFFINED COUPLED HANGING
(— WITH) ABOUT
(ELECTRICALLY —) ALIVE
(NOT —) FOREIGN ASYNARTETE
(SYNTACTICALLY —) ABSOLUTE
(SUFF.) (— WITH) ARIA ARIUM AST ORIAL

CONNECTICUT
CAPITAL: HARTFORD
COLLEGE: TRINITY
COUNTY: TOLLAND WINDHAM
INDIAN: PEQUOT MOHEGAN
　　NIANTIC
STATE BIRD: ROBIN
STATE FLOWER: LAUREL
STATE NICKNAME: NUTMEG
STATE TREE: OAK
TOWN: AVON BETHEL CANAAN
　　COSCOB DARIEN MYSTIC
　　SHARON STORRS WILTON
　　DANBURY MERIDEN NIANTIC
　　NORWALK NORWICH TOLLAND
　　WINDSOR NEWHAVEN
　　RINGDUNN WESTPORT
　　GREENWICH RIDGEFIELD
UNIVERSITY: YALE WESLEYAN

CONNECTING BETWEEN SYNDETIC
CONNECTION Y HUB TAP TIE BOND LINK HITCH NEXUS UNION BUCKLE CLEVIS FAMILY GROUND REPORT SUTURE SWIVEL BEARING BOLSTER CONTACT DESCENT FERRULE HOLDING KINSHIP LIAISON RAPPORT SIAMESE SIBNESS SOCIETY AFFINITY ALLIANCE COMMERCE CONNEXUS INTIMACY JUNCTION LIGATION RELATIVE SYNDETIC RELATIONSHIP
(ELECTRICAL —) GROUND
(FORKED —) BRANCH
(MECHANICAL —S) LEADOUT
CONNECTIVE IZAFAT SUTURAL JUNCTION LIGATIVE SYNDETIC VINCULAR
CONNING TOWER SAIL
CONNIVANCE CAHOOT CAHOOTS
CONNIVE ABET PLOT WINK BLINK CABAL ASSENT FOMENT INCITE COLLUDE
(— AT MEDICAL TREATMENT) COVER
CONNOISSEUR JUDGE CRITIC EXPERT CAMEIST EPICURE GOURMET CIDERIST DILETANT LAPIDARY COGNOSCENTE MEDIEVALIST
CONNOTATION DEPTH INTENT MEANING
CONNUBIAL MARITAL

CONJUGAL DOMESTIC
CONQUER GET WIN BEAT BEST DOWN FIRK GAIN LICK ROUT TAME WHIP CRUSH DAUNT DEBEL EVICT DEBELL DEFEAT EVINCE HUMBLE IMPORT MASTER REDUCE SUBDUE VICTOR ACQUIRE PREVAIL SUBJECT SURPASS TRIUMPH OVERCOME OVERGANG SURMOUNT VANQUISH
CONQUEROR HERO MASTER VICTOR WINNER TRIUMPHER
CONQUEST MASTERY SCALING TRIUMPH VICTORY WINNING
CONSANGUINEOUS AKIN CARNAL KINDRED NATURAL RELATED
CONSANGUINITY BLOOD NASAB KINSHIP AFFINITY
CONSCIENCE WORD DAENA HEART INWIT SENSE SCRUPLE THOUGHT
CONSCIENTIOUS FAIR JUST EXACT RIGID EIDENT HONEST STRICT DUTIFUL UPRIGHT FAITHFUL
CONSCIENTIOUSNESS RELIGION
CONSCIOUS KEEN WARE ALIVE AWAKE AWARE JERRY GUILTY FEELING KNOWING WITTING RATIONAL SENSIBLE SENTIENT CONSCIENT
CONSCIOUSNESS EGO HEART SENSE SPIRIT ANOESIS FEELING THOUGHT SENTIENT AWARENESS PERCEPTION
(HALF —) DOVER
CONSCRIPT LEVY CHOCO DRAFT ENROL ENLIST MUSTER DRAFTEE DRAUGHT RECRUIT JEANJEAN
CONSCRIPTION LEVY
CONSECRATE VOW FAIN HOLY SAIN SEAL BLESS DEIFY HEAVE SACRE ANOINT DEVOTE HALLOW ORDAIN SACRATE CONSACRE DEDICATE SANCTIFY
CONSECRATED BLEST OBLATE SACRED VOTARY VOTIVE BLESSED SACRATE HALLOWED HIERATIC
CONSECRATION IHRAM SACRE SACRY SACRING DEVOTION HOLINESS
CONSECUTIVELY TOGETHER
CONSECUTIVENESS SEQUENCE
CONSENT HEAR AGREE ALLOW GRANT YIELD ACCEDE ACCORD AFFORD ASSENT BETEEM COMPLY CONCUR PERMIT APPROVE GOODWILL PERMISSION
CONSENTIENT UNANIMOUS
CONSEQUENCE AND END BORE EVENT FORCE FRUIT ISSUE SUITE WORTH BROWST CHARGE EFFECT ENTAIL FIGURE GROWTH IMPORT MOMENT REPUTE RESULT SEQUEL WEIGHT CONCERN OUTCOME PRODUCE PURPOSE SEQUELA SEQUENT BACKLASH INTEREST MISCHIEF OCCASION SEQUITUR COROLLARY OUTGROWTH CONSECTARY RAMIFICATION
(DONE IN —) PURSUANT

(HARMFUL —) EVIL
(PERSON OF —) HEAVY
(PL.) AFTERINGS
CONSEQUENT COMES THESIS ADJUNCT
CONSEQUENTIAL HEAVY POMPOUS COROLLARY MOMENTOUS
CONSEQUENTLY SO ERGO THEN THUS HENCE LATER PURSUANT PRESENTLY
CONSERTAL SUTURAL
CONSERVATION HUSBANDRY
CONSERVATISM BOURBONISM
CONSERVATIVE SAFE TORY FUSTY QUIET STAID FABIAN HUNKER STABLE BOURBON DIEHARD HARDHAT MODERATE UNIONIST
CONSERVATORY STOVE SCHOOL ACADEMY
CONSERVE CAN JAM SAVE GUARD GUMBO JELLY DEFEND SECURE SHIELD UPHOLD HUSBAND PROTECT SEATRON SUSTAIN MAINTAIN PRESERVE
(GRAPE —) UVATE
CONSIDER AIM BAT LET SEE CALL CAST DEEM GAUM GIVE HASH HEED HOLD MULL MUSE RATE SEEM TAKE TALE VIEW VISE WISE ALLOW BESEE COUNT ENTER ETTLE JUDGE PANSE POISE SPELL STUDY THINK VERSE VOLVE WEIGH ADVERT ADVISE BEHOLD DEBATE DEVISE DIGEST ESTEEM EXPEND FIGURE IMPUTE PONDER REASON RECKON REGARD REWARD SURVEY ACCOUNT BELIEVE BETHINK CANVASS CONSULT EXAMINE INSPECT PERPEND PREPEND REFLECT RESPECT REVOLVE SUPPOSE COGITATE ESTIMATE MEDITATE PERPENSE RUMINATE
(— FAVORABLY) CREDIT
(— PROS AND CONS) ARGUE
(— SEPARATELY) SPECIALIZE
CONSIDERABLE GAY GEY FAIR GOOD TIDY BONNY CANNY GEYAN GREAT LARGE SMART STARK GOODLY PRETTY GOODISH HEALTHY INTENSE NOTABLE SEVERAL HANDSOME POWERFUL SENSIBLE UNLITTLE
CONSIDERABLY GAY GEY WELL GEYAN PRETTY SMARTLY
CONSIDERATE KIND MILD NICE GENTLE TENDER CAREFUL HEEDFUL PRUDENT SERIOUS TACTFUL DELICATE GRACIOUS ATTENTIVE
CONSIDERATENESS GRACE
(MUTUAL —) SHU
CONSIDERATION GUT GUTS SAKE COUNT PRICE STUDY TOPIC ADVICE ASPECT COMITY DEBATE ESTEEM MOMENT MOTIVE NOTICE REASON REFLEX REGARD SURVEY ACCOUNT INSIGHT PREMIUM RESPECT THOUGHT ALTRUISM COURTESY DELICACY EMINENCE EMPHASIS GRATUITY PROSPECT SANCTION

(BASIC —) BEDROCK
(ETHICAL —) SCRUPLE
(THOUGHTFUL —) THEORIA
CONSIDERED ADVISED DELIBERATE
CONSIDERING IF FOR SINCE SEEING
CONSIGN DOOM GIVE MAIL SEND SHIP ALLOT AWARD CHECK DIGHT REMIT SHIFT YIELD ASSIGN COMMIT DESIGN DEVOTE REMAND RESIGN ADDRESS BETEACH CONFIDE DELIVER DEPOSIT ENTRUST INTRUST BEQUEATH DELEGATE RELEGATE TRANSFER
(— FOR DESTRUCTION) ACCURSE
(— TO OBLIVION) BURY EXPUNGE
(— TO PERDITION) DAMN CONDEMN
CONSIGNEE AGENT FACTOR SHIPPER RECEIVER
CONSIGNMENT INVOICE FOREDOOM SHIPMENT
(— OF TEA) BREAK
CONSIST LIE HOLD RELY REST DWELL EXIST STAND INHERE RESIDE CONTAIN EMBRACE COMPRISE
CONSISTENCY BODY UNION DEGREE CONCENT CONCORD HARMONY KEEPING COMPAGES EVENNESS FIRMNESS SOLIDITY SYMMETRY
CONSISTENT EVEN FIRM STEADY DURABLE LOGICAL REGULAR UNIFORM COHERENT ENDURING SUITABLE COMPATIBLE SEQUACIOUS
(— WITH NATURE) KIND KINDLY
(BE —) ACCORD
(MAKE —) CLEAR
CONSISTING
(PREF.) DIA
(SUFF.) (— OF) IC(AL)
CONSOCIES
(SUFF.) ETUM
CONSOLATION SOP FINE RELIEF SOLACE COMFORT SPIRITING
CONSOLE CALM ALLAY ANCON CHEER ORGAN TABLE SOLACE SOOTHE BRACKET CABINET COMFORT RELIEVE SUPPORT SUSTAIN CARTOUCH
CONSOLER PARACLETE
CONSOLIDATE COG MIX KNIT MASS POOL WELD BLEND CLOSE MERGE UNIFY UNITE HARDEN MINGLE SETTLE COMBINE COMPACT ANKYLOSE COALESCE COMPRESS CONDENSE ORGANIZE SOLIDIFY
CONSOLIDATED CONFLATE
CONSOLS GOSCHENS
CONSOMME MADRILENE
CONSONANCE ACCORD UNISON HARMONY DIAPASON DIAPENTE SYMPATHY SYMPHONY
CONSONANT WAW MUTE STOP DENTAL FORTIS LABIAL LETTER LIQUID SONANT UNISON LATERAL MUTABLE PALATAL PLOSIVE SPIRANT UNIFIED ALVEOLAR

ASPIRATA ASPIRATE BILABIAL EJECTIVE GEMINATE HARMONIC SUITABLE
(CONSECUTIVE —S) CLUSTER
(SMOOTH —) LENE LENIS
(TENSE AND STRONG —) FORTIS
(VOICELESS —) SURD SPIRATE
CONSORT COT AIDE ALLY JOIN MATE MOUP WIFE YOKE GROUP TROOP UNITE ACCORD ATTEND ESCORT MINGLE SPOUSE COMPANY COMRADE CONCERT DAMKINA EMPRESS HUSBAND PARTNER ACCUSTOM ASSEMBLY PRINCESS
(VISHNU'S —) LAKSHMI
CONSPECTUS LIST APERCU SURVEY OUTLINE THEATER THEORIC SPECTRUM SYNOPSIS
CONSPICUOUS BIG BOLD RANK CLEAR FAMED PLAIN STARY EXTANT FAMOUS MARKED PATENT SIGNAL BLATANT EMINENT GLARING NOTABLE OBVIOUS POINTED SALIENT SIGHTLY STARING VISIBLE APPARENT EMPHATIC FLAGRANT KENSPECK MANIFEST STRIKING PROMINENT NOTICEABLE OUTSTANDING
CONSPIRACY COUP PLAN PLOT RING CABAL COVIN JUNTO PARTY COVINE SCHEME COMPACT COMPLOT INTRIGUE CATILINISM
CONSPIRATOR PACKER PLOTTER SCHEMER
CONSPIRE ABET PACK PLOT CABAL UNITE LEAGUE SCHEME COLLUDE COMPLOT CONJURE CONNIVE COLLOGUE CONTRIVE
CONSTABLE COP BULL PEON SLOP BEADLE BEAGLE HARMAN KAVASS KEEPER KOTWAL WARDEN BAILIFF CORONER DOZENER NUTHOOK OFFICER STALLER SUBASHI ALGUAZIL DOGBERRY TIPSTAFF CASTELLAN CATCHPOLE CATCHPOLL BORSHOLDER
CONSTANCE (FATHER OF —) FONDLOVE NONESUCH
(HUSBAND OF —) ALLA
(SON OF —) ARTHUR
CONSTANCY ZEAL ARDOR FAITH TRUTH FEALTY HONESTY LOYALTY ONENESS PURPOSE DEVOTION FIDELITY
CONSTANT K SET EVEN FIRM JUST LEAL TRUE FIXED LOYAL SOLID STILL TIGHT TRIED ITHAND STABLE STEADY CERTAIN CHRONIC DURABLE FOREVER LASTING REGULAR STAUNCH UNIFORM DEFINITE ENDURING FAITHFUL POSITIVE RESOLUTE SEDULOUS STANDING PERENNIAL
CONSTANTLY AWAY EVER ALWAYS THRONG
CONSTANT NYMPH (AUTHOR OF —) KENNEDY
(CHARACTER IN —) DODD KATE CARYL LEWIS SUSAN TESSA ALBERT SANGER TERESA

ANTONIA PAULINA FLORENCE CHURCHILL SEBASTIAN
CONSTELLATION ARA CUP FLY FOX LEO APUS ARGO COLT CROW CRUX DOVE GOAT GRUS HARE HARP LION LYNX LYRA MAST PAVO PLOW SIGN SWAN TAUR URSA VELA WAIN WOLF ALTAR ARIES CAMEL CETUS CLOCK CRANE DRACO EAGLE GROUP HYDRA INDUS LEPUS LIBRA LUPUS MALUS MENSA MUSCA NORMA ORION PYXIS RAVEN TABLE VIRGO WAGON WHALE ANTLIA AQUILA AURIGA BOOTES CAELUM CANCER CARINA CORVUS CRATER CYGNUS DIPPER DORADO FORNAX GEMINI HYDRUS INDIAN LIZARD OBELUS OCTANS OKNARI PICTOR PISCES PISCIS PLOUGH PUPPIS SCALES SCUTUM TAURUS TIGRIS TOUCAN TUCANA VOLANS ALGEBAR CEPHEUS CLUSTER COLUMBA COMPASS DOLPHIN FURNACE GIRAFFE LACERTA MONARCH OETAEUS PATTERN PEACOCK PEGASUS PERSEUS PHOENIX RHOMBUS SAGITTA SCORPIO SERPENS SERPENT SEXTANS SEXTANT XIPHIAS AQUARIUS ASTERISM CHAMPION CIRCINUS CYNOSURE EQUULEUS ERIDANUS HERCULES HERDSMAN KASHYAPA QUADRANS REINDEER RETICULE SCORPION SCORPIUS SCULPTOR TRIANGLE
CONSTERNATION FEAR ALARM PANIC DISMAY FRIGHT HORROR TERROR TREPIDITY
CONSTIPATE BIND ASTRICT
CONSTIPATED BOUND COSTIVE STENOTIC
CONSTITUENCY BOROUGH
CONSTITUENT ATOM ITEM PART PIECE VOTER DETAIL FACTOR FUSAIN MATTER MEMBER SIMPLE ELECTOR ELEMENT FEATURE TAGMEME INTEGRAL
(— OF BLOOD SERUM) OPSONIN
(— OF CLINKER) ALITE CELITE
(— OF COAL) DURAIN FUSAIN
(— OF DURAIN) ATTRITUS
(— OF MUSCLE) CREATINE
(— OF STEEL) PEARLITE
(—S OF BEER) EXTRACT
(NECESSARY —) ESSENCE
(PL.) MATTER BIOSESTON
CONSTITUTE BE FIX SET FORM MAKE ENACT ERECT FORGE FOUND SHAPE SPELL CREATE DEPUTE GRAITH ORDAIN APPOINT COMPOSE FASHION STATION COMPOUND COMPRISE
CONSTITUTION LAW SET CODE SETT BEING CANON FRAME FUERO HUMOR SETUP STATE CHARTE CRASIS CUSTOM DESIGN ESTATE HEALTH NATURE TEMPER CHARTER HABITUS SYNODAL GRONDWET GRUNDLOV HABITUDE PHYSIQUE POLITEIA
(— STATE) CONNECTICUT

(BODILY —) HABIT SPIRITS
(GERMINAL —) HEREDITY
CONSTITUTIONAL WALK HECTIC INNATE RIKKEN EXERCISE
CONSTITUTIVE FORMAL
CONSTRAIN ART PUT TIE ARCT BEND BIND CURB DOOM FAIN HALE HOLD LEAD URGE CHAIN CHECK CLASP COART CRAMP DETER DRIVE FORCE IMPEL LIMIT PRESS COERCE COMPEL EVINCE OBLIGE RAVISH SECURE STRAIN THRAST ASTRICT CONFINE CONJURE ENFORCE MANACLE OPPRESS REPRESS VIOLATE COMPRESS CONCLUDE DISTRESS OBLIGATE PERFORCE POUNDAGE RELIGATE RESTRAIN
CONSTRAINED FAIN TIED VAIN BOUND FORCED FORMAL UNEASY COACTED
CONSTRAINING UNEASY COMPELLENT
CONSTRAINT BOND CRAMP FORCE BRIDLE DURESS STRESS RESERVE STRAINT COERCION DISTRESS PRESSURE
CONSTRICT TIE BIND CURB GRIP CHOKE CRAMP LIMIT STRAP HAMPER SHRINK STRAIN STRAIT ASTRICT DEFLATE SQUEEZE STIFFEN TIGHTEN ASTRINGE COMPRESS CONDENSE CONTRACT DISTRAIN RESTRICT
CONSTRICTED STRAIT STRICT ADENOID
(— AT INTERVALS) MONILIFORM
CONSTRICTION KNOT CHOKE ISTHMUS STENOSIS THLIPSIS
CONSTRICTOR BOA ABOMA GUAVINA
CONSTRUCT UP BIG ATOM FORM IDEA LEVY MAKE REAR BUILD CRAFT DIGHT EDIFY ERECT FRAME MODEL WEAVE BURROW DEDUCE DESIGN DEVISE FABRIC ARRANGE CARPENT COMBINE COMPILE COMPOSE CONCEPT CONFECT CONTOUR EXTRUCT FASHION CONSTRUE ENGINEER PRACTISE
(— ARCH) TURN
CONSTRUCTED BUILT EDIFICATE
(CAREFULLY —) CLEVER
(HASTILY —) GIMCRACK JIMCRACK
CONSTRUCTION BOOM ALTAR FRAME FABRIC MONSTER SYNESIS APPROACH BUILDING DWELLING ERECTION
(— OF NAME) ABSTRACTION
(ABSTRACT —) STABILE
(GRAMMATICAL —) SYNESIS APPOSITION
(POINTED —) BEAK
CONSTRUCTIVE PONENT FACTIVE HELPFUL VIRTUAL CREATIVE IMPLICIT INFERRED
CONSTRUCTOR ENGINEER
CONSTRUE INFER PARSE STRUE INTEND RENDER ANALYZE CONSTER DISSECT EXPLAIN EXPOUND RESOLVE
CONSUL SUFFECT

CONSULT LOOK SEEK TALK ADVISE CONFER EMPARL IMPARL COUNSEL RESOLVE
CONSULTANT EXPERT ADVISER COUNSEL
CONSULTATION ADVICE COUNCIL COUNSEL
CONSUL, THE (CHARACTER IN —) JOHN MAGDA SOREL
(COMPOSER OF —) MENOTTI
CONSUME EAT SUP USE BOLT BURN CHEW FANG FARE FEED FRET GULP IDLE KILL RUST TAKE TUCK WEAR DALLY DRINK FLAME LURCH RAVEN SHIFT SPEND TOOTH WASTE ABSORB BEZZLE BROWSE CANKER DEVOUR ENGAGE EXPEND FINISH IMBIBE INHALE PERISH PUNISH VANISH CORRODE DESTROY DWINDLE ENGROSS EXHAUST SWALLOW CONTRIVE SQUANDER
(— TOTALLY) KILL
(— VORACIOUSLY) HOG
CONSUMED ALL PAU DOWN BURNT SPENT COMBUST OUTWORN
CONSUMING EATING SACRED BURNING FLAMING
CONSUMMATE END FINE FULL RIPE CLOSE IDEAL SHEER ARRANT EFFECT FINISH FULFIL RATIFY ACHIEVE CONSUME CROWNED FULFILL PERFECT PERFORM ABSOLUTE COMPLETE MERIDIAN THOROUGH
CONSUMMATION CROWN PERIOD UPSHOT
CONSUMPTION USE DECAY WASTE EXPENSE WASTING PHTHISIS SPENDING
(PREF.) PHTHISIO
CONSUMPTIVE LUNGY HECTIC PREDATORY
CONTACT ABUT JOIN KISS MEET SLED CROSS TOUCH TRUCK UNION ARRIVE IMPACT SYZYGY EPHAPSE HOLDING MEETING TACTION JUNCTION TANGENCY TOUCHING
(— OF TELEGRAPH KEY) ANVIL
(ELECTRICAL —) HUB HUBB POINT
(EVIL —) CONTAGION
(FLEETING —) BRUSH
(FORCIBLE —) IMPACT
(3-POINT —) OSCNODE
(PREF.) HAPT(O) THIGMO
CONTAGION POX TAINT VIRUS MIASMA POISON
CONTAGIOUS TAKING NOXIOUS SMITTLE CATCHING EPIDEMIC
CONTAIN RUN HAVE HOLD KEEP STOW TAKE CARRY CHECK CLOSE COVER HOUSE EMBODY ENFOLD ENSEAM HARBOR RETAIN COMPILE EMBRACE ENCLOSE INCLUDE INVOLVE RECEIVE SUBSUME SUSTAIN COMPRISE RESTRAIN
(PREF.) CHADA
CONTAINED IN
CONTAINER BAG BOX CAN CUP HAT JAR JUG KEG LUG NIN PAN

POD POT TIN TUB URN VAT BAIL
BOMB CAGE CASE CASK CRIB
DRUM EWER FILE FLAT JACK
SACK SALT SILO SINK SKIP TANK
TUBE VASE ALBUM BASIN BILLY
CADDY CHEST CRATE CRUET
DEWAR EMPTY FLASK GLASS
GOURD POUCH SCOOP SCRAY
STAND STOOP STOUP BARREL
BASKET BOTTLE BUCKET BUSHEL
CARBOY CARTON CASTER
CASTOR COOLER CRADLE DUSTER
HAMPER HATBOX HOLDER
INKPOT MAILER PICNIC RABBIT
RIDDLE SHAKER WITJAR AEROSOL
AMPULLA BANDBOX BLADDER
CAPSULE COASTER COSTREL
CRISPER FEEDBOX HANAPER
HOLDALL INKWELL PACKAGE
SEEDLIP SHIPPER STEEPER
CANISTER DECANTER DEMIJOHN
ENVELOPE HOGSHEAD HONEYPOT
INHOLDER KNAPSACK PUNCHEON
SLIPCASE RELIQUARY
POCKETBOOK
(— FOR BEER) GROWLER
(— FOR BOBBINS) BUFFALO
(— FOR COINS) BANK
(— FOR EXPLOSIVE CHARGE) CAP
(— FOR FISH) BASS
(— FOR GOLD DUST) SHAMMY
(— FOR HOLY OIL) STOCK
(— FOR PLANTS) BAND
(— MADE OF HOLLOW LOG) GUM
(COFFEE —) INSET
(DESSERT —) COUPE
(DRINK —) DOP
(EARTHENWARE —) STEAN
(FIRECLAY —) SETTER
(RAILROAD —S) BUNKER
(SHELVED —) CABIN
(SHIPPING —) KIT
(SNUFF —) WEASAND
(TOBACCO —) SARATOGA
(VENTILATED —) CHIP
(5-GALLON —) JERICAN JERRICAN
(PL.) CONVEYER CONVEYOR
CONTAINING
(SUFF.) IC(AL)
CONTAMINATE FOUL HARM SLUR
SMIT SOIL STAIN SULLY TAINT
BEFOUL DEBASE DEFILE INFECT
INJURE POISON ATTAINT
CORRUPT DEBAUCH FLYBLOW
POLLUTE TARNISH VITIATE
DISHONOR
CONTAMINATED DIRTY
DEGRADED INFECTED
CONTAMINATION INFECTION
TAINTMENT
(— IN GLASS) STONE
CONTE TALE CRAYON
CONTEMN HATE FLOUT SCORN
SPURN REJECT SLIGHT DESPISE
DISDAIN CONTEMPT INDIGNIFY
CONTEMPLATE FACE MUSE PLAN
SCAN VIEW DEIGN STUDY THINK
WEIGH BEHOLD DESIGN PONDER
REGARD SURVEY CHERISH
PROPOSE REFLECT CONSIDER
ENVISAGE ENVISION MEDITATE
CONTEMPLATION MUSE STUDY
DHYANA MUSING PRAYER

REGARD THEORY INSIGHT
MOONING REQUEST THEORIA
PETITION RECOLLECTION
CONTEMPLATIVE BROODY
PENSIVE THEORIC STUDIOUS
CONTEMPORANEOUS COEVAL
LIVING MODERN CURRENT
EXISTING
CONTEMPORARY EQUAL COEVAL
FELLOW CURRENT PRESENT
YEALING EXISTENT
SIMULTANEOUS
CONTEMPT PRUT SCORN SHAME
SNEER SLIGHT CONTEMN
DESPECT DESPITE DISDAIN
HETHING MOCKERY DEFIANCE
DERISION DESPISAL DISGRACE
MISPRIZE MISPRISION
OPPROBRIUM
(ONE HELD IN —) FINK
CONTEMPTIBLE LOW BASE MEAN
POOR VILE BALLY CHEAP DIRTY
DUSTY LOUSY MANGY MUCKY
PETTY POCKY RUDDY SCALD
SORRY ABJECT BLOODY CRUDDY
GRUBBY MEASLY PALTRY SCABBY
SCUMMY SCURVY SHABBY
SNOTTY SORDID YELLOW
BROKING LIGHTLY PEEVISH
PELTING PITIFUL SCALLED
SCORNED SHITTEN SLAVISH
SQUALID BAUBLING BEGGARLY
FRIPPERY INFAMOUS INFERIOR
PICAYUNE PITIABLE PRECIOUS
SNEAKING UNWORTHY
WRETCHED MISBEGOTTEN
(SUFF.) (— ONE) EEN EER
CONTEMPTIBLENESS BEGGARY
CONTEMPTUOUS SLIGHT SNEERY
SNOOTY HAUGHTY LIGHTLY
SLIGHTY SPITOUS ARROGANT
FLOUTING INSOLENT SCOFFING
SCORNFUL
CONTEND TUG VIE WAR WIN
CAMP COCK COPE DEAL FRAB
KEMP PLEA RACE WAGE ARGUE
BANDY BRAWL CHIDE CLAIM
FIGHT FLITE PRESS ASSERT
BATTLE BICKER BREAST BUCKLE
BUFFET BUSTLE COMBAT DEBATE
DIFFER JOSTLE JUSTLE MEDDLE
OPPOSE PINGLE REASON STRIVE
BARGAIN COMPETE CONTEST
COUNTER DISPUTE PROPUGN
QUARREL SCUFFLE STICKLE
SUSTAIN WRESTLE CONFLICT
CONTRAST CONTRIVE MAINTAIN
MILITATE SQUABBLE STRUGGLE
CONTENT PAY CALM EASE GIST
GLAD PAID RATH APPAY HAPPY
HUMOR RATHE SERVE AMOUNT
CUBAGE PLEASE APPEASE
CONTENU GRATIFY PERFECT
REPLETE SATIATE SATISFY
SUFFICE WILLING BLISSFUL
CAPACITY CONTENU WILCWEME
(-S OF SACK) BUDGET
(—S OF STOMACH) COOKIES
(ENERGY —) STRENGTH
(HEAT —) ENTHALPY
(SUPERFICIAL —S) AREA
(PL.) LINING

CONTENTED COZY FAIN VAIN
QUIET SATED CONTENT PLEASED
CHEERFUL
CONTENTION WAR BAIT BATE
CASE FEUD PLEA RIOT TIFF TOIL
BROIL CHEST STRUT BICKER
COMBAT DEBATE ESTRIF JANGLE
STRIFE CHIDING CONTEKE
CONTEST DISCORD DISPUTE
OPINION QUARREL RIVALRY
WRANGLE ARGUMENT CONFLICT
SQUABBLE STRUGGLE VARIANCE
COLLUCTATION
CONTENTIOUS CROSS BATEFUL
PEEVISH PERVERSE BELLICOSE
CONTENTMENT EASE BLISS
HEAVEN PLEASURE
SATISFACTION
CONTERMINOUS NEXT ADJACENT
FRONTIER PROXIMAL
CONTEST GO IT BEE FIX RUN SUE
TRY VIE AGON BOUT CAMP COPE
DUEL FEUD FRAY GAME HOLD
KEMP LAKE MART PULL RACE
SHOW SPAR TIFF TILT TURN
YOKE AGONY ARGUE BROIL
CLASH DERBY EVENT FIGHT
MATCH PLATE PRIZE ROLEO
SCRUB SPORT TRIAL WAGER
ACTION ADJURE AFFRAY BATTLE
BISLEY COMBAT DEBATE DEFEND
FLIGHT OPPOSE RESIST RUBBER
SEESAW STRIFE STRIVE TUSSLE
YOKING BARGAIN BRABBLE
CLASSIC COMPETE CONTECK
CONTEND DERAIGN DISPUTE
GRAPPLE PROTEST SHUTOUT
TOURNEY WARFARE ARGUMENT
CONCOURS CONFLICT DOGFIGHT
HANDICAP LITIGATE SKIRMISH
SLUGFEST STRIVING STRUGGLE
WALKAWAY WALKOVER
PANCRATIUM PENTATHLON
(— IN WORDS) SPAR
(— NARROWLY WON) SQUEAKER
(ATHLETIC —) BIATHLON
(AUTOMOBILE — ON FROZEN LAKE)
ICEKHANA
(CLOSE —) DICE
(DRAWN —) TIE DRAW STALEMATE
(MOCK —) SCIAMACHY
(RACING —) DRAG
(REAPING —) KEMP
(PREF.) MACHO
(SUFF.) AGONIST(IC) MACHIA
MACHY
CONTESTANT VIER RIVAL WAGER
PLAYER AGONIST ENTRANT
SCRATCH FINALIST PROSPECT
CONTIGUITY ADJACENCY
CONFINITY IMMEDIACY
CONTIGUOUS NEXT NIGH NEARBY
TANGENT ABUTTING ADJACENT
TOUCHING
CONTINENT ASIA MASS PORE
SOBER AFRICA CHASTE EUROPE
CONTENT CAPACITY MAINLAND
MODERATE ABSTINENT
CONTINGENCY BOOK CASE EVENT
CHANCE ADJUNCT CONTACT
VENTURE ACCIDENT CASUALTY
FORTUITY INCIDENT JUNCTURE
PROSPECT

CONTINGENT CASUAL CHANCE
DOUBTFUL EVENTUAL INCHOATE
TOUCHING
CONTINUAL STILL HOURLY
ABIDING ENDLESS ETERNAL
LASTING REGULAR UNDYING
UNIFORM CONSTANT ENDURING
UNBROKEN
CONTINUALLY AY AYE EVER STILL
ALWAYS EVERLY HOURLY STEADY
ENDLESS ETERNAL FOREVER
MINUTELY
CONTINUANCE STAY WHEN
DELAY LEASE SEQUEL ABIDING
DURANCE LASTING ABIDANCE
DURATION STANDING SURVIVAL
CONTINUANT OPEN LIQUID
DURATIVE
CONTINUATION SEQUEL
CONTANGO DURATION
PROLONGATION PERSEVERATION
(— OF DOUBLET) BASQUE
CONTINUE BE DO ABY SUE ABYE
BIDE DURE HOLD JUMP KEEP
LAST LIVE STAY TIDE ABIDE
CARRY EXIST PERGE STICK UNITE
ABEGGE BELEVE ENDURE EXTEND
PURSUE REMAIN RESUME
BELEAVE CONNECT CONTUNE
PERSIST PROCEED PROLONG
SUBSIST SURVIVE SUSTAIN
PROTRACT
(— UNALTERED) TARRY
CONTINUED STILL SERIAL
CHRONIC CONSTANT
CONTINUING ABIDING DURABLE
LASTING DURATIVE PERPETUAL
PERSISTENT OUTSTANDING
(— FOR LONG TIME) CHRONIC
(— TO BE) YET
CONTINUITY TRACT SCRIPT
COHESION SCENARIO
CONTINUUM
(PREF.) SYNECHIO
CONTINUOUS RUN EVEN ANEND
EIDENT ENTIRE EYDENT STEADY
CHRONIC ENDLESS RUNNING
UNBROKEN PERENNIAL
PERPETUAL
CONTINUOUSLY AWAY EVER FAST
ANEND OUTRIGHT
CONTORT WRY BEND COIL CURL
TURN WARP GNARL SCREW
TWIST WREST CRINGE DEFORM
WRITHE DISTORT PERVERT
SQUINCH WREATHE OBVOLUTE
CONTORTED WRY WRIED KNOTTY
CRISPED KNOTTED SCREWED
WRITHEN OBVOLUTE
CONTORTION SCREW STITCH
WRITHE MURGEON WORKING
CONTOUR FORM LINE CURVE
GRAPH SHAPE SWEEP AMOEBA
FIGURE OUTLINE PROFILE
CARTOUCH CONTORNO
MANDORLA PLANFORM
TOURNURE
(— ON SHIP) HANCE
CONTRA CONTRE AGAINST
COUNTER OPPOSED
CONTRABAND HOT GOODS
ILLEGAL ILLICIT SMUGGLED
UNLAWFUL

CONTRABASS BASS OCTOBASS
CONTRACEPTIVE (ORAL —) PILL
CONTRACT GET BOND DRAW
FARM FORM HALE KNIT PACT
SALE TACK CATCH CLOSE COACT
COUCH CRAMP FEVER INCUR
LEASE LIMIT NEXUM PINCH
SHRUG SNURP CARTEL COCKLE
COMMIT CRINGE ENGAGE FUTURE
GATHER HIRING INDENT LESSEN
MUTUUM NARROW PIGNUS
PLEDGE POLICY PROMPT PUCKER
REDUCE SHRIMP SHRINK SUBLET
TREATY ABRIDGE APPALTO
BARGAIN BUMMERY CHARTER
COMPACT CRIMPLE CRUMPLE
CURTAIL DEFLATE FIDUCIA
MANDATE PROMISE SCRUNCH
SHORTEN SHRIVEL SOCIETY
WRINKLE ASSIENTO BOTTOMRY
CONDENSE COVENANT
HANDFAST HARDNESS LOCATION
RESTRICT STEELBOW STRAITEN
SYNGRAPH ABBREVIATE
OBLIGATION
(— BROW) FROWN
(— INTO WRINKLES) KNIT
(BRIDGE —) SOLO AUCTION
(MARRIAGE —) KETUBA AFFIANCE
HANDFAST BETROTHAL
SPONSALIA
CONTRACTED BOXY CRAMP
BOOKED ASTRICT INGROWN
INSULAR SCREWED CONTRACT
CONTRACTILITY MOTILITY
CONTRACTION HM ANT NIP TIC
TIS AINT CANT ISNT KNIT MAAM
WONT CRAMP HADNT HASNT
NISUS SPASM CRASIS GATHER
INTAKE MUSTNT SHRINK TWITCH
ELISION EPITOME WOULDNT
APNEUSIS TRACTION
ABRIDGMENT ABRIDGEMENT
(— OF HEART) SYSTOLE
(— OF SYLLABLES) SYNIZESIS
(PL.) TREPPE
CONTRACTOR KHOT BUTTY
BUILDER REMOVER SUPPLIER
CONTRADICT DENY BELIE CROSS
REBUT FORBID IMPUGN NEGATE
OPPOSE RECANT REFUTE THREAP
COUNTER GAINSAY REVERSE
WITHSAY CONTRARY DISPROVE
DOWNFACE NEGATIVE
OUTSTAND
CONTRADICTION CLASH DENIAL
DEMENTI PARADOX WITHSAW
ANTILOGY ANTIMONY ANTILOQUY
(LUDICROUS —) BULL
CONTRADICTORY OPPOSE
ANTINOME OPPOSITE
THWARTING
CONTRAPTION RIG TOOL DEVICE
GADGET JIGGER CONCERN
MACHINE
CONTRARILY BACKWARD
CRISSCROSS
CONTRARIWISE CONTRA
CONTRARY
CONTRARY BALKY CROSS KICKY
SNIVY AVERSE CONTRA ORNERY
SNIVEY THRAWN ADVERSE
COUNTER CRABBED FROWARD

HOSTILE INVERSE OPPOSED
PEEVISH RESTIVE REVERSE
WAYWARD ABSONANT ANTIPODE
CAPTIOUS CONTRAIR INIMICAL
OPPOSITE PERVERSE PETULANT
SINGULAR ABHORRENT
(— TO) BESIDE AGAINST
ATHWART
(— TO HAPPINESS) ILL
(— TO REASON) SILLY ABSONANT
(PREF.) CONTRA COUNTER DIS
RETRO
CONTRAST CLASH STRIFE
COMPARE CONTEND DISCORD
ANTIMONY DIVISION DYNAMICS
OPPOSITE
CONTRASTING
(PREF.) CONTRA
CONTRAVENE DEFY DENY HINDER
OPPOSE THWART DISPUTE
VIOLATE INFRINGE OBSTRUCT
CONTRAVENTION SIN VICE CRIME
BREACH OFFENSE
CONTRETEMPS SLIP BONER HITCH
MISHAP SCRAPE ACCIDENT
INCIDENT
CONTRIBUTE AID ANTE FORK GIVE
HELP MAKE TEND CAUSE ENTER
GROUT SERVE ASSIST BESTOW
CONCUR CONFER DONATE
PUNGLE RENDER SUPPLY TENDER
ANIMATE CONDUCE FURNISH
FURTHER PROVIDE
CONTRIBUTING ACCESSORY
CONTRIBUTION BIT SUM TAX
ALMS BOON GIFT SCOT SHOT
ESSAY INPUT SHARE IMPOST
SYMBOL ARTICLE LARGESS
PAYMENT PRESENT RENEWAL
WRITING DONATION EXACTION
OFFERING ROMESHOT
CONTRITE WORN SORRY HUMBLE
RUEFUL PENITENT SORROWFUL
CONTRITION SORE SORROW
PENANCE PENITENCE
CONTRIVANCE (ALSO SEE DEVICE)
ART BOW FLY GIN JET JIG LEG
DROP GEAR HARP JACK KITE
LURE PAGE PLAN PLOT RASP
REED TOOL ALARM BRAKE CARRY
CHECK DOLLY DRAFT FLOAT
FRAME GUIDE HICKY KNACK
MIXER QUIPU SHIFT SNARE
STOCK ANCHOR DAMPER DECEIT
DESIGN DEVICE DOCTOR DOLLIE
ENGINE FABRIC FANGLE GABION
GADGET GIMBAL HANGER
HARROW HEATER HICKEY
HOLDER JIGGER JINKER MARKER
MORTAR MUZZLE POLICY RATTLE
SCHEME SLUICE SPIDER TEASEL
WEIGHT WHEEZE WINDAS
WRENCH BOLSTER CLEANER
CLEARER CONCERN COUPLER
CUNNING DINGBAT DRAUGHT
FICTION FISHWAY HUMIDOR
KNOCKER MACHINE PAGEANT
PROJECT REDUCER ROASTER
SCRAPER SHEBANG SPANNER
STOPPER TOASTER TRIPPER
VOLVELL ADAPTION ARTIFICE
CROTCHET DUTCHMAN EUPYRION
FAKEMENT FORECAST GOVERNOR

INDUSTRY MOLITION OXIDATOR
REGISTER RESOURCE SCISSORS
SQUEEZER SUBTLETY WITCRAFT
CONTRIVE GET LAY BREW CAST
DRAW FIND FIRK MAKE PLAN
PLOT WORK FRAME FUDGE
HATCH SHAPE STAGE WEAVE
AFFORD DESIGN DEVISE DIVINE
ENGINE FIGURE INVENT MANAGE
SCHEME WANGLE ACHIEVE
AGITATE COMMENT COMPASS
CONCOCT CONJURE CONSULT
CONTEND FASHION IMAGINE
MACHINE PROCURE PROJECT
REPAREL CONSPIRE ENGINEER
FORECAST INTRIGUE PURCHASE
CONTRIVED PAT SLICK STAGED
TIMBERED
CONTRIVER DAEDAL DAEDALUS
ENGINEER
CONTRIVING FASHION SCHEMERY
CONTROL BIT LAP LAW MAN POT
RUN CONN CURB EGIS GRIP
HAND HANK HAVE HOLD REDE
REIN RULE STAY SWAY WIND
AEGIS BOOST CHARM CHECK
COACT DAUNT DUMMY GRASP
GUIDE LEASH ORDER POWER
STEER SWING THEAT TREAT
TUTOR VERGE WIELD BANDON
BRIDLE CHARGE CLUTCH COERCE
CORNER DANGER DIRECT EMPERY
GOVERN HANDLE MANAGE
POCKET TEMPER AMENAGE
COMMAND CONDUCT CONTAIN
CUSTODY FORBEAR MASTERY
QUALIFY STRINGS COACTION
DOMINATE DOMINIUM IMPERIUM
MODERATE REGULATE SERVOTAB
POSSESSION
(— A BULL) MANDAR
(— OF RESOURCES) HUSBANDRY
(— OVER WIFE) MANUS
(ABSOLUTE —) BECK
(FIRE —) BLANKET
(GOVERNMENT —) DIRIGISM
SQUADRISM
(MANUAL —) JOYSTICK
(NONCLERICAL —) LAICISM LAICITY
CONTROLLED STEADY SERVILE
CONTAINED
CONTROLLER FENCER GERENT
MASTER STARTER
(SPEED —) GOVERNOR RHEOCRAT
CONTROLLING MASTER LEADING
DOMINANT HEGEMONIC
CONTROVERSIAL ERISTIC
POLEMIC
CONTROVERSIALIST ERISTIC
POLEMIC DISPUTANT GLADIATOR
CONTROVERSY PLEA SPAT SUIT
CHEST FUROR BATTLE COMBAT
DEBATE FURORE HASSEL HASSLE
HOORAH HURRAH STRIFE TUSSLE
DISPUTE POLEMIC QUARREL
WRANGLE ARGUMENT TRAVERSE
CONTENTION
(ART OF —) POLEMICS
CONTROVERT DENY FACE MOOT
ARGUE DEBATE DEFEND OPPOSE
OPPUGN REFUTE CONTEST
DISPUTE GAINSAY DISPROVE
CONTUMACIOUS UNRULY

RIOTOUS CONTUMAX INSOLENT
MUTINOUS PERVERSE STUBBORN
CONTUMELY ABUSE SCORN
INSULT CONTECK DISDAIN
REPROOF UPBRAID CONTEMPT
RUDENESS
CONTUSE BEAT POUND THUMP
BRUISE INJURE SQUEEZE
CONTUSION POUND BRUISE
CONUNDRUM PUN WHIM GUESS
ENIGMA PUZZLE RIDDLE CONCEIT
CROTCHET
CONURE ARATINGA
CONVALESCE MEND GUARISH
RECOVER
CONVENANCE FORM
CONVENE SIT CALL HOLD MEET
UNITE GATHER MUSTER SUMMON
CONVENT CONVOKE ASSEMBLE
CONVERGE
CONVENIENCE GAIN BEHOOF
URINAL LEISURE COMMODITY
CONVENIENT FIT GAIN HEND NIGH
HANDY HENDE READY CLEVER
FITTED PROPER SUITED USEFUL
ADAPTED AVENANT COMMODE
HELPFUL BECOMING EXPEDITE
SUITABLE OPPORTUNE
COMMODIOUS
CONVENIENTLY HANDILY
CLEVERLY
CONVENT ABBEY HOUSE TEKKE
TEKYA CENOBY COVENT FRIARY
PRIORY CONVENT MEETING
RECLUSE CLOISTER LAMASERY
MOTHERHOUSE
CONVENTION DIET FEIS FORM
MISE RULE TABU SYNOD TABOO
USAGE CARTEL CAUCUS CUSTOM
TREATY DECORUM MEETING
ASSEMBLY ASSIENTO CONCLAVE
CONGRESS CONTRACT COVENANT
PRACTICE PRECEDENT
(LONG-ESTABLISHED —) TRADITION
(STAGE —) ASIDE
(PL.) DECENCIES
CONVENTIONAL MORE NOMIC
RIGHT TRITE USUAL DECENT
FORMAL MODISH PROPER
CORRECT POMPIER REGULAR
ACADEMIC ACCEPTED COPYBOOK
ORTHODOX CUSTOMARY
(RIGIDLY —) UPTIGHT
CONVENTIONALITY FORM
ACADEMISM FORMALITY
GRUNDYISM
CONVENTIONALIZE STYLIZE
CONVERGE JOIN MEET FOCUS
CONCUR CORNER CONNIVE
DESCEND APPROACH FOCALIZE
CONVERSANT ADEPT BUSIED
EXPERT VERSED SKILLED
FAMILIAR OCCUPIED
CONVERSATION RAP SAY CALL
CHAT CHIN RUNE TALE TALK
BOARD CRACK PROSE CACKLE
CONFAB DEVICE GOSSIP PARLEY
POWWOW SPEECH YABBER
CEILIDH COMMUNE CONDUCT
PALAVER PURPOSE BACKCHAT
BEHAVIOR CAUSERIE CHITCHAT
COLLOGUE COLLOQUY DIALOGUE
GIFFGAFF HARANGUE PARLANCE

QUESTION COLLOCUTION
(— BETWEEN WHALERS) GAM
CONVERSATIONALIST TALKER
CAUSEUR
CONVERSE CHAT CHIN LIVE MOVE
TALK DWELL SPEAK CACKLE
COMMON CONFER DEVISE
HOMILY PARLEY REASON
COMMUNE CONVERT DISCUSS
OBVERSE PROPOSE REVERSE
COLLOQUE EXCHANGE OPPOSITE
QUESTION
CONVERSION CHANGE EXCHANGE
METRICATION PROSELYTISM
(— INTO VAPOR) FLASH
(— OF IRON) FINING
CONVERT TAW TURN WEND
ALTER AMEND APPLY MAULA
RENEW CHANGE DECODE DETECT
DIRECT MAWALI NOVICE SHAIKH
SOUPER COMMUTE CONCOCT
RESOLVE RESTORE REVERSE
ACTIVATE CONVERSE DISCIPLE
NEOPHYTE PERSUADE PROSELYTE
(— COTTON) LAP
(— INTO CASH) NEGOTIATE
(— INTO LEATHER) TAN TAW
(— INTO LIQUID) BREW
(— INTO PELLETS) PRILL
(— INTO SOAP) SAPONIFY
(— INTO STEEL) ACIERATE
(— INTO STONE) LAPIDIFY
(— SOAP) CLOSE
(— TO CARBON) CHAR
CONVERTER ROTARY SELECTOR
CONVERTIBLE AUTO DROPHEAD
CONVEX BOWED ARCHED CAMBER
CURVED BULGING EMBOWED
GIBBOUS ROUNDED
CONVEXITY CAMBER ARCUATION
CONVEY JAG BEAR BOOK CART
CEDE DEED DUCT HAVE LEAD
MEAN PASS SEND SIGN TAKE
TOTE WAIN WILL BRING CARRY
DRIVE FETCH GRANT GUIDE
HURRY STEAL ARRIVE ASSIGN
CONVOY DEDUCE DELATE DEMISE
DEVISE ELOIGN GIGGIT IMPART
IMPORT REMOVE YMMOTE
AUCTION CHANNEL CHARIOT
CHARTER CONDUCT DELIVER
DERRICK DISPONE DISPOSE
LIGHTER RESTORE ALIENATE
BEQUEATH DESCRIBE TRANSFER
TRANSMIT
(— AN ESTATE) DEMISE
(— BY ALLUSION) IMPLY
(— FORCIBLY) HUSTLE
(— LEGALLY) DEED GRANT LEASE
DEMISE ELOIGN DISPONE
(— NEARER) BRING
(— SECRETLY) CRIM
CONVEYANCE BUS CAR AUTO
CART DEED DRAG GIFT LOAD
SLED TAXI TRAM GRANT SEDAN
STAGE TAUGA THEFT TRAIN
WAGON DEMISE JINGLE CHARTER
CONDUCT COURIER MACHINE
RATTLER TRAILER TRAJECT
TRANSIT TROLLEY VECTURE
VEHICLE WAFTAGE CARRIAGE
CARRYING CONVEYAL DELATION
FERRIAGE STEALING TRANSFER

CONVEYOR LIFT WORM DRAPER
LADDER SHAKER CARRIER
CREEPER HURRIER SCRAPER
CAROUSEL CONVEYER ELEVATOR
CONVICT LAG CAST FIND STAR
ARGUE EXILE FELON LIFER PROVE
TAINT ATTAIN FORCAT LAGGER
TERMER TRUSTY APPROVE
ATTAINT CAPTIVE CONDEMN
CULPRIT EXPIREE IMPEACH
REPROVE CRIMINAL JAILBIRD
PRISONER REDARGUE SENTENCE
CONVICT FISH MANINI HINALEA
CONVICTION CREDO CREED
DOGMA FAITH SENSE TAINT
TENET BELIEF CREDIT CONCERN
OPINION SENTENCE
CONVINCE EVICT FETCH ASSURE
EVINCE REPROVE RESOLVE
SATISFY CONCLUDE
(— OF ERROR) CONVICT
CONVINCED FIRM SOLD SURE
CERTAIN ABSOLUTE POSITIVE
CONVINCING SOUND VALID
COGENT POTENT EVIDENT
TELLING FORCIBLE LUCULENT
POWERFUL PREGNANT
CONVIVIAL GAY BOON FESTAL
GENIAL JOVIAL SOCIAL FESTIVE
HOLIDAY JOCULAR REVELING
ANACREONTIC
CONVIVIALITY REVEL FESTIVAL
MERRYMAKING
CONVOCATION DIET SYNOD
CALLING COUNCIL MEETING
SUMMONS ASSEMBLY CONGRESS
VOCATION
CONVOKE CALL HOLD GATHER
SUMMON CONVENE ASSEMBLE
CONVOLUTE COIL ROLL WIND
TWIST TANGLE WRITHE CONTORT
INVOLUTE OBVOLUTE
CONVOLUTED GYRATE
CONVOLUTION COIL CURL FOLD
TURN WRAP GYRUS SWIRL TWINE
TWIRL TWIST WHORL CUNEUS
GYROMA VOLUME VOLUTION
CONVOLVE TURN WIND TWIST
ENFOLD ENWRAP INFOLD
WRITHE
CONVOLVULUS BINDWEED
SCAMMONY
CONVOY LEAD WAFT CARRY
GUARD GUIDE PILOT TRADE
WATCH ATTEND CONVEY ESCORT
MANAGE CONDUCT WAFTAGE
SAFEGUARD
CONVULSE ROCK STIR SHAKE
EXCITE AGITATE DISTURB
CONVULSION FIT SHRUG SPASM
THROE ATTACK TUMULT UPROAR
CONVULSE LAUGHTER PAROXYSM
COMMOTION
CONVULSIVE FITFUL EPILEPTIC
CONY DAS HARE PIKA CONEY
CUNNY DAMAN DASSY GANAM
HUTIA HYRAX BURBOT CONEEN
DASSIE GAZABO GAZEBO RABBIT
WABBER ASHKOKO BOOMDAS
HYRACID KLIPDAS HYRACOID
KLIPDACH
COO CROO CURR WOOT CHIRR
CHIZZ CROOD MURMUR

CROODLE CRUDDLE
COOEE BIRD KOEL
COOK DO FIX FRY BAKE BOIL CHEF
COCT FAKE MAKE SEAR STEW
BROIL CUSIE FRIZZ GRILL POACH
ROAST SCALD SHIRR STEAM
BRAISE CODDLE COOKIE COOPER
DECOCT DIGEST PORTER SAUTEE
SEETHE SIMMER ARTISTE BROILER
FRIZZLE GRIDDLE PASTLER
PERCOCT POTAGER PREPARE
PROCESS SERVANT SMOTHER
SWAMPER BAWARCHI BOBACHEE
COCINERO CUSINERO GRILLADE
MAGIRIST PASTERER
(— TOO LONG) OVERDO
(— UP) BUILD
(BULL —) FLUNKY FLUNKEY
GREASER
(SHIP'S —) DOCTOR SLUSHY
SKILLET SLUSHER
(PREF.) MAGIRO
COOKED DONE FRIED BOILED
(— BY BOILING) AUBLEU
(— WITH SUGAR) CANDIED
(PREF.) COCTO
COOKEE FLUNKY HASHER
FLUNKEY
COOKER CANNER HAYBOX
DIGESTER
COOKERY CURY CUISINE KITCHEN
MAGIRICS
COOKHOUSE GALLEY
COOKIE CAKE ROCK SNAP COOKY
HERMIT KIPFEL BISCUIT BROWNIE
OATCAKE PLACENT CRESCENT
SEEDCAKE
COOKING COCTION
COOKROOM CUDDY
COOL AIR FAN ICE CALM COLD
KEEL AKELE ALGID ALLAY CHILL
EVENT FRESH GELID NERVY
QUEEL SOBER STAID WHOLE
AIRISH CALLER CHILLY PLACID
QUENCH SEDATE SERENE TEMPER
UNWARM COOLISH REFROID
UNMOVED CARELESS CAUTIOUS
COMPOSED MITIGATE MODERATE
TRANQUIL NERVELESS
POSSESSED NONCHALANT
UNFLAPPABLE
(— IN WATER) SLACK SLACKEN
(— OF EVENING) SERENE
COOLED COLD FRAPPE
COOLER COLA ICER JAIL KEEL
OLLA SINK ICEBOX LOCKUP
PRISON SINKER KEELFAT
ALCOGENE
(WINE —) GLACIER
COOLIE CHANGAR MADRASI
MAZDOOR
COOLNESS COOL FROST NERVE
SWALE APLOMB PHLEGM
SERENITY
COOM CULM GAUM SMUT SOOT
COOMB GRIME SLACK
COONTIE SAGO ZAMIA COMPTIE
COOP COT CUB CUP MEW PEN POT
RIP CAGE COOB COTE JAIL
CRAMP HUTCH BASKET CORRAL
CONFINE
(— UP) PEN IMMEW INCOUP
(HEN —) CAVEY CAVIE BARTON

COOPER BUNGS COPER COWPER
HEADER HOOPER TUBBER TUBBIE
TUBMAN
COOPERATE HAND TEND AGREE
COACT UNITE CONCUR COMBINE
CONDUCE CONNIVE COADJUTE
CONSPIRE
COOPERATION SOCIETY
COURTESY TEAMWORK
COOPERATIVE COOP SOCIAL
SYNERGIC
COORDINATE SINE ADAPT EQUAL
ADJUST ARRANGE SYNTONY
ABSCISSA CLASSIFY ENSEMBLE
COORDINATION BOND SKILL
HARMONY LIAISON
COORG KADAGA
COOT CUIT DUCK RAIL QUEET
SMYTH BELTIE GORHEN PELICK
SCOTER HENBILL LOBIPED
PULLDOO LOBEFOOT RAILBIRD
SWAMPHEN
COP BAG NAB ROB BANK BLOW
BULL HEAD HEAP JOHN LIFT PILE
TRAP TUBE CATCH CREST FILCH
MOUNT QUILL SHOCK SNARE
STEAL STOCK SWIPE BOBBIN
COPPIN PEELER SPIDER STRIKE
CAPTURE
COPA YAYA COPITA
COPAL BOEA LOBA ANIME CONGO
KAURI KAURY RESIN COWRIE
DAMMAR CHAKAZI
COPE VIE WAR CAPE DUTY FACE
LIFT MEET CAPPA CLOAK COVER
DRESS EQUAL FIGHT MATCH
NOTCH RIVAL VAULT WIELD
BARTER CANOPY CHAPEL
COMBAT MANTEL MUZZLE
OPPOSE SEMBLE STRIKE STRIVE
ANABATA CHLAMYS CONTEND
CONTEST GRAPPLE MANDYAS
PLUVIAL COMPLETE EXCHANGE
FACTABLE SEMICOPE STRUGGLE
VESTMENT
COPEHAN WINTUN
COPEPOD CALANID CAYENNE
DIAPTOMID
COPIAPITE MISY MISSY IHLEITE
COPIER COPIST SCRIBE
JOHNSONIAN
COPING CAP COPE FLUE SKEW
CORDON CAPSTONE FACTABLE
COPING STONE TABLET TABLING
COPIOUS FREE FULL GOOD LUSH
RANK RICH AMPLE LARGE
FLUENT LAVISH DIFFUSE
FLOWING FULSOME LENGTHY
PROFUSE REPLETE TEEMING
UBEROUS ABUNDANT AFFLUENT
FRUITFUL GENEROUS NUMEROUS
PLENTIFUL
COPIOUSNESS COPY PLENTY
COPPER AES COP BULL CENT
BOBBY METAL PENNY VENUS
CUPRUM PEELER VELLON BLISTER
CARNELIAN
(GILDED —) VERMEIL
(OF —) AEN
(PREF.) CHALC(O) CHALK(O)
CUPR(I)(O)
(SUFF.) CHALCITE
COPPERAS COPEROSE

INKSTONE COQUIMBITE
COPPERHEAD REDEYE MOCCASIN
COPPERSMITH TINKERBIRD
COPPER SULFATE BLUESTONE
COPPER SULFIDE FERRETTO
COVELLINE COVELLITE
COPPERY CUPREOUS
COPPICE COP BROW WOOD COPPY
COPSE FIRTH FRITH GROVE
COVERT FOREST GROWTH
SPROUT THICKET ARBUSTUM
(SUFF.) DRYMIUM
COPREUS (FATHER OF —) PELOPS
(HORSE OF —) ARION
(MOTHER OF —) HIPPODAMIA
COPSE CUT HAG HASP HEWT HOLT
MOTT SHAW TRIM DROKE HURST
CLEVIS SPINNY COPPICE
LOWWOOD SHACKLE SPINNEY
ARBUSTUM COPEWOOD
COPULA BAND LINK UNION
COPY APE CALK CAST ECHO EDIT
MIME MOCK NICK DITTO DUMMY
GROSS IMAGE MIMIC MODEL
PRINT REVIE STICK STUFF TRACE
CALQUE DOUBLE ECTYPE EFFIGY
FILLER FLIMSY FOLLOW MATTER
RECORD REFLEX SAMPLE
SHADOW EDITION EMULATE
ENGROSS ESTREAT EXTRACT
IMITATE PATTERN REDRAFT
REPLICA REPRINT RUBBING
TRACING VIDIMUS APOGRAPH
AUTOTYPE EXEMPLAR EXSCRIBE
EXSCRIPT KNOCKOFF LIKENESS
MANIFOLD POROTYPE PORTRAIT
RESEMBLE SPECIMEN MICROCOPY
MINIATURE PHOTOSTAT
(— EDITOR) SLOT
(— IN COMPUTER) DUMP
(— OF DOCUMENT) EXTRACT
PROTOCOL
(— OF DRESS) FORD
(DUPLICATE — OF PROGRAM)
BACKUP
(EXACT —) TENOR
(PRINTING —) KILL BOGUS
(UNREMUNERATIVE —) LEAN
(WORTHLESS —) BALAAM
COPYING MIMICRY INSINUATION
COPYIST COPIER PENMAN SCRIBE
COPYCAT SCRIVENER
COPYREAD EDIT SUBEDIT
COQUET TOY VAMP COPPY DALLY
FLIRT TRIFLE BLINKER CELIMENE
COQUETRY AGACERIE
COQUILLE SHELL
COQUINA DONAX
CORA NAYARIT
(HUSBAND OF —) ALONZO
CORACIIFORM NONPASSERINE
CORACLE SCOW CURAGH
CURRACH CURRANE
CORAL RED PINK AKORI BLOOD
POLYP ALCYON PALULE PORITE
FUNGIAN OCULINA ACROPORE
ASTRAEAN CORALLUM FAVOSITE
POLYPITE STAGHORN TUBIPORE
ZOOPHYTE MADREPORE
MILLEPORE
CORAL BEAN SOPHORA
FRIJOLILLO
CORAL-BELLS HEUCHERA

CORALBERRY BUCKBUSH
CORALFISH DOLLFISH
CORALROOT ORCHID CRAWLEY
CORAL SNAKE ELAPID ROLLER
ELAPOID SCYTALE
CORAL TREE GABGAB ERYTHRINA
CORBEIL PANNIER
CORBEL KNOT ANCON CORBET
TIMBER BRAGGER RESPOND
CARTOUCH SPRINGER
CORBELING SQUINCH
CORBIESTEP CATSTEP CROWSTEP
CORCIR CORKE ARCHIL CORKER
ORCHIL ARCHILLA
CORD AEA RIB AGAL BAND BIND
BOND FILE LACE LASH LINE ROPE
WELT BRAID CHORD FUNIS
GUARD LEASH LIGNE MATCH
NERVE OLONA TWINE TWIST
BINDER BOBBIN BRIDLE BUNGEE
CATGUT CHORDA CORDON
FIADOR GIRDLE LASHER LISERE
RACHIS SENNET STRING TENDON
TOGGLE AMENTUM BOWYANG
BULLION CORDING FUNICLE
LANIARD LANYARD MACRAME
SEAMING SEIZING SKIRREH
TIEBACK URACHUS BELLPULL
CHENILLE DRAWCORD HAIRLINE
SHOELACE WHIPCORD
(— AROUND BOWSTRING) SERVING
(— FOR PIPING) BOBBIN
(— OF CANDLENUT BARK) AEA
(CROCHETING —) CORDE
(ELECTRIC —) FLEX
(EMBROIDERY —) ARRASENE
(FRINGED —) LLAUTU
(HAMMOCK —S) CLEW
(HAWK'S —) CREANCE
(MASON'S —) SKIRREH
(ORNAMENTED —) AGLET AIGLET
(PARACHUTE —) SHROUD
(SACRED —) KUSTI
(SPINAL —) EON AEON NUKE
(TWISTED —) TORSADE
(PREF.) CHORD(O)
CORDAGE DA COIR ERUC FERU
HEMP IMBE JUTE KYAR ROPE
HAMBER SENNIT RIGGING
(LENGTH OF —) CATENARY
CORDATE HEARTED
CORDED TIED JETTED REPPED
RIBBED WELTED TWILLED
COR-DE-NUIT PASTORITA
CORDER RUFFER
CORDIAL REAL WARM CREAM
ARDENT CASSIS CLOVES DEVOUT
ELIXIR GENIAL HEARTY PASTIS
CORDATE DIAMBER LIQUEUR
PERSICO RATAFIA ROSOLIO
SINCERE ZEALOUS ANISETTE
FRIENDLY GRACIOUS PERSICOT
VIGOROUS BENEDICTINE
(NOT —) DISTANT STANDOFF
(PL.) SWEETS
CORDIERITE IOLITE FAHLUNITE
CORDON BLEU BENGALEE
CORDONNET CRESCENT
CORDWOOD BODYWOOD
CORE AME COB HUB NUT BONE
COKE COLK GIST KNOT NAVE
PITH BLOCK FOCUS HEART
NOWSE RUMPF SPOOL BARREL

CENTER CENTRE HEATER KERNEL
MATRIX MIDDLE NODULE POCKET
STAPLE CENTRUM CHEMISE
COMPANY CORNCOB ESSENCE
NUCLEUS FILAMENT HEARTING
(— OF COAL) STOCK
(— OF COLUMN) BELL HEART
(— OF CRICKET BALL) QUILT
(— OF LOG) PITH
(— OF MOLD) NOWEL
(EARTH'S HYPOTHETICAL —) NIFE
(WATER —) GLASSINESS
CORE ARBOR STALK
COREE CORANINE
CORELIGIONIST BROTHER
COREMIUM SYNEMA SYNNEMA
COREOPSIS TICKSEED TICKWEED
LEPTOSYNE
CORF TUB CAGE CAWF COFF CORB
SKIP CREEL BASKET DOSSER
CORGI CARDIGAN PEMBROKE
CORIANDER (— LEAVES) CILANTRO
CORIOLANUS (AUTHOR OF —)
SHAKESPEARE
(CHARACTER IN —) CAIUS TITUS
BRUTUS JUNIUS TULLUS LARTIUS
MARCIUS VALERIA AUFIDIUS
COMINIUS MENENIUS SICINIUS
VIRGILIA VOLUMNIA
CORIUM CUTIS DERMA LAYER
DERMIS
CORK BUNG PLUG FLOAT SHIVE
SUBER BOBBER BOUCHON
CRINKLE PHELLEM SOBERIN
STOPPER STOPPLE
(PREF.) PHELL(O) SUBERI
CORKED BOUCHE
CORKER WHIZ RAKER WHIZZ
CUTTER HUMDINGER
CORKSCREW WORMER
CORKWING CONNER
CORKWOOD BALSA GUANO
HAREFOOT
CORM SET BULB SEED CORMEL
CORMUS FREESIA UINTJIE
CORMEL BULBLET
(PL.) SPAWN
CORMORANT SHAG CRANE
GORMA NORIE SCARF SCART
DUIKER DUYKER GORMAW
GUANAY SCARFE SCARTH
GLUTTON SHAGLET
CORN ZEA DANA DENT SALT SAMP
GRAIN MAIZE SPIKE WYROK
AGNAIL CALLUS CLAVUS HELOMA
INDIAN KERNEL MEALIE NOCAKE
NUBBIN POWDER WYROCK
FORMITY FRUMENT FRUMENTY
PRESERVE SAUTERNE
(— SPURREY) YARR
(CROW —) COLICROOT
(CRUSHED —) STAMP
(DECORATED EAR OF —) TIPONI
(EAR OF —) ICKER
(GUINEA —) DURRA DHURRA
(INDIAN —) MAIZE INDIAN NOCAKE
(PARCHED —) ROKEE NOCAKE
PINOLE YOKAGE GRADDAN
ROKEAGE YOKEAGE
(STRING OF —) TRACE
(UNRIPE EAR OF —) TUCKET
CORNAGE HORNGELD
CORN BREAD PONE

KANKIE BANNOCK
CORN COCKLE GITH COCKLE
POPPLE COCKWEED HARDHEAD
MELANTHY
CORNCRACKER STATE
KENTUCKY
CORNCRAKE RAIL CORNBIRD
CORN CROWFOOT JOY
GOLDWEED HELLWEED
JACKWEED
CORNEL DOGWOOD REDBRUSH
CORNEOUS HORNLIKE KERASINE
CORNER IN GET OUT WRO BEND
CANT COIN HALK HERN JAMB
NOOK POOL TRAP TREE WICK
ANCON ANGLE BIGHT CATCH
COIGN ELBOW HERNE INGLE
JAMBE NICHE QUOIN TRUST
BOTTLE CANTLE CANTON COLLAR
CORNEL CRANNY RECESS SQUARE
OUTSIDE QUINYIE TURNING
MONOPOLY
(— IN A DRIFT) ARRAGE
(— OF EYE) CANTHUS
(— OF GUNSTOCK) TOE
(— OF MOLDBOARD) SHIN
(— OF SAIL) CLEW CLUE TACK
GOOSEWING
(CHIMNEY —) LUG
(LOWER —) CLEW CLUE
(RE-ENTRANT —) DIEDRE
(ROUNDED —) FILET FILLET
(SECRET —) CREEK
(TIGHT —) BOX
(PREF.) (— OF EYE) CANTH(O)
CORNERPIECE BUMPER CANTLE
CORNERSTONE COIN BASIS COIGN
QUOIN HEADSTONE
CORNET CONE HORN ZINK TWIST
ZINKE ZINCKE CORONET
CORNETTO CORNOPEAN
CORNETFISH FLUTEMOUTH
HEMIBRANCH
CORNFIELD MOW
CORN FLAG LEVERS
CORNFLOWER BLUET BLAVER
BARBEAU BLUECAP BLUECUP
BLAEWORT
CORN GROMWELL SALFERN
CORNHUSK CAP
CORNHUSKER STATE NEBRASKA
CORNHUSKING SHUCKING
CORNICE CAP BAND DRIP EAVE
JOPY ANCON CROWN JOWPY
DETAIL GEISON PELMET ANTEFIX
MOLDING SURBASE ASTRAGAL
SWANNECK
(UNDER SIDE OF —) PLANCIER
(PREF.) GEISSO
CORNICLE SIPHON SYPHON
CORNISHMAN CELT KELT
CORN MARIGOLD GOLD GOOLS
BODDLE BOODLE BUDDLE
GOWLAN GOLDING GOLLAND
CORN MEAL MASA SAMP ATOLE
HOECAKE
CORN PARSLEY UMBEL
CORN POPPY BLAVER CANKER
COCKLE COPROSE EARACHE
PONCEAU REDWEED SOLDIER
CORN SALAD FETTICUS
MILKGRASS
CORN SPURREY YARR

CORN STACK HOVEL
CORNSTALKS KARBI
CORNSTARCH BINDER
CORNU HORN THYROHYAL
CORNUCOPIA HORN CORNU
COFFIN
CORNUS CORNIN REDBRUSH
CORN VIOLET SPECULARIA
CORN WOUNDWORT STACHYS
CORNY BANAL STALE TRITE
MICKEY BUCKEYE
COROADO BORORO
CORODY CONRED
COROEBUS (FATHER OF —)
MYGDON
(SLAYER OF —) DIOMEDES
COROLLA CUP BELL COROL
CUPULE LIGULE PERIANTH
COROLLARY DOGMA PORISM
RESULT TRUISM ADJUNCT
THEOREM CONSECTARY
COROMANDEL COLCOTHAR
CORONA BUR BURR CIGAR CROWN
GLORY AURORA FILLET ROSARY
WREATH AUREOLE CIRCLET
CORONET GARLAND LARMIER
SCYPHUS
CORONAL CRONET CORONEL
CROWNAL
CORONATION ABHISEKA
CROWNMENT
CORONATION OF POPPAEA
(CHARACTER IN —) NERONE
OTTONE SENECA OTTAVIA
POPPAEA DRUSILLA
(COMPOSER OF —) MONTEVERDI
CORONER ELISOR CROWNER
EXAMINER SEARCHER
CORONET BAND BURR CROWN
TIARA ANADEM CIRCLE CRONET
DIADEM TIMBRE WREATH
CHAPLET CORONAL CROWNAL
CROWNET GARLAND CROWNLET
CORONIS (FATHER OF —) PHLEGYAS
PHORONEUS
(HUSBAND OF —) BUTES
(LOVER OF —) APOLLO ISCHYS
(SON OF —) ASCLEPIUS
CORONOPUS CARARA
CORPORAL NYM FANO NAIG NAIK
PALL FANON FANUM NAYAK
PHANO BODILY EXEMPT GUNNER
NAIGUE NAIQUE SINDON TINDAL
CORPORATE UNITED COMBINED
CORPORATION BODY CITY FIRM
POUCH TRUST SCHOLA BOROUGH
COLLEGE COMMUNE FREEDOM
GUILDRY SOCIETY SPONSOR
CORPOREAL REAL HYLIC SOMAL
ACTUAL BODILY CARNAL FLESHLY
SOMATIC MATERIAL PHYSICAL
TANGIBLE
CORPOSANT HERMO
CORPS CORE ORDU VELITES
SERAGLIO
(— DE BALLET) ENSEMBLE
CORPSE BIER BODY CLAY DUST
LICH MORT GHOST MUMMY RELIC
STIFF TRUCK ZOMBI CORPUS
DEADER ZOMBIE ANATOMY
CADAVER CARCASS CARRION
CROAKER DEADMAN FLOATER
(— WASHING) TAHARAH

(PREF.) NECR(O)
CORPSMAN MEDIC BEARER
CORPULENCE FAT FATNESS
STOUTNESS
CORPULENT FAT BULKY BURLY
FATTY GROSS HUSKY OBESE
PLUMP STOUT TUBBY FLESHY
GREASY PORTLY ROTUND
ADIPOSE BELLIED WEIGHTY
CORPUSCLE CELL GHOST
GLOBULE HEMATID HAEMATID
HEMOCYTE
CORRAL PEN STY COOP ATAJO
POUND TAMBO CONFINE
ENCLOSE STOCKAGE SURROUND
(ELEPHANT —) KRAAL KEDDAH
CORRECT DUE FIT FIX TIC BEET
BOOK EDIT JAKE JUST LEAL LEAN
MARK MEND NICE OKAY SMUG
TRUE AMEND CHECK CLEAN
EMEND EXACT ORDER RIGHT
SOUND SPILL ADJUST BETTER
CHANGE INFORM PROPER PUNISH
REBUKE REFORM REMEDY REPAIR
REVAMP REVISE SEEMLY STRICT
ADDRESS CHAPTER CHASTEN
CORRIGE ELEGANT IMPROVE
PERFECT PRECISE RECLAIM
RECTIFY REDRESS REGULAR
REPROVE SINCERE ACCURATE
CHASTISE DEFINITE EMENDATE
EQUALIZE REGULATE RIGOROUS
STRAIGHT TRUTHFUL CASTIGATE
(APPROXIMATELY —) BALLPARK
(GRAMMATICALLY —) CONGRUE
(MATHEMATICALLY —) PURE
(PREF.) ORTH(O)
CORRECTABLE CORRIGIBLE
CORRECTION YARD REFORM
CENSURE FLEXURE IMPRINT
REDRESS SCOURGE FUGACITY
(— IN COMPUTER PROGRAM)
PATCH
CORRECTIVE SALT REMEDY
CORRECTLY JUST RIGHT ARIGHT
RIGHTLY SOUNDLY PROPERLY
CORRECTNESS TRUTH DECORUM
FITNESS JUSTICE ACCURACY
JUSTNESS VERACITY
**CORREGIDOR, DER (CHARACTER IN
—)** TIO LUCAS MERCEDES
FRASQUITA CORREGIDOR
(COMPOSER OF —) WOLF
CORRELATE PARALLEL
HARMONIZE
CORRELATIVE OR NOR THEN
EQUAL STILL EITHER MUTUAL
NEITHER ANALOGUE CONJOINT
REDDITIVE
CORRESPOND FIT GEE JIBE SUIT
AGREE MATCH TALLY WRITE
ACCORD ANSWER CONCUR
SQUARE COMPORT RESPOND
COINCIDE PARALLEL QUADRATE
(— IN SOUND) ASSONATE
(— TO) ENSUE
CORRESPONDENCE MAIL TALLY
ANALOGY CONSENT HARMONY
KEEPING LETTERS
TRAFFIC FUNCTION
HOMOGENY HOMOLOGY
SYMMETRY SYMPATHY
SIMILARITY SIMILITUDE

PARALLELISM RESEMBLANCE
(INCOMPLETE —) ASSONANCE
(OFFICIAL —) BUMF
CORRESPONDENT NEWSMAN
QUADRATE RELEVANT STRINGER
SUITABLE STRINGMAN
CORRESPONDING LIKE SIMILAR
PARALLEL ACCORDANT
CONGRUENT
(PREF.) COUNTER
CORRESPONDINGLY SORTLY
SIMILARLY
CORRIDA BULLFIGHT
CORRIDOR HALL AISLE ORIEL
VISTA ARCADE COULOIR GALLERY
PASSAGE COULISSE HALLCIST
TRESANCE
CORRIE CIRQUE
CORRIGENDUM ERRATUM
CORROBORATE PROVE SECOND
APPROVE COMFORT CONFIRM
SUPPORT SUSTAIN ROBORATE
CORRODE EAT BITE BURN ETCH
FRET GNAW RUST DECAY ERODE
EXEDE TOUCH WASTE BEGNAW
CANKER IMPAIR CONSUME
GRAPHITE
CORRODING BITE RODENT
ESURINE
CORROSION EROSION
EMBAYMENT
CORROSIVE ACID ACRID ARDENT
BITING CORSIE EATING CAUSTIC
EROSIVE ESURINE FRETFUL
MORDANT DIERETIC
CORRUGATE GIMP CRIMP CRISP
FURROW RUMPLE CRINKLE
CRUMPLE WRINKLE
CORRUGATED PLAITED WRINKLY
FURROWED WRINKLED
CORRUGATION BAT FOLD GILL
REED RUGA CREASE PUCKER
CRINKLE WRINKLE
CORRUPT BAD ILL LOW ROT WEM
EVIL RANK SICK SOIL VILE ADDLE
BLEND BRIBE FALSE SPOIL STAIN
SULLY TAINT VENAL VENOM
WEMMY AUGEAN CANKER
DEBASE DEFILE FESTER IMPURE
INFECT PALTER POISON PUTRID
RAVISH ROTTEN SEPTIC ABUSIVE
ATTAINT BEDEVIL BEGRIME
BESHREW CARRION CORRUMP
CROOKED DEBAUCH DEFINED
DEGRADE DEPRAVE ENVENOM
FALSIFY IMMORAL PECCANT
PERVERT POLLUTE PUTREFY
SUBVERT TRADING VIOLATE
VITIATE CONFOUND DEPRAVED
EMPOISON PERVERSE POLLUTED
PRACTICE PRACTISE SINISTER
VITIATED PERVERTED
ADULTERATE CONTAMINATE
PECKSNIFFIAN
CORRUPTED SICK
CORRUPTION DIRT SOIL VICE
DECAY SPOIL TAINT JOBBERY
PRAVITY SQUALOR ADULTERY
BARRATRY INFECTION
MALVERSATION PUTREFACTION
CORSAC ADIVE KARAGAN
CORSAGE WAIST BODICE
BOUQUET CANEZOU

CORSAIR BUG CAPER PIRATE
ROBBER CURSARO PICAROON
ROCKFISH
CORSAIR, THE (CHARACTER IN —)
SEID MEDORA CORRADO
GULNARA
(COMPOSER OF —) VERDI
CORSELET LORICA THORAX
ALLECRET HALECRET
CORSET BELT BUSK STAY STAYS
GIRDLE SUPPORT
CORSICA (CAPITAL OF —) AJACCIO
(HARBOR OF —) BASTIA
(MOUNTAIN OF —) CINTO
ROTONDO
(RIVER OF —) GOLO TARAVO
GRAVONE
(TOWERLIKE STRUCTURES OF —)
TORRI
(TOWN OF —) CALVI CORTE ALERIA
BASTIA AJACCIO SARTENE
(VEGETATION OF —) MAQUIS
CORSICAN PINE LARCH
CORTEGE POMP SUITE TRAIN
PARADE RETINUE
CORTEX BARK PEEL RIND MANTLE
PALLIUM PERIBLEM PERIDIUM
CORUNDUM RUBY SAND EMERY
ADAMAS ALUMINA ABRASIVE
AMETHYST CORINDON SAPPHIRE
BARKLYITE
(SYNTHETIC —) EMERALD
CORUSCATE BLAZE FLASH GLEAM
SHINE GLANCE GLISTEN GLITTER
RADIATE SPARKLE BRANDISH
CORVEE POLO
CORVINO (WIFE OF —) CELIA
CORYPHENE DORADO
CORYTHUS (FATHER OF —) ZEUS
PARIS JUPITER
(SON OF —) DARDANUS
(WIFE OF —) ELECTRA
CORYZA COLD
COSAM (FATHER OF —) ELMODAM
**COSA RARA, UNA (CHARACTER IN
—)** TITA LILLA CORRADO LISARGO
GIOVANNI
(COMPOSER OF —) SOLER
COSCET COTTAR COTARIUS
COTSETLE
COSETTE (MOTHER OF —) FANTINE
**COSI FAN TUTTE (CHARACTER IN —
)** ALFONSO DESPINA FERRANDO
DORABELLA GUGLIELMO
FIORDILIGI
(COMPOSER OF —) MOZART
COSMETIC KOHL WASH CREAM
FUCUS HENNA LINER PAINT
PETER ROUGE BLANCH CERUSE
CRAYON ENAMEL POMADE
POWDER BLUSHER MASCARA
STIBIUM AMANDINE LIPSTICK
STIBNITE
COSMIC VAST MUNDANE ORDERLY
CATHOLIC INFINITE
COSMOLABE PANTACOSM
COSMOPOLITAN URBAN
ECUMENIC PANDEMIC
AMPHIGEAN
COSMOS EARTH GLOBE ORDER
REALM WORLD FLOWER HEAVEN
HARMONY UNIVERSE
COSSACK TURK TATAR ATAMAN

HETMAN TARTAR ZAPOROGUE

COSSET MUD PET LAMB CARESS
CODDLE CUDDLE FONDLE
PAMPER TIDDLE

COSSETTE CHIP SLICE STRIP
SCHNITZEL

COST SIT GAFF LOSS PAIN SOAK
BASIS PRICE SPEND STAND
VALUE CHARGE DAMAGE OUTLAY
SCATHE EXPENSE REPRISE
ESTIMATE SPENDING

COSTA RICA

CAPE: ELENA VELAS BLANCO
CAPITAL: SANJOSE
COIN: COLON CENTIMO
DANCE: PUNTO TORITO
GULF: DULCE NICOYA PAPAGAYO
INDIAN: BORUCA GUAYMI
ISLAND: COCO
LAKE: ARENAL
MEASURE: VARA CAFIZ CAHIZ
    FANEGA TERCIA CAJUELA
    CANTARO MANZANA
MOUNTAIN: BLANCO CHIRRIPO
PENINSULA: OSA NICOYA
POINT: QUEPOS CAHUITA
    GALONOS LLERENA
PORT: LIMON PUNTARENAS
RIVER: POAS IRAZU MATINA
    SIXAOLA TENORIA TARCOLES
TOWN: CANAS LIMON VESTA
    BORUCA NICOYA BAGACES
    CARTAGO GOLFITO HEREDIA
    LIBERIA NEGRITA ALAJUELA
    COLORADO GUAPILES
VOLCANO: POAS IRAZU
WEIGHT: BAG CAJA LIBRA

COSTERMONGER COSTER
HAWKER NIPPER PEARLY
PEDDLER BARROWMAN

COSTIVE BOUND EMPLASTIC

COSTLINESS DEARTH DEARNESS

COSTLY DEAR FINE HIGH RICH
SALT DAINTY LAVISH SILVER
COSTFUL COSTLEW GORGEOUS
PLATINUM PRECIOUS PRODIGAL
SPLENDID PRICELESS

COSTMARY TANSY ALECOST
MAUDLIN ROSEMARY

COSTREL KEG HEAD FLASK BOTTLE
COYSTREL

COSTUME RIG GARB ROBE SARI
SUIT BURKA DRESS GETUP HABIT
SHAPE TRUSS ATTIRE DOMINO
FORMAL SETOUT TOILET
APPAREL BLOOMER CLOTHES
POLLERA RAIMENT SCARLET
UNIFORM CHARSHAF CLOTHING
ENSEMBLE TOILETTE VENETIAN
(ACADEMIC —) GUISE

COSTUSROOT PACHAK PUTCHOCK

COSY FEEL FEIL SNUG INTIME

COT BED HUT MAT PEN BOAT
COOP COTE FOLD ABODE BOTHY
CABIN COUCH COVER HOUSE
STALL COTEEN CRADLE GURNEY
PALLET SHEATH TANGLE
CHARPAI CHARPOY COTTAGE
SHELTER BEDSTEAD COTHOUSE
DWELLING STRETCHER

COTERIE SET RING CABAL JUNTO

MONDE CIRCLE CLIQUE GALAXY
SETOUT CENACLE CIRCUIT
COLLEGE PLATOON SOCIETY

COTHURNUS BOOT BUSKIN
COTHURN

COTILLION GERMAN

COTO OREJON

COTTA KATHA STOLE MANTLE
BLANKET SURPLICE VESTMENT

COTTAGE BOX COT HUT BACH
BARI COSH CRIB SHED WALK
BOTHY BOWER CABIN HOUSE
HOVEL LODGE SHACK BOHAWN
BOTHIE CABANA CHALET
SHELTER BUNGALOW COTHOUSE
SHEELING SHIELING THALTHAN

COTTAGE CHEESE SKYR
SMEARCASE SMIERCASE

COTTAGER MAILER

COTTER KEY MAT PIN VEX CLOT
BOWPIN COTMAN FASTEN
MAILER POTTER PUCKER SHRINK
TOGGLE WITHER CONGEAL
COTTIER PEASANT SHRIVEL
VILLEIN COTARIUS COTTAGER
COTTEREL ENTANGLE FORELOCK
LINCHPIN

COTTON SAK BEAT DRAB FLOG
MALO PIMA AGREE BAYAL BOLLY
DERRY MATTA SAKEL SURAT
BOMBACE BROACH CODDLE
COMBER DHURRY FABRIC
MAARAD MALLOW NANKIN
PEELER STAPLE ALGODON
BENDERS CANTOON DHURRIE
GARMENT GINNING SILESIA
SUCCEED
(— SQUARE) TZUT TZUTE
(BOLL OF —) SNAP
(NAPPED —) LAMBSKIN
(PAINTED —) INDIENNE
(PIECE OF —) SPONGE
(PRINTED —) SARONG
(RAW —) LINT BAYAL
(SILK —) FLOSS
(STRIPED —) BENGAL
(TREE —) MACO
(TWILLED —) JEAN SALLO SALLOO
(WAD OF —) TAMPON
(WASTE —) GRABBOTS
(PREF.) BYSSI BYSSO

COTTON GRASS CANNA
CANNACH DRAWLING

COTTON PLANT LAMB
(— FLOWER) SQUARE

COTTON TREEE SIMAL

COTTONWOOD ALAMO

COTYLEDON BUTTON PICHURIM
SARCOLOBE

COUCH BED COT KIP LAY LIE HIDE
LAIR LURK SOFA SUNK DIVAN
INLAY LODGE PRESS SKULK SLINK
SNEAK SNOOP SQUAB SQUAT
UTTER BURROW CLOTHE DAYBED
LITTER PALLET PLINTH SETTEE
CONCEAL EXPRESS HAMMOCK
OTTOMAN OVERLAY RECLINE
TRANSOM
(NUPTIAL —) THORE
(WOODEN —) RUSTBANK
(PREF.) CLIN(O) STROMATI
STROMATO
(SUFF.) STROMA

COUCH GRASS CUTCH KUTCH
QUACK QUICK TWICH QUITCH
SCOTCH SCUTCH STROIL QUICKEN
WITHVINE

COUGAR CAT PUMA PAINTER
PANTHER CARCAJOU

COUGH YEX YOX BAFF BARK HACK
HOST KINK CHINK CROUP HOAST
HOOSE HOOZE TISICK TUSSIS

COUGH DROP PASTIL TROCHE
LOZENGE PASTILLE

COUGH SYRUP LINCTUS

COULEE DRAW GORGE GULCH
COOLEY RAVINE

COULOMB WEBER

COUMA SORVA HYAHYA

COUNCIL BODY BULE DAEL DIET
DUMA FONO RAAD REDE YUAN
BOARD BOULE BUNGA CABAL
CAPUT DIVAN DIWAN DOUMA
JIRGA JUNTA JUNTO SABHA
SOBOR STATE SYNOD THING
JIRGAH LUKIKO MAJLIS
POWWOW QUORUM SENATE
SOVIET TARYBA CABILDO
CABINET CHAMBER CONSULT
GERUSIA HUSTING MEETING
PENSION WHITLEY ASSEMBLY
CONCLAVE CONGRESS FOLKMOOT
FOLKMOTE HEEMRAAD
HEEMRAAT MINISTRY PLACITUM
RIGSRAAD CAMARILLA
PARLIAMENT AMPHICTYONS
(MORMON —) PRESIDENCY

COUNCILLOR RAT VIZIR ENDUNA
INDUNA VIZIER FAIPULE SENATOR
WISEMAN DECURION
(PL.) ANZIANI

COUNSEL RAD LORE REDE RULE
RUNE SILK WARD WARN AREED
CHIDE DEVIL GUIDE ADVICE
ADVISE CONFER LEADER
ABOGADO CAUTION COUNCIL
LECTURE ADMONISH ADVOCATE
PRUDENCE
(JUNIOR LEGAL —) DEVIL
(KING'S —) SILK
(SACRED —) TORAH

COUNSELOR RAT SAGE WITE
CONSUL LAWYER MENTOR
NESTOR ADVISER ADVISOR
COUNSEL ECHEVIN GONZALO
PROCTOR STARETS ADVOCATE
ATTORNEY REDESMAN
UCALEGON

COUNT ADD GAN SUM TOT BANK
CAST EARL FOOT GANO GRAF
NAME RELY RIME SIZE TALE TELL
TOTE COMES COMPT COMTE
GRAVE JUDGE RHYME SCORE
TALLY WEIGH CENSUS CONSUL
COUNTY DEPEND ESTEEM FIGURE
IMPUTE NUMBER RECKON
TOTTLE ACCOUNT ARTICLE
ASCRIBE COMPUTE GANELON
ADNUMBER NUMERATE
SANCTION CALCULATE
PALSGRAVE
(— IN BILLIARDS) DOUBLE
(— OF A FIBER) GRIST
(— OF SHEEP OR CATTLE) BREAK
(— ON) LITE RELY
(— UNIT) WARP

COUNTABLE DISCRETE

COUNTENANCE AID MUG OWN
RUD ABET BROW FACE GIZZ LEER
MIEN PUSS SHOW VULT CHEER
FAVOR FRONT GRACE ASPECT
ENDURE UPHOLD VISAGE
APPROVE BEARING CONDUCT
ENDORSE FEATURE PROFFER
SUPPORT BEFRIEND DEMEANOR
FOREHEAD SANCTION
SEMBLANCE
(PREF.) PROSOP(O)

COUNTER BAR DIB LOT BANK
BUCK CENT CHIP DESK DUMP
EDDY FISH JACK KIST PAWN
STOP CAROM CHECK FORCE
HATCH JETON MERIL PIECE SHELF
STALL STAND TABLE TOTER
BUFFET COMBAT GEIGER ISLAND
JETTON MARKER OPPOSE SQUAIL
ADVERSE BUTTOCK CONTEND
CURRENT FANTAIL SHAMBLE
CONTRARY MAHOGANY OPPOSITE
TELLTALE
(— TO) AGAINST
(LEADEN —) DUMP
(LUNCH —) PLACE
(PREF.) ANTI GAIN

COUNTERACT CHECK CANCEL
OPPOSE RESIST THWART
BALANCE CORRECT DESTROY
NULLIFY ANTIDOTE NEGATIVE

COUNTERACTION DEADLOCK

COUNTERACTIVE REMEDY
ADVERSE

COUNTERBALANCE COVER WEIGH
CANCEL SETOFF BALANCE

COUNTERCLOCKWISE DIRECT
DIRECTLY

COUNTERCURRENT BACKSET

COUNTEREARTH ANTICHTHON

COUNTERFEIT ACT BASE COIN
COPY DAUB DUFF FAKE IDOL
MOCK SHAM BELIE BOGUS
DUMMY FALSE FEIGN FLASH
FORGE FUDGE GAMMY MIMIC
PHONY QUEER SNIDE AFFECT
ASSUME CHEMIC ERSATZ FORGED
PSEUDO TINSEL BASTARD
CHEMICK DUFFING FALSIFY
FASHION FEIGNED FORGERY
IMITANT IMITATE SIMULAR
BORROWED DEFORMED
PHANTASM POSTICHE POSTIQUE
RESEMBLE SIMILIZE SIMULATE
SPURIOUS SUPPOSED
(PREF.) PSEUD(O)

COUNTERFEITER COINER
JACKMAN JARKMAN SCRATCHER

COUNTERFEITERS (AUTHOR OF —)
GIDE
(CHARACTER IN —) LAURA VEDEL
ARMAND GEORGE ROBERT
BERNARD EDOUARD LILLIAN
OLIVIER VINCENT DOUVIERS
GRIFFITH MOLINIER PASSAVANT
GHERIDANISOL PROFITENDIEU

COUNTERFEITING COINING
FICTION POSTICHE POSTIQUE

COUNTERFOIL FOIL STUB CHECK

COUNTERFORT SCONCE BUTTRESS

COUNTERION GEGENION

COUNTERIRRITANT MOXA GINGER
IODINE PEPPER MUSTARD
CANTHARIS
COUNTERMAND STOP ANNUL
CANCEL FORBID RECALL REVOKE
ABOLISH RESCIND REVERSE
UNORDER ABROGATE PROHIBIT
COUNTERMOVE DEMARCHE
COUNTERMOVEMENT BACKFIRE
COUNTERPANE PANE LIGGER
BEDSPREAD
COUNTERPART COPY LIKE MATE
SPIT TWIN FETCH IMAGE MATCH
MORAL SHELL TALLY COUSIN
DOUBLE SHADOW BALANCE
COUNTER OBVERSE PENDANT
SIMILAR ANTIPART PARALLEL
RESCRIPT SIMILITUDE
(SPEECH —) A
COUNTERPOINT FOIL DESCANT
CONTRAST FABURDEN
COUNTERPOISE POISE OFFSET
BALANCE EQUALIZE MAKEWEIGHT
COUNTERPOISON ORVIETAN
COUNTERSIGN BACK MARK SEAL
SIGN SIGNAL CONFIRM
ENDORSE PASSWORD SANCTION
COUNTERSINK DISH REAM BEVEL
CHAMFER
COUNTERSTATEMENT ANSWER
COUNTERSUN ANTHELION
COUNTERWEIGHT TARE
MAKEWEIGHT
COUNTERWORD ANIMAL
COUNTER
COUNTESS OLIVIA COMTESSE
CONTESSA
COUNTING ACCOUNT
COUNTLESS INFINITE
NUMBERLESS
(PREF.) MYRI(A)(O)
COUNT OF MONTE CRISTO
(AUTHOR OF —) DUMAS
(CHARACTER IN —) FARIA ALBERT
DANTES EDMOND HAIDEE
MONDEGO MORRELL DANGLARS
MERCEDES FERDINAND
VALENTINE VILLEFORT
CADEROUSSE MAXIMILIAN
COUNTRIFIED JAY BUCOLIC
LOBBISH AGRESTIC HOBNAILED
COUNTRY SOD DESH EARD HICK
HOME KITH LAND PAIS SOIL
ADDLE CLIME EARTH FAIRY FRITH
MARCH PLAGE REALM STATE
TRACT WEALD GROUND KINTRA
KINTRY NATION PEOPLE REGION
STICKS UPLAND IMAMATE
KWINTRA MONKERY MUFASAL
BACKVELD DISTRICT DOMINION
ELDORADO LANDWARD
MAGAZINE MOFUSSIL REGALITY
PRINCIPALITY
(— OF ETHIOPIA) SEBA
(— OF ORIGIN) HOMELAND
(— OF PERFECTION) EUTOPIA
(— ON SEA) SEABOARD
(— STYLE) PAYSANNE
(ANCIENT —) ARAM
(CABIN —) LOBBY
(FRONTIER —) BORDER
(HOME —) BLIGHTY

(IMAGINARY —) EREWHON
LILLIPUT RURITANIA
(LIMESTONE —) KARST
(MARITIME —) MAREMMA
(MYTHICAL —) UTOPIA LEONNOYS
SVITHIOD SWITHIOD TEUTONIA
(OPEN —) BLED VELD FIELD VELDT
WEALD CAMPAIGN
(PETTY —) TOPARCHY
(ROUGH —) BOONDOCK
BUNDOCKS
(RURAL —) OUTBACK
(PREF.) RURI
(SUFF.) STAN
COUNTRYMAN HOB BOOR HIND
KERN TIKE CHURL CLOWN HODGE
KERNE SWAIN YOKEL GAFFER
GIBARO JIBARO GRANGER
HAYSEED LANDMAN PAESANO
PAISANO PEASANT PLOWMAN
LANDSMAN
(PL.) KITH
COUNTRYSIDE BLED BOCAGE
MOFUSSIL
COUNTRY WIFE (AUTHOR OF —)
WYCHERLEY
(CHARACTER IN —) HORNER
ALITHEA HARCOURT SPARKISH
PINCHWIFE
COUNTY AMT LAN SEAT FYLKE
SHIRE DOMAIN PARISH BOROUGH
COMITAT NORFOLK DISTRICT
COUP BUY BLOW DEAL PLAN PLAY
COUPE FAULT SCOOP UPSET
ATTACK BARTER PUTSCH REFAIT
STRIKE STROKE CAPSIZE TRAFFIC
OVERTURN
COUP DE POING BOUCHER
HANDSTONE
COUPE CUT CABRIOLET
LANDAULET
COUPED HUMETTY HUMETTEE
COUPLE DUO TIE TWO BOND CASE
DYAD JOIN LINK MATE PAIR SPAN
TEAM TWIN YOKE BRACE LEASH
MARRY TWAIN UNITE GEMINI
SPLINE SWINGE BRACKET
CONNECT COUPLER COUPLET
DOUBLET SHACKLE TWOSOME
VOLTAIC ACCOUPLE ASSEMBLE
COPULATE ACCOMPANY
(— OF HAWKS) CAST
COUPLED GEMEL YOKED JOINED
WEDDED GEMELED COPULATE
GEMINATE
COUPLER LINK RING BOBBER
COPULA JANNEY LINKER SUTURE
UNITER DRAGBAR DRAWBAR
REDUCER SHACKLE SNAPPER
TIRASSE DRAGBOLT DRAWBOLT
DRAWGEAR SHACKLER
COUPLET BAIT COPLA ELEGIAC
COUPLING HUB HICKY UNION
CLUTCH HICKEY NIPPLE SHACKLE
SHACKLER
COUPON TWOFER
COURAGE BIEL FIRE GRIT GUTS
MIND MOOD PROW SAND SOUL
BIELD CREST HEART HONOR
MOXIE NERVE PLUCK SPUNK
VALOR DARING DAUBER METTLE
PECKER SPIRIT VIRTUE VIRTUS

BRAVERY COJONES CORAGIO
HEROISM MANHEAD MANHOOD
MANSHIP PROWESS STOMACH
VENTURE AUDACITY BOLDNESS
CORRAGIO FIRMNESS TENACITY
(— OF CONVICTION) STAMINA
(MORAL —) STRENGTH
(PREF.) THYM(O)
(SUFF.) THYMIA
COURAGEOUS BOLD GAME GOOD
TALL BRAVE GUTSY HARDY LUSTY
MANLY STOUT WIGHT DARING
HEROIC MANFUL PLUCKY SPUNKY
CORIAUS GALLANT SPARTAN
STAUNCH VALIANT FEARLESS
GENEROUS INTREPID VALOROUS
COURAGEOUSLY BIG BRAVELY
COURANT ROMP CAPER DANCE
LETTER CORANTO CURRENT
GAZETTE RUNNING
COURBARIL JATOBA LOCUST
GUAPINOL CUAPINOLE
COURGETTE ZUCCHINI
COURIER NEWS POST GUIDE
SCOUT KAVASS NEWING POSTER
ESTAFET ORDERLY PATAMAR
POSTBOY POSTMAN SOILAGE
CICERONE CURSITOR DRAGOMAN
HORSEMAN ORDINARY
PATTAMAR
COURLAN LIMPKIN
COURONNE CROWN
COURSE FLY LAP RUN WAY BEAT
BENT FLOW GAGE GAME GANG
GATE HEAT HUNT LANE LINE
LODE MESS MODE PACE PATH
RACE RACK RAIK RAND RILL RING
RINK ROAD ROTA ROTE WENT
CLASS COURS CRUST CURRY
CURVE CYCLE DRAFT DRIFT
DRIVE EMBER GAUGE GREAT
LAPSE LAYER LEDGE MARCH
MOYEN ORBIT PLATE POINT
ROUTE SENSE SITHE SPACE STEPS
SWELT SWING TENOR TRACK
TRACT TRADE TRAIL TREND
WEENT ARTERY CAREER COPING
CURSUS DROMOS FURROW
GALLOP GIRDER GUTTER HONORS
MANNER METHOD MOTION
RESACA SCHOOL SERIES SPHERE
STREAM STREET SYSTEM TRIPOS
ZODIAC AZIMUTH BEELINE
CHANNEL CIRCUIT CONDUCT
DIAULOS DRAUGHT HIGHWAY
LECTURE PASSADE PASSAGE
PATHWAY PROCESS ROUTINE
RUNNING SEMINAR SERVICE
STRETCH SUBJECT SUCCESS
TIDEWAY TRAJECT TRUNDLE
CURRENCY CURRICLE DIADROME
DISTANCE ELECTIVE PROGRESS
RECOURSE SEQUENCE STEERAGE
TENDENCY MOTORDROME
(— OF A ROPE) LEAD
(— OF ACTION) LARK TACK TROD
VEIN DANCE CUSTOM ROUTINE
DEMARCHE
(— OF ACTIVITY) SIDELINE
(— OF BOAT) LEG
(— OF BRICK) BED ROWLOCK
SCINTLE CREASING

(— OF FEEDING) DIET
(— OF KNITTING) BOUT
(— OF LIFE) GOINGS PILGRIMAGE
(— OF LUCK) FORTUNE
(— OF MASONRY) BAHUT STILT
COPING HEADING SKEWBACK
(— OF NATURE) TAO
(— OF PROCEDURE) RULE
(— OF PROCEEDING) FORE
(— OF PURSUIT) SCENT
(— OF ROADBED) SUBCRUST
(— OF STONES) BED PLINTH
(— OF STUDY) DEBATE COLLEGE
LECTURE SEMINAR ELECTIVE
(— OF SUN) JOURNEY
(— OF TREATMENT) CURE
(— OF WALL) CORNICE
(— WITH GREYHOUNDS) GREW
(BELL-RINGING —) HUNT
(CIRCULAR —) SWEEP CHUKKAR
CHUKKER COMPASS
(COLLEGE —) PRECEPTORIAL
(CURVING —) SWING
(CUSTOMARY —) GUISE
(DOWNWARD —) DIP DECLINE
TOBOGGAN
(DUE —) TRAIN
(EASY —) PIPE
(EXACT —) BEAM
(FIRST —) ANTEPAST
(FREE —) FORTH
(IRREGULAR —) ERROR
(LAST —) VOID
(MIDDLE —) MIDS TEMPER
(NATURAL —) RITA
(OBLIQUE —) SKEW
(OVERHANGING —) JET
(PREDETERMINED —) DESTINY
(ROUNDABOUT —) DETOUR
WINDLASS
(SETTLED —) BIAS GROOVE
(SKIING —) SCHUSS
(PREF.) DROM(O)
COURSER HORSE RACER STEED
CUSSER CHARGER
COURSING CURSIVE
COURT BAR BID HOF SEE SUE WOO
AREA BAIL BODY CLAW FUSS
GATE GIRL LEET QUAD ROTA
SEAT SEEK SUIT TOWN WALE
WARD WYND YARD ARENA
BENCH BUREO CURIA CURRY
DAIRI DIVAN FAVOR FORUM
FUERO GARTH JUDGE PATIO
SHIRE SPACE SPARK SPOON
SWEET TEMPT THING THINK
TOURN TRAIN YAMEN ADALAT
ALLURE ATRIUM BAILEY COUNTY
DARGAH DURBAR DURGAH
GEMOTE HOMAGE INVITE PALACE
PARVIS PURSUE SPLUNT SUITOR
TOLSEY ADAWLUT ADDRESS
ASSIZES ATTRACT BARMOTE
DUOVIRI EPHETAE FOREIGN
HELIAEA HUSTING JUSTICE
PARVISE RETINUE SOLICIT
TEMENOS TOURNEL AUDIENCE
BURHMOOT CHANCERY
FOUJDARY LAWCOURT
MARKMOOT MARKMOTE
QUARANTY SERENADE SESSIONS
SWANMOTE TRIBUNAL

WOODMOTE PERIBOLOS PARLIAMENT
(— **FAVOR**) FAWN
(— **OF A HUNDRED**) MALL MALLUM MALLUS
(— **OF CIRCUIT JUDGES**) EYRE
(— **OF FORTRESS**) PEEL
(— **OF MIKADO**) DAIRI
(— **ORDER**) VACATUR
(— **THE GREAT**) LEVEE
(**ECCLESIASTICAL** —) ROTA CURIA SYNOD COLLOQUY AUDIENCIA
(**EXERCISE** —) EPHEBEUM
(**FORTIFIED** —) BAWN
(**GERMAN** —) FEHM VEHM
(**INNER** —) PATIO
(**MUSLIM** —) DIVAN DIWAN
(**REFORMED** —) CLASIS
(**SMALL** —) WIND WYND CORTILE
(**SUPREME** —) SUDDER
(**TURKISH** —) GATE

COURTEOUS FAIR HEND BUXOM CIVIL GENTY SUAVE BONAIR GENTLE POLITE SMOOTH URBANE AFFABLE CORDIAL GALLANT GENTEEL GENTILE REFINED DEBONAIR FAMILIAR GRACIOUS OBLIGING

COURTEOUSLY FAIR FAIRLY GENTLY KINDLY AFFABLY

COURTEOUSNESS COMITY

COURTESAN MADAM QUAIL THAIS WHORE COURTY GEISHA LALAGE MADAME PLOVER AMOROSA ASPASIA CANIDIA DELILAH LORETTE PUCELLE DEVADASI (PL.) DEMIMONDE

COURTESY MENSK COMITY EXTENT GENTRY MANSHIP TASHRIF BREEDING CALIDORE CORTEISE ELEGANCE GENTRICE GRATUITY URBANITY (PL.) HONORS

COURTHOUSE CUTCHERY KACHAHRI

COURTIER CURAN OSRIC WOOER OSRICK COURTER IACHIMO COURTMAN POLONIUS

COURTING SUING SPLUNT

COURTLY HEND AULIC CIVIL HENDE POLITE AULICAL ELEGANT REFINED STATELY POLISHED DIGNIFIED

COURT-NOUE RONCET

COURTSHIP SUIT AMOUR DRURY SPARKING

COURTYARD AREA WYND CLOSE CURIA PATIO TRANCE BALLIUM CORTILE TETRAGON CURTILAGE

COUSIN COZ KIN AKIN HERO ALLIED NEPHEW

COUSIN BETTE (**AUTHOR OF** —) BALZAC
(**CHARACTER IN** —) HULOT AGATHE CREVEL MONTES ADELINE LISBETH HORTENSE MARNEFFE VICTORIN CELESTINE STEINBOCK

COVE CO BAY DEN CAVE CHAP FILE GILL HOLE NOOK PASS SUMP BASIN BAYOU BIGHT CREEK INLET COVING FELLOW HOLLOW RECESS VALLEY MOLDING CALANQUE GUNKHOLE

COVENANT BIND BOND BRIS MISE PACT TRUE AGREE BERIT BRITH TOUCH ACCORD BERITH CARTEL COMART CONAND ENGAGE INDENT LEAGUE PATISE PLEDGE TREATY BARGAIN COMPACT CONCORD PROMISE ALLIANCE CONTRACT DOCUMENT HANDFAST TREATISE

COVENANTER HILLMAN TRUEBLUE

COVER DO CAP COT HAP LAP LAY LID NAP TOP TUP WRY BIND CEIL CLAD COAT COOM CURE DAUB . DECK FACE FADE FALL FURL GARB GATE HEAD HEAL HEEL HIDE HILL HOOD LATH LEAD LEAP LINE MASK PAVE ROOF SILE SPAN TELD TICK TIDE TILT VEIL WRAP APRON BATHE BOARD CLOAK CLOUT COPSE CROWN DRAPE DRESS FENCE FLESH FLOOD GUISE HATCH KIVER MOUNT RECTO SCARF SERVE SHADE STREW STUDY THEAK THEEK TOWEL TREAD VERSO WELME WHALM AWNING BATTER BINDER BLAZON CANOPY CHALON CLOTHE DOUBLE EARLAP ENAMEL ENCASE ENFOLD ENTIRE ENVEIL FOLDER HACKLE IMMASK INVEST JACKET KIRTLE MANTLE OVERGO POTLID RUNNER SCONCE SCREEN SHADOW SHEATH SHIELD SLEEVE SPREAD SPRING SWATHE TOILET TOPPER WHAUVE APPAREL ASPHALT BANDAGE BESTREW BLANKET CAPSULE CONCEAL CONTECT COUVERT ELYTRON EMBRACE ENCRUST FASCINE HEADCAP HOUSING INCRUST KNEECAP MANHEAD OBSCURE OMNIBUS OVERLAY PRETEXT SHEATHE SHELTER SHUTTER TAMPION THIMBLE BEDCOVER COMPRISE COVERCLE DEBRUISE ENCLOTHE ENSCONCE HOODWINK IMMANTLE OVERHAIL OVERSILE OVERWEND PALLIATE PRETENCE PRETENSE SLIPOVER SURPOOSE
(— **A FIRE**) BANK DAMP
(— **AROUND FLOWER**) CYMBA
(— **BRICKS**) SCOVE
(— **BY EXCUSES**) ALIBI PALLIATE
(— **FOR ALEMBIC**) HEAD
(— **FOR CHALICE**) PALL
(— **FOR DIAPER**) SOAKER
(— **FOR ENGINE**) COWLING
(— **FOR FOOD**) BELL
(— **FOR GUN**) TAMPION
(— **FOR MILITARY CAPE**) HAVELOCK
(— **FOR PISTON**) FOLLOWER
(— **FOR POWDER PAN**) HAMMER
(— **FOR WIRES**) BOOTLEG
(— **GROUND**) HEAT
(— **HEARTH**) FETTLE
(— **OF BALL**) CARCASS
(— **OF BOILER**) VOMIT
(— **OF COFFIN**) COOM
(— **OF HAWSEHOLE**) BUCKLER
(— **OF MINE CAGE**) BONNET
(— **OF RIFLE MAGAZINE**) GATE

(— **OF SPORANGIUM**) EPIGONE
(— **OF VEGETATION**) GROWTH
(— **OPPRESSIVELY**) SMOTHER
(— **OVER**) RAKE WELME WHELM QUELME SHEUGH BECLOUD OVERDECK WITHHELE OVERWHELM
(— **PLANTS**) BAG
(— **PROTECTIVELY**) SHROUD SHEATHE
(— **ROAD**) BLIND
(— **SOIL WITH CLAY**) GAULT
(— **UP**) HAP BELY FOLD BELIE SALVE SLEEK HUDDLE
(— **WITH ASHES**) SOIL
(— **WITH BACON**) BARD
(— **WITH CLAY**) CLOAM
(— **WITH COWL**) MOB
(— **WITH CRUMBS**) BREAD
(— **WITH DOTS**) CRIBBLE
(— **WITH DROPS**) DAG
(— **WITH EARTH**) BURY HEAL INTER
(— **WITH FILM**) SKIM
(— **WITH FLESH**) INCARN
(— **WITH FOAM**) EMBOSS
(— **WITH GOLD**) GILD
(— **WITH MEAL**) MELVIE
(— **WITH MUD**) BEMUD BELUTE
(— **WITH OAKUM**) FOTHER
(— **WITH PITCH**) PAY
(— **WITH PLASTER**) PARGET
(— **WITH SHEATH**) GLOVE
(— **WITH SOLDER**) SPLASH
(— **WITH STONE**) ASHLAR
(— **WITH STRAW**) THATCH
(— **WITH TIN**) BLANCH
(— **WITH TOPSOIL**) KELLY
(— **WITH WATER**) DOUSE DOWSE FLOOD WHELM OVERFLOW
(— **WITH WAX**) CERE
(— **WITH WEAVING**) GRAFT
(— **WITH WINGS**) BROOD
(**BED** —**S**) HEALING
(**BEEHIVE** —) QUILT
(**BOOK** —) CASE SIDE
(**GLASS** —) STRIKE
(**PACK** —) MANTA
(**POSTAL** —) ENTIRE
(**POT** —) BRED
(**SADDLE** —) PILCH HOUSING
(**SLIDING** —) BRIDGE
(**TABLE** —) BAIZE DUCHESSE
(**WING** — **OF BEETLE**) SHARD
(**PREF.**) OPERCULI

COVERAGE PROTECTION

COVERALL GOWN JUMPER

COVERED CLAD FULL SHOD TECT BLIND MOSSY CLOSED COVERT HIDDEN ENCASED OBTECTED SCREENED
(— **WITH CRYSTALS**) DRUSY
(— **WITH FEATHERS**) HIRSUTE
(— **WITH FOREST**) HYLEAN
(— **WITH HAIRS**) COMATE VILLOUS
(— **WITH PROTUBERANCES**) HUMPY
(— **WITH SCALES**) SCUTATE
(— **WITH SEAWEED**) TANGLY
(— **WITH WHITE DUST**) PRUINOSE
(**THINLY** —) BARISH
(**PREF.**) CALYPT(O) CRYPT(O) KRYPT(O)

COVERED WAGON WHITETOP BUCKWAGON

COVERER DECKER

COVERING (**ALSO SEE COVER**) BOX COT FUR HAP KEX LAG ARIL BARB BARK BOOT CASE CAUL COAT CUFF DECK FILM HAME HEAD HOOD HULL HUSK KELL MASK OVER PALL PUFF ROBE ROOF SLIP SPAT TARP TILE TILT TRAP VEIL APRON ARMOR BRAID BURSE CRUST DRESS GLOBE GLOVE HATCH QUILT SCALE SHELL SKIRT STALL SWARD TESTA TUNIC TWEEL WREIL ARMING ATTIRE AWNING BANCAL BANKER CANOPY CANVAS COVERT DRAPET EMBRYO ENAMEL FACING FENDER GAITER GANOIN HACKLE HATCAP HELMET JACKET MUZZLE PELAGE SADDLE SCREEN SHEATH SHROUD SINDON TEGMEN VERNIX BLANKET BUFFONT CAMISIA CAPPING CAPSULE CEILING COATING COWLING EARFLAP ENVELOP EXCIPLE GRATING HAPPING HEALING HEELCAP HOUSING MUFFLER OVERLAY PURPORT SARPLER SHADING SHELTER SHOEING SLIPPER TECTURE TEGMENT VESTURE WRAPPER ARMGUARD BLAZONRY BOARDING CASEMENT CLEADING CLOTHING COMPRESS COVERLET EGGSHELL EPISPORE INDUMENT INDUSIUM MANTELET MANTLING OVERCAST PAVILION PERICARP SETATION UMBRELLA TECTORIAL PILLOWCASE
(— **FOR ANTENNA**) RADOME
(— **FOR BENCH**) BANKER
(— **FOR BOXERS' HANDS**) CESTUS
(— **FOR EGG**) COSY
(— **FOR FOREHEAD**) BONGRACE
(— **FOR NECK**) TUCKER PARTLET
(— **FOR ROOF APEX**) EPI
(— **FOR SHOULDERS**) STOLE
(— **FOR SKI**) SKIN
(— **FOR STIRRUP**) HOOD
(— **OF BED**) TIKE
(— **OF BELL ROPE**) GRIP
(— **OF BIRD**) INDUMENT
(— **OF BOW HANDLE**) ARMING
(— **OF CASH SHORTAGE**) LAPPING
(— **OF FEATHERS**) DOWN
(— **OF GILLS**) OPERCULUM
(— **OF NUTMEG**) MACE
(— **OF ROOT**) CALYPTRA
(— **OF ROPE**) SERVICE
(— **OF VEGETATION**) FLEECE
(— **WITH IRON**) ACIERAGE
(—**S FOR NIPPLES**) PASTIES
(**CAST** —**S**) EXUVIAE
(**CHIMNEY** —) COWL
(**CLOTH** —) TOILET
(**COARSE** —) CADDOW TILLET
(**DEFENSIVE** —) ARMOR KICKER
(**EAR** —) EARLAP EARFLAP EARMUFF OREILET
(**EYE** —**S**) GOGGLES
(**FLOOR** —) RUG TILE CRASH CARPET LINOLEUM OILCLOTH
(**FOUL** —) SCUM
(**HEAD** —) CAP HAT WIG HAIR HIVE

HOOD CURCH BONNET HELMET
BIRETTA CHAPEAU CHAPERON
HAVELOCK HEADRAIL TROTCOZY
(LEG —) BOOT HOSE STOCK
GAITER LEGGIN PEDULE KNEELET
LEGGING STOCKING
(LIGHT —) GRIMING
(LINEN —) BARB
(OUTER —) BARK HIDE HULL HUSK
CRUST TESTA JACKET CARAPACE
(PLANT —) PERIDERM
(PROTECTIVE —) APRON ARMOR
SHELL COCOON
(SADDLE —) MOCHILA
(SEED —) PERIGONE
(SLIGHT —) CYMAR
(STAGE —) HEAVENS
(STERILE —) DRAPE
(STICKY DAMP —) GLET
(THIN —) FILM SCRUFF WASHING
(PREF.) CALYPT(O) COLE STEG(O)
STRATI STRATO
(— OF EYEBALL) CORNE
(SUFF.) DERM(A)(ATOUS)(IA)(IS)(Y)
(— PLATE) STEGE
COVERLET PANE HELER HOUSE
QUILT REZAI THROW AFGHAN
CADDOW CHALON COLCHA
LIGGER SPREAD BLANKET
BUFFALO COVERLID DAGSWAIN
COVER-SHAME SAVIN SAVINE
COVERT DEN LAY LIE SLY LAIR
VERT EARTH NICHE PRIVY
ASYLUM HARBOR HIDDEN
LATENT MASKED MYSTIC REFUGE
SECRET COVERED DEFENSE
PRIVATE SHELTER TECTRIX
THICKET DISGUISE INVOLVED
(PL.) CRISSUM
COVERTLY CLOSE CLOSELY
COVET ACHE ENVY PANT WANT
WISH CRAVE YEARN YISSE DESIRE
GRUDGE HANKER
COVETOUS AVID GAIR GARE
EAGER FRUGAL GREEDY SORDID
STINGY ENVIOUS GRIPPLE
MISERLY DESIROUS GRASPING
COVETOUSNESS GREED MISERY
AVARICE YISSING COVETISE
CUPIDITY PLEONEXIA
COVEY BEVY FALL BROOD FLOCK
HATCH COVERT COMPANY
COVIN BAND CREW FRAUD COVINE
COMPANY CONVENE ASSEMBLY
TRICKERY
COW AWE KEY NOT BEEF BOGY
BOSS COWL CUSH FAZE MOIL
MULL NOTT ROAN RUNT VACA
ABASH ALARM BEEVE BOSSY
BROCK BULLY CUSHA DAUNT
DOMPT DRAPE MOGGY QUAIL
SCARE SNOOL VACHA BOVINE
BULLER COLLOP CRUMMY GOBLIN
HAWKEY HAWKIE HEIFER MAILIE
MILKER MULLEY ROTHER SUBDUE
BOARDER BUGBEAR BULLOCK
CRITTER CRUMMIE DEPRESS
MESTENO MILCHER OVERTOP
SQUELCH TERRIFY ALDERNEY
AUDHUMLA BROWBEAT
COWBRUTE DISPIRIT FRIGHTEN
STRIPPER THREATEN
(— ABOUT 3 FEET HIGH) GYNEE

(— BEFORE CALVING) SPRINGER
(BAD-TEMPERED —) RAGER
(BARREN —) DRAPE BARRENER
(DRY —) KEY SEW
(HORNLESS —) NOT MOIL NOTT
DODDY MULEY DODDIE HUMLIE
MAILIE HUMBLIE POLLARD
MOULLEEN
(PART OF —) HIP JAW RIB CROP
HOCK HOOF HORN KNEE LOIN
NECK POLL RUMP TAIL TEAT
CHEST CHINE FLANK GIRTH
PLATE THIGH THURL UDDER
BARREL BRIDGE DEWLAP MUZZLE
SWITCH THROAT BRISKET
DEWCLAW PASTERN PINBONE
WITHERS FOREHEAD
(PREGNANT —) CALVER INCALVER
(WHITE-FACED —) HAWKEY
HAWKIE
(YOUNG —) QUEY STIRK HEIFER
(PL.) KYE KINE DAIRY
(PREF.) VACCI(NI)(NO)
COWARD COW COOF DAFF FUNK
FUGIE LACHE PIKER CRAVEN
FUNKER PIGEON BUZZARD
CAITIFF CHICKEN COUCHER
DASTARD MEACOCK NITHING
PANURGE QUITTER NIDERING
POLTROON RECREANT TURNBACK
TURNTAIL VILLIAGO
COWARDICE DASTARDY
LASHNESS POLTROONERY
COWARDLINESS PUSILLANIMITY
COWARDLY SHY ARGH FAINT
LACHE TIMID AFRAID COWARD
COWISH CRAVEN TURPID YELLOW
CAITIFF CHICKEN GUTLESS
HILDING MEACOCK FACELESS
NIDERING POLTROON RECREANT
SNEAKING POLTROONISH
PIGEONHEARTED
COW BARN BYRE SAUR BARTH
SHIPPON VACCARY
COWBIRD BECCO BUNTING
CUCKOLD OXBITER COKEWOLD
LAZYBIRD
COWBOY HAZER RIDER ROPER
SCREW WADDY CHARRO GAUCHO
GINETE HERDER JINETE WADDIE
COWHAND COWHERD COWPOKE
GRAZIER HERDBOY LLANERO
PANIOLO PUNCHER REFUGEE
VAQUERO BUCKAROO DALLYMAN
JACKAROO NEATHERD
NOWTHERD OUTRIDER PASTORAL
RANCHERO SWINGMAN
WRANGLER
COWCATCHER GUARD LASSO
PILOT FENDER
COWED HANGDOG DOWNCAST
COWER HUG COUR FAWN RUCK
HOVER QUAIL SHRUG SNOOL
SQUAT STOOP TOADY WINCE
COORIE CRINGE CROUCH HURKLE
SHRINK CROODLE CRUDDLE
COWFISH TORO BECCO CUCKOLD
MANATEE SIRENIA
COWHAGE KIWACH
COWHAND PEELER FLANKER
STOCKMAN
COWHERB COCKLE SOAPWORT
COWHERD HERDSMAN NEATHERD

COWHOUSE BYRE SHIPPEN
SHIPPON
COWL CAP COW LID SOE TUB
COUL HOOD MONK MITER
BONNET CUCULE CAPUCHE
SCUTTLE CAPUCHIN
COW PARSNIP MADNEP
CADWEED HOGWEED PIGWEED
BEARWORT BUNDWEED
COWPEA SITAO FRIJOL FRIJOLE
TOWCOCK BLACKEYE BLACKPEA
COWPEN CUPPEN CUPPIN
COW PILOT PINTANO
COWPOX PAPPOX KINEPOX
VACCINA VACCINIA
COWRIE COWRY VENUS ZIMBI
CYPRAEID
COWSLIP PAIGLE PRIMULA
SHOOTER AURICULA CYCLAMEN
MARIGOLD PRIMROSE
COXA HIP HAUNCH
COXCOMB FOP NOB BUCK DUDE
FOOL PRIG TOFF CLEAT DANDY
HINGE PRINCOX POPINJAY
PRINCOCK
COXCOMBRY FOPPERY
COXSWAIN PATROON
COY PAL SHY ARCH COAX NICE
ALOOF CHARY DECOY QUIET
SQUAB STILL ALLURE CARESS
DEMURE MODEST PROPER
SKEIGH BASHFUL DISTANT
PEEVISH STRANGE RESERVED
SKITTISH VERECUND KITTENISH
COYNESS SHYNESS
COYO CHININ
COYOL COROJO COROZO
COYOTE VARMINT
(— STATE) SOUTHDAKOTA
COYPU DEGU NUTRIA
COZBI (FATHER OF —) ZUR
COZEN COG CON BILK GULL POOP
CHEAT TRICK CHISEL GREASE
BEGUILE DECEIVE DEFRAUD
SWINDLE HOODWINK
COZENER SNAP SNECKDRAW
COZENING SIMILATE
COZIER CADGER CODGER COSIER
COZY RUG BEIN BIEN COSY EASY
HOMY SAFE SNUG BIELD CANNY
CUSHY HOMEY CHATTY PENTIT
SECURE TOASTY COVERING
FAMILIAR HOMELIKE SOCIABLE
CPU CHIP
CRAB GIN UCA BOCO JUEY MAJA
ZOEA ANGER ARROW AYUYU
BLUEY MAIAN MAIID MAJID
RACER SANDY THIEF WINCH
BUSTER CANCER GROUSE
HARPER HERMIT KABURI NIPPER
PARTAN PEELER PUNGAR
PUNGER RACING SCRAWL SPRITE
BUCKLER BUCKLUM BURSTER
CABOUCA CANCRID FIDDLER
GRUMBLE INACHID OCYPODE
PANFISH POLYPOD SHEDDER
SOLDIER SPECTER SPECTRE
SURIQUE ARACHNID CRABFISH
DORIPPID GRAPSOID HORSEMAN
IRRITATE LIMULOID LITHODID
OCHIDORE OXYSTOME PAGURIAN
PORTUNID RANINIAN TRAVELER
WINDLASS BRACHYURA

(MATING —) DOUBLER
(PREF.) CANCERI CANCERO
CANCRI CARCIN(I)(O)
CRAB APPLE CRAB SCRAB SCROG
COLING
CRABBED SOUR UGLY CABBY
CRANK CROSS SURLY TESTY
BITTER COPPED CROOSE CROUSE
CRUSTY MOROSE RUGGED
SULLEN TEETHY TRYING BOORISH
CANKERY CRABBIT CRAMPED
CRONISH CROOKED FRABBIT
GNARLED KNOTTED OBSCURE
PEEVISH CANKERED CHURLISH
CONTRARY CRABBISH LIVERISH
PETULANT VINEGARY
CRABBEDNESS ACRIMONY
ASPERITY
CRABCATCHER CRABIER
CRABER VOLE AGOUARA
CRABGRASS DRAWK FONIO PANIC
DARNEL PANICLE CRABWEED
ELEUSINE
CRAB LOUSE CRAB MORPION
MOREPEON
CRAB PLOVER DROME
CRAB TREE GRIBBLE
CRABWOOD ANDIROBA
POISONWOOD
CRACK GAG KIN POP BANG BLOW
CHAP CHIP CHOP CLAP CONE
DOKE FENT FLAW GAIG JEST JIBE
JOKE KIBE LEAK LICK QUIP REND
RIFT RIME RIVE SCAR SLAT SNAP
YERK BRACK BREAK CHARK
CHECK CHICK CHINE CHINK
CLACK CLEFT CRAKE CRAZE
FLAKE FLANK FLASH GRIKE
KNACK KNICK SCORE SHAKE
SLASH SOLVE SPANG SPLIT
CLEAVE CRANNY SLITER SPIDER
SPRING BLEMISH CRACKLE
CREVICE FISSURE SLIFTER
SLITHER FRACTURE HAIRLINE
STRAMASH
(— A WHIP) YERK FLANK
(— IN FLESH) KIN CHAP KIBE
(— IN FLOOR) STRAKE
(— IN INGOT) SPILL
(— IN MAST) SPRING
(— IN ROCK) GRIKE JOINT
(— IN SEA ICE) RIFTER
(— IN STEEL) CHECK SPILL
(— OPEN) SEAM
(— PETROLEUM) BURN
(— WHILE FIRING) DUNT
(PL.) CRAZE
(PREF.) RIMI
CRACKAJACK NAILER NAILING
CRACKBRAINED BATS CRAZY
NUTTY CRACKY ERRATIC
CRACKED BATS FLED NECKED
CHAPPED COMICAL TOUCHED
CRACKERS
CRACKER BAKE LIAR WAFER
BONBON POPPER BISCUIT
BOASTER BREAKER BURSTER
COSAQUE REDNECK SALTINE
SNAPPER
(— STATE) GEORGIA
(BOILED —S) CUSH
(BROKEN —S) DUNDERFUNK
CRACKERJACK TRUMP

CRACKING CRAZE SHIVERING
(PL.) SCRAP
CRACKLE SNAP BREAK CRACK
CRISP BRUSTLE CRINKLE SPARKLE
SPUTTER CREPITATE
CRACKLING CRISP GREAVE
SNAPPY CRACKEL CRACKLE
CREMANT GREAVES CRACKNEL
CRITLING CREPITANT
(PL.) SCRAPS GRIEBEN
CRACKNEL SIMNEL CRACKLING
CRACKPOT CRACK ERRATIC
LUNATIC CRANKISH
CRACKSMAN YEGG BURGLAR
PETEMAN
CRADLE BED COT CRIB REST ROCK
WOMB CRATE FRAME CRECHE
MATRIX ROCKER SADDLE
TROUGH BERCEAU SHELTER
BASSINET CUNABULA
(— FOR SHIP) BED SLEE
(— FOR VATS) STILLING STILLION
(— IN ARCHERY) PURSE
(CERAMICS —) CHUM
(GRAIN —) CADAR CADER
(PL.) CHOCKS
CRADLESONG BERCEUSE
CRADLING BRACK
CRAFT ART BARK BOAT SAIL
FRAUD GUILE SKILL TRADE
BARQUE BATEAU CAUTEL DECEIT
DROGER METIER MISTER POLICE
ROADER STRUSE TALENT VESSEL
ABILITY CUNNING DROGHER
MYSTERY PANURGY SLEIGHT
APTITUDE ARTIFICE BASKETRY
VOCATION
(ANTIQUATED OR CLUMSY —)
HOOKER
(LANDING —) DUCK
(PREF.) TECHNI TECHNO
(SUFF.) TECT
CRAFTILY FOXILY
CRAFTINESS DESIGN SLEIGHT
SLYNESS
CRAFTSMAN CARL HAND CARLE
CRAFT NAVVY ARTIST WRITER
ARTISAN TOHUNGA WORKMAN
LETTERER MECHANIC ARTIFICER
MACHINIST
CRAFTY SLY ARCH DEEP DERN
FINE FOXY NOUP SLIM WILY WISE
ADEPT COONY PAWKY SLAPE
SLEEK ADROIT ARTFUL ASTUTE
CALLID QUAINT SHREWD SOLERT
SUBTLE TRICKY CUNNING POLITIC
SLEEKIT SLEIGHT SUBTILE
VAFROUS VERSUTE VULPINE
CAPTIOUS DEXTROUS ENGINOUS
FETCHING JESUITIC SLEIGHTY
CAUTELOUS
CRAG TOR CRAW KNEE NECK ROCK
SCAR SPUR ARETE BRACK CLIFF
CLINT CRAIG HEUCH HEUGH
THROAT
(PREF.) CREMNO
CRAGGY ROUGH ABRUPT CLIFFY
CLIFTY KNOTTY PAMPER RUGGED
CRAGGED KNAGGED
CRAKE CROW RAIL ROOK RAVEN
CORNBIRD RAILBIRD
CRAKOW BEAKER CRACOWE
POULAINE

CRAM BAG MUG RAM WAD BONE
CRAP FILL GLUT LADE PACK
PANG PORR PURR STOW TRIG
TUCK URGE CROWD CRUSH
DRIVE FARCE FORCE FRANK
GORGE GRIND LEARN PRESS
SCRAM STECH STUDY STUFF
TEACH AGROTE CROMME PESTER
STEEVE STODGE THRACK
(— WITH RICH FOOD) PAMPER
CRAMMED PANG STODGY
CHOCKFUL JAMPACKED
CRAMMER CRAM FEEDER
CRAMMING GAVAGE
CRAMP ART ARCT COOP CRIB KINK
PAIN TUCK CRICK CRIMP CROWD
DOWEL PINCH STUNT TRAMP
AGRAFE DOGTIE HAMPER HINDER
KNOTTY PESTER CONFINE
CRAMPER CRAMPET COMPRESS
CONTRACT RESTRAIN RESTRICT
CRAMPED POKY CRIMP POKEY
BOUNDED CRIMPED SQUEEZY
CRAMPFISH TORPEDO
CRAMPING UNEASY
CRAMPON CRAMP CRAMPET
CRAMPOON
CRANBERRY BERRY CRANE
ERICAD BOGWORT PEMBINA
ACROSARC BILBERRY BOGBERRY
COWBERRY FENBERRY FOXBERRY
CROWBERRY
(— BUSH) PIMBINA
CRANBERRY TREE PEMBINA
SNOWBALL VIBURNUM
CRANE JOB GRUS HOOK SWAY
CYRUS DAVIT HERON HOIST
JENNY RAISE SARUS TITAN
WADER BROLGA COOLEN JIGGER
KULANG SAHRAS COOLUNG
CRAWLER DERRICK GOLIATH
KAIKARA WHOOPER ADJUTANT
GRUIFORM TRAVELER
(— FOR FIREPLACE) COTTREL
COTTEREL
CRANE ARM GIB JIB GIBBET
RAMHEAD COTTEREL
CRANESBILL ALUMROOT
DOVEFOOT FLUXWEED
CRANIUM PAN HEAD CRANE
CRANY SKULL BRAINPAN
CRANK NUT WIT BENT SICK WALT
WEAK WHIM WIND BRACE LOOSE
ROGUE SHAKY THROW WALTY
WINCH AILING BOLDLY CRANKY
EVENER GROUCH HANDLE INFIRM
AWKWARD BRACKET FANATIC
LUSTILY
(SOMEWHAT —) TENDER
CRANKCASE SUMP
CRANKINESS ANGULARITY
CRANKY UGLY CRAZY CRONK
CROSS LUSTY SHAKY TESTY
AILING CRANNY FIFISH INFIRM
SICKLY CROOKED GROUCHY
PERVERSE TORTUOUS
CRANNY HOLE NOOK CHINK CLEFT
CRACK CORNER CRANNEL
CREVICE FISSURE
CRANTARA TARIE
CRANTS WREATH CORANCE
GARLAND
CRAPE BAND CURL FRIZ CREPE

CRIMP DRAPE GAUZE SHROUD
MOURNING
CRAPE MYRTLE JAPONICA
ASTROMEDA
CRAPPIE BACH SHAD BATCH
CALICO CROPPIE BACHELOR
BACULERE NEWLIGHT SACALAIT
TINMOUTH CHINKAPIN
CRAPS CRAP HAZARD
CRASH BASH FAIL FALL RACK
BLAST BURST CLOTH CRUSH
FRUSH PRANG SHOCK SMASH
SOUND FIASCO FRAGOR HURTLE
FAILURE SHATTER STENTER
COLLAPSE ICEQUAKE SPLINTER
STRAMASH
(— OF THUNDER) CLAP
CRASHING ROPAND SMASHING
CRASH-LAND DITCH
CRASS RAW DULL LOUD RUDE
CRUDE DENSE GROSS ROUGH
THICK COARSE OBTUSE STUPID
CRASSNESS SQUALOR
CRATCH CRIB RACK CRITCH
MANGER GRATING
CRATE BOX CAR CASE CRIB FLAT
PLANE SERON BASKET CRADLE
ENCASE HAMPER HURDLE
CACAXTE CANASTA CARRIER
PACKAGE VEHICLE
(EMPTY —) EMPTY
CRATER CUP PIT CONE HOLE
DINOS FOVEA NICHE CELEBE
HOLLOW CALDERA
(— FORMED BY STEAM) MAAR
(LUNAR —) LINNE
(VOLCANIC —) MAAR
CRATUS (FATHER OF —) PALLAS
URANUS
(MOTHER OF —) GAEA STYX
CRAUNCH CRANCH SCRANCH
CRAVAT TIE TECK ASCOT FRONT
SCARF STOCK CHOKER GRAVAT
BANDAGE NECKTIE OVERLAY
SOUBISE CRUMPLER
CRAVE ASK BEG GAPE ITCH LONG
NEED PRAY SEEK WISH COVET
GREED YEARN DESIRE HANKER
HUNGER LINGER THIRST YAMMER
BESEECH ENTREAT IMPLORE
REQUEST REQUIRE SOLICIT
APPETITE
CRAVEN AFRAID COWARD SCARED
DASTARD COWARDLY DEFEATED
OVERCOME POLTROON RECREANT
SNEAKING
CRAVING AVID ITCH WANT LETCH
DESIRE HUNGER THIRST LONGING
APPETITE LIKEROUS TICKLING
APPETENCE
(— FOR LIQUOR) DRY
(— FOR UNNATURAL FOOD) PICA
(ABNORMAL —) BULIMY BULIMIA
BOULIMIA
CRAW MAW CRAG CROP STOMACH
CRAWFISH KREEF
CRAWL LAG COON DRAG FAWN
INCH LOOP RAMP SHUG SWIM
CREEP KRAAL SLIDE SLIME SNAKE
TRAIL BUSTLE CRINGE GROVEL
SCRAWL SCRIDE CLAMBER
SLITHER SNIGGLE TRUDGEN
INCHWORM SCRABBLE

CRAWLING
(SUFF.) (— CREATURE) ERPETON
CRAWLY CREEPY
CRAYFISH DAD CRAB YABBY
YABBIE CAMARON CRAWDAD
LOBSTER CAMBARUS CRABFISH
CRAWFISH
CRAYON KEEL PLAN CHALK CONTE
SAUCE PASTEL PENCIL SKETCH
SANGUINE
CRAZE BUG FAD FLAW MAZE
MODE RAGE BREAK CRACK
CRUSH FEVER FUROR MANIA
VOGUE DEFECT IMPAIR MADDEN
MADDLE WEAKEN WHIMSY
DERANGE DESTROY FASHION
SHATTER WHIMSEY DISTRACT
(PREF.) MANIC
CRAZED MAD REE AMOK LOCO
WILD WOOD WOWF ZANY BALMY
BATTY DAFFY DOTTY GIDDY
MANIC NUTTY POTTY WACKY
COOCOO DOTTLE INSANE LOONEY
BERSERK FANATIC LUNATIC
DATELESS DELEERIT DEMENTED
DERANGED POSSESSED
CRAZINESS CRAZE LUNACY
DEMENTIA
CRAZY (ALSO SEE CRAZED) APE
OFF REE WET BATS BUGS GYTE
HITE LOCO NUTS WILD ZANY
BATTY BEANY BUGGY DAFFY
DIPPY DOILT DOTTY FLAKY
GOOFY KOOKY LOOLY LOONY
POTTY CRANKY CUCKOO DOTTLE
FLAKEY FRUITY INSANE LOCKET
MENTAL SCATTY SCREWY
BANANAS BONKERS CRACKED
LUNATIC PEEVISH SCRANNY
BUGHOUSE COCKEYED CRACKERS
DERANGED HALLICET HALUCKET
MESHUGGA
CREAK CRY GIG GEIG GIRG JARG
RASP YIRR CHARK CHEEP CHIRK
CRAIK CRANK CROAK GRIND
GROAN FRATCH SCREAK SCRIKE
SCROOP SKRAIK SQUEAK
COMPLAIN
CREAKING JARG SCREAK SCRIKE
CREAKY ARTHRITIC
CREAM DIP BEAT BEST FOOL HEAD
REAM CREME ELITE FROTH
REAME SAUCE BONBON CHOICE
TRIFLE COLOGNE FATNESS
EMULSION OINTMENT
CREAMING MANTLING
CREAM PUFF PUFF DUCHESSE
CREAMY RICH REAMY ACREAM
SMOOTH LUSCIOUS
CREASE GAW CLAM FOLD LINE
LIRK RUCK RUGA SEAM BLOCK
CRESS CRIMP PLAIT PLEAT PRESS
SCARF SCORE FURROW SCARPA
SUTURE WREATH CRUMPLE
CRUNKLE WRIMPLE WRINKLE
(SERIES OF —S) BREAK
(PL.) RASCETA
CREASED CRUMPLED ACCORDION
CREATE COIN CREE FORM MAKE
PLAN BUILD CAUSE ERECT FORGE
IMPEL RAISE SHAPE WRITE
AUTHOR DESIGN IMPOSE INVENT
COMPACT COMPOSE CONJURE

FASHION IMAGINE PRODUCE COMPOUND GENERATE CONSTRUCT
(— A DISTURBANCE) RIOT
(— CONFUSION) GARBOIL
CREATION WORLD COSMOS EFFECT NATURE POETRY EDITION FACTURE FASHION POIESIS PRODUCT SHAPING BERESHIT BUSINESS CREATURE UNIVERSE
(MENTAL —) FANTASY PHANTASY
(VISIONARY —) DREAM
CREATIVE FERTILE FORMFUL PLASTIC POIETIC FORGEFUL GERMINAL NATURING POMATIVE PROMETHEAN ORIGINATIVE
CREATOR MAKER AUTHOR FATHER FORMER VARUNA WORKER KHEPERA TAGALOA DESIGNER INVENTOR OPERATOR PRODUCER TANGALOA
CREATURE MAN FOOD TOOL BEAST BEING DABBA JOKER SLAVE THING TRICK WIGHT ANIMAL FELLOW MINION PERSON WRETCH CRITTER GANGREL MINIKIN MINIMUS SHAPING CRAYTHUR CREATION HELLICAT
(— OF LITTLE VALUE) SHOT
(CANNIBALISTIC —) WENDIGO WINDIGO
(DISORDERLY —) ROIT ROYT
(DWARF —) FAIRY GNOME
(ELFLIKE —) PERI
(EVIL —) HELLICAT
(FABLED —) LUNG SIREN MERMAN WIVERN ALBORAK MERMAID
(LITTLE —) MITING
(MANGY —) RONION RONYON
(MANLIKE —) HOMINID HOMONID HOMINIAN
(MEAN —) LEFT
(MECHANICAL —) GOLEM
(MISERABLE —) SNAKE
(NONSENSE —) SNARK
(SILLY —) GOOSE
(SMALL —) ATOM GRIG BEASTIE
(SPRY —) WHIPPET
(STUNTED —) WIRL URLING WIRLING
(SUPERNATURAL —) MAN DRAGON
(TINY —) ELF ATOMY
(UNDERDEVELOPED —) SLINK
(UNDERSIZED —) DURGAN
(USELESS —) HUSHION
(VICIOUS —) DEVIL
(WORTHLESS —) SCULPIN SNIPJACK
(WRETCHED —) ARMINE
(3 —S OF A KIND) LEASH
(PL.) CREATION
CRECHE CRIB PUTZ MANGER NURSERY
CREDENCE FAITH TRUST BELIEF BUFFET CREDIT CREANCE CREDENZA
CREDENTIAL VOUCHER CREDENCE
CREDENZA NICHE SHELF TABLE BUFFET SERVER CREDENCE CUPBOARD
CREDIBILITY FAITH CREDIT
CREDIBLE LIKELY CREDENT FAITHFUL PROBABLE

TROWABLE PLAUSIBLE
CREDIT LOAN TICK ASSET CHALK ENDOW FAITH HONOR IZZAT MENSK MERIT STRAP TENET TRUST BELIEF CHARGE ESTEEM IMPUTE RENOWN REPUTE TICKET WEIGHT ACCOUNT ASCRIBE BELIEVE CREANCE JAWBONE OPINION WORSHIP ACCREDIT CREDENCE HEADMARK PRESTIGE
(HOCKEY —) ASSIST
CREDITABLE HONEST CREDIBLE REPUTABLE
CREDITOR DEBTEE SHYLOCK TRUSTER ADJUDGER APPRIZER CRANSIER CREANCER
(TROUBLESOME —) DUN
CREDO FAITH
CREDULITY EASINESS
CREDULOUS FOND SIMPLE SPOONY SPOONEY BOOBYISH CREDIBLE GULLIBLE
CREED ISM LAY CULT SECT CREDO DOGMA FAITH TENET BELIEF KELIMA SYMBOL CREANCE KALIMAH TROWING DOCTRINE SYMBOLUM
CREEK BAY CUT GEO GIO GUT POW RIA RIO RUN VLY VOE BURN COVE HOPE KILL PILL RILL SLEW SLUE VLEI VLEY WASH WICK BACHE BAYOU BIGHT BOGUE BROOK CRICK DRAFT FLEET INLET ZANJA ARROYO BRANCH BREACH CANADA ESTERO SLOUGH STREAM DRAUGHT ESTUARY RIVULET ZANJONA MUSKOGEE
(AUSTRALIAN —) COWAL
(TIDE —) SLAKE
CREEK SEDGE THATCH
CREEL RIP CAUL CAWL HASK JACK KELL RACK TRAP HARSK BASKET JUNKET
(— FOR BOBBINS) BANK SKEWER
CREELER TUBER LIGGER
CREEP COON FAWN INCH RAMP CRAWL CROPE DRIFT GLIDE PROWL SKULK SLINK SMOOT STEAL TRAIL CRINGE GROVEL SCRIDE SPRAWL CRAMBLE CRAMMEL SNIGGLE TAURANGA
(— AS IVY) RIZZLE
(PL.) WILLIES
(PREF.) HERPETI HERPETO
CREEPER IVY JITI SHOE VINE WORM CREEP CROPE SNAKE COWAGE CRADLE IPECAC REPENT ROMPER TECOMA CLAMPER CLIMBER COWHAGE COWITCH CRAWLER REPTANT REPTILE RUNNING TRAILER FOXGLOVE GUITGUIT PICUCULE WOODBINE PERIWINKLE
CREEPING SLOW REPTANT REPTILE SERVILE SERPIGINOUS
(PREF.) HERPET(I)(O)
(SUFF.) **(— CREATURE)** ERPETON
CREEPING CROWFOOT SITFAST CRAWFOOT
CREEPING SNOWBERRY MOXA TEABERRY
CREESE KRIS STAB CRESS CRISE SWORD DAGGER

CREMATE BURN
CRENEL LOOP CORNEL KERNEL CRENELET
CREOLE PATOIS CRIOLLO DIALECT HAITIAN MESTIZO
(— STATE) LOUISIANA
CREON (DAUGHTER OF —) GLAUCE
(FATHER OF —) MENOECEUS
(SISTER OF —) JOCASTA HIPPONOME
CREOSOTE BUSH LARREA
CREPE CRAPE FRIZZED NACARAT PANCAKE CHIRIMEN CRINKLED WRINKLED
CREPITATE SNAP GRATE RATTLE CRACKLE
CRESCENT HORN LUNE MOON ROOL CURVE LUNAR LUNOID LUNULE MOONED SICKLE WAXAND LUNETTE DEMILUNE MENISCUS
(END OF —) CUSP HORN
(PREF.) MENISCI MENISCO
CRESCENTLIKE BICORN
CRESCENT-SHAPED MOONY LUNATE LUNATED
(PREF.) SELEN(O)
CRESOL FROTHER
CRESPHONTES (BROTHER OF —) TEMENUS ARISTODEMUS
(FATHER OF —) ARISTOMACHUS
(SON OF —) AEPYTUS
CRESS EKER KERSE CUCKOO MADWORT CRUCIFER WHITETOP PEPPERGRASS
CRESSET TORCH BASKET BEACON SIGNAL CRISSET FLAMBEAU
CREST COP TIP TOP ACME APEX COMB EDGE HOOD KNAP PEAK RUFF SEAL TUFT CHINE CROWN PLUME RIDGE COPPLE CREASE CRISTA CUMBRE FINIAL HEIGHT HELMET SUMMIT TIMBER TIMBRE BEARING FEATHER TOPKNOT CENTROID CRESTING ECTOLOPH METALOPH PINNACLE WHITECAP
(— OF BREAKER) SEEGE
(— OF HELMET) COMB CIMIER
(— OF HILL) KNAP
(— OF MINERAL VEIN) APEX
(— OF MOUNTAIN RANGE) ARETE SAWBACK
(— OF PEACOCK) CHAPLET
(— OF RIDGE) EDGE
(— OF SNOW) CORNICE
(— ON BIRD) CROWN ECKLE COPPLE
(IMPERIAL —) KIKUMON
(WAVE —) FEATHER WHITECAP
(PREF.) CRISTI LOPH(I)(IO)(O)
(SUFF.) LOPH(US)
CRESTED COMBED MUFFED TAPPET TAPPIT COPPLED CRISATE CROWNED CRISTATE PILEATED CRISTATED
CRESTED GREBE CARGOOSE
CRESTED QUAIL COPPY
CRESTFALLEN COWED DEJECTED
CRESTING CHENEAU
CRETACEOUS CHALKY
CRETAN KEFTI MINOAN CANDIOT
CRETAN SPIKENARD PHU

CRETE
BAY: SUDA KANCA KISAMO MESARA
CAPE: BUZA LIANO SALOME SIDERO SPATHA STAVROS LITHINON SIDHEROS
CAPITAL: CANEA
GULF: KHANIA MERABELLO
MOUNTAIN: IDA DIKTE JUKTAS LASITHI THEODORE
NAME: CRETA KRETE CANDIA
TOWN: HAG LATO CANEA KHORA SITIA ZAKRO ANOYIA CANDIA KHANIA KISAMO RETIMO KISAMOS KASTELLI HERAKLION

CRETHEUS (FATHER OF —) AEOLUS
(MOTHER OF —) ENARETE
(SLAYER OF —) TURNUS
(SON OF —) AESON PHERES AMYTHAON
(WIFE OF —) TYRO
CRETIN IDIOT
CREUSA GLAUCE GLAUKE
(FATHER OF —) CREON PRIAM ERECHTHEUS
(HUSBAND OF —) AENEAS XUTHUS
(MOTHER OF —) HECUBA PRAXITHEA
(SLAYER OF —) MEDEA
(SON OF —) ION DORUS ACHAEUS ASCANIUS
CREVALLE JACK JUREL
CREVASSE CHASM SPLIT MOULIN SCHRUND CLEAVAGE BERGSCHRUND
CREVICE KIN BORE LEAK NOOK PEEP SEAM VEIN BREAK CHINE CHINK CLEFT CRACK CREEK CUNNE GRIKE CRANNY STRAKE CRANNEL FISSURE GUNNIES KRAVERS OPENING SLIFTER CREVASSE PEEPHOLE
(VOLCANIC —) SOLFATARA
CREW LOT MEN MOB SET BAND GANG GING HERD OARS SHIP TEAM COVIN EIGHT HANDS MEINY PARTY SQUAD STAFF COVINE MEINIE SEAMEN THRONG AIRCREW COMPANY FACULTY MANNING MEMBERS RETINUE EQUIPAGE
(— OF SHEARERS) BOARD
CREWEL CRUEL CADDIS CADDICE
CRIB BED BIN BOX CAB COT CUB HUT KEY BOOM CRUB CURB DIVE JACK PONY RACK RAFT SKIN TROT BOOSE BOOSY CHEAT CRATE FRAME HOVEL STALL STEAL BUNKER CRATCH CRECHE CRITCH MANGER PIGSTY PILFER CABBAGE ENGLISH PURLOIN BASSINET CORNCRIB CRIBBAGE CRIBBING CRIBWORK
CRIBBER SHORER STUMPSUCKER
CRICK KINK CREEK HITCH SPASM TWIST
CRICKET GRIG MOLE SNOB CHANGA SADDLE GRYLLID TWIDDLER ORTHOPTERAN
(— HIT) SLOG

(— SCORE OF 100 RUNS) TON
(PREF.) GRYLLO
CRICKETER CUT COLT PLAYER
RABBIT GENTLEMAN
CRICKET ON THE HEARTH
(AUTHOR OF —) DICKENS
(CHARACTER IN —) DOT MAY JOHN
CALEB BERTHA EDWARD
PLUMMER FIELDING TACKLETON
PERRYBINGLE
CRIER HUER CRYER BEADLE
HERALD WAILER BELLMAN
MUEZZIN WRAWLER OUTCRIER
CRIME ACT SIN EVIL FACT LACK
ABUSE ARSON BLAME CAPER
FOLLY LIBEL WRONG FALSUM
FELONY INCEST MURDER PIACLE
FORFEIT FORGERY MISDEED
OFFENCE OFFENSE INIQUITY
SABOTAGE VILLAINY
MALEFACTION MISDEMEANOR
(ORGANIZED —) GANGLAND
CRIME AND PUNISHMENT
(AUTHOR OF —) DOSTOEVSKI
(CHARACTER IN —) SONIA DOUNIA
LUZHIN PORFIRY PETROVICH
RAZUMIHIN MARMELADOV
RASKOLNIKOV SVIDRIGAILOV
CRIMINAL BAD SORE YEGG CROOK
FELON TOUGH APACHE BASHER
DACOIT GUILTY GUNMAN INMATE
KILLER NOCENT SLAYER WARGUS
WICKED CONVICT CULPRIT
HEINOUS HOODLUM ILLEGAL
MOBSTER NOXIOUS SEVENER
VAUTRIN CRIMEFUL CULPABLE
GANGSTER GAOLBIRD HABITUAL
HARDCASE JAILBIRD PIACULAR
SCELERAT
(HABITUAL —) RECIDIVIST
(PETTY —) ROUNDER
(VIOLENT —) DESPERADO
(PL.) AMALAITA
CRIMINATE IMPEACH
CRIMP BEND CURL FOLD FRIZ
POKE POTE WAVE WEAK CLAMP
CRISP FLUTÉ FRILL FRIZZ PINCH
PLAIT BUCKLE GOFFER RUFFLE
CRIMPER CRIMPLE CRINKLE
FRIABLE GAUFFER WRINKLE
OBSTACLE
CRIMSON LAC RED PINK GRAIN
BLOODY JOCKEY MAROON
MODENA CARMINE SCARLET
CRAMOISY CREMOSIN
CRIMSON CLOVER NAPOLEON
CRIMSON LAKE SULTAN
CRINED MANED
CRINGE BOW BEND CURB CURR
DUCK FAWN JOUK BINGE COWER
CRAWL CREEP QUAIL SNEAK
SNOOL STOOP WINCE YIELD
BUCKLE CROUCH GROVEL SHRINK
SUBMIT ADULATE CRINKLE
DISTORT SCRINGE TRUCKLE
CRINGER FLUNKEY
CRINGING ABJECT HANGDOG
SERVILE SPANIEL
CRINKLE BEND CURL KINK TURN
WIND CREPE CRISP PUCKER
RIPPLE RUMPLE RUSTLE CRACKLE
CRANKLE FRIZZLE WRINKLE
CRINKLED CRIMP CURLY BUCKLED

ENCOMIC CRISPATE
CRINKLY CREPY CREPEY
CRINOID POLYP CRINITE
CAMERATE COMATULA
(BODY OF —) CROWN
CRINOLINE CRIN HOOP
CRIPPLE MAR CRIP GIMP HARM
HURT LAME MAIM BACACH
HOBBLE IMPAIR INJURE SCOTCH
WEAKEN CRAPPLE CRUMPET
DISABLE LAMETER LAMIGER
LAMITER HANDICAP LAMESTER
MUTILATE PARALYZE
(PL.) LAMZIEKTE
CRIPPLED GIMPY COUPLED
DISABLED
CRIPPLING MAIM MAYHEM
CRISIS FIT ACME CRUX FLAP HEAD
JUMP PASS TURN BRUNT CARDO
CRISE PANIC PERIL PINCH POINT
STATE STORM TRIAL STRAIT
DUNKIRK DECISION JUNCTURE
MOUNTAIN
(AUTHOR OF —) CHURCHILL
(CHARACTER IN —) BRICE GRANT
CARVEL COLFAX ABRAHAM
LINCOLN STEPHEN WHIPPLE
CLARENCE VIRGINIA
CRISP NEW COLD CURL FRIZ FROW
HARD BRISK CLEAR CRIPS CRUMP
CURLY FRESH FRIZZ NIPPY PITHY
SHARP SHORT SPALT STIFF TERSE
BITING BRIGHT CRISPY LIVELY
SNAPPY BRACING BRITTLE
CONCISE CRACKLY CRUNCHY
CUTTING FRIABLE FRIZZLE
SMOPPLE INCISIVE
CRISPED FUZZY FRIZZLY CRISPATE
CRISPINELLA (SISTER OF —)
BEATRICE
CRISPNESS SNAP
CRISSCROSS AWRY CROSS
NETWORK CONFUSED
CRITERION LAW NORM RULE TEST
TYPE AXIOM CANON CHECK
GAUGE MODEL PROOF TOUCH
CRISIS METRIC INDICIA MEASURE
PLUMMET STANDARD
SHIBBOLETH
CRITIC MOME BOOER JUDGE
MOMUS CARPER CENSOR CORNER
EXPERT PUNDIT SLATER SYNDIC
ZOILUS STYLIST ZOILIST
COLLATOR CRITIQUE DEBUNKER
OVERSEER REVIEWER THONGMAN
ARISTARCH
AMERICAN CARY MORE TATE
AIKEN BROWN ELSON FINCK
FISKE KOBBE MABIE POUND
WHITE BECKER BROOKS CHENEY
DOWNES FULLER GILMAN
HUTTON KRUTCH LEDOUX
LOWELL MANTLE MILLER
MUNSON NATHAN PARKER
PHELPS TAYLOR WILSON ALDRICH
ANDREWS HUNEKER WHIPPLE
ATKINSON HAGEDORN
ROSENFELD WOOLLCOTT
CHOTZINOFF
AUSTRALIAN TURNER
AUSTRIAN KUH KRAUS
DANISH LANGE BRANDES
GERSTENBERG

DUTCH BRINK BILDERDIJK
JONCKBLOET VALCKENAER
ENGLISH BELL LAMB READ SHAW
WEST AGATE DILKE ELWIN
GOULD GREIN PAGET PATER
RYMER SCOTT WAUGH ARNOLD
COLLES COLVIN DENNIS HUXLEY
MORGAN PALMER RUSKIN
SYMONS THOMAS WALKER
WARTON AINSLIE BENTLEY
BRADLEY COLLIER COLLINS
FREEMAN GIFFORD JOHNSON
RALEIGH SHORTER SITWELL
STEPHEN WALKLEY WHIBLEY
BEERBOHM MARRIOTT SECCOMBE
STEPHENS MACCARTHY
PARTRIDGE SAINTSBURY
SWINNERTON
FRENCH BIDOU BLAZE GILLE TAINE
FAGUET FRANCE LANSON
BATTEUX BOURGET BREMOND
GAUTIER REGNIER AUBIGNAC
MEZIERES MONTEGUT VALLETTE
BRUNETIERE
GERMAN BAB EYE KERR MERCK
MUNDT OPITZ MENZEL SCHOLL
WAAGEN LESSING NICOLAI
RIBBECK ZARNCKE ACIDALIUS
GREEK ZOILUS ARISTARCHUS
HUNGARIAN KOLCSEY
ICELANDIC BLONDAL
INDIAN ANAND
IRISH BOYD MARTYN
ITALIAN OJETTI OVIDIO BARETTI
CAPUANA ZANELLA CHIARINI
ALGAROTTI CASTELVETRO
CAVALCASELLE
NORWEGIAN WELHAVEN
POLISH LANGE
PORTUGUESE VASCONCELLOS
RUSSIAN PYPIN STASOV BELINSKI
SCOTTISH ARCHER WILSON
JEFFREY
SPANISH CANETE
SWEDISH SIREN LEOPOLD
KELLGREN LEVERTIN
SWISS BODMER
CRITICAL EDGY HIGH NICE ACERB
ACUTE CHILLY CRITIC NASUTE
SEVERE URGENT ACERBIC
ADVERSE CARPING EXIGENT
NERVOUS PARLOUS CAPTIOUS
CARDINAL CAVILING DECISIVE
EXACTING JUDICIAL PRESSING
SLASHING TICKLISH CLIMACTERIC
CRITICISM RAP FIRE FLAK GAFF
SLAM BLAME KNOCK SLATE
ATTACK CRITIC REVIEW CENSURE
COMMENT DESCANT PANNING
QUIBBLE SLASHER SLATING
ZOILISM BLUDGEON CRITIQUE
DIATRIBE JUDGMENT STRICTURE
(PETTY —) NITPICKING
CRITICIZE HIT PAN RAP RIP CARP
CRAB FLAY FLOG SKIN SLAM
SLUR TIDE YELP BLAME BLAST
CAVIL DECRY GRIPE JUDGE
KNOCK ROAST SCORE SLASH
SLATE BERATE CRITIC REBUKE
REVIEW CENSURE COMMENT
CONDEMN CRITIZE EXAMINE
SCARIFY BADMOUTH CRITIQUE
DENOUNCE TOMAHAWK

(— MINUTELY) NITPICK
(— SEVERELY) FLAY JUMP
(— SLASHINGLY) SLASH SLATE
CRITIQUE CRITIC REVIEW
CRITICISM
CRIUS (FATHER OF —) URANUS
(MOTHER OF —) GAEA
(SON OF —) PALLAS PERSES
ASTRAEUS
CRO CROY PAYMENT
CROAK CAW DIE GASP KILL PORK
ROUP CRAKE CREAK CRONK
PLUNK QUALM QUARK SPEAK
CROAPE GRUMBLE COMPLAIN
FOREBODE
CROAKER SPOT RONCO CROCUS
RONCHO TOMCOD BUBBLER
CABEZON CORBINA CORVINA
CABEZONE HARDHEAD KINGFISH
SCIAENID
CROAKING CROAKY HOARSE
RANARIAN COAXATION
CROAT CHORWAT CHROBAT
SYRMIAN
(PL.) HRVATI HERVATI
CROCARD BRABANT SCALDING
SLEEPING
CROCHET HOOK KNIT BRAID PLAIT
WEAVE CROTCHET
CROCK JAR PIG POT SMUT SOIL
SOOT STEAN STEEN STOOL
CHATTY CRITCH GOOLAH
PANMUG SMUDGE CRAGGAN
TERRINE POTSHERD
CROCKERY CHINA CLOAM DISHES
PIGGERY POTWARE CLAYWARE
CROCODILE GOA CROC GATOR
MAGAR CAYMAN GAVIAL JACARE
LIZARD MUGGER YACARE
CRAWLER CREEPER DIAPSID
REPTILE SAURIAN SERPENT
LORICATE
CROCODILE BIRD SICSAC TROCHIL
MESSMATE
CROCUS IRID LILY SAFFRON
COLCHICUM
CROFT FARM TORP CRAFT CRYPT
FIELD GARTH VAULT BLEACH
CAVERN PARROCK PIGHTLE
CROMLECH QUOIT CIRCLE
DOLMEN CROMMEL GORSEDD
CROMORNA CREMONA
KRUMHORN
CRONE HAG AUNT TROT CRONY
WITCH BELDAM RIBIBE BELDAME
CRONY PAL CHUM BILLY GOSSY
NETOP GIMMER GOSSIP
CROOK BEND HOOK TURN WARP
CHEAT CHINK CLEEK CRANK
CROMB CROOM CRUMP CURVE
HUNCH NIBBY PEDUM STAFF
THIEF TRICK CRUMMY INDENT
TWICER CAMBUCA CROSIER
CROZIER CRUMMIE INCURVE
POTHOOK SLICKER ARTIFICE
CHISELER CRUMMOCK SWINDLER
(— IN BRANCH) KNEE
(— OF HEAD) HEEL
(SHEPHERD'S —) CROTCH KEBBIE
CROOKBACKED CROUCHIE
CROOKED CAM WRY AGEE AWRY
BENT GAME WOGH AGLEY ASKEW
BANDY BOWLY CRANK CRUMP

FALSE GLEED KINKY SNIDE
THRAW TIPSY WRONG ACROOK
AKIMBO ARTFUL ASLANT
CAMMED CAMSHO CRABBY
CRAFTY CRANKY CURVED
DOGLEG HURLED THRAWN
TRICKY WEEWAW WEEWOW
ZIGZAG ASKANCE ASQUINT
CORRUPT CRABBED CURVOUS
OBLIQUE TURNING TWISTED
WINDING CAMSHACH THRAWART
TORTUOUS
(PREF.) ANKYL(O) CROM
CROOKEDNESS PRAVITY
RHEBOSIS
CROOKNECK CASHAW CUSHAW
CROON HUM LOW BOOM LULL
SING WAIL CHIRM CRONY WHINE
LAMENT MURMUR TEEDLE
COMPLAIN
CROP BOB COW CUT MAW SET
TOP CLIP CRAP CRAW KNAP MINE
REAP SETT STOW TRAP TRIM
WHIP FRUIT GRAZE PLANT QUIRT
SHAVE SHEAR SHIFT SWATH
TILTH TRASH BROWSE BURDEN
DECERP GATHER GEBBIE SILAGE
BEARING BURTHEN CRAPPIN
CURTAIL CUTTING HARVEST
MAMMONI MASHLUM TILLAGE
GLEANING PROFICHI TRASHIFY
INGLUVIES
(— CANDLEWICK) SNUFF
(— OF A HAWK) GORGE
(— OF FRUIT) HANG
(— OF GRASS) LEA LEY SWATH
SWARTH SWATHE
(— OF OYSTERS) SET
(— OF POTATOES) GARDEN
(— OUT) BASSET
(GREEN —S) SOILAGE
(INDIAN —) RABI KHARIF
(LARGE —) HIT
(RIDING —) ROP
(SECOND-GROWTH —) ROWEN
AFTERMATH
(PL.) FEED TILLAGE
CROPPED GOTCH SHAVED
GOTCHED
CROPPER CARVER MUCKER
PURLER GRINDER PLUMPER
CROPPING EARMARK
CROQUET ROQUE BOMBARD
CROQUETTE CECIL OYSTER
KROMESKI KROMESKY
CROSIER BAGLE CROCE CROOK
PEDUM STAFF POTENT BACULUS
CAMBUCA CROZIER PASTORAL
CROSS GO CAM CUT MIX TAU
ANKH CRUX FORD FUNK MARK
PASS ROOD SIGN SOUR SPAN
TREE WOOD ANGRY CANGY
CHUFF CORSE GAMMY GURLY
SURLY TEATY TESTY THRAW
TRAVE TRIAL YAPPY BISECT
CHUFFY CRABBY CRANKY
CROUCH DENIAL EMBLEM
FRANZY GIBBET GROUTY GRUMPY
HIPPED OUTWIT PATCHY SIGNUM
SNAGGY SNASTY SNUFFY SULLEN
SYMBOL TEETHY THWART
TOUCHY WICKED WOOLLY
ATHWART BECROSS CALVARY

CRABBED CROSIER CROZIER
CRUSADE CRUSADO FRABOUS
FRETFUL FROWARD OBLIQUE
PASSAGE PATIBLE PEEVISH
PETTISH POTENCE SALTIER
SALTIRE CAMSHACH CRANTARA
CROCIATE CROISADE CROSSLET
CROTCHED CRUCIFIX DEBRUISE
DEMISANG FRAMPOLD FRATCHED
FRUMPISH OVERPASS PECTORAL
PETULANT PHRAMPEL SNAPPISH
SWASTIKA THUNDERY TRAVERSE
VEXILLUM WINDMILL
(— BETWEEN GRAPEFRUIT AND
TANGERINE) UGLI
(— BY PLANE) HOP
(— ONESELF) SAIN
(— OVER) SPAN TRAJECT
(DOUBLE —) BUSINESS
(MALTESE —) FIREBALL
(PREF.) CRUCI STAUR(O)
CROSSARM WISHBONE
CROSSBAR RUNG CROWN JUGUM
DRIVER TRANSOM
(— IN GATE) SWORD
(— IN SHAFT) STEMPEL STEMPLE
(— OF BALANCE) BEAM
(— OF DOOR) SLOAT
(— OF WINDOW) LOCKET
CROSSBEAM BAR BUNK SPUR
TRAVE GIRDER BOLSTER
DORMANT TRANSOM TRAVERSE
CROSSBEARER CRUCIFER
SPREADER
CROSSBILL FINCH
CROSSBOW PROD RODD BRAKE
LATCH PIECE PRODD TILLER
SLURBOW ARBALEST BALISTER
BALLISTA STEELBOW STOCKBOW
STONEBOW
(PART OF —) NUT IRON LOCK
GUARD SIGHT STOCK WEDGE
GROOVE STIRRUP TRIGGER
BOWSTRING
CROSSBREED HUSKY METIS
SANGA SANGU HYBRID
CROSS CARRIER CRUCIFER
CROSSCURRENT SURGING
CROSSCUT DRIFT OFFSET TUNNEL
COUPURE
CROSSCUT SAW BRIAR
CROSSCUTTER BUCKER
CROSSE STICK
CROSSED ACROSS SQUINT
WOOFED CRUCIAL THWARTING
(PREF.) CHIASTO
CROSSER STICKER
CROSSETTE EAR ANCON ELBOW
ANCONE CROSET
CROSSEXAMINE TARGE
CROSS-EYE ESOTROPIA
CROSS-EYED SQUINT
CROSS-FERTILIZATION
ALLOGAMY PHYTOGAMY
CROSS FORM URDE URDY
CROSS-GRAINED UGLY NURLY
GNARLED HICKORY CONTRARY
FRAMPOLD
CROSSHEAD YOKE
CROSSING XG PASS CROSS LACED
MIXTURE PASSAGE TRAJECT
CRUCIATE OPPOSING OVERPASS
TRAVERSE CROSSOVER

(KIND OF —) ZEBRA
CROSSPATCH BEAR CRAB
CRANK GROUCH
CROSSPIECE BAR BAIL SPAR STEP
YOKE BEARD GLAND GRILL
ROUND STOCK PUTLOG THWART
TOGGEL TOGGLE BOLSTER
TRANSOM CROSSARM CROWFOOT
FOOTRAIL HEADRAIL TRAVERSE
CHOPSTICK
(PL.) CROSSTREE
CROSS-QUESTION TARGE TAIRGE
CROSSROAD LEET VENT WENT
WEENT CAREFOX CARFOUR
COMPITUM CROSSWAY
(PL.) TRIVIA
CROSSRUFF SAW SEESAW
CROSS-SHAPED CRUCIAL
CRUCIATE
CROSS-STAFF CROSS RADIUS
CROSIER CROZIER ARBALEST
CROSS STROKE BIND
CROSS-TEMPERED FRUMPISH
CROSSWISE CROSS ACROSS
ATHWART ACROSTIC DIAGONAL
OVERWART TRAVERSE WEFTWISE
CROSSWAYS
CROSSWORT MAYWORT
MUGWEED MUGWORT
CROTALUM CROTAL CYMBAL
CROTCH FORK POLE POST CLEFT
NOTCH STAKE CRATCH CRUTCH
GRAINS CROTCHET
CROTCHET FAD TOY HOOK KINK
WHIM CRANK FANCY FREAK
FIZGIG MAGGOT VAGARY
CORCHAT CRANKUM
CROTCHETY KINKY CRANKY
CROUCH HUG BEND CLAP COOK
CURB DARE DROP FAWN FORM
ROOK RUCK COWER HOVER
SQUAT STOOP COORIE CRINGE
CROOCH HUDDLE HUNKER
HURKLE HURTLE SCOOCH
SCOUCH CROODLE CROWDLE
SCROOCH SCRUNCH SQUATTER
CROUCHING SQUAT CROUCHANT
CROUD SCROUGE
CROUP CRUP HIVES CRUPPER
CROUPIER DEALER TOURNEUR
CROUTON DIABLOTIN
CROW AGA CAW CRY DAW BRAG
BRAN CRAW DOWP ROOK AYLET
BOAST CRAKE CROWD EXULT
HOODY KELLY RAVEN VAUNT
CARNAL CHOUGH CORBIE
CORVUS HOODIE KOKAKO
GORCROW GRAPNEL JACKDAW
SWAGGER ABSAROKA BALDHEAD
BLACKNEB GAVELOCK GRAYBACK
GREYBACK
(PREF.) CORACO CORVI
(SUFF.) CORAX
CROWBAR PRY SET CROW BETTY
JEMMY JIMMY LEVER SETUP
SWAPE FORCER GABLOCK
PITCHER GAVELOCK HANDSPEC
CROWBERRY HEATH HEATHER
CROWD FRY HUG JAM MOB SET
TAG TIP BIKE CRAM CRUT FARE
HEAP HERD HOST JOSS MONG
PACK PAVE PILE PUSH RAFT
ROCK ROTE ROUT RUCK SERR

SKIT SLUE SORT STOW SWAD
TURB WOOD BUNCH CLOUD
COHUE COVEY CRAMP CRUSH
CRWTH DROVE FLOCK GROUP
HORDE HURRY PLUMP POSSE
PRESS ROTTA SERRY SHACK
SHOAL STECH STIVE STUFF
SWARM THREE VOLGE WEDGE
BOODLE CHORUS CLIQUE HUBBLE
HUDDLE HUSTLE IMPACT JOSTLE
MITHER MOIDER OUTFIT PESTER
RABBLE RESORT SCRUZE THRAVE
THREAD THRIMP THRONG
THRUST TOURBE TYMPAN
VOLLEY BOUROCK CHROTTA
CLUSTER COMPANY CONGEST
IMPRESS JIMBANG SCROOGE
SCROUGE SQUEEZE THICKEN
THRUTCH CABOODLE ENTHRONG
FREQUENT JINGBANG SANDWICH
SATURATE VARLETRY
CONCOURSE GATHERING
MULTITUDE CLAMJAMFRY
(— ABOUT) FLOCK
(— AROUND) BESIEGE
(— OUT) DISPLACE
(— TOGETHER) HUG HOTTER
HOWDER HUDDLE CLUTTER
CONTRUDE
(CONFUSED —) HURRY
(MOVING —) DROVE
(NOISY —) ROUT
(PREF.) OCHLO
CROWDED PANG CLOSE DENSE
SPISS STIFF THICK FILLED SPISSY
THRONG BUNCHED COMPACT
OPPLETE POPULAR SERRIED
STIPATE STUFFED TEEMING
NUMEROUS POPULOUS
CROWFOOT JOY PAGLE CREATE
EXOGEN PAIGLE EELWARE
GOLDCUP GOLLAND GOWLAND
BANEWORT CRAWFOOT
GOLDWEED HELLWEED
CROWING COCK
CROWN CAP TAJ TIP TOP BULL
COIN GULL HELM PALE PATE
PEAK POLL RIGO TIAR ADORN
BASIL BEZEL BEZIL CREST MITER
MITRE MURAL POLOS REGAL
ROUND ROYAL TIARA ANADEM
CANTLE CIRCLE CLIMAX CORONA
DIADEM DOLLAR FILLET INVEST
LAUREL POTONG REWARD
SUMMIT TIMBER TROPHY
UPWARD VALLAR VERTEX
WREATH AUREOLE CHAPLET
CORNICE CORONAL CORONET
FORETOP GARLAND INSTALL
PSCHENT STEPHEN TONSURE
CORONATE CORONULE
ENTHRONE PINNACLE SURMOUNT
TURNPIKE
(— OF CHICORY) ENDIVE
(— OF EGYPT) ATEF PSCHENT
(— OF HEAD) NOLL PATE SKULL
CANTLE POMMEL FORETOP
(— OF HILL) KNAP
(— OF LAUREL) BAY
(— OF ROCK) KRANTZ
(HALF —) GEORGE ALDERMAN
(PIECE OF —) BULL
(PLANT —) STOOL

(PREF.) CORONI CORONO STEPHAN(O)
CROWNED CORONATE LAURELED
(**— WITH ROSES**) ROSATED
CROW SHRIKE MAGPIE SQUEAKER
CROW'S NEST LOOKOUT
CROZER CHUCKER
CRUCIAL KEY ACUTE PIVOT NEEDLE SEVERE TRYING PIVOTAL SUPREME TELLING CRITICAL DECISIVE
CRUCIAN CARP GIBEL
CRUCIBLE POT DISH ETNA SHOE TEST CRUCE FOYER CRUSET HEARTH MONKEY RETORT FURNACE CROSSLET
CRUCIFIX PAX ROOD CROSS
CRUCIFIXION RANSOM
CRUCIFY VEX HANG KILL HARRY MORTIFY TORMENT TORTURE CRUCIATE
CRUDE ILL RAW BALD BARE RUDE BRUTE CRASS GREEN GROSS HAIRY HARSH ROUGH TACKY CALLOW COARSE DOUGHY INCULT KUTCHA SAVAGE UNRIPE VULGAR ARTLESS GLARING SQUALID UNCOUTH AGRESTIC IGNORANT IMMATURE IMPOLITE INDIGEST PRIMITIVE
(**NOT —**) DELICATE
CRUDELY HARSHLY GAUCHELY
CRUDITY BARBARITY CRASSNESS GAUCHERIE ROUGHNESS
CRUEL ILL FELL GRIL GRIM HARD BLACK BREEM BREME BRUTE FELON HARSH RETHE SADIC STERN WROTH BITTER BLOODY BRUTAL DIVERS DREARY FIERCE IMMANE SAVAGE SEVERE UNJUST UNKIND UNMEEK UNMILD UNRIDE WANTON WICKED BESTIAL BOARISH BRUTISH GRIMFUL INHUMAN NERONIC SCADDLE SPITOUS WILROUN BARBARIC DIABOLIC FELONOUS FIENDISH INHUMANE PITILESS RUTHLESS SADISTIC TYRANNIC TRUCULENT
CRUELLY FELL HARD CRUEL FELLY HARSHLY
CRUELTY RIGOR DURESS SADISM DEVILRY DEVILTRY FELLNESS SEVERITY
CRUET AMA JAR JUG VIAL BURET CRUSE BOTTLE CASTER CREVET CREWET GUTTUS AMPULLA BURETTE URCEOLE
CRUISE SAIL TRIP JUNKET STOOGE
(**— AS A PIRATE**) BUSK
CRUISER SHIP VALUER VESSEL WARSHIP ESTIMATOR
CRULLER WONDER OLYCOOK OLYKOEK TWISTER DOUGHNUT
CRUMB BIT ORT MURL NIRL PIECE LITTLE MORSEL CRIMBLE CRUMBLE MEALOCK MURLACK REMNANT FRAGMENT
(PL.) PANADA PANURE MOOLINGS
CRUMBLE ROT CRIM MULL MURL MUSH BREAK BROCK CRUSH DECAY RAVEL SLAKE SPALL SPOIL

BUCKLE MOLDER MYRTLE PERISH SLOUGH CORRADE CRIMBLE MOULDER COLLAPSE
(**— DOWN**) GRUSH
(**— UNDER OVERWEIGHT**) FLUSH
CRUMBLED UNDURE
(**EASILY —**) CRIMP BRUCKLE CRUMBLY
CRUMBLING SAMEL SAMMEL POWDERY
CRUMBLY NESH MURLY CRUMBY CRUMMY FRIABLE PULVERULENT
CRUMPET CAKE MUFFIN PIKELET
CRUMPLE FOLD MOOL MUSS ROOL WISP CRUSH SCREW BUCKLE CREASE FURROW RAFFLE RUCKLE RUMPLE CRIZZLE CRUNKLE FRUMPLE SCRUNCH WRINKLE COLLAPSE CONTRACT SCRUMPLE
CRUNCH BITE CHEW CRUMP CRUSH CHOMP CRASH CRUMP CRUSH GNASH GRIND PRESS RUNCH CRANCH CRINCH GRANCH GROWSE CRAUNCH SCRANCH SCRUNCH
CRUPPER CROUP CURPEL CURPIN TAILBAND
CRUSADE WAR JEHAD JIHAD CROISEE CAMPAIGN CROCIATE
CRUSADER PILGRIM TEMPLAR EQUITIST REFORMER
(PL.) CROISES
CRUSADER IN EGYPT (**CHARACTER IN —**) ADRIANO ALADINO ARMANDO PALMIDE DORVILLE ELMIRENO
(**COMPOSER OF —**) MEYERBEER
CRUSH BOW HUG JAM BEND BORE BRAY CASE CHEW CRAM DASH MASH MILL MULL PASH RAVE STUB BRAKE BREAK BRIZZ CHAMP CHECK CRASH CRAZE CREEM CROWD FORCE FRUSH GRIND GRUSH PRESS QUASH QUELL SMASH SMUSH SQUAB SQUAT STAMP TREAD UNMAN BRUISE BURDEN CRUNCH DEFOIL DEFOUL KNATCH KNETCH SCOTCH SCRUSH SCRUZE SQUASH SQUISS SUBDUE THRING THRONG THWACK ACCABLE BECRUSH CONQUER CONTUSE CRACKLE CRUMPLE DEPRESS DESTROY OPPRESS OVERRUN REPRESS SCRUNCH SCRUNGE SHATTER SQUEEZE SQUELCH SUCCUMB TRAMPLE COMPRESS FORBREAK OVERCOME SQUABASH SUPPRESS OVERWHELM
(**— BEANS**) NIB
(**— HAT**) BONNET
(**— IN**) STAVE
(**— ROCK**) DOLLY DOLLEY DOLLIE
(**— SPIRIT**) BREAK
CRUSHABLE QUASHY
CRUSHED TAME BROKEN ECRASE MUSHED CONTRITE CRUMPLED
CRUSHER NIBBER
CRUSHING FIERCE BRUISING SMASHING SQUABASH
(SUFF.) TRIPSY
CRUST FUR PIP CAKE HULL RIND SCAB SHELL SKULL COFFIN

CRUSTA ESCHAR GRATIN HARDEN RONDLE SCRUFF ABAISSE CALICHE COATING ENCRUST INCRUST CARAPACE PELLICLE SCUTULUM WINEBALL DURICRUST
(**— OF DIKE**) SALBAND
(**— ON WINE**) ARGAL ARGOL
(**PIE —**) HUFF COFFIN
(PL.) SORDES
CRUSTA PES
CRUSTACEAN BUG APUS CRAB FLEA SCUD ZOEA ALIMA CARID KRILL LOUSE PRAWN SCREW SCROW CYPRID ENDITE ISOPOD SHRIMP SLATER SQUILL ARTEMIA COPEPOD CRAYLET DAPHNID DECAPOD GRIBBLE HAYSEED LOBSTER SQUAGGA SQUILLA AMPHIPOD BARNACLE CIRRIPED CRAYFISH GAMMARID LERNAEAN MONOCULE OSTRACOD PAGURIAN SQUILLID BRACHYURA PHYLLOPOD SCHIZOPOD SHELLFISH MALACOSTRACAN RHIZOCEPHALAN
CRUSTADE DARIOLE
CRUSTY CURT BLUFF BLUNT RUSTY TESTY MOROSE SULLEN CRABBED PEEVISH PETTISH STARCHY SNAPPISH
CRUTCH FORK STILT CLUTCH CRATCH CROTCH POTENT SADDLE SCATCH STADDLE
CRUX NUB GIST HALF PITH CROSS POINT PUZZLE RIDDLE PROBLEM
CRUX ANSATA ANKH
CRWTH ROTA ROTE CROWD CRUTH ROTTA ROTTE CROUTH CHROTTA
CRY HO BOO CAW CRI FAD HOA HUE OLE PIP SOB YIP BAWL BELL BUMP CALL COWL CROW EVOE FALL GLAM GOWL HAIL HAWK HOOT HOWL KEEN MEWL NOTE OYES OYEZ PULE RAGE RAME RANE REEM RERD ROOP SCRY SIKE TOOT WAIL WEEP YELL YELP BARLA BLART BLORE CHEVY CLEPE CRAKE CROUP CRUNK GREDE GREET GROAN QUEAK RUMOR SHOUT SOUND TROAT UTTER VOGUE WHEWL WHINE WHULE WRAWL BARLEY BELLOW BOOHOO CHIVVY CLAMOR DEMAND ENSIGN LAMENT OUTCRY QUETHE SCREAM SHRIEK SLOGAN SNIVEL SQUALL SQUAWL SQUEAL TONGUE WIMICK YAMMER EXCLAIM FASHION HOSHANA SCREECH SPRAICH GARDYLOO PROCLAIM SCRONACH
(**— ALOUD**) BLART GREDE
(**— AT SIGHT OF WHALE**) FALL
(**— DOWN**) DOWNCRY BERATTLE
(**— FOR TRUCE**) BARLA BARLY BARLEY
(**— HOARSELY**) CROUP
(**— LIKE ELEPHANT**) BARR TRUMPET
(**— LIKE PIG**) WRINE
(**— OF A BAT**) CHIP
(**— OF ABORIGINES**) COOEE

(**— OF BACCHANALS**) EVOE
(**— OF BIRD**) CAW COO PEW BOOM CAWK CLANG BIRDCALL
(**— OF BITTERN**) BILL
(**— OF CAT**) MEW MEWL MIAOU MIAOW MIAUL MIAUW CALLING
(**— OF CONTEMPT**) BOO
(**— OF DEER**) BELL
(**— OF ENTHUSIASM**) BANZAI
(**— OF GOOSE**) HONK YANG
(**— OF GUINEA HEN**) POTRACK
(**— OF HOUND**) MUTE MUSIC
(**— OF JACKAL**) PHEAL PHEALE PHEEAL
(**— OF MOURNING**) KEEN TANGI
(**— OF NEWBORN CHILD**) VAGITUS
(**— OF RAVEN**) QUALM
(**— OF SHEEP**) BAA BLAT BLEAT
(**— OF SNIPE**) SCAPE
(**— OF SORROW**) ULLAGONE
(**— OF SURRENDER**) KAMERAD
(**— OF WATCHMAN**) WATCH
(**— OUT**) BAY BAWL BRAY GALE GAPE HOOT HOWL JERK SCRY BLORE CHIRM CLAIM ESCRY SHOUT HALLOO HOLLER SCREAM SHRIEK THREAP THROPE BREATHE EXCLAIM RECLAIM DISCLAIM PROCLAIM
(**— TO CLEAR PASSAGE**) HALL
(**— TO COMBATANTS**) BAILE
(**— UP**) CRACK
(**BATTLE —**) CRY ENSIGN MONTJOY GERONIMO MONTJOYE
(**DRINKING —**) RIVO
(**HOARSE —**) CROAK
(**HUNTING —**) TIVY CHEVY CHIVY CHEVVY STABOY YOICKS TALLYHO TANTARA TANTIVY PILILLOO
(**PROLONGED —**) RANE
(**RALLYING —**) SLOGAN
(**RAUCOUS —**) CATCALL
(**SHRILL —**) SKIRL SQUEAK SQUEAL SCREECH YALLOCK
(**WAR —**) DIN ALALA HAVOC BANZAI SLOGAN
(**WORDLESS —**) KEEN ULULU
CRYING PIPING URGING CLAMANT HEINOUS VAGIENT PRESSING RECREANT
(**— OF HOUND**) BELLING
CRYPT PIT CRAFT CROFT CROWD VAULT CAVERN GROTTO RECESS SHROUD CHAMBER RECESS
CRYPTIC DARK VAGUE HIDDEN OCCILT SECRET OBSCURE ELLIPTIC MYSTICAL SIBYLLIC
CRYPTOGAM ACROGEN
CRYPTOGAMOUS AGAMIC AGAMOUS
CRYPTOGRAM CODE CRYPT CIPHER
CRYPTOGRAPH GEMATRIA
CRYPTOGRAPHER VIGENERE
CRYPTORCHID RIDGLING
CRYSOPHANIC RHEUMIC
CRYSTAL XL ICE DIAL DOME HARD IRIS SEED XTAL CLEAR GLASS GRAIN LUCID LUNET NICOL TABLE GLASSY LIMPID MIRROR NEEDLE PEBBLE QUARTZ TABLET ACICULA DIAMOND DIPLOID GLASSIE LUNETTE ORTHITE TWOLING

ULEXITE YAJEINE ZOISITE
FIVELING FOURLING PELLUCID
TRICHITE TRILLING PERIMORPH
PHENOCRYST
(— FOREIGN TO ROCK) XENOCYST
(— OF GREAT STRENGTH) WHISKER
(FINE —) BERYL
(ICE —S IN WATER) FRAZIL
(NEEDLE-SHAPED —S) RAPHIDES
(ROCK —) BRISTOL CITRINE
(TWIN —) TWIN MACLE TWINDLE
TWOLING FOURLING
(PL.) DRUSE GRAIN
(PREF.) CHRYSTO
(SUFF.) BLAST(IC)(Y) HEDRON
CRYSTAL GAZE SCRY
CRYSTAL GAZER SEER SCRYER
SKRYER
CRYSTALLINE PURE CRYSTAL
PELLUCID
CRYSTALLITE BELONITE TRICHITE
BACILLITE SCOPULITE
CRYSTALLIZE FIX FIRM JELL
CANDY SUGAR NEEDLE CONGEAL
SOLIDIFY
CRYSTALLOGRAPHY LEPTOLOGY
C-SHAPED SIGMATE
CTENIDIUM COMB
CTENOPHORE RIB NUDA CESTOID
CYDIPPID JELLYFISH
CUADRA MANZANA
CUB FRY PEN BEAR CHIT COOP
SHED TOTO STALL WHELP LIONET
NOVICE CODLING REPORTER
(— SCOUT) WEBELOS

CUBA

BAY: NIPE PIGS
CAPE: CRUZ MAISI LUCRECIA
CAPITAL: HAVANA
CIGAR: HAVANA
COIN: PESO CENTAVO CUARENTA
DANCE: CONGA RUMBA DANZON
RHUMBA GUARACHA
PACHANGA
FALLS: TOA AGABAMA CABURNI
GULF: MEXICO ANAMARIA
BATABANO
INDIAN: CARIB TAINO ARAWAK
ISLAND: PINES
ISLANDS: SABANA CAMAGUEY
MEASURE: VARA BOCOY TAREA
CORDEL FANEGA
MOUNTAIN: TURQUINO
MOUNTAINS: CRISTAL MAESTRA
ORGANOS TRINIDAD
PROVINCE: HAVANA ORIENTE
CAMAGUEY MATANZAS
RIVER: ZAZA CAUTO
SWAMP: ZAPATA
TOWN: COLON MANES ALAMAR
BAYAMO GUINES HAVANA
BARACOA HOLGUIN PALMIRA
ARTEMISA CAMAGUEY
GUAYABAL MATANZAS
SANTIAGO
TREE: JIQUE JIQUI
WEIGHT: LIBRA TERCIO

CUBAN LILY SCILLA
CUBBYHOLE NOOK CUBBY
CUBE CUT DIE NOB KNOB BLOCK
EIGHT SOLID TIMBO BABASCO

CUBELET TESSERA BARBASCO
QUADRATE TESSELLA
(— OF BREAD) CROUTON
(MEAT —S) CABOB KABOB KEBOB
(PL.) DICE
CUBIC SOLID CUBOID CUBICAL
CUBICALLY DIEWISE
CUBIC CENTIMETER FLUIGRAM
CUBICLE BAY CELL ROOM BOOTH
CABIN NICHE STALL ALCOVE
CARREL CARRELL
CUBIC METER STERE
CUBIT ELL CODO HATH COVID
HASTA COUDEE
CUB SHARK LAMIA GALEID
REQUIEM
CUCKING STOOL THEW TUMBLER
TUMBREL TUMBRIL
CUCKOLD TUP HORN BECCO
VULCAN WITTOL ACTAEON
CORNUTE CORNUTO HORNIFY
RAMHEAD COKEWOLD
CUCKOLDED FORKED UNICORN
CUCKOLDRY HORNWORK
CUCKOO ANI COWK CUCK FOOL
GOUK GOWK KOEL KOIL CLOCK
CRAZY KOKIL SILLY COUCAL
DIDRIC HUNTER KOBIRD
BOOBOOK CHATAKA DIEDRIC
KOWBIRD SIRKEER CHOWCHOW
PICARIAN RAINBIRD RAINFOWL
(PREF.) CUCULI
CUCKOOFLOWER HEAD PAGLE
SPINK CUCKOO PAIGLE
HEADACHE MILKMAID
CUCKOOPINT ARUM RAMP AARON
BOBBIN DRAGON BUCKRAM
OXBERRY MANDRAKE
CUCKOO SPIT WOODSERE
CUCULLATE COWLED HOODED
COVERED
CUCUMBER CUKE PEPO GOURD
CONGER CUCURB PEPINO PICKLE
GHERKIN PICKLER CUCURBIT
PEPONIDA PEPONIUM
(BITTER —) COLOCYNTH
(SHRIVELED —) CRUMPLING
(WILD —) SICYOS CREEPER
(PREF.) CUCUMI
CUCURBIT BODY FLASK GOURD
CUCURB ALEMBIC MATRASS
CUD CHEW QUID BOLUS QUEED
RUMEN CUDGEL
CUDBEAR CORK PERSIO PERSIS
CUDWEED
CUDDLE HUG LAP PET CARESS
COSSET FONDLE HUGGLE KIDDLE
KIUTLE NESTLE PETTLE CROODLE
CRUDDLE EMBRACE SMUGGLE
SNOOZLE SNUGGLE CANOODLE
CUDDLESOME HUGGABLE
CUDDY ASS LOUT BRIBE CABIN
DONKEY GALLEY PANTRY
CUDEIGH
(BELOVED OF —) BUXOMA
CUDGEL BAT CUD BEAT CANE
CLUB CRAB DRUB KENT MACE
RACK RUNG TREE BASTE BATON
BILLY DRIVE KEBBY KEVEL LINCH
LINGE SHRUB STAFF STAVE STICK
THUMP TOWEL ALPEEN BALLOW
BASTON BILLET GIBBET KEBBIE
LIBBET THRASH WASTER

BELABOR BOURDON DRUBBER
SWADDLE SWINGLE TROUNCE
BLUDGEON SHILLALA THWACKER
CUDWEED ENAENA CATFOOT
CUE QU NOD TAG TIP HINT MAST
TAIL WINK BRAID CLUFF PLAIT
QUEUE TWIST PROMPT SIGNAL
PIGTAIL
(BILLIARD —) MACE MAST STICK
(MUSICAL —) PRESA
(PART OF —) TIP BUTT HILT JOINT
POINT SHAFT BUMPER FERRULE
(SHUFFLEBOARD —) SHOVEL
(TIP OF —) LEATHER
CUFF BOX BANK BLOW GOWF
SLAM SLAP SLUG SWAT TURF
CLOUT FIGHT GOWFF MISER
SCUFF SCUFT SMITE SOUSE
BUFFET CODGER FENDER MITTEN
STRIKE TURNUP COLPHEG
SCUFFLE WHERRET GAUNTLET
HANDBLOW HANDCUFF
TURNBACK
CUIR DORADO
CUIRASS CURACE CURATE CURIET
LORICA THORAX
CUIRASSIER LOBSTER
CUISINE FOOD MENU TABLE
COOKERY KITCHEN
CUITLATEC TECO
CUL-DE-SAC POCKET STRAIT
IMPASSE
CULL OPT CAST COIL DUPE GULL
PICK PIKE SIFT SORT ELECT
GLEAN PLUCK ASSORT CHOOSE
GARBLE GATHER REMOVE SELECT
CULLING SEPARATE
CULLET SCRAP
CULM COOM HAULM SLACK
COOMBE REFUSE DEPOSIT
(PL.) SIRKI SIRKY
CULMINATION END ACME APEX
AUGE CULM NOON ROOF BLOOM
CREST CROWN HIGHT POINT
APOGEE CLIMAX CULMEN
CUMBLE HEIGHT PERIOD SUMMIT
VERTEX ZENITH BLOWOFF
CULPABILITY BLAME FAULT GUILT
DEMERIT
CULPABLE FAULTY GUILTY
LACHES SINFUL IMMORAL
BLAMABLE CRIMINAL
CULPRIT FELON CONVICT
CRIMINAL OFFENDER
CULT CLAN DADA SECT CREED
KUKSU CHURCH CULTUS DOMNEI
MANISM NUDISM RITUAL SCHOOL
SHINTO AMIDISM DADAISM
ICONISM MYALISM MYSTERY
WORSHIP DEVILISM HUMANISM
SATANISM
(SUFF.) ISM
CULTCH CUTCH STOOL SCULCH
CULTIVATE EAR HOE CROP DISC
DISK FARM GROW PLOW REAR
TEND TILL WORK DRESS EARTH
LABOR NURSE RAISE STUDY
TRAIN AFFECT FOSTER FURROW
HARROW MANAGE MANURE
PLOUGH RATOON SARCLE
SCHOOL ACQUIRE CHERISH
CONTOUR CULTURE EDUCATE
EMBRACE EXPLOIT HUSBAND

IMPROVE NOURISH PREPARE
SCRATCH CIVILIZE
(— FAVOR) BOOTLICK
CULTIVATED ABAD TAME CIVIL
GROWN POLITE SATIVE TOILED
POLITIC REFINED CULTURED
ARTIFICIAL
(ARTIFICIALLY —) HOTHOUSE
CULTIVATION CROP TILTH FINISH
GROWTH CULTURE TILLAGE
TILTURE LABORAGE MANURAGE
REFINEMENT
(— IN MANNERS) FINISH
(MENTAL —) HUMANITY
CULTIVATOR JAT KMET RYOT
ILAVA SULKY FARMER GADABA
HARROW ILAVAN MAMOTY
MILLER RIDGER TILLER FLORIST
GRUBBER HUSBAND MEADOWER
ROSARIAN SCUFFLER
(— GANG) RIG
(PL.) LAETI
CULTURAL HUMANIST
CULTURE ART AGAR STAB KULLI
NASCA NAZCA SHAKE SLANT
SLOPE TAJIN TASTE TILTH
JHUKAR KULTUR POLISH STREAK
WILTON ABASHEV ANANINO
AZILIAN IRANISM JHANGAR
KAYENTA SOCIETY STARTER
TILLAGE HUMANISM LEARNING
(ESKIMO —) DORSET
(MEXICAN —) MAZAPAN
CULTURED CIVIL POLITE LETTERED
CULVERIN SLING CULVER
LANTACA PELICAN SPIROLE
CULVERT FOX GOUT DRAIN SLUIT
BRIDGE CONDUIT CULBERT
PINNOCK PONCEAU OVERPASS
CUMBER BURDEN CUMMER
SHACKLE
CUMBERSOME GOURD HEAVY
CLUMSY UNRIDE AWKWARD
LUGSOME ONEROUS WEIGHTY
CUMBROUS UNWIELDY
CUMMER GIRL LASS WOMAN
KIMMER
CUMMERBUND BAND BELT SASH
CUMULATE HEAP GATHER
COMBINE
CUMULATIVE CHAIN SUMMATIVE
CUNA CUEVA DARIEN
CUNEIFORM ULNARE WEDGED
CUNNER CANOE NIPPER WRASSE
BURGALL CHOGSET GOLDNEY
NIBBLER BERGGYLT
BLUEFISH CORKWING
GILTHEAD
CUNNING ART OLD SHY SLY WIT
ARCH CUTE DEEP FAST FINE
FOXY KEEN SLIM SNOD TRAP
WILY WISE CANNY CRAFT
DOWNY FAVEL GUILE LOOPY
PAUKY PAWKY POKEY SHARP
SMART ADROIT ARTFUL ASTUTE
CALLID CLEVER CRAFTY DAEDAL
DECEIT ENGINE FOXERY PRETTY
QUAINT SHREWD SUBTLE SUPPLE
TRICKY WISDOM COMPASS
CRAFTLY CURIOUS FINESSE
KNOWING PARLISH PARLOUS
POLITIC PRACTIC SLEIGHT
SUBTILE VARMINT VULPINE

CONTOISE DEXTROUS MANAGERY QUENTISE SKILLFUL SLEIGHTY STEALTHY YEPELEIC
CUNNING LITTLE VIXEN
(CHARACTER IN —) LAPAK PRIEST HARASTA TERYNKA FORESTER SHARPEARS GOLDENMANE SCHOOLMASTER
(COMPOSER OF —) JANACEK
CUNNINGLY YEPLY YEPELY
CUP AMA BOX CAN DOP MUG NOG POT TOT TUN TYG CELL DOPP HORN LOTA PECE SHOE SKEW TASS TOSS BOUSE CALIX CHARK COGUE COPPE CRUSE CYLIX DEPAS GLASS GODET GRAIL KITTY PHIAL SCALE STEIN STOOP STOUP TAZZA THECA BEAKER BICKER BUCKET BUMPER CAPPIE CHOANA COTYLA CRATER CUPULA DOBBIN EGGCUP EYECUP FALSIE FESSEL FINJAN GOBLET JICARA KOTYLE MAZARD NAGGIN NOGGIN OXHORN POTION RUMKIN TASSIE VESSEL BRIMMER CAPSULE CHALICE CHEERER CYATHUS GODDARD KYATHOS QUONIAM SCYPHUS SHERBET STIRRUP THIMBLE TRINKET VENTOSE BRIDECUP GRADUATE PANNIKIN STANDARD TJANTING
(— FOR HOLDING DIAMOND) DOP DOPP
(— FOR PERFUMES) CONCH
(— FOR YEAST) SKEP
(— IN SAUCER OF ALCOHOL) ETNA
(— OF FLOWER) BELL
(— OF TEA) DISH SPEED OYSTER
(— ON BULLET) GASCHECK
(— WITH COVER) HANAP
(ASSAYING —) CUPEL
(DRINKING —) CAN MUG NUT TIG TUN TYG CANN HORN TASS TOSS GODET BEAKER GOBLET HOLMOS QUAICH RUMMER CHALICE GODDARD TRINKET
(FAIRY —) COOLWORT
(FILLED —) BUMPER
(IRISH —) MADDER METHER
(IRON —) CULOT MUSHROOM
(LARGE —) FACER BLACKJACK
(LEATHER —) WELL GISPIN
(LONG-HANDLED —) CYATH DIPPER CYATHUS KYATHOS
(MAPLE —) MAZER
(NAUTICAL —) THIEF
(ORNAMENTAL —) TAZZA
(PAPER —) DIXIE
(PASTRY —) DARIOLE
(PRIZE —) PEWTER
(SACRED —) GRAIL
(SHALLOW —) CYLIX TAZZA TASTER CAPSULE
(SMALL —) DOP NOG TOT DOPP TASS DOBBIN NAGGIN NOGGIN TASSIE
(SQUARE —) MADDER METHER
(STIRRUP —) BONAILIE
(WOODEN —) COG COGUE CAPPER CAPPIE METHER QUAICH
(PL.) VALONIA
(PREF.) CALATHI CALICI COTYL(I)(O) CUPULI CYATH(I)(O)

POCILLI SCYPH(I)(O)
(SUFF.) COTYL(LY)(OUS)
CUPBEARER HEBE SAKI CUPPER GANYMEDE
CUPBOARD CUB KAS BOLE CASE COIN SAFE AMBRY CHEST CUBBY CUDDY HUTCH PRESS ABACUS AUMBRY BUFFET CLOSET LARDER LOCKER PANTRY SPENCE ALMIRAH ARMOIRE CABINET DRESSER SKIBBET ALHACENA CREDENCE CREDENZA TROSTERA
(ARCHERY —) ASCHAM
CUPEL TEST
CUPFUL CUP CAROUSE
CUP HOLDER ZARF
CUPID DAN AMOR EROS LOVE PUTTO CHERUB AMORINO AMOURET AMORETTO
(PL.) PUTTI
CUPIDITY LUST GREED DESIRE AVARICE AVIDITY LONGING APPETITE RAPACITY
CUPOLA DOME KILN TYPE VAULT BELFRY TURRET CALOTTE FURNACE LANTERN LOOKOUT CIMBORIO COCKLOFT
(ROUND —) THOLUS
CUPOLAMAN HEATER
CUPPED GLENOID
CUPPING GLASS VENTOSE
CUPSEED NUTSEED
CUP-SHAPED PEZIZOID SCYPHATE
CUPULE CUP BOLSTER CYATHUS THUMBMARK
CUR DOG YAP FICE FIST FYCE MUTT TIKE TYKE FEIST KEOUT BRAKJE MESSAN MESSIN BOBTAIL MONGREL WHAPPET
CURABLE SANABLE
CURARE URARE URARI OORALI WOORALI
CURASSOW MITU COPPY HOCCO MITUA PAUXI
CURATE ABBE CURA AGENT VICAIRE MINISTER
CURATIVE HEALING IATRICAL PHYSICAL REMEDIAL SALUTARY SANATIVE
CURATOR KEEPER STEWARD GUARDIAN OVERSEER
CURB BIT LID CRUB FOIL KERB REIN SKID SNIP SNUB BRAKE CHECK CRIMP CURVE GUARD LIMIT MOUND ARREST BOTTLE BRIDLE COERCE COLLAR DECKLE GOVERN HAMPER STIFLE STRAIN SUBDUE THWART CONTROL CURBING INHIBIT REFRAIN REPRESS SHACKLE ATTEMPER COMPESCE MODERATE RESTRAIN RESTRICT WITHHOLD
(OFFICIAL —) LID
(WELL —) PUTEAL
CURCULIO TURK WEEVIL
CURCUMA ZEDOARY
CURD CRUD DAHI CHEESE CURDLE CASEINE CLABBER CONGEAL COAGULUM
(— IN MILK) ZIEGA
(—S AND WHEY) SLIP PINJANE
(BEAN —) TOFU
(PL.) SKYR FLEETINGS

(PREF.) THROMB(O)
CURDLE CAP LOP RUN SAM SET CRIM CURD EARN LEEP QUAR SAMM SOUR TURN WHIG YERN CARVE QUAIL QUARL SPOIL YEARN CAILLE LAPPER LOBBER LOPPER POSSET QUARLE CLABBER CONGEAL CRIDDLE CRUDDLE THICKEN CONDENSE
CURDLED CURDLY QUARRED SHOTTEN
(NOT —) UNCRUDDED
CURE DIP DRY DUN FIX BEEF BOOT CARE CORN HEAL HEED HELP JERK MEND SALT SANE SAVE AMEND BLOAT BOTEN LEECH REEST SMEEK SMOKE CHARGE CURATE KIPPER PHYSIC PRIEST RECURE REMEDY SEASON SUCCOR TEMPER WARISH BESMOKE RECOVER RESTORE THERAPY TREACLE ANTIDOTE BARBECUE CURATION GUERISON PRESERVE REVOCERY
(— A HABIT) BREAK
(— BY SMOKING) GAMMON SMUDGE
(— FISH) DUN ROUSE
(— GRASS) HAY
(— HAY) WIN
(— HERRINGS) BLOAT
(— IN SUN) RIZZAR
(— SKINS) DRESS
(COUGH —) SAPA SAPE
CURE-ALL BALM AVENS ELIXIR REMEDY PANACEA THERIAC
CURED SALT BLOATED
CURIOSITY CURIO ODDITY INTEREST
(— OF SMALL VALUE) GABION
(—S OF THE CITY) LIONS
(PL.) CURIOSA
CURIOUS ODD NOSY RARE SELI QUEER SELLE SELLY PRYING QUAINT SNOOPY CUNNING STRANGE UNUSUAL FREAKISH MEDDLING PECULIAR SINGULAR
CURL BOB BEND COIL FEAK FURL KINK LOCK PURL ROLL TUBE WAVE WIND ACKER CANON CRIMP CRISP DILDO FRILL FRIZZ QUIRL SPIRE TRESS TWIRE TWIST BERGER BUCKLE CANNON CRUCHE CURDLE FROWSE MULLET RIPPLE SPIRAL TUNNEL WRITHE CRIDDLE CRIMPLE CRINKLE CROCKET CRUDDLE EARLOCK FLEXURE FRIZZLE FROUNCE RINGLET SERPENT TENDRIL WHISKER FAVORITE LOVELOCK SQUIGGLE
(— HAIR) CROOK
(— OF SMOKE) WREATH
(— OF WIG) SNAKE
(— ON FOREHEAD) CRUCHE CROUCHE
(— OVER) BREAK
(— UP) CRUMP HUNCH SNIRL HUDDLE SHRINK SNUGGLE
(FRINGE OF —S) FRISETTE FRIZETTE
(METAL —) CHIP
(SMALL —) CROCK
(PREF.) CIRR(I)(O) CIRRH(I)(O)

CURLED CRISP FUZZY KINKY SPIRY CIRRATE COCKLED CRISPED FRIZZLY SAVOYED WREATHY CRISPATE CRUMPLED GAUFFRED GOFFERED HELICINE SCROLLED
CURLER GOFFER TEASER CRIMPER FRIZZER MULLETS
CURLEW FUTE JACK SPOW KIOEA SNIPE SPOWE WHAAP WHAUP DIKKOP MARLIN SMOKER BANKERA BUSTARD DOEBIRD BLUELEGS WHIMBREL SICKLEBILL
CURLICUE ESS CAPER CURVE CASSIS PARAPH SQUIRL FLOURISH PURLICUE SCRIGGLE SQUIGGLE
CURLING MARK TEE
CURLING MATCH SPIEL
CURLING STONE IRON STONE LOOFIE GRANITE
(— SPIN) RAISE
CURLY WAVY CRISP CRULL OUNDY CRIMPY RIPPLED CRINKLED
(— HAIR) VEDDOID
CURMUDGEON CRAB CHURL HUNKS MISER GLEYDE GROUCH NIGGARD
CURMUDGEONLY STINGY
CURRANT PASA BERRY CASSIS RAISIN RIZZAR RIZZLE CORINTH
(PL.) RIBES SPICE
CURRANT BUN WIG WIGG
CURRAWONG SQUEAKER STREPERA
CURRENCY CASH COIN PASS BILLS CATER MONEY SCRIP SERIES SPECIE PASSAGE WILDCAT
(FRACTIONAL —) SPONDULIX
(SHELL —) UHLLO
CURRENT NOW WAY EDDY FLOW FLUX FORD RACE RIFE TIDE VEIN WAFT ALIVE DRIFT GOING RAPID ROUST SCOUR SWIFT TENOR TESLA TREND USUAL ABROAD ACTUAL COEVAL COMMON COURSE DOUCHE DURANT FLUENT LATEST LIVING MOTION MOVING OFFSET OUTSET RECENT RIZZER RULING SLUICE STRAND STREAM TONGUE VOLANT COUNTER DRAUGHT FLOWING FRESHET GENERAL INDRAFT INSTANT PASSANT PRESENT RUNNING STICKLE THERMAL TORRENT BACKWASH CURRANCE DOWNCAST FREQUENT MILLRACE OCCURENT PASSABLE TIDERACE TODAYISH UNDERTOW
(— IN SPEECH) WAIF
(AIR —) DRAFT SHEET SPLIT BREEZE DRAUGHT DOWNCAST DOWNFLOW
(ELECTRIC —) STRAY
(HOT —) BACK
(JAPAN —) KUROSHIO KUROSIWO
(PREVAILING —) MAINSTREAM
(RAPID —) SWIFT TONGUE
(SOUND —) DISTORTION
(STRONG —) GALE ROOST ROUST
(PREF.) RHEO
CURRENTLY ANYMORE
CURRICULUM STREAM PROGRAM PROGRAMME

CURRISH BASE CYNICAL DOGGISH IGNOBLE SNARLING

CURRY COMB DRUB KARI CLEAN DRESS GROOM BRUISE CAJOLE CARREE POWDER PREPARE TARKEEAN

(— FAVOR) HUG NUT QUILL COTTON SMOOGE CUITTLE SMOODGE

CURSE BAN POX BANE BLOW CUSS DAMN OATH PIZE WARY BLAST BLESS CORSE SHREW SPELL SWEAR WEARY WINZE DETEST DEVOTE GOOFER GUFFER MAKUTU MALIGN MAUGER MAUGRE ACCURSE BESHREW MALISON ANATHEMA EXECRATE FORSPEAK MALEDICTION

CURSED DASH CUSSED DAMNED DASHED ACCURSED

CURSER WARIER

CURSING BLESSING BLASPHEMY

CURSIVE RUNNING

CURSORY FAST BRIEF HASTY QUICK SHORT FITFUL ROVING SPEEDY PASSANT PASSING SHALLOW CARELESS RAMBLING

CURT BUFF RUDE TART BLUFF BLUNT BRIEF BRUSK NIPPY SHORT SQUAB TERSE ABRUPT CURTAL CUTTED SNIPPY BRUSQUE CONCISE CRYPTIC LACONIC CAVALIER SNAPPISH SNIPPETY SUCCINCT

CURTAIL CUT LOP CLIP CROP DOCK PARE STOP ABATE ELIDE SHORT SLASH STUNT TRUNK DECURT LESSEN REDUCE ABRIDGE BOBTAIL CRACKLE SHORTEN DIMINISH MINORATE RETRENCH

CURTAILED TAIL CUTTY SHORT STUNT CURTAL BOBTAIL CONCISE ABRIDGED

CURTAIN END BOOM DROP IRIS MASK VEIL WALL BLIND DRAPE SCENE SHADE SHEET VELUM COSTER HANGER PURDAH SCREEN SHROUD CEILING CONCEAL CORTINE DRAPERY HANGING VITRAGE ASBESTOS PORTIERE TRAVERSE

(CHURCH —) CLOTH RIDDEL ENDOTYS ENDOTHYS

(THEATER —) IRON SCRIM TEASER TRAVELER TORMENTER

CURTAIN ROD TRINGLE

CURTAIN STRETCHER SCRAY STRAINER

CURTAL CRAPE COURTAL CURTLAX

CURTSY BOB BOW DIP DOP BECK DROP JOUK KNEE CONGE HONOR CURCHY

CURUBA CASSA BANANA

CURVATED STUNT HOOKED

CURVATURE ARC PLY ARCH BENT BOOL CURL CURVE SHEER SINUS CAMBER CURVITY ADUNCITY APOPHYGE CYRTOSIS GRYPOSIS KYPHOSIS LORDOSIS

(— OF BONE) ARCUATION

(— OF DECK) SHEER

(— OF LEGS) RHEBOSIS

(— OF SHOE SOLE) SWING

(— OF SPINE) KYPHOSIS SCOLIOSIS

(— OF STOMACH) FUNDUS

(— OF STRAKE) SPILING

CURVE ARC BOW CUP ESS SAG ARCH BEND BOUT COME CURB FADE HOOK KNEE LINE OGEE TURN VEER WIND AMBIT BIGHT BREAK CONIC CROOK CRUMP CUBIC HELIX NONIC OGIVE PEDAL POLAR QUIRK SLICE SWEEP SWIRL TARVE TREND TWIST WITCH BOUGHT CAMBER CIRCLE DEFLEX JORDAN LITUUS SOLVUS SPIRAL SPRING TOROID WIMPLE ADIABAT BRACKET CAUSTIC CIRCUIT CISSOID COMPASS CONCAVE CONTOUR COSEISM CURVITY CYCLOID ELLIPSE ENVELOP FESTOON FLEXURE INCURVE INFLECT LIMACON PHUGOID PROFILE QUARTIC SCALLOP SINUATE SOLIDUS CARDIOID CATENARY CONCHOID DYGOGRAM ELASTICA EXTRADOS FADEAWAY INTRADOS INVOLUTE LIGATURE LIQUIDUS OPHIURID PARABOLA SINUSOID TONOGRAM TRACTRIX TROCHOID CATACAUSTIC

(— DESCRIBED BY GRAPH) GRAM

(— IN HANDRAIL) KNEE

(— IN PLANKING) HANG

(— IN SAIL) ROACH

(— OF ARCH) INTRADOS

(— OF BALL) DROP

(— OF BIT) LIBERTY

(— OF COLUMN) APOPHYGE

(— OF FINGERNAIL) GRYPOSIS

(— OF HORSE'S NECK) CREST

(— OF PLANK) SNY

(— OF SHIP'S BOW) FLAIR FLARE

(— OF TIMBER) CUP

(— SATISFYING EQUATION) BRANCH

(— SPACE) KNOT

(— WHEN DRAWN) COME

(BASEBALL —) SNAKE

(CRICKET —) SWERVE

(DOUBLE —) CIMA CYMA

(PLANE —) ROSE STROPHOID

(PLANE CUBIC —) WITCH

(VERTICAL —) RAMP

CURVED BENT SOFT ADUNC CORBE CURVE CURVY ROUND WOUND CONVEX CURVEY GYRATE HAMATE TURNED ARCUATE ARRONDI CONCAVE CROOKED CURVANT EMBOWED FALCATE SIGMOID ADUNCOUS ANCHORAL AQUILINE ARCIFORM CRUMPLED CYGNEOUS DECURVED EXCURVED SCROLLED ARCHIFORM

(PREF.) ANCYLO ANKYLO CAMPTO CAMPYL(O) CURVI CURVO CYRT(O)

(SUFF.) CLASTIC

CURVET HOP LEAP LOPE SKIP TURN BOUND CAPER FRISK PRANK VAULT CAVORT CROUPE FROLIC GAMBOL PRANCE

PANNADE CORVETTO CROUPADE

CURVING SPIRY SIMOUS TWISTY AQUILINE DRAWDOWN

(— IN) CONCAVE

(DOWN —) EPINASTY

(SMOOTHLY —) FAIR

CUSH (FATHER OF —) HAM

CUSH-CUSH CARA YAMPEE

CUSHION BAG COD MAT PAD PIG BALL BANK BOSS PUFF SEAT SUNK TRIM GADDI GADHI PANEL SQUAB TRUSH BUFFER INSOLE JOCKEY MUSNUD PILLOW SACHET BOLSTER BRIOCHE COSSHEN HASSOCK KNEELER MUFFLER PILLION REPOSAL ROOTCAP CUTIDURE OREILLER PULVINAR PINCUSHION

(LACE-MAKERS —) BOTT

(PIN —) PRINCOD

(SEAT —) BANKER

(TAILOR'S —) HAM

(PREF.) PULVILLI PULVINI

CUSHIONING DUNNAGE

CUSHIONLIKE PULVINAR

CUSHION PLANT POLSTER

CUSHIONY PADDY

CUSHITIC NUBIAN

CUSK COD TUSK TORSK BURBOT CATFISH

CUSP APEX CONE HORN PEAK ANGLE POINT STYLE TOOTH CORNER SPINODE ENTOCONE HYPOCONE METACONE PARACONE

CUSPID CANINE

CUSPIDOR GABOON CRACHOIR SPITTOON

CUSSO KOSO KOUSSO BRAYERA BRAZERA

CUSTARD FLAN FOOL CREME FLAWN DOUCET DOWCET CHARLET PARFAIT FLUMMERY DIABLOTIN ZABAGLIONE

CUSTARD APPLE ANONA ANNONA PAWPAW CORAZON SWEETSOP

CUSTODIAN HACK GUARD BAILEE CUSTOS KEEPER SEXTON WARDEN WARDER CURATOR JANITOR CERBERUS CLAVIGER GUARDIAN CONCIERGE

CUSTODY LAP BAIL CARE HOLD KEEP WARD TRUST ARREST CHARGE SAFETY YEMSEL CONTROL DURANCE KEEPING TUITION COMMENDA CUSTODIA HANDFAST SECURITY WARDSHIP

CUSTOM FAD LAW MOS PAD TAX URE USE WON ASAL DUTY FORM GARB MODE MORE RITE ROTE RULE THEW TOLL WONE WONT FUERO GUISE HABIT HAUNT RITUS STYLE SUNNA TRADE TREAD TRICK USAGE VOGUE BYRLAW DASTUR DHARMA GROOVE IMPOST MANNER MINHAG MONTEM PRAXIS SUNNAH USANCE COSTUME DUSTOOR DUSTOUR FASHION FORMULA HALAKAH TRIBUTE USAUNCE WARNOTH BUSINESS ENDOGAMY HABITUDE PRACTICE

ASSUETUDE CONSUETUDE PRESCRIPTION

(BINDING —) LAW

(BUSINESS —) TRADE GOODWILL

(CHILDBIRTH —) COUVADE

(CHURCH —) COMITY

(CORRUPT —) ABUSE

(FESTIVAL —) HOCKING

(OUTMODED —) ARCHAISM

(PRIMITIVE —) COUVADE

(RURAL —) HEAVING

(SECRET —) SANDE

(TEMPORARY —) FAD VOGUE

(PL.) MORES MOEURS HAIKWAN FOLKLORE PROPRIETIES

CUSTOMARILY USUALLY CUSTOMLY

CUSTOMARY PER RIFE TAME USED NOMIC USUAL BEATEN COMMON SOLEMN VULGAR WONTED CLASSIC GENERAL REGULAR USITATE EVERYDAY FAMILIAR HABITUAL ORTHODOX

(NOT —) INSOLENT

CUSTOMER CHAP COVE BUYER CLIENT PATRON SUCKER ACCOUNT CALLANT CHAPMAN PATIENT SHOPPER MERCHANT PROSPECT

(PRINTER'S —) AUTHOR

(TOUGH —) HARDCASE

(PL.) CUSTOM CLIENTELE

CUSTOMHOUSE ADUANA DOGANA DOUANE

CUSTOM-MADE BESPOKE BESPOKEN

CUSTOMS OFFICER SHARK WAITER

CUT AX ADZ AXE BOB DAG DAP DIE HAG HEW KIT LOP MOW NIP RIT SAW SNY TAP ADZE BANG BITE BOLO BOLT BUZZ CHIP CHOP CLIP CROP DADO DOCK FACE FELL FILE GASH GIRD HACK HASH HEWN JERK KNAP LIMB MAKE MODE MUSH NICK OCHE PARE RACE RASH RAZE REAP SIDE SKIN SLIT SLOT SMIT SNEE SNEG SNIP SNUB STOW SUMP SWAP SWOP TAME TRIM VELL VIDE BEVEL BLOCK BREAK CANAL CANCH CARVE CHIVE CHYND CLEFT COPSE COUPE CRIMP DRESS FLICK FRAZE FRITH GOUGE GRAVE GRIDE GROOP HOWEL KITTE KNIFE LANCE LATHE MINCE NOTCH PLATE PRUNE RAZEE SABER SABRE SCALP SCARP SCIND SCORE SEVER SHAPE SHARE SHEAR SHIVE SHRED SKICE SKISE SLASH SLICE SLICK SLISH SLIVE SNICK SLIP STAMP SWEEP SWIPE SWISH TOUCH TWITE VOGUE WHITE ABLATE AJOURE BARBER BISECT BROACH CAMBER CHISEL CLEAVE CORNER CUTTED DIVIDE EXCISE FIGURE FLETCH FLITCH FRENCH GROOVE GULLET HACKLE HAGGLE IGNORE INCIDE INCISE INDENT LESSEN MANGLE OUTPUT RASURE REDUCE RIPPLE SCORCH SCOTCH SCRIBE SCYTHE SLIGHT SLIVER SNATHE STRAIT

STREAK SULLET SWINGE TAILYE THWITE TRENCH AFFRONT CONVERT CURTAIL CUTTING DIACOPE DISCIDE DISSECT DRAWCUT ENGRAVE FASHION FRITTER HATCHET SCALPEL SCISSOR SCUTTLE SECTILE TAILZEE WHITTLE DISSEVER FRACTION INCISION INCISURE INTAGLIO LACERATE MALAHACK RETRENCH THWITTLE
(— A THREAD) CHASE
(— AN OPENING) BREACH
(— AT ANGLE) CANT BEVEL
(— AT RANDOM) SLASH
(— AWAY) COPE SLIT UNDO ABATE CONCISE
(— BACK) HEAD SPUR
(— BARK) CHIP
(— BEAM) KERF
(— CARS) LIFT
(— CHEESE) HARP
(— CLAY) SLING
(— CORNERS) SKIRT CHAMFER CHAMPHER
(— CRUST) CHIP
(— DEEPLY) DIG SHANK
(— DIAGONALLY) CATER SLANT
(— DOWN) MOW FELL STAG STUB RAZEE SCANT SCARP ABRIDGE SHORTEN RETRENCH
(— FANCY FIGURE) DASH
(— FISH) SOLAY STEAK
(— FOR FODDER) CHAFF
(— GEAR TEETH) RATCH
(— GLASS) SPLIT
(— GRAIN) BAG FAG CRADLE SWINGE
(— HAIR) DOD
(— IN) INSECT INCISED
(— IN A TREE) FACE
(— IN BARREL STAVE) HOWEL
(— IN EXCAVATIONS) GULLET
(— IN RELIEF) ENCHASE
(— IN SOFT ROCK) CAVATE
(— IN SQUARES) CHECK
(— INTO LARGE SLICES) WHANG
(— INTO SLIPS) ZEST
(— INTO STRIPS) JERK FLETCH FLITCH JULIENNE
(— INTO TREE) BOX
(— JAGGEDLY) HACK SNAG
(— LEDGES) BENCH
(— LOGS) LUMBER
(— OF FISH) JOWL
(— OF GEM) STAR
(— OF GRAIN) MILL
(— OF MEAT) ARM SEY CROP HOCK SHIN SIDE CHUCK SHANK STEAK BRISKET FORESEY ICEBONE SIRLOIN EDGEBONE FORERIBS
(— OF RIFLING) GROOVE
(— OFF) BOB LOP CLIP CROP DOCK KILL PARE SHUT SLIT STAG BELEE CROSS ELIDE PRUNE SCIND SEVER SHAVE SHEAR SKIVE SLIPE SPIKE COUPED DECIDE EXEMPT FORCUT RESECT SHIELD STIFLE SWATCH ABJOINT ABSCIND ABSCISE ABSCISS CURTAIL EXSCIND ISOLATE PRECIDE RESCIND AMPUTATE CLEIDOIC DESECATE RESECATE

RETRENCH TRUNCATE
(— OFF BY BITS) DRIB
(— OFF END) BUTT
(— OFF WOOL) DOD DODD
(— OPEN) SPLAY
(— OUT) DESS DINK CLICK BROACH EXCIDE EXCISE EXSECT
(— PATH) FRAY
(— SALMON) CHINE
(— SHEEP) TOMAHAWK
(— SHORT) BOB COW HOG LOP BANG CROP DOCK JIMP SNIB BOBBED CURTAL HOGGED BOBTAIL CHAPPED CONCISE SCANTLE PRESCIND
(— TENDONS) ENERVATE
(— THE THROAT) JUGULATE
(— THE WAVES) SNORE
(— THINLY) CURL
(— TO PIECES) CHOP DICE MINCE BRITTLE FRITTER
(— TO SIZE) TAIL
(— TURF) VELL
(— UNDER) KIRVE
(— UNEVENLY) CHATTER
(— UP) TUSK CARVE CHINE JOINT PRANK SPOIL TRAIN GOBBET COLLOPED
(— UP SWAN) LIFT
(— WHALE BLUBBER) LEAN FLENSE
(— WITH BACKWARD SLOPE) COOT
(— WITH DIE) DINK BLANK
(— WITH SHEARS) SHIRL
(— WITH SICKLE) BAG REAP
(COLD —S) ASSIETTE
(CREW —) BUTCH FLATTOP
(DEEP NARROW —) JAD
(FENCING —) STRAMAZON
(LARGE — OF FOOD) DODGE
(NOT —) UNCORVEN
(SHORT —) ATAJO
(SLIGHT —) SNICK SCOTCH
(THIN —) TARGET
(PREF.) SEC(O) TEMNO TOMO
(SUFF.) COPATE COPE SECT SECTED TOMA TOME TOMIC TOMOUS TOMY
CUT-AND-DRIED CANNED
CUTANEOUS DERMAL
CUTCH GAMBIR CATECHU GAMBIER
CUTE COY KEEN COONY DINKY DUCKY SHARP CLEVER PRETTY SHREWD CUNNING DARLING
CUTICLE DERM HIDE SKIN SHUCK THECA MEMBRANE PELLICLE
(— OF EGGSHELL) BLOOM
CUTLASS SWORD CURTAL DUSACK HANGER TESACK CURTAXE MACHETE SHABBLE CAMPILAN
CUTLASS FISH HIKU SAVOLA KALKVIS MACHETE HAIRTAIL
CUTLET SCHNITZEL
CUTOVER COUPE
CUTPURSE NIP BUNG THIEF HORNTHUMB
CUTTER DIE BEEF BOAT IRON MILL PONE SLED BRAVO FACER FRAZE SLOOP SMACK BAYMAN CHERRY COLTER COTTER DOCKER EDITOR FRAZER MINCER SLEIGH SLICER CLIPPER COULTER DROMOND INCISOR RUFFIAN KNIFEMAN

REVENUER SCHOKKER SHEPSTER
(— OF STONES) LAPIDARY
(BRICK —) RUBBER
(PEAT —) PINER
(WIRE —) SECATEUR
CUTTERHEAD WABBLER WOBBLER
CUTTHROAT THUG BRAVO CUTTER RUFFIAN SWORDER
CUTTHROAT TROUT MYKISS
CUTTING CUT HAG RAW SET ACID CARF CURT KEEN KERF SECT SETT SLIP TART TWIG ACUTE BLEAK CHECK CRISP EAGER EDGED GRIDE SCION SCRAP SCROW SHARP SMART BITING BITTER BORING ENTAIL GODOWN GORING JAGGED PHYTON PIPING SECANT SEVERE SNITHE BURNING CAUSTIC GRIBBLE INCISAL MORDANT NICKING OVERCUT PAINFUL PIQUANT POLLING SARMENT SATIRIC SECTION SLICING CHILLING CLEARING INCISIVE PIERCING POIGNANT QUICKSET SCATHING SCISSION SNAPPISH WOUNDING TRENCHANT
(— FOR DIRT-CAR TRACK) GULLET
(— FOR WATER) TAJO
(— FROM PLANT) SLIP SHROUD SARMENT PROPAGULE TRUNCHEON
(— OF DEER) SAY
(— OF TREES) HAG
(— OFF) AVULSION
(— SHORT) ABORTIVE
(DRILL —S) MUD
(OBLIQUE —) BARBING
(SECOND —) ROWEN
(WASTE —) SELVAGE SELVEDGE
(SUFF.) THEMA THESIS TOMA TOME TOMIC TOMOUS TOMY
(— OUT) ECTOMY
CUTTLEBONE SEPIA SEPION SEPIUM GLADIUS SEPIARY
CUTTLEFISH SEPIA SHELL SQUID CUDDLE CUTTLE SCRIBE CATFISH DECAPOD INKFISH MOLLUSK OCTOPUS SCUTTLE
(PREF.) TEUTHIS
CUVETTE POT TUB TANK BASIN BUCKET TRENCH CISTERN
CYANEE (DAUGHTER OF —) BYBLIS
(FATHER OF —) MAEANDER
(HUSBAND OF —) MILETUS
(SON OF —) CAUNUS
CYANIDE NITRILE CYANURET PRUSSIATE
CYANIPPUS (FATHER OF —) PHARAX
(WIFE OF —) LEUCONE
CYANITE SAPPARE DISTHENE
CYANOGEN PRUSSIN PRUSSINE
CYBELE RHEA KYBELE AGDISTIS
(DAUGHTER OF —) JUNO
(FATHER OF —) URANUS
(HUSBAND OF —) SATURN
(MOTHER OF —) GAEA
(SON OF —) JUPITER NEPTUNE
CYCAD BANGA CICAD ZAMIA COONTIE CYCADITE
CYCHREUS (DAUGHTER OF —) GLAUCE

(FATHER OF —) NEPTUNE POSEIDON
(MOTHER OF —) SALAMIS
CYCLADES (ISLAND OF —) IOS KEOS DELOS MELOS NAXOS PAROS SYROS TENOS ANDROS AMORGOS KYTHNOS SANTORIN SERIPHOS
CYCLAMEN BACCHAR PRIMWORT SOWBREAD
CYCLE AGE EON ERA AEON BIKE EPOCH KALPA PEDAL PRIME ROUND SAROS SECLE WHEEL BAKTUN CIRCLE COURSE CYCLUS PERIOD BICYCLE CIRCUIT DICYCLE TRICYCLE
(— OF WORK) ROTA JOURNEY
(—S CAUSED BY KARMA) SAMSARA SANSARA
(BUSINESS —) JUGLAR KITCHIN
(LUNAR —) SAROS
(ONE — PER SECOND) HERTZ
(SECONDARY —) EPICYCLE
CYCLIC CYCLAR ANNULAR CYCLICAL PERIODIC
CYCLIST CYCLER WHEELER WHEELMAN
CYCLOLITH CROMLECH
CYCLOMETER ODOGRAPH VIAMETER
CYCLONE GALE GUST WIND BLAST STORM BAGUIO TORNADO TWISTER TYPHOON SECONDARY NEUTERCANE
CYCLOPARAFFIN NAPHTHENE
CYCLOPEAN HUGE VAST STRONG MASSIVE COLOSSAL GIGANTIC
CYCLOPS ARGES BRONTES COPEPOD STEROPES
CYCLORAMA CYKE PANORAMA
CYCLOSIS STREAMING
CYCLOSTOME HAGFISH
CYCNUS (DAUGHTER OF —) HEMITHEA
(FATHER OF —) ARES MARS NEPTUNE POSEIDON
(MOTHER OF —) CALYCE PYRENE PELOPIA
(SON OF —) TENES
(WIFE OF —) PROCLEA PHYLONOME
CYLINDER CAN EKE GIG TIN BEAM BOMB BURR CAGE CANE DRUM LEAD MUFF PIPE PRIM ROLL SLUG TUBE WELL BLOCK CORER DRAIN FIBER FIBRE FUDGE SCREW SHELL SPOOL STELA STELE SWIFT BARREL BOBBIN BUTTON COLUMN COPPER DECKER DOFFER DUSTER FILTER GABION PISTON PLATEN ROLLER SCREEN TIPITI TUMBLE URCHIN WORKER CUTCHER SLEEVER SLUDGER SUCCULA FOLLOWER GRADUATE NEURAXIS SPARKLET
(— AROUND MOLD) COTTLE
(— FOR DANCE RHYTHM) CLAVE
(— OF STEAM WHISTLE) BELL
(— OF TISSUE) CORTEX
(— OF YARN) CAKE
(— ON LOOM) BEAM
(— WITH PERFORATIONS) FLUSHER
(—S PULLED THROUGH DUCT) MANDREL

(ARMORED —) BARBETTE
(GLASS —) MUFF
(HOLLOW —) PIPE TUBE
(MARKING —) LEAD
(NAPPING —) GIG
(RELAY —) BATON
(REVOLVING —) BEATER ROLLER
(TOOTHED —) SPROCKET
(WATERMARK —) DANDY
CYLINDRICAL ROUND TERETE
TOROSE CENTRIC TUBULAR
TERETIAL
(PREF.) TERETI
CYMA GOLA GULA OGEE DOUCINE
MOLDING CYMATIUM
CYMA REVERSA HEEL
CYMBA YET
CYMBAL ZEL CHIME TARGET
CROTALUM KYMBALON
(PL.) TAL BECKEN PIATTI
CYMBELINE (AUTHOR OF —)
SHAKESPEARE
(CHARACTER IN —) CAIUS HELEN
CLOTEN IMOGEN LUCIUS
MORGAN IACHIMO PISANIO
BELARIUS LEONATUS PHILARIO
ARVIRAGUS CORNELIUS
CYMBELINE GUIDERIUS
POSTHUMUS
(SON OF —) ARVIRAGUS
GUIDERIUS
CYMBIUM MELO
CYME CYMULE BOSTRYX
CYMLING SIMNEL CYMBLIN

SCALLOP PATTYPAN
CYMOSE DEFINITE SYMPODIAL
CYMRY KYMRI WELSH
CYNIC SATYR TIMON DOUBTER
APEMANTUS
CYNICAL CYNIC SULLEN CURRISH
DOGGISH DOGLIKE CAPTIOUS
SARDONIC SNARLING JAQUESIAN
MISOGYNIC PESSIMISTIC
MISANTHROPIC
CYNOCEPHALUS AANI
CYNORTES (BROTHER OF —)
HYACINTHUS
(FATHER OF —) AMYCLAS
(MOTHER OF —) DIOMEDE
(SON OF —) PERIERES
CYNOSURE SHOW LODESTAR
CYPRESS CULL SABINO SIPERS
FIREBALL AHUEHUETE
BELVEDERE
CYPRESS SPURGE BALSAM
NAPOLEON
CYPRIPEDIUM CYP DUCK
NERVINE

CYPRUS
CAPE: GATA GRECO ANDREAS
ARNAUTI ZEVGARI
CAPITAL: NICOSIA
COIN: PARA
MEASURE: OKA OKE PIK CASS
DONUM KOUZA GOMARI
KARTOS MEDIMNO
MOUNTAIN: TROODOS

RIVER: PEDIAS PEDIEOS
TOWN: POLIS CITIUM PAPHOS
KYRENIA LARNACA MORPHOU
NICOSIA LIMASSOL FAMAGUSTA
WEIGHT: OKA OKE MOOSA
KANTAR

CYRANO DE BERGERAC (AUTHOR
OF —) ROSTAND
(CHARACTER IN —) CYRANO
ROXANE VALVERT DEGUICHE
CHRISTIAN
CYRENE (FATHER OF) HYPSEUS
(MOTHER OF —) CHLIDANOPE
(SON OF —) IDMON DIOMEDES
ARISTAEUS
CYRILLA TITI
CYRUS KORESH
CYST BAG SAC WEN POUCH
CYSTUS RANULA DERMOID
HYDATID HYGROMA SACCULE
VESICLE ATHEROMA DACRYOPS
MUCOCELE STEATOMA
CYSTOPTERIS FILIX
CYTOKININ ZEATIN
CYTOLYSIN AMBOCEPTOR
CYTOME SPHEROME
CYTOPLASM MASSULA OOPLASM
PLASMON DIASTEMA
(PREF.) PLASTO
CZAR CSAR IVAN TSAR TZAR
PETER NICHOLAS
CZARDAS CSARDAS
(SECTION OF —) FRISS

LASSU FRISZKA
CZECH CECH TSECH TSCEKH
BOHEMIAN

CZECHOSLOVAKIA
BEER: PILSEN
CAPITAL: PRAHA PRAGUE
CASTLE: HRADCANY
COIN: CROWN DUCAT HALER
HELLER KORUNA
DANCE: POLKA REDOWA FURIANT
MEASURE: LAN SAH MIRA KOREC
LATRO STOPA MERICE STRYCH
MOUNTAIN: ORE TATRA SUDETEN
PROVINCE: BOHEMIA MORAVIA
SLOVAKIA
REGION: BOHEMIA MORAVIA
SLOVAKIA
RIVER: UH MZE VAG VAH DYJE
EGER ELBE GRAU HRON IPEL
ISAR ISER LABE NISA ODER
OHRE OLSE OPPA WAAG BECVA
DUNAJ MARCH NITRA SLANA
TISZA DANUBE HORNAD
MOLDAU MORAVA ONDAVA
SAZAVA TORYSA VLTAVA
LABOREC LUZNICE BEROUNKA
TOWN: AS ASCH BRNO CHEB EGER
MOST BRUNN OPAVA PLZEN
TABOR TUZLA AUSSIG BILINA
KLADUS PILSEN PRESOV VSETIN
ZVOLEN BUDWEIS JIHLAVA
OSTRAVA TEPLITZ

D

D DE DEE DOG DELTA

DAB DAP DOB DOT DUB HIT PAT BLOW CHIT DAUB LICK LUMP PECK SPOT CLOUT DHABB DIGHT LEMON SMEAR BLOTCH EXPERT STRIKE DABSTER PORTION SPLOTCH FLATFISH FLOUNDER MARYSOLE SANDLING

DABBER BALL PROD TAMPON

DABBING PICKING

DABBLE DAB DIB MESS DALLY DIBBLE MEDDLE MUDDLE PADDLE POTTER SOSSLE SPLASH TAMPER TRIFLE DRABBLE MOISTEN PLOUTER PLUTTER SMATTER SPATTER DELIBATE SPRINKLE **(— WITH BLOOD)** ENGORE

DABBLER AMATEUR DABSTER

DABCHICK GREBE DIPPER DOBBER DOPPER PUFFER HENBILL DIDAPPER DOPCHICK

DACE CHUB DARE DART CYPRINID GRAYLING

DACHSHUND DACHS TECKEL BADGERER

DACOIT DAKU DAKOO ROBBER CRIMINAL

DACTYL TOE FOOT FINGER

DACTYLOPODITE POLLEX

DACTYLOZOOID PALPON

DACTYLUS DACTYL DIGITUS

DAD BEAT BLOW DAUD HUNK LUMP PAPA KNOCK THUMP FATHER STRIKE

DADDY BABBO DEDDY

DADDY LONGLEGS SPINNER LONGLEGS PHALANGID

DADO DIE GROOVE SOLIDUM

DAEDALUS (ANCESTOR OF —) ERECHTHEUS **(NEPHEW OF —)** TALUS **(SON OF —)** ICARUS

DAEMON (ALSO SEE DEMON) GHOST DAIMON PYTHON EUDAEMON MISTRESS **(PL.)** CURETES

DAFFODIL GLEN LILY DAFFY DILLY JONQUIL ASPHODEL BELLWORT CROWBELL

DAFT GAY WILD BALMY BATTY CRAZY DAFFY GIDDY LOONY POTTY SILLY INSANE FOOLISH IDIOTIC IMBECILE

DAG JAG DAGG STAB SLASH DAGGLE PIERCE DAGGING DAGLOCK PRICKET

DAGAME SALAMO MADRONA LEMONWOOD

DAGGER DAG SAX DIRK ITAC KRIS SAEX SNEE SPUD STAB TANG CRISE DAGUE KATAR KREES POINT PRICK SKEAN STEEL ANLACE BODKIN COUTEL CREESE DIESIS HANGER KIRPAN KUTTAR PANADE PINKER POPPER SKHIAN STYLET BALARAO BAYONET COUTEAU DUDGEON HANDJAR KANDJAR KHANJAR OBELISK PONIARD SLASHER STABBER BASELARD PUNCHEON PUNTILLA STILETTO **(— AS CERAMICS COVER)** HILLER **(— REFERENCE MARK)** SPIT **(— WITH WAVY BLADE)** KRIS CREESE KREESE **(DOUBLE —)** DIESIS **(SACRED —)** KIRPAN **(PREF.)** MACHAIRO

DAGOMBA DAGBANE DAGBANI

DAH DAO DOW DHAO

DAHLIA JICAMA POMPON

DAHOMEY (CAPITAL OF —) PORTONOVO **(PEOPLE OF —)** FON FONG BARIBA **(RIVER OF —)** NIGER OUEME **(TOWN IN —)** KANDI NIKKI ABOMEY OUIDAH COTONOU

DAILY ADAY ADAYS DIARY DIURNAL

DAINCHA NARDOO

DAINTIES EST ESTE SOCK CATES DIABLOTIN

DAINTILY CHOICELY GINGERLY MINIONLY

DAINTINESS FLUTTER DELICACY

DAINTY CATE FINE NICE RARE TEAR ACATE DAINT DENTY FRILL GENTY NAISH BONBON CHOICE COSTLY FRIAND MIGNON MINION PICKED REGALO SCARCE SPICED SUNKET CURIOUS ELEGANT FINICAL FINICKY MINIKIN REGALIA TAFFETA TAFFETY DAINTITH DAINTREL DELICACY DELICATE ETHEREAL LIKEROUS MIGNIARD TRYPHOSA **(PREF.)** ABRO HABRO

DAIRY TAMBO LACTARY VACCARY CREAMERY DEYHOUSE **(— PRODUCTS)** MILCHIGS

DAIRYMAID DEE DEY DEYWOMAN MILKMAID

DAIRYMAN AHIR MILKMAN

DAIS PACE SEAT BENCH LEWAN STAGE TABLE CANOPY ESTATE LISSOM PODIUM PULPIT SETTLE ESTRADE TERRACE TRIBUNE CHABUTRA FOOTPACE HALFPACE HATHPACE HUSTINGS PLATFORM

DAISY BULL GOLD DANDY GOWAN OXEYE BENNET MORGAN SHASTA BONESET BOWWORT COMFREY DOGBLOW BACKWORT BONEWORT COMPOSIT HEXAFOIL KNITBACK PISSABED MOONPENNY BRUISEWORT MARGUERITE

DAISY CUTTER GRUB

DAISY FLEABANE ERIGERON SCABIOUS

DAKOTA SIOUX LAKOTA

DALE HAW DELL DENE GLEN VALE SPOUT BOTTOM DINGLE TROUGH VALLEY

DALEA PAROSELA

DALIBOR (CHARACTER IN —) BENES ZDENEK DALIBOR MAILADA **(COMPOSER OF —)** SMETANA

DALLES DELLS RAPIDS

DALLIANCE TOY CHAT PLAY TALK SPORT GOSSIP TOUSEL TOUSLE TRIFLE COLLING

DALLIER PINGLER

DALLY TOY CHAT DAFF FOOL IDLE JAKE JAUK PLAY SWAN WAIT DELAY FLIRT SPORT TARRY COQUET DABBLE DAWDLE LINGER LOITER PINGLE TRIFLE WANTON DRINGLE SLIDDER

DALLYING COQUETRY SISSETON

DALMATIC TUNICLE

DALPHON (FATHER OF —) HAMAN

DAM BAR BAY PEN REE BUND DAME HEAD POND SADD SPUR STAY STEM STOP SUDD WEIR BLOCK CAULD CHECK CHOKE GARTH MOUND POUND STANK ANICUT CAUSEY HINDER MOTHER PARENT ANNICUT BARRAGE BARRIER BURROCK MILLDAM PENHEAD RAMPIRE TAPPOON ABOIDEAU BLOCKADE GRANDDAM OBSTACLE OBSTRUCT RESTRAIN **(PART OF —)** GATE PIER POOL SILL WALL BASIN CREST OUTLET SLUICE ROADWAY TAINTOR OVERFLOW SPILLWAY POWERHOUSE

DAMAGE MAR BLOT BURN COST HARM HURT JEEL LOSS RUIN SKIN TEEN BLITZ BURST CLOUD CRACK HAVOC PRANG SPOIL WOUND WRONG BATTER CHARGE DANGER DEFACE DEFECT HINDER IMPAIR INJURE INJURY INSULT LESION SCATHE SORROW AFFLICT DAMNIFY DEGRADE DISTURB EXPENSE FOUNDER OFFENCE OFFENSE PAYMENT SCRATCH SCUTTLE SHATTER ACCIDENT BUSINESS DISSERVE FRACTURE FRETTING MISCHIEF SABOTAGE **(PREF.)** DAMNI

DAMAGED HURT CRAZY LESED BROKEN CRACKED INJURED

DAMAGES INTEREST HAMESUCKEN

DAMAGING HARMFUL HURTFUL SCATHING

DAMAN DAS CONY CONEY CUNNY DASSY GANAM HYRAX DASSIE WABBER ASHKOKO CHEROGRIL

DAMA PADEMELON TAMMAR WALLABY

DAMASCENED WATERED

DAMASCENE WORK KOFTGARI

DAMASK LINEN DARNEX DORNIC DORNICK VALANCE DAMASSIN DRAWLOOM

DAMAYANTI (HUSBAND OF —) NALA

DAME DINT LADY DAMIE WOMAN MATRON

DAME BLANCHE, LA (CHARACTER IN —) ANNA BROWN JENNY GEORGE DICKSON GAVESTON **(COMPOSER OF —)** BOIELDIEU

DAME'S VIOLET EVEWEED

DAMKINA (HUSBAND OF —) EA

DAMMARA AGATHIS

DAMN DEE DEM DOG RAT BLOW BURN DANG DARN DASH DING DRAT DUMB DURN BLAME BLANK BLAST BLESS CURSE FETCH TARAL WHOOP BEDAMN BUGGER DEMPNE DEVOTE GODDAM CONDEMN CONSARN DOGGONE GODDAMN GOLDARN GOLDURN CONFOUND EXECRATE

DAMNABLE RUDDY DAMNED ODIOUS ACCURSED INFERNAL

DAMNABLY DEUCED CURSEDLY DEUCEDLY

DAMNATION NATION PERDITION

DAMNATION DE FAUST (CHARACTER IN —) FAUST MARGUERITE MEPHISTOPHELES **(COMPOSER OF —)** BERLIOZ

DAMNED DEE DAMN DARN DEED DURN LOST BALLY DOOMS BLAMED BLOODY DARNED DASHED DURNED GODDAM GORMED TARNAL BLASTED BLESSED CONSARN DOGGONE ETERNAL GOLDARN GOLDURN MUCKING ACCURSED BLANKETY BLINKING DASHEDLY INFERNAL JIGGERED

DAMO (FATHER OF —) PYTHAGORAS **(MOTHER OF —)** THEANO

DAMP DEG FOG RAW WAK WET CLAM DANK DEWY DULL MIST ROKY SOFT WACK BLUNT DABBY HUMID JUICY MALMY MOCHY MOIST MOOTH MUGGY MUNGY MUSTY RAFTY RAINY RAWKY SAPPY SEEPY SOBBY SOGGY THONE WAUGH WEAKY BLIGHT CLAMMY DAMPEN DEADEN MUFFLE QUENCH RHEUMY STUPOR BEDEWED DAMPISH DEPRESS MOISTEN SQUIDGY

142

DEJECTED DISPIRIT HUMIDIFY
HUMIDITY MOISTURE
(— OF EVENING) SERENE
(CHOKE —) STYTHE
(PREF.) HUMI(DI)
DAMPEN DEG DAMP MOIL CHILL
CRAMP FREEZE SPONGE
MOISTURE
DAMPENER MULLER
DAMPER DAMP MUTE BREAD
CHECK CHECKER SORDINE
REGISTER
DAMPNESS CLAM DAMP
HUMIDITY
DAMSEL GIRL WENCH MAIDEN
MOPPET DAMOSEL DAMOZEL
PUCELLE DONZELLA PRINCESS
DAMSELFISH PINTANO
DAMSELFLY NAIAD ODONATE
DAN GI DEN
(MOTHER OF —) BILHAH
DANAKIL AFAR
DANAUS ANOSIA
(BROTHER OF —) AEGYPTUS
(DAUGHTER OF —) AMYMONE
(FATHER OF —) BELUS
(MOTHER OF —) ANCHINOE
DANCE BAL BOB HOP JIG MAI SON
BALL DRAG DUET DUMP FISH
FOOT FRUG HEEL HOOF HORA
JAZZ JIVE JUBA JUKE KOLO LEAP
LOPE LOUP MASK MILL MOVE
PROM REEL SAIL SHAG SKIT STEP
BAILE BAMBA BONGO BRAWL
CANON CAPER CAROL CONGA
DANZA ENTRY FLING FLISK FRIKE
FRISK GOPAK LASYA LIMBO LINDY
MAMBO PAVAN POLKA RINKA
RUMBA SALLY SAMBA STOMP
SWING TANGO TRACE TREAD
TWIST VOLTA WALTZ ALTHEA
AREITO BALLET BALTER BOLERO
BOOGIE BOSTON BRANLE CANARY
CANCAN CEBELL CORDAX
DANZON DIDDLE DREHER FADING
FORMAL FROLIC GERMAN
HORMOS MASQUE MINUET
MOBBLE MONKEY MORRIS NRITTA
PASSAY RACKET RHUMBA
SHIMMY TODDLE TRESCA TUMBLE
VALETA VELETA ANTHEMA
BEGUINE CALINDA CANTICO
COURANT CZARDAS DANSANT
FADDING FARRUCA FOOTING
FOXTROT FURLANA GAVOTTE
MEASURE MORISCO PATTERN
SALTATE SARDANA SHUFFLE
TEMPETE TRESCHE TRIPPLE
VOLTIZE ZIGANKA ANGLAISE
AURRESCU BAMBOULA
BUNNYHUG CACHUCHA
CAKEWALK CHACONNE
COMPARSA COONJINE COTILLON
ENTRACTE ESTAMPIE FANDANGO
FANTASIA FLAMENCO GALLIARD
GALOPADE GUARACHA
HABANERA HEYDEGUY HORNPIPE
KOLATTAM MATELOTE
MERENGUE SALTATION
SHAKEDOWN CARMAGNOLE
SCHOTTISCHE
(— ART) NATYA ORCHESIS

(— ATTENDANCE) LACKEY
LACQUEY
(— CLUMSILY) BALTER
(— DRAMA) NO NOH
(— FACE TO FACE) SET
(— FORM) PIVA
(— IN CIRCLE) JIGGER
(— METHOD) LABAN
(— NIMBLY) CANARY
(— RESEMBLING THE POLKA)
BERLIN
(— STEP) RIFF PICKUP
(— STYLE) ABHINAYA
(— TYPE) TANDAVA
(ACROBATIC —) ADAGIO
(AFRICAN —) SHOUT
(ARGENTINE —) CUANDO
(AUSTRIAN —) LANDLER
(BALINESE —) KEBYAR LEGONG
(BALLROOM —) SON CONGO
COTILLON
(BOHEMIAN —) REDOWA FURIANT
(CARNIVAL —) COOCH FOLIA
COOTCH
(CEREMONIAL —) AREITO CANTICO
DUTUBURI
(COQUETTISH —) PURPOSE
(COUNTRY —) HAY RANT CONFESS
LANDLER MUSETTE ANGLAISE
SARABAND
(COURTSHIP —) CUECA BATUQUE
LEZGINKA
(DANISH —) SEXTUR
(FIESTA —S) AKRIEROS
(FLAMENCO —) ALEGRIAS
(FRENCH —) BAL BOREE BRAWL
GAVOT BRANLE BOURREE
BOUTADE BRANSLE GAVOTTE
LAVOLTA
(GAY —) RANT GAILLARD
GALLIARD
(GESTURE —) SIVA
(GREEK —) CORDAX KORDAX
ROMAIKA SIKINNIS
(GYPSY —) FARRUCA
(HAITIAN —) JUBA
(HOBBYHORSE —) CALUSAR
(HOLIDAY —) PATTERN
(HUNGARIAN —) KOS
(IMPROMPTU —) BOUTADE
(INDIAN —) IRUSKA KATHAK
KANTIKOY
(IRISH —) FADING PLANXTY
(ITALIAN —) FORLANA FURLANA
BERGAMASK SALTARELLO
(JAPANESE —) BUGAKU KAGURA
(JAVANESE —) SERIMPI
(LIVELY —) JIG REEL GALOP GIGUE
POLKA RUMBA BOLERO CANARY
RHUMBA SPRING BOURREE
CORANTO FURLANA HOEDOWN
GALLIARD GALOPADE HORNPIPE
(MAORI —) HAKA
(MARTIAL —) PYRRHIC
(MEXICAN —) JARABE HUAPANGO
SANDUNGA
(MOURNFUL —) DUMP
(NORWEGIAN —) HALLING
(OLD ENGLISH —) CEBELL MORRIS
ARGEERS ANGLAISE
(OLD-FASHIONED —) LOURE
PASSACAGLIA
(PEASANT —) JOTA

DANZON BALITAO
(PERUVIAN —) CUECA KASWA
CACHUA
(POLISH —) POLACCA KUJAWIAK
POLONAISE VARSOVIENNE
(POLYNESIAN —) HULA
(PORTUGUESE —) FADO
(ROMAN —) TRIPUDIUM
(ROUND —) RAY BRAUL CAROL
WALTZ CAROLE MAXIXE
(RUSSIAN —) ZIGANKA
(RUSTIC —) HAY HEY HAYMAKER
(SPANISH —) JOTA POLO JALEO
BOLERO JARABE CHACONNE
FLAMENCO GUARACHA
MALAGUENA ZAPATEADO
SEGUIDILLA
(SPEAR —) BARIS
(SQUARE —) SQUARE ARGEERS
HOEDOWN LANCERS QUADRILLE
(STATELY —) PAVAN PAVANE
EMMELEIA SARABAND POLONAISE
(SWORD —) BACUBERT MATACHIN
(VENEZUELAN —) JOROPO
(WEDDING —) CANACUAS
(WEST INDIAN —) LIMBO
(PREF.) CHORE(I)(O) CHORO
ORCHESO
DANCER PONY CLOWN PONEY
ARTIST CORNER HOOFER HOPPER
MAENAD APSARAS CLOGGER
DANSEUR PASCOLA PRANCER
PRANKER SAILOUR STEPPER
TODDLER BALADINE BAYADERE
DANSEUSE DEVADASI FIGURANT
MURRICER
(BALLET —) ETOILE SOLISTE
CORYPHEE
(EGYPTIAN —S) GHAWAZI
GHAWAZEE
(JAVANESE —) SERIMPI
(JAVANESE —S) BEDOYO
(MASKED —S) GAHE
(SQUARE —S) FLOOR
(SWORD —) MATACHIN
(ZUNI —) SHALAKO
DANCING SWING ADANCE BALLET
CHANGE FROLIC MORRIS
SALTANT SURGING STEPPING
TRIPSOME
(— MANIA) TARANTISM
DANDELION BLOW BLOWER
CANKER DINDLE CHICORY
HAWKBIT BLOWBALL COMPOSIT
PISSABED
(RUSSIAN —) KOKSAGYZ
DANDELION HEAD PUFF CLOCK
BUFFBALL BULLFICE BULLFIST
PUFFBALL
DANDER ANGER DUTCH SCURF
STROLL TEMPER WANDER
HACKLES PASSION SAUNTER
DANDRUFF
DANDIFIED SPRUCE BUCKISH
ADONIZED
DANDIFY ADONIZE DANDYIZE
DANDLE DANCE DIDDLE DOODLE
FADDLE FONDLE PAMPER
DANDRUFF SCURF DANDER
FURFUR PORRIGO
DANDY FOP JAY ADON BEAU BUCK
DAND DUDE FINE JAKE MAJO
PRIG TOFF TRIG YAWL BLOOD

DILDO JEMMY SWELL ADONIS
MIZZEN BUCKEEN CAPSTAN
COXCOMB ELEGANT FOPPISH
JESSAMY MACARONI MUSCADIN
SAILBOAT
DANDY HORSE HOBBY DRAISINE
DANDYISHNESS SPIFF
DANDYISM BUCKISM
DANE DANSKER LOCHLIN
DUBHGALL
DANEWORT EBULUS LOCHLIN
DANEBALL DANEWEED
DEADWORT WALLWORT
DANGER FEAR RISK DOUBT PERIL
WATHE HAZARD PLIGHT
EXTREME PITFALL VENTURE
DISTRESS JEOPARDY
DANGEROUS BAD HOT ILL RUM
DEAR FOUL GRAVE NASTY RISKY
FICKLE KITTLE SCATHY SHREWD
UNSURE AWKWARD FEARFUL
PARLOUS UNCANNY DOUBTFUL
INSECURE PERILOUS UNCHANCY
BREAKNECK WANCHANCY
PRECARIOUS PESTIFEROUS
(MAKE LESS —) DEFUSE
DANGLE BOB LOP HANG LOLL
DROOP SWING DANDLE SHOGGLE
SHOOGLE SUSPEND SWINGLE
TROLLOP
DANGLIN DANLI
DANGLING VERSATILE
DANIEL (FATHER OF —) DAVID
(MOTHER OF —) ABIGAIL
DANK WET DAMP DONK HUMID
MADID MOIST CLAMMY COARSE
DAMPEN DANKISH DRIZZLE
WETNESS MOISTURE
DANSEUSE DANCER BALLERINA
DANZIG GDANSK
(— LIQUEUR) RATAFIA
DAPHNE (CHARACTER IN —) GAEA
APOLLO DAPHNE PENEIOS
LEUKIPPOS
(COMPOSER OF —) STRAUSS
DAPPER NEAT TRIM NATTY
SPRUCE FINICAL FOPPISH
SPARKISH
DAPPLE COVER FLECK FRECK
DAPPLED BLOCKY DOTTED
POMELY FLECKED MOTTLED
SPOTTED FRECKLED
DARBHA KUSA KUSHA
DARDA (FATHER OF —) MAHOL
DARDANUS (CHARACTER IN —)
VENUS IPHISE TEUCER ANTENOR
ISMENOR DARDANUS
(COMPOSER OF —) RAMEAU
(DAUGHTER OF —) IDAEA
(FATHER OF —) ZEUS JUPITER
(MOTHER OF —) ELECTRA
(SON OF —) ILUS DEIMAS IDAEUS
ERICHTHONIUS
DARE OSS DAST DEFU FACE OSSE
RISK BRAVE STUMP ASSUME
BANTER DACKER ATTEMPT
BRAVADE FASHION PRESUME
VENTURE
(— NOT) DASSNT DAURNA
DASSENT
DAREDEVIL MADCAP
HARDYDARDY
DARING BOLD DARE DERF PERT

RASH WILD BRAVE HARDY MANLY
NERVE PREST FELONY HEROIC
COURAGE DAIROUS DAREFUL
BOLDNESS DEVILISH FEARLESS
STALWART

DARIOLE MADELINE

DARK DIM DUN MUM SAD WAN
BASE BLAE DEEP DERK DERN
DUSK EBON HARD MALE MIRK
MURK BLACK BLIND BROWN
CLOUD DINGY DUSKY FAINT
MIRKY MURKY ROOKY SHADY
SOOTY SWART UMBER UNLIT
VAGUE CLOSED CLOUDY CYPRUS
DIMPSY DISMAL DRUMLY
GLOOMY OPAQUE SOMBER
SOMBRE SWARTH WICKED
APHOTIC DARKISH DUSKISH
MELANIC OBSCURE PITMIRK
RAYLESS STYGIAN SUNLESS
SWARTHY THESTER UNCLEAR
ABSTRUSE DARKLING DARKSOME
GLOOMFUL GLOOMING IGNORANT
LOWERING SINISTER CIMMERIAN
CALIGINOUS
(PREF.) AITHO MAVRO MEL(A)
MELAN(O)
(SUFF.) MELANE

DARK BEAVER PRALINE

DARK-COLORED SAD SWART
SOMBER SOMBRE SWARTH
SWARTHY
(PREF.) FUSCO

DARKEN DIM DUN BLUR DULL
DUSK BEDIM BLIND CLOUD
GLOAM GLOOM POCHE SHADE
SULLY SWART UMBER DEEPEN
ENDARK SHADOW BECLOUD
BENIGHT BLACKEN ECLIPSE
EMBROWN OBSCURE OPACATE
PERPLEX SLUBBER TARNISH
OVERCAST OBFUSCATE
OVERSHADOW
(— HAIR) BLEND

DARKENED SABLE CLOUDY
BLINDED LAMPLESS

DARKENING SCURF

DARK HORSE MOREL

DARKISH DIM

DARKLY DARK CLOSE SABLY
MISTILY

DARKNESS DARK DERN DUSK
MIRK MURK BLACK GLOOM NIGHT
SHADE TAMAS SHADOW DIMNESS
PITMIRK PRIVACY SECRECY
TENEBRA GLOAMING INIQUITY
MIDNIGHT TENEBRES TWILIGHT
NIGRITUDE
(PREF.) SCOTO TENEBRI

DARKNESS AT NOON (AUTHOR OF
—) KOESTLER
(CHARACTER IN —) ARLOVA
BOGRAV IVANOV GLETKIN
HARELIP KIEFFER MICHAEL
NICHOLAS RUBASHOV

DARLING JO JOE PET CHOU CONY
DEAR DUCK LIFE LOVE NOBS
PEAT ROON AROON ARUIN BULLY
CHERI DEARY DUCKS LIEVE
SWEET WHITE CHERIE DAUTIE
DAWTIE MINION MOPPET OCHREE
POPPET ACUSHLA ASTHORE
BUNTING CUSHLAM DILLING

MINIKIN PIGSNEY PINKENY
QUERIDA STOREEN DEARLING
DUMPLING FAVORITE LIEBCHEN
LOVELING MACUSHLA PRECIOUS
SWEETING MAVOURNIN
MAVOURNEEN

DARLING PEA INDICO INDIGO

DARN DOG BLOW DERN DURN
MEND PATCH BUGGER RENTER
REPAIR DOGGONE

DARNED BLAME BLAMED DEUCED
DURNED BLESSED BLINDING
DOWNGONE

DARNEL RAY CRAP TARE WEED
CHEAT CHESS DRANK DRAWK
DRUNK EAVER GRASS IVRAY
NEELE COCKLE EGILOPS AEGILOPS

DART JET POP BOLT BUZZ CANE
CHOP COLP FLIT JOUK LEAP LICK
PILE PLAN PLAY ROUT ARROW
BOUND FLAME FLING FLIRT
GLEAM GLINT LANCE SCAMP
SCOOT SHAFT SHOOT SKITE SKIVE
SPEAR SPEED SPRIT START
ANCHOR BULTEN DARTLE ELANCE
GLANCE LANCET LAUNCH
METHOD SCHEME SPRING SQUIRT
STRIKE SUMPIT THRUST JAVELIN
MISSILE STRALET VERUTUM
BRANDISH GAVELOCK JACULATE
SPICULUM BANDERILLA
(— ABOUT) SPRINKLE
(— OF LIGHTNING) STREAK
(— OF MOLDING) ANCHOR
(— REPEATEDLY) DARTLE
(PART OF —) POINT SHAFT BARREL
FLIGHT
(PREF.) JACULI TELI

DARTER SPECK

DARTING SALLY ARROWY

DARTLIKE SPICULAR

DASH DAD DAH PEP ZIP BANG
BOLT CAST DING DIVE ELAN GIFT
HINT HURL LASH LINE LUSH PASH
PELT POSS RACE RASH RUIN
RULE RUSH SHOW SLAM SOSH
TICK VEIN WHAP WHOP ABASH
ARDOR BLANK BREAK CHAFE
CLASH CRASH CRUSH DRIVE
ECLAT FLASH FLING FRUSH
KNOCK PLASH PLOUT SKITE
SLASH SLOSH SMASH SPEED
SPEND SPICE SPURN START
STYLE SWASH SWELL TASTE
THROW TOUCH TRICK BEDASH
DALLOP DASHEE DOLLOP ENERGY
HURTLE HYPHEN JABBLE RELISH
SHIVER SPIRIT SPLASH SPRINT
STRAIN STROKE THRUST
ABANDON BRAVURA BREENGE
COLLIDE DEPRESS DISPLAY
HUNDRED IMPINGE PANACHE
SHATTER SPATTER SPLOTCH
TANTIVY VIRETOT CONFOUND
GRATUITY SPLINTER
(— ABOUT WILDLY) GAD REEL
(— AGAINST) BEAT
(— DOWN) QUELL STRAM
STRAMASH
(— IN PIECES) CRASH
(— OF LIQUID) JAW
(— OF SPIRITS) LACE LACING
(— OUT) QUELL

(— TOGETHER) COLLIDE
(— UP) FLURR
(— WITH WATER) JAW BLASH
SLASH

DASHARATHA (FATHER OF —) AJA
(SON OF —) RAMA BHARATA
LAKSHMANA SHATRUGHNA
(WIFE OF —) KAIKEYI SUMITRA
KAUSHALYA

DASHBOARD DASH FACIA DASHER
FASCIA

DASHED SWITCHED

DASHEEN TARO

DASHER DASH BEATER PLUNGER

DASHING BOLD BULLY DASHY
DOGGY SHOWY SMART SPICY
SWASH JABBLE SPANKY SWANKY
VELOCE DOGGISH GALLOWS
LARKING STYLISH SWAGGER
VARMINT SLASHING SPANKING
SPIRITED

DASTARD CAD SOT DAFF SNEAK
COWARD CRAVEN DULLARD
HILDING WITHING POLTROON

DASTARDLY FOUL VILLAIN
COWARDLY POLTROON SNEAKING

DASYLIRION SOTOL

DASYPUS TATU

DASYURE TIGER YABBI DAPPLE

DATA DOPE FILE FACTS IMPUT
INPUT MATERIAL
(INACCURATE —) GARBAGE
(STORE OF —) PUSHDOWN
(USELESS —) GARBAGE

DATE DAY ERA DRAG FARD FUSS
DATUM EPOCH FARDH FRUIT
SAIDI CUTOFF FRIEND HALAWI
JUJUBE RECKON GALLANT
ANTEDATE ASHARASI DEADLINE
(— FIXED UPON) TERM
(— RIPENING) KIMRI RUTAB
KHALAL
(CHINESE —) BER

DATED GIVEN PASSE OUTMODED

DATE PLUM LOTUS SAPOTE
ZAPOTE

DATHAN (FATHER OF —) ELIAB

DATOLITE BAKERITE
HUMBOLDTITE

DATUM FACT ITEM GIVEN DONNEE

DATURA DUTRA STRAMONY
TOGUACHA

DAUB DAB DOB MUD BALM BLOB
BLOT CLAG CLAM CLAT CLAY
COAT GAUM MOIL SOIL TEER
CLAIK CLART CLEAM COVER
DITCH FLICK PAINT SLAKE SLAUM
SMEAR BEDAUB CLATCH GREASE
LABBER SMUDGE SPLASH
BESMEAR DRIBBLE PLASTER
SCLATCH SLUBBER SPLATCH
SPLOTCH SLAISTER

DAUBED GAUMY

DAUBING DUBBING MOILING

DAUBY BLOTTY

DAUGHTER ANAC BINT DAME GIRL
CHILD FILLE FILLY KIBEI REGAN
ALUMNA CADETTE DOCHTER
GONERIL CORDELIA
(PANTALOON'S —) COLUMBINE
(PREF.) FILI

DAUGHTER OF THE REGIMENT
(CHARACTER IN —) MARIE TONZIO

SULPICE COUNTESS
(COMPOSER OF —) DONIZETTI

DAUNT AWE COW DAW ADAW
DARE DAZE FAZE MATE PALL
STUN TAME ABASH ACCOY
AMATE BREAK CHECK DETER
DOMPT QUAIL DANTON DISMAY
SUBDUE CONQUER CONTROL
OVERAWE REPRESS STUPEFY
TERRIFY DISPIRIT OVERCOME

DAUNTLESS BOLD GOOD BRAVE
AWELESS SPARTAN FEARLESS
INTREPID

DAUNUS (DAUGHTER OF —) EUIPPE
(FATHER OF —) PILUMNUS
(MOTHER OF —) DANAE
(SON OF —) TURNUS
(WIFE OF —) VENILIA

DAVENPORT DESK SOFA COUCH
DIVAN

DAVID TAFFY DAWKIN
(COMPANION OF —) JONATHAN
(DAUGHTER OF —) TAMAR
(FATHER OF —) JESSE
(SON OF —) AMNON ABSALOM
(WIFE OF —) ABIGAIL AHINOAM

DAVID COPPERFIELD (AUTHOR OF
—) DICKENS
(CHARACTER IN —) HAM DICK
DORA HEEP JANE MICK ROSA
AGNES BETSY CLARA DAVID
EMILY JAMES MEALY TOMMY
URIAH BARKIS DARTLE GRINBY
STRONG WALKER CREAKLE
SPENLOW WILKINS MICAWBER
PEGGOTTY TRADDLES
TROTWOOD MURDSTONE
WICKFIELD STEERFORTH

DAVIDIST JORIST

DAVIT CRANE

DAW DA DAWN DRAB DAUNT
MAGPIE DAWPATE JACKDAW
SLATTERN SLUGGARD

DAWDLE LAG IDLE JAUK LOAF
MUCK MULL POKE TOIT DALLY
DELAY DRILL KNOCK DADDLE
DAIDLE DIDDLE DOODLE DRETCH
FADDLE LINGER LOITER MUCKER
PICKLE PIDDLE PINGLE POTTER
PUTTER TANTLE TRIFLE DRIDDLE
FINNICK QUIDDLE SAUNTER
LALLYGAG LOLLYGAG SHAMMOCK
SLUMMOCK

DAWDLER DAWDLE MUSARD
LOUTHER

DAWN DAW ROW EOAN MORN
BREAK CREEK LIGHT PRIME SHINE
SUNUP AURORA MORROW
ORIENT SPRING UPRISE DAWNING
GREKING MORNING SUNRISE
COCKCROW DAYBREAK
(PREF.) EO EOSINO

DAY DA DEI ERA SUN YOM DATE
DIEM DIES DIET TIME EPOCH
LIGHT FRIDAY MONDAY PERIOD
SUNDAY JOURNEY TUESDAY
LIFETIME SATURDAY THURSDAY
WEDNESDAY
(— AND NIGHT) KALPA
(— BEFORE) EVE
(— OF JUDGMENT) INQUEST
DOOMSDAY
(— OF ORIGIN) BIRTHDAY

(— OF REST) SABBATH
(— OF ROMAN MONTH) IDES
NONES CALENDS KALENDS
(DOG —S) CANICULE
(EVERY —) ALDAY
(EVIL —S) DISMAL
(FAST —) ASHURA FASTEN
(FIRST — OF AUGUST) LAMMAS
(FIRST — OF MAY) BELTANE
BEALTINE
(HOLY —) FEAST HOLIDAY
(HOT —) BROILER ROASTER
SCORCHER
(LAST — OF FESTIVAL) APODOSIS
(MARKET —) NUNDINE TIANGUE
(NO FLESH —) MAIGRE
(PATRON SAINT'S —) PATTERN
(QUARTER —) TERM
(TWELFTH —) EPIPHANY
(UNLUCKY —S) DISMAL
(WEEK —) FERIA
(WORK —) WARDAY
(5 NAMELESS —S) UAYEB
(60TH OF —) GHURRY
(8TH — AFTER FEAST) UTAS
(PREF.) HEMER(O)
(LASTING BUT A —) EPHEMERO
DAYAK DYAK IBAN BAHAU DUSUN
KAYAN KENYA KENYAH KELABIT
DAYBOOK BOOK DIURNAL
JOURNAL
DAYBREAK DAWN MORN SUNUP
DAWNING DAYDAWN DAYLIGHT
(PREF.) EO EOSINO
DAYDREAM DWAM MUSE DREAM
DWALM FANCY VISION FANTASY
REVERIE PHANTASY
DAYDREAMER REVEUR
DAYFLOWER COHITRE
DAYLIGHT DAY LIGHT DAYSHINE
(BROAD —) FUIRDAYS
DAYWORKER DILKER
DAZE FOG DAMP DARE MAZE ROCK
STUN DAUNT DAVER DIZZY
DOZEN GALLY SWOON ASTONY
BEDAZE BEMUSE BENUMB
DAZZLE DEAFEN MUDDLE
TRANCE CONFUSE PETRIFY
STUPEFY TORPIFY ASTONISH
BEWILDER DUMFOUND PARALYZE
DAZED MAD ASEA DAMP ASSOT
DIZZY DOYLT MUZZY SILLY TOTTY
WOOZY CUCKOO DOILED GROGGY
ROTTEN BEMUSED DONNERT
SPOILED WITLESS ASTONIED
BESOTTED DITHERED DONNERED
WITHERED
DAZEDLY GROGGILY
DAZZLE DARE DAZE BLEND BLIND
DROWN GLAIK SHINE FULGOR
ECLIPSE BEWILDER OUTSHINE
SURPRISE
DAZZLED BLINDED
DAZZLING FLARE FLASH GLAIK
FLASHY GARISH ADAZZLE
FLARING FULGENT GLARING
RADIANT DIZZYING GORGEOUS
DDT TDE DICOPHANE
DEACON ADEPT CLERIC DOCTOR
LAYMAN LEVITE MASTER PHILIP
MINISTER
DEACONESS WIDOW
DEAD FEY LOW AWAY BONG BUNG

COLD DEAF DOWD DULL FLAT
GONE MORT NUMB POKY SURE
TAME ADEAD AMORT BLIND
DEEDS INERT NAPOO POKEY
QUIET SLAIN STARK VAPID
ASLEEP BYGONE FALLEN LAPSED
NAPOOH PARTED REFUSE
DEADISH DEFUNCT EXACTLY
EXPIRED EXTINCT INSIPID
SAINTED STERILE TEDIOUS
ABSOLUTE COMPLETE DECEASED
DEPARTED INACTIVE LIFELESS
OBSOLETE SCUPPERED
(— AT TOP) RAMPICK
(PREF.) NECR(O)
DEAD-ARM NECROSIS
DEAD-DRUNK BLIND
DEADEN DAMP DULL DUMB KILL
MULL MUTE NUMB SEAR STUN
BLUNT SLAKE BENUMB DAMPEN
MUFFLE OBTUND OPIATE RETARD
STIFLE WEAKEN MORTIFY
PETRIFY REPRESS SLUMBER
SMOTHER AMORTIZE ASTONISH
ENFEEBLE
(— A SCENT) FOIL
DEAD END PLACE
(AUTHOR OF —) KINGSLEY
(CHARACTER IN —) KAY JACK
DRINA TOMMY GIMPTY HILTON
MARTIN BABYFACE
DEADENED DEAD DEAF SEAR SERE
DEADENING PUGGING
DEADHEAD SINK BOBBER SINKER
DEADHOUSE MORGUE MORTUARY
DEAD LETTER NIX
DEADLINE DATELINE
DEADLINESS LETHALITY
DEADLOCK TIE LOGJAM IMPASSE
STANDOFF STOPPAGE
DEADLY WAN DIRE FELL MORT
FATAL FERAL TUANT DEATHY
FUNEST LETHAL MORTAL
CAPITAL DEATHLY FATEFUL
RUINOUS MORTIFIC VENOMOUS
VIRULENT PESTILENT THANATOID
PERNICIOUS
DEADLY CARROT DRIAS THAPSIA
DEAD NETTLE HENBIT
DEADS MULLOCK
DEAD SOULS (AUTHOR OF —)
GOGOL
(CHARACTER IN —) PAVEL ALEXEI
PLATON KLOBUEFF KOPEYKIN
MANILOFF NOZDREFF LYENITZEN
PLATONOFF PLIUSHKIN
SOBAKEVITCH KOSTANZHOGLO
TCHITCHIKOFF TENTETNIKOFF
BETRISHTCHEFF
DEAF SURD DUNCH DUNNY SORDA
SORDO
(PREF.) SURDI SURDO
DEAFEN DIN DORR DEAVE DEADEN
DEAFENING DEEVEY
DEAF-MUTE FENELLA SURDOMUTE
DEAFNESS ASONIA SURDITY
ANACUSIA ANACUSIS COPHOSIS
DEAL GO END JOB DAIL DOLE
LEND PART SALE TALE WHIZ
ALLOT BOARD BROKE FETCH
PLANK SERVE SEVER SHAKE
SHARE SHIFT TRADE TREAT
TROKE TRUCK WIELD YIELD

BATTEN BESTOW DIVIDE HANDLE
MEDDLE NUMBER PARCEL
BARGAIN DELIVER INFLICT
PIANOLA PORTION SCATTER
TRUCKLE WRESTLE DISPENSE
SEPARATE
(— CARDS) DRAW TALLY
(— CLANDESTINELY) TRINKET
(— IN A TRIFLING WAY) PIDDLE
(— IN BRIDGE) BOARD
(— IN GRAIN) SWALE
(— OF CARDS) COUP SPOIL
GOULASH
(— SHREWDLY) JOCKEY
(— WITH) HAND COVER DIGHT
TOUCH TREAT BUCKET CUSTOM
DEMEAN HANDLE ENTREAT
NEGOTIATE
(GREAT —) MORT LOADS MIGHT
SIGHT JUGFUL OODLES SKINFUL
(POLITICAL —) DICKER
DEALER BANK CHAP AGENT COPER
BADGER BANKER BROKER
CADGER EGGLER GROCER JOBBER
JUNIOR MONGER SELLER TRADER
BUTCHER CHAPMAN KEELMAN
YOUNGER CHANDLER MERCHANT
OCCUPIER OPERATOR STICKMAN
TAILLEUR
(— IN CATTLE) COUPER COWPER
DROVER
(— IN CHEMICALS) SALTER
DRYSALTER
(— IN DRY GOODS) DRAPER
(— IN GRAIN) SWALER
(— IN OLD CLOTHES) FRIPPER
(— IN PAINTS) COLORMAN
(— IN TEXTILES) MERCER
(CARDS —) FARMER
(COAL —) COLLIER
(HORSE —) COPER COUPER
COWPER CHANTER SCORSER
(SLAVE —) MANGO
(STOCK —) STAG JOBBER
OUTSIDER
DEALFISH VAAGMAR VAAGMAER
RIBBONFISH
DEALING DOLE PRICE TRUCK
TAFFIC TRADING EXCHANGE
(BUSINESS —S) TROKE
(JUST —) DOOM
(TRICKY —) BROKING
(PL.) DEAL TRAFFIC BUSINESS
COMMERCE PRACTICE PRACTISE
(SUFF.) (—WITH) IC(AL)
DEAN DECAN DOYEN DEANER
SENIOR VERGER PREFECT
PROVOST SUBDEAN ARCHDEAN
PRAEFECT
DEAR JO GRA HON JOE PET AGRA
CARA CHER CHOU CONY FAIR
FOND GOOD HIGH LAMB LIEF
LOVE NEAR NOBS SALT ANGEL
BOSOM CHARY CHERE CHUCK
DEARY HONEY LOVED SWEET
TIGHT COSTLY DAUTIE DAWTIE
DEARIE DEARLY POPPET SCARCE
SEVERE SQUALL TENDER
WORTHY BELOVED DARLING
LOVABLE PIGSNEY QUERIDA
SPECIAL TOOTSIE ESPECIAL
ESTEEMED GLORIOUS PRECIOUS
VALUABLE

(SUFF.) (— ONE) EEN
DEARLY DEAR ALIFE DEEPLY
KEENLY RICHLY HEARTILY
DEARNESS CHERTE DEARTH
DEARTH LACK WANT CHERTE
FAMINE PAUCITY POVERTY
DEARNESS SCARCITY SOLITUDE
(SUFF.) PENIA
DEASPIRATION PSILOSIS
DEATH DEE END BALE BANE DEAD
DOOM EXIT FAIL FATE KILL MORS
MORT OBIT PASS REST WINK
ANKOU DECAY GRAVE GRUEL
LETHE NIGHT SLEEP CHAROS
CHARUS DEMISE DEPART ENDING
EXITUS EXPIRY MURDER PERIOD
REAPER WAGANG ACHERON
CURTAIN DECEASE FUNERAL
PARTING PASSAGE QUIETUS
SILENCE BIOLYSIS CASUALTY
CURTAINS FATALITY NECROSIS
RAWBONES THANATOS
MORTALITY NOTHINGNESS
(— ANGEL) AZRAEL
(— BY HANGING) HALTER
(— OF TISSUE) GANGRENE
(PREF.) LETHI THANAT(O)
(SUFF.) THANASIA
DEATH ADDER ELAPID ELAPOID
DEATH CAMASS LOBELIA
**DEATH IN VENICE (CHARACTER IN
—)** TADZIO ASCHENBACH
(COMPOSER OF —) BRITTEN
DEATHLESS ETERNAL UNDYING
IMMORTAL
DEATHLESSNESS ATHANASY
DEATHLIKE CHARNEL DEATHLY
GHASTLY MACABRE GHASTFUL
MORIBUND MORTUOUS
DEATHLY DEAD FATAL DEADLY
MORTAL GHASTLY STYGIAN
DEATHFUL MORTALLY
**DEATH OF A SALESMAN (AUTHOR
OF —)** MILLER
(CHARACTER IN —) BIFF HAPPY
LINDA LOMAN WILLY
DEATH'S-HEAD SKULL
DEBACLE ROUT STAMPEDE
COLLAPSE
DEBAR DENY TABU CROSS ESTOP
REPEL TABOO DISBAR FORBID
HINDER REFUSE BOYCOTT
DEPRIVE EXCLUDE OUTSHUT
PREVENT SECLUDE SUSPEND
PRECLUDE PROHIBIT
DEBARK LAND
DEBARRED FROZEN OUTSHUT
DEBASE SINK ABASE ALLAY ALLOY
AVILE DIRTY LOWER STOOP
BEMEAN DEFILE DEMEAN DILUTE
EMBASE IMPAIR NIDDER NITHER
REDUCE REVILE VILIFY CORRUPT
DEBAUCH DECLINE DEGRADE
DEPRAVE PERVERT PROFANE
TRADUCE VILLAIN VITIATE
PROSTITUTE
DEBASED BASE VILE HEDGE
BASTARD CORRUPT SQUALID
CANKERED DEGRADED DEROGATE
DEBASEMENT TARNISH
PROSTITUTION
DEBASING DOWNWARD
DEBATABLE MOOT DISPUTABLE

DEBATE AGON BEAT FRAY MOOT ARGUE FIGHT PLEAD STUDY ARGUFY COMBAT HASSEL HASSLE REASON STRIFE AGITATE CANVASS CONTEND CONTEST DISCEPT DISCUSS DISPUTE EXAMINE MOOTING PALAVER QUARREL WRANGLE ARGUMENT COLLOQUY CONSIDER CONTRARY MILITATE PARLANCE QUESTION CONTENTION

DEBATER PICADOR

DEBAUCH BUM BOUT FILE SPREE TAINT WHORE DEBASE DEBOSH DEFILE GUZZLE MISUSE SEDUCE SPLORE VILIFY CORRUPT DEBOISE DEPRAVE MISLEAD POLLUTE VIOLATE DISHONOR SQUANDER STRUMPET STUPRATE

DEBAUCHED LEWD RAKELY RAKISH DEBOIST DEBOSHED RAKEHELL

DEBAUCHEE RIP RAKE ROUE HOLOUR LECHER RAKEHELL

DEBAUCHERY RIOT RAKERY DEBAUCH PRIAPISM

DEBENTURE BOND SECURITY

DEBENZOLIZE STRIP

DEBILITATE SINK

DEBILITATED WEAK SEEDY FEEBLE INFIRM SAPPED ASTHENIC

DEBILITY ATONY ADYNAMY ASTHENY LANGUOR ADYNAMIA ASTHENIA WEAKNESS MYASTHENIA
(PREF.) ASTHEN(O)
(SUFF.) ASTHENIA

DEBIR (SLAYER OF —) JOSHUA

DEBIT DEBT LOSS CHARGE

DEBONAIR AIRY JAUNTY POLITE CAVALIER GRACEFUL GRACIOUS

DEBORA E JAELE (CHARACTER IN —) JAELE DEBORA SISERA
(COMPOSER OF —) PIZZETTI

DEBOUCH FALL MOUTH

DEBOUCHMENT INFLUX INFLUXION

DEBRIS GUCK SLAG DECAY FRUSH TRADE TRASH WASTE RAFFLE REFUSE RUBBLE RUDERA CRUMBLE ELUVIUM RUBBISH SLIDDER DETRITUS
(— IN WOOL) BUR BURR
(— OF INSECTS) FRASS
(— OF ROCKS) HEAD DRIFT SCREE TALUS ELUVIUM
(FLUFFY —) FLUE
(FOREST —) SLASH

DEBT DUE SIN POST DEBIT FAULT STOCK ARREARS DEBITUM JUDGMENT TRESPASS
(PL.) OBLATA WANIGAN ARREARAGE

DEBTOR OWER PEON SKIP DYVOUR DEBITOR YIELDER

DEBUT OPENING ENTRANCE

DEBUTANTE BUD DEB DEBBY INGENUE ROSEBUD

DECADENT EFFETE DECAYED HOTHOUSE OVERRIPE

DECAHYDRATE SODA

DECALOGUE WITNESS

DECAMP GUY PUT BOLT HIKE KITE ELOPE MOSEY SCOOT SCOUR SLOPE VAMOS DEPART ESCAPE LEVANT MIZZLE MORRIS POWDER VAMOSE ABSCOND DISCAMP VAMOOSE ABSQUATULATE

DECAMPING GUY

DECAN DECURION

DECANT EMIT POUR RACK UNLOAD TRANSFER

DECANTER CARAFE CARAFON URCEOLE GARDEVIN INGESTER

DECAPITATE BEHEAD DECOLLATE

DECAPITATION DECOLL HEADING

DECAPOD BUSTER

DECARBONIZE DECOKE

DECATING SPONGING

DECAY EBB ROT ROX BLET CONK DOAT DOTE DOZE FADE RUIN SEED WANE WEAR CROCK DEATH FAILL SHANK SLOOM SLOUM SPOIL WASTE BLIGHT CANKER CARIES FADING MARCOR MILDEW MOLDER MOSKER SICKEN WITHER CRUMBLE DECLINE FAILURE FORFAIR MORTIFY PUTREFY DECREASE FORDWINE
(— IN WOOD) CONK DOZE
(— OF FRUIT) BLETTING
(INCIPIENT —) BLET
(PREF.) (TOOTH —) CARIO

DECAYED BAD DEAF DOZY ROXY FRUSH SEEDY DAISED MARCID PUTRID ROTTEN SPAKED CARIOUS RUINOUS SNAGGLED

DECAYING COLD DOTY SHABBY CARIOUS

DECEASE DIE FAIL OBIT PASS DEATH DEMISE PASSAGE

DECEASED DEAD LATE PARTED DEFUNCT EXTINCT UMWHILE DEPARTED UMQUHILE

DECEIT GAB DOLE FLUM GAFF GULL RUSE SHAM TRAP TRAY WILE ABUSE COVIN CRAFT DOLUS FRAUD GUILE SARAB SWICK SWIKE CAUTEL FELONY WOIDRE CUNNING DISSAIT FAITERY FICTION ARTIFICE COZENAGE FALSEDAD INTRIGUE SPOOFERY SUBTLETY TRICKERY TRUMPERY WILINESS

DECEITFUL JIVE BLIND BRAID FALSE GAUDY JANUS LOOPY PUNIC SLAPE SNAKY ARTFUL COVERT CRAFTY DOUBLE FICKLE HOLLOW ROTTEN TRICKY CUNNING EVASIVE FICTIVE SIRENIC SLEEKIT SLIDDER UNWREST WINDING COVINOUS GUILEFUL ILLUSIVE INDIRECT SHAMMISH TORTUOUS MENDACIOUS

DECEITFULLY DOUBLE FALSELY

DECEITFULNESS SHAM DECEIT FALSITY

DECEIVE BOB COG CON DOR FOB FUB GAB GAS GUM KID LIE BILK BRAG BUNK CRAP DUPE FAKE FLAM FOOL GAFF GULL HAVE HOAX HYPE JILT JOUK MOCK SELL SHAM SILE SNOW TURN WILE ABUSE AMUSE BLEAR BLEND BLENK BLIND BLINK BLUFF CATCH CHEAT COZEN CROSS CULLY DODGE DORRE FEINT GLEEK GLOZE HOCUS LURCH PATCH SHUCK SPOOF SWICK SWIKE TRICK TROIL TRUFF TRUMP TRYST BAFFLE BARRAT BEDOTE BEFLUM BEFOOL BETRAY BLANCH BUBBLE CAJOLE CLOINE CLOYNE DELUDE DIVERT EUCHRE GAMMON HUMBUG ILLUDE JUGGLE MISLEAD NIGGLE SUCKER WIMPLE BEGUILE DEFRAUD MISLEAD OVERSEE TRAITOR BEJUGGLE FLIMFLAM HOODWINK OUTREACH

DECEIVER ANGLE CHEAT HOCUS COGGER FAITOR FALSER GUILER MOCKER TRAPAN TREPAN FALSARY ILLUSOR JUGGLER SHARPER SPOOFER TRUMPER WARLOCK WERNARD IMPOSTOR LOSENGER LOTHARIO MAGICIAN TREGETOUR

DECELERATE SLOW

DECENCY GRACE DECORUM HONESTY MODESTY CHASTITY

DECENNIUM DECADE

DECENT FAIR CHASTE COMELY HONEST MODEST PRETTY PROPER SEEMLY FITTING GRADELY JANNOCK SHAPELY SIGHTLY DECOROUS GRAITHLY WISELIKE

DECENTLY WHITE

DECEPTION BAM COG DOR GAG LIE DOLE FLAM FLUM GAFF GULL HOAX HYPE MAZE RIDE RUSE SELL SHAM WILE ABUSE BLIND BLUFF CHEAT COVIN CRAFT CURVE DOLUS DORRE FAVEL FRAUD GLAIK GLEEK GUILE MAGIC SHUCK SNARE SPOOF TRICK BARRAT CAUTEL DECEIT DUPERY HUMBUG JUGGLE ABUSION BLAFLUM CHICANE CUNNING EVASION FALLACY FALSERY FICTION GULLAGE GULLERY KNAVERY PRETEXT SLYNESS ARTIFICE DISGUISE FALSEDAD FLIMFLAM ILLUSION INTRIGUE PHANTASM PRESTIGE SUBTLETY TRICKERY TRUMPERY WILINESS

DECEPTIVE FLAM FALSE ARTFUL BUBBLE SIRENIC TRICKSY DELUSIVE DELUSORY FLIMFLAM ILLUSORY IMPOSING SHAMMISH UNSICKER

DECEPTIVENESS FANTASTRY

DECIBEL (10 —S) BEL

DECIDE FIX CAST DEEM HOLD RULE TELL WILL AWARD JUDGE PATCH PITCH DECERN DECISE DECREE FIGURE REWARD SETTLE ADJUDGE DERAIGN RESOLVE CONCLUDE SENTENCE
(— UPON) SET ELECT CHOOSE TERMINE

DECIDED FIRM FLAT MAIN FORMED SETTLED DECISIVE RESOLUTE

DECIDEDLY DIRECTLY DISTINCTLY

DECIDUA CADUCA

DECIGRAM LI

DECIMA TENTH TITHE

DECIMAL DENARY REPEATER
(— PART) MANTISSA

DECIMATE TENTH DESTROY

DECIPHER READ SOLVE CIPHER DECODE DETECT REVEAL DECRYPT DISCOVER INDICATE UNPUZZLE

DECIPHERING EPIGRAPHY

DECISION ACT END CALL DOOM FIAT GRIT ARRET AWARD CANON FAITH ISSUE PARTY PLUCK POINT ACTION CHOICE CRISIS DECREE DIKTAT RULING ACUERDO CONSULT INTERIM PRACTIC VERDICT FINALITY JUDGMENT PLACITUM SENTENCE SUFFRAGE UMPIRAGE
(— OF COURT) HOLDING ABSOLVITOR
(EXISTENTIAL —) LEAP
(FINAL —) ISSUE
(LEGAL —) FETWA

DECISIVE FATAL FINAL CRISIC PAYOFF VIRILE CRUCIAL DECIDED CRITICAL CRUSHING DECRETAL POSITIVE

DECISIVELY FINALLY

DECK FIG TOG BANK BUSK BUSS DAUB DINK FLAT HEAP PINK POOP PROW TRIG ADORN ARRAY COVER DIZEN DRESS EQUIP FLOOR HATCH PRANK PRINK STORE AWNING BEDECK BETRIM BLAZON CLOTHE ENRICH FETTLE FOCSLE LAUREL APPAREL BEDIGHT BEDIZEN FEATHER FLOUNCE GEMMATE BEAUTIFY DECORATE EMBLAZON PLATFORM
(— OF CARDS) BOOK
(— OUT) BARB TIFF DIZEN SPICK BEDECK DAIKER FANGLE FINIFY BEDIGHT
(HIGH —) POOP
(LOWEST —) ORLOP

DECKED CLAD BESEEN ARMORIED LAURELED
(— OUT) SPIFFED

DECKHAND BOATMAN TRIMMER BARGEMAN ROUSTABOUT

DECKHOUSE CABOOSE CAMBOOSE PILOTHOUSE

DECKLE DECKEL FEATHEREDGE

DECKMAN TRIPPER LEVERMAN

DECLAIM GALE RANT RAVE ROLL MOUTH ORATE SPEAK SPOUT BLEEZE RECITE ELOCUTE INVEIGH DENOUNCE DISCLAIM HARANGUE PERORATE SINGSONG

DECLAIMER BARD SPEECHIFIER

DECLAMATION FROTHING HARANGUE RHETORIC SPOUTING PHILIPPIC

DECLARATION BILL CALL DICK NARR TALE WORD COUNT FUERO LIBEL PAROL AVOWAL DECEIT MISERE ORACLE PAROLE PLACET SAYING EXPRESS PROMISE RESOLVE MANIFEST PLATFORM
(— IN BRIDGE) MAKE AUCTION
(— OF HOSTILITIES) DEFIANCE
(OFFICIAL —) AUTHORITY

DECLARE BID KEN LAY SAY VOW

AVER AVOW DENY MAKE READ
SHOW SNUM SWAN TROW VOTE
AREAD AREED BRUIT KEETH
KITHE KYTHE POSIT SNORE
SOUND SPEAK STATE TRUTH
VOUCH AFFIRM ALLEGE ASSERT
ASSURE AUTHOR AVOUCH
BLAZON COUTHE DEPONE
DESCRY EXPONE HERALD INDICT
NOTIFY PATEFY RELATE SPRING
UPGIVE ACCLAIM BEHIGHT
DISCUSS EXPRESS OUTTELL
PROFESS PROTEST PUBLISH
SIGNIFY TERMINE TESTIFY
ANNOUNCE DENOUNCE DESCRIBE
INDICATE INTIMATE MAINTAIN
MANIFEST NUNCIATE PROCLAIM
RENOUNCE PREDICATE
(— A SAINT) CANONIZE
(— ARBITRARILY) GAVEL
(— INVALID) ANNUL
(— PUBLICLY) CRY
(— UNTRUE) DENY
(— WAR) DEFY
(SOLEMNLY —) AFFY SWEAR
DECLARED AVOWED STATED
DECLARER LAWMAN VIVANT
DECLINATION BIAS DECAY SLOPE
REGRET DECLINE DESCENT
REFUSAL SOUTHING SWERVING
DECLINE BEG DIP EBB SAG SET
BALK BEND BUST DENY DIVE
DOWN DROP FADE FAIL FALL
FLAG FLOP HELD SINK SLIP TURN
VAIL WANE WELK BAULK CHUTE
DECAY DROLL DROOP DWINE
FAINT HEALD HIELD LAPSE
LOWER QUAIL REPEL SLACK
SLOPE SLUMP SPURN STOOP
STRAY TABES WAIVE DEBASE
DEVALL FALTER REFUSE REJECT
RENEGE SICKEN WEAKEN
ATROPHY DESCEND DESCENT
DETRECT DEVIATE DISAVOW
DWINDLE ECLIPSE FAILURE
FALLOFF FORBEAR INFLECT
LETDOWN SINKAGE DECREASE
DOWNBEAT DOWNTURN
FOREBEAR LANGUISH TOBOGGAN
WITHDRAW REPUDIATE
(— IN MARKET PRICE) SPILL
(— IN POPULATION) CRASH
(PREF.) CLIN
DECLINING DOWN AWANE
BEARISH FALLING WESTERN
DECADENT
DECLIVITY BENT BREW FALL
HANG SIDE SKUG CLIFF COAST
DEVEX PITCH SCARP SLENT
SLOPE CALADE HANGER DECLINE
DESCENT HANGING DOWNHILL
DECLIVOUS PRONE SLOPING
DECOCT BOIL COOK SMELT EXCITE
KINDLE REFINE EXTRACT
DECOCTION BANG OOZE SAVE
BHANG APOZEM CREMOR PTISAN
TISANE APOZEMA DECOCTUM
DECOHERER TAPPER
DECOLLETE LOW
DECOMPOSE ROT FOUL FRIT
DECAY ATTACK DIGEST DEGRADE
DISSOLVE
DECOMPOSED PUTRID

DECOMPOSITION DECAY
BREAKUP BIOLYSIS EXCHANGE
(DOUBLE —) METATHESIS
(SUFF.) LYSE LYSIS LYST LYTE
LYTIC LYZE
DECORATE DO BIND BUSK CHIP
CITE DECK EDGE FRET GAUD PINK
RAIL RULE TIFF TIRE TRIM ADORN
DRESS FLOCK FRILL GRAIN INLAY
MENSE PANEL POKER TRAIL
TRICK BEDECK BUTTON DAIKER
DAMASK DECORE EMBOSS
FLOWER FRESCO PARGET
POUNCE PURFLE SPONGE
SUBORN BECROSS CORONET
ENCHASE FESTOON FURNISH
GADROON GARNISH HISTORY
IMPASTE INWEAVE MINIATE
PERFORM BELETTER FLOURISH
ORNAMENT OVERWORK TITIVATE
DECORATED GIDDY LACED
AJOURE FLAMBE ORNATE
ADORNED DAMASSE FROGGED
INCISED WROUGHT COCKADED
DISTINCT FLORETED
DECORATING LIMNERY
DECORATION KEY BUHL FALL
FUSS IKAT BOULE DECOR DODAD
HONOR MEDAL PRIDE BOULLE
DECKER DECORE DESIGN DOODAB
DOODAD FINERY FLORET FRIEZE
GOTHIC NIELLO PLAQUE SETOFF
TINSEL ARTWORK BARBOLA
DECKING EPERGNE FLUTING
GARNISH TRACERY BAYADERE
DENTELLE DIAMANTE ESCALLOP
FLOURISH FRETTING FRETWORK
INTARSIA ORNAMENT
(— IN GUEST CHAMBER) XENIUM
(— OF LEAVES) VIGNETTE
(— OF MONKEYS) SINGERIE
(— TECHNIQUE) PLANGI
(BOOK-COVER —) DENTELLE
(CUTOUT —) APPLIQUE
(ENAMEL —) WUTSAI
(FESTIVE —) GALA
(INESSENTIAL —) SPINACH
(MURAL —) TOPIA
(MUSICAL —) GRACE
(PORCELAIN —) KAKIEMON
(POTTERY —) BRODERIE
(RICH —) PARAMENT
(SCANDINAVIAN —) ROSEMALING
(WALL —S) TENTURE
(PL.) COLORS BUNTING
GREENERY
DECORATIVE FANCY FIKIE
DECOROUS CALM DONE GOOD
NICE PRIM DOUCE GRAVE QUIET
SOBER STAID CHASTE DECENT
DEMURE MODEST POLITE PROPER
SEDATE SEEMLY SERENE STEADY
BECOMED FITTING ORDERLY
REGULAR SETTLED BECOMING
COMPOSED MANNERLY
DECOROUSLY FITLY
DECOROUSNESS CHASTITY
POLITESSE
DECORTICATE FLAY HULL HUSK
PARE PEEL PILL SKIN STRIP
DENUDE
DECORUM DECENCY DIGNITY
FITNESS HONESTY

MODESTY PROPRIETY
DECOY COY BAIT CALL GOAD LURE
TOLE TOLL COACH CRIMP DRILL
PLANT ROPER SHILL STALE STALL
STOOL TEMPT TRAIN ALLURE
BUTTON CALLER CAPPER ENTICE
ENTRAP PIGEON SEDUCE TOLLER
TREPAN BARNARD BERNARD
DECOYER INVEIGLE SQUAWKER
(— FOR GAMBLERS) CAPPER
(— FOR SWINDLERS) BARNARD
BERNARD
(AUCTIONEER'S —) BONNET
BUTTON
DECREASE EBB BATE DROP FALL
LOSS SINK WANE WELK WILK
ABATE CROCK DECAY LAPSE
SWAGE TAPER WANZE WASTE
CHANGE DECESS DECREW IMPAIR
LESSEN NARROW REDUCE SHRINK
ATROPHY CUTDOWN DECLINE
DWINDLE SHORTEN SLACKEN
SUBSIDE ABLATION DECIMATE
DIMINISH DOWNTURN MODERATE
RETRENCH
(— IN FORCE) LAY
(— IN VOLUME) ABLATION
(— OF EFFICIENCY) FATIGUE
(— STITCHES) FASHION
DECREE ACT DIT LAW SAW SET
DOOM FIAT REDE RULE WILL
WITE AREAD AREED ARRET
CANON EDICT ENACT FIANT
GRACE HATTI IRADE JUDGE
ORDER POINT SHAPE TENET
UKASE WRITE ARREST ASSIZE
DECERN DICTUM FIRMAN INDICT
MODIFY ORDAIN PLACIT RECESS
ADJUDGE APPOINT BESLUIT
COMMAND CONSULT DECREET
DICTATE DIVORCE ESCRIPT
GEZERAH MANDATE SETNESS
STATUTE WORKING DECISION
DECRETUM JUDGMENT PLACITUM
PSEPHISM RESCRIPT ROGATION
SANCTION SENTENCE ORDINANCE
ABSOLVITOR
(— BEFOREHAND) DESTINE
(ECCLESIASTICAL —) CANON
SYNODICAL
(JUDICIAL —) AUTO
(MOHAMMEDAN —) IRADE
(OFFICIAL —) RESCRIPT
(PAPAL —) DECRETAL
DECREPIT LAME WEAK UNORN
BEDRID CREAKY FEEBLE INFIRM
SENILE FAILING INVALID
FORFAIRN
DECRY BOO CRAB SLUR LOWER
ROGUE DESCRY LESSEN ASPERSE
BARRACK CENSURE CONDEMN
DEBAUCH DEGRADE DETRACT
BELITTLE DEROGATE MINIMIZE
DECRYPT BREAK DECODE
DECURRENT DEFLUENT
DECUSSATION CHIASM CHIASMA
DEDAN (FATHER OF —) RAAMAH
JOKSHAN
(MOTHER OF —) KETURAH
DEDANS HAZARD
DEDICATE VOW VOTE DEVOW
SACRE SACRI DEVOTE DEVOVE
DIRECT HALLOW OBLATE ASCRIBE

ENTITLE CHRISTEN INSCRIBE
INTITULE SEPARATE NUNCUPATE
DEDICATED HOLY OBLATE SACRED
VOTIVE
DEDICATION CULT WAKF
DEVOTION
DEDUCE PUT DRAW LEAD TAKE
BRING DRIVE FETCH GUESS INFER
TRACE DEDUCT DERIVE ELICIT
EVOLVE GATHER COLLECT
EXPLAIN EXTRACT SUBSUME
CONCLUDE
DEDUCT BATE DOCK TAKE ABATE
ALLOW SHAVE DEFALK REBATE
RECOUP REDUCT REMOVE
CURTAIL SUBDUCT TRADUCE
ABSTRACT DISCOUNT SEPARATE
SUBTRACT
DEDUCTION AGIO SALT CREDIT
DEDUCT REBATE BEAMAGE
DOCKAGE IMPRESS OFFTAKE
REPRISE DISCOUNT ERGOTISM
ILLATION STOPPAGE ABATEMENT
COROLLARY
DEDUCTIVE DOGMATIC
DEE DUANT
DEED DO ACT BILL BOOK CASE
FACT FAIT FEAT FIAT GEST HARD
JEST TURN WORK ACTUM ACTUS
BROAD CHART DOING GESTE
ISSUE SANAD THING TITLE
ACTION CONVEY ESCROW
FACTUM POTTAH REMISE SASINE
SUNNUD TAILYE CHARTER
EXPLOIT FACTION TAILZIE
CHIVALRY HEIRLOOM PARERGON
PRACTICE PRACTISE TRANSFER
PERFORMANCE
(BRUTAL —) ATROCITY
(CHARITABLE —S) ALMS
(EVIL —) MALEFACTION
(GOOD —) BENEFIT MITZVAH
(HEBREW —) STARR
(PART OF —) HABENDUM
(VALIANT —) VALIANCE
(WICKED —) ILL
(PL.) DOINGS SERVICE
MUNIMENTS
DEEM LET SAY SEE GIVE HOPE
RECK SEEM TELL JUDGE OPINE
THINK ESTEEM EXPECT ORDAIN
RECKON REGARD ACCOUNT
ADJUDGE BELIEVE RECOUNT
RESPECT SURMISE ANNOUNCE
CONSIDER JUDGMENT PROCLAIM
DE-EMPHASIZE DOWNPLAY
DEEMSTER DOOMSMAN
DE-ENERGIZE KILL CLEAR
DEEP LOW SAD SEA BASS BOLD
DUAT HOLL HOWE NEAL RAPT
ABYSS BROAD DEWAT GRAVE
GREAT GRUFF HEAVY OCEAN
SOUND STIFF STOOR STOUR
HOLLOW INTENT STRONG SULLEN
ABYSMAL INTENSE SERIOUS
UNMIXED ABSORBED ABSTRUSE
COMPLETE POWERFUL
PROFOUND THOROUGH
RECONDITE
(PREF.) **(— SEA)** BATH(O)(Y)
DEEP-DYED ENGRAINED
DEEPEN CLOUD DARKEN DREDGE
ENHANCE THICKEN HEIGHTEN

DEEPEST INMOST DEEPMOST
DEEPLY DEEP ADEEP DEARLY
SOUNDLY DEVOUTLY GROUNDLY
INWARDLY
DEEP-SEA DIPSY BATHYL DIPSEY
BATHYAL
DEEP-SEATED DEEP INTIMATE
PROFOUND INGRAINED
DEEP-TONED STOUR
DEER ELK RED ROE AXIS BUCK
DAIM HART HIND MILU MUSK
OLEN PARA PUDU RUSA SHOU
SIKA STAG WILD BROCK GEMUL
MARAL MOOSE SABIR SPADE
STAIG CERVID CHITAL CHITRA
FALLOW GUEMAL HANGUL
HEARST HUEMUL PARRAH
RASCAL SAMBAR SAMBUR
THAMIN VENADA BROCKET
BROWZER CARIBOU CERVINE
CERVOID CHEETAL DEERLET
FANTAIL GUAZUTI KASTURA
MUNTJAC PLANDOK SAMBHAR
THAMENG VENISON BOBOLINK
CARIACOU CARJACOU ELAPHURE
RUMINANT
(— IN 3RD YEAR) SPAY SOREL
SPAYAD SPAYAD
(— UNDER 1 YEAR) KID
(CASTRATED —) HAVIER
(FEMALE —) DOE ROE HIND
(FEMALE — IN 2ND YEAR) TEG
HEARST
(HINDQUARTERS OF —) FOUCH
FOURCHE
(MALE — IN 2ND YEAR) PRICKET
(MALE — IN 4TH YEAR) SORE
STAGGARD STAGGART
(MALE — OVER 5 YEARS) HART
STAG
(RED —) OLEN SPAY MARAL
BROCKET
(RUSINE —) AXIS
(YOUNG —) KID FAWN SPITTER
(2-YEAR OLD —) KNOBBER
(PREF.) CERVI
DEER BUSH SOAPBUSH
DEER FERN HARDFERN
DEERFLY TABANID
DEERHAIR SEDGE BULRUSH
DEERHOUND DEERDOG
BUCKHOUND
DEERSKIN BUCK DEER
DEERSLAYER (AUTHOR OF —)
COOPER
(CHARACTER IN —) HARRY HETTY
NATTY UNCAS BUMPPO HUTTER
JUDITH THOMAS CHINGACHGOOK
DEFACE MAR FOUL RUIN SCAR
ERASE SHAME SPOIL CANCEL
DAMAGE DAMASK DEFAME
DEFOIL DEFORM DEFOUL EFFACE
INJURE INJURY DESTROY
DETRACT DISTORT SLANDER
DISGRACE DISHONOR MALAHACK
MUTILATE OUTSHINE
DEFACED FOUL
DEFACING DIMINUTION
DEFALCATE DRIB DEFALK
DEFAMATION LIBEL DEFAME
DEFAMY DEPRAVE SCANDAL
SLANDER ASPERSION
DEFAMATORY SCANDALOUS

DEFAME FOUL ABASE BELIE
CLOUD LIBEL NOISE SMEAR
ACCUSE CHARGE DEFACE DEFOIL
DEFOUL FORGAB INFAME INJURE
MALIGN REVILE SUGGIL VILIFY
ASPERSE BLACKEN BLEMISH
DEBAUCH DETRACT DIFFAME
PUBLISH SCANDAL SLANDER
SPATTER TRADUCE DISHONOR
INFAMIZE VILIPEND
DEFAMER SYCOPHANT
DEFAULT FAIL FLAW LOSS MORA
ERROR FAULT OFFEND BLEMISH
FAILURE MISTAKE NEGLECT
OFFENSE OMISSION
(— ON DEBT) LEVANT
DEFAULTER DUCK
(PL.) JANKERS
DEFEASANCE DEFEAT UNDOING
DEFEASIBLE IMPERFECT
DEFEAT EAT PIP WIN BALK BEAT
BEST BOWL CAST DING DOWN
DRUB FOIL HAVE JINK KILL LACE
LICK LOSS ROUT RUIN RUSH SINK
SKIN STOP TOLL TOSS TRAP TRIM
UNDO WHAP WHIP WHOP AVOID
BREAK CHECK FACER FALSE
FLING FLOOR OUTDO PASTE
SHEND SKUNK SMITE SWAMP
THROW WASTE WHACK WORSE
WORST WRACK BAFFLE CUMBER
DEROUT EUCHRE LARRUP
MASTER MURDER OUTGUN
REBUFF STOUSH THWACK
THWART WAGGLE WEAKEN
CLOBBER CONQUER DEPRIVE
DESTROY LICKING OVERSET
PEREMPT REVERSE SCOMFIT
SETBACK SHELLAC SNOOKER
SUBVERT TROUNCE INFRINGE
IRRITATE OUTFIGHT OVERCOME
SLOSHING VANQUISH WATERLOO
OVERPOWER OVERTHROW
(— COMPLETELY) SKUNK
(— DECISIVELY) EAT DRUB SACK
BLAST CLEAN FLATTEN SHELLAC
(— IN BRIDGE) SET
(— IN LAWSUIT) CAST
(DECISIVE —) CLEANUP CLEANING
PLASTERING
(INTO —) DOWN
(UTTER —) MATE ROUT DEROUT
DEFEATED DOWN LOST KAPUT
BEATEN CRAVEN WHIPPED
DEFEATIST BOLO FATALIST
DEFECT BUG FLAW LACK MAIM
MOTE TWIT VICE WANE WANT
BOTCH CLOUD CRAZE ERROR
FAULT MINUS MULCT TOUCH
DAMAGE DESERT HIATUS INJURY
LACUNA MALADY MAYHEM
PLIGHT VICETY VITIUM ABSENCE
BLEMISH DEMERIT FAILING
MISPICK PEELING PINHOLE
COLOBOMA CRESCENT
DRAWBACK WEAKNESS
SHORTCOMING
(— IN ARTICULATION) PSELLISM
(— IN CRYSTAL) HOLE
(— IN ENAMEL) SCAB SAGGING
SCUMMING
(— IN FABRIC) GOUT SCOB BARRE
BRACK SMASH

(— IN GLASS) KNOT TEAR STONE
WREATH THREADS
(— IN IRON) SEAM
(— IN MARBLE) TERRAS TERRACE
TERRASSE
(— IN METAL) SNAKE BLOWHOLE
(— IN PRINTING PLATE) HICKY
HICKEY
(— IN STEEL) LAP
(— IN TIMBER) LAG SHAN
COLLAPSE
(— IN YARN) SINGLING
CORKSCREW
(— OF CHARACTER) HOLE SHADE
HAMARTIA
(LINT —) SPOT
(SPEECH —) BALBUTIES
CLUTTERING
(TELEVISION —) FLOPOVER
DEFECTION LETDOWN APOSTASY
DESERTION
DEFECTIVE BAD ILL EVIL FOXY
LACK LAME MANK POOR SICK
BAUCH BAUGH BLIND FALSE
FLAWY PASUL COMMON FAULTY
FLAWED MANGUE MEAGER
MEAGRE RAGGED HALTING
TOMFOOL VICIOUS DISGENIC
DYSGENIC MUTILOUS VITIATED
(PREF.) ATEL(O)
DEFEND FEND HOLD KEEP SAVE
WARD WARN WEAR COVER
GUARD SHEND WATCH ASSERT
FORBID SCREEN SECURE SHIELD
UPHOLD WARISH BUCKLER
BULWARK CONTEST DERAIGN
ESPOUSE EXPOUND FLANKER
JUSTIFY PREVENT PROPUGN
PROTECT SHELTER SUPPORT
WARRANT ADVOCATE CHAMPION
CONSERVE GARRISON MAINTAIN
PRESERVE PROHIBIT SAFEGUARD
DEFENDANT REA REUS ACCUSED
AVOWANT APPELLEE
DEFENDER FENDER PATRON
ADVOCATE ASSERTER ASSERTOR
CHAMPION GUARDIAN UPHOLDER
DEFENSE EGIS FORT PALE ROCK
WALL WARD WEAR AEGIS ALIBI
FENCE GRITH GUARD TOWER
ABATIS ANSWER BEHALF COVERT
FRAISE SCONCE BARRACE
BARRIER BASTION BULWARK
CONTEST COUNTER DEFENCE
DILATOR OUTWORK PARADOS
RAMPART SHELTER WARDING
WARRANT ADVOCACY APOLOGIA
BOUNDARY FRONTIER GALAPAGO
GARRISON MUNITION SECURITY
SEPIMENT
DEFENSELESS BARE COLD NAKED
SILLY UNARMED HELPLESS
DEFENSIBLE TENABLE JUSTIFIABLE
DEFER BOW RISE STAY WAIT
DELAY DRIVE HONOR REFER
REMIT STAVE TARRY TRACK
WAIVE YIELD ESTEEM HUMBLE
RETARD REVERE SUBMIT
ADJOURN SUSPEND CONSIDER
INTERMIT POSTPONE PROROGUE
PROTRACT SUSPENSE
DEFERENCE VAIL COURT HONOR
CRINGE ESTEEM HOMAGE

REGARD RESPECT WORSHIP
CIVILITY OBEISANCE
DEFERENT ECCENTRIC
DEFERENTIAL DUTIFUL OBEISANT
DEFERMENT STAY
DEFERVESCENCE LYSIS DECLINE
DEFIANCE DARE DEFI DEFY GAGE
BRAVE DEFIAL CHALLENGE
DEFIANT BOLD BARDY BRAVE
STOUT DARING STOCKY
INSOLENT STUBBORN
OBSTREPEROUS
DEFIANTLY ACOCK
DEFICIENCY FAIL LACK WANT
ANOIA ERROR FAULT MINUS
DEARTH DEFECT INLAIK ULLAGE
ABSENCE ANOESIA BLEMISH
DEFICIT FAILING FAILURE
POVERTY DELETION SCARCITY
SHORTAGE SHORTFALL
SHORTCOMING
(— OF BLOOD) ISCHEMIA
(— OF NERVOUS ENERGY) ANEURIA
(— OF OXYGEN) ASPHYXIA
(CARBON DIOXIDE —) ACAPNIA
(MENTAL —) IDIOCY AMENTIA
(PL.) SHORTS
(PREF.) ISCH
(SUFF.) PENIA
DEFICIENT BAD LEAN WANE
BLUNT MINUS SCANT BARREN
FEEBLE MEAGER MEAGRE SCARCE
SCRIMP SKIMPY BOBTAIL
DISGENIC DYSGENIC INDIGENT
(— IN TURGOR) FLACCID
(MENTALLY —) SOFT
(SUFF.) PRIVIC
DEFICIT SHORTAGE UNDERAGE
DEFILE GUT RAY ABRA BAWD
BEDO FILE FOIL FOUL GATE GOWL
HALS LIME MOIL MUCK PACE
PASS SLIP SLOT SLUT SMUT SOIL
ABUSE BERAY CLEFT CROCK
DIRTY FILTH GLACK GORGE
HALSE NOTCH SLACK SMEAR
STAIN SULLY TAINT BEWRAY
DEBASE GULLET IMBRUE INFECT
RAVISH SMOUCH SMUTCH
CORRUPT DEBAUCH DEPRAVE
DISTAIN PASSAGE POLLUTE
PROFANE SLOTTER SMATTER
TARNISH VIOLATE DISHONOR
MACULATE
DEFILED DIRTY IMPURE SPOTTY
UNCLEAN MACULATE
DEFILEMENT MOIL SOIL SULLAGE
TAINTURE
(PREF.) MEASMATO MIASMO
MYS(O)
DEFILING PIKY PITCHY
DEFINE END FIX SET MERE TERM
BOUND LIMIT DECIDE CLARIFY
DELIMIT EXPLAIN EXPOUND
DESCRIBE DISCOVER
DEFINED FORMED STRICT
(SHARPLY —) HARD
DEFINITE SET FIRM HARD SURE
CLEAR FINAL FIXED SHARP FINITE
FORMED LIQUID STRAIT CERTAIN
EXPRESS LIMITED POINTED
PRECISE DISTINCT EMPHATIC
EXPLICIT LIMITING POSITIVE
PUNCTUAL SPECIFIC

DEFINITELY BUT WELL FAIRLY
EVERMORE
DEFINITION GLOSS CLARITY
DIORISM
(— OF FORM) SFUMATO
(PREF.) ORISMO
DEFINITIVE LAST FINAL GRAND
ORISTIC DEFINITE
DEFLATE EMPALE IMPALE
CONTRACT
DEFLATED FLAT
DEFLATING SETDOWN
DEFLATION HANGOVER
DEFLECT CUT WRY BEND COCK
SWAY WARP PARRY WREST
WRING BAFFLE DETOUR DIVERT
SWERVE DEVIATE DIVERGE
INFLECT REFLECT REFRACT
DEFLECTION DROOP SWEEP
WINDAGE
(— ON METER) KICK
(PREF.) SPHINGO
DEFLECTOR (AIR —) SPOILER
DEFLOWER FRAY DEFOIL DEFOUL
FORLIE RAVAGE RAVISH DEFLORE
DESPOIL VIOLATE UNMAIDEN
UNVIRGIN
DEFORM MAR FLOW WARP GNARL
DEFACE BLEMISH CONTORT
DISFORM DISTORT DIFFORME
DISGUISE DISHONOR MISSHAPE
SHAUCHLE
DEFORMATION CREEP SPRING
STRAIN FLEXURE FLOWAGE
DEFORMED GAMMY WRONG
INFORM PAULIE CROOKED
HIDEOUS MISBORN FORMLESS
UNMACKLY
(PREF.) CAC(O) CACH
(SUFF.) CACE
DEFORMITY GALL VICE BLEMISH
HARELIP PRAVITY CLUBFOOT
CLUBHAND FLATFOOT
WANSHAPE
DEFRAUD ROB BEAT BILK FAKE
GULL NICK ROOK TRIM WIPE
CHEAT COZEN GOUGE LURCH
MULCT SLICK STICK TRICK
WRONG BOODLE CHOUSE
CHOWSE DECEIVE SKELDER
SWINDLE
DEFRAY PAY BEAR AVERT COVER
ABSORB EXPEND PREPAY
APPEASE REQUITE SATISFY
DISBURSE
DEFT FEAT GAIN NEAT TALL TRIM
AGILE HANDY NATTY QUICK SLICK
ADROIT EXPERT HEPPEN NIMBLE
SPRACK SPRUCE DELIVER
DEXTROUS SKILLFUL
DEFTEST EFTEST
DEFTLY LIGHTLY SLICKLY
DELIVERLY
DEFTNESS SLEIGHT
DEFUNCT DEAD EXTINCT
DECEASED DEPARTED FINISHED
DEFY BRAG DARE DEFI FACE MOCK
BEARD BRAVE STUMP TEMPT
CARTEL FORBID MAUGER
MAUGRE REJECT AFFRONT
BRAVADE DESPISE DISDAIN
OUTDARE OUTFACE CHAMPION
DEFIANCE OUTSCOUT RENOUNCE

CHALLENGE
DEGENERATE ROT SINK DEBADE
EFFETE UNKIND DEGENER
DEGRADE DEPRAVE DESCEND
DEGENDER DEROGATE
(— IN IDLENESS) RUST
(— TOWARD BARBARISM) WILDER
DEGENERATION WALLER
ATROPHY ADIPOSIS PEJORATION
DEGRADATION FALL WOHL
SHAME DEMISS DECLINE
DESCENT ADULTERY COMEDOWN
DEPOSURE IGNOMINY ABJECTION
DEGRADE BUST SINK ABASE
BREAK DECRY LOWER SHAME
SHEND STOOP STRIP UNMAN
DEBASE DEMEAN DEMOTE
DEPOSE EMBASE HUMBLE LESSEN
REDUCE VILIFY CORRUPT
DECLINE DEPRESS IMBRUTE
REGRADE VILLAIN DIMINISH
DISGRACE DISHONOR DISMOUNT
DISPLUME SUPPLANT
DEGRADED BASE BROKE SEAMY
ABJECT DEMISS FALLEN SORDID
DEBASED DEGREED GRIECED
OUTCAST
DEGRADING BASE VILE MENIAL
SHAMEFUL
DEGRAS MOELLON
DEGREE PEG PIP POL BANK CAST
DEAL FORM GREE HEAT PEEP
POLL RANK RATE RUNG STEP
TERM TIER CLASS GRADE GRADO
GRECE GRICE HONOR LEVEL
NOTCH ORDER PITCH PLACE
POINT PRICK SHADE STAGE STAIR
EXTENT GRIECE LENGTH MEDIUM
SOEVER DESCENT DIGNITY
MEASURE SAENGER STATION
ACCURACY AEGROTAT QUANTITY
STANDING STRENGTH
(— OF CLOSENESS) FIT
(— OF COMBINING POWER)
VALENCE
(— OF CONTRAST) GAMMA
(— OF DEVIATION) LEEWAY
(— OF ELEVATION) ASCENT
(— OF ENGAGEMENT) DEPTH
(— OF FLAWLESSNESS) CLARITY
(— OF FORCE) KICK
(— OF HEIGHT) GRADE
(— OF IMPORTANCE) CALIBER
CALIBRE
(— OF INFESTATION) BURDEN
(— OF INTOXICATION) EDGE
(— OF KNOWLEDGE) SCIENTER
(— OF LIGHTNESS) VALUE
(— OF MIXTURE) ALLOY
(— OF OPACITY) DENSITY
(— OF PLENTIFULNESS)
ABUNDANCE
(— OF PRESTIGE) PLACE
(— OF SLOPE) PITCH SPLAY
(— OF STREAMLINING) FAIRNESS
(— OF THE SOUL) RUACH
(— OF WATER HARDNESS) GRAIN
(— OF WHITENESS) BLEACH
(EXCESSIVE —) EXTREME
(GREATEST —) UTMOST OPTIMUM
(HIGHEST —) PINK SUMMIT
SUPREME SUBLIMITY
(INDEFINITE —) SEEM

(MINUTE —) DROP SHADE
(MUSICAL —) SPACE SUBTONIC
(RABBINICAL —) SEMICHA
SEMIKAH SEMICHAH
(SMALL —) ACE TAD HAIR INCH
IOTA SHADOW GLIMMER
(SOME —) BIT
(UTMOST —) SUM ACME HEIGHT
EXTREME EXTREMITY
(10 —S OF LONGITUDE) FACE
(15 —S) HOUR
(PREF.) (OF THE THIRD ALGEBRAIC
—) CUB(I)(O)
(SUFF.) ANCE ANT ENCE ITY NESS
TY
DEGU OCTODONT
DEGUM STRIP
(— SILK) SOUPLE
DEHGAN SWAT SWATI
DEHORN SNUB DISBUD
DEHWAR DEHKAN
DEHYDRATE DRY DESICCATE
DEIANIRA (BROTHER OF —) TYDEUS
MELEAGER
(FATHER OF —) OENEUS
(HUSBAND OF —) HERCULES
(MOTHER OF —) ALTHAEA
DEIDAMIA HIPPODAMIA
(FATHER OF —) LYCOMEDES
(LOVER OF —) ACHILLES
(SON OF —) PYRRHUS
NEOPTOLEMUS
DEIFICATION APOTHEOSIS
DEIFY GOD BEGOD DIVINE
GODDIZE DIVINIFY DIVINIZE
DEIGN STOOP VOUCHSAFE
DEILEON (BROTHER OF —)
PHLOGIUS AUTOLYCUS
(FATHER OF —) DEIMACHUS
DEION (DAUGHTER OF —)
ASTERODIA
(FATHER OF —) AEOLUS
(MOTHER OF —) ENARETE
(SON OF —) ACTOR AENETUS
CEPHALUS PHYLACUS
(WIFE OF —) DIOMEDE
DEIPHOBUS (BROTHER OF —) PARIS
HECTOR
(FATHER OF —) PRIAM
(MOTHER OF —) HECUBA
(WIFE OF —) HELEN
DEIPYLE (FATHER OF —) ADRASTUS
(HUSBAND OF —) TYDEUS
(SISTER OF —) AEGIA ARGIA
(SON OF —) DIOMEDES
DEIPYLUS (FATHER OF —)
POLYMNESTOR
(MOTHER OF —) ILIONE
DEITY (ALSO SEE GOD AND
GODDESS) EA EL KA RA RE SU
ABU BEL GAD GOD RAN SHU SOL
AKAL AMEN AMON BAAL CAGN
DEVA FAUN FURY GWYN MIND
MORS RANA SIVA SOBK ALALA
ALALU AMIDA AMITA AMMON
DAGAN DAGON HAOMA HOBAL
HORUS HUBAL INUUS JANUS
MIDER MITRA MONAD SATYR
SEBEK SHIVA SIRIS SURYA ZOMBI
ASHIMA ATHTAR BATALA
BUNENE CAISSA FATHER FAUNUS
IASION MARDUK MOLOCH NIBHAZ
OANNES ORISHA ORMAZD

ORMUZD RIMMON SOMNUS
SUCHOS SYLVAN VARUNA
ZOMBIE ALASTOR FORSETE
FORSETI GODDESS GODHEAD
GODLING GODSHIP HERSHEF
IAPETUS KHEPERA MANITOU
NINURTA NISROCH PHORCUS
PHORKYS RESHEPH SETEBOS
SILENUS TAGALOA TARANIS
VIRBIUS BAALPEOR BEELPEOR
BELFAGOR DEVARAJA DIVINITY
ELAGABAL GOVERNOR HACHIMAN
MELKARTH MERODACH
PICUMNUS PILUMNUS SEILENOS
SILVANUS TANGALOA
TUTELARY ZEPHYRUS
ZOOMORPH
(AVENGING —) ALASTOR
(HEATHEN —) IDOL
(INFERIOR —) GODKIN GODLING
DEMIURGE PETTYGOD
(SHINTO —) KAMI
(SUPREME —) HANSA
(TUTELARY —) NUMEN GENIUS
(PL.) CABIRI PENATES
DEJECT ABASE LOWER HUMBLE
LESSEN FLATTEN DISPIRIT
DOWNCAST
DEJECTA EGESTA
DEJECTED BAD LOW SAD DAMP
DOWN GLUM POOR SUNK AMORT
MUDDY WAPED ABASED ABATTU
DEJECT DEMISS DROOPY GLOOMY
PINING SOMBER SOMBRE
ALAMORT DUMPISH HANGDOG
HANGING HUMBLED LUMPISH
UNHAPPY DOWNCAST
DOWNWARD REPINING
WOBEGONE WRETCHED
MELANCHOLY
DEJECTEDLY HEAVILY
DEJECTION CRAB DAMP GLOOM
SLOTH DISMAY DISMALS
HUMDRUM SADNESS
MELANCHOLY
DEJEUNER LUNCH BREAKFAST
COLAZIONE COLLATION
DEKASTERE (ABBR.) DAS
DEL NABLA
DELAIAH (FATHER OF —)
MEHETABEEL
(SON OF —) SHEMAIAH

DELAWARE
CAPITAL: DOVER
COUNTY: KENT SUSSEX
NEWCASTLE
INDIAN: LENAPE
STATE BIRD: BLUEHEN
STATE FLOWER: PEACH
STATE NICKNAME: FIRST BLUEHEN
DIAMOND
STATE TREE: HOLLY
TOWN: LEWES NEWARK SMYRNA
ELSMERE CLAYMONT
WILMINGTON

DELAY LAG LET BLIN BODE HOLD
HONE LENG LING LITE MORA SIST
SLOW SLUG STAY STOP WAIT
ABIDE ABODE ALLAY BLINE
CHECK DALLY DEFER DEMUR
DETER DRIFT DWELL FRIST

PAUSE REPRY SLOTH STALL STENT STICK STINT TARDY TARRY TRACT ARREST ATTEND BACKEN BELATE DAWDLE DETAIN DILATE DILUTE DRETCH ESSOIN FUTURE HINDER HOLDUP IMPEDE LINGER LOITER QUENCH REMORE RETARD TAIGLE TARROW TEMPER WEAKEN ADJOURN ASSUAGE BARRACE CONFINE DRUTTLE FORSLOW PROLONG RESPECT RESPITE SLACKEN SOJOURN DEMURRAL DILATION FORESLOW FOURCHER HANGFIRE HESITATE MACERATE MITIGATE MORATION OBSTRUCT POSTPONE PROTRACT REPRIEVE STOPPAGE CUNCTATION OBSTRUCTION
(— IN COUNTDOWN) HOLD
(— TRIAL) TRAVERSE
(LEGAL —) DILATOR INDUCIAE
(UNDUE —) LACHES
(PL.) AMBAGES

DELAYED LATE TARDY LAGGED BELATED OVERDUE
DELAYING TRAIN DILATORY
DELECTABLE TASTY DESIROUS PLEASING BEAUTIFUL EXQUISITE
DELEGATE NAME SEND ASSIGN COMMIT DELATE DEPUTE DEPUTY LEGATE NUNCIO APPOINT CONSIGN EMPOWER ENTRUST EMISSARY RELEGATE TRANSFER
DELEGATION MISSION DELEGACY
(ATHENIAN —) DELIA
DELETE DELE EDIT OMIT BLACK ERASE PURGE SLASH CANCEL CENSOR DELATE REMOVE STRIKE DESTROY EXPUNGE STONKER CASTRATE
DELETERIOUS BAD PRAVE HARMFUL HURTFUL NOXIOUS PRAVOUS DAMAGING DELETERY PERNICIOUS
DELIBERATE COOL PORE RUNE SLOW STUDY THINK VOULU ADVISE CONFER DEBATE PONDER REGARD ADVISED BALANCE BETHINK CONSULT COUNCIL COUNSEL DELIBER DELIVER REFLECT RESOLVE STUDIED WILLING WITTING CONSIDER DESIGNED MEASURED MEDITATE PERPENSE PREPENSE PROPENSE STUDIOUS
DELIBERATELY COOLY COOLLY APURPOSE ADVISEDLY
DELIBERATENESS MATURITY
DELIBERATION ADVICE COUNCIL COUNSEL LEISURE THOUGHT VISEMENT
DELICACY BIT ROE CATE EASE NORI TACT ACATE FRILL KNACK TASTE CAVIAR DAINTY DELICE JUNKET LUXURY NICETY REGALO FINESSE RAREBIT REGALIA TENUITY TRINKET AIRINESS DAINTITH DAINTREL DELICATE KICKSHAW LEGERETE NICENESS PLEASURE SUBTLETY
(PL.) CATES ACATES
DELICATE SLY AIRY FINE LACY NESH NICE SOFT TEAR ZART

DELIE DORTY ELFIN FAIRY FRAIL LIGHT SILKY TEWLY CASHIE CHOICE DAINTY FLIMSY GENTLE GINGER INCONY KITTLE MINION PASTEL PETITE PULING QUEASY SILKEN SLIGHT SUBTLE TENDER TICKLE TWIGGY ELEGANT EPICENE FINICAL FRAGILE MINIKIN REFINED SLIMMER SUBTILE SUMMERY TAFFETA TAFFETY TENUOUS TIFFANY WILLOWY ARANEOUS CHARMING ETHEREAL FEATHERY GOSSAMER GRACEFUL HOTHOUSE LUSCIOUS MIGNIARD PINDLING PLEASANT SENSIBLE SUMMERLY TICKLISH UNLUSTIE
(— IN APPEARANCE) HUNGRY
(AFFECTEDLY —) ROSEWATER
(PREF.) ABRO HABRO
DELICATELY FINE SMALLY FAIRLY MELTINGLY
DELICATESSEN GASTRONOME CHARCUTERIE
DELICIOUS DAINTY FRIAND DELICATE SCRUMPTIOUS
DELIGHT JOY GLEE GUST LITE LOVE SEND TAKE BLESS BLISS CHARM EXULT FEAST GRACE GUSTO MIRTH REVEL SAVOR SMACK ADMIRE ARRIDE DELICE DIVERT LIKING PLEASE RAVISH REGALE RELISH TICKLE DISPORT ECSTASY ENCHANT GLADDEN GRATIFY JOYANCE JOYANCY LECHERY RAPTURE REJOICE DELICATE ENTRANCE GLADNESS PLEASURE SAVORING
(— IN) LOVE SAVOR
(PL.) DELICIAE
DELIGHTED GLAD
DELIGHTFUL NICE GREAT JAMMY JOLLY MERRY SOOTH DREAMY SAVORY ELYSIAN LEESOME ADORABLE CHARMING DELICATE DELITOUS GLORIOUS GORGEOUS HEAVENLY LUSCIOUS SCRUMPTIOUS
DELIMER DRENCHER
DELIMIT FIX DEFINE SUBTEND
DELIMITATION
(PREF.) HORISMO
DELIMITED MERED MEERED
DELINEATE MAP DRAW ETCH LIMN LINE CHALK CHART FENCE IMAGE PAINT STELL TABLE TOUCH TRACE TRICK BLAZON CIPHER DELINE DEPICT DESIGN DEVISE SKETCH SURVEY DEPAINT EXPRESS LINEATE OUTLINE PICTURE PORTRAY DECIPHER DEFIGURE DESCRIBE TRAVERSE
DELINEATION DRAFT DESIGN SKETCH SURVEY DRAUGHT
(CARELESS —) PERIGRAPH
DELINQUENCY FAULT GUILT FAILURE MISDEED OFFENSE OMISSION
DELINQUENT CRIMINAL
(PL.) KALANG
DELIQUESCE MELT LIQUEFY DISSOLVE
DELIRIOUS FEY MAD OFF REE

GYTE LIGHT MANIC INSANE RAVING FLIGHTY FRANTIC LUNATIC MADDING BRAINISH DELEERIT DELIERET DERANGED FRENETIC FRENZIED
DELIRIUM FURY MAZE MANIA FRENZY LUNACY RAVERY RAVING MADNESS DELIRACY IDLENESS INSANITY
DELIRIUM TREMENS JUMP HORRORS JIMJAMS JIMMIES POTOMANIA
DELIVER DO HIT LAY LET RID BAIL BORN DEAL FREE GIVE LEND REDD SAVE SELL SEND TAKE BEKEN BRING COUGH LIVER SERVE SPEAK UTTER ADDICT ASSIZE ASSOIL BETRAY COMMIT CONVEY EXEMPT PREACH RANSOM REDEEM RENDER RESCUE RESIGN SUCCOR UNBIND BETEACH BITECHE COMMEND CONSIGN DECLAIM DICTATE OUTTAKE PRESENT RECOVER RELEASE RELIEVE DISPATCH EXORCISE EXORCIZE LIBERATE
(— BALL) BOWL
(— BLOW) LEND POKE SEND
(— BLOWS ON HEAD) NOB
(— CHILD) LIGHT
(— FORCEFULLY) FASTEN
(— LOGS) STOCK
(— MERCHANDISE) UTTER
(— OVER) BETAKE CONSIGN
(— RHETORICALLY) DECLAIM
(— SPEECH) ADDRESS
DELIVERANCE BOOT ESCAPE RESCUE SAVING DELIVERY RIDDANCE SOLUTION VOIDANCE SALVATION
DELIVERED LANDED
(— FREE) FRANCO
(PRECISELY —) FLUSH
DELIVERER SOTER DRAYMAN SAOSHYANT
DELIVERY FLY BAIL FLIER FLYER ISSUE LIVERY RESCUE ADDRESS AIRDROP BAILMENT SHIPMENT ACCOUCHEMENT
(— IN SPEAKING) DICTION
(— OF BALL) BOWL
(— WAGON) FLY
(MAIL —) TAPPALL TAPPAUL
(PREF.) TOCO TOKO
(SUFF.) TOCIA TOCO(US) TOKIA TOKO(US) TOKY
DELL DEN HOW DALE DEAN DENE DILL DRAB GLEN VALE SLACK SLADE TRULL WENCH DARGLE DIMBLE DINGLE RAVINE VALLEY
(PL.) DALLES
DELPHINIUM DAUPHIN DOLPHIN LARKSPUR
DELPHUS (FATHER OF —) APOLLO NEPTUNE POSEIDON
(MOTHER OF —) CELAENO MELANTHO
DELUDE BOB JIG BILK DUPE FOOL HOAX MOCK AMUSE CHEAT COZEN ELUDE EVADE GLAIK SPOOF TRICK BAFFLE BANTER BEFOOL BUBBLE CAJOLE DIDDLE ILLUDE BEGUILE DECEIVE

ENCHANT MISLEAD OVERSEE BEJUGGLE HOODWINK INVEIGLE OVERSILE
DELUGE SEA FLOW FLOOD SWAMP DILUVY CATARACT INUNDATE OVERFLOW SATURATE SUBMERGE CATACLYSM
DELUNDUNG LINSANG ZINSANG VIVERRINE
DELUSION MAZE MOHA ABUSE DWALE FRAUD TRICK MIRAGE VISION CHIMERA FALLACY FANTASM PHANTOM WANHOPE ILLUSION NIHILISM PHANTASM
DELUSTER DULL
DELUXE PALACE ELEGANT ELABORATE SUMPTUOUS
DELVE DEN DIG DIP PIT CAVE DINT MINE DITCH PLUMB BRUISE BURROW EXHUME FATHOM INDENT IMPRESS EXCAVATE INSCRIBE
DEMAGNETIZE DEPERM DEPOLARIZE
DEMAGOGUE CLEON LEADER ORATOR ROUSER DEMAGOG JACOBIN SPEAKER TRIBUNE JAWSMITH OCHLOCRAT
DEMAND ASK CRY TAX USE CALL NEED RAME SALE CLAIM CRAVE DRAFT EXACT GAVEL ORDER QUERY SIGHT BEHEST CHARGE DESIRE ELICIT EXPECT SNATCH SUMMON ARRAIGN COMMAND CONSIST DRAUGHT INQUIRE MANDATE REQUEST REQUIRE SOLICIT INSTANCE QUESTION POSTULATE SCISCITATION
(— PAYMENT) DUN CALL
(— RECOGNITION) CLAIM ASSERT
(PL.) EXIGENCE EXIGENCY
DEMANDABLE DUE EXIGIBLE
DEMANDED COMPULSORY
DEMANDING HEFTY EXIGENT
(— ATTENTION) ACUTE
DEMANTOID EMERALD OLIVINE
DEMARCATE DELIMIT SEPARATE
DEMARCATION CELL
DEMEAN ABASE CARRY LOWER BEHAVE DEBASE DEPORT CONTAIN DEGRADE DESCEND MALTREAT
DEMEANOR AIR GARB MIEN PORT FRONT HABIT ACTION HAVIOR BEARING CONDUCT DISPOSE FASHION CARRIAGE PORTANCE
(COLD —) MORGUE
DEMENTED MAD NUTS BUGGY CRAZY LOONY NUTTY INSANE SKEWED FATUOUS
DEMENTIA FATUITY INSANITY
DEMERIT MARK FAULT DESERT BROWNIE
(PL.) GIG
DEMESNE MANOR PLACE REALM DOMAIN ESTATE REGION DISTRICT
DEMETER CERES MISTRESS
DEMETRIUS (BELOVED OF —) CELIA HERMIA
(MOTHER OF —) TAMORA
DEMIGOD AITU HERO KAMI YIMA ADAPA SATYR GARUDA PAGODA

TRITON GODLING
(PL.) NEPHILIM
DEMIGODDESS URD NORN
HEROINE
DEMILUNE RAVELIN
DEMISE WILL DEATH CONVEY
DECEASE BEQUEATH
DEMISED LETTEN
DEMIT LOWER HUMBLE RESIGN
ABDICATE
DEMOCRACY POPULACY
COMMONALTY
DEMOCRAT DEMO DANITE
HUNKER SNAPPER DEMOCRAW
LOCOFOCO POPOCRAT
(CONSERVATIVE —) HARD
DEMODULATE DETECT
DEMOISELLE KULM CRANE
COOLEN KAIKARA
DEMOLISH RASE RAZE RUIN
ABATE BREAK ELIDE LEVEL
WASTE WRECK BATTER SLIGHT
DESTROY RUINATE SHATTER
SUBVERT UNBUILD DOWNCAST
STRAMASH PULVERIZE
DEMOLITION END FALL
DEMON ALP DEV HAG IMP NAT OKI
AITU ATUA BADB BALI BHUT
DEVA DOOK OGRE OKEE PUCK
RAHU SURT WADE ASURA DEVIL
DHOUL FIEND GENIE GHOST
JUMBY LAMIA LESHY LESIY
OTKON SATAN SATYR SHEDU
SURTR TAIPO WITCH ABIGOR
AFREET ARIOCH BILWIS DAEMON
DAIMON DAITTA GENIUS JUMBIE
MAMMON PILWIZ PISACA THURSE
VRITRA YAKSHA YAKSHI ASMADAI
ASMODAY DEMONIO HARPIER
PISACHA VILLAIN WARLOCK
ALICHINO ASHMODAI ASMODEUS
BAALPEOR BEELPEOR CURUPIRA
EUDAEMON OBIDICUT SUCCUBUS
WATERMAN
(— OF WOODS) LESHY LESIY
LESHEY
(ARABIC —) AFRIT AFREET AFRITE
EFREET
(EVIL —) SHEDU
(FEMALE —) HAG LAMIA PISACHI
SUCCUBUS
(NATURE —) GENIUS
(PETTY —) IMP
(WATER —) NICKER
(PL.) DASYUS
DEMONASSA (FATHER OF —)
AMPHIARAUS
(HUSBAND OF —) THERSANDER
(MOTHER OF —) ERIPHYLE
(SON OF —) TISAMENUS
DEMONIAC DEMONIC LUNATIC
SATANIC DEVILISH DIABOLIC
FIENDISH INFERNAL
DEMONIACAL DEMONIAC
INFERNAL
DEMONICE (FATHER OF —) AGENOR
(MOTHER OF —) EPICASTE
(SON OF —) MOLUS EVENUS
PHYLUS THESTIUS
DEMONSTRABLE ACTUAL
DEMONSTRATE GIVE SHOW
CLEAR PROVE SPEAK CONVICT
DISPLAY PORTRAY CONVINCE

INSTANCE MANIFEST
DEMONSTRATION SHOW SIGN
TIME PROOF OVATION APODIXIS
BALLYHOO DARSHANA MANIFEST
(— OF POWER) MANIFESTATION
(OSTENTATION —) SPLURGE
DEMONSTRATIVE THAT THIS
THESE THOSE EFFUSIVE EVINCIVE
DEMOPHON (FATHER OF —) CELEUS
THESEUS
(MOTHER OF —) PHAEDRA
METANIRA
(NURSE OF —) DEMETER
DEMORALIZE WEAKEN CONFUSE
CORRUPT DEPRAVE PERVERT
DEMORALIZING INFECTIOUS
SHATTERING
DEMOTE BUMP BUST REDUCE
UNRANK DEGRADE DISRATE
DEMOTIC POPULAR ENCHORIAL
DEMOTION BUMP
DEMULCENT MANNA SALEB SALEP
BORAGE GINSENG EMULSION
SOOTHING
DEMUR COY GIB JIB SHY BALK
STAY DELAY DOUBT PAUSE
QUALM STICK BOGGLE LINGER
OBJECT STRAIN DEMEORE
SCRUPLE STICKLE STUMBLE
SUSPEND DEMURRER HESITATE
SUSPENSE
DEMURE COY MIM SHY MURE
PRIM GRAVE SPAKE STAID SUANT
SUENT MODEST SEDATE PRENZIE
PRIMSIE COMPOSED DECOROUS
DEN MEW CAVE COVE DEAN DELL
DIVE GLEN HELL HOLE HOLT
HUNK LAIR LAKE NEST ROOM
SHED SINK BIELD CABIN CAVEA
COUCH DELVE HAUNT LODGE
SLADE STUDY BURROW CAVERN
COVERT GROTTO HOLLOW
KENNEL RAVINE SHROUD
RETREAT SPELUNK HIDEAWAY
SNUGGERY WORKROOM
(— OF BEAR) WASH
(— OF INIQUITY) DOMDANIEL
(DRINKING —) BOTHAN
(FOUL —) SPITAL
(GAMBLING —) DEADFALL
DENARIUS DENAR PENNY DINDER
DENATURANT PYRIDINE
DENDRITE PROCESS
DENIAL NO NAY WARN DENAY
DENIER NAYSAY DEFENSE
DEMENTI REFUSAL REPULSE
CONTRARY NEGATION TRAVERSE
(— OF AUTHORITY) ANARCHY
(— OF TRUTH) HERESY
DENIED LOST
DENIER DINERO NEGATOR
DENARIUS DINHEIRO
(HALF —) MAIL MAILLE
DENIGRATE BEFOUL CRUCIFY
DENIM DUNGAREE
DENIZEN CITIZEN RESIDENT
(— BY BIRTH) NATIVE
(— OF HELL) HELLION

COUNTY: AMT FYN RIBE SORO
VEJLE AARHUS MARIBO
ODENSE TONDER VIBORG
AALBORG RANDERS AABENRAA
BORNHOLM
INLET: ISE LIM FJORD VEJLE
NISSUM ODENSE HORSENS
LOGSTOR MARIAGER
ISLAND: OE ALS FYN MON AARO
AERO FANO FOHR MORS ROMO
BAAGO FAROE LAESO SAMSO
SANDO AMAGER SEJERO
SUDERO FALSTER SEELAND
ZEALAND
MEASURE: ELL FOD MIL POT ALEN
FAVN RODE ALBUM KANDE
LINJE PAEGL TOMME ACHTEL
PAEGEL SKEPPE LANDMIL
OLTONDE SKIEPPE VIERTEL
FJERDING
PARLIAMENT: RIGSRAAD
FOLKETING LANDSTING
PENINSULA: JUTLAND
POSSESSION: FAROE ICELAND
GREENLAND
RIVER: ASA HOLM OMME STOR
GUDEN SKIVE SUSAA VARDE
GELSAA STORAA VORGOD
GUDENAA LILLEAA LONBORG
SETTLERS: OSTMEN
STRAIT: KATTEGAT SKAGERRAK
TOWN: ARS HOV HALS KOGE NIBE
SORO VRAA FARUM HOBRO
SKIVE AARHUS DRAGOR
KORSOR NYBORG ODENSE
SKAGEN STRUER VIBORG
AALBORG HERNING HORSENS
KOLDING RANDERS ALSINORE
BALLERUP GENTOFTE
GLOSTRUP ROSKILDE
HELSINGOR COPENHAGEN
TRIBE: DANES JUTES ANGLES
CIMBRI TEUTONS
TRIBUNAL: RIGSRAD RIGSRET
WEIGHT: ES LOD ORT VOG LAST
MARK PUND UNZE CARAT
KVINT POUND QUINT TONDE
CENTNER LISPUND QUINTIN
LISPOUND SKIPPUND

DENOMINATE CALL NAME STYLE
TITLE DENOTE CHRISTEN
INDICATE NOMINATE
DENOMINATION CULT NAME SECT
CLASS FAITH TITLE VALUE
CHURCH SCHOOL SOCIETY
CATEGORY
DENOMINATIONAL SECTARIAN
CONFESSIONAL
DENOTATION SIGN TOKEN EXTENT
NOTION SPHERE AMBITUS
BREADTH REFERENCE
DENOTE GIVE MARK MEAN NAME
NOTE SHOW SOUND IMPORT
NOTIFY BETOKEN CONNOTE
EXPRESS SIGNIFY DENOTATE
DESCRIBE INDICATE
DENOUEMENT END ENVOY ISSUE
PAYOFF OUTCOME SOLUTION
ANAGNOSIS
DENOUNCE BAN DAMN WRAY
ASCRY BASTE BLAST DECRY
TAUNT ACCUSE DELATE DESCRY

DETEST MENACE SCATHE
ARRAIGN CONDEMN DECLAIM
DECLARE UPBRAID EXECRATE
PROCLAIM THREATEN
OBJURGATE
DENOUNCEMENT DELATION
DENSE SAD FAST FIRM CLOSE
CRASS DUNCH FOGGY GROSS
HEAVY MASSY MURKY SILLY
SOLID SOUND SPISS STIFF THEET
THICK TIGHT WOOFY OBTUSE
OPAQUE SPISSY STUPID THICKY
THIGHT COMPACT
CROWDED INTENSE
SERRIED CONDENSE
(NOT —) TENUOUS
(PREF.) PACHY PYCN(O) PYKN(O)
DENSITY FOG CANDY FASTNESS
GAUSSAGE SOLIDITY
(UNIT OF —) TESLA
(PREF.) DASY
DENT BASH BURT DINT DOKE
DUNT FAZE NICK CLOUR DELVE
DINGE NOTCH STOVE TOOTH
BATTER DUNTLE HALLOW INDENT
BLEMISH DEPRESS
(— OF REED) SPLIT
(PL.) BEER
DENTAL POINT
DENTICULATE SERRATE SERRATED
DENTICULATION JAG JAGG
DENTIFRICE WASH
DENTIL DENTEL DENTELLO
DENTICLE
DENTINE IVORY DENTIN
DENTIST ODONTIST OPERATOR
DENTISTRY PROSTHODONTICS
DENTURE PLATE BRIDGE
DENUDE BARE SCALP SHAVE STRIP
DIVEST NUDATE DESPOIL
DENUDATE
DENUNCIATION BAN THREAT
THUNDER ANATHEMA DIATRIBE
DENY NAY NAIT NICK NITE WARN
BELIE DEBAR NITTE RENAY REPEL
WERNE ABJURE DISOWN FORBID
IMPUGN NEGATE REFUSE REFUTE
REJECT RENEGE CONFUTE
DEPRIVE DISAVOW DISPUTE
FORSAKE GAINSAY PROTEST
SUBLATE WITHSAY ABNEGATE
DENEGATE DISALLOW
DISCLAIM FORSWEAR
NEGATIVE RENOUNCE
TRAVERSE WITHHOLD
(— ACCESS) CLOSE
(— RECOGNITION) BLINK
DEOXIDIZE REDUCE
DEOXIDIZED
(PREF.) DESOXY
DEPART GO DIE MOG OFF WAG
BLOW EXIT FLIT HOOK MOVE
PACK PART PASS PIKE QUIT SHED
STEP VADE VARY VOID WALK
WEND WITE AVOID BREAK
FOUND LEAVE MOSEY SEVER
SHAKE SHIFT START TRUSS
AVAUNT BEGONE DECAMP
DECEDE DEMISE DESIST DIVIDE
PERISH RECEDE REMOVE RETIRE
SKIDOO SUNDER SWERVE
WANDER ABSCOND DEVIATE
DISCEDE FORSAKE RETREAT

SKIDDOO VAMOOSE DISCOAST FAREWELL SEPARATE TRESPASS WITHDRAW
(— FROM HARBOR) SORTIE
(— FROM LIFE) DECEASE
(— IN HASTE) BREEZE
(— IN HURRY) SKIVE LAMMAS
(— SECRETLY) ABSCOND ABSQUATULATE
(— SUDDENLY) FLEE DECAMP MIZZLE
(— WITH SPEED) VAMOOSE
DEPARTED DEAD BYGONE DEFUNCT DECEASED DECEDENT
DEPARTMENT END PART OKRUG REALM AGENCY BRANCH BUREAU EXCISE MEMBER OKROOG SPHERE FOUNDRY HANAPER PORTION REVENUE SPICERY AGITPROP CHANCERY DIVISION INDUSTRY NOMARCHY PROVINCE SCULLERY
(— IN CHINA) FU
(— OF CHANCERY) HAMPER
(NEWSPAPER —) COLUMN FEATURE
(TREASURY —) CAMERA
DEPARTURE BUNK EXIT BREAK DEATH EXODE GOING LEAVE LUCKY OUTGO CHANGE CONGEE DEPART EGRESS EXODUS HEGIRA SETOFF WAGANG WAYING DECEASE EASTING OUTGANG PARTING PARTURE RETREAT SAILING TRUNDLE WAYGATE DEPARTER FAREWELL OFFGOING REMOTION
(— FROM CORRECTNESS) ATROCITY
(— FROM SUBJECT) ASIDE
(— FROM THEME) CADENZA
(— OF SHIP) SORTIE
(CHARACTER IN —) LUISE TROTT GILFEN
(COMPOSER OF —) D'ALBERT
(EMERGENCY —) BAILOUT
(GEOLOGICAL —) ANOMALY
(SECRET —) GUY SLIP
DEPEND BANK HANG LEAN PEND RELY REST RIDE STAY TURN BUILD COUNT FOUND HINGE TRUST LIPPEN CONFIDE
DEPENDABILITY SECURITY
DEPENDABLE GOOD SURE TRIG SIKER SOLID SOUND THERE SECURE SICCAR SICKER STANCH STEADY CERTAIN STAUNCH RELIABLE SILVENDY SUREFIRE
DEPENDENCE MAINSTAY RELIANCE SERVILITY
DEPENDENCY TALUK COLONY APANAGE APPANAGE
DEPENDENT CHILD CLIENT HANGBY MINION SPONGE VASSAL FEODARY FEUDARY PRONEUR RELIANT SERVILE SPONGER SUBJECT WRAPPED BEHOLDEN CLINGING CREATURE ENCLITIC EVENTUAL FOLLOWER RETAINER
(— ON) ILLATIVE
(NOT —) ABSOLUTE
DEPENDING ATTENDANT
(— ON UNCERTAIN EVENTS) ALEATORY
DEPICT HUE DRAW ETCH LIMN

PICT UNDO ENTER IMAGE PAINT SPEAK WRITE BLAZON SHADOW DEPAINT DISPLAY EXPRESS IMPAINT PICTURE PORTRAY DESCRIBE EMBLAZON RESEMBLE
DEPICTED DEPAINT
(— AS BROKEN) ROMPU
DEPICTION SCAN SCHEMA
DEPILATION PSILOSIS
DEPILATORY RUSMA EPILATOR PELADORE PSILATRO
DEPLETE DRAIN EMPTY PUNISH REDUCE UNLOAD EXHAUST BANKRUPT DIMINISH
DEPLETED WASTE BANKRUPT
DEPLETION DRAIN EROSION
DEPLORABLE SAD WOFUL WOEFUL DOLOROUS GRIEVOUS WAILSOME WRETCHED
DEPLORABLY SADLY
DEPLORE RUE MOAN SIGH WAIL MOURN BEMOAN BEWAIL GRIEVE LAMENT REGRET COMPLAIN
DEPLOY UNFOLD DISPLAY
DEPLOYMENT FORMATION
DEPOLYMERIZE DEGRADE
DEPONE SWEAR DEPOSE TESTIFY
DEPONENT AFFIANT DEPONER EXAMINATE
DEPOPULATE RAVAGE DESOLATE DISPEOPLE
DEPORT BEAR EXILE EXPEL BANISH BEHAVE DEMEAN BEARING CONDUCT DISPORT RELEGATE
DEPORTMENT AIR GEST MIEN PORT GESTE HABIT ACTION DEPORT HAVING MANNER ADDRESS BEARING COMPORT CONDUCT GESTURE HAVANCE BREEDING CARRIAGE DEMEANOR MAINTAIN PORTANCE
DEPOSE AVER ABASE PRIVE SWEAR AFFIRM ASSERT BANISH DEPONE DIVEST REDUCE REMOVE DEGRADE DEPOSIT DESTOOL TESTIFY DETHRONE DISCROWN DISPLACE
DEPOSIT FUR LAY PUT SET ADHI BANK CAKE CAST CRUD DROP DUMP FUND HIDE HOCK PAWN BLOOM CHEST COUCH COVER DEPOT LODGE PLACE SCURF STORE TOSCA BESTOW DEPONE DEPOSE ENTOMB ESCROW FLYSCH GARNER IMPOSE INHUME PLEDGE REPOSE SALINE SCORIA SCROLL SETTLE SINTER TOPHUS ASHFALL CONSIGN HORIZON DILUVIUM FOULNESS SANDBANK PRECIPITATION
(— BALLOT) CAST
(— DRIFT-SAND) SUD
(— EGGS) BLOW SPAWN
(— FOR COPYRIGHT) ENTER
(— IN CHAMPAGNE) GRIFFE
(— IN EARTH) INTER INHUME
(— IN GUN BORE) FOULING
(— IN WINE CASK) CRUST TARTAR
(— OF DEBRIS) BRECCIA
(— OF LOAM) LOESS
(— OF ORE) BANK FLAT
(— OF PEBBLES AND SAND) BEACH CASCALHO

(— OF SALT WATER) SOAK
(— ON LEATHER) BLOOM
(— ON LEAVES) HONEYDEW
(— STOLEN ARTICLES) FENCE
(— USED AS FERTILIZER) FALUN
(ALLUVIAL —) APRON DELTA
(ARCHAEOLOGICAL —) LENS LENSE
(BANK —S) CASH
(BLACK —) STUPP
(CORNEA —) ARCUS
(EARTHY —) GUHR MARL
(GEOLOGIC —) BLANKET HORIZON
(GLACIAL —) TILL DRIFT ESKAR ESKER SHEET PLACER MORAINE
(GRAVEL —) LEAD
(KIDNEY —) GRAVEL
(MASS OF SEDIMENTARY —S) GOBI
(MINERAL —) FLAT LODE CARBONA
(MUDDY —) SLUDGE SLUMGULLION
(POWDERY —) BERGMEHL
(SEDIMENTARY —) SILT VARVE
(SHELLY —) CRAG
(SHOAL-WATER —) CULM
(SKELETAL —) CORAL
(STOMACH —) SABURRA
(TARRY —) GUM
(WELDING —) TACK
(PREF.) THESO
DEPOSITARY POSITOR SEQUESTER
DEPOSITION PAD BURIAL DEPOSIT OPINION SILTING DEPOSURE SEDIMENT
DEPOSITORY BANK DROP SAFE AMBRY ATTIC VAULT DEPOSIT OSSUARY SENTINE DEPOSITO ESCROWEE OSSARIUM
DEPOT BANK BASE GARE AURANG AURUNG STAPLE STATION MAGAZINE TERMINAL TERMINUS
DEPRAVE TAINT DEBASE DEFILE INFECT MALIGN REVILE BESHREW CORRUPT PERVERT VITIATE
DEPRAVED BAD EVIL UGLY VILE PRAVE ROTTEN SHREWD WICKED BESTIAL CORRUPT IMMORAL PRAVOUS VICIOUS MISCREANT
DEPRAVITY VICE ABYSS ILLNESS PRAVITY VILLAINY TURPITUDE
DEPRECATE PRAY INVOKE BESEECH
DEPRECATORY PEJORATIVE
DEPRECIATE FALL LACK SLUR ABASE AVILE DECRY SLUMP DEBASE EMBASE LESSEN MINISH REDUCE SHRINK CHEAPEN DEBAUCH DEGRADE DEPRAVE DEPRESS DETRACT DISABLE SLANDER SMALLEN BELITTLE DEROGATE DISCOUNT DISPRIZE DISVALUE MINIMIZE PEJORATE VILIPEND
DEPRECIATION AGIO DECRIAL DISCOUNT
DEPREDATION PREY RAPINE PILLAGE
DEPRESS BOW COW HIP LOW BATE BEAR BORE DAMP DASH DENT FALL FLAT SINK SUMP ABASE APPAL BREAK CHILL COUCH CRUSH FAINT LOWER SLUMP VAPOR WEIGH APPALL DAMPEN DEBOSS DISMAY

HUMBLE INDENT LESSEN MURDER SADDEN SETTLE SICKEN SLOUCH STRIKE WEAKEN DECLINE DEGRADE DESTROY FLATTEN OPPRESS REPRESS BROWBEAT DIMINISH DISPIRIT DOWNBEAR ENFEEBLE
(— STRINGS OF INSTRUMENT) FRET
DEPRESSANT HELLEBORE
DEPRESSED LOW SAD BLUE DAMP DULL FLAT SICK SUNK COWED WROTH BROODY DISHED GLOOMY HIPPED HOLLOW LONELY OBLATE SOMBER TRISTE ACCABLE LETDOWN DEJECTED DOWNCAST DOWNSOME
(— AT THE POLES) OBLATE
(ECONOMICALLY —) HARD
DEPRESSING SAD BLUE COLD BLEAK CHILL DREAR DUSKY MUZZY OURIE DISMAL DREARY GLOOMY SOMBER SOMBRE TRISTE OPPRESSIVE
DEPRESSION COL DIP EYE GAT PAN PIT BUST CROP DAMP DELK DENT DOKE DOWN FALL FOSS GASH GLEN HOLL HOWE SLEW SLOT SLUE WELL ATRIO BASIN BLUES BOSOM CANON COWAL CRYPT DELVE DINGE FOSSA FOSSE FOVEA GLOOM GROIN NADIR NAVEL ORBIT POLJE SALAR SCOOP SELLA SINUS SLUMP SWALE AMPHID BLIGHT BUCKLE CAFARD CANYON CAVITY CRATER CUPULE DIMPLE DISMAY FURROW GROOVE GULLEY GUTTER INDENT LACUNA RAVINE SAUCER SLOUGH SPLEEN VALLEY WALLOW ALVEOLA BLOWOUT BOGHOLE CHAGRIN CLAYPAN CONCAVE COUNTER FOSSULA FOSSULE FOVEOLA JIMMIES SADNESS SALTPAN SINKAGE SINKING VARIOLE BOTHRIUM DOLDRUMS DOWNBEND FAINTING FOLLICLE FOREDEEP FOSSETTE FOSSULET PUNCTURE SINKHOLE SOAKAWAY EPHIPPIUM MELANCHOLY OPPRESSION
(— BEHIND COW'S SHOULDERS) CROP
(— BETWEEN BREASTS) CLEAVAGE
(— BETWEEN HILLS) SWIRE
(— IN BOARD) SKIP
(— IN BOTTLE BOTTOM) KICK
(— IN DECK) COCKPIT
(— IN DOG'S FACE) STOP
(— IN FRUITS) EYE
(— IN GROUND) DALK DELK SOAK SWAG WELL SWALE CHARCO
(— IN MILLSTONE) BOSOM
(— IN NILE VALLEY) KORE
(— IN RANGE) PASS
(— IN RIDGE) COL
(— IN SNOW) SITZMARK
(— IN VELD) COMITJE KOMMETJE
(— OF EAR) SCAPHA
(— OF SPIRITS) JAWFALL
(— PRONE) VAPORISH
(ARTICULAR —) GLENE
(OBLONG —) CIRCUS
(SMALL —) DENT DIMPLE

LACUNA FOLLICLE

DEPRIVATION COST LOSS MAIM
WANT MAYHEM AMOTION
MISTURE DEPRIVAL
(— OF SIGHT) DARKNESS
(SUFF.) STERESIS

DEPRIVE BAR ROB BATE DENY
DOCK EASE GELD TWIN ABATE
BENIM BREAK DEBAR EMPTY
EXUTE PREVE SPOIL STRIP
WRONG AMERCE DEFEAT
DENUDE DEPOSE DEVEST DISMAY
DIVEST FAMISH FORBAR HINDER
HUSTLE REMOVE ABRIDGE
BEGUILE BEREAVE CASHIER
CURTAIL DECEIVE DEFORCE
DEPRAVE DESPOIL DESTROY
DISABLE EXHAUST FOREBAR
GUDGEON PRIVATE UNDRESS
BANKRUPT DENATURE DESOLATE
DISANNUL EVACUATE
(— BY TRICKERY) NOSE MULCT
(— FRAUDULENTLY) GUDGEON
(— OF BRILLIANCE) DEADEN
(— OF COURAGE) UNNERVE
(— OF FREEDOM) FETTER
(— OF INDIVIDUALITY) FORDIZE
(— OF LIFE) DEADEN
(— OF OFFICE) DEPOSE
(— OF POSSESSIONS) FLAY
(— OF REASON) DEMENT
(— OF SENSATION) BENUMB
(— OF SENSE) INEBRIATE
(— OF SIGHT) SEEL
(— OF STRENGTH) ENERVATE
(— OF VIRGINITY) DEFLOWER
(PREF.) DE DIS

DEPRIVED REFT SANS BANKRUPT
DESOLATE

DEPTH DIP BURY DEEP DROP
MOHO ABYSS MIDST SIDTH
FATHOM HEIGHT ALTITUDE
DEEPNESS PROFOUND SOUNDING
STRENGTH PENETRATION
(— OF NIGHT OR WINTER) HOLL
HOWE
(— OF SAIL) HOIST
(— OF SHIP) GAGE GAUGE
(— OF SIN) SLOUGH
(— OF SPADE) SPIT GRAFT
(— OF WATER) DRAFT DRAUGHT
(-S OF SEA) PROFOUND
(LOWEST —) GROUND
(MORAL —) ABYSS
(PL.) MUD ABYSS HEART
(PREF.) BATH(O)(Y)

DEPUTATION MISSION THEORIA
LEGATION

DEPUTE SEND ALLOT ASSIGN
DEVOTE APPOINT DELEGATE

DEPUTY AIDE VICE AGENT ENVOY
NABOB PROXY VICAR ANGELO
COMMIS CURATE DEPUTE
EXARCH FACTOR KEHAYA LEGATE
MINION ADJOINT BAILIFF
ESCALUS SUBDEAN CAIMACAM
DELEGATE ORDINARY PYLAGORE
QAIMAQAM TENIENTE VICARIAN
(— OF BISHOP) VICAR VIDAME
(PREF.) CO

DERAIL TOAD DERAILER
THROWOFF

DERANGE TURN CRAZE UNWIT

UPSET HAMPER RUFFLE CONFUSE
DERAIGN DISEASE DISTURB
PERTURB UNSHAPE DISORDER
DISPLACE UNSETTLE

DERANGED OUT GYTE CRAZY
CRAZED SKIVIE FRANTIC FURIOUS
BUGHOUSE DEMENTED
DETRAQUE INFORMAL

DERANGEMENT MANIA UPSET
FRENZY LUNACY DISEASE
MADNESS PHRENSY RUMMAGE
DELIRIUM DISORDER INSANITY

DERBY POT CADY KATY RACE
BOXER CADDY DICER KELLY SHIRE
BOWLER

DERBY BLUE ELDERBERRY

DERELICT STREET FAILURE
BETRAYER CASTAWAY

DERELICTION FAILURE RELICTION

DERIDE BOO GECK GIBE HOOT
JAPE JEER JIBE LOUT MOCK TWIT
DRAPE FLEER FLOUT KNACK
LAUGH RALLY SCOFF SCORN
SCOUT TAUNT EXPOSE ILLUDE
IRRIDE CATCALL LOWBELL
RIDICULE

DERIDER IRRISOR

DERISION GECK JEER MOCK
HOKER SCORN SPORT MOWING
ASTEISM MOCKERY CONTEMPT
IRRISION RIDICULE

DERISIVE JEERY SNIDE MOWING
SATANIC DERISORY IRRISORY
SARDONIC SCOFFING

DERIVATION ORIGIN DESCENT
PEDIGREE PARENTAGE

DERIVATIVE FURAN LININ SLOPE
ACOINE ACYLAL BORANE FURANE
INDOLE PHENOL RETENE ALKYLOL
ANALGEN DERIVED ENOLATE
FLAVONE FLUXION FULGIDE
FULVENE GERMANE SUCRATE
ALBUMOSE ANALGENE FLAVONOL
FORMAZAN HEMATINE INDAZOLE
STANNANE SECONDHAND
ADSCITITIOUS

DERIVE GET DRAW STEM TAKE
BRING CARRY DRIVE FETCH INFER
TRACE BORROW CONVEY DEDUCE
DESUME ELICIT EVOLVE GATHER
OBTAIN SPRING DESCEND
EXTRACT PROCEED RECEIVE
TRADUCE

DERIVED
(SUFF.) **(— FROM)** IC(AL)

DERMA LAYER CORIUM DERMIS
KISHKE

DERMATITIS ICH ICK CASCADO
CUTITIS

DERMATOGEN PROTODERM

DERMIS CUTIS DERMA CORIUM

DERNIER LAST FINAL DARREIN

DERNIER CRI FASHION

DEROGATE ANNUL DECRY LESSEN
REPEAL DETRACT SLANDER
RESTRICT WITHDRAW

DEROGATORY BAD

DERRICK JIB RIG LIFT SPAR CRANE
DAVIT HOIST STEEVE TACKLE
ERECTER ERECTOR GALLOWS
HANGING HANGMAN STIFFLEG
JINNYWINK

DERRIS TUBA DEGUELIA

DERVISH AGIB FAKIR FAKEER
SADITE SANTON DARWESH
WHIRLER CALENDER

DESALT DEIONIZE

DESATURATE SADDEN

DESCANT SING SONG COPULA
MELODY REMARK WARBLE
COMMENT QUINIBLE

DESCEND DIP SYE DIVE DROP
DUCK FALL SHED SINK SKIN VAIL
AVALE LIGHT LOWER SQUAT
STOOP SWOOP ALIGHT DERIVE
DEVALL DEVAUL SETTLE DECLINE
DELAPSE DEVOLVE SUBSIDE
SUCCEED DISMOUNT
PREPONDERATE
(— INTO HELL) HARROW

DESCENDANT SON CION GHUZ
HEIR SEED SLIP CHILD GHUZZ
SCION BRANCH LINEAL DESCENT
AARONITE ASHERITE DAUGHTER
EPIGONUS
(— OF IMMIGRANTS) BRAVA
(— OF JEW) CHUETA
(— OF MOHAMMED) EMIR
(— OF NOAH) AD
(—S OF MOHAMMED) ASHRAF
(INSIGNIFICANT —) TAG
(PL.) SEED DONMEH DUNMEH
STRAIN PROGENY OFFSPRING
POSTERITY
(SUFF.) ITE

DESCENDING FALL CADENT
DOWNWARD
(— FROM COMMON ANCESTOR)
AKIN

DESCENT JET KIN SET DIVE DOWN
DROP FALL KIND VAIL BIRTH
BLOOD CANCH CHUTE ISSUE
PITCH SCARP SHUTE SLOPE
STOCK CLEUCH CLEUGH ESCARP
RAPPEL STRAIN ASSAULT
DECLINE DISSENT EXTRACT
FALLOUT INCLINE KINDRED
LINEAGE PROGENY ANCESTRY
BREEDING COMEDOWN
DOWNCOME DOWNFALL
DOWNGATE DOWNHILL GLISSADE
INVASION PEDIGREE PARENTAGE
(— IN MOUNTAINEERING) ABSEIL
(— OF AIRPLANE) LETDOWN
APPROACH
(— OF BIRD) STOOP
(— OF DEITY) AVATAR AVATARA
(— OF LIQUID) DRIBBLE
(— OF MASS) SLIDE
(— OF RIVER) LEAP
(FAMILIAR —) HAVAGE
(OVERWHELMING —) AVALANCHE
(PARACHUTE —) JUMP BAILOUT
(PLUNGING —) SPIN

DESCHAMPSIA AIRA

DESCRIBE GIVE READ TELL BLAZE
IMAGE PAINT POINT STYLE WRITE
DEFINE DENOTE DEPICT DEVISE
DILATE RELATE DEPAINT SKETCH
TITULE DECLARE DEPAINT
DISPLAY EXPLAIN EXPRESS
NARRATE OUTLINE PICTURE
PORTRAY PRESENT RECOUNT
STORIFY DESCRIVE INSCRIBE
REHEARSE
(— A LINE) CUT

(— AS) CALL
(— BRIEFLY) KODAK
(— GRAMMATICALLY) PARSE

DESCRIPTION KIN IMAGE BLAZON
SKETCH SURVEY ACCOUNT
DICTION DISPLAY PICTURE
LANDSKIP RELATION TREATISE
(— OF A COUNTRY) FACE
(— OF VISION) AISLING
(BRIEF —) LEGEND
(RUSTIC —) IDYL IDYLL

DESCRY SEE SPY ESPY MAKE SCRY
ASCRY SIGHT BEHOLD BETRAY
DETECT REVEAL DISCERN
DISPLAY DENOUNCE DESCRIBE
DISCLOSE DISCOVER PERCEIVE

DESDEMONA (FATHER OF —)
BRABANTIO
(HUSBAND OF —) OTHELLO

DESECRATE ABUSE DEFILE
POLLUTE PROFANE VIOLATE
TEMERATE UNHALLOW

DESECRATION PROFANATION

DESERT DUE ERG RAT RUN AREG
ARID BOLT FAIL FLEE MEED SAND
SERT TURN VAST GUILT LEAVE
LURCH MERIT PLANT SERIR
START WAIVE WASTE WORTH
BARREN BETRAY DEFECT EXPOSE
LONELY RENEGE REWARD SHRINK
THIRST WESTEN ABANDON
ABSCOND CHICKEN DEMERIT
FORSAKE HORNADA OVERRUN
WASTERN WASTINE DESOLATE
RENOUNCE SOLITARY SOLITUDE
WASTABLE
(PL.) GUILT
(PREF.) EREM(O)

DESERTED DEAD LONE WYSTY
LONELY FORLORN DESOLATE
FORSAKEN SOLITARY
(— WOMAN) AGUNAH

DESERTER RAT BOLTER BUGOUT
APOSTATE BUSHWACK FUGITIVE
RECREANT RENEGADE RUNAGATE
TURNTAIL

DESERTION BUGOUT RATTERY
APOSTASY

DESERT LEMON KUMQUAT

DESERVE EARN MEED RATE MERIT
REPAY SERVE ASSERVE BENEFIT
DEMERIT DISSERVE PROMERIT

DESERVED JUST COMING WORTHY
CONDIGN

DESERVING WORTHY CONDIGN
WORTHFUL ADMIRABLE
MERITORIOUS

DESICCATE DRY ARID SEAR SERE
DRAIN DEHYDRATE

DESICCATION XERANSIS

DESIDERATUM NEED DESIRE

DESIGN AIM END MAP CAST DRAW
GOAL IDEA MARK MEAN PLAN
PLAT PLOT TREE WORK ALLOT
CHECK DECAL DECOR DODAD
DRAFT DRIFT ETTLE FANCY
MODEL MOTIF NOTAN QUILT
SHAPE STAMP STUDY STYLE
BOWPOT CACHET CORNER
CREATE DEVICE DEVISE DOODAD
DOODLE EMBLEM FIGURE FLORAL
FLOWER INCUSE INTEND INTENT
INVENT LAYOUT MODULE OBJECT

OBTENT PROJET SCHEME SKETCH SYSTEM VERVER ALLOVER BOSCAGE CARTOON CARVING CHASING COMPOSE CONCERT COUNSEL CROQUIS DESTINE DIAGRAM DRAUGHT ETCHING FANTASY FASHION OUTLINE PATTERN PRETEND PROJECT PROPOSE PURPORT PURPOSE REVERSE SCALLOP SLEIGHT THOUGHT APPLIQUE BAYADERE BOUGHPOT CONTRIVE CYMATION CYMATIUM ENGINEER FILIGREE FLOCKING FORECAST GRAFFITO GROOVING INTAGLIO PHANTASY PLATFORM REMARQUE SINGERIE STRIPING SUNBURST GOFFERING SCHEMATISM
(— AS TITLE PAGE) VIGNETTE
(— ON BOOK) TOOL
(— ON CARPET) MEDALLION
(— ON COIN) BEADING
(— ON FABRIC) BATIK BATTIK
(ARTFUL —) MACHINATION
(BOOK —) FILET FILLET
(CUP-SHAPED —) HUSK
(EMBLEMATIC —) IMPRESS
(ESSENTIAL —) BONES
(FASHION —) FORD
(OUTLINE —) KEYSTONE
(PERFORATED —) POUNCE
(STRIPED —) STRIA STRIE
(TESSELLATED —) MOSAIC
(TEXTILE —) STRIPE HAIRLINE

DESIGNATE SET HAIL MARK MEAN NAME SHOW ELECT LABEL SPEAK STYLE TITLE ANOINT ASSIGN DENOTE DESIGN FINGER INTEND SETTLE APPOINT EARMARK ENTITLE EXPRESS SPECIFY SURNAME ALLOCATE DESCRIBE IDENTIFY INDICATE NOMINATE PRESCRIBE

DESIGNATION NAME TYPE LABEL STYLE TITLE CAPTION HOMONYM ADDITION
(— OF PLACE) ADDRESS

DESIGNED PREPENSE SUPPOSED
(— FOR MALE AND FEMALE) UNISEX

DESIGNER STYLER FANCIER PLANNER PLOTTER SCHEMER STYLIST COLORIST ENGINEER MEDALIST MOSAICIST
(PL.) COUTURE

DESIGNING ARTFUL CUNNING JESUITIC PLANNING PLOTTING SCHEMING

DESIRABLE FAIR GOOD KEEN WORTH PLUMMY AMIABLE GRADELY HEALTHY OPTABLE WELCOME WISHFUL DESIROUS ELIGIBLE ENVIABLE PLEASING SALUTARY

DESIRE YEN ACHE CARE ENVY EROS FAIN HAVE HOPE ITCH KAMA KEEP LEST LIST LOAD LUST MIND NEED PANT URGE WANT WILL WISH WIST ARDOR BOSOM BRAME COVET CRAVE FANCY GIMME GREED GROAN HEART MANGE MANIA NISUS QUEST STUDY TANHA TASTE WILNE YEARN YISSE AFFECT APPETE

ASPIRE BEHEST BESOLN DEMAND DEVICE HANKER HUNGER OREXIS POTHOS PREFER TALENT THIRST UTINAM YAMMER AVARICE AVIDITY CONATUS COURAGE CRAVING EROTISM FANTASY HIMEROS INKLING LONGING PASSION STOMACH VOLUNTY WILLING AMBITION APPETITE COVETISE CUPIDITY PLEASING NECESSITY
(— FOR LIFE) TANHA
(— WITH EAGERNESS) ASPIRE
(ARDENT —) THIRST
(IRRITATING —) ITCH
(SEXUAL —) HOTS PRIDE
(STRONG —) CUPIDITY SLAVERING
(UNCONTROLLABLE —) CACOETHES
(PREF.) **(SEXUAL —)** ERO EROTO
(SUFF.) OREXIA

DESIRE UNDER THE ELMS
(AUTHOR OF —) ONEILL
(CHARACTER IN —) EBEN ABBIE CABOT PUTNAM EPHRAIM

DESIROUS AVID FAIN FOND LIEF VAIN EAGER FRACK FRECK LUSTY ARDENT WILFUL ANXIOUS THIRSTY WILLFUL WILLING WISHING APPETENT COVETOUS LIKEROUS PRURIENT SPIRITED

DESIST HO LIN EASE HALT QUIT REST SIST STOP WHOA CEASE LEAVE SPARE STINT SWICK SWIKE WONDE DEPART ABANDON FORBEAR FORFEIT RESPITE SUBSIST SURCEASE
(— FROM) CUT LEAVE REMIT FORBEAR

DESK PEW AMBO SCOB BOARD DESSE TABLE BUREAU CAISSE PULPIT CONSOLE LECTERN PLUTEUS COPYDESK STANDISH VARGUENO

DESMA CLON CLONE

DESMAN MOLE SQUASH MUSKRAT ONDATRA

DESMANTHUS ACUAN

DESOLATE SAD BARE LORN RUIN SACK SOLE VAST WILD ALONE BLEAK DREAR GAUNT GUBAT OURIE STARK UNKED UNKET UNKID WASTE WASTY WYSTY BARREN DESERT DISMAL DREARY GLOOMY GOUSTY LONELY RAVAGE DESTROY FORLORN GOUSTIE HOWLING LACKING UNCOUTH WIDOWED WILSOME DEPRIVED DESERTED FORSAKEN SOLITARY WASTEFUL WOBEGONE

DESOLATION WOE RUIN GLOOM GRIEF HAVOC WASTE RAVAGE SADNESS

DESPAIR GLOOM UNHOPE WANHOPE

DESPAIRING HOPELESS

DESPERADO BRAVO BADMAN BANDIT RUFFIAN CRIMINAL RESOLUTE

DESPERATE MAD DIRE RASH ACHARNE DESPERT EXTREME FORLORN FRANTIC HEADLONG HOPELESS PERILOUS RECKLESS

DESPERATELY BONE

DESPICABLE BUM BASE MEAN ORRA VILE CHEAP DIRTY FOUTY SCALY ABJECT PALTRY SHABBY SORDID CAITIFF IGNOBLE PITIFUL REPTILE PITIABLE UNWORTHY WRETCHED

DESPICABLY DIRTILY

DESPISE DEFY HATE SCORN SCOUT SPISE SPURN DETEST FORHOO LOATHE SLIGHT VILIFY CONTEMN DESPITE DISDAIN DISPRIZE MISPRIZE VILIPEND

DESPITE BY VEX SPITE MALGRE DESPISE

DESPOIL ROB PELF PILL POLL RAID RAPE RUIN SKIN BOOTY HARRY PLUME RAVEN REAVE RIFLE SPOIL STRIP STRUB TRICE BEZZLE DIVEST FLEECE HESPEL HUSPEL RAVAGE RAVISH REMOVE BEREAVE DEPRIVE DISROBE PILLAGE PLUNDER UNSPOIL DEFLOWER DISARRAY SPOLIATE SPUILZIE UNCLOTHE

DESPOINA KORE PERSEPHONE

DESPONDENCY DUMP HUMP BLUES DUMPS GLOOM ATHYMY MISERY ATHUMIA ATHYMIA DESPAIR DESPOND

DESPONDENT SAD BLUE GLOOMY FORLORN DEJECTED DOWNCAST HOPELESS

DESPOT CZAR TSAR TZAR ANARCH SATRAP TYRANT AUTARCH MONARCH AUTOCRAT

DESPOTIC LORDLY ABSOLUTE DOMINANT

DESPOTISM TYRANNY AUTARCHY SULTANISM

DESQUAMATE PEEL

DESSERT ICE PIE CAKE FOOL SKYR SNOW VOID BETTY BOMBE COUPE DOLCE FRUIT GLACE GRUNT JELLY LACTO SLUMP AFTERS ECLAIR JUNKET MOUSSE PASTRY POSTRE SPONGE SWEETS TRIFLE BAKLAVA BANQUET PARFAIT PUDDING SHERBET SOUFFLE SPUMONE STRUDEL SUPREME DUMPLING FLUMMERY FRUMENTY NAPOLEON PANDOWDY SILLABUB

DESTINATION END GOAL PORT BOURN BILLET BOURNE

DESTINE DOOM EURE FATE MARK ALLOT SHAPE SLATE WEIRD DEPUTE DESIGN DEVOTE INTEND ORDAIN APPOINT PURPOSE SENTENCE

DESTINY LOT DOLE DOOM EURE FATE SORT KARMA MOIRA STARS WEIRD KHARMA KISMET DESTINE FORTUNE PORTION FOREDOOM

DESTITUTE BARE NACE POOR SANS VOID CLEAN EMPTY NAKED NEEDY WASTE BEREFT DEVOID VACANT WASTED FORLORN LACKING NAUGHTY VIDUATE WANTING BANKRUPT BEGGARED DEFEATED DEPRIVED DESOLATE FORSAKEN HELPLESS INDIGENT INNOCENT VIDUATED PENNILESS

(— OF) BUT
(— OF FEATHERS) DEPLUMATE
(— OF LEAVES) APHYLLOUS
(— OF LIGHT) DARK
(— OF TEETH) EDENTATE
(— OF WATER) ANHYDROUS
(SUFF.) **(— OF)** LESS

DESTITUTION NEED WANT FAMINE PENURY BEGGARY DEFAULT POVERTY

DESTROY BAG EAT END GUT MOW RID ZAP BLOW CHEW FRAP FULL KILL NULL RASE RAZE RUIN RUSH SINK SLAY SMIT STRY TINE UNDO VOID BREAK CRACK CRAZE DECAY ELIDE ERASE ERODE FORDO HAVOC MISDO PRANG QUADE QUAIL QUELL SHEND SHOOT SMASH SMITE SPEED SPEND SPILL SPLIT SPOIL STROY SWAMP TOTAL TRASH WASTY WRACK WRECK BLIGHT CANCEL CUMBER DEFACE DEFEAT DELETE DEVOID DEVOUR EFFACE FAMISH FOREDO MURDER PERISH QUENCH RANKLE RAVAGE STARVE STIFLE UNMAKE UNPILE UNWORK UPROOT UPTEAR ABOLISH CONSUME CORRODE DEPRIVE DISTURB ENECATE EXPUNGE FLATTEN FORFARE FORLESE MORTIFY NULLIFY OVERRUN PEREMPT RUINATE SHAMASH SHATTER SMOTHER SUBVERT TERRIFY UNBUILD WHITTLE AMORTIZE CONFOUND DECIMATE DEMOLISH DESOLATE DESTRUCT DISANNUL DISPLANT DISSOLVE FRACTURE FRAGMENT IMMOLATE INFRINGE MUTILATE OVERTURN PARALYZE SABOTAGE STRAMASH OBLITERATE
(— BARK) GIRDLE
(— BY FIRE) CONSUME
(— FERTILITY) EXHAUST
(— SELF-POSSESSION) ABASH
(— TOTALLY) SMASH SWEEP CUMBER SCUTTLE
(SUFF.) CLASE CLASIA CLAST(IC)

DESTROYED FLAT BLOWN KAPUT KAPUTT

DESTROYER CAN HUN DEATH TINCAN UNDOER VANDAL VICTOR FLIVVER STROYER UNMAKER WARSHIP APOLLYON DEVOURER SABOTEUR
(SUFF.) CIDAL CIDE PHTHORA

DESTROYING FELL
(PREF.) ANTI
(SUFF.) CLASTIC

DESTRUCTIBLE FRAIL

DESTRUCTION BAR END HEW BANE DOGS DOOM FIRE LOSS RACK RUIN STRY TALA CRUSH DEATH DECAY GRAVE HAVOC SMASH STRIP STROY WASTE WRACK DEFEAT DISMAY ENDING EXPIRY WONDER ABADDON CARNAGE EROSION UNDOING COLLAPSE DELETION DISPOSAL DOWNFALL EVERSION EXCISION SHAMBLES SMASHERY RUINATION
(— OF BONES) CARIES

(— OF ENVIRONMENT) ECOCIDE
(— OF SHIP'S PAPERS) SPOLIATION
(CELL —) LYSIS
(GRADUAL —) CORROSION
(MALICIOUS —) SABOTAGE
(UTTER —) PERDITION
(SUFF.) LYSE LYSIS LYST LYTE LYTIC LYZE
DESTRUCTIVE FELL FATAL DEADLY MORTAL BALEFUL BANEFUL DEATHLY EXITIAL FATEFUL HARMFUL HUMLIKE HURTFUL NOISOME NOXIOUS RUINOUS ANERETIC DEATHFUL EXITIOUS WASTEFUL WRACKFUL WREAKFUL ANAERETIC PESTILENT
DESUETUDE BREACH DISUSE
DESULTORY IDLE HASTY LOOSE ROVING AIMLESS CURSORY RAMBLING UNSTEADY WAVERING IRREGULAR
DETACH CUT DRAFT LOOSE SEVER LOOSEN UNBIND UNGLUE UNWORK CRACKLE DISJOIN DRAUGHT ISOLATE UNHINGE UNRIVET UNSEIZE ABSTRACT DISSOLVE DISUNITE PRESCIND SEPARATE UNFASTEN WITHDRAW
DETACHABLE SLIP
DETACHED CUT COLD FREE ALONE ALOOF DEADPAN INSULAR PORTATO SCIOLTO ABSTRACT CLINICAL DISCRETE ISOLATED OUTLYING SEPARATE SPICCATO UNBIASED
(PREF.) APH APO
DETACHMENT POINT POSSE ATARAXY OUTPOST ATARAXIA AVULSION OUTGUARD
(SUFF.) LYSE LYSIS LYST LYTE LYTIC LYZE
DETAIL CREW ITEM DODAD POINT ACCENT ASSIGN DOODAB DOODAD NICETY PARCEL RELATE RETAIL ACCOUNT APPOINT ARTICLE ITEMIZE MINUTIA NARRATE NULLING RESPECT SEVERAL SPECIFY INSTANCE REHEARSE SALIENCE PARTICULAR PARTICULARITY
(—S OF MAP) CULTURE
(CLIMACTIC —) BEAUTY
(PETTY —) CHICKEN
(PL.) DOPE FROUFROU FURNITURE
DETAILED NARROW PROLIX CLOSEUP SPECIAL PUNCTUAL TIRESOME
DETAIN BAIL HOLD KEEP STAY STOP CHECK DELAY TARRY ARREST ATHOLD COLLAR HINDER RETARD TAIGLE IMPRISON RESTRAIN WITHHOLD
DETECT SEE SPY ESPY FIND NOSE SPOT CATCH SCENT SENSE SMOKE TRACE DESCRY DIVINE EXPOSE REVEAL DEVELOP DISCERN UNCOVER DECIPHER DISCOVER OVERTAKE
DETECTIVE EYE TEC BULL BUSY DICK JACK TRAP PLANT SNOOP BEAGLE MOUSER RUNNER

SHADOW SHAMUS SLEUTH TAILER TRACER GUMSHOE SCENTER SNOOPER SPOTTER TRAILER DETECTOR FLATFOOT HAWKSHAW HOUSEMAN OPERATOR SHERLOCK OPERATIVE PINKERTON PLAINCLOTHESMAN
DETECTOR ASDIC COHERER REAGENT SFERICS SPHERICS
(LIE —) POLYGRAPH
DETENT DOG PALL PAWL CATCH CLICK RATCH PALLET RATCHET
DETENTION DELAY ARREST CAPTURE DETINUE JANKERS DETAINER STOPPAGE
DETER BAR FEAR BLOCK BLUFF CHECK DELAY DEHORT HINDER RETARD PREVENT TERRIFY DISSUADE PRECLUDE RESTRAIN
DETERGE PURGE CLEANSE MUNDIFY
DETERGENT SOAP SYNDET ABLUENT PURGING RHYPTIC SMECTIC SOLVENT CLEANSER GARDINOL
DETERIORATE GO FAIL GIVE SLIP SOUR WEAR DECAY ERODE SPILL WORST APPAIR APPERE DEBASE IMPAIR SICKEN WORSEN DECLINE PERVERT FIREFANG
DETERIORATING DECADENT
DETERIORATION DECAY IMPAIR MALADY DECLINE EROSION FAILURE DOLDRUMS PEJORATION
DETERMINABLE FIXED DEFINITE DEFINABLE GAUGEABLE
DETERMINANT CYTOGENE JACOBIAN CIRCULANT WRONSKIAN PLASTOGENE
DETERMINATE CERTAIN ORISTIC DEFINITE RESOLUTE RESOLVED SPECIFIC
DETERMINATION ACT HEST WILL ASSAY BLANK CAUSE ADVICE BEARING CONSULT PURPOSE RESOLVE ANALYSIS BACKBONE BIOASSAY DECISION DIVISION FIRMNESS FORECAST JUDGMENT JUDICIAL SENTENCE VOLITION
DETERMINATIVE FINAL FORMANT SHAPING LIMITING
(MOST —) DOMINANT
DETERMINE END FIT FIX GET RUN TEST WILL ASSAY AWARD JUDGE PITCH WIELD ADJUST ASSESS ASSIGN ASSOIL CHOOSE DECERN DECIDE DECREE DEFINE DESCRY DETECT DETERM DEVISE FIGURE GOVERN PERFIX SETTLE ACCOUNT ADJUDGE ANALYZE APPOINT ARRANGE COMPUTE DELIMIT DERAIGN DISPOSE RESOLVE TERMINE COGNOSCE CONCLUDE DISCOVER PINPOINT INFLUENCE
(— FINENESS) SET SETT
(— PATERNITY) AFFILIATE
(— RATE) ASSESS
(— ROOT) EXTRACT
DETERMINED SET BENT DERN FIRM GRIM BOUND GIVEN STOUT UPSET BITTER DOGGED GRITTY INTENT MULISH STURDY DECIDED

SETTLED DECISIVE FOREGONE PERVERSE RESOLUTE RESOLVED STUBBORN
DETERMINER GENE CHANCE PLASMAGENE
DETERMINIST JABARITE
DETEST DAMN HATE ABHOR CURSE LOATHE CONDEMN DESPISE DISLIKE DENOUNCE EXECRATE ABOMINATE
DETESTABLE FOUL HORRID ODIOUS BLASTED HATABLE HATEFUL HELLISH HIDEOUS ACCURSED DAMNABLE HATEABLE INFAMOUS INFERNAL MALEDICT ABHORRENT ABOMINABLE
DETESTATION ODIUM HATRED HORROR LOATHING ANTIPATHY
DETHRONE DEPOSE DIVEST UNCROWN
DETONATE FIRE BELCH BLAST SHOOT EXPLODE DETONIZE
DETONATION BLAST KNOCK AMBITUS PINGING PINKING
DETONATOR CAP FUSE FUZE FUSEE FUZEE SQUIB TORPEDO INITIATOR
DETOUR BYPASS CIRCUIT DIVERSION ROUNDABOUT
DETRACT TAKE DECRY DEDUCT DEFAME DETRAY DIVERT VILIFY ASPERSE TRADUCE BELITTLE DEROGATE DIMINISH DISTRACT MINIMIZE PROTRACT SUBTRACT WITHDRAW
(— FROM) IMPEDE
DETRACTION CALUMNY SCANDAL SLANDER ZOILISM
DETRIMENT COST HARM HURT LOSS SORE WOUND DAMAGE DAMNUM DENIAL INJURY BEATING EXPENSE JACTURE DISFAVOR MISCHIEF
DETRIMENTAL ADVERSE CAPITAL HARMFUL HURTFUL LOSSFUL DAMAGING INVIDIOUS PERNICIOUS PREJUDICIAL
(— TO HEALTH) HARD
DETRITUS OUTWASH SHINGLE SHEETWASH
DEUCALION (FATHER OF —) PROMETHEUS
(MOTHER OF —) CLYMENE
(SON OF —) HELLEN ORESTHEUS AMPHICTYON
(WIFE OF —) PYRRHA
DEUCE DIANTRE DICKENS
(WILD —) FREAK
DEUCEDLY BLAME BLAMED
DEUEL (SON OF —) ELIASAPH
DEUTERIUM DIPLOGEN
DEUTEROGAMY DIGAMY
DEUTOMALA LABIUM
DEUX JOURNEES, LES
(CHARACTER IN —) ARMAND MIKELI MAZARIN
(COMPOSER OF —) CHERUBINI
DEVA DEV DEWA SURA ANGEL DEITY
DEVASTATE EXILE HARRY HAVOC WASTE DEVAST RAVAGE ATOMIZE DESTROY PILLAGE PLUNDER SCOURGE DEMOLISH

DEVASTATED WASTE
DEVASTATING DEADLY LETHAL SAVAGE CRUSHING FEROCIOUS MURDEROUS
DEVASTATION RUIN SACK EXILE HAVOC WASTE WRACK HARASS RAVAGE SACCAGE SACKAGE SACCAGE
DEVELOP BUD RUN BOOM COOK FORM GROW STEM TILL ARISE BREAK BREED BUILD ERECT RIPEN SHOOT APPEAR BRANCH DETECT EVOLVE EXPAND FLOWER FULFIL MATURE REVEAL UNFOLD UNFURL BURGEON BURNISH EDUCATE ENLARGE EVOLUTE EXPOUND FULFILL UNCOVER DEVELOPE DISCLOSE DISCOVER DISVELOP ENGENDER GENERATE INCUBATE MANIFEST
(— A HEAD) HEART
(— BULB) BOTTOM
(— COLOR) AGE
(— CRACKS) ALLIGATOR
(— WELL) COTTON
DEVELOPABLE TORSE
DEVELOPED DEEP FORWARD
(— AFTER BIRTH) ACQUIRED
(FULLY —) BOLD ADULT FLORID FORMED SUMMED
(GREATLY —) ADVANCED
(IMPERFECTLY —) ABORTIVE
(INCOMPLETELY —) SEED
DEVELOPER ELON SOUP METOL ORTOL AMIDOL GLYCIN KACHIN QUINOL BUILDER GLYCINE RODINAL
DEVELOPING
(SUFF.) PLASTIC
DEVELOPMENT WAX DRIFT EVENT HATCH ESTATE GROWTH DESCENT GENESIS PROCESS STATURE BREEDING INCREASE ONTOGENY PEDIGREE UPGROWTH UPSPRING
(— OF SEX) DIOECISM
(FULL —) BLOW MATURITY
(HIGHEST —) BLOOM
(NORMAL —) APHANISIA
(SUBSEQUENT —) SEQUEL
(THEMATIC —) CONTINUITY
(UNEXPECTED —) ACCIDENT
(PREF.) PLASTO
(SUFF.) PLASIA PLASIS PLASM(A)(IA)(IC) PLAST(IC)(Y) PLASY
DEVI UMA KALI DURGA GAURI CHANDI SHAKTI BHAVANI BHOWANI HIMAVAT MAHADEVI HAIMAVATI
(FATHER OF —) HIMAVAT
(HUSBAND OF —) SHIVA
DEVIANT KINKY ABERRANT DIVERGENT
DEVIATE ERR RUN WRY YAW LEAN MISS VARY VEER BEVEL BREAK DRIFT LAPSE SHEER SPORT START STRAY WAIVE CHANGE DEPART DETOUR DIVERT RECEDE SQUINT SWERVE WANDER DECLINE DEFLECT DIGRESS DIVERGE INCLINE REFLECT ABERRANT ABERRATE DEROGATE

(**— FROM VERTICAL**) HADE
DEVIATING SKEW DEVIANT
DEVIOUS ERRATIC SINUOUS
ABERRANT INDIRECT
DEVIATION BOW YAW HELM JUMP
SKEW TURN DRIFT LAPSE QUIRK
SHEER TWIST ABRASH BATTER
CHANGE DETOUR FIGURE SPREAD
ANOMALY BRISURE LICENCE
LICENSE ACCURACY DRIFTAGE
LATITUDE SOLECISM VARIANCE
ABERRATION
(**— OF COLOR**) ABRASH
(**STANDARD —**) SIGMA
DEVICE (ALSO SEE INSTRUMENT)
ARM ART DIE DOG DOP EYE FAN
FLY FOB GAG GIN GUN HOG JIG
KEY MOP MOT PEN SET TIP TUP
WAY WIT ARCH BELL BOND
BOOM BUFF COIN COMB COUP
DARE DOPP DRAG DRIP FAKE
FIRE FLAG FORK FROG FUSE FUZE
GAGE GATE GOBO GRAB GRIP
GYRO HASP HAUL HEAD HECK
HORN IRIS IRON JACK KEEP KITE
LAMP LENS LOCK MOVE MULE
MUTE NAIL PACE PAGE PAWK
PLOW POKE PUMP REEL SEAL
SHOE SHUT SIGN SLAY SLEY SLUR
SNAP SPUD STOP STUD SUMP
TOOL TRAP TRIP VICE WEIR
WHIM WHIP WIND WING WOLF
ALARM APRON BADGE BALUN
BITCH BLOCK BREAK BRUSH
CHECK CLAMP CODER COVIN
CRAMP CROSS DODGE DRIER
DRIFT DRYER DUMMY FADER
FANCY FLAIL FLARE FLASH FLIRT
FLOAT GAUGE GLAND GORGE
GRIPE GUARD GUIDE GUILE HICKY
HINGE HOKUM IMAGE KAZOO
KEYER LADLE LASER LATCH LEVEL
MATCH OTTER PARER PLATE
PUNKA SCREW SHADE SHANK
SHIFT SIEVE SIGHT SIGIL SIREN
SIZER SKATE SLAVE SLICK SLIDE
SLING SONDE SPOOL SPOUT
SQUIB STAMP STILL STOOL STOVE
SWEEP SWELL TABLE TABUT
TAMER THIEF TIMER TORCH
TRUER TUNER UNION VERGE
AGRAFE AIRWAY ALARUM ALINER
ANCHOR ARREST BAILER BASTER
BEACON BEATER BECKET BEDDER
BEEPER BINDER BLOWER BOBBIN
BOOMER BRIDLE BROOCH BUCKLE
BUFFER BULLEN BUMPER
BUNGEE BUNTER BURNER
BUTTON CHARGE CIPHER COOKER
DASHER DECEIT DERAIL DESIGN
DIMMER DOFFER DOTTER DRIVER
DROGUE DUMPER EMBLEM
ENGINE EVENER FABRIC FALLER
FEEDER FENDER FILLER FILTER
FINDAL FINDER FORMER GADGET
GLAZER GOFFER GOGGLE GRADER
GRATER GRISLY GUIDER HANGER
HEATER HICKEY HOLDER HOOTER
INVENT JIGGER JOGGER KEEPER
KICKER LAYBOY LETOFF LIFTER
LOOPER MARKER MIRROR
MODULE MORTAR MOTHER
NAVAID NIPPLE NONIUS NOTION

PACKER PEELER PICKUP PLAYER
PLOUGH PORTER POTEYE PULLER
PUNKAH REROLL RINGER ROCKET
ROLLER ROOTER ROTULA ROUTER
SACKER SADDLE SAFETY SANDER
SCALER SCHEME SCREEN SEALER
SEEKER SENSOR SETTER SHAKER
SHIELD SIFTER SIGNAL SINKER
SIPPER SLEIGH SLICER SLIDER
SLIMER SLOPER SLUICE SOCKET
SOLION SORTER SPACER SPRING
STONER STYLUS SUCKER SWITCH
TACTIC TAGGER TAPPER TELLER
TEMPLE TESTER TILLER TRACER
TUCKER TUNNEL TURNER
WARMER WASHER WEANER
WEEDER WHEEZE WINDER
WINNOW WORKER ADAPTER
ADJUNCT AERATOR AGRAFFE
ALIGNER AUTOCUE BALANCE
BECKETT BIMETAL BIMORPH
BINDING BLEEDER BLEEPER
BLENDER BLINKER BLOCKER
BLOWOFF BLOWOUT BOOKEND
BOOSTER BREAKER CALTROP
CHIPPER CLAPPER COMPASS
DASHPOT DISHMOP DIVISOR
DRAWOFF DRESSER DRINKER
EARPICK EDUCTOR EJECTOR
EMPRESA EXCITER FACEBOW
FASHION FETLOCK FICELLE
FICTION FITMENT FIXTURE
FLASHER FLIPPER FLUSHER
FLYFLAP FRISKET GAUFFER
GIMMICK GLASSES GRAINER
GRENADE GRIDDLE GRILLER
GRINDER GRIPPER GRIZZLY
GROMMET GROOVER GROWLER
GUDGEON GUZZLER HATCHER
HELIDON IGNITER IMAGINE
IMPRESA IMPRESS INFUSER
INHALER IRONMAN KICKOFF
KNOTTER LIGHTER MACHINE
MUFFLER OOGRAPH PIGTAIL
PLOTTER POINTER PRESSER
RATCHET RATTLER RECEDER
REDUCER RELEASE ROASTER
ROSETTE SAMPLER SCALPER
SCANNER SCOGGAN SCRAPER
SCUPPER SERVANT SETBACK
SETOVER SETWORK SHACKLE
SHEDDER SHIFTER SHIPPER
SHOOFLY SHUTTER SHUTTLE
SINKBOX SKIMMER SLAPPER
SLEEVER SLINGER SLITTER
SLUDGER SLUSHER SNAPPER
SNIFFER SNIGGLE SNORKEL
SNUBBER SNUFFER SNUGGER
SONOVOX SOUNDER SPARGER
SPEEDER SPLICER SPOTTER
SPRAYER SQUEEZE STACKER
STAPLER STARTER STEMMER
STENTER STIRRER STOPPER
STRIKER STRIPER SUCTION
SWATTER SWEEPER SYRINGE
TAMBOUR TENDRIL TENSION
THEORIC THINNER TICKLER
TREADLE TRINDLE TRIPPER
TRIPPET TUMBLER TURNOUT
TWISTER WASHOUT WRINGER
ABSORBER ADJUSTER AQUASTAT
BACKSTAY BAROSTAT BIOMETER
BLOCKING BOOTJACK BRAILLER

BREATHER BRONTEUM BUSINESS
BUSYBODY CATAPULT CATHETER
COLOPHON CONTOISE COUPLING
CROTCHET CRYOTRON
DAMPENER DEHORNER DERAILER
DIFFUSER DIRECTOR DISPOSER
DOORSTOP DROPHEAD DUPLEXER
EARPHONE EPISEMON ESPRESSO
EXPLODER FAIRLEAD FAKEMENT
FASTENER FLASHGUN FLYBRUSH
FUELIZER GASCHECK GATHERER
GIMCRACK GUNSTICK GYROSTAT
HALLMARK HANDTRAP
HEADGEAR HOLDBACK IMPROVER
INKSTAND IRENICON IRISCOPE
ISOLATOR KNOCKOUT LAUNCHER
LEEBOARD LOXOCOSM LUNARIUM
MNEMONIC MOLITION NEOSTYLE
ODOGRAPH OVERLIFT OVERRIDE
PACIFIER PARAVANE PENWIPER
PINWHEEL PULSATOR PYROSTAT
QUADRANT QUENTISE REFILTER
REHEATER REPEATER RETARDER
REVERSER SCORCHER SCOTCHER
SCRAWLER SCUTCHER SELECTOR
SHRINKER SILENCER SILVERER
SINKBOAT SMOOTHER
SNOWPLOW SNOWSHOE
SPLITTER SPREADER SPROUTER
SQUEEGEE SQUEEZER STOPWORK
STRAINER STRINGER STRIPPER
STROPPER SURFACER SWEATBOX
TELETYPE TELLTALE TERMINAL
THROWOFF THROWOUT
TRAVELER TRAVERSE TRIANGLE
NEURISTOR PINSETTER
PROJECTOR STRATAGEM
MARTINGALE PERIPHERAL
PINSPOTTER ACCELERATOR
(**— FOR BENDING PIPE**) HICKEY
(**— FOR BORING WELLS**) TIGER
(**— FOR CONCENTRATING ORE**)
JIGGER
(**— FOR PUTTING IN GEAR**) STRIKER
(**— IN LOOM**) FEELER TEMPLE
(**— ON FLAG**) UNION
(**— PLACED OVER CHIMNEY**) JACK
(**— PROTECTING DENTIST'S HAND**)
THIMBLE
(**— THAT CONVERTS SIGNALS**)
MODEM
(**— TO LOCATE AN OBJECT**) LIDAR
(**— TO RETAIN COFFEE GROUNDS**)
GRECQUE
(**ARTIFICIAL —**) PROSTHESIS
(**CENTRIFUGAL —**) CYCLONE
(**CLEVER —**) COUP KNACK
(**COMPUTER —**) TERMINAL
ACCUMULATOR
(**DISTINGUISHING —**) SPOT
(**ELECTRICAL —**) OVONIC
(**GAMBLING —**) HOLDOUT
(**GLASSBLOWER'S —**) DUMMY
(**HAMPERING —**) HOBBLES
(**HEATING —**) ETNA
(**HERALDIC —S**) ARMS
(**LITERARY —**) FRAME
(**MAGICIAN'S —**) FAKE FEKE CRAFT
(**MIXING —**) CRUTCHER
(**POLISHING —**) WAGWAG
(**PYROTECHNIC —**) FOUNTAIN
(**RHETORICAL —**) ANAPHORA
(**ROTATION —**) TACH

(**SIGHTING —**) ALIDADE
(**SIGNALLING —**) CRICKET
(**SKILLFUL —**) ART
(**SPEECH —**) ITALICS
(**THEATRICAL —**) SLOAT SLOTE
(**TIMEKEEPING —**) HOROLOGE
(**TOROIDAL —**) TOKAMAK
(**WATER-RAISING —**) JANTU SWEEP
CHURRUS
(**WEAVING —**) BOAT ENGINERY
(**SUFF.**) STAT(IC)(ICS)
(**MUSICAL —**) INA INE
DEVIL DEL IMP BENG BHUT BOGY
DEIL HAZE MAHU NICK PUCK
QUED WOLF WOND ANNOY
BOBBY BOGEY BOGIE CHORT
CLOOT DEMON DEUCE EBLIS
FIEND HARRY SATAN SCRAT
SHEDU TAIPO TEASE AMAMON
BELIAL DAEMON DIABLE DIABLO
HORNIE NICKIE PESTER RAGMAN
SORROW THURSE AMAIMON
ANHANGA CLOOTIE DIANTRE
DICKENS GREMLIN LUCIFER
MAHOUND RUFFIAN SERPENT
SHAITAN TORMENT WARLOCK
WENDIGO WINDIGO APOLLYON
BAALPEOR BEELPEOR BELFAGOR
CAGNAZZO CURUPIRA DEVILING
DEVILKIN DIABOLUS MEPHISTO
MISCHIEF OBIDICUT PLOTCOCK
WIRRICOW WORRICOW
WORRYCOW
(**BLUE —S**) MARE
(**PREF.**) DIABOL(O)
DEVILFISH RAY MANTA
DEVILISH DARING DEUCED DEVILY
RAKISH WICKED DEMONIC
EXTREME FIENDLY HELLISH
INHUMAN SATANIC DEMONIAC
DIABOLIC FIENDISH INFERNAL
SATURNINE
DEVILISHLY DEUCED DEUCEDLY
DEVIL'S CLUB FATSIA
DEVIL'S COACHHORSE DARDAOL
DEVIL'S DISCIPLE (AUTHOR OF —)
SHAW
(**CHARACTER IN —**) DICK ESSIE
JUDITH DUDGEON ANDERSON
BURGOYNE
DEVIL'S-MILK WARTWEED
WARTWORT
DEVIL'S-TREE DITA
DEVIOUS DEEP ERRING LOUCHE
ROVING SHIFTY SUBTLE TRICKY
OBLIQUE PLAITED VAGRANT
WINDING HAVERING INDIRECT
RAMBLING SCHEMING TORTUOUS
AMBAGIOUS MEALYMOUTHED
DEVISE AIM CAST COOK FIND GIVE
PLAN PLOT WARP WILL ARRAY
FANCY FRAME FUDGE IMAGE
LEAVE SHAPE WEAVE ADVISE
CONVEY DECOCT DESIGN DEVICE
DIVIDE DIVINE INVENT SCHEME
AGITATE APPOINT ARRANGE
BETHINK COMMENT COMPASS
CONCERT CONCOCT CONSULT
IMAGINE PREPARE PROJECT
BEQUEATH CONTRIVE
DEVISER FINDER ARTIFICER
DEVISING DEVICE DEVISAL
FORGERY

DEVITALIZE DULL DEADEN
DEVITALIZED DEGENERATE
DEVITRIFIED AMBITTY
DEVOID FREE VAIN VOID EMPTY
BARREN EXPERT VACANT
SINCERE WANTING DESOLATE
(— OF) BOUT EMPTY
(— OF HELP) AIDLESS
(— OF KINDNESS) CRUEL
(— OF MERCY) BRUTAL
(— OF MIND) AMENTAL
(— OF VALUE) HOLLOW
DEVOLUTION DESCENT
DEVOLVE FALL PASS VEST RESULT
BLOSSOM SUCCEED OVERTURN
TRANSFER TRANSMIT
DEVOTE VOW ALLY AVOW DOOM
GIVE LEND TAKE TURN APPLY
DEVOW ADDICT ATTACH BESTOW
DEPUTE DESIGN DEVOVE DIRECT
EMPLOY INTEND RESIGN
ADDRESS APPOINT CONSIGN
DESTINE DEDICATE VENERATE
(— TIME) BOTHER
(— TO MISERY) ACCURSE
DEVOTED MAD HIGH TRUE LIEGE
LOYAL PIOUS ARDENT DEVOUT
DOOMED ENTIRE FERVID LOVING
OBLATE VOTARY VOTIVE
ADORING ARDUOUS JEALOUS
SERIOUS ZEALOUS ADDICTED
ATTACHED CONSTANT FAITHFUL
(— TO COUNTRY) PATRIOTIC
(— TO ENJOYMENT) APOLAUSTIC
(OVERLY —) SUPERSTITIOUS
DEVOTEE OAT FAN NUN DUFF
MONK YATI ADEPT JNANI ADDICT
BHAGAT BHAKTA DEVOTO
DEVOUT HEPCAT VOTARY
VOTEEN ZEALOT ADMIRER
AMATEUR BOPPIST BOPSTER
CINEAST FANATIC HEPSTER
HIPSTER SHAVIAN TARTUFE
AMOURIST BURNSIAN CABALIST
DEVOTARY FOLLOWER IBSENITE
PARTISAN PRIAPIAN SAVOYARD
SIMPLIST TARTUFFE VOTARESS
VOTARIST ALLIGATOR
AFICIONADO
DEVOTION CULT ZEAL ARDOR
PIETY BHAKTI NOVENA ANGELUS
ARABISM CULTISM LOYALTY
PIETISM FIDELITY IDOLATRY
JEALOUSY KAVVANAH
KAWWANAH RELIGION
NATIONALISM
(— OF ONESELF) VOW NARCISSISM
(— TO HUMAN WELFARE)
HUMANISM
(FERVENT —) ADORATION
(PARENTAL —) PROGENITY
(PL.) HOLIES
(SUFF.) LATER LATRIA LATROUS
LATRY
DEVOTIONAL PIOUS SOLEMN
DEVOUR EAT JAW FRET GULP
SWAP SWOP VOUR GORGE
RAVEN SCOFF WASTE AFRETE
ENGULF CONSUME ENGORGE
FRAUNCH SWALLOW
(— GREEDILY) SWILL
(SUFF.) VORA VORE VOROUS
DEVOURING PREY EATING GREEDY

VORANT EDACIOUS
DEVOUT GOOD HOLY WARM
FROOM GODLY GRACY PIOUS
HEARTY INWARD SOLEMN
CORDIAL DEVOTED GODLIKE
PITEOUS SAINTLY SINCERE
REVERENT PIETISTIC PRAYERFUL
RELIGIOUS PIETISTICAL
SANCTIMONIOUS
(NOT —) LINK
DEVOUTNESS PIETY DEVOTION
DEW DAG RIME BLOOM FROST
MOISTEN REFRESH MOISTURE
(— METER) PAGOSCOPE
(NIGHT —) SERENE
(PREF.) DROSO RORI
DEWBERRY MAYES
DEWDROP PEARL
DEWLAP JOWL GULLET JOLLOP
CHOLLER WATTLES
(— OF MALE MOOSE) BELL
DEWY DAMP RORY MOIST RORAL
RORIC RORID GENTLE ROSCID
DEXTERITY ART CHIC CRAFT
KNACK SKILL STROIL ABILITY
ADDRESS AGILITY APTNESS
CUNNING FINESSE SLEIGHT
APTITUDE DEFTNESS FACILITY
(— IN ARMS) CHIVALRY
DEXTEROUS APT FLY DEFT FEAT
HEND NEAT WISE ADEPT CANNY
CLEAN FEATY HANDY HAPPY
HENDE JIMMY QUICK READY
SMART TIGHT ADROIT ARTFUL
CLEVER DRAFTY CUNNING
OLEIGHT DEXTROUS HANDSOME
SKILLFUL SLEIGHTY
DEXTEROUSLY YARELY HANDILY
DEXTRAN GLUCOSAN
DEXTROROTATORY POSITIVE
DEXTRORSE EUTROPIC
DEXTROSE AME CEROLOSE
DHAK DAK PALAS PULAS
DHAVA BAKLI
DHOLE KOLSUN
DHOW BUGALA LATEEN SAMBUK
SAMBOUK LATEENER
DHRITARASHTRA (BROTHER OF —)
PANDU
(FATHER OF —) VYASA
VICHITRAVIRYA
(SON OF —) DURYODHANA
(WIFE OF —) GANDHARI
DHYANA JHANA
DIABASE OPHITE DOLERITE
THOLEITE
DIABOLICAL CRUEL WICKED
DEMONIC HELLISH INHUMAN
SATANIC VIOLENT DEMONIAC
DEVILISH DIABOLIC FIENDISH
INFERNAL
DIABOLISM SATANISM
DIACETATE ACETIN
DIACONATE DEACONRY
DIACONICON PARABEMA
DIACRITIC HACEK TILDE UMLAUT
MODIFIER
DIAD DIGONAL TWOFOLD
DIADEM TAJ MIND CROWN TIARA
ANADEM CIRCLE EMBLEM FILLET
CIRCUIT CORONET HEADBAND
DIAERESIS TREMA CESURA
CAESURA DIALYSIS

DIAGNOSE ANALYZE IDENTIFY
KNOWLEDGE
DIAGONAL BIAS SLANT SLASH
COUNTER SOLIDUS VIRGULE
BENDWISE DIAGONIC
DIAGONALLY BIAS ASLOPE
BENDWAYS BENDWISE
DIAGRAM MAP PLAN PLOT TREE
CARTE CHART EPURE GRAPH
DESIGN FIGURE SCHEMA SCHEME
SYMBOL YANTRA ISOGRAM
ISOTYPE SECTION VIAGRAM
PICTOGRAM PICTOGRAPH
DIAGRAMMATIC GRAPHIC
DIAGRAPH OE
DIAL NOB FACE KNOB WATCH
DIACLE JIGGER AZIMUTH
CRYSTAL DECLINER HOROLOGE
INCLINER RECLINER
DIAL BIRD DAYAL DHYAL
DIALECT (ALSO SEE LANGUAGE)
HO KA WU GEG GIZ KHA LAI SAC
TWI AMOY CANI CANT DRAA EFIK
EGBA EPIC GEEZ GHEG GONA
GUEG IOWA ITZA KORA MANX
NAMA NORN OGAM PALI SAUK
SHOR SOGA TALK TCHI TOSK
TUBA ALTAI ARGOT ASURI ATTIC
CONOY DORIC FANTI GHEEZ
GHESE HAKKA IDIOM IONIC
IOWAY IRAQI KANSA KAREL
KOINE LADIN LINGO MAZUR
MOPAN MUKRI NGOKO OGHAM
PARSI PUNIC SABIR SAXON SCOTS
SLANG TIGRE TSCHI VALVE
VOGUL ZMUDZ AEOLIC AGNEAN
ASANTE ATSINA AWADHI
BADAGA BRETON BROGUE
CANTON CREOLE DEBATE
DUNGAN FAEROE FANTEE
FURLAN GASCON GULLAH
GUTNIC HARARI HARAYA IBANAG
ISINAI ITAVES JARGON KABYLE
KANSAS KHAMIR KORANA KVITSH
LADAKI LADINO LAHULI LALLAN
LEDDEN LIBYAN PARSEE PATOIS
PATTER PICARD SANTEE SCOTCH
SHARRA SKAGIT SPEECH SUDANI
SWATOW SYRIAC SZEKEL TAVAST
TONGUE TUSCAN YANKEE
ZENAGA ACADIAN AEOLIAN
AMOYESE ANGLIAN ASHANTI
BHOTANI BHUTANI BUNDELI
CATALAN CHILULA CHUVASH
CLATSOP COCKNEY CORNISH
CUZCENO CYPRIOT FAYUMIC
FOOCHOW GEECHEE GHEGISH
GUTNISH JAIPURI KARAITE
KENTISH KITKSAN KONKANI
LADAKHI LALLAND LEONESE
LESBIAN MALTESE MARSIAN
MARWARI MERCIAN MIDLAND
MULTANI MUNDARI OLONETS
PANAYAN PRAKRIT SAHIDIC
SANROIL SHORTZY SOKOTRI
SPOKANE SQUAXON SWABIAN
SZEKLER TIGRINA VAUDOIS
WALLOON ABANEEME ACHMIMIC
AKHMIMIC ALGERINE ARCADIAN
ASSYRIAN BASILECT BAVARIAN
BHOJPURI BISCAYAN BOEOTIAN
BOHAIRIC CLAKAMAS COLVILLE
CORSICAN CYPRIOTE FALERIAN

FALISCAN FAROEISH FRANCIEN
FRIULIAN GARHWALI HARARESE
IZCATECO KANESIAN KARELIAN
KERMANJI KICKAPOO KINGWANA
LACANDON LANGUAGE
LAWLANTS MAGHREBI MAGHRIBI
MAITHILI MANDAEAN MANDARIN
MANISIAN MAZATECO MAZURIAN
MEMPHITE NABATEAN
NEENGATU PANAYANO PEKINESE
RABBINIC SALTEAUX SOULETIN
SOUTHERN TAUNGTHU TIGRINYA
TIRHUTIA TUNISIAN VENERIAN
VIENNESE NORTHUMBRIAN
(ENGLISH — IN LIVERPOOL) SCOUSE
(STRANGE —) GIBBERISH
(PL.) WU ANGLIAN
DIALECTIC PILPUL
DIALOGUE ION CRITO DIALOG
EPILOG PATTER PHAEDO
TIMAEUS COLLOQUY DUOLOGUE
EPILOGUE EXCHANGE PHAEDRUS
COLLOCUTION
(—S OF BUDDHA) SUTRA SUTTA
(COMIC —) LAZZO
DIAMETER BORE GAGE GEAR
MOOT GAUGE WIDTH MODULE
(— OF BULLET) CALIBER CALIBRE
(— OF PELVIS) CONJUGATA
(— OF PUPIL) APERTURE
(— OF WIRE) GAGE GAUGE
DIAMOND GEM ICE BORT LASK
PICK ROCK ROSE BAHIA BOORT
BORTZ DORJE FANCY FIELD
JAGER JEWEL LOZEN MELEE
POINT RHOMB RIVER SANCY
SPARK TABLE VAJRA ADAMAS
BOARTS CANARY CARBON
JAEGER LASQUE ORLOFF PENCIL
REGENT RONDEL SHINER TABLET
ADAMANT BRIOLET CARREAU
CRYSTAL FISHEYE INFIELD
LOZENGE PREMIER RHOMBUS
SPARKLE CORUNDUM KOHINOOR
RONDELLE SPARKLER BRIOLETTE
(— CUT TOO THIN) FISHEYE
(— MOLDER) DOP
(— STATE) DELAWARE
(— USED FOR ENGRAVING) SHARP
(BLACK —) CARBONADO
(FLAT —) LASQUE
(GLAZIER'S —) QUARREL
(IMITATION —) SCHLENTER
(INFERIOR GRADE OF —) FLAT
(PERFECT —) PARAGON
(PURE WHITE —) RIVER
(ROUGH —) BRAIT
(SINGLE —) SOLITAIRE
(TRANSPARENT —) CRYSTAL
(YELLOW —) CANARY
(PL.) MELANGE
DIAMOND BIRD PARDALOTE
DIAMORPHINE HEROIN
DIANA LUCINA TRIVIA ARTEMIS
(BROTHER OF —) APOLLO
(FATHER OF —) JUPITER
(MOTHER OF —) LATONA
DIANA MONKEY ROLOWAY
DIAPASON MONTRE DIAPASE
DIAPAUSE BLOCK
DIAPER FUR DIDY CLOUT DIDIE
NAPPY HIPPEN HIPPIN NAPKIN
NAPPIE DIAPERY

DIAPHANOUS CLEAR SHEER FRAGILE DIAPHANE VAPOROUS

DIAPHONY ORGANUM TRIPHONY

DIAPHORETIC BUCCO BUCHU BUCKU BORAGE DIAPNOIC HIDROTIC SUDATORY SASSAFRAS PILOCARPINE

DIAPHRAGM IRIS RIFF SLIT APRON PHREN SKIRT WAFER DECKER PLATEN MIDRIFF PHRAGMA SKIRTING TRAVERSE TYMPANUM (PREF.) PHREN(O)

DIAPHRAGMATIC PHRENIC

DIARRHEA LAX FLUX LASK GURRY RELAX SCOUR SPRUE PURGING SQUIRTS LIENTERY

DIARY LOG RECORD DAYBOOK DIURNAL JOURNAL REGISTER EPHEMERIS

DIASKEUAST EDITOR REVISER

DIASPORA GALUT GOLAH GALUTH

DIASPORE MIGRULE

DIASTASE MALT ENZYME AMYLASE

DIATOM BRITTLEWORT ASTERIONELLA

DIATOMITE TRIPOLI

DIATONIC ACHROMATIC

DIATRIBE SATIRE SCREED HARANGUE INVECTIVE

DIB DAP DIP DIBBLE DIBSTONE

DIBBLE DAP DIB DABBLE DIBBER KIPPIN TRIFLE DIBBLER KIPPEEN

DIBRI (SON OF —) SHELOMITH

DIBS COCKAL

DICAST HELIAST JURYMAN

DICE CHOP CUBE DEES BONES CRAPS FLATS LOWMEN REJECT CHECKER IVORIES
(— GAME) SET RAPHE MUMCHANCE
(— HAVING FOUR SPOTS) QUATRE
(FALSE —) GOAD TATS GOURD GRAVIERS SQUARIER STOPDICE
(HIGHEST THROW AT —) APHRODITE
(LOADED —) TOPS DOCTOR
(LOWEST THROW AT —) AMBSACE
(PAIRED NUMBERS AT —) DUPLET DOUBLETS
(2, 3, OR 12 ON 1ST —) MISSOUT
(PREF.) ASTRAGAL(O)

DICE PLAYER THROWSTER

DICER HAT DERBY GAMBLER GRAINER

DICERION DYKER

DICHASIAL BIPAROUS

DICHLORVOS DDVP

DICHONDRA LAWNLEAF

DICHOTOMY DUALITY

DICHROITE IOLITE

DICKENS HECK DEUCE

DICKER ICRE SWAP DAKER BARTER HAGGLE BARGAIN CHAFFER EXCHANGE

DICKEY POOP WEAK DICKY FRONT GILET SHAKY DONKEY RUMBLE VESTEE HADDOCK PLASTRON

DICKIE SHAM DICKY FRONT SQUARE TUCKER STARCHER

DICLINOUS IMPERFECT

DICTATE SAW SAY DITE TELL UTTER WRITE DECREE DICTUM ENJOIN IMPOSE INDITE OCTROY ORDAIN IMPOSE SCHOOL COMMAND DELIVER REQUIRE SUGGEST WARRANT DICTAMEN PRESCRIBE

DICTATION DICTAMEN

DICTATOR CHAM CZAR DUCE TSAR CAESAR PENDRAGON

DICTATORIAL BOSSY LORDLY CZARIST POMPOUS TSARIST ARROGANT DOGMATIC ORACULAR POSITIVE ARBITRARY MAGISTERIAL

DICTION STYLE TERMS PHRASE IMAGERY LANGUAGE PARLANCE VERBIAGE
(BAD —) CACOLOGY
(SUFF.) ESE

DICTIONARY GRADUS ALVEARY CALEPIN LEXICON GLOSSARY WORDBOOK THESAURUS
(PREF.) LEXICO

DICTUM SAY ADAGE AXIOM EDICT DECREE SAYING DICTATE EFFATUM OPINION APOTHEGM PRINCIPLE STATEMENT
(— NOT) DIDNA DIDNT

DIDACTIC DRY PREACHY SERMONIC

DIDO ANTIC CAPER TRICK
(BROTHER OF —) PYGMALION
(FATHER OF —) BELUS
(HUSBAND OF —) SICHAEUS
(LOVER OF —) AENEAS

DIDO AND AENEAS (CHARACTER IN —) DIDO AENEAS BELINDA MERCURY
(COMPOSER OF —) PURCELL

DIE GO BED DEE DOD END HOB HUB PIP ROT SIX TAT BOSS COIN CONK CUBE DADO DEAD DICE DROP EXIT FADE FAIL FALL FINE FIVE FLIT KICK MARK MOLD PART PASS PIKE PILE SEAL TATT TINE WANE CROAK FORCE FUDGE GHOST IVORY NAPOO PATAY PRINT PUNCH QUAIL SHAPE SNUFF SOUGH SPILL STALL STAMP STOCK SWELT CHANCE DEMISE DEPART DOCTOR EXPIRE FAMISH FINISH FORCER FORMER FULLAM MATRIX MULLAR PATRIX PERISH ROLLER STARVE STRIKE TORFEL TORFLE TRANCE VANISH WITHER BLOCKER DECEASE SUCCUMB TESSERA INTAGLIO LANGUISH MISCARRY PUNCHEON TRESPASS TRUSSELL
(— AWAY) FAIL SWOON
(— BEFORE) PREDECEASE
(— BY HANGING) SWING
(— DOWN) FLIT SINK ABATE
(— FOR DRAWING WIRE) WHIRTLE WHORTLE
(— FOR MAKING DRAINPIPE) DOD
(— FOR MOLDING BRICK) KICK
(— FROM HUNGER) AFFAMISH
(— OF COLD) STARVE
(— OF PEDESTAL) SOLIDUM
(— WITH 4 SPOTS) QUATRE
(— WITH 6 SPOTS) CISE SICE SISE SIZE
(COINING —) SICCA

(FRAUDULENT —) FULHAM FULLAM FULLOM
(HOLLOW —) GOURD
(IMPROPER —) FLAT
(LOADED —) TAT DOCTOR FULHAM HIGHMAN LANGRET
(LOWER —) BED
(REVOLVING —) DREIDEL

DIEBACK STAGHEAD EXANTHEMA

DIED DYDE OBIIT WRATE

DIEHARD TORY BLIMP

DIESIS FEINT

DIET BANT FARE FAST FOOD SEIM SEYM BOARD HOFTAG REDUCE SEIMAS VIANDS VICTUS DIETINE LANDTAG REGIMEN RIKSDAG CONGRESS KREISTAG VOLKSTAG

DIETARY (— LAWS) KASHRUTH

DIETETICS SITOLOGY

DIETHER APIOL APIOLE DIOXANE

DIETING BANTING

DIFFER VARY RECEDE SQUARE COMPARE DISCORD DISSENT DIVERGE DISAGREE

DIFFERENCE SHED CHASM CLASH FAVOR BREACH CHANGE DIFFER ANOMALY BRISURE DISCORD DISPUTE QUALITY VARIETY DISTANCE DIVISION IMPARITY VARIANCE
(— IN ELEVATION) HEAD
(— IN EXCHANGE) AGIO
(— IN LATITUDE) SOUTHING
(— IN LONGITUDE) EASTING
(— IN PITCH) COMMA INTERVAL
(— IN PRESSURE) DRAFT DRAUGHT
(— IN WIDTH) BILGE
(— OF OPINION) DISSENT ARGUMENT
(— OF VESSEL'S DRAFT) DRAG
(ANGULAR —) EXPLEMENT
(GRADED —) GRADIENT
(MINUTE —) SHADE
(PRICE —) BASIS
(SMALL —) HAIRLINE

DIFFERENT FAR MANY SERE FRESH OTHER PARTY DIVERS SCREWY SUNDRY UNLIKE ANOTHER DISTANT DIVERSE SEVERAL STRANGE UNALIKE UNUSUAL VARIANT VARIOUS CONTRARY DISTINCT MANIFOLD SEPARATE OTHERWISE OTHERGUESS NONIDENTICAL
(PREF.) DIVERSI HETER(O)

DIFFERENTIA MARK LIMIT

DIFFERENTIAL FLUXION

DIFFERENTIATE APLITE DIFFER DISCERN HAPLITE CONTRAST SPECIATE

DIFFERENTIATION ANABOLY DEVIATION DICHOTOMY
(PREF.) ALL(O)

DIFFERING DIVERSE SINGULAR DIVERGENT

DIFFICULT ILL HARD WICK CRAMP CRANK GREAT HEAVY SPINY STEEP STIFF AUGEAN CRABBY CRANKY KNOTTY SEVERE STICKY STRAIT STRONG TICKLE TRAPPY UNEASY UNEATH UPHILL WENETH WICKED ARDUOUS AWKWARD BRITTLE COMPLEX CRABBED DIFFUSE LABORED NERVOUS OBSCURE PAINFUL PERPLEX PRACTIC SERIOUS STICKLE UNNETHE ABSTRACT CUMBROUS FIENDISH PUZZLING SCABROUS STRUGGLE STUBBORN TICKLISH
(— TO BEAR) BITTER
(— TO COMPREHEND) STRANGE
(— TO FOLLOW) DIRTY
(— TO GRASP) FUGITIVE
(— TO HANDLE) SPINOUS
(— TO MANAGE) SURLY STURDY
(— TO OBTAIN) CLOSE
(— TO PLEASE) CURIOUS
(— TO RAISE) DORTY
(— TO SATISFY) CHOOSY CHOOSEY
(— TO UNDERSTAND) DEEP HIGH SUBTLE CRABBED ABSTRACT ABSTRUSE ESOTERIC
(PREF.) DYS MOGI

DIFFICULTY ADO BAR BOX ILL JAM RUB BUMP CLOG COIL HEAT JAMB KNOT LOCK NODE PAIN PINE SNAG SORE WERE CHECK DOUBT GRIEF NODUS PRESS RIGOR STAND STOUR TRADE APORIA BOGGLE BUNKER HABBLE HOBBLE PLIGHT PLUNGE RUBBER SCRAPE STRAIT TIFTER BARRIER DICKENS GORDIAN PITFALL PROBLEM SQUEEZE ASPERITY DISTRESS HARDNESS HARDSHIP OBSTACLE SEVERITY STRUGGLE
(UNEXPECTED —) SNAG
(WITH —) SCARCELY
(PREF.) **(WITH —)** DYS MOGI

DIFFIDENCE DOUBT MODESTY RESERVE SHYNESS DISTRUST HUMILITY TIMIDITY

DIFFIDENT SHY BLATE CHARY MODEST BACKWARD RESERVED RETIRING SHEEPISH

DIFFUSE FULL SHED BLEED EXUDE LARGE STREW WORDY DEFUSE DERIVE DILATE DIVIDE EXPAND EXTEND OSMOSE PROLIX SPREAD SPRING COPIOUS DIALYSE DIALYZE DIFFUND PERFUSE PERPLEX PERVADE PUBLISH RADIATE SCATTER SPARKLE SPRAWLY SPRENGE SUFFUSE VERBOSE CONFUSED DIFFUSED DIOSMOSE DISPERSE PATULENT PATULOUS SPRANGLE
(NOT —) STRICT COMPACT

DIFFUSION SPREAD OSMOSIS BLEEDING DEFUSION

DIG HOE JOB NIP CLAW DIKE DYKE GIRD GORE GRUB HOWK MINE MOOT PICK PION POKE PROD ROOT SINK SLAM SMUG SPIT SPUD SUMP SWOT DELVE DITCH DWELL GAULT GRAFT GRAVE LODGE POACH PROBE SNOUT SPADE START STOCK BURROW DREDGE EXHUME GRAVEL HOLLOW PLUNGE SHOVEL THRUST TUNNEL BEDELVE COSTEAN SPUDDLE UNEARTH EXCAVATE
(— OUT) SCOOP STUMP EXHUME
(— OUT CREVICES) FOSSICK

(— PEAT) SHEUGH
(— POTATOES) LIFT
(— TRENCHES) GRIP COSTEAN COSTEEN
(— UP) CAST GRUB STUB SPADE STOCK EXHUME UPGRAVE DISINTER
(— WITH NAILS) SCRAPE
(— WITH SNOUT) GROUT
(— WITH STICK) CROW
DIGAMMA VAU
DIGEST COCT CODE DEFY ENDEW ENDUE INDUE RIPEN CODIFY DECOCT DOCKET MATURE SEETHE CONCOCT EPITOME PANDECT SUMMARY CONDENSE SYLLABUS
DIGESTION PEPSIS COCTION EUPEPSY EUPEPSIA
(SUFF.) PEPSIA PEPTIC
DIGESTIVE PEPSIN PEPTIC DIGERENT
DIGGER DIG PAL PLOW MINER BANKER BILDAR DRUDGE PLOUGH COMRADE PEATMAN PIONEER PLODDER TRENCHER
(POST HOLE —) LOY
DIGGING DIG DIKAGE DYKAGE STRIPPING
DIGHT DAB RUB DECK DINK DITE WIPE ADORN DICHT DRESS EQUIP ORDER RAISE TREAT MANAGE REPAIR WINNOW APPOINT CONSIGN PERFORM PREPARE
DIGIT TOE UNIT DOIGT POINT THUMB DACTYL FIGURE FINGER HALLUX MEDIUS NUMBER DEWCLAW DIGITAL
(BINARY —) BIT BINIT
(EXTRA —) PREPOLLEX
(PREF.) DACTYL(O) DACTYLIO
(SUFF.) DACTYLIA DACTYLOUS
DIGITAL KEY MANUAL
DIGITATE DIGITAL FINGERED
DIGNIFIED GRAND LOFTY MANLY NOBLE STAID AUGUST LORDLY SEDATE SOLEMN COURTLY EXALTED STATELY TOGATED ELEVATED ENNOBLED MAJESTIC
DIGNIFY DUB ADORN CROWN EXALT GRACE HONOR RAISE ELEVATE ENNOBLE PROMOTE
DIGNITARY DON WIG BABA RAJA CANON RAJAH PRIEST SHERIF DIGNITY HUTUKTU PRELATE PROVOST SHEREEF ALDERMAN HUTUKHTU VESTIARY
DIGNITY DOG CHIC FACE RANK BENCH DINES HONOR IZZAT PRIDE STATE AFFAIR BARONY LAUREL REPOSE BARONRY BEARING DECORUM DUKEDOM EARLDOM FITNESS GRAVITY MAJESTY SHAHDOM STATION WORSHIP CHIVALRY EARLSHIP GRANDEUR NOBILITY
(— OF BISHOP) LAWN
(ACCIDENTAL —) JOY HAYZ
(PAPAL —) TIARA
(SUFF.) DOM SHIP
DIGRAPH CH OE PH RH TH RRH BIGRAM LIGATURE DIPHTHONG
DIGRESS VEER EXCUR DIVERT

SWERVE WANDER DEVIATE DIVERGE EXCURSE DISGRESS DIVAGATE
DIGRESSION ASIDE VAGARY DIGRESS ECBASIS EPISODE EXCURSE PASSAGE TANGENT DISGRESS EXCURSUS SIDESLIP PARENTHESIS
(RHETORICAL —) ECBOLE
DIKE BAR RIB BANK BUND DICE DICK DYKE GALL POND POOL DIGUE DITCH LEVEE CAUSEY CRADGE CHANNEL DIKELET POWDIKE ABOIDEAU CAUSEWAY ESTACADE SPREADER
DIKER COWAN COWEN
DIKETONE BENZIL BIACETYL DIMEDONE
DIKLAH (FATHER OF —) JOKTAN
DILACTONE LACTIDE ANEMONIN
DILAPIDATE DESTROY
DILAPIDATED BAD BEATEN CREAKY RAGGED RUINED SHABBY WRECKY CRAICHY CREACHY RUINOUS DESOLATE TATTERED WOBEGONE
DILAPIDATION RUIN DECAY DECREPITY DISREPAIR
DILATATION BULB SINUS VARIX JARBOT SPREAD AMPULLA ECTASIA ECTASIS ANEURISM DILATION MYDRIASIS
(SUFF.) ECTASIA ECTASIS
DILATE TENT DELAY PLUMP SWELL WIDEN RELATE EXPAND EXTEND SPREAD AMPLIFY BROADEN DESCANT DIFFUSE DISTEND ENLARGE INFLATE PROLONG STRETCH DISPERSE INCREASE LENGTHEN PROTRACT DISCOURSE
DILATING
(SUFF.) EURYSIS
DILATOR DIOPTER DIOPTRA DIOPTRY DIVULSOR SPECULUM
DILATORY LATE SLOW SLACK SPARE TARDY FABIAN REMISS DILATOR LAGGARD LATREDE TEDIOUS BACKWARD DELAYING INACTIVE SLUGGISH
DILEMMA FIX FORK LOCK NODE BRIKE CHOICE PLUNGE CORNUTE SNIFTER JEOPARDY QUANDARY
DILETTANTE LOVER SUNDAY ADMIRER AMATEUR DABBLER DABSTER ESTHETE AESTHETE
DILIGENCE HIE CARE HEED DILLY EFFORT CAUTION HORNING BUSINESS INDUSTRY SEDULITY ASSIDUITY
DILIGENT BUSY HARD TIDY ACTIVE EIDENT ITHAND STEADY CAREFUL EARNEST HEEDFUL OPEROSE PAINFUL PATIENT WORKFUL CAUTIOUS CONSTANT LABOROUS SEDULOUS STUDIOUS
DILL ANET CALM SOYA ANISE UMBEL PICKLE SOOTHE DILLWEED
DILLYDALLY LAG TOY LOAF DELAY DILLY STALL LOITER TRIFLE
DILOGY ECHO
DILUENT CARRIER VEHICLE
DILUTE CUT BREW FUSE LEAN THIN WEAK ALLAY BLUNT DELAY

WATER RAREFY REDUCE WEAKEN WHITISH DIMINISH LENGTHEN WATERISH
(— LIQUOR) BREW SPLIT
(— WINE) GALLIZE
(VERY —) SMALL
DILUTED WASHY DILUTE REMISS
DILUTING ATTENUANT
DIM DIP WAN BLUR DARK DULL FADE GRAY HAZY MIST PALE PALL VEIL BEDIM BLEAK BLEAR BLIND DUSKY DUSTY FAINT FOGGY MISTY STAIN UNLIT BEMIST BLEARY CLOUDY DARKEN DASWEN DIMPSY GLOOMY OBTUSE SHADOW TWILIT BECLOUD DARKISH DISLIMN ECLIPSE OBSCURE OPACATE SHADOWY TARNISH DARKLING OVERCAST CALIGINOUS CREPUSCULAR
(NOT —) FRESH
DIME HOG HOGG DISME TENPENCE TENPENNY
(HALF —) PICAYUNE
DIMEDON METHONE
DIMENHYDRINATE DRAMAMINE
DIMENSION BODY BULK SIZE SCOPE WIDTH ASSIZE DEGREE EXTENT HEIGHT LENGTH MOISON BREADTH PROPORTION MEASUREMENT
(COLOR —) CHROMA
(TYPE —) EM EN
(PL.) GAGE SIZE GAUGE GIRTH EXTENT SIDING MEASURE
DIMENSIONS
(PREF.) (THREE —) STERE(O)
DIMER (— IN EXCITED STATE) EXCIMER
DIMIDIATE HALVED
DIMINISH GO CUT EBB SAP BATE BURN CHOP DAMP DROP EASE FADE FAIL FINE FRET MELT PARE PINK SINK WANE WEAR ABATE ALLAY BREAK CLOSE DRAFT DWARF ELIDE ERODE LOWER MINCE PETER SLACK SMALL TAPER DAMPEN DEBATE DECOCT DEDUCT DILUTE IMPAIR LESSEN MINISH REBATE REDUCE SLOUGH VANISH WITHER ABRIDGE ASSUAGE CORRODE CURTAIL DEGRADE DEPLETE DEPRESS DETRACT DIMINUE DRAUGHT DWINDLE FRITTER INHIBIT QUALIFY REFRACT RELIEVE TARNISH ADMINISH AMOINDER CONDENSE DECREASE DIMINUTE DISCOUNT MINORATE MITIGATE MODERATE RETRENCH
(— FRONT) PLOY
DIMINISHED SLACK ABATED GRAYED DIMINUTE
DIMINISHING TAPER CRITICAL FLAGGING
(— IN LOUDNESS) CALANDO
DIMINUTION FALL WASTE RABATE DECREASE PERDITION
DIMINUTIVE TOY WEE BABY TINY BANTY DWARF PETTY RUNTY SMALL YOUNG BANTAM LITTLE MIDGET PETITE POCKET MANIKIN

MIDGETY MINIKIN SHRIMPY EXIGUOUS
(— OF BAR) SCARP CLOSET SCARPE
(SUFF.) CLE CULE CULUS EL ET ETTE KIN OCK SY ULA ULE
DIMLY DULLY DARKLY FEEBLY SHADOWY
DIMMED BLEARY CLOUDY GRAYED BLEARED
DIMMING GRAYOUT
DIMNESS DIM HAZE MIST SLUR GLOOM CALIGO DARKNESS
DIMPLE DOKE AHMADI AHMEDI RIPPLE GELASIN FOSSETTE
DIM-SIGHTED PURBLIND
DIN BUM DUN REEL RERD RIOT UTIS ALARM BABEL BRUIT CHIME CHIRM CLANG DEAVE DEEVE FRUSH NOISE RERDE ALARUM BELDER CLAMOR FRAGOR HUBBUB RACKET RANDAN RATTLE STEVEN TUMULT UPROAR CLANGOR CLATTER DISCORD TURMOIL DINGDONG TINTAMAR
DINAH (BROTHER OF —) LEVI SIMEON
(FATHER OF —) JACOB
(MOTHER OF —) LEAH
DINAR DENARE MARAVEDI
DINARZADE (SISTER OF —) SCHEHERAZADE
DINDLE RING QUIVER THRILL TINGLE TINKLE TREMOR STAGGER VIBRATE
DINE EAT SUP FARE FEAST REGALE
DINER EPICURE GOURMAND
DING DIN BEAT DANG DASH KICK PUSH RING WHIP CLANG DRIVE EXCEL FLING KNOCK PITCH POUND PUNCH THUMP STROKE THRASH THRUST
DINGE DENT DINT BATTER BRUISE TARNISH
DINGHY PRAM SKIFF DINGEY ROWBOAT SHALLOP SNOWBIRD
DINGLE DEN DALE DELL GLEN VALE DIMBLE DUMBLE HOLLOW VALLEY
DINGMAN BUMPER
DINGO WARRAGAL WARRIGAL
DINGUS GADGET DOOHICKEY
DINGY DUN DARK BLACK DIRTY DUSKY GRIMY OURIE SMOKY DINGHY FUSCOUS SUBFUSC SMIRCHED
DINING CENATION
(PREF.) DEIPNO
DINING ROOM TRICLINIUM
DINKA JANGHEY
DINNER DINE HALL KALE MEAL MEAT NOON BEANO FEAST DINING REPAST BANQUET PUCHERO FUNCTION
(CEREMONIAL —) SEDER
(PERTAINING TO —) PRANDIAL
(PREF.) DEIPNO
DINOSAUR DIAPSID SAURIAN DUCKBILL NODOSAUR SAUROPOD TROODONT ORNITHISCHIAN
DINT BEAT BLOW DENT DUNT NICK CLOUR DELVE DINGE FORCE

NOTCH ONSET POWER PRESS
SHOCK ATTACK CHANCE EFFORT
STRIKE STROKE IMPRINT
EFFICACY STRIKING
DIOCESAN EPISCOPAL
DIOCESE SEE EPARCHY DISTRICT
BISHOPRIC
DIODE KENOTRON
(— THAT EMITS LIGHT) LED
(TYPE OF —) ZENER
DIOLEFIN DIENE ALLENE
HEXADIENE
DIOMEDES (FATHER OF —) MARS
TYDEUS
(MOTHER OF —) CYRENE DEIPYLE
(WIFE OF —) AEGIALE
DION (DAUGHTER OF —) EUPHRASIA
(FATHER OF —) HIPPARINUS
(SISTER OF —) ARISTOMACHE
(SLAYER OF —) CALLIPPUS
(TEACHER OF —) PLATO
(WIFE OF —) ARETE
DIONYSUS BACCHUS BROMIOS
BROMIUS LENAEUS LIKNITES
DIONYZA (HUSBAND OF —) CLEON
DIOPSIDE VIOLAN ALALITE
PYROXENE
DIORITE CORSITE DIABASE
ORNOITE APPINITE TONALITE
DIOSCURI ALCIS ANACES ANAKES
CASTORES
DIOXIDE SILICA BINOXIDE
DIP DAP DIB DOP SOP BAIL DROP
DUCK DUNK LADE LAVE SINK
SOAK BATHE DELVE LADLE
LOWER MERSE PITCH SCOOP
SLOPE SOUSE SWOOP TAINT
CANDLE HOLLOW PLUNGE
BAPTIZE DECLINE IMMERGE
IMMERSE INCLINE MOISTEN
DIPSTICK SUBMERGE GUACAMOLE
(— AND THROW) BAIL BALE
(— IN DANCING) CORTE
(— INTO) SAMPLE
(— OUT) KEACH
DIPENTENE CINENE CAJUPUTENE
DIPHTHONG BIVOCAL
DIPHTHONGIZED BROKEN
DIPLOIDIZE SPERMATIZE
DIPLOMA SANAD DEGREE
SUNNUD CHARTER CODICIL
PARCHMENT SHEEPSKIN
DIPLOMACY TACT POLICE TREATY
DIPLOMAT DEAN ENVOY CONSUL
ATTACHE MINISTER
DIPLOMATIC SUAVE FECIAL
FETIAL
DIPLOPIA POLYOBA AMBIOPIA
DIPNOAN DIPNOID MUDFISH
DIPODY METER METRE DIIAMB
SYZYGY
DIPPER BAIL GAWN PIET PLOW
GOURD HANDY LADLE SCOOP
SPOON BUCKET DUNKER PIGGIN
PLOUGH TUNKER DUNKARD
PICKLER CALABASH
(ASTRONOMICAL —) WAGON
WAGGON
DIPPING
(SUFF.) CLINIC CLINOUS
DIPSOMANIA ENOMANIA
POTOMANIA
DIPTERAN SYRPHID

DIPTEROCARP GURJUN
DIPTERON DIPTER
DIPTEROUS BIALATE
DIRDUM BLOW BLAME DURDUM
OUTCRY REBUKE TUMULT
UPROAR SCOLDING
DIRE DERN EVIL FELL AWFUL
FATAL DEADLY DISMAL DREARY
FUNEST TRAGIC WOEFUL
DIREFUL DOLEFUL DRASTIC
FEARFUL DREADFUL FUNESTAL
HORRIBLE TERRIBLE ULTIMATE
DIRECT AIM BID CON KEN SAY SET
WIS AGYE AIRT BAIN BEAM BEND
BOSS CAST DEAD EDIT EVEN
FLAT FULL GAIN HEAD HELM
HOLD LEAD NEAR NIGH OPEN
REIN SEND SOON SWAY TELL
TURN WAFT WEND WILL WISE
AIRTH APPLY AREAD AREED
BLANK BOUND BURLY COACH
DRESS ETTLE FLUSH FRAME
FRANK GUIDA GUIDE HIGHT
INDEX LEVEL ORDER PLUMP
POINT REFER RIGHT SPEED STEER
TEACH TRAIN UTTER WEISE
WRITE ADVERT ARRECT CUSTOS
DEVOTE ENJOIN ENSIGN FASTEN
GOVERN GRAITH HANDLE
HOMELY HONEST IMPART INDITE
INFORM INTEND LINEAL MANAGE
MASTER MOSTRA REFORM
SQUARE STEADY STRECK TEMPER
WITTER ADDRESS APPOINT
COMMAND CONDUCT CONTROL
CONVERT DEICTIC DESTINE
EXECUTE EXPRESS FRONTAL
GENERAL INSTANT MARSHAL
OFFICER PRESIDE SPADISH
ABSOLUTE ADMONISH CONVERSE
DEDICATE DIRECTOR HOMESPUN
IMMEDIAL INSTRUCT INTIMATE
MANUDUCE MANUDUCT
MINISTER OUTRIGHT REGULATE
STRAIGHT
(— AGAINST) LAUNCH
(— ATTENTION) ATTEND
(— BLOW) MARK
(— DOGS) BLOW
(— FALL OF TREE) GUN
(— HELMSMAN) CON CONN
(— HORSE) HUP
(— ITSELF) TENT
(— ONE'S COURSE) HIT
(— PROCEEDINGS) PRESIDE
(— SECRETLY) STEAL
(— SIDEWAYS) SKLENT
(— TO GO) ADDRESS
(— UPWARD) MOUNT
DIRECTED FAST COMPULSORY
(— FORWARD) ANTRORSE
(— TOWARD GOAL) HORMIC
(— UPWARD) ERECT
DIRECTING AIM LEADING
PRINCIPAL
DIRECTION (ALSO SEE MUSICAL
DIRECTION) AIM RUN WAY AIRT
BENT CARE DUCT EAST EGIS
GATE HAND LEFT PART ROAD
RULE WEST WORD YARD AEGIS
ANGLE COAST DRIFT EAVER
KIBLA NORTH ORDER PARTY
POINT QIBLA RANGE ROUTE

SENSE SOUTH TENOR TREND
ASPECT COURSE DESIGN
ADDRESS BEARING BIDDING
CHANNEL COMMAND CONDUCT
CONTROL COUNSEL DICTATE
HEADING HELMAGE MANDATE
PRECEPT STRETCH BEARINGS
CALENDAR DELEATUR DIAGONAL
GUIDANCE STEERAGE STEERING
TENDENCY ORDINANCE
ORIENTATION PRESCRIPTION
(— OF CURRENT) AXIS
(— OF FLOW) SET
(— OF ROCK CLEAVAGE) GRAIN
(— OF WIND) EYE CORNER
(— OUTWARD) BEAM
(—S FOR DELIVERY) ADDRESS
(DANCE —) CALL
(HORIZONTAL —) COURSE
AZIMUTH
(OBLIQUE —) SKEW
(OPPOSITE —) EYE COUNTER
(SINGING —) GIMEL GYMEL
(PREF.) PHORO
(SUFF.) ERLY ERN
(— TO) WARD
DIRECTIVE DICTATE CIRCULAR
DIRECTLY DUE BANG BOLT DEAD
FLAT GAIN JUST MEAN PLAT
PLUM SLAP SOON PLAIN PLUMB
PLUNK POINT ROUND SHEER
SMACK SOUSE SPANG STANG
ARIGHT CLEVER SIMPLY SQUARE
RIGHTLY SHEERLY OUTRIGHT
PROMPTLY SLAPDASH STRAIGHT
PRESENTLY
DIRECTNESS CLARITY IMMEDIACY
DIRECTOR BOSS HEAD COACH
GUIDE PILOT STAFF ARCHON
AUTEUR BISHOP LEADER MASTER
RECTOR WARDEN CURATOR
DESKMAN MANAGER PREFECT
STARETS STERNER TRAINER
ACCENTOR DISPOSER GOVERNOR
PRAEFECT PRODUCER TETRARCH
(FILM —) AUTEUR
DIRECTORY PIE BOOK
DIRGE KEEN SONG ELEGY KINAH
LINOS LINUS QINAH TANGI
HEARSE LAMENT MONODY
THRENE EPICEDE REQUIEM
CORONACH THRENODY
ULLAGONE
(PREF.) THREN(O)
DIRIGIBLE BLIMP AIRSHIP
DIRK SNEE SKEAN SWORD DAGGER
SKHIAN SKIVER WHINGER
WHINIARD
DIRT FEN MUD PAY DUST GORE
GUCK MOOL MUCK NAST SOIL
SUMP CROCK EARTH FILTH GRIME
GROUT SEUCH SEUGH TRASH
FULYIE FULZIE GRAVEL GROUND
REFUSE MULLOCK SLOTTER
MUCKMENT
DIRTINESS GRIME JAKES
DIRTY LOW RAY BASE CLAT DIRT
FOUL MOIL MUSS SOIL WORY
BAWDY BLACK CABBY DINGY
FOGGY GRIMY GUSTY HORRY
MUDDY NASTY POUSY SOILY
SULLY BEMIRE CLARTY CLATTY
DEFILE DIRTEN FILTHY FULYIE

FULZIE GREASY GRUBBY IMPURE
MUSSED POUCEY REECHY SCRIMY
SLASHY SLURRY SMIRCH SMUTTY
SOILED SORDID STORMY BEGRIME
BROOKED BROOKIE BRUCKLE
CLOUDED GRUFTED IMBROIN
MUDDIED PIGGISH ROYNOUS
SCRUFFY SLOTTER SMUTCHY
SQUALID SULLIED TARNISH
UNCLEAN AMURCOUS SLOBBERY
SLOTTERY SOAPLESS
DISABLE OUT HOCK LAME MAIM
BREAK CHINK CROCK GRUEL
UNFIT WRECK BRUISE DISMAY
UNABLE WEAKEN CRIPPLE
(— CANNON) SPIKE
(— HORSE) NOBBLE
(— TANK) BELLY
DISABLED LAME INVALID
DISABLING BUM
DISACCHARIDE BIOSE LACTOSE
MALTOSE SUCROSE
DISACCUSTOM DISUSE
DISACKNOWLEDGE DISCLAIM
DISADVANTAGE HURT MISS RISK
LURCH WORRY DAMAGE DENIAL
INJURY STRIKE DICKENS PENALTY
UNSELTH UNSPEED DISAVAIL
DISFAVOR HANDICAP
DISADVANTAGEOUS HURTFUL
INCONVENIENT
DISAFFECT DEBAUCH ESTRANGE
DISAFFECTED FALSE UNTRUE
DISEASED DISLOYAL FORSWORN
PERJURED RECREANT
DISAFFECTION DECEIT MUTINY
DISEASE DISGUST DISLIKE
DISORDER HOSTILITY
DISAFFIRM DENY ANNUL REVERSE
DISCLAIM
DISAGREE VARY ARGUE CLASH
DIFFER DISCEPT DISCORD
DISSENT QUARREL CONFLICT
DISAGREEABLE BAD ILL ACID EVIL
FOUL PERT SOUR UGLY VILE
AWFUL CROSS HARSH NASTY
STIFF GREASY PUTRID ROTTEN
SNUFFY STICKY UNEASY UNGAIN
BEASTLY CHRONIC COMICAL
GHASTLY HATEFUL INGRATE
IRKSOME NAUGHTY UNLUSTY
CHISELLY KINDLESS TERRIBLE
UNGENIAL UNLIKELY UNLOVELY
UNSAVORY
DISAGREEABLENESS ILLNESS
ASPERITY
DISAGREEABLY HARSHLY
DISAGREEING ODD DISSENTIVE
DISAGREEMENT BREE CLASH
CROSS FIGHT BREACH FRATCH
DISCORD DISGUST DISPUTE
DISSENT FISSURE MISLIKE
QUARREL WRANGLE ARGUMENT
CLASHING DISTANCY DIVISION
FRICTION SQUABBLE VARIANCE
MISUNDERSTANDING
(IN —) APART
DISALLOW FORBID REJECT
CENSURE DISCLAIM DISPROVE
PROHIBIT
DISAPPEAR DIE FLY DROP FADE
FALL FLEE LIFT PASS SINK WEND
WHOP BREAK CLEAR FAINT LAPSE

SLIDE SLOPE SNUFF REMOVE
RETIRE VANISH EVANISH
IMMERGE DISSOLVE EVANESCE
(— GRADUALLY) ELY FADE DRAIN
EVANESCE
(— SUDDENLY) COOK DUCK BURST
MIZZLE
(— UNEXPECTEDLY) LEVANT
DISAPPEARANCE ECLIPSE
FADEAWAY
DISAPPOINT BALK BILK FAIL FALL
MOCK SOUR UNDO CHEAT SNAPE
BAFFLE DEFEAT DELUDE OUTWIT
THWART BEGUILE DECEIVE
DESTROY FALSIFY NULLIFY
DISPOINT
DISAPPOINTED OUTED THROWN
SOREHEAD
DISAPPOINTING FIERCE
FALLACIOUS
DISAPPOINTMENT RUE BALK
SUCK BAULK LURCH DENIAL
LETDOWN COMEDOWN
DISAPPROBATION ODIUM DISLIKE
DISAPPROVAL BAN BOOH HISS
VETO CATCALL CENSURE
DISFAVOR DISGRACE
DISAPPROVE NIX GROAN REJECT
RESENT CENSURE CONDEMN
DISLIKE MISTAKE PROTEST
DISALLOW DISPROVE HARRUMPH
DISAPPROVED DISTASTED
DISAPPROVER WOWSER
DISARM SUBDUE UNSTEEL
DISARRANGE MESS MUSS
DEFORM GARBLE RUFFLE TIPPLE
UNTIDY UNTUNE CLUTTER
CONFUSE DERANGE DISTURB
RUMMAGE SLATTER TROUBLE
COCKBILL DISHEVEL DISORDER
UNSETTLE
(— TYPE) SQUABBLE
DISARRANGEMENT DISARRAY
DISARRAY MESS TASH RIFLE
STRIP CADDLE DISRAY FUFFLE
HUDDLE DESPOIL UNDIGHT
DISHEVEL DISORDER
DISARRAYED UNKEMPT
DISASSEMBLE STRIP DEMOUNT
DISMOUNT
(— CASK) SHAKE
DISASSEMBLY TAKEDOWN
TEARDOWN
DISASSOCIATE SEVER SEPARATE
DISASTER ILL WOE BALE BLOW
EVIL FATE RUIN GRIEF MISHAP
STROKE REVERSE ACCIDENT
CALAMITY CASUALTY EXIGENCY
FATALITY
DISASTROUS BAD ILL FATAL
WEARY SINISTER
DISAVOW DENY DEVOW ABJURE
DISOWN RECANT REFUSE
DECLINE RETRACT ABNEGATE
DISCLAIM DISVOUCH RENOUNCE
DISAVOWAL DENIAL
DISBAND BREAK REDUCE REFORM
ADJOURN CASHIER DISMISS
RELEASE SCATTER DISSOLVE
DISBAR EXCLUDE
DISBELIEF ATHEISM SCRUPLE
ACOSMISM
DISBELIEVE DOUBT REJECT

SUSPECT DISCOUNT DISCREDIT
DISBELIEVER ATHEIST HERETIC
INFIDEL
DISBURDEN RID EASE CLEAR
UNLOAD DELIVER DISLOAD
RELIEVE
DISBURSE SPEND DEFRAY EXPEND
OUTLAY DEBURSE
DISC (ALSO SEE DISK) DIAL DISK
BLANK MEDAL PATEN PLATE
QUOIT COLTER RECORD RONDEL
SQUAIL COULTER DISCOID
PLATTER TROCHUS
(— FOR PRESSING HERRINGS)
DAUNT
(FLOPPY —) DISKETTE
DISCANT HOCKET
DISCARD CAST DECK DEFY JILT
JUNK MOLT OMIT OUST SHED
CHUCK DITCH FLING SCRAP
SHUCK SLUFF THROW TRASH
CHANGE DECARD DISUSE DIVEST
EXCUSS REJECT SLOUGH
ABANDON CASHIER DISMISS
EXPUNGE FORSAKE ABDICATE
JETTISON
(— IN BRIDGE) ECHO
DISCARDED DORMANT OFFCAST
DISCARDING DISPOSAL
DISCERN KEN SEE SPY WIT DEEM
ESPY KNOW READ SCAN JUDGE
SIGHT BEHOLD DESCRY DETECT
DEVISE NOTICE PIERCE SCERNE
DIGNOSCE DISCOVER PERCEIVE
DISCERNIBLE EVIDENT VISIBLE
APPARENT MANIFEST
OBSERVABLE
DISCERNING SAGE WISE NASUTE
SHREWD SUBTLE SAPIENT
SAGACIOUS PERCEPTIVE
PERCIPIENT PENETRATING
DISCERNMENT EYE DOOM GOUT
TACT FLAIR SENSE SKILL TASTE
ACUMEN INSIGHT ELECTION
JUDGMENT SAGACITY SAPIENCE
PERCEPTION PENETRATION
DISCHARGE AX DO AXE CAN GUN
LET RUN BOLT BOOT CASS DUMP
EMIT FIRE FLOW FLUX FREE GIVE
KICK PASS POUR QUIT RIFF SACK
SEND SHOT VENT VOID BLAST
BLEED BRUSH CLEAR DRAIN
EJECT EMPTY EXPEL EXUDE
FRUSH GLEET GRASS ICHOR ISSUE
LOOSE OZENA PURGE RHEUM
SHOOT SPEED START VOMIT
WHIFF YIELD ACQUIT ASSOIL
BOUNCE DEFRAY EFFECT EXCERN
EXEMPT EXHALE FEEDER LOCHIA
OZAENA TICKET UNLADE UNLOAD
ABSOLVE CASHIER DEBOUCH
DEFEASE DEHISCE DELIVER
DERAIGN DISBAND DISMISS
EXCRETE EXHAUST MISSION
PAYMENT PERFORM QUIETUS
RELEASE RELIEVE SATISFY
SKITTER SOLUTIO CATAPULT
COMPOUND DEFECATE
DESPATCH DISGORGE DISPATCH
DISPLACE DISPLODE EMISSION
EVACUATE MITTIMUS OUTSHOOT
PERSOLVE SEPARATE SOLUTION
STREAMER

(— ARROW) TWANG
(— BULLET) DRIVE
(— CARGO) STRIKE
(— DEBT) MEET CLEAR ACQUIT
LOOSING
(— DUTY) SERVE
(— FROM HORSE'S FOOT) FRUSH
(— FROM RESERVOIR) HUSHING
(— MATTER) WEEP
(— OF DEBT) SETOFF
(— OF GAS) FEEDER
(— OF STREAM) FALL SPOUT
(— SUDDENLY) HIKE
(BLOODY —) SHOW SANIES
(CANNON —) TIRE CANNON
(CONCENTRATED —) BARRAGE
(DISHONORABLE —) BOBTAIL
(ELECTRIC —) ARC SPARK LEADER
EFFLUVE STREAMER LIGHTNING
(ELECTRIC —S) STATIC
(HEAVY —) STORM
(SIMULTANEOUS —) SALVO
BROADSIDE FUSILLADE
(SUFF.) CENOSIS RRHAGIA RRHEA
RRHOEA
DISCHARGED SPED SATISFIED
DISCHARGER EXCITATOR
DISCHARGING LABILE
DISCIPLE SON JOHN MARK CHELA
JUDAS MURID PETER PUPIL
TEACH TRAIN ANANDA DISPLE
DORCAS HEARER PUNISH
APOSTLE AUDITOR MATTHEW
OVIDIAN SCHOLAR SECTARY
SRAVAKA STUDENT ADHERENT
FOLLOWER GALENIST SECTATOR
DISCIPLINARIAN RAMROD
TRAINER MARTINET
DISCIPLINARY STRICT
DISCIPLINE THEW WHIP BREAK
DRILL INURE TEACH TRAIN
TUTOR CHURCH ETHICS FERULA
FERULE GOVERN INFORM PUNISH
SEASON TAIRGE VIRTUE CHASTEN
CORRECT CULTURE EDUCATE
FURNACE NURTURE SCOURGE
DISCIPLE DOCTRINE EXERCISE
INSTRUCT LEARNING MATHESIS
PEDAGOGY REGULATE RESTRAIN
TEACHING TRAINING TUTORING
PHILOSOPHY CASTIGATION
(MENTAL —) YOGA
(RELIGIOUS —) CHURCH PENANCE
SADHANA
DISCIPLINED INURED STEADY
DISCLAIM DENY DEVOW ABJURE
DISOWN REFUSE DISAVOW
ABDICATE ABNEGATE DISALLOW
RENOUNCE
DISCLOSE OPE RIP BARE BLOW
CALL KNOW OPEN TELL BREAK
COUGH UNRIP UNWRY UTTER
BETRAY BEWRAY DESCRY DIVINE
EVOLVE EXPOSE IMPART REVEAL
SHRIVE UNBURY UNCASE
UNHASP UNHIDE UNLOCK
UNROLL UNSEAL UNSHUT UNVEIL
UNWRAP CONFESS DEVELOP
DISCUSS DISPLAY DIVULGE
EXHIBIT EXPLAIN PROPALE
UNCLOSE UNCOVER DISCOVER
INDICATE MANIFEST UNBUNDLE
UNKENNEL UNSECRET UNTHATCH

(— PARTIALLY) ADUMBRATE
DISCLOSED OUT
DISCLOSURE REVEAL SHRIFT
COLORING DESCRIAL DISCLOSE
OVERTURE APOCALYPSE
DISCOLOR FOX BURN FADE SPOT
BLACK SMOKE STAIN TINGE
SMIRCH STREAK DISTAIN
TARNISH BESMIRCH
DISCOLORATION CORN BLEED
SCALD SPECK STAIN TINGE
FOXING LIVEDO MILDEW ARGYRIA
BURNING MELASMA BRONZING
BROWNING CHLOASMA CYANOSIS
DYSCHROA SCALDING
(— OF FRUIT) SUNBURN
(— OF TURKEYS) BLUEBACK
(— ON CHOCOLATE) BLOOM
(— ON CURED FISH) RUST
(SMALL —) FRECKLE
(SUFF.) CHROIA
DISCOLORED HAW FOUL DINGY
FOXED RUSTY STAINED
SCORCHED USTULATE
(— BY DECAY) DOTY FOXED
DISCOMFIT MATE ROIT ABASH
ABAVE AFLEY SHEND SHENT
UPSET WORST BAFFLE DEFEAT
FEAGUE SQUASH CONFUSE
CONQUER DISTURB
DISCOMFITURE LURCH
DISCOMFORT (FEELING OF —)
BLAHS
DISCOMPOSE FEEZE PERTURB
DISCONCERT BASH BOWL FAZE
FUSS HACK ABASH BLANK DAUNT
FEEZE PHASE UPSET WORRY
BAFFLE BLENCH MISPUT PUZZLE
RATTLE SQUASH CONFUSE
DISTURB FLUMMOX NONPLUS
PERTURB SQUELCH BROWBEAT
DISORDER
DISCONCERTED BLANK ASHAMED
RATTLED CONFUSED
DISCONCERTING BAFFLING
DISCONNECT UNDO SEVER DIVIDE
UNDOCK UNYOKE DISJOIN
DISSOLVE DISUNITE SEPARATE
UNCOUPLE
DISCONNECTED LOOSE ABRUPT
BROKEN CHOPPY CURSORY
DECOUSU RAMBLING STACCATO
ASYNARTETE
DISCONSOLATE SAD GLOOMY
WOEFUL DOLEFUL FORLORN
UNCOUTH DEJECTED DESOLATE
DOWNCAST HOPELESS
DISCONTENT ENVY DISQUIET
SOURNESS
DISCONTENTED DUMPY RESTLESS
MALCONTENT
DISCONTINUANCE BREAK LAPSE
DEMISE CUTBACK DISUNION
SHUTDOWN CESSATION
DISCONTINUE END DROP HALT
QUIT STOP BREAK CEASE CLOSE
LETUP DESIST DISUSE SUNDER
DISRUPT SUSPEND INTERMIT
SURCEASE
DISCONTINUITY JAR BREAK
COMMA BREACH
DISCONTINUOUS BROKEN
DISJUNCT SALTATORY

DISCORD DIN JAR BROIL JANGLE
SCHISM STRIFE DISLIKE FACTION
FISSURE JARRING MISTONE
CONFLICT DISTANCE DIVISION
FRACTION MISCHIEF UNSAUGHT
VARIANCE CACOPHONY
DISCORDANT AJAR RUDE CRONK
HARSH FROWZY HOARSE JANGLY
HIDEOUS JARRING SQUAWKY
ABSONANT CONTRARY JANGLING
SCORDATO
DISCOTHEQUE AGOGO
DISCOUNT AGIO BATTA SHAVE
REBATE REDUCE DISCOMPT
DISCOURAGE CARP DAMP CHILL
DAUNT DETER FROST DAMPEN
DEJECT DISMAY FREEZE STIFLE
DEPRESS FLATTEN INHIBIT
DISPIRIT DISSUADE
DISCOURAGEMENT COLD DAMP
CHILL DAUNT REBUFF LETDOWN
PUTBACK
DISCOURAGING CHILL DREARY
DISCOURSE SAW CARP RANT
READ TALE TALK TELL WORD
DROOL FABLE ORATE PAPER
SPEAK SPELL THEME TRACT
TREAT COMMON DILATE EULOGY
HOMILY PARLEY PREACH REASON
SCREED SERMON THESIS TONGUE
TREATY ACCOUNT ADDRESS
COMMENT CONTEXT DECLAIM
DELIVER DESCANT DIETARY
DISCANT DISCUSS DISSERT
ENTREAT EXPOUND GRAMMAR
LECTURE NARRATE ORATION
PARABLE PRATING PRELECT
PURPOSE RECITAL TALKING
ARGUMENT COLLOQUY
CONVERSE EXERCISE LOCUTION
LOQUENCE PARLANCE SPEAKING
SPELLING TRACTATE TREATISE
PHILIPPIC PROLUSION
(— OF LITTLE VALUE) STUFF
(LAUDATORY —) PANEGYRIC
(LONG —) SCREED
(PROLONGED —) DIATRIBE
(RAMBLING —) RHAPSODY
(SERIOUS —) HOMILY
(SIMPLE —) PAP
(UNIMAGINATIVE —) PROSE
(PL.) EXOTERICS
(PREF.) LOG(O)
(SUFF.) LOG(ER)(IA)(IAN)(IC)(ICAL)
(IST)(UE)(Y)
DISCOURTEOUS RUDE SCURVY
UNCIVIL UNHENDE CAVALIER
IMPOLITE UNGENTLE
DISCOURTESY CUT SLIGHT
DISCOVER RIP SEE SPY WIT ESPY
FEEL FIND PICK TWIG CATCH
LEARN SPELL DEFINE DESCRY
DETECT DIVINE EXPOSE IMPART
INVENT LOCATE OVERGO REVEAL
STRIKE UNHIDE CONFESS
DESCURE DEVELOP DISCERN
DISCURE DISPLAY DIVULGE
EXHIBIT EXPLORE UNCOVER
UNEARTH CONTRIVE DECIPHER
DESCRIBE DISCUREN MANIFEST
UNKENNEL
DISCOVERABLE VISIBLE
DISCOVERER SPY SCOUT

DISCOVERY COLUMBUS EXPLORER INVENTOR
FIND TROVE DESCRY
ESPIAL STRIKE DESCRIAL
DISCREDIT FOUL SLUT DECRY
DOUBT REFEL DEFACE DEFECT
ASPERSE BLEMISH DESTROY
IMPEACH SCANDAL SUSPECT
BELITTLE DISGRACE DISHONOR
DISTRUST REPROACH UNCREDIT
(SUFF.) ARD ART
DISCREDITABLE BLACK
UNHONEST
DISCREET SAGE WARY WISE CIVIL
WITTY HUSHED POLITE SILENT
CAREFUL GUARDED POLITIC
PRUDENT CAUTIOUS RESERVED
RETICENT
DISCREETLY SENSIBLY
DISCREPANCY VARIANCE
DISCREPANT VARIANT CONTRARY
DISSONANT
DISCRETE ETERNAL DISTINCT
DISCRETION TACT OPTION
WISDOM CONDUCT RETENUE
COURTESY JUDGMENT PRUDENCE
DISCRETIONARY ARBITRARY
DISCRIMINATE PART SEVER
SECERN DISCERN PERCEIVE
SEPARATE
DISCRIMINATED DISTINCT
DISCRIMINATING GOOD NICE
ACUTE SHARP ASTUTE CHOICE
NASUTE SELECT CHOOSEY
CRITICAL EXPLICIT
DISCRIMINATINGLY CHOICE
FINELY
DISCRIMINATION EYE DOOM
TACT TASTE ACUMEN AGEISM
CHOICE SEXISM FINESSE RESPECT
DELICACY SAPIENCE
(SYMBOL OF —) HANSA
DISCRIMINATIVE RESPECTIVE
DISCURSIVE ROVING CURSORY
RAMBLING DESULTORY
DISCURSIVELY WIDE
DISCUS DISC DISK QUOIT DISKOS
DISCOID
DISCUSS AIR BANDY MOOT RUNE TALK
ARGUE BANDY COVER DANDY
TRACT TREAT COMMON CONFER
DEBATE DICKER EMPARL EXCUSS
IMPARL PARLEY AGITATE
BESPEAK CANVASS COMMENT
CONSULT DESCANT DISCANT
DISCEPT DISCUTE DISPUTE
DISSERT EXAMINE NARRATE
TRAVERSE CONJOBBLE
(— AT LENGTH) BAT
(— CASUALLY) MENTION
(— EXCITEDLY) AGITATE
(— LIGHTLY) BANDY
(— QUICKLY) SKIP
(— SECRETLY) ROUN
(— TERMS) CHAFFER
(— THOROUGHLY) EXHAUST
(— TO EXCESS) VEX
DISCUSSION MOOT DEBAT FORUM
COMMON CONFAB DEBATE
HASSEL HOMILY HUDDLE PARLEY
TREATY BARGAIN CANVASS
COMMENT COUNSEL DISCUSS
DISPUTE MOOTING PALAVER
PRIBBLE ARGUMENT CAUSERIE

CHINFEST COLLOQUY DIATRIBE
ENTREATY EXCURSUS QUESTION
(CONTROVERSIAL —) DISPUTE
(DIDACTIC —) HARANGUE
(HEATED —) FLAK
DISDAIN COY TUT DAIN DEFY
PRIDE SCORN SDAIN SPURN
SDEIGN SLIGHT CONTEMN
DESPISE CONTEMPT
DISDAINFUL COY DIGNE PROUD
SAUCY TOSSY SCORNY SLIGHT
SNIFFY SNUFFY DAINFUL
HAUGHTY ARROGANT DEIGNOUS
PROUDFUL SCORNFUL SNIFFISH
TOPLOFTY
DISDAINFULLY SMALL SNIFFILY
DISEASE BUG FLU MAL ROT AIDS
BATS COTH CRUD EVIL FLAW
GOUT GRIP NOMA PEST PHOS
SORE AGROM BATTS BEJEL
BENDS CAUSE COTHE CROUP
DECAY DOLOR FEVER GRIEF
LUPUS PHOSS PINTA PINTO
SCALL SHAKE SPRUE SURRA
AINHUM ANGINA CANCER
CARATE CORYZA COURAP
DENGUE GRAVEL GRIPPE HERPES
MALADY MORBUS PALMUS
PIEDRA POPEYE SCURVY SICKEN
SURRAH UROSIS ZOOSIS AILMENT
CHOLERA COXALGY DECLINE
ENDEMIC ENTASIA LANGUOR
LEPROSY MALEASE MISLIKE
MYCOSIS MYIASIS PATHEMA
RAPHANY SCOURGE SEQUELA
SERPIGO SIBBENS SORANCE
SYCOSIS XERASIA ZYMOTIC
ALASTRIM ATHEROMA BERIBERI
COXALGIA CRIPPLER CYNANCHE
DIAMONDS ENZOOTIC JAUNDICE
LEUKEMIA PALUDISM PANDEMIC
PELLAGRA RAPHANIA SCABBADO
SICKNESS SMALLPOX SORRANCE
STAGGERS SYPHILIS UNHEALTH
XANTHOMA ZOONOSIS
(— OF ANIMALS, GENERAL) ROT
CLAP CORE FIRE GOUT HUSK LICK
WEED APTHA CLEFT CLING
CLOSH COTHE CROOK DRUSE
FARCY FLAPS NENTA NGANA
PAINS SPEED SWEAT TAINT
APHTHA AVIVES BROSOT CANKER
CARNEY CREEPS FARCIN GARGET
GRAPES LAMPAS NAGANA
ROUGET SPAVIN SURRAH
WOBBLE ANTHRAX BIGHEAD
CALCINO CALORIS CARCEAG
DOURING EARWORM EQUINIA
FASHION FISTULA FOUNDER
FROUNCE KETOSIS LAMPERS
MURRAIN MURRINA QUITTER
QUITTOR SLOBBER SOLDIER
TAKOSIS BULLNOSE CRATCHES
CRIPPLES FERNSICK FOOTHALT
HORSEPOX HYSTERIA
MAWBOUND SLOBBERS SNUFFLES
THWARTER VACCINIA EPIZOOTIC
(— OF APPLES) CORK BLOTCH
(— OF BANANAS) SIGATOKA
SQUIRTER
(— OF BARLEY) STRIPE
(— OF BEES) SACBROOD
(— OF BEETS) HEARTROT

(— OF BIRDS) GOUT
(— OF BLUEBERRY) BLUESTEM
(— OF CABBAGE) ANBURY
CLUBROOT
(— OF CATERPILLARS) WILT
FLACHERY
(— OF CATS) PANLEUCOPENIA
(— OF CATTLE) PUCK TURN BARBS
BLAIN CLOSH FARCY HOOVE
HOOZE SLOWS COWPOX GARGET
GRAPES HAMMER HEAVES
ANTHRAX BLACKLEG BLOATING
(— OF CEREALS) BRAND ERGOT
(— OF CHICKEN) PIP CORYZA
(— OF CHILDREN) PROGERIA
(— OF COTTON) HYBOSIS CYRTOSIS
STENOSIS
(— OF DUCKLING) KEEL
(— OF EYES) WALL GLAUCOMA
SYNECHIA TRACHOMA
(— OF FIGS) SMUT
(— OF FINGERNAILS) FLAW
(— OF FLAX) BROWNING
(— OF FOWLS) PIP CRAY ROUP
GAPES SOREHEAD
(— OF GRAIN) ILIAU ICTERUS
(— OF GRAPES) COLEUR ERINOSE
ROUGEAU ROUGEOT SHELLING
(— OF HAWKS) RYE CRAY CROAK
CROAKS FROUNCE FILANDER
(— OF HORSES) HAW CLAP CURB
MOSE MULE WEED FARCY LEUMA
VIVES APHTA SCALMA THRUSH
BARBELS DOURINE QUITTOR
SARCOID AZOTURIA GLANDERS
HORSEPOX STRANGLES
(— OF INSECTS) POLYHEDROSIS
(— OF LAMB) SWAYBACK
(— OF LETTUCE) STUNT
(— OF NARCISSUS) SMOLDER
SMOULDER
(— OF ONION) SMUDGE
(— OF ORANGE) LEPROSIS
(— OF PALMS) KOLEROGA
(— OF PLANTS) SCAB NECROSIS
(— OF PLANTS, GENERAL) POX ROT
BUNT CORK DROP FIRE GOUT
KNOT PULP SMUT BLAST DWARF
EDEMA ERGOT FLECK FLOCK
GRUBS SCALD SCALE SCURF
SEREH SPIKE STUNT TUKRA
TWIST AUCUBA BLIGHT BLOTCH
BLUING BRAUNE CALICO CANKER
COLEUR GIRDLE OEDEMA OIDIUM
PETECA SMUDGE STREAK STRIPE
VIROSE BLISTER BLUEING
BRINDLE CRINKLE DIEBACK
ERINOSE EYESPOT FROGEYE
HYBOSIS MEASLES PRURIGO
ROSETTE SHATTER SMOLDER
STIPPEN TIPBURN TOMOSIS
VIRUELA WALLOON BLUESTEM
BREAKING BROWNING BUCKSKIN
CLUBROOT CYRTOSIS DARTROSE
EXANTHEMA FLYSPECK GUMMOSIS
KOLEROGA LEPROSIS MELANOSE
MELAXUMA POLEBURN PSOROSIS
RAPHANIA SMOULDER STENOSIS
VIROSITY WHIPTAIL WILDFIRE
CHLOROSIS
(— OF POTATO) CURL HAYWIRE
(— OF RABBITS) SNUFFLES
(— OF RICE) BLAST SPECK

(— OF SHEEP) CAW COE GID MAD RAY ROT BANE BELT CORE HALT SHAB WIND BLAST BLOOD BRAXY GILLAR OVINIA PINING STURDY ANTHRAX BRADSOT DAISING RUBBERS SCRAPIE THWARTER WILDFIRE BREAKSHARE
(— OF SILKWORM) UJI CALCINO GATTINE PEBRINE FLACHERY
(— OF SUGARCANE) ILIAU SEREH EYESPOT
(— OF SWINE) GARGET
(— OF TOBACCO) ETCH CALICO BRINDLE FROGEYE
(— OF TOMATO) FERNLEAF GRAYWALL
(— OF TONGUE) AGROM
(— OF TREES) KNOT CANKER
(— OF TULIPS) SHANKING
(— OF UNKNOWN ORIGIN) AINHUM ACRODYNIA
(CAISSON —) CHOKES
(FATAL — OF NERVOUS SYSTEM) KURU
(FOOT-AND-MOUTH —) AFTOSA
(FUNGUS —) PECK MYCOSIS
(KIDNEY —) RIPPLE
(LUNG —) CON
(MUSHROOM —) FLOCK
(PINK —) ACRODYNIA
(PLANT —) ESCA YAWS
(SKIN —) ACNE SCAB FAVUS HIVES LEPRA MANGE PSORA RUPIA SCALL TINEA ECZEMA LICHEN TETTER EXORMIA PORRIGO PRURIGO PURPURA SERPIGO VERRUGA CHLOASMA IMPETIGO MILIARIA MYCETOMA SHINGLES VERRUGAS VITILIGO PEMPHIGUS
(SWELLING —) EDEMA
(VENEREAL —) BURNING SYPHILIS
(WINE —) GRAISSE
(WOOLSORTER'S —) ANTHRAX
(PREF.) MORBI NOS(O) PATH(O)
(SUFF.) IASIS ITIS NOSUS OMATOSIS OSIS SIS
(FUNGUS —) OSIS
DISEASED BAD EVIL SICKLY MORBOSE PECCANT VICIOUS MORBIFIC
(PREF.) CAC(O) CACH DYS
(SUFF.) CACE
DISEMBARK LAND ALIGHT DEBARK UNBARK UNBOAT DISBOARD
DISEMBARRASS EXTRICATE
DISEMBODIED SEPARATE DISBODIED FLESHLESS
DISEMBODIMENT SOUL SPIRIT
DISEMBOGUE MOUTH
DISEMBOWEL GUT HULK PAUNCH DEBOWEL EMBOWEL GARBAGE UNTRIPE GRALLOCH
DISEMIC DIMORIC DICHRONOUS
DISENCHANT DISMAY
DISENCHANTED SOUR
DISENCUMBER RID FREE REDD UNCUMBER
DISENGAGE FREE CLEAR EDUCE UNTIE DETACH EVOLVE LOOSEN CUTOVER DISGAGE RELEASE UNRAVEL LIBERATE UNCLUTCH
DISENTANGLE CARD COMB FREE

REED TOSE TOZE CLEAR LOOSE RAVEL TEASE EVOLVE SCUTCH SLEAVE UNMAZE UNMESH RESOLVE UNRAVEL UNREAVE UNTWINE UNTWIST OUTTWINE UNTANGLE
DISENTANGLEMENT SOLUTION
DISESTEEM UMBRAGE DISVALUE
DISFAVOR DUTCH ODIUM DISLIKE OFFENCE OFFENSE UMBRAGE MALGRACE
DISFIGURE MAR BLUR FOUL MAIM SCAR TASH AGRISE DEFACE DEFEAT DEFORM INJURE MANGLE BLEMISH DISGRACE DISGUISE MUTILATE
DISFIGURED FOUL DEFET DEFEIT DEFORMED
DISFIGUREMENT SCAR BLEMISH CATFACE DEFORMITY
DISGORGE SPEW VENT EJECT EMPTY VOMIT
DISGRACE BLOT FOIL FOUL HISS LACK SLUR SMIT SOIL SPOT TASH ABASE CRIME ODIUM SCORN SHAME SHEND SPITE STAIN TAINT BAFFLE BEFOUL BISMER HUMBLE INFAMY REBUKE STIGMA VILIFY AFFRONT ATTAINT DEGRADE OBLOQUY OFFENCE OFFENSE REPROOF SCANDAL SLANDER UMBRAGE CONTEMPT DISHONOR IGNOMINY REPROACH SHENDING UNWORTHY VILLAINY OPPROBRIUM
(PUBLIC —) ATIMY
DISGRACEFUL MEAN SOUR FILTHY INDIGN IGNOBLE CRIMINAL DEFAMOUS INHONEST SHAMEFUL
DISGRUNTLED SORE PEEVISH
DISGUISE DAUB FACE HIDE LAIN LEAN MASK VEIL BELIE CLOAK COLOR COUCH COVER FEIGN GLOZE GUISE SHADE VISOR VIZOR COVERT DEFORM IMMASK MANTLE MASQUE VIZARD CONCEAL OBSCURE PRETEND PURPORT COLORING DISLIKEN MISGUISE PALLIATE PRETENCE PRETENSE TRAVESTY UMBRELLA
(— INFORMATION) LAYNE
DISGUISED COVERT FUCATE GILDED LATENT MYSTIC FEIGNED PALLIATE TRAVESTY
DISGUST IRK CLOY PALL LOATH REPEL SHOCK STALL DEGOUT HORROR NAUSEA OFFEND REVOLT SICKEN SCUNNER STOMACH SURFEIT AVERSION DISTASTE KREISTLE LOATHING NAUSEATE SCOMFISH SICKNESS
DISGUSTED IRK SICK IRKSOME
DISGUSTING FOUL PERT VILE LOUSY MUCKY NASTY FILTHY SCRIMY SICKLY BEASTLY CLOYING FULSOME HATEFUL LOATHLY MAWKISH NOISOME OBSCENE SHITTEN FOULSOME LOATHFUL NAUSEOUS SHOCKING
DISH CAP CAUP CUSH DISC DISK FOOL MEAT MOLD PLAT SOLE BASIN BATEA COMAL DEVIL MOULD NAPPY PATEN PINAX

PLATE SHAPE BASQUE BASSIE BICKER BLAZER BUTTER CHAFER CRITCH CUSCUS ENTREE FONDUE LUGGIE OLIVES PADDLE PANADA PATERA PATINA PHIALE RECIPE SAUCER SUNDAE TAMALE TUREEN BALANCE BOBOTEE BOBOTIE CAPSULE CEVICHE CHARGER COCOTTE COMPORT COMPOTE CRESSET DORMANT DOUBLER EPERGNE PAPBOAT PATELLA PLATEAU PLATTER RAMEKIN SCUTTLE SUPREME TERRINE TIMBALE AMATORIO CIOPPINO CLAPDISH COQUILLE COUSCOUS GALATINE KEDGEREE MAZARINE POWSODDY STANDARD ENTREMETS
(— IN PYRAMID STYLE) BUISSON
(— OF MEAT AND EGGPLANT) MOUSSAKA
(BAKING —) SCALLOP SCOLLOP
(BRAISED —) HASLET
(CHAFING —) CHAFER CHOFFER SCALDINO
(CONE-SHAPED —) BOMBE
(EXQUISITE —) AMBROSIA
(FANCY —) SURPRISE
(FLAT —) ASHET COMAL CHARGER
(HIGH-FLAVORED —) HOGO
(JAPANESE —) SUSHI TERIYAKI
(JEWISH —) CHOLENT
(PHILIPPINE —) BURO
(PIE —) COFFIN
(PILE OF —S) BING
(ROMAN —) LANX PATERA PATINA
(SAILOR'S —) BURGOO SCOUSE
(SCOTTISH —) BROSE
(SIDE —) OUTWORK
(SWEET —) JUNKET FLUMMERY
(TASTY —) MORSEL
(WOODEN —) CUP CAUP BOWIE GOGGAN LUGGIE KICKSHAW
(PL.) GARNISH BAKEWARE FLATWARE ENTREMETS
(PREF.) LECO
DISHABILLE MOB DISARRAY DISORDER NEGLIGEE
DISHAN (FATHER OF —) SEIR
DISHARMONY SCHISM ADHARMA FRACTION
DISHCLOTH DISHRAG TORCHON
DISHCLOTH GOURD LOOFAH PATOLA DISHRAG
DISHEARTEN AMATE DAUNT FAINT DEJECT DEPRESS FLATTEN UNHEART UNNERVE DISHEART DISPIRIT
DISHEARTENED DULL GLOOMY DOWNCAST DEPRESSED
DISHEARTENING GLOOMY DESOLATE
DISHEVEL MUSS TOWSE RUFFLE TOUSEL TOUSLE TUMBLE TRACHLE DISARRAY DISORDER
DISHEVELED ROOKY BLOUSY BLOWZY FROWZY TUMBLED UNKEMPT FROWZLED SHEVELED SLIPSHOD TATTERED
DISHON (FATHER OF —) ANAH
DISHONEST FOUL LEWD CRONK CROSS FALSE LYING QUEER SNIDE TWISTY UNFAIR UNJUST

CORRUPT CROOKED JACKLEG KNAVISH INDECENT INDIRECT SHAMEFUL SINISTER UNCHASTE UNHONEST MENDACIOUS
DISHONESTLY DOUBLY FALSELY
DISHONESTY IMPROBITY
DISHONOR FILE FOUL ABASE ABUSE ATIMY ODIUM SHAME SPITE STAIN WRONG DEFAME DEFILE DEFORM INFAMY VILIFY DEGRADE DISTAIN OBLOQUY SLANDER VIOLATE DISGLORY DISGRACE DISPLUME IGNOMINY REPROACH VILLAINY ATTAINDER
DISHONORABLE BASE FOUL MEAN BLACK NASTY SHABBY YELLOW DISLEAL IGNOBLE SHAMEFUL UNHONEST UNWORTHY
DISHONORED DEFAMED
DISHPAN KEELER
DISH RACK FIDDLE
DISHWASHER SWILLER
DISILLUSION SOUR DISMAY
DISINCLINATION NILL UNLUST UNWILL DISLIKE QUARREL AVERSION DISTASTE
DISINCLINED LOTH LOATH AFRAID AVERSE HESITANT
(— TO) ABOVE
DISINFECT SCRUB SEASON CLEANSE SWEETEN
DISINFECTANT LYSOL IODINE PHENOL CREOLIN EUGENOL TACHIOL FUMIGANT HALAZONE PARAFORM
DISINGENUOUS FALSE UNFAIR OBLIQUE
DISINHERIT DEPRIVE DISHEIR ABDICATE DISHERIT
DISINTEGRATE BEAT DUST MELT BREAK DECAY ERODE GRUSH SLAKE SPLIT MOLDER CRUMBLE DISBAND RESOLVE SHATTER COLLAPSE DISSOLVE SEPARATE
DISINTEGRATING ROTTEN SCHIZOID
(SUFF.) CLASTIC
DISINTEGRATION DECAY BREAKUP EROSION BIOLYSIS COLLAPSE HEARTROT SOLUTION
(SUFF.) LYSE LYSIS LYST LYTE LYTIC LYZE
DISINTER EXHUME UNBURY UNTOMB UNGRAVE
DISINTERESTED FAIR CANDID APATHETIC IMPARTIAL
DISJOIN PART UNDO SEVER DETACH SUNDER UNTACK UNYOKE DISSOLVE DISUNITE SEPARATE
DISJOINED BITTY SEJOINED DIAZEUTIC
DISK (ALSO SEE DISC) EYE NOB ORB PAN SAW WAX WEB BURR CHAD DIAL DISC FLAN FLAT KNOB PALM PUCK STAR TUFT CAKRA DAUNT MEDAL PATEN PLATE ROUND SABLE SABOT SPILL TOKEN TRUCK WAFER WHEEL WHORL BEZANT BOTTOM BUCKET BUMPER BUTTON CACHET CARTON CHAKRA CONCHA CONCHO CORONA DISCUS

GHURRY HARROW PALLET PELLET
RECORD RIFFLE RONDEL SEQUIN
SHEAVE SQUAIL WASHER WEIGHT
ZEQUIN ACETATE BLOTTER
BOBECHE CHECKER CHIPPER
CLIPEUS DIOPTER DISCOID
GOGGLES KNICKER MEDALET
PHALERA ROSETTE SLITTER
SPINNER SPOTTER TONDINO
DIFFUSER EYEPIECE HOLDFAST
PLANCHET RONDELLE ROUNDLET
ZECCHINO
(— FOR BARRELING HERRING)
DAUNT
(— FOR CHEESE) FOLLOWER
(— FOR STRIKING HOURS) GHURRY
(— OF JELLYFISH) BELL
(— OF WAX) AGNUS
(— ON WOODEN ROD) SPILL
(BULL'S-EYE —) CARTON
(COIN-MAKING —) FLAN PLANCHET
(ECCENTRIC —) SHEAVE
(FLESHY —) SARCOMA
(HANDLED —) RIFFLE
(MEDICATED —) LAMELLA
(METAL —) SLUG MEDAL
(ORNAMENTAL —) BANGLE
SPANGLE
(PADDED IRON —) SPINNER
(PAPER —S) CONFETTI
(POTTER'S —) BAT
(REVOLVING —) WAFTER
(ROTATING —) SCANNER
(SOLAR —) ATEN ATON
(SUN —) CAKRA CHAKRA
(TROCHAL —) CORONA
(WINGED —) FEROHER
(PREF.) DISC(I)(O)
DISLIKE DEFY DOWN HATE LOTH
LUMP MIND DERRY LOATH SPITE
DETEST PHOBIA REGRET SPLEEN
UNLIKE DESPISE MISLIKE
QUARREL SCUNDER SCUNNER
STOMACH AVERSION DESPISAL
DISFAVOR DISTASTE DYSPATHY
(— OF CHILDREN) MISOPEDIA
(FOOLISH —) TOY
DISLOCATE LUX SLIP BREAK
SPLAY UNSET LUXATE DISLOCK
UNWREST DISJOINT DISPLACE
DISLOCATED SHOTTEN DISLOCATE
DISLOCATION BREAK SHIFT SLIDE
THROW
(PL.) SETTLEMENTS
DISLODGE BEAT BOLT BUCK BUMP
EXPEL SHAKE SHIFT SWOOP
REMOVE DISROOT UNHORSE
UNHOUSE UNLODGE DISHABIT
(— BY BLASTING) BRUSH
DISLODGING BULLING
DISLOYAL FALSE FELON UNTRUE
DISLEAL
DISLOYALTY SWICK SWIKE
UNLEWTY UNTRUTH
DISMAL SAD WAN BLUE DARK
DIRE DOWF DREE DULL EERY
GASH GLUM GRAY GREY BLACK
BLEAK DOWFF DREAR EERIE
LURID MORNE OURIE SABLE
SORRY SURLY SWART WASTE
WISHT DREARY DREICH DREIGH
GLOOMY GOUSTY LENTEN
SULLEN TRISTE DIREFUL DOLEFUL

FUNERAL GASHFUL GHASTLY
GOUSTIE JOYLESS OMINOUS
POCOSIN STYGIAN UNCOUTH
UNHAPPY DESOLATE DOLESOME
DOLOROUS FUNEREAL GROANFUL
LONESOME NOVEMBRY SOLITARY
WEARIFUL MELANCHOLY
DISMAL-LOOKING GASH
WOBEGONE
DISMALLY DERNLY DIRELY
DISMANTLE RASE RAZE STRIP
DIVEST STRIKE DEPRIVE DESTROY
UNCLOAK DISMOUNT
DISMAY BOWL FEAR RUIN ALARM
AMATE APPAL DAUNT DREAD
FLUNK APPALL ASTONY CHASSE
FRIGHT SUBDUE TERROR
DEPRESS DEPRIVE FOUNDER
HORRIFY TERRIFY AFFRIGHT
CONFOUND CONSTERNATION
DISMAYED ASTONIED
DISMAYING HIDEOUS
DISMEMBER LIMB MAIM PART
REND SEVER MANGLE UNLIMB
DISCERP DISLIMB DISSECT
QUARTER DISJOINT MUTILATE
DISMISS AX AXE CAN PUT BOOT
BUMP BUST CASH CAST DAFF
DROP DRUM FIRE KICK OUST
QUIT SACK SEND SHAB SWAP
SWOP TURN VAIK VOID AMAND
AMOVE BREAK BRUSH CHUCK
DEMIT DIMIT DITCH EJECT EXPEL
FLIRT FLUNK LOOSE SCOUT
BANISH BOUNCE CHASSE CONGEE
DISMIT DISOWN REJECT REMOVE
SHELVE CASHIER DISBAND
DISCARD LICENCE LICENSE
DISGRACE DISPATCH DISPOINT
RELEGATE WITHDRAW
DISMISSAL AX BOOT SACK BRUSH
CHUCK CONGE SHAKE AVAUNT
BOUNCE KICKAXE REMOVAL
DISPATCH MITTIMUS
REDUNDANCY
(UNCEREMONIOUS —) CONGE
CONGEE
DISMISSED DEGOMME
DISMOUNT AVALE AVOID LIGHT
ALIGHT DEVOID DESCEND
FLYAWAY UNHORSE UNMOUNT
DISHORSE UNSTRIDE
DISOBEDIENCE CONTEMPT
DISOBEDIENT BAD FORWARD
FROWARD NAUGHTY UNBUXOM
UNGODLY WAYWARD MUTINOUS
DISOBEY SIT REJECT
DISOBLIGE OFFEND REFUSE
AFFRONT NEGLECT
DISOBLIGING MEAN UNBAIN
UNBANE
DISORDER ILL MUX PIE CRUD
FLAW MESS MUSS RIOT RUFF
STIR TOUT CHAOS CRACK DERAY
GRIME HAVOC REVEL SNAFU
SPLIT TOUSE TUKRA UPSET
BURBLE CHOREA DEFUSE DESRAY
HUDDLE JUMBLE LITTER MALADY
MASTIC MUCKER MUDDLE
RUFFLE TOUSLE TROPPO TUMULT
UNTIDY WALTER AILMENT
CLUTTER COBWEBS CONFUSE
DERANGE DISEASE DISTURB

EMBROIL FERMENT FLUTTER
GARBOIL ILLNESS MISDEED
MISRULE OUTRAGE PERTURB
SHATTER TROUBLE UNRAVEL
UNSHAPE DISARRAY DISHEVEL
EPILEPSY MILIARIA MISORDER
NEUROSIS ROWDYISM SICKNESS
UNSETTLE COMMOTION
CONFUSION POLLINOSIS
(— OF BIRDS) PIP
(— OF EYES) HIPPUS
(— OF VISION) DIPLOPIA
(— OF WINES) CASSE
(COMPLETE —) CHAOS ANARCHY
(MENTAL —) INSANITY PARANOIA
(SPEECH —) LALOPATHY
(SUFF.) (SPEECH —) PHASIA
PHEMIA PHRASIA
DISORDERED ILL SICK WILD CRAZY
GAUMY LIGHT MESSY UNRID
BLOTTO FROUZY FROWSY
FROWZY INCULT INSANE MUSSED
TURBID CHAOTIC CLOUDED
FORLORN TUMBLED UNSIDED
CONFUSED DERANGED DISEASED
FEVERISH FLURRIED INCHOATE
DISORDERING CRIMP
DISORDERLY RAND RANDY
ROWDY RABBLE UNRULY
BUNTING LAWLESS ROARING
CONFUSED FAROUCHE LARRIKIN
SLIPSHOD SLOVENLY SLUTTISH
SLATTERNLY
DISORGANIZE SHOCK UPSET
CONFUSE CONTUSE DERANGE
DISBAND DISRUPT DISORDER
DISSOLVE
DISOWN DENY RENAY UNOWN
REJECT DISAVOW RETRACT
ABDICATE DISALLOW DISCLAIM
RENOUNCE REPUDIATE
DISPARAGE LACK SLUR ABUSE
DECRY LOWER TRASH DEBASE
LESSEN SLIGHT BACKCAP
DEBAUCH DEGRADE DEMERIT
DEPRESS DETRACT DISABLE
DOWNCRY IMPEACH BELITTLE
DEROGATE DIMINISH DISCOUNT
DISHONOR DISPRIZE MINIMIZE
MISLIKEN VILIPEND
DISPARAGEMENT DIASYRM
SNIDERY WASHWAY
DISPARAGING SNIDE SLIGHTING
PEJORATIVE
DISPARATE UNEQUAL SEPARATE
DISPARITY DISSENT DISTANCE
IMPARITY
DISPASSIONATE CALM COOL FAIR
STOIC SEDATE SERENE CLINICAL
COMPOSED MODERATE
DISPATCH RID FREE KILL MAIL
NOTE POST SEND SLAY WING
BRIEF ENVOY FLASH HASTE
HURRY SHOOT SPEED DIRECT
EMPLOY HASTEN ADDRESS
COMMAND DELIVER DISPEED
EXPRESS HATCHET BREVIATE
CELERITY CONCLUDE DESPATCH
EXPEDITE TELEGRAM
DISPATCH BOAT AVISO PACKET
DISPATCHER STARTER
DISPEL FRAY SHOO CHASE ASSOIL
BANISH DISCUSS SATISFY

SCATTER DISPERSE
DISPENSATION LAW LILA GRACE
LIVERY ECONOMY FACULTY
QUIENAL TOTQUOT COVENANT
DISPOSAL
DISPENSE DEAL DOLE HELP SHED
WEIGH EFFUSE EXCUSE EXEMPT
FOREGO MANAGE SPREAD
ABSOLVE ARRANGE DISPEND
DRIBBLE MINISTER
(— WITH) MISS WANT SPARE
SUSPENSE
DISPENSER BOMB MANAGER
STEWARD
DISPERSE DOT SOW FRAY MELT
PART ROUT SHED LOOSE SCALE
SEVER SKAIL STREW BAFFLE
DEFEAT DILATE DISPEL SKIVER
SPARSE SPERSE SPREAD UNKNIT
VANISH WINNOW DIFFUSE
DISBAND DISJECT DISMISS
DRIBBLE FRITTER SCATTER
SHATTER SPARKLE SPARPLE
SPERPLE DISSOLVE DISTRACT
SEPARATE SQUANDER STAMPEDE
DISPERSEDLY PASSIM
DISPERSING SCALE
(— SHADOWS) SCIALYTIC
DISPERSION CUT FOAM STAIN
SPREAD DEBACLE SCATTER
DIASPORA EMULSOID SOLUTION
STAMPEDE
(PREF.) LYO
DISPIRIT COW DAMP MATE MULL
CHILL DAUNT DEJECT DEPRESS
FLATTEN OPPRESS
DISPIRITED DOWY DOWIE ABATTU
ABATTUE LETDOWN SHOTTEN
DOWNCAST DOWNSOME
SACKLESS UNHEARTY WOBEGONE
DISPIRITING COLD CHILL DISMAL
DISPLACE BUMP EDGE MOVE STIR
BANISH DEPOSE LUXATE MISLAY
REMOVE WINKLE DERANGE
SWALLOW UNHINGE UNPLACE
ANTEVERT DISLODGE DISPLANT
MISPLACE SUPPLACE SUPPLANT
UNSETTLE
(— LATERALLY) HEAVE
DISPLACED ATOPIC DEPAYSE
DISPLACEMENT JEE BUMP SLIP
HEAVE SCEND SHIFT START
CUBAGE OFFSET UPSLIP FALLING
EVECTION
(— OF STAR) ABERRATION
(DOWNWARD —) PTOSIS
(OPTICAL —) PARALLAX
DISPLAY ACT AIR BRAG DASH
GAUD ORGY POMP SHOW SIGN
STAR WEAR AGONY ARRAY BINGE
BLAZE BOAST DERAY ECLAT
EMOTE FLASH PRIDE SCENE
SHINE SIGHT SPLAY SPORT STAGE
VAUNT BLAZON DEPLOY DESCRY
ESTATE EVINCE EXPOSE EXTEND
FLAUNT MUSTER OSTENT
OUTLAY PARADE REVEAL RUFFLE
SETOUT SPLASH SPRANK SPREAD
UNCASE APPROVE BALLOON
BRAVERY ETALAGE EXHIBIT
EXPRESS FANFARE FLUTTER
GAUDERY PAGEANT PRESENT
SHOWING SPLURGE TRADUCE

UNCOVER BEEFCAKE BLAZONRY
BOOKFAIR CEREMONY DISCLOSE
DISCOVER EMBLAZON EQUIPAGE
EVIDENCE EXERCISE EXPOSURE
FLOURISH INDICATE MANIFEST
PARAFFLE SPLENDOR TINSELRY
(— EXCITEMENT) FAUNCH
(— OF COMPUTER TASKS) MENU
(— OF EMOTION) GUSH
(— OF SKILL) APPERTISE
(BOASTFUL —) JACTATION
(DARING —) BRAVURA
(EMPTY —) GAUD EYEWASH
(EXCESSIVE —) OSTENTATION
(FLORAL —) BLOW BLANKET
(IMPRESSIVE —) SWELL
(LAVISH —) PROFUSION
(OSTENTATIOUS —) DOG GAUDERY
SWAGGER
(RADAR —) SCAN
DISPLAYED SPLAY EXPANDED
DISPLEASE VEX MIFF ANGER
ANNOY PIQUE MISPAY MISSET
OFFEND DISLIKE DISSUIT MISLIKE
PROVOKE IRRITATE
DISPLEASED MAD GLUM UNEASY
UNFAIN
DISPLEASING BAD DRY PUTRID
IRKSOME TEDIOUS UNLOVELY
DISPLEASURE IRE ANGER MUMPS
PIQUE INJURY STRUNT UNLUST
UNWILL DISLIKE OFFENSE
TROUBLE UMBRAGE UNTHANK
DISFAVOR DISGRACE DISTASTE
DISPORT PLAY AMUSE FRISK
SPORT DIVERT FROLIC GAMBOL
DISPLAY
DISPOSAL SALE BANDON
CLEANUP PROPINE BESTOWAL
DEVOTION DISPATCH
(QUICK —) WASHWAY
DISPOSE APT SET BEND CAST
DUMP GIVE MIND TRIM YARK
ARRAY BRUSH DIGHT ORDER
PLACE POSIT ADJUST ATTIRE
BESTOW DIGEST SETTLE TEMPER
APPOINT ARRANGE DISPONE
GESTURE INCLINE PREPARE
RESOLVE DISPATCH REGULATE
(— OF) JOB SELL SCRAP FINISH
HANDLE
DISPOSED APT FIT SET SIB LIEF
DIGHT GIVEN PRONE READY
WRAST MINDED MINDFUL
SUBJECT WILLING ADDICTED
AFFECTED PREGNANT PROCLIVE
PROPENSE PROTENSE TALENTED
(— AT INTERVALS) ALTERNATE
(— TO ACTION) ACTIVE
**(— TO ASSOCIATE WITH ONE
GROUP)** CLANNISH
(— TOWARD) AFFECTED
(FAIRLY —) CANDID
(FAVORABLY —) PROPITIOUS
(WELL —) FAIN INCLINED
DISPOSITION BENT BIAS MAKE
MIND MOOD RACE SORT TRIM
TURN DRIVE ETHOS FRAME
GRAIN HABIT HEART HUMOR
SPITE TACHE AFFECT ANIMUS
DESIGN GENIUS HEALTH KIDNEY
NATURE PTYXIS SPIRIT SPRITE
STRIND TALENT TEMPER

CONCEPT COURAGE DISPOSE
FACULTY STOMACH APTITUDE
ATTITUDE DISPOSAL POSITURE
PERSONALITY
(— OF DRAPERIES) CAST
(— OF PAWNS) SKELETON
(— TO ANGER) CHOLER
(— TO RESIST) DEFIANCE
(GENEROUS —) HEART
(GENIAL —) BONHOMIE
(KINDLY —) CHARITY HUMANITY
(NATURAL —) KIND GRAIN TARAGE
INDOLES
(ORNAMENTAL —) DECOR
(ULTIMATE —) FATE
DISPOSSESS OUST EJECT EVICT
EXPEL STRIP WRONG DEPOSE
DIVEST BEREAVE CASHIER
DEPRIVE DISSEIZE SEPARATE
DISPOSSESSED LUMPEN
DISPOSSESSION OUSTER
DISPRAISE BLAME CENSURE
DISPROOF ELENCH REFUTE
IMPROOF REPROOF
DISPROPORTIONATE UNEQUAL
DISPROVE BREAK REBUT REFEL
NEGATE REFUTE CONFUTE
EXPLODE IMPROVE REPROVE
DISALLOW NEGATIVE REDARGUE
DISPUTABLE MOOT VAGUE
UNSURE DUBIOUS FALLIBLE
DISPUTANT FENCER POLEMIC
WRANGLER
DISPUTATION PARVIS PILPUL
POLEMIC PROBLEM WRANGLE
ARGUMENT COURSING DEBATING
EXERCISE QUODLIBET
DISPUTATIOUS POLEMIC
LITIGIOUS POLEMICAL
DISPUTE JAR ROW TAX CALL
CHOP DENY FEUD FRAY FUSS
HOLD MOOT ODDS RIOT SAKE
SPAR SPAT TILT ARGUE BRAWL
BROIL CABAL CHEST FLITE FLYTE
HURRY PLEAD SPUTE SQUIB
ARGUFY BARNEY BICKER CAMPLE
CANGLE DABBER DACKER DAIKER
DEBATE DIFFER FITTER FRATCH
HAGGLE HASSLE IMPUGN
MATTER NAGGLE SHARRY
SQUALL SQUEAL THREAP
BRABBLE CONTEND CONTEST
DERAIGN DISCEPT DISCUSS
DISSERT FACTION GAINSAY
PRIBBLE QUARREL WRANGLE
ARGUMENT CATFIGHT CONTRARY
POLEMIZE QUESTION SKIRMISH
SPARRING SPLUTTER SQUABBLE
(POETICAL —) FLYTING PARTIMEN
DISQUALIFY DEBAR UNFIT
OUTLAW DISABLE
DISQUIET VEX FEAR FRET PAIN
TOSS UNRO EXCITE UNCALM
UNEASE UNREST AGITATE
ANXIETY DISREST DISTURB
INQUIET PERTURB SOLICIT
TROUBLE TURMOIL UNPEACE
UNQUIET
DISQUIETED UNEASY
DISQUIETINGLY UGLY
DISQUIETUDE CHAGRIN WANREST
WANRUFE
DISRAELI DIZZY

DISREGARD BY SIT BLOW MOCK
OMIT PASS WANE BELAY FLING
WAIVE FORGET HUBRIS IGNORE
SLIGHT UNHEED CASHIER
DESPISE FORHEED LICENCE
LICENSE NEGLECT OVERSEE
DISCOUNT DISFAVOR DISPENSE
DISVALUE EASINESS OVERHALE
OVERLOOK OVERPASS UNREGARD
DISRELISH DISLIKE DISTASTE
DISREPUTABLE LOW BASE GAMY
HARD WAFF GAMEY SEAMY
SEEDY SHADY TOUGH LOUCHE
SHODDY RAFFISH SHAMEFUL
UNHONEST
DISREPUTABLENESS BEGGARY
DISREPUTE DISFAME DISFAVOR
DISHONOR REPROACH
DISRESPECT AFFRONT CONTEMPT
RUDENESS
DISRESPECTFUL HARM SAUCY
UNCIVIL IMPOLITE IMPUDENT
INSOLENT
DISROBE STRIP CHANGE DIVEST
DESPOIL UNDRESS
DISRUPT GASH REND TEAR BREAK
CROSS HAMPER DISRUMP
DISTRACT
DISRUPTED BROKEN DISRUPT
DISRUPTION BREACH BREAKUP
DEBACLE RUPTURE SOLUTION
DISSATISFACTION PAIN DISTASTE
VEXATION
(FEELING OF —) BLAHS
DISSATISFIED UNEASY
MALCONTENT
DISSATISFY MISPAY
DISSECT BAR ANALYZE DISJOIN
SCALPEL UNPIECE
DISSECTED MATURE
DISSECTION ANATOMY ANALYSIS
DISSEMBLE ACT FOX HIDE MASK
CLOAK FEIGN BOGGLE SEMBLE
CONCEAL DISGUISE SIMULATE
SIMULIZE
DISSEMBLER SIMULAR
DISSEMBLING SLY BRAIDE IRONIC
FICTION AESOPIAN IRONICAL
DISSEMINATE SOW BEAR BLAZE
STREW EFFUSE SPREAD DIFFUSE
PUBLISH SCATTER SPARPLE
DISPERSE SEMINATE
DISSEMINATION PROPAGATION
DISSENSION JAR ODDS DEBATE
STRIFE DISCORD DISLIKE DISSENT
FACTION MISLIKE BROILERY
DISPEACE DISTANCE DISUNION
DISUNITY DIVISION FRACTION
FRICTION SEDITION
DISSENT VARY DIFFER HERESY
CONTEND PROTEST DISAGREE
DISSENTER HERETIC SECTARY
RECUSANT SEPARATE RASKOLNIK
(PL.) SEPARATION
DISSENTING PANTILE
DISSEPIMENT REPLUM SEPTUM
PHRAGMA
DISSERTATION ESSAY THEME
TRACT DEBATE MEMOIR SCREED
THESIS DESCANT LECTURE
MEMOIRS EXCURSUS EXERCISE
TRACTATE TREATISE
(— ON TEA) TSIOLOGY

DISSERVICE HARM DAMAGE
INJURY MISCHIEF
DISSIDENT FRONDEUR
DISSIMILAR UNLIKE DIFFORM
DIVERSE UNLIKEN
DISSIMILATE UNLIKEN
DISSIMULATION IRONY DECEIT
DISSIPATE BURN FRAY SPEND
WASTE BANISH DISPEL EXPEND
CONSUME DIFFUSE DISCUSS
FRITTER RESOLVE SCAMBLE
SCATTER SHATTER SWATTLE
TARNISH DISPERSE DISSOLVE
EMBEZZLE EVANESCE SQUANDER
DISSIPATED FAST HIGH LOST
SPORTY OUTWARD RACKETY
DISSIPATION RAKERY
DISSOLUTE LAX LEWD WILD
LOOSE SLACK RAKELY RAKISH
SUBURB UNTIED WANTON
IMMORAL LAWLESS VICIOUS
DESOLATE RAKEHELL RECKLESS
RESOLUTE SUBURBAN UNCURBED
DISSOLUTION END RUIN DECAY
BREAKUP DECEASE DIVORCE
DIALYSIS
(PREF.) LYS(I)
DISSOLVE CUT END DEFY FADE
FUSE MELT SOLV THAW BREAK
FLEET LOOSE SOLVE UNFIX
DIGEST DISTIL RELENT SOLUTE
UNBIND UNGLUE UNKNIT
ADJOURN DESTROY DISBAND
DISJOIN DISTILL DIVORCE
LIQUEFY RESOLVE DISCANDY
DISUNITE SEPARATE
(— OUT) LEACH
(PREF.) LY(O)
DISSOLVED SOLUT REMISS
SOLUTE RESOLUTE
DISSOLVING
(SUFF.) LYSE LYSIS LYST LYTE
LYTIC LYZE
DISSONANCE WOLF DISCORD
DIAPHONY
DISSONANT HARSH RAGGED
GRATING JARRING JANGLING
DISSUADE BLUFF DETER DEHORT
DIVERT RETIRE
DISTAFF ROCK
DISTAFFINA (LOVER OF —)
BOMBASTES
DISTANCE DX WAY BLUE GAIT
GATE LOOK PIPE SPAN STEP
DEPTH DRAFT RANGE SPACE
GROUND HEIGHT LENGTH
SPREAD STANCE STITCH
BOWSHOT BREADTH DRAUGHT
FARNESS JOURNEY MILEAGE
MILEWAY RESERVE STRETCH
YARDAGE COLDNESS COSECANT
DIAMETER FOOTSTEP HANDSPAN
INTERVAL LATITUDE OFFSCAPE
OUTSTRIP
(— ALONG TRACK) LEAD
(— BETWEEN BATTENS) GAG
(— BETWEEN GEAR TEETH) PITCH
(— BETWEEN MASTS) INTERVAL
(— BETWEEN RAILS) GAGE GAUGE
(— BETWEEN RIVET-HEADS) GRIP
(— FOR PUTTING COAL) RENK
(— FROM BELLY TO BACK) BODY
(— FROM EQUATOR) HEIGHT

(— FROM LOCK FACE) BACKSET
(— FROM THE EYE) DEPTH
(— IN ADVANCE) START
(— OF ARCHERY RANGE) BUTT
(— OF BOW SHOT) CAST
(— OF HAUL) LEAD LEADAGE
(— OF TURNING SHIP) ADVANCE
(— OF VISION) KEN
(— ON FISHHOOK) BITE
(— ON GEAR WHEEL) ADDENDUM
(— OVER WHICH WIND BLOWS)
FETCH
(ANGULAR —) ANOMALY
(AT A —) LARGE
(GREAT —) INFINITY
(INTERVENING —) GAP
(PERPENDICULAR —) DROP
CAMBER ALTITUDE
(SAFE —) BERTH
(SEA —) OUTING STEAMING
(SHOOTING —) SHOOT
(SHORT —) INCH SPIT STEP SPELL
BITTIE FOOTSTEP
(SHORT — AWAY) OUTBYE
(SMALL —) HAIR STEP
(UNIT OF —) LI YOJAN PARASANG
DISTANT DX COY FAR OFF AFAR
AWAY BACK COLD SIDE YOND
ALOOF CHILL FERNE HENCE
FERREN REMOTE YONDER
FARAWAY FOREIGN FROSTED
REMOVED STRANGE RESERVED
(— IN TIME) EARLY
(— PART) OFFSCAPE
(MORE —) YOND YONDER
ULTERIOR
(PREF.) TEL(E)(EO)
DISTASTE HATE DEGOUT UNLUST
DISGUST DISLIKE MISLIKE
AVERSION MISTASTE
(— FOR FOOD) APOSITIA
DISTASTEFUL SOUR AUGEAN
BITTER BEASTLY HATEFUL
BRACKISH NAUSEOUS SHOCKING
UNSAVORY REPUGNANT
DISTEMPER SOAK STEEP CHOLER
DILUTE GARGET GARGIL GARGLE
MALADY PANTAS AILMENT
DISEASE ILLNESS DISORDER
DYSCRASE SICKNESS UNSETTLE
(— OF COLT) STRANGLES
DISTEND BAG BLOW FILL GROW
HEFT BLOAT PLUMP STRUT
SWELL WIDEN DILATE EXPAND
EXTEND INTEND SPREAD
BALLOON ENLARGE INFLATE
STRETCH
DISTENDED BIG FULL PENT TAUT
TRIG WIDE BLOWN POOCH TUMID
ASTRUT GRAVID BLOATED
DISTENT SWOLLEN INFLATED
PATULENT PATULOUS
DISTENDEDLY ASTRUT
DISTENTION BLOAT DISTENT
TYMPANY
DISTHENE CYANITE KYANITE
DISTICH SLOKA PROODE COUPLET
DISTILL DROP ELIX EMIT RATE
STILL DISTIL EXTILL INFUSE
ALEMBIC LIMBECK TRICKLE
DISTILLATE GUNDY ROSIN BENZIN
ALCOHOL BENZINE
DISTILLATION RUN DESCENT

DISTILLER ABKAR STILLER
DISTILLERY STILL JIGGER STILLERY
DISTINCT HOT FAIR FREE VIVE
BREME BRISK CLEAR PLAIN
SHARP VIVID PLUCKY PROPER
SECRET SUNDRY ANOTHER
ASUNDER DIVERSE EVIDENT
LEGIBLE OBVIOUS PRECISE
SCIOLTO SEVERAL SPECIAL
APPARENT DISCRETE DIVIDUAL
PALPABLE PECULIAR SEPARATE
TRENCHANT
(PREF.) CHORI CHORIST(O) IDIO
DISTINCTION MARK NOTE RANK
SHED TEST CLASS GLORY HONOR
FIGURE LAUREL LUSTER LUSTRE
RENOWN DIORISM QUALITY
QUILLET ACCESSIT DIVISION
GRANDEZA SUBTLETY
REFINEMENT
(ACADEMIC —) HONORS HONOURS
(LACKING —) VANILLA
(WITHOUT —) COMMON
DISTINCTIVE JUICY DIRECT
PROPER SIGNAL PECULIAR
PHONEMIC SEPARATE SPANKING
TALENTED
DISTINCTIVENESS EMPHASIS
DISTINCTLY CLEAR REDLY FAIRLY
CLEARLY
DISTINCTNESS PLUCK CLARITY
SEVERALTY
(LACKING —) SMUDGY
DISTINGUISH DEEM KNOW MARK
SORT BADGE JUDGE LABEL SEVER
SKILL STAMP DECERN DEFINE
DESCRY DEVISE DIVIDE ENSIGN
SECERN SINGLE CONCERN
DISCERN DESCRIBE PERCEIVE
SEPARATE
DISTINGUISHED CLEAR GREAT
NOTED SWELL BANNER FAMOUS
GENTLE MARKED SOLEMN
EMINENT INSIGNE NOTABLE
SIGNATE SPECIAL TOPPING
DISTINCT ESPECIAL LAUREATE
RENOWNED SPLENDID
CONSPICUOUS
DISTINGUISHING BETWEEN
DISTORT WRY SKEW WARP CLOUD
COLOR FUDGE SCREW TWIST
WREST WRING CRINGE DEFACE
DEFORM DETORT GARBLE
MANGLE SHEVEL WRENCH
WRITHE BLUBBER CONTORT
FALSIFY GRIMACE PERVERT
SHACHLE SHACKLE SLANDER
OUTIMAGE WIREDRAW
DISTORTED WRY AWRY SKEW
ASKEW CRANK SKEWED WARPED
CROOKED DISTORT GNARLED
LOXOTIC WRITHEN CAMSHACH
DEFORMED DEGRADED STRAINED
TORTIOUS PERVERTED
DISTORTING CONVULSION
DISTORTION FIB HOG SAG WOW
WREST STRAIN FLUTTER
GRIMACE GARBLING SKEWNESS
(— IN WOOD) WARP DIAMONDING
DISTRACT MAD AMUSE CRAZE
STROY BEMUSE DETRAY DIVERT
HARASS INSANE MADDEN MITHER
MOIDER PUZZLE TWITCH AGITATE

CONFUSE DETRACT DISTURB
EMBROIL PERPLEX SCATTER
BEWILDER CONFOUND FORHAILE
DISTRACTED GYTE WILD CRAZY
EPERDU STRACT FRANTIC
SCRANNY FRENETIC
DISTRACTION ALARM BLIND
ALARUM ESCAPE FRENZY
TUMULT ECSTASY
DISTRAIN NAM NAAM DRIVE
POIND STRAIN STRESS DISTRESS
POUNDAGE
DISTRAINT NAM NAAM POIND
DISTRAUGHT MAD CRAZED
FRANTIC DERANGED DISTRACT
DISTRAIT STRAUGHT
DISTRESS AIL ILL MAR VEX BITE
CARK GNAW HURT MOAN NEED
PAIN PORT PUSH TEAR TEEN
AGONY ANGER ANNOY DOLOR
GRATE GRIEF GRILL GRIPE LABOR
PINCH PRESS SMART TRYST
TWEAK WORRY WOUND WRING
BARRAT DANGER DURESS GRIEVE
GRUDGE HARASS HARROW
LAMENT MISERY SORROW STRESS
TAKING THRONG WORRIT
AFFLICT ANGUISH ANXIETY
CHAGRIN DAYMARE DESTROY
DISEASE EXTREME HERSHIP
MISEASE OPPRESS PASSION
PENANCE PERPLEX STURBLE
TORMENT TORTURE TRAVAIL
TROUBLE UNQUERT AGGRIEVE
CALAMITY DARKNESS DISTASTE
DISTRAIN EXIGENCE FORHAILE
PRESSURE SORENESS STRAITEN
WANDRETH GRIEVANCE
DISTRESSED WRUNG DOWNGONE
DISTRESSFUL STRAIT
DISTRESSING BAD HOT SAD GRIM
HARD SORE BLEAK CHARY CRUEL
DIRTY SHARP BITTER SEVERE
SHREWD THORNY CARKING
FEARFUL GRIPING PAINFUL
GRIEVOUS
DISTRIBUTE DOT SOW CAST DEAL
DOLE GRID METE SEED SORT
TAME ALLOT CLASS DIVVY ISSUE
PLACE SHARE SHIFT SPEND
ASSIGN ASSORT DEPART DEVISE
DIGEST DIVIDE EXPEND IMPART
PARCEL REPART SPARSE SPREAD
ARRANGE DISPEND DISPOSE
EROGATE PRORATE SCATTER
ALLOCATE CLASSIFY DESCRIBE
DISBURSE DISPENSE DISPERSE
SEPARATE SPRINKLE
(— GUNFIRE) SEARCH
(— SEED) SOW SEED DRILL
(— TYPE) DISH THROW
DISTRIBUTED BALANCED
DISPERSE
DISTRIBUTION DOLE SALE ARRAY
DIVVY DETAIL DIVIDE PARTING
DISPOSAL DIVIDEND
DISTRIBUTIVELY EACH APIECE
DISTRIBUTOR SOWER SHARER
CARRIER ZANJERO
DISTRICT DO AMT GAU LAN SOC
WAY WON AREA COIL FARM
HUNT LEET LIWA PALE PART SIDE
SLUM SOKE TEMA WARD WENE

WICK WOON AIMAK ANNEX COILA
EXURB HARSH JAGIR JEWRY
MAHAL OKRUG PAGUS PARTY
SHIRE SOKEN TALUK TEMAN
TRACT VICUS AGENCY BARRIO
BOWERY CANTON CERCLE CIRCLE
COUNTY FOREST JAGHIR MARKAZ
MEMBER MERINA OKROOG
PARAMO PARISH POLLAM
REGARD REGION SIRCAR STAPLE
STREET SYSSEL VINTRY ZILLAH
CALABAR CIRCUIT CLASSIS
COMARCA COMMUNE COUNTRY
CURRAGH DEMESNE DIOCESE
ENCLAVE FREEDOM LIBERTY
MAHALLA MALACCA MAYFAIR
MELIZKI MISSION PIMLICO
PURLIEU QUARTER SEASIDE
SLUMDOM THANAGE THEBAID
UPRIVER CHAPELRY CIMARRON
DISTRITO DIVISION FAUBOURG
GILDABLE LEGATION MACASSAR
MAGAZINE MONTANAS PRECINCT
PROVINCE REGIMENT
MAGISTRACY PREFECTURE
(— BORDERING RIVER) WATER
(— OF COURT) LEET
(— OF JAPAN) DO KEN
(BROTHEL —) STEW
(BURNED —) QUEMADO
(CHINESE —) HIEN
(COASTAL —) RIVIERA
(ECCLESIASTICAL —) SYNOD
CLASSIS DIOCESE
(HUNTING —) WALK
(ICELANDIC —) SYSSEL
(JUDICIAL —) CIRCUIT
(OUTWARD —) END
(POOR —) SLUM SLUMS
(POSTAL —) RAYON
(RURAL —) WAYBACK
(RURAL —S) STICKS
(RUSSIAN —) OBLAST STANITSA
STANITZA
(TENANT —) THIRL
(TRIBAL —) GAU
(TURKISH —) ORDU SANJAK
(PL.) GAELTACHT
DISTRUST FEAR DOUBT DREAD
STRIFE DIFFIDE SUSPECT
UNFAITH UNTRUST DEFIANCE
DISFAITH MISFAITH MISTRUST
QUESTION WANTRUST
DISTRUSTFUL SHY LEERY JEALOUS
DISTURB JEE VEX BUSY FAZE FRET
FUSS JOLT RILE ROCK ROIL STIR
TOSS ALARM ANNOY BRASH
DROVE FEEZE KNOCK PHASE
ROUSE SHAKE STEER UPSET
AFFRAY BOTHER HARASS JOSTLE
MOLEST RUFFLE SQUEAK
UNCALM UNEASE AGITATE
COMMOTE COMMOVE CONCUSS
DERANGE DISREST DRUMBLE
FRAZZLE GARBOIL INQUIET
MISMAKE PERTURB SCUFFLE
SOLICIT STURBLE TEMPEST
TROUBLE CONVULSE DISJOINT
DISORDER DISQUIET DISTRACT
DISTRESS FRIGHTEN
(— BY HANDLING) TOUCH
(— SUDDENLY) START
(— THE PEACE) RIOT INQUIET

DISTURBANCE VEX BOIL BREE CAIN COIL DUST RIOT ROUT STIR WIND WORK ALARM BEANO BRAWL BROIL DERAY FUGUE FUROR HURRY SHINE SHOCK STEER STORM STROW STURT TOUSE AFFRAY BOTHER BREEZE CATHRO DESRAY FRACAS FRAISE FURORE HUBBUB KICKUP POTHER RUCKUS RUMBLE RUMPUS SHINDY SQUALL STATIC TUMULT TURNUP UPROAR BLUNDER BOBBERY BRULYIE BRULZIE CHAGRIN CLATTER CLUTTER DISTURB EMOTION FERMENT GRINDER MADNESS ROOKERY RUCTION TROUBLE TURMOIL BROILERY BUSINESS DISORDER FOOFARAW INCIDENT REELRALL STRAMASH TRAVALLY RABBLEMENT PERTURBATION
(— OF OCEAN) SEA
(ATMOSPHERIC —) STORM GRINDER
(DIGESTIVE —) BLOAT
(MENTAL —) FRENZY PHRENSY DELIRIUM
(SEISMIC —) SEAQUAKE
DISTURBED CRACKED INQUIET MAKADOO TROUBLE AGITATED FLURRIED STREAKED
DISTURBING BREAK NASTY HAUNTING
DISUNION DIVORCE
DISUNITE RIP PART SEVER UNTIE DETACH DIVIDE SUNDER UNKNIT UNLIME DISBAND DISJOIN DISLINK DISSENT DIVORCE UNRAVEL ALIENATE DISSEVER DISSOLVE ESTRANGE SEPARATE UNSOLDER
DISUNITY DISCORD DISUNION DIVISION
DISUSE MISUSE OUTAGE ABANDON DISCARD DISUSAGE MISAPPLY
DISUSED DEAD WASTE DESUETE EXOLETE OBSOLETE
DITCH GAW RUT SAP SOW DELF DICK DIKE DYKE FOSS GOOL GOUT GRIP GURT HOLL LEET LODE MOAT SEEK SICK SIKE SINK TRIG CANAL CLAUD DELFT DELVE FENCE FLEAM FOSSA FOSSE GRAFF GRAFT GRAVE GRIPE GROOP GULLY PUDGE RHEEN RHINE RIGOL SEWER SHORE SLONK SLUIT SOUGH STANK STELL ZANJA GUTTER GUZZLE HOLLOW RELAIS SHEUCH SHEUGH TRENCH ZANJON ABANDON ACEQUIA CHANNEL GRINDLE GRIPPLE LATERAL VANFOSS ZANJONA WATERING
(MUDDY —) LETCH
(NARROW —) RELAIS
(OPEN —) STELL
(WIDE —) SLOT
(PREF.) FOSSI
DITCH GRASS ENALID
DITCH MILLET HUREEK PASPALUM
DITCH REED SPIRE BENNEL
DITHER SHAKE TIZZY BOTHER

LATHER SHIVER TROUBLE
DITI (FATHER OF —) DAKSHA
(HUSBAND OF —) KASHYAPA
DITROCHEE DIPODY
DITTO SAME REPEAT LIKEWISE
DITTY DIT LAY DITE DYTE POEM SING SONG THEME VERSE SAYING DICTATE VINETTA
DIURETIC ZEA CAVA KAVA BUCCO BUCHU CUBEB LAPPA PICHI SABAL NASROL DROSERA EMICTORY PIPSISSEWA
DIVAN SOFA OTTOMAN SOCIABLE
DIVE BAR DEN DASH DUMP JOINT SOUSE GAINER HEADER PLUNGE SALOON BROTHEL JACKNIFE SUBMERGE
(KIND OF —) SWAN TWIST GAINER JACKKNIFE
(MAKE A NOSE —) PEARL
DIVER AMA LOON DUCKER PEARLER PLUNGER PLUNGEON
(SCUBA —) AQUANAUT
(SUFF.) DYTA DYTES
DIVERGE LEAVE BRANCH DIFFER DIVIDE RAMIFY SPREAD SQUARE SWERVE DEVIATE DIGRESS DIVERSE DISAGREE DIVAGATE
DIVERGENCE DIP ERROR CHANGE SPREAD SWERVE VAGARY CONTRAST OBLIQUITY
DIVERGENT OFF APART REMOTE TANGENT VARIANT
(MORE —) FARTHER
DIVERS EVIL MANY CRUEL SUNDRY SEVERAL VARIOUS PERVERSE DIFFERING
(PREF.) PARTI PARTY
DIVERSE EVIL SERE MOTLEY SUNDRY UNLIKE VARIED ADVERSE SEVERAL VARIOUS DISTINCT PERVERSE SEPARATE VARIETAL
(PREF.) PARTI PARTY POLY VARI(O)
DIVERSIFIED MOTLEY EXTENDED
DIVERSIFY DOT FRET VARY CHECK FRECK BEGARIE CHECKER VARIATE SPRINKLE
DIVERSION JEU GAME MASK PLAY ALARM FEINT FRISK HOBBY SPORT ATTACK DEDUIT DIVERT LAUGHS SCHEME SOLACE DISPORT PASTIME ESCAPISM PLEASURE SIDESHOW VARIORUM
(— OF STREAM) CAPTURE
DIVERSITY CHANGE DISCORD DISSENT VARIETY CONTRAST
(PREF.) POLY
DIVERT SWAY AMUSE BLANK RELAX SHUNT SPORT WRING DERAIL DERIVE DETURN SIPHON SWITCH SYPHON TICKLE BEGUILE CELIGHT DECEIVE DEFLECT DETRACT DISPORT PASTIME PERVERT REFLECT ABSTRACT DISSUADE DISTRACT ESTRANGE RECREATE
(— ATTENTION) COVER
(— HEADWATERS) BEHEAD
(— STREAM) CAPTURE
(— WATER) FLUME
DIVERTED MERRY

AMUSED DISTRACT
DIVERTICULUM UTERUS OLEOCYST
DIVERTING DROLL AMUSING FOOLISH PLEASANT SPORTFUL LAUGHABLE
DIVEST BARE DOFF REFT TIRL EMPTY EXUTE REAVE SHEAR SPOIL STRIP DELAWN DENUDE DEPOSE DEVEST DISMIT UNVEST BEREAVE DEPRIVE DESPOIL DISROBE UNCOVER UNDRESS DENATURE DETHRONE UNCLOTHE
(— OF) ABDICATE
(— OF ARMOR) DEMAIL
(— OF VALUE) DEVALUE
DIVIDE CUT LOT CAST DEAL FORK MERE PART RIFT SHED SLIP TEAR ZONE BREAK CARVE CLASS CLEFT DIVVY GAVEL JOINT SCALE SCIND SEVER SHARE SHIFT SLICE SNACK SPACE SPLIT SPRIT WHACK BEPART BISECT BRANCH CANTLE CANTON CLEAVE COTEAU DEPART DEVISE DIFFER DOMIFY INDENT PARCEL RAMIFY SECTOR SEJOIN SLEAVE SUNDER ALIQUOT ANALYZE ATOMIZE AVERAGE BRITTEN COMPART DIFFUSE DIREMPT DISCIDE DISPART DISSECT DIVERGE FISSURE FRITTER PARTAKE PRORATE ALLOCATE CLASSIFY CROSSCUT DISCRETE DISSEVER DISTRACT DISUNITE FRACTION FRAGMENT GRADUATE HEMISECT MEDISECT SEPARATE STRATIFY UNSEEDER
(— BEEF) BLOCK
(— FILAMENTS) SLEAVE
(— INTO DISTRICTS) CANTON
(— INTO MEASURES) BAR
(— INTO PIECES) GOBBET
(— INTO 2 PARTS) HALVE BISECT
(— INTO 4 PARTS) QUARTER
(— LAND) STINT
(— NATURALLY) FALL
(— SMALL) SCANTLE
DIVIDED ENTE REFT SIDE CLEFT FORKY SPLIT ATOMIC CLOVEN PRONGY FISSATE FOURCHE GYRONNY PARTITE SEPTATE AEROLATE CAMERATE DIVIDUAL FOURCHEE
(— IN TWO) FOURCHE DIMIDIATE
(— INTO 4 PARTS) PALY QUARTERED
(— TWICE) RETAILLE
(NOT —) GLOBAL
(PREF.) CHORI(ST)(STO) FISSI PARTI PARTY SCHIZ(O)
(SUFF.) FID FIDATE SECT SECTED TOMOUS
DIVIDEND BONUS SHARE
DIVIDER BUNTON MERIST SHARER BUNTING COMPASS SEVERER DIVIDANT
DIVI-DIVI LIBIDIBI
DIVINATION OMEN SORS SORT AUGURY MANTIC SORTES AUSPICE SCRYING SORCERY GEOMANCY TAGHAIRM
(— SCIENCE) MANTIC

(PREF.) MANTO
(SUFF.) MANCER MANCY MANTIC
DIVINE HOLY SORT SPAE TWIG AREAD AREED ATMAN AUGUR DIVUS GUESS PIOUS DEIFIC DETECT DEVISE GODFUL HALSEN PRIEST SACRED BLESSED FORESEE GODLIKE PORTEND PREDICT PRESAGE ARIOLATE CONTRIVE FOREBODE FOREKNOW FORETELL HEAVENLY IMMORTAL MINISTER PERCEIVE UBIQUIST SPIRITUAL
DIVINER SEER AUGUR SIBYL ARUSPEX AUGURER PROPHET HARUSPEX
DIVING BELL NAUTILUS
DIVING BOARD RISE
DIVING SUIT GANGAVA
DIVINING ROD TWIG DOWSER
DIVINITY (ALSO SEE GOD AND GODDESS) JOSS LLEU LLEW TIEN AHURA DEITY HYBLA NUADA NUADU NYMPH POWER ATHTAR VEDUIS GLAUCUS GODDESS GODHEAD GODSHIP HYBLAEA TARANIS VIRBIUS TEUTATES VEDIOVIS
(— CIRCUIT BINDING) YAPP
(PL.) CABIRI ELOHIM
DIVISIBLE SECABLE DIVIDUAL PARTIBLE
(— BY 2) AIM
DIVISION BAY BOX CUT DAG FIT JAG LEG CHAP CLAN DOLE FARM FAUN FORK GELD GELT GORE HOLD LITH NEAT PACE PANE PART RANK RAPE RIFT CAPUT CHASM CLASS CLEFT CURIA DIGOR DIVVY DULAN DULAT FIELD FIGHT GENOS GRANT GROUP IJORE MURUT PERES REALM SHARD SHARE SUBAH TAXIS THEME TOMAN WHEEN BARONY CANTON COHORT DECADE DECURY DEGREE DIVIDE EOGAEA HAWIYA IMAHAL JHURIA PORTIO SCHISM SEASON SECTOR SUNDER VOLOST ZILLAH BREAKUP COMARCA CUSTODY DIOCESE DUALISM ENOMOTY FISSURE FURLONG HASHIYA KINGDOM KITKSAN NATUARY PARTAGE PARTING ROULADE SECTION SEGMENT SUBRACE ARPEGGIO CATEGORY CLEAVAGE DECANATE DIERESIS DISTRICT FASCICLE MEROTOMY PARGANNA PRECINCT SCISSION SCISSURE SHEDDING SQUADRON SUBCLASS
(— BETWEEN PIERS) BAY
(— BETWEEN STALLS) BAIL
(— FOR TAXATION) GELD
(— IN DENMARK) AMT
(— IN HUNGARY) COMITAT
(— IN MINING BED) CLEAVE
(— OF ANGELS) CHOIR
(— OF ARMY) BATTLE LOCHUS
(— OF BEJA) BISHARIN
(— OF BOOK) CHAPTER FASCICLE
(— OF BUILDING) STORY STOREY
(— OF CHARIOTEERS) FACTION
(— OF CHURCH) AISLE

(— OF CONTEST) HEAT INNING
(— OF COUNTY) RAPE BARONY HUNDRED
(— OF CROPLAND) FLAT
(— OF DISCOURSE) HEADING
(— OF DRAMA) ACT SCENE
(— OF FAMILY) BRANCH
(— OF FIELD) RIG
(— OF FOOT) SEMEION
(— OF FOREST) WARD
(— OF GEOLOGICAL TIME) ERA EPOCH PERIOD
(— OF GRASS) SPRIG
(— OF GREAT HORDE) DULAN DULAT KANGLA KANGLI
(— OF HEADLINE) BANK DECK
(— OF HERALDIC SHIELD) POINT
(— OF ISLE OF MAN) SHEADING
(— OF KENT) LATHE
(— OF LAND) LAINE KONOHIKI
(— OF LEGION) COHORT HASTATI MANIPLE TRIARII
(— OF LOG LINE) KNOT
(— OF MANCHU ARMY) BANNER
(— OF MANKIND) RACE
(— OF MEAL) COURSE
(— OF NIGHT) WATCH
(— OF ORANGE) LITH
(— OF POEM) FIT DUAN CANTO STANZA STROPHE
(— OF PROCESS) STAGING
(— OF ROCKS) SYSTEM
(— OF ROSARY) DECADE CHAPLET
(— OF SOCIETY) CASTE ATOMISM
(— OF SONG) FIT
(— OF STOPE) FLOOR
(— OF STRUCTURE) STAGE
(— OF SUSSEX) RAPE
(— OF TREF) RANDIR
(— OF UTTERANCE) COLON
(— OF WINDOW) DAY
(— OF YORKSHIRE) RIDING
(— OF ZILLAH) PARGANA
(— OF ZODIAC) SIGN DECAN
(— OVER ISSUE) BREACH
(ADMINISTRATIVE —) FU LATHE CHARGE CIRCLE COUNTY EYALET CUSTODY DIOCESE TOWNSHIP
(ANTHROPOLOGICAL —) STOCK
(ARMY —) MORA
(ASTROLOGICAL —) FACE
(CELL —) MITOSIS AMITOSIS
(ECCLESIASTICAL —) SCHISM SOCIETY PRECINCT
(GEOLOGICAL —) ERA LIAS MALM BUNTER KEUPER LUDIAN SERIES LARAMIE ARNUSIAN RICHMOND
(HINGED —) LEAF
(ISLE OF MAN —) SHEADING
(MUSICAL —) ALLEGRO
(NUCLEAR —) FISSION
(PHILIPPINE —) ATO
(POLICE —) TANA THANA
(POLITICAL —) ATO CITY LATHE STATE COUNTY PARISH BOROUGH HUNDRED SURPLUS DISTRICT PURCHASE WAPENTAKE
(POPULATION —) STRATUM
(SOCIAL —) HORDE
(TRIBAL —) CLAN
(SUFF.) KINESIS
DIVITIACUS (BROTHER OF —) DUMNORIX

DIVORCE GET GETT AHSAN HASAN KHULA SEVER TALAK SUNDER ASUNDER DISBAND DISMISS MUBARAT UNMARRY DISSOLVE DISUNION DISUNITE SEPARATE
DIVOT CLOD TURF
DIVULGE BARE CALL SHOW TELL BLURT BREAK SPILL UTTER VOICE BABBLE BEWRAY EVULGE IMPART REVEAL SPREAD UNFOLD PROPALE PUBLISH UNCOVER DISCLOSE DISCOVER EVULGATE PROCLAIM
DIZZINESS HILO SWIM DINUS TIEGO MEGRIM VANITY MERLIGO SCOTOMY VERTIGO SWIMMING WILLNESS
DIZZY DUNT CRAZY FAINT GIDDY LIGHT TOTTY WESTY WOOZY FICKLE STUPID FOOLISH SWIMMING UNSTEADY
DJIBOUTI (GULF OF —) TADJOURA
DNA (— SEGMENT) CISTRON
DO D ACT DIV FAY TRY BILK BURN CHAR COME DEAL DOST MAKE PASS SUIT AVAIL BITCH CHEAT EXERT GUISE SERVE SHIFT TRICK ANSWER COMMIT NOBBLE RENDER ACHIEVE EXECUTE PERFORM PRODUCE SATISFY SUFFICE TRANSACT
(— AWAY WITH) BURK ABATE BURKE FORDO BANISH FOREDO ABOLISH AMOLISH CASHIER CONSUME ABROGATE DEMOLISH DISSOLVE IMBOLISH RETRENCH
(— BUSINESS) CHAFFER
(— CARELESSLY) SLIM
(— CASUAL WORK) GRASS
(— FOR) FIX GET JACK POOP SINK FETCH NAPOO DIDDLE SCUPPER
(— IMPERFECTLY) HUDDLE
(— IN SLOVENLY WAY) SLUBBER
(— INJURY) BANE
(— NOT) DONT DINNA
(— PENANCE) SATISFY
(— PIECEWORK) DACKER
(— SMARTLY) LINK
(— THOROUGHLY) FLOOR
(— WITHOUT) LACK SPARE FORBEAR DISPENSE
(— WRONG) ERR SIN MISCARRY
(— YE) DEE
DOABLE AGIBLE
DOBLON ISABELLA
DOBRA JO JOE OCTAVE
DOCENT TUTOR TEACHER LECTURER
DOCILE CALM MEEK TALL TAME TAWIE FACILE GENTLE DOCIOUS DUCTILE DUTIFUL BIDDABLE OBEDIENT TOWARDLY
DOCK BOB CUT PEN BANG CLIP MOOR PIER QUAY RUMP SCUT BASIN SHORE WHARF CAMBER COFFER DOCKEN FIDDLE HAMBLE MARINA SORREL STRUNT BOBTAIL CURTAIL PARELLA PARELLE SHORTEN CANAIGRE PATIENCE SHIPSIDE
DOCKAGE BERTHAGE
DOCKMACKIE VIBURNUM
DOCKYARD ARSENAL

(— WORKMAN) MATEY
DOCTOR (ALSO SEE PHYSICIAN) DOC COOK DOPE DOSE FAKE PILL BRUJO HAKIM LEECH SUGAR TREAT CROCUS DEACON EXTERN HAIKUN HEALER INTERN MAULVI POWWOW CROAKER KORADJI TEACHER MEDICATE PHYSICIAN MANIPULATE
(— OF CANON LAW) JCD
(— OF LAWS) JD
(— UP) COOK FAKE EYEWASH
(PLAY —) FIXER
(QUACK —) CROCUS
(WITCH —) BOCOR BOKOR GOOFER GUFFER WIZARD WITCHMAN
DOCTOR'S DILEMMA (AUTHOR OF —) SHAW
(CHARACTER IN —) LOUIS RALPH CULLEN COLENSO DUBEDAT PATRICK RIDGEON WALPOLE JENNIFER BONINGTON BLENKINSOP
DOCTRINAIRE ISMY.
DOCTRINE ISM DOXY LEAR LORE RULE CREDO CREED DOGMA LIGHT MAXIM TABLE TENET ZOISM AHIMSA BABISM BELIEF DHARMA EGOISM EROTIC GOSPEL HOLISM MALISM MONISM NOETIC THEORY ACROAMA AMIDISM ANIMISM ARTICLE ATAVISM ATHEISM ATOMISM BAHAISM DUALISM EGOTISM EVANGEL KARAISM KRYPSIS MISHNAH NEOLOGY NOETICS OPINION PEELISM PRECEPT PROGRAM REALISM SENSISM TRIKAYA ACTIVISM AGATHISM ANALYTIC ARIANISM ARYANISM BAJANISM CHILIASM CYNICISM DARBYISM DEVILISM DOCETISM DYNAMISM ENERGISM FATALISM FINALISM GOBINISM HEDONISM HYLOLOGY IDENTISM IDEOLOGY ISLAMISM MOLINISM NIHILISM PAJONISM PAMNESIA PEJORISM POSITION POSOLOGY PSYCHISM REGALISM RHEMATIC SIDERISM SOLIDISM SPHERICS TYPOLOGY UBIQUITY VITALISM DITHEISM MECHANISM MUTUALISM PANTHEISM PESSIMISM PLURALISM NATURALISM
(BAD —) CACODOXY
(BUDDHIST —) ANATTA ANATMAN
(CONTRARY —) HERESY
(ESOTERIC —) CABALA QABBALA CABALISM
(EVIL —) MOLOCH
(PL.) ESOTERY SCOTISM CREDENDA DONATISM LABADISM SCRIBISM
(SUFF.) ISM LOGER LOGIA(N) LOGIC(AL) LOGIST LOGUE LOGY OLOGY
DOCUMENT DOC GET BILL BOND BOOK CALL CHOP DEED FORM GETT OLLA SEAL WRIT CHART DEMIT DIMIT GRIEF LEASE PAPER PROOF SCRIP SCRIT STIFF TARGE TEACH TITLE BILLET BREVET CADJAN CAJANG CEDULA COCKET DOCKET PATENT RAGMAN SCHOOL SCRIPT SOURCE SURVEY TICKET VOLUME ARCHIVE CONDUCT DIPLOMA ELOHIST ESCRIPT EXHIBIT INQUEST LICENSE MISSIVE PLACARD PRECEPT WARRANT WAYBILL WHEREAS WRITING CITATION CONTRACT COVENANT FURLOUGH INSTRUCT MORTGAGE SCHEDULE SECURITY TRANSIRE BORDEREAU
(CONDITIONAL —) SCRIP
(COPY OF —) VIDIMUS
(PL.) BUMF ARCHIVE ARCHIVES PALAPALA
DODAVAH (SON OF —) ELIEZER
DODDER SCAD SCALD SHAKE DODDLE DOTHER FIDEOS TOTTER TREMBLE FLAXDROP HAIRWEED HALEWEED HELLWEED MULBERRY
DODDERING OLD ANILE INANE INFIRM SENILE FOOLISH
DODDER LAUREL WOEVINE MISTLETOE
DODDIE HUMLIE
DODECANESE (— ISLAND) KOS SYME KASOS LEROS TELOS KHALKE LIPSOS PATMOS NISYROS KALYMNOS
DODGE RIG SHY BILK DUCK GAME JINK JOUK LURK RUSE AVOID CHEAT ELUDE EVADE FENCE FUDGE GLOSS LURCH PARRY PLANT SHIFT SHIRK SHUNT STALL TRICK ESCAPE FIDDLE PALTER RACKET WHEEZE DECEIVE EVASION PROFFER ARTIFICE CROTCHET GILENYIE MALINGER SIDESTEP
DODGER FLIER FLYER SOGER HAGGLER HANDBILL
(DRAFT —) BUSHWACK
DODGING JINK
DODO (SON OF —) ELEAZAR ELHANAN
DOE DA ROE TEG FAUN HIND NANNY ALMOND BISCUIT
(— IN 1ST YEAR) FAWN
(BLUE —) FLIER FLYER
DOER ACTOR AGENT MAKER AUTHOR FACTOR FEASOR WORKER FACIENT MANAGER ATTORNEY EXECUTOR
(— OF ODD JOBS) JACK
(SUFF.) AST ATOR IST OR STER STRESS
DOES S DOTH DUSE
(— NOT) DONT DISNA DOESNT
DOFF OFF DAFF VAIL AVALE DOUSE DOWSE STRIP DIVEST REMOVE UNDRESS
DOFFER DRUM DUFFER
DOFFING CAP
DOG CUR MUT PUG PUP YAP ALAN ALCO CHOW DANE FAUS GOER KIYI MONG MUTT PAWL STAG TIKE TRAY TYKE ALAND ALANT ARGOS BAWTY BEDOG BESET BOUCH BOXER CALEB CANID CORGI DERBY DODGE HOUND HUSKY LIMER PELON POOCH

PUPPY RACHE RAKER RATCH
SILKY SLING SPITZ STALK WHELP
AFGHAN BANDOG BARBET
BARKER BASSET BAWTIE BEAGLE
BELTON BORZOI BOSTON
BOWWOW BRIARD BUFFER
CANINE COCKER COLLIE COONER
DANCER DETENT DRIVER ESKIMO
FINDER GUNDOG HEADER HEELER
HUNTER JOWLER KELPIE KENNET
MISSET POODLE RANGER RATTER
SALUKI SEIZER SETTER SHOUGH
SIRIUS SUSSEX TALBOT TOLLER
TOWSER VIZSLA YAPPER YAUPER
YELPER BASENJI BOARDER
BULLDOG CARRIER COURSER
CRAMPON CREEPER DOGGESS
DROPPER GRIFFON HARRIER
LURCHER MALTESE MASTIFF
MONGREL OWTCHAH POINTER
SCOTTIE SKIRTER SLEUGHI
SPANIEL SPORTER STARTER
TERRIER TUMBLER WHIPPET
YAPSTER ABERDEEN AIREDALE
ALEUTIAN ALSATIAN CERBERUS
COACHDOG CYNHYENA
DEMIWOLF DOBERMAN
ELKHOUND FISSIPED FOXHOUND
KEESHOND LABRADOR LANDSEER
LONGTAIL MALEMUTE MALINOIS
PAPILLON PEKINESE SAMOYEDE
SEALYHAM SHEPHERD SIBERIAN
SPRINGER TURNSPIT VERMINER
WATCHDOG WATERRUG
PEKINGESE POMERANIAN
AFFENPINSCHER
(— OF INDIA) PARIAH
(— OF LATHE) DRIVER
(— TRAINED AS DECOY) TOLLER
(BELGIAN —) SCHIPPERKE
(BIRD —) BOLTER
(CHAINED —) BANDOG
(CHINESE —) SHIHTZU
(DECOY —) PIPER
(ESKIMO —) HUSKY SIWASH
(FARM —) KOMONDOR
(FEMALE —) GYP SLUT BITCH
DOGGESS
(FOXLIKE —) COLPEO
(GERMAN —) ROTTWEILER
(HOUSE —) WAP WAPP
(HUNGARIAN —) PULI KUVASZ
(HUNTING —) ALAN BRACH RACHE
RATCH ALAUND BASSET HUNTER
KENNET LUCERN RACCHE SALUKI
SEIZER SETTER SLOUGH COURSER
DROPPER HARRIER POINTER
STRIKER
(JAPANESE —) AKITA
(LAP —) MESSAN SHOUGH
(LARGE —) DANE TOWSER
MASTIFF KOMONDOR
(LIKE A —) CYNIC
(LONG-HAIRED —) ALCO SHOCK
(MONGREL —) CUR BRAKJE
DEMIWOLF
(NON-BARKING —) BASENJI
(PART OF —) PAD PAW TOE ARCH
BACK DOME HOCK KNEE LOIN
RUMP STOP CHEEK CHEST CREST
CROUP ELBOW FLEWS THIGH
CARPUS DEWLAP MUZZLE STIFLE
BRISKET CUSHION KNUCKLE

LEATHER OCCIPUT PASTERN
WITHERS FOREHEAD HEELKNOB
(PARTI-COLORED —) PIE PYE
(PET —) MINX LAPDOG MOPPET
(PUG —) MOPS
(PUNCH'S —) TOBY
(SHAGGY —) RUG OWTCHAH
(SHEEP —) CUR COLLIE KELPIE
BEARDIE MALINOIS SHEPHERD
(SMALL —) TOY FICE FIST DOGGY
FEIST LAIKA PIPER DOGGIE
AMERTOY SPANIEL PAPILLON
PEKINESE
(VICIOUS —) TAEPO
(WATCH —) CUR GARM GARMR
(WILD —) ADJAG DHOLE DINGO
GUARA JACKAL AGOUARA
CIMARRON
(YELPING —) WAPPET
(PL.) DOGGERY
(PREF.) CYN(O)
DOGBANE KENDIR KENDYR
ECHITES FLYTRAP ALSTONIA
MILKWEED OLEANDER
PERIWINKLE
DOGBOAT PIG
DOGCART GADDER TUMTUM
BOUNDER GADABOUT
DOG COLLAR TRASH
DOG DAYS CANICULE
DOG EAR LEATHER
DOG FENNEL HOGWEED
DOGFIGHT SCRAMBLE
DOGFISH DOG HOE HUSS TOPE
FLAKE HOUND HURSE MANGO
TOPER BOUNCE DAGGAR GALEID
MORGAY BONEDOG GABBACK
SPURDOG TRIAKID GRAYFISH
SEAHOUND
(PREF.) SCYLLIO SQUALI SQUALO
DOGGED DOUR SULLEN DOGGISH
DOGLIKE STUBBORN OBSTINATE
DOGGEREL NOMINY TRIVIA
DOGGREL SINGSONG
DOGGONE BLESSED DOWNGONE
DOGIE LEPPY STRAY
DOG KEEPER FEWTERER
DOGLIKE CYNIC CYNOID DOGGED
DOGMA CREED TENET DICTUM
DOCTRINE DOCUMENT
DOGMATIC THETIC PONTIFIC
POSITIVE ARBITRARY CONFIDENT
PONTIFICAL
DOGMATISM BOWWOW
DOGMATIST BIGOT PHILODOX
DOG POUND GREENYARD
DOG ROSE BUCKY CANKER
BEDEGUAR DOGBERRY
DOG SALMON CHUM KETA
MORGAY DOGFISH
DOGSHORE DOG DAGGER
DOG'S MERCURY SAPWORT
DOG SNAPPER JOCU
DOGSTAIL BENT
DOGWOOD OSIER SUMAC CORNEL
CORNUS GAITER WIDBIN
BARBASCO FISHWOOD
DOILY MAT TIDE TIDY NAPKIN
DOING ACT DEED FACT STIR EVENT
ACTION FUNCTION PRACTIVE
(PL.) FARE GEAR
(SUFF.) ANT ENT PRACTIC PRAXIA
PRAXIS

DOIT DODKIN
DOLE LOT ALMS DEAL DOOL GIFT
GOAL METE PART VAIL ALLOT
FRAUD GRIEF GUILE MOURN
POGEY SHARE DECEIT GRIEVE
RELIEF SORROW CHARITY
DEALING DESTINY HANDOUT
PAYMENT PORTION BOUNDARY
DIMENSUM DISPENSE DIVISION
GRATUITY LANDMARK PITTANCE
DOLEFUL SAD DOWY DOWIE
DREAR HEAVY DISMAL DOOLFU
DREARY FUNEST RUEFUL FLEBILE
DOLESOME DOLOROUS FUNESTAL
MOURNFUL TRAGICAL
DOLERITE DIABASE
DOLL TOY BABE BABY MOLL ARRAY
DOLLY DOLLIE KEWPIE MAIDEN
MAUMET MOPPET MUNECA
POPPET POUPEE PUPPET
KACHINA KATCINA KATCHINA
MISTRESS
(— UP) SWANK
(PASTEBOARD —) PANTINE
(PREF.) PUPI
DOLLAR BALL BEAN BONE BUCK
CASE DURO FISH ROCK SCAD
SKIN SPOT ADOBE BERRY DALER
EAGLE PLONK PLUNK WHEEL
GOURDE PATACA DAALDER
SMACKER FROGSKIN PATACOON
SIMOLEON
(ONE MILLION —S) MEGABUCK
(SILVER —) SINKER
(SPANISH —) COB DURO COBBE
(THOUSAND —S) GEE THOU GRAND
DOLLARFISH SHINER MOONFISH
STARFISH
DOLL'S HOUSE (AUTHOR OF —)
IBSEN
(CHARACTER IN —) NORA RANK
HELMER LINDEN TORVALD
KROGSTAD CHRISTINA
DOLLY DRAB HOBBY PEGGY
PUNCH SWAGE MAIDEN
FOLLOWER MISTRESS SLATTERN
DOLLYMAN BUCKER
DOLLYWAY DOCK
DOLMEN SENAM TOLMEN
CROMMEL CROMLECH MEGALITH
DOLOMITE ANKERITE PEARLSPAR
DOLOR CALOR GRIEF SORROW
ANGUISH SADNESS DISTRESS
MOURNING
DOLOROUS SAD DISMAL DOLEFUL
GRIEVOUS PATHETIC
DOLPHIN INIA SUSU BOUTO
WHALE DORADO KILLER PALACH
TURSIO BOLLARD COWFISH
PELLOCK PULLOCK SNUFFER
CETACEAN MAHIMAHI MUTILATE
PORPOISE
(PREF.) DELPHIN DELPHO
(SUFF.) DELPHIS
DOLPHIN STRIKER MARTINGALE
DOLT ASS OAF PUT ASSE CALF
CHUB CLOD COOF DULT FOOL
GOFF MOKE PEAK POOP STUB
BOOBY CHUMP CLUNK DOBBY
DUMMY DUNCE FUNGE GOLEM
IDIOT NUMPS PATCH THICK
BEFOOL CUDDEN DOODLE DULTIE
HOBBIL OXHEAD BLUNTIE

DAWCOCK DULLARD JACKASS
SAPHEAD SCHNOOK BONEHEAD
BOSTHOON CLODPATE CLODPOLL
DUMBBELL IMBECILE LUNKHEAD
MACAROON MOONCALF
NUMSKULL LAMEBRAIN
DOLTISH DULL STUPID FOOLISH
PEAKISH SOTTISH TOMFOOL
BESOTTED BLOCKISH DOLTLIKE
DOMAIN LAND BOUND BOURN
REALM SCOPE STATE WORLD
BARONY BOURNE COUNTY
DEMAIN EMPERY EMPIRE ESTATE
SPHERE DEMESNE EARLDOM
BIRTHDOM DOMINION LORDSHIP
PROVINCE SEIGNORY STAROSTY
(— OF SULTAN) SOLDAN
(— OF THE UNCONSCIOUS)
SHADOWLAND
(MATHEMATICAL —) FIELD
(NETHER —) HELL
(TRANSCENDENT —) HEAVEN
(WOMAN'S —) DISTAFF
DOMBEYA ASSONIA
DOMBEY AND SON (AUTHOR OF —
) DICKENS
(CHARACTER IN —) GAY PAUL
EDITH CARKER CUTTLE DOMBEY
WALTER GRANGER FLORENCE
DOME CAP CIMA TYPE CROWN
VAULT COCKLE CUPOLA THOLOS
CALOTTE EDIFICE CIMBORIO
HEMIDOME
(— OVER TOMB) WELI
(BUDDHIST —) TOPE
(OBSERVATION —) BLISTER
(ROUND —) THOLUS
(SNOW-CAPPED —) CALOTTE
DOMER CLASPER
DOMESTIC HIND HOME MAID
MOZO DOMAL TABBY FAMILY
HAMEIL HAMELT HEYDUC
HOMELY HOMISH HOUSAL
INLAND INMATE INWARD MENIAL
NATIVE FAMELIC HEYDUCK
ONSHORE SCALDER SERVANT
FAMILIAR HOMEBRED HOMEMADE
INTIMATE
(PL.) FOLK
DOMESTICALLY ONSHORE
DOMESTICATE TAME ENTAME
AMENAGE RECLAIM CIVILIZE
DOMESTICATED CADE TAME
GENTLE INWARD DOMESTIC
FAMILIAR
DOMICILE CRIB HOME SHED
ABODE HOUSE MENAGE
DWELLING RESIDENCE
DOMINANCE SWAY INFLUENCE
DOMINANT BOSSY CHIEF FIFTH
TENOR MASTER RULING SOVRAN
CENTRAL REGNANT SUPREME
DOMINULE SUPERIOR
PARAMOUNT OVERBEARING
PREPONDERANT
DOMINATE TOP HAVE RULE
CHARM REIGN COERCE DIRECT
GOVERN VASSAL BEWITCH
COMMAND CONTROL ENVELOP
POSSESS BESTRIDE DOMINEER
OVERRIDE OVERSWAY OVERTONE
DOMINATING SUPERIOR
BREATHLESS

DOMINATION EMPIRE CONTROL STRINGS BOVARISM BOVARYSM DOMINION POSSESSION
DOMINEER BOSS BRAG LORD RULE BULLY FEAST REVEL TOWER COMPEL COMMAND SWAGGER DOMINATE OVERBEAR OVERLEAD OVERLORD
(— OVER) RIDE HECTOR
DOMINEERING SURLY LORDLY HAUGHTY ARROGANT DESPOTIC MASTERLY MASTERFUL
DOMINICA (CAPITAL OF —) ROSEAU
(MOUNTAIN PEAK IN —) MORNEDIABLOTIN
DOMINICAN JACOBIN JACOBITE PREACHER PREDICANT

DOMINICAN REPUBLIC
BAY: OCOA YUMA NEIBA RINCON SAMANA ISABELA CALDERAS ESCOCESA
CAPE: BEATA FALSO CABRON ENGANO CAUCEDO ISABELA MACORIS
CAPITAL: SANTODOMINGO
COIN: ORO PESO
INDIAN: TAINO
ISLAND: BEATA SAONA ALTOVELO CATALINA HISPANIOLA
LOWLAND: CIBAO
MEASURE: ONA TAREA FANEGA
MOUNTAIN: TINA GALLO DUARTE
MOUNTAINS: NEIBA BAHORUCO ORIENTAL
RIVER: YUNA OZAMA
TOWN: AZUA BANI MOCA PENA POLO BONAO COTUI NAGUA NEIBA NIZAO SOSUA HIGUEY OVIEDO SANCHEZ BARAHONA SANTIAGO
VALLEY: REAL NEYBA

DOMINIE MASTER PASTOR
DOMINION RULE SWAY CROWN REALM REIGN DITION DOMAIN EMPERY EMPIRE REGNUM CONTROL DIOCESE DYNASTY KHANATE MASTERY POUSTIE REGENCY CALIFATE IMPERIUM LORDSHIP SEIGNORY SIGNORIA SOVRANTY OBEDIENCE
(PL.) DUCHY
DOMINO DIE BONE CARD FIVE MASK TILE BLANK JETON STONE DOUBLE JETTON MATADOR VENETIAN
(FIRST — PLAYED) SET
(PL.) MATADOR MUGGINS BONEYARD
DOMINO NOIR, LE (COMPOSER OF —) AUBER
DOMITILLA (DAUGHTER OF —) DOMITILLA
(HUSBAND OF —) VESPASIAN
(SON OF —) TITUS DOMITIAN
DOM PEDRO SNOOZER
DON WEAR ARRAY DRESS ENDUE INDUE THROW ASSUME CLOTHE INVEST ADDRESS NOBLEMAN
DONALBAIN (FATHER OF —) DUNCAN

DONATE GIE GIFT GIVE BESTOW PRESENT
DONATION GIFT GRANT DONATIO PRESENT DONATIVE BENEFACTION
(—S RECEIVED BY SINGERS) CARL
DON CARLOS (CHARACTER IN —) EBOLI CARLOS PHILIP VALOIS CHARLES RODRIGO ELISABETH
(COMPOSER OF —) VERDI
DONE GAR DEEN OVER BAKED ENDED GIVEN COOKED THROUGH FINISHED
(— BY WORD OF MOUTH) PAROL PAROLE
(— CARELESSLY) SCAMBLING
(— FOR) GONE SUNK KAPUT KAPUTT FINISHED
(— IN FAITH) AF
(— IN PLAIN SIGHT) BRAZEN
(— POORLY) BOTCHY
(— TOGETHER) CONCERTED
(— WITH) BY
(— WITHOUT DELIBERATION) SNAP
(— WRONG WAY) AWK
(TO BE —) PASS
DONEE DONATOR HERITOR RECEIVER
DON GIOVANNI (CHARACTER IN —) ANNA ELVIRA MASETTO OTTAVIO ZERLINA GIOVANNI LEPORELLO
(COMPOSER OF —) MOZART
DONJON KEEP ROCCA DUNGEON
DONKEY ASS BUSS DONK FUSS MOKE BURRO CHUMP CUDDY DICKY EQUID GENET GUDDA HINNY HORSE JENNY NEDDY BRAYER CUDDLE DICKEY JENNET ONAGER ASINEGO BUSSOCK FUSSOCK JACKASS LONGEAR CARDOPHAGUS
DONKEY ENGINE DOCTOR DONKEY ROADER YARDER DOLLBEER
DONNA DEL LAGO (CHARACTER IN —) ELENA DOUGLAS GIACOMO MALCOLM RODERICK
(COMPOSER OF —) ROSSINI
DONNA DIANA (COMPOSER OF —) REZNICEK
DONOR GIVER DONATOR
DO-NOTHING DONNOT DONOUGHT FAINEANT
DON PASQUALE (CHARACTER IN —) NORINA ERNESTO PASQUALE SOFRONIA MALATESTA
(COMPOSER OF —) DONIZETTI
DON QUIXOTE (AUTHOR OF —) CERVANTES
(CHARACTER IN —) PANZA PEDRO PEREZ ALONZO DAPPLE SAMSON SANCHO TOBOSO GUINART QUIXOTE CARRASCO DULCINEA NICHOLAS ROSINANTE
DONUM GIVER DEUNAM
DOODAD DODAD DOODAB DOFUNNY GIMCRACK JIMCRACK
DOOM KER LAW LOT DAMN FATE RUIN CURSE DEATH JUDGE ADDEEM DECREE DEVOTE STEVEN CONDEMN DESTINE DESTINY FORTUNE STATUTE DECISION FOREDOOM SENTENCE

DOOMED FEY DEAD DONE LORN FATAL DAMNED FORLORN ACCURSED FINISHED
DOOM PALM DOUM
DOOMSMAN LAWMAN
DOOR LID DROP EXIT FOLD GATE HECK SHUT TRAP ENTRY HATCH JANUA VALVE DAMPER JIGGER PORTAL RADDLE WICKET BARRIER DOORWAY INGRESS OPENING OUTDOOR PASSAGE POSTERN ANTEPORT ENTRANCE FOREDOOR POSTICUM SERVIDOR STOPPING TRAVERSE VOMITORY
(— IN MINE) STOPPING
(— OF ASH PIT) ARCH
(— OF MASONIC LODGE) TILE
(AIRPLANE —) CLAMSHELL
(HALF —) HECK HATCH
(PART OF —) RAIL SILL STILE LINTEL MULLION
(ROMAN —S) FORES
(SLIDING —) SHUT SHOJI FUSUMA TRAVERSE
(STORM —) DINGLE
(STRONG —) OAK
(TRAP —) SLOT SCRUTO VAMPIRE VAMPYRE
(PREF.) THYRE(O) THYRO
(SUFF.) THYRIS
DOORFRAME BUCK
DOORHEAD DERNER
DOORKEEPER TILER TILIA USHER DURWAN PORTER WARDEN DOORMAN JANITOR OSTIARY DOORWARD HUISSIER JANITRIX PORTRESS WISKINKY
DOOR KNOCKER HAMMER RAPPER
DOOR LATCH SNECK HAGGADAY
DOORMAN FOOTMAN HALLMAN DOORWARD
DOORMAT COCOMAT
DOORPOST DURN JAMB PIER POST ALETTE POSTEL
DOORSILL SOIL
DOORSTOP BUMPER HOLDBACK
DOORWAY DOOR EXIT PORTAL OPENING
DOOZER LULU SNORTER HUMDINGER
DOOZY LULU HUMDINGER
DOPATTA UPARNA DOOPUTTY
DOPE HOP LUG BOOB DRUG GOFF GOON GOOP INFO BOOBY OPIUM PASTE STUPE HEROIN INSIDE OPIATE LOWDOWN PREDICT STUPEFY NARCOTIC
DOPED CRONK
DOPER GREASER
DOR BEE DORR JOKE MOCK BONGO CLOCK DORRE JOKER SCOFF TRICK BEETLE DRONER BUFFOON DECEIVE MOCKERY
DORADO CUIR XIPHIAS GOLDFISH
DORALICE (HUSBAND OF —) PHODOPHIL MANDRICARDO
(LOVER OF —) RODOMONT
DORBEETLE DOR CLOCK DRONER BUZZARD BUMCLOCK
DORIGEN (HUSBAND OF —) ARVIRAGUS
(LOVER OF —) AURELIUS

DORIMENE (HUSBAND OF —) SGANARELLE
(LOVER OF —) DORANTE
DORINDA (HUSBAND OF —) AIMWELL
(SISTER OF —) MIRANDA
DORIS (BROTHER AND HUSBAND OF —) NEREUS
(FATHER OF —) OCEANUS
(MOTHER OF —) TETHYS
DORMANCY TORPOR ABEYANCE
DORMANT FIXED INERT ASLEEP LATENT TORPID RESTING SLEEPER INACTIVE LATITANT SLEEPING CONNIVENT
DORMER WINDOW LUCOMB MEMBER DORMANT EYEBROW LUCARNE LUTHERN
DORMITORY DORM HALL HOUSE DORMER DORTER HOSTEL BULLPEN COLLEGE DORTOUR CUBATORY QUARTERS
DORMOUSE LOIR DRYAD LEROT GLIRID SLEEPER
(PREF.) GLIRI
DORNICK DONEY LINEN DARNEX DONACK DONNICK
DORPER DORSIAN
DORSAL NOTAL DORSER DOSSER NEURAL TERGAL ABAXIAL HANGING SUPERIOR POSTERIOR
(PREF.) OPISTH(O)
DORSUM BACK
DORUS (BROTHER OF —) LAODOCUS POLYPOETES
(FATHER OF —) APOLLO HELLEN XUTHUS
(MOTHER OF —) CREUSA ORSEIS PHTHIA
(SLAYER OF —) AETOLUS
DOSAGE (SCIENCE OF —) POSOLOGY
DOSE BOLE DOST SHOT BROMO DATIO DOSIS DRAFT STORE TREAT DATION DOCTOR DOSAGE DRENCH POTION BOOSTER BROMIDE CAPSULE DRAUGHT QUANTITY
(NARCOTIC —) LOCUS BINDLE LOCUST
DOSS BOW DOS KNOT TUFT BUNCH
DOSSERET PULVINO
DOT SET CLOT DOTE LUMP MOTE PECK SPOT STAR TICK COVER DOWER DOWRY POINT PRICK PUNTO SPECK BULLET CENTER CENTRE DOTLET PERIOD STIGME TITTLE TOCHER PUNCTUM PUNCTUS SPECKLE SPOTTLE STIPPLE FLYSPECK PARTICLE SPRINKLE
(— IN CODE) DIT
(— ON FOREHEAD) BOTTU
(— ON PATCH OF DIFFERENT COLOR) ISLET
(BLACK —) DARTROSE
(PL.) LEADERS
DOTAGE DOTE FOLLY DRIVEL SENILITY TWICHILD
DOTARD DOBBY DOTER SILLY DOBBIE DOTANT SENILE DOTTREL DOTTEREL IMBECILE LIRIPIPE LIRIPOOP

DOTCHIN STEELYARD
DOTE ROT DOVE DOZE FOND LIKE LOVE TIRE ADORE DECAY ENDOW BESTOW DOTAGE DOTARD DRIVEL STUPOR IMBECILE
DOTING FON FOND GAGA DOTAGE PAWING
DOTTED SEME CRIBLE SEMEED TICKED TOUCHY SPOTTED PUNCTATE SPECKLED STIPPLED STELLATED
(— SWISS) LAPPET
DOTTER SPOTTER
DOTTEREL DUPE GULL WIND PLOVER DOTTREL MORINEL
DOTTY TOTY CRAZY TOTTY FEEBLE SPOTTY
DOUBLE KA BOW PLY DUAL FOLD SORE TWIN CRACK DUPLE FETCH ROUND SOSIE BIFOLD BINARY BINATE DOPPIO DUPLEX MIDDLE DIPLOID DOUBLET TWOFOLD BIVALENT GEMINATE BIFARIOUS SIMILITUDE
(— IMPRESSION) MACKLE
(— IN POKER) STRADDLE
(— MUSICAL NOTES) AUGMENT
(— UP) BUCK JACKKNIFE
(PHANTOM —) FETCH
(PREF.) BI BIN(I)(O) DI(S) DIPHY DIPL(O) DISS(O) DITTO GEMINI
DOUBLE BASSOON FAGOTTONE
DOUBLE CHIN CHOLLER
DOUBLECROSS BITCH CHEAT BETRAY DECEIVE SWINDLE BUSINESS
DOUBLE-CROSSER RAT HEEL
DOUBLED GEMEL GEMINOUS
(PREF.) BIS
DOUBLE DAGGER DIESIS
DOUBLE-DEALING DECEIT DUPLICITY
DOUBLE FLUTE DIAULOS
DOUBLENESS DUALITY PLENITUDE
DOUBLE-RIPPER BOBSLED BOBSLEIGH
DOUBLE-RUNNER SKATE
DOUBLET SNIFF DOUBLE DUPLET PALTOCK PLACCATE POURPOINT
DOUBLE-TALK NEWSPEAK RAZZMATAZZ
DOUBLETREE EVENER SPREADER
DOUBLING LAP FOLD HEAD LOOP
(— OF THE BLIND) STRADDLE
DOUBLOON ONZA
DOUBLY
(PREF.) BI
DOUBT FEAR WEIR DEMUR DREAD DWERE QUERY WAVER BALANCE DIFFIDE DUBIETY SCRUPLE SKEPSIS SUSPECT SWITHER UMBRAGE DISTRUST DUBITATE HESITATE MISTRUST QUESTION STAGGERS MISLIPPEN
DOUBTER CYNIC SKEPTIC DUBITANTE
DOUBTFUL JUBUS DOUBTY UNSURE DUBIOUS FEARFUL JEALOUS PERHAPS WILSOME BOGGLISH DREADFUL JUBEROUS PERILOUS WAVERING QUESTIONABLE PROBLEMATICAL
DOUBTING DUBIOUS DUBITANT

DOUBTLESS WITTERLY
DOUCEUR BONUS POURBOIRE
DOUCHE RINSE EYEWASH
DOUGH CASH DUFF MASA CRUST DAIGH MONEY PASTE PUPPY CHANGE HALLAH NOODLE SPONGE BRIOCHE MANDLEN TEIGLACH
(BISCUIT —) CAKE
(BREAD —) SPONGE
(FERMENTING —) LEAVEN
(FRIED —) SPUD
(NOODLE —) FARFEL FERFEL
DOUGHNUT NUT SINK DONUT CYMBAL SINKER CRULLER FATCAKE NUTCAKE OLYCOOK OLYKOEK SIMBALL TWISTER BISMARCK FASNACHT
(SHAPED LIKE —) TOROIDAL
DOUGHTY FELL PREU TALL BRAVE VALIANT INTREPID
DOUGHY SAD DUNCH SODDEN
DOUR DERN GLUM GRIM HARD SOUR ROUGH STERN GLOOMY MOROSE SEVERE STRONG SULLEN OMINOUS TACITURN
DOUSE BEAT BLOW DOFF DUCK QUIT STOW CEASE DOWSE RINSE SOUSE DRENCH PLUNGE SLUICE STRIKE STROKE IMMERSE DOWNPOUR
DOUZEPER ANSEIS PALADIN
DOVE DOO DOW DOZE KUKU JONAH CULVER CUSHAT JEMIMA PIGEON COLUMBA DOVELET LAUGHER NAMAQUA SLUMBER DOVELING RINGDOVE
(— SOUND) CURR
(GROUND —) ROLA
(RING —) TOOZOO
(ROCK —) SOD
(SCALE —) INCA
DOVECOTE DOOCOT LOUVER DOVECOT DOWCOTE PIGEONRY COLUMBARY
DOVEKIE AUK ALLE BULL ROTCH ROTGE DOVEKEY BULLBIRD DOVELIKE
DOVETAIL COG JAG JAGG MESH MERGE TENON
DOWDINESS FRUMPERY
DOWDY POKY FRUMP MOPSY POKEY TACKY BLOWZY SHABBY STODGY UNTIDY FRUMPISH SLOVENLY
DOWEL NOG PEG PIN COAK STUD SPRIG JOGGLE PINTLE DULEDGE
DOWER DOS DOWRY ENDOW TOCHER DOARIUM PORTION HERITAGE MARITAGE
DOWITCHER SNIPE DRIVER SLEEPER GRAYBACK GREYBACK LONGBEAK
DOWN HUP OFF BETE CAST DOON DOWL FELL FLIX FLUE FUZZ HILL LINT MOXA PILE SOUR ADOWN BELOW DOWLE EIDER FLOOR FLUFF BEDOWN FRIEZE LANUGO PAPPUS HANDOUT HILLOCK PLUMAGE DOWNLAND
(— AND OUT) QUISBY
(— AT THE HEEL) SLIPSHOD

(— THAT WAY) DOWNBY DOWNBYE
(— THE LINE) ALONG
(FAR —) DEEP DEEPLY
(FARTHEST —) BOTTOMMOST
(STRAIGHT —) DOWNRIGHT
(PREF.) CAT(A)(O) CATH DE HYPO KAT(A) LACHN(O) OB PTIL(O) SUB
DOWNBEAT THESIS
DOWNCAST BAD SAD DOWN ABJECT GLOOMY HANGING DEJECTED HOPELESS
DOWNFALL PIT FALL FATE RUIN TRAP ABYSS DECAY FINISH DESCENT ECLIPSE UNDOING COLLAPSE DOWNCOME
(AUTHOR OF —) ZOLA
(CHARACTER IN —) JEAN WEISS HONORE GOLIATH GUNTHER MAURICE SILVINE FOUCHARD MACQUART HENRIETTE LEVASSEUR DELAHERCHE GARTLAUBEN
DOWNFEED OVERHEAD
DOWNFLOW VAIL DEFLUX
DOWNFOLD SADDLE DOWNWARP
DOWNHILL DOWNDALE
(SKI —) WEDEL
DOWNPOUR POUR RAIN BRASH DOUSE DOWSE FLOOD PLASH SPILL SPOUT DELUGE TORRENT CATARACT AVALANCHE
DOWNRIGHT FAIR FLAT PURE RANK BLANK BLUNT PLAIN PLUMB PLUMP ROUND SHEER STARK ARRANT DIRECT FAIRLY STURDY REGULAR ABSOLUTE EVENDOWN POSITIVE THOROUGH
DOWNSPOUT SPOUT DOWNPIPE DOWNTAKE
DOWNSTAIRS BELOW
DOWNSTROKE DOWNBEAT
DOWNSWING DOLDRUMS
DOWNWARD ADOWN BELOW LOWER PRONE DEORSUM DOWNWITH
(— ON ONE SIDE) SIDEWAYS
(PREF.) BATH(O)(Y) CAT(A)(O) CATH
DOWNWIND LEEWARD
DOWNY SOFT FLUEY MOSSY NAPPY PILAR PLUMY QUIET CALLOW FLEDGY FLOSSY FLUFFY PILARY PLACID COTTONY CUNNING KNOWING SOOTHING
(PREF.) HEBE
DOWRY DOS DOT GIFT DOWER SULKA DOWAGE LOBOLA LOBOLO TALENT PORTION
DOWSE WITCH
DOXOLOGIZE LAUD
DOXOLOGY GLORIA KADDISH
DOXY WENCH HARLOT
DOYEN DEAN DOYENNE
DOZE NAP NOD ROT DARE DORM DOTE DOVE DECAY DOVER SLEEP SLOOM CATNAP DROWSE MUDDLE SNOOZE MEMENTO PERPLEX SLUMBER SNOOZLE STUPEFY
DOZEN DIZZEN DOSAIN
(FIVE —) TALLY
(TWO —) THRAVE

DOZING DOGSLEEP
DRAB BOX DAW FOX SAD DELL DRUG DULL BESOM BLEAK DINGY DOLLY GRAVE GRAZE HEAVY TRULL WENCH WHORE FRUMPY ISABEL MALKIN POISON PUSSEL STODGY PROSAIC PUCELLE SUBFUSC DOLLYMOP EVERYDAY POMPLESS
(CHAETURA —) BEAR
DRABBLE DRAGGLE
DRACHM DRAM
DRACO ANGUIS DRAGON
DRAFT NIP SIP CHIT DOSE DRAG DRAM DRAW GLUT GULF GUST ITEM LEVY PLAN PLOT SUCK SWIG TOOT WORK BLAST CHECK DRINK EPURE SLOCK SWILL SWIPE TAPER WRITE DESIGN DRENCH GODOWN MINUTE POTION PROJET REDACT RETURN SCHEME SCROLL SKETCH WAUCHT WAUGHT ABBOZZO DRAUGHT DRAWING OUTLINE PATTERN PHILTER PROJECT BEVERAGE POTATION PROTOCOL
(— OF A VESSEL) GAGE GAUGE
(— OF AIR) COOKE
(— OF COMPOSITION) SCORE
(— OF LAW) BILL
(— OF PATTERN) STRIP
(— OFF) SHED
(HEAVY —) WHITTER
(LARGE —) SCOUR CAROUSE
(MIDDAY —) NOONING
(ORIGINAL —) PROTOCOL
(ROUGH —) EBAUCHE BROUILLON SCANTLING
(SLEEPING —) DORTER
(SMALL —) NIP SIP SUCK TIFF TIFT
DRAFTER HORSER
DRAFTSMAN DRAWER TRACER TIPPLER
DRAG DOG LAG DRUG HALE HONE HOOK KITE RASH SHOE SKID SLUR TOLE TOLL TUMP CREEP DEVIL DRAWL DRIFT FLOAT LURRY NOWEL PLUCK RALLY SLIDE SNAKE SWEEP TEASE TRAIL TRAIN TRAWL TRICE DAGGLE DROGUE LINGER REMORA SCHOOL TAIGLE TRAYNE DRAGBAR DRAGGLE GRAPNEL GRAPPLE SCHLEPP SKIDPAN ARRASTRA DRAGSHOE
(— ALONG) LUG CRAWL SHOOL TRAYNE TRACHLE TRAUCHLE
(— CARELESSLY) HIKE
(— DOWN) DEGRADE
(— FEET) SLODGE
(— FORCIBLY) SNAKE
(— HOME CARCASS OF GAME) TUMP
(— IN DEEP WATER) CREEP
(— JERKILY) SNIG
(— LOGS) SKID
(— OFF) HARRY
(— OUT) DRAWL
(PLANK —) RUBBER
DRAGGING LEADEN
(— DEAD BULL FROM RING) ARRASTRE
DRAGGLE LAG DRAIL DAGGLE

DRABBLE TRACHLE
DRAGNET FLUE TRAIN TRAWL DRAWNET TRAINEL
DRAGON AHI LUNG WORM DRAKE RAHAB NIDHOG VRITRA WYVERN BASILISK DRAGONET NIDHOGGR NITHHOGG
(— WITH 7 HEADS) HYDRA
(SEA —) QUAVIVER
(WINGLESS —) LINDWORM
(PREF.) DRACO(NT)(NTO)
DRAGONET FOX ILLECK FOXFISH GOWDNIE GURNARD JUGULAR SCULPIN LORICATE QUAVIVER
DRAGONFLY NAIAD ODONATE SKIMMER LIBELLULA
DRAGON TREE DRACAENA
DRAGROPE DRAG GUSS
DRAGSTER FUELER SLINGSHOT
DRAIN DRY FRY GAN GAW SAP SEW TOP BUZZ COUP DAIL DALE DELF DIKE DRAG DRAW GOUT GRIP GURT LADE LODE MILK SIKE SINK SOAK SUFF SUMP TEEM TILE BLEED BUNNY CANAL DELFT DRAFT DREEN DRILL DROVE EMPTY FLEET GROOP GULLY LEECH RHINE SEUCH SEUGH SEWER SHORE SIVER STANK STELL EMULGE FILTER FURROW GUZZLE RIGGOT SHEUCH SHEUGH SIPHON SPONGE SWOUGH SYPHON TRENCH TROGUE TROUGH ZANJON ACEQUIA ALBERCA CAROUSE CARRIER CHANNEL CULVERT DEPLETE DRAUGHT EXHAUST GRINDLE GRIPPLE SCUPPER ZANJONA CANALIZE CARRIAGE SINKHOLE SUBDRAIN THURROCK
(— DRY) JIB
(— IN FEN) LEAM
(— IN MINE) SOUGH
(— IN STABLE) GROOP
(COVERED —) THURROCK
(OPEN —) SIVER STELL
(SMALL —) TRONE
DRAINAGE ADIT SAUR SOCK SULLAGE SUMPAGE
DRAINAGEWAY DRAW
DRAINING SEEPAGE DRAINAGE EMULGENT
DRAINPIPE SINK SHELL WHELM LEADER QUELME
DRAKE STAG STAIG DRAKELET
DRAM GO NIP MITE SLUG TIFF TIFT DRAFT DRINK SOPIE CALKER CHASSE DRACHM JIGGER CAULKER SNIFTER MERIDIAN POTATION QUANTITY
(— OF LIQUOR) TOT SLUG SNIFTER
(— OF SPIRITS) NOBBLER
DRAMA RAS AUTO MIME PLAY LEGIT OPERA COMEDY NATAKA SCENES SOAPER TRAGIC ATELLAN COMEDIA HISTORY PROVERB THEATRE TRAGEDY DUODRAMA MONODRAM OPERETTA PASTORAL
(DANCE —) KATHAKALI
(JAPANESE —) NO KABUKI
(MUSICAL —) OPERA SAYNETE OPERETTA

DRAMATIC WILD VIVID SCENIC THESPIAN
(— REPRESENTATION) WAYANG
(HAVING LYRIC AND — QUALITIES) SPINTO
DRAMATIST (ALSO SEE PLAYWRIGHT) OG ACTOR IBSENITE
DRAMSHOP GROGSHOP
DRAPE HANG PALL VEST ADORN COVER CRAPE WEAVE CURTAIN FESTOON HANGING VALANCE
DRAPED BEHUNG
DRAPER TAILOR LINENMAN
DRAPERY SWAG BAIZE DRAPE SCENE CURTAIN REREDOS VALANCE MOURNING
(— ON BEDSTEAD) PAND
(PIECE OF —) HANGING
DRAPING BLOUSE DRAPERY
DRASTIC DIRE HARSH EXTREME RADICAL RIGOROUS
(NOT —) BLAND
DRAT RABBIT DOGGONE
DRATTED BLESSED
DRAUGHT (ALSO SEE DRAFT) SLUG WAUGHT OENOMEL
DRAUPADI (FATHER OF —) DRUPADA
DRAVIDIAN GOND KOTA TODA TULU ARAVA COORG GONDI KHOND KLING MALTO ORAON TAMIL ANDHRA BADAGA BIRHOR BRAHUI KODAGU KURUKH TELEGU TELUGU COLLERY DRAVIDA TAMILIC KANARESE TAMILIAN
DRAW LUG TEE TIE TOW TUG DRAG DUCT HALE HAUL LADE LIMN LINE LURE PUFF PULL RAKE SPAN TILL TIRE TOLL TREK VENT CATCH DRAFT DRILL EDUCE ENDUE EXACT HEAVE PAINT SKINK TRACE TRAIN TRECK ALLURE BUCKET DEDUCE DEPICT DERIVE DESIGN DEVISE ELICIT ENGAGE ENTICE INDUCE INHALE SELECT SKETCH STRIKE ATTRACT BEGUILE CONTOUR DETRACT DOGFALL DRAUGHT EXTRACT INSPIRE PORTRAY SCREEVE SCUMBLE INSCRIBE INVEIGLE OUTBRAID STANDOFF
(— A CARD) CUT
(— AIR) BREATHE
(— ALONG) TRACK TRAIN
(— APART) REAM DIVEL DIDUCE DIVERGE
(— AT A PIPE) SHOOH SHAUGH
(— AWAY) ARACE DRAFT ABDUCT ARACHE DRAUGHT ENTRAIN ABSTRACT DISTRACT
(— AWKWARDLY) SCRAWL
(— BACK) FADE REVEL START WINCE ARREAR RETIRE REVOKE SHRINK CRINKLE RECLAIM WITHEE
(— BACK FROM) BLENCH FLINCH RESILE TORFEL TORFLE DETRECT
(— BACK LIPS) GRIN
(— BOLT) SLOT
(— BY SUCTION) ASPIRATE
(— DEEP BREATH) SUSPIRE

(— DRINK) BIRL
(— EARTH AROUND) HILL
(— FIRST FURROW) FEER
(— FORTH) EDUCE EVOKE FETCH ELICIT DEPROME EXHAUST
(— IN) PINK
(— OFF) BROACH
(— ON) INDUE INDUCE SOLICIT
(— OUT) MILK SLUB EXACT SKINK TRACT ELICIT EXHALE EXTEND
(— TIGHT) FRAP THRAP STRAIN
(— TOGETHER) COWL LACE COART GATHER CRIMPLE
(— UP) FORM MAKE HUCKLE INKNIT UPWALE
DRAWBACK OUT LETDOWN TAKEOFF DISCOUNT PULLBACK
DRAWBAR DRAGBAR BULLNOSE DRAWLINK SLIPRAIL
DRAWBRIDGE PONTLEVIS
DRAWEE ACCEPTER
DRAWER TILL LIMNER LOCKER TILLER ENTERER INTAKER SHUTTLE
(— OF WATER) GIBEONITE
(COAL —) PUTTER
(TYPEWRITER —) BED
DRAWER-DOWN KNOBBLER
DRAWER-IN ENTERER HEALDER HEDDLER
DRAWER-OFF RACKER
DRAWERS PANTS SHORTS LININGS PANTIES SHALWAR CALSOONS CALZOONS SHINTYAN PANTELETS SHULWAURS
DRAWGATE SLACKER
DRAWING DRAW CHALK DRAFT ENVOI EPURE SEPIA TUSHE CRAYON DESIGN DETAIL FIGURE FUSAIN SKETCH CAMAIEU CARTOON CROQUIS DIAGRAM DRAUGHT HAULING ISOTYPE PULLING RETRAIT TOUSCHE ADDUCENT CHARCOAL CROSSING DOODLING FREEHAND FROTTAGE HATCHING LINEWORK SANGUINE SLUBBING SPECULUM STICKMAN TRACTION TRANSFER TRICKING
(— BACK) ABDUCENT
(— IN) INDRAFT
(— OF LOTS) BALLOT
(— OUT) BATTUE
(COMIC —) CARTOON DROLLERY
(PREHISTORIC —) PICTOGRAM PICTOGRAPH
(SIDEWALK —) SCREEVE
(PREF.) GRAMO
(SUFF.) GRAM
DRAWING-IN DRAW ENTERING
DRAWKNIFE SHAVE JIGGER
DRAWL DRANT DRATE DRUNT TRAIN LOITER PROLATE
DRAWN DRAFT STREIT DRAUGHT GRAPHIC HAGGARD
(— APART) DISTRACT
(— AWAY) ABSTRACT
(— CLOSE) STRICT
(— OFF) DRAINED
(— OUT) DREE DREICH DREIGH EXTENDED
DRAWPLATE AGATE FLATTER
DRAWSHEET TYMPAN
DRAWSTRING LATCH STRING

DRAY CART LORRY SCOOT SLOOP WAGON CAMION JIGGER ROLLEY RULLEY SLOVEN WHEERY
DREAD AWE DREE FEAR FRAY FUNK WARD WERE ANGST AWFUL DOUBT GRISE TIMOR ADREAD AGRISE DISMAY ESCHEW HORROR TERROR ANXIETY DISMISS DRIDDER REDOUBT AFFRIGHT DREDDOUR GASTNESS MISDREAD TERRIBLE
(SUFF.) PHOBE PHOBIA(C) PHOBIC PHOBOUS
DREADED AWESOME BEDREAD
DREADFUL DERN DIRE AWFUL CRUEL DISMAL GRISLY HORRID AWESOME CAREFUL DIREFUL DRIDDER FEARFUL GHASTLY GRIMFUL HIDEOUS UNCOUTH DOUBTFUL DOUBTOUS GHASTFUL HORRIBLE HORRIFIC PERILOUS SCAREFUL SHOCKING TERRIBLE TERRIFIC
DREADFULLY DIRELY GRISLY ABYSMALLY
DREADNOUGHT TANK DAREALL WARSHIP FEARLESS
DREAM METE MOON MUSE REVE FANCY SWEVEN VISION AISLING AVISION CHIMERA FANTASY IMAGINE NIRVANA REVERIE ROMANCE CHIMAERA DAYDREAM PHANTASM SOMNIATE
(FRIGHTENING —) NIGHTMARE
(PREF.) ONEIR(O) ONIR(O)
DREAMER POET METER MUSARD FANTAST IDEALIST PHANTAST
DREAMINESS LANGUOR
DREAMING ADREAM TRAUMEREI
DREAMTIME ALCHERA
DREAMY KEF SOFT MOONY VAGUE POETIC FARAWAY LANGUID MUSEFUL ONEIRIC PENSIVE DREAMFUL FANCIFUL SOOTHING
DREAR DERN BLEAK DISMAL GLOOMY DOLEFUL
DREARY SAD DIRE DOWY DREE DULL FLAT GLUM BLEAK CRUEL DOWIE DRURY OURIE WASTE WISHT DISMAL DREICH ELENGE GLOOMY GOUSTY LONELY DOLEFUL GOUSTIE HOWLING WILSOME GRIEVOUS WEARIFUL
DREDGE MOP DRAG DREG SIFT SCOOP TRAIN DEEPEN DRUDGE SCRAPE SPONGE TANGLE GANGAVA SCALLOP EXCAVATE SPRINKLE
DREDGER DUSTER HEDGEHOG
DREDGING JILLING
DREGS LAG MUD CRAP FAEX LAGS LEES SCUT SILT SUDS TAIL DRAFF DREST DROSS DRUGS FECES FOOTS GROUT JAUPS MAGMA BOTTOM DRAINS DUNDER FECULA MOTHER REFUSE SORDES SORDOR ULLAGE DRIBBLE GROUNDS GRUMMEL HEELTAP OUTWALE RESIDUE RINSING GRUMMELS REMNANTS SEDIMENT SETTLING
(— OF LIQUOR) TAPLASH
(— OF MOLTEN GLASS) DRIBBLE

(— OF SOCIETY) WASH LEGGE CANAILLE

(— OF TALLOW) GREAVES

DREIBUND TRIPLICE

DREIDEL TRENDEL

DREI PINTOS, DIE (CHARACTER IN —) GOMEZ PINTO GASTON AMBROSIO CLARISSA PANTALEONE

(COMPOSER OF —) MAHLER

DRENCH DOSE HOSE SIND SINK SOAK TOSH BLASH DOUSE DOWSE DRAFT DRINK DROKE DROUK DROWN SLOCK SLUSH SOUSE STEEP SWILL BUCKET DELUGE DOUCHE IMBRUE INFUSE POTION SLUICE DRUNKEN EMBATHE IMMERSE INDRENCH PERMEATE SATURATE SUBMERGE

DRENCHED DRUNKEN

DRENCHER INFUSER

DRENCHING DOUSE DOWSE DOWNPOUR

DRESS AX AXE BED DON DUB FIG FIT HOE KIT RAG RAY RIG TOG BARB BEGO BOWN BUSK BUSS CLAY COAT COMB DESK DILL DINK GALA GARB GEAR GORE GOWN HONE HUKE KNAP MIDI MILL MINI RAIL ROBE SUIT TIFF TIRE TRIM TUBE TUCK VEST WEAR ADORN ARRAY BIGAN BRAWS CLEAN CLOTH CRUMB CRUSH CURRY DIGHT DIZEN EQUIP FLOAT FROCK GUISE HABIT IHRAM MAGMA PREEN PRICK PRIMP PRINK PRUNE SHAPE THING TRICK AGUISE ATTIRE ATTRAP BARBER BETRIM BROACH CLOTHE ENROBE FANGLE FETTLE FRAISE GRAITH INVEST JELICK JUMPER KIRTLE MAGPIE MULLET MUUMUU OUTFIT PLIGHT REVEST SARONG SHEATH SHROUD TOILET ADDRESS AFFAITE APPAREL BANDAGE BEDIZEN CHEMISE CLOTHES COSTUME DALLACK DUBBING GARMENT GARNISH HARNESS HATCHEL RAIMENT TOGGERY VESTURE ACCOUTER ACCOUTRE CLEADING CLOTHING DECORATE FEATHERS HANDMADE ORNAMENT SUNDRESS TAILLEUR VESTMENT EMBELLISH

(— A SKIN) WHEEL

(— DOWN) BRACE

(— ELEGANTLY) DINK

(— FISH) CALVER

(— FLAX) TED

(— FLINT) NAP KNAP

(— FOOD) SAUCE

(— FOR FELTING) CARROT

(— HAIR) TIRE TRUSS BARBER

(— HIDES) BEAM

(— HURRIEDLY) HUDDLE

(— IN FINE CLOTHES) DIKE BRANK

(— MEAT) LARD SHROUD

(— NEGLIGENTLY) MOB

(— ORE) VAN

(— OVER) STOP

(— SHEEPSKINS) TAW

(— SMARTLY) DALLACK

(— STONE) DAB NIG DAUB DRAG

FACE GAGE HACK GAUGE NIDGE POINT SCABBLE SCAPPLE

(— TAWDRILY) BEDIZEN

(— UNTIDILY) MAB

(— UP) BUSK DILL ADORN ARRAY PRANK PRIMP PRINK SPICK WATER FETTLE TOGGLE BECLOUT BEDRESS TITIVATE

(— VULGARLY) DAUB

(— WITH CHISEL) DROVE

(— WITH TROWEL) STRIKE

(— WORN BY MAN) DRAG

(— WOUND) PANSE BANDAGE

(COAT —) SIMAR SYMAR SIMARRE

(EVENING —) FORMAL

(FESTIVE —) GALA

(INCOMPLETE —) DISARRAY

(LONG —) MAXI

(LOOSE —) SACK SACQUE

(MORNING —) PEIGNOIR

(ONE-PIECE —) CAGE

(PECULIAR —) LIVERY

(POPLIN —) TABINET TABBINET

(RUSSIAN NATIONAL —) SARAFAN

(SHOWY —) BRAVERY

(SLEEVELESS —) SKIMMER

(STYLE OF —) GETUP

(SUFF.) ESTHES

DRESSED CLAD DONE BOUND BECLAD COATED COMBED HABITED GOFFERED

(— GAILY) FRESH SPARKISH

(— IN WHITE) CANDIDATE

(LOOSELY —) DISCINCT

(RICHLY —) BROCADED

(ROUGHLY —) HEWN

(SHOWILY —) BEPRANKED

(STYLISHLY —) SMART

(WELL —) BRAW GASH

DRESSER AMBRY ROBER TAWER BUREAU FRAMER MODISTE CUPBOARD

(LEATHER —) LEVANTER

DRESSING CAST GRAVY BEATING BLANKET IODOFORM RAVIGOTE REMOLADE SCOLDING STUFFING MAYONNAISE

(— FOR WOUNDS) LINT SPONGE

(— OF STONE) SKIFFLING

(HAIR —) LACKER LACQUER

DRESSING ROOM SHIFT VESTRY CAMARIN VESTUARY

DRESSMAKER SEWER SEAMER MODISTE STITCHER COUTURIER TIREWOMAN

DRESSMAKING COUTURE

DRESS RACK FRIPPERY

DRESSY SHARP

DRIBBLE DRIB DRIP DROP CARRY DRIVEL DRIBLET DRIPPLE DRIZZLE SLABBER

DRIBLET CLOT PIECE

(PL.) SMALLS

DRIED SEAR SERE ADUST GIZZEN TORRID WIZENED GIZZENED

DRIFT FAN JET SAG DENE DUNE FORD HERD PLOT RACK SILT TIDE TILL DRIVE DROVE FLEET FLOAT FLOCK IOWAN SENSE SLIDE SLOOM SLOUM TENOR TREND BROACH COURSE DESIGN DEVICE DRIVER OFFSET PODGER SCHEME STREAM TUNNEL WINDLE

CURRENT DIPHEAD DRIBBLE GALLERY HEADING IMPETUS IMPULSE LATERAL OUTWASH PASTURE PROCESS PURPORT SETBOLT DILUVIUM DRIFTPIN TENDENCY

(— LANGUIDLY) SWOON

(— OF CLOUDS) CARRY

(— OF SAND OR SNOW) WREATH

(— SIDEWISE) CRAB

(— WITH ANCHOR DOWN) CLUB

(DOWNWARD —) DROOP

(GLACIAL —) CARY TILL IOWAN

(RUBBLE —) HEAD

DRIFTER DROVER

DRIFTING ADRIFT DRIFTAGE

DRIFT PLUG DUMMY

DRIFTWAY DROVE

DRIFTWOOD WAFTURE

DRILL GAD JAR JIG RIG SOW TAP BORE CORE SPUD AUGER BORER CHARK CHURN DECOY DREEL PADDY THIRL TRAIN TUTOR TWIRL WHIRL ALLURE BROACH ENTICE FURROW JUMPER PIERCE SCHOOL SEEDER SINKER STOPER THRILL CHANNEL DRIFTER JANKERS PLUGGER STARTER EXERCISE INSTRUCT

(— SYSTEM) MARTINET

(MASONRY —) AIGUILLE

DRILLMAN STOPER

DRINK GO ADE ALE BIB BUM FIX GIN HUM LAP MOP PEG POT RUM RYE SIP SUP TEA TOT WET BALL BEER BEND BENO BOLL BOSA BOZA BREW BULL BUMP CHIA COKE COLA DRAG DRAM FIZZ FLIP GROG HAVE HORN JAKE LUSH MEAD NIPA NOGG PULL PURL SHOT SIND SLUG SOAK SOMA SOPE SPOT SWIG TIFF TOOT TOPE WHET AIRAH ASSAI BEVER BINGE BLAND BOMBO BOOZE BOUSE BOZAH BUBUD BUMBO CIDER CRUSH DAISY DRAFT FLOAT GLOGG HAOMA JULEP LAGER MORAT NEGUS PAINT POSCA PUNCH QUAFF ROUSE SETUP SKINK SLING SLOCK SMACH SMASH SMILE SMOKE SNIFF SNORT SOPIE SOUSE SWATS SWILL THING TOAST TODDY VODKA WHIFF ZOMBI ABSORB BEZZLE BRACER BRANDY BUMPER BURTON CALKER CASIRI CATLAP CAUDLE CHASER COFFEE COOPER DIBBLE DRENCH EGGHOT EGGNOG FUDDLE GIMLET GODOWN GUGGLE GUZZLE HOOKER IMBIBE MESCAL POSSET POTION PTISAN RICKEY SCREED SHANDY SIPPLE SIRPLE SWANKY SWINGE TACKLE TAMPOY TASTER TIPPLE VELVET WAUCHT WAUGHT ZOMBIE BRAGGET BRIMMER CAROUSE CHEERER CHIRPER COBBLER COLLINS CONSUME CORDIAL DILUENT DRAUGHT EXHAUST FLANNEL GUARANA GUARAPO INHAUST MORNING NOONING PROPOMA SHERBET SIDECAR SNEEZER

SNIFTER SUCTION SUPPAGE SWALLOW TANKARD TRILLIL APERITIF BEVERAGE BRIDECUP COCKTAIL HIGHBALL LIBATION MAHOGANY NIGHTCAP POTATION QUENCHER REFRESCO RUMBARGE SANGAREE SPRITZER SYLLABUB TEQUILA PHOSPHATE

(— AT DRAFT) TOP

(— EXCESSIVELY) TOPE BIBLE SOUSE BEZZLE BIBBLE SWIZZLE

(— FROM FERMENTED MILK) AIRAN KEFIR

(— GREEDILY) SLOP SWACK SWILL GUTTLE GUZZLE

(— HEAVILY) TOOT SWINK

(— INTOXICATING LIQUOR) IRRIGATE

(— LIQUOR) TIP DRAM SOAK BOOZE PAINT

(— NOISILY) SLURP

(— OF BEER) BUTCHER

(— OF BEER AND BUTTERMILK) BONNY CLABBER

(— OF BEER AND GINGERALE) SHANDYGAFF

(— OF IMMORTALITY) SOMA

(— OF INDIA) SHRAB

(— OF LIQUEUR) FRAPPE

(— OF LIQUOR) WET DRAM JOLT SHOT SPOT TASS WHET SETUP WHIFF CALKER JIGGER TASTER WETTING HIGHBALL NIGHTCAP

(— OF MOLASSES) SWITCHEL

(— OF THE GODS) AMRITA NECTAR

(— OF VINEGAR AND WATER) POSCA

(— OFF) COUP

(— SOCIALLY) BIRL HOBNOB

(— SPARINGLY) BLEB

(— TO LAST DROP) BUZZ

(— UP) CRUSH EPOTE CAROUSE EXHAUST

(— WITHOUT PAUSE) CHUGALUG

(ADDITIONAL —) EIK EKE

(ALCOHOLIC —) BENO BINO MIST NIPA BOMBO BUDGE BUMBO DRAIN JOUGH SHRAB SLING SNORT SNIFTER

(AUSTRALIAN —) BEAL

(BRAZILIAN —) ASSAI ASSAHY

(BUTTERMILK AND WATER —) BLAND

(CURRANT —) CASSIS

(DRUGGED —) HOCUS

(FARINACEOUS —) PTISAN

(FERMENTED —) BOSA MEAD BALCHE MUSHLA PULQUE CASSIRI GUARAPO

(FREE —) SHOUT

(GREAT —) JORUM

(HALF-SIZED —) CHOTAPEG

(HEADY —) HUFFCAP

(HOT —) COPUS SALOP TODDY BISHOP EGGHOT PLOTTY SALOOP CARDINAL

(INCLINED TO —) OUTWARD

(INSIPID —) SLUM

(INTOXICATING —) AVA GROG SUCK BOOZE KUMISS SCOTCH DRAPPIE PAIWARI SWIZZLE SKOKIAAN

(INTOXICATING —S) SAUCE BOTTLE

(LONG —) SWIPE HIGHBALL
(MEAN —) LAP
(MEDICINAL —) ADVOCAAT
(MIDDAY —) NOONING MERIDIAN
(NARCOTIC —) KAVA
(NON-ALCOHOLIC —) GAZOZ COOLER
(PALM —) ASSAI
(PARTING —) BONAILIE
(POISONOUS —) DRENCH
(RUSSIAN —) OBARNE OBARNI
(SACRED —) HOMA AMRIT HAOMA AMRITA
(SACRIFICIAL —) HOMA SOMA
(SMALL —) PEG DRAM SOPIE DALLOP WETTING
(SOUR —) ALEGAR
(STRONG —) BUB HUM BENO SICER FUDDLE SHICKER
(TASTELESS —) SLOP
(THIN —) SLOSH
(WEAK —) LAP BOOL BULL CATLAP
DRINKER SOT LUSH TANK POTER TOAST TOPER BARFLY BENDER CUPMAN LUSHER SOAKER SPONGE IMBIBER INTAKER QUAFFER DRUNKARD
(EXCESSIVE — OF TEA) THEIC
(HEAVY —) JUICEHEAD
(WATER —) HYDROPOT
DRINKING BEVER DRAFT DRINKY GUZZLE DRAUGHT POTTING CAROUSAL POTATION
(CONTINUOUS —) BOUT
DRIP LIP SIE SYE DROP LEAK SEGE SILE WEEP CANAL DRILL EAVES LABEL STILL DRIBBLE DRIPPLE LARMIER TRICKLE TRINKLE TRINTLE
(— WITH TINKLING SOUND) PINK
(PREF.) STALACTI(TI) STALAGMO
DRIPPING ADRIP STAXIS WEEPING
DRIPSTONE BAT DING LABEL HOODMOLD
DRIVE CA CAW COT FOG HOY JOG AUTO BANG BEAR BEAT BUTT CALL CRAM DING DRUB DRUM FIRE FIRK FLOG GOAD HACK HERD HUNT HURL JASM JEHU KICK LASH MOVE PICK PILE POSS PUSH RACK RIDE SEND SERR SINK SLOG SPUR STAB STUB TOOL TOUR TURN TRAM BRAWL CHASE CHECK COACT CROWD DRIFT DROVE FEEZE FLAIL FORCE HORSE HURRY IMPEL INFER LODGE MOTOR PEDAL POACH PRESS PULSE PUNCH REPEL ROUST SHOVE SLASH SMITE SPANK SWEEP TEASE ATTACK BATTER BEETLE BENSEL CHARGE COMPEL CUDGEL DEDUCE DERIVE FERRET HAMMER HASTEN IMPACT JARVEY JOSTLE PLUNGE PROPEL BLUSTER ENFORCE IMPULSE OVERTAX SETDOWN TRAVAIL CATAPULT CONATION SHEPHERD TENDENCY MOTIVATION
(— A BALL) LACE SEND
(— A HORSE ONWARD) WHIG
(— AIR) BLOW
(— ANIMALS) HAZE

(— AT TOP SPEED) BARREL CAREER
(— AWAY) RID FIRK HUSH SHOO BANDY EXILE FEEZE FLEME HOOSH REPEL SMOKE SWEEP AROINT BANISH DEFEND DISPEL ENCHASE DISPLACE EXORCISE
(— BACK) RUSH REBUT REPEL CULBUT DEFEND REBATE REBUFF RETUND REPULSE REFRINGE
(— BACK AND FORTH) TENNIS
(— BEFORE STRONG WIND) SPOON
(— BRISKLY) JUNE
(— CLOSE BEHIND WHILE RACING) DRAFT
(— CRAZY) BUG
(— DISTRACTED) BEDEVIL
(— FORTH) ISH
(— HARD) SWEAT HACKNEY
(— HOME) CLINCH
(— HURRIEDLY) BUM BUCKET
(— IN) CRAM DINT PILE TAMP INJECT
(— IN A PARK) TOUR
(— INTO THE GROUND) STUB
(— INTO WATER) ENEW
(— LOGS) SPLASH
(— OFF) KEEP LIFT EXCOCT
(— OFF STAGE) EXPLODE
(— OUT) BOLT FIRE DEPEL DROWN EJECT EXPEL KNOCK WREAK AROINT EXTURB ABANDON DISLODGE EXORCISE PROPULSE
(— RECKLESSLY) COWBOY
(— ROUGHLY) CHOUSE
(— SLANTINGLY) TOE
(— TO BAY) EMBOSS
(— TO MADNESS) FRENZY
(— VIOLENTLY) THUD SMASH HURTLE
(— WITH BLOWS) SKELP COURSE
(— WITH SHOUTS) HOY HUE
(FREE GOLF —) MULLIGAN
DRIVEL BLAH DOTE DRIP MUSH DROOL SLUSH DOTAGE DRUDGE FOOTLE HUMBUG MENIAL SLAVER DRIBBLE EYEWASH MAUNDER SLABBER TWADDLE NONSENSE SALIVATE CODSWALLOP
DRIVELING SLAVERY FOOTLING IMBECILE SLOBBERY BLITHERING
DRIVEPIPE POINT
DRIVER MUG HACK JEHU MUSH WHIP DRABI URGER CABMAN CALLER COWBOY DROVER FLYMAN HAULER JARVEY JOCKEY MALLET MIZZEN MUSHER PONIER STAGER VANMAN WAINER CATCHER COCHERO FLANKER HACKMAN HOODLUM HURRIER JITNEUR PHAETON SPANKER SPEEDER SUMPTER TOPSMAN TRUCKER WHIPMAN BANDYMAN BULLOCKY CALESERO CAMELEER COACHMAN DRAGSMAN ENGINEER GALLOWAY GOADSMAN IMPULSOR JITNEUSE MOTORMAN OVERSEER REINSMAN TEAMSTER WHIPSTER
(— OF ANIMALS) DROVER SKINNER
(— OF ELEPHANT) MAHOUT
(— OF OMNIBUS) PIRATE
(CAMEL —) SARWAN CAMELEER
(FAST —) JEHU SPEEDER

(FIELD —) HAYWARD
(PACK-HORSE —) SUMPTER
(SKILLFUL —) REINSMAN
(TOWPATH —) HOGGY HOGGEE
(PREF.) ELATRO
DRIVEWAY DRIVE SWEEP AVENUE DRIFTWAY
DRIVING PELTING COACHING SLASHING
(— ALONG) SCUD
(— OF GAME) BATTUE
(— OF WIND) GUST
(— TOGETHER) DRIFT
(— TOWARD) APPULSE
DRIZZLE DEG MUG DANK DRIP DROW HAZE LING RAIN SMUR STEW DRISK MISLE SMURR MIZZLE DRISSEL SCOUTHER SPRINKLE
(— OF RAIN) SKEW
DRIZZLY SOFT DRIPPY MIZZLY
DROGUE DRAG DRUG SLEEVE
DROLL ODD RUM COMIC DROLE FUNNY MERRY QUEER WITTY JESTER JOCOSE AMUSING BUFFOON COMICAL JOCULAR STRANGE WAGGISH FARCICAL HUMOROUS
DROLLERY WIT JEST FARCE HUMOR DROLERIE
DROMEDARY OONT CAMEL DELUL DELOUL HAGEEN HAGEIN HYGEEN MEHARI CAMAILE CAMELUS DROMOND
DRONE BEE BUM HUM DRUM SLUG SPIV DRANT DROLL IDLER SNAIL THRUM BUMBLE BURDEN CHORUS DRAUNT DRONEL DRONET LUBBER BAGPIPE BUMBARD BUMBASS HUMMING SHIRKER SLEEPER SOLDIER SPEAKER LOITERER SLUGGARD
DRONE BASS FOOT
DRONGO FORKTAIL
DRONING BOURDON HUMDRUM HUMMING SINGSONG
DRONISH SLOW INDOLENT SLUGGISH
DROOL FLAT DRIVEL SLAVER DRIBBLE SLABBER SLOBBER SALIVATE
DROOP FAG LOB LOP SAG BEND DROP FADE FLAG HANG LAVE LOLL PEAK PINE SINK SWAG WEEP WILT DAVER DREEP DROWK FLACK HEALD HIELD MOURN BANGLE BLOUSE DANGLE DEPEND NUTATE SLOUCH CURTAIN DECLINE FLITTER LANGUISH PENDENCY
DROOPING LOP DRAG FLAG LANK LAZY LIMP GOTCH OURIE ADROOP DROOPY FLAGGY NUTANT SLOUCH SOPITE GOTCHED HANGING LANGUID NODDING POPPIED CERNUOUS TRAILING
(— OF EARS) LAVE
(— OF EYELID) PTOSIS
DROOPY DREEPY SLIMPSY
DROP DAP DIP SIE SYE BEAD BEDE BLOB CAST DRIB DRIP DUMP FALL GLOB GOUT OMIT SEGE SHED

SILE SINK SPOT STOP TEAR BREAK CLOTH DROOP FLUMP GUTTA LAPSE LOWER MINIM PEARL PLUMP PLUNK SLUMP STILL SWOOP CANCEL DISTIL DRAPPY EXTILL FUMBLE GOBBET GOUTTE PLUNGE SINKER SLOUGH SPRINK TUMBLE ABANDON CURTAIN DESCENT DEWDROP DISCARD DISMISS DISTILL DRAPPIE DRIBBLE DRIBLET DROPLET EXPUNGE FORSAKE GLOBULE GUTTULA GUTTULE INCURVE LETDOWN MELDROP PLUMMET RELEASE SPATTER DECREASE DROPLING
(— ANCHOR) SLIP
(— ARGENT) LARME
(— AS SEEDS FROM A POD) ROSE
(— AWAY) DESERT
(— BAIT IN WATER) DAP
(— BY DROP) DROPWISE GUTTATIM
(— DOWN) VAIL
(— IN) STOP HAPPEN INSTIL INSTILL
(— OF GIN) DAFFY
(— OUT) FLOUNCE
(CHOCOLATE —) DRAGEE
(THEATRICAL —) TAB SCRIM
(UNEXPECTED —) DOYST
(PL.) GTT GUTT
(PREF.) GUTTI STAGMO STAGONO STILLI
DROP-CURTAIN GREENY
DROP ELBOW PIERDROP
DROPLET GLOBULE
(PL.) DEW
DROPLIGHT PENDANT
DROPPER SINK BOBBER SINKER PIPETTE
DROPPING FALL SCAT SKAT SHARD COWSHARD
(— ABRUPTLY) BOLD
(— SHARPLY) ABRUPT
(PL.) SOIL SPOOR FLYINGS
DROPSICAL PUFFY EDEMIC DROPSIED HYDROPIC
DROPSY EDEMA ASCITES ANASARCA
DROPWORT HORSEBANE DEADTONGUE
DROSS KISH LEES SCUM SLAG CHAFF DREGS DRUSH SCOBS SLACK SPRUE WASTE GARBLE REFUSE SCORIA SCRUFF SHRUFF SINTER CINDERS LEAVING OFFSCUM
DROSSEL SLUT HUSSY DRAZEL DRAZIL
DROUGHT DRYTH DROUTH THIRST ARIDITY DRYNESS
DROVE MOB SENT ATAJO CROWD DRIFT FLOCK MANADA BOASTER DISTURB TROUBLE DRIFTWAY
DROVER DEALER DRIVER TOPMAN TOPSMAN WHACKER HERDSMAN
DROWN DEAFEN DRENCH STIFLE ADRENCH DRUNKEN INDRENCH INUNDATE OVERTONE
DROWNED ADRENT
DROWNING NOYADE
DROWSE NOD SOG DOZE DOVER

DRONE SLEEP SNOOZE SLUMBER
DROWSINESS COMA DULLNESS
LETHARGY
DROWSING DORMANT
DROWSY DOZY DULL LOGY HEAVY
NODDY SLEEPY SNOOZY SOPITE
STUPID SUPINE SWOONY
DORMANT LULLING NODDING
POPPIED COMATOSE COMATOUS
OSCITANT SLUGGISH LETHARGIC
DRUB TAP WAP BANG BEAT BLOW
DRUM PAIK ARRAY CURRY STAMP
THUMP WHALE ANOINT CUDGEL
SCUTCH THRASH BELABOR
DRYBEAT SHELLAC
DRUBBING PAIK LICKING SACKING
DRUDGE DIG FAG TUG DROY DRUG
GRUB HACK MOIL PLOD SERF
TOIL DROIL GRIND SCRAT SCRUB
SLAVE SWEAT DIGGER DRIVEL
ENDURE JACKAL MOILER SCODGY
SCOGIE SLAVEY SLUDGE SUFFER
GRUBBER HACKNEY PLODDER
SLAVERY SWEATER TRACHLE
DRUDGERY FAG MOIL SLOG TOIL
WORK LABOR SWEAT SWINK
FAGGERY SLAVERY TRACHLE
TURMOIL DRUDGISM
DRUG (ALSO SEE NARCOTIC) HOP
ACID ALOE ALUM BUKU CURE
DOPE DRAB DULL HEMP LOAD
NUMB SINA BUCHU HOCUS JALAP
LOCUS MECON OPIUM RUTIN
SALOL SENNA SPECE SPEED
SULFA TONGA TRUCK COOLER
DEWTRY FINGER HEROIN IPECAC
JAMBUL LOCUST MYOTIC NOBBLE
OPIATE PEYOTE PEYOTL PITURI
POTION SIDDHI SIMPLE SULPHA
ANODYNE ASPIRIN ATEBRIN
BOTANIC CUSHION DAMIANA
DAPSONE DILATER ECBOLIC
ETHICAL HASHISH JAMBOOL
METOPON PHILTER PHILTRE
QUASSIA STUPEFY STYPTIC
SURAMIN ZEDOARY ADJUVANT
AROMATIC ASPIDIUM ATARAXIC
BANTHINE HYPNOTIC KOROMIKO
LAXATIVE MEDICATE MEDICINE
MERSALYL NARCOTIC NEPENTHE
PEMOLINE SALIVANT SEDATIVE
SPECIFIC TOXICANT ZERUMBET
ATARACTIC BARBITONE
COLCHICUM SALURETIC
PAINKILLER
(— DOSE) HIT
(— IN TABLET OF VARIOUS COLORS)
RAINBOW
(— SMUGGLER) MULE
(— USER) ACIDHEAD JOYPOPPER
(BITUMINOUS —) MUMMY
(DEPRESSANT —) DOWNER
(FREE FROM — ADDICTION) CLEAN
(INHALE A —) SNORT
(NONUSER OF —S) STRAIGHT
(ONE WHO USES A —) HEAD
(ONE WHO USES ILLICIT —S) FREAK
(ORAL DIURETIC —) THIAZIDE
(STIMULANT —) UPPER
(STRENGTHENING —) ROBORANT
(TAKE A — THROUGH THE MOUTH)
DROP
(TAKE —S ORALLY) POP

(TO INJECT —) SHOOT
(VEGETABLE —) FINGER
(PL.) DRUGGERY
(PREF.) PHARMACO
DRUGGED POPPIED
DRUGGET BAUGE BOCKING
DRUGGIST CHEMIST DRUGGER
GALLIPOT
DRUGSTORE APOTHEC PHARMACY
DRUID SARONIDE
DRUM GIN GOO BOWL CAGE DRUB
LALI ROUT SKIN SPOT TOPH TRAP
BONGO CONGA CRAWL DRONE
GUMBE GUMBY SHAPE SNARE
SWASH TABOR THRUM TOMBE
ATABAL BARREL CROCUS RIGGER
TABRET TAMBOR TIMBRE TUMBLE
TUMMER TYMPAN ANACARA
BUBBLER CROAKER FRUSTUM
GRUNTER RATTLER REDFISH
SNUBBER TABORIN TAMBOUR
TEMPEST TIMBREL TUMBLER
BAMBOULA BARBUKKA CANISTER
CYLINDER DERBUKKA DRUMFISH
HUEHUETL MOULINET MRIDANGA
TYMPANUM MRIDANGAM
(— AS SHIP'S SIGNAL) SHAPE
(— FOR WINDING ROPE) CAGE
(— IN WINCH) GIPSY GYPSY
(— MADE FROM HOLLOW TREE)
GUMBE GUMBY
(— OF CAPSTAN) RUNDLE
MOULINE
(— OF INDIA) MRIDANGA
MRIDANGAM
(— ON WINDLASS) WILDCAT
(— UP BUSINESS) HUSTLE
(— UP INTEREST) BALLYHOO
(HEATED —) DRIER DRYER
(IGOROT —) GANGSA
(PAIR OF HINDU —S) TABLA
(REVOLVING —) GURDY RATTLER
(SUMERIAN —) ALA ALAL
DRUMBEAT DUB FLAM RUFF TUCK
MARCH RUFFLE ASSEMBLY
BERLOQUE BRELOQUE
(— SOUND) TUCK
DRUMFISH SPOT CROCUS
BUBBLER CROAKER DRUMMER
DRUMSLER SCIAENID
DRUMLIN DRUM SOWBACK
DRUMMER DRUM TABOR STICKS
TABRET ROADMAN SWASHER
TAMBOUR TUMBLER DRUMSLER
SALESMAN
DRUMMING TATTOO
DRUM ROLL DIAN DIANA
DRUMS ALONG THE MOHAWK
(AUTHOR OF —) EDMONDS
(CHARACTER IN —) HON JOHN
LANA MARK YOST BRANT JURRY
NANCY WOLFF ARNOLD GAHOTA
JOSEPH MARTIN DEMOOTH
GILBERT MCLONIS SCHUYLER
MAGDELANA MCKLENNAR
DRUMSTICK LEG STICK BAGUET
TAMPON BAGUETTE
DRUNK CUT FAP FOU REE WET
GONE HIGH LUSH NASE PAID RIPE
SOSH BLIND BOOZE BOSKY CLEAR
DRINK LUMPY LUSHY MALTY
MOPPY OILED QUEER SHICK STIFF
TIGHT TIPSY BAGGED BLOTTO

BOILED BOMBED BUZZED
CANNED FLUFFY GROGGY
JAGGED LOADED LOOPED
MORTAL POTTED SLOPPY
SODDEN SOSHED SOUSED SOZZLY
SPONGY SPRUNG STEWED
STINKO STONED TIDDLY UPPISH
UPPITY ZONKED BLOTTER
BONKERS BOTTLED CROCKED
DRUNKEN JINGLED MAUDLIN
PICKLED SCREWED SHICKER
SLOPPED SMASHED SOZZLED
SQUIFFY SWACKED COCKEYED
GLORIOUS MUCKIBUS PLEASANT
SQUIFFED STINKING BLITHERED
PIXILATED
DRUNKARD SOT LUSH SOAK
BLOAT DIPSO DRUNK GULCH
RUMMY SOUSE TOPER LUSHER
SOAKER SPONGE DRUNKER
FUDDLER POTSHOT SHICKER
STEWBUM TIPPLER TOSSPOT
BORACHIO HABITUAL SWILLTUB
DRUNKEN REE WAT GONE WINY
BLIND BOUSY DROWN DRUNK
BLOTTO FLUFFY SODDEN
BACCHIC DRUCKEN PICKLED
SOTTISH WHIPCAT DRENCHED
SATURATE SQUIFFED VINOLENT
WOODSERE
DRUNKENNESS BUN IVRESSE
POTSHOT METHYSIS
DRUPE TRYMA DRUPEL DRUPELET
DRUPEOLE
DRUPELET GRAIN ACINUS
DRUPE STONE NUTLET
DRUSILLA (BROTHER OF —)
CALIGULA
(FATHER OF —) HEROD CALIGULA
GERMANICUS
(HUSBAND OF —) FELIX AZIZUS
AUGUSTUS
(MOTHER OF —) CYPROS CAESONIA
AGRIPPINA
(SON OF —) AGRIPPA TIBERIUS
DRY EBB KEX SEC TED WIN ADRY
ARID BAKE BLOT BRUT DULL EILD
GELD HASK KEXY KILN PINE SAVE
SERE SOUR WELT WIPE AREFY
CORKY DRAIN FROST GUESS
HASKY JUSKY MEALY PARCH
PROSY SANDY SECCO SMEEK
SWEAT VAPID WIZEN BARKEN
BARREN BIRSLE BORING CHIPPY
ENSEAR GIZZEN HISTIE JEJUNE
SCORCH STARKY AREFACT
BRUSTLE INSIPID SAPLESS
SICCATE SQUALID STERILE
THIRSTY TORREFY XEROTIC
BARBECUE DROUGHTY INFUMATE
TIRESOME WOODSERE
(— HERRINGS) DEESE
(— IN SUN) RIZZAR
(— OF MILK) SEW EILD
(— PARTLY) SAMMY
(— UP) SERE WELK WITHER
AREFACT FORWELK SKELLER
(— WOOD) BEATH SWEAT SEASON
(NOT —) SWEET
(PREF.) DEHYDR(O) JEJUN(O)
SCLER(O) SICCI TORRE XER(O)
(— PLACE OR PROCESS) XER(O)
DRYAD DRYAS NYMPH CAISSA

YAKSHA YAKSHI WOODMAID
DRYER DRIER STOVE SIROCCO
DRY GOODS DRAPERY
DRYING SICCANT
DRYING RACK CRIB
DRYNESS DROUTH ARIDITY
DROUGHT SICCITY XEROSIS
XEROTES HASKNESS AREFACTION
DRYOPE (FATHER OF —) EURYTUS
(HUSBAND OF —) ANDRAEMON
(SISTER OF —) IOLE
(SON OF —) AMPHISSUS
DUAL TWIN BINARY DOUBLE
DUALIST TWOFOLD
DUALISM DVAITA
DUALITY DUAD TWINE TWONESS
DUANT DE DEE
DUB DIB RUB ADUB BLOW CALL
NAME POOL ADORN ARRAY
DRESS STYLE THUMP CLOTHE
KNIGHT PUDDLE SMOOTH STRIKE
ENTITLE BEGINNER DRUMBEAT
ORNAMENT
DUBBIN DAUBING
DUBIOUS DICKY FISHY JUBUS
DOUBTY BEARISH DOUBTFUL
DOUBTING JUBEROUS
PRECARIOUS QUESTIONABLE
(NOT —) EXPRESS
DUCA D'ALBA, IL (CHARACTER
IN —) AMELIA EGMONT MARCELLO
(COMPOSER OF —) DONIZETTI
DUCHY SAVOY DUCATUS DUCHERY
DUKEDOM PARMESAN
DUCK AIX BOB BOW CAN DIG DIP
DOP MIG PET WIO CHAP COLK
COOT DIVE DOGS DOGY DOKE
DUKW JOUK LADY LORD PATO
ROOK SMEE SMEW TEAL TEUK
BOOBY BUNTY CRICK DILLY
DODGE DOUSE DOWSE DUCKY
EIDER HOUND MOMMY NODDY
PADDY POKER RODGE ROUEN
SCAUP SHIRK SOUSE SPIKE SPRIG
STOOL BOBBER CALLOO CALLOW
CANARD CANNET DUCKIE
FELLOW GARROT HARELD PEKING
PERSON PLUNGE QUANDY
RUNNER SCOTER SMETHE
ANATINE BARWING BLACKIE
BOWSSEN BUMMALO CANETTE
CRACKER DABBLER DARLING
DRABBLE DUCKING DUCKLET
DUNBIRD FIDDLER FLAPPER
GADWALL GEELBEC GREASER
MALLARD OLDWIFE PENTAIL
PINKEYE PINTAIL POCHARD
REDHEAD REDLEGS REDWING
SCOOTER SLEEPER SPATTER
WADDLER WIDGEON YAGUAZA
BALDPATE BLUEBILL BLUEWING
BOATBILL BULLNECK DUCKLING
DUCKWING GARGANEY
GRAYBACK GREYBACK HARDHEAD
IRONHEAD MOONBILL MORILLON
PIKETAIL REDSHANK RINGBILL
RINGNECK SHOVELER SHUFFLER
SQUEALER WIRETAIL BERGANDER
(— AT CRICKET) BLOB
(— EGGS) PIDAN
(MALE —) DRAKE
(PART OF —) EAR EYE WEB BEAN
BILL CAPE HEAD NECK RUMP TAIL

WING FLUFF SHANK BREAST
SADDLE COVERTS NOSTRIL
SHOULDER PRIMARIES
SECONDARIES
(STUFFED —) DUMPOKE
(YOUNG —) CANETON FLAPPER
FLOPPER
DUCKBILL OOTOCOID PLATYPUS
TAMBREET MONOTREME
DUCKWEED GLIT GRAIN LEMNAD
LENTIL DIGMEAT DUCKMEAT
FROGFOOT
DUCT VAS MAIN PIPE TUBE VEIN
CANAL ALVEUS BUSWAY DUCTUS
MEATUS URETER CHANNEL
CONDUIT DUCTULE DUCTURE
LACTEAL LEADING PASSAGE
TRACHEA AQUEDUCT CALIDUCT
DOWNTAKE EFFERENT EMISSARY
EXHALANT GONADUCT GUIDANCE
OLEODUCT
(PREF.) RHYN(O) VAS(I)(O)
DUCTILE SOFT DOCILE FACILE
PLIANT PLASTIC PLIABLE TENSILE
FLEXIBLE TRACTILE
(PREF.) ELAST(O)
DUD FLOP LEMON STUMER
STUMOR FAILURE
DUDE FOP DANDY DUDINE
JOHNNY COXCOMB JACKEEN
DUDGEON PIQUE OFFENSE
DUE HAK LOT OWE BACK CENS
DEBT FAIR FARM FLAT HAKH
JUST MEED OWED TOLL DROIT
ENDOW ENDUE FATED MERIT
OWING COMING CUSTOM DESERT
EXTENT LAWFUL MATURE
PROPER UNPAID CONDIGN
EXACTLY FALDFEE FITTING
JETTAGE TALLAGE ADEQUATE
DIRECTLY HEREGELD HEREZELD
RIGHTFUL SUITABLE TRUNCAGE
DUEL TILT FENCE FIGHT AFFAIR
COMBAT DUELLO MENSUR
CONTEST MEETING CONFLICT
DUELLIZE HOLMGANG
DUELIST FIGHTER SPADASSIN
DUENNA DRAGON GRIFFIN
CHAPERON
DUES TOLLS DROITS CHIEFRY
INWARDS JETTAGE PAYMENT
PENSION QUAYAGE ALTARAGE
HAVENAGE SOUNDAGE THIRLAGE
WHARFAGE
DUET DUO TWO DUETTO
TWOSOME
(BALLET —) ADAGIO
DUFF ALTER BRAND CHEAT FLOOR
PUDDING
DUFFER DUB MUFF SHAM CHEAT
BUFFER HAWKER RABBIT SHICER
PEDDLER
DUG TEAT
(— UP) HOWKIT
(PREF.) ORYCTO
DUGONG SEACOW YUNGAN
COWFISH HALICORE MUTILATE
SIRENIAN
DUGOUT ABRI BOAT BURY CAVE
BANCA BONGO BUNGO CANOE
DONGA DUNGA SHELL BAROTO
BUNKER CAYUCA CAYUCO CORIAL
TROUGH BANTING PIRAGUA

PIROGUE SHELTER BLINDAGE
LIPALIPA
DUHSHASANA (FATHER OF —)
DHRITARASHTRA
DUIKER IPITI DUYKER BLAUBOK
DUKE DUC DUX KNEZ PEER AYMON
CHIEF KNIAZ HERZOG LEADER
ORSINO AUMERLE GORLOIS
SOLINUS STEENIE HERETOGA
PROSPERO
DUKEDOM DUCHY ALBANY
DUCATUS
DULCET SWEET DULCID SIRUPY
SYRUPY SOOTHING
DULCIAN CURTAL
DULCIMER ROTA CANUN CITOLE
SANTIR CEMBALO MAGADIS
SANTOUR CYMBALOM PANTALON
SAUTERIE ZIMBALON
DULIA ADORATION
DULL DIM DOW DRY FAT LAX MAT
SAD ARID BLAH CLOD COLD
DAMP DEAD DILL DOWD DOWF
DOWY DRAB DREE DRUG DUMB
FLAT GRAY GREY LOGY MOPE
MULL POKY SLOW TAME THIN
TURN BESOT BLACK BLAND
BLATE BLEAR BLIND BLUNT
BRUTE CRASS DENSE DINGY
DOWFF DOWIE DOWLY DREAR
DUBBY DUNCH DUNNY DUSTY
FISHY FOGGY GLAZY GRAVE
GROSS HEAVY INERT LOURD
MATTE MORON MOSSY MUDDY
MUSTY MUZZY NOOSE PLUMP
POKEY PROSE PROSY SHADE
SLACK SOGGY STARY STILL SULKY
TERNE THICK UNAPT VAPID
WASTE BARREN BLEARY BOVINE
CLOUDY DAMPEN DARKEN
DEADEN DISMAL DRAGGY
DREARY DRIECH DRIEGH DROWSY
EARTHY FRIGID FRUMPY GLASSY
HEBETE JEJUNE LEADEN LOURDY
MUFFLE OBTUND OBTUSE
OPAQUE PALLID REBATE RETUND
SLEEPY SLOOMY SODDEN
SOMBER SOMBRE STODGY STOLID
STUFFY STUPID SULLEN TIMBER
TORPID TRISTE TURBID URLUCH
WOODEN ADENOID BLUNTED
CONFUSE DEADISH DISEDGE
DOLTISH DOWFART DRAINED
DULLISH DUMPISH HUMDRUM
INSIPID IRKSOME LANGUID
LUMPISH MUMPISH PEAKISH
PINHEAD PROSAIC SHEATHE
SOTTISH STUPEFY TEDIOUS
UNLUSTY VACUOUS BACKWARD
BANAUSIC BEFUDDLE BLOCKISH
BOEOTIAN BROMIDIC COMATOSE
COMATOUS DIDACTIC DISCOLOR
DULLSOME EDGELESS FRUMPISH
GAUMLESS HEBETATE INFICETE
LIFELESS LISTLESS LOURDISH
OVERCAST PLODDING SLOTTERY
SLUGGISH SOULLESS STAGNANT
TIRESOME PINHEADED
PONDEROUS SATURNINE
(— EDGE OF) ABATE
(— IN MOTION) LOGY
(— SCENT) FOIL
(— WITH LIQUOR) SEETHE

(BECOME —) PALL RUST
(MENTALLY —) DOPY DOPEY
BARREN
(PREF.) AMBLY(O) BRADY
DULLARD DOLT BOOBY DUNCE
IDIOT MORON DODUNK STUPID
BROMIDE DASTARD DOLDRUM
DULBERT POTHEAD BLINKARD
DULLHEAD
DULLED EMPTY HEAVY JADED
BROKEN CLOUDY GRAYED
SODDEN STUPID BLEARED
DULLISH DIRTY
DULLNESS DRAB HAZE YAWN
CLOUD TAMAS FADEUR PHLEGM
TORPOR DIMNESS DOLDRUM
DULLITY DUNCERY FATUITY
LANGUOR OPACITY DUMBNESS
HEBETUDE SLOWNESS SOPITION
VAPIDITY SEGNITUDE STOLIDITY
DULL-SPIRITED MUZZY
DULL-WITTED FOZY WITLESS
BESOTTED DONNERED
(— PERSON) MOREPORK
DULLY FLATLY HEAVILY
DULSE DILLESK DILLISK SEAWEED
DULY DUE FITLY RIGHT RITELY
PROPERLY
DUMAH (FATHER OF —) ISHMAEL
DUMB DULL MUTE STONY SILENT
STONEY STUPID
DUMBBELL DUMMY DUNCE
HALTER KNOTHEAD
DUMBFOUND DAZE STUN AMAZE
CONFUSE CONFOUND SURPRISE
DUMBFOUNDED STUPENT
DUMBNESS SILENCE APHRASIA
DUMBWAITER LIFT DUMMY
DUMMY COPY DOLT MUTE SHAM
DUMBY FAGOT EFFIGY FAGGOT
PONTIC SHADOW SILENT
PHANTOM DUMBBELL
(SWORDSMAN'S —) PEL
DUMNORIX (BROTHER OF —)
DIVITIACUS
DUMP SUM TIP BEAT CASH COIN
COUP FALL HOLE JAIL MUSE NAIL
TOOM EMPTY HOUSE SHOOT
GRIEVE PLUNGE TIPPLE UNLOAD
BOGHOLE COUNTER DEPOSIT
REVERIE SADNESS STORAGE
(MINE —) BURROW
(PL.) SUDS MOPES SADNESS
DUMPCART DUMPER TUMBREL
TUMBRIL
DUMPER TIPMAN
DUMPLING COB CRUST KNODEL
KNAIDEL NOCKERL DOUGHBOY
QUENELLE
(PL.) KLOSSE GNOCCHI
DUMPY DUNCH GROSS PUDGY
SQUAB SQUAT DUMPTY STOCKY
SQUATTY
DUN BUM TAN FORT KICK URGE
ANNOY BROWN CRAVE CROWD
DINGY FAVEL MOUND SEPIA
DUNNER LEADEN PESTER PLAGUE
DUNNISH SWARTHY
DUNCE ASS DOLT DULT GABY
GONY BOBBY BOOBY DOBBY
IDIOT NINNY DULTIE HOBBIL
PEDANT DULLARD SOPHIST
NUMSKULL STUNPOLL

TOMNODDY WISEACRE
DUN-COLORED
(PREF.) PHAEO PHEO
(SUFF.) PHAEIN PHEIN
DUNDERHEAD OAF CLOD DOLT
DUNCE TURNIP GOMERIL
DUNE BAR DENE MEAL MOUND
TOWAN TWINE BARKAN
BARCHAN BARKHAN
(SAND —) DRAB SAIF SEIF
DUNG MIS CACK CHIP DOLL FIME
GORE MERD MUCK MUTE SOIL
TATH ARGAL ARGOL FECES FILTH
FUMET MIXEN SCARN SHARN
BILLET CASSON FIANTS LESSES
MANURE ORDURE SCUMBER
SCUMMER TREDDLE COWSHARD
DROPPING STALLAGE
(— AS FUEL) ARGOL CASSON
CASSONS
(— OF BEAST OF PREY) LESSES
(— OF DEER) FUMET FEWMET
(COW —) MIST UPLA COWSHARD
COWSHARN
(OTTER'S —) SPRAINTS
(SHEEP —) BUTTONS TREDDLE
TROTTERS
(PREF.) COPR(O) FIMI GUANI
GUANO MERDI SCAT(O) SCORI
SPATILO STERCO STERCOR(I)
DUNGEON PIT CELL HELL HOLE
LAKE VAULT CACHOT DONJON
PRISON CONFINE OUBLIET
REVOLVER OUBLIETTE
DUNGHILL MIXEN MIDDEN MIXHILL
DUNGON DONGON SUNDARI
DUNK DIP SOP SOAK STEEP
IMMERSE MOISTEN
DUNKER DIPPER TAUFER TUNKER
DUMPLER DUNKARD TUMBLER
DUNLIN STIB OXEYE PURRE STINT
DORBIE OXBIRD REDBACK
LEADBACK
DUNNAGE FARDAGE
DUODECIMO TWELVEMO
DUPE APE BAM FOB FOP MUG
BOOB COAX CONY CULL DUST
FOOL GECK GULL HOAX LAMB
ROOK TOOL CHEAT CHUMP
COKES CONEY CULLY HEALD
MOOTH MOUTH SLANG STALE
TRICK BEFOOL BUBBLE CHOOSE
CHOUSE COUSIN DELUDE DERIDE
MONKEY PIGEON PLOVER SQUARE
SUCKER VICTIM BECASSE
CATSPAW CHICANE CULLION
DECEIVE GUDGEON MISLEAD
SAPHEAD SWINDLE YOUNKER
DOTTEREL HOODWINK RODERIGO
DUPERY RAMP
DUPLE BINARY DOUBLE TWOFOLD
DUPLEX DOUBLE TWOFOLD
DUPLEXITY EQUIVOKE
DUPLICATE BIS COPY DUPE ALIKE
DITTO SPARE TALLY DOUBLE
FLIMSY REPEAT COUNTER
ESTREAT MISLEAD REPLICA
TWOFOLD LIKENESS
(PREF.) COUNTER
DUPLICATION DISOMATY
DUPLICATOR MIMEOGRAPH
DUPLICITY ART GUILE DECEIT
TRICKERY

DUPONDIUS BRONZE
DURABILITY WEAR FIBER FIBRE
STEEL DURANCE STAMINA
DURABLE FIRM HARD LASTY
STOUT STABLE STAPLE LASTING
SERVICE CONSTANT ENDURING
LIVELONG
DURABLENESS DURATION
DURAMEN HEARTWOOD
DURANCE DURANT DURESS
CUSTODY
DURANGO CARTOUCH
DURATION AGE DATE LAST LIFE
SPAN TERM TIME WHEN DUREE
KALPA SPACE LENGTH PERIOD
DURANCE LASTING INFINITE
LIFETIME STANDING
(— BREEZE) SLATCH
(BOUNDLESS —) INFINITE
(INFINITE —) ETERNITY
DURAZZO (WARD OF —) CALDORO
DURESS FORCE DANGER CRUELTY
DURANCE COERCION HARDNESS
PRESSURE
DURGA KALI CHAMUNDA
(HUSBAND OF —) SHIVA
DURIAN JAK JACK JAKFRUIT
DURING IN ON BIN AMID OVER
TIME AMONG INTRA WHILE
AMIDST WHILST WITHIN
AMONGST DURANTE PENDING
ENDURING
(PREF.) DIA INTRA
DURRA DARI DURA MILO JOWAR
CHOLUM DHURRA JONDLA
SORGHUM FETERITA
DURYODHANA (BROTHER OF —)
PANDU
(FATHER OF —) DHRITARASHTRA
(SON OF —) LAKSHMANA
(WIFE OF —) DRAUPADI
DUSACK TESACK
DUSHYANTA (SON OF —) BHARATA
(WIFE OF —) SHAKUNTALA
DUSK DIM EVE DARK DIMPS
GLOAM GLOOM DIMMET DIMPSY
DIMNESS DUCKISH DARKNESS
GLOAMING OWLLIGHT TWILIGHT
NIGHTFALL
DUSKY DIM DUN SAD WAN DARK
DUSK ADUSK BLACK BROWN
DINGY GRIMY MOORY TAWNY
GLOOMY PHAEIC SMUTTY
SOMBER SOMBRE SWARTH
DARKISH DARLING OBSCURE
SUBFUSC SUBFUSK SWARTHY
BLACKISH
(PREF.) PERCNO PHAEO
DUST ROW COOM DIRT FOGO
MUCK MULL PILM SMUT BRISS
CLEAN COOMB FLOUR POUCE
STIVE STOUR DREDGE FILLER
KITTEN POLLEN POWDER SMEECH
BEFLOUR EBURINE REMAINS
SAWDUST SMEDDUM TURMOIL
ANTELOPE BULLDUST PUMICITE
(— IN FLOUR MILLS) STIVE
(— IN QUARTZ MILL) SLICKENS
(BLOOD —) HEMOCONIA
(CHOKING —) POTHER
(COAL —) COOM CULM DUFF
COOMB
(COKE —) BREEZE

(COSMIC —) STARDUST
(DIAMOND —) SEASONING
(FIBER —) FLOCK
(FLAX —) POUCE POUSE
(THICK —) SMOTHER
(PREF.) CON(I)(ICO)(IDIO)(O)
(SUFF.) CONITE
DUST CLOUD STEW
DUST COVER WRAPPER
DUSTER DEVIL WILLOW ZEPHYR
TORCHON DUSTCOAT
DUSTY ADUST MOTTY MOTTLE
POUCEY STOURY POWDERY
UNDUSTED
DUTCH (SEE NETHERLANDS)
HOGEN HOLLAND
DUTCH FOIL ORSEDE ORSEDUE
DUTCH GOLD CLINQUANT
DUTCHMAN HANS HOGEN
BLANDA DUTCHY BELANDA
DUTCHER MYNHEER BATAVIAN
DUTCHMAN'S-BREECHES
DICENTRA
DUTIFUL PIOUS DOCILE LAWFUL
DEBTFUL DUTEOUS OBEDIENT
OFFICIAL REVERENT OFFICIOUS
DUTIFULNESS PIETY
DUTY DO END JOB LOT TAX CALL
CARE FYRD ONUS PART PROW
ROLE TAIL TASK TOLL WIKE
CHORE DEVER ERMIN LADLE LIKIN
OUGHT PREST RIGHT STINT
WIKEN BLANCH BURDEN CHARGE
COCKET DEVOIR DHARMA EXCISE
EXITUS HERIOT IMPOSE IMPOST
INGATE OFFICE RIVAGE TARIFF
AVERAGE BAILAGE BOOMAGE
FOSSAGE FURDUNG GRANAGE
INDULTO KEELAGE LASTAGE
PONTAGE PRIMAGE ROYALTY
SCAVAGE SERVICE STATION
TONNAGE TRIBUTE TRONAGE
TUNNAGE BALLIAGE BUSINESS
FUNCTION MALIKANA MALTOLTE
REDDENDO WEIGHAGE
OBLIGATION
(— FOR LEAD ORE) COPE
(CUSTOMS —) OCTROI
(FEUDAL —) HERIOT
(IMPORT —) ERMIN INDULTO
(MILITARY —) STABLES
(TIRING —) FATIGUE
(PL.) CUSTOMS INGATES
ACTIVITY
DUX CHIEF LEADER SUBJECT
HERETOGA
DWARF ELF PUG URF AETA CRUT
GRIG GRUB NANA RUNT CRILE
CROWL GALAR GNOME KNURL
MIDGE PIGMY PYGMY SCRUB
STUNT TROLL ABLACH ALVISS
CONJON DROICH DURGAN
DURGEN MIDGET SHRIMP
ANDVARI ANDWARI BLASTIE
CONGEON MANIKIN OVERTOP
PACOLET WRATACK ALBERICH
BELITTLE HOMUNCIO HOMUNCLE
HUCKMUCK KNURLING
MENEHUNE NANANDER
(PL.) CERCOPES NIBLUNGS
NIBELUNGS
(PREF.) NAN(O) NANN(O)
DWARF DANDELION KRIGIA

DWARFED STUNTY STUNTED
DWARF ELDER WALLWORT
DWARFING BRACHYSM
DWARFISH ELFIN PIGMY PYGMY
GRUBBY KNURLY NANOID
RUNTISH STUNTED
DWARFISHNESS NANISM
DWARFISM NANISM ATELIOSIS
DWARF MALLOW CHEESE PELLAS
DWARF RASPBERRY PLUMBOG
DWELL BIG COT DIG SIT WIN WON
BIDE BIGG HAFT HARP LIVE STAY
TELD WINE WONT ABIDE BIELD
BOWER BROOD BUILD DELAY
HOUSE LODGE PAUSE SHACK
STALL TARRY LINGER REMAIN
RESIDE TENANT CLIMATE
COHABIT INHABIT CONVERSE
(— IN) BIG BIGG BEDWELL INHABIT
(— IRRITATINGLY) GRATE
(— ON) HARP BROOD GLOAT
DWELLER TENANT WONNER
DENIZEN PALEMAN DOWNSMAN
HABITANT OCCUPANT RESIDENT
(— BY SEA) PARALIAN
(BUSH —) CAVEMAN TROGLODYTE
(CAVE —) CAVEMAN TROGLODYTE
(CITY —) SLICKER
(COAST —) BUFFALO ORARIAN
(LAKE —) LACUSTRIAN
(PL.) HUTHOLD
(SUFF.) ITE
DWELLING DAR HUT INN SEE WON
CASA FARM FLAT FORT HAFT
HALL HOME NEST ROOF SLUM
TENT WIKE WONE ABODE BOWER
CABIN DOMUS HOGAN HOOCH
HOTEL HOUSE HOVEL JOINT
MANSE MOTEL PLACE CASTLE
DUGOUT DUPLEX HOMING
HOOTCH MALOCA SHANTY
TEEPEE WIGWAM WONING
COTTAGE LODGING MANSION
SALTBOX TRAILER TRIPLEX
WONNING BUILDING BUNGALOW
DOMICILE TENEMENT PENTHOUSE
RESIDENCE
(— IN UNDERWORLD) CHTHONIC
(— PLACE) HOWF HOWFF
(— WITH ANOTHER) INMATE
(ATTRACTIVE —) BOWER
(CRUDE —) SHED SHEBANG
(LAKE —) CRANNOG PALAFITTE
(MEAN —) SHANTY
(MISERABLE —) BURROW
DOGHOLE
(NAVAJO —) HOGAN
(NEOLITHIC —) TERRAMARA
(ONE-ROOM —) CELL
(PORTABLE —) CAMPER
(RAMSHACKLE —) HUMPY
(RUDE —) BOTHY BOTHIE
(SMALL —) CRIB
(SUBTERRANEAN —) WEEM
(SWISS —) CHALET
(PL.) HOUSING
DWINDLE FADE FAIL FINE MELT
PINE WANE DECAY DRAIN PETER
TAPER TRAIL WASTE MOLDER
SHRINK CONSUME DECLINE
FRITTER MOULDER DECREASE
DIMINISH FORDWINE
DWINDLING DOWN FLAGGING

DYAD PAIR
DYBBUK GILGUL
DYE (ALSO SEE DYESTUFF) AAL DIP
LIT ANIL BLUE COLOR EMBUE
FUCUS IMBUE LOKAO STAIN
SUDAN TINCT VENOM ARCHIL
IMBRUE INFECT MADDER TINGER
ENGRAIN INTINCT LACMOID
LOGWOOD PUCCOON ZAMBESI
AMARANTH COLORANT DYESTUFF
FUGITIVE INDIGOID TINCTURE
(— FUR) FEATHER
(— NOT FAST) FUGITIVE
(BLACK —) GUAKO
(BLUE —) RUM ROOM SAXE WOAD
CYANINE DICYANINE
(BROWN —) CACHOU
(GENERAL —S) NIL NILL AZINE
BROWN EOSIN GREEN DIANIL
EOSINE ISAMIN ORANGE PURPLE
VIOLET CYANINE FUCHSIN
METANIL PONCEAU PRIMULA
ALIZARIN AURANTIA CIBACRON
DICYANIN EURHODOL FUCHSINE
HYPERNIC INDULINE NIGROSIN
TURNSOLE VIRIDINE NIGROSINE
SAFRANINE
(HAIR —) RASTIK
(KIND OF —) SRA
(ORANGE —) KAMALA ROUCOU
(PURPLE —) CASSIUS GALLEIN
TURNSOLE
(RED —) AAL ANATO AURIN EOSIN
GRAIN HENNA RUBIN ANATTO
AURINE CERISE EOSINE RELBUN
RUBINE ALKANET ANNATTO
CORINTH CRIMSON MAGENTA
PONCEAU SAFFLOR ALIZARIN
AMARANTH BORDEAUX CORALLIN
CROCEINE
(SCARLET —) TULY GRAIN
(VIOLET —) MAUVE ARCHIL ORCHIL
LACMOID ARCHILLA
(YELLOW —) ARUSA FLAVIN
CHRYSIN FISETIN FLAVINE
LAWSONE WONGSHY AURAMINE
DYED INGRAIN
(PERMANENTLY —) FAST
DYEING TINCTION
DYER LISTER TINGER TINTER
DYESTER FIELDER SKEINER
TAINTOR TINTIST
DYERMA ZARMA ZAREMA
DYERS' MULBERRY FUSTIC
DYERS'-WEED SOLIDAGO
DYESTUFF (ALSO SEE DYE) DYE
LIT WELD WOAD CHICA LOKAO
WOULD ANATTO BRAZIL KAMALA
LITMUS ORCEIN RELBUN
ALKANET ARNATTO CUDBEAR
DYEWARE SAFFRON INDULINE
LUTEOLIN PITTACAL PURPURIN
DYEWEED WOODWAX
DYEWOOD FUSTET FUSTIC
BARWOOD CAMWOOD HYPERNIC
DYING FEY DEATH MORENDO
PARTING MORIBUND
(— AWAY) CALANDO DILUENDO
MANCANDO PERDENDO
SMORZATO
DYNAMIC POTENT DRIVING
KINETIC FORCEFUL
DYNAMITE BLAST DUALIN

SAWDUST RENDROCK GELIGNITE
DYNAMO EXCITER TORNADO
(PART OF —) BRUSH FIELD FRAME
RIGGING ARMATURE COUPLING
COMMUTATOR
DYNASTY (OR MEMBER THEREOF)
KIN SUI WEI YIN CHIN CHOU HSIA
RACE SUNG TANG YUAN BUYID

CHING PIAST REALM RULER
SHANG HAFSID PRINCE SAFAVI
SELJUK ABBASID ALMOHAD
ARSACID ATTALID AYUBITE
AYYUBID BOUIDES FATIMID
HAFSITE IDRISID JAGELLO
LAKHMID MONARCH OMAYYAD
ROMANOV SAADIAN SAFAWID

SAMANID TULUNID ABBASIDE
AGHLABID AGLABITE ASMONEAN
BUWAIHID CAPETIAN CHALUKYA
DOMINION EDRISITE GOVERNOR
IDRISITE JAGIELLO LORDSHIP
SAFFARID SARGONID SASANIAN
SELEUCID SOFFARID SASSANIDE
DYSENTERY FLUX SCOUR

MENISON TOXEMIA DIARRHEA
DYSPEPTIC CACOGASTRIC
DYSPHORIA FIDGET
DYSSODIA BOEBERA
DZIGGETAI HEMIONUS

E

E EASY ECHO

EA HEA ENKI

EACH A EA UP ALL ILK THE UCH ILKA UCHE EVERY APIECE EITHER EVERYONE
(OF —) ANA

EAGER HOT RAD YAN ACID AGOG AVID EDGY FAIN FELL FOND FREE GAIR HIGH KEEN RATH SOUR TARE THRO VAIN WARM WAVE YARE YERN AFIRE AGASP ANTSY BRIEF FIRST FRACK FRECK HASTY HIGRE ITCHY PRIME READY SHARP SNELL YIVER ARDENT FIERCE GREEDY HETTER INTENT STRONG TIPTOE ANXIOUS ATHIRST BRITTLE BURNING EXCITED FERVENT FORWARD ITCHING PROVOKE DESIROUS IRRITATE SPIRITED VIGOROUS YEARNING SOLICITOUS
(— IN PURSUIT) SHARP
(WILDLY —) CRAZY

EAGERLY FAST FELL YERN HOTLY BELIVE TIPTOE YARELY YEPELY PRESTLY HUNGRILY INTENTLY

EAGERNESS GOG ELAN GARE ZEAL ARDOUR DESIRE FERVOR ARDENCY AVIDITY ALACRITY CUPIDITY DEVOTION FAINNESS FERVENCY

EAGLE AAR ERN CROW ERNE GIER TERN HARPY AQUILA BERGUT EAGLET FALCON FORMAL FORMEL RAPTOR ALLERION BATALEUR BATELEUR BEARCOOT BERGHAAN RINGTAIL
(SEA —) ERN ERNE PYGARG PYGARGUS
(PREF.) AET(O)
(SUFF.) AETUS

EAGLE OWL KATOGLE

EAGLESTONE AETITES

EAGLET BIRD LAIGLON

EAGLEWOOD AGAR AGILA ALOES AGALLOCH AQUILARI

EAGRE BORE WAVE AEGIR HYGRE

EANFLED (FATHER OF —) EADWINE
(HUSBAND OF —) OSWIU

EAR LUG NEB CLIP HEAR HEED HOOK LIST OBEY PLOW TILL AURIS BRACE PINNA SENSE SOUSE SOWSE SPIKE CANNON CONCHA CROSET EARLET LISTEN AURICLE HEARING SENSORY AUDIENCE PAVILION RECEPTOR
(— OF BELL) CANON CANNON
(— OF CORN) COB ICKER MEALIE NUBBIN CORNCOB
(— OF GRAIN) RISOM SPIKE RIZZOM
(— OF WHEAT) SPICA WHEATEAR
(—S OF GRAIN) CAPES EARHEAD
(PART OF —) LOBE TUBE CANAL

HELIX INCUS PINNA CONCHA MEATUS SCAPHA STAPES TRAGUS COCHLEA MALLEUS MEMBRANE TYMPANUM ANTIHELIX ANTITRAGUS
(UNRIPE — OF CORN) TUCKET
(PREF.) AUR(I) AURICULO OT(ICO)(IO)(O) SPICI SPICULI SPICULO
(— OF CORN) ATHERO STACHY(O)
(SUFF.) OTIC

EARACHE OTALGY OTALGIA

EARCOCKLE PURPLES

EARDRUM TABOR TABOUR TYMPAN MYRINGA DRUMHEAD TYMPANUM
(PREF.) TRYPAN(O) TYMPAN(O)

EARFLAP LUG EARLAP EARTAB EARMUFF

EARINE (LOVER OF —) AEGLAMOUR

EARL EORL GRAF JARL LORD PEER COMES NOBLE CONSUL SIWARD
(— OF COVENTRY) SNIPSNAPSNORUM

EARLDOM DERBY COUNTY

EARLIER ERE OLD ERST FORE ELDER UPPER BEFORE FORMER HITHER RATHER SOONER FIRSTER FURTHER PIONEER PREMIER PREVIOUS
(PREF.) FORE PROTER(O)
(— THAN) PRE PRO

EARLIEST ERST FIRST ELDEST MAIDEN PIONEER PREMIER RATHEST FURTHEST PRIMROSE ABORIGINAL
(PREF.) EO

EAR LOBE LUG EARLAP
(— PEOPLE) OREJON

EARLY AIR ERE OLD GOOD HIGH RARE RATH SOON FORME PRIMY RATHE VERTY REARLY SUDDEN TIMELY ANCIENT BETIMES ERLICHE FORWARD YOUTHFUL MATUTINAL
(PREF.) EO PALAE(O) PALE(O)

EARMARK BIT CROP SPLIT LUGMARK OVERBIT SLEEPER ALLOCATE OVERCROP UNDERBIT

EAR MUFF OREILET

EARN GET WIN FANG GAIN TILL VANG ADDLE ETTLE GLEAR MERIT GARNER HUSTLE OBTAIN ACHIEVE ACQUIRE CHEVISE DEMERIT DESERVE
(— BY LABOR) ADDLE SWINK BESWINK

EARNEST ARRA DEAR DERN HARD PAWN ARLES EAGER GRAVE SMART SOBER STAID ARDENT ENTIRE HANSEL HEARTY INTENT SEDATE SOLEMN EMULOUS ENGAGED FERVENT FORWARD

HANDSEL INTENSE SERIOUS SINCERE ZEALOUS DILIGENT EMPHATIC STUDIOUS
(IN —) AGOOD

EARNESTLY HARD DEARLY WISHLY WISTLY EARNEST DEVOUTLY DINGDONG ENTIRELY HEARTILY INTENTLY INWARDLY

EARNESTNESS GLOW FERVOR WARMTH GRAVITY DEVOTION DILIGENCE

EARNINGS GET MAKING ADDLINS PICKING ADDLINGS

EARPIECE BUTTON

EARPLUG STOPPLE TEMBETA EARSPOOL

EARRING DROP GRIP EARBOB EARLET PENDLE EARCLIP EARDROP PENDANT EARSCREW

EAR SHELL ORMER ABALONE

EARSHOT SOUND HEARING EARREACH

EARTH ERD ORB SET BALL BANK BURY BYON CLAY CLOD DIRT DUST FLAG FOLD GRIT LAND LOAM MARL MASS MEAL MOLD MOOL MUCK ROCK SOIL SORY STAR VALE YIRD ADOBE CRUMB FLOSS GLEBE GLOBE GROOT INTER LOESS MOULD REGUR TERRA TRASS UMBER WORLD CENTER CENTRE COARSE GROUND YACATA KOKOWAI MIDGARD TERRENE TIERRAS TOPSOIL TRIPOLI MAGNESIA MIDGARTH
(— FOR RAMPART) REMBLAI
(— INHABITANT) TERRAN
(— PROVIDING OCHER) KOKOWAI
(— SUITABLE FOR CULTIVATION) LAYER
(BLACK —) MUCK SORY KILLOW AMPELITE CHERNOZEM
(BLUE —) KIMBERLITE
(BROWN —) UMBER
(CLAYEY —) LAME LOAM
(DRY —) MOOL GROOT
(FULLER'S —) CRETA CIMOLITE SMECTITE
(GEM-BEARING —) BYON
(HEAVY —) BARYTA
(LOOSE —) CRUMB GEEST
(MOIST —) SLAB SLIME
(POOR —) RAMMEL
(RAMMED —) PISE
(RED —) RUDDLE
(REFUSE —) MURGEON
(RIVER-BANK —) GREWT
(SMALL —) TERRELLA
(SOAP —) SOAPROCK
(STRAW-YELLOW —) BISMITE
(SUN-DRIED —) SWISH
(VITRIFIED —) FLOSS

(VOLCANIC —) TRASS TARRASS
(PREF.) GE(O) TELLUR(I) TERR(A)(E)(I)
(SUFF.) GAEA GEA

EARTHEN FICT DIRTEN EARTHLY YARTHEN

EARTHENWARE PIG POT DELF CHINA CLOAM CROCK DELFT CLAYEN JASPER ASTBURY BISCUIT FAIENCE POTTERY TICKNEY BUFFWARE CROCKERY MAJOLICA TALAVERA
(BROKEN PIECE OF —) CROCK

EARTHINESS SALT TERREITY

EARTHKIN TERRELLA

EARTHLY LAIRY CARNAL EARTHY MORTAL EARTHEN GLEBOUS MUNDANE SECULAR TERRAIN TERRENE WORLDLY SUBLUNAR TELLURIC TEMPORAL

EARTHNUT ARNOT ARNUT CHUFA HOGNUT JARNUT PEANUT PIGNUT HARENUT HAWKNUT TRUFFLE

EARTH PIG ERDVARK AARDVARK

EARTHQUAKE QUAKE SEISM SHAKE SHOCK TEMBLOR SEAQUAKE
(PREF.) SEISMO SISMO
(SUFF.) SEISM SEISMAL SEISMIC

EARTHSTAR GEASTER

EARTHWALL TRINCHERA

EARTH WOLF AARDWOLF

EARTHWORK BANK RATH AGGER CASTLE SCONCE RAMPART TERRACE
(PL.) PARADOS

EARTHWORM ESS MAD WORM ANNELID DEWWORM IPOMOEA MADDOCK ANGLEDOG BRANDLIN EACEWORM FISHWORM RAINWORM TWATCHEL BRANDLING LUMBRICID OLIGOCHATE

EARTHY GROSS SALTY WORMY CLODDY VULGAR EARTHLY TERRENE BARNYARD TERREOUS VISCERAL

EAR TICK PINOLIA

EAR TRUMPET CORNET AEROPHONE

EARWAX CERUMEN
(PREF.) CERUMINI

EARWIG GOLACH GOLOCH TOUCHBELL

EARWORM BOLLWORM

EASE CALM COSY COZY EASY REST ALLAY KNACK PEACE QUIET RELAX SLAKE LOOSEN PACIFY REDUCE RELIEF REPOSE SAUGHT SMOOTH SOFTEN SOOTHE APPEASE ASSUAGE COMFORT CONTENT FACILITY FLUENCY

FREEDOM LEISURE LIBERTY
LIGHTEN RELIEVE SLACKEN
SUBSIDE DIMINISH FACILITY
MITIGATE MODERATE PALLIATE
PLEASURE SECURITY UNBURDEN
(— OF A BURDEN) LIGHT
(— OFF) FLOW CHECK START
SLOUGH
(APATHETIC —) INDOLENCE
(AT —) OTIOSE
(CAREFREE —) ABANDON
EASEL FRAME SUPPORT SCAFFOLD
EASEMENT EASE EASING RELIEF
HERBAGE TURBARY SERVITUS
WAYLEAVE
EASE-TAKING PICKTOOTH
EASIEST EFTEST
EASILY EASY EATH WELL LIGHT
EATHLY GENTLY GLIBLY HANDILY
LIGHTLY READILY SLIGHTLY
SMOOTHLY
(PREF.) EU
EASINESS GRACE FACILITY
EASING DETENTE
EAST ASIA MORN LEVANT ORIENT
SUNRISE EASTWARD
(— OF) FOLLOWING
EAST AFRICA (— TREE) PODO
EASTER PT PACE PASCH EOSTRE
PASCHA PASQUE
EASTERN LEVANT ORTIVE
AURORAL ORIENTAL
EASTERNER DUDE

EAST GERMANY
CAPITAL: EASTBERLIN
DISTRICT: GERA SUHL HALLE
ERFURT ROSTOCK
RIVER: ELBE ODER HAVEL SAALE
SPREE
TOWN: GERA SUHL HALLE ERFURT
COTTBUS DRESDEN LEIPZIG
POTSDAM ROSTOCK SCHWERIN
MAGDEBURG

EAST INDIAN (— TREE) SAL AMLA
DHAK TEAK KOKAN LANSA
MAHUA MOHWA NIEPA PALAS
PULAS ROHAN ROHUN SALAI
SIMAL
EASTLAND ESTRICHE
EASTWARD EAST EASEL EASSEL
EASY CALM COZY CRIP EATH EITH
GAIN GLIB MILD RIFE SNAP SOFT
CUSHY JAMMY LARGE LIGHT
PLAIN PRONE ROYAL SUAVE
YEZZY CASUAL COMODO FACILE
FLUENT FRUITY GENTLE GENTLY
SECURE SIMPLE SMOOTH
UNHARD ARTLESS GRADUAL
LENIENT NATURAL CAREFREE
CARELESS CAVALIER EXPEDITE
FAMILIAR GRACEFUL HOMELIKE
MODERATE TRANQUIL UNFORCED
(— IN MIND) SECURE
(— TO HANDLE) HANDSOME
(— TO UNDERSTAND) PELLUCID
(— TO USE) CLEVER
EASYGOING LAX QUIET DEGAGE
EAT FOG KAI SUP BITE CHOP
CHOW DINE FARE FEED FRET
GNAW GRUB HAVE HEYT MAKE
PECK RUST TUCK ERODE FEAST

GRAZE MANGE MUNCH SCOFF
STOKE TASTE WASTE ABSORB
BEGNAW DEVOUR INGEST NIBBLE
RAVAGE CONSUME CORRODE
DESTROY SWALLOW VICTUAL
(— A MEAL) GRUB
(— A SNACK) NOSH
(— AS HOGS) SLUICE
(— AWAY) GNAW ERODE RANKLE
CORRODE
(— BETWEEN MEALS) NOSH
(— BIG MEAL) STOKE
(— CRUNCHINGLY) GROUZE
(— GLUTTONOUSLY) GUDGE STUFF
(— GREEDILY) GAMP GAWP SLAB
SLOP TUCK CHAUM MOOCH
SCOFF GOBBLE GOFFLE GUTTLE
GUZZLE RAUNGE GLUTTON
GOURMAND
(— HEARTILY) THORN
(— IN GULPS) LAB
(— MINCINGLY) PICK PICKLE
PIDDLE
(— NOISILY) SLOP GULCH SLURP
GUTTLE SLOTTER
(— OUT) EXEDE
(— RUDELY) TROUGH
(— SLOVENLY) SLUP MUMMICK
(— SPARINGLY) DIET
(— TO EXCESS) COLF BEZZLE
(— UP) DEMOLISH
(— VORACIOUSLY) CRAM WORRY
(— WITH GUSTO) SMOUSE
(— WITHOUT CHEWING) BOLT
(SUFF.) ESTES PHAG(A)(E)(IA)(ISM)
(IST)(O)(OUS)(US)(Y) VORA VORE
VOROUS
EATABLE FOODY COOKER EDIBLE
ESCULENT
EATEN CANKERED
(HALF —) SEMESE
(PREF.) BROTO
EATER PECKER DEVOURER
(GREEDY —) GOURMAND
EATING BIT FOOD ESURINE
(— BETWEEN MEALS) TIFFIN
(— COARSE FOOD) FOUL
(— INTO) CANKEROUS
(— OUT) EXESION
(PREF.) PHAG(O)
EAVES EASE EASING
EAVESDROP DARK HARKEN
LISTEN HEARKEN
EAVESDROPPER COWAN EARWIG
DRAWLATCH
EAVES TROUGH CHENEAU
EBAL (FATHER OF —) SHOBAL
EBB FAIL FALL SINK WANE ABATE
DECAY RECEDE REFLOW REFLUX
RETIRE TIDING DECLINE REFLOAT
SUBSIDE DECREASE DIMINISH
(— AND FLOW) ESTUS AESTUS
FLUIDITY
EBBING AWANE REFLUENT
REFLUOUS
(— AND FLOWING) TIDAL
EBED (FATHER OF —) JONATHAN
(SON OF —) GAAL
EBER (FATHER OF —) SALAH ELPAAL
EBLIS JANN IBLIS
EBONY EBON BLACK GABON
GABOON WAMARA HEBENON
IRONWOOD

EBULLIENCE OVERFLOW
ELEVATION
EBULLIENT BRASH FERVID BOILING
EBULLIOSCOPE ZEOSCOPE
EBULLITION SEETHE FERMENT
OUTBURST
ECAD ECOPHENE
ECCENTRIC FEY ODD OFF CARD
DOER NUTS CRANK DOTTY KINKY
OUTRE QUEER WIPER CRANKY
LOCOED OUTISH PSYCHO SCREWY
SHAGGY BIZARRE CURIOUS
DEVIOUS ERRATIC STRANGE
TOUCHED ABNORMAL FITIFIED
PECULIAR SINGULAR
(— PERSON) KOOK
ECCENTRICITY KINK FERLY
ODDITY ANOMALY CROTCHET
QUIDDITY
(— OF CURVE) E
ECCLESIASTES KOHELETH
QOHELETH
ECCLESIASTIC ABBE ABBOT CLERK
VICAR ARCHON FATHER LECTOR
LEGATE PRIEST KIRKMAN
PRELATE SECULAR EPISTLER
SUBDEACON
ECCLESIASTICAL CHURCH
CANONIC CHURCHLY CHRISTIAN
SPIRITUAL
ECHELES (FATHER OF —) ACTOR
(FOSTER SON OF —) EUDORUS
(WIFE OF —) POLYMELA
ECHEVIN SCABINE SCABINUS
ECHIDNA NODIAK ANTEATER
EDENTATE MONOTREME
PORCUPINE
(CHILD OF —) HYDRA LADON
ORTHUS SPHINX CERBERUS
CHIMAERA
(FATHER OF —) PHORCYS
CHRYSAOR
(MOTHER OF —) CETO CALLIRRHOE
(SLAYER OF —) ARGUS
ECHINODERM CYSTID CRINOID
BLASTOID STARFISH
ECHINOPANAX FATSIA
ECHINO-SOREX GYMNURA
ECHION (FATHER OF —) MERCURY
(MOTHER OF —) ANTIANIRA
(SON OF —) PENTHEUS
(WIFE OF —) AGAVE
ECHO ECO RING SING CHORUS
REPEAT REVERB SECOND IMITATE
ITERATE RESOUND RESPEAK
RESPOND REVOICE REDOUBLE
RESPONSE
(— EFFECT) REVERB
(RADAR —) ANGEL
ECLAT FAME GLORY RENOWN
ACCLAIM SCANDAL APPLAUSE
FACILITY PRESTIGE SPLENDOR
ECLECTIC BROAD LIBERAL
ECLIPSE DIM BIND BLOT HIDE
BLIND CLOUD SHADE STAIN
SULLY DARKEN DAZZLE DEFECT
EXCEED OCCULT DEFAULT
OBSCURE PRODIGY TRAVAIL
OUTRIVAL OCCULTATION
ECLOGUE IDYL IDYLL BUCOLIC
ECOLOGIST BIONOMIST
ECOLOGY BIOLOGY BIONOMY
MESOLOGY

ECOMOMIST GERMAN GESELL
ECONOMIC
(PREF.) EC(O) OEC(O) OIKO
ECONOMICAL WARY CHARY
FENDY FRUGAL SAVING CAREFUL
PRUDENT SPARING THRIFTY
SCREWING
ECONOMICS PLUTONOMY
ECONOMIST HUSBAND MANAGER
PHYSIOCRAT
AMERICAN DAY ELY GRAY POOR
ADAMS ARROW BALCH CAREY
CLARK DEWEY HANEY HICKS
LUBIN MEYER WELLS YOUNG
CARVER DUNBAR DURAND
ECCLES FISHER FOSTER GEORGE
HADLEY HARVEY MILLIS RAGUET
RIPLEY SPLAWN SUMNER TUCKER
TURNER WALKER WEAVER WILLIS
BULLOCK COMMONS CROWELL
GARRETT JOHNSON KUZNETS
TAUSSIG TUGWELL ANDERSON
FRIEDMAN KEMMERER
KOOPMANS LAUGHLIN LEONTIEF
MITCHELL GALBRAITH
HENDERSON HOLLANDER
SAMUELSON WILLOUGHBY
AUSTRALIAN DONALD
AUSTRIAN HAYEK MISES SPANN
MENGER
BELGIAN ZEELAND LEVELEYE
MOLINARI
CANADIAN MAVOR LEACOCK
DUTCH TINBERGEN
ENGLISH COLE MILL WARD WEBB
WEST HICKS HIRST JAMES MEADE
PAISH PETTY PRICE STAMP
ASHLEY BARBON BAXTER
COBDEN FARRER GIFFEN HOBSON
JEVONS KEYNES KIRKUP LAYTON
LESLIE REEVES ROGERS SALTER
SENIOR TUCKER WILSON
BAGEHOT CHAPMAN CLAPHAM
FAWCETT MALTHUS MALYNES
RICARDO TOYNBEE BELLERBY
MARSHALL BEVERIDGE
EDGEWORTH MACMILLAN
MARTINEAU NICHOLSON
OVERSTONE CUNNINGHAM
FINNISH PROCOPE
FRENCH SAY LEVY RIST BODIN
GUYOT CAMBON HAUSER
BASTIAT BLANQUI BLONDEL
COURNOT FAUCHER GARNIER
GOURNAY MONTYON QUESNAY
MIRABEAU PECQUEUR ROEDERER
WOLOWSKI CHEVALIER
LEVASSEUR SIEGFRIED
GERMAN RAU BONN HAHN ENGEL
FUCHS HARMS JUSTI KNIES
LANGE BRIEFS BUCHER CONRAD
ECKERT ERHARD GOSSEN HIRSCH
SERING ANDREAE DUHRING
EHEBERG GERLOFF HEIMANN
JASTROW LEDERER MICHELS
ROSCHER HUFELAND SCHAFFLE
BAMBERGER RODBERTUS
SCHMOLLER FLURSCHEIM
HAXTHAUSEN HELFFERICH
RAIFFEISEN SCHUMPETER
OPPENHEIMER
GREEK ANDREADES
IRISH SMIDDY CAIRNES

BASTABLE CANTILLON
ITALIAN BODIO CARLI GIOJA
LORIA NITTI ROSSI BOTERO
PARETO BECCARIA GENOVESI
LUZZATTI SCIALOIA CERNUSCHI
PANTALEONI
NORWEGIAN FRISCH
POLISH GRABSKI WOJCIECHOWSKI
RUSSIAN BUNGE KANTOROVICH
VOZNESENSKI
SCOTTISH MILL SMITH
MACLEOD ANDERSON
MCCULLOCH
SWEDISH OHLIN CASSEL MYRDAL
SWISS SISMONDI CHERBULIEZ
URUGUAYAN COSIO
ECONOMIZE HAIN SAVE SKIMP
STINT SCRIMP HUSBAND UTILIZE
RETRENCH
ECONOMY SPARE SAVING SYSTEM
THRIFT MANAGERY PARSIMONY
ECOTONE EDGE
ECSTASY JOY BLISS POWER
SWOON TRANCE DELIGHT
EMOTION MADNESS RAPTURE
RHAPSODY
ECSTATIC HOT RAPT PYTHIAN
GLORIOUS
ECTENE IRENICON
ECTODERM EXODERM EPIBLAST
ECTOMORPHIC LINEAR ASTHENIC
LEPTOSOME
ECTROPION EVERSION
ECU CROWN SCUTE SHIELD

ECUADOR

ANCIENT NAME: QUITO
CAPE: ROSA PASADO PUNTILLA
CAPITAL: QUITO
COIN: SUCRE CONDOR CENTAVO
INDIAN: CARA INCA PALTA
CANELO JIVARO
ISLAND: PUNA WOLF MOCHA
PINTA BALTRA CHAVES
DARWIN PINZON WENMAN
ISABELA
ISLANDS: COLON GALAPAGOS
LANGUAGE: JIBARO QUECHUA
SPANISH
MEASURE: CUADRA FANEGA
MOUNTAIN: ANDES SANGAY
CAYAMBE ANTISANA COTOPAXI
NATIVE: MONTUVIO
PROVINCE: LOJA AZUAY CANAR
COLON ELORO CARCHI GUAYAS
MANABI BOLIVAR LOSRIOS
COTOPAXI IMBABURA
RIVER: COCA MIRA NAPO DAULE
PINDO TIGRE GUAYAS TUMBES
ZAMORA CURARAY PASTAZA
AGUARICO BOBONAZA
CONONACO NARANJAL
PUTUMAYO
TOWN: JAMA LOJA MERA NAPO
PUYO TENA CANAR GUANO
MANTA PAJAN PINAS PIURA
QUITO YAUPI AMBATO CUENCA
IBARRA PUJILI TULCAN
ZARUMA AZOGUES CAYAMBE
GUAMOTE MACHALA PELILEO
PILLARO SALINAS BABAHOYO
GUARANDA RIOBAMBA
WATERFALL: AGOYAN

WEIGHT: LIBRA

ECUMENE HEARTH
ECUMENICAL LIBERAL CATHOLIC
ECZEMA TETTER EARWORM
MALANDERS
EDACITY GREED APPETITE
VORACITY
EDDA SAGA
EDDISH ETCH ARRISH EEGRASS
EDDO TARO COCOYAM
EDDY CURL GULF PURL WASH
WEEL WELL ACKER GURGE SHIFT
SWIRL TWIRL WHIRL SWOOSH
VORTEX WIRBLE BACKSET
WREATHE
(PREF.) DINO
EDDYING WALE
EDEMA BRAXY TUMOR DROPSY
BIGHEAD HYDROPS ANASARCA
SWELLING
EDEMATOUS BLOATED HYDROPIC
EDEN ADEN HEAVEN UTOPIA
ARCADIA ELYSIUM PARADISE
(FATHER OF —) JOAH
EDENTATA BRUTA
EDENTATE SLOTH AARDVARK
ANTEATER
EDGE AGE BIT HEM JAG LIP RIM
BANK BERM BRIM BROW CURB
DRAW FACE KANT LIMB LIST
RAND SIDE TRIM WELL WHET
ARRIS BERME BEVEL BLADE
BOARD BRINK CHIMB CHIME
CREST EAVES FRILL KNIFE LABEL
LEDGE MARGE PEARL RULER
SHARP SIDLE SPLAY VERGE
BORDER CANTLE DECKLE FLANGE
FORAGE IMPALE LABRUM MARGIN
NOSING PLANGE MARGENT
SELVAGE SHARPEN VANDYKE
BOUNDARY EMBORDER KEENNESS
MAJORITY OUTSKIRT SELVEDGE
STICKING UMSTROKE
(— FORWARD) CREEP
(— IN MINING DRIFT) ARRAGE
(— OF BASKET) FOOT
(— OF BED) STOCK
(— OF BIRD'S BILL) TOMIUM
(— OF BOOK) FERRULE BACKBONE
(— OF BOOK COVER) FLAP
(— OF BRILLIANT) GIRDLE
(— OF CASK) CHIME CHINE
(— OF COAL PILE) RUN
(— OF DAM) CREST
(— OF DUMP) TOE
(— OF FLAG) HOIST
(— OF MESA) CEJA
(— OF MINERAL VEIN) APEX
(— OF ROADWAY) SHOULDER
(— OF RUDDER) BEARDING
(— OF RUFFLE) HEADING
(— OF SAIL) FOOT HEAD LEACH
LEECH
(— OF SAW) SAFE
(— OF SHELL) HINGE
(— OF STRATUM) BASSET
(— OF STREAM) HAG
(— OF TOOL) BEZEL BEZIL
(— OF TOOTH) SCALPRUM
(— OF TROUSERS) CREASE
(— OF VAULT) GROIN
(— OF WOOD) WOODRIME

(—S OF COAT) LAP
(BEVELED —) CHAMFER
(CUTTING —) SHOE
(DOUBLE —) FLAT
(EMBROIDERED —) SURFLE
SURPHUL
(EXTERIOR —) AMBITUS
(FRONT — OF BOOK) FACE
(ORNAMENTAL —) FRILL
(RAGGED —) RAG
(ROCKY —) ARETE
(ROUGH —S) FASH
(SHARP —) ARRIS BEARD
(UNPLOWED — OF FIELD) RAND
(UNTRIMMED —) DECKLE
(PREF.) AMBO
EDGED EDGY EROSE SHARP
CRENATE CUTTING
(— BY ARCS) INVECTED
EDGER WHETTER STRANDER
EDGING HEM CURB EDGE LACE
LIST FILET FRILL LEDGE PICOT
BORDER FILLET FRINGE LIMBUS
BEADING BINDING GIMPING
HAMBURG COQUILLE FRILLING
PUNTILLA RICKRACK SKIRTING
SURROUND PASSEMENTERIE
EDGY EAGER SHARP ANGULAR
CRITICAL SNAPPISH
EDIBLE EDULE EATABLE ESCULENT
EDICT ACT BAN LAW BULL FIAT
TYPE ARRET BANDO BULLA IRADE
ORDER SANAD UKASE ASSIZE
DECREE DICTUM NOTICE
COMMAND EMBARGO PLACARD
PROCESS PROGRAM STATUTE
ECTHESIS RESCRIPT
EDIFICE DOME CHURCH TURBEH
BUILDING ERECTION TETRAGON
EDIFY GROW BUILD FAVOR TEACH
BENEFIT IMPROVE PROSPER
CONVINCE INSTRUCT ORGANIZE
EDIFYING HIGH SAVORY ELEVATED
EDIT CUT EMEND DIRECT REDACT
REVIEW REVISE ARRANGE
COMPILE CORRECT PREPARE
PUBLISH REWRITE COPYREAD
EDITION KIND EXTRA FINAL FIRST
ISSUE PRINT STAMP ALDINE
DIGLOT SOURCE AUSGABE
BULLDOG HEXAPLA OCTAPLA
VERSION PRINCEPS VARIORUM
(FIRST —) PRINCEPS
EDITOR AUTHOR OVERSEER
REDACTOR
AMERICAN BOK BURR CARY DANA
DELL DUNN FOSS FUNK HILL
LUCE REID SHAW WARE YUST
ALLEN CANBY CLARK COLBY
DEBOW FENNO GRADY KNOTT
MABIE MOORE NILES PAINE
PRATT RIDER WHITE ABBOTT
AIKENS BARRON BOWKER
BOWLES CAPPER CATTON
CHURCH CLARKE COWLEY DANIEL
DENNIE DUBOIS FINLEY FLOWER
GILDER HANSEN HOOPER LARSEN
LUMMIS MALONE MANTLE
MARTIN MERWIN MONROE
MUNSON NATHAN PALLEN
RASCOE WILLIS ALDRICH
BURNETT COUSINS EASTMAN
FADIMAN FERNALD FREEMAN

GANNETT HAPGOOD HAZLITT
HOFFMAN HOLLAND HUBBARD
JOHNSON LINCOLN LITTELL
MENCKEN STEDMAN VIERECK
WALLACE ALLIBONE ANDERSON
BARSOTTI BENJAMIN CRAWFORD
GRINNELL GRUENING LIPPMANN
PETERSON SEDGWICK STRUNSKY
THOMPSON VANDOREN
WHEELOCK ALTSHELER
BARTHOLDT BLACKWELL
KAEMPFFERT UNTERMEYER
CHAMBERLAIN CROWNINSHIELD
ENGLISH LEE MEE READ RHYS
TODD CRAIG GIBBS WAUGH
ALLOTT BARNES DELANE GARVIN
HUTTON HUXLEY KELTIE SEAMAN
BOWDLER BURNAND CHAPMAN
HYAMSON KNOWLES VERRALL
CHISHOLM GOLDRING MUIRHEAD
PROTHERO SPEDDING
BOTTOMLEY CUSHENDUN
PEMBERTON RAPPOPORT
MONTGOMERY
FRENCH MIGNE MORTIER YRIARTE
CHAUMEIX HACHETTE
GERMAN BARTH HUBER MULLER
HUNGARIAN HARSANYI
SCOTTISH CURRIE HERVEY
ANDERSON HASTINGS LOCKHART
FINDLATER
EDITORIAL LEADER
EDO BENI BINI
EDRED (BROTHER OF —) EDMUND
(FATHER OF —) EDWARD
(MOTHER OF —) EADGIFU
EDUCATE REAR BREED TEACH
TRADE TRAIN EXPAND INFORM
SCHOOL DEVELOP NURTURE
INSTRUCT
EDUCATED BRED CIVIL TAUGHT
TRAINED INFORMED LETTERED
LITERATE
EDUCATION CLERGY NURTURE
BREEDING LEARNING NORTELRY
PEDAGOGY TRAINING
(LIBERAL —) HUMANITY
(PHYSICAL —) GYM
EDUCATOR TEACHER
AMERICAN DAY FEW HAM AMES
BLOW CASE CHEW COLN CONE
FORD FRYE HALL HART HILL HOLT
HOPE HULL HYDE LYON MANN
MOON PAGE RAND ROOT RUGG
TARR TRUE WARD WARE WEST
ADAMS ADLER AVERY AYRES
BAKER BATES BEARD BEERS
BERRY BROWN BRYAN BYRNE
CAPEN CAPPS CHASE CLARK
CROSS CURRY DAMON DENNY
DEWEY DOBIE ELIOT FRANK
FUESS GATES GAUSS GOULD
HEDGE JAMES JENKS JONES
KNOTT KRAPP KRAUS LANGE
LOCKE LOWES MANLY MEYER
MEZES ORTON PATRI PERRY
POUND ROLFE SCOTT SMITH
SMYTH TYLER UPHAM WHITE
YOUNG ANGELL BAGLEY BAILEY
BARNES BASCOM BAXTER
BOVARD BOWMAN BRIGGS
BUMPUS BUTLER CARTER
CONANT COOPER CORSON

COUNTS DABNEY DAVIES
DONHAM DRAPER DUBOIS
DURANT FERRIS FINLEY FINNEY
FOWLER GAYLEY GEDDES GILMAN
GOEBEL GRAVES HADLEY HARPER
HARRIS HAWKES HAZARD HIBBEN
HOWARD JESSUP JEWETT
JUDSON KELLER KEPPEL LANDIS
LERNER LOVETT LOWELL MARTIN
MATHER MCAFEE MEARNS MILLIS
MONROE NORTON PALMER
PARKER PEFFER PEIRCE PHELPS
PORTER SARETT SCOPES SLOANE
SPARKS STRONG STUART
THOMAS THWING WIGGIN
WILDER WRIGHT ANAGNOS
ANDREWS BABBITT BARBOUR
BARNARD BARROWS BENEZET
BETHUNE BRADLEY BRAWLEY
CALKINS CLAXTON COFFMAN
COLBURN COMFORT CONNELY
DENNETT DOHERTY DYKSTRA
ERSKINE FARRAND GARNETT
GILMORE GOODNOW GOODWIN
GOUCHER GUMMERE HASKINS
HERRICK HOPKINS HOUSTON
HUEBNER HULBERT HULBURT
JACKSON JARDINE JOHNSON
KIMBALL KIMPTON LEONARD
LINCOLN LINDSAY MATHEWS
MCMURRY PATRICK PEABODY
RAYMOND RICKERT ROLLINS
SCUDDER SHUSTER TATLOCK
TAUSSIG THACHER VANDYKE
VANHISE WALLACE WHEELER
WILLARD WOOLSEY ZEITLIN
ALDERMAN BANCROFT
BASHFORD BREWSTER BRITTAIN
CALLAHAN CHANDLER
COMMAGER COMSTOCK
COPELAND FLETCHER FOERSTER
GRISWOLD HARRISON HOLLOWAY
HUTCHINS LANGSTON LAWRENCE
MARQUAND MATTHEWS
MCGUFFEY MCKNIGHT PENNIMAN
PHILLIPS ROBINSON SCHURMAN
SEASHORE STODDARD SUZZALLO
TUTWILER WHEELOCK WILLIAMS
WOODBURN WOODWARD
ARMSTRONG AYDELOTTE
CARPENTER CHAUVENET
FAIRBANKS FAIRCHILD
GOODSPEED GRANDGENT
GREENOUGH HENDERSON
KITTREDGE LOUNSBURY
PARTRIDGE PATTERSON
PENDLETON SCHELLING
SHARPLESS SPAULDING
THORNDIKE WENTWORTH
BLOOMFIELD CHADBOURNE
KILPATRICK LONGSTREET
PARRINGTON STURTEVANT
WASHINGTON GILDERSLEEVE
ARGENTINIAN AVELLANEDA
AUSTRALIAN HOLME
CANADIAN GRANT PRATT CAPPON
HUTTON MACKAY MURRAY
MACLEAN
CZECH COMENIUS
DANISH LUND
ECUADORIAN ROCAFUERTE
ENGLISH DENT KING ALLEN BEALE
ELTON FITCH GRANT LUCAS

OGDEN ROUSE SMITH ARNOLD
BARNES COTTON FARMER
HADDON HOGBEN KEYNES
MORANT RIPMAN SADLER
BALFOUR BALLARD STARKIE
CHAMBERS CUNLIFFE SPURGEON
MANSBRIDGE
FRENCH ANDLER BOUTMY
CAMPAN FONCIN WAILLY
BELJAME BIDAULT BUISSON
BOUTROUX COMPAYRE
GERMAN AHN ALER KERN REIN
CAMPE GRAFE LANGE STURM
GEDIKE NATORP ZIMMER
BECKMAN FISCHER FROEBEL
DORPFELD DIESTERWEG
TROTZENDORF
HUNGARIAN BEOTHY
INDIAN HUSAIN GOKHALE
ITALIAN FEDELE VILLARI
GALLENGA MONTESSORI
JAPANESE ASAKAWA NEESIMA
FUKUZAWA
MEXICAN CAMPOS
SCOTTISH BELL DALGARNO
SWEDISH SIREN
SWISS GIRARD TOPFFER
FELLENBERG
EDUCE DRAW EVOKE ELICIT
EVOLVE EXTORT EXTRACT
EEL ELE GRIG LING OPAH SNIG
TUNA ELVER MORAY SIREN
APODAN CARAPO CONGER
FAUSEN MOREIA MURENE
CONGRIO KWATUMA LAMPREY
MURAENA SNIGGLE WRIGGLE
CONGEREE GYMNOTID KINGKLIP
(YOUNG —) ELVER OLIVER YELVER
(25 —S) STICK SWARM
EELGRASS DREW WRACK ENALID
EELPOUT BARD LING POUT QUAB
BURBOT CONGER GUFFER
YOWLER LYCODOID
EELSKIN (10 —S) TIMBER
EELSPEAR PILGER
EELWORM EEL NEMA
EERIE EERY SCARY TIMID WEIRD
WISHT CREEPY DISMAL GLOOMY
GOUSTY SPOOKY AWESOME
GHOSTLY GOUSTIE MACABRE
STRANGE UNCANNY ELDRITCH
GHOULISH POKERISH
EFFACE BLOT DASH DELE RASE
RAZE WEAR ERASE CANCEL
DEFACE SPONGE STRIKE DESTROY
DISLIMN EXPUNGE NULLIFY
UNPAINT
EFFECT DO SEE DENT DOES FECK
HAVE PRAY PREY TEEM WORK
CAUSE CLOSE ECLAT ENACT
ETTLE EVENT FORCE FRUIT ISSUE
STAMP ACTION ENERGY GROWTH
INDUCE INTENT OBTAIN RESULT
SECURE SEQUEL STEREO UPSHOT
ACHIEVE ACQUIRE ARRANGE
COMPASS CONDUCE EMOTION
EXECUTE FULFILL IMPRESS
IMPRINT OPERATE OUTCOME
PERFORM PROCURE PRODUCE
PURPORT REALIZE CAUSATUM
COMPLETE CONCLUDE CONTRIVE
FRUITAGE CONSEQUENT
(— OF PAST EXPERIENCE) MNEME

(BLURRED —) FUZZ
(COUNTERBALANCING —)
STANDOFF
(DAZZLING —) ECLAT
(DECORATIVE —) CHIPPING
(ELECTRICAL —) STRAY
(ESTHETIC —) ATMOSPHERE
(FALSE —) FACADE
(FINAL —) AMOUNT
(ILL —) EVIL
(INTENSE —) STRESS
(MOTTLED —) SPRINKLE
(MUSICAL —) BEND SHADING
(OPTICAL —) PHANTASMAGORIA
(PAINFUL —) JAR
(PAINTING —) STIPPLE
(PENETRATING —) SEARCH
(PERNICIOUS —) BLAST
(PERSONAL —S) DUNNAGE
(SECONDARY —) OVERTONE
(SHATTERING —) BRISANCE
(THEATRICAL —) CURTAIN
(TO HAVE —) MILITATE
(TOTAL —) ENSEMBLE
(TOXIC —S) THEISM
(TREMOLO —) BEBUNG
(VISIBLE —) TOUCH
(SUFF.) ERGATE ERGY
EFFECTIVE ABLE HOME MEAN
REAL ALIVE GREAT HAPPY PITHY
SIKER SOUND VALID ACTIVE
ACTUAL CAUSAL DEADLY DIRECT
FRUITY POTENT SEVERE SICKER
SOVRAN CAPABLE FECKFUL
OPERANT TELLING VIRTUAL
ADEQUATE FORCEFUL POWERFUL
SMASHING STRIKING VIGOROUS
TRENCHANT
EFFECTIVELY NAITLY
EFFECTIVENESS AIM BANG CHIC
EDGE VOLTAGE EFFICACY
LEVERAGE
EFFECTUAL ACTUAL TOOTHY
ADEQUATE POWERFUL
MAGISTRAL
EFFECTUATE FULFIL FULFILL
COMPLETE
EFFEMINATE NICE SOFT MILKY
MISSY SAPPY SISSY BITCHY
FEMALE LYDIAN NIMINY PRISSY
SILKEN TENDER WANTON
WEAKLY CITIZEN EPICENE
MEACOCK WOMANLY FEMINATE
FEMININE LADYLIKE OVERSOFT
WOMANISH
EFFERENT EXODIC
EFFERVESCE FIZZ HUFF KNIT
BUBBLE SPARKLE
EFFERVESCENCE FRET CRACKLE
SPARKLE
EFFERVESCENT UP BRISK FIZZY
QUICK BUBBLY ABUBBLE ELASTIC
BUBBLING
EFFERVESCING BRISK
EFFETE SERE PASSE SPENT
BARREN DECADENT ETIOLATE
MORIBUND
EFFICACIOUS VALID MIGHTY
POTENT FORCIBLE POWERFUL
SINGULAR VIGOROUS VIRTUOUS
OPERATIVE
EFFICACY DINT FECK DEVIL FORCE
GRACE MIGHT POWER DEGREE

VIRTUE POTENCY VALIDITY
OPERATION
EFFICIENCY POWER SKILL AGENCY
ABILITY FACULTY DISPATCH
EFFICACY PERFORMANCE
EFFICIENT ABLE GOOD SMART
VALID POTENT CAPABLE FECKFUL
POWERFUL SPEEDFUL
EFFIGY GUY IDOL POPE SIGN
DUMMY IMAGE LIKENESS
MONUMENT
EFFLORESCE GERMINATE
EFFLORESCENCE RASH BLOOM
BLOSSOM ROSEOLA ANTHESIS
ERUPTION WHITEWASH
EFFLUENCE ISSUE EFFLUX ELAPSE
EMANATE
EFFLUVIA SCENT
EFFLUVIUM AURA MIASMA
FLUXION SPECIES APORRHEA
EMISSION OUTGOING EMANATION
EFFLUX OUTGO OUTFLOW
EFFUSION
EFFORT JOB TRY TUG DINT FIST
HUMP JUMP MINT PASS SHOT
TOIL ASSAY BRUNT BURST CRACK
DRIVE ESSAY FLING LABOR NISUS
PAINS POWER REACH STUDY
THROE TRIAL ANIMUS DEVOIR
FAVORS FIZZLE FUFFLE PINGLE
STRAIN STROKE THRIFT ATTEMPT
CONATUS MOLIMEN NITENCY
SPLURGE STRETCH TENSURE
TROUBLE WORKING ENDEAVOR
EXERTION GOODWILL INDUSTRY
MOLITION REACHING STRIVING
STRUGGLE
(— FOR ONESELF) FEND
(ABORTIVE —) FIZZLE
(AGONIZED —) THROE
(ARTICULATIVE —) ACCENT
(EARNEST —) STUDY
(EFFECTIVE —) LICK
(FINAL —) CHARETTE
(INITIAL —) ASSAY
(MAXIMUM —) BEST
(SALVATIONIST —) ATTACK
(SINGLE —) HEAT TRICE
(STRENUOUS —) HASSEL HASSLE
(UNSUCCESSFUL —) ATTEMPT
(UTMOST —) DEVOIR BUSINESS
(VIOLENT —) BURST STRAIN
OUTRAGE STRUGGLE
EFFORTLESS EASY
EFFORTLESSNESS EASE
EFFRONTERY BROW FACE GALL
BRASS FRONT BRONZE AUDACITY
BOLDNESS CHUTZPAH FOREHEAD
TEMERITY
EFFULGENCE BLAZE GLORY
RADIANT RADIANCE SPLENDOR
EFFULGENT BRIGHT FULGENT
RADIANT SHINING
EFFUSE GUSH SHED FLING EFFUND
EMANATE DISPENSE
EFFUSION EFFLUX FOISON SCREED
SPILTH STREAM
EFFUSIVE GOOEY GUSHY LAVISH
SLOPPY GUSHING BUBBLING
EFFUSIVENESS SLOP
EFT ASK EVET NEWT LIZARD
TRITON
EGAD ADAD ECOD IGAD SGAD

EGEST VOID EXCRETE ELIMINATE
EGEUS (DAUGHTER OF —) HERMIA
EGG AI ABET GOAD GOOG OVUM
PROD SEED SPUR URGE CHECK
HUEVO OVULE SPORE DARNER
INCITE OOCYTE PEEWEE ZYGOTE
ACTUATE COCKNEY COKENEY
OOPLAST OOSPERM PROTOVUM
(— CASE) POD
(— CLUTCH) LAUGHTER
(— OF FISH OR LOBSTER) BERRY
(— ON) HAG EDGE GOAD URGE
(— PRODUCT) ZOON
(— WITH BACON) COLLOP
(—S OF BEES) BROOD
(—S OF SILKWORM) GRAINE
(ACID —) SLOWCASE
(CRACKED —) CHECK CRACK
LEAKER
(DRIED —S) AHUATLE
(DUCK —S) PIDAN
(FLY'S —) BLOW FLYBLOW
(FOSSIL —) OVULITE
(GOLDEN —S) SUNCUP
(GOOSE —) BLOB
(HUNT BIRDS' —S) OOLOGIZE
(INFERTILE —) CLEAR
(INSECT —) BLOW
(PART OF —) YOLK SHELL WHITE
ALBUMEN CHALAZA MEMBRANE
BLASTODISC
(SMALL —) OVULE OVULUM
(PL.) OVA ROE SEED EYREN
SPAWN CLUTCH ETTING
AHUATLE
(PREF.) OARI(O) OIDIO OO OV(I)(O)(U)
(— CASE) OOTHEC(O)
EGG AND DART ECHINUS
EGGFRUIT LUCUMA CANISTEL
EGGHEAD HIGHBROW
INTELLECTUAL
EGGNOG NOG CAUDLE ADVOCAAT
EGGPLANT BRINJAL SOLANUM
BRINGELA EGGFRUIT
EGG-SHAPED OOID OVAL OVATE
OVOID OOIDAL OBOVOID
OVALOID OVIFORM
EGGSHELL SHARD CASCARON
EGG WHITE GLAIR ALBUMEN
EGG YOLK YELLOW VITELLUS
EGLAH (HUSBAND OF —) DAVID
EGLANTINE (FATHER OF —) PEPIN
(HUSBAND OF —) VALENTINE
EGO I ATTA SELF ATMAN EGOITY
FYLGJA CONCEIT SUBJECT
EGOCENTRIC INSEEING
EGOISM PRIDE ONEISM VANITY
CONCEIT EGOTISM OWNHOOD
SELFNESS NARCISSISM
EGOIST (AUTHOR OF —) MEREDITH
(CHARACTER IN —) DALE LUCY
CLARA HARRY OXFORD VERNON
DECRAYE CROSSJAY DARLETON
LAETITIA PATTERNE WHITFORD
MIDDLETON CONSTANTIA
WILLOUGHBY
EGOTISM EGO PRIDE EGOISM
VANITY CONCEIT EGOMANIA
EGREGIOUS FINE GROSS CAPITAL
EMINENT FLAGRANT PRECIOUS
SHOCKING
EGREGIOUSLY BEASTLY
EGRESS EXIT ISSUE OUTGO

OUTLET EXITURE OUTCOME
OUTGATE PASSAGE REGRESS
OUTGOING
EGRET HERON PLUME GAULIN
KOTUKU AIGRETTE GAULDING
EGYPT MIZRAIM

EGYPT

BAY: FOUL
CALENDAR: AHET APAP TYBI
PAYNI SHEMU THOTH CHOIAK
HATHOR MECHIR MESORE
PAOPHI PACHONS
CANAL: SUEZ
CAPE: BANAS RASBANAS
CAPITAL: CAIRO ELQAHIRA
CHRISTIAN: COPT COPTIC
COIN: FILS DINAR GIRSH POUND
DIRHAM GUINEA JUNAYH
PIASTER MILLIEME
DAM: ASWAN
DESERT: LIBYAN
GOVERNORATE: SUEZ CAIRO
CANAL SINAI BAHARIYA
BAHRIYAH ALEXANDRIA
GULF: AQABA
ISTHMUS: SUEZ
KING: AY IB KA ITI ITY TUT DJER
DJET HUNY PAMI PEPI SETI
TEOS TETI UNIS ARSES BEBTI
FOUAD ITETI KEBEH KHUFU
KNIAN MENES NEBKA NECHO
NEFER UDIMU ZEMTI ZOSER
CHEOPS DARIUS FAROUK
KHAFRE NARMER RANSES
SENEDJ XERXES MENKURE
PHARAOH PTOLEMY RAMESES
SALADIN CHEPHREN THUTMOSE
LAKE: EDKU IDKU MARYUT
MOERIS MANZALA BURULLUS
MAREOTIS
LAKES: BITTER
MEASURE: APT DRA HEN PIK ROB
DRAA KHET ROUB THEB ABDAT
ARDAB CUBIT FARDE KELEH
KILAH SAHME ARTABA AURURE
FEDDAN KEDDAH ROBHAH
SCHENE CHORYOS DARIBAH
MALOUAH ROUBOUH
TOUMNAH KASSABAH
KHAROUBA
MOUNTAIN: SINAI GHARIB
KATHERINA
NAME: UAR
NATIVE: ARAB COPT NILOT
BERBER MUSLIM NUBIAN
OASIS: SIWA DAKHLA KHARGA
FARAFRA BAHARIYA
PENINSULA: SINAI
PORT: TOR SUEZ ATTUR DUMYAT
QUSEIR RASHID SAFAGA
SALLUM ROSETTA DAMIETTA
HURGHADA PORTSAID
ALEXANDRIA
PROVINCE: GIZA QENA QINA
ASWAN ASYUT MINYA SOHAG
DUMYAT FAIYUM SAWHAJ
TAHRIR ALJIZAH BEHEIRA
BENISUEF DAMIETTA GHARBIYA
MINUFIYA SHARQIYA
RESERVOIR: ASWAN
RIVER: NILE
RUINS: ABYDOS THEBES

MEMPHIS PYRAMIDS
SUN GOD: RA RE ATUM
TOWN: NO MUT DUSH GIZA IDFU
ISNA QENA SAIS SIWA SUEZ
ZOAN ASWAN ASYUT BENHA
BULAQ CAIRO ELTUR FAYID
GIRGA GIZEH LUXOR NAKHL
SALUM SOHAG TAHTA TANIS
TANTA ABYDOW AKHMIN
DUMYAT ELQASR HELWAN
RASHID THEBES BURSAID
ROSETTA ZAGAZIG BENISUEF
DAMIETTA ISMAILIA
WEIGHT: KAT KET OKA OKE HEML
KHAR OKIA ROTL ARTAL ARTEL
DEBEN KERAT MINAE MINAS
OKIEH POUND RATEL UCKIA
HAMLAH KANTAR DRACHMA
QUINTAL
WELL: BIRTABA
WIND: KAMSIN SIROCCO
KHAMSEEN

EGYPTIAN ARAB COPT GIPPY
GYPPY TASIAN PHARIAN
BADARIAN MEMPHIAN
EHUD (FATHER OF —) GERA BILHAN
EIDER COLK WAMP DIVER EDDER
DUCKER SHOREYER
EIDOLON ICON GHOST IMAGE
IDOLUM PHANTOM LIKENESS
EIGHT ETA ECHT AUGHT CHETH
OCTAD OCTET OCTAVE OGDOAD
OCTONARY
(PREF.) OCT(A)(O)(U)
EIGHTEENMO OCTODECIMO
EIGHTH AUGHT
EIGHTH NOTE UNCA CROMA
CHROMA QUAVER
EIRE (SEE IRELAND)
EITHER ANY EDDER ITHER OTHER
WHETHER
EJACULATE BELCH BLURT EJECT
FLING EXCLAIM EMISSION
EJACULATION HOW COADS
ZOWIE BEGORRA CRIMINE
UTTERING
(MYSTIC —) OM
EJACULATORY SPUTTERY
EJECT OUT BLOW BOOT CAST EMIT
FIRE HOOF OUST SHED SPAT
SPEW SPIT VOID WARP AVOID
BELCH CHUCK ERUCT ERUPT
EVICT EXPEL SHAKE SHOOT
SPOUT SPURT VOMIT BANISH
BOUNCE REJECT SQUIRT
DEFORCE DISMISS EXCLUDE
EXTRUDE OBTRUDE DISGORGE
OUTBRAID
EJECTION BLOW OUSTER OUTING
EVICTION
EJECTOR LIFTER EDUCTOR
EKE IMP ALSO YEKE AUGMENT
ENLARGE HUSBAND STRETCH
APPENDIX INCREASE LENGTHEN
LIKEWISE UNDERLAY
ELABORATE LUSH FIKIE GREAT
LABOR DELUXE DRESSY ELABOR
ORNATE QUAINT REFINE CURIOUS
DEVELOP ENLARGE LABORED
PERFECT
(OVERLY —) NIGGLING
ELABORATED WROUGHT

ELABORATELY FANCILY
ELABORATENESS FINENESS
CURIOSITY
ELAH (FATHER OF —) UZZI CALEB
BAASHA
(SLAYER OF —) ZIMRI
(SON OF —) HOSHEA
ELAINE (FATHER OF —) PELLES
BRANDEGORIS
(SON OF —) GALAHAD
ELAIS (FATHER OF —) ANIUS
(MOTHER OF —) DORIPPE
(SISTER OF —) OENE SPERMO
ELAMITE SUSIAN ANZANITE
ELAN DASH ARDOR DRIVE GUSTO
VERVE SPIRIT WARMTH POTENCY
ELAND ORYX IMPOFO
ELAN VITAL ZOISM
ELAPS MICRURUS
ELAPSE GO RUN PASS ROLL SLIP
GLIDE SPEND EXPIRE
ELAPSING CURRENT
ELASAH (FATHER OF —) SHAPHAN
ELASMOBRANCH PLACOID
ELASTIC QUICK GARTER RUBATO
SPONGY BUOYANT SPRINGY
STRETCH CHEVEREL CHEVERIL
FLEXIBLE STRETCHY VOLATILE
ELASTICITY GIVE LIFE ELATER
SPRING STRETCH
ELATE BYOU PUFF CHEER EXALT
EXULT FLUSH LOFTY RAISE
ELATED EXCITE PLEASE THRILL
ELEVATE GLADDEN INFLATE
SUBLIME SUCCESS ELEVATED
HEIGHTEN INSPIRIT JUBILATE
ELATED RAD HIGH RADE CHUFF
ELATE HAPPY PROUD VAUDY
VOGIE WLONK CHUFFY JOVIAL
UPPISH UPPITY EXCITED
EXULTED JOCULAR SUBLIME
EXULTANT GLORIOUS INFLATED
JUBILANT PRIDEFUL UPLIFTED
ELATER BEETLE CRINULA SKIPJACK
ELATION JOY GLEE RUFF
BUOYANCY
ELATUS (FATHER OF —) ARCAS
(MOTHER OF —) ERATO
CHRYSOPELIA
(SON OF —) CYLLEN ISCHYS
PEREUS AEPYTUS STYMPHALUS
(WIFE OF —) LAODICE
ELBOW ELL BEND ANCON JOINT
NUDGE SHOVE CROSET ELBUCK
JOSTLE JUSTLE SPRING PIERDROP
(PREF.) CUBITO ULNO
ELCAJA MAFURA
ELDER AIN IVA AINE WITE ELLER
OLDER PRIOR MAHANT PRIMUS
SENIOR ANCIENT NEGUNDO
STAROST TRAMMON ANCESTOR
BOUNTREE BOURTREE CARELESS
DANEWORT ELDERMAN
PRESBYTER
ELDERLY AGED GRAY ALDER
ELDERN SENILE BADGERLY
ELDEST AYNE EIGNE OLDEST
PRIMUS
ELEASAH (FATHER OF —) HELEZ
RAPHA
ELEAZAR (BROTHER OF —) ABIHU
NADAB ITHAMAR
(FATHER OF —) AARON ELIUD

MAHLI PAROSH ABINADAB PHINEHAS
(GRANDFATHER OF —) MERARI
ELECAMPANE INULA CANADA ELFWORT SCABWORT
ELECT CALL PICK VOICE ASSUME CHOOSE CHOSEN DECIDE ISRAEL PREFER SELECT
ELECTION PROXY CHOICE LECTION PRIMARY
ELECTIONEERING HUSTINGS
ELECTIVE OPTION OPTIONAL
ELECTOR VOTER ELISOR CHOOSER ELIGENT INTRANT ELECTANT
ELECTORATE PEOPLE COUNTRY
ELECTRA LAODICE
(BROTHER OF —) ORESTES
(DAUGHTER OF —) IRIS AELLO OCYPETE
(FATHER OF —) ATLAS OCEANUS AGAMEMNON
(HUSBAND OF —) PYLADES THAUMAS
(MOTHER OF —) ERATO TETHYS PLEIONE CLYTEMNESTRA
(SON OF —) IASION DARDANUS
ELECTRIC
(PREF.) POTAM(O)
(— RAY) NARC(O)
ELECTRICIAN GAFFER JUICER BOARDMAN
ELECTRICITY JUICE POWER PYROGEN ELECTRIC GALVANISM
ELECTRIFY EXCITE THRILL STARTLE
ELECTROCUTE BURN EXECUTE
ELECTRODE DE DEE GRID ANODE PLATE DYNODE CATHODE IGNITER CROWFOOT REOPHORE
(PL.) ELEMENT
ELECTRODEPOSIT STRIKE REGULINE
ELECTROLYTE STRIKE IONOGEN
ELECTROMAGNETIC (— UNIT) OERSTED ABAMPERE
ELECTRON ION NEGATON POLARON NEGATRON POSITRON CORPUSCLE
ELECTRONIC RADIONIC
ELECTRONOGRAPHY ONSET
ELECTRON TUBE TRIODE
ELECTROPHONE MARTENOT
ELECTROPLATE SILVER
ELECTROTYPE PATCH CLICHE WORKER ELECTRO
ELECTRUM AMBER ELECTRE ORICHALC
ELECTRYON (DAUGHTER OF —) ALCMENE
(FATHER OF —) PERSEUS
(MOTHER OF —) ANDROMEDA
ELECTUARY DIASCORD LECTUARY THERIACA MITHRIDATE
ELEGANCE CHIC GARB LUXE TONE CLASP GRACE STYLE SWANK TASTE FINERY GAIETY GAYETY LUXURY NICETY POLISH COURTESY EUPHUISM FINENESS FRIPPERY GRANDEUR SPLENDOR
ELEGANT CHIC DINK FAIR FEAT FINE FIXY GENT JIMP POSH CIVIL COMPT FANCY NOBBY RITZY SHARP SLEEK SWANK SWISH

CHOICE CLASSY DAINTY DELUXE DRESSY FACETE MINION POLITE PRETTY QUAINT SUPERB SWANKY URBANE VENUST CAPITAL CLEANLY COURTLY FEATISH FEATOUS GENTEEL MINIKIN REFINED SMICKER DEBONAIR DELICATE GINGERLY GRACEFUL GRAZIOSO HANDSOME POLISHED TASTEFUL CONCINNOUS
ELEGANTLY FINE TALLY FAIRLY GENTLY GINGERLY
ELEGIAC MOURNFUL EPICEDIAL
ELEGY POEM SONG DIRGE KINAH QINAH LAMENT MONODY EPICEDE
ELEKTRA (CHARACTER IN —) OREST AEGISTH ELEKTRA CHRYSOTHEMIS KLYTEMNESTRA
(COMPOSER OF —) STRAUSS
ELEMENT AIR ATOM DIAD DYAD RECT WOOF BEARD ETHER FIBER FIBRE METAL MONAD PUNCT STUFF AETHER ARTIAD COSTAL FACTOR HEPTAD LOSSER MATTER MOMENT SIMPLE ACTINON ADAPTER BUNCHER CARRIER CATCHER ESSENCE FEATURE ACTINIDE BACKBONE CEREBRAL EQUATION PERISSAD RUDIMENT SELECTOR THERBLIG
(— IN GRAPH) SPIKE
(— IN WAVE) DART
(— IN WORD GROUP) KOINON
(— OF ALCHEMIST) AIR FIRE EARTH WATER
(— OF EXISTENCE) DHARMA
(— OF MACHINE) HORN SPIDER
(— OF WEALTH) COMMODITY
(ALIEN —) ALLOY
(ARCHITECTURAL —) SLAB
(BINDING —) CEMENT
(CHARACTERISTIC —) PARAMETER
(CHEMICAL —) TIN GOLD IRON LEAD NEON ZINC ARGON BORON RADON XENON BARIUM CARBON CERIUM CESIUM COBALT COPPER CURIUM ERBIUM HELIUM INDIUM IODINE MURIUM NICKEL OSMIUM OXYGEN RADIUM SILVER SODIUM SULFUR ARSENIC BISMUTH BROMINE CADMIUM CALCIUM FERMIUM GALLIUM HAFNIUM HOLMIUM IRIDIUM KRYPTON LITHIUM MERCURY NIOBIUM RHENIUM RHODIUM SILICON TERBIUM THORIUM THULIUM URANIUM WOLFRAM YTTRIUM ACTINIDE ACTINIUM ANTIMONY ASTATINE CHLORINE CHROMIUM EUROPIUM FLUORINE FRANCIUM HYDROGEN LUTETIUM MASURIUM NITROGEN NOBELIUM NONMETAL PLATINUM POLONIUM RUBIDIUM SAMARIUM SCANDIUM SELENIUM TANTALUM THALLIUM TITANIUM TUNGSTEN VANADIUM METALLOID PALLADIUM PLUTONIUM
(COMMUNION —) GIFT
(CRIMINAL —) GANGLAND
(DECORATIVE —S) ART
(DOMINANT —) CAPSHEAF

(ELECTRIC —) IMPEDOR
(ESSENTIAL —) CORPUS
(EUCHARISTIC —S) HAGIA SPECIES
(FATAL —) BANE
(FUNDAMENTAL —) STAMEN KEYSTONE
(GLOOMY —) PALL
(HEATING —) CALANDRIA
(HYPOTHETICAL —) CORONIUM
(INTERFERING —) CRIMP
(LAMP —) GLOWER
(LEADING —) HEAD
(LINGUISTIC—) SERVILE INTENSIVE
(MILITARY —) SUPPORT
(MODIFYING —) LEAVENING
(MORAL —) DAENA
(MOST IMPORTANT —) CAPSTONE
(PRIMAL —) GUNA SALT ARCHE
(PRINCIPAL —) STAPLE
(SKELETAL —) SCLERE
(STRUCTURAL —) ARCUALE
(SUPPOSED —) PROTYLE WELSIUM VICTORIUM
(SUSTAINING —) BREAD STAPLE
(TRACE —) MICRONUTRIENT
(TRANSITORY —S) SKANDHAS
(UNITING —) BOND
(PL.) DETAIL ALPHABET
(PREF.) **(FIRST —)** STOICHIO
(SUFF.) AD IUM
(CHEMICAL —) ID IDE INE IUM
ELEMENTAL PURE BASIC PRIMAL SIMPLE PRIMARY ULTIMATE PRIMITIVE
ELEMENTARY PRIMAL SIMPLE INITIAL PRIMARY INCHOATE ULTIMATE RUDIMENTARY
ELEMI ANEMI ANIME MATTI RESIN CONIMA
ELEPHANT COW BULL CALF HINE PUNK HATHI HATTY JUMBO ROGUE MUCKNA TUSKER KOOMKIE AIRAVATA LOXODONT MASTODON OLIPHANT PROBOSCIDEAN
ELEPHANT FISH JOSEF JOSUP JOSEPH
ELEPHANTIASIS TYRIASIS
ELEPHANTINE HUGE ENORMOUS
ELEPHANT'S-EAR TARO
ELEPHANT SHREW JUMPER
ELEUT KALMUK KALMYK KALMUCK
ELEVATE HAIN JUMP LIFT REAR RISE EDIFY ELATE ENSKY ERECT EXALT EXTOL GRIMP HEAVE HOIST MOUNT RAISE TOWER REFINE UPLIFT ADVANCE DIGNIFY ENHANCE ENNOBLE GLORIFY PROMOTE SUBLIME UPRAISE HEIGHTEN INSPIRIT
ELEVATED EL FINE HIGH GREAT LOFTY NOBLE RISEN STEEP AERIAL AMOTUS ELATED RAISED RISING WINGED BULLATE ELEVATO EXALTED MOUNTED STILTED SUBLIME MAJESTIC UPLIFTED
(— IN CHARACTER) HIGH
(NOT —) COMICAL
ELEVATION UP ARM BAND BANK DOME DRUM GLEE HIGH HILL HUMP LIFT RISE SPUR TOFT TOOT UMBO AGGER BULLA GRADE

KNOLL MOUND PITCH RAISE RIDGE SHOAL SWELL TOWER WHEAL CONULE CRISTA HEIGHT PAPULE UPLIFT DIGNITY FURCULA MAJESTY UPRIGHT ALTITUDE EMINENCE EVECTION HIGHNESS LEVATION MOUNTAIN SWELLING MONTICULE
(— OF CARTILAGE) ANTHELIX
(— OF CUTICLE) BLEB
(— OF SKIN) BLISTER
(— ON TOOTH) STYLE
(— SEPARATING CREEKS) BUGOR
(GUN —) RANDOM
(TURRET —) HOOD
(PREF.) ORO
ELEVATOR BIN CAGE LIFT SILO HOIST BRIDGE LIFTER TEAGLE HOISTER STACKER UPTAKER UPLIFTER UPRAISER
ELEVEN
(PREF.) HENDEC(A) UNDEC(A)
ELEVENTH ELFT
ELF FAY HAG HOB IMP OAF PUG DROW FANE OUPH PERI PIXY PUCK DWARF ELFIN FAIRY GNOME OUPHE PIGMY PIXIE ELFKIN GOBLIN SPIRIT SPRITE URCHIN BLASTIE BROWNIE INCUBUS SUCCUBUS
ELFIN ELF FEY CHILD ELFIC ELFISH URCHIN
ELFISH ELFIN ELVAN ELVISH IMPISH URCHIN ELFLIKE TRICKSY
ELFRIDA (HUSBAND OF —) EDGAR
(SON OF —) AETHELRED
ELIAB (BROTHER OF —) DAVID
(DAUGHTER OF —) ABIHAIL
(FATHER OF —) HELON NAHATH
(SON OF —) ABIRAM DATHAN
ELIADA (FATHER OF —) DAVID
ELIADAH (SON OF —) REZON
ELIAKIM (FATHER OF —) ABIUD MELEA HILKIAH
(SON OF —) AZOR JONAN
ELIAM (DAUGHTER OF —) BATHSHEBA
ELIASAPH (FATHER OF —) LAEL
ELIASHIB (FATHER OF —) BANI ZATTU
ELICIT DRAW MILK PUMP CLAIM EDUCE EVOKE EXACT FETCH WREST WRING DEDUCE DEMAND ENTICE EXTORT INDUCE EXTRACT PROVOKE SOLICIT
ELIDE OMIT SKIP ANNUL IGNORE DESTROY NULLIFY DEMOLISH SUPPRESS
ELIEZER (FATHER OF —) JORIM MOSES BECHER ZICHRI DODAVAH
ELIGIBILITY FITNESS
ELIGIBLE FIT ACTIVE WORTHY SUITABLE
(— IN POKER) ACTIVE
ELIMELECH (SON OF —) MAHLON CHILION
(WIFE OF —) NAOMI
ELIMINATE FAN COMB EDIT KILL EDUCE EXPEL PURGE SCRUB DELETE EFFACE EXCEPT IGNORE REMOVE SCREEN WINNOW BLANKET BRACKET DIVULGE EXCLUDE EXCRETE RELEASE

SCISSOR SILENCE SUBLATE
SEPARATE
ELIMINATION STRIP
ELIOENAI (FATHER OF —) NEARIAH
ELIPHAL (FATHER OF —) UR
ELIPHALET (FATHER OF —) DAVID
ELIPHAZ (FATHER OF —) ESAU
   (MOTHER OF —) ADAH
   (SON OF —) TEMAN
ELIPHELET (FATHER OF —) DAVID
   ESHEK
ELISABETH (HUSBAND OF —)
   ZACHARIAS
   (SON OF —) JOHN
ELISHA (FATHER OF —) SHAPHAT
ELISHAH (FATHER OF —) JAVAN
ELISHAMA (FATHER OF —) DAVID
   (SON OF —) NETHANIAH
ELISHAPHAT (FATHER OF —) ZICHRI
ELISHEBA (BROTHER OF —)
   NAHSHON
   (FATHER OF —) AMMINADAB
   (HUSBAND OF —) AARON
ELISHUA (FATHER OF —) DAVID
ELISION SYNCOPE
ELISIR D'AMORE (CHARACTER IN —
) ADINA BELCORE NEMORINO
   DULCAMARA
   (COMPOSER OF —) DONIZETTI
ELISSA (BROTHER OF —)
   PYGMALION
   (FATHER OF —) BELUS METGEN
   (HUSBAND OF —) ACERBAS
   SYCHAEUS SICHARBAAL
   (SISTER OF —) ANNA
ELITE BEST LITE FINK CREAM
   CHOICE CIRCLE FLOWER GENTRY
   SELECT PERFECTI
ELIUD (FATHER OF —) ACHIM
ELIXIR DAFFY AMRITA SPIRIT
   AMREETA ARCANUM CORDIAL
   CUREALL ESSENCE PANACEA
   MEDICINE
ELIZAPHAN (FATHER OF —) UZZIEL
ELK ALCE DEER LAMA LOSH ALAND
   ALCES ELAND LOSHE MOOSE
   CERVID SAMBAR WAPITI
   SAMBHUR WAMPOOSE
   (— HIDE) LOSH
   (YOUNG —) DEACON
ELKANAH (FATHER OF —) KORAH
   (SON OF —) SAMUEL
   (SLAYER OF —) ZICHRI
ELK BARK BIGBLOOM
ELL ULNA ELBOW ALNAGE
   ADDITION
ELLIPSE OVAL
ELLIPSIS BRING ELLIPSE
ELLIPSOGRAPH TRAMMEL
ELLIPSOID CONOID ELLIPTIC
   SPHEROID
ELLIPTICAL OVAL OVATE OBLONG
ELLOBIUM AURICULA
ELM ULME ELVEN ULMUS WAHOO
   MEZCAL CHEWBARK
   ORHAMWOOD
ELMODAM (FATHER OF —) ER
ELMSEED
   (PREF.) SAMARI
ELNAAM (SON OF —) JERIBAI
   JOSHAVIAH
ELOCUTION SPEECH DICTION
   ORATORY

ELOCUTIONIST READER RECITER
ELOIGN CONVEY REMOVE
   ABSCOND CONCEAL
ELON (FATHER OF —) ZEBULUN
ELONGATE EXTEND REMOVE
   STRETCH LENGTHEN PROTRACT
ELONGATED LANK LONG LINEAR
   OBLONG PROLATE SLENDER
   HAIRLIKE PRODUCED
ELOPE DECAMP ESCAPE ABSCOND
ELOQUENCE FACUND FLUENCY
   ORATORY
ELOQUENT VOCAL DISERT
   FACUND FERVID FLUENT SILVER
   RENABLE SPEAKING ORATORICAL
ELPAAL (BROTHER OF —) ABITUB
   (FATHER OF —) SHAHARAIM
   (MOTHER OF —) HUSHIM
ELPALET (FATHER OF —) DAVID

EL SALVADOR

CAPITAL: SANSALVADOR
COIN: PESO COLON CENTAVO
DANCE: PASILLO
DEPARTMENT: LAPAZ CABANAS
   MORAZAN SONSONATE
GULF: FONSECA
INDIAN: PIPIL
LAKE: GUIJA ILOPANGO
MEASURE: VARA CAFIZ CAHIZ
   FANEGA TERCIA BOTELLA
   CAJUELA CANTARO MANZANA
POINT: REMEDIOS
PORT: CUTUCO ACAJUTLA
RIVER: JIBOA LAPAZ LEMPA
RUINS: TAZUMAL
TOWN: CUTUCO IZALCO CORINTO
   METAPAN ACAJUTLA
   USULUTAN SONSONATE
   AHUACHAPAN
VOLCANO: IZALCO
WEIGHT: BAG CAJA LIBRA

ELSE OR ENS ENSE OTHER BESIDES
   INSTEAD
ELSEWHERE ALIBI EXCEPT THENCE
   (FROM —) ALIUNDE
ELUCIDATE CLEAR LUCID EXPLAIN
   SIMPLIFY
ELUDE BEAT FLEE FOIL JINK MISS
   MOCK SLIP AVOID DODGE EVADE
   BAFFLE BEFOOL DELUDE DOUBLE
   ESCAPE BEGUILE DECEIVE
   HEDGEHOP
ELUSIVE EELY LUBRIC SHIFTY
   SUBTLE TRICKY TWISTY EVASIVE
   BAFFLING FUGITIVE SLIPPERY
ELYSIUM EDEN ANNWFN
   PARADISE
ELYTRON HUSK SCUTE SHARD
   SHERD SHEATH
ELYTRUM SHARD TEGMEN
ELZAPHAN (FATHER OF —) UZZIEL
EM EMMA
   (HALF —) EN
EMACIATED LEAN POOR EMPTY
   GAUNT MEAGER PEAKED SKINNY
   WASTED TABETIC WASTREL
   MARASMIC SKELETAL
   WANTHRIVEN
EMACIATING MARCID
EMACIATION NITON TABES
   MACIES ATROPHY POVERTY

ASTHENIA MARASMUS
EMANATE FLOW ARISE EMANE
   EXUDE ISSUE DERIVE EFFUSE
   EXHALE OUTRAY SPRING
   BREATHE OUTCOME PROCEED
   RADIATE
EMANATING EFFLUENT
EMANATION FUG AURA BEAM
   BLAS GLORY NITON AZILUT
   BREATH EFFLUX ELAPSE EIDOLON
   MOFETTE OUTCOME PROCESS
   SEPHIRA EMISSION PROCESSION
   (— FROM A MEDIUM) ECTOPLASM
   (SENSED —) KARMA
   (PL.) SCENT
EMANCIPATE FREE MANUMIT
   RELEASE LIBERATE UNFETTER
EMANCIPATION FREEDOM
   RELEASE
   (FINAL —) NIRVANA
EMASCULATE GELD SOFTEN
   EVIRATE CASTRATE ENERVATE
EMATHION (BROTHER OF —)
   MEMNON
   (FATHER OF —) TITHONUS
   (MOTHER OF —) EOS
   (SLAYER OF —) HERCULES
EMBALM BALM CERE MUMMY
   SPICE BALSAM SEASON CONDITE
   MUMMIFY
EMBANK BUND
EMBANKMENT BAY BAND BANK
   BUND DIKE DYKE FILL QUAY
   ARGIN DIGUE LEVEE MOUND
   REVET BUNKER STAITH BACKING
   BANKING PARADOS PILAPIL
   RAMPART RAMPIRE SEAWALL
   APPROACH STRENGTH
   REVETMENT
EMBARGO EDICT ORDER IMBARGE
   BLOCKADE STOPPAGE
EMBARK BANK SAIL SHIP ENGAGE
   ENLIST INSHIP INVEST LAUNCH
   IMBARGE
EMBARRASS SET CHAW CLOG
   FAZE HACK LAND POSE ABASH
   ANNOY SHAME UPSET BOGGLE
   CUMBER GRAVEL HAMPER
   HINDER HOBBLE IMPEDE PLUNGE
   PUZZLE RATTLE CONFUSE
   ENTRIKE FLUMMOX INVOLVE
   NONPLUS BEWILDER CONFOUND
   DUMFOUND ENCUMBER
   ENTANGLE HANDICAP IMPESTER
   OBSTRUCT STRAITEN
EMBARRASSED AWKWARD
   FLURRIED SHEEPISH
EMBARRASSING STICKY
   AWKWARD HIDEOUS
EMBARRASSINGLY AWKWARDLY
EMBARRASSMENT FIX GENE
   LURCH SHAME STAND CADDLE
   CUMBER HOBBLE PUZZLE
   NONPLUS CONFUSION
EMBASSY SAND ERRAND
   AMBASSY MESSAGE MISSION
   INBASSAT LEGATION
EMBATTLED BATTLED CRENELE
   BRETESSE CRENELEE
EMBAY BATHE DETAIN ENCLOSE
   SHELTER SUFFUSE ENCIRCLE
   SURROUND
EMBAYMENT FIORD FJORD

EMBED BED SET BOND IMBED
   STAMP CHARGE ENGAGE
   EMBOWEL IMMERSE
   (— IN SAND) DOCK
EMBEDDED INNATE ENGAGED
   IMMERSED
EMBELLISH GEM DECK GILD TRIM
   ADORN DRESS FUDGE GRACE
   BEDECK BETRIM BLAZON EMBOSS
   ENRICH FIGURE FLOWER
   APPAREL BEDRAPE EMBLAZE
   GARNISH MYSTIFY VARNISH
   BEAUTIFY DECORATE FLOURISH
   ORNAMENT
EMBELLISHED FLORID GESTED
   ORNATE COLORED FUCUSED
   BROCADED SPLENDID
EMBELLISHMENT FILIP GRACE
   FILLIP RELISH AGREMEN GARNISH
   GILDING WINDING AGREMENT
   FLOURISH MOUNTING ORNAMENT
   PARERGON TRAPPING TRICKING
   PASSAGGIO
   (MUSICAL —) MELISMA ROULADE
   ARABESQUE
   (PL.) FIXINGS
EMBER ASH COAL AIZLE GLEED
   IMBER CINDER
   (RED-HOT —S) BAGA
EMBEZZLE STEAL PECULATE
   SQUANDER
EMBEZZLEMENT THEFT
   PLUNDERAGE
EMBITTER SOUR BITTER CURDLE
   ACIDIFY ENVENOM ACERBATE
   EMPOISON VERJUICE
EMBITTERED SOURED ACERBATE
   ENFESTED
EMBLAZON LAUD ADORN EXTOL
   BLAZON DISPLAY EMBLAZE
   EXHIBIT GLORIFY
EMBLAZONED CLOUE CLOUEE
   CRINED CRESTED BRISTLED
   (— WITH ANTLERS) ATTIRED
   (— WITH BEARD) BARBED
EMBLAZONMENT HERALDRY
EMBLEM BAR ANKH ATEN LOGO
   MACE ORLE SEAL SIGN STAR
   TYPE AWARD BADGE CREST
   CROSS EAGLE FAVOR IMAGE
   TIARA TOKEN DEVICE DIADEM
   ENSIGN FIGURE KAHILI SABCAT
   SHIELD SIGNAL SYMBOL TRISUL
   CHARACT IMPRESA IMPRESE
   SCEPTER SCEPTRE ALLEGORY
   CADUCEUS COLOPHON INSIGNIA
   (— OF CUCKOLD) HORN
   (— OF IMMORTALITY) AMARANTH
   (— OF IRELAND) SHAMROCK
   (— OF WALES) LEEK
   (AUTOMOBILE —) MARQUE
   (PRINTING —) COLOPHON
   (SACRED —) HIEROGRAM
EMBLEMATIC TYPAL FIGURAL
   TYPICAL SYMBOLIC
EMBLIC AMLA AULA MYROBALAN
EMBODIMENT MAP SON SELF
   AVATAR GENIUS EPITOME
   IMAGERY BODIMENT
EMBODY BODY UNITE INBODY
   CONTAIN EXPRESS COALESCE
   ORGANIZE
EMBOLDEN BOLD BIELD BRAVE

ERECT NERVE ASSURE BOWDEN
ENHARDY HEARTEN STOMACH

EMBOLUS CLOT STYLE

EMBOSOM BOSOM FOSTER
CHERISH ENCLOSE IMBOSOM
SHELTER SURROUND

EMBOSS BOSS HIDE KNOB KNOT
ADORN BLOCK CHASE GOFFER
INDENT POUNCE ANTIQUE
CONCEAL ENCLOSE EXHAUST
GAUFFER INFLATE ORNAMENT

EMBOSSED BOSSED RAISED
ANTIQUE CHAMPED MATELASSE

EMBOSSING CELATURE

EMBOUCHURE LIP CHOPS LIPPING

EMBOWER BOWER

EMBOWERED ARBORED

EMBRACE ARM HUG CLIP COLL
FOLD LOVE NECK PLAT SIDE
ZONE ADOPT BOSOM BRACE
CHAIN CLASP CLING CRUSH
ENARM GRASP HALCH HALSE
INARM OXTER PRESS TWINE
ABRAZO ACCEPT ACCOLL AMPLEX
BECLIP CARESS CLINCH COMPLY
CUDDLE ENFOLD FATHOM
HUDDLE INCLIP INFOLD PLIGHT
SHRINE AMPLECT CHERISH
CONTAIN ENCLOSE ESPOUSE
INCLUDE INVOLVE ACCOLADE
AMPLEXUS CANOODLE COMPLECT
COMPRESS COMPRISE CONCLUDE
ENCIRCLE

EMBRACING COLLING OSCULANT
AMPLECTANT

EMBRASURE LOOP PORT VENT
CRENEL CRENELLE PORTHOLE

EMBROCATION ARNICA
EMBROCHE LINIMENT

EMBROIDER RUN TAT DARN FRET
LACE BROUD COUCH FAGOT
PANEL SMOCK BEWORK EMBOSS
FAGGOT FRIEZE NEEDLE PURFLE
STITCH SURFLE TISSUE BROIDER
TAMBOUR ORNAMENT

EMBROIDERED BRODE BRODEE
BROWDEN BROCADED

EMBROIDERER SPRIGGER

EMBROIDERY KANT LACE OPUS
WORK BREDE ASSISI BONNAZ
CREWEL EDGING HEDEBO
APPAREL CHICKEN CUTWORK
ORPHREY SETWORK TAMBOUR
ARRASENE BRODERIE BROIDERY
COUCHING FAGOTING LISTWORK
PHULKARI SMOCKING TAPESTRY
CREWELLERY NEEDLEPOINT

EMBROIL BROIL JUMBLE INVOLVE
PERPLEX TROUBLE DISORDER
DISTRACT ENTANGLE

EMBRYO GERM CADET FETUS
OVULE FOETUS EMBRYON
NEURULA PLANULA ACANTHOR
BLASTULA GASTRULA PRINCIPE
(PREF.) BLAST(O)

EMBRYONIC GERMINAL

EMCEE HOST

EME AUNT YEME UNCLE FRIEND
NEIGHBOR

EMEND (ALSO SEE AMEND) EDIT
MEND ALTER AMEND BETTER
REFORM REPEAL REVISE
CORRECT IMPROVE RECTIFY

REDRESS EMENDATE

EMERALD BERYL GREEN EMRAUD
EMERANT PRASINE SMARAGD

EMERALD FISH ESMERALDA

EMERGE BOB DIP BOLT LOOM
PEER RISE BREAK ERUPT EXUDE
ISSUE START APPEAR BECOME
PLUNGE SPRING DEBOUCH
EXTRUDE

(— FROM EGGSHELL) HATCH
ECLOSE

(— FROM SLEEP) AWAKE

(— SLOWLY) PEEK

EMERGENCE NEED BIRTH PINCH
EGRESS GROWTH PRICKLE
BECOMING DEBOUCHE ECLOSION
EMERSION ERUPTION EXIGENCE
TENTACLE

(— FROM DARKNESS) BREAK

EMERGENCY NEED PEND PUSH
PINCH CRISIS STRAIT SUDDEN
EMERGENT EXIGENCY JUNCTURE

EMERGENT RISING ONCOMING

EMERGING EMANANT EMERGENT

EMERITA HIPPA

EMERY EMERIL SMIRIS ABRASIVE
CORUNDUM

EMETIC ALUM PICK PUKE PUKER
VOMIT EVACUANT VOMITIVE
VOMITORY

EMIGRANT EMIGRE EXODIST
PATARIN SETTLER COLONIST
PATERINE STRANGER

(— FROM MECCA) COMPANION

EMIGRATE MOVE REMOVE
MIGRATE

EMIGRATION EXODUS HEGIRA
HEJIRA SWARMING

EMILIA (HUSBAND OF —) IAGO
PALAMON

EMINENCE DUN NAB BALL BERG
CRAG KNOT MONS MOTE NOTE
POLE RANK RISE SCAR TOOT
CHIEF HOYLE KNOLL PERCH
STATE WHEAL WORTH ASCENT
HEIGHT KRANTZ RENOWN
RIDEAU ALTITUDE GRANDEUR
TUBERCLE

(— OF HAND) SUBVOLA

EMINENT BIG ARCH HIGH CHIEF
GRAND GREAT LOFTY NOBLE
NOTED FAMOUS MARKED SIGNAL
EXCELSE SUBLIME TOPPING
GLORIOUS RENOWNED SINGULAR
TOWERING PROMINENT
CONSPICUOUS

EMIR AMIR AMEER NOBLE RULER
LEADER PRINCE ADMIRAL
GOVERNOR

EMISSARY SPY AGENT SCOUT
LEGATE DELEGATE

EMISSION FUME GUST VENT

EMISSIVE EMITTENT EXHALANT

EMIT RUN BARK BEAM CAST DRIP
GIVE GUSH HURL LASH MOVE
OOZE PASS POUR REEK SEND
SHED SPIT VENT VOID WARP
AVOID BELCH EJECT ERUCT
EXERT EXUDE FLASH FLING ISSUE
UTTER YIELD DECANT DONATE
EVOLVE EXHALE EXPIRE SPREAD
BREATHE DISTILL EMANATE
EXHAUST OUTSEND RADIATE

REFLAIR ERUCTATE TRANSMIT

(— COHERENT LIGHT) LASE

(— FOAM) SPURGE

(— FORCEFULLY) FIRE

(— IN PUFFS) PLUFF

(— LIGHT) GLOW

(— ODOR) REEK STEAM

(— OUTCRIES) CHUNNER CHUNTER

(— PLAY OF COLORS) OPALESCE

(— RAYS) RADIATE IRRADIATE

(— SMOKE) SMEECH

(— SOUND) BUFF MOVE

(— SPARKS) SNAP

EMITTING EMISSIVE SOUNDING
(SUFF.) (— LIGHT) ESCENT

EMMA (AUTHOR OF —) AUSTEN
(CHARACTER IN —) EMMA JANE
BATES ELTON FRANK SMITH
GEORGE MARTIN ROBERT
WESTON FAIRFAX HARRIET
CHURCHILL KNIGHTLEY
WOODHOUSE

EMMENAGOGUE ALOE SAFFRON
GROUNDSEL

EMMER SPELTZ AMELCORN

EMMET ANT ENEMY PISMIRE
FORMICID

EMMOR (SON OF —) SHECHEM

EMOLLIATE SOFTEN

EMOLLIENT LENIENT ICHTHYOL
LENITIVE MALACTIC MOLLIENT
SUPPLING

EMOLUMENT FEES WAGES
INCOME PROFIT SALARY BENEFIT
STIPEND

EMOTION IRE LOVE ONDE PANG
STIR AGONY ANGER CHORD GRIEF
HEART SHAME AFFECT EFFECT
MOTION RAPTUS SNIVEL SPLEEN
ECSTASY FEELING PASSION
VULTURE GRAMERCY MOVEMENT
SURPRISE SENTIMENT

(CONTROLLING —) LEITMOTIF
LEITMOTIV

(EVIL —) DEMON DAEMON

(PREF.) THYM(O)

(SUFF.) THYMIA

EMOTIONAL MUSHY DRIPPY
EMOTIVE AFFECTIVE

(UNDULY —) SPOONY SPOONEY
RHAPSODIC

EMOTIONLESS COLD

EMPATHY SYMPATHY

EMPEROR I IMP CZAR INCA KING
TSAR AKBAR RULER TENNO
CAESAR DESPOT KABAKA KAISER
SULTAN BAGINDA MONARCH
VIKRAMA AUGUSTUS IMPERIAL
PADISHAH

EMPERY DOMAIN EMPIRE EMPIRY
DOMINION

EMPHASIS ANGLE ACCENT STRESS
WEIGHT EMPIRISM SALIENCE

EMPHASIZE HIT CLICK PINCH
PRESS ACCENT BETONE CHARGE
STRESS

EMPHATIC LOUD STRONG
EARNEST MARCATO SERIOUS
ENFATICO FORCIBLE MARCANDO
POSITIVE RESOUNDING

EMPHATICALLY FLATLY
STRONGLY POINTEDLY

EMPHYSEMA HEAVES

EMPIRE RULE SWAY POWER
REALM REIGN STATE DIADEM
DOMAIN EMPERY CONTROL
KINGDOM IMPERIUM

(— STATE) NEWYORK

(— STATE OF SOUTH) GEORGIA

(SELJUK —) RUM ROUM

EMPIRIC QUACK IMPOSTOR

EMPIRICAL POSITIVE

EMPIRICIST VIRTUOSO

EMPLACEMENT BATTERY
GALLERY PLATFORM

EMPLOY FEE PAY USE BUSK BUSY
HIRE PLOY TAKE WAGE WISE
ADOPT APPLY BESET IMPLY
SPEND BESTOW ENGAGE ENLIST
INFOLD INVOKE OCCUPY SUPPLY
CONCERN CONDUCT ENCLOSE
IMPROVE INVOLVE SERVICE
UTILIZE PRACTICE

(— FLATTERY) COLLOGUE

(— ONESELF ABOUT) TOSS

(— SHIFTS) CHICANE

EMPLOYED APPLIED ENGAGED

EMPLOYEE HAND HELP BOOTS
CLERK FACTOR LEADER BELLBOY
BOOTBOY CALLBOY CARRIER
SERVANT CHASSEUR CIVILIAN
FLOORMAN IMPROVER

(— WHO RUNS ERRANDS) GOFER
GOPHER

EMPLOYER BOSS JOSS BLOKE
GAFFER ENGAGER MANAGER
PADRONE GOVERNOR

(SMALL —) CORK

EMPLOYMENT FEE JOB USE CALL
HIRE NOTE TASK TOIL USER
WORK CRAFT TRADE TREAD
USAGE MISTER THRIFT CALLING
PURPOSE PURSUIT SERVICE
USAUNCE BUSINESS EXERCISE
POSITION RETAINER VOCATION

(CASUAL —) GRASS

EMPORIUM MART SHOP BAZAR
STORE BAZAAR EMPORY MARKET
STAPLE MONOPOLE

EMPOWER POWER ENABLE
ENTITLE DELEGATE DEPUTIZE

EMPRESS IMPX EMPERESS
IMPERIAL KAISERIN

EMPTIED DRAINED

EMPTILY TOOMLY

EMPTINESS VAIN VOID INANE
ANEMIA VACUUM VANITY
ANAEMIA INANITY VACANCY
VACUITY LEERNESS

(— OF SPIRIT) ENNUI

EMPTY DRY FAT RID TIM AIRY
BARE BOSS BUZZ CANT DEAF
DUMP EMPT FALL FARM FREE
GLIB HOWE IDLE LEER NEAR
POUR ROOM TEEM TOOM VAIN
VIDE VOID ADDLE AVOID BLANK
BLEED CLEAN CLEAR DRAIN
EQUAL EXPEL HUSKY INANE
LEERY MOUTH SCOOP SHOOT
SKAIL STARK START STRIP
SWAMP TINNY WINDY BARREN
BUBBLE CHAFFY DEVOID GOUSTY
HOLLOW JEJUNE STRIKE SWASTY
UNEMPT UNLOAD VACANT
VACATE DELIVER DEPLETE
EXHAUST EXPRESS UNTAKEN

VACUATE VACUOUS VIDUOUS DISGORGE EVACUATE EVANESCE NEGATION UNFILLED
(— AN EGG) BLOW
(PREF.) CEN(O) JEJUN(O) KEN(O)
EMPTY-HEADED VAIN DOLLISH
EMPTYING EVACUANT
(ACT OF —) KENOSIS
EMPTY-SOUNDING TOOM
EMPUSA MONSTER SPECTER SPECTRE
EMPYREAN ETHER AETHER HEAVENS EMPYREUM
EMU EMEU RHEA RATITE
EMU APPLE COLANE
EMU BUSH BERRIGAN
EMULATE APE VIE COPY EMULE EQUAL EXCEL RIVAL COMPETE IMITATE
EMULATION STRIFE CONTEST PARAGON RIVALRY
EMULATOR RIVAL
EMULOUS EMULATE ENVIOUS CORRIVAL
EMULOUSLY AVIE
EMULSIFIABLE SOLUBLE
EMULSION PAP LATEX
EMU WREN STIPITURE
EN NUT
ENABLE ABLE EMPOWER ENTITLE QUALIFY INHABILE
ENACT LIVE MAKE PASS ADOPT DECREE EFFECT ORDAIN ACTUATE APPOINT PERFORM PORTRAY
ENACTMENT LAW DOOM ENACT NOVEL ASSIZE DECREE MEASURE PASSAGE STATUTE ENACTION ENACTURE
ENAMEL AMEL FLUX SLIP EMAIL GLAZE GLOSS PAINT SLUSH AUMAIL SHIPPO SMALTO DENTINE LIMOGES SCHMELZ
ENAMOR LOVE CHARM SMITE CAPTIVE
ENAMORED FOND EPRIS EPRISE MASHED AMOROUS CHARMED SMITTEN
(VAINLY —) FOOLISH
ENARCHUS (NEPHEW OF —) MUSIDORUS
(SON OF —) PYROCLES
ENCAMP TELD TENT LODGE PITCH INCAMP LAAGER BIVOUAC LEAGUER
ENCAMPMENT CAMP DOUAR ETAPE SIEGE LAAGER BIVOUAC CASTRUM HUTMENT TOLDERIA
ENCASE CASE HOUSE SHELL INCASE ENCHASE INCLOSE SURROUND ENCAPSULE
ENCELIA INCIENSO
ENCEPHALON CEREBRUM
ENCHAIN FETTER INCHAIN
ENCHANT CHARM DELUDE GLAMOR INCANT ATTRACT BECHARM BESPELL BEWITCH DELIGHT GLAMOUR BEDAZZLE ENSORCEL CAPTIVATE
ENCHANTED RAPT HAGGED CAPTIVE
ENCHANTER MAUGIS CHARMER MAGICIAN MALAGIGI ARCHIMAGE

ENCHANTING ORPHIC WIZARD HEAVENLY SPELLFUL
ENCHANTMENT HEX TAKE CHARM FAIRY MAGIC SPELL SPOKE CARACT CHANTRY DEVILRY GRAMARY SORCERY SORTIARY WITCHERY
ENCHANTRESS CIRCE FAIRY MEDEA ACRASIA URGANDA
ENCHARGE ENJOIN ENTRUST
ENCHASE INFIX ENRICH ENGRAVE
ENCHIRIDION MANUAL HANDBOOK TREATISE
ENCHORIAL NATIVE DEMOTIC DOMESTIC
ENCIPHER CODE CIPHER ENCRYPT
ENCIRCLE ORB BAND BELT BIND CLIP COIL GIRD GIRT HALO HOOP PALE RING RINK STEM WIRE ZONE BELAY BESET BRACE CLASP CROWN EMBAY EMBOW GIRTH HEDGE INORB ROUND TWINE TWIST BECLIP CIRCLE EMBALL ENGIRT ENLACE ENRING ENWIND FATHOM GIRDLE IMPALE SWATHE WRITHE BETREND COMPASS EMBRACE ENCLAVE ENCLOSE ENTWINE ENVIRON ENWHEEL SERPENT WREATHE CINCTURE CORSELET ENSPHERE IMMANTLE SURROUND
ENCIRCLED GIRT CINCT BELTED SUCCINCT
ENCIRCLEMENT EMBRACE
ENCIRCLING AROUND EMBRACE CORONARY ENCYCLIC
(PREF.) AMPLEXI
ENCLAVE INLIER
(— IN SOUTH AFRICA) BANTUSTAN
ENCLOAK MANTLE
ENCLOSE IN BAY BOX CAN HEM LAP MEW ORB PAR PEN PIN RIM BANK BUNG CAGE CASE COOP FORT GIRD HAIN HOOP PALE SPAR TINE WALL WARD WOMB YARD BOSOM BOUND BOWER BRICK CHEST CLOSE DITCH EMBAR EMBED EMBOX FENCE FRAME GARTH GRIPE HEDGE HOUSE IMBED INURN BOUGHT CARTON CASTLE CAVERN CIRCLE CORDON CORRAL EMBANK EMBOSS EMPALE EMPARK EMPLOY ENCASE ENCYST ENFOLD ENGULF ENLOCK FASTEN IMMURE IMPALE IMPARK INCASE INCLIP INHOOP INSACK INWALL JACKET PICKET POCKET TACKLE APPROVE CAPSULE COMPASS CONFIDE CONTAIN CURTAIN EMBOSOM EMBWELL EMBOWER EMBRACE ENCHASE ENCLAVE ENGLOBE ENHEDGE ENVELOP HARNESS IMBOSOM IMMERSE IMPOUND INBOUND INCLUDE INFIELD PARROCK PINFOLD SHEATHE BULKHEAD COMPRISE COMPRIZE CONCLUDE CONVOLVE EMBORDER ENCIRCLE ENSHRINE ENSPHERE IMPRISON LANDLOCK PALISADE PARCLOSE SURROUND
(— IN ARMOR) EMPANOPLY
(— LOGS) CRIB

ENCLOSED BOUND CLOSED OBTECT INGROWN INTERNAL
ENCLOSING LIMITARY
(PREF.) PERI
ENCLOSURE HAG HAW HOK MEW PAR PEN REE STY TYE BAWN BOMA BYTH CAGE CAVE CELL COOP DOCK FOLD HAIN HOCK HOPE KILN LIST PALE PEEL SEPT SKIT SLOT TIGH TOWN WALL WEIR YARD ALTIS ATAJO BASIN BLIND BOOLY BOOTH BOSOM CAROL CLOSE COURT CRAWL CREEP CUBBY FENCE FRANK GARTH GOTRA HOARD KENCH KRAAL LOBBY MARAI PLECK POUND REEVE STALL STELL AVIARY BOOLEY BOXING CANCHA CARREL CORRAL COWPEN CRUIVE DRYLOT GARDEN HURDLE INTAKE KENNEL OUTSET PALING PRISON SERAIL TAMBOR TEOPAN TINING VIVARY WARREN BELLOWS BOROUGH BULLPEN CLOSURE COCKPIT EMBRACE GALLERY GONDOLA HAINING HENNERY HOUSING HUMIDOR LANTERN PADDOCK PIGHTLE PUDDOCK SEVERAL STUFFER TAMBOUR AEDICULA CASEMATE CHIPYARD CINCTURE CLAPNEST CLAUSURE CLOISTER COMPOUND DELUBRUM ENCEINTE ENCHASER PARADISE POUNDAGE PRECINCT PURPRISE SEPIMENT SERAGLIO SKIRTING STOCKADE VIVARIUM
(— ABOUT ALTAR) BEMA
(— FOR BOWLING) ALLEY
(— FOR COCKPIT) CANOPY
(— FOR FISH) CROY YAIR YARE KENCH SPILLER SPILLET
(— FOR JURY) BOX
(— FOR KNIGHTLY ENCOUNTERS) BARRACE
(— FOR LIGHT) LANTERN
(— FOR ROASTING ORE) STALL
(— OF HOUSE) RAWN
(— SURROUNDED BY DITCH) COP
(ELEPHANT —) KEDDAH
(OBLONG —) CIRCUS
(PORTABLE —) PLAYPEN
(POULTRY —) HENNERY
(SACRED —) SECOS SEKOS
(PREF.) CLAUSTRO SEPTATO
(SUFF.) SEPTATE
ENCOLPION PANAGIA
ENCOMIAST EULOGIST
ENCOMIUM ELOGE ENCOMY EULOGY PRAISE PLAUDIT TRIBUTE PANEGYRIC
ENCOMPASS BEGO BELT CLIP GIRD PALE RING SPAN WALL WRAP BELIE BERUN BESET BIGAN BRACE CLOSE CROWN ROUND BEGIRD BEGIRT CIRCLE ENGIRD BESEIGE COMPASS EMBOWEL EMBRACE ENCLOSE ENVIRON INCLUDE SUBSUME UMBESET CINCTURE ENCIRCLE ENGIRDLE PURPRISE SURROUND
(— WITH ARMS) FATHOM
ENCOMPASSED AMID BAYED AMIDST BEGIRT

ENCOMPASSING ROUND AMBIENT CINCTURE PROFOUND INCLUSIVE
ENCORE BIS AGAIN ANCORA RECALL REPEAT
ENCOUNTER BIDE BUMP COIL COPE FACE FIND KEEP MEET MOOT RINK BRUSH CLOSE FIGHT FORCE GREET INCUR OCCUR ONSET SHOCK STOUR VENUE ACCOST AFFRAY ANSWER ASSAIL ATTACK BATTLE BREAST CAREER COMBAT JOSTLE JUSTLE OPPOSE RUFFLE ADDRESS AFFRONT CONTEST COUNTER DISPUTE HOSTING JOINING PASSAGE CONFLICT CONFRONT CONGRESS REANSWER RECONTER SKIRMISH COLLISION
(— HOSTILELY) CROSS
(HOSTILE —) CLOSE
(PUGILISTIC —) MILL
ENCOURAGE DAW EGG ABET BACK FIRM URGE BOOST CHEER ERECT FAVOR FLUSH HEART IMPEL NERVE SERVE STEEL ADVISE ASSURE EXHORT FOMENT FOSTER HALLOO HARDEN INCITE INDUCE INVITE NUZZLE REHETE SECOND SPIRIT UPHOLD ADVANCE ANIMATE CHERISH COMFORT CONFIRM CONSOLE ENFORCE ENLIVEN FLATTER FORTIFY FORWARD HEARTEN INSPIRE PROMOTE STOMACH UPCHEER UPRAISE EMBOLDEN INSPIRIT REASSURE
ENCOURAGED BUCKED CONFIRMED
ENCOURAGEMENT BOOST FLUSH HURRAH COMFORT FOMENTO IMPETUS BLESSING SANCTION
ENCOURAGING HELPFUL FAVORING
ENCRATITE TATIAN AQUARIAN
ENCROACH JET PINCH POACH IMPOSE INVADE TRENCH IMPINGE INTRUDE SHINGLE ENTRENCH INFRINGE INTRENCH TRESPASS
ENCROACHING INVASIVE
ENCROACHMENT BREACH INROAD ENCROACH INVASION
ENCRUST CAKE CANDY BARKEN BARKLE INCRUST
ENCRUSTED CAKED SCABROUS
ENCUMBER CLOG LOAD PACK BESET CHECK CROWD TRASH ACCLOY BEMOIL BURDEN FELTER HAMPER HINDER IMPEDE LUMBER MITHER MOIDER RETARD SADDLE WEIGHT BEPAPER INVOLVE OPPRESS ACCUMBER ENTANGLE HANDICAP OBSTRUCT OVERCOME OVERLOAD
ENCUMBERED HEAVY CONGESTED
ENCUMBRANCE CLOG LIEN LOAD CLAIM BURDEN CHARGE CUMBER TROUBLE MORTGAGE ALBATROSS
ENCYCLICAL PASCENDI
ENCYCLOPEDIA TOME
(GAME —) HOYLE
ENCYSTED CYSTIC SACCATE SACCATED
END EN AIM DAG EAR FAG TIP

BUTT DATE DOUP FACE FATE
FINE FOOT GOAL HALT HEEL LAST
MAIN MARK SAKE STOP TAIL
TERM VIEW AMEND ARTHA
BLOCK BREAK CAUSE CEASE
CLOSE DEATH ENSUE EVENT
FINIS ISSUE LIMIT LOOSE NAPOO
OMEGA POINT PRICK RAISE
SCOPE SCRAP SHANK START
STASH THULE DECIDE DEFINE
DESIGN DOMINO EFFECT EFFLUX
ENDING EXITUS EXPIRE EXPIRY
FINALE FINISH INTENT NAPOOH
OBJECT PERIOD RESULT THIRTY
UPSHOT UTMOST WINDUP
ABOLISH ACHIEVE CLOSURE
CURTAIN DESTROY FANTAIL
FINANCE LINEMAN MEANING
OUTGIVE PURPOSE REMNANT
BOUNDARY COMPLETE
CONCLUDE DESITION DISSOLVE
FINALITY SURCEASE TERMINAL
TERMINUS ULTIMATE
(— DEBATE) CLOTURE
(— OF ANTENNA) CLAVA
(— OF ANVIL) BICKIRON
(— OF ARCHERY PILE) STOPPING
(— OF ARROW) NOCK
(— OF BEEF LOIN) BUTT
(— OF BLANKET) DAGON
(— OF BONE) EPIPHYSIS
(— OF BOOM) JAW
(— OF BOW) EAR
(— OF BRICK) HEADING
(— OF BRISTLE) FLAG
(— OF BUILDING) GABLE
(— OF CAN) BREAST
(— OF CANE) FRAZE
(— OF CART) TIB
(— OF CRESCENT) HORN
(— OF EAR CANAL) AMPULLA
(— OF EGG) DOUP
(— OF EXISTENCE) DEMISE
(— OF FABRIC) FENT
(— OF FISHHOOK) SPEAR
(— OF FLAG) FLY
(— OF FROG) TOE
(— OF HALTER) CAPITULUM
(— OF HAMMER) CLAW POLL
(— OF HAMMERHEAD) PEEN
(— OF HORSE-COLLAR) GULLET
(— OF INGOT) CROP
(— OF KEEL) GRIPE
(— OF LEVER) FORK
(— OF LOAF) HEEL
(— OF MINE TUNNEL) FACE
(— OF MINERAL LODE) SLOVAN
(— OF MINING LEVEL) DEAN
(— OF MUZZLE) MUFFLE
(— OF NAIL) CLENCH
(— OF ONE'S LIFE) DOOM
(— OF PIER) CUTWATER
(— OF PIPE) TAFT SPIGOT
(— OF POCKETKNIFE HANDLE)
BOLSTER
(— OF RAILROAD CAR) BEND
(— OF ROAD) ROADHEAD
(— OF ROD) FORKHEAD
(— OF SHEEP SHEARING) CUTOUT
(— OF SHIP) STERN
(— OF SPINE) ACRUMION
(— OF TENON) HAUNCH
(— OF TOOL) BUTT

(— OF UTERUS) FUNDUS
(— OF WORLD) PRALAYA
(— OF YARD) ARM YARDARM
(— ON) ABUT
(— ON POND) FOREBAY
(—S OF RIBBONS) FATTRELS
(—S OF SATURN'S RINGS) ANSA
(CANDLE —) DOUP SNUFF
(DOMINO —) ACE
(FAG —) RUMP
(HANGING —) DAG DAGGE
(JAGGED —) SHRAG
(NARROWED —) NEB
(NORTH — OF COMPASS NEEDLE)
LILY
(POINTED —) APEX
(POSTERIOR —) BOTTOM
(REEF —S) DEADMAN
(ROPE'S —) COLT FEAZE PIGTAIL
FEAZINGS
(SPECIAL —) SAKE
(TAPERING —) POINT
(TATTERED —) FRAZZLE
(ULTIMATE —) SUM TELOS
(UNPLEASANT —) GRIEF
(UPPER —) HEAD
(WARP —S) ACCIDENTAL
(PREF.) ACR(O) FINI TEL(IO)
ENDANGER DANGER HAZARD
IMPERIL SCUPPER
ENDANGERED BESTED BESTEAD
FRAUGHT
ENDANGERER MARPLOT
ENDEARMENT LOVE CARESS
ENDEAVOR DO AIM PUT TRY WIN
BEST MINT SEEK WORK ASSAY
ESSAY ETTLE EXERT OFFER
STUDY TEMPT TRIAL AFFAIR
ASSAIL DEVOIR EFFORT INTEND
STRIFE STRIVE AFFORCE
ATTEMPT CONATUS CONTEND
CULTURE EMPRISE EMULATE
IMITATE MOLIMEN NITENCY
WORKING EXERTION PURCHASE
STRUGGLE
(— TO CONCLUSION) STUDY
(BEST —) DEVOIR
(EARNESTLY —) FEND
ENDED DONE OVER PAST FINISHED
(— BY CONSONANT) CHECKED
ENDEMIC LOCAL ENDEMIAL
ENDING END CLOSE DEATH GRAVE
FINALE BREAKUP FINANCE
DESITION
(NERVE —) SPINDLE
ENDIVE CHICORY WITLOOF
ESCAROLE SCARIOLE
ENDLESS ANANTA ETERNE
ETERNAL FOREVER UNDYING
UNENDED UNENDLY DATELESS
FINELESS IMMORTAL INFINITE
UNENDING
ENDMOST TIPMOST FARTHEST
REMOTEST
ENDOCARP STONE PYRENA
PUTAMEN
ENDOGENOUS INNATE
AUTOGENIC
ENDOMORPHIC PYCNIC PYKNIC
ENDOPITE PETASMA
ENDOPLEURA TEGMEN
ENDORSE BACK SIGN ADOPT
BOOST DOCKET ENDOSS SECOND

APPROVE CERTIFY INDORSE
SPONSOR SUPPORT ADVOCATE
SANCTION RECOMMEND
ENDORSEE HOLDER
ENDORSEMENT FIAT FORM VISA
RIDER BACKING APPROVAL
HECHSHER SANCTION
ENDOSPERM FARINA ALBUMEN
ENDOSPORIUM INTINE
ENDOW DOW DUE DOTE GIFT
RENT VEST BLESS CROWN
DOWER ENDUE EQUIP FOUND
INDUE SEIZE STATE STUFF
ASSIGN CLOTHE DOTATE ENABLE
ENRICH ENSOUL ESTATE INVEST
CHARTER ENLARGE FURNISH
INSTATE APPANAGE BENEFICE
BEQUEATH ENTALENT
(— WITH FORCE) DYNAMIZE
ENDOWED ABLE GIFTED FAVORED
ENDOWMENT CLAY FINE GIFT
WAKF WAQF DOWER DOWRY
GRACE CORPSE GENIUS TALENT
APANAGE CHANTRY CHARISM
FACULTY APPANAGE DOTATION
PATRIMONY BENEFACTION
(NATURAL —S) BUMP DOTES
TALENT
(PL.) ALTARAGE
ENDPAPER FLYLEAF
ENDPIECE BRACE CHUMP
(— OF STETHOSCOPE) BELL
ENDUE DUE ENDOW INDUE TEACH
CLOTHE INVEST INSTRUCT
ENDURABLE LIVABLE BEARABLE
LIVEABLE PORTABLE
ENDURANCE GAME LAST TACK
PLUCK BOTTOM BEARING
COMFORT DURANCE GRANITE
LASTING STAMINA BEARANCE
DURATION GAMENESS HARDSHIP
PATIENCE STRENGTH
ENDURE GO ABY SIT VIE ABYE
BEAR BIDE DREE DURE HOLD
KEEP LAST TAKE TIDE WEAR
ABEAR ABIDE ALLOW BROOK
CARRY DRIVE POUCH SPARE
STAND STICK STOUT THOLE
TOUGH WIELD ABROOK ACCEPT
DRUDGE HARDEN REMAIN
SUFFER ABROOKE COMFORT
FORBEAR PERSIST STOMACH
SUPPORT SUSTAIN SWALLOW
TOUGHEN UNDERGO WEARING
CONTINUE FOREBEAR TOLERATE
ENDURING FAST SURE STOUT
BIDING DURING STABLE STURDY
ABIDING DURABLE ETERNAL
LASTING PATIENT IMMORTAL
REMANENT STUBBORN
PERENNIAL
ENDWAYS ANEND ENDWISE
ENDYMION (DAUGHTER OF —)
EURYDICE
(FATHER OF —) ZEUS JUPITER
AETHELIUS
(MOTHER OF —) CALYCE
(SON OF —) EPEUS PAEON
AETOLUS
(WIFE OF —) CROMIA ASTERODIA
HYPARIPPE
ENEMA CLYSMA CLYSTER
LAVEMENT

ENEMY FOE AXIS BOYG FEID DEVIL
FIEND SATAN FOEMAN HOSTILE
CONTRARY OPPONENT
(— OF MANKIND) DEVIL FIEND
SATAN
(PERSONAL —) HATER
**ENEMY OF THE PEOPLE (AUTHOR
OF —)** IBSEN
(CHARACTER IN —) KIIL PETER
MORTEN HORSTER HOVSTAD
ASLAKSEN STOCKMANN
ENERGETIC BUSY FAST FELL HARD
LIVE RASH BRISK DASHY LUSTY
PITHY STOUT TIGHT VITAL YAULD
ZIPPY ACTIVE HEARTY HUSTLE
LIVELY SPROIL ACTIOUS ANIMOSO
ARDUOUS DASHING DRIVING
DYNAMIC ENERGIC FURIOUS
NERVOUS PUSHFUL PUSHING
VIBRANT EMPHATIC ENERGICO
FORCEFUL FORCIBLE HUSTLING
VIGOROUS
(— PERSON) TOWSER
ENERGETICALLY MANLY
FURIOUSLY
ENERGID PROTOPLAST
ENERGIZE EXCITE ANIMATE
ENERGIZING KINETIC VIRTUAL
ENERGY U W GO PEP VIM ZIP
BANG BENT BIRR DASH EDGE
JASM LIFE SAKT SNAP TUCK ZING
ARDOR ECLAT FORCE INPUT
NERVE POWER STEAM VIGOR
EFFORT FOISON INTAKE ORGONE
OUTPUT SPIRIT SPRAWL SPRING
SPROIL STARCH VIRTUE POTENCY
SPIRITS ACTIVITY AMBITION
DYNAMISM ENERGEIA MOTIVITY
PRAKRITI STRENGTH VIVACITY
(— PEAK) NUCLEUS
(EMOTIONAL —) LIBIDO
(LIBINAL —) CATHEXIS
(LIFE —) JIVA SAKTI SHAKTI
(LIGHT —) RAD
(MENTAL —) DOCITY PSYCHURGY
(POTENTIAL —) ERGAL
(QUANTUM OF —) PLASMON
(RADIANT —) SOUND ACTINISM
EINSTEIN
(VITAL —) HORME PANZOISM
(PREF.) (RADIANT —) PENETRO
(SOLAR -) HELI(O)
ENERVATE SAP COOK FLAG MELT
SOFTEN WEAKEN MOLLIFY
UNNERVE UNSINEW ENFEEBLE
ENERVATED BEDRID EFFETE
LANGUID BEDRIDDEN
ENERVATING MUGGY DREARY
ENERVATION COLLAPSE
ENFEEBLE NUMB FAINT SHAKE
APPALL DEADEN FEEBLE IMPAIR
SOFTEN WEAKEN DEPRESS
UNSINEW AFFEEBLE ENERVATE
IMBECILE UNSTRONG
ENFEEBLED FEY NUMB
ENFOLD (ALSO SEE INFOLD) LAP
FURL ROLL WRAP CLASP COVER
DRAPE ENROL IMPLY COMPLY
ENLACE ENROLL ENWIND
ENWRAP INCLIP INFOLD INWIND
SHADOW SWATHE WATTLE
EMBRACE ENCLOSE ENVELOP
ENVIRON INCLUDE INVOLVE

UMBELAP CONVOLVE
ENFORCE BULL LEVY EXACT FORCE
PRESS COERCE COMPEL EFFECT
FOLLOW INVOKE EXECUTE
IMPLANT
ENFORCED COMPULSORY
ENFORCER EXECUTOR
MUSCLEMAN
ENFRAMEMENT CARTOUCH
ENG AGMA
ENGAGE DIP WED BOOK BUSY
GAGE HAVE HIRE JOIN LIST MESH
RENT SIGN TAKE WAGE AGREE
AMUSE CATCH ENTER LEASE
PITCH TRADE TRYST ABSORB
ARREST EMBARK EMPLOY ENLIST
INDUCE OBLIGE OCCUPY PLEDGE
PLIGHT BESPEAK BETROTH
CONCERN CONDUCE CONSUME
ENGROSS IMMERSE INVOLVE
PROMISE AFFIANCE CONTRACT
COVENANT ENTANGLE INTEREST
INTRIGUE PERSUADE PREOCCUPY
(— DEEPLY) DROWN
(— IN) GO CUT SUE HAVE JOIN
LEAD PROSECUTE
(— IN ARGUMENT) BALK BAULK
(— IN COMBAT) DEBATE STRIKE
(— IN DEBATE) STONEWALL
(— IN DISCUSSION) CONTEND
(— IN PRANKS) LARK
(— IN TILT) JUST JOUST
(— WHOLLY) ABSORB CONSUME
IMMERSE
(SUFF.) (— IN) IZE
ENGAGED DENT DUGY FAGT GONE
HIRED ACTIVE BONDED BOOKED
MESHED ASSURED BESPOKE
EARNEST ENTERED PLEDGED
TOKENED VERSANT ABSORBED
ATTACHED EMBEDDED
EMPLOYED INSERTED INTEREST
INVOLVED OCCUPIED PROMISED
(— IN) ABOUT
(— IN CONTROVERSY) DISPUTANT
(MENTALLY —) VERSANT
(WARMLY —) ZEALOUS
ENGAGEMENT AVAL DATE COWLE
SPURN ACTION AFFAIR BATTLE
COMBAT ESCROW PLIGHT
STANZA SURETY BARGAIN
BOOKING DUSTING SERVICE
CONFLICT RETAINER SKIRMISH
WARRANTY
(— TO MARRY) TRYST
(MILITARY —) DO SHOW
(SHORT —) SNAP
(SINGLE —) GIG
(THEATRICAL —) SHOP
(WRITTEN —) COWLE
ENGAGING SOFT SAPID SWEET
TAKING
ENGENDER BEGET BREED CAUSE
EXCITE GENDER DEVELOP
PRODUCE GENERATE INGENDER
OCCASION
ENGIDU EABANI
ENGINE GAS JET SIX FOUR GOAT
TANK EIGHT JINNY MOTOR OILER
STEAM BANKER DIESEL DOCTOR
DUDLER DUDLEY INGENE JORDAN
KICKER PUFFER RADIAL ROADER
YARDER MACHINE POACHER

POTCHER SKIDDER STEAMER
TRACTOR TURBINE BULLGINE
COMPOUND DOLLBEER
EXPANDER GASOLINE IMPULSOR
(— FOR HAULING LOGS) DUDLER
DUDLEY
(— FOR THROWING MISSILES) GIN
PETRARY SPRINGAL
(— OF TORTURE) GIN RACK
(— OF WAR) RAM SWEEP
HELEPOLE
(AIRPLANE —) SCRAMJET
(DONKEY —) DOCTOR
(FIRE —) TUB
(JET —) ATHODYD
(MILITARY —) BOAR TOWER
BRICOL FABRIC TREPAN BRICOLE
DONDINE PERRIER PETRARY
TORMENT WARWOLF BALLISTA
DONDAINE MANGONEL MARTINET
SCORPION
(RAILROAD —) HOG GOAT YARDER
SWITCHER
(REACTION —) THRUSTER
THRUSTOR
(ROCKET —) ARCJET VERNIER
(TYPE OF ROTARY —) WANKEL
ENGINEER PLAN GUIDE DRIVER
FANNER HOGGER MANAGE
SAPPER HOGHEAD PLANNER
PLOTTER CONTRIVE DESIGNER
INGENIER INVENTOR MANEUVER
AMERICAN AMY BURR BUSH DORR
DUNN EADS HERR HILL KRUG
LAKE PECK RICE ALLEN CARTY
ELLET GANTT HAUPT LAMME
MILLS MOORE OWENS PRATT
STOUT ARNOLD BOGART CONRAD
COOPER COWLES CRAVEN FERRIS
GREENE HAMMER HOLLEY HOLLIS
HOUDRY HUTTON JACOBY
LAMONT LITTLE MORGAN
NEWELL PARKER PENDER PORTER
RUMSEY WILSON BALDWIN
BARRELL BEHREND CLEMSON
CROCKER FANNING FREEMAN
GODFREY HASWELL KINEALY
KINTNER KNOWLES LATROBE
LEONARD PACKARD PARSONS
PATRICK SERRELL STRAUSS
WHIPPLE AMSTRUTZ EDGERTON
ELLSBERG ERICSSON GOETHALS
HARRISON HARTNESS HUNSAKER
KENNELLY MCALPINE OVINGTON
REYNOLDS RICHARDS ROEBLING
ARMSTRONG CARPENTER
GILLESPIE KETTERING STEINMETZ
TRAUTWINE FARNSWORTH
LINDENTHAL RIESENBERG
STRICKLAND WORTHINGTON
ALEXANDERSON BRECKENRIDGE
AUSTRALIAN CLAPP
AUSTRIAN BIRAGO ENGERTH
MANNLICHER
CANADIAN KLOTZ
CUBAN MENOCAL
CZECH SKODA
DANISH POULSEN
DUTCH MUSSERT
ENGLISH FOX AIRD PAUL BAKER
BOYLE CLARK COOKE GOOCH
GROVE KEMPE MANCE ROYCE
AYRTON BRAMAH BRUNEL

CLARKE CUBITT DONKIN FOWLER
HARRIS HEDGES MCADAM
BERKLEY BOULTON CAUTLEY
DUDDELL FLEMING HARTLEY
MURDOCK SMEATON ANDERSON
BRINDLEY BUCHANAN CRAMPTON
FERRANTI HAWKSHAW
REDMAYNE GREATHEAD
GRIFFITHS HOPKINSON
WILLCOCKS WIMSHURST
HORNBLOWER TREVITHICK
BRAITHWAITE FITZMAURICE
FRENCH LAME ARCON MALUS
PRONY BERTIN CHAPPE CUGNOT
DEPREZ EIFFEL LEPLAY MARTIN
RATEAU RIQUET ALPHAND
BELIDOR BERLIER BERNARD
BIERIOT CLERGET GIFFARD
LEBLANC LENFANT TELLIER
BELGRAND PONCELET
FOURNEYRON HENNEBIQUE
GERMAN BACH BENZ BOSCH
KNORR CRELLE DIESEL GERBER
LANGEN CARNALL CULMANN
DAIMLER SIEMENS FLETTNER
EYTELWEIN LILIENTHAL
BAUERNFEIND GOLDSCHMIDT
HASELWANDER
ITALIAN VINCI CODAZZI FABRONI
MARCONI
POLISH NARUTOWICZ
RUSSIAN THEREMIN
SCOTTISH BARR BELL WATT
CLERK ELDER EWING MURRAY
NAPIER RANKINE TELFORD
BRUNLEES FAIRBAIRN
STEVENSON SYMINGTON
SPANISH CIERVA
SWEDISH LAVAL POLHEM BRINELL
DAHLBERG
SWISS ILG FAVRE
ENGINEMAN HOISTER HOISTMAN
ENGINERY TIRE
ENGIRDLED CINCT
ENGLAND HOME ALBION LOGRIA
BLIGHTY BRITAIN LOEGRIA
HOMELAND

ENGLAND

AIRFORCE: RAF
BAY: TOR LYME WASH START
MOUNTS BIGBURY BIDEFORD
CARDIGAN FALMOUTH
TREMADOC WEYMOUTH
CAPITAL: LONDON
CHANNEL: SOLENT BRISTOL
ENGLISH SPITHEAD
CHANNEL ISLAND: HERM SARK
JERSEY ALDERNEY GUERNSEY
COIN: ORA RIAL RYAL ACKEY
ANGEL CROWN GROAT NOBLE
PENCE PENNY POUND SPRAT
UNITE BAWBEE FLORIN GUINEA
SESKIN TESTON ANGELET
CAROLUS HAPENNY TUPPENY
FARTHING SHILLING SIXPENCE
TUPPENCE
CONSERVATIVE: TORY
COUNTY: KENT DEVON ESSEX
HANTS NOTTS SALOP WIGHT
DORSET DURHAM LONDON
SURREY SUSSEX NORFOLK
RUTLAND SUFFOLK CHESHIRE

CORNWALL SOMERSET
DANCE: MORRIS
FIRTH: SOLWAY
FOREST: ARDEN EXMOOR
DARTMOOR SHERWOOD
HEAD: SPURN BEACHY FORMBY
LIZARD CEMMAES TREVOSE
HILLS: MENDIP BRENDON CHEVIOT
MALVERN CHILTERN
COTSWOLD
INVADER: DANE PICT ROMAN
SAXON NORMAN
ISLAND: HOLY LUNDY WIGHT
COQUET MERSEA THANET
TRESCO WALNEY BARDSEY
HAYLING IRELAND SHEPPEY
ANGLESEA ANGLESEY
FOULNESS HOLYHEAD
ISLANDS: FARNE SCILLY CHANNEL
KING: HAL LUD BRAN BRUT CNUT
COLE KNUT LEAR HENRY JAMES
SWEYN ALFRED BLADUD
BRUTUS CANUTE EDWARD
EGBERT GEORGE ARTEGAL
ELIDURE RICHARD WILLIAM
GORBODUC
LAKE: CONISTON
LIBERAL: WHIG
MEASURE: CUT ELL LEA MIL PIN
ROD RUN TON TUN VAT ACRE
BIND BOLL BUTT CADE COMB
COOM CRAN FOOT GILL GOAD
HAND HANK HEER HIDE INCH
LAST LINE MILE NAIL PACE
PALM PECK PINT PIPE POLE
POOL ROOD ROPE SACK SEAM
SPAN TRUG TYPP WIST YARD
YOKE BODGE CABOT CHAIN
COOMB CUBIT DIGIT FLOAT
FLOOR FLUID HUTCH JUGUM
MINIM OUNCE PERCH POINT
PRIME QUART SKEIN STACK
TRUSS BARREL BOVATE BUSHEL
CRANNE FATHOM FIRKIN
GALLON HOBBET HOBBIT
LEAGUE MANENT OXGANG
POTTLE RUNLET SECOND
SQUARE STRIKE SULUNG
THREAD TIERCE AUCHLET
FURLONG KENNING QUARTER
RUNDLET SEAMILE SPINDLE
TERTIAN VIRGATE CARUCATE
CHALDRON HOGSHEAD
LANDYARD PUNCHEON
QUADRANT QUARTERN
STANDARD
MOUNTAIN: PEAK SCAFELL
SKIDDAW SNOWDON
MOUNTAINS: BLACK PENNINE
SNOWDON CAMBRIAN
CUMBRIAN
NAME: ALBION BRITAIN
BRITANNIA
PENINSULA: PORTLAND
POINT: NAZE LYNAS MORTE SALES
DODMAN LIZARD PRAWLE
HARTLAND LANDSEND
GIBRALTAR
POLICEMAN: BOBBY COPPER
PEELER
RACE TRACK: ASCOT
RESORT: BATH BRIGHTON
BLACKPOOL

RIVER: CAM DEE DON ESK EXE LEA NEN URE WYE AIRE AVON EDEN LUNE NENE NIDD OUSE PENK TAME TEES TILL TYNE WEAR YARE ANKER COLNE DEBEN STOUR SWALE TAMAR TAWAR TRENT TWEED HUMBER KENNET MERSEY RIBBLE ROTHER SEVERN THAMES WENSUM WHARFE WITHAM DERWENT PARRETT WAVENEY WELLAND TORRIDGE

ROCKS: MANACLES

ROYAL HOUSE: YORK TUDOR STUART HANOVER WINDSOR LANCASTER PLANTAGENET

SCHOOL: ETON RUGBY HARROW

SEA: IRISH NORTH

SETTLER: JUTE PICT ANGLE SAXON NORMAN

SOLDIER: TOMMY REDCOAT FUSILEER

STRAIT: DOVER

TOWN: ELY BATH DEAL HULL RYDE WARE YORK BLYTH BRENT DERBY DOVER ERITH FLINT LEEDS RIPON TRURO WIGAN BARNET BOLTON BOOTLE CAMDEN DURHAM EALING EXETER HANLEY JARROW LEYTON LONDON OLDHAM OXFORD YEOVIL BRISTOL BROMLEY BURNLEY CHELSEA CROYDON ENFIELD GRIMSBY HALIFAX HORNSEY IPSWICH LAMBETH NEWPORT NORWICH PRESTON SALFORD SEAFORD WESTHAM BRADFORD BRIGHTON CORNWALL COVENTRY DEWSBURY HASTINGS PLYMOUTH ROCHDALE WALLASEY WALLSALL GREENWICH LIVERPOOL SHEFFIELD BIRMINGHAM MANCHESTER

TRIBE: ICENI

UNIVERSITY: LONDON OXFORD CAMBRIDGE

VALLEY: COOM EDEN TEES TYNE COMBE COOMB COQUET

WEIGHT: BAG KIP TOD TON KEEL LAST MAST MAUN BARGE FAGOT GRAIN MAUND POUND SCORE STAND STONE TRUSS BUSHEL CENTAL FANGOT FIRKIN FOTHER FOTMAL POCKET QUARTER QUINTAL SARPLER

ENGLISH SAXON AUSTRAL BRITISH ENGLAND SAXONISH SOUTHRON STANDARD
(— DIALECT IN LIVERPOOL) SCOUSE
(— MIXED WITH SPANISH) SPANGLISH
(IN —) ANGLICE
(PREF.) ANGLO

ENGLISHMAN SAXON BRITON BRONCO GODDAM GRINGO JOHNNY ROOINEK MACARONI SOUTHRON ENGLISHER

ENGLISHWOMAN INGLESA

ENGORGE GLUT GORGE DEVOUR SWALLOW

ENGRAFT INSET

ENGRAM TRACE
(— PATTERN) MEANING

ENGRAVE CUT ETCH RIST CARVE CHASE GRAVE HATCH PRINT SCULP CHISEL INCISE SCULPT CRIBBLE ENCHASE EXARATE IMPRESS IMPRINT INSCULP STIPPLE INSCRIBE ORNAMENT

ENGRAVED GRAVEN GRAPHIC INCISED
(PREF.) GRAPTO

ENGRAVER POINT CHASER ETCHER GRAVER ARTISAN INSCULP BURINIST MEDALIST SCULLION WRIGGLER
(— OF STONES) LAPIDARY

ENGRAVING CUT PRINT SCULP STAMP GRAVERY GRAVING GRAVURE WOODCUT AQUATINT DRYPOINT HATCHING INTAGLIO LINEWORK MEZZOTINT
(PREF.) GLYPHO GLYPT(O)

ENGROSS BURY SINK SOAK AMASS GROSS ABSORB ENGAGE ENROLL ENWRAP OCCUPY SCROLL COLLECT CONSUME IMMERSE INVOLVE PREOCCUPY

ENGROSSED DEEP FULL RAPT INTENT BEMUSED WRAPPED ABSORBED IMMERSED PREOCCUPIED

ENGULF GULF ABYSM ABYSS SOUSE SWAMP WHELM ABSORB DEVOUR INVADE QUELME SLOUGH ENGORGE SWALLOW SUBMERGE

ENHANCE FOIL LIFT BUILD ENARM ENDOW EXALT RAISE DEEPEN AUGMENT ELEVATE ENLARGE EXHANCE GREATEN IMPROVE SHARPEN HEIGHTEN INCREASE

ENHANCEMENT SAKE

ENHYDRA LATAX

ENID (HUSBAND OF —) GERAINT

ENIGMA WHY EGMA GRIPH REBUS PUZZLE RIDDLE SPHINX GRIPHUS MYSTERY PROBLEM PROVERB

ENIGMATIC HUMAN MYSTIC CRYPTIC OBSCURE ELLIPTIC MYSTICAL ORACULAR PUZZLING RIDDLING

ENJAMBMENT OVERFLOW

ENJOIN BID JOIN WILL ENIUN ORDER CHARGE DECREE DIRECT FORBID COMMAND DICTATE REQUIRE ADMONISH PROHIBIT

ENJOY GO JOY FAIN HAVE LIKE BROOK FANCY PROVE SAVOR TASTE WIELD ADMIRE DEVOUR GROOVE RELISH DELIGHT
(— ONESELF) FEAST LAUGH

ENJOYABLE GOOD FRUITY AMIABLE BLESSED CAPITAL GLORIOUS SAVOROUS SPLENDID

ENJOYING FRUITIVE

ENJOYMENT FUN JOY USE BANG BASK BOOT EASE GUST KAMA PLAY ZEST FEAST GUSTO LIKING RELISH COMFORT DELIGHT JOLLITY JOYANCE JOYANCY

FELICITY FRUITION PLEASURE SKITTLES
(— FROM OTHERS' TROUBLES) SCHADENFREUDE

ENKINDLE WARM INCENSE INFLAME

ENLARGE ADD EKE BORE GROW HONE HUFF OPEN REAM ROOM BUILD FARCE LARGE SWELL WIDEN BIGGEN BRANCH BROACH DIDUCE DILATE EXPAND EXTEND FRAISE GATHER LARGEN OMNIFY SPREAD AMPLIFY AUGMENT DISTEND ENHANCE GREATEN IMPROVE INGREAT MAGNIFY STRETCH AMPLIATE CUMULATE FLOURISH INCREASE
(— COAL MINE) SNUB

ENLARGED TUMID BLOATED CLUBBED SWELLED SWOLLEN AMPLIATE CAPITATE EXPANDED EXTENDED VARICOSE ACCRESCENT

ENLARGEMENT BULB DISC DISK KNOP NODE CLAVA SWELL BLOWUP BUNION GIBBER GROWTH SCYPHA ENLARGE FOOTING SCYPHUS STATION ANEURYSM INCREASE SWELLING PROPAGATION
(— IN MINE SHAFT) STATION
(— IN MUSCLE) KNOT
(— OF GLAND) GOITER GOITRE
(— OF GULLET) CROP
(— OF MOLD) RAPPAGE
(— OF NERVE FIBER) BOUTON
(— OF ORGAN) STRUMA
(BONY —) SPAVIN SPAVINE
(PREF.) MACR(O) MEG(A) MEGAL(O) PLETHYSMO
(SUFF.) AUXE MEGALY

ENLARGING EVASE SWELLING
(PREF.) MICR(O)

ENLIGHTEN OPEN CLEAR EDIFY TEACH ILLUME INFORM UNSEEL EDUCATE LIGHTEN CIVILIZE ENKINDLE INSTRUCT

ENLIGHTENED WISE LUMINOUS

ENLIGHTENMENT BODHI LIGHT SATORI WISDOM CULTURE INSIGHT SAMADHI AUFKLARUNG

ENLIST DRUM JOIN LEVY SOUD ENROL ENTER HITCH PREST ENGAGE ENROLL INDUCT IMPRESS RECRUIT REGISTER

ENLISTMENT LEVY HITCH PREST LISTING

ENLIVEN DASH JAZZ WARM BRACE BRISK CHEER QUICK RAISE ROUSE KITTLE REVIVE ANIMATE COMFORT INSPIRE REFRESH SMARTEN BRIGHTEN INSPIRIT RECREATE

ENLIVENING GENIAL LIVELY VIVIFIC CHIRPING

ENMESH TRAP CATCH SNARL IMMESH ENSNARE ENTANGLE

ENMITY WAR FEUD SPITE WRAKE ANIMUS HATRED MALICE RANCOR STRIFE FOEHOOD AVERSION

ENNEAGON NONAGON

ENNOBLE LORD EXALT HONOR

NOBLE RAISE GENTLE UPLIFT DIGNIFY ELEVATE GLORIFY GREATEN NOBLIFY SUBLIME

ENNUI BORE TEDIUM ACCIDIE BOREDOM DOLDRUM

ENOCH (FATHER OF —) CAIN JARED
(SON OF —) METHUSALEH

ENOCH ARDEN (AUTHOR OF —) TENNYSON
(CHARACTER IN —) LEE RAY LANE ANNIE ARDEN ENOCH MIRIAM PHILIP

ENORMITY GRAVITY

ENORMOUS BIG GOB HUGE REAM VAST ENORM GREAT HEROIC MIGHTY UNRIDE IMMENSE ABNORMAL COLOSSAL FLAGRANT GIGANTIC WHAPPING WHOPPING

ENOS (FATHER OF —) SETH
(GRANDFATHER OF —) ADAM
(SON OF —) CAINAN

ENOUGH BAS ENOW WELL WHEN AMPLE ASSAI BASTA BELAY ANEUCH PLENTY APLENTY SUFFICE ADEQUATE
(HARDLY —) SKIMP

ENOUNCE STATE UTTER AFFIRM DECLARE PROCLAIM

ENRAGE RAGE ANGER GRIEVE MADDEN INCENSE INFLAME STOMACH

ENRAGED MAD ASHY WODE WOOD ANGRY IRATE LIVID SAVAGE AGRAMED BERSERK CHOLERIC INCENSED MADDENED

ENRAPTURE RAVISH TRANCE ECSTASY ENCHANT ENRAVISH ENTRANCE

ENRAPTURED RAPT ENRAPT TRANCED ECSTATIC

ENRICH FAT BOOT FEED FRET LARD RICH ADORN CROWN ENDOW GUANO BATTEN FATTEN INVEST FEATHER FORTIFY FURNISH GUANIZE INCREASE ORNAMENT TREASURE
(— A GAS) CARBURET
(— A MINE) SALT
(— FUEL MIXTURE) CHOKE

ENRICHED FLORID

ENRICHMENT DITATION

ENROLL BEAR JOIN LIST POLL ENROL ENTER WRITE ATTEST BILLET ENFOLD ENLIST INDUCT MUSTER RECORD ASCRIBE IMPANEL INITIATE INSCRIBE REGISTER

ENROLLMENT LISTING REGISTRY

ENROOT ENRACE IMPLANT

ENSCONCE HIDE COVER SETTLE CONCEAL SHELTER

ENSEMBLE CORPS DECOR WHOLE COSTUME PANTSUIT
(— OF ARMS) ARMORY
(WOMAN'S —) PANTSUIT

ENSHEATHE EMBOSS

ENSHRINE SAINT SHRINE ENCHASE ENTEMPLE

ENSHROUD WRAP

ENSIFORM ENSATE XIPHOID GLADIATE

ENSIGN FLAG IAGO SIGN BADGE COLOR SENYE AQUILA BANNER

BEACON PENNON PISTOL SIGNAL
SYMBOL ALFEREZ ANCIENT
INSIGNE DANEBROG GONFALON
ORIFLAMB PAVILION STANDARD
(—S ARMORIAL) ARMS
(IMPERIAL —) TUT
(JAPANESE —) SUNBURST
(PL.) ENSIGNRY HERALDRY
ENSILE SILO SILAGE
ENSLAVE THEW CHAIN SLAVE
THIRL ENTHRAL NESLAVE
SLAVISH ENTHRALL
ENSLAVED SLAVE THRALL
ENSLAVEMENT DULOSIS SLAVERY
ENSNARE NET WEB GIRN LACE
LIME MESH TOIL TRAP WRAP
BENET CATCH NOOSE SNARE
SNARL ALLURE ATTRAP ENGINE
ENMESH ENTOIL ENTRAP TANGLE
TREPAN BEGUILE DECEIVE
ENGLEIM SNIGGLE SPRINGE
BIRDLIME INVEIGLE OVERTAKE
SURPRISE
ENSNARL ENTANGLE
ENSPHERE INORB SPHERE
ENSTATITE BRONZITE
ENSUE FOLLOW RESULT SUCCEED
(— UPON) SUE
ENSUING NEXT SUING SEQUENT
ENSURE ASSURE INSURE SECURE
BETROTH ESPOUSE WARRANT
AFFIANCE
ENTABLATURE (PART OF —)
CORONA FRIEZE TAENIA CORNICE
CYMATIUM ARCHITRAVE
ENTADA LENS
ENTAIL TAIL INCUR IMPOSE
CONTAIN INVOLVE REQUIRE
TAILZIE
ENTAILED AYNE TAIL EIGNE
ENTAMOEBA LOSCHIA
ENTANGLE ELF LAP MAT TAT WEB
BALL CAST COLL FOUL HARL KNIT
KNOT LIME MESH MIRE TOIL
WRAP BROIL CATCH HALCH
RAVEL SNAFU SNARE SNARL
TWIST BEFOUL COMMIT COTTER
ENGAGE ENLACE ENMESH
ENTRAP ENWRAP FANKLE FELTER
HAMPER HANKLE HATTER
INMAZE INMESH PESTER PUZZLE
RAFFLE RANGLE TACKLE TAIGLE
TANGLE WRAPLE CONFUSE
EMBRAKE EMBROIL ENSNARL
ENTRIKE IMBRIER INVOLVE
PERPLEX TRAMMEL BEWILDER
ENCUMBER IMPESTER INTRIGUE
STRAPPLE
ENTANGLED DEEP FOUL COTTY
TANGLY COMPLEX KNOTTED
IMPLICIT
ENTANGLEMENT FOUL KNOT
TWIT HITCH BUNKER COBWEB
ENTRAIL HEDGEHOG OBSTACLE
PERPLEXITY
ENTASIS SWELL
ENTENTE TREATY ALLIANCE
ENTER BOX DIP SET BEAR BOOK
JOIN POST ADMIT BEGIN BOARD
BREVE ENROL INCUR PROBE
SHARE START ACCEDE APPEAR
BILLET ENGAGE ENLIST ENROLL
ENTRER INCEPT INVADE PIERCE

RECORD SPREAD INGRESS
INTRUDE COMMENCE ENCROACH
INITIATE INSCRIBE NOMINATE
REGISTER PENETRATE
(— BY FORCE) BREAK IRRUPT
INTRUDE
(— DATA) INPUT
(— HASTILY) BULGE
(— IN ATTACK) FORCE
(— IN BOOK) ACCESS
(— IN BOOKS) ACCRUE
(— INFORMATION INTO COMPUTER)
WRITE
(— INTO) JOIN INTERN
(— PROGRAM INTO COMPUTER)
LOAD
(— SLOWLY) SEEP
(— UNNOTICED) CREEP
(— UPON CAREER) INCEPT
(— UPON DUTIES) ASSUME
(— WITHOUT RIGHT) ABATE
ENTERING ENTRY INGOING
INGRESS INTRANT INCOMING
ENTEROTOXEMIA STRUCK
ENTERPRISE FIRM IRON PUSH
TOGT DRIVE ESSAY ACTION
EMPIRE SPIRIT VOYAGE ATTEMPT
EMPRISE HOLDING PROJECT
VENTURE BUSINESS CARNIVAL
GUMPTION VIRITOOT
(CRIMINAL —) JOB
(HARD —) DIFFICULTY
(REMEDIAL —) CRUSADE
(SPECULATIVE —) ADVENTURE
(UNPROFITABLE —) SINKHOLE
ENTERPRISING BOLD FORTHY
PUSHFUL PUSHING
ENTERTAIN INN BEAR BUSK EASE
FETE HAVE HOLD HOST AMUSE
ENJOY FEAST GUEST SPORT
TREAT DIVERT FROLIC GESTEN
HARBOR JUNKET RECULE REGALE
RETAIN SOLACE TICKLE ACCOURT
BEGUILE CHERISH DISPORT
KITCHEN CONSIDER INTEREST
RECREATE
(— WITHOUT CHARGE) DEFRAY
ENTERTAINED OUGHT
ENTERTAINER BHAT HOST ACTOR
AMUSER ARTIST BUSKER DANCER
FIDDLE HARLOT SINGER ACTRESS
ARTISTE DISEUSE GLEEMAN
HETAERA HOSTESS REGALER
SPEAKER BEACHBOY COMEDIAN
HOSTELER MAGICIAN MINSTREL
ENTERTAINING GOOD RICH TREAT
PRETTY AMUSING BEDSIDE
GUESTING SPORTFUL
ENTERTAINMENT BASH BILL FARE
FETE GALA GLEE PLAY SHOW
BOARD CHEER FEAST GAUDY
OPERA REVUE SPORT CIRCUS
DIVERT DOMENT GAIETY GAYETY
HOSTEL INFARE KERMIS NAUTCH
SETOUT SHIVOO WATTLE
BANQUET BENEFIT BUMMACK
BUMMOCK BURLESK CEILIDH
CONCERT COSHERY FESTINE
FESTINO JOLLITY KERMESS
PASTIME RIDOTTO TAMASHA
CAKEWALK CARNIVAL
COMMORTH DROLLERY
EASEMENT ENTREATY ENTREMES

FUNCTION GESTNING GESTONIE
GUESTING HOGMANAY JONGLERY
MUSICALE WAYZGOOSE
(FAREWELL —) FOY
ENTHALPY H
ENTHRALL SEND CHARM THIRL
THRALL ENSLAVE ENTHRAL
CAPTIVATE
ENTHRONE CROWN EXALT STALL
ENSEAT THRONE THRONIZE
ENTHUSIASM BUG ELAN FIRE
FURY ZEAL ZEST ZING ARDOR
ESTRO FEVER FLAME FUROR
HEART MANIA OOMPH VERVE
FERVOR HURRAH SPIRIT WARMTH
ABANDON ARDENCY AVIDITY
MADNESS MUSTARD DEVOTION
LYRICISM
(— IN BATTLE) EARNEST
(CONTAGIOUS —) FUROR FURORE
(EXCESSIVE —) MANIA
(WILD —) DELIRIUM
ENTHUSIAST BUG FAN NUT BUFF
BIGOT FREAK ROOTER VOTARY
ZEALOT DEVOTEE EUCHITE
FANATIC FANCIER FOLLOWER
VOTARESS VOTARIST
(PL.) ARDITI
ENTHUSIASTIC GAGA KEEN NUTS
WARM HAPPY NUTTY RABID
ARDENT HEARTY CRACKED
FERVENT GLOWING CRACKERS
PASSIONATE
(BECOME —) FLIP
(EXCESSIVELY —) FANATIC
(VAINLY —) FOOLISH
ENTICE COG COY PUT WIN BAIT
COAX DRAW DRIB LEAD LOCK
LURE TICE TOLE TOLL WILE
CHARM DECOY DRILL LATHE
SIREN SLOCK STEAL TEMPT TRAIN
TROLL TULLE ALLECT ALLURE
ATTICE CAJOLE ENLURE INCITE
INDUCE INVITE SEDUCE ATTRACT
BEWITCH SOLICIT SUGGEST
INVEIGLE PERSUADE
ENTICEMENT BAIT CORD LURE
TICE
ENTICING SIREN ALLURING
ENTIRE ALL DEAD EVEN FULL HALE
MEAR MERE SOLE CLEAN EVERY
GROSS PLAIN QUITE ROUND
SOUND STARK TOTAL TUTTO
UTTER WHOLE VERSAL PERFECT
PLENARY ABSOLUTE COMPLETE
ENDURING GLOBULAR INTEGRAL
LIVELONG OUTRIGHT TEETOTAL
UNBROKEN
(PREF.) HOL(O) INTEGRI
ENTIRELY DEAD DEIN FAIR FULL
PURE CLEAN CLEAR FULLY PLAIN
QUITE STARK WHOLE BODILY
WHOLLY EXACTLY QUIETLY
THROUGH CLEVERLY ABSOLUTELY
ENTIRETY WHOLE ENTIRE
TOTALITY
(PREF.) PAM PAN
ENTITLE DUB CALL NAME TERM
AFFIX STYLE ENABLE CAPTION
EMPOWER QUALIFY INTITULE
NOMINATE
ENTITLED APPARENT ELIGIBLE
ENTITY ENS BODY FORM UNIT

BEING HABIT OUSIA SPACE THING
ENERGY ESSENCE INTEGER
TOTALITY
ENTOMB BURY TOMB INTER INURN
ENCAVE HEARSE IMMURE
INHUME SHRINE
ENTOMBMENT BURIAL
ENTOMOLOGIST AMERICAN SAY
DYAR HORN BANKS BRUES RILEY
FORBES HARRIS HOWARD
MORGAN BURGESS PACKARD
POLLARD SCHWARZ COMSTOCK
COQUILLETT
DANISH FABRICIUS
DUTCH LYONNET
ENGLISH SCOTT LEFROY
HAWORTH ORMEROD
WESTWOOD
FRENCH FABRE AUDOUIN
LATREILLE LACORDAIRE
GERMAN BRAUER
SWISS FOREL SAUSSURE
ENTOMOLOGY BUGOLOGY
ENTOMOPHTHORA EMPUSA
ENTOTROPHI DIPLURA
ENTOURAGE TRAIN COMITES
RETINUE
ENTRACTE INTERACT INTERVAL
ENTRAIL BOWEL TRAIL INTRAIL
(PREF.) SPLANCHN(O)
ENTRAILS GUT GUTS DRAFT TRIPE
FIBERS GIBLET HALLOW HASLET
INWARD JAUDIE MUGGET
PAUNCH QUARRY QUERRE
UMBLES INSIDES NUMBLES
CHAWDRON GRALLOCH
PURTENANCE
ENTRANCE ADIT BOCA CUSP
DOOR GATE HALL PEND BOCCA
CHARM DEBUT ENTER ENTRY
FOYER GORGE INLET MOUTH
PORCH STULM THIRL TORAN
ACCESS ATRIUM ENTREE INFAIR
INGANG INGATE INROAD PORTAL
RAVISH TORANA TRANCE
ZAGUAN DELIGHT GATEWAY
HALLWAY INGOING INGRESS
INITIAL INTRADO INTROIT
PASSAGE POSTERN ENTRESSE
FOREGATE VOMITORY
PROPYLAEUM
(— TO SEWER) JAWHOLE
(— TO VALLEY) CHOPS
(ASTROLOGICAL —) CUSP
(CELLAR —) ROLLWAY
(FORCIBLE —) INROAD
(FORMAL —) DEBUT
(HARBOR —) BOCA
(HOSTILE —) INVASION
(HURRIED —) BOUT
(MINE —) EYE ADIT
(PRIVATE —) POSTERN
ENTRANCED RAPT CHARMED
TRANCED ECSTATIC
ENTRANCEMENT SPELL
ENTRANCING ORPHIC
ENTRANT INTRANT STARTER
BEGINNER
ENTRAP BAG EBB NET HOOK SNIB
TOIL TRAP CATCH CRIMP DECOY
NOOSE SNARE ALLURE AMBUSH
ATTRAP CAJOLE ENGAGE ENTOIL
TAIGLE TANGLE TREPAN BEGUILE

ENSNARE PITFALL ENTANGLE INVEIGLE
ENTRAPPED (— IN SEDIMENT) CONNATE
ENTREAT ASK BEG BID SUE WOO PRAY PRIG SEEK URGE CRAVE HALSE PLEAD PRESS TREAT ADJURE APPEAL DESIRE INVOKE BESEECH CONJURE EXORATE IMPLORE PREVAIL PROCURE REQUEST SOLICIT PERSUADE PETITION
ENTREATING TREAT CRAVING
ENTREATY DO CRY PLEA SUIT APPEAL DEESIS PRAYER TREATY BESEECH BIDDING ENTREAT PURSUIT REQUEST URGENCY PETITION PLEADING
ENTREE ENTRY ACCESS BOUDIN OSTIUM ENTRADA INTRADA SOUFFLE ENTRANCE FRICANDO MAZARINE
ENTREMES SAINETE SAYNETE
ENTRENCH INVADE SCONCE TRENCH ENCROACH TRESPASS
ENTRENCHMENT CLOSURE COUPURE LODGMENT
ENTROPY S
ENTRUST ARET FIDE GIVE STOW BEKEN TRUST CHARGE COMMIT CREDIT LIPPEN ADDRESS BEHIGHT COMMEND CONFIDE CONSIGN DEPOSIT INTRUST BEQUEATH DELEGATE ENCHARGE RECOMMEND
(— TO DEPUTY) DEVIL
ENTRY ADIT HALL ITEM STET BREAK CLOSE DEBIT AUTHOR CREDIT DOCKET ENTREE PORTAL POSTEA RECORD RINGER TRANCE ENTRADA INGRESS INTRADO PASSAGE ENTRANCE ENTRESSE ENTRYWAY NOTANDUM REGISTER VOCATION
(— IN CHRONICLE) ANNAL
ENTWINE FOLD LACE WIND BRAID CLASP IMPLY PLASH TWINE TWIST WEAVE ENLACE INWIND ENTWIST INVOLVE SERPENT WREATHE
ENTWINED ACCOLLE BRAIDED INWOVEN ACCOLLEE
ENUMERATE POLL TELL COUNT SCORE DETAIL NUMBER RECITE RECKON RELATE COMPILE COMPUTE ITEMIZE RECOUNT ESTIMATE REHEARSE
ENUMERATION LIST TALE COUNT SCORE CENSUS ACCOUNT CATALOG RECITAL CITATION
ENUNCIATE SAY UTTER DECLARE DELIVER ENOUNCE ANNOUNCE PROCLAIM
ENUNCIATION DICTION DELIVERY
(IMPERFECT —) LALLATION
ENVELOP BUR FOG LAP LOT POD WEB BURR CASE COMA FOLD HUSK MAIL ROLL BRACE CLOUD COVER KNIFE ROUND BEGIRD BEGIRT BEMIST BINDLE CLOTHE COCOON CORONA CUPULE ENFOLD ENGIRT ENTIRE ENWRAP FARDEL FOLDER INFOLD INVEST

JACKET MANTLE MUFFLE POCKET SHEATH SHROUD STIFLE SWATHE WRIXLE CALYMMA CAPSULE CHORION ENCLOSE ENVIRON INVOLVE SWADDLE SWALLOW VESTURE WRAPPER ENSPHERE ENVELOPE MANTLING PERIANTH PERIDIUM POCHETTE SURROUND WRAPPAGE
(— IN SMOKE) ENFUME
(GLASS —) BULB
(LUMINOUS —) CORONA
(NEBULOUS —) CHEVELURE
(OPEN —) JACKET
(PAY —) PACKET
(STAMPED —) ENTIRE
(VEGETABLE —) COD
ENVELOPE
(PREF.) **(OUTER —)** PERIDI
(SUFF.) LEMMA
ENVELOPED WOMPLIT
ENVELOPING AMBIENT
ENVENOM VENOM CORRUPT VITIATE EMBITTER EMPOISON
ENVIOUS YELLOW EMULOUS JEALOUS ENVIABLE
ENVIRON HEM BEGO GIRD BIGAN LIMIT VIRON ENVIRE GIRDLE SUBURB COMPASS ENVELOP INCLOSE INVOLVE PURLIEU DISTRICT ENCIRCLE SURROUND
(PL.) SKIRT UMLAND BANLIEU SUBURBS PRECINCT
ENVIRONMENT HOTBED MEDIUM MILIEU AMBIENT CONTEXT ELEMENT HABITAT SETTING TERRAIN AMBIANCE CINCTURE PRECINCT
(— OF NURTURE) LAP
(ACADEMIC —) ACADEME
(DOMESTIC —) INTERIEUR
(NORMAL —) HOME
(PREF.) EC(O) OEC(O) OIK(O)
ENVISAGE FACE CONFRONT ENVISION
ENVOY AGENT ELCHI ENVOI DEPUTY ELCHEE LEGATE LENVOY NUNCIO EMBASSY TORNADA ABLEGATE LEGATION METATRON
ENVY CHAW ONDE COVET GRUDGE EMULATE BEGRUDGE GRUDGERY JEALOUSY
ENWRAP FOLD ROLL CLASP IMPLY ENFOLD INFOLD KIRTLE ENGROSS ENVELOP OBVOLVE CONVOLVE ENVELOPE INSWATHE
ENZOOTIC RABIES
ENZU SIN
ENZYME ASE ZYM ZYMO LYASE RENIN CYTASE KINASE LIGASE LIPASE LOTASE MUTASE OLEASE PAPAIN PEPSIN RENNIN UREASE ZYMASE ACYLASE ADENASE AMIDASE AMINASE AMYLASE APYRASE CASEASE EMULSIN ENOLASE EREPSIN FERMENT GUANASE HYDRASE INULASE LACCASE LACTASE MALTASE MYROSIN OXIDASE PECTASE PEPSINE PHYTASE PLASMIN PRUNASE TANNASE TRYPSIN ALDOLASE ARGINASE BROMELIN CATALASE CATALYST CYTOLIST

DIASTASE ELASTASE EREPTASE ESTERASE FUMARASE INVERTIN LYSOZYME NUCLEASE PERMEASE PROTEASE RACEMASE SEMINASE SYNTHASE THROMBIN TRYPTASE
(PREF.) ZYM(O)
(SUFF.) ASE EIN EINE IN INE
EOS MORNING
EPAPHUS (DAUGHTER OF —) LIBYA
(FATHER OF —) ZEUS JUPITER
(MOTHER OF —) IO
(WIFE OF —) MEMPHIS
EPAULET KNOT SWAB SWOB WING SCALE SHELL
EPENDYTES HAPLOMA
EPENTHESIS ANAPTYXIS
EPEUS (BROTHER OF —) AETOLUS
(DAUGHTER OF —) HYRMINA
(FATHER OF —) ENDYMION PANOPEUS
(WIFE OF —) ANAXIROE
EPHAH BATH
(FATHER OF —) JAHDAI MIDIAN
EPHELIS FRECKLE
EPHEMERAL BRIEF VAGUE HORARY DIURNAL FUNGOUS PASSANT PASSING EPISODAL EPISODIC FUGITIVE MUSHROOM STAYLESS MOMENTARY
EPHEMERIS DIARY TABLE RECORD ALMANAC JOURNAL CALENDAR
EPHER (FATHER OF —) EZRA MIDIAN
EPHIPPIUM SADDLE
EPHOD VAKASS
(SON OF —) HANNIEL
EPHRAIM (FATHER OF —) JOSEPH
(MOTHER OF —) ASENATH
EPHRATAH (HUSBAND OF —) CALEB
(SON OF —) HUR
EPHRON (FATHER OF —) ZOAR
EPHTHALITE HAITHAL
EPI PEAK SPIRE FINIAL PINNACLE
EPIBLAST ECTODERM
EPIC EDDA EPOS SAGA GRAND ILIAD NOBLE BYLINA EPOPEE HEROIC LUSIAD BEOWULF EPYLLION KALEVALA RAMAYANA
(SUFF.) AD
EPICALYX CALYCLE
EPICARP HUSK RIND EXOCARP
EPICENE SEXLESS
EPICURE FRIAND FEASTER GLUTTON GOURMET GOURMAND PALATIST
EPICUREAN APICIAN SENSUOUS
EPIDEMIC FLU PLAGUE POPULAR PANDEMIA PANDEMIC
EPIDERMIS SKIN CUTICLE ECDERON VELAMEN
EPIDOTE SCORZA
EPIGLOTTIS FLAP WEEZLE
EPIGRAM POEM ENGLYN EPITAPH
EPIGRAMMATIC LACONIC POINTED
EPIGRAPH EPIGRAM IMPRINT
EPILEPTIC FITIFIED
EPILOGUE CLOSE APPENDIX
EPIMANIKION CUFF
EPINAOS POSTICUM
EPINEPHRINE ADRENINE
EPIPACTIS SERAPIAS
EPIPHANY TWELFTH
EPIPHARYNX PALATE EPIGLOTTIS

EPIPHRAGM TYMPANUM
EPIPHYTE KARO EPIPHYLL
EPIPHYTOTIC EPIDEMIC
EPIRUS (KING OF —) PYRRHUS
EPISCOPACY BISHOPRIC PRELATISM
EPISCOPAL PRELATIC
EPISODE GAG EPOCH EVENT SCENE STORY AFFAIR INCIDENT SEQUENCE OCCURRENCE
(COMIC —) BURLA
(MUSICAL —) COUPLET
EPISPASTIC VESICANT
EPISPERM TESTA
EPISTAXIS NOSEBLEED
EPISTERNUM MANUBRIUM
EPISTLE CANON JAMES LETTER PISTLE MISSIVE WRITING DECRETAL
EPISTLER SUBDEACON
EPISTOLOGRAPHIC DEMOTIC
EPISTROPHE EPODE ABGESANG
EPISTYLE PLATBAND
EPITHELIUM ENDODERM
EPITHET AKAL GOOD NAME TERM LABEL SMEAR TITLE BYWORD MONETA PHRASE AGNOMEN JAPHETIC MULCIBER
(PL.) LANGUAGE
EPITOME MAP SUM FLETA DIGEST PRECIS SCHEME COMPEND PITOMIE SUMMARY SUMMULA ABSTRACT BREVIARY LANDSKIP SYLLABUS SYNOPSIS ABRIDGMENT CONSPECTUS
EPITOMIZE RESUME ABRIDGE CURTAIL ABSTRACT COMPRESS CONDENSE CONTRACT DIMINISH
EPITONIUM SCALA
EPIZOA PARASITA
EPOCH AGE ERA DATE ECCA TIME DWYKA EVENT EOCENE PERIOD CLINTON OLIGOCENE
EPONYM LIMMU ANCIENT
EPOPEUS (BROTHERS OF —) ALOIDAE
(FATHER OF —) ALOEUS POSEIDON
(MOTHER OF —) CANACE IPHIMEDIA
(WIFE OF —) ANTIOPE
EQUABLE EVEN JUST EQUAL SUANT SMOOTH STEADY UNIFORM TRANQUIL
EQUAL AEQ PAR TIE COPE EGAL EVEN FERE JUST LIKE MAKE MATE MEET PEEL PEER SAME ALIKE LEVEL MATCH PARTY RIVAL TOUCH DOUBLE EQUATE EVENLY FELLOW MARROW PAREIL ABREAST BALANCE COMPEER EMULATE EQUABLE IDENTIC PARAGON PAREGAL UNIFORM ADEQUATE EQUALIZE EVENHAND PATCHING TRANQUIL
(— IN MEANING) BE
(— QUANTITY) ANA
(— TO) ANOTHER
(NOT —) UNMEET UNMETE
(PREF.) AEQUI EQUI IS(O) PARI
EQUALING TO
EQUALITY PAR TIE EQUITY OWELTY PARAGE PAREIL PARITY BALANCE EGALITE EGALITY

ISOTELY EQUATION EVENHAND
EVENNESS FAIRNESS
(— BEFORE THE LAW) ISONOMY
(— OF ELEVATION) ISOMETRY
(— OF POWER) ISOCRACY
(— OF RATIOS) ANALOGY
(— STATE) WYOMING
EQUALIZATION EQUATION
DISCHARGE
EQUALIZE EVEN KNOT EQUAL
LEVEL EQUATE BALANCE
ADEQUATE
EQUALIZER EVENER
EQUALLY AS BOTH LIKE ONCE
SAME ALIKE EGALLY EVENLY
JUSTLY EMFORTH
EQUANIMITY POISE PHLEGM
TEMPER BALANCE EGALITY
CALMNESS EVENNESS SERENITY
SANGFROID
EQUATE EQUAL BALANCE
EQUALIZE
EQUATING COMPARISON
EQUATION CUBIC IDENTITY
EQUATOR LINE GIRDLE EQUINOX
(— CROSSER) POLLIWOG
EQUATORIAL GUINEA (CAPITAL OF
—) MALABO
(RIVER OF —) MUNI CAMPO BENITO
(TOWN OF —) BATA NSOK
SANTAISABEL
EQUES KNIGHT
EQUIDISTANT CENTRAL HALFWAY
EQUILIBRIUM POISE APLOMB
BALANCE STATION EQUATION
EVENHAND ISOSTASY
(— OF FLUID) LEVEL
(PREF.) STATO
EQUINE COLT FOAL MARE FILLY
HORSE ZEBRA EQUOID EQUINAL
HORSELY
EQUINIA MALLEUS
EQUIP ARM FIT IMP KIT RAY RIG
ABLE BEAM DECK FEAT FIND
GEAR GIRD GIRT HEEL REEK TRIM
ARRAY DIGHT DRESS ENARM
ENDOW POINT SPEED STUFF
AGUISE ATTIRE BUCKLE ORDAIN
OUTFIT SUBORN APPAREL
APPOINT BEDIGHT FORTIFY
FRAUGHT FURNISH GARNISH
HARNESS PLENISH PREPARE
QUALIFY ACCOUTER ACCOUTRE
ACCOMPLISH
(— FOR ACTION) ARM
EQUIPAGE RIG CREW SAMAN
SUITE TRAIN SUPPLY RETINUE
TURNOUT UNICORN CARRIAGE
EQUIPMENT KIT FARE GEAR TIRE
STOCK STUFF ATTIRE CONREY
DUFFEL DUFFLE FITOUT GRAITH
OUTFIT SETOUT TACKLE APPAREL
BAGGAGE FITMENT HARNESS
PANOPLY ARMAMENT EQUIPAGE
MATERIAL MATERIEL MOUNTING
SUPELLEX
(— FOR CATCHING FISH) CRAFT
(— FOR JOURNEY) FARE
EQUIPOISE POISE BALANCE
EQUIPOTENTIAL LEVEL
EQUIPPED SEEN ARMED BODEN
THERE EQUIPT ARMORED
INSTRUCT WEAPONED

(FULLY —) SUMMED
(INADEQUATELY —) HAYWIRE
(LIGHTLY —) EXPEDITE
EQUISETUM CANDOCK
EQUITABLE EVEN FAIR JUST
EQUAL RIGHT EVENLY HONEST
EQUABLE UPRIGHT BONITARY
RATIONAL RIGHTFUL
EQUITY LAW EPIKY MARGIN
EPIKEIA HONESTY JUSTICE
EQUALITY EVENHAND FAIRNESS
EQUIVALENT KIND SAME EQUAL
COUSIN UNISON ANALOGUE
EVENHAND
(— IN MONEY) CHANGE
(— OF TWO BUSHELS) HUTCH
EQUIVOCAL FISHY SHADY DOUBLE
FORKED DUBIOUS EVASIVE
HALFWAY OBSCURE DOUBTFUL
HAVERING PUZZLING SIBYLLIC
EQUIVOCATE LIE DODGE EVADE
SHIFT BOGGLE ESCAPE PALTER
TRIFLE WAFFLE WEASEL QUIBBLE
SHUFFLE SCRAFFLE PREVARICATE
EQUIVOCATION QUIP QUIRK
EVASION QUIBBLE SHUFFLE
EQUIVOKE
EQUULEUS FOAL
ER (FATHER OF —) JOSE
(SON OF —) ELMODAM
ERA AGE AEON DATE TIME EPOCH
STAGE PERIOD CENOZOIC
PROTEROZOIC
(EMPEROR'S —) KIMIGAYO
(HINDU —) SAMVAT
(MUSLIM —) HEGIRA HEJIRA
ERADICATE DELE ROOT SLAY
WEED CROSS ERASE STAMP
DELETE EFFACE REMOVE UNROOT
UPROOT ABOLISH DESTROY
EXPUNGE OUTROOT SUPPLANT
(— HAIR) EPILATE
ERADICATOR ERASER
ERAL MOINE
ERAN (GRANDFATHER OF —)
EPHRAIM
ERASE BLOT DASH DELE RACE
RASE RASH RAZE ANNUL PLANE
CANCEL DEFACE DELETE EFFACE
EXCISE REMOVE SCRAPE SPONGE
DESTROY EXPUNGE OUTRAZE
SCRATCH UNWRITE OBLITERATE
ERASER RASER RUBBER
ERASTE (LOVER OF —) JULIE
LUCILLE ORPHISE
ERASURE RASURE ERASION
DELETION EXCISION
ERD SHREW RANNY
ERE OR AIR SOON EARLY PRIOR
BEFORE EREWHILE FORMERLY
EREBUS (FATHER OF —) CHAOS
(SISTER OF —) NOX
(SON OF —) CHARON
ERECHTHEUS (DAUGHTER OF —)
CREUSA PROCRIS CHTHONIA
ORITHYIA
(FATHER OF —) PANDION
(SLAYER OF —) JUPITER
(SON OF —) MERION CECROPS
PANDORUS
(WIFE OF —) PRAXITHEA
ERECT BIG SET BIGG LEVY REAR
RECT STEP STEY SWAY TELD

AREAR BRANT BUILD DRESS
EXALT FRAME MOUNT RAISE
SETUP STAND ARRECT UPLIFT
UPREAR ADDRESS ATROPAL
BRISTLE ELEVATE STATELY
UPRAISE UPRIGHT UPSTART
STANDING STRAIGHT VERTICAL
(— TENT) PITCH
(NOT —) LAZY COUCHED
ERECTED UPSET
ERECTION DOME HARD FABRIC
CHORDEE MACHINE
ERELONG ANON SOON
EREMITE HERMIT ASCETIC
RECLUSE ANCHORET
EREWHILE ERE WHILOM
EREWHON (AUTHOR OF —) BUTLER
(CHARACTER IN —) HIGGS GEORGE
STRONG ZULORA CHOWBOK
AROWHENA NOSNIBOR
ERG REG EROGON
(PL.) AREG
ERGINUS (FATHER OF —) CLYMENUS
POSEIDON
(SON OF —) AGAMEDES
TROPHONIUS
ERGO SO ARGO ARGAL HENCE
ERGOT SPUR CLAVUS ECBOLIC
(STAGE OF —) SPHACELIA
ERI (FATHER OF —) GAD
ERICHTHONIUS (FATHER OF —)
VULCAN DARDANUS
(MOTHER OF —) ATTHIS
(SON OF —) PANDION
ERIDANUS (FATHER OF —)
OCEANUS
(MOTHER OF —) TETHYS
ERIE WENRO
ERIGONE (FATHER OF —) ICARIUS
AEGISTHUS
(MOTHER OF —) CLYTEMNESTRA
ERINYS FURY ALECTO MEGAERA
(PL.) DIRAE FURIAE SEMNAE
EUMENIDES
ERIOPHORUM DRAWLING
ERIPHYLE (FATHER OF —) TALAUS
(HUSBAND OF —) AMPHIARAUS
(SON & SLAYER OF —) ALCMAEON
ERISTIC DIALECTIC
ERMINE VAIR VARE STOAT WEASEL
ERMELIN FUTERET FUTTRAT
MINIVER CLUBSTER WHITRACK
WHITTRET
ERNANI (CHARACTER IN —) CARLO
GOMEZ SILVA ELVIRA ERNANI
(COMPOSER OF —) VERDI
ERODE EAT COMB ETCH GNAW
GULL WEAR CLIFF GULLY SCOUR
ABRADE DENUDE CORRODE
DESTROY
ERODIUM HERONBILL
EROS AMOR CUPID AENGUS
POTHOS
EROSE ERODED UNEVEN
EROSION PIPING CHIMNEY
NIVATION SCOURING
(MECHANICAL —) PLANATION
ERO THE JOKER (COMPOSER OF —)
GOTOVAC
EROTIC LOVING AMATORY
AMOROUS CURIOUS LESBIAN
THERMAL
EROTICA CURIOSA FACETIAE

ERR MAR SIN BOOT FAIL MISS SLIP
ABERR LAPSE MISGO STRAY
BUNGLE FORVAY WANDER
BLUNDER DEVIATE MISPLAY
MISTAKE SCRITHE STUMBLE
MISCARRY MISJUDGE
ERRAND CHORE ENVOY JOURNEY
MISSION LEGATION
(— BOY) LOBBYGOW
ERRANT STRAY ASTRAY ERRING
DEVIOUS PRICKANT
ERRATIC WILD CRAZY HUMAN
LOONY QUEER WACKY CRANKY
WHACKY STRANGE TANGENT
VAGRANT ACROSTIC ERRABUND
FITIFIED PLANETAL PLANETIC
TRAVELED VAGABOND
PLANETARY
ERRATUM ERROR
ERRING ASTRAY ERRANT DEVIOUS
ERRINGLY FALSE
ERRONEOUS AMISS FALSE WRONG
UNTRUE ERRATIC MISTAKEN
STRAYING WRONGFUL
(PREF.) PSEUD(O)
ERRONEOUSLY AWRY
ERRONEOUSNESS FALLACY
ERROR X HOB SIN BALK BUBU
BULL FLUB HELL MUFF SLIP TRIP
BEARD BEVUE BONER DEVIL
FAULT FLUFF LAPSE SCAPE
BOBBLE BOOBOO FUMBLE GARBLE
HOWLER LAPSUS MISCUE
NAUGHT SPHALM BLOOMER
BLUNDER BOTTLE ERRATUM
FALLACY FALSITY LITERAL
MISPLAY MISSTEP MISTAKE
OFFENSE RHUBARB SNAPPER
STUMBLE DELUSION HAMARTIA
MISPRINT MISSMENT SOLECISM
OVERSIGHT MISPRISION
(— IN PLEADINGS) JEOFAIL
ERS VETCH KERSANNE
ERSE ERSCH IRISH CELTIC GAELIC
SCOTTISH
ERST ONCE FORMERLY RECENTLY
ERSTWHILE ONCE FORMER
FORMERLY
ERUCT RASP BELCH
ERUCTATION BRASH
ERUDITE LEARNED CLERGIAL
DIDACTIC
ERUDITION WIT LORE WISDOM
LETTERS LEARNING
ERUPT BOIL BELCH BURST EJECT
IRRUPT
ERUPTING ACTIVE
ERUPTION ITCH RASH REEF RUSH
AGRIA BLAIN BRASH BURST
RUPIA SALLY SALVO STORM
BLOTCH HYDROA NIRLES ACTERID
BLOWOUT ECTHYMA MORPHEA
MORPHEW PUSTULE SAWFLOM
SUDAMEN SYCOSIS EMPYESIS
ENANTHEM EXANTHEM
MALANDER OUTBREAK
OUTBURST
(— ON CHIN) MENTAGRA
(CUTANEOUS —) HUMOR
(SUFF.) ANTHEMA PHLYSIS
ERVUM LENS LENTILLA
ERYSICHTHON (FATHER OF —)
CECROPS TRIOPAS

(MOTHER OF —) AGRAULOS
(SISTER OF —) IPHIMEDIA
ERYSIPELAS POX ROSE BLAST
WILDFIRE
ERYTHROBLASTOSIS HYDROPSY
ERYX (FATHER OF —) BUTES
(MOTHER OF —) VENUS
(SLAYER OF —) HERCULES
ESAU EDOM
(BROTHER OF —) JACOB
(FATHER OF —) ISAAC
(MOTHER OF —) REBEKAH
(SON OF —) JEUSH KORAH REUEL
JAALAM ELIPHAZ
(WIFE OF —) ADAH BASHEMATH
ESCALADE SCALE SCALADE
SCALADO ESCALADO
ESCAPADE CAPER PRANK SALLY
SCHEME SPLORE RUNAWAY
FREDAINE
ESCAPE FLY GUY LAM RUN BAIL
BALE BEAT BLOW BOLT FLEE
GATE HISS JINK JUMP LEAK MISS
SHUN SKEW SLIP VENT AVOID
BREAK CHAPE DODGE ELOPE
ELUDE EVADE FLANK ISSUE
SCAPE SHIFT SKIRT SMOKE SPILL
ASTERT DECAMP ESCHEW
OUTLET POWDER SQUEAK
ABSCOND AVOLATE BLOWOUT
ELUSION EXHAUST GETAWAY
LEAKAGE MISTAKE OUTFLOW
SCRITHE SQUEEZE WILDING
BLOWBACK ESCAPADE ESCAPAGE
EXSHEATH OUTSCAPE OVERSLIP
RIDDANCE WITHSLIP
(— FROM) FLY SHUN ILLUDE
(— FROM WORK) SNIB
(— LEGAL PROCESS) ABSCOND
(— NOTICE) ELUDE
(— OF FLUID) EFFUSION
(NARROW —) SHAVE
ESCAPEMENT SCAPE CRUTCH
ESCAPE FOLIOT VIRGULE
KARRUSEL
ESCARGOT SNAIL
ESCAROLE ENDIVE SCAROLA
ESCARPMENT EDGE
ESCHAR SCAB CRUST ASCHER
ESCHAROTIC CAUSTIC
ESCHEAT FALL LAPSE REVERT
EXCHEAT FORFEIT
ESCHEW SHUN ABHOR AVOID
FORGO ESCAPE FOREGO ABSTAIN
ESCOLAR PALU ROVET OILFISH
ROVETTO MACKEREL
ESCORT MAN SEE SET TRY BEAR
BEAU COND LEAD SHOW TEND
WAIT BRING CARRY GUARD
USHER ATTEND CONVEY CONVOY
FOLLOW SQUIRE COLLECT
CONDUCT CONSORT ESQUIRE
GALLANT CAVALIER CHAPERON
SHEPHERD SAFEGUARD
(PAID —) GIGOLO
ESCRITOIRE DESK BUREAU
LECTERN
ESCULENT EDIBLE EATABLE
ESCUTCHEON CREST SHIELD
(CENTER OF —) NOMBRIL
ESHBAN (FATHER OF —) DISHON
ESHCOL (BROTHER OF —) ANER
MAMRE

(COMPANION OF —) ABRAHAM
ESKER AS OS OSE KAME ESKAR
HOGBACK
ESKIMO ITA HUSKY INUIT INNUIT
AGOMIUT AMERIND ANGAKOK
KUNMIUT OKOMIUT ORARIAN
AGLEMIUT ESQUIMAU IKOGMIUT
KIDNELIK KINIPETU MAGEMIUT
MALEMIUT NUGUMIUT SINIMIUT
(— ASSEMBLY HOUSE) KASHIM
(— CULTURE) PUNUK
(— TENT) TUPEK TUPIK
ESLI (FATHER OF —) NAGGE
ESOPHAGUS GULLET SWALLOW
WEASAND
(PREF.) LAEMO LEMO
ESOTERIC INNER MYSTIC ORPHIC
SECRET PRIVATE ABSTRUSE
RAREFIED RARIFIED
ESPADON ESPADA SPADON
SPADROON
ESPALIER CORDON LATTICE
RAILING TRELLIS PALISADE
ESPARTO ALFA HALFA SPART
STIPA ATOCHA
ESPAVE CARACOLI
ESPECIAL VERY CHIEF SPECIAL
PECULIAR UNCOMMON
ESPECIALLY SUCH EXTRA RATHER
CHIEFLY OVERALL SPECIAL
ESPIAL SPY ESPY SCOUT NOTICE
ESPINAL MONTE
ESPIONAGE SPYING
ESPLANADE BUND WALK DRIVE
MAIDAN MARINA
ESPOUSAL CEREMONY SPOUSAGE
BETROTHAL
ESPOUSE WED AFFY MATE ADOPT
MARRY DEFEND ENSURE SPOUSE
BETROTH EMBRACE HUSBAND
SUPPORT ADVOCATE MAINTAIN
ESPOUSED HANDFAST
ESPUNDIA UTA
ESPY SEE ASPY SPOT ASCRY SIGHT
WATCH BEHOLD DESCRY DETECT
LOCATE NOTICE DISCERN
OBSERVE DESCRIBE DISCOVER
ESQUIRE RADMAN ARMIGER
ESCUDERO SERGEANT
ESSAY TRY SEEK ASSAY CHRIA
OFFER PAPER PROVE TASTE
THEME TRACT TRAIL CASUAL
EFFORT MEMOIR SAILYE SATIRE
SCREED THESIS ARTICLE
ATTEMPT PROFFER VENTURE
WRITING CAUSERIE ENDEAVOR
EXERCISE EXERTION TRACTATE
TREATISE TURNOVER
ESSAYIST AMERICAN MORE VERY
ADAMS GRANT WHITE YOUNG
BROOKS COFFIN FISHER GUINEY
HOLMES HUTTON KRUTCH
LOWELL EMERSON LAZARUS
WHIPPLE STRUNSKY TUCKERMAN
AUSTRIAN BLEI
BELGIAN MAETERLINCK
CANADIAN MACMECHAN
ENGLISH HUNT LAMB DRAKE
MUNRO MYERS PAGET PATER
GARROD MACHEN MARTIN
SEELEY STEELE TEMPLE ADDISON
BUDGELL CHAPONE HAYWARD
HAZLITT HEWLETT SYMONDS

CONGREVE NEVINSON STERLING
DICKINSON
FRENCH CAMUS ARAGON MOUREY
CHAMSON STAPFER CHARTIER
SCHOPEN MONTAIGNE
GERMAN ZWEIG FONTANE
GREEK XENOPHON
IRISH BOYD LECKY MAGEE
ITALIAN BRACCO
POLISH BELCIKOWSKI
MAKUSZYNSKI
SCOTTISH WILSON CARLYLE
STEVENSON
SWEDISH EKELUND
ESSE BEING
ESSENCE ENS NET ALMA ATAR
BASE BONE CORE CRUX DRAW
ESSE GIST GUTS KIND ODOR
OTTO PITH QUID RASA SOUL
YOLK ATTAR BASIC BASIS BEING
EIDOS FIBER FIBRE FUMET HEART
JUICE OTTAR OUSIA STUFF
BOTTOM EFFECT ENTITY FLOWER
INWARD MARROW NATURE
SPRITE ALCOHOL ELEMENT
EXTRACT FUMETTE GODHEAD
INBEING MEDULLA PERFUME
RATAFIA BERGAMOT CONCRETE
ESSENTIA
(— OF BEING) SAT
(— OF FLOWERS) CONCRETE
(— OF GOD) SPIRIT DIVINITY
(— OF MEAT) BLOND
(— OF TEA) DRAW
(— OF VITAL MATTER) GLAME
(INNERMOST —) ATMAN
(UNIVERSAL —) FORM
(VITAL —) STAMINA
ESSENE ESSEE ASCETIC
ESSENTIAL KEY REAL BASAL BASIC
VITAL ENTIRE FORMAL INWARD
CENTRAL CRUCIAL NEEDFUL
CARDINAL CRITICAL INHERENT
MATERIAL OBLIGATE NECESSARY
(— TO LIFE) BIOGENOUS
(NOT —) ACCIDENTAL
ESSENTIALLY AUFOND
ESSONITE GARNET HYACINTH
ESTABLISH BED FIX PUT SET BASE
FAST FIRM FOOT MAKE REAR
REST ROOT SEAT BUILD DEFIX
EDIFY ENACT ERECT EVICT
FOUND PLANT PROVE RAISE
SEIZE SETUP START STATE STELL
ATTEST AVOUCH BOTTOM
CEMENT CLINCH CREATE ENROOT
FASTEN FICCHE GROUND INVENT
INVEST LOCATE ORDAIN RATIFY
SETTLE STABLE VERIFY ACCOUNT
APPOINT APPROVE CONFIRM
ENSTATE INSTALL INSTATE
INSTORE POSSESS PREEMPT
SUSTAIN COLONIZE CONSTATE
CONTRACT ENSCONCE ENTRENCH
IDENTIFY INITIATE INSTRUCT
RADICATE REGULATE STABLISH
VALIDATE ASCERTAIN
(— FACT) APPROVE
(— FIRMLY) HAFT INDURATE
(— MORALS) ETHIZE
(— TRUMP) PITCH
ESTABLISHED SAD FAST FIRM
SURE LEGAL ROOTED SEATED

SICCAR STABLE STAPLE STATED
STRONG CERTAIN SETTLED
STANDING
ESTABLISHMENT HONG MILL
SHOP STAB DAIRY FORGE JOINT
PLANT POWER SALON STORE
AGENCY CAISSE CENOBY ECESIS
LAYOUT MENAGE SALOON
SCHOOL ARSENAL ATELIER
BROTHEL COENOBY CONCERN
DOWNSET FACTORY FISHERY
FOUNDRY FUNDUCK SHEBANG
AQUARIUM AVERMENT BUSINESS
CHEESERY CREAMERY ERECTION
HACIENDA
(— IN NEW HABITAT) ECESIS
(— OF COLONY) DEDUCTION
(BATHING —) THERM
(DOMESTIC —) MENAGE
(DRINKING —) STUBE SALOON
BARROOM SHEBEEN
(GAMBLING —) HOUSE TRIPOT
(HORSE-BREEDING —) HARAS
(MONASTIC —) CLOISTER
(WHITE —) MAN
ESTAFETTE COURIER STAFETTE
ESTATE FEE ALOD COPY FEOD FIEF
HOME LAND POMP RANK UDAL
ACRES ALLOD DAIRA DOWER
DOWRY ESTER ESTRE ETHEL
FINCA FUNDO HABIT HOUSE
MANOR STATE TALUK ABBACY
BARONY DEMISE DOMAIN ENTAIL
GROUND LIVING MISTER QUINTA
TALUKA ALODIUM CHATEAU
COMMONS DEMESNE DIGNITY
DISPLAY FORTUNE HAVINGS
MAJORAT ALLODIUM BENEFICE
COPYHOLD DOMINION EXECUTRY
FREEHOLD HACIENDA JOINTURE
LIFEHOLD LONGACRE MESNALTY
POSITION PROPERTY SENATORY
STANDING STAROSTY PATRIMONY
PERPETUITY
(— OF REBEL) FISC FISK
(— WITH SERFS) HAM
(CATTLE —) ESTANCIA
(HINDU —) CHAK
(PORTION OF —) LEGITIM
(REAL —) FUNDUS
(PL.) AMANI
ESTEEM AIM LET USE DEEM HOLD
RATE TALE ADORE COUNT FAVOR
HONOR PRICE PRIDE STEEM
THINK VALUE WEIGH WORTH
ADMIRE CREDIT EXTIME REGARD
REPUTE REVERE TENDER
WONDER ACCOUNT CONCEIT
OPINION RESPECT SUSPECT
APPRAISE CONSIDER ESTIMATE
VENERATE
ESTEEMED DEAR PRECIOUS
ESTER FMN BIXIN ETHER OLEIN
SARIN TABUN BORATE CAPRIN
ERUCIN HUMATE LAURIN MALATE
OLEATE ACETATE ADIPATE
ANISATE AZELATE CINERIN
ELAIDIN FORMATE FUROATE
GALLATE HEPARIN INDICAN
LACTATE LACTONE LAURATE
MALEATE MELLATE NITRATE
OCTOATE OXALATE OXAMATE
PECTATE PEPSIDE PICRATE

SORBATE STEARIN SULTONE
ABIETATE ACRYLATE ARSENATE
ARSENITE ARSONATE BEHENATE
BENZOATE CAFFEATE CONGENER
DIPHENAN ESTOLIDE FLUORIDE
FUCOIDIN KETIPATE LINOLATE
LINOLEIN MALONATE MARGARIN
MYRISTIN NUCLEATE PALMITIN
PIMELATE PIPERATE RACEMATE
SEBACATE SELENATE SILICATE
SINAPATE STEARATE SUBERATE
TARTRATE PYRETHRIN
(SUFF.) OATE
ESTHER (COUSIN OF —) MORDECAI
(FATHER OF —) ABIHAIL
(HUSBAND OF —) AHASUERUS
ESTHER WATERS (AUTHOR OF —)
MOORE
(CHARACTER IN —) FRED RICE
LATCH SARAH ESTHER JACKIE
PEGGIE TUCKER WATERS
PARSONS WILLIAM BARFIELD
ESTIMABLE GOOD SOLID WORTH
GENTLE HONEST WORTHY
THRIFTY VALUABLE
ESTIMATE AIM SET CALL CAST
GAGE RANK RATE READ RECK
ASSAY AUDIT CARAT CENSE
COUNT GAUGE GUESS JUDGE
MOUNT PLACE PRIZE SCALE
STOCK TALLY VALUE WEIGH
ASSESS BUDGET ESTEEM RECKON
REGARD SURVEY ACCOUNT
AVERAGE BALANCE CENSURE
COMPUTE CONCEIT MEASURE
APPRAISE CONSIDER CRITIQUE
CALCULATE
(— OF ONE'S SELF) OPINION
(— TOO HIGHLY) OVERRATE
(LOW COST —) LOWBALL
ESTIMATION AIM EYE CESS FAME
NAME ODOR PASS RATE COUNT
HONOR PRICE SIEGE VALUE
CHOICE ESTEEM REGARD REPUTE
ACCOUNT OPINION JUDGMENT
PRESTIGE
(— OF STRAIGHTNESS) BONING
(HIGH —) CONCEIT
(LOW —) DISREPUTE
ESTIMATOR RATER CRUISER
ESTOC STOCK SWORD
ESTOILE STAR ETOILE

ESTONIA
CAPITAL: TALLINN
COIN: SENT KROON ESTMARK
DIALECT: TARTU
ISLAND: DAGO MUHU OESEL
SAARE VORMSI HIIUMAA
SAAREMAA
LAKE: PEIPUS
MEASURE: TUN ELLE LIIN PANG
SUND TOLL TOOP FADEN VERST
SAGENE VERSTA KULIMET
VERCHOC TONNLAND
NATIVE: ESTH AESTI
PROVINCE: SAARE
RIVER: EMA NARVA PARNU
KASARI
TOWN: NARVA PARNU REVAL
TARTU TALLINN
WEIGHT: LOOD NAEL PUUD

ESTONIAN ESTH
ESTOP BAR FILL PLUG STOP DEBAR
PREVENT
ESTRANGE PART WEAN ALIEN
AVERT DIVERT ALIENATE
DISUNITE STRANGER
ESTRANGED ALIEN
ESTRANGEMENT STANCE
DISTASTE
ESTRAY STRAY WANDER
ESTREAT COPY FINE EXACT
RECORD STREET EXTRACT
EXTREAT
ESTREPEMENT STRIP
E STRING QUINT
ESTRIOL THEELOL
ESTROGEN MESTRANOL
ESTRONE THEELIN
ESTRUS HEAT SEASON
ESTUARY PARA WASH CREEK
FIRTH FLEET FRITH INLET LIMAN
ESTERO
ETCETERA ETC KTL
ETCH BITE FROST ENGRAVE
AQUATINT INSCRIBE
ETCHED FROSTED
ETCHER POINT
ETCHING ETCH AQUATINT
ETEOCLES (BROTHER OF —)
POLYNICES
(FATHER OF —) OEDIPUS
(MOTHER OF —) JOCASTA
ETERNAL ETERNE TARNAL
AGELESS ENDLESS LASTING
UNAGING ENDURING IMMORTAL
TIMELESS UNCAUSED
ETERNALLY AKE EER EVER
ALWAYS ETERNE FOREVER
ETERNITY AGE EON AEON OLAM
GLORY ETERNE ETERNAL
EWIGKEIT INFINITY PERPETUITY
ETESIAN ANNUAL PERIODIC
ETHAN (FATHER OF —) KISHI MAHOL
ETHANE DIMETHYL
ETHAN FROME (AUTHOR OF —)
WHARTON
(CHARACTER IN —) ETHAN FROME
ZEENA MATTIE PIERCE SILVER
ZENOBIA
ETHBAAL (DAUGHTER OF —)
JEZEBEL
ETHER AIR SKY APIOL ESTER
PINOLE ANISOLE ASARONE
EPOXIDE ETHYLIN HARMINE
SAFROLE SESAMIN SESAMOL
SOLVENT ACACETIN ELEMICIN
EMPYREAN GUAIACOL
PHENETOLE
ETHEREAL AERY AIRY SKYEY
AERIAL SKYISH AIRLIKE ETHERIC
FRAGILE SLENDER DELICATE
HEAVENLY SUPERNAL VAPOROUS
ETHICAL ETHIC MORAL
HONORABLE
ETHICS HEDONICS PHILOSOPHY

ETHIOPIA
ANCIENT CAPITAL: AXUM AKSUM
CAPITAL: ADDISABABA
COIN: BESA BIRR AMOLE GIRSH
DOLLAR TALARI ASHRAFI
PIASTER
DEPRESSION: DANAKIL

FALLS: TISISAT BLUENILE
ISLANDS: DAHLAK
LAKE: ABE TANA ABAYA SHOLA
ZEWAY RUDOLF STEFANIE
LANGUAGE: GEEZ TIGRE SOMALI
AMHARIC GALLINYA TIGRINYA
MARRIAGE: DAMOZ QURBAN
SEMANYA
MEASURE: TAT KUBA SINJER
SINZER FARSAKH FARSANG
MOUNTAIN: BATUGUGEGUNATALO
MOUNTAINS: AHMAR CHOKE
NAME: ABYSSINIA
NATIVE: AFAR GALLA ABIGAR
AMHARA ANNUAK HAMITE
SEMITE SOMALI TIGRAI CUSHITE
DANAKIL FALASHA
PORT: ASSAB MASSAWA
PRINCE: RAS
PROVINCE: BALE KEFA WELO
ARUSI GOJAM HARER SHEWA
TIGRE SIDAMO ERITREA
RIVER: OMO WEB BARO DAWA
GILA ABBAI AKOBO AWASH
FAFAN TAKKAZE
TOWN: EDD DESE GOBA GORE
JIMA THIO ADOLA ADUWA
AKSUM ASSAB AWASH DIMTU
HARAR HARER JIMMA MOJJO
ASMARA DESSYE DUNKUR
GONDAR MAKALE MEKELE
GARDULA MASSAWA NAKAMTI
NEKEMTE DIREDAWA LALIBALA
MUSTAHIL
VALLEY: RIFT
WATERFALL: FINCHA DALVERME
TESISSAT
WEIGHT: KASM NATR OKET ALADA
NETER WAKEA WOGIET
FARASULA

ETHIOPIAN SIDI HAMITE HARARI
AETHIOP AFRICAN CUSHITE
FALASHA
ETHIOPIC GIZ GEEZ GHEEZ
ETHNAN (FATHER OF —) ASHUR
(MOTHER OF —) HELAH
ETHNIC (— GROUP) ACHANG
ETHNOLOGIST AMERICAN GIBBS
HODGE LOWIE MASON SMITH
FEWKES MOONEY MORGAN
THOMAS BARROWS GODDARD
HENSHAW PILLING FLETCHER
GATSCHET GRINNELL CHURCHILL
SCHOOLCRAFT
AUSTRIAN MULLER LUSCHAN
WINTERNITZ
DANISH RASMUSSEN
DUTCH STEINMETZ NIEUWENHUIS
ENGLISH HADDON LATHAM
PRICHARD
FINNISH CASTREN
GERMAN BOEHM FINSCH GROSSE
KRAUSE BASTIAN GERLAND
STEINEN FROBENIUS FRIEDERICI
RUSSIAN KOPPEN
ETHOS MANNER
ETHYLENE ELAYL ETHENE ETHERIN
ETIQUETTE FORM DECORUM
MANNERS
(— OF DRINKING TEA) CHANOYU
ETRUSCAN TUSCAN RASENNA
ETRURIAN TYRRHENE

(PL.) TURSENOI TYRRHENI
ETUDE STUDY
ETUI CASE ETWEE TWEEZE
TWEEZER EQUIPAGE RETICULE
ETYMOLOGY ORIGIN DERIVATION
ETYMON RADIX
EUAECHME (DAUGHTER OF —)
PERIBOEA
(FATHER OF —) MEGAREUS
(HUSBAND OF —) ALCATHOUS
EUBOEANS ABANTES
EUCALYPT GUM YATE APPLE
BIMBIL CARBUN JARRAH MALLEE
MYRTAL CARBEEN CUTTAIL
MESSMAN COOLABAH IRONBARK
MESSMATE WHITETOP YERTCHUK
EUCALYPTOLE CINEOL CINEOLE
EUCALYPTUS BLUEGUM
EUCALYPT WHIPSTICK
EUCHARIST HOUSEL MAUNDY
SUPPER MYSTERY VIATICUM
EUCHARISTIC (— ELEMENTS) HAGIA
EUCHITE SATANIST ADELPHIAN
MESSALIAN
EUCHRE LOVE
(— HAND) JAMBONE JAMBOREE
EUDAEMONIA HAPPINESS
EUDOCIMUS GUARA
EUDOXIA (FATHER OF —) BAUTO
(HUSBAND OF —) ARCADIUS
(SON OF —) THEODOSIUS
EUGENE ONEGIN (CHARACTER IN —
) OLGA GREMIN LARINA ONEGIN
OLENSKY TATYANA TRIQUET
(COMPOSER OF —) TCHAIKOVSKY
EUGENIE GRANDET (AUTHOR OF —)
BALZAC
(CHARACTER IN —) NANON
CHARLES CRUCHOT EUGENIE
GRANDET DEGRASSINS
EULALIA NETI
EULENSPIEGEL OWLGLASS
EULOGIST PRAISER LAUREATE
PANEGYRIST
EULOGISTIC EULOGIC EPENETIC
MAGNIFIC LAUDATORY
EULOGY PRAISE TONGUE ADDRESS
ELOGIUM ORATION ENCOMIUM
PANEGYRE
EUMOLPUS (FATHER OF —)
NEPTUNE
(MOTHER OF —) CHIONE
(SON OF —) ISMARUS
EUNEUS (BROTHER OF —) THOAS
(FATHER OF —) JASON
(MOTHER OF —) HYPSIPYLE
EUNICE (SON OF —) TIMOTHEUS
EUNUCH CAPON SPORUS WETHER
GELDING HALFMAN CASTRATE
EUPHAUSID SHRIMP
EUPHEMISM DEE FIB GEE GOR
DASH GOSH GOLES GOLLY LAWKS
DIANTRE DICKENS GRACIOUS
EUPHEMUS (FATHER OF —)
NEPTUNE POSEIDON
(MOTHER OF —) EUROPA
(SON OF —) BATTUS
EUPHONIOUS TUNEFUL
EUPHORIA ELATION
EUPHROSYNE JOY
EUPHUISM GONGORISM
EURASIAN BURGHER FERINGI
EUREKA RED PUCE

EURO WALLAROO
EUROPA (BROTHER OF —) CILIX CADMUS THASUS PHINEUS PHOENIX
(FATHER OF —) AGENOR
(HUSBAND OF —) ASTERIUS
(MOTHER OF —) TELEPHASSA
(SON OF —) MINOS SARPEDON RHADAMANTHYS
EUROPE BELAIT CONTINENT

EUROPE
(ALSO SEE SPECIFIC COUNTRIES)
LAKE: COMO GARDA ONEGA VANEM GENEVA LADOGA LUGANO PEIPUS VANERN ZURICH BALATON MALAREN SCUTARI VATTERN MAGGIORE CONSTANCE NEUCHATEL
MOUNTAIN: DOM ETNA ELBRUS KAZBEK LYSKAMM SHKHARA JUNGFRAU NADELHORN WEISSHORN ZUGSPITZE MATTERHORN
NATION: ITALY SPAIN FRANCE GREECE MONACO NORWAY POLAND RUSSIA SWEDEN ALBANIA ANDORRA AUSTRIA BELGIUM DENMARK ENGLAND FINLAND GERMANY HOLLAND HUNGARY IRELAND ROMANIA BULGARIA PORTUGAL SCOTLAND SANMARINO LUXEMBOURG YUGOSLAVIA EASTGERMANY NETHERLANDS SOVIETUNION SWITZERLAND VATICANCITY WESTGERMANY GREATBRITAIN LIECHTENSTEIN UNITEDKINGDOM CZECHOSLOVAKIA
RANGE: ALPS URAL BALKAN KJOLEN RHODOPE SUDETEN CAUCASUS PYRENEES APENNINES CARPATHIAN
RIVER: PO AAR DON AARE EBRO ELBE ODER DOURO DVINA LOIRE RHINE RHONE SEINE TAGUS TIBER VOLGA DANUBE THAMES DNIEPER VISTULA DNIESTER

EUROPEAN FRANK SAHIB BOHUNK EUROPE FRINGE INDIAN FERINGI TOPIWALA
(— IN INDIES) BLIJVER
(WESTERN —) FRANK
EUROPEAN BARRACUDA SPET
EUROPEAN BASS BRASSE
EUROPEAN BISON AUROCHS
EUROPEAN CLOVER ALSIKE
EUROPEAN GULL MEW
EUROPEAN HERRING SPRAT
EUROPEAN JUNIPER CADE
EUROPEAN KITE GLEDE
EUROPEAN LAVENDER ASPIC
EUROPEAN LINDEN TEIL
EUROPEAN MINT HYSSOP
EUROPEAN OAK DURMAST
EUROPEAN PERCH RUFF RUFFE
EUROPEAN POLECAT FITCHEW
EUROPEAN PORGY BESUGO
EUROPEAN RABBIT CONY
EUROPEAN SHARK TOPE

EUROPEAN SPARROW WHITECAP
EUROPEAN STARLING STARNEL
EUROPEAN SWALLOW MARTIN
EUROPEAN THRUSH MAVIS OUZEL
EUROPEAN WIDGEON WHIM WHEWER
EUROPEAN WREN STAG
EURYANTHE (CHARACTER IN —) ADOLAR LYSIART EGLANTINE EURYANTHE
(COMPOSER OF —) WEBER
EURYBIA (FATHER OF —) PONTUS
(MOTHER OF —) GAEA
(SON OF —) PALLAS PERSES ASTRAEUS
EURYNOME (DAUGHTERS OF —) GRACES CHARITES
(FATHER OF —) CHAOS OCEANUS
EURYPTERID SERAPHIM
EURYPYLUS (FATHER OF —) NEPTUNE TELEPHUS
(MOTHER OF —) ASTYOCHE
(SLAYER OF —) PYRRHUS HERCULES
EURYSACES (FATHER OF —) AJAX
(MOTHER OF —) TECMESSA
EURYSTHEUS (FATHER OF —) STHENELUS
(MOTHER OF —) NICIPPE
(SLAYER OF —) HYLLUS
EURYTUS (DAUGHTER OF —) IOLE
(FATHER OF —) ACTOR AUGEAS MELANEUS
(MOTHER OF —) GAEA
(SLAYER OF —) HERCULES
EUTECTIC STEADITE
EUTERPE (FATHER OF —) JUPITER
(MOTHER OF —) MNEMOSYNE
EUXANTHONE PURRONE
EUXOA AGROTIS
EVACUATE PASS VENT VOID AVOID EMPTY EXPEL STOOL VACATE DEPRIVE EXCRETE EXHAUST NULLIFY VACUATE PERSPIRE
EVACUATION OFFICE DUNKIRK
EVADE BEG GEE BILK DUCK FLEE FOIL JOUK JUMP SHUN SLIP VOID AVERT AVOID BLINK DALLY DODGE ELUDE FENCE FLANK PARRY SHIRK SKIRT SKIVE BAFFLE BLENCH BYPASS COPOUT DELUDE ESCAPE ILLUDE BEGUILE FINESSE OUTSLIP QUIBBLE HEDGEHOP LEAPFROG SIDESTEP
(— LEGAL PROCESS) ABSCOND
(— PAYMENT) BILK
(— WORK) JOUK BLUDGE
EVADNE (FATHER OF —) PELIAS NEPTUNE POSEIDON
(HUSBAND OF —) CAPANEUS
(MOTHER OF —) IPHIS PITANA
(SON OF —) IAMUS
EVALUATE RATE ASSESS PONDER RECKON DISSECT APPRAISE ESTIMATE
EVALUATION STOCK ESTIMATE
EVANDER (FATHER OF —) HERMES
(MOTHER OF —) CARMENTA
EVANESCE FADE VANISH
EVANESCENCE ANICCA
EVANESCENT FLEET EVANID

BRITTLE CURSORY EVASIVE FRAGILE DELICATE FLEETING FLITTING FUGITIVE STAYLESS
EVANGELICAL GOSPEL SIMEONITE
(— ACTIVITY) WARFARE
EVANGELIST LUKE MARK EVANGEL GOSPELER SALVATIONIST
EVAPORATE DRY EXHALE AVOLATE CONDENSE VAPORIZE
EVAPORATOR BOILER EFFECT
EVASION JINK SLIP DODGE QUIRK SALVE SHIFT AMBAGE ESCAPE SNATCH ELUSION OFFCOME SHUFFLE TWISTER ARTIFICE ESCAPISM VOIDANCE
EVASIVE SLY EELY DODGY SHIFTY SUBTLE TWISTY ELUSIVE ELUSORY TRICKSY SLIPPERY SLIPSKIN
(TO BE —) STONEWALL
EVE DUSK EREB EREV EVEN VIGIL SUNSET SUNDOWN
(NEW YEAR'S —) HAGMENA HOGMANAY
EVELINA (AUTHOR OF —) BURNEY
(CHARACTER IN —) JOHN DUVAL ARTHUR HOWARD ANVILLE BELMONT CLEMENT EVELINA ORVILLE VILLARS WILLOUGHBY
EVEN ALL DEN EEN TIE YET FAIR HUNK JUST PAIR TIED TILL ALINE CLEAN EQUAL EVERY EXACT FLUSH GRADE HUNKY LEVEL MATCH PLAIN RIVAL STILL SUANT SUENT SWEET DIRECT ITSELF PLACID SILKEN SMOOTH SQUARE STEADY ABREAST BALANCE EQUABLE FLATTEN REGULAR UNIFORM UPSIDES EQUALIZE MODERATE PARALLEL
(— NUMBERS) PAIR
(— OFF) LEVEL
(— THOUGH) IF ALTHO ALBEIT ALTHOUGH
(MAKE —) WEIGH STEADY
(PREF.) ARTIO HOMAL(O) LEUR(O)
EVENING DEN EVE EREB EVEN ABEND TARDE SUNSET VESPER EVENTIDE VESPERAL
(— BEFORE PASSOVER) PARASCEVE
(— OF SONG) CEILIDH
(AT —) TEEN
(YESTERDAY —) STREEN
EVENING PRIMROSE SUNCUP SCABIOUS
EVENING STAR VENUS HESPER VESPER EVESTAR HESPERUS
EVENLY FAIR PLAIN FLATLY EQUALLY
EVENNESS EQUALITY
EVENT HAP CASE FACT FATE FEAT TILT CASUS DOING EPOCH FRAME ISSUE THING ACTION EFFECT FACTUM RESULT TIDING TIMING EPISODE FIXTURE MIRACLE PORTENT TRAGEDY INCIDENT OCCASION OCCURRENCE
(AMUSING —) COMEDY
(CHANCE —) ACCIDENT FORTUITY
(EXTRAORDINARY —) MIRACLE
(FORTUITOUS —) HAZARD
(GRAVE —) CALAMITY
(HAPPY —) GODSEND

(IMPORTANT —) ACE ERA
(PAST —S) HISTORY
(SEISMIC —) STARQUAKE
(SET OF —S) EPISODE
(SIGNIFICANT —) CRISIS
(SKI —) DOWNHILL
(SOCIAL —) BENEFIT
(SPORTING —) STAKE
(THEATRICAL —) DRAW
(TURNING-POINT —) LANDMARK
(UNEXPECTED —) STUNNER ACCIDENT AFTERCLAP
(UNPLEASANT —) BUMMER
(YEARLY —) ANNUAL
EVENTFUL LIVELY NOTABLE
EVENTIDE VESPER EVENING
EVENTUAL LAST FINAL ULTIMATE
EVENTUALITY EVENT
EVENTUALLY YET FINALLY
EVENTUATE GO LEAD ISSUE RESULT SUCCEED ULTIMATE
EVENUS (DAUGHTER OF —) MARPESSA
(FATHER OF —) ARES MARS
EVER O AY SO AYE EER ONCE STILL ALWAYS ETERNE FOREVER
EVERGLADE STATE FLORIDA
EVERGREEN BOX FIR IVY YEW ASIS BAGO ILEX PINE TAWA BOLDO CAROB CEDAR HEATH HOLLY LARCH SAVIN THUYA TOYON BAUERA COIGUE DAHOON LAUREL MASTIC SPRUCE BANKSIA BARETTA BEBEERU BILIMBI GOWIDDE HEMLOCK JASMINE TARATAH BOXTHORN CALFKILL CARAUNDA IRONWOOD TILESEED
(PL.) CHRISTMAS
EVER-INCREASING ACCRESCENT
EVERLASTING ETERNE AEONIAL AEONIAN AGELONG DURABLE ENDLESS ETERNAL FOREVER LASTING TEDIOUS ENDURING IMMORTAL INFINITE TIMELESS PERPETUAL
EVERLASTINGLY ALWAYS FOREVER
EVERSION BLOWOUT BEARINGS
EVERT UPSET EVERSE SUBVERT OVERTURN
EVERY ALL ANY ILK PER THE EACH EVER ILKA ENTIRE EVERICH COMPLETE
(— DAY) QD QUOTID
(— HOUR) QH
(— NIGHT) QN
(PREF.) PAM PAN
EVERYBODY ALL EACH EVERYMAN EVERYONE
EVERYDAY USUAL HOMELY PROSAIC ORDINARY WORKADAY
EVERY MAN IN HIS HUMOUR
(AUTHOR OF —) JONSON
(CHARACTER IN —) EDWARD KITELY BOBADIL BRIDGET CLEMENT KNOWELL MATTHEW WELLBRED BRAINWORM
EVERYTHING ALL ATHING
EVERYWHERE PASSIM UBIQUE ALGATES AYWHERE OVERALL ALLWHERE
EVICT OUST EJECT EXPEL
EVIDENCE MARK SHOW SIGN TEST

PROOF SCRIP SMOKE TOKEN
TRACE TRIAL ATTEST AVOUCH
BETOKE RECORD REVEAL
CHARTER EXHIBIT HEARSAY
SHOWING SUPPORT ARGUMENT
DISPROOF DOCUMENT EVICTION
INDICATE MANIFEST MONUMENT
MUNIMENT WARRANTY
ADMINICLE
(— OF DISEASE) SYMPTOM
(— OF FRESHNESS) BLOOM
(— OF WRONGDOING) GOODS
(POSITIVE —) CONSTAT

EVIDENT LOUD OPEN PERT APERT
BROAD CLEAR FRANK GROSS
NAKED PLAIN EXTANT LIQUID
PATENT WITTER EMINENT
GLARING OBVIOUS PROBATE
VISIBLE APPARENT DISTINCT
FLAGRANT LUCULENT MANIFEST
PALPABLE
(PREF.) DELO

EVIL BAD DER ILL SIN BALE BASE
DIRE HARM LEWD PAPA POOR
SORE VICE VILE WICK YELL CRIME
CURSE DEVIL FELON FOLLY
HYDRA MALUM QUEDE SORRY
WATHE WRONG CANCEL DIVERS
INJURY MALIGN MENACE
NAUGHT PLAGUE ROTTEN
SHREWD SINFUL UNFEEL UNFELE
UNGOOD UNWELL WICKED
WONDER ADVERSE BALEFUL
CORRUPT DISEASE DIVERSE
HEINOUS HURTFUL IMMORAL
MISDEED NOXIOUS SATANIC
UNHAPPY UNSOUND VICIOUS
CALAMITY DEPRAVED DEVILISH
DISASTER GANGRENE IMPROPER
INIQUITY MISCHIEF QUEDSHIP
SINISTER NEFARIOUS
(— BEING) MARF
(— OF MANY PHASES) HYDRA
(— SPIRIT) JUMBIE
(IMAGINARY —) WINDMILL
(IMPENDING —) MENACE
IMMINENCE
(SOCIAL —) SCOURGE
(SPIRITUAL —) SCAB
(PREF.) MAL(E) PONERO

EVILDOER BADMASH BUDMASH
SLASHER

EVIL EYE DROCHUIL MALOCCHIO

EVINCE SHOW ARGUE PROVE
SUBDUE BREATHE CONQUER
DISPLAY EXHIBIT EVIDENCE
INDICATE MANIFEST

EVISCERATE GUT DRAW BOWEL
PAUNCH GARBAGE

EVOCATION SADHANA

EVOCATIVE REDOLENT

EVOKE FIT MOVE STIR EDUCE
AROUSE ELICIT SUMMON
EVOCATE PROVOKE SUGGEST

EVOLUTION DRIFT GROWTH
BIOGENY DIOECISM HOROTELY
MANEUVER BRADYTELY
(PL.) AEROBATICS

EVOLUTIONISM DARWINISM

EVOLVE COOK EMIT EDUCE DERIVE
UNFOLD UNROLL BLOSSOM
DEVELOP EVOLUTE CONCEIVE
UNPLIGHT

EWE KEB TEG CROCK CRONE
DRAPE SHEEP GIMMER LAMBER
RACHEL THEAVE CHILVER
(— AND LAMB) COUPLE
(OLD —) BIDDY CROCK CRONE
BIDDIE
(YOUNG —) THEAVE

EWER JUG CREW LAIR BASIN
UDDER PITCHER URCEOLE

EXACERBATE SOUR ENRAGE
FERMENT EMBITTER IRRITATE

EXACERBATION PAROXYSM

EXACT ASK DUE DEAD EVEN FINE
FLAT HAVE JUMP JUST LEVY
NEAT NICE TRUE VERY PRESS
SCREW WREAK WREST COMPEL
DEMAND ELICIT EVINCE EXTORT
FORMAL GRAITH MINUTE
NARROW PROPER SEVERE
SQUARE STRAIT STRICT CAREFUL
CERTAIN COLLECT COMMAND
CORRECT ENFORCE ESTREAT
EXPRESS EXTRACT LITERAL
PARTILE PERFECT POINTED
PRECISE PRECISO REFINED
REGULAR REQUIRE ACCURATE
CRITICAL EXPLICIT FAITHFUL
RIGOROUS SPECIFIC
(— BY FINE) ESTREAT
(— SATISFACTION) AVENGE
(NOT —) PLATIC
(PREF.) ORTH(O)

EXACTING NICE HARSH PICKY
STERN STIFF TIGHT SCREWY
SEVERE STRAIT STRICT ARDUOUS
EXIGENT FINICKY ONEROUS
CRITICAL IMPOSING IRONCLAD
PRESSING SCREWING
PARTICULAR PERSNICKETY
(— EXCLUSIVE DEVOTION) JEALOUS

EXACTION TAX MART GOUGE
GRIPE
(— OF PROVISIONS) CESS COYNE
COIGNY
(UNDUE —) EXTORTION

EXACTLY DUE BANG DEAD EVEN
FLAT FLOP FULL JUMP JUST
VERY PLUMB PLUNK QUITE RIGHT
SHARP SPANG TRULY ARIGHT
EVENLY ITSELF JUSTLY NICELY
PERFECT SLAPDAB DIRECTLY
MINUTELY SMACKDAB

EXACTNESS RIGOR TRUTH NICETY
ACCURACY DELICACY DISPATCH
FIDELITY IDENTITY JUSTNESS
SAPIENCE SEVERITY PRECISION
PARTICULARITY
(FUSSY —) FIKE

EXAGGERATE GAB MORE COLOR
BOUNCE CHARGE COLOUR
EXTEND OVERDO AMPLIFY
ENHANCE ENLARGE MAGNIFY
OUTLASH ROMANCE STRETCH
INCREASE OVERDRAW OVERLASH
OVERPLAY OVERTELL OVERSTATE
OVERCHARGE
(— OPENING OF MOUTH) CHINK

EXAGGERATED CAMP SLAB TALL
COLORED FUSTIAN FABULOUS
INFLATED OVERDONE OVERSHOT
OVERWEENING

EXAGGERATING ARROGANT

EXAGGERATION BLAH

REACHER HYPERBOLE

EXALT HAUT REAR AREAR BUILD
DEIFY ELATE ERECT EXTOL HEAVE
HEEZE HONOR MOUNT RAISE
TOWER ALTIFY ASCEND EXHALE
PREFER REFINE THRONE UPREAR
WORTHY ADVANCE AUGMENT
DIGNIFY ELEVATE ENHANCE
ENNOBLE FEATHER GLORIFY
GREATEN INSPIRE MAGNIFY
PROMOTE SUBLIME DIVINIZE
ENTHRONE GRADUATE HEIGHTEN
INHEAVEN PEDESTAL

EXALTATION LAUD AVATAR
ANAGOGE ANAGOGY ELATION
RAPTURE ERECTION

EXALTED HAUT HIGH ELATE
GRAND LOFTY NOBLE SHEEN
SKYEY SOARY ASTRAL TIPTOE
TOPFUL HAUGHTY SUBLIME
ELEVATED EXALTATE MAGNIFIC

EXALTING HUMAN

EXAM MUG

EXAMINATION EX MAY EXAM
FACE QUIZ TEST ASSAY AUDIT
BOARD CHECK FINAL GREAT
POINT PROBE STUDY TRIAL
BIOPSY EXAMEN NOTICE REVIEW
SCHOOL SEARCH SURVEY TRIPOS
AUTOPSY BEARING CANVASS
CHECKUP DIVVERS EXAMINE
HEARING INQUEST INQUIRY
MIDYEAR OPPOSAL TUGGERY
ANALYSIS CRITIQUE DOCIMASY
EXERCISE NECROPSY PHYSICAL
RESEARCH SCANNING SCRUTINY
PRACTICAL PRELIMINARY
(PL.) HOURS
(SUFF.) SCOPE SCOPIC SCOPUS
SCOPY

EXAMINE ASK CON FAN SEE SPY
TRY BOLT CASE COMB FEEL LAIT
LINE LOOK OGLE QUIZ RIPE SCAN
SEEK SIFT TEST VIEW ASSAY
AUDIT CHECK ENTER GROPE
PROBE QUEST QUOTE SAMEN
SENSE SOUND STUDY VISIT
APPOSE BEHOLD CANDLE DEBATE
PERUSE PONDER REVIEW SCREEN
SEARCH SURVEY ANALYZE
CANVASS COLLATE DISCUSS
EXPLORE INQUIRE INSPECT
OVERSEE PALPATE RUMMAGE
COGNOSCE CONSIDER OVERHAUL
TRAVERSE
(— BY TOUCH) PALPATE
(— CAREFULLY) SCAN SIFT
PONDER
(— LAND) SOUM

EXAMINER POSER TRIER CENSOR
CONNER SABORA ANALYST
APPOSER AUDITOR CORONER
PROBATOR SEARCHER

EXAMPLE A CASE CAST COPY
LEAD NORM TYPE BEAUT BYSEN
ESSAY LIGHT MODEL PIECE
EMBLEM PRAXIS SAMPLE
BOUNCER LEADING LECTURE
PATTERN PURPOSE SAMPLER
THEATER CALENDAR ENSAMPLE
EXEMPLAR EXEMPLUM FORBYSEN
FOREGOER INSTANCE PARADIGM
SPECIMEN

(DISGRACEFUL —) BIZEN BYSEN
BYZEN MONSTROSITY
(EXTREME —) CAUTION
(FINEST —) PEARL
(INFERIOR —) EXCUSE
(INSTRUCTIVE —) LESSON
(OLDEST —) DOYEN
(PERFECT —) APOTHEOSIS
(STANDARD —) PROTOTYPE
(SUPERLATIVE —) BLINGER

EXANTHEMA DIEBACK ERUPTION

EXASPERATE IRE IRK MAD BAIT
GALL HEAT URGE ANNOY BLOOD
ENRAGE EXCITE NETTLE EXASPER
INFLAME PROVOKE ROUGHEN
ACERBATE IRRITATE

EXASPERATED SNAKY WROTH
SNAKEY SNAKISH ACERBATE

EXASPERATION GALL HEAT
WRATH

EXCAVATE CUT DIG PIT HOLE
HOWK MINE MOLE MUCK PION
SINK DELVE DRILL DRIVE GRAVE
NAVVY SCOOP STOPE BURROW
DREDGE EXCAVE GULLET
HOLLOW QUARRY

EXCAVATION CUT DIG PIT HOLE
MINE REDD SINK SUMP BERRY
DELFT DELPH DITCH GRAFT
GRAVE HEUGH PILOT STOPE
BURROW CAVITY DUGOUT
GROOVE TRENCH BREAKUP
CUTTING PADDOCK TUTWORK
WORKING DENEHOLE SLUSHPIT

EXCAVATOR DIG BUDAR GLFOID
DIGGER DIPPER DRIFTER
HATCHET PIONEER

EXCEED COW TOP BEST PASS
EXCEL OUTDO OUTGO BETTER
OUTRUN OUTVIE OVERDO
OVERGO ECLIPSE OUTPASS
OVERRUN OVERTAX PRECEDE
SURPASS OUTRANGE OUTREACH
OUTSTRIP OVERCOME OVERGANG
OVERSTEP OVERWEND
SURMOUNT PREPONDERATE
(— IN IMPORTANCE) OVERSHADOW
(— THE RESOURCES) BEGGAR

EXCEEDING VILE

EXCEEDINGLY ALL DONE PURE
TRES VERY AMAIN BLAME
BLAMED MASTER PROPER
PURELY AWFULLY LICKING
PARLOUS PASSING HEARTILY
HEAVENLY HORRIBLE PROPERLY
(PREF.) PRE ULTRA

EXCEL CAP COB TOP BANG BEAT
BEST DING FLOG MEND PASS
STAR BLECK OUTDO OUTGO
SHINE TRUMP BETTER EXCEED
MASTER OUTRAY OVERDO
OVERGO PRECEL ECLIPSE
EMULATE OUTPEER SURPASS
OUTCLASS OUTRANGE OUTRIVAL
OUTSHINE OUTSTRIP OVERPEER
SUPERATE SURMOUNT

EXCELLENCE ARETE MERIT PRICE
VIRTU WORTH BEAUTY DESERT
HEIGHT VIRTUE DIGNITY
PROWESS GOODNESS SPLENDOR
BRILLIANCE PREROGATIVE
(— OF QUALITY) STRIKE
(MORAL —) GRACE

(PL.) SANCTITIES

EXCELLENT FAB GAY RUM BEST
BOSS BRAW COOL FINE GOOD
HEND HIGH PURE RARE RIAL
SLAP TALL TRIM ATHEL BONNY
BONZA BRAVE BULLY BURLY
CRACK GREAT JAMMY JOLLY
LUMMY PIOUS PRIME SOLID
SUPER SWELL TOUGH TRIED
WALLY BONNIE BONZER BOSKER
BUMPER CHEESY CHOICE CLASSY
FAMOUS FREELY GENTLE GOODLY
PRETTY PROPER SELECT SPIFFY
WICKED WIZARD WORTHY
YANKEE BLIGHTY BOSHTER
CAPITAL CORKING CURIOUS
ELEGANT GALLANT IMMENSE
QUALITY SNIFTER STAVING
TOPPING CLIPPING COLOSSAL
EXIMIOUS GENEROUS KNOCKOUT
SPIFFING STUNNING SUPERIOR
VALUABLE VIRTUOUS WAUREGAN
YNGOODLY
(— IN QUALITY) FRANK
(MOST —) BEST

EXCELLENTLY BRAWLY CLEVER
FINELY FREELY PROUDLY
DIVINELY FAMOUSLY

EXCELLING BEST PASSANT

EXCEPT BAR BUT CEP NOT BATE
BOUT OMIT ONLY SAVE ABATE
FORBY SEVER EXEMPT FORBYE
NOBBUT SAVING SCUSIN UNLESS
BARRING BESIDES EXCLUDE
OUTCEPT OUTSIDE OUTTAKE
OUTWITH RESERVE WITHOUT
FORPRISE OUTTAKEN RESERVED
(PREF.) PRETER

EXCEPTING BATING EXCEPT
SAVING UNLESS BARRING

EXCEPTION DEMUR SALVO SAVING
DISSENT OFFENSE DEMURRER
FALLENCY FORPRISE INSTANCE

EXCEPTIONAL RARE EXEMPT
ROUSING STRANGE UNUSUAL
ABERRANT ABNORMAL ESPECIAL
SINGULAR UNCOMMON

EXCEPTIONALLY AMAZING
SPANKING

EXCERPT CITE PATCH QUOTE
SCRAP EXTRACT OFFPRINT
(— FROM SONG) SNATCH

EXCESS OVER PLUS RIOT FLOOD
INORD LUXUS PRIDE ACRASY
SPILTH ACRASIA BALANCE
DEBAUCH EXTREME MISRULE
NIMIETY OUTRAGE OVERAGE
OVERSET PROFUSE RIOTISE
SURFEIT SURPLUS EXCEDENT
GLUTTONY INTEREST OVERLASH
OVERMUCH OVERPLUS
PLEONASM PLETHORA PLEURISY
SATURNALIA OVERABUNDANCE
(— OF ACTION) OVERKILL
(— OF LOGS) BANK
(— OF METAL) FEEDHEAD
(— OF SOLAR MONTH) EPACT
(— OF VOTES) PLURALITY
(SUFF.) ARD ART

EXCESSIVE TOO OVER RANK
ENORM FANCY STEEP STIFF
THICK UNDUE DEADLY DEUCED
WOUNDY BURNING EXTREME

FURIOUS NIMIOUS OVERDUE
SURFEIT ABNORMAL CRIMINAL
DEVILISH ENORMOUS HORRIBLE
INSOLENT OVERMUCH TERRIBLE
TERRIFIC PLETHORIC
(PREF.) POLY SUR

EXCESSIVELY TOO SUPER DEADLY
OVERLY STRONG UNDULY
PARLISH PARLOUS PASSING
PLAGUEY WOUNDLY DEVILISH
PLAGUILY
(PREF.) HYPER

EXCHANGE RAP SET CASH CAUP
CHOP CODE COPE COUP KULA
MART SELL SWAP SWOP BANDY
BOARD BOLSA CORSE SHIFT
STORE TRADE TROKE TRUCK
BARTER BOURSE CAMBIO
CHANGE DICKER EXCAMB
MARKET NIFFER RESALE RIALTO
SCORSE SHOPPE TOLSEL TOLZEY
VALUTA WISSEL WRIXLE
BARROOM CAMBIUM CHAFFER
COMMUTE CONVERT DEALING
PERMUTE TRAFFIC COMMERCE
TRUCKAGE
(— IN CHECKERS) CUT SHOT
(— OF BLOWS) HANDPLAY
(— OF PRISONERS) CARTEL
(— OF SYLLABLES) ANACLASIS
(— SMALL TALK) CHAFFER
(— THOUGHTS) CONVERSE
(— VISITS) GAM
(DANCE —) CROSSOVER
(FAIR —) GIFFGAFF
(FOREIGN —) DEVISE
(POETICAL —) FLYTING
(POST —) CANTEEN
(TELEPHONE —) CENTRAL
(PREF.) CAMBI(O)

EXCHEQUER FISC PURSE COFFER
KHALSA CHECKER FINANCE
TREASURY

EXCIPIENT OXYMEL

EXCISE CUT TAX CROP DUTY GELD
TOLL SLASH EXCIDE EXSECT
IMPOST RESECT EXSCIND
ALCABALA RETRENCH

EXCISEMAN GAGER GAUGER
EXCISOR

EXCISION CUT ERASURE ABLATION

EXCITABLE NERVY NERVOUS

EXCITATION LASH

EXCITE HOT CITE FIRE HEAT HYPO
SEND SPUR STIR URGE WAKE
WHET WORK YERK ALARM
AMOVE ANGER CHAFE ELATE
ERECT FLAME FLUSH IMPEL
PIQUE RAISE ROUSE SCALD
SPOOK AROUSE AWAKEN BOTHER
DAZZLE DECOCT FLURRY FOMENT
GROOVE IGNITE INCEND INCITE
INVOKE JANGLE KINDLE LATHER
PROMPT SALUTE TICKLE UPREAR
WECCHE AGITATE ANIMATE
COMMOVE ENCHAFE FERMENT
INCENSE INFLAME PHILTER
PROVOKE QUICKEN STARTLE
WHITTLE DISQUIET ENGENDER
EXCITATE IRRITATE
(— MIRTH) DIVERT

EXCITED UP GAY HOT AGOG GYTE
PINK ABOIL AGLOW CADGY

EAGER PROUD RANTY SKEER
BLEEZY ELATED HEATED STEAMY
ATHRILL FEVERED HAYWIRE
SKEERED WAKENED AGITATED
ATWITTER ELEVATED FEVERISH
FLURRIED FRENETIC STARTLED
OVERWROUGHT
(EASILY —) KITTLE
(INTENSELY —) MAD

EXCITEMENT ADO GOG BUZZ
FUME FUSS GLOW HEAT KICK
RUFF STIR TOSS UNCO FEEZE
FEVER FUROR KICKS LARRY
MANIA SETUP STOUR UNCOW
FRENZY SPLASH WARMTH
FERMENT FRISSON NERVISM
TAMASHA WIDDRIM BROUHAHA
DELIRIUM INTEREST RACKETRY
(FILLED WITH —) HECTIC
(GREAT —) FEVER
(MENTAL —) WIDDRIM
(PLEASANT —) SUSPENSE
(VIOLENT —) GARE

EXCITING HOT HIGH ZINGY HECTIC
AGACANT BURNING PARLOUS
RACKETY ROUSING EXCITANT
EXCITIVE PATHETIC STIRRING
TERRIFIC
(— HORROR) DIRE DIREFUL

EXCLAIM CRY HOWL BLURT ESCRY
SNORT CLAMOR OUTCRY
BESPEAK

EXCLAMATION (ALSO SEE
INTERJECTION) O AH AI AY BO
EH EY HA HI HO LA LO MY OH
OW SO ST YO AHA AIE BAH BAM
BOO FEN FIE FOH GEE GIP GRR
GUP HAI HAW HAY HEM HEP HEY
HIC HOY HUH NOW OCH OFF OHO
OUF OUT PAH PEW POH POX ROT
SEE SUZ TCH TCK TUT UGH VOW
WEE WOW YAH YOW AHEM ALAS
AVOY BUFF DEAR DRAT EGAD
EVOE FAST GARN GOOD HAIL
HECH HECK HIST HOLA HUFF
HUNH HUSH HYKE OONS OUGH
PHEW PHOO PHUT PIFF PISH
POOH PRUT PUGH RATS RIVO
SCAT SIRS SOFT SOHO TCHU
TUSH WALY WEEK WEET WELL
WHAM WHAT WHEE WHEW WHIR
WHIT WUGG YOOP YULE ALACK
BRAVO EWHOW FAINS FANCY
FAUGH FEIGH GLORY GOODY
HEIGH HELLO HOLLA HUFFA
HULLO HUMPH HUZZA JOSSA
OHONE PSHAW RIGHT SALVE
SHISH SKOAL SORRY SUGAR
TEREU WAUGH WELOO WHING
WHISK WHIST WHOOP WIRRA
WOONS CARAJO CLAMOR
ENCORE HALLOO HEYDAY
HOOTAY HURRAH INDEED
OUTCRY PERFAY QUOTHA
RATHER RIGHTO SHUCKS STEADY
WALKER WHOOSH CARAMBA
DOGGONE GODSAKE HOSANNA
JEEPERS JIGGERS KERCHOO
KERWHAM NICHEVO PRITHEE
RUBBISH SALAMAT TANTIVY
THUNDER WELCOME WHOOPEE
FAREWELL WAESUCKS
WELLAWAY

(— OF DISGUST) AUH FIE FOH PAH
UGH AUGH AVOY PHEW PISH
POOT PSHA PUGH FAUGH FEICH
FEIGH PSHAW WELOO
(— OF DISTRESS) AI AIE HARO
HARROW
(— OF DOUBT) HUM HUMPH
(— OF IMPATIENCE) GIP PHEW
(— OF INCREDULITY) AHEM INDEED
WALKER
(— OF REPUGNANCE) UGH
(— OF SURPRISE) HA OW GIP LAW
HEIN HUNH LACK LAND LAWK
LORD ODSO BABAI HEUGH LAWKS
MARRY CRIMINE CRIMINY
HEAVENS JUCKIES GORBLIMY
GRAMERCY
(— OF TRIUMPH) AH IO GRIG
HEUCH HOOCH HURRAH
(PROFANE —) BAN

EXCLAMATION POINT BANG
SHOUT SCREAMER

EXCLUDE BAR SHUT SINK CLOSE
DEBAR EJECT EXPEL FENCE
BANISH DISBAR EXCEPT EXEMPT
FORBAR FORBID REJECT BLANKET
DEFAULT EXPUNGE FOREBAR
FOREIGN OUTTAKE OUTWALL
REPULSE SECLUDE SUSPEND
OSTRACIZE
(PREF.) DIS

EXCLUDED EXEMPT FOREIGN

EXCLUDING BAR BUT LESS
BARRING

EXCLUSION OSTRACISM

EXCLUSIVE ALL ONLY RARE SOLE
VERY ALONE ELECT WHOLE
NARROW SELECT CLIQUISH
ENTIRELY RECHERCHE
(— OF) BEFORE

EXCLUSIVELY ALL ONLY ALONE
SINGLY ENTIRELY

EXCOGITATE CONSIDER

EXCOMMUNICATE CURSE
UNCHURCH

EXCOMMUNICATION BAN CURSE
HEREM EXCISION

EX-CONVICT LAG LAGGER

EXCORIATE FLAY GALL SCORE
STRIP ABRADE SCATHE SCORCH
BLISTER LAMBASTE

EXCREMENT LEE CRAP DIRT DREG
DUNG FRASS JAKES SIEGE
HOCKEY ORDURE REFUSE
VOIDING CROTTELS COLLUVIES
(— OF EARTHWORM) CAST
(— OF FOXES) SCUMBER
(— OF HARES) CROTTELS
(— OF INSECTS) FRASS
(PL.) DEJECTA
(PREF.) COPR(O) MERDI

EXCRESCENCE NOB PIN WEN
BURL BURR GALL HORN KNOB
KNOT KNUR LUMP SCAB WART
FUSEE FUZEE KNURL THORN
EXCESS HURTLE MORULA NUBBLE
PIMPLE BOLSTER PUSTULE
RATTAIL SPINACH CARUNCLE
EPITHEMA TUBERCLE
(— ON HORSE'S FOOT) FIG TWITTER
(— ON WHALE'S HEAD) BONNET
(PREF.) GANGLI GANGLO

EXCRETA EGESTA

EXCRETE EGEST SWEAT EXCERN SECERN DEFECATE PERSPIRE

EXCRETION SORDES ECRISIS PERISARC

EXCRUCIATE RACK GRIND AGONIZE TORMENT TORTURE

EXCRUCIATING GRINDING

EXCULPATE FREE CLEAR REMIT ACQUIT EXCUSE PARDON ABSOLVE FORGIVE JUSTIFY RELEASE PALLIATE

EXCULPATION EXCUSE

EXCURSION DIP HOP ROW DIET RIDE SAIL SPIN TOUR TRIP ESSAY JAUNT RANGE SALLY START TRAMP AIRING CANTER CRUISE FLIGHT JUNKET OUTING PASEAR RAMBLE SASHAY VAGARY VOYAGE JOURNEY OUTLOPE OUTRIDE OUTROAD CAMPAIGN ESCAPADE

EXCURSIONIST TRIPPER

EXCUSABLE VENIAL

EXCUSE FAIK PLEA ALIBI COLOR GLOSS PLANE REMIT SALVO SCUSE ACQUIT ESSOIN EXEMPT PARDON REASON REFUGE SCONCE SECURE SUNYIE ABSOLVE APARDON APOLOGY CONDONE ESSOIGN EVASION EXCUSAL FORGIVE OFFCOME PRETEXT DISPENSE OCCASION OVERLOOK PALLIATE PRETENCE (**CONSCIENTIOUSLY —**) SCRUPLE

EXCUSS SHAKE DISCARD DISCUSS

EXECRABLE BAD CURST CURSED DAMNED HEINOUS ACCURSED DAMNABLE WRETCHED

EXECRATE BAN DAMN ABHOR CURSE DEVOTE

EXECRATION CURSE ANATHEMA MALEDICTION

EXECUTE DO ACT CUT TOP BURN DASH FILL GIVE HANG HAVE KILL OBEY PASS PLAY SLAY FRAME GANCH LYNCH SCRAG YIELD DESIGN DIRECT EFFECT FINISH FULFIL GARROT GIBBET MANAGE ACHIEVE CONDUCT ENFORCE FULFILL GAROTTE PERFORM STRETCH COMPLETE DISPATCH EXPEDITE PRACTICE PRACTISE (**— BOW**) WREATHE (**— POORLY**) DUB (**— SUCCESSFULLY**) COMPLETE

EXECUTED GIVEN (**— EXQUISITELY**) CURIOUS (**— WITH CARE**) ACCURATE (**CRUDELY —**) DAUBY

EXECUTION GANCH TOUCH EFFECT FACTURE GARROTE HANGING TECHNIC CARRIAGE GARROTTE PRACTICE PERFORMANCE (**— BY BURNING**) STAKE (**— BY DROWNING**) NOYADE (**— OF WILL**) FACTUM

EXECUTIONER BURRIO HEADER TORTOR BUTCHER HANGMAN HEADMAN LOCKMAN CARNIFEX EXECUTOR HEADSMAN CRUCIFIER

EXECUTIVE BOSS DEAN MAYOR WARDEN CASHIER MANAGER

PODESTA PREMIER GOVERNOR OFFICIAL

EXECUTOR DOER AGENT ALBACEA SECUTOR ENFORCER MINISTER

EXEGESIS ANAGOGE ANAGOGY MIDRASH HAGGADAH

EXEMPLAR COPY TYPE MODEL FATHER MIRROR MODULE EIDOLON EXAMPLE PARABLE PATTERN PARADIGM

EXEMPLARY LAUDABLE

EXEMPLIFICATION SOUL SAMPLE CONSTAT EXAMPLE

EXEMPLIFY SAMPLE SATISFY ENSAMPLE MODELIZE

EXEMPT EXON FREE EXEEM EXEME FRANK SEVER SPARE EXPERT FIDATE IMMUNE EXCLUDE RELEASE DISPENSE EXCEPTED PRIVILEGE (**PREF.**) IMMUNO

EXEMPTION GRACE CHARTER FREEDOM LIBERTY SWEATER BLOODWIT IMMUNITY IMPUNITY

EXEQUATUR PLACET

EXERCISE ACT AIR DIP PLY URE USE BEAR HAVE DRILL ETUDE EXERT HALMA LATIN LONGE SWEAT AIRING BREATH CAREER EMPLOY EXERCE LESSON MANUAL PARADE PRAXIS SCHOOL AUFGABE BREATHE DISPLAY ENHAUNT JOGGING PROBLEM ACTIVITY EXERTION FORENSIC PALESTRA PRACTICE PRACTISE (**— CONTROL**) BOSS PRESIDE (**— HORSE**) BREEZE (**—S TO REDUCE WEIGHT**) SLIMNASTICS (**ACADEMIC —**) PRACTICUM (**CAVALRY —**) MELEE (**DEVOTIONAL —**) ANGELUS (**MUSICAL —**) ETUDE SOLFEGE VOCALISE (**PRELIMINARY —**) WARMUP PROLUSION (**PUNISHMENT —**) PENSUM (**STRONG —**) INTENSION (**SYSTEM OF —**) AEROBICS (**UNWARRANTED —**) STRETCH (**PL.**) ALLEGRO ATHLETICS

EXERT DO PLY PUT DRAW EMIT HUMP STIR DRIVE SPEND SWING BESTIR EXTEND REVEAL STRAIN AFFORCE ENFORCE IMPRESS CHARETTE ENDEAVOR EXERCISE (**— A SPELL**) TAKE (**— POWER**) ACT BEAR (**— PRESSURE**) PRESS SQUEEZE (**— TRACTION**) HAUL

EXERTING (**— POWER**) AGENT

EXERTION DINT HEFT BURST ESSAY LABOR TRIAL WHILE ACTION EFFORT MOTION PINGLE STRESS STRIFE ATTEMPT TROUBLE ENDEAVOR EXERCISE STRUGGLE (**EXCESSIVE —**) STRAIN (**STRENUOUS —**) HUMP

EXFOLIATE SCALE SPALL SPAWL

EXFOLIATION FURFUR

EXHALATION AURA FUME REEK

STEAM BREATH EXPIRY MIASMA HALITUS MALARIA FUMOSITY MEPHITIS

EXHALE CAST EMIT REEK EXUDE STEAM WHIFF EXPIRE BREATHE FURNACE REFLAIR RESPIRE EXHALATE PERSPIRE

EXHALED SFOGATO

EXHAUST DO FAG SAP BEAT BURN COOK COWL EMIT FAIL FLAG FLOG JADE KILL MATE SOAK TIRE TUCK BLAST BREAK CLEAN DRAFT DRAIN EMPTY FORDO GRUEL LEECH PETER SHOOT SPEND SWINK WASTE WEARY ABRADE BETOIL BOTTOM BUGGER EMBOSS FINISH FOREDO HARASS HATTER OVERDO TAIGLE TUCKER BREATHE CONSUME DEPLETE DEPRIVE DRAUGHT EXTRACT FATIGUE OUTWEAR SCOURGE SURREIN TRACHLE DISTRESS EDUCTION EVACUATE FORSPEND FORSWINK FORWEARY OVERWEAR OVERSPEND

EXHAUSTED TAM BEAT DEAD DONE DUNG GONE WEAK WORN BLOWN EMPTY JADED SPENT STANK TIRED BARREN BEATEN BUSHED EFFETE GROGGY MARCID PLAYED TOILED TRAIKY ATTAINT DRAINED EMPTIED FORDONE FORSUNG FORWORN TEDIOUS WHACKED BANKRUPT CONSUMED FOREDONE FOREWORN FORFAIRN FORSPENT FOUGHTEN HARASSED OUTSPENT OVERWORN (**— OF AIR**) HIGH

EXHAUSTING ARDUOUS IRKSOME PREYING

EXHAUSTION EXHAUST FATIGUE SELLOUT SOOREYN DISTRESS GONENESS PROSTRATION

EXHAUSTIVE FULL MINUTE THOROUGH

EXHIBIT AIR PEN FAIR HAVE SHEW SHOW TURN WEAR CARRY SPORT STAGE BLAZON DEMEAN EVINCE EXPOSE OPPOSE OSTEND PARADE REVEAL APPROVE CONCENE DIORAMA DISPLAY EXPRESS MONSTER PERFORM PRESENT PRODUCE PROJECT PROPOSE TRADUCE BOOKFAIR BRANDISH CONCEIVE DISCLOSE DISCOVER EMBLAZON EVIDENCE FORTHSET MANIFEST SHOWCASE (**— ALARM**) GLOFF (**— DOGS**) BENCH (**— IN SNARLING**) GRIN

EXHIBITION EXPO FAIR SALE SHOW DROLL ENTRY SALON SIGHT ANNUAL PARADE SALARY ACADEMY DISPLAY EXHIBIT PAGEANT PENSION PRESENT SHOWING STAGERY EXERCISE PERFORMANCE (**— OF DOGS**) BENCH (**— ON STAGE**) STAGERY (**PUBLIC —**) SPECIES (**RIDING —**) CAROUSEL

EXHIBITIONER SERVITOR

EXHIBITIONIST HAM HAMFATTER

EXHIBITOR SHOWER

EXHILARATE AMUSE CHEER ELATE ANIMATE ELEVATE ENLIVEN GLADDEN

EXHILARATED RAD GLAD HAPPY HEADY ELEVATED

EXHILARATING SAPID

EXHILARATION GAIETY JOLLITY GLADNESS HILARITY

EXHORT URGE WARN CHARM ADHORT ADVISE CHARGE DEHORT ENGAGE INCITE PREACH CAUTION ADMONISH DISSUADE

EXHORTATION ADVICE EXHORT HOMILY COUNSEL PROPHECY PREACHMENT

EXHORTER HORTATOR PREACHER

EXHUME DIG DELVE UNBURY UNTOMB UNEARTH DISINTER EXHUMATE

EXIGENCY NEED PUSH WANT EXIGENT URGENCY JUNCTURE OCCASION PRESSURE

EXIGENT DIRE VITAL URGENT CRITICAL EXACTING PRESSING

EXIGUITY PAUCITY

EXIGUOUS MEAGER MEAGRE

EXILE EXUL POOR RUIN THIN EXPEL GALUT WREAK BANISH DEPORT GALUTH OUTLAW SCANTY WRETCH EXULATE GERSHOM OUTCAST PILGRIM REFUGEE SLENDER DIASPORA FUGITIVE OUTLAWRY OSTRACIZE

EXILED FORFIGN FUGITIVE

EXIST AM BE IS ARE LIE COME GROW LIVE MOVE PASS DWELL CONSIST SUBSIST (**— IN FULL SUPPLY**) FLOW

EXISTENCE ENS ESSE LIFE SEIN BEING DASEIN ENTITY IDEATE INESSE ESSENCE IDEATUM REALITY ENERGEIA IDENTITY STANDING SURVIVAL PERSONALITY (**— AFTER DEATH**) AFTERLIFE (**DULL —**) DEATH (**ETERNAL —**) SAT (**EVER-CHANGING —**) SAMSARA SANSARA (**IN —**) GOING AROUND EXTANT (**INDEPENDENT —**) ASEITY PERSEITY (**PERMANENT —**) INHERENCE (**WAKING —**) JAGRATA (**PREF.**) ONTO

EXISTENT HARD REAL ALIVE BEING ACTUAL EXTANT EXISTING (**— IN DIFFERENT FORMS**) ALLOTROPIC (**CONTINUALLY —**) STUBBORN

EXISTING GOING ACTUAL EXTANT PRESENT EXISTENT (**— IN NAME ONLY**) DUMMY (**SUFF.**) ANT ENT

EXIT ISH DOOR GATE VENT GOING ISSUE LEAVE EGRESS EXITUS OUTLET OUTWAY EXITION OUTGATE OUTPORT PASSAGE DEBOUCHE (**HURRIED —**) BOUT

EXITE BRACT

EX LIBRIS BOOKPLATE

EXOCYCLIC IRREGULAR
EXODUS EXODY EXITUS HEGIRA
HEJIRA EXODIUM
EXON EXEMPT
EXONERATE FREE ALIBI CLEAR
ACQUIT EXCUSE EXONER UNLOAD
ABSOLVE RELIEVE
EXOPODITE EXOPOD SQUAMA
EXORABLE PRAYABLE
EXORBITANT STEEP UNDUE
ABNORMAL
EXORCIST BENET
EXORDIUM PREFACE PRELUDE
EXOSKELETON CORSLET
CORSELET
EXOSPORIUM EXINE EXTINE
EXOSPERM
EXOSTOSIS POROMA SPLINT
OSSELET RINGBONE
EXOTIC ALIEN FOREIGN STRANGE
ADVENTIVE RECHERCHE
EXOTOSPORE BLAST
EXOTROPIA WALLEYE
EXPAND OPE WAX BLOW BULK
FLAN FLUE FOAM GROW HUFF
OPEN FARCE FLASH RETCH SPLAY
SWELL WIDEN DIDUCE DILATE
EXTEND INTEND SPREAD SPROUT
UNFOLD UNFURL AMPLIFY
BALLOON BLOSSOM BOLSTER
BROADEN BURGEON DEVELOP
DIFFUSE DISPAND DISPLAY
DISTEND EDUCATE ENLARGE
EXPANSE EXPLAIN INFLATE
STRETCH DISPREAD INCREASE
LENGTHEN OUTREACH
(— AS A VESSEL) FLAN
(— FEATHERS) PRIDE
(— INTO PODS) KID
EXPANDED NOWY OPEN OVERT
DILATE PATENT SPREAD DILATED
SWOLLEN INFLATED PATULENT
PATULOUS
EXPANDER EXTENDER
EXPANDING BOSOMY
EXPANSE AREA ROOM BOSOM
BURST FIELD REACH TRACT
EXTENT LENGTH SPREAD
COUNTRY STRETCH DISTANCE
EXPANSUM SEPARATE
(— OF ICE) SHEET
(— OF SEA ICE) FIELD
(BROAD —) ACRE MAIN
(FLAT —) LEVEL
(IMMEASURABLE — OF TIME)
ETERNITY
(IMMENSE —) OCEAN
(INDEFINITE —) VAGUE
(VAST —) SEA
(WIDE —) BREADTH
EXPANSIBILITY ELATER
EXPANSION ALA BULB WING
FLUSH SPLAY GROWTH SPREAD
ECTASIA ECTASIS EXPANSE
HASTULA ACROCYST COQUILLE
DIASTOLE DILATION INCREASE
SWELLING
(— IN SEEDS) ALA WING
(— OF RIVER) BROAD
(FOLIOSE —) LAMINA
(LITURGICAL —) EMBOLISM
EXPANSIVE FREE WIDE BROAD
GENIAL ELASTIC LIBERAL

GENEROUS SPACIOUS SWELLING
EXPATIATE DWELL DILATE
EXPAND SPREAD AMPLIFY
BROADEN DESCANT DIFFUSE
ENLARGE SATISFY
EXPATRIATE EXILE EXPEL BANISH
OUTLAW OUTCAST
EXPATRIATION EXILE
EXPECT ASK DEEM HOPE LITE
LOOK STAY TEND TROW WAIT
WEEN ABIDE AWAIT THINK
ATTEND DEMAND INTEND LIPPEN
RECKON PRESUME REQUIRE
SUPPOSE SUSPECT CALCULATE
EXPECTANT ATIPTOE CHARGED
HOPEFUL INCHOATE
EXPECTANTLY AGOG TIPTOE
EXPECTATION HOPE VIEW WAIT
WEEN TRUST EXPECT FUTURE
ESPEIRE OPINION SUPPOSE
THOUGHT WEENING PROSPECT
EXPECTED DUE NATURAL
SUPPOSED
EXPECTORANT CINEOL STORAX
CINEOLE EMETINE AMMONIAC
CREOSOTE GUAIACOL TEREBENE
EXPECTORATE SPIT
EXPECTORATION EMPTYSIS
EXPEDIENCE ARTIFICE
EXPEDIENT FIT WISE ATAJO
CRAFT DODGE JOKER KNACK
SALVO SHIFT DEVICE RESORT
STRING DODGERY POLITIC
STOPGAP ARTIFICE RESOURCE
DESIRABLE MAKESHIFT
EXPEDITATE LAW
EXPEDITION LAWING
EXPEDITE HIE EASY FREE HURRY
SPEED EXPEDE GREASE HASTEN
QUICKEN DISPATCH
EXPEDITION CAMP FARE PLOY
ROAD TREK DRAVE HASTE HURRY
RANGE SCOUT TRADE SAFARI
VOYAGE CARAVAN CRUSADE
ENTRADA JOURNEY OUTLOPE
SERVICE WARFARE WARPATH
COMMANDO HEADHUNT
PROGRESS
(FISHING —) DRAVE
(HUNTING —) SAFARI
(MILITARY —) HARKA CRUSADE
HOSTING JOURNEY WARPATH
EXPEDITIOUS FAST HASTY QUICK
RAPID READY SHORT PROMPT
SPEEDY
EXPEL CAN OUT USH BLOW BOLT
DRUM DUMP FIRE OUST VOID
WARP AVOID CHASE CHECK
DEPEL EJECT ERUPT EVICT EXILE
KNOCK SPURT BANISH BOUNCE
DEBOUT DEPORT DEVOID DISBAR
DISOWN OUTPUT OUTRAY
REFUSE ABANDON EXCLUDE
EXPULSE EXTRUDE OBTRUDE
SCRATCH SECLUDE SUSPEND
DISLODGE DISPLACE EVACUATE
FORJUDGE
(— AIR) COUGH
(— FROM MEMBERSHIP) HAMMER
(— GAS) BELCH
(— SUDDENLY) SLIRT
(PREF.) DIS
EXPEND USE LEND SPEND SPORT

WASTE WREAK DEFRAY IMPEND
OCCUPY OUTLAY PONDER
CONSUME DISPEND EROGATE
EXHAUST OVERUSE DISBURSE
SQUANDER
EXPENDITURE COST MISE OUTGO
PENSE CHARGE OUTLAY EXPENSE
PENSION SPENDING
(— OF ENERGY) EFFORT
EXPENSE EX COST GAFF LOSS
BATTA PRICE SUMPT CHARGE
DAMAGE GERSUM ONCOST
OUTLAY OUTSET AVERAGE
OVERHEAD SUMPTURE
(— OF CARRYING) CARRIAGE
(— OF TREAT) SAM
(PL.) BATTA COSTS MISES
EXPENSIVE DEAR HIGH SALT
PRICY STIFF COSTLY LAVISH
PRICEY APICIAN LIBERAL THRIFTY
EXPERIENCE SEE TRY FEEL FIND
GUST HAVE HENT HOLD KNOW
LIVE TEST ASSAY EVENT PROOF
PROVE SKILL TASTE TRIAL USAGE
BEHOLD EXPERT FRAIST ORDEAL
SAMPLE SUFFER APPROVE
CALVARY CONTACT FEELING
FURNACE KNOWING REALIZE
SUSTAIN UNDERGO ESCAPADE
(— GOOD OR ILL FORTUNE) SPEED
(— OF INTENSE SUFFERING)
CALVARY
(— WITH BITTERNESS) BEAR
(CALAMITOUS —) ADVERSITY
(DRUG —) TRIP
(ENJOYABLE —) GROOVE
(EXCITING —) TRIP
(FIRST —) TIROCINIUM
(HALLUCINATORY —) TRIP
(ORDINARY —) USE
(PAINFUL —) FIT
(PARTIAL —) GUST
(TRYING —) ORDEAL
EXPERIENCED HAD MET OLD SEEN
USED SALTY EXPERT SALTED
TRADED ANCIENT PRACTIC
THRIVEN VETERAN WEIGHED
SEASONED
(— INTENSIVELY) ACUTE
(ACTUALLY —) SPECIOUS
EXPERIENTIAL EMPIRIC
EXPERIMENT SHY TRY TEST ASSAY
ESSAY TRIAL ATTEMPT CONTROL
(PREF.) EMPIRICO EMPIRIO
EXPERIMENTAL SAMPLE
(NOT —) STANDARD
EXPERT ACE DAB DEFT FULL GOOD
PERT ADEPT CRACK FLASH
MAVEN MAVIN READY SHARP
SWELL ADROIT ARTIST CLEVER
FACILE HABILE KAHUNA MASTER
MAYVIN PANDIT PERTLY QUAINT
SUBTLE WIZARD ARTISTE
ATTACHE CAPABLE DABSTER
PERFECT PERITUS SKILLED
DEXTROUS GAINSOME SKILLFUL
SPEEDFUL VIRTUOSO PROFESSED
PROFICIENT
(— IN JEWISH LAW) DAYAN
(— ON DRIVING LOGS) LAKER
(BANK —) SHROFF
(GREAT —) ONER
(SCIENTIFIC —) BOFFIN

(SUFF.) ICIAN
EXPERTNESS SAVVY SKILL
FACILITY HABILITY
EXPIATE ABY SKUG ATONE AVERT
ASSOIL RANSOM
EXPIATORY PIACULAR
EXPIRATION END DEATH BREATH
EFFLUX ELAPSE EXPIRE EXPIRY
(SPASMODIC —) SNEEZE
EXPIRE DIE END EMIT FALL EXPEL
GHOST LAPSE ELAPSE EXHALE
INLAIK OUTRUN PERISH
EXPIRED UP DEAD EXPIATE
EXPIRING DYING
EXPIRY ISH CLOSE DEATH EFFLUX
EXPLAIN OPEN REDE SAVE SCAN
UNDO WISE AREAD AREED CLEAR
GLOSS GLOZE PLANE RECHE
SOLVE SPEED TOUCH DEFINE
EXPAND EXPLAT EXPONE
REMENE RIDDLE UNFOLD
ABSOLVE ACCOUNT AMPLIFY
CLARIFY COMMENT CONTRUE
DECLARE DEVELOP DISCUSS
EXHIBIT EXPOUND JUSTIFY
RESOLVE CONSTRUE DESCRIBE
MANIFEST SIMPLIFY UNPLIGHT
UNWONDER
EXPLAINER EXPONENT
EXPLAINING EXPONENT
EXPLANATION KEY NOTE FARSE
GLOSS SALVE SALVO ANSWER
CAVEAT ACCOUNT APOLOGY
ADDENDUM EXEGESIS INNUENDO
NOTATION SOLUTION
EXPLETIVE AND GEE BOSH EGAD
GOSH OATH BEGAD MODAL
BEHEAR SDEATH TUNKET
DAMMISH MORBLEU GOODYEAR
GRACIOUS
EXPLICATE OPEN CLEAR EXPAND
UNFOLD ACCOUNT EXPLAIN
EXPLICATION CRIB ANALYSIS
EXPLICIT OPEN CLEAR EXACT
FIXED PLAIN EXPRESS PRECISE
ABSOLUTE DEFINITE IMPLICIT
POSITIVE PUNCTUAL SPECIFIC
EXPLICITLY BARELY DIRECT
FORMALLY
EXPLODE POP BLOW FIRE BELCH
BLAST BURST CRUMP ERUPT
PLUFF SHOOT SQUIB SPRING
BACKFIRE DETONATE DISPLODE
EXPLOIT ACT DEED FEAT GEST
JEST MILK WORK GESTE GOUGE
STUNT PERFORM SUCCESS
CHIVALRY PARERGON PROPERTY
(— FINANCIALLY) RIPOFF
(— SUCCESSFULLY) PARLAY
EXPLOITER KULAK
EXPLORATION SPY PROBE
SEARCH EXPLORE
EXPLORATORY FRONTIER
PROBATIVE PROBATORY
EXPLORE DO DIP MAP SPY DIVE
DRAG FEEL VIEW CHART COAST
DELVE RANGE SCOUT SOUND
SEARCH EXAMINE PALPATE
BOTANIZE DISCOVER
(— FOR MINERALS) PROSPECT
EXPLORER CAVEMAN PIONEER
COLUMBUS
AMERICAN BYRD COOK GRAY

HALL KANE LONG PIKE BEEBE
CLARK FIALA HAYES JAMES
LEWIS MUSIL NILES PEARY
AKELEY ASHLEY BRYANT CARVER
DELONG GREELY HERVEY RAINEY
ANDREWS BALDWIN BURNHAM
FREMONT STANLEY WELLMAN
WORKMAN BRAINARD BRIDGMAN
LOCKWOOD MELVILLE SCHWATKA
ELLSWORTH MACMILLAN
DANENHOWER HUNTINGTON
HALLIBURTON
AUSTRALIAN WILLS STUART
FORREST KENNEDY LINDSAY
WILKINS BERNACCHI
AUSTRIAN HUGEL PAYER GLASER
BAUMANN PAULITSCHKE
BELGIAN GERLACHE
CANADIAN MACKAY JOLLIET
SIMPSON BARTLETT PALLISER
STEFANSSON
COLOMBIAN REYES
DANISH BOCK HOLM KOCH
MIKKELSEN RASMUSSEN
DUTCH NIEUWENHUIS
ENGLISH BACK BASS BENT COOK
EYRE BAKER BRUCE DAVYS
EVANS GRANT OATES PARRY
SCOTT SPEKE STURT YOUNG
BURTON CONDER GROGAN
HEARNE HOWITT LANDER
MAWSON OSBORN PHILBY SABINE
WILSON CAMERON CHESNEY
DEWINDT GREGORY HOLDICH
JACKSON WICKHAM FRANKLIN
GRENFELL JOHNSTON SCORESBY
ALEXANDER WARBURTON
INGLEFIELD MCCLINTOCK
SCHOMBURGK SHACKLETON
LIVINGSTONE YOUNGHUSBAND
FRENCH BONIN MONTS BINGER
BRAZZA CALLIE DULUTH GENTIL
HAARDT ABBADIE CARTIER
CRAMPEL CREVAUX FOUREAU
GARNIER LASALLE NICOLET
BONVALOT COUDREAU
MARCHAND CAILLIAUD
CHAMPLAIN IBERVILLE
MARQUETTE VINCENNES
GERMAN LENZ BARTH PFEIL
POGGE REISS VOGEL DECKEN
FLEGEL JUNKER PETERS ROHLFS
FISCHER NEUWIED NIEBUHR
OVERWEG DENHARDT FILCHNER
FRANCOIS KOLDEWEY KOTZEBUE
WISSMANN FEDERMANN
GUSSFELDT WEYPRECHT
LEICHHARDT SCHLAGINTWEIT
IRISH BURKE
ITALIAN ZENO CABOT CAGNI
GESSI CASATI NOBILE BELZONI
CODAZZI FILIPPI PIAGGIA
ALBERTIS ANTINORI COLUMBUS
NEW ZEALAND HAAST HILLARY
NORWEGIAN ASTRUP NANSEN
WISTING AMUNDSEN JOHANSEN
SVERDRUP JOHANNESEN
BORCHGREVINK
PORTUGUESE CABRILLO COVILHAO
FERNANDES
RUSSIAN TOLL POTANIN
WRANGEL PRZHEVALSKI
BELLINGSHAUSEN

SCOTTISH RAE PARK ROSS BRUCE
LAING LAIRD CADELL FORBES
THOMSON MITCHELL MACKENZIE
CLAPPERTON
SPANISH ANZA OJEDA AYLLON
BALBOA CORTES DESOTO
AGUIRRE ALARCON CORDOBA
MENDOZA PIZARRO BASTIDAS
CARDENAS CORONADO GRIJALVA
ORELLANA VIZCAINO ESCALANTE
SWEDISH HEDIN NATHORST
PALANDER ANDERSSON
NORDENSKJOLD
SWISS MUNZINGER
EXPLOSION POP BANG BLOW
BLAST BURST CRUMP SALVO
BLOWUP BOUNCE REPORT
PLOSION INCIDENT OUTBURST
(FUEL —) BACKFIRE
(SLIGHT —) PLUFF
EXPLOSIVE EGG TNT MINE AMVIS
AMATOL JOVITE LIMPET POWDER
TETRYL TONITE TORPEX TOUCHY
TRITON ABELITE AMMONAL
AZOTINE DUNNITE LIGNOSE
LYDDITE PLOSIVE PRIMING
PUDDING SHIMOSE THORITE
AMMONITE CHEDDITE DYNAMITE
ECRASITE ERUPTIVE GELATINE
MAXIMITE MELINITE PYROLITE
ROBURITE SABULITE SAXONITE
SECURITE RACKAROCK
SAMSONITE
(CHARGE OF —) TULIP RESPONDER
EXPONENT INDEX POWER
(SUFF.) ICIAN
EXPORT OUTCARRY
EXPORTATION EXPORT OUTPORT
EXPOSE AIR BARE GIVE OPEN RISK
SHOW STRIP BEWRAY DEBUNK
DETECT EXPONE GIBBET OBJECT
OPPOSE REVEAL UNHUSK
UNMASK DISPLAY EXHIBIT
EXPOUND PILLORY PROPINE
PUBLISH SUBJECT UNCOVER
UNEARTH UNTRUSS BRANDISH
DISCLOSE DISCOVER MUCKRAKE
RIDICULE SATIRIZE UNCLOTHE
UNSHROUD
(— FOR BLEACHING) CROFT
(— ORE) HUSH
(— PLAYING CARD) BURN
(— SELF TO) WAGE
(— SUDDENLY) FLASH
(— TO AIR) AERATE
(— TO DANGER) JUMP COMMIT
SUBMIT
(— TO HEAT) AIR
(— TO INFAMY) GIBBET
(— TO MOISTURE) RET
(— TO SCORN) PILLORY
(— TO SULFUR DIOXIDE) STOVE
(— TO SUN) INSOLATE SOLARIZE
(— TO SUN AND AIR) FIELD
EXPOSED AIRY BARE OPEN BLEAK
LIABLE PUBLIC UNSAFE SUBJECT
VEILLESS
(— TO) AGAINST
(— TO DANGER) INSECURE
EXPOSITION FAIR GECK SHOW
ZEND TRACT APERCU EXPOSE
METHOD SURVEY ACCOUNT
EXPOSAL MIDRASH ANALYSIS

EXEGESIS EXPOSURE EXTHESIS
HAGGADAH TREATISE
(— OF FEAST) SYNAXARY
EXPOSITORY EXEGETIC
EXPOSTULATE ARGUE OBJECT
DISCUSS EXAMINE PROTEST
EXPOSTULATION PROTEST
EXPOSURE ASPECT EXPOSE
EXPOSAL FLASHING FRONTAGE
PROSPECT
(— OF CARDS) SPREAD
(— OF KING) CHECK
(— TO AIR) AERATE AIRING
(BODY —) FLASH
EXPOUND OPEN REDE UNDO
GLOZE SENSE TREAT DEFINE
EXPONE EXPOSE COMMENT
DEVELOP DISCUSS EXPLAIN
EXPOSIT EXPRESS CONSTRUE
SIMPLIFY PHILOSOPHIZE
EXPOUNDER MUFTI MULLAH
EXPRESS EXPONENT HERMETIC
(— OF THEORY) ALFAQUI
PHILOSOPHER
EXPRESS AIR BID PUT SAY CAST
EMIT PASS POST VENT COUCH
EMOTE FRAME OPINE SPEAK
STATE UTTER VOICE WIELD
BROACH DEMEAN DENOTE
DIRECT EVINCE IMPORT PHRASE
ABREACT BREATHE DECLARE
DICTATE EXPOUND EXPREME
TESTIFY DEFINITE DESCRIBE
DISPATCH EXPLICIT INTIMATE
MANIFEST
(— APPROVAL) AGREE ACCEDE
APPLAUD
(— AS LANGUAGE) LAY
(— BY GESTURE) BECK
(— BY LAUGHTER) LAUGH
(— CONCERN) CLUCK
(— DISAPPROVAL) BOO CHIDE
DECRY GROAN CATCALL
(— DISDAIN) TUT
(— EFFERVESCENTLY) CHORTLE
(— FOLLY) EXPAND
(— GRATITUDE) THANK AGGRATE
(— GRIEF) DEPLORE
(— IN WORDS) SAY DRAW SPEAK
PHRASE
(— NUMERICALLY) EVALUATE
(— ONE'S FEELINGS) FLOW
(— SORROW) LAMENT COMPLAIN
(— WILLINGNESS) CONSENT
EXPRESSION DIT HIT SAY CAST
EUGE FACE FORM POSE SHOW
SIGN TERM VULT WORD ADIEU
GLIFF IDIOM SNEER TOKEN VOICE
BYWORD DILOGY DIVERB EFFECT
FACIES ORACLE PHRASE SPEECH
SYMBOL COMMENT DESCANT
EPITHET EXPRESS GRIMACE
ALLEGORY AUSDRUCK DANICISM
FELICITY LACONISM MONOMIAL
(— IN FEW WORDS) BREVITY
(— OF ANNOYANCE) SOH
(— OF APPROVAL) EUGE PLACET
(— OF ASSENT) CONTENT
(— OF BEAUTY) ART
(— OF CHOICE) VOTE
(— OF CONTEMPT) COBLOAF
(— OF DISPLEASURE) FROWN
(— OF DISTASTE) FACE

(— OF HOMAGE) OVATION
(— OF JOY) GREETING
(— OF OPINION) EDITORIAL
(— OF RESPECT) DUTY
(— OF SADNESS) SHADE
(— OF SCORN) GECK
(— OF SINGLE IDEA) RHEME
(APT —) FELICITY
(CHEMICAL —) EQUATION
(COMMONPLACE —) BROMIDE
(CORRECT —) SUMPSIMUS
(CURT —) LACONIC
(FACIAL —) GRIN CHEER SCOWL
SMILE
(INCONGRUOUS —) BULL
(LOUD) CLAMOR
(MATHEMATICAL —) INDEX SERIES
BINOMIAL EQUATION FUNCTION
INTEGRAL
(MOCKING —) SCOFF
(PECULIAR —) IDIOM
(PET —) CANT
(PUERILE —) BOYISM
(SARCASTIC —) GIBE JIBE
(SERIOUS —) EARNEST
(SINCERE —) CANDOR
(SYMBOLIC —) FORMULA
(TENDER —) LANGUISH
(TRITE —) CLICHE
(UNRESTRAINED —) EFFUSION
(VERBAL —) LETTER
(VULGAR —) SOLECISM
(WISE —) ORACLE
(SUFF.) LOG(ER)(IA)(IAN)(IC)(ICAL)
(IST)(IJE)(Y)
EXPRESSIONLESS BLANK STONY
LEADEN SODDEN VACANT
WOODEN TONELESS
EXPRESSIVE POETIC TONGUED
ELOQUENT EMPHATIC SPEAKING
EXPRESSIVENESS DICTION
DELICACY TOURNURE
ELOQUENCE
EXPRESSLY NAMELY EXPRESS
PRESSLY FORMALLY
EXPRESSWAY FREEWAY
SPEEDWAY
EXPROBATE CENSURE UPBRAID
EXPULSION EXILE BOUNCE
OUSTER BANNIMUS EJECTION
EXCISION
(— OF SPORES) ABJECTION
EXPUNGE BLOT DELE ERASE SLASH
CANCEL DELETE EFFACE EXCISE
SCRAPE DESTROY SCRATCH
DISPUNGE
EXPURGATE GELD PURGE
CASTRATE
EXPURGATION BOWDLERISM
EXQUISITE FOP DUDE FINE NICE
PERT PINK RARE DANDY EXACT
CHOICE DAINTY CAREFUL
ELEGANT GEMLIKE PERFECT
REFINED AFFECTED DELICATE
ETHEREAL MACARONI
RECHERCHE
EXQUISITELY CHOICELY
EXSCIND CUT SEVER EXCISE
EXTANT ALIVE BEING LIVING
VISIBLE EXISTING MANIFEST
(PREF.) NEO
EXTEMPORE SUDDEN OFFHAND
IMPROVISO

EXTEND GO EKE LIE RUN BEAR
BUSH COME DATE DRAW GROW
LAST OPEN PASS PUSH RISE ROLL
SPAN SPIN BREDE BULGE CARRY
COVER FARCE REACH RENEW
RETCH SEIZE SHOOT STENT
VERGE WIDEN AMOUNT DEEPEN
DEPLOY DILATE EXPAND INTEND
OUTLIE SPREAD SPRING STRAIN
STREAK THRUST TRENCH
AMPLIFY BROADEN DIFFUSE
DISPLAY DISTEND ENLARGE
OVERLAP OVERRUN PORRECT
PORTEND PRODUCE PROFFER
PROJECT PROLONG PROMOTE
PROTEND RADIATE STRETCH
CONTINUE ELONGATE INCREASE
LENGTHEN OUTREACH
PROROGUE PROTRACT PROTRUDE
OUTSPREAD PROPAGATE
OUTSTRETCH
(— ACTIVITIES) BRANCH
(— AROUND) GIRTH
(— HAND) RAX
(— IN SPACE) DURE
(— IRREGULARLY) TRAIL
(— OVER) SPAN COVER CROSS
CONTAIN OVERLAP OVERRIDE
(— SAIL) SHEET
(— THE FRONT) DEPLOY
(— TO) LINE REACH
EXTENDED FAT LONG OPEN
BROAD EXTENT SPREAD EXTENSE
LENGTHY PROLATE SPLAYED
EXPANDED INTENDED
(PREF.) MEG(A) MEGAL(O)
EXTENDER INERT FILLER LIGNIN
EXTENDING BROAD
(— OVER) ASTRIDE
EXTENSION ARM EKE ELL AREA
CAPE SCOPE POCKET SATTVA
SPHERE SPREAD BREADTH
STRETCH ADDENDUM ADDITION
DURATION INCREASE PROTENSE
(— OF BUILDING MATERIAL) APRON
(— OF CREDIT) DATING
(— OF MINERAL VEIN) FLAT
(— OF RACE TRACK) CHUTE SHUTE
(— OF SHELL) LAPPET
(— OF TIME) RESPITE
(— OF WAGON FRAME) THRIPPLE
(BALLET —) BATTEMENT
EXTENSIVE HUGE VAST WIDE
AMPLE BROAD LARGE EXTENSE
IMMENSE EXPANDED INFINITE
SWEEPING
EXTENT DUE RUN TAX AREA BODY
BULK DEAL GAGE LEVY PASS SIZE
WRIT AMBIT DEPTH FIELD GAUGE
LIMIT RANGE REACH SCOPE
SPACE STENT SWEEP TRACK
AMOUNT ASSIZE ATTACK DEGREE
LENGTH SPREAD STREEK
ACREAGE ASSAULT BREADTH
COMPASS CONTENT EXPANSE
PURVIEW SEIZURE STRETCH
VARIETY DISTANCE INCREASE
LATITUDE OUTREACH QUANTITY
STRAIGHT
(— OF FRONT) FRONTAGE
(— OF LAND) HEIGHT CONTINENT
(— OF SPACE) ROOM
(BROAD —) SWEEP MAGNITUDE

(RELATIVE —) SCALE
(SOME —) BIT
(UNLIMITED —) INFINITY
(UTMOST —) FULL
(VAST —) DEEP
(VERTICAL —) ALTITUDE
EXTENUATE THIN GLOZE MINCE
EXCUSE LESSEN SOOTHE WEAKEN
DIMINISH PALLIATE
EXTERIOR CRUST ECTAD ECTAL
OUTER SHELL EXTERN OUTSIDE
OUTWARD SURFACE EXOTERIC
EXTERNAL OUTLYING
(PREF.) OUT
EXTERMINATE WIPE EXPEL
UPROOT ABOLISH DESTROY
EXTERNAL OUT OUTER EXTERN
OUTSIDE OUTWARD STRANGE
EXOTERIC EXTERIOR INCIDENT
PHYSICAL PERIPHERAL
(PREF.) ECT(O) OUT
EXTERNALITY OUTNESS
EXTERNALIZE OBJECTIFY
EXTERNALLY OUTWARD WITHOUT
EXTINCT DEAD BYGONE DEFUNCT
QUENCHED
(— MAN) KANJERA
(PREF.) NECR(O)
EXTINCTION DOOM FINE DEATH
EXPIRY DELETION
EXTINGUISH OUT DAMP DOUT
REDD STUB ANNUL CHOKE
CRUSH DOUSE DOWSE DROWN
QUELL REPEL SLAKE SNUFF
STAMP ASLAKE QUENCH STANCH
STIFLE ABOLISH BLANKET
DESTROY ECLIPSE EXPIATE
EXTINCT OBSCURE OPPRESS
SLOCKEN STAUNCH SUPPRESS
(— BY CRUSHING) DINCH
(— CIGARETTE) SNUB
EXTINGUISHED OUT DEAD
EXTINCT
EXTINGUISHER DOUTER STAUNCH
BACKPACK QUENCHER STANCHER
EXTIRPATE DELE ROOT STUB
ERASE EXPEL STAMP STOCK
EXCISE EXTIRP UPROOT DESTROY
EXSCIND OUTROOT SUPPLANT
EXTIRPATION ROOTAGE EXCISION
EXTOL CRY FETE HYMN LAUD
BLESS CRACK EXALT KUDOS
ROOSE SPEAK EXTOLL PRAISE
ADVANCE APPLAUD COLLAUD
COMMEND ELEVATE ENHANCE
GLORIFY MAGNIFY RESOUND
UPRAISE EMBLAZON EULOGIZE
PROCLAIM
EXTOLMENT PRECONY
EXTORT PEEL PILL RAMP BLEED
BRIBE EDUCE EXACT FORCE
PINCH WREST WRING COMPEL
ELICIT SPONGE STRAIN WRENCH
WRITHE EXTRACT OUTWREST
EXTORTION CHOUT GOUGE
EXTORT HOLDUP SCOTAL
BRIBERY PILLAGE CHANTAGE
EXACTION RAPACITY
SHAKEDOWN
EXTORTIONATE HARD CRIMINAL
GRINDING
EXTORTIONER BRIBER POLLER
SHAVER BLEEDER VAMPIRE

EXTORTIONIST POLLER
EXTRA ODD GASH MORE ORRA
OVER PLUS ADDED SPARE
SPECIAL SURPLUS SUPERIOR
LAGNIAPPE
(PREF.) HYPER SUPER
EXTRACT DIG PRY CITE COPY
DRAW KINO KOLA PULL SOAK
ANIMA BLEED CUTCH DRAFT
EDUCE ELUTE EXACT KUTCH
KYPOO QUOTE RENES RUSOT
SCRAP STEEP WRING CORTIN
CURARE DECOCT DEDUCE DERIVE
DEWTRY DISTIL ELICIT ELIXIR
EVULSE EXTORT GOBBET GUACIN
MULIUM OVARIN REMOVE
RENDER RUSWUT TRIPOS
UZARON ABORTIN AMALTAS
ARCANUM CATECHU DESCENT
DISTILL DRAUGHT ERGOTIN
ESSENCE ESTREAT EXCERPT
EXHAUST FUMARIA INTRAIT
LIMBECK MONESIA PASSEWA
SUMMARY VANILLA ACETRACT
AMBRETTE GINGERIN HYPERNIC
INFUSION LICORICE PERICOPE
SEPARATE TIKITIKI TINCTURE
WITHDRAW
(— BY BOILING) DECOCT ELIXATE
(— BY DIGGING) GRUB
(— DATA FROM COMPUTER) READ
(— FORCIBLY) EVULSE
(— FROM ACACIA) KATH CASHOO
CATECHU
(— FROM BERBERIS) RUSOT
RUSWUT
(— OF BARK) EUONYMIN
(— OF GINGER) JAKE JAKEY
(— ORE) STOPE
(TANNING —) AMALTAS
EXTRACTION KIN BIRTH BROOD
STOCK ORIGIN DESCENT EDITION
ESSENCE EXTRACT EXTREAT
BREEDING TINCTURE
(— OF ROOTS) EVOLUTION
(— OF STEAM) BLEEDING
EXTRACTIVE AGAR BANG BHANG
AMAROID CARAGEEN
EXTRADITE BANISH
EXTRANEOUS ALIEN OUTER
EXOTIC FOREIGN OUTLYING
SPURIOUS
EXTRAORDINARILY BYOUS
EXTRAORDINARY ODD FREM
ONCO RARE BYOUS ENORM
SMASH DAMNED EXEMPT MIGHTY
RAGING SIGNAL CORKING
CURIOUS HUMMING NOTABLE
SPECIAL STRANGE UNUSUAL
ABNORMAL EXIMIOUS FORINSEC
SINGULAR SMASHING
UNCOMMON PHENOMINAL
PRODIGIOUS
EXTRARETINAL PAROPTIC
EXTRAVAGANCE CAMP FRILL
PRIDE WASTE LUXURY EXPENSE
RAMPANCY SQUANDER UNTHRIFT
WILDNESS PROFUSION
SATURNALIA
(MENTAL —) MADNESS
EXTRAVAGANT MAD HIGH LUSH
WILD FANCY FISHY FOLLE LARGE
OUTRE COSTLY GOTHIC HEROIC

LAVISH SHRILL WANTON
BAROQUE BIZARRE COSTLEW
FANATIC FLAMING FURIOUS
NIMIOUS PROFUSE RAMPANT
VAGRANT INSOLENT PRODIGAL
RECKLESS ROMANTIC UNTHRIFT
WANDERER WASTEFUL
BOMBASTIC PROFLIGATE
EXTRAVAGANTLY LARGE
EXTRAVAGANZA FEERIE
EXTRAVAGATION VIBEX
EXTRAVASATION EFFUSION
EXTREME NTH BLUE DEEP DIRE
HIGH LAST RANK SORE VILE
ACUTE BLACK CLOSE CRUEL
DENSE DIZZY FINAL GREAT LIMIT
PITCH STEEP ULTRA UNDUE
UTTER ARDENT ARRANT BRAZEN
DEADLY FAROUT FIERCE HEROIC
LENGTH MORTAL SAVAGE SEVERE
STRONG UTMOST WOUNDY
ABYSMAL DRASTIC FEARFUL
FORWARD FRANTIC HOWLING
INTENSE OUTWARD PROFUSE
RADICAL SURFEIT VICIOUS
VIOLENT ALMIGHTY DEVILISH
DREADFUL EGYPTIAN ENORMOUS
FABULOUS FARTHEST GREATEST
MERCIFUL SPENDFUL TERRIBLE
TERRIFIC ULTIMATE EXQUISITE
(NOT —) SWEET
(PL.) PASO
(PREF.) ACR(O) ARCH
EXTREMELY SO BIG DOG TOO
WAY BONE DEAD EVER FULL
MAIN RANK SELI THAT UNCO
VERY AWFUL BLACK BULLY
BYOUS CRAZY CRUEL EXTRA
HEAPS RIGHT SELLE SOWAN
SUPER BITTER DAMNED DEADLY
DEUCED HIGHLY MIGHTY NATION
POISON SORELY SURELY UNCOLY
APLENTY AWFULLY BOILING
CRUELLY EXTREME GALLOWS
HOPPING INNERLY SOPPING
STAVING ALMIGHTY ENORMOUS
MORTALLY PRECIOUS PROPERLY
EXTREMISM JACOBINISM
EXTREMIST JACOBIN RADICAL
SANSCULOTTE
EXTREMITY END TIP HEAD NEED
PUSH TAIL CLOSE LIMIT SHIFT
START VERGE BORDER FINGER
EXIGENT EXTREME ACROSTIC
ALTITUDE DISASTER JUNCTURE
OUTRANCE TERMINAL
(— OF MOON) HORN
(— OF TENDRIL) HOLDFAST
(— OF TOOTH ROOT) APEX
(REMOTEST —) CORNER
(PREF.) ACR(O)
EXTRICATE FREE HELP WIND
CLEAR LOOSE RESCUE SQUIRM
OUTWIND EXPEDITE LIBERATE
UNTANGLE
(— ONESELF) WANGLE
EXTRINSIC ALIEN EVERY FOREIGN
OUTWARD EXTERNAL OUTLYING
EXTROVERT SYNTONIC
EXTRUDE BEAR SPEW EJECT
EXPEL SHOOT PROJECT
PROTRUDE
EXUBERANCE PRICE EXCESS

LUXURY PLENTY ABANDON
LAUGHTER OVERFLOW
RAMPANCY
EXUBERANT RANK BOUNCY
FEISTY LAVISH COPIOUS FERTILE
GLOWING PROFUSE RAMPANT
EFFUSIVE
EXUDATE GUM SPEW SPUE
MANNA DIKAMALI GUAIACUM
HONEYDEW SARCOCOL
EXUDATION DIP GUM LAC SAP
TAR BALM KINO COPAL PITCH
RESIN ROSIN SUDOR ULMIN
CHARAS MASTIC SANIES
CHURRUS GALIPOT MOCHRAS
SPEWING BLEEDING EXUDENCE
LAITANCE MOISTURE
EXUDE GUM DRIP EMIT OOZE REEK
SPEW BLEED STILL SWEAT EXTILL
STRAIN STREAM EXUDATE
GUTTATE SCREEVE SECRETE
SWELTER PERSPIRE
EXULT JOY CROW LEAP BOAST
GLOAT GLORY INSULT SPRING
MAFFICK REJOICE TRIUMPH
EXULTANT PROUD ELATED
PRIDEFUL
EXULTATION JOY PAEAN OVATION
RAPTURE
EXULTING EXULTANT JUBILANT
EYALET VILLAYET
EYAS NESTLING
EYE O EE HE ORB SPY DISC GAZE

GLIM LAMP LOOP MIEN OGLE
SCAN UVEA VIEW GLARE GLASS
GLENE NAVEL OPTIC SENSE
SHANK SIGHT TOISE WATCH
BEHOLD COLLAR EUCONE EYELET
GOGGLE OCULAR OCULUS OILLET
PEEPER POPEYE REGARD ROLLER
SHINER STEMMA VISION WINDOW
WINKER BLINKER EUCONIC
EXOCONE EYEBALL EYEHOLE
OBSERVE OCELLUS PIERCER
PIGSNEY PINKANY PINKENY
SENSORY WITNESS LATCHING
NOISETTE OMMATEUM RECEPTOR
(— AMOROUSLY) OGLE
(— FORMED BY ROPE) TONGUE
(— IN BIGHT) COLLAR
(— IN EGYPTIAN SYMBOLISM) UTA
(— OF BEAN) HILUM
(— OF FRUIT) NOSE
(— OF HINGE) GUDGEON
(— OF INSECT) STEMMA
(— OF RA) SEKHET
(— SORENESS) LIPPITUDE
(BLACK —) KEEK MOUSE SHINER
(EVIL —) DROCHUIL MALOCCHIO
(JERKY — MOVEMENT) SACCADE
(METAL —) HONDA
(PART OF —) IRIS LENS FOVEA
PUPIL CORNEA MACULA SCLERA
CHAMBER CHOROID LIGAMENT
CONJUNCTIVA
(PL.) EEN EES NIE YEN YES EYNE

LAMPS LIGHTS SEEING GOGGLES
KEEKERS GLAZIERS GLIMMERS
(PREF.) OCELLI OCUL(I)(O)
OMMA(TO) OPHTHALM(O)
OPTI(CO) OPTO
(SUFF.) OMMA OPHTHALMA
OPHTHALMUS OPIS OPS
(DEFECT OR CONDITION OF —) OPE
OPIA OPIC OPIS OPS OPY
EYEBALL EYE BALL GLASS GLOBE
(— MOVEMENT) VERGENCE
(PREF.) OPHTHALM(O)
EYEBOLT SPRIG RINGBOLT
(INTERLOCKING —S) SNIBEL
EYEBRIGHT EYEWORT EUPHRASY
EYEBROW BREE BROW EEBREE
WINBROW WRIGGLE
EYE-CATCHING BOLD
EYE-CORNER
(PREF.) CANTH(O)
EYECUP EYEGLASS
EYED
(SUFF.) OPIS OPS
EYEGLASS QUIZ NIPPER MONOCLE
EYEGLASSES GLIMS SPECS LENSES
GLASSES LORGNON NIPPERS
BIFOCALS
EYEHOLE EYELET EYEPIT
EYELASH BREE LASH CILIUM
WINKER EYEBREE
(LOSS OF —S) MADAROSIS
(PL.) CILIA EAVES
(PREF.) CILI(I)(O)

EYELET MAIL PINK OELET AGRAFE
OILLET POUNCE AGRAFFE
CRINGLE GROMMET PEEPHOLE
EYELID HAW LID BREE WINDOW
EYEBREE PALPEBRA
(PL.) EAVES
(PREF.) BLEPHAR(O) CILI(I)(O)
(SUFF.) BLEPHARON CIL
EYEPIECE OCULAR EYEGLASS
(— OF TELESCOPE) POWER
EYESHADE VISOR OPAQUE
EYESHOT RANGE REACH EYESIGHT
EYESIGHT VIEW LIGHT SIGHT
EYE SOCKET ORBIT
EYESORE DESIGHT
EYESPOT EYEDOT STIGMA
EYEHOLE OCELLUS EYEPOINT
EYESTALK STIPES
EYETOOTH CUSPID DOGTOOTH
EYEWASH COLLYRIE EYEWATER
COLLYRIUM
EYOT AIT EIGHT ISLET
EYRE AIR ITER
EZBAI (SON OF —) NAARAI
EZBON (FATHER OF —) GAD BELA
EZEKIEL (FATHER OF —) BUZI
EZER (FATHER OF —) EPHRAIM
(SON OF —) HUSHAH
EZRA (SON OF —) EPHER
EZRI (FATHER OF —) CHELUB

F

F EF FF EFF FOX DIGAMMA FOXTROT
FABA VICIA
FABLE MYTH TALE FEIGN STORY LEGEND TRIFLE FICTION PARABLE POETIZE UNTRUTH ALLEGORY APOLOGUE FABULATE FABULIZE
(— OF GOLD COAST) NANCY
(MORAL —) EMBLEM
(PREF.) MYTHO
FABRIC ABA BAN ACCA CORD DUCK GOLD GROS HAIR HUCK IKAT SILK SUSI TAPA TARS TUKE CHECK CREPE DHOTI DOBBY DYNEL FANCY MOIRE NINOW PRINT RUMAL SCRIM SPLIT STUFF SUPER SURAH SURAT TABBY TAMMY TARSE TERRY TEWKE TWEED TWILL UNION VICHY VOILE WEAVE WIGAN AGARIC ALACHA BENGAL BROCHE BYSSUS CAFFOY CARPET COTTON CREPON CYPRUS DACRON DAMASK DIAPER DOBBIE EPONGE ESTRON FLEECE HARDEN LAPPET LUSTER LUSTRE MARBLE MASHRU MURREY POODLE SENNIT STRIPE TAMINY TANJIB TARTAN TRICOT TUSSAH VELURE VELVET WADMAL WINCEY ZENANA ACETATE ALEPINE ALLOVER BANDALA BANDING BELTING BEWPERS BINDING BUCKRAM CANILLE CHALLIS CHEKMAK CHIFFON CYPRESS DAMASSE DOESKIN DRABBET EDIFICE ELASTIC EPINGLE FACONNE FUSTIAN MIXTURE MORELLA PAISLEY PLUMBET SAYETTE SEGATHY SILESIA SUITING TABARET TABINET TAFFETA TEXTILE TIFFANY VESSETS AGABANEE BARRACAN BOCASINE BOURETTE BROCATEL CAMELINE CANNELLE CASEMENT CHAMBRAY CRETONNE DIAMANTE DUCHESSE HAIRLINE HANDMADE HARATEEN JACQUARD KNITTING LUSTRINE MATERIAL MOLESKIN OSNABURG SHANTUNG SHIRTING SICILIAN SKIRTING SWANSKIN TAPESTRY TARLATAN VALENCIA
(— CONTAINING GOLD OR SILVER THREAD) ACCA TASH TASS KINCOB
(— FOR STIFFENING) WIGAN
(— OF TWO OR MORE MATERIALS) UNION
(— RESEMBLING TOWELING) AGARIC
(— WITH INWOVEN SCENES) ARRAS
(ABSORBENT —) HUCK

(BROCADED —) LAME LAMPAS
(CARPET —) DURRIE
(COARSE —) TAT BAFT CRASH HAIRE DUFFEL RATINE STAMIN BAGGING BOCKING DRABBET SACKING STAMMEL DAGSWAIN
(CORDED —) REP PIQUE DUCAPE POPLIN OTTOMAN BENGALINE
(COTTON —) CREA DUCK JEAN LENO LINO SUSI BAIZE BASIN DENIM DRILL RUMAL SUPER SWISS VICHY WIGAN BURRAH CALICO CANVAS CATGUT CHILLO CHINTZ COUTIL COVERT DIMITY MADRAS MUSLIN PENANG SATEEN BLANKET BUSTIAN CANTOON DAMASSE ETAMINE FLANNEL GALATEA GINGHAM HICKORY HOLLAND JACONET ORLEANS PERCALE TICKING BOCASINE BUCKSKIN COTELINE COUTILLE CRETONNE DRILLING DUNGAREE INDIENNE SHEETING SILKALINE MARSEILLES
(DECORATED —) DIAMANTE
(DELICATE —) HUSI JUSI
(DURABLE —) SCRIM SERGE
(ELASTIC —) GORING ELASTIC
(EMBOSSED —) CLOKY CLOQUE
(EMBROIDERED —) BALDAQUIN
(FIGURED —) BROCADE BROCATEL
(FINE —) PIMA SILK SUSI LINEN DIMITY MERINO MOHAIR BATISTE PERCALE
(GAUZELIKE —) BAREGE GOSSAMER
(GLAZED —) CIRE
(GLOSSY —) SATIN GLORIA SATEEN PERCALINE
(GOAT'S-HAIR —) ABA TIBET
(HEAVY —) GROS CRASH DENIM DRILL BURLAP CATGUT FRIEZE LINENE TOBINE WHITNEY
(JUTE —) BALINE BURLAP
(KNITTED —) SUEDE BOUCLE JERSEY TRICOT CHIFFON
(LIGHTWEIGHT —) GLORIA BUNTING DELAINE FORTISAN PARAMATTA SEERSUCKER
(LINEN —) HARN SINDON BEWPERS BUCKRAM CAMBRIC DRABBET HOLLAND NACARAT CRETONNE
(MOTTLED —) CHINE
(MOURNING —) ALMA
(MUSLIN —) TANJIB
(OPENWORK —) LACE SKIPDENT
(ORNAMENTAL —) GIMP LACE LAMPAS GALLOON
(PEBBLY-SURFACED —) ARMURE
(PILED —) TERRY BOLIVIA KRIMMER CHENILLE
(PRINTED —) BATIK CALICO

ALLOVER PERCALE TOURNAY
(RAFFIA —) RABANNA
(RIBBED —) CORD GROS PIQUE COTELE FAILLE SOLEIL DROGUET CORDUROY MAROCAIN MOGADORE WHIPCORD
(RICH —) SAMITE
(ROUGH —) TERRY HOPSACK HOMESPUN
(SATIN —) CAMLET ETOILE CHARMEUSE
(SHEER —) LAWN NINON SHEER SWISS BAREGE DIMITY BATISTE SOUFFLE VALENCE GOSSAMER MOUSSELINE MARQUISETTE
(SHORT-NAPPED —) RAS
(SILK —) ACCA ALMA FUGI FUJI GROS IKAT MOFF RASH ATLAS CARDE NINON PEKIN RAJAH RUMAL SATIN SHIKH SURAH TIRAZ ARMURE BROCHE CAMACA CHAPPE CREPON DIAPER DUCAPE FAILLE KHAIKI MANTUA PONGEE SENDAL ALACHAH ALAMODE BROCADE EPINGLE GROGRAM SCHAPPE YESTING BARATHEA DUPPIONI EOLIENNE IMPERIAL ORMUZINE SHAGREEN SIAMOISE MARCELINE MESSALINE BROCATELLE
(SOFT SILK —) KASHA BARATHEA
(SOFT-NAPPED —) PANNE DUVETYN
(STRIPED —) ABA STRIPE BAYADERE MERALINE
(THIN —) CRISP GAUZE VOILE PONGEE TAMISE HERNANI MARABOU PERSIAN
(TWILLED —) REP SAY DENIM KASHA SERGE SURAH COUTIL RUSSEL BOLIVIA ESTAMIN FLANNEL ZANELLA CAMELINE CASHMERE CORDUROY DIAGONAL MARCELLA SHALLOON VENETIAN
(UNBLEACHED —) DRABBET
(UNGLAZED —) CRETONNE
(UPHOLSTERY —) FRISE FRIEZE BROCATEL MOQUETTE
(VELVETY —) TRIPE DUVETYN
(WATERPROOF —) MACINTOSH MACKINTOSH
(WOOLEN —) REPP BAIZE DOILY OSSET SERGE TAMIS TWEED BUFFIN BURNET COTTON DJERSA DUFFEL FRISCA MANTLE MOREEN MOTLEY PERPET SAXONY SHAYAK SHODDY STAMIN TAMISE VICUNA WADMAL WITNEY BATISTE BOCKING BOLIVIA CHEVIOT CHEYNEY CRYSTAL DELAINE DRUGGET FRISADO HEATHER RATTEEN STAMMEL ALGERINE BATSWING BURBERRY CASHMERE

CATALOON CHIVERET HARATEEN LAMBSKIN PRUNELLA RATTINET SHALLOON SHETLAND WOOLENET ZIBELINE
(WORSTED —) TABBY COBURG ESTAMIN ETAMINE SAGATHY BARATHEA
(WOVEN —) LENO TWEED TWILL SOLBIL TISSUE GROGRAM TEXTURE VALENCIA
FABRICATE COIN COOK FAKE FORM MAKE MINT VAMP WARP BUILD FORGE FRAME FRUMP WEAVE DEVISE FANGLE INVENT CONCOCT FASHION IMAGINE PRODUCE CONTRIVE
(— CLOTH) DRAPE
(— PAPER) CONVERT
FABRICATION LIE WEB TRIFLE CHIMERA FICTION FINGURE FORGERY UNTRUTH BASKETRY PRETENSE
(PL.) INVENTARY
FABRICATOR LIAR COINER FORGER
FABULIST LIAR AESOP FABLER
FABULOUS FEIGNED MYTHICAL ROMANTIC
FACADE FACE FRONT FUCUS FRONTAL FRONTLET
FACE JIB MAP MUG NEB PAN BIDE CHIV CLAD COPE DARE DEFY DIAL GIZZ HEAD LEER LINE MASK MEET MOUE MUNS PHIZ PUSS SIDE ABIDE BEARD BRAVE BRICK BRUNT CASTE CHECK CHEER COVER FACET FAVOR FRONT GUARD INDEX REVET STAND STONE VISOR VIZOR ASPECT BRAZEN FACADE FACIES KISSER MAZARD MUZZLE OPPOSE PHIZOG VENEER VISAGE AFFRONT BAZOOKA COMMAND DIGLYPH FASHION FEATURE GRIMACE GRUNTLE PROPOSE RESPECT REVERSE SURFACE UPRIGHT CONFRONT ENVISAGE EXTRADOS FEATURES FROGFACE FRONTAGE FRONTIER PROSPECT SEMBLANT PERPENDICULAR
(— DOWN) DEFACE
(— IN DEFIANCE) AFFRONT
(— OF ANIMAL) MASK
(— OF CUBE) SQUARE
(— OF CUTTING TOOL) BEZEL BEZIL
(— OF GLACIER) SNOUT
(— OF STUMP) SCARF SCARPH
(— ON DOOR KNOCKER) MASCARON
(— ONE'S DANCING PARTNER) SET
(— THE EAST) ORIENTATE
(— TO FACE) AFRONT BEFORE FACIAL DIRECTLY
(— WITH MARBLE) PIN

(— WITH STONE) BATCH
(CLOCK —) DIAL TABLE WATCH
(CRYSTAL —) PINAKOU
(CURVED —) EXTRADOS INTRADOS
(DIE —) ACE
(FANTASTIC —) ANTIC
(HALF DOMINO —) END
(HAVING SHORT BROAD —)
LATERAL
(INNER —) CONCAVE
(MADE-UP —) MOP
(MINING —) BANK BREAST
FOREHEAD LONGWALL
(MOCKING —) MOE MOWE
(QUARRY —) HEUGH
(ROCK —) CLIFF
(UPPER —) BROW
(WRY —) MOUTH GRIMACE
(PREF.) FACIO PROSOP(O)
FACE-ARBOR KNIFE
FACED
(SUFF.) PROSOPOUS
FACE GUARD FRONTAL
FACEMAN HAGGER WINNER
FACEPLATE FRONT DOGPLATE
FACER BUMPER DRIFTER TANKARD
FACET PANE STAR BEZEL CULET
PHASE COLLET STEMMA FACETTE
LOZENGE TEMPLET
FACETIAE CURIOSA
FACETIOUS FUNNY MERRY SMART
WITTY FACETE JOCOSE JOCULAR
HUMOROUS POLISHED
FACIAL
(PREF.) FACIO
FACILE PAT ABLE EASY QUICK
READY EXPERT FLUENT GENTLE
AFFABLE DUCTILE LENIENT
FACILITATE AID EASE HELP FAVOR
SPEED ASSIST GREASE EXPEDITE
FACILITY ART EASE FEEL HELP
ECLAT KNACK SKILL ADDRESS
COMMAND FREEDOM PROWESS
EASINESS
(PL.) ADDITIONS
FACING DADO HARL FRONT HARLE
LAPEL LINER PANEL SKIRT
BEFORE TOWARD VENEER
AGAINST FORNENT SURFACE
BLACKING CAMPSHOT CONFRONT
COVERING FACEWORK FORNENST
OPPOSITE PITCHING
(— AGAINST GLACIER) STOSS
(— AHEAD) FULL
(— APEX) ACROSCOPIC
(— AUDIENCE OBLIQUELY) EFFACE
AFFRONTY
(— FOR WALLS) CASE
(— FROM GLACIER) STOSS
(— INWARD) INTRORSE
(— OUTWARDS) EXTRORSE
(PREF.) OB
FACSIMILE FAX COPY MODEL
REPLICA AUTOTYPE
FACT CASE DEED FAIT DATUM
EVENT SOOTH TRUTH DONNEE
EFFECT FACTUM VERITY
COMPERT FORMULA GENERAL
INDICIA KEYNOTE LOWDOWN
REALITY PARTICULAR
(CONCLUSIVE —) CRUSHER
(DECISIVE —) CLINCHER

(FUNDAMENTAL —) KEYNOTE
(TRUE —S) STRENGTH
(PL.) DATA FEAT
FACTION BLOC NERI PART SECT
SIDE WING CABAL JUNTO PARTY
BRIGUE CLIQUE SCHISM BIANCHI
DISPUTE PINFOLD QUARREL
INTRIGUE SPLINTER
(— OF SECEDERS) CAVE
(PARTY —) STASIS
FACTITIOUS SHAM WHIPPED
KRITRIMA
FACTOR GEN DOER GENE ITEM
AGENT ALLEL CAUSE MAKER
ALLELE AUTHOR CENTER DETAIL
BAILIFF CONTROL GOUCHER
CUSHION ELEMENT ENTROPY
FACTRIX ISOLATE STEWARD
ADHERENT AUMILDAR COFACTOR
DOMINANT EQUATION
GOMASHTA INCIDENT INCITANT
PARAMETER
(—S IN EVOLUTION) ANTICHANCE
(CYTOPLASMIC —) KAPPA
(DECISIVE —) CAPSTONE
(ECOLOGICAL —) INFLUENT
(ENVIRONMENTAL —) GEOGEN
(HEREDITY —) GENE INSTINCT
(HINDERING —) CRIMP
(INTELLIGENCE —) G
(PERSONALITY —) SURGENCY
(RESTRICTIVE —) BARRIER
FACTORY HONG MILL SHOP PLANT
USINE AURANG AURUNG FABRIC
SUGARY CANNERY HATTERY
HOSIERY OFICINA SOAPERY
BUILDING COMPTOIR FABRIQUE
FILATURE HACIENDA OFFICINA
STAMPERY WORKSHOP
MANUFACTORY
FACTOTUM SIRCAR FAMULUS
COMPRADOR
FACTUAL HARD REAL TRUE
ACTUAL BEDROCK EARTHLY
EMPIRIC LITERAL PROSAIC
(INSUFFICIENTLY —) ABSTRACT
FACTUALLY INSOOTH
FACULTY ART WIT BOOM BUMP
EASE GIFT WILL FANCY POWER
SENSE BREATH BUDDHI GIFTIE
SEEING TALENT ABILITY COLLEGE
COUNSEL HABITUS APTITUDE
CAPACITY FELICITY
(— OF EXPRESSION) LANGUAGE
(CRITICAL —) JUDGMENT
(MENTAL —) HEADPIECE
(POETIC OR CREATIVE —) IDEALITY
PRINCIPLE
(REASONING —) DISCOURSE
(PL.) INDULTS
FAD BUG CULT FIKE RAGE WHIM
CRAZE FANCY HOBBY FOIBLE
MAGGOT CROCHET FASHION
WRINKLE
FADDIST CRANK
FADE DIE DIM DOW FLY WAN BRIT
CAST FATE FLAT GIVE PALE PEAK
PINE PINK VADE WELK WILK WILT
BLANK DAVER DECAY FLEET
PASSE PETER QUAIL SWING
SWOON DARKLE PERISH VANISH
WITHER DECLINE INSIPID
LIGHTEN DIMINISH DISCOLOR

DISSOLVE EVANESCE LANGUISH
(— AWAY) DOW BREAK FLEET
WALLOW
FADED PASSE SHABBY EXOLETE
SHOPWORN
FADGE FAY FIT SUIT
FADING FUGITIVE MANCANDO
SWINGING
FAERIE QUEENE (AUTHOR OF —)
SPENSER
(CHARACTER IN —) UNA GUYON
IRENE TALUS ACRASY AMORET
ARTHUR DUESSA TIMIAS
ASTRAEA MALEGER ARTEGALL
CALIDORE GLORIANA ORGOGLIO
RADIGUND ARCHIMAGO
BELPHOEBE BRITOMART
FLORIMELL GRANTORTO
SCUDAMOUR
FAFNIR (FATHER OF —) HREIDMAR
(SLAYER OF —) SIGURD
FAG FLAG JADE TIRE TOIL DROOP
WEARY DRUDGE HARASS MENIAL
EXHAUST FATIGUE FRAZZLE
FAGGED TASKIT
FAGGOT BROSNA CHUMPA
FAGALD
FAGOT KID BUNT PILE PIMP BAVIN
FADGE NICKY NITCH FAGGOT
KNITCH GARBAGE
FAIL GO CUT EBB ERR PIP BANK
BUST CONK FALL FLAG FLOP
FOLD LACK LOSE MISS SINK SKEW
SPIN WANE APPAL BREAK BURST
CRACK FAULT FLUFF FLUKE
FLUNK PETER QUAIL SLAKE
SMASH SPILL VAILE APPALL
BETRAY DEFAIL DEFECT DESERT
FALTER FIZZLE REPINE WINDER
DECLINE DEFAULT EXHAUST
FALSIFY FLICKER FLUMMOX
FOUNDER MISFARE MISGIVE
SCANTLE LANGUISH
(— AT) FLUB
(— IN DUTY) LAPSE
(— IN EARLY STAGES) ABORT
(— IN HEALTH) SINK BREAK
(— IN STUDIES) BILGE
(— ON RIFLE RANGE) BOLO
(— TO GAIN ALTITUDE) MUSH
(— TO GROW) MISS
FAILING BAD ILL BLOT FAULT
FOIBLE BLEMISH FAILURE FRAILTY
ABORTIVE WEAKNESS
FAILURE DUD BALK BOMB BUST
FAIL FLOP FLUB FOIL LACK LOSS
MISS MUFF TRIP BAULK BILGE
CRASH DECAY ERROR FAULT
FLUKE FLUNK FROST GRIEF GUILT
LAPSE LEMON PLUCK SMASH
BRODIE FIASCO FIZZLE OUTAGE
STUMER STUMOR BLOOMER
CROPPER DEBACLE DECLINE
DEFAULT FLIVVER FLUMMOX
NEGLECT STUMBLE ABORTION
COLLAPSE DISASTER FAILANCE
FLOPEROO OMISSION
(— OF DAM) BLOW
(— OF FIREARM) STOPPAGE
(— OF MILK SECRETION) AGALAXY
AGALAXIA
(— OF MUSCLE) ACHALASIA
(— OF PAVEMENT) BLOWUP

(— OF PRIMER) HANGFIRE
(— OF VITALITY) DELIQUIUM
(— TO RAISE OAR) CRAB
(COMPUTER —) CRASH
(FLAT —) DUD
(RIDICULOUS —) FIASCO
FAIN FOND GLAD LIEF EAGER
PLEASED WILLING DESIROUS
INCLINED
FAINEANT IDLE LAZY
FAINT GO DIM LOW WAN WAW
COLD CONK COOL DARK PALE
PALL SOFT THIN WEAK LIGHT
QUEAL QUEER SHADY SWELT
SWOON TIMID WAUFF WAUGH
WERSH EVANID FEEBLE REMISS
REMOTE SICKLY WAMBLY
FEIGNED FORGONE LANGUID
OBSCURE SWITHER SYNCOPE
WEARISH COWARDLY DELICATE
LANGUISH LISTLESS SLUGGISH
TIMOROUS
(— FROM HEAT) SWELTER
(— FROM HUNGER) LEERY
(— OF SCENT) COLD WAUGH
FAINTHEARTED TIMID COWARD
CRAVEN COWARDLY UNHEARTY
FAINTHEARTEDNESS QUALM
FAINTING AFAINT SYNCOPE
DELIQUIUM
(— SPELL) DROW DWAM DWALM
FAINTLY DIMLY FAINT SMALL
FAINTNESS TENUITY GONENESS
WEAKNESS
FAINT-VOICED INWARD
FAIR GAY GEY MOP BEAU BELL
CALM EVEN FINE GAFF GALA
GOOD HEND JUST MART PLAY
TIDE TIDY BAZAR BLOND CLEAN
CLEAR EQUAL FERIA HENDE
LARGE RIGHT ROUND SHEER
TRYST WHITE AONACH BAZAAR
BLONDE CANDID COMELY
DECENT DINKUM HONEST KERMIS
PRETTY SERENE SQUARE EXHIBIT
JANNOCK KERMESS STATUTE
BOOKFAIR DISTINCT FESTIVAL
HORNFAIR MIDDLING RATIONAL
STRAIGHT UNBIASED OBJECTIVE
REASONABLE
(— AND CALM) SETTLED
(— AND SQUARE) DINKUM
(HINDU —) MELA
(VILLAGE —) WALK
FAIRER SHIPWRIGHT
FAIRING SPAT SPINNER FAIRLING
FAIR-LEAD WAPP
FAIRLY WELL GAILY GAYLY GEYAN
EVENLY JUSTLY MEANLY
HANDILY PLAINLY RIGHTLY
MIDDLING PROPERLY SUITABLY
FAIRNESS FAIR CANDOR EQUITY
HONESTY JUSTICE EQUALITY
EVENNESS FAIRHEAD FAIRHOOD
FAIRWAY HOLE WATERWAY
FAIR-WEATHER SUNSHINE
FAIRY ELF FAY FEE HOB IMP FAIN
PERI PIXY PUCK SHEE VILA
OUPHE PECHT PIXIE SIDHE
WIGHT COURIL FAERIE HATHOR
KEWPIE SPIRIT SPRITE YAKSHA
YAKSHI ARGANTE BANSHEE
ORIANDA SHEOGUE SYLPHID

URGANDA FOLLETTO MELUSINA
(IRISH —) SHEE SIDHE
(TRICKSY —) PUCK
(PL.) GENTRY
FAIRY BELL FOXGLOVE
FAIRYFOLK SHEE SIDHE
FAIRYLAND ANNWN ANNWFN
FEERIE ELFLAND
FAITH DIN FAY FOY LAW LAY VAY
FACK FAIX FEGS SLAM TROW
CERTY CREED HAITH STOCK
TOUCH TROTH TRUST TRUTH
BELIEF CERTIE CREDIT GOSPEL
CREANCE FACKINS AFFIANCE
RELIANCE RELIGION
(BAD —) DUPLICITY
(RELIGIOUS —) SRADH SRADDHA
SHRADDHA
(PREF.) FIDE(I) PISTIO PISTO
FAITHFUL FAST FEAL FIRM GOOD
JUST LEAL LIKE REAL TRIG TRUE
FALSE HEMAN LIEGE LOYAL
PIOUS SOOTH SWEER TIGHT
TREST TRIED AEFALD ARDENT
ENTIRE FIDELE HONEST LAWFUL
PISTIC STANCH STEADY TRUSTY
DEVOTED SINCERE STAUNCH
ACCURATE CONSTANT RESOLUTE
SPEAKING RELIGIOUS
FAITHFULNESS HSIN FEALTY
VERITY LOYALTY FIDELITY
TRUENESS
FAITHFUL SHEPHERDESS
(AUTHOR OF —) FLETCHER
(CHARACTER IN —) CHLOE ALEXIS
AMORET CLORIN THENOT
DAPHNIS PERIGOT AMARILLIS
FAITHLESS FALSE PUNIC FICKLE
HOLLOW ROTTEN UNJUST
UNTRUE ATHEIST APOSTATE
DELUSIVE DISLOYAL SHIFTING
UNSTABLE NIDDERING
PERFIDIOUS
FAITHLESSNESS FALSITY PERFIDY
UNTRUTH
FAKE DUD DUFF FEKE HOAX HOKE
SHAM BOGUS CHEAT FALSE
FEIGN FLAKE FRAUD FUDGE
PHONY WANGLE DUFFING
FALSIFY FURBISH GUNDECK
PRETEND SWINDLE SIMULATE
SPURIOUS ADULTERINE
(— OF STOWED ROPE) FLEET
(FOOTBALL —) JUKE
(PREF.) PSEUD(O)
FAKER FAKIR QUACK HUMBUG
CAMELOT PEDDLER
(— OF ART) TRUQUEUR
FAKIR FAKIH FAQUIR DERVISH
FALCHION FALX
FALCON EYAS HAWK SORE BESRA
HOBBY SAKER STOOP GENTLE
JAGGER JUGGER LANNER
LUGGAR LUGGER MERLIN
MUSKET PREYER RAPTOR SHAHIN
TERCEL KESTREL SAKERET
BERIGORA BOCKEREL FALCONET
PEREGRIN SOREHAWK
(— BOARD) HACK
(— IN FIRST YEAR) SORE
SOREHAWK
(FEMALE —) FORMAL FORMEL
LANNER

(MALE —) TASSEL TERCEL
SAKERET
(SMALL —) HOBBY MERLIN
KESTREL
(WHITE —) ICELANDER
FALCONER HAWKER OSTREGER
FALCONRY HAWKING
FALDSTOOL ORATORY
FALL GO EBB SAG SYE TIP BACK
BAND COME COUP DIVE DRIP
DROP DUNT FLOP HANG PICK
PLOP RASH RUIN RUSE SHED SILE
SINK SLIP SWAK SWAP SWAY
SWOP TILT WHAP WHOP ABATE
CHUTE CLOIT CRASH DROOP
HANCE INCUR JABOT LAPSE
LIGHT LODGE PITCH PLUMB
PLUMP RAPID SAULT SHAKE
SHOOT SKITE SLIPE SLUMP SPILL
SQUAB SQUAT THROW TRACE
TWINE ALIGHT AUTUMN BRODIE
DEVALL DOUNCE DRYSNE
FOOTER HAPPEN HEADER
JOUNCE PERISH PLUNGE RECEDE
SEASON SLOUGH STREEK STRIKE
TOPPLE TUMBLE CASCADE
CROPPER CROWNER DECLINE
DEGRADE DEPRESS DESCEND
DEVOLVE DRIBBLE ESCHEAT
ILLAPSE PLUMMET RELAPSE
RETREAT SQUELCH STUMBLE
SUBSIDE CATARACT COLLAPSE
COMMENCE DECREASE
DOWNCOME PRECIPITATE
(— ABRUPTLY) DUMP
(— APART) BREAK SHIVER
COLLAPSE DISUNITE
(— AWAY) DEFECT
(— BACK) RECEDE RESORT
(— BEHIND) LAG
(— DIZZILY) SPIN
(— DOWN) CAVE FLOP SWAP
SLUMP REVERSE SWITHER
(— DUE) ACCRUE BEFALL
(— FAST) HOP
(— FLAT) PLAT FLIVVER
(— FORWARD) PECK PITCH
PROLAPSE
(— FROM A HORSE) PURL
VOLUNTARY
(— FROM SURFBOARD) WIPEOUT
(— FROM UNDERMINING) CALVE
(— FROM VIRTUE) LAPSE
(— GRADUALLY) EBB SAG
(— HEAVILY) DING LUMP SOSS
CLOIT CLYTE GULCH PLOUT
PLUMP SOUSE SWACK THROW
(— ILL) TRAIK
(— IN) CAVE FOUNDER
(— IN DROPS) DRIP STILL DRIBBLE
(— IN FLURRIES) SPIT
(— IN FOLDS) BLOUSE
(— IN RIVER) SAULT
(— IN WITH) INCUR
(— INTO) STRIKE
(— INTO ERROR) SLIP STUMBLE
(— INTO FAINT) DWAM DWALM
(— INTO RUIN) DECAY
(— INTO SLUMBER) DROWSE
(— INTO TRAP) DECOY
(— INTO WATER) DOP
(— OF DEW) SEREIN SERENE
(— OF RAIN) SKIFF SKIFT

ONDING SHOWER
(— OF SNOW) SKIFF SKIFT
ONCOME SCOUTHER SNOWFALL
(— OF WICKETS) ROT
(— OFF) BATE SLIP SLACK
(— ON BACK) BACKER
(— ON SUCCESSIVE DAYS) CONCUR
(— ON THE NOSE) NOSER
(— OUT) BREAK LIGHT FORTUNE
QUARREL
(— PRONE) GRABBLE
(— RAPIDLY) SKID
(— SHORT) DROP FAIL FAULT
(— SLOWLY) SETTLE
(— SUDDENLY) BOLT PLOP SLUMP
(— THROWING HORSE AND RIDER)
CRUMPLER
(— TO NOTHING) DISSOLVE
(— TO PIECES) BUCKLE CRUMBLE
(— UPON) WARP
(— VIOLENTLY) BEAT
(BAD —) BUSTER
(HEAVY —) PASH POUR SWAG
BLASH CLOIT GULCH SKELP
SOUSE SQUAT MUCKER
(INCOMPLETE WRESTLING —) FOIL
(SOFT —) SCLAFF
(SUDDEN —) HANCE SQUAT
SQUASH
FALLACIOUS SLY WILY ABSURD
CRAFTY UNTRUE DELUSIVE
GUILEFUL ILLUSORY
FALLACY IDOL ERROR FALLAX
IDOLUM SOPHISM EQUIVOKE
ILLUSION
(PL.) IDOLA
FALLEN DOWN FAUN FLAT SHED
LAPSED DECLASSE
(— IN) SUNKEN
FALLER GILL FLATHEAD
FALLFISH CHUB DACE CORPORAL
FALL HERRING TAILOR
FALLIBLE HUMAN ERRANT
ERRABLE
FALLING SIT CADENT CAVING
PROLAPSE WINDFALL
(— BACK) ESCHEAT
(— DOWN) RUIN
(— INTO) INFALL
(— OF MINE ROOF) SIT
(— OF RAIN) SPIT
(— OFF) CADUCE LEEWAY
CADUCOUS
(— ON SOMETHING) INCIDENT
(— OUT) DIFFICULTY
(— SHORT) DEFICIT
(PREF.) CADUCI
(SUFF.) PTOMA PTOSIS
FALLOPIAN TUBE TUBAL
(PREF.) FALL(O)
FALLOVER OSTREGER
FALLOW LEA PALE HOBBY BARREN
VALEWE
(PREF.) POLI(O)
FALLOW DEER DAMINE DAPPLE
FALLOWING ARDER
FALSE DEAD FAKE FLAM SHAM
BOGUS FAUSE LYING PASTE
PHONY WRONG FICKLE HOLLOW
LUTHER PSEUDO UNTRUE
ASSUMED BASTARD CROOKED
FEIGNED APOSTATE DISLOYAL
ILLUSIVE RECREANT RENEGADE

SPECTRAL SPURIOUS
MENDACIOUS
(PREF.) PSEUD(O)
FALSE BEACHDROPS PINESAP
FALSE CRAWLEY PINEDROPS
FALSE FOXGLOVE FEVERWEED
FALSE HELLEBORE EARTHGALL
FALSEHOOD COG FIB LIE BUNG
CRAM FLAM TALE CRACK ERROR
FABLE STORY FALSET UNFACT
YANKER CRAMMER CRETISM
FALSAGE FALSERY FALSITY
FIBBERY FICTION LEASING
PERFIDY PHANTOM ROMANCE
UNTRUTH FALSHEDE ROORBACK
STRAPPER
FALSE MERMAID FLOERKEA
LIMNANTH
FALSENESS SHAM DECEIT
FALSE WINTERGREEN PYROLA
FALSEWORK CENTERING
FALSIES CHEATERS
FALSIFIER LIAR FALSER FORGER
FALSARY
FALSIFY LIE COOK FAKE WARP
ABUSE BELIE FEINT FORGE
BETRAY DOCTOR FIDDLE
GUNDECK VIOLATE EMBEZZLE
MISREPRESENT
FALSITY LIE ERROR VANITY
UNTRUTH INVERITY
FALSTAFF (CHARACTER IN —) MEG
FORD JOHN PAGE ALICE BROOK
CAIUS FENTON QUICKLY
FALSTAFF NANNETTA
(COMPOSER OF —) VERDI
FALTER FAIL HALT PAUSE WAVER
BOGGLE FLINCH TOTTER FRIBBLE
STAMMER STUMBLE TREMBLE
HESITATE
FALTERING HINK HALTING
FALX FALCULA
FAME BAY CRY LOSE NAME STAR
WORD BRUIT ECLAT GLORY
HONOR KUDOS PRICE RUMOR
VOICE ESTEEM LAUREL RENOWN
REPORT REPUTE TONGUE
HEARSAY WORSHIP
(EVIL —)
(HALL OF —) (SEE HALL OF FAME)
(ILL —) OPPROBRIUM
FAMED RIFE KNOWN NOTED
EMINENT RENOMEE RENOWNED
FAMILIAR FLY BAKA BOKO BOLD
COZY EASY FREE FULL HOMY
TAME TOSH CLOSE CONNU
GREAT HOMEY KNOWN PRIVY
THICK USUAL BEATEN CHUMMY
COMMON ENTIRE FOLKSY
GERMAN HOMELY INWARD
KENNED STRAIT THRONG VERSED
AFFABLE FAMULAR FOLKSEY
POPULAR FREQUENT HABITUAL
INTIMATE SOCIABLE
STANDARD
(— WITH) KNOWING
(MAKE —) POST
(PRESUMPTUOUSLY —) INSOLENT
FAMILIARITY HABIT FREEDOM
LIBERTY PRIVACY PRIVITY
TRAFFIC HABITUDE INTIMACY
CONSUETUDE
FAMILIARIZE HAFT VERSE

ACCUSTOM ACQUAINT FREQUENT
FAMILIARLY HOMELY
FAMILY ILK KIN AIGA CLAN GING
KIND LINE NAME RACE TEAM
TRIP CINEL CLASS FLESH GOTRA
GROUP HOUSE MEINY STIRP
STOCK CLETCH FAIMLY PARAGE
STEMMA STIRPS STRAIN ZEGRIS
DYNASTY KINDRED LINEAGE
ORLEANS PROGENY CATEGORY
FIRESIDE
(COSMOPOLITAN —) FELIDAE
FABACEAE
(FIRST —) FF
(LANGUAGE —) CHON BANTU
CLICK COCHE CUNAN KADAI
STOCK AIMARA ATALAN AYMARA
CHOLON GILIAK HUARPE LENCAN
SERIAN BOTOYAN CADDOAN
CARIBAN CATIBAN CHINOOK
CHOLONA CHUMASH COPEHAN
ESSELEN KARTHLI KARTVEL
KERESAN SHASTAN ATAKAPAN
CHANGOAN
(LARGE —) QUIVERFUL
(ONE-PARAMETER —) PENCIL
(SUPER —) APINA APOIDEA
FAMINE LACK PINE WOLF DEARTH
HUNGER SCARCITY
FAMISH KILL STARVE DESTROY
ENFAMISH
FAMOUS MERE BREME FAMED
GRAND NOBLE NOTED FAMOSE
NAMELY EMINENT NAMABLE
NOTABLE RENOWNED
FAMULUS WAGNER SERVANT
FAN ONE RUN VAN BEAT BLOW
BUFF COOL WASH DELTA PUNKA
WHIFF BASKET BLOWER CHAMAR
COLMAR FANNER FLABEL FLIGHT
PUNKAH ROOTER SHOVEL
SPREAD VENTOY WINNOW
ADMIRER DEVOTEE FLABRUM
FLYFLAP MPANGWE PAHOUIN
WHISKER EVENTAIL FOLLOWER
RHIPIDION
(— FOR BLOWER) WAFTER
(ALLUVIAL —) CONE APRON DELTA
(FEMALE — OF ROCK MUSICIAN)
GROUPIE
(FOOTBALL —) GRIDDER
(JAZZ —) CAT
(WINNOWING —) SAIL LIKNON
(PL.) FOLLOWING
(PREF.) FLABELLI RHIPI(D)(DO)
FANALOKA FOSSA FOUSSA
FANATIC MAD BIGOT CRAZY FIEND
RABID ULTRA ZEALOT DEVOTEE
FURIOSO PHANTIC PULAHAN
PULIJAN BABAYLAN FRENETIC
FANATICAL RABID ULTRA
EXTREME FURIOUS
FANCIED UNREAL DREAMED
AFFECTED
FANCIFUL ODD ANTIC FAIRY IDEAL
QUEER VIEWY DREAMY QUAINT
UNREAL BIZARRE CURIOUS
FANCIED LAPUTAN STRANGE
WHIMSIC CHIMERIC FANCICAL
FILIGREE NOTIONAL ROMANTIC
FANCY BEE FAD GIG IDEA ITEM
LIKE LOVE MAZE TROW WEEN
WHIM BRAID BRAIN DREAM

FREAK GUESS HUMOR SHINE
AFFECT BEGUIN FANGLE FIGURE
FLOSSY IDEATE LIKING MAGGOT
MEGRIM NOTION ORNATE SHINDY
VAGARY VISION WHIMSY CAPRICE
CHIMERA CONCEIT CONCEPT
CROCHET FANCIED FANCIFY
FANTASY PROPOSE ROMANCE
SUSPECT THOUGHT WRINKLE
CHIMAERA CONCEIVE CROTCHET
DAYDREAM ILLUSION PHANTASM
PHANTASY
(FOOLISH —) CHIMERA CHIMAERA
(PASSING —) FIKE
(PERVERSE —) CROTCHET
(WILD —) TOY MAZE
(PL.) DREAMERY
FANDANGO MURCIANA
FANE FLAG BANNER FANACLE
FANFARE TUSCH HOORAY
HURRAH TUCKET TANTARA
FANFARON FLOURISH
FANFARONADE BLUSTER
FANFARE SWAGGER BOASTING
FANFLOWER TACCADA
FANG FAN EARN FALX TAKE TANG
TUSK VANG BEGIN PRONG SEIZE
SNARE TOOTH ASSUME OBTAIN
PANGWE CAPTURE PAHOUIN
PROCURE
FANON CAPE ORALE PHANO
FANNEL MANIPLE
FAN PALM YARAY ERYTHEA
FANTREE TALIPOT
FAN-SHAPED ALARY RHIPIDATE
FANTAIL COMET SHAKER WAGTAIL
FAN-TAN PARLIAMENT
FANTASIA FANTASY QUODLIBET
FANTASTIC ODD WILD ANTIC
LUCIO OUTRE QUEER ABSURD
GOTHIC ROCOCO TOYISH UNREAL
ANTICAL BAROQUE BIZARRE
WHIMSIC FANCIFUL FREAKISH
ROMANTIC SINGULAR
(— PERSON) KICKSHAW
FANTASY IDEA DREAM FANCY
DESIRE VISION CAPRICE CHIMERA
PHANTOM ROMANCE CHIMAERA
PHANTASM PHANTASY
FANTINE (DAUGHTER OF —)
COSETTE
FAR AWAY LONG MUCH ROOM
SIDE WELL WIDE CLEAN SIZES
WIDEN REMOTE DISTANT
FARAWAY ROOMWARD
(— AND AWAY) STREETS
(— OFF) OUTBYE
(— ON) ADVANCED
(PREF.) TEL(E) TELOTERO
FARAMONDO (COMPOSER OF —)
HANDEL
FARCE MIME DROLL EXODE FORCE
STUFF COMEDY GARLIC SOTTIE
EXODIUM MOCKERY TEMACHA
BURLETTA DROLLERY FARCETTA
(RELATING TO —) ATELLAN
FARCEUR WAG JOKER FORCER
FARCICAL BUFFO COMIC DROLL
ATELLAN
FARCTATE STUFFED
FARCY FARCIN EQUINIA FASHION
FARE DO GO EAT TRY COME DIET
FEND FOOD PATH RATE TIME

WEND CHEER CHEFE CHIVE
FRAME GOING LIGHT PRICE
SPEED TABLE TOKEN TRACK
VIAND COMMON FARING FETTLE
HAPPEN TRAVEL CARFARE
JOURNEY PASSAGE PROCEED
PROSPER WAFTAGE WAYFARE
FERRYAGE PROGRESS
(— FOR FERRY) NAULUM
FERRYAGE
(— WELL) SPEED
(COARSE —) HAWEBAKE
FAREWELL AVE VALE ADIEU ADIOS
ALOHA CONGE FINAL LEAVE
CHEERO BONALLY CHEERIO
GOODBYE LEAVING LULLABY
PARTING
FAREWELL TO ARMS (AUTHOR OF
—) HEMINGWAY
(CHARACTER IN —) HENRY
BARKLEY RINALDI FREDERIC
CATHERINE
FARFETCHED FARFET FORCED
DEVIOUS STRAINED EXQUISITE
FAR-FLUNG EXTENDED
FAR FROM THE MADDING
CROWD (AUTHOR OF —) HARDY
(CHARACTER IN —) OAK TROY
FANNY ROBIN GABRIEL
BOLDWOOD EVERDENE
BATHSHEBA
FARIDUN (FATHER OF —) ABTIN
(MOTHER OF —) FIRANAK
(SON OF —) TUR IRAJ SALM
FARINA MEAL FLOUR FARINE
POLLEN STARCH
FARKLEBERRY BLUET
FARL PARLY FARREL
FARM FEU PEN CROP TACK TILL
TORP TOWN WALK CROFT DAIRY
EMPTY FIRMA HARAS MAINS
MILPA PLACE RANCH RANGE
STEAD BARTON BOWERY CHACRA
ESTATE FURROW GRANGE
RANCHO TYDDEN TYDDYN
CLEANSE HENNERY KOLKHOZ
MAILING POTRERO POULTRY
SOVKHOS VACCARY ESTANCIA
HACIENDA HATCHERY LABORING
LOCATION STEADING TOWNSHIP
(— OUT) DIMIT ARRENT
(COLLECTIVE —) KIBBUTZ KOLKHOZ
(COMMUNAL —) KVUTZA KVUTZAH
(DAIRY —) WICK
(LARGE —) RANCH BARTON
(RENTED —) MAILING
(SMALL —) CHACRA
(STOCK —) ESTANCIA
(STUD —) STUD HARAS
FARMER HOB CARL FARM HOBB
KHOT KYLE RUBE RYOT TATE
AILLT AUMIL BOWER CARLE CEILE
CLOWN COLON HODGE KISAN
COCKIE GROWER HOGMAN
JIBARO TILLER YEOMAN BUCOLIC
BUSHMAN BYWONER COTTIER
CROFTER GRANGER HAYSEED
HUSBAND LANDMAN METAYER
PLANTER PLOWMAN RANCHER
SCULLOG TILLMAN TRUCKER
COCKATOO PRODUCER PUBLICAN
RURALIST SELECTOR
(AUSTRALIAN —) SELECTOR

(NORWEGIAN —) BONDER
(POOR —) PIKE
(PROSPEROUS —) KULAK
(SMALL —) BOOR COCKIE
(TENANT —) AILLT GEBUR SIRDAR
COLONUS SHAREMAN
SHARECROPPER
FARMHAND HAND HELP
FARMHOLD CROFT
FARMHOUSE FARM TOWN ONSET
GRANGE QUINTA CASERIO
ONSTEAD STEADING
FARMING SOIL FARMERY
HUSBANDRY
(— SYSTEM) METAYAGE
FARMLAND ACREAGE
FARMSTEAD TOWN WICK STEAD
FARMERY ONSTEAD
FARMYARD WERF CLOSE BARTON
RICKYARD
FARO MONTE STUSS TIGER
PHARAOH
(— CARD) SODA
FARO BANK TIGER
FAR-OFF DISTANT
FAR-OUT KINKY
FAR-REACHING GREAT FARGOING
FARRIER SHOER SMITH MARSHAL
FARROW PIG ROW RAKE DRAPE
LITTER
FARSEEING ORACULAR
FARSIGHTED SHREWD SIGHTY
FARTHER YOND AHEAD STILL
LONGER FURTHER REMOTER
THITHER
FARTHEST ULTIMA ENDMOST
EXTREME FARMOST LONGEST
OUTMOST DOWNMOST FURTHEST
REMOTEST ULTIMATE
FARTHING RAG GRIG JACK QUAD
FADGE FERLING QUARTER
QUADRANS QUADRANT
(HALF —) CUE
(THREE —S) GILL
FARTHINGALE FERDEGEW
VERTUGAL
FASCIA BAND SASH FACIA FILLET
BANDAGE MOLDING LIGATURE
PLATBAND
FASCICLE BUNDLE PHALANGE
FASCICULUS HEFT BUNDLE
COLUMN TRACTUS
FASCINATE DARE CHARM SEIZE
WITCH ALLURE ENAMOR
ATTRACT BEWITCH ENCHANT
ENGROSS GLAMOUR PHILTER
PHILTRE ENSORCEL ENTRANCE
INTEREST INTRIGUE SIRENIZE
CAPTIVATE
FASCINATED BESOTTED
FASCINATING NUTTY ORPHIC
TAKING SIRENIC CHARMING
FETCHING MESMERIC
FASCINATION CHARM SPELL
WITCHERY
FASCINE FAGOT FAGGOT
SAUCISSE
FASCIOLA DISTOMA DISTOMUM
FASCIOLE SEMITA
FASCIST BLACK FASCISTA
FASHION GO CRY CUT FAD LAT
TON WAY CHIC FEAT FORM GARB
GATE KICK MAKE MODE MOLD

RAGE RATE SORT TURN TWIG
WEAR WISE BUILD CRAZE FEIGN
FORGE FRAME GUISE MODEL
MOULD SHAPE STYLE VOGUE
WEAVE AGUISE ASSIZE BUSTLE
CAMBER CREATE CUSTOM
DESIGN FANGLE INVENT MANNER
METHOD ALAMODE COMPOSE
IMAGERY PORTRAY QUALITY
CONTRIVE
(LATEST —) KICK
(PREVAILING —) CRY
(SPECIAL —) TOUCH
FASHIONABLE CHIC PINK POSH
TONY DASHY DOGGY DOSSY
NOBBY RITZY SMART SWELL
SWISH VOGUE GIGOLO JAUNTY
MODISH TIMISH TONISH TRENDY
DASHING GALLANT GENTEEL
STYLISH SWAGGER BELGRAVIAN
(NOT —) DEMODE
FASHIONABLY SMARTLY
FASHIONED HUED CARVED
SHAPED WROUGHT FEATURED
FASHIONING FINGENT
FASHION PLATE SWELL
FASSAITE PYRGOM
FAST HOT HUT COLD FIRM HARD
LENT SOON SURE WIDE AGILE
APACE BRISK CHEAP FIXED FLASH
FLEET HASTY QUICK RAPID
ROUND SADLY STUCK SWIFT
TIGHT TOSTO CARENE ESTHER
FASTLY LIVELY SECURE SPEEDY
SPORTY STABLE STARVE ABIDING
EXPRESS HOTSHOT HURRIED
PROVISO RASPING SETTLED
SIKERLY STATION TAANITH
ENDURING FAITHFUL SPINNING
SPORTING WIKIWIKI
(— DAY) ASHURA
(SUFF.) **(MAKING —)** PEXIA PEXIS
PEXY
FAST-DYED INGRAIN
FASTEN BAR DOG FAY FIX GAD GIB
KEY LAG PEN PIN SEW TAG TIE
YOT BELT BEND BIND BITT BOLT
BRAD CLIP FRET GIRD GIRT GLUE
GRIP HANG HANK HASP HOOK
HOOP HORN KILT KNIT KNOT
LACE LASH LINK LOCK MOOR
NAIL ROPE SEAL SNIB SOUD SPAN
SPAR STAY WELD WIRE AFFIX
ANNEX BELAY BIGHT BRACE
CABLE CATCH CHAIN CHOCK
CINCH CLAMP CLASP CLING
COPSE CRAMP DEFIX GIRTH
HALSH HITCH INFIX LATCH PASTE
RIVET SCREW SEIZE SLOUR SNECK
STEEK STICK STRAP TRUSS WITHE
ANCHOR ATTACH BATTEN
BUCKLE BUTTON CEMENT CLINCH
COTTER COUPLE ENGAGE ENTAIL
FATHER GARTER HAMPER
HANKLE INKNOT PICKET SECURE
SKEWER SOLDER STAPLE STITCH
STRAIN TETHER BRACKET
CONFINE CONNECT EMBRACE
GRAPPLE GROMMET PADLOCK
BARNACLE FORELOCK INTERTIE
OBLIGATE TRANSFIX
(— A SAIL) CROSS
(— ABOUT) THRAP

(— ANCHOR) SCOW
(— AS SPURS) SPEND
(— IN) EMBAR
(— PROMPTLY) CLAP
(— TO) TAG
(— TOGETHER) COAPT SEIZE
SPLICE CONNECT
(— WINGS ON) IMP
(— WITH A GIRTH) WARRICK
(— WITH NOTCHES) GAIN
(PREF.) HAPT(O)
FASTENED FAST SHUT BOUND
FIXED BOUNDEN
(PREF.) **(— TOGETHER)** SYNAPTO
FASTENER BAR GIB GIN NUT PIN
AGAL BOLT DOME FAST FROG
HASP LOCK NAIL SNAP TACK
CATCH CLAMP CLASP LATCH
RIVET SCREW SPIKE STRAP
TATCH THONG BUCKLE BUTTON
HATPIN STAPLE ZIPPER FIXATOR
LATCHET PADLOCK SNAPPER
TENDRIL FASTNESS STAYLACE
FASTENING TEE TIE FROG HASP
SEAL SNAP SNIB STAY TACK
TACHE BUCKLE CLINCH LACING
MUZZLE STRIKE TINGLE BINDING
CLOSURE LATCHET MOUSING
PINNING SEIZING FORELOCK
KNITTING
(— FOR HAWK'S WING) BRAIL
(— OF COPE) MORSE
(— ON HARPOON IRON) HITCH
(HOOK AND LOOP —) AGRAFE
AGRAFFE
(PL.) GRIPES
(PREF.) DESM(A)(IDI)(IDIO)(O)
(SUFF.) PEXIA PEXIS PEXY
FASTIDIOUS FINE NEAT NICE
CHARY DONCY FEEST FUSSY
NAISH NATTY PAWKY PICKY
CHOICE CHOICY CHOOSY DAINTY
DONSIE MOROSE PICKED QUAINT
QUEASY SPRUCE CHOOSEY
CURIOUS ELEGANT FINICAL
FINICKY HAUGHTY PICKING
REFINED TAFFETA TAFFETY
CRITICAL DELICATE EXACTING
GINGERLY OVERNICE PICKSOME
PRECIOUS SCORNFUL SQUEAMISH
PARTICULAR PERSNICKETY
SCRUMPTIOUS
(NOT —) GROSS
(OVERLY —) SAUCY
FASTIDIOUSNESS DAINTY NICETY
DELICACY
FASTING RAMADAN
(PREF.) NEST(I)
FAST-MOVING SUDDEN
FASTNESS FORT CASTLE CITADEL
RETREAT FORTRESS
FAST-WORKING HOTSHOT
FAT GHI OIL TUB FOZY GHEE LARD
LIPA MORT RICH SAIM SUET
ADEPS BROSY CETIN CHUFF
COCUM ESTER FLECK FLICK
FOGGY GROSS JUICY KEDGE
KOKUM LARDY LIPID LIPIN LUSTY
OBESE PLUMP PODGY PORKY
PUDDY PUDGY PURSY SAAME
SPICK SQUAB STOUT SUMEN
THICK WASTY AXUNGE BLOWSY
CHOATY CHUBBY CHUFFY

DEGRAS FATTED FINISH FLESHY
GREASE LIPIDE LIPOID PLUFFY
PORTLY PUBBLE PUNCHY PYKNIC
ROTUND STOCKY STUFFY
TALLOW UCUUBA ADIPOSE
BLOATED BLUBBER CEROTIN
FATNESS FERTILE FLESHLY
FULSOME LANOLIN OPULENT
PINGUID PURSIVE REPLETE
STEARIN EXTENDED FRUITFUL
MARROWED MURUMURU
PALMITIN UNCTUOUS
(— AROUND WHALE'S NECK) KENT
(— MEAT) SPECK
(— OF HIPPOPOTAMUS) SPECK
(— PERSON) SQUAB
(ANIMAL —) GLOR SAIM SUET
ADEPS GLORE GREASE TALLOW
(FLOATING —) FLOT
(LARD —) FLARE FLECK FLICK
(LUMP OF —) KEECH
(NATURAL —) ESTER
(POULTRY —) SCHMALZ SCHMALTZ
(SOLID —) LARD KIKUEL STEARIN
(PREF.) LIP(O) LIPAR(O) PI(O)
PIA(R)(RO) PINGUE PINGUI SEBI
STEAR(O) STEAT(O)
FATAL FEY DIRE MORT FERAL
VITAL DEADLY DISMAL DOOMED
FUNEST LETHAL MORTAL TRAGIC
CAPITAL DEATHLY EXITIAL
FATEFUL KILLING OMINOUS
RUINOUS UNSONSY BASILISK
DESTINED EXITIOUS FUNESTAL
MORTIFIC
FATALITY DOOM ACCIDENT
CALAMITY DISASTER
FAT-BELLIED GUTTY
FATE DIE END KER LOT CAST DOLE
DOOM EURE NORN RUIN SORT
STAR CAVEL EVENT GRACE
KARMA MOIRA MORTA WEIRD
WHATE WRITE ANANKE CHANCE
KISMET DESTINY FORTUNE
OUTCOME PORTION DOWNFALL
FATALITY
(INEXORABLE —) HEAVEN
(PREF.) FATI
FATED DUE FEY FATAL DOOMED
DECREED DESTINED
FATEFUL FATAL FATED DEADLY
DOOMFUL OMINOUS DOOMLIKE
FATES CLOTHO MOERAE PARCAE
ATROPOS LACHESIS
(ONE OF —) URD NONA PARCA
SKULD CLOTHO DECUMA
ATROPOS LACHESIS VERDANDE
FATHEAD REDFISH
FATHEADED FOZY
FATHEADEDNESS FOZINESS
FATHER BU DA PA ABU AMA DAD
POP TAT ABBA ABOU AMBA
ANBA ATEF BABA BAPU DADA
PAPA PERE SIRE ADOPT BABBO
BEGET DADDY FRIAR PADRE
PATER VADER PARENT PRIEST
SUBORN ELKANAH GENITOR
TATINEK BEAUPERE GENERATE
GOVERNOR PATRIARCH
PATERFAMILIAS
(CHURCH —) APOLOGIST
(SEMIDIVINE —) PITRI
(SIDE OF —) AGNATE

(PL.) PP
(PREF.) PARRI PATR(I)(IO)(O)
FATHER GORIOT (AUTHOR OF —)
BALZAC
(CHARACTER IN —) EUGENE
GORIOT VAUTRIN DELPHINE
ANASTASIE DERESTAUD
TAILLEFER VICTORINE
DENUCINGEN DEBEAUSEANT
DERASTIGNAC
FATHERLAND KITH HOMELAND
FATHER-LASHER GUNDIE COTTOID
SCULPIN BULLHEAD LORICATE
FATHERLESS ORBATE SIRELESS
**FATHERS AND SONS (AUTHOR OF
—)** TURGENEV
(CHARACTER IN —) KATYA PAVEL
ARKADY VASILY NIKOLAI
BAZAROFF FENICHKA KIRSANOFF
ODINTZOFF SITNIKOFF
FATHOM BRACE BRASS DELVE
FADME PLUMB SOLVE SOUND
TOUCH BOTTOM MEASURE
PLUMMET
FATIGUE FAG HAG TEU BEAT BORE
COOK JADE TASH TIRE TRAY
SPEND STALL TARRY THRIE TRAIK
TRASH WEARY HARASS OVERDO
TAIGLE TUCKER EXHAUST
LANGUOR TRACHLE FATIGATE
VEXATION
FATIGUED BEAT GONE JADED
TIRED WEARY TASKIT OUTWORN
WEARIED FATIGATE HARASSED
OVERDONE TUCKERED
FATIGUING HARD IRKSOME
FATLIKE LIPOID
FATNESS BLOOM GREASE
FATTEN FAT BEEF LARD SOIL
BRAWN FARCE FLESH FRANK
PROVE SMEAR STALL BATTEN
BATTLE ENRICH FINISH TALLOW
THRIVE PINGUEFY SAGINATE
FATTENING FRANK BATTEL
BATTABLE
FATTY SUETY BACONY GREASY
ADIPOSE ADIPOUS FATLIKE
PINGUID SEBIFIC LIPAROID
LIPAROUS UNCTUOUS ALIPHATIC
(PREF.) LIPAR(O)
FATUOUS DOPY GAGA DOPEY
INANE SILLY SIMPLE STUPID
UNREAL FATUATE FOOLISH
IDIOTIC WITLESS DEMENTED
ILLUSORY IMBECILE
FAUCES JAWS
FAUCET BIB TAP BIBB COCK QUILL
SPOUT VALVE CUTOFF DOSSIL
DOZZLE OFFLET SPIGOT BIBCOCK
HYDRANT PETCOCK TURNCOCK
(WOODEN —) HORSE
FAUGH BAH FOH VAH
FAUJDAR PHOUSDAR
FAULT BUG RUB SIN BEAM CLAG
COUP DEBT FAIL FLAW FLUB
GALL HOLE LACK LAST MOLE
SAKE SLIP SPOT VICE WANT WITE
ABUSE AMISS BLAME BREAK
CULPA ERROR FLUFF GUILT
LAPSE SCAPE SHIFT SLIDE SWICK
TACHE BLOTCH DEFECT FOIBLE
RUNNER THRUST VICETY VITIUM
BLEMISH BLISTER BLUNDER

DEFAULT DEMERIT EYELAST
FAILING FAILURE FRAILTY
MISTAKE NEGLECT OFFENSE
FAULTING PECCANCY WEAKNESS
(— IN BADMINTON) SLING
(MINING —) COUP LEAP CHECK
HITCH
(PL.) FAULTAGE
FAULTFINDER MOMUS CARPER
CRITIC MOMIST CAPTION
KNOCKER NAGSTER
FAULTFINDING CARPING
CAPTIOUS CRITICAL
FAULTILY BADLY
FAULTLESS PURE CLEAN RIGHT
CORRECT PERFECT PRECISE
FLAWLESS
FAULTY BAD ILL SICK AMISS UNFIT
WRONG FLAWED FAULTED
PECCANT VICIOUS BLAMABLE
CULPABLE SPURIOUS
(PREF.) DYS PARA
FAUN SATYR WOODMAN
WOODWOSE
FAUNA FAUNULA FAUNULE
ZOOLOGY
(FOSSIL —) BIOCHRON
FAUSSEBRAIE VAMURE VAUMURE
FAUST (AUTHOR OF —) GOETHE
(CHARACTER IN —) FAUST HELEN
SIEBEL WAGNER GRETCHEN
VALENTINE HOMUNCULUS
MARGUERITE MEPHISTOPHELES
(COMPOSER OF —) GOUNOD
FAUX PAS GAFF SLIP BONER
ERROR GAFFE BLOOMER FLOATER
MISSTEP MISTAKE SNAPPER
**FAVOLA D'ORFEO (CHARACTER IN
—)** PLUTO APOLLO CHARON
ORPHEUS MESSENGER
PROSERPINA
(COMPOSER OF —) MONTEVERDI
FAVOR AID FOR ORE PRO BOON
ESTE FACE GREE HEAR HELP LIKE
MAKE BLESS BRIBE GRACE LEAVE
MENSK SERVE SPARE SPEED
THANK TREAT ASSIST ERRAND
ESTEEM FAVOUR LETTER NOTICE
PENCEL UPHOLD ADVANCE
AGGRACE BENEFIT ENFAVOR
FEATURE FORWARD GRATIFY
INDULGE RESPECT SUPPORT
ADVOCACY BEFRIEND COURTESY
FAVORIZE GOODWILL KINDNESS
RESEMBLE SYMPATHY
ACCEPTANCE
FAVORABLE HOT BOON FAIR FREE
GOOD HIGH KIND ROSY TIDY
CIVIL CLEAR HAPPY LARGE
MERRY TRINE WHITE WILLY
BENIGN DEXTER GENIAL GOLDEN
KINDLY TOWARD BENEFIC
EXALTED OPTIMAL POPULAR
PRESENT FAVONIAN FRIENDLY
GRACIOUS PLEASING PROPENSE
SPEEDFUL TOWARDLY
BENIGNANT PROPITIOUS
PROSPEROUS
(— TO PURCHASER) KEEN
(NOT —) INFAUST
FAVORABLY FAIR WELL HIGHLY
FAVORED WELL FAURD HAPPY
FAURED GIFTED BLESSED

FAVOURED
FAVORER FAUTOR FRIEND
FAVORITE
FAVORING FAVONIAN
(PREF.) PRO
(SUFF.) ABLE IBLE
FAVORITE BOY PET POT PEAT
CHALK GREAT INGLE WHITE
MINION DARLING FANCIED
MINIKIN POPULAR SPECIAL
GRACIOSO WHITEBOY
FAVORITE, LA (CHARACTER IN —)
GUSMAN ALFONSO LEONORA
FERNANDO
(COMPOSER OF —) DONIZETTI
FAVORITISM BIAS FAVOR
NEPOTISM
FAVUS WHITECOMB
FAWN COG BUCK CLAW DEER
FAON JOUK ROOT COWER CRAWL
CREEP GLOZE HONEY SMARM
TOADY WHELP CRINGE CROUCH
GROVEL KOWTOW SHRINK
SLAVER ADULATE CROODLE
CRUDDLE FLATTER FLETHER
HANGDOG SERVILE SPANIEL
TOADEAT TRUCKLE WHEATEN
BOOTLICK
(— UPON) SUCK SMOOGE
ADULATE
FAWNIA (LOVER OF —) DORASTUS
FAWNING SLEEK CRINGE GREASE
MENIAL SLEEKY SMARMY SUPPLE
FLETHER GLOZING HANGDOG
SERVILE SPANIEL FLATTERY
FAWNSKIN NEBRIS
FAY ELF FEY FAIRY FEIGH
FAZE DAUNT FEEZE PHASE WORRY
FEALTY FEE FEWTE HOMAGE
LOYALTY SERVICE TREWAGE
FIDELITY
FEAR UG AWE DREE FLAY FUNK
WARD ALARM DOUBT DREAD
JELLY PANIC AFFRAY ALARUM
DANGER DISMAY FRIGHT HORROR
PHOBIA TERROR ANXIETY
SUSPECT AFFRIGHT DISQUIET
DISTRUST EERINESS MISDOUBT
VENERATE
(PREF.) PHOB(O)
(SUFF.) PHOBE PHOBIA(C) PHOBIC
PHOBOUS
FEARFUL ARGH DIRE AWFUL
FERLY PAVID TIMID WINDY
WROTH AFRAID COWISH FRIGHTY
GHASTLY NERVOUS PANICKY
WORRIED CAUTIOUS DOUBTFUL
DREADFUL GREWSOME
GRUESOME HORRIBLE HORRIFIC
SHOCKING SKITTISH TERRIBLE
TERRIFIC TIMOROUS
(PREF.) DEIN(O) DIN(O)
FEARLESS BOLD BRAVE DARING
HEROIC AWELESS IMPAVID
INTREPID
FEASIBLE FIT LIKELY POSSIBLE
PROBABLE SUITABLE
FEAST (ALSO SEE FESTIVAL) EAT
FOY PIG SUP DINE FARM FETE
LUAU MEAL TUCK UTAS AZYME
CHEER CHOES CITUA DIRGY
FESTA FESTY GAUDY REVEL
TREAT ARTHEL AVERIL BRIDAL

DEVOUR DINNER DOUBLE INFARE
ISODIA JUNKET MAUNDY REGALE
REPAST SIMPLE SMOUSE SPREAD
AHAAINA BANQUET BRIDALE
DELIGHT FESTINO GRATIFY
GREGORY LAMBALE LEMURIA
SHEVUOS SYNAXIS ANALEPSY
CAROUSAL DOMINEER EPIPHANY
FESTIVAL GESTNING GESTONIE
HANUKKAH KOIMESIS PASSOVER
POTLATCH SHABUOTH VESTALIA
(— BEFORE JOURNEY) FOY
(— OF BOOTHS) SUCCOS SUKKOTH
(— OF LANTERNS) HON
(— OF LOTS) PURIM
(— OF WEEKS) SHEVUOS
SHABUOTH
(— PLACE) IDGAH
(DRINKING —) BANQUET
(FUNERAL —) ARVAL ARVEL DIRGY
DIRGIE DREDGIE
(HARVEST —) BUSK
(JEWISH —) SENDAH
(RELIGIOUS —) CANAO KANYAW
PENTECOST
(VILLAGE —) TANSY
(PREF.) DAPI FESTI FESTO
HEORTO
(SUFF.) (— DAY) MAS
FEASTER CONVIVE
FEASTING FEAST CARNIVAL
FEAT ACT KIP DEED FATE GEST
WORK GESTE SPLIT STUNT TRICK
CRADDY CUTOFF EXPLOIT
MASTERY MIRACLE WORSHIP
DEXTROUS PERFORMANCE
(— IN SURFING) SPINNER
QUASIMODO
(CRICKETER'S —) DOUBLE
(TUMBLING —) SCISSORS
(PL.) DAGS
FEATHER BOO PEN TAB DECK
DOWN FLAG HERL SETA STUB
VANE ADORN AXIAL PENNA
PINNA PLUMA PLUME QUILL
REMEX CLOTHE COVERT CRINET
FLEDGE FLETCH FLIGHT HACKLE
MANUAL PINION SARCEL SICKLE
SQUAMA TIPPET TONGUE
AXILLAR BRISTLE FLEMISH
IMPLUME PRIMARY RECTRIX
REMICLE STIPULE TECTRIX
TERTIAL TOPPING AXILLARY
SCAPULAR STREAMER TERTIARY
(BRISTLELIKE —) VIBRISSA
(HAWK'S —S) BRAIL BRAILS
(HORSE —) SPEAR
(NEW —) STIPULE
(OSTRICH TAIL —) BOO
(PINION —) SARCEL
(TAIL —) SICKLE RECTRIX
(YELLOW —S) HULU
(PL.) GIG BOOT CAPE DOWN FLUE
MAIL BRAIL CRISSUM CUSHION
FLIGHTS PLUMAGE REMIGES
SPURIAE
(PREF.) PENNAT(I)(O) PENNI
PENNO PINN(I)(O) PINNAT(I)(O)
PLUMI PTER(O) PTIL(O)
(SUFF.) PENNATE PENNINE PTILE
PTILUS
FEATHER BED TYE
FEATHER CLOAK AHUULA TEMIAK

FEATHERED FLEDGE FLEDGY
PENNATE PINNATE FLIGHTED
(PREF.) PTENO
(SUFF.) PINNATE
FEATHERING STOCKING
FEATHER KEY FIN STOP SPLINE
FEATHER
FEATHER-LEGGED COOTY COOTIE
FEATHERLIKE PINNATE
FEATHERY PLUMY FLEDGY FLUFFY
PLUMOSE PLUMEOUS
FEATLY NEATLY FOOTINGLY
FEATURE WAY FACE ITEM NOTE
STAR BREAK FAVOR GRACE
MOTIF TOKEN TRACT TRAIT
TREAT ASPECT CACHET
FAVOUR SPLASH AMENITY
OUTLINE HALLMARK
SALIENCE
(— OF WORD FORM) ASPECT
(ATTRACTIVE —) AMENITY
(DETERMINING —) LIMIT
(DISTINGUISHING —) TRAIT STROKE
HALLMARK
(ESSENTIAL —) CHARACTER
(FATAL —) BANE
(LINGUISTIC —) ISOGLOSS
SURVIVAL
(MAIN —) CRUX
(MOST COGENT —) BEAUTY
(OBJECTIONABLE —) DISCOUNT
DRAWBACK
(SALIENT —) MOTIF
(TOPOGRAPHIC —) ARC
(TOPOGRAPHIC —S) LIE
(PL.) LAY FACE CONTOUR
FASHION GEOLOGY RETRAIT
FEAZE FRAY FAIZE ROUGHEN
FEBRIFUGE PEREIRA ANGOSTURA
FEBRILE PYRETIC FEVERISH
FECES DRAST HOCKEY ORDURE
(PREF.) COPR(O)
FECKLESS WEAK FEEBLE
FECULENCE DREG
FECULENT DREGGY
FECUND FERTILE FRUITFUL
PROLIFIC
FED FAT MEATED
FEDERATION BUND CROM UNION
LEAGUE NATION
COUNCIL ALLIANCE
FEDERACY TRIALISM
FEDORA (CHARACTER IN —) LORIS
FEDORA IPANOV ROMANOV
(COMPOSER OF —) GIORDANO
FEE FEU DUES DUTY FEAL FEUL
FIEF FIER HIRE RATE WAGE
CAULP EXTRA HANSE PRICE
RIGHT ALNAGE AMOBER BARONY
CHARGE DASTUR EMPLOY EXCISE
REWARD SALARY SHEKEL
BUOYAGE DASTURI DUMPAGE
DUSTOOR FALDAGE FIRNAGE
FURNAGE GAOLAGE GARNISH
GRATIFY GUIDAGE HALLAGE
HOUSAGE JAILAGE MULTURE
PAYMENT PINLOCK PREFINE
STIPEND STORAGE TALLAGE
TRIBUTE VANTAGE BOOTHAGE
BOUNTITH CHUMMAGE EXACTION
FAREWELL GRATUITY MALIKANA
POUNDAGE REREFIEF RETAINER
SHIPPAGE WHARFAGE

(— TO LANDOWNER) TERRAGE
(— TO TEACHER) MINERVAL
(CUSTOMARY —) DASTUR
(CUSTOMS —) LOT
(ENTRANCE —) HANSA HANSE
INCOME
(GRINDING —) THIRLAGE
(INITIATION —) FOOTING
(PHYSICIAN'S —) SOSTRUM
(ROAD —) PIKE
(UNAUTHORIZED —) GARNISH
(PL.) EXHIBITS

FEEBLE LOW WAN FLUE LAME
MEAN PALE POOR PUNY SOFT
WEAK DONCY DOTTY FAINT
SEELY SILLY SOBER UNORN
WANKY WASHY WERSH WONKY
CADUKE DEBILE DONSIE DOTAGE
FAINTY FLABBY FLIMSY FOIBLE
INFIRM PAULIE PUISNE SCANTY
SEMMIT SICKLY SIMPLE TANGLE
UNFIRM WANKLE WEANLY
DWAIBLY DWEEBLE FRAGILE
INVALID LANGUID QUEECHY
RICKETY SAPLESS SHILPIT
SLENDER SLIMPSY THREADY
UNWIELD UNWREST WEARISH
DECREPIT DROGHLIN FEATLESS
IMBECILE IMPOTENT INFERIOR
LUSTLESS MALADIVE RESOLUTE
SACKLESS THEWLESS THOWLESS
UNSTRONG UNWIELDY WATERISH
YIELDING NERVELESS

FEEBLE-MINDED ANILE DOTTY
DOTTLE FOOLISH MORONIC
WANTING IMBECILE

FEEBLENESS DOTAGE FEEBLE
POVERTY CADUCITY DEBILITY
WEAKNESS

FEED EAT HAY BAIT BEET BRAN
CROP DIET DINE FILL FOOD GLUT
GRUB MEAL MEAT OATS SATE
AGIST FLESH FLUSH GORGE
GRASS GRAZE NURSE SERVE
STOKE TABLE BATTLE BROWSE
FODDER FOSTER INFEED NOODLE
REFETE REPAST SUCKLE SUPPLY
BLOWOUT FURNISH GRATIFY
HERBAGE INDULGE KEEPING
NOURISH NURTURE PASTURE
PROVENT SATIATE SATISFY
SUBSIST SURFEIT SUSTAIN
VICTUAL PROVENDER
(— ABUNDANTLY) STOKE
(— ANIMAL) SORT SERVE
(— AT NIGHT) SUP
(— CATTLE) SOIL
(— FOR CATTLE) FODDER STOVER
TACKLE
(— FORCIBLY) CRAM
(— GLUTTONOUSLY) BATTEN
(— GREEN FOOD TO CATTLE) SOIL
(— HIGH) FRANK
(— IN STUBBLE) SHACK
(— ON FLIES) SMUT
(— RAVENOUSLY) FRAUNCH
(— STOCK) FOG SOIL SOILING
(— TO REPLETION) ENGORGE
(— TO THE FULL) SATIATE
(— WELL) BATTLE
(GROUND —) CHOP
(POULTRY —) SCRATCH
(RED —) HAYSEED

(STOCK —) BRAN
(WHALE —) GRIT
(PREF.) THREP(SO)
FEEDBOARD DECK
FEEDER HOGGER HOPPER PECKER
STOCKER
(YARN —) CARRIER
FEEDHEAD RISER FEEDER
SINKHEAD
FEEDING RELIEF FOLDAGE
PANNAGE
(— GROUND FOR FISH) MEADOW
(— THROUGH TUBE) GAVAGE
(FREE-CHOICE —) CAFETERIA
(PREF.) PHAG(O)
FEEL FIND PALP GROPE SENSE
THINK TOUCH FIMBLE FINGER
HANDLE RESENT EXAMINE
EXPLORE FEELING SENSATE
PERCEIVE
(— ACUTELY) SUFFER
(— AVERSION FOR) HATE LOATHE
(— CHILLY) CREEM
(— COMPASSION) PITY YEARN
(— DEJECTION) REPINE
(— FEAR) UG GRUE UGGE
TREMBLE
(— GRIEF) GRIEVE DEPLORE
(— HAPPY OR BETTER) LIGHT
(— NAUSEA) WAMBLE
(— OF CLOTH) HAND
(— ONE'S WAY) GROPE FUMBLE
GRAMMEL
(— OUT) SOUND
(— PAIN) URN
(— REPUGNANCE) ABHOR
(— SHAME) BLUSH
(— WANT OF) MISS
FEELER DRAW KITE PALP SNIFF
PALPUS TACTOR ANTENNA
SMELLER PROPOSAL TENTACLE
(PREF.) ANTENNI
FEELING FEEL PITY TACT VIEW
CHEER HEART HUMOR SENSE
SORGE TOUCH AFFECT CEMENT
MORALE CONSENT EMOTION
OPINION PASSION VELUNGE
ATTITUDE SENTIENT SENSATION
PRESENTIMENT
(— ILL) HOWISH
(— MIRTH) JOCUND
(— OF ACCORD) SYMPATHY
(— OF AMUSEMENT) CHARGE
(— OF ANTIPATHY) ALLERGY
(— OF ANXIETY) ANGST
(— OF CONTEMPT) DISDAIN
(— OF DISGUST) UG
(— OF DOUBT) SCRUPLE
(— OF HORROR) CREEP CREEPS
(— OF HOSTILITY) ANIMUS
(— OF JOY) GLOAT
(— OF OPPOSITION) KICK
(— OF RESENTMENT) GRUDGE
(— OF ROMANCE) STARDUST
(— OF UNEASINESS) MALAISE
(— OF WEARINESS) ENNUI
(— OF WELL-BEING) EUPHORIA
(— PRODUCED BY DRUG) RUSH
(ANGERED —) DUDGEON
(BODILY —) TABET
(CONCEITED —) SWELLING
(ILL —) HARDNESS
(INTUITIVE —) HUNCH

(KINDLY —) GOODWILL
(REPRESSION OF —) STOICISM
(STRONG —) STAB
(STRONG, POSITIVE —) SOUL
(PL.) HEART WITHERS
(PREF.) SENSI
(SUFF.) PATH(IA)(IC)(Y)
FEEN, DIE (CHARACTER IN —) ADA
GROMA ARINDAL
(COMPOSER OF —) WAGNER
FEET DOGS TONGS STAMPS
WALKERS GUNBOATS TRILBIES
PETTITOES
(— WASHING) MAUNDY
(BOARD —) FOOTAGE
(LARGE —) GUFFINS
(PREF.) PED(I)
(SUFF.) PEDE
(MEASURE OF —) METER
FEIGN ACT FAKE MINT MOCK SEEM
SHAM VEYN AVOID FABLE FALSE
FORGE PAINT SHAPE SHIRK
AFFECT ASSUME GAMMON
INVENT POSSUM CONCEAL
FALSIFY FASHION IMAGINE
POETIZE PRETEND ROMANCE
DISGUISE SIMULATE
(— ASSENT) COLLOGUE
(— IGNORANCE) CONNIVE
(— ILLNESS) MALINGER
FEIGNED SHAM FALSE FEINT
POETIC PSEUDO ASSUMED
COLORED FICTIVE FICTIOUS
SIMULATE
(PREF.) PSEUD(O)
FEIGNING FICTION FORGERY
SIMULATION
FEIJOA ANDRE
FEINT FAKE MINT RUSE APPEL
FAINT SHIFT SPOOF TRICK
FALSIFY FEIGNED FEINTER
FINCTURE PRETENSE REVIRADO
FELDSPAR ALBITE AMBITE GNEISS
CELSIAN SYENITE ADULARIA
ANDESINE FELSPATH PERTHITE
PETUNTZE SANIDINE
MOONSTONE
FELICIA AGATHAEA
FELICITATE HUG BLESS MACARIZE
FELICITOUS FIT HAPPY
FELICITOUSLY HAPPILY
FELICITY JOY BLISS SONSE
HEAVEN
FELINE CATTISH
FELL CUR FEN HEW COSH DOWN
DROP FALL HIDE HILL MOOR PELT
RUIN SKIN VERY CRUEL EAGER
FIELD GRASS GREAT SHARP
DEADLY FIERCE FLEECE INTENT
MIGHTY SAVAGE SHREWD
TUMBLE BRUTISH CRASHED
DOUGHTY HIDEOUS INHUMAN
STRETCH TUMBLED MOUNTAIN
SPIRITED VIGOROUS
(— A TREE) HEW LODGE
FELLER GIDEON
FELLING FALL CUTTING
FELLOE BOD FELF FALLY
FELLOW S BO BOY COD DON EGG
FOX GUY JOE LAD MAC MAN
MUN NUT WAG WAT YOB BALL
BEAN BEAU BIRD BOZO BUFF
CARL CHAL CHAP COVE CUSS

DEAN DICK DUCK DUDE DULL
GENT GILL GINK HIND HUSK JACK
JAKE JOHN LOON MATE NABS
PEER PRIG SNAP BILLY BIMBO
BLOKE BROCK BUDDY BULLY
CARLE CHIEL COVEY CULLY FRUIT
GROOM GUEST JOKER MATCH
PARTY SCOUT SKATE SLAVE
SPORT SPRIG SWIPE BEGGAR
BILLIE BIRKIE BOHUNK BOOGER
BUDDIE BUFFER BUGGER BUSTER
CALLAN CHIELD CODGER CUFFIN
CUTTER FELLER FOOTER FOUTER
FOUTRA GALOOT GAZABO
HOMBRE JASPER JOCKEY JOHNNY
JOSSER KIPPER PERSON SHAVER
SINNER SIRRAH SISTER SOCIUS
TURNIP BASTARD BROTHER
CALLANT CHAPPIE COMRADE
CULLIES CULLION CUSTRON
KNOCKER PARTNER SCROYLE
SNOOZER BLIGHTER CONFRERE
DOTTEREL MERCHANT NEIGHBOR
SYNODITE
(AWKWARD —) JAY OAF CLUB
GAWK CLOWN LOOBY GALOOT
SLOUCH
(BASE —) CARL CARLE CULLION
(BASHFUL —) SHEEP
(BOLD —) HEARTY
(BRUTAL —) CLUBFIST
(CLOWNISH —) COOF BAYARD
LOBLOLLY
(CLUMSY —) BOOB FILE CAMEL
FARMER LUBBER PALOOKA
(COMMON —) JACK LOUT
(CONCEITED —) JEMMY DALTEEN
PRINCOX
(CONTEMPTIBLE —) DOG SCUT
SMAIL SNAKE RABBIT SMATCH
PEASANT
(CONTENTIOUS —) SQUARER
(CORPULENT —) POMPION
(COUNTRY —) JAKE JASPER
(CRUDE —) STIFF
(DASHING —) BUCK BLADE
(DASTARDLY —) HOUND
(DESPICABLE —) FOUTER FOUTRA
HANGDOG SMATCHET
(DIRTY —) SCAB BROCK
(DISAGREEABLE —) GLEYDE
(DISSOLUTE —) RAKE ROUE
RAKEHELL
(DROLL —) CARD
(DROWSY —) LUNGIS
(DRUNKEN —) BORACHIO
(DULL —) BUFF DRIP FOGY CHUFF
SUMPH LUNGIS HUMDRUM
(FAT —) HIND GULCH GLUTTON
(FIERCE-LOOKING —) KILLBUCK
(FINE —) BAWCOCK
(FOOLISH —) SOP GABY GOFF
ZANY GANDER JACKSON
WIDGEON
(GAY —) GALLIARD
(GOOD —) BRICK BULLY TRUMP
HEARTY TROJAN
(GOOD-FOR-NOTHING —) JACKEEN
(GREEDY —) SLOTE
(IDLE —) FANION FOOTER STOCAH
LOLLARD SKULKER
(IGNORANT —) GOBBIN
(ILLBRED —) LARRIKIN

(IMPERTINENT —) JACK WHISK
(INSIGNIFICANT —) SQUIB
(JOLLY —) VAVASOR VAVASOUR
(LAZY —) BUM LUSK TOOL LENTO
(LOW —) RAG WAFF SWEEP
LIMMER VARLET MECHANIC
WHORESON
(MEAN —) CAD DOG BOOR BOUCH
BUCKO CAVEL CHURL SCURF
RASCAL CULLION BEZONIAN
COISTREL COISTRIL SNEAKSBY
SPALPEEN STINKARD
(NIGGARDLY —) SNUDGE
(NOISY —) MOUTH
(OLD —) GLYDE GAFFER GEEZER
(OLD-FASHIONED —) FOGY
(OVERBEARING —) GRIMSIR
(PROSAIC —) PRUNE
(PUNY —) SMAIK
(QUARRELSOME —) HECTOR
(QUEER OLD —) CODGER GEEZER
(RESIDENTIAL —) DON
(ROGUISH —) DOG
(RUDE —) BOOR JACK ROUGH
(SHABBY —) SHAB SQUEEF
(SHEEPISH —) SUMPH
(SHIFTLESS —) PROG SHACK
PROGGER
(SHREWD —) COLT
(SILLY —) TOT GUMP ZANY SHEEP
SMAIK BUFFER DOTTEREL
MUSHHEAD
(SIMPLE —) DOODLE
(SLOVENLY —) SLUTE
(SLY —) FOX COON
(SNEAKING —) SNUDGE
(SORDID —) HUNKS
(SOUTH AFRICAN —) KEREL
(SPIRITED —) BRICK
(SPORTY —) PLAYBOY
(STRANGE —) CODGER
(STRAPPING —) SWANKY SWANKIE
(STUPID —) ASS BOOB CLOD COOF
DAFF DOLT GUMP HASH MUFF
SIMP BOOBY CUDDY DUNCE
MORON STIRK BAYARD BUFFER
FARMER FOOZLE GANDER
ASINOCO DOWFART HUMDRUM
CLODPOLL CODSHEAD SOCKHEAD
(SULLEN —) GLUMP
(SURLY —) CHUFF CHOUGH
(TRICKISH —) HUMBUG
(TRICKY —) ROOK GREEK KNAVE
SCAMP DODGER RASCAL
(UNCIVIL —) RUDESBY
(UNCOUTH —) JAKE KEMP TIKE
(VILE —) RAT SKUNK
(VULGAR —) TIGER
(WORTHLESS —) BUM CUR DOG
HASH PROG RAFF WAFF JAVEL
ROGUE SCAMP SHOAT SNAKE
STUMER BROTHEL BUDMASH
PROGGER VAURIEN TARTARET
(WRETCHED —) DEVIL DOGBOLT
(YOUNG —) BILLY BUCKO CADIE
CADDIE
(PREF.) CO
(SUFF.) ENGRO
FELLOWMAN BROTHER NEIGHBOR
FELLOWSHIP GUILD HAUNT
UNION FAMILY COMPANY
ALLIANCE SODALITY
(CHRISTIAN —) KOINONIA

FELLY RIM FELF FELLOE KEENLY
CRUELLY BITTERLY FIERCELY
SAVAGELY TERRIBLY
FELO-DE-SE SUICIDE
FELON WILD CRUEL FETLOW
FIERCE WICKED CONVICT
CULPRIT PANARIS VILLAIN
WHITLOW PHLEGMON
RUNROUND MALEFACTOR
FELONY ARSON CRIME OFFENSE
FELT JIG PLAIT FILTER NUMNAH
SENSED SOLEIL VELOUR DOUBLER
FELTING PANNOSE
(— INTENSIVELY) ACUTE
(— THROUGH SENSES) SENSATE
(DEEPLY --) CORDIAL INTENSE
(PERSONALLY —) CONSCIOUS
(PL.) CLOTHING
(PREF.) PIL(O)
FELTWORK NEUROPIL
FEMALE DOE EWE HEN HER SHE
SOW DAME GIRL GYNE LADY
MORT ADULT JENNY SMOCK
SQUAW WOMAN WAHINE
WEAKLY DISTAFF FEMINAL
WOMANLY DAUGHTER FEMININE
GYNAECIC LADYLIKE WOMANISH
PETTICOAT
(— ANCESTOR) TAPROOT
(IMPERFECT —) FREEMARTIN
(PARTHOGENETIC —) AMAZON
(PREF.) FEMINO GYN(AE)(AECO)
(AEO)(ANDRO)(E)(ECO)(EO)(O)
THELY
(SUFF.) ESS ETTE GYN(E)(IST)(OUS)
INE TRIX
FEMININE FAIR SOFT WEAK
WOMAN FEMALE TENDER
WAHINE FEMINAL WOMANLY
WOMANISH PETTICOAT
(SUFF.) INA INE
FEMININE WILES (CHARACTER IN —
) BELLINA LEONORA FILANDRO
GIAMPOLO ROMUALDO
(COMPOSER OF —) CIMAROSA
FEMININITY MUSLIN FEMINITY
MULIEBRITY
FEMME FATALE SIREN
FEMORAL CRURAL
(PREF.) CRURO
FEMUR THIGH
FEN BOG CARR FAIN FELL FOWL
MERE MOOR WASH BROAD FAINS
MARSH SNIPE SWAMP VENTS
MORASS QUAGMIRE
FENCE BAR HAW HAY BANK DIKE
DUEL DYKE HAHA HAIN PALE
PLAY RAIL STUB WALL WEIR
WIRE BEARD DODGE FRITH
GUARD HEDGE MOUND PALIS
STICK STUMP DETENT FENDER
FRAISE GLANCE HURDLE LEADER
PALING PICKET RADDLE RASPER
SCHERM SCRIME TIMBER BARRIER
BULWARK CYCLONE DEFENSE
ENCLOSE FENCING FENSURE
IMPALER PASSAGE RAILING
SWAGMAN BACKSTOP ENCHASER
ENCLOSER GRAFFAGE HOARDING
PALISADE PALISADO SEPIMENT
SKIRMISH BRANDRETH
BRANDRITH
(— AROUND BULLRING) BARRERA

(— AROUND MACHINERY) BRATTICE
(— CLOSING DITCH) WOLF
(— OF LOCK) STUB
(— OF LOGS) GLANCE
(CATTLE —) OXER WIPE SKERM
SCHERM
(FISH —) WEIR KIDDLE LEADER
(METAL —) RAIL RAILING
(PREF.) HERCO PHRAGMO
SEPTATO
(SUFF.) SEPTATE
FENCER DUELIST IMPALER
PARRIER PROVOST SCRIMER
SWORDER FOILSMAN
BACKSWORD
FENCE RAIL DRAWBAR
FENCE SECTION PANE
FENCE-SITTER MUGWUMP
FENCING WIRE FENCE PALING
ESCRIME PASSAGE SCIENCE
SWORDING
FEND WARD PARRY SHIRK DEFEND
FORBID RESIST SUPPORT
FENDER SKID WING CAMEL GUARD
SKATE BUFFER BUMPER SHIELD
DOLPHIN PUDDING BOWGRACE
MUDGUARD SPLASHER
(— FOR FIREPLACE) CURB KERB
(— NEAR HOLE) TELLTALE
(ROPE —) PUDDENING
FENDER SKID GLANCER
FENESTRA FORAMEN
FENGHUANG FUM PHOENIX
FENKS FRITTERS
FENMAN WEBFOOT
FENNEC ZERDA
FENNEL ANIS DILL HEMP SOYA
FERULE FINKEL COWBANE
HOGWEED SPINGEL FINOCHIO
FLORENCE CAROSELLA
FENNER ZERDA
FENRIS (FATHER OF —) LOKI
(MOTHER OF —) ANGURBODA
(SISTER OF —) HEL
(SLAYER OF —) VIDAR
FENSTER WINDOW
FENUGREEK BAUMIER MELLILOT
(SEEDS OF —) HELBEH
FERAL WILD BRUTAL DEADLY
FERINE SAVAGE BESTIAL
UNTAMED FUNEREAL UNBROKEN
FER-DE-LANCE BONETAIL
JARARACA
FERMATA HOLD PAUSE TENOR
CORONA
FERMENT FRY LOB ZYM BARM
FRET HEAT SOUR TURN WORK
ZYME FEVER SWEAT YEAST
DANDER ENZYME FLOWER
FOMENT SEETHE SIMMER
TUMULT UPROAR AGITATE
QUICKEN TURMOIL DISORDER
(PREF.) ZYM(O)
(SUFF.) ZYME
FERMENTATION SWEAT CUVAGE
FERMENT MOWBURN WORKING
ZYMOSIS
FERMENTED SOD
(IMPROPERLY —) FOXY
FERMENTING BARMY WORKING
FERN HEII NITO PULU TARA WEKI
BRAKE DUGAL EKAHA FROND
NARDO PITAU PONGA ULUHI

WHEKI AMAMAU DOODIA
NARDOO OSMUND PTERIS
ACROGEN ATERACH BOGFERN
BRACKEN OSMUNDA SYNANGE
WOODSIA ADIANTUM ASPIDIUM
BAROMETZ BUCKHORN
BUNGWALL CETERACH DAVALLIA
DENDRITE FERNWORT FILICITE
GOLDBACK HARDFERN KOLOKOLO
MOONWORT MULEWORT
PARAREKA PILLWORT POLYPODY
SPOROGEN STAGHORN
MAIDENHAIR
(PART OF —) AXIS CASE LEAF
STEM BLADE FROND PINNA STIPE
TOOTH MIDRIB RACHIS LEAFLET
PETIOLE PINNULE SUBLEAFLET
(PL.) FILICES
(PREF.) PTERID(O)
(SUFF.) PTERIS
FERN LEAF FROND CROSIER
FERNLIKE FERNY PTEROID
FEROCIOUS ILL FELL GRIM RUDE
WILD BRUTE CRUEL FERAL
BLOODY BRUTAL FEROCE FIERCE
GOTHIC RAGING SAVAGE
ACHARNE INHUMAN OMINOUS
VIOLENT WOLFISH PITILESS
RAVENOUS RUTHLESS TARTARLY
FEROCITY FERITY SAVAGERY
VIOLENCE ACHARNEMENT
FERRARA ANDREW
FERRET HOB MONK TAPE PADOU
MONACH WEASEL POLECAT
(— OUT) FOSSICK
(FEMALE —) GIL GILL JILL BITCH
(MALE —) HOB HOBB
FERRIAGE WAFTAGE
FERRIC OXIDE CROCUS
FERROCYANIDE PRUSSIATE
FERROTYPE GLAZE TINTYPE
FERROUS SIDEROUS
FERRULE CAP TIP CUFF RING SHOE
VIRL COLLET PULLEY RUNNER
VERREL VIROLE ARMGARN
BUSHING CRAMPET
FERRY FORD PASS PONT SCOW
PASSAGE TRAJECT TRANECT
TRANSFER
FERRYBOAT BAC PONT SCOW
FERRY
FERRYMAN CHARON FERRIER
WATERMAN
FERTILE FAT GOOD RANK RICH
GLEBY BATFUL BATTLE FECUND
HEARTY STRONG TEEMING
ABUNDANT BATTABLE FRUITFUL
GENEROUS PREGNANT PROLIFIC
SPAWNING
FERTILITY HEART FATNESS
(PATRON OF —) YAKSHA
FERTILIZATION ENDOGAMY
POROGAMY
FERTILIZE FAT DUNG FISH LIME
MARL CHALK BATTEN ENRICH
FRUCTIFY
FERTILIZER FAT MARL GUANO
HUMUS ALINIT FLOATS MANURE
POLLEN POTASH CARRIER
COMPOTE HUMOGEN KAINITE
NITRATE TANKAGE AMMONITE
CINEREAL NITROGEN
FERULA NARTHEX

FERULE ROD RULER COLLET
   FENNEL FERULA PALMER
FERVENCY WARMTH CANDENCY
FERVENT HOT KEEN WARM EAGER
   FIERY ARDENT BITTER FERVID
   FIERCE INWARD RAGING SAVAGE
   BOILING BURNING GLOWING
   INTENSE PECTORAL ROMANTIC
   VEHEMENT RELIGIOUS
FERVID HOT ARDENT TROPIC
   BOILING BURNING FERVENT
   GLOWING ZEALOUS UNCTUOUS
   VEHEMENT
FERVOR FIRE HEAT HWYL RAGE
   SOUL ZEAL ARDOR WARMTH
   PASSION CANDENCY DEVOTION
   STRENGTH VIOLENCE
   (— IN PRAYER) KAVVANAH
   KAWWANAH
FESCUE VESTER
FESS BAR BAND PERT DANCE
   HUMET
   (DIMINUTIVE —) TRANGLE
FESTAL GAY GALA GAUDY FESTIVE
   FESTUAL FEASTFUL
FESTER ROT BEAL RANK SCAR
   RANKLE PUSTULE PUTREFY
FESTERING RANK FRETTY
FESTIVAL (ALSO SEE FEAST) ALE
   BON PWE BUSK FAIR FEIS FETE
   GALA HOLI MELA PUJA TIDE
   UTAS WAKE DELIA FEAST FERIA
   FESTA GAUDY HALOA PURIM
   REVEL ROUSE SEDAR ADONIA
   BAIRAM BRIDAL CARNEA DEWALI
   DIASIA DIPALA FIESTA HOHLEE
   HUFFLE KERMIS LAMMAS LENAEA
   OPALIA PONGOL POOJAH
   POSADA SUCCOS AGONIUM
   AGRANIA BANQUET BELTANE
   DASAHRA EQUIRIA FESTIAL
   HILARIA KERMESS MATSURI
   PALILIA SUKKOTH THIASOS
   TOXCATL UPHELYA VINALIA
   AGRIONIA AIANTEIA APATURIA
   ATHENAEA BEALTINE BRUMALIA
   CARNIVAL COTYTTIA DASAHARA
   DIIPOLIA DIONYSIA DUSSERAH
   ENCAENIA FASNACHT FLORALIA
   HANUKKAH HIGHTIDE KALENDAE
   LUPERCAL MARYMASS MATRALIA
   MITHRIAC MUHARRAM
   MUNYCHIA NATIVITY NEOMENIA
   POTLATCH STAMPEDE TAARGELIA
   SATURNALIA
   (HIGHLAND —) MOD
   (MUSICAL —) EISTEDDFOD
   (PL.) MOED VOTA
   (SUFF.) MAS
FESTIVE GAY GALA JOLLY FESTAL
   GENIAL JOYOUS FEASTLY
   HOLIDAY JOCULAR CONVIVAL
   FEASTFUL MIRTHFUL SPORTIVE
   CONVIVIAL
FESTIVITY GALA GAUD UTAS UTIS
   BEANO FEAST MIRTH RANDY
   REVEL GAIETY GAYETY SPLORE
   HOLIDAY JOLLITY JOYANCE
   PATTERN FESTIVAL FUNCTION
   MERRIMENT MERRYMAKING
FESTOON SWAG WREATH
   GARLAND DECORATE
   (PL.) ENCARPUS

FETCH FET FESH GASP GIVE SHAG
   TACK TAKE TEEM WAIN BRING
   SWEEP TRICK DOUBLE STROKE
   WRAITH ACHIEVE ATTRACT
   ARTIFICE FETCHING INTEREST
FETCHED FOSH
FETCHING SWEET CRAFTY
   CUNNING ALLURING PLEASING
   SCHEMING
FETE FAIR GALA FEAST HONOR
   BAZAAR FIESTA HOLIDAY
FETID OLID RANK MUSTY PUTID
   ROTTEN VIROSE NOISOME
   SANIOUS MALODOROUS
FETIDLY FOULLY
FETISH OBI IDOL JUJU OBIA ZEME
   ZEMI ZOGO ANITO ASCON CHARM
   GUACA HUACA OBEAH OBIAH
   TOTEM AMULET FETICH GRIGRI
   NAGUAL VOODOO SHINTAI
   SORCERY FETISHRY GREEGREE
   TALISMAN
FETLOCK COOT FOOTLOCK
FETTER BAND BEND BOLT BOND
   FIND GYVE IRON SPAN BASIL
   BEWET BILBO CHAIN SLANG
   SWATH ANKLET GARTER HALTER
   HAMPER HOBBLE HOPPLE IMPEDE
   LANGEL RACKAN SWATHE
   CLINKER CONFINE ENCHAIN
   FETLOCK GARNISH MANACLE
   SHACKLE SPANCEL TRAMMEL
   RESTRAIN
   (PL.) IRONS LINKS DARBIES
   GARNISH GARTERS
FETTERBUSH PIPESTEM
   PIPEWOOD
FETTLE BEAT DECK FUSS MULL
   TIDY TWIG VEIN DRESS GROOM
   WHACK YARAK GIRDLE REPAIR
   SETTLE STRIKE ARRANGE
   BANDAGE FEATHER HARNESS
FETTLER BILLYER NOBBLER
FETTLING FIX FETTLE FIXING
FETUS BIRTH CHILD YOUNG
   AMELUS BREECH EMBRYO
   FOETUS ABORTUS CYCLOPS
   FEATURE AMORPHUS
   (PREF.) EMBRY(O) FETI FETO
   FOETI FOETO
FEUD FIEF FRAY BROIL AFFRAY
   ENMITY FEODUM FEUDUM STRIFE
   CONTEST DISPUTE QUARREL
   VENDETTA
FEUDATORY FIEF VASSAL
   ZAMINDAR ZEMINDAR
FEUILLE MORTE PHILAMOT
FEVER AGUE FIRE ARDOR CAUMA
   DANDY LEUMA OCTAN CAUSUS
   DENGUE FEBRIS HECTIC SEPTAN
   SEXTAN SODOKU TYPHIA TYPHUS
   VOMITO AMAKEBE FERMENT
   FEVERET HELODES MALARIA
   PINKEYE PYREXIA QUARTAN
   TERTIAN TYPHOID SYNOCHUS
   TERTIANA TYPHINIA CALENTURE
   (— OF HORSE) WEED SCALMA
   (— OF PERU) VERRUGA
   (— OF SHEEP) BRAXY
   (BRAIN —) PHRENITIS
   (HAY —) RHINITIS
   (MALARIAL —) TAP
   (MARSH —) HELODES

   (TEXAS —) TRISTEZA
   (WITHOUT —) APYRETIC
   (PREF.) FEBRI PYR(ET)(ETO)
   (SUFF.) PYRA
FEVERED DISEASED
FEVERFEW MAYWEED MUGWORT
   PELLITORY
FEVERISH HOT FIERY FEVERY
   HECTIC EXCITED FEBRILE
   FRANTIC RESTLESS
FEVERLESS APYREXIA
FEVERROOT GENSON
FEVER TREE BITTERBARK
FEVERWEED FITWEED
FEVERWORT BONESET
FEW LIT CURN LESS SOME SCANT
   THREE WHEEN WHONE CURRAN
   PICKLE LIMITED SEVERAL
   EXIGUOUS
   (PREF.) OLIG(O) PAUCI
FEWER LESS
   (PREF.) MI(O)
FEWNESS PAUCITY
FEY DEAD DYING ELFIN FATAL
   UNLUCKY PIXILATED
FEZ TARBOOSH
FIADOR THEODORE
FIANCE TRUST SPOUSE FIANCEE
   PROMISE AFFIANCE
FIASCO CRASH FLASK FROST
   FIZZLE FAILURE DISASTER
FIAT EDICT ORDER UKASE DECREE
   COMMAND DECISION SANCTION
FIB LIE YED FLAW WHID SLANT
   STORY FITTEN PUMMEL SKLENT
   TARADIDDLE
FIBBER LIAR
FIBER TAL ADAD BASS BAST COIR
   ERUC FERU FLAX HARL HEMP
   IMBE JUTE LINE PITA SILK SUNN
   TULA ABACA AGUST AZLON
   CAJUN CAROA CHOEL ERIZO
   FIBRE GRAIN HARLE ISOTE ISTLE
   IXTLE IZOTE KENAF KITUL MURVA
   OAKUM RAMIE RAPHE SIMAL
   SISAL STRAW TERAP TOSSA
   TUCUM VIVER AMIRAY ARGHAN
   BINDER BUNTAL BURITI CABUYA
   CATENA DACRON EMBIRA FIBRIL
   FIMBLE HINOKI KANAFF KENDIR
   KOHEMP MUCUNA NYTRIL RAFFIA
   SALAGO STAPLE STRAND STRING
   SUTURE THREAD TUCUMA
   TURURI VINYON YACHAN ZAPUPE
   ACETATE ACRYLIC ANONANG
   ARAMINA BASSINE CANTALA
   CASCARA CHANDUL CHINGMA
   COQUITA ESPARTO FILASSE
   FUNICLE GEBANGA GRAVATA
   GUAXIMA GUMIHAN HUARIZO
   KERATTO KITTOOL MOCMAIN
   PALMITE PANGANE PAUKPAN
   POCHOTE SABUTAN CANAPINA
   CURRATOW FILAMENT HARAKEKE
   HENEQUEN PIASSAVA TOQUILLA
   TRONADOR
   (— FROM PEACOCK FEATHERS)
   MARL
   (— OF PALM) DOH LIF ERUC
   COYOL COROZO GOMUTI KITTUL
   COQUITA GEBANGA
   (—S OF FLAX) HARE
   (CLUSTER OF —S) NEP

   (COARSE —) KEMP
   (COCONUT —) COIR KYAR
   (COTTON —) LINT STAPLE
   (FLAX —) TOW
   (KNOT OF —) NOIL
   (MANUFACTURED —) DYNEL
   ORLON ESTRON ACRILAN
   SPANDEX
   (MATTED —) SHAG
   (MINERAL —) ASBESTOS
   (MUSCLE —) RHABDIUM
   (NERVE —) EFFERENT DEPRESSOR
   (PULVERIZED —) FLOCK
   (SILKY —) PULU KAPOK KUMBI
   YACHAN CASTULI
   (TWISTED —S) STRAND
   (WASTE —) FLY GOUT
   (WASTE —S) FLOSS
   (WOODY —) BAST GRAIN SCUTCH
   (PL.) FUZZ KERATTO
   (PREF.) FIBRO IN(O)
FIBRIL AXONEME DESMOSE
   MYONEME MYOPHAN
FIBRILS
   (SUFF.) **(NETWORK —)**
   SPONGIA(E)(N) SPONGIUM
FIBRIN GLUTEN MYOSIN
FIBROCARTILAGE FABELLA
   MENISCUS
FIBROID DESMOID
FIBROMA INOMA FIBROID
FIBROUS FIBROSE STRINGY
   NEMALINE
FIBULA LACE CLASP BROOCH
   BUCKLE PERONE SPLINT
   (PREF.) PERONEO PERONO
FICHE FILMCARD
FICKLE GERY DIZZY FALSE GIDDY
   LIGHT UNSAD HARLOT KITTLE
   MOBILE PUZZLE SHIFTY VOLAGE
   WANKLE WANKLY CASALTY
   CASELTY FLATTER MOONISH
   MOVABLE MUTABLE VAINFUL
   VARIANT VOLUBLE GOSSAMER
   MOVEABLE SKITTISH STIRRING
   UNSTABLE UNSTEADY VARIABLE
   VOLATILE WAVERING
FICKLENESS CHANGE LEVITY
   EASINESS FICKLETY VARIANCE
FICO FIG FIGO TANTI
FICTILE FIGULINE
FICTION BAM TALE FABLE FALSE
   NOVEL ROMAN STORY DECEIT
   DEVICE FABULA FITTEN LEGEND
   COINAGE FANTASY FIGMENT
   FORGERY MARCHEN NOVELRY
   ROMANCE ROMANZA KAILYARD
   PHANTASY PRETENCE PRETENSE
FICTITIOUS MADE BOGUS DUMMY
   FALSE PHONY FABLED POETIC
   ASSUMED FEIGNED PHANTOM
   FABULOUS FICTIOUS MYTHICAL
   ROMANTIC SIMULATE SPURIOUS
   LEGENDARY
   (PREF.) PSEUD(O)
FICUS PYRULA
FID PRICK NORMAN PRICKER
   SPLICER
FIDDLE BOW BOX GIG SAW VIOL
   CHEAT CROWD GEIGE GIGUE
   GUDOK CHORUS FITHEL POTTER
   TRIFLE URHEEN VIOLIN CHROTTA
   SARANGI SWINDLE HUMSTRUM

(— STRING) THAIRM
(— WITH) TWIDDLE
FIDDLER CRAB VIOLER VIOLIN
CROWDER SCRAPER SIXPENCE
FIDDLER CRAB RACER FIDDLER
OCYPODE SOLDIER
FIDDLESTICKS PSHAW FIDDLE
FIDELIO (CHARACTER IN —) ROCCO
FIDELIO LEONORE PIZARRO
JACQUINO FLORESTAN
MARZELLINE
(COMPOSER OF —) BEETHOVEN
FIDELITY TRUE ARDOR FAITH
PIETY TROTH TRUTH FEALTY
HONESTY LOYALTY ADHESION
DEVOTION RELIGION VERACITY
CONSTANCY
FIDGET MOP FIKE FIRK FUSS ROIL
FIDGE FITCH HOTCH SHRUB
SHRUG WORRY BREVIT FIGGLE
FISSLE FISTLE FRIDGE FUSSER
HIRSEL JIFFLE JIGGET NESTLE
NIBBLE NIGGLE TIDDLE TRIFLE
VIGGLE WORRIT NERVOUS
RESTLESS TWITCHET
(— ABOUT TRIFLES) SPOFFLE
(STATE OF —) FANTAD FANTOD
(PL.) JUMPS
FIDGETY FIKIE FUSSY ITEMY
FEISTY FIGENT FLISKY KITTLE
UNEASY RESTIVE TWITCHY
RESTLESS
FIDUCIARY TRUSTEE TRUSTFUL
FIE SISS FAUGH
FIEF FEE HAN FEUD FEOFF TIMAR
ZIAMET SATSUMA SUBFIEF
BENEFICE
(— HOLDER) TIMARIOT
FIELD LEA LOT ACRE AGER AREA
BENT CAMP FELL FLAT HADE
INAM LAND LIST MEAD PALE
PARK RAND TOWN WONG BRECK
CAMPO CHAMP CLOUR CROFT
EARTH GLEBE INNAM LAYER
MILPA NILPA PADDY RANGE
ROWEN SAWAH TILTH VELDE
ARRISH CAMPUS CAREER
CHAMPE DOMAIN FURROW
GARDEN GROUND MACHAR
MATTER MEADOW PADANG
PINGLE SHIELD SPHERE CHARMEL
COMPASS CULTURE DIAMOND
FERRING GARSTON INFIELD
MOWLAND NEWTAKE PADDOCK
PARROCK PIGHTLE PURVIEW
QUILLET TERRAIN THWAITE
TILLAGE CLEARING PROVINCE
(— ADJOINING HOUSE) CROFT
(— AT CRICKET) SCOUT
(— OF ACTIVITY) GAME ARENA
BARONY SPHERE TERRAIN
(— OF BATTLE) PLAIN
(— OF BLOODSHED) ACELDAMA
AKELDAMA
(— OF CONTROL) DOMAIN
(— OF ENDEAVOR) BUSINESS
(— OF SNOW) NEVE SNOWPACK
(— OF STUDY) GROUND
(— ON WHICH GRASS IS GROWN)
MEAD MEADOW
**(— SOWN FOR TWO SUCCESSIVE
YEARS)** HOOK
(ENCLOSED —) AGER TOWN

CLOSE CROFT
(FOOTBALL —) GRIDIRON
(FRUITFUL —) CHARMEL
(GRASSY —) LEA PEN GARSTON
(HOP —) HOPYARD
(LAVA —) PEDREGAL
(LITTLE-KNOWN —) BYWAY
(NEW GOLD —) RUSH
(PLOWED —) FURROW
(RICE —) SAWAH
(SMALL —) HAW CLOSE CROFT
PADDOCK
(SPORTS —) ARENA PITCH
(STUBBLE —) HIRSH ROWEN
ARRISH GRATTEN GRATTON
(TILTING —) LISTS
(TOBACCO —) VEGA
(UNEXPLOITED —) FRONTIER
(UNPLOWED EDGE OF —) RAND
(PL.) AGRI AGRO ARVI CAMPI
(PREF.) AGRI AGRO ARVI CAMPI
FIELD BALM SHEEPMINT
FIELD CAMOMILE OXEYE
FIELDER GLOVEMAN
(CRICKET —) SLIP COVER FIELD
GULLY POINT SCOUT GULLEY
INFIELDER
FIELDFARE FELT JACK REDLEG
FELLFARE HILLBIRD JACKBIRD
REDSHANK SNOWBIRD VELTFARE
FIELD MADDER SPURWORT
FIELD MOUSE VOLE MIGALE
FIELDPIECE GUN AMUSETTE
GALLOPER
FIELD SCABIOUS BLUECAP
FIELDWORK LUNET REDAN
LUNETTE
FIEND FEN FOE PUG FEND FYND
DEMON DEVIL ENEMY SATAN
TRULL WIZARD SHAITAN
SUCCUBA TITIVIL BARBASON
SUCCUBUS
FIENDISH CRUEL WICKED
DEMONIC FIENDLY SATANIC
DEMONIAC DEVILISH DIABOLIC
INFERNAL
FIERCE ILL BOLD FELL GRIM KEEN
RUDE THRO WILD WOOD ASPER
BREME CRUEL EAGER FELON
HATEL ORPED RETHE SHARP
SMART STARK STERN STOUR
STOUT WROTH ARDENT FEROCE
GOTHIC HETTER IMMANE LUPINE
RAGING RUGGED SAVAGE
STURDY UNMEEK UNMILD
WICKED BRUTISH FERVENT
FURIOSO FURIOUS GRIMFUL
INHUMAN MANKIND RABIOUS
RAMPANT SCADDLE VICIOUS
VIOLENT STERNFUL TIGERISH
(PREF.) LABRO
FIERCE-EYED WALLEYED
FIERCELY FELL HARD FELLY FIERCE
FIERCENESS FURY FEROCITY
FIERY HOT RED ADUST FIRED
QUICK SHARP ARDENT FLASHY
IGNITE BURNING FERVENT
FLAMING FURIOUS GLOWING
HOTHEAD IGNEOUS PARCHED
PEPPERY VIOLENT ADUSTIVE
CHOLERIC FEVERISH FRAMPOLD
INFLAMED PHRAMPEL SPIRITED
SPITFIRE VEHEMENT

FIERY ANGEL (CHARACTER IN —)
RENATA AGRIPPA HEINRICH
RUPPRECHT MEPHISTOPHELES
(COMPOSER OF —) PROKOFIEV
FIERY RED SANDIX
FIESTA FETE FERIA PARTY
HOLIDAY
(— COSTUME) POLLERA
FIFE STICK PIFERO PIFFERO
FIFTEEN FIVE
(PREF.) PENTADEC(A)
FIFTEENTH DOUBLETTE
FIFTH QUINT QUINTIN HEMIOLA
(PREF.) QUINT(I)
FIFTY (— YEAR ANNIVERSARY)
JUBILEE
FIFTY-FIFTY EVEN
FIG RIG FICO ARRAY BREBA DRESS
ELEME ELEMI PIPAL SABRA TANTI
BALETE BALITI FOUTER FOUTRA
GINGER LOBFIG PEEPUL TRIFLE
FURBISH GONDANG SICONUS
SYCONUS WARINGIN
(— CROP) MAMME
(PREF.) FICI SYCO
FIG BASKET CABAS
FIGHT BOX MIX WAP WAR WIN
BEAT BEEF BLUE BOUT CAMP
CLEM COCK COPE COWP CRAB
CUFF DUEL FLOG FRAY LAKE
MEET MELL MILL SHOW SLUG
SPAR TILT WAGE YOKE BANDY
BRAWL CLASH FIELD FLOLT
HURRY JOUST MATCH MELEE
RAMMY SCRAP SHINE SPURN
STOUR TOUSE AFFAIR AFFRAY
BARNEY BATTLE BICKER BLOWUP
COMBAT DEBATE FEUCHT
FRACAS FRAISE HASSLE IMPUGN
MEDDLE OPPOSE RELUCT
REPUGN RESIST RIPPIT RUFFLE
SHOWER STOUSH STRIFE STRIKE
STRIVE TOUSEL TURNUP
BARGAIN BRABBLE CONTEND
CONTEST COUNTER JOURNEY
QUARREL RUCTION SIMULTY
TUILYIE WARFARE CONFLICT
DOGFIGHT DUOMACHY FINISHER
GUNFIGHT MILITATE SKIRMISH
SLUGFEST SQUABBLE STRUGGLE
TIRRIVEE TIRRWIRR TRAVERSE
(— AGAINST) BUCK OPPUGN
(— BETWEEN TWO) DUEL
DUOMACHY
(— FOR) SERVE CHAMPION
(— WITH CLUB) TIMBER
(FIST —) RIPPIT TURNUP
(SEA —) NAUMACHY
(STREET —) HABBLE
(SUFF.) MACHIA MACHY
FIGHTER PUG VAMP BOXER
COCKER BATTLER DUELIST
SLUGGER SOLDIER WARRIOR
ANDABATA BARRATER BARRATOR
CHAMPION GUERILLA PUGILIST
SCRAPPER
(FIRE —) EXEMPT HOTSHOT
(GUERILLA —) MAQUIS
FIGHTING BLOW ACTION AFFRAY
DEBATE WARLIKE CONFLICT
MILITANT
(— WITH SHADOW) SCIAMACHY
FIGHTING FISH PLAKAT

**FIGLIA DI JORIO, LA (CHARACTER
IN —)** MILA ALIGI LAZARO
(COMPOSER OF —) PIZZETTI
FIG MARIGOLD SAMH MESEM
FICOID FOXCHOP FICOIDAL
FIGMENT IDEA FICTION
FIGPECKER BECCAFICO
FIGURATE FLORID FIGURAL
FIGURED FIGURATO
FIGURATION FORM SHAPE DESIGN
OUTLINE
FIGURATIVE FLORID FIGURAL
FIGURED FLOWERY TYPICAL
ALLUSIVE TROPICAL
FIGURE FIG HUE VOL BOSH DOLL
FORM IDEA SIGN STAR ANGLE
ANTIC DATUM DIGIT FLIRT
FRAME IMAGE MAGOT MOTIF
SHAPE SPADE SPRIG AUMAIL
BABOON CHANGE CIPHER
COCKUP CUTOUT DEVICE EFFIGY
EMBLEM ENTAIL FIGGER GOOGOL
INCUSE NUMBER PERSON
SCHEME SYMBOL TAILLE TATTOO
CHASSIS CHEVRON CHIFFER
CHIFFRE COMPUTE CONTOUR
DRAWING GESTALT IMPRESS
NUMERAL OUTLINE STATURE
DIHEDRAL FIGURATE GRAFFITO
HEXAGRAM LIKENESS SEMBLANT
MARIONETTE
**(— FORMED BY INTERSECTING
LINES)** KNOT
(— IN PRAYER) ORANT
(— IN WOOD GRAIN) BURL FLAKE
(— MADE OF CORN) KNACK
(— MADE OF 3 LINES) TRIGRAM
TRIANGLE
(— OF SPEECH) IMAGE IRONY
TROPE APORIA CLIMAX FLOWER
SCHEME SIMILE VISION ZEUGMA
ANALOGY IMAGERY CHIASMUS
DIALLAGE METAPHOR METONYMY
OXYMORON SYLLEPSIS
ABSCISSION
(— OUT) BOTTOM
(— UP) ITEM
(— USED AS COLUMN) ATLAS
TELAMON CARYATID
(— USED AS MAGIC SYMBOL)
PENTACLE
(—S OF SPEECH) COLORS
(ANATOMICAL —) ECORCHE
(ARTIFICIAL —) GOLEM
(BIBLICAL —) ANGEL CHERUB
(CARVED —) GLYPH FIGURINE
(CENTRAL —) HERO
(CIRCULAR —) HOOP
(COMIC —) BILLIKEN
(CONSPICUOUS —) MARK
(CRESCENT-SHAPED —) LUNE
(DANCE —) SWING TRACE SQUARE
PURPOSE ASSEMBLE PROMENADE
(DOMINANT —) CAPTAIN
(FEMALE —) ORANTE
(FOLDED PAPER —) FLEXAGON
(GEOMETRICAL —) BODY CONE
CUBE LUNE PRISM RHOMB SOLID
CIRCLE GNOMON ISAGON ISOGON
OBLONG SECTOR SQUARE
DIAGRAM ELLIPSE LOZENGE
PELCOID RHOMBUS SECTION
HEXAFOIL SPHEROID

(GREEK —) KOUROS
(GROTESQUE —) MAGOT BABOON MAXIMON
(HAVING FULL ROUNDED —) ZAFTIG ZOFTIG
(IDEAL —) EIDOLON
(IMAGINARY —) BOGEYMAN
(INCISED —) INTAGLIO
(JAPANESE — ON GRAVE) HANIWA
(MUMMYLIKE —) USHABTI
(MUSICAL —) IDEA LICK OSTINATO
(ODD —) MAUMET
(OVAL —) SWASH ELLIPSE
(PREHISTORIC —) CHACMOL CHACMOOL
(QUADRILLE —) POULE
(QUEER —) GIG
(RHETORICAL —) COLOR COLOUR
(RHYTHMIC —) SNAP
(SCULPTURED —) CANEPHOR
(SHADOW —) SKIAGRAM
(SKATING —) SPIRAL BRACKET COUNTER
(SPINDLE-SHAPED —) FUSEE FUZEE
(STUFFED —) DUMMY
(SYLLOGISTIC —) SCHEMA
(SYMBOLIC —) MORAL EMBLEM
(TAILOR'S —) MANNEQ MANNEQUIN
(TRIANGULAR —) TRIQUET
(UNDRAPED —) NUDE
(WINGED —) ANGEL EIDOLON
(PL.) SPILING
(PREF.) EID(O)
(SUFF.) HEDRON
FIGURED FIGURY FACONNE
FIGUREHEAD DUMMY FRONT SCROLL
FIGURINE TANAGRA CRIOPHORE
FIGWORT BARTSIA PILEWORT PAULOWNIA PENSTEMON BLUEHEARTS

FIJI
BAY: MBYA NATEWA NGALOA SAVUSAVU
CAPITAL: SUVA
EASTERN GROUP: LAU
ISLAND: ELD KIA ONO AIWA KIOA KORO MALI NGAU VIWA WAIA AGATA MANGO MOALA NAIAU RAMBI MAMOLO MATUKU MBENGA MBULIA NAIRAI NAVITI KIA HIT PAD BUNG CLOY TOTOYA YASAWA YENDUA KAMBARA KANDAVU LAKEMBA TAVEUNI VITILEVU
MOUNTAIN: NARARU MONAVATU
NIECE OR NEPHEW: VASU
POINT: VUYA
TOWN: BA MAU MBA MOMI NADI REWA SUVA TUVU NANDI THUVU ETUMBA LABASA NALOTO NAMOLI NARATA NASALA NAVOLA SAGARA LAUTOKA VATUKOULA

FIJIAN VITIAN
FILAGO GIFOLA
FILAMENT BRIN DOWL HAIR HARL NEMA PILE SILK CHIVE CHORD FIBER FIBRE FILUM TWIRE CIRRUS ELATER HEATER MANTLE STRAND

THREAD CIRRHUS FIMBRIA FLIMMER RHIZOID TEXTILE PARANEMA PHACELLA STERIGMA PARAPHYSIS
(— OF FEATHER) BARB DOWL DOWLE
(— OF MINERAL) STRINGER
(— OF SILK) BRIN
(—S OF FLAX OR HEMP) HARL
(TWISTED —S) STRAND
(PL.) HACKLE
FILAMENTOUS BYSSOID STRINGY HAIRLIKE
FILANDERS BACKWORM
FILARIASIS MUMU
FILBERT HAZEL COBNUT HAZELNUT
(SIEVE OF —S) PRICKLE
FILCH BOB FUB NIM ROB BEAT DRIB FAKE PILK PRIG SMUG SNIP FETCH LURCH PILCH SNAKE SNEAK STEAL CLOYNE PILFER SMOUCH STRIKE CABBAGE PURLOIN
FILE BOX ROW BARB DECK LINE LIST RANK RASP RATE RISP ROLL SLIP STUB EMERY ENTER FLOAT FOUND GRAIL INDEX LABEL RIFLE TRACK TRAIN ACCUSE ANSWER BEFOUL CARLET DEFILE FILACE RASCAL RUBBER STRING TOPPER ARCHIVE ARRANGE CHOILER CONDEMN DOSSIER EXHIBIT GRAILLE QUANNET TICKLER DRAWFILE
(— DOWN SAW TEETH) JOINT
(— OF SIX SOLDIERS) ROT
(— OFF) DEFILE
(— USED BY COMBMAKERS) GRAIL TOPPER GRAILER GRAILLE
(— WITH COURT OF LAW) BOX
(COARSE —) RAPE
(CURVED —) RIFFLER
FILE BOX SOLANDER
FILEFISH LIJA UNIE TURBOT UNICORN BALISTID FOOLFISH PLECTOGNATH
FILIAL PIUS SONLY
FILIBUSTER FLIBUTOR STONEWALL
FILING RASION LIMATION
(PL.) LEMEL SCOBS LIMAIL
FILIPENDULA ULMARIA
FILIPINO KALINGA KANKANAI
FILL EKE HIT PAD BUNG CLOY CRAM FEED GLUT HOLD LADE LINE MEET PANG QUAR SATE STOP TEEM BELLY BLOAT BULGE CHOKE ESTOP FLOCK GORGE KEDGE PITCH PRIME STORE STUFF CHARGE FULFIL INFUSE OCCUPY QUERRE SUPPLY AGGRADE DISTEND ENLARGE EXECUTE IMPLETE INFLATE INVOLVE PERFECT PERFORM PERVADE PLENISH SATIATE SATISFY SUFFUSE COMPLETE COMPOUND FREQUENT PERMEATE
(— COMPLETELY) SATURATE
(— CUP TO BRIM) BRIM CROWN BUMPER
(— FULL) FARCE STUFF

(— HORSES' TEETH) BISHOP
(— IN) NOG KILL STOP SLUSH INFILL BALLAST
(— IN CHINKS) LIP
(— IN WITH RUBBLE) HEART
(— INTERSTICES) BLIND
(— LEATHER WITH OIL) FAT
(— OUT) BUNCH SWELL
(— TO EXCESS) CROWD FLOOD CONGEST SURFEIT
(— TO OVERFLOWING) FLOW THWACK
(— UP) STOP BRICK CHOKE CLOSE ESTOP STOAK FULFIL IMPACT STODGE PLENISH
(— UP HOLE) STIFLE
(— WITH) SWILL
(— WITH ALE) RACK
(— WITH ANXIETY) ALARM ALARUM
(— WITH CARGO) STOW
(— WITH CLAY) CAT PUG
(— WITH FEAR) APPAL APPALL
(— WITH HORROR) ABHOR
(— WITH LIGHT) GLUT
(— WITH LIQUOR) TUN SKINK
(— WITH METAL) BACK
(— WITH MORTAR) GROUT
(— WITH ODORS) EMBALM
(— WITH RUBBISH) BASH
(— WITH TERROR) AMAZE
(ONE'S —) SLITHERS
FILLED BIG ALIVE FLUSH QUICK SATED SOLID GRAVID LOADED CROWDED HAUNTED IMPLETE OPPLETE REPLETE SWOLLEN FREQUENT INSTINCT POPULOUS
(— OUT) BOLD FULL
(— TO EXCESS) FLOWN
(— WITH EXCITEMENT) ABUZZ
(— WITH FEAR) AFRAID
(— WITH INTERSTICES) AREOLAR
(— WITH MOISTURE) FAT
(— WITH PRIDE) YNPRIDID
FILLER GARA BOGUS SILEX SILKA SQUIB BALAAM LIGNIN FILLING LOADING WRAPPER
FILLET BAND BONE GIRT LIST ORLE ORLO SOLE TAPE AMPYX CROWN FACET FILET GORGE LABEL LEDGE MITER MITRE QUIRK SCROD SNOOD STRAP STRIA TIARA VITTA ANADEM BENDEL BINDER CIMBIA COMBLE CORONA DIADEM FASCIA INFULA LISTEL NORSEL POTONG QUADRA REGLET REGULA RIBBON ROLLER TAENIA TURBAN TURBOT ANNULET BANDAGE BANDEAU CLOISON CORONET EYEBROW FACETTE FRONTAL GARLAND LAMBEAU MOLDING TRESSON TRINGLE BANDELET CINCTURE FRONTLET HAIRLACE HEADBAND PLATBAND TRESSOUR TRESSURE UNDERCUT
(PREF.) TAENI(A)(O)
FILLIFORM CATENOID
FILL-IN MODESTY
FILLING GOB FILL MODE PLUG WEFT WOOF INLAY STUFF FILLER STOPPING STUFFING
(— OF GAPS) CONFAB
(— UP) CLOSURE RIPIENO

(BASKET —) SLEW
(DENTAL —) INLAY
(SILK —) SHIKII
FILLIP BLOW FLIP SNAP SPUR TOSS URGE FILIP FLASH FLIRT FLISK IMPEL BUFFET INCITE MOMENT PROJECT STIMULATE
FILLY COLT FOAL GIRL
FILM H BRAT HAZE HULL KELL MIST SCUM SKIM SKIN VEIL WEFT BLEAR COVER FLAKE FLICK GLAZE LAYER PEARL PLATE SCALE SHOOT SHORT BUBBLE MOTHER PATINA SCRUFF CUTICLE FEATURE PHILOME TAFFETA TOPICAL TRAILER BEESWING FIRECOAT NEGATIVE PELLICLE MICROFILM MONOLAYER
(— OF AIR) PLASTRON
(— OF ICE) VERGLAS
(— OF OIL) SLICK
(— OF TARTAR) SCALE PLAQUE
(— ON COPPER) PATINA
(— ON PORRIDGE) BRAT
(— ON WINE) BEESWING
(— OVER EYE) WEB
(DISCARDED —) OUTTAKE
(POLYESTER —) MYLAR
(X-RAY —) BITEWING
FILMY FINE HAZY GAUZY MISTY SHEER WISPY CLOUDY CLOUDED TIFFANY FILMLIKE GOSSAMER
FILOSOFO DI CAMPAGNA, IL
(CHARACTER IN —) NARDO EUGENIA LESBINA RINALDO TRITEMIO
(COMPOSER OF —) GALUPPI
FILTER CLAY RAPE SIFT SILE DRAIN SEITZ SIEVE BOUGIE CANDLE COLATE CONTEX LAUTER MEDIUM PURIFY REFINE STRAIN BAGHOUSE COLATURE FILTRATE INFILTER STRAINER
FILTERER CLARIFIER
FILTH FEN KET DIRT DUNG GORE MUCK NAST SLUT SOIL SUDS ADDLE BILGE DRECK GLEAM GLEET JAKES POUCE SWILL DEFILE FULYIE FULZIE IMMUND ORDURE SORDES SORDOR VERMIN SLOTTER SQUALOR SULLAGE FOULNESS MUCKMENT SNOTTERY WORTHING COLLUVIES
(PREF.) COPR(O)
FILTHINESS MUCOR SQUALOR SULLAGE CENOSITY
FILTHY LOW FOUL MIRY VILE BAWDY DIRTY DROVY DUNGY GROSS LAIRY MUCKY NASTY AUGEAN BAWDRY CRUMBY CRUMMY CRUSTY DIRTEN IMMUND IMPURE SORDID BEASTLY BESTIAL HOGGISH OBSCENE PIGGISH SQUALID UNCLEAN ORDUROUS SLUTTISH
FILTRATE MALLEIN
FILTRATION BAGGING COLATURE
FIN ARM RAG RIB ANAL BURR FANG HAND KEEL SAIL FLASH PINNA CAUDAL FINLET ACANTHA FEATHER FLIPPER PINNULE VENTRAL FORELIMB PECTORAL
(BOMB —) VANE

(PREF.) PTER(O) PTERYG(O)

FINAGLE CHEAT TRICK REVOKE DECEIVE FENAGLE

FINAL LAST UTTER FINIAL LATTER RUNOFF ULTIMA UTMOST DARREIN DERNIER EXTREME FINALIS OUTMOST PARTING SUPREME ABSOLUTE DECISIVE DECRETAL DEFINITE EVENTUAL FAREWELL ULTIMATE
(— STANZA) ENVOI
(NOT —) NISI

FINALE END CODA FINIS ENDING CLOSING

FINALITY END ERGO

FINALLY YET LAST AFINE LASTLY

FINANCE TAX BACK BANK FUND GOODS REVENUE TAXATION TREASURE

FINANCIAL FISCAL MONETARY PECUNIARY

FINANCIER BANIAN BANYAN MONEYMAN
(AUTHOR OF —) DREISER
(CHARACTER IN —) FRANK HENRY AILEEN BUTLER EDWARD SEMPLE STENER LILLIAN WINGATE COWPERWOOD

FINBACK WHALE FINNER GIBBAR FINFISH RORQUAL JUBARTAS

FINCH FINK MORO PAPE JUNCO SERIN TERIN BURION CANARY CITRIL LINNET PALILA SISKIN TOWHEE BUNTING CHEWINK PEEWEEP REDHEAD REDPOLL OENEOAL ORANNOW TANAGER WAXBILL AMADAVAT COMBASOU FIRETAIL GOULDIAN GROSBEAK HAWFINCH LONGSPUR SNOWBIRD BRAMBLING SEEDEATER
(— FLOCK) CHARM

FIND GET RUG MEET VAIL CATCH INVENT LOCATE STRIKE ADJUDGE FINDING DISCOVER SCROUNGE
(— FAULT) CARP BARGE BLAME CAVIL GRONT KNOCK PINCH SCOLD NATTER ARRAIGN
(— GUILTY) ATTAINT CONVICT
(— OUT) AFIND CHECK ESSAY LEARN SPELL TROVE DETECT CONTRIVE DECIPHER DISCOVER
(— REFUGE) BIEL BIELD
(— SOLUTION) SOLVE
(— THE SUM) SUMMATE
(— TIME) EEM

FINDER SIGHT SEEKER FOUNDER

FINDING TROVER INQUEST VERDICT

FINE CRO GAY RUM TAX BEIN BIEN BOTE BRAW CAIN CROP DIRE ERIC FAIR GENT GOOD HUNK JAKE LEVY MOOI NICE PURE RARE SEPT SLAP TALL TEAR TINE TRIM ABWAB BONNY BRAVE BULLY CHECK DAISY DANDY DELIE DUCKY FRAIL GAUDY GRAND GREAT HUNKY ISSUE KELTY MULCT NIFTY NOBLE RORTY SHARP SHEER SMALL SPALE SWANK SWEET UNLAW WALLY WHITE AMENDE AMERCE BONNIE BONZER BRAWLY BRIGHT CHEESY

CHOICE CLEVER COSTLY CRAFTY DAINTY FACETE FINISH FLUTED GERSUM HERIOT HUNGRY INCONY ORNATE PEACHY PRETTY PROPER QUAINT RANSOM SARAAD SCONCE SERENE SILKEN SLIGHT SPIFFY TENDER CLARIFY CONDEMN CORKING CREANCE CUNNING ELEGANT ESTREAT FERDWIT FINICAL FORFEIT FRAGILE GALANAS GALLANT GALLOWS GRADELY GRASSUM IMMENSE MARCHET MERCHET MURDRUM ORFGILD PENALTY PERFECT REFINED SCUTAGE STAVING TENUOUS TOPPING VALIANT WERGILD ABSOLUTE BLOODWIT BUDGEREE CAVALIER CLINKING DELICATE DUSTLIKE FLITWITE FOOTGELD HANDSOME LASHLITE MARITAGE PENALIZE PESHKASH PINPOINT PLEASANT SKILLFUL SPLENDID SUPERIOR WARDWITE WIRESPUN MAGNIFICENT
(— AGAINST SERVANTS) CHECK
(— FOR KILLING) BOTE
(— IN LIEU OF FLOGGING) HIDE
(BLOOD —) ERIC WITE
(OSTENTATIOUSLY —) GAUDY
(PRINTING OFFICE —) SOLACE
(VERY —) BUNKUM SPLENDID
(PL.) SILT FLOUR
(PREF.) LEPT(O)

FINE-DRAW RANTER

FINE-LOOKING SPICY WALLY SPIFFY

FINELY FINE GAILY GAYLY WALLY BRAGLY RARELY SMALLY BRAVELY SMICKLY SWEETLY

FINENESS ALLOY GRAIN TRICK DENIER FINERY PURITY THREAD EXILITY FINESSE DELICACY
(— AS RECKONED BY CARATS) TITLE
(— OF FABRIC) CUT GAGE GAUGE
(— OF METAL) STANDARD
(— OF PITCH) COUNTS

FINERY GAUD WALY ARRAY BRAWS WALLY BAUBLE BAWDRY BEAUTY FEGARY GAIETY GAYETY TAWDRY BRAVERY GAUDERY REGALIA BEAUETRY ELEGANCE FINENESS FOFARRAW FOLDEROL FOOFARAW FRIPPERY ORNAMENT RIBANDRY

FINESPUN HAIR THIN TWITTERY

FINESSE ART CHEAT SKILL TRICK PURITY SERENE CUNNING ARTIFICE DELICACY SUBTLETY THINNESS

FINFOOT SUNBIRD

FINGER TOY PAUT PLAY DIGIT INDEX PINKY DACTYL HANDLE MEDDLE MEDIUS PADDLE PILFER PINKIE POLLEX ANNULAR DIGITAL MINIMUM MINIMUS PURLOIN DIGITIZE THRIMBLE
(— INFECTION) FELON
(FORE —) INDEX
(LITTLE —) PINKY PINKIE PIRLIE MINIMUS AURICULAR
(RING —) ANNULAR

RINGMAN ANNULARY
(PL.) HOOKS
(PREF.) DACTYL(IO)(O) DIGITI DIGITO
(SUFF.) DACTYLIA DACTYLOUS

FINGERFLOWER FOXGLOVE

FINGERING DOIGTE

FINGERLING PARR TROUTLET

FINGERNAIL DIGGER
(RELATING TO —) ONYCHOID
(SUFF.) ONYCHA ONYCHES ONYCHIA ONYCHIUM ONYCHUS ONYX

FINGERPRINT DAB ARCH LOOP WHORL LATENT

FINGERROOT FOXGLOVE

FINGERSTALL COT

FINIAL EPI NOB TEE TOP CROP KNOB KNOP KNOT BUNCH CREST CROWN FINAL POPPY PRICKET ORNAMENT PINNACLE

FINICAL NICE FUSSY CHOOSY DAINTY DAPPER JAUNTY PRETTY PRISSY SPRUCE CHOOSEY FINICKY FINIKIN FOPPISH MINCING PERJINK PICKING SMICKER DELICATE

FINICALLY SMICKLY GINGERLY

FINICKY NICE DINKY FIKEY FIKIE PRISSY FINICAL FINIKIN PRECISE

FINISH DO DIE END CHAR EDGE FACE FINE MILL OVER PASS SINK SNUG STOP BLOOM BOUND CEASE CHARE CHEVE CLOSE CROWN FEEZE GLACE GLAZE LIMIT SPEED UPPER BOTTOM BUSHEL FULFIL FULLDO PLISSE POLISH SETTLE WINDUP ABSOLVE ACHIEVE DEPETER EXECUTE FLUTING FULFILL PERFECT SURFACE COMPLETE CONCLUDE DEPRETER DRESSING FINALIZE FROSTING TERMINAL
(— CAREFULLY) NEATEN
(— CLOTH) BURL CONVERT
(— METAL) PLANISH
(— OF FABRIC) CIRE HOLLAND
(— OF PAPER) STIPPLE
(— OFF) DASH CRUSH ABSOLVE ACCOMPLISH
(— STONE) COMB BOAST DROVE
(— WITH A SEAM) FELL
(— WORK) FLOOR
(CALENDERED —) CHASING
(DULL —) MAT MATTE
(GLAZED —) GLACE LACKER LACQUER
(STUCCO —) SPATTER
(SUPERFICIAL —) BLAZONRY

FINISHED BY DID OER PAU ARCH DONE DOWN FINE GONE OVER PURE RIPE SHOT ENDED EXACT KAPUT NAPOO ROUND CLOSED NAPOOH ORNATE PERFECT REFINED ROUNDED STOPPED THROUGH BANKRUPT CLIMAXED GOFFERED LUSTERED POLISHED
(— IN NATURAL COLOR) FAIR
(— WITH NAP) BRUSHED
(ABSOLUTELY —) SUNK
(HIGHLY —) SUAVE
(IMPERFECTLY —) RUDE

FINISHER EYER ENDER CORKER

GAFFER BEETLER CEMENTER ENAMELER SOCKDOLOGER

FINISHING CRUSHING

FINITE LIMITED

FINLAND	
CAPITAL:	HELSINKI HELSINGFORS
COIN:	PENNI MARKKA
DIVISION:	IJORE VILLIPURI
GOD:	TAPIO JUMALA
ISLAND:	ALAND KARLO AALAND HAILUTO VALLGRUND
ISTHMUS:	KARELIA
LAKE:	JUO MUO KEMI KIVI NASI OULU PURU PYHA SIMO ENARE HAUKI INARI KALLA LAPPA LESTI PUULA LENTUA SAIMAA SOUNNE SYVARI KOITERE NILAKKA PIELINEN
LANGUAGE:	AVAR LAPP UGRIC MAGYAR OSTYAK TAVAST SAMOYED ESTONIAN
MEASURE:	KANNU TUNNA VERST FATHOM SJOMIL OTTINGER SKALPUND TUNNLAND
MOUNTAIN:	HALTIA
NAME:	SUOMI
PARLIAMENT:	EDUSKUNTA
PROVINCE:	HAME KYMI OULU LAPPI VAASA KUOPIO MIKKELI UUSIMAA
RIVER:	II KALA OULU SIMO TENO IVALO LOTTA OUNAS SIIKA IIJOKI LAPUAN MUONIO PASVIK TORNIO KITINEN KOKEMAKI
TOWN:	ABA ABO KEM KEMI OULU PORI VASA ENARE ESPOO KOTKA LAHTI TURKU VAASA IMATRA KUOPIO MIKKELI TAMPERE HELSINKI
TRIBE:	HAME VEPS VEPSE UGRIAN KARJALAISET SUOMALAISET

FINLET PINNULE

FINN FIOUN INGER OSTIAK OSTYAK TAVAST INGRIAN CHEREMIS INGERMAN SWEKOMAN
(PL.) SUOMI

FINNISH
(PREF.) FENNO

FINNOCK HERLING

FINTA GIARDINIERA, LA
(CHARACTER IN —) ONESTI ANCHISE ARMINDA BELFIORE SANDRINA SERPETTA VIOLANTE
(COMPOSER OF —) MOZART

FIORD FJORD INLET

FIORIN KNOTGRASS

FIORITURA ORNAMENT

FIPPLE FLUTE RECORDER

FIR VER LARCH SAPIN BAUMIER LASHORN PINABETE

FIR CLUB MOSS FOXFEET

FIRE CAN FEU LOW AGNI APOY BALE BRIO BURN HEAT KILN LOWE POOP SWAP SWOP ZEAL ARDOR ARSON BLAST BLAZE BREAK BURST EMPTY FEVER GLEED INGLE LIGHT LOGHE LOOSE LOUGH PLUFF SERVE SHOOT SQUIB STOKE AROUSE ENGHLE EXCITE FERVOR IGNITE INCITE KINDLE SMUDGE SPIRIT

SPLEEN VULCAN ANIMATE
BONFIRE BURNING BURNOUT
CHIMNEY DISMISS EMITTER
EXPLODE FURNACE GLIMMER
INFLAME INSPIRE SMOLDER
BACKFIRE BALEFIRE CAMPFIRE
DETONATE HELLFIRE ILLUMINE
IRRITATE NEEDFIRE SMOULDER
VIVACITY PORCELAINIZE
(— A REVOLVER) FAN
(— ON) AFIRE
(— THE CHARGE) HIT
(— TWO ROUNDS) DOUBLE
(— UPON) GUN SPRAY
(CROSS —) GANTLET GAUNTLET
(DAMPENED —) SMOTHER
(FOREST —) BREAK
(LITTLE —) SPONK SPUNK
(MASSED —) ARTILLERY
(PEAT —) GREESAGH
(RUNNING-OUT —) DANDY
(SIGNAL —) BALE BEACON
BALEFIRE
(PREF.) EMPYRO IGNEO IGNI
PHLOGO PYR(ET)(ETO)(ITI)(O)
(SUFF.) PYRA
FIRE ALARM FIREBOX
FIREARM ARM GUN IRON SHOT
TUBE FIRER ORGAN PIECE RIFLE
JEZAIL MAGNUM MAUSER
MUSKET PISTOL POPPER
BOMBARD CARBINE CURRIER
DEMIHAG HANDGUN PINFIRE
SHOOTER SPANNER ARQUEBUS
BROWNING CULVERIN EXPELLER
EXPLODER PETRONEL REVOLVER
(PL.) HARDWARE ARTILLERY
FIRE ARROW MALLEOLUS
FIREBACK REREDOS MACARTNEY
FIREBALL BOLIDE
FIRE BEETLE COCUYO CUCUYO
ELATER ELATERID
FIREBOAT PALANDER
FIREBRAND BLAZE BRAND BLEERY
BOUTEFEU
FIREBRICK QUARLE
(PL.) GROG
FIREBUG BUG ARSONIST
FIRE CARRIER PORTFIRE
FIRECLAY THILL
FIRE COVER CURFEW CURPHEW
FIRECRACKER DEVIL SQUIB
BANGER PETARD SALUTE
CRACKER SNAPPER FIREWORK
WHIZBANG
FIRE-CURED DARK
FIREDAMP GAS FOULNESS
WILDFIRE
FIREDART PHALARICA
FIREDOG DOG IRON
FIRE ENGINE RIG TUB MANUAL
FIRE EXTINGUISHER SQUIRT
EXTINCTOR
FIRE FIGHTER EXEMPT HOTSHOT
FIREFLY CUCUYO FIREBUG
GLOWFLY LAMPFLY FIREWORM
GLOWWORM LAMPYRID
FIREGUARD FENDER
FIRELINE GUTTER
FIRELOCK FUSEE FUZEE SPANNER
FIREMAN VAMP FIRER FUELER
STOKER TEASER TIZEUR FIREBOY
HOSEMAN BAKEHEAD FURNACER

FIREPLACE FOCUS FOGON FORGE
FOYER GRATE INGLE TISAR
HEARTH CHIMNEY CHEMINEE
(— AND CHIMNEY) STACK
(— STONE) MANTEL
(PORTABLE —) BARBECUE
BARBEQUE
FIREPLUG PLUG HYDRANT
FIRER STOKER BLASTER
FIRESIDE SMOKE HEARTH
FIRESTAND HASTER HASTENER
FIRE THORN PYRACANTH
FIREWEED FIRETOP ROSEBAY
PILEWEED PILEWORT
FIREWOOD FIRE LENA SLAB WOOD
CHUNK FAGOT BILLET BILLOT
ELDING FIRING TALWOOD
FIREBOTE TALLWOOD TALSHIDE
FIREWORK JET SUN GERB DEVIL
GERBE PEEOY SAXON SHELL
WHEEL FIZGIG MAROON PETARD
ROCKET SALUTE SHOWER
TRACER CASCADE SERPENT
SPARKER TORPEDO FOUNTAIN
SPARKLER
(PL.) FUN FIRE
FIRE WORSHIPPER PARSI GHEBER
GHEBRE PARSEE
FIRING FIRE FUEL COUGH SALVO
BURNING DRUMFIRE
FIRKIN VESSEL
FIRM HUI PAT BUFF FAST HARD
IRON NASH SURE TAUT TRIG
TRIM CHAMP CORKY CRISP DENSE
FIRMA FIXED HARDY HOUSE
LOYAL RIGID SOLID SOUND STARK
STIFF STITH STOUT SWITH TIGHT
TOUGH HARDEN HEARTY SECURE
SETTLE SICCAR SICKER SINEWY
STABLE STANCH STEADY STEEVE
STOLID STRONG STURDY TRUSTY
ADAMANT CERTAIN COMPACT
COMPANY CONCERN CONFIRM
CONTEXT DECIDED DURABLE
STAUNCH UNMOVED CONSTANT
FAITHFUL FIDUCIAL OBDURATE
RESOLUTE SUBSTANT UNSHAKEN
(— BUT EASILY CUT) SEMISOFT
(NOT —) FUZZY
(PREF.) PAGIO
FIRMAMENT SKY DEEP POLE
CARRY CANOPY HEAVEN
EXPANSE EMPYREAN EMPYREUM
EXPANSUM
FIRMLY BUFF FAST FIRM HARD
SADLY STARK TIGHT HARDLY
SQUARE SURELY SOLIDLY
SECURELY STRONGLY
FIRMNESS BODY GRIT IRON
ETHAN PROOF FIXTURE COURAGE
FIRMITY GRANITE BACKBONE
DECISION FASTNESS SECURITY
SOLIDITY STRENGTH TENACITY
FIRN NEVE
FIRST ERST FUST GULE HEAD HIGH
MAIN ALPHA CHIEF FORME NIEVE
PRIMA PRIME PRIMO MAIDEN
PRIMAL PRIMUS VIRGIN FIRSTLY
HIGHEST INITIAL LEADING
PREMIER PRIMARY EARLIEST
FOREHAND FOREMOST FORMERLY
ORIGINAL PARAVANT PREMIERE
PRINCEPS

(— PRIZE) BLUE
(— SERGEANT) TOP
(— STATE) DELAWARE
(PREF.) PRIMI PRIMO PROT(O)
(— IN TIME) ARCH
FIRSTBORN AYNE EIGNE ELDEST
FIRST-CLASS GAY TOP BOSS POSH
FLASH PRIME PUKKA BUNKUM
STUNNING
FIRST-FRUITS ANNATES
FIRSTHAND DIRECT PRIMARY
ORIGINAL
FIRST-RATE BOSS BRAG GOOD
JAKE MAIN SLAP BULLY DANDY
LUMMY PRIME SLEEK SLICK
SUPER SWELL BONSER BONZER
BOSKER CHEESY FAMOUS TIPTOP
BLIGHTY BOSHTER CAPITAL
SKOOKUM STELLAR TOPPING
CHAMPION CLINKING CLIPPING
TOPNOTCH
FIRTH ARM KYLE FRITH INLET
COPPICE ESTUARY
FISCAL BURSAL MONETARY
FISH AU ID AKU AWA AYU BIB CAT
COD DAB DAP DIB EEL FIN GAR
GIG GOO HEN IDE IHI JIG JUG
ORF RAY SAR TAI UKU BANK
BARB BASS BLAY BOCE BOGA
CARP CAST CERO CHUB CHUG
CHUM CLOD CRAB CUSK DACE
DORY DRAG DRAW DRUM ERSE
FUGU GADE GHOL GOBY GRIG
HAKE HIND HUCH HUSO JACK
JUNK LINE LING LOTE MADO
MERO MOLA OPAH PEAL PEGA
PIKE POOR POUT PRIM QUAB
RAIL RUDD RUFF SCAD SCUP
SEER SHAD SOLE SPET SPIN SPOT
TILE TORO TUNA ACARA AHOLE
AKULE ANGLE ATULE BEGTI
BETTA BINNY BLAIN BLEAK BOLTI
BOLTY BREAM BULLY BULTI
CABIO CATLA CHIO CISCO COBIA
CONEY DANIO DORAB DRAIL
DRIFT DRIVE ELOPS ERIZO FLOAT
FLUKE FOGAS FRIAR GADID
GRUNT GUPPY HILSA HUCHO
JUREL KILLY LAKER LANCE
MANTA MIDGE MINIM MORAY
OTTER PERCH PIABA PLATY
PORGY POWAN POWER REINA
ROACH SAIDE SARGO SAURY
SEINE SHARK SKATE SMELT
SNOEK SNOOK SPRAT SQUID
SULEA SWEEP TENCH TETRA
TRABU TROLL TROUT TUNNY
UMBRA VIUVA VORAZ WAHOO
WHIFF AIMARA ALEVIN ANABAS
ANGLER BARBEL BARBER BENNET
BICHIR BISKOP BLENNY BONITO
BOWFIN BUMPER BURBOT
CALLOP CANDIL CAPLIN CARANX
CARIBE COELHO COTTID CREOLE
CUCHIA CUNNER DARTER DASSIE
DENTEX FISHET GANOID GINNEL
GULPER GUNNEL HAMLET
HAPUKU HILSAH HUSSAR INANGA
KOKOPU LAUNCE LEDGER LIGGER
LOUVAR MAIGRE MARLIN MENISE
MILTER MINNOW MOLLIE MOLOID
MULLET NONNAT PHOEBE PLAICE
POMPON PUFFER PUNECA

REDFIN REMORA ROBALO
ROUGHY RUNNER SABALO SALELE
SALEMA SALMON SAPSAP SARDEL
SAUGER SAUREL SERRAN SHINER
SIERRA SIMARA SPARID SUCKER
TAILER TAIMEN TANDAN TARPON
TAUTOG TESTAR TETARD TINOSA
TOMCOD TURBOT VENDIS
WALLER WEAVER WIRRAH
WRASSE ZINGEL ALEWIFE
ALFIONA ANCHOVY BACALAO
BARBUDO BATFISH BEARDIE
BERGYLT BERYCID BOXFISH
BRAGGLE BUFFALO BUMMALO
CABEZON CANDIRU CAPELIN
CAPLING CATFISH CAVALLA
CAVALLY CHIMERA CHROMID
CICHLID CLUPEID CONVICT
CORVINA COWFISH CRAPPIE
CROAKER CTENOID CUTLIPS
CYCLOID DRABBLE DREPANE
DRUMMER EELPOUT ESCOLAR
FATHEAD FINFISH GALJOEN
GEELBEC GEELBEK GOBIOID
GOGGLER GOLDEYE GOURAMI
GRAYSBY GROUPER GRUNION
GRUNTER GUAPENA GUAVINA
GUDGEON GULARIS GURNARD
GWYNIAD HADDOCK HAGFISH
HALIBUT HARMOOT HERRING
HINALEA HOGFISH HOUTING
ICEFISH ICHTHUS INCONNU
JAWFISH JEWFISH JUGULAR
LABROID LAGARTO LONGFIN
MACHETE MAHSEER MAYFISH
MOJARRA MOONEYE MORWONG
OARFISH OLDWIFE OQUASSA
PEGASUS PIGFOOT PINTADO
PIRANHA POISSON POLLACK
POMFRET POMPANO PUPFISH
RONQUIL SANCORD SARDINE
SAUROID SAVELHA SAWFISH
SCALARE SCAROID SCHELLY
SCULPIN SENNETT SILURUS
SLEEPER SMUTTER SNAPPER
SOLDIER SPAWNER STERLET
SUNFISH TELEOST TOMTATE
TOPKNOT TORPEDO TUBFISH
UMBRANA UNICORN VENDACE
VIAJACA WAREHOU WAUBEEN
WHAPUKA WHAPUKU WHITING
ALBACORE ALFONSIN APOGONID
ARAPAIMA ATHERINE BAITFISH
BALISTID BIGMOUTH BILLFISH
BLENNOID BLUEBACK BLUEFISH
BOARFISH BONEFISH BRISLING
BROTULID BULLHEAD CACKEREL
CANCHITO CARANGID CARANGIN
CARDINAL CATALINA CATALUFA
CHANCITO CHIMAERA CHOANATE
CHROMIDE CORACINE CROSSOPT
CYPRINID DEALFISH DIPNEUST
DITREMID DONCELLA DRAGONET
DRUMFISH DUMBFISH ECHENEID
ELEOTRID EPISCATE FALLFISH
FILEFISH FLAGFISH FLATFISH
FLATHEAD FLOUNDER FOOLFISH
FROGFISH FUNDULUS GAMBUSIA
GEELBECK GILTHEAD GOATFISH
GOLDFISH GRAINING GRAYFISH
GRAYLING GREYSKIN HAIRFISH
HALFBEAK HANDFISH HANDLINE
HAPLOMID HARDHEAD HARDTAIL

HOMOCERC HORNFISH
HORSEMAN JACKFISH JUMPROCK
KABELJOU KARMOUTH KELPFISH
KINGFISH LADYFISH LUMPFISH
MACKEREL MENHADEN MILKFISH
MOONFISH PICKEREL PILCHARD
PIRARUCU PORKFISH QUERIMAN
ROBALITO ROCKFISH ROCKLING
ROSEFISH SAILFISH SALANGID
SANDFISH SANDGOBY SCIAENID
SCOMBRID SCOTSMAN SEERFISH
SKILFISH SKIPJACK SOAPFISH
STUDFISH STURGEON TALLYWAG
TARWHINE TERAGLIN TILEFISH
TOADFISH TREEFISH TREVALLY
WARMOUTH WEAKFISH
WHISTLER WRYMOUTH
QUILLBACK SCORPAENO
NEEDLEFISH SHEEPSHEAD
SHOVELHEAD SHOVELNOSE
SILVERSIDES MOUTHBREEDER
(— BY TROLLING) DRAIL
(— FOR EELS) GRIG SNIGGLE
(— FOR SALMON) SNIGGER
(— NETTED) LIFT
(— NOT UNDERSIZED) COUNT
KEEPER
(— TAPE) SNAKE
(— THROUGH ICE) CHUG
(— UNDERWATER) GOGGLE
(— WITH HANDS) GUMP GUDDLE
(AQUARIUM —) GUPPY RASBORA
(BLIND —) PINKFISH
(CURED —) DUNFISH
(FABLED —) MAH
(FEMALE —) RAUN SPAWNER
(FIGHTING —) PLAKAT
(HAWAIIAN —) AU
(HERALDIC —) CHABOT
(INDIAN —) ROHU
(NUMBER OF —) SCHOOL
(OLD —) MOSSBACK
(PART OF —) EYE FIN JAW ANUS
CHEEK NARIS SCALE MAXILLA
MANDIBLE OPERCULUM
PREMAXILLA
(PULPED —) POMACE
(QUANTITY OF —) MAZE
(RAW —) SASHIMI
(REFUSE —) CHUM SHACK
(SALTED —) COR
(SMOKED —) FUMADO
(SPLIT —) KLIPFISH
(STEWED —) MATELOTE
(THIN —) RACER
(YOUNG —) FRY ALEVIN
(25 LBS. OF —) STICK
(PREF.) ICHTHY(O) ISCI
(SUFF.) CHROMIS ICHTHYS
FISH BASKET POT CAUL CREEL
SLATH
FISH BOX TRUNK
FISH BRINER COBBERER
FISH CLEANER GILLER
FISH DRESSER IDLER
FISHER MART EELER PEKAN SABLE
SOBOL TAIRA TAYRA MARTEN
SEINER WEJACK MARTRIX
TRAWLER TROLLER
(SPONGE —) HOOKER
FISHERMAN (ALSO SEE ANGLER)
TOTY EELER ANGLER GIGMAN
GILLER KEDGER MAIMUL SEINER

WORMER ADMIRAL DORYMAN
DRAGMAN DRIFTER PRAWNER
RODSTER SHANKER SMELTER
STRIKER TRAWLER TROTTER
TROWMAN PETERMAN PISCATOR
SEASONER SHRIMPER
FISHERY FISHING PISCARY
SEALERY
FISHGARTH WEIR
FISHHOOK FLY GIG HOOK LARI
ANGLE DRAIL KIRBY LARIN SLEEK
ANGULE SPROAT KENDALL
ABERDEEN BARBLESS CARLISLE
LIMERICK
(PART OF —) EYE GAP BARB BEND
POINT SHANK
(PL.) PULLDEVIL
FISHING PIKING ANGLING BANKING
BASSING GRAINING SNOEKING
(— TOOL) OVERSHOT
FISHING GROUNDS HAAF
FISHING ROD GAD
FISHING TACKLE TEW LEDGER
FISHLINE GIMP TROT SNELL
TRAWL DIPSEY LIGGER BOULTER
GANGION OUTLINE SETLINE
TRIMMER HAIRLINE TROTLINE
FISH LOUSE GISLER
FISHMONGER PESSONER
FISH NEST REDD
FISHNET FLUE SEINE SETNET
FISHPOND STEW VIVER PISCINA
VIVARIUM
FISHPOUND MADRAGUE
FISH SPEAR GRANES WASTER
LEISTER
FISHTAIL UROSOME
FISHWAY PASS RACEWAY
FISHY DULL FUNNY GLASSY
VACANT
FISSION BREAKING CLEAVAGE
CLEAVING GAMOGENY SCISSION
FISSURE GAP CHAP CONE FLAW
GOOL GULL LEAK LOCH LODE
RENT RIFT RIMA RIME SEAM SLIT
TEAR VEIN VENT CHASM CHINE
CHINK CLEFT CRACK FLAKE GRIKE
PIPER PORTA SHAKE SPLIT ZYGON
CLEAVE CRANNY DIVIDE LESION
RICTUS RIMULA SPRING SULCUS
BLEMISH CREVICE FISSURA
MOFETTE OPENING SWALLET
APERTURE BLOWHOLE CLEAVAGE
COLOBOMA CREVASSE INCISURE
QUEBRADA SCISSURA TRAVERSE
(— IN BUILDING STONE) DRY
(— IN HEEL) GAUG
(— IN MAST) SPRING
(— IN PLATEAU) ABRA
(PL.) RHAGADES
(PREF.) RHAGADI
(SUFF.) SCHISIS SCHIST
FISSURED RIMATE CHAPPED
CLEFTED FISSATE
FIST JOB PUD DUKE NAVE NEIF
NIEF FOIST GRASP INDEX NIEVE
CLENCH CLUTCH DADDLE EFFORT
MAULER MAULEY PINKER STRIKE
ATTEMPT CLUBFIST FISTNOTE
PUFFBALL TIGHTWAD
FISTFIGHT TURNUP
FISTICUFF BOX NEVEL FISTIFY
FISTULA EGILOPS

(PREF.) SYRING(O)
FISTULOUS TUBULAR
FIT GO APT FAY GEE JAG PAN RIG
SET SIT ABLE AGUE BOUT FEAT
FURY GOOD HARD KINK MEET
PANG RIPE SORT SUIT TRIM TURN
WELL WHIM ADAPT ADEPT APPLY
BESIT CHINK CLICK DIGNE EXIES
FADGE FANCY FITLY FRAME FRISK
FUROR HAPPY ICTUS MATCH
PITCH QUEME QUIRK READY
RIGHT SERVE SPASM SPELL
START STOUR SWOON TALLY
ACCESS ADJUST ANSWER
ATTACK BECOME BEHOVE BESORT
DUEFUL FINISH FITTEN HABILE
HEPPEN LIABLE PROPER SEASON
SEEMLY SPLEEN SQUARE STREAK
STROKE STRONG SUITED WORTHY
ADAPTED BEHOOVE CAPABLE
CONCENT CONDIGN CONFORM
CORRECT DESPAIR FASHION
FITTING HEALTHY PREPARE
QUALIFY SEIZURE TANTRUM
WIDDRIM ADEQUATE BECOMING
DOVETAIL ELIGIBLE GLOOMING
IDONEOUS OUTBREAK PAROXYSM
PASSABLE SUITABLE SYNCOPES
(— CLOSELY) FAY CHOCK
(— CORNER TO CORNER) BUTT
(— FOR THE GALLOWS) WIDDIFOW
(— IN) GO
(— INTO SOCKET) FANG
(— LOOSELY) SLOP
(— OF ANGER) WAX FRAP FUME
HUFF RAGE TIFF FLING RAVERY
SPLEEN
(— OF DEPRESSION) HUMP
(— OF ILL HUMOR) DOD PET TIG
FUNK POUT TOUT GRUMPS
(— OF ILL TEMPER) MAD TANTRUM
(— OF ILLNESS) DROW TOUT FLING
(— OF LAUGHTER) GIRD KINK
(— OF NERVOUSNESS) TWITCHET
(— OF RESENTMENT) PIQUE SNUFF
(— OF SHIVERING) AGUE GROOSE
(— OF STUBBORNNESS) REEST
(— OF SULKS) GEE STRUM
(— OF SULLENNESS) DOD
(— OF TEMPER) WAX BAIT BIRSE
HISSY PADDY TETCH GROUCH
SPLEEN SQUALL BRAINGE
(— OF WEEPING) CRY
(— OF YAWNING) GAPE
(— ONE WITHIN ANOTHER) NEST
(— OUT) ARM BUSK BEFIT EQUIP
ASTORE CLOTHE OUTFIT APPAREL
APPOINT FURNISH HABILLE
ACCOUTER
(— RIFLE BARREL) BED
(— TIGHTLY) STUFF
(— TO BE DRUNK) SORBILE
(— TOGETHER) MESH NEST COAPT
JOINT COHERE ASSEMBLE
(— UP) RIG
(— WITH COMPACTNESS) BOX
(— WITH FETTERS) GARNISH
(RITUALLY —) KOSHER
(PL.) LUNES
(SUFF.) ABLE IBLE
FITCH LINER
FITFUL GERY CATCHY GERFUL
GLEAMY CURSORY FLIGHTY

RESTLESS UNSTABLE VARIABLE
SPASMODIC
FITLY FIT PAT DULY FEATLY
GLADLY MEETLY TIDELY APROPOS
HAPPILY PROPERLY SUITABLY
FITNESS FORM APTNESS DECENCY
DECORUM DIGNITY APTITUDE
CAPACITY IDONEITY JUSTNESS
PROPERTY CONGRUITY
FITTED APT ABLE ADAPT KEYED
SUITED ADAPTED ENGAGED
ADJUSTED ASSORTED ELIGIBLE
FITTER TUBER GASMAN
FITTING TO APT CAP DUE LUG PAT
BUTT FAIR FEAT FORK HARP
JUMP JUST KIND MEET CLEAT
HAPPY QUEME WORTH BECOME
CLENCH CLEVIS LEADER PROPER
SADDLE SEEMLY WASHER
ADAPTER CONGRUE PENDANT
SERVING SHACKLE SUCTION
TACTFUL CONDULET DECOROUS
GRACEFUL RIGHTFUL SUITABLE
RECEPTACLE
(— TIGHTLY) CLOSE
(PIPE —) CROSS ELBOW
(PL.) BRASS COVER REPAREL
FITMENTS
FIVE CINQ FUNF CINQUE EPSILON
QUINQUE
(— CENTS) JITNEY NICKEL
(— HUNDRED DOLLARS, POUNDS)
MONKEY
(— IN CRAPS) PHOEBE
(— OF TRUMPS) PEDRO
(— YEARS) LUSTRUM
(TWO —S) QUINAS
(PREF.) CINQUE LEPT(O)
PEN(T)(TA)(TH) QUINQU(E)
FIVES BALL SNACK
FIVESTONES SNOBS
FIX BOX JAM PEG PIN SET CLEW
CLUE FAST FIRM GAFF GLUE
HOLD HOLE JAMB LOCK MEND
MOOR NAIL PICK RELY SEAL SPOT
STAY AFFIX ALLOT DEFIX FOUND
GRAFT GRAVE IMBED INFIX LIMIT
PLACE PLANT POINT POSIT SEIZE
STATE STEEK STELL STICK TRYST
ADJUST ANCHOR ARREST ASSIGN
ASSIZE ATTACH CEMENT CLINCH
DEFINE ENROOT ENTAIL FASTEN
FICCHE FIXATE FREEZE GROUND
IMPALE REPAIR REVAMP SETTLE
SQUARE TEMPER APPOINT
ARRANGE CALCIFY CONFIRM
DELIMIT DESTINE DILEMMA
GRAPPLE IMPLANT IMPRESS
IMPRINT PREPARE STATION
PINPOINT RENOVATE TRANSFIX
(— AMOUNT) AFFEER
(— ATTENTION) NAIL
(— FIRMLY) SEAL FREEZE IMPACT
INCUBE RAMPIRE
(— PRICE) ASSIZE CHARGE SETTLE
(— UPON) CHAP AFFIX
FIXATION FETICH FETISH
(SUFF.) PAGUS PEXIA PEXIS PEXY
FIXATIVE FIXER SKATOLE
AMBRETTE EUDESMOL
HYRACEUM LABDANUM
FIXED PAT PUT SAD SET SOT FAST
FIRM FLAT HARD GIVEN SIKER

STAID UPSET FINITE FROZEN
INTENT MENDED SICKER STABLE
STATED STEADY STRONG
CERTAIN DORMANT EMPIGHT
HABITED LIMITED SETTLED
SITFAST STATARY STATIVE
STELLED ACCURATE ARRANGED
ATTACHED CONSTANT DEFINITE
EXPLICIT FASTENED IMMOBILE
IRONCLAD MOVELESS RESIDENT
RESOLUTE STANDING STUBBORN
(NOT —) FLUID SHIFTY FUGITIVE
(PREF.) APLANO
FIXEDLY SAD FAST FIRM FIXLY
INTENTLY
FIXEDNESS FASTNESS
FIXER PATCH
FIXTURE ANNEX EVENT GUARD
FAUCET SHIELD BRACKET
CREEPER KNOCKER THIMBLE
(LIGHTING —) SCONCE
(STORE —) GONDOLA
FIZZING FIZZY GASSING
FIZZLE FLOP FUSS BARNEY
FAILURE FLIVVER
FLABBINESS MYATONIA
FLABBY LAX FOZY LASH LIMP
WEAK BAGGY FLASH FOGGY
FRUSH SAPPY WOOZY CASHIE
DOUGHY FEEBLE FLAGGY FLAPPY
LIMBER QUAGGY WATERY
FLACCID YIELDING
FLABELLUM RHIPIDION
FLACCID LIMP WOOZY FLABBY
FLAGGY EMARCID FLACKED
YIELDING
FLAG FAG LAG SAG SOD FAIL FANE
FLAT HOOK JACK JADE LECK PINE
TURF WAFT WAIF WILT CREST
DROOP FAINT FLAKE SEDGE
SLAKE UNION VEXIL WHEFT
WHIFF BANNER BOUGEE BURGEE
COLORS CORNET EMBLEM ENSIGN
FANION GUIDON LEVERS PENCEL
PENNON SIGNAL TABARD WIMPLE
ANCIENT BEEWORT CALAMUS
CATTAIL CURTAIN DECLINE
DRAPEAU FANACLE LABARUM
PENDANT PENNANT SCOURGE
BANDEROL BRATTACH GONFALON
HANDFLAG LANGUISH PAVILION
STANDARD STREAMER TRICOLOR
VEXILLUM WATCHMAN
(— CORNER) UNION
(— OF DENMARK) DANEBROG
(— OF TRANSVAAL) VIERKLEUR
(— OF TRUCE) KARTEL
(— OF U.S.) GRIDIRON
(— ON LANCE) PAVON
(BLUE — WITH WHITE SQUARE)
PETER
(CAVALRY —) STANDARD
(KNOTTED —) WAFT
(PIRATE —) ROGER BLACKJACK
(SERPENT-LIKE —) DRACO ANGUIS
(SHIP'S —) DUSTER
(TURKISH —) ALEM
(WATER —) SAG
(PL.) BUNTING
FLAG BEARER GUIDON ANCIENT
FLAGELLANT WHIPPER SCOURGER
(PL.) ALBI
FLAGELLATE MONAS NOCTILUCA

FLAGELLUM WHIP CILIUM
RUNNER KONSEAL WHIPLASH
(PREF.) BLEPHAR(O) MASTIG(O)
(SUFF.) KONT
FLAGEOLET PIPE ZUFOLO BASAREE
LARIGOT SIBILUS ZUFFOLO
MONAULOS
FLAGGING WEAK LANGUID
FLAGITIOUS WICKED CORRUPT
HEINOUS CRIMINAL FLAGRANT
GRIEVOUS
FLAGON GUN STOUP BOTTLE
VESSEL FLACKET FLAGONET
REHOBOAM
FLAGRANT BAD RED RANK GROSS
ODIOUS STRONG WANTON
WICKED BLATANT GLARING
HATEFUL HEINOUS SCARLET
VIOLENT SHAMEFUL
FLAGSHIP FLAG ADMIRAL
FLAGSTONE FLAG LECK SLAB
FAVUS
FLAIL BEAT FLOG WHIP DRASH
FRAIL THRAIL THRASH THRESH
SWINGLE SWIPPLE STRICKLE
THRESHEL
FLAIR RAY BENT NOSE ODOR
SMELL GENIUS LEANING
FLAKE CHIP FILM FLAG FLAW RACK
SNOW FLANK FLECK FLOCK
LAMIN SCALE SLATE SPALL
SPAWL STRIP APHTHA HURDLE
LAMINA PALING FLAUGHT
SHAVING FLOCCULE FRAGMENT
(— OF METAL) FLITTER
(— OF SNOW) FLAG
(PREF.) LEPID(O)
(SUFF.) LEPIS
FLAKY SCALY SHIVERY
FLAMBE JUBILEE
FLAMBEAU TORCH
FLAMBOYANCE BLARE PANACHE
FLAMBOYANT BAROCK FLORID
GARISH ORNATE BAROQUE
BUCKEYE FLAMING GORGEOUS
FLAME LOW FIRE GLOW LOWE
LUNT ARDOR BLAZE FLARE FLASH
GLARE GLEED INGLE LIGHT
RESEPH TONGUE BURNING
FLAMELET INKINDLE
(ACETYLENE —) CALCIUM
(SMALL —) SPUNK FLAMELET
FLAMMULE
(PL.) GLEED
FLAME SCARLET FLORENTINE
FLAME TREE KURRAJONG
FLAMING LIVE AFIRE FIERY FLAMY
VIVID AFLARE ARDENT BLAZING
BURNING FLARING FLAGRANT
FLAMMA, LA (CHARACTER IN —)
AGNES CERVIA BASILIO DONELLO
SILVANA
(COMPOSER OF —) RESPIGHI
FLAN PLANCHET
FLANGE BEAD BOSS BEZEL COLLAR
COLLET FLANCH SHROUD
FEATHER DUCKBILL FOLLOWER
(— OF GIRDER) BOOM
(WITHOUT —) BALD
FLANGER FLAYER GOUGER
FLANK LEER LISK SIDE WING
CHEEK SKIRT THIGH BORDER
FLITCH

(PREF.) LAPAR(O)
FLANNEL LANA DOMETT SAXONY
STAMIN WHITTLE MOLLETON
SWANSKIN
FLAP FAN LUG ROB TAB TAG TAP
WAP BATE BEAT BLOW CLAP FLIP
FLOG FLOP GILL LOBE LOMA
SLAM SLAT WAFF WELT ALARM
APRON FLACK FLAFF FLICK
BALLUP BANGLE LAPPET LIBBET
STRIKE TONGUE WAFFLE WALLOP
WINNOW AILERON BLINDER
CLICKET FLACKER FLAPPET
FLICKER FLOUNCE FLUTTER
SWINDLE VALANCE AVENTAIL
BACKFLAP COATTAIL CODPIECE
TURNOVER AGITATION
COMMOTION CONFUSION
(— OF BOOTEE) FLY
(— OF GARMENT) LAP
(— OF HAT OR CAP) VALANCE
(— OF HINGE) LEAF
(— ON HOLSTER) FLOUNCE
(— ON SADDLE) SKIRT JOCKEY
(— VIOLENTLY) FLOG SLAT
(CARDIAC —) CUSP
(FLESHY —) GILL
(MUD —) BOOT
(TROUSERS' —) FALL
FLAPPER FLAP FLOPPER SNICKET
FLAPPING WAFF WHUTTER
FLARE BELL FLUE BLAZE FLAME
FLASH FLECK FUSEE LIGHT SPIRT
TORCH FLANCH SIGNAL SPREAD
FLICKER TRUMPET OUTBURST
(— ON SHIPBOARD) DUCK
(— UP) KINDLE
FLARING BELL FLUE EVASE GAUDY
AFLARE FLAMING GLARING
SWAGGER BOUFFANT DAZZLING
FLASH DOT BEAT DASH LAIT LAMP
LASH LEAM POOL SHOT STAB
WINK BLASH BLAZE BURST FLAME
FLARE FLOSH FLUFF GLADE GLAIK
GLEAM GLENT GLINT LEVIN
MARSH SPARK STEAM BOTTLE
FILLIP GLANCE QUIVER BLUETTE
FLAUGHT FOULDRE GLIMMER
GLIMPSE GLISTEN GLITTER
INSTANT LIGHTEN QUICKEN
SHIMMER SPARKLE TWINKLE
SPLINTER SUNBURST CORUSCATE
SCINTILLATION
(— FORTH) OUTRAY
(HOT —) FLUSHING
(NEWS —) FUDGE
FLASHBACK THROWBACK
FLASHING CURB FLASH STEEP
ARDENT BRIGHT FLASHY
FORWARD LAMPING SHINING
CREASING METEORIC SLASHING
SNAPPING
FLASHLIGHT BUG GLIM FLASH
TORCH PENLITE PENLIGHT
FLASHY GAY FLAT GAUD LOUD
BAVIN FIERY GAUDY NOBBY
SHOWY SLEEK FLOSSY FROTHY
GARISH SLANGY SPORTY STUNTY
INSIPID RAFFISH TINHORN
DAZZLING FLASHING SPORTING
TIGERISH VEHEMENT
FLASK BOX PIG BODY HEAD HELM
JACK OLPE SNAP BETTY BULGE

FRAME GIRBA GOURD BOTTLE
FIASCO FLACON GUTTUS HELMET
LAGENA AMPULLA BOMBOLA
CANTEEN FLASKET MATRASS
TICKLER WARBURG CHRISMAL
CUCURBIT
(POCKET —) TICKLER
(PREF.) OLPIDI
FLAT DEAD DOWD DULL EVEN
FADE FLUE PLAT SLOB TAME
ABODE AFLAT BANAL BLAND
BLUNT DUSTY HAUGH LEVEL
MOLLE MUSTY PLAIN PLANE
PRONE ROOMS SEBKA SLAKE
VAPID WALSH AGRUFE BORING
CALLOW DREARY FLASHY JEJUNE
LEADEN PLANAR QUATCH
SEBKHA SILENT SIMOUS DECIDED
FLIPPER INSIPID INSULSE
PLATOID PROSAIC SHILPIT
TABULAR UNIFORM DIRECTLY
LIFELESS UNBROKEN WATERISH
CHAMPAIGN POINTLESS
PROSTRATE
(— AND CIRCULAR) DISCOID
(— AND SHORT) CAMUS CAMUSE
(— IN MUSIC) BEMOL MOLLE
(— OF SWORD) PLAT
(MUD —) SLOB SLAKE CORCASS
(NOT —) BRISK
(SALT —) SALINA
(THEATRICAL —) JOG
(PREF.) PLAN(I) PLAT(Y)
FLATBOAT ARK SCOW PULLBOAT
FLATCAR FLAT IDLER LORRY
(ON A —) PIGGYBACK
FLATFISH DAB RAY BUTT DACE
KITE SLIP SOLE TONG BREAM
BRILL FLUKE QUIFF RHINA WHIFF
ACEDIA CARTER PLAICE TURBOT
HALIBUT SUNFISH TORPEDO
FLOUNDER MARYSOLE
FLATHEAD SALISH
FLATIRON IRON GOOSE STEEL
SADIRON
FLATLY
(PREF.) PLANO
FLATNESS BATHOS SILENCE
EVENNESS KURTOSIS
(— OF NOSE) SIMITY
FLAT-NOSED CAMUS
FLATTEN BEAT COMB DECK EVEN
PLAT CRUSH LEVEL PLUSH SPLAT
BEETLE CLINCH DEJECT SMOOTH
SPREAD SQUASH DEPRESS
EXPLAIN PANCAKE PLANISH
SUBSIDE SURBASE COMPRESS
DISPIRIT
FLATTENED ECRASE OBLATE
DILATED PLANATE TABULAR
FLATTER BULL CLAW COAX DAUB
FAGE FUME PALP SOAP WORD
CHARM FLOAT GLOZE HONEY
PAINT ROOSE SLEEK SMALM
BECOME BUTTER CAJOLE CRINGE
FICKLE FLEECH FRAISE GLAVER
KITTLE PEPPER PHRASE SAWDER
SLAVER SMOOGE SOOTHE STROKE
ADULATE BEGUILE BEHONEY
BLARNEY FLETHER FLUTTER
INCENSE PALAVER SOOTHER
SWEETEN WHEEDLE BESLAVER
BLANDISH BOOTLICK COLLOGUE

FLATTERER FLOIT COGGER DAUBER EARWIG GLOZER JENKINS PRONEUR SOOTHER BOOTLICK CLAWBACK COURTIER DAMOCLES INCENSER LOSENGER SLAVERER SMOOTHER

FLATTERING SOAPY SMARMY SMOOTH BUTTERY CANDIED COURTLY GLAVERING

FLATTERY BULL BUNK DAUB FLUM MUSH SOAP FRAIK GLOZE SALVE TAFFY BUTTER CARNEY FLEECH GREASE PHRASE SAWDER SLAVER BLARNEY DAUBING EYEWASH FAWNING FLETHER INCENSE PALAVER CAJOLERY ADULATION

FLATULENCE WIND VAPOR

FLATULENT GASSY WINDY TURGID POMPOUS VENTOSE FLATUOUS INFLATED

FLATWARE SILVER

FLATWORM ACOEL FLUKE PLATODE RADIATE POLYCLAD

FLAUNT BOSH SHOW WAVE BOAST SKYRE STOUT VAUNT PARADE DISPLAY FLUTTER TRAIPSE BRANDISH FLOURISH

FLAUNTING GAUDY PURPLE SKYRIN FLAGGERY

FLAVONE CHROMONE

FLAVOR GAMY GOUT MASK ODOR RASA SALT TANG ZEST AROMA ASSAI CURRY DEVIL SAPID SAPOR SAUCE SAVOR SCENT SMACK SPICE TASTE TINGE ASARUM ASSAHY INFUSE RANCIO RELISH SEASON TARAGE FLAVOUR PERFUME SUPTION HAUTGOUT PIQUANCY
(HIGH —) HOGO
(SPECIAL —) GUST
(UNPLEASANT —) TACK

FLAVORED SPICY TINCT SPICED

FLAVORFUL SAVOROUS

FLAVORING DIP ALMOND CASSIS MIREPOIS

FLAVORLESS BLAND STALE SILENT WATERISH

FLAW BUG FIB GAP LIE MAR RUB WEM BANE BLOT CHIP FLEE GALL HOLE RASE RIFT SPOT WIND BOTCH BRACK BURST CHICK CLEFT CRACK CRAZE FAULT FLAKE PLUME SPECK BLOTCH BREACH DEFECT FOIBLE LACUNA LESION BLEMISH BLISTER DEFAULT EYELAST FEATHER FISSURE NULLIFY SUNSPOT VIOLATE WHITLOW FRACTURE FRAGMENT GENDARME WINDFLAW
(— IN CASTING) BUCKLE
(— IN CLOTH) BRACK
(— IN DIAMOND) GENDARME
(— IN MARBLE) TERRACE
(— IN METAL) SNAKE
(— IN PRECIOUS STONE) FEATHER
(— IN STEEL) STAR
(— IN STONE) DRY
(— IN WICK) THIEF
(MORAL —) SMIRCH

FLAWED CRACKED

FLAWLESS CLEAN

SOUND PERFECT

FLAX LIN POB TOW CARD FLIX HARL LINE LINT ROCK GRAIN HURDS BREADS BYSSUS KORARI PEANUT PEBBLE SCUTCH LINSEED FLAXWORT HARAKEKE
(— DISEASE) PASMO
(PREF.) BYSSI BYSSO LINO

FLAXEN FLAXY BLONDE

FLAXWEED TOADFLAX

FLAY SKIN SCULP STRIP FLEECE UNCASE CENSURE PILLAGE REPROVE SCARIFY

FLEA LOP SCUD FLECH FLECK PULEX TUNGA CHEGRE CHIGOE VERMIN PULICID SANDBOY
(— INFESTED) PULICOSE
(PREF.) PULI

FLEABANE SKEVISH SCABIOUS WHITETOP

FLEA BEETLE THRIPS

FLEAM BEVEL

FLEAWORT CAMMOCK FLEASEED PSYLLIUM

FLECHE SPIRELET

FLECK FLAKE FREAK DAPPLE FLEECE POUNCE STREAK STIPPLE

FLEDERMAUS, DIE (CHARACTER IN —) ADELE FALKE FRANK ALFRED ORLOFSKY ROSALINDE EISENSTEIN
(COMPOSER OF —) STRAUSS

FLEDGED FLUSH FLIGGED

FLEDGLING SQUAB NESTER FLIGGER BIRDLING

FLEE FLY LAM RUN BOLT FLEG LOUP SCUR SHUN TURN ELOPE ELUDE SKIRR SPEED ESCAPE VANISH ABANDON ABSCOND FORSAKE SCAMPER LIBERATE SKEDADDLE
(SUFF.) FUGAL FUGE

FLEECE JIB KET TEG BUCK CAST FELL GAFF MORT PLOT ROOK SKIN TEGG TEGS FLICK PASHM PLOAT SHAVE SHEAR SHEEP SWEAT PASHIM PIGEON PUSHUM TOISON SHEARING
(— OF MEDIUM GRADE) SUPER
(POOREST PART OF —) ABB

FLEEING FUGIENT HOTFOOT RUNNING FUGITIVE

FLEER GIBE JIBE LEER FLIRE FLOUT SCOFF SNEER

FLEET BAY FAST FLIT NAVY SAIL SKIM SWIM CREEK DRAIN DRIFT EVAND FLOAT FLOTA HASTY INLET POWER QUICK RAPID SWIFT ARGOSY ARMADA FLIGHT HASTEN NIMBLE SPEEDY CARAVAN COMPANY FLOTILLA NAVARCHY WARCRAFT

FLEETING BRIEF BUBBLE CADUCE FLYING VOLAGE CURSIVE FLIGHTY PASSING POSTING SHADOWY VOLATIC CADUCOUS FUGITIVE VOLATILE

FLESH KIN BEEF BODY FELL GAME LAMB LIRE MEAT RACE WEED SLATE STOCK FAMILY MUSCLE SEASON CARNAGE KINDRED MANKIND NATURAL HUMANITY MOONLIGHT

(— ABOUT CHIN AND JAWS) GILL
(— OF CALF) SLINK
(— OF GOAT) CHEVON
(— OF KID) CABRITO
(— OF SHEEP) TRAIK
(— ON LOWER JAW) CHOLLER
(— OUT) CLOTHE
(— UNDER SKIN) FELL
(ANIMAL —) BRAWN
(DEAD —) MURRAIN
(HORSE —) JACK
(LIFELESS —) MUMMY
(PUTREFYING —) CARRION
(SUN-DRIED —) TAPA
(SUPERFLUOUS —) LUMBER
(PREF.) CARNI CRE(O) CREATO KRE(O) SARC(O)
(SUFF.) SARC

FLESHBRUSH STRIGIL

FLESH-COLORED SARCOLINE

FLESHER LINING

FLESHINESS FULLNESS CORPULENCE

FLESHLY CARNAL FLESHY SENSUAL SARKICAL

FLESHY FAT BEEFY LUSTY OBESE PLUMP PULPY STOUT ANIMAL BODILY BRAWNY CARNAL BUNTING CARNOSE SARCOUS CARNEOUS

FLETCH WING FLIGHT

FLEUR-DE-LIS LIS LYS LILY LUCY FLEUR

FLEX BEND

FLEXED PENCHE

FLEXIBILITY WHIP FLUIDITY

FLEXIBLE LIMP LUSH SOFT BUXOM LIMSY LITHE WANDY WITHY FLOPPY LIMBER LITHER PLIANT SUPPLE DUCTILE ELASTIC FINGENT FLEXILE FLEXIVE LISSOME PLIABLE SPRINGY WILLOWY WINDING WRIGGLE BENDSOME YIELDING
(PREF.) CAMPTO

FLEXURE ARCH BEND BENT CURL FOLD CURVE TWIST SIGMOID WINDING

FLICK FILM FLIP CLICK FLACK FLANK FLECK FLIRT FLISK MOVIE CINEMA

FLICKER FAIL FLIT LICK WINK BLINK FLAME FLARE FLICK FLUNK WAVER BICKER FITTER SHIVER YUCKER BLINTER FLIMMER FLITTER FLUTTER SKIMMER TREMBLE TWINKLE WHIFFLE FLICHTER HIGHHOLE

FLICKERING FLICKY FLUTTER LAMBENT FLEXUOUS UNSTEADY

FLICKERTAIL STATE NORTHDAKOTA

FLIER ACE BIRD KIWI FLYER PILOT AIRMAN AVIATOR

FLIGHT FLY GUY HOP LAM BOLT BUNK LAKE PAIR ROUT WING CHEVY FLOCK GLIDE GRICE SCRAP VOLEE CHIVVY EXODUS FUGACY HEGIRA HEJIRA JOYHOP SPIRAL BOUQUET EVASION FLAUGHT FLYOVER MIGRATE MISSION SCAMPER STEPWAY REGIFUGE STAMPEDE SWARMING

(— OF BALL) HOOK DRIVE SLICE
(— OF BIRDS) VOLARY VOLERY VOLLEY
(— OF FANCY) SALLY
(— OF GEESE) SKEIN
(— OF SNIPE) WISP
(— OF STEPS) RISE TRAP GRECE PITCH SCALE STOOP PERRON STAIRS STEPWAY STAIRWAY
(— OF WILD FOWL) SKEIN
(— OF WOODCOCK) RODING
(ABORTIVE —) ABORT
(HASTY —) TIFT
(HAWK'S —) CAREER
(HIGH —) TOWER
(IN —) ALOFT
(SUDDEN —) START STAMPEDE
(UNAUTHORIZED —) BUGOUT
(UPWARD —) SOAR
(SUFF.) FUGAL FUGE PHOBE PHOBI(A)(AC)(C) PHOBUS

FLIGHTY ANILE BARMY GIDDY LIGHT SWIFT FITFUL GARISH UNFIRM VOLAGE WHISKY FLYAWAY FOOLISH GIGGISH MOONISH ROCKETY FLEETING FREAKISH HELLICAT
(— PERSON) TRIVVET

FLIMSINESS INANITY

FLIMSY LIMP THIN VAIN WEAK FRAIL GAUDY JERRY FEEBLE PALTRY SLEAZY SLIGHT SLIMSY HAYWIRE SHALLOW TENUOUS TIFFANY GIMCRACK GOSSAMER JIMCRACK TWITTERY

FLINCH FUNK GAME JARG BLUNK BUDGE FEIGN QUAIL SHUNT START WINCE WONDE BLANCH BLENCH FALTER FLENSE RECOIL SHRINK SCRINGE SCUNNER SQUINCH

FLINCHER VELLINCH

FLINDER FLITTER SMITHERS

FLINDERSIA SILKWOOD

FLINDOSA CUDGERIE

FLING SHY BUZZ CAST DART DASH DING EMIT FLAP FLEG GIBE HURL KICK LASH PECK PICK SLAT TOSS WARP BRAID CHEAT DANCE FLIRT LANCE PITCH SHOOT SLING SNEER SWING THROW WHANG BAFFLE EFFUSE HURTLE LAUNCH PLUNGE REBUFF SPIRIT ENFORCE FLOUNCE REPULSE SARCASM SCATTER SWINDLE SHYLANCE SPANGHEW
(— MISSILES) CHUNK
(— UPWARD) HAUNCH
(HIGHLAND —) WALLOCH

FLINT CORE BLANK CHERT MISER SILEX EOLITH QUARTZ REJECT ESLABON FURISON SCRAPER GRATTOIR GUNFLINT
(PREF.) SILICEO SILICI SILICO

FLINTINESS HEART

FLINTLOCK FUSEE FUSIL FUZEE MUSKET SPANNER FIRELOCK MIQUELET SNAPHAAN

FLINTWOOD WHITETOP

FLIP SKY TAP FLAP SNAP TOSS TRIP FLANK FLICK FLIRT SLIRT SMART FILLIP FLITCH LIMBER NIMBLE PLIANT PROPEL

FLIPPANT AIRY FLIP GLIB FLUENT LIMBER NIMBLE
FLIPPER ARM FIN PAW HAND SWELL PADDLE FLAPPER SPRINGER
FLIRT TOY FIKE FLIP MASH TICK VAMP FLICK ROVER SLIRT JILLET MASHER TRIFLE GALLANT PICKEER TWINKLE COQUETTE PHILANDER
FLIRTATION FIKE PASSADE COQUETRY PHILANDER
FLIT DART FLOW SCUD FLECK FLEET FLICK FLIRT FLOAT FLURR HOVER QUICK SCOOT SKIFF SWIFT NIMBLE FLICKER FLUTTER
FLITCH FLICK GAMMON LONGWOOD MIDDLING
FLOAT BOB FLY KIT SEA BOOM BUOY CORK DRAG FLOW FLUX HAWK HONE HOVE LIVE PONT RAFT RIDE SAIL SCOW SOAR SWIM TILT WAFT WAVE BALSA BLADE CAMEL DERBY DRIFT DRIVE FLEET FLOOD FLUSH GRAIL HOVER LADLE QUILL SHOAD SWOON BILLOW BOBBER BUCKET BUNGEY CANNEL DOBBER PADDLE PONTON RADEAU STREEL TOPPER CAISSON DRINGLE FLATTER FLOTTER FRESHEN OROPESA PAGEANT PLANKER PLUMMET PONTOON SLICKER LEVITATE PICKOVER
(— AIMLESSLY) DRIFT
(— DELIGHTFULLY) COWD
(— FOR HERRING NET) BOWL
(— FOR RING BUOY) LEMON
(— LOGS) DRIVE
(— OF REEDS) KELEK LIGGER
(— PAST) GLACE
(— PROPERLY) WATCH
(CANOE —) AMA
(FISHLINE —) BOB CORK BOBBER DOBBER TRIMMER
(PLASTERER'S —) DARBY
FLOATBOARD BLADE FLOAT LADLE
FLOATER STIFF
FLOATING FREE WAFT AWASH LOOSE ADRIFT AFLOAT FLYING NATANT BUOYANT FLYAWAY PENDENT DRIFTING FLUITANT SHIFTING UNFUNDED
FLOCCILATION TILMUS
FLOCK MOB POD BAND BANK BEVY FOLD GAME GANG HERD MANY PACK ROUT SAIL SORT TEAM TRIP WISP BROOD BUNCH CHARM COVEY CROWD DRIFT DROVE FLAKE FLECK GROUP PLUMP SEDGE SHOAL SWARM TRIBE TROOP COVERT FLIGHT GAGGLE HIRSEL MANADA MEINIE RAFTER SCHOOL SCURRY VOLERY COMPANY GOOSERY THICKEN PADDLING
(— OF BIRDS) POD BANK HERD TEAM WISP BROWN COVEY SEDGE SIEGE TRIBE FLIGHT VOLERY
(— OF BITTERNS) SEDGE SIEGE
(— OF DUCKS) PADDLING

(— OF FINCHES) CHARM CHIRM
(— OF GEESE) SKEIN GAGGLE
(— OF HERONS) SEDGE SIEGE
(— OF LARKS) EXALTATION
(— OF LIONS) PRIDE
(— OF MALLARDS) SORD SUTE
(— OF NIGHTINGALES) WATCH
(— OF PARTRIDGE) COVEY
(— OF PEACOCKS) MUSTER
(— OF PIGEONS) KIT LOFT
(— OF PLOVER) WING
(— OF ROOKS) ROOKERY
(— OF SANDPIPERS) FLING
(— OF SHEEP) FOLD HIRSEL
(— OF SHELDRAKE) DOPPING
(— OF SNIPE) WISP
(— OF SWANS) BANK GAME MARK
(— OF TURTLE-DOVES) DOLE
(— OF WIDGEONS) COMPANY
(— OF WILDFOWL) SCRY SKEIN
(— TOGETHER) RAFT
(SMALL —) SPRING
(PREF.) **(— OF WOOL)** FLOCCI
FLOCKING REPAIR
FLOE PAN
FLOG CAT TAN TAW BEAT CANE CHOP HIDE LASH LICK LUMP TOCO WALE WARM WELK WHIP YANK BIRCH EXCEL FIGHT FLAIL HORSE KNOUT LINGE QUILT SAUCE SKEEG SWISH WHANG BREECH COTTON LARRUP LATHER STRIKE SWITCH THRASH WALLOP WATTLE BALEISE BELABOR COWHIDE SCOURGE SJAMBOK TROUNCE CARTWHIP CHAWBUCK SLAISTER URTICATE VAPULATE
(— WATER) SCRINGE
FLOGGER HORSING SWISHER
FLOGGING TOCO TOKO TANNING BIRCHING WHIPPING
FLOOD SEA BORE BUOY FLOW FLUX POUR TIDE EAGRE FLOAT FLUSH SPATE SWAMP SWILL WATER DELUGE EXCESS RAVINE SLUICE SPLASH DEBACLE FLOTTER FRESHET NIAGARA TORRENT ALLUVION CATARACT INUNDATE OVERFLOW SURROUND
FLOODED AWASH AFLOAT
FLOODGATE CLOW DRAG GOLE HATCH SLUICE STAUNCH CATARACT PENSTOCK
FLOODING UP PROUD FLOWAGE DILUVIAL FLOATING
FLOODLIGHT OLIVET
FLOODPLAIN BENCH DAMBO
FLOOR BECK DROP FLAT LAND LOFT PAVE SEAT BOARD FLOAT GRASS PIANO PIECE SOLAR STAGE STORY BELFRY FLIGHT GROUND SOLLAR PLANCHE BARBECUE FLOORING HALFPACE PAVEMENT SUBFLOOR
(— OF COAL MINE) SOLE THILL
(— OF COAL SEAM) SILL
(— OF FORGE) HEARTH
(— OF GLASS FURNACE) SIEGE
(— OF OCEAN) SEABED
(— OF SPORTS RING) CANVAS
(— OF WOOLSHED) BOARD
(FOREST —) SEEDBED

(GROUND —) TERRENO BASEMENT
(OPENWORK —S) GRATINGS
(RAISED —) LEEWAN HALFPACE
(THRESHING —) MOWSTEAD
FLOORBOARD FOOTLING
(BOAT'S —) BURDEN
FLOORING STAGE PARQUET TERRAZZO
FLOORMAN CALLBOY
FLOP DOG BOMB SWOP WHOP SQUAB BUMMER TURKEY TRAGEDY
FLORA CYBELE FLORULA
(— AND FAUNA) BIOTA
FLORAL TREE LEAF
FLORENCE FLASK BETTY
FLORENCE IRIS ORRIS TREOS
FLORESTAN (WIFE OF —) LEONORA
FLORID FINE HIGH BUXOM FRESH RUDDY ORNATE ROCOCO RUBIED ASIATIC FLOWERY TAFFETA BLOOMING FIGURATE RUBICUND SANGUINE SPLENDID VIGOROUS

FLORIDA
BAY: BISCAYNE APALACHEE WACCASASSA
CAPITAL: TALLAHASSEE
COLLEGE: ROLLINS
COUNTY: BAY LEE DADE GULF LEON POLK BAKER DIXIE HARDEE HENDRY NASSAU ORANGE ALACHUA BREVARD BROWARD MANATEE OSCEOLA VOLUSIA PINELLAS SARASOTA
INDIAN: AIS OCALE UTINA CALUSA CHATOT POTANO TIMUCUA SEMINOLE
ISLANDS: KEYS
KEY: WEST LARGO BISCAYNE
LAKE: DORA APOPKA HARNEY JESSUP NEWNAN LEDWITH ARBUCKLE KISSIMMEE OKEECHOBEE
NATIVE: CONCH CRACKER
RIVER: BANANA INDIAN AUCILLA MANATEE SCAMBIA SUWANEE OCHLAWAHA
STATE BIRD: MOCKINGBIRD
STATE NICKNAME: SUNSHINE
STATE TREE: PALMETTO
TOWN: TICE COCOA MIAMI OCALA TAMPA ORLANDO PALATKA SEBRING SARASOTA PENSACOLA
UNIVERSITY: STETSON
WETLANDS: GLADES

FLORIDIAN CRACKER
FLORIMEL (HUSBAND OF —) MARINEL
FLORIPES (BROTHER OF —) FIERABRAS
(HUSBAND OF —) GUY
FLOSS FLUFF SKEIN WASTE CADDIS SLEAVE CADDICE
FLOSSER FANNER
FLOSS-SILK TREE SAMOHU
FLOTSAM JETSAM WILSAM WAFTURE WAVESON DRIFTAGE FLOATAGE
FLOUNCE FLAP HUFF SKIT SLAM FLING FRILL RUCHE PEPLUM

RIPPLE ROBING ROUNCE RUFFLE VOLANT FALBALA FALBELO FROUNCE RUCHING FLOUNDER FURBELOW STRUGGLE
FLOUNDER DAB GAD BUTT KEEL POLE ROLL TOSS BREAM FLUKE SLOSH WITCH WRELE GADOID GROVEL MEGRIM MUDDLE PLAICE TOLTER TURBOT WALLOP WALLOW WARSLE BLUNDER FLASKER FLOUNCE PLOUNCE STUMBLE SUNFISH TOPKNOT VAAGMAR ANACANTH FLATFISH FOOLFISH PLUNTHER SANDLING
FLOUR AMYL ATTA DUST CONES HOVIS BINDER CLEARS FARINA FLOWER PATENT POLLEN SICKEN TSAMBA WHITES BOXINGS BRAVURA CRIBBLE CANAILLE
(— OF MALT) SMEDDUM
(COARSE —) THIRD CHISEL BOXINGS CRIBBLE
(FINE —) CONES SUJEE
(LOW-GRADE —) TAIL
(PARTICLE OF —) CHOP
(POTATO —) FROW
(UNSORTED —) ATTA
(PREF.) ALEURO
FLOURISH TAG WAG BOOM BRAG FUSS GROW LICK RIOT RISE SHOW TUCK WAVE ADORN BLOOM BOAST CHEVE GLOSS QUIRK REIGN SHAKE SWASH SWING SWISH TUSCH VAUNT CATTER PARADE PARAPH QUAVER SQUIRL THRIVE BLOSSOM BURGEON CADENZA DISPLAY ENLARGE FANFARE GAMBADE GAMBADO PASSAGE PROSPER ROULADE SUCCEED TRIUMPH WAMPISH ARPEGGIO BRANDISH CURLICUE INCREASE ORNAMENT SKIRMISH
(— OF BAGPIPE) WARBLER
(— OF TRUMPET) MORT SENNET TUCKET
FLOURISHING FAR FRIM FRUM PERT GREEN PALMY PEART VITAL BLOOMY FLORID GOLDEN FLORENT HEALTHY VERNANT THRIVING VEGETOUS PROSPEROUS
FLOURY MEALY
FLOUT BOB GIBE JEER JERK JIBE LOUT MOCK FLEER FLITE FRUMP SCOFF SCOMM SCORN SCOUT SNEER TAUNT DERIDE INSULT BETONGUE
FLOW GO EBB ERN JET PUT RUN SET SUE BORE COMB FLIT FLUX FUSE GUSH HALE LAVA LAVE MELT PASS POUR RAIL ROLL SEND SHED SILE SLIP SOAK SWIG TAIL TEEM TIDE WELL AVALE DRAIN DRIFT EAGRE EXUDE FLEAM FLEET FLOAT FLOOD FLUSH FRESH GLIDE ISSUE QUELL RIVER SCOOT SLIDE SPEND SPILL SPURT SWILL TRILL ABOUND AFFLUX COURSE CURSUS DELUGE GUGGLE GUTTER POPPLE RECEDE RINDLE SPRING STREAM CURRENT DEVOLVE DISTILL

DRIBBLE EMANATE FLOWAGE
FLUTTER FLUXION ILLAPSE
INDRAFT MEANDER SPURTLE
TRINKLE TRINTLE ALLUVION
BACKWASH CURRANCE
CURRENCY DOWNFLOW EMISSION
FOUNTAIN INUNDATE
(— **AGAINST**) LAP LAVE BATHE
(— **BACK**) EBB
(— **BEYOND BANKS**) DEBORD
SURROUND
(— **DOWN**) AVALE
(— **IN**) INFLOW INFLOOD
(— **IN RILLS**) DRILL
(— **IN RIVULETS**) GUTTER
(— **IN SPURTS**) SALTATION
(— **INTERMITTENTLY**) HEAD
(— **NOISILY**) BICKER
(— **OF AIR**) SIDEWASH
(— **OF ELECTRICITY**) BOLT
OSCILLATION
(— **OF METAL**) CREEP
(— **OF RADIO SIGNAL**) BEAM
(— **OF SOUNDS**) CADENCE
(— **OUT**) EMIT ISSUE EFFUSE
SPREAD EXHAUST RESOLVE
(— **OVER**) BERUN
(— **SLOWLY**) SEEP EXUDE GLEET
(— **TOGETHER**) CONCUR CONFLOW
(— **WITH**) FLEET
(**CONTINUOUS** —) LAPSE
(**COPIOUS** —) HALE RIVER
(**LAVA** —) COULE COULEE
(**RHYTHMICAL** —) LILT
(**TIDAL** —) BORE AEGIR EAGER
EAGRE
(PREF.) RHEO RHYSI
(SUFF.) FLUENCE FLUENT
FLUOUS FLUX RRHAGIA RRHEA
RRHOEA
FLOWER (ALSO SEE PLANT AND
HERB) BUD GAY BEST BLOW
FLAG IRIS IXIA PINK POLE POSY
ROSE ARROW ASTER BLOOM
BLUET BREAK DAISY ELITE FANCY
FLOOR GOWAN LILAC PANSY
PHLOX TRUSS TULIP TUTTY
AZALIA CHOICE CORYMB CROCUS
CYMULE DAHLIA DATURA FLORET
MAYPOP ORCHID SCILLA SEASON
SHOWER SINGLE STEVIA UNFOLD
AMELLUS ANEMONE ARBUTUS
BLETHIA BLOSSOM BOSTRYX
CAMPANA DEVELOP ESSENCE
FLEURET FLOSCLE GAZANIA
GENTIAN GERBERA IPOMOEA
PETUNIA PICOTEE TORENIA
BELAMOUR CAMELLIA CYCLAMEN
DAFFODIL DIANTHUS GARDENIA
GERANIUM HEPATICA HIBISCUS
HYACINTH PRIMROSE SPARAXIS
(— **STATE**) FLORIDA
(— **WITH 6 SEGMENTS**) SEXFOIL
(**COTTON** —) SQUARE
(**DEFORMED** —) BULLHEAD
(**DOUBLE** —) BURSTER
(**DRIED** —**S**) BRAYERA
(**IMAGINARY** —) AMARANTH
(**PART OF** —) OVARY PETAL SEPAL
STALK STYLE ANTHER PISTIL
STAMEN STIGMA PEDICEL
FILAMENT PEDUNCLE PERIANTH
RECEPTACLE

(**SHOWY** —) ORCHIS
(**STRIPED** —) BIZARRE
(**UNFADING** —) AMARANTH
(PL.) BOUQUET
(PREF.) ANTH(O) FLORI
(SUFF.) ANTHEMA ANTHEMUM
ANTHERA ANTHEROUS ANTHERY
ANTHES ANTHOUS ANTHUS
FLORAL FLOROUS
FLOWERFLY SYRPHID
FLOWERHEAD CALATHUS
FLOWERING AFLOWER FLOWERY
ANTHESIS BLOOMING
FLOWERING GLUME LEMMA
FLOWERLESS ANANTHOUS
FLOWER-OF-AN-HOUR SHOOFLY
FLOWER-PECKER KAKAWAHIE
FLOWERPOT POT CACHEPOT
FLOWERY BLOWN BLOOMY FLORID
POSIED FLORENT PRIMROSE
FLOWING FAIR FLUX LAVE SIDE
AFLOW FLOAT FLUID FLUOR
QUICK TIDAL AFFLUX DEFLUX
FLUENT FUSILE LIVING COPIOUS
CURRENT CURSIVE EMANANT
FLUXING FLUXION FLUXIVE
RUNNING SLIDING DEFLUENT
DILUENDO FLUVIOSE
(— **AT LOW SPEED**) SLACK
(— **BACK**) EBB
(— **IN**) INFLUX INFLUENT
INFLUXION
(— **OF GLAZE**) STREAMING
(— **OF TIDE**) FLOOD
(— **OUT**) ELAPSE EFFLUENT
(— **SMOOTHLY**) PROFLUENT
(PREF.) (— **OUT**) EFFLUVIO
FLOWOFF RUNOFF
FLUCAN SELVAGE SELVEDGE
FLUCTUATE SWAY VARY VEER
FLEET SWING WAVER BALANCE
VIBRATE WAMPISH UNDULATE
UNSTEADY VACILLATE
FLUCTUATING WAVY HECTIC
LABILE RUBATO ERRATIC FLUXIVE
WAYWARD UNSTABLE UNSTEADY
FLUCTUATION CYCLE FADING
JIGGLE FLICKER FLUTTER
VIBRATO OSCILLATION
(— **IN LAKES**) SEICHE
FLUE NET BARB DOWN OPEN PIPE
THIN VENT FLARE FLUFF FLUKE
TEWEL FUNNEL TUNNEL UPTAKE
CHIMNEY OUTTAKE PASSAGE
DOWNTAKE
FLUE-CURED BRIGHT
FLUENCY SKILL
FLUENT GASH GLIB FLUID READY
FACILE LIQUID SMOOTH STREAM
COPIOUS CURRENT FLOWING
FLUIDIC RENABLE VERBOSE
VOLUBLE ELOQUENT FLIPPANT
FLUFF FUG FLUE LINT OOZE PUFF
BEARD ERROR FLOSS WHEEL
MISTAKE
FLUFFING WHEELING
FLUFFY SOFT DOWNY DRUNK
FILMY FLUEY FUZZY LIGHT
LINTEN PLUFFY FEATHERY
UNSTEADY
(**NOT** —) CLOSE
FLUID INK SAP MASS RASA BLOOD
FLUOR HUMOR JUICE LATEX

SERUM SPERM SWEAT WATER
FLUENT LIQUID WATERY
COOLANT FLOWING FLUIBLE
FLUXILE GASEOUS SYNOVIA
EMULSION FLOATING FLUXIBLE
FORESHOT PERSPERATION
(**ANIMAL** —) SERUM
(**BODY** —) CHYLE
(**EAR** —) PERILYMPH
(**EGYPTIAN PRIMEVAL** —) NU NUN
(**ELECTRIC** —) VRIL
(**ETHEREAL** —) ICHOR
(**LIVER** —) BILE
(**LUBRICATING** —) SYNOVIA
(**MAMMARY** —) MILK
(**SOLDERING** —) FAKE
(**THICK VISCOUS** —) GRUME
(**WATERY** —) LYE SANIES SEROSITY
(**WORKING** —) AIR
(PREF.) SERO
FLUIDITY LENGTH
(— **UNIT**) RHE
FLUKE FLUE PALM BLADE GRASP
SCALE PLAICE DISTOME PLATODE
SCRATCH FLATWORM FLOUNDER
BILHARZIA
(— **OF ANCHOR**) HOOK KILLICK
(— **OF WHALE'S TAIL**) BLADE
FLUME CHUTE DITCH SHUTE
SLUICE
FLUMMERY SOWENS WASHBREW
FLUNK BUST FAIL SKEW SPIN
FLICKER
FLUNKY SNOB TOADY COOKEE
JEAMES LACKEY FOOTMAN
SERVANT STEWARD
FLUORESCENCE BLOOM
FLUORESCENT PSYCHEDELIC
FLUORINE PHTOR PHTHOR
FLUORITE CAND FLUX FLUOR
FLURRY ADO FIT FACT FRET GUST
PIRR SPIT STIR TEAR HASTE SKIFF
SKIRL BOTHER BUSTLE SCURRY
SQUALL CONFUSE FLUSKER
FLUSTER FLUTTER FOOSTER
SWITHER WHITHER SPITTING
FLUSH JET EVEN GLOW HUSH
JUMP POOL ROSE BLOOM BLUSH
COLOR ELATE FLASH FLUSK
FRESH KNOCK LEVEL RAISE
ROUGE SCOUR START VIGOR
AFLUSH EXCITE HECTIC LAVISH
MANTLE MORASS REDDEN
RUDDLE SLUICE SPRING THRILL
ANIMATE BOBTAIL CRIMSON
SUFFUSE ABUNDANT AFFLUENT
PRODIGAL ROSINESS
(— **GAME**) SERVE
(— **IN SKY**) SUNGLOW
(**NOT** —) FLAT
FLUSHED RED ROSY BEAMY FIERY
FLOWN FLORID FLUSHY HECTIC
CRIMSON RUBICUND
FLUSTER PAVIE SHAKE BOTHER
FLURRY FUDDLE MUDDLE
POTHER RATTLE CONFUSE
FLUSKER FOOSTER SWITHER
BEFUDDLE FLOWSTER FLUSTRUM
FLUTE NAY FIFE FUYE PIPE AULOS
CRIMP CUENA PUNGI QUENA
STICK STYKE TIBIA TWILL CANNEL
DOUCET FLAUTO GEWGAW
GOFFER POOGYE ZUFOLO

CHAMFER DIAULOS FLAMFEW
FLUTING GAUFFER HEMIOPE
MAGADIS MATALAN PICCOLO
SIBILUS SIFFLOT TONETTE
TRANGAM WHISTLE ZUFFOLO
FLAUTINO MONAULOS RECORDER
(— **OF A COLUMN**) STRIGA
CHANNEL
(— **STOP**) VENTAGE
(**CHINESE** —) TCHE
(**EAST INDIAN** —) MATALAN
(**EUNUCH** —) KAZOO
(**JAPANESE** —) FUYE SHAKUHACHI
(**LYDIAN** —) MAGADIS
(**MOSLEM** —) NAY
(**PHOENICIAN** —) GINGRAS
(PL.) NEHILOTH
(PREF.) AUL(O)
FLUTED QUILLED
FLUTEMOUTH CORNETFISH
FLUTE PLAYER AULETE FLUTER
FLUTIST TIBICEN TOOTLER
AULETRIS FLAUTIST
FLUTING STRIX FULLER GADROON
STRIGIL COULISSE QUILLING
FLUTTER BAT FAN FUG BATE
BLOW BUZZ FLAP FLIT FLOW
FLUE OOZE PLAY WAFF WAVE
FLACK FLAFF FLARE FLECK FLICK
FLOSS FLURR HOVER SHAKE
WAVER BANGLE FLAUNT FLURRY
RUFFLE SWIVET WAFFLE WALLOP
WINNOW FLACKER FLAFFER
FLASKER FLATTER FLAUGHT
FLICKER FLITTER FLUSKER
SKIMMER WAGTAIL WHIFFLE
FLICHTER SQUATTER VOLITATE
(**IN A** —) PITAPAT
FLUTTERING AWING FLITTY
WHUTTER AFLUTTER FLICKERY
FLUTTERINGLY PITAPAT
FLUTTER-TONGUING GROWL
FLUX FLOW FUSE LASK MELT
BORAX FLOAT FLOOD ISSUE
RESIN ROSIN SMEAR SMELT
FUSION CURRENT EURIPUS
FLOWING LEAKAGE OUTFLOW
(— **UNIT**) WEBER MAXWELL
FLY BEE FAG FAN GAD HOP RUN
FIRK FLEA FLEE FLEG FLIT FRIT
GNAT KITE KIVU LASH LEAP MELT
RACK RAKE SAIL SCUD SMUT
SOAR SOLO WHEW WHIR WHIZ
WIND WING ZIMB AGILE ALERT
EMPID FLEET FLIER FLOAT FLURR
FLUSH FLYER GLIDE LATCH
MIDGE MUSCA OXFLY PERLA
PHORA PILOT QUICK SEDGE
SHARP SKIRL SKIRR STOUR
WHAME WHIRR ZEBUB ASILID
AVIATE BANGLE BLOWER BOTFLY
BREEZE DAYFLY ESCAPE FLIGHT
FLYBOY GADFLY GORFLY JARFLY
LEPTID MOTUCA NIMBLE PALMER
PHORID PUNKIE RANDON ROBBER
SEPSID SEROOT SPRING TIPULA
TSETSE VANISH VERMIN WINNOW
AVIGATE AVOLATE BROMMER
CANOPID CHALCID CONOPID
FORMATE GRANNOM KNOWING
LOVEBUG ORTALID PYRALIS
SCIARID TYRPHID AIRPLANE
BIBIONID BRACONID COACHMAN

DIPTERAN DROPPING EPHYDRID
EULOPHID GLOSSINA HORSEFLY
HOUSEFLY RUBYTAIL SIMULIID
TACHINID TATUKIRA VOLITATE
(— AFTER GAME) RAKE
(— AIMLESSLY) BANGLE
(— ALOFT) SOAR TOWER
(— AWAY) CARRY
(— CLUMSILY) FLIGHTER
(— ERRATICALLY) GAD
(— INTO RAGE) FUFF RARE
(— LOW) DICE DRAG HEDGEHOP
(— NEAR THE GROUND) ACCOST
(— OUT) EXPIRE
(— RAPIDLY) SCUR SKIRR
(— TOO HIGH) SCUD
(— WIDE) MISS
(BITING —) PIUM
(FISHING —) BEE DUN OAK BUZZ
GNAT HARL HERL SMUT WASP
ZULU ABBEY ALDER BAKER FAIRY
NYMPH SEDGE BADGER BOBFLY
CADDIS CAHILL CANARY CLARET
DOCTOR HACKLE MILLER ORIOLE
WILLOW BABCOCK BUTCHER
CADDICE COLONEL DROPPER
DUBBING GRANNOM HUZZARD
SPINNER WATCHED WATCHET
BUCKTAIL CATSKILL COACHMAN
FERGUSON GOVERNOR STREAMER
WOODRUFF WRENTAIL
(MAY —) DUN DRAKE
(SHEEP —) FAG KED
(STONE —) SALLY
(PREF.) MUSCI MYI(O)
(SUFF.) MYI(A)(O)
FLYBLOWN BLOWN STRUCK
FLYBOAT FLUTE FLIGHT
FLYCATCHER TODY PEWEE PEWIT
CHEBEC COBWEB MILLER PEEWEE
PHOEBE PIPIRI RAFTER TYRANT
YETAPA ELEPAIO FANTAIL
GRIGNET GRINDER PITIRRI
TOMFOOL TYRANNI BEAMBIRD
FIREBALL FIREBIRD FLYEATER
FORKTAIL GERYGONE KINGBIRD
KISKADEE PITANGUA WALLBIRD
SCISSORTAIL
FLY, FISHING (PART OF —) EYE TAG
BODY BUTT HEAD HORN TAIL
WING CHEEK JOINT HACKLE
RIBBING TOPPING
FLYING AWING FLIGHT VOLANT
WAVING FLOTANT VOLATIC
AVIATION FLOATING
(— MANEUVER) LUFBERY
FLYING DUTCHMAN, THE
(CHARACTER IN —) ERIK SENTA
DALAND
(COMPOSER OF —) WAGNER
FLYING FISH SKIPPER VOLADOR
FLYING FOX KALONG PTEROPID
FLYING GURNARD ANGLER
BATFISH LATCHET LOPHIID
VOLADOR
FLYING LEMUR COBEGO COLUGO
KUBONG
FLYING MACHINE AVIATOR
AEROSTAT
FLYING PHALANGER CUSCUS
SQUIRREL
FLYING SQUIRREL TAGUAN
ASSAPAN

FLYMAN LOFTMAN
FLYSCH MACIGNO
FLYWHEEL FLY FLIER FLYER
WHORL WHARVE
FOAL CADE COLT FILLY PODDY
SLEEPER
FOAM FOB SUD BARM BEES BOIL
FUME HEAD KNIT REAM SCUD
SCUM SUDS WORK CREAM FROST
FROTH SPUME YEAST BUBBLE
FLOWER FLURRY FREATH IMBOST
LATHER SEETHE BLUBBER
DESPUME MELDROP
(PREF.) APHR(O) SPUMI
FOAMING AFOAM NAPPY YEASTY
SPUMOUS MANTLING
FOAMY BARMY BEADY SPUMY
SUDSY FROTHY SPUMOSE
FOB FUB SPUNG POCKET
FOCAL POINT OMPHALOS
FOCUS FIX PUT POINT PURSE
TRAIN CENTER CLIMAX DIRECT
FASTEN FIXATE HEARTH TEMPLE
NUCLEUS CONVERGE FOCALIZE
GANGLION
FODDER HAY FEED FOOD SOIL
VERT GOOMA MANGE EATAGE
FORAGE FOTHER PODDER SILAGE
STOVER FARRAGE PODWARE
PROVAND BROWSING ENSILAGE
ROUGHAGE
FODDERCAGE TUMBREL
FODDERER FOGGER
FOE ENEMY FIEND RIVAL FOEMAN
HOSTILE OPPOSER OPPONENT
WRANGLER
FOG FF DAG RAG DAMP DAZE
HAAR HAZE MIST MOKE MOSS
MURK PRIG RACK ROKE SMOG
SMUR SOUP BEDIM BRUME
CLOUD GRASS HUMOR MUDDY
SMIRR SPRAY STOUR VAPOR
MUDDLE NEBULA SALMON
STUPOR FOGGAGE OBSCURE
POGONIP SMOTHER BEWILDER
MOISTURE
(— OF THE NILE) QOBAR
(FROZEN —) BARBER
(LIGHT —) GAUZE
(SEA —) HAAR HARR
FOGBOW DOG FOGDOG SEADOG
MISTBOW FOGEATER
FOGDOG DOG STUBB FOGBOW
SEADOG FOGEATER
FOGGINESS CLOUDING
FOGGY DIM DULL HAZY MIRK
MOKY MURK ROKY DENSE DIRTY
GROSS MISKY MISTY MURKY
ROOKY ROUKY SPEWY CLOUDY
GREASY GROGGY MARSHY
MILKEN SMURRY BRUMOUS
MUDDLED OBSCURE CONFUSED
NUBILOUS VAPOROUS
FOGHORN SIREN TYFON RIPPER
MEGAFOG
FOGY FOGEY DUFFER FOGRAM
FOOZLE STODGER MOSSBACK
FOGYISH MUSTY
FOIBLE VICE FAULT FERLY FEEBLE
FAILING FRAILTY WEAKNESS
FOIL BACK BALK EPEE FILE FOIN
SOIL TAIN BLADE BLANK BLUNT
CHEAT ELUDE EVADE FALSE

STAIN STUMP SWORD TRACK
TRAIL BAFFLE BLENCH BOGGLE
CHATON DEFEAT DEFILE FLORET
OFFSET OUTWIT STIGMA STOOGE
THWART BEGUILE FAILURE
FOILING FOLIATE LAMETTA
PAILLON POLLUTE REPULSE
STONKER TRAMPLE DISGRACE
(— STRIPS) WINDOW
(FENCING —) EPEE BLUNT FLORET
FLEURET
(PART OF —) END TIP BELL GRIP
HILT BLADE FORTE GUARD POINT
BUTTON FOIBLE HANDLE
POMMEL MOUNTING
(POINTED —) TANG
(TIN —) TAIN
FOIST WISH FUDGE FATHER
SUBORN FOISTER SHOEHORN
FOLD BOW FLY LAP PEN PLY SET
WAP BEND COTE CREW CRUE
DART FAIL FALX FAUN FELD FLAP
FURL HANK HOOD LIRK LOOP
RUCK RUGA SWAG TUCK WRAP
BREAK CLASP CRIMP CRISP
CROZE DRAPE FAULD FLIPE
FLOCK FLYPE FRILL GROIN LAYER
PARMA PINCH PLAIT PLEAT PLICA
PRANK QUILL SINUS YIELD
BOUGHT BUCKLE COLLOP CREASE
CRISTA CUTTLE DEWLAP DIAPIR
DOUBLE ENFOLD FORNIX
FRENUM FURDLE GATHER
GUSSET HURDLE INFOLD LABIUM
LAPPET MANTLE PIPING PLIGHT
PUCKER RIMPLE RUMPLE WIMPLE
CAPSIZE CRINKLE CRUMPLE
EMBRACE ENVELOP FLEXION
FLEXURE PINFOLD PLACATE
PLICATE REVERSE ROLLING
ROULEAU TURNING VALVULA
CRIMPING FLECTION FLITFOLD
QUILLING SCAPULET SPLENIUM
SURROUND PLICATION REPLICATE
REFLECTION
(— CLOTH) RAG
(— DOWN) COLLAPSE
(— FOR CATTLE) BAWN
(— IN HOOD) SHOVE
(— INWARD) CRIMP
(— OF MEMBRANE) CRISTA
(— OF SKIN) APRON DEWLAP
SHEATH OMENTUM FORESKIN
MESENTERY
(— ROCKS) DEFORM
(—S OF TOGA) SINUS
(CARDIAC —) CUSP
(GEOLOGICAL —) DIAPIR CLOSURE
EXOCLINE SYNCLINE MONOCLINE
(LOOSE —) LAPPET
(RESTRAINING —) FRENUM
FRAENUM
(SHEEP —) REEVE
(PREF.) PLEXI PLICATO PLICI
PTYCH(O) SINU(ATO) VALVI VALVO
(SUFF.) FARIOUS PLEX PLICATE
PLOID
(COVERING —) STEGE STEGITE
FOLDAGE SOC SOKE
FOLDED SHUT DOUBLE FANLIKE
PLICATE PLICATED REFLEXED
WREATHED
(— AND WAVED) GYROSE

(PREF.) PLICATO
FOLDER KIT BOOK FILE FOLD
ATLAS COVER FOLIO BINDER
CLEANER HANDOUT LEAFLET
STROKER PAMPHLET
FOLDING KNOT
(— OF LEAF) PTYXIS
(— PAPER) ORIGAMI
FOLIACEOUS PHYLLOID
FOLIAGE HERB SHADE GREENS
LEAVES SHROUD BOSCAGE
GILLERY LEAFAGE LEAFERY
UMBRAGE FRONDAGE GREENERY
(CARVED —) KNOT
FOLIATED SPATHIC
FOLIATION SEXFOIL TREFOIL
CINQFOIL SEPTFOIL
FOLIC ACID PGA
FOLIO CASE ATLAS FOLIUM
FOLK DAIONE PEOPLE
(FAIRY —) SHEE SIDHE
(PL.) GENTRY
FOLKSONG SON TONADA
VOLKSLIED
FOLKSY HOMY HOMEY HOMESPUN
FOLKTALE DROLL FABULA
MARCHEN
FOLLETTO DUSIO
FOLLICLE CRYPT LACUNA OVISAC
CONCEPTACLE
FOLLOW GO PAD SUE TAG COME
COPY HUNT NEXT SEEK SHAG
TAIL TAKE TOUT ADOPT AFTER
CHASE DODGE ENSUE SNAKE
SPOOR TRACE TRACK TRAIL
TREAD ADHERE ATTEND DANGLE
FOLLER OCCUPY PURSUE RESULT
SECOND SHADOW SUIVEZ
TAGGLE HOTFOOT IMITATE
OBSERVE PROFESS REPLACE
SUCCEED VALOUWE PRACTICE
SUPPLANT
(— A POINTER'S LEAD) BACK
(— IN SUCCESSION) VARY
(— INSIDIOUSLY) DOG
(— SCENT) ROAD CARRY
(— SLOWLY) DRAGGLE
(— THROUGH) PRESS
(— TRACK) SLEUTH
(— UP) SUE ATTEND
(— UPON) WAIT
FOLLOWER FAN IST SON APER
BEAU ZANY ADEPT CHELA GILLY
BILDAR COHORT DRIVEN ENSUER
GILLIE GUDGET KNIGHT LACKEY
SEQUEL SUITOR SULTER VOTARY
ACACIAN ACOLYTE CARRIER
DEVOTEE EPIGONE FLATTER
GRIFTER POLIGAR PURSUER
RETINUE SECTARY SEQUENT
SPANIEL SUPPOST TRAILER
ADHERENT DISCIPLE FAITHFUL
FAVORITE HENCHMAN
MYRMIDON OBSERVER OFFSIDER
PARTISAN RETAINER SECTATOR
SERVITOR SATELLITE
PURSUIVANT
(— OF ART) BOHEMIAN
(— OF CELEBRITY) GROUPIE
(CAMP —) BUMMER GUDGET
LASCAR
(CRANE —) SPOTTER
(SERVILE —) SLAVE

LACKEY ANTHONY
(PL.) FOLK SECTA SEQUACES
(SUFF.) ITE

FOLLOWING LAST NEXT SECT SUIT
AFTER FIRST SUANT TRACE
TRAIN BEHIND SEQUEL ENSUANT
ENSUING SEQUENT AUDIENCE
BUSINESS SECUNDUM SEGUENDO
TRAILING VOCATION

FOLLOW-UP FOLO

FOLLY ATE SIN RAGE LAPSE MORIA
SOTIE BETISE DOTAGE LUNACY
NICETY WANWIT DAFFERY
DAFFING FOOLERY FOPPERY
IDIOTCY MADNESS MISTAKE
SOTTAGE UNSKILL FONDNESS
FOOLHEAD IDLENESS LEWDNESS
MOROLOGY NONSENSE RASHNESS
SURQUIDY UNTHRIFT UNWISDOM
WILLNESS WOODNESS SIMPLICITY

FOMALHAUT DIFDA DIPHDA

FOMENT SOW ABET BREW SPUR
ROUSE STUPE AROUSE EXCITE
INCITE AGITATE FERMENT
INSPIRE

FOND TID DAFT DEAR DOTE FAIN
FOOL FUND KIND VAIN WEAK
CRAZY SILLY STOCK STORE
ARDENT BEFOOL CARESS CHOICE
DEARLY DOTING FONDLE FONDLY
LOVING SIMPLE TENDER
AMATORY AMOROUS BEGUILE
BROWDEN FONDISH FOOLISH
INSIPID PARTIAL DESIROUS
ENAMORED SANGUINE TRIFLING
UXORIOUS
(PREF.) (— OF) PHIL(O)
(SUFF.) (— OF)
PHIL(A)(AE)(E)(OUS)(US)

FONDLE PET BABY BILL CLAP COAX
DAUT DAWT FOND NECK TICK
WALY DAUNT INGLE NURSE
WALLY CARESS COCKER CODDLE
COSSET CUDDLE CUTTER DANDLE
GENTLE KIUTLE MUZZLE PAMPER
SLAVER STROKE TANTLE TIDDLE
CHERISH FLATTER SMUGGLE
TWATTLE BLANDISH CANOODLE

FONDLING NINNY NURSLING

FONDLY DEAR FOND DEARLY
FOOLISH

FONDNESS GRA LOVE FANCY
FOLLY TASTE DOTAGE NOTION
FEELING DEARNESS WEAKNESS
(— FOR WOMEN) PHILOGYNY
(SUFF.) (— FOR) ITIS

FONS (FATHER OF —) JANUS
(MOTHER OF —) JUTURNA

FONT BILL FUND PILA BASIN
FOUNT SOURCE SPRING LAVACRE
PISCINA BENITIER DELUBRUM

FONTANEL MOLD MOULD
FENESTRA

FOOD BIT KAI PAP SAP BAIT BITE
BUNK CATE CHIH CHOP CHOW
CRAM DIET DISH EATS FARE
FARM FUEL GEAR GRUB HASH
JOCK KAIL KALE MEAT NOSH
PECK PLAT PROG SALT SOCK
STEW TACK TOKE TUCK BREAD
BROMA CHEER CHUCK FLUFF
FORAY GRILL SCAFF SCOFF
SCRAN TABLE THING TOMMY

TREAT TRIPE APPAST BUTTER
DODGER DOINGS EATING FODDER
FOSTER LIVING MAIGRE MORSEL
MUKTUK REFETE STOVER SUNKET
TACKLE TUCKER VIANDS VIVERS
WRAITH ALIMENT FAUSTER
HANDOUT INGESTA KEEPING
KITCHEN NURTURE PABULUM
PASTURE PECKAGE PROVANT
PULTURE EATABLES FLUMMERY
GRUBBERY NUTRIENT PEMMICAN
PROVIANT TRENCHER VICTUALS
PROVENDER NOURISHMENT
(— AND DRINK) BOUGE CHEER
LOWANCE
(— AND LIQUOR) GEAR
(— AND LODGING) FOUND
EASEMENT
(— BANNED DURING PASSOVER)
HAMETZ CHAMETZ
(— EATEN AS RELISH) KITCHEN
(— EATEN BETWEEN MEALS)
BAGGING
(— FOR ANIMALS) FODDER
FORAGE
(— FOR CATTLE) BROWSE TACKLE
(— FROM KELP) KOMBU
(— IN SLICES) LEACH
(— IN STOCK) LARDER
(— NOT RITUALLY CLEAN)
TEREPHAH
(— OF DUCK EGGS) BALUT
(— OF RUMINANTS) CUD
(— OF THE GODS) AMRITA
AMREETA AMBROSIA
(— OF WHALE) KRILL
(— OF WORKMEN) TOMMY
(— ON TABLE AT ONE TIME) MESS
(ASIATIC —) TEMPEH
(BEE —) CANDY
(COOKED —) CURY BAKEMEAT
(DAILY —) TUCKER
(EXTRA —) GASH
(FILLING —) STODGE
(FLAVORLESS —) HOGWASH
(GROUND —) DUST
(HAWAIIAN —) POI
(INDIGESTIBLE —) STODGE
(JAPANESE —) TERIYAKI
(LIQUID —) LAP SLOP SOUP GRUEL
LEBAN LEBEN SUPPING
(LUXURIOUS —) CATE CATES
JUNKET
(MADE OF SEVERAL —S) PANACHE
(MIRACULOUS —) MANNA
(RICH —) CHEER
(SEMILIQUID —) SWILL
(SOFT —) PAP
(STARCHY —) AMYLOID
(TAPIOCA-LIKE —) SALEP
(WATERY —) SLIPSLOP
(PREF.) SITIO SITO TROPH(O)
(SUFF.) PHAGA PHAGE PHAGIA
PHAGOUS PHAGUS PHAGY
TROPHIA TROPHIC TROPHY
(WANT OF —) ATROPHIA

FOODLESS JEJUNE VICTLESS

FOODSTUFF TRADE CEREAL
COOKABLE

FOOL APE ASS BAM BOB COD CON
DAW DOR FON FOP FOX FUN GIG
KID MUG NIT NUP POT RIG SAP
SOT TOY BULL BUTT CAKE CHUB

CLOT COLT DOLT DUPE FOND
GECK GOER GOFF GOOP GOWK
GYPE HARE HAVE HOIT JAPE JEST
JOKE JOSH MOME MUCK NIZY
POOP RACA RACH SIMP TONY
TOOT TWIT ZANY BLIND BLUFF
BUFFO CHUMP CLOWN DALLY
FUNGE GALAH GLAIK GOOSE
GREEN HORSE IDIOT KNAVE
MORON NINNY NIZEY NODDY
PATCH PATSY SAMMY SCREW
SILLY SNIPE SPOOF STICK STIFF
STIRK TOMMY TRICK BUFFLE
COUSIN CUCKOO CUDDEN
DELUDE DIMWIT DISARD DOTARD
DOTTLE FOLEYE FOOTER
GAMMON JESTER MOTLEY
MUCKER MUSARD NIDGET NIMSHI
NINCOM NUPSON SAWNEY
SHMUCK STRING TAMPER WITTOL
ASINEGO BECASSE BUFFOON
COXCOMB DAGONET DECEIVE
DIZZARD FATHEAD FOOLISH
FRIBBLE GOMERAL GOMERIL
HAVERAL JACKASS LACKWIT
MADLING MISLEAD NATURAL
OMADAWN PINHEAD PLAYBOY
SCHMUCK STOOKIE TOMFOOL
WANTWIT WITLING ABDERITE
BADINAGE DRIVELER FONDLING
HOODWINK IMBECILE MONUMENT
OMADHAUN TOMNODDY
NINCOMPOOP
(— AROUND) JIVE SKYLARK
LALLYGAG
(— AWAY) FRIBBLE
(BORN —) MOONCALF
(LEARNED —) MOROSOPH
(NATURAL —) INNOCENT
(PL.) FOOLERY

FOOLERY GAME FOLLY BARNEY
MOTLEY BAUBLERY

FOOLHARDY RASH BRASH
FOOLATUM

FOOLISH FAT SOT BETE DAFT
DUMB FOND FOOL GAGA GYPE
IDLE MADE NICE RASH SOFT VAIN
VOID WEAK ZANY BALMY BARMY
BATTY BOGGY BUGGY DILLY
DIPPY DIZZY DOILT EMPTY FONNE
GAWKY GOOFY GOOSY INANE
INEPT JERKY LOONY NODDY
POTTY SAPPY SAWNY SCREW
SEELY SILLY YAPPY ABSURD
CUDDEN DOTISH DOTTLE FONDLY
GLAKED GOTHAM GOWKIT
HARISH INSANE MOMISH MOPISH
SHANNY SIMPLE SLIGHT SOFTLY
SPOONY STOLID STULTY STUPID
TAWPIE UNWISE VACANT
ASININE DAMFOOL DOLTISH
ETOURDI FANGLED FATUOUS
FLIGHTY FOLLIAL FOPPISH
GLAIKIT GOOSISH GULLISH
IDIOTIC PEEVISH PUERILE
SOTTISH TOMFOOL UNWITTY
WANTWIT WITLESS ABDERIAN
FOOTLING FOPPERLY HEADLESS
HEEDLESS HIGHLAND IMBECILE
SENSELESS
(PREF.) STULT(I)

FOOLISHLY IDLY FONDLY SIMPLE
SIMPLY

FOOLISHNESS JAZZ PUNK FOLLY
BARNEY BUNKUM FADDLE LEVITY
LUNACY RUBBLE VANITY FATUITY
PORANGI BUNCOMBE FONDNESS
INSANITY TOMMYROT ABSURDITY
SAPPINESS

FOOT FIT PAT PAW PEG PES BASE
COOT FUSS GOER HEEL HOOF
PIED SOLE TAIL BASIS PIECE
BOTTOM CLUTCH GAMMON
PATTEN PODIUM RHYTHM
TOOTSY TRILBY WALKER FOOTING
GAMBONE MEASURE METREME
PEDICEL FOREFOOT
(— OF ANIMAL) PAD PAW HOOF
TROTTER
(— OF APE) HAND
(— OF INSECT) TARSUS
(— OF WINE GLASS) MULE
(CHINESE —) CHEK CHIH
(HALF —) SEMIPED
(LARGE AWKWARD —) CAVE
(METRIC —) IAMB BASIS DIAMB
IONIC PAEAN CHOREE DACTYL
DIIAMB IAMBUS SYZYGY ANAPEST
BACCHIC PYRRHIC SPONDEE
TROCHEE ANAPAEST BACCHIUS
CHORIAMB DOCHMIUS EPITRITE
MOLOSSUS TRIBRACH TRIMACER
(STEWED OX —) COWHEEL
(TUBE —) SUCKER
(PREF.) PED(I)(O) PEDATI
PEDICULO PEZO POD(O)
(SUFF.) PED(E)
POD(A)(AL)(E)(IA)(IUM)(OUS) PUS

FOOTAGE SETUP

FOOTBALL GRID HURLY ROUGE
FOOTER HURLING LEATHER
PIGSKIN KICKBALL
(— FORMATION) SHOTGUN
WISHBONE
(— PLAY) DELAY SWING AUDIBLE
ROLLOUT SCRAMBLE
(— PLAYER) FLANKER SLOTBACK
(KIND OF —) CAMP

FOOTBOY PAGE PEDES

FOOTBRIDGE PLANK LIGGER
FOOTLOG

FOOTED FITTIT PEDATE
(SUFF.) PEDE PODOUS

FOOTFALL PAD STEP TREAD
FOOTSTEP

FOOTGEAR PATTEN FOOTWEAR

FOOTHOLD TIP HACK STEP
FOOTING TOEHOLD

FOOTING PAR FOOT TROD BASIS
EARTH TRACK HEADING PIECING
TOEHOLD FOOTHOLD

FOOTLESS APODAL

FOOTLIGHTS FOOTS FLOATS
LIGHTS

FOOTLIKE PEDATE

FOOTMAN SKIP FLUNKY JEAMES
LACKEY VARLET DOORMAN
FOOTPAD BOTTOMER CHASSEUR
HIRCARRA WAGONMAN

FOOTPACE HALFPACE PREDELLA

FOOTPAD PAD WHYO PADDER
ROBBER FOOTMAN PADFOOT
SCOURER LANDRAKER

FOOTPATH LANE TROD JETTY
SENDA TRAIL FOOTWAY
HIGHWAY PARAPET RAMPIRE

SIDEWALK TROTTOIR
(— TO A PASTURE) DRUNG
(RAISED —) CLAPPER
FOOTPICK CASCROM
FOOTPIECE STEP
FOOTPRINT PAD PUG STEP TROD
PRICK SPOOR TRACE TRACK
TRADE TREAD FOOTING ICHNITE
PUGMARK FOOTMARK
(PREF.) ICHN(O)
FOOTREST COASTER HASSOCK
STIRRUP
FOOTROPE HORSE
FOOTS SEDIMENT
FOOTSCRAPING SAND
FOOTSORENESS SURBATE
FOOTSTALK STRIG PODIUM
PEDICEL PETIOLE PEDUNCLE
(PREF.) PEDICULO
FOOTSTEP PAD STEP TROD CLAMP
VESTIGE FOOTBEAT FORESTEP
(PREF.) ICHN(O)
FOOTSTOOL TUT LOVE MORA
STOOL BUFFET SAMBLE CRICKET
HASSOCK OTTOMAN FOOTREST
FOOT-WASHING NIPTER
FOOTWAY PATH CATWALK
FOOTPATH
(— ALONGSIDE BRIDGE)
BANQUETTE
FOOTWEAR FEET
FOP TO ADON BEAU BUCK DUDE
DUPE FOOL KNUT PRIG TOFF
DANDY FLASH PUPPY MASHER
MOPPET VANITY COXCOMB
JESSAMY GIMCRACK MACARONI
MACAROON MUSCADIN POPINJAY
SKIPJACK
FOPPISH APISH DANDY FOPPY
SAPPY SILLY DAPPER PRETTY
SPRUCE STUPID BEAUISH
BUCKISH FANGLED FINICAL
FOOLISH DANDYISH SKIPJACK
FOR P IN TO PRO TIL VER TILL
SINCE FORWHY BECAUSE
FORNENT FAVORING
(— A LONG TIME) YORE
(— CASH) SPOT
(— EXAMPLE) EG VG
(— FEAR THAT) LEST
(— INSTANCE) AS SAY
(— THE EMERGENCY) PRN
(— THE MOST PART) FECKLY
GENERALLY
(— TIME BEING) ACTUALLY
(PREF.) PRO
FORAGE ERS OAT RYE CORN GUAR
MAST PROG RAID ETAPE FORAY
BREVIT RUSSUD ZACATE
GOITCHO HAYLAGE PICKEER
BOOTHALE SCROUNGE
FORAGER OUTRIDER
FORAMEN PORE EXOSTOME
METAPORE TROCHLEA
FORAMINIFER NUMMULITE
FORAY RAID MELEE CREAGH
FURROW INROAD MARAUD
RAVAGE RAZZIA SORTIE
CHAPPOW HERSHIP PILLAGE
SPREAGH SPREATH
FORBEAR LET BEAR HELP HOLD
SHUN SIRE AVOID FORGO SPARE
WAIVE DEPORT DESIST ENDURE

PARENT RETAIN ABSTAIN
DECLINE REFRAIN RESPITE
ANCESTOR FOREBEAR
WITHDRAW
(— PROSECUTION) COMPOUND
FORBEARANCE MERCY LENITY
NONACT PARDON QUARTER
MILDNESS PATIENCE
FORBEARING CLEMENT LENIENT
PATIENT MERCIFUL TOLERANT
FORBID BAN BAR NIX DEFY DENY
FEND TABU VETO WARN DEBAR
TABOO BANISH DEFEND ENJOIN
IMPEDE OPPOSE REFUSE SHIELD
FORFEND FORWARN GAINSAY
INHIBIT WITHSAY DISALLOW
FORSPEAK PRECLUDE PROHIBIT
PROSCRIBE
FORBIDDANCE BAN VETO
FORBODE
FORBIDDEN TABU TABOO BANNED
DENIED VERBOTEN
(SOMETHING —) NONO
FORBIDDING DOUR GRIM HARD
BLACK GAUNT STERN FIERCE
GLASSY GLOOMY GRISLY ODIOUS
STRICT FORBODE GRIZZLY
REPULSIVE
FORCE GAR GUT HAP JAM LID VIM
VIS ZIP BANG BEAR BEAT BEND
BIRR BODY CLIP CRAM DINT
DOOM DRAG EDGE FECK FOSS
GRIP GUTS HEAD JAMB JINX
MAIN MAKE MANA SNAP SOCK
ABATE AGENT ARDOR BRAWL
BRING BRUSH CLAMP COACT
CRAFT CROWD CRUSH DEMON
DRAFT DRIVE EXACT EXERT
FOHAT GAVEL IMPEL KARMA
MIGHT PAINT PEISE POACH POINT
POWER PRESS PRIZE PUNCH
REPEL SHEAR SHOVE SINEW
STEAM STUFF THROW WAKAN
WREST CHARGE COERCE COMPEL
CUDGEL DURESS EFFECT EFFORT
ENERGY EXTORT HIJACK HOTBED
IMPACT IMPOSE JOSTLE OBLIGE
POWDER RAVISH SHAKTI STRAIN
STRESS WRENCH ABILITY
AFFORCE BLUSTER CASCADE
COGENCE COGENCY CONCUSS
DRAUGHT DYNAMIC IMPETUS
IMPRESS IMPULSE LASHKAR
OPPRESS REQUIRE SQUEEZE
TORMENT VIOLATE WAKANDA
ACTIVITY ADHESION AFFINITY
BULLDOZE COACTION COERCION
DYNAMISM EFFICACY HOTHOUSE
MOMENTUM PRESSURE
STRENGTH VALIDITY VIOLENCE
VIRILITY NECESSITATE
(— AIR UPON) BLOW
(— AN ENTRANCE) RANDOM
THRUST
(— APART) SUNDER DISPART
(— BACK) REPEL RAMBARRE
(— BY THREAT) SWAGGER
(— DOWN) CLEW CLUE DETRUDE
DISMOUNT
(— IN) INJECT INTRUDE
(— OPEN) BURST JIMMY SPORT
RANFORCE
(— OUT) SPEW EJECT ERUPT

EVICT EXPEL KNOCK WRING
EXTUND EXPRESS
(— PASSAGE) SQUEEZE
(— WAY) CROWD WREST WRING
(— WITH LEGAL AUTHORITY) POSSE
(ALLEGED —) OD
(ARMED —) CREW HEAD POWER
CONREY ARMAMENT BATTALIA
(CONCENTRATED —) PITH
(CONFINING —) LID
(CONSTRAINING —) STRESS
(COSMIC —) EVIL
(CREATIVE —) NATURE
(DRIVING —) STEAM SWINGE
(EVOLUTIONARY —) BATHMISM
(EXPLOSIVE —) MEGATON
(HYPOTHETICAL —) FORTUNE
(LACK OF — TO DEFEAT) UNDERKILL
(LIFE —) SHAKTI
(MAIN —) BRUNT
(MILITANT —) SWORD
(MILITARY —) FYRD LEGION
WERING BAYONET OCCUPATION
(MOVING —) SOLICITATION
(NAVAL —) FLEET
(PHYSICAL —) NERVE
(PREPONDERATING —) SWAY
(PROTECTIVE —) CONVOY
(RELIGIOUS —) SANCTITY
(SACRED —) KAMI
(SPIRITUAL —) SOUL
(UNRESTRAINED —) FURY
(UPWARD —) BUOYANCY
(PL.) ARMY WILL COLORS
(SUFF.) (UNIT OF —) DYNE
FORCED LABORED ENFORCED
FALSETTO SARDONIC SPURIOUS
STRAINED
FORCEFUL RUDE GREAT GUTSY
PITHY STIFF STOUT MIGHTY
PUNCHY STRONG VIRILE
DYNAMIC STHENIC VIOLENT
BRUISING ELOQUENT EMPHATIC
ENFATICO FORCIBLE VIGOROUS
TRENCHANT
FORCEFULNESS PUNCH EMPHASIS
FORCEMEAT FARCE BOUDIN
GODIVEAU QUENELLE STUFFING
FORCEPS DOG FURCA TONGS
TENAIL BULLDOG CLAMMER
PINCERS PINSONS RONGEUR
CROWBILL DENTAGRA PINCETTE
VULSELLA TENACULUM
(PREF.) FORCI LABID(O)
FORCIBLE VIVE STOUT VALID
COGENT MIGHTY POTENT
STRONG FORCIVE NERVOUS
VIOLENT WEIGHTY EMPHATIC
FORCEFUL POWERFUL PREGNANT
PUISSANT VEHEMENT VIGOROUS
FORCIBLY AMAIN SADLY HARDLY
MAINLY HEAVILY STRONGLY
FORD PASS RACK RIFT WADE
WATH DRIFT STREAM CURRENT
FORDING PASSAGE PASSING
CROSSING
(PAVED —) STEAN STEENING
FORE VAN WAY AFORE AHEAD
FRONT PRIOR FORMER FURTHER
FOREARM CUBIT CUBITAL
CUBITUS
FOREBEAR ANCESTOR
FOREBODE BODE GIVE OMEN

ABODE AUGUR CROAK BETIDE
DIVINE BETOKEN MISBODE
OMINATE PORTEND PREDICT
PRESAGE FORETELL
(— EVIL) CROAK
FOREBODING OMEN BLACK FATAL
AUGURY BODING DISMAL
GLOOMY ANXIETY BALEFUL
BANEFUL DRUTHER OMINOUS
PRESAGE BODEMENT SINISTER
ABODEMENT PROGNOSTICATION
FOREBODINGLY DIRELY
FOREBRAIN CEREBRUM
PROENCEPHALON
FORECAST BODE CAST SCHEME
CAUTION FORESEE FORESET
PREDICT FOREDEEM FOREDOOM
FORETELL PROPHESY
ADUMBRATE PREVISION
PROGNOSIS PREDICTION
PROGNOSTICATION
FORECASTLE FOCSLE ISLAND
FORECOURT VESTIBULE
FOREDOOM JINX DESTINY
FOREFACE CUSHION
FOREFATHER AYEL SIRE ELDER
PITRI PARENT ANCESTOR
FOREBEAR PROGENITOR
PRIMOGENITOR
FOREFINGER INDEX
FOREFOOT PAW PUD GRIPE
FOREFOOTING MANGANA
FOREFRONT VAN FRONT VAWARD
FOREGO FORGO WAIVE ESCHEW
ABSTAIN NEGLECT PRECEDE
REFRAIN ABNEGATE DISPENSE
RENOUNCE
FOREGOING PAST ABOVE
ANTERIOR PREVIOUS PRECEDING
FOREGROUND PROSCENIUM
FOREHEAD BROW FRONS FRONT
FRONTLET SINCIPUT
(— INDENTATION) STOP
(— MARK) KUMKUM
(HIGH —) LEPTENE
(PREF.) FRONTI FRONTO METOPO
FOREHEARTH SETTLER
FOREIGN UNCO ALIEN FREMD
WELSH ALANGE EXILED EXOTIC
FRENCH REMOTE UNKIND
DISTANT ECDEMIC EPIGENE
EXCLUDE FRAMMIT HEATHEN
OUTBORN OUTLAND OUTWARD
STRANGE BARBARIC EPIGENIC
EXTERIOR EXTERNAL FORINSEC
OVERSEAS PEREGRIN STRANGER
BARBAROUS OUTLANDISH
TRAMONTANE
(— TO) DEHORS
(PREF.) ALIENI EXOTO
FOREIGNER ALIEN HAOLE ALLTUD
GRINGO PAKEHA GREENER
OUTBORN OUTLAND PARDESI
ETRANGER OUTSIDER PEREGRIN
PORTUGEE STRANGER
MLECHCHHA OUTLANDER
(PREF.) XEN(O)
(SUFF.) XENE XENOUS XENY
FOREKNOW DIVINE FORESEE
FOREWIT
FOREKNOWLEDGE PRESAGE
FORELEG GAMB
FORELOCK TOP BANG QUIFF

COTTER TOUPET FORETOP
TOPPING FOREBUSH
FOREMAN BOSS BULL CORK JOSS
LUNA PUSH CHIEF DOGGY
BUNTER GAFFER GANGER LEADER
RAMROD SIRDAR TENTER
CAPATAZ CAPORAL CAPTAIN
FOUNDER HEADMAN MANAGER
MANDOER OVERMAN SHOOFLY
SKIDDER STEWARD FOREHAND
GANGSMAN OVERSEER
(— OF JURY) CHANCELLOR
FOREMOST TOP HEAD HIGH MAIN
CHIEF FIRST FORME FRONT
GRAND BANNER FORMER
LEADING RANKING SUPREME
VANMOST CHAMPION
(— PART) VAWARD
FOREORDAIN FATE SLATE
DESTINE FORESAY PREDOOM
FORECAST
FOREORDINATION FATE
FOREPART FRONT FOREHEAD
(— OF FACE) CHAP
(— OF HORSE'S HEAD) CHANFRIN
(— OF SHIP) STEM FORWARD
CUTWATER ENTRANCE
FOREPOLE LATH SPILE SPILING
FORERUN HERALD OUTRUN
PRECEDE PRELUDE ANNOUNCE
FORESHOT
FORERUNNER OMEN SIGN USHER
AUGURY HERALD ANCESTOR
FOREGOER FOURRIER OUTRIDER
PRODROME MESSENGER
PRECURSOR
FORERUNNING PRECURSE
FORESADDLE RACK
FORESEE SEE READ DIVINE
PURVEY PREVISE PROVIDE
ENVISAGE ENVISION FORECAST
FOREKNOW PROSPECT
PREFIGURE
FORESHADOW HINT FIGURE
HERALD FORERUN PATTERN
PRELUDE PRESAGE UMBRATE
FORETYPE ADUMBRATE
FORESHORE HARD SHORE
HARDWAY SEASHORE
FORESHOW BODE ABODE AUGUR
BETOKEN PORTEND SIGNIFY
FORETELL PROPHESY
FORESIGHT FEAR VISION FOREWIT
FORECAST FORELOOK PROSPECT
PRUDENCE
FORESIGHTED CAGY CAGEY
CANNY
FOREST BUSH GAPO MATA RUKH
WOLD WOOD FIRTH GLADE
GUBAT MATTA MATTO MONTE
SYLVA TAIGA WASTE WEALD
JUNGLE TIMBER BOSCAGE
CALYDON COPPICE CAATINGA
WOODLAND
(— CITY) PORTLAND SAVANNAH
CLEVELAND
(— FOR DEER) FIRTH
(IMMENSE —) MONTANA
(RAIN —) SELVA
(SIBERIAN —) URMAN
(STUNTED —) CAATINGA
KRUMMHOLZ
(PREF.) HYL(O) SILVI SYLVI

FORESTAGE APRON
FORESTALL BEAT HELP LURCH
STALL DEVANCE FORERUN
OBVIATE PREVENE PREVENT
FORSTEAL ANTICIPATE
FORESTALLER KIDDER GROSSER
FORESTAYSAIL JUMBO
FORESTER FOSTER WALKER
MONTERO TINEMAN TREEMAN
WOODMAN WOODSMAN
FORETASTE GUST HANSEL TEASER
EARNEST HANDSEL ANTEPAST
PROSPECT PRELIBATION
FORETELL BODE ERST READ SPAE
AUGUR INSEE WEIRD WRITE
DIVINE HALSEN HERALD RESPEAK
FORESAY PORTEND PREDICT
PRESAGE ANNOUNCE FOREBODE
FORECAST FORESHOW PROPHESY
SOOTHSAY
FORETELLING PROPHECY
FORETHOUGHT CAUTION
FORECAST PREPENSE PRUDENCE
FORETOKEN OMEN AUGUR
PORTEND PROMISE FORECAST
FORESHOW FORESIGN
FOREVER AY AKE AYE EVER ETERN
ALWAYS ETERNE ENDLESS
ETERNITY EVERMORE
FOREWARN WEIRD PREMONISH
FOREWARNING HINT PORTENT
PREMONITION
FOREWING PRIMARY
FOREWORD PROEM PREFACE
PREAMBLE
FORFEIT WED FINE LOSE TINE
WITE CHEAT CRIME DEDIT FORGO
LAPSE FOREGO SCONCE DEFAULT
ESCHEAT FORWORK PENALTY
FORFAULT
FORFEITURE FINE BLIND MULCT
TINSEL ESCHEAT FORFEIT
PENALTY
FORGE FOGE MINT TILT WELL
CLICK FALSE FEIGN SMITH STOVE
HAMMER SMITHY STEADY STITCH
STITHY SWINGE CHAFERY FALSIFY
FASHION BLOOMERY
FORGED BOGUS SPURIOUS
FORGER SMITH FALSER FALSARY
LEVERMAN
FORGERY SHAM FALSUM FICTION
BLOOMERY
FORGET LOSE OMIT WANT FLUFF
BILEVE UNKNOW UNMIND
NEGLECT OVERLOOK
FORGETFUL OBLIVIOUS
FORGETFULNESS SWIM FLUFF
LETHE AMNESIA AMNESTY
OBLIVION
(PREF.) LETHO
FORGET-ME-NOT MYOSOTE
FORGETTING
(PREF.) LETHO
FORGING HOOP CLICK JACKET
FORGIVE REMIT SPARE ASSOIL
EXCUSE PARDON ABSOLVE
CONDONE OVERLOOK
FORGIVENESS GRACE PARDON
FORGIFT
FORGIVING GRACE HUMANE
CLEMENT MERCIFUL
MAGNANIMOUS

FORGOTTEN DERELICT UNMINDED
FORINT FLORIN
FORK CROC EVIL HOOK TANG TINE
CLEFT CLOFF FURCA GLACK
GRAIN GRAIP PRONG TWIST
BISECT BRANCH CLITCH CROTCH
DIVIDE FEEDER GAFFLE HACKER
OFFSET TWISEL BIPRONG
FOURCHE FRUGGIN HAYFORK
TOASTER CROTCHET EQUULEUS
GRAINING PITCHFORK
(— OF BODY) SHARE
(— OF PENNON) FANON
(— OF WINDPIPE) BRONCHUS
(MEAT —) TORMENTOR
(THATCHER'S —) GROM
(TUNING —) DIAPASON
(PREF.) FURCI
FORKED BIFID FORKY FURCAL
PRONGY DIVIDED FURCATE
LITUATE BIFORKED BIRAMOUS
BRANCHED FOURCHEE SUBBIFID
FORKING STAR
FORLORN LORN LOST REFT ALONE
ABJECT FORFAIRN FORSAKEN
HELPLESS HOPELESS PITIABLE
WITLOSEN
FORM AME DIG FIG HEW HUE SET
BLEE BODY CASE CAST CAUL
DOME FLOW GARB IDEA KERN
KITE MAKE MODE MOLD PLAN
RITE SEAT THEW TURN BENCH
BLANK BLOCK BOARD BUILD
BUNCH CHART CHECK CRUSH
DUMMY EIDOS ERECT FORCE
FORMA FORME FRAME GALBE
GUISE IMAGE MATCH MEUSE
MODEL SHAPE SPELL STAMP
THROW USAGE ADJUST CHALAN
COUPON CREATE CUSTOM DEVISE
DOCKET FIGURE FILLER HANGER
INVENT MANNER REMOVE RITUAL
SCHEMA SCHOOL SPONGE STRIKE
SYSTEM TAILLE AGENDUM
ARRANGE COMPOSE CONFECT
CONTOUR DEVELOP FASHION
FEATURE FORMULA GESTALT
IMPANEL INVOICE LITURGY
MAKEDOM OUTLINE PATTERN
PORTRAY PORTURE PRODUCE
PROFILE SPECIES STATURE
BILLHEAD CEREMONY COMPOUND
CONCEIVE CONTRIVE FORMWORK
INSTRUCT LIKENESS MODALITY
ORGANIZE SEMBLANCE
(— A HEAD) POME
(— A NETWORK) PLEX
(— A RING) ENVIRON
(— ASSUMED AFTER DEATH)
KAMARUPA
(— BRANCHES) BREAK
(— BY CUTTING OFF) ABJOINT
(— CONNECTION) ALLY
(— FOR BELL FOUNDING) SWEEP
(— FOR CONCRETE) BOXING
(— FOR HOLDING BARREL) SQUAW
(— FOR MOLD) JACKET
(— FOR PRESSING VENEERS) CAUL
(— FRUIT) KNIT
(— INTO A CHAIN) CATENATE
(— INTO BALL) CONGLOBE
(— INTO RINGLETS) CRISP
(— LEATHER) CRIMP

(— MOUND) TUMP
(— OF GOVERNMENT) ESTATE
KINGSHIP
(— OF PREDICATION) CATEGORY
(— POLITICAL SUCCESSION) CAVE
(— WITH PLASTER) RUN
(— YARN INTO THREAD) CABLE
(ANCESTRAL —) BLASTAEA
STEMFORM
(CONVENTIONAL —) AMENITY
(DEXTROROTATORY —) CAMPHOR
(DISPLAY —) MANNEQUIN
(IMPERFECT —) SEMIFORM
(IRREGULAR —) PSEUDOMORPH
(ISOMETRIC —) DIPLOID
(LINGUISTIC —) FOSSIL GERUND
(LITERARY —) KNACK
(LYRICAL —) SESTINA
(MUSICAL —) RAGA SUITE
(POETIC —) CINQUAIN
(POINTED —) ANGLE
(SCHOOL —) SHELL
(SHOE —) LAST FILLER
(SHORTENED —) ABBREVIATION
(SONG —) BAR
(SPECTRAL —) SHADOW
(SPEECH —) LEXEME IDIOLECT
(SPIRAL OR CIRCULAR —) GYRE
(STRUCTURE —) MORPHOLOGY
(TOP —) GROOVE
(VERB —) FUTURE CONATIVE
DEFINITE DURATIVE
(VERSE —) EPODE BALLAD
PANTUM SONNET KYRIELLE
LIMERICK
(VISIBLE —) RUPA
(WILD —) AGRIOTYPE
(WORD —) ETYMON ANOMALY
(PREF.) IDO MORPH(O) PLASMATO
(SUFF.) FY GEN(E)(ESIA)(ESIS)
(ETIC)(IC)(IN)(OUS)(Y) IFY
MORPH(A)(AE)(IC)(ISM)(OSIS)(OTIC)
(OUS)(Y) PLASIA PLASIS
PLASM(A)(IA)(IC) PLAST(IC)(Y)
PLASY
(HAVING — OF) IC(AL)
(IN THE — OF) OID(AL)
FORMAL DRY SET BOOK PRIM
BUDGE CHILL COURT EXACT
STIFF SOCIAL SOLEMN STOCKY
ANGULAR BOOKISH LOGICAL
NOMINAL ORDERLY OUTWARD
PRECISE REGULAR SOLWARD
STARCHY STATELY STILTED
ABSTRACT ACADEMIC AFFECTED
ELEVATED FORMULAR OFFICIAL
PUNCTUAL STARCHED
FORMALDEHYDE FORMAL
MONOSE HARDENER METHANAL
FORMALISM ACADEMISM
FORMALIST PEDANT SCHOLASTIC
FORMALISTIC COURT ACADEMIC
FORMALITY FORM SASINE STARCH
BUCKRAM DECENCY WIGGERY
CEREMONY PHARISAISM
FORMALIZE STIFFEN
FORMALLY FORMLY STARCHLY
FORMAT SIZE GETUP SHAPE STYLE
FORMATION FORM RANK SPUR
BIOME FLIGHT GROWTH HARROW
MASSIF SPREAD POTENCE
BOTRYOID

(**— ENCLOSING MINE WORKING**) GROUND
(**— ENCOUNTERED IN DRILLING**) STRAY
(**— OF BRAIN**) FORNIX
(**— OF BRANCHES**) CANOPY
(**— OF CRYSTAL**) SHOOT
(**— OF JOINT**) ANKYLOSIS
(**— OF PLANES**) JAVELIN
(**— ON TOAD**) SPADE
(**— RESEMBLING ICICLE**) STIRIA
(**BATTLE —**) HERSE
(**CLOUD —**) NUBECULA
(**DANCE —**) SET
(**DIAGONAL —**) HARROW
(**DRIPSTONE —**) COLUMN
(**ECOLOGICAL —**) BIOME
(**FLIGHT —**) SQUADRON
(**FOOTBALL —**) SHOTGUN WISHBONE
(**GEOLOGIC —**) BOEL CULM CHICO STRAY MARKER MEDINA CURTAIN MANLIUS MATAWAN POTOMAC TERRAIN AQUIFUGE FERNANDO KOOTANIE KOOTENAI LOCKPORT TOPATOPA YORKTOWN
(**HABIT —**) FIXATION
(**INDENTED —**) CLEFT
(**INFANTRY —**) TERTIA ECHELON
(**LAND —**) BOOTHEEL
(**MILITARY —**) SNAIL FLIGHT
(**NAVAL —**) SCREEN
(**POINTED —**) BEAK
(PREF.) PLASTO
(**TAIL —**) CERC(O)
(SUFF.) GENESIA GENESIS OSIS POEIA POESIS POIEISIS POIETIC
FORMATIVE CREANT PLASTIC DEMIURGIC
(SUFF.) POEIA POESIS POIEISIS POIETIC
FORMED BUILT BOOKIT DECIDED MATURED SETTLED WROUGHT TIMBERED
(**— AT BASE OF MOUNTAIN**) PIEDMONT
(**— INTO STEPS**) GRADY
(**— ON SURFACE OF EARTH**) EPIGENE
(**IMPERFECTLY —**) ABORTIVE
(**STURDILY —**) BUXOM
(PREF.) APO PLASTO
FORMEE PATE PATTEE
FORMER DIE OLD ERER ERST FERN FORE LATE ONCE PAST ELDER FORME GAUGE GUIDE MAKER OTHER PRIOR BYGONE RATHER WHILOM ANCIENT ANOTHER CREATOR EARLIER FIRSTER FURTHER ONETIME PRIDIAN QUONDAM TEMPLET UMWHILE PRETERIT PREVIOUS PRISTINE SOMETIME STRICKLE UMQUHILE PRECEDING
(PREF.) PROTER(O)
FORMERLY ERE NEE OLD ERST FORE ONCE THEN YORE GRAVE WHILOM WHILST ONETIME QUONDAM SOMETIME UMQUHILE
FORMIDABLE MEAN FEARFUL ALARMING DREADFUL MENACING TERRIBLE FEROCIOUS REDOUBTABLE

(**— PERSON**) TARTAR
FORMING
(SUFF.) GENIC GEROUS
FORMLESS ARUPA DOUGHY ANIDIAN CHAOTIC DEFORMED INDIGEST
FORMOSA (SEE TAIWAN)
FORMULA LAW MIX DATE FIAT FORM RULE CANON CREED DHIKR GRAPH INDEX LURRY KEKULE MANTRA METHOD RECIPE THEORY RECEIPT APOLYSIS CLAUSULE DOXOLOGY EXORCISM
(**— OF FAITH**) KELIMA
(**MAGICAL —**) CARACT
(**WORD —**) PATERNOSTER
(PL.) RAKA RAKAH
FORMULARY SYMBOL
FORMULATE PUT CAST DRAW FRAME DEVISE CAPSULE COMPOSE FORMULE PLATFORM
FORMULATED STATED WRITTEN
FORMULATION (**— OF A TRUTH**) COUNT CREED DOGMA APHORISM APOTHEGM DOCTRINE
(SUFF.) (**SYSTEMATIC —**) ICS
FORMWORK SHUTTERING
FORNIX VAULT PSALIS
FORSAKE DENY DROP FLEE QUIT SHUN ABAND AVOID FORGO LEAVE WAIVE DEFECT DEPART DESERT FOREGO FORHOO FORLET REFUSE REJECT ABANDON DISCARD FORLESE DESOLATE FORHOOIE RENOUNCE WITHDRAW
FORSAKEN LORN FORLORN DESERTED DESOLATE LASSLORN
FORSETE (**FATHER OF —**) BALDER
FORSOOTH EVEN MARRY QUOTH
FORSWEAR DENY ABJURE REJECT ABANDON PERJURE ABNEGATE MANSWEAR RENOUNCE
FORSYTE SAGA (**AUTHOR OF —**) GALSWORTHY
(**CHARACTER IN —**) JON VAL JUNE MONT FLEUR HOLLY IRENE JOLLY MONTY DARTIE JOLYON PHILIP SOAMES ANNETTE FORSYTE LAMOTTE MICHAEL PROFOND PROSPER SWITHIN TIMOTHY BOSINNEY WINIFRED
FORT PA DUN LIS PAH LISS PEEL SHEE SPUR WORK COTTA REDAN SIDHE CASTLE SANGAR SCHERM SCONCE STRONG BASTION BULWARK CITADEL CLOSURE REDOUBT BASTILLE CASTILLO FASTHOLD FASTNESS FORTRESS MARTELLO PRESIDIO
(**FAIRY —**) LIS LIOS LISS SHEE SIDHE
(**HILL —**) RATH
(**RUINS OF —**) ZIMBABWE
(**SMALL —**) GURRY FORTIN BASTIDE FORTLET FORCELET
FORTE FORT STARK METIER STRONG EMINENCY STRENGTH
FORTESCUE COBBLER SCORPION
FORTH OUT AWAY FURTH
(PREF.) E OUT
FORTHCOMING PROXIMATE
FORTHRIGHT BALD BURLY

GUTTY CANDID
FORTHRIGHTLY FRANKLY
FORTHRIGHTNESS PLUMPNESS
FORTHWITH EFT NOW ANON AWAY BEDENE DIRECT BETIMES FORTHON DIRECTLY
FORTIFICATION BAWN BOMA FORT MOAT WALL REDAN TOWER ABATIS CASHEL CASTLE GLACIS LAAGER BASTION BULWARK CITADEL DEFENCE DEFENSE PARAPET PILLBOX RAMPART RAVELIN REDOUBT FORTRESS MUNITION RONDELLE STRENGTH
(**LINE OF —S**) TROCHA
(**PART OF —**) BERM MOAT ANGLE DITCH FLANK GORGE SCARP SLOPE COVERT ESCARP GLACIS PARADE BASTION CURTAIN PARAPET RAMPART SALIENT BANQUETTE TERREPLEIN COUNTERSCARP
FORTIFIED ARMED CONFIRMED
FORTIFY ARM MAN BANK FORT LINE WALL WARD FENCE SPIKE STANK BATTLE IMMURE MUNIFY MUNITE BULWARK COMFORT DEFENSE GARNISH RAMPIRE BASTILE EMBATTLE FORTRESS RAMFORCE STOCKADE
FORTITUDE GRIT GUTS SAND FIBER FIBRE NERVE PLUCK METTLE BRAVERY COURAGE HEROISM STAMINA BACKBONE PATIENCE STRENGTH
(**AUTHOR OF —**) WALPOLE
(**CHARACTER IN —**) TAN HANZ NORA BOBBY BRANT CLARE JERRY PETER ZANTI EMILIO LAUNCE GALLEON JERRARD MONOGUE STEPHEN ZACHARY BROCKETT ROSSITER WESTCOTT CARDILLAC GOTTFRIED AITCHINSON
FORTNIGHTLY BIWEEKLY
FORTRESS (**ALSO SEE FORT**) BURG KEEP KASBA PIECE PLACE ROCCA CASBAH CASTLE ALCAZAR BARRIER BOROUGH CASTRUM CHATEAU CITADEL KREMLIN ZWINGER ALCAZAVA BASTILLE FASTNESS STRENGTH
(**AUTHOR OF —**) WALPOLE
(**CHARACTER IN —**) ADAM JOHN KRAFT PARIS ROGUE BENJIE CAESAR JUDITH REUBEN TEMPLE UHLAND WALTER HERRIES SUNWOOD JENNIFER MARGARET ELIZABETH GOLIGHTLY CHRISTABEL
FORTUITOUS CASUAL CHANCE RANDOM FORTUIT FORTUNEL
FORTUITY LUCK CHANCE
FORTUNATE EDI FAT HAP SRI GOOD SHRI WELL CANNY FAUST HAPPY LUCKY RIGHT WHITE DEXTER EUROUS BLESSED FAVORED WEIRDLY GRACIOUS
FORTUNATELY FAIR HAPPILY
FORTUNE DIE HAP LOT URE BAHI DOOM FALL FARE FATE HAIL LUCK PILE SEEL STAR EVENT GRACE ISSUE LINES SONSE SPEED

WEIRD WHATE CHANCE ESTATE MISHAP RICHES WEALTH DESTINY SUCCESS THEEDOM VENTURE ACCIDENT CASUALTY FELICITY STOCKING
(**GOOD —**) SELE SONSE SPEED THRIFT FURTHER GOODHAP BONCHIEF FELICITY
(**ILL —**) DOOM THRAW
(PREF.) TYCH(O)
FORTUNES OF RICHARD MAHONY (**AUTHOR OF —**) RICHARDSON
(**CHARACTER IN —**) TOM JOHN LUCY MARY ZARA CUFFY OCOCK POLLY SARAH LALLIE MAHONY RICHARD TURNHAM CUTHBERT
FORTUNE-TELLER SEER SIBYL SYBIL SPAEMAN SORTIARY SPAEWIFE
(PL.) CHALDAEI
FORTY DAYS OF MUSA DAGH
(**AUTHOR OF —**) WERFEL
(**CHARACTER IN —**) TER HAIK MARIS SARKIS BEREKET GABRIEL STEPHAN GONZAGUE HAIGASUN HULIETTE KILIKIAN BAGRADIAN NOKHUDIAN
FORUM COURT PLATFORM TRIBUNAL
FORWARD ON TO AID BOG BUG GAY ABET BAIN BOLD FORE FREE HELP PERT SEND SHIP STEP AHEAD ALONG AVANT BARDY BRASH CAGER EAGER FAVOR FORTH FRACK FRECK FRONT HASTY PAWKY PUSHY RANDY READY RELAY REMIT SAUCY SERVE SPACK ULTRA AFFORD ARDENT AVAUNT BEFORE BRIGHT COMING DEVANT FORRIT FORTHY HASTEN NUZZLE ONWARD PROMPT ROUDAS SECOND TOWARD ADVANCE BETIMES EARNEST EXTREME FURTHER PROMOTE PUSHING RADICAL SOLICIT ADELANTE ARROGANT FROMWARD IMMODEST IMPUDENT MALAPERT ONCOMING PERVERSE PETULANT TELLSOME TOWARDLY TRANSMIT OBTRUSIVE
(**MOST —**) HEADMOST
(PREF.) ANTE
(**LEANING —**) PRONO
FORWARDNESS IMMODESTY
FOR WHOM THE BELL TOLLS
(**AUTHOR OF —**) HEMINGWAY
(**CHARACTER IN —**) MARIA PABLO PILAR JORDAN ROBERT ANSELMO
FORZA DEL DESTINO, LA
(**CHARACTER IN —**) CARLO ALVARO LEONORA CALATRAVA
(**COMPOSER OF —**) VERDI
FOSSA FOSS FOVEA GALET TRENCH VALLIS FOSSULA FOSSETTE
FOSSE DITCH GRAFF
FOSSIL CYCAD CYSTID DOLITE EOZOON FUCOID ICHITE PINITE AMBRITE BLASTID CHAMITE CRINITE ICHNITE JUNCITE LITUITE NEREITE OVULITE REMANIE

TYLOPOD ZOOLITE ZOOLITH
AISTOPOD AMMONITE
ANCODONT ASTROITE BACULITE
BALANITE BIOCHRON BLASTOID
BUFONITE CALAMITE CERATITE
CONCHITE CONODONT ECHINITE
EOHIPPUS FAVOSITE FILICITE
FUSULINA GEDANITE GYROLITH
MIMOSITE PEUCITES POLYPITE
SALIGRAM SCAPHITE SERAPHIM
SPONGOID SYNAPSID TARSIOID
CARPOLITE OSTRACODERM
(PREF.) NECR(O) ORYCT(O)
(SUFF.) LITE LITH(IC) LITIC
FOSTER REAR NURSE COCKER
HARBOR NUZZLE SUCKLE
CHERISH DEPOSIT EMBOSOM
GRATIFY INDULGE NOURISH
NOURSLE NURTURE BEFRIEND
CULTIVATE
FOSTERAGE NURSERY
FOSTERER NORRY
FOUL BAD BASE EVIL HORY RANK
ROIL VILE BAWDY BLACK DIRTY
DITCH FUNKY GRIMY GURRY
HORRY KETTY LOUSY MUDDY
MUSTY NASTY RUSTY SULLY
WEEDY CLARTY DEFAME DIRTEN
DREGGY FILTHY GREASY IMPURE
MALIGN ODIOUS PUTRID ROTTEN
SOILED SORDID UNFAIR VIROSE
ABUSIVE BEASTLY DEFACED
FULSOME HATEFUL ILLEGAL
IMBROIN NOISOME OBSCENE
PROFANE SLOTTER SMEARED
SQUALID TETROUS UNCLEAN
VICIOUS AMURCOUS ENTANGLE
FECULENT INDECENT MEPHITIC
SLOTTERY STAGNANT STINKING
TRAUCHLE WRETCHED
(— UP) BOTCH
FOULMOUTHED RIBALD ROUDAS
ABUSIVE OBSCENE PROFANE
FOULNESS FEDITY PRAVITY
(— OF MOUTH) SABURRA
FOUL-SMELLING FUNKY
FOUND FIX TRY YET BASE CAST
REST STAY BEGIN BOARD BUILD
ENDOW ERECT PLANT START
ATTACH BOTTOM DEPART
GROUND INVENT EQUIPPED
PRACTICE PROVIDED SUPPLIED
FOUNDATION BED BASE BODY
FIRM FOND FUND GIST ROOT SILL
SOLE BASIS FOUND STOCK STOOL
ANLAGE BOTTOM CRADLE
GROUND LEGACY MATRIX
PODIUM RIPRAP BEDDING
BEDROCK CHANTRY COLLEGE
MORTISE PINNING RADICAL
ROADBED SUBBASE WARRANT
BACKBONE DONATION MATTRESS
MIREPOIX PEDESTAL PLATFORM
STANDARD UNDERLAY
(— FOR WIG) CAUL
(— OF BASKET) SLATH SLARTH
(FLOATING —) CRIB
(LACE —) RESEAU
(PRECARIOUS —) STILT
FOUNDATIONER GOWNBOY
COLLEGER
FOUNDED FUSILE
FOUNDER FAIL IMAM AUTHOR

CASTER DYNAST EPONYM HELLEN
YETTER AFOUNDE STUMBLE
BELLETER MISCARRY LAMINITIS
PATRIARCH
(— OF COLONY) OECIST
FOUNT FONS FONT SOURCE
FOUNTAIN URN AQUA FOND HEAD
KELD PANT PILA SYKE WELL
DIRCE FOUNT GURGE QUELL
SURGE ORIGIN PHIALE PIRENE
SOURCE SPRING BUBBLER
CONDUIT SPRUDEL AGANIPPE
SALMACIS UPSPRING WELLHEAD
(INK —) DUCT
(SODA —) SPA
(PREF.) PEGO
(SUFF.) CRENE
FOUNTAINHEAD ORIGIN SOURCE
FOUNTAIN PEN STICK STYLO
FOUR MESS CATER DELTA DALETH
FEOWER TETRAD QUARTET
QUATRAL MURNIVAL QUADRATE
(— OF ANYTHING) GUNDA
(— OF TRUMPS) TIDDY
(— TIMES A DAY) QD QID
(— YEAR PERIOD) PYTHIAD
(GROUP OF —) TETRAD
(PREF.) QUADR(I)(U) QUADRATO
QUATER TESSARA TETR(A)
(— ATOMS OF HYDROGEN)
TETRAZ(O)
(— TIMES) QUATER TETRAKIS
(HAVING — PARTS) TETR(A)
FOURCHETTE FORGET SIDEWALL
WISHBONE
FOURFOLD FOURBLE QUATERN
**FOUR HORSEMEN OF
APOCALYPSE (AUTHOR OF —)**
IBANEZ
(CHARACTER IN —) JULIO CHICHI
MARCELO DESNOYER HARTROTT
FOURIERISM SOCIALISM
FOUR-O'CLOCK FRIARBIRD
FOURPENNY BIT JOE FLAG JOEY
GROAT
FOURTEENER SEPTENAR
FOURTH DELTA QUART FARDEL
FORPIT FERLING QUARTER
QUADRANT
(— HOUR) SEXT
(— OF BAHMANI EMPIRE) TARAF
(— OF CAKE) FARL FARLE
(— OF YEAR) RAITH
(AUGMENTED —) TRITONE
(PREF.) QUART(I) TETART(O)
FOUSSA CIVET GALET
FOVEOLA VARIOLE
FOWL HEN RED COCK GAME GRIG
JAVA ROCK SLIP BIDDY CHUCK
CLUCK COPPY DUMPY MALAY
MANOC MARAN SILKY ANCONA
ASHURA BANTAM BRAHMA
CAMBAR COCHIN HOUDAN
LAMONA LEGBAR POLISH REDCAP
SULTAN SUSSEX BUFFBAR
CAMPINE CHICKEN CORNISH
DORKING FRIZZLE HAMBURG
LEGHORN MINORCA OKLABAR
POULTRY ROOSTER SPANISH
SUMATRA COCKEREL CUBALAYA
DELAWARE DUCKWING DUNGHILL
GAMECOCK LANGSHAN
SHANGHAI SHOWBIRD VOLAILLE

(AGGREGATION OF —) RAFT
(CASTRATED —) CAPETTE
(CRESTED —) TOPKNOT
(GUINEA —) KEEL COMEBACK
(MALE —) STAG
(STUFFED —) FARCI
(TAILLESS —) RUMKIN
(5-TOED —) SILKY SILKIE
FOWLER BIRDMAN
FOX DOG KIT PUG TOD ASSE FOOL
STAG WILD ADIVE BRANT CAAMA
SWIFT TRICK VIXEN ZORRO
ARCTIC BAGMAN CANDUC
COLFOX CORSAC FENNEC LOWRIE
OUTWIT RENARD RUSSEL
BEGUILE CHARLEY CHARLIE
KARAGAN REYNARD STUPEFY
VULPINE CUSTOMER MUSKWAKI
OUTAGAMI PLATINUM
FOX-AND-GEESE MERELS
FOXGLOVE POPPY POPDOCK
THIMBLE FLAPDOCK POPGLOVE
FOX GRAPE ISABELLA LABRUSCA
FOXHOUND WALKER
FOX HUNTER PINK
FOXTAIL CAUDA CHAPE COUGH
KNEED TWITCH SETARIA
GAMELOTE
FOXY SLY WILY COONY SHREWD
CUNNING VULPINE DEXTROUS
FOYER HALL LOBBY ANTEROOM
FRACAS BOUT BRAWL MELEE
MUSIC BICKER RUMPUS SHINDY
UPROAR QUARREL SHINDIG
FRACTION INCIDENT
FRACTION BIT CUT PYO FLUX
PART BREAK PIECE SCRAP
BREACH LITTLE MOIETY DECIMAL
GLUTOSE WETNESS
(— OF RADIATION) ALBEDO
(NAPHTHA —) LIGROIN
(PREF.) MER(I)(O)
(SUFF.) MER(E)(IC)(OUS)(Y)
FRACTIONAL ALIQUOT FRACTED
PARTIAL
FRACTIOUS MEAN UGLY CROSS
UNRULY CRABBED PEEVISH
WASPISH PERVERSE SNAPPISH
FRACTURE BUST FLAW REND
BILGE BREAK CLEFT CRACK FAULT
JOINT BREACH DEFORM HACKLE
DIACOPE FISSURE RUPTURE
DIACLASE FRACTION
(PREF.) RHEGMA RHEGNO
(SUFF.) CLASE RHEXIS RRHEXIS
FRACTURED SPLIT BROKEN
FRACTURING SLIP STRAIN
FAILURE
FRA DIAVOLO (CHARACTER IN —)
PAMELA DIAVOLO LORENZO
ZERLINA COCKBURN
(COMPOSER OF —) AUBER
FRAGILE FINE FROW WEAK FRAIL
FROWY LIGHT SWACK FEEBLE
FROUGH INFIRM SLIGHT TENDER
BRICKLE BRITTLE FROUGHY
SLENDER TIFFANY DELICATE
EGGSHELL ETHEREAL FRACTILE
SLATTERY BREAKABLE
FRAGILITY DELICACY
FRAGMENT BIT ORT ATOM BLAD
CHIP DRIB FLAW GROT MOIT
MOTE PART RUMP SHED SNIP

WISP ANGLE BLAUD BRACK
BREAK BROKE CATCH CHUNK
CLOUT CRUMB FRUST GIGOT
PIECE RELIC SCRAP SHARD SHERD
SHIVE SHRED SPALL SPELL SPLIT
CANTLE FARDEL FILING GOBBET
MORSEL REMAIN SCREED SHIVER
SIPPET SLIVER CANTLET EXCERPT
FLINDER FLITTER FRITTER
FRUSTUM MACERAL MAMMOCK
REMANIE REMNANT SEGMENT
SHATTER SHAVING SNIPPET
AVULSION CHIPPING DETRITUS
FRACTION OARTICLE POTSHERD
SCANTLET SKERRICK SPLINTER
(— CUT OFF) CANTLE
(— OF BONE) SEQUESTER
SEQUESTRUM
(— OF BRICK) BRICKBAT
(— OF DIAMOND) CLEAVAGE
(— OF ICE) CALF
(— OF LAVA) FAVILLA LAPILLUS
(— OF MELODY) LAY
(— OF ROCK) CRAG AUTOLITH
LAPILLUS
(— OF SAIL) HULLOCK
(— OF SOD) TAB
(— OF STONE) SCABBLING
(— OF UNFINISHED WORK) TORSO
(— OF VEIN MATERIAL) SHOAD
SHODE
(—S OF CLOUD) SCUD
(-S OF DIAMOND) BORT
(—S OF SAND) FINES
(CAST IRON —) POTLEG
(ICE —S) BRASH
(JAGGED —) BROCK
(LITERARY —) ANALECTA
(MASS OF —S) BRASH
(PLANT —) SHIVE
(SHELL —S) SHRAPNEL
(WOODY —S FOUND IN FOOD) CHAD
(PL.) BRASH FRUSH SCRAPS
CINDERS FITTERS GUBBINS
SMATTER FLINDERS LEFTOVER
SMITHERS SMITHEREENS
FRAGMENTAL CLASTIC
FRAGMENTARY HASHY SNIPPY
SCRAPPY DIVIDUAL
FRAGRANCE BALM ODOR AROMA
SCENT SMELL SWEET BREATH
FLAVOR FRAGOR BOUQUET
INCENSE PERFUME SUAVITY
FRAGRANT NOSY RICH BALMY
OLENT SPICY SWEET SAVORY
SPICED ODORANT ODOROUS
PERFUMY SCENTED AROMATIC
FLAGRANT NECTARED ODORIFIC
REDOLENT
FRAIL FINE POOR PUNY WEAK
CRAZY REEDY SEELY SILLY
BASKET BROTEL CROCKY FLIMSY
INFIRM SICKLY SINGLE SLIGHT
SLIMSY SQUEAL TICKLE TOPNET
BRITTLE BRUCKLE FRAGILE
SLENDER SLIMPSY UNHARDY
DELICATE PINDLING
FRAILTY FAULT FOIBLE INVENT
FAILING DELICACY WEAKNESS
(HUMAN —) ADAM
FRAMBESIA PIAN YAWS BUBAS
MORULA
FRAME BED BIN BOW BOX FLY

GYM MAT SET BAIL BEAM BIER
BUCK BULK BUNK CANT CASE
CAUM CELL CLAM CRIB CURB
DESK DRAG FORM FROG GATE
GILL HACK HARP HECK JACK
MOLD PORT RACK SASH SLEY
SOLE STEP AIRER ANGLE BANJO
BLADE BLIND BLOCK BUILD
CADRE CHASE CLEAT CRATE
CROOK DRAFT EASEL FLAKE
FLASK FLEAK FLOAT GRATE
HERSE HORSE MOUNT OXBOW
PERCH PRESS SCRAY SHAPE
STAND STATE STEAD STOCK
STOOL TRAIL BARROW BATTEN
BINDER BUCCAN BUCKET CASING
CHEVAL COFFIN CRADLE CRATCH
CRUTCH DECKLE DREDGE FABRIC
FENDER GANTRY GRILLE HANGER
HARROW HOTBED HURDLE
PERSON PILLAR QUADRA REDACT
REEDER SCREEN SETTLE SLEDGE
SPIDER SQUARE STAPLE TANGLE
TENTER TESTER ARMRACK
BREAKER CABINET CARRIER
CASEBOX CHASSIS COAMING
COASTER CRAMPON CRIMPER
DRAUGHT DROSSER FASHION
FRAMING FRISKET GALLOWS
GARLAND GATEWAY GIGTREE
GRATING HAYRACK HOUSING
ICEBOAT MACHINE MONTURE
OXBRAKE PORTRAY SETTING
STADDLE TRANSOM TRESTLE
TRIBBLE BARBECUE BOWGRACE
CARRIAGE CASEMENT CONCEIVE
CONTRIVE DOORCASE GRAFFAGE
GRIDIRON GRILLAGE HALBERDS
HOGFRAME PLOWHEAD
RAILROAD RECEIVER RETAINER
SKELETON THRIPPLE TRIANGLE
TURNPIKE BRANDRITH
OUTRIGGER
(— FOR ARCH) COOM COOMB
(— FOR BEEHIVE) SECTION
(— FOR CANDLES) HEARSE
(— FOR CARRYING STRAW) KNAPE
(— FOR CASK) GANTRY STALDER
(— FOR CATCHING FISH) HATCH
(— FOR CLOTHES DRYING) AIRER
(— FOR CONFINING HORSE) TRAVE
TRAVAIL
(— FOR COW'S HEAD) BAIL
(— FOR DRYING FISH) HACK HAIK
(— FOR DRYING SKINS) HERSE
(— FOR FISHING LINE) CADAR
CADER
(— FOR GLAZING LEATHER) BUCK
(— FOR HAWKS) CADGE
(— FOR KILLING PIGS) CREEL
(— FOR LENS) BOW
(— FOR ROLLER BEARINGS) CAGE
(— FOR SMOKING MEAT) BOUCAN
BUCCAN
(— FOR STACK) HAYRACK STADDLE
(— FOR WASHING ORE) BUDDLE
(— OF A VESSEL) HULL
(— OF MIND) HAZE SPITE SPIRIT
TEMPER FEELING POSTURE
(— OF PIER) JETTY
(— OF SAW) HUSK
(— OF SPINNING MULE) SQUARE
(— OF STRAW) SIME

(— OF TINWORK) MARQUITO
(— ON STAGE) CEILING
(— TO CATCH STARFISH) TANGLE
(— TO CLEAN SHIP'S BOTTOM) HOG
(— TO DRY CLOTHES) AIRER
(BELL —) SWEEP
(BOBBIN —) BANK
(CARRIAGE —) BRAKE BREAK
(COUNTING —) ABACUS
(DIVING —) LUNET LUNETTE
(EMBROIDERY —) TENT TABORET
TAMBOUR
(FISHING —) DREDGE
(GLAZIER'S —) FRAIL
(HARNESS —) HEALD
(LOOM —) SLAY SLEY LATHE
BATTEN SLEIGH
(MINING —) APRON
(PHOTOGRAPHY —) BUTTERFLY
(PORTABLE —) BIER CACAXTE
(PRINTING —) CHASE PRESS
(SHIP'S —) CANT
(SLUBBING —) BILLY
(STRETCHING —) TENT SLEDGE
TENTER
(TANNING —) BEAM
(WINDOW —) CHESS
(2-WHEELED —) GILL
(PL.) PROFILE
FRAMED NATE NATED ENGAGED
FRAMEWORK BED BENT BIER
BONE BUCK BULK CAGE CRIB
DURN GRID RACK SASH BONES
CADRE CHUTE COPSE CREEL
FLAKE SHELL STOCK BELFRY
BRIDGE BUSTLE CABANE CRADLE
DESIGN FABRIC GOCART GUARDS
HARROW HEARSE REBATO SHIELD
STROMA WATTLE CABINET
CARCASS CLIMBER COMMODE
DERRICK FRAMING FULCRUM
JACKBOX LATTICE PANNIER
REBATER RETABLE STADDLE
TRESTLE BARBECUE BEDSTEAD
BULKHEAD CARRIAGE CRADLING
CRIBWORK GRIDIRON GRILLAGE
OSSATURE SCAFFOLD SHELVING
SHOWCASE SKELETON
(— AROUND HATCHWAY) FIDDLEY
(— FOR CORNSTACK) HOVEL
(— FOR PEAL OF BELLS) CAGE
(— OF REFERENCE) SCHEMA
(— TO EXPAND SKIRTS) BUSTLE
PANNIER
(EMPTY —) HUSK
(SCULPTOR'S —) ARMATURE
FRAMING CURB LEAD BELFRY
ARMATURE BEDPLATE
**FRAMLEY PARSONAGE (AUTHOR
OF —)** TROLLOPE
(CHARACTER IN —) LUCY MARK
FANNY SMITH LUFTON THORNE
CRAWLEY ROBARTS SOWERBY
DUNSTABLE
FRANCE
(PREF.) GALLO

FRANCE
BAY: BISCAY ARACHON
CAPE: HAGUE
CAPITAL: PARIS
CHEESE: BLEU BRIE BONBEL
BOURSIN MUNSTER

CAMEMBERT MARCILLAT
ROQUEFORT
COIN: ECU SOL SOU GROS AGNEL
BLANC BLANK FRANC LIARD
LIVRE LOUIS OBOLE SAIGA
SCUTE BLANCA BLANCO DENIER
DIZAIN TESTON AGNEAUX
CENTIME TESTOON CAVALIER
NAPOLEON
DANCE: GAVOT BRANLE CANARY
CANCAN BOUTADE GAVOTTE
DEPARTMENT: AIN LOT VAR AUBE
AUDE CHER EURE GARD GERS
JURA NORD OISE ORNE TARN
AISNE INDRE ISERE LOIRE
RHONE YONNE ARIEGE CANTAL
CREUSE LOZERE NIEVRE
CORREZE GIRONDE MOSELLE
DIVISION, ANCIENT: ARLES PERCHE
NEUSTRIA AQUITAINE
AQUITANIA
DYNASTY: CAPET VALOIS
BOURBON ORLEANS CAPETIAN
MEROVINGIAN
FOOD: PATE CREPE CANAPE
MOUSSE QUICHE BRIOCHE
SOUFFLE ESCARGOT PIPERADE
POTAUFEU TOURNEDO
ISLAND: RE YEU CITE CORSE
GROIX HYERE OLERON USHANT
CORSICA
KING: ODO EUDES PEPIN CLOVIS
LOTHAIR
LAKE: ANNECY CAZAUX
MEASURE: POT SAC AUNE LINE
MINE MUID PIED VELT ARPEN
CARAT LIEUE LIGNE MINOT
PERCH PINTE POINT POUCE
TOISE VELTE ARPENT HEMINE
LEAGUE QUARTE SETIER
CHOPINE HEMINEE POISSON
SEPTIER BOISSEAU QUARTAUT
ROQUILLE QUARTERON
MILITARY ACADEMY: STCYR
SAINTCYR
MOUNTAIN: PUY DORE BLANC
CINTO FOREZ PELAT COTEDOR
MOUNIER VENTOUX
VIGNEMALE CHAMBEYRON
MOUNTAIN RANGE: ALPS ECRINS
VOSGES CEVENNES PYRENEES
MARITIMES
NAME: GAUL GAULE GALLIA
NATIONAL ANTHEM: MARSEILLAISE
NATIVE: CELT GAUL FRANK
BASQUE BRETON GASCON
NORMAN PICARD CATALAN
GALLOIS LORRAIN FRANCIEN
LIGURIAN PROVENCAL
BURGUNDIAN
PORT: CAEN BREST CALAIS
TOULON LEHAVRE BORDEAUX
CHERBOURG DUNKERQUE
MARSEILLE
PROTESTANT: HUGUENOT
PROVINCE: FOIX ANJOU AUNIS
BEARN ALSACE ARTOIS
COMTAT POITOU AUVERGNE
BRETAGNE BRITTANY LIMOUSIN
LORRAINE PROVENCE
TOURAINE
RACE TRACK: AUTEUIL
LONGCHAMPS

REPUBLIC CALENDAR: NIVOSE
FLOREAL VENTOSE BRUMAIRE
FERVIDOR FRIMAIRE GERMINAL
MESSIDOR PLUVIOSE PRAIRIAL
FRUCTIDOR THERMIDOR
VENDEMIAIRE
RESORT: PAU NICE CANNES
MENTON RIVIERA
RIVER: AIN LOT LUY LYS VAR AIRE
AUBE AUDE CHER DRAC EURE
GARD GERS LOIR OISE ORNE
TARN VIRE ADOUR AISNE
AULNE DROME INDRE ISERE
LOIRE MARNE MEUSE RHONE
RISLE SAONE SEINE SOMME
VIAUR YONNE ALLIER ARIEGE
ESCAUT SAMBRE SCARPE
VEZERE VIENNE DURANCE
GARONNE GIRONDE MAYENNE
MOSELLE CHARENTE
DORDOGNE
STOCK EXCHANGE: BOURSE
STRAIT: BONIFACIO
TOWN: AY EU AIX DAX GEX PAU
AGDE AGEN ALBI AUBY AUCH
BRON CAEN LAON LOOS METZ
NICE OPPY ORLY RIOM SENS
SETE STLO TOUL UZES VAUX
VIMY VIRE ARLES ARRAS BLOIS
BREST DIJON DINAN DOUAI
ERNEE LAVAL LILLE LISLE
LYONS NANCY NERAC NESLE
NIMES ORNES PARIS REIMS
ROUEN SEDAN TOURS TULLE
VICHY AMIENS ANGERS CALAIS
LEMANS LONGWY NANTES
PANTIN RENNES RHEIMS
SARLAT SENLIS SEVRES TARARE
TARBES TOULON TROYES
TULLUM VALOIS VERDUN
BAREGES CASTRES LIMOGES
ORLEANS ROUBAIX VALENCE
BORDEAUX CLERMONT
GRENOBLE MULHOUSE
ROCHELLE TOULOUSE
MARSEILLE STRASBOURG
TRIBE: REMI AEDUI ARVERNI
SALUVII ALLOBROGES
VERSE FORM: LAI ALBA AUBADE
RONDEL BALLADE DESCORT
RONDEAU VIRELAI VIRELAY
WATERFALL: GAVARNIE
WEIGHT: GROS MARC ONCE
CARAT LIVRE POUND TONNE
TONNEAU ESTERLIN
WIND: MISTRAL
WINE: MACON MEDOC GRAVES
CHABLIS POMEROL BORDEAUX
BURGUNDY MUSCADET
SAUTERNE CHAMPAGNE
WINE DISTRICT: MEDOC ALSACE
BORDEAUX BURGUNDY
CHAMPAGNE

FRANCESCA DA RIMINI
(CHARACTER IN —) PAOLO
FRANCESCA GIANCIOTTO
MALATESTINO
(COMPOSER OF —) ZANDONAI
FRANCHISE SOC SOKE VOTE
CHASE FERRY HONOR INFANG
CHARTER FREEDOM LIBERTY
CONTRACT FREELAGE

SUFFRAGE TENEMENT
FRANCISCAN MINOR MINORITE
FRANCOLIN COQUI TETUR TITAR
REDWING PHEASANT
FRANCOPHILE GALLOMAN
FRANGIBLE BRITTLE
FRANGIPANI SHAKEWOOD
FRANK FREE OPEN RANK BLUFF
BLUNT BURLY LUSTY NAIVE
PLAIN BRAZEN CANDID DIRECT
FORTHY HONEST SALIAN ARTLESS
GENUINE LIBERAL PROFUSE
SINCERE CAREFREE CAVALIER
GENEROUS STRAIGHT VIGOROUS
OUTSPOKEN OPENHEARTED
PLAINSPOKEN
FRANKENSTEIN (AUTHOR OF —)
SHELLEY
(CHARACTER IN —) HENRY ROBERT
VICTOR WALTON CLERVAL
JUSTINE WILLIAM ELIZABETH
FRANKENSTEIN
FRANKINCENSE THUS OLIBAN
OLIBANUM
FRANKINCENSE (— TREE)
(PREF.) LIBO
FRANKLY FREELY OPENLY PLAINLY
CANDIDLY
FRANKNESS CANDOR FREEDOM
OPENNESS
FRANKPLEDGE BORROW FRIBORG
FRANSERIA RAGWEED
FRANTIC MAD WOOD RABID
INSANE MANIAC FURIOUS
LUNATIC VIOLENT DERANGED
FEVERISH FRENETIC FRENZIED
MANIACAL
FRAPPE ICE GRANITE
FRATERCULA MORMON
FRATERNAL BROTHERLY
DIZYGOTIC NONIDENTICAL
FRATERNITY FRAT FRARY HOUSE
ORDER FRATRY QUALITY SOCIETY
SODALITY
FRATERNIZE FRAT COTTON
FRAUD GYP DOLE FAKE GAFF
GAUD GULL JAPE JUNT LURK
RUSE SHAM SKIN WILE CHEAT
COVIN CRAFT DOLUS FAKER
FAVEL GLAIK GUILE HOCUS
LURCH SHARK SHIFT SHUCK
SWICK SWIKE TRICK BROGUE
DECEIT FIDDLE FULLAM HUMBUG
INTAKE STUMER WRENCH
FLIVVER KNAVERY ROGUERY
STUMOUR SWINDLE BOODLING
COZENAGE IMPOSTER OPERATOR
SUBTLETY TRUMPERY
FRAUDULENT SKIN WILY CRONK
COGGED CRAFTY QUACKY
ABUSIVE CROOKED CUNNING
KNAVISH CHEATING COVINOUS
FRAUDFUL GUILEFUL QUACKISH
SINISTER SPURIOUS
FRAXINELLA DITTANY RUEWORT
FRAY FRET BROIL BROOM FEAZE
MELEE RAVEL AFFRAY BUSTLE
CHAUVE FRIDGE TIFFLE CONTEST
FRAZZLE
FRAYED WORN FLAGGY RAVELED
FRAZER FINNER
FREAK FIRK FLAM WHIM FANCY
HUMOR LUSUS MOODS SCAPE

SPORT MEGRIM SPLEEN WHIMSY
CAPRICE CROTCHET ESCAPADE
FLIMFLAM WHIMWHAM
MONSTROSITY
(CRAZY —S) LUNES
FREAKISH FREAKY BIZARRE
FLIGHTY MAGGOTY WHIMSIC
CRANKISH
FRECKLE CHIT EPHELIS FRECKEN
LENTIGO SUNSPOT HEATSPOT
FRECKLED FRECKLY FLECKLED
FREE LAX LET MOD RID BOLD EASE
LISS OPEN PERT REDD SHED
SHUT CLEAN CLEAR FLUID FRANK
LARGE LISSE LOOSE READY
SCOUR SLAKE SPARE ACQUIT
DEGAGE DEVOID EXEMPT FACILE
FLUENT FREELY GRATIS IMMUNE
LOOSEN SOLUTE UNSLIP VACANT
VAGILE CLEANSE DELIVER
GRIVOIS INEXACT LASKING
LIBERAL MANUMIT RELEASE
SCIOLTO UNBOUND UNSLAVE
UNTWIST WILLING ABSOLUTE
AUTARKIC BUCKSHEE EASINESS
EXPEDITE FACILITY FREEHAND
GRIVOISE INDIGENT LAXATIVE
LIBERATE UNBRIDLE
(— AND EASY) GLIB CAVALIER
FAMILIAR
(— BROOK OF WEEDS) RODE
(— FROM) EX REDD DEVOID
DISPATCH
(— FROM ABIGUITY) HOMELY
DECIDED
(— FROM ACCUSATION) SACKLESS
(— FROM ACIDITY) DULCIFY
(— FROM ANXIETY) CONTENT
(— FROM ARTIFICIAL) ARTLESS
(— FROM BIAS) CANDID
(— FROM CARE) EASY CARELESS
(— FROM CHARGE) FDD PURGE
FRANCO
(— FROM CONSTRAINT) CASUAL
(— FROM DEDUCTIONS) NET
(— FROM DEFECT) HAIL HALE
SOUND
(— FROM DIRT) BRIGHT
(— FROM DOUBT) RESOLVE
(— FROM ELECTRICAL CHARGE)
DEAD
(— FROM ERROR) LEAL SOUND
CORRECT ACCURATE
(— FROM EVIL) RESCUE
(— FROM EXTREMES) EQUABLE
(— FROM FLAWS) GOOD
(— FROM FROST) FRESH
(— FROM IMPURITIES) FINE DRESS
DEFECATE DEPURATE
(— FROM KNOTS) ENODE ENODATE
(— FROM MARKS) BLANK
(— FROM MICROORGANISMS)
ASEPTIC STERILE
(— FROM OBLIGATION) ACQUIT
EXCUSE
(— FROM PENALTY) ABSOLVE
(— FROM RESTRAINT) ABANDONED
(— FROM STONES) CHESSOM
(— OF DIFFICULTIES) AFLOAT
(— OF FAT) ENSEAM
(— OF OVERTONES) PURE
(— OF TAR) WRECK
(— ONE'S SELF) SOLVE

(— PLUNGER) ARM
(— THROW AREA) KEYHOLE
(PREF.) ELEUTHER(O) IMMUNO
LIBRO
(— FROM) DE
FREEBOARD QUICKSIDE
FREEBOOTER TORY RIDER ROVER
THIEF PIRATE BRIGAND CATERAN
CORSAIR PINDARI PILLAGER
RAPPAREE SNAPHANCE
FREEBORN INGENUOUS
FREEDMAN LEYSING TITYRUS
(PL.) LAET
FREEDOM RUN EASE FRITH LARGE
UHURU ACCESS STREET APATHIA
BREADTH LEISURE LIBERTY
LICENCE LICENSE RELEASE
AUTONOMY FREELAGE FREENESS
IMMUNITY IMPUNITY LARGESSE
WITHGATE
(— FROM BIAS) CANDOR
(— FROM CONSTRAINT) ABANDON
(— FROM DANGER) SECURITY
(— FROM ERROR) ACCURACY
(— FROM GUILT) SHRIVE
(— OF ACCESS) ENTREE
(— OF ACTION) SWINGE LATITUDE
(— OF SPEECH) PARISIA
(— TO PROCEED) HEAD
(CARELESS —) ABANDON
(PREF.) ELEUTHER(O)
FREEHOLD BARONY
FREEHOLDER SWAIN BONDER
YEOMAN FRANKLIN
FREEING LIVERY ACQUITAL
FREE LANCE ROUTIER
FREELY FREE LIEF LARGE LARGELY
READILY HEARTILY
FREEMAN BUR AIRE BARON CEORL
HAULD BONDER CITIZEN
FRANKLIN ROTURIER
(POOR —) THETE
FREEMASON FRATER MORGAN
NOACHITE
(ONE NOT A —) COWAN
FREESTONE HAZEL
(— STATE) CONNECTICUT
FREETHINKER INFIDEL SKEPTIC
AGNOSTIC
FREEZE ICE RIME CATCH CHILL
FROST CURDLE FRAPPE HARDEN
STARVE STEEVE CONGEAL
GLACIATE
FREEZING COLD FREEZY FRIGID
FROSTY GLACIAL CRYONICS
GELATION
(PREF.) CRY(O) KRY(O)
FREIGHT LOAD CARGO GOODS
ASTRAY BURDEN LADING
FRAUGHT HOTSHOT PLUNDER
PORTAGE TRUCKAGE
(— CAR) TRUCK
**FREISCHUTZ, DER (CHARACTER IN
—)** MAX CUNO AGATHE HERMIT
KASPAR SAMIEL AENNCHEN
(COMPOSER OF —) WEBER
FREMD FRAIM FRAMMIT
FRENCH CREOLE FRANCO
GALLIC GALLIAN
GALLICAN
(— MIXED WITH ENGLISH)
FRANGLAIS
(PREF.) FRANCO GALLO

FRENCH GUIANA (CAPE OF —)
ORANGE
(CAPITAL OF —) CAYENNE
(RIVER OF —) MARONI
(TOWN OF —) MANA KOUROU
FRENCH HONEYSUCKLE SULLA
FRENCH LAVENDER STECHADOS
FRENCHMAN GAUL PICARD
FRENCHY MONSIEUR PARLEYVOO
FRENCH MULBERRY SOURBUSH
FRENCH NUDE ALESAN
FRENCH REPUBLIC MARIANNA
MARIANNE
FRENCH SUDAN (SEE MALI)
FRENULUM TENDON
FRENUM BRIDLE FRAENUM
FRENULUM VINCULUM
FRENZIED MAD MUST RABID
RAMAGE BERSERK FANATIC
FRANTIC MADDING FRENETIC
FURIBUND POSSESSED
FRENZY AMOK FURY GERE MOON
MUST RAGE AMUCK FUROR
MANIA MUSTH FURORE RAVING
MADNESS OESTRUS SWIVVET
DELIRIUM INSANITY
FREQUENCY HERTZ PITCH
CREBRITY
FREQUENT USE BANG KEEP
HAUNT HOWFF OFTEN THICK
AFFECT COMMON HOURLY
INFEST RESORT ENHAUNT
OFTTIME CREBROUS FAMILIAR
PRACTICE ACCUSTOMED
(PREF.) SYCHNO
FREQUENTLY OFT OFTEN HOURLY
UNSELDOM
FRESH GAY HOT NEW WET FLIP
GOOD RACY SMUG WARM BRISK
CRISP GREEN MOIST QUICK
RUDDY SASSY SMART SOUND
SWEET VIVID CALLER CALVER
FLORID LIVELY MAIDEN STRONG
UNUSED VERNAL VIRENT VIRGIN
ANOTHER NOUVEAU UNFADED
VERDANT NOUVELLE ORIGINAL
SPANKING YOUTHFUL
(PREF.) CENO
(SUFF.) CENE
FRESHEN BRACE FRESH RENEW
BREEZE CALLER REVIVE CHOUNCE
PEARTEN REFRESH SWEETEN
FRENCHEN
FRESHENER BRACER
FRESHET TIDE FLOOD FRESH
SPATE TORNADO
FRESHMAN FOX BEJAN FROSH
BEJANT GREENY PENNAL
FRESHER
FRESHNESS DEW VERD NOVELTY
VERDURE VIRIDITY ORIGINALITY
FRET DIK NAG ORP RUB RUX VEX
CARK FASH FRAY FUSS GALL
GNAW RAGE STEW YIRM CHAFE
CRAKE CRISP FLISK GRATE PIQUE
WORRY WREAK ABRADE CORSIE
CRYSAL HARASS MUCKLE NETTLE
PLAGUE REPINE RIPPLE RUFFLE
CHRYSAL GRECQUE GRIZZLE
MEANDER SCRUPLE SQUINNY
ALIGREEK IRRITATE
FRETFUL CROSS GIRNY ORPIT
TEATY TEENY TESTY FRETTY

PENCEY SULLEN TATCHY TWISTY
FRECKET PEEVISH PETTISH
SPLEENY CAPTIOUS CRANKOUS
FRETSOME FROPPISH PETULANT
PINDLING QUERULOUS
FRETTED FRETTY MAGGED
FRETTING FRET EATING
FREY FREYR YNGVI
(FATHER OF —) NJORD
(SISTER OF —) FREYA
FREYA (BROTHER OF —) FREY
(FATHER OF —) NJORD
(HUSBAND OF —) ODIN
FRIABLE CRIMP CRISP CRUMP
FLAKY FRUSH MEALY SHORT
CRUMBY CRUMMY FLUFFY
PUTRID CHESSOM CRUMBLY
MOLDERY POWDERY RESOLUTE
ROTTENLY SHATTERY
(NOT —) SAD
FRIAR FRATE FREER MINIM MINOR
BHIKKU FRATER GELONG GOSAIN
LISTER BHIKSHU JACOBIN
LIMITER SERVITE BREVIGER
CAPUCHIN JACOBITE MINORIST
MINORITE PREACHER AUGUSTINE
CARMELITE CORDELIER
MENDICANT BENEDICTINE
FRIARBIRD COLDONG PIMLICO
MONKBIRD
FRIAR SKATE DOCTOR
FRICANDEAU GRENADINE
FRICASSEE POTPIE
FRICATIVE BUZZ HISS OPEN YOGH
DURATIVE
FRICTION BUZZ DRAG HISS CHAFE
WINDAGE
(PREF.) TRIBO
(SUFF.) TRIPSIS
FRICTIONLESS SMOOTH
FRIED FRIT SAUTE
FRIEDCAKE WONDER CRULLER
FATCAKE DOUGHNUT
FRIEND AME AMI AMY BOR CAD
EME PAX BHAI CHUM NABS OPPO
PARD WINE AMIGO BRICK BUDDY
INGLE NETOP TROUT AIKANE
BELAMY COBBER COUSIN
CUMMER GOSSIP INWARD
KIMMER PRINCE QUAKER
ACHATES COMRADE SOCIETY
COCKMATE COMPADRE
DEMOPHIL FEDERATE HICKSITE
INTIMADO INTIMATE TILLICUM
(— OF BRIDEGROOM) PARANYMPH
(—S NOT SPEAKING) CUTS
(CLOSE —) PRIVY COBBER
COMPADRE
(DIVINE —) SOCIUS
(FAMILIAR —) CRONY GREMIAL
SPECIAL
(GIRL —) DOXY DRAG DONEY
DOXIE STEADY
(INTIMATE FEMALE —) CUMMER
(PRIVATE —) PRIVADO
(WOMAN —) GIMMER
(PL.) FOLK KITH SOCE FOLKS
SOCIETY
FRIENDLESS FORLORN
FRIENDLINESS AMITY AFFINITY
BONHOMIE GOODWILL
FRIENDLY COSH GOOD HOLD
HOMY KIND TOSH CADGY CHIEF

COUTH GREAT HOMEY MATEY
THICK AMICAL CHATTY CHUMMY
FOLKSY FORTHY HOMELY KINDLY
SMOOTH AFFABLE AMIABLE
AMICOUS COUTHIE AMICABLE
HOMELIKE INTIMATE SOCIABLE
NEIGHBORLY
FRIENDSHIP PAX AMITY AMOUR
FRIEZE KELT FRISE CUSHION
FALDING FRISADO FRIEZING
FRIGATE ZABRA
FRIGATE BIRD IOA IWA ALCATRAS
FRIGATE MACKEREL BONITO
TASSARD
FRIGG FREA FRIJA
FRIGGA (HUSBAND OF —) ODIN
(SON OF —) BALDER
FRIGHT COW BOOF FEAR FLEG
FRAY ALARM GHAST GLIFF GLOFF
PANIC SCARE AFFRAY GASTER
GLIFFY SCHRIK TERROR STARTLE
SWITHER FRIGHTEN GASTNESS
GLIFFING
FRIGHTEN AWE COW FLY SHY SOB
BAZE BREE DARE DOSS FEAR
FLEG FLEY FRAY FUNK HARE
HAZE SHOO AFEAR AFLEY ALARM
APPAL BLUFF GALLY GHOST GLIFF
HAZEN SCARE SHORE SPOOK
AFFRAY ALARUM APPALL BOGGLE
BOOGER COWARD FLAITE FLIGHT
FRIGHT GALLEY GALLOW
AFFREUX FRECKEN SCARIFY
STARTLE TERRIFY AFFRIGHT
MISTRYST
(— BIRDS) KEEP
(PREF.) TERRI TERRORI
FRIGHTENED RAD EERY FRIT GAST
EERIE GHAST WINDY AFRAID
AGHAST SCARED SCAREY
STURTIN GHASTFUL
(EASILY —) TIMID SKITTISH
FRIGHTENING EERY DREAD EERIE
GOURY HAIRY FRIGHTY GHASTLY
SHIVERY DREADFUL FLEYSOME
FRIGHTFUL WAN GRIM UGLY
AWFUL FERLY HORRID UGSOME
AFFREUX DIREFUL FEARFUL
GASHFUL GHASTLY HIDEOUS
ALARMING DREADFUL ELDRITCH
FEARSOME GHASTFUL HORRIBLE
HORRIFIC TERRIBLE TERRIFIC
FRIGID DRY ICY COLD BLEAK FISHY
ARCTIC FROSTY FROZEN WINTRY
GLACIAL FREEZING SIBERIAN
FRIGIDITY GLARE
FRILL DIDO PURL JABOT RUCHE
RUFFLE ARMILLA FLOUNCE
SPINACH SPINAGE CHITLING
CRIMPING FRILLERY FURBELOW
(— OF HAIR) APRON
(PL.) PUFFERY FOOFARAW
FRILLERY
FRILLINESS CHICHI
FRILLING RUCHE ROUCHE
SWEEPER
FRILLY CHICHI
FRINGE WLO EDGE GILL LOMA
RUFF WELT BEARD THRUM
BORDER EDGING MARGIN PELMET
TASSEL BULLION CREPINE
EYELASH FEATHER FIMBRIA
MACRAME SELVAGE TRAILER

VALANCE WHISKER CILIELLA
FRISETTE INDUSIUM PENUMBRA
SELVEDGE TRIMMING
(— OF TEETH) PERISTOME
(SOFT —S) THRUM
(PL.) ZIZITH
(PREF.) CROSS(O) FIMBRI(O)
LACINI THYSAN(O)
FRINGED JUBATE CILIATE
LACINIATE
FRINGEFOOT UMA
FRINGEPOD LACEPOD
FRINGETAIL VEILTAIL
FRINGE TREE SHAVINGS
FRIPPERY FLIPPERY TRINKUMS
(PL.) GAUDERY
FRISK COLT FISK PLAY ROLL SKIP
WHID BOUND CAPER SKICE
CAREER CAVORT CURVET FRISCO
FROLIC TITTUP WANTON FRISCAL
FRISKLE
FRISKY GAY PERT FRISK CROUSE
FEISTY KIPPER LIVELY WANTON
BUCKISH COLTISH JIGGISH
PLAYFUL SKITTISH SPORTIVE
FRISON KNUB
FRIT FRETT CALCINE
FRITTER FOOL FRIT TEAR BOLLO
DRILL BANGLE DRIVEL LOUNGE
BEIGNET DRIBBLE FLITTER
SLATTERN
FRIVOLITY LEVITY FRIBBLE
INANITY ITEMING FUTILITY
NONSENSE NUGACITY
FRIVOLOUS GAY DAFT VAIN GIDDY
INANE LIGHT PETTY SILLY WASHY
FLIMSY FRILLY FRIVOL FROTHY
FUTILE TOYISH YEASTY FATUOUS
FRIBBLE LIGHTLY NIDGETY
SHALLOW TRIVIAL GIMCRACK
JIMCRACK SKITTISH TRIFLING
FRIVOLOUSNESS FUTILITY
FRIZZ FRIZ CREPE FRIZE FRIZZLE
FROUNCE
FRIZZED CRISPY
FRIZZLE CRAPE CREPE
FRIZZLY FUZZY CRIMPY FRIZZY
FRIZZY FUZZY CRIMPY FRIZZLY
FROCK DUD JAM GOWN JUMP
SLIP SLOP WRAP LAMMY SMOCK
TRUSS TUNIC CLERIC JERSEY
LAMMIE MANTLE ROCHET
SUKKENYE
FROCK COAT CRISPIN
FROG PAD POD KICK FROSH FROSK
FROUD PADDO PADDY RANID
RONCO ANURAN PEEPER TOGGLE
CHARLIE CRAWLER CREEPER
CROAKER CUSHION FRESHER
FROGLET PADDOCK PODDOCK
QUILKIN BULLFROG FERREIRO
FROGGING PLATANNA REPLACER
(— IN LOOM) HEATER
(— OF HORSE'S HOOF) FRUSH
CUSHION
(TREE —) NOTOTREMA
(PREF.) BATRACH(O) RANI
FROG CRAB RANINIAN
FROGFISH ANGLER SLIMER
TOADFISH
FROGGER CHASER TRAILER
ZOOGLER
FROGGY RANARIAN

FROGHOPPER HOPPER CERCOPID
FROGMOUTH MOPOKE MOREPORK
PODARGUE
FROGS (AUTHOR OF —)
ARISTOPHANES
(CHARACTER IN —) AEACUS
CHARON BACCHUS DIONYSUS
HERCULES XANTHIAS AESCHYLUS
EURIPIDES
(SUFF.) BATRACH(O)(US)
FROLIC BUM GAY RIG BLOW COLT
GAME GELL HAZE JINK LAKE LARK
ORGY PLAY PLOY RANT REEK
ROMP TEAR CAPER FREAK FRISK
MERRY PRANK RANDY ROUSE
SALLY SPORT SPREE BUSTER
CAVORT CURVET FRATCH
GAMBOL PLISKY POWWOW
PRANCE ROLLIX SHINDY SPLORE
VAGARY WANTON DISPORT
GAMMOCK MARLOCK PLISKIE
ROLLICK SCAMPER SKYLARK
SPANIEL STASHIE WASSAIL
CAROUSAL JAMBOREE
FROLICSOME GAY DAFT ROID
ANTIC BUXOM CADGY FRISK
GILPY LARKY FRISKY LIVELY
WANTON ANTICAL JOCULAR
LARKING LARKISH PLAYFUL
WAGGISH ESPIEGLE FRISKFUL
FROLICKY GAMESOME LARKSOME
PRANKISH SPORTFUL SPORTIVE
FROLICSOMENESS HEYDAY
FROM A AB DE EX OF FAE FRA FRO
VAN VON THROM AGAINST
(— A DISTANCE) ALOOF
(— BEGINNING TO END) THROUGH
(— ELSEWHERE) ALIUNDE
(— OFF) AFFA
(— SIDE TO SIDE) OVER CROSS
ATHWART
(— THIS PLACE) HENCE
(PREF.) AP APH APO
FROND FERN TRESS CROSIER
FRONDLET
FRONT BOW VAN BROW FACE
FORE HEAD PROW THIN AFORE
VAUNT BEFORE DEVANT FACADE
FACING FORMER OPPOSE SECTOR
VAWARD ADVANCE FORWARD
FRONTAL FURTHER OBVERSE
PALATAL PREFACE RESPECT
SLENDER FOREHEAD FOREMOST
FOREPART FORESIDE FRONTAGE
(— OF ASTROLABE) WOMBSIDE
(— OF BARN) FOREBAY
(— OF BIRD'S NECK) GUTTUR
(— OF BODY) GROUF
(— OF HEAD) VISAGE FORETOP
(— OF HELMET) VENTAIL
(— OF SHIRT) BOSOM
(— OF WATERWHEEL BUCKET)
START
(— UPON) AFFRONT
(PREF.) ANTER(O) PRO
(IN —) FORE PRO(S)(SO)
(IN — OF) ANTE ANTER(O) PRAE
PRE
FRONTAL PALL FRONT SINDON
TABULA FRONTON METOPIC
FRONTLET SUFFRONT
FRONTIER BOUND COAST FRONT
MARCH BORDER BARRIER

FRONTURE OUTLYING
(FORTIFIED —) LIMES
FRONTING OBVIOUS
FRONTISPIECE FRONT UNWAN
FRONTIS
FRONTLET TIARA FRONTAL
CHAMFRON
FRONT PAGE (AUTHOR OF —)
HECHT MACARTHUR
(CHARACTER IN —) EARL BURNS
GRANT HILDY PEGGY WALTER
HARTMAN JOHNSON WILLIAMS
FRONTPIECE GORE
FROST ICE COLD HOAR RIME RIND
(PREF.) CRYMO PAGO RHIGO
(HOAR —) PACHNO
FROSTED PRUINOSE
FROSTING ICING DIVINITY
FROSTWEED ROCKROSE
FROSTY ICY COLD RIMY CHILL
CRISP FRORE GELID GLARY
HUNCH BOREAL FRIGID FROREN
CHILLING INIMICAL PRUINOUS
(NOT —) OPEN
FROTH FOB BARM FOAM HEAD
REAM SCUM SUDS WORK CREAM
SPUME YEAST FLOWER FREATH
LATHER SPURGE
FROTHER CREOSOTE
FROTHING HUMMING MANTLING
FROTHY BARMY FOAMY REAMY
SPEWY SPUMY SUDSY FLASHY
YEASTY SPUMOSE SPUMOUS
WHIPPED
FROWARD RANK CROSS
AWKWARD PEEVISH WAYWARD
CONTRARY FROPPISH PERVERSE
PETULANT PROTERVE SHREWISH
UNTOWARD
FROWN GLUM LOUR GLOOM
GLOUT GLUMP LOWER SCOWL
GLOWER GLUNCH FROUNCE
FRONTLET
FROWNING GLUM GLUNCH
FROWZY BLOUSY BLOWSY
BLOWZY RAFFISH FROWZLED
SCABROUS SLOVENLY
FROZEN FAST FIXED FRORE FRORY
GELID GLARY FRAPPE FROREN
FRUCTIFICATION CONK AECIDIUM
BASIDIUM APOTHECIUM
FRUCTOSE ACROSE
FRUGAL EASY MILD CANNY CHARY
ROMAN SCANT SPARE SAVING
SCARCE SCOTCH CAREFUL
PRUDENT SLENDER SPARING
THRIFTY PROVIDENT
PARSIMONIOUS
FRUGALITY SPARE THRIFT
ECONOMY PARCITY MANAGERY
FRUGALLY HARD CHARILY
SAVINGLY
FRUIT BEL FIG HAW UVA AKEE
ATTA BAEL BITO COYO DATE
DIKA DROP GEAN JACK LIME
NOOP PEAR PLUM POME SEED
SLOE SNAP SORB AKENE ANISE
APPLE BERRY CLING COUMA
DRUPE GENIP GOURD GRAPE
GUAVA HAZEL ILAMA LEMON
LIMON MANGO MELON OLIVE
PAPAW PEACH RIPER SORVA
TRYMA ACHENE ACINUS ALMOND

BANANA BUTTON CEDRON
CEREZA CHERRY CITRON CITRUS
COBNUT COCHAL COCONA
DAMSON DURIAN EMBLIC
EMBOLO GUARRI JUJUBE KEEPER
LEGUME LONGAN LOQUAT
MAMMEE MARANG MAYPOP
MUYUSA NARRAS ORANGE
PAPAYA PAWPAW PELLAS
POMATO RESULT SAPOTA
SQUASH UVALHA WAMPEE
WESTME ZAPOTE APRICOT
ATEMOYA AVOCADO AZAROLE
BILIMBI BLOATER CARAWAY
CHAYOTE CHECKER CIRUELA
COCONUT CURRANT DESSERT
GEEBUNG GENIPAP GHERKIN
KUMQUAT MURCOTT PIGFACE
PRODUCT RIPENER SERVICE
SHALLON SOROSIS SOURSOP
TANGELO ACHENIUM BAYBERRY
BELLERIC BILBERRY CALABASH
CANISTEL CAPSICUM CARDAMUM
CITRANGE COCOPLUM
CUCUMBER DEWBERRY
DOGBERRY EGGFRUIT FOLLICLE
FRUITAGE FRUITERY FRUITLET
GOLKAKRA INKBERRY LIMEQUAT
OSOBERRY PIEPRINT PODOCARP
RAMBUTAN SEBESTEN SEEDBALL
SHADDOCK SWEETSOP
SYCONIUM CARYOPSIS
NECTARINE PINEAPPLE
SAPODILLA CHERIMOYER
MANGOSTEEN
(— OF CACTUS) SABRA
(— OF CAPER) CAPOT
(— OF CITRON) ETROG ETHROG
(— OF HEMLOCK) CONIUM
(— OF OAK) ACORN
(— OF PALM) SALAK PUPUNHA
(— OF ROSE) HEP HIP BUTTON
(— ON TREES) HANG
(—S COOKED IN SYRUP) COMPOTE
(AGGREGATE —) ETAERIO
DRUPETUM HETAERIO
(ASTRINGENT —) GAB GAUB
CHEBULE
(AVOCADO-LIKE —) ANAY
(CANDIED —) CONSERVE
(CARMINATIVE —) BADIAN
(COILED —) STROMBUS
(COLLECTIVE —) SYNCARP
(DRIED —) PASA CUBEB MUMMY
SABAL OREJON CAPSULE
EMBELIA
(EARLY —) PRIMEUR HASTINGS
(FALLEN —) SHEDDER WINDFALL
(FIRST —S) ANNATES BIKKURIM
PRIMICES
(FLESHY —) SYCONIUM
SARCOCARP
(GOURD —) PEPO
(GRAPEFRUIT-LIKE —) SUHA
(GRAPELIKE —) WAMPEE
(HAWTHORN —) PEGGLE
(IMPERFECT —) SPECH NUBBIN
(MASHED —) FOOL
(MEDICINAL —) AIWAIN AJOWAN
EMBELIA
(ONE-SEEDED —) AKENE ACHENE
(PALMYRA —) PUNATOO
(PLUMLIKE —) CARISSA CIRUELA

(PRESERVED —) SUCCADE
CONFITURE
(PRICKLY —) HEDGEHOG
(SELF-FERTILIZED —) AUTOCARP
(SLICED DRIED —) SNITS SNITZ
SCHNITZ
(SPURGE —) TAMPOE
(SUPERIOR —) TOPPER
(UNRIPE OAK —) CAMATA
(WINGED —) SAMARA
(WOODY —) XYLOCARP
(PREF.) CARP(O) FRUCTI FRUGI
(BEAK-LIKE —) RYNCO
(SUFF.) CARP(OUS)(US)(Y)
FRUIT BAT KALONG
FRUIT-BEARING FERTILE
FRUIT DOVE KUKU
FRUITFUL FAT FOODY BATTEL
FECUND FRUITY GRAVID FERTILE
TEEMFUL UBEROUS ABUNDANT
CHILDING FRUITIVE PREGNANT
PROLIFIC PLENTEOUS
FRUITFULNESS UBERTY FATNESS
FRUITGROWER FRUITIST
FRUITLESS DRY GELD VAIN ADDLE
BARREN FUTILE STERILE USELESS
ABORTIVE BOOTLESS
FRUIT PIGEON KUKU LUPE
KUKUPA MANUMA MANUTAGI
FRUIT STONE COB PYRENE
PUTAMEN
(PREF.) PYREN(O)
FRUMP JUDY
FRUSTRATE BALK BEAT BILK CRAB
DASH DISH FOIL LAME BAULK
BLANK BLOCK CHECK CROSS
ELUDE SMEAR THRAW WRECK
BAFFLE BLIGHT BUGGER DEFEAT
DELUDE KIBOSH OUTWIT SCOTCH
THWART ANIENTE DECEIVE
FALSIFY PREVENT CONFOUND
INFRINGE STULTIFY
FRUSTRATED DISHED MANQUE
FRUSTRATER MARPLOT
FRUSTRATING BOOTLESS
FRUSTRATION FOIL SUCK DEFEAT
FIASCO
FRUSTULE TESTULE HYPOTHECA
FRY SILE BROOD FRIZZ KRILL
SAUTE FRIZZLE GREYFISH
FRYER FRIER FRIZZER SPRINGER
FRYING PAN FRYPAN SPIDER
CREEPER SKILLET
FUCHSIA CORREA KONINI FUCHSIN
EARDROPS
FUCHSIN ROSEINE SOLFERINO
FUCHSINE RUBIN RUBINE
MAGENTA ROSANILINE
FUDDLE FUZZLE FLUSTER
FUDDLED FAP REE DOPY BOSKY
DOPEY SWASH TIPSY MAUDLIN
TOSTICATED
FUDGE HUNCH SNUDGE PENUCHE
DIVINITY
FUEL GAS OIL POB COAL COKE FIRE
PEAT UPLA ARGOL ACETOL
BUNKER ELDING FIRING SHRUFF
TIMBER COALITE PABULUM
SYNTHOL FIREBOOT FIREBOTE
GASOGENE GAZOGENE TRIPTANE
(JELLED —) NAPALM
(ROCKET —) HYDYNE
FUGITIVE HOT FLEME FLYER FUGIE

SCAMP OUTLAW FLEEING
LAMSTER REFUGEE RUNAWAY
FLEETING RUNAGATE UNSTABLE
(PL.) MANZAS
FUGUE FUGA RICERCAR
(— THEME) DUX
(PART OF —) STRETTA
FULA PEUL PEUHL FELLANI
FELLATA
FULANI PEUL PEUHL
FULCRUM BAIT GLUT
FULFILL FILL FULL KEEP MEET
HONOR ANSWER COMPLY FULFIL
REDEEM ACHIEVE PERFORM
SATISFY COMPLETE COMPLISH
ACCOMPLISH
(— A TERM) EXPIRE
FULFILLMENT PASS EFFECT
FUNCTION PERFORMANCE
(— OF GOD'S WILL) KINGDOM
(IMAGINARY —) FANTASY
FULGURATION BLICK
FULL BAD BIG FAT FOW COOL
DEEP FAIR GOOD JUST PANG
RANK TRIG TUCK AMPLE AWASH
BROAD CLEAR FLUSH LARGE
LUCKY PIENO PLAIN PLENY
ROUND SATED SOLID TIGHT
TOTAL WHOLE ENTIRE GOGGLE
HONEST STRONG BAPTIZE
BRIMFUL COPIOUS DESTROY
DIFFUSE FULFILL FULSOME
LIBERAL OROTUND PERFORM
PLENARY REPLETE TEEMING
TRAMPLE WEALTHY ABSOLUTE
ADEQUATE BOUFFANT BRIMMING
CHOCKFUL COMPLETE EXTENDED
FREQUENT PREGNANT RESONANT
THOROUGH
(— CLOTH OR YARN) WALK
(— OF AIR) LIGHT
(— OF BLANKS) LACUNOSE
(— OF CHINKS) RIMOSE
(— OF DELAY) MOROSE
(— OF DEVILTRY) HEMPY HEMPIE
(— OF DIRT) FOUL
(— OF EGGS) GRAVID
(— OF ENERGY) STOUT SWANK
(— OF FLAWS) CRAZY
(— OF FUN) FROLIC
(— OF HAPPINESS) SUNSHINY
(— OF INTEREST) AGOG
(— OF IRON) SIDEROSE
(— OF LIFE) SPUNKY ANIMATE
(— OF LOOPS) KINKY
(— OF MATTER FOR THOUGHT)
MEATY
(— OF RUSHES) SPRITTY
(— OF SAND) ARENOSE
(— OF SLEEP) SOPOROSE
(— OF SMALL OPENINGS) POROUS
(— OF SPIRIT) GENEROUS
(— OF VIGOR) FLUSH GREEN LUSTY
ANIMATED SPIRITED
(— OF ZEST) RACY
(PREF.) PLENI PLERO
(SUFF.) **(— OF)** IOUS OSE OUS
FULL-BLOODED PLETHORIC
FULL-BLOWN JUICY
FULLBODIED FAT LOFTY HEARTY
ROBUST
FULL-BOSOMED BUXOM
FULLER GAG HARDY HARDIE

ROLLER TUCKER WALKER
BLOCKER CREASER
THICKER CLOTHIER
FULL-FACED AFFRONTE AFFRONTY
FULL-FLAVORED BOLD RACY
FULL-FLEDGED SUMMED
FULL-GROWN RIPE GROWN
MATURE SEEDED
FULLNESS BODY FLAIR FLARE
FULTH PLENUM FULNESS
PLEROMA SATIETY
FULLY ALL DOWN EVEN INLY WELL
AMPLY LARGE ENOUGH FAIRLY
THRICE WHOLLY CLEARLY
LARGELY UTTERLY CLEVERLY
ENTIRELY INWARDLY MATURELY
FULMAR HAG NELLY NODDY
HAGDON NELLIE MALDUCK
MALMOCK STINKER MALLEMUCK
FULMINATE BLOW FULMINE
FULSOME FAT SUAVE FOULSOME
FUMARIC BOLETIC LICHENIC
FUMAROLE HORNITO
FUMBLE BOOT MUFF MULL PIRL
BOBBLE BOGGLE FAFFLE MUMBLE
PRODDLE MISFIELD THRUMBLE
FUMBLER STUMER BUNGLER
STUMOUR
FUMBLING HALTING
FUME FUFF RAGE REEK EWDER
SMOKE STIFE STORM SNUFFLE
FUMIGATE
FUMID SMOKY SMOKEY
FUMIGATE SMEEK SMOKE PASTIL
CYANIDE PASTILLE
FUMIGATION GASSING
FUMIGATOR AERATOR
FUMITORY FUMARIA FUMEROOT
FUMEWORT
FUN GIG GAME GELL JEST JOKE
LAKE PLAY BORAK BOURD
HUMOR KICKS MIRTH MUSIC
SPORT FROLIC GAIETY GAYETY
DAFFERY DAFFING GAMMOCK
WHOOPEE
(MAKE — OF) JAPE RIDE
(UNRESTRAINED —) HELL
FUNCTION ACT JOB RUN USE
DUTY FORM ROLE WORK POWER
ACTION AGENCY MATRIX MISTER
OFFICE SQUASH CONCEPT
FACULTY ISOLATE PERFORM
SERVICE WORKING ACTIVITY
BUSINESS MINISTRY PROVINCE
(— EFFECTIVELY) AVAIL
(—S OF JUDGES) ERMINE
(APPARENT —) STUDY
(CHEMICAL —) PARACHOR
(ECCLESIASTICAL —) DIET
(ESSENTIAL —) DHARMA
(MATHEMATICAL —) DEL FORM
METRIC INVERSE QUARTIC
(SPECIAL —) CEREMONY
(SUFF.) CY URE
FUNCTIONAL DYNAMIC
FUNCTIONARY BEADLE FLUNKY
CAPTAIN FLUNKEY CHAPRASI
FUNCTIONING AFLOAT
FUNCTIONLESS OTIOSE
FUND BOX BANK FOND MASS
CHEST KITTY MOUNT SLUSH
STOCK STORE ESCROW CHALUKA
JACKPOT RESERVE

HALUKKAH PECULIUM
(COMMON —) POT POOL
(POLITICAL —S) BARREL
(PL.) CAJA PURSE COFFER
FUNDAMENT NOCK TAIL BOTTOM
FUNDUS
FUNDAMENTAL NET BASE BASAL
BASIC KLANG PRIME VITAL
BOTTOM PRIMAL SIMPLE BASILAR
BEDROCK ORGANIC PRIMARY
RADICAL ABSOLUTE CARDINAL
ORIGINAL RUDIMENT SUBSTRAT
ULTIMATE PRIMORDIAL
RUDIMENTARY
FUNDAMENTALLY AUFOND
FUNDUS FORNIX
FUNERAL TANGI BURIAL EXEQUY
BURYING CORTEGE FUNEBRE
FUNERARY MORTUARY
FUNERAL DIRECTOR BLACKMAN
FUNEREAL BLACK FERAL DISMAL
SOLEMN FUNEBRE FUNERAL
DIRGEFUL EXEQUIAL MOURNFUL
SEPULCHRAL
FUNGI MYCOFLORA
FUNGICIDE MANEB NABAM ZINEB
FERBAM CALOMEL BORDEAUX
DICHLONE
FUNGOID MYCOID FUNGOUS
FUNGOSO (FATHER OF —) SORDIDO
FUNGUS BUNT MOLD SMUT BLACK
BRAND ERGOT FUNGE HYPHO
MOREL MOULD PHOMA SPUNK
SWARD TRUFF VALSA VERPI
AGARIC BOLETE FUNGAL MILDEW
OIDIUM AMANITA BOLETUS
CHYTRID FUNGOID GEASTER
LEPIOTA TRUFFLE AECIDIUM
CLATHRUS CORNBELL EUMYCETE
FUSARIUM HELVELLA MUCEDINE
MUSHROOM OOMYCETE
OTOMYCES PHALLOID POLYPORE
PUFFBALL RHIZOPUS SAPROGEN
SPOROGEN TREMELLA TUCKAHOE
NEUROSPORA PENICILLIUM
(UNICELLULAR —) BEES EAST
YEAST
(PREF.) AGARICI BASIDIO HYDNO
MYC(ET)(ETO)(O)
(SUFF.) MYCES MYCET(O)
MYCETE(S) MYCOSIS
(— DISEASE) OSIS
FUNK FUNG NESH
FUNNEL CAST STACK TEWEL
TRUNK FILLER FUMMEL HOPPER
SIPHON SYPHON TUNNEL
TUNNER TRUMPET TUNDISH
HYPONOME WINDSAIL
(PREF.) CHOAN(O)
(SUFF.) CHOANITE CHOANITIC
FUNNY ODD GOOD COMIC DROLL
MERRY QUEER COMICAL JOCULAR
RISIBLE STRANGE HUMOROUS
(VERY —) SPLITTING
SIDESPLITTING
FUR FOX BEAR CALF COON FLIX
FLUE FOIN GRAY GREY GRIS MINK
PEAN PELF PELL PILE SEAL VAIR
BUDGE COYPU CROSS FITCH
FLICK GENET GRISE OTTER PAHMI
SABLE SCARF SHUBA BADGER
BEAVER COUGAR DESMAN
ERMINE FISHER GALYAC JACKET

MARTIN NUTRIA PELAGE POTENT
RABBIT SPRING SUSLIK CALABER
CARACAL FITCHET FITCHEW
FURRURE MINIVER TOPCOAT
CACOMIXL ERMINOIS KOLINSKI
(— OF LAMBSKIN AND WOOL)
BUDGE
(— RESEMBLING PERSIAN LAMB)
KRIMMER
(BEAVER —) WOOM CASTOR
(GRAY —) GRAY GREY GRIS GRISE
CRIMMER LETTICE
(LAMB —) CARACUL KARAKUL
(NUMBER OF — SKINS) TIMBER
TIMMER
(RABBIT —) CONY SCUT CONEY
FLICK LAPIN HATTER SEALINE
ERMILINE
(SQUIRREL —) CALABAR
(SQUIRREL OR MARTIN —) AMICE
POPEL
(STONE MARTEN'S —) FOIN
(PL.) PELTRY FURRIERY
(PREF.) DORA
FURBEARER PLATINUM
FURBELOW DIDO FRILL FALBALA
FURBISH DO FIG RUB FAKE FINE
VAMP CLEAN SCOUR FINIFY
POLISH BURNISH VARNISH
RENOVATE
FURCATE FORKY BRANCH FURCAL
FURCULA SPRING FURCULUM
FURCULUM WISHBONE
FURFOOZ GRENELLE
FURIES ALECTO ERINYS ERINYES
MEGAERA ERINNYES TISIPHONE
FURIOUS MAD GRIM WOOD YOND
ANGRY BRAIN GIDDY IRATE LIVID
RABID SHARP FIERCE FURIAL
FURIED INSANE RENISH STORMY
ACHARNE FRANTIC HOPPING
MADDING MANKIND PELTING
RAGEOUS REDWOOD RUSHING
TEARING VIOLENT FRENZIED
MAENADIC TOWERING VEHEMENT
VESUVIAN WRATHFUL
FURIOUSLY CRAZY ANGERLY
TEARING
FURL FOLD HAND ROLL STOW
WRAP FRESE TRUSS FARDEL
FURDLE
FURLED IN
FURLONG SHOT STADE
FURLOUGH LEAVE BLIGHTY
FURNACE ARC KILN OVEN TANK
BENCH CUPEL DRIER DRYER
FORGE MOUTH TISAR BURNER
CALCÄR COCKLE CUPOLA HEATER
ATHANOR CHAFERY CRESSET
FIREPOT PUDDLER ROASTER
BESSEMER BLOOMERY CALCINER
CHAUFFER FIREWORK IRONCLAD
LIMEKILN PRODUCER REFINERY
TRYWORKS
(— DOOR) TWEEL
(ALMOND —) ALMAN
(ARC —) HEROULT
(GLASS-HEATING —) TISAR
(PORTABLE —) DANDY CRESSET
FURNACEMAN BUSTLER DROSSER
SMELTER IMPROVER REHEATER
FURNISH ARM SOW DECK FEAT
FEED FILL FRET FRUB GIVE LEND

TRIM VEST ARRAY BESEE ENDOW
EQUIP FRAME INDUE PITCH
POINT SERVE SPEED STOCK
STORE STUFF AFFORD GRAITH
INSURE INVEST OUTFIT RENDER
SUPPLY ADVANCE APPAREL
APPOINT BRACKET GARNISH
INSTORE PERFORM PLENISH
PRESENT PRODUCE PROVIDE
SUFFICE ACCOUTER DECORATE
FRUBBISH MINISTER
ACCOMMODATE
(— ABUNDANTLY) FREQUENT
(— ANALYSIS) ACCOUNT
(— FULLY) CHARGE
(— REFRESHMENT) EASE
(— WITH) BESEE
(— WITH DRINK) BIRL BYRL
(— WITH MEALS) BOARD
(— WITH NEW PARTS) RETROFIT
(— WITH STEEP SLOPE) ESCARP
(— WITH STRENGTH) MAN
(— WITH WINGS) IMP
FURNISHED ARMED BODEN GARNI
(COMFORTABLY —) BEIN
FURNISHING ADVANCE FITMENT
(PL.) STUFF BAGGAGE PENATES
FURNITURE ADAM BUHL STOOL
SAMAN STOOL STUFF GRAITH
FITMENT INSIGHT MEUBLES
MOVABLE EQUIPAGE ORNAMENT
SUPELLEX TACKLING
(CHEAP —) BORAX
(SHIP'S —) HARNESS
(STORED —) LUMBER
FURORE FUROR BROUHAHA
FURRED PURED LOADED
FURRING PACKING
FURROW FUR GAP GAW RIB RUT
FURR GRIP HINT LINE PLOW RAIN
RILL ROUT RUCK SEAM SULK
CHASE DRAIN DRILL EARTH FIELD
RIGOL SCORE SEUGH STRIA
GROOVE GUTTER INDENT SULCUS
SUTURE TRENCH BREAKER
CHAMFER CHANNEL CRUMPLE
FEERING PLOWING QUILLET
SCRATCH WINDROW WRINKLE
CARRIAGE NOTAULIX THOROUGH
VALLECULA
(PREF.) AULAC(O) HOLC(O) LIRELLI
SULCI SULCO
FURROWED SEAMED EXARATE
FURROWY SULCATE TRENCHED
FURROWING KNOT DRESS
FURRY SHAGGY
FUR SEAL URSAL
FURTHER MO AID YET ALSO HELP
YOND ADDED AGAIN FRESH
SPEED SUPRA BEYOND EXTEND
SECOND ADVANCE DEVELOP
FARTHER FORWARD PROMOTE
MOREOVER REMANENT ULTERIOR
FURTHERMORE BESIDES FURTHER
OVERMORE
FURTIVE SLY PRIVY CLAMMY
SECRET SHIFTY SNEAKY
HANGDOG MEACHING MYSTICAL
SNEAKING STEALTHY THIEVISH
CLANDESTINE
FURTIVELY SLILY SLYLY SIDELINS
FURTIVENESS STEALTH
FURUNCLE BOIL

FURY HAG IRE MAD WAX BURN
RAGE ANGER BRETH DREAD
FUROR IRISH RIGOR WRATH
ALECTO BELDAM CHOLER FRENZY
FURORE MADNESS MEGAERA
WIDDRIM DELIRIUM FEROCITY
VIOLENCE WOODNESS TISIPHONE
FURZE FUN FUZZ LING ULEX WHIN
GORSE WHINCOW
FUSE RUN CAKE FLOW FLUX FRIT
FUZE MELT BLEND FOUND FUSEE
FUZEE QUILL SMELT SQUIB
SWAGE TRAIN UNITE MINGLE
SPITTER COALESCE CONCRETE
CONFLATE COPULATE PORTFIRE
SAUCISSE COLLIQUATE
FUSED CONNATE
FUSEE FUZEE SPINDLE VESUVIAN
VESUVIUS

FUSELAGE BODY
(— MEMBER) LONGERON
FUSIFORM FUSATE SPINDLE
FUSIL (DIVIDED INTO —S) PLUMETE
FUSION ZYG FLUX FUSURE
CHIASMA FLUXION CYTOGAMY
MITAPSIS PLASMOGAMY
(PREF.) ZYG(O)(OTO)
(SUFF.) APSIS
FUSS DO ADO ROW TEW COIL FAFF
FIKE FIRK FIZZ FRET ROUT SONG
STIR TIME TOUSE TOWSE TRADE
WHAUP BOTHER CADDLE
DIRDUM FANTAD FETTLE FISSLE
FISTLE FIZZLE FRAISE FUFFLE
FUSTLE HOORAY HURRAH
PHRASE POTHER RACKET SETOUT
STROTH TURNUP FOOSTER
FRIGGLE FUSSIFY NAUNTLE

POOTHER SPUFFLE SPUTTER
TAMASHA BUSINESS FOOFARAW
SCRONACH
FUSSBUDGETY SPOFFISH
FUSSINESS DAINTY FADDLE
FIKERY FOOSTER
FUSSING BOTHER
FUSSY BUSY FIKY FIXY FUDGY
PICKY CHICHI FIDFAD PROSSY
SPOFFY SPRUCE STICKY FIDGETY
NIGGLING NOTIONAL SPOFFISH
SQUEAMISH PERSNICKETY
FUSTET ZANTE FUSTIC
FUSTIAN HOLMES PILLOW
BOMBAST TWADDLE CORDUROY
MOLESKIN
FUSTIC LIME MORA FUSTET
DYEWOOD AMARILLO
FUSTINESS FOIST FROWST

FUSTY FOIST MOLDY MUSTY
FOISTY RANCID
FROWSTY MALODOROUS
FUTILE IDLE TOOM VAIN OTIOSE
USELESS BOOTLESS FECKLESS
FOOTLESS FUTILOUS HELPLESS
NUGATORY
FUTILITY VANITY NUGACITY
VAINESSE
FUTTAH WHATA
FUTURE LATER SKULD AVENIR
COMING ONWARD OPTION
TOCOME TOWARD LAVENIR
FUTURITY ONCOMING
(— TIME) MANANA
FUZZ LINTERS
FUZZY LOUSY MUZZY WOOLY
WOOLLY
FYTTE PASSUS

G

G GEE GOLF GEORGE
GA AKRA ACCRA INKRA
GAAL (FATHER OF —) EBED
GAB GOB YAP BLAB CHIN
CHINFEST
GABBLE WAB CANK CHAT CONK
JAVER BABBLE GAGGLE HABBLE
PATTER RABBLE TATTER YABBLE
CLATTER JAUNDER TWADDLE
TWITTER SLIPSLOP SLUMMOCK
GABBRO BOJITE NORITE EUCRITE
GABION KISH KEESH BASKET
WALING CORBEIL
GABLE GAVEL GOFOL DETAIL
DORMER GABLET KENNEL
MEMBER PINION AILERON
PEDIMENT
GABON (CAPITAL OF —) LIBREVILLE
(LAKE OF —) ANENGUE AZINGUO
(MOUNTAIN OF —) MPELE
IBOUNDJI
(NATIVE OF —) FANG ADOUMA
ECHIRA OKANDE
(RIVER OF —) ABANGA IVINDA
OGOOUE NGOUNIE
(TOWN OF —) OYEM BONGO
KANGO MITZIC OMVANE
MAKOKOU
GABOON OKOUME
GABRIELINO TOBIKHAR
GAD GAR RUN FISK GAUD JAZZ
RAKE JINKET GADLING TRAIPSE
VIRETOT
(— ABOUT) HAIK ROLL STRAM
GALLANT TROLLOP
(BROTHER OF —) ASHER
(FATHER OF —) JACOB
(MOTHER OF —) ZILPAH
GADABOUT GAD GADDER TRAIPSE
GADDI (FATHER OF —) SUSI
GADFLY GAD CLEG GLEG BRIZE
CLEGG STOUT WHAME BOTFLY
BREEZE GADBEE OESTRID
TABANID HORSEFLY
(PREF.) ESTRA ESTRI ESTRO
OESTR(I)
GADGET DODAD GISMO GIZMO
HICKY DINGUS DOODAD GILGUY
HICKEY JIGGER JIMJAM WIDGET
CONCERN DOFUNNY GIMMICK
BUSINESS GIMCRACK JIMCRACK
CONTRAPTION
(PL.) GIBBLES GUBBINS
GADGETRY
GADI (SON OF —) MENAHEM
GADUS MORRHUA
GADWALL RODGE VOLANT
GADWELL REDWING SHUTTLE
GAEL CELT KELT SCOT GOIDEL
GAEDHEAL
GAELIC ERSE IRISH
GAFF CLIP SPAR SPUR YARD
GAFFLE GABLOCK GAFFLET

SLASHER GAVELOCK
(— MACKEREL) GAMBEER
GAFFER STAGEHAND
GAG BOFF GEGG JOKE PONG SCOB
HEAVE KEVEL SCOBE AGUAJI
MUZZLE WHEEZE
GAGE (ALSO SEE GAUGE) LAY
PAWN WAGE GAUGE JEDGE
NORMA WAGER FEELER PLEDGE
SPIDER SCANTLE STANDARD
UDOMETER
GAHAM (FATHER OF —) NAHOR
(MOTHER OF —) REUMAH
GAHERIS (MOTHER OF —)
MORGANSE
GAIETY JOY GALA JEST RANT
CHEER MIRTH BAWDRY FROLIC
GAYETY LEVITY BAUDERY
BEGONIA DAFFERY DAFFING
GAYNESS JOLLITY JOYANCE
ROLLICK BUOYANCY FESTIVAL
HILARITY VIVACITY
GAILY GAY GAYLY BRAVELY
LIGHTLY
GAIN BAG DAP GET NET POT WIN
BEAR BOOT DRAW GROW HAVE
LAND MAKE PELF SACK TILL
ADDLE BOOTY CATCH LATCH
LUCRE REACH SCORE ARRIVE
ATTAIN CHIEVE DERIVE GATHER
INCOME OBTAIN PROFIT STRAIN
CAPTURE CONQUER EMBRACE
GAYMENT GETTING HARVEST
POSSESS PROCURE REALIZE
VANTAGE WINNING CLEANING
CONQUEST PURCHASE
PERQUISITE
(— ADMISSION) ENTER
(— ADVANTAGE) GLEEK
(— ASCENDANCY) PREVAIL
(— BY EXTORTION) SQUEEZE
(— BY FORTUNE) DRAW HAZARD
(— COMMAND OF) MASTER
(— IN FAVOR) PROPITIATE
(— KNOWLEDGE) EDIFY LEARN
(— OVER) ENGAGE
(— UNDERSTANDING) SMOKE
(— WITHOUT DEDUCTION) CLEAR
(DISHONEST —) MEED
(ESTIMATED —) ESTEEM
(ILL-GOTTEN —) PELF BOODLE
(ILLICIT —) SPLOSH
(MATERIAL —) PUDDING
(UNEXPECTED —) BUNCE
(PL.) PICKING PLUNDER
GANANCIAS
GAINFUL LUCROUS GAINSOME
GAINSAY DENY FORBID IMPUGN
OPPOSE REFUTE RESIST DISPUTE
RECLAIM WITHSAY AGAINSAY
GAIT BAT JOG GANG LOPE PACE
RACK SKIP STEP TROT VOLT
WALK AMBLE AUBIN GOING

STALK TRAIN ALLURE CANTER
GALLOP LOUNGE SLOUCH
SWINGE TODDLE WADDLE
WALLOW WAMBLE WOBBLE
DOGTROT HICKORY PIAFFER
SAUNTER SCUTTLE SHAMBLE
SHUFFLE WALKING WAUCHLE
(— OF ILL-BROKEN HORSE) CHACK
(DEFECTIVE —) WINDING
(LIMPING —) HIRPLE
(UNSTEADY —) STAGGER
(4-BEAT —) AMBLE
GAITER SPAT VAMP STRAD
BONNET BRAGAS COCKER GASKIN
GUETRE HOGGER HUGGER
LEGGIN PUTTEE GAMBADE
GAMBADO LEGGING STARTUP
BOOTIKIN CUTTIKIN
(PL.) UPPERS GASKINS
GAMASHES GRAMOCHES
GAIZE MALMSTONE
GAJO GORGIO
GALACTITE MILKSTONE
GALACTOSIDE IDEIN IDAEIN
GALAGO LEMUR LEMUROID
GALAL (FATHER OF —) ASAPH
JEDUTHUN
GALANAS GAINES
GALAOR (BROTHER OF —) AMADIS
GALATEA (DAUGHTER OF —)
LEUCIPPUS
(FATHER OF —) NEREUS
(HUSBAND OF —) PYGMALION
(LOVER OF —) ACIS
(MOTHER OF —) DORIS
(SON OF —) PAPHUS METHARME
GALAX COLTSFOOT
GALAXY NEBULA SPIRAL
(KIND OF —) SEYFERT
(PREF.) GALACT(O)
GALBANUM FERULA GALBAN
ALBETAD
GALCHA PAMIR
GALE BLOW GELL HELM WIND
GAGEL PERRY STOUR BUSTER
EASTER BAYBUSH BURSTER
GALEAGE TEMPEST FLEAWOOD
GALEWORT NORWESTER
GALEA MITRA HELMET
GALGA INGUSH
GALIBI CARIBI KALINA
GALINGALE CYPRESS WANHORN
CHINAROOT
GALIPOT BARRAS GALLIPOT
TACAMAHAC
GALJOEN BLACKFISH
GALL GA GAW BAIT FELL FRET
NERVE WRING ANBURY COCKLE
HARASS HUTZPA ANBERRY
BEDEGAR CHUTZPA GALLNUT
HUTZPAH KNOPPER NUTGALL
BEDEGUAR CECIDIUM CHUTZPAH
FLEASEED IRRITATE OAKBERRY

SEEDGALL SPURGALL TACAHOUT
(SAND —) SALT NATRON
SANDIVER
(PL.) PURPLES
(PREF.) CHOL(E)(O)
(SUFF.) CHOLIA CHOLY
GALLANT GAY BEAU PROW BLADE
BRAVE BULLY CIVIL JOLLY LOVER
NOBLE PREUX SHOWY SPARK
SWAIN DONZEL ESCORT HEROIC
POLITE RUTTER SPARKY SQUIRE
SUITOR AMATORY AMORIST
AMOROSO AMOROUS CONDUCT
GALANTE GREGORY SPARKER
STATELY TOPPING YOUNKER
BELAMOUR CAVALIER CICISBEO
FEMALIST GALLIARD HANDSOME
POLISHED
GALLANTRY GAME DRURY
DRUERY BRAVERY COURAGE
PROWESS CHIVALRY PARAMOUR
GALLBERRY INKBERRY
GALLED RAW
GALLEON CARAC CARRACK
GALLOON
GALLERY POY SAP COOP GODS
JUBE LOFT PAWN ALURE BOYAU
ORIEL PRADO ARCADE BURROW
DEDANS NARROW PIAZZA
SCHOOL SOLLAR SUBWAY
TUNNEL BALCONY GALERIE
HEADWAY MIRADOR TERRACE
VERANDA BARTISAN BRATTICE
CANTORIA CORRIDOR HOARDING
PARADISE PERAMBLE SCAFFOLD
TRAVERSE VERANDAH
BLINDSTORY
(— IN BAZAAR) PAWN
(— IN HOUSE OF COMMONS)
VENTILATOR
(— MADE BY INSECT) MINE
(— OF FORT) CASEMATE
(CHURCH —) JUBE LAFT LOFT
(MINE —) BORD BROW SLOVAN
(MINSTREL'S —) ORIEL
(OPEN —) LOGGIA
(UNDERGROUND —) HYPOGEE
HYPOGEUM
GALLEY FUST CUDDY DRAKE FOIST
STICK BIREME GALIOT HEARTH
ZYGITE BASTARD CABOOSE
DROMOND GALLIOT HEXERIS
LYMPHAD TRIREME UNIREME
CAMBOOSE COOKROOM
CROMSTER GALLEASS RAMBERGE
(— BOTTOM) SLICE
(CHIEFTAIN'S —) BIRLING BIRLINN
(PHILIPPINE —) CALAN
(VIKING —) AESC DRAKE
GALLEY SLAVE FORSADO
SFORZATO
GALLFLY CYNIPID
GALLIMAUFRY HASH

234

GALLINACEOUS RASORIAL
GALLINAE RASORES
GALLINAZO VIRU VULTURE
GALLING BITTER
GALLINULE COOT KORA MOHO
RAIL GORHEN PUKEKO SKITTY
MOORHEN STANKIE SULTANA
DABCHICK HYACINTH
MANUALII RAILBIRD
RICEBIRD SWAMPHEN
GALLIVANT KITE ROAM ROVE
GALLANT
GALLNUT
(PREF.) CECIDIO CEDIDO
GALLON GAWN CONGIUS
(— OF ORE) DISH
(EIGHTH) OCTARIUS
(HALF —) POTTLE
(128 —S) LEAGUER
GALLOON ORRIS
GALLOP FOG RUN AUBIN PRICK
CANTER CAREER COURSE TITTUP
WALLOP TANTIVY
GALLOWS NUB CRAP DROP FORK
TREE BOUGH CHEAT FURCA
WIDDY GIBBET WOODIE DERRICK
FORCHES JUSTICE POTENCE
STIFLER WARYTREE
GALLOWS BIRD HEMPY WIDDY
HEMPIE HEMPSEED WIDDIFOW
CRACKROPE
GALOSH ARCTIC ZIPPER EXCLUDER
OVERSHOE
GALUTH GOLUS GOLAHI
GALVANIC VOLTAIC
GALVANIZE ZINCIFY SHERADISE
GALVANOMETER DETECTOR
REOMETER
GAMBESON WAMBAIS
GAMBIA (CAPITAL OF —) BANJUL
(COIN OF —) BUTUT DALASI
(LANGUAGE OF —) JOLA WOLOF
FULANI MALINKE
(MONEY OF —) DALASI
(NATIVE OF —) JOLA PEUL WOLOF
DIOLAS FULANI MANDINGO
SERAHULI
(TOWN OF —) KAUUR MANSA
FATOTO BINTANG BRIKAMA
KUNTAUR
GAMBIA POD BABLOH
GAMBIER CATECHU
GAMBIT MANEUVER
GAMBLE BET DICE GAFF GAME
NICK PLAY PUNT RISK SPORT
STAKE WAGER CHANCE
GAMMON HAZARD PLUNGE
FLUTTER
(— AGAINST) BUCK
GAMBLER PIKER SPORT CARROW
DEALER PLAYER PUNTER
HUSTLER PLAYMAN PLUNGER
SLICKER THROWER BLACKLEG
GAMESTER HAZARDER
GAMBLER, THE (CHARACTER IN —)
ALEXEY BLANCHE PAULINE
(COMPOSER OF —) PROKOFIEV
GAMBLING GAMING HAZARDRY
(— DEVICE) PACHINKO
GAMBLING HOUSE HELL TRIPOT
GAMBO GOOSE SPURWING
GAMBOL HOP PLAY CAPER FRISK
KEVEL PRANK CAREER CAVORT

FROLIC PRANCE GAMBADO
CAPRIOLE
GAMBREL CAMMOCK SPREADER
GAME COB FUN JEU JIG GAMY
LAKE MAIL PLAY DANCE GAMEY
PARTY SPIEL SPORT WATHE
BATTUE MORRIS QUARRY
RAMSCH VENERY JENKINS
KNICKER BREATHER FIGHTING
FOREGAME
(— FOR FISHERMEN) SKISH
(— LIKE HANDBALL) FIVES
(— LIKE HOCKEY) DODDART
(— NARROWLY WON) SQUEAKER
(— OF CAT) BILLET
(— OF FOOTBALL) BOWL CAMP
(— OF FORFEITS) KEN
(— OF HOCKEY) BANDY SHINNY
(— OF INSULTS) DOZENS
(— OF MARBLES) TAW BOWL
BONCE GULLY KEEPS KNUCKS
MIGGLES
(— OF MENTAL SKILL) GO CHESS
CHECKERS
(— OF NINEPINS) KAILS KAYLES
(— OF PRISONER'S BASE) CHEVY
CHIVVY
(— WITH BOOMERANG) BRIST
(— WITH COUNTERS) DUMPS
GOOSE
(— WITH SHUTTLECOCK) TAHYING
(BACKGAMMON —) HIT IRISH
(BALL —) CAT TUT SNOB CATCH
RUGBY SOCCER SQUASH TENNIS
CRICKET KNAPPAN BASEBALL
FOOTBALL HANDBALL SLUGFEST
SOFTBALL
(CARD —) AS HOC LOO MAW NAP
PAM PIT PUT SET BRAG CENT
FARO FISH FROG GRAB JASS
LANT PINK POOL POPE POST
RUFF SANT SKAT SLAM SNAP
SOLO STUD VINT BEAST BUNCO
BUNKO CARDS CARIE CHICO
CINCH COMET CRIMP DECOY
GILET GLEEK GRAND LEAST
MONTE NODDY OMBER OMBRE
PEDRO PITCH POKER PRIME
RUMMY SCOPA SLAMM STOPS
STUSS TRUMP WHIST BANKER
BASSET BIRKIE BOODLE BOSTON
BRIDGE CASINO CHEMMY
COMMIT ECARTE EIGHTS EUCHRE
FARMER FLINCH HEARTS HOWELL
LOADUM PANFIL PIQUET QUINZE
RAMSCH ROUNCE SLOUGH
SMUDGE SPIDER TOURNE
AUCTION AUTHORS BELOTTE
BEZIQUE CANASTA CASSINO
CAYENNE CHICAGO COONCAN
GARBAGE HUNDRED JACKPOT
PLAFOND PONTOON PRIMERO
REVERSI SCOPONE SETBACK
TRIUMPH VINGTUN VITESSE
BACCARAT BASEBALL BRISCOLA
COMMERCE CONQUIAN
CONTRACT CRIBBAGE FREAKPOT
HANDICAP IMPERIAL NAPOLEON
PATIENCE PENCHANT PENNEECH
PINOCHLE SHOWDOWN SKINBALL
SKINNING SLAPJACK TREDILLE
TRESILLO VERQUERE VIDERUFF
(CARNIVAL —) HOOPLA

(CHILDREN'S —) TAG DIBS JACKS
KICKBALL PEEKABOO
(CONFIDENCE —) RAMP BIGMITT
(COURT —) PELOTA SQUASH
TENNIS HANDBALL
(DICE —) FARE TRAY BINGO CRAPS
NOVUM RAPHE HAZARD BARBUDI
ADDITION BARBOTTE CAMEROON
HOOLIGAN
(DRAWN —) SPOIL REFAIT
(DRINKING —) HIJINKS
(EGYPTIAN —) SENT SENIT
(GAMBLING —) EO TAN FARO
HAND PICO BOULE CRAPS MACAO
MONTE POKER PROPS RONDO
STUSS BRELAN HAZARD
RONDEAU ROULETTE
(GENERAL —) HEI HIM HIT HOB
TAG TIG BALL BASE BULL BUNT
BUZZ CENT DIBS DUCK FARE
GOLF HOLE JOWL KENO MALL
POLO POOL SLAM SNOB TICK
BANDY BINGO BONCE BOULE
CHESS CHUBA CHUNK CLOSH
DARTS DOLOS FIVES GOOSE
HALMA HOUSE IRISH JACKS
LOTTO LURCH NOVUM NULLO
PITCH PUSSY RUGBY SALTA
SALVO SCRUB TROCO WHOOP
BEAVER BEETLE CAROMS CHIVVY
CHUNKY CLUMPS COBNUT
COCKAL COOTIE CRAMBO FEEDER
GOBANG GRACES HAZARD
HOOPLA HUBBUB JEREED KAYLES
MERELE PELOTA PLUMPS
RAGMAN RINGER SEESAW
SHINNY SIPPIO SKILLO STICKS
TENNIS TIGTAG TIPCAT TIVOLI
TRIGON TRUCKS BALLOON
BEANBAG BEEBALL BOWLING
COBBLER CONKERS CROQUET
CURLING DIABOLO DODDART
DOUBLES DREIDEL ENDBALL
GOGGANS HANGMAN HURLBAT
LOGGATS MAHJONG MATADOR
MUGGINS NETBALL PALLONE
PASSAGE PEEVERS PUSHPIN
QUINTET RINGTAW SARDINE
SQUAILS STATUES TENPINS
TOMBOLA ANAGRAMS BALKLINE
BASEBALL CHARADES CHECKERS
CHOUETTE DOMINOES DOUBLETS
DRAUGHTS DUCKPINS FIVEPINS
FOOTBALL FORFEITS GIVEAWAY
HARDHEAD KICKBALL KORFBALL
LEAPFROG PARCHESI PEEKABOO
PETANQUE PURPOSES PUSHBALL
PYRAMIDS RINGTOSS ROULETTE
ROUNDERS SCRABBLE SKITTLES
STOBBALL STOWBALL
TRAPBALL VERQUERE
PARCHEESI PHILOPENA
SHUFFLEBOARD
(GUESSING —) LOVE MORA
CANUTE
(INDIAN —) CHUNKY HUBBUB
(INFERIOR —) CHECK
(JAPANESE —) GO
(MEXICAN —) FRONTENIS
(NUMBERS —) BUG
(OUTDOOR —) GOLF POLO HURLY
ROQUE RUGBY SOCCER CROQUET
HURLING BASEBALL

FOOTBALL LACROSSE
(PROGRESSIVE —) DRIVE
(PUZZLE —) GLAIK
(REHEATED —) SALMI SALMIS
(SWISS —) JASS
(THREE BOWLING —S) SERIES
(TRAPSHOOTING —) SCOOT
(WAR —) BARRIERS
(WORD —) GHOST ANAGRAMS
(PL.) LUDI
(PREF.) LUDI
GAMECOCK STAG STAIG
GAMEKEEPER GAMIE KEEPER
WALKER WARNER VENERER
WARRENER
GAMESTER DICER PLAYER
GAMBLER PLAYMAN SHARPER
HAZARDER TABLEMAN
GAMETE SPERM OOCYTE ZYGOTE
GAMETOID OOGAMETE OOSPHERE
GAMETOCYTE GAMONT
CRESCENT GONOCYTE
GAMETOPHYTE GERMLING
GAMIN TAD ARAB URCHIN
GAVROCHE
GAMMA AGMA
GAMMON BAM
GAMUT GAMME RANGE SCALE
SERIES COMPASS DIAGRAM
GANDAREWA (SLAYER OF —)
KERESASPA
GANDER STEG STAIG GANNER
(— AND GEESE) SET
GANDHARI (HUSBAND OF —)
DHRITARASHTRA
GANESA GUNPUT GANAPATI
GANG MOB SET BAND BUND CORE
CREW GING PACK PAIR PUSH
TEAM BATCH BUNCH GROUP
HORDE SPELL SQUAD CHIURM
COFFLE GAGGLE LAYOUT
MOHOCK SCHOOL COMPANY
(— MEMBER) WHYO
(— OF FISHHOOKS) PULLDEVIL
(— OF MINERS) CORE
(— OF WITCHES) COVEN
(ROWDY —) TRIBULATION
GANGLING GAWKY GANGLY
GANGLION TUMOR CEREBRUM
GANGPLANK BROW GANGWAY
GANGRENE NOMA CANKER
GANGER SPHACEL NECROSIS
MORTIFICATION
(PREF.) NECR(O) SPHACELO
GANGSTER HOOD PUNK WHYO
APACHE BANDIT COWBOY
CHOPPER
GANGUE MATRIX LODESTUFF
VEINSTONE
GANGWAY BROW ROAD SLIP
LOGWAY TUNNEL CATWALK
COULOIR GATEWAY
GANJA GUNJAH CANNABIS
GANNET BOOBY GAUNT SOLAN
PIQUERO SEAFOWL ALCATRAS
GANTRYMAN DROPMAN
GANYMEDE (BROTHER OF —) ILUS
ASSARACUS
(FATHER OF —) TROS
(MOTHER OF —) CALLIRRHOE
GAOLER (ALSO SEE JAILER) ADAM
ALCAIDE
GAP SAG FLAW GAPE GOWL GULF

MUSE NICK SLAP SLOP WANT
BREAK BRECK CHASM CHAUM
CHAWN CLOVE FRITH MEUSE
MUSET NOTCH SHARD SHERD
VUIDE BREACH GULLET HIATUS
LACUNA SPREAD THROAT
VACUUM CLOSING OPENING
VACANCY VACUITY APERTURE
DIASTEMA ENTREFER INTERVAL
MULTIGAP QUEBRADA
(— IN BANK OF STREAM) GAT
(— IN FOOTBALL LINE) SLOT
(— IN MEMORY) AMNESIA
(— SERVING AS PASS) COL
(PREF.) CHASMO
GAPE GAN GAP GANT GAUP GAWK
GAWP GAZE GOVE GRIN YAWN
CHAUN GERNE HIATE STARE
RICTUS DEHISCE INHIATE
(PREF.) CHAEN(O)
GAPER COMBER
GAPING GALP AGAPE HIANT
CHAPPY CHASMA GAWISH
MOUTHED RINGENT ADENOIDAL
GAR HOUND SNOOK AGUJON
CHERNA GARFISH GARPIKE
BILLFISH GOREFISH GURDFISH
HORNBEAK HORNFISH HORNKECK
LONGJAWS LONGNOSE
GARAGE HANGAR LOCKUP SIDING
GARRIDGE
(ROW OF —S) MEWS
GARAVANCE CARAUNA
GARBANZO
GARB (ALSO SEE APPAREL AND
DRESS) COWL GEAR TOGA VEST
DRESS GUISE HABIT APPAREL
CLOTHES COSTUME RAIMENT
(UNIVERSITY —) ACADEMICALS
GARBAGE GASH SLOP OFFAL
TRASH WASTE GIBLET REFUSE
SCRAPS
(— IN, OUT) GIGO
GARBAGEMAN DUSTMAN
GARBLE GELD JUMBLE MANGLE
DISTORT GARBLING MUTILATE
MISREPRESENT
GARDANT AFFRONTE
GARDEN HAW EDEN KNOT YARD
ARBOR GARTH CIRCLE POMACY
POMARY QUINTA ROSARY
SHAMBA VERGER VIHARA
ACADEMY HERBARY OLITORY
ORCHARD ROCKERY TOPIARY
CHINAMPA FLORETUM HORTYARD
KALEYARD LEIGHTON PARADISE
PARTERRE POTAGERE ROSARIUM
(— CITY) CHICAGO
(— STATE) NEWJERSEY
(BEER —) BRASSERIE
(SECLUDED —) PLEASANCE
(PREF.) HORT(I) TOPI
(SUFF.) ETUM
GARDENER MALI PONICA
CROPPER PLANNER BOSTANGI
GARDEN HELIOTROPE VALERIAN
GARDENIA TIARA
GARDENING TOPIARY
GARDEN ROCKET EVEWEED
GARDEN WARBLER JACK
HAYBIRD BECAFICO FAUVETTE
FIGEATER
GARFISH (SEE GAR)

GARGAMELLE (SON OF —)
GARGANTUA
GARGANEY TEAL CRICK
GARGANTUA AND PANTAGRUEL
(AUTHOR OF —) RABELAIS
(CHARACTER IN —) JOHN BRIDE
BACBUC TRIPPE BADEBEC
PANURGE ANARCHUS JOBERLIN
GARGANTUA TRIBOULET
GARGAMELLE GRANGOSIER
HOLOFERNES PANTAGRUEL
PICROCHOLE PONOCRATES
ENTOMMEURES TROUILLOGAN
RAMINAGROBIS
GARGANTUAN HUGE VAST GIANT
HOMERIC TITANIC ENORMOUS
GIGANTIC HOMERIAN
GARGET MASTITIS
GARGLE GURGLE COLLUTORY
GARGOYLE BOSS
GARIBALDI GOLDFISH
GARISH GAUDY GIDDY SHOWY
CRIANT GLARING
GARISHNESS GLARE
GARLAND BAY LEI CROWN TORAN
VITTA ANADEM CORONA CRANTS
ROSARY WREATH CHAPLET
CORANCE CORONAL FESTOON
(PREF.) STEMMATI STEPHAN(O)
GARLIC AJO MOLY RAMP CHIVE
PORET ALLIUM PORRET RAMSON
GARMENT DUD TOG BACK BRAT
COAT GOWN PELL PELT RAIL
ROBE SARK SHAG SILK SLIP SLOP
SULU VEST WEED ABAYA BUREL
BURKA CENTO CLOAK CLOTH
COTTE CYMAR DRESS FROCK
HABIT HAORI JOSEY JUPON
KHAKI MANGA NABOB SHAWL
SHIFT SHIRT SIMAR SKIRT STOLE
WRIEL ALPACA ATTIRE BARROW
BLOUSE BURKHA CAFTAN
CAMLET CAPOTE CHAMMA
COTTON CYCLAS ERMINE EXOMIS
FECKET HUIPIL JACKET JERSEY
JUMPER KERSEY KIRTLE MOHAIR
MOTLEY SARONG SHORTY
SHROUD STROUD TAMEIN ZIZITH
AMICTUS BROIGNE BUNTING
CAMBLET CASSOCK CHIRIPA
CRAWLER CUCULLA CULOTTE
DOUBLET FALDING FLOCKET
GROGRAM PALETOT PELISSE
RAIMENT SHORTIE SURCOAT
SWEATER VESTURE WRAPPER
BATHROBE CAMELINE CAPUCHIN
CHAUSSES COLOBIUM CORSELET
COVERALL DEERSKIN EPIBLEMA
GAMBESON GUERNSEY HIMATION
INDUMENT PADUASOY PULLOVER
SCAPULAR SEALSKIN SLIPOVER
SNOWSUIT VESTMENT WEARABLE
PETTICOAT REDINGOTE
STROUDING
(— OF DERVISH) KHIRKAH
(— OF HERALD) TABARD
(— OF HIGH PRIEST) EPHOD
(— OF PATCHES) CENTO
(ARABIAN —) ABA
(BABY'S —) BARROW CRAWLER
CREEPER
(BADLY-MADE —) DRECK
(BLUE —) MAZARINE

(BURIAL —) SHROUD
(COARSE —) BRAT STROUD
(DEFENSIVE —) JACK BROIGNE
GAMBESON
(ECCLESIASTICAL —) STOLE
RHASON ROCHET CASSOCK
(ETHIOPIAN —) CHAMMA
(HINDU —) SARI SAREE
(INFANT'S —) BARRY BARROW
DIAPER BUNTING SLEEPER
PANTYWAIST
(JAPANESE —) HAORI
(LEATHER —) BUFF
(LINEN —) LINE
(LONG —) JIBBA KANZU STOLE
JIBBEH MANDYAS PELISSE
HIMATION
(MEDIEVAL —) ROCHET CHAUSSES
DALMATIC GAMBESON
(MONK'S —) SCAPULAR
(MOURNING —) SABLE
(ONE-PIECE —) BODYSUIT
(ONE-PIECE WOMAN'S —) CATSUIT
(OUTER —) BRAT COAT GOWN
HAIK HYKE SLOP WRAP FROCK
HAORI NABOB PALLA PILCH
SMOCK DOLMAN ROCHET
CHEMISE GALABIA PALETOT
SURCOAT SWEATER HIMATION
OVERSLOP
(PADDED —) TRUSS
(PENITENTIAL —) CILICE
(PULLOVER —) DASHIKI
(SLEEVELESS —) ABA CAPE COWL
VEST MANTLE CUCULLA
GANDURAH
(SQUARE —) KAROSS
(SYRIAN —) ABAYA
(THIN —) GOSSAMER
(TIGHT-FITTING —) HOSE COTTE
TRICOT LEOTARD
(WOMAN'S —) IZAR BURKA CYMAR
NABOB SIMAR BURKHA CHITON
JOSEPH PEPLOS PEPLUM VISITE
BLOUSON BURNOUS
(PL.) GEAR COSTUME GARNISH
FLANNELS
(PREF.) RHACO
GARNER REAP STORE GATHER
IMBARN COLLECT
GARNET GRENAT PYROPE
ANTHRAX GRANATE OLIVINE
VERMEIL ESSONITE MELANITE
ROSOLITE YANOLITE CARBUNCLE
RHODOLITE UVAROVITE
(YTTRIUM IRON —) YIG
GARNISH LARD TRIM ADORN
DRESS EQUIP MENSE STICK
FURNISH PARSLEY TOPPING
CHUMMAGE DECORATE
DUXELLES ORNAMENT
GARNISHED GARNI
GARNISHEE CHECK FACTOR
GARNISH
GARRET ATTIC SOLAR SOLLAR
MANSARD COCKLOFT
GARRISON WARD STUFF PRESIDY
WARNISON
GARROTE STRANGLE
GARRULITY POLYLOGY
GARRULOUS GABBY TALKY
WORDY BABBLY TONGUY
VOLUBLE

GARTER GARTEN LEGLET ELASTIC
STRAPPLE
GARTH CORTILE OUTGARTH
GARUM LIQUAMEN
GAS DAMP XENON FLATUS
GENAPP LEAVEN OXYGEN PETROL
EXHAUST KRYPTON YPERITE
AFTERGAS ETHERION FIREDAMP
HYDROGEN STANNANE VESICANT
(— CONSTANT) R
(COLORLESS —) OXAN OXANE
KETENE GERMANE STIBINE
(EXPLOSIVE —) METHYLAMINE
(NERVE —) SARIN
(NONCOMBUSTIBLE —) INERT
(POISONOUS —) ARSINE ADAMSITE
AQUINITE CYANOGEN PHOSGENE
BRETONITE PHOSPHINE
(TEAR —) ACROLEIN
(VOLCANIC —) MOFETTE
(PREF.) MANO
PNEUM(O)(ON)(ONO) PNEUMA
PNEUMAT(O)
(CONTAINING —) PYOPNEUMO
(PRESENCE OF —) PHYS(O)
(SUFF.) **(INERT —)** ON
GASCONADE BRAG CROW BOAST
BLUSTER
GASEOUS AERIFORM GASIFORM
VOLATILE
GASH CUT CHOP LASH BLASH
CRIMP GANCH GRIDE SCORE
SLASH SLISH SCOTCH SLUICE
TRENCH INCISION INCISURE
(— A FISH) RIM
GASKET LUTE CASKET GASKIN
GROMMET SCISSIL
GASKIN BRAGAS
GASOLINE AVGAS JUICE PETROL
BENZINE NATURAL
GASP FOB BLOW GAPE KINK PANK
PANT CHINK CROAK FETCH
THRATCH
GASPING CHINK
GASTRONOME EPICURE
GASTROPOD SLUG DRILL HARPA
OLIVA SNAIL BUCKIE NERITE
ABALONE MOLLUSK TOXIFER
UNIVALVE VELUTINA PULMONATE
PROSOBRANCH
GATAM (FATHER OF —) ELIPHAZ
GATE BAB BAR JET HEAD LIFT
PORT SASH SLAP YATE YETT
ENTRY HATCH JANUA SALLY
SPRAY STICK TORAN ENAJIM
ESCAPE FENDER FUNNEL
HARROW INGATE LIGGAT PADDLE
PORTAL RUNNER TIMBER
TORANA WICKET ZAGUAN
BARRIER CLICKET FIVEBAR
GATEWAY LIDGATE POSTERN
SHUTTER ABOIDEAU ANTEPORT
DECUMANA ENTRANCE
FOREGATE GURDWARA
PENSTOCK TOLLGATE TOWNGATE
TRIMTRAM TURNPIKE
(— OF CASTLE) BAR
(— OF DRYDOCK) CAISSON
(BACK —) POSTERN
(CUSTOMS —) BARRIER
(IRRIGATION —) CHECK TAPON
TAPPOON
(LICH —) SCALLAGE TRIMTRAM

(RUNNING —) FUNNEL
(SAW —) FRAME
(SAWMILL —) SASH
(SLALOM —S) HAIRPIN
(SLUICE —) HATCH VALVE
(TEMPLE —) VIMANA
(TIDE —) ABOIDEAU ABOITEAU
(WATER —) SLUICE
(PREF.) PYL(E)
(SUFF.) PYL(E)
GATEADO DIOMATE
GATEHOUSE BAR LODGE
GATEKEEPER WARDEN CERBERUS
GATEWARD PORTITOR STILEMAN
GATEMAN GUARD
GATEPOST DURN HARR HEEL PIER
POST SHAFT POSTEL
GATEWAY DAR DOOR GATE LOKE
PORT TORU PYLON TORAN TORII
BARWAY GOPURA TORANA
PROPYLON
(COMPUTER —) PORT
GATHER GET LEK POD WIN BAND
BREW CLAN CLOT CROP CULL
FURL HERD HIVE HOST PICK REAP
RELY TUCK AMASS BANGE
BROOM BUNCH FLOCK GLEAN
GUESS INFER LEASE PLUCK RAISE
SWEEP ACCRUE COMPEL CORRAL
DECERP DERIVE GARNER HUDDLE
HUSTLE IMBARN MUSTER
RAMASS SCRAPE CLUSTER
COLLATE COLLECT COMPILE
CONGEST CONVENE CONVOKE
HARVEST RAMMASS RECRUIT
ASSEMBLE CUMULATE SHEPHERD
(— AS ARMY) HOST
(— BY SCRAPING) SCRATCH
(— GRASS SEED) STRIP
(— HEADWAY) SET
(— HERBS) SIMPLE
(— IN A HEAP) HATTER
(— IN RAGS) TAT
(— SEWING) GAGE GAUGE
(— UP) KILT
(SUFF.) LEGE
GATHERED KILTED CUMULATE
GATHERER GEDDER TUCKER
RUFFLER CHICLERO PLICATOR
PUCKERER
GATHERING HUI LED LEK SUM
FAIR FEST KNOT SING SIVA LEVEE
SHINE TRYST AFFLUX INDABA
MUDDLE PLISSE POWWOW
RUELLE SMOKER COLLECT
COMMERS COMPANY FUNFEST
HARVEST HOSTING HUSKING
JOLLITY KLATSCH MEETING
MOOTING NYMPHAL ROCKING
TURNOUT ASSEMBLY CONCLAVE
FUNCTION JAMBOREE PANIONIA
POTATION RECOURSE SINGSONG
SOCIABLE STAMPEDE
(— OF ANIMALS) DRIVE
(— OF ARMED MEN) HOSTING
(— OF CLOTH) SHIRR SHIRRING
(— OF FILM) CISSING
(— OF SCOUTS) CAMPOREE
JAMBOREE
(— PLACE) LESCHE
(BASUTO —) PITSO
(FORMAL —) HALL
(RELIGIOUS —) SHOUT

(SOCIAL —) BEE FRY BAKE BALL
CLUB DRUM STAG WINE BAILE
BINGE BINGO DANCE MIXER
SHIVOO SMOKER CANTICO
KLATSCH SHINDIG SQUEEZE
BARBECUE CAMPFIRE CLAMBAKE
TALKFEST RECEPTION
SYMPOSIUM
(STUDENTS' —) KOMMERS
(SUFF.) (FESTIVE —) FEST
GAU BANT
GAUCHE CLUMSY AWKWARD
GAUD GAY GAUDY FANGLE VANITY
TRINKET
GAUDINESS GLARE GLITTER
GAUDY GAY LOUD CHEAP FLARY
SHOWY VAUDY BRAZEN FLASHY
FLIMSY FLORID GARISH GAWISH
SKYRIN TAWDRY TINSEL BRANKIE
CHINTZY FLARING GAUDISH
GLARING MERETRICIOUS
GAUGE (ALSO SEE GAGE) BORE
GAGE MOOT PLUG SIZE TRAM
GADGE NORMA RANGE DENTIN
FEELER FORMER GABARI
DEPTHEN TEMPLET TRAMMEL
ESTIMATE INDICANT MEASURER
STANDARD SURFACER TEMPLATE
MANOMETER
(— FOR SLATES) SCANTLE
(RAIN —) UDOMETER
GAUGER SURVEYOR
GAUL GALLIA
(PL.) PICTONES
GAULISH
(PREF.) GALLO
GAUNT BONY GRIM LANK LEAN
SLIM THIN PINED SPARE THIRL
BARREN HAGGED HOLLOW
MEAGER MEAGRE SHELLY
HAGGARD SLENDER DESOLATE
RAWBONED CADAVEROUS
GAUNTLET TOP CUFF GLOVE
GANTLET GAINPAIN GANTLOPE
GAUR BISON SELADANG
GAUZE LISSE MARLI MARLY UMPLE
CYPRUS CYPRESS TIFFANY
CARBASUS
GAUZY FILMY
GAVE GIN GUV YAF YAFE
GAVEL HAMMER GAVELAGE
GAVIAL NAKOO LIZARD GHARIAL
LORICATE
GAVOTTE MUSETTE
GAWK GAWKY GAWNEY LUMPKIN
RAMMACK
GAWKY GOWKIT ANGULAR
AWKWARD GAWKISH
GAY MAD AIRY BOON DAFT GLAD
GLEG HIGH RORY TRIM WILD
BONNY BUXOM GAUDY JOLLY
LIGHT MERRY NITID RIANT RORTY
SUNNY VAUDY WLONK ALEGER
BLITHE CHEERY FLASHY FRISKY
FROLIC GARISH JOCUND JOVIAL
JOYFUL JOYOUS KIPPER LIVELY
SOCIAL SPORTY WANTON
BOBBISH CHIPPER FESTIVE
GALLANT GIOJOSO GLEEFUL
LARKING RACKETY SMICKER
SMILING TITTUPY WINSOME
CAVALIER DEBONAIR FROHLICH
GAMESOME PLEASANT PRIMROSE

SPARKISH SPLENDID SPORTIVE
GAY-FEATHER LIATRIS
GAYUMART (SLAYER OF —)
ANGROMAINYUS
(SON OF —) SIYAMAK
GAYWINGS MAYWINGS
GAZE EYE PRY CAPE GAPE GOUK
GOWK LEER LOOK MOON OGLE
PEER PORE SCAN TOOT GLAIK
GLARE GLOAT GLORE SIGHT
STARE TWIRE VISIE WLITE
ASPECT GLOWER REGARD
AFTEREYE
GAZELLE AHU GOA ADMI AOUL
CORA DAMA MOHR ADDRA ARIEL
KORIN MHORR DZEREN GROUSE
ALGAZEL CHIKARA CORINNE
DIBATAG TABITHA CHINKARA
GAZELLE HOUND SALUKI
GAZETTE COURANT JOURNAL
(— OF CRIMES) HUE
GAZEZ (FATHER OF —) CALEB
HARAN
(MOTHER OF —) EPHAH
GE TAPUYAN
GEAN MERRY MURIE MURRY
GUIGNE GASKINS
GEAR KIT SPUR TACK TRIM IDLER
TOOTH FOURTH GRAITH HYPOID
PINION TACKLE CLOBBER
GEARING HARNESS REVERSE
RIGGING SEGMENT TRILOBE
BACKPACK HEADGEAR
OVERDRIVE
(— OF DIVER) ARMOR
(CHAFING —) SCOTCHMAN
(DEFENSIVE —) ARMORY
(RUNNING —) CARRIAGE
(TRANSMISSION —) HIGH FIRST
SPEED FOURTH SECOND REVERSE
GEARED GIRT
GEARWHEEL UNILOBE WABBLER
WOBBLER
GEB KEB SEB
GEBER (FATHER OF —) URI
GECKO FANFOOT TARENTE
GEKKONID LACERTID
GEDALIAH (FATHER OF —) AHIKAM
(SLAYER OF —) ISHMAEL
GEELBEC SALMON TERAGLIN
GEEPOUND SLUG
GEESE SET
GEIGER TREE ALOEWOOD
SEBESTEN
GEL JELL JELLY LIVER GELATE
ALCOGEL
GELATIN AGAR GLUE COLLIN
GLUTIN GLUTOID HAITSAI
NORGINE ISINGLASS
GELATINOUS COLLOID MUCULENT
JELLYLIKE
GELD LIB GELT ALTER CASTRATE
GELDING HORSE SPADE SPADO
GEM GIM JADE ONYX OPAL RUBY
AGATE BERYL BIJOU CAMEO
JAZEL JEWEL PEARL SPARK
STONE TOPAZ ZIMME AMULET
BAGUET CRUSTA GARNET IOLITE
JASPER PEBBLE PYROPE RONDEL
ZIRCON CITRINE DIAMOND
DOUBLET EMERALD JACINTH
KUNZITE ONEGITE PERIDOT
SPARKLE ACHROITE AMATRICE

AMETHYST BAGUETTE HYACINTH
INTAGLIO MARQUISE ORIENTAL
RONDELLE SAPPHIRE SARDONYX
HIDDENITE MOONSTONE
RUBICELLE
(— CARVED IN RELIEF) CAMEO
INTAGLIO
(— ENGRAVED WITH CHARM)
ABRAXAS
(— OF IMPERFECT BRILLIANCY)
LOUPE
(— REFLECTING LIGHT IN 6 RAYS)
ASTERIA
(— STATE) IDAHO
(IMITATION —) PASTE
(UNCUT —) ROUGH CABOCHON
GEMALLI (SON OF —) AMMIEL
GEMARIAH (FATHER OF —) HILKIAH
SHAPHAN
(SON OF —) MICHAIAH
GEMMA BUD GEMMULE SOREDIUM
GEMMULE SPORE BROODSAC
GEMMY EMERALD
GEMSBOK ORYX KOKAMA
GEMSBUCK
GEMSTONE JADE STAR CHEVEE
PYROPE SPINEL EMERALD
FISHEYE CROSSCUT HYALITHE
MORGANITE
(PART OF —) BEZEL CROWN CULET
FACET TABLE GIRDLE PAVILION
GENA CHEEK
GENDER SEX KIND CLASS
FEMININE
GENE GEN ALLEL AMORPH FACTOR
LETHAL PRIMER CYTOGENE
MODIFIER POLYGENE RECESSIVE
GENERAL (ALSO SEE SOLDIER)
MAIN MOST BROAD GROSS
ATAMAN COMMON HETMAN
PUBLIC VULGAR CURRENT
GENERIC MARSHAL SUMMARY
AUFIDIUS CANIDIUS CATHOLIC
ECUMENIC ENCYCLIC OVERHEAD
PANDEMIC PUFIDIUS STRATEGE
BRIGADIER
(PL.) DIADOCHI
(PREF.) CAEN(O) CEN(O) COEN(O)
PAN
GENERALITY CREDO GENERALE
GENERALIZATION LAW AXIOM
BROMIDE
GENERALIZE WIDEN EXTEND
SPREAD BROADEN
GENERALIZED GROSS GLOBAL
GENERALLY BROADLY LARGELY
OVERALL ROUNDLY MOSTWHAT
GENERATE MAKE SIRE TEEM
BEGET BREED IMPEL SPAWN
STEAM CREATE FATHER GENDER
IMPOSE KITTLE DEVELOP INBREED
PRODUCE ENGENDER
(— PUS) DIGEST
GENERATION AGE KIND TIME
WORLD STRAIN STRIND DESCENT
DIPLOID GETTING KINDRED
GAMOBIUM GENITURE SAECULUM
THEOGONY TRIPLOID UPSPRING
OFFSPRING
(FUTURE —S) POSTERITY
(SPONTANEOUS —) ABIOGENESIS
(SUFF.)
GON(E)(IDIUM)(IMO)(IUM)(Y)

GENERATIVE GENIAL GAMETIC GENESIC GENETIC SEEDFUL SEMINAL PROLIFIC

GENERATOR KIPP BUZZER DYNAMO RULING ELEMENT DIPHASER GENERANT OSCILLATOR

GENEROSITY GRACE LARGE BOUNTY GENTRY BREADTH FREEDOM HONESTY COURTESY GOODNESS KINDNESS LARGESSE

GENEROUS BIG FREE OPEN SOFT FRANK HEFTY LARGE NOBLE LIBERAL GRACIOUS HANDSOME INSORDID LARGEOUS MAGNIFIC OPENHANDED

GENEROUSLY LUCKY MANLY KINDLY FRANKLY

GENESIS BIRTH ORIGIN BERESHIT GENETICS

GENET BERBE CIVET DAPPLE VIVERRINE

GENIAL BEIN BIEN WARM DOUCE SONSY DOULCE FORTHY FURTHY HEARTY KINDLY MELLOW MENTAL CHEERFUL GRACIOUS PLEASANT

GENIALITY BONHOMIE

GENICULATE KNEED ELBOWED

GENIE GENIUS HATHOR SANDMAN

GENII XIN JANN

GENIN BUFAGIN

GENIP GINEP JAGUA IRONWOOD

GENIPAP LANA GENIP JAGUA GUENEPE

GENISTA FURZE RETAMA

GENITAL SECRET
(PL.) HARNESS PRIVITY GENITURE

GENITALS
(PREF.) EDE(O)

GENIUS KA FIRE GIFT HAPI KALI TURN ANGEL BRAIN DEMON GENIO NUMEN DAEMON INGENY INGINE TALENT WIZARD DUSTMAN DUAMUTEF EINSTEIN FRAVASHI SILVANUS
(— OF LANGUAGE) IDIOM

GENOA GEANE

GENOTYPE BIOTYPE LOGOTYPE

GENOUILLERE KNEELET

GENRE EPIC KIND SORT TYPE CLASS STYLE FABLIAU SPECIES CATEGORY

GENS HOUSE

GENSERIC (BROTHER OF —) GONDERIC GONTHARIS
(FATHER OF —) GODIGISDUS

GENTEEL NICE GENTY GENTIL JAUNTY POLITE STYLISH GRACEFUL

GENTIAN BIT FELWORT AGUEWEED GALLWEED BALDMONEY PENNYWORT

GENTILE GOI GOY ARIAN ARYAN GOYISH HEATHEN

GENTILITY POLISH CIVILITY GENTRICE NICENESS

GENTLE MOY CALM DEFT DEWY FAIR HEND KIND MEEK MILD MURE NESH SLOW SOFT SOOT TAME BLAND CANNY LIGHT LITHE MILKY QUIET SMALL SOBER SWEET BENIGN BONAIR CADISH

DOCILE FACILE LYDIAN MODEST PLACID REMISS SILKEN SILVER SOFTLY TENDER AFFABLE AMABILE CLEMENT GRADUAL SOAKING SUBDUED DEBONAIR DELICATE DOVELIKE EGGSHELL LAMBLIKE LENITIVE MAIDENLY MANSUETE MODERATE PEACEFUL SARCENET TOWARDLY TRANQUIL
(— AS OF THE WIND) LOOM

GENTLEFOLK GENTRY GENTILITY

GENTLEMAN NIB SIR BABU GENT TOFF BABOO CURIO DORAY SAHIB SENOR GEMMAN MILORD SENHOR SIGNOR YONKER BRAVERY GALLANT GENTMAN MYNHEER CAVALIER MIRABELL SEIGNEUR SEIGNIOR SQUIREEN
(— COMMONER) HAT
(— TRAINING FOR KNIGHTHOOD) DONZEL
(COUNTRY —) SQUIRE
(GIPSY —) RYE
(MILITARY —) CADET
(POOR —) BUCKEEN
(WOULD-BE —) SHONEEN
(PL.) HERREN CHIVALRY

GENTLEMAN-AT-ARMS PENSIONER

GENTLEMANLY JAUNTY

GENTLENESS FLESH LENITY AMENITY DOUCEUR CLEMENCY KINDNESS MANSUETUDE

GENTLY SOFT CANNY SOAVE EASILY FAIRLY LIGHTLY EASYLIKE PRETTILY TENDERLY

GENTRY COUNTY GENTRICE SQUIRAGE SZLACHTA

GENUBATH (FATHER OF —) HADAD

GENUFLECTION VENIE KNEELING

GENUINE ECHT GOOD LEAL PURE REAL TRUE VRAI PLAIN PUKKA SOLID ACTUAL ARRANT DINKUM DIRECT HONEST KOSHER PISTIC CURRENT GERMANE GRADELY SINCERE VERIDIC GRAITHLY STERLING
(NOT —) TIN SHAM BOGUS PLASTIC PRETENDED
(SEEMINGLY —) COLORABLE
(SUFF.) (NOT —) ASTER

GENUINENESS VERIDITY

GENUS KIND CLASS ANALOG GENDER GENERAL
(— OF ALGAE) DASYA FUCUS BANGIA CHORDA CODIUM HYPNEA NOSTOC PADINA DIATOMA LEMANEA LIAGORA PTILOTA VALONIA ZYGNEMA ANABAENA BRYOPSIS CAULERPA CERAMIUM CHONDRUS CONFERVA CUTLERIA DICTYOTA DUMONTIA GELIDIUM GOMONTIA HALIMEDA LERAMIUM LESSONIA NEMALION OOCYSTIS PALMELLA PORPHYRA STRIARIA TAONURUS ULOTHRIX
(— OF AMOEBA) CHAOS
(— OF AMPHIBIAN) HYLA RANA SIREN PROTEUS AMPHIUMA NECTURUS
(— OF ANT) ATTA ECITON LASIUS

PONERA TERMES FORMICA PHEIDOLE TAPINOMA
(— OF ANTELOPE) ORYX KOBUS BUBALIS GAZELLA MADOQUA REDUNCA ANTILOPE EGOCERUS
(— OF APE) PAN PONGO SIMIA
(— OF APHID) ADELGES CHERMES
(— OF ARACHNID) ACARUS GALEODES
(— OF ARMADILLO) DASYPUS XENURUS
(— OF ASCIDIAN) CIONA MOLGULA BOLTENIA PYROSOMA
(— OF ASCLEPIAD) STAPELIA
(— OF AUK) ALCA ALLE
(— OF BABOON) PAPIO
(— OF BACTERIA) VIBRIO EIMERIA ERWINIA GAFFKYA PROTEUS SARCINA BACILLUS BRUCELLA SERRATIA SHIGELLA
(— OF BADGER) MELES ARCTONYX HELICTIS
(— OF BARNACLE) LEPAS BALANUS ELMINIUS
(— OF BASIDIOMYCETE) BOVISTA
(— OF BAT) EUDERMA PETALIA DESMODUS DIPHYLLA MOLOSSUS MORMOOPS NOCTILIO NYCTERIS PLECOTUS PTEROPUS VAMPYRUM
(— OF BEAN) ABRUS
(— OF BEAR) URSUS EUARCTOS MELURSUS
(— OF BEAVER) CASTOR
(— OF BEE) APIA APIS BOMBUS ANDRENA TRIGONA COLLETES HALICTUS MELIPONA
(— OF BEETLE) AMARA FIDIA HISPA LAMIA LARIA LYTTA MELOE SAGRA ALTICA ASILUS CLERUS ELATER LYCTUS PTINUS SILPHA ACILIUS ADELOPS AGRILUS ANOBIUM ANOMALA BRUCHUS CARABUS CASSIDA EPITRIX PRIONUS SAPERDA SITARIS ADORETUS AGRIOTES APHODIUS CALOSOMA CATORAMA CYBISTER DYNASTES DYTISCUS EPICAUTA EUMOLPUS HARPALUS LAMPYRIS MEGASOMA PASSALUS POPILLIA SCOLYTUS SPHINDUS TENEBRIO DERMESTES
(— OF BIRD) ARA ALCA APUS CRAX CREX GYPS JYNX MIRO MITU MOHO OTIS PICA RHEA SULA TYTO XEMA AJAJA ANOUS ANSER ARDEA ARGUS ASTUR BUCCO FALCO GAVIA GOURA GUARA GYGIS IRENA JUNCO LARUS LERWA LOXIA MIMUS MITUA MUNIA PIPRA PITTA SITTA TODUS UPUPA VIDUA VIREO ALAUDA ALCEDO ANHIMA ANTHUS AQUILA BONASA BRANTA CAPITO CIRCUS COLIUS CORVUS DACELO ELANUS FULICA GALLUS JACANA LANIUS LEIPOA LIMOSA MARECA MENURA MEROPS MILVUS MONASA NESTOR NUMIDA PASSER PASTOR PERDIX PERNIS PROGNE QUELEA RALLUS SAPPHO SCOPUS SIALIA SPINUS STERNA SYLVIA TETRAO TRERON TRINGA TROGON TURDUS TURNIX

VULTUR ANHINGA APTERYX ARTAMUS BUCEROS CACICUS CAPELLA CARIAMA CERTHIA CHIONIS CICONIA CINCLUS COLINUS COLUMBA COTINGA CUCULUS ELAENIA GALBULA GARRUPA HALCYON HIRUNDO IBYCTER ICTERUS KAKATOE LAGOPUS LOPHURA LYRURUS MALURUS MANACUS MESITES MILVAGO MOMOTUS ORIOLUS PANDION PAROTIA PIRANGA PITYLUS PLAUTUS PLOCEUS PORZANA REGULUS SEIURUS SERINUS STURNUS TANAGRA TIMALIA TOTANUS XENICUS ZENAIDA ACCENTOR ACCIPTER ACREDULA AFROPAVO AGELAIUS AMIZILIA BOTAURUS BUCORVUS BURHINUS CHAETURA COLYMBUS CORACIAS COTURNIX DELICHON DIATRYMA DINORNIS DIOMEDEA DREPANIS EMBERIZA EUPHONIA EURYPYGA FULMARUS GARRULUS GEOSPIZA GERYGONE GLAREOLA GRALLINA GYPAETUS IONORNIS LUSCINIA MACHETES MYCTERIA NEOPHRON NOTORNIS NUMENIUS OREORTYX PENELOPE PHAETHON PITANGUS PLATALEA PLEGADIS PODARGUS PRIONOPS PRUNELLA PUFFINUS RUPICOLA SALTATOR SAXICOLA SCOLOPAX SPEOTYTO SPIZELLA STRUTHIO TRAGOPAN TYRANNUS
(— OF BIVALVES) MYA PINNA ANOMIA MACTRA NUCULA ETHERIA MYTILUS PANDORA COLYMBUS HINNITES PISIDIUM SAXICAVA TRIDACNA XYLOTRYA SPHAERIUM
(— OF BOWFIN) AMIA
(— OF BRACHIOPOD) ATRYPA CRANIA ATHYRIS DISCINA SPIRIFER
(— OF BRYOZOAN) BUGULA ESCHARA FLUSTRA RETEPORA
(— OF BUG) ANASA CIMEX EMESA CORIXA TINGIS
(— OF BUTTERFLY) CALIGO COLIAS DANAUS MORPHO PIERIS THECLA EURYMUS JUNONIA KALLIMA LYCAENA PAPILIO STRYMON VANESSA ARGYNNIS HESPERIA LEMONIAS MELITAEA SPEYERIA
(— OF CABBAGE) COS
(— OF CACTUS) CEREUS NOPALEA OPUNTIA HARRISIA
(— OF CANTELOUPE) CUCUMIS
(— OF CAT) FELIS ACINONYX HEMIGALE
(— OF CATTLE) BOS NEAT TAURUS
(— OF CEPHALOPOD) SEPIA SPIRULA
(— OF CETACEAN) INIA
(— OF CHINK) LACUNA
(— OF CHIPMUNK) EUTAMIAS
(— OF CILIATE) COLPODA CHILODON EUPLOTES
(— OF CIVET) FOSSA PAGUMA
(— OF CLAM) ENSIS GEMMA SOLEN SPISULA
(— OF COCKLE) CHIONE

(**— OF COCKROACH**) BLATTA
(**— OF CODFISH**) GADUS
(**— OF CORAL**) ASTREA FUNGIA
MAENDRA OCULINA PORITES
ACROPORA TUBIPORA
(**— OF CRAB**) UCA MAIA BIRGUS
CANCER GRAPSUS OCYPODE
PAGURUS LITHODES PORTUNUS
(**— OF CRANE**) GRUS
(**— OF CRAYFISH**) CAMBARUS
(**— OF CRICKET**) ACHETA GRYLLUS
(**— OF CRUSTACEAN**) APUS HIPPA
JASUS LIGIA MYSIS CYPRIS
LIGYDA SELLUS TRIOPS ARGULUS
ARTEMIA ASTACUS BOPYRUS
CALAPPA CHELURA DAPHNIA
EMERITA HOMARUS IDOTHEA
LERNAEA NEBALIA SQUILLA
CAPRELLA ESTHERIA GAMMARUS
LEUCIFER LIMNETIS LIMNORIA
NEPHROPS PHRONIMA
(**— OF CTENOPHORE**) BEROE
CESTUM
(**— OF CUCUMBER**) CUCUMIS
(**— OF CURASSOW**) CRAX
(**— OF DEER**) AXIS DAMA PUDU
RUSA CERVUS MAZAMA
MOSCHUS RUCERVUS
(**— OF DIATOM**) DIATOMA
SYNEDRA MERIDION NAVICULA
(**— OF DODO**) DIDUS
(**— OF DOG**) CUON CANIS LYCAON
(**— OF DORMOUSE**) GLIS
(**— OF DRAGONFLY**) AESCHNA
(**— OF DUCK**) AIX ANAS AYTHYA
MERGUS NYROCA NETTION
SPATULA CLANGULA FULIGULA
(**— OF EAGLE**) AQUILA
(**— OF ECHINODERM**) ASTERIAS
(**— OF EDENTATE**) MANIS
(**— OF EEL**) CONGER ECHIDNA
MURAENA ANGUILLA GYMNOTUS
MORINGUA
(**— OF FERN**) FILIX TODEA ANEMIA
AZOLLA DOODIA CYATHEA
ISOETES ONOCLEA OSMUNDA
PELLAEA WOODSIA ADIANTUM
ASPIDIUM ATHYRIUM BLECHNUM
CETERACH CIBOTIUM CLEMATIS
DAVALLIA LYGODIUM MARATTIA
SALVINIA SCHIZAEA VITTARIA
(**— OF FIREFLY**) LAMPYRIS
(**— OF FISH**) AMIA ESOX HURO
LOTA MOLA RAJA ZEUS ALOSA
BADIS BERYX BETTA DORAS
ELOPS GADUS GOBIO HUCHO
LATES MANTA MUGIL PERCA
SALMO SARDA SOLEA UMBRA
ALBULA ANABAS APOGON BAIGRE
BARBUS BELONE CARANX CLUPEA
COTTUS DIODON GERRES GOBIUS
HIODON KUHLIA LABRUS LATRIS
MOBULA MYXINE NOMEUS
PAGRUS PSETTA REMORA
SCARUS SPARUS TRIGLA TRUTTA
TURSIO WEEVER ABRAMIS
ALOPHAS ALOPIAS ARACANA
ASPREDO BROTULA CARAPUS
CLARIAS DREPANE ECHIDNA
GARRUPA GIRELLA GYMNORA
LEPOMIS LIMANDA LUCANIA
LYCODES OSMERUS PEGASUS
PRISTIS SCIAENA SCOMBER

SEPIOLA SERIOLA SIGANUS
SILLAGO SILURUS SPHYRNA
SQUALUS SYNODUS THUNNUS
TORPEDO TOXOTES TRIODON
XIPHIAS ZOARCES AMEIURUS
ANABLEPS ANGUILLA ARAPAIMA
ASTYANAX ATHERINA BALISTES
BODIANUS CARANGUS CHIMAERA
CLADODUS CTENODUS CYPRINUS
DAPEDIUS DIPLODUS DIPTERUS
DOROSOMA ECHENEIS ETRUMEUS
FUNDULUS GADOPSIS GALAXIAS
GAMBUSIA GOBIESOX HAEMULON
ICOSTEUS KYPHOSUS LEBISTES
LUTIANUS MEGALOPS MORMYRUS
MUSTELUS NOTROPIS OPHIDION
PALOMETA PANTODON
PHOCAENA POLYODON PYGIDIUM
SERRANUS SQUATINA
COREGONUS MYCTOPHUM
(**— OF FLAGELLATE**) COCOS
GONIUM OPHION SYNURA
VOLVOX ATTALEA CARYOTA
EUGLENA GIARDIA BORASSUS
CERATIUM EUDORINA HEXAMITA
HYDRURUS
(**— OF FLEA**) PULEX BOSMINA
(**— OF FLY**) DACUS MUSCA MYMAR
PERLA PHORA ASILUS CEPHUS
FANNIA PIMPLA RHYSSA SCIARA
TIPULA CALIROA CHALCIS DIOPSIS
EPHYDRA HYLEMYA MIASTOR
ORTALIS OSCINIS PANORPA
TACHINA THEREVA ACROCERA
AGROMYZA ANOMALON APHIDIUS
BOMBOMUS SITELONUS SITINYGGRA
CHRYSOPS GLOSSINA PSYCHODA
SCHEDIUS SIMULIUM STOMOXYS
(**— OF FLYING SQUIRREL**) BELOMYS
(**— OF FOSSIL**) AMPYX ERYON
ADAPIS ATRYPA BAIERA ERYOPS
GEIKIA HYENIA KLUKIA MAMMUT
OLENUS ORTHIS RHYNIA ANDRIAS
ANTEDON APTIANA ASAPHUS
DICERAS EXOGYRA GANODUS
HAMITES HYBODUS KNORRIA
LESKEYA LESLEYA LOXOMMA
MESONYX MOROPUS MYLODON
OTOZOUM PHACOPS PHIOMIA
PROAVIS PROETUS WALCHIA
AGLASPIS AGNOSTUS AMYNODON
APHELOPS ARCHELON BIRKENIA
BRONTOPS CALIPPUS CALYMENE
CAYTONIA CERATOPS CLYMENIA
CTENODUS DAPEDIUS DEINODON
DIATRYMA DINOHYUS DIPLODUS
DIPTERUS ENCHODUS ENCRINUS
EODISCUS EOHIPPUS EOSAURUS
EUSMILUS GORDONIA GRYPHAEA
HALLOPUS HELIGMUS ILLAENUS
LANARKIA LEBACHIA LECROSIA
LEGUATIA LESTODON LITUITES
MACLUREA MARRELLA METOPIAS
OLDHAMIA PLACODUS PORTHEUS
RUTIODON SMILODON SPIRIFER
STEGODON STEGOMUS
TAONURUS THELODUS XIPHODON
ZAMICRUS CONULARIA
(**— OF FOX**) ALOPEX VULPES
UROCYON
(**— OF FROG**) RANA ANURA
HYLODES
(**— OF FUNGUS**) FOMES IRPEX

PHOMA TUBER VALSA VERPA
ALBUGO BREMIA CAEOMA
EMPUSA FUMAGO HYDNUM
ISARIA OIDIUM PEZIZA TORULA
ZYTHIA ACRASIA AMANITA
BOLETUS CANDIDA CHALARA
CYATHUS ELSINOE ERYSIBE
FABRAEA GEASTER LEPIOTA
MONILIA NECTRIA OZONIUM
PACHYMA PYTHIUM RHIZINA
RUSSULA SIMBLUM STEREUM
STICTIS STILBUM TYPHULA
XYLARIA ACHORION AECIDIUM
AGARICUS BOTRYTIS CALVATIA
CLATHRUS CLAVARIA COLLYBIA
COPRINUS CORYNEUM CYPHELLA
CYTTARIA DAEDALEA DIPLODIA
ENDOTHIA ENTOLOMA ENTYLOMA
ERYSIPHE EXOASCUS FUSARIUM
GEASTRUM GNOMONIA
GRAPHIUM HELOTIUM HELVELLA
LENZITES MERULIUS MYCOGONE
PAXILLUS PHOLIOTA PUCCINIA
RHIZOPUS RHYTISMA SEPTORIA
SORDARIA SPICARIA TAPHRINA
TERFEZIA TRAMETES TREMELLA
TROCHILA USTILAGO USTULINA
VENTURIA CORDICEPS
(**— OF GALLFLY**) CYNIPS
(**— OF GASTROPOD**) FICUS HARPA
LIMAX OLIVA EBURNA PATELLA
TENEBRA SCYLLAEA STROMBUS
(**— OF GEESE**) CHEN ANSER
NETTAPUS
(**— OF GNAT**) SCIARA
(**— OF GOAT**) IBEX CAPRA
OREAMNOS
(**— OF GRASS**) POA ZEA AIRA COIX
AVENA BRIZA ORYZA STIPA
APLUDA ARUNDO BROMUS
ELYMUS HOLCUS LOLIUM
LYGEUM MELICA MILIUM NARDUS
PHLEUM SECALE UNIOLA ZOYSIA
BAMBUSA BUCHLOE CHLORIS
CYNODON FESTUCA HILARIA
HORDEUM LAGURUS LEERSIA
MELINIS MOLINIA PANICUM
SETARIA SORGHUM ZIZANIA
AEGILOPS AGROSTIS ARISTIDA
AXONOPUS BULBILIS CENCHRUS
DACTYLIS ELEUSINE GLYCERIA
GYNERIUM IMPERATA PASPALUM
PHALARIS SPARTINA SPINIFEX
TRISETUM TRITICUM
(**— OF GRASSHOPPER**) LOCUSTA
(**— OF GUAN**) CRAX
(**— OF GULL**) XEMA LARUS
(**— OF HAWK**) BUTEO CIRCUS
(**— OF HERB**) GYP IVA AMMI ARUM
BETA GEUM GLAX HEBE LENS
MEUM MUSA OLAX RUTA SIDA
SIUM ADOXA AJUGA APIOS
APIUM CALLA CANNA CAREX
CARUM CICER DALEA DRABA
ERUCA ERVUM FEDIA GALAX
GAURA GILIA GLAUX HOSTA
INULA LAPPA LAVIA LAYIA LEMNA
LINUM LOASA LOTUS LUFFA
MADIA MALVA NAPEA PANAX
PARIS PHACA PHLOX PILEA
RHEUM RHOEO RUBIA SEDUM
TACCA URENA VICIA VIGNA
VINCA VIOLA ZIZIA ACAENA

ACNIDA ACORUS ACTAEA ADONIS
ALISMA ALLIUM ALSINE AMOMUM
ANOGRA ARABIS ARALIA ARNICA
ASARUM ATROPA BACOPA
BAERIA BASSIA BELLIS BIDENS
BLITUM BLUMEA BORAGO CAKILE
CALTHA CASSIA CELSIA CICUTA
CISTUS CLEOME CNICUS COLEUS
CONIUM COPTIS COSMOS
CRAMBE CREPIS CRINUM CROCUS
CROTON CUNILA CYNARA DAHLIA
DATURA DAUCUS DIODIA DONDIA
ECHIUM ELODEA ELODES EMILIA
EUCLEA FILAGO GALEGA GALIUM
GIFOLA GYNURA ISATIS ISMENE
KOCHIA KRIGIA KUHNIA LAMIUM
LEDUEA LUZULA MALOPE
MENTHA MIMOSA MONTIA
MUCUNA MUILLA NERINE
NERIUM NESLIA ONONIS OTHAKE
OXALIS PICRIS PISTIA PYROLA
RESEDA RESTIO RHEXIA RIVINA
RUPPIA SAGINA SALVIA SCILLA
SESBAN SESELI STEVIA SUAEDA
THALIA TULIPA VIORNA ZINNIA
ABRONIA ADLUMIA AETHUSA
ALEGRIA ALETRIS ALKANNA
ALPINIA ALTHAEA ALYSSUM
AMORPHA AMSONIA ANCHUSA
ANEMONE ANETHUM ANYCHIA
APHANES ARACHIS ARCTIUM
ARNEBIA ARUNCUS BABIANA
BARTSIA BEGONIA BOEBERA
BUTOMUS CACALIA CAJANUS
CALYPSO CARLINA CELOSIA
CHELONE CINGAEA CIRCIUM
CLARKIA COMARUM CROOMIA
CURCUMA CUSCUTA CYTINUS
DATISCA DECODON DERINGA
DIASCIA DROSERA ELATINE
EOMECON EPISCIA ERODIUM
FELICIA FICARIA FRASERA
FREESIA FUMARIA GAZANIA
GERBERA GLECOMA GLYCINE
GUNNERA HALENIA HECHTIA
HEDEOMA HOMERIA HUGELIA
HYPOXIS IRESINE JASIONE
KICKXIA KNAUTIA KOELLIA
LACTUCA LAPPULA LAPSANA
LEWISIA LIATRIS LINARIA
LINNAEA LOGANIA LOPEZIA
LUNARIA LUPINUS LYCHNIS
LYTHRUM MARANTA MEDEOLA
MIMULUS MITELLA MOLLUGO
MONESES MUSCARI NEMESIA
NIGELLA OTHONNA PAEONIA
PAPAVER PAVONIA PEGANUM
PETUNIA PLUCHEA PRIMULA
RORIPPA ROTALIA RUELLIA
SALSOLA SAMOLUS SCANDIX
SENECIO SESAMUM SHORTIA
SILYBUM SINAPIS SOLANUM
SONCHUS STACHYS STATICE
SUCCISA SWERTIA TAGETES
TALINUM THALIA THAPSIA
THESIUM THLASPI THURNIA
TORENIA TORILIS TOVARIA
TRILISA URGINEA VALLOTA
VERBENA ZEBRINA ACALYPHA
ACANTHUS ACHILLEA ACONITUM
AGALINIS AGERATUM ALLIARIA
ALLIONIA ALOCASIA AMBROSIA
AMMOBIUM ANDRYALA ANGELICA

ANTHEMIS ANTICLEA APOCYNUM
ARCTOTIS ARENARIA ARGEMONE
ARISAEMA ASPERULA ATRIPLEX
BAPTISIA BARBAREA BARTONIA
BERGENIA BERTEROA BETONICA
BISTORTA BOLTONIA BORRERIA
BRASSICA BRUNONIA BUCHNERA
CALATHEA CAMASSIA CAMELINA
CANNABIS CAPSICUM CERINTHE
CLEMATIS COCHARUS COLLOMIA
COLUMNEA COMANDRA
COOPERIA CRASSULA CUBELIUM
DENTARIA DIANTHUS DICENTRA
DIPSACUS DISPORUM DYSSODIA
ECHINOPS EPIFAGUS ERANTHIS
EREMURUS ERIGENIA ERIGERON
ERYNGIUM ERYSIMUM EUCHARIS
EUTHAMIA FITTONIA FLAVERIA
FLOERKEA FRAGARIA GALACTIA
GENTIANA GERARDIA GESNERIA
GILLENIA GLAUCIUM GLECHOMA
GLORIOSA GLOXINIA GOODENIA
GRATIOLA GUZMANIA HELENIUM
HELONIAS HEPATICA HESPERIS
HEUCHERA HIBISCUS HIPPURIS
HOSACKIA HOTTONIA HUDSONIA
HYDROLES HYSSOPUS IONIDIUM
ISNARDIA JATROPHA JUSSIAEA
JUSTICIA KNEIFFIA KOHLERIA
LAPORTEA LAVATERA LEONOTIS
LEONURUS LEPIDIUM LEPTILON
LIMONIUM LOPHIOLA LYCOPSIS
MACLEAYA MANFREDA MANTISIA
MEDICAGO MEIBOMIA MYOSOTIS
MYOSURUS OBOLARIA OENANTHE
OPOPANAX ORONTIUM PAROSELA
PHACELIA PHORMIUM PHYMOSIA
PHYSALIS PHYSARIA PLANTAGO
PLUMBAGO POLYGALA POLYMNIA
POTERIUM PRUNELLA PSORALEA
RAPHANUS RHAGODIA SABBATIA
SAMBUCUS SANICULA SARCODES
SAROTHRA SATUREIA SCABIOSA
SCOLYMUS SESBANIA SESUVIUM
SEYMERIA SIDALCEA SILPHIUM
SOLIDAGO SPERGULA SPIGELIA
SPINACIA STOKESIA TAENIDIA
THASPIUM TIARELLA TRIBULUS
TRILLIUM TROLLIUS TUECRIUM
UVULARIA VACCARIA VALERIAN
VANELLUS VERATRUM VERNONIA
VERONICA VISCARIA WATSONIA
XANTHIUM RUDBECKIA
(— OF HERON) ARDEA EGRETTA
(— OF HORSE) EQUUS CALIPPUS
EOHIPPUS
(— OF HYDROZOAN) DIPHYES
PHYSALIA
(— OF HYENA) HYAENA CROCUTA
(— OF INSECT) NEPA APHIS EMESA
JAPYX SIREX BOREUS CICADA
COCCUS CORIXA EMPUSA ICERYA
KERMES MANTIS PHASMA
PODURA SIALIS THRIPS CHALCIS
FORMICA FULGORA LEPISMA
ORYSSUS RANATRA STYLOPS
VEDALIA BACILLUS CAMPODEA
EPHEMERA LABIDURA LACCIFER
LECANIUM LYONETIA MACHILIS
MANTISPA NERTHRUS REDUVIUS
(— OF ISOPOD) IDOTEA IDOTHEA
CIROLANA
(— OF JAY) GARRULUS

(— OF JELLYFISH) CYANEA
AURELIA AEQUOREA
(— OF JERBOA) DIPUS
(— OF KELP) AGARUM
(— OF LANGUR) SIMIAS
(— OF LEAFHOPPER) AGALLIA
EMPOASCA
(— OF LEECH) HIRUDO HAEMOPIS
(— OF LEMUR) INDRI GALAGO
(— OF LIANA) BAUHINIA
(— OF LICE) APHIS PSYLLA
ARGULUS ONISCUS BOVICOLA
ERIOSOMA GONIODES LIPEURUS
(— OF LICHEN) CORA USNEA
STICTA EVERNIA GRAPHIS
LECIDEA LOBARIA PHYSCIA
CETRARIA CLADONIA LECANORA
PARMELIA ROCCELLA STRIGULA
(— OF LIMPET) ACMAEA
(— OF LIZARD) UTA AGAMA
DRACO GEKKO AMEIVA ANGUIS
ANOLIS IGUANA EUMECES
LACERTA PYGOPUS SCINCUS
ACONTIAS CHIROTES COLEONYX
LYGOSOMA RHINEURA
(— OF LOCUST) TETRIX TETTIX
(— OF MACAW) ARA
(— OF MAMMAL) BOS SUS HOMO
LAMA ALCES BISON CAPRA
TAYRA DUGONG FRISON
AELURUS AILURUS BUBALUS
GALIDIA GYMNURA LINSANG
OTOCYON AUCHENIA CYCLOPES
CYNOGALE SURICATA TRAGULUS
(— OF MAPLE) ACER
(— OF MARSUPIAL) DASYURUS
MACROPUS POTOROUS TARSIPES
(— OF MARTEN) MARTES MUSTELA
(— OF MEDUSA) SARSIA GERYONIA
(— OF MICROSPORIDIAN) GLUGEA
(— OF MILDEW) ERYSIPHE
UNCINULA
(— OF MILLIPEDE) JULUS
(— OF MINT) ICIMUM NEPETA
MELISSA PERILLA PHLOMIS
ORIGANUM
(— OF MITE) ACARUS ACERIA
LEPTUS DEMODEX ACARAPIS
(— OF MOLD) MUCOR FULIGO
MELIOLA
(— OF MOLE) TALPA SCALOPS
SCALOPUS
(— OF MOLLUSK) ARCA DOTO LEDA
LIMA CHAMA DONAX EOLIS FICUS
HARPA LIMAX MUREX OLIVA
VENUS AEOLIS ANOMIA BANKIA
CASSIS CHITON LEPTON LUCINA
OSTREA PECTEN PHOLAS PYRULA
SEMELE TEREDO TETHYS
ACTAEON ASTARTE ATLANTA
CARDITA CARDIUM CYPRAEA
CYPRINA DOSINIA ETHERIA
EXOGYRA LINGULA TELLINA
BUCCINUM GRYPHAEA HALIOTIS
LIMACINA LUTRARIA MODIOLUS
NAUTILUS PINCTADA SCYLLAEA
STROMBUS
(— OF MONGOOSE) GALIDIA
(— OF MONKEY) AOTES AOTUS
CEBUS ATELES MACACA CACAJAO
COLOBUS NASALIS SAIMIRI
PITHECIA
(— OF MOOSE) ALCES

(— OF MOSQUITO) AEDES CULEX
EUXOA MNIUM SAMIA SESIA
TINEA ACTIAS ALYPIA ARCTIA
BOMBYX COSSUS DATANA
HYPNUM LESKEA PLUSIA PSYCHE
SPHINX THYRIS URANIA AGROTIS
ALABAMA APATELA ARCHIPS
ATTACUS BARBULA CRAMBUS
FUNARIA GRIMMIA PHASCUM
PRONUBA PYRALIS SESAMIA
TORTRIX ZEUZERA ZYGAENA
ANDREAEA CATOCALA
DAWSONIA DIATRAEA DICRANUM
ENDROMIS EPHESTIA EUPREPIA
GALLERIA GELECHIA HEPIALUS
PLUTELLA PRODENIA PYRAUSTA
SATURNIA SPHAGNUM THUIDIUM
(— OF MOTH) CHILO ABRAXAS
(— OF MOUSE) MUS APODEMUS
(— OF MUSKMELON) CUCUMIS
(— OF MUSKRAT) FIBER ONDATRA
(— OF NARWHAL) MONODON
(— OF NEMATODE) ACUARIA
ALAIMUS ANGUINA NECATOR
(— OF NUDIBRANCH) GLAUCUS
(— OF OATS) AVENA
(— OF OPOSSUM) MARMOSA
(— OF ORCHID) DISA VANDA
BLETIA LAELIA PHAJUS ACINETA
AERIDES ANGULOA BRASSIA
CORDULA EUCOSIA IBIDIUM
ISOTRIA LIPARIS LISTERA
MALAXIS POGONIA VANILLA
ANGRECUM ARETHUSA BLETILLA
CALANTHE CATTLEYA CYTHEREA
FISSIPES GOODYERA MILTONIA
ONCIDIUM PERAMIUM SERAPIAS
SOBRALIA TRIPHORA
(— OF OTTER) LUTRA
(— OF OWL) BUBO NINOX STRIX
KETUPA NYCTEA AEGOLIUS
SPEOTYTO
(— OF OXEN) BIBOS
(— OF OYSTER) OSTREA AVICULA
(— OF PALM) NIPA ARECA ASSAI
COCOS HOWEA SABAL ARENGA
ELAEIS INODES KENTIA RAPHIA
RHAPIS ATTALEA BACTRIS
CALAMUS CARYOTA CORYPHA
ERYTHEA EUTERPE GEONOMA
LATANIA LICUALA PHOENIX
SERENOA THRINAX BORASSUS
HYPHAENE IRIARTEA LODOICEA
MAURITIA
(— OF PARASITE) STRIGA CUSCOTA
CUSCUTA HYDNORA OLPIDIUM
CASSYTHIA
(— OF PARRAKEET) ARATINGA
(— OF PARROT) NESTER AMAZONA
KAKATOE
(— OF PEACOCK) PAVO
(— OF PENGUIN) EUDYPTES
(— OF PHALANGER) DROMICIA
(— OF PIGEON) GOURA DUCULA
COLUMBA
(— OF PLANT) ALOE ARUM COLA
DION FABA IRIS IXIA PUYA SOJA
ADOXA AGAVE ASTER BATIS
CANNA CHARA DIOON DRYAS
INULA NAIAS PIPER RUMEX
TRAPA TYPHA XYRIS YUCCA ZILLA
ABROMA ACACIA AIZOON ALBUCA

ANANAS CACTUS CUPHEA
DATURA EXACUM FERULA IBERIS
JAMBOS JUNCUS LICHEN LILIUM
MAYACA MORAEA NUPHAR
PHRYMA RICCIA SILENE SMILAX
STRIGA URTICA VISCUM ALONSOA
ASTILBE BALLOTA CABOMBA
CUCUMIS CYPERUS DIONAEA
DROSERA ENCELIA EPACRIS
EPIGAEA EURYALE FAGELIA
GLYCINE GODETIA HELXINE
HOOKERA ISOETES ISOLOMA
KARATAS LYCOPUS MANIHOT
MONARDA NELUMBO NITELLA
RAOULIA RICINUS STEMONA
SYRINGA TRIURUS TURNERA
WOLFFIA WYETHIA ZOSTERA
ABUTILON ACANTHUS ADIANTUM
ANABASIS ANTHYLIS BRASENIA
BRODIAEA BROMELIA CALADIUM
CAPSICUM CYCLAMEN FORCRAEA
FURCRAEA GALTONIA GASTERIA
GERANIUM LATHRAEA LATHYRUS
MARSILEA MONSTERA NYMPHAEA
PANDANUS PEDALIUM PELVETIA
PERESKIA SAURURUS SPARAXIS
THEVETIA TIGRIDIA TRITONIA
VELLOZIA VICTORIA ZINGIBER
(— OF POLYZOAN) LEPRALIA
LOXOSOMA
(— OF POPLAR) ALAMO
(— OF PORCUPINE) COENDOU
HYSTRIX
(— OF PORPOISE) INIA PHOCAENA
(— OF PRAWN) PALAEMON
(— OF PROTOZOAN) BODO HYDRA
MONAS ADELEA AMOEBA
ACINETA ARCELLA EIMERIA
STENTOR DIDINIUM EUGLYPHA
ISOSPORA UROGLENA
(— OF RABBIT) LEPUS
(— OF RACCOON) OLINGO
(— OF RAT) ANISOMYS
(— OF RHIZOPOD) AMOEBA
GROMIA LAGENA HATTERIA
PELOMYXA
(— OF RODENT) MUS CAVIA DIPUS
LEPUS ZAPUS GEOMYS LEMMUS
SPALAX CYNOMYS DINOMYS
ECHIMYS LEGGADA MERINES
NESOKIA ZYZOMYS ALACTAGA
ARVICOLA CAPROMYS CITELLUS
CRICETUS HAPLODON HYDROMYS
LAGIDIUM MICROTUS MYOTALPA
ORYZOMYS
(— OF ROTIFER) HYDATINA
PEDALION
(— OF RUST) UREDO HEMILEIA
UROMYCES
(— OF SALAMANDER) ANDRIAS
EURYCEA SIREDON TRITURUS
(— OF SCALE) KERMES LECANIUM
(— OF SCALLOP) HINNITES
(— OF SCORPION) BUTHUS
SCORPIO CHELIFER
(— OF SEA ANEMONE) MINYAS
ACTINIA
(— OF SEA FAN) GORGONIA
(— OF SEA OTTER) ENHYDRA
(— OF SEA SLUG) ELYSIA
(— OF SEA URCHIN) ARBACIA
CIDARIS DIADEMA ECHINUS
(— OF SEAL) PHOCA HYDRURGA

MIROUNGA ZALOPHUS
(— OF SEAWEED) ULVA ALARIA
(— OF SEDGE) FUIRENA SCIRPUS
SCLERIA SCHOENUS
(— OF SHARK) LAMNA GALEUS
ISURUS ACRODUS ALOPIAS
SPHYRNA SQUALUS CLADODUS
MENASPIS SQUATINA
(— OF SHEEP) OVIS
(— OF SHELL) PUPA LAMBIS
EXOGYRA LATIRUS MALLEUS
TROCHUS HAMINOEA MACLUREA
OLIVELLA TRIGONIA UMBRELLA
(— OF SHREW) SOREX BLARINA
(— OF SHRIMP) CRAGO CRANGON
(— OF SHRUB) IVA ACER BIXA
BRYA HOYA ILEX INGA ITEA MABA
OLEA RHUS ROSA SIDA THEA
ULEX ALNUS ANONA BIOTA
BUTEA BUXUS CATHA DALEA
DIRCA ERICA EURYA FICUS
HAKEA IXORA LEDUM MALUS
OCHNA PADUS RIBES RUBUS
SABIA SALIX TAXUS THUJA
TREMA UNONA URENA VITEX
ABELIA ACAENA ADELIA ALHAGI
AMYRIS ANNONA ARALIA ARONIA
AUCUBA AZALEA BAPHIA BAUERA
BETULA BLUMEA BYBLIS CANTUA
CASSIA CELTIS CERCIS CISTUS
CITRUS CLEOME CLUSIA COFFEA
CORDIA COREMA CORNUS
CORREA CROTON DAPHNE
DATURA DERRIS DIOSMA DONDIA
DRIMYS ECHIUM EVODIA FATSIA
FEIJOA GARRYA GNETUM GREWIA
GUAREA KALMIA KERRIA LARREA
LIPPIA LITSEA LUCUMA LYCIUM
MIMOSA MYRCIA MYRICA
MYRTUS OCOTEA OLINIA OPILIA
PENAEA PERSEA PIERIS PROTEA
PTELEA PUNICA QUIINA RAMONA
RANDIA ROCHEA ROYENA
RUSCUS SALVIA SAPIUM SCHIMA
SELAGO SESBAN SORBUS STEVIA
STYRAX SUAEDA TECOMA
AECULUS AMORPHA ARBUTUS
ARDISIA ARMERIA ASIMINA
ASSONIA BANKSIA BAROSMA
BENZOIN BORONIA BUMELIA
BURSERA CALLUNA CARISSA
CASASIA CERASUS CESTRUM
CLETHRA CNEORUM COLUTEA
CORYLUS COTINUS CUNONIA
CYRILLA CYTISUS DEUTZIA
DOMBEYA DURANTA EHRETIA
ENCELIA EPACRIS EPHEDRA
EUCHLEA EUGENIA EURSERA
FABIANA FUCHSIA GENISTA
GMELINA GYMINDA HAMELIA
HOVENIA KARATAS LAGETTA
LANTANA MAHONIA MERATIA
MONIMIA MORINDA MUTISIA
MYRRHIS NANDINA NEMESIA
OLEARIA OTHONNA PAVETTA
PAVONIA PENTZIA PIMELEA
PISONIA PURSHIA QUASSIA
QUERCUS RAPANEA REMIJIA
RHAMNUS RHODORA ROBINIA
ROMNEYA RUELLIA SALSOLA
SENECIO SKIMMIA SOLANUM
SOPHORA SPIRAEA SURIANA
SYRINGA TAMARIX TELOPEA

XIMENIA XYLOPIA XYLOSMA
ZELKOVA ACALYPHA ALANGIUM
ALSTONIA ANAGYRIS ATRIPLEX
BALOGHIA BAUHINIA BERBERIS
BORRERIA BUCKLEYA BUDDLEIA
CAMELLIA CAPPARIS CAPSICUM
CARAGANA CASSIOPE CASTANEA
CODIAEUM COLLETIA CONDALIA
CONNARUS COPROSMA CORIARIA
CRATAEVA DAVIESIA DENDRIUM
DILLENIA DODONAEA DOVYALIS
DRACAENA DUBOISIA EMPETRUM
EUONYMUS EUPTELEA EXOSTEMA
FRAXINUS GALACTIA GOODENIA
GORDONIA GUAIACUM HIBISCUS
HIRTELLA IONIDIUM JASMINUM
JATROPHA JUSTICIA KNIGHTIA
KRAMERIA LABURNUM LAVATERA
LAWSONIA LEONOTIS MAGNOLIA
MAYTENUS MICHELIA MYOPORUM
NOTELAEA PALIURUS PAROSELA
PHILESIA PHOTINIA PHYMOSIA
PLUMIERA POLYGALA POTERIUM
PROSOPIS PSORALEA RHAGODIA
ROLLINIA RORIDULA RUSSELIA
SAMBUCUS SATUREIA SAURAUIA
SESBANIA SOLANDRA SORBARIA
SPARTIUM TABEBUIA TORRUBIA
TRECULIA VARRONIA VERNONIA
VERONICA VIBURNUM VOCHYSIA
WITHANIA ZIZYPHUS MENZIESIA
(— OF SILKWORM) BOMBYX
(— OF SKUNK) MEPHITIS
(— OF SLOTH) BRADYPUS
(— OF SLUG) DOTO ARION DORIS
LIMAX ELYSIA GLAUCUS
(— OF SNAIL) HUA PILA CONUS
FUSUS GALBA HELIX MITRA
OVULA PHYSA THAIS TURBO
CERION EULIMA NATICA NERITA
RISSOA TRITON ANCYLUS
BITTIUM BULINUS BUSYCON
CYMBIUM LATIRUS LITIOPA
LYMNARA MELANIA MODULUS
PURPURA RANELLA VALVATA
VERTIGO VITRINA ZONITES
ACHATINA ALOCINMA ELLOBIUM
FOSSARIA GYRAULUS HELICINA
HELISOMA JANTHINA KATAYAMA
LITORINA NERITINA OLEACINA
SUCCINEA
(— OF SNAKE) BOA ERYX NAIA
NAJA ASPIS BITIS BOIGA ECHIS
ELAPS CAUSUS DABOIA ELAPHE
HURRIA ILYSIA LIGUUS NATRIX
PYTHON VIPERA ATHERIS
BOAEDON COLUBER ECHIDNA
MEHELYA OPHIDIA ZAMENIS
BOTHROPS BUNGARUS CERBERUS
CROTALUS DEMANSIA EUNECTES
FARANCIA LAVHESIS MICRURUS
STORERIA TYPHLOPS
(— OF SPIDER) ARANEA LYCOSA
MYGALE AGALENA ARGIOPE
ATTIDAE NEPHILA PHOLCUS
LINYPHIA ULOBORUS
(— OF SPIROCHETE) BORRELIA
(— OF SPONGE) SYCON GEODIA
SCYPHA ASCETTA CHALINA
GRANTIA SPONGIA SYCETTA
LEUCETTA
(— OF SPOROZOAN) NOSEMA
(— OF SQUID) LOLIGO SEPIOLA

(— OF SQUIRREL) SCIURUS
(— OF SUBSHRUB) LECHEA
ARMERIA ASCYRUM BEGONIA
FELICIA ATRIPLEX COLUMNEA
(— OF SWAN) OLOR CYGNUS
(— OF TAKIN) BUDORCAS
(— OF TAPEWORM) BERTIA LIGULA
DAVAINEA HARRISIA
(— OF TAYRA) GALERA GALICTIS
(— OF TELEDU) MYDAUS
(— OF TERN) GYGIS STERNA
(— OF THISTLE) CNICUS CARDUUS
(— OF TICK) ARGAS ARGUS IXODES
HYALOMMA
(— OF TOAD) BUFO HYLA PIPA
ALYTES XENOPUS ASCAPHUS
(— OF TREE) ACER BIXA BRYA
COLA HURA ILEX INGA MABA
OLAX OLEA RHUS THEA ABIES
BUTEA BUXUS CARYA CEIBA
CYCAS DURIO EURYA FAGUS
FICUS HAKEA HEVEA HOPEA
IXORA KHAYA LARIX MALUS
MELIA MESUA MORUS NYSSA
OCHNA PADUS PICEA PINUS
PYRUS SALIX TAXUS THUJA TILIA
TOONA TREMA TSUGA ULMUS
UNONA VITEX XYLIA ABROMA
ACHRAS AKANIA AMOMIS AMYRIS
ANDIRA ANNONA ARALIA
AUCUBA AZALEA BAPHIA BETULA
BOMBAX CANTUA CARAPA
CARICA CASSIA CEDRUS CELTIS
CERCIS CITRUS CLUSIA COFFEA
CORDIA CORNUS DATURA
DRIMYS EPERUA EPERVA EUCLEA
EVODIA FEIJOA GARRYA GENIPA
GINKGO GNETUM GREWIA
GUAREA IDESIA ILLIPE LAURUS
LITCHI LITSEA LUCUMA LYCIUM
MAMMEA MIMOSA MYRCIA
MYRICA OCOTEA OLNEYA OSTRYA
OWENIA PAPPEA PARITI PERSEA
PRUNUS PTELEA QUIINA RANDIA
ROYENA SAPIUM SAPOTA SCHIMA
SENCIO SESBAN SHOREA SIMABA
SORBUS STYRAX TECOMA
AGATHIS ARBUTUS ARDISIA
ASIMINA ASSONIA BANKSIA
BUMELIA BURSERA CANANGA
CANELLA CASASIA CATALPA
CEDRELA CERASUS CLETHRA
COPAIVA CORYLUS COTINUS
CUNONIA CUPANIA CYDONIA
CYRILLA DOMBEYA ECHINUS
EHRETIA EPACRIS EUGENIA
FERONIA GMELINA GUAZUMA
GYMINDA HAGENIA HALESIA
HICORIA HOVENIA HUMIRIA
JUGLANS KADELIA KOKOONA
LAGETTA LICANIA LINGOUM
MACLURA MICONIA MORINDA
MORINGA MURRAYA OCHROMA
OLEARIA PANGIUM PIMENTA
PISONIA PLANERA POPULUS
PROTIUM PSIDIUM QUASSIA
QUERCUS RAPANEA REMIJIA
RHAMNUS ROBINIA SCHINUS
SENECIO SEQUOIA SLOANEA
SOLANUM SOPHORA SURIANA
SYRINGA TAMARIX TECTONA
TELOPEA TORREYA TROPHIS

VATERIA XIMENIA XYLOPIA
XYLOSMA ZELKOVA AESCULUS
ALANGIUM ALBIZZIA ALSTONIA
ANTIARIS AVERRHOA BALANOPS
BALOGHIA BAUHINIA BRABEJUM
BROSIMUM BUDDLEIA CABRALEA
CAMELLIA CANARIUM CAPPARIS
CARAGANA CARPINUS CARYOCAR
CASEARIA CASTANEA CASTILLA
CECROPIA CINCHONA CODIAEUM
CONDALIA CYBISTAX DILLENIA
DIPTERYX DODONAEA DOVYALIS
DRACAENA DUBOISIA EUCOMMIA
EUONYMUS EUPTELEA EXOSTEMA
FITZROYA FRAXINUS FUNTUMIA
GARCINIA GARDENIA GORDONIA
GUAIACUM HIBISCUS HIRTELLA
HOMALIUM HYMENAEA ILLICIUM
JATROPHA KANDELIA KNIGHTIA
LABURNUM LAPORTEA LAVATERA
LECYTHIS LEUCAENA LYSILOMA
MAGNOLIA MALLOTUS MAYTENUS
MESPILUS MICHELIA MIMUSOPS
MYOPORUM NOTELAEA PHOTINIA
PISCIDIA PISTACIA PLATANUS
PLUMIERA PONCIRUS PROSOPIS
QUILLAJA RAVENALA ROLLINIA
SAMADERA SAMBUCUS
SANTALUM SAPINDUS SAURAUIA
SESBANIA SIMARUBA SPONDIAS
SWARTZIA TABEBUIA TAXODIUM
TORRUBIA TRECULIA VARRONIA
VERONICA VIBURNUM VIRGILIA
VOCHYSIA
(— OF TUNICATE) SALPA ASCIDIA
DOLIOLUM
(— OF TURTLE) EMYS AMYDA
CHELUS CHELYS CARETTA
CHELONE CLEMMYS TESTUDO
TRIONYX ARCHELON CHELONIA
CHELYDRA PELUSIOS
(— OF TWINER) STEMONA
(— OF UNIVALVE) DOLIUM
(— OF VINE) ROSA ABRUS ABUTA
PISUM TAMUS UNONA VIGNA
VITIS AKEBIA CISSUS COBAEA
DERRIS ENTADA HEDERA
MUCUNA PETREA POTHOS
SICANA SICYOS SOLLYA VIORNA
ARAUJIA BASELLA BOMAREA
BRYONIA ECHITES EMBELIA
EPACRIS FALCATA HUMULUS
IPOMOEA MIKANIA PISONIA
SECHIUM UNCARIA ZANONIA
ANAMIRTA ATRAGENE BIGNONIA
CLEMATIS COCCULUS DEGUELIA
DOLICHOS EUONYMUS JASMINUM
KENNEDYA PANDOREA PUERARIA
SECAMONE SERJANIA TACSONIA
WISTARIA
(— OF WALRUS) ODOBENUS
(— OF WASP) SPHEX VESPA
BEMBEX CYNIPS SCOLIA TIPHIA
CHRYSIS EUMENES MASARIS
MUTILLA ANDRICUS CHLORION
ODYNERUS POLISTES POMPILUS
SPHECIUS
(— OF WEASEL) MUSTELA
(— OF WEED) CAPSELLA
(— OF WEEVIL) APION HYPERA
SITONA CLEONUS CALANDRA
CALENDRA CURCULIO
(— OF WHALE) CETE ARETA KOGIA

BALAENA ORCINUS ZIPHIUS
PHYSETER
(— OF WOLVERINE) GULO
(— OF WORM) DERO SPIO ALARIA
EUNICE KERRIA MERMIS NEREIS
SYLLIS ACHAETA ACHOLOE
ASCARIS DUGESIA EISENIA
FILARIA GLYCERA GORDIUS
HESIONE LEODICE POLYNOE
SABELLA SAGITTA SERPULA
SETARIA SPIRURA TUBIFEX
ARABELLA ASCAROPS BIPALIUM
BONELLIA COOPERIA DOCHMIUS
ECHIURUS FASCIOLA GEOPLANA
PHORONIS SPADELLA SUBULURA
SYNGAMUS SYPHACIA
(— OF ZORIL) ICTONYX
(PREF.) GEN(O)
(SUFF.) IA
GEODE DRUSE
GEOGRAPHER **AMERICAN** BAKER
DAVIS GUYOT ATWOOD BOWMAN
BRYANT SEMPLE DAVIDSON
MITCHELL HUNTINGTON
ARAB BAKRI
AUSTRIAN KORISTKA
PAULITSCHKE
CANADIAN PALLISER
DUTCH BLAEU
EGYPTIAN PTOLEMY
ENGLISH BEKE KEANE BEAZLEY
HAKLUYT MARKHAM RENNELL
GREENOUGH MACKINDER
FRESHFIELD
FRENCH JOMARD RECLUS VALLOT
ANVILLE DELISLE DEMANGEON
GERMAN BEHM KOHL BANSE
PENCK VOGEL ANDREE BEHAIM
CLUVER RATZEL RITTER APIANUS
EBELING GERLAND HETTNER
KIEPERT KRUMMEL PESCHEL
SCHONER BERGHAUS BRUCKNER
BUSCHING DRYGALSKI
PETERMANN RICHTHOFEN
GREEK SCYLAX STRABO MARINUS
PYTHEAS DIONYSIUS PAUSANIAS
ERATOSTHENES
HUNGARIAN TELEKI
ICELANDIC THORODDSEN
ITALIAN BALBI CODAZZI AMORETTI
MARSIGLI
POLISH LELEWEL
PORTUGUESE CORDEIRO
RUSSIAN SEMENOV KROPOTKIN
SHOKALSKI
SCOTTISH MILL BROWN
JOHNSTON
SPANISH COSA
SWEDISH HEDIN
GEOLOGIST **AMERICAN** DALY DANA
HALL KEMP KING REID TARR
CROSS GUYOT HAGUE HOBBS
LEITH MCGEE ORTON SCOTT
SMITH SPURR WHITE ARNOLD
ATWOOD BAYLEY DUTTON
FOSTER HAYDEN HOLMES IRVING
JAGGAR LAWSON LESLEY
MARCOU MATHER POWELL
SHALER UPJOHN WRIGHT
BARRELL BRANNER GILBERT
HOLLICK IDDINGS JOHNSON
MACLURE MERRILL PIRSSON
RANSOME RUSSELL TALMAGE

VANHISE LEVERETT MITCHELL
NEWBERRY PUMPELLY SILLIMAN
WINCHELL HITCHCOCK
JOHANNSEN SALISBURY
TWENHOFEL CHAMBERLIN
LOUDERBACK WASHINGTON
AUSTRALIAN DAVID
AUSTRIAN BECKE HAUER SUESS
HAIDINGER HOCHSTETTER
MOJSISOVICS
BELGIAN RENARD
CANADIAN BELL ADAMS LOGAN
WALLACE
DANISH KOCH
ENGLISH BELT TATE JUKES LYELL
SORBY ANSTED BONNEY CLARKE
FORBES HOLMES MAWSON
SCROPE DAWKINS GREGORY
HOLLAND MANTELL BUCKLAND
LYDEKKER PHILLIPS SEDGWICK
GREENOUGH MURCHISON
PRESTWICH STRICKLAND
FRENCH FOUQUE ARCHIAC
DAUBREE DELESSE BARRANDE
BEAUMONT BERTRAND
DOLOMIEU DUFRENOY
LAPPARENT
GERMAN BUCH ABICH COHEN
DECHEN ROEMER WERNER ZITTEL
ALBERTI BISCHOF CREDNER
GEINITZ LEONHARD QUENSTEDT
KEYSERLING ROSENBUSCH
ICELANDIC THORODDSEN
IRISH OLDHAM
ITALIAN MERCALLI
NEW ZEALAND HAAST
NORWEGIAN BROGGER KJERULF
RUSSIAN OBRUCHEV
SCOTTISH HALL CROLL GEIKIE
HUTTON MILLER RAMSAY
OGLIVIE PLAYFAIR
MACCULLOCH
SWEDISH ANTEVS TORELL
HISINGER NATHORST
NORDENSKJOLD
SWISS HEIM DELUC
GEOMETRIC CUBIST CUBISTIC
GEOMETRY EUCLID SPHERICS
GEOPHAGY PICA

GEORGIA
CAPITAL: ATLANTA
COLLEGE: SPELMAN MOREHOUSE
COUNTY: BIBB CLAY COBB COOK
HALL TIFT WARE BANKS BRYAN
BUTTS DOOLY EARLY FLOYD
GRADY PEACH RABUN TROUP
WORTH COFFEE COWETA
DEKALB ECHOLS ELBERT
FANNIN FULTON JASPER
LANIER OCONEE TWIGGS
WILKES CATOOSA LAURENS
LUMPKIN GWINNETT
MUSCOGEE
INDIAN: GUALE YUCHI CHIAHA
OCONEE YAMASEE
LAKE: LANIER MARTIN HARDING
NOTTELY BANKHEAD
HARTWELL SINCLAIR
MOUNTAIN: STONE KENNESAW
NATIVE: CRACKER
PRESIDENT: CARTER
RIVER: PEA FLINT ETOWAH

OCONEE PIGEON CONECUH
SATILLA ALTAMAHA
OCMULGEE
STATE BIRD: THRASHER
STATE NICKNAME: PEACH
STATE TREE: LIVEOAK
TOWN: JESUP MACON JASPER
OCILLA AUGUSTA CONYERS
DECATUR ELLIJAY GRIFFIN
VIDALIA MARIETTA
MOULTRIE SAVANNAH
VALDOSTA WAYCROSS
UNIVERSITY: EMORY GATECH
MERCER

GEORGIAN ADZHAR CRACKER
GEORGIA PINE LONGLEAF
GEPHYREAN STARWORM
GER STRANGER
GERAINT (WIFE OF —) ENID
GERANIUM DOVEFOOT FLUXWEED
SHAMEFACE
GERANIUM LAKE SPARK
NACARAT
GERANIUM PINK BERMUDA
GERBIL JIRD
GERIANOL ISOLATE
GERM BUG CHIT SEED SPARK
SPAWN SPERM GERMEN
GERMULE MICROBE SEMINAL
RUDIMENT SEEDLING SEMINARY
SEMINIUM
(— CELL) GONE
(PREF.) BLAST(O) SPERM(A)(ATI)
(ATIO)(ATO)(I)(IO)(O)
(SUFF.) BLAST(IC)(Y) SPERM(A)(AE)
(AL)(IA)(IC)(OUS)(UM)(Y)
GERMAN BALT HANS ALMAN
HEINE JERRY ALMAIN DUTCHY
HEINIE TEUTON TEDESCO
COTILLON GERMANIC TUDESQUE
(PREF.) TEUTO
GERMANDER POLY BETONY
FOXTAIL SOVENEZ
SCORDIUM
GERMANE GERMAN RELEVANT
PERTINENT
GERMANIC GOTHIC GOTHONIC
TEUTONIC
GERMAN SHEPHERD ALSATIAN

GERMANY
ANCIENT: ALMAIN ALMAINE
ANCIENT TRIBESMAN: JUTE
TEUTON VISIGOTH OSTROGOTH
CANAL: KIEL WESER LUDWIG
CAPITAL: BONN BERLIN
CHEESE: MUENSTER TILSITER
LIMBURGER
COAL REGION: RUHR SAAR SARRE
COIN: MARK KRONE TALER
GULDEN KRONEN THALER
PFENNIG GROSCHEN
DIALECT: KOLSCH KOELSCH
BALTISCH HESSISCH
DYNASTY: HOHENSTAUFEN
HOHENZOLLERN
FOOD: WURST KNODEL SPATZLE
STRUDEL MARZIPAN ROULADEN
HANSEATIC CITY: KOLN LUBECK
COLOGNE HAMBURG
LUEBECK
ISLAND: USEDOM WOLLIN

FEHMARN FRISIAN
LAKE: DUMMER WURMSEE
AMMERSEE BODENSEE
CHIEMSEE MURITZEE
CONSTANCE
LANGUAGE: DEUTSCH
MEASURE: AAM IMI OHM FASS
FUSS LAST RUTE SACK STAB
CARAT EIMER KANNE KETTE
LINIE MAASS METZE RUTHE
SIMRI MASSEL MORGEN
OXHOFT SEIDEL STRICH
JUCHART KLAFTER TAGWERK
SCHEFFEL SCHOPPEN
STUBCHEN VIERLING
MOUNTAIN: FELDBERG
WATZMANN
MOUNTAIN RANGE: ORE ALPS
HARZ RHON HARDT HUNSRUCK
NAME: REICH ASHKENAZ
GERMANIA DEUTSCHLAND
NATIVE: GOTH SAXON TEUTON
PORT: EMDEN BREMEN HAMBURG
ROSTOCK STETTIN
RESORT: EMS BADEN AACHEN
RIVER: ALZ EMS INN EDER EGER
ELBE ISAR LAHN LECH MAIN
NAAB NAHE ODER OKER REMS
RUHR SAAR SIEG ALLER DONAU
EIDER FULDA HAVEL HUNTE
ILLER LEINE LIPPE MOSEL
MULDE PEENE REGEN RHEIN
RHINE SAALE SAUER SPREE
UCKER VECHT WERRA WESER
DANUBE ELSTER KOCHER
NECKAR NEISSE RANDOW
TAUBER WARNOW ALTMUHL
JEETZEL PEGNITZ SALZACH
UNSTRUT
STATE: BADEN HESSE LIPPE
BAYERN BREMEN HESSEN
SAXONY BAVARIA HAMBURG
PRUSSIA SAARLAND
BRUNSWICK
TOWN: AUE EMS HOF ULM BONN
GERA GOCH HAAR HAMM JENA
KIEL KOLN LAHR AALEN AHLEN
EMDEN ESSEN FURTH GOTHA
HAGEN HALLE HERNE MAINZ
MOLLN NEUSS PIRNA TRIER
AACHEN ALTENA ALTONA
BARMEN BERLIN BREMEN
CASSEL DACHAU DESSAU
ERFURT KASSEL LINDEN
LUBECK MUNICH PLAUEN
TREVES BAMBERG BRESLAU
COBLENZ COLOGNE CREFELD
DRESDEN GORLITZ HAMBURG
HANOVER LEIPZIG MAYENCE
MUNCHEN MUNSTER POTSDAM
ROSTOCK SPANDAU ZWICKAU
AUGSBURG CHEMNITZ
DORTMUND DUISBURG
FREIBURG LIEGNITZ MANNHEIM
NURNBERG WURSELEN
WURZBURG DARMSTADT
KARLSRUHE MAGDEBURG
NUREMBERG OSNABRUCK
STUTTGART WUPPERTAL
DUSSELDORF HEIDELBERG
OBERHAUSEN
UNIVERSITY TOWN: FREIBURG
HEIDELBERG

WEIGHT: LOT GRAN LOTE LOTH UNZE LOTHE PFUND STEIN PRUNDE DRACHMA ZENTNER VIERLING
WINE: MOSELLE RIESLING

GERMICIDE KRELOS MERBROMIN
GERMINABLE PREGNANT
GERMINATE BUD HIT CHIP CHIT GERM SHOOT SPIRE SPRIT BRAIRD SPROUT STRIKE PULLULATE
GERMINATION CATCH
GERSHOM (FATHER OF —) LEVI MOSES
(MOTHER OF —) ZIPPORAH
GERYON (DOG OF —) ORTHUS
(FATHER OF —) CHRYSAOR
(MOTHER OF —) CALLIRRHOE
(SLAYER OF —) HERCULES
GESAN TAPUYAN CHAVANTE
GESHAM (FATHER OF —) JAHDAI
GESTATION GOING BREEDING PREGNANCY
GESTICULATE GESTURE
GESTURE CUT FIG BECK BERE GEST SIGN FILIP GESTE HONOR SANNA ACTION BECKON BREATH CUTOFF FILLIP MOTION SALUTE SIGNAL CURTSEY FASHION FLICKER MURGEON ACCOLADE CEREMONY
(— OF DERISION) SNOOK
(AFFECTED —) GAATCH
(HINDU —) NAMASTE
(OBSCENE —) BIRD
(OSTENTATIOUS —) POMP
(USELESS —) FUTILITY
GET COP GIT WIN EARN FALL GAIN GRAB HAVE HENT TAKE TILL AFONG ANNEX CATCH COVER FETCH LATCH DERIVE OBTAIN PUZZLE SECURE ACQUIRE COMPARE CONQUER PROCURE PRODUCE RECEIVE PERCEIVE
(— ABOARD) FLIP
(— ABOUT) BEGO NAVIGATE
(— ALONG) DO GEE FARE FEND AGREE FADGE FODGE SPEED FETTLE
(— AROUND) BYPASS COMPASS FINESSE FLUMMER OUTFLANK
(— AT) ATTAIN
(— AWAY) LAM RYNT SLIP EVADE CHEESE ESCAPE
(— BACK) REDEEM RETIRE RECOVER
(— BETTER OF) WAX BEST DING DOWN DAUNT FLING SHEND SHENT STICK STING JOCKEY OVERGO RECOVER OVERCOME SURMOUNT
(— BY ARTIFICE) WIND
(— BY ASKING) KICK
(— BY CUNNING) WHIZZLE
(— BY EXTORTION) GRATE
(— BY FLATTERY) COG
(— CLEAR OF) STRIP
(— DISHONESTLY) FIRK
(— DOWN) ALIGHT
(— ON) FARE BOARD CHEFE CHEVE FRAME SHIFT EXPLOIT
(— ON WELL) LIKE

(— OUT) LEAK SCRAM CHEESE OUTWIN VOETSAK
(— PAST) BEAT HURDLE
(— POSSESSION) CARRY
(— READY) GET BOUN PARE RANK BOWNE BRACE FRAME FETTLE ORDAIN APPAREL
(— RID) CAST DISH DUMP FREE JUNK SHAB TOSS ERASE SHAKE SHIFT SHOOT SLOUGH UNLOAD DELIVER DISCARD EXTRUDE DISPATCH DISSOLVE
(— SURREPTITIOUSLY) SNEAK
(— THE POINT) SAVVY
(— TO BOTTOM OF) FATHOM
(— UNDER CONTROL) RAIM
(— UP) ARISE HUDDUP UPRISE HAIRPIN
(PREF.) (— OFF) DE
GETA SABOT
GETHER (FATHER OF —) ARAM
GET-TOGETHER DO DRINK HOBNOB BAMBOCHE POTLATCH
GETUP SETOUT
GEWGAW DIE TOY WALY KNACK WALLY BAUBLE FANGLE FEGARY JIGGER FLAMFEW TRANGAM TRINKET FOLDEROL GIMCRACK JIMCRACK TRIMTRAM
GEYSER BORE JETTER

GHANA
CAPITAL: ACCRA
COIN: PESEWA
DAM: AKOSOMBO
LAKE: VOLTA BOSUMTWI
LANGUAGE: GA EWE TWI FANTI HAUSA DAGBANI DAGOMBA
MONEY: CEDI NEWCEDI
MOUNTAIN: AFADJATO
NATIVE: GA EWE AHAFO BRONG FANTI ASHANTI DAGOMBA MAMPRUSI
REGION: VOLTA ASHANTI BRONGAHAFO
RIVER: OTI PRA DAKA TANO AFRAM VOLTA ANKOBRA KULPAWN
TOWN: HO WA ODA AXIM FIAN KETA TALA TEMA ACCRA BAWKU ENCHI LAWRA LEGON SAMPA YAPEI DUNKWA KARAGA KPANDU KUMASI NSAWAM OBUASI SWEDRU TAMALE TARKWA WASIPE ANTUBIA DAMONGO MAMPONG PRESTEA SEKONDI SUNYANI WINNEBA AKOSOMBO KINTAMPO TAKORADI
WIND: HARMATTAN

GHARRY SHIGRAM
GHASTLY WAN GASH GRIM PALE BLATE GHAST LURID UNKET UNKID DISMAL GOUSTY GRISLY PALLID CHARNEL DEATHLY FEARFUL GASHFUL GRIZZLY GRUGOUS HIDEOUS MACABRE DREADFUL GRUESOME HORRIBLE SHOCKING TERRIBLE
GHAWAZI BARAMIKA
GHERKIN CUCUMBER
GHETTO JEWRY JUDAISM

GHIBELLINE WAIBLING
GHOST HAG KER BHUT HANT JUBA WAFF BUGAN CADDY DUFFY DUPPY FETCH GAIST GUEST HAUNT JUMBY LARVA PRETA SHADE SPOOK UMBRA CHUREL SOWLTH SPIRIT SPRITE TAISCH ANTAEUS ANTAIOS BOGGART BUGGANE GYTRASH PHANTOM SPECTER SPECTRE VAMPIRE BARGHEST GUYTRASH PHANTASM REVENANT
(PREF.) SPECTRO SPOOKO
GHOSTFISH WRYMOUTH
GHOSTLY EERY EERIE GOUSTY SHADOWY UNCANNY WEIRDLY CHTHONIC GHASTFUL SPECTRAL
GHOST MOTH SWIFT HEPIALID
GHOSTS (AUTHOR OF —) IBSEN
(CHARACTER IN —) HELEN JACOB ALVING OSWALD REGINA MANDERS ENGSTRAND
GHOST-WRITER SPOOK
GHOULISH SATANIC
GHUZ OGHUZ
GIAI NHANG
GIANNI SCHICCHI (CHARACTER IN —) BUOSO DONATI LAURETTA RINUCCIO SCHICCHI
(COMPOSER OF —) PUCCINI
GIANT ORC ETEN HUGE OGRE OTUS WATE YMER YMIR AFRIT BALOR CACUS HYMIR JOTUN MIMAS MIMER THRYM TITAN TROLL AFRFET ALBION FAFNIR GIGANT GOEMOT PALLAS THJAZI THURSE TITYUS WARLOW ANTAEUS CYCLOPS GOLIATH WARLOCK ASCOPART BELLERUS COLBRAND GIGANTIC GOEMAGOT GOGMAGOG MASTODON MORGANTE ORGOGLIO TYPHOEUS PROCRUSTES
(1-EYED —) CYCLOPS
(100-HANDED —) GYGES COTTUS BRIAREUS
(1000-ARMED —) BANA
(PL.) ANAK ANAKIM COTTUS ALOADAE REPHAIM NEPHILIM ZAMZUMMIM
(PREF.) GIGANT(I)(O)
GIANTESS NORN ARGANTE
GIANT FULMAR NELLY STINKER STINKPOT
GIANT GRASS OTATE
GIANT HERON GOLIATH
GIANTISM ACROMEGALY
GIANT LILY FIGUE MAGUEY
GIANT PUFFBALL FUZZ FUZZBALL
GIANTS IN THE EARTH (AUTHOR OF —) ROLVAAG
(CHARACTER IN —) OLE PER ANNA HANS OLSA BERET HANSA PEDER
GIARDIA LAMBLIA
GIB JIB SHOE DEMUR SLIPPER
GIBBAR GIBBERT JUBARTAS
GIBBER CHAT CHATTER
GIBBERISH GREEK JABBER JARGON CHOCTAW ABRACADABRA
GIBBET STOB TREE CROOK JEBAT GALLOWS POTENCE EQUULEUS
GIBBON LAR WAWA UNGKA

WUYEN CAMPER HULOCK HOOLOCK SIAMANG HYLOBATE
GIBBOUS CONVEX HULCHY HUMPED SACCATE
GIBE (ALSO SEE JIBE) BOB RUB GIRD JAPE JEST JIBE PROG QUIB QUIP SKIT WIPE FLEER FLING FLIRT FRUMP GLEEK KNACK SCOFF SCOMM SCORN SLANT SNEER DERIDE GLANCE HECKLE BROCARD SARCASM RIDICULE
GIBING SNASH
GID DUNT GIDDY STURDY GOGGLES POTHERY VERTIGO
GIDDALTI (FATHER OF —) HEMAN
GIDDINESS LUNACY SOORAWN
GIDDY BARMY GLAKY LIGHT WESTY GIGLET GLAKED GOWKED GOWKIT SHANNY STURDY VOLAGE GLAIKET LARKING HALUCKET HELLICAT
GIDDY-HEADED HELLICAT
GIDEON (FATHER OF —) JOASH
GIDEONI (SON OF —) ABIDAN
GIFT BOX FOY QUO SOP BENT BOON DASH ENAM MEED SAND BONUS BRIBE CAULP CUDDY DONUM GRANT KNACK TOKEN BEFANA CADEAU DASHEE DONARY GENIUS GERSUM GIFTIE GIVING HANSEL LEGACY RECADO REGALO TALENT XENIUM APTNESS BEFFANA BENEFIT CHARISM CHARITY DEODATE DONATIO DOUCEUR ETRENNE FACULTY FAIRING GIFTURE HANDSEL PRESENT PROPINE REGALIO SUBSIDY TASHRIF TRIBUTE AMATORIO APTITUDE BENEFICE BESTOWAL BLESSING COURTESY DONATION DONATIVE GARRISON GIVEAWAY GRATUITY MORTUARY OBLATION OFFERING POTLATCH SPORTULA BENEFACTION REMEMBRANCE PHILANTHROPY PRESENTATION
(— FROM HUSBAND TO WIFE) ARRAS
(— OF GOD) GRACE
(— OF MONEY) POUCH BAKSHISH
(— OF NATURE) DOWER DOWRY
(— TO ROMAN PEOPLE) CONGIARY
(CHARITABLE —) ALMS ENAM PITTANCE
(COMPULSORY —) SIXENIA
(LIBERAL —) LARGESSE
(NATURAL —) TALENT
(NEW YEAR'S EVE —) ETRENNE HAGMENA HOGMANAY
(SPIRITUAL —) CHARISM CHARISMA
(PL.) OBLATA MISSILES
GIFTBOOK ANNUAL KEEPSAKE
GIG TUB MOZE BANDY BUGGY CHAIR GIGGE CHAISE CLATCH DENNET WHISKY CALESIN TILBURY STANHOPE
GIGANTIC HUGE GIANT MAMMOTH TITANIC COLOSSAL ENORMOUS GIGANTAL ATLANTEAN MONSTROUS BROBDINGNAGIAN
GIGGER TEASELER
GIGGLE TEHEE KECKLE NICKER

TEEHEE TITTER SNICKER TWITTER
GIGLET JIG
GIL BLAS
GIL BLAS (AUTHOR OF —) LESAGE
  (CHARACTER IN —) GIL BLAS LEWIS
  PEREZ AURORA MENCIA SCIPIO
  ANTONIA ARSENIA ROLANDO
  ALPHONSO DOROTHEA FABRICIO
  MATTHIAS OLIVAREZ SANGRADO
GILD GILT BEGILD ENGILD ORFGILD
GILDED GILT AURATE INAURATE
GILDER TRACER
GILEAD (FATHER OF —) MACHIR
  (SON OF —) JEPHTHAH
GILGAMESH IZDUBAR
GILL JILL QUAD GHYLL PLICA
  GILLIE LAMELLA BRANCHIA
  QUADRANT
  (—S OF BIVALVE) BEARD
  (PL.) GINNERS CHOLLERS
  BRANCHIAE
  (SUFF.) BRANCH(IA)(IATE)
GILLAR PITTO
GILLIE GILLY HENCHMAN
GILLS
  (PREF.) BRANCHI(O)
GILLYFLOWER STOCK GILVER
  GELOFRE GILLIVER
GILTHEAD CONNER MELANURE
GIMBAL GEMEL JEMBLE
GIMCRACK QUIP BAUBLE FIZGIG
  GEWGAW JIMJAM TRIFLE
  TRANGAM TRINKET JIMCRACK
  WHIMWHAM
GIMLET SCREW WIMBLE PIERCEL
  PIERCER
GIMMICK GAFF
GIMP TAR ORRIS GUIMPE GIMPING
GIN MAX CRAB GRIN LACE RUIN
  TAPE CLEAN JACKY SNARE SNARL
  DIDDLE GENEVA JAMBER
  JAMMER SPRINGE TITTERY
  TWANKAY EYEWATER HOLLANDS
  SCHIEDAM SCHNAPPS
  (DROP OF —) DAFFY
GINATH (SON OF —) TIBNI
GINGER PEPPER RATOON
  AROMATIC ZINZIBER COLTSFOOT
GINGERBREAD SPICE PARKIN
GINGERLY GINGER WARILY
  CHARILY EDGINGLY
GINGERROOT HAND RACE
  (PL.) ASARUM
GINGHAM CHAMBRAY
GINKGO ICHO
GINSENG SANG FATIL PANAX
  ARALIA IVYWORT REDBERRY
GIOCONDA, LA (CHARACTER IN —)
  ENZO CIECA LAURA ALVISE
  BARNABA GIOCONDA GRIMALDO
  (COMPOSER OF —) PONCHIELLI
GIRAFFE OONT CAMEL DAPPLE
  KAMEEL SERAPH CAMAILE
  RUMINANT
GIRASOL OPAL
GIRD BELT BIND GIRR GIRT HASP
  YERK CLOSE SCOFF ENGIRD
  FASTEN GIRDLE SECURE ACCINGE
  ENVIRON CINCTURE SURROUND
GIRDER BEAM GIRD GIRT GIRTH
  TABLE TRUSS BINDER SUMMER
  WARREN GIRDING TWISTER
  BUCKSTAY STRINGER

GIRDING CINCTURE
GIRDLE OBI ZON BARK BELT CEST
  GIRD HOOP SASH ZONA ZONE
  CEINT GIRTH MITER PATTE SARPE
  WAIST BODICE CESTUS CINGLE
  CIRCLE MOOCHA TISSUE ZODIAC
  ZONULA ZOSTER BALDRIC
  BALTEUS CENTRUM CENTURE
  COMPASS GIRDING SHINGLE
  CEINTURE CINCTURE CINGULUM
  SURROUND
  (— FOR HELMET) TISSUE
  (— OF DIATOM) HOOP
  (BRIDE'S —) CEST CESTUS
  (LITTLE —) ZONULE ZONELET
  (ROYAL —) MALO
  (SACRED —) KUSTI
  (PREF.) ZON(I)(O) ZOSTERI
  ZOSTERO
  (SUFF.) PLEURA
GIRDLED RUNG
GIRL BIT GAL HER KIT POP SHE SIS
  TIB TID TIT BABE BABY BINT BIRD
  CHIT DAME DEEM DELL GILL JANE
  JILL JUDY LASS MARY MOPS
  MORT PERI PUSS SLUT WREN
  BEAST FILLY FLUFF GUIDE KITTY
  LUBRA QUEAN SISSY SKIRT TIDDY
  TITTY TOOTS TRULL BURDIE
  CALICO CLINER CUMMER DALAGA
  DAMSEL DEEMIE FEMALE FIZGIG
  GEISHA GIRLIE LASSIE LOVELY
  MAGGIE NUMBER PIGEON SHEILA
  SISTER SUBDEB TOMATO
  CAMILLA COLLEEN CRUMPET
  DAMOSEL MADCHEN MAUTHER
  TENDREL BONNIBEL FARMETTE
  FEMININE GRISETTE MUCHACHA
  (AGILE —) YANKER
  (AWKWARD —) HOIT
  (BEATIFIED —) BEATA
  (BEAUTIFUL —) BELLE
  (BOLD —) HOIDEN HOYDEN
  (CAMP FIRE —) ARTISAN
  (CHORUS —) CHORINE CORYPHEE
  (CLUMSY —) TAWPIE
  (COUNTRY —) MEG JOAN
  (DANCING —) ALMA DASI ALMAH
  KISANG KISAENG BAYADERE
  DEVADASI
  (DANCING —S) GHAWAZI
  (DEAR —) PEAT
  (DUMPY —) CUTTY
  (FLIGHTY —) GOOSECAP
  (FLIRTATIOUS —) JADE JILLET
  (FLOWER —) NYDIA
  (FORWARD —) STRAP
  (FROLICSOME —) GILPY
  (GIDDY —) GIG GIGLET GIGLOT
  JILLET
  (GREEK —) HAIDEE
  (GYPSY —) GITANA
  (HIRED —) BIDDY BIDDIE
  (IMPUDENT —) STRAP
  (JAPANESE —) GEISHA
  (LITTLE —) SIS COOKY SISSY
  COOKIE LASSOCK
  (MISCHIEVOUS —) CUTTY HUSSY
  (MODEST —) BLUSHET
  (NAIVE —) INGENUE
  (NON-JEWISH —) SHIKSE SHIKSA
  (PERT —) MINX HUSSY
  (PRETTY —) PRIM BUNNY

CUTEY CUTIE
  (ROMPING —) STAG TOMBOY
  (SAUCY —) SNIP
  (SERVANT —) SLUT
  (SHIFTLESS —) MYSTERY
  (SILLY —) SKIT
  (SINGING —) ALMA ALMEH
  (SLENDER —) SYLPH
  (SMALL —) PINAFORE
  (SPIRITED —) FILLY
  (UNATTRACTIVE —) FRUMP
  (UNMARRIED —) MOUSME TOWDIE
  MUSUMEE MADEMOISELLE
  (WANTON —) GIG FILLOCK
  (WILD —) BLOWZE
  (WORKING —) ORISETTE
  (WORTHLESS —) HUSSY
  (YOUNG —) BUD MODER TITTY
  MAIDEN MOTHER BAGGAGE
  COLLEEN FLAPPER GIRLEEN
  ROSEBUD
  (PL.) GIRLERY GIRLHOOD
  (PREF.) PUPI
GIRL OF THE GOLDEN WEST
  (CHARACTER IN —) DICK JACK
  RANCE MINNIE JOHNSON
  RAMERREZ
  (COMPOSER OF —) PUCCINI
GIRT CINCT
GIRTH GIRD GIRT TAPE CINCH
  GARTH GIRSE GRETH WANTY
  CINGLE WARROK COMPASS
  GIRDING SHINGLE WEBBING
GIST JET NET NUB SUM CHAT
  CORE GITE KNOT MEAT PITH
  GREAT HEART JOIST POINT SENSE
  BURDEN KERNEL PURPORT
  SUMMARY STRENGTH
GITH MELANTHY
GIVE ADD GIE HOB TIP BEAR DEAL
  DOLE HAND METE SELL TAKE
  WEVE WHIP YEVE ALLOW AWARD
  COUGH GRANT REFER YIELD
  ACCORD AFFORD BESTOW
  CONFER DEMISE DOTATE FASTEN
  IMPART IMPOSE IMPUTE RENDER
  SUPPLY CONSIGN DELIVER
  FORGIVE FURNISH PRESENT
  PROPINE BEQUEATH DISPENSE
  (— A BOOST) BOLSTER
  (— A PLACE TO) SITUATE
  (— A REASON) ACCOUNT
  (— A REMEDY) MINISTER
  (— ADHERENCE) ASSENT
  (— ADMITTANCE) ACCEPT
  (— ADVICE) READ ADVISE
  (— AN ACCOUNT) TELL RELATE
  REPORT
  (— AND TAKE) GIFFGAFF
  (— ANYTHING NAUSEOUS TO) DOSE
  (— APPROVAL) CONSENT
  (— AS CONCESSION) YETTE
  (— AS EXPLANATION) ASSIGN
  (— ASSURANCE) EFFRONT
  (— ATTENTION TO) HEED
  (— AUTHORITY) ENABLE EMPOWER
  ACCREDIT
  (— AWAY) PART
  (— BACK) REFUND RETURN
  RESTORE
  (— BIRTH) KIT BEAR BORN DROP
  FIND MAKE BEGET BREED ISSUE
  WORLD FARROW KINDLE LITTER

DELIVER FRESHEN
  (— BY WILL) DEVISE
  (— CARE) NURSE
  (— CLAIM TO) REMISE
  (— COUNSEL) AREAD AREED
  (— CREDIT FOR) FRIST
  (— CURRENCY TO) PASS
  (— EAR) HARK HARKEN LISTEN
  HEARKEN
  (— EXPRESSION TO) EMOTE FRAME
  VOICE
  (— FORM) CUT
  (— FORTH) WARP YIELD AFFORD
  CONCEIVE
  (— GROUND) RETIRE
  (— HEED) LOOK ATTEND
  (— IN) BOW CONCEDE COLLAPSE
  (— IN EXCHANGE) SWAP SWOP
  (— IN MARRIAGE) BESTOW SPOUSE
  (— INFORMATION) WARN
  (— INSTRUCTION) LEAR
  (— NAME TO) BAPTIZE
  (— NOTICE) WARN HERALD
  APPRISE PUBLISH ANNOUNCE
  INTIMATE
  (— NOTICE TO APPEAR) GARNISH
  (— OBLIQUE EDGE) CANT
  (— OFF) EMIT SEND SHED EXUDE
  FLING DIVIDE EFFUSE EVOLVE
  EXHALE EXPIRE EXCRETE
  SEPARATE
  (— ONE'S SELF OVER TO) ADDICT
  (— ONE'S WORD) PROMISE
  (— OUT) BOOM LEAK EXUDE ISSUE
  PETAL EVOLVE EMANATE
  OUTGIVE
  (— OVER) LIN
  (— PAIN) AGGRIEVE
  (— PLACE) VAIL BACCARE
  (— PLEDGE) GAGE
  (— PROMINENCE TO) FEATURE
  (— RELUCTANTLY) BEGRUDGE
  (— SATISFACTION) ABY ABYE
  ABEGGE
  (— SPARINGLY) INCH
  (— STRENGTH TO) NERVE
  (— SUPPORT) ASSIST ANIMATE
  (— TEMPORARILY) LEND
  (— TIP) TOUT
  (— TONGUE) CRY YEARN
  (— UP) PUT BURY DROP PART
  CHUCK DEMIT DEVOW FORGO
  LEAVE RAISE REMIT SHOOT
  SPARE SPEND ABJURE ADDICT
  BETRAY DESERT DEVOTE FOREGO
  MIZZLE REFUSE RELENT RENDER
  RESIGN VACATE ABANDON
  DEPOSIT DESPAIR FLUMMOX
  FORBEAR FORGIVE REFRAIN
  RELEASE ABDICATE RENOUNCE
  (— VENT TO) EMIT ISSUE
  DISCHARGE
  (— VOICE) BOLT ACCENT
  (— WARNING) ALERT
  (— WAY) GO FAIL FOLD KEEL SINK
  VAIL BREAK BUDGE BURST FAINT
  SLAKE YIELD BUCKLE FALTER
  RELENT SWERVE FOUNDER
  RECLAIM SUCCUMB
  (— WITNESS) DEPOSE
GIVEN APT DONEE NATHAN
  PROMPT
  (— TO) ALL AFTER

(SUFF.) (— TO) ABLE IBLE LEW
GIVER DONOR
(— OF LIFE) APHETA
(NAME —) EPONYM
GIVING DOLE BOUNTY DATION
REMISE
(— HELP) ADJUTANT
(— MILK) FRESH
(— NO MILK) YELD YELL
(— TROUBLE) CUMBROUS
GIZZARD GIGERIUM
GIZZARD SHAD SKIPJACK
GLABROUS BALD SMOOTH
GLABRATE LEVIGATE
GLACIATION MINDEL
(— STAGE) RISS WURM
GLACIER BRAE ICECAP STREAM
CALOTTE ICEBERG PIEDMONT
(PREF.) GLACIO
GLACIOLOGY CRYOLOGY
GLACIS ESPLANADE
GLAD GAY FAIN LIEF VAIN CANTY
HAPPY PROUD BLITHE FESTUS
GLADLY JOCUND JOYFUL JOYOUS
GLADFUL GLEEFUL JOCULAR
ANIMATED CHEERFUL CHEERING
FESTIVAL GLADSOME PLEASING
GLADDEN JOY GLAD BLESS BLISS
CHEER EXULT MIRTH BLITHE
COMFORT GLADIFY LIGHTEN
REJOICE
(PREF.) TERP(I)(SI)
GLADE LAWN LAUND SLADE
SHRADD SUNGLADE SUNSCALD
(PREF.) NEMO
GLADIATOR THRAX RETIARY
SAMNITE SECUTOR ANDABATA
GLADIOLUS GLAD IRID LILY
LEVERS LILIUM GLADIOLA
GLADLY GLAD LIEF FAINLY LIEFLY
LOVELY HAPPILY
GLADNESS JOY GLAD GLEE BLISS
MIRTH BLITHE FAINNESS
GLADSHIP PLEASURE
GLADSOME BLITHE
GLAGA KASA KUSA TALTHIB
GLAMOR SCRY UTIS OOMPH
PIZAZZ BRABBLE PIZZAZZ
BALLYHOO
GLAMORIZE POT GLORIFY
GLAMOROUS EXOTIC ALLURING
CHARMING
GLAMOUR PAZAZZ PIZAZZ PIZZAZZ
GLANCE EYE RAY SEE BEAM CAST
GLIM LEER PEEK SCRY SKEG VIEW
WINK BLENK BLINK SLIPS
CAROM FLASH GLEEK GLENT
GLIDE GLIFF GLINT GLISK GRAZE
PRINK SCREW SIGHT SKIME
SLANT SQUIZ TWIRE APERCU
ASPECT CARROM GANDER
REGARD SCANCE STRIKE VISION
EYEBEAM EYESHOT EYEWINK
GLIMPSE BELAMOUR GLIFFING
OEILLADE
(— OFF) GLACE
(— THROUGH) SAMPLE
(LOVE —) AMORET
(MELANCHOLY —) DOWNCAST
(SHARP —) DART
(SIDELONG —) SHEW SLENT
SKLENT
(SLY —) GLEG GLIME GLOAT

GLAND MILT NOIX SETA CLYER
CRYPT GONAD LIVER MAMMA
ACINUS BREAST KERNEL THYMUS
ADRENAL CRUMENA NECTARY
PAROTID PAROTIS TEARPIT
THYROID CONARIUM ENDOCRIN
FOLLICLE FOLLOWER GANGLION
GLANDULA GLANDULE
HOOFWORM PROSTATE SCIRRHUS
SPERMARY
(PREF.) ADEN(O) SCIRRH(O)
(SUFF.) ADEN SCIRRHUS
GLANDERS FARCY MALLEUS
GLANDULAR EARTHY INNATE
SEXUAL ADENOID PHYSICAL
ADENOIDAL
GLANS NUT GLAND
GLARE BEAT GAZE BLARE BLAZE
BLOOM FLAME GLAZE STARE
GLITTER ICEBLINK RADIANCE
GLARING HARD RANK GLARY
AGLARE GARISH BURNING
FLARING STARING FLAGRANT
GLASS CUP VER CALX FLAT FLUX
FRIT JENA MOIL PONY VITA
CHARK FACER FLINT GLAZE
STOOP STOUP VERRE VITRE
CALGON CEMENT CULLET
RUMMER SPECKS VITRUM
ALEYARD BIFOCAL BRIMMER
CHIRPER CRYSTAL PERLITE
SCHMELZ TALLBOY VITRITE
FROSTING OBSIDIAN SCHOPPEN
PERSPECTIVE
(— IN STATE OF FUSION) METAL
(— OF A MIRROR) STONE
(— OF BEER) BREW
(— OF BRANDY) SNEAKER
(— OF SPIRITS) CHASSE
(— OF WHISKY) KELTY RUBDOWN
(— OF WINE) APERITIF
(— STICKING TO PUNTY) COLLET
(BEER —) SHELL SEIDEL PILSNER
PILSENER
(BELL-SHAPED —) CUP CLOCHE
(BURNING —) SUNGLASS
(CHEVAL —) PSYCHE
(COLORED —) SMALT SMALTO
TINTER SCHMELZ
(COLORED —S) GOGGLES
(CUPPING —) VENTOSE
(CURVED —) LENS
(DESSERT —) COUPE
(DRINKING —) GOBLET RUMKIN
PILSNER PIMLICO SCUTTLE
TUMBLER SCHOONER
(EUROPEAN ORNAMENTAL —)
PELOTON
(EXAMINATION —) SLIDE
(FULL —) BUMPER
(FUSIBLE —) FLUX
(HALF —) SPLIT
(ICE CREAM —) SLIDER
(LEAD —) STRASS
(LIQUEUR —) PONY PONEY
(LIQUOR —) GUN
(MAGNIFYING —) LOUPE
(MASS OF MOLTEN —) PARISON
(METEORITIC —) MOLDAVITE
(OPALESCENT —) OPALINE
(OPAQUE —) HYALITHE
(PIECE OF HOT —) BIT
(PULVERIZED —) FROSTING

(REFUSE —) CALX CULLET
(RUBY —) SCHMELZE
(RUSSIAN —) CHARK
(SHERBET —) SUPREME
(SHERRY —) COPITA
(SMOKED —) SHADE
(STAINED —) VITRAIL
(TALL —) RUMMER
(THIN —) MOUSSELINE
(VOLCANIC —) PUMICE PERLITE
(WINDOW —) PANE
(WINE —) FLUTE
(PL.) SHELLS
(PREF.) HYAL(O) VITR(EO)(I)(O)
GLASSBLOWER MUMBLER
GLASS CRAB SPECTER SPECTRE
GLASSES (TINTED —) SHADES
GLASSHOUSE STOVE HOTHOUSE
GLASS-LIKE VITRIC
GLASS MENAGERIE (AUTHOR OF —)
(WILLIAMS)
(CHARACTER IN —) TOM JAMES
LAURA AMANDA OCONNOR
GLASSWARE AGATA AURENE
BURMESE FAVRILE OPALINE
STEUBEN VITRICS AMBERINA
GLASSWORK GLAZING GLAZIERY
GLASSWORKER GANGMAN
GLAZIER SNAPPER GLASSMAN
SERVITOR
GLASSWORT KALI KELPWORT
SALTWORT SAMPHIRE
GLASSY GLIB FILMY GLAZY
GLAZEN GLASSEN HYALINE
HYALOID VITREAL VITREOUS
(PREF.) HYAL(O)
GLAUCE (FATHER OF —) CREON
(HUSBAND OF —) JASON
GLAUCUS (FATHER OF —) MINOS
ANTHEDON SISYPHUS
HIPPOLOCHUS
(MOTHER OF —) MEROPE
PASIPHAE
GLAZE DIP LEAD SIZE SLIP GLASS
SLEET SMEAR ENAMEL QUARRY
CELADON COPERTA EELSKIN
GLASSEN GLAZING GLIDDER
COUVERTE TIGEREYE
(— OF ICE) GLARE
GLAZED FILMY GLACE GLASSEN
GLOSSED
GLAZED WARE GLOST
GLAZIER PUTTIER
(TOOL OF —) SPRIG LADKIN
GLEAM RAY BEAM GLOW LEAM
WAFT WINK BLENK BLINK BLUSH
FLASH GLAIK GLEEN GLENT GLINT
GLISK GLIST GLOSE SHINE SKIME
SPUNK STARE STEEM TWIRE
GLANCE SCANCE FOULDRE
GLIMMER GLITTER SHIMMER
CORUSCATE SCINTILLA
(— FAINTLY) SHIMMER
(— OF LIGHT) LEAM PINK GLAIK
SCANCE
(FAINT —) SCAD
GLEAMING FAW GLOW CLEAR
GLINT STEEP ABLAZE BRIGHT
GLEAMY ADAZZLE SHINING
GLOOMING
GLEAN CULL EARN REAP LEASE
GATHER COLLECT SCRINGE
GLEANER STIBBLER

GLEANING CROP GATHERING
(LITERARY —S) ANALECTA
ANALECTS
GLEBE SOD CLOD LAND SOIL
TERMON KIRKTOWN
GLEE GLY JOY SONG MIRTH SPORT
GAIETY DELIGHT ELATION
WASSAIL HILARITY MADRIGAL
GLEEFUL GAY MERRY JOYOUS
JOCULAR GLEESOME
GLEEMAN SONGMAN MINSTREL
GLEN DEN GILL GLYN GRIFF HEUCH
HEUGH KLOOF SLACK SLADE
TEMPE CANADA DINGLE POCKET
GLIADIN GLUTIN PROLAMIN
GLIB PAT FLIP SLICK CASUAL
GLOSSY OFFHAND RENABLE
SHALLOW VOLUBLE FLIPPANT
GLIDE GO SKI FLOW SAIL SILE SKIM
SLIP SLUR SOAR SWIM COAST
CREEP DANCE FLEET GLACE
GRAZE LAPSE MERGE PLANE
SCOOP SHIRL SKATE SKIFF SKIRR
SKITE SLADE SLEEK SLICK SLIDE
SLIPE STEAL GLANCE GLIDER
SASHAY SNOOVE ILLAPSE
SCRIEVE SCRITHE SKITTER
SLITHER AIRPLANE GLISSADE
VOLPLANE SEMIVOWEL
(— AWAY) ELAPSE
(— BY) PASS FLEET
(— OFF) EXIT
GLIDER BIPLANE SCOOTER
SAILPLANE
GLIDING LAPSE TRAIL SLIDING
(— OF THE VOICE) DRAG
(— OVER) LAMBENT
GLIMMER FIRE GLIM GLOW LEAM
STIM BLINK FLASH GLEAM GLOOM
STIME SIMPER BLINTER FLIMMER
GLIMPSE GLITTER SHIMMER
SPARKLE TWINKLE SUNBLINK
GLIMMERING GHOST AGLIMMER
GLOOMING
GLIMPSE IDEA WAFF WAFT BLINK
BLUSH FLASH GLIFF GLINT GLISK
SIGHT STIME TINGE TRACE WHIFF
GLANCE GLEDGE LUSTER SCANCE
GLIMMER INKLING
(BRIEF —) APERCU
(FLEETING —) SHIM SNATCH
GLINT PEEP FLASH GLEAM GLENT
GLANCE SPARKLE
GLIS MYOXUS
GLISSANDO GLISS SMEAR
GLISSADE
GLISTEN FLASH GLISK GLISS GLIST
SHINE GLISTER GLITTER SHIMMER
SPANGLE SPARKLE RUTILATE
GLISTENING SHINY AGLISTEN
GLITTER FLASH GLARE GLEAM
GLEIT GLINT GLORE SHEEN SHINE
SKYRE STARE BICKER LUSTER
SCANCE GLIMMER GLISTEN
GLISTER SKINKLE SPANGLE
SPARKLE TWINKLE BRANDISH
RADIANCE RUTILATE CORUSCATE
(FALSE —) GILT
GLITTERING GEMMY SHEEN SHINY
STEEP FULGID SPANGLY
AGLITTER GLITTERY RUTILANT
BRILLIANT CLINQUANT
GLOAMING EVE DUSK GLOAM

GLOOMING TWILIGHT
GLOAT GAZE GLUT TIRE EXULT
PREEN
GLOBAL PLANETARY
GLOBE ORB BALL BOWL CLEW
CLUE POME AGGER GEOID
MONDE MOUND ROUND SPHERE
COMPASS GEORAMA GLOBULE
GRENADE AQUARIUM ROUNDURE
GLOBEFISH FUGU TOBY TOADO
ATINGA BOTETE PUFFER
BLAASOP BURFISH OOPUHUE
BLOWFISH
GLOBEFLOWER BOLT GOLLAND
GOWLAND CORCHORUS
GLOBE THISTLE ECHINOPS
GLOBOSE COCCOID COCCOUS
CAPITATE GLOBULAR
GLOBULAR GLOBED ROTUND
GLOBATE GLOBOSE GLOBICAL
GLOBULE BEAD BLOB DROP GLOB
PEARL BUBBLE BUTTON REGULUS
GLOBULET SPHERULE
(— OF TAPIOCA) FISHEYE
GLOBULIN MAYSIN MYOSIN VIGNIN
ARACHIN CORYLIN EDESTIN
LEGUMIN TUBERIN VICILIN
ANTIBODY BIOLOGIC EXCELSIN
GLYCININ MUSCULIN ORYZENIN
GLOCKENSPIEL BELL LYRA
CARILLON
GLOMERULE GLOME FASCICLE
GLOOM DAMP DUSK MURK CLOUD
DREAR FROWN SOMBER DESPAIR
DIMNESS GLOOMTH SADNESS
DARKNESS MIDNIGHT
GLOOMY DUN SAD WAN BLUE
COLD DARK DOUR DREE DULL
EERY GLUM MIRK MURK ADUSK
ADUST BLACK BROWN DOWFF
DREAR DUSKY EERIE FERAL
GUMLY HEAVY LURID MOODY
MORNE MUDDY MUNGY MUSTY
MUZZY ROOKY SABLE SORRY
STERN SULKY SURLY SWART
TRIST CLOUDY DISMAL DREARY
DREICH DROOPY DRUMLY
GLUMMY MOROSE SOLEMN
SOMBER SULLEN TETRIC THRAWN
OBSCURE STYGIAN THESTER
DARKSOME DESOLATE DOLESOME
DOWNBEAT DOWNCAST
FUNEREAL GLOOMING LOWERING
OVERCAST TRISTFUL PESSIMISTIC
GLORIA GLORY AUREOLE
GLORIFICATION AVATAR
GLORIFY HERY LAUD BLESS DEIFY
EXALT EXTOL HERSE HONOR
PRIDE WURTH KUDIZE PRAISE
CLARIFY ELEVATE MAGNIFY
DIVINIZE EMBLAZON EULOGIZE
PROCLAIM STELLIFY
GLORIOLE HALO AUREOLE
GLORIOUS SRI DEAR DERE MERE
SHRI GRAND PROUD BRIGHT
EMINENT RENOWNED
GLORY JOY ORE SUN FACE FAME
GLOR HALO HORN BLAZE BOAST
EXULT HONOR KUDOS PRIDE
WULDER AUREOLA CLARITY
GARLAND GLORIFY RADIANCE
SPLENDOR WORTHING
GLORY-PEA KOWHAI

GLOSS GILL COLOR DUNCE GLASS
GLAZE GLOZE JAPAN SHEEN
SHINE BLANCH LUSTER LUSTRE
POSTIL REMARK VENEER BURNISH
EXPOUND VARNISH FLOURISH
PALLIATE POLITURE
(— OVER) FARD HUSH SALVE
SLEEK SOOTHE
GLOSSA LINGUA
GLOSSARY GLOSS CLAVIS
GLOSSIPHONIA CLEPSINE
GLOSSY GLOZE NITID SHINY SILKY
SLEEK SLICK SATINY SMOOTH
GLOVE KID CUFF GAGE MITT
COFFE BERLIN MITTEN CHEVRON
DANNOCK GANTLET GOMUKHI
GAUNTLET
(— FOR RUBBING SKIN) STRIGIL
(BISHOP'S —) GWANTUS
(BODY OF —) TRANK
(BOXING —) MUFFLE
(HEDGER'S —) DANNOCK
(HUSKING —) HUSKER
(PART OF —) THUMB TRANK
GUSSET BINDING FOURCHETTE
GLOVEMAKER DOMER GLOVER
CLASPER FINGERER
GLOVER TRANKER
GLOW ARC LOW AURA BURN FIRE
LEAM LOOM LOWE BLAZE BLOOM
BLUSH FLAME FLASH FLUSH
GLAZE GLEAM GLEED GLORY
GLOSS GLOZE SHINE STEAM
CORONA KINDLE WARMTH
FLUSTER LIGHTEN
(— OF PASSION) ESTUS AESTUS
(— WITH INTENSE HEAT) IGNITE
GLOWER GAZE GLOW GLARE
GLOOM GLORE
GLOWING HOT LIVE WARM
AGLOW FIERY LIGHT QUICK
RUDDY VIVID ABLAZE ARDENT
ORIENT BURNING CANDENT
FERVENT RADIANT SHINING
FLAGRANT RUTILANT
GLOWWORM FIREFLY FIREWORM
GLOWBIRD LAMPYRID
GLOZE FAWN PAINT SMOOTH
FLATTERY
GLUCINUM BERYLLIUM
GLUCOSE AME GLYCOSE
DEXTROSE
GLUCOSIDE GEIN APIIN RUTIN
TUTIN ADONIN BINDER CORNIN
DURRIN FRAXIN FUSTIN IRIDIN
PICEIN UZARIN ACACIIN ARBUTIN
DAPHNIN DIOSMIN ESCULIN
ESTEVIN GITALIN GITONIN
GITOXIN HEDERIN HELECIN
INDICAN LOGANIN LOTUSIN
LUPININ OUABAIN POPULIN
ROBININ SALICIN TABACIN
TEUCRIN ADONIDIN CARTHAME
ERICOLIN GENISTIN GOSSYPIN
MORINDIN NARINGIN PARIGLIN
PARILLIN PRUNASIN QUINOVIN
SAPONINE SCILLAIN SINIGRIN
SYRINGIN THEVETIN VERNONIN
VIBURNIN VICIANIN
GLUE PAD EPOXY MOUNT STICK
BEGLEW CEMENT FUNORI
FUNORIN STICKER STICKUM
TAUROCOL

(BEE —) PROPOLIS
(PREF.) COLL(A)(O)(OIDIO)(OIDO)
GLOEO
(SUFF.) COLL GLIA GLOEA
GLUE-LIKE
(PREF.) (— SUBSTANCE) GLI
GLUEY GLUISH STICKY STRINGY
VISCOUS ADHESIVE
GLUM CLUM DOUR GRUM SURLY
GLOOMY GLUMPY MOROSE
SULLEN DEJECTED
GLUMALES POALES
GLUME PILE FLIGHT
(FLOWERING —) LEMMA
(PL.) CHAFF
GLUSIDE SACCHARIN
GLUT CLOY FILL GULP QUAT SATE
CHOKE DRAFT GORGE BATTEN
ENGLUT EXCESS MARROW
PAMPER PAUNCH ENGORGE
GLUTTON SATIATE SURFEIT
SWALLOW OVERFEED SAGINATE
SATURATE
GLUTEAL NATAL
GLUTELIN AVENINE ORYZENIN
GLUTENIN AVENIN ZYMOME
ZYMOMIN
GLUTINOUS ROPY SIZY ROPEY
SLIMY TOUGH STICKY VISCID
(PREF.) GLOEO GLOIO
GLUTTED QUAT GORGED SATIATED
GLUTTER VEER
GLUTTON HOG PIG GLUT GORB
GUTS GULCH MIKER GLOTUM
HELLUO MACCUS EPICURE
GUTLING LURCHER MOOCHER
RAVENER SWILLER CARCAJOU
DRAFFMAN GOURMAND
GULLYGUT
(STUPID —) GRUB
GLUTTONIZE BIZLE BEZZLE
GLUTTONOUS GREEDY GLUTTON
HOGGISH GOURMAND
GLUTTONY GULE EDACITY
SURFEIT
GLYCERIDE BUTYRIN
GLYCINE SOJA
GLYCOL CARBOWAX
GLYCOPROTEIN MUCIN MUCOID
GLYCOSIDE APIIN CROCIN ACACIIN
CYMARIN DIGOXIN GITALIN
GITOXIN HEDERIN HYPERIN
LOGANIN LOTUSIN SAPONIN
ALDESIDE ANDROSIN ANTIARIN
HOLOSIDE KETOSIDE
GNARL NOB KNOB KNUR KNARL
KNURR SNIRL WARRE DEFORM
GNARLED GNARLY KNARRY
KNOTTY CRABBED KNOTTED
KNURLED
GNASH TUSK CHAMP CRASH
GANCH GRASH GRATE KNASH
GNAT KNAW SMUT MIDGE PUNKY
STOUT KNATTE SCIARA SCIARID
SCINIPH BLACKFLY DIPTERAN
GNATLING
(PREF.) CULIC(I)
GNATCATCHER SYLVIID
GNATHION MENTON
GNAW EAT NAB BITE FRET TIRE
CHELE GNARL MOUSE SHEAR
ARRODE BEFRET BEGNAW
CANKER CHAVEL NATTLE NIGGLE

ROUNGE CHIMBLE CHUMBLE
CORRODE
GNAWED
(PREF.) BROTO
GNAWING EATING RODENT
FRETFUL ARROSION ROSORIAL
GNOME NIS NISSE PECHT PYGMY
KOBOLD VAKSHA YAKSHI
GNOMIDE GREMLIN HODEKEN
ERDGEIST
GNOMON COCK INDEX STILE STYLE
FESCUE STYLUS
GNOSTIC CLEVER SHREWD
KNOWING PERATES EBIONITE
MANDAEAN SEVERIAN SIMONIAN
SIMONITE
GNU KOKOON BRINDLE
GO BE DO ACT GAE HOP ISH LAY
NIM PEP TEE WAG BANG BEAR
BING BOWN BUSK DRAW FAND
FARE FOND GANG HARK HAUL
HUMP MOVE QUIT RAIK ROAM
ROLL SEEK SHOT SILE SLAP SNAP
STAB STEP TAKE TEEM TOUR
WADE WANE WEAR WEND WEVE
WIND WISE WORK YEAD YEDE
AMBLE BOUND CARRY CHEVE
DEMON DRESS FETCH FRAME
HAUNT KNOCK LEAVE MOSEY
PLUCK REACH SCRAM SHAKE
SLOPE SPEED TOUCH TRACE
TRACK TRENE TRINE TRUSS
WHIZZ YONGE BECOME BETAKE
CHIEVE CRUISE DEPART EXTEND
QUATCH QUETCH REPAIR RESORT
RESULT RETIRE SASHAY STRAKE
STRIKE TODDLE TRAVEL WEAKEN
JOURNEY SCRITHE DIMINISH
WITHDRAW
(— ABOUT) JET BEGO BIGAN
(— ABOUT DEJECTEDLY) PEAK
(— ABOUT GOSSIPING) COURANT
(— AHEAD) HOLD
(— AIMLESSLY) ERR BUMMLE
(— ALONG) PATH
(— ALONG WITH) ACCOMPANY
(— AROUND) SKIRT BYPASS
CIRCUE
(— ASHORE) LAND
(— ASTRAY) ERR MAR WRY MANG
WILL MISGO DELIRE FORVAY
MISWEND DEROGATE MISCARRY
(— AWAY) AGO HOP OFF BEAT
BUNK HIKE NASH PART SHOO
VADE CLEAR HENCE IMSHI LEAVE
SCRAM SHIFT BEGONE BUGGER
DEPART REMOVE VACATE
SKIDDOO ELONGATE
(— BACK IN TIME) MOUNT
(— BAD) SOUR
(— BEFORE) LEAD FOREGO
PRECEDE ANTECEDE PREAMBLE
(— BEYOND) SURPASS FOREPASS
(— BRISKLY) JUNE
(— BROKE) BUST
(— COURTING) WENCH
(— DOWN) SET SINK VAIL DROOP
SOUND DESCEND
(— EASILY) AMBLE
(— ERRATICALLY) KICK
(— FAST) HURRY SPLIT BARREL
BEELINE
(— FORTH) AGO DEPART FORTHGO

(— **FORWARD**) HUP HUPP
ADVANCE AGGRESS PROCEED
(— **FOWLING**) AUCUPATE
(— **FURTIVELY**) SLINK SNEAK STEAL
(— **HANG**) SNICK
(— **HEAVILY**) LOB LAMPER
(— **IN**) ENTER INGRESS
(— **IN A HURRY**) SCUFFLE
(— **IN HASTE**) LEN LAMMAS
(— **IN PURSUIT**) SUE
(— **INTO BUSINESS**) EMBARK
(— **LAME**) FOUNDER
(— **LEISURELY**) BUMMEL JIGGET
JIGGIT
(— **LIGHTLY**) TIPTOE
(— **MAD**) CRAZE MADDLE
(— **NEAR**) APPROACH
(— **NOISILY**) LARUM
(— **OFF**) MOG DISCHARGE
(— **ON**) DO GARN LAST PASS
PERGE FURTHER PROCEED
(— **ON BOARD**) BOARD EMBARK
ENTRAIN
(— **ON FOOT**) SHANK
(— **ON TO SAY**) ADD
(— **OUT**) EXIT ISSUE SLOCK
EGRESS EXEUNT QUENCH SORTIE
(— **OVER**) KNEE REVOLT SURPASS
OVERGANG
(— **OVER AGAIN**) RENEW REVISE
RETRACE
(— **PROSPEROUSLY**) COTTON
(— **QUICKLY**) GET HIE BUZZ LAMP
PIKE SCAT SPEED
(— **RAPIDLY**) LAMP SPLIT
(— **SHARES**) SNACK
(— **SLOWLY**) CRAWL CREEP
(— **SLUGGISHLY**) SHACK
(— **SMOOTHLY**) SLIP
(— **STEALTHILY**) SHIRK SLINK
SNEAK GUMSHOE
(— **SUDDENLY**) CLAP SCOOT
(— **SWIFTLY**) SKISE STRIP
HIGHBALL
(— **THE ROUNDS**) PATROL
(— **THROUGH**) SUFFER
(— **THROUGH WATER**) SQUATTER
(— **THROUGHOUT**) COAST
(— **TO BED**) KIP DOSS FLOP SNUG
(— **TO EXCESS**) DEBORD
(— **TO HARBOR**) VERT
(— **TO PIECES**) SNURP
(— **TO SCHOOL**) SCOLEY
(— **TO SLEEP**) HUSHABY
(— **TO WAR**) RISE
(— **TOO FAR**) OUTREACH
(— **UP**) CLIMB AMOUNT ASCEND
(— **WEARILY**) HAGGLE
(— **WITH EFFORT**) HIKE
(— **WRONG**) MISS FAULT CURDLE
MISFARE BACKFIRE
GOAD EGG GAD GIG HAG BAIT
BROD BROG DARE EDGE GAUD
LASH MOVE PROD SPUR URGE
WHIP YERK ANKUS HARRY IMPEL
PIQUE PRICK PROGG PUNGE
STING VALET INCITE NEEDLE
OXGOAD ANKUSHA HOTFOOT
INFLAME PROVOKE IRRITATE
SLAPJACK STIMULUS
GOADMAN GADMAN GAUDSMAN
GOADSTER
GOAL RYF DEN END BASE BUTT

DOLE DOOL HAIL HALE MARK
METE PORT BOURN FINIS IDEAL
SCOOP SCOPE SCORE STING
DESIGN OBJECT SIGHTS
DESTINY HORIZON
TERMINUS OBJECTIVE
(— **IN GAMES**) HUNK
(**FIELD —**) BASKET
(**REMOTE —**) THULE
(**UNATTAINABLE —**) STAR
GO-ASHORE KOHUA
GOAT BOK TUR IBEX TAHR BEDEN
BILLY BOVID EVECK SEROW
ALPINE ANGORA AOUDAD CAPRID
CHAMAL JEMLAH MAZAME
NUBIAN PASANG SAANEN
WETHER CHAMOIS AEGAGRUS
CAPRIPED MARKHOOR
BOUQUETIN
(**DOMESTIC —**) HIRCUS
(**FEMALE —**) NANNY DOELING
(**MALE —**) BUCK BUCKLING
(**YOUNG —**) KID KIDDY TICCHEN
GOATLING
(**PREF.**) AEG(I)(O) CAPRI EGO
GOAT ANTELOPE GORAL SEROW
GOORAL
GOATEE TUFT
GOATFISH MOANO
GOATHERD DAMON
GOAT-LIKE CAPRINE GOATISH
HIRCINE
GOAT MOTH COSSID
GOATSBEARD ROSACEAN
GOATSKIN CRUST CASTOR
CHEVRETTE
GOATSUCKER PUCK PEWKE
POTOO EVEJAR BULLBAT
DORHAWK GRINDER SPINNER
DOORHAWK EVECHURR
NIGHTJAR PAURAQUE
GOB CLOT GOAF SWAB SWOB
WASTE GOBBET SWABBY
GOBBET BIT CHUNK MORSEL
GOBBLE MOP BOLT SLOP GOFFLE
GORBLE
GOBBLEDYGOOK PEDAGESE
GO-BETWEEN BAWD FIXER MEANS
BROKER DEALER PANDAR
CONTACT MEDIATOR
GOBLET DINOS GLASS HANAP
POKAL SKULL STOOP STOUP
BUMPER HOLMOS RUMKIN
CHALICE SCYPHUS SNIFTER
TALLBOY JEROBOAM STANDARD
STEMWARE
(**PREF.**) CALICI
GOBLIN (ALSO SEE HOBGOBLIN)
COW HAG NIS PUG BHUT BOGY
MARE PUCK BOGEY NISSE OUPHE
POOKA BODACH BOGGLE BOOGER
CHUREL EMPUSA FOLIOT SPRITE
BOGGARD BOGGART BROWNIE
BUGBEAR KNOCKER PADFOOT
BARGHEST BOGEYMAN FOLLETTO
GOBY MAPO BULLY BIGHEAD
CHALACO GOBIOID GUAVINA
GUDGEON MUDFISH BULLHEAD
PINKFISH SANDGOBY
GOCART SULKY WALKER
STROLLER
GOD (ALSO SEE DEITY) AS EA EL
ER RA VE BEL BES COG DAD DES

DEV DIS DOD EAR GAR GAW GEB
GOG GOL GOM GUM ING KEB LAR
LOK MEN MIN ODD ORO SEB SUN
TEM TYR ULL UTU VAN AITU
AMEN AMON ARES ASUR ATEO
ATUA ATYS BAAL BEER BRAN
BURE CHAC COCK DEUS DEVA
DIEU ESUS FONS FREY GAWD
GOSH HAPI HOLY HOTH INTI JOVE
KANE KING LIFE LLEU LOKE LOKI
LOVE LUGH MARS MIND NABU
NEBO NUDD ODIN PTAH SHEN
SHIN SOMA SOUL TANE THOR
TIKI ULLR UTUG VAYU XIPE YAMA
ZEUS ARAWN ASHUR ASURA
ATTES ATTIS COMUS DAGDA
DEITY DEOTA DUVEL DYAUS
DYLAN EBISU ELOAH FREYR
GHOST GOLES GOLLY GRAVE
GUACA HESUS HIEMS HORUS
HOTHR HUACA HYMEN INDRA
JUDGE KINGU LADON LIBER
LLUDD MENTU MIDER MOMUS
NJORD NUMEN PALES PICUS
SILEN TAMUZ THOTH TINIA
TRUTH TYCHE URASH WAKEA
WODIN WOTAN ZOMBI ADITYA
ADONAI ADONAY ANSHAR
ANUBIS APOLLO ASEITY AUTHOR
CHAMOS CONSUS DEVATA
DHARMA ELATHA ELOHIM
FATHER FAUNUS GANESA
HEAVEN HERMES HOENIR MEZTLI
MILCOM MITHRA NEREUS NERGAL
OSIRIS PATRON PENEUS PLUTUS
PUSHAN SESHAT SOCIUS SOURCE
SPIRIT SUTEKH SYLENE TAAROA
TAMMUZ TARTAK TERAPH
TRITON TRIVIA VARUNA VEDUIS
VERITY VISHNU VULCAN WISDOM
YAKSHA YAKSHI ZOMBIE
ABRAXAS ADRANUS ALPHEUS
ANTEROS BELENUS CHEMOSH
DAIKOKU DELLING ETERNAL
GODHEAD HANUMAN IAPETUS
JEHOVAH JUPITER KANALOA
MERCURY MITHRAS MUTINUS
NEPTUNE NJORTHR PROTEUS
PRYDERI REMPHAN ROBIGUS
SAVITAR SERAPIS TRIGLAV
VATICAN VEJOVIS ZAGREUS
ALMIGHTY ASTRAEUS BISHAMON
CAMAXTLI DEMIURGE DEVOTION
DIVINITY GUCUMATZ INFINITE
JIUROJIN KUKULKAN MIXCOATL
MORPHEUS POSEIDON SABAZIOS
SUMMANUS TANGAROA
TERMINUS TUTELARY VEDIOVIS
ZEPHYRUS OMNIPOTENT
(— **OF AGRICULTURE**) PICUS URASH
FAUNUS AMAETHON NINGIRSU
(— **OF ARTS**) SIVA
(— **OF ATMOSPHERE**) HADAD
(— **OF COMMERCE**) MERCURY
(— **OF CORN**) CAT
(— **OF DAY**) HORUS
(— **OF EARTH**) BEL GEB KEB SEB
DAGAN
(— **OF EVIL**) SET FOMOR
FOMORIAN ZERNEBOCK
(— **OF FERTILITY**) SHANGO
(— **OF FIRE**) AGNI GIRRU NUSKU
RUDRA VULCAN

(— **OF FLOCKS**) PAN
(— **OF HAPPINESS**) HOTEI JUROJIN
(— **OF HEAVENS**) ANU JUMALA
(— **OF JUSTICE**) FORSETE FORSETI
(— **OF LEARNING**) IMHOTEP
(— **OF LOVE**) AMOR ARES EROS
KAMA BHAGA CUPID AENGUS
(— **OF MOON**) SIN ENZU NANNAR
(— **OF NATURE**) MARSYAS
(— **OF POETRY**) BRAGE BRAGI
(— **OF RAIN**) PARJANYA
(— **OF SEA**) LER VAN AEGIR DYAUS
NEPTUNE PROTEUS PALAEMON
POSEIDON
(— **OF SKY**) ANU GWYDION
(— **OF SLEEP**) HYPNOS HYPNUS
MORPHEUS
(— **OF SOUTHEAST WIND**) EURUS
(— **OF STORM**) ZU ADAD ADDA
ADDU MARUT RUDRA TESHUP
(— **OF SUN**) RA RE SHU SOL TEM
TUM UTU AMON ATMU ATUM
BAAL LLEU UTUG SAMAS SEKER
SURYA APOLLO HELIOS SOKARI
KHEPERA PHOEBUS SHAMASH
PHAETHON TONATIUH
(— **OF THUNDER**) THOR DONAR
PERUN PERKUN PEROUN SHANGO
TLALOC HURAKAN TARANIS
(— **OF UNDERWORLD**) DIS BRAN
GWYN YAMA HADES ORCUS
PLUTO
(— **OF VEGETATION**) ATYS ATTIS
(— **OF WAR**) ER IRA ORO TIU TYR
ARES GOFI IRRA MARS MENT
ODIN THOR MONTU NINIB MEXITL
SKANDA CAMULUS MEXITLI
NINURTA ENYALIUS NINGIRSU
QUIRINUS
(— **OF WEALTH**) BHAGA KUBERA
KUVERA PLUTUS
(— **OF WIND**) ADAD ADDA ADDU
VAYU MARUT AEOLUS BOREAS
EECATL
(— **OF WISDOM**) TAT THOTH
(— **WILLING**) DV
(**BLIND —**) HOTH HOTHR
(**FALSE —**) BAAL IDOL MAUMET
(**FEMALE —**) GODDESS
(**HAWAIIAN —**) AUMAKUA
(**IMMORTAL —**) AKAL
(**INFERIOR —**) PANISK
(**PAGAN —**) DEMON
(**RAM-HEADED —**) AMON KHNUM
KHNEMU
(**TIMELESS —**) AKAL
(**TUTELARY —**) LAR
(**UNKNOWN —**) KA
(**WOOD —**) SILEN SILENUS
(**PL.**) DI DII KAMI AESIR IGIGI
SUPERI PANTHEON TRIMURTI
(**PREF.**) DEI DEO THE(O)
GODDESS (ALSO SEE DEITY) AI NU
ANA ANU ATE AYA DEA DON NUT
OPS UNI VAC ANTA BADB BODB
CACA DANA DANU ERIS ERUA
FRIA HELA HERA JORD JUNO
MAIA MEDB NIKE NINA NONA
PELE SAGA SATI TARA UPIS
ALLAT AMENT ANATH ANTUM
ARURU BAUBO CERES CHLOE
DEESS DIANA DIANE DIRGA
DOLMA DOMNU EPONA FRIGG

HYBLA IAMBE ISTAR KOTYS
MAEVE NANAI NINTU PAKHT
PALES PARCA SALUS SEDNA
SKADI TANIT TYCHE USHAS
VENUS VESTA ADEONA AESTAS
ANATUM ANUKIT APHAIA
ATHENA BELILI BENDIS BOOPIS
BRIGIT CYRENE EOSTRE FRIGGA
GEFJON HELENA HESTIA HYGEIA
INNINA KISHAR LIBERA MOTHER
NINGAL PEITHO PHOBOS
POMONA PRORSA RUMINA
SEKHET SEMELE SKATHI SOTHIS
TANITH TEFNUT TRIVIA URANIA
VACUNA YDGRUN ANAHITA
ANAITIS ARTEMIS ASHERAH
DEMETER DERCETO FERONIA
FJORGYN GODHEAD KOTYTTO
LARENTA LARUNDA MAJAGGA
MAJESTA MINERVA MORNING
MORRIGU MYLITTA NEKHEBT
NEMESIS PALATUA PARBATI
PARVATI SALACIA ADRASTEA
AGLAUROS ANGERONA BELISAMA
CARMENTA CENTEOTL
COCAMAMA DESPOINA DICTYNNA
GULLVEIG MORRIGAN NEPHTHYS
PARBUTTY PRAKRITI RHIANNON
SEFEKHET THOUERIS VICTORIA
(— OF AGRICULTURE) BAU OPS
DEMETER CENTEOTL
(— OF AIR) AURA
(— OF BEAUTY) VENUS LAKSHMI
(— OF BURIAL) LIBITINA
(— OF CHILDBIRTH) LEVANA
LUCINA
(— OF DAWN) EOS USAS USHAS
AURORA MATUTA
(— OF DEW) HERSE
(— OF DISCORD) ATE ERIS
(— OF EARTH) GE LUA SEB ERDA
GAEA GAIA TARI ARURU DIONE
JORTH TERRA SEMELE TELLUS
THEMIS DAMKINA PERCHTA
(— OF FERTILITY) MA ISIS MAMA
NERTHUS
(— OF FLOWERS) FLORA CHLORIS
(— OF FORTUNE) TYCHE FORTUNA
(— OF GRAIN) CERES
(— OF HEALING) EIR GULA
(— OF HEALTH) DAMIA HYGEIA
VALETUDO
(— OF HEARTH) VESTA HESTIA
(— OF HISTORY) SAGA
(— OF HOPE) SPES
(— OF INFATUATION) ATE
(— OF JUSTICE) DIKE MAAT
THEMIS ASTRAEA NEMESIS
JUSTITIA
(— OF LEGISLATION) EUNOMIA
(— OF LOVE) ATHOR FREYA VENUS
FREYJA HATHOR
(— OF MAGIC) HECATE
(— OF MARRIAGE) HERA
(— OF MATERNITY) APET
(— OF MERCY) KWANNON
(— OF MOTHERHOOD) ISIS
(— OF NIGHT) NOX NYX
(— OF OCEAN) NINA
(— OF OVENS) FORNAX
(— OF PEACE) PAX IRENE
NERTHUS
(— OF PLEASURE) BES

(— OF RAINBOW) IRIS
(— OF SEASONS) DIKE HORA
(— OF THE DEAD) HEL HELA
(— OF THE HUNT) DIANA VACUNA
ARTEMIS
(— OF THE MOON) LUNA MOON
DIANA SELENA TANITH ARTEMIS
(— OF THE SEA) INO RAN DORIS
BRANWEN EURYNOME
(— OF TRUTH) MAAT
(— OF VEGETATION) OPS CERES
COTYS COTYTTO
(— OF VENGEANCE) ARA NEMESIS
(— OF VICTORY) NIKE
(— OF WAR) ENYO ANATH ANATU
ANUNIT BELLONA
(— OF WATER) ANAHITA
(— OF WEALTH) LAKSHMI
(— OF WISDOM) ATHENA MINERVA
(— OF YOUTH) HEBE JUVENTAS
(COW-HEADED —) ISIS
(ESKIMO —) SEDNA
(FERTILITY —) ASTARTE
(MARRIAGE —) VOR
(SUBORDINATE —) DEMIURGE
(THUNDER-SMITTEN —) SEMELE
KERAUNIA
(3-HEADED —) HECATE
(PL.) HORAE MATRIS POINAE
ASYNJUR
GO-DEVIL TRAVOIS ALLIGATOR
GODFATHER GOSSIP GODPAPA
PADRINO SPONSOR GODPHERE
GODHEAD DEITY GODHOOD
DIVINITY
GODLESS WICKED ATHEIST
IMPIOUS PROFANE UNGODLY
GODLESSNESS ATHEISM
GODLIKE DEIFIC DIVINE IMMORTAL
OLYMPIAN
GODLINESS PIETISM SANCTITY
GODLING DEVATA GENIUS GODKIN
GODLET PANISC DEMIGOD
PANISCUS
GODLY HOLY WISE PIOUS DEVOUT
GRACIOUS
GODMOTHER CUMMER GOSSIP
SPONSOR GODMAMMA MARRAINE
GODPARENT SPONSOR
GOD'S S
GODSON FILLEUL GODCHILD
GOD TREE CEIBA
GODWIT PICK PRINE BARKER
MARLIN SCAMMEL YARWHIP
RINGTAIL SHRIEKER SPOTRUMP
YARDKEEP YARWHELP
GOFFER QUILL FULLER GAUFFER
GOG (FATHER OF —) SHEMAIAH
GO-GETTER HUSTLER
GOGGLER SCAD
GOGLET COOJA SERAI MONKEY
SURAHI GURGLET SURAHEE
GOING FARE GAIT BOUND AGOING
WAYING PASSADO SLEDDING
(— ABOUT) AROUND
(— BEYOND OTHERS) ULTRA
(— IN) INEUNT INFARE INGOING
(— ON) FARE AGATE TOWARD
(— OUT) EGRESS
(— UP) ANABASIS
(SUFF.) GRESS
GOITER WEN GLANS GOITRE
STRUMA BRONCHOCELE

GOITERED ANTELOPE ZENU
GOITROUS STRUMOUS
GOLD OR ORO RED SOL DORE GILT
GULL ALTUN AURUM GUILD
METAL OCHER OCHRE RIDGE
SHINY GOLDEN OBRIZE ORMOLU
YELLOW BULLION SPANKER
(— PIECE) TALI
(GREENISH —) AENEUS AENEOUS
(IMITATION —) PINCHBECK
(PREF.) AUR(I) AUREO CHRYS(O)
ORI
GOLDBEATER (TOOL OF —) WAGON
GOLDCREST MOON TIDLEY
MUDDLER TROCHIL
GOLDEN RED DORE GOLD BLEST
DURRY GOLDY SUNNY AUREAL
BLONDE GILDEN GILTEN AUREATE
AUREOUS HALCYON AURULENT
DEAURATE
(— STATE) CALIFORNIA
GOLDEN ASS (AUTHOR OF —)
APULEIUS
(CHARACTER IN —) ISIS MILO FOTIS
LUCIUS CHARITES PAMPHILE
SOCRATES BYRRHAENA
LEPOLEMUS THRASILLUS
ARISTOMENES
GOLDEN BOWL (AUTHOR OF —)
JAMES
(CHARACTER IN —) ADAM STANT
MAGGIE VERVER AMERIGO
CHARLOTTE
GOLDEN CHAIN LABURNUM
GOLDEN CLUB TAWKEE TAWKIN
TUCKAHOE
GOLDEN EAGLE RINGTAIL
GOLDENEYE CUR GARROT
COBHEAD GOWDNIE BULLHEAD
IRONHEAD MORILLON WHIFFLER
WHISTLER
GOLDEN ORIOLE PIROL WITWALL
GOLDEN PLOVER KOLEA
FROGSKIN SQUEALER WHISTLER
GOLDEN RAGWORT LIFEROOT
GOLDENROD BONEWORT
SOLIDAGO JIMMYWEED
GOLDENSEAL EYEBALM EYEROOT
ICEROOT PUCCOON
GOLDEN SHINER CHUB DACE
WINDFISH
GOLDFINCH JACK FINCH GOLDY
GOWDY CANARY REDCAP
FLAXBIRD GRAYPATE
GOLDFINNY CONNER GOLDNEY
CORKWING
GOLDFISH FUNA MOOR COMET
CALICO FANTAIL CYPRINID
VEILTAIL
GOLD-OF-PLEASURE FLAX
MADWORT OILSEED
GOLDSMITH SONAR AURIFEX
ENGLISH HILLIARD
FRENCH MEISSONIER
GERMAN JAMNITZER
ITALIAN LEONI ROBBIA
WELSH MYDDELTON
GOLFER TEER
GOMER (FATHER OF —) JAPHETH
(HUSBAND OF —) HOSEA
GOMUTI EJOO IROK ARENG KITTUL
SAGWIRE SAGOWEER
GONAD GERMEN

GONCALO ALVES KINGWOOD
GONDOLA GON BARGE
GUNDALOW
GONE AWAY LOST NAPOO
(— BY) AGO DONE PAST AGONE
PASSE BEHIND BYGONE
(— OUT OF USE) EXTINCT
(— TO PIECES) HAYWIRE
**GONE WITH THE WIND (AUTHOR
OF —)** MITCHELL
(CHARACTER IN —) FRANK OHARA
RHETT ASHLEY BUTLER WILKES
CHARLES KENNEDY MELANIE
HAMILTON SCARLETT
GONG BELL CLOCK GANGSA
DOORBELL
(SERIES OF —S) BONANG
GONGORISM CULTISM
GONOPHORE MEDUSOID
SPOROSAC
GOOD BON GAY TOP TRY ABLE
BEAU BEIN BIEN BOON BRAW
FINE GAIN HEND NICE NOTE
PROW SAKE BONNY BONUM
BRAVE BULLY CANNY FRESH
GWEED JELLY KAPAI PAKKA
PUKKA SEELY SOUND VALID
BENIGN BRAWLY BUCKRA DIVINE
EXPERT FACTOR FORBYE HONEST
MABUTI PRETTY PROFIT PROPER
WEALTH BENEFIT COPIOUS
CORKING FAIRISH FORTHBY
GODLIKE GRADELY HELPFUL
LIBERAL SNIFTER STAVING
TRAINED UPRIGHT BUDGEREE
GRAITHLY INTEREST LAUDABLE
PLEASING SALUTARY SKILLFUL
SUITABLE
(EXCEPTIONALLY —) SLAMBANG
(EXTREMELY —) SLICK
(HOLD —) BEAR
(INFINITELY —) HOLY
(MIGHTY —) SKOOKUM
(NO —) DUFF NAPOO NAPOOH
(PRETTY —) FAIR TIDY
(RELATIVELY —) SMOOTH
(SUPERLATIVELY —) BRAG
BEAUTIFUL
(SUPREMELY —) IMMENSE
GORGEOUS
(SURPASSINGLY —) SUPERIOR
(VERY —) HOT TOP DANDY DICTY
GRAND NIFTY BONZER BOSHTA
BOSKER BOSHTER NAILING
SPLENDID SWINGING
(PREF.) AGATH(O) BENI EU
GOOD-BYE BY BYE TATA ADDIO
ADIEU ADIOS LULLABY FAREWELL
SAYONARA
**GOOD COMPANIONS (AUTHOR OF
—)** PRIESTLEY
(CHARACTER IN —) DEAN HUGH
NUNN ELSIE INIGO JERRY JIMMY
SUSIE TRANT JESIAH OAKROYD
ELIZABETH JOLLIFANT
LONGSTAFF MCFARLANE
JERNINGHAM
GOOD EARTH (AUTHOR OF —)
BUCK
(CHARACTER IN —) LIU LUNG
NUNG OLAN PEAR WANG CHING
HWANG LOTUS
GOOD-FOR-NAUGHT LOSEL

GOOD-FOR-NOTHING BUM ORRA SLIM SLINK DONNOT KEFFEL RIBALD STUMER BRETHEL FUSTIAN SCROYLE SHOTTEN SKEEZIX SKELLUM SKYBALD VAURIEN WOSBIRD VAGABOND
GOOD-HUMORED SONSY
GOOD-KING-HENRY BLITE ALLGOOD MARKERY MERCURY CHENOPOD
GOOD-LOOKING BRAW FAIR FOXY MOOI BONNY GAWSY COMELY PRETTY SEEMLY EYESOME GRADELY WINSOME GOODLIKE HANDSOME STUNNING
GOODLY BOON PROPER GOODLIKE
GOOD-NATURED SONSY CLEVER AMIABLE
GOODNESS BONTE BONUM MENSK PROOF BONITY BOUNTY SATTVA VIRTUE KINDNESS
GOODS FEE BONA GEAR KIND PELF CARGO STUFF TRADE WORLD WRACK ADVANCE CAPITAL CHATTEL EFFECTS FINANCE HAVINGS INSIGHT TRAFFIC CHAFFERY HIGGLERY PROPERTY
(— BARTERED) DICKER
(— CAST OVERBOARD) JETSAM
(— SUNK IN SEA) LAGAN LIGAN LAGEND
(DRY —) DRAPERY
(HOUSEHOLD —) INSIGHT
(IMPERFECT —) FENT
(INFERIOR —) BRACK
(PIECE —) CUTTANEE
(SECONDHAND —) BROKERY
(SLOW-SELLING —) JOBS
(STOLEN — THROWN AWAY) WAIF
(SURPLUS —) OVERAGE
(VALUABLE —) SWAG
GOOD-SIZED HEFTY GAWSIE
GOOD-TASTING DAINTY
GOODWILL GREE PHILANTHROPY
GOODY-GOODY PI MOLLYCODDLE
GOOEY CLARTY
GOOF BOOB GOOFER
GOOGLY BOSEY WRONGUN
GOON MUSCLEMAN
GOOSANDER JACKSAW RANTOCK
GOOSE ELK LAMA NENE ROUT BRANT BRENT EMDEN HANSA HOBBY ROMAN SOLAN WAVEY CAGMAG CANADA EMBDEN GALOOT GANDER GOSLET HISSER HONKER SOLAND AFRICAN BLACKIE BUSTARD GAGGLER GOSLING GRAYLAG GREASER GREYLAG OUTARDE WIDGEON BALDHEAD BARGOOSE BARNACLE BERNICLE SPURWING TOULOUSE
(MYTHICAL —) GANZA
(PART OF —) BOW EAR EYE TOE WEB BEAN BILL CAPE FOOT KEEL RUMP WING FLUFF SHANK BREAST COVERT DEWLAP SADDLE FEATHER NOSTRIL SHOULDER SECONDARY
(PREF.) CHEN(O)
GOOSEBERRY BLOB FABE FAPE POHA BRAGAS GOBLIN GOZILL GROZER DOWNING GASKINS GROZART CARBERRY CATBERRY

DOGBERRY EATBERRY FEABERRY GOOSEGOG HOUGHTON INDUSTRY
(PL.) THAPES
GOOSE EGG DUCK
GOOSEFOOT BLITE ORACH BASSIA KOCHIA ORACHE QUINOA ALLSEED PIGWEED
GOOSEGIRL GOSSARD
GOOSE GRASS HERIF HARIFFE CLEAVERS
GOOSEHERD GOZZARD GOOSEBOY
GOOSENECK ROOSTER
GOPHER TUZA GAUFFRE GEOMYID MUNGOFA QUACHIL SALAMICH TUCOTUCO
(— STATE) MINNESOTA
GOPHERMAN SWAMPER
GOPHERWOOD FUSTIC
GORBODUC (SON OF —) FERREX PORREX
GORDIUS (SON OF —) MIDAS
GORE CLY CLOY GARE HIKE HIPE HOOK HORN PICK PIKE SHOT CRUOR GODET STICK GORING GUSSET
GOREVAN AUBURN
GORGE GAP JAM FILL GASH GAUM GLUT JAMB KHOR RENT BREAK CAJON CANON CHASM CHINE CLUSE DRAFT FARCE FLUME GULLY GURGE KLOOF PONGO POUCH STECH STRID STUFF TANGI CANYON DEFILE NULLAH RAVINE STODGE STRAIT THROAT COULOIR DATIATE DRAUGHT ENGORGE SATIATE SLABBER BARRANCA QUEBRADA
GORGED ACCOLLE
GORGEOUS VAIN GRAND SHOWY COSTLY DAZZLING GLORIOUS SPLENDID
GORGERIN NECK NECKING
GORGIBUS (DAUGHTER OF —) CELIE
GORGING STODGE
GORGON MEDUSA STHENO EURYALE
GORGOPHONE (FATHER OF —) PERSEUS
(HUSBAND OF —) OEBALUS PERIERES
(MOTHER OF —) ANDROMEDA
(SON OF —) ICARIUS APHAREUS LEUCIPPUS TYNDAREUS
GORILLA APE PIGMY PYGMY
GORING CORNUPETE
GORMANDIZE STECH STEGH GUTTLE
GORMANDIZER HELLUO GLUTTON
GORSE ULEX WHIN FURZE GORST
GORY BLOODY
GOSHAWK GOS ASTUR TERCEL
GOSLING GULL
GOSPEL SPELL DHARMA EVANGEL KERUGMA KERYGMA SYNOPTIC
(— OF REDEMPTION) CROSS
(PL.) TEXT
GOSSAMER MOUSEWEB STARDUST
GOSSIP EME GUP PIE AUNT BLAB BUZZ CANT CLAT CONK COZE DIRT NEWS TALK CAUSE CLACK CLASH CLYPE COOSE CRACK

FERLY FRUMP GOSSY SIEVE YENTA BABBLE CACKLE CADDLE CALLET CAMPER CLAVER CUMMER FERLIE JANGLE KIMMER NORATE TATTLE TITTLE CLATTER COMPERE GOSTHER HASHGOB NASHGAB SCANDAL TATTLER TRATTLE CAUSERIE CHITCHAT GOSSIPRY QUIDNUNC SCHMOOZE NEWSMONGER
GOSSIPY BUZZY NEWSY CHATTY
GOTH GOTHIAN SUIOGOTH VISIGOTH
GOTHAM ABDERA
GOTHAMITE ABDERITE
GOTHIC OGIVAL
GOTTERDAMMERUNG
(CHARACTER IN —) HAGEN GUNTHER GUTRUNE SIEGFRIED WALTRAUTE BRUNNHILDE
(COMPOSER OF —) WAGNER
GOUGE DIG PUG BENT SCUFF CHISEL FLUKAN GOUGER HOLLOW SCRIBE FLOOKAN SCORPER SELVAGE SELVEDGE STICKING
(— OUT) BULLDOZE
(V-TYPE —) VEINER
GOUGER CHISELLER
GOURD MATE PEPO LUFFA ABOBRA JICARA PATOLA ANGURIA DISHRAG HECHIMA CALABASH CUCURBIT PEPONIDA PEPONIUM
GOURMAND EPICURE GLUTTON GORMAND
GOURMET PALATE EPICURE GOURMAND
GOUT GUT CLOT DROP SPLASH PODAGRA PODAGRY CHIRAGRA ARTHRITIS
(SUFF.) AGRA
GOUTTE DROP ICICLE
GOUTWEED AXWEED ASHWEED ACHWEED AISEWEED BOLEWORT GOATWEED GOUTWORT
GOUTY PODAGRAL PODAGRIC
GOVERN RUN WIN CURB KING LEAD REDE REIN RULE SWAY WALD WARD WIND YEME GUIDE JUDGE REGLE STEER TREAT WIELD BRIDLE DIRECT MANAGE ORDAIN POLICE POLICY TEMPER COMMAND CONDUCT CONTROL PRESIDE REFRAIN DISPENSE DOMINATE IMPERATE MODERATE OVERRULE OVERSWAY POLICIZE REGULATE RESTRAIN
GOVERNED BENT
GOVERNESS ABBESS DUENNA FRAULEIN MISTRESS MADEMOISELLE
GOVERNING REGENT REGITIVE
GOVERNMENT GATE LAND RULE KREIS METRO POWER STATE STEER DURBAR HAVANA POLICY RULING CABINET CZARISM DIARCHY DYARCHY RECTION REGENCY REGIMEN TSARISM CIVILITY ENDARCHY GOBIERNO HEGEMONY ISOCRACY ISOCRYME KINGSHIP STEERING ABSOLUTISM
(— BY FEW) OLIGARCHY

(— BY GOD) THEONOMY
(— BY MOB) OCHLOCRACY
(— BY WEALTHY) PLUTOCRACY
(— BY WOMEN) GYNARCHY
(— BY 10) DECARCHY
(— BY 2) DIARCHY DUARCHY
(— OF CEYLON) DISSAVA
(— OF TURKEY) GATE PORTE
(ARBITRARY —) ABSOLUTISM
(CHURCH —) PRELACY
(INDIAN —) CIRCAR SIRCAR
(MALAYSIAN —) KOMPENI
(MOROCCAN —) MAGHZEN MAKHZAN
(PREF.) CRATO
(WITHOUT —) ANARCH(O)
(SUFF.) ARCH ARCHIC ARCHY CRACY CRAT(IC)
GOVERNMENTAL ARCHICAL
GOVERNOR BAN BEY DEY EARL KAID LORD NAIK TUTU VALI BANUS CLEON DEWAN DIWAN HAKIM NABOB NAZIM SHEIK SUBAH TUPAN AUTHOR DYNAST GRIEVE LEGATE MOODIR MYOWUN NAIGUE NAIQUE PATESI PENLOP RECTOR REGENT SACHEM SATRAP SHEIKH SHERIF TUCHUN WARDEN CATAPAN DAROGHA LEONATO PODESTA RECTRIX SERKALI SHEREEF TOPARCH TSUNGTU VICEROY WIELDER AUTOCRAT BURGRAVE ETHNARCH HOSPODAR LANDVOGT MISTRESS RESIDENT SUBAHDAR TETRARCH CASTELLAN PRESIDENT PROCONSUL
(— OF ALGIERS) DEY DISAWA
(— OF BURMA) WUN WOON
(— OF EGYPT) MUDIR
(— OF FORTRESS) ALCAIDE ALCAYDE
(— OF SHIRE) ALDERMAN
(— OF TAMMANY) SACHEM
(BYZANTINE —) EXARCH CATAPAN
(CEYLON —) DISAWA
(GERMAN —) LANDVOGT
(GREEK —) ETHNARCH
(JAPANESE —) SHOGUN TYCOON
(PAPAL —) LEGATE
(ROMAN —) TETRARCH
(SELJUK —) ATABEG ATABEK
(SPARTAN —) HARMOST
(TURKISH —) BEY WALI MUDIR KEHAYA
GOVERNOR-GENERAL VALI
GOWDIE SCULPIN
GOWK CUCKOO
GOWN GOR SAC GITE GORE HUKE JAMA RAIL SACK SILK TOGA BANIA DRESS FROCK GOUND HABIT JAMAH MANTO TABBY TOOSII BANIAN BANIYA CAFTAN CAMISE CANDYS CHITON JESUIT JOHNNY KIMONO KIRTLE KITTEL LEVITE MANTUA ARISARD CASSOCK GARMENT JOHNNIE SLAMKIN SULTANA SULTANE WRAPPER CAMISOLE GANDOURA MAZARINE PEIGNOIR
(HAWAIIAN —) MOLOKU MUUMUU

GOYA CURRANT
GOYIM GENTES
GRAB NAB NAP RAP GLAM GOPE GLAUM SCRAB CLUTCH COLLAR CRATCH DIPPER NIPPER NOBBLE SNATCH CRAPPLE GRABBLE GRAPNEL GRAPPLE NIPPERS
GRABEN TROUGH
GRABWEED BISHOPWEED
GRACE EST ORE BEAT ESTE GARB HELD SWAY ADORN COULE FAVOR HONOR MENSE MENSK MERCY SLIDE THANK VENUS BEAUTY BECOME BEDECK CHARIS POLISH RELISH THALIA AGGRACE CHARISM COMMEND DIGNITY FINESSE GRATIFY MELISMA MORDENT BACKFALL BEAUTIFY BLESSING DECORATE EASINESS ELEGANCE FELICITY GRATUITY LEVATION ORNAMENT
(— OF FORM) FLOW SWAY TOURNURE
GRACEFUL AIRY FEAT GENT BONNY GENTY GRATE COMELY FEATLY FELINE FLUENT GAINLY QUAINT SEEMLY SILKEN VENUST ELEGANT FITTING GENTEEL GRACILE SYLPHID WILLOWY CHARMING DELICATE GRACIOUS LEGGIERO MACEVOLE SWANLIKE SYLPHISH
(PREF.) ABRO HABRO
GRACEFULLY FAIR FEATLY HAPPILY LEGGIERO
GRACEFULNESS JOLLITY ELEGANCE
GRACELESS AWKWARD
GRACES CHARITES
GRACIOUS GOOD HEND HOLD KIND MILD CIVIL GODLY HAPPY LUCKY SUAVE WINLY BENIGN GENIAL GENTLE GOODLY KINDLY AFFABLE CORDIAL WINSOME BENEDICT DEBONAIR GENEROUS HANDSOME MERCIFUL PLEASING SOCIABLE BENIGNANT
GRACIOUSLY FAIR SWEETLY
GRACIOUSNESS GRACE MENSK FACILITY GRATUITY
GRACKLE BEO DAW JACKDAW BOATTAIL TINKLING TROOPIAL
GRADATION HUE CLINE ABLAUT CLIMAX NUANCE GEOCLINE STRENGTH
GRADE CUT BANK CHOP EVEN FORM MARK RANK SIZE STEP GLIDE LEVEL ORDER PLANE SCORE SIEGE STAGE ASCENT DEGREE RATING STAPLE TRIAGE FAILURE INCLINE INSPECT DEMISANG GRADIENT GRADUATE MERIDIAN STANDARD
(— DOWN) FAULT
(— LUMBER) SURVEY
(— OF BEEF) GOOD CUTTER
(— OF LUMBER) CULL
(— OF OAK) WAINSCOT
(— OF OFFICER) CORNET
(— ROAD) IMPROVE
(ABLAUT —) GUNA
(DESIGNED FOR USE IN —S 1-12) ELHI

(SUPERIOR —) SUPER
(THIRD —) FAIR
GRADER PLANER CLASSER SCRAPER
GRADIENT GRADE LAPSE SLOPE ASCENT INCLINE DOWNHILL
(SUFF.) CLINAL CLINE
GRADIN GRADINO PREDELLA
GRADUAL EASY FLAT SLOW GRAIL GENTLE LENTOUS STEPWISE PIECEMEAL
GRADUALLY GENTLY EDGINGLY GRADATIM INCHMEAL PIECEMEAL
GRADUATE GRAD GRADE ALUMNA DIVIDE FELLOW ALUMNUS GRADATE BACHELOR
(EISTEDDFOD —) OVATE
GRADUATED SCALAR MEASURED
GRADUATION CLICK
GRAFT BUD IMP PIE CION WORK GRAFF GRAVY INEYE SCION BOODLE INARCH PAYOLÂ SPLICE ENGRAFT IMPLANT JOBBERY SQUEEZE TOPWORK APPROACH BOODLING GRAFTING INSITION
GRAFTED ENTE
GRAFTER BOODLER
GRAFTING GRAFTAGE INSITION
(PREF.) GREFFO
GRAIL CUP GRAAL CHALICE SANGRAAL
GRAIN JOT RUN RYE WAY CORN CURN DANA KERN PILE RICE SAND SEED WALE WOOD EMMER FIBER FIBRE FUNDI GAVEL GLEBE GRIST PANIC SCRAP SPARK STUFF TRACE WHEAT ANNONA BARLEY BRAINS CEREAL CURRAN GROATS KERNEL FRUMENT GRANULE - PANICLE VICTUAL GRAINING PARTICLE STRAIGHT SWEEPAGE
(— FOR MUSH) KASHA
(— FROM MASH TUN) DRAINS
(— LEFT AFTER HARVEST) GAVEL SHACK
(— MEASURE) THRAVE
(— OF BOARD) BEAT
(— OF CORN) PICKLE
(— OF GOLD) PIPPIN
(— OF WOOD) BATE
(CHAFF OF —) BRAN
(COARSE —) THIRD
(COARSELY GROUND —) MEAL GRITS KIBBLE
(DAMAGED —) SALVAGE
(EAR OF —) SPIKE RISSOM RIZZON
(GERMINATED —) MALT
(GROUND —) GRIST
(HANDFUL OF —) REAP
(HULLED —) GRITS GROUT GROATS SHELLING
(HUSKED —) SHEALING SHILLING
(MILLET —) CUSCUS
(MIXED —) MASLIN
(MIXED —S) DREDGE
(PARCHED —) GRADDAN
(REFUSE —) SHAG DRAFF
(SACRIFICIAL —) ADOR
(SHOCK OF —) COP
(STACK OF —) HOVEL
(STORED —) MOW
(STREAKED —) ROEY
(PL.) PICKLES RAGGING

(PREF.) CHONDR(I)(IO)(O) COCC(O) GRANI GRANUL(I)(O) SITIO SITO
(SUFF.) COCCAL COCCIC
GRAIN BEETLE CADELLE
GRAINER DICER BOARDER
GRAINSMAN THROWER DRAFFMAN
GRAIN SORGHUM DURRA SHALLU
GRAM KHESARI
(MILLIONTH —) GAMMA
GRAMMAR DONAT SYNTAX GRAMARY PRISCIAN
(TYPE OF —) TAGMEMIC
GRAMMARIAN PRISCIAN
GRAMPUS ORC COWFISH DOLPHIN SPRINGER
GRANARY GOLA GUNJ SILO GOLAH GUNGE LATHE GARNER GIRNEL GRANGE HORREUM RESERVE CORNLOFT GRAINERY
GRAND OLD AIRY BRAW EPIC MAIN TALL CHIEF GREAT LOFTY NOBLE PROUD SHOWY SWELL WLONK ANDEAN AUGUST COSMIC EPICAL FAMOUS GLOBAL KINGLY LORDLY SIGHTY SUPERB SWANKY EXALTER IMMENSE STATELY SUBLIME COSMICAL FOREMOST GLORIOUS GORGEOUS IMPOSING MAJESTIC SPLENDID MAGNIFICENT
(PREF.) BEL
GRAND CANYON STATE ARIZONA
GRANDCHILD OE OY OYE
(GREAT —) IEROE
GRANDDAUGHTER NIECE
GRANDEE DON GRAND OMRAH BASHAW GRANDO MAGNATE
GRANDEUR POMP STATE ESTATE FIGURE PARADE MAJESTY ELEGANCE GRANDEZA HAUTESSE NOBILITY SPLENDOR VASTNESS
GRANDFATHER AIEL NONO BOBBY GRAMP ATAVUS GRAMPS BELSIRE GRANDAD GRANDPA GRANDFER GUIDSIRE
(GREAT —) NONO
(GREAT-GREAT-GREAT —) QUATRAYLE
GRAND HOTEL (AUTHOR OF —) BAUM
(CHARACTER IN —) ANNA OTTO FLAMM GAIGERN PREYSING ELISAVETA FLAEMMCHEN KRINGELEIN GRUSINSKAYA OTTERNSCHLAG
GRANDILOQUENT TALL HEROIC TURGID BOMBAST MAGNIFIC RHETORICAL
GRANDIOSE GRAND COSMIC TURGID SUBLIME COSMICAL IMPERIAL
GRANDISSIMUS (AUTHOR OF —) CABLE
(CHARACTER IN —) KEENE AURORA HONORE JOSEPH PALMYRE AGRICOLA CLOTILDE FUSILIER NANCANOU FROWENFIELD GRANDISSIMUS
GRANDMOTHER GRAM GRAN LUCKY NANNY GRANNY GUDAME LUCKIE BELDAME NOKOMIS BABUSHKA GRANDAME

GRANDMOTHERS (AUTHOR OF —) WESTCOTT
(CHARACTER IN —) JIM EVAN ROSE ALWYN FLORA HENRY NANCY RALPH TOWER CANNON SERENA LEANDER MARIANNE
GRANDPARENT TUTU TUPUNA
GRAND SLAM VOLE
GRANDSON NEPHEW NEPOTE
GRANITE MOYITE RUNITE GREISEN SYENITE ALASKITE RAPAKIVI PEGMATITE
(— STATE) NEWHAMPSHIRE
(DECOMPOSED —) GROWAN
(PREF.) PEGMATO SYENO
GRANITEWARE GRAYWARE
GRANNY TUTU BABUSHKA
GRANT AID FEU BOOK BOON CEDE ENAM GALE GIFT GIVE HEAR LEND LOAN MISE SEND STOW YARK ADMIT ALLOT ALLOW AWARD BONUS CHART COWLE FLOAT FUERO LEASE SEIZE SPARE TITHE YETTE YIELD ACCEDE ACCORD AFFORD ASSENT BESTOW BETAKE BETEEM BOUNTY CONFER DESIGN EXTEND FIRMAN IMPART JAGEER NOVATE OCTROI PATENT PERMIT REMISE ADJUDGE APPOINT COLLATE CONCEDE CONSENT DISPONE INDULGE LICENSE PRESENT PROMISE SUBSIDY TRIBUTE APPANAGE BESTOWAL CONTRACT DONATION EXCHANGE MONOPOLY PITTANCE TRANSFER CONCESSION ACKNOWLEDGE
(— AS PROPER) ACCORD
(— OF LAND) FEU ENAM GALE PATA SASAN CASATE
(— PERMISSION) ALLOW DISPENSE
(— RELIEF) FORGIVE
(— TIME) FRIST
(INDIAN —) ENAM COWLE SASAN JAGEER JAGHIR
(PL.) PORK
GRANTING IF ALTHO REMISE ALTHOUGH ACCORDANCE
GRANTOR LESSOR
GRANULAR CORN OPEN GRAINY
GRANULATE CORN KERN GRAIN SUGAR
GRANULATED CORN GRANULAR
GRANULATION SUGARING
GRANULE GRIT GRANUM LUCULE NODULE BIOBLAST GONIDIUM GRANULET
(ALTMANN'S —S) BIOPLAST
(ICE —S) FRAZIL
(SUFF.) PLAST
GRAPE UVA VINE BERRY GRAIN PINOT TOKAY ACINUS AGAWAM ISABEL MALAGA MONICA MUSCAT RAISIN VERDEA WORDEN CATAWBA CONCORD HAMBURG MALMSEY MISSION NIAGARA SULTANA CABERNET DELAWARE GRAPELET HANEPOOT ISABELLA LABRUSCA MALVASIA MORILLON MOUNTAIN MUSCATEL NUCULANE RIESLING SLIPSKIN SYLVANER THOMPSON VINIFERA MUSCADINE

(PL.) RAPE UVAE
(PREF.) ACINI UVI UVULO
GRAPEFRUIT POMELO POMOLO
POMMELO TORONJA
GRAPE HYACINTH MUSK
GRAPE JUICE MUST SAPA STUM
GRAPENUTS TERRAPIN
GRAPEROOT BERBERIS
GRAPES
(PREF.) (BUNCH OF —) BOTRY(O)
STAPHYL(O)
GRAPES OF WRATH (AUTHOR OF
—) STEINBECK
(CHARACTER IN —) AL JIM TOM
JOAD NOAH ROSE CASEY MULEY
CONNIE GRAVES RUTHIE
WINFIELD
GRAPESTONE
(PREF.) ACINI
GRAPEVINE
(PREF.) AMPEL(O)
GRAPH CHART CURVE OGIVE
TRACE CONTOUR DIAGRAM
PROFILE ISOPLETH
GRAPHIC PICTORIAL PICTURESQUE
GRAPHITE WAD KISH LEAD WADD
KEESH PENCIL PLUMBAGO
MODERATOR
GRAPNEL CROW DRAG GRAB
CREEP CREEPER GRABBLE
GRAPPLE SNIGGER GRABHOOK
GRAPPLE DOG CLOSE GRASP
GRIPE LATCH BUCKLE CLINCH
GRABBLE GRAPNEL GRIPPLE
SNIGGER SNIGGLE WRESTLE
(— QUARRY) BIND
GRAPPLING IRON CLIP DRAG
CLASP CRAMP CORVUS CRAMPER
CRAMPON CREEPER GRAPNEL
GRAPPLE HARPAGO
GRAPTOLITHA XYLINA
GRASP HUG NAP SEE CLAM CLAW
CLUM FAKE FANG FIST GLAM
GRAB GRIP HAND HENT HOLD
SNAP SPAN TAKE VICE CATCH
CINCH CLAMP CLASP CLAUT
CLEUK GRIPE GROPE LATCH
SAVVY SEIZE SENSE SHAKE
SPEND CLENCH CLINCH CLUTCH
COLLAR FATHOM GOUPEN
RUMBLE SNATCH CLAUGHT
COMPASS ENCLOSE GRAPPLE
GRIPPLE SMITTLE CONCEIVE
HANDFAST HOLDFAST
(— FULLY) SWALLOW
(— MENTALLY) ENVISAGE
(— OF REALITY) EPIPHANY
(PREF.) CHADA
GRASPING HARD NIPPY SNACK
GRABBY GREEDY GRIPPY HAVING
TAKING BROKING MISERLY
PUGGING COVETOUS HANDGRIP
AVARICIOUS
GRASS BON FAG FOG POA RAY
BENT COIX DISS DOOB GAMA
HERB ICHU KANS KUSA MUNJ
MUSK RAGI TARE TORE USAR
ANKEE BARIT BROME COGON
COUCH CROFT DRAWK DRINN
FLAWN FUNDI GARSE GIRSE
GLAGA GRAMA HARIF HAVER
HICHU ILLUK KOGON KUSHA
KWEEK MELIC MUHLY PANIC

QUILA REESK ROOSA SEREH SPIRE
STIPA SUDAN ZORRA BARLEY
BHABAR BHARTI DARNEL
EMOLOA FESCUE FIORIN GLUMAL
KIKUYU QUITCH RAGGEE REDTOP
RIPGUT SCUTCH TOETOE TWITCH
ZACATE AMOURET CANNACH
DOGFOOT ESPARTO EULALIA
FESTUCA FINETOP FOXTAIL
GALLETA GOLDEYE HERBAGE
HORDEUM JARAGUA MATWEED
MUSCOVY PANICLE PASTURE
PIGROOT SETARIA SORGHUM
TIMOTHY TOCUSSO TUSSOCK
VETIVER ZACATON AEGILOPS
BLUESTEM BROWNTOP CALFKILL
CAMALOTE CELERITY COCKSPUR
DOGSTAIL DRAWLING DROPSEED
EELGRASS ELEUSINE FINEBENT
GAMELOTE MANGRASS
MATGRASS PASPALUM
SANDBURR SANDSPUR SANDSTAY
SPANIARD SPARTINA SPINIFEX
SWEEPAGE TEOSINTE WHITETOP
MARIJUANA
(— AMONG GRAIN) DRAWK
(— FOR STOCK) EATAGE
(— FOR THATCHING) BANGO
(— ON BORDER OF FIELD) RAND
(— READY FOR REAPING) SWATH
SWATHE
(AROMATIC —) KHUS CUSCUS
KHUSKHUS
(BEACH —) STAR
(BERMUDA —) DOOB SCUTCH
(COARSE —) FAG DISS TATH
COGON REESK LALANG SNIDDLE
(COUCH —) CUTCH KWEEK QUITCH
SCUTCH STROIL SQUITCH
(CURED —) HAY
(DEAD —) FOG FOGGAGE
(DITCH —) ENALID
(GOOSE —) CLIVERS CLEAVERS
(MEADOW —) POA
(NUT —) COCO COCOA
(ORCHARD —) DOGFOOT
(PART OF —) AWN TIP APEX CULM
LEAF NODE ROOT STEM BLADE
BRACT GLUME SHOOT FLORET
FLOWER LIGULE SHEATH TILLER
PEDICEL RHIZOME SPIKELET
(PASTURE —) TORE GRAMMA
(POVERTY —) HEATH
(QUAKING —) SHAKER
(REED —) CARRIZO
(REEDLIKE —) BENT DISS
(SUDAN —) GARAWI
(SWEET —) SORGO
(PREF.) CHORTO GRAMIN(I)(O)
HERBI
GRASS-EATING
(PREF.) POE
GRASSERIE JAUNDICE
GRASSHOPPER GRIG CICADA
HOPPER QUAKER SAWYER TETTIX
ACRIDID CRICKET KATYDID
SKIPPER ACRIDIAN LANGOSTA
GRASSLAND HAM LEA RAKH VELD
VELDT BOTTOM MEADOW
PATANA LEYLAND PASTURE
SAVANNA
(TRACT OF —) PRAIRIE
(PL.) SCHIH

GRASS PEA LANG KHESARI
GRASSQUIT QUAT QUIT CIVITE
GRASS TREE BLACKBOY
GRASSY HERBY
GRATE JAR FRET GRIT RASP
CHARK CHIRK DANDY DEVIL
GRIDE GRIND RANGE STOVE
ABRADE CHAFER SCRAPE SCREAR
SCREEK SCROOP GRATING
MANGRATE
(FALSE —) DANDY
GRATEFUL KIND SAPID WELCOME
THANKFUL
GRATEFULNESS GRATUITY
GRATIANO (BROTHER OF —)
BRABANTIO
(WIFE OF —) NERISSA
GRATIFICATION GLUT GUST
LUXURY RELISH REWARD SATIETY
DELICACY GRATUITY PLEASURE
TICKLING SATISFACTION
GRATIFIED GLAD PROUD
CHARMED CONTENT PLEASED
GRATIFY PAY BABY FEED LUST
AMUSE FEAST FLESH GRACE
HUMOR MIRTH QUEME SAVOR
SERVE STILL WREAK ARRIDE
FOSTER OBLIGE PAMPER PLEASE
REGALE SALUTE TICKLE AGGRATE
CONTENT DELIGHT FLATTER
GLADDEN INDULGE SATISFY
PLEASURE
(— THE PALATE) SEASON
GRATIFYING GOOD COMELY
DELICATE GRATEFUL
GRATING GRID HACK HARD HOCK
JACK RACK CRATE CRUDE GRILL
HARSH RANGE RASPY TRAIL
BAFFLE CRATCH GITTER GRILLE
HOARSE RUGGED WICKET
BAFFLER ECHELLE ECHELON
BABRACOT CATAPULT GRIDIRON
METALLIC SCRANNEL STRIDENT
PORTCULLIS
GRATIS FREE FREELY BUCKSHEE
GRATITUDE THANK THANKS
GRATUITY
GRATUITOUS FREE WANTON
BASELESS NEEDLESS
GRATUITY FEE TIP BOON DASH
VAIL PILON SPIFF SPILL BOUNTY
CUMSHAW DASTURI DOUCEUR
PRESENT PRIMAGE BAKSHISH
BONAMANO BUCKSHEE
COURTESY DUSTOORI GRATUITO
REAPDOLE PERQUISITE
(CHRISTMAS —) BOX
(PL.) LARGESSE
GRAVE BED DRY LOW PIT SAD
URN BALK BASS BIER CELL CIST
DEEP DELF FOSS GRIT HIGH
HOME KIST LAIR LAKE MOLD
MOOL RUDE SADE SAGE TOMB
URNA DELFT FOSSE GRAFF
GROVE HEAVY MOULD SHEOL
SOBER STAID STIFF SUANT VAULT
BURIAL DEMURE GRIEVE HEARSE
SEDATE SEVERE SOLEMN SOMBER
SOMBRE STEADY AUSTERE
EARNEST FUNERAL PITHOLE
SERIOSO SERIOUS
SOBERLY CATONIAN
DECOROUS MATRONAL

SERMONIC SATURNINE
GRAVECLOTHES LINEN
CEREMENTS
GRAVEDIGGER RATEL BEDRAL
BURIER FOSSOR PITMAN BEDERAL
GRAVEL GRIT ARENA GEEST GRAIL
CHESIL RANGLE SAMMEL SHILLA
BALLAST CALICHE CHANNEL
RATCHEL SHINGLE STANNER
BLINDING
(— AND SAND) DOBBIN
(— DEPOSIT) LEAD
(— IN KIDNEYS) ARENA
(LOOSE —) SLITHER
(SCREENED —) HOGGINS
(PREF.) CROCO
GRAVELLY HASKY CHISELLY
GLAREOUS
GRAVELY SADLY DEEPLY
GRAVE MOUND TUMULUS
GRAVER BURIN STYLE PLASTIC
SCORPER
GRAVESTONE BAUTA PLANK
STELA STELE STONE TABLE
CIPPUS JUMPER THROUGH
GRAVEYARD CEMETERY
GRAVID HEAVY WOMBED
PREGNANT
GRAVIMETER DOODLEBUG
GRAVITATIONAL UNIT SLUG
GRAVITY WEIGHT DIGNITY
EARNEST SOBRIETY
GRAVY JUS SOP BREE FOND LEAR
BLANC BUNCE JIPPER
GRAY ASH BAT FOG ASHY BEAR
BLAE BLUE DOVE DUSK GREW
GRIS GULL HOAR IRON LEAD SALT
ACIER CAMEL CRANE HOARY
LYART MOUSE STEEL WHITE
CASTOR CINDER DENVER FROSTY
FRUSTY GREIGE GRISLY ISABEL
LEADEN NICKEL NUTRIA PEWTER
QUAKER STRING BLUNKET
CRUISER GRANITE GRIZARD
GRIZZLE GRIZZLY HUELESS
MURINUS NEUTRAL PELICAN
PILGRIM SARKARA SPARROW
ALUMINUM BLONCKET CHARCOAL
CINEREAL CINEROUS EVENGLOW
FELDGRAU PLATINUM PLYMOUTH
(DARKEST —) BLACK
(GOOSE —) LAMA
(MOLE —) TAUPE
(MOTH —) SHEEPSKIN
(STREAKED WITH —) LYARD
(VIOLET —) GRIDELIN
(PREF.) GLAUC(O) POLI(O)
GRAYBACK DOWITCH GRAYCOAT
GREYBACK
GRAY CRANE COOLEN COOLUNG
GRAY DRAB ACIER
GRAYISH NEUTRAL
GRAYLING PINK OMBRE UMBER
HERRING UMBRANA BLUEFISH
SALMONID
GRAYNESS CANITIES
GRAY PARROT JAKO
GRAYSBY CONY CONEY
GRAY WHALE RIPSACK GRAYBACK
HARDHEAD
GRAZE BITE CROP FEED SCUR SKIM
AGIST BRUSH GRASS GRIDE
RANGE SCAMP SCUFF SHAVE

SKIFF SKIRR STOCK BROWSE
CREASE FODDER GLANCE RIPPLE
SCRAPE SCRAZE PASTURE
GRAZIER PASTURER SQUATTER
TREKBOER
GRAZING BIT FEED GRASS COLLOP
RASANT FOLDING PASCUAGE
GREASE COOM SAIM SEAM ADEPS
BLECK COOMB SMEAR SPICK
ARMING AXUNGE CREESH
ENSEAM LIQUOR POMATE
ALEMITE SAINDOUX
(— IN HARD CAKES) SEAK
(PIG'S —) MORT
(WOOL —) YOK DEGRAS LANOLIN
(PREF.) SEBI
GREASE-HEELS GRAPES
GREASER DOPER
GREASEWOOD CHICO CHEMIZO
GREASY FAT GLET OILY RICH
FATTY PORKY YOLKY SMEARY
TRAINY CREESHY PINGUID
TALLOWY UNCTUOUS
GREAT BIG FAR FAT FIT OLD BARO
DEEP DREE FELL FINE GONE
GURT HUGE KEEN MAIN MUCH
RIAL SOME TALL UNCO VAST VILE
AMPLE BURRA CHIEF FELON
GRAND LARGE MEKIL STOUR
SWEET SWELL TOUGH YEDER
FIERCE GAPING HEROIC MICKLE
NATION STRONG CAPITAL
EMINENT EXTREME GALLOWS
HOWLING IMMENSE INTENSE
STAVING TITANIC VIOLENT
VOLUMED ALMIGHTY CRACKING
ELEVATED ENORMOUS FAVORITE
GALACTIC GALAXIAN GIGANTIC
HORRIBLE INFINITE PRECIOUS
TERRIFIC MONSTROUS
MAGNIFICENT
(— LAND) ALASKA
(IMMEASURABLY —) ABYSMAL
(TOO —) OVERDUE
(VERY —) MAIN SORE AWFUL
STEEP ARDENT DEADLY IMMANE
INGENT MORTAL EXTREME
FRANTIC GHASTLY HOWLING
SUBLIME DREADFUL MOUNTAIN
MONUMENTAL
(PREF.) ARCH MAGN(I) MAHA
MEG(A) MEGAL(O)
(HOW —) QUANTI
(SUFF.) MEGALY
GREAT AUK PENGUIN PINWING
GAREFOWL
GREAT BRITAIN (SEE ENGLAND)
GREATCOAT GREGO JEMMY
JOSEPH POSTEEN OVERCOAT
GREATER SUPERIOR
(PREF.) MEIZO
GREATER STITCHWORT HEAD
SNAPPER HEADACHE SNAPJACK
SNAPWORT
GREATER YELLOWLEGS YELPER
GREATEST UTMOST EXTREME
MAXIMAL
(— POSSIBLE) ALL SUPREME
**GREAT EXPECTATIONS (AUTHOR
OF —)** DICKENS
(CHARACTER IN —) JOE PIP ABEL
BIDDY DOLGE SARAH ORLICK
PHILIP PIRRIP POCKET PROVIS

BENTLEY DRUMMLE ESTELLA
GARGERY HERBERT JAGGERS
MATTHEW HAVISHAM MAGWITCH
COMPEYSON PUMBLECHOOK
GREAT GATSBY (AUTHOR OF —)
FITZGERALD
(CHARACTER IN —) JAY TOM NICK
BAKER DAISY MCKEE GATSBY
GEORGE JORDAN MYRTLE
WILSON BUCHANAN CARRAWAY
CATHERINE WOLFSHIEM
GREAT-GRANDCHILD IEROE
GREAT GRANDFATHER NONO
BESAIEL GRANDSIR
GREAT LAKE ERIE HURON
ONTARIO MICHIGAN SUPERIOR
GREATLY FAR MUY FELL MUCH
AMAIN SWITH FINELY MAINLY
STRONG SWYTHE SWEETLY
WOUNDLY MIGHTILY
GREAT MOLE RAT ZEMMI ZEMNI
GREATNESS FORCE GRANDEUR
GRANDEZA MUCHNESS
GREAT RAGWEED KINGHEAD
GREAT TITMOUSE SHARPSAW
GREAVE JAMB JAMBE JAMBEAU
(PL.) CRAP HOSE GRAVES
GREBE LEAD LOON DIVER GAUNT
WITCH DIPPER DOBBER DUCKER
FINFOOT HENBILL PYGOPOD
ARSEFOOT CARGOOSE DABCHICK
DIDAPPER GRUIFORM
GRECE GRICE DEGREE GRISSEN

GREECE

ANCIENT LOCATIONS: ELIS DORIS
PYLOS ACHAEA ACTIUM ATTICA
DELPHI EPIRUS HELLAS LOCRIS
PHOCIS SPARTA THEBES TIRYNS
BOEOTIA CORINTH EPEIROS
LACONIA MACEDON MEGARIS
MYCENAE PAESTUM
ARMY UNIT: TAXIS
BAY: ELEUSIS SALAMIS PHALERON
CAPE: KRIOS MALEA SPADA
AKRITAS MATAPAN SIDEROS
DREPANON GRAMBYSA
TAINARON
CAPITAL: ATHENS ATHENAI
COIN: OBOL HECTE DIOBOL
LEPTON STATER DRACHMA
DIOBOLON
COLUMN: DORIC IONIC
CORINTHIAN
DANCE: PYRRHIC ROMAIKA
DIALECT: COAN ATTIC DORIC
ELEAN EOLIC IONIC AEOLIC
MELIAN THERAN ACHAEAN
ARCADIAN
DISTRICT: ARTA ELIS CANEA CHIOS
CORFU CRETE DRAMA EVROS
KHIOS PELLA SAMOS ZANTE
ACHAEA ACHAIA ATTICA
EPIRUS EUBOEA KILKIS KNANIA
KOZANE LARISA LESBOS
LEUKAS PHOCIS PIERIA SERRAI
THRACE XANTHE AETOLIA
ARCADIA ARGOLIS BOEOTIA
CORINTH KAVALLA LACONIA
LARISSA LASETHI MTATHOS
PREVEZA RHODOS CYCLADES
IOANNINA KARDITSA KASTORIA
MAGNESIA MESSENIA

PHLORINA RETHYMNE
SALONIKA THESSALY TRIKKALA
MACEDONIA
GULF: VOLOS ATHENS MESARA
PATRAI PATRAS ARGOLIS
CORINTH KAVALLA KNANION
LACONIA LEPANTO MESSINI
RENDINA SARONIC STRIMON
MESSENIA SALONIKA SINGITIC
THERMAIC TORONAIC
HOME OF GODS: OLYMPUS
ISLAND: DIA IOS KEA KOS NIO
CEOS KEOS MILO SYME SYRA
CHIOS CORFU CRETE DELOS
KASOS KHIOS LEROS MELOS
MILOS NAXOS PAROS PAXOI
PAXOS PSARA RODOS SAMOS
SARIA SYROS TELOS TENOS
THERA THIRA TINOS ZANTE
ANAPHE ANDROS CANDIA
CERIGO CHALKE EUBOEA
EVVOIA GAVDOS IKARIA ITHACA
ITHAKI LEMNOS LESBOS LEUKAS
LEVKAS PATMOS RHENEA
RHODES SIFNOS SKYROS
THASOS AMORGOS CIMOLUS
CYTHERA KERKYRA KIMOLOS
KYTHERA KYTHNOS LEVITHA
MYKONOS NISYROS SALAMIS
SIPHNOS KALYMNOS MYTILENE
SANTORIN SERIPHOS
ISLANDS: IONIAN CYCLADES
SPORADES DODECANESE
STROPHADES
LAKE: KARLA VOLVE COPAIS
KOPAIS PRESPA TOPOLIA
KASTORIA TACHINOS VISTONIS
LETTER: MU NU PI XI CHI ETA PHI
PSI RHO TAU BETA IOTA ZETA
ALPHA DELTA GAMMA KAPPA
OMEGA SIGMA THETA LAMBDA
EPSILON OMICRON UPSILON
MARKET PLACE: AGORA
MEASURE: PIK BEMA PIKI POUS
BARIL CADOS CHOUS CUBIT
DIGIT MARIS PEKHE PODOS
PYGON XYLON ACAENA BACHEL
BACILE BARILE COTULA DICHAS
GRAMME HEMINA KOILON
ORGYIA PALAME PECHYS
SCHENE AMPHORA CHENICA
CHOENIX CYATHOS DIAULOS
HEKTEUS METRETA STADION
STADIUM STREMMA CONDYLOS
DAKTYLOS DEKAPODE
DOLICHOS MEDIMNOS
METRETES PALAISTE PLETHRON
PLETHRUM SPITHAME
STATHMOS
MOUNTAIN: IDA IDHI OSSA ATHOS
PAROS ELIKON PARNON PELION
PILION WITSCH HELICON
OLYMPUS VURANON
KRAGNOVO SMOLIKAS
TAYGETOS PARNASSUS
MOUNTAINS: OETA OTHRYS
PINDUS RODOPI RHODOPE
HYMETTOS TAYGETUS
NAME: ELLAS HELLAS
PENINSULA: ACTE AKTE AKTI
MOREA SITHONIA
PELOPONNESE
PORT: SYRA CORFU PYLOS SYROS

VOLOS MEGARA PATRAI
PATRAS KAVALLA KERKYRA
PIRAEUS SALONIKA
RIVER: IRI ARDA ARTA AURO
AXIOS DOONA EVROS LERNA
ALFIOS NESTOS PENEUS PINIOS
STRUMA VARDAR ALPHEUS
EUROTAS EVROTAS ILISSOS
PENEIOS ROUFIAS SARANTA
STRIMON ACHELOUS AKHELOOS
ALIAKMON KEPHISOS
RHOUPHIA
RUINS: DELOS PELLA SAMOS
CORINTH ELEUSIS ELEVSIS
ACROPOLIS
SEA: CRETE AEGEAN IONIAN
MIRTOON
STATE: PHOCIS
TOWN: IOS KEA KOS ARTA ELIS
KYME PETA SYME YDRA ADREA
AGYIA ARGOS CANEA CHIOS
CORFU DRAMA KARYA MELOS
NAXOS NEMEA PELLA POROS
PSARI PYLOS PYRGI SAMOS
SYROS TENOS VAMOS VATHY
VOLOS VYRON ZANTE ACTIUM
ATHENS CANDIA DAPHNI
DELPHI EDESSA ITHACA JANINA
KOZANE LARISA MEGARA
NIKHIA PATRAS RHODES SERRAI
SERRES SPARTA THEBES TIRYNS
XANTHE ATHENAI CORINTH
ELEUSIS KERKYRA LARISSA
MYCENAE PIRAEUS IOANNINA
KOMOTINE MARATHON
PHARSALA SALONIKA TRIKKALA
PERISTERI
VALLEY: NEMEA
VERNACULAR: DEMOTIC
WEIGHT: MNA OKA OKE MINA
OBOL LITRA LIVRE MANEH
POUND DIOBOL DRAMME
KANTAR OBOLOS OBOLUS
STATER TALENT CHALCON
CHALQUE DRACHMA DIOBOLON
TALANTON
WOMEN: THYIAD

GREED AVARICE AVIDITY HOGGERY
CUPIDITY
GREEDINESS AVARICE AVIDITY
GULOSITY
GREEDY AVID GAIR GORB YELP
EAGER GUTTY YIVER GRABBY
GUNDIE KITISH STINGY GLUTTON
GRIPPLE HOODOCK MISERLY
PIGGISH COVETOUS ESURIENT
GRASPING RAVENOUS LICKERISH
(PREF.) LICHNO
GREEK GREW ATTIC HADJI KOINE
METIC ARGIVE IONIAN KLEPHT
ACHAIAN AEOLIAN GRECIAN
GRIFFON HELLENE GRECANIC
HELLADIC HELLENIC ITALIOTE
SICELIOT
(PREF.) GRAECO GRECO HELLENO
GREEN (ALSO SEE COLOR) LEEK
VERD VERT CRUDE FRESH
CALLOW VIRENT NOUVEAU
SINOPLE UNFIRED VERDANT
BAYBERRY IMMATURE NOUVELLE
VAGABOND VIRIDIAN
WEDGWOOD WOODLAND

(— MOUNTAIN STATE) VERMONT
(COOKED —S) SALAD
(NILE —) BOA
(PALE —) ALOE ALOES
(YELLOWISH —) GLAUZY ABSINTHE
GLAUCOUS
(PREF.) CHLOR(O) PRASEO PRASO
VERD(O) VIRID(I)
GREEN AMARANTH REDROOT
GREENBACK FROGSKIN
(PL.) GREEN LETTUCE
GREEN BAY TREE (AUTHOR OF —)
BROMFIELD
(CHARACTER IN —) CYON LILY
ELLEN GIGON IRENE JULIA SHANE
HATTIE WILLIE HARRISON
KRYLENKO TOLLIVER
GREENBRIER SMILAX
SARSAPARILLA
GREEN CORMORANT SHAG
GREENFISH BLUEFISH
GREENHEART BIBIRU BEBEERU
GREEN HERON KIALEE
GREENHORN JAY MUG YAP JAKE
PUTT IKONA GREENY SUCKER
SOFTHORN
GREENHOUSE STOVE GREENERY
HOTHOUSE ORANGERY
COOLHOUSE
GREENISH BERYL SANIOUS
GREENISH-YELLOW RESEDA

GREENLAND
AIR BASE: THULE
BAY: DISKO BAFFIN MELVILLE
CAPE: JAAL GRIVEL WALKER
BISMARCK BREWSTER
FAREWELL LOWENORN
CAPITAL: GODTHAAB
DISCOVERER: ERIC
MOUNTAIN: FOREL PAYER
KHARDYU GUNNBJORN
STRAIT: DAVIS DENMARK
TOWN: ETAH NORD THULE
UMANAK GODHAVN IVIGTUT
GODTHAAB JULIANEHAB
EGEDESMINDE SUKKERTOPPEN
HOLSTEINSBORG

GREENLING TROUT BOREGAT
BODIERON LORICATE ROCKFISH
GREEN MANSIONS (AUTHOR OF —)
HUDSON
(CHARACTER IN —) ABEL RIMA
NUFLO
GREEN MONKEY GUENON
GREENNESS VERD VERT VERDURE
VERDANCY VIRIDITY
GREEN ONION RARERIPE
GREEN PIKE JACK
GREENROOM FOYER
GREENSHANK TATTLER
GREENSTONE POUNAMU
GREEN SUNFISH REDEYE
GREENWEED WOODWAX
GREEN WOODPECKER ECCLE
SPRITE YAFFLE YOCKEL YUKKEL
HEWHALL HEWHOLE SNAPPER
SPEIGHT YAFFLER POPINJAY
WOODHACK WOODWALL
GREET CRY JOY CROW HAIL HALSE
ACCOST HERALD SALAAM SALUTE
ADDRESS RECEIVE WELCOME

GREETING HOW CIAO HIYA ALOHA
GREET HELLO HOWDY KOMBO
ACCOST CHEERO SALAAM SALUTE
SHALOM ADDRESS CHEERIO
COMMEND SLAINTE WELCOME
REMEMBRANCE
GREGARIOUS GREGAL SOCIAL
GREGE NUTRIA
GRENADA (CAPITAL OF —)
STGEORGES
(ISLAND OF —) CARRIACON
GRENADE EGG TROMBE GRENADO
FIREBALL PINEAPPLE
GRENADIER RATTAIL WHIPTAIL
GRENADINE FLORENCE
GRENDEL (SLAYER OF —) BEOWULF
GRETCHEN (BELOVED OF) FAUST
**GRETTIR THE STRONG (AUTHOR
OF —)** UNKNOWN
(CHARACTER IN —) ATLI GEST
GLAM GRIM JARL ANGLE BJORN
EINAR ASMUND ILLUGI OGMUND
OXMAIN SKEGGI STEINN THORIR
DROMUND GRETTIR MAKSSON
HALLMUND LONGHAIR REDBEARD
SNAEKOLL STEINVOR THORFINN
THORGILS SLOWCOACH
THORBJORN THORSTEINN
GREY (SEE GRAY)
GREYHOUND GREW SALUKI
BANJARA SAPLING TUMBLER
WHIPPET
GRID BOUCAN BUCCAN GRIDDLE
GRIDIRON
(CIRCULAR —) DISC DISK
GRIDDLE COMAL GRILL GIRDLE
GRILLE BRANDER
GRIDDLE CAKE AREPA LATKE
CHAPATTY CORNCAKE FLAPJACK
SLAPJACK
GRIDIRON GRID GRILL TRAIL
BRANDER BROILER GRIDDLE
GRIEF VEX WOE CARE DILL DOLE
DOOL DREE HARM HURT MOAN
MOOD PAIN RUTH SORE TEEN
TINE AGONY DOLOR GRAME
RUING TRIAL WRONG BARRAT
DESIRE MISHAP REGRET SORROW
STOUND WONDER ANGUISH
CHAGRIN EMOTION FAILURE
OFFENSE SADNESS THOUGHT
TROUBLE WAESUCK WAYMENT
DISASTER DISTRESS HARDSHIP
(— STEM) KELLY
(SECRET —) CANKER
(PREF.) DOLORI LYPO
GRIESEN ZWITTER
GRIEVANCE BEEF GRIEF PEEVE
BURDEN BYGONE GRAVAMEN
HARDSHIP
GRIEVE VEX CARE DOLE DUMP
EARN ERME HONE HURT PAIN
PINE SIGH WAIL GRAME GRIPE
MOURN SORRY WOUND YEARN
ATHINK CORSIE LAMENT REPINE
SORROW AFFLICT CHAGRIN
CONDOLE GRIZZLE TROUBLE
WAYMENT COMPLAIN DISTRESS
GRIEVED WOE GRAME SORRY
GRIEVING SORRY
GRIEVOUS SAD DEAR DEEP DERF
HARD SORE CHARY DIRTY GRIEF
HEAVY SORRY WEARY BITTER

DREARY SEVERE SHREWD
CAREFUL HEINOUS WEIGHTY
DOLOROUS ATROCIOUS
GRIEVOUSLY DERNLY FOULLY
SORELY HEAVILY
GRIFFE SPUR
GRIFFIN GRIPE GRYPHON
EPIMACUS
GRILL REJA BRACE BROIL DEVIL
TRAIL AFFLICT BROILER GRILLADE
GRILLE FACE REJA HAZARD
GRILLROOM GROOM
GRILSE PEAL SEWIN FINNAC
GRAWLS BOTCHER FORKTAIL
GRIM DOUR GASH SOUR BLEAK
CRUEL GAUNT STERN GRIMLY
GRISLY HORRID SULLEN TORVID
GHASTLY GRIZZLY HIDEOUS
MACABRE TORVOUS PITILESS
RUTHLESS
GRIMACE MOP MOW MUG POT
FACE GIRN IRPE MOUE MUMP
YIRN FLEER MOUTH SNEER
SNOOT GIMBLE SHEYLE STITCH
MURGEON SIMAGRE
GRIMALKIN CAT HAG MOLL WITCH
BELDAM HARRIDAN
GRIME DIRT SMUT COLLY SMOUCH
SMUTCH
GRIMME COQUETOON
GRIMNESS TORVITY
GRIMP CLIMB
GRIMY DINGY GRUBBY SCABROUS
GRIN DRAD GIRN MUMP FLEER
RISUS SNEER SIMPER GRIZZLE
GRIND DIG GAP DONE DRAY CHEW
FILE GRUN MILL MULL MUZZ
SMUG SWOT CRUSH FLOAT
FLOUR GRATE GRIDE GRIST
QUERN CRUNCH DRUDGE
POWDER EMERIZE GRISTLE
SWOTTER LEVIGATE
(— COARSELY) KIBBLE
(— DIAMONDS) SKIVE
(— SMALL) BRAY
(— TEETH) GNASH GRATE GRINT
GRISBET
GRINDER CRASH MULLER BRUISER
GRINDING BREAK MOLAR
ABRASION
(— OF CORN) MULTURE
(— OF MEAL) BREAK GRIST
(— OF TEETH) BRUXISM
GRINDSTONE MANO PAVER
STONE
GRIP BITE BURR CLIP FANG FIST
HOLD HOLT TAKE VICE CHOKE
CINCH CLAMP CLASP GRASP
GRIPE PINCH SALLY SEIZE BARREL
CLINCH CLUTCH CRADLE FREEZE
EMBRACE HANDBAG HOLDING
SEIZURE ADHESION FOOTLOCK
HANDFAST HANDGRIP
HANDHOLD STAGEHAND
(— OF A SWORD) FUSEAU
(— OF BELL ROPE) SALLY
(— TO A SPAR) DOG
GRIPE CRAB FRIB BITCH CREATE
GROUSE HOLLER KVETCH NATTER
SNATCH GRIZZLE COMPLAIN
GRIPER GRIZZLER
GRIPES TORMINA
GRIPING GRIPPLE PINCHING

GRIPPER KEEPER NIPPER
GRIPPING STONY STONEY
GRIQUA BASTARD BASTAARD
GRISKINISSA (HUSBAND OF —)
ARTAXAMINOUS
GRISLY GRIM GHASTLY GRIZZLY
HIDEOUS GRUESOME
GRISON HURON GALICTIS
GRIST PABULUM
GRISTLE CARTILAGE
GRIT SAND GRIND PLUCK BOTTOM
BRAVERY DECISION GRITROCK
BURSTONE
(PL.) CUTLINGS
GRITH MUND GYRTH
GRITTY SANDY SHARP GRISTY
CHISELLY SABULINE SABULOUS
GRIVET TOTA WAAG GEUNON
NISNAS
GRIZZLED GRISLY STREAKED
GRIZZLY BEAR (— STATE)
CALIFORNIA
GROAN MOAN ROME GRANK
GRUNT STECH COMPLAIN
GROAT BIT FLAG GILL HARP
GROATS
(PREF.) ATHERO
GROCER SPICER EPICIER PEPPERER
GROCERY BODEGA PULPERIA
GROG RUMBO TEMPER CHAMOTTE
GROGGERY SHANTY GROGSHOP
GROGGY SHAKY UNSTEADY
WAVERING
GROGSHOP SHANTY DOGGERY
GROGGERY
GROIN LISK PIER SHARE CLUTCH
INGUEN GRUNZIE
(PREF.) INGUIN(O)
GROMMET BECKET COLLAR
EYELET CRINGLE GARLAND
GROMWELL PUCCOON REDROOT
SALFERN GRAYMILL
GROOM LAD MAFU NEAT SYCE
CURRY DRESS MAFOO STRAP
SWIPE TIGER BARBER BATMAN
FETTLE FOGGER GUINEA MEHTAR
OSTLER HOSTLER MARSHAL
COISTREL COISTRIL GROOMLET
STRAPPER
GROOVE RUT BEAD DADO GAIN
KERF LUCE PORT RAKE SLOT
CANAL CHASE CROZE FLUTE
GLYPH GORGE GOUGE GUIDE
JOINT QUIRK REGAL RIFLE RIGOL
SCARF SCORE STRIA SWAGE
CREASE CULLIS FULLER FURROW
GUTTER KEYWAY RABBET
RAGGLE RAGLET REBATE RIFFLE
RUNNER SCROBE SULCUS
THROAT TRENCH CHAMFER
CHANNEL GARLAND KEYHOLE
PLOWING SULCATE BOTHRIUM
GROOVING PHILTRUM
CANNELURE VALLECULA
(— IN AUGER) POD
(— IN COLUMN) FLUTE
(— IN MASONRY) RAGGLE
(— IN STAVES) CROZE
(— IN STONE) JAD
(— IN TIRE) SIPE
(— ON UPPER LIP) PHILTRUM
(— ON WEEVIL) SCROBE
(— ON WHALE) SCARF

(— UNDER COPING) GORGE
(—S ON ROCK) LAPIES
(RECTANGULAR —) REGLET
GROOVED FLUTED MILLED
EXARATE SULCATE
GROOVER FLUTER
GROPE CLAM CLAW FEEL POKE
RIPE GLAUM GRAIP FUMBLE
GUDDLE GRABBLE GRAPPLE
GROPPLE GRUBBLE SCRABBLE
GROSBEAK FINCH HAWFINCH
GROSGRAIN ROYALE
GROSS FAT DULL FOUL LUMP
RANK BROAD CRASS FOGGY
GREAT GUTTY LARGE MACRO
SLUMP THICK WHOLE ANIMAL
COARSE EARTHY FILTHY GREASY
SORDID STRONG BLOATED
FULSOME CLODDISH FLAGRANT
INDECENT SLUTTISH
GROSSO MATAPAN
GROTESQUE ANTIC WOOZY
ROCOCO BAROQUE BIZARRE
CROTESCO FANCIFUL
GROTTO CAVE GROT ANTRE SPEOS
CAVERN LUPERCAL
CROUCH SULK CRANK GROUSE
SOURBALL SOURPUSS
GROUND SEW SOD SUE BASE
CLOD DIRT FOLD FOND GIST
LAND MOLD REST ROOT SOIL
STAY WOLD EARTH FIELD FIRTH
FOUND MOULD PLACE SCORE
SOLUM TRAIN TUTOR VENUE
CREASE MATTER REASON
SMACKED FORELAND INITIATE
(— AT TOP OF SHAFT) BANK
(— COVERED WITH RUBBLE) TITI
(— FOR COMPLAINT) BEEF
(— OF FLAG) FIELD
(— OF LACE) FOND
(— OVERLYING TIN DEPOSIT)
BURDEN
(BOGGY —) SOG CARR SNAPE
(BROKEN —) HAG
(BURYING —) CEMETERY
(CAMPING —) AUTOCAMP
(COLLEGE —S) CAMPUS
(DUMPING —) TIP TOOM
(FALLOW —) BRISE
(FEEDING —) HAUNT
(FIRM-HOLDING —) LANDFANG
(FISHING —) HAAF
(FROZEN —) TJAELE
(GRASSY —) LAWN CLOWRE
(GRAZING —) HERDWICK
(HARD —) HARDPAN
(HUNTING —) CHASE
(LOW —) INCH SWALE TALAO
(MIDDLE —) LIMBO
(MUDDY —) SLOB
(NEW ENCLOSED —) TINING
(ORIGINAL —) URGRUND
(PARADE —) MAIDAN
(PASTURE —) HIRSEL
(RECREATION —) PARK
(RISING —) HURST HYRST
(SLOPING —) CLEVE
(SOLID —) HILL
(SPONGY —) BOG
(SWAMPY —) PUXY CRIPPLE
(UNCULTIVATED —) JUNGLE
(UNUSED —) AREA

(WET WASTE —) MOOR REESK
(PL.) GROUT STOCK
(PREF.) CHAMAE CHAME GE(O)
PEDO SOLI
(ON THE —) HUMI
GROUND HEMLOCK SHINWOOD
GROUND HOG MARMOT
GROUND IVY GILL HEWE HOVE
JILL YARROW ALEHOOF CATFOOT
GAGROOT MILFOIL TUNHOOF
FOALFOOT
GROUNDLESS IDLE FALSE
BASELESS
GROUNDLINE SETLINE
GROUNDMAN GRUNT
GROUNDMASS PASTE CEMENT
MATRIX
GROUNDNUT GOBBE PEANUT
PIGNUT
GROUND PINE FOXTAIL
STAGHORN
GROUNDSEL SIMSON DOGBUSH
SENCION SENECIO BINDWEED
BIRDSEED
GROUNDSMAN CURATOR
GROUND SQUIRREL GOPHER
GRINNY SUSLIK MEERKAT
SCIURID SOUSLIK SCIURINE
GROUND THRUSH PITTA
GROUNDWORK BASE FOND FUND
BASIS BOTTOM FUNDUS
GROUP MOB SET BAND BEVY BODY
CREW DECK FOLD GANG KNOT
PAIR RING SECT SORT STEW TREF
ARRAY BATCH BREED BUNCH
CLASS CLUMP COVEY FIRCA
FLOCK GENUS GLOBE PLUMP
SABHA SKULK SQUAD STACK
TALLY WHEEN CIRCLE CLUTCH
COHORT FAMILY GRUPPO PARCEL
RUBRIC AGGROUP BATTERY
BOILING BOUROCK BRACKET
CLASSIS CLUSTER COLLEGE
COMMUNE COMPANY CONSORT
FELLOWS FLUTTER QUOTITY
SECTION SEVERAL SOCIETY
ALLIANCE CATEGORY CLASSIFY
DIVISION FAISCEAU FLOTILLA
GROUPING
(— OF ANGELS) FLIGHT
(— OF ARTIFACTS) CACHE
(— OF BADGERS) CETE
(— OF BUILDINGS) BLOCK
(— OF CASTINGS) SPRAY
(— OF CATS) CLOWDER
(— OF CELLS) GLAND ISLET LAURA
CENTER CORONA EPITHEM
SEMILUNE
(— OF COMPUTER JOBS) BATCH
(— OF DECOYS) STOOL
(— OF DEITIES) CABEIRI
(— OF DIALECTS) AEOLIC
(— OF EELS) SWARM
(— OF EIGHT) OCTAD OCTET
OCTETTE
(— OF FAMILIES) FINE
(— OF FIVE) PENTAD CINQUAIN
(— OF FOUR) MESS QUARTET
(— OF FRIENDS) BUNCH
(— OF FURNISHINGS) ENSEMBLE
(— OF HAITIANS) COMBITE
COUMBITE
(— OF HOUSES) BOROUGH

(— OF HUTS) BUSTI KRAAL BUSTEE
(— OF ILLUSTRIOUS PERSONS)
PANTHEON
(— OF INDIAN STATES) AGENCY
(— OF ISOGLOSSES) BUNDLE
(— OF KINDRED) SIOL
(— OF KINSMEN) AHL
(— OF LAYMEN) COFRADIA
(— OF LIONS) PRIDE
(— OF LISTENERS) AUDIENCE
(— OF MARTENS) RICHESSE
(— OF MILITARY VEHICLES)
DEADLINE
(— OF MOLDINGS) DANCETTE
(— OF NINE) ENNEAD NONARY
(— OF NUCLEONS) SHELL
(— OF OFFSPRING) CLUTCH
(— OF ORGANISMS) FORM STRAIN
(— OF PARACHUTISTS) STICK
(— OF PERSONS) BAG CLUB KNOT
SWAD CROWD DROVE CIRCLE
GAGGLE KENNEL
(— OF RETORTS) BENCH SETTING
(— OF RUFFIANS) PUSH
(— OF SCHOLARS) ULAMA
(— OF SCULPTURE) MORTORIO
(— OF SEVEN) HEPTAD SEPTET
HEBDOMAD
(— OF SIX) HEXAD SENARY
(— OF SLAVES) COFFLE
(— OF SOILS) LATERITE
(— OF SOLDIERS) DRAFT COHORT
(— OF STARS) ASTERISM
(— OF STRATIFIED BEDS) FACIES
(— OF STUDENTS) SEMINAR
(— OF SYLLABLES) FOOT
(— OF SYMBOLS) FORMULA
(— OF SYMPTOMS) SYNDROME
(— OF TEN) DECADE DENARY
(— OF TENTS) CAMP CANVAS
(— OF THEATERS) CIRCUIT
(— OF THREE) TRIO GLEEK TRIAD
TRINE
(— OF TRAITS) COMPLEX
(— OF TROUT) HOVER
(— OF VERSES) SYSTEM
(— OF WEAPONS) NEST
(— OF WINGS) RUFFLE
(— OF WIRES) DROP
(— OF WORDS) ACCENT GENITIVE
(— OF 10 NOTES) DECUPLET
(— OF 1000) CHILIAD
(— OF 12) DOZEN
(— OF 2 VOWELS) DIGRAM
DIGRAPH
(— OF 40 THREADS) BEER BIER
(— OF 60 PIECES) SHOCK
(ASSISTANCE —) AINI
(ATOMIC —) LIGAND
(AUTHORITATIVE —) CONCLAVE
(AVANT-GARDE —) UNDERGROUND
(CONFUSED —) SNARL
(CORE —) CADRE
(CRIME SYNDICATE —) FAMILY
(ECOLOGICAL —) GUILD
(ETHNIC —) LI ACHANG BALAHI
BATTAK ETHNOS CHINGPAW
(ETHNOLOGICAL —) ISLAND
(EXCLUSIVE —) ELECT
(FAMILY —) GWELY
(HARMONIOUS —) DOVECOTE
(INTIMATE —) COTERIE
(KINSHIP —) SUSU

(LANGUAGE —) ATALAN
(LARGE —) PASSEL
(LINKED —) NEXUS
(LIVELY —) GALA
(NON-MOSLEM —) MILLET
(PAGAN —) BATAK BATANGAN
(PHILOSOPHICAL —) CENACLE
(POLITICAL —) BLOC PARTY
FASCIO COMMONS MACHINE
(SEGREGATED —) GHETTO
(SMALL —) PLUMP
(SOCIAL —) KITH SEPT TRIBE
FAMILY INGROUP
(PREF.) (CULTURAL —) ETHNO
(SUFF.) AD ET OME SOME
GROUPED AGMINATE
GROUPER GAG HIND MERO GUASA
HAMEL SCAMP AGUAJI BONACI
CHERNA GROPER HAMLET
WARSAW BACALAO GARLOPA
GARRUPA GOURAMI JEWFISH
REDFISH LAPULAPU REDBELLY
ROCKFISH SCIRENGA SERRANID
(YOUNG —) SNAPPER
GROUPING KIND ARRAY BATTERY
KINDRED DIVISION GROUPAGE
SODALITY SYNTAGMA
(— OF POTTERY) SERIES
GROUSE CRAB BITCH GANGA
PEEVE GORHEN GROUCH HOOTER
ATTAGEN CHEEPER GAZELLE
GORCOCK PINTAIL COMPLAIN
MOORBIRD MOORFOWL
PTARMIGAN
(YOUNG —) POULT SQUEALER
GROUT GROOT LARRY SLUSH
GROUTING
GROUTER GUNITER
GROVE CAMP HEWT HOLT MOTT
SHAW TOFT TOPE WONG ALTIS
BLUFF COPSE GLADE HURST
HYRST GARDEN GREAVE GROVET
ISLAND OLIVET SCROBE SPRING
ACADEMY ARBORET BOSCAGE
COPPICE SPINNEY THICKET
WOODING SERINGAL WODELEIE
(— OF ALDERS) CARR
(— OF MANGO TREES) TOPE
(— OF OAKS) ENCINAL
(— OF OSIERS) HOLT
(— OF SUGAR MAPLES) CAMP
(SACRED —) ALTIS SARNA
(SMALL —) SHAW
(PREF.) NAEMOR
(SUFF.) ETUM
GROVEL FAWN ROLL CREEP
CRINGE TUMBLE WALLOW
WELTER GRABBLE FLOUNDER
GROVELING PRONE WORMY
ABJECT HANGDOG REPTILE
GROW AGE BUD GET HIT ICH WAX
BOLL COME CROP ECHE ITCH
MAKE RISE SEED THEE THRO
WEAR EDIFY ISSUE PLANT PROVE
RAISE SHOOT SWELL ACCRUE
BATTEN BECOME DOUBLE
EXPAND EXTEND GATHER SPRING
SPROUT THRIVE AUGMENT
BROADEN BURGEON DEVELOP
DISTEND ENLARGE IMPROVE
NOURISH ADOLESCE FLOURISH
HEIGHTEN INCREASE THRODDEN
PROLIFERATE

(— ANGRY) STIVER
(— BETTER) IMPROVE
(— DARK) GLOAM GLOOM NIGHT DARKEN DARKLE
(— FAINT) DIE APPAL APPALL
(— FAT) FEED BATTEN
(— IN LENGTH) ELONGATE
(— IRREGULARLY) SCRAMBLE
(— LESS) ABATE SLAKE ASSUAGE DECREASE
(— LIGHT) DAWN
(— LUXURIANTLY) THRIVE
(— MAD) WOOD
(— MILD) GIVE
(— OLD) AGE OLD SENESCE
(— OVER) INVADE
(— PLUMP) PLIM
(— RICH) FATTEN
(— SOUND) HEAL
(— SPIRITLESS) FLAG
(— STILL) HUSH
(— STRONG) FORTIFY STORKEN
(— THIN) PEAK
(— TO HEAD) CABBAGE
(— TO STALK) SPINDLE
(— TOGETHER) KNIT ACCRETE CONCREW COOSIFY COALESCE
(— UNDER GLASS) GLASS
(— UP) STEM ACCRUE
(— WEAK) FAINT
(PREF.) (— TOGETHER) SYMPHY(O)

GROWING GROWY ONGOING CRESCENT CRESCIVE ACCRESCENT
(— ANGRY) IRASCENT
(— IN AIR) AERIAL
(— IN CLUSTERS) RACEMOSE
(— IN GRAIN FIELDS) SEGETAL
(— IN HEAPS) ACERVATE
(— IN MEADOW) PRATAL
(— IN PAIRS) BINATE
(— IN RUBBISH) RUDERAL
(— IN WATER) AQUATIC
(— ON A STEM) CAULINE
(— OUT) ENATE
(— RAPIDLY) BOOMING
(— THICKLY) HOUSY
(— VIGOROUSLY) THRIFTY
(— WILD) SAVAGE AGRARIAN AGRESTAL
(SUFF.) PLASIA PLASIS PLASM(A)(IA)(IC) PLAST(IC)(Y) PLASY
(— IN OR ON) COLE COLINE COLOUS

GROWL YAR GNAR GURL GURR NARR RASE ROIN ROME WIRR YARR YIRR GARRE GNARL GNARR GROIN SNARL GOLLAR HABBLE GRUMBLE MAUNDER

GROWLER CLARENCE

GROWLING GROIN SURLY

GROWN THRIVEN
(— COLD) DEAD
(— HIGH) LOGGY
(— TOGETHER) ADNATE ACCRETE
(FULL —) GREAT MATURE
(WELL —) THRODDY

GROWN-UP ADULT GROWN MATURE

GROWTH FUR WAX BUSH COAT CORN FILM GROW JUBA RISE SPUR SUIT DUVET FLUSH GUMMA
MAQUI STAND STOCK STOOL SWELL BUTTON CALLUS CANCER CLAVUS EATAGE EPULIS FRINGE FUNGUS LANUGO SCREEN SPROUT TYLOSE UPCOME WASTME AUXESIS BRACKEN COPPICE ERINEUM FUNGOID MACCHIE SARCOID STATURE TYLOSIS BEARDING CARUNCLE ENDOGENY INCREASE SETATION SWELLING UPSPRING ACCRETION
(— IN EYE) FILM
(— OF BEARD) DOWN
(— OF HAIR) SUIT
(— OF HORN) BUTTON SPIDER
(— OF PLANKTON) BLOOM
(— OF TREES) MOTTE BOSQUE BOSCAGE COPPICE SHINNERY
(— ON HORSE'S LEG) FUSEE FUZEE
(— ON VESSEL'S BOTTOM) GARR
(ABUNDANT —) FLUSH
(DENSE —) BRUSH FOREST SHINNERY
(DOWNY —) LANUGO
(GREEN —) GREENTH
(HARD —) STONE
(LUXURIANT —) FLOURISH
(ROUGH —) STUBBLE
(RUDIMENTARY —) STUB STUMP
(SIDE —) SPRIG
(SPARSE —) SCRAGGLE
(SUPERFICIAL —) MILDEW
(TRANSPARENT —) DRUSE
(VIGOROUS —) THRIFT
(WOODY —) BURL
(2ND — OF GRASS) FOG
(PREF.) AUXANO AUXO
(SUFF.) PHYTA PHYTE(S) PHYTIC PHYTUM PLASTY TROPHIA TROPHIC TROPHY
(INHIBITION OF —) STASIA STASIS

GROWTH OF THE SOIL (AUTHOR OF —) HAMSUN
(CHARACTER IN —) AXEL ISAK BREDE INGER OLINE OLSEN STROM BARBRO SIVERT ARONSEN ELESEUS REBECCA GEISSLER LEOPOLDINE

GRUB BOB DIG EATS HUHU MOIL MOOT ROUT STUB WORM CHUCK GROUT MATHE SCRAN SNOUT WROTE ASSART ESSART GRUGRU MAGGOT MUZZLE ROOTLE NEASCUS PIGROOT FLAGWORM GRUBWORM MUCKWORM SKINWORM

GRUBROOT STARWORT

GRUDGE DOWN ENVY DERRY PEEVE SCORE SPITE ANIMUS GROUCH GRUNCH GRUTCH MALICE MALIGN SPLEEN DESPITE EYELAST SIMULTY

GRUDGING JEALOUSY

GRUEL SLOP BLEERY BURGOO CAUDLE CONGEE CROWDY SKILLY SOFKEE BROCHAN CROWDIE LOBLOLLY WANGRACE

GRUESOME UGLY GRISLY GROOLY HORRID SORDID FEARFUL GHASTLY HIDEOUS MACABRE

GRUFF BLUFF ROUGH CLUMSE SULLEN AUSTERE BEARING BRUSQUE CLUMPST
(PL.) TAILINGS

GRUIFORMES GRALLAE

GRUMBLE CARP GIRN GREX HONE KREX ROIN BLEAT BROCK CROAK DRUNT GROIN GROWL GRUMP GRUNT MUNGE GROUCH GROUSE GRUDGE GRUNCH MUMBLE MUNGER MURMUR MUTTER NOLLER PEENGE REPINE RUMBLE SQUEAL TARROW YAMMER CHANNER CHUNNER CHUNTER GNATTER GRIZZLE GRUNTLE MAUNDER MURGEON QUADDLE SWAGGER COMPLAIN

GRUMBLER GROUCH QUADDLE GROGNARD

GRUMBLING BITCH DRUNT GRIPE GROIN GRUDGE MURMUR MURGEON

GRUMPY ILL CROSS GLUMPY GLUMPISH GRUMPISH

GRUNION SMELT

GRUNT OINK BURRO GROIN HUMPH RONCO SARGO GRUMPH RONCO BURRITO CROAKER GRUNTER GRUNTLE PIGFISH PINFISH TOMTATE KNORHAAN KOORHAAN PORKFISH REDMOUTH RONCADOR

GUACHARO FATBIRD OILBIRD

GUAICURU CADUVEO

GUAM (BAY OF —) AGAT YLIG CETTI AJAYAN UMATAC
(CAPITAL OF —) AGANA
(HARBOR OF —) APRA
(ISLAND OF —) CABRAS
(MOUNTAIN OF —) TENJO LAMLAM
(PENINSULA OF —) OROTE
(TOWN OF —) UPI ARRA ASAN TOTO YONA AGANA LUPOG MAGUA MERIZO UMATAC MALOLOS

GUAMA INGA PACAY

GUAN JACU ORTALIS PHEASANT

GUANA CHANE

GUANABANA SOURSOP

GUANCHE CANARIAN

GUANO OSITE

GUAPENA SERRAN SERRANA AGUAVINA

GUARANTEE (ALSO SEE GUARANTY) BAIL BAND SEAL CINCH COVER AVOUCH ENGAGE ENSURE INSURE RATIFY SECURE SURETY CAUTION CERTIFY HOSTAGE WARRANT AWARRANT GUARANTY PRESTATE SECURITY WARRANTY

GUARANTEED ASSURED CERTIFIED FOOLPROOF

GUARANTOR ENGAGER GRANTOR GUARAND SPONSOR GUARANTY

GUARANTY (ALSO SEE GUARANTEE) ANDI AVAL PAWN SEAL CAUTIO PLEDGE WARRANT SECURITY WARRANTY

GUARD BOW LEG NIT PAD SEE CARE CURB HERD HOLD KEEP KNOW LOOK REDE SAVE STOP STUB TENT TILE WAIT WEAR WERE WITE YEME ASKAR AWARD BLESS BLOCK CHECK COVER FENCE FORAY HEDGE HINGE
PILOT SCREW SKIRT TUTOR WAKEN WATCH ASKARI BANTAY BASKET BRACER BRIDLE BUMPER BUTTON CONVOY DEFEND DRAGON ESCORT FENDER GHAFIR GUNMAN JAILER KAVASS KEEPER MIDDLE POLICE SCREEN SECURE SENTRY SHIELD SHROUD WAITER WARDER YEMING BULWARK CHERISH ESGUARD FRONTAL GHAFFIR GHATWAL GUARDER KEEPING PANDOUR PRESIDY PROTECT SOULACK TRABANT WARDAGE WARRANT CHAPERON GARRISON MUDGUARD OUTGUARD PEDESTAL PILOTMAN PRESERVE SECURITY SENTINEL SHEPHERD SPLASHER WARDSMAN WATCHMAN
(— ON FOIL) BUTTON
(— WHILE IN TRANSIT) RIDE
(AXLE —) HOUSING
(COACH —) SHOOTER
(CONSULAR —) KAVASS
(IMPERIAL —) BOSTANGI BOSTANJI
(KEYHOLE —) LAPPET
(MOUNTED —) SHOMER
(NECK —) CAMAIL
(ON —) AWARE EXCUBANT
(PRISON —) HACK SCREW CHASER JAILER
(STIRRUP —) TAPADERA
(SWORD —) BOW TSUBA
(WRIST —) BRACER
(PL.) HEAVIES

GUARDED WARY IMMUNE MANNED

GUARDEDLY GINGERLY

GUARDHOUSE BRIG CLINK BULLPEN HOOSEGOW

GUARDIAN HERD ANGEL ARGUS TUTOR YEMER CUSTOS KEEPER MIMING PASTOR PATRON SHOMER WARDEN CORONER CURATOR GARDANT GARDEEN GRIFFIN BARTHOLO BELLERUS CERBERUS CREANCER DEFENDER ECKEHART FRAVASHI GOVERNOR GUARDANT PROTUTOR TUTELARY
(— OF HOME) SIF
(WORLD —) LOKAPALA MAHARAJA
(PL.) SELLI SELLOI

GUARDIANSHIP WARD TUTELA CUSTODY KEEPING TUITION WARDAGE WARDING CUSTODIA GUARDAGE TUTELAGE WARDENRY WARDSHIP

GUARDROOM WARDROOM

GUARDSMAN GUARDEE

GUASA MERO

GUATEMALA

CAPITAL: GUATEMALA
COIN: PESO CENTAVO QUETZAL
DANCE: ELSON GUARIMBA
DEPARTMENT: PETEN IZABAL JALAPA QUICHE SOLOLA ZACAPA JUTIAPA ESCUINTLA
GULF: HONDURAS
INDIAN: MAM CHOL ITZA IXIL MAYA XINCA CARIBE QUICHE POKOMAM
LAKE: DULCE GUIJA PETEN

GUAVA ARACA MYRTAL GUAYABA
GUAYABO GOIABADA
GUAYCURU MBAYA
GUDDLE GUMP NOODLE HANDFISH
GUDGEON PIN QUAB CHALDER
TRUNNION
GUDRUN (FATHER OF —) HETEL
GUELDER-ROSE GAITER OPULUS
DOGWOOD WHITTEN DOGBERRY
SNOWBALL VIBURNUM
GUENDOLEN (HUSBAND OF —)
LOCRINE
GUENON GRIVET NISNAS VERVET
TALAPOIN TALLAPOI MOUSTACHE
GUEREZA COLOBIN COLOBUS
GUERRILLA COWBOY GORILLA
JAYHAWK SKINNER BUSHWACK
FELLAGHA KOMITAJI
GUERRILLERO KOMITAJI
GUESS AIM CALL HARP REDE SHOT
WEEN AREAD COUNT ETTLE
FANCY INFER TWANG DEVISE
DIVINE RECKON IMAGINE
SURMISE SUSPECT
(— CORRECTLY) TOUCH
GUEST COME GOER HOST DINER
INVITEE VISITOR SYMPHILE
VISITANT
(— AT RANCH) DUDE
(UNINVITED —) SHADOW
(PL.) LEVEE COMPANY
(PREF.) XEN(O)
(SUFF.) XENE XENOUS XENY
GUFA KUFA GOOFAH KUPHAR
GUFFAW GAFF ROAR HEEHAW
GUIDANCE AIM DUCT EGIS AEGIS
STEER CONDUCT GUIDAGE
HELMAGE LEADING WISSING
AUSPICES ENGINERY REGIMENT
STEERAGE
GUIDE GUY LAY PIR TIP AIRT BEAD
CURB GAGE GATE LEAD PASS
REIN RULE SWAY WISE CARRY
CHARM DRESS FRAME GAUGE
LIGHT MAHDI MOROC PILOT
STEER TEACH WEISE ADALID
BARKER BEACON BEDWAY
CONVOY DIRECT ESCORT FORMER
GILLIE GOVERN INFORM LEADER
MANAGE POPPET CONDUCE

CONDUCT COURIER GHILLIE
INSPIRE MARSHAL MERCURY
PIONEER SHIKARI STERNER
TRACKER CALENDAR CICERONE
DIRECTOR DRAGOMAN ENGINEER
FAIRLEAD LODESMAN PEDESTAL
POLESTAR PRACTICO REPEATER
SHIKAREE SIGNPOST
(MORAL —) LABARUM
(RAILWAY —) ABC BRADSHAW
(SPIRITUAL —) PIR GURU BISHOP
DIVINE
(TRAFFIC —) MUSHROOM
(SUFF.) AGOGUE AGOGY
GUIDEBOOK ABC GUIDE WAYBOOK
BAEDEKER HANDBOOK
ROADBOOK
GUIDELINE SLUG PARAMETER
GUIDEPOST GUIDE PARSON
WAYMARK WAYPOST SIGNPOST
GUIDERIUS (FATHER OF —)
CYMBELINE
GUIDEWAY SLAY SLEY SLEIGH
SLIDEWAY SWANNECK
GUIDING POLAR BEHIND HOMING
LEADING
GUIDO (WIFE OF —) ALERIA
GUILD HUI GILD HOEY HONG YELD
CRAFT HANSA HANSE GREMIO
GUIDRY SCHOLA BASOCHE
COLLEGE COMPANY MYSTERY
GUILE DOLE WILE CHEAT CRAFT
FRAUD TRAIN CAUTEL DECEIT
HUMBUG CUNNING FALLACY
ARTIFICE
GUILELESS PLAIN CANDID HONEST
ARTLESS ONEFOLD IGNORANT
INNOCENT SACKLESS UNNOOKED
GUILLEMOT AUK COOT LARY LAVY
LOOM QUET TURR URIA ARRIE
CUTTY FROWL MURRE SCOUT
TOIST TYSTE GRYLLE LUNGIE
MAGGIE MARROT SCRABE TINKER
DOVEKEY DOVEKIE SEACOOT
SKIDDAW TARROCK WILLOCK
PUFFINET ROCKBIRD SCUTTOCK
SPRATTER
GUILT SIN SAKE WITE BLAME
CULPA FAULT PIACLE PLIGHT
NOCENCE OFFENSE HAMARTIA
INIQUITY
GUILTLESS FREE PURE CLEAN
UNSAKED INNOCENT SACKLESS
GUILTY FAULTY NOCENT WICKED
CORREAL HANGDOG NOXIOUS
PECCANT BLAMEFUL CRIMINAL
CULPABLE GUILTFUL
(— OF ERROR) LAPSED
GUINEA MEG BEAN QUID QUEED
GEORGE SHINER GEORDIE
(HALF —) SMELT

**GUINEA-BISSAU (ARCHIPELAGO OF
—)** BIJAGOS
(CAPITAL OF —) BISSAU
(RIVER OF —) GEBA CACHEU
MANSOA CORUBAL
GUINEA FOWL KEEL KEET PEARL
MEBACK GALEENY PINTADO
COMEBACK GALLINEY
(SOUND OF —) POTRACK
GUINEA GRASS PANIC PANICLE
SACATON ZACATON GAMELOTE
GUINEA PEPPER PIMENTO
GUINEA PIG CAVY
(MALE —) BOAR BUCK
GUINEA RUSH ADRUE
GUISE HUE FORM GARB COLOR
COVER SHAPE MANNER PERSON
APPAREL CLOTHES GUISARD
LIKENESS
GUISER MUMMER
GUITAR AX AXE BOX KIT PIPA
DOBRO JAMON KITAR SITAR
TIPLE GIMBRI KITTAR SANCHO
SATTAR CITHERN CITTERN
MACHETE UKULELE CHARANGO
CHITARRA
(PART OF —) KEY NUT PEG BASE
BODY BONE FRET HEAD HEEL
HOLE NECK BRACE GUARD WAIST
BRIDGE SADDLE STRING ROSETTE
FINGERBOARD
GUITARFISH RAY BATOID
PURAQUE
GUITGUIT PITPIT
GULANCHA GILO GILOE
GULCH COULE GULLY SLUIT
CANYON COULEE RAVINE
GULDEN FLORIN GUILDER
(100,000 —) TUN
GULES MARS RUBY TORTEAU
GULF SINE CHAOS GULPH VORAGE
VORAGO
(BOTTOMLESS —) ABYSM ABYSS
GULFWEED SARGASSO
GULL COB COX MEW COBB CONY
COOT CULL DUPE FOOL GOLL
LARI MALL PINT PIRR SELL SKUA
XEME ALLAN ALLEN ANNET
BOSUN CHEAT CHUMP COBBE
COKES CROCK CULLY HOODY
JAGER LARID LARUS PEWIT
SCULL SMELT YAGER BONXIE
BUBBLE CHOUSE COUSIN JOCKEY
PEEWIT PIGEON SIMPLE TEASER
TULIAC VICTIM WAGGEL WHILLY
CROCKER DECEIVE MEDRICK
PICKMAW POPELER SCAURIE
SEABIRD SEAFOWL SWARBIE

TARROCK TRUMPIE BLACKCAP
DIRTBIRD DOTTEREL DUNGBIRD
SEEDBIRD
(LIKE A —) LAROID
GULLET MAW GULE LANE GORGE
GARGLE PECHAN THROAT
KEACORN STOMACH SWALLOW
WEASAND GURGULIO
(PREF.) ESOPHAG(O) LAEMO
LEMO RUMENO
GULLIBLE GOOFY GREEN SIMPLE
CULLIBLE
GULLIVER GRILDRIG
GULLY BOX GEO GUT DRAW GULL
RAIK RAKE SICK SIKE DONGA
DRAFT GOYLE GULCH SLAKE
SLUIT ZANJA ARROYO GULLET
GULLEY GUTTER NULLAH RAVINE
SHEUCH SHEUGH CHIMNEY
COULOIR DRAUGHT BARRANCA
GULP BOLT GAUP GLUT GULL
POOP SOPE SWIG GULCH QUILT
SLOSH SWIPE ENGLUT GLUTCH
GOBBLE GOLLOP PAUNCH
SLABBER SWALLOW SWATTLE
SLUMMOCK
(— NOISILY) SLORP
GUM ASA AMRA BLOB FILL GOOM
LOAD TUNO ALGIN AMAPA BABUL
CUMAY DHAVA ACAJOU ANGICO
BARRAS CHICLE KARAYA TOUART
TUPELO CARANNA CARAUNA
GINGIVA GUMWOOD PERRIER
BORRACHA CARABEEN DEXTRINE
DRESSING FEVERGUM
CALENDULIN
(ACACIA —) GEDDA
(AROMATIC —) MYRRH
(ASTRINGENT —) KINO
(CHEWING —) WAX
(FRAGRANT —) BUMBO
(RED —) JARRAH
(UNGRADED —) SORTS
(WOOD —) XYLAN
(PL.) ULA
(PREF.) COMMI GUMMI GUTTI
GUM ARABIC KIKAR ACACIA
ACACIN
GUMBO OKRA
GUMBOIL PARULIS
GUMBO-LIMBO JOBO BIRCH
GOMART MASTIC NEGRITO
ALMACIGO ARCHIPIN
GUMDROP GUM JUJUBE
GUMMER BIDDY BIDDIE SCRAPER
SCUFFER SCUFFLER SCUPPLER
GUMMY GLUEY CLAGGY MASTIC
GUMMOUS
GUMPTION NOUS SENSE SPRAWL
GUMS
(PREF.) GINGIV(O) ULEMO ULO
GUM SUCCORY HOGBITE
GUM TREE KARI KARRI TOOART
TOUART TUPELO EUCALYPT
GUMWEED GRINDELIA
SUNFLOWER
GUN GAT POP BREN HAKE PIAT
ROER STEN TUBE BARIL FIFTY
FIRER FUSEE FUZEE RAKER
REWET RIFLE ARCHIE BERTHA
CANNON CHASER CULVER
DUCKER INCHER JEZAIL MINNIE
QUAKER RANDOM SPIGOT SWIVEL

TUPARA CALIVER FIREARM
HACKBUT HANDGUN JINGALL
LANTACA MUZZLER AMUSETTE
ARQUEBUS CHAUCHAT CULVERIN
FIRELOCK GALLOPER OERLIKON
PEDERERO SHAGBUSH
TROMBONE
(BOAT —) BASE
(LOWER-DECK —) BARKER
(MACHINE —) CHOPPER GATLING
(SPRING —) STEL
(TOY —) SPARKLER
(PL.) FLAK CHASE ARTILLERY
GUNA RAJAS TAMAS SATTVA
GUNBOAT SKIP BARCA GONDOLA
TINCLAD
GUN CARRIAGE PANEL MADRIER
GALLOPER
GUNCREWMAN PLUGMAN
GUNDOBAD (BROTHER OF —)
GODOMAR CHILPERIC GODEGISEL
(FATHER OF —) GUNDIOCH
GUNDOG POINTER
GUNFLINT STONE
GUNI (FATHER OF —) NAPHTALI
GUNITE SHOTCRETE
GUNLOCK ROWET FIRELOCK
GUNMAN HOOD GUNSEL
GUNSMAN TORPEDO ENFORCER
GANGSTER
GUNNEL BLENNY SWORDICK
GUNNER GUN POPPER FIREMAN
SHOOTER ENGINEER
GUNNY TAT BURLAP BAGGING
SACKING
GUNNYSACK CORNSACK
GUNPOWDER SULFUR SULPHUR
GUNSIGHT VISIE HAUSSE
GUNSTOCK BLANK TIPSTOCK
GUNSTONE OGRESS PELLET
GUNTHER (SISTER OF —) KRIEMHILD
(WIFE OF —) BRUNEHILDE
GUNTRAM (BROTHER OF —)
SIGEBERT CHARIBERT CHILPERIC
(CHARACTER IN —) ROBERT
GUNTRAM FREIHILD FRIEHOLD

(COMPOSER OF —) STRAUSS
(FATHER OF —) CLOTAIRE
GUNWALE GUNNEL PORTOISE
GUNZ SCANIAN
GUPPY MILLIONS BELLYFISH
GUR GOOR KHAUR JAGGERY
VOLTAIC
GURGLE GLOX BRAWL CLUNK
QUARK SLOSH BICKER BUBBLE
BULLER BURBLE GOLLER GUGGLE
RUCKLE
GURGLINGLY TRILLIL
GURJUN YANG
GURNARD CUR TUB PIPER ELLECK
ROCHET BATFISH CAPTAIN
GRUNTER LATCHET SOLDIER
TRIGLID TUBFISH VOLADOR
HARDHEAD KNORHAAN LORICATE
GURO KWENI
GUSH JET BOIL FLOW FOAM HUSH
RAIL SLOP WALM BELCH SLUSH
SMALM SMARM SPIRT SPURT
STOUR SWOSH BURBLE PHRASE
SWOOSH WALLOW WHOOSH
SLOBBER
(SENTIMENTAL —) SLOSH
GUSHING SLOPPY SMARMY
EFFUSIVE
GUSSET GORE MITER MITRE QUIRK
PIECETTE
GUST BUB FLAN GALE GUSH WAFF
WAFT WIND BLAST FRESH SLANT
FLURRY HUFFLE SQUALL
FLAUGHT WILLIWAW WINDFLAW
(— OF RAIN) SKIT
(— OF WIND) FLAM FLAN FUFF
GALE GUSH PIRR SCUD TIFT
BERRY BLAST BLORE FLAFF
THODE SQUALL WINDFLAW
GUSTATION TASTE
GUSTO GUST ZEST VERVE RELISH
UNCTION
GUSTY DIRTY PUFFY BLASHY
BLASTY FRETFUL GUSTFUL
SQUALLY
GUT GIB BOWEL CECUM CLEAN

CAECUM CATGUT HOLLOW
STRING ELISION GRALLOCH
(FISH —) GIP GILL
(TWISTED —) THARM THERM
(PL.) MOXIE BOWELS COJONES
PUDDING ENTRAILS
GUTSY BALLSY
GUTTA SOH DROP PUAN SIAK
SUSU DUJAN GERIP SANGE
SUNDIK CAMPANA JANGKAR
SEMARUM TRENAIL TRUNNEL
HANGKANG KETAPANG
GUTTER GRIP REAN SIKE GRIPE
GULLY RIGOL SIVER SPOUT
SWEAL BOTTOM CANNEL CULLIS
GROOVE GUZZLE KENNEL RIGGOT
RUNNEL STRAND TROUGH
VENNEL CHANNEL CHENEAU
GRIZZLE
(— OF STREET) KENNEL
(MINING —) BOTTOM HASSING
(ROOF —) RONE
(PL.) LIMBERS
GUTTERMAN SWAMPER
GUTTURAL GRUM BURRY HARSH
THICK
GUY BOD CAT EGG JOE NUT BIRD
BOZO DUDE GENT GINK HUSK
JACK JOHN BLOKE COOKY JOKER
SCOUT SPOOF BUFFER COOKIE
GAZABO GAZEBO GAZOOK GILGUY
HOMBRE JASPER JIGGER MALKIN
MAUMET MAWKIN KNOCKER
BLIGHTER
GUYANA (CAPITAL OF —)
GEORGETOWN
(RIVER OF —) CUYUNI BERBICE
DEMERARA MAZARUNI
ESSEQUIBO
(TOWN OF —) ITUNI BILOKU
ISSANO MACKENZIE
(WATERFALL IN —) MARINA
KAIETEUR
GUY MANNERING (AUTHOR OF —)
SCOTT
(CHARACTER IN —) GUY MEG LUCY

BROWN DANDY HARRY JULIA
BERTRAM DINMONT GLOSSIN
SAMPSON MANNERING MERRILIES
ELLANGOWAN HATTERAICK
GUY ROPE STAY VANG
GUZ GAZ GEZ ZAR ZER GUDGE
GUZERAT KANKREJ
GUZZLE BUM GUM SOT TUN BEND
GULL SLOSH SWILL GOOZLE
GUDDLE SWATTLE SWIZZLE
GUZZLER BENDER
GWYNIAD SCHELLY
GYASCUTUS PROCK
GYLE BEER GAIL BREWING
GYMKHANA AUTOCROSS
GYMNASIUM GYM PALESTRA
TURNHALL PALAESTRA
GYMNAST SOKOL BENDER
TURNER ACROBAT TUMBLER
GYMNASTIC (— SOCIETY) SOKOL
GYNOECIUM BRUSH APOCARP
GYNOPHORE PODOGYN
GYPSUM GYP GYPS YESO GESSO
LUDIAN PARGET GYPSITE
SATINITE SELENITE ALABASTER
GYPSY FAW CALO APTAL CAIRD
GIPSY ROMNI BOSHAS GITANO
ROMANY TINKER AZUCENA
CZIGANY MOONMAN TINKLER
TZIGANE ZINCALO ZINGARO
BOHEMIAN EGYPTIAN FLAMENCO
ZIGEUNER
(NON —) GORGIO
(SEA —) BAJAU
(PL.) ROMANESE
GYRATE GYRE SPIN TURN TWIRL
WHIRL CURVET INGYRE ROTATE
REVOLVE SQUIRREL
GYRATION PRECESSION
GYRATORY GIDDY GYRAL
GYRFALCON JERKIN
GYRON GIRON ESQUIRE
GYROSE SINUATE

H

H HOW AITCH HOTEL ASPIRATE
HABERDASHER OUTFITTER
HABERDASHERY TOGGERY
HABERGEON HAUBERK
HABILIMENT GARB HABIT
APPAREL RAIMENT CLOTHING
(PL.) CLOTHES EQUIPAGE
HABILITATE ENABLE
HABIT LAW PAD SET USE WON
COAT GARB GATE SUIT THEW
WONT FROCK HAUNT TACHE
TRADE TRICK USAGE CUSTOM
GROOVE MANNER PRAXIS TALENT
CLOTHES FOLKWAY HABITUS
WONTING CROTCHET HABITUDE
PHYSIQUE PRACTICE PRACTISE
ASSUETUDE CONSUETUDE
(— OF GRINDING TEETH) BRUXISM
(BAD —) HANK VICE MISTETCH
CACOETHES
(DEPRAVED —) CACHEXY
(SPEECH —S) ACCENT
(PL.) DAPS
(PREF.) HEXICO
HABITABLE BIGLY LIVABLE
HABITAT ECE HOME RANGE
PATRIA STATION LOCALITY
(PREF.) EC(O) OEC(O) OIKO
HABITATION HOLD TELD TENT
ABODE BIELD HABIT HOUSE
BIDING WONING DOMICILE
DWELLING PANTHEON TENEMENT
RESIDENCE
(— SITE) YACATA
(QUIET —) SHADE
(UNDERGROUND —) HOLE
HABITUAL USUAL COMMON
HECTIC CHRONIC REGULAR
FREQUENT ORDINARY
HABITUATE USE HOWF ENURE
FLESH HABIT INURE ADDICT
SEASON HACKNEY ACCUSTOM
ACQUAINT OCCASION
HABITUATED WONT SEASONED
ACCUSTOMED
HABITUDE HABIT SCHESIS
HABITUE DENIZEN COURTIER
HABRONEMIASIS BURSATI
BURSATTEE
HACEK WEDGE
HACHALIAH (SON OF —) NEHEMIAH
HACK HAG HEW BOLO CHIP HAKE
DEVIL HATCH DRUDGE FIACRE
HACKLE HAGGLE HODMAN
JOBBER MANGLE SCOTCH
HACKNEY MATTOCK VETTURA
MUTILATE
(LITERARY —) GRUB DEVIL
HACKBERRY EGGBERRY HACKTREE
HAGBERRY ONEBERRY
HACKBUT HAGBUT DEMIHAG
HACKBUSH
HACK GHARRI SHIGRAM

HACKLE COMB RUFF HECKLE
NAPPER RUFFER HATCHEL
ROUGHER
HACKNEY HACK MIDGE NODDY
HACKNEY CARRIAGE MIDGE
FIACRE JARVEY VETTURA
HACKNEYED HACK WORN BANAL
HOARY TRITE CANNED CLICHE
COMMON FOREWORN
HAD D HED HEDDE
(— NOT) HADNA HADNT
HADAD (FATHER OF —) ISHMAEL
HADADEZER (FATHER OF —) REHOB
HADDOCK GADE GADID SCROD
DICKEY HADDIE
(DRIED —) CRAIL RIZZAR SPELDING
SPELDRIN
HADE UNDERLIE
HADES PIT ADES HELL AIDES
ORCUS PLUTO SHEOL SHADES
TARTAR ACHERON AIDONEUS
TARTARUS
(FATHER OF —) SATURN
(WIFE OF —) PROSERPINA
HADORAM (FATHER OF —) TOU
JOKTAN
HAECCEITY THISNESS
HAEMON (FATHER OF —) CREON
PELASGUS
(SON OF —) THESSALUS
HAEMUS (FATHER OF —) BOREAS
(MOTHER OF —) ORITHYIA
(SON OF —) HEBRUS
(WIFE OF —) RHODOPE
HAFF LAGOON
HAFNIUM CELTIUM
HAFT HEFT HOVE HELVE DUDGEON
HAFTER HANDLER
HAG ATE MARE REBEC RUDAS
SIBYL VECKE WITCH BELDAM
HECATE ROUDAS BELDAME
HAGGARD HELLCAT HARRIDAN
HAGAR (MISTRESS OF —) SARAH
(SON OF —) ISHMAEL
HAGBOAT HOGGET HOGGIE
HAGFISH HAG BORER VECKE
MYZONT SUCKER PLACOID
MYXINOID
HAGGARD PALE THIN GAUNT
WISHT HAGGED
HAGGI (FATHER OF —) GAD
HAGGITH (HUSBAND OF —) DAVID
(SON OF —) ADONIJAH
HAGGLE CHOP PRIG DODGE
BADGER BANTER BOGGLE DICKER
HACKER HIGGLE HUCKLE NAGGLE
NIFFER PALTER SCOTCH THREEP
BARGAIN CHAFFER HUCKSTER
HAGGLER DODGER
HAGGLING BARGAIN CHAFFER
HAGIOGRAPHA KETUBIM
HAGIOSCOPE SQUINT SQUINCH
HAIDA SKITTAGET

HAIL AVE HOY HALE GREET SALVE
SPEAK STORM ACCOST BAYETE
HAGGLE HALLOO HERALD SALUTE
ACCLAIM
(SOFT —) GRESIL GRAUPEL
(PREF.) CHALAZI CHALAZO
HAILSTONE STONE
HAINAI IONI
HAIR FAX JAG RIB WIG BARB CROP
FLUE GLIB HEAD KEMP PELF PILE
SETA WIRE BEARD CRIMP CRINE
FRIZZ FRONT PILUS QUIFF
ANGORA BRILLS BRUTUS CRINET
FIBRIL FROWZE MERKIN SETULA
THATCH TRAGUS CULOTTE
ELFLOCK GLOCHIS TOPKNOT
WHISKER CAPILLUS COLLETER
PALPOCIL TENTACLE TRICHODE
TRICHOME VIBRISSA
(— BROWN) ARGALI
(— OF ANIMALS) FUR PELF
(— OF HORSES OR COWS) CERDA
(— OF TERRIER) FALL
(— ON HORSE'S HOOF) CRONET
(— ON LEAF) GLAND
(— ON TEMPLES) HAFFET HAFFIT
(— ON THIGHS) CULOTTE
(— OVER EYES) BROW GLIB
EYELASH
(BARBED —) GLOCHIS
(BRAID OF —) QUEUE PIGTAIL
(BUNDLE OF —) LEECH
(CAMEL'S —) DEER
(COARSE —) KEMP BRISTLE
(CURLED —) FRIZZ
(CUTDOWN —) STUMPS
(FALSE —) WIG JANE FRONT
PERUKE
(FRIZZED —) FROWZE
(GRAY —) GRIZZLE
(LOCK OF —) TUZ FEAK TATE
FLOCK TRESS
(LONG HEAVY —) MANE
(LOOSE —) COMBINGS
(MATTED —) SHAG ELFLOCK
(MOP OF —) TOUSLE
(NOSE —) VIBRISSA
(PLANT —) COLLETER
(ROOT —) FIBRIL
(SNARL OF —) TANGLE
(SOFT —) DOWN LANUGO
(STINGING —) STING STIMULUS
(STINGING —S) COWHAGE
(STRAY LOCK OF —) TAG
(STYLE —) CORNROW
(TUFT OF —) PLUME KROBYLOS
(WAVING LOCK OF —) WIMPLER
(WHITE —) SNOW SNOWS
(PL.) SETAE COWAGE COWHAGE
HACKLES
(PREF.) CAPILLI CHAET(I)(O)
CHETO COME COMI CRINI
HIRSUTO LACHN(O) PIL(I)(O)

TRICH(O) TRICHINO VILLI
(SUFF.) CHAETA CHAETES
CHAETUS COMA THRICHOUS
THRIX TRICHA TRICHI(A) TRICHY
HAIRBREADTH HERMELE WHISKER
HAIR BROWN QUAIL
HAIRBRUSH TOILETRY
HAIRCLOTH HAIR CILICE
HAIRCUT BOB CUT CROP BUTCH
SHINGLE DUCKTAIL
HAIRDO AFRO FRISURE
HAIRDRESSER WAVER FRISEUR
COIFFEUR
HAIRDRESSING FRISURE
BANDOLINE
HAIR FRAME PALISADE
HAIRINESS PILOSISM PILOSITY
HAIRLESS BALD PELON CALLOW
ATRICHIC DEPILOUS GLABROUS
HAIRLIKE TRICHOID
HAIRLINE WHISKER
HAIRPIN ACUS BODKIN SKEWER
HAIRSPLITTING FINE PILPUL
HAIRSTYLE AFRO BINGLE
HAIRWORM GORDIID GORDIOID
HAIRY FAXED MOSEY PILAR
ROUGH COMATE COMOUS PILARY
PILINE CRINITE CRINOSE HIRSUTE
PILEOUS VILLOUS UNSHAVEN
(PREF.) DASI DASY HEBE

HAITI

CAPE: FOUX
CAPITAL: PORTAUPRINCE
CHANNEL: SUD STMARC
COIN: GOURDE
DEITY: LOA
GULF: GONAVE
INDIAN: TAINO
ISLAND: VACHE GONAVE TORTUE
NAVASSA TORTUGA
ISLAND GROUP: CAYMITES
LAKE: SAUMATRE
MAGIC: OBI OBEAH
MOUNTAIN: NORD CAHOS NOIRES
LAHOTTE LASELLE TROUDEAU
PLAIN: NORD CAYES JACMEL
LEOGANE ARCAHAIE CULDESAC
GONAIVES
PRIEST: BOCOR HOUNGAN
RIVER: GUAYAMOUC ARTIBONITE
SPIRIT: LOA BAKA BOKO
TOWN: AQUIN CAYES FURCY
LIMBE HINCHE JACMEL JEREMIE
LEOGANE SALTROU GONAIVES
KENSCOFF

HAKAM CACAM HAHAM CHOCHEM
KHAKHAM
HAKE GADE HAIK LING GADOID
CODLING HADDOCK WHITING
ANACANTH QUODLING
HAKENKREUZLER SWASTIKA

HALBERD BILL PIKE GLAIVE
GLEAVE POLEARM PARTISAN
(PART OF —) BEAK BUTT BLADE
SPIKE
HALBERDIER DRABANT
HALCYON CALM ALCYON GOLDEN
HALE YELL FRACK FRECK TRAIL
ROBUST STRONG HEALTHY
VIGOROUS
HALER HELLER
HALF M ARF ELF DEMI HAUF HOVE
SEMI SIDE MEDIO HALFEN HALFLY
MOIETY MEDIETY
(— GALLON) POTTLE
(— OF DRAW) BRACKET
(OF EM) EN
(— OF INNING) BOTTOM
(— OF MOLD) VALVE
(FRUIT —S) SLABS
(PREF.) DEMI HEMI SAM SEMI
(ONE AND A —) SESQUI
HALFBACK (OFFENSIVE —)
SLOTBACK
HALFBEAK GAR IHI BALAO PIPER
BALLYHOO
HALF-BLOOD DEMISANG
HALF BOOT BUSKIN BOTTINE
HALF-BREED BREED METIF METIS
SAMBO MUSTEE RAMONA
CABOCLO MESTIZO METISSE
DEMISANG HARRATIN MIXBLOOD
HALF-CASTE TOPAZ TOPASS
HALF-CRAZY FIFISH
HALF CROWN GEORGE ALDERMAN
HALF-DEAD ALAMORT
HALF DENIER MAILE MAILLE
HALF DOBRA PECA
HALF-EATEN SEMESE
HALF-FARTHING CUE MITE
MINUTE
HALF-GABLE AILERON
HALF GAINER ISANDER
HALF-GROWN HALFLIN
HALF-GUINEA SMELT
HALF HITCH ROLLING
HALF MASK LOUP DOMINO
HALF-MOON LUNETTE DEMILUNE
HALF NOTE MINIM
HALFPENCE GROCERY
HALFPENNY OB MAG MEG DUMP
GRAY GREY MAIK MAIL MAKE
MEKE OBOL SOUSE STAMP
BAUBEE BAWBEE MAILLE
HAPENNY PATRICK STUIVER
(COUNTERFEIT —) RAP GRAY
(THICK —) DUMP
HALF-PIKE SPONTON DEMIPIKE
SPONTOON
HALF-PINT CUP JACK CUPFUL
HALF REST SOSPIRO
HALF SOLE TAP
HALF STEP CHROMA
HALFTONE DROPOUT
HALF TURN DEMIVOLT
HALF-WIT DOLT DUNCE HAVEREL
TOMFOOL STAUMREL UNDERWIT
HALF-WITTED SOFT DOTTY SIMPLE
HALUCKET IMBECILE STAUMREL
HALIBUT BUT BUTT FLITCH
TURBOT FLATFISH
HALIFAX BALLYHACK
HALIOTIS ABALONE

HALIRRHOTHIUS (FATHER OF —)
NEPTUNE
(MOTHER OF —) EURYTE
(SLAYER OF —) MARS
HALL HA AULA HELL IWAN SALA
AIWAN ATRIO BALAI BURSA
CURIA DIVAN ENTRY FOYER
HOUSE OECUS SALLE SALON
ATRIUM CAMERA DURBAR
EXEDRA GARDEN LESCHE SALOON
SCHOOL SENATE TOLSEY TRANCE
APADANA CHAMBER DANCERY
GALLERY HALLWAY KURHAUS
KURSAAL MEGARON PASSAGE
VINGOLF ANTEROOM ARCHEION
ASSEMBLY BASILICA CHOULTRY
COLISEUM CORRIDOR FOREHALL
HASTROND HOSPITAL RAADZAAL
TOLBOOTH VALHALLA
(— FOR PERFORMANCES) ODEON
ODEUM
(— OF JUSTICE) COURT
(— WITH STATUES) VALHALLA
(DINING —) COMMON REFECTORY
(LECTURE —) SCHOLA
(MISSION —) CITADEL
(MUSIC —) GAFF
(TOWN —) CABILDO RATHAUS
TRIBUNAL
(UNIVERSITY —) BURSA
HALLMARK CROWN SHOPMARK
HALL OF FAME (AVIATION —) ELY
SIX BYRD LAHM LEAR LINK LUKE
MOSS POST RYAN WADE EAKER
GLENN LEMAY PIPER REEVE
ARNOLD BOEING CESSNA FOKKER
HUGHES LEVIER MARTIN ROGERS
SPAATZ SPERRY TOWERS TRIPPE
TURNER WALDEN WRIGHT
YAEGER CHANUTE EARHART
GRUMMAN LANGLEY LOENING
SHEPARD TWINING MITCHELL
NORTHROP SIKORSKY
ARMSTRONG LINDBERGH
MCDONNELL RICKENBACKER
(BASEBALL —) OTT COBB DEAN
FORD FOXX HOYT KELL KLEM
MACK MAYS MIZE RUTH WYNN
AARON BANKS BERRA COMBS
EVERS FRICK GOMEZ GROVE
HAFEY KINER LEMON LOPEZ
LYONS PAIGE PLANK RUSIE
SPAHN TERRY VANCE WALSH
WANER WHEAT YOUNG ALSTON
CHANCE CRONIN CUYLER FELLER
FRISCH GEHRIG GOSLIN KALINE
KOUFAX LAJOIE LANDIS MANTLE
MANUSH MCGRAW MUSIAL
RICKEY SISLER TINKER WAGNER
WILSON WRIGHT YAWKEY
APPLING AVERILL BURKETT
HORNSBY HUBBARD HUGGINS
JOHNSON PENNOCK RUFFING
SIMMONS SPEAKER STENGEL
TRAYNOR BOUDREAU COMISKEY
DIMAGGIO GRIFFITH MACPHAIL
MARICHAL MCCARTHY ROBINSON
WILLIAMS COVELESKI
BRICKHOUSE MARANVILLE
(BASKETBALL —) GALE GOLA PAGE
REED WEST COUSY FULKS GREER
HAGAN HYATT LUCAS MIKAN
ARIZIN BARLOW BAYLOR COOPER

FOSTER HANSON HOLMAN
KRAUSE MURPHY PETTIT PHILIP
RAMSEY ROOSMA SEDRAN
TWYMAN WOODEN BECKMAN
BRADLEY BRENNAN DEHNERT
GRUENIG KURLAND POLLARD
SCHAYES SCHMIDT SHARMAN
WACHTER BORGMANN
ENDACOTT LAPCHICK LUISETTI
MACAULEY SCHOMMER
MCCRACKEN STEINMETZ
VANDIVIER DEBERNARDI
DEBUSSCHERE
(BUSINESS —) FORD HAAS LUCE
OCHS VAIL GARST HEINZ ROUSE
SLOAN BATTEN DISNEY DORIOT
DUPONT HILTON KAISER LASKER
MELLON MORGAN OGILVY
PENNEY SCHIFF SCHWAB
EASTMAN SARNOFF WHITNEY
CARNEGIE FRANKLIN MCCORMICK
VANDERBILT ROCKEFELLER
WESTINGHOUSE WEYERHAEUSER
(FOOTBALL —) MIX RAY BELL HEIN
HUFF LARY MARA OTTO FEARS
GROZA GUYON HALAS HAYES
LAYNE LILLY LYMAN MUSSO
NEALE RINGO ROYAL BADGRO
BLANDA BUTKUS GRANGE HINKLE
KINARD MATSON MCAFEE
ROONEY THORPE TITTLE TRIPPI
UNITAS ALWORTH GILLMAN
LUCKMAN MILLNER LOMBARDI
MITCHELL WARFIELD JURGENSEN
PARSEGHIAN
(GOLF —) BERG FORD HOPE
BOROS BURKE DUTRA EVANS
HAGEN HOGAN JONES SHUTE
SMITH SNEAD ARMOUR COOPER
DIEGEL GHEZZI LITTLE NELSON
OUIMET PALMER PICARD RUNYAN
TRAVIS DEMARET GULDAHL
HARBERT MANGRUM REVOLTA
SARAZEN ZAHARIAS DEVICENZO
(THEATER —) DREW KERR BROOK
HECHT KELLY SIMON PRINCE
DUNNOCK CHAMPION KINGSLEY
LANSBURY MCARTHUR MEREDITH
SONDHEIM STRASBERG
YOUNGMANS BLOOMGARDEN
HALLOO HO HOO LOO ALEW BAWL
LURE WHOOP ACCOST TALLYHO
HALLOW BLESS HALWE DEDICATE
SANCTIFY
HALLOWED HOLY SACRED
BLESSED
HALLUCINATION DWALE
ACOASMA ACOUASM ACOUSMA
FANTASY PHONEME DELUSION
ILLUSION PHANTASY ZOOSCOPY
HALLUCINOGEN ACID
HALLUX TALON
HALLWAY ENTRY FOYER TRANCE
HALMA HOPPITY
HALMALILLE PETWOOD
HALO DOG BURR GLOR NIMB
GLORY SHINE AREOLA CIRCLE
CORONA GLORIA NIMBUS
SUNDOG AREOLET AUREOLE
BOROUGH CINCTURE
HALOHESH (SON OF —) SHALLUM
HALT HO HOP ALTO BAIT BALK
HOLD LIMP SKID STAY STOP TRIP

WAIT BAULK BLOCK BREAK CEASE
CHECK HILCH HITCH STAND STICK
ARREST BARLEY SCOTCH STANCE
CONTAIN CRIPPLE STATION
STOPPAGE
(— GAME) CALL
(— TO DOGS) TOHO
HALTER EVIL SOLE BRANK TRASH
WANTY WIDDY WITHE POISER
CAUSSON CAVESON JAQUIMA
POINTEL BALANCER NECKLACE
HALTING BODE LAME ZOPPA
CRIPPLE LIMPING
HALVE DIMIDIATE
(PL.) HALVERS
HALVING HAPLOSIS
HAM PIG GAMMON JAMBON
JARRET PESTLE GAMBONE
PROSCIUTTO
(BROTHER OF —) SHEM JAPHET
(FATHER OF —) NOAH
(PICNIC —) CALA CALI
(SON OF —) CUSH PHUT CANAAN
MIZRAIM
HAMATUM UNCIFORM
HAMESUCKEN HAMFARE
HAMITE BORAN BORANA DANAKIL
DANKALI
HAMLET KOM DORP TOON TOWN
TREF VILL ALDEA CASAL HAMEL
SITIO STEAD THORP VICUS
ALDEIA BUSTEE THORPE
CLACHAN KAMPONG KIRKTON
KIRKTOWN
(AUTHOR OF —) SHAKESPEARE
(CHARACTER IN —) OSRIC HAMLET
HORATIO LAERTES OPHELIA
BERNARDO CLAUDIUS GERTRUDE
POLONIUS REYNALDO CORNELIUS
FRANCISCO MARCELLUS
VOLTIMAND FORTINBRAS
ROSENCRANTZ GUILDENSTERN
HAMMEDATHA (SON OF —)
HAMAN
HAMMER AX AXE BIT DOG PEG
SET CALL COCK DROP HORN
MALL MASH MAUL MELL SETT
TILT CAVIL KEVEL KNOCK MADGE
POUND SMITE THUMP BEETLE
BUCKER CLOYER DRIVER FALLER
FULLER MALLET MARTEL NOPPER
OLIVER PLEXOR SCUTCH SLEDGE
TACKER TILTER KNAPPER
KNOCKER MALLEUS PLESSOR
STRIKER CRANDALL MALLEATE
MJOLLNIR SCUTCHER TREMBLER
(— FOR DRESSING STONE) KEVEL
(— OF GUNLOCK) DOG COCK
DOGHEAD
(— OUT) ANVIL
(BRICKLAYER'S —) SCOTCH
SCUTCH SCUTCHER
(LEADEN —) MADGE
(MINER'S —) BULLY
(PART OF —) BELL CLAW FACE
GRIP HEAD NECK PEEN POLL
CHEEK HANDLE
(PAVING —) REEL
(PNEUMATIC —) GUN BUSTER
(SLATE-CUTTER'S —) SAX
(STEAM —) IMPACTER IMPACTOR
(TUNING —) KEY
HAMMERED BEATEN WROUGHT

HAMMERHEAD CORNUDA
HAMMERKOP UMBER UMBRETTE
HAMMERLOCK BAR ARMLOCK
HAMMERMAN STRIKER
HAMMOCK SACK HUMMOCK
  (— CARRIED BY BEARERS) DANDY
  (— SLUNG ON POLE) MACHILA
  (WOODEN —) KATEL KARTEL
HAMMOLEKETH (BROTHER OF —)
  GILEAD
  (FATHER OF —) MACHIR
HAMPER BIN COT MAR PED TUB
  BEAT BIND CLOG CURB FLAT
  HURT LOAD SLOW TUCK BLOCK
  CABIN CRAMP CRATE MAUND
  RUSKY SERON BASKET BURDEN
  FETTER HALTER HINDER HOBBLE
  HOPPLE IMPEDE TANGLE
  BUFFALO CONFINE HANAPER
  MANACLE PANNIER PERPLEX
  SHACKLE TRAMMEL ENCUMBER
  ENTANGLE OBSTRUCT RESTRAIN
  RESTRICT STRAITEN
HAMPERING STIFLING DIFFICULT
HAMSTER CRICETID
HAMSTRING HOX HOCK LAME
  HOUGH ENERVATE
HAMUL (FATHER OF —) PHAREZ
HAMUTAL (FATHER OF —)
  JEREMIAH
  (HUSBAND OF —) JOSIAH
  (SON OF —) JEHOAHAZ ZEDEKIAH
HANAMEEL (COUSIN OF —)
  JEREMIAH
  (FATHER OF —) SHALLUM
HANAN (FATHER OF —) AZEL
  ZACCUR MAACHAH IGDALIAH
HANANI (FATHER OF —) HEMAN
  (SON OF —) JEHU
HANANIAH (FATHER OF —) AZUR
  BEBAI HEMAN ZERUBBABEL
  (GRANDSON OF —) IRIJAH
  (SON OF —) ZEDEKIAH
HANAPER HAMPER
HAND M CAT DAB FAM FIN HAN
  PAW PUD CLAW DEAL DUKE GIVE
  GOLL HALF JACK LOOF MAIN
  MANO MITT PART PASS SPAN
  CAMAY CLAUT CLEUK FLUSH
  GLAUM GRASP GRIPE INDEX
  MANUS NIEVE POWER SHARE
  STIFF STOCK BRIDGE CLUNCH
  CLUTCH DADDLE DOUBLE
  FAMBLE GOWPEN HANDLE
  MAULEY MINNIE STAGER
  WORKER CLAWKER FAMELEN
  FLAPPER FLIPPER POINTER
  WORKMAN GRAPPLER MORTMAIN
  (— COUNTING ZERO) BACCARA
  BACCARAT
  (— DOWN) DEVOLVE TRADUCE
  BEQUEATH TRANSMIT
  (— GESTURES) MUDRA
  (— IN POKER) FULL SKIP BLAZE
  FLUSH SKEET TIGER BICYCLE
  JACKPOT SKIPPER IMMORTAL
  STRAIGHT
  (— IN WHIST) MORT TENACE
  (— ON) BUCK SPREAD
  (— ON HIP) AKIMBO
  (— OVER) GIVE REACH BETEACH
  BITECHE DELIVER
  (— UP STRAW) SERVE

(— WITH 5 HIGHEST TRUMPS)
JAMBOREE
(BABY'S —) SPUD
(BIG AND UNGAINLY —) MAIG
(BRIDGE —) BID DUMMY DOUBLE
CHICANE LAYDOWN
(CLENCHED —) FIST
(COLD —S) SHOWDOWN
(CURSIVE —) CIVILITE
(DECK —) HAWSEMAN
(DUMMY —) BOARD
(ELDEST —) EDGE SENIOR
(EUCHRE —) JAMBONE
(EXTRA — IN LOO) MISS
(FRENCH —) COULEE
(GRASPING —) CLAUT
(GREEN —) FARMER JACKEROO
(LEFT —) SINISTRA
(LONE —) JAMBONE
(PART OF —) PAD BALL HEEL PALM
DIGIT INDEX THUMB PINKIE
CARPUS CREASE FINGER PINKIE
THENAR MINIMUS BRACELET
LIFELINE FINGERTIP FOREFINGER
HYPOTHENAR TRANSVERSE
(PERSIAN —) SHIKASTA
(POKER —S) BOARD
(RANCH —) COWBOY
(REEL —) SPINDLER
(RIGHT —) DEXTER
(ROUND —) RONDE
(SECTION —) SNIPE
(SKILLFUL —) DAB
(SPARE — IN CARDS) CAT
JAMBOREE
(UNSKILLED —) DABSTER
(UPPER —) BULGE EMINENCE
(WEAK CARD —) BUST
(PREF.) CHEIR(O) CHIR(O) MANI
MANU PALMATI PALMI
(SUFF.) CHEIRIA CHIRIA
HANDBAG BAG CABA NEIF CABAS
  PURSE SATCHEL ENVELOPE
  GRIPSACK POCHETTE RETICULE
  POCKETBOOK
HANDBALL PALM
HANDBARROW BIER HANDY
  TRUCK BARROW
HANDBELL SKELLAT TANTONY
HANDBILL BILL FLIER FLYER LIBEL
  DODGER
HANDBOOK VADY GRADUS
  MANUAL BAEDEKER
HANDBOW STONEBOW
HANDCAR DRAG
HANDCART PRAM DANDY HURLY
  TRUCK GOCART TROLLY TROLLEY
HANDCUFF CUFF STAY LINKER
  NIPPER STAYER MANACLE
  TRAMMEL WRISTER BRACELET
  HANDBOLT HANDLOCK LIGAMENT
  SNITCHER WRISTLET
  (PL.) IRONS SNAPS DARBIES
  NIPPERS
HANDEDNESS
  (SUFF.) CHEIRIA CHIRIA
HANDER-IN INGIVER
HANDFUL M MAN GRIP LOCK WISP
  YELM CLAUT GRIPE LITCH
  GOUPIN GOWPEN HANTLE
  YAFFLE FISTFUL MANIPLE
  (— OF GRAIN) RIP REAP SINGLE
  SONGLE

(— OF LEAVES) PATRIN
(DOUBLE —) GOWPEN
(LAST — OF HARVEST) KIRN
(SMALL —) PUGIL
HANDFUL OF DUST (AUTHOR OF —
) WAUGH
  (CHARACTER IN —) JOCK JOHN
  LAST TODD TONY BEAVER
  BRENDA MENZIES MESSINGER
HANDGRIP TUFFING
HANDGUN HAKE CALIVER
  HANDARM
HANDICAP START BURDEN DENIAL
  HAMPER HINDER IMPEDE STRIKE
  PENALTY ENCUMBER PENALIZE
HANDICAPPED CRIMP CRIMPED
HANDICRAFT MYSTERY ARTIFICE
  MECHANIC HANDCRAFT
HANDICRAFTSMAN ARTISAN
HANDILY HANDY GAINLY
HANDINESS YARAGE
HANDIWORK MACHINE
HANDKERCHIEF WIPE CLOUT
  FOGLE HANKY ROMAL STOOK
  WIPER HANKIE MADRAS NAPKIN
  SUDARY TIGNON BANDANA
  BELCHER FOULARD KERCHER
  MANIPLE ORARIUM SNEEZER
  BANDANNA KERCHIEF MOCKETER
  MONTEITH MOUCHOIR SUDARIUM
  VERNACLE VERONICA
HANDLE BOW EAR FAN LUG NIB
  NOB PAD PIN PLY USE ANSA BAIL
  BALE BOOL BUTT CROP FEEL FIST
  GAUM GRIP HAFT HALE HAND
  HANK HILT KILP KNOB LIFT RAPE
  RUNG STOP GRASP GRIPE GROPE
  HELVE MOUNT SHAFT SPOKE
  STAIL STALE START STEAL STELE
  STOCK SWING TREAT WIELD
  BECKET FETTLE FINGER FUSEAU
  HANGER LIFTER MANAGE
  MANURE POMMEL ROUNCE
  TILLER CONDUCT DUDGEON
  WOOLDER BEERPULL BELLPULL
  BITSTALK BITSTOCK DISPENSE
  HANDGRIP HANDHOLD HANDLING
  MOPSTICK STAGHORN
  PENHOLDER MANIPULATE
  (— AWKWARDLY) FUMBLE
  THUMBLE
  (— BADLY) ILLGUIDE
  (— CLUMSILY) PAW FUMBLE
  (— IMPROPERLY) GAUM
  (— MODISHLY) GALLANT
  (— OF AXE) HELVE
  (— OF BENCH PLANE) TOAT TOTE
  (— OF CANNON) MANIGLION
  (— OF DAGGER) DUDGEON
  (— OF KETTLE) BAIL
  (— OF LADLE) SHANK
  (— OF OAR) GRASP
  (— OF PLOW) HALE STAFF START
  STILT PLOWTAIL
  (— OF PRINTING PRESS) ROUNCE
  (— OF RAKE) STALE
  (— OF SCYTHE) TACK SNATH
  SNEAD THOLE SNATHE SNEATH
  (— OF SWORD) HAFT HILT
  (— OF WHIP) CROP
  (— RECKLESSLY) FOOL
  (— ROUGHLY) MALL MAUL TOWSE
  MUZZLE GRABBLE MANHANDLE

(— VIOLENTLY) BOUNCE
(CRANK —) WINK
(CROSSBOW —) TILLER
(CURVED —) BOOL BOUL
(DETACHABLE —) KILP
(LIFTING — OF GUN) DOLPHIN
(PUMP —) BRAKE SWIPE
(ROPE —) SHACKLE
(WOODEN —) TREE
(PL.) HALES
HANDLED (EASILY —) BANTAM
HANDLER DOCKHAND
  (AIRPLANE —) AIREDALE
  (SUFF.) STER STRESS
HANDLEY CROSS (AUTHOR OF —)
  SURTEES
  (CHARACTER IN —) JOHN PIGG
  HARDY MELLO BELINDA BRAMBER
  DOLEFUL MICHAEL SWIZZLE
  JORROCKS FLEECEALL
  BARNINGTON
HANDLING USE CONTROL
  (SKILLFUL —) CONDUCT
  (UNSKILLFUL —) BUNGLING
HANDMAID ANCILLA
HANDOUT DOWN
HANDRAIL BAR RAIL MANROPE
  BANISTER EASEMENT MOPSTICK
  TOADBACK
HANDSHAKE SHAKE SHRUG
HAND-SHAPED PALMATE
HANDSOME BRAW FAIR FINE
  MOOI NICE PERT TALL BONNY
  FETIS FITTY FUSOM LUSTY
  ADONIC BRAWLY CLEVER COMELY
  FARAND GOODLY HEPPEN LIKELY
  PROPER SEEMLY ADONIAN
  AVENANT ELEGANT FEATISH
  FEATOUS FEWSOME GALLANT
  LIBERAL SMICKER GOODLIKE
  STUNNING VENEREAN WEELFARD
HANDSOMELY FAIRLY HANDSOME
HANDSTONE MANO
HAND STRAP TOGGEL TOGGLE
HANDSTROKE TALLY
HANDWORK TOOLING
HANDWRITING PAW FIST HAND
  WRITE DUCTUS NESHKI NIGGLE
  SCRIPT SCRIVE BATARDE
  WRITING BACKHAND HANDWRIT
HANDY DAB DEFT GAIN NEAT
  WEME JEMMY LUSTY QUEME
  READY TIGHT ADROIT CLEVER
  HEPPEN KNACKY DEXTROUS
  EXPEDITE HANDSOME SKILLFUL
HANDYMAN MOZO JUMPER
  GREASER SWAMPER
HANG NUB TOP CRAP DRAG FALL
  HANK KILT PEND TREE TUCK
  DRAPE DROOP HOVER KETCH
  NOOSE SCRAG STRAP SWING
  TRINE TRUSS TWIST ANHANG
  APPEND DEPEND GIBBET HALTER
  IMPEND SLOUCH STRING TALTER
  DOGGONE HANGING LANTERN
  STRETCH SUSPEND
  (— ABOUT) DRING HOVER
  (— AROUND) KNOCK HANKER
  SLINGE
  (— BACK) LAG BOGGLE
  (— BEHIND) PLOD
  (— CRIMINAL) STRAP TOTTER
  (— DOWN) DIP LOP LAVE DROOP

DEPEND FESTOON PROPEND
(— HEAVILY) SWAG
(— LOOSELY) BAG SAG FLAG FLOW
LOLL BANGLE DANGLE PAGGLE
(— ONE'S HEAD) SLINK
(— OUT) LILL
(— OVER) WAUVE IMPEND
WHAUVE
(— PICTURE NEAR CEILING) SKY
(— SOGGILY) TROLLOP
(— WITH TAPESTRY) TAPIS
(PREF.) CREMO
HANGAR DOCK GARAGE AIRDOCK
HANGER PASSIVE SHABBLE
BASELARD WHINYARD
(— FOR CARCASSES) STANG
(COAT —) SHOULDER
(CRANK —) BRACKET
(LACE-MAKING —) WORKER
(SWORD —) CARRIAGE
HANGER-ON BUR CAD BURR SPIV
LEECH TOADY CLIENT HANGBY
HEELER LACKEY SPONGE
LACQUEY PENDING PARASITE
(— OF CELEBRITY) GROUPIE
HANGING FLAG HEMP TURN
ARRAS BAGGY DRAPE SWING
CELURE DORSEL DOSSER DERRICK
DRAPERY PENDENT PENSILE
ANTEPORT HANGMENT
PARAMENT
(— LOOSE) LOPPY BAGGED
(— LOW) SIDE
(— THREATENINGLY) IMMINENT
(LIMPLY —) FLAGGY SLIMPSY
(WALL —) CEILING TENTURE
KAKEMONO
(PL.) TAPIT TAPPET DRAPERY
PARAMENT
HANGMAN KETCH HANGER
HANGIE TOPMAN DERRICK
GREGORY TOPSMAN VERDUGO
CARNIFEX SCRAGGER
(HALTER OF —) TOW
HANGMAN'S DAY FRIDAY
HANGNAIL AGNAIL
HANGOUT NEST JOINT SCATTER
HANGOVER HOLDOVER RESIDUUM
HANG-UP BAG
HANIEL (FATHER OF —) ULLA
HANK HASP SKEIN BOBBIN
SELVAGEE
(— OF FLAX) HEAD
(— OF TWINE) RAN
(— OF YARN) SLIP
HANKER HANK LONG LINGER
HANKERING ITCH HANKER
HANKUL ENMUN ONMUN
HANNAH (HUSBAND OF —)
ELKANAH
(SON OF —) SAMUEL
HANNIEL (FATHER OF —) EPHOD
HANOCH (FATHER OF —) REUBEN
HANS BRINKER (AUTHOR OF —)
DODGE
(CHARACTER IN —) HANS RAFF
GLECK HILDA GRETEL BOEKMAN
BRINKER MEVROUW
HANSOM CAB SHOFUL SHOWFUL
HANUMAN ENTELLUS
HANUN (FATHER OF —) NAHASH
ZALAPH
HAP REDE CHANCE

FORTUNE HAPPING
HAPHAZARD CASUAL CHANCE
CHANCY RANDOM BUCKEYE
SCRATCH CARELESS SCRAMBLY
SLAPDASH TUMULTUARY
HAPHAZARDLY ANYHOW
HAPLESS POOR UNLUCKY
HAPLY HAPS HAPPILY
HAPPEN BE DO GO HAP COME
COOK FALL FARE GIVE LUCK PASS
RISE TIDE TIME BREAK EVENE
EVENT LIGHT OCCUR SHAPE
ARRIVE BECOME BEFALL BETIDE
CHANCE TUMBLE FORTUNE
STUMBLE SUCCEED BECHANCE
OVERCOME
(— TOGETHER) CONCUR
HAPPENING HAP FACT EVENT
THING CHANCE TIDING TIMING
INCIDENT OCCASION
OCCURRENCE
(ACTUAL —) FACT
(UNEXPECTED —) ACCIDENT
HAPPILY FAIN FITLY GLADLY
JOYOUSLY
HAPPINESS JOY WIN GLEE SELE
SONS WEAL BLISS GLORY MIRTH
SOOTH FELICE WEALTH DELIGHT
ECSTASY FELICIA RAPTURE
UTILITY FELICITY GLADNESS
HILARITY
HAPPY FIT COSH FAIN GLAD GLEG
SELI WELY BONNY FAUST FELIX
LIGHT LUCKY MERRY PROUD
SEELY SONSY SUNNY WHITE
BLITHE BONNIE BRIGHT JOYFUL
COMICAL GLEEFUL HALCYON
JOCULAR PERFECT SEELFUL
WEALFUL WEIRDLY BLISSFUL
CAREFREE DISPOSED FROHLICH
GRACIOUS SUNSHINE
(PREF.) FELICI
HARA-KIRI SEPPUKU
HARAN (BROTHER OF —) ABRAHAM
(DAUGHTER OF —) ISCAH MILCAH
(FATHER OF —) CALEB TERAH
(MOTHER OF —) EPHAH
(SON OF —) LOT
HARANGUE ORATE CONCIO
PATTER SERMON SPEECH TIRADE
ADDRESS DECLAIM EARBASH
DIATRIBE PERORATE
HARASS FAG GIG HAG HOX MAG
NAG RAG TAW VEX BAIT CARK
FRAB FRET GALL GNAW HAKE
HALE HARE HAZE HOCK JADE
PAIL PUSH RIDE SEEK TIRE TOIL
TOSS WORK ANNOY BESET BULLY
CHAFE CHASE CHEVY CHIVY
CURSE FLISK GRIND GRIPE HARRY
HURRY PRESS TARGE TEASE
TRASH WEARY WORRY BADGER
BOTHER CHIVVY CHOUSE
CUMBER FERRET HASSLE HATTER
HECKLE HECTOR HESPEL HOORAY
HURRAH INFEST MOLEST
MURDER OBSESS PESTER PINGLE
PLAGUE POTHER PURSUE
AFFLICT AGITATE BEDEVIL
DRAGOON HAGRIDE HARRAGE
OPPRESS PERPLEX PROVOKE
TERRIFY TORMENT TRAVAIL
TROUBLE TURMOIL BULLYRAG

DISTRACT DISTRESS EXERCISE
FORHAILE IRRITATE SPURGALL
SUPPRESS PERSECUTE
(— MENTALLY) GRUDGE
HARASSED BESTEAD HARRIED
HAUNTED
(— BY) BEFORE
HARASSING WARM
HARBINGER ANGEL USHER
HERALD FORAGER FORAYER
FURRIER OUTRIDER PRODROME
(— OF SUMMER) SWALLOW
HARBOR REE BEAR DOCK HOLD
PIER PORT BASIN BAYOU CHUCK
CREEK HAVEN HITHE SLADE
BREACH BUNDER COTHON
FOSTER REFUGE OUTPORT
PORTLET SEAPORT SHELTER
CARENAGE ENHARBOR SHIPRADE
(— A CRIMINAL) RESET
(SUBMARINE —) PEN
HARBOR SEAL DOTANT DOTARD
RANGER SEALCH TANGFISH
HARD DRY FIT ILL COLD DEAR
DOUR DURE FAST FIRM IRON
MEAN NASH OPEN CHAMP CLOSE
CORKY HARSH HORNY ROCKY
SMART SNELL SOLID SOUND
STEEL STERN STIFF STONY STOOR
STOUT TIGHT BOARDY BRAWNY
COARSE FLINTY GLASSY KITTLE
KNOBBY KNOTTY ROBUST
RUGGED SEVERE STARKY STINGY
STRICT STRONG STURDY UNEATH
UNNETH WOODEN ADAMANT
ARDUOUS AUSTERE CALLOUS
HARDWAY HORNISH ONEROUS
SUBDURE CORNEOUS DILIGENT
HARDBACK HARDENED
IRONHARD OBDURATE PETROSAL
RIGOROUS SCLEROID SCLEROSE
TOILSOME
(— BY) FORBY FORTHBY
(— TO BEAR) FIERCE
(— TO MANAGE) SALTY
(— TO PLEASE) FINICKY CONCEITY
(— TO REACH) CUMBROUS
(— TO READ) BLIND
(— TO SATISFY) EXIGENT
EXIGEANT
(— TO SELL) STICKY
(— TO UNDERSTAND) DIFFUSE
(PREF.) DURO SCLER(O) STERE(O)
HARD-BILL SEEDEATER
HARD-BITTEN GNARLED
HARDEN SET TAW BAKE BEEK
CAKE FIRM HARN KERN SEAR
BRAZE ENURE FLESH INURE
STEEL STONE BRONZE ENDURE
FREEZE OBDURE OSSIFY POTASH
SEASON TEMPER CALCIFY
EMBRAWN PETRIFY STIFFEN
THICKEN CONCRETE ENHARDEN
INDURATE SOLIDIFY
(— QUILL) DUTCH
(CASE —) STEEL
HARDENED DRAW HARD LOST
SALTED CALLOUS COCTILE
CRUSTED FIBROUS INDURATE
OBDURATE
HARDENING SET POROMA
SCLEROMA OSSIFICATION
HARDHACK SPIREA

IRONBUSH WHITECAP
HARDHEAD LION BOCHE
HARDHEARTED STERN STONY
OBDURATE
HARDICANUTE (FATHER OF —)
CANUTE
(HALF-BROTHER OF —) HAROLD
(MOTHER OF —) EMMA
HARDIHOOD PLUCK COURAGE
AUDACITY
HARDLY ILL SCANT BARELY
RARELY SCARCE UNEATH
SCARCELY
HARDNESS SEG GRAIN PROOF
RIGOR STEEL DURESS DURITY
ADAMANT HARDSHIP SEVERITY
SOLIDITY
(— OF CHARACTER) HEART
HARD-OF-HEARING DULL DUNCH
DEAFISH
HARDPAN PAN CLAYPAN
MOORPAN MOORBAND ORTSTEIN
HARDSHIP HARD GRIEF PINCH
RIGOR STOUR THRONG UNWEAL
SQUEEZE ASPERITY HARDNESS
(PL.) EXTREMES
HARDTACK PANTILE
(— AND MOLASSES) BURGOO
HARD TIMES (AUTHOR OF —)
DICKENS
(CHARACTER IN —) JUPE JAMES
SISSY JOSIAH LOUISA SLEARY
THOMAS SPARSIT STEPHEN
GRAGRIND BLACKPOOL
BOUNDERBY HARTHOUSE
MCCHOAKUMCHILD
HARDWARE TRIM IRONWARE
(COMPUTER —) MONITOR
HARDWOOD HARD BREAKAX
LEAFWOOD
HARDWORKING EIDENT
HARDY DOUR HARD WIRY LUSTY
MANLY STOUR STOUT TOUGH
GARDEN INURED RUGGED
STURDY SPARTAN STUBBED
GAILLARD GALLIARD STUBBORN
HARE PUG WAT BAWD CONY PUSS
SCUT BAWTY CUTTY LEPUS
PUSSY MALKIN MAUKIN BELGIAN
LEPORID POUSSIE VENISON
BAUDRONS KLIPHAAS LEPORINE
(— IN FIRST YEAR) LEVERET
(— TRACK) PRICK
(FEMALE —) DOE
(GREAT —) MANABOZHO
(LITTLE CHIEF —) CONY PIKA
(MALE —) BUCK
(PATAGONIAN —) MARA
(SIBERIAN —) TOLAL
(PL.) FLICK
(PREF.) LAG(O) LEPORI
HAREBELL BLAWORT THIMBLE
BLAEWORT BLUEBELL
HAREBRAINED GIDDY WINDY
HARELIP LAGOSTOMA
HAREM SERAI ZENANA ANDERUN
HAREMLIK SERAGLIO
HAREPH (FATHER OF —) CALEB
(SON OF —) BETHGADER
HARE'S-EAR MODESTY BUPLEVER
HARHAIAH (SON OF —) UZZIEL
HARIJAN PANCHAMA
HARL WHIRL

HARLEQUIN DUCK SQUEALER
(FEMALE —) LADY
(MALE —) LORD
HARLOT PUG DRAB LOON SLUT
HIREN PAGAN QUEAN RAHAB
STRAP TWEAK WHORE RIBALD
TOMBOY DELILAH MERMAID
WAGTAIL MERETRIX MISWOMAN
STRUMPET
(PREF.) PORN(O)
HARLOTRY PUTAGE BITCHERY
HARM NEY NOY NYE WEM ARME
BALE BANE DERE HURT SCAT
SORE TEEN WERD ANNOY GRAME
HERME LOATH QUALM SHEND
SPOIL TOUCH WATHE WEMMY
WOUGH WOUND WRAKE WREAK
WRONG DAMAGE DAMNUM
DANGER GRIEVE INJURE INJURY
SCATHE SORROW WONDER
DESPITE DISEASE FORFEIT
IMPEACH TROUBLE UNQUERT
BUSINESS DISAVAIL DISSERVE
ENDAMAGE MISCHIEF NOCUMENT
NUISANCE
(— REPUTATION) DEFAME
(DO —) ENVY
(PREF.) NOCI
HARMFUL BAD EVIL HARM NASTY
NOXAL NOCENT NOCIVE NOYFUL
UNSELY BANEFUL HURTFUL
NOISOME NOXIOUS DAMAGING
INIMICAL SINISTER PERNICIOUS
HARMFULNESS VICE MALICE
HARMINE BANISTERINE
HARMLESS SAFE SELI TAME
CANNY SEELY SILLY WHITE
DOVISH FEARLESS HURTLESS
INNOCENT SACKLESS UNHARMED
HARMONIA (DAUGHTER OF —) INO
AGAVE SEMELE AUTONOE
(FATHER OF —) MARS
(HUSBAND OF —) CADMUS
(MOTHER OF —) VENUS
(SON OF —) POLYDORUS
HARMONIC OVERTONE
HARMONICA HARP EUPHON
SYRINX AEOLINE PANPIPE
ARMONICA ZAMPOGNA
HARMONIOUS HAPPY SWEET
COSMIC SILKEN UNITED MUSICAL
SPHERAL TUNEFUL BALANCED
CHARMING HARMONIC PEACEFUL
ACCORDING CONCINNOUS
CONCORDANT
(PREF.) SYMPHO
HARMONITE RAPPIST RAPPITE
HARMONIUM ORGAN VOCALION
HARMONIZE GO FIT GEE KEY JIBE
SORT TUNE AGREE ATONE BLEND
CHORD GROUP HITCH RHYME
ACCORD ASSORT COTTON
COMPORT CONCENT CONCORD
CONSORT ORDINATE
ACCOMMODATE
HARMONIZING HENOTIC
HARMONY SUIT TUNE CHIME
CHORD UNITY ACCORD ATTUNE
COSMOS HEAVEN MELODY
UNISON BALANCE CONCENT
CONCERT CONCORD CONSENT
CONSORT KEEPING RAPPORT
DIAPASON FABURDEN SYMPATHY

SYMPHONY CONGRUITY
HARNEPHER (FATHER OF —)
ZOPHAH
HARNESS TUG GEAR HAME LEAF
REIN BRACE CROWN DRAFT
FRONT GEARS SLING TRACE
COLLAR FETTLE GULLET INSPAN
TACKLE DRAUGHT GEARING
GIGTREE LORMERY SIMBLOT
TOGGERY DRAWGEAR ENCLOSER
HEADGEAR TACKLING TURNBACK
(— FOR LOOM) LEAF HEALD
MOUNTING
(— FOR PULLING GUNS) BRICOLE
(DECORATIVE —) CAPARISON
(PART OF —) BIT REIN GIRTH
TRACE COLLAR BLINDER
CRUPPER BELLYBAND BREECHING
CHECKREIN
(WEAVING —) HEADLE HEDDLE
HARNESSED ANTELOPE GUIB
GUIBA BOSCHBOK BUSHBUCK
HARNESS MAKER KNACKER
WHITTAW
HAROLD I HAREFOOT
HARP ARPA FORK LYRE VINA
NABLA NANGA HARPER SABECA
CHROTTA DECHORD SAMBUKE
AUTOHARP CLARSACH
(CELTIC —) TELYN CLARSACH
(FINNISH —) KANTELA KANTELE
(ICELANDIC —) LANGSPIL
(JAPANESE —) KOTO
(JEW'S —) TRUMP
(PART OF —) BASE BODY FOOT
NECK BOARD PEDAL PILLAR
STRING
(PERSIAN —) SANG
(TRIANGULAR —) TRIGON
TRIGONON
HARPOON IRON FIZGIG GRAINS
FISHGIG HARPAGO STRIKER
HARPAGON
HARPOONED FAST
HARPOONER STRIKER
HARP SEAL HARP BEATER
SADDLER
HARPSICHORD SPINET CEMBALO
CLAVIER CLAVECIN HASPICOL
HARPY HAG AELLO CELAENO
OCYPETE PODARGE
HARQUEBUS HAGBUT CALIVER
HACKBUT ARQUEBUS
HARQUEBUSIER CARABIN
HARRIER HAWK KAHU BEAGLE
FALLER MILLER PUTTOCK
HARROWER
HARROW COG CHIP DISC DISK
DRAG HARO TINE BRAKE BREAK
HERSE DREDGE DRUDGE FALLOW
LADDER SPADER CUTAWAY
LACERATE OXHARROW
HARROWED HAGGARD
HARROWING TINE TINING
TEARING
(— OF HELL) ANASTASIS
HARRY HAG BRACE CHIVEY
CHIVVY FERRET HARASS CRUCIFY
HARSH ILL ACID BULL DOUR FOUL
HARD HASH HASK IRON RUDE
SOUR ACERB ACRID ASPER BRUTE
CRONK CRUDE GRILL GRUFF
HEAVY HUSKY RASPY ROUGH

ROUND RUVID SHARP SNELL
STARK STERN STIFF STOUR
STOUT BRUTAL COARSE FLINTY
GRAVEL GRISLY HOARSE RAGGED
RASPED RUGGED SEVERE
SHREWD STURDY SULLEN TETRIC
UNKIND UNRIDE AUSTERE
CRABBED RASPING RAUCOUS
SQUAWKY VIOLENT ABRASIVE
ACERBATE ASPERATE ASPEROUS
CATONIAN CLASHING DRACONIC
GRAVELLY GRINDING GUTTURAL
JANGLING OBDURATE RIGOROUS
SCABROUS SCRANNEL STRIDENT
STROUNGE STUBBORN TETRICAL
UNGENTLE UNKINDLY
(— OF VOICE) STEER
HARSHLY HARD HARSH SHORTLY
HARSHNESS WOLF RIGOR DURESS
CATOISM CRUDITY CRUELTY
DUREZZA RAUCITY ACERBITY
ACRIMONY ASPERITY FELLNESS
HARDNESS HASKNESS
MORDANCY SEVERITY
HART SPADE VENISON
HARTEBEEST ASSE TORA TORI
BUBAL CAAMA KAAMA KONZE
LECAMA BUBALIS CONGONI
KONGONI SASSABY
HART'S-TONGUE LONGLEAF
HARUM (SON OF —) AHARHEL
HARUMAPH (SON OF —) JEDAIAH
HARUSPEX ARUSPEX ARUSPICE
EXTISPEX
HARUZ (DAUGHTER OF —)
MESHULLEMETH
HARVEST IN WIN CROP HEAP RABI
REAP SLED SNAP FOISON GATHER
HAIRST RUBBEE COMBINE
GRABBLE INGATHER SHEARING
HARVESTER COMBINE
HARVEST FISH WHITING
MOONFISH STARFISH
HARVEST HOME KIRN MELL
HOCKEY HORKEY
HARVESTING SLEDDING
HARVESTMAN CARTER CARTARE
HARY JANOS (COMPOSER OF —)
KODALY
HAS S AS HATH
(— NOT) NAS AINT
HASADIAH (FATHER OF —)
ZERUBBABEL
HAS-BEEN WUZZER
HASH RAPE MINCE HACHIS
MUDDLE RAGOUT
HASHABIAH (COMPANION OF —)
EZRA
(FATHER OF —) BUNNI KEMUEL
JEDUTHUN MATTANIAH
HASHABNIAH (SON OF —)
HATTUSH
HASHISH HEMP ASSIS
HASHUBAH (FATHER OF —)
ZERUBBABEL
HASID ASSIDEAN
HASKALAH (FOLLOWER OF —)
MASKIL
HASP COP HAPS COPSE SPRENT
HASSAR DORAD
HASSOCK TUT BOSS PESS POUF
TOIT TRUSH BUFFET TUFFET
HASTE HIE POST RACE RAGE RAPE

CHASE FEVER HASTY HURRY
SPEED BUSTLE FLURRY SWIVET
DISPATCH RAPIDITY STROTHER
PRECIPITATION
(HEADLONG —) SPURN
(IN —) HOTFOOT
(IN GREAT —) AMAIN
HASTEN HIE RAP RUN BUSK DUST
FIRK PELL PLAT POST RACE RAPE
RUSH SPUR URGE CATCH CHASE
DRIVE FLEET HASTE HURRY
PRESS PREST SLATE SPEED STEER
EXPEDE SCURRY STREAK SWITHE
ADVANCE FORWARD HACKNEY
HOTFOOT PREVENT QUICKEN
SLITHER SWIFTEN WITHHIE
DISPATCH EXPEDITE ACCELERATE
(— AWAY) FLEE SHERRY SQUIRR
HASTILY HOTLY RAPELY RASHLY
FOOTHOT HOTFOOT HYINGLY
HEADLONG
HASTY FAST RAPE RASH BRASH
FLEET QUICK FLYING RAPELY
CURSORY HOTHEAD HURRIED
PEPPERY TEARING HASTEFUL
HEADLONG SUBITANE
(TACTLESSLY —) BRASH
HAT DIP FEZ LID NAB ATTE BAKU
COIF DISC DISK FELT FLAT HIVE
HOOD KNAB MOAB SLOP TILE
TOPI BEANY BENJY BENNY BERET
BOXER CADDI CORDY DERBY
DICER GIBUS JERRY KELLY MILAN
MITER MITRE SHELL TARAI TERAI
TOPEE TOQUE TRUSH ABACOT
BEANIE BEAVER BOATER BOWLER
BRETON BUMPER CADDIE
CASQUE CLAQUE CLOCHE
COCKUP COIFFE FEDORA HELMET
PANAMA PILEUS RAFFIA SAILOR
SHOVEL SLOUCH TOPPER
TURBAN VIGONE BANDEAU
BANGKOK BLOOMER BRIMMER
BYCOKET CATSKIN CAUBEEN
CHAPEAU FANTAIL HATTING
HATTOCK HOMBURG LEGHORN
PETASOS PILLBOX PLATEAU
PLATTER SALACOT SCRAPER
SHALLOW SKIMMER SMASHER
STETSON BONGRACE CAPELINE
GOSSAMER HEADGEAR JIPIJAPA
MONTABYN MUSHROOM
NABCHEAT RAMILIES REHOBOAM
ROUNDLET SOMBRERO
(— BLOCKER) ROPER
(— OF MERCURY) PETASUS
(BEAVER —) CASTOR
(CLERGYMAN'S —) SHOVEL
(COCKED —) BICORNE RAMILIE
SCRAPER
(COWBOY —) STETSON
(FABRIC —) TOQUE
(FELT —) DERBY JERRY TARAI
TERAI ALPINE BOWLER TRILBY
BILLYCOCK
(HIGH —) KYL PLUG TILE TOPPER
(IRON —) GOSSAN GOZZAN
(MILITARY —) BUSBY BEARSKIN
(OILSKIN —) SQUAM
(OPERA —) GIBUS CLAQUE
(PART OF —) BOW BRIM CROWN
PINCH LINING BINDING HATBAND
SWEATBAND

(PITH —) TOPI TOPEE
(SILK —) KYL BEAVER SHINER CATSKIN
(STIFF —) TILE DERBY KELLY BOATER BOWLER SAILOR
(STOVEPIPE —) CAROLINE
(STRAW —) BAKU FLAT HOOD KADY KATY TOYO BENJY BENNY CADDY STRAW BASHER BOATER PANAMA LEGHORN
(TOP —) PLUG TOPPER
(UNBLOCKED —) CONE
(WATERPROOF —) TARPAULIN
(WIDE-BRIMMED —) FLAT BENJY TARAI SMASHER SUNDOWN
(3-CORNERED —) TRICORN
HATBAND BAND WEED WEEPER
HAT BRIM LEAF TARFE TURNUP
HATCH HECK BREED BROOD CLECK CLOCK COVEY GUICHET UNSHELL DISCLOSE INCUBATE
HATCHERY CHICKERY
HATCHET MOGO HACHE GWEEON THIXLE FRANCISC TOMAHAWK
(PREF.) SECURI
HATCHING CLETCH BREEDING ECLISION
HATCHWAY HATCH SCUTTLE
HATE FIRE TEEN ABHOR SPITE DETEST HATRED LOATHE UNLOVE DESPITE
HATEFUL FOUL LOTH BLACK CURST DIRTY HATEL LOATH CURSED ODIOUS HEINOUS HIDEOUS ACCURSED FLAGRANT ABOMINABLE
HATER ULYSSES
HATH MOOLUM
HATHATH (FATHER OF —) OTHNIEL
HATING
(PREF.) MIS(O)
HAT MONEY TAMPANG
HATRED DOSA ENVY HATE HELL ONDE HAINE ODIUM SPITE ENMITY RANCOR AVERSION ABHORRENCE
(— OF CHILDREN) MISOPEDIA
(— OF MARRIAGE) MISOGAMY
(— OF MEN) MISANDRY MISANTHROPY
(— OF NEW IDEAS) MISCAINEA
(— OF REASONING) MISOLOGY
(— OF WOMEN) MISOGYNY
(PREF.) MIS(O)
HATTER GADGER HURRER
HATTUSH (FATHER OF —) HASHABNIAH
HAUBERK BYRNIE
HAUGHTILY BIGLY
HAUGHTINESS AIR PRIDE HEIGHT MORGUE ORGUIL DISDAIN HAUTEUR STOMACH HAUTESSE
HAUGHTY DAIN HIGH RANK STAY DIGNE DORTY HUFFY LOFTY LUSTY POTTY PROUD STOUT SURLY TAUNT FEISTY FIERCE HAUGHT QUAINT DISTANT HAUTAIN HONTISH PAUGHTY STATELY SUBLIME ARROGANT CAVALIER DEIGNOUS FASTUOUS GLORIOUS IMPERIAL INSOLENT ORGULOUS PRIDEFUL SCORNFUL SNIFFISH SUPERIOR

TOPLOFTY PEREMPTORY
HAUL KEP LUG RUG TEW TOW TUG DRAG DRAW DRAY HALE HURL JUNK PULL SKID TAKE TOTE TRAM BOUSE DRAVE HEAVE LIGHT ROUSE SNAKE TRACT TRICE TRAVOY DRAUGHT SCHLEPP CORDELLE HANDBANK
(— AFT) TALLY
(— DOWN) STRIKE
(— IN) GATHER
(— LOGS) TODE SLOOP SWAMP SIWASH HANDBANK
(— OF FISH) TACK DRAVE
(— OF NET) LIFT
(— SAIL) BUNT CLEW CLUE
(— SHIP) SPRING
(— TO DECK) BOARD
(— UP AND FASTEN) TRICE
(— WITH TACKLE) BOUSE
HAULAGE DOOK
HAULAGEWAY GANGWAY
HAULING HALE CARTAGE
HAUNCH HIP HOOK HUCK HANCE HUCKLE
(PL.) GRUG HUNKERS
HAUNT DEN HANT HOME HOWF KEEP NEST WALK GHOST HOWFF SPOOK STALK INFEST KENNEL OBSESS OUTLAY PURSUE REPAIR PURLIEU FREQUENT PRACTICE
(— OF ANIMALS) LIE HOME
(FAMILIAR —) SLAIT
HAUNTED SPOOKY
HAUNTING BESETTING
HAUSTELLATE GLOSSATE
HAUSTORIUM SINK SINKER SUCKER
HAUTBOY OBOE WAIT
HAUTEUR PRIDE HEIGHT MORGUE
HAVE A AN OF OWN HOLD BOAST ENJOY OUGHT WIELD POSSESS
HAVEN ARK HOPE PIER PORT HITHE HARBOR HAVENET
HAVILAH (FATHER OF —) CUSH JOKTAN
HAVING
(SUFF.) IOUS OSE OUS
HAVOC HOB HELL WASTE RAVAGE
HAW HOI HECK SLOE WIND WYND BOOTS PEGGLE ALISIER

KAMAKOU MAUNAKEA LANAIHALE
MOUNTAIN RANGE: KOHALA KOOLAU WAIANAE
NATIVE: KANAKA
STATE BIRD: GOOSE
STATE FLOWER: HIBISCUS
STATE NICKNAME: ALOHA
STATE TREE: CANDLENUT
TOWN: EWA AIEA HANA HILO LAIE PAIA KAPAA KEAAU LIHUE MAILI KAILUA KEKAHA PAHALA HONOKAA KAHULUI KANEOHE WAHIAWA WAIANAE WAILUKU HONOLULU PAPAIKOU
TREE: KOA NAIO WILIWILI
VALLEY: MANOA
VOLCANO: KILAUEA HUALALAI MAUNAKEA MAUNALOA

HAWAIIAN KANAKA KAMAAINA
HAWFINCH KATE GROSBEAK
HAWK IO EYAS KITE ALLAN BATER BUTEO CADGE EYESS HOICK HOUGH REACH RIVER STOOP BAWREL FALCON FOOTER HIGGLE KEELIE MERLIN MUSKET OSPREY PALLET PEDDLE RAMAGE RAPTOR RIFLER SHIKRA VERMIN BUZZARD GOSHAWK HAGGARD HARRIER HERONER KESTREL LENTNER STANIEL SWOOPER BRANCHER CARACARA HARROWER LENTINER PASSAGER ROUGHLEG SPARHAWK TALENTER TARTARET MORTARBOARD
(— FIGHT) CRAB
(CAGE FOR —S) MEW
(CROP OF —) GORGE
(FEMALE —) FORMAL FORMEL
(MALE —) JACK TASSEL TERCEL
(YOUNG —) EYAS NIAS BOWET BOWESS BRANCHER
(PREF.) HIERACO
HAWKER CRIER CRYER BADGER CADGER COSTER DUFFER JOWTER PEDDER PETHER CAMELOT CHAPMAN HIGGLER MERCURY PEDDLER CRATEMAN GLASSMAN HUCKSTER
HAWKEYE STATE IOWA
HAWKING FALCONRY
HAWK PARROT HIA
HAWKWEED DINDLE BUGLOSS FIREWEED OXTONGUE
HAWSE BAG JACKASS
HAWSER FAST WARP HEADLINE
HAWTHORN HAW MAY QUICK THORN AIGLET MAYBUSH COCKSPUR MAYBLOOM MAYTHORN QUICKSET
(FRUIT OF —) HAZEL PEGGLE
HAY HEI RIP MATH RAKH RISP FETTLE STOVER WINDLIN SWEEPAGE
(— CUT FINE) CHAFF
(— PUT IN BARN) END
(BUNDLE OF —) TRUSS
(PILE OF —) TUMBLE
(ROW OF —) WINDROW
(SECOND-GROWTH —) EDDISH
(SMALL LOAD OF —) HURRY
(SMALL PIECE OF —) TATE

HAYCOCK MOW COIL HOVEL QUILE SHOCK DOODLE HIPPLE LAPCOCK HAYSHOCK
HAYFIELD PARK RAKH MOWING
HAYFORK PIKE PICKEL
HAYLOFT LOFT TALLET SCAFFOLD
HAYMAKER PICKMAN
HAYMOW GOAF HAYLOFT OVERDEN OVERHEAD
HAYRACK HECK HAYRIG THRIPPLE
HAYSTACK COB PIKE RICK HOVEL HAYRICK STACKAGE
HAYSUCK EYSOGE
HAY SWEEP BUCK
HAYWARD MEADSMAN
HAZAN CANTOR CHAZZAN
HAZARD DIE LAY LOT JUMP PAWN RISK WAGE JENNY LOSER PERIL CHANCE DANGER NIFFER BALANCE IMPERIL VENTURE ENDANGER JEOPARDY
HAZARDOUS NICE NASTY RISKY CHANCY QUEASY RISQUE UNSAFE UNSURE PARLOUS PERILOUS
HAZARDOUSLY CHANCILY
HAZE FOG URE FILM GLIN MIST REEK SMOG TRUB DEVIL GAUZE HAZLE SMEETH
(— AND SMOKE) SMAZE
HAZEL AGLET AIGLET COBNUT MUFFIN FILBERT HAZELNUT NOISETTE
(— FOR THATCHING) SPRAYS
HAZEL HOE PULASKI
HAZELNUT NIT HAZEL FILBERT
HAZEL TREE AVELLANO
HAZILY DIMLY
HAZINESS HAZE GRAYOUT
HAZO (FATHER OF —) NAHOR
(MOTHER OF —) MILCAH
HAZY DIM FOGGY MISTY MUZZY SMOKY THICK VAGUE CLOUDY DREAMY OBSCURE SMUISTY NEBULOUS
HE A E HI HO HEH HEY HIM HYE SHE ILLE THON CESTUI
(— DIED) OB
(— GAVE AND DEDICATED) DDD
(— MADE) F FEC
(— PAINTED IT) PNXT
(— READS) LEG
(— WAS NOT FOUND) NEI
HEAD BIT BUT COP DON FAT MIR NAB NOB PEN POW TOP BEAN BOSS CAPE COCO CONK COSP CROP DATU DEAN DOME HELM JOLE JOWL KAID KNOB LEAD MAKE MASK NOLL PASH PATE POLL RAIS TURN YEAD ALDER ATTIC BLADE BLOCK BONCE CHIEF CHUMP CROWN DATTO MAZER ONION RISER SCALP SHODE SKULL START TIBBY TROPE BELFRY BLANCH CABEZA CENTER CHAULE COBBRA COCKER DAROGA EXARCH GARRET GATHER HEADER KAISER MAHANT MAZARD NAPPER NODDLE PALLET RUBRIC SCONCE CAPITAL CAPTAIN COCONUT COSTARD COSTREL COXCOMB CRUMPET CUPHEAD GENARCH HEADING HEGUMEN NUCLEUS

PRELATE TOPKNOT CALABASH
CEPHALON DECURION DIRECTOR
DUFFADAR FOUNTAIN HEADLINE
INITIATE PHYLARCH POINTING
TOPPIECE CAPERNOITIE
(— IN PARTICULAR DIRECTION)
STEM
(— OF ABBEY) ABBOT
(— OF ALEMBIC) MITER MITRE
(— OF BEAR, WOLF OR BOAR) HURE
(— OF CABBAGE) LOAF
(— OF CEREAL) EAR
(— OF CHAIR) MAKER
(— OF CLOVER) COB SUCKER
(— OF COLUMN) CHAPITER
(— OF COMET) COMA
(— OF CONVENT) ABBESS
SUPERIOR
(— OF CRIME SYNDICATE) CAPO
(— OF DANDELION) BLOWBALL
(— OF DRILL BRACE) CUSHION
(— OF FAMILY) ALDER COARB
COMARB GOODMAN
(— OF FISH) JOWL
(— OF GANG) TINDAL
(— OF GOVERNMENT) MUKHTAR
(— OF GRAIN) ICKER
(— OF GUILD) ALDERMAN
(— OF HAIR) SUIT CRINE FLEECE
CHEVELURE
(— OF HARPOON) BOMB
(— OF HERRING) COB
(— OF JEWISH ACADEMY) GAON
(— OF LANCE) MORNE MOURNE
(— OF LOOM) JACQUARD
(— OF MONASTERY) HEGUMEN
(— OF MUSHROOM) BUTTON
(— OF MUSICAL INSTRUMENT)
SCROLL
(— OF NUNNERY) DAME
(— OF ORDER) MURSHID
(— OF PROJECTILE) OGIVE
(— OF RING) CHATON
(— OF RIVET) BULLHEAD
FLATHEAD SNAPHEAD
(— OF SEPT) COARB COMARB
(— OF STATE) CAUDILLO PRINCEPS
(— OF TAPEWORM) SCOLEX
(— OF TREE) COMA
(— OF 10 MONKS) DEAN
(— ON) SQUARE
(— PREMATURELY) BUTTON
(— USED AS TARGET) SARACEN
(BAKED SHEEP'S —) JAMES JEMMY
(BALD —) PILGARLIC
(BARBED —) FLUKE
(DRAGON'S —) RAHU
(FLOWER —) DAISY ARNICA
BUTTON PINBALL
(FLOWER —S) CURD ANTHEMIS
(FROM — TO FOOT) CANAPE
(LATHE —) POPPET
(NAIL —) ROSEHEAD
(POPPY —) POST
(PRINTED —) BOXHEAD
(SEED — OF FLAX) HOPPE
(SHRUNKEN —) TSANTSA
(PL.) GEONIM
(PREF.) CEPHAL(O) CORY(PH)(PHO)
CRANIO
(SUFF.) CEPHALIC CEPHALOUS
CEPHALUS CEPHALY PATE
HEADACHE HEAD SODA

BUSTHEAD HEADWARK MIGRAINE
CEPHALALGY
HEADBAND MITER MITRE VITTA
CARCAN DIADEM TAENIA CIRCLET
GARLAND CARCANET FOOTBAND
STEPHANE
HEADBOROUGH VERGES
HEADCAP SETHEAD CAPELINE
HEADDRESS FLY TOP TOY APEX
COIF FRET HEAD HORN KELL
PARE POUF TETE TIRE TOUR
AEGIS AMPYX CROWN GABLE
LAUTU PASTE POLOS PSHEM
SHAKO TIARA TOWER VITTA
ALMUCE ATTIRE ATTOUR BONNET
CASQUE CORNET FAILLE HENNIN
KENNEL KULLAH MOBCAP PINNER
TIRING TUINGA BANDORE
COMMODE FLANDAN MORTIER
PSCHENT STEEPLE TABLITA
THERESE TRESSON TUTULUS
BILIMENT BINNOGUE BYCOCKET
CAPRIOLE COIFFURE HEADGEAR
HEADTIRE KAFFIYEH MASKETTE
STEPHANE TRESSURE
(— OF DOGES) TOQUE
(— OF GODS) MODIUS
(— OF POPE) REGNUM
(— WITH LONG LAPPET) PINNER
(HIGH —) TOWER STEEPLE
FONTANGE
(WIDOW'S —) BANDORE
HEADED KNOTTED
(— OUT) RIZZOMED
(SUFF.) PATED
HEADER BINDER BONDER NOBBER
SADDLE KNOBBER HEADSMAN
STRETMAN
HEADFAST HEADROPE
HEADFIRST HEADLONG
HEADFOREMOST TOPSAIL
HEADFRAME POPPET GALLOWS
HEADGEAR (ALSO SEE
HEADDRESS) HIVE PASTE
BONNET BRIDLE HEADWEAR
HEADHUNTER LAKHER TAIYAL
ATAIYAL QUIANGAN
HEADING END HEAD STOW
LEMMA PILOT TROPE WICKET
CAPTION DIPHEAD HEADILY
STENTON WITCHET FOREHAND
STENTING
HEADLAND KOP PEN RAS BILL
CAPE HEAD MULL NASE NAZE
NESS NOOK NOUP PEAK SCAW
THRUM FORELAND PROMONTORY
HEADLESS ACEPHALOUS
(PREF.) ACEPHALO
HEADLINE HEAD LABEL BANNER
CAPTION DROPLINE SCREAMER
STREAMER SCAREMONGER
HEADLONG FULL RANK AHEAD
HASTY PRONE STEEP SUDDEN
RAMSTAM TANTIVY GADARENE
HEADLING RECKLESS
PRECIPITATE
HEADMAN BAAS JARL CHIEF
DATTO MALIK PATEL POMBO
VIDAN ATAMAN CABEZA HETMAN
INDUNA LOWDAH LULUAI POTAIL
TOPMAN KOMARCH ALDERMAN
CABOCEER CAPITANO HEADSMAN
KONOHIKI MALGUZAR

MOKADDAM PENGHULU
PRINCEPS STAROSTA TENIENTE
HEADMASTER HEAD RECTOR
REGENT PRECEPTOR
HEADMOST FOREMOST
HEADNOTE SYLLABUS
HEADPIECE CAP POT BASKET
CASQUE HELMET PALLET TESTER
TREMOR BASINET BRASSET
CASQUET CHAMFRON TESTIERE
HEADPIN KINGPIN
HEADQUARTERS BASE DEPOT
YAMEN AGENCY FONDACO
EXCHANGE BATTALION
HEADROPE BALK BAULK HEADLINE
HEADSET PHONES
HEADSHIP CHIEFTY
(SPIRITUAL —) KHALIFAT
HEADSPACE OUTAGE
HEADSTALL HALTER BRADOON
BRIDOON JAQUIMA
HEADSTOCK POPPET
HEADSTRONG RASH COBBY
RACKLE STOCKY UNRULY
HOTSPUR RAMSTAM VIOLENT
WAYWARD PERVERSE STUBBORN
HEADWAITER CAPTAIN
HEADWAY WAY DENT SEAWAY
WAYGATE HEADROOM
HEADWORD ENTRY
HEADY BOLD NAPPY HUFFCAP
HEAL CURE HALE MEND SAIN
AMEND COVER LEECH SALVE
SOUND WHOLE PHYSIC RECURE
SUPPLE TEMPER WARISH
CLEANSE GUARISH RECOVER
REDRESS RESTORE MEDICATE
(— OVER) INCARN
HEALD CAMB DUPE HAVEL
HEALER CURER ALTHEA SHAMAN
POWWOWER PRACTITIONER
(SUFF.) IATRIST
HEALING IATRIC POWWOW
BALSAMIC CURATION IATRICAL
SANATION
(PREF.) IATR(O)
(SUFF.) IATRIA IATRIC(S) IATRIST
IATRY
HEALTH SAP HAIL HEAL SONS
QUART SALEW LIKING PLEDGE
SALUTE SANITY EUCRASY
SLAINTE EUCRASIA TONICITY
VALETUDE VALIDITY
(GOOD —) PLIGHT VERDURE
(ILL —) SICKNESS
(NORMAL —) USUAL
(PREF.) HYGE(I) HYGI SALUTI
HEALTHFUL HEALTHY HYGIENIC
SALUTARY SANATORY SANITARY
HEALTHY FIT FIER FIRM HALE
IRON SAFE SANE TIDY WELL
BONNY HODDY QUART SOUND
STOUT VALID ENTIRE HEARTY
ROBUST BOUNCING LAUDABLE
SALUTARY SANITARY VEGETOUS
VIGOROUS
(PREF.) SANI
HEAP COP CUB HOT MOW PIE SOW
TON BALE BING BULK DECK DESS
HILL HOTT LEET PILE POKE POOK
RAFF REEK RUCK SESS TASS
TUMP AMASS CLAMP CLUMP
COUCH CROWD SHOCK SORUS

STACK WOPSE BURROW HIPPLE
HOTTER ISLAND JALOPY MEILER
OODLES QUARRY RICKLE RUCKLE
SCRAPE SORITE TOORIE BOUROCK
CUMULUS ENDORSE HAYCOCK
HAYRICK HURROCK TOOROCK
TUMMELS WINDROW BASURALE
CONGERIES ACCUMULATE
ACCUMULATION
(— HAY) UNCOCK
(— OF DEAD BODIES) CARNAGE
(— OF GAME) QUARRY
(— OF GRAIN) BING
(— OF MORTAR) BINK
(— OF ORE) PANEL MONTON
(— OF PRODUCE) BURY CLAMP
(— OF REFUSE) BURROW BASURAL
(— OF RUBBISH) GAGING
(— OF SILVER ORE) TORTA
(— OF SLAIN) CARNAGE
(— OF STONES) AHU MAN CAIRN
SCRAE SCREE HURROCK
MONTJOY
(— OF VEGETABLES) HOG
(— REPROACHES) KICK
(— TOGETHER) AGGEST HOWDER
LUMBER CUMULATE
(— UP) HILL SACK AGGEST
ACERVATE AGGERATE OVERHEAP
(COMBUSTIBLE —) PYRE
(MANURE —) HOTT MIXEN
(PROMISCUOUS —) RAFF
(PREF.) CUMULI CUMULO SOREDI
SORI SORO THOMO
HEAPED COCKED ACERVATE
CUMULATE
HEAR EAR LIST OYES OYEZ LEARN
LITHE HARKEN LISTEN HEARKEN
(— DIRECTLY) IMPINGE
(PREF.) ACOU(O) AUDIO
HEARD AUDIBLE
(EASILY —) CLEAR
HEARER AUDIENT AUDITOR
HEARING EAR LIST OYER AUDIT
SOUND ASSIZE AUDIENCE
AUDITION
(PREF.) ACOU(O)
(SUFF.) ACOUSIA ACOUSIS
ACUSIA ACUSIS
HEARKEN HARK HEAR HEED LIST
TEND LITHE ATTEND HARKEN
INTEND
HEARSAY REPORT ACCOUNT
HEARSE HACK CATAFALCO
HEART AB COR CORE GIST HATI
PUMP RAAN SOUL YOLK BOSOM
BOWEL CHEER JARTA QUICK
BREAST CENTER CENTRE DEPTHS
HASLET MIDDLE NATURE TICKER
VISCUS COURAGE EMOTION
ESSENCE FEELING
(— OF DIXIE) ALABAMA
(— OF ROTTEN TREE) DADDOCK
(DEAR —) DILIS
(PREF.) CARDI(A)(O) CORDI
PHREN(O)
(AROUND THE —) PERICARDI(O)
(SUFF.) CARDIA CARDIUM
HEARTACHE SORROW
HEARTBEAT STROKE
(SUFF.) CROTIC
HEARTBREAK HOUSE (AUTHOR OF
—) SHAW

(CHARACTER IN —) DUNN ELLIE MANGAN HESIONE MAZZINI HUSHABYE SHOTOVER UTTERWORD
HEARTBURN PYRÒSIS
HEART CHERRY GASKINS
HEARTEN BIELD CHEER HEART SPIRIT EMBOLDEN INSPIRIT
HEARTFELT DEAR DEEP REAL TRUE INFELT INWARD CORDIAL GENUINE SINCERE
HEARTH EARD SOLE TEST ASTRE CUPEL EARTH FOCUS FOGON FOYER SMOKE CHIMNEY
(— GODDESS) VESTA
HEARTILY INLY AGOOD DEARLY FREELY WARMLY SHEERLY DINGDONG INWARDLY STRONGLY
HEARTINESS GOODWILL
HEARTLESS SARDONIC
HEARTLESSNESS CYNICISM
HEART OF MIDLOTHIAN (AUTHOR OF —) SCOTT
(CHARACTER IN —) MEG JOHN DAVID DEANS EFFIE MADGE BUTLER GEORGE JEANIE REUBEN GEORDIE PORTEUS STAUNTON ROBERTSON MURDOCKSON
HEARTSEASE PANSY
HEARTTHROB DUNT
HEARTWOOD ALOES HEART SAPAN SPINE GUAYAB BUBINGA DURAMEN TRUEWOOD
HEARTY REAL WARM BUXOM CORBY FRECK HEAVY STOUT DEVOUT ENTIRE ROBUST STANCH BOBBISH CORDIAL EARNEST HEALTHY RAFFING SINCERE HEARTFUL VIGOROUS BOISTEROUS
HEAT HET HOT RUT SUN TAP BOIL FIRE GLOW SALT WARM ARDOR BEATH BROIL CALOR CAUMA CHAFE FEVER PRIDE PROUD STECH TEPOR TRIAL ACHAFE ANNEAL DEGREE DIGEST FERVOR HEATEN IGNITE SCORCH SEASON SIZZLE SPARGE WARMTH CALCINE CALORIC ENCHAFE FERMENT FLUSTER INCENSE INFERNO PASSION SWELTER UPERIZE CALIDITY
(— GENTLY) SOAK
(— OF BATTLE) PRESS
(— SCRAP IRON) BUSHEL
(— SWEETEN, AND SPICE) MULL
(— TOBACCO) SAP
(ROWING —) REPECHAGE
(SCORCHING —) EWDER
(PREF.) CALORI PYR(O) THERM(ATO)(O)
(BURNING —) KAUMO
(MODIFIED BY —) COCTO
(SUFF.) THERM(Y)
HEATED WARM FIERCE STEAMY
HEATER GAT GUN FIRE COCKLE PISTOL SMOKER CHAFFER CHOFFER LATROBE
HEATH BENT YETH BESOM BRIAR BRIER ERICA ERICAD COMMONS HEATHER RHODORA CRAKEBERRY
(PREF.) ERICO
HEATHEN AKKUM PAGAN ETHNIC

PAYNIM GENTILE PROFANE SARACEN GENTILIC
HEATHENISM ODINISM OTHINISM PAGANISM
HEATHER BENT GRIG LING BROOM ERICA HEATH HADDER
HEATHERY LINGY
HEATH PEA CARMELE
HEATING BAKEOUT BURNING
HEATLESS ATHERMIC
HEAVE GAG BUNG HEFT HOVE KECK LIFE QUAP FETCH HOIST SCEND SURGE BUCKLE KECKLE POPPLE ESTUATE
HEAVEN SKY HIGH ABOVE BLISS DYAUS ETHER GLORY ASGARD CANAAN HIMMEL SVARGA SWARGA URANUS WELKIN KINGDOM OLYMPUS DEVALOKA EMPYREAL EMPYREAN PARADISE SVARLOKA
(12TH PART OF —) HOUSE
(PL.) ARCH LIFT LANGI HEIGHT REGION SPHERE ELEMENT TENGERE EMPYREAN KAMALOKA
(PREF.) URAN(I)(O) URANOSO
HEAVENLY ABOVE DIVINE ANGELIC BLESSED URANIAN ETHEREAL OLYMPIAN AMBROSIAL
HEAVEN'S MY DESTINATION
(AUTHOR OF —) WILDER
(CHARACTER IN —) BAT HERB BRUSH COREY EFRIM LOUIE MCCOY BURKIN CROFUT GEORGE JESSIE MARGIE MORRIE DOREMUS QUEENIE ROBERTA BLODGETT ELIZABETH
HEAVENWARD ZIONWARD
HEAVER COALY DANNER HEFTER
HEAVILY SOSS CLOIT CLYTE HEAVY PLUMP SADLY SOUSE SWACK
HEAVINESS DOLE HEFT GLOOM POISE WEIGHT GRAVITY
HEAVY FAT HOT SAD CLIT DEEP DOWF DULL HARD BEEFY BURLY DENSE DOWFF DUNCH GRAVE GREAT GROSS HEFTY HOGGY STIFF THARF THERF THICK WROTH CHARGE CLUMPY CLUMSY DOUGHY DRAGGY HEARTY LEADEN LIVERY LOGGER SODDEN STODGY STRONG STUPID WOODEN INSIPID LABORED LIVERED LUMPING MASSIVE ONEROUS OUTSIZE PESANTE WEIGHTY CUMBROUS GRIEVOUS PERSANTE PREGNANT THUMPING PONDEROUS SATURNINE
(PREF.) BARY GRAVI HADR(O)
HEAVY-FOOTED SOGGY LEADEN INFICETE
HEBDOMADARY WEEKLY
HEBE (FATHER OF —) JUPITER
(HUSBAND OF —) HERCULES
(MOTHER OF —) JUNO
HEBER (GRANDFATHER OF —) ASHER
(SON OF —) SOCHO
(WIFE OF —) JAEL
HEBREW RABBINIC
HEBRIDES
(ISLAND OF H) IONA
HEBRON (FATHER OF —) KOHATH

HECATE TRIVIA
(FATHER OF —) PERSES
(MOTHER OF —) ASTERIA
HECKLE BAIT GIBE HACK BADGER HARASS HECTOR HATCHEL
HECTIC ETIK SEPTIC HECTIVE FEVERISH FRENETIC FRENZIED
HECTOLITER VAT
(5.82 —S) LEAGUER
HECTOR BAIT HUFF BULLY HARRY TEASE WORRY HARASS HECKLE BLUSTER BRAVADO BROWBEAT
(FATHER OF —) PRIAM
(MOTHER OF —) HECUBA
(SLAYER OF —) ACHILLES
(WIFE OF —) ANDROMACHE
HECUBA (DAUGHTER OF —) POLYXENA
(FATHER OF —) DYMAS CISSEUS
(HUSBAND OF —) PRIAM
(SON OF —) PARIS HECTOR HELENUS POLYDORUS
HEDDA GABLER (AUTHOR OF —) IBSEN
(CHARACTER IN —) THEA BRACK DIANA HEDDA EILERT GABLER GEORGE TESMAN ELVSTED JULIANA LOVBERG
HEDDLE CAMB DOUP HAVEL HEALD
(PL.) CAAM
HEDGE BAR HAW HAY HYE OXER SAVE BEARD EDDER FENCE FRITH FUDGE HOVER MOUND QUICK COPPER FRIGHT RADDLE ENCLOSE QUICKSET RUFFMANS SEPIMENT SURROUND THICKSET
(PREF.) SEPI SEPTATO
(SUFF.) SEPTATE
HEDGE BINDWEED CREEPER HELLWEED WOODBINE
HEDGEHOG ORCHEN URCHIN ECHINUS ERICIUS YLESPIL HEDGEPIG HERISSON
HEDGE LAUREL TARATA
HEDGE MUSTARD BANKWEED FLUXWEED
HEDGE NETTLE STACHYS
HEDGE PARSLEY HOGWEED
HEDGE-PRIEST PATRICO
HEDGE SPARROW DICKY DONEY DICKEY EYSOGE PHILIP CHANTER DUNNOCK HAYSUCK PINNOCK TITLING ACCENTOR
HEDGEWOOD LAYER
HEED CARK COME CURE GAUM HEAR KEEP LOOK MIND NOTE RECK TEND TENT VISE WARE YEME AWAIT TASTE VALUE ATTEND INTENT NOTICE REGARD REMARK REWARD CAUTION OBSERVE RESPECT SUSPECT THOUGHT OBSERVATION
HEEDFUL WARE ATTENT DILIGENT VIGILANT REGARDFUL
HEEDLESS RASH BLIND DIZZY GIDDY BLITHE REMISS UNWARY LANGUID UNHEEDY CARELESS LISTLESS MINDLESS RECKLESS WISTLESS NEGLECTFUL
HEEDLESSLY BLIND HEADLONG
HEEL TIP BUTT CALX FROG HIELD

SPIKE TALON DOTTLE INCLINE BOOTHEEL
(— IN) SHOUGH
(— OF GATE) HARR
(— OF HORSESHOE) SPONGE
(— OF SWORD BLADE) TALON RICASSO
(— OVER) SEEL TILT CAREEN
(PREF.) CALCANEO TAL(I)(O)
HEEL BEVEL RAND
HEEL PLATE SHOD CLEAT
HEFT WEIGHT
HEFTY HEAVY
HE-GOAT
(PREF.) HIRCO
HEIFER IO QUI QUEE QUEY QUOY BULLER STOCKER
(— IN 2ND YEAR) STIRK
(YEARLING —) BURLING
HEIGH-HO HECH
HEIGHT SUM ACME ALTO APEX FELL HIGH LOFT MOTE PINK TUNE CREST HICHT STATE ALTURE INCHES SUMMIT CEILING COMMAND HEIGHTH STATURE SUPREME ALTITUDE EMINENCE HAUTESSE SIDENESS VERTICAL ACROPOLIS
(— OF FASHION) GO
(— OF PROSPERITY) GLORY
(— OF ROOM) STUD STUDDING
(— OF SAIL) HOIST
(GREATEST —) NOON SUMMIT ZENITH
(ROCKY —) KNOT
(PREF.) ACR(O) BATHO BATHY BATO HYPS(I)(O)
HEIGHTEN ENDOW EXALT FORCE RAISE ACCENT BOLSTER ENHANCE SUBLIME
(— FLAVOR) PETUNE
HEINOUS SWART CRYING WICKED SCARLET FLAGRANT GRIEVOUS
HEIR SCION SPRIG COHEIR HERITOR APPARENT PARCENER
(— APPARENT) ATHELING ETHELING
(CELTIC —) TANIST
(FEMALE —) DISTAFF
(PREF.) HEREDI HEREDO
HEIRESS BEGUM PORTIA FORTUNE HERITRIX
HEIRLOOM
(PL.) CIMELIA
HEL (FATHER OF —) LOKI
(MOTHER OF —) ANGURBODA
HELAH (HUSBAND OF —) ASHUR
(SON OF —) TEKOA
HELEB (FATHER OF —) BAANAH
HELEK (FATHER OF —) GILEAD
HELENUS (FATHER OF —) PRIAM
(MOTHER OF —) HECUBA
(SON OF —) CESTRINUS
(WIFE OF —) ANDROMACHE
HELEZ (FATHER OF —) AZARIAH
HELI (SON OF —) JOSEPH
HELIANTHEMUM SUNROSE
HELICAL SPIRAL
HELICAON (FATHER OF —) ANTENOR
(MOTHER OF —) THEANO
(WIFE OF —) LAODICE
HELICOPTER HOVER COPTER

CHOPPER WINDMILL
(— TO REMOVE CASUALTIES)
DUSTOFF
(ARMED —) GUNSHIP
HELIOPOLIS ON
HELIOS HYPERION PHAETHON
(DAUGHTER OF —) CIRCE PASIPHAE
(FATHER OF —) HYPERION
(MOTHER OF —) THEIA
(SISTER OF —) EOS SELENE
(SON OF —) AEETES PHAETHON
HELIOSIS SUNBURN
HELIOTROPE HELIO BENNET
SETWALL GIRASOLE TURNSOLE
VALERIAN
HELIPORT SKYPORT
HELIX COIL SPIRAL
HELIXIN HEDERIN
HELL PIT POT HECK PAIN ABYSS
AVICI BLAZE DEUCE HADES
SHEOL BLAZES NARAKA TARTAR
TOPHET TUNKET ABADDON
GEHENNA HELLBOX INFERNO
TORMENT TARTARUS
BARATHRUM PERDITION
PANDEMONIUM
(PREF.) TARTARO
HELLBENDER TWEEG MENOPOME
HELLE (BROTHER OF —) PHRIXUS
(FATHER OF —) ATHAMAS
(MOTHER OF —) NEPHELE
HELLEBORE POKE BUGBANE
ITCHWEED LINGWORT
LUNGWORT NOSEWORT
POKEROOT VERATRUM
EARTHGALL
HELLEN (FATHER OF —) DEUCALION
(MOTHER OF —) PYRRHA
(SON OF —) DORUS AEOLUS
XUTHUS
(WIFE OF —) ORSEIS
HELLER HALER HALERZ
HELLERI SWORDTAIL
HELL-FIRE BRIMSTONE
HELLGRAMMITE DOBSON SIALID
CLIPPER CRAWLER SPRAWLER
HELLISH HELLY SATANIC STYGIAN
DEVILISH INFERNAL TOPHETIC
HELLO HALLO HILLO HULLO HILLOA
HELM KEY STEER STERN TIMON
HELMET TIMBER STEERAGE
HELMET CAP POT CASK HELM
HOOD ARMET CREST GALEA
MAZER MOUND BARBEL BEAVER
CASQUE CASTLE GALERA
HEAUME MORION PALLET SALADE
SALLET TESTER BASINET
CASQUET GALERUM GALERUS
AVENTAIL BURGANET BURGONET
HEADGEAR KNAPSCAP SCHAPSKA
SKULLCAP TARNHELM TESTIERE
(— PART) VENTAIL
(PITH —) TOPI TOPEE
(PREF.) GALEI
HELMET-SHAPED GALEATE
HELMSMAN PILOT STEER
GLAUCUS TIMONEER
HELON (SON OF —) ELIAB
HELP AID BOT ABET BACK BOOT
CAST LIFT STOP AVAIL BOOST
FAVOR FRITH HEEZE RESET
SPEED START STEAD YELDE
ASSIST HELPER RELIEF REMEDY

SECOND SUCCOR UPTAKE
BENEFIT BESPEED BESTEAD
CHEVISE COMFORT FORWARD
FURTHER HELPING IMPROVE
PRESIDY PROMOTE REDRESS
RELIEVE SUPPORT SUSTAIN
ADJUMENT BEFRIEND SUFFRAGE
(— FORWARD) FRANK FURTHER
(— ON) ADVANCE
(— ONWARD) FORWARD
(— OUT) FIRK
(HIRED —) LABOR
HELPER AID CAD FOAL HELP MATE
PAGE ANSAR AIDANT BARBOY
COOKEE DIENER FLUNKY JUMPER
NIPPER TENTER WAITER ADJOINT
ADJUNCT ADJUTOR ANCILLA
CASHBOY GALOPIN SUMPMAN
SWAMPER HELPMATE OFFSIDER
SCULLION TROUNCER
(— IN GLASSWORKS) SNAPPER
(BLACKSMITH'S —) STRIKER
(CHIMNEY SWEEP'S —) CHUMMY
(COOK'S —) SLUSHY
(COOPER'S —) TUBBIE
(HORSESHOER'S —) FLOORMAN
(PICKPOCKET'S —) BULKER
(YOUNG —) FOAL
HELPFUL GOOD AIDANT AIDFUL
HELPLY SECOND SPEEDY USEFUL
ADJUVANT HELPSOME OBLIGING
SINGULAR SERVICEABLE
HELPING HELP AIDANT PORTION
SERVING ADJUTORY ADJUVANT
HELPLESS NUMB SILLY ABJECT
UNABLE AIDLESS FORLORN
FECKLESS HAVELESS REDELESS
HELPLESSNESS ADYNAMIA
HELTER-SKELTER TAGRAG
PELLMELL
HELVE HELM SHAFT
HELVE HAMMER OLIVER
HEM HUM WLO FELL SLIP WELT
HEDGE SPLAY PURFLE TURNUP
HEMMING TURNING SURROUND
(— AND HAW) HAVER
(— GLOVE) WRIST
(— IN) BOX LAP BEBAY BESET
IMPALE BESIEGE COMPASS
ENCLOSE ENVIRON STRAITEN
SURROUND
(— IN FISH) EBB
(— OF SAIL) TABLING
(— OF TROUSERS) CUFF
(PREF.) LIMBI
HEMAM (BROTHER OF —) HORI
(FATHER OF —) LOTAN
HEMAN (FATHER OF —) JOEL ZERAH
(GRANDFATHER OF —) SAMUEL
HEMATITE ORE OLIGIST SANGUINE
HEMDAN (FATHER OF —) DISHON
HEMICRANIA MIGRAINE
HEMIEPES ENOPLION
HEMIMORPHITE CALAMINE
HEMIOLIC SESCUPLE
HEMISTICH SECTION
HEMITHEA (BROTHER OF —) TENES
(FATHER OF —) CYCNUS
(MOTHER OF —) PROCLEA
HEMLOCK BUNK CASH KELK
BENNET CICUTA COWBANE
DEATHIN SHINWOOD
HEMOPHILIAC BLEEDER

HEMORRHAGE STAXIS APOPLEXY
BLEEDING HEMOPTOE PETECHIA
HEMOSTATIC RHATANY ERIGERON
HEMP IFE KEF KIF TOW BANG CARL
POOA RINE SANA SUNN ABACA
BHANG DACHA DAGGA FIQUE
GANJA HURDS MURVA RAMIE
SABZI SISAL AMBARY CABUYA
FIMBLE LIAMBA NALITA SINAWA
AMYROOT CABULA GAGROOT
NIYANDA PANGANE PITEIRA
SOSQUIL BIRDSEED CANNABIS
CHUCKING LOCOWEED
NECKWEED NEPENTHE
MARIJUANA
(PREF.) CANNABI
HEMP AGRIMONY EUPATORY
HEMPWEED
HEMPEN NOGGEN
HEMP NETTLE IRONWORT
HEMPWEED BONESET DUCKBLIND
HEN FOWL BIDDY CHUCK LAYER
BROODY MABYER PULLET
CLOCKER HOVERER PARTLET
LANGSHAN
(— THAT HAS NOT LAID) TOWDIE
(— WITH CHICKENS) CLUCK
(— WITH SHORT LEGS) GRIG
(BROODY —) SITTER
(FATHER OF —) ZEPHANIAH
(FATTENED —) POULARD
(1-YEAR-OLD —) YEAROCK
HENBANE HEBENON CHENILLE
HENCE AWAY ERGO HYNE THUS
AVAUNT HETHEN HEREOUT
HENCEFORTH YET HENCE
HENCHMAN FELLOW SATRAP
SERVANT FOLLOWER RETAINER
UNDERLING
HEN COOP CAVY CAVIE
HENGEST (BROTHER OF —) HORSA
(KINGDOM FOUNDED BY —) KENT
(SON OF —) AESC
HEN HARRIER FALLER KATABELLA
(IMMATURE —) RINGTAIL
(MALE —) MILLER
HENNA MENDY ALCANNA
ALHENNA CAMPHIRE
HENNIN STEEPLE
HENPECK NAG
HENRY QUAD HAWKIN SECOHM
HEINRICH QUADRANT
HENRY ESMOND (AUTHOR OF —)
THACKERAY
(CHARACTER IN —) HOLT FRANK
HENRY JAMES MOHUN ESMOND
RACHEL STUART BEATRIX
FRANCIS
HENRY IV-PART I (AUTHOR OF —)
SHAKESPEARE
(CHARACTER IN —) JOHN OWEN
PETO BLUNT HENRY PERCY POINS
EDMUND SCROOP THOMAS
VERNON WALTER DOUGLAS
HOTSPUR MICHAEL QUICKLY
RICHARD BARDOLPH FALSTAFF
GADSHILL MORTIMER ARCHIBALD
GLENDOWER LANCASTER
WESTMORELAND
HENRY IV-PART II (AUTHOR OF —)
SHAKESPEARE
(CHARACTER IN —) DAVY DOLL
FANG JOHN PETO WART BLUNT

GOWER HENRY POINS RUMOR
SNARE FEEBLE MORTON MOULDY
PISTOL SCROOP SHADOW SURREY
THOMAS MOWBRAY QUICKLY
SHALLOW SILENCE TRAVERS
WARWICK BARDOLPH BULLCALF
CLARENCE FALSTAFF HARCOURT
HASTINGS HUMPHREY COLEVILLE
LANCASTER TEARSHEET
WESTMORELAND
NORTHUMBERLAND
HENRY V (AUTHOR OF —)
SHAKESPEARE
(CHARACTER IN —) NYM GREY
JAMY YORK ALICE BATES COURT
GOWER HENRY LEWIS EXETER
ISABEL PISTOL SCROOP THOMAS
BEDFORD BOURBON CHARLES
MONTJOY ORLEANS WARWICK
BARDOLPH BURGUNDY FLUELLEN
GRANDPRE RAMBURES WILLIAMS
ERPINGHAM KATHARINE
MACMORRIS SALISBURY
GLOUCESTER WESTMORELAND
HENRY VIII (AUTHOR OF —)
SHAKESPEARE
(CHARACTER IN —) ANNE VAUX
BUTTS DENNY HENRY SANDS
BULLEN LOVELL SURREY THOMAS
WOLSEY ANTHONY BRANDON
CRANMER NORFOLK SUFFOLK
CAMPEIUS CAPUCIUS CROMWELL
GARDINER GRIFFITH NICHOLAS
PATIENCE GUILDFORD
KATHARINE BUCKINGHAM
ABERGAVENNY
HENRY VI-PART I (AUTHOR OF —)
SHAKESPEARE
(CHARACTER IN —) JOAN JOHN
LUCY HENRY BASSET EDMUND
TALBOT THOMAS VERNON
ALENCON BEDFORD CHARLES
RICHARD SUFFOLK WARWICK
WILLIAM BEAUFORT BURGUNDY
FASTOLFE GARGRAVE MARGARET
MORTIMER REIGNIER GLANSDALE
LAPUCELLE SALISBURY
WOODVILLE GLOUCESTER
PLANTAGENET
HENRY VI-PART II (AUTHOR OF —)
SHAKESPEARE
(CHARACTER IN —) SAY CADE DICK
HUME IDEN JACK JOHN VAUX
BEVIS GOFFE HENRY PETER
SMITH EDWARD GEORGE HORNER
SCALES ELEANOR HOLLAND
MATTHEW MICHAEL RICHARD
SIMPCOX STANLEY SUFFOLK
WARWICK BEAUFORT CLIFFORD
HUMPHREY JOURDAIN
MARGARET SOMERSET STAFFORD
ALEXANDER SALISBURY
SOUTHWELL BUCKINGHAM
BOLINGBROKE PLANTAGENET
HENRY VI-PART III (AUTHOR OF —)
SHAKESPEARE
(CHARACTER IN —) BONA HUGH
JOHN HENRY LEWIS MARCH
EDMUND EDWARD EXETER
GEORGE OXFORD RIVERS
BOURBON NORFOLK RICHARD
RUTLAND STANLEY WARWICK
CLIFFORD HASTINGS MARGARET

MONTAGUE MORTIMER
PEMBROKE SOMERSET STAFFORD
MONTGOMERY PLANTAGENET
WESTMORELAND
NORTHUMBERLAND
HEP (NOT —) ICKY
HEPATICA AI TRINITY
HEPATITIS FAVISM JAUNDICE
HEPHAESTUS LEMNIAN
  (FATHER OF —) ZEUS
  (MOTHER OF —) HERA
  (WIFE OF —) CHARIS
HEPHZIBAH (HUSBAND OF —)
  HEZEKIAH
  (SON OF —) MANASSEH
HER A ARE SHE HARE HERS HURF
HERA JUNO
  (FATHER OF —) KRONOS
  (HUSBAND OF —) ZEUS
HERALD BODE LYON USHER
  BEADLE DECLARE FORERUN
  PREFACE STENTOR BLAZONER
  PRECURSE PROCLAIM ROTHESAY
  MESSENGER
HERALDIC FECIAL FETIAL
HERALDRY ARMORY
HERB ANU APE PIA RUE UDO WAD
  ALOE ANET ANYU ARUM COUS
  DILL HEMP IRID LEEK MINT MOLY
  POLY RAPE SAGE SOLA WOAD
  WORT YAMP YARB AWIWI BLITE
  BRUSH CHIVE CREAT CROUT
  DAGGA DAISY DRABA GALAX
  GAURA GILIA GRASS HOSTA
  LOASA LUFFA MEDIC MUNGO
  NANCY SEDGE SOLAH STOCK
  SULLA THYME ZIZIA ALLIUM
  ARALIA ARNICA AXSEED BAGPOD
  BAMBAN BANANA BLINKS
  BORAGE CANCER CATGUT CATNIP
  CENIZO CICELY CISTUS CLOVER
  COCASH COLEUS CONIUM
  COWISH COWPEA ELODEA
  ENDIVE ERYNGO FENNEL GALAXY
  GINGER HARMEL HYSSOP KOCHIA
  KRIGIA KRIGLA LOOFAH LOVAGE
  RAMTIL RATTLE ROBERT SESAME
  SESELI SHEVRI WASABI ABRONIA
  ALPINIA ALTHAEA ALYSSUM
  AMORPHA AMSONIA ANCHUSA
  ANEMONE ANGELON ARACHIS
  BABIANA BABROOT BARTSIA
  BIRDEYE BLINKER BONESET
  BUGSEED BUGWEED CHICORY
  CUDWEED CULVERS DEWDROP
  DYEWEED EPISCIA ERODIUM
  FREESIA FROGBIT FUMMORY
  GERBERA GINSENG GOITCHO
  GOSMORE GOUAREE GUAYULE
  GUNNERA HARMALA HEDEOMA
  HENBANE HERBLET IRESINE
  ISOLOMA JONQUIL LABIATE
  LEWISIA LINNAEA MARANTA
  MIMULUS MUDWEED MUDWORT
  MULLEIN MUSTARD NAILROD
  NEMESIA NIEVETA PAVONIA
  PETUNIA PINESAP PINWEED
  PUCHERA ROSELLE SAFFLOR
.SALSIFY SEEDBOX SKIRRET
  SOWBANE SPIGNEL STACHYS
  ABELMOSK ABELMUSK ACANTHUS
  ACONITUM AGERATUM ALOCASIA
  ALUMROOT AMBROSIA

AMMOBIUM ANGELICA
ARGEMONE ASPHODEL
BEDSTRAW CALATHEA
CAPEWEED CARELESS CENTAURY
CHENILLE COLLOMIA COSTMARY
COWWHEAT CRASSULA
CROMWELL DANEWEED
DEERWEED DROPWORT
ECHINOPS EGGPLANT EREMURUS
ERIGERON EUCHARIS FEVERFEW
FLEABANE FOWLFOOT GAYWINGS
GERARDIA GESNERAD GESNERIA
GHETCHOO GLOXINIA GOATROOT
GUZMANIA HAREBELL HEPATICA
HEUCHERA HIBISCUS HOLEWORT
HONEWORT HOROKAKA
HUDSONIA IRONWEED LICORICE
LOCOWEED MANDRAKE
MANFREDA MANYROOT
MARDOWRT MARJORAM
MARTYNIA MURRNONG PHACELIA
PINKROOT PLUMBAGO
POKEWEED SACALINE SAINFOIN
SALICORN SAMPHIRE SANDBURR
SCABIOUS SHINLEAF SMALLAGE
SNOWDROP SOAPROOT
SOAPWORT STAPELIA SUNDROPS
TETRIFOL TOCALOTE WOODRUFF
MONEYWORT PUSSYTOES
RUDBECKIA SAXIFRAGE
NASTURTIUM PENNYCRESS
PERIWINKLE SARRACENIA
(— COUNTERACTING POISON)
CANCER
(— OTHER THAN GRASS) FORB
(AROMATIC —) MINT ANISE CLARY
CATNIP CAAPEBA CHERVIL
DITTANY
(BIENNIAL —) LEEK PARSLEY
ANGELICA
(BULBOUS —) LILY CANNA ALLIUM
CRINUM GARLIC NERINE SQUILL
BABIANA SHALLOT DOGTOOTH
SLANGKOP
(FABULOUS —) MOLY PANAX
PANACE
(FLOATING —) FROGBIT
(FORAGE —) FITCHES GOITCHO
(MEDITERRANEAN —) CRAMBE
(POISONOUS —) CONIUM HEMLOCK
MONKSHOOD
(PL.) POTAGERIE
HERBAGE HAY BITE GRASS GRAZE
PICHI ADONIS SACATE ZACATE
GRAZING
HERB EVE IVA IVY
HERB GRACE RUE
HERBICIDE IPE DIURON SILVEX
DALAPON MONURON PARAQUAT
PICLORAM PROPANIL SIMAZINE
HERB IMPIOUS DOWNWEED
HOARWORT
HERB PARIS TRUE ONEBERRY
TRUELOVE
HERB ROBERT JENNY ROBIN
ROBERT
HERCULEAN HUGE
HERCULES ERCLES ALCIDES
HERSHEF OETAEUS OVILLUS
HERAKLES
(BROTHER OF —) IPHICLES
(CAPTIVE OF —) IOLE
(FATHER OF —) JUPITER

(MOTHER OF —) ALCMENA
(WIFE OF —) HEBE MEGARA
DEIANIRA
HERCULES ALLHEAL OPOPANAX
HERCULES-CLUB ARALIA IVYWORT
RUEWORT SHOTBUSH
HERD BOW GAM MOB BAND CREW
GAME GANG HEAD RACE ROUT
RUCK TAIL TEAM TRIP DROVE
FLOCK HEARD TROOP CAVIYA
CHOUSE HIRSEL HUDDLE
MANADA MEINIE REMUDA
SPREAD THRAVE CREAGHT
RANGALE SHEPHERD
(— CATTLE) TAIL WRANGLE
(— OF CATTLE) FLOTE
(— OF COLTS) RAG
(— OF HORSES) RACE HARAS
HARRAS
(— OF SEALS) PATCH
(— OF WHALES) GAM
(— OF WILD SWINE) SOUNDER
HERDBOY BOUCHAL
HERDER DROVER FEEDER
HERDBOY
HERDSMAN AMOS SENN GAUCHO
HERDER LOOKER PASTOR
HERDBOY LLANERO THYRSIS
VAQUERO BEASTMAN DAMOETAS
GARTHMAN NEATHERD
PASTORAL PASTURER RANCHERO
SWANHERD WRANGLER
HERE ADSUM READY WHERE
HEREAT HITHER PRESENT
(— AND THERE) ABOUT ABROAD
AROUND PASSIM SPARSIM
HEREAFTER BEYOND
HEREDITAMENT LAND
HEREDITARY INBORN INNATE
KINDLY LINEAL PATERNAL
HEREIN WITHIN
HERESY DOCETISM KETZEREI
MISBELIEF
HERETIC BUGGER KETZER ZINDIQ
LOLLARD PATARIN PROFANE
SECTARY JUDAIZER MISCREANT
SABELLIUS MISBELIEVER
(PL.) ACEPHALI
HERETICAL HERETIC HETERODOX
MISCREANT
HERETO HITHER
HERETOFORE ERST BEFORE
ERENOW EREWHILE FORMERLY
**HEREWARD THE WAKE (AUTHOR
OF —)** KINGSLEY
(CHARACTER IN —) BRAND GODIVA
MARTIN WILLIAM ALFTRUDA
HEREWARD TORFRIDA
LIGHTFOOT
HERITAGE HEIRDOM HEIRSHIP
PATRIMONY
HERMA MERCURY
HERMAPHRODITE MOPH SCRAT
ANDROGYNOUS
HERMAPHRODITIC BISEXED
BISEXUAL MONOECIOUS
HERMAPHRODITISM GYNANDRY
HERMAPHRODITUS (FATHER OF —)
MERCURY
(MOTHER OF —) VENUS
HERMENEGILD (FATHER OF —)
LEOVIGILD
HERMES MERCURY

AGORAIOS CYLLENIUS
(FATHER OF —) ZEUS
(MOTHER OF —) MAIA
HERMIA (BELOVED OF —) LYSANDER
(FATHER OF —) EGEUS
HERMIONE (FATHER OF —)
MENELAUS
(HUSBAND OF —) PYRRHUS
(MOTHER OF —) HELEN
HERMIT ARME MUNI HANIF MINIM
ANCHOR SANTON SULLEN
ASCETIC EREMITE RECLUSE
TAPASVI ANCHORET MARABOUT
SOLITARY
HERMITAGE ASHRAM ASHRAMA
RECLUSE
HERNIA BURST RAMEX BREACH
RUPTURE MEROCELE
(SUFF.) CELE COELE COELUS
HERO CID KIM RAB AJAX EGIL IDAS
KAMI MAUI NALA NATA OFFA
RINK YIMA ADAPA BERNE DEBON
ETANA FAUST GHAZI HODER
HOTHR IRAYA KIPPS MARKO
ORSON TASSO TIMON VOTAN
EGMONT FIGARO GIDEON GOLIAS
HEROIC IASION IOLAUS MAUGIS
MINYAS OSSIAN PELHAM PENROD
RIENZI ROLAND RUSTAM SIGURD
TARZAN USHEEN VATHEK
ALCESTE BOGATYR DEMIGOD
FAUSTUS GLUSKAP INGOMAR
JAMSHID MACBETH MANRICO
MARMION MAZEPPA ORLANDO
OTHELLO PALADIN RAFFLES
TANCRED THALABA THESEUS
TROILUS ULYSSES VOLPONE
WERTHER WIDSITH WIELAND
ACADEMUS ARGONAUT
CHAMPION FANSHAWE
FERUMBAS FRITHJOF GAEDHEAL
GILGAMES LAMMIKIN MALAGIGI
MORGANTE OROONOKO
PALMERIN PARSIFAL PERICLES
RASSELAS RODOMONT
SUPERMAN TRISTRAM WAVERLEY
(LOVER OF —) LEANDER
(TRIBAL —) JUDGE
HERODIAS (BROTHER OF —)
AGRIPPA
(FATHER OF —) ARISTOBULUS
(HUSBAND OF —) HEROD
HEROIC EPIC FELL GREAT NOBLE
EPICAL FEATLY EXTREME
GALLANT VALIANT FEARLESS
HEROICAL HOMERIAN INTREPID
SPLENDID
HEROIN JUNK SCAG SKAG SNOW
HORSE SMACK
HEROINE AIDA EMMA MIMI RUTH
JULIE MEDEA NORMA SEDNA
THAIS ESTHER FEDORA GUDRUN
HELENA JUDITH JULIET MARTHA
MIGNON PAMELA PHEDRE
RAMONA ROMOLA SALOME SILVIA
TRILBY UNDINE ERMINIA EVELINA
GALATEA GINEVRA GRAINNE
HEROESS MONIMIA SHIRLEY
ZENOBIA ZULEIKA ATALANTA
ISABELLA MARGARET PATIENCE
POMPILIA ROSMUNDA SOFRONIA
HEROISM VALOR BRAVERY
COURAGE PROWESS

HERON QUA POKE SOCO CRAIG CRANE EGRET FRANK HERNE PADDY QUAWK YABOA AIGRET GAULIN KIALEE KOTUKU QUAKER SQUAWK BITTERN CRABIER GOLIATH HANDSAW QUABIRD SQUACCO BOATBILL GAULDING HERONSEW UMBRETTE
(— FLOCK) SIEGE
HERON'S-BILL ERODIUM
HERPES DARTRE TETTER
HERPES ZOSTER ZONA SHINGLES
HERRING ALEC BRIT CHUB SILD BLOAT CAPON CISCO DORAB HILSA MARAY MATIE SPRAT KIPPER POLLAN TAILOR BLOATER CLUPEID NAILROD ROLLMOP SHADINE BLUEBACK BRISLING BUCKLING CROPSHIN GRAYBACK QUODDIES SCUDDAWN STRADINE
(— SEASON) DRAVE
(— UNIT) LAST MAZE
(FEMALE —) RAUN
(LAKE —) KIYI CISCO
(RED —) CAPON SOLDIER
(SMOKED —) BLOATER
(YOUNG —) COB BRIT SILD SILE SILL SOIL WILE BRITT COBBE MATIE SPRAT SARDINE SPERLING
(2, 3 OR 4 —S) WARP
HERS HERN SHISN
HERSE (FATHER OF —) CECROPS
(SISTER OF —) AGRAULOS
(SON OF —) CEPHALUS
HERSELF HI HER SELF ITSELF
HERSHEF ARSAPHES
HESHVAN BUL CHESHVAN
HESIONE (FATHER OF —) LAOMEDON
(HUSBAND OF —) TELAMON
(RESCUER OF —) HERCULES
HESITANCY HANG
(— IN SPEECH) BALBUTIES
HESITANT SHY CAGY CHARY GROPING HALTING SUSPENSE
(NOT —) FACILE
HESITATE COY HEM STAY STOP CHECK CRANE DEMUR DOUBT FORCE PAUSE STAND STICK SUSSY WAVER BOGGLE FALTER HANKER LINGER MAMMER RELUCT SCOTCH TARROW TARTLE BALANCE PROFFER SCRUPLE STAGGER STAMMER SWITHER THRIMBLE
(— IN SPEAKING) HACKER
HESITATING JUBUS HALTING BACKWARD DOUBTFUL JUBEROUS TIMOROSO
HESITATION HANG HINK WAND PAUSE STAND STICK SUSSY SWITHER
HESPERUS VESPER
HESRON (FATHER OF —) REUBEN
HESSIAN BURLAP
HESTIA (FATHER OF —) KRONOS
(MOTHER OF —) RHEA
HETAERA LAIS THAIS PHRYNE MISTRESS
HETER-
(PREF.) XEN(O)
HETERODOX HERETIC SINISTRAL
HETERODOXY HERESY CACODOXY

HETEROGENEOUS MIXED MOTLEY UNLIKE DIVERSE PIEBALD ASSORTED
HETEROMYS SACCOMYS
HETEROSEXUAL STRAIGHT
HETEROTROPHIC HOLOZOIC
HETEROXENOUS INDIRECT
HETEROZYGOUS CROSS SPLIT IMPURE
HETMAN ATAMAN
HEW CUT HAG CHIP SNAG STUB SHRED SLICE
(— OUT) CARVE
(— STONE) CHAR
HEWER JOEY GETTER GIDEON FACEMAN
HE WHO GETS SLAPPED (AUTHOR OF —) ANDREYEV
(CHARACTER IN —) ALFRED ZINIDA BENZANO BRIQUET JACKSON MANCINI REGNARD CONSUELO
HEX WITCH VOODOO WHAMMY
HEXAGON SEXANGLE
HEXAGONAL HEX DIMETRIC
HEXAGRAM PENTACLE
HEXAMETER MIURUS RHOPALIC
(DACTYLIC —) EPOS HEROIC
HEXOBARBITAL EVIPAL
HEXOSAN MANNAN GLUCOSAN MANNOSAN
HEYDAY MAY HIGHDAY
HEZEKIAH (FATHER OF —) AHAZ NEARIAH
(MOTHER OF —) ABI
HEZION (SON OF —) TABRIMON
HEZRON (FATHER OF —) PHAREZ REUBEN
HIATUS GAP BREAK CHASM BREACH HIATAL LACUNA
HIBERNATE SHACK WINTER SLUMBER
HIBERNATING LATITANT
HIBERNIA EIRE ERIN IRELAND JUVERNA
HIBERNIAN IRISHMAN IVERNIAN
HIBISCUS ROSELLE
HICCUP YEX YOX HICK HOCKET HOQUET SINGULTUS
HICK BOOR HIND JAKE BACON BUSHMAN CORNBALL
HICKORY NOGAL PIGNUT BULLNUT SHAGBARK
HICKORY NUT TRYMA PIGNUT BULLNUT KISKITOM
HICKWALL ECCLE HECKLE HICKWAY
HIDDEN HID SHY DEEP DERN LOST TECT BLIND CLOSE DOGGO DUSKY PERDU PRIVY ARCANE BURIED COVERT INNATE LATENT MASKED MYSTIC OCCULT SECRET VEILED BOSOMED CLOUDED COVERED CRYPTIC OBSCURE RECLUSE SUBTILE ABDITIVE ABSTRUSE CRYPTOUS HIDEAWAY PALLIATE SCREENED SECLUDED SNEAKING CRYPTICAL RECONDITE
(PREF.) CRYPT(O) KRYPT(O)
HIDE HOD WRY BUFF BURY CASE CROP DARK DERN FELL FELT HILL HOOD JOUK LEAN MASK PELL PELT SCAB SKIN SKUG SNUG STOW VEIL WELL BELIE BELLY

BLIND CACHE CLOAK CLOUD COUCH COVER DITCH EARTH FLANK GLOSS LAYNE LOSHE MANSE PLANT SHADE SPOIL STASH STEER TAPIS BURROW BUSHEL CASATE EMBOSS ENCAVE ENWOMB FOREST HUDDLE IMBOSK MANENT PELAGE SCREEN SHADOW SHIELD SHROUD ABSCOND CONCEAL COWHIDE EMBOWEL FLAUGHT OBCLUDE OVERLAY SECLUDE SECRETE SPREADY TAPPICE CARUCATE DISGUISE ENSCONCE HIDELAND HOODWINK PALLIATE PLOWLAND SQUIRREL SUPPRESS CLANDESTINE
(— AS AN EEL) MUD
(— IN WOODS) WOOD BUSHWACK
(— UNDER) BUSHEL
(CALF'S —) DEACON
(DRESSED —S) LEATHER
(HALF OF —) BEND
(HAVING SOFT —) MELLOW
(SHEEP'S —) SLAT
(TANNED —) CROP
(THICKEST —S) BACKS
(UNDRESSED —) KIP
(PL.) JUFTI JUFTS
(PREF.) DERM(AT)(ATO)(O) DORA
(SUFF.) DERM(A)(ATOUS)(IA)(IS)(Y)
HIDE-AND-GO-SEEK BOGLE WHOOP BOGGLE
HIDEAWAY MEW LAIR
HIDEBOUND BORNE NARROW BIGOTED
HIDEOUS FELL GASH GRIM UGLY AWFUL TOADY DEFORM GRIMLY GRISLY HORRID ODIOUS OGRISH GHASTLY DEFORMED DREADFUL FIENDISH GRUESOME HORRIBLE SHOCKING TERRIBLE MONSTROUS
HIDEOUSLY FOULLY
HIDING DERN MICHING SECRECY ABDITIVE HIDEAWAY
HIEMAL WINTRY
HIERACIUM DINALE HAWKWEED
HIERARCHY SATRAPY
HIEROGLYPH CIPHER
(PL.) SIGNARY
HIGGLE HUCK HAGGLE
HIGH UP ALT AIRY DEAR HAUT MAIN MUCH RANK TALL ACUTE ALOFT BRENT CHIEF CLOSE FIRST GREAT LOFTY MERRY NOBLE SHARP STEEP BOMBED COSTLY SHRILL ZONKED EMINENT EXALTED HAUGHTY STICKLE SUBLIME TOPPING VIOLENT ELEVATED FOREMOST PIERCING TOWERING
(— AND MIGHTY) HOGEN
(— IN CHROMA) STRONG
(— IN PITCH) ALT ACUTE
(— IN RANK) MUCH
(— PITCH) ORTHIAN
(MOST —) SERENE
(PRETTY —) STIFFISH
(VERY —) TAUNT RAREFIED RARIFIED
(PREF.) ALTI HYPS(I)(O)
(ON —) HYPS(I)(O)
HIGHBORN NOBLE GENEROUS

HIGHBOY TALLBOY
HIGHBRED SOFT REFINED
HIGHBROW EGGHEAD
HIGH-CLASS CLASSY UPSTAGE
HIGH-CLIMBER TOPPER
HIGH-COLORED BLOWSY BLOWZY
HIGH-CROWNED COPATAIN
HIGHER OVER ABOVE SENIOR SUPERIOR
(PREF.) SUPER(O) SUPRA
HIGHEST ACE TOP HEXT FIRST EXTREME MAXIMAL SUPREME BUNEMOST HIGHMOST OVERMOST
(— IN DEGREE) LAST
HIGHFALUTIN PAUGHTY
HIGH-FED BEANY
HIGH-FLAVORED GAMY
HIGH-FLOWN TALL TUMID
HIGH-HANDED CAVALIER
HIGHLAND RAND CERRO
HIGHLANDER GAEL TARTAN NAINSEL PLAIDMAN REDSHANK TREWSMAN UPLANDER
(PL.) TREWS TARTAN
HIGHLIGHT ADORN HEIGHTEN PINPOINT SALIENCE
HIGHLY THRICE
HIGH-MINDED HAUGHT
HIGHNESS ALTESSE ALTEZZA ALTITUDE
(— OF PRICE) DEARTH
HIGH-PITCHED ACUTE PROUD PIPING TREBLE ORTHIAN SHRIEKY
HIGH-POWERED MAGNUM
HIGH-PRICED DEAR
HIGH-RIGGER TOPPER
HIGH-SOUNDING BIG BOMBAST MAGNIFIC SONORANT SONOROUS SOUNDING
HIGH-SPIRITED CRANK FIERY FIERCE LIVELY GALLANT GINGERY RAMPANT CAVALIER VASCULAR
HIGH-SPIRITEDNESS SPLEEN
HIGH-STRUNG TENSE NERVOUS
HIGH-TONED TONY DICTY DICKTY
HIGHWAY VIA WAY BELT ITER PATH PIKE ROAD TOBY BOLOS ARTERY CAUSEY COURSE RUMPAD SKYWAY STREET BELTWAY CALZADA FREEWAY RAMPIRE THRUWAY ARTERIAL AUTOBAHN BROADWAY CAUSEWAY CHAUSSEE HIGHROAD MOTORWAY SPEEDWAY
(— ROBBERY) TOBY
(LOCATED OFF THE —) DEVIOUS
(PART OF —) EXIT GORE LANE LOOP RAMP ACCESS BRIDGE ISLAND MEDIAN DIVIDER ROADWAY JUNCTION OVERPASS SHOULDER UNDERPASS INTERSECTION
HIGHWAYMAN PAD RIDER SCAMP BANDIT CUTTER PADDER RODMAN BRIGAND FOOTPAD LADRONE PRANCER RODSMAN TOBYMAN BIDSTAND DAMASTES HIGHTOBY HIJACKER LANCEMAN OUTRIDER BANDOLERO
HIGH-WROUGHT INTENSE
HIKE MUSH MARCH TRAMP RAMBLE

HILARIOUS MAD RORTY JOVIAL JOCULAR RAUGHTY CHIRPING GLORIOUS

HILARITY GIG JOY GLEE LAUGH MIRTH GAIETY GAYETY DEVILRY JOLLITY WHOOPEE MERRIMENT

HILKIAH (FATHER OF —) AMZI HOSAH
(SON OF —) ELIAKIM GEMARIAH JEREMIAH

HILL BEN DEN DUN HOE HOW KOP LOW PUY VAN ALTO BANK BERG BRAE BULT BUMP COTE DAGH DENE DOWN DRUM FELL HIGH HONE KNAP LOMA LUMP MESA MOOR MOTE NOUP PAHA TOFT ZION BARGH BUTTE CERRO CLIFF COAST HEUGH KNOCK KNOLL KOPJE MORRO MOUND MOUNT STILL SWELL TELLE WATCH ASCENT BARROW BEACON COBBLE COLLIS COPPLE CUESTA HEIGHT HEUVEL LOMITA SPRUNT STRONE CAELIAN CAPITOL COLLINE DRUMLIN HILLOCK NUNATAK PICACHO SOWBACK VIMINAL AREOPAGY CATOCTIN DRUMLOID FOOTHILL MONTICLE QUIRINAL MONADNOCK
(— OF SAND) DENE DUNE
(— OF STRATIFIED DRIFT) KAME
(— UP) MOLD
(BROAD-TOPPED —) LOMA
(CONICAL —) LAW PAP PINGO
(CRAGGY —) TOR
(FORTIFIED —) RATH
(HIGH —) BEN
(ISOLATED —) HUM TOFT BARGH BUTTE
(LAST —) STRONE
(LOW —) HOW BAND WOLD KOPPIE SOWBACK
(NIPPLELIKE —) PAP
(NORTH AFRICAN —) JEBEL DJEBEL
(RESIDUAL —) CATOCTIN
(ROUNDED —) DODD HONE MAMELON
(SHARP-POINTED —) KIP KIPP PIKE
(SMALL —) KNAP KNOLL KOPJE KOPPIE HILLOCK MOLEHILL
(STEEP —) BREW BROW STILL
(STONY —) ROACH
(SUGAR-LOAF —) SPITZKOP
(WOODED —) HOLT HURST
(PREF.) BUNO

HILLOCK HOW LOW NOB BOSS BULT DOWN KAME KNAP KNOB TERP TOFT TUMP BERRY HEAVE HURST KNOCK KNOLL KOPJE MOUND TOMAN BARROW BURROW COPPET HILLET HUMMOCK MAMELON TUMMOCK TUMULUS MOLEHILL

HILLSIDE BENT BRAE COTE EDGE CLEVE FALDA SLADE FELLSIDE SIDEHILL

HILLTOP DOD NAB PIKE RISE KNOLL

HILLY KNOBBY

HILT HAFT BASKET POIGNET HANDGRIP
(— OF DAGGER) DUDGEON
(PART OF —) BOW CUT GRIP RING

GUARD BUTTON POMMEL CAPSTAN LANGUET QUILLON RICASSO CROSSPIECE COUNTERGUARD

HILUM EYE SCAR HILUS PORTA NUCLEUS CICATRIX

HIM A EN HE HEM HIN MUN

HIMATION PALLION PALLIUM

HIMERUS (FATHER OF —) LACEDAEMON
(MOTHER OF —) TAYGETE
(SISTER OF —) CLEODICE

HIMSELF HIM IPSE SELF HISSEL ITSELF HERSELF HISSELF

HIND ROE CONY HINE HINT CONEY HEARST HINDER VENISON CABRILLA

HIND-BODY ABDOMEN

HINDBRAIN RHOMBENCEPHALON

HINDER BAR DAM KEP LET MAR ROB CLOG HELP SLOW SLUG STAY STOP TENT WARN AFTER BLOCK CHEAT CHECK CHOKE CRAMP DEBAR DELAY DETER EMBAR ESTOP HEDGE SLOTH THROW TRASH ARREST CUMBER DETAIN FORBID FORLET HAMPER HARASS HINNER IMPEDE IMPEND INJURE RETARD RETRAL SCOTCH TAIGLE UNHELP ABSTAIN DEPRIVE FORELAY IMPEACH INHIBIT OCCLUDE PREVENT TRACHLE ENCUMBER HANDICAP IMPEDITE OBSTRUCT PRECLUDE PROHIBIT POSTICOUS
(PREF.) POSTERO

HINDERED FOUL

HINDERER LETTER

HINDERMOST LAG ACHTER

HINDQUARTER HIND HAUNCH
(HALF —) LEG
(PL.) FOUCH CRUPPER HAUNCHES

HINDRANCE BAR LET RUB BALK CURB REIN SLUG STAY STOP BLOCK CHECK DELAY HITCH TRASH ARREST CUMBER DENIAL HINDER OBJECT UNHELP SHACKLE UNSPEED DISCOUNT DRAWBACK HOLDBACK OBSTACLE PULLBACK

HINDU BABU BABOO SUDRA BABHAN BANIAN BANYAN GENTOO JAJMAN KALWAR KHATRI NAYADI SHUDRA THAKUR VAISYA MUSAHAR VAIRAGI
(— ASCETIC) SADHU
(— ASSOCIATION) SANGH
(— CASTE) TELI VARNA
(— CUSTOM) SATI SUTTEE
(— ENERGY) SAKTI SHAKTI
(— IDOL) SWAMI
(— INTERJECTION) OM AUM
(— PHILOSOPHY) VEDANTA
(— PRACTICE) PURDAH
(— RITE) PUJA POOJA
(— SAGE) RSI RISHI
(— SCRIPTURE) VEDA
(— VARNA MEMBER) SUDRA
(— WORSHIPER) SAKTA
(— WRITING) VEDA
(— WRITINGS) SMRTI TANTRA
(TWICE-BORN —) KSATRIYA

HINDUSTANI URDU HINDI OORDOO DAKHINI

HINDWING BALANCER

HINGE RUN BAND BUTT FLAP HARR TRIM TURN CARDO CROOK GEMEL JOINT MOUNT NODUS SKELL SKEWL TWIST DEPEND GARNET GEMMEL GIMMER HANGLE JIMMER SNIBEL CHARNEL COXCOMB FULCRUM HOLDBACK
(— OF BIVALVE SHELL) CARDO
(— OF HELMET) CHARNEL
(— TOGETHER) SCISSOR
(HALF OF —) FLAP
(PHILATELIC —) STICKER
(PREF.) GINGLYMO

HINGED SWING
(SUFF.) POMATOUS

HINNY BURDON FUNNEL JENNET

HINT CUE ASTE ITEM MINT TANG WIND WINK CHEEP IMPLY INFER POINT SPELL STEER TOUCH TRACE WHIFF ALLUDE GLANCE OFFICE SMATCH TIPOFF WHEEZE INKLING LEADING MEMENTO POINTER SUGGEST UMBRAGE WHISPER WRINKLE ALLUSION INDICATE INNUENDO INTIMATE TELLTALE

HINTERLAND BLED BACKLAND

HIP HEP COXA HUCK PITCH SHOOP HAUNCH HUCKLE HIPBERRY
(— JOINT) THURL
(— OF ROSE) BERRY CHOOP SHOOP
(— OF TARGET) SPOT
(PREF.) COX(O) ISCHI(O) OSPHY(O)

HIPBONE FINBONE PINBONE EDGEBONE SIDEBONE

HIPPARCHUS (BROTHER OF —) HIPPIAS
(FATHER OF —) PISISTRATUS

HIPPARETE (BROTHER OF —) CALLIAS
(FATHER OF —) HIPPONICUS
(HUSBAND OF —) ALCINIADES

HIPPEUS KNIGHT

HIPPIE FREAK

HIPPOCAMPUS ERGOT HIPPO

HIPPOCOON (BROTHER OF —) TYNDAREUS
(FATHER OF —) OEBALUS
(MOTHER OF —) GORGOPHONE
(SLAYER OF —) HERCULES

HIPPODAMIA (FATHER OF —) ADRASTUS OENOMAUS
(HUSBAND OF —) PELOPS PEIRITHOUS
(SON OF —) ATREUS TROEZEN PITTHEUS THYESTES

HIPPOLYTUS (FATHER OF —) THESEUS
(MOTHER OF —) HIPPOLYTE
(STEPMOTHER OF —) PHAEDRA

HIPPOMENES (FATHER OF —) MEGAREUS
(MOTHER OF —) MEROPE
(WIFE OF —) ATALANTA

HIPPONACTEAN SCAZON

HIPPOPOTAMUS HIPPO ZEEKOE BEHEMOTH BUNODONT

HIPPOTHOE (FATHER OF —) MESTOR

(MOTHER OF —) LYSIDICE
(SON OF —) TAPHIUS

HIPPOTRAGUS OZANNA EGOCERUS

HIRAH (COMPANION OF —) JUDAH

HIRE FEE JOB HAVE MEED RENT SIGN WAGE PREST WAGES EMPLOY ENGAGE RETAIN SALARY BESPEAK CHARTER CONDUCE CONDUCT FREIGHT STIPEND
(— CATTLE) TACK

HIRED PAID TEEKA TICCA WAGED

HIRELING HACK VENAL HACKNEY MYRMIDON WAGELING MERCENARY PENSIONER PENSIONARY

HIRSUTE HAIRY SHAGGY

HIS S AS ES IS HISN

HISPID STRIGOSE STRIGOUS

HISS BLOW FUFF HISH HIZZ QUIZ SISS SIZZ GOOSE WHISS FISSLE FIZZLE SIFFLE WHOOSH WHISTLE SIBILATE
(— OF SWORD) SOUGH

HISSING BIRD AFFLATUS SIBILANT

HISTONE GLOBIN

HISTORIAN MORONI STORIER ANNALIST
AMERICAN FAY FOX BEER DODD FISH HART SHEA ADAMS BEARD BEMIS ELSON FORCE GIBBS GROSS HAZEN MAHAN MOORE MUNRO MYERS SMITH STONE USHER ABBOTT BARBER BARZUN BECKER BEESLY BOURNE BOWERS FISHER GREENE HANSEN LATANE LOWELL MALONE MOTLEY MUZZEY NEVINS PAXSON REEVES RHODES SLOANE SPARKS STILES TURNER WINSOR ANDREWS BASSETT CHAPMAN CHEYNEY CLELAND DUNNING GAYARRE HEADLEY HULBERT JAMESON LEARNED MCELROY MORISON PALFREY PARKMAN RIDPATH SCHMITT SHANNON VANTYNE BANCROFT BOTSFORD BRODHEAD COMMAGER COOLIDGE HILDRETH JOHNSTON MCMASTER PENNIMAN PHILLIPS PRESCOTT ROBINSON STEPHENS THWAITES TRUMBULL BEVERIDGE GROSVENOR MACDONALD PRIESTLEY STEVENSON MCLAUGHLIN WESTERMANN OBERHOLTZER ROSTOVTZEFF SCHLESINGER
ARGENTINIAN FUNES LOPEZ MITRE CARBIA
AUSTRIAN BIBI SRBIK ARNETH LORENZ HORMAYR LOSERTH MENGHIN PRIBRAM ASCHBACH HELLWALD WURZBACH
BELGIAN JUSTE HYMANS GACHARD HASSELT LAURENT PIRENNE
CANADIAN BEGG BRYCE WRONG GARNEAU BOURINOT CASGRAIN
CHINESE PANKU
COLOMBIAN ACOSTA RESTREPO
CZECH GOLL PALACKY

DANISH HOLM ALLEN BARFOD AAGESEN AAGESON BRANDES MOLBECH WORSAAE PEDERSEN HAMMERICH NEERGAARD
DUTCH BOR BLOK GEYL FRUIN HOOFT JAPIKSE BARLEAUS HUIZINGA
ENGLISH COXE DYER HALL HYDE MUIR OMAN PAUL ROSE STOW TOUT WARD ACTON BIRCH BROWN CARTE DAVIS DIXON DORAN DOYLE EDMER FIRTH FYFFE GOOCH GREEN GUEST HELPS INNES PARIS SMITH TERRY TOOKE WELLS BARKER BUCKLE BURNET CAMDEN COLOMB CREASY FINLAY FISHER FROUDE GIBBON GILDAS HALLAM MILMAN POWELL ROSCOE SEELEY STRYPE STUBBS TURNER WARNER WILSON BEAZLEY BOULGER COULTON DOUGLAS FORSTER FREEMAN HASSALL HAYWARD KNOLLES LANGTON LINGARD MITFORD POLLARD RALEIGH SYMONDS ADOLPHUS GAIRDNER GARDINER KINGLAKE MACAULAY MAITLAND MARRIOTT OLDMIXON PALGRAVE PHILLIPS PROTHERO ARMSTRONG KINGSFORD ROBERTSON TEMPERLEY TREVELYAN HAVERFIELD
FINNISH FORSMAN
FRENCH FAY SEE DROZ FAIN DURUY FILON FLACH GIDEL GLOTZ GOYAU MABLY MONOD NAUDE RENAN SOREL AULARD BALUZE BEMONT BONNET DANIEL DAUDET GERARD GUIZOT HAUSER MARTIN MASSON MATTER MIGNET OZANAM ROMIER THIERS VANDAL VERTOT ZELLER BARANTE BLONDEL CHENIER CHERUEL FAGNIEZ FAURIEL JULLIAN LAGORCE LANFREY LAVISSE LERMINA MADELIN MEZERAY PFISTER RAMBAUD THIERRY DEBIDOUR DUCHESNE GODEFROY HANOTAUX LUCHAIRE MICHELET PARFAICT RULHIERE BEAUCOURT BONNEMERE BOURGEOIS HERICAULT SEIGNOBOS SIEGFRIED TILLEMONT DESJARDINS GUIGNEBERT ROHRBACHER CHANTELAUZE
GERMAN DAHN HEHN KAPP KOCH LENZ NIEM ALZOG FALKE JAFFE KLOPP KOSER LUDEN MEYER MOSER PERTZ RANKE RIEHL SYBEL VEHSE VOGEL VOIGT WAITZ WEBER ZEUSS ABELIN BELOCH BOHMER HEEREN KUGLER MENZEL ONCKEN PREUSS ANDREAS DROYSEN DUMMLER ECKHART FISCHER FORSTER HAEBLER HELMOLT HETTNER KEUTGEN LEHMANN LINDNER ROTTECK RUVILLE SCHAFER SCHMIDT SCHULTE BRESSLAU DELBRUCK DONNIGES FLEMMING GALLETTI GERVINUS HOETZSCH

HOFFMANN KAUFMANN KROMAYER LEDEBOUR SCHLOZER FREIDRICH LAMPRECHT SCHIEMANN SCHMOLLER SLEIDANUS ARCHENHOLZ BAUMGARTEN BIEDERMANN HIRSCHFELD LAPPENBERG MARHEINEKE POSCHINGER TREITSCHKE ZIMMERMANN BRANDENBURG FALLMERAYER GARDTHAUSEN GREGOROVIUS SECKENDORFF
GREEK DURIS GREEN ARRIAN BIKELAS EPHORUS LAMBROS SOZOMEN TIMEAUS DEXIPPUS HERODIAN POLYBIUS XENOPHON CRATIPPUS HERODOTUS HESYCHIUS PHILISTUS TIMAGENES ANAXIMENES CLITARCHUS HELLANICUS HIERONYMUS PHYLARCHUS THEOPOMPUS THUCYDIDES ARISTOBULUS MEGASTHENES OLYMPIODORUS AGATHARCHIDES
HUNGARIAN FEJER TOLDY PAULER TELEKI FESSLER FRAKNOI MAILATH MARCZALI SZILAGYI
IRISH BURY LECKY GILBERT WADDING
ITALIAN AMARI CANTU VOLPE CANALE CIAMPI DENINA EMILIO FEDELE GIOVIO NOVATI VASARI ACCOLTI FERRERO VILLANI VILLARI AMMIRATO CIBRARIO GIANNONE MOLMENTI MURATORI BERTOLINI LIUTPRAND SALVEMINI
MEXICAN ALAMAN PEREYRA CLAVIJERO BUSTAMANTE
NORWEGIAN KOHT LANGE MUNCH DIETRICHSON
PERUVIAN ULLOA
POLISH KUBALA BIELSKI CHODZKO DIUGOSZ LELEWEL SZUJSKI ASKENAZY BOBRZYNSKI KUCHARZEWSKI
PORTUGUESE GOES MELO LOPES BARROS CASTANHEDA
ROMAN LIVY CORDUS FLORUS TROGUS SALLUST TACITUS APPIANUS VALERIUS EUTROPIUS SUETONIUS FENESTELLA
RUMANIAN IORGA KOGALNICEANU
RUSSIAN KAVELIN POGODIN BRUCKNER KARAMZIN MILYUKOV TURGENEV VENGEROV POKROVSKI HRUSHEVSKY KOSTOMAROV
SCOTTISH MILL BOECE BROWN LAING BURTON TYTLER CARLYLE GILLIES NEILSON SPALDING MACKINTOSH
SPANISH AVILA XEREZ PINELO PULGAR TORENO DESCLOT GOMARRA HERRERA MARIANA MONCADA FERRERAS LAFUENTE SEPULVEDA MONTESINOS
SWEDISH DALIN BESKOW GEIJER CARLSON FRYXELL FORSSELL MESSENIUS
SWISS KOPP BLUMER GELZER MULLER STUMPF TSCHUDI SISMONDI GAGLIARDI BURCKHARDT

HISTORICAL GENETIC
HISTORIOGRAPHER SCALD SKALD
HISTORY STORY ANNALS LEGEND RECORD SURVEY ACCOUNT ANCESTRY PROPHECY RELATION
(**— OF EXPERIENCES**) MEMOIRS
(**— OF JAPAN**) KOJIKI
(**LIFE —**) COURSE
(**TRIBAL —**) PHYLOGENY
HISTRIONIC ACTORY ACTORISH ACTRESSY
HIT BAT BOP BOX DOT GET HAT JOB PEG PIP WOW BASH BEAN BEAT BELT BIFF BLOW BOFF BUST CHOP CONK DONG FOUR GOLD NAIL PINK POKE PUCK PUNT RUFF SLAM SOCK SWAT SWIP TAKE TANK TUNK WART WIPE ANGLE CHECK CLOUT CLUNK CROWN FIVER FLICK GOUFF KNOCK POTCH PRANG PUNTA PUNTO SCORE SLASH SLOSH SMASH SMITE SNICK SWIPE TAINT TOUCH VENUE ATTAIN DOUBLE FOURER HURTLE SCLAFF STRIKE VOLLEY ATTAINT BOFFOLA CONNECT MUZZLER SANDBAG WHERRET BLUDGEON BOUNDARY LENGTHER STRICKEN
(**— A KEY**) STRIKE
(**— BALL**) CUR FLY DINK DRIVE SHOOL SKITE SNICK
(**— BUNT**) DRAG
(**— GAME**) STOP
(**— GENTLY**) BABY
(**— GOLF BALL**) CAN BLAST EXPLODE
(**— HARD**) DUMP SLOG SLUG PASTE SKELP SOUSE DEVVEL STOUSH STONKER
(**— IN BOXING**) LEADOFF
(**— IN FIELD HOCKEY**) CORNER
(**— IN TILTING**) TAINT
(**— IT OFF**) CLICK
(**— LIGHTLY**) KISS
(**— ON BULL'S-EYE**) GOLD
(**— POORLY**) DUB
(**— SHARPLY**) CLIP
(**— SUDDENLY**) ZAP
(**— TOGETHER**) CLASH
(**— UPON**) FIND
(**— WITH FOOT**) KICK SPURN
(**BASE —**) BINGLE DOUBLE SAFETY SINGLE TRIPLE SCRATCH SMOTHER
(**CRICKET —**) SLOG BOUNDARY
(**EASILY —**) SITTING
(**FENCING —**) HAI HAY VENUE
(**SHARP —**) LICK
(**SMASH —**) SOCKEROO
HITCH JET TUG HALT HIKE ITCH KNOT PULL CATCH HOTCH SPELL TRACE HIRSLE INSPAN MAGNUS CONTRETEMPS
(**NOSE —**) BOZAL
HITCHHIKE HOP THUMB
HITCHHIKER PICKUP
HITCHING KNOT SHRUG
HITHER HERE
HITHERTO YET BEFORE
HIT-OR-MISS CASUAL CHANCE HOBNOB CARELESS
HITTER SWATTER

HITTING BATTING SLOGGING
HITTITE HATTI KHATTI TABALIAN
HIVE GUM BIKE SKEP PYCHE STAND STATE STOCK SWARM APIARY ALVEARY BEEHIVE SWARMER
(**— PLACED OVER ANOTHER**) SUPER
HIVES CROUP UREDO
HLORRITHI THOR THORR
HOAGIE TORPEDO
HOAR GRAY RIME HOARY
HOARD HEAM POSE SAVE AMASS HUTCH MISER STOCK COFFER MAGPIE MUCKER STOUTH GENIZAH HUSBAND SQUIRREL TREASURE
HOARDER MUCKER STORER HUSBAND
HOARFROST RAG HOAR RIME RIND
HOARINESS HOAR ROOP MUCOR
HOARSE RAW FOGGY GRUFF HEAZY HUSKY RAWKY ROKEY ROUGH ROUPY STOUR CROAKY CROUPY RASPED ROUPIT GRATING RAUCOUS
HOARSENESS FROG ROUP QUACK RAUCITY HASKNESS BARYPHONIA
HOARY AGED GRAY GREY HOAR WHITE FROSTY ANCIENT HOARISH INCANOUS
HOATZIN ANNA HANA HOACTZIN
HOAX BAM COD FUN GAG HUM KID RAG RIG BILK DUPE FAKE GAFF GEGG GUNK JOSH QUIZ RAMP RUSE SELL SHAM SKIT CHEAT FRAUD GREEN SHAVE SPOOF TRICK WINDY CANARD DIDDLE HUMBUG STRING BLAFLUM DECEIVE FLIVVER ARTIFICE
HOB HUB PUNCH MATRIX
HOBAB (**BROTHER-IN-LAW OF —**) MOSES
HOBBER LEANER
HOBBLE GIMP LOCK SPAN BUNCH HILCH HITCH STILT STUMP HABBLE HIRPLE HOPPLE LANGLE LANKET TOLTER CRAMBLE CRAMMEL CRIPPLE SHACKLE SHAFFLE SPANCEL STAGGER TRAMMEL SIDELINE
HOBBLEBUSH DOGWOOD
HOBBY BUG FAD HOBBLER AVOCATION
HOBBYHORSE HOBBY PLAYMARE
HOBBYIST BUG
HOBGOBLIN (**ALSO SEE GOBLIN**) COW HAG HOB PUG BOGY PUCK BOGEY BUCCA BUGAN POKER SCRAT SPOOK BOODIE BOWSIE EMPUSA SPOORN BUGABOO RAWHEAD BOGGLEBO COLTPIXY POPLEMAN PUCKEREL WORRICOW
HOBNAIL HOB HUB PUNCH TACKET
HOBNAILED TACKETY
HOBO BO BOE BUM STIFF
HOCK HAM HOX HEEL HOUGH HUXEN SINEW SKINK JARRET CAMBREL GAMBREL HOCKSHIN SUFFRAGO

HOCKEY HURLY HORKEY HURLEY
SHINNY CAMMOCK HURLBAT
(— STAR) ORR
HOCKEY STICK HOOKY HURLY
STICK BULGER SHINNY CAMBUCA
CAMMOCK DODDART HURLBAT
HOCUS-POCUS FAKERY HUMBUG
FLIMFLAM QUACKERY
HOD TRAY
(FATHER OF —) ZOPHAH
HODAVIAH (FATHER OF —)
HASSENUAH
HOD CARRIER PADDY
HODESH (HUSBAND OF —)
SHAHARAIM
HODGEPODGE CHOW HASH MESS
OLIO RAFF SALAD BOLLIX JUSSEL
MAGPIE MEDLEY MELANGE
CHIVAREE CHOWCHOW
HOTCHPOT KEDGEREE MISHMASH
PASTICHE PORRIDGE SCRAMPUM
PATCHWORK
HODOMETER VIAMETER
HOE BROD CHIP CLAT HACK HOWE
SHIM CLAUT LARRY THIRD
CHONTA HACKER PAIDLE PECKER
SARCLE GRUBBER PULASKI
SCRAPER SCUFFLE GRIFFAUN
(— HANDLE) STAIL
(HORSE —) NIDGET NIGGET
(PART OF —) BLADE SHANK
HANDLE FERRULE
HOECAKE CORNCAKE
HOG BEN SOW BOAR GALT GILT
PORK DUROC GRUNT SHOAT
BARROW HOGGET HOGGIE
PORKER PORKET YORKER
BACONER BUTCHER GRUNTER
HOGLING MONTANA BABIRUSA
BUNODONT HEREFORD
LANDRACE VICTORIA RAZORBACK
(PREF.) SUI
HOGAN LODGE TEPEE DWELLING
HOGBACK FLATIRON HOGFRAME
HOGCHOKER SOLE
HOGFISH CAPITAN LADYFISH
LORICATE SCORPION
HOGGER HUGGER HOGHEAD
HOGGISHNESS GRILL GRYLL
HOGLAH (FATHER OF —)
ZELOPHEHAD
HOGNOSE SNAKE ADDER
FLATHEAD
HOG PLUM AMRA JOBO
HOGSHEAD CASK CARDEL
HOG'S-MEAT TOSTON HOGWEED
HOG-TIE HAMPER
HOGWASH DRAFF SWASH SWILL
PIGWASH
HOIST FID HEFT KILT LIFT SWAY
SWIG WHIM WHIP CRANE ERECT
HEAVE HEEZE HEIST HOICK
HOOSH HORSE RAISE WEIGH
JAMMER LAUNCH LIFTER TUGGER
WHIMSY DERRICK
(— A LOG) CANNON
(— ANCHOR) CAT
(— FISH) BRAIL
(— FLUKES) FISH FANCHER
HOISTED (— TIGHT) ATRIP
HOISTMAN CAGEMAN
HOKUM BLAA BLAH HOKE JUNK
HOLD HOD OWN BULK DEEM FEEL

FILL GAUM GIVE GRIT HANK HAVE
HELD HEND HILT HOLE HOLT
HOOK KEEP LOCK NAIL RELY SOFT
STOW AFONG AHOLD AHOLT
BELAY CARRY CINCH CLAMP
CLING GRASP GRIPE LATCH LEASE
PAUSE POISE ROCCA STORE
WOULD ADHERE ADSORB ARREST
CLUTCH DETAIN HANDLE INTERN
MANURE OCCUPY REGARD
REPUTE RETAIN ADJUDGE
CAPTURE CLAUGHT CONFINE
CONTAIN ENCLOSE FERMATA
GRAPPLE HOLDING RECEIVE
SEIZURE SUBSIST SUSPEND
COMPRISE FOOTHOLD FOREHOLD
HANDFAST HANDHOLD
HEADLOCK HOLDFAST PURCHASE
THURROCK
(— A BELIEF) SUPPOSE
(— AS PRECIOUS) TREASURE
(— AS TRUE) ACCEPT
(— AT BAY) DOMPT
(— BACK) STOP WELL BELAY
LAYNE BOGGLE DETAIN FLINCH
HINDER RETIRE SHRINK CONTAIN
DETRACT FORBEAR INGIBIT
RECLAIM REFRAIN SLACKEN
HESITATE SUPPRESS WITHDRAW
(— BACK ON LEASH) TRASH
(— CLOSELY) CRADLE CUDDLE
(— CONSULTATION) ADVISE
(— CORONER'S INQUEST) CROWN
(— DEAR) CHERISH
(— DOWN) PINION CONTAIN
(— FAST) FIX BAIL BITE CLING
SNARL CLENCH CLINCH SECURE
STABLE
(— FIRMLY) CLIP INSIST
(— FOR FOOD) COZY COSEY
(— FORTH) SPIEL
(— FROM) ABSTAIN
(— GOOD) APPLY SERVE
(— IN CHECK) REIN GOVERN
REPRESS COMPESCE
(— IN CONTEMPT) SMILE DISPRIZE
(— IN PLACE) ANCHOR
(— OF PLASTER) KEY
(— ON COURSE) STEM FETCH
STAND
(— ON FINAL NOTE) TENOR
(— ON SHORE) LANDFAST
(— OUT) DREE LAST STAY OFFER
EXTEND PROTEND STRETCH
SUSTAIN
(— PROTECTIVELY) LAP
(— TIGHTLY) CLIP STICK
(— TOGETHER) BOND COHERE
CONSIST
(— UP) BEAR HALT STAY ERECT
HEIST IMPEDE UPHOLD RUMPADE
SUPPORT SUSTAIN TRADUCE
(— UP BY LEADING STRINGS) DADE
(— UP TO CONTEMPT) FLEER
(— UP TO PUBLIC NOTICE) GIBBET
(SHIP'S —) HOLE HOLL HHHOLD
(WRESTLING —) CROTCH KEYLOCK
CHANCERY HEADLOCK SCISSORS
SIDEHOLD
(PREF.) CHADA
HOLDBACK DAM
HOLDER WYE HAVER STOCK
DIPPER SOCKET CRACKER

CASSETTE JAGIRDAR
(— FOR CARRYING GLASS) FRAIL
(— FOR COIL) SPOOL
(— FOR CUP) ZARF
(— FOR FLOWERS) FROG
(— FOR TOOLS) TURRET
(— FOR WHIP) BUCKET
(— OF GRANT) ENAMDAR
(ALLOTMENT —) CLERUCH
(CANDLE —) SPIDER GIRANDOLE
(LAMP —) BODY
(PL.) GRIPPERS
(PREF.) PORTE
HOLDFAST CLINCH HAPTERON
HOLDIKEN HADDIN
HOLDING HAL COPY COTE HOLD
TAKE GRASP HONOR HADDIN
POFFLE TENANT TENURE
TENANCY COMMENDA
(— DIFFERENT OPINIONS) APART
(— FAST) IRON
(— OF OFFICE) OCCUPATION
(— OF SECURITIES) CARRY
(PL.) FLOCKS PROPERTY
HOLDUP HEIST STICKUP
HOLE CAN CUP EYE GAP PIT TAP
BORE BURY LEAK MAIL MUSE
PECK PINK POCK PUKA WANT
CHINK DITCH FLOSS FOSSE
MEUSE SINUS SLACK SPRUE
SQUAT TEWEL THIRL THURL
BURROW CAVITY CENTER CENTRE
CRANNY CRATER EYELET
HOLLOW LACUNA OBTAIN OILLET
PIERCE POCKET POUNCE WEEPER
BLOWOUT BOGHOLE BOTHROS
DIBHOLE EYEHOLE KEYHOLE
MORTICE MORTISE OILHOLE
OPENING PINHOLE POTHOLE
SCUTTLE SWALLET VENTAGE
ACCEPTER APERTURE BLOWHOLE
BOREHOLE COALHOLE CRABHOLE
FUMAROLE HANDHOLE
KNOCKOUT KNOTHOLE OVERTURE
PEEPHOLE POSTHOLE PUNCTURE
WELLHOLE WINDHOLE
PERTUSION PERFORATION
(— CAUSED BY LEAK) GIME
(— FOR WIRE) HUB HUBB
(— IN BANK OF STREAM) GAT
(— IN GARMENT) FRACK
(— IN GUILLOTINE) LUNET LUNETTE
(— IN HEDGE) SMEUSE
(— IN HIDE) BOTHOLE
(— IN KEEL) LIMBER RUFFLE
(— IN KIVA) SIPAPU
(— IN ONE STROKE) ACE
(— IN STREAM BED) DUMP
(— IN WIND INSTRUMENT) LILL
(— INTO MOLD) GEAT SPRUE
(— THREE BELOW PAR) ALBATROSS
(AIR —) SPIRACLE
(BREATHING —) SUSPIRAL
(DEEP —) POT GOURD
(FOX —) KENNEL
(GOLF —) CUP DOGLEG
(MELON —) GILGAI
(RABBIT —) CLAPPER
(SAND —) BUNKER
(SINK —) SOAKAWAY
(SPY —) JUDAS
(TO —) GOBBLE HAZARD
(VOLCANIC —) FUMAROLE

(WATER —) DUB CHARCO
(WELL-LIKE —) CASCAN
(PREF.) TREMATO TROGLO
HOLIDAY HOL PLAY TIDE WAKE
FERIE FESTA MERRY FIESTA
JOVIAL FESTIVE HALEDAY
PLAYDAY YEARDAY PASSOVER
SHABUOTH WAYGOOSE
(HALF —) REMEDY
(PL.) FERIA
HOLINESS PIETY HALIDOM
SANCTITY SANCTIMONY
HOLLA SOLA
HOLLAND (ALSO SEE
NETHERLANDS) FROGLAND
HOLLANDAISE GULASH GOULASH
HOLLAND BLUE ORION
HOLLANDER DUTCHMAN
HOLLANDS GIN GENEVA
HOLLER HALLO HOLLO HALLOO
KYOODLE
HOLLO SOLA
HOLLOW DEN DIP KEX BOSS BOWL
CAVE COMB COOM COVE DALK
DELL DENT DINT DISH DOCK
DOKE FOLD GORE HOLE HOLL
HOWE KEXY KHUD SINK SLOT
THIN VOID WAME BASIN BIGHT
CAVUM CHASE CLEFT CUPPY
DELVE DOWFF EMPTY GAUNT
GOYLE GULCH GULLY HEUCH
LAIGH NOTCH SCOOP SINUS
SLOCK SWAMP WOMBY ARMPIT
BULLAN CAVITY CORRIE DIMPLE
HOLLER INDENT KETTLE MATRIX
POCKET RECESS SOCKET SUNKEN
VACANT WALLOW BOXLIKE
CONCAVE UNSOUND VACUITY
CAVITARY CHELIDON CORELESS
CRUCIBLE FISTULAR FOSSETTE
NOTCHING SPECIOUS
(— AMONG HILLS) SWAG SLOCK
(— IN COIL OF CABLE) TIER
(— IN HILL) COOM CLASH COMBE
COOMB CORRIE
(— IN TILE) KEY
(— OF ARM) LEAD ARMPIT
(— OF EAR) ALVEARY
(— OF HANDS) GOUPEN GOWPEN
(— OF HORSE'S TOOTH) MARK
(— OF KNEE) HAM
(— OF ROOF) VALLEY
(— OUT) CUT DIG BORE HOWK
KERF CAVERN EXCISE
(LONG —) GROOVE
(NOT —) SOLID FARCTATE
(PASSING —) CRESCENT
(ROUND —) CIRQUE
(SECLUDED —) GLEN
(SPRINGY —) GAW
(WOODED —) GULLY
(PREF.) CAEL(I)(O) CAVI CAVO
CEL(O) COEL(I)(O)
(SUFF.) COELOUS COELUS
HOLLOWED HOWKIT CONCAVE
SPOUTED
HOLLOW-EYED HAGGARD
HOLLOWNESS VANITY INANITY
VACUITY CONCAVITY
HOLLY HOLM HULL ILEX MATE
DAHOON HOLLIN HULVER
TOLLON YAUPON CATBERRY
INKBERRY MILKMAID

HOLLYHOCK HOCK ALTHEA MALLOW
HOLM ISLET ISLAND BOTTOMS
HOLOFERNES (SLAYER OF —) JUDITH
HOLOTHURIAN TREPANG
HOLY SRI SHRI HUACA SAINT SANTO DEVOUT DIVINE SACRAL SACRED BLESSED PERFECT SAINTLY SINLESS BLISSFUL INNOCENT REVEREND SPIRITUAL SANCTIMONIOUS
  (— MAN) SADHU
  (— OF HOLIES) ADYT ADYTUM
  (ALL —) PANAGIA
  (PREF.) HAGI(O) HIER(O) HIERATICO HOSIO SANCTI SANCTO SEMNO
  (SUFF.) HIERIC
HOLY BASIL TULCE TOOLSY
HOLY SPIRIT PARACLETE
HOLY STONE BEAR BIBLE
HOLY WOOD LIGNUM
HOMAGE FEE COURT HONOR YMAGE FEALTY MANRED INCENSE LOYALTY MANRENT MANSHIP OVATION SERVICE TREWAGE EMINENCE OBEISANCE
  (SUPREME —) LATRIA
HOME BYE DEN HAM BASE HAME HUNK WIKE ABODE ASTRE BEING DOMUS FOYER HAUNT SMOKE HEARTH BLIGHTY SHELTER DOMICILE FIRESIDE ROOFTREE
  (— FOR THE POOR) HOSPICE
  (— OF THE BLESSED) GIMLE
  (FUNERAL —) CHAPEL
  (HARVEST —) KERN KIRN MELL HOCKEY
  (REST —) FARM HOSTEL
  (PREF.) (RETURN —) NOST(O)
HOMELAND HAVAIKI
HOMELESS ROOFLESS VAGABOND
HOMELIKE HOMEY HAMEIL HAMILT HOMISH HOMESOME
HOMELINESS YEOMANRY
HOMELY FOUL UGLY PLAIN DUDGEN RUGGED PLAINLY EVERYDAY FAMILIAR HOMELIKE
HOME PLATE RUBBER
HOMER KOR CHOMER
HOME RUN SWAT SWOT BLAST
HOMESICKNESS HEIMWEH NOSTALGIA
HOMESPUN KERSEY RUSSET RAPLOCH
HOMESTEAD TOFT TREF ONSET PLACE WORTH TYDDYN FARMERY ONSTEAD STEADING
HOMESTEADER NESTER
HOMETHRUST HAI HAY
HOMEWORK PREP
HOMICIDE DEATH MORTH KILLING
HOMILETIC KERYSTIC
HOMILY PRONE OMELIE POSTIL SERMON
HOMINY SAMP NASAUMP
HOMOEOMERY GERM SEED
  (PL.) SPERMATA
HOMOGENEITY SAMENESS
HOMOGENEOUS LIKE SOLID GLOBAL SIMPLE COMPACT MASSIVE SIMILAR

HOMOGENOUS ENTIRE
HOMOLOGUE CYANINE HOMOTYPE
  (PREF.) NOR
HOMOPHONY MONODY
HOMORGANIC COGNATE
HOMOSEXUAL (FEMALE —) DIKE DYKE
HOMOZYGOUS PURE ISOGENIC

HONDURAS
CAPITAL: TEGUCIGALPA
COIN: PESO CENTAVO LEMPIRA
DEPARTMENT: YORO COLON COPAN VALLE OLANCHO
GULF: FONSECA
INDIAN: MAYA PAYA SUMO ULVA CARIB LENCA PIPIL TAUIRA JICAQUE MISKITO MOSQUITO
ISLAND: ROATAN
ISLANDS: BAY BAHIA
LAKE: CRIBA YOJOA BREWER
MEASURE: VARA MILLA MECATE TERCIA CAJUELA MANZANA
MOUNTAINS: PIJA AGALTA CELAQUE
PORT: LACEIBA TRUJILLO
RIVER: COCO SICO ULUA AGUAN LEMPA NEGRO TINTO WANKS PATUCA SULACO GUAYAPE OLANCHO SEGOVIA SANTIAGO
RUINS: TENAMPUA
TOWN: TELA YORO COPAN LAPAZ ROATAN GRACIAS LACEIBA TRUJILLO YUSCARAN JUTICALPA
WEIGHT: CAJA LIBRA

HONE HO STROP STROKE STRICKLE
HONEST FAIR GOOD JAKE TRUE AFALD FRANK ROUND SOUND WHITE CANDID DEXTER DINKUM ENTIRE PROPER RUSTIC SINGLE SQUARE SINCERE UPRIGHT RIGHTFUL STRAIGHT
HONESTLY TRULY DINKUM HONEST INDEED SINGLY SQUARE SQUARELY
HONESTY FAITH HONOR SATIN EQUITY LUNARY REALTY VERITY JUSTICE LUNARIA PROBITY BOLBONAC FAIRNESS FIDELITY MOONWORT SATINPOD YEOMANRY
HONEY MEL MELL HINNY HONEYBUN
  (— BEVERAGE) MULSE
  (ROSE-FLAVORED —) RODOMEL
  (PREF.) MELI(TTO) MELL(I)
HONEYBEE (ALSO SEE BEE) BEE GYNE KING DRANE DRONE QUEEN DINGAR DRONER EGATES CYPRIAN DEBORAH DESERET KOOTCHA MELISSA STINGER ACULEATE ANGELITO
HONEY BUZZARD PERN
HONEYCOMB COMB FRAME WAXCOMB
  (PREF.) CERIO FAVI
HONEYCREEPER IIWI MAMO PALILA DREPANID GUITGUIT
HONEYDEW MANNA MILDEW
HONEY EATER OO IAO TUI MOHO

MINER TENUI MANUAO MAOMAO ROSTER BELLBIRD WURRALUH
HONEYED SWEET HYBLAN SUGARY SUGARED HYBLAEAN LUSCIOUS
HONEY GUIDE MOROC
HONEY MESQUITE ALGAROBA HONEYPOD
HONEY PLANT HOYA HUAJILLO
HONEYSUCKLE VINE SUCKLE WEIGELA BINDWEED SUCKLING WOODBINE

HONG KONG
BAY: SHEKO REPULSE
CAPITAL: VICTORIA
COIN: CENT DOLLAR
DISTRICT: WANCHAI
GARDENS: TIGERBALM
ISLAND: LANTAO
MOUNTAIN: CASTLE VICTORIA
PENINSULA: KOWLOON
TOWN: KOWLOON

HONK KONK YANG CRONK
HONOR BAY ORE FAME FETE HORN KUDO ADORE CROWN GLORY GRACE HERRY IZZAT MENSE MENSK SPEAK TREAT CREDIT DECORE ENHALO ESTEEM HOMAGE HONOUR LAUREL PRAISE REVERE SALUTE WORTHY DIGNITY EMBLAZE GLORIFY HONESTY MANSHIP RESPECT WORSHIP ACCOLADE DECORATE GRANDEZA TASHREEF
  (PL.) ACES
  (PREF.) TIMO
HONORABLE DEAR FREE GOOD DIGNE NOBLE OPIME WHITE GENTLE HONEST HONORA LORDLY SQUARE HONORA GENEROUS HANDSOME HONORARY
HONORABLENESS HONESTY
HONORABLY GENTLY
HONORARIUM SALARY DOUCEUR ALTARAGE HONORARY
HONORED GOOD FAMOUS LAUREL LAURELED PRESTIGIOUS
HONORIFIC MAGNIFIC
HOOD HOW COIF COWL HEAD HUDE JACK AMICE ALMUCE BIGGIN BONNET BURLET CALASH CAMAIL CANOPY CAPOTE CUTOFF DOMINO FUNNEL MANTLE RAFFIA BANGKOK BASHLYK CALOTTE CAPUCHE BLINDAGE CALYPTRA CAPUCCIO CAPUTIUM CHAPERON CUCULLUS FOOLSCAP LIRIPIPE LIRIPOOP MAZARINE TROTCOZY NITHSDALE
  (— AND CAPE COMBINED) FALDETTA
  (— FOR EVENING WEAR) CAPELINE
  (— OF BOILER) VOMIT
  (— OF CARRIAGE) HEAD
  (— OF MAIL) COIF CAMAIL COIFFE
  (— OF VEHICLE) TOP CAPOTE
  (— ON CUPBOARD) TREMOR
  (— ON HORSES) BLINKER
  (— OVER DOOR) MARQUISE
  (LENS —) SUNSHADE
  (MONK'S —) COWL

  (STIRRUP —) TAPADERO
  (STRAW —) JAVA
  (WOMAN'S —) SURTOUT VOLUPER
HOODED COWLED GALEATE CUCULLATE
HOODED CROW HOODIE GRAYBACK GREYBACK
HOODED MERGANSER SMEW SNOWL SPIKE TADPOLE TOWHEAD MOSSHEAD
HOODED SEAL WIG HOOD HOODCAP
HOODLUM HOOD PUNK BADDY BADDIE SKOLLY LURCHER HOOLIGAN LARRIKIN
HOODOO JINX
HOODWINK MOP DUPE FOOL SEEL BLEAR BLIND BLUFF CHEAT BAFFLE CLOYNE DELUDE GAMMON WIMPLE AVEUGLE BEGUILE BLINKER DECEIVE MISLEAD INVEIGLE
HOOEY BUSHWAH
HOOF CLOOF CLOOT COFFIN UNGUIS UNGULA CLOOTIE HOOFLET FOREHOOF
  (PREF.) UNGULI
HOOK DOG GAB JIG PEW TUG CLIP DRAG FLAG GAFF HAKE HUCK KILP MEAK NOCK PEVY PRIN PUGH SETT SKID STAY TACK CATCH CHAPE CLEEK CLICK CRAMP CROME CROOK DRAIL HAMUS ONCIN PEAVY PREEN SARPE SPOON TACHE UNCUS BECKET DETENT HANGLE HINGLE PINTLE TENTER AGRAFFE GAMBREL GRUNTER HAMULUS HITCHER HOOKLET KNUCKLE NUTHOOK PELICAN PENNANT PINHOOK POTHOOK RAMHEAD SNIGGLE SPERKET UNCINUS BOATHOOK CROTCHET GRABHOOK PORTHOOK PULLBACK VULSELLA WEEDHOOK
  (— FISH) FOUL HANG SNAG DRAIL HITCH STRIKE SNIGGLE FISHHOOK
  (— FOR BACON) COMB
  (— FOR KETTLE) KILP HANGLE TRAMMEL
  (— FOR POT) DRACKEN POTHOOK SLOWRIE
  (— FOR TWISTING HEMP) WHIRL WHIRLER
  (BENCH —) JACK
  (BOAT —) HITCHER
  (BOXING —) CROSS
  (COUPLING —) JIGGER
  (LONG-HANDLED —) HOCK MEAK
  (MUSICAL —) FLAG PENNANT
  (PRUNING —) SARPE CALABOZO
  (REAPING —) HINK TWIBILL
  (SAFETY —) CLEVIS
  (SKIDDING —S) GRAB
  (2 —S FASTENED AT SHANKS) DOUBLES
HOOKAH KALIAN CHILLUM
HOOKED ADUNC UNCATE UNCOUS ADUNCAL FALCATE HAMATED HAMULAR ADUNCATE ADUNCOUS AQUILINE HAMIFORM UNCINATE
HOOKEDNESS ADUNCITY
HOOKER-OUT STICKMAN

HOOK-SHAPED ANKYROID
HOOKUP CIRCUIT
HOOKWORM STRONGYL
HOOLIGAN ROUGH ROWDY TOUGH
APACHE GOONDA LARRIKIN
(PL.) AMALAITA
HOOP RIB BAIL BAND BOND BOOL
CLIP GIRD GIRR PASS RING TIRE
GARTH GIRTH FRETTE HOOPLE
LAGGIN WICKET CIRCLET
GARLAND TROCHUS TRUNDLE
(— FOR A SPAR) BANGLE
(— FOR BARREL) BAND GIRD GIRTH
(— FOR LAMPSHADE) HARP
(— FOR ORE BUCKET) CLEVIS
(— FOR WINNOWING GRAIN)
WEIGHT
(— NET) TRUNK
(— OF WHEEL) STRAKE
(— TO STRENGTHEN GUN) FRETTE
(HALF —) BAIL BALE
HOOPED RUNG
HOOPOE HOOP UPUPA WHOOP
IRRISOR DUNGBIRD PICARIAN
HOOPSKIRT TUBTAIL
HOOP SNAKE WAMPUM
HOOSE HUSK
HOOSIER SCHOOLMASTER
(AUTHOR OF —) EGGLESTON
(CHARACTER IN —) BUD PETE
JONES MEANS RALPH SMALL
WHITE HANNAH MARTHA
SANDER SHOCKY WALTER
HAWKINS JOHNSON MATILDA
PEARSON THOMSON
HOOSIER STATE INDIANA
HOOT CURR WHOO WHOOP
WHOOT EXPLODE ULULATE
HOOVE BLOAT
HOP HIP NIP FLIP JUMP LEAP
BOUND HITCH SWINE FLIERS
GAMBOL SPRING TITTUP
CROWHOP HOPBIND HOPVINE
LUPULUS SKIPPER
HOPBUSH AKE AKEAKE
HOP CLOVER SHAMROCK
SUCKLING
HOPE WON DEEM SPES TROW
COMBE THINK TRUST DESIRE
EXPECT PERDUE ESPEIRE
THOUGHT SPERANZA VELLEITY
(VAIN —) PIPE WANHOPE
HOPEFUL FOND BUOYANT
SANGUINE WENLICHE
HOPELESS DULL ABJECT FORLORN
DOWNCAST
HOPELESSNESS ANOMIE DESPAIR
HOPHNI (BROTHER OF —) PHINEHAS
(FATHER OF —) ELI
HOP HORNBEAM DEERWOOD
HARDHACK IRONWOOD
HOPI MOKI MOQUI
HOP-LIKE LUPULINE
HOPPER CURB JACK BUNKER
CLOSET HAPPER MACARONI
HOPPLE HOBBLE PASTERN
SIDELANG
HOPS SHATTER
(— BETWEEN 2 AND 4 YEARS) OLDS
HOPSCOTCH POTSY HOPPERS
PALLALL PEEVERS
HOP TREE RUEWORT WINGSEED
HORDE ARMY CAMP CLAN PACK

CROWD GROUP SWARM LEGION
THRONG
(INNER —) BUKEYEF
HOREHOUND HENBIT MARVEL
WONDER MARRUBE
HORI (FATHER OF —) LOTAN
(SON OF —) SHAPHAT
HORIZON LAYER VERGE COMPASS
FINITOR ORTERDE SKYLINE
HORIZONTAL LEVEL LINEAR
NAIANT ACLINAL STRAIGHT
HORIZONTALLY FLATLY BARWAYS
BARWISE ENDLONG FESSWAYS
FESSWISE
HORMIGO QUIRA
HORMONE CORTIN LUTEIN
EQUILIN ESTRIOL ESTRONE
GASTRIN INSULIN RELAXIN
STEROID THEELIN THEELOL
ANDROGEN ENDOCRIN ESTROGEN
FLORIGEN GALACTIN LACTOGEN
OESTRIOL SECRETIN CORTISONE
HORN BEAK BATON BUGLE CONCH
CORNO CORNU SHOOT ANTLER
CLAXON KLAXON OXHORN
TOOTER ALPHORN ALTHORN
ANTENNA BUFFALO CLARONE
FOGHORN HELICON HUTCHET
OUTHORN PRICKET SHOPHAR
UNICORN BEAKIRON BUCKHORN
CLAVICOR CORNICLE OLIPHANT
SLUGHORN STAGHORN
WALDHORN NOISEMAKER
(— NOTE) MORT
(— OF COW) SCUR
(— OF CRESCENT MOON) CUSP
(— OF DILEMMA) PIKE
(— OF DRINK) SLOSH
(— OF YOUNG STAG) BUNCH
(BUDDING —) SHOOT
(DRINKING —) RHYTON
(ENGLISH —) CA
(FRENCH —) CORNO
(GREY —) COLUMN
(HUNTER'S —) HUTCHET
WALDHORN
(INSECT'S —) ANTENNA
(IVORY —) OLIFANT
(RAM'S —) SHOPHAR
(RUDIMENTARY —) SLUG
(STUNTED —) SCUR
(PREF.) CORNEO CORNI CORNU
(SUFF.) CERA(S) CEROS CEROUS
CERUS CORN
HORNBEAM HARDBEAM
HARDHACK HORNWOOD
IRONWOOD
HORNBILL TOCK CALAO TOUCAN
BUCEROS HOMURAI BROMVOEL
PICARIAN YEARBIRD
HORNBLENDE SIDERITE
HORNED FORKED CORNUTE
(PREF.) CERA CERVI CORNEO
CORNI CORNU
HORNED DACE CHUB
HORNED POUT CATFISH
HORNED SCREAMER ANHIMA
KAMACHI KAMICHI UNICORN
HORNED VIPER WAMPUM
CERASTES
HORNET VESPA VESPID STINGER
HORNGELD CORNAGE
HORNLESS NAT NOT MOIL POLL

DODDY MULEY POLEY DODDED
HUMBLE HUMMEL MAILIE MULLEY
POLLED ACEROUS
HORNPIPE MATELOTE
HORN POPPY SQUATMORE
HORNSTONE CHERT KERALITE
HORNTAIL SIREX ORYSSID
UROCERID WOODWORM
HORNWORT COONTAIL
HORNWEED
HORNY WAUKIT CALLOUS
CERATOID CORNEOUS KERASINE
KERATOID
HORNYHEAD CHUB
HOROSCOPE SCOPE THEME
FIGURE GENESIS NATIVITY
HORRIBLE DIRE GRIM UGLY
AWFUL BLACK GREAT GRISLY
HORRID GEARFUL GHASTLY
HIDEOUS HORRENT UNSLOGH
DREADFUL GRUESOME HORRIFIC
SHOCKING TERRIBLE MONSTROUS
HORRID GRIM UGLY AWFUL
ROUGH RUGGED SNUFFY
UGSOME WICKED HIDEOUS
DREADFUL GRUESOME HORRIBLE
SHOCKING
HORRIFIC FEARFUL
HORRIFIED AGHAST GHASTLY
HORRENT
HORRIFY APPAL AGRISE DISMAY
ENHORROR
HORROR FEAR DREAD TERROR
CONSTERNATION
(PL.) JIM JAMS
HORSA (BROTHER OF —) HENGIST
HORS D'OEUVRE CANAPE RELISH
OUTWORK ZAKUSKA
(PL.) ASSIETTE
HORSE BAY CUT DUN GEE GRI NAG
PAD POT RIP TIT ARAB AVER
BARB DOON GOER GROG HACK
HAND HOSS JADE MARE MOKE
PRAD PROD QUAD RACK RIDE
ROAN ROIL SKIN STUD TEAM
TURK WEED YAWD ZAIN AIVER
ARION ARVAK BEAST BIDET
BLACK BROCK CAPLE CAPUL
CHUNK CREAM CROCK DUMMY
EQUID FAVEL GLYDE GRANI
HAIRY HOBBY MILER MOREL
PACER PINTO PIPER POLER
PUNCH RACER ROGUE RUNSY
SCREW SHIER SHIRE SKATE
SOMER STEED STIFF TACKY
WALER WIDGE ALEZAN AMBLER
BANKER BOLTER BRONCO
BRUMBY BUCKER BUSSER CABBER
CALICO CASTER CHASER CHEVAL
COLLOP CURTAL CUSSER DAPPLE
DOBBIN DRIVER ENTIRE EQUINE
FENCER FILLER GANGER GARRON
GLEYDE GRULLA HUNTER
JUMPER KEFFEL LEADER MAIDEN
MORGAN NUBIAN ORLOFF
OUTLAW PELTER PLATER POSTER
PULLER RACKER ROARER ROUNCY
RUNNER SAVAGE SORREL STAGER
TARPAN TRACER TURKEY
VANNER WARPER WEAVER
ALSVINN ALSVITH ARABIAN
BARBARY BELGIAN BOARDER
CABALLO CHARGER CLICKER

CLIPPER COACHER COCOTTE
COURSER CRIBBER CRIOLLA
CRITTER DRAFTER FLEMISH
GALATHE GELDING GIGSTER
GRUNTER HACKNEY KNACKER
LEEFANG MONTURE MUSTANG
NEIGHER PACOLET PALFREY
PIEBALD PRANCER PRANKER
RATTLER REESTER REFUSER
REMOUNT RUNAWAY SADDLER
SLEDDER SLEEPER SPANKER
STAGGIE STEPPER SUFFOLK
SUMPTER TRAPPER TRESTLE
TROOPER TROTTER WHEELER
ARDENNES BATHORSE BUCKSKIN
CHESTNUT CHEVALET COCKTAIL
COLICKER CREATURE CYLLAROS
DEMISANG DESTRIER EOHIPPUS
FOOTROPE FRIPPERY GALLOPER
GALLOWAY HRIMFAXI KADISCHI
MACHINER OUTSIDER PALOMINO
RIDGLING ROADSTER SKEWBALD
STIBBLER TRIPPLER WHISTLER
YARRAMAN
(— ACT) MANAGE
(— CERTAIN NOT TO WIN) STIFF
(— ESTABLISHMENT) HARAS
(— LOSING FIXED RACE) STUMER
STUMOUR
(— OF UNIFORM DARK COLOR) ZAIN
(— RACE) WALKOVER
(— THAT WON'T START) STICK
(—S RUNNING BEHIND) RUCK
(ARABIAN —) ARAB KOHL ARABIAN
(BALKY —) JIB JIBBER
(BROKEN-DOWN —) JADE CROCK
SCREW DURGAN GARRAN
(CALICO —) PINTO
(CASTRATED —) GELDING
(CLUMSY —) STAMMEL
(DECREPIT —) SKATE GLEYDE
(DRAFT —) HAIRY PUNCH SHIRE
BEETEWK BELGIAN SUFFOLK
PERCHERON
(DROVE OF —S) ATAJO
(EASY-PACED —) PAD
(FALLOW —) FAVEL
(FAMILY —) DOBBIN
(FAST —) GANGER
(FEMALE —) MARE FILLY
(FLEMISH —) ROIL
(GRAY —) SCHIMMEL
(HIGH-SPIRITED —) STEPPER
(IMAGINARY —) AULLAY
(IMMUNIZED —) BLEEDER
(INFERIOR —) PLUG CAYUSE
PLATER
(JUMPING —) LEPPER
(MALE —) STALLION
(NEAR —) HAND
(OLD —) JADE PROD YAUD AIVER
CROCK
(PACK —) BIDET SUMPTER
(PART OF —) EAR EYE JAW RIB
FACE HOCK HOOF KNEE LOIN
MANE NECK NOSE POLL TAIL
BELLY CHEEK CROUP ELBOW
FLANK MOUTH THIGH BREAST
CANNON GASKIN HAUNCH STIFLE
BUTTOCK CORONET FETLOCK
FOREARM NOSTRIL PASTERN
WITHERS FOREHEAD FORELOCK
SHOULDER THROATLATCH

(RANGE —) FANTAIL
(ROAN —) SCHIMMEL
(SADDLE —) MOUNT
(SHAFT —) SHAFTER THILLER
(SHAGGY —) ALTAI
(SLUGGISH —) HOG
(SMALL —) NAG TIT BIDET GENET
HOBBY CANUCK JENNET
GALLOWAY
(STOCKY —) COB
(TEAM OF —S) CARTWARE
(TEAM OF 3 —S WITH LEADER)
UNICORN
(TRICK —) SIMON
(UNBROKEN —) BRONCO
(VICIOUS —) LADINO
(WILD —) FUZZY BRUMBY
KUMRAH OUTLAW TARPAN
JUGHEAD BANGTAIL FUZZTAIL
WARRIGAL
(WINGED —) PEGASUS
(WORN-OUT —) HACK GARRAN
KNACKER CROWBAIT
(WORTHLESS —) JADE SHACK
KEFFEL
(YOUNG —) TIT COLT FOAL STAG
STOT STAGGIE
(2-YEAR OLD —) TWINTER
(3 —S ABREAST) TROIKA
(3 —S ONE BEHIND ANOTHER)
RANDOM
(4 —S ABREAST) QUADRIGA
(PL.) MANADA STABLE UNICORN
(PREF.) HIPP(O)
(SUFF.) HIPPUS
HORSE BALM KNOBWEED
KNOTROOT RICHWEED
HORSE BLANKET RUG MANTA
HORSE BOY TRACER
HORSE CHESTNUT CONKER
HORSECLOTH HOUSE HOUSING
HORSE DEALER COPER CHANTER
COURSER
HORSE-EYE JACK XUREL
HORSE FENNEL SESELI
HORSEFLESH JACK
HORSEFLY BOT GAD CLEG CLEGG
STOUT BOTFLY BREEZE GADBEE
GADFLY BULLDOG DEERFLY
TABANID
HORSEHAIR SETON
HORSELAUGH GUFFAW
HORSELEECH ALUKAH
HORSELOAD SEAM
HORSE MACKEREL TUNNY
SAUREL
HORSEMAN RIDER CHARRO
COWBOY HUSSAR KNIGHT
RUTTER COURIER PICADOR
PRICKER CAVALIER GALLOPER
(PL.) HORSE CAVALRY
HORSEMANSHIP CAVALRY
HORSEMINT RIGNUM
HORSE MUSHROOM WHITECAP
HORSE NETTLE SOLANUM
HORSEPLAY HIJINKS
(PANTOMIME —) RALLY
HORSEPOWER SOUP
HORSEPOX GREASE
HORSE-RADISH MAROR MOROR
REDCOLL
HORSE-RADISH TREE BEN BEHN
BEHEN

HORSESHOE TIP SHOE PLATE
HOBBER LUNETTE
HORSETAIL TAIL PRELE TOADPIPE
HORSETAIL LICHEN TREEHAIR
HORSETAIL TREE AGOHO AGOJO
HORSEWEED COCASH COWTAIL
HOGWEED FIREWEED
SCABIOUS
HORTATORY EMOTIVE
HORTICULTURIST (ALSO SEE
BOTANIST)
HORUS SEPT SOPT SEPTI
HORMAKHU
(FATHER OF —) OSIRIS
(MOTHER OF —) ISIS
HOSACKIA ACMISPON
HOSE LINE VAMP HOSEN GASKIN
BROGUES BULLION HOSIERY
CHAUSSES HANDLINE HOSEPIPE
HOSEA (FATHER OF —) BEERI
HOSHAIAH (SON OF —) AZARIAH
JEZANIAH
HOSHEA (FATHER OF —) NUN
AZAZIAH
HOSIERY HOSE KNITWEAR
(— WORKER) LOOPER
HOSPICE IMARET DIACONIA
HOSPITAL
HOSPITABLE DOUCE CLEVER
DOULCE SOCIAL CORDIAL
FRIENDLY
HOSPITAL BEDLAM CRECHE
SPITAL COLLEGE LAZARET
PESTHOUSE POLYCLINIC
HOSPITALITY SALT MENSE
XENODOCHY
HOSPODAR VOIVOD GOSPODAR
HOST SUM ARMY FYRD WARE
CROWD JASON MAKER POWER
SWARM WERED LEGION LODGER
NATION THRONG BALEBOS
COMPANY FYRDUNG SACRING
VIANDER LANDLORD PARTICLE
MULTITUDE
(— OF INVADERS) HERE
(EUCHARISTIC —) LAMB SACRING
(PL.) SABAOTH
(SUFF.) XENOUS XENY
HOSTA NIOBE FUNKIA
HOSTAGE BORROW PLEDGE
SURETY RANSOMER
HOSTEL INN ENTRY HOSTAGE
KINGDOM HOSPITAL
HOSTELRY AUBERGE
HOSTESS TAUPO LANDLADY
CHATELAINE
HOSTILE FOE HARD ALIEN BLACK
ENEMY FREMT HATEL STOUT
DEADLY FRIGID INFEST ADVERSE
ASOCIAL FIENDLY OPPOSED
UNQUERT WARLIKE CONTRARY
INIMICAL OPPOSITE
HOSTILITY WAR FEID FEUD HATE
ANIMUS ENMITY HATRED
RANCOR SCHISM DAGGERS
RUPTURE
(PL.) WAR ARMS ARMOR
WARFARE
HOSTLER NAGMAN OSTLER
HORSEBOY
HOT WARM ADUST CALID EAGER
FIERY ARDENT ESTIVE FERVID
IGNITE SULTRY TORRID ANIMOSE

ANIMOUS BOILING BURNING
CANDENT FERVENT PEPPERY
THERMAL CAYENNED FEVERISH
SEETHING SIZZLING
(— WATER) SOUP
HOTBED BED NEST HOTHOUSE
HOT-BLOODED VASCULAR
HOTBOX SMOKER STINKER
HOTEL INN SPA FLOP FONDA
HOUSE HYDRO HOSTEL HOTTLE
POSADA FLEABAG FONDACO
FUNDUCK GASTHOF HOSTELRY
(— NEAR AIRPORT) AIRTEL
(WATERSIDE —) BOATEL
HOTELKEEPER HOTELIER
HOTHAM (FATHER OF —) HEBER
HOTHAN (SON OF —) SHAMA
JEHIEL
HOT-HEADED BRAINISH MADBRAIN
HOTHIR (FATHER OF —) HEMAN
HOTHOUSE STEW STOVE PINERY
FRUITERY
HOT ROD DRAGSTER
HOT-TEMPERED PEPPERY
CHOLERIC SPITFIRE
HOTTENTOT NAMA TOTTY
HOTNOT KOKANA WITBOOI
QUAEQUAE
(PL.) BALAO BALAWU
HOUND DOG PIE BAIT HARL HUNT
MUTE BRACE BRACH ENTRY
HARRY LEASH LIMER SLATE
AFGHAN BASSET BEAGLE HUNTER
JOWLER LEAMER LUCERN SLEUTH
TUFTER CURTISE ENTRADA
GELLERT REDBONE SKIRTER
BARUKHZY BLUETICK BRATCHET
COURSING FOXHOUND
(BITCH —) BRACH
(CRY OF —) MUSIC
(EXTINCT —) TALBOT
(RELAY OF —S) VANLAY
(SLEUTH —) TALBOT
(SPECTRAL —) SHUCK
(PL.) RACHES
HOUND'S-TONGUE TORYWEED
HOUR URE TIDE TIME CURFEW
GHURRY
(CANONICAL —) NONE SEXT PRIME
MATINS TIERCE ORTHROS
VESPERS COMPLINE EVENSONG
(HALF —) BELL
(KILOWATT —) KELVIN
(LAST —S) DEATHBED
(STUDY —) PREP
(6 —S) QUADRANT
(PREF.) HORO
HOURGLASS (PART OF —) BULB
SAND FRAME WAIST
HOURLY HORAL HORARY
HOUSE BOX KEN CASA CRIB DOME
DUMP FIRM FLET HALL HELL
HOLE HOME RACE ROOF STOW
ABODE ADOBE AERIE BAHAY
BANDA COVER DACHA DOMUS
HOOCH HOUSE JACAL LODGE
MEESE PLACE STAGE WHARE
BESTOW BIGGIN BOTTLE CAMARA
CASITA CASTLE CHEMIS CLOTHE
DUPLEX FAMILY HEARTH HOOTCH
MAISON PALACE PARISH SINGLE
STABLE WIGWAM BASTIDE
BIGGING CABOOSE CASSINE

EUDEMON FAZENDA HOGGERY
HOUSING MESUAGE QUARTER
SHELTER AEDICULA BARADARI
BUNGALOW DOMICILE DOVECOTE
DWELLING MEDSTEAD MESSUAGE
TENEMENT NOVITIATE
(— AND LAND) DEMESNE
(— AND 5 ACRES) COTE
(— FOR DOGS) KENNEL
(— FOR WOMEN) HAREM
(— IN BOROUGH) HAW
(— OF A MARABOUT) KOUBA
(— OF CORRECTION) BRIDEWELL
(— OF KNIGHTS TEMPLARS)
PRECEPTORY
(— OF LEGISLATURE) SEANAD
CHAMBER ASSEMBLY
(— OF PARLIAMENT) COMMONS
LAGTING
(— OF PROSTITUTION) CRIB BAGNIO
BORDEL
(— OF REFUGE) MAGDALEN
MAGDALENE
(— OF THIEVES) KEN
(— OF WORSHIP) BETHEL CHURCH
(— WITH TRIANGULAR FRONT)
AFRAME
(APARTMENT —) INSULA
(ASTROLOGICAL —) ANGLE
(AUSTRALIAN —) HUMPY
(CHANGE —) DRY
(CHAPTER —) CABILDO
(CLAY —) ADOBE TEMBE
(COACH —) REMISE
(COMMUNAL —) MORONG
(COUNTRY —) PEN DACHA CASINO
GRANGE QUINTA BASTIDE
CHATEAU
(COW —) VACCARY
(DAIRY —) WICK
(EATING —) COOKSHOP
(ESKIMO —) IGLU IGLOO TOPEK
KASHGA KASHIMA
(FIJI —) BURE
(FORTIFIED —) GARRISON
(GAMBLING —) BANK HELL
RIDOTTO
(GOVERNMENT —) KONAK
(GRINDING —) HULL
(GROUP OF —S) CLUSTER
(HAWAIIAN —) HALE
(LODGING —) INN KIP HOST ENTRY
HOTEL HOSTEL
(LOG —) TILT
(MANOR —) HAM HALL COURT
PLACE SCHLOSS SEIGNEURY
(PLANETARY —) TOWER
(POULTRY —) ARK HENNERY
(PUBLIC —) INN HOSTEL SHANTY
CANTEEN SNUGGERY
(RANCH —) HUT
(RELIGIOUS —) CELL CONVENT
KELLION MONASTERY
PRESBYTERY
(RENTED —) LET
(REST —) DAK KHAN SERAI
(RETREAT —) CENACLE
(ROOMING —) DOSS FLOP
FLEABAG
(ROYAL —) AERIE
(SENATE —) CURIA
(SMALL —) COT HUT BACH CELL
CABIN HOVEL SHACK CASITA

COTTAGE MAISONETTE
(SOD —) SODDY
(STILT —) CHIKEE CHICKEE
(SUMMER —) TRELLIS
(TENEMENT —) LAND CHAWL
(THATCHED —) BANDA
(TOY —) COBHOUSE
(TURKISH —) KONAK
(PREF.) DOMI ECO OECO OIKO
STEG(O)
(SUFF.) OECA OECIA STEGE
STEGITE
HOUSEBOAT BARGE HOUSER
WANGAN WANIGAN DAHABEAH
HOUSEBREAKER MILL JACOB
MILLKEN
HOUSEBREAKING CRACK
HOUSECARL THINGMAN
HOUSECOAT DUSTER
HOUSEFINCH BURION LINNET
REDHEAD
HOUSEHOLD HIRED HOUSE
FAMILY HOUSAL MEINIE MENAGE
FIRESIDE MAINPAST
(PREF.) EC(O) OEC(O) OIKO
HOUSEHOLDER ASTRER
GOODMAN GUIDMAN NAUKRAR
FRANKLIN
HOUSEKEEPER HUSSY MATRON
HOUSELEEK JUBARB AYEGREEN
HOMEWORT SENGREEN SILGREEN
HOUSEMATE DOMESTIC
HOUSE OF MIRTH (AUTHOR OF —)
WHARTON
(CHARACTER IN —) GUS BART
JUDY LILY GRYCE PERCY SIMON
BERTHA DORSET GEORGE SELDEN
TRENOR LAURENCE PENISTON
ROSEDALE
HOUSE OF SEVEN GABLES
(AUTHOR OF —) HAWTHORNE
(CHARACTER IN —) MAULE PHOEBE
VENNER JAFFREY CLIFFORD
HEPZIBAH HOLGRAVE PYNCHEON
HOUSEWARMING INFARE
HOUSEWIFE DAME FRAU FROW
WIFE HUSSY VROUW BUSHWIFE
HAUSFRAU
(MEAN —) NIP
HOUSEY-HOUSEY BINGO
HOUSING BOX BASE CASE DRUM
TRAP BANJO BLIMP GLOBE
HOUSE KIOSK BARREL RADOME
SHIELD HOUSAGE SHELTER
DOGHOUSE PADCLOTH PECTORAL
PEDESTAL SHABRACK
(HORSE'S —) BASE
(RADAR —) BLISTER
(PL.) HOLSTERS
HOVA IMERINA
HOVEL HUT COSH CREW CRIB
CRUE HELM HULK HULL BOTHY
CHOZA HUTCH LODGE BOTHIE
BURROW CRUIVE PONDOK
HOVELER HOBBLER HUFFLER
HOVEN BLOATING
HOVER BAIT FLIT HANG HOVE
BROOD POISE FLUTTER HOVERER
HOW AS FOO HOO HOWE HOWEER
HOWEVER QUOMODO WHEREBY
HOWDAH TOWER AMBARI
AMBAREE
HOWEVER BUT THO YET ONLY

HOWSO STILL THOUGH
HOW GREEN WAS MY VALLEY
(AUTHOR OF —) LLEWELLYN
(CHARACTER IN —) HUW BETA
DAVY IVOR OWEN EVANS IANTO
GWILYM IESTYN MARGED
MORGAN BRONWEN ANGHARAD
GRUFFYDD
HOWITZER HOWITZ LICORN
UNICORN
HOWITZER SHELL OBUS
HOWL WAP WOW BAWL GOWL
GURL HURL RAVE WAUL WAWL
YAWL YOLL YOUT YOWL TIGER
WHEWL WRAWL BEHOWL
STEVEN ULULATE
(— VOCIFEROUSLY) TONGUE
HOWLER BONER ERROR
ARAGUATO
HOWLER MONKEY MONO ARABA
HOWLER GUARIBA GUEREBA
STENTOR ALOUATTE
HOWLING ULULANT
HOY TJALK BILANDER CRUMSTER
HOYDEN MEG BLOWZE RIGSBY
TOMBOY
HREIDMAR (SON OF —) REGIN
FAFNER FAFNIR
H-SHAPED ZYGAL
HUAMUCHIL INGA
HUAVE WABI HUABI
HUB HOB BOSS NAVE STOCK
CENTER CENTRE FAUCET HUBBLE
SOCKET SPIDER OMPHALOS
(— AND SPOKES) SPEECH
HUBBLE-BUBBLE CALEAN KALIAN
CALAHAN
HUBBUB DIN COIL STIR CLAMOR
FRAISE HUBBLE RABBLE RACKET
TUMULT BOBBERY CLUTTER
BROUHAHA HUBBABOO
ROWDYDOW SPLATTER
HUCHEN HUSO
HUCHNOM TATU
HUCKLEBERRY HURT ERICAD
CRACKERS
HUCKLEBERRY FINN (AUTHOR OF
—) TWAIN CLEMENS
(CHARACTER IN —) JIM TOM DUKE
FINN HUCK JANE KING POLLY
SALLY SUSAN WILKS JOANNA
PHELPS SAWYER WATSON
DOUGLAS GRANGERFORD
SHEPHERDSON
HUCKSTER BADGER CADGER
KIDDER HAGGLER KIDDIER
TRUCKER OUTCRIER
HUDDLE RUCK HUNCH CRINGE
CROUCH FUMBLE HOWDER
HURTLE SCRUMP SHRIMP SHRINK
CROODLE SCRINCH SCROOCH
SCRUNCH SHUFFLE
HUDIBRAS (AUTHOR OF —) BUTLER
(CHARACTER IN —) RALPHO
CROWDERO HUDIBRAS
SIDROPHEL
HUE RUD BLEE BLUE COND CYAN
CHLOR COLOR GREEN LEMON
SHOUT TAINT TINCT CHROMA
(DULL —) DRAB
(SOMBER —) DARK
HUELESS GRAY GREY
HUFF DOD BLOW RUFF TIFF

DRUNT SNUFF OFFENSE
HUFFY FUFFY SHIRTY
HUG CLIP COLL COUL MOLD CREEM
CRUSH HALSE PRESS CUDDLE
HUDDLE HUGGLE STRAIN
CHERISH EMBRACE SQUEEZE
HUGE BIG FELL MAIN VAST ENORM
GIANT GREAT JUMBO LARGE
STOUR HEROIC IMMANE BANGING
BUMPING DECUMAN HIDEOUS
IMMENSE MASSIVE MONSTER
TITANIC COLOSSAL ENORMOUS
GALACTIC GIGANTIC MOUNTAIN
PYTHONIC SLASHING SWAPPING
THUMPING THWACKING
MOUNTAINOUS
HUGENESS ENORMITY
HUGUENOT CAMISARD
HUGUENOTS, LES (COMPOSER OF
—) MEYERBEER
HUISACHE WABI AROMO CASSIE
POPINAC OPOPANAX
HUL (FATHER OF —) ARAM
(GRANDFATHER OF —) SHEM
HULDAH (HUSBAND OF —)
SHALLUM
HULK CHOP HULL CORSE
HULL HUD POD BODY BULK HULK
HUSK PILL BURSE CASCO SWELL
(— OF COTTON BOLL) BUR BURR
(— OF SHIP) BODY HULK BOTTOM
(PART OF —) BEAM DECK KEEL
RAIL BATTEN RABBET CEILING
FUTTOCK KEELSON GARBOARD
PLANKING STRINGER WATERWAY
STANCHION SHELFPIECE
SPIRKETING
HULLABALOO DIN FLAP CLAMOR
HUBBUB RACKET BROUHAHA
HUM BUM BLUR BRUM BUZZ HUSS
TUNE CHIRM CROON DRONE
FFIGN SOUGH SOWFF
HUMBLE TEEDLE FREDDON
TRUMPET
HUMAN BEING MANLY FINITE
FLESHY HUMANE MORTAL
MANNISH HOMININE HUMANIST
(PREF.) HOMI HOMIN(I)
HUMAN BEING MAN WIGHT
MORTAL PERSON ADAMITE
CREATURE RATIONAL
(PREF.) ANTHROP(O)
HUMAN COMEDY (AUTHOR OF —)
SAROYAN
(CHARACTER IN —) BESS MARY
ARENA HOMER KATEY TOBEY
ACKLEY GEORGE GROGAN
HUBERT LIONEL MARCUS
THOMAS BYFIELD ULYSSES
MACAULEY SPANGLER
HUMANE CIVIL KINDLY TENDER
MERCIFUL
HUMANELY MANLY
HUMANITARIAN (ALSO SEE
PHILANTHROPIST) PUBLIC
PHILANTHROPIC
HUMANITY FLESH MENSK WORLD
MANHEAD MANHOOD MANSHIP
SPECIES ADAMHOOD HUMANISM
KINDNESS LENITUDE
HUMBLE LOW BASE HOWE MEAN
MEEK MILD MURE POOR TAME
VAIL ABASE ABATE BUXOM DEMIT

DIMIT LOWER LOWLY PLAIN SILLY
SMALL SOBER WORMY ATTERR
DEJECT DEMEAN DEMISS EMBASE
HONEST MASTER MODEST
REDUCE SIMPLE SLIGHT UNPUFF
AFFLICT DEGRADE DEPRESS
FOOLISH IGNOBLE MORTIFY
OBSCURE CONTRITE DISGRACE
(— ONESELF) STOOP GROVEL
HUMBLED SMALL ABASED
DEJECTED
HUMBLENESS HUMILITY
HUMBLER INFERIOR
HUMBLING SETDOWN ABJECTION
HUMBLY SIMPLE
HUMBUG GAS GUM HUM KID
BUNK FLAM GAFF GAME GUFF
JAZZ SHAM CHEAT FRAUD FUDGE
GUILE JOLLY SPOOF SPOOK TRICK
BARNEY BLAGUE GAMMON
BLARNEY FLUMMER VERNEUK
FLIMFLAM FLUMMERY
HUCKMUCK IMPOSTER NONSENSE
HUMDINGER LULU ONER DOOZY
DINGER HUMMER SNORTER
RIPSNORTER
HUMDRUM IRKSOME PROSAIC
BOURGEOIS
HUMERUS ARM
HUMID WET DAMP DANK MOIST
SOGGY STICKY SULTRY WETTISH
HUMOROUS
HUMIDITY
(PREF.) HYGR(O)
HUMILIATE ABASE ABASH SCALP
SHAME NIDDER NITHER DEGRADE
MORTIFY UNPLUME DISGRACE
HUMILIATED SMALL ASHAMED
HUMILIATION DUST COMEDOWN
DISGRACE
HUMILITY MODESTY MEEKNESS
MILDNESS
HUMIN MELANIN
HUMMEL FALTER
HUMMING AHUM BROOL SINGING
HUMMINGBIRD RUBY STAR
MANGO SYLPH TENUI TOPAZ
AMAZON COQUET HERMIT
HUMMER ROSTER SAPPHO
COLIBRI EMERALD HUMBIRD
JACOBIN RAINBOW SNOWCAP
TROCHIL WARRIOR CALLIOPE
COQUETTE FIRETAIL FROUFROU
MIMOTYPE PICARIAN SAPPHIRE
WHITETIP
HUMMOCK HUMP CHENIER
HAMMOCK TUSSOCK
HUMOR CUE PIN TID WIT BABY
BILE CANT COAX MOOD TIFF VEIN
WHIM FRAME IRONY TUTOR
MEGRIM PAMPER PHLEGM SANIES
SOOTHE SPLEEN SPRITE TEMPER
FOOLING GRATIFY INDULGE
VITREUM VITRINA ARCHNESS
DISHUMOR DROLLERY EYEWATER
FUMOSITY SANGUINE VITREOUS
(BAD —) BATS THROW
(ILL —) BILE DUDGEON
(QUIET —) DRYNESS
(SLIMY —) HIPPOMANES
HUMORIST JOKER FUNSTER
FUNMAKER FUNNYMAN
AMERICAN NYE LEAF SHAW WARD

LEWIS SHUTE SMITH LELAND
LOOMIS MASSON ROGERS
MARQUIS THOMSON PERELMAN
STREETER SULLIVAN SHILLABER
AUSTRIAN SAPHIR
CANADIAN LEACOCK
ENGLISH PAIN WARD SEAMAN
FRENCH RABELAIS
GERMAN RICHTER
IRISH MAHONY
HUMOROUS DROLL FUNNY
PAWKY QUEER JOCOSE COMICAL
GIOCOSO PLAYFUL WAGGISH
PLEASANT SARDONIC
HUMP BOSS HUNK BULGE BUNCH
CROUP CRUMP HULCH HUNCH
GIBBER GIBBUS HUMMIE GIBBOUS
(PREF.) HYB(O)
HUMPBACK LORD CRUMP PUNCH
KYPHOSIS
HUMPBACKED HUMPED HUMPTY
GIBBOSE GIBBOUS
(PREF.) CYPH(O) HYB(O)
HUMPBACKED SALMON HADDO
HOLIA
HUMPED HULCH HUMPY HUTCH
HUMPTY HUNCHY BUNCHED
HUMPHRY CLINKER (AUTHOR OF —
) SMOLLETT
(CHARACTER IN —) JERRY LYDIA
GEORGE WILSON BRAMBLE
CLINKER HUMPHRY JENKINS
MATTHEW MELFORD OBADIAH
TABITHA DENNISON WINIFRED
LISMAHAGO
HUMUS MOR MOLD MULL HUMIN
MOULD
HUNCH HUMP HUNK HULCH
HUNCHET SCRUNCH
HUNCHBACK URCHIN HUMPBACK
HUNCHBACK OF NOTRE DAME
(AUTHOR OF —) HUGO
(CHARACTER IN —) CLAUDE
FROLLO PHOEBUS ESMERALDA
GRINGOIRE QUASIMODO
CHATEAUPERS
HUNDRED RHO CENT CENTUM
HUNDER HUNNER CANTRED
CANTREF CENTARY
(— THOUSAND) LAC LAKH
(NINE —) SAN SAMPI
(5 —) D
(PREF.) CENT(I) HECATO
HECATOM HECATON HECT(O)
HUNDREDFOLD CENTUPLE
HUNDRED-HANDED BRIAREAN
HUNDREDTH CENTESIMAL
(— OF INCH) POINT
(— OF RIGHT ANGLE) GRAD GRADE
HUNDREDWEIGHT CENT CENTAL
CENTENA CENTNER HUNDRED
QUINTAL
HUNGARIAN HUN KUMAN
MAGYAR
(PREF.) UGRO

HUNGARY
CANAL: SIO SARVIZ
CAPITAL: BUDAPEST
COIN: GARA BALAS LENGO FILLER
FORINT KORONA
COUNTY: VAS PEST ZALA BEKES
FEJER HEVES TOLNA NOGRAD

SOMOGY BARANYA
DANCE: CZARDAS
DYNASTY: ARPAD ANGEVIN
FOREST: BAKONY
GYPSY: SZIGANE TZIGANE
KING: BELA GEZA IMRE ARPAD
ISTVAN KALMAN MATTHIAS
LAKE: FERTO BALATON VELENCE
BLATENSEE
MEASURE: AKO HOLD JOCH YOKE
ANTAL ITCZE MAROK METZE
HUVELYK MERFOLD
MOUNTAIN: KEKES BAKONY
MECSEK BORZSONY KORISHEGY
MOUNTAIN RANGE: BUKK MATRA
MECSEK CARPATHIAN
MUSICAL INSTRUMENT: TAROGATO
NATIVE: HUN SERB CROAT GYPSY
MAGYAR SLOVAK UGRIAN
PLAIN: PUSZTA
REGIME: KADAR
RIVER: DUNA MURA RAAB RABA
SAJO ZALA BODVA DRAVA
DRAVE IPOLY KAPOS KOROS
MAROS RABCA TARNA TISZA
DANUBE HENRAD POPRAD
SZAMOS THEISS ZAGYVA
VISTULA BERRETYO
TOWN: ABA ACS OZD VAC BUDA
EGER GYOR MAKO PAPA PECS
PEST TATA ZIRC KOMLO
CEGLED MOHACS SOPRON
SZEGED DBRECEN MISKOLC
SZENTES DEBRECEN SZEGEDIN
WEIGHT: VAMFONT VAMMAZSA
WINE: EGER TOKAJ TOKAY
SZEKSZARD

HUNGER BELL CLEM WANT ACORIA
DESIRE FAMINE CRAVING
HUNGRY YAP HOWE KEEN LEER
YAUP EMPTY THIRL HOLLOW
JEJUNE PECKISH YAPPISH
ANHUNGRY ESURIENT
HUNK DAD DAUD JUNK MOUNTAIN
(— OF BREAD) TOMMY
HUNT DOG GUN JAG MOB RUN
GREW JACK LARK PUMP SEAL
SEEK SHOP CHASE CHEVY DRIVE
HOUND REVAY TRACK TRAIL
BATTUE BEAGLE BREVIT CHEVVY
COURSE FALCON FERRET SEARCH
SHIKAR VANLAY ENCHASE
AUCUPATE PIGSTICK SCROUNGE
VENATION
(— BIG GAME) GHOOM
(— DEER) FLOAT
(— DOWN) QUARRY
(— DUCKS) TOLL
(— FOX) CUB
(— WITH HAWK) FLY
(— WITH SPEAR) STICK
HUNTER GUN HUNT PINK JAGER
BIRDER CHASER GUNNER JAEGER
NIMROD THERON ACTAEON
BUSHMAN CATCHER COURSER
MONTERO SHIKARI SHOOTER
SKIRTER STALKER TRAILER
VENERER CEPHALUS CHASSEUR
FIELDMAN HUNTSMAN TRAILMAN
(— ON SNOW) CRUSTER
(BUFFALO —) CIBOLERO
(MYTHOLOGICAL —) GWYN ORION

(RING OF —S) TINCHEL TINCHILL
HUNTING DRAG HANK AHUNT
WATHE SHIKAR VENERY CUBBING
GUNNING BEAGLING PURCHASE
SHOOTING SURROUND VENATION
(— SIGNAL) SEEK
HUNTSMAN WHIP HUNTER
JAEGER ACTAEON CATCHER
COURSER MONTERO SCARLET
VENATOR VENERER CHASSEUR
HUPHAM (FATHER OF —) BENJAMIN
HUR (GRANDSON OF —) BEZALEEL
(SON OF —) REPHAIAH
HURAM (FATHER OF —) BELA
HURDLE TRAY FLAKE FRITH PANEL
STALE STICK DOUBLE RADDLE
SLEDGE WATTLE
HURDS TOW
HURDY-GURDY LIRA ROTA
LANTUM VIELLE SAMBUKE
HUMSTRUM SYMPHONY
HURI (SON OF —) ABIHAIL
HURL BUM BUN CAST CLOD DASH
DUST FIRE PASH PELT PICK SLAT
SOAK SOCK DRIVE FLING HEAVE
LANCE PITCH SLING SMITE SPANG
SWING THIRL THROW WHIRL
THRILL HURLBAT SWITHER
WHITHER JACULATE PRECIPITATE
HURLY-BURLY HURL RACKET
UPROAR
HURRAH HAIL HUZZA HOORAY
HURRAY BRAVISSIMO
HURRICANE BAGUIO PRESTER
FURACANA FURICANE WILDWIND
HURRIED HASTY RAPID THRONG
HASTEFUL SNATCHED
HURRY ADO FOG NIP RAP RUB
RUN BUSK DUST HUMP PELL
PLAT POST RAPE RESE RUSH STIR
TIFT TROT URGE WHIR CHASE
CROWD HASTE HYPER LURRY
MOSEY PRESS SESSA SKIRT SPEED
STAVE STOUR WHIRL BUCKET
BUNDLE BUSTLE HASTEN HUSTLE
POWDER STROTH TATTER
WHORRY HOTFOOT QUICKEN
SCUDDLE SKELTER SLITHER
WHITHER DISPATCH EXPEDITE
SPLUTTER ACCELERATE
(— A HORSE) SPUR
(— ABOUT) SCOUR
(— AWAY) FLEE BUNCH SCREW
SKIRT
(— CLUMSILY) TAVE TEAVE
(— NOISILY) SPLUTTER
(— OFF) DUST
(— UP) BUSK
HURT CUT HOT NOY DERE FIKE
GALL HARM PAIN SCAT ABUSE
BLAME GRIEF GRIPE PINCH SORRY
SPITE THORN WATHE WOUND
BRUISE DAMAGE GRIEVE IMPAIR
INJURE INJURY LESION MIFFED
MITTLE PAINED PUNISH SCATHE
STRAIN STROKE WINGED AFFLICT
HURTING OFFENCE OFFENSE
SCADDLE MISCHIEF NUISANCE
(— EASILY) FROISSE
(— FEELINGS) CUT TOUCH
(— REPUTATION) LIBEL
(— SEVERELY) KILL
(EASILY —) GINGER

(PREF.) NOCI
HURTFUL BAD ILL EVIL MALIGN
NOCENT NOCIVE NOUGHT
SHREWD TAKING BALEFUL
BANEFUL HARMFUL MALEFIC
NOCUOUS NOXIOUS SCADDLE
UNQUERT GRIEVOUS HURTSOME
SCATHFUL
HURTLE HURL FLING THIRL
HUSBAND EKE MAN WER BOND
CHAP FERE KEEP LORD MAKE
MATE SAVE SIRE BARON CHURL
HOARD HUBBY MATCH STORE
MANAGE MASTER MISTER
SPOUSE CONSORT GOODMAN
GUIDMAN HENPECK PARTNER
CONSERVE
(— OF ADULTRESS) CUCKOLD
(AFFIANCED —) FUTURE
(SUPPLEMENTARY —) PIRRAURU
(PL.) PUNALUA
(PREF.) MARITI
HUSBANDMAN BOND BOOR CARL
CLOWN COLON RUSTIC TILLER
ACREMAN HUSBAND PLOWMAN
TILLMAN AGRICOLE
HUSBANDRY GAINER GAINOR
THRIFT ECONOMY MANAGERY
HUSH SH HSH MUM PAX HESH
HOOT LULL BURKE SHUSH STILL
WHISH WHIST WHUSH HUDDLE
BESTILL HUSHABY SILENCE
HUSHED QUIET STILL GENTLE
WHISHT
HUSHIM (HUSBAND OF —)
SHAHARAIM
HUSK BUR COD HUD KEX SID ARIL
BARK BURR COAT COSH HOSE
HUCK HULK PILL SEED SHIV SKIN
HOOSE SCALE SHACK SHALE
SHAUP SHELL SHILL SHOOD
SHUCK SHUDE COLDER DEHUSK
FLIGHT SLOUGH BOLSTER
CARCASS CASCARA
(— OF NUT) SHACK BOLSTER
(— OF OATS) SHUD SHOOD FLIGHT
(CORN —) HOJA
(PL.) BHUSA CHAFF BHOOSA
HULKAGE SHELLING
(PREF.) LEMMO LEPO LOPO
SILIQUI
(SUFF.) LEMMA
HUSKY HUSK CODDY FOGGY THICK
FURRED BUIRDLY HULKING
BOUNCING SIBERIAN
HUSSITE TABORITE
HUSSY MINX SLUT BESOM CUTTY
GIPSY GYPSY MADAM STRAP
HIZZIE LIMMER DROSSEL
HUSTINGS BEMA
HUSTLE FAN PEG HUMP JUMP
BLITZ SKELP BUCKET BUNDLE
BUSTLE JOSTLE RABBLE RUSTLE
SCUFTER
HUSTLECAP PINCH
HUSTLER HUSTLE PEELER BUSTLER
FIREBALL
HUT COE COT BARI BUTT COSH
COTE CREW CRIB HALE HULK
HULL ISBA IZBA SHED SKEO TENT
TILT BASHA BENAB BOHIO BOOTH
BOTHY CABIN CHAWL CHOZA
HOVEL HUMPY HUTCH JACAL

KRAAL LODGE SCALE SETER
SHACK SHIEL TOLDO TOPEK
WHARE WURLY BOHAWN
BOTHAN CANABA CHALET
GUNYAH GUNYEH MIAMIA
PONDOK RANCHO REFUGE
SAETER SCONCE SHANTY SHELTY
WIGWAM WIKIUP BALAGAN
BARRACK BOUROCK CAMALIG
COTTAGE GOONDIE HUDDOCK
HUTMENT SHEBANG YAKUTAT
BARABARA CHANTIER RONDAWEL
SHIELING THOLTHAN TUGURIUM
(— FOR TEMPORARY USE) CORF
(— IN VIETNAM) HOOCH HOOTCH
(— OVER MINING SHAFT) COE
(ABORIGINAL —) MIMI WURLY
GUNYAH MIAMIA WURLEY
GOONDIE
(FISHERMAN'S —) SKEO SKIO
(HEATED —) HOTHOUSE
(HERMIT'S —) CELL
(NAVAJO —) HOGAN
(POULTRY —) IGLOO
(SAMOYED —) CHUM
(SENTRY —) BOX
(SIBERIAN —) JURT
(SOUTH AFRICAN —) STRUIS
(PREF.) CALIO
HUTCH ARK BUDDLE RABBITRY
HUTIA UTIA JUTIA PILORI
HUZ (FATHER OF —) NAHOR
HYACINTH LILY MUSK LILIUM
CROWTOE FLOATER GREGGLE
JACINTH BLUEBELL CROWFOOT
HAREBELL JACOUNCE
HYACINTH BEAN LABLAB
BONAVIST BONNYVIS DOLICHOS
HYACINTHUS (FATHER OF —)
AMYCLAS
(MOTHER OF —) DIOMEDE
HYALOGEN NEOSSIN
HYBRID DZO ZHO MULE ZOBO
CROSS GRADE HINNY LIGER
COYDOG GALYAK MOSAIC MULISH
SPLAKE TURKEN BASTARD
BIGENER CATTALO JERSIAN
MONGREL PLUMCOT ZEBRASS
ZEBRULA ZEBURRO CARIDEER
CITRANGE KAFERITA LIMEQUAT
ZEBRINNY
(PREF.) NOTH(O)
HYBRIDIZE CROSS
HYDRANT CHUCK FIREPLUG
(PART OF —) NUT CHAIN BARREL
BONNET STANDPIPE
CONNECTION
HYDRANTH SIPHON SYPHON
HYDRATE SLAKE
HYDRAULIC

(PREF.) HYDR(I)(O)
HYDRAZINE DIAMIDE
HYDRAZOATE AZIDE
HYDRIA KALPIS
HYDROCARBON ARENE CUMOL
FREON GUTTA IDRYL INDAN
IRENE TOLAN XYLOL ALKANE
ALKYNE ALLENE BUTANE BUTYNE
CARANE CETANE CETENE
CYMENE DECANE ETHANE
ETHENE HEXINE INDANE INDENE
MELENE NONENE OCTANE
OCTENE OCTINE PICENE PINENE
PYRENE RETENE TOLANE TOLUOL
XYLENE AMYLENE AZULENE
BENZENE CHOLANE CYCLENE
DECALIN ETHERIN FULVENE
HEPTANE HEPTENE HEPTYNE
LYCOPIN MUCKITE MYRCENE
OLEFINE PENTINE PENTYNE
PHYTANE PROPANE STYRENE
TETROLE TOLUENE BIPHENYL
CADALENE CADINENE CAMPHANE
CARBURAN CEROTENE CETYLENE
CHRYSENE CORONENE
CUMULENE DECYLENE DIOLEFIN
DIPHENYL DOCOSANE DYSODILE
EICOSANE ETHYLENE EUDALENE
FLUORENE HEXYLENE ILLIPENE
ISOPRENE LYCOPENE MENTHENE
NONYLENE OCTYLENE PARAFFIN
PRISTANE PYRACENE RUTYLENE
SABINENE SQUALENE STILBENE
(SUFF.) YLENE
HYDROCHLORIC ACID
(SUFF.) CHLORHYDRIA
HYDROCYANIC PRUSSIC
HYDRODAMALIS RHYTINA
HYDROEXTRACTOR BUZZER
WHIZZER
HYDROFLUORIC PHTHORIC
HYDROGEN HYDRO PROTIUM
HYDROGRAPHER AMERICAN
MAURY MITCHELL
ENGLISH SMYTH MURRAY
GERMAN NEUMAYER
NORWEGIAN SVERDRUP
HYDROHEMATITE TURGITE
HYDROID POLYP OBELIA ACALEPH
ZOOPHYTE
HYDROLEA NAMA
HYDROMEL ALOJA
HYDROMETER SPINDLE
HYDROPERITONEUM ASCITES
HYDROPHOBIA LYSSA RABIES
HYDROPHOBIC LYSSIC
HYDROPHYLLIUM BRACT
HYDROXIDE ALKALI HYDRATE
HYDRIDE
HYDROXYL

(SUFF.) (CONTAINING —) OLIC
HYDROZINCITE CALAMINE
HYENA HINE DABUH SIMIR
HYAENID
HYGIENIC SANITARY
HYGRODEIK PAGOSCOPE
HYLAS (FATHER OF —) THIODAMAS
(LOVER OF —) DRYOPE
(MOTHER OF —) MENODICE
HYLLUS (FATHER OF —) HERCULES
(MOTHER OF —) DEIANIRA
(SLAYER OF —) ECHEMUS
(WIFE OF —) IOLE
HYLOZOIST PHYSICIST
HYMEN CHERRY BRIDEGOD
MAIDENHEAD
HYMENIUM THECIUM
HYMENOCALLIS ISMENE
HYMN ODE FUGE LAUD SING
DIRGE GATHA PAEAN PSALM
YASHT YMPNE ANTHEM CARVAL
CHORAL HIMENE HIRMOS
MANTRA ORPHIC THEODY VESPER
CHORALE EXULTET HEIRMOS
INTROIT CANTICLE CATHISMA
DOXOLOGY ENCOMIUM
PSALMODY SEQUENCE TRISAGION
TROPARION
(— COLLECTION) MENAION
(MEXICAN —) ALABADO
(PL.) HYMNODY
HYMNAL HYMNARY HYMNBOOK
HYPATIA (AUTHOR OF —) KINGSLEY
(CHARACTER IN —) AMAL MIRIAM
AUFUGUS HYPATIA ORESTES
PELAGIA RAPHAEL VICTORIA
HERACLIAN PHILAMMON
HYPERBOLE AUXESIS
HYPERCORACOID RADIAL
SCAPULA
HYPERCRITICAL NICE CAPTIOUS
CRITICAL
HYPERDULIA ADORATION
HYPEREMIA RUBOR
HYPEREMIC CONGESTED
HYPERENOR (BROTHER OF —)
EUPHORBUS POLYDAMAS
(FATHER OF —) PANTHOUS
(MOTHER OF —) PHRONTIS
(SLAYER OF —) MENELAUS
HYPERICUM TUTSAN
HYPERION (DAUGHTER OF —)
AURORA
(FATHER OF —) URANUS
(MOTHER OF —) GAEA
(WIFE OF —) THEA
HYPERON BARYON
HYPEROPIC FARSIGHTED
HYPERSENSITIVITY ATOPY
ALLERGY

HYPHA STOLON
HYPHEN BAND
(PL.) LEADERS
HYPNOTIC AMYTAL BROMAL
CHLORAL SECONAL BARBITAL
NARCEINE SOPORIFIC
HYPNOTISM DEVIL BRAIDISM
HYPNOSIS MESMERISM
HYPNOTIST OPERATOR SVENGALI
HYPOBLAST ENDODERM
HYPODERM
HYPOCHONDRIA HIP HYP HYPO
MEGRIM
HYPOCHONDRIAC ARGAN HIPPY
HIPPIST ATRABILIAR
HYPOCOTYL RADICLE TIGELLA
TIGELLUS
HYPOCRISY SHAM POPEHOLY
PHARISAISM
HYPOCRITE CANT BIGOT CHEAT
FACER FRAUD BLIFIL CAFARD
HUMBUG MUCKER MAWWORM
SIMULAR CHADBAND DECEIVER
TARTUFFE
HYPOCRITICAL FALSE SLAPE
DOUBLE CANTING PLASTER
POPEHOLY SPECIOUS
HYPOCYCLOID ASTROID
HYPODERMIS SKIN
HYPOPHARYNX LINGUA LABIELLA
HYPOSTASIS PERSON
HYPOSTATIZE ENTIFY
HYPOSTOME MANUBRIUM
HYPOTENUSE SUBTENSE
HYPOTHESIS SYSTEM THEORY
PREMISE WEGENER SUPPOSAL
POSTULATE
HYPOTHETICAL IDEAL
HYPOTRACHELIUM GORGERIN
HYPSEUS (DAUGHTER OF —)
CYRENE
(FATHER OF —) PENEUS
(MOTHER OF —) CREUSA
(WIFE OF —) CHLIDANOPE
HYPTIS OREGANO
HYRAX DAS CONY CONEY DAMAN
WABUR DASSIE WABBER
ASHKOKO KLIPDAS HYRACOID
HYRMINA (FATHER OF —) EPEUS
(HUSBAND OF —) PHORBAS
(SON OF —) ACTOR
HYRNETHO (BROTHER OF —)
AGELAUS CALLIAS EURYPYLUS
(FATHER OF —) TEMENUS
(HUSBAND OF —) DEIPHONTES
HYSTERIA MOTHER NERVES
PIBLOKTO TARASSIS
(PRONE TO —) VAPORISH
(RELIGIOUS —) LATA
HYSTERICAL NERVOUS SHRIEKY

I A Y HI HY CHE ICH ISS SHE ITEM
UTCH INDIA UTCHY
(— AM) ISE CHAM ICHAM
(— HAD) CHAD
(— WILL) CHILL ICHULLE
(— WOULD) CHUD
IALEMUS (FATHER OF —) APOLLO
(MOTHER OF —) CALLIOPE
IALMENUS (BROTHER OF —)
ASCALAPHUS
(FATHER OF —) ARES APOLLO
(MOTHER OF —) ASTYOCHE
CALLIOPE
IAMB IAMBIC IAMBUS
(DOUBLE —) DIIAMB
IAMUS (FATHER OF —) APOLLO
(MOTHER OF —) EVADNE
IAPETUS (FATHER OF —) URANUS
(MOTHER OF —) GAEA
(SON OF —) ATLAS MENOETIUS
(WIFE OF —) ASIA CLYMENE
IAPYGIANS MESSAPII
IAPYX (BROTHER OF —) DAUNIUS
PEUCETIUS
(FATHER OF —) LYCAON DAEDALUS
IASION (BROTHER OF —) DARDANUS
(FATHER OF —) ZEUS JUPITER
(LOVER OF —) CERES DEMETER
(MOTHER OF —) ELECTRA
(SON OF —) PLUTUS
IATROCHEMICAL SPAGYRIC
IATROCHEMISTRY SPAGYRIC
IBANAG CAGAYAN
IBEX KYL TEK TUR ZAC KAIL BEDEN
EVECK IZARD JAELA EVICKE
SAKEEN
IBHAR (FATHER OF —) DAVID
IBIS GUARA GANNET HADADA
JABIRU TURKEY CICONIID
IRONHEAD
IBNEIAH (FATHER OF —) JEROHAM
ICARIUS (BROTHER OF —)
TYNDAREUS
(DAUGHTER OF —) ERIGONE
PENELOPE
(FAITHFUL DOG OF —) MOERA
(FATHER OF —) OEBALUS
(MOTHER OF —) GORGOPHONE
ICARUS (FATHER OF —) DAEDALUS
(MOTHER OF —) NAUCRATE
ICE YS GEAL FROST
GLACE CRYSTAL
VERGLAS
(— IN ROUGH BLOCKS) RUBBLE
(ANCHOR —) FRAZIL
(DRIFTING FRAGMENT OF —) PAN
CALF
(PATCH OF —) RONE
(PINNACLE OF —) SERAC
(RIDGE OF —) HAMMOCK
HUMMOCK
(SEA —) GLACON SLUDGE
(SHORE —) FAST

(SLUSHY —) SISH
(SOFT —) SLOB LOLLY
(THIN NEW —) DISH PANCAKE
(THIN OR FLOATING —) FLOE GRUE
BRASH
(WATER —) SHERBET
(PREF.) CRYSTALL(I)(O) GLACI(O)
(SUFF.) CRYST
ICEBERG BERG GROWLER
FLOEBERG
ICEBOAT SKEETER
ICE CREAM BISK CREAM GLACE
AUFAIT BISQUE NOUGAT
TASTER SPUMONI
TORTONI
ICE CREAM CONE CORNET
ICED COLD GLACE FRAPPE
ICEFISH SALANGID
ICEHOUSE (— WORKER) AIRMAN

ICELAND
BALLAD: RIMUR
BAY: FAXA HUNA
CAPITAL: REIKJAVIK REYKJAVIK
COIN: AURAR EYRIR KRONA
DISH: SKYR SVIO BLOOMOR
HAROFISK
EPIC: EDDA SAGA
FIRST SETTLER: ARNARSON
FJORD: BREIDHA
GEYSER: GRYLA
GIANT: ATLI
GLACIER: HOFSJOKULL
LANGJOKULL VATNAJOKULL
HERO: BELE ERIC LEIF
SIGUROSSON
LAKE: MYVATN THORISVATN
MEASURE: SET ALIN LINA ALMUD
TURMA ALMENN ALMUDE
FERFET POTTUR FATHMUR
FERALIN FERMILA OLTUNNA
SJOMILA
MOUNTAIN: JOKUL
PARLIAMENT: ALTHING
REPUBLIC: LYOVELDIO
RIVER: HVITA JOKULSA THJORSA
TOWN: AKRANES AKUREYRI
KEFLAVIK KOPAVOGUR
VOLCANIC ISLAND: SURTSEY
VOLCANO: LAKI ASKJA HEKLA
ELDFELL
WATERFALL: GULL DETTI
GULLFOSS DETTIFOSS
WEIGHT: PUND POUND

ICHABOD (FATHER OF —) PHINEHAS
(GRANDFATHER OF —) ELI
ICHNEUMON URVA NYMSS
MEERKAT VANSIRE
ICHOROUS GLEETY
ICHU HICHU STIPA
ICICLE ICARY ICKLE YOKEL TANGLE
SHOGGLE SHOOGLE COCKBELL

ICINESS GLARE
ICING ICE PIPING ALCORZA
FROSTING MERINGUE
ICON IKON EIKON IMAGE DEESIS
ICONOCLAST DEBUNKER
ICONOSTASIS DIASTYLE
ICTEROHEMATURIA CARCEAG
ICTONYX ZORILLA
ICTUS ACCENT DOWNBEAT
ICY GELID BOREAL FRIGID WINTRY
GLACIAL
ID ES ORF GARDON SYPHILID

IDAHO
CAPITAL: BOISE
COUNTY: ADA GEM BUTTE CAMAS
LATAH LEMHI POWER TETON
BLAINE BONNER CARNAS
CASSIA JEROME OWYHEE
BENEWAH KOOTENAI
DAM: OXBOW BROWNLEE
INDIAN: BANNOCK KALISPEL
NEZPERCE SHOSHONI
LAKE: BEAR GRAYS PRIEST
MOUNTAIN: RYAN BORAH RHODES
TAYLOR BIGBALDY BLUENOSE
MOUNTAIN RANGE: CABINET
SELKIRK
NICKNAME: GEM
RIVER: SNAKE LOCHSA SALMON
PAYETTE
SPRINGS: SODA HOOPER LAVAHOT
STATE BIRD: BLUEBIRD
STATE FLOWER: SYRINGA
TOWN: BUHL MALAD NAMPA
BURLEY DRIGGS DUBOIS
MOSCOW WEISER CASCADE
CHALLIS ORIFINO REXBURG
POCATELLO

IDAS (BROTHER OF —) LYNCEUS
(FATHER OF —) APHAREUS
(MOTHER OF —) ARENE
(WIFE OF —) MARPESSA
IDDO (FATHER OF —) ZECHARIAH
(SON OF —) AHINADAB
IDE ORFE
IDEA EGG GIG KINK EIDOS IMAGE
THING ANONYM DHARMA ECTYPE
FIGURE INTENT NOTICE NOTION
RECEPT THREAP THROPE BEGRIFF
CONCEIT CONCEPT GIMMICK
GLIMPSE MAROTTE OPINION
PROJECT SPECIES SURMISE
THOUGHT GIMCRACK NOTIONAL
PRECONCEPTION
(—S OF LITTLE VALUE) STUFF
(CENTRAL —) ARGUMENT
(COMMONPLACE —) SHIBBOLETH
(CONSERVATIVE —S) FOGYISM
(DOMINANT —) CLOU
(DULL STUPID —S) STODGE
(FAINT —) GLIMMER

(FALSE —) FALLACY
(FANTASTIC —) VAPOR MAGGOT
(FAVORITE —) HORSE
(FIXED —) TICK
(FUNDAMENTAL —) KEYNOTE
(IRRATIONAL —) FOLLY
(MAIN —) POINT
(MUSICAL —) SENTENCE
(ODD —) FREAK
(OVERWORKED —) CLICHE
(PLATONIC —) ESSENCE
(RECURRING —) BURDEN
(STALE —S) BILGE
(SUPERSTITIOUS —) FREIT
(TRANSCENDENT —) FORM
(PL.) EIDE THOUGHT
(PREF.) IDEO
IDEAL ISM IDEA DREAM AERIAL
BEAUTY DOMNEI DREAMY
MENTAL UNREAL PATTERN
PERFECT UTOPIAN ABSTRACT
FANCIFUL IDEALITY NOTIONAL
QUADRATE ORIFLAMME
(— OF BEAUTY) KALON
IDEALISM IDEOLOGY
IDEALIST IDEIST UTOPIAN
FICHTEAN UTOPIAST
IDEALIZE PLATONIZE
IDEALIZED POETICAL
IDENTICAL LIKE SAME SELF VERY
ALIKE EQUAL EVENLY PROPER
CORRECT IDENTIC NUMERIC
SELFSAME
IDENTIFICATION IDENT
DOCUMENT EQUATION
RECOGNITION
IDENTIFIED SIGNATE
IDENTIFIER BIRDER
IDENTIFY PEG TAB MARK NAME
RANK SPOT IDENT PLACE TALLY
FINGER DISCERN DIAGNOSE
PINPOINT
(— WITH) ENTER
IDENTITY SEITY UNITY IPSEITY
ONENESS EQUALITY SAMENESS
IDEOGRAPH CHARACTER
(PL.) KANJI
IDEOGRAPHIC REAL
IDEOLOGICAL MENTAL
IDIOBLAST SPHERE IDIOSOME
IDIOCY ANOIA ANOESIA FATUITY
IDIOTRY MOROSIS IDIOTISM
IDIOM CANT ARGOT JUANG
DORISM IFUGAO JARGON MEDISM
SPEECH AEOLISM ANOMALY
GRECISM PEHLEVI TURKISM
DANICISM DORICISM IDIOTISM
IONICISM LANGUAGE
LOCALISM PARLANCE
RURALISM
IDIOMORPHIC EUHEDRAL
IDIOPHONE RATTLE
IDIOSOME SPHERE

IDIOSYNCRASY WAY IDIASM RUMNESS

IDIOT FON OAF SOT DAFF DOLT FOOL AMENT BOOBY DUNCE FONNE CRETIN HOBBIL NIDGET NIDIOT DULLARD NATURAL OMADAWN PINHEAD IMBECILE INNOCENT SLAVERER
(AUTHOR OF —) DOSTOEVSKI
(CHARACTER IN —) LEF GANYA AGLAYA PARFEN MYSHKIN NATASYA EPANCHIN ROGOZHIN ΓILIPOVNA ARDALIONOVITCH

IDIOTIC DAFT ZANY IDIOT FATUOUS FOOLISH WANTWIT IMBECILE

IDLE COLD DEAD HACK HAKE HANG HULL JAUK LAKE LAZE LAZY LUSK MUZZ SOFT SORN TICK VAIN VOID DALLY EMPTY SHOOL SLIVE THOKE WASTE COOTER DAIDLE DANDER DREAMY FOOTER GAMMER LOUNGY OTIANT OTIOSE SLIMSY TEETER TIDDIE TIFFLE TRIFLE TRUANT UNUSED VACANT DRONISH IDLEFUL IDLESET LOAFING SAUNTER SHACKLE SLUMBER SLUTHER UNLUSTY VACUOUS WHIFFLE BASELESS BOOTLESS FAINEANT INACTIVE INDOLENT SHAMMOCK SLAISTER SLOTHFUL TRIFLING WORKLESS
(TO BE —) SLOTH

IDLENESS LAZE RUST SLOTH IDLETΓ IDLESET IDLESSE IGNAVIA VACANCY VACUITY FLANERIE IDLEHOOD INACTION
(— PERSONIFED) LAURENCE LAWRENCE
(LIVE IN —) MAROON

IDLER BUM GAUM HAKE JAUK KERN LOON DRONE BADAUD BUMBLE DONNOT IDLEBY LUBBER PLAYER QUISBY RODNEY STALKO TRUANT BLELLUM BUCKEEN DAWDLER FAITOUR FRANION IDLESBY LOLLARD LOUNGER LOUTHER LURDANE SLOUNGE TRIFLER DOLITTLE FAINEANT IDLESHIP LAYABOUT LAZARONE UNWORKER WHIFFLER

IDLE WHEEL IDLER RUNNER
IDLY TOOMLY VAGUELY
IDMON (DAUGHTER OF —) ARACHNE
(FATHER OF —) APOLLO
(MOTHER OF —) CYRENE ASTERIA

IDOCRASE EGERAN CYPRINE VESUVIAN

IDOL GOD BAAL ICON JOSS TIKI WOOD ZEMI ANITO BESAN EIKON GUACA HOBAL HUACA IMAGE STOCK SWAMI IDOLET IDOLUM MAMMET MAUMET MINION PAGODA POPPET PUPPET TERAPH EIDOLON MAHOMET BAPHOMET MAUMETRY PANTHEUM
(HEATHEN —) DEVIL
(PREF.) EIDOLO IDOLO

IDOLATER AKKUM PAGAN HEATHEN IDOLIST

IDOLATROUS PAGAN IDOLISH

IDOLATRY BAALISM IMAGERY ADULTERY MAUMETRY

IDOLIZE GOD IDOL ADORE ADMIRE WORSHIP

IDUMAEAN EDOMITE
IDUN (HUSBAND OF —) BRAGI
IDYIA (DAUGHTER OF —) MEDEA
(FATHER OF —) OCEANUS
(HUSBAND OF —) AEETES
(MOTHER OF —) TETHYS
(SON OF —) APSYRTUS

IDYL IDYLL BUCOLIC ECLOGUE
IDYLLIC HALCYON PASTORAL THEOCRITEAN

IDYLLS OF THE KING (AUTHOR OF —) TENNYSON
(CHARACTER IN —) BORS ENID BALAN BALIN ISOLT ARTHUR ELAINE GARETH GAWAIN MERLIN MODRED VIVIEN ETTARRE GALAHAD GERAINT LYNETTE PELLEAS BEDIVERE LANCELOT TRISTRAM GUINEVERE PERCIVALE

IF AN AND GIF GIN THO GEVE IFFEN SOBEIT THOUGH PROVIDED
(— EVER) ONCE
(— NOT) BUT ELSE NISI
(PREF.) QUASI

IF WINTER COMES (AUTHOR OF —) HUTCHINSON
(CHARACTER IN —) MARK NONA EFFIE MABEL PERCH SABRE TYBAR BRIGHT FARGUS HAROLD FORTUNE TWYNING

IGAL (FATHER OF —) JOSEPH NATHAN

IGDALIAH (SON OF —) HANAN
IGEAL (FATHER OF —) SHEMAIAH
IGERNA (HUSBAND OF —) UTHER GORLOIS
(SON OF —) ARTHUR

IGNEOUS PLUTONIC
(PREF.) PLUTONO

IGNIS FATUUS WISP SPUNKIE WILDFIRE

IGNITE TIND FLASH LIGHT SHOOT ILLUME KINDLE CALCINE LIGHTEN

IGNITED LIVING BURNING
IGNITER SPARKER
IGNITION FIRE LIGHTING
IGNOBLE LOW BASE MEAN VILE ABJECT GRUBBY SORDID CURRISH SERVILE UNNOBLE BASEBORN SHAMEFUL

IGNOBLY BASELY
IGNOMINIOUS BASE VILE INFAMOUS SHAMEFUL

IGNOMINY SHAME REBUKE SCANDAL DISGRACE DISHONOR

IGNORAMUS IDIOT IGNARO SIMPLE AMHAAREZ

IGNORANCE IRONY TAMAS AGNOSY AVIDYA AVIJJA BETISE NICETY RUDITY UNSKILL DARKNESS IDIOTISM NESCIENCE
(BOLD —) BAYARD
(FEIGNED —) IRONY
(PREF.) AGNOIO

IGNORANT LAY DARK NICE RUDE VAIN GREEN GROSS SILLY INGRAM SIMPLE ARTLESS SECULAR UNAWARE UNCOUTH UNKNOWN IMPERITE INNOCENT

INSCIENT INSCIOUS NESCIENT UNTAUGHT BENIGHTED

IGNORANTLY SIMPLY
IGNORE BALK BLOW SINK SNUB VAIN BAULK BLINK ELIDE BYPASS MISKEN SLIGHT DESPISE MISKNOW NEGLECT CONFOUND OVERJUMP OVERLEAP OVERLOOK OVERPASS

IGOROT BONTOK NABALOI KANKANAI

IGUANA GUANA GUANO LEGUAN
IGUVINE UMBRIAN
IJO DJO BONI BONNY
IKKESH (SON OF —) IRA
ILAIRA (FATHER OF —) LEUCIPPUS
(HUSBAND OF —) CASTOR
(MOTHER OF —) PHILODICE
(SISTER OF —) PHOEBE

ILEUM
(PREF.) ILEO

ILEUS MISERERE
ILIA RHEA
(FATHER OF —) NUMITOR
(SON OF —) REMUS ROMULUS

ILIAD (AUTHOR OF —) HOMER
(CHARACTER IN —) AIAS HELEN PARIS PRIAM ATHENA HECTOR NESTOR ACHILLES DIOMEDES MENELAUS ODYSSEUS PANDARUS AGAMEMNON APHRODITE PATROCLUS ANDROMACHE

ILIONE (BROTHER OF —) POLYDORUS
(FATHER OF —) PRIAM
(HUSBAND OF —) POLYMNESTOR
(MOTHER OF —) HECUBA
(SON OF —) DEIPYLUS

ILK KIN
ILL BAD EVIL ILLY SICK AEGER CRONK CROOK DONCY FUNNY WISHT GROGGY INJURY POORLY SICKLY UNWELL SICKISH VICIOUS MISCHIEF PHYSICAL
(— AT EASE) ASHAMED AWKWARD FAROUCHE
(PREF.) MAL(E) MIS

ILL-ADVISED FOOLISH
ILL-BEHAVED UNTHEWED
ILL-BEING ILLTH
ILL-BODING DIRE DISMAL
ILL-BRED HOYDEN CADDISH CHURLISH PLEBEIAN MISLEARED

ILL-CHOSEN UNSORTED
ILL-CONSIDERED HASTY
ILL-DEFINED BLIND VAGUE MONGREL

ILLEGAL BLACK LAWLESS UNLAWFUL WRONGOUS ADULTERINE
(NOT —) COLD

ILLEGALITY UNLAW
ILLEGIBLE BLIND
ILLEGITIMACY BASTARDY
ILLEGITIMATE BASE BASTARD BOOTLEG NATURAL NOTHOUS MISBEGOT NAMELESS UNLAWFUL WRONGFUL MISBEGOTTEN
(PREF.) NOTH(O)

ILL-FATED UNHAPPY UNSONCY UNCHANCY

ILL-FAVORED UGLY UNSONCY
ILL-FORMED SCRAWLY INFORMED
ILL HUMOR TID BILE DRUNT

GRUMP THRAW FANTEE SPLEEN DUDGEON FANTIGUE

ILL-HUMORED FOUL GLUM CROOK DUDDY GRUMPY MOROSE STUFFY SULLEN CROOKED FRETFUL PEEVISH

ILLIBERAL LITTLE NARROW INSULAR BANAUSIC GRUDGING

ILLICIT SLY BLACK ILLEGAL UNLAWFUL

ILLIMITABLE INFINITE

ILLINOIS
CAPITAL: SPRINGFIELD
COLLEGE: AURORA EUREKA OLIVET QUINCY SHIMER
COUNTY: BOND CASS COOK KANE OGLE COLES MACON BUREAU DUPAGE GRUNDY HARDIN MASSAC PEORIA IROQUOIS MACOUPIN SANGAMON
FRENCH SETTLEMENT: CAHOKIA
HILLS: SHAWNEE
INDIAN: FOX SAUK
LAKE: MICHIGAN
NICKNAME: SUCKER PRAIRIE
PRESIDENT: REAGAN
RIVER: OHIO ROCK WABASH ELKHORN MACKINAW SANGAMON
STATE BIRD: CARDINAL
STATE FLOWER: VIOLET
STATE TREE: OAK
TOWN: PANA ALEDO ALTON CAIRO CARMI DIXON FLORA LACON OLNEY PARIS PEKIN ALBION CANTON EUREKA GALENA HARDIN HAVANA HERRIN JOLIET OTTAWA PEORIA QUINCY SKOKIE URBANA VIENNA CHICAGO DECATUR GENESEO MENDOTA NOKOMIS TAMPICO ROCKFORD

ILLINOISIAN SUCKER
ILLIPE BASSIA VIDORICUM
ILLITERATE UNREAD IGNORANT MUSELESS UNTAUGHT

ILL-MADE AWKWARD
ILL-NATURED ACID UGLY NASTY SURLY CRABBY SNARLY SULLEN THWART CANKERY PEEVISH

ILLNESS DROW TOUT BRASH CHILL TRAIK MORBUS PLUNGE DISEASE SICKNESS
(MENTAL —) MONOMANIA
(MINOR —) HURRY
(MOMENTARY —) DROW
(SUDDEN —) WEED SWEAM

ILL-NOURISHED SHELLY
ILLOGICAL MAD SPURIOUS
ILL-OMENED DISMAL UNLUCKY
ILL-SHAPED WEEDY
ILL-SMELLING FUSTY STINKING
ILL-TEMPERED ILL FESS MEAN PUXY ACRID CHUFF NURLY RATTY CAMMED CHUFFY CURSED GIRNIE SHRILL SNAGGY RAMPANT ROPABLE VICIOUS CAMSHACH LUNGEOUS SHREWISH VIXENISH MALODOROUS

ILL-TREAT FOB HOIN MISDO AFFRONT

ILLUMINATE FIRE LIMN CLEAR
LIGHT ENLIMN ILLUME KINDLE
BESHINE CLARIFY EMBLAZE
LIGHTEN MINIATE RADIATE
EMBRIGHT FLOURISH ILLUMINE
LUMINATE
(**— FAINTLY**) TWILIGHT
ILLUMINATION E GLIM GLORY
LIGHT SHINE LIGHTING LUMINARY
(**— INCREASE**) WOMP
(**— UNIT**) PHOT
ILLUMINE SUN FIRE LAMP CLEAR
LUMINE ENLIGHT
ILL-USAGE ABUSE
ILLUSION MAYA DEATH ERROR
FAIRY FANCY FLESH TRICK
MATTER CHIMERA ELUSION
FALLACY FICTION MOCKERY
PHANTOM RAINBOW ZOLLNER
DELUSION PHANTASM PRESTIGE
ILLUSIVE PHANTOM
ILLUSORY FALSE EVANID
FATUOUS PHANTOM TRICKSY
APPARENT ILLUSIVE SPECTRAL
ILLUSTRATE INSTANCE
ILLUSTRATION CUT GAY ICON
IKON SHOW SPOT INSET FIGURE
COMPARE DISIMILE EXEMPLUM
INSTANCE VIGNETTE
ILLUSTRATIVE CLASSIC
ILLUSTRIOUS GRAND NOBLE
NOTED SHEEN BRIGHT CANDID
HEROIC EMINENT EXALTED
GLORIED SHINING GLORIOUS
HEROICAL LUCULENT MAGNIFIC
PRECLARE RENOWNED SPLENDID
STARLIKE BRILLIANT
REDOUBTABLE
(**MOST —**) ILMO ILLMO
ILL WILL SPITE ENMITY GRUDGE
MALICE MAUGER MAUGRE
RANCOR DESPITE AMBITION
ILL-WISHER FOE
ILUS (**FATHER OF —**) TROS
(**MOTHER OF —**) CALLIRRHOE
(**SON OF —**) LAOMEDON
ILVAITE YENITE LIEVRITE
ILYSIA TORTRIX
IMAGE DAP GOD MAP FORM ICON
IDOL IKON JOSS MAKE SEAL SIGN
SPIT TIKI AGNUS DITTO EPHOD
FANCY HERMA IMAGO MEDAL
MORAL PAINT PRINT SAMMY
SANTO SHAPE SIGIL SWAMI
SWAMY TOTEM AGALMA ALRAUN
EFFIGY EMBLEM FIGURE MAUMET
MODULE POPPET RECEPT REFLEX
SHRINE SPHINX STATUE SVAMIN
TERAPH VISAGE WEEPER
EIDOLON EXPRESS FANTASY
GODLING IMAGERY KATCINA
PICTURE PROPOSE CONCEIVE
DAIBUTSU OPTOGRAM PORTRAIT
SURPRINT ZOOMORPH
SEMBLANCE SIMILITUDE
SIMULACRUM RESEMBLANCE
(**— IN CHINESE COSTUME**)
MANDARIN
(**— OF CHRIST**) SUDARIUM
(**— OF DEITY**) SWAMI GODKIN
SVAMIN GODLING
(**— OF SAINT**) BULTO SAINT SANTO
GEORGE SANTON

(**— OF WOOD**) XOANON
(**— RECALLED BY MEMORY**) IDEA
(**CULT —**) JOSS
(**FALSE —**) GHOST
(**GOOD-LUCK —**) ALRAUN ALRUNA
(**HEAVENLY —**) FRAVASHI
(**LINGERING —**) SHADE
(**MENTAL —**) FANCY IMAGO
RECEPT CONCEPT FANTASY
SPECIES PHANTASM
(**RADAR —**) BLIP
(**REFLECTED —**) SHADOW SPECIES
(**SEQUENCE OF —S**) REVERIE
(**VAGUE —S**) FRINGE
(PL.) IMAGERY TERAPHIM
(PREF.) EID(O)(OLO) EIKON(O)
ICON(O) IDOLO IKON(O) TYP(I)(O)
IMAGERY ICONISM
IMAGINARY IDEAL AERIAL
FEIGNED FICTIVE SHADOWY
CHIMERAL CHIMERIC FANCIFUL
FICTIOUS MYTHICAL NOTIONAL
QUIXOTIC ROMANTIC SCENICAL
VISIONAL BARMECIDE
IMAGINATION CHIC BRAIN FANCY
FLAME NOTION FANTASY
PROJECT THOUGHT
(**DROLL —**) HUMOR
IMAGINATIVE FORMFUL CREATIVE
FANCIFUL POETICAL
IMAGINE SEE WIS REDE WEEN
DREAM FANCY FEIGN FRAME
GUESS IMAGE THINK DEVISE
FIGURE IDEATE INVENT RECKON
COMPASS CONCEIT CONJURE
FANCIFY FANTASY FEATURE
PICTURE PORTRAY PROJECT
PROPOSE SUPPOSE SURMISE
SUSPECT CONCEIVE DAYDREAM
JEALOUSE
IMAGINED FANCIED SUPPOSED
IMAGINER FANCIER
IMAGINING FICTION PHANTOM
IMAM IMAUM MAHDI
IMBALANCE DRIVE DYSCRASIA
IMBECILE MAD DOTE FOOL AMENT
ANILE DAFFY IDIOT CRANKY
DOTARD DOTING DOTISH
CONGEON FATUOUS
IMBECILITY AMENTIA FATUITY
IMBIBE DRINK SMACK ABSORB
SPONGE INHAUST SWALLOW
IRRIGATE
IMBIBING SUCTION
IMBIBITORY SPONGY
IMBRIUS (**FATHER OF —**) MENTOR
(**SLAYER OF —**) AJAX
(**WIFE OF —**) MEDESICASTE
IMBRUE EMBREW INSTEEP
IMBUE SOAK STEW COLOR CROWN
EMBUE INDUE SCENT STEEP
TINCT ENSOUL IMBIBE INFUSE
LEAVEN SEASON ANIMATE
INGRAIN INSENSE INSTILL
SATURATE TINCTURE
IMBUED INSTINCT REDOLENT
IMHOTEP (**FATHER OF —**) PTAH
(**MOTHER OF —**) SEKHMET
IMIDE LACTIM SACCHARIN
IMITATE APE COPY ECHO MIME
MOCK ZANY ENSUE FORGE IMAGE
MIMIC AFFECT ANSWER FOLLOW
SEMBLE COPYCAT EMULATE

PAGEANT PATTERN PASTICHE
RESEMBLE SIMULATE
(PREF.) MIMO
IMITATION COPY FAKE SHAM
DUMMY IMAGE MIMIC ALPACA
ANSWER BUMPER ECTYPE
SHADOW CAMBLET FOULARD
IMITANT MIMESIS MOCKAGE
MOCKERY CHENILLE PARROTRY
PASTICHE POSTIQUE
(**— OF COIN**) COUNTER
(**BURLESQUE —**) TRAVESTY
(**COTTON —**) CAMBRIC
(**EXAGGERATED —**) BURLESQUE
(**UNSUBSTANTIAL —**) GHOST
(PREF.) NE
(SUFF.) EEN ETTE
IMITATIVE ARTY MIMIC ARTFUL
ECHOIC SHODDY MIMETIC
SIMULAR SLAVISH APATETIC
EPIGONAL
IMITATOR APE MIME ZANY MIMIC
COPIER COPYIST EPIGONE
EMULATOR EPIGONUS HOMERIST
(SUFF.) MIMUS
IMMACULATE CLEAN CANDID
CHASTE BLOTLESS SPOTLESS
UNSOILED
IMMANENCE INBEING
IMMATERIAL MENTAL SLIGHT
ETHEREAL FORMLESS SEPARATE
TRIFLING
IMMATURE RAW CRUDE GREEN
SAPPY SMALL VEALY YOUNG
BOYISH CALLOW JEJUNE LARVAL
NEANIC TENDER GIRLISH HALFLIN
IMPUBIC LADDISH NOUVEAU
PUERILE UNBAKED JUVENILE
NEPIONIC UNWEANED SHIRTTAIL
IMMATURITY NONAGE
IMMEASURABLE UNTOLD
ABYSMAL INFINITE
IMMEDIACY HERE
IMMEDIATE DIRECT MODERN
PARATE SUDDEN INSTANT
PRESENT PROXIMAL SYNECTIC
POSTHASTE
IMMEDIATELY PDQ TIT ANON
AWAY FAST JUST ONCE SOON
PLUMB RIGHT ASTITE DIRECT
PRESTO PRONTO SUBITO
DIRECTLY HEREUPON OUTRIGHT
STRAIGHT
IMMEDIATENESS INSTANCY
IMMEMORIAL DATELESS
IMMENSE HUGE VAST GRAND
GREAT LARGE UNMEET UNRIDE
TITANIC ENORMOUS GIGANTIC
INFINITE SLASHING WHOOPING
PLANETARY
IMMENSELY EVER
IMMENSITY VAST IMMANE
IMMENSE ENORMITY GRANDEUR
HUGENESS
IMMERSE DIP SINK SOAK COVER
DOUSE MERGE MERSE SOUSE
STEEP DRENCH PLUNGE BAPTIZE
BOWSSEN DEMERGE EMBATHE
ENSTEEP IMMERGE DISSOLVE
IMMERSED DEEP INNATE
IMMERSION DIP DUNKING
MERSION
IMMERSIONIST DIPPER

IMMIGRANT LAG BALT ISSEI
JIMMY METIC POMMY GUINEA
HALUTZ CHALUTZ INCOMER
PILGRIM COMELING
IMMINENCE INSTANCY
IMMINENT TOWARD PENDING
PROXIMATE
IMMOBILE FIXED STILL FROZEN
DORMANT GLACIAL TRANCED
MOVELESS
(PREF.) ANKYL(O)
IMMOBILIZATION FUSION
FIXATION
IMMOBILIZE FREEZE SPLINT
STIFFEN
IMMOBILIZED STIFF
IMMODERATE FREE DIZZY UNDUE
LAVISH UNMETH EXTREME
OVERWEENING
IMMODERATENESS EXCESS
IMMODEST FREE BRAZEN
OBSCENE INDECENT PETULANT
UNCHASTE
IMMORAL BAD ILL EVIL IDLE
LOOSE WRONG WANTON
CORRUPT VICIOUS CULPABLE
DEPRAVED INDECENT SLIPPERY
IMMORTAL DIVINE ENDLESS
ETERNAL GODLIKE UNDYING
ENDURING UNDEADLY
IMMORTALITY AMRITA ATHANASY
ETERNITY
IMMOVABLE PAT SET FAST FIRM
FIXED RIGID ADAMANT SITFAST
CONSTANT IMMOBILE IMMOTIVE
OBDURATE
IMMUNE FREE SALTED
REFRACTORY
IMMUNITY SOC CHARTER
FREEDOM LIBERTY WOODGELD
PROTECTION
IMMURE MURE WALL CONFINE
CLOISTER IMPRISON
IMMUTABILITY ONENESS
IMMUTABLE ETERNAL
IMNAH (**FATHER OF —**) ASHER
IMOGEN (**FATHER OF —**) CYMBELINE
(**HUSBAND OF —**) POSTHUMUS
IMP PUG LIMB DEMON DEVILET
DEVILING DEVILKIN FOLLETTO
IMPACT HIT JAR BEAT BITE BLOW
BUMP DASH DUSH JOLT SLAM
BRUNT CLASH FEEZE PEISE POISE
PULSE SHOCK SKITE GLANCE
STROKE CONTACT IMPULSE
COLLISION
(**HAVING STRONG —**) GUT
IMPAIR MAR BLOT HARM HURT
MAIM MANK SOUR WEAR ALLOY
CLOUD CRACK CRAZE DECAY
ERODE QUAIL SPOIL TAINT
ACRAZE DAMAGE DEADEN
DEFACE HINDER INJURE LABEFY
LESSEN REDUCE SICKEN WEAKEN
WORSEN BLEMISH CRIPPLE
DISABLE IMPEACH REFRACT
SHATTER STRETCH VITIATE
DECREASE ENFEEBLE IMBECILE
IMPERISH INFRINGE LABEFACT
(**— BY INACTIVITY**) RUST
(**— ESSENTIALLY**) RUIN
IMPAIRED HURT STALE CROCKY
FLYBLOWN

(**— BY AGE**) FUSTY
(**— IN TONE**) BREATHY
(PREF.) DYS
IMPAIRMENT ALLAY FAULT SPOIL
DOTAGE IMPAIR INJURY LESION
BEATING DEFICIT DISEASE
EROSION WEARING AKINESIA
PAIRMENT
(**— OF CONSCIOUSNESS**) ABSENCE
IMPALA PALLA PALLAH REDBUCK
ROOIBOK ROODEBOK ROOYEBOK
IMPALE BAIT SPIT GANCH GANSH
SPEAR SPIKE STAKE STICK STING
SKIVER TRANSFIX
IMPALPABLE ELUSIVE
IMPART GIVE SHED TELL BREAK
DRILL SHARE YIELD BESTOW
COMMON CONFER CONVEY
DIRECT IMPUTE INSTIL PARTEN
REVEAL DELIVER DIVULGE
PURPORT DISCOVER INSTRUCT
INTIMATE
(**— TONE**) TONE
(**— ZEST**) ANIMATE
IMPARTIAL EVEN FAIR JUST
EQUAL LEVEL CANDID NEUTER
UNBIASED
IMPARTIALITY CANDOR EQUITY
EQUACITY EVENNESS
IMPARTIALLY FAIRLY EQUALLY
IMPASSABLE WICKED INVIOUS
PASSLESS ROADLESS TRACKLESS
IMPASSE LOGJAM DEADLOCK
IMPASSION COMMOVE
IMPASSIONED ARDENT FERVID
FERVENT FEVERISH PERFERVID
IMPASSIVE FROZEN STOLID
PASSIVE STOICAL PHLEGMATIC
IMPASSIVENESS APATHY
MORGUE STOICISM
IMPATIENT HOT ANTSY EAGER
HASTY SHARP TESTY FRETFUL
PEEVISH RESTIVE TIDIOSE
CHOLERIC PETULANT
IMPATIENTLY HASTILY
IMPEACH CALL ACCUSE CHARGE
INDICT ARRAIGN CENSURE
IMPLEAD TRAVERSE
IMPEACHMENT APPEAL
IMPECCABLE SINLESS
IMPECUNIOUS POOR
IMPEDE BOG DAM GUM JAM LET
MAR CLOG GRAB JAMB KILL SLUG
SNAG ANNOY BLOCK CHECK
CHOKE DELAY EMBAR ESTOP
HITCH SLOTH SPOKE BAFFLE
FETTER FORBID FORSET HAMPER
HARASS HINDER HOBBLE PESTER
RETARD STYMIE IMPEACH
PREVENT SHACKLE ENCUMBER
HANDICAP OBSTRUCT PRECLUDE
IMPEDIMENT BAR RUB CLOG
SNAG STOP BLEAR BLOCK HITCH
SPOKE STICK BURDEN RUBBER
SCOTCH BLINDER EMBARGO
OBSTACLE OBSTANCY
(**— IN SPEECH**) HAAR HALT
IMPEDIMENTA STUFF
IMPEDING CATCH HEAVY FOULING
IMPEL PAT PUT BEAR BEAT CALL
CAST GOAD HURL MOVE SEND
URGE WHIP CARRY DRIVE FEEZE
FORCE KNOCK PRESS PRICK

PULSE COMPEL EXCITE INCITE
INDUCE PROPEL ACTUATE
DESTINE INSPIRE INSTINCT
MOTIVATE
(**— TO GREATER SPEED**) GATHER
IMPELLER RUNNER
IMPEND BREW HANG DEPEND
OVERHANG
IMPENDING TOWARD PENDENT
PENDING IMMINENT MENACING
IMPENETRABLE HARD DENSE
MURKY PROOF THICK AIRTIGHT
HARDENED
IMPENITENT OBDURATE
IMPERATIVE VITAL PRESSING
MASTERFUL
IMPERCEPTIBLE OCCULT SUBTLE
IMPERFECT ILL HALF POOR AMISS
BLIND FUZZY ROUGH BOTCHY
FAULTY PLATIC ATELENE STICKIT
UNWHOLE VICIOUS INPARFIT
MUTILOUS
(PREF.) ATEL(O)
IMPERFECTED INCHOATE
IMPERFECTION BUG RUB WEN
FLAW KINK MOLE SLUR VICE
ERROR FAULT BLOTCH DEFECT
FOIBLE BLEMISH CRUDITY
DEFAULT DEMERIT FAILING
FRAILTY WEAKNESS
(**— IN BOTTLE**) HEELTAP
(**— IN GLASS**) STRIA STREAK
(**— IN LEATHER**) FRIEZE
(**— IN SILK**) CORKSCREW
(**— IN WICK**) THIEF WASTER
IMPERFECTIVE ATELIC
IMPERFECTLY ILL HALF AMISS
ROUGHLY
IMPERFORATION ATRESIA
IMPERIAL TUFT ROYAL KINGLY
PURPLE MAJESTIC
IMPERIALIST CAESAR
IMPERIL RISK EXPONE EMPERIL
ENDANGER JEOPARDY
IMPERIOUS SURLY LORDLY
HAUGHTY DESPOTIC IMPERIAL
MASTERLY PRESSING MASTERFUL
IMPERISHABLE ETERNAL
UNDYING ENDURING IMMORTAL
IMPERMANENCE ANICCA
IMPERMANENT FLEETING
IMPERSONAL COLD DEADPAN
INHUMAN ABSTRACT
IMPERSONATE POSE TYPIFY
PERSONIFY
IMPERSONATION GENIUS
IMPERSONATOR ACTOR CACHINA
KACHINA KATCINA
IMPERTINENCE PAWK SNASH
AUDACITY
IMPERTINENT GAY FREE PERT
RUDE FRESH SASSY SAUCY
PUSHING IMPERENT IMPUDENT
OBTRUSIVE OFFICIOUS
MEDDLESOME
IMPERTURBABILITY ATARAXY
ATARAXIA SANGFROID
IMPERTURBABLE COOL PLACID
GLACIAL TRANQUIL
UNFLAPPABLE
IMPERVIOUS DEAD GASTIGHT
HARDENED HERMETIC
MOTHPROOF

(SUFF.) PROOF
IMPETUOSITY BIRR FURY HASTE
WRATH FOUGUE POWDER
RANDOM SPLEEN
IMPETUOUS HOT RAMP RUDE
BRASH EAGER FIERY FRECK
HASTY HEADY SHARP ARDENT
BROTHE FIERCE FLASHY LAVISH
RACKLE STRONG BUCKISH
FURIOUS HOTHEAD HOTSPUR
RAMSTAM VIOLENT BRAINISH
EMPRESSE HEADLONG SLAPDASH
VEHEMENT PRECIPITATE
IMPETUS BIRR FARD SEND DRIFT
GRACE SWING YMPET BENSEL
IMPACT POWDER RAVINE SWINGE
SWOUGH IMPULSE MOMENTUM
IMPINGE FALL IMPACT ASSAULT
CROSSCUT
IMPINGEMENT IMPACT
IMPIOUS UNHOLY ATHEIST
ATHEOUS GODLESS UNGODLY
DOWNWEED HOARWORT
NEFANDOUS NEFARIOUS
IMPISH IMPY ELFISH PUCKISH
WARLOCK
IMPLACABLE STOUT DEADLY
MORTAL
IMPLACABLY FATALLY
IMPLANT FIX IMP SOW HAFT ROOT
GRAFT INFIX INLAY ENRACE
ENROOT FASTEN INFUSE INSTIL
ENFORCE ENGRAFT IMPRESS
INSPIRE ENTRENCH INSTINCT
IMPLANTED INBORN INSITE
IMPLEMENT (**ALSO SEE TOOL**) AX
AXE BAT CARD DISC DISK FORK
GRAB HACK HONE HOOK LOOM
PLOW SPUD SPUR TOOL CROOK
DRILL FLINT LANCE SCRUB SHEAR
SLICK SPADE SPOON STEEL STICK
TRIER AMGARN BEAMER BLADER
BROACH COLLAR COOLER DIBBLE
DREDGE DRIVER DUSTER EOLITH
FLAKER FLUTER HACKER
HARROW INVOKE LADDER LIPPER
LUNATE MARKER MEALER
PACKER PADDLE PALLET PESTLE
PLOUGH RIMMER SCREEN SCYTHE
SEATER SEEDER SERVER SHEARS
SHOVEL SICKLE SLICER SMOOTH
BREAKER CHOPPER CLEANER
CLEAVER ENFORCE FLESHER
FLYFLAP GAROTTE GRUBBER
HARPOON HUSTLER KNAPPER
MATTOCK NUTPICK SKIMMER
SLABBER SLASHER SLEEKER
SLICKER SPATTLE SPATULA
SPITTLE SPURTLE STAMPER
STICKER SWATHER UTENSIL
AGITATOR BUSHWACK MEASURER
SCUTCHER SEARCHER SHREDDER
SKETCHER SPLITTER SPREADER
STRIPPER TERRACER THWACKER
TOLLIKER TRANCHET TWEEZERS
WARKLOOM WORKLOOM
NUTCRACKER
(**— FOR CUTTING CHEESE**) HARP
(**— FOR HANGING POT**) HALE
(**— TO PREVENT MALT FROM
OVERFLOWING**) STROM
(**—S OF HUSBANDRY**) WAINAGE
(**ANCIENT —**) POINT SLICE

AMGARN EOLITH NEOLITH
RACLOIR PALEOLITH
(**BAKER'S —**) PEEL
(**CLIMBING —**) CREEPER
(**ESKIMO —**) ULU
(**GARDENING —**) HOE RAKE SEEDER
SICKLE
(**HEDGING —**) TRAMP
(**IRRIGATION —**) CROWDER
(**LOGGING —**) TODE
(**POTTER'S —**) PALLET SPATTLE
(**PREHISTORIC —**) CELT FLAKER
(**SHOVEL-LIKE —**) SCOOP
(**SOLDERING —**) DOCTOR
(**TORTURE —**) ENGINE
(**UPROOTING —**) MAKE
(**WINNOWING —**) FAN
(PL.) GEAR CUTLERY GAINAGE
FLAUGHTS
(SUFF.) LABE
IMPLEMENTATION PERFORMANCE
IMPLICATE DIP ENWRAP CONCERN
EMBROIL INCLUDE INVOLVE
IMPLICATION CLAIM IMPLIAL
INNUENDO
IMPLICIT COVERT
IMPLIED TACIT IMPLICIT
IMPLORATION PETITION
IMPLORE ASK BEG CRY PRAY
CHARM CRAVE PLEAD INVOKE
OBTEST BESEECH CONJURE
ENTREAT SOLICIT PETITION
IMPLY HINT ARGUE CARRY COUCH
INFER EMPLOY ENTAIL IMPORT
INDUCE CONNOTE CONTAIN
INCLUDE INVOLVE PRESUME
SIGNIFY SUGGEST SUPPOSE
PREDICATE
IMPOLITE RUDE UNCIVIL
IMPOLITENESS CRUDITY
IMPONDERABLE FRIGORIC
IMPORT SAY WIT BEAR BODY
TOUR DRIFT FORCE IMPLY MORAL
SCOPE SENSE SOUND SPELL
VALOR AMOUNT CHARGE
DENOTE INGATE INTENT MATTER
SPIRIT BETOKEN MEANING
PRETEND SIGNIFY CARRIAGE
INDICATE
(PL.) INWARDS
IMPORTANCE BORE MARK PITH
FORCE POISE WORTH CHARGE
IMPORT MATTER MOMENT
REMARK STRESS STROKE WEIGHT
ACCOUNT ESSENCE GRAVITY
VALENCY EMPHASIS MAGNITUDE
SIGNIFICANCE
**IMPORTANCE OF BEING
EARNEST** (**AUTHOR OF —**) WILDE
(**CHARACTER IN —**) JACK ALGIE
PRISM CECILY EARNEST
ALGERNON WORTHING
BRACKNELL GWENDOLEN
MONCRIEFF
IMPORTANT BIG DEAR DREE HIGH
MAIN REAL GRAVE GREAT
GAPING NEEDLE STRONG URGENT
VALOUR CAPITAL CENTRAL
CRUCIAL EMINENT MATTERY
PIVOTAL SERIOUS EVENTFUL
MATERIAL PRESSING
MOMENTOUS OVERBEARING
SIGNIFICANT

(MOST — ONE OF GROUP) FLAGSHIP
IMPORTER MILLINER
IMPORTUNATE URGENT INSTANT
DEVILING EXIGEANT PRESSING
IMPORTUNE BEG WOO BEAT BONE
PRIG TOUT PRESS TEASE
BESEECH BESIEGE INSTANT
SOLICIT TERRIFY INSTANCE
IMPORTUNITY BRASS URGENCY
IMPOSE LAY SET TOP CLAP GIVE
LEVY MUMP POLE SORN ABUSE
APPLY CLAMP INPUT STAMP
TRUMP BURDEN CHARGE ENJOIN
ENTAIL FASTEN FATHER IMPONE
IMPUTE BLAFLUM DICTATE
INFLICT IRROGATE
(— UPON) FOB GAG HUM LAY
DUPE SELL CULLY TRAIL BLUDGE
DELUDE EXCISE HUMBUG NUZZLE
CULLION DECEIVE HOODWINK
IMPOSED BOUNDEN
IMPOSING BIG EPIC BUDGE BURLY
GRAND HEFTY NOBLE PROUD
AUGUST EPICAL FEUDAL PORTLY
HAUGHTY POMPOUS STATELY
HANDSOME MAGNIFIC SONORANT
SONOROUS
(— UPON) PRACTICE PRACTISE
IMPOSITION BAM COD HUM LEVY
SELL TAIL GOUGE IMPOT CHOUSE
GAMMON INTAKE TAILLE
IMPOSAL ARTIFICE IMPOSURE
(MILITARY —) CESS
(SCHOOL —) PENSUM
IMPOSSIBLE OUT HOPELESS
IMPOST LAY TAX CAST LEVY TAIL
TASK TOLL ABWAB ANNALE
AVANIA EXCISE GABELLE
POUNAMU TALLAGE TONNAGE
TRIBUTE CHAPTREL SPRINGER
(PL.) CUSTOMS
IMPOSTOR FOB FAKE GULL IDOL
CHEAT FAKER FRAUD GOUGE
QUACK BUNYIP FOURBE HUMBUG
MUMPER EMPIRIC FAITOUR
PROCTOR SHAMMER PHANTASM
IMPOSTURE BAM GAG FAKE HOAX
SHAM CHEAT FRAUD TRICK
DECEIT HUMBUG JUGGLE
ARTIFICE DELUSION JUGGLERY
IMPOTENCE ACRATIA UNMIGHT
WEAKNESS
IMPOTENCY UNWELTH
IMPOTENT WEAK FRIGID PAULIE
UNABLE STERILE UNMIGHTY
IMPOUND FIND POIND POUND
INTERN PINFOLD
IMPOVERISH PILL CLOUD BEGGAR
IMPOOR SICKEN DEPLETE
DEPRESS EMPOVER BANKRUPT
POVERISH
IMPOVERISHED POOR OBOLARY
BANKRUPT INDIGENT
IMPRACTICAL CRAZY FECKLESS
IMPRECATE WISH
IMPRECATION DASH OATH PIZE
WISH BLAME CURSE DAMME
DAMMIT CONSARN ANATHEMA
IMPREGNABILITY STRENGTH
IMPREGNABLE FAST PROOF
IMPREGNATE BIG HOP DOPE FILL
LIME MILT BREED IMBUE STOCK
STUFF TINCT AERATE CHARGE

INFORM INFUSE LEAVEN SEASON
SETTLE ASPHALT ENVENOM
IMPREGN CHROMATE CONCEIVE
CREOSOTE FRICTION FRUCTIFY
GRAPHITE MEDICATE PERMEATE
SATURATE SILICATE TINCTURE
(SUFF.) **(— WITH)** URET(UM)
IMPREGNATED BRED COATED
IMPRESS FIX BITE COIN DING DINT
ETCH MARK AFFIX BRAND CLAMP
CRIMP DRIVE GRAVE GRILL INFIX
PRESS PRINT REACH SEIZE STAMP
STEAD WRITE AFFECT ENSEAL
FASTEN INCUSE INDENT SALUTE
STRIKE ANTIQUE ENGRAVE
ENSTAMP IMPLANT IMPREST
IMPRINT INSENSE AUTOTYPE
INSCRIBE NEGATIVE
(— DEEPLY) DELVE ENGRAVE
(— SUDDENLY) SMITE
(— WITH FEAR) AFFRIGHT
(FAIL TO —) UNDERWHELM
IMPRESSED BLIND ANTIQUE
INDENTED
IMPRESSIBLE WAXY
IMPRESSION CUT HIT AURA CAST
CHOP DENT DINT IDEA MARK
MOLD SEAL STEP STIR FANCY
GOUGE IMAGE MOULD PRINT
STAMP STATE ECTYPE EFFECT
ENGRAM FIGURE INCUSE OFFSET
SIGNET STRIKE EOPHYTE
ETCHING FANTASY IMPRESS
MOULAGE OPINION SEALING
SQUEEZE STENCIL TOOLING
BLANKING ENGRAMMA NEGATIVE
PRESSION PRESSURE STAMPAGE
TOOLMARK PHOTOGENE
(— OF DIE) CLICHE
(— ON COIN) CROSS
(— WITHOUT INK) ALBINO
(AUDITORY —) SOUND
(DOUBLE —) MACKLE MACULE
(IMMEDIATE —) APERCU
(LUMINOUS —) PHOSPHENE
(MAKE AN — ON) GRAB
(MENTAL —) GRAVING
(STRONG —) HUNCH
(TRANSITORY —) SNAPSHOT
(VIVID —) SPLASH
(PREF.) TYP(I)(O)
(SUFF.) TYPAL TYPE TYPIC TYPY
IMPRESSIONABLE SOFT WAXY
WAXEN TENDER PLASTIC
PASSIBLE
IMPRESSIONIST LUMINIST
IMPRESSIVE BIG FAT EPIC AWFUL
GRAND NOBLE PROUD EPICAL
SOLEMN PESANTE STATELY
TEARING TELLING WEIGHTY
FORCIBLE IMPOSING SMASHING
SONORANT SONOROUS
STUNNING MAGNIFICENT
IMPRINT DINT ETCH SIGN STEP
PRESS STAMP CUTOFF FASTEN
STRIKE ENGRAVE ENSTAMP
IMPRESS APREYNTE COLOPHON
EPIGRAPH PRESSION PRESSURE
STAMPAGE
(— ON CHEEK) FASTEN
IMPRISON JUG LAG NUN BOND
GAOL HULK JAIL QUOD SEAL
SHOP WARD CROWD EMBAR

GRATE COMMIT IMMURE JIGGER
PRISON SLOUGH CONFINE
INTOWER BASTILLE
IMPRISONED FAST
IMPRISONMENT BAND BOND
ARREST CHAINS DURESS PRISON
CUSTODY DURANCE
IMPROBABLE FISHY UNLIKE
UNLIKELY
IMPROMPTU GLIB MAGGOT
SUDDEN OFFHAND
IMPROPER BAD PAH PAW AMISS
LARGE SPICY UNDUE UNFELE
UNJUST ILLICIT INDECENT
PERVERSE TORTIOUS UNSEEMLY
WRONGOUS MALODOROUS
IMPROPERLY AMISS
IMPROPRIETY SOLECISM
IMPROVE FIX BEET GAIN GOOD
GROW HELP MEND AMEND EDIFY
EMEND GRADE MOISE SMART
TOUCH BETTER ENRICH PROFIT
ADVANCE BENEFIT CORRECT
CULTURE ELEVATE PERFECT
PROMOTE RECTIFY UPSWING
(— APPEARANCE OF HORSE)
BISHOP
(— APPEARANCE OF TEA) FACE
(— CONDUCTIVITY) AGE
IMPROVED BETTER
IMPROVEMENT AMENDS PICKUP
POLICY PROFIT REFORM REDRESS
UPSWING
IMPROVIDENT PRODIGAL
WASTEFUL
(— PERSON) MICAWBER
IMPROVISATION THEME CALYPSO
IMPROVISE JAM COOK FAKE PONG
VAMP ADLIB FANTASY
(— MUSICALLY) JAM FAKE
NOODLE
IMPRUDENCE FOLLY
IMPRUDENT FESS RASH FALSE
UNWARY FOOLISH RECKLESS
IMPUDENCE GALL BRASS CHEEK
MOUTH NERVE SLACK BRONZE
PUPPYISM
IMPUDENT BOLD COXY FACY RUDE
BANTY BARDY BRASH FRESH
GALLY LIPPY SASSY SAUCY
BRASSY BRAZEN CHEEKY STOCKY
BIGGETY CHUNKED FORWARD
GALLOWS PERKING INSOLENT
MALAPERT AUDACIOUS
BAREFACED
IMPUDENTLY COOLY COOLLY
FRESHLY
IMPUGN DENY FALSE DISPUTE
IMPEACH
IMPULSE FIT BIAS RESE SEND
URGE DRIVE NISUS SPEND START
DESIRE MOTIVE SIGNAL SPLEEN
YETZER CALLING CONATUS
IMPETUS INSTINCT MOVEMENT
STIRRING
(BLIND —) ATE
(ELECTRICAL —) KICK
(SPONTANEOUS —) ACCORD
(SUDDEN —) SPLEEN
(SUPERNATURAL —) AFFLATUS
(PREF.) OSMO
IMPULSION SWING IMPULSE
IMPULSIVE QUICK

FITFUL HEADLONG
IMPURE DRY FOUL LEWD GROSS
HORRY MUDDY FILTHY TURBID
UNPURE MONGREL SCABBED
UNCLEAN VICIOUS INDECENT
MACULATE PRURIENT
MACULATED
IMPURITY CRUD DONOR DROSS
FEDITY ACCEPTER ACCEPTOR
FOULNESS
(— IN LINT) SHALE
(— IN MINERAL) GANG GANGUE
(PL.) SCUM GARBLE SLUMMAGE
IMPUTABLE OWING
IMPUTATION SCANDAL
IMPUTE LAY PUT RET ARET EVEN
WITE COUNT REFER ARRECT
CHARGE FASTEN IMPOSE OBJECT
RECKON REPUTE ASCRIBE
ENTITLE IMPEACH
IN A I N Y AT TO BAJO INBY INTO
UPON ALONG INTIL
(— A FAINT) AWAY
(— A SERIES) SERIATIM
(— A STATE OF ACTION) ENERGIC
(— ACCORDANCE) AFTER
(— ADDITION) EKE TOO ALSO
ABOVE AGAIN ALONG FORBY
STILL BEYOND BESIDES FARTHER
FURTHER MOREOVER OVERPLUS
THERETIL
(— ADVANCE) AHEAD FORTH
BEFORE
(— ANY CASE) EVER HOWEVER
(— BEHALF OF) PRO
(— CASE THAT) AUNTERS
(— CIRCULATION) ABROAD
(— CONNECTION WITH) FORNENT
FERNINST
(— EARNEST) AGOOD
(— EXCESS OF) OVER
(— FACT) SOOTH TRULY INDEED
ITSELF MERELY VERILY ACTUALLY
VERAMENT
(— FAITH) IVADS EFECKS YFACKS
(— FRONT) FORE AFACE FORNE
AGAINST PARAVANT
(— FULL) ALONG
(— GOOD SEASON) BETIMES
(— GOOD SPIRITS) BOBBISH
(— GRACEFUL MANNER) ADAGIO
(— JEST) AGAME
(— NO MANNER) NOWISE
NAEGATES
(— ONE DIRECTION) ANON
(— ORDER) FOR ATAUNT
ATAUNTO
(— PLACE OF) FOR WITH INSTEAD
(— POSSESSION) WITHIN
(— PROGRESS) AFOOT TOWARD
(— PROPER MANNER) DULY
(— RESPECT TO) ANENT
(— RETURN FOR) AGAINST
(— ROTATION) ABOUT
(— SO FAR AS) AS QUA
(— SOLE CONTROL) ABSOLUTE
(— SOOTH) PARFEY PERFAY
(— SPITE OF) FOR ALTHO MALGRE
AGAINST DESPITE MALGRADO
(— SUSPENSE) PENDING
(— THE DOING OF) WITH
(— THE FIELD) ABROAD
(— THE FIRST PLACE) IMP IMPRIMIS

(— THE FUTURE) HENCE
(— THE MORNING) MANE
(— THE REAR) AREAR ASTERN
(— THE REGIONS OF UNBELIEVERS)
IPI
(— THE SAME PLACE) IBID IBIDEM
(— THE SAME WAY) AS
(— TOWARD) INOWER
(— TRUTH) MARRY SOOTH CERTES
INDEED VERILY SOOTHLY
FORSOOTH
(— VAIN) WASTELY
(— VIEW OF THE FACT THAT)
SEEING
(— WHAT MANNER) HOW
QUOMODO
(NOT —) OUT
(PREF.) A IL IM IN INTRO IR
INABILITY (— TO FEED) APHAGIA
(— TO MASTICATE) AMASESIS
(— TO SPEAK) ALOGIA ANEPIA
DUMBNESS
(— TO WALK) ABASIA
INACCESSIBILITY FASTNESS
INACCESSIBLE COY REMOTE
UNGAIN WICKED SHADOWY
INACCURATE SOUR FALSE LOOSE
FAULTY UNJUST INEXACT
IMPROPER SLIPSHOD
INACHUS (DAUGHTER OF —) IO
(FATHER OF —) OCEANUS
(MOTHER OF —) TETHYS
(SON OF —) PHORONEUS
INACTION RUST
INACTIVATE MOTHBALL
INACTIVE LAX DEAD DRUG FLAT
IDLE LAZY MESO SLOW HEAVY
INERT NOBLE SLACK SULKY
ASLEEP SEDENT STATIC SUPINE
TORPID CESSANT DORMANT
PASSIVE RESTIVE COMATOSE
COMATOUS DEEDLESS DILATORY
FAINEANT SLOTHFUL SLUGGISH
THEWLESS THOWLESS
QUIESCENT
INACTIVITY SLOTH ANERGY
TORPOR ANERGIA ABEYANCE
IDLENESS CESSATION SEGNITUDE
INADEQUACY DEFECT FRAILTY
SCARCITY
INADEQUATE BAD BARE POOR
THIN INEPT SCANT SHORT SLACK
FEEBLE STRAIT FOOLISH INVALID
SLENDER HIGHLAND INFERIOR
MISERABLE
(PREF.) MAL
INADEQUATELY BADLY SLACK
SLACKLY
INADVERTENCE LAPSUS
INADVERTENT CARELESS
INAJA JAGUA
INALIENABLE INHERENT
INAMORATA AMORADO
AMORETTO
INANE DIZZY EMPTY JERKY SILLY
VAPID JEJUNE VACANT FATUOUS
FOOLISH INSIPID VACUOUS
IMBECILE SLIPSLOP TRIFLING
INANGA MINNOW
INANIMATE DEAD DULL BRUTE
INERT DEADLY STOLID STUPID
LIFELESS
INANIMITY CONSENSUS

INANITY FATUITY VACUITY
INAPPLICABLE SPURIOUS
INAPPROPRIATE INEPT UNAPT
UNDUE FOREIGN UNHAPPY
(SOMETHING —) CAMP
INAPT BACKWARD FOOTLESS
INARTICULATA LYOPOMA
INARTICULATE DUMB LAME THICK
INARTISTIC CRUDE ARTLESS
INATTENTION ABSENCE NEGLECT
APROSEXIA
INATTENTIVE DEAF SLACK ABSENT
REMISS SUPINE DREAMSY
UNTENTY CARELESS DISTRAIT
HEEDLESS MINDLESS
INAUDIBLE SECRET
INAUDIBLY INWARDLY SECRETLY
INAUGURATE AUGUR BEGIN
HANDSEL INITIATE
INAUGURATION HANDSEL
INAUSPICIOUS BAD ILL EVIL FOUL
ADVERSE OBSCENE OMINOUS
UNHAPPY UNLUCKY SINISTER
INAUTHENTIC SPURIOUS
INBORN GENIAL INBRED INNATE
NATIVE CONNATE NATURAL
HABITUAL INHERENT
INBRED INBORN INNATE
INBREED SELF
INBREEDING ENDOGAMY
INCA INGUA OREJON
INCALCULABLE UNTOLD SUMLESS
UNKNOWN
INCA MAGIC FLOWER CANTUT
CANTUTA
INCANDESCENCE GLOW
INCANDESCENT BRIGHT
INCANTATION CHARM DAWUT
SPELL CARMEN FETISH MANTRA
CANTION CHANTRY GREEGREE
INCAPABLE DEAD NUMB UNABLE
HANDLESS
INCAPACITATE NAPOO UNFIT
NOBBLE UNABLE DISABLE
INCAPACITATED FLAT DISABLED
STRICKEN
INCARCERATE IMMURE CONFINE
IMPRISON
INCARNATE BODIED EMBODY
CARNATE ENFLESH HUMANIFY
PERSONIFY
INCARNATION RAMA IMAGE
ADVENT AVATAR GENIUS MNEVIS
TERTON HUTUKTU EPIPHANY
PERSONIFICATION
INCAUTIOUS RASH UNWARY
UNCHARY UNTENTY CAREFREE
RECKLESS
INCENDIARY FIREBUG ARSONIST
BOUTEFEU
INCENSE CENSE INFLAME
KETURAH PROVOKE IRRITATE
THYMIAMA
(— INGREDIENT) ONYCHA
(— VESSEL) SHIP
(PREF.) THURI
INCENSED RAW IRATE WROTH
WRATHFUL
INCENTIVE BROD GOAD SPUR
PRICK MOTIVE IMPETUS IMPULSE
INCITIVE STIMULUS MOTIVATION
INCEPTION ORIGIN ANCESTRY
INCESSANT STEADY

ENDLESS CONSTANT
INCESSANTLY FOREVER
INCH UNCH PRIME UNCIA
(ABOUT 7 —S) FISTMELE
(100TH OF —) POINT
(4 —S) HANDFUL
(48TH OF —) IRON
(9 —S) SPAN
INCHOATE FORMLESS
INCIDENT GO EVENT LIABLE
CAUTION EPISODE PASSAGE
SUBJECT ACCIDENT CASUALTY
OCCASION OCCURRENCE
(AMUSING —) BAR BREAK
(LITERARY —) BIT
INCIDENTAL BY BYE SIDE STRAY
CASUAL EPISODIC GLANCING
INCIDENT OCCURRENT
INCIDENTALLY BYHAND OBITER
APROPOS
INCINERATE COMBUST CREMATE
INCINERATOR BURNER
SALAMANDER
INCIPIENCE BUD
INCIPIENT INITIAL GERMINAL
INCHOATE
INCISE CHOP RASE LANCE INCIDE
CHANNEL ENGRAVE
INCISION CUT GASH SLIT SNIP
ISSUE SCORE BROACH SCOTCH
STREAK CUTDOWN DIACOPE
APLOTOMY CECOTOMY
COLOTOMY
(SUFF.) TOMY
INCISIVE ACID KEEN CRISP SHARP
BITING BRUTAL CUTTING
ACULEATE PIERCING TRENCHANT
INCISIVENESS MORDANCY
INCISOR CUTTER NIPPER
GATHERER
INCITE EGG HIE HOY PUT SIC TAR
ABET BEET BUZZ EDGE FIRE
GOAD LASH MOVE PROD SICK
SNIP SPUR STIR URGE WHET
AWAKE CHIRK IMPEL PRICK
PROKE SPARK SPURN STING
TEMPT AROUSE BESTIR ENTICE
EXCITE EXHORT FILLIP FOMENT
HALLOO INDUCE KINDLE NETTLE
PROMPT UPSTIR ACTUATE
ANIMATE COMMOVE INCENSE
INSPIRE PROMOVE PROVOKE
QUICKEN SOLICIT INCITATE
MOTIVATE
(— SECRETLY) SUBORN
(— TO ATTACK) SET HIRR SOOL
INCITEMENT GOAD PROD SPUR
STING MOTIVE EGGMENT
STIRRING
(— OF LITIGATION) BARRATRY
INCITER FEEDER MONITOR
INCENSOR INCENTOR
INCLEMENCY RIGOR CRUELTY
TYRANNY ASPERITY HARDNESS
SEVERITY
INCLEMENT RAW HARD RUDE
SOUR GURLY STARK COARSE
RUGGED SEVERE UNFINE
UNKINDLY
(NOT —) OPEN CIVIL
INCLINATION DIP GEE MAW PLY
SET BENT BIAS BROO CANT CARE
DRAG DRAW EDGE FALL GUST

HANG LEAN LIKE LIST LOVE LUST
MIND SLEW TURN VEIN WILL
BEVEL BOSOM DRAFT DRIFT
FANCY GRAIN HABIT HIELD
HUMOR KNACK LURCH PITCH
POISE SLANT SLOPE STUDY
SWING TASTE THEAT TREND
AFFECT ANIMUS ANLAGE ASCENT
DESIRE DEVICE GATHER GENIUS
INTENT LIKING MOTION NOTION
PONDUS RELISH SQUINT TALENT
YETZER APTNESS CONATUS
COURAGE CURRENT DESCENT
DRAUGHT FANTASY INKLING
LEANING STOMACH VERSANT
WILLING APPETITE APTITUDE
CLINAMEN DEVOTION GRADIENT
PENCHANT TENDENCY VELLEITY
VERGENCY WOULDING
PROCLIVITY PROPENSITY
(— DOWNWARD) DIP DESCENT
HANGING
(— OF OARSMAN'S BODY) LAYBACK
(INWARD —) BATTER
(PREDOMINATE —) STRENGTH
INCLINE APT BOW DIP KIP TIP
WRY BEAR BEND BIAS BREW
CANT CAST DOCK DOOK DOOR
DROP GIVE HANG HEEL HELD
HILL LEAN LIKE LIST PECK PEND
RAKE SEEL STAY SWAY TILT
TURN BEVEL CLIMB CLINE DROOP
FLECT HIELD JINNY OFFER PITCH
SHAPE SLANT SLOPE SOUND
VERGE AFFECT GLACIS INTEND
SHELVE STEEVE UPBROW
DECLINE DESCEND GANGWAY
PROPEND PROCLINE PROCLIVE
(— SKI) EDGE
(PREF.) CLIN(O)
INCLINED APT SIB BENT CANT
FAIN LIEF RIFE VAIN ARAKE
GIVEN PRONE READY COUCHE
MINDED PROMPT SLOPED SUPINE
FORWARD HANGING OBLIQUE
PRONATE STUDIED AFFECTED
DISPOSED ENCLITIC PREGNANT
PROPENSE SIDELING TALENTED
(— TO DRINK) BIBULOUS
INCLINING HILLY SHELVY SLOPING
CERNUOUS PROPENSE SIDELING
(SUFF.) CLINIC CLINOUS
INCLUDE ADD LAP HAVE TAKE
ANNEX COUCH COVER IMPLY
EMPLOY ENSEAM RECKON
BELOUKE COLLECT CONNOTE
CONTAIN EMBRACE IMMERSE
INVOLVE RECOUNT SUBSUME
COMPRISE CONCLUDE
(— IN LIST) ENGROSS
INCLUDING TO CUM
INCLUSIVE GRAND CAPABLE
CATHOLIC
INCLUSIVELY BROADLY
INCLUSUS RECLUSE
INCOHERENT FUZZY BROKEN
RAVING INCHOATE
INCOHERENTLY IDLY
INCOMBUSTIBLE APYROUS
ASBESTIC
INCOME GAIN PORT RENT LIVING
PEWAGE PEWING PROFIT SALARY
FACULTY INTRADO INTRATE

PRODUCE REVENUE STIPEND
INTEREST PROCEEDS
POCKETBOOK
(— OF BENEFICE) ANNAT
(ANNUAL —) RENTE
(UNFORESEEN —) GRAVY
INCOMMENSURATE UNEQUAL
INCOMMODE VEX ANNOY MOLEST
PLAGUE TROUBLE DISQUIET
INCOMPARABLE ALONE
INCOMPATIBILITY SOLECISM
ANTIPATHY
INCOMPATIBLE ALIEN
REPUGNANT
INCOMPETENT INEPT UNFIT
SLOUCH UNABLE UNMEET
FECKLESS HANDLESS HELPLESS
SPLITTER
INCOMPLETE WANE BLIND ROUGH
BROKEN UNDONE DIVIDED
LACKING PARTIAL IMMATURE
INCHOATE SEGMENTAL
(PREF.) ATEL(O) DEMI SEMI
INCOMPLETELY BADLY HALVES
INCOMPOSITE PRIME
INCOMPREHENSIBILITY
ACATALEPSY
INCOMPREHENSIBLE PARTIAL
COCKEYED
INCONCLUSIVE FUZZY
INCONGRUITY JAR ANOMALY
SOLECISM
INCONGRUOUS ALIEN ABSURD
ANOMALOUS
INCONNU CONY NELMA CONNIE
SHEEFISH
INCONSEQUENTIAL NUGATORY
INCONSIDERABLE WEAK LIGHT
PETTY LITTLE
INCONSIDERATE RASH UNKIND
ASOCIAL RECKLESS
INCONSISTENCY HOLE
INCONSISTENT ALIEN
REPUGNANT
INCONSPICUOUS OBSCURE
INCONSTANCY CHANGE LEVITY
INCONSTANT FICKLE BRUCKLE
FLUXILE MOONISH MUTABLE
SLIDING VARIOUS FLUXIBLE
MOVEABLE STRUMPET VARIABLE
CHAMELEON MERCURIAL
VERSATILE
INCONTESTABLE SURE CLEAN
CERTAIN POSITIVE
INCONTINENCE ENURESIS
INCONTINENT LOOSE LAXATIVE
INCONTROVERTIBLE GRAND
INCONVENIENCE FASH BOTHER
CUMBER STRESS SQUEEZE
DISQUIET
INCONVENIENT UNKED CLUMSY
UNBANE UNGAIN AWKWARD
UNHANDY ANNOYING UNCHANCY
UNTOWARD
INCOORDINATION ASTASIA
INCORPORATE MIX FOLD FUSE
JOIN ANNEX KNEAD MERGE
UNITE ABSORB EMBODY ENGRAIN
ENTRAIN INWEAVE INCORPSE
(— IN WALL) ENGAGE
INCORPOREAL AERY BODILESS
ASOMATOUS
INCORRECT BAD ILL OFF FALSE

WRONG PECCANT UNRIGHT
UNSOUND VICIOUS PERVERSE
(PREF.) CAC(O)
INCORRIGIBLE HARD
INCORRUPTIBLE IMMORTAL
INCREASE UP ADD EIK EKE IMP
WAX BUMP ECHE GAIN GROW
HELP HIKE ITCH JACK JUMP
MEND MORE MUCH PLUS PUSH
RISE SOAR THEE THRO BOOST
BUILD BULGE CLIMB CROWD
FLUSH FRESH HEAVE LARGE
RAISE SPURT SWELL ACCENT
ACCESS ACCRUE BETTER BIGGEN
CHANGE CREASE DEEPEN
DOUBLE EXPAND EXTEND
EXTENT GATHER GROWTH
SPREAD SPRING ADVANCE
AMPLIFY AUCTION AUGMENT
AUXESIS BALLOON DISTEND
ELEVATE ENGROSS ENHANCE
ENLARGE GREATEN IMPROVE
INFLATE MAGNIFY STEEPEN
SURCRUE ACCRESCE ADDITION
COMPOUND FLOURISH HEIGHTEN
LENGTHEN MAJORATE MAXIMATE
MAXIMIZE MULTIPLY THRODDEN
PROPAGATE PROLIFERATE
(— AT USURY) OCKER
(— GREATLY) ACCUMULATE
(— HEAT OF KILN) RUSTLE GLISTER
(— IN BUSINESS) UPBEAT
(— IN PAY) FOGY FOGIE
(— IN STRENGTH) FRESHEN
(— KNOWLEDGE) ENRICH
(— POWER) SOUP
(— PRICE BY BIDDING) CANT
(— SPEED) JAZZ ACCELERATE
(— STITCHES) FASHION
(— SUDDENLY) LEAP
(PRICE —) RIST
(SHORT-TERM —) BOOMLET
(PREF.) AUXO
(SUFF.) AUXE OSIS
INCREASING GROWING CRESCENT
CRESCIVE DILATANT SWELLING
(— RAPIDLY) BOOMING
INCREDIBLE TALL STEEP DAMNED
FABULOUS
INCREDULITY UNBELIEF
INCREDULOUS INFIDEL
INCREMENT DOSE DELTA
INCREASE
INCRIMINATE ACCUSE
INCRUST FOUL
INCRUSTATION CRUD MOSS
CRUST SCALE TARTAR FOULING
FURRING
INCUBATE SIT BROOD CLOCK
COVER HATCH
INCUBATION PASSAGE
INCUBATOR FURNACE HATCHER
COUVEUSE ISOLETTE
INCUBUS DUSE MARE DUSIO
NIGHTMARE
INCULCATE BREED INFIX INCULK
INFUSE IMPLANT IMPRESS
INSTILL
INCULCATED BRED
INCUMBENT COARB BEARER
INCUR RUN BEAR GAIN WAGE
CONTRACT
INCURABLE BOOTLESS HOPELESS

INCURRENT INHALANT
INCURSION RAID ROAD FORAY
INFALL INROAD RAZZIA DESCENT
HOSTING INBREAK INCURSE
ANABASIS INVASION
INCUS AMBOS ANVIL
INDEBTED DEBTFUL BEHOLDEN
INDEBTEDNESS DEBT SCORE
INDECENCY IMPURITY PRIAPISM
RIBALDRY
INDECENT PAW BLUE FOUL LEWD
RANK BAWDY GROSS NASTY
SAUCY GREASY IMPURE PAWPAW
SMUTTY CURIOUS GRIVOIS
IMMORAL OBSCENE IMMODEST
IMPROPER SHAMEFUL UNCOMELY
INDECISION DEMUR DOUBT
MAYBE POISE SWITHER
INDECISIVE DRAWN HALTING
INDECISIVENESS SUSPENSE
INDECOROUS RUDE COARSE
FORWARD UNCIVIL IMMODEST
IMPOLITE IMPROPER INDECENT
UNSEEMLY UNTOWARD
INDEED SO ARU NAY TOO WIS YEA
AWAT DEED EVEN IWIS JUST
SURE MARRY QUOTH TIENS
ATWEEL ITSELF PARDIE SURELY
FAITHLY FRANKLY FORSOOTH
VERAMENT
INDEFATIGABLE TIRELESS
INDEFENSIBLE INVALID
INDEFINABLE NAMELESS
INDEFINITE HAZY FUZZY GROSS
LOOSE VAGUE DIVERS INEXACT
AORISTIC
INDEFINITELY IN
INDELIBLE FAST FIXED
INDELICATE RAW FREE WARM
BROAD GROSS ROUGH COARSE
GREASY IMPOLITE IMPROPER
UNSEEMLY
INDEMNIFICATION RELIEF
INDEMNIFY PAY RECOUP SATISFY
WARRANT
INDENT JAG BRIT DENT GIMP
MUSH NICK CHASE DELVE NOTCH
STAMP TOOTH WHEEL BRUISE
CRENEL ENGRAIL GAUFFER
INDENTATION CHOP DENT DINT
DOKE FOIL KINK SCAR BOSOM
BULGE CLEFT CRENA DINGE
NOTCH SINUS DIMPLE FURROW
GROOVE INDENT RECESS IMPRESS
CRENELLE TOOTHING
(— IN BOTTLE) KICK
(— IN DOG'S FACE) STOP
(— IN SHELL) EYE
INDENTED WAVED CRENATE
NOTCHED SINUATE
INDENTURE BIND INDENT
ESCALLOP SYNGRAPH
INDEPENDENCE AUTARKY
FREEDOM AUTARCHY
(— OF GOD) ASEITY ASEITAS
(POLITICAL —) SWARAJ
INDEPENDENT FREE PROUD
SEEKER BIGGITY DIVIDED
MUGWUMP SECTARY ABSOLUTE
PECULIAR POSITIVE SEPARATE
(STATISTICALLY —) ORTHOGONAL
(PREF.) SELF
INDEPENDENTLY APART

INDESCRIBABLE TERMLESS
INEFFABLE
INDETERMINATE AORISTIC
FORMLESS INFINITE
INDEX PIE FIST HAND ARNETH
ELENCH PIGNET TONGUE
POINTER ALPHABET EXPONENT
REGISTER
(COMPUTER —) KWIC KWOC
INDIA BHARAT

INDIA
CAPE: COMORIN
CAPITAL: NEWDELHI
CASTE: JAT MAL AHIR GOLA JATI
MALI DHOBI SANSI SUDRA
VARNA DACOIT DHANUK
LOHANA VAISYA AGARWAL
BRAHMAN DHANGAR
COAST: MALABAR
COIN: LAC PIE ANNA FELS LAKH
PICE TARA ABIDI CRORE PAISA
RUPEE
COLLEGE: TOL
DESERT: THAR
DISTRICT: SIBI NASIK PATNA
SIMLA ZILLAH MALABAR
NELLORE MOFUSSIL
GULF: KUTCH CAMBAY MANNAR
ISLAND: CHILKA
LAKE: WULAR CHILKA COLAIR
DHEBAR SAMBAHR
LANGUAGE: URDU HINDI TAMIL
TELUGU SANSKRIT
MEASURE: ADY DHA GAZ GUZ
JOW KOS LAN SER BYEE COSS
DAIN DHAN HATH JAOB KUNK
MOOT PARA RAIK RATI SEIT
TAUN TENG TOLA AMUNA
BIGHA CAHAR COVID CROSA
DANDA DRONA GARCE GIREH
HASTA PALLY PARAH RATTI
SALAY YOJAN ADHAKA ANGULA
COVIDO CUDAVA CUMBHA
GEERAH LAMANY MOOLUM
MUSHTI PALGAT PARRAH
ROPANI TIPREE UNGLEE
YOJANA ADOULIE DHANUSH
GAVYUTI KHAHOON NIRANGA
PRASTHA VITASTI OKTHABAH
MOUNTAIN: MERU GHATS KAMET
MASTUJ TANKSE KALAHOI
SIWALIK VINDHYA SULEIMAN
MOUNTAIN RANGE: SATPURA
VINDHYA ARAVALLI HIMALAYA
NATIVE: TODA HINDU TAMIL
PROVINCE: HAR ASSAM BIHAR
ANDHRA BENGAL KERALA
MADRAS MYSORE ORISSA
PUNJAB GUJARAT HARYANA
KASHMIR MANIPUR
REGION: MALABAR
RIVER: AI DOR SON TEL KOSI KUSI
NIRA REHR SIND BETWA BHIMA
DAMOH GOGRA INDUS JAWAI
RAPTI SANKH SONAR TAPTI
TUNGA CHENAB GANGES
KISTNA PENNER SUTLEJ
WARDHA CAUVERY CHAMBAL
IRAWADI KRISHNA NARMADA
NARMEDA HEMAVATI
HYDASPES MAHANADI
NERBUDDA VINDHYAS

SEAPORT: DAMAN BOMBAY COCHIN MADRAS CALCUTTA
STATE: ASSAM BIHAR KERALA MYSORE ORISSA PUNJAB GUJARAT MANIPUR
STRAIT: PALK
TERRITORY: DIU GOA DAMAN MINICOY AMINDIVI
TOWN: DIU AGRA DAMA GAYA PUNA REWA ADONI AKOLA ALWAR ARCOT BHERA DACCA DATIA DELHI GIROT KALPI PAIAN PAINA POONA SALEM SIMLA SURAT TEHRI AJMERE AMBALA BARELI BARODA BHOPAL BOMBAY CHAMBA COCHIN DUMDUM HOWRAH INDORE JAIPUR KANPUR LAHORE MADIRA MADRAS MADURA MEERUT MULTAN MUTTRA MYSORE NAGPUR RAMPUR UJJAIN ALIGARH BENARES BIKANER CALICUT CAWNPUR DINAPUR GWALIOR JODHPUR KARACHI KURNOOL LASWARI LUCKNOW RANGOON RANGPUR AMRITSAR BHATINDA BHATPARA CALCUTTA DINAPORE JABALPUR KOLHAPUR MANDALAY MIRZAPUR PESHAWAR SHOLAPUR SRINAGAR VARANASI
TRIBE: AO GOR BHIL BADAGA SHERANI
WATERFALL: JOG GOKAK CAUVERY
WEIGHT: MOD PAI SER VIS DHAN DRUM KONA MYAT PALA PANK PICE RAIK RATI RUAY SEER TANK TOLA YAVA ADPAD BAHAR CANDY CATTY HUBBA MASHA MAUND PALLY POUAH RATTI RETTI RUTEE TICAL TICUL TIKAL ABUCCO DHURRA KARSHA CHITTAK PEIKTHA

INDIAN LO RED ROJO INJUN TAWNY ABNAKI INDISH BHARATI HOSTILE NAIKPOD REDSKIN LONGHAIR MUSKOGEE PENOBSCOT SHAHAPTIAN NARRAGANSET
(AMERICAN —) AIS AUK FOX HOH KAW OTO REE SAC SIA UTE WEA ZIA ADAI COOS CREE CROW DOEG ERIE EYAK HANO HOPI HUPA IOWA KATO KOSO MOKI MONO OTOE OTTO PIMA PIRO SAUK TANO TAOS TEWA TIOU TOAG UTAH WACO YUMA ZUNI ACOMA ALSEA BANAK BIDAI CADDO CHAUI COMOX CONOY COREE CREEK HANIS HOOPA HUECO HURON JEMEZ KANIA KANSA KAROK KERES KIOWA KOROA KUSAN LENCA LIPAN MAKAH MANSO MIAMI MINGO MODOC MOQUI NAMBE OMAHA OSAGE OSTIC OZARK PECOS PINAL PIUTE PONCA SAMBO SARSI SEWEE SIOUX SITKA SKIDI SLAVE SNAKE SOOKE TETON TEXAS TIGUA TONTO TWANA TYIGH UINTA UNAMI WAPPO WASCO WASHO WIYOT YAMEL YAZOO YUCHI YUROK AGAWAM AHTENA APACHE ATSINA ATUAMI AVOYEL BILOXI CALUSA CAYUGA CAYUSE CHATOT CHERAW CHETCO COOSUC CUPENO DAKOTA DIGGER EYEISH FARAON GILENO HAINAI HAISLA ISLETA KAIBAB KAINAH KANSAS KICHAI KOSIMO KUITSH LAGUNA LENAPE MANDAN MAUMEE MAYEYE METOAC MICMAC MIKMAK MOHAVE MOHAWK MUNSEE NASHUA NATICK NAUSET NAVAHO NAVAJO NEUTER NOOTKA OGLALA ONEIDA OREJON OTTAWA PAIUTE PAPAJO PATWIN PAWNEE PEORIA PEQUOD PEQUOT PIEGAN PODUNK PUEBLO QUAPAW QUERES RIKARI SALISH SAMISH SANTEE SAPONI SATSOP SENECA SHASTA SILETZ SIOUAN SIWASH SKAGIT SOKOKI SUMASS SUMDUM SUTAIO SYLVID TAPOSA TENINO TOHOME TOLOWA TONGAS TUNICA TUTELO UMPQUA WALAPI WAPATO WATALA WAXHAW WEANOC WIKENO WINTUN YAKIMA YAMASI ZUNIAN ABENAKI ALABAMA ALIBAMU AMERIND ANDARKO ANDASTE ARIKARA ATAKAPA AYAHUCA BANNOCK CAHOKIA CALOOSA CATAWBA CHILCAT CHILULA CHINOOK CHOCTAW CHUMASH CHUMAWI CIBECUE CLALLAM CLATSOP COCHITI COLCINE COWLITZ DEADOSE DHEGIHA DWAMISH ESSELEN GOSHUTE HELLELT HIDATSA HUCHNOM HUICHOL INGALIK JUANENO KANAWHA KLAMATH KOASATI KOHUANA KOPRINO KUNESTE KUTCHIN KUTENAI LUISENO MASHPEE MASKOKI MOHEGAN MOHICAN MONACAN MONSONI MONTAUK MOUSONI NANAIMO NASCAPI NATCHEZ NIANTIC NIMKISH NIPMUCK OJIBWAY PACIFID PADUCAH PAMLICO PICURUS QUAITSO SALIAN SANETCH SANPOIL SERRANO SHAPTAN SHAWANO SHAWNEE SIKSIKA SIUSLAW SONGISH SPOKANE SQUAXON STIKINE TAMAROA TESUQUE TIMUCUA TLINGIT TONKAWA TUALATI TULALIP TUTUTNI UGARONO WAILAKI WALPAPI WAMESIT WANAPUM WASHAKI WEWENOC WHILKUT WICHITA WISHOSK WITUMKI WYANDOT YANKTON YAQUINA YAVAPAI YOJUANE YONKALA ABSAROKA ACHOMAWI ACHUMAWI ALGONKIN AMERICAN AMOSKEAG APALACHI ARIVAIPA ARKANSAS ASTAKIWI ATFALATI ATSUGEWI CAHINNIO CAHUILLA CANARSIE CHAWASHA CHEHALIS CHEMAKUM CHEROKEE CHEYENNE CHIMAKUM CHOPTANK CHOWANOC CLACKAMA COLUMBIA COLVILLE COMANCHE COQUILLE COYOTERO DELAWARE DIEGUENO ETCHIMIN FLATHEAD HITCHITI HUNKPAPA ILLINOIS IROQUOIS KALISPEL KAWAIISU KICKAPOO KIKATSIK KLASKINO KLIKITAT KONOMIHU LAMANITE MALECITE MASCOTIN MENOMINI MIKASUKI MINITARI MISSOURI MOGOLLON MUSCOGEE MUSKWAKI NEHANTIC NESPELIM NOTTOWAY OKINAGAN ONONDAGA PAMUNKEY PANAMINT PATUXENT PAVIOTSO PENACOOK PISHQUOW POWHATAN PUYALLUP QUATSINO QUERECHO QUILEUTE QUINAULT ROCKAWAY SAHAPTIN SAULTEUR SAVANNAH SEMINOLE SHIVWITS SHOSHONE SIHASAPA SINGSING SINKIUSE SINKYONE SINTSINK SISSETON SOUHEGAN SQUAMISH SQUEDUNK TLAKLUIT TOBIKHAR TOPINISH TSIHALIS TUSHEPAW TUSKEGEE UMATILLA WABANAKI WACHUSET WAHPETON WETUMPKA YAHUSKIN YAMACRAW DOUSTIONI SQUAWTITS
(BRAZILIAN —) BUGRE
(CANADIAN —) DENE COMOX HAIDA SLAVE TINNE DOGRIB HAISLA LASSIK MICMAC SARSEE BEOTHUK GOASILA KHOTANA KOYUKON CHISEDEC COWICHAN HEILTSUK KIMSQUIT KWAKIUTL LILLOOET SALTEAUX SHUSHWAP
(FEMALE —) SQUAW KLOOCH
(MALE —) BUCK SANNUP SIWASH
(MEXICAN —) MAM OVA CHOL CORA JOVA MAYA MAYO ROTO SERI TECA TECO XOVA AZTEC CHIZO CHORA HUABI HUAVE KAMIA NAHUA OPATA OTOMI YAQUI ZOQUE CAHITA CHOCHO CONCHO EUDEVE KILIWI NEVOME OTONIA PAKAWA TARASC TOLTEC ZOTZIL ACOLHUA AKWAALA AMISHGO CHATINO CHINCHA CHINIPA CHONTAL COTONAM COUHIMI GUASAVE HUASTEC HUAXTEC MAZATEC MISTECA MIXTECA NAYARIT SINALOA TEGUIMA TEHUECO TEPANEC TEPEHUA TZENTAL TZOTZIL ZACATEC ZAPOTEC CHANABAL CHAPANEC CHUCHONA COLOTLAN COMANITO CONICARI GUASAPAR HUASTECO IRRITILA JACALTEC JANAMBRE LACANDON LAGUNERO TARUMARI TECPANEC TEXCOCAN TEZCUCAN TOTONACO TZAPOTEC YUCATECO
(OTHER —) GE ITE ONA URO URU YAO AGAZ ANDE ANTA ANTI AUCA BABU CAME CANA CARA CHUJ COTO CUNA DENE DIAU DUIT INCA ITZA IXIL MOJO MOXO MURA MUSO MUZO PEBA PIRO RAMA TAMA TAPE TATU TOBA TRIO TUPI TUPY ULUA ULVA ACROA ARARA ARAUA ARUAC AUETO BAURE BETOI BRAVO BUGRE CAITE CAMPA CANCA CARIB CHANE CHIMU CHITA CHOCO CHOKO CHOLA CHOLO CHONO COCTO COLAN CUEVA DIRIA GUANA GUATO HUARI JAVAH KASKA LENCA MOCOA MOZCA OPATA OYANA PALTA PAMPA PASSE PETEN PINTO PIOJE PIOXE PIPIL POKAN POKOM QUITU SENCI SIUSI SMOOS TAINO UAUPE UMAUA VEJOZ WAURA XINCA YAGUA YAMEO YUNCA YUNGA AGUANO AIMARA AKAVAI AKAWAI AMORUA ANDOKE ANTISI APANTO APARAI APIACA ARAWAK AROACO ATORAI AYMARA BABINE BANIVA BETOYA BORORO BRIBRI BRUNKA CAHETE CAIGUA CANCHI CANELO CARAHO CARAJA CARAYA CARIRI CAUQUI CAVINA CAYAPA CHAIMA CHARCA CHAYMA CHICHA CHISCA CHOCOI CHORTI COCAMA COCOMA COCORA COFANE COLIMA COTOXO CUCAMA CULINO CUMANA DOGRIB DORASK GALIBI GOYANA GUAIMI GUAQUE GUAYMI HUARPE HUBABO IGNERI INCERI IXIAMA JIVARO JUCUNA JUMANA JURUNA KARAYA KEKCHI KUCHIN LENGUA LUCAYO MACUSI MAKUSI MANGUE MANIVA MIRANA MUYSCA NAHANE NASCAN OMAGUA OTOMAC PAPAGO PKOMAM PURUHA QUICHE SABUJA SACCHA SALIBA SALIVA SAMUCU SEKANE SETIBO SIPIBO SUERRE TACANA TAGISH TAHAMI TAMOYO TAPAJO TAPUYA TARUMA TECUNA TICUNA TIMOTE TOTORO TUCANO TUNEBO UIRINA UITOTO VILELA WAIWAI WITOTO WOOLWA YAHGAN YAHUNA YARURO YURUNA ZAPARA ACHAGUA ACKAWOI AKAMNIK ANDAQUI ANGAITE APALAII APINAGE ARECUNA ARHUACO BEOTHUK BILQULA CACHIBO CAINGUA CALIANA CAMACAN CARANGA CARIBAN CARIBEE CARRIER CASHIBO CHARRUA CHIBCHA CHIMANE CHIMILA CHIRINO CHONCHO CHOROTE CHUMULU CHUNCHO CHURAPA CHUROYA CIBONEY CJACOGO COROADO FRENTON FUEGIAN GITKSAN GOAHIVO GOAJIRA GUAHIVO GUARANI GUARAYO GUARANY GUARRAU GUARUAN GUATUSO GUETARE HUANUCO HUATUSO ITONAMA JACUNDA JICAQUE KALIANA KOPRINO KULIANA LUCAYAN MAIPURE MISKITO MONGOYO MORCOTE NICARAO PAMPERO PAYAGUA PEDRAZA PIARROA POKOMAM PUELCHE PUQUINA QUECHUA QUEKCHI

RANQUEL SARIGUE SATIENO
SHUSWAP SINSIGA SIRIONE
TAHLTAN TALUCHE TALUHET
TAMANAC TARIANA TARRABA
TAYRONA TELEMBI TIMBIRA
TIRRIBI TSONECA UARAYCU
UCAYALE VOYAVAI WOYAWAY
YUSTAGA ZUTUHIL AGUARUNA
AHOUSAHT AKIYENIK ALACALUF
AMAHUACA APOLISTA ARAQUAJU
AWISHIRA BOTOCUDO CAINGANG
CALINAGO CANAMARY CANOEIRO
CAQUETIO CARIBISI CARIJONA
CARIPUNA CAYUBABA CHAMBOIA
CHANDALA CHAVANTE CHIQUITO
CHIRIANA COLORADO COMIAKIN
CONCHUCU CORABECA
CUSTENAU GUAYAQUI
GUAYCURU JAVITERO KANHOBAL
KLASKINO LOROKOTO MACARANI
MAYORUNA MISSKITO MOSQUITO
NIQUIRAN OCHOZOMA OROTINAN
PACAVARA PALENQUE
PARUKUTU PINALENO POIGUARA
POKONCHI POPOLOCO POTYUARA
PUPULUCA QUATSINO QUERENDY
QUIMBAYA SHIRIANA SNONOWAS
SUBTIABA TADOUSAC TAPACURA
TENAKTAK TOCOBAGA
TOROMONA TSATTINE
TUMUPASA UAREKENA
URUKUENA USPANTEC
YURUCARE
(SPANISH-AMERICAN —) CHOLO

INDIANA
CAPITAL: INDIANAPOLIS
COLLEGE: BALL BETHEL DEPAUW
GOSHEN MARIAN PURDUE
WABASH
COUNTY: JAY CASS CLAY KNOX
OWEN PIKE RUSH VIGO BOONE
FLOYD WELLS JASPER TIPTON
DAVIESS PULASKI
INDIAN: MIAMI HAWNEE
LAKE: MONROE MANITOU
WAWASEE MICHIGAN
NATIVE: HOOSIER
RIVER: OHIO WHITE WABASH
STATE BIRD: CARDINAL
STATE FLOWER: PEONY
STATE TREE: TULIP
TOWN: GARY PERU PAOLI VEVAY
ALBION ANGOLA BRAZIL
GOSHEN JASPER KOKOMO
MUNCIE SHOALS WABASH

INDIAN BEECH KURUNJ
INDIAN BREAD TUCKAHOE
INDIAN CORN KANGA MAIZE
CHOLUM JAGONG MEALIES
INDIAN FIG SABRA
INDIAN FISH FLATFISH
INDIAN GOOSEBERRY EMBLIC
INDIAN HEMP KEF KIF SANA
DAGGA SABZI AMYROOT
DOGBANE
INDIANIAN HOOSIER
INDIAN JALAP TURPETH
INDIAN LICORICE JEQUIRITY
INDIAN MADDER MUNJEET
INDIAN MALLOW SIDA DAGGA
PIEPRINT

INDIAN MILLET JONDLA
INDIAN MULBERRY AL AAL ACH
ALROOT
INDIAN PIPE FITROOT EYEBRIGHT
WAXFLOWER
INDIAN POKE ITCHWEED
INDIAN RED BOLE
INDIAN SHOT ALIIPOE
INDIAN TOBACCO GAGROOT
LOBELIA PUKEWEED SOURBUSH
INDIAN YELLOW PIOURY PURREE
INDIC (— LANGUAGE) URDU VEDIC
INDICATE RUN SAY BODY CITE
HINT LOOK MAKE MARK READ
SHOW ARGUE INDEX INFER POINT
PROVE SPEAK ALLUDE ATTEST
BETRAY DENOTE DESIGN EVINCE
FINGER IMPORT NOTIFY REVEAL
BESPEAK BETOKEN CONNOTE
DECLARE DISPLAY PORTEND
SIGNIFY SPECIFY ADMONISH
ANNOUNCE DECIPHER DISCLOSE
EVIDENCE MANIFEST OUTPOINT
REGISTER SIGNALIZE
(— BY SOUNDING) STRIKE
(— WILLINGNESS) AGREE
INDICATION BECK CLEW CLUE
HINT LEAD MARK NOTE SHOW
SIGN CURVE INDEX PROOF SCENT
TOKEN AUGURY BEACON INDICE
REMARK SAMPLE SIGNAL
AUSPICE MENTION PROFFER
SYMPTOM ALLUSION ARGUMENT
EVIDENCE MONITION MONUMENT
NOTATION SIGNANCE TELLTALE
(— OF APPROVAL) CACHET
(— OF CONTROL) COLLAR
(— OF LIGHT) AUREOLE
(— OF OFFICE) SEAL
(OBSCURE —) SHADOW
(VAGUE —) GLIMMER
(PL.) INDICIA
INDICATOR PIN HAND SIGN FLOAT
INDEX LITMUS SHOWER STYLUS
TARGET LACMOID POINTER
DETECTOR TELLTALE
(— OF BALANCE) COCK
(— OF HOUR) GNOMON
(ECONOMIC —) LAGGER LEADER
INDICIA POSTAGE
INDICT DITE CRIME PANEL ACCUSE
ATTACH CHARGE INDITE
ARRAIGN ARTICLE IMPEACH
TROUNCE WARRANT
INDICTMENT CHARGE DITTAY
INDIFFERENCE APATHY PHLEGM
ATARAXY DISDAIN ATARAXIA
COLDNESS EASINESS FROIDEUR
INDIFFERENT COLD COOL DEAD
DRAM EASY SOSO ALOOF BLASE
EQUAL SOBER CASUAL DEGAGE
FRIGID SUPINE CALLOUS
LANGUID NEUTRAL DETACHED
LISTLESS LUKEWARM MEDIOCRE
RECKLESS SUPERIOR UPSITTEN
APATHIC
INDIFFERENTIST POLITIC
INDIFFERENTLY DRYLY HUMDRUM
INDIGENCE NEED WANT PENURY
BEGGARY POVERTY TENUITY
INDIGENE ENDEMIC
INDIGENOUS DESI
NATIVE DOMESTIC

HOMEBORN ABORIGINAL
INDIGENT POOR BEGGARLY
INDIGESTIBLE STUDGY
INDIGESTION APEPSY APEPSIA
DYSPEPSY
INDIGNANT ANGRY WROTH
ANNOYED UPTIGHT INCENSED
INDIGNATION IRE ANGER WRATH
DESPITE DISDAIN DUDGEON
JEALOUSY
INDIGNITY CUT SLUR SCORN
INSULT SLIGHT AFFRONT
OFFENCE CONTUMELY
INDIGO ANIL NILL SHOOFLY
(PREF.) INDI(CO)
INDIRECT SLY SIDE DEVIOUS
OBLIQUE CIRCULAR GLANCING
OVERHEAD OVERWART SIDELONG
SIDEWAYS SIDEWISE
ROUNDABOUT
(— WAY) AMBAGE
INDIRECTION CIRCUITY
INDIRECTLY SECONDHAND
INDIRECTNESS OBLIQUITY
INDISCREET RASH HASTY SILLY
WITLESS CARELESS HEEDLESS
INDISCRETION FOLLY FRÉDAINE
INDISCRIMINATE MIXED MINGLED
SWEEPING PROMISCUOUS
INDISCRIMINATELY PELLMELL
INDISPENSABLE NEEDFUL
CRITICAL
INDISPOSED ILL MEAN SICK ILLISH
UNWELL
INDISPOSITION AIL BRASH
MALADY AILMENT SICKNESS
(— TO MOTION) INERTIA
INDISPUTABLE SURE CERTAIN
EVIDENT MANIFEST POSITIVE
APODICTIC
INDISTINCT DIM DARK DULL HAZY
FAINT FUZZY INNER LIGHT MISTY
MUDDY SHADY THICK VAGUE
BLEARY CLOUDY DREAMY
INWARD SLURRY WOOLLY
BLEARED BLURRED OBSCURE
SHADOWY UNCLEAR NEBULOUS
(— IN UTTERANCE) CHOKING
INDISTINCTNESS BLUR
CONFUSION
INDITE PEN DITE DRAW
INDIVIDUAL GEE MAN ONE HEAD
SORT UNIT BEING MONAD THING
PROPER SINGLE SPIRIT VERSAL
APOMICT ATAVISM AZYGOTE
BIONTIC DIPLOID EIDETIC ISOLATE
MONADIC NUMERIC SEVERAL
SPECIAL EVERYONE IDENTITY
SEPARATE SINGULAR SOLITARY
SPECIMEN PERSONAGE
(COLOR-BLIND —) MONOCHROMAT
(COUNTRIFIED —) HOBNAIL
(DESPICABLE —) HEEL
(DULL —) BOEOTIAN
(FOOLISH —) SOP
(HAUGHTY —) POT
(IDENTICAL —) CLONE
(IMMATURE —) ADULTOID
(IMPUDENT —) BOLDFACE
(INDEPENDENT —) MAVERICK
(IRRITABLE —) SNAPPER
(LEADING —) KEY
(MOSAIC —) GYNANDER

(MUTANT —) SALTANT
(PHYSIOLOGICAL —) BION
(PROSAIC —) PHILISTINE
(ROUGH-LOOKING —) BOHUNK
(SKILLED —) ADEPT
(SLOVENLY —) GROBIAN
(STUPID —) HOBBIL
(TRICKY —) BILK
(UNDERSIZED —) KIT KITT
(WINGED —) ALATE
(YOUNG —) KID
(PL.) FRY
INDIVIDUALITY KA SEITY QUALITY
SELFDOM HECCEITY IDENTITY
SELFHOOD
INDIVIDUALIZE ATOMIZE
INDIVIDUALLY APART APIECE
SINGLY PROPERLY
INDIVIDUATION AHANKARA
INDIVISIBLE PUNCTUAL
INDO-CHINESE SERIFORM
INDOCTRINATE BRIEF INSTRUCT
INDO-EUROPEAN ARIAN ARYAN
JAPHETIC
INDOLE KETOLE
INDOLENCE SLOTH LANGUOR
IDLESHIP MUSARDRY SLUGGING
(— PERSONIFIED) LAURENCE
LAWRENCE
INDOLENT IDLE LAZY FAINT INERT
SWEER DROWSY OTIOSE SUPINE
DRONISH LABGUID WILSOME
FAINEANT INACTIVE LISTLESS
LOUNGING SLOTHFUL SLUGGISH
PICKTOOTH
INDO-MALAYAN (— TREE) SUPA

INDONESIA
CAPITAL: DJAKARTA
COIN: RUPIAH
GULF: BONE TOLO TOMINI
ISLAND: ALOR BALI BURU JAVA
CERAM IRIAN SUMBA WETAR
BAWEAN BORNEO BUTUNG
FLORES KOMODO LOMBOK
MADURA PELENG CELEBES
SALAJAR SUMATRA SUMBAWA
SULAWESI
ISLAND GROUP: EWAB SUNDA
BANJAK NATUNA ANAMBAS
MOLUCCA TABELAN SABALANA
LAKE: RANAU TOWUTI
LANGUAGE: BAHASA MALAYAN
MOUNTAIN: BULU NIUT RAJA
DEMPO MURJO NIAPA LEUSER
SLAMET MENJAPA OGOAMAS
SAMOSIR KATOPASA KERINTJI
MAHAMERU RINDJANI
TALAKMAU
MOUNTAINS: MULLER BARISAN
QUARLES SCHWANER
NATIVE: BUGI
PROVINCE: RIAU ATJEH DJAMBI
MALUKU LAMPUNG BENGKULU
RIVER: HARI MUSI DIGUL KAJAN
PAWAN BARITO KAMPAR
KAPUAS MAHAKAM
SEA: JAVA BANDA CERAM TIMOR
FLORES ARAFURA CELEBES
STRAIT: SUNDA LOMBOK
MAKASSAR
TOWN: PALU MEDAN MALANG
MANADO BANDUNG KENDARI

MAKASAR SEMARANG SURABAJA PALEMBANG SURAKARTA
VOLCANO: GEDE AGUNG DEMPO RAUNG MARAPI MERAPI SINILA SLAMET SUNDORO TAMBORA KERINTJE RINDJANI
WEIGHT: CATTY OUNCE THAIL

INDONESIAN NESIOT SADANG
INDOORS WITHIN
INDRA SAKKA SAKRA
INDUBITABLE SURE EVIDENT APPARENT MANIFEST UNIVOCAL
INDUCE GET DRAW LEAD MOVE URGE WORK ARGUE BRIBE BRING CAUSE IMPEL INFER TEMPT WEIGH ADDICT ADJURE ALLURE ENGAGE ENTICE IMPORT INCITE INVITE OBTAIN REDUCE SEDUCE SUBORN ACTUATE PREVAIL PROCURE PROVOKE SOLICIT MOTIVATE PERSUADE WIREDRAW
(— BY BRIBERY) FIX
INDUCEMENT MOTIVE REASON FEATURE PERSUASION
INDUCT STALL INSTAL INITIATE
INDUCTANCE HENRY
INDUCTION EPAGOGE
INDULGE PET BABY CADE CANT FEED GLUT ALLOW HUMOR JOLLY SPOIL TUTOR WALLY WREAK COCKER FOSTER PAMPER PETTLE DEBAUCH GRATIFY
(— IN PRIDE) PRIDE
(— TO EXCESS) PAMPER DEBAUCH SURFEIT
INDULGED CADE
INDULGENCE LAW BINGE FAVOR FOLLY MERCY SPREE EXCESS INDULT PARDON PATENT JUBILEE QUIENAL SURFEIT COURTESY DELICACY EASINESS GLUTTONY POCULARY
(SEXUAL —) LECHERY
INDULGENT FOND GOOD MEEK MILD SPOONY LENIENT TOLERANT
INDURATE HARDEN INDURE
INDURATED SCLEROID SCLEROUS
INDURATION SCLEROMA
INDUSTRIOUS BUSY DEEDY EIDENT STEADY OPEROSE PAINFUL DILIGENT SEDULOUS VIRTUOUS WORKSOME
INDUSTRY TOIL LABOR SCREEN VIRTUE CERAMICS SEDULITY
INDWELLING IMMANENT INHERENT
INE (WIFE OF —) AETHELBURH
INEBRIATE SOUSE EBRIATED
INEBRIATED DRUNK DRINKY
INEFFACEABLE INBURNT INDELIBLE
INEFFECTIVE DUD WEAK CLUMSY DREEPY FLABBY FUTILE FLACCID HALTING STERILE BUMBLING
INEFFECTIVELY ILL BADLY FEEBLY
INEFFECTUAL WAN DEAD IDLE TAME VAIN VOID JERKY FUTILE SPINDLY USELESS BOOTLESS FAINEANT FIDDLING NUGATORY
INEFFICIENT ILL LAME POOR

CLUMSY DOLESS ROTTEN UNABLE SLOUCHY USELESS FECKLESS HANDLESS
INELEGANT RUDE HOYDEN AWKWARD
INELOQUENT WANMOL
INEPT INAPT ABSURD AWKWARD FOOTLESS MALADROIT
INEPTITUDE PIFFLE
INEQUAL ROUGH
INEQUALITY ODDS CAHOT ANOMALY EVECTION IMPARITY NUTATION
INEQUITABLE HARD
INERADICABLE LASTING INDELIBLE PERMANENT
INERT DEAD DULL LAZY SLOW HEAVY NOBLE SULKY LEADEN SODDEN STUPID SUPINE TORPID PASSIVE INACTIVE INDOLENT LIFELESS SLOTHFUL SLUGGISH STAGNANT THEWLESS THOWLESS
INERTIA TAMAS
INESCAPABLE DEAD NECESSARY
INESTIMABLE SUMLESS PRICELESS
INEVITABILITY FINALITY
INEVITABLE DUE SURE DIRECT CERTAIN FATEFUL
INEXACT FREE ROUGH CLOUDY
INEXHAUSTIBLE INFINITE
INEXORABLE STERN STONY STRICT RIGOROUS
INEXPEDIENCY IMPOLICY
INEXPEDIENT UNWISE
INEXPENSIVE LOW CHEAP REASONABLE
INEXPERIENCED RAW PUNY CRUDE FRESH YOUNG UNSEEN KITLING STRANGE INEXPERT INSOLENT PRENTICE UNTRADED
INEXPERT ILL RUDE CRUDE GREEN SIMPLE
INEXPLICABLE FELL
INFAMOUS BASE RUDDY BLOODY NOTOUR ODIOUS BLEEDING FLAGRANT NIDERING SHAMEFUL NEFARIOUS OPPROBRIOUS
INFAMY STAIN BAFFLE DEFAME SHONDE DISHONOR IGNOMINY OPPROBRIUM
INFANCY CRADLE BABYHOOD
INFANT BABE BABY TINY WEAN CHILD MINOR PREMIE CHRISOM MILKSOP PREEMIE BALDLING BANTLING
(NAKED —) SCUDDY
(NEWLY-BORN —) NEONATUS
(VORACIOUS -) KILLCROP
INFANTILE BABYISH
INFANTRY FOOT FANTERIE FOOTFOLK
INFANTRYMAN ASKAR ZOUAVE DOGFACE DRAGOON DOUGHBOY PIOUPIOU SOREFOOT VOETGANGER
INFATUATE FOOL ASSOT BESOT
INFATUATED MAD FOND GONE ASSOT CRAZY DOTTY ENTETE ENGOUEE FOOLISH BESOTTED
INFATUATION ATE PASH RAVE CRUSH FOLLY BEGUIN
(TRANSIENT —) CRAZE
(SUFF.) (— FOR) MANE MANIA(C)

(— WITH) ITIS
INFECT SMIT TAINT CANKER DEFILE EMPEST ENTACH INFEST POISON CORRUPT DISEASE POLLUTE SMITTLE CONTAMINATE
INFECTED FUNGUSED
(NOT —) BLAND
INFECTION COLD DOSE SMIT FELON TAINT FUNGUS
INFECTIOUS TAKING SMITTLE CATCHING SMITABLE SMITTING VIRULENT
INFEFTMENT SASINE
INFER DRAW PICK TAKE GUESS JUDGE DECIDE DEDUCE DEDUCT DERIVE DIVINE GATHER INDUCE REASON COLLECT INCLUDE PRESUME SURMISE CONCLUDE CONSTRUE
INFERENCE EDUCT SEQUEL ANALOGY SEQUELA ILLATION SEQUENCE SEQUITUR OBSERVATION PRESUMPTION
INFERIOR BAD BUM DOG ILL JAY LOW OFF SAD EVIL LESS MEAN POOR PUNK SLIM SOUR WAFF BASER BAUCH BELOW CHEAP DOGGY GROSS LOUSY LOWER PETTY PLAIN SCALY SCRUB WORRY BEHIND CAGMAG COARSE COMMON CRAPPY FEEBLE FEMALE IMPURE LESSER MEASLY PALTRY PEDARY PUISNE PUISNY ROTTEN SECOND SHABBY SHODDY WOODEN BADDISH CRIPPLE HUMBLER NAGGISH POPULAR SCRUBBY SUBJECT ABNORMAL ANTERIOR DEROGATE ORDINARY PARAVAIL TERRIBLE
(PREF.) DEMI INFRA SUB
(SUFF.) ASTER EEN
(— ONE) LING
INFERIORITY LESSNESS MEANNESS
INFERNAL BLACK AVERNAL BLASTED ETERNAL HELLISH SATANIC SHEOLIC STYGIAN CHTHONIC DAMNABLE DEVILISH PLUTONIC PLUTONIAN
INFERTILE DEAD DEAF DOUR LEAN POOR THIN CLEAR STERILE
INFEST COE VEX BESET INFECT PESTER PLAGUE OVERRUN TORMENT
INFESTATION SCALE PLAGUE STRIKE MYIASIS LOAIASIS PEDICULOSIS
INFESTED MITY BLOWN BROOD BUGGY FLUKY FLUKED GRUBBY HAUNTED FLYBLOWN
INFIDEL DEIST KAFIR GIAOUR PAYNIM ATHEIST SARACEN SKEPTIC AGNOSTIC MISCREANT MISBELIEVER
INFIDELITY PERFIDY ADULTERY TRAHISON
INFIELD INTOWN DIAMOND
INFILTRATE FILTER CRETIFY COLONIZE
INFILTRATION SEEPAGE ADIPOSIS SATURATION
INFINITE CHAOS COSMIC ENDLESS ETERNAL IMMENSE
INFINITENESS ETERNITY

INFINITESIMAL PUNCTUAL
INFINITIVE SUPINE VERBID
(FRENCH —) ETRE
INFINITY OLAM ANANTA ETERNITY
INFIRM LAME WEAK ANILE CRAZY CRONK SHAKY CRANKY FEEBLE SICKLY UNFIRM UNSURE CASALTY CRAICHY DOWLESS DWAIBLE FRAGILE INVALID SAPLESS UNFEARY DODDERED FIRMLESS INSECURE RESOLUTE UNSTRONG
INFIRMITY WOE CRAZE DOTAGE FOIBLE UNHEAL DISEASE FAILING FRAILTY UNMIGHT DEBILITY SICKNESS WEAKNESS
INFIX INLAY INSET ENGRAVE IMPLANT INGRAIN
INFIXED INHERENT
INFLAME BURN FIRE GOAD HEAT STIR ANGER BLAIN FLAME SCALD SHAME AROUSE ENAMOR EXCITE FESTER IGNITE INCEND KINDLE MADDEN RANKLE EMBRASE FLUSTER INCENSE ESCHAUFE
INFLAMED RED ANGRY FIERY ABLAZE FRETTY TORRID FLAGRANT
INFLAMMABLE FIERY ARDENT TOUCHY PICEOUS TINDERY
INFLAMMATION ACNE FIRE ANGER FELON GLEET SCALD SEBEL AGNAIL ANCOME BLIGHT CANKER DEFLUX GREASE IRITIS CATARRH CECITIS CHAFING COLITIS COXITIS FISTULA GONITIS ILEITIS QUITTOR SUNBURN ADENITIS ANGIITIS AORTITIS BURSITIS CHILITIS CYCLITIS CYSTITIS SHINGLES
(SUFF.) ITIS
INFLATE HOVE HUFF KITE PLIM PUFF BLOAT BOLNE HEAVE SWELL DILATE EMBOSS EXPAND HUFFLE INBLOW TUMEFY BLADDER BOMBAST DISTEND FORBLOW OUTSWELL SUFFLATE
INFLATED TRIG BLOWN FLOWN GASSY PUFFY TUMID TURGID BOMBAST BULLATE FUSTIAN OROTUND STILTED SWOLLEN TURGENT BLADDERY OUTBLOWN TOPLOFTY TUMOROUS VANITOUS BOMBASTIC OVERBLOWN PLETHORIC
INFLATION FLATUS CADENCE TYMPANY
INFLECT COMPARE DECLINE
INFLECTION SIGN TONE ARSIS ACCENT FLEXION LATINISM MODULATION
INFLECTIONAL FORMAL
INFLEXIBILITY ACAMPSIA
INFLEXIBLE ACID DOUR FIRM HARD IRON EAGER SOLID STERN STIFF STONY STOUR SEVERE STRICT STUFFY ADAMANT RESTIVE GRANITIC IRONCLAD OBDURATE PREFRACT RESOLUTE RIGOROUS STIFFISH STUBBORN ADAMANTINE
INFLICT DO ADD PUT SET GIVE SEND INFER YIELD IMPOSE RAMROD STRIKE

(— CHASTISEMENT) WREAK
(— HURT) BRUISE
(— INJURY) AGGRIEVE
(— PAIN) LAY CHASTISE
INFLORESCENCE CHAT CYME
AMENT ARROW BRUSH SPIKE
UMBEL CORYMB FLOWER RACEME
SPADIX TASSEL BOSTRYX
PANICLE THYRSIS CYATHIUM
FASCICLE NUCAMENT
INFLOW INSET AFFLUX INCOME
INFLUX INCOURSE
INFLOWING AFFLUENT
INFLUENCE IN WIN BEND BIAS
COAX DRAG DRAW HAND HANK
HEFT LEAD MOVE PULL PUSH
RULE SUCK SWAY BRIBE CHARM
CLOUT COLOR ENACT FORCE
GRACE IMPEL MOYEN POWER
REACH SPELL VAPOR VOGUE
WEIGH AFFECT ALLURE CREDIT
EFFECT GOVERN IMPORT INDUCE
INFLOW INFLUX MOTIVE OBSESS
PONDUS SALUTE SHADOW
STROKE WEIGHT ACTUATE
ATTINGE ATTRACT BEARING
BEWITCH BLARNEY BOSSDOM
CAPTURE CONCUSS CONTROL
DISPUTE ENCHANT GRAVITY
IMPRINT INCLINE INSPIRE
MASTERY SUASION TENDRIL
DOMINION HEGEMONY INTEREST
LEVERAGE MEDICINE PRESTIGE
SANCTION STRENGTH CAPTIVATE
(— BY GIFTS) GREASE
(— CORRUPTLY) BRIBE
(— OF GODS) MANA
(— OF THE STARS) BLAS
(— UNREASONABLY) OBSESS
(ATTEMPT TO —) JAWBONE
(BENIGN —) UNCTION
(CONTROLLING —) SWAY
(CORRUPTING —) SMOUCH
SMUTCH
(DEPRESSING —) CHILL
(DIABOLICAL —) DEVILDOM
(DISRUPTIVE —) GREMLIN
(DOMINANT —) GENIUS STREAM
(DULLING —) DAMPER
(ELEVATING —) LIFT
(HARMFUL —) UPAS GRUDGE
(INJURIOUS —) RUST
(MALEVOLENT —) DISASTER
(MALIGN —) TAKING
(PERNICIOUS —) BALE BLAST
(SINISTER —) MALICE
(SOOTHING —) SALVE
(SURROUNDING —) AIR AMBIENCE
(UNDER — OF ALCOHOL OR DRUGS)
ZONKED
INFLUENCING INFUSIVE
INFLUENTIAL BIG GRAVE
POWERFUL
INFLUENZA FLU LEUMA GRIPPE
PINKEYE
INFLUX STORM INCOME INFLOW
INRUSH ILLAPSE
(— IN A MINE) COURSE
(— OF TIDE) INSET
INFOLD WRAP IMPLY TWINE
EMPLOY INWRAP ENVELOP
INVOLVE CONVOLVE
INFORM KEN BEEF BLOW FINK

NOSE POST SHOP SHOW TELL
WARN WISE LEARN PEACH
ADVISE ASSURE DELATE DETECT
NOTIFY PREACH SNITCH WITTER
APPRISE EDUCATE IMPEACH
INSENSE PARTAKE POSSESS
RESOLVE SIGNIFY SUGGEST
ACQUAINT DENOUNCE INFORMED
INSTRUCT SPARSILE
INFORMAL BREEZY CASUAL
CHATTY COMMON FOLKSY
TWEEDY INTIMATE SLIPSHOD
SOCIABLE NEGLIGENT OFFICIOUS
INFORMANT AUTHOR INFORMER
SYCOPHANT
INFORMATION AIR GEN OIL WIT
CLEW CLUE DOPE INFO LORE
NEWS NOTE TALE WIRE WORD
DATUM GRIFF SCOOP SKILL
ADVICE INSIDE LIGHTS NOTICE
APPRISE PEMICAN READOUT
TIDINGS WITTING BRIEFING
NOTITION PEMMICAN
(— ON VIDEO SCREEN) DISPLAY
(BODY OF —) DIGEST
(INCIDENTAL —) SIDELIGHT
(SECRET —) ARCANUM
(SUFF.) ANA IANA
INFORMED UP HEP WISE AWARE
WITTY KNOWING LEARNED
INFORMER FINK NARK NOSE PIMP
SPIV STAG RUSTY SNEAK SPLIT
BEAGLE CANARY FINGER SETTER
SNITCH TELLER DELATOR
STOOLIE TANQUAM APPROVER
PROMOTER SQUAWKER
SQUEAKER SQUEALER TELLTALE
INFORTUNE MARS SATURN
INFRACTION BREACH OFFENCE
TRESPASS
INFRARED ULTRARED
INFREQUENCY SELDOMCY
INFREQUENT RARE SELDOM
FUGITIVE UNCOMMON
INFRINGE IMPOSE INVADE TRENCH
IMPINGE INFRACT INTRUDE
ENCROACH REFRINGE TRESPASS
INFRINGEMENT FOUL BREACH
TRESPASS VIOLENCE
INFRINGER PIRATE
INFULA FANON LABEL LAPPET
HEADBAND
INFUNDIBULUM FUNNEL PAVILION
INFURIATE ENRAGE ENFELON
INFUSE DRAW MASK IMBUE IMMIT
SPOIL STEEP AERATE AERIFY
IMMISS INFLOW INFORM INFUND
INVEST LEAVEN BREATHE DISTILL
ENGRAIN IMPLANT INFOUND
INSPIRE INSTILL SUFFUSE
SATURATE
(— TEA) TRACK
(— WITH HATRED) TURN
INFUSED SHOT
INFUSION SHADE CARDIN INCOME
TISANE HORDEATE
(— OF MALT) WORT GROUT
(BITTER —) RUE
INFUSORIAN LEPOCYTE
INGA GUAVA
INGATE GATE LEDGE TEDGE
INGATHERING HARVEST
INGENIOUS SLY CUTE FAST FEAT

FINE ACUTE SHARP SMART WITTY
ADROIT BRAINY CLEVER CRAFTY
DAEDAL GIFTED KNACKY PRETTY
QUAINT SUBTLE CUNNING
POLITIC SKILLFUL
INGENUITY ART WIT ENGINE
ADDRESS COMPASS ARTIFICE
CONTOISE INDUSTRY QUENTISE
INGENUOUS FREE FRANK NAIVE
PLAIN CANDID HONEST SUBTLE
ARTLESS NATURAL SINCERE
INNOCENT
INGENUOUSNESS NAIVETE
INGEST EAT INCEPT ENGLOBE
SWALLOW
INGESTION SLURP
INGOT GAD SOW WEDGE LINGOT
NIGGOT CROPHEAD
(— OF BRASS) STRIP
(— OF SILVER) SHOE TING SCHUYT
(SILVER —S) SYCEE
(SOAKING —S) HEAT
INGRAIN GRAIN INFUSE ENFLESH
INGRAINED INWORN
INGRATE SNAKE
INGRATIATE FLATTER
INGRATIATING BLAND SILKY
SLEEK SLICK SOAPY SILKEN
SMOOTH
INGRATITUDE UNTHANK
INGREDIENT FACTOR AMALGAM
BINDING ELEMENT ADJUVANT
(ACTIVE —) ANIMA
(FUNDAMENTAL —) BASIS
(FUSIBLE —) BOND
(MAIN —) BASE
INGRESS ENTRY ENTRANCE
INGROWTH APODEMA
INGUEN GROIN
INHABIT BIG WIN WON COVER
DWELL HABIT OCCUPY BEDWELL
INDWELL POSSESS POPULATE
INHABITANT INMATE BURGHER
CITIZEN DENIZEN DWELLER
PEOPLER BORDERER CONFINER
DEMESMAN HABITANT INCOLANT
INHOLDER
(— OF ALASKA) SOURDOUGH
(— OF BORDER REGION) MARCHER
(— OF CITY) CIT CITIZEN
(— OF INDIA) BHARATA
(— OF JUNGLE) JUNGLI
(— OF SWISS ALPS) GRISON
(— OF TORRID ZONE) ASCIAN
(— OF VIRGINIA) COOHEE
(— OF WISCONSIN) BADGER
(EARTH —) TERRAN
(PL.) SIDE WARE
(SUFF.) COLA ITE OT OTE
INHABITING
(SUFF.) COLE COLINE COLOUS
INHALATION SNUFF BREATH
(PREF.) ANEM(O)
INHALE DRAW TAKE SMOKE SNIFF
SNUFF ATTRACT BREATHE
INHAUST INSPIRE RESPIRE
ASPIRATE
(— A DRUG) SNORT
(PREF.) INSPIRO
INHALER SNIFTER
INHARMONIOUS ABSURD RUGGED
ABSONANT
INHERE CONSIST INEXIST

INHERENCE INBEING
INHERENT KIND INBORN INNATE
INWARD NATIVE PROPER INGENIT
HABITUAL IMMANENT INTEGRAL
INTERNAL RESIDENT
INHERIT HEIR SUCCEED
INHERITANCE KIND ENTAIL
HEIRDOM HEIRSHIP HEREDITY
HERITAGE LANDFALL VACANTIA
(— OF CATTLE) ERF
(PARTICULATE —) MENDELISM
INHERITED INBORN INNATE
CONGENITAL
(SUFF.) CLINOUS CLINY
INHIBIT COOP CURB SNUB CRIMP
DETER FORBID STIFLE SUPPRESS
INHIBITED COLD
INHIBITION AKINESIS
INHIBITOR PARGYLINE
PHENELZINE
INHIBITORY COLYTIC
INHOSPITABLE STERN DESERT
INHUMAN FELL CRUEL BRUTAL
FIERCE IMMANE SAVAGE BESTIAL
MANLESS DEVILISH KINDLESS
INHUMANE WANTON
INHUMANITY CRUELTY
INHUME BURY INTER ENTOMB
INIMICAL BAD FROSTY HOSTILE
INIQUITOUS ILL DARK WRONG
SINFUL WICKED NEFARIOUS
INIQUITY SIN EVIL VICE CRIME
GUILT DARKNESS MISCHIEF
INITIAL LETTER VIRGIN ASPIREE
PRINCIPAL
(INTERWOVEN —S) CIPHER
(PL.) PERFINS
INITIATE HEAD MYST OPEN ADEPT
ADMIT BEGIN BREAK ENTER
EPOPT FOUND START GROUND
INDUCE INDUCT INVENT LAUNCH
MYSTES ORPHIC BAPTIZE INSTALL
INSTATE OPERATE ORPHEAN
SYMMIST YTIGGER COMMENCE
ESOTERIC INCHOATE ORIGINATE
INITIATION DIKSHA OPENING
ENTRANCE
(— OF GROWTH) BUDBREAK
INITIATIVE PEP LEAD GETUP
ACTION AMBITION GUMPTION
OVERTURE
INJECT DRIVE IMMIT
(— DRUGS) MAINLINE
INJECTION JAG HYPO SHOT
BOOSTER CLYSTER INSERTION
INJUDICIOUS UNWISE
INJUDICIOUSNESS ACRISY
INJUNCTION HEST BEHEST
CHARGE IMPOSE RUBRIC BIDDING
DICTATE EXPRESS MANDATE
PRECEPT
INJURE DO GAS ILL MAR BURN
CHEW DERE ENVY GALL HARM
HURT MAUL TEAR TEEN WERD
ABUSE BLAST CRAZE DIRTY
MISDO RIFLE SCALD SHEND
SMITE SPOIL STEER WOUND
WRONG BRUISE DAMAGE DEFACE
DEFECT DEPAIR GRIEVE HINDER
IMPAIR INJURY MANGLE NOBBLE
PUNISH RANKLE SCATHE SCOTCH
STRAIN AFFLICT AFFRONT
CONTUSE DAMNIFY DESPITE

FORWORK MISBEDE TERRIFY
AGGRIEVE DISASTER DISSERVE
FORSLACK IMPERISH INTERESS
MISCHIEF MISGUIDE MUTILATE
PREJUDGE SPURGALL
(— BY ASPERSION) SPATTER
(— BY FALSE REPORT) SLANDER
(— BY GLANCE OF BASILISK) STRIKE
(— BY TREADING UPON) FITTER
(— SCENT) STAIN
(— SERIOUSLY) DO KILL SPOIL
(— SLIGHTLY) ANNOY
(— THE BACK) CHINK
(— WITH GRENADE) FRAG
(SEVERELY —) WASTE
INJURED HURT LESED BLASTED
INJURIOUS BAD ILL EVIL NOCENT
NOYANT NOYFUL SHREWD
ABUSIVE HARMFUL HURTFUL
NOXIOUS SCADDLE DAMAGING
GRIEVOUS SINISTER TORTIOUS
TORTUOUS WRACKFUL
WRONGFUL PERNICIOUS
INJURIOUSLY HEAVILY
INJURY ILL JAM MAR BALE BANE
BURN EVIL HARM HURT JEEL
LOSS RUIN SCAT TEEN TORT
WITE ABUSE BLAME CHAFE
CRUSH GRIEF SCALD SCORE SPITE
SPOIL TOUCH WATHE WRACK
WRONG BREACH BRUISE DAMAGE
DANGER IMPAIR LESION SCATHE
STRAIN STROKE TRAUMA
BEATING DESPITE EXPENSE
OFFENSE OUTRAGE PAYMENT
SCADDLE SCRATCH SURANCE
BUSINESS CASUALTY CREPANCE
INTEREST MISCHIEF NUISANCE
(— OF HORSES) TREAD CREPANCE
(— OF PLANTS) SUNSCALD
(CHIEF —) FOCUS
(SERIOUS —) MAYHEM
INJUSTICE WRONG INJURY
INJURIA UNRIGHT HARDSHIP
INEQUITY
(GROSS —) INIQUITY
INK BEAT COLOR ARNEMENT
ATRAMENT
(PRINTER'S —) CYAN
INK-BALL DABBER PUMPET
INKER SLOSHER
INKING PAD TOMPION
INKLE SPINEL
INKLING HINT ITEM SCENT
GLIMMER GLIMPSE UMBRAGE
INKSTAND STANDISH
INKWELL FOUNT INKSTAND
INKY BLACK ATRAMENTOUS
INLAID PIQUE CONTISE
(— WORK) KOFTGARI
INLAND MAUKA INMORE INWARD
MIDLAND INTERIOR
INLAY PICK PIKE COUCH HATCH
INLET PIQUE SPELL CRUSTA
ENAMEL IMPAVE INDENT NIELLO
TARSIA ENCHASE ENCRUST
INCRUST COMMESSO
INLAYING TARKASHI
INLET ARM BAY CUT GEO RIA VOE
COVE DOCK HOPE MERE SLEW
WICK BAYOU BRACE CHUCK
CREEK FIORD FJORD FLEET
HAVEN LOGAN LOUGH STOMA

ESTERO HARBOR INFALL SLOUGH
TONGUE DOGHOLE INDRAFT
SUCTION CALANQUE SEAPOOSE
(— OF THE SEA) EA
(MUDDY —) SUMP
(TIDAL —) GAP
INLIER WINDOW
INLYING INNERLY
INMATE FISH LODGER TENANT
BEADSMAN DOMESTIC PRISONER
INMOST SECRET RETIRED
INN PUB KHAN STOP VENT ANGEL
FONDA HOTEL MESON TAMBO
VENTA CABACK HARBOR HOSTEL
HOSTRY IMARET POSADA PUBLIC
SHANTY ALBERGE AUBERGE
BOLICHE CAFENEH CAFENET
FONDACO FONDOUK HOSTAGE
LOCANDA OSTERIA SOJOURN
SURAHEE CHOULTRY GASTHAUS
HOSTELRY ORDINARY SERAGLIO
WAYHOUSE ROADHOUSE
INNARDS GIZZARD INWARDS
STUFFING
INNATE BORN KIND INBORN
INBRED CONNATE INGRAIN
NATURAL INSTINCT
(— QUALITY) LARGESS
INNER BEN ENTAL INSIDE INWARD
INWITH MENTAL INTERIOR
INTERNAL PECTORAL
(— LIGHT) SEED
(PREF.) ENT(O) ESO
(— PARTS OF BODY) BATHY
INNER MONGOLIA (CAPITAL OF —)
HOHHOT HUHEHOT
INNERMOST UPPER INMOST
MIDMOST INTIMATE
INNINA ISHTAR
INNING END HAND HEAD FRAME
(PL.) KNOCK WICKET
INNKEEPER HOST DUENA TAPPER
VENTER GOODMAN HOSTESS
HOSTLER PADRONE BONIFACE
(PL.) CAUPONES
INNOCENCE BLUET WHITE
CANDOR PURITY SIMPLICITY
INNOCENT SOT FREE NAIF PURE
CANNY CLEAR NAIVE SEELY SILLY
WHITE CHASTE DOVISH HONEST
SIMPLE CHRISOM LAMBKIN
UPRIGHT ARCADIAN HARMLESS
IGNORANT PASTORAL PRIMROSE
SACKLESS UNGUILTY ZACCHEUS
INNOCUOUS HARMLESS INNOCENT
INNOVATE NOVELIZE
INNOVATION NOVEL NOVELTY
INNOVATOR HERETIC
INNUENDO HINT SLUR SLIPE
INNUMERABLE MYRIAD
NUMBERLESS
INO (BROTHER OF —) POLYDORUS
(FATHER OF —) CADMUS
(HUSBAND OF —) ATHAMAS
(MOTHER OF —) HARMONIA
(SISTER OF —) AGAVE SEMELE
AUTONOE
(SON OF —) LEARCHUS PALAEMON
MELICERTES
INOCULATE SEED PLANT INFUSE
ENGRAFT EQUINATE
INOCULATION JAG
INOCULUM STAR STREAK

INOFFENSIVE HARMLESS
INOPERATIVE OFF DEAD
NUGATORY
INOPPORTUNE UNTIMELY
INORDINATE WILD UNDUE
ENORMOUS
INORGANIC MINERAL
INOSITOL DAMBOSE
INPOURING INFLUX
INQUEST CROWN QUEST ASSIZE
OFFICE INQUIRY
INQUIET UNEASY
INQUILINE GUEST
INQUIRE ASK AXE SEEK QUERY
SPERE DEMAND FRAYNE SEARCH
EXAMINE HEARKEN QUESTION
INQUIRER ASKER QUERENT
INQUIRY PROBE QUERY THANK
TRIAL DEMAND EXAMEN TRACER
DOCIMASY QUESTION RESEARCH
SCRUTINY SPEERING
INQUISITION CUSTOM INQUIRY
QUAESTIO
INQUISITIVE NOSY PEERY PRYING
CURIOUS MEDDLING QUIZZICAL
INROAD RAID BREACH INBREAK
INVASION
INSALUBRIOUS NOXIOUS
INSANE MAD WUD DAFT WOOD
BALMY BATTY BUGGY CRAZY
DIPPY QUEER WRONG CRANKY
LOCOED SCREWY FLIGHTY
FRANTIC FURIOUS LUNATIC
WITLESS BUGHOUSE DEMENTED
DERANGED DISTRACT
INSANITY RAGE CRACK CRAZE
FOLIE MANIA FRENZY LUNACY
MADNESS VESANIA DELIRIUM
DEMENTIA WOODNESS
ACROMANIA PSYCHOSIS
INSATIABLE GREEDY
INSCRIBE DELVE ENTER WRITE
BLAZON DOCKET ENDOSS INDITE
LEGEND LETTER SCRIBE SCRIVE
SCROLL ASCRIBE ENDORSE
ENGROSS DEDICATE DESCRIBE
EMBLAZON ENSCROLL INTITULE
INSCRIBED INWRIT WRITTEN
DESCRIPT
INSCRIPTION HEAD ELOGY
CACHET LEGEND LETTER
ELOGIUM EPIGRAM EPITAPH
MENTION TITULUS WRITING
COLOPHON EPIGRAPH GRAFFITO
INSCRIPT SCRIBING
(— ON ROCK) PETROGLYPH
(— ON TOMBSTONE) ELOGE
ELOGIUM
(3-LETTER —) TRIGRAM
INSCRUTABLE EQUIVOCAL
MYSTERIOUS
INSECT ANT BEE BUG DOR DUN
ELF FLY NIT ANER FLEA GNAT
GOGO GYNE MOTH PELA PEST
PUPA SPIT WASP WETA ZIMB
APHID APHIS BICHO BORER FLYER
GOGGA GUEST IMAGO LOUSE
MINER ROACH SCALE BEETLE
BLIGHT CALLOW CICADA CIXIID
EARWIG EMBIID HAWKER HOPPER
INSTAR MANTIS NITTER PODURA
PSOCID SAPPER SAWFLY THRIPS
VERMIN WALKER WEEVIL

ATTACUS BLATTID BOATMAN
BRUMMER BUZZARD CRAWLER
CREEPER CRICKET CYNIPID
DEALATE DRUMMER EARWORM
FIREBUG FIREFLY GALLFLY
GIRDLER GRAYFLY HEXAPOD
JAPYGID KATYDID PHASMID
SANDBOY SCINIPH SKIPPER
SPECTRE STAINER STYLOPS
TERMITE VAGRANT WEBWORM
ALDERFLY ALKERMES BLACKFLY
BRACONID DIPTERAN FIREBRAT
FULGORID GLOWWORM
HOMOPTER HORNTAIL LACEWING
LECANIUM MEALYBUG
PRONYMPH SEMIPUPA SEXUPARA
SPHECOID STINKBUG STYLOPID
SYMPHILE
(PART OF —) EYE CLAW COXA
WING FEMUR TIBIA CERCUS
LABRUM PALPUS TARSUS
THORAX ABDOMEN ANTENNA
OCELLUS MANDIBLE SPIRACLE
OVIPOSTOR PROTHORAX
TYMPANIUM MESOTHORAX
METATHORAX OVIPOSITER
TROCHANTER
(PREF.) ENTOM(O)
(SUFF.) CORIS
INSECTICIDE DDD DDT DIP CUBE
FLIT MIREX NALED TIMBO ALDRIN
DERRIS ENDRIN RONNEL
CALOMEL ISODRIN LINDANE
MENAZON OVICIDE PHORATE
CHLORDAN CULICIDE DIELDRIN
FENTHION NICOTINE ROTENONE
SCHRADAN ANTRYCIDE
MALATHION PARATHION
PYRETHRUM
INSECTIVORE AGOUTA DESMAN
MOONRAT ALAMIQUI
INSECURE DICKY EEMIS LOOSE
SHAKY INFIRM TICKLE UNFAST
UNSAFE UNSURE CASALTY
INSEMINATE BREED
INSENSATE SURD FATUOUS
INSENSIBILITY DAMP APATHY
STUPOR TORPOR
INSENSIBLE DEAR DULL LOST
NUMB BRUTE DENSE MARBLE
SEARED WOODEN DATELESS
APATHETIC
INSENSITIVE DEAD BLUNT STONY
OBTUSE STUPID BOORISH
INSEPARABLE WRAPPED
INSERT SLIP SPUD STOP BOTCH
DICKY ENROL ENTER FUDGE
IMMIT INFER INFIX INLET INSET
STUFF COLLET GUSSET INWORK
INWEAVE GATEFOLD INTROMIT
SANDWICH SLASHING SUBTRUDE
THROWOUT
(— IN SHOE) CUSHION
(SKIRT —) GORE
(— SURREPTITIOUSLY) FOIST
INSERTION FLOWER BEADING
INSET GODET INSERT
(DRESS —) MOTIF
INSHEATHE EMBOSS
INSIDE IN BEN ATHIN INBYE INNER
INWITH KEYHOLE INTERIOR
(— OF ANGLE BAR) BOSOM
(— OF OUTER EAR) BUR BURR

(PREF.) END(O)

INSIDIOUS SLY SNARY COVERT SUBTLE GUILEFUL

INSIGHT KEN SIGHT APERCU THEORY NOSTRIL

INSIGNIA TYPE ORDER SIGNS COLLAR GEORGE CADUCEUS COMMENDA HERALDRY OPINICUS PONTIFICALS

INSIGNIFICANCE NOTHINGNESS

INSIGNIFICANT NULL POOR PUNY DINKY FOOTY PETIT PETTY POTTY SCRUB SMALL HUMBLE NAUGHT PALTRY PUISNE SIMPLE SLIGHT FOOLISH NAUGHTY NIFLING NOMINAL PELTING PIMPING SCRUBBY TENUOUS TRIVIAL BAUBLING INFERIOR PEDDLING PITIABLE SNIPPING TRIFLING TRIPENNY

INSINCERE FALSE DOUBLE FEIGNED ARTIFICIAL

INSINCERITY ARTIFICE DISGUISE

INSINUATE HINT MINT WIND CRAWL SCREW TWIST ALLUDE GLANCE INFUSE INSTIL WRITHE IMPLANT INNUATE

INSINUATING SNIDE SILKEN SMARMY

INSINUATION HINT INKLING

INSIPID DRY WAW DEAD FADE FLAT FOND FOZY LASH TAME BANAL BAUCH BLAND FLASH INANE PROSY STALE VAPID WALSH WAUGH FLASHY FRIGID JEJUNE SWASHY THREEP WAIRSH WALLOW EXOLETE FATUOUS INSULSE MAWKISH PROSAIC SAPLESS SHILPIT WEARISH WEERISH LIFELESS UNSAVORY WATERISH

INSIST AVER PRESS THREAP CONSIST

(— PEEVISHLY) CRAIK

(— UPON) SOLICIT

INSISTENCE URGENCY INSTANCY

INSISTENT LOUD ADAMANT INSTANT EMPHATIC FRENZIED IMPOSING

INSOLE CUSHION SLIPSOLE

INSOLENCE GUM CHEEK PRIDE SNASH HUBRIS DISDAIN AUDACITY SURQUIDY CONTUMELY PETULANCE

INSOLENT FACY PERT RUDE WISE BARDY BRASH LUSTY PROUD CHEEKY LORDLY WANTON ABUSIVE DEFIANT PAUGHTY ARROGANT IMPUDENT PETULANT SCORNFUL AUDACIOUS

INSOLUBLE HOPELESS

INSOMNIA AHYPNIA AGRYPNIA

INSOUCIANT CAVALIER

INSPECT SEE VET CASE ESPY LOOK BRACK CHECK SIGHT VISIT INLOOK PERUSE SURVEY EXAMINE OVERSEE CONSIDER OVERLOOK OVERVIEW

(— CASUALLY) BROWSE

(— COINS) SHROFF

(— MERCHANDISE IN BALTIC) BRACK

INSPECTION EYE PRY VIEW CHECK

SIGHT REVIEW SURVEY BEDIKAH CHECKUP INSIGHT INSPECT PERUSAL VIDIMUS OVERHAUL OVERVIEW SCRUTINY

(— OF CLOTH) ALNAGE

INSPECTOR SAYER SNOOP BISHOP CENSOR CONNER JUMPER LOOKER VIEWER GRAINER MOOCHER PERCHER SAMPLER SNOOPER VEADORE EXAMINER SEARCHER

(— OF COAL) KEEKER

(— OF COTTON LOOMS) TACKLER

(— OF ELECTRIC LAMPS) AGER

(ECCLESIASTICAL —) EXARCH

INSPIRATION FIRE SIGH POESY ANIMUS SPIRIT SPRITE IMPULSE MADNESS PEGASUS AFFLATUS AGANIPPE INFLATUS

(— IN ORATORY) HWYL

INSPIRE FIRE MOVE CHEER ELATE EXALT SPARK BEACON INBLOW INCUSS INDUCE INFORM INFUSE KINDLE PROMPT ACTUATE ANIMATE EMBRAVE ENFORCE ENLIVEN HEARTEN IMPLANT PREMOVE QUICKEN SUGGEST CATALYZE ENTALENT INSPIRIT MOTIVATE SUFFLATE

INSPIRED VATIC AFFLATED DAEMONIC ENTHEATE VISIONED

INSPIRER SOUL

INSPIRING INFUSIVE SPLENDID STIRRING

INSPIRIT CHEER HEART ROUSE SPIRIT ANIMATE CHERISH COMFORT ENLIVEN HEARTEN INSPIRE QUICKEN ALACRIFY

INSPISSATE STIFFEN THICKEN

INSPISSATED STIFF THICK

INSTABILITY SLIDDER FLUIDITY

INSTALL SEAT CHAIR STALL INDUCT INVEST ENSTOOL POSSESS ENTHRONE INITIATE

INSTALLATION INDUCTION

(— OF MINISTER) INFARE

(MILITARY —) GARRISON

INSTALLMENT KIST SERIAL EARNEST CONTRACT

(— OF SERIAL) HEFT

(— OF WAGES) COMPO

(— SELLER) TALLYMAN

(FIRST —) HANDSEL

(NEXT —) SEQUEL

INSTANCE CASE PINK SAMPLE EXAMPLE PURPOSE ENSAMPLE EXEMPLAR

(EXTREME —) CAPSHEAF

INSTANT POP HINT WHIP WINK BLICK CLINK CRACK FLASH GLENT GLIFF GLISK JIFFY POINT SHAKE SOUND START TRICE WHIFF WIGHT BREATH FLIFFY MINUTE MOMENT SECOND PRESENT CLIFFING

(PRECISE —) TIME

INSTANTANEOUS PRESTO DIRECTLY

INSTANTANEOUSLY OUTRIGHT

INSTANTLY SLAP SWITH PRONTO SWITHE DIRECTLY MOMENTLY

INSTAR STAGE

INSTEAD EITHER

(PREF.) ANTI PRO

INSTEP WRIST TARSUS

(PREF.) PEDI(O)

INSTIGATE EGG ABET GOAD MOVE SPUR URGE IMPEL ATTICE ENTICE EXCITE FOMENT INCITE INDUCE INVOKE PROMPT SPIRIT SUBORN ACTUATE INCENSE INSTINCT

INSTIGATION MOTION MOTIVE EGGMENT INSTANCE INSTINCT

INSTIGATOR AUTHOR MOTIVE SOURCE MONITOR

INSTILL GRAFT INFIX IMPART INFUSE INSTIL BREATHE IMPLANT

INSTINCT KIND FILLED NATURE CHARGED IMPULSE CAPACITY TENDENCY

INSTINCTIVE INNATE NATURAL INHERENT ORIGINAL

INSTITUTE BEGIN BRING ERECT FOUND RAISE STUDY FOMENT INVENT KINDLE ORDAIN ACTIVATE

(— MEMBER) PIARIST

INSTITUTION BANK CAMP FOLD CLINIC FRIARY SCHOOL ACADEMY CHARITY COLLEGE GALLERY JUBILEE LIBRARY SHELTER STATION VERITAS SEMINARY ORPHANAGE OBSERVATORY PENITENTIARY

(— FOR HOMELESS CHILDREN) PROTECTORY

(— FOR INSANE) ASYLUM

(CHARITABLE —) SPITTLE DEACONRY HOSPITAL

(DRUIDICAL —) GORSEDD

INSTRUCT KEN REAR SHOW WISE BREED COACH DRILL EDIFY ENDUE GUIDE TEACH TRAIN CHARGE DIRECT GROUND INDUCE INFORM LESSON PREACH REFORM SCHOOL COMMAND EDUCATE INSENSE POSSESS ADMONISH DOCUMENT

(— BEFOREHAND) PRIME

INSTRUCTED SCIENCED

INSTRUCTION LORE ADVICE ASSIZE CHARGE LESSON COUNSEL PRECEPT TUITION WISSING COACHING DOCTRINE DOCUMENT MONITION PEDAGOGY PROPHECY TEACHING TUTELAGE

(COMPUTER —) MACRO

(DIVINE —) LAW

(SACRED —) TORAH

(SERIES OF COMPUTER —S) LOOP

(PL.) BRIEF BRIEFING

INSTRUCTIVE DOCENT DIDACTIC

INSTRUCTOR DON SOAK SCREW TUTOR MENTOR REGENT ACHARYA CRAMMER MONITOR TEACHER BEACHBOY CHAIRMAN ELDERMAN

INSTRUMENT (ALSO SEE MUSICAL INSTRUMENT) DEED TOOL WRIT AGENT SLANG THEME FACTUM UTENSIL SYNGRAPH

(— FOR ACQUIRING KNOWLEDGE) ORGANON

(— NOT UNDER SEAL) PAROL

(— OF DESTRUCTION) SWORD

(— OF DIVINATION) EPHOD

(— OF TORTURE) BOOT RACK BRAKE BRANK FURCA GADGE WHEEL TUMBREL BARNACLE SQUEEZER SCARPINES PILLIWINKS

(—S OF WAR) ENGINERY

(CALCULATING —) ABACUS

(FINANCIAL —) ITEM

(LEGAL —) DEED GRANT FACTUM SASINE SCRIPT CHARTER CODICIL DUPLICATE

(METEOROGICAL —) LIDAR

(NEGOTIABLE —) HUNDI HOONDEE

(OFFICIAL —) SLANG

(PREHISTORIC —) CELT

(SCIENTIFIC OR OTHER —) AWL FAN HOE KEY MET RAX SAX BROG CLAM COMB DIAL DRAG FILE FORK GAGE HOOK PALM PLOW RACK RING SPAR ARMIL BEVEL BLADE BRACE BRAKE CHAIN CLAMP CORER DATER DOLLY DRILL FLAIL FLOAT FLUKE GAUGE GLASS INDEX KNIFE LADLE LEVER METER MISER PILOT RAZOR SCALE SCOPE SLATE SLICE SLING SPADE SPEAR SPRAY STAMP STEEL SWIFT THROW TONGS TUNER WHISK ABACUS BEATER BEETLE BODKIN BRIDGE CHOWRY CIRCLE DOUCHE ENGINE ERASER FERULE FOLDER GRATER LEAPER MORTAR NEEDLE PALLET PESTLE PICKER PLOUGH PULLER PUMPER RAMMER RASPER RATTLE RUBBER SCALER SCORER SCRIBE SCUTCH SCYTHE SHEARS SQUARE SQUIRT STADIA STRAIK STROBE STYLET STYLUS TACKLE TICKER WIMBLE ALIDADE BELLOWS BREAKER CADRANS CLEAVER COMPASS DIOPTER DOLABRA DOUBLER FISTUCA GRAFTER GRAINER GRAPPLE HATCHEL LAYOVER MASSEUR MEASURE OOMETER OOSCOPE PAVIOUR PELORUS PIERCER PINCERS PRICKER PRINTER PYROPEN QUADRAT SCRAPER SEXTANT SHOCKER SHUTTLE SLITTER SOUNDER SPLAYER SPRAYER STRIGIL SUNDIAL SWINGLE TRAMMEL TRIMMER WHISTLE ANALEMMA ATOMIZER BARNACLE BIRDCALL BLOWPIPE BUTTERIS CALLIPER COALRAKE DECAPPER DETECTOR DIAGRAPH DIPMETER DIVIDERS EQUULEUS ERGMETER EXPLORER FATHOMER GEOPHONE HOROLOGE IMPINGER IRISCOPE ISOGRAPH ISOSCOPE JOVILABE MESOLABE MHOMETER ODOMETER OHMMETER PHOTOMER QUADRANT RECORDER RINGHEAD RUMMAGER SCISSORS SEARCHER SQUEEGEE STILETTO STRICKLE TJANTING TRIANGLE VELLINCH VIAGRAPH YAWMETER

(SURGICAL OR MEDICAL —) GAG HOOK SPUD FLEAM PROBE SCALA SCOOP SNARE SOUND STAFF STYLE BILABE BOUGIE BROACH GORGET LANCET SEEKER TREPAN

TROCAR UNGULA VECTIS XYSTER
AGRAFFE AIRDENT DILATER
FORCEPS HARPOON LEVATOR
LIGATOR MYOTOME PELICAN
PLUGGER RONGEUR SCALPEL
SOUNDER SYRINGE TRACTOR
TRILABE TURNKEY ANOSCOPE
AURILAVE AXOMETER BISTOURY
DIRECTOR DIVULSOR ECRASEUR
ELEVATOR EXSECTOR HEMOSTAT
KERATOME MYOGRAPH
SPECULUM TREPHINE
(VOID —) NULLITY
(PREF.) **(POINTED —)** SCOLO
(WIND —) AEOLO
(SUFF.) LABE METER
METR(E)(O)(Y) STAT(IC)
(MUSICAL —) INA
(SURGICAL REMOVAL —) ECTOME
INSTRUMENTAL MEDIATE
ORGANIC SERVILE SERVIENT
MINISTERIAL
INSTRUMENTALIST KLEZMER
SIDEMAN
INSTRUMENTALITY HAND MEANS
AGENCY MEDIUM CHANNEL
COUNCIL MINISTRY
**(— FOR ACQUISITION OF
KNOWLEDGE)** ORGANON
(NAVAL —S) BEACH
INSUBORDINATE FACTIOUS
MUTINOUS UNWIELDY
INSUBORDINATION MUTINY
INSUBSTANTIAL AIRY INANE
FROTHY SLENDER SPECTRAL
INSUBSTANTIALITY FRAILTY
INSUFFICIENCY PAUCITY
(PREF.) OLIG(O)
INSUFFICIENT POOR WANE SHORT
SCANTY
INSUFFICIENTLY BARELY FEEBLY
THINLY
INSULATE ISLE ISLAND ISOLATE
INSULATION LAGGING ISOLATION
INSULATOR NOB KNOB CLEAT
TAPLET VITRITE MEGOHMIT
STANDOFF
(PL.) STRING
INSULT CAG FIG JOEY RUMP SLAP
SLUR ABUSE CHECK FLOUT
FRUMP SLANG INJURE INJURY
OFFEND OUTRAY RUFFLE SCRAPE
ABUSION AFFRONT OFFENCE
OUTRAGE BRICKBAT DISHONOR
CONTUMELY
INSULTING RUDE ABUSIVE
ARROGANT INSOLENT
INSULTINGLY FOULLY
INSURANCE LINE CHOMAGE
COVERAGE INDEMNITY
(— AGENT) TWISTER
(UNEMPLOYMENT —) DOLE POGEY
INSURE COVER ASSURE ENSURE
FURNISH
INSURER ABANDONEE
INSURGENT REBEL RISER CHOUAN
OAKBOY TAIPING BARRABAS
CAMISARD STEELBOY
INSURRECTION RIST MUTINY
REVOLT UPROAR OUTBREAK
SEDITION UPRISING REBELLION
INSURRECTO GUGU
INTACT SOUND WHOLE

ENTIRE MAIDEN
(PREF.) INTEGRI
INTAGLIO ENTAIL DIAGLYPH
(PART OF —) INCAVO
INTANGIBLE VAGUE SUBTLE
AERIFORM SLIPPERY
INTEGER SUM NORM TOTITIVE
INTEGRAL FLUX NEEDFUL
INTEGRANT ELEMENT
INTEGRATE FUSE PIECE COMBINE
FULFILL ORGANIZE
INTEGRATED FUSED INTEGRAL
INTEGRATION BALANCE
HARMONY
INTEGRITY HONOR TRUTH
HONESTY JUSTICE PROBITY
CHASTITY STRENGTH SINCERITY
INTEGUMENT KEX ARIL PILL SKIN
TESTA TUNIC SWATHE CUTICLE
ENVELOP EPIDERM EXODERM
PRIMINE TUNICLE VELAMEN
EPISPERM PERISARC SCABBARD
SECUNDINE
(PREF.) SCYT(O)
(SUFF.) DERM(A)(ATOUS)(IA)(IS)(Y)
INTELLECT MIND NOUS HEART
INWIT MAHAT SKILL BRAINS
NOTICE REASON SPIRITS
THINKING
(HIGHEST —) NOUS
INTELLECTUAL BLUE GAON IDEAL
BOOKSY MENTAL NOETIC SOPHIC
BRAHMIN EGGHEAD GNOSTIC
CEREBRAL LONGHAIR SOPHICAL
DIANOETIC SPIRITUAL
INTELLIGENCE AIR CIT SAT CHIT
KNOW MIND NEWS NOTE NOUS
WORD AGIEL SAVVY SENSE
ADVICE BRAINS ESPRIT INGENY
NOTICE PSYCHE WITTING
MENTALITY
(— IN EGYPTIAN LORE) CHU
(— OF PLANET JUPITER) JOPHIEL
(LACKING —) VACUOUS
(LIVELY —) WIT
INTELLIGENT APT GASH PERT
ACUTE ALERT SMART SPACK
AKAMAI BRAINY BRIGHT CLEVER
MENTAL SHREWD SPRACK
WITFUL KNOWING INFORMED
LUMINOUS RATIONAL SKILLFUL
INTELLIGENTSIA CLERISY
INTELLIGIBLE CLEAR PLAIN
LUMINOUS PELLUCID PERVIOUS
REVELANT PERCEIVABLE
INTELLIGIBLY SIMPLY
INTEMPERANCE ACRASY EXCESS
ACRASIA OUTRAGE
INTEMPERATE SHRILL SURFEIT
(NOT —) SWEET
INTEND GO AIM FIX CAST MEAN
MIND MINT PLAN PLOT TEND
ALLOT ALLOW ETTLE TIGHT
ATTEND DESIGN RECKON
BEHIGHT DESTINE FORELAY
PRETEND PROPOSE PURPORT
PURPOSE FOREMIND MEDITATE
PRETENSE
INTENDED ON SUPPOSED
INTENSE HOT ACID COLD DEEP
HARD HIGH KEEN BLANK DENSE
GREAT HEAVY QUICK SHARP
TENSE VIVID ARDENT BRAZEN

FIERCE INTENT PITCHY SEVERE
STRONG BURNING CHARGED
CHRONIC CUTTING EXTREME
FERVENT FRANTIC FURIOUS
VICIOUS VIOLENT EGYPTIAN
GRIEVOUS POWERFUL PROFOUND
SEETHING TERRIFIC VEHEMENT
INTENSELY STIFF HIGHLY ACUTELY
CURSEDLY FERVIDLY MORTALLY
SHREWDLY
INTENSIFICATION
(PREF.) DE
INTENSIFIED ACUTE
INTENSIFY RISE URGE EXALT
RAISE ACCENT DEEPEN BOLSTER
ENFORCE ENHANCE IMPROVE
INFLAME MAGNIFY SHARPEN
THICKEN CONDENSE HEIGHTEN
INCREASE REDOUBLE
INTENSION INTENT MEANING
INTENSITY EDGE HEAT ARDOR
DEPTH DRIVE FEVER FIELD VIGOR
ACCENT DEGREE DOSAGE FERVOR
FRENZY STRESS CURRENT
FEROCITY STRENGTH VIOLENCE
(— OF DISEASE) ACUITY
(— OF EMOTION) ARDENCY
INTENSIVE HARD HIGH EXTENDED
INTENSIVELY HARD SOLIDLY
INTENT SET DEEP DOLE FELL HENT
MIND RAPT TENT BEADY CAUSE
DRIFT ETTLE FIXED HEART PRICK
SCOPE TENOR TENSE EFFECT
SPIRIT COUNSEL INTENSE
PRESENT PURPOSE STUDIED
WISTFUL
(CRIMINAL —) DOLE
(EVIL —) DOLUS
INTENTION AIM END GOAL HENT
MIND VIEW WILL HEART SCOPE
ANIMUS ATTENT DESIGN DEVICE
EFFECT INTENT OBJECT REGARD
COUNSEL COURAGE EARNEST
FORESET MEANING PROPOSE
PURPORT PURPOSE SUPPOSE
THOUGHT PRETENSE OBJECTIVE
(CRIMINAL —) DOLE
INTENTIONAL SET WILLFUL
WILLING WITTING INTENDED
INTENTLY BUSILY WISHLY
EAGERLY FIXEDLY
INTER BURY EARTH ENTER GRAVE
PLANT ENTOMB INHUME
INEARTH
INTERACTION COUPLING
INTERAGENT MEDIUM MIDDLER
INTERBREED CROSS
INTERBREEDING APOGAMY
MIXTURE PANMIXY CROSSING
INTERCALATE INSERT
INTERCALATION EMBOLISM
INTERCEPT KEP HEAD KEEP STOP
CATCH NORMAL ABSCISS
TRAMMEL GAINCOPE INTERPEL
RETRENCH
INTERCEPTION CUTOFF
INTERCESSION MOYEN DIPTYCH
PLEADING
INTERCESSOR MEANS PLEADER
ADVOCATE MEDIATOR
INTERCHANGE CHANGE ANAGRAM
COMMUTE PASSAGE PERMUTE
COMMERCE EXCHANGE

(— OF OPINION) COUNSEL
(— OF WORDS) SPEECH
(PREF.) TRANS
INTERCHANGEABLE FUNGIBLE
INTERCHANGED CROSS
INTERCOLUMNIATION EUSTYLE
SYSTYLE DIASTYLE
INTERCOMMUNICATION LIAISON
INTERCONNECTED SYNDETIC
INTERCONNECTION BONDING
INTERCOURSE GAM DEAL MANG
MONG TRADE TRUCK TURGY
BAWDRY HOBNOB NEGOCE
COITION DEALING MIXTURE
QUARTER SOCIETY TRAFFIC
BUSINESS COMMERCE CONVERSE
RECOURSE RELATIONS
INTERDICT BAN TABU TABOO
FORBID UTRUBI INHIBIT PROHIBIT
SUPPRESS
INTERDICTION VETO
INTEREST BUG DIP FAD USE BENT
GOOD HAND HOLD PART CLOSE
COLOR DRIVE FAVOR FETCH
GAVEL HOBBY RENTE RIGHT
STAKE STUDY USAGE USURA
USURY BEHALF ENGAGE EQUITY
ESTATE FAENUS FERVOR FINGER
INCOME USANCE ATTRACT
CONCERN RESPECT USAUNCE
CONTANGO INCREASE VIGORISH
(— OF HUSBAND) CURTESY
(— ON LAND) CLOSE
(ACTIVE —) SYMPATHY
(EXORBITANT —) JUICE
(LEGAL —) EASEMENT
(POLITICAL —) FENCE
(SECURITY —) LIEN
(SPECIAL —) MEAT ANGLE
INTERESTED HIPPED ENGAGED
SERIOUS CONCERNED
(— IN) INTO
INTERESTING FRUITY CURIOUS
PIQUANT STORIED ABSORBING
INTERFERE CUT MAKE ANNOY
BLOCK CHECK HITCH POACH
BAFFLE HAMPER HINDER HOBBLE
IMPEDE MEDDLE STRIKE TAMPER
INTRUDE INTROMIT
(— SLIGHTLY) BRUSH
(— WITH) AIL JOLT MESS CROSS
HECKLE BLANKET DISTURB
INTERFERENCE BALK CHOKE
THUMP HINDER JOSTLE MEDDLE
CONFLICT FREINAGE
INTERFERING CUT
INTERFEROMETER ETALON
INTERFLUVE DOAB
INTERGROWTH PERTHITE
INTERIM BREAK VACANCY
INTERIOR BEN BELLY BOSOM
INNER ENTIRE INLAND INWARD
INWITH MIDDLE GIZZARD
ENTRAILS INTERNAL
(— OF CUPOLA) CALOTTE
(— OF TEMPLE) CELLA
(— OF VESSEL) HOLD
(— PART) MANTLE
INTERJECT POKE ENTER SQUIB
INJECT THRUST
INTERJECTION (ALSO SEE OATH)
AW ER HA LO BAH COO FIE GEE
GIP GUP HAH HEH HEY OOH

AHEM AHOY ALAS ANAN CHUT EGAD FORE GOSH HECH HOLA JOVE ODSO OOPS OUCH PISH ADIOS ALACK ARRAH FAUGH GOODY HEIGH MAFEY MARRY MUSHA OHONE PROST PSHAW SUGAR TENEZ ATWEEL BARLEY CRIKEY CRIPES EUREKA HARROW OUTCRY PHOOEY PROSIT CARAMBA CRIMINE LACKADAY

INTERLACE LACE WARP BRAID WEAVE ENLACE PLEACH ENTRAIL INWEAVE WREATHE
INTERLACED BRACED FRETTED PLEACHED
INTERLACEMENT KNOT
INTERLACING RETE TWINY
INTERLINING DOUBLER
INTERLOCK KNIT LOCK MESH PITCH ENGAGE FINGER TANGLE DOVETAIL
INTERLOPE INTRUDE
INTERLUDE JIG JEST LETUP COMEDY VERSET TEMACHA TRIUMPH ANTIMASK ENTRACTE ENTREMES RITORNEL VERSETTE PARENTHESIS
(OPERATIC —) RITORNELLO
(ROMANTIC —) IDYL IDYLL
INTERMEDDLER STRANGER
INTERMEDDLING GESTION
INTERMEDIARY MEAN AGENT MOYENER MEDIATOR TRAMPLER MIDDLEMAN
INTERMEDIATE MEAN MESNE FILLER ISATIN MEDIAL MEDIUM MIDDLE NEUTRAL MIDDLING
(PREF.) MEDI MES(O)
INTERMEDIATOR BROKER
INTERMENT BURIAL BURYING DEPOSIT HUMATION
INTERMINABLE ETERNAL INFINITE TIMELESS UNENDING
INTERMINGLE MIX BRAID COALESCE IMMINGLE INTERMIT INTERMIX
INTERMINGLED AMONG AMONGST
INTERMINGLING
(SUFF.) MIXIS
INTERMISSION REST WAIT BREAK DWELL PAUSE DEVALL RECESS NOONING RELACHE RESPITE INTERVAL SURCEASE VACATION
(— OF FEVER) APYREXIA
(— OF PAIN) SABBATH
INTERMISSIVE CESSANT
INTERMIT CEASE DEFER DEVAUL SUSPEND
INTERMITTENT BROKEN FITFUL PERIODIC
INTERMIX BLEND MEDLEY MINGLE
INTERMIXTURE CROSS INTIMACY
INTERNAL INLY INNER ENTIRE INLAND INNATE INSIDE INWARD DOMESTIC
(PREF.) INTRA
INTERNALLY INLY INSIDE INWARD INWARDLY
INTERNODE ROSETTE
INTERPELLATION FLOWER
INTERPENETRATED SHOT
INTERPLAY AUSPICE
INTERPOLATE FARCE FARSE FOIST

FUDGE INSERT THRUST
INTERPOLATION GAG FARSE
INTERPOSE BAR CHOP POKE DEMUR OBJECT THRUST THWART MEDIATE
INTERPRET MAKE OPEN READ SCAN TAKE AREAD AREED FANCY GLOSS GLOZE RECHE DEFINE DIVINE INTEND CLARIFY COMMENT DECLARE ENGLISH EXPLAIN EXPOUND CONSTRUE DECIPHER SIMPLIFY
INTERPRETATION REDE GLOSS SENSE GOSPEL STRAIN ANAGOGE BARAITA COMMENT DOBHASH EPIKEIA MEANING CABALISM EXEGESIS INNUENDO MOONSHEE SOLARISM SOLUTION
INTERPRETER BROKER DUBASH UNDOER EXEGETE LATINER MUNCHEE CABALIST DRAGOMAN EXPONENT LINKSTER TRUCHMAN
(— OF SCRIPTURE) TROPIST
(PL.) HAHAM SELLI SELLOI CHOCHEM HAKAMIM
INTERRELATED INTIMATE
INTERRELATIONSHIP ACCORD LIAISON COMMERCE
INTERROGATE ASK TARGE DEBRIEF EXAMINE INQUIRE
INTERROGATION EROTESIS QUESTION
INTERROGATORY EROTETIC
INTERRUPT CUT MAR NIP CHOP STOP TAKE BREAK CHECK CRACK EMBAR ARREST DERAIL DERANGE DISRUPT FORBREAK INTERMIT INTERPEL OBSTRUCT
INTERRUPTED BROKEN CHOPPY SNATCHY
INTERRUPTER BUZZER
INTERRUPTION CESS JUMP STOP BLOCK BREAK CHECK DWELL LAPSE PAUSE BREACH HIATUS HOCKET HOQUET ISLAND OUTAGE CAESURA CUTBACK DIASTEM BLOCKING BREAKAGE SOLUTION STOPOVER
(WITHOUT —) FLUSH
INTERRUPTOR TIKKER BREAKER CHOPPER RHEOTOME
INTERSECT CUT CROSS BISECT INCISE CROSSCUT
INTERSECTING CRUCIAL COMPITAL
INTERSECTION LEET CHINE CROSS CURVE CHIASMA CROSSING CROSSWAY JUNCTION
INTERSEXUAL EPICENE
INTERSEXUALITY GYNANDRY
INTERSPACE SPACE POCKET
INTERSPERSE DOT SALT SHED MEDDLE THREAD CHECKER INTERSOW SPRINKLE
INTERSTICE PORE SEAM CHINK GRATE SPACE AREOLA AREOLE RIFFLE CELLULE VACUITY
(PL.) CANCELLI
INTERSTRATIFY INTERBED
INTERTWINE KNIT LACE WARP TWINE FELTER TANGLE WAMPLE WARPLE WRITHE ENSNARL COMPLECT IMPLEACH INTERTEX

INTERTWINED INWOUND
INTERTWIST RADDLE
INTERVAL GAP LAG CENT GULF REST SAND SEXT SPOT STEP BLANK BREAK COMMA CYCLE FIFTH LAPSE PRIME QUINT SIXTH SPACE SWING TENTH THIRD BREACH DECIMA DEGREE DIESIS DITONE FOURTH MERLON SECOND SLATCH SYSTEM ADVANCE DIASTEM DISCORD HEADWAY HEMIOLA INTERIM PASTIME RESPITE SCHISMA SETTIMO STADIUM TRITONE DIAPASON DIAPENTE DISTANCE ELEVENTH ENTRACTE FONTANEL INTERACT MICROTONE PARENTHESIS
(— BETWEEN FINGERS) SUBVOLA
(— BETWEEN ROPE STRANDS) CONTLINE
(— OF BRIGHTNESS) FLICKER
(— OF FAIR WEATHER) SLATCH
(— OF HARSH WEATHER) SNAP
(— OF SEMITONE) APOTOME
(— OF TIME) WINDOW
(REST —) SOB
(SHORT —) STREAK
(TIME —) HEADWAY
INTERVALE BOTTOM
INTERVENE CHOP STEP STRIKE MEDIATE OBVIATE STICKLE INTERCUR
INTERVENING MESNE MIDDLE MEDIANT
(PREF.) INTER
INTERVIEW BUZZ CONTACT AUDIENCE CONGRESS
INTERWEAVE MAT PLAT CRISP PLAIT PLASH PLEACH RADDLE TANGLE WATTLE ENTWINE TEXTURE TRELLIS COMPLECT ENTANGLE IMPLEACH INTERTEX
INTERWEAVING BREDE CROWN INTIMATE
(— OF INITIALS) CIPHER
INTERWOVEN INWOVEN IMPLICIT INTIMATE
INTESTINAL INNER ENTERAL ENTERIC SPLANCHNIC
INTESTINE GUT ROPE BOWEL INNER THARM INWARD MIDDLE THAIRM
(PORTION OF —) JEJUNUM
(PL.) VISCUS INGANGS CHITLINS
(PREF.) COL(O) ENTER(O)
INTHROW RIDGE
INTIMACY LIAISON PRIVACY AFFINITY CHUMMERY GOSSIPRY INTRIGUE MUTUALITY
(UNDUE —) LIBERTY
INTIMATE SIB BOON GRIT HINT HOME HOMY KIND NEAR NEXT PACK TOSH BOSOM CHIEF CLOSE GREAT HOMEY PALLY PRIVY THICK ALLUDE ENTIRE FRIEND HOMELY INTIME INWARD NOTICE SECRET STRAIT STRICT THRANG THRONG CHAMBER CLOSEUP GREMIAL INNERLY INNUATE KEYHOLE PRIVADO PRIVATE SIGNIFY SPECIAL SUGGEST COCKMATE ESPECIAL FAMILIAR

FREQUENT FRIENDLY INDICATE INTIMADO
(MOST —) MIDMOST
(PL.) FOLKS
INTIMATELY INLY NEAR TOSH WELL COZILY CLOSELY INWARDLY
INTIMATION CUE HINT ITEM WARN WIND SCENT NOTICE OFFICE GLIMMER INKLING CIRCULAR INNUENDO MONITION
INTIMIDATE COW HAZE ABASH BULLY COWER DAUNT DETER PSYCH HECTOR PSYCHE TERRIFY BROWBEAT BULLDOZE BULLYRAG FRIGHTEN
INTO IN INTIL WITHIN
(PREF.) IL IM IN INTRO IR
INTOLERABLY PLAGUY
INTOLERANCE BIGOTRY
INTOLERANT CLOSED BIGOTED
INTONATION FALL ITALICS
INTONE CANT SING TONE CHANT CHAUNT ENTUNE MODULATE CANTILLATE
INTOXICANT BOZA
INTOXICATE FOX TIP TOX CORN FLAW GOOF SOAK TODDY FUDDLE MUDDLE SOZZLE SPRING TIPSIFY DISGUISE OVERTAKE SPRINKLE
INTOXICATED CUT FAP LIT WET HIGH LUSH RIPE SHOT SOSH TOFT TOSY BOSKY BUFFY DRUNK FRESH FRIED FUNNY HEADY LACED NAPPY PIPED TIGHT BLOTTO BOILED GROGGY LOADED LOOPED MELLOW PIPPED QUAINT SCREWY SKEWED SLEWED SLOPPY SODDEN SOSHED SOZZLE STEWED TANKED UPPISH UPPITY ZONKED EBRIATE EXALTED FLECKED JINGLED POTSHOT SCREWED SLOPPED SMASHED SPIFFED SQUIFFY UNSOBER BESOTTED COCKEYED DELEERIT ELEVATED OVERSEEN OVERSHOT PLEASANT SQUIFFED TEMULENT TOXICATE
INTOXICATING HARD HEADY STARK HUFFCAP
INTOXICATION WINE FUDDLE IVRESSE LOCOISM DISGUISE EBRIOSITY TEMULENCE
(— OF ANIMALS) DUNZIEKTE
INTRACTABLE BAD HARD SALTY STACK SURLY FIERCE KITTLE SULLEN THWART UNRULY CRABBED HAGGARD RESTIVE ROPABLE WAYWARD CHURLISH INDOCILE MUTINOUS OBDURATE PERVERSE SHREWISH
INTRADOS SOFFIT
INTRANSITIVE NEUTER
INTREPID BOLD BRAVE HARDY HEROIC PRETTY SAVAGE DOUGHTY VALIANT RESOLUTE
INTREPIDITY GAME COURAGE
INTRICACY KNOT INTRIGUE
INTRICATE HARD MAZY BLIND DAEDAL IMPLEX KNOBBY KNOTTY SUBTLE TANGLY TRICKY COMPLEX CRABBED CURIOUS GORDIAN PERPLEX PUZZLED

SINUOUS INVOLUTE INVOLVED
ANFRACTUOUS
INTRIGUE PLOT ANGLE CABAL
CLOAK STORY AFFAIR AMOUNT
BRIGUE DECEIT SCHEME CONNIVE
FACTION FINAGLE JOBBERY
TRINKET TRINKLE ARTIFICE
CHEATING COLLOGUE PRACTICE
PRACTISE STRATEGY TRIPOTER
INTRIGUER JESUIT SCHEMER
DESIGNER TRINKETER
INTRIGUING EXCITING SCHEMING
INTRINSIC REAL TRUE INBORN
INBRED INNATE INWARD NATIVE
GENUINE NATURAL ABSOLUTE
IMMANENT INHERENT INTERNAL
INTIMATE
INTRINSICALLY PERSE PROPERLY
INTRODUCE READ DEBUT ENTER
FRONT IMMIT INFER PLANT
START USHER BROACH HERALD
INDUCE INDUCT INFUSE INJECT
INSERT INVECT INVOKE LAUNCH
PREFER FORERUN IMPLANT
INSTILL INVEIGH PRECEDE
PREFACE PRELUDE PRESENT
SHUFFLE SPONSOR ACQUAINT
INNOVATE INTROMIT WIREDRAW
(— AIR INTO) AERATE
(— AS FIRST ACT) INITIATE
(— FROM WITHOUT) IMPORT
(— SURREPTITIOUSLY) FOIST
INTRODUCTION LASSU PROEM
PRONE INTRADA INTROIT
ISAGOGE MENTION PREFACE
ENTRANCE EXORDIUM PREAMBLE
PROLOGUE PRELUSION
(— INTO STOMACH) GAVAGE
(— OF DRAMA) PROTASIS
(— OF NOVELTY) CHANGE
(MUSICAL —) INTRO INTRADA
OVERTURE
(SUFF.) PHORESIS
INTRODUCTORY EXORDIAL
ISAGOGIC LIMINARY PROTATIC
SYSTATIC PRELUSIVE
PRELIMINARY
INTROIT REQUIEM
INTRORSE ANTICAL
INTROSPECTION INLOOK REFLEX
INTRUDE JET ABATE BARGE CRASH
POACH BOTHER CHISEL INGYRE
INJECT INVADE IRRUPT THRUST
AGGRESS OBTRUDE ENCROACH
INFRINGE TRESPASS
INTRUDER INTRUS INCOMER
INVADER STRANGER
INTRUSION INVASION
INTRUSIVE NOSY FRESH NOSEY
SPURIOUS
(PREF.) XEN(O)
INTUITION HUNCH PRESAGE
INSTINCT
INTUITIONIST EIDETIC
INULIN ALANTIN
INUNDATE FLOW DROWN FLOOD
INUND SWAMP DELUGE
OVERFLOW SUBMERGE
SURROUND
INUNDATION FLOW FLOOD
WATER DELUGE ALLUVIO
FRESHET ALLUVION FLOODAGE
OVERFLOW

INURE URE BREAK ENURE STEEL
HARDEN SCHOOL SEASON
ACCUSTOM INDURATE
ACCLIMATIZE
INVADE ASSAIL INTRUDE
ENCROACH INTRENCH TRESPASS
INVADER HUN PICT
INVADING INGRUENT
INVAGINATION GULLET
INVALID BAD BUM NULL CHRONIC
NUGATORY
INVALIDATE UNDO AVOID BREAK
CANCEL INFIRM IMPROVE
INVALID VITIATE
INVALUABLE COSTLY PRECIOUS
PRICELESS
INVARIABLE STEADY UNIFORM
CONSTANT
INVARIABLENESS ONENESS
INVARIABLY EVER ALWAYS
INVASION RAID INROAD DESCENT
INBREAK INJURIA
INVECTIVE ABUSE HOKER SATIRE
RAILING DIATRIBE REPROACH
INVEIGH RANT INVECT DECLAIM
DENOUNCE
INVEIGLE COAX ROPE WILE CHARM
DECOY SNARE ALLURE ENTICE
SEDUCE
INVENT COIN FIND FORM MINT
VAMP FEIGN FRAME FRUMP
CREATE DESIGN DEVISE IDEATE
CONCOCT CONJURE CONTRIVE
DISCOVER
INVENTED MADE
INVENTION FANCY DEVICE FINDAL
NOTION FANTASY FICTION
FIGMENT FORGERY WITCRAFT
(DRAMATIC —) IBSENISM
INVENTIVE ADROIT FERTILE
CREATIVE MECHANIC ORIGINAL
PREGNANT
INVENTIVENESS WIT ARTIFICE
INVENTOR TALOS COINER FINDER
FRAMER MINTER CREATOR
MINTMAN ENGINEER ARTIFICER
AMERICAN LEE BELL COLT FELT
GRAY HALL HOWE HUNT IVES
LAND LOWE OTIS READ WOOD
ADAMS ALLEN BLAKE BROWN
DAVIS EARLE EVANS FIELD FITCH
GIBBS HYATT LOCKE MCKAY
MOODY MOREY MORSE NOYES
PRATT TESLA WHITE BENDIX
BORDEN BORTON BOYDEN CAHILL
CHURCH CLYMER CURTIS DURYEA
EDISON FOLMER FRENCH FULTON
GARAND GAYLEY GORDON
GORRIE HAMLIN HAYNES
HORGAN HUGHES HUSSEY
JANNEY JUDSON PORTER
SAXTON SHOLES SINGER SPERRY
WESSON WILCOX WILSON
ACHESON APPLEBY BABBITT
BETHELL BIGELOW BRADLEY
CORLISS EASTMAN GODFREY
HAMMOND HOLLAND JENKINS
KNOWLES LANSTON PERKINS
PULLMAN SELLERS STEVENS
TAINTER WHITNEY BACHRACH
BERLINER BIRDSEYE BOGARDUS
BUSHNELL DEFOREST ELLSBERG
ERICSSON GILLETTE GOODYEAR

WATERMAN BURROUGHS
BUTTERICK DRAWBAUGH
HOTCHKISS MCCORMICK
HERRESHOFF WESTINGHOUSE
AUSTRIAN KEMPELEN
BELGIAN BAEKELAND
DUTCH DREBBEL
ENGLISH KAY MOON WATT MILLS
SMITH AYRTON BRUNEL DONKIN
GURNEY HOLDEN LISTER
BESEMER BURGESS GAUDENS
MORLAND MURDOCK STARLEY
CROMPTON STURGEON
ACKERMANN APPLEGATH
ARKWRIGHT ARMSTRONG
HEATHCOAT WHITWORTH
CARTWRIGHT HARGREAVES
STEPHENSON
FRENCH FOUCHE GIRARD LENOIR
MONIER PROGIN DAGUERRE
DELSARTE JACQUARD
CHASSEPOT MONTGOLFIER
GERMAN DREYSE MAUSER
FLETTNER
GREEK CTESIBIUS ARCHIMEDES
IRISH BRENNAN
ITALIAN MARCONI
NORWEGIAN KRAG
SCOTTISH BARR WATT BAIRD
DUNLOP MILLER GREGORY
NEILSON TWADDELL SYMINGTON
SWEDISH DALEN POLHEM
SWISS VETTERLI
INVENTORY BILL LIST STOCK
ACCOUNT INVOICE TERRIER
ANAGRAPH DATABASE REGISTER
SCHEDULE
INVERSE
(PREF.) OB
INVERSION WALDEN CHIASMUS
ENTROPION
(— OF STITCHES) PURL
INVERT CANT TURN REVERT
REVERSE
INVERTASE SUCRASE
INVERTED AWKWARD
INVEST DON DUB PUT BELT FUND
GARB GIFT GIRD GIRT GOWN
LOCK SINK VEST WRAP BELAY
BLOCK ENDOW ENDUE FEOFF
INDUE CLOTHE EMBODY ENROBE
FORSET OCCUPY ORDAIN BESIEGE
COMPASS ENFEOFF ENVELOP
INSTATE OBSERVE BENEFICE
BLOCKADE SURROUND
(— ONESELF) COVER ASSUME
(— WITH) INFEFT
(— WITH AUTHORITY) SCEPTER
ACCREDIT
(— WITH ENERGY) CATHECT
(— WITH SOVEREIGN DIGNITY)
ENTHRONE
(SUFF.) (— WITH ATTRIBUTES OF)
FY IFY
INVESTED GARTERED
INVESTIGATE SPY SIFT CHECK
PROBE SOUND STUDY EXCUSS
FATHOM SEARCH DISCUSS
EXAMINE EXPLORE INQUIRE
INDAGATE SCRUTATE
(— QUICKLY) SKIP
INVESTIGATION CHECK PROBE
TRIAL EXAMEN PILPUL SEARCH

DELVING INQUEST INQUIRY
LEGWORK ZETETIC ANALYSIS
QUESTION RESEARCH SCRUTINY
SOUNDING
INVESTIGATOR SNOOP TRIER
SLEUTH GUMSHOE SPOTTER
FIELDMAN
INVESTING AMBIENT
INVESTITURE VESTURE INDUMENT
INVESTMENT DOG FLIER CUTICLE
CATHEXIS PANNICLE
INVETERATE BLACK SWORN
ROOTED CHRONIC HARDENED
INVIDIOUS ENVIOUS HATEFUL
INVIGORATE PEP BRACE CHEER
RAISE RENEW VIGOR VIVIFY
COMFORT ENFORCE ENLIVEN
FORTIFY INNERVE INSINEW
REFRESH INSPIRIT
INVIGORATING BRISK CRISP
FRESH TONIC VITAL HEARTY
LIVELY BRACING CORDIAL
VEGETANT
INVIOLABILITY SANCTITY
INVIOLABLE SACRED SECURE
STYGIAN
INVIOLATE SACRED
INVISIBLE HID BLIND SECRET
UNSEEN VIEWLESS SIGHTLESS
(PREF.) APHAN(O) CRYPT(O)
KRYPT(O)
INVITATION BID CALL CARD
INVITE BIDDING CALLING
(— TO CONTEND) DARE
INVITE ASK BID WOO BEAR CALL
LURE PRAY TOLL CLEPE COURT
LATHE TEMPT TRYST ALLURE
DESIRE ENTICE INDITE ATTRACT
CONVITE PROVOKE REQUEST
SOLICIT
INVITING ADORABLE HOMELIKE
INVOCATION WISH DAWUT NANDI
BISMILLAH
INVOICE BILL BRIEF CHALAN
FACTURE MANIFEST BORDEREAU
INVOKE WISH CLEPE EVOKE
APPEAL ATTEST OBTEST
CONJURE ENTREAT PROVOKE
SOLICIT INVOCATE
INVOLUCRE HULL HUSK CUPULE
CALYCLE CALYCULE EPICALYX
INVOLUNTARY FORCED REFLEX
HELPLESS
INVOLUTE INVOLVED
INVOLUTED SCREWY
INVOLUTION ATRESIA
INVOLVE DIP LAP MIX MIRE WRAP
BROIL CARRY COUCH IMPLY
RAVEL DIRECT EMPLOY ENGAGE
ENTAIL HANKLE INWRAP TANGLE
COMPORT CONCERN CONNOTE
EMBRACE EMBROIL ENSNARE
ENTWINE ENVIRON IMMERSE
INCLUDE ENCUMBER ENTANGLE
INTEREST
(— IN DIFFICULTY) STEAD
INVOLVED IN DEEP GONE INTO
BLIND KNOTTY COMPLEX
ENGAGED PLAITED IMPLICIT
INVOLUTE CONCERNED
ANFRACTUOUS
INWARD ENTAD INNER INWITH
BENWARD INNERLY HOMEFELT

(PREF.) IL IM IN INTRO IR OB
INWICK INRING
IO (BROTHER OF —) PHORONEUS
  (FATHER OF —) INACHUS
  (SON OF —) EPAPHUS
IODINE
  (PREF.) **(REMOVAL OF —)** DESIODO
IOLAUS (COMPANION OF —)
  HERCULES
  (FATHER OF —) IPHICLES
  (MOTHER OF —) AUTOMEDUSA
  (WIFE OF —) MEGARA
IOLE (FATHER OF —) EURYTUS
  (HUSBAND OF —) HYLLUS
IOLITE IBERITE PELIOMA
ION ACID ADION ANION CATION
  ISOMER KATION LIGAND
  AMPHION HYDRION OXONIUM
  SPECIES ZWITTERION
  (— DURATION) LIFETIME
  (FATHER OF —) XUTHUS
  (MOTHER OF —) CREUSA
  (SON OF —) GELEON ARGADES
  HOPLETES AEGICORES
  (PREF.) IONTO
  (SUFF.) **(CHARGED —)** ONIUM
IONIA (GULF OF —) ARTA
IONIZATION BURST
IOPHON (FATHER OF —) SOCRATES
  (MOTHER OF —) NICOSTRATE
IOTA JOT WHIT GHOST TITTLE
  SCRUPLE
IOU MARKER

IOWA
CAPITAL: DESMOINES
COLLEGE: COE DORDT LORAS
  CORNELL PARSONS GRINNELL
  WARTBURG
COUNTY: IDA LEE SAC CASS LINN
  PAGE POLK TAMA ADAIR
  BOONE CEDAR EMMET FLOYD
  LUCAS SIOUX BREMER KEOKUK
  OBRIEN DUBUQUE KOSSUTH
  MAHASKA OSCEOLA
LAKE: CLEAR STORM SPIRIT
NICKNAME: HAWKEYE
PRESIDENT: HOOVER
RIVER: CEDAR SKUNK BIGSIOUX
  MISSOURI
STATE BIRD: GOLDFINCH
STATE FLOWER: WILDROSE
STATE TREE: OAK
TOWN: ADEL AMES LEON ALBIA
  MASON ONAWA OSAGE PERRY
  SIOUX ALGONA ELDORA
  KEOKUK LEMARS MARION
  SIBLEY VINTON ANAMOSA
  OTTUMWA WATERLOO
  DAVENPORT

IOWAN HAWKEYE
IPECAC ITOUBOU
IPHIANASSA (FATHER OF —)
  PRŒTIUS
  (HUSBAND OF —) BIAS
  (MOTHER OF —) ANTIA
IPHICLUS (BROTHER OF —)
  HERCULES
  (FATHER OF —) PHYLACUS
  AMPHITRYON
  (MOTHER OF —) ALCMENA

(SON OF —) PODARCES
  PROTESILAUS
  (WIFE OF —) CLYMENE
IPHIDAMAS (FATHER OF —)
  ANTENOR
  (MOTHER OF —) THEANO
  (SLAYER OF —) AGAMEMNON
IPHIGENIA (BROTHER OF —)
  ORESTES
  (FATHER OF —) AGAMEMNON
  (MOTHER OF —) CLYTEMNESTRA
  (SISTER OF —) ELECTRA
IPHIMEDIA (HUSBAND OF —)
  ALOEUS
  (SON OF —) OTUS EPHIALTES
IPHINOE (FATHER OF —) PROETUS
  (MOTHER OF —) ANTIA
  (SISTER OF —) LYSIPPE
  IPHIANASSA
IPHIS (FATHER OF —) LIGDUS
  (MOTHER OF —) TELETHUSA
  (WIFE OF —) IANTHE
IPHITUS (BROTHER OF —) CLYTIUS
  (FATHER OF —) EURYTUS
  (SISTER OF —) IOLE
  (SLAYER OF —) HERCULES
IPIL VESI
IPOMOEA NIL NILL BATATAS
  MANROOT TURBITH TURPETH
  SCAMMONY
IPSEITY SELFHOOD
IRA (FATHER OF —) IKKESH
IRACUND IREFUL
IRAD (FATHER OF —) ENOCH
  (GRANDFATHER OF —) CAIN
  (SON OF —) MEHUJAEL

IRAN
CAPE: HALILEH
CAPITAL: TEHRAN TEHERAN
COIN: PUL ASAR CRAN LARI RIAL
  BISTI DARIC DINAR LARIN
  SHAHI TOMAN STATER ASHRAFI
  KASBEKE PAHLAVI
DESERT: KERMAN
FORMER NAME: PERSIA
GOVERNORSHIP: ILAM YAZD
  SEMNAN ZANJAN HAMADAN
  LORESTAN
LAKE: NIRIS NIRIZ TASHT TUZLU
  URMIA SAHWEH SISTAN
  MAHARLU NEMEKSER
  URUMIYEH
LANGUAGE: ZEND PAHLAVI
MEASURE: GAZ GUZ MOV ZAR ZER
  CANE FOOT GAREH JERIB KAFIZ
  MAKUK QASAB ARTABA
  CHARAC CHEBEL GARIBA
  GHALVA OUROUB CAPICHA
  CHENICA FARSAKH FARSANG
  MANSION MISHARA PAIMANEH
  PARASANG SABBITHA
  STATHMOS
MOUNTAIN: CUSH KUSH HINDU
  KHOSF ARARAT HAMUNT
  BINALUD KHORMUJ SABALAN
  DEMAVEND
MOUNTAIN RANGE: ELBURZ
  SIAHAN ZAGROS JAGATAL
PEOPLE: LUR KURD MEDE SART
  KAJAR MUKRI PERSE TAJIK
  HADJEMI PERSIAN
PORT: JASK BUSHIRE PAHLEVI

PROVINCE: FARS GILAN KERMAN
  TEHRAN ESFAHAN KHORASAN
  KORDESTAN
RIVER: MAND MUND SHUR ARAKS
  JAGIN KARUN RABCH SEFID
  BAMPUR GORGAN HALIRI
  TIGRIS KARKHEH MASHKEL
  SAFIDRUD ZAYENDEH
  EUPHRATES
STRAIT: HORMUZ
TOWN: FAO KOM AMOL SARI YAZD
  AHVAZ KHVOY NIRIZ RASHT
  RESHT ABADAN DEZFUL
  GORGAN KASVIN KERMAN
  MASHAD MESHED SHIRAZ
  TABRIZ TAURIS HAMADAN
  ISFAHAN SANANDAJ
WEIGHT: SER DRAM DUNG ROTL
  SANG SEER ABBAS ARTEL
  MAUND PINAR RATEL BATMAN
  DIRHEM GANDUM KARWAR
  MISCAL NAKHOD NIMMAN
  ABBASSI TCHEIREK

IRANIAN TAT SART GALCHA
  SHUGNI BACTRIAN BARTANGI
  (— SOVEREIGN) SHAH

IRAQ
CAPITAL: BAGDAD BAGHDAD
COIN: DINAR DIRHAM
DISTRICT: BASRA KURDISTAN
FORMER NAME: MESOPOTAMIA
MOUNTAINS: ZARGOS KURDISTAN
OASIS: MANIYA
PEOPLE: ARAB KURD
PORT: FAO BASRA
RIVER: ZAB TIGRIS EUPHRATES
TOWN: ANA HIT AFAQ AMARA
  BAIJI BASRA ERBIL HILLA
  MOSUL NAJAF HILLAH KIRKUK
  TIKRIT KARBALA

IRASCIBILITY BILE CHOLER
IRASCIBLE WARM ANGRY CROSS
  FIERY GASSY HASTY IRATE SHARP
  TECHY TESTY CRANKY IREFUL
  SPUNKY TETCHY TOUCHY
  ANGULAR BILIOUS FRETFUL
  IRACUND PEEVISH TINDERY
  TOUSTIE WASPISH CAPTIOUS
  CHOLERIC PETULANT SNAPPISH
  STOMACHY
IRATE ANGRY HEATED CHOLERIC
  WRATHFUL
IRE FURY ANGER WRATH
IREFUL ANGRY JEALOUS

IRELAND
BAY: MAL CLEW SLIGO BANTRY
  DINGLE GALWAY TRALEE
  DONEGAL DUNDALK KILLALA
  BLACKSOD DROGHEDA
CAPE: CLEAR
CAPITAL: TARA DUBLIN BELFAST
COIN: RAP REAL
COUNTY: CORK DOWN LEIX MAYO
  CAVAN CLARE KERRY LOUTH
  MEATH SLIGO ANTRIM ARMAGH
  CARLOW GALWAY OFFALY
  TYRONE ULSTER DONEGAL
  KILDARE LEITRIM WEXFORD
  WICKLOW KILKENNY LIMERICK

  MONAGHAN FERMANAGH
  LONDONDERRY
ISLAND: ARAN TORY SALTEE
  RATHLIN
LAKE: DOO KEY REE TAY CONN
  DERG ERNE MASK CARRA
  GOWNA LEANE RAMOR BODERG
  COOTER ENNELL DROMORE
  OUGHTER SHEELIN
MEASURE: MILE BANDLE
MOUNTAIN: OX CAHA ANTRIM
  GALTEE KEEPER MOURNE
  MULREA DONEGAL ERRIGAL
  KENNEDY KIPPURE WICKLOW
  LEINSTER
MOUNTAIN RANGE: GALTY STACKS
  COMERAGH
OTHER NAME: EIRE ERIN BANBA
  IERNE IRENA ULSTER BOGLAND
  HIBERNIA INISFAIL
PEOPLE: CELT ERSE GAEL CELTIC
  HIBERNIAN
PERTAINING TO: CELTIC GAELIC
POINT: CAHORE CARNSORE
PORT: COBH
PROVINCE: ULSTER MUNSTER
  LEINSTER CONNAUGHT
RIVER: LEE BANN DEEL ERNE
  NORE SUIR BOYNE CLARE
  FEALE FLESK FOYLE LAUNE
  BANDON BARROW LIFFEY
  KENMARE MUNSTER SHANNON
TOWN: CORK NAAS TRIM ADARE
  CAVAN ENNIS OMAGH SLIGO
  ARMAGH CARLOW DUBLIN
  GALWAY LURGAN TRALEE
  LIMERICK TIPPERARY

IRENE (FATHER OF —) JUPITER
  (MOTHER OF —) THEMIS
IRENIC CALM HENOTIC PEACEFUL
IRENICA AITESIS
IRI (FATHER OF —) BELA
IRIDESCENCE LUSTER LUSTRE
  REFLET
IRIDESCENT SHOT IRISED IRIDINE
  IRISATE OPALINE PAVONINE
IRIS EYE SET FLAG LILY LUCE LUCY
  SEGG AZURE IREOS ORRIS SEDGE
  FLAGON LEVERS LILIAL LILIUM
  SHADOW SUNBOW ALCAZAR
  BABIANA FLAGGER GLADDON
  FLAGLEAF
  (FATHER OF —) THAUMAS
  (MOTHER OF —) ELECTRA
  (PREF.) IRID(O) IRIDICO IRIDIO
IRISH ERSE EIRANN IRISHRY
  MILESIAN
  (— KING) RIG
  (ILLITERATE —) KEELMAN
  (PREF.) HIBERNO
IRISHMAN MAC PAT CELT GAEL
  KELT SCOT GREEK IRISH PADDY
  YREIS TEAGUE GRECIAN IRISHER
  MILESIAN ORANGEMAN
  (LEARNED —) OLLAMH
IRISH MOSS SLOKE CHONDRUS
IRISHWOMAN HARP
IRK BORE ITCH ANNOY WEARY
  BOTHER
IRKSOME DULL WARM WEARY
  HUMDRUM OPEROSE PAINFUL
  TEDIOUS ANNOYING TIRESOME

IROKO ODUM ODOOM MUVULE KAMBALA

IRON BIT DOG IRE AIRN MARS WIRE ANGLE ANVIL BASIL BRAND DRAIL DRIFT FLOSS HORSE NEGRO PRESS SPIKE STEEL WAVER ANCONY BEATER CALKER CAUTER FERRUM GAGGER GOFFER JAGGER OSMUND CAUTERY COBIRON CRAMPER FERRITE FURISON GAMBREL GAUFFER PRICKER SADIRON FLATIRON TRICOUNI
(— FOR CLOSING STAVES) HORSE
(— OF MILLSTONE) RIND RYND
(— ORE) LIMNITE
(— PIECES) POTLEG
(— PLATE) TRAMP
(— SUPPORTING SPIT) COBIRON
(— TO SUPPORT BEAM) TORSEL
(ANGLE —) LATH STIFFENER
(BASKETWORK —) BEATER
(BOOM —) WITHE WYTHE
(BRANDING —) BURN
(CAST —) METAL YETLIN SPIEGEL YETLING PROMETAL SEMISTEEL
(CLIMBING —) GAFF SPUR CREEPER
(CRUDE CASTING OF —) PIG
(DRIVING —) CLEEK
(GLASSBLOWING —) BAIT
(GOLF —) JIGGER
(GRAPPLING —) CRAMPON CRAMPOON
(HATTER'S —) SLUG
(MASS OF WROUGHT —) BLOOM
(METEORIC —) SIDERITE
(PASTY —) SPONGE
(PIG —) SPIEGEL KENTLEDGE
(PRIMING —) DRIFT
(PUDDLING —) RABBLE
(RUSSIAN —) SABLE
(SHEET —) TERNE
(SOLDERING —) COPPER
(SPECULAR —) HEMATITE
(TAILOR'S —) GOOSE
(TAMPING —) DRIVER
(8 PIGS OF CAST —) FODDER
(PL.) GARTERS
(PREF.) FERRI FERRO SIDER(O)
(SUFF.) SIDERITE

IRONBARK MUGGA
IRON BROWN NEGRO
IRONCLAD ARMORED IRONSIDE
IRON, GOLF (PART OF —) TOE FACE GRIP HEAD HEEL NECK NOSE SOLE HOSEL SHAFT
IRON GRAY BAT
IRON HAT GOSSAN
IRONIC ACERB ACERBIC SATIRIC SARCASTIC
IRONICAL BLAND CRUEL PAWKY
IRON-LIKE MARTIAL
IRON MAN TALUS
IRONMONGERY HARDWARE
IRON-OXIDE RED TARRAGONA
IRONSMITH FERRER
IRONSTONE DOGGER SIDERITE
IRONWEED FLATTOP VERNONIA WINGSTEM
IRONWOOD TITI COLIMA MOPANE MOPANI PURIRI WAMARA CYRILLA JOEWOOD AXMASTER

BURNWOOD FIREWOOD
IRONWORKER LOHAR MOSCHI
IRONWORT SIDERITE
IRONY SATIRE ASTEISM SARCASM RIDICULE
IROQUOIS HURON MINGO CAYUGA MENGWE
IRRADIATE XRAY EMBEAM
IRRATIONAL MAD REE SURD WILD BRUTE SILLY ABSURD RAVING STUPID BESTIAL FOOLISH
IRRECONCILABLE HOSTILE FRONDEUR
IRREDUCIBLE BASIC
IRREGULAR ODD DUMB WILD BUMPY EROSE FANCY MIXED WOPSY ATYPIC CATCHY FITFUL PATCHY RAGGED RUGGED SPOTTY UNEVEN UNLIKE WEEWAW ANAXIAL ATACTIC BAROQUE CATERAN CRABBED CROOKED CURSORY DEVIOUS DIFFORM ERRATIC FRECKET MUTABLE SCRAWLY SNATCHY UNEQUAL WAYWARD ABNORMAL ATYPICAL DOGGEREL INFORMAL PINDARIC SCRAGGLY SCRAMBLY UNLAWFUL UNSTABLE UNSTEADY VARIABLE AMORPHOUS PROMISCUOUS
(— IN SHAPE) BAROQUE
(PREF.) AMETR(O) ANOM ANOMAL(O)
IRREGULARITY SNAG DEFECT RUFFLE ANOMALY ACCIDENT
(— IN YARN) SNICK
IRREGULARLY UNDULY
IRRELIGIOUS PAGAN WICKED HEATHEN IMPIOUS PROFANE SENSUAL
IRREMEDIABLE HELPLESS HOPELESS
IRREPROACHABLE SPOTLESS
IRRESISTIBLE MESMERIC OPPOSELESS
IRRESISTIBLY FATALLY
IRRESOLUTE FICKLE INFIRM UNSURE WANKLE DOUBTFUL UNSTABLE
IRRESPONSIBLE WILDCAT CAREFREE FECKLESS SKITTISH
IRRESPONSIVE LEADEN
IRRETRIEVABLE HOPELESS
IRREVERENCE IMPIETY
IRREVERENT ATHEIST AWELESS IMPIOUS PROFANE
IRREVOCABLE DEAD
IRREVOCABLY FATALLY FINALLY
IRRIGATE FLOAT WATER SYRINGE
IRRIGATION KAREZ
IRRIGATOR FLOATER
IRRITABILITY BATE NERVES SPLEEN ERETHISM SORENESS VAGOTONY SENSITIVITY
IRRITABLE BAD EDGY BIRSY CROOK FIERY FUSSY HASTY HUFFY JUMPY MUSTY NAGGY RASPY TETTY TILTY TOITY CRANKY GROWLY NETTLY PATCHY SNUFFY SPUNKY STOCKY TEETHY TETCHY TOUCHY CRABBED FRATCHY FRETFUL HORNETY HUFFISH KICKISH

PECKISH PEEVISH SPLEENY TEDIOUS TWITCHY WASPISH LIVERISH PETULANT SNAPPING SNAPPISH STOMACHY SPLENETIC
IRRITANT PHOSGENE
IRRITATE BUG EAT GET IRE IRK NAG RUB TAR TEW TRY VEX BURN CRAB FIRE FRET GALL GOAD GRIG GRIT ITCH NARK RILE ROIL SOUR TEEN ANGER ANNOY CHAFE EAGER FRUMP GRATE GRILL GRIPE PEEVE PIQUE STING TARRY ABRADE BOTHER FRIDGE GRAVEL HARASS HECTOR NETTLE RUFFLE AFFRONT INCENSE INFLAME NERVOUS PROVOKE STOMACH ACERBATE
IRRITATED RILY SORE HUFFY RAGGY MUFFED SHIRTY EMPORTE FRATCHED SOREHEAD
(EASILY —) TESTY
IRRITATING ACRID HARSH CORSIE ELVISH GRAVEL FRETFUL GALLING IRKSOME PUNGENT RASPING ANNOYING FRETSOME GRAVELLY NETTLING SCRATCHY SPITEFUL STINGING TIRESOME MADDENING NETTLESOME
IRRITATION FRET TEEN BIRSE PIQUE STEAM NEEDLE RUFFLE TEMPER WARMTH ANTPRICK FLEABITE PINPRICK VEXATION
IRRUPTION BREAK INROAD INBREAK INBURST ERUPTION INVASION
IRU (FATHER OF —) CALEB
IS S YS BEES
(— NOT) NIS AINT ISNT
ISAAC (FATHER OF —) ABRAHAM
(MOTHER OF —) SARAH
(SON OF —) ESAU JACOB
(WIFE OF —) REBEKAH
ISABELLA (BROTHER OF —) CLAUDIO
(HUSBAND OF —) BIRON VILLEROY VINCENTIO
(LOVER OF —) ZERBINO
(SLAYER OF —) RODOMONT
ISABELLE (GUARDIAN OF —) SGANARELLE
(HUSBAND OF —) VALERE
ISAIAH ESAY ESAIAS
(FATHER OF —) AMOZ
ISANDER (BROTHER OF —) HIPPOLOCHUS
(FATHER OF —) BELLEROPHON
(SISTER OF —) LAODAMIA
ISCAH (BROTHER OF —) LOT
(FATHER OF —) HARAN
(SISTER OF —) MILCAH
ISCHEMIA ANEMIA
ISCHIAL SCIATIC
ISEULT (FATHER OF —) HOEL ANGUISH
(HUSBAND OF —) MARK
(LOVER OF —) TRISTAN
ISFENDIYAR (BROTHER OF —) BISHUTAN
(FATHER OF —) GUSHTASP
(SLAYER OF —) RUSTAM
(SON OF —) BAHMAN
ISHBAK (FATHER OF —) ABRAHAM
(MOTHER OF —) KETURAH

ISHBOSHETH (FATHER OF —) SAUL
ISHI (SON OF —) ZOHETH
ISHIAH (FATHER OF —) IZRAHIAH
ISHMAEL (FATHER OF —) AZEL ABRAHAM JEHOHANAN NETHANIAH
(MOTHER OF —) HAGAR
(SON OF —) ZEBADIAH
ISHMAIAH (FATHER OF —) OBADIAH
ISHPINGO CINNAMON
ISHSHAKKU PATESI
ISHTAR NINNI
ISHUAH (FATHER OF —) ASHER
ISHUI (FATHER OF —) SAUL
(MOTHER OF —) AHINOAM
ISINGLASS AGAR LEAF MICA PIPE KANTEN CARLOCK
ISIS (BROTHER OF —) OSIRIS
(FATHER OF —) SATURN
(MOTHER OF —) RHEA
ISLAM ABBASID
ISLAMIC (— CUSTOM) SUNNA
ISLAND CALF CAYO HOLM INCH ISLE JAVA POLO ENNIS MALTA MAYDA AVALON ITHACA OGYGIA REFUGE RIALTO CIPANGO JAMAICA MADEIRA TOWHEAD BLEFUSCU CALAURIA DOMINICA GUERNSEY LILLIPUT LUGGNAGG
(— IN EVERGLADES) HAMMOCK
(— OF REIL) INSULA
(ARTIFICIAL —) CRANNOG
(CORAL —) ATOLL
(FABLED —) MERU UTOPIA
(FLOATING —) HOVER
(FLYING —) LAPUTA
(FORTIFIED —) CRANNOG
(LEGENDARY —) BRAZIL OBRAZIL
(LITTLE —) AIT KAY KEY ISLET
(LOW —) KEY
(ROCKY —) SKERRY
(SANDY —) BEACH BARRIER
(SMALL —) CAY ISLE ISLET NUBBLE SANDKEY
(PREF.) NESO
ISLANDER KANAKA ISLEMAN INSULARY
ISLE IZLE ISLET SKERRY
ISLET OE AIT CAY KEY EYOT HAFT HOLM ILOT MOTU ROCK ISLOT STACK NUBBLE
ISMENE (FATHER OF —) OEDIPUS
(MOTHER OF —) JOCASTA
(SISTER OF —) ANTIGONE
ISOBAR MEIOBAR MESOBAR PLEIOBAR
ISOGRAM ISOPLETH
ISOLATE SPORE ENISLE ISLAND DISSECT SECLUDE COLONIZE INSULATE PRESCIND SEPARATE SEQUESTER
ISOLATED LONE POCKET UNIQUE OUTLYING SOLITARY STRANDED SECESSIVE
ISOLATION HERMITRY LONENESS SOLITUDE SEQUESTER
ISOMER PYRAN TOSYL XYLENE CUMIDINE DECOSANE DODECANE
ISOMERIC ISO ALLO
ISOMETRIC ALLO CUBIC REGULAR TESSULAR
ISOPLETH GEOTHERM
ISOPOD SLATER ASELLUS BOPYRID

GRIBBLE EPICARID
ISOTOPE IONIUM THORON
ACTINON CARRIER PROTIUM
TRITIUM
ISOTYPE COTYPE SYNTYPE
ISPAGHUL SPOGEL
ISPAHAN HERAT HERATI

ISRAEL
CAPITAL: JERUSALEM
COIN: AGORA POUND SHEKEL
COLLECTIVE FARM: KIBBUTZ
DESERT: NEGEV
FORMER NAME: CANAAN
PALESTINE
GULF: AQABA
LAKE: HULEH TIBERIAS
MEASURE: CAB HIN KOR LOG
BATH EPHA EZBA OMER REED
SEAH CUBIT EPHAH HOMER
KANEH QANEH
MOUNTAIN: NAFH SAGI HARIF
MERON RAMON ATZMON
CARMEL
PLAIN: ESDRAELON
RIVER: FARIA MALIK SOREQ
JORDAN QISHON SARIDA
YARKON LAKHISH
SEA: DEAD GALILEE
SEAPORT: EILAT ELATH ASHDOD
TELAVIV
TOWN: ACRE RAMA HAIFA HOLON
JAFFA JENIN JOPPA RAMLE
SAFAD BATYAM HEBRON
NABLUS JERICHO NATANYA
TELAVIV TULKARM NAZARETH

ISRAELI SABRA
(— STUDY CENTER) ULPAN
ISRAELITE JEW SAINT HEBREW
JACOBITE
(PL.) ZION
ISSUE END ISH COME EMIT FALL
FLOW GIVE GUSH HEAD MISE
REEK TERM VENT ARISE COUNT
EVENT FRUIT LOOSE OUTGO
SETON SOURD UTTER EFFECT
EFFUSE EGRESS EMERGE ESCAPE
EXITUS MUTTON RESULT SEQUEL
SETTER SPRING UPPING BALLOON
DEBOUCH DESCENT DRIZZLE
EMANATE ESSENCE EXSURGE
OUTCOME PROCEED PROGENY
REDOUND REFLAIR SUCCESS
EXPEDITE FONTANEL INCREASE
ISSUANCE KINDLING OUTGOING
(— AND ORDER) BID
(— SLOWLY) EXUDE
(— SPASMODICALLY) BELCH
(— SUDDENLY) SALLY
(— WITH FORCE) SPOUT
(BOND —) CONSOL
(FAVORABLE —) SPEED FORTUNE
(FINAL —) FATE UPSHOT UTMOST
(NUMEROUS —) SPAWN
(REAL —) CRUX
ISSUED OUT
ISSUING EMANANT JESSANT
MANATION
ISTHMUS BALK STRAIT TARBET
ISTLE PITA IXTLE JUAMAVE
GUAPILLA
IT HE HIT MUN TAGGER

(— FOLLOWS) SEQ SEQU
(— HAS BEEN SWORN) JURAT
ITALIAN ITALIC AUSONIAN
MACARONI
ITALIANA IN ALGIERI, L'
(CHARACTER IN —) ELVIRA
TADDEO LINDPRO ISABELLA
MUSTAPHA
(COMPOSER OF —) ROSSINI
ITALITE VESBITE
ITALY AUSONIA HESPERIA
SATURNIA

ITALY
CAPE: TESTA CIRCEO LICOSA
LINARO COLONNE FALCONE
PASSERO RIZZUTO SANVITO
TEULADA VATICANO
CAPITAL: ROMA ROME
CHEESE: ROMANO FONTINA
RICOTTA BELPAESE PARMESAN
TALEGGIO
COIN: LIRA LIRE TARI GRANO
PAOLI PAOLO SCUDO SOLDO
DANARO DENARO DUCATO
SEQUIN TESTONE ZECCHINO
FAMILY: ASTI ESTE AMATI CENCE
DORIA BORGIA MEDICI SFORZA
FOOD: PASTA PIZZA SCAMPI
GNOCCHI LASAGNE POLENTA
RAVIOLI RISOTTO SPUMONI
TORTONI CAPONATA LINGUINE
MACARONI PEPERONI
GULF: GAETA GENOA OROSEI
SALERNO TARANTO CAGLIARI
ORISTANO
ISLAND: ELBA LERO CAPRI LEROS
PONZA GIGLIO ISCHIA LINOSA
SALINA SICILY USTICA ALICUDI
ASINARA CAPRAIA GORGONA
LEVANZO PANAREA PIANOSA
SICILIA VULCANO FILICUDI
SARDINIA
ISLANDS: EGADI LIPARI TUSCAN
PELAGIE PONTINE TREMITI
LAKE: COMO ISEO NEMI GARDA
ALBANO LESINA LUGANO
VARANO BOLSENA PERUGIA
MAGGIORE BRACCIANO
MEASURE: PIE ORNA CANNA
PALMA PALMO PIEDE PUNTO
SALMA STAIO STERO BARILE
MIGLIE MIGLIO MOGGIO RUBBIO
TAVOLA TOMOLO BOCCALE
BRACCIO SECCHIO GIORNATA
POLONICK QUADRATO
MOUNTAIN: ETNA ROSA VISO
AMARO BLANC CORNO SOMMA
CIMONE BERNINA VESUVIUS
MOUNTAIN RANGE: ALPS ORTLES
APENNINES MARITIMES
NATIVE: ITALO LATIN OSCAN
ROMAN SABINE TIRANO
TUSCAN LOMBARD SIENESE
LIGURIAN VENETIAN
PASS: FREJUS BERNINA BRENNER
SPLUGEN
PORT: BARI POLA ZARA GENOA
TRANI ZADAR RIMINI SALERNO
TRIESTE
PROVINCE: ASTI COMO ENNA PISA
AOSTA CUNEO FORLI LECCE
NUORO PARMA PAVIA RIETI

SIENA UDINE FOGGIA MATERA
MODENA PADOVA RAGUSA
TRENTO VERONA BRESCIA
PISTOIA SASSARI VITERBO
REGION: CARSO APULIA LATIUM
MARCHE MOLISE PUGLIA SICILY
UMBRIA ABRUZZI LIGURIA
TUSCANY VENETIA CALABRIA
CAMPANIA LOMBARDY
PIEMONTE SARDINIA
RESORT: LIDO SANREMO
TAORMINA
RIVER: PO ADDA AGRI ANIO ARNO
LIRI NERA RENO SELE TARO
ADIGE CRATI MANNU OGLIO
PARMA PIAVE SALSO STURA
TIBER TIRSO ANIENE BELICE
MINCIO OFANTO PANARO
RAPIDO SANGRO SIMETO
TANARO TEVERE TICINO
BIFERNO BRADANO CHIENTI
METAURO MONTONE OMBRONE
PESCARA RUBICON SECCHIA
TREBBIA VOLTURNO
SEA: IONIAN ADRIATIC LIGURIAN
STRAIT: MESSINA OTRANTO
BONIFACIO
TOWN: BRA RHO ACRI ALBA ASTI
BARI COMO DEGO ELEA ENNA
ESTE FANO GELA IESI LODI
NARO NOLA PISA POLA ROMA
ROME ACQUI ANZIO AOSTA
ASOLA AVOLA CAPUA CUNEO
EBOLI FIUME FORLI GENOA
IMOLA LECCE LUCCA MASSA
MILAN MONZA OSTIA PADUA
PARMA PAVIA SIENA TEANO
TRENT TURIN UDINE VELIA
ALCAMO AMALFI ANCONA
ANDRIA AREZZO CEFALU
FAENZA FOGGIA GENOVA
MANTUA MESTRE MILANO
MODENA NAPLES NAPOLI
NOVARA RIVOLI SPEZIA TRENTO
VARESE VENICE VERONA
BERGAMO BOLOGNA BOLZANO
BRESCIA CARRARA CASERTA
CATANIA COSENZA CREMONA
FERRARA FIRENZE GORIZIA
IMPERIA LEGHORN LIVORNO
MARSALA MESSINA PALERMO
PERUGIA PISTOIA POMPEII
RAVENNA TARANTO TRIESTE
BRINDISI CAGLIARI FLORENCE
PIACENZA SORRENTO
SYRACUSE
VOLCANO: ETNA SOMMA
VULCANO VESUVIUS
STROMBOLI
WATERFALL: FRUA TOCE
WEIGHT: CARAT LIBRA ONCIA
POUND CARATO DENARO
LIBBRA OTTAVA
WINE: SOAVE CHIANTI MARSALA
ORVIETO

ITCH EWK EACH REEF RIFF YEUK
YEWK YUKE PSORA TICKLE
ITCHING SCABIES PRURITUS
CACOETHES VANILLISM
(PREF.) ACARI ACARO PSOR(O)
ITCHING ITCHY YEUKY PRURIENT
PRURITUS URTICANT

ITEM ANA JOB TOT ENTRY POINT
THING DETAIL PARCEL ARTICLE
SEVERAL PARTICULAR
(— IN SERIES) COURSE
(— OF PROPERTY) CHATTEL
(— OF VALUE) ASSET
(APPENDED —) ADDENDUM
(COLLECTOR'S —) SPOIL
(DECORATIVE —) CONCEIT
(LUXURY —) BOUTIQUE
(NEWS —) DISPATCH
(UNPUBLISHED —S) ANECDOTE
(VALUELESS —) BEAN
(PL.) CHECKAGE
ITEMIZE DETAIL
ITERATION PLEONASM
ITHIEL (FATHER OF —) JESAIAH
ITHRA (SON OF —) AMASA
(WIFE OF —) ABIGAIL
ITHRAN (FATHER OF —) DISHON
ITHREAM (FATHER OF —) DAVID
(MOTHER OF —) EGLAH
ITHURIEL'S-SPEAR GRASSNUT
ITINERANT ERRANT AMBULANT
STROLLING PERIPATETIC
ITINERARY DIET JOURNAL
WAYBILL
(— OF ROYAL PROGRESS) GEST
ITINERATION EYRE
ITS HIS
ITSELF IT HERSELF
ITTAI (FATHER OF —) RIBAI
ITYS (FATHER OF —) TEREUS
(MOTHER OF —) PROCNE
ITZA PETEN
IULUS ASCANIUS
IVANHOE (AUTHOR OF —) SCOTT
(CHARACTER IN —) JOHN BRIAN
GIRTH ISAAC LUCAS ROBIN
WAMBA CEDRIC ROWENA ULRICA
MAURICE REBECCA RICHARD
WILFRED REGINALD BEAUMANOIR
IVATAN BATAN
IVORY EBURE DENTINE ELEPHANT
(DUST OF —) EBURINE
(WALRUS —) RIBZUBA RIBAZUBA
IVORY BLACK ABAISER

IVORY COAST
CAPE: PALMAS
CAPITAL: ABIDJAN
DAM: BANDAMA
LANGUAGE: DIOULA
MOUNTAIN: NIMBA
PEOPLE: ABE AKAN ATLE KOUA
KROU MANDE ABOURE LAGOON
MALINKE VOLTAIC
RIVER: KOMOE BANDAMA
CAVALLY SASSANDRA
TOWN: MAN DALOA TABOU
BOUAKE GAGNOA KORHOGO
SASSANDRA

IVORY GULL SNOWBIRD
IVORY NUT ANTA TAGUA JARINA
IVORY PALM TAGUA COROJO
COROZO
IVORY TREE PALAY
IVY TOD GILL HOVE IVIN JILL PICRY
ARALIA HEDERA HIBBIN ALEHOOF
ARALIAD IVYWORT BINDWEED
FOALFOOT
(PREF.) HEDERI

IWW WOBBLY
IXION (FATHER OF —) PHLEGYAS

(SISTER OF —) CORONIS
(WIFE OF —) DIA

IYNX (FATHER OF —) PAN
(MOTHER OF —) ECHO

IZHAR (FATHER OF —) KOHATH
IZMIR SMYRNA

J

J JAY JIG JULIETT
JAALAM (FATHER OF —) ESAU
JAAL GOAT BEDEN JAELA
JAASIEL (FATHER OF —) ABNER
JAAZANIAH (FATHER OF —) AZUR
SHAPHAN JEREMIAH
JAB GAG GIG JAG JOB POKE STAB
STICK
JABAL (BROTHER OF —) JUBAL
(FATHER OF —) LAMECH
(MOTHER OF —) ADAH
JABBER CHAT JAVER BURBLE
GABBER GABBLE JOBBER YABBER
YATTER CHATTER
JABESH (SON OF —) SHALLUM
JABIRU STORK CICONIID
JABOT RUFFLE
JACANA PARRA
JACARANDA BROWN DATE
TALLYHO
JACARE CAIMAN CAYMAN
JACHIN (FATHER OF —) SIMEON
JACINTH LIGURE
JACK DIB FLAG JACA CRICK DICKY
KNAVE NANCA COLORS KATHAL
SCALET SETTER WENZEL
MATADOR BLOCKING JACKFISH
POLIGNAL SOURJACK TURNSPIT
UPLIFTER
(— IN BOWLS) BABY MARK KITTY
MASTER MISTRESS
(— IN CARDS) PAM PUR TOM
BOWER CNAFE KITTY KNAPE
KNAVE MAKER KNIGHT VARLET
WENZEL VARLETTO
(— OF CLUBS) NODDY BRAGGER
MATADOR
(— OF SAME SUIT) NOB
(— OF TRUMPS) TOM JASS JASZ
BOWER HONOR PLAYBOY
(PIANO —) HOPPER STICKER
SAUTEREAU
(SPINNING —) BEAT
JACKAL DIEB JACK KOLA THOS
CANID CANINE DRAGON SILVER
THOOID SIACALLE
JACKAROO RINGNECK
JACKASS JACK
JACKASS FISH MORWONG
TERAKIHI
JACK BEAN OVERLOOK
JACK CREVALLE TORO
JACKDAW DAW KAE JACK SHELL
CADDOW CARDER CHOUGH
KADDER CADESSE DAWCOCK
DAWPATE GRACKLE
JACKER SLIPMAN TORCHER
JACKET SAC COAT ETON JACK
JUMP JUPE SACK VEST ACTON
COVER DICKY JUPON PARKA
POLKA SHRUG WAMUS BANIAN
BASQUE BIETLE BLAZER BOLERO
CARACO CORSET DOLMAN
FECKET GANSEY JERKIN JERSEY
JUMPER RAILLY REEFER SACQUE
SADDLE SLEEVE SLIVER SONTAG
TABARD TEMIAK WAMPUS
WARMUS ZOUAVE BEDGOWN
CANEZOU LOUNGER NORFOLK
PALETOT PALTOCK PEACOAT
RISTORI SPENCER SURCOAT
SWEATER CAMISOLE CARDIGAN
CHAQUETA HANSELIN JIRKINET
MACKINAW OVERSLOP PENELOPE
SEALSKIN CARMAGNOLE
ROUNDABOUT
(— FOR TURKEY) APRON
(— LINED WITH STEEL) PLACCATE
(— OF INDIA) BANIAN BANIYA
(— UNDER ARMOR) ACTON TRUSS
HAQUETON
(CROCHETED —) SONTAG
(HOODED —) GREGO ANORAK
GRIEKO
(HUSSAR'S —) PELISSE
(KIND OF —) MAO NEHRU
(LADY'S —) BRUNSWICK
(LOOSE —) VAREUSE
(MALAY —) BAJU BADJU KABAYA
(PART OF —) FOB HEM DART FLAP
SEAM VENT GORGE LAPEL
BUTTON COLLAR INSEAM PIPING
POCKET REVERS SLEEVE
ARMHOLE OUTSEAM
BUTTONHOLE
(PEASANT'S —) SAYON
(UNDRESS MILITARY —) SHELL
(WORK —) BAWNEEN
JACKFRUIT JACA KATHAL
SOURJACK
JACKHAMMER SINKER PLUGGER
JACKKNIFE JACK PIKE BARLOW
JACKMAN SHELLMAN
JACK-OF-ALL-TRADES DOCTOR
TINKER GIMCRACK
JACKSCREW CRICK
JACKSMELT PEIXEREY
JACKSNIPE GID JED JACK PEERT
SCAPE SNIPE SNIGHT CHOROOK
CREAKER JUDCOCK SQUATTER
JACKSTAY JACK HORSE PARREL
JACKROD RAILWAY
JACKSTRAW SPILIKIN
JACK TREE NANGKA
JACOB ISRAEL
(BROTHER OF —) ESAU
(DAUGHTER OF —) RACHEL
DEBORAH
(FATHER OF —) ISAAC
(MOTHER OF —) REBEKAH
(SON OF —) JOSEPH
JACOB'S LADDER POLEMONIUM
JACQUARD FACONNE
JADA (BROTHER OF —) SHAMMAI
(FATHER OF —) ONAM
JADE YU DUN TIT HACK JAUD
MINX PLUG SLUT TIRE HUSSY
QUEAN TRASH BEJADE HARASS
RANNEL AXSTONE HILDING
POUNAMU
(DIRTY —) SLAISTER
JADED FORGONE SHOPWORN
DISJASKIT
JADEITE YU
JAEGER LARI SKUA ALLAN BOSUN
LARID SHOOL BONXIE TEASER
TULIAC TRUMPIE DIRTBIRD
DUNGBIRD
JAEL (HUSBAND OF —) HEBER
(VICTIM OF —) SISERA
JAFFIER (WIFE OF —) BELVIDERA
JAG BUN JOG BARB GIMP JAUG
LOAD SOSH TOOT SKATE TOOTH
INDENT
JAGELLO (WIFE OF —) HEDWIG
JAGGED JAGGY HACKLY RAGGED
RUGGED SCRAGGY SHAGGED
SNAGGED INDENTED SCRAGGLY
TATTERED
JAGGERY GUR GOOR GOUR
KHAUR KHAJUR KITTUL
JAGUAR CAT OUNCE TIGER
PANTHER UTURUNCU
JAHANGIR (FATHER OF —) AKBAR
JAHATH (FATHER OF —) LIBNI
SHIMEI SHELOMOTH
JAHAZIAH (FATHER OF —) TIKVAH
JAHAZIEL (FATHER OF —) HEBRON
ZECHARIAH
JAHDO (FATHER OF —) BUZ
(SON OF —) JESHISHAI
JAHLEEL (FATHER OF —) ZEBULUN
JAHZEEL (FATHER OF —) NAPHTALI
JAI ALAI PELOTA
(— COURT) FRONTON
JAIL CAN GIB JUG BOOB CAGE
COOP CRIB DUMP GAOL HELL
HOLD HOLE KEEP LAKE LOCK
NICK STIR WARD CHOKY CLINK
GRATE KITTY LIMBO LODGE
POKEY TENCH TRONK BUCKET
CARCEL COOLER ENJAIL JIGGER
LIMBUS LOCKUP TOLZEY FREEZER
FURNACE GEHENNA KIDCOTE
PINFOLD SLAMMER TOLLERY
BASTILLE CALABOZO HOOSEGOW
IMPRISON MILLDOLL TOLLHALL
BRIDEWELL CALABOOSE
(— TERM) JOLT
JAILBIRD LAG
JAILER ADAM GAOLER KEEPER
WARDEN ALCAIDE TURNKEY
INCLUDER
JAIR (FATHER OF —) KISH
(SON OF —) ELHANAN MORDECAI
JAKAN (FATHER OF —) EZER
JAKE FINE HICK FELLOW
JAKES AJAX GONG
JALAP MECHOACAN
JALON (FATHER OF —) EZRA
JALOPY HEAP CLUNKER
JAM DIP CRAM JAMB BLOCK
CHOKE CROWD STICK KONFYT
THRONG JACKPOT
JAMAICA (CAPITAL OF —)
KINGSTON
(RIVER OF —) BLACK COBRE
MINHO
(TOWN OF —) MAYPEN
PORTANTONIO SPANISHTOWN
JAMAICA COBNUT OUABE
PIGNUT
JAMAICA DOGWOOD BABASCO
BARBASCO FISHWOOD
JAMAICAN RAINBIRD TOMFOOL
JAMAICA VERVAIN GERVAO
JAMAICIN BERBERINE
JAMB DURN ALETTE HAUNCH
REVEAL DOORPOST
(PL.) COVING
JAMES JEM JIM JIMMY SEAMAS
SHAMUS
(BROTHER OF —) JOHN JESUS
JOSES
(COUSIN OF —) JESUS
(FATHER OF —) CLOPAS
(MOTHER OF —) MARY SALOME
JAMIN (FATHER OF —) RAM SIMEON
JANAKA (DAUGHTER OF —) SITA
JANAMEJAYA (FATHER OF —)
PARIKSHIT
JANE EYRE (AUTHOR OF —)
BRONTE
(CHARACTER IN —) EYRE JANE
JOHN MARY REED ADELE DIANA
ELIZA GRACE POOLE BERTHA
BESSIE EDWARD ELLIOT INGRAM
LEAVEN RIVERS TEMPLE VARENS
BLANCHE FAIRFAX GEORGIANA
ROCHESTER
JANGLE CLAM SQUABBLE
JANGLING HARSH JANGLY
AJANGLE
JANISSARY CREOLE RABIRUBIA
JANITOR DURWAN PORTER
SERVITOR
JANIZARY SOLAK SOLACH
JANNA (FATHER OF —) JOSEPH
(SON OF —) MELCHI
JANSENIST RIGORIST
JANUARY (— IN SPANISH) ENERO
JANUS IANUS BIFRONT
JAOB JOW
JAPAN NIPPON YAMATO CIPANGO

JAPAN
BAY: ISE MUTSU OTARU ARIAKE
ATSUMI SENDAI SURUGA
TOYAMA WAKASA UCHIURA
CAPE: TOI ESAN MINO NOMA SHIO
SOYA SUZU ERIMO KYOGA
RURUI MUROTO NOJIMA

TODOGA SHIRIYA ASHIZURI SHAKOTAN
CAPITAL: TOKIO TOKYO
COIN: BU RIN SEN YEN OBAN KOBAN OBANG TEMPO ICHEBU ITZEBU KOBANG
ISLAND: IKI SADO AWAJI BONIN HONDO KURIL REBUN HONSHU KIUSHU KURILE KYUSHU RYUKYU CIPANGO LOOCHOO RISHIRI SKIKOKU HOKKAIDO IKISHIMA OKIGUNTO OKUSHIRI TSUSHIMA YAKUJIMA
ISLAND GROUP: OKI GOTO BONIN VOLCANO
LAKE: BIWA TOYA TOWADA CHUZENJI KUTCHAWA SHIKOTSU INAWASHIRO
MEASURE: BU JO SE BOO CHO KEN TAN HIRO SHAKU TSUBO
MOUNTAIN: ZAO FUJI ASAHI ASAMA YESSO ASOSAN ENASAN HIUCHI KIUSIU YARIGA FUJISAN HAKUSAN KUJUSAN TOKACHI FUJIYAMA
PORT: OTARU YAHATA YAWATA
PREFECTURE: MIE GIFU NARA OITA SAGA AICHI AKITA CHIBA EHIME FUKUI GUMMA HYOGO IWATE KOCHI KYOTO SHIGA AOMORI KAGAWA MIYAGI NAGANO TOYAMA NIIGATA OKINAWA SAITAMA TOTTORI NAGASAKI WAKAYAMA YAMAGATA TOKUSHIMA
SEA: SUU AMAKUSA
STRAIT: KII BUNGO OSUMI NEMURO TANEGA TOKARA TSUGARU TSUSHIMA
STREET: GINZA
TOWN: OME TSU GIFU KOBE KURA MITO NAHA NARA OITA OTSU SAGA UEDA AKITA ATAMI CHIBA FUKUI KIOTO KOCHI NIKKO OSAKA OTARU SAKAI UJINA URAWA CHOSHI MATSUE NAGOYA SASEBO SENDAI TAKADA TOYAMA FUKUOKA NIIGATA OKAYAMA OKAZAKI SAPPORO HAKODATE KAMAKURA KANAZAWA KAWASAKI KUMAMOTO NAGASAKI YOKOHAMA YOKOSUKA HIROSHIMA
VOLCANO: ASO USU FUJI ASAMA ASOSAN HAKUSAN FUJIYAMA
WATERFALL: KEGON
WEIGHT: MO FUN KIN KON RIN SHI KATI KWAN NIYO CARAT CATTY MOMME PICUL KWAMME HIYAKKIN

JAPAN CEDAR SUGI
JAPANESE JAP JAPONIC
JAPANESE APRICOT UME
JAPANESE CHERRY SAKURA
JAPANESE DEER SIKA
JAPANESE GELATIN AGAR
JAPANESE IRIS SHADOW
JAPANESE PERSIMMON KAKI
JAPANESE PLUM KELSEY
JAPANESE PORGIE TAI
JAPANESE QUINCE JAPONICA

JAPANESE VELVET BIRODO
JAPE GAUD JOKE BEGUNK
JAPHETH (BROTHER OF —) HAM SHEM
(FATHER OF —) NOAH
(SON OF —) JAVAN
JAPHIA (FATHER OF —) DAVID
JAPONICA ASTILBE
JAQUENETTA (LOVER OF —) ARMADO
JAR TUN CELL JANG JARG JOLT JURR OLLA BANGA BOCAL CADUS CRUSE KADOS SHOCK DOLIUM HUSTLE HYDRIA IMPACT JUDDER KALPIS PANKIN PINATA PITHOS TINAJA CANOPUS CONCUSS POTICHE PSYKTER STAMNOS TERRINE MARTABAN STINKPOT
(BELL —) CLOCHE
(BULGING —) OLLA
(EARTHENWARE —) CAN NAN CROCK GAMLA PIPKIN PITHOS TERRINE
(POROUS —) GURGLET
(SQUAT —) KORO
(STONE —) STEEN STONE CROPPA
(WATER —) KANG BANGA CHATTI CHATTY GUMLAH HYDRIA
(2-HANDLED —) AMPHORA
(PREF.) DOLIO URCEI
JARASANDHA (FATHER OF —) BRIHADRATHA
(SLAYER OF —) BHIMA
JARED (SON OF —) ENOCH
JARGON CANT JIVE RANE SLUM ARGOT LINGO SLANG LINGUA LINSEY PATOIS PATTER PIDGIN SHELTA SIWASH CHINOOK CHOCTAW DIALECT JARGOON PALAVER BARRIKIN KEDGEREE PARLANCE POLYGLOT SCHMOOZE SHOPTALK
(THIEVES' —) FLASH
(TINKER'S —) KENNICK
(UNINTELLIGIBLE —) BARAGOUIN
JARHA (MASTER OF —) SHESHAN
JARIB (FATHER OF —) SIMEON
JARRING JARG RUDE SOUR HARSH ROUGH DARING STRIDENT
JASHUB (FATHER OF —) BANI ISSACHAR
JASMINE BELA MALATI PIKAKE JESSAMY WOODBINE
JASPER JASPIS MORLOP DIASPER BASANITE CREOLITE
JATAYU (FATHER OF —) GARUDA
(SLAYER OF —) RAVANA
JAUNDICE AURIGO GULSACH ICTERUS JANDERS YELLOWS JAUNDERS GRASSERIE
(PREF.) ICTER(O)
JAUNDICED ICTERODE
JAUNT TRIP SALLY JAUNCE VAGARY JOURNEY
JAUNTILY AIRILY BOUNCILY
JAUNTING CAR SIDECAR OUTSIDER
JAUNTY PERK PERT TRIM COCKY PERKY SASSY DAPPER JANTEE SHANTY FINICAL PERKING DEBONAIR

JAVA
INDONESIAN NAME: DJAWA
ISLAND: BALI LOMBOK MADURA
MEASURE: PAAL
MOUNTAIN: GEDE MURJO RAOENG SEMERU SLAMET SEMEROE SOEMBING
PORT: BATAVIA SURABAJA TJILATJAP
RIVER: SOLO LIWUNG BRANTAS
TOWN: BOGOR DESSA KEDIRI MALANG BANDUNG BATAVIA JAKARTA SEMARANG SURABAJA
WEIGHT: POND TALI

JAVA ALMOND PILI CANARI KANARI TALISAY
JAVA COTTON KAPOK
JAVA HEAD (AUTHOR OF —) HERGESHEIMER
(CHARACTER IN —) TAOU YUEN RHODA EDWARD GERRIT JEREMY NETTIE VOLLAR AMMIDON DUNSACK WILLIAM
JAVAN (FATHER OF —) JAPHETH
JAVANESE KRAMA KRAMA
JAVANESE SKUNK TELEDU
JAVA PLUM DUHAT JAMBUL LOMBOY JAMBOOL
JAVA SPARROW MUNIA PADDY RICEBIRD
JAVELIN COLP DART PILE ACLYS PILUM JAREED LANCET ASSAGAI HARPOON HURLBAT JAVELOT ACONTIUM GAVELOCK
JAW JIB BEAK CHAP CHAW CHOP JOWL WANG ANVIL CHAFT CHEEK CHOKE SCOLD CHAWLE FEELER JAWBONE MAXILLA MANDIBLE
(— OF FORCEPS) BEAK
(— OF SPIDER) FANG
(— OF VISE) CHAP
(—S OF BIRD) BILL
(FALSE —) CLAMP
(RECEDING NOSE AND UNDERSHOT —) LAYBACK
(PL.) MAW BITS THROAT
(PREF.) (UNDER —) GENYO
(SUFF.) GNATHA(E) GNATHI(A)(C)(SM) GNATHOUS GNATHUS
JAWBONE JOWL WANG MAXILLA CHAWBONE
(PREF.) MAXILLI MAXILLO
JAWBREAKING CRACKJAW
JAY JAYPIET SIRGANG BLUECOAT MEATBIRD
JAYHAWKER KANSAN
JAZERANT GESSERON
JAZZ BOP JIVE HOTCHA
JEALOUS YELLOW EMULOUS ENVIOUS
JEALOUSY ENVY YELLOWS EMULATION ZELOTYPIA
JEAN FROCKING
JEAN-CHRISTOPHE (AUTHOR OF —) ROLLAND
(CHARACTER IN —) ADA JEAN GRAZIA KRAFFT LOUISA MICHEL COLETTE LORCHEN OLIVIER STEVENS MELCHIOR GRUNEBAUM

JEANPAULIA BAIERA
JEATERAI (FATHER OF —) ZERAH
JECHOLIAH (HUSBAND OF —) AMAZIAH
(SON OF —) UZZIAH AZARIAH
JEDAIAH (FATHER OF —) HARUMAPH
JEDIAEL (FATHER OF —) SHIMRI MESHELEMIAH
JEDIDAH (HUSBAND OF —) AMON
(SON OF —) JOSIAH
JEEP PEEP SEEP BANTAM
JEER BOB BOO MOB GECK GIBE GIRD JAPE JEST JIBE MOCK SKIT WIPE FLIRT FLOUT FLUTE FLYTE FRUMP GLAIK LAUGH SCOFF SCOMM SNEER TAUNT CHIACK DERIDE BARRACK RIDICULE
JEERING BIRD FLOUT DERISIVE
JEHALELEL (SON OF —) AZARIAH
JEHIEL (BROTHER OF —) JEHORAM
(FATHER OF —) HOTHAN HACHMONI JEHOSHAPHAT
(SON OF —) GIBEON OBADIAH SHECHANIAH
JEHIZKIAH (FATHER OF —) SHALLUM
JEHOADDAN (HUSBAND OF —) JOASH
(SON OF —) AMAZIAH
JEHOAHAZ (FATHER OF —) JEHU JOSIAH JEHORAM
(SON OF —) JEHOASH
JEHOASH (FATHER OF —) AHAZIAH JEHOAHAZ
JEHOIIANAN (SON OF —) ISHMAEL
JEHOIACHIN (FATHER OF —) JEHOIAKIM
JEHOIADA (FATHER OF —) PASEACH
(SON OF —) BENAIAH
(WIFE OF —) JEHOSHEBA
JEHOIAKIM (FATHER OF —) JOSIAH
(SON OF —) JEHOIACHIN
JEHONADAB (FATHER OF —) RECHAB
JEHONATHAN (FATHER OF —) UZZIAH
JEHORAM (BROTHER OF —) AHAZIAH
(FATHER OF —) AHAB JEHOSHAPHAT
(SLAYER OF —) JEHU
(WIFE OF —) ATHALIAH
JEHOSHAPHAT (FATHER OF —) ASA AHILUD NIMSHI PARUAH
(SON OF —) JEHU JEHORAM
JEHOSHEBA (FATHER OF —) JORAM
(HUSBAND OF —) JEHOIADA
(SON OF —) JOASH
JEHOVAH JAH LORD JAHVE YAHWEH
(— WITNESS) PIONEER
JEHOZABAD (FATHER OF —) OBEDEDOM
(MOTHER OF —) SHOMER SHIMRITH
JEHOZADAK (FATHER OF —) SERAIAH
(SON OF —) JESHUA
JEHU (FATHER OF —) HANANI JOSIBIAH JEHOSHAPHAT
(SON OF —) JEHOAHAZ
(VICTIM OF —) JEHORAM

JEHUDI (FATHER OF —) NETHANIAH
JEHUSH (FATHER OF —) ESHEK
JEJUNE DRY ARID MEAGER INSIPID
JEKAMIAH (FATHER OF —)
SHALLUM
JELL COME FIRM
JELLY GEAL JEEL JELL GELEE
CULLIS JUJUBE ALCOGEL
FISNOGA GELATIN JELLIFY
FLUMMERY HYDROGEL QUIDDANY
MARMALADE
  (AGAR-AGAR —) KANTEN
  (CALF'S-FOOT —) SULZE
  (FRUIT —) ROB
  (MEAT —) ASPIC
  (PREF.) GELATI
JELLYFISH JELLY QUARL CARVEL
MEDUSA ACALEPH AURELIA
BLUBBER MEDUSAN SLOBBER
SUNFISH SCYPHULA SEACROSS
STROBILA
  (PART OF —) ARM BELL MOUTH
MARGIN STOMACH TENTACLE
UMBRELLA MANUBRIUM
  (PREF.) MEDUSI
JELLYLIKE SLABBY
JEMIMA (FATHER OF —) JOB
JEMMY BETTY
JEMUEL (FATHER OF —) SIMEON
JENNY MULE BETTY JINNY
JEOPARDIZE STAKE EXPOSE
HAZARD IMPERIL ENDANGER
JEOPARDY RISK PERIL DANGER
HAZARD
JEPHTHAH (FATHER OF —) GILEAD
JEPHUNNEH (SON OF —) CALEB
JEQUIRITY BEAN EYEN RUTTEE
JERAH (FATHER OF —) JOKTAN
JERAHMEEL (FATHER OF —) MAHLI
HEZRON HAMMELECH
JERBOA GERBIL JUMPER
JERED (FATHER OF —) MAHALALEEL
  (SON OF —) ENOCH
JEREED TZIRID
JEREMIAD TRAGEDY
JEREMIAH (DAUGHTER OF —)
HAMUTAL
  (FATHER OF —) HILKIAH
  (SON OF —) JAZANIAH
JEREMOTH (SON OF —) ELAM
HEMAN MUSHI ZATTU
JERIMOTH (DAUGHTER OF —)
MAHALATH
  (FATHER OF —) BELA DAVID
HEMAN MUSHI AZRIEL BECHER
JERIOTH (HUSBAND OF —) CALEB
JERK BOB GAG JET NUD TIT BOUT
CANT FIRK GIRD HIKE JERT JIRT
JOLT JOUK KICK PECK SNAP SNIG
YANK YERK BRAID CHUCK FLIRT
HITCH HOICK SCHMO SLIRT
SNAKE SPANG SURGE TWEAK
TWICK FILLIP JIGGER SWITCH
TWITCH WRENCH FLOUNCE
SACCADE SCHMUCK SPANGHEW
JERKED MEAT TASAJO
JERKILY HITCHILY
JERKIN SAYON JACKET
JERKY NERVY SHARP CHOPPY
ELBOIC FLICKY FLINGY HITCHY
JIGGETY CHOPPING PALMODIC
RATCHETY SACCADIC
JEROBOAM REHOBOAM

(FATHER OF —) JOASH NEBAT
  (WIFE OF —) ANO
JEROHAM (FATHER OF —) PASHUR
  (SON OF —) ADAIAH AZAREEL
AZARIAH ELKANAH IBNEIAH
JERSEY FROCK SHIRT GANSEY
TRICOT ZEPHYR MAILLOT SINGLET
CAMISOLE GUERNSEY
JERUSALEM ZION ARIEL SOLYMA
AHOLIBAH
JERUSALEM ARTICHOKE TUBER
CANADA GIRASOL
JERUSALEM CHERRY SOLANUM
JERUSALEM DELIVERED (AUTHOR
OF —) TASSO
  (CHARACTER IN —) HUGH OTHO
SWENO ARMIDA OLINDO ALADINE
ERMINIA GODFREY RINALDO
TANCRED ARGANTES BOUILLON
CLORINDA SOLIMANO SOPHRONIA
JERUSALEM OAK AMBROSIA
JERUSALEM SAGE PHLOMIS
SAGELEAF
JERUSALEM THORN CASCOL
RETAMA
JERUSHA (FATHER OF —) ZADOK
  (HUSBAND OF —) UZZIAH
JESAIAH (BROTHER OF —) PELATIAH
  (FATHER OF —) HANANIAH
JESHAIAH (FATHER OF —)
JEDUTHUN REHABIAH
  (MOTHER OF —) ATHALIAH
JESHARELAH (FATHER OF —)
ASAPH
JESHER (FATHER OF —) CALEB
  (MOTHER OF —) AZUBAH
JESIAH (FATHER OF —) UZZIEL
JESSAMINE JASMINE WOODBINE
JESSE (FATHER OF —) OBED
  (SON OF —) DAVID
JESSICA (FATHER OF —) SHYLOCK
  (HUSBAND OF —) LORENZO
JEST BAR BOG COD COG FUN GAB
JOE TAX BULL GAME GAUD GIRD
JAPE JOKE JOSH PLAY QUIP QUIZ
RAIL SKIT BOURD BREAK CHAFF
CLOWN DROLL FLIRT GESTE
GLEEK SPORT THING BANTER
GLANCE JAPERY RAILLY TRIFLE
DICTERY GAMMOCK JOLLITY
WAGGERY DROLLERY RAILLERY
  (— SPITEFULLY) SLENT
JESTER FOOL MIME BUFFO CLOWN
DROLL IDIOT JAPER JOKER PATCH
WAMBA DISOUR MOTLEY YORICK
BADCHAN BOURDER BUFFOON
DIZZARD DROLLER JOCULAR
JUGGLER PICADOR SCOFFER
SCOGGIN TOMTRAM MERRYMAN
OWLGLASS PLEASANT RAILLEUR
TRINCULO
JESTING DROLL JAPERY SCOPTIC
WAGGISH
  (RUDELY —) INFICETE
JESUI (FATHER OF —) ASHER
JESUIT PAULIST TERTIAN
IGNATIAN LOYOLITE
JESUS GEE GIS IHC IHS JHS YHS
JESU WISDOM
  (SAYINGS OF —) AGRAPHA
JET BOLT TAIL TANG BREAK
DUMBY DUMMY JETTO SALLY
SCOOT SPOUT SPRAY SPURT

CANDLE DELUGE DOUCHE
GAGATE SQUIRT FANTAIL
JETTEAU SPATTER SPURTER
FOUNTAIN SOFFIONE UPSPRING
  (— OF FLAME) TONGUE
  (— OF METAL) BREAK
  (— OF VOLCANIC STEAM) STUFA
  (SMALL —) SQUIB
  (SUBSONIC —) AIRBUS
JET-BLACK BUGLE
JETHER (FATHER OF —) EZRA JADA
GIDEON
  (SON OF —) AMASA
  (SON-IN-LAW OF —) MOSES
JETHRO (DAUGHTER OF —)
ZIPPORAH
  (SON-IN-LAW OF —) MOSES
JETTING SALIENT
JETTISON DUMP JETSAM
JETTY JET PEN DIKE GROIN JUTTY
BRIDGE OVERHANG
JEUSH (FATHER OF —) ESAU BILHAN
REHOBOAM
  (MOTHER OF —) AHOLIBAMAH
JEW SAINT ESSENE JUDEAN
LITVAK SEMITE SMOUCH SMOUSE
TOBIAD BARABAS GRECIAN
KARAITE MARRANO APIKOROS
CONVERSO GALICIAN JUDAHITE
LANDSMAN SEPHARDI
  (—S OUT OF ISRAEL) DIASPORA
  (BALKAN —) LADINO
JEWEL GEM JOY DROP OUCH
BIJOU REGAL STONE BROOCH
GEORGE TRIFLE CRAPAUD
GARLAND POUNDER
  (PL.) BULSE PERRIE
JEWELER GEMMARY LAPIDARY
JEWELRY ICE JUNK OUCH PARURE
COLLARET LAPIDARY
  (MOCK —) LOGIE
  (PIECE OF —) GAUD
JEWELS OF THE MADONNA
  (CHARACTER IN —) GENNARO
MALIELLA RAFFAELE
  (COMPOSER OF —) WOLFFERRARI
JEWELWEED CEROLINE EARJEWEL
SNAPWEED
JEWFISH MERO GUASA WARSAW
PERCOID JUNEFISH MULLOWAY
SERRANID
JEWISH JUDAIC SEMITIC
  (— BODY) VAAD
  (— COMMUNITY) KEHILLAH
  (— QUARTER) MELLAH
  (— SCHOOL) ALJAMA
  (PREF.) JUDAEO JUDEO
JEW OF MALTA (AUTHOR OF —)
MARLOWE
  (CHARACTER IN —) JACOMO
MARTIN ABIGAIL BARABAS
MATHIAS CALYMATH ITHAMORE
LODOWICK BELLAMIRA
BERNARDINE
JEWRY GHETTO JUDAISM
JEW'S-HARP HARP TROMP TRUMP
GEWGAW FLAMFEW TRANGAM
GUIMBARD
JEW'S MALLOW DESI
JEZANIAH (FATHER OF —)
HOSHAIAH
JEZEBEL GILLIVER
  (FATHER OF —) ETHBAAL

  (HUSBAND OF —) AHAB
  (SLAYER OF —) JEHU
JEZER (FATHER OF —) NAPHTALI
JEZOAR (FATHER OF —) ASHER
  (MOTHER OF —) HELAH
JEZREEL (FATHER OF —) HOSEA
JIB GIB BALK BAULK DEMUR GIGUE
STICK GIBBET SPITFIRE
JIBE (ALSO SEE GIBE) GEE KAY
GAFF GIBE JAPE JERK MOCK SKIT
AGREE FLIRD MARCH SNACK
THRUST
JIBSAM (FATHER OF —) TOLA
JIDLAPH (FATHER OF —) NAHOR
JIFFY JIFF BRAID FLISK WHIFF
GLIFFY GLIFFING
JIG BUCK FRISK GIGUE SQUID
GARLIC JIGGER JIGGET JITTER
LOCATOR
  (— FOR WASHING ORE) HUTCH
  (FISHING —) PILK
JIGGER SHOT DANDY PIQUE
DOODAD GADGET JIGMAN
VATMAN CHIGGER
JIGGLE DIDDLE JUGGLE TEETER
JILT GUNK KICK SACK BEGOWK
BEGUNK MITTEN
JIMMY BETTY JAMES JEMMY
JIMNA (FATHER OF —) ASHER
JIMSONWEED DATURA DEWTRY
JIMSON FIREWEED STRAMONY
JINGLE TUNE CHIME CHINK CLINK
DINGLE RICKLE TINKLE CHINKLE
CLERIHEW DINGDONG JINGLING
  (MEANINGLESS —) SPORT
JINGLING SMIT JANGLE RIGADIG
TINKLING
JINGO WARRIOR WARMONGER
JINGOISM CHAUVINISM
JINKER WHIM
JINN DJIN JANN AFRIT EBLIS GENIE
AFREET DJINNI SHAITAN
  (PL.) JINNI
JINNI MARID AFREET ALUKAH
GENIUS YAKSHA YAKSHI JINNIYEH
JINRIKIMAN KURUMAYA
JINRIKISHA GOCART KURUMA
RICKSHAW
JINX HEX JONAH HOODOO
JIPIJAPA CHIDRA PANAMA
PALMILLA TOQUILLA
JITTERBUG TRUCKING
JITTERY EDGY JUMPY TENSE
SPOOKY AJITTER
JIVARO JIBARO SHUARA XIBARO
JOAB (BROTHER OF —) ASAHEL
ABISHAI
  (MOTHER OF —) ZERUIAH
  (SLAYER OF —) BENAIAH
  (UNCLE OF —) DAVID
  (VICTIM OF —) ABNER
JOAH (FATHER OF —) ASAPH
JOAHAZ ZIMMAH OBEDEDOM
  (SON OF —) EDEN
JOAHAZ (SON OF —) JOAH
JOAN JUG JONE
  (— OF ARC) PUCELLE
JOANNA (FATHER OF —) RHESA
  (HUSBAND OF —) CHUZA
JOASH (FATHER OF —) AHAB
BECHER AHAZIAH SHEMAAH
JEHOAHAZ
  (SON OF —) GIDEON

(VICTIM OF —) ZECHARIAH
JOB LAY TUT CHAR CRIB FIST
SHOP TURN BERTH CHORE FIRST
PLACE BILLET HOBJOB HUSTLE
JOBSITE SWEATER BUSINESS
POSITION
(EASY —) BLUDGE
(FATHER OF —) ISSACHAR
(SMALL —) CHORE JOBBLE
JOBAB (FATHER OF —) JOKTAN
JOBBER BRAGER DEALER FLUNKY
BROGGER COURSER
JOB'S TEARS COIX ADLAI ADLAY
JOCHEBED (HUSBAND OF —)
AMRAM
(SON OF —) AARON MOSES
JOCKEY JOCK ROPER WASTER
CHANTER EQUISON TURFITE
SKIPJACK
(— FOR POSITION) DICE
(DISC —) DEEJAY
JOCOSE JOCO LEPID JOCULAR
JOCOTE MOMBIN
JOCOTE DE MICO BARBAS
JOCULAR GAY AIRY GLAD JOKY
DROLL FUNNY HAPPY JOLLY
MERRY WITTY BLITHE ELATED
JAPISH JOCOSE JOCUND JOKISH
JOVIAL JOYFUL JOYOUS LIVELY
BUOYANT COMICAL FESTIVE
GLEEFUL PLAYFUL WAGGISH
ANIMATED CHEERFUL DEBONAIR
GLADSOME HUMOROUS
JOCATORY JOKESOME
LAUGHING MIRTHFUL
BURLESQUE
JOCULARITY FUN WAGGERY
JOCUND BUDGE MERRY JOCANT
JOCULAR
JOE JO
(HALF —) JOANNES JOHANNES
JOED (FATHER OF —) PEDAIAH
JOEL (BROTHER OF —) NATHAN
(FATHER OF —) NEBO SAMUEL
ZICHRI PEDAIAH PETHUEL
IZRAHIAH
(SON OF —) HEMAN
JOELAH (FATHER OF —) JEROHAM
JOE-PYE WEED EUPATORY
JOEWOOD JOEBUSH BARBASCO
IRONWOOD
JOG BOB HOD JAG JIG JOT MOG
KICK POKE SHOG SPUD STIR TROT
WHIG DUNCH HOTCH MOSEY
NUDGE TWEAK DIDDLE JITTER
JOGGLE JUNDIE
(— ALONG) FADGE FODGE
(— AWKWARDLY) DODGE
(— WITH ELBOW) DUNCH
JOGGER LAYBOY
JOGGLE HOTCH JUGGLE SHOGGLE
SHOOGLE
JOGLI (SON OF —) BUKKI
JOHA (FATHER OF —) BERIAH
JOHANAN (FATHER OF —) JOSIAH
KAREAH TOBIAH AZARIAH
ELIOENAI HAKKATAN
(SON OF —) AZARIAH
JOHANNES JOE PECA
JOHN IAN JEAN JOCK JONE JUAN
SEAN JOHANN SEAGHAN
GIOVANNI
(BROTHER OF —) JAMES

(FATHER OF —) ZEBEDEE
ZACHARIAS
(MOTHER OF —) SALOME
ELISABETH
JOHN BROWN'S BODY (AUTHOR
OF —) BENET
(CHARACTER IN —) CLAY JACK
LUCY LUKE DUPRE SALLY SOPHY
SPADE VILAS ELLYAT MELORA
SHIPPY WINGATE WEATHERBY
BRECKINRIDGE
JOHNNYCAKE CORNCAKE
JOIADA (FATHER OF —) ELIASHIB
JOIAKIM (FATHER OF —) JESHUA
JOIN ADD COP FAY MIX OUP PAN
TAG TIE UNY ALLY COPE FAIR
FUSE GAIN GLUE KNIT LINK MEET
MELL SEAM SOUD TAIL TEAM
YOKE ANNEX BLEND ENTER
FRANK GRAFT JOINT MERGE
TENON UNITE WRING ACCEDE
ADJECT ADJOIN ASSIST ATTACH
CEMENT COCKET COMMIT
CONCUR ENGAGE INDENT
JOGGLE MARROW MINGLE PIECEN
RELATE RELIDE SPLICE STITCH
STRIKE COMBINE CONJOIN
CONNECT CONTACT INJOINT
JOINING SHACKLE ACCOUPLE
COALESCE COMPOUND COPULATE
DOVETAIL JUNCTION
ACCOMPANY
(— BATTLE) JOUST ENGAGE
(— BY SEWING) STITCH SUTURE
(— CLOSELY) FAY AFFY WELD
GRAFT
(— IN COMBAT) BUCKLE
(— IN MARRIAGE) WED TACK
HITCH COUPLE
(— THE PARTS OF) PIECE
(— TOGETHER) CLOSE COAPT
FRANK HITCH COUPLE ENGLUE
ENJOIN ASSEMBLE COAGMENT
COALESCE
(— UP) ACCEDE
(PREF.) ARTIO
JOINED JOINT ALLIED DIRECT
SEAMED ACCOLLE ADJUNCT
APPINED EMBOITE ADJUGATE
COMBINED CONJUNCT COPULATE
INTEGRAL
(PREF.) GAM(ETO)(O) ZEUCTO
ZEUGLO
JOINER SNUG WRIGHT JOINTER
JOINING BAR JOIN SEAM BRIDE
CLOSE SPLICE BETWEEN JOINDER
ADDITION JUNCTION JUNCTIVE
JUNCTURE SYNECTIC
JOINT BED HAR HIP BUTT COXA
FISH HEAD HELL HOCK JOIN KNEE
LITH LOCK SEAL SEAM TUCK
ANKLE BRAZE BUILD CARDO
CHASE ELBOW MITER MITRE
PLACE SCAPE SCARF SPALD
UNION UNITE WRIST BOXING
COMMON HAUNCH MUTUAL
SCARPH SPLICE STIFLE SUTURE
TOGGLE UNITER ARTHRON
ARTICLE COGGING DIGITAL
FETLOCK FLEXURE ISCHIUM
JOINING KNUCKLE SCATTER
SHIPLAP SIAMESE CONJOINT
CONJUNCT COUPLING DIACLASE

DOVETAIL FLASHING JOINTURE
JUNCTURE SUBJOINT SUFFRAGO
TROCHOID VARIATOR
(— ABOVE HOCK) STIFLE
(— OF BIRD'S WING) FLEXURE
(— OF FLAIL) CAPEL
(— OF MEAT) BARON SADDLE
(— OF SHIP) CHASE
(— OF STEM) NODE
(ANKLE —) COOT
(ELBOW —) NOOP
(FLEXIBLE —) HINGE
(GROOVED —) RABBET
(HIP —) COXA THURL
(MASONRY —) JOGGLE
(MINING —) CLEAT SLINE
(QUARRYING —) CUTTER
(SCARF —) BOXING
(UNIVERSAL —) CARDAN
(VERTICAL —) BUILD
(WHEEL-LIKE —) TROCHITE
(PREF.) ARTHR(O) ARTI CO
CONDYL(O) HARMO HOM(O)
JOINTED ARTHROUS
JOINTED CHARLOCK KRAUT
RUNCH
JOINTER JOINER SKIMMER
JOINT FIR EPHEDRA
JOINT GRASS PASPALUM
JOINTLY
(PREF.) CO COL COM CON COR
JOIST GEEST LEDGE BRIDGE
RAGLIN DORMANT SLEEPER
CARRIAGE
(PL.) PIGGIN JOISTING
JOJOBA PIGNUT SHEEPNUT
JOKE BAR DOR FUN GAB GAG GIG
JOE KID ROT WIT FOOL GAFF
GAME GAUD GEGG JAPE JEST
JOSH LICE NOTE QUIP QUIZ TYPE
BREAK CRACK FLIRT GLEEK GRIND
LAUGH PRANK RALLY SPORT
TRICK BANTER JAPERY PLISKY
WHEEZE JOKELET WAGGERY
CHESTNUT
(PRACTICAL —) BAR FUN GAG RIG
HOAX REAK SHAVIE HOTFOOT
(STALE —) CHESTNUT
(PL.) JAPERY
JOKER BUG DOR WAG CARD
CLOWN GRIND SLAVE FARCER
FOOLER GAGGER JOKIST
FARCEUR GIMMICK FUNNYMAN
HUMORIST JOKESTER
JOKESTER WAG WIT
JOKIM (FATHER OF —) SHELAH
JOKING JOSH BANTER JOCOSE
(PRACTICAL —) GAME
JOKSHAN (FATHER OF —)
ABRAHAM
(MOTHER OF —) KETURAH
(SON OF —) DEDAN SHEBA
JOKTAN (FATHER OF —) EBER
JOLLIFICATION RAG RANT BEANO
JOLLY SINDIG
JOLLITY MIRTH GAIETY HILARITY
JOLLITRY
JOLLY GAY KID BOON BUXOM
GAWSY MERRY RORTY SONSY
WALLY BLITHE CROUSE JOVIAL
STRING JOCULAR RAUGHTY
DISPOSED
JOLLY BOAT YAWL DANDY

JOLT JET JIG JOG JOT JUT BELT
BUMP DIRD DIRL HIKE JOWL
JUMP KICK SHOG JAUNT HOTTER
IMPACT JOGGLE JOSTLE JOUNCE
JUMBLE
JOLTING JERKY BUMPITY HOTTERY
JONA (SON OF —) PETER
JONADAB (COUSIN OF —) AMNON
(FATHER OF —) SHIMEAH
(UNCLE OF —) DAVID
JONAH JINX JONAS HOODOO
(FATHER OF —) AMITTAI
JONAN (FATHER OF —) ELIAKIM
JONATHAN (BROTHER OF —)
JOHANAN
(COMPANION OF —) DAVID
(FATHER OF —) SAUL ASAHEL
JOIADA KAREAH ABIATHAR
(SON OF —) MEPHIBOSHETH
JONQUIL JONK LILY DAFFODIL
JORAM (FATHER OF —) TOI AHAB
JEHOSHAPHAT

JORDAN
CAPITAL: AMMAN
COIN: DINAR
GULF: AQABA
MOUNTAIN: BUKKA DABAB ATAIBA
MUBRAK
REGION: PEREA BASHAN PERAEA
RIVER: JORDAN YARMUK
TOWN: AQABA ARIHA IRBID
KARAK ZARQA ZERKE NABLUS
JERICHO

JORIM (FATHER OF —) MATTHAT
JOSE (FATHER OF —) ELIEZER
JOSEPH JOSEY GIUSEPPE
(FATHER OF —) HELI JACOB JUDAH
MATTHIAS
(MOTHER OF —) RACHEL
(SON OF —) IGAL JESUS
(WIFE OF —) MARY ASENATH
JOSEPH ANDREWS (AUTHOR OF —
) FIELDING
(CHARACTER IN —) ADAMS BOOBY
FANNY PETER JOSEPH PAMELA
POUNCE THOMAS WILSON
ANDREWS GOODWILL SLIPSLOP
JOSEPHINE BLUSH PHENY
JOSEPH VANCE (AUTHOR OF —)
DEMORGAN
(CHARACTER IN —) JOE BONY
JANEY NOLLY SIBYL VANCE
JOSEPH LOSSIE THORPE VIOLET
BEPPINO DESPREZ PHEENER
RANDALL SPENCER PERCEVAL
CHRISTOPHER MACALLISTER
JOSES (BROTHER OF —) JESUS
(FATHER OF —) ELIEZER
JOSH GUY KID RIB JOKE CHAFF
STRING
JOSHAVIAH (FATHER OF —)
ELNAAM
JOSHBEKASHAH (FATHER OF —)
HEMAN
JOSHI JOTI JOTISARU
JOSHUA JESUS
(FATHER OF —) NUN JOZADAK
JOSIAH (FATHER OF —) AMON
ZEPHANIAH
(MOTHER OF —) JEDIDAH
JOSIBIAH (SON OF —) JEHU

JOSTLE JOG JOLT JOSS PUSH SHOG CROWD ELBOW HUNCH JUNDY SHOVE HURTLE HUSTLE JOGGLE JUNDIE JUSTLE SHOULDER
JOSTLING SCRAMBLE
JOT ACE DOT ATOM IOTA MARK MITE TARE WHIT GRAIN MINIM POINT TWINT WIGHT TITTLE SCRUPLE SYLLABLE
(— DOWN) NICK
JOTHAM (FATHER OF —) GIDEON UZZIAH
(MOTHER OF —) JERUSHAH
JOTTING TOT
JOTUNN GEIRROTH
JOUNCE HIKE JOLT JAUNT
JOURNAL TOE BOOK DIARY PAPER BLAZER SERIAL DAYBOOK DIURNAL GAZETTE GUDGEON JOURNEY CASHBOOK NOCTUARY TRUNNION
(SEA —) LOGBOOK
JOURNAL BEARING RHODING
JOURNALISM NEWSWRITING
JOURNALIST SCRIBE WRITER BYLINER DIARIAN
AMERICAN NEW BAUM CAIN COBB CROW DALY EDGE HOWE HUNT KENT MOTT OTIS OWEN PAGE PECK PRAY REED REID ROSS SNOW WEBB WEED ADAMS BACHE BAKER BEACH BEALS BEEBE BRANN BROUN CREEL DUANE EARLY ELSER FISKE FLYNN GREEN GUILD HARTE HOUSE IRWIN JAMES KROCK LEWIS LOCKE MCCOY MOLEY MOORE MORSE NOYES OGDEN OHARA PAINE PIATT POORE PRIME RALPH REEDY SAXON STONE STOWE SWING SWOPE TOWLE UPTON WALSH WHITE YOUNG ZEVIN ASBURY BAILEY BIERCE BISHOP BLIVEN BONSAL BOWERS BURMAN CHILDS CROUSE FOWLER GILDER GILMER GODWIN GRAHAM GRAVES GREENE HARVEY HASKIN HATTON HERSEY HOWARD HOWELL KEIRAN KENNAN LAFFAN LAWSON LELAND MANTLE MARDEN MEDILL MILLER MILLIS MORRIS MORTON MOWRER NELSON NEWELL PEGLER REDMAN RESTON RIDDER RUNYON SAVAGE SEAMAN SEATON SELDES SHIRER STREIT TAYLOR TILTON TUCKER TURNER WALKER WALTER WARMAN WILCOX WILSON ANTHONY BARRETT BIGELOW BRENNAN BULLARD CARROLL DANIELS EASTMAN EDWARDS FARRELL FEARING FISCHER FREEMAN GALLICO GARRETT GIBBONS GREELEY GUNTHER HALLOCK HASSARD KENDALL LOSSING MANNING MARQUIS MELONEY OCONNOR OURSLER OVERTON POLLARD PRINGLE RANDALL RAYMOND REDPATH RITCHIE RUSSELL SANBORN SERVISS

SMALLEY STANTON VANLOON VEILLER VILLARD WELLMAN WHEELER WOLFERT BROWNELL CREELMAN JOHNSTON LAWRENCE LIPPMANN MCINTYRE MCKELWAY MEREDITH PULITZER ROBINSON STARRETT STEFFENS STILLMAN STODDARD SULLIVAN THOMPSON TOWNSEND WESTCOTT WHITLOCK WILLIAMS BENEFIELD BERNSTEIN MACDONALD MARCOSSON MCCORMICK MOREHOUSE PATTERSON WATTERSON WOOLLCOTT CHAMBERLIN WEITZENKORN
ARGENTINIAN AVELLANEDA
AUSTRALIAN DONALD FAWKNER PATERSON
AUSTRIAN BAHR SEIDL HEVESI SAPHIR CASTELLI
CANADIAN LAUT BROWN DAFOE PAASSEN DECELLES FRECHETTE
CZECH CAPEK NERUDA HAVLICEK
DANISH JORGENSEN GOLDSCHMIDT
DUTCH SCHIMMEL
ENGLISH LOW MEE BELL FYFE GORE LANE LUCY MAIS SIMS BANKS BLAKE COTES CROWE DICEY DORAN GIBBS LEWIS MIALL MOULT SCOTT SHIEL STEAD STEED WERTH ARKELL ARNOLD BAINES BARKER BEGBIE BENHAM BOADEN BROOKS BUCKLE CANTON CASTLE CHIROL DILLON FORBES GARVIN GIBBON HANNAY MACKAY MANNIN MAYHEW MURRAY NORMAN REEVES SQUIRE TRAILL WATSON BOLITHO BYWATER CHORLEY COBBETT ENNEVER HAMMOND HERBERT HORABIN LEHMANN MEYNELL ROBERTS SHORTER SPENDER WALLACE BAERLEIN CARSWELL CHISHOLM COURTNEY FLETCHER HOBHOUSE LAWRENCE LOCKHART MONTAGUE MORRISON ROBINSON SLOCOMBE STEEVENS STRACHEY TOWNSEND WOODFALL BLANCHARD COLQUHOUN GREENWOOD LESTRANGE MACDONELL MONYPENNY THORNBURY BALLANTYNE BRAILSFORD CHATTERTON CHESTERTON FONBLANQUE HUDDLESTON MASSINGHAM THURSFIELD HOLLINGSHEAD
FRENCH BLUM KARR MACE PUJO BULOZ CAPUS CLAIR DUPUY GOSSE GRIMM HAMEL HAVES HERVE MEYER MILLE SOREL STEEG VERON BERTIN CARNOT CARREL DAUDET DELORD DUCAMP FONTAN FRERON GOZLAN HEBERT LEROUX MAZADE NISARD PICHON ROMIER SARCEY UZANNE BRISSOT CARRERE CHARMES GENOUDE HAUREAU LARBAUD LINGUET MICHAUD MIRBEAU NALECHE RECOULY REINACH REYBAUD

SCHERER SIMONDS TABOUIS TILLIER VIARDOT CALMETTE CLARETIE DUJARDIN GIRARDIN GUEROULT JOUVENEL MAZELINE NEFFTZER PELLETAN PERTINAX PROUDHON QUILLARD RENAUDOT RIVAROLI VEUILLOT BAINVILLE CAILLAVET CAVAIGNAC DESCHAMPS MIRECOURT ROCHEFORT SAUERWEIN VACQUERIE BARTHELEMY DESMOULINS LACRETELLE MONTLOSIER TASCHEREAU TAILLANDIER MONTALEMBERT
GERMAN LONS BUSCH THOMA BECKER DREYER EISNER GORRES GROSSE GUBITZ HARDEN BARTELS FRANZOS GUTZKOW HAMMANN KALISCH MARTENS BERNHARD ROHRBACH LIEBNECHT SCHUCKING STREICHER BEUMELBURG POSCHINGER
HUNGARIAN BAJZA BALAZS HUSZAR MORICZ RAKOSI
IRISH BELL LYND LESLIE OBRIEN OKELLY PIGOTT DESMOND OCONNOR ROLLESTON
ITALIAN ANCONA MONETA BATTISTI ALBERTINI FEDERZONI
JAPANESE INUKAI FUKUZAWA KAWAKAMI
NEW ZEALAND BALLANCE
NORWEGIAN FINNE VINJE
PARAGUAYAN BENITEZ
PERUVIAN CANDAMO
RUSSIAN KATKOV CHERNOV NOVIKOV DOBROLYUBOV
SCOTTISH BELL REID BLACK MUNRO CHALMERS CARRUTHERS
SWEDISH THORILD STRANDBERG
SWISS DROZ FAZY MEYER MURET DUCOMMUN
WELSH EVANS
JOURNEY BE GO JOG RUN WAY DIET EYRE FARE FORE GAIT GANG GATE HIKE JUMP RACE RAIK RIDE ROAD STEP TOUR TREK TRIP TURN WENT BROAD COVER DRIVE JAUNT REISE SITHE TRAIK TRAIL TURUS WEENT COMINO ERRAND FLIGHT HEGIRA JUNKET TRAVEL VAGARY EMBASSY ENTRADA EXCURSE JORNADA JOURNAL MEANDER PASSAGE STRETCH TRAVAIL TROUNCE WALKING WAYFARE GODSPEED PROGRESS PILGRIMAGE
(— BY SEA) VOYAGE
(— DOWNSTREAM) DESCEND
(DAY'S —) DIET
(DESERT —) JORNADA
(FATIGUING —) TRAIK
(LONG —) TREK
(TEDIOUS —) TRANCE
(PL.) PERIPATETICS
JOURNEYING CRUISE
JOURNEYMAN YEOMAN
JOUST PLAY TILT JOSTLE JUSTLE TOURNEY
JOUSTER TILTER
JOVIAL GAY BOON JOVY BULLY JOLLY MERRY GENIAL HEARTY

MELLOW WANTON BACCHIC HOLIDAY JOCULAR CONVIVIAL RANTIPOLE
JOVIALITY JOLLITY ROLLICK HILARITY
JOWL CHOW CHAULE
(PL.) CHOPS
JOY JO WIN GLEE LIST PLAY BLISS CHEER DREAM EXULT MIRTH REVEL GAIETY HEYDAY DELIGHT ECSTASY ELATION JOYANCE RAPTURE REVELRY FELICITY GLADNESS HILARITY PLEASURE
JOYFUL GAY GLAD BEAMY JOLLY BLITHE FESTUS JOCUND JOVIAL JOYANT JOYOUS GAUDFUL GLADFUL GLEEFUL JOCULAR GLADSOME
JOYFULLY FAIN FAINLY GLADLY JOYOUSLY
JOYLESS DESOLATE LUSTLESS UNBLITHE
JOYOUS GAY GLAD JOLLY MERRY YOUSE BLITHE JOVIAL FESTIVE GIOJOSO GLEEFUL JOCULAR SMILING FRABJOUS FROHLICH SUNSHINY
JOYOUSNESS HILARITY
JOZABAD (FATHER OF —) JESHUA
JOZACHAR (VICTIM OF —) JOASH
JUBAL (FATHER OF —) LAMECH
(MOTHER OF —) ADAH
JUBILANT ELATED JOYFUL EXULTANT
JUBILATION JOY JOYANCE JUBILEE
JUDA (FATHER OF —) JOSEPH HANANIAH
(MOTHER OF —) JOANNA
JUDAH (FATHER OF —) JACOB
(MOTHER OF —) LEAH
JUDAHITE JEW
JUDAISM JEWISM HEBRAISM
JUDAS TREE CERCIS
JUDEA JEWRY
JUDEO-SPANISH LADINO
JUDE THE OBSCURE (AUTHOR OF —) HARDY
(CHARACTER IN —) SUE DONN JUDE FAWLEY RICHARD ARABELLA DRUSILLA BRIDEHEAD PHILLOTSON
JUDGE (ALSO SEE JURIST) DAN JUS SEE WIG CADI CAID CAZY DEEM DOOM HOLD IMAM JUEZ JURY KAZI QADI RATE RULE SCAN AWARD COUNT COURT DAYAN GAUGE HAKIM INFER JUDEX MINOS OPINE PUNEE TRIER WEIGH BREHON CENSOR CRITIC DANIEL DECERN DEEMER DICAST DOOMER INTEND JUDGER JURIST OPINER PUISNE SAMSON SAMUEL SETTLE SQUIRE ACCOUNT ADJUDGE ALCALDE ARBITER BENCHER BRIDOYE CENSURE DISCERN FLAGMAN FOUJDAR HELIAST JURYMAN JUSTICE MUNSIFF PODESTA REFEREE SCABINE SHAMGAR SUPPOSE APPRAISE CENTENAR CONCLUDE CONSIDER DEEMSTER DEMPSTER DIRECTOR DOOMSMAN

DOOMSTER ESTIMATE FOREDEEM JEPHTHAH JUDGMENT JUDICATE LINESMAN MINISTER MITTIMUS ORDINARY QUAESTOR RECORDER REGICIDE SCABINUS STRADICO **(— OF UNDERWORLD)** AEACUS **(PREF.)** KRIT(O)

JUDGMENT ACT EYE BOOK DEEM DOME DOOM REDE VIEW ARRET AWARD FANCY JUISE SENSE SIGHT SKILL TASTE ADVICE ASSIZE DECREE ESTEEM JUWISE OUSTER STEVEN ACCOUNT CENSURE CONCEIT HOLDING OPINION THOUGHT VERDICT WITTING DECISION ESTIMATE JUDICIAL JUDICIUM SAGACITY SAPIENCE SENTENCE THINKING PREJUDICE OBSERVATION **(PREF.)** GNOMO

JUDICATORY SYNOD

JUDICIOUS SAGE WISE POLITIC PRUDENT CRITICAL JUDICIAL MODERATE SENSEFUL SENSIBLE WISELIKE

JUDITH (FATHER OF —) BEERI **(HUSBAND OF —)** ESAU

JUDITH PARIS (AUTHOR OF —) WALPOLE **(CHARACTER IN —)** ADAM EMMA JOHN CARDS DAVID PARIS STANE JUDITH REUBEN WALTER WARREN DOROTHY FRANCIS GAUNTRY GEORGES HERRIES SUNWOOD WILLIAM FORESTER JENNIFER CHRISTADEL FERNYHIRST

JUDO (— EXERCISES) KATA **(— PRACTICE)** RANDORI **(— SCHOOL)** DOJO **(EXPERT LEVEL IN —)** DAN

JUG CAN EWER JACK JUST ASCUS ASKOS BUIRE GAMLA GOTCH JORUM JUBBE STEAN BOGGLE CROUKE GOGLET GOMLAH HYDRIA CREAMER PITCHER CRUISKEN LECYTHUS LEKYTHOS OENOCHOE PROCHOOS **(— WITH SPOUT)** BUIRE DOLLIN **(ALE —)** TOBY **(BEER —)** BOCK **(BULGING —)** GOTCH **(LEATHER —)** JACK BOMBARD **(ONE-HANDLED —)** URCEUS **(SPOUTLESS —)** OLPE

JUGATED BAJOIRE

JUGGLE TRICK BAFFLE FUMBLE CONJURE SHUFFLE

JUGGLER HARLOT CONJURER JONGLEUR TREGETOUR

JUGLONE NUCIN

JUGULARES DERIPIA

JUGUM FIBULA JUGULUM

JUICE JUS SEW BREE BROO FOND OOZE SUCK ANIMA BLOND BLOOD GRAVY HUMOR LASER MOBBY PERRY CASIRI CREMOR JIPPER SUCCUS CAMBIUM AGUAMIEL HYPOCIST VERJUICE **(— OF COCONUT)** MILK **(— OF TREE)** SAP LYCIUM JELUTONG **(— OF UNRIPE FRUIT)** OMPHACY

(APPLE —) CIDER **(CANE —)** SLING **(CASSAVA —)** CASSAREEP CASSARIPE **(CONCENTRATED —)** SIRUP SYRUP **(DRIED —)** ALOE KINO **(FERMENTED —)** SURA GRAPE **(FRUIT —)** ROB ROHOB **(GRAPE —)** MUST SAPA STUM **(INSPISSATED —)** HYPOCIST **(INTOXICATING —)** SOMA **(LETTUCE —)** THRIDACE **(MEAT —)** BLOND **(POPPY —)** CHICK MECONIUM **(TOBACCO —)** AMBEER AMBIER **(PL.)** ESSENCE HUMIDITY **(PREF.)** CHYL(I)(O) MYRO OPO **(SUFF.)** CIDAL CIDE

JUICY FAT FRIM FRUM NAISH SAPPY FRUITY SUCCOSE WATERISH

JUJUBE BER ELB TSAO LOTUS LOTEBUSH LOTEWOOD ZIZYPHUS

JUKEBOX PICCOLO NICKELODEON

JULIUS CAESAR (AUTHOR OF —) SHAKESPEARE **(CHARACTER IN —)** CATO CASCA CINNA CLITO PORTA VARRO BRUTUS CAESAR CICERO CIMBER DECIUS JULIUS LUCIUS MARCUS STRATO CASSIUS FLAVIUS LEPIDUS MESSALA PUBLIUS ANTONIUS CLAUDIUS LIGARIUS LUCILIUS MARULLUS METELLUS OCTAVIUS PINDARUS POPILIUS TITINIUS CALPURNIA DARDANIUS TREBONIUS VOLUMNIUS ARTEMIDORUS

JUMBLE PI PIE ROG HASH MESS MUSS RAFF BOTCH BOLLIX BUMBLE FUDDLE GARBLE HUDDLE JABBLE JUMPER JUNGLE MEDLEY MOMBLE MUDDLE PALTER RAFFLE WELTER WUZZLE CLUTTER CONFUSE EMBROIL GOULASH SHUFFLE DISORDER MISHMASH PASTICHE RHAPSODY SMACHRIE **(— OF SOUNDS)** LURRY

JUMBLED CRAZY HASHY JUMBLY MEDLEY HUDDLING MACARONIC

JUMP HOP LEP NIP DART JETE LEAP LUTZ SKIP SKIT STEN STOT TUMB BOUND CAPER FENCE HALMA SALTO SAULT SPANG SPEND START STOIT VAULT DOUBLE FOOTER HURDLE INSULT LAUNCH SPRING SPRUNT STARRE WALLOP CISEAUX CROWHOP SALTATE SKYLARK BALLONNE **(— ABOUT)** SKIT CAPER **(— FROM AIRCRAFT)** BAIL BALE **(— IN FENCING)** BALESTRA **(— ON HORSEBACK)** LARK **(— ON SKATES)** AXEL SALCHOW **(— TO CONCLUSION)** SALTUS **(PL.)** ALLEGRO

JUMPER LAMMY SWAGE BARKER LEPPER HANDYMAN

JUMPING SALIENT SALTANT

JUMPING JACK PANTINE

JUMPY ITCHY NERVOUS

JUNCO SNOWBIRD

JUNCTION HIP FROG JOIN CLOSE CROWN RAPHE UNION FILLET INFALL CONTACT JOINING MEETING UNITION ABUTMENT JUNCTURE CONSERTION **(— OF EARTH AND SKY)** HORIZON **(— OF STREAMS)** GRAINS **(— OF THREADS)** FELL STOP **(— ON TOOTH)** CERVIX

JUNCTURE PASS PINCH CRISIS STRAIT ARTICLE BRACKET JOINING OPHRYON EXIGENCY JOINTAGE JOINTURE OCCASION QUANDARY

JUNEBERRY SHADBLOW SHADBUSH SERVICEBERRY

JUNE BUG DUZZARD DUMCLOCK

JUNGLE BUSH RUKH SHOLA BOONDOCK **(AUTHOR OF —)** SINCLAIR **(CHARACTER IN —)** ONA JACK DUANE JONAS CONNOR JURGIS MARIJA RUDKUS ANTANAS ELZBIETA STANISLOVAS

JUNGLE BENDY WEENONG

JUNGLE BOOK (AUTHOR OF —) KIPLING **(CHARACTER IN —)** KAA KHAN AKELA BALOO HATHI SHERE BULDEO MESSUA MOWGLI TABAQUI BAGHEERA BANDARLOG

JUNIOR PUNY CADET YOUNG PUISNE YOUNGER

JUNIPER CADE EZEL GORSE GORST RETEM SAVIN SABINE

JUNK GNAM GEAN GOOK TOPE DRECK REFUSE SCULCH DISCARD PLUNDER TONGKANG **(WORTHLESS —)** SLUM

JUNKET TRIP KNACK JINKET SAFARI

JUNKMAN TATTER SCRAPMAN SCAVENGER

JUNO MONETA PRONUBA

JUNO AND THE PAYCOCK (AUTHOR OF —) OCASEY **(CHARACTER IN —)** JACK JUNO MARY BOYLE JERRY JOXER DEVINE JOHNNY BENTHAM CHARLIE TANCRED

JUPITER JOVE STATOR FORTUNE MUSHTARI TERMINUS **(PREF.)** JOVI ZENO

JUPITER'S BEARD JOUBARB SENGREEN

JUR LWO LUOH

JUREL RUNNER CREVALLE HARDTAIL

JURGEN (AUTHOR OF —) CABELL **(CHARACTER IN —)** LISA HELEN JURGEN MERLIN SEREDA ANAITIS CHLORIS DESIREE DOLORES DOROTHY KOSHCHEI GUENEVERE

JURISDICTION SOC BAIL SOKE FUERO HONOR REALM VERGE ABBACY BANDON BEYLIK DANGER DIWANI RIDING SPHERE DEANERY DEWANEE DROSTDY EMIRATE FOUDRIE KHANATE BAILIERY CHAPELRY FOUJDARY LIGEANCE PASHALIC PROVINCE **(— OF BISHOP)** SEE **(COERCIVE —)** SWORD

(MORMON —) KEYS **(SUFF.)** DOM

JURISPRUDENCE LAW BYRLAW REPORTS

JURIST JUDGE MUFTI BREHON LAWYER DOTTORE **AMERICAN** DAY JAY LEE BOND DANA DANE DYER GOFF GRAY HALL HUNT KENT NOTT POPE REED RUSK SHAW TAFT TAIT WARE ZANE BETTS BLACK BLAIR BROWN CASEY CHASE DAVIS DAWES DUANE EATON FIELD FREAR GRIER LAMAR LOGAN MOODY MOORE PAINE RANDA SMITH STONE STORY TANEY TYLER WAITE WAYNE WEARE WHITE WYTHE YATES BAYLOR BREWER BURGER BURTON BUTLER BYRNES CATRON CLARKE COOLEY CURTIS DANIEL DARROW DULLES FOLGER FORTAS FULLER GASTON GIBSON HARLAN HOLMES HUDSON HUGHES JEROME KENYON LANDIS LOWELL LURTON MARTIN MILLER MINTON MORRIS MURPHY NELSON PARKER PECORA PETERS PITNEY POWELL SEWALL STRONG SUMNER SWAYNE UPSHUR VINSON WARREN WILBUR BALDWIN BRADLEY CARDOZO CLAYTON CUSHING DOUGLAS DRAYTON GRIFFIN JACKSON JOHNSON LINDSEY MCKENNA PARSONS PODERTO PANDOON SANFORD SHERMAN STEVENS STOWELL TRIMBLE WHARTON WHEATON ANDERSON BLACKMUN BRANDEIS CLIFFORD GOLDBERG GRISWOLD GROSSCUP KIRCHWAY LAWRENCE MACVEAGH MARSHALL MATTHEWS MCKINLEY MITCHELL PENFIELD ROSENMAN RUTLEDGE SEDGWICK STAFFORD WALWORTH WOODBURY ELLSWORTH GREENLEAF GROESBECK HOPKINSON PENDLETON SHARSWOOD UNDERWOOD WHITTAKER BLATCHFORD MCREYNOLDS POINDEXTER TROWBRIDGE WASHINGTON FRANKFURTER VANDEVANTER **ARGENTINIAN** CALVO DRAGO ALBERDI CASADO CASTILLO **AUSTRIAN** GROSS UNGER GLASER ZELLER REDLICH LAMMASCH RINTELEN SCHMERLING **BELGIAN** NYS PICARD LAURENT DESCAMPS GERLACHE **BOLIVIAN** SILES SAAVEDRA **BRAZILIAN** PESSOA BARBOSA BARROSO PECANHA **CANADIAN** CARON JETTE ARMOUR DAVIES MULOCK STUART DOHERTY LACOSTE FOURNIER HAULTAIN NEWCOMBE RICHARDS ROBINSON HALIBURTON FITZPATRICK **CHILEAN** EGANA DONOSO **COSTA RICAN** CARRILLO

CZECH HACHA

DUTCH GEER ASSER LODER GROTIUS OPZOOMER BYNKERSHOEK

ENGLISH MAY AMOS CAVE COKE HALE HOLT KING REID ANSON BOWEN BRYCE GROVE HURST IMPEY JAMES MAINE PRATT SCOTT TWISS VINER ABBOTT ATKYNS AUSTIN BARNES CARSON DAVIES FINLAY GATLEY HENLEY HEWART HUGHES MERSEY NORTON PALMER SANKEY SELDEN AMULREE DARLING GODFREY HOLLAND JENKINS MOULTON PLOWDEN CAMPBELL CHALMERS HAILSHAM JEFFREYS CALDECOTE FORTESCUE HERSCHELL LITTLETON OPPENHEIM BLACKSTONE FITZHERBERT

FRENCH ADAM GIDE MOLE DOMAT FLACH WEISS COCHIN DEMETZ DONEAU DUGUIT GOHIER HOTMAN MERLIN PITHOU DECAZES HENAULT LECONTE NOGARET RENAULT CUJACIUS DUMOULIN GODEFROY PASQUIER PORTALIS AGUESSEAU BEAUMANOIR EPREMESNIL LAFERRIERE

GERMAN UZ BAR FALK GANS HUGO KAHL POST WACH ZORN CROME FRANK HANEL KRAUS MOSER SPAHN TEMME WITTE AEGIDI AHRENS FICKER GERBER GNEIST HITZIG KELSEN LABAND

MEZGER PREUSS BOCKING COCCEJI GOLDAST GOSCHEL HEFFTER KOSTLIN RICHTER THIBAUT WICHERT ANCILLON DERNBURG EICHRODT FISCHART GEFFCKEN HABERLIN HEDEMANN HUFELAND ALTHUSIUS EBERMAYER FEUERBACH HINSCHIUS KIRCHMANN PUFENDORF HEINECCIUS KOHLRAUSCH GOLDSCHMIDT KANTOROWICZ MITTERMAIER HOLTZENDORFF

GREEK POLITES

INDIAN SAPRU

IRISH BALL MORRIS OHAGAN MACNEILL FITZGIBBON

ITALIAN AZO FIORE ROCCO ACCORSO ALCIATI CARRARA GRAVINA MANCINI TANUCCI BARTOLUS BULGARUS GAROFALO IRNERIUS ANZILOTTI ROMAGNOSI FILANGIERI PIERANTONI

JAPANESE ADACHI

MEXICAN IGLESIAS

NEW ZEALAND STOUT BULLER MANING

NORWEGIAN FALSEN HAGERUP

PANAMANIAN PORRAS

PARAGUAYAN BAEZ

PERUVIAN CORNEJO

ROMAN GAIUS LABEO CELSUS FRONTO PAULUS ULPIAN SABINUS SALVIUS PAPINIAN PROCULUS SCAEVOLA SULPICIUS TRIBONIAN MODESTINUS GREGORIANUS

RUSSIAN KAVELIN MARTENS MUROMTSEV MEYENDORFF VINOGRADOFF POBEDONOSTSEV

SCOTTISH HOME CRAIG FORBES ERSKINE GIFFORD JEFFREY LORIMER BROUGHAM

SPANISH GALVEZ PINELO AGUSTIN

SWEDISH UNDEN

SWISS DUBS MUSY HILTY HUBER LARDY MEILI BLUMER DELOLME

URAGUAYAN BRUM

JUROR JURAT ASSIZER JURYMAN CENTUMVIR

JURY ARRAY PANEL QUEST ASSIZE JURATA COUNTRY EMPANEL INQUEST

(— COUNTY) VISNE

JURYMAN DICAST JURIST ASSIZER

JURY-RIGGED HAYWIRE

JUST ALL DUE EVEN FAIR FLOP LEAL ONLY TRUE EQUAL FIRST LEVEL NOBUT ROUND VALID ZADOC CANDID GIUSTO HONEST JUSTIN JUSTUS MERELY SQUARE EQUABLE LEESOME UPRIGHT ACCURATE LIEFSOME RATIONAL RIGHTFUL SKILLFUL UNBIASED

(— AS) AFTER

(— HOVE CLEAR) ATRIP

(— IN TIME) SONICA

(ONLY —) HARDLY SCARCELY

JUSTAUCORPS JUSTICO

JUSTICE LAW DOOM RIGHT SKILL DHARMA EQUITY REASON HONESTY SHALLOW SILENCE DEEMSTER JUDGMENT JUSTITIA JUSTNESS RECORDER

(— OF PEACE) BEAK SQUIRE

(AUTHOR OF —) GALSWORTHY

(CHARACTER IN —) HOW RUTH DAVIS FROME JAMES FALDER WALTER CLEAVER COKESON WILLIAM HONEYWILL

(PREF.) DICAEO

JUSTIFIABLY FAIRLY

JUSTIFICATION CALL COLOR EXCUSE APOLOGY DEFENCE WARRANT APOLOGIA

JUSTIFIED FAIR JUST

JUSTIFY AVOW CLEAR PROVE SALVE DEFEND EXCUSE HONEST EXPLAIN RECTIFY SUPPORT WARRANT DARRAIGN MAINTAIN SANCTION UNDERPIN VINDICATE

JUSTLY WELL TRULY EVENLY FAIRLY EQUALLY HANDILY SQUARELY

JUSTNESS SQUARE FITNESS JUSTICE ACCURACY

JUSTUS JESUS

JUT HANG BULGE JETTY JUTTY BEETLE EXTEND IMPEND EXTRUDE

JUTE PAT DESI PAUT DAISEE ARAMINA CHINGMA

JUTTING HANGING

JUVENILE TEEN YOUNG JEJUNE PUERILE YOUTHFUL

JUXTAPOSED ADJACENT

JUXTAPOSITION BALANCE CONTACT CONTRAST NEARNESS

K

K KA KAY KILO KING
KAABA CAABA ALCAABA
KABAYA BADJU CABIE
KABELJOU KOB
KABISTAN KUBA
KABOB KEBOB SHASLIK
KABUKALLI CUPIUBA
KACHA (FATHER OF —) BRIHASPATI
KACHARI BODO
KACHIN SINGFO SINGPO
 CHINGPAW
KADAGA COORG
KADAMBARI (FATHER OF —)
 CHITRARATHA
 (MOTHER OF —) MADIRA
KAFFIR KATI XOSA FINGO TEMBU
 CAFFRE INFIDEL TAMBUKI
 WAIGULI
 (— BOY) UMFAAN
KAGU GRUIFORM
KAHODA (SON OF —) ASHTAVAKRA
KAIKAWAKA CEDAR
KAIKAWUS (FATHER OF —)
 KAIQUBAD
 (WIFE OF —) SAUDABAH
KAIKEYI (HUSBAND OF —)
 DASHARATHA
 (SON OF —) BHARATA
KAIKHUSRAU (FATHER OF —)
 SYAWAUSH
 (MOTHER OF —) FARANGIS
KAINGIN SWIDDEN
KAKI TRIUMPH
KAKU (GRANDFATHER OF —) ZOHAK
 (SLAYER OF —) MINUCHIHR
KALAPOOIAN LAKMIUT
KALE COLE KAIL COLLARD
 SPROUTS BORECOLE ·
KALEVALA (AUTHOR OF —)
 UNKNOWN
 (CHARACTER IN —) KULLERVO
 ILMARINEN VAINAMOINEN
 LEMMINKAINEN
KALI (HUSBAND OF —) SIVA SHIVA
KALMASHAPADA (FATHER OF —)
 SUDASA
KALMUCK ELEUT UIRAD KHOSHOT
KALPA EON AEON
KALUMPIT ANAGEP
KAMA (DAUGHTER OF —) TRISHA
 (FATHER OF —) DHARMA
 (MOTHER OF —) LAKSHMI
 SHRADDHA
 (SON OF —) ANIRUDDHA
 (WIFE OF —) RATI PRITI
KAMAHI BIRCH TOWAI
KAMALA WURRUS ROTTLERA
KAME AS
KAMICHI SCREAMER
KAMPUCHEA (SEE CAMBODIA)
KANA IROFA IROHA
KANGAROO ROO EURO BILBI FLIER
 FLYER TUNGO BOOMER FOSTER
 WOILIE DIDELPH POTOROO
 WALLABY BETTONGA BOONGARY
 FILANDER FORESTER WALLAROO
 (FEMALE —) DOE GIN
 (YOUNG —) JOEY
KANGAROO APPLE GUNYANG
 POROPORO
KANGAROO RAT JERBOA
 BETTONG POTOROO
KANHOBAL CONOB
KANKANAI IGOROT
KANS KUSA GLAGA KUSHA
 GLAGAH
KANSA (FATHER OF —) UGRASENA
 (SLAYER OF —) KRISHNA
KANSAN JAYHAWK

KANSAS
CAPITAL: TOPEKA
COLLEGE: BAKER TABOR BETHANY
 STERLING WASHBURN
COUNTY: ELK GOVE LINN LYON
 NESS RENO GEARY PRATT
 ROOKS TREGO BARTON COFFEY
 NEMAHA NEOSHO BOURBON
 LABETTE ATCHISON
FORT: RILEY SCOTT
INDIAN: KANSA KIOWA PAWNEE
 WICHITA COMANCHE
LAKE: CHENEY KIRWIN NEOSHO
 MILFORD
MOUNTAIN: SUNFLOWER
NATIVE: JAYHAWK
NICKNAME: JAYHAWKER
 SUNFLOWER
PRESIDENT: EISENHOWER
RIVER: SALINE SOLOMON
 ARKANSAS MISSOURI
STATE BIRD: MEADOWLARK
STATE FLOWER: SUNFLOWER
STATE TREE: COTTONWOOD
TOWN: ALMA GOVE HAYS IOLA
 COLBY DODGE HOXIE LAKIN
 LEOTI SEDAN LARNED SALINA
 ABILENE CHANUTE LIBERAL
 ULYSSES WICHITA

KAOLIANG SORGHUM
KAPOK CEIBO FLOSS
KARAISM ANANISM
KARAKA KOPI
KARA KIRGHIZ BURUT BOUROUT
KARATAS PITA
KARATE (— SCHOOL) DOJO
 (EXPERT LEVEL IN —) DAN
KAREN SGAU SGAW
KARENNI PADAUNG
KARMA FATE
 (BAD —) DEMERIT
KARNA (FATHER OF —) SURYA
 (MOTHER OF —) KUNTI PRITHA
 (SLAYER OF —) ARJUNA
KARTTIKEYA (FATHER OF —)

 RUDRA SHIVA
KASKA NAHANE
KAT KHAT QUAT CAFTA
KATE KAI
KATHERINE (HUSBAND OF —)
 PETRUCHIO
KAUNAS KOVNO
KAURI COWRIE BERAIROU
KAUSHALYA (HUSBAND OF —)
 DASHARATHA
 (SON OF —) RAMA
KAVA AVA AWA YAQONA
 KAVAKAVA YANGGONA
KAW AKHA
KAYANUSH (BROTHER OF —)
 FARIDUN PURMAYAH
KAZOO BAZOO GAZOO ZARAH
 HEWGAG MIRLITON
KEEL FIN BACK SEEL BARGE
 CARINA CRISTA RADDLE SERRULA
 (— OF BIRD'S MANDIBLE) GONYS
 (AFTERPART OF —) SKAG SKEG
 (PREF.) CARINI
KEEN DRY FLY GAY SHY YAP ACID
 DEAR FINE GAIR GLEG HIGH
 HOWL NUTS PERT TART TEEN
 WAIL WARM WILD ACUTE BREME
 BRIEF BRISK EAGER QUICK SHARP
 SMART SNELL SPICY VIVID
 ARGUTE ASTUTE BITTER CAOINE
 GREEDY LIVELY SEVERE SHREWD
 SHRILL CUNNING HAWKING
 MORDANT PARLISH PARLOUS
 PUNGENT SERIOUS THIRSTY
 OBSERVANT SAGACIOUS
 TRENCHANT PERSPICACIOUS
 (PREF.) OXY
KEENER HOWLER
KEENLY KEEN FELLY DEARLY
 ACUTELY
KEENNESS EDGE ACUITY ACUMEN
 PUNGENCY
 (— OF SIGHT) ACIES
KEEN-SCENTED NASUTE
 NOSEWISE
KEEN-SIGHTED EAGLE
KEEP HUG HAVE HOLD SALT SAVE
 WAIT WITE BLESS ROCCA WITIE
 COFFER DETAIN REDUIT CONFINE
 CONTAIN DEFORCE HUSBAND
 KEEPING OBSERVE RESERVE
 CONSERVE MAINTAIN PRESERVE
 RESTRAIN WITHHOLD
 (— A COURSE) CAPE
 (— A SMALL SHOP) CRAME
 (— A WOUND OPEN) TENT
 (— ABREAST) FOLLOW
 (— AFLOAT) BUOY
 (— AN EYE ON) STAG
 (— APART) DOTTLE ISOLATE
 SEPARATE
 (— AT A DISTANCE) ESTRANGE
 (— AWAY) ABSENT

 (— AWAY FROM) ABHOR AVOID
 (— BACK) DAM HAP ROB STAY
 ARREAR DETAIN RETARD
 RESERVE
 (— COMPANY WITH) GANG MOOP
 CONSORT
 (— FREE) ESCHEW
 (— FROM BOILING OVER) KEEL
 (— FROM BURNING) REDD
 (— HIDDEN) HOARD SECRETE
 (— IN) CAGE
 (— IN CIRCULATION) WIND
 (— IN EXCITEMENT) ALARM
 ALARUM
 (— IN MIND) RETAIN
 (— IN ORDER) TARGE
 (— IN STOCK) CARRY
 (— IN THE TRACK) GATHER
 (— OFF) FEND WEAR EXPEL
 SHIELD
 (— OUT) BAR EXPEL
 (— POSSESSION) HARBOR
 (— SCORELESS) BLANK
 (— SECRET) HUSH WHIST
 (— STRAIGHT) DIRECT
 (— TABS ON) FINGER
 (— TIME) GO
 (— TO ONESELF) BOSOM
 (— UNTIL YEAR OLD) HOG
 (— UP) SUBSIST SUSTAIN
 CONTINUE
 (— WAITING) DELAY
 (— WARM) STIVE STOVE FOSTER
 (— WATCH) BARK TOUT WAIT
 BEWAKE
 (PREF.) SOZ(O)
 (— OFF) ALEXI
KEEPER NAB KEEP SCREW TUTOR
 YEMER CUSTOS GAOLER JAILER
 LIFTER LOOKER PARKER PASTOR
 RAHDAR RANGER WARDEN
 BAILIFF CURATOR GEARMAN
 PIKEMAN PROVOST BEARWARD
 DEERHERD DOLLYMAN
 ELDERMAN FEWTERER
 GUARDANT GUARDIAN
 HOUNDMAN TRAITEUR
 WARRENER
 (— OF CATTLE) HAYWARD
 (— OF DOGS) FEWTERER
 (— OF ELEPHANT) MAHOUT
 (— OF PRISON) GAOLER JAILER
 WARDEN ALCAIDE PROVOST
 (DOOR —) DURWAN
KEEPING CARE WARD TRUST
 CHARGE CUSTODY DETAINER
KEEPSAKE DRURY TOKEN
 GIFTBOOK SOUVENIR
KEEVE TUB KIEVE
KEG CAG PIN TUB CADE CASK
 KNAG WOOD ANKER BARRICO
 COSTREL
KELP KILP LEAG VAREC WRACK

GIRDLE SEAWEED BELLWARE
KELPIE NIX BARB
KELT SLAT LIGGER
KENAF DA GOMBO MESTA AMBARI
KANAFF PAPOULA STOKROOS
KENILWORTH (AUTHOR OF —)
SCOTT
(CHARACTER IN —) AMY HUGH
TONY GILES JANET SMITH
ALASCO DICKIE DUDLEY EDMUND
FOSTER SLUDGE SUSSEX VARNEY
WALTER GOSLING MICHAEL
RALEIGH RICHARD ROBSART
WAYLAND DOBOOBIE ELIZABETH
LAMBOURNE LEICESTER
TRESSILIAN FLIBBERTIGIBBET
KENNEL STALL VENERY VENISON
DOGHOUSE
KENO HOUSE
KENTISH (— UNIT) YOKE

KENTUCKY

CAPITAL: FRANKFORT
COLLEGE: BEREA ASBURY CENTRE
BRESCIA URSULINE
COUNTY: BATH BELL BOYD HART
TODD ADAIR BOYLE TRIGG
WOLFE ESTILL MENIFEE
MAGOFFIN
INDIAN: SHAWNEE CHEROKEE
IROQUOIS
LAKE: CUMBERLAND
RIVER: DIX OHIO SALT BARREN
STATE BIRD: CARDINAL
STATE FLOWER: GOLDENROD
STATE NICKNAME: BLUEGRASS
STATE TREE: TULIP
TOWN: INEZ BEREA CADIZ DIXON
HYDEN MCKEE PARIS CORBIN
HARLAN HAZARD GLASGOW
GREENUP PADUCAH DANVILLE
COVINGTON LEXINGTON
OWENSBORO

KENYA

BAY: FORMOSA
CAPITAL: NAIROBI
COIN: SHILLING
LAKE: MAGADI RUDOLF NAIVASHA
VICTORIA
LANGUAGE: LUO KIKUYU SWAHILI
MEASURE: WARI
MOUNTAIN: ELGON KENYA KULAL
NYIRU MATIAN LOGONOT
PEOPLE: LUO MERU BANTU
KAMBA KISII LUHYA MASAI
NANDI KIKUYU OGADEN
BALUHYA HAMITIC HILOTIC
TURKANA KIPSIGIS
RIVER: LAK ATHI TANA KEIRO
TURKWELL
TOWN: MERU KITUI NAROK KIPINI
KISUMU MOYALE NAKURU
NAYUKI ELDORET MALINDI
MOMBASA

KERCHIEF CURCH ROMAL RUMAL
ANALAV CYPRUS MADRAS
NAPKIN PEPLUM CYPRESS
KERCHER PANUELO THERESE
BABUSHKA BANDANNA HEADRAIL
KAFFIYEH KINGSMAN

KERESAPA (BROTHER OF —)
URVAKHSHAYA
(FATHER OF —) THRITA
KERF CARF SKAFF GROOVE
UNDERCUT
KERI QRI KERE
KERMANSHAH COCONUT
KERMES GRAIN
KERNEL NUT BUNT CORE KERN
MEAT PITH BERRY GOODY GROAT
ACINUS ALMOND CARNEL PICKLE
NUCLEUS PICHURIM
(CORN —S) HOMINY
(UNHUSKED —S) CAPES
(PL.) NIXTAMAL
(PREF.) CARY(O) KARY(O)
KEROGEN SAPROPEL
KEROSINE PARAFFIN
KERSENNEH ERS ERVIL
KERSEY WASHER ORDINARY
KESTREL FANNER KEELIE STANIEL
STANNEL STANCHEL WINDHOVER
KETA CHUM
KETCH SAIC
KETONE IRONE ACETOL ARMONE
CARONE CARVOL COTOIN
HEXONE IONONE QUINOL
ACETOIN ACETONE ACYLOIN
BENZOIN CAMPHOR CARVONE
DYPNONE FLAVONE JASMONE
MUSCONE PHORONE SHOGAOL
THUJONE ACRIDONE ANTHRONE
BAECKEOL BUTANONE BUTYRONE
CHALCONE CHALKONE
CHROMONE DEGUELIN EXALIONE
FENCHONE MENTHONE PROPIONE
PULEGONE ROTENONE STEARONE
TAGETONE THIENONE VALERONE
XANTHONE
KETTLE LEAD STEW DIXIE BOILER
CANNER FESSEL MARMIT MASLIN
TRIPOD VESSEL CALDRON SKILLET
STEWPOT CALABASH FLAMBEAU
KETTLEDRUM NAKER ATABAL
KETTLE TIMBAL TYMBAL TIMBALE
TYMPANY
KEVEL CAVEL KNAPPER
KEX KECKSY
KEY CAY KAY CLEW CLUE CRIB
FLAT JACK KING NOTE PLUG
PONY DITAL SCREW TASTO
WREST BUTTON CHIAVE CIPHER
CLAVIS COTTER SAMARA SPLINE
WINDER DIGITAL LANGUET
PASSKEY SPEAKER LATCHKEY
TONALITY
(— FOR TUNING HARP) WREST
(— OF KEYBOARD INSTRUMENT)
CHIP MANUAL
(— OF LIFE) ANKH
(— OF ORGAN) TASTO DIGITAL
(— OF PIANO) IVORY NATURAL
(— OF SPINET) CHIP
(— ON WOODWIND INSTRUMENT)
LANGUET SPEAKER
(— UP) STRING
(—S OF CARILLON) CLAVECIN
(ARITHMETICAL —) ADDITIVE
(ASH —) PIGEON
(FALSE —) GLUT
(FEATHER —) FIN STOP SPLINE
FEATHER
(PART OF —) BOW BLADE

WARDING SHOULDER SERRATION
(SKELETON —) GILT TWIRLER
(TELEGRAPH —) BUG TAPPER
(WHITE —) NATURAL
(PREF.) CLAVI CLEID(O) CLEIST(O)
(SUFF.) CLEISIS CLISIS
KEYBOARD CLAVIER PEDALIER
(PREF.) CLAVI
KEYHOLE KEY LOCKHOLE
KEYNOTE A B D E KEY MESE TONIC
FINALIS
KEYSTONE KEY QUOIN VERTEX
SAGITTA VOUSSOIR
(— STATE) PENNSYLVANIA
KEYWAY SPLINE KEYSLOT
KEZIA (FATHER OF —) JOB
KHA KA KHMU KACHE LAMET
KHALAT SEERPAW
KHAN CAN CHAM HAWN SERAI
TACON CHAGAN KHAKAN
KHAS-KURA NEPALI PAHARI
PARBATI GORKHALI
KHATTISH HATTIC
KHEDIVE QUITEVE
KHELLIN VISAMMIN
KHOTANA KOYUKON
KHUSKHUS CUSCUS VETIVER
KIANG ONAGER CHIGETAI
HEMIONUS
KIBBLE GIG KETTLE
KIBBLER CRACKER
KICK BOOT FICK FLEG FLIG FOOT
FUNK HEEL HOOF LASH PORR
POTE PUNT SHIN TURF YERK
ANGLE BUNCH FLING KEVEL
PAUSE PUNCH SKELP SPANG
SPURN CHARGE CORNER FITTER
KICKER KICKUP OBJECT SPIRAL
VOLLEY DROPOUT FOUETTE
KICKOFF DROPKICK PLACEKICK
(— ABOUT) SPARTLE
(— AS A HORSE) FLING WINCE
(— HEELS UP) SPURN
(— ON SHINS) HACK SHINNER
(BALLET —) BRUSH
(SOCCER —) CORNER
(SWIMMING —) THRASH
KICKER TEDDER WINCER
KID COD FUN POD TUB FAWN
FOOL JIVE JOKE CHILD FAGOT
HORSE JOLLY KIDDY SPOOF
KIDLET SQUIRT DECEIVE EANLING
FATLING TICCHEN YOUNGER
CHEVEREL YEANLING
KIDDING JOKE SPOOFERY
KIDNAP STEAL ABDUCT PANYAR
SPIRIT
KIDNAPER PLAGIARY SNATCHER
SPIRITER
KIDNAPING SNATCH PLAGIUM
PLAGIARY
KIDNAPPED (AUTHOR OF —)
STEVENSON
(CHARACTER IN —) ALAN BRECK
COLIN DAVID RIACH SHUAN
BALFOUR RANSOME CAMPBELL
EBENEZER HOSEASON
RANKEILLOR
KIDNEY NEAR NEER REIN TYPE
NEPHRON
(PL.) REINS ROGNONS
(PREF.) NEPHR(O) RENI RENO
(SUFF.) NEPHRITIS NEPHROSIS

KIDNEY BEAN FRIJOLE
(PL.) FASELS
KIER KEEVE PUFFER
KIESELGUHR DOPE GUHR
KILL DO BAG END GET MOW OFF
OUT PIP ZAP BANE BOLO COOK
COOL DOWN FELL MORT NECK
SLAY TAME WING BLAST BRAIN
CROAK CULLE FETCH FORDO
GANCH MISDO NAPOO QUELL
SABER SCRAG SHOOT SMITE
SNUFF SPEED SPEND SPILL SPOIL
STALL STICK SWELT SWORD
WASTE CORPSE DEADEN DIDDLE
FAMISH FINISH HANDLE IMPALE
MARTYR MURDER POISON
STARVE UNLIVE ACHIEVE
BUTCHER DESTROY EXECUTE
FLATTEN HATCHET KILLING
MORTIFY SMOTHER STONKER
SUICIDE DEATHIFY DISPATCH
DISSOLVE IMMOLATE JUGULATE
STILETTO
(— ANIMALS) CONTROL
(— BY STONING) LAPIDATE
(— BY SUBMERSION) STIFLE
(— CALF AFTER BIRTH) DEACON
(— CATTLE) PITH
(— EVERY TENTH) DECIMATE
(— GAME) SATCHEL
(— OFF) ENECATE
(— SMALL GAME) BARK
(— TIME) GOOF
(— WITH GRENADE) FRAG
KILLDEER KILLDEE DEERKILL
KILLED KILT WINGED SKITTLED
(FRESHLY —) GREEN
KILLER GUN BRAVO GUNMAN
SLAYER TORPEDO MURDERER
THRESHER
(SUFF.) CIDAL CIDE
KILLER WHALE ORCA DOLPHIN
GRAMPUS
KILLIFISH KELLY KILLY MINNOW
COBBLER GUDGEON MAYFISH
MUDFISH PANCHAX FUNDULUS
ROCKFISH SACALAIT STUDFISH
SWAMPINE MUMMICHOG
KILLING FELL KILL MORT QUELL
TUANT MURDER CLEANUP
HANGING CLEANING DISPATCH
FELICIDE HOMICIDE
MANSLAUGHTER
(MERCY —) EUTHANASIA
KILLJOY NARK GLOOM LEMON
SOURPUSS
KILN BING KEEL LEHR OAST CULLE
DRIER GLAZE STOVE TILER
COCKLE CUPOLA TILERY
FURNACE CALCINER LIMEKILN
**KILOGRAM (— OF MARIJUANA OR
HEROIN)** KEY
(— OF NARCOTIC) KEY
KILOMETER LI
KILORAD KRAD
KILT QUELT PIUPIU FILIBEG
PHILIBEG PETTICOAT
KILTER SKEET
KIM (AUTHOR OF —) KIPLING
(CHARACTER IN —) ALI KIM OHARA
ARTHUR HURREE LURGAN
MAHBUB BENNETT KIMBALL
CREIGHTON MOOKERJEE

KIN SIB KATI KITH CATTY CUNNE
FLESH FAMILY AFFINITY
RELATION
KIND ILK KIN LOT BOON CAST FAIR
FORM GOOD HAIR HEND LIKE
MAKE MEEK MILD MODE MOLD
NICE RATE SELY SOFT SORT SUIT
TRIM TYPE WING BREED BROOD
CLASS GENRE GENUS GESTE
ORDER SPICE STAMP BENIGN
BLITHE FACILE GENDER GENTLE
GOODLY HUMANE KIDNEY KINDLY
MANNER MISTER NATURE SPEECE
STRAIN STRIPE TENDER CLEMENT
EDITION FASHION FEATHER
FLESHLY LENIENT QUALITY
REGIMEN SPECIAL SPECIES
SPECKLE FRIENDLY GENEROUS
MANSUETE OBLIGING BENIGNANT
INDULGENT OFFICIOUS
PERSUASION
(— OF) A
(— OF PEOPLE) FOLK
(DIFFERENT IN —) DIVERS
(DISTINCTIVE —) BRAND
(OF EVERY —) ALKIN
(PREF.) GEN(O)
KINDLE BEET BLOW FIRE LUNT
MOVE TAKE TEND TIND FLAME
LIGHT QUICK SPUNK ACCEND
ALIGHT DECOCT ENFIRE EXCITE
IGNITE ILLUME EMBLAZE ESPRISE
INCENSE INFLAME SOLICIT
KINDLING
KINDLINESS CANDOR
KINDLING FIRE BAVIN FAGOT
TINDER IGNITION
KINDLY FAIR GAIN KIND NESH
AGREE COUTH HENDE NAISH
BENIGN BLITHE COUTHY GENIAL
HOMELY AMIABLE BENEFIC
INNERLY FAVOROUS GENEROUS
GRACIOUS QUEMEFUL TOWARDLY
KINDNESS LOVE ALOHA FAVOR
BOUNTY CANDOR LENITY
BENEFIT SERVICE CLEMENCY
EASINESS GOODNESS HUMANITY
LENITUDE MILDNESS
KIND OF
(SUFF.) EE
KINDRED KIN SIB KIND KITH
BLOOD FLESH HOUSE FAMILY
KOBONG NATION STRIND
COGNATE KINFOLK KINSMENS
RELATED SIBSHIP AFFINITY
COGNATION CONGENIAL
CONGENEROUS
KINE KYE COWS
KINETIC ACTUAL
(— POTENTIAL) L
KING RI SO BAN DAM LOT LUD PUL
REX REY RIG ROY AGAG AMON
ATLI BALI BELI BIJA BORS BRAN
BRES CRAL CZAR JEHU KRAL LEIR
MARK NUDD NUMA OMRI OTTO
PHUL RAJA RIAL TSAR TZAR
WANG YIMA ARDRI BALOR BELUS
CONOR CREON DAGDA DAHAK
EGLON ETZEL GYGES HIRAM
HOGNI HOSEA IPHIS IXION JOASH
LAIUS LLUDD LYCUS MESHA
MIDAS MINOS NADAB NEGUS
NORSE NUADA PEKAH PRIAM

RAJAH SAMMY SWAMI ZIMRI
ZOHAK AEOLUS AGENOR AILILL
ALBOIN ALONSO ALOROS ARIOCH
BLADUD CODRUS DIOMED
DUNCAN ELATHA FINGAL FRODHI
FROTHI GOEMOT INKOSI KABAKA
LEMUEL LYCAON MEMNON
MINYAS NESTOR NODONS
OENEUS OGYGES PELEUS PELIAS
SAUGHT SHESHA SVAMIN TEUCER
URIENS UZZIAH VASUKI ADMETUS
AHAZIAH AMAIMON AMYCLAS
ANGEVIN ARDRIGU ARTEGAL
ATHAMAS BAGINDA BELINUS
BUSIRIS CACIQUE CEPHEUS
CROESUS ELIDURE EPAPHUS
EPOPEUS ETHBAAL EURYTUS
GUNTHER HYGELAC INACHUS
JAMSHID JEHOASH JEHORAM
KINGLET LAERTES LATINUS
LEONTES MENAHEM MONARCH
PANDION PHINEUS POLYBUS
REGULUS ROMULUS ROYALET
SMERDIS SOLOMON VOLSUNG
ACRISIUS ADRASTUS AEGYPTUS
ALBERICH AMRAPHEL ASNAPPER
BAHMANID BRENNIUS CLAUDIUS
COPHETUA ELDORADO ETEOCLES
GILGAMES GOEMAGOT
GOGMAGOG GORBODUC
HEZEKIAH HROTHGAR JEHOAHAZ
JEROBOAM KINGLING LAOMEDON
LISUARTE MANASSEH MELIADUS
MENELAUS ODYSSEUS
ORCHAMUS OSNAPPAR OVERKING
PADISHAH PEKAHIAH PENTHEUS
RAMESSID REHOBOAM RODERICK
RODOMONT ROITELET SARPEDON
SHEPHERD SISYPHUS TANTALUS
(— AND QUEEN OF TRUMPS) BELLA
(— CHANGED TO WOLF) LYCAON
(— OF ARMS) GARTER NORROY
(— OF BEASTS) LION
(— OF DWARFS) ALBERICH
(— OF FAIRIES) OBERON
(— OF TRUMPS) HONOR
(IRISH —) RI RIG ARDRI ARDRIGH
(POLYNESIAN —) ALII ARII ARIKI
(PREF.) REGI
KINGBIRD PIPIRI PETCHARY
KINGBOLT KING KINGPIN MAINPIN
KING CRAB LIMULID LIMULUS
PANFISH
KINGDOM WEI REALM REIGN
WORLD ESTATE MONERA
MORVEN REGION SAXONY
MITANNI
KINGFISH BARB CERO HAKE HAKU
MINK OPAH TOMCOD CHENFISH
SCIAENID TOMMYCOD
KINGFISHER HALCYON PODITTI
TOROTORO
KING JOHN (AUTHOR OF —)
SHAKESPEARE
(CHARACTER IN —) JOHN BIGOT
ESSEX HENRY JAMES LEWIS
MELUN PETER ARTHUR BLANCH
ELINOR GURNEY HUBERT PHILIP
ROBERT DEBURGH LYMOGES
BRETAGNE PANDULPH
PEMBROKE CHATILLON
CONSTANCE SALISBURY
FAULCONBRIDGE

KING LEAR (AUTHOR OF —)
SHAKESPEARE
(CHARACTER IN —) KENT LEAR
CURAN EDGAR REGAN ALBANY
EDMUND OSWALD GONERIL
BURGUNDY CORDELIA CORNWALL
GLOUCESTER
KINGLET REGULI
KINGLY REGAL ROYAL REGNAL
BASILIC IMPERIAL MAJESTIC
PRINCELY
KING PARAKEET WELLAT
KING'S HENCHMAN, THE
(CHARACTER IN —) EADGAR
AELFRIDA AETHELWOLD
(COMPOSER OF —) TAYLOR
KINGSHIP STOOL THRONE
KINGDOM ROYALTY DEVARAJA
KINGHOOD
KING SOLOMON'S MINES
(AUTHOR OF —) HAGGARD
(CHARACTER IN —) GOOD JOHN
JOSE ALLAN HENRY KHIVA
TWALA CURTIS GAGOOL GEORGE
IGNOSI UMBOPA FOULATA
SCRAGGA INFADOOS SILVESTRE
VENTVOGEL QUATERMAIN
KING'S PEACE GRITH
KING'S ROW (AUTHOR OF —)
BELLAMANN
(CHARACTER IN —) DRAKE ELISE
JAMIE NOLAN RANDY RENEE
TOWER CASSIE GORDON LOUISE
MCHUGH PARRIS SANDOR
PERDOFF MONAGHAN
CASSANDRA WAKEFIELD
KING'S SCHOLAR TUG
KING VULTURE PAP PAPA
KININ KALLIDIN
KINK NIB SNICK BUCKLE DOGLEG
KINKLE
(— IN ROPE) GRIND
KINKAJOU POTTO HEYRAT
APOROSO
KINKING FLUTING
KINKY NAPPY ENCOMIC KINKLED
KINO BIJA BIJASAL
KINSHIP SIB BLOOD NASAB STOOL
ENATION KINDRED SIBNESS
SIBSHIP AFFINITY AGNATION
RELATION PROPINQUITY
KINSMAN KIN SIB ALLY BLOOD
AFFINE AGNATE COUSIN FRIEND
BROTHER GOTRAJA KINDRED
WINEMAY BANDHAVA RELATION
RELATIVE COLLATERAL
KINSWOMAN SISTER KINDRED
RELATIVE
KIP SKIP GRASSER KIPSKIN
UPSTART
KIRGHIZ QYRGHYZ
KIRGIZ (MOUNTAIN RANGE IN —)
ALAI
KIRIBATI (CAPITAL OF —) TARAWA
BAIRIKI
(FORMER NAME OF —)
GILBERTISLANDS
(ISLAND OF —) BERU MAKIN
ABAIANG ABEMAMA NONOUTI
TABITEUEA
KIRN MELL
KISH (FATHER OF —) JEHIEL
(SON OF —) SAUL

KISS BA LIP NEB BASS BUSS PECK
PREE MOUTH POGUE SLAKE
SMACK BEKISS CARESS SALUTE
SLAVER SMOOCH SMOUCH
OSCULATE
(— OF PEACE) PAX
(— WETLY) SLOBBER
(STOLEN —) SMOORICH
KISSING LIPWORK
KIT CHIT DUFFEL KITTEN OUTFIT
POCHETTE
(LUMBERMAN'S —) TURKEY
(MESS —) CANTEEN
KITCHEN BUT GALLEY CABOOSE
CUISINE KITCHIE COOKROOM
KITE LAP CHIL CYTE HAWK GLEDE
CHILLA DRACHE DRAGON ELANET
FALCON PREYER SENTRY MILVINE
PUDDOCK PUTTOCK FORKTAIL
HELLKITE
KITTEN KIT KITTY KITTLE CATLING
KITLING
KITTIWAKE GULL WAEG ANNET
KITTY PICKUP HACKLET TARROCK
TIRRLIE
KITTY CAT POT BADRANS
BAUDRONS
KIVA ESTUFA
KIWI APTERYX
(BROWN —) ROA
KLAMATH WEED AMBER
GOATWEED
KLANG PHONE
KLIPSPRINGER KAINSI KLIPBOK
KLONDIKE CANFIELD SOLITAIRE
KNACK ART FEAT FEEL GATE GIFT
HANG CATCH QUIRK SKILL TRICK
SLEIGHT WRINKLE INSTINCT
KNACKER CLAPPER
(PL.) BONES
KNAPSACK WALLET MOCHILA
MUSETTE SNAPBAG SNAPSACK
KNAPWEED SWEEP BLUETOP
FLATTOP BALLWEED BELLWEED
BOLEWEED BULLWEED
BUNDWEED CENTAURY
CLUBWEED CROPWEED
HARDHEAD IRONHEAD IRONWEED
KNOTWEED MATFELON
KNAVE BOY ELF LAD NOB PAM
PUR TOM JACK BOWER CHEAT
DROLE MAKER NODDY ROGUE
TIGER COQUIN FRIPON HARLOT
KNIGHT PICARO RASCAL VARLET
WENZEL CAMOOCH CUSTREL
PEASANT VILLAIN BEZONIAN
COISTREL SWINDLER VARLETTO
KNAVERY ROPERY CATZERIE
PATCHERY RASCALITY
KNAVISH ROGUISH SCAMPISH
KNAWEL KNOTWEED KNOTWORT
KNEAD ELT TEW MOLD POST
BRAKE STOCK PETRIE MASSAGE
(— HIDES) STOCK
KNEADING (— MACHINE) BRAKE
KNEE GENU HOCK CROOK
KNAPPER SLEEPER SUFFRAGO
(— HOLLOW) HAM
(— OF COMPOSING STICK) SLIDE
(PREF.) GENU GONY
KNEECAP CAP ROTULA PATELLA
(PL.) MARROWBONES
KNEEL SIT KNEE COUCH

SHIKO KOWTOW
KNEELER SPRINGER
KNEELING SHIKO BENDED
KNEEPAN ROTULA PATELLA
KNELL BELL RING TOLL KNOLL
STROKE
KNICKKNACK TOY KNACK TRICK
GEWGAW NOTION PRETTY
BIBELOT GIMCRACK
KNIFE DAH DIE PIN SAX ULU BOLO
BUCK MOON SAEX SHIM SHIV
SPUD TANG BOWIE BURIN CHIVE
CUTTO FACON GULLY KNIVE
KUKRI PANGA SHANK SHAVE
SKEAN SLICE BARLOW BARONG
CAMPIT CARVER COLTER COUTEL
CUTTLE CUTTOE DAGGER
DOCTOR JIGGER PANADE
PARANG PAVADE PORKER PULLER
RIMMER SICKLE SLICER TREVET
TRIVAT WORKER BREAKER
CATLING CHOPPER COUTEAU
FIPENNY KIOTOME MACHETE
PALETTE SCALPEL SEVERER
SKINNER SLASHER SNICKER
STICKER SUNDANG TICKLER
WHITTLE BELDUQUE BILLHOOK
CALABOZO JOCTELEG SERPETTE
THWITTLE YATAGHAN
SNICKERSNEE
(— FOR BREAKING FLAX) BEATER
(— FOR LEATHER) PIN
(— FOR RUBBER DOUGH) DOCTOR
(BLACKSMITH'S —) BUTTERIS
(BURMESE —) DAH DAO DOW
(CURRIER'S —) CLEANER
(ENGRAVER'S —) CRADLE
(ESKIMO —) ULU
(MORO —) BARONG
(PART OF —) NEB TIP WEB BACK
EDGE HEEL HILT BLADE CHOIL
GUARD POINT RIVET FULLER
HANDLE POMMEL BOLSTER
QUILLON ROCASSO
(SHOEMAKER'S —) BUTT
(SURGICAL —) CATLING SCALPEL
BISTOURY EXSECTOR
(TANNER'S —) GRAINER
KNIFE-PLEATED KILTED
KNIGHT N ELF SIR ADUB GANO
TULK EQUES EQUIS HORSE LANCE
RIDER THANE TOLKE CABALL
ERRANT KEMPER PENCEL RITTER
ROGERO GENILON PALADIN
YOUNKER ALMANZOR BACHELOR
BANNERET CAVALIER COLVILLE
GANELONE IRONCLAD ISENBRAS
PALMERIN RUGGIERO
(— IN CHESS) HORSE
(— OF ROUND TABLE) GAN BORS
OWEN GARETH GAWAIN MODRED
CARADOC CRADOCK GALAHAD
GANELON EGLAMORE LANCELOT
PALMERIN PERCIVAL TRISTRAM
(CARPET —) DAMMARET
KNIGHTHOOD CAVALRY
KNIGHTS (AUTHOR OF —)
ARISTOPHANES
(CHARACTER IN —) CLEON DEMUS
NICIAS AGORACRITUS
DEMOSTHENES
KNIPHOFIA TRITOMA
KNIT SET BIND KNOT PLAIT PURSE

UNITE WEAVE COMPACT
CONNECT WRINKLE CONTRACT
(— STOCKINGS) SHANK
KNITTED FLAT WOVEN
KNITTING (— OF BONES) POROSIS
KNITTING LOOP STEEK
KNITTING NEEDLE WIRE
KNOB BOB BUR NOB NUB BEAD
BOLL BOSS BURR CLUB DENT
HEAD HEEL KNOP KNOT KNUB
LIFT NODE NOOP PULL SNUG
STUD TORE BERRY BULLA BUNCH
FORTE GEMMA KNURL NATCH
ONION PLOOK PLUKE BUTTON
CROCHE EMBOSS NOBBLE
NUBBLE PIMPLE PISTON POMMEL
FERRULE HORNTIP KNOBBLE
BELLPULL DOORKNOB DRAWSTOP
OMPHALOS
(— OF HAIR) TOORIE
(— OF ROCK) BUHR BURR
KNUCKLE
(— ON BILL OF SWAN) BERRY
(— ON BUTT OF CANNON) GRAPE
(— ON CHAIR) POMMEL
(— ON DEER'S ANTLER) OFFER
CROCHE
(— ON ROPE) MOUSE
(PREF.) CONDYL(O) TYL(O)
KNOBBED NODOSE TOROSE
BULLATE TUBEROUS TYLOTATE
KNOBBY GOUTY KNOTTY TOROSE
WHELKY GOUTISH KNOBBLY
SCRAGGED
KNOCK CON DAD HIT JOW JUT
POP PUN RAP WAP BANG BASH
BEAT BUMP CALL CHAP CHOP
DASH DAUD DING DUMP DUNT
HACK JOLT JOWL KNAP NOCK
NOIT PINK PLUG POLT POSS
PUSH ROUT SLAM SLAY SNOP
TANK TIRL WHAP WHOP CLOUR
CLUMP KNOIT POUND SMITE
SNOCK STAVE STRAM THUMP
BOUNCE DUNTLE KNATCH
KNETCH STOTER CANVASS
PINKING
(— ABOUT) RUMBLE
(— DOWN) MOW DROP DUMP FELL
FLOOR GRASS LEVEL SMITE
SOUSE HURTLE RAFFLE UNPILE
(— OFF) SECURE
(— ON HEAD) MAZER MAZARD
(— OUT) OUT SAP CONK COOL
KAYO FLATTEN STIFFEN
(— UNCONSCIOUS) COLDCOCK
(— WITH THE HORNS) DISH
(IGNITION —) PING
KNOCKER CROW RISP HAMMER
WHACKER
(DOOR —) CROW HAMMER
RAPPER
KNOCK-KNEED VARUS VALGUS
KNOCKOUT KO KAYO CRUSHER
NOBBLER
(PRETENDED —) DIVE
KNOLL NOB HIGH KNAP KNOB
KNOW TOFT HEAVE HURST
HYRST MOUND SHOAL COPPLE
BOUROCK HUMMOCK
KNOP NOB KNOB KNOSP KNAPPE
KNOT BOB BOW BUN FAG NIB NOB
NUB PIN TIE BEND BURR CHOU

CLOD CLOT CLUB HARL KILL
KNAG KNAR KNOB NODE NOIL
NURL SLUG SNUB TRUE WAFT
WALL BUNCH CROWN DUNNE
GNARL GNARR HALCH HALSH
HATCH HITCH KNURL MOUSE
NODUS NOEUD SNARL SNICK
SWIRL TWIST WARRE BOUGHT
BUTTON CLINCH CROCHE FINIAL
GRANNY MASCLE SORTIE TANGLE
BOWKNOT BOWLINE CHIGNON
COCKADE GORDIAN MAYBIRD
CICISBEO DRAWKNOT GRAYBACK
KNITTING SLIPKNOT TRUELOVE
SHEEPSHANK
(— IN CLOTH) FAG NEP BURL
(— IN COTTON FIBERS) NEP
(— IN SIGNAL FLAG) WAFT WEFT
WHEFT
(— IN WOOD) PIN BURL BURR
KNAG KNAR SNUB GNARL KNAUR
KNURL
(— IN YARN) SLUG SNICK
(— OF HAIR) BOB BUN COB PUG
CLUB KNURL CHIGNON
(— OF RIBBONS) FAVOR
(EMBROIDERY —) PICOT
(LOVE —) AMORET
(ORNAMENTAL —) BOW
(SHOULDER —) WING
(WALL —) WALE
(PREF.) NODI
KNOTGRASS LIGNUM HOGWEED
PIGWEED BINDWEED BIRDWEED
DOORWEED KNOTWEED
KNOTWORT PINKWEED
POLYGONY WIREWEED
KNOTTED KNIT NOUE TIED NOWED
NODOSE SWIRLY CRABBED
NODATED SCRAGGY
KNOTTY HARD CRAMP GOUTY
NODAL COMMON CRAGGY
GNARLY KNAGGY KNOBBY
KNURRY NODOSE NODOUS
COMPLEX GNARLED GOUTISH
JOINTED KNARRED KNOTTED
SCABROUS
KNOTWEED LIGNUM ALLSEED
HOGWEED JUMPSEED POLYGONY
POLYGONUM
KNOW CAN CON KEN WIS WIT
WOT CITE HAVE SABE WEET WIST
WOTH SAVVY SKILL COGNIZE
(— NOT) NOOT
(—S NOT) NOTE
(DID NOT —) KENDNA
(DO NOT —) KENNA
KNOWABLE SENSABLE
KNOW-HOW SAVVY SKILL
KNOWING FLY HEP HIP SLY FOXY
GASH SPRY WISE AWARE CANNY
DOWNY JERRY LEERY SPACK
WITTY EXPERT SCIENT SCIOUS
SHREWD WITFUL WITTER
GNOSTIC SAPIENT
(— SUPERFICIALLY) SCIOLOUS
(SUFF.) GNOSIA GNOSIS GNOSTIC
GNOSY
KNOWINGLY CANNILY SCIENTER
SHREWDLY WITTERLY
KNOWLEDGE CAN WIT BOOK KITH
KNOW LAIR LEAR LORE NOTE
INWIT JNANA SKILL VIDYA

ADVICE AVIDYA CLERGY GNOSIS
NOESIS NOTICE WISDOM
CUNNING DIANOIA HEARING
KNOWING MEANING SCIENCE
WITTING DAYLIGHT DOCTRINE
EPISTEME LEARNING LETTRURE
NOTITION PRUDENCE SAPIENCE
SCIENTIA COGNIZANCE
(— OF SPIRITUAL TRUTH) GNOSIS
(FAMILIAR —) HANG
(LATER —) AFTERWIT
(MYSTERIOUS —) ARCANUM
(PIECEMEAL —) SMATTER
(PRIVATE —) PRIVITY
(PUBLIC —) LIGHT
(SLICK —) ANGLE
(SLIGHT —) INKLING SMATTER
(SUPERFICIAL —) SCIOLISM
(SUPERIOR —) MASTERY
(SUPREME —) PRAJNA
(SYSTEMATIZED —) SCIENCE
(UNIVERSAL —) PANSOPHY
(PREF.) EPISTEMO GNOSIO
(SUFF.) GNOSIA GNOSIS GNOSTIC
GNOSY ICS SOPH(ER)(IC)(IST)(Y)
KNOWLEDGEABLE KNOWING
SKILLED STUDIED
KNOWN EVER COUTH COMMON
(ACTUALLY —) SPECIOUS
(LITTLE —) FAMELESS
(NOT —) DARK SILENT
(OTHERWISE — AS) ALIAS
(PUBLICLY —) EXOTERIC
(UNMISTAKABLY —) STATED
(WIDELY —) COMMON
KNOW-NOTHING SAM
KNUCKLE KNUCK JARRET
(PREF.) CONDYL(O)
KNUCKLEBONE DIB DOLOS TALUS
COCKAL SHACKLE
KNURL MILL NULL DWARF SNARL
KNURLING NULLING REEDING
KNULLING
KOALA BEAR BAALU BALOO SLOTH
KOOLAH WOMBAT CARBORA
PHALANGER
KOANGA (CHARACTER IN —) JOSE
PEREZ SIMON KOANGA PALMYRA
MARTINEZ
(COMPOSER OF —) DELIUS
KOBOLD NIS GNOME NISSE
HODEKEN HUTCHEN
KOEL KOIL KOKIL RAINBIRD
KOHATH (FATHER OF —) LEVI
(SISTER OF —) JOCHEBED
KOHL COHOL ALCOHOL
KOHLRABI BROMATIUM
KOKAN LAMPATIA
KOKO LEBBEK
KOKUM GARCINIA
KOKUMIN BAN
KOLA COLA BICHY GOORANUT
KOLAIAH (SON OF —) AHAB
KOMBU KOBU KAMBOU CHAKOBU
KOMMETJE WALLOW COMITJE
KONAK YALI
KOOKABURRA KOOKA JACKASS
KOPECK KAPEIKA
KORAH (FATHER OF —) ESAU IZHAR
ELIPHAZ
(MOTHER OF —) AHOLIBAMAH
KORAKAN RAGI RAGGI RAGGY
KORAN KITAB QURAN ALCORAN

(SECTION OF —) SURA SURAH
KORE DESPOINA
  (FATHER OF —) IMNAH
KOREA (SEE NORTH KOREA OR SOUTH KOREA)
KOREC MIRA
KORINA LIMBA
KOS COAN
KOSHER (NOT —) TREF
KOSIN KOUSSIN TAENNIN BRAYERIN
KOSO PANAMINT
KOULAN GOUR
KOVANSHCHINA (CHARACTER IN —) ENNA IVAN MARFA ANDREY DOSIFEY GOLITSYN KHOVANSKY
  (COMPOSER OF —) MUSSORGSKY
KOWHAI GOAI PELU LOCUST SOPHORA
KOWTOW KNEEL SHIKO
KOYUKON TENA KHOTANA
KRAAL CRAW MANYATTA ZIMBABWE
KRAIT ADDER KORAIT BUNGARUM

KRATER KELEBE
KRAUNHIA WISTARIA
KREIS CIRCLE
KREUTZER SONATA (AUTHOR OF —) TOLSTOY
  (CHARACTER IN —) LIZA VASYLA POZDNISHEF TRUKHASHEVSKY
KRIEMHILD (BROTHER OF —) GERNOT GUNTHER GISELHER
  (FATHER OF —) GIBICH
  (HUSBAND OF —) ATTILA SIEGFRIED
KRIS CREASE CREESE DAGGER
KRISHNA VASUDEVA
  (BROTHER OF —) BALARAMA
  (FATHER OF —) VASUDEVA
  (FOSTER FATHER OF —) NANDA
  (FOSTER MOTHER OF —) YASHODA
  (MOTHER OF —) DEVAKI
  (UNCLE OF —) KANSA
KRISTIN LAVRANSDATTER
  (AUTHOR OF —) UNDSET
  (CHARACTER IN —) ULF IVAR GAUTE MUNAN SIMON SKULE

ERLEND JOFRID NAAKVE AASHILD HALVARD KRISTIN LAVRANS RAMBORG ULVHILD BJORGULF JARDTRUD NIKULAUS RAGNFRID ANDRESSON BJORGULFSON IVARSDATTER LAVRANSDATTER
KRONE CROWN CORONA
KRU KROOBOY KROOMAN
KRUMMHORN CREMONA CROMORNE
KSHATRIYA THAKUR
KUA MAKUA MAKWA
KUBA BUSHONGO KABISTAN
KUDZU VINE KOHEMP
KUI KHONDI
KU KLUXER KLUXER KLUCKER KLANSMAN
KUKURUKU IKPERE
KULANAPAN POMO
KUMAN POLOVTZY
KUMBUK ARJAN ARJUN
KUMMEL ALLASCH
KUMQUAT NAGAMI

KUNTI
  (FATHER OF —) PANDU SHURA
  (SON OF —) BHIMA KARNA ARJUNA YUDHISHTHIRA
KURRAJONG CALOOL LACEBARK
KURUKH ORAON
KUSA DARBHA
KUSHAIAH (SON OF —) ETHAN
KUSIMANSEL MANGUE
KUTCHIN LOUCHEUX
KUWAIT (CAPITAL OF —) ALKUWAIT
  (OIL FIELD OF —) WAFRA BAHRAH BURGAN SABRIYA MINAGISH RAUDHATAIN
  (OTHER NAME OF —) KOWEIT KUWEIT
  (TOWN OF —) MAGWA AHMADI HAWALLI ABDULLAH FAHAHEEL
KVASS BEER QUASH
KWENI GURO
KYANITE DISTHENE
KYPHOSIS HUMPBACK
KYURINISH LESGHIN LEZGHIAN

L

L EL LIMA FIFTY
LAADAH (FATHER OF —) SHELAH
  (GRANDFATHER OF —) JUDAH
LAADAN (FATHER OF —) GERSHOM
LAAGER LEEGTE LEAGUER
LABAN (DAUGHTER OF —) LEAH
  RACHEL
  (FATHER OF —) BETHUEL
  (SISTER OF —) REBEKAH
LABDACUS (FATHER OF —)
  POLYDORUS
  (MOTHER OF —) NYCTEIS
  (SON OF —) LAIUS
LABDANUM MYRRH
LABEL TAG BILL FILE MARK FICHE
  STAMP TALLY TITLE DIRECT
  DOCKET TICKET ENDSEAL
  LAMBEAU STICKER
  (— ON SUIT OF CLOTHES) ETIQUET
LABELLUM LIP LABEL
  (PART OF —) HYPOCHIL
LABIAL ROUND
LABIATE HOREHOUND
LABIUM LIP LABRUM
LABOR ADO FAG TUG WIN CARK
  MOIL TASK TAVE TILL TOIL WORK
  BEGAR DELVE GRAFT GRIND
  HEAVE PAINS SWEAT SWINK
  TEAVE TREAD WHILE YAKKA
  CORVEE DRUDGE EFFORT
  HAMMER STRIVE BULLOCK
  FATIGUE MANUARY OPIFICE
  PROCURE SERVICE SLAVERY
  TRAVAIL TROUBLE TURMOIL
  BUSINESS DRUDGERY EXERTION
  GROANING INDUSTRY LABORAGE
  STRUGGLE
  (— ARDUOUSLY) BILDER
  (— HARD) THRASH THRIPPLE
  (— UNDER) SUFFER
  (DAY'S —) DARG JOURNEY
  (DIFFICULT —) DYSTOCIA
  (EXCESSIVE —) STRAIN
  (FORCED —) BEGAR CORVEE
  (HARD —) HARD BULLWORK
  (HIRED —) TOGT
  (IMPOSED —) TASKAGE
  (MENTAL —) HEADWORK
  (SEVERE —) AGON
  (UNPAID —) CORVEE
LABORATORY LAB SHOP KITCHEN
  OFFICINA WORKSHOP
LABORED HEAVY FORCED SWEATY
  STRAINED
LABORER (ALSO SEE WORKER AND
  WORKMAN) BOY BHAR ESNE
  HIND JACK JOEY MOZO PEON
  TOTY BAGDI CHURL GUASO
  HUNKY NAVVY PALLI PINER STIFF
  BALAHI BEGARI BOHUNK COALER
  COOLIE DAYMAN DILKER DOCKER
  FELLAH FLUNKY FOGGER HEAVER
  HODMAN HOLEYA JIBARO

LUMPER RAFTER TASKER
WAYMAN WORKER BRACERO
BYWONER CREWMAN DAYSMAN
DIGGORY DIRGLER DRAINER
DVORNIK GRECIAN HOBBLER
MANUARY MAZDOOR PICKMAN
PIONEER PIPEMAN PLOWMAN
SANDHOG SCOURER SHIPPER
SMASHER SOUGHER SPALLER
STOCKER SWINKER TOTYMAN
WORKMAN BIJWONER CHAINMAN
COTTAGER DOLLYMAN
FARMHAND FLOORMAN
GANGSMAN HOLDSMAN
SPADEMAN SPALPEEN STRAPPER
TIDESMAN ROUSTABOUT
  (INEXPERIENCED —) GREENER
LABORIOUS HARD HEAVY STIFF
  TOUGH SWEATY UPHILL
  ARDUOUS OPEROSE SLAVISH
  TOILFUL DILIGENT LABOROUS
  TOILSOME
LABRADOR TEA LEDUM
  GOWIDDIE
LABURNUM AWBER
LABYRINTH MAZE CIRCUIT
  MEANDER
LABYRINTHINE TORTUOUS
LAC LACCA LACQUER
LACE VAL BEAT BEST FOND GOTA
  LASH PEAK FILET LACIS LIVEN
  ORRIS POINT SCREW SPRIG
  WEAVE BLONDE CADDIS CORDON
  DEFEAT EDGING GINLE LACING
  LASHER THRASH TUCKER VENISE
  ALENCON ALLOVER BULLION
  CURRAGH CUTWORK FOOTING
  GALLOON GUIPURE HONITON
  LATCHET MACRAME MALINES
  MECHLIN MELANGE NANDUTI
  TAMBOUR TATTING TORCHON
  TROLLEY ARGENTAN BOBBINET
  BONEWORK BOOTLACE BRUSSELS
  DENTELLE ILLUSION LACEWORK
  LIMERICK PEARLING STAYLACE
  COLBERTINE NEEDLEPOINT
  (— EDGING) PUNTILLA
  (— IN PLACE OF COLLAR) RUCHE
  (— MAKER) TWISTHAND
  (— PATTERN) TOILE
  (KIND OF —) CLUNY
  (KNOTTED —) TATTING
LACEBARK LAGETTO DAGUILLA
  LACEWOOD
LACE BUG TINGITID
LACEDAEMON (DAUGHTER OF —)
  CLEODICE
  (FATHER OF —) ZEUS JUPITER
  (MOTHER OF —) TAYGETE
  (SON OF —) HIMERUS
  (WIFE OF —) SPARTA
LACERATE REND TEAR GANCH
  ENGORE HARROW MANGLE

SCARIFY FRACTURE
LACERATION RIP TEAR WOUND
LACEWING NEUROPTERAN
LACEWOOD SYCAMORE
LACEWORK DENTELLE
LACHRYMOSE SAD TEARY WEEPY
  MAUDLIN
LACINARIA LIATRIS
LACING LACET LINGEL ECHELLE
  LANGUET
  (RAWHIDE —S) BABICHE
LACINIATION DAG
LACK FAIL LANK LIKE LOSS MAIM
  MISS NEED VOID WANE WANT
  FAULT MINUS DEARTH DEFECT
  INLAIK ABSENCE BLEMISH
  DEFAULT FAILURE PAUCITY
  VACANCY SCARCITY SOLITUDE
  WANTROKE
  (— CONFIDENCE) DOUBT
  (— FAITH) DIFFIDE
  (— HARMONY) DISAGREE
  (— OF APPETITE) ANOREXIA
  (— OF CLARITY) DARKNESS
  (— OF CONFIDENCE) MISTRUST
  (— OF COORDINATION) ASYNERGY
  DYSERGIA
  (— OF DEVELOPMENT) AGENESIS
  (— OF EARNESTNESS) ITEMING
  (— OF EFFUSIVENESS) RESERVE
  (— OF EMOTION) APATHY
  (— OF ENERGY) ATONY ANERGY
  ATONIA
  (— OF FLAVOR) SILENCE
  (— OF FORESIGHT) MYOPIA
  (— OF HARMONY) DISCORD
  DISUNITY
  (— OF INTENTION) ACCIDENT
  (— OF INVOLVEMENT) DISTANCE
  (— OF ORDER) ATAXY ATAXIA
  DISARRAY
  (— OF PATRIOTISM) INCIVISM
  (— OF REFINEMENT) CRUDITY
  (— OF SENSE) FOLLY
  (— OF SENSE OF SMELL) ANOSMIA
  (— OF STEADINESS) LEVITY
  (— OF SYMPATHY) DYSPATHY
  (— OF VIGOR) LANGUOR
  (— OF VITALITY) ANEMIA
  ADYNAMIA
  (— OF WIND) CALM
  (— OF WORTH) IMMERIT
  (— STRENGTH) DROOP
LACKADAISICAL LANGUID
  LISTLESS
LACKEY SKIP SLAVE LACQUEY
  STAFFIER
LACKING BUT SHY BARE FREE
  SANS WANT ALACK GNEDE
  MINUS SHORT ABSENT BARREN
  DEVOID WITHIN WANTING
  DESOLATE INDIGENT
  (PREF.) LONCH(O)

LACKLUSTER DULL FISHY CLOUDY
  GLASSY
LACONIC CURT SHORT CONCISE
  POINTED SPARTAN SUCCINCT
LA CORUNA GROIN
LACQUER LAC DOPE DUCO JAPAN
  CHATON LACKER URUSHI
  VARNISH
LACRIMAL
  (PREF.) DACRY(O)
LACTATION (— PERIOD) NOTE
LACTONE CUMARIN LIMONIN
  MECONIN DIKETENE
LACTOSCOPE PIOSCOPE
LACUNA GAP BREAK
LACUSTRINE LAKISH
LAD BOY BUB MAN BOYO CARL
  CHAP DICK HIND JOCK LOON
  SNAP BILLY BUCKO CADDY CHIEL
  GROOM YOUTH BURSCH CADDIE
  CALLAN FELLOW LADDIE LADKIN
  MANNIE NIPPER SHAVER
  CALLANT MUCHACHO SPRINGER
  STRIPLING
  (AWKWARD —) GROMET
  GRUMMET
  (MISCHIEVOUS —) GAMIN
  (MY —) AVICK
  (SERVING —) GILLIE GOSSOON
LADDER STY STEE JACOB SCALE
  AERIAL BANGOR ESCAPE PULEYN
  GANGWAY POLEYNE POMPIER
  (FIREMAN'S —) STICK
  (FISH —) FISHWAY
  (JACOB'S —) CHARITY
  (REVOLVING —) POTENCE
  (ROPE —) ETRIER
LADDIE JOCKEY LATHIE LADDOCK
  LADDIKIE
LADE BAIL LAVE LADEN TRUSS
  BURDEN FRAUGHT
  (— INTO COOLER) STRIKE
LADEN HEAVY BELAST LOADED
  FRAUGHT FREIGHT GESTANT
LADING LOAD CARGO BURDEN
  FREIGHT
LADINO SPANIOL
LADLE DIP JET GAWN SKEP CLATH
  CYATH KEACH STOOP DIPPER
  LADING CUVETTE CYATHUS
  KYATHOS POTSTICK
  (— OUT SOUP) SLEECH
  (— WITH HANDLES) CYATH SHANK
  CYATHUS KYATHOS SKIPPET
  (BRINE —) LOOT
  (LARGE —) SCOOP
  (PREF.) ARYTENO
LADRONE TULISAN LATHERIN
LADY BIBI BURD DAME RANI
  DONNA HANUM BEEBEE DOMINO
  FEMALE KADINE KHANUM
  RAWNIE SAHIBA SENORA
  LADYKIN MADONNA SENHORA

BELAMOUR SINEBADA
(— OF HIGH RANK) BEGUM
(— OF HOUSE) GOODWIFE
(BEAUTIFUL —) CLEAR
(LEADING —) PREMIERE
(TURKISH —) KHANUM
(PL.) LADYHOOD
LADYBUG VEDALIA
LADYFISH WRASSE PUDIANO
BONEFISH BONYFISH DONCELLA
LADYLIKE FEMALE
LADYLOVE LADY DELIA MINION
MISTRESS
LADY'S-COMB NEEDLES
LADY'S-MANTLE DEWCUP
PADELION
LADY'S-SLIPPER DUCK YELLOW
NERVINE YELLOWS UMBILROOT
(PREF.) CYPRI CYPRO
LADY WINDERMERE'S FAN
(AUTHOR OF —) WILDE
(CHARACTER IN —) LORTON
ERLYNNE AUGUSTUS MARGARET
DARLINGTON WINDERMERE
LAEL (SON OF —) ELIASAPH
LAERTES (FATHER OF —) ARCESIUS
(MOTHER OF —) CHALCOMEDUSA
(SON OF —) ULYSSES
(WIFE OF —) ANTICLEA
LAG DRAG DRAW SLOG DELAY
TRAIL HOCKER LAGGER LINGER
LOITER STRING DRIDDLE LAGGING
(— IN PRODUCTION) SLIPPAGE
LAGGARD SLOW TARDY LAGGER
TORTOISE
LAGGING TARDY JACKET DEADING
LAGGARD CLEADING DRAWLING
FOREPOLE
LAGNIAPPE TIP GIFT BONUS
PILON PRESENT
LAGOMORPH PIKA RABBIT
LAGOON HAFF POOL BAYOU
LIMAN LAGUNA SALINA
LAHAD (FATHER OF —) JAHATH
LAHMI (BROTHER OF —) GOLIATH
LAID (— ACROSS WALL) INBOND
(— DOWN) THETIC THETICAL
(— WASTE) BARE
LAIR DEN LAY FORM HOLD SHED
COUCH EARTH HAUNT LODGE
MEUSE SQUAT HARBOR KENNEL
SPELUNK
(— OF FOX) KENNEL
(— OF OTTER) HOLT HOVER
(— OF WILD BOAR) SOUNDER
LAISH (SON OF —) PHALTIEL
LAISSE TIRADE
LAITY FOLK LAYMEN PEOPLE
LAIUS (FATHER OF —) LABDACUS
(SON OF —) OEDIPUS
(WIFE OF —) JOCASTA
LAKE LAY SEA VLY BAHR JAIL JHIL
LAGO LLYN LOCH MERE MOAT
SHOR TANK TARN VLEI VLEY
BAYOU CHOTT JHEEL LERNA
LIMAN LOUGH SPARK TUBIG
LAGOON NYANZA STROND
ANCYLUS CARMINE LAKELET
TURLOUGH
(CASHEW —) AUBURN
(DRY —) PLAYA
(FENNY —) BROAD
(MOUNTAIN —) TARN

(RELATING TO —S) LIMNAL
(SALT —) SHOT CHOTT SHOTT
SALINA SALINE
(SMALL —) GURGES MARIGOT
(TEMPORARY —) PINAG
(YELLOW —) PINK
(PREF.) LIMN(I)(O)
(SUFF.) LIMNION
LAKE CARP DRUM LAKER
LAKE HERRING KIYI CISCO
GRAYBACK
LAKE TROUT POGY TOGUE
LAKE WHITEFISH POLLAN
LAKME (CHARACTER IN —) LAKME
GERALD NILAKANTHA
(COMPOSER OF —) DELIBES
LAKSHMANA (FATHER OF —)
DURYODHANA
(SLAYER OF —) ABHIMANYU
LAKSHMI SRI SHREE
(HUSBAND OF —) VISHNU
LAMA ELK AUCHENIA
LAMB BUM PET PUR CADE DEAR
DUPE LOME SOCK YEAN AGNUS
PESAH PODDY AGNEAU COSSET
HIEDER LAMBIE LAMKIN PESACH
SUCKER WASTER WEANER
CHILVER EANLING FATLING
HOGLING PASCHAL PERSIAN
RUFFIAN TWAGGER BAAHLING
LAMBLING PASSOVER YEANLING
(— AND WHEAT) KIBBE
(SCYTHIAN —) BAROMETZ
(SHOULDER OF —) BANJO
(SIDE OF —) CONCERTINA
LAMBASTE CREAM SQUABASH
LAMBENT BRIGHT RADIANT
LAMBREQUIN MANTLING
LAMBSKIN LAMB BAGDAD
BAGHDAD SALZFELLE
LAMB'S QUARTERS MUCKWEED
LAMB'S WOOL WASSAIL
LAME BUM GAME HALT LAHN
GAMMY GIMPY GRAVEL TINSEL
CRIPPLE CRIPPLY HALTING
HIPHALT GORGERIN SPAVINED
(— A HORSE) STUB NOBBLE
(— WITH HORSESHOE NAIL) ACCLOY
LAMECH (DAUGHTER OF —)
NAAMAH
(SON OF —) NOAH JABAL JUBAL
TUBALCAIN
(WIFE OF —) ADAH ZILLAH
LAMELLA PLICA FOLIUM FORNIX
LAMELLIBRANCH PELECYPOD
LAMENESS HALT
LAMENT CRY WEY CARE DOLE
HONE HOWL KEEN MEAN MOAN
PINE SIGH TEAR WAIL WALY
WEEP CROON DUMKA GREET
KINAH MOURN PLAIN QINAH
BEHOWL BEMOAN BEWAIL
BEWEEP COMMOS KOMMOS
PLAINT REGRET REPINE SORROW
SQUAWK THREAP YAMMER
BEMOURN CONDOLE DEPLORE
EJULATE ELEGIZE GRIZZLE
REGRATE THRENOS WAYMENT
COMPLAIN CORONACH
MOURNING THRENODY
ULLAGONE WELLAWAY
LAMENTABLE YEMER FUNEST
RUEFUL DOLEFUL PITIFUL

PITIABLE PLAINFUL YAMMERLY
LAMENTATION KEEN MOAN WAIL
DOLOR LINOS RUING TANGI
LAMENT PLAINT REGRET
SORROW THRENE PLANGOR
TRAGEDY WAYMENT WILLAWA
CORONACH MOURNING PATHETIC
WAILMENT WELLAWAY
LAMENTING
LAMINA FILM LAME LAMP LEAF
OBEX BLADE FLAKE LAMIN PLATE
SCALE SHELL TABLE FOLIUM
CAPSULE
LAMINATE LEAFY FLAGGY
LAMINATED BUILT FOLIATE
TABULAR
LAMINATION SLABBING
LAMINITIS FOUNDER
LAMMAS DAY GULE TERM
LAMMERGEIER AREND OSSIFRAGE
LAMP ARC EYE SEE DAVY GLIM
INKY JACK SLUT ALDIS ARGAND
ASTRAL BULLET HELION LAMPAD
TARGET ILLUMER LAMPION
LAMPLET LANTERN LUCERNE
LUCIGEN SUNLAMP SUNSPOT
AEOLIGHT CIRCLINE GASLIGHT
SIDELAMP TORCHERE
PHOTOFLASH PHOTOFLOOD
(— FOR FIREPLACE) KYLE
(CHIMNEYLESS —) TORCH
(DARKROOM —) SAFELIGHT
(IRON —) CRUSIE
(MAKESHIFT —) BITCH
(NIGHT —) VEILLEUSE
(PART OF —) CAP CORD HARP
SHELL FINIAL NIPPLE SOCKET
SWITCH WASHER NECKWING
(SAFETY —) DAVY GEORDIE
(STAGE —S) BATTEN
(4-CORNERED —) CHILL
(PL.) CLUSTER
(PREF.) LYCHNO
LAMPBLACK LINK SOOT
LAMPETIA (FATHER OF —) APOLLO
HELIOS
(MOTHER OF —) NEAERA
(SISTER OF —) PHAETHUSA
LAMP HOLDER HUSK
LAMPLIGHTER LEERIE
LAMPOON PIPE SKIT GESTE LIBEL
SQUIB IAMBIC SATIRE BERHYME
PASQUIN COCKALAN RIDICULE
SATIRIZE PASQUINADE
LAMPOONER PASQUIL PASQUIN
LAMPREY PRIDE LAMPER MYZONT
RAMPER SAYNAY SUCKER
LAMPERN
LAMP RING CRIC
LAMPSHADE GLOBE
(PART OF —) RIB RING SHADE
SPIDER
LAMPSTAND TORCHERE
LAMPWICK MATCH
LANATE WOOLY LANOSE WOOLLY
LANCE PIC CANE DART SHAFT
SPEAR STAFF BROACH ELANCE
GLAIVE GLEAVE LANCET ROCKET
LANCELET SPICULUM
(KING ARTHUR'S —) RON
LANCE GUARD VAMPLATE
LANCE HEAD MORNE SOCKET
LANCELET AMPHIOXUS

LANCER LANCE SOWAR UHLAN
LANCE REST QUEUE FEWTER
LANCET FLEAM FLEEM LANCELET
LANCEWOOD YAYA CIGUA
CANELA YARIYARI
LAND ERD ERF NOD RIB AGER DIRT
FOLD GALE GISH GORE JODO
MARK SITE SOIL EARTH EJIDO
ETHEL FIELD GLEBE JUGER PLANT
SHORE SOLUM ALIGHT ASSART
FUNDUS GROUND COMMONS
COUNTRY DEMESNE ELLASAR
HOLDING LANDING LIBRATE
QUILLET TERRENE ALLODIAL
BOOKLAND COMMONTY
FARMLAND FLEYLAND FOLKLAND
POMERIUM PRAEDIUM
(— A PLANE) GREASE
(— BETWEEN FURROWS) SELION
(— BETWEEN RIVERS) DOAB
(— CLEARING) KAINGIN
(— CONVERTED TO TILLAGE)
TWAITE THWAITE
**(— HAVING VALUE OF POUND PER
YEAR)** LIBRATE
(— IN CONACRE) MOCK
(— IN GRASS) LAYER
(— LEFT FALLOW) ARDER
(— MEASURE) RIG
(— OF BLISS) GOKURAKU
(— OF GIANTS) UTGARTHAR
(— OF MANSION) DEMESNE
(— OF OPPORTUNITY) ARKANSAS
(— OF PLENTY) GOSHEN
(— OF REGION) MOLD MOULD
(— PLOWED IN A DAY) JORNADA
(— RECOVERED FROM SEA) INTAKE
INNINGS
(— REGULARLY FLOODED) SALTING
(— SURROUNDED BY WASTE) HOPE
(— UNIT) URE KIPUKA MECATE
MORGEN MANZANA VIRGATE
(ALLUVIAL —) BATTURE
(ANCESTRAL —) ETHEL
(ARABLE —) LEA LEY LAINE
(ARID —) DESERT STEPPE
(BOTTOM —) SLASH CALLOW
STRATH
(CHURCH —) GLEBE TERMON
(CHURCH —S) CROSS
(CLEARED —) ASSART
(COMMON —) EJIDO EXIDO STRAY
(CONTINENTAL —) MAIN
(CULTIVATED —) FARM ARADA
TILTH CULTURE FEERING
WAINAGE LABORAGE METAIRIE
(ENCLOSED —) CLOSE INTAKE
(FREEHOLD —) MULK
(GRAVELLY —) GEEST GRAVES
(GRAZING —) GRASS HIRSEL
HIRSLE FEEDING
(HEATHY —) ROSLAND
(HERITABLE —) ODAL UDAL
(IMAGINARY —) FAERIE COCKAYNE
LILLIPUT
(LEASED —) TACK
(LONG STRIP OF —) SLANG SPONG
(LOW —) BOG FEN GALL INKS
CARSE BOTTOM
(LOW RICH —) CARSE
(NATIVE —) SOD KITH BLIGHTY
BIRTHDOM HOMELAND
(OBDURATE —) TILL

(PARCEL OF —) FEU LOT MOCK
(PASTURE —) HA ALP FEED HOGA
WALK GRASS VELDT LEASON
SCATHOLD SCATLAND
(PLATEAU —) HIGHVELD
(PLOWED —) ARADA FALLOW
FURROW BREAKING
(PRIVATE —) SEVERAL
(PROMISED —) CANAAN
(PURE —) JODO SUKHAVATI
(RECLAIMED —) POLDER
(RESOWN —) HOOKLAND
(ROUGH —) BRAKE
(SAVANNAH —S) LALANG
(SCRUBBY —) SCROG SCROGS
(SMALL PARCEL OF —) SUERTE
(SWAMPY —) WOODSERE
(TIMBER —S) STICKS
(WASTE —) HEATH
(WESTERN —) HESPERIA
(WET —) SOAK SWAMP SWANG
(WOODED —S) STICKS
(PL.) ACRES SUCKEN LAENDER
NOVALIA
(PREF.) CHERSO CHOR(O)
(SUFF.) GAEA GEA
LANDBOOK TERRIER
LANDED PRAEDIAL
LANDFORM CUSP CUESTA
LANDHOLDER LAIRD COSCET
TALUKDAR
LANDHOLDING BARONY
LANDING BANK YARD STAITH
LANDAGE ARRIVAGE FOOTPACE
HALFPACE LANDFALL
(ABRUPT —) PANCAKE
(CRASH —) PRANG
(SMOOTH —) GREASER
LANDING PLACE GHAT HARD
SCALE PALACE ARRIVAGE
LANDING STAGE MEAR STAGE
STAIR STAITH STELLING
LANDLADY WIFE DUENA
PADRONA GOODWIFE
LANDLOCK EMBAY
LANDLORD HOST LESSOR
GOODMAN PADRONE ZAMINDAR
LANDMARK COPA DOLE DOOL
MARK MERE BAKEN BOUND
CAIRN MARCH MEITH SENAL
CIPPUS SEAMARK
LANDMASS BULGE
LANDOWNER THANE BONDER
SQUIRE CACIQUE EFFENDI
FREEMAN BHUMIDAR FRANKLIN
ZAMINDAR
(PL.) GAMORI GEOMOROI
LANDSCAPE VIEW BOCAGE
PAYSAGE SCENERY LANDSKIP
LANDSLIDE SLUMP LANDFALL
LANDSLIP
LANDSMAL MAL NYNORSK
LAND SPRING LAVANT
LANDVOGT BAILIFF
LANE GUT WAY GANG LOAN LOKE
PASS RACE VEIN WIND WYND
ALLEY CHASE DRANG DRONG
ENTRY BOREEN VENNEL
LANEWAY LOANING TWITTEN
DRIFTWAY
(AIR TRAFFIC —) CORRIDOR
(NARROW —) CHAR CHARE TEWER
BOREEN RUELLE

(OCEAN —) SEAWAY
LANGUAGE (ALSO SEE DIALECT)
BAT LIP CHIB CODE LEED RUNE
TALE TESO LEDEN LINGO SLANG
LANGUS LINGUA SPEECH TONGUE
YABBER ACCENTS CABLESE
DIALECT IDIOLECT LEGALESE
PARLANCE PILIPINO
(— THAT CONDEMNS) ABUSE
(ARTIFICIAL —) RO IDO NEO ARULO
NOVIAL VOLAPUK ESPERANTO
(BANTU —) KIRUNDI
(COMPUTER —) BAL ALGOL BASIC
COBOL SNOBOL FORTRAN
(FIGURATIVE —) IMAGERY
(FLORID —) SILLABUB
(FOOLISH —) STUFF FLUMMERY
(FOUL —) SMUT ORDURE
(GYPSY —) CALO
(IMPUDENT —) SNASH
(INCOMPREHENSIBLE —) CHOCTAW
(INTERNATIONAL —) ANGLIC
(LATIN —) GRAMMAR HUMANITY
(NONSENSICAL —) BANTER
(OBSCENE —) BAWDY BAWDRY
(ORDINARY —) PROSE
(OVERPRETENTIOUS —) BOMBAST
(PERT —) SAUCE
(PIDGIN —) SABIR CAVITENO
FANAKALO
(PLAIN —) CLEAR
(PROPAGANDISTIC —) NEWSPEAK
(SECRET —) ARGOT
(SHOWY —) FLUBDUB
(SPECIFIC —) GA GE HO MO VU AIS
AKA ATA EDO EFE EPE EVE EWE
FAN FON FOX FUL GEG HET ICA
IJO ILA KAI KAU KOL KOT KRU
KUI LAB LAI LAZ MON MRU SIA
TWI UDI YAO ZIA AFAR AGAO
AGAU AGNI AHOM AINU AKAN
AKIM ALUR AMBO ANDI ANTA
ARUA AVAR BARI BEJA BIAK
BODO BONI BORA BUBE BUGI
BULU CARA CHAM CHIN CHOL
CHUJ COOS CORA COTO CREE
CROW CUNA DENE DOBU DYAK
EFIK EKOI ERIE EYAK FANG FIJI
FULA FUNG GARO GEEZ GHEG
GOLA GOLD HARE HEHE HOPI
HOVA HULA HUPA IBAN IDJO
IJAW IXIL KADU KAFA KAMI KAVI
KAWI KELE KOCH KOMI KONO
KOTA KUKI KURI LAHU LAKH
LAPP LASI LATI LAZI LESU LETT
LUBA MANX MAYA MOLE MORO
NAGA NAMA NIAS NIUE NUBA
NUPE OGOR PALA PALI PEGU
PEUL PUME RAMA SAHO SERB
SERI SGAW SHAN SIUS SORB
SULU SUMO SUMU SUSU TAAL
TIAM TIBU TINO TODA TSHI TUPI
TUPY VEPS VOTE XOSA ZULU
ALEUT ALSEA ARAUA AUETO
AZTEC BAJAU BALTI BANTU
BASSA BATAK BATTA BAURE
BEMBA BHILI BICOL BILIN BONNY
CAMPA CARIB CAYUA CHANE
CHIMU CHOCO CHOPE COFAN
COIBA COMAN CUEVA CUMAN
CUNZA CZECH DAFLA DAYAK
DIERI DINKA DUALA DUTCH
DYULA EMPEO FANTI FINGO

FUNJI GAFAT GALLA GANDA
GETAN GETIC GOLDI GONDI
GREBO GREEK GUAMO GUATO
GURMA GYPSY HABAB HAIDA
HAIKH HATSA HAUSA HINDI
HUABI HUARI HURON HUSKY
HYLAM IGALA ILOKO IRAYA IRISH
JAKUN JATKI JUANG JUTIC
KABYL KAMBA KAMIA KANDH
KAREN KAROK KHASI KHMER
KHOND KHUZI KIOWA KISSI KIWAI
KOINE KOLIS KONDE KONGO
KORKU KORWA KOTAR KUMUK
KUMYK KUSAN KWOMA LAMBA
LAMUT LANGO LATIN LENCA
LENDU LHOKE LHOTA LIMBA
LIMBU LUIAN LUNDA MAGHI
MAHRA MAHRI MALAY MALTO
MAORI MAZUR MBUBA MEDIC
MENDI MIKIR MODOC MOSSI
MUONG MURMI MURUT NAHUA
NOGAI NORSE NYORO ORAON
ORIYA OROMO OSAGE OSCAN
PALAU PAMIR PELEW PEUHL
PLATT PUNIC RONGA SAKAI
SAMAL SANTO SAXON SCOTS
SERER SHILH SHINA SHONA SICEL
SIKEL SLAVE SOTHO SOYOT
SUOMI SWAZI TAINO TAMIL TELEI
TONGA TURKI UDISH UIGUR
URIYA UZBEK VOGUL WAYAO
WELSH WOLOF YAKUT YUNCA
ZERMA ABIPON ABKHAS ACAWAI
ACHOLI ADIGHE ADZHAR AFGHAN
AHTENA ALTAIC ANDAKI ANDHRA
ANDOKE ANGAMI APACHE
APANTO APIACA ARABIC ARANDA
ARAONA ARAWAK ARUNTA
ATAROI AVANTI AYMARA
BAGOBO BAHASA BAITSI BAKELE
BANIVA BASQUE BASUTO BEAVER
BHOTIA BHUMIJ BIHARI BILAAN
BILOXI BOHUNK BONTOC BORORO
BRAHUI BRETON BRIBRI BUKAUA
BULGAR BURIAT CAGABA CANITA
CARAJA CARIAN CARIRI CAUQUI
CAVINA CAYAPA CAYUGA CAYUSE
CEBUAN CHAGGA CHAIMA
CHANGO CHOCHO CHOKWE
COCAMA CONIBO COPTIC CREOLE
DAKOTA DANISH DOGRIB
DYERMA ESKIMO EUDEVE
FRENCH FULANI FULNIO FUTUNA
GADDAN GALCHA GALIBI GATHIC
GENTOO GERMAN GILAKI GILIAK
GILYAK GOTHIC GUAIMI GUETAR
GUINAU GULLAH GURIAN HAINAN
HANTIK HARARI HATTIC HEBREW
HERERO HIBITO IBANAG IBIBIO
IFUGAO IGNERI IGOROT INDIAN
INDOIS INNUIT INUPIK ISINAI
ISLETA IVATAN KABARD KACHIN
KAFFIR KAIBAL KALMUK KAMASS
KANAKA KANURI KATIRI KEKCHI
KHALKA KHAMTI KHARIA
KHOWAR KIKUYU KILIWA
KODAGA KODAGU KOIARI KOIBAL
KOLAMI KOREAN KORYAK KOTIAK
KPELLE KUNAMA KURNAI
KURUKH KYURIN LADINO LAGUNA
LAHNDA LAHULI LENAPE LEPCHA
LIBYAN LIUKIU LIVIAN LUSHAI
LUVIAN LUWIAN LYCIAN LYDIAN

MAGAHI MAGYAR MANCHU
MANOBO MBONDO MBUNDA
MEDIAN MEGREL MICMAC
MINOAN MISHMI MISIMA
MOHAWK MONTES MUYSCA
MYSIAN NEPALI NEWARI NINGPO
NOOTKA NUBIAN NYANJA
OJIBWA ONEIDA OORIVA OSTIAK
OTOMAC OVAMPO PAHARI
PAIUTE PALAIC PAPAGO PAPUAN
PASHTO PAZAND POLISH PUSHTO
PUSHTU RASHTI REJANG
ROMANY SAFINE SAKIAN SALISH
SAMOAN SANGIL SANGIR SARCEE
SASSAK SAVARA SEDANG SEKANI
SELKUP SELUNG SEMANG SENECA
SENUFO SESUTO SHARRA SHASTA
SILETZ SINDHI SLOVAK SOMALI
SONRAI SUBIYA SURHAI SUSIAN
TARTAR TAVGHI TELEGU TELEUT
TETTUM THONGA TIPURA
TUNGUS VANNIC VOTYAK
YANKEE YARURA YORUBA
ZAREMA ABENAKI ACHAGUA
AEQUIAN AKWAALA AKWAPIM
ALABAMA ALTAIAN AMANAYE
AMHARIC AMORITE AMUESHA
APINAYE ARAMAIC ARAPAHO
ARAUCAN ARECUNA ARGOBBA
ARICARA ARMORIC ASHANTI
ASURINI ATACAMA ATAKAPA
AUSTRAL AVESTAN AXUMITE
BAGHELI BAGIRMI BAINING
BAKONGO BALANTE BALUCHI
BAMBARA BANGALA BANNACK
BASHKIR BENGALI BEOTHUK
BERBERI BHOTIYA BHUTANI
BOSNIAN BRITISH BULANDA
BUNDELI BUNYORO BURMESE
BUSHMAN CALIANA CALINGA
CARRIER CASHIBO CATALAN
CATAWBA CAWAHIB CHACOBO
CHARRUA CHATINO CHEBERO
CHECHEN CHIBCHA CHIMILA
CHINOOK CHIRINO CHIWERE
CHONTAL CHOROTI CHUKCHI
CHUMASH CHUROYA CHUVASH
CIBONEY CIMBRIC CLALLAM
COCHIMI CORNISH COTONAM
COWLITZ CYMRAEG DAGBANE
DAGOMBA DANAKIL DANKALI
DARGHIN DEUTSCH DHEGIHA
DRAVIDA ENGLISH ESCUARA
ESSELEN EUSKERA FINNISH
FLEMISH FOOCHOW FRIESIC
FRISIAN GAULISH GOAJIRO
GUAHIBO GUARANI GUAYAKI
GURUNSI GYARUNG HAITIAN
HANUNOC HIDATSA HITTITE
HUASTEC HUCHNOM HUICHOL
HURRIAN IBERIAN ILOKANO
ILONGOT INGALIK IPURINA
ITALIAN ITELMES ITONAMA
JACUNDA JAGATAI KAKHYEN
KALINGA KALMUCK KAMASIN
KANAUJI KANNADA KASHUBE
KASSITE KIKONGO KIPCHAK
KIRANTI KIRGHIZ KIRUNDI
KLAMATH KOASATI KONKANI
KOYUKON KUBACHI KULAMAN
KURDISH KUTCHIN KUTENAI
LAMPONG LATVIAN LESGHIN
LINGALA LOATUKO LUGANDA

MAGADHI MAHICAN MALINKE
MALTESE MAPUCHE MARATHI
MASKOKI MERCIAN MEXICAN
MINAEAN MINGREL MISKITO
MITANNI MOABITE MOCHICA
MONUMBO MORATTY MORISCO
NAHUATL NICOBAR OJIBWAY
OSMANLI OSSETIC PAHLAVI
PALAUNG PANJABI PARBATE
PERMIAK PERMIAN PERSIAN
PICTISH PRAKRIT PUNJABI
PUQUINA QUECHUA QUERCHI
SABAEAN SALINAN SAMBALI
SAMNANI SAMNITE SAMOYED
SANDAWE SANTALI SANTANA
SEMITIC SERBIAN SHAWANO
SHAWNEE SHILLUH SHIPIBO
SHUSWAP SIAMESE SIRIONO
SIUSLAW SOGDIAN SONGHAI
SONGISH SORBIAN SPANIOL
SPANISH STIKINE SUBANUN
SVANISH SWAHILI SWEDISH
TAGALOG TIBETAN TUAMOTU
TURKISH UMBRIAN UMBUNDU
VISAYAN WALLOON WENDISH
YENISEI YIDDISH ZABERMA
ZONGORA ABANEEME ACHINESE
ACHUMAWI AKKADIAN AKSUMITE
ALACALUF ALBANIAN ALFURESE
AMAHUACA AMERICAN
AMMONITE ANGOLESE
ANNAMESE ANZANIAN APALACHI
ARMENIAN ASSAMESE ASSYRIAN
ATJINESE AWISHIRA BACTRIAN
BALINESE BARBACOA BECHUANA
BIIOJPURI BISCAYAN BOSNISCH
BOTOCUDO CAHUILLA CAINGANG
CANARESE CANOEIRO CAQUETIO
CARELIAN CARIJONA CAYUBABA
CHALDEAN CHAMORRO CHEHALIS
CHEMAKUM CHEYENNE
CHINGPAW CHIQUITO CHITRALI
COCONUCA COLUMBIA
COMANCHE CORAVECA
CROATIAN CUSTENAU DELAWARE
DIEGUENO EGYPTIAN ELAMITIC
ETHIOPIC ETRUSCAN FALISBAN
FORMOSAN FRANKISH FULFULDE
GALICIAN GALLEGAN GEORGIAN
GERMANIC GORKHALI GUAICURU
GUJARATI HADENDOA HAWAIIAN
HITCHITI ILLINOIS ILLYRIAN
IROQUOIS JAPANESE JAVANESE
KANARESE KANAWARI KANKANAI
KASHMIRI KASUBIAN KERMANJI
KIMBUNDU KOLARIAN LANDSMAL
LANUVIAN LIGURIAN LIHYANIC
LILLOOET LIVONIAN LUSATIAN
MADURESE MAHRATTI MAKASSAR
MALAGASY MANDINGO
MARSHALL MASOVIAN
MAYATHAN MAZOVIAN
MONGOLIC MUSKOGEE NUMIDIAN
NYAMWEZI ONONDAGA OSSETIAN
PAMPANGO PHRYGIAN PILIPINO
POLABIAN PORTUGAL PRUSSIAN
RABBINIC ROMANIAN SABELLIC
SANSKRIT SAWAIORI SCOTTISH
SCYTHIAN SEBUNDOY SEECHELT
SHAMBALA SHIRIANA SHOSHONE
SICILIAN SKIPETAR SLAVONIC
SOUTHRON SQUAMISH SUBARIAN
SUBTIABA SUMATRAN SUMERIAN

TAHITIAN TALMUDIC TAMASHEK
THRACIAN TURCOMAN VENETIAN
VOLSCIAN WOGULIAN YUGOSLAV
YUKAGHIR CANAANITE
MONGOLIAN
(SWAHILI —) KISWAHILI
(UNCLEAN —) SEWERAGE
(UNIVERSAL —) PASILALY
(WELSH —) CYMRAEG
(PL.) BALTIC FINNIC MAHORI
SEMITIC SUDANIC ILLYRIAN
(PREF.) GLOSS(O) GLOTT(I)(O) KI
(SUFF.) ESE GLOT
LANGUE D'OC LEMOSI LIMOSI
LANGUET LANGUID LANGUAGE
LANGUID WAN LANK DOWIE FAINT
DREAMY FEEBLE SICKLY SUPINE
TORPID CARELESS FLAGGING
HEEDLESS INDOLENT LISTLESS
SLUGGISH
LANGUISH DIE FADE FALL FLAG
PINE WILT DROOP DWINE FAINT
QUAIL SWOON SICKEN WITHER
DECLINE
LANGUISHING FADE SICK
LANGUID
LANGUOR KEF KIF ENNUI DEBILITY
LASSITUDE
LANGUR DOUC MAHA LOTONG
LUTONG SIMPAI WANDEROO
LANK LEAN THIN GAUNT LANKY
SLANK MEAGER MEAGRE
SCRANKY SLUNKEN
LANKY LEAN RENKY SLINK GANGLY
GANGLING
LANOLIN LANUM DEGRAS
LANSEH DUKU LANSA LANZON
LANTANA OREGANO
LANTERN (ALSO SEE LAMP) BUAT
BOUET BOWET CROWN DARKY
LIGHT CUPOLA LOUVER PHAROS
SCONCE THOLUS CIMBORIO
LANTHORN
(— ON ROOF) FEMEREIL
(DARK —) DARKY ABSCONCE
ABSCONSA
(ELEVATED —) PHAROS
(OPTICAL —) EPISCOPE
LANTERN FISH INIOME
LANTERN FLOUNDER MEGRIM
LANTERN FLY FULGORID
LANTERN PINION RUNDLE
TRUNDLE
LANYARD CORD WAPP
GILGUY LANIARD
BACKROPE
LAODAMIA (BROTHER OF —)
ISANDER HIPPOLOCHUS
(FATHER OF —) ACASTUS
BELLEROPHON
(HUSBAND OF —) PROTESILAUS
(MOTHER OF —) HIPPOLYTE
(SLAYER OF —) ARTEMIS
(SON OF —) SARPEDON
LAODICE (FATHER OF —) PRIAM
(HUSBAND OF —) HELICAON
(MOTHER OF —) HECUBA
LAOIGHIS LEIX
LAOMEDON (DAUGHTER OF —)
HESIONE
(FATHER OF —) ILUS
(MOTHER OF —) EURYDICE
(SON OF —) PRIAM CLYTIUS

LAOS
CAPITAL: VIENTIANE
COIN: KIP
MEASURE: BAK
MOUNTAIN: BIA LAI LOI SAN COPI
KHAT ATWAT KHOUNG TIUBIA
PEOPLE: LU KHA LAO MEO YAO
THAI
RIVER: NOI DONE KHONG MEKONG
NAMHOU SEBANG
TOWN: NAPE PAKSE XIENG
PAKLAY THAKHEK
SAVANNAKHET
LUANGPRABANG
WATERFALL: MEKONG

LAP LEP LIP BARM FOLD GORE LICK
SLAP SLOD SOSS SUCK WASH
WELT SKIVE LAPPER LAPPET
SHOVEL INTERLAP
(— IN STEEL) SPILL
(— OF STRAKES) LAND
LAPACHOL TECOMIN
LAPBOARD PANEL
LAPDOG MESSAN MESSET SHOUGH
LAPEL LAPPET REVERE REVERS
LAPIDARY STONER GEMMARY
LAPIDIST
LAPIDOTH (WIFE OF —) DEBORAH
LAPILLUS RAPILLO
(PL.) CINDER
LAPIS LAZULI AZURE
LAP-JOINTED CLINCH
LAPP LAPPISH LAPPONIC
LAPPED FOLIATED
LAPPET LAP PAN BARBE FANON
LABEL CORNET INFULA PINNER
(PREF.) LACINI
LAPSE DROP FADE FALL HALT SLIP
ERROR FAULT FOLLY SPACE
TRACT EFFLUX HIATUS LAPSUS
DELAPSE ESCHEAT FAILURE
PASSAGE PROCESS RELAPSE
RESOLVE SLIDING ABEYANCE
CADUCITY
(— OF MEMORY) BLACKOUT
(MENTAL —) ABERRATION
(PL.) LACHES
LAPSED CADUCOUS
LAPSING CADUCOUS
LAPSTRAKE CLINCH
LAPWING WEEP WYPE PEWIT
PEEWEE PEEWIT PLOVER TIRWIT
HORNPIE PEEWEEP PIEWIPE
TEUCHIT FLOPWING PEESWEEP
TEEWHAAP TERUTERU
LARBOARD PORT BABURD
LARCENY THEFT FELONY ROBBERY
BURGLARY STEALAGE
LARCH ALERCE LARICK JUNIPER
EPINETTE TAMARACK
LARD MORT SAIM ADEPS DAUBE
ENARM FLARE FLECK FLICK
AXUNGE ENLARD INLARD
NEUTRAL SAINDOUX
LARDED PIQUE CADUCE
CADUCOUS
LARDER CAVE PANTRY SPENCE
BUTTERY LARDINER
LARGE BIG BULL FEAT GOOD LONG
MAIN ROOM TALL AMPLE BULKY
BURLY GRAND GREAT GROSS

HUSKY JOLLY LARGY MACRO
MAXIM RENKY ROUND SMART
SPACY WALLY GAWSIE GOODLY
HEROIC MAXIMA STRONG TRABAL
BOWERLY CAPITAL COPIOUS
FAIRISH FEARFUL HEALTHY
HULKING LASKING LIBERAL
MASSIVE OUTSIZE SIZABLE
BOUNCING CHOPPING OUTSIZED
PLUMPING SENSIBLE SWACKING
(— AND HOLLOW) CAVAL
(— AND ROUND) SIDE
(— IN DIAMETER) STOUT
(APPALLINGLY —) HIDEOUS
(EXTRA —) MAXI
(EXTREMELY —) GIANT DECUMAN
GIGANTIC
(FAIRLY —) SMART
(INDEFINITELY —) NTH INFINITE
(MODERATELY —) FAIR TIDY
PRETTY
(UNUSUALLY —) HEAVY SKELPIN
SKELPING
(VERY —) HUGE JUMBO ROYAL
BOXCAR BUMPER INGENT NATION
GOLIATH INTENSE BEHEMOTH
SLAPPING SPANKING SWINGING
WHACKING
(PREF.) MACR(O) MEGA MEGAL(O)
(HOW —) QUANTI
LARGE-FOOTED MEGAPOD
LARGE-FRAMED ROOMY
LARGE-LETTERED UNCIAL
LARGELY BIG HARD BIGLY
LARGENESS BULK MICKLE
BREADTH FREEDOM GIANTISM
LARGEOUR
LARGEST BEST MAXIMUS
LARIA BRUCHUS
LARIAT ROPE LASSO RIATA
CABESTRO
LARK GAME ROMP FROLIC PEEWEE
SCHEME GAMMOCK LAVROCK
LAYROCK SKYLARK CALANDER
LAVEROCK
LARKA KOLS HO
LARKSPUR LOCOWEED
LARNITE BELITE
LARRIGAN PAC
LARRIKIN NUT ROWDY HOODLUM
LARVA BOT BLOW BOTT CRAB
GRUB HUHU SLUG TURK WOLF
WORM ALIMA ASCON BARDY
BRUKE ERUCA LEECH OTTER
REDIA SYCON CORBIE COSSID
DRAGON EPHYRA GRUGRU
HOPPER LEPTUS LEUCON LOOPER
MAGGOT MEASLE NIGGER
PEDLAR TORCEL WABBLE
WORMIL WOUBIT ATROCHA
BUDWORM CADELLE CREEPER
DIPORPA FIGWORM FLYBLOW
GORDIAN HYDATID HYPOPUS
PEDDLER PLANULA PLUTEUS
PREPUPA VELIGER WIGGLER
ACTINULA ANTIZOEA ARMYWORM
BOLLWORM BOMBYCID
BOOKWORM CASEWORM
CERCARIA COENURUS CYRTOPIA
DEUTOVUM DROPWORM
EPHYRULA FIREWORM FURCILIA
GEOMETER GILTTAIL GLOWWORM
GNATWORM LEAFTIER

LEAFWORM MEALWORM MUCKWORM NAUPLIUS PILIDIUM ROOTWORM SCYPHULA SEMIPUPA SILKWORM SKINWORM SPANWORM SPRAWLER STAGWORM SUBIMAGO TORNARIA VERMICLE WASPLING WIREWORM WOODGRUB WOODWORM

LARVACEA ATREMATA COPELATA

LARVAL NEPIONIC

LARYNGITIS CROUP

LARYNX
(PREF.) LARYNG(O)

LASCIVIOUS LEWD NICE SALT HORNY LUBRIC WANTON BLISSOM FLESHLY GOATISH PAPHIAN PRURIENT SALACIOUS

LASCIVIOUSNESS LECHERY ASELGEIA LUXURITY LUBRICITY

LASERWORT SILPHIUM

LASH CUT BEAT FIRK FLOG JERK LACE WELT WHIP WIRE YERK LEASE LEASH SCORE SKEEG SLASH THONG TRICE WHALE CANVAS CILIUM LAINER LAUNCH STRIPE SWINGE SWITCH FLYFLAP KURBASH SCOURGE
(— BOWSPRIT) GAMMON
(— TOGETHER) RACK

LASHER THONGMAN

LASHING YARK YERK GAMMON LISTING MOUSING SEIZING SLATING FRAPPING
(PL.) OODLES OODLINS SLITHERS

LASS TIB GILL PRIM TRULL DAMSEL KUMMER LASSIE DAMOZEL LASSIKY TENDREL MUCHACHA

LASSITUDE COPOS LANGUOR LETHARGY

LASSO LASH LAZO ROPE RIATA LARIAT CABESTRO

LAST ABY LAG DURE HOLD KEEP RIDE SAVE ABIDE FINAL SERVE ABEGGE ENDURE LATEST LATTER REMAIN ULTIMA UTMOST DARREIN DERNIER EXTREME PERDURE SUPREME CONTINUE EVENTUAL HINDMOST LATEMOST REARMOST TERMINAL ULTIMATE AFTERMOST
(— BUT ONE) PENULT
(— OUT) SPIN STAY
(AT —) FINALLY
(THE —) OMEGA
(PREF.) ESCHATO POSTREMO ULTIMO

LAST DAYS OF POMPEII (AUTHOR OF —) BULWER LYTTON
(CHARACTER IN —) IONE BURBO JULIA NYDIA DIOMED ARBACES CLODIUS GLAUCUS SALLUST APAECIDES

LASTING FIXED LASTY DURANT DURING STABLE ABIDING DURABLE DUREFUL CONSTANT ENDURING LIVELONG REMANENT STANDING
(— FOR LONG PERIOD) AEONIC AEONIAL
(— FOR ONE DAY) DIARY DIURNAL

LASTINGNESS STAY DURATION

LAST OF THE MOHICANS

(AUTHOR OF —) COOPER
(CHARACTER IN —) CORA WEBB ALICE DAVID GAMUT MAGUA MUNRO NATTY UNCAS BUMPPO DUNCAN HAWKEYE HEYWARD MONTCALM CHINGACHGOOK

LAST PURITAN (AUTHOR OF —) SANTAYANA
(CHARACTER IN —) JIM IRMA ROSE ALDEN BOBBY EDITH MARIO PETER WEYER BOWLER OLIVER DARNLEY HARRIET SCHLOTE BUMSTEAD

LAST SUPPER CENA COENA MAUNDY

LAT STAMBHA

LATCH FLY PIN HASP RISP CATCH CHAIR CLICK CLINK SNECK SNICK KEEPER CLICKET

LATCHET DAG TAB SANDAL LANGUET

LATCHING LASKET

LATCHKEY CLICKET PASSKEY

LATE LAG NEW DEEP RIPE SLOW TARDY TARDIVE UMWHILE ADVANCED LATEWARD SOMETIME UMQUHILE
(— IN DEVELOPING) SEROTINOUS

LATE GEORGE APLEY (AUTHOR OF —) MARQUAND
(CHARACTER IN —) JOHN MARY APLEY AMELIA GEORGE ELEANOR HORATIO MONAHAN OREILLY WILLIAM WILLING BOSWORTH PRENTISS CATHARINE

LATELY LATE ALATE NEWLY

LA TENE MARNEAN

LATENT HIDDEN MASKED ABEYANT DORMANT PASSIVE LATITANT QUIESCENT
(PREF.) CRYPT(O) KRYPT(O)

LATER POI SIN ANON POST SYNE AFTER ELDER BEHIND FUTURE LATTER PUISNE ANOTHER INFERIOR UMQUHILE
(PREF.) HYSTERO INFRA META POST

LATERAL SIDE
(PREF.) PLEUR(O)

LATERALLY SIDELONG

LATERITE CABOOK KUNKUR

LATEST LAST LATTER FARTHEST FURTHEST

LATEX GUTTA SORVA ANTIAR SENAMBY

LATH BAT LAG SLAT SPAIL·SPALE SPELL SWALE REEPER SPLENT SPLINT STOOTH LATHING FOREPOLE LATHWORK

LATHE LAY SLEY TURN LAITH THROW BEATER WISKET
(— FOR CYLINDERS) BROAD
(— OF LOOM) LAY
(TURNING —) THROW
(WATCHMAKER'S —) TURN TURNS MANDREL

LATHER FOAM SUDS FROTH FREATH SAPPLES

LATHERED SOAPY

LATIN ROMAN HISPERIC LATINITY SCATTERMOUCH
(— COMPOSITION) VULGUS

LATIN-AMERICAN LATIN LADINO

LATINO HISPANIC

LATINUS (DAUGHTER OF —) LAVINIA
(FATHER OF —) FAUNUS
(SON-IN-LAW OF —) AENEAS
(WIFE OF —) AMATA

LATITUDE SCOPE WIDTH EXTENT HEIGHT
(HELIOCENTRIC —) LIMIT

LATONA (DAUGHTER OF —) DIANA
(FATHER OF —) COEUS
(MOTHER OF —) PHOEBE
(SON OF —) APOLLO

LATRIA ADORATION

LATRINE BOG REAR PRIVY TOILET BOGGARD

LATTER LAST FINAL RECENT SECOND PRESENT
(— PORTION) AUTUMN

LATTICE GRATE HERSE TWINE PINJRA UMBREL GRATING CANCELLI
(— OF POINTS) SATIN
(MOVING —) APRON
(PREF.) CLATHR

LATTICED CLATHRATE

LATTICE PLANT LACELEAF

LATTICEWORK ARBOR GRATE GRATING ESPALIER TUKUTUKU

<table>
<tr><td colspan="2" align="center">**LATVIA**</td></tr>
<tr><td>**CAPITAL:**</td><td>RIGA</td></tr>
<tr><td>**COIN:**</td><td>LAT RUBLIS KAPEIKA SANTIMS</td></tr>
<tr><td>**MEASURE:**</td><td>STOF KANNE STOFF STOOF VERST ARSHIN KULMET SAGENE VERCHOC KROUCHKA POURVETE</td></tr>
<tr><td>**NAME:**</td><td>LATVIJA LETTLAND LETTONIE</td></tr>
<tr><td>**PEOPLE:**</td><td>LETT</td></tr>
<tr><td>**RIVER:**</td><td>AA OGRE DVINA GAUJA VENTA SALACA LIELUPE</td></tr>
<tr><td>**TOWN:**</td><td>CESIS LIBAU DVINSK LIBAVA TUKUMS JELGAVA LIEPAJA REZEKNE DUNABURG VALMIERA DAUGAVPILS</td></tr>
<tr><td>**WEIGHT:**</td><td>LIESPFUND</td></tr>
</table>

LAUAN KALUNTI

LAUD EXTOL PRAISE ADVANCE APPLAUD COMMEND GLORIFY MAGNIFY EMBLAZON EULOGIZE MACARIZE

LAUDATION PUFF EULOGY PRAISE PANEGYRIC

LAUDATORY SNEER EPENETIC PRAISING

LAUGH GAFF CHUCK FLEER LEUGH RISUS ARRIDE NICKER TITTER CHORTLE GRIZZLE SNICKER SNIGGER SNIRTLE TWITTER LAUGHTER
(— CONTEMPTUOUSLY) SNORT DERIDE
(— GLEEFULLY) CHECKLE
(— HYSTERICALLY) CHECKLE
(— IN AFFECTED MANNER) GIGGLE
(— IN COARSE MANNER) FLEER GUFFAW
(— LIKE HEN) CACKLE
(— LOUDLY) GAFF GUFFAW
(— QUIETLY) GULE SMUDGE CHUCKLE SNIRTLE

(BELLY —) BOFF BOFFOLA
(LOUD —) GAUSTER

LAUGHABLE ODD RICH COMIC DROLL FUNNY MERRY QUEER WITTY AMUSING COMICAL RISIBLE STRANGE WAGGISH FARCICAL HUMOROUS LAUGHING PLEASANT SPORTIVE RIDICULOUS

LAUGHING RIANT RIDENT IRRISION
(— MATTER) MOWS

LAUGHING GULL PEWIT

LAUGHING OWL WEKAU WHEKAU

LAUGHINGSTOCK GUY BUTT JEST JOKE SONG SPORT DERISION RIDICULE

LAUGHTER JOKE MIRTH RISUS SNIRT CACKLE LAWTER SPLEEN HILARITY RISIBILITY
(HYSTERICAL —) CACHINNATION
(PREF.) GELOTO

LAUNCE LANT LANCE SMELT AMMODYTE SANDLING

LAUNCH PUT BURST DRIVE LANCE ELANCE STRIKE BAPTIZE PINNACE PROMOTE STEAMER VIBRATE CATAPULT
(— HOSTILELY) DIRECT

LAUNCHER (ROCKET —) BAZOOKA

LAUNDER TYE WASH TRUNK SLUICE STRAKE LAUNDRY

LAUNDRESS TRILBY LAVENDER

LAUNDRY WASH LAVATORY

LAUREL BAY IVY LAURY UNITE WICKY DAPHNE KALMIA MALLET MYRTLE CAJEPUT IVYWOOD WOEVINE BREWSTER CALFKILL
(GROUND —) ARBUTUS

LAUREL OAK ACAJOU

LAURIC PICHURIC

LAURUSTINE VIBURNUM

LAUSUS (FATHER OF —) NUMITOR MEZENTIUS
(SISTER OF —) ILIA
(SLAYER OF —) AMULIUS

LAUTVERSCHIEBUNG SHIFT

LAVA AA ASHES SPINE COULEE LATITE SCORIA VERITE FAVILLA LAPILLO MALPAIS ASPERITE ORENDITE PAHOEHOE
(MUD —) MOYA LAHAR
(SCORIACEOUS —) AA SLAG
(SLAGGY —) SCORIA

LAVABO LAVATORY

LAVAGE LAVATION LAVEMENT

LAVALAVA SULU

LAVAN KALUNTI

LAVATORY BASIN CHALET CLOSET LAVETTE WASHROOM CLOAKROOM

LAVE LIP WASH BATHE SPLASH

LAVENDER BEHN ASPIC BEHEN SPICK SPIKE INKROOT LAVANDIN STICHADO

LAVENGRO (AUTHOR OF —) BORROW
(CHARACTER IN —) JOHN MOLL ARDRY HERNE PETER ISOPEL JASPER BERNERS FRANCIS LEONORA TAGGART LAVENGRO SAPENGRO SLINGSBY WILLIAMS WINIFRED PETULENGRO

LAVER SION SLAKE SLOKE LOUTER PHIALE AMANORI CISTERN CANTHARUS

LAVINIA (FATHER OF —) LATINUS **(HUSBAND OF —)** AENEAS **(MOTHER OF —)** AMATA

LAVISH FREE LASH LUSH FLUSH LARGE SPEND SPORT WASTE COSTLY WANTON COPIOUS OPULENT PROFUSE GENEROUS LUCULLAN PRODIGAL SQUANDER WASTEFUL REDUNDANT MUNIFICENT

LAVISHNESS WASTE FINERY LAVISH

LAW ACT FAS IUS JUS LAY LEX ADAT DOOM JURE RULE CANON DROIT NOMOS TORAH BYELAW BYRLAW DECREE DHARMA EQUITY BROCARD DANELAW DERECHO HALACHA HALAKAH JUSTICE PRECEPT SETNESS STATUTE JUDGMENT JUDICIAL ROGATION STATEWAY TANISTRY ORDINANCE **(—S OF MANU)** SUTRA SUTTA **(BEDOUIN —)** THAR **(DIETARY —S)** KASHRUTH **(ISLAMIC —)** ADA BAI ADAT SHERI SHARIA SHERIAT **(MARRIAGE —)** LEVIRATE **(OPPOSING —)** ANTINOMY **(PROPOSED —)** BILL **(UNIVERSAL —)** HEAVEN **(PL.)** LORS **(PREF.)** JURIS LEGI LEGO NOMI(O) THESMO **(SUFF.)** LEGE NOMY

LAW-ABIDING LAWFUL

LAWBREAKER FELON HOUGHER

LAWFUL DUE LEAL TRUE VERY LEGAL LICIT LOYAL VALID KINDLY LEEFUL ENNOMIC LEESOME INNOCENT LIEFSOME RIGHTFUL

LAWGIVER MINOS MOSES SOLON LAWYER LAWMAKER

LAWLESS LEWD UNRULY ILLEGAL MOBBISH ANARCHIC

LAWLESSNESS ANOMY ANOMIE ANARCHY

LAWMAKER LEGIFER

LAWN ARBOR GRASS LINON SWARD UMPLE CYPRUS BATISTE QUINTIN TIFFANY

LAWSUIT LIS CASE SAKE SECTA ACTION BRABBLE

LAWYER **(ALSO SEE JURIST)** JET PEAT AVOUE PATCH SHARK BREHON JURIST LAWMAN LEGIST SQUIRE WRITER COUNSEL MUKHTAR TEMPLAR DEFENDER LEGISTER TRAMPLER BARRISTER MOUTHPIECE PETTIFOGGER

LAX DULL FREE LASH LAZY LINK SLOW SWAG WIDE LARGE LOOSE RELAX SLACK TARDY REMISS BACKWARD INACTIVE DISSOLUTE NEGLIGENT

LAXATIVE LAX LASK CASCARA APERIENT HYDROMEL LAPACTIC RELAXANT SOLUTIVE TARAXACUM

LAXITY LASCHETY LATITUDE

LAY LIE SET CLAP LAIC LEWD SLEY SONG WAGE BIGHT CIVIL COUCH DITTY LATHE LEDGE QUIET STAKE STILL COMMON HAZARD IMPOSE IMPUTE APPEASE ASCRIBE LAYDOWN POPULAR SECULAR SIRVENTE TEMPORAL **(— ASIDE)** DOFF DOWN DUMP SHUCK DEPOSE DIVEST DEPOSIT PIGEONHOLE **(— AWAY)** STORE **(— BARE)** BARE NAKE TIRL TIRVE DENUDE DETECT OPPOSE UNCOVER DENUDATE **(— CLAIM)** ASSERT BESPEAK ARROGATE **(— CROSSWISE)** COB **(— DOWN)** ABDICATE PRESCRIBE **(— EGGS)** BLOW WARP LEDGE OVIPOSIT **(— FLAT)** SQUAT ADPRESS **(— HOLD OF)** FANG GRIP HENT TAKE GRIPE LATCH ATHOLD ATTACH COLLAR COMPRISE **(— IN BIGHTS)** JAG **(— IN COIL)** FLEMISH **(— IN PLEATS)** FOLD **(— LOW)** STREW STRIKE **(— OF LOOM)** BEATER **(— ON)** APPLY INFLICT **(— OPEN)** BREAK CHINE EXPOSE UNMASK **(— OUT)** FRAY PLAT RANGE SPELD SPEND BEWARE DESIGN EXTEND SPREAD STREAK STREEK CHECKER DEVELOP STRETCH CONTRIVE **(— PRONE)** LEVEL **(— RUBBLEWORK)** SNECK **(— SIEGE)** INVEST **(— SMOOTH)** EVEN **(— SNARE FOR RABBITS)** HAY **(— STONE)** PAVE **(— STRAIGHT)** COMB **(— TYPE)** CASE **(— UP)** HEAP HIVE ADDLE HOARD HUTCH STOCK TREASURE **(— WASTE)** PEEL WEST HARRY HAVOC HARASS RAVAGE DESTROY DESOLATE FORWASTE

LAYBOY JOGGER

LAYDOWN LAYOUT SPREAD

LAYER BED LAY BARK CAKE COAT DASS FACE FILM FLAP FOLD LAIR LOFT RIND SEAM SKIN WEFT ZONA CHESS COUCH COVER CRUST CUTIS FLAKE FLASH LEDGE SCALE CARPET COURSE FASCIA FILLER FOLIUM INTINE LAMINA LISSOM STREAK BLANKET COATING CUTICLE EPICARP FEATHER FLAVEDO GANGMAN INLAYER LAMELLA PACKING PHELLEM PROPAGO PROVINE STRATUM SUBCOAT SUPPORT ECTOCYST ECTOSARC ENDOCYST ENDODERM EPIBLAST EPIBLEMA EPISPORE EPITHECA INTERBED MOLLISOL PERIOPLE PERISARC SUBCRUST PERIPLAST PHELLODERM **(— IN FUNGI)** HYMENIUM

(— OF ATMOSPHERE) MESOSPHERE OZONOSPHERE **(— OF BLOOD VESSEL)** EXTIMA EXTERNA **(— OF CELLS)** EXINE CORTEX EXTINE CAMBIUM PHELLEM TAPETUM PERICYCLE **(— OF CLAY)** GLEY VARVE SELVAGE SELVEDGE **(— OF EARTH)** SPIT **(— OF FAT)** LEAF FINISH **(— OF FELT)** BAT BATT **(— OF FIBER)** LAP **(— OF FINE MATERIAL)** CUSHION **(— OF FOREST GROWTH)** SUBSTORY OVERSTORY **(— OF FUEL)** FIREBED **(— OF GLASS)** CASING **(— OF IRIS)** UVEA **(— OF MEAT)** SPINE **(— OF MORTAR)** SCREED **(— OF NERVE FIBERS)** ALVEUS **(— OF ORGANIC MATTER)** FLOOR **(— OF PLASMA)** BUFFCOAT **(— OF ROCK)** CAP SHELF SHELL SLATE FOLIUM SEPTUM BLISTER SKULLCAP **(— OF ROOTS)** SOLE **(— OF SEDIMENT)** WARP **(— OF SHALE)** BONE **(— OF SHEEPSKIN)** FLESHER **(— OF SHOE HEEL)** LIFT **(— OF SILT)** VARVE **(— OF SKIN)** DERM DERMA EPIDERM **(— OF SOIL)** SOLUM GALLOW CASING HARDPAN HORIZON **(— OF STONES)** DASS DESS **(— OF TANBARK)** HAT **(— OF TISSUE)** BED DARTOS FASCIA SEROSA ELASTICA EPIBLEMA PERIDERM **(— OF TOBACCO LEAVES)** HANGER **(— OF TURF)** FLAW KERF **(— OF WHITE MATTER)** CAPSULE **(— OF WOOD)** CORE **(BONY —)** LAMELLA CEMENTUM **(BOTTOM —)** BEDDING **(FLAT —)** BED FLAP FLAKE **(FROZEN —)** PERMAFROST **(GERM —)** MESODERM **(IMPERVIOUS —)** LINING **(OUTER —)** HUSK **(PREF.)** LAMELLI LAMIN(I) PTYCH(O) STRATI **(SUFF.)** CLINAL CLINE LAMIN **(— OF SKIN)** DERMIS **(GERM —)** BLAST(IC)(Y)

LAYERING LAP GOOTEE STOOLING

LAYMAN LAIC CLERK IDIOT DEACON SECULAR DEFENSOR EXHORTER EXOTERIC FAMILIAR STRANGER WORLDMAN

LAYOFF FURLOUGH

LAYOUT MISE DUMMY SETOUT **(— OF CARDS)** TABLEAU

LAZARETTO SPITAL SPITTLE

LAZARUS (SISTER OF —) MARY MARTHA

LAZINESS LAZE SLOTH SLOUCH OISIVITY

LAZULITE SIDERITE

LAZY ARGH IDLE LASS DOXIE

DRONY FAINT INERT LINGY LUSKY RESTY SLOAN SLOTH CLUMSY LIMPSY LURDAN LUTHER ORNERY SWEERT TRAILY CLUMPST DRONISH LUSKISH PEAKISH SLIVING DROGHLIN FAINEANT FECKLESS INDOLENT LITHERLY OSCITANT SLOTHFUL SLUGGARD THOWLESS TRIFLING SHIFTLESS

LEA LAY GRASS LAYER LAYLAND LEALAND

LEACH TAP LETCH SOFTEN

LEAD GO TEE VAN WIN BEAR DADE GIVE GROW HAVE HEAD HERD LEED SLIP TAKE TEEM WORK BLAZE BOUND BRING CARRY GREBE GUIDE MAYNE PILOT PRESA SOUND START TRAIN TREAT CONVEY DEDUCE DIRECT ESCORT INDUCE INDUCT LEADER SATURN BEGUILE CAPTAIN CONDUCE CONDUCT LEADING MARSHAL PIGTAIL PIONEER PLUMBUM PLUMMET LEADSMAN MANUDUCE MANUDUCT SQUIRREL **(— A BAND)** BATON **(— AND SUPPORT)** DADE **(— ASIDE)** CHAR SINGLE **(— ASTRAY)** ERR MANG TURN WARP BEFOOL BETRAY ENTICE WANDER WILDER DEBAUCH MISLEAD MISWEND PERVERT SOLICIT TRADUCE BEWILDER INVEIGLE MISGUIDE **(— AWAY)** CHAR ABDUCT DIVERGE **(— BACK)** REDUCT **(— FORCIBLY)** ESCORT **(— IN CARD GAME)** SNEAK WHITECHAPEL **(— IN RACE)** LAP **(— IN SINGING)** PRECENT **(— INTO ERROR)** ABUSE DELUDE **(— MONOXIDE)** MASSICOT **(— ON)** TRAIL **(— PASSIVE EXISTENCE)** VEGETATE **(— POISONING)** PLUMBISM **(BLACK —)** WAD WADD GRAPHITE **(COLOR —)** PLOMB **(DEEP-SEA —)** DIPSY DIPSEY **(MOCK —)** BLENDE **(OVERLAPPING —)** DRIP **(PLUMBING —)** BLUEY **(SYMBOL FOR —)** PB **(WHITE —)** KREMS CERUSE **(PREF.)** GALENO MOLYBD(O) PLUMB(I)(O) **(SUFF.)** AGOGUE AGOGY

LEAD-COLORED WAN BLAE

LEADEN HEAVY PLUMBEAN

LEADER BO BOH COB DUX HOB MIR CAST COCK DUCE DUKE HEAD HOBB JEFE NAIG NAIK OMDA SOUL TYEE CHIEF DOYEN ELDER FIRST MAHDI MOSES OMDEH PILOT SEYID TRACE ARCHON CALIPH DESPOT HEADER HONCHO RECTOR SAYYID TYCOON ACREMAN ADVISER CAPTAIN CONDUCT DEMAGOG DRUNGAR FOREMAN FUEHRER INDUCER PRIMATE ACCENTOR CAUDILLO DIRECTOR FUGLEMAN

HEADSMAN HERETOGA
LODESMAN PANDARUS STRATEGE
PENDRAGON PROTAGONIST
(— ARMY) VAIYODE VOIVODE
(— OF DACOITS) BOH
(— OF GUISERS) SKUDLER
(— OF MINING GANG) CORPORAL
(— OF MUTINEERS) ELECTO
(— OF REVOLT) ANARCH
(BAND —) BATONEER
(CHOIR —) CANTOR PRECENTOR
(CHORUS —) CHORAGUS
(COSSACK —) HETMAN
(FASCIST —) RAS
(INTELLECTUAL —) BRAIN
(MOB —) MOBOCRAT
(POLITICAL —) SACHEM
(PRAYER —) IMAM
(RELIGIOUS —) AGA AGHA SHEIKH
(SCOUT —) AKELA SIXER
(SPIRITUAL —) GURU SADDIK
GUARDIAN
(SUFF.) ARCH ARCHIC ARCHY
LEADERSHIP LEAD AEGIS MANRED
CONDUCT IMAMATE LEADING
MANRENT CHIEFDOM GUIDANCE
HEADSHIP HEGEMONY
(— BY TALENTED) MERITOCRACY
LEADING BIG BEST COCK DUCT
HEAD LEAD MAIN CHIEF FIRST
BANNER PREMIER STELLAR
GUIDANCE PROMINENT
(— OUTWARD) EMISSARY
(— TO NOTHING) IDLE
LEADSMAN SOUNDER
LEADWORK PLUMBAGE PLUMBING
LEADWORT CROWTOE PLUMBAGO
LEAF PAD BACK BARB BUYO FLAG
FLAP FOIL FOLD GEAR PAGE
PALM STUB BLADE BLANK FLIER
FLYER FOLIO FROND GRASS
GUARD LEAVE SCALE SEPAL
SIGHT SPILL TEPAL BONNET
CADJAN CARPEL COUPON
FOLIUM FRAISE FULZIE NEEDLE
PEPPER DAMIANA FOLDOUT
HARNESS LEAFLET TREFOIL
WITNESS PHYLLADE PHYLLOME
MICROPHYLL
(— FAT) FLICK
(— FROM AXIL) BRACT
(— OF BOOK) PAGE FOLIO INSET
PLATE FLYLEAF
(— OF CALYX) BARB
(— OF CORN) HUSK
(— OF COROLLA) PETAL
(— OF DOOR) VALVE
(— OF HEDDLES) GEAR
(— OF PALM) FAN OLA PAN CHIP
OLLA FROND LATANIER
(— OF SPRING) BACK
(BETEL —) PAN SIRIH
(BIBLE —) COSTMARY
(DEAD —) FLAG
(HOLLOW —) PHYLLODE
(PART OF —) RIB TIP APEX BASE
LOBE STEM VEIN BLADE SINUS
LAMINA MARGIN MIDRIB PETIOLE
LEAFSTALK
(RUDIMENTARY —) CATAPHYLL
(SPRING —) WRAPPER
(STRAWBERRY —) FRAISE
(THIN —) LAMELLA

(TOBACCO —) LUGS STRIP CUTTER
WRAPPER
(WASTE GOLD —) SKEWING
(PREF.) FOLI(O) PETAL(I)(O)
PHYLL(I)(O)
(SUFF.) FOLIATE FOLIOUS
PETALOUS PHYLL(A)(OUS)(UM)(Y)
LEAFAGE FOLIAGE
LEAFHOPPER HOPPER JASSID
THRIPS HOMPTER
LEAFLET PINNA TRACT MAILER
FOLIOLE STUFFER
(-S DROPPED FROM AIR) BUMF
(PAIR OF —S) JUGUM
(PL.) SENNA CAROBA
LEAFLIKE PHYLLINE
LEAFMOLD KOLINSKY
LEAFY GREEN LEAVY FOLIATE
FOLIOSE FRONDOSE
LEAGUE BOND BUND BANDY
BOARD GUEUX HANSA PARTY
UNION WHEEL CIRCUIT COMPACT
ALLIANCE SYSTASIS COALITION
(— OF NATIONS) GENEVA
(BUSH —S) STICKS
LEAGUED FEDERATE
LEAH (DAUGHTER OF —) DINAH
(FATHER OF —) LABAN
(HUSBAND OF —) JACOB
(SISTER OF —) RACHEL
(SON OF —) LEVI JUDAH REUBEN
SIMEON ZEBULUN ISSACHAR
LEAK BLOW SEEP WEEP GEYZE
SPUNK INLEAK SIGGER SPRING
ZIGGER LEAKAGE MELTERS
SCREEVE
(— IN ELECTRIC CIRCUIT) FAULT
LEAKAGE ESCAPE SEEPAGE
(— OF ELECTRICITY) CREEPAGE
(— OF GAS) SLIP
(— OF WIND) RUNNING
LEAKING ALEAK DRIBBLE NAILSICK
LEAKY LEAK UNTIGHT GIZZENED
LEAL FAITHFUL
LEAN BEAR BEND BONY HANG
HEEL LANK PEND POOR PRIN
RACY RELY REST SEEL STAY
SWAY THIN TOOM EMPTY GAUNT
HIELD LANKY LEANY SLANK
SOUND SPARE STOOP HOLLOW
MEAGER RECUMB SKINNY SPRING
UPLEAN ANGULAR FATLESS
HAGGARD INCLINE SCRAGGY
SCRAWNY SLUNKEN STRINGY
MACILENT SCRAGGED SCRANNEL
(— FOR SUPPORT) ABUT
(— FORWARD) PROCLINE
(— OVER) WHAUVE
(PREF.) CLIN(O)
LEANDER (LOVE OF —) HERO
LEANDRE (FATHER OF —) GERONTE
(LOVER OF —) LUCINDE ·
LEANER HOBBER
LEANING DRIFT FLAIR PENCHE
HANGING ACCLINAL ENCLITIC
FROMWARD PROPENSE
PROCLIVITY PROPENSITY
(— BACKWARD) SUPINE
(STRONG —) GENIUS PENCHANT
LEANNESS LANK POVERTY
SPARENESS
LEAN-TO SHED LINTER OUTSHOT
SKILLION

LEAP FLY HOP POP BEND DART
DIVE FALL GIVE JUMP LOPE LOUP
RAMP RISE SKIT WIND BOUND
BREAK CAPER DANCE EXULT
FLIER FLYER FRISK LUNGE PRIME
SALTO SAULT SCOPE SCOUP
SPANG STEND VAULT BOUNCE
BREACH CURVET INSULT LAUNCH
SPRENT SPRING SPRUNT WALLOP
REBOUND SALTARY SALTATE
SUBSULT BUCKJUMP LEAPFROG
SPANGHEW UPSPRING
(— BACK) RESULT SPRUNT
(— FOR JOY) EXULT
(— IN DANCING) STOT
(— LIGHTLY) SKIP
(— OF HORSE) CURVET BALOTADE
CAPRIOLE CROUPADE
(— OF WHALE) BREACH
(— OUT) SALLY
(— OVER) FREE OVER SKIP CLEAR
HURDLE
(— UPON) ASSAIL
(BALLET —) JETE ASSEMBLE
CABRIOLE
(FROLICSOME —) CAPER
(SUICIDAL —) BRODIE
(PL.) ALLEGRO
(PREF.) SCIRTO
LEAPING GAMBOL SPRING
RAMPANT SALIENT SALTANT
LEARCHUS (BROTHER OF —)
MELICERTA
(FATHER OF —) ATHAMAS
(MOTHER OF —) INO
LEARN DO CON GET SEE WIT ARAL
FIND HAVE HEAR LEAR LERE
EDIFY GLEAN STUDY RECORD
REALIZE RECEIVE DISCOVER
ASCERTAIN
(— FROM EXPERIENCE) ASSAY
LEARNED BLUE SEEN LERED
LORED DUCTUS BOOKISH
CLERKLY CUNNING ERUDITE
STUDIED TUITIVE ACADEMIC
CLERGIAL LETTERED OVERSEEN
POLYMATH PROFOUND SCIENCED
(— MAN) OLLAV
(AFFECTEDLY —) INKHORN
(SOMETHING TO BE —) LIRIPIPE
LEARNEDLY CLERKLY
LEARNER PUPIL NOVICE SCHOLAR
TRAINEE PRENTICE ABECEDARIAN
(LATE —) OPSIMATH
LEARNING ART WIT BOOK LEIR
LERE LORE CLERGY WISDOM
APPRISE CUNNING GRAMMAR
INSIGHT LETTERS WISTING
BOOKLEAR BOOKLORE DOCTRINE
HUMANISM LETTRURE MATHESIS
PEDANTRY
(SUFF.) MATHY
LEASE FEU FEW LET SET FARM
HIRE RENT TACK COWLE DIMIT
FIRMA LISSE DEMISE POTTAH
RENTAL ASSEDAT CHARTER
SETTING BACKTACK SUBLEASE
LEASEHOLDER LIVIER
LEASH LEAD LYME SLIP LEASE
TRASH COUPLE STRING SWINGE
(— OF HOUNDS) HARL
(DOG —) SLIP TRASH TIRRET
(HAWK'S —) LOYN LUNE

TIRRET CREANCE
LEASING LOCATIO
LEAST LEST MINIMAL MINIMUM
MINIMUS
(AT —) HURE
LEAST FLYCATCHER CHEBEC
LEAST SANDPIPER PEEP OXEYE
STINT
LEATHER ELK KID BEND BOCK
BUFF CALF CAPE HIDE NAPA
SEAL ADUST ALUTA BALAT FLANK
NIGER RETAN SUEDE BULGAR
CASTOR CHROME LIZARD ORIOLE
OXHIDE PEBBLE RUSSET SKIVER
TURKEY BELTING BUFFING
CANEPIN CHAMOIS COWHIDE
COWSKIN DEGRAIN DOGSKIN
DONGOLA HEADCAP HOGSKIN
KIDSKIN MURRAIN PANCAKE
PECCARY PERSIAN SAFFIAN
ANTELOPE BUCKSKIN BULLNECK
CABRETTA CALFSKIN CAPESKIN
CHEVEREL COLTSKIN CORDOBAN
CORDWAIN DEERSKIN GOATSKIN
KANGAROO LAMBSKIN SHAGREEN
SHEEPSKIN
(— FOR DRESSING FLAX) RIBSKIN
(— FROM SHEEPSKIN) ROAN
(— SHREDS) MOSLINGS
(— STRIP) RAND
(ARABIAN —) MOCHA
(ARTIFICIAL —) KERATOL
PEGAMOID
(BOARDED —) BOX
(CORDOVAN —) CORDOBAN
CORDWAIN
(GRAINED —) ROAN
(MOROCCO —) LEVANT MAROQUIN
(PATCH OF —) CLOUT
(PRUSSIAN —) SPRUCE
(RUSSIAN —) YUFT BULGAR
RUSSIA JUCHTEN
(SHEEPSKIN —) BOCK BUCK
MOCHA
(SOFT —) OOZE ALUTA
(SUPERIOR —) BUFF
(THICK —) BUTT
(WASH —) LOSH LOSHE
(PREF.) SCYT(O)
LEATHERBACK LUTH
LEATHERFISH LIJA FOOLFISH
LEATHERJACKET FILEFISH
ZAPATERO
LEATHERLEAF CASSANDRA
LEATHERWOOD DIRCA WICOPY
BURNWOOD FIREWOOD
IRONWOOD LEADWOOD
ROPEBARK
LEATHERWORKER TAWER
BEDDER CHAMAR MADIGA
FLUFFER CHUCKLER
LEAVE GO GET LET BUNK DROP
FADE FLEE HOOK LEAF PART
QUIT VADE VOID WALK AVOID
CONGE FAVOR FORGO GRACE
SHOVE WAIVE BUGGER BUGOFF
DEPART DESERT DEVOID FORLET
PERMIT RETIRE SECEDE STRAND
VACATE FORLEIT FORLESE
FORSAKE LARGESS LIBERTY
LICENSE FAREWELL PATIENCE
UNTENANT PERMISSION
SABBATICAL

(— ALONE) FORBEAR DESOLATE
(— BEHIND) LET PLANT DISTANCE
OUTSTRIP
(— BRIGHT TRAIL) STREAM
(— BY WILL) BEQUEATH
(— COVER) BREAK
(— HASTILY) SCUR SKIRR
(— HURRIEDLY) CUT BLOW FLEE
JUMP SCAT SKIP
(— IN ISOLATION) MAROON
(— IN SAFEKEEPING) CHECK
(— NOTHING TO BE DESIRED)
SATISFY
(— OF ABSENCE) ABSIT EXEAT
LIBERTY FURLOUGH
(— OFF) CEASE DEVAL PETER
BILEVE CHEESE DESIST SURCEASE
(— OUT) BATE OMIT SKIP SLIP
ELIDE
(— PORT) CLEAR
(— QUICKLY) SCREW
(— SECRETLY) STEAL
(— SUDDENLY) KITE
(— UNDONE) PRETERMIT
LEAVED
(SUFF.) PHYLLOUS
LEAVEN ZYM ZYMO RAISE YEAST
INFUSE RAISING SOURING
(PREF.) ZYM(O)
LEAVENING EMPTINGS
LEAVES PATRIN FOLIAGE LEAFAGE
LEAFERY
(— OF BAOBAB TREE) LALO
(— OF ORCHID) FAHAM
(— OF TOBACCO) LEAF FLYINGS
SECUNDS
(— ON STEM AFTER WITHERING)
INDUVIAE
(— USED AS STYPTIC) MATICO
(BOILED — OF POTHERB) CHARD
(DRIED —) LAUHALA
(FALLEN —) DUFF
(MEDICINAL —) COCA FILE BUCCO
BUCKU FARFARA FUMARIA
(PALM —) ATAP ATTAP CADJAN
CAJANG
(TEA —) SOUCHONG
(WITHERED —) PININGS
(SUFF.) **(HAVING —)** CLEMA
PHYLLOUS
(NUMBER OF —) MO
LEAVE-TAKING VALE ADIEU
CONGEE PARTING WAYGANG
FAREWELL WAYGOING
LEAVING BIT ORT TAG
(PL.) RAFF SNUFF REFUSE
RESIDUE RESIDUUM
(PREF.) LIPO

LEBANON
CAPITAL: BEIRUT BEYROUTH
COIN: LIVRE PIASTRE
MOUNTAIN: ARUBA HERMON
SANNINE KENISSEH
PLAIN: ELBIKA
RIVER: JOZ LYCOS DAMOUR
LITANI HASBANI LEONTES
ORONTES KASEMIEH
SEAPORT: TYRE SAIDA SIDON
BEIRUT
TOWN: SUR TYRE ALEIH HALBA
SAIDA SIDON ZAHLE
JUNIYE ZAHLAH QARTABA

TRIPOLI MERJUYUN
VALLEY: BEQAA

LEBBEK KOKO KOKKO SIRIS
LEBKUCHEN LEKACH
LECHER GOAT LUXUR PALLIARD
LECHEROUS LEWD SALT PRIME
RANDY WANTON BOARISH
CODDING GOATISH LUSTFUL
LIKEROUS SCABROUS SPORTIVE
STUPROUS SALACIOUS
(PREF.) LUBRI
LECHERY LUXURY
LECTERN DESK EAGLE LUTRIN
LATERAN LATTERIN
LECTION GOSPEL EPISTLE READING
PERICOPE PROPHECY
LECTIONARY LEGEND
LECTOR LISTER READER
LECTURE JOBE CREED FORUM
HOMILY LECTOR LESSON SERMON
ADDRESS EARBASH HEARING
PRELECT READING JOBATION
ORDINARY
LECTURER DOCENT LECTOR
READER DRYASDUST
LEDGEMAN BREAKER
LEDGER BOOK SLAB LIEGER
JOURNAL OVERLIER
LEDGER BOARD RIBBON
LEE LEW LEEWARD
LEECH GILL HARPY LEACH APODAN
SANGSUE BDELLOID HELMINTH
(PREF.) BDELL(A) HIRUDINI
(SUFF.) BDELLA
LEEK FOUAT ALLIUM PORRET
SCALLION SENGREEN ROCAMBOLE
(— COLORED) PRASINE
(PREF.) PRASEO PRASO
LEEK GREEN RESEDA
LEER LEAR LOOK OGLE FLEER
LEERY SKIME SMIRK TWIRE
LEERFISH GARRICK
LEES LAGS ADDLE DRAFF DREGS
DROSS GROUT AMURCA BOTTOM
DUNDER MOTHER ULLAGE
GROUNDS EMPTINGS SEDIMENT
WINEDRAF
LEEWAN SOFA DIVAN
LEEWARD DOWNWIND
LEEWAY DRIFT
LEFT G CAR KAY GAWK NEAR PORT
OTHER TOWARD DESERTED
(— EYE) OL OS
(PREF.) LAEV(O) LEV(O) SINISTR(O)
LEFT HAND MG MS SM SIN
GAUCHE
(— PAGE) VERSO
LEFTHANDED CAR GAUCHE
AWKWARD DUBIOUS OBLIQUE
KITHOGUE SOUTHPAW
LEFT-HANDER SOUTHPAW
LEFTOVER END ORT REMNANT

SURPLUS REMAINDER
(TOBACCO —) TOPPER
(PL.) SCRAN ANALECTS
LEG ARM GAM PEG PIN CRUS
GAMB JAMB LIMB TRAM BOUGH
GAMBE JAMBE REACH SHANK
STICK STUMP BENDER GAMBON
GAMMON LEGLET MOGGAN
OVIGER PESTLE PLANTA PROLEG
WALKER FORELEG TRESTLE
FORELIMB
(— OF CRUSTACEAN) PODITE
(— OF HAWK) ARM
(— OF LAMB) GIGOT WABBLER
WOBBLER
(— OF TABLE) BALUSTER
(— OF WHEELBARROW) STILT
(— USED FOR FOOD) PESTLE
(—S OF ARTIFICIAL FLY) HACKLE
(ARTIFICIAL —) PYLON
(FURNITURE —) CABRIOLE
(MILK —) WEED
(TROUSER —) SLOP
(WIRE —S) SLING
(WOODEN —) PEG STUMP TIMBER
(PL.) PROPS TONGS STAMPS
STICKS
(PREF.) SCEL(O)
(SUFF.) SCELES
(LOWER —) CNEMA CNEMIA
CNEMIC CNEMUS
LEGACY ENTAIL LEGATE BEQUEST
HERITAGE WINDFALL
LEGAL LEAL LICIT SOUND VALID
LAWFUL SQUARE JURIDIC
RIGHTFUL
LEGALISM NOMISM SCRIBISM
LEGALISTIC COURT
LEGATE ENVOY DEPUTY EXARCH
LEGATUS CONSULAR LEGATARY
PANDULPH
LEGATION MISSION
LEGATO SMOOTH
LEGEND EDDA MYTH POSY SAGA
TALE FABLE STORY TITLE THREAP
CAPTION CUTLINE HAGGADA
(MAP —) KEY
(PREF.) MYTHO
LEGENDARY FABLED FICTIOUS
LEGERDEMAIN PRESTIDIGITATION
LEGERDEMAINIST JUGGLER
LEGGING SPAT COCKER BOTTINE
GAMBADO JAMBEAU BALATONG
BOOTIKIN CHIVARRA
(LEATHER —) STRAD
(PL.) CHAPS SHANKS BROGUES
COGGERS GAMASHES LEATHERS
OVERALLS
LEGIBLE FAIR READABLE
LEGION HOST TERZO TERZIO
LEGIONARY ANT DRIVER
FORAGER
LEGISLATION DYSNOMY
LAWMAKING
LEGISLATOR SOLON LAWGIVER
LAWMAKER
LEGISLATURE DIET COURT THING
LAGTING RIKSDAG LANDRATH
RIGSRAAD
LEGITIMATE JUST TRUE VERY
LEGAL LEGIT LOYAL HONEST
KINDLY KOSHER LAWFUL REABLE
SQUARE NATURAL LEGITIME

LEGITIMATELY FAIRLY MULIERLY
LEGPIECE JAMBEAU
LEGUME POD GUAR PULSE
LOMENT PODDER COCHLEA
LEGUMEN PODWARE SOYBEAN
STROMBUS
LEHUA OHIA
LEIPOA LOWAN MEGAPOD
PHEASANT
LEISHMANIASIS UTA ESPUNDIA
LEISTER SPEAR WASTER
LEISURE TIME TOOM VOID OTIUM
RESPITE VACANCY VACATION
LEISURELY SLOW SOODLY TIMELY
TOOMLY GRADUAL PICKTOOTH
LELEX (FATHER OF —) NEPTUNE
POSEIDON
(MOTHER OF —) LIBYA
(SON OF —) MYLES
LEMAN UNDERPUP
LEMMING CRICETID
LEMMUS MYODES
LEMNISCUS FILET FILLET
LAQUEUS
LEMON DOG DUD CEDRA CHLOR
LEMONY CEDRATE FAILURE
KUMQUAT
LEMONADE COOLER
LEMON GRASS TANGLAD
LEMON SOLE MARYSOLE
LEMON VERBENA ALOYSIA
LEMUR MAKI VARI AVAHI INDRI
KOKAM LORIS POTTO SIFAC
ADAPID COBEGO COLUGO
GALAGO KUBONG MACACO
MAHOLI MONKEY SIFAKA
APOSORO MEERKAT NATTOCK
PRIMATE SEMIAPE TARSIER
AMPONGUE BABAKOTO
MONGOOSE PRIMATAL TARSIOID
LEND OCKER PREST SECOND
ADVANCE IMPREST
(— AT INTEREST) GAVEL
(— ITSELF) ALLOY
LENDING (— AGENCY) MOUNT
LENGTH LUG DREE TOWT PITCH
SCOPE SIDTH COURSE EXTENT
TOWGHT FOOTAGE DISTANCE
LEGITUDE SIDENESS
(— ATHWARTSHIP) ABURTON
(— OF BRIDGE) BAY
(— OF CABLE) SCOPE SHACKLE
(— OF CHAIN) SHOT
(— OF CLOTH) CUT
(— OF FIBER) STAPLE
(— OF FISHING LINE) CAST
(— OF GEAR TOOTH) FACE
(— OF HAIR) KNOT
(— OF HAIR IN FISHING LINE) IMP
(— OF LINE) LOYN
(— OF METAL) SHAPE
(— OF MOUTH) GAPE
(— OF NET) LEAD
(— OF PISTON STROKE) TRAVEL
(— OF ROPE) DRIFT SPOKE BRIDLE
COURSE STOPPER
(— OF SERVICE) STANDING
(— OF SHOEMAKER'S THREAD) END
(— OF THREAD) STITCH
(— OF TILE) GAUGE
(— OF TIMBER) BALK FLITCH
(— OF TRIP) GATE
(— OF WINDMILL ARM) WHIP

(— OF YARN) KNOT TAPE CHASE SKEIN
(— UNIT) FERMI
(AT FULL —) ALONG
(CONTINUOUS —) STRETCH
(FOCAL —) FOCUS
(UNIT OF —) PIC PIK ROD FOOT INCH KILO PIKE REED VARA WRAP YARD METER SHAKU POLLEX FURLONG PLETHRON
(UTMOST —) EXTREME
(PREF.) MEC(O)
LENGTHEN EKE LONG DILATE EXPAND EXTEND LENGTH AMPLIFY DISTEND PRODUCE PROLONG STRETCH ELONGATE INCREASE PROTRACT
(— BY INTERPOLATION) FARSE
LENGTHENING HOLD ECTASIS DIASTOLE
LENGTHWISE ALONG ALENGTH ENDLONG ENDWAYS ENDWISE VERTICAL
LENGTHY LONG LARGE PROLIX LONGFUL EXTENDED
LENIENCY FAVOR MERCY LENITY CHARITY CLEMENCY LENIENCE
LENIENT LAX EASY KIND MILD SOFT FACILE GENTLE HUMANE LENITIVE
LENITIVE MILD MITIGANT SEDATIVE
LENITY MERCY HUMANITY KINDNESS LENITUDE
LENO GAUZE
LENS EYE CROWN GLASS OPTIC FLASER PEBBLE READER APLANAT BIFOCAL CONCAVE CONTACT DOUBLET ACHROMAT EYEGLASS EYEPIECE HYPERGON LENTICLE LUNETTES MENISCUS MAGNIFIER
(WITHOUT —) APHAKIA
(PREF.) PHAC(O)
LENT CAREME IMPREST
LENTICULAR PHACOID
LENTIGO FRECKLE
LENTIL LENS LINT TILL LENTILE LENTICLE
(PREF.) PHAC(O)
LEOFRIC (FATHER OF —) LEOFWINE
(WIFE OF —) GODIVA
LEONORE (GUARDIAN OF —) ARISTE
(SISTER OF —) ISABELLE
LEONTOCEBUS MIDAS
LEOPARD PARD TIGER PARDAL WAGATI LIBBARD PAINTER PANTHER PARDALE CATAMOUNT
(SNOW —) IRBIS OUNCE
LEOVIGILD (SON OF —) ERMENEGILD
(WIFE OF —) GOISWINTHA
LEPCHA RONG RONGPA
LEPER LAZAR MESEL LAZARUS
LEPIDOMELANE ANNITE
LEPIDOPTERA GLOSSATA
LEPIDOPTERIST AURELIAN
LEPIDOSIS SCALING
LEPRECHAUN ELF SPRITE LURACAN
LEPROSY LEPRA MESEL SCALL ALPHOS LAZARY MESELRY
LEPROUS MESELY MESELED

LEPTON MITE MUON
LEPTOSPIROSIS JAUNDICE
LERP LAAP
LESBIAN EROTIC SAPPHIC TRIBADE SAPPHIST
LESION PIT GALL HIVE SORE CRATER ESCHAR LEPRID ANTHRAX CHANCRE FISSURE LEPROMA BEESTING ERUPTION LEUKEMID TERTIARY

LESOTHO
CAPITAL: MASERU
COIN: RAND
FORMER NAME: BASUTOLAND
LANGUAGE: SOTHO SESOTHO
MOUNTAINS: MALUTI
PEOPLE: BASOTHO
RIVER: ORANGE CALEDON
TOWN: LERIBE MASHAI MORIJA PITSENG QUTHING SEKAKES MAFETENG
WATERFALL: MALETSUNYANE

LESPEDEZA SERICEA
LESS FEW MIN MENO FEWER MINOR LESSER SMALLER WANTING
(— BY A COMMA) MINOR
(PREF.) HYPO MEIO MIMIO MIO
(— THAN NORMAL) HYPO
LESSEE FARMER TERMOR HUURDER TACKSMAN
LESSEN CUT EBB BATE DOCK EASE FAIK FRET KILL LESS SINK WANE ABATE BREAK LOWER MINCE SMALL TAPER BUFFER DEADEN DEJECT IMPAIR INLESS MINIFY MINISH NARROW REBATE REDUCE WEAKEN AMENUSE ASSUAGE CURTAIL DEPLETE DEPRESS ELEVATE LIGHTEN RELIEVE SHORTEN CONTRACT DECREASE DEROGATE DIMINISH DISCOUNT EMBEZZLE MITIGATE MODERATE PALLIATE
(— FORCE) GELD
(— IN VALUE) SHRINK CHEAPEN
(— SENSITIVITY) DULL
(— STRENGTH) WEAR
(— TENSION) RELAX
(— VELOCITY) DEADEN
LESSENING LETUP PERDITION
LESSER PETIT MINUTE SMALLER INFERIOR
(PREF.) MI(O) MINI
(SUFF.) (— ONE) ET ETTE
LESSER CELANDINE PILEWORT
LESSON TAX LEAR TASK STUDY EXAMPLE LECTURE PRECEPT READING DOCUMENT LIRIPOOP
(DIFFICULT —) SOAK
(TORAH —) PARASHAH
LESSOR SETTER
LEST UNLESS ANANTER ANAUNTERS
LET LAT SET HIRE ALLOW LEASE LEAVE LETTEN PERMIT SUFFER TENANT
(— BAIT BOB) DIB
(— BECOME KNOWN) SPILL
(— BURN) BISHOP
(— CONTINUE) DRILL

(— DOWN) VAIL DEMIT DIMIT LOWER STOOP STRIKE SUBMIT
(— DOWN ROCK FACE) ABSEIL
(— FALL) DROP VAIL AVALE AWALE DEPOSE
(— FLY) PEG BOLT FIRE WING
(— GO) DROP FAIK QUIT DEMIT BILEVE DEMISE DISMIT UNHAND DISCARD UNSEIZE
(— HIM TAKE) SUM
(— IN) IMMIT INLET IMMISS ADHIBIT
(— IT BE REPEATED) REPET
(— IT STAND) STET
(— KNOW) ACQUAINT
(— LAND) GAVEL
(— LOOSE) FREE SLIP LIBERATE
(— OUT) BLAB TEAM WAGE BREAK SPILL ARRENT BROACH
(— SLIP) BALK BAULK CHECK FOREGO
LETDOWN HANGOVER
LETHAL FATAL DEADLY MORTAL
LETHARGIC INERT DROWSY SLEEPY TORPID DORMANT PASSIVE COMATOSE COMATOUS SLUGGISH SLUMBROUS
LETHARGY COMA SLOTH STUPOR TORPOR SLUMBER HEBETUDE INACTION SOPITION
LETO LATONA
LETT BALT
LETTER EF EL EM EN EX HE PE AIN AYN BEE CEE CHI DAK DEE EDH ESS ETA ETH GEE HET JAY KAY LIL MEM NUN PEE SIN TAV TAW TEE VEE WAW YOD YOK ZED ZEE ALEF ALIF AYIN BETA BETH BILL BULL CHIT DEAD HETH IOTA KAPH RESH SHIN SORT TETH YODH YOGH AITCH ALEPH BLIND BREVE CAPON DELTA DEMIT FAVOR GAMMA GIMEL GRAPH KAPPA KNOWN KOPPA SADHE SIGMA STAVE STIFF ZAYIN ACCENT ADVICE ANSWER BILLET CADJAN CARTEL CHARTA COCKUP DALETH FAVVER ITALIC LAMBDA LAMEDH MEDIAL SAMEKH SCRIPT SIGLUM SUNNUD SYMBOL VERSAL CODICIL COLLINS CONTROL DIGAMMA DIPLOMA EPISTLE EPSILON KAREETA MISSIVE SPECIAL AEROGRAM ASCENDER ENCYCLIC MONITORY NUNDINAL PASTORAL
(— OF DEFIANCE) CARTEL
(— OF PERMISSION) EXEAT
(—S DIMISSORY) APOSTOLI
(—S OF MARQUE) MART
(ANGLO-SAXON —) EDH ETH THORN
(AUTHORIZING —) BREVE
(BEGGING —) SCREEVE
(BLACK —) GOTHIC
(BREAD AND BUTTER —) COLLINS
(CAPITAL —) CAP UNCIAL CAPITAL FACTOTUM MAJUSCULE
(FRIENDLY —) SCREED
(INITIAL —) BLOOMER
(LOVE —) POULET
(LOWERCASE —) MINISCULE
(OBSOLETE —) EPISEMON

(OFFICIAL —) BRIEF
(PAPAL —) BULL TOME BREVE ENCYCLIC
(PRIVATE —) BOOK
(SHORT —) CHIT LINE NOTE BILLET LETTERET
(SILENT —) MUTE
(SMUGGLED —) KITE
(SUBSCRIPT —) SUBFIX
(WORD —) LOGOGRAM
(PL.) MAIL APOSTOLI
(PREF.) EPISTOLO
LETTER BOX APARTADO
LETTER CARRIER CORREO MAILMAN POSTMAN
LETTERER SKETCHER
LETTERING FAC WRITE INCUSE
LETTERPRESS TEXT CAPTION
LETTING FIRMA LOCATIO
LETTING-OUT DROPPING
LETTUCE COS BIBB GRASS SALAD KARPAS SALLET ICEBERG ROMAINE FIREWEED MILKWEED
LETUSHIM (FATHER OF —) DEDAN
LEUCIPPE (BROTHER OF —) CALCHAS
(FATHER OF —) MINYAS THESTOR
(SISTER OF —) THEONOE
(SON OF —) TEUTHRAS
LEUCIPPUS (BROTHER OF —) APHAREUS
(DAUGHTER OF —) PHOEBE HILAIRA
(FATHER OF —) OENOMAUS PERIERES
(MOTHER OF —) GORGOPHONE
(WIFE OF —) PHILODICE
LEUCITE LENAD
LEUCITITE ITALITE SPERONE ALBANITE CECILITE
LEUCOCYTE POLY NEOCYTE HEMAMEBA MONOCYTE OXYPHILE
LEUCOMA ALBUGO WALLEYE
LEUCORRHEA WHITES
LEUCOTHEA (FATHER OF —) ORCHAMUS
(MOTHER OF —) EURYNOME
LEUKEMIA CHLOROMA LEUKOSIS
LEVANT EASTERN WORMSEED
LEVANTINE SCATTERMOUCH
LEVEE DIKE DYKE WALL WEIR DURBAR STOPBANK
LEVEL BONE EVEN FAIR FLAT GLAD LUTE PLAT RAZE SHIM VIAL COUCH EQUAL FLUSH GRADE PLAIN PLANE POINT SLICK SOLID CHARGE DOUBLE EVENLY FIELDY NIVEAU SLIGHT SMOOTH STRIKE TUNNEL FLATTEN GALLERY GANGWAY REGULAR DEMOLISH LEVELLER SUBGRADE
(— A RAFTER) EDGE
(— AFTER PLOWING) BUSH
(— AND SCATTER) GELD
(— OF SOCIETY) STRATUM
(— OF STAGE) STUDY
(— OFF) HAMMER BULLDOZE
(— PLACE) PLANILLA
(COMMON —) PAR
(ENERGY —) SINGLET
(EYE —) EYELINE
(HIGHER —S) BRASS
(HIGHEST —) SUMMIT

(LOWEST —) FLOOR BOTTOM HARDPAN
(MINING —) KIP HEAD GALLERY GANGWAY
(STRATIGRAPHIC —) HORIZON
(TOP —) HIGH CEILING
(PREF.) PLAN(I)
LEVELED BENT
LEVELER DIGGER
  (PL.) ACEPHALI
LEVELING EGALITE EGALITY
LEVER KEY PRY BEAM GAUL HOOK HORN JACK SWAY TREE BRAKE FLAIL FLIRT HELVE PEDAL PINCH PLUTO PRIZE SPOON STANG STANK SWIPE THROW BINDER CLUTCH SWIPE COUPER DETENT FEELER GAFFLE HAMMER HEAVER HOPPER LOWDER PORTER ROCKER TAPPET TILLER BALANCE BOOTLEG POINTER RAMHEAD SHIPPER SWINGLE TREADLE TRIGGER TUMBLER BACKFALL GAVELOCK SELECTOR THROTTLE
  (— ARM) NIGGER
  (— FOR CROSSBOW) GAFFLE GARROT
  (— FOR TURNING RUDDER) HELM TILLER
  (— IN KNITTING MACHINE) JACK
  (— IN TIMEPIECE) PALLET
  (— LIKE CANTHOOK) PEAVY PEAVIE
  (— OF GIN) START
  (GEARSHIFT —) STICK
  (ORGAN —) BACKFALL
  (SPINNING —) BOOTLEG
  (SPOKELIKE —) SWINGLE
  (THROTTLE —) GUN
  (WEAVING —) LAM LAMM SWELL BINDER TIPPLER
LEVERAGE PRY PRIZE
LEVI (FATHER OF —) JACOB ALPHAEUS
  (MOTHER OF —) LEAH
  (SON OF —) KOHATH MERARI GERSHON
LEVIGATE DUST
LEVITY FOLLY HUMOR GAIETY WHIFFLERY
LEVOROTATORY LAEVO LEVOGYRE NEGATIVE
LEVY CUT TAX CESS MISE REAR LEVEL RAISE ASSESS EXTEND EXTENT IMPOSE IMPOST UPTAKE IMPRESS TRIBUTE DISTRAIN DISTRESS SHIPPAGE
  (— A TAX) GELD GELT TAIL STENT
  (— DISTRESS) DRIVE
  (IRISH —) MART
LEVYING EXACTION
LEWD NICE BAWDY FOLLY PRIME RANDY HARLOT IMPURE LACHES LUBRIC RAKISH WANTON HIRCINE LEERING LUSTFUL OBSCENE RAMMISH RIGGISH SCARLET SENSUAL WHORISH PRURIENT SLUTTISH UNCHASTE SALACIOUS
LEWDNESS FOLLY RAKERY LECHERY HARLOTRY PUTANISM LUBRICITY SCULDUDDERY
LEXICOGRAPHER AMERICAN GOVE ALLEN CARHART WEBSTER WHEELER WORCESTER

BRAZILIAN MORAES
ENGLISH WYLD COLES DYCHE SCOTT SMITH BAILEY BLOUNT CRAGIE FARMER FLORIO FOWLER MURRAY ONIONS WALKER BRADLEY CAWDREY JOHNSON MINSHEU WITHALS BULLOKAR COCKERAM COTGRAVE AINSWORTH COCKERELL PARTRIDGE STORMONTH RICHARDSON
FRENCH LITTRE BEAUJAN GODEFROY LAROUSSE FURETIERE
GERMAN ERMAN MURET SACHS FLUGEL SCHNEIDER
GREEK POLLUX SUIDAS PAMPHILUS
ICELANDIC BLONDAL
ITALIAN CESARI CALENUS FANFANI FACCIOLATI FORCELLINI
POLISH LINDE
SCOTTISH GRANT OGILVY
LEXICON CALEPIN WORDBOOK
LIABILITY DEBT DEBIT CHARGE TRIBUTE OBLIGATION
LIABLE APT ABLE OPEN GUILTY EXPOSED OBVIOUS ONEROUS SUBJECT AMENABLE INCIDENT
  (SUFF.) ABLE IBLE
LIAISON BOND AFFAIR AFFAIRE LINKING INTIMACY INTRIGUE
LIANA CIPO BEJUCO GUARANA BUSHROPE
LIANG TAEL
LIAR LEAR ANANIAS BOUNCER CRACKER CRAMMER PROCTOR WARLOCK WERNARD FABULIST
LIBATION AMBROSIA
LIBEL DEFAME MALIGN VILIFY SLANDER
LIBELOUS FAMOUS SCANDALOUS
LIBER PHLOEM
LIBERAL FAIR FREE GOOD OPEN WHIG BROAD FRANK LARGE NOBLE SOLUTE JANNOCK PROFUSE ADVANCED CATHOLIC GENEROUS HANDSOME LARGEOUS PRODIGAL SEPARATE MUNIFICENT
  (CANADIAN —) GRIT
  (NOT —) CHARY SPARE
LIBERAL ARTS MUSES
LIBERALITY LARGE BOUNTY BREADTH CHARITY FREEDOM HONESTY LARGESS
LIBERALLY LARGE BROADLY
LIBERATE FREE QUIT FRITH REMIT UNGYVE UNWRAP DELIVER MANUMIT RELEASE UNSLAVE UNFETTER UNTHRALL
LIBERATION FREEDOM RELEASE DELIVERY KAIVALYA DISCHARGE
  (— OF SPORE) ABSCISSION

LIBERIA
CAPITAL: MONROVIA
CUSTOM: SANDE
HILLS: BOMI
MEASURE: KUBA
MOUNTAIN: UNI NIETE NIMBA WUTIVI
MOUNTAINS: BONG SATRO
PEOPLE: GI KRU KWA VAI VEI

GOLA KROO KROU TOMA BASSA GIBBI GISSI GREBO KPELLE KROOBY KRUMAN KROOBOY MANDINGO
RIVER: CESS LOFA MANO LOFFA MANNA MORRO CESTOS DOUOBE STJOHN STPAUL CAVALLY SANPEDRO
TOWN: GANTA GRIBO REBBO HARPER ZORZOR NANAKRU TAPPITA BUCHANAN MARSHALL SASSTOWN

LIBERTINE ROUE PUNKER PANURGE STRIKER LOTHARIO LOVELACE STRINGER
LIBERTY MAY SOC EASE LARGE LEAVE SCOPE ACCESS SCOUTH STREET FREEDOM LARGESS LICENSE WITHGANG
  (— OF ACTION) PLAY SWING
  (— OF ENTRANCE) INGRESS
  (— OF GOING OUT) ISH
  (— OF TURNING PIGS INTO FIELDS) SHACK
  (— TO BUY AND SELL) TOLL
  (— TO HUNT) CHASE
  (PARTIAL — OF HAWK) HACK
  (SEXUAL —) INTIMACY
  (UNDUE —) HEAD
LIBERTY CAP PILLEUS
LIBIDINIZATION EGOISM
LIBIDINOUS FLESHY FLESHLY
LIBNI (FATHER OF —) MAHLI GERSHON
LIBRA AS PONDUS
LIBRARIAN AMERICAN COLE DANA HILL HUNT KOCH LANE DEWEY EAMES GREEN MUDGE POOLE SMITH CUTTER FOLSOM HUMMEL JEWETT PUTNAM WINSOR EDMANDS SONNECK VANNAME WELLMAN BARTLETT BOSTWICK COGSWELL MACLEISH SAUNDERS SPOFFORD YARMOLINSKY
ENGLISH BOND COXE PANIZZI THOMPSON
FRENCH DUPUY OMONT BONNECHOSE TASCHEREAU
GERMAN EBERT BURGER
PERUVIAN ULLOA
SPANISH MACHADO
LIBRARY AMBRY BIBLE MUSEUM BHANDAR BOOKERY ATHENEUM
LIBRETTO BOOK WORD TESTO TEXTBOOK

LIBYA
ALPHABET: TIFINAGH
CAPITAL: BENGASI BENGAZI TRIPOLI
COIN: DIRHAM
DESERT: FEZZAN MURZUK MURZUCH
GULF: SIDRA SIRTE
MEASURE: SAA BOZZE DONUM JABIA TEMAN BARILE MISURA MATTARO
MOUNTAIN: BETTE
OASIS: JALO KUFRA SEBHA FEZZAN GIOFRA TAZERBO GIARABUB
SEAPORT: HOMS DERNA SIDRI

TOBRUK BENGAZI
TOWN: BRAK DERJ HOMS BARKA DERNA SEBHA SIDRI UBARI ZAWIA ELMARJ GARIAN MURZUQ REMADA TOBRUK MISURATA
WEIGHT: KELE UCKIA GORRAF TERMINO KHAROUBA

LICE CREEPERS
  (FISH —) EPIZOA
LICENSE CHOP GALE HEAD EXEAT LEAVE SLANG SWING BANDON CAROON FIRMAN INDULT PATENT PERMIT READER TICKET CAROOME CERTIFY CROTTLE FACULTY FREEDOM INDULTO LIBERTY LICENCE PLACARD WARRANT ESCAMBIO IMMUNITY MORTMAIN PASSPORT TEZKIRAH
  (— FOR CART) CAROOME
  (— PLATE) NUMBER
  (PEDDLER'S —) SLANG
LICENTIOUS GAY LAX FREE LEWD WILD FRANK LARGE LOOSE FILTHY RIBALD UNRULY WANTON CYPRIAN FLESHLY IMMORAL LAWLESS LIBERAL UNYOKED
LICENTIOUSNESS DIRT LICENSE
LICHEN RAG MOSS MANNA USNEA ARCHIL CORKIR KORKIR ORCHIL CROTTAL CROTTLE CUDBEAR EVERNIA OAKMOSS PARELLA ARCHILLA CAPEWEED LECANORA LUNGWORT PARMELIA ROCKHAIR TREEHAIR WARTWORT
LICIT LEGAL LAWFUL LEEFUL
LICK LAP LIKE SUCK MOUTH SLAKE CONQUER
LICKER-IN TUMBLE
LICKING LAMBENT GRUELING
LICKSPITTLE LACKEY
LICORICE POMFRET SWEETROOT
LICORICE PILL CACHOU
LICYMNIUS (FATHER OF —) ELECTRYON
  (MOTHER OF —) MIDEA
  (SISTER OF —) ALCMENA
  (SLAYER OF —) TLEPOLEMUS
  (WIFE OF —) PERIMEDE
LID DIP BRED DECK TYMP COVER BRIDLE EYELID POTLID CLAPPER CLICKET CLOSURE SCUTTLE SHUTTER COVERCLE OPERCULUM
  (SUFF.) POMATOUS
LIE FIB GAB KIP LAY LIG LIN SIT YED CRAM FALL FLAW LIGG REST RIDE WHID DEVIL DWELL FABLE FEIGN LEASE STAND STORY BOUNCE FITTEN PALTER RAPPER RESIDE SPRAWL VANITY YANKER BOUNCER CONSIST CRACKER CRAMMER CRUMPER FALSITY GRABBLE LEASING PLUMPER TWISTER UNTRUTH WHACKER WHISKER WHOPPER MENDACITY TARADIDDLE PREVARICATE
  (— ALONGSIDE) ACCOST
  (— AROUND) COMPASS
  (— AT ANCHOR) HOVE
  (— AT FULL LENGTH) STRETCH
  (— CONCEALED) DARKLE
  (— CONTIGUOUS) CONFINE

(— DETECTOR) POLYGRAPH
(— DORMANT) SLEEP
(— DOWN) LEAN COUCH CHARGE
(— FLAT ON BELLY) GROVEL
(— HEAD TO WIND) TRY
(— HIDDEN) LURK MICHE TAPPISH
(— IN AMBUSH) HUGGER
(— IN BED) KIP THOKE
(— IN WAIT) AWAIT LOWER
AMBUSH FORELAY
(— IN WATER) DOUSE DROWN
(— LOW) TAPPICE
(— NEXT TO) ADJOIN
(— OPPOSITE TO) SUBTEND
(— OVER) COVER
(— PRONE) GROVEL GRABBLE
(— PROSTRATE) STREEK
(— QUIET) SNUDGE
(— SNUG) CUDDLE
(— UNEVENLY) SAG
(— WITH SAILS FURLED) HULL
(BIG —) CAULKER
(IMPUDENT —) BOUNCE
(MONSTROUS —) STRAMMER
(PREF.) (— HID) LANTHAN(O)
LANTHO

LIECHTENSTEIN
CAPITAL: VADUZ
CASTLE: GUTEMBURG
MOUNTAIN: RHATIKON
RIVER: RHINE SAMINA
ROMAN NAME: RHAETIA
TOWN: HAAG BALZER SCHAAN
NENDELN
TRIBE: ALAMANNI

LIED BALLAD
LIEF DEAR LEAVE LEEVE LIEVE
FREELY GLADLY BELOVED
LIEUTENANT LUFF ZANY LOUEY
JAYGEE KEHAYA CAIMAKAM
QAIMAQAM TENIENTE WOODVILE
LIFE IT VIE ZOE HIDE JIVA PUFF
SNAP TUCK VALE ANIMA BEING
BLOOD DEMON HEART LIFER
QUICK SWEAT BIOSIS BREATH
CANDLE COURSE ENERGY SPIRIT
SPRITE LIFELET LIFEWAY VITALITY
VIVACITY
(— AFTER DEATH) FUTURITY
(— IN HEAVEN) GLORY
(— IN SOCIETY) SAMSARA
SANSARA
(— OF FURNACE LINING) CAMPAIGN
(— OF THE SEA) HALIBIOS
(ACADEMIC —) ACADEMIA
(ANIMAL —) FLESH
(ANIMAL AND PLANT —) BIOS
BIOTA BIOLOGY EDAPHON
(CLOISTERED —) VEIL
(INTELLECTUAL —) JIVATMA
(MONASTIC —) CLOISTER
(MORAL —) DAENA
(MOSS —) BRYOLOGY
(PLANT —) FLORA BOTANY
(ROBUST —) JUICE
(SINGLE —) CELIBACY
(TERRESTRIAL —) GEOBIOS
(WAY OF —) BAG SCENE
(WITHOUT —) AZOIC
(PREF.) BI(O) EMBIO PSYCH(O)
VIT(A)(O)

(NOT —) ABIO
(SUFF.) BIA BIONT BIOSIS BIOTIC
BIOUS BIUM BIUS BY PSYCHE
LIFE BELT SAFETY
LIFEBLOOD BLOOD SWEAT
LIFE-FORCE KUNDALINI
LIFE FOR THE TSAR, A
(CHARACTER IN —) SOBININ
SUSANIN ANTONIDA
(COMPOSER OF —) GLINKA
LIFELESS ARID DEAD DULL FLAT
AMORT HEAVY INERT VAPID
ANEMIC TORPID SAPLESS
DESOLATE GRIPLESS INACTIVE
(PREF.) ABIO
LIFELESSLY DEADLY INERTLY
LIFELESSNESS ANEMIA
LIFELIKE VIVE QUICK EIDETIC
NATURAL ANIMATED SPEAKING
LIFE PRESERVER FLOAT NEDDY
LIFETIME AGE DAY WORLD LIVING
LIFEDAY DURATION LIFELONG
LIFE WITH FATHER (AUTHOR OF —)
DAY
(CHARACTER IN —) DELIA GULICK
CLARENCE MARGARET
LIFT WIN BOOM BUOY CAST COCK
HEFT JACK REAR TOSS WEVE
ARSIS BOOST BREAK ELATE
HEAVE HITCH HOICK HOIST
HOOSH MOUNT PRESS RAISE
SPOUT STEAL WEIGH BUCKET
CLEECH SNATCH ELEVATE
ENHANCE HEELTAP NAUNTLE
BOOKLIFT CHAIRWAY ELEVATOR
LEVITATE
(— HAT) DOFF
(— IN VEHICLE) SETDOWN
(— OF WAVE) SCEND
(— ONESELF) SOAR
(— QUICKLY) PERK
(— UP) HOVE CRANE ERECT EXALT
EXTOL HORSE WEIGH ADVANCE
ELEVATE NAUNTLE
(— WITH BLOCK AND TACKLE)
BOUSE
LIFTED ARRECT SUBLIME
LIFTER GAGGER SERVER HOISTER
HOISTMAN
LIFTING HIKE UPTAKE
LIFT VALVE POPPET
LIGAMENT BAND BOND ARTERY
FRENUM PAXWAX STRING
ZONULE ARMILLA LIGATURE
(PREF.) DESM(A)(IDI)(IDIO)(O)
SYNDESM(O)
LIGAMENTOUS DESMOID
LIGATE BAR
LIGATURE CLAM PLICA DIGRAM
PNEUMA STIGMA DIGRAPH
FUNICLE LIGAMENT LIGATION
(— OE) ASH
LIGGER TRIMMER
LIGHT BUG DAY GAY HAP LAW SHY
SUN AIRY EASY FAIR FALL FINE
FIRE FLIT FLUX GLIM LAMP LEET
LUNT MILD SLUT SOFT BAVIN
BLAZE CORKY FANAL FILMY
FLAME FLEET FUFFY LEGER
LOUGH MERRY PITCH QUICK
SHEER SPILL WHITE BEACON
BRIGHT CHAFFY FLOATY FLOSSY
FLUFFY FROTHY GENTLE HAPPEN

ILLUME KINDLE LANCET LUSTER
LUSTRE MARKER PASTEL PHAROS
SIGNAL SLUSHY STINGY STRIKE
SUTTLE VOLAGE BENGOLA
BUOYANT CRESSET FRAGILE
GLITTER LAMBENT SFOGATO
SMITHER SUMMERY TORTAYS
TRIVIAL UNGRAVE BACKFIRE
DAYLIGHT DELICATE DIAPHANE
ELECTRIC EXPEDITE FEATHERY
GASLIGHT GOSSAMER LEGGIERO
LUMINARY PALOUSER SUNLIGHT
SUNSHINE
(— AND BRILLIANT) LAMBENT
(— AND FIRE ON HORSE'S MANE)
HAG
(— AND FREE) FLYAWAY
(— AND QUICK) VOLANT
(— CANDLES) TOLLY
(— FROM NIGHT SKY) AIRGLOW
(— IN WINDOW) LANCET
(— OF MORNING) AURORA
(— ON TV SCREEN) SNOW
(— UP) FLASH GLOZE ILLUME
RELUME GLORIFY
(— UPON) STRIKE
(BRIGHT —) GLARE GLEAM
(BURST OF —) FLASH
(CIRCLE OF —) HALO NIMBUS
(EMIT COHERENT —) LASE
(FAINT —) GLIMMER SCARROW
(FEEBLE —) TAPER GLIMMER
(FITFUL —) SHIMMER
(HARBOR —) BUG
(INDICATOR —) BEZEL
(INNER —) SEED
(NEBULOUS —) CHEVELURE
(NEW —) SEPARATE
(NIGHT —) MORTAR
(PARKING —S) DIMMERS
(PATCH OF —) CURSOR
(PERSIAN GOD OF —) MITHRAS
(REFLECTED —) SKYME
(SHIP'S —) FANAL
(SMALL —) TAPER
(TRAFFIC —) BLINKER
(WAVERING —) FLICKER
(PL.) BUFF
(PREF.) LUCI LUMIN(I)(O) PHOS
PHOT(O)
LIGHT-COLORED BLONDE
LIGHTEN ALAY CLEAR LEVIN LIGHT
RAISE ALLEGE BLEACH ENCLEAR
FOULDRE MOLLIFY SWEETEN
THUNDER LEVIGATE
LIGHTENING BREAK
(— OF HAIR) FROSTING
LIGHTER KEEL SCOW ACCON
BARGE CASCO PRAAM WHERRY
DROGHER GABBARD GONDOLA
PONTOON CHOPBOAT
LIGHTERMAN KEELER KEELMAN
LIGHT-GREEN
(PREF.) CHLOR(O)
LIGHT-HEADED IDLE BARMY LIGHT
LIVELY CARRIED GLAIKET
SKITTISH
LIGHT-HEARTED GAY GLAD GIDDY
BUOYANT WINSOME CAREFREE
DEBONAIR VOLATILE
LIGHTHEARTEDNESS BUOYANCY
LIGHTHOUSE FANAL LIGHT MINAR
BEACON PHAROS LANTERN

(PREF.) PHARO
LIGHT IN AUGUST (AUTHOR OF —)
FAULKNER
(CHARACTER IN —) DOC JOE GAIL
LENA ALLEN BROWN BURCH
BYRON GROVE HINES LUCAS
BOBBIE BURDEN JOANNA
EUPHEUS CHRISTMAS
HIGHTOWER
LIGHTLESS APHOTIC
(PREF.) APHOTO
LIGHTLY LIGHT AIRILY FAIRILY
HOVERLY LEGGIERO SLIGHTLY
LIGHT-MINDED BLITHE ETOURDI
LIGHTNESS CHEER VALUE GAIETY
LEVITY AIRINESS BUOYANCY
LEGERETE LEGERITY
(— OF MOVEMENT) BALLON
LIGHTNING BOLT FIRE LAIT LEVIN
FULMEN METEOR FOULDRE
SULPHUR THUNDER FIREBALL
FIREBOLT WILDFIRE
LIGHT-O'-LOVE COCOTTE LEVERET
LIGHT-TEXTURED FOZY
LIGHTWOOD FATWOOD
LIGIA LIGYDA
LIGNEOUS WOODY XYLOID
LIGNIN LIGNOSE XYLOGEN
LIGNITE JET
LIGNUM VITAE GUAYACAN
POCKWOOD
LIGROIN BENZINE CANADOL
LIGULA LANGUET
LIGULE STRAP LIGULA
LIKE AS DIG DOTE LIST LOVE ALIKE
ENJOY EQUAL FANCY SAVOR
TASTE ADMIRE AFFECT BELIKE
LIKELY MATTER PLEASE SEMBLE
SIMILE CONCEIT SIMILAR
SEMBLANT SUITABLE SEMBLABLE
(— A GLAND) ADEMOSE ADENOUS
(— BETTER) PREFER
(— HAIR) CRINITE
(VERY —) SIAMESE
(PREF.) HOME(O) HOMOE HOMOI
SYM
(SUFF.) AR EOUS IC(AL) INE IS ISH
ISTIC LY ODE OID(AL) SOME
LIKELIHOOD APTNESS
LIKELY APT FAIR LIKE READY
LIABLE PROOFY SEEMLY GRADELY
SMITTLE APPARENT FEASIBLE
POSSIBLE PROBABLE
PROSPECTIVE
(MOST —) BELIKE
LIKEN EVEN LIKE REMENE SEMBLE
COMPARE ASSEMBLE CREDIBLE
RESEMBLE SIMILIZE
LIKENESS DAP BLEE ICON IDOL
MAKE SECT BLUSH DUMMY GLIFF
IMAGE MORAL SHAPE EFFIGY
FIGURE STATUE ANALOGY
KINSHIP PATTERN PICTURE
RETRAIT EQUALITY HOMOLOGY
PARALLEL PORTRAIT SEMBLANCE
SIMILARITY
(PERFECT —) SPIT
LIKEWISE EKE TOO ALSO ITEM
EITHER EQUALLY LIKEWAYS
(— NOT) NOR
LIKHI (FATHER OF —) SHEMIDAH
LIKING GOO GRA PAY GOUT GUST
LIKE LIST LUST FANCY FLAIR

GUSTO HEART SHINE SKILL
SMACK TASTE THEAT SWALLOW
AFFINITY APPETITE FONDNESS
PENCHANT
(ECCENTRIC —) FOIBLE
(SUFF.) (— FOR) PHIL(A)(AE)(E)
(IA)(ISM)(IST)(OUS)(US)(Y)
LIKUTA
(PL.) MAKUTA
LILAC LILAS MAUVE LAYLOCK
LILACIN SYRINGIN
LILIOM (AUTHOR OF —) MOLNAR
(CHARACTER IN —) WOLF JULIE
MARIE FICSUR LILIOM LOUISE
MUSKAT LINZMAN HOLLUNDER
LILY ALOE IXIA KELP SEGO AZTEC
CALLA CLOTE AUGUST LILIUM
VALLEY COCUISA MONOCOT
ASPHODEL LILYWORT MARTAGON
NENUPHAR
(AFRICAN —) AGAPANTHUS
(CLIMBING —) GLORIOSA
(PALM —) TI
(SEA —) CRINOID
(WATER —) CANDOCK CAMALOTE
(PREF.) LIRIO
(SUFF.) CRINUS
LILY OF THE VALLEY LILIUM
MUGGET MUGUET MUGWET
LILYWORT SHINLEAF
LIMA BEAN HABA LIMA
LIMB ARM LEG CLAW FOOT KNOT
LITH TRAM WING ARTUS BOUGH
SPALD SPAUL SWAMP BRANCH
MEMBER PODITE FEATURE
FLIPPER FORCEPS PLEOPOD
NECTOPOD
(PREF.) MEL
(SUFF.) (CONDITION OF —) MELIA
LIMBA AFARA FRAKE
LIMBER BAIN FLIP LIMP LUSH
LINGY LITHE LISSOM SEMMIT
SUPPLE SWANKY BRUSHER
BRUTTER KNOTTER LIMMOCK
PLIABLE FLEXIBLE FLIPPANT
LIME CALX LIMA CEDRA CEDRAT
CHUNAM CITRON FUSTIC
(— IN BRICK) BOND
(WILD —) COLIMA
(PREF.) CAL(AREO)(I)(IO)(O)
LIMEN THRESHOLD
LIMESTONE CAM HUM CALP CAUK
CAUM LIAS LYAS MALM POROS
ROACH CLUNCH KUNKUR OOLITE
CIPOLIN SCAGLIA PISOLITE
TRAVERTINE
(— REGION) KARST
(DECOMPOSED —) ROTTENSTONE
LIME TREE LIME TEIL LINDEN
LIMIT END FIX BIND BUTT FINE
HOLD LINE LIST MARK MERE PALE
TAIL BLOCK BOUND COAST
GAUGE HEDGE SCANT STENT
STINT VERGE BORDER BOURNE
DEFINE EFFLUX EXTENT FINISH
FINITE HAMPER LENGTH MODIFY
NARROW PALING SCRIMP TROPIC
UPSHOT ASTRICT CLOSURE
COMPASS CONFINE CONTENT
HORIZON MAXIMUM MEASURE
OUTSIDE BOUNDARY CONTRACT
DEADLINE IMPRISON LIMITARY
LIMITATE OUTGOING OUTREACH

RESTRAIN RESTRICT SOLSTICE
TERMINUS PARAMETER
(— EFFECT) ALLAY
(— IN A FOREST) BAIL
(— MOTION) HOLD
(— OF STATUTE) PURVIEW
(— OF VISION AT SEA) KENNING
(EXTREME —) HEIGHT
(LOWER —) FLOOR
(UPPER —) CEILING
(UTTER —) EXTREME
(PL.) AMBIT CANCELS ENVIRONS
PERIMETER
(PREF.) ORI
LIMITATION TAIL FRAME STINT
DENIAL CLOTURE RESERVE
(PL.) SWADDLE
LIMITED MILD TAIL BORNE BRIEF
SHORT SMALL FINITE NARROW
STINTY STRAIT BOUNDED
SPECIAL CONFINED DEFINITE
LIMITARY PAROCHIAL SECTARIAN
MEASURABLE PROVINCIAL
RESTRICTED
(— IN APPEAL) CHICHI
(— IN SCOPE) MODERATE
LIMITING DEFINITE ADJECTIVE
EXCLUSIVE
LIMITS (NEAR OUTER — OF PLAY)
DEEP
LIMMA DIESIS
LIMMU EPONYM
LIMON (BROTHER OF —) SCEPHRUS
(FATHER OF —) TEGEATES
(MOTHER OF —) MAERA
LIMONENE CINENE CARVENE
CITRENE
LIMONIUM STATICE
LIMOUSINE BERLIN SALOON
SUBURBAN
LIMP HIP HOP CLOP GIMP HALT
HIMP HOIT SOFT THIN HENCH
HILCH HITCH LINGY LOOSE LOPPY
SLAMP STILT FLABBY FLIMSY
HAMBLE HIMPLE HIRPLE HOBBLE
LENNOW LIMBER LIMPSY FLACCID
LIMMOCK SHAFFLE UNSMART
DRAGGLED DROOPING
CLAUDICATION
LIMPET CHINK OPIHI SHELL
ACMAEA LIMPIN FLIDDER
LIMPID PURE CLEAR LUCID BRIGHT
CRYSTAL PELLUCID
LIMPING LAME GIMPY LIMPY
ZOPPA HALTING
LIMPLY LANKLY
LINAGE SPACE
LINALOOL LICAREOL
LINCHPIN FORELOCK
LINCTUS LOOCH LOHOCH LOHOCK
LINDEN LIN LIME LYNE TEIL TILIA
TILLET LINWOOD BASSWOOD
DADDYNUT WOODLIND
LINE BAR BOX FIX RAY ROW TAW
BOFF CASE CEIL COLA CRIB DASH
FACE FILE GAME GAPE LACE
LARD LATH LEAD LING MAIN
MARK RACE RANK RULE STOP
TAUM WHIP AGONE FAINT FEINT
FLEET HATCH LIGNE LINEA
METER RANGE SCORE STRIA
TOUCH TRACE TRAIL TRAIN
TWIST BINDER CABURN CEVIAN

CREASE DEGREE DOUBLE EARING
GASKET ISOBAR ISOHEL ISOPAG
ISOTAC METIER NETTLE SECANT
SECOND SPRING STRING STRIPE
AZIMUTH BABBITT CATLINE
CONTOUR CREANCE ENVELOP
GUNLINE HIPLINE ISOCHOR
ISOGRAM ISOHYET ISONEPH
ISORITH ISOSTER ISOTOME
KNITTLE MARLINE NACARAT
SCRATCH WINDROW BALKLINE
BISECTOR BOUNDARY BUSINESS
CHAMPAIN DATELINE DEADLINE
DIAGONAL DIAMETER DRAGLINE
DRUMLINE FISHBACK GANTLINE
GEODESIC GIRTLINE HAIRLINE
HANDLINE HEXAPODY ISOGLOSS
ISOGONIC ISOPHANE ISOPHENE
ISOPLERE ISOTHERE ISOTHERM
LANDWIRE LIFELINE MARTINET
SLIPBAND STRINGER SUBCLONE
SUBSTILE SUBSTYLE UPSTROKE
PERPENDICULAR
(— AROUND STAMP) FRAME
(— AS CENTER FOR REVOLVING)
AXIS
(— HEARTH) FIX FETTLE
(— IN GLASS) STRING
(— IN HAT) HEADLINE
(— MINESHAFT) TUB
(— OF ACTION) LAY
(— OF BATTLE) FRONT
(— OF BUSINESS) WAY
(— OF CELLS) ANNULUS
(— OF CLIFFS) SCARP BREAKS
(— OF COLOR) SLASH STREAK
(— OF DANCERS) CHAIN
(— OF DESCENT) SIDE STEM STIRP
STOCK PHYLUM STRAIN
ANCESTRY BREEDING
(— OF DETERMINANT) COLUMN
(— OF DEVELOPMENT) STREET
(— OF DEVOLUTION) ENTAIL
(— OF FIBERS) CHRYSAL
(— OF FIRE HOSE) LEAD
(— OF FLOTATION) BEARINGS
(— OF FORTIFICATION) LIMES
ENCEINTE
(— OF HAY) WAKE WALLOW
(— OF HEALTH) HEPATICA
(— OF HIGH TIDE) LANDWASH
(— OF HOUSES) BLOCK
(— OF INTERSECTION) GROIN
BUTTOCK
(— OF JUNCTION) MEET SEAM
(— OF MERCHANDISE) NAMEPLATE
(— OF MERCURY) HEPATICA
(— OF PERSONS) QUEUE CORDON
STICKLE
(— OF PORES) HATCHING
(— OF SOLDIERS) RAY FILE RANK
WAVE CORDON
(— OF STITCHING) BASTING
(— OF TIMBERS) BOOM STOCKADE
(— OF TREES) SCREEN
(— OF TYPE) SLUG KICKER
(— OF UNION) SUTURE
(— ON A LETTER) SERIF
(— ON BOOK COVER) BAND
(— ON COAT) GORGE
(— ON DOLPHIN) STOP
(— ON HIGHWAY) BARRIER
(— THAT CUTS ANOTHER) SECANT

(— TO BIND CABLES) CABURN
(— TO FASTEN SAIL) EARING
GASKET
(— TO RAISE FLAG) LANIARD
LANYARD
(— TO START RACE) TRIG
(— TOUCHING ARC) TANGENT
(— UP) LAY
(— WITH BRICKS) GINGE
(— WITH PANELLING) WAINSCOT
(— WITH STONES) STEEN STEYN
(— WITH TIMBER) CRIB
(ANCHOR —) RODING
(BEARING —) CUT
(BOUNDARY —) MERE FENCE
BORDER ISOGLOSS
(BOUNDING　) SIDE BOUNDARY
PERIMETER
(BRIEF —) ITEM
(COASTAL —) SEAMARK
(CONNECTING —) LIGATURE
(CONTINUOUS —) STRETCH
(CURVED —) ARC SLUR SWEEP
(DEMARCATION —) BOMBLINE
(DIAGONAL —) BIAS
(DIVIDING —) EDGE MIDRIB
DIVISION FRONTIER
(ELECTRIC —) HIGHLINE
(FACIAL —) TRAIT
(FINISHING —) TAPE WIRE
(FISHING —) TOME TROT FLEET
SNELL SNOOD LEADER LEDGER
NORSEL BACKING BOULTER
OUTLINE SPILLER SPILLET
TRIMMER BLOWLINE CORKLINE
FISHLINE SNAGLINE TROTLINE
(HORIZONTAL —) LEVEL
(IMAGINARY —) AGONE HINGE
GROOVE ISOBAR ISOGAM ISOHEL
ISOPAG HORIZON ISOBASE
ISOBATH ISOGRIV ISOHYET
ISOLINE ISOTACH ISOBRONT
ISOCHASM ISOCHEIM ISOCHLOR
ISOCHORE ISOCRYME ISOGLOSS
ISOPHOTE ISOPLETH ISOSTERE
ISOTHERM
(INCLINED —) CANT
(LONGITUDINAL —) MERIDIAN
(MEDIAN —) RAPHE
(METRICAL —) EIGHT STAFF STICH
DIMETER SAPPHIC STICHOS
MONOMETER OCTAMETER
PENTAMETER
(MINESHAFT —) BRATTICE
(MUSICAL —) ACCOLADE
(NAUTICAL —) EARING LACING
GESWARP MARLINE PAINTER
RATLINE DOWNHAUL MESSENGER
(ONE-TENTH OF —) GRY
(PERPENDICULAR —) CATHETUS
(PLOTTED —) ADIABAT
(RADIATING —) BEAM
(RAILROAD —) STEM STUB
(RAISED —) RIDGE
(SPECTRUM —) GHOST DOUBLET
SINGLET TRIPLET MULTIPLET
(STARTING —) SCRATCH
(STRAIGHT —) CHORD BEELINE
STRAIGHT
(SUPPLY —) AIRLIFT UMBILICAL
(SURVEYING —) WAD BASE CHAIN
(THEATRICAL —S) FAT
(TOW —) CORDELLE

(TRANSPORTATION —) FEEDER CARRIER
(WAVY —) SQUIGGLE
(ZIGZAG —) DANCETTE
(42 —S) LENGTH
(PREF.) LINEO STICHO
(SUFF.) STICH(OUS)
(STRAIGHT —) TRIX
LINEAGE GET KIN KIND RACE TEAM BIRTH BLOOD SPACE STIRP STOCK FAMILY HAVAGE NATION PARAGE SOURCE SPRING STRAIN DESCENT KINDRED PROGENY SUCCESS ANCESTRY PEDIGREE PARENTAGE
LINEAL DIRECT
LINEAMENT LINE TRACT TRAIT FEATURE
LINEAR RUNNING
LINECUT ZINCO
LINED MASONED
LINEMAN FORWARD WIREMAN CHAINMAN
LINEN LIN BUCK LAWN CRASH IRISH TOILE BARRAS DAMASK DIAPER RAINES SENDAL BATISTE DORNICK HOLLAND LOCKRAM TABLING BARANDOS OSNABURG PLATILLA
(— CLOSET) LOCKER
(— FOR SHIRTS) SARKING
(— TO COVER CHALICE) PALL
(CHINESE —) KOMPOW
(COARSE —) HARN BARRAS
(FINE —) LAKE LAWN BYSSUS DAMASK DIAPER RAINES
(HOUSEHOLD —) NAPERY TABLING
(SCRAPED —) LINT
(SPANISH —) CREA
(PREF.) BYSSI BYSSO LINO
LINER SHIP BASKET SCRIBER STEAMER
LINES
(PREF.) (TWO CROSSED —) CHIASMO CHIASTO
LINET (BROTHER OF —) LIONES
(HUSBAND OF —) GARETH
LINEUP SHOWUP
LING BURBOT DRIZZLE STOKVIS
LINGA DILDO
LINGCOD CULTUS
LINGER LAG HANG HOVE LING STAY CLING DALLY DELAY DEMUR DWELL HAUNT HOVER PAUSE TARRY DRETCH HANKER LOITER TAIGLE TARROW DRINGLE
LINGERER LUNGIS LAGGARD
LINGERIE FRILLIES PRETTIES
LINGERING SLOW DELAY MOROSE TARDANT DRAGGING
LINGO BAT CANT JARGON LINGUA PATTER DIALECT
LINGUA GLOSSA TONGUE
LINGUAL GLOSSAL
LINGUIST (ALSO SEE PHILOLOGIST)
LINGUISTIC GLOTTIC
LINGUISTICS GRAMMAR PHILOLOGY
LINIMENT EIK EMBROCHE OPODELDOC
LININ PLASTIN
LINING FUR BACK COAT BAIZE BRASS FACING PANNEL BABBITT

BUSHING CEILING FURRING FURRURE THIMBLE TINNING TUBBING CLEADING DOUBLING DOUBLURE FIREBACK SHEETING UNDERLAY WAINSCOT PERCALINE
(— FOR WELL) STEENING STEYNING
(— OF BEARING) JEWEL
(— OF CYLINDER) BUSH
(— OF FURNACE) BASQUE FIREBACK
(— OF HAT) TIP
(— OF SMELTING LADLE) SCULL
(MINESHAFT —) CRIB
(WOODEN —) LAG BRATTICE
(SUFF.) PLEURA
LINK JAR TIE TOW JOIN KNIT LUNT SHUT YOKE CLEEK COMMA NEXUS COPULA COUPLE FASTEN FETTER TOUGHT CODETTA CONNECT COUPLER ENCHAIN INVOLVE LIAISON SHACKLE CATENATE IDENTIFY VINCULUM COLLIGATE
(— ARMS) CLEEK
(— IN NETWORK) LEG
(COMPOUND —) SWIVEL
(WOODEN —) LAG
LINKAGE BOND CELL COUPLING LINKWORK
LINKED CONNEX CATENATE INTEGRAL
LINKING HOOKUP ANNECTANT
(— DEVICE) LINCHPIN
LINKMAN LINKBOY LIGHTMAN
LINKS MACHAIR
LINNET FINCH TWITE LENARD LINTIE REDPOLL REDFINCH
LINSANG CIVET ZINSANG
LINSEED LINGET
LINSEY-WOOLSEY WINCEY
LINT FLY FLUE FLICK CADDIS CADDICE CHARPIE CARBASUS
(SCRAPED —) XYSTUS
LINTEL CAP CLAVY HANCE CLAVEL DARNER SUMMER SQUINCH TRANSOM BRESSUMMER
LINUS (BROTHER OF —) ORPHEUS
(FATHER OF —) APOLLO OEAGRUS ISMENIUS
(MOTHER OF —) CALLIOPE PSAMATHE
LION CAT LLEW MORNE SHEDU SIMBA LIONEL LIONET LEOPARD
(MOUNTAIN —) PUMA COUGAR
(PREF.) LEON LEONT(O)
LION MONKEY LEONCITO
LION-TAILED MONKEY MACACO MACAQUE WANDEROO
LIP BLOB EDGE MASK PUSS APRON CHOPS GROIN MOUTH SPOUT TUTEL LABIUM LABRUM ROUTER CHILOMA LABELLUM UNDERLIP
(— DISEASE) PERLECHE
(— OF BELL) SKIRT
(— OF COROLLA) GALEA
(— OF FLOWER) HELM
(— OF ORCHID) SLIPPER
(— OF PITCHER) BEAK
(—S OF MOOSE) MUFFLE
(FLAT —) APRON
(LOWER —) JIB FIPPLE
(PL.) LABRAS CUSHION

(PREF.) CHEIL(O) CHIL(O)
(SUFF.) CHIL(IA)(O)(US)
LIPARITE RHYOLITE
LIPASE PIALYN
LIPIDE CERIDE ADIPOID STERIDE TETHELIN
LIPOCHROME LUTEIN
LIPOID FAT
LIPOMA STEATOMA
LIPPED LABIATE
(SUFF.) LABIATE
LIPPIA WRIGHT ALOYSIA
LIP PLUG LABRET TEMETA
LIPPY STIMPART
LIPS
(PREF.) LABIO
LIQUEFIED FUSILE POTATE REMISS RESOLVED
LIQUEFY RUN FUSE MELT RELENT LIQUATE DISSOLVE ELIQUATE
LIQUEUR EAU OUZO RAKI AURUM CREME NOYAU CHASSE GENEPI KUMMEL PASTIS PERNOD RACKEE STREGA ANESONE CORDIAL CURACAO PERSICO RATAFIA RATIFIA ABSINTHE ADVOCAAT ALKERMES ANGELICA ANISETTE CALVADOS MANDARIN PRUNELLE VESPETRO MARASCHINO BENEDICTINE
(PL.) EAUX
LIQUID AQUA BREE BLASH DRINK FLUID LEACH MOIST ACETAL FLUENT FURANE AEROSOL BUCKING CINEOLE EYEWASH FLOWAGE VINASSE BLACKING EFFLUENT EFFUSION EXCITANT FURFURAN LEACHATE LIBATION SOLUTION
(— AFTER SALT CRYSTALLIZATION) BITTERN
(— IN CELL) EXCITANT
(— UNIT) TUN CHENG SHENG SHING POTTLE MUTCHKIN PUNCHEON
(ACID-RESISTANT —) GROUND
(COLORING —) HENNA
(COOKING —) BREE BROO BROTH STOCK
(DISABLING —) MACE
(DISTILLED —) SPIRIT
(FILTHY —) ADDLE
(INSULATING —) ASKAREL
(OILY —) ANILINE CHLORAL PICAMAR CARDANOL CREOSOTE
(PERFUMED —) COLLEN COLOGNE
(REFUSE —) SCOURAGE
(REFUSE —S) SEWAGE
(SIZING —) GLAIK
(STERILIZED —) JOHNIN
(STINKING —) CACODYL
(SYRUPY —) HONEY
(TANNING —) LIME
(THICK —) DOPE SIRUP SYRUP
(THICK, STICKY —) GLOP
(VISCOUS —) TAR SCHRADAN
(VOLATILE —) ETHER ALCOHOL DILUENT LIGROIN
(WEAK —) BLASH SLIPSLOP
(PREF.) LATICI
LIQUIDATE SINK SETTLE
LIQUIDATION CLEANUP
LIQUOR ALE BUB DEW GAS LAP

OKE PAD POT RUM SUP TAP WET BEER BREE FIRE FIZZ GEAR GROG LUSH PURL SUCK SWIG TAPE TIFF BOGUS BUDGE CEBUR DRINK GLASS HOOCH JUICE KEFIR MOBBY NAPPY PERRY PISCO SAUCE SHRAB SHRUB SICER SKINK STICK BOTTLE CASSIS CHICHA DIDDLE DOCTOR FOGRAM FUDDLE GATTER GENEVA GUZZLE HYDROL KIRSCH MASTIC MESCAL POTTLE ROTGUT SAMSHU STRUNT TIPPLE WHISKY BITTERN BRACKET BRAGGET GROCERY PHLEGMA SPUNKIE SUCTION TAPLASH TEQUILA WAIPIRO WHISKEY ABSINTHE BRAGWORT EYEWATER HYDROMEL MEDICINE OKOLEHAO POTATION RUMBOOZE FIREWATER
(— CABINET) TANTALUS
(— CASE) GARDEVIN
(— FROM MUST) ARROPE
(— FROM PEARS) PERRY PERRIE
(— FROM WOOL-SCOURING) SUD SUDS
(— MIXED WITH WINE) DOCTOR
(— SALE) ABKARI
(— TAKEN IN SODA WATER) CINDER
(ACID —) VERJUICE
(ALCOHOLIC —) GIN ARAK HOOCH ARRACK BRANDY SAMSHU AQUAVIT BITTERS SNOOTFUL
(ALCOHOLIC —S) ARDENT
(BITTER —) TIRE
(CHEAP —) SMOKE
(COLORLESS —) GLYCID GLYCOL GLYCIDOL GUAIACOL
(CRAB APPLE —) WHERRY
(DISTILLED —) DEW SOTOL GRAPPA PHLEGM SCHNAPPS
(DRUGGED —) HOCUS
(HARD —) BOOZE
(INTOXICATING —) GROG LOAD LUSH TAPE BUDGE GUZZLE KUMISS HASHISH MOONSHINE
(MALT —) ALE BUB BEER STOUT ENTIRE PORTER STINGO
(MOTHER —) HYDROL BITTERN
(POT —) BREWIS
(RICE —) SAMSHU
(SPIRITUOUS —) DEW GROG MOBBY STRUNT WAIPIRO KAOLIANG
(STRAIGHT —) SHORT
(STRONG —) RUG TUBA VINO HOGAN RUMBO STINGO
(TAN —) OOZE
(TANNING —) LAYAWAY TAILING
(WATERED —) BLASH
(WEAK —) BULL SLIPSLOP
LIRA LIRE ZWANZIGER
(ONE-TWENTIETH —) SOLDO
LIRIPIPE TIPPET
LISSOME LITHE LIMBER NIMBLE SUPPLE SVELTE FLEXIBLE
LIST TIP BILL FILE HEEL LEET NOTE POLL ROLL ROON ROTA SWAG BRIEF CANON GISTS INDEX PANEL SCORE SCRIP SCROW SLATE AGENDA CENSUS COLUMN DETAIL DOCKET ERRATA HUDDLE LEGEND PURREL RAGGER

RAGMAN RECORD ROSTER SCREED SCROLL SERIES CATALOG CITATOR COMPILE DIPTYCH ITEMIZE LISTING NOTITIA WAYBILL CALENDAR CINCTURE HANDLIST PLATBAND REGISTER SCHEDULE SYNONYMY TITULARY
(— OF BOOKS) CANON
(— OF CANDIDATES) LEET SLATE TERNA
(— OF CONTESTANTS) DRAW SEEDING
(— OF DISEASES) NOSOLOGY
(— OF JURORS) TALES
(— OF MAP SYMBOLS) LEGEND
(— OF PASSERS WITHOUT HONORS) GULF
(— OF RATES) TARIFF
(— OF THEATRICAL PARTS) CAST
(GENEALOGICAL —) BEGATS
(IMPRESSIVE —) ARRAY
(LEGAL —) TABLEAU
(PRAYER —) BEADROLL
(WINE —) CARD
(PL.) CAREER BARRACE
LISTEL QUADRA
LISTEN HARK HEAR LIST TEND TENEZ ATTEND HARKEN INTEND WHISPER
(— TO) DIG EAR HARK HEAR CATCH ATTEND
LISTENER AUDITOR OTACUST
LISTENING PRICK AUDIENT HEARING
(PREF.) ACOU
LISTER SULKY RIDGER
LISTERA OPHRYS
LISTING ITEM FRAME PARADE LASHING
(— OF JURORS) ARRAY
LISTLESS DOPY DULL WOFF DOWFF FAINT DONSIE SUPINE LANGUID UNLISTY UNLUSTY CARELESS INDOLENT THOWLESS TONELESS UNHEARTY
LISTLESSLY DAVIELY
LISTLESSNESS ACEDIA APATHY UNLUST VACUITY
LISUARTE (DAUGHTER OF —) ORIANA
(FATHER OF —) ESPLANDIAN
LITANY AITESIS ROGATION
LITERAL VERBAL TEXTUAL
LITERALLY SIMPLY
LITERARY BLUE BOOKISH LITERATE
(— MATERIAL) KITSCH
(SUFF.) (— STYLE) ESE
LITERATE LETTERED
LITERATI CLERISY
LITERATURE FICTION LETTERS CLAPTRAP
(— CLANDESTINELY DISTRIBUTED) SAMIZDAT
(SACRED —) VEDA SRUTI
(WISDOM —) CHOKMAH HOKHMAH
LITHE BAIN SWACK CLEVER LIMBER SILKEN SUPPLE SVELTE WANDLE LISSOME FLEXIBLE

LITHUANIA
CAPITAL: VILNA WILNA VILNIUS
COIN: LIT LITAS MARKA CENTAS

FENNIG OSTMARK AUKSINAS SKATIKAS
FORMER CAPITAL: KOVNO KAUNAS
NAME: LITVA LIETUVA
PEOPLE: BALT LETT ZHMUD LITVAK YATVYAG
RIVER: NEMAN NERIS RUSNE VENTA DUBYSA LIELUPE NEMUNAS PREGOLYA
TOWN: MEMEL VILNA JELGAVA VILNIUS KAPSUKAS KLAIPEDA SIAULIAI

LITHUANIAN BALT ZHMUD
LITIGANT SUITOR
LITIGATE LAW PLEAD CONTEST
LITIGATION LAW LIS MOOT SUIT LAWING PLEADING PLEASHIP
LITMUS LAKMUS TURNSOLE
LITOTES MEIOSIS
LITTER DIG PIG BIER RAFF REDD BREED CABIN CLECK DOOLY DRECK HAULM MULCH SEDAN DOOLIE FARROW GOCART KINDLE KITTEN MAHMAL REFUSE CLUTTER LETTIGA LOUSTER MAMMOCK NORIMON RUBBISH RUMMAGE SCAMBLE BRANCARD CARRIAGE KINDLING MUNCHEEL PAVILION STRETCHER
(— FOR LIVESTOCK) BEDDING
(— OF PIGS) FAR FARE FARROW
(— ON PACK ANIMAL) CACOLET
(CAMEL —) KAJAWAH
(FOREST —) DUFF
LITTERED FOUL
LITTLE FEW LIL WEE CURN LITE TINY VEEN CHOTA CRUMB SMALL TASTE WHONE BITTIE DAPPER LEETLE MINUTE PETITE PICKLE PUSILL KENNING MODICUM THOUGHT FRACTION SNIPPING
(— BY LITTLE) EDGINGLY INCHMEAL
(— LESS THAN) ABOUT
(— MUSICALLY) POCO
(— ONE) BUTCHA POPPET
(A —) SOMEWHAT
(INDEFINITELY —) NTH
(PREF.) OLIG(O) PARVI PAUCI PUSILL(I) STEN(O)
(SUFF.) ISK KIN STENOSIS
(— ONE) CLE ELLA ETTE IE ILLA
LITTLE DEMON (AUTHOR OF —) SOLOGUB
(CHARACTER IN —) SASHA LIUDMILA PYLNIKOV PEREDONOV RUSTILOVA NEDOTYKOMKA
LITTLE DORRIT (AUTHOR OF —) DICKENS
(CHARACTER IN —) AMY JOHN CASBY FANNY FLORA ARTHUR DORRIT EDWARD PANCKS CHIVERY CLENNAM MEAGLES WILLIAM BLANDOIS PLORNISH BARNACLES
LITTLE MINISTER (AUTHOR OF —) BARRIE
(CHARACTER IN —) DOW ROB ADAM GAVIN MICAH NANNY BABBIE OGILVY DISHART MCQUEEN RINTOUL WEBSTER MARGARET

LITTLENESS ATOMITY
LITTLE WOMEN (AUTHOR OF —) ALCOTT
(CHARACTER IN —) JO AMY MEG BETH DEMI JOHN BHAER DAISY FRITZ KIRKE MARCH BROOKE CARROL LAURIE MARMEE LAURENCE THEODORE
LITTORAL COAST
LITURGY FORM RITE ABODAH MAARIB MINHAG NEILAH MINCHAH MYSTERY HIERURGY SHAHARIT
LIVE BE USE WIN KEEP LEAD STAY ALERT ALIVE DWELL EXIST GREEN HABIT LEEVE QUICK SHACK VITAL HARBOR LIVELY LIVING REMAIN RESIDE BREATHE INHABIT SUBSIST CONTINUE CONVERSE VIGOROUS
(— AT ANOTHER'S EXPENSE) COSHER
(— BY BEGGING) CADGE SKELDER
(— BY STRATAGEMS) SHARK
(— FROM DAY TO DAY) EKE
(— IN CONTINENCE) CONTAIN
(— IN LUXURY) STATE
(— IN PEACE) COEXIST
(— IN SAME PLACE) STALL
(— ON) SURVIVE
(— RIOTOUSLY) JET
(— TEMPORARILY) CAMP
(— THROUGH) PASS TIDE
(— TOGETHER) AGREE COHABIT
(— WELL) BATTEN
LIVE-BOX CAR
LIVE-FOREVER LULANG ORPINE
LIVELIHOOD BEING BREAD LIVING LIFEHOOD
LIVELINESS PEP BRIO FIRE FIZZ LIFE PUNCH SPUNK BOUNCE ESPRIT GAIETY SPIRIT ENTRAIN SPARKLE ACTIVITY VITALITY VIVACITY
LIVELONG LEELANG ENDURING
LIVELY GAY TID AIRY BRAG CANT FAST FESS GLEG KECK LIVE PERT RACY TAIT TRIG VITE VIVE WARM YARE AGILE ALERT ALIVE BONNY BRISK BUXOM CANTY CHIRK COBBY CORKY CRISP DESTO FRESH FRISK JAZZY KEDGE KINKY MERRY PAWKY PEART PEPPY POKEY RUDDY SASSY SMART VIVID WHICK ACTIVE BLITHE BOUNCY BRIGHT CHEERY CHIRPY COCKET CROOSE CROUSE DAPPER FIERCE FRISCH GINGER JOCUND KIPPER LIVING NIMBLE QUIVER SEMMIT SPARKY SPRACK TROTTY VEGETE WHISKY WIMBLE ALLEGRO ANIMATE ANIMOSE BOBBISH BUCKISH BUOYANT GIGGISH GIOCOSO JOCULAR KINETIC LEBHAFT POINTED ROUSING SPIRITY SPRINGY TITTUMY TITTUPY WINCING ANIMATED BOUNCING CHIRRUPY FRISKFUL FRISKING GALLIARD SANGUINE SKITTISH SMACKING SPANKING SPIRITED SPORTIVE STEERING STIRRING TRIPSOME VEGETOUS VOLATILE SPARKLING

(— PERSON) SWINGER
(TO BE —) SWING
LIVEN LACE CHEER ANIMATE
LIVE OAK ENCINA
LIVER MAW FOIE HEPAR VISCUS PUDDING
(— ATROPHY) LUPINOSIS
(— OF LOBSTER) TOMALLEY
(PREF.) HEPAT(O) HEPATICO
LIVERPOOL (NATIVE OF —) SCOUSER
LIVERWORT HEPATICA MOSSWORT
LIVERY SUIT CLOTH LIVRE UNIFORM CLOTHING
LIVESTOCK FEE WARE STOCK STORE STUFF CHATTEL BESTIALS FATSTOCK
LIVE WIRE HUSTLER
LIVID HAW WAN BLAE BLUE
LIVING KEEP ALIVE BEING BREAD GOING QUICK VITAL WHICK AROUND LIVELY VIABLE ZOETIC ANIMATE SUPPORT ANIMATED BENEFICE
(— IN THE WORLD) SECULAR
(— IN WAVES) LOTIC
(— NEAR THE GROUND) EPIGEAN
(— ON BANKS OF STREAMS) RIPAL RIPARIAN
(— THING) QUICK
(BARE —) CRUST
(ECCLESIASTICAL —) BENEFICE
(PREF.) ONT(O) VIVI
(— ORGANISMS) BIO
(SUFF.) (— IN OR ON) COLE COLINE COLOUS
LIVRE FRANC
LIXIVIATE LEACH
LIXIVIUM LYE
LIZARD DAB EFT GOH UMA UTA DABB GILA IBIT SEPS TEGU TEJU URAN AGAMA ANOLE BLUEY DRACO GECKO GUANO SKINK SNAKE SWIFT TEIID TOKAY TWEEG VARAN AMEIVA ANGUID ARBALO DRAGON GOANNA HARDIM IGUANA LACERT LEGUAN MOLOCH TEIOID WORRAL ZONURE BUMMAJO CAUDATE CHEECHA DIAPSID MONITOR REPTILE SAURIAN SCINCID SCINCUS TUATARA TUCKTOO BASILISK KAKARIKI MOKAMOKA SCINCOID SCORPION SLOWWORM TEGUEXIN WHIPTAIL ZONUROID CHAMELEON PLEURODONT
(PREF.) LACERTI SAUR(O)
(SUFF.) SAUR(A)(IA)(IAN)(US)
LIZARD FISH ULAE INIOME SOAPFISH SPEARING
LLAMA ALPACA VICUNA GUANACO
LLUDD NUDD
LO SEE ECCE
LOACH DOJO BEARDIE MUDFISH
LOAD JAG LUG TON BUCK CARK CRAM DECK DRAW FILL HAUL LADE LAST LUMP PACK RAKE SEAM STEM STOW TOTE TURN BARTH CARGO DRAFT PITCH PRIME STACK TRUSS TURSE BURDEN CHARGE COMBLE DEMAND FODDER FOTHER

HAMPER LADING LOADEN THRACK WEIGHT BALLAST CARLOAD DERRICK DRAUGHT ENDORSE FRAUGHT FREIGHT ONERATE OPPRESS BACKPACK CARRIAGE ENCUMBER HEADLOAD SHIPLOAD PLANELOAD
(— A DIE FOR CHEATING) COG
(— FABRICS) WEIGHT
(— OF COAL) KEEL
(— OF HAY OR CORN) HURRY
(— OF LAMBS) DECK
(— OF LOGS) PEAKER BUNKLOAD
(— OF WOOL) TOD
(— ON BACK) ENDORSE INDORSE
(— SHIP) STEM
(— TO CAPACITY) SATURATE
(— TO EXCESS) ENCUMBER
(ELECTRIC —) DEMAND
(HORSE —) SEAM SUMAGE
(LAST — OF GRAIN) WINTER
(SMALL —) JAG JAGG JOBBLE
(PL.) BUSHEL
LOADER CHARGER
LOADING LADING MARGIN ARRASTRE
LOADSTONE MAGNET SIDERITE LODESTONE
LOAF BAP BUM COB AZYM HACK HAKE HULL LAKE MIKE SLIM SORN BANGE BREAD BRICK DRING MOUCH SHOOL SLIVE SLOSH BLUDGE BROGUE CADDLE DIDDLE GEORGE HALLAH RODNEY SLINGE WASTEL HOOSIER MANCHET SHACKLE SLOUNGE SOLDIER OBLATION PANHAGIA QUARTERN SHAMMOCK
(— AROUND) HULL HOWFF SLOSH RODNEY
(— OF BREAD) COB BATON FADGE MICHE TOMMY HALLAH TAMMIE
(BROWN —) GEORGE
(ROUND —) BUN COBURG
(SMALL —) BAP COB NACKET
(SUGAR —) TITLER
LOAFER BUM CAD YOB BEAT GRUB STIFF BUMBLE BUMMER CADGER KEELIE SLOUCH SLOVEN BLUDGER COASTER FAITOUR HOODLUM SLINKER SOLDIER COBERGER HOOLIGAN LARRIKIN LAYABOUT SEASONER
LOAFING IDLE MIKE
LOAM RAB LAME MALM MARL SLIP LOESS REGUR CLEDGE
LOAMY MELLOW
LOAN DHAN LEND LENT PREST CREDIT DONATE MUTUUM ADVANCE FIXTURE IMPREST
LOANBLEND HYBRID
LOATH LOTH LAITH LEATH SWEER DAINTY BACKWARD
LOATHE UG HATE SHUN ABHOR LAITH WLATE AGRISE DETEST DESPISE SCUNDER SCUNNER NAUSEATE
LOATHING NAUSEA REVOLT DISGUST SCUNNER
LOATHLY LAIDLY
LOATHSOME FOUL UGLY VILE POCKY LAIDLY UNLIEF HATEFUL LOATHLY MAWKISH OBSCENE

TETROUS WLATFUL DEFORMED NAUSEOUS WLATSOME NEFANDOUS ABOMINABLE
LOBBY HALL FOYER NARTHEX PASSAGE TAMBOUR ANTEROOM COULISSE
LOBBYIST PROMOTER
LOBE ALA FIN LAP AXIS LIST MALA ALULA EXITE FIBER FIBRE FLUKE GALEA LOBUS THECA TOOTH UVULA EARLAP FILLET FOLIUM GLOSSA INSULA LAPPET LIGULE LOBING MANTLE VANNUS VERMIS AROLIUM AURICLE HEMAPOD LACINIA LOBULUS AMYGDALA EPICHILE GLABELLA LABELLUM PALPIFER PHYLLOID SQUAMULE
(PREF.) (— OF BRAIN) LEUC(O)
LOBED CUT LOMATINE
(SUFF.) FID FIDATE
LOBSTER CRAY HOMARD DECAPOD SHEDDER CRAWFISH CRAYFISH LANGOSTA MACRURAN
(— ENCLOSURE) CRAWL
(— LESS THAN 10 INCHES LONG) JOE
(FEMALE —) HEN
(NORWAY —) SCAMPO
(SMALL —) PAWK NANCY
(UNDERSIZED —) SHORT
LOBSTER POT COY CRAIL CREEL TRUNK FISHPOT
LOBULARIA KONIGA
LOCAL HOME NATIVE LIMITED TOPICAL VICINAL REGIONAL EPICHORIC
(NOT —) AZONIC
(PREF.) TOP(O)
LOCALE SITE LOCAL PLACE SCENE
LOCALITY SPA HAND PLAT SPOT LOCUS PLACE POINT SITIO SITUS STEAD HABITAT LATITUDE POSITURE SITUATION
(BARREN —) GALL
(BEAUTIFUL —) XANADU
(GUARDED —) POST
LOCALIZE SITUATE POSITION
LOCATE SITE SPOT PITCH PLACE BESTOW BILLET SETTLE SITUATE PINPOINT
(— AT INTERVALS) SPOT
(— WATER) DIVINE
LOCATED SET FIXED SEATED SITUATED
(— OFF THE HIGHWAY) DEVIOUS
LOCATING SYSTEM SOFAR
LOCATION FALL HOME PLOT SEAT PLACE SITUS WHERE UBIETY AMENITY STATION HOMESITE STANDING
(ESSENTIAL —) EYE
(FOREST —) CHANCE
(GEOGRAPHIC —) SEAT
(MINING —) MYNPACHT
(NATURAL —) HABITAT
(SUFF.) TOPE TOPY
LOCH LOUGH LOCHAN
LOCK COT KEY FEAK FRIB HOLD TRIM YALE CHUBB CLASP SASSE DUBBEH ENLOCK LUCKEN DAGLOCK EARLOCK KEYLOCK PINLOCK SPANNER DEADLOCK FORELOCK

(— IMPROPERLY) BIND
(— IN RIVER) SASSE
(— OF HAIR) COT TAG TUZ COTT CURL FEAK TATE FLAKE FLOCK FLUKE QUIFF TRESS TANGLE COWLICK EARLOCK FRIZZLE SERPENT WIMPLER FORELOCK SIDELOCK
(— OF WOOL) TAG COTT FRIB FLOCK STAPLE HASLOCK
(— UP) JAIL STOW CABINET
(CANAL —) COFFER CHAMBER
(DIRTY —) FRIB
(MATTED —) COT COTT DAGLOCK
(MUSKET —) ROWET
(PART OF —) REWET STRIKE
(WHEEL —) REWET
LOCKED FAST LUCKEN
LOCKER HUTCH ASCHAM
LOCKERMAN NIBBLER SCOTCHER SNIBBLER
LOCKET BRELOQUE
LOCKJAW TETANUS TRISMUS
LOCKNUT JAMNUT KEEPER
LOCKOUT SHUTOUT
LOCKSMITH LOCKYER
LOCKUP JUG GAOL JAIL LOCK LOGS CHOKY CLINK TRONK COOLER HOOSEGOW ROUNDHOUSE
LOCOMOTION FLYING LATION
LOCOMOTIVE HOG PIG PUG BOGY GOAT HOGG MULE SHAG TANK BOGIE DINKY DUMMY MOGUL PILOT DIESEL DOCTOR DOLLIE DONKEY ENGINE LOADER PUSHER SMOKER YARDER BOBTAIL BOOSTER SHUNTER STEAMER CALLIOPE CHOOCHOO COMPOUND DOLLBEER
(— WITHOUT CARS) WILDCAT
(EXTRA —) HELPER
(PART OF —) CAB ROD BELL DOME HOSE LAMP STEP BRACE HINGE PILOT TRUCK BOILER JACKET TENDER COUPLER SANDBOX WHISTLE CYLINDER HANDRAIL INJECTOR SANDPIPE HEADLIGHT RESERVOIR DRIVEWHEEL SMOKESTACK
LOCOMOTOR ATAXIA TABES
LOCOWEED LOCO LEGUME PEAVINE
LOCRINE (DAUGHTER OF —) SABRINA
(FATHER OF —) BRUTE BRUTUS
LOCULUS THECA
LOCUS PLACE EVOLUTE SURFACE SYNAPSE CONCHOID ENVELOPE HOROPTER
LOCUST WETA BRUKE CICAD HONEY ACACIA CICADA QUAKER SKIPPER TETRIGID VOETGANGER
LOCUST TREE CAROB ACACIA LOCUST ROBINIA ALGAROBA
LODE LEAD REEF VEIN LEDGE COURSE FEEDER QUARRY SCOVAN COUNTER
LODESTONE MAGNET SIDERITE TERRELLA
LODGE DIG HUT INN LIE BEAT CAMP HOST KEEP ROOM STAY STOW TENT BOWER CABIN

COUCH COURT GROVE GUEST HOGAN HOTEL HOUSE HOWFF LAYER LOGIS STICK TARRY ALIGHT BESTOW BILLET BURROW COSHER GESTEN GRANGE HOSTEL RESIDE SETTLE BARRACK LODGING QUARTER SOJOURN EMBOLIZE HARBINGE
(— AND EAT) COSHER
(— FOR SAFEKEEPING) DEPOSIT
(— IN COURT) BOX
(LOCAL —) COURT
(SPORTSMAN'S —) SHEAL
LODGEPOLE PINE TAMARACK
LODGER INMATE ROOMER TENANT
LODGING BED CRIB FERM GIST HAFT HOST NEST GEAST LOGIS HARBOR HOSTEL LIVERY HOSPICE HOUSING COUCHANT GUESTING
(— FOR SOLDIERS) CASERN
(— OF MARABOUT) KOUBA
(VILE —) KENNEL
(PL.) PAD DIGS DIGGINGS
LODGINGHOUSE INN KIP GITE STOP HOTEL LOGIA LOCANDA PENSION HOSTELRY
LODICULE SQUAMULA SQUAMULE
LODOLETTA (CHARACTER IN —) ANTONIO FLAMMEN LODOLETTA
(COMPOSER OF —) MASCAGNI
LOESS LIMON
LOFT BALK FLAT GOLF JUBE LAFT ATTIC SOLAR GARRET SOLLAR HAYLOFT COCKLOFT SCAFFOLD TRAVERSE
(HAY —) TALLET TALLIT
LOFTIEST SUPREME
LOFTINESS PRIDE HEIGHT DIGNITY MAJESTY EMINENCE GRANDEUR HIGHNESS CELSITUDE
(— OF SPIRIT) MAGNANIMITY
LOFTSMAN LINESMAN
LOFTY AIRY HIGH LOFT TALL BRENT ELATE GRAND GREAT NOBLE PROUD SKYEY STEEP WINGY AERIAL ANDEAN HAUGHT TOPFUL TOWERY UPWARD WINGED ANDESIC ARDUOUS EMINENT EXCELSE HAUGHTY SUBLIME ARROGANT ELEVATED GENEROUS MAJESTIC OLYMPIAN TOWERING
LOG NOG BUNK CLOG DRAG SKID CHOCK CHUCK CHUNK PIECE STICK STOCK BATTEN BILLET PEAKER PEELER SADDLE SAWLOG BACKLOG DAYBOOK DEADMAN DEGRADE JOURNAL LOGBOOK DEADHEAD
(— AS ANCHOR) DEADMAN
(— AS RAFTER) VIGA
(— BINDING A RAFT) SWIFTER
(— CAR) BUNK
(— FASTENED TO TRAP) DRAG
(— SUPPORTING MINE ROOF) NOG
(— WITH SPIKES IN END) DEADENER
(— WITHOUT BARK) BUCKSKIN
(ENCLOSED —S) BOOM
(FLOATING —S) DRIVE
(LOAD OF —S) PEAKER
(PILE OF —S) DECK ROLLWAY
(SAWED —) BOULE

(SLABBED —) CANT
(SMALL —) LOGGET
(SPLIT —) PUNCHEON
(STRIPPED —) BATTEN
(SUNKEN —) DEADHEAD
LOGANIN MELIATIN
LOGARITHM DENSITY
(— SYMBOL) PF PH PK RH
(NEGATIVE —) PH
LOGBOOK LOG JOURNAL
LOGE BOX BOOTH LODGE STALL
LOGGER RIDER BOWMAN DECKER
FALLER GOPHER HOOKER LIMBER
MARKER SCORER CHOPPER
FROGGER GRABBER SPOTTER
CATTYMAN
LOGGIA LODGE BALCONY
MIRADOR
LOGIC NYAYA LOGICS CANONIC
WITCRAFT
(— OF DISCOVERY) HEURETIC
LOGICAL SANE RAISONNE
RATIONAL
LOGISTILLA (SISTER OF —) ALCINA
MORGANA
LOGMAN CHASER CHOPPER
LOGO EMBLEM
LOGOGRAM IDEOGRAM
LOGOS WORD
LOGOTYPE SIG
LOG PERCH DARTER HOGFISH
ROCKFISH
LOGROLLING BIRLING
(— TOURNAMENT) ROLEO
LOGWOOD BRAZIL ADMIRAL
DYEWOOD BLUEWOOD HYPERNIC
CAMPEACHY
LOGY DROWSY GROGGY
LOHAN RAKAN
LOHENGRIN (CHARACTER IN —)
ELSA HENRY ORTRUD FREDERICK
GOTTFRIED LOHENGRIN
TELRAMUND
(COMPOSER OF —) WAGNER
(FATHER OF —) PARSIFAL
(WIFE OF —) ELSA
LOIN LEER LISK ALOYAU LUNYIE
(PORK —) GRISKIN
(2 UNCUT —S) BARON
(PL.) REINS FILLET SADDLE
(PREF.) LUMB(O) OSPHY(O)
LOINCLOTH IZAR MALO MARO
DHOTI LUNGI PAGNE PAREU
MOOCHA PANUNG DHOOTIE
LOIS (DAUGHTER OF —) EUNICE
(GRANDSON OF —) TIMOTHY
LOITER LAG CLUG FOOL HAKE
HANG HAWM HAZE HOVE LOUT
MIKE MUCK SLUG COOSE DELAY
DRAWL KNOCK MOUCH SHOOL
SIDLE TARRY COOTER DAWDLE
LAGGER LINGER MUCKER STRAKE
TAIGLE PROJECT SHAFFLE
LALLYGAG LOLLYGAG SCOWBANK
SLAMMOCK SLUMMOCK
LOITERER DRONE IDLER LAGGER
LAGGARD LURCHER
LOITERING SLIMSY LAGGARD
LOKAPALA MAHARAJA
LOKI (DAUGHTER OF —) HEL
(FATHER OF —) FARBAUTI
(MOTHER OF —) NAL LAUFEY
ANGRBODHA

(SLAYER OF —) HEIMDALL
(WIFE OF —) SIGYN ANGURBODA
LOLL FUG LOUT FROWST LOLLUP
LOUNGE SOZZLE SPRAWL
RECLINE SCAMBLE SCOWBANK
LOLLAPALOOZA LULU ONER
LOLLIPOP LOLLY SUCKER
SUCKABOB
LOLO NOSU
LONDON SMOKE COCKAGNE
(BRIDGE IN —) TOWER ALBERT
PUTNEY CHELSEA WATERLOO
(DISTRICT OF —) SOHO ACTON
ADELPHI ALSATIA BRIXTON
CHELSEA MAYFAIR
(MONUMENT IN —) GOG MAGOG
NELSON CENOTAPH VICTORIA
(RIVER OF —) THAMES
(STREET OF —) BOND FLEET
CANNON SAVILE DOWNING
WARDOUR HAYMARKET
(SUBURB OF —) KEW FINCHLEY
LONDONER FLATCAP
LONE LANE SOLE ALONE APART
SINGLE SOLITARY
(— STAR STATE) TEXAS
LONELINESS ONENESS VACANCY
SOLITUDE
LONELY LORN ONLY SOLE VAST
ALONE UNKET UNKID WISHT
ALANGE DEAFLY SULLEN
DEAVELY FORLORN LONEFUL
SOLEYNE DESOLATE SECLUDED
SOLITARY
(PREF.) EREM(O)
LONESOME ALONE DOLEY LONELY
LANESOME SOLITARY
LONG HO DIE FAR FIT YEN ACHE
DREE HANK HONE ITCH LANG
SIDE TALL WILN WISH YAWN
CRAVE DREAM GREEN LANGY
LONGA MOURN STARK WEARY
YEARN ARIGUE ASPIRE DESIRE
DREICH HANKER HUNGER LINGER
LONGUS PROLIX STOUND THIRST
LENGTHY TEDIOUS WEILANG
GEMINATE INFINITE
(— AGO) FERN LANGSYNE
(— AND SLENDER) REEDY SQUINNY
(— AND UNIFORM IN WIDTH)
LINEAR
(— FOR) CARE HONE COVET
CRAVE TASTE ASPIRE DESIRE
SUSPIRE
(— RESTLESSLY) ITCH
(— SINCE) YORE
(EXTRA —) MAXI
(TEDIOUSLY —) MORTAL
(PREF.) DOLICH(O) LONGI LONGO
MACR(O) MEC(O)
LONG-BILLED CURLEW SMOKER
LONGBOAT SLOOP
LONG-BODIED RACY RANGY
LONGERON SPAR
LONGEVITY VIVACITY
(— CHARACTER) SHOU
LONGING YEN ENVY ITCH LUST
PINE WISH BRAME YEARN DESIRE
HANKER TALENT THIRST ATHIRST
CRAVING THIRSTY WILLING
WISHFUL WISTFUL APPETENT
APPETITE CUPIDITY HOMESICK
PRURIENT

LONGINGLY WISTLY
LONGITUDINALLY ENDLONG
LONG-LASTING CHRONIC
LONGLEGS STILT
LONGLINE BULTOW
LONG-LIVED LONGEVE MACROBIAN
LONGSHOREMAN DOCKER
HOBBLER WHARFIE DOCKHAND
ROUSTABOUT
LONG-STANDING OLD
LONG-SUFFERING MEEK PATIENT
ENDURING PATIENCE
LONG-TAILED WHIDAH REDBILL
LONG TOM SKIPPER
LONG-WINDED PROLIX PROSAIC
LOOK LA LO AIR EYE KEN SEE SPY
CAST GAWK GAZE GIVE GLOM
HEED KEEK LATE LUCK MARK
MIEN POKE SEEM SWAP VIEW
WAIT ACIES BLUSH DEKKO FAVOR
FLASH GLEAM GLEER GLIFF GLINT
SCREW SIGHT SQUIZ VIZZY WLITE
APPEAR ASPECT EYEFUL GANDER
GLANCE REGARD REWARD VISION
EYESHOT EYEWINK INSIGHT
SEEMING DISCOVER LANGUISH
OEILLADE
(— ABOUT) BELOOK SPECTATE
(— AFTER) TENT ATTEND FATHER
FETTLE PROCURE
(— ASKANCE) GLIM LEER SKEW
BAGGE GLENT GLEDGE SKLENT
(— AT) DIG SEE GLOM LAMP VIEW
VISE GLISK ADVISE BEHOLD
REGARD REWARD CONSIDER
SPECTATE
(— CLOSELY) PRY ESPY SCAN
(— CROSS-EYED) SHEYLE
(— DOWN UPON) SNOB DESPISE
(— DULLY) BLEAR
(— FIXEDLY) GAZE KYKE GLORE
STARE
(— FOR) SPY FOND SEEK GROPE
EXPECT PROPOSE RESPECT
(— FORWARD) EXPECT FORESEE
ENVISAGE ENVISION
(— GLANCINGLY) BLINK
(— IN SNEAKING MANNER) SNOOP
(— INTENTLY) GLOSE VISIE
GLOWER EYEBALL
(— INTO) SOUND SEARCH
(— OBLIQUELY) GLIME GOGGLE
SQUINT
(— OF DERISION) FLEER
(— OF PLANETS) ASPECTS
(— OUT) FEND MIND CHEESE
JIGGERS OUTLOOK
(— OVER) SCAN TOISE BROWSE
SURVEY EXAMINE
(— SEARCHINGLY) PEER PORE
TOOT
(— SLYLY) PEEP GLINK
(— SOUR) GLUNCH
(— STEADFASTLY) GLOAT
(— SULKY) LUMP
(— SULLEN) LOUR LOWER
(— UPON AS) ACCOUNT
(— WILDLY) GLOP WAUL WHAWL
(— WITH FAVOR) SMILE
(AMOROUS —) SMICKER
(ANGRY —) SCOWL
(BRIEF —) GLIM GLINT GLIMPSE
(LOVING —) BELGARD

(QUICK —) SCRY GLENT
(SEARCHING —) SCRUTINY
(SEVERE —) FROWN
(SIDELONG —) GLEE GLIME
(SLY —) GLEG GLIME TWIRE
(SULLEN —) GLOOM GLOUT
GLUNCH
(TENDER —) LANGUISH
(WANTON —) LEER
(PL.) DAPS
(PREF.) **(— THROUGH)** PERSPECTO
LOOKER BEAUTY HERDSMAN
SEARCHER
LOOKER-ON BEHOLDER
LOOK HOMEWARD ANGEL
(AUTHOR OF —) WOLFE
(CHARACTER IN —) BEN GANT
LUKE DAISY ELIZA HELEN JAMES
LAURA EUGENE GROVER OLIVER
LEONARD MARGARET
**LOOKING BACKWARD (AUTHOR
OF —)** BELLAMY
(CHARACTER IN —) WEST EDITH
LEETE JULIAN BARTLETT
PILLSBURY
LOOKOUT HUER TOUT SCOUT
WATCH BANTAY CONNER
TOOTER FUNERAL OUTLOOK
ATALAYAN BANTAYAN BARTIZAN
COCKATOO PROSPECT
TOWERMAN WATCHOUT
OBSERVATORY
LOOM BEAM BULK HULK LEEM
DOBBY FRAME GLOOM BEETLE
DOBBIE DRAWLOOM HANDLOOM
JACQUARD OVERPICK
(— ATTACHMENT) LAPPET
(PREF.) HIST(O)
LOOM AXLE ROCKTREE
LOOM BAR EASER DAGGER
LOOMFIXER TACKLER
LOOM HARNESS LEAF HEADLE
SIMBLOT MOUNTING
LOON DIVER IMBER WABBY
COBBLE DUCKER GUNNER
WHABBY PYGOPOD
LOOP BOW EYE LUG NOB TAB TAG
ANSA BEND COIL FAKE HANK
KINK KNOB KNOP LEAF LINK
LOUP PURL BIGHT BRIDE CHAPE
COQUE GUIDE KINCH LACET
LATCH NOOSE PEARL PICOT
SHANK STRAP TERRY WITHY
BECKET BILLET BUCKLE FOLIUM
HANGER HOLDER KEEPER KINKLE
PARRAL SPIRAL STAPLE STITCH
TWITCH COCKEYE COUPURE
CRINGLE CRUPPER GROMMET
KNUCKLE LATCHET SEGMENT
ANTINODE COURONNE
(— AND THIMBLES) CLEW CLUE
(— BY ICESKATER) SPOON
(— IN KNITTING) STEEK
(— IN MINER'S ROPE) SLUG
(— IN NEEDLEWORK) BRIDE
(— OF INTESTINES) KNUCKLE
(— OF IRON) OOLLY
(— OF ROPE) FAKE BIGHT FLAKE
KINCH NOOSE ANCHOR BECKET
PARRAL SNORTER SNOTTER
(— OF SCABBARD) FROG
(— OF TUBING) SCROLL
(— ON ARMOR) VERVELLE

(**— ON SAIL**) LASKET
(**— ON SPINNING FRAME**) BAND
(**— ON SWORD BELT**) HANGER
(**HANGING —**) FESTOON
(**HEDDLE —**) DOUP
(**ORNAMENTAL —**) PICOT
(**SHOULDER —**) EPAULET
(**SURGICAL —**) CURET CURETTE
(**TIGHT —**) KINK KINKLE
(**PREF.**) FUNDI
LOOPER INCHWORM SPANWORM
LOOPHOLE LOOP CHINK MEUSE
EYELET OILLET WICKET BARBICAN
PORTHOLE
LOOSE GAY LAX EMIT FREE GLAD
LASH LIMP OPEN SOFT UNDO
WIDE WILD BAGGY CRANK FRANK
LARGE LIGHT RELAX SLACK
VAGUE WASHY ADRIFT FLUFFY
LIMBER SLOPPY SOLUTE SPORTY
SUBURB UNBIND UNGIRT UNLASH
WOBBLY ABSOLVE CHESSOM
FLYAWAY IMMORAL MOVABLE
RELAXED SHOGGLY STRINGY
UNBOUND UNHITCH UNTIGHT
DIFFUSED DISCINCT FLOATING
INSECURE LAXATIVE SHATTERY
UNSTABLE
(**— ARROW**) BOLT
(**MORALLY —**) FRANK
(**PREF.**) LAXI
LOOSE-JOINTED LANKY SHACKLY
LOOSELY SLACK LARGELY SLACKLY
LOOSEN LAX BREAK SLACK UNTIE
LAXATE LIMBER UNBEND
RESOLVE SLACKEN UNGRIPE
UNLOOSE UNSCREW DISHEVEL
UNSTRING
(**— ANCHOR**) TRIP
(**— ROCK**) GAD
LOOSENESS SLACK LAXITY
LATITUDE
(**PREF.**) LYO
LOOSENING START SOLUTIVE
SOLUTORY
(**PREF.**) LYS(I)
LOOSESTRIFE KILLWEED
PEATWEED PEATWOOD
PRIMWORT
LOOSING
(**SUFF.**) LYSE LYSIS LYST LYTE
LYTIC LYZE
LOOT SACK SWAG BOOTY HARRY
SPOIL STEAL THEFT BOODLE
MARAUD HERSHIP PILLAGE
PLUNDER SNAFFLE
LOOTING SACK
LOP DOD LAP CLIP DODD OCHE
SNED SNIG TRIM SHRAG SHRED
SHRUB STUMP TRASH TWINE
SHROUD SNATHE TRASHIFY
TRUNCATE
(**— OFF**) COW DOD CROP DODD
HEAD SNAG SNED PRUNE SHRED
TRUNK DEFALK AMPUTATE
LOPE SHAG
LOPPED
(**PREF.**) (**— OFF**) TRUNCATO
LOPPER CLABBER
LOPPINGS SHROUD
LOQUACIOUS GABBY FUTILE
LOQUACITY PRATE PRATTLE
FUTILITY

LOQUAT BIWA NISPERO
LORAL FRENAL
LORD BEL DAM DEN DON GOD HER
LOR MAR SID SIR DION DOMN
EROS HERR LAUK LOSH NAIK SIRE
TUAN ANGUS ARAWN BARON
LAFEU LIEGE LUDDY NIGEL
OMRAH RABBI SAHIB SWAMI
DOMINE DUMAIN KYRIOS PRABHU
SAYYID SIGNOR TANIST THAKUR
CAMILLO CERIMON JACQUES
JEHOVAH MARCHER OGTIERN
VAVASOR BHAGAVAT DESPOTES
DRIGHTEN GRANDPRE LORDLING
MARGRAVE OVERLORD PALATINE
SEIGNEUR SEIGNIOR SUPERIOR
SUZERAIN THALIARD
(**— OF DARKNESS**) HYLE
(**— OF WORLD**) LOKINDRA
(**FEUDAL —**) DAUPHIN VAVASOR
SUZERAIN
(**JAPANESE —**) KAMI
LORD CHANCELLOR WOOLPACK
LORD JIM (**AUTHOR OF —**) CONRAD
(**CHARACTER IN —**) JIM DAIN
BROWN STEIN WARIS MARLOW
DORAMIN
LORDLINESS PRIDE
LORDLY PROUD SUPERB
ARROGANT DESPOTIC
LORDOSIS SWAYBACK
LORDSHIP NAVY DYNASTY
ERECTION SEIGNORY SIGNORIA
LORE LEAR LORUM MASTAX
LEARNING
LORGNETTE STARER
LORICA LORIC SHEATH SHIELD
LORIKEET PARROT WARRIN
CORELLA WEROOLE
LORIS KOKAM LEMUR SLOTH
LEMUROID
LORN ALONE
LORNA DOONE (**AUTHOR OF —**)
BLACKMORE
(**CHARACTER IN —**) FRY TOM ALAN
JOHN RIDD ANNIE DOONE DUGAL
ENSOR LORNA CARVER FAGGUS
JEREMY REUBEN BRANDIR
STICKLES HUCKABACK
LORRY DRAG RULLY CAMION
ROLLEY
LORY LOORY CORELLA LORIKEET
LOSE LET TIN AMIT DROP TINE
WANT FORGO LAPSE LEASE TRAIL
GAMBLE MISLAY FORBEAR
FORFEIT FORLESE SLATTER
(**— AT CARDS**) BUST
(**— BET**) WRONG
(**— BRILLIANCE**) FAINT
(**— BY DEATH**) BURY
(**— BY GAMING**) GAME
(**— BY STUPIDITY**) BLUNDER
(**— CONTROL**) BLOW CRACK
(**— COURAGE**) DREEP TAINT
(**— FLAVOR**) FOZE APPAL APPALL
(**— FORCE**) COLLAPSE
(**— FRESHNESS**) FADE WILT
WITHER
(**— HEART**) JADE FAINT QUAIL
COLLAPSE
(**— HOPE**) DESPAIR DESPOND
(**— LUSTER**) TARNISH
(**— MOISTURE**) GUTTATE

(**— NERVE**) CHICKEN
(**— OFFICE**) FALL
(**— ONE'S BREATH**) CHINK
(**— ONE'S WAY**) STRAY
(**— POWER**) FAIL DISSOLVE
(**— SELF-POSSESSION**) ABASH
(**— SPIRIT**) JADE
(**— STRENGTH**) GO FADE FAIL PALL
WEAKEN LANGUISH
(**— VISION**) DAZZLE
(**— WARMTH**) COOL CONGEAL
(**— WEIGHT**) ENSEAM
LOSS ACE COST HARM LEAK LOST
MISS LAPSE QUALM WASTE
BURIAL DAMAGE DAMNUM
DEFEAT INJURY TINSEL AVERAGE
DEBACLE DEFICIT EXPENSE
JACTURE LEAKAGE LEESING
MISTURE REPRISE AMISSION
BREAKAGE CLEANING MISSMENT
PERDITION SACRIFICE
(**— BY EVAPORATION**) ULLAGE
(**— BY SIFTING**) ULLAGE
(**— IN WORKING**) SLIPPAGE
(**— OF ABILITIES**) COLLAPSE
(**— OF ACTIVITY**) AKINESIA
(**— OF APPETITE**) ASITIA ANOREXIA
(**— OF CONSCIOUSNESS**) SWOON
ABSENCE APOPLEXY BLACKOUT
FAINTING
(**— OF ELASTICITY**) SET
(**— OF ELECTRICITY**) EFFLUVE
(**— OF EXPRESSION**) AMIMIA
(**— OF HAIR**) DEFLUX ALOPECIA
PTILOSIS
(**— OF HONOR**) ATIMY
(**— OF HOPE**) DESPAIR
(**— OF MEMORY**) AMNESIA
BLACKOUT
(**— OF PRESTIGE**) DISHONOR
(**— OF SCENT**) CHECK
(**— OF SENSE OF SMELL**) ANOSMIA
(**— OF SIGHT**) ANOPSY ANOPSIA
(**— OF SIZE**) WANE
(**— OF SOUND**) APOCOPE SYNCOPE
APHERESIS
(**— OF SPEECH**) ALALIA APHASIA
APHONIA
(**— OF VOICE**) ANAUDIA APHONIA
(**— OF VOWEL**) APHESIS
(**— OF WILL POWER**) ABULIA
(**CONTRACT —**) LESION
(**SUFF.**) ZEMIA
LOST ASEA GONE LORN TINT
STRAY WASTE ASTRAY BUSHED
HIDDEN NAUGHT FORFEIT
FORLORN MISSING CONFUSED
OBSCURED BENIGHTED
(**— IN THOUGHT**) PREOCCUPIED
LOST HORIZON (**AUTHOR OF —**)
HILTON
(**CHARACTER IN —**) HUGH BRIAC
CHANG HENRY CONWAY LOTSEN
BARNARD CHARLES ROBERTA
BRINKLOW MALLISON PERRAULT
RUTHERFORD
LOST LADY (**AUTHOR OF —**)
CATHER
(**CHARACTER IN —**) IVY BLUM NIEL
FRANK OGDEN PETERS HERBERT
ELLINGER POMMEROY
CONSTANCE FORRESTER
LOT CUT HAP PEW CHOP CROP

DEAL DOLE DOOM DRAW FALL
FATE HEAP PACK PART PILE REDE
SKIT SLEW SLUE SORS SORT
BATCH BLOCK BREAK BUNCH
CAVEL FIELD GRACE GRIST GROSS
LINES SHARE SHOOT SIGHT SITHE
STAND TEEMS TROOP WEIRD
AMOUNT BARREL BOODLE
BUNDLE CHANCE DICKER FARDEL
OODLES PARCEL TICHEL BOILING
DESTINY FEEDLOT FORTUNE
OODLINS PORTION SANDLOT
BACKYARD CABOODLE JINGBANG
MOUTHFUL RIMPTION
WOODLAND
(**— OF PERSONS**) BOODLE
(**— OF TEA**) BREAK
(**— OF 60 PIECES**) SHOCK
(**BUILDING —**) ERF
(**BURIAL —**) LAIR
(**FATHER OF —**) HARAN
(**GREAT —**) SWAG
(**MISCELLANEOUS —**) RAFT
(**SISTER OF —**) ISCAH MILCAH
(**UNCLE OF —**) ABRAHAM
(**VACANT —**) COMMON COMMONS
(**PREF.**) CLERO SORTI
LOTAN (**FATHER OF —**) SEIR
LOTION WASH EYEWASH
EYEWATER LAVATORY
LOTS HEAPS TEEMS BUSHEL
HODFUL
LOTTERY AMBO LOTTO TERNO
RAFFLE TOMBOLA
LOTTO KENO BINGO TOMBOLA
(**— GAME**) HOUSE
LOTUS LOTE LOTOS PADMA
NELUMBO WANKAPIN
LOTUS TREE SADR ZIZYPHUS
LOUCHEUX KUTCHIN
LOUD HARD HIGH MAIN CRUDE
FORTE GAUDY GREAT HEAVY
SHOWY STARK STOUR WIGHT
BRASSY BRAZEN COARSE CRIANT
FLASHY GARISH HOARSE VULGAR
BLATANT CLAMANT HAUTAIN
VIOLENT BIGMOUTH FRENZIED
PIERCING SLAMBANG STREPENT
STRIDENT VEHEMENT
STREPITANT
LOUDLY BOST ALOUD FORTE
STARK
LOUDNESS STRESS SONORITY
MAGNITUDE
(**— UNIT**) PHON SONE
LOUDSPEAKER WOOFER SPEAKER
TWEETER BULLHORN SQUAWKER
LOUD-SPOKEN RANDY
LOUIS LUIGI LODOWIC

NATIVE: CAJUN CREOLE ACADIAN
NICKNAME: CREOLE PELICAN
PARISH: WINN CADDO ACADIA
  IBERIA SABINE TENSAS
  ORLEANS RAPIDES OUACHITA
  CALCASIEU
RIVER: RED AMITE BOEUF SABINE
  TENSAS OUACHITA
STATE BIRD: PELICAN
STATE FLOWER: MAGNOLIA
STATE TREE: CYPRESS
STREAM: BAYOU
TOWN: JENA MANY HOMER
  HOUMA EDGARD GRETNA
  MINDEN MONROE RUSTON
  BASTROP VIDALIA BOGALUSA
  TALLULAH NEWORLEANS

LOUISIANIAN CAJUN ACADIAN
LOUNGE HAWM LOAF LOLL SORN
  SOSS BANGE TRAIK DACKER
  FROUST FROWST GLIDER LOLLUP
  LOPPET RIZZLE SLINGE SOZZLE
  LAMMOCK SAUNTER SLOUNGE
LOUNGER IDLER SLOUNGER
LOUSE BOB BUG SOW CRAB
  CRUMB BOOGER BRAULA COOTIE
  GISLER PALMER SISTEN VERMIN
  MORPION PUCERON GRAYBACK
  (FISH —) GISLER ARGULUS
  (PLANT —) APHID APHIS
  (WOOD —) SOW SLATER
  (YOUNG —) NIT
  (PREF.) ONISCI PEDICUL(I)(O)
LOUSEWORT RATTLE SNAFFLES
LOUSINESS PEDICULOSIS
LOUSY SEEDY CRAPPY CRUMMY
  PEDICULOUS
LOUT HOB LOB LUG YOB BOOR
  CHUB COOF GAUM GAWK JAKE
  LOON NOWT SWAB SWAD BOOBY
  CHUMP CUDDY GNOFF LOOBY
  LOURD ROBIN THRUM WHAUP
  YAHOO BOHUNK CLUNCH GOBBIN
  HOBLOB LOURDY LUBBER LUNGIS
  SLOUCH TRIPAL BUMPKIN
  GROBIAN HALLION HAWBUCK
  LOBCOCK PALOOKA
  LOBLOLLY
  (COUNTRY —) KERN BUMPKIN
LOUTISH SWAB HULKY SLOOMY
  BOORISH HULKING VILLAIN
  BOEOTIAN CLOWNISH
LOUVER SLAT LOUVRE LUFFER
  DIFFUSER FEMERELL
  (PL.) SHUTTER
LOVABLE AMABEL CUDDLY
  AMIABLE ADORABLE DOVELIKE
  LOVESOME
LOVABLENESS DEARNESS
LOVAGE SMELLAGE
LOVE GRA LOO AMOR EROS KAMA
  LIKE ALOHA AMOUR CUPID
  DRURY FANCY HEART MINNE
  AFFECT TENDRE CHARITY
  EMBRACE FEELING PASSION
  DEVOTION KINDNESS LOVEHOOD
  PARAMOUR
  (— IN RETURN) REDAME
  (— OF COUNTRY) PATRIOTISM
  (— OF MARVELOUS) TERATISM
  (— TO EXCESS) IDOLIZE
  (— TOWARD DEITY) BHAKTI

  (CHRISTIAN —) CHARITY
  (INTENSE —) FIRE
  (NATURAL —) STORGE
  (SELF-GIVING —) AGAPE
  (UNLAWFUL —) LEMANRY
  (PREF.) ERO(TO)
  (SUFF.) PHIL(A)(AE)(E)(IA)
  (ISM)(IST)(OUS)(US)(Y)
LOVED DEAR BELOVED
  (MUCH —) SWEET
LOVE FEAST AGAPE
LOVE KNOT AMORET
LOVELINESS BEAUTY
LOVELOCK EARLOCK
LOVELY DREAMY LOVING TENDER
  AMIABLE AMOROUS ADORABLE
  LOVESOME
LOVEMAKING AMOUR
LOVER GRA LAD MAN BEAU CHAP
  AMANT AMOUR DRURY LEMAN
  ROMEO SPARK SWAIN AMADIS
  AMANTE MARROW MINION
  SQUIRE ADMIRER AMORIST
  AMOROSO CELADON GALLANT
  PATRIOT SPARKER SPECIAL
  SPRUNNY AMORETTO BELAMOUR
  CASANOVA CICISBEO PARAMOUR
  STREPHON
  (MODEL —) LEILAH
  (SILLY —) SPOON
LOVE SEAT CAUSEUSE
LOVE'S LABOR'S LOST (AUTHOR
  OF —) SHAKESPEARE
  (CHARACTER IN —) DULL MOTH
  BOYET MARIA ARMADO DUMAIN
  ADRIANO BEROWNE COSTARD
  MERCADE ROSALINE FERDINAND
  KATHERINE NATHANIEL
  HOLOFERNES JAQUENETTA
  LONGAVILLE
LOVING DEAR FOND TENDER
  AMATORY AMOROUS
  (PREF.) PHIL(O)
  (SUFF.) PHIL(A)(AE)(E)(OUS)(US)
LOW BAS BOO LAW MOO BASE
  BASS KEEN MEAN NEAP OPEN
  ORRA ROUT SLOW VILE WEAK
  BLORE DIRTY GROSS HEDGE
  LAICH PUTID SHORT SMALL
  SNIDE THIRD CALLOW EARTHY
  FILTHY GENTLE GRUBBY HARLOT
  HUMBLE LIMMER MENIAL ORNERY
  RASCAL RIBALD SECRET SHABBY
  SILKEN TURPID VULGAR BESTIAL
  IGNOBLE RAFFISH REPTILE
  SLAVISH SUBMISS SOUTERLY
  (— AS OF A VOWEL) OPEN
  (— DOWN) SIDE
  (— IN LIGHTNESS) DULL
  (— IN PERCEPTION) CRUDE
  (— IN PITCH) GRAVE
  (— IN PRICE) MODERATE
  (— IN QUALITY) HEDGE
  (— IN SATURATION) GRAYISH
  (— IN SPIRITS) BLUE DOWN
  GLOOMY DOWNCAST
  (— IN TONE) SOFT SUBMISS
  (— IN WATER) RACE
  (— NUMBERS) MANQUE
  (— POINT) TROUGH
  (IMMEASURABLY —) ABYSMAL
  (PREF.) CHAMAE CHAME TAPIN(O)
LOWBORN WAFF

LOWBRED BASTARD PLEBEIAN
LOW-DOWN BUCKASS
LOWER CUT DIP LOW BASE BATE
  DOWN DROP DUCK FELL SINK
  VAIL ABASE ABATE ALLOY AVALE
  BELOW BLAME COUCH COWER
  DECRY DEMIT DOUSE FROWN
  GLOOM LEVEL SCOWL STOOP
  BEMEAN DEBASE DEJECT
  DEMEAN EMBASE GLOWER
  HUMBLE JUNIOR LESSEN MODIFY
  NETHER REDUCE SETTLE STRIKE
  SUBDUE SUBMIT BENEATH
  DECLASS DEGRADE DEPRESS
  SHORTEN DIMINISH DOWNWARD
  INFERIOR MODERATE
  (— BANNER) VAIL
  (— BY HALF STEP) FLAT
  (— IN ESTEEM) CHEAPEN
  DEROGATE
  (— IN PITCH) FLAT SHADE
  (— ONESELF) SINK BEMEAN
  DESCEND
  (— PRICES) BEAR
  (— SAIL) AMAIN
  (— THE HEAD) STOOP
  (PREF.) BATH(O)(Y) CATO INFERO
  INFRA NERTERO
  (— IN STATUS) INFRA
  (MAKE —) DE
LOWERING DIP DUCK DOWLY
  HEAVY LAPSE BEETLE SULLEN
  PEJORATION
  (— OF BODY) FONDU
  (— OF LAND) ABLATION
LOWEST LAST LEAST EXTREME
  LOWMOST PRIMARY PARAVAIL
  NETHERMOST
  (— CLASS) LAG
  (— POSSIBLE) KNOWDOWN
LOWING MUGIENT
LOWLAND LAICH POLDER
  LALLAND DOWNLAND
  (— BESIDE RIVER) INKS
  (BARREN —) LANDES
LOWLANDER SAXON ZHMUD
  SASSENACH
LOWLIER LESS
LOWLY LOW BASE SILLY HUMBLE
  BASEBORN
LOW-LYING CALLOW LALLAN
  INFERIAL SUBJECTED
LOW-MINDED BASE MEAN
LOWNESS LOWTH
  (— OF PITCH) GRAVITY
  (— OF SPIRITS) GLOOM SPLEEN
  MEGRIMS
LOW-PITCHED GRUFF
LOW-SPIRITED HIPPED DEJECTED
LOW SUNDAY QUASIMODO
LOY SLICK
LOYAL FAST FEAL FIRM HOLD LEAL
  REAL TRUE LIEGE PIOUS SOUND
  ARDENT HEARTY LAWFUL SECRET
  STANCH CONSTANT FAITHFUL
  STALWART YEOMANLY
LOYALIST TORY
LOYALLY SURELY
LOYALTY ARDOR FAITH FEALTY
  HOMAGE LEALTY REALTY SPIRIT
  REALITY DEVOTION FIDELITY
  CONSTANCY NATIONALISM
LOZENGE TAB JUBE COIGN QUOIN

  CACHOU JUJUBE MASCLE PASTIL
  QUARRY ROTULA RUSTRE TABLET
  TABULE TROCHE CREMULE
  DIAMOND TABELLA PASTILLE
  ROSEDROP
  (— OF CEMENT) WAFER
LOZI ROZI BAROTSE
LSD ACID
LUBBER LOUT SWAB LOOBY
  SLOUCH LOBCOCK LILBURNE
LUBBERLY AWKWARD
LUBRICANT DOPE GREASE
  AQUADAG UNGUENT
LUBRICATE OIL DOPE GLIB GREASE
  LUBRIFY
LUBRICATOR OILER OILCAN
LUCARNE LUCOMBE
LUCE GED
LUCENT BRIGHT LUCIBLE
LUCERNE LEGUME ALFALFA
LUCIA DI LAMMERMOOR
  (CHARACTER IN —) LUCY EDGAR
  HENRY ARTHUR ASHTON
  BUCKLOW RAVENSWOOD
  (COMPOSER OF —) DONIZETTI
LUCIANA (SISTER OF —) ADRIANA
LUCID SANE CLEAR AERIAL BRIGHT
  LIMPID CRYSTAL DILUCID
  LITERATE LUCULENT LUMINOUS
LUCIDITY SANITY CLARITY
LUCIFER DEVIL PHOSPHOR
LUCK HAP CESS EURE SONS SPIN
  GRACE ISSUE CHANCE THRIFT
  FORTUNE HANDSEL SUCCESS
  VENTURE HAMINGJA
  (BAD —) ACE DOLE DEUCE
  HOODOO UNLUCK AMBSACE
  MISCHANCE
  (BAD — TO YOU) YLAHAYLL
  (GOOD —) HAP FORTUNE
  THEEDOM
  (ILL —) UNHAP DIRDUM DISGRACE
  MISHANTER
  (RELATING TO —) ALEATORY
  (UNEXPECTED —) BUNCE
LUCKILY HAPPILY
LUCKY HOT CANNY HAPPY JAMMY
  SEELY SONSY CHANCY LUCKLY
  LUCKFUL GRACIOUS
  PROVIDENTIAL
LUCRATIVE FAT GOOD GAINFUL
LUCRE SWAG DROSS
LUCREZIA BORGIA (CHARACTER IN
  —) ALFONSO GENNARO LUCREZIA
  (COMPOSER OF —) DONIZETTI
LUD (FATHER OF —) SHEM
LUDICROUS AWFUL COMIC DROLL
  ABSURD COMICAL FOOLISH
  HIDEOUS RISIBLE FARCICAL
  BURLESQUE
LUDO UCKERS
LUFF DERRICK
LUFFA LOOFAH SPONGE
LUG EAR HUG TUG WAG SNUG
  SPUD TOTE ZULU PATCH WALTZ
LUGGAGE SWAG TRAPS HATBOX
  BAGGAGE TRUSSERY
  (AIRPLANE —) CARRYON
LUGGAGE CASE IMPERIAL
LUGGAR JAGGAR JUGGER LAGGAR
LUGGER CAT TOUP ZULU FIFIE
LUGUBRIOUS BLACK TEARY
  BALEFUL DOLEFUL DOLOROUS

LUGWORM LOB LUG LOBWORM SANDWORM
LUIGINO TEMIN
LUISA MILLER (CHARACTER IN —) WURM LUISA MILLER WALTER RODOLFO FREDERICA
(COMPOSER OF —) VERDI
LUKEWARM LEW LUKE TEPID WLACH
LULL CALM DRUG FODE HUSH ROCK CROON HUSHO LETUP SLACK STILL SOPITE HUSHABY HUSHEEN
LULLABY LULL BALOO BALOW LULLAY HUSHABY HUSHEEN ROCKABY
LULLING DROWSY CIRCEAN
LULU DOOZY DOOZER SNORTER HUMDINGER
LUMBER BURR DEAL RAFF NANMU STOCK STRIP CUMBER FINISH FLITCH RAFFLE REFUSE SAMCHU SHORTS TIMBER DEGRADE DUNNAGE GUMWOOD RUMMAGE TRUNDLE STEPPING
(INFERIOR —) SAPS SCOOT
LUMBERING AWKWARD LUMBERLY LUMBROUS
LUMBERJACK JACK LOGGER TOPPER TIMBERER
LUMBERMAN PINER DOGGER SCORER CHOPPER GIRDLER TIMBERER
LUMINANCE HELIOS
LUMINARY LIGHT CANDLE PLANET
LUMINESCENCE FLAME
LUMINOSITY FIRE GLOW LIGHT VALUE
LUMINOUS LIGHT LUCID SHINY BRIGHT LUMINANT
LUMMOX LOBSTER PALOOKA
LUMP BAT BOB COB CUB DAB DAD FID GOB JOB LOB NIB NOB NUB WAD BLOB BURL CLAG CLAM CLOT COOL COWL DUNT JUNK KNOB KNOT NIRL PONE SWAD TOKE BLOOM BUNCH CHUCK CHUNK CLAUT CLUMP CLUNK GLEBE HUNCH KNOLL KNURL MOUSE SLUMP STONE WEDGE WODGE CLUNCH DOLLOP GOBBET HUBBLE HUDDLE LUMPET NUBBLE NUGGET CLUMPER CLUNTER PUMPKNOT
(— IN CLOTH) BURL
(— IN GLASS) YOLK
(— OF BLACK LEAD) SOP
(— OF BLOOD) CLOD
(— OF CLAY) BAT
(— OF COAL) NUBBLING
(— OF DOUGH) DIP
(— OF FAT) KEECH
(— OF GLASS) BLOOM
(— OF IRON) OOLLY
(— OF LAVA) BOMB
(— OF LINT) SLUG
(— OF MEAT) OLIVE
(— OF METAL) MASS SLUG
(— OF ORE) ROCK HARDHEAD
(— OF RUBBER) THIMBLE
(— OF SALT) SALTCAT
(— OF WOOD) CHUMP
(— OF YEAST) BEE

(— ON HORSE'S BACK) SITFAST
(— ON SKIN) MILIUM
(LARGE —) BLAD DOLL HUNK
(LITTLE —) NODULE KNOBBLE
(ROUNDED —) CLOT
(PREF.) THROMB(O)
LUMPFISH GROSS PADDLE SUCKER
LUMPISH STODGY CHUCKLE
LUMPSUCKER PADDLE
LUMPY GOBBY CHUNKY CLOGGY CLUNCH COBBLY STODGY BUNCHED
LUNACY MOON FOLLY MADNESS DELIRIUM INSANITY
LUNARIA SATINPOD
LUNARY VOLVELLE
LUNATIC GELT LOONY BEDLAM MADMAN MANIAC FANATIC FRANTIC CRACKPOT MOONLING MOONSICK
LUNCH CUT BAIT CRIB TIFF BEVER PIECE SNACK BRUNCH NACKET TIFFIN UNDERN BAGGING ELEVENS DEJEUNER DRINKING ELEVENER LUNCHEON NUNCHEON COLLATION
(DAIRY —) CREMERIE
(MINER'S —) SNAP
LUNCHEON CRIB LUNCH STULL TIFFIN DEJEUNE DINETTE NOONMEAT
LUNCHROOM EATERY
LUNETTE OUTWORK
LUNG PULMO DRAGON LONGUE
(PREF.) PNEO PNEUM(A)(ATO)(O)(ON)(ONO) PULMO PULMON(I)
LUNGE FOIN PASS SPAR POINT VENUE CHARGE ALLONGE
LUNGFISH CYCLOID DIPNOAN MUDFISH SIRENOID
LUNGS LIGHTS VISCUS BELLOWS
(PERTAINING TO —) PULMONIC
LUNKHEAD DOLT JUGHEAD
LUNULE ALBEDO
LUO DHOLUO
LUPINE SUNDIAL
LURCH JOLL STOT SWAG PITCH STOIT CAREEN STOITER STUMBLE SWAGGER
LURCHING DRUNKEN ROLLING
LURE CON JAY BAIT HOOK ROPE TOLL WISE DECOY DRILL FEINT SLOCK SNARE SNOOK SPOON SQUID STALE TEMPT TROLL ALLURE CAPPER CLARET ENTICE ENTRAP RABATE SEDUCE TREPAN VELURE GUDGEON INVEIGH PHANTOM PITFALL WOBBLER BUCKTAIL INVEIGLE LUREMENT
(— INTO GAMBLING) HUSTLE
(— OF CARRION) TRAIN
(— WILDFOWL) STOOL
LURI ALUR
LURID RED PURPLE SULTRY CRIMSON GHASTLY
LURK DARE LOUT COUCH LOWER SKULK SLINK SNEAK AMBUSH DARKLE
LURKING LURKY GRASSANT LATITANT
LUSCIOUS FOND RICH SWEET CREAMY DULCET DELICATE

LUSH RICH GREEN LUSTY MOIST SAVORY FERTILE OPULENT PROFUSE THRIVING
LUST HELL KAMA BLOOD PRIDE DESIRE LIBIDO LIKING LUXURY NICETY PASSION COVETISE CUPIDITY CARNALITY
(SUFF.) LAGNIA
LUSTER NAIF GLASS GLINT GLOSS SHEEN SHINE WATER LUSTRE POLISH REFLET BURNISH GLIMPSE GLISTER LUSTRUM NITENCY FULGENCE LUSTRATE RADIANCY SPLENDOR
(— OF FIBER) BLOOM
(BRONZE-LIKE —) SCHILLER
LUSTERLESS WAN DEAD DULL FISHY STARY
LUSTFUL HOT GAMY GOLE LEWD RANK SALT CADGY LUSTY PRIME RANDY RUTTY WANTON BEASTLY CODDING FLESHLY FULSOME GOATISH JEALOUS RAMMISH RUTTISH LIKEROUS SALACIOUS
LUSTFULNESS SATYRISM
LUSTILY CRANK HOTLY
LUSTING ITCHY
LUSTRATION ABHISEKA
LUSTROUS CLEAR DOGGY NITID BRIGHT GLOSSY ORIENT SHEENY SILKEN SILVER SHINING SPLENDID
LUSTY BRAG CANT BURLY CRANK FLUSH FRACK FRANK FRECK GUTSY HARDY JUICY RANDY STIFF STOUT GAWSIE ROBUST STURDY LUSTFUL LUSTICK BOUNCING PHYSICAL SKELPING SPORTIVE VIGOROUS
LUTE TAR BIWA LAUD DOMRA NABIA NABLE REBAB REBEC SAROD CITOLE ENLUTE LORICA LUTING SCREED VIELLE ANGELOT BANDORE DICHORD DYPHONE MANDOLA MANDORE MINIKIN PANDORE THEORBO VIHUELA ANGELICA ARCHLUTE PENORCON TAMBOURA TEMPLATE TRICHORD
LUTER DAUBER PASTER
LUTJANID JEWFISH

LUXEMBOURG

CAPITAL: LUXEMBOURG
HIGHEST POINT: BURGPLATZ
LOWLAND: BONPAYS GUTLAND
MEASURE: FUDER
MOUNTAIN RANGE: ARDENNES
PLATEAU: ARDENNES
RIVER: OUR SURE SAUER ALZETTE MOSELLE
TOWN: BOUS EICH ROODT WILTZ PETANGE VIANDEN DIEKIRCH DUDELANGE ETTELBRUCK DIFFERDANGE

LUXURIANT GOLE LUSH RANK RICH FRANK PROUD LAVISH WANTON OPULENT PROFUSE RAMPANT TEEMING PAMPERED PRODIGAL
LUXURIANTLY FATLY
LUXURIATE BASK REVEL FROWST WALLOW WANTON
LUXURIOUS HIGH LUSH NICE

POSH RANK SOFT GAUDY PLUSH SWANK CAPUAN DELUXE GILDED PALACE SILKEN SWANKY WANTON APICIAN ELEGANT DELICATE LUCULLAN PRODIGAL REGALADO SENSUOUS TRYPHENA TRYPHOSA
LUXURIOUSLY HIGH DELUXE
LUXURY FRILL FINERY OUTRAGE DELICACY ELEGANCE PLEASURE RICHNESS PRINCELINESS
LUXURY-LOVING DELICATE
LYCANTHROPE WEREWOLF
LYCAON (DAUGHTER OF —) CALLISTO
(FATHER OF —) PELASGUS
LYCEUM PLATFORM
LYCHNIS FIREBALL NONESUCH
LYCIUM RUSOT
LYCOPODIUM MOSS FOXTAIL CROWFOOT STAGHORN
LYCURGUS (BROTHER OF —) POLYDECTES
(FATHER OF —) DRYAS EUNOMUS
(SON OF —) OPHELTES
LYCUS (BROTHER OF —) AEGEUS PALLAS IPHINOE
(FATHER OF —) PANDION
(MOTHER OF —) PYLIA
(WIFE OF —) DIRCE
LYDIA MAEONIA
LYE LEY BOUK BUCK STRAKE LESSIVE LIXIVIUM SOAPLEES
LYING FLAT FALSE LEASE CRETISM LEASING MENTERY ACCUBATION MENDACIOUS
(— APART) DISSITE
(— AT BASE OF MOUNTAINS) PIEDMONT
(— CLOSE) QUAT
(— DOWN) DOWN LODGED CUMBENT DORMANT COUCHANT
(— HID) LATITANT
(— IDLE) INACTIVE
(— ON BACK) SUPINE
(— ON FACE) PRONE PROCUMBENT
(— OVER) JACENT
(— UNDER GRASS) LEA
LYING-IN INLYING CHILDBED GROANING
LYMPH CHYLE VIRUS
(PREF.) CHYL(O)
(SUFF.) CHYLIA
LYMPHAD GALLEY
LYMPHANGITIS WEED FILLING
LYMPHATIC LACTEAL
LYMPHOGRANULOMA BUBO
LYMPHOMATOSIS FISHEYE
LYNCEUS (BROTHER OF —) IDAS
(FATHER OF —) AEGYPTUS APHAREUS
(WIFE OF —) HYPERMNESTRA
LYNCH HANG DEWITT
LYNX LOSSE OUNCE PISHU BOBCAT GORKUN LUCERN CARACAL LUCIVEE WILDCAT CARCAJOU
LYRE ASOR HARP LYRA SHELL CHELYS KINNOR KISSAR TRIGON CITHARA TESTUDO BARBITON PHORMINX TRICHORD TRIGONON
LYREBIRD LYRETAIL PHEASANT
LYRIC LAY LIED HOKKU LAEAN MELIC GHAZEL TENSON CANCION

CHANSON DESCORT MADRIGAL
(HAVING — AND DRAMATIC
QUALITIES) SPINTO

(LOVE —) ALBA
(PL.) SONG
LYSIPPE (FATHER OF —) PROETUS

(HUSBAND OF —) MELAMPUS
(MOTHER OF —) ANTIA
(SISTER OF —) IPHINOE IPHINASSA

LYTTA WORM

M

M EM EMMA MIKE METRO
  (WRONG USE OF —) MYTACISM
M-1 GARAND
MAACAH (HUSBAND OF —) DAVID
  (SON OF —) ABSALOM
MAACHAH (FATHER OF —) NAHOR
  URIEL TALMAI
  (HUSBAND OF —) JEHIEL MACHIR
  REHOBOAM
  (MOTHER OF —) REUMAH
  (SON OF —) HANAN ABIJAH
  ACHISH ABSALOM SHEPHATIAH
MAADAI (FATHER OF —) BANI
MA'AM MARM MISTRESS
MAARIB ARBIT ARBITH
MAASEIAH (FATHER OF —) ADAIAH
  BARUCH SHALLUM
  (SON OF —) AZARIAH ZEDEKIAH
  ZEPHANIAH
MAATH (FATHER OF —)
  MATTATHIAS
MAAZ (FATHER OF —) RAM
MACA ENIMAGA
MACABRE SICK HORRIBLE
MACACA PITHECUS
MACADAMIZE METAL
MACAO (CHINESE NAME OF —)
  AOMEN
  (ISLAND OF —) TAIPA COLOANE
MACAQUE KRA BROH BRUH
  MACAC TOQUE MACHIN RHESUS
  RILAWA WANDEROO
MACARIA (FATHER OF —)
  HERCULES
  (MOTHER OF —) DEIANIRA
MACARIZE LAUD
MACARONI DITALI
MACARONIC SKEW
MACAW ARA ARARA PARROT
  MARACAN ARACANGA COCKATOO
MACBETH (AUTHOR OF —)
  SHAKESPEARE
  (CHARACTER IN —) ROSS ANGUS
  BANQUO DUNCAN HECATE
  LENNOX SEYTON SIWARD
  FLEANCE MACBETH MACDUFF
  MALCOLM MENTEITH CAITHNESS
  DONALBAIN
MACE CROC MALL MAUL POKER
  VERGE MALLET SPARTH CATTAIL
  (PART OF —) HEAD HILT SPIKE
  FLANGE HANDLE
  (REED —) DOD DODD
  (ROYAL —) SCEPTER SCEPTRE
MACE-BEARER BEADLE VERGER
  MACEMAN
MACERATE RET SOUR STEEP
MACHAON (BROTHER OF —)
  PODALIRIUS
  (FATHER OF —) AESCULAPIUS
  (MOTHER OF —) CORONIS
MACHETE GULOC PARANG
  CURTAXE CUTLASH CUTLASS

MACHI (COMPANION OF —) CALEB
  JOSHUA
  (SON OF —) GEUEL
MACHIAVELLIAN CRAFTY
  CUNNING GUILEFUL
MACHINATION ARTIFICE INTRIGUE
  SCHEMERY
MACHINE (ALSO SEE DEVICE AND
  ENGINE) GIN HOG JIG SAW AGER
  BABY COMB GEAR JACK LIFT
  MULE PUMP RASP TRAY WHIM
  WINK ADDER AWNER BALER
  BENCH BILLY BOARD BRAKE
  BREAK COPER CRANE DEVIL
  EDGER ERNIE FRAME FUDGE
  FUGAL JENNY JERRY JOLLY
  LATHE LAYER METER MIXER
  MOWER NAVVY RAKER RESAW
  ROVER SCREW SETUP SHEEN
  SIZER STAMP SULKY TRONE
  VINER WILLY BARKER BEADER
  BEAMER BEATER BEETLE BENDER
  BILLER BINDER BOLTER BUCKLE
  BUMPER BUTTER CANTER
  CAPPER CARDER CONCHE
  COOLER CREWER DECKER
  DOFFER DONKEY DRAPER
  DREDGE DUSTER ENGINE FLAKER
  FOLDER FOOTER FORMER
  GADDER GAPPER GLAZER
  GRADER GRATER GUMMER
  HEADER HEMMER HOBBER
  HOGGER HOOPER HULLER
  HUSKER IRONER JIGGER JORDAN
  KICKER LEGGER LIFTER LINTER
  LOGGER MAILER MANGLE MILLER
  MITRER NAPPER NETTER NIBBER
  NIPPER PACKER PEGGER PINNER
  PLATER PUMPER RIPPER ROSSER
  ROTARY ROUTER SANDER
  SCUTCH SEALER SEAMER SHAKER
  SHAPER SHAVER SINGER SKIVER
  SLICER SORTER SPACER STOCKS
  STOKER TEDDER TENTER TWINER
  VANNER WASHER WELDER
  WILLOW ABRADER AUTOMAT
  AVIATOR BACKHOE BATCHER
  BELLOWS BLENDER BLUNGER
  BOTTLER BRANNER BREAKER
  CANDROY CAPSTAN CHIPPER
  COMBINE CRUSHER DIBBLER
  DRESSER EMULSOR ENCODER
  ENROBER ERECTOR EXOSTRA
  FLANGER FLOSSER FREEZER
  GARNETT GLASSER GRAINER
  GRINDER GROOVER GROUTER
  HUMIDOR IRONMAN JOINTER
  KNITTER KNOTTER MACHINA
  MANGLER MATCHER MITERER
  PERRIER PLODDER PLUCKER
  POTCHER PRINTER QUILLER
  REPRESS RIVETER ROASTER
  SAMMIER SCALPER SHEARER

  SHEETER SIROCCO SLABBER
  SLASHER SLITTER SLOTTER
  SLUBBER SLUGGER SMASHER
  SPALLER SPEEDER SPINNER
  SPONGER SPOOLER SPRAYER
  STACKER STAMPER STAPLER
  STEAMER STEMMER STICKER
  TENONER TEREBRA TOOTHER
  TRAMPER TREATER TRIMMER
  TRUSSER TWILLER TWISTER
  TYPOBAR WHIPPER WHIZZER
  AERIFIER AIRCRAFT BROACHER
  CALENDER CANCELER CARTONER
  CLINCHER COLLATOR COMPRESS
  DUNGBECK ELEPHANT EXPLODER
  EXTRUDER FILATORY FINISHER
  FLYWINCH FORKLIFT GATHERER
  HARDENER HAYMAKER HERCULES
  HUMMELER IMPACTER KILLIFER
  MORTISER MOULINET ODOGRAPH
  OROGRAPH PROFILER PULSATOR
  SCHIFFLI SCUTCHER SHREDDER
  SOFTENER SPLITTER SPREADER
  SPRIGGER SQUEEZER STITCHER
  STRANDER STRIPPER SURFACER
  TEMPERER THREADER THRESHER
  THROSTLE TRAVELER TRISPAST
  TUNNELER UPSETTER WINNOWER
  ADDRESSER
MACHINE GUN STINGER
  CHAUCHAT
MACHINERY MINT TOPCAP
  SUCCULA APPARATUS
MACHINE SHOP TURNERY
MACHINIST FRILLER THINNER
  MACHINER
MACHIR (FATHER OF —) AMMIEL
  MANASSEH
MACHISMO MACHO
MACHNADEBAI (FATHER OF —)
  BANI
MACKEREL CHAD PETO SCAD TINK
  BLINK OPELU SNOEK TUNNY
  BONITO SAUREL TINKER BLINKER
  BLOATER SCOMBER TASSARD
  ALBACORE HARDHEAD SCOMBRID
  SEERFISH
  (— ABOUT 8 OR 9 INCHES) TINK
  TINKER
  (PICKLED —) SCALPEEN
  (POOR BONY —) SLINK SLINKER
  (YOUNG —) SPIKE
  (PREF.) SCOMBRI
MACKLE SLUR SHAKE MACULA
MACROGAMETE OVUM
MACROSCOPIC GROSS
MACROSPECIES LINNEON
MAD FEY AWAY GITE GYTE HYTE
  WOOD YOND ANGRY BATTY
  BRAIN CRAZY DIPPY FOLLE RABID
  BEDLAM FRENZY INSANE MANIAC
  WOODEN BERSERK BONKERS
  FANATIC FRANTIC FURIOUS

  LUNATIC MADDING MADDOCK
  MANKIND REDWOOD WITLESS
  DELIRANT DEMENTED DISTRACT
  INFORMAL MANIACAL MINDLESS
  RAVENING POSSESSED

MADAGASCAR

CAPITAL: ANTANANARIVO
FORMER NAME:
  MALAGASYREPUBLIC
ISLAND GROUP: ALDABRA
LAKE: ITASY ALAOTRA
MEASURE: GANTANG
NATIVE: HOVA SAKALAVA
PEOPLE: HOVA COTIER MARINA
RIVER: IKOPA MANIA SOFIA
  MANGOKY MANGORO ONYLAHY
TOWN: IHOSY MANJA TULEAR
  MAJANGA NOSSIBE TSIVORY
  TAMATAVE ANTISIRABE

MADAI (FATHER OF —) JAPHET
MADAM MEM MUM BAWD MAAM
  PANI DONNA MADAME SENORA
  SENHORA SIGNORA GOODWIFE
  MISTRESS SINEBADA
MADAMA BUTTERFLY
  (CHARACTER IN —) SUZUKI
  CIOCIOSAN PINKERTON
  SHARPLESS
  (COMPOSER OF —) PUCCINI
MADAME BOVARY (AUTHOR OF —)
  FLAUBERT
  (CHARACTER IN —) EMMA LEON
  BOVARY DUPUIS HOMAIS
  CHARLES HELOISE ROUAULT
  LHEUREUX RODOLPHE
  BOULANGER
MADAR YERCUM
MADDEN ENRAGE INCENSE
  INFLAME DISTRACT
MADDENED ENRAGED FRENZIED
MADDER GAMENE LIZARY ALIZARI
  GARANCE MUNJEET TANAGRA
  GARANCIN SPURWORT
  WOODRUFF
MAD-DOG SKULLCAP MADWEED
  HOODWORT
MADE SET BUILT COMPACT
  PREPARED TIMBERED
  (— FLUID BY HEAT) FUSILE
  (— OF DISSIMILAR PARTS) MIXED
  (— OF FLAX) LINEN
  (— OF GRAIN) OATEN CEREAL
  (— OF IVORY) EBURNEAN
  (— OF SILVER) ARGENT
  (— OF STONE) STONEN
  (— OF TWIGS) VIRGAL
  (— SHORT) CURTAL
  (— TART) EUCHRED
  (— TO ORDER) BESPOKEN
  (— TRANSLUCENT) AJOURE
  (— UP) ACCRETE

(— WITH CEDAR) CEDARN
(PREF.) (— OF) DIA
(SUFF.) (— OF) INE
MADE-BEAVER SKIN CASTOR
MADEIRA ISLANDS (ISLAND OF —)
GRANDE DEZERTE
(TOWN OF —) FUNCHAL
(WINE OF —) BUAL TINTA
MALMSEY SERCIAL VERDELHO
MADELON POLIXENE
MADHOUSE ASYLUM BEDLAM
MADHUCA BASSIA ILLIPE
MADLY WOOD CRAZY
MADMAN GELT BEDLAM MANIAC
FURIOSO LUNATIC WOODMAN
MADNESS MAD FURY MOON
WOOD FOLIE FOLLY FUROR
MANIA BEDLAM FRENZY LUNACY
DEWANEE ECSTASY MOONERY
WIDDRIM DELIRIUM DEMENTIA
PIBLOKTO WILLNESS WOODNESS
WOODSHIP
(PREF.) LYSSO MANIC
(SUFF.) MANE MANIA(C)
MADONNA LADY VIRGIN
MADREPORE FUNGID
MADRIGAL ENSALADA
MADRONA LAUREL MANZANITA
MADTOM TADPOLE
MADWORT ALYSSUM BUGLOSS
MAENAD FROW BASSARID
BACCHANTE
(PL.) BACCHAE
MAFIC FEMIC
MAFURA ROKA ELOAJA
MAGANI BAGANI
MAGAZINE BOOK DRUM FLAT
IGLOO SLICK STORE RETORT
ALMACEN JOURNAL CASSETTE
(BLACKWOOD'S —) MAGA
MAGDALEN MAUDLIN
MAGGOT MAD GRUB MAWK
WORM METHE GENTLE WARBLE
WORMIL MADDOCK SKIPPER
MUCKWORM
MAGIC JUJU MAYA RUNE CRAFT
FAIRY GOETY SPELL TURGY
GOETIC TREGET VOODOO
ALCHEMY CANTRIP CONJURY
DEVILRY GLAMOUR GRAMARY
MAGICAL SORCERY BRUJERIA
HECATEAN WIZARDRY
NECROMANCY
(BLACK —) GOETY GOETIC
MALEFICE
(WHITE —) TURGY
MAGICAL WIZARD WONDER
HERMETIC NUMINOUS THEURGIC
**MAGIC FLUTE, THE (CHARACTER
IN —)** PAMINA TAMINO
PAPAGENA PAPAGENO SARASTRO
MONOSTATOS
(COMPOSER OF —) MOZART
MAGICIAN MAGE BOKOR MAGUS
UTHER CUNJAH GOETIC GOOFER
GUFFER MAGIAN MERLIN
WABENO WIZARD CHARMER
GWYDION KOSCHEI WARLOCK
WIELARE WISEMAN CONJURER
FETISHER SORCERER THEURGIC
TROLLMAN ARCHIMAGE
MAGIC MOUNTAIN (AUTHOR OF —)
MANN

(CHARACTER IN —) HANS NAPHTA
BEHRENS CASTORP CAUCHAT
CLAVDIA JOACHIM ZIEMSSEN
KROKOWSKI PEEPERKORN
SETTEMBRINI
MAGISTERIAL LOFTY PROUD
AUGUST CURULE LORDLY
HAUGHTY STATELY ARROGANT
DOGMATIC
MAGISTERY MASTERY
MAGISTRACY AMT PRYTANY
MAGISTRATE BEAK FOUD EPHOR
JUDGE JURAT MAYOR PRIOR
REEVE AMTMAN ARCHON
AVOYER BAILIE BAILLI CENSOR
CONSUL FISCAL KOTWAL SYNDIC
ALCALDE BAILIFF BURGESS
DUUMVIR ECHEVIN EPHORUS
JUSTICE NOMARCH PODESTA
PRAETOR PREFECT PROVOST
STEWARD SUFFETE TRIBUNE
ALABARCH ALDERMAN CAPITOUL
DEFENSOR DEMIURGE DICTATOR
GOVERNOR MITTIMUS PHYLARCH
PRYTANIS RECORDER STRADICO
STRATEGE HUNDREDER
CORREGIDOR
(— IN CHANNEL ISLANDS) JURAT
(— OF ANCIENT ROME) EDILE
(— OF VENICE AND GENOA) DOGE
(MOHAMMEDAN —) CADI CADY
SHERIF
(SCOTCH —) PROVOST STEWARD
MAGMA ICHOR
MAGMATIC JUVENILE
MAGNANIMITY HEIGHT FREEDOM
MAGNANIMOUS BIG FREE GREAT
LARGE LOFTY NOBLE HEROIC
EXALTED GENEROUS
MAGNATE BARON MOGUL
BASHAW TYCOON
MAGNESIA PULVIL
MAGNET FIELD ADAMAS MAGNES
ADAMANT SOLENOID TERRELLA
MAGNETISM IT DEVIL OOMPH
MAGNETITE LOADSTONE
LODESTONE
MAGNETIZE TOUCH SATURATE
MAGNETOMETER DOODLEBUG
MAGNIFICATION POWER
MAGNIFICENCE GITE POMP FLARE
GLORY STATE PARADE JOLLITY
ROYALTY GRANDEUR SPLENDOR
MAGNIFICENT RIAL GRAND NOBLE
PROUD ROYAL AUGUST LAVISH
IMMENSE POMPOUS STATELY
SUBLIME GLORIOUS GORGEOUS
MAGNIFIC PALATIAL PRINCELY
SPLENDID
**MAGNIFICENT OBSESSION
(AUTHOR OF —)** DOUGLAS
(CHARACTER IN —) BRENT HELEN
JOYCE NANCY WAYNE DAWSON
HUDSON ROBERT ASHFORD
MERRICK
MAGNIFY LAUD BLESS ERECT
EXALT PRAISE ADVANCE DISTEND
ENLARGE GLORIFY GREATEN
INCREASE MAXIMIZE MULTIPLY
**MAGNIFYING
(PREF.)** MICR(O)
MAGNIFYING GLASS LOUPE
READER

MAGNILOQUENT TURGID
BOMBAST
MAGNITUDE BULK MASS SIZE
DATUM LEVEL SOLID EXTENT
FIGURE PERIOD EXTREME
CONSTANT FUNCTION INFINITE
MAGNOLIA YULAN BIGBLOOM
CUCUMBER MAURICIO
(— STATE) MISSISSIPPI
MAGOG (FATHER OF —) JAPHETH
MAGPIE MAG PIE PIET PYAT CISSA
KOTRI MADGE NINUT MARGET
NANPIE PIANET PIEMAG SIRGANG
HAGISTER MARGARET PHEASANT
PIENANNY
MAGPIE LARK PEEWEE GRALLINA
MAGPIE ROBIN DAYAL DHYAL
MAGUEY AGAVE MESCAL
CANTALA
MAGYAR SZEKEL SZEKLER
MAHALAH (MOTHER OF —)
HAMMOLEKETH
(UNCLE OF —) GILEAD
MAHALATH (FATHER OF —)
ISHMAEL JERIMOTH
(HUSBAND OF —) ESAU REHOBOAM
MAHALI (FATHER OF —) MERARI
MAHATMA SAGE ARHAT
MAHAZIOTH (FATHER OF —)
HEMAN
MAH-JONGG WOO
MAHLAH (FATHER OF —)
ZELOPHEHAD
MAHLI (FATHER OF —) MUSHI
MERARI
MAHLON (DAUGHTER OF —) NAOMI
(SON OF —) ELIMELECH
(WIFE OF —) RUTH
MAHOE EMAJAGUA
MAHOGANY SIPO ALMON CAOBA
CEDAR ROHAN ACAJOU AGUANO
SAPELE THITKA ALBARCO
AVODIRE BAYWOOD GUNNUNG
MADEIRA RATTEEN TABASCO
BANGALAY HARDTACK TANGUILE
(INDIAN —) TOON
(PHILIPPINE —) BAGTIKAN
MAHONIA ASHBERRY ODOSTEMON
MAHOUND MACON
MAHUA FULWA MOWHA MOWRA
MADHUCA PHULWARA
MAHUANG EPHEDRA
MAIA (FATHER OF —) ATLAS
(MOTHER OF —) PLEIONE
(SON OF —) MERCURY
MAID MAY AYAH GIRL LASS MEDE
SLUT CHINA WENCH WOMAN
MAIDEN SLAVEY TWEENY VIRGIN
ANCILLA GENERAL MAIDKIN
PHYLLIS PUCELLE WENCHEL
BONIBELL BRANGANE HANDMAID
SUIVANTE TIREMAID
(— IN WAITING) DAMSEL DAMOZEL
(— OF HONOR) MARIE
(— OF-ALL-WORK) SLAVEY
GENERAL
(KITCHEN —) SCOGIE
(LADY'S —) AYAH ABIGAIL
TIREMAID
(NURSE —) BONNE
(OLD —) TABBY SPINSTER
(WAITING —) ABIGAIL SUIVANTE
MAIDEN MAY BIRD BURD DAME

GIRL MAID DALAGA DAMSEL
FROKIN MEISJE COLLEEN CYDIPPE
DAMOZEL MADCHEN
DAUGHTER
(— WITH BASKET ON HEAD)
CANEPHOR
(PREF.) PARTHENO
MAIDENHAIR GINGKO ADIANTUM
MAIDENLY VIRGIN GIRLISH
VIRGINAL
MAIDEN PINK SPINK DIANTHUS
MAIDSERVANT LASS BIDDY
BONNE SKIVVY ANCILLA LISETTE
MAIEUTIC HEBAMIC
MAIGRE BAR SCIAENID WEAKFISH
MAIL BAG DAK HOOD POST
MATTER AIRMAIL JACKPOT
MAILBAG ORDINAR POSTAGE
POSTBAG SEAPOST TAPPALL
ORDINARY
(IMPROPERLY ADDRESSED —) NIX
NIXY
MAILBAG BAG POUCH POSTBAG
MAILBOX POST PILLAR POSTBOX
MAILLECHORT ARGENTON
MAILLOT SWIMSUIT
MAILMAN POSTMAN BREVIGER
MAIM LAME BREAK TRUNK
HAMBLE MANGLE MAYHEM
SCOTCH CRIPPLE MUTILATE
TRUNCATE
(— AN ANIMAL) LAW MANK
MAIMED GAMMY SPAVINED
(PREF.) PERO
MAIN HIGH LINE MOST CHIEF
GRAND GREAT PRIME SHEER
MIGHTY CAPITAL LEADING
CARDINAL FOREMOST

MAINE
CAPITAL: AUGUSTA
COLLEGE: BATES COLBY BOWDOIN
COUNTY: KNOX WALDO KENNEBEC
AROOSTOOK PENOBSCOT
SAGADAHOC PISCATAQUIS
INDIAN: ABNAKI
LAKE: GRAND SEBEC SEBAGO
RANGELEY SCHOODIC
MOOSEHEAD CHESUNCOOK
MOUNTAIN: BIGELOW CADILLAC
KATAHDIN
NATIVE: MANIAC
RIVER: SACO KENNEBEC
AROOSTOOK KENNEBAGO
PENOBSCOT
STATE BIRD: CHICKADEE
STATE FLOWER: PINECONE
STATE NICKNAME: LUMBER
PINETREE
STATE TREE: PINE
TOWN: BATH ORONO AUBURN
BANGOR BELFAST HOULTON
KITTERY MACHIAS BOOTHBAY
LEWISTON OGUNQUIT
PORTLAND SKOWHEGAN

**MAINLAND
(PREF.)** EPEIRO
MAINLY BROADLY CHIEFLY
LARGELY
MAINSTAY KEY ATLAS SINEW
STOOP PILLAR BACKBONE
RELIANCE

MAIN STREET (AUTHOR OF —)
LEWIS
(CHARACTER IN —) ERIK HUGH
WILL CAROL MILFORD VALBORG
KENNICOTT
MAINTAIN AVOW BEAR FEND FIND
HOLD KEEP LAST SAVE ADOPT
ARGUE CARRY CLAIM ESCOT
SALVE ADHERE ALLEGE ASSERT
AVOUCH DEFEND INTEND RETAIN
THREAP UPHOLD UPKEEP
CONFIRM CONTEND DECLARE
DISPUTE JUSTIFY NOURISH
SUBSIST SUPPORT SUSTAIN
CONTINUE PRESERVE
(— AS TRUE) AVOUCH SOOTHE
(— POSITION) STALL
(— WITHOUT REASON) ARROGATE
MAINTAINER FOUNDER RETAINER
MAINTENANCE KEEP LIVING
UPKEEP ALIMONY CUSTODY
FINDING KEEPING PREBEND
SERVICE
(— OF POPULATION) BALANCE
MAITHILI TIRHUTIA
MAIZE CORN GRAIN CEREAL
INDIAN JAGONG STAPLE MEALIES
DJAGOONG
(— CRUSHED WITH PESTLE) STAMP
MAJAGUA HAU BARU BOLA MAHO
MOJO BURAO GUANA MAHOE
PURAU BALIBAGO CORKWOOD
EMAJAGUA
MAJESTIC HIGH AWFUL GRAND
LOFTY REGAL ROYAL AUGUST
KINGLY SUPERB STATELY
SUBLIME ELEVATED IMPERIAL
MAESTOSO SPLENDID
MAJESTY DIGNITY AUGUSTUS
GRANDEUR KINGSHIP
MAJOON BANG BHANG
MAJOR BEY DUR DURUM SHARP
CAPITAL GREATER MAGGIORE
MAJOR BARBARA (AUTHOR OF —)
SHAW
(CHARACTER IN —) LOMAX SARAH
CUSINS BARBARA CHARLES
STEPHEN ADOLPHUS BRITOMART
UNDERSHAFT
MAJORITY BODY BULK FECK
CORPSE SUBSTANCE
(ABSOLUTE —) QUORUM
MAKARAKA IDDIO
MAKARI KOTOKO
MAKE DO CUT GAR LET MAY FORM
GIVE LEVY BRAND BUILD CAUSE
COVER FETCH FORGE FRAME
SEIZE SHAPE STAMP AUTHOR
COBBLE CREATE GRAITH INDUCE
RENDER CONFECT FASHION
IMAGERY IWURCHE PERFORM
PRODUCE CONTRIVE GENERATE
(— A DIFFERENCE) SKILL
(— A MESS OF) PIE
(— A RUG) HOOK
(— A VISIT) COSHER
(— ACKNOWLEDGMENT) CONFESS
(— ACTIVE) ENERGIZE
(— AMENDS) ABYE ATONE ABEGGE
ANSWER REDEEM EXPIATE
REDRESS
(— ANGRY) GRAMY WRATH
(— ATTRACTIVE) GILD

(— AWAY WITH) ABOLISH
EMBEZZLE
(— BARE) STRIP DENUDE
(— BELIEVE) LET PRETEND
(— BETTER) AMEND HEIGHTEN
(— BLUE) HIP
(— BRIGHT) ENGILD ILLUME
CLARIFY
(— BRISK) PERK
(— BROWN) TAN
(— BY STAMPING) MINT
(— CANDLE) DIP DRAW
(— CERTAIN) ASSURE ENSURE
(— CHANNEL IN) THROAT
(— CHEERFUL) SOLACE
(— CHOICE) OPT CHOOSE SELECT
(— CLAMMY) ENGLEUM
(— CLEAR) DECLARE DEVELOP
DISCUSS EXHIBIT EXPOUND
LIGHTEN DESCRIBE
(— COLD) REFRIGID
(— COMPLETE) SPHERE
(— CONSPICUOUS) ENNOBLE
(— CONTENT) SATISFY
(— CULTIVABLE) EMPOLDER
(— CUT PRIOR TO LAYERING)
TONGUE
(— DESTITUTE) BEREAVE
(— DIFFERENT) ALTER CHANGE
(— DIRTY) MOIL GRIME
(— DISPLAY OF) AFFECT DISCOVER
(— DRUNK) FOX SOUSE FUDDLE
SOZZLE
(— DRY) HAZLE HAZZLE
(— EARLIER) ADVANCE
(— EFFERVESCENT) AERATE
(— EFFIGY) GUY
(— END OF) SNIB FETCH
(— ENDURING) ANNEAL
(— EQUAL) WEIGH EQUATE
(— EVEN) GLAZE LEVEL WEIGH
SQUARE
(— FACES) GIMBLE MURGEON
(— FALSE PRETENSES) SHAM
(— FAST) FIX BAIL FAST GIRD KNIT
MAKE STOP BELAY HITCH BUCKLE
FASTEN SECURE
(— FAT) BATTEN
(— FIRM) FIX BRACE FASTEN
(— FIT) APTATE STRIKE
(— FOOL OF) DOR BORE DOLT
DORRE BEGOWK DOODLE
(— FOOLISH) DAFF GREEN NUGIFY
STULTIFY
(— FOOTSORE) SURBATE
(— FROTHY) MILL
(— FULL) FARCE FULFILL
(— FUN OF) GUY KID GAFF JAPE
JEST JOSH RIDE DROLL GLAIK
SCOUT SMOKE
(— FUSS OVER NOTHING) FAFF
(— GLAD) FAIN
(— GLASS) FOUND
(— GLOSSY) SLEEK
(— GLOW) FURNACE
(— GOLDEN) ENDORE
(— GOOD) ABET
(— GRINDING NOISE) GRINCH
(— GURGLING SOUND) CROOL
(— HAPPY) BLESS ENJOY REFORM
BEATIFY SATISFY FELICIFY
(— HARD) TAW STEEL ENDURE
HORNIFY

(— HARDY) FASTEN
(— HEADWAY) STEM WALK
ENFORCE
(— HELPLESS) STAGGER
(— HOLY) BLESS SACRE HALLOW
SANCTIFY
(— HORSE SEEM YOUNGER) BISHOP
(— ILL) MORBIFY
(— IMMOBILE) FREEZE
(— IMPACT) ASSAIL
(— INCURSION) HARRY
(— INSIGNIFICANT) MICRIFY
(— INTO BUNDLE) FARDEL
(— INTO LAW) ENACT
(— INVALID) DAMASK
(— JOINT) SYPHER
(— KNOWN) BID OUT GIVE WISE
AREAD BEKEN BREAK KITHE
SOUND SPEAK BEWRAY BROACH
COUTHE DENOTE DESCRY EXPOSE
INFORM REVEAL SPREAD
CONFESS DECLARE DELIVER
DIVULGE PUBLISH SIGNIFY
UNCOVER ANNOUNCE DECIPHER
DISCLOSE DISCOVER INDICATE
PROCLAIM PROMULGE
(— LESS DENSE) THIN RAREFY
(— LESS SEVERE) MITIGATE
(— LIABLE) DANGER
(— LOVE) WOO COURT SPOON
GALLANT
(— LUKEWARM) WLECCHE
(— LUSTERLESS) FLATTEN
(— MANIFEST) EVINCE EXPLAIN
(— MELANCHOLY) HYP
(— MELODIOUS) ATTUNE
(— MELODY) DREAM
(— MENTION) SPEAK
(— MERRY) JET GAUD CHEER
SPORT FROLIC SHROVE DISPORT
REHAYTE
(— METALLIC SOUND) CHINK
(— MISTAKE) ERR BOOB GOOF
(— MONOTONOUS NOISE) DRONE
(— MORAL) ETHICIZE
(— MUCH OF) DAWT DANDLE
(— MURMURING NOISE) BUM
(— NEAT) FEAT SMUG TIDY
GROOM
(— NEST) TIMBER
(— NONMAGNETIC) DEGAUSS
(— NUMB) DAZE ETHERIZE
(— OFF) BAG BOLT HOOK ANNEX
HEIST MOSEY SLOPE SPIRIT
SCARPER
(— ONE) UNE
(— ONE'S WAY) AIRT BORE TRADE
(— OPEN) AIR PATEFY
(— OUT) FARE FILL GLEAN SKILL
DISCERN DECIPHER
(— OVER) TURN ALIEN CHANGE
RECOCT DELIVER REFORGE
(— PALE) CHALK
(— PLEASANT) SWEETEN
(— POIGNANT) SAUCE
(— PREGNANT) ENWOMB
(— PROGRESS) GAIN STEM
GATHER
(— PROUD) WLENCH
(— PUBLIC) BLOW BLAZE BREAK
BLAZON DELATE DIVULGE
FANFARE PUBLISH BULLETIN
(— QUIET) ALLAY QUIET APPEASE

(— RATTLING NOISE) TIRL
(— READY) DO BUN GET BOUN
BOWN BUSK YARK BELAY BOWNE
DRESS PREST PRIME FETTLE
GRAITH ADDRESS APPAREL
DISPOSE PREPARE
(— RECORD OF) REFER
(— REFERENCE) MENTION
(— RESISTANCE) REBEL
(— RESOLUTE) STEEL
(— RETURN FOR) REQUITE
(— RICH) FREIGHT IMBURSE
(— ROSY) FLUSH
(— RUSTLING SOUND) FISSLE
FISTLE
(— RUTTING CRY) FREAM
(— SCANTY LIVING) EKE
(— SERIES OF NOTES) TINKLE
(— SHIFT) SCAMBLE
(— SIGN OF CROSS) BLESS
(— SMALL) MICRIFY BELITTLE
(— SMALLER) MINIFY COMPRESS
(— SMOOTH) SLAB GLAZE SLEEK
GENTLE HAMMER SCRAPE
LEVIGATE
(— SOFT) NESH GENTLE
(— SOGGY) SOP
(— SOUR) FOX WIND
(— SPIRITLESS) MOPE
(— SPORT OF) LARK
(— SPRUCE) PERK SMARTEN
(— STRAIGHT) ADDRESS
(— STRONG) STEEL FASTEN
FORTIFY
(— STUPID) MOIDER STULTIFY
(— SUITABLE) ADAPT
(— SURE) SEE INSURE
(— TIPSY) FLUSTER
(— TRANSITION TO) MODULATE
(— UP) UP COOK FORM SPELL
INDITE SETTLE ANALYZE
COMPACT COMPOSE COMPUTE
CONCOCT CONFECT FASHION
COMPOUND COMPRISE DISPENSE
(— UP ACCOUNTS) BREVE
(— USE OF) FEE BUSK APPLY AVAIL
BROOK SERVE SPEND EMPLOY
EXECUTE IMPROVE UTILIZE
(— VIBRANT SOUND) CHIRR
(— VOID) ABATE ANNUL
(— WAR) WARRAY
(— WET) DRAGGLE
(— WHISTLING NOISE) WHEW
(— WHITE) BLANCH BLEACH
CANDIFY
(— WORSE) IMPAIR PEJORATE
(PREF.) POETICO POETO
(SUFF.) EN FECT FEIT
FIC(AL)(ATE)(ATION)(ATIVE)(ATOR)
(ATORY)(E)(ENCE)(ENT)(IAL)(IARY)
(IENT) FIER FIQUE FY IFY POEIA
POESIS POIESIS POIETIC
MAKE-BELIEVE BORAK DUMMY
ASSUMED PRETENCE
MAKER DOER JACK KNAVE SMITH
FACTOR FORGER FORMER
WORKER WRIGHT CREATOR
DECLARER OPERATOR
(— OF ARROWS) FLETCHER
(— OF BARRELS) COOPER
(— OF POTS) POTTER
(— OF SADDLETREES) FUSTER
(— OF SONGS) BULBUL

(— OF TALLOW) CHANDLER
(DRIP-COFFEE —) MACCHINETTA
(SUFF.) STER STRESS
MAKESHIFT JURY RUDE JERRY
TOUSY BEWITH CUTCHA KUTCHA
APOLOGY JACKLEG STOPGAP
RESOURCE TIMENOGUY
MAKEUP FACE BUILD GETUP
HABIT PAINT ROUGE SETUP
SHAPE FACIES FORMAT ANATOMY
CONSIST FEATURE EYELINER
PHYSIQUE TRAVESTY
MAQUILLAGE
MAKING FACT
(SUFF.) FACIENT
FACT(ION)(IVE)(ORY)
MALABAR BAY
MALABAR ALMOND KAMANI
ALMENDRO
MALACEAE POMACEAE PYRACEAE
MALADJUSTMENT SCAR
MALADROIT ILL INEPT AWKWARD
UNHANDY BUNGLING
MALADY AMOK EVIL MORB CAUSE
GRIEF ONCOME AILMENT DISEASE
ILLNESS DISORDER MISCHIEF
SICKNESS
(SUFF.) (— ARISING FROM) ITIS
MALAGASY LEMURIAN
MALAGASY REPUBLIC (SEE
MADAGASCAR)
MALAGIGI (COUSIN OF —) RINALDO
MALAPROPISM SLIPSLOP
MALAR JUGAL
MALARIA AGUE MIASMA SHAKES
QUARTAN PALUDISM
(— PARASITE) VIVAX
MALARIAL PALUDAL PALUDOSE
PALUDOUS

MALAWI
CAPITAL: LILONGWE
COIN: KWACHA TAMBALA
FORMER CAPITAL: ZOMBA
FORMER NAME: NYASALAND
HIGHLANDS: SHIRE
LAKE: NYASA
LANGUAGE: YAO CEWA BANTU
NGONI TONGA NYANJA
TUMBUKA
MOUNTAIN: MLANJE
PEOPLE: YAO BANTU CHEWA
NGURU NYANJA
RIVER: SHIRE
TOWN: DOWA CHOLO MZUZU
NCHEU ZOMBA KARONGA
BLANTYRE LILONGWE
VALLEY: RIFT

MALAY AMOK ASIL AMUCK BAJAU
ILOCO JAKUN MANOBO ILOKANO
MALAYAN (— TREE) TERAP
MALAY APPLE OHIA JAMBO
KAVIKA

MALAYSIA
CAPITAL: KUALALUMPUR
COIN: TRA TRAH
ISLAND: ARU GOA KAI OBI OMA
ALOR BALI GAGA JAVA MUNA
MURU SULU AMBON BANDA
BOHOL BUTON CERAM LUZON
MISOL PANAY SANGI SUMBA

TIMOR WETAR BANGKA
BOEFON BOEROE BORNEO
BUTUNG FLORES LOMBOK
MADURA PELENG SANGIR
TALAUR WAIGEU AMBOINA
CELEBES JAMDENA MINDORO
MOROTAI PALAWAN SALAJAR
SALWATI SUMATRA SUMBAWA
BELITONG DJAILOLO TANIMBAR
ISTHMUS: KRA
LANGUAGE: TAGALOG
MOUNTAIN: BULU NIUT RAJA
MURJO NIAPA LEUSER SLAMET
BINAIJA RINDJANI
PEOPLE: ATA BAJAU SEMANG
BISAYAN TAGALOG VISAYAN
RIVER: KUTAI PERAK BARITO
PAHANG
STATE: KEDAH PERAK SABAH
JOHORE PAHANG PENANG
PERLIS MALACCA SARAWAK
TOWN: IPOH DAVAO ILOILO
KANGAR KUPANG MANADO
KUANTAN KUCHING MALACCA
SANDAKAN SEREMBAN
WEIGHT: TAEL WANG TAMPANG

MALCHAM (FATHER OF —)
SHAHARAHIM
(MOTHER OF —) HODESH
MALCHIAH (FATHER OF —) HARIM
PAROSH RECHAB
MALCHIEL (FATHER OF —) BERIAH
MALCHIRAM (FATHER OF —)
JEHOIACHIN
MALCHISHUA (FATHER OF —) SAUL
MALCONTENT FRONDEUR
MALDIVES (CAPITAL OF —) MALE
MALE HE DOG HIM MAN BUCK
BULL COCK JACK ADULT MANLY
SPEAR JOHNNY MANFUL MASCLE
VIRILE LALAQUI MANKIND
MANLIKE MANNISH PURUSHA
(— OF ANIMALS) TOM BUCK BULL
JACK STUD STALLION
(EFFEMINATE —) NANCE
(GELDED —) GALT
(YOUNG —) GROOM
(PREF.) ANDR(O)
(SUFF.) ANDRIA ANDROUS
ANDRY
MALECITE ETCHEMIN
MALEDICTION BAN WISH CURSE
MALISON ANATHEMA
MALEFACTOR BADDY FELON
BADDIE CULPRIT CRIMINAL
EVILDOER
MALEFIC TAKING
MALEFICENT BALEFUL
MALELEEL (FATHER OF —) CAINAN
MALEO MEGAPOD
MALE ORCHIS CUCKOO CROWTOE
CULLION PURPLES RAGWORT
CROWFOOT
MALEVOLENCE SPITE ENMITY
GRUDGE HATRED MALICE
RANCOR SPLEEN MALIGNITY
MALEVOLENT ILL EVIL FELL
MALIGN HATEFUL HOSTILE
SPITEFUL RANCOROUS
MALFEASANCE MISCONDUCT
MALPRACTICE
MALFORMATION CURL ERROR

HEMITERY MONSTROSITY
(— OF CARNATION) TWITTER
(— OF FRUIT) CATFACE
MALFORMED SHAMBLE
MALFUNCTION GLITCH

MALI
ANCIENT CITY: TIMBUKTU
CAPITAL: BAMAKO
FORMER NAME: FRENCHSUDAN
LAKE: DO DEBO GAROU KORAROU
LANGUAGE: DOGON DYULA
MANDE MARKA PEULH
BAMBARA MALINKE SENOUFO
SONGHAI
MOUNTAIN: MINA MANDING
PEOPLE: MOOR PEUL TUAREG
BAMBARA MALINKE SONGHAI
SENOULFO
RIVER: BANI BAGOE BAKOY NIGER
BAOULE AZAOUAK SENEGAL
TOWN: GAO SAN KATI KITA NARA
BAMBA KAYES MOPTI NIONO
NIORO SEGOU SIKASSO

MALICE DOLE ENVY HAIN PIQUE
SPITE VENOM VIRUS ENMITY
GRUDGE RANCOR SPLEEN
DESPITE AMBITION MALIGNITY
MALEVOLENCE
MALICIOUS SHREW TEENY BITTER
DOGGED MALIGN WANTON
HATEFUL HEINOUS LEERING
SPITOUS VICIOUS CANKERED
NARQUOIS SINISTER SPITEFUL
VENOMOUS VIPEROUS
MALIGN ILL FOUL ABUSE LIBEL
WRONG BEWRAY DEFAME REVILE
VILIFY ASPERSE DEPRAVE
HURTFUL SLANDER BLASPHEME
MALIGNANCY FEROCITY
MALIGNANT EVIL ATTRY BLACK
FELON FERAL SWART ATTERY
MALIGN BALEFUL ENVIOUS
HATEFUL HELLISH PEEVISH
REPTILE VICIOUS WARLOCK
CANKERED SHREWISH SPITEFUL
VENOMOUS VIPEROUS VIRULENT
WRATHFUL RANCOROUS
MALIGNITY GALL LIVER VENOM
VIRUS HATRED MALICE RANCOR
DESPITE
MALINGER MIKE DODGE SKULK
MALINGERER SCONCER
MALL WALK ALLEE
MALLARD TWISTER
(FLOCK OF —S) SORD SUTE
PADDLING
MALLEABLE MILD SOFT DUCTILE
PLASTIC BATTABLE
MALLEIN MORVIN
MALLEMUCK MOLLIE MALMARSH
MALLET MALL MAUL MELL GAVEL
BEATER BEETLE DRIVER HAMMER
DRESSER FLOGGER STRIKER
PLOWMELL
(— FOR BREAKING CLODS) BILDER
(CURRIER'S —) MACE
(HATTER'S —) BEATER
(PAVER'S —) TUP
(PREF.) MALLEI MALLEO SPHYRA
MALLEUS HAMMER OSSICLE
PLECTRUM

MALLOTHI (FATHER OF —) HEMAN
MALLOW MAW DOCK HOCK ALTEA
KOKIO MALVA MAUVE TAUPE
CHEESE ESCOBA GEMAUVE
ABUTILON PIEPRINT
MALLUCH (FATHER OF —) BANI
MALMSEY MALVASIA MALVOISIE
MALNUTRITION CACHEXY
CACHEXIA CACOTROPHY
MALODOROUS GAMY HIGH NOSY
RANK FETID SMELLY VIROSE
VIROUS NOISOME
MALT WORT
(GROUND —) GRIST
(REMAINS OF —) DRAFF
MALTA (ANCIENT NAME OF —)
MELITA
(CAPITAL OF —) VALLETTA
(ISLAND OF —) GOZO COMINO
(TOWN OF —) QORMI RABAT
HAMRUN SLIEMA XAGHRA
ZABBAR BIRKIRKARA
MALTASE GLUCASE
MALTHA BREA
MALTHOUSE MALTING
MALTOSE AMYLON
MALTREAT MAUL ABUSE DIGHT
DEFOUL DEMEAN HESPIL HUSPEL
MISUSE THREAT BEDEVIL
MISGUIDE MANHANDLE
MALTREATMENT ABUSE
MALVA DOCK MALLOW
MAMAMU MU
MAMBA COBRA ELAPOID
MAMMA MA MOM MAMA WIFE
MOMMA WOMAN MOTHER
MAMMAL OX ASS BAT CAT COW
DOG FOX PIG YAK BEAR BOAR
COON DEER GOAT HARE LION
LYNX MINK MOLE PUMA SEAL
ZEBU BEAST BISON CAMEL COATI
COYPU GENET HORSE HYENA
LEMUR LLAMA MOOSE OKAPI
OTTER PANDA RATEL SABLE
SHEEP SHREW SKUNK SLOTH
SWINE TAPIR TIGER WHALE ZORIL
ALPACA ANIMAL BADGER
COUGAR CULPEO DESMAN
DUGONG FISHER FOUSSA
GOPHER GRISON JAGUAR
MARTEN MONKEY OCELOT
TENREC VICUNA WALRUS
WOMBAT BUFFALO CARIBOU
DOLPHIN ECHIDNA GIRAFFE
GLUTTON GUANACO HIPPOID
HUANACO MANATEE OPOSSUM
PECCARY POLECAT PRIMATE
RACCOON SUCKLER SURICAT
TARSIER TYLOPOD WILDCAT
AARDVARK AARDWOLF
ANTELOPE BANXRING CACOMIXL
CREODONT ELEPHANT FALANAKA
HEDGEHOG KINKAJOU MAMMIFER
PANGOLIN PINNIPED REINDEER
SQUIRREL PRONGHORN
RHINOCEROS
MAMMALIA MASTOZOA
MAMMEE ABRICO ABRICOT
MAMMILLA PAP TEAT NIPPLE
MAMMOTH HUGE LARGE GIGANTIC
MAMRE (BROTHER OF —) ANER
ESHCOL
MAN BO HE BOY GEE GUY HIM LAD

TAO WAT WER BUCK CHAL CHAP
COVE DICK EARL GENT GOME
HOMO JACK JONG MALE RINK
TULK BERNE BIMBO BIPED BLOKE
CHURL COVEY CULLY FORCE
FREKE GROOM GUEST HEART
HOMME HORSE JOKER SEGGE
SWAIN WIGHT BIMANE CHIELD
CUFFIN FELLOW HOMBRE
MANTZU WEPMAN BIMANUS
HOMONID KINSMAN MANKIND
(— AFFECTING FOREIGN WAYS)
MACARONI
(— DRESSED AS WOMAN) BESSY
MALINCHE
(— IN DEBT) DYVOUR
(— IN PRIVATE STATION) IDIOT
(— IN TUG-OF-WAR) ANCHOR
(— LEADING 12TH NIGHT) BEAN
(— OF ALL WORK) MOZO
(— OF AUTHORITY) AGHA SEIGNIOR
(— OF BEAUTY) APOLLO
(— OF BRASS) TALOS
(— OF GREAT WEALTH) NABOB
(— OF HIGH RANK) CHAM KHAN
THAKUR GRANDEE
(— OF SUBSTANCE) IDLEMAN
(— OF THE COMMON PEOPLE) JACK
(— OF VIGOR) WYE
(— OF VIOLENCE) RABIATOR
(— OF WAR) ANDREW CARAVEL
CRUISER
(— TO MAN) SINGLE
(ARTIFICIAL —) GOLEM
(BACKGAMMON —) BLOT BUILDER
(BALD —) PILGARLIC
(BEST —) BRIDEMAN PARANYMPH
(BIG —) COB BRUISER MUGWUMP
(BRISK —) SPARK
(CASTRATED —) SPADO EUNUCH
(CHIEF —) FOREMAN FORMAN
(CHURLISH —) NABAL BODACH
(CLEANING —) BUSBOY
(COMMON —) CARL STREET
YEOMAN
(COVETOUS —) HUNKS
(CRAFTY —) FOX
(CRUEL —) OGRE BRUTE
(DISAGREEABLE —) GLEYDE
(DISLIKED —) CUT
(DISSOLUTE —) RAKE
(ECCENTRIC —) GEEZER
(EDUCATED —) EFFENDI
(EFFEMINATE —) DILDO FAIRY
NANCE PUNCE SISSY JESSIE
COCKNEY MEACOCK MIDWIFE
MILKSOP ANDROGYN
MOLLYCODDLE
(END —) BONES BRAKE
(ENLISTED —) GI SNIPE AIDMAN
AIRMAN KEEPER STORES
ARMORER STRIKER SONARMAN
(ENTIRE —) EGO
(EXTINCT —) TEPEXPAN
(FAITHFUL —) TRUEMAN
(FANCY —) PONCE
(FASHIONABLE —) TOUPET
ELEGANT FOPLING GALLANT
(FIRST —) ASK ADAM ASKR TIKI
FOREMAN
(FLASHILY-DRESSED —) LAIR
(FOPPISH —) BLOOD
(FREE —) LIBER

(GRAY-HAIRED —) GRIZZLE
(GREAT —) VAVASOR
(HARDHEARTED —) KNARK
(HAUGHTY —) BASHAW
(HOLDUP —) FOOTPAD
(HOLY —) SADHU SAINT SANNYASI
(HONORS —) WRANGLER
(IDEAL —) SUPERMAN
(IMMORAL —) REP
(INEFFECTUAL —) DUFFER
(INSANE —) FURIOSO
(LADY'S —) FOPLING DAMMARET
(LAME —) BACACH
(LEARNED —) ULEMA LAMDAN
OLLAMH PUNDIT SAVANT
SOPHIST
(LECHEROUS —) SATYR
(LEWD —) BROTHEL
(LIAISON —) COURIER
(LITERARY —) GIGADIBS
(LITTLE —) MANNET SHRIMP
MANNIKIN
(LUSTFUL —) GOAT
(MAINTENANCE —) CAMPMAN
(MARRIED —) HUSBAND BENEDICT
(MEDICINE —) PEAI DOCTOR
SHAMAN ANGAKOK
(MEEK —) MOSES
(MIGHTY —) SAMSON
(ODD-JOB —) JOEY
(OLD —) HAG OLD BOOL CUFF
GAFF CRONE DOBBY UNCLE
BODACH DUFFER FATHER GAFFER
NESTOR GERONTE STARETS
ECKEHART VELYARDE PATRIARCH
(OLD-CLOTHES —) POCO
(ONE-ARMED —) WINGY
(ONE-EYED —) ARIMASP
(OVERFASTIDIOUS —) DUDE
(PARTY —) SIDESMAN
(PRIMITIVE —) URMENSCH
(PRINCIPAL —) HERO TOPARCH
(RASH —) HOTSPUR
(RICH —) DIVES CROESUS
(RIGHTEOUS —) SADDIK
(RIGHT-HAND —) HENCHMAN
(SERVING —) GARCON
(SOUND-EFFECTS —) CRAWK
(STERN —) GRIMSIRE
(STRAIGHT —) STOOGE
(STRONG —) KWASIND
(STRONG-ARM —) HOOD GORILLA
(STUPID —) SUBMAN
(THICKSET —) GRUB KNAR SPUD
(TOUGH —) KNAR
(UNEMPLOYED —) BATLAN
(UTILITY —) JUMPER
(VICIOUS —) YAHOO
(WHITE —) BOSTON BUCKRA
PAKEHA CACHILA
(WHITE — LIVING WITH ABORIGINE)
COMBO
(WILD —) WOODMAN WOODWOSE
(WISE —) NAB HAKAM SABIO
SOLON SOPHY NESTOR WIZARD
SOLOMON TOHUNGA
(WIZENED —) GNOME
(WOMANISH —) JENNY
(WRETCHED —) CAITIFF
(YOUNG —) BOY LAD JONG PUNK
YOUTH BOCHUR DAMSEL EPHEBE
KNIGHT BOUCHAL BUCKEEN
YOUNKER COCKEREL SPRINGAL

(PREF.) ANDR(O) ANTHROP(O)
HOMI(NI)
(SUFF.) ANDRIA ANDROUS
ANDRY ENGRO VIR(ATE)
MAN-ABOUT-TOWN FLANEUR
MANABOZHO MICHABOU
WINABOJO
MANACLE BAND BOND DARBY
HAMPER TIRRET SHACKLE
HANDCUFF HANDLOCK
(PL.) IRONS CHAINS
MANAGE DO GET MAN RUN BEAR
BOSS CURB FEND HACK HOLD
KEEP LEAD MAKE RULE TEND
TOOL WIND WORK BROOK CARRY
DIGHT FORTH FRAME GUIDE
MAYNE ORDER SHIFT SPEND
STEER SWING WIELD CONVEY
DEMEAN DEVISE DIRECT FETTLE
GOVERN HANDLE INTEND
MANURE TEMPER AGITATE
CONDUCT DISPOSE EXECUTE
FINAGLE HUSBAND MINSTER
OFFICER OPERATE SOLICIT
STEWARD CONTRIVE ENGINEER
NEGOTIATE
(— AWKWARDLY) FOOZLE
(— CLUMSILY) KEVEL
(— SKILLFULLY) MANIPULATE
(— TO BEAR) AFFORD
MANAGEABLE EASY YARE
BANTAM DOCILE WIELDY
DUCTILE FLEXIBLE YIELDING
MANAGEMENT CARE HEEL WORK
CHARGE CONDUCT CONTROL
ECONOMY GESTION RUNNING
CARRIAGE DEMEANOR ENGINERY
MANAGERY MANEUVER
REGIMENT STEERAGE STEERING
(DOMESTIC —) MENAGE
HUSBANDRY
(GOOD —) EUTAXY
(SKILLFUL —) PRACTICE PRACTISE
MANAGER BOSS DOER AGENT
DAROGA DEPUTY PURSER SYNDIC
AMILDAR CURATOR ERENACH
HUSBAND STEWARD WIELDER
AUMILDAR DIRECTOR DISPOSER
ENGINEER HERENACH INSTITOR
(— OF ENTERTAINERS) ROADIE
(— OF FARM) HIND GRIEVE
(ASSISTANT —) CAPORAL
(MINE —) CAPTAIN
(POLITICAL —) FUGLEMAN
(SUFF.) EER
MANAHATH (FATHER OF —)
SHOBAL
MANAKIN PIPRA
MAN-AT-ARMS KNIGHT
MANATEE COWFISH HOGFISH
MERMAID LAMANTIN MUTILATE
SIRENIAN
MANBARKLAK JARANA KAKARAL
MANCALA WARI
MANCHU SHERRY
MANCHURIA (CHINESE NAME
FOR —) MANCHOW
(PENINSULA OF —) LIAOTUNG
(PROVINCE OF —) JILIN LIAONING
HEILONGJIANG
(RIVER OF —) AMUR LIAO YALU
ARGUN USSURI SUNGARI
MANDAEAN SABAEAN

MANDANE (FATHER OF —)
ASTYAGES
(HUSBAND OF —) CAMBYSES
(SON OF —) CYRUS
MANDARIN TOWKAY CHINESE
MANDARIN ORANGE SATSUMA
MANDATE BREVE ORDER BEHEST
CHARGE DECREE FIRMAN
BIDDING COMMAND PRECEPT
PROCESS MANDAMUS
MANDATUM WARRANTY
(— OF GOD) JUDGMENT
MANDATORY OBLIGATORY
MANDIBLE BEAK JOWL SETA
RAMUS JAWBONE GNATHITE
(— PART) MALA
MANDINGO MANDE MALINKE
WANGARA
MANDOLIN OUD MANDORA
MANDRAKE ALRAUN DUDAIM
MANDREL BALL STUD SLEEVE
CHEMISE SPINDLE TRIBLET
MANDRICARDO (BELOVED OF —)
ANGELICA
(FATHER OF —) AGRICAN
(SLAYER OF —) ORLANDO
MANDRILL MAIMON MORMON
MANE JUBA MONE CREST PITRI
ENCOLURE
MAN-EATER REQUIN REQUIEM
MANEGE TRAIN
MANEUVER PLAY TURN WISE
GAMBIT JOCKEY MANURE PESADE
VRILLE FINAGLE FINESSE
ARTIFICE DEMARCHE ENGINEER
EXERCISE STRATEGY WINDLASS
(— IN AUTO RACING) SLINGSHOT
(— IN SPACE) DOCK
(— IN SURFING) CUTBACK
(— OF MOTORCYCLE OR BICYCLE)
WHEELIE
(- GENTLY) EASE
(AERIAL —) BUNT LOOP SPIN
FISHTAIL WINGOVER
(BULLFIGHTING —) VERONICA
(ILLEGAL —) GAME
(ROCK-CLIMBING —) LAYBACK
(SKIING —) SNOWPLOW
(WRESTLING —) ESCAPE BUTTOCK
MANEUVERABLE YARE
MANEUVERING FINESSE
FLANKING
MANGE ITCH REEF SCAB CANKER
DARTARS SCABIES
MANGER BIN BUNK CRIB HECK
STALL CRATCH
MANGLE MAR HACK MOUTH
BRUISE GARBLE HACKLE IRONER
MAGGLE MURDER MAMMOCK
LACERATE MUTILATE
MANGO DIKA AMHAR AMINI
BAUNO AMCHOOR CARABAO
PAHUTAN
(POINT OF —) NAK
MANGOSTEEN SANTOL GARCINIA
MANGROVE BACAO GORAN
MANGLE MYRTAL BACAUAN
CERIOPS COURIDA HANGALAI
LANGARAI
MANGUE CHOLUTECA CHOROTEGA
MANGY SCABBY ROINISH
SCABETIC
MANHANDLE MESS ROUGH SCRAG

MANHATTAN TRANSFER (AUTHOR OF —) DOSPASSOS
(CHARACTER IN —) BUD GUS JOE HERF JOHN RUTH STAN CONGO ELLEN EMERY EMILE HARRY JIMMY SUSIE GEORGE MCNIEL NELLIE OKEEFE PRYNNE BALDWIN HARLAND MERIVALE PEARLINE THATCHER GOLDWEISER OGLETHORPE
MANHOOD ADAMHOOD
MANIA RAGE CRAZE FUROR FRENZY DELIRIUM HYSTERIA INSANITY CACOETHES
MANIAC KILLER MADMAN FANATIC LUNATIC
MANIFEST HAVE NUDE OPEN RIFE SENE SHOW APERT CLEAR FRANK GROSS KITHE NAKED OVERT PLAIN PROVE SPEAK SUTEL ARRANT ATTEST COUTHE EVINCE EXTANT GRAITH LIQUID OSTEND PATENT PHANIC APPROVE BETOKEN CONFESS DECLARE EVIDENT EXHIBIT EXPRESS OBVIOUS SIGNIFY VISIBLE APPARENT DISCLOSE DISCOVER INDICATE PALPABLE PROCLAIM
(NOT —) LATENT
(PREF.) PHANER(O) PHANTA(SMO) PHANTO
MANIFESTATION ACT SON BEAM COMA SIGN GLINT AVATAR COMING EFFECT OSTENT ADVANCE DISPLAY EXPRESS OUTSIDE SHOWING EPIPHANY MANIFEST
(BARELY PERCEPTIBLE —) SCINTIL
(BRIEF —) GLEAM
(DIVINE —) SPIRIT SHEKINAH
(HORRIBLE —) CHIMAERA
(MORAL —) SOUL
(VAGUE —) GLIMMER
(SUFF.) PHANE PHANOUS PHANT PHANY
MANIFESTLY WITTERLY
MANIFESTO PLACARD
MANIFOLD MANY TURRET VARIOUS FELEFOLD MANYFOLD MULTIPLE MULTIPLEX REPLICATE
(SUFF.) PLOID
MANIKIN ECORCHE PANTINE PHANTOM HOMUNCIO HOMUNCLE MANNIKIN
MANILA HEMP ABACA
MANIOC CASSAVA CATELLA MANDIOCA
MANIPLE FANON ORALE FANNEL COMPANY HANDFUL SUDARIUM
MANIPULATE COG COAX COOK DIAL FAKE HAND STIR TOOL CROOK HUMOR KNEAD SHAPE TREAT WIELD CHIVVY GOVERN HANDLE JOCKEY MANAGE WANGLE SHUFFLE
(— BY DECEPTIVE MEANS) RIG
MANIPULATION PASS JUGGLERY MANAGERY
MANITO ORENDA POKUNT MANITOU TAMANOAS
MANITOBA (CAPITAL OF —) WINNIPEG

(RIVER OF —) RED SEAL SWAN NELSON ROSEAU SOURIS PEMBINA CHURCHILL SASKACHEWAN
(TOWN OF —) CARMAN BRANDON DAUPHIN KILLARNEY SWANRIVER
MANKIND MAN FLESH SHEEP WORLD BIMANA SPECIES HUMANITY UNIVERSE MORTALITY
MANLIKE MALE MANLY MANNISH HOMINOID
MANLINESS ARETE VIRTUS MANSHIP
MANLY BOLD MALE HARDY MANNY DARING VIRILE MANLIKE
MAN-MADE CULTURAL SYNTHETIC
MANNA TREHALA WINDFALL
MANNER AIR BAT JET LAT WAY FORM GAET GARB GATE KIND MAKE MIEN MODE RATE SORT THEW TOUR WISE WONE GUISE LATES SHAPE STYLE TENUE TRICK COURSE CUSTOM METHOD MISTER STRAIN ADDRESS AMENITY FASHION QUALITY QUOMODO CARAPACE DEMEANOR LANGUAGE
(— OF APPROACH) ABORD
(— OF DOING) ACTION
(— OF HANDLING) HAND
(— OF MAKING ANYTHING) FACTURE
(— OF SITTING) ASANA
(— OF SPEAKING) SLUR SOUGH ACCENT GRAMMAR PARLANCE
(— OF WALKING) STEP
(AFFECTED —) AIR
(AMUSING —) DROLLERY
(ARROGANT —) BRAG HAUTEUR
(FORBIDDING —) SHELL
(FORMAL —) STARCH
(HABITUAL —) SONG
(OUTWARD —) TOUR FRONT
(SMOOTH —) JAPAN
(SWAGGERING —) SIDE PANACHE
(UNUSUAL —) SINGULARITY
(USUAL —) HABIT
(PL.) ADDRESS CORNERS HAVINGS BREEDING
(SUFF.) WISE
(AFTER THE — OF) FASHION
(IN A —) LY
(IN THE — OF) IC(AL)
MANNERED CUTE MORATE THEWED
MANNERISM POSE TRICK IDIASM
(PL.) DAPS
MANNERLY CIVIL POLITE
MANNERS MORES HAVANCE HAVINGS BEAUETRY BREEDING
MANNITOL MANNITE PUNICIN
MANOAH (SON OF —) SAMSON
MAN-OF-WAR CARAVEL
MAN-OF-WAR FISH PASTOR
MANON (CHARACTER IN —) MANON GRIEUX LESCAUT BRETIGNY
(COMPOSER OF —) MASSENET
MANON LESCAUT (CHARACTER IN —) MANON GRIEUX GERONTE
(COMPOSER OF —) PUCCINI
MANOR HAM HOF BURY HALL

TOWN VILL BARONY COMMOTE MANSION LORDSHIP TOWNSHIP
MANPOWER BRAWN LABOR
MANROOT IPOMOEA
MANROPE LIMMER
MANSERVANT (ALSO SEE SERVANT) LAD MOZO GROOM VALET ANDREW BUTLER TEABOY
MANSFIELD PARK (AUTHOR OF —) AUSTEN
(CHARACTER IN —) TOM MARY WARD FANNY HENRY JULIA MARIA PRICE YATES EDMUND NORRIS THOMAS BERTRAM CRAWFORD RUSHWORTH
MANSION DOME SEAT HOTEL HOUSE MANSE SIEGE TOWER CASTLE HARBOR HOSTEL CHATEAU
(— OF THE MOON) ALNATH
MANSLAUGHTER BLOOD FELONY HOMICIDE
MANTEL CLAVY CLAVEL
MANTELET MANTA MANTLE MANTLET GALAPAGO
MANTELPIECE BRACE PAREL CLAVEL MANTEL MANTLING
MANTICORE MONTEGRE
MANTIS CAGN RACER REARER MANTOID PROPHET
MANTIS CRAB SQUILLA
MANTLE CAPA HOSE PALL REAM ROBE CLOAK CREAM FROCK JABUL LAMBA PALLA TUNIC CAMAIL CAPOTE KHIRKA KIRTLE ROCHET SLAVIN SULMAN TABARD CHLAMYS CHRISOM CHUDDAR FERIDJI MANTEAU PAENULA PALLIUM SLEEVES WHITTLE WRAPPER BARRACAN CHRYSOME MANTELET REGOLITH RICINIUM STOCKING
(PREF.) CHLAMYD(O) PHARO
MANTLEROCK REGOLITH
MANTO (DAUGHTER OF —) TISIPHONE
(FATHER OF —) HERCULES TIRESIAS
(HUSBAND OF —) RHACIUS
(SON OF —) OCNUS MOPSUS AMPHILOCHUS
MANTRA OM DHARANI GAYATRI MANTRAM SAVITRI
MANTUA MANTY SEMAR
MANTZU MIAOTZE
MANUAL VADY COACH GREAT TUTOR PORTAS CAMBIST CEMBALO DIDACHE MANUARY BOMBARDE HANDBOOK KEYBOARD ORDINARY PORTHORS SYNOPSIS
(MAGICIAN'S —) GRIMOIRE
(NAVIGATION —) BOWDITCH
MANUAO IAO
MANUBRIUM HYPOSTOME
MANUFACTURE COIN FAKE MAKE FORGE PERFORM PRODUCE WORKING BOOKWORK
(— OF LIQUOR OR DRUGS) ABKARI
(ILLEGAL —) COINING
MANUFACTURED STORE
MANUFACTURER BRAND MAKER WRIGHT DISKERY

SPINNER SUPPLIER
MANUMIT FREE LIBERATE
MANURE HOT MIG DUNG LIME MUCK SAUR SOIL TATH FECES GUANO MIXEN FULZIE SEASON SLEECH COMPOST FOLDING GOODING POUDRET DRESSING WORTHING
MANURED BONED
MANUS HAND
MANUSCRIPT CODEX FLIMSY MATTER SCRIPT UNCIAL CURSIVE PANDECT PAPYRUS PINTURA WITNESS EXEMPLAR PARCHMENT
MANX CAT RUMPY
MANX SHEARWATER CREW PUFFIN SCRABE SCRABER
MANY TEN FELE MUCH SERE FORTY GREAT MAINT MOULT OODLES TWENTY ENDLESS JILLION SEVERAL VARIOUS MANIFOLD COUNTLESS
(BEING —) NUMEROUS
(GOOD —) HANTLE
(GREAT —) MORT RAFF SWITH
(PREF.) MULT(I) PLURI POLY
(HOW —) POSO QUOT
MANYATTA KRAAL
MANY-COLORED BONT
MANY-HANDED BRIAREAN
MANYPLIES FARDEL OMASUM
MANYROOT RUELLIA
MANY-SIDED VARIOUS
MAO NEHRU
MAOCH (SON OF —) ACHISH
MAORI (— IMAGE) TIKI
(— LAW) UTU
(— VILLAGE) PA PAH KAINGA
(NOT —) PAKEMA
MAP KEY CARD DICE PLAT PLOT CARTE CENTO CHART DRAFT INSET QUART STILL DRAUGHT GRAPHIC CARTGRAM GATEFOLD PLATFORM
(PREF.) CARTO CHARTO
MAPAU MAPLE MATIPO TARATA PIRIPIRI
MAPLE MAZER DOGWOOD SYCAMORE WINGSEED
(FLOWERING —) ABUTILON
(GROVE OF —) SAPBUSH
MAR BLOT SCAR SMIT SNIP BLOOM BOTCH SHEND SPILL SPOIL BLOTCH DEFACE DEFEAT DEFORM EFFACE IMPAIR INJURE MANGLE BLEMISH DISGRACE
MARABOU STORK ARGALA MORABIT ADJUTANT
MARANAO LANAO
MARASMUS MARCOR ATHREPSIA
MARAUD RAID DACOIT PICKEER PILLAGE
MARAUDER TORY BANDIT BUMMER LOOTIE PIRATE CATERAN LADRONE
(PL.) BLACKS
MARAUDING BANDITRY OUTRIDING
MARBLE MIB MIG PEA POT TAW ALLY BOOL BOWL DUCK DUMP MARL AGATE AGGIE ALLEY RONCE COMMY IMMIE IVORY LINER PUREY RANCE DOGGLE

MARMOR MARVEL MIGGLE PARIAN PEEWEE STEELY CARRARA CIPOLIN GLASSIE GRIOTTE KNICKER PARAGON PITCHER SHOOTER BROCATEL DOLOMITE KNUCKLER
(BLACK —) JET
(IMITATION —) SCAGLIOLA
(SIENA —) BROCATELLO
(PL.) TAW BOWLS PLUMPS HUNDRED
MARBLED MIRLY
MARCH FILE HIKE LIDE MARK MUSH SLOG ROUTE TRACE TRINE TROOP WALTZ DEFILE DOUBLE PARADE REVIEW DEBOUCH STRETCH FOOTSLOG PROGRESS
(— BEHIND) COVER
(— IN FRONT OF) LEAD
(— OBLIQUELY) INCLINE
(DAY'S —) ETAPE
(PL.) FRONTIER
MARCHING (— UP) ANABASIS
MARCHIONESS MARCHESA MARQUISE
MARCOT GOOTE
MARCOTTAGE GOOTEE
MARE SEA YAD YADE YAUD GILLIE GILLOT GRASNI HUNTRESS
MARE'S-TAIL HIPPURID
MARGARET MEG META MARGET MARGOT GRETCHEN
MARGATE PORGY
MARGAY TIGER
MARGIN HEM RIM VAT BANK BRIM BROW CURB EDGE FOLD HAIR INCH LIMB LIST RAND BRINK EAVES MARGE VERGE BORDER FRINGE LABRUM LACING CUSHION DRAUGHT MARGENT SELVAGE HAIRLINE
(— OF CARAPACE) DOUBLURE
(— OF CIRCLE) LIMB
(— OF LIP) PROLABIUM
(— OF PAGE) BACK
(— OF SAFETY) LEEWAY
(— OF SHELL) LABRUM LIMBUS
(— OF SUPERIORITY) LEAD
(— OF WING) TERMEN
(—S OF HERD) SWING
(NARROW —) ACE NECK
(SEA —) COAST
MARGOSA NIM NEEM NEEMBA
MARGRAVE RUDIGER MARKGRAF
MARIA (FATHER OF —) OCTAVIO PETROBIUS
(HUSBAND OF —) PETRUCHIO
MARIANA SILYBUM
MARIGOLD GOLD GULL SAMH AZTEC BOOTS GOLDE GOOLS HELIO BACLIN BUDDLE GOLDCUP GOLDING GOLLAND KINGCUP MARYBUD TAGETES
MARIJUANA BOO POT WEED DAGGA GRASS MOOCAH LOCOWEED MARYJANE
(ONE OUNCE OF —) LID
(ONE WHO TAKES —) POTHEAD
(OUNCE OF —) CAN
(PUFF ON — CIGARETTE) TOKE
MARINE JOLLY GALOOT GULPIN GYRENE TOPMAN MARINAL HALIMOUS MARITIME NAUTICAL

AEQUOREAL THALASSIC
(PREF.) ENALI(O) THALASS(O) THALASSI(O) THALATTO
MARINER MARINE SAILOR SEALER SEAMAN BUSCARLE SEAFARER WARRENER
(PL.) SEAFOLK
MARINHEIRO ACAJOU
MARIONETTE PUPPY POPPET PUPPET
MARITAL INTIMATE HUSBANDLY
MARITIME MARINE HALIMOUS NAUTICAL
MARJORAM AMARACUS
MARK AIM END HOB HUB MOT POP BELT BLOT BUOY BUTT CHOP CLIP DELE DINT FAZE FIST GOAL KEEL LINE MIND NOTE RIST SCAR SEAR SIGN SMOT SMUT SPOT TEND TEXT TICK VIRE WAND WIND BADGE BOTTU BRAND BREVE CHANT CHECK CLOUD DATUM DITTO DRAFT FLECK FRANK GHOST GRADE HILUM KNIFE LABEL MARCH MARCO MEITH NOKTA POINT PRINT PROOF ROVER SCART SCOPE SCORE SCUFF SPOOR STAMP SWIRL TOKEN TOUCH TRACE TRACK TRACT WATCH WHITE ACCENT ALPIEU BEACON BESPOT BLOTCH BUTTON CARACT DAGGER DAPPLE DENOTE DIRECT INDICE LETTER MARKER NOTICE OBJECT SMUTCH STREAK STRIKE STROKE SUCKER SYMBOL TARGET UPSHOT WICKER WITTER BETOKEN CHARBON COCKSHY DEMERIT DIAMOND DRAUGHT EROTEME EXCUDIT FINMARK IMPRESS IMPRINT INSIGNE KENMARK SCARIFY SERRATE SIGNARY SPECKLE STRIATE SYMPTOM VESTIGE WAYMARK BRACELET CROWFOOT DATEMARK DIASTOLE DISPUNCT EVIDENCE FOOTMARK FOOTSTEP IDENTIFY IDEOGRAM MONUMENT NOTATION
(— A BIRD) BAND
(— AFTER ASSAY) TOUCH
(— AS SPURIOUS) ATHETIZE
(— BY BURNING) CHAR
(— BY CUTTING) SCRIBE
(— BY PLOWING) STRIKE
(— CROSSWISE) CRANK
(— DENOTING CORRUPT PASSAGE) OBELUS
(— DIRECTIONS) ADDRESS
(— IN ARCHERY) CLOUT HOYLE ROVER WHITE
(— IN BOOK) PRESSMARK
(— IN CANON) LEAD
(— IN CURLING) TEE COCK
(— IN QUOITS) MOT
(— INDICATING CONTRACTION) CORONIS
(— INDICATING DIRECTION) ARROW
(— OF ACKNOWLEDGEMENT) ACCOLADE
(— OF DISGRACE) STAIN STIGMA
(— OF DISHONOR) ABATEMENT
(— OF DISTINCTION) BELT

(— OF ESTEEM) LAUREL GARLAND
(— OF OFFICE) SEAL
(— OF OWNERSHIP) SWANMARK
(— OF PURITY) HALLMARK
(— OF REFERENCE) OBELISK
(— OF SIGNATURE) CROSS
(— OF SUPERIORITY) BELL
(— OF WEAVER) KEEL
(— OFF) SUBTEND
(— OFF LAND) FEER PHEER
(— ON ANIMAL'S FACE) BLAZE STRIPE
(— ON CHART) VIGIA
(— ON EXAM) PASS
(— ON FEATHER) BAR SPANGLE
(— ON FOREHEAD) KUMKUM
(— ON PENNSYLVANIA BARNS) HEXAFOOS
(— ON SHEEP) SMIT BUIST
(— ON SHIP) SURMARK
(— ON SKIN) PLOT CREASE
(— ON STAMP) CONTROL
(— OUT) RUN CANCEL DELINE AIRMARK APPOINT COMPART DESCRIBE
(— OVER GERMAN VOWEL) UMLAUT
(— OVER LETTER N) TILDE
(— OVER LONG VOWELS) MACRON
(— RIGS) FEER
(— SHEEP OR CATTLE) BASTE BUIST DEWLAP
(— TIME) BEAT COUNT
(— TO BE ATTAINED) BOGEY BOGIE
(— TO GUIDE VESSELS) MYTH
(— TO SCARE DEER) SHEWEL
(— TRANSVERSELY) LADDER
(— UNDER LETTER C) CEDILLA
(— WITH LINES) HATCH CAMLET
(— WITH POINTED ROLLER) GRILL
(— WITH RIDGES) RIB
(— WITH STRIPES) WALE STREAM
(— WITH TAR) BASTE
(ACCENT —) VERGE
(ANGULAR —) HOOK
(BALLOT —) SCRATCH
(BOUNDARY —) DOOL MEAR MERE TERM WIKE MEITH STAKE LANDMARK
(CADENCY —) BRISURE
(CANCELLATION —) BUMPER KILLER
(DIACRITICAL —) TIL TILDE TITTLE
(DIRTY —) SMIRCH
(DISTINCTIVE —) BADGE INDICIA
(DISTINGUISHING —) ITEM COCARDE EARMARK INSIGNE
(DOUBLE-DAGGER —) DIESIS
(EASY —) YAP SMELT PIGEON
(EIGHTH —) URE
(EXACT —) NICK
(EXCLAMATION —) SCREAMER
(IDENTIFICATION —) MOLE CREST SPLIT SIGNET WATTLE EARMARK KENMARK LUGMARK COLOPHON
(LOW-WATER —) DATUM
(MAGICAL —) SIGIL
(MERIDIAN —) MIRE
(MUSICAL —) PRESA CORONA
(PARAGRAPH —) PILCROW
(PROOFREADER'S —) STET CARET
(PUNCTUATION —) DASH STOP BRACE BREVE COLON COMMA HYPHEN PERIOD BRACKET

DIERESIS ELLIPSIS DIACRITIC SEMICOLON PARENTHESIS
(RED —) HICKEY
(SECTARIAN —) BOTTU TILAKA
(SKATE —) CUSP
(SMALL ROUND —) DOT
(TRAMP'S —) MONICA MONNIKER
(WHITE —) RACHE
(PL.) POINTING
(PREF.) STIGONO
MARKED FAR GREAT SCORED SEVERE SPOTTY COLORED EMINENT MARCATO POINTED SCARRED SPECKED SPOTTED
(— BY COLORED RINGS) AREOLATE
(— BY FURROWS) RIVOSE
(— BY INTELLIGENCE) ABLE
(— BY PROSTRATION) ALGID
(— BY REFINEMENT) ELEGANT
(— BY RIDGES) SERRIED
(— BY SHREWDNESS) ADROIT
(— BY SIMILARITY) AKIN
(— BY SIMPLICITY) ATTIC
(— BY WAVY LINES) GYROSE
(— OUT) DISTINCT
(— SPOTS OR LINES) MACULATE
(— UP) FOUL
(— WITH BANDS) ZONATE
(— WITH SMALLPOX) FRETTEN
(— WITH SPOTS OR LINES) NOTATE
(— WITH WHITE) BAUSOND
(EXTREMELY —) INTENSE
MARKEDLY BYOUS
MARKER HOB HUB IOU DOLE FLAG MARK SPAD STUMP TYPER BUTTON GUIDON HOBBLE HUBBLE TABBER DAYMARK SCRIBER
MARKET CURB GUNJ MART PORT SALE SOOK VEND VENT CHEAP CROSS GUNGE HALLE PASAR PRICE TRONE TRYST BAZAAR BOURSE MERCAT OUTLET PARIAN RIALTO STAPLE POULTRY CHEAPING DEBOUCHE EMPORIUM EXCHANGE MACELLUM
(CATTLE —) TRISTE
(MEAT —) SHAMBLES
MARKETABLE SUK SUQ SOUK STAPLE SALABLE VENDIBLE
MARKETING (SYSTEM OF —) ADMASS
MARKETPLACE SUK SUQ SOUK TRON AGORA CHAWK CHOWK HALLE PLAZA BAZAAR RIALTO EMPORIUM
MARKING EYE HOOD COLLAR CLOUDING SCARRING SCRIBING
(— OF WOOD) CURL GRAIN
(— ON FEATHER) SPANGLE
(— ON MARS) CANAL
(—S ON STEEL) DAMASK
(ANIMAL —) SADDLE SHIELD
(CATTLE —) JINGLEBOB
(CRESCENT-SHAPED —) LUNULA LUNULE
(DROP-SHAPED —) GUTTA
(POSTAL —) INDICIA OVERPRINT
(RINGLIKE —) ANNULUS
(STRIPED —) STRAKE
MARKKA FINMARK

MARKSMAN SHOT MARKER PLUFFER SHOOTER SHOTMAN SHOOTIST

MARL MALM MARLITE

MARLI MARIE

MARLIN AU AGUJA

MARLINESPIKE FID JAEGER PRICKER STABBER

MARMALADE CHEESE SQUISH CODINIAC

MARMALADE TREE CHICO MAMEY MAMMIE SAPOTE ZAPOTE

MARMOSET MICO TITI SAGOIN JACCHUS OUITITI QUIRCAL SAIMIRI TAMARIN WISTITI ORABASSU

MARMOT BOBAC PAHMI GOPHER SUSLIK SCIURID SIFFLEUR WHISTLER

MARMOTA ARCTOMYS

MAROON AZTEC PICNIC CIMARRON

MARQUEE CANOPY MARQUISE

MARQUISE NAVETTE

MARQUISETTE LENO

MARRANOS ANUSIM

MARRED CUPPY SCABBY SLURRED SPECKED

MARRIAGE MUTA DAIVA HYMEN KARAO BEENAH BRIDAL BUCKLE SPLICE SPOUSE EXOGAMY NUPTIAL PUNALUA SPOUSAL WEDDING WEDLOCK CONUBIUM LEVIRATE OPSIGAMY
(— AFTER DEATH OF FIRST SPOUSE) DIGAMY
(— AT ADVANCED AGE) OPSIGAMY
(— BELOW POSITION) HYPOGAMY
(— CONTRACT) KETUBAH
(— OUTSIDE FAMILY) EXOGAMY
(— PORTION) TOCHER
(— WITH AN INFERIOR) MESALLIANCE
(— WITHIN GROUP) ENDOGAMY
(PREF.) GAMO
(SUFF.) GAM(AE)(IST)(OUS)(Y) GAMETE

MARRIAGEABLE NUBILE

MARRIED COVERT WEDDED ESPOUSED
(NOT —) SOLE

MARROW KEEST MARIE MERCH MERGH MEDULLA
(PREF.) MEDULLI MYEL(O) MYELINO
(SUFF.) MYELIA MYELITIS

MARRY TIE WED FAST WIFE WIVE CLEEK MATCH BUCKLE CROTCH ENSURE MARROW SPLICE HUSBAND NUPTIAL WEDLOCK DESPOUSE
(— OFF) BESTOW
(PREF.) GAMETO GAMO
(SUFF.) GAM(AE)(IST)(OUS)(Y) GAMETE

MARS ARES MAMERS MARMAR MAVORS MASPITER TEUTATES
(FATHER OF —) JUPITER
(MOTHER OF —) JUNO
(SON OF —) REMUS ROMULUS
(PREF.) AREO

MARSH BOG FEN HAG CARR DANK FELL FLAM FLAT HOPE JHIL MASH MIRE OOZE QUAG ROSS SOIL SUDS TARN VLEI VLEY WASH WHAM FLASH GLADE JHEEL LIMAN SLACK SLASH SLUMP SWAMP MORASS PALUDE PUDDLE CIENAGA CORCASS POCOSIN PONTINE QUAGMIRE STROTHER TURLOUGH
(SALT —) SALT SEBKA SALINA SALINE
(PREF.) ELO HELO LIMN(I)(O) PALUDI

MARSHAL ARRAY ORDER MUSTER PARADE JERONIMO MARECHAL MOBILIZE
(— FACTS) HASH

MARSHBUCK SITUTUNGA

MARSH ELDER JACKO

MARSH FEVER HELODES

MARSH GAS METHANE

MARSH HARRIER PUDDOCK PUTTOCK

MARSHLAND MAREMMA

MARSHMALLOW MALLOW WYMOTE

MARSH MARIGOLD BOOTS CAPER CRAZY GOOLS DRAGON GAMOND GOWLAN COWSLIP ELKSLIP GOLDCUP KINGCOB KINGCUP MARYBUD DRUNKARD

MARSH PENNYWORT PENNYROT WATERCUP

MARSH PINK SABBATIA

MARSH TEA LEDUM

MARSH TREFOIL BUCKBEAN

MARSH WREN LONGBILL

MARSHY BOGGY FOGGY MOORY MOSSY PONDY SNAPY SPEWY CALLOW MARISH PLASHY QUAGGY QUASHY SLUMPY HELODES MOORISH PALUDAL QUEACHY PALUDINE WATERISH

MARSILEA NARDOO

MARSUPIAL KOALA QUOLL CUSCUS POSSUM WOMBAT BETTONG DASYURE OPOSSUM KANGAROO BANDICOOT PETAURIST

MART STAPLE EMPORIUM

MARTEN FOIN PEKAN SABLE SOBOL FISHER MARTRIX MUSTELID MUSTELIN
(GROUP OF —S) RICHESSE
(SUFF.) ICTIS

MARTENSITE SORBITE

MARTHA (CHARACTER IN —) JULIA NANCY LIONEL MARTHA HARRIET PLONKETT
(COMPOSER OF —) FLOTOW

MARTIAL BELLIC WARLIKE WARRIOR BELLICAL MILITARY

MARTIN MARTLET SWALLOW MARTINET

MARTIN CHUZZLEWIT (AUTHOR OF —) DICKENS
(CHARACTER IN —) GAMP MARK MARY SETH JONAS MERCY SARAH GRAHAM MARTIN TAPLEY ANTHONY CHARITY PECKSNIFF CHUZZLEWIT

MARTINMAS TERM

MARTYR STEPHEN WITNESS SUFFERER

MARTYRDOM MARTYRY PASSION

MARVEL MARL MUSE FERLY SELLY ADMIRE WONDER MAGNALE MIRACLE MONSTER PORTENT PRODIGY SELCOUTH ADMIRATION

MARVELOUS FAB EPATANT MIRIFIC STRANGE FABULOUS WONDROUS MIRACULOUS

MARY MOLL POLL MAMIE MAURA MOLLY MIRIAM MARILLA

MARYLAND
BATTLESITE: ANTIETAM
CAPITAL: ANNAPOLIS
COLLEGE: HOOD GOUCHER STJOHNS
COUNTY: KENT CECIL TALBOT CALVERT HARFORD ALLEGANY SOMERSET
INDIAN: CONOY NANTICOKE
LAKE: PRETTYBOY
MOUNTAIN: BACKBONE
NATIVE: WESORT TERRAPIN
NICKNAME: COCKADE OLDLINE
RIVER: CHESTER POTOMAC CHOPTANK PATUXENT
STATE BIRD: ORIOLE
STATE TREE: OAK
TOWN: BELAIR DENTON EASTON ELKTON TOWSON LAPLATA ABERDEEN BETHESDA POCOMOKE BALTIMORE

MARYSOLE CARTER LEADER CARTARE

MARZIPAN MARCHPANE

MASAI WAKWAFI WAKWAVI

MASCEZEL (BROTHER OF —) GILDO

MASCOT BILLIKEN

MASCULINE MALE BUTCH DOGGY MACHO RUDAS VIRILE LALAQUI MANLIKE
(EXAGGERATEDLY —) MACHO
(PREF.) ANDR(O) MASCULO
(SUFF.) ANDRIA ANDROUS ANDRY

MASCULINITY (EXAGGERATED AWARENESS OF —) MACHISMO

MASH PAP BEER CHAP MASA MASK MESH SLOP CHAMP CREEM SMASH SMUSH MUDDLE STILLAGE
(FATHER OF —) ARAM

MASHED CHAPPED DAUPHINE

MASHER FLIRT BEETLE

MASJID MOSQUE

MASK FACE HIDE JEST LOUP SLUR VEIL BLOCK BLOOP CLOAK COVER GRILL GUISE LARVE POINT VIZOR DOMINO GRILLE MUZZLE SCREEN VEILER VIZARD BECLOUD CONCEAL CURTAIN MASKOID ANTEMASK DEFILADE DISGUISE MASCARON PRETENSE
(— OUT) CROP
(GAS —) CANARY
(HALF —) LOO LOUP DOMINO
(PL.) AREITO

MASKED LARVATED VIZARDED

MASKED BALL (CHARACTER IN —) HORN ANGRI AMELIA RENATO TOMASI ULRICA ARMANDO RIBBING SAMUELE ARVIDSON GUSTAVUS RICCARDO ANCKERSTROEM
(COMPOSER OF —) VERDI

MASKER GUISARD MASQUER

MASKING MUMMERY MUMMING COLORING

MASKLIKE PERSONATE

MASLIN MESTLEN MASHLOCH MUNGCORN MASSELGEM

MASNADIERI, I (CHARACTER IN —) CARLO AMALIA FRANCESCO MASSIMILIAN
(COMPOSER OF —) VERDI

MASON LAYER BUILDER MASONER COMACINE KNOBBLER LAMMIKIN SCUTCHER

MASONRY ASHLAR MANTLE BACKING BLOCAGE MOELLON NOGGING ISODOMUM QUOINING ROCKWORK RUBBLEWORK

MASQUE MASK COMUS DEVICE ANTIMASK DISGUISE

MASQUER REX

MASQUERADE MASK GUISE DOMINO MASQUE PARADE MASKERY DISGUISE

MASQUERADER RAGSHAG

MASQUERADING CARNIVAL

MASS BAT BED GOB SOP WAD BODY BULK CLOD GOUT HEAP HEFT KNOT LEAD LUMP MOLE OBIT STOW SWAD AMASS BATCH BLOOM CLAMP CLASH CLUMP CROWD CRUST DIRGE GLOBE GORGE GROSS MATTE MISSA PRESS SLUMP SOLID SPIRE STORE WODGE COMMON GOBBET NUGGET PROPER VOLUME WEIGHT BOUROCK CONGEST DENSITY MASKIN MESKINS MYSTERY REQUIEM SALOMON CALAPITE CONGERIE ENDOSOME FLOCCULE MOUNTAIN MYCETOMA SOULMASS ACCUMULATION
(— IN THE WHITE NILE) SUDD
(— OF BACTERIA) SLIME BAREGINE SYMPLASM
(— OF BLOSSOMS) BLOW
(— OF BLUBBER) MELON
(— OF BRANCHES) SPRAY
(— OF BUBBLES) FOAM
(— OF BUSHES) SHAG
(— OF CARPELS) SOREMA
(— OF CELLS) COMB CANCER MORULA CUMULUS STALACE PULVINUS
(— OF CLOUDS) BANK
(— OF COAL) JUD
(— OF COLORS) BLOB
(— OF COTTON) FUSSOCK
(— OF CURED RUBBER) LOAF
(— OF DEBRIS) SLIDE
(— OF DOUGH) DUMPLING
(— OF FIBERS) KAPOK
(— OF FILAMENTS) FLOCCUS MYCELIUM
(— OF FILTH) GORE
(— OF FRAGMENTS) BRASH
(— OF GAS) PROMINENCE
(— OF GOLD) BONANZA
(— OF HAIR) GLIB TOUPET
(— OF HYPHAE) MEDULLA

(— OF ICE) BERG CALF FLOE FLAKE PATCH ICICLE STURIS GROWLER ICEBERG FLOEBERG
(— OF INSECTS) CACHE
(— OF IRON) BALL BLOB CORE BLOOM INDUCTOR
(— OF LAVA) BOMB SPINE
(— OF LEAVES) FOLIAGE
(— OF LIMESTONE) HUM
(— OF LOOSE BOULDERS) CLATTER
(— OF METAL) SOW INGOT BUTTON
(— OF MOLTEN GLASS) GOB BLOOM GATHER PARISON
(— OF MUD) CLASH
(— OF ORE) BACK SLUG BUNNY SQUAT REGULUS
(— OF PEOPLE) CROWD HORDE
(— OF POMACE) CHEESE
(— OF ROCK) DOME NECK HORSE LEDGE NAPPE SCALP SNOUT INLIER SARSEN BOULDER FOOTWALL
(— OF SAND) PAAR
(— OF SOAP) CURD
(— OF SPORES) SORUS
(— OF SUGAR) FONDANT
(— OF SUGAR CRYSTALS) STRIKE
(— OF TISSUE) COLLAR GANGLION NUCELLUS
(— OF WATER) HEAD
(— OF YARN) COP BALLOON
(— OF YOLK) LATEBRA
(— OVERHANGING) CORNICE
(— TOGETHER) HUDDLE
(—S OF DRIFTWOOD) EMBARRAS
(ALPINE —) FLYSCH
(AMORPHOUS —) JUMBLE SYMPLASM
(BILLOWY —) CLOUD
(BUSHY —) SHOCK
(COMPACT —) BRIQUET
(CONCENTRATION OF MOON —) MASCON
(CONFUSED —) COT JUMBLE JUNGLE PILEUP CLUTTER RUMMAGE SHUFFLE
(DISORDERLY —) SCRAMBLE
(EGG —) BUNION CULTCH SPONGE
(FATTY —) BEAN HEADSKIN
(FECAL —) SCYBALUM
(FLATTISH —) DAB
(FLUFFY —) PUFF
(FLUID —) FLUOR
(GLASSY —) SLAG
(GLOBULAR —) MOORBALL
(INDISTINCT —) SMUDGE
(IRREGULAR —) CUB
(LIVING —) BLASTEMA
(MOIST —) PULP
(MOUNTAIN —) OROGEN
(NUCLEAR —) SHIELD
(OVERSPREADING —) PALL
(PART OF —) INTROIT
(PEAR-SHAPED —) BOULE
(POROUS —) FILTER
(PROJECTING —) BOSS
(PULPY —) SQUELCH
(RECTANGULAR —) BRICK
(ROOT —) SOLE
(ROUNDED —) COB NOB KNOB BOLUS KUGEL BULLET RONDLE
(SEDIMENTARY —) GOBI

(SHAPED —) PAT LOAF
(SHAPELESS —) JELLY
(SLIPPERY —) SIND SLUD SLUDDER
(SLUSHY —) POSH
(SOFT —) MASH MOXA MUMMY
(STICKY —) CLAG
(SWOLLEN —) CERE
(TANGLED — OF HAIR) MOP KNURL
(UNCTUOUS —) LANOLIN
(UNIT OF —) DALTON
(UPRIGHT —) COLUMN
(PL.) MEINY MEINIE TRENTAL POPULACE
(PREF.) ONCO
(SUFF.) IUM OME
MASSA (FATHER OF —) ISHMAEL

MASSACHUSETTS
CAPE: ANN COD
CAPITAL: BOSTON
COLLEGE: SMITH AMHERST SIMMONS WHEATON WILLIAMS RADCLIFFE WELLESLEY
COUNTY: DUKES ESSEX BRISTOL NORFOLK SUFFOLK BERKSHIRE NANTUCKET BARNSTABLE
INDIAN: NAUSET POCOMTUC
ISLAND: DUKES NANTUCKET
LAKE: ONOTA QUABBIN ROHUNTA WEBSTER
MOUNTAIN: BRODIE POTTER ALANDER EVERETT GREYLOCK
MOUNTAIN RANGE: BERKSHIRE
POND: WALDEN
PRESIDENT: KENNEDY
RIVER: NASHUA CHARLES CONCORD QUABOAG TAUNTON CHICOPEE DEERFIELD MERRIMACK
STATE BIRD: CHICKADEE
STATE FLOWER: MAYFLOWER
STATE NICKNAME: BAY OLDBAY OLDCOLONY
STATE TREE: ELM
TOWN: AYER LYNN OTIS ATHOL BARRE LENOX AGAWAM DEDHAM GROTON LOWELL NAHANT NATICK REVERE SAUGUS WOBURN HOLYOKE IPSWICH PEABODY TAUNTON BROCKTON CHICOPEE COHASSET SCITUATE UXBRIDGE YARMOUTH CAMBRIDGE NANTUCKET WORCESTER PITTSFIELD SPRINGFIELD
UNIVERSITY: CLARK TUFTS HARVARD BRANDEIS

MASSACRE SLAY POGROM CARNAGE SCUPPER BUTCHERY SLAUGHTER
MASSAGE WISP KNEAD FACIAL PETRIE SHAMPOO TRIPSIS LOMILOMI ANATRIPSIS
MASSAGER MASSEUR VIBRATOR
MASSECUITE GUR FILLMASS
MASSED DENSE
MASSENA QUAIL COPPY
MASSIVE BIG BEAMY BULKY GROSS HEAVY LUSTY MASSY SOUND STERN STRONG HEALTHY HULKING VOLUMED TIMBERED MONUMENTAL

MAST BUCK MAIN POLE SPAR OVEST STICK STING DRIVER JIGGER MIZZEN ARTEMON ASHERAH MASTAGE PANNAGE SPANKER FOREMAST JURYMAST MAINMAST SHIPMAST MIZZENMAST
(FALLEN —) SHACK
(SIXTH —) DRIVER
MASTAX TROPHI
MASTER DON HER JOE MAS RAB SAB SIR ARCH BAAS BEAK BOSS COCK FACE HERR JOSS KING LORD MIAN SIRE TUAN BWANA MARSE MASSA RABBI SAHIB SWAMI SWAMY SWELL BRIDLE BUCKRA CASTER DEACON DOMINE HUMBLE MAITRE PATRON RECTOR RHETOR SIRCAR WAFTER CAPTAIN CONQUER DOMINIE DOMINUS EFFENDI MAESTRO NAKHODA OGTIERN PADRONE RABBONI AMAISTER BARGEMAN BEMASTER KINGFISH LANDLORD MAGISTER OVERCOME SLOOPMAN SURMOUNT VANQUISH
(— OF CEREMONIES) EMCEE VERGER COMPERE CHAIRMAN
(— OF CRAFT) KAHUNA
(— OF HOUSEHOLD) BALABOS GOODMAN
(— OF REVELS) ALYTARCH
(— OF WHALER) SPOUTER
(FENCING —) LANISTA
(INFERIOR —) KNIFER
(PREF.) ARCH
MASTER-AT-ARMS JAUNTY JAUNTIE
MASTER BUILDER (AUTHOR OF —) IBSEN
(CHARACTER IN —) ALINE HILDA BROVIK RAGNAR SOLNESS
MASTERFUL BOSSY LORDLY VIRILE HAUGHTY ARROGANT MAGERFUL PEREMPTORY
MASTER OF BALLANTRAE
(AUTHOR OF —) STEVENSON
(CHARACTER IN —) CHEW DASS BALLY BURKE HENRY JAMES TEACH ALISON DURRIE GRAEME FRANCIS SECUNDRA MACKELLAR DURRISDEER
MASTERPIECE TOPPIECE
MASTERY GREE GRIP GRIPE COMMAND MAISTRY OVERHAND
MASTHEAD FLAG HIGHTOP
MASTICATE GUM CHAW CHEW
MASTICATORY PAN BUYO
MASTIC BULLY JOCUM JOCUMA
MASTIC TREE ACOMA AUSUBO COCUYO COCULLO LENTISK
MASTIFF ALAN MASTY BANDOG TIEDOG
MASTIGONEME FLIMMER
MASTITIS CLAP WEED GARGET
MAST TREE ASAK
MASTURBATE ABUSE
MASTURBATION ONANISM FROTTAGE
MASTWOOD POON KAMANI
MAT COT RUG TOD BASS FLAT FLET FOOT HAIR MOSS NIPA

PACE RAFT SHAG TAUT DOILY KILIM TATTY COTTER FELTER FOOTER PAUNCH PETATE TARGET COASTER CUSHION DOORMAT KAITAKA MATTING FOOTPACE FROSTING MATTRESS SPANDREL
(— BORDER) TANIKO
(BOWLING —) FOOTER
(FIBER —) IE BASS
(PALM-LEAF —) YAPA
(PICTURE-FRAME —) FLAT
(POLYNESIAN —) LAUHALA
(SCOURING —) BEAR
(TABLECLOTH —) GARDNAP
(PL.) DUNNAGE
MATACHIN BOUFFON
MATACO CORONADO
MATADOR MAT ESPADA CAPEADOR
(— MOVEMENT) PASE
MATCH GO CAP VIE BOUT COPE EVEN FERE LUNT MAKE MATE MEET MILL MOTE PAIR PEEL PEER SIDE SUIT AMATE EQUAL FIRER FUSEE FUZEE MOUSE PARTY RIVAL SPUNK TALLY VENUE VESTA ASSORT BESORT CANCEL COMMIT FELLOW KIPPIN MARROW QUADER RUBBER SAMPLE SWATCH COMPEER EXAMPLE IGNITER ILLUMER KINDLER KIPPEEN LIGHTER LUCIFER PARAGON PAREGAL PATTERN PENDANT SINGLES APPROACH BONSPIEL BREATHER CONGREVE EUPYRION FOURSOME INFLAMER LOCOFOCO PARALLEL PORTFIRE REANSWER VESUVIAN VESUVIUS SEMIFINAL PREMINIARY QUARTERFINAL
(— AT DICE) MAIN
(BOXING —) SPAR FIGHT PRELIM SLUGFEST
(CURLING —) SPIEL BONSPIEL
(DANCING —) KANTIKEY
(DISHONEST —) CROSS
(GOLF —) NASSAU FOURSOME
(SCOLDING —) FLYTE
(SHOOTING —) TIR SHOOT
(SLOW —) LUNT SMIFT SQUIB
(TILTING —) CAROUSEL
(PL.) LIGHTS
MATCHED ASSORTED
MATCHING MARROW SUITABLE
MATCHLESS ALONE UNIQUE NONESUCH PEERLESS
MATCHMAKER SHADCHAN
MATE CAWK FERE METE PAIR PEER BILLY BREED BUDDY BULLY CHINA CLASP CULLY DICKY MATCH PARTY TALLY YERBA BUNKIE COBBER FELLOW FUTURE MARROW PAREIL BROTHER COMPEER COMRADE CONSORT HUSBAND PARAGON NEIGHBOR PIRRAURA
(BOATSWAIN'S —) BUFFER
(GUNNER'S —) LADY
(SECOND —) DICKY
MATERIAL FINE MOLD GAUZE GOUGE HYLIC METAL MOULD PASTE PLASS STUFF THING TRADE BORROW CARNAL CYANUS

FABRIC GRAITH HOGGIN MATTER
PAPREG PUBLIC THINGY APPAREL
FOOTING SUBJECT TEXTILE
UNIDEAL WEIGHTY ADDITIVE
CORPORAL ECONOMIC EQUIPAGE
RELEVANT SENSIBLE SNOODING
TANGIBLE THINGISH OBJECTIVE
PHENOMENAL
(— ELIMINATED) CULLAGE
(— FOR FERMENTING) GUILE
(— FOR OYSTER BEDS) CULCH
CULTCH
(— IN GRAIN) DOCKAGE
(— IN MAKING CEMENT) ADDITION
(— IN NEEDLEWORK) INKLE
(— OF CORDED SILK) CRYSTAL
(— OF SCREENINGS) HOGGIN
HOGGING
(— REMOVED BY SAW CUT) KERF
(— USED IN WAXING) BALL
(— WEIGHED) DRAFT DRAUGHT
(—S FOR MAKING GLASS) FRIT
(ABSORBENT —) DOPE
(ALLUVIAL —) SHINGLE
(ANCIENT —) MURRA MURRHA
(ARTISTIC —) KITSCH
(BAGGING —) HOPSACK
(BITUMINOUS —) KEROGEN
(BONY —) COSMINE
(BUILDING —) LATH ADOBE BRICK
STAFF SWISH TABBY TAPIA
SILLAR CONCRETE
(BUILDING —S) TIGNUM
(CLAY —) TAPIA
(CLAYEY —) GOUGE
(COLORING —) TINCTION
(COMBUSTIBLE —) KINDLING
(CONSTRUCTION —) BREEZE
(CORE —) NIFF
(CUSHIONING —) AIRFOAM
(DEPOSITED —) FOOTS
(DIAMOND —) BORT
(DOWNY —) FLUE
(DRESS —) FOULE VOILE PEELING
COTILLON EOLIENNE
(DYEING —) SUMAC SUMACH
(EMBOSSED —) CLOQUE
(EMROIDERY —) ARRASENE
(EXCAVATED —) SPOIL
(FACING —) ENAMEL
(FISSIONABLE —) STUFF
(FOUNDATION —) UNDERLAY
(GLUTINOUS —) GELATIN
(GRANULAR —) BASIS
(HARD —) CARBIDE
(HEAT-RESISTANT —) ALSIFILM
(ILLUSTRATIVE —) ART
(INSECTICIDAL —) SCABRIN
(INSULATING —) KERITE PECITE
BLANKET LAGGING OKONITE
MEGOTALC
(LEFTOVER —S) ARISINGS
(LOOSE —) SAND GRAVEL
DETRITUS
(MINING REFUSE —) ATTLE
(MINUTE —) SESTON
(NUTRITIVE —) FUEL
(ORGANIC —) EXINITE
(PAPER-THIN —) FOIL
(PATCHING —) BOTCH
(PETRIFIED —) GEMSTONE
(POLISHING —) RABAT
(POWDERED —) FINES

(PRIMORDIAL —) BLASTEMA
(RAW —) STOCK STAPLE
(REFRACTORY —) GROG BULLDOG
CASTABLE
(RESIDUAL —) CEMENT
(RESOURCE —) SWIPE
(REVERSIBLE —) DAMASK
(SEDIMENTARY —) SILT
(SILK —) HONAN PEKIN FOULARD
SARCENET
(SLIMY —) GLIT SWARF
(SMOKING —) KEF KIF
(STIFF —) CANVAS
(STIFFENING —) BOXING
(TANNING —) BADAN SYNTAN
(THIN SLICE OF —) WAFER
(TILE STRENGTHENING —) WEB
(TRASHY —) SLUSH
(TWEEDY —) HOMESPUN
(TYPE-HIGH —) BEARER
(UNPUBLISHED —) INEDITA
(UPHOLSTERY —) LAMPAS
(VOLCANIC —) EJECTA
(WATERPROOF —) KERATOL
(WORTHLESS —) GARBLE
(WOVEN —) LAPPET
(PL.) STOCK STUFF
(PREF.) HYL(O)
(SUFF.) (PLASTIC —) PLASM(A)
MATERIALISM HYLISM SOMATISM
(DIALECTICAL —) DIAMAT
MATERIALISTIC SENSATE
SENSUAL BANAUSIC
MATERIALIZE REIFY DESCEND
MATER LECTIONIS GRAPHY
MATERNITY WARD NATUARY
MATGRASS NARD MATWEED
MATH MUTH MONASTERY
MATHEMATICIAN ALGORIST
GEOMETER
AMERICAN SEE FINE WEST WEYL
BROWN FISKE HARDY MASON
MOORE SMITH YOUNG CAJORI
KASNER KEYSER LEHMER LOOMIS
MILLER NEWTON OSGOOD PEIRCE
RUNKLE VEBLEN DICKSON
GODFREY METZLER NEUMANN
SAFFORD BANNEKER BIRKHOFF
BOWDITCH COOLIDGE FRANKLIN
MURNAGHAN HUNTINGTON
WILCZYNSKI
AUSTRIAN HAGEN DOPPLER
PURBACH
BELGIAN LEMAITRE
BRAZILIAN GUSMAO
DUTCH BLAEU VLACQ CEULEN
STEVIN HUYGENS SNELLIUS
GRAVESANDE MUSSCHENBROEK
EGYPTIAN PTOLEMY
ENGLISH DEE LAMB MUIR PELL
ALLEN BOOLE COTES ELLIS
HARDY MURIS ROUTH SHARP
SMITH WALES ATWOOD BARLOW
BARNES BARROW BRIGGS CAYLEY
COCKLE DARWIN DIGGES GUNTER
HADLEY HUTTON KELVIN LARMOR
NEWTON ROBINS STOKES TAYLOR
WALLIS WEDDLE BABBAGE
DODGSON HARRIOT LUBBOCK
MAKEHAM MASERES PEACOCK
RECORDE RUSSELL WHEWELL
WHISTON CLIFFORD GLAISHER
GOMPERTZ LEYBOURN

MACMAHON OUGHTRED
RAYLEIGH DUNSTABLE GREENHILL
NICHOLSON TODHUNTER
WHITEHEAD WHITTAKER
WOODHOUSE CODDINGTON
GELLIBRAND SACROBOSCO
SAUNDERSON
FRENCH BIOT FINE LAME LEVY
BORDA BOREL CHEZY COMTE
LEROY MONGE PRONY RAMUS
STURM VIETE BEAUNE BEZOUT
BOSSUT CAUCHY FERMAT FERNEL
GALOIS JORDAN MOIGNO PICARD
BOUGUER BROCARD CHASLES
CHUQUET COURNOT DARBOUX
GERMAIN GOURSAT HERMITE
KOENIGS LACROIX LAPLACE
POINSOT POISSON PUISEUX
VERNIER ALEMBERT BERTRAND
CLAIRAUT CORIOLIS DEMOIVRE
GERGONNE HACHETTE
HADAMARD LAGUERRE LEBESGUE
LEGENDRE MERSENNE MONTUCLA
PAINLEVE POINCARE PONCELET
ROBERVAL BRIANCHON
CONDORCET DESARGUES
DESCARTES LIOUVILLE
BURCKHARDT DEPARCIEUX
MAUPERTUIS
GERMAN GAUSS HESSE KLEIN
MAYER MISES PASCH PFAFF
RUNGE WOLFF BALMER CANTOR
JACOBI KUMMER MOBIUS
MULLER STIFEL APIANUS
CLEBSCH FRIESEN HILBERT
KASTNER LAMBERT PLUCKER
RIEMANN WIDMANN ARONHOLD
BLASCHKE DEDEKIND DROBISCH
LEIBNITZ MERCATOR RHATICUS
SCHOTTKY SCHUBERT DIRICHLET
GRASSMANN KRONECKER
LINDEMANN BIEBERBACH
EISENSTEIN HINDENBURG
PRINGSHEIM TSCHIRNHAUS
WEIERSTRASS KONIGSBERGER
GREEK CONON PAPPUS DIOCLES
ANTIPHON AUTOLYCUS
OENOPIDES SOSIGENES
ARCHIMEDES DIOPHANTUS
PYTHAGORAS DINOSTRATUS
HUNGARIAN BOLYAI
INDIAN ARYABHATA RAMANUJAN
IRISH BALL SALMON HAMILTON
BROUNCKER
ITALIAN CEVA BALDI FRISI PEANO
AGNESI GRANDI CARDANO
CREMONA PACIOLI RICCATI
BRIOSCHI CAMPANUS MALFATTI
BOSCOVICH CAVALIERI FIBONACCI
TARTAGLIA BELLAVITIS
MASCHERONI TORRICELLI
JAPANESE SEKI
NORWEGIAN LIE ABEL STORMER
GULDBERG
POLISH BARTEL CIOLEK WRONSKI
PORTUGUESE NUNES
RUSSIAN KRYLOV LIAPUNOV
CHEBYSHEV KOVALEVSKI
LOBACHEVSKI
SCOTTISH TAIT IVORY KEILL
LESLIE NAPIER BURGESS FORSYTH
GREGORY PLAYFAIR STIRLING
SWISS EULER AMSLER CRAMER

GULDIN BYRGIUS STEINER
BERNOULLI CHRISTOFFEL
MATHEMATICS MATHESIS
MATING NICK COUPLE DIALLEL
BREEDING HOMOGAMY PANMIXIA
(RANDOM —) PANGAMY
MATRASS BOLTHEAD CUCURBIT
MATRED (DAUGHTER OF —)
MEHETABEL
(FATHER OF —) MEZAHAB
MATRIMONIAL MARITAL NUPTIAL
SPOUSAL CONJUGAL
MATRIMONIO SEGRETO, IL
(CHARACTER IN —) FIDALMA
PAOLINO CAROLINA ELISETTA
GERONIMO ROBINSON
(COMPOSER OF —) CIMAROSA
MATRIMONY WEDLOCK
MARRIAGE
MATRIMONY VINE JASMINE
JESSAMY BOXTHORN
MATRIX PI BED MAT SORT PLASM
SHELL SLIDE DYADIC MASTER
MOTHER STRIKE STROMA
CALYMMA FORMULA MATRICE
PATTERN PROPLASM
MATRON DAME
MATTAN (SON OF —) SHEPHATIAH
MATTANIAH (FATHER OF —) BANI
ELAM HEMAN ZATTU
(SON OF —) ZACCUR
MATTE SLURRY REGULUS
MATTED COTTY FELTY PINNY
FELTED TAGGED TAUTED WAUKIT
STRINGY FELTLIKE CESPITOSE
MATTENAI (FATHER OF —) JOIARIB
MATTER RES BONE CASE GEAR
HYLE ITEM RECK WHAT AMPER
FORCE PARTY SKILL STUFF
THEME TOPIC AFFAIR ARGUFY
BEHALF DITTAY IMPORT ARTICLE
CONCERN MATERIA SHEBANG
SIGNIFY SUBJECT BUSINESS
COMETHER MATERIAL
(— ADDED TO BOOK) APPENDIX
(— AROUND THE TEETH) TOPHUS
(— CONSTITUTING PERFUME)
ESSENCE
(— IN DISPUTE) ISSUE
(— OF BUSINESS) SHAURI
(— OF CONCERN) FUNERAL
(— OF INTEREST) GRIST
(— TO) CONCERN
(ALLUVIAL —) GEEST
(BRAIN —) ALBA
(CARTILAGINOUS —) GRISTLE
(COLORING —) DYE COLOR CROCK
EOSIN MORIN PIURI ALNEIN
BUTEIN FUSTIC INDIGO ORCEIN
PIOURY CARMINE CASTORY
CUDBEAR LIGULIN OENOLIN
PIGMENT PUNICIN XANTHIN
ALGOCYAN ALIZARIN BRAZILIN
FUSTERIC LAPACHOL SCOPARIN
TINCTION
(CORRUPT —) PUS ATTER
(DECAYED ORGANIC —) DUFF
(ESSENTIAL —) POINT
(EXPLANATORY —) HAGGADA
(FATTY —) SEBUM
(FECAL —) SIEGE
(FILTHY —) GUNK
(FOREIGN —) SOIL DROSS

(FOUL —) FILTH SORDES
(FRONT —) FOREWORD
(GELATINOUS —) BREAK SPAWN
(GRAY —) GLIOSA CINEREA
(HYPOTHETICAL —) PROTYLE
(INANIMATE —) AJIVA
(INFECTIOUS —) MIASMA
(MINERAL —) FLOAT FLOATS
(NERVE —) CINEREA
(POTENTIAL —) PRAKRITI
(PRIMARY —) PRADHANA
(PRINTED —) BOX DISPLAY
(PULVERIZED —) ATTRITUS
(READING —) BODY
(SLIMY —) GLAIR
(SMALL —) MINUTIA
(SOFT —) PASH
(SUBJECT —) SCOPE CONTENT
(SUPPURATIVE —) PUS
(TRIVIAL —) JOKE
(TYPESET —) CHASE
(WASTE —) DIRT DRAFF DROSS
RAMMEL SEWAGE EXCRETA
(WORTHLESS —) SLAG CHAFF
GARBAGE
(WRITTEN —) SCRIVE
(PL.) HARNESS SQUARES
(PREF.) HYL(O)
(SUFF.) **(COLORING —)** PHYLL
MATTER-OF-FACT DRY PROSE
LITERAL PROSAIC
MATTER-OF-FACTNESS PROSE
MATTHAN (GRANDSON OF —)
JOSEPH
MATTHEW (FATHER OF —)
ALPHAEUS
MATTING MAT TAT BAST BEAR
BUMP SIRKI TATTY SAWALI
TATAMI COCOMAT RABANNA
MATTOCK MAT BILL HACK MATAX
PICKAX TUBBAL TWIBIL GRUBBER
MATTRESS BED MAT TICK DIVAN
QUILT RESAI REZAI PALLET
BISCUIT MATRACE PALLIASSE
MATURATE MATTER
MATURE AGE OLD BOLD FULL
GRAY RIPE ADULT MANLY RIPEN
SHOOT ACCRUE AUTUMN
DECOCT DIGEST MELLOW SEASON
SEEDED CONCOCT DEVELOP
FURNISH PERFECT PROVECT
MATURATE
(PREF.) TEL(E)(O)
MATURED ADULT GROWN
FORMED HEADED MELLOW
SEEDED HOMOGAMY
(SEXUALLY —) HIGH
MATURING (— EARLY) RATHRIPE
MATURITY AGE RIPENESS
MATWEED NARDUS
MATZOTH MATZOS AFIKOMEN
MAUDLIN BEERY MOIST FUDDLED
MAUDLINISM BATHOS
MAUL FAN PAW TUG MALL MELL
GAVEL GLAUM BEATER BEETLE
BEMAUL MUZZLE SCAMBLE
MAUND MAO MEIN MAHAN
MAUNDER HAVER
MAUNDY NIPTER MANDATE
MAURITANIA (CAPITAL OF —)
NOUAKCHOTT
(MONEY OF —) OUGUIYA
(RIVER OF —) SENEGAL

(TOWN OF —) ATAR NEMA AGMAR
KAEDI OUJAF
MAURITIUS (CAPITAL OF —)
PORTLOUIS
(CHANNEL OF —) QUOIN
(ISLAND OF —) AGALEGA GABRIEL
RODRIGUEZ
(RIVER OF —) GRAND POSTE
REMPART
(TOWN OF —) VACOAS TRIOLET
CUREPIPE SOUILLAC
MAUSOLEUM MOLE TOMB SHRINE
TURBEH BARADARI
MAUVE MALLOW PURPLE
MAUVINE
MAVEN EXPERT
MAW MAA CROP GORGE CROPPY
THROAT
MAWKISH CUTE SAPPY SOPPY
SOUPY WALSH DRIPPY SICKLY
VANILLA
MAXILLA SETA GNATHITE
CULTELLUS
MAXILLIPED JAWFOOT GNATHITE
MAXIM SAW SAY DICT ITEM NORM
RULE TEXT WORD ADAGE AXIOM
GNOME LARGE MOTTO DICTUM
SAYING SYMBOL BROCARD
DICTATE IMPRESA PRECEPT
PROVERB APHORISM APOTHEGM
DOCTRINE MORALISM PROTASIS
SENTENCE
(PL.) LOGIA
MAXIMUM FULL MOST PEAK
CREST EXTREME OUTSIDE
SUMMARY ULTIMATE
MAXIXE CARIOCA
MAXWELL LINE WEBER
MAY CAN MUN MOTE MOWE MUST
PRIME SHALL HEYDAY
HAWTHORN SYCAMORE
(3D OF —) RUDMASDAY
MAYA PRAKRITI
MAYAN COCOM
(— CALENDAR PERIOD) UAYEB
UINAL
(— GOD) CHAC CHAAC
MAYAPPLE MANDRAKE
MAYBE MEBBE HAPPEN PERHAPS
POSSIBLY
MAY DAY BELTANE
MAYFISH ROCKFISH
MAYFLOWER ARBUTUS
MAYFLY DUN DOON DRAKE NAIAD
DAYFLY SPINNER EPHEMERA
MAYHEM FELONY
MAYONNAISE MAYO GOULASH
DRESSING
(GARLIC —) AIOLI
MAYOR MAIRE BAILIFF DEMARCH
PODESTA PROVOST PALATINE
(BULGARIAN —) KMET
(SPANISH —) ALCALDE
MAYOR OF CASTERBRIDGE
(AUTHOR OF —) HARDY
(CHARACTER IN —) JOPP SUSAN
DONALD NEWSON FARFRAE
LESUEUR LUCETTA MICHAEL
RICHARD HENCHARD ELIZABETH
TEMPLEMAN
MAYORSHIP CHAIR
MAYPOLE SHAFT
MAYPOP MAYCOCK MARACOCK

MAYWEED BALDER COTULA
MATHER HOGWEED COMPOSIT
DILLWEED
MAZE JUNGLE WARREN CONFUSE
BEWILDER LABYRINTH
MAZEPPA (CHARACTER IN —)
MARIA ANDREY MAZEPPA
KOCHUBEY
(COMPOSER OF —) TCHAIKOVSKY
MAZUMA (ALSO SEE MONEY)
LUCRE
MCCOY QUILL
ME I MA US
MEAD MEATHE BRAGGET
HYDROMEL METHEGLIN
MEADOW LEA ABEL MEAD VEGA
WISH WONG FIELD GRASS LEASE
MARSH SWALE WARTH CALLOW
PARAMO SAETER SMOOTH
POTRERO THWAITE CHINAMPA
(ARTIFICIAL —) CHINAMPA
(IRISH —) BAAN
(LOW —) ING INCH INGE HAUGH
CALLOW
(PREF.) PRATI
(SUFF.) ING
MEADOW CROWFOOT
FROGWORT
MEADOW GRASS POA
MEADOWLAND ALP MOWING
MOWLAND
MEADOWLARK ACORN MEDLAR
MEADOW MOUSE VOLE
MEADOW PEA COWPEA
MEADOW PIPIT WEKEEN CHEEPER
TIETICK TITLING LINGBIRD
TWITLARK
MEADOW SAFFRON UPSTART
COLCHICUM
MEADOW SAXIFRAGE SESELI
MEADOWSWEET SPIREA
MEADWORT
MEAGER BALD BARE LANK LEAN
NICE POOR THIN GAUNT NAKED
SCANT SILLY SKIMP SOBER SPARE
JEJUNE LEEPIT LENTEN MEAGRE
NARROW PILLED SCANTY SLIGHT
SPARSE STINGY SCRAGGY
SCRANNY SCRIMPY SCRUBBY
SLENDER SPARING STARVED
STERILE MARGINAL SCRANNEL
SCRATCHY MISERABLE
MEAGERLY BARELY SPARELY
SPARINGLY
MEAGERNESS ECONOMY EXILITY
TENUITY SPARENESS
MEAL AMYL ATTA BAKE CENA
CHOW FARM FEED HASH KAIL
MEAT MONG NOSH TUCK COENA
FLOUR MANGE SCOFF BUFFET
COMIDA DINNER FARINA MANGER
POLLEN REPAST SPREAD SQUARE
SUPPER UNDERN BLOWOUT
COOKOUT CRIBBLE MELTITH
NAGMAAL NOONING SETDOWN
ALMUERZO CORNMEAL
EVENMETE MEALTIDE ORDINARY
TRENCHER
(— AND WATER) DRAMMOCK
(— FROM CASSAVA ROOT) FARINE
FARINHA
(— GROUND BY HAND) GRADDAN
(— OF FELLOWSHIP) AGAPE

(— STIRRED WITH MILK) STUROCH
(ACORN —) RACAHOUT
(COARSE —) GRIT GROUT KIBBLE
CRIBBLE GURGEONS
(COLLEGE —) HALL
(CORN —) MASA ATOLE NOCAKE
(ELABORATE —) FEAST BANQUET
(FIRST —) ALMUERZO
(FULL —) GORGE
(HASTY —) SNAP CHACK
(HEARTY —) AIT
(IMPROMPTU —) BITE CHECK
(LIGHT —) BAIT BEVER CHACK
CHECK FOURS NUNCHEON
(MIDDAY —) NOON
(MORNING —) BRUNCH
(PERTAINING TO —) PRANDIAL
(PURIM —) SEUDAH
(SCANTY —) PICK
(SMALL —) SNAP MORSEL
(SOLITARY —) SULLEN
(UNSORTED —) ATTA
(PL.) TUCKER
(PREF.) ATHERO
MEALTIDE MELTITH
MEALTIME CHOW MELTETH
MEALY FLOURY FARINOSE
PERONATE
MEALYBUG COCCID
MEAN LOW BASE CLAM HARD
LEAN MIDS NICE POKY POOR SLIM
VILE AGENT ARGUE DINGY DIRTY
DUSTY FOOTY GRIMY KETTY
LOUSY MANGY MESNE MEZZO
MIDST MINGY MOYEN MUCKY
NASTY PETIT PETTY RATTY
RUNTY SCALD SCALL SCALY
SCRUB SEEDY SILLY SMALL SNIDE
SNIVY SORRY SOUND SPELL
ABJECT BEMEAN COMMON
DENOTE DESIGN DIRTEN FEEBLE
FROWZY FRUGAL GRUBBY
HUMBLE HUNGRY IMPORT INSECT
INTEND LEADEN LITTLE MEASLY
MEDIAL MEDIUM MENIAL MIDDLE
NARROW ORNERY PALTRY
PEANUT PILLED POKING RASCAL
SCABBY SCREWY SCUMMY
SCURVY SHABBY SLIGHT SNIFTY
SNIPPY SORDID SQUALL STRAIT
TEMPER YELLOW AVERAGE
CAITIFF CHANNEL CHETIVE
COMICAL CONNOTE HACKNEY
HILDING IGNOBLE MESQUIN
MISERLY MOTETUS OBSCURE
PEAKING PELTING PIGGISH
PIMPING PITIFUL PORTEND
REPTILE ROINISH SCABBED
SHABBED SIGNIFY VICIOUS
BEGGARLY CHURLISH DOGGEREL
MEDIOCRE MIDDLING NIGGLING
PICAYUNE PITIABLE RASCALLY
RIFFRAFF SHAMEFUL SNEAKING
TWOPENNY WRETCHED
MEANDER WIND STRAY TWINE
CIRCLE WIMPLE WINDLE SERPENT
WINDING STRAGGLE
MEANING WIT HANG DRIFT SENSE
SOUND IMPORT INTENT SEMEME
PURPORT PURPOSE CARRIAGE
INNUENDO SENTENCE STRENGTH
REFERENCE SIGNIFICANCE
(BASIC —) EFFECT

(DOUBLE —) WHIM EQUIVOKE
(ESSENTIAL —) CORE CONTENT
(IMPLIED —) EMPHASIS
(MANIFEST —) FACE
(REAL —) SPIRIT
(SECONDARY —) OVERTONE
(SECRET —) HEART
(SENSE THE — OF) READ
MEANINGFUL RICH PREGNANT
MEANINGFULNESS BODY
MEANINGLESS BANAL ABSURD
FECKLESS SENSELESS
(— LETTER OR CODE) NULL
MEANNESS BEGGARY
MEANS MIDS AGENT DRIVE MESNE
MOYEN PURSE THEME AGENCY
AVENUE ENGINE MATTER MIDDES
POCKET STRING WRENCH
BALANCE BENEFIT DEMESNE
FACULTY FASHION QUOMODO
COURTESY
(— OF COMMUNICATION) CANAL
COMMERCE
(— OF DEFENSE) HORN HEDGE
SHIELD BULWARK
(— OF ESCAPE) CHINK SCAPE
FLIGHT
(— OF LIVING) ALIMONY
(— OF OFFENSE) ARM
(— OF PROTECTION) SAFETY
(— OF SUPPORT) HOLD ALIMENT
SUPPORT
MEANSPIRITED POOR SUPINE
CURRISH BANAUSIC RECREANT
MEANTIME MEAN WHILE WHILES
INTERIM
MEANTONE TERTIAN
MEANWHILE WHILST INTERIM
MEANTIME
MEASLES RUBEOLA MORBILLI
(BLACK —) ESCA APOPLEXY
MEASURE (ALSO SEE UNIT AND
WEIGHT) AR BU EM EN HO KO LI
MO RI SE TU AAM ARE AUM BAG
CAB CHO DRA ELL FAT FEN FIT
FOU FUN GAD GAZ GUZ HIN HOB
IMI KAB KAN KIP KOR KOS LEA
LOG LUG MAU MIL MOY PIK RIG
RIN ROD SAA SHO TON TUN VAT
VOG WEY ACRE ALMA AUNE
BARN BATH BEKA BOLL BOUW
BUTT CADE CENT CHIH COOM
COSS DEPA DOSE DRAA DRAM
DYNE EPHA EPHI FALL FANG
FOOT FULL GAGE GERA GILL GIRT
GOAD GRAM GREX HAND HATT
HIDE HOOP HOUR IMMI INCH
KNOT KOKU LAST MEAL METE
MILE MUID NAIL NOOK OMER
PACE PINT PIPE POLL REAM RIME
ROOD ROPE ROTL SAAH SACK
SALM SEAH SEAM SIZE SKEP
SPAN STEP TAKT TAPE TIME
TRAM TRUG TSUN VARA WIST
YARD ALMUD AMBER ANKER
ARDAB ARDEB ARURA BEKAH
BIGHA BLANK BODGE BRASS
CABAN CABLE CABOT CANDY
CARAT CARGA CATTY CAVAN
CHAIN CHANG CHING CLOVE
COOMB CRANS CUBIT CUMAL
CUNIT DENUM DEPOH DIGIT
DRAFT DUNAM DUNUM EPHAH

GAUGE GERAH GIRTH HOMER
HUTCH JUGER LABOR LAGEN
LIANG LIBRA LIGNE LIPPY LITER
LITRE MEITH METER METRE
MINIM MODEL OUNCE PEISE
PERCH PLANK POUND QUIRE
RASER RHYME SALMA SCALE
SCORE SHAKU SHENG SHING
SIEVE SLEEP STACK STERE STONE
STOOP STOUP THERM TOISE
TOVET TRACE VERST YOJAN
APATAN ARCHIN ARPENT ARSHIN
ASSIZE BARREL BATMAN BEMETE
BOVATE BUNDLE BUSHEL
CANADA CANTAR CHOMER
CHOPIN COLLOP COUDEE COVIDO
CUERDA DAVACH DAVOCH
DECARE DEGREE DENIER DIPODY
DIRHAM DRACHM ENGLER
EXTENT FANEGA FATHOM
FEDDAN FINGER FIRKIN FIRLOT
FLAGON FODDER FORPET FOTHER
GALLON GRAMME HALEBI HIDAGE
KISHEN LEAGUE MICRON MODIUS
MODULE MOGGIO MORGEN
NUMBER OITAVA OUROUB
OXHIDE QANTAR REASON
SAZHEN SETIER SQUARE STERAD
STRIKE SULUNG TERMIN THRAVE
WINDLE YOJANA ADOULIE
AMPHORA ANAPEST ARSHINE
BATTUTA BRACCIO BREADTH
CADENCE CALIPER CALORIE
CENTARE CENTNER CENTRAD
CHITTAK COMPASS CONGIUS
CONTAIN DECIARE DIOPTER
DRACHMA DRAUGHT ENTROPY
FARSAKH FARSANG FRUNDEL
FURLONG HECTARE HEMINEE
KILIARE NOCKTAT QUARTAN
QUARTER SCHEPEL SCRUPLE
SECCHIO SKEPFUL SKIPPLE
SPANGLE SPINDLE STADION
STADIUM TERTIAN VIRGATE
ALQUEIRE CAPACITY CARUCATE
CENTIAVE CHETVERT CRANNOCK
DACTYLIC DECAGRAM DECIGRAM
DESIATIN DIAPASON HOGSHEAD
INNOCENT LANDYARD
METEWAND MUTCHKIN
PARASANG PLOWGANG
PLOWGATE SCHOONER
SCHOPPEN STANDARD
PRECAUTION
(— DEPTH) SOUND
(— FOR DRINKS) JIGGER
(— FOR FISH) COT VOG CRAN LAST
DRAFT HAMPER DRAUGHT
(— FOR SHELLFISH) WASH
(— OF BEER) HANDLE
(— OF BUTTER) SPAN
(— OF CHAFF) FAN
(— OF COAL) TEN CORF KEEL
CHALDER CHALDRON
(— OF DEVELOPMENT) AGE
(— OF DIAMONDS) BULSE
(— OF DISCREPANCY) LEEWAY
(— OF EELS) BIND STICK
(— OF EFFICIENCY) DUTY
(— OF FURS) MANTLE
(— OF GRAIN) MOY COOP
(— OF HERRINGS) MEASE
(— OF LIQUOR) FIFTH

(— OF MERCURY) FLASK
(— OF MINING CLAIMS) MERE
(— OF PEAS) COP
(— OF RAISINS) FRAIL
(— OF ROTATION) ANGLE
(— OF SILK) DRAMMAGE
(— OF STRAW) KEMPLE
(— OF SUPERIORITY) LEAD
(— OF TIMBER) TON STANDARD
(— OF WAR) BLOCKADE
(— OF WATCHES) LIGNE
(— OF WATERCRESS) HAND
(— OF WEIGHT FOR ARROWS)
SHILLING
(— OF WHISKY) CRUISKEN
CRUISKEEN
(— OF WOOD) CORD STACK
(— OF WOOL FINENESS) BLOOD
(— OF WORK) POOL
(— OF YARN) LEA RAP CLEW HEER
THREAD SPANGLE SPINDLE
(— OUT) BATCH
(ANGULAR —) ARC
(COERCIVE —) SANCTION
(COUNTERFEIT —) SLANG
(DANCE —) TRACE
(DUE —) MANNER
(FULL —) SATIETY
(QUANTITATIVE —) MAGNITUDE
(ROAD —) SCHENE
(RUSSIAN —) VERST SAGENE
(SANCTIONED —) STANDARD
(PREF.) METR(O)
(SUFF.) METER METR(E)(O)(Y)
(BY A SPECIFIED —) MEAL
MEASURED NUMEROUS
MEASURE FOR MEASURE
(AUTHOR OF —) SHAKESPEARE
(CHARACTER IN —) ELBOW FROTH
LUCIO PETER ANGELO JULIET
POMPEY THOMAS CLAUDIO
ESCALUS MARIANA VARRIUS
ABHORSON ISABELLA OVERDONE
FRANCISCA VINCENTIO
BARNARDINE
MEASURELESS ENDLESS INFINITE
MEASUREMENT GAGE DEPTH
GAUGE LEVEL MEITH METAGE
DIALING MEASURE SOUNDING
(— FOR TAXATION) HIDE HIDAGE
(— OF CLOTH) ALNAGE
(— OF FINENESS) SET SETT
(LUMBER —) LAST
MEASURER METER
MEASURING
(SUFF.) METRY
MEAT BEEF FISH FOOD LAMB LEAN
LIFT PORK FLESH STEAK VIFDA
VIVDA BUCCAN CAGMAG FLEECE
MATTER NUTTON TARGET
PECKAGE
(— AND FISH) LAULAU
(— COOKED WITH SKEWERS)
SASSATIE
(— DRIED IN SUN) JERKY CHARQUI
PEMMICAN
(— OF CONCH) SCUNGILI
(— OF KID) CAPRETTO
(— WITH VEGETABLES) STEW
MULLIGAN
(BOILED —) SOD SODDEN BOUILLI
(BROILED —) GRISKIN GRILLADE
(BUFFALO —) FLEECE

(CANNED —) SPAM
(CHOPPED —) BURGER
(COCONUT —) COPRA
(CURED —) HAM
(CUT OF —) ARM
(DRIED —) MUMMY
(FAT —) SPECK
(FROZEN —) FRIGO
(INFERIOR —) CAGMAG STICKING
(JERKED —) BILTONG CHARQUI
(LEAN —) MUSCLE
(MINCED —) CHUET JIGOTE
RISSOLE SANDERS
(POTTED —) RILLETT
(RABBIT —) LAPAN
(RAGOUT OF —) HARICOT
(ROAST —) BREDE CABOB
(ROLLED —) BIRD
(SALTED —) JUNK MART
(SIDE —) SOWBELLY
(SMOKED —) BUCCAN
MEAT CURER BATHMAN
MEAT HOOK GAMBREL
MEAT JELLY ASPIC
MEATLESS PARVE LENTEN PAREVE
MEAT PIE PASTY
MEATUS BUR BURR ALVEARY
MEATY PITHY
MECATE MCCARTY
MECHANIC JOINER WRIGHT
ARTISAN FELTMAN SHOPMAN
WORKMAN BANAUSIC OPERATIVE
MECHANICAL FROZEN INHUMAN
METALLIC AUTOMATIC
(NOT —) HORMIC
MECHANICALLY BLINDLY
MECHANISM FAN BOND FEED
GEAR KITE LIFT MOTE APRON
CATCH CROWD FORCE ORGAN
SHAKE SLIDE SPARK STEER
ACTION BOTTOM CUTOFF INFEED
MOTION SICKLE STRIKE AUTOVAC
BUILDER CHANNEL CONTROL
EJECTOR GIGBACK GRIPPER
GUNLOCK HOLDOUT SETTING
TRIPPER ACTUATOR ELEVATOR
KINETICS RACKWORK SELECTOR
SETWORKS SIGNALER STEERING
STOPWORK THROWOUT
(— OF HEREDITY) PANGENESIS
MECHANIZE DESKILL AUTOMATE
MECHLIN MALINES
MECONIN OPIANYL
MEDAL STAR AWARD STAMP
PLAQUE MEDALET OSCELLA
VERNICLE MEDALLION
MEDALLION CAMEO TONDO
PADUAN PATERA PANHAGIA
MEDAN (FATHER OF —) ABRAHAM
(MOTHER OF —) KETURAH
MEDDLE TIG FOOL MELL MESS
MIRD POKE TOUCH DABBLE
FIDDLE FINGER HECKLE POTTER
PUTTER TAMPER TANGLE TINKER
MEDDLER SNOOP SNOOPER
BUSYBODY KIBITZER STICKLER
STIFFLER BUTTINSKY
MEDDLESOME FRESH NEBBY
MEDDLING BUSY
MEDEA (BROTHER OF —) ABSYRTUS
APSYRTUS
(FATHER OF —) AEETES
(HUSBAND OF —) JASON AEGEUS

(MOTHER OF —) IDYIA
(SISTER OF —) CHALCOPE
CHALCIOPE
MEDIA ELASTICA
MEDIAL MEDIAN MEDIUM MIDDLE
AVERGAGE
MEDIAN MEDIAL MESIAL AVERAGE
(— STRIP) MALL TERRACE
MEDIANT THIRD
MEDIATE MEAN REFEREE
MEDIATING MIDDLE MIDWAY
MEDIATOR MEANS MEDIUM
DAYSMAN MIDDLER PLACATER
STICKLER MODERATOR
MEDIC HOP NONESUCH
SHAMROCK
MEDICAL IATRIC PHYSIC IATRICAL
PAEONIAN
(— WORK) ALMONING
(PREF.) (— TREATMENT) IATR(O)
MEDICAMENT SMEGMA FRONTAL
EPULOTIC
MEDICINAL IATRIC PHYSIC
MEDICAL THERIAL PHYSICAL
SALUTARY THERICAL OFFICINAL
MEDICINE DRUG MUTI PEAI DROPS
GRUEL STEEL STUFF TONIC
TRADE AMULET ECLEGM ELIXIR
MAGUAL PHYSIC POWDER
REMEDY SIMPLE ALOETIC
ANODYNE ANTACID CORDIAL
HEPATIC LUCHDOM MIXTURE
OPORICE PLACEBO POROTIC
PYROTIC SPLENIC AROMATIC
DIAPENTE DIGESTER DRUGGERY
EARDROPS ECCRITIC EMULGENT
LAXATIVE LEECHDOM LENITIVE
LOBLOLLY PECTORAL PHARMACY
PULMONIC RELAXANT SPECIFIC
STOMATIC PRESCRIPTION
(CHINESE —) SENSO
(QUACK —) NOSTRUM
(SYSTEM OF —) AYURVEDA
(UNIVERSAL —) PANACEA
(PL.) GALIANES
(PREF.) IAMATO IATRO
PHARMACO
MEDICINE MAN PEAI DOCTOR
KAHUNA PIACHE POWWOW
SHAMAN SINGER ANGEKOK
TOHUNGA CONTRARY
POWWOWER
MEDIEVAL OLD GOTHIC
MEDIOCRE HACK MEAN SUCH
MEDIUM AVERAGE INFERIOR
MIDDLING MODERATE PASSABLE
MEDITATE CAST CHEW MUSE
BROOD GLOAT STUDY THINK
WEIGH PONDER RECORD BETHINK
COMMENT IMAGINE PREPEND
REFLECT REVOLVE COGITATE
CONSIDER PURPENSE RUMINATE
MEDITATION MOYEN STUDY
THINK DHYANA MUSING REVERIE
THOUGHT HIGGAION
MEDITATIVE MUSING MUSEFUL
PENSIVE RUMINANT
MEDITERRANEAN MIDLAND
MEDIUM BATH EVEN LENS MEAN
ETHER JUICE MIDST MOYEN
ORGAN BALIAN BISTER BISTRE
DIGEST MIDDLE MIDWAY ORACLE
SLUDGE TEMPER PSYCHIC

VEHICLE MEDIOCRE SHOWCASE
CONTINUUM
(— OF EXCHANGE) CURRENCY
(— OF TRANSMISSION) AIR
AIRWAVE
(CULTURE —) AGAR STAB BROTH
HYRAX SLANT CULTURE
BOUILLON
(ENVELOPING —) SWATH
(REFINING —) ALEMBIC
MEDIUM, THE (CHARACTER IN —)
FLORA MONICA
(COMPOSER OF —) MENOTTI
MEDLAR MESPIL LAZAROLE
MEDLEY OLIO BABEL REVUE
JUMBLE CHIVARI CLANGOR
FARRAGO GOULASH MELANGE
MIXTURE BROUHAHA KEDGEREE
MACARONI MISHMASH RHAPSODY
SLAMPAMP VARIORUM
CHARIVARI MACEDOINE
MEDOC WINE LAFITTE
MEDREGAL BONITO
MEDULLA PITH MARROW
MEDULLA OBLONGATA BULB
MEDUSA JELLY QUARL GORGON
BLUBBER GERYONID
(FATHER OF —) PHORCYS
(MOTHER OF —) CETO
(SLAYER OF —) PERSEUS
(PL.) BRACT
MEEK LOW DAFT MURE LOWLY
GENTLE HUMBLE PACIFIC
LAMBLIKE YIELDING
MEEKNESS MANSUETUDE
MEERSCHAUM PIPE GRAVEL
KIEFEKIL SEPIOLITE
MEET FIT KEP SEE COPE FACE FILL
HENT NOSE ABIDE CLOSE CROSS
FRONT GREET INCUR OCCUR
PIECE TOUCH ANSWER BATTLE
BEMEET COMBAT CONCUR FULFIL
INVENT SEMBLE CONTACT
CONVENE CONVENT COUNCIL
FULFILL SATISFY ASSEMBLE
CONFRONT CONVERGE GAINCOPE
(— A BET) SEE
(— A NEED) SUFFICE
(— AT END) BUTT
(— FACE TO FACE) AFFRONT
(— SQUARELY) ENVISAGE
(— VIOLENTLY) CHECK HURTLE
(— WITH) GET SEE BUMP FIND
STRIKE
(ATHLETIC —) GALA GYMKHANA
MEETING MOD FEIS MOOT CLOSE
FORUM SABHA SHINE STOUR
SYNOD TRYST ACCESS AUMAGA
CAUCUS CHAPEL CLINIC HUDDLE
POWWOW SEANCE CABINET
CHAPTER COLLEGE CONTACT
CONVENT COUNCIL JOLLITY
MOOTING OCCURSE REVIVAL
SEMINAR SITTING SYNAXIS
ASSEMBLY CONGRESS CONSULTA
DELEGACY ECCLESIA EXERCISE
JUNCTION OSCULANT TERTULIA
WARDMOTE CONCOURSE
COLLOQUIUM
(— OF BARDS) GORSEDD
(— OF NEIGHBORS) HUSKING
(— OF SCHOLARS) LEVY
(— OF WITCHES) ESBAT

(— OF WORSHIPERS) SERVICE
(ANGLO-SAXON —) GEMOTE
(GENERAL —) PRIME
(NOT —) PARALLEL
(POLITICAL —) CAUCUS
(PRIVATE —) CONCLAVE
(SECRET —) CABAL CONSULT
CONCLAVE
(SOCIAL —) CLUB JOLLY HOBNOB
(TOWN —) TUNMOOT
MEETINGHOUSE MORADA
MEETING PLACE AMBALAM
CENACLE TINWALD
MEGAPHONE VAMPHORN
MEGAPODE MALEO LEIPOA
MEGARA (FATHER OF —) CREON
(HUSBAND OF —) HERCULES
MEGAREUS (FATHER OF —)
HIPPOMENES
(MOTHER OF —) OENOPE
(SON OF —) EUIPPUS
(WIFE OF —) IPHINOE
MEGILP GUMPTION
MEHETABEL (HUSBAND OF —)
HADAD
(MOTHER OF —) MATRED
MEHIR (FATHER OF —) CHELUB
MEHTAR BUNGY BHUNGI
MEHUJAEL (FATHER OF —) IRAD
MEIOSIS LITOTES REDUCTION
**MEISTERSINGER VON
NURNBERG, DI** (CHARACTER IN —
) EVA HANS VEIT DAVID FRITZ
SACHS POGNER KOTHNER
WALTHER STOLZING MAGDALENE
BECKMESSER
(COMPOSER OF —) WAGNER
MELAMPUS (BROTHER OF —) BIAS
(FATHER OF —) AMYTHAON
(MOTHER OF —) IDOMENE
(SON OF —) MANTIUS ANTIPHATES
(WIFE OF —) LYSIPPE
MELANCHOLIA ATHYMY ATHYMIA
SADNESS
MELANCHOLIC HYPPISH
MELANCHOLY WO LOW SAD WOE
BLUE DRAM DULL DUMP MARE
ADUST BLUES DEARN DOWIE
DREAR DUSKY GLOOM SORRY
WISHT GLOOMY SOMBER SOMBRE
SORROW SPLEEN SULLEN
YELLOW CHAGRIN DOLEFUL
DUMPISH ELEGIAC SADNESS
SPLEENY THOUGHT ATRABILE
LIVERISH TRISTFUL
MELANESIAN DOBUAN KANAGA
KANAKA EFATESE
MELANGE GOMBO GUMBO
SMORGASBORD
MELANIPPUS (FATHER OF —)
THESEUS HICETAON
(LOVER OF —) COMAETHO
(MOTHER OF —) PERIGUNE
(SON OF —) IOXUS
MELANISM PHAEISM
MELANTERITE INKSTONE
MELANTIUS (SISTER OF —) EVADNE
MELATOPE EYE
MELCHI (FATHER OF —) ADDI
JANNA
MELCHIAH (SON OF —) PASHUR
MELD SET SAMBA SPREAD BOLIVIA
DECLARE

MELEA (FATHER OF —) MENAN
MELEAGER (FATHER OF —) OENEUS
(MOTHER OF —) ALTHAEA
MELECH (FATHER OF —) MICAH
MELEE BRAWL MEDLEY DOGFIGHT
PELLMELL WINGDING
MELIA (FATHER OF —) OCEANUS
(SON OF —) ISMENUS TENERUS
AEGIALEUS PHORONEUS
MELIBOEA (FATHER OF —)
AMPHION
(HUSBAND OF —) NELEUS
(MOTHER OF —) NIOBE
MELIORATE MITIGATE
MELISMA JUBILUS
MELL KIRN
MELLIFLUOUS SUGARED
HYBLAEAN
MELLOW AGE OMY HAZE LUSH
MALM PLUM RICH RIPE SOFT
FRUSH RIPEN FLUTED GOLDEN
MATURE
MELLOWED BEERY
MELODIOUS SOFT SOOT TUNY
SWEET TUNED ARIOSO DULCET
MELODIC MUSICAL SIRENIC
SONGFUL TUNABLE TUNEFUL
CANOROUS CHARMING
NUMEROUS SOUNDFUL
(EXCESSIVELY —) SIRUPY SYRUPY
MELODRAMA HAM TANK
MELODY AIR HUM LAY ARIA NOTE
TUNE CANTO CHANT CHARM
DREAD MELOS MIRTH NIGUN
CANTUS CHORAL GHAZEL
MONODY NIGGUN STROKE
CANZONA CANZONE CHORALE
DESCANT HARMONY MEASURE
MELISMA PLANXTY ROSALIA
CARILLON CAVATINA DIAPASON
VOCALISE
(— COMPASS) AMBITUS
(MOURNFUL —) DUMP
(SYNAGOGAL —S) CHAZANUT
HAZANUTH
MELON PEPO GOURD MANGO
CASABA CITRON DUDAIM
MAYCOCK CUCURBIT HONEYDEW
PEPONIDA PEPONIUM
MELT FLY RIN RUN BLOW FADE
FLOW FLUX FUSE THAW FOUND
LEACH SMELT SWEAL SWELT
TOUCH GUTTER RELENT SOFTEN
DISTILL FORMELT RESOLVE
DISCANDY DISSOLVE ELIQUATE
COLLIQUATE
(— AWAY) SWEAL
(— DOWN) RENDER
(— IRREGULARLY) DROZE
MELTED RUN FONDU FUSED
FUSILE
MELTING SOFT FUSILE FUSION
MELTWATER OUTWASH
MEMBER LIMB LITH PART BRANCH
FELLOW FILLET GIRDER SOCIUS
AMANIST COMPART ERANIST
FAIRING ALBRIGHT AULARIAN
BRIDLING
(— OF ANSAR) HELPER
(— OF BALLET) FIGURANT
(— OF BAND) SIDEMAN
(— OF BODYGUARD) HUSCARL

(— OF BROTHERHOOD) ESSENE SENUSSI

(— OF CLAN) CHILD CALEBITE

(— OF CLERGY) DEFENSOR

(— OF COAST GUARD) SPAR

(— OF COUNCIL) CONSUL HEEMRAAD

(— OF COURT) DICAST EPHETE

(— OF CREW) HAND IDLER LAYER DRIVER STROKE BOWSMAN FORETOP BRAKEMAN SHAREMAN

(— OF CULT) ANGEL AMIDIST

(— OF FACULTY) COUNSEL LECTURER

(— OF FAMILY) FETII

(— OF FRATERNAL ORDER) ELK SHRINER FORESTER KIWANIAN

(— OF FRATERNITY) GREEK

(— OF FRENCH ACADEMY) IMMORTAL

(— OF GANG) HENCHMAN

(— OF GENTRY) SEIGNEUR

(— OF GIRL SCOUTS) BROWNIE

(— OF GREEK ARMY) EVZONE

(— OF GUILD) COMACINE HOASTMAN

(— OF HOUSEHOLD) FAMILIAR

(— OF HUNTING PARTY) STANDER

(— OF INN OF COURT) ANCIENT BENCHER

(— OF ITALIAN ARMY) ALPINO

(— OF KNOW-NOTHING PARTY) SAM

(— OF LEGISLATURE) SOLON DEPUTY DELEGATE

(— OF LITERARY GROUP) FELIBRE

(— OF MIDDLE CLASS) BURGHER

(— OF PARLIAMENT) CONTENT THINGMAN

(— OF PRIMROSE LEAGUE) KNIGHT

(— OF RELIGIOUS ORDER) DAME FRIAR EUDIST FRAILE FRATER HERMIT JESUIT SISTER ALEXIAN BEGUINE BRINSER DERVISH HUSSITE SEPARTE SERVANT SERVITE CENOBITE EXORCIST HUMANIST SALESIAN

(— OF RETINUE) SEQUEL SEQUENT

(— OF RUSSIAN ARISTOCRACY) BOIAR BOYAR BOYARD

(— OF SAME GENUS) CONGENER

(— OF SECRET ORGANIZATION) DEMOLAY

(— OF SECRET SOCIETY) BOXER DANITE

(— OF SECT) BABI BABEE DRUSE HASID KHOJA AUDIAN BEREAN BRAHMO CATHAR DIPPER DOPPER IBADHI JUMPER KHLYST SMARTA AISSAWA AJIVIKA AUDAEAN CAINITE CHASSID DREAMER EMPIRIC EUCHITE IBADITE ISAWIYA ISMAILI RAPPIST SENUSSI SEVENER AQUARIAN CALIXTIN DARBYITE DUKHOBOR EBIONITE FAMILIST GLASSITE LABADIST MANDAEAN SADDUCEE SEVERIAN SHAFIITE SIMONIAN

(— OF STAFF) ATTACHE

(— OF STATE) CITIZEN

(— OF STOCK EXCHANGE) BOARDMAN

(— OF TEAM) SPARE BOBBER KICKER

(— OF TRIBE) LEVITE JUDAHITE LAMANITE

(— OF UPPER CLASS) EFFENDI

(— OF VARNA) SUDRA SHUDRA

(— OF WHITE RACE) HAOLE

(— OF WINDOW) APRON

(—S OF CLASS) FRY

(—S OF PROFESSION) FACULTY

(—S OF SECT) SKOPTSY

(—S OF TRIBUNAL) ACUERDO

(ARCHITECTURAL —) FAN ARCH FLAT SILL SPAN GABLE SOCLE STILE STILT CORBEL FASCIA CONSOLE CORNICE

(CHURCH —) GREEK LATIN DANITE DUNKER KIRKER TUNKER AZYMITE BAPTIST BEGHARD BROTHER DUNKARD KIRKMAN SECEDER ARMENIAN BRYANITE CATHOLIC DISCIPLE DOWIEITE JACOBITE

(CHURCH —S) FAITHFUL

(EVERY —) ALL

(FEEBLEST —) WRIG

(FULL —) GREMIAL

(OLDEST —) FATHER

(OVERHANGING —) BRACKET

(POLITICAL —) CADET ENDEK SHIRT GUELPH HUNKER LEADER APRISTA LEFTIST LIBERAL ABHORRENT BUCKTAIL DEMOCRAT HERODIAN LABORITE

(PROJECTING —) TENON

(SECRET —) CRYPTO

(SENIOR —) DOYEN

(TENSION —) HANGER

(TERMINAL —) TOE

(SUFF.) AD CRAT

(— OF A CLASS) ANDER MER(E)(IC)(IS)(OUS)(Y)

MEMBERS
(SUFF.) (— OF THE FAMILY) IDAE
(— OF THE SUBFAMILY OF) INAE

MEMBERSHIP SEAT GARTER GUILDRY

MEMBRANE RIM WEB CAUL COAT DURA FELL HEAD TELA GALEA HYMEN VELUM AMNION AMNIOS EXTINE INTINE MENINX MOTHER MUCOSA PLEURA RETINA SEPTUM SEROSA TIMBAL TUNICA TYMPAN BLANKET CAPSULE CHORION CHOROID CUTICLE DECIDUA EPICYTE HYALOID OOLEMMA PUTAMEN STRATUM VELAMEN ECTODERM ENDOCYST ENVELOPE EPENDYMA EPISPORE EXOLEMMA INDUSIUM INTEXINE LABELLUM PATAGIUM PELLICLE STRIFFEN ALLANTOIS PERIPLAST PERITONEUM

(— OF ORANGE) ZEST

(NICTITATING —) HAW

(TYMPANIC —) TYMPAN MYRINGA DRUMHEAD DRUMSKIN

(PL.) ADNEXA ANNEXA MENINGES

(PREF.) CHORI(O) HYMEN(O) MENING(O) MYRINGO VEL(I)

(SUFF.) YMENITIS

MEMBRANOUS HUSKY SKINNY

HYMENOID SCARIOSE SCARIOUS

MEMENTO RELIC TOKEN MEMORY TROPHY KEEPSAKE REMINDER SOUVENIR

MEMINNA PEESOREH

MEMNON (FATHER OF —) TITHONUS

(MOTHER OF —) AURORA

(SLAYER OF —) ACHILLES

MEMOIR ELOGE RECORD HISTORY MEMORIAL

MEMORABLE GRAND SIGNAL CLASSIC NOTABLE MEMORIAL NAMEABLE NOTEWORTHY

MEMORANDA (SET OF —) TICKLER

MEMORANDUM BILL CHIT NOTE SLIP BRIEF JURAT CAHIER CIPHER DOCKET MEMOIR MINUTE TICKET JOTTING MEMORIAL NOTANDUM PROTOCOL BORDEREAU

MEMORIAL AHU AGALMA CAHIER FACTUM MEMOIR MEMORY RECORD TROPHY DENKMAL MEMENTO MENTION EBENEZER MONUMENT REMEMBRANCE

MEMORIZE LEARN MANDATE REMEMBER

MEMORY MIND HEART IMAGE STORE RECALL RECORD MEMENTO STORAGE MEMORIAL SOUVENIR

(— ON COMPUTER CHIP) RAM ROM

(— SUBDIVISION) PAGE

(COMPUTER —) STACK

(OF POOR —) FLUFFY

(PAINFUL —) SCAR

(SMALL COMPUTER —) SCRATCHPAD

(PREF.) MNEM(I)(O)

(SUFF.) MNESIA(C) MNESIS MNETIC

MEN THEY ORANG INNUIT MANHEAD MANHOOD MANKIND MENFOLK HUMANITY

MENACE BOAST IMPEND THREAT BOGEYMAN MINATORY THREATEN

MENACING STOUT SURLY FIERCE TOWARD MINATORY MINACIOUS

MENAHEM (FATHER OF —) GADI

(VICTIM OF —) SHALLUM

MEN-AT-ARMS CHIVALRY

MEND DO FIX BEET DARN HEAL HELP STOP TINK AMEND CLOUT EMEND GRAFT MOISE PALCH COBBLE DOCTOR FETTLE RANTER REFORM REPAIR SOLDER SPETCH TINKLE IMPROVE INWEAVE REDRESS RIGHTLE

(— BY ADDING FEATHERS) IMP

(— CLUMSILY) BOTCH

(— MEN'S CLOTHES) BUSHEL

MENDACIOUS FALSE DISHONEST

MENDACITY LYING DECEIT FALSITY UNTRUTH

MENDER TINKER KETTLER BEATSTER

MENDICANCY BEGGARY

MENDICANT NAGA DANDI FAKIR FRIAR UDASI BEGGAR BHIKKU FAKEER FRATER GOSAIN AJIVIKA BAIRAGI EUCHITE VAIRAGI PANDARAM SANNYASI PASSIONIST

MENDING COBBLE

MENEL NELL

MENELAUS (BROTHER OF —) AGAMEMNON

(FATHER OF —) ATREUS PLISTHENES

(MOTHER OF —) AEROPE

(SISTER OF —) ANAXIBIA

(WIFE OF —) HELEN

MENHADEN POGY PORGY BUNKER CHEBOG SHINER ALEWIFE BUGFISH BUGHEAD CLUPEID ELLFISH FATBACK OLDWIFE SAVELHA SHADINE WHITING BONYFISH HARDHEAD

MENHIR BOUTA GORSEDD PEULVAN CATSTONE HAGIOLITH

MENIAL FAG BASE LOON PAGE KNAVE DRIVEL HARLOT POTBOY VARLET SERVILE SLAVISH BANAUSIC SCULLION SERVITOR

MENISCOID CRESCENT

MENNONITE HOOKER AMISHMAN AMMANITE HUTERITE

MENOETIUS (BROTHER OF —) ATLAS PROMETHEUS

(FATHER OF —) ACTOR

(MOTHER OF —) AEGINA

(SON OF —) PATROCLUS

MENOPAUSE CLIMAX

MENSTRUATE FLOW

MENSTRUATING SICK

MENSTRUATION FLOW CURSE FLUOR CRAMPS PERIOD COURSES

(FIRST —) MENARCHE

(PREF.) MENO

(SUFF.) (— CONDITION) MENIA

MENSTRUUM SOLVENT

MENTAL IDEAL GENIAL INWARD MINDLY PHRENIC PSYCHIC CEREBRAL

MENTALITY MIND SENSE ACUMEN REASON SPIRIT PSYCHISM

MENTHA LABIATE

MENTHANE TERPANE

MENTHOL CAMPHOR

MENTION CALL CITE HINT MIND MING MINT NAME CHEEP CLEPE SPEAK TOUCH MEMBER NOTICE SPEECH MEANING SPECIFY SUGGEST CITATION INSTANCE MEMORATE REHEARSE REMEMBER REFERENCE REPETITION

(— BY NAME) NEMN NEMME NEMPNE

(— CASUALLY) DROP

(HONORABLE —) ACCESSIT

MENTOR TEACHER CICERONE

MENTUM PERULA

MENU CARD CARTE

(COMPUTER —) DISPLAY

MEONOTHAI (FATHER OF —) OTHNIEL

MEPACRINE ATABRIN ATABRINE

MEPERIDINE DEMEROL

MEPHIBOSHETH (BROTHER OF —) ARMONI

(FATHER OF —) SAUL JONATHAN

(MOTHER OF —) RIZPAH

(SON OF —) MICHA

MEPHISTOPHELIAN SATANIC

MEPROBAMATE MILTOWN
MERAB (FATHER OF —) SAUL
(HUSBAND OF —) ADRIEL
MERARI (FATHER OF —) LEVI
MERCAPTAN THIOL
MERCEDARIAN NOLASCAN
RANSOMER
MERCENARY HACK VENAL JACKAL
HESSIAN PINDARI HIRELING
WAGELING
MERCER SILKMAN
MERCERIZE SCHREINER
MERCHANDISE CARGO CHEAP
GOODS STUFF WARES ARTWARE
CHAFFER SHIPPER TRAFFIC
CHAFFERY SALEWARE
(CHEAP SHODDY —) BORAX
(RETURNED —) COMEBACK
MERCHANT ARAB SETH SETT TELI
WALLA BADGER FACTOR KITELY
NEPMAN RETAIL TAIPAN TRADER
ANTONIO CHAPMAN GOLADAR
HANSARD HOWADJI CHANDLER
HUCKSTER MARCHAND
POVINDAH SOUDAGUR
(GRAIN —) LAMBADI
(GREAT —) TAIPAN
(HINDU —) BUNIA BUNNIA
(WINE —) VINTNER
MERCHANT OF VENICE (AUTHOR
OF —) SHAKESPEARE
(CHARACTER IN —) GOBBO TUBAL
PORTIA ANTONIO JESSICA
LORENZO NERISSA SALANIO
SALERIO SHYLOCK BASSANIO
GRATIANO LEONARDO SALARINO
STEPHANO BALTHASAR
LAUNCELOT
MERCIFUL KIND MILD HUMANE
RUEFUL TENDER CLEMENT
LENIENT MILDFUL PITIFUL
SPARING GRACIOUS QUEMEFUL
MERCILESS GRIM CRUEL SHARP
BLOODY FIERCE SAVAGE
WANTON PITILESS
MERCURY HG AZOCH AZOTH
DRAGON HERMES SPIRIT CHIBRIT
MARKERY TEUTATES
QUICKSILVER
(FATHER OF —) JUPITER
(MOTHER OF —) MAIA
MERCY LAW ORE HORE PITY RUTH
GRACE GRITH BLITHE LENITY
CHARITY CLEMENCY LENIENCY
COMPASSION
(PREF.) MISERI
MERE BARE NUDE ONLY PURE
PUTE SOLE VERY NAKED SHEER
SINGLE
(PREF.) PSIL(O)
MEREL PIN
MERELY BUT JUST ONLY BARELY
PURELY SIMPLY SINGLY SOLELY
ALONELY UTTERLY ENTIRELY
SCARCELY
MEREMOTH (FATHER OF —) BANI
URIAH
MERETRICIOUS CHEAP GAUDY
GILDED TAWDRY PUNKISH
MERGANSER SMEE SMEW HARLE
SNOWL SPIKE HERALD SAWNEB
WEASER BRACKET GARBILL
JACKSAW RANTOCK SAWBILL

TADPOLE TOWHEAD TWEEZER
WHEEZER EARLDUCK MOSSHEAD
SHELDRAKE
MERGE FUSE JOIN MELD BLEND
ENTER GLIDE UNIFY VERGE
MINGLE COALESCE COMMERGE
CONFLATE LIQUESCE
MERGING BLEND FUSION
MERICARP COCCUS
MERIDIAN (THOSE LIVING UNDER
SAME —) ANTOECI
MERINGUE KISS
MERINO DELAINE
MERISTEM PERIBLEM
MERIT DUE EARN MEED PUNY
BROOK FOUND THANK WORTH
DESERT PRAISE VIRTUE WRIHTE
DEMERIT DESERVE PUDDING
(— CONSIDERATION) COUNT
(POSSESSING —) WORTHY
MERITED JUST
(NOT —) INDIGN
MERITORIOUS CAPITAL MERITORY
THANKFUL VALOROUS
MERL BLACKIE
MERLIN (MISTRESS OF —) VIVIEN
MERLON COP
MERMAID NIXIE SIREN MERROW
MERWOMAN
MERMAN SEAMAN MANFISH
MERODACH (FATHER OF —) EA
(WIFE OF —) ZARPAINT
MEROPE (BROTHER OF —)
PHAETHON
(FATHER OF —) ATLAS OENOPION
PANDAREUS CRESPHONTES
(HUSBAND OF —) POLYBUS
SISYPHUS POLYPHONTES
(MOTHER OF —) PLEIONE
CYPSELUS HARMOTHOE
(SISTER OF —) AEDON CLEOTHERA
(SON OF —) AEPYTUS
MEROPODITE FEMUR MEROS
MEROZOITE AGAMETE
MERRILY GAILY GAMELY LIGHTLY
LUSTICK JOYOUSLY
MERRIMENT FUN JOY GALE GLEE
JEST UTAS DERAY MIRTH FROLIC
SPLEEN DAFFERY DAFFING
FESTIVE JOLLITY WAGGERY
HILARITY
MERRY GAY BOON CANT GLAD
GOLE BONNY BUXOM CADGY
CRANK DROLL JOLLY LIGHT
LUSTY MURRY SUNNY VOGIE
VOKIE BLITHE COCKET FROLIC
JOCANT JOCOSE JOCUND JOVIAL
JOYOUS LIVELY FEASTLY GLEEFUL
HOLIDAY JOCULAR LUSTICK
RAFFING WINSOME CHIRPING
DISPOSED FESTIVAL GAMESOME
GLEESOME LAUGHING PLEASANT
SPANKING SPORTFUL SPORTIVE
CONVIVIAL
(UNREASONABLY —) DAFT
MERRY-ANDREW AIRY ZANY
ANTIC DROLL JESTER BUFFOON
MERRY-GO-ROUND CAROUSEL
TURNABOUT ROUNDABOUT
MERRYMAKING ALE MAY RAG
KIRN PLOY REVEL GAIETY JUNKET
RACKET SPLORE CARNIVAL
MERRYTHOUGHT WISHBONE

MERRY WIDOW (CHARACTER IN —)
ZETA HANNA MIRKO DANILO
GLAWARI
(COMPOSER OF —) LEHAR
MERRY WIVES OF WINDSOR
(AUTHOR OF —) SHAKESPEARE
(CHARACTER IN —) NYM ANNE
FORD HUGH JOHN PAGE CAIUS
EVANS ROBIN RUGBY FENTON
PISTOL SIMPLE QUICKLY
SHALLOW SLENDER WILLIAM
BARDOLPH FALSTAFF
MERUS PALM
MESA HILL LOMA BENCH MESILLA
PLATEAU TERRACE CARTOUCH
MESADENIA CACALIA
MESCAL PEYOTE PEYOTL WOKOWI
MEXICAL CHALLOTE
MESCALERO FARAON
MESECH (FATHER OF —) JAPHET
MESENTERY CROW RUFFLE
MESH MASK MOKE CHAIN PITCH
SHALE ACCRUE ENGAGE MASCLE
SCREEN INTERLOCK SCREENING
(— IMPROPERLY) BUTT
(IN —) DIRECT
MESHA (FATHER OF —) CALEB
SHAHARAIM
(MOTHER OF —) HODESH
MESHED ENGAGED
MESHEZABEEL (FATHER OF —)
ZERAH
(SON OF —) PETHAHIAH
MESHILLEMOTH (FATHER OF —)
IMMER
MESHULLAM (FATHER OF —)
BERECHIAH BESODEIAH
ZERUBBABEL
(SON OF —) SALLU
MESHULLEMETH (FATHER OF —)
HARUZ
(HUSBAND OF —) MANASSEH
(SON OF —) AMON
MESOCARP FLESH
MESOMORPHIC SOMAL SOMATIC
ATHLETIC
MESON RHO KAON PION
BARYTRON MESOTRON
MESOPODIUM PETIOLE
MESOPOTAMIA (TREE OF —) HOMA
MESOTONIC TERTIAN MEANTONE
MESQUITE HONEY KEAWE PACAY
CASHAW ALGAROBA HONEYPOD
IRONWOOD MOSQUITO
MESS JAG JAM MIX MUX PIE SOP
CLAT FIST HASH JAMB MUCK
MULL MUSS SLUB SOSS STEW
SUSS BOTCH CAUCH JAKES
STREW SWILL BOLLIX BUNGLE
CADDLE CLATCH JUMBLE
MUCKER PICKLE PUDDLE SOZZLE
TUMBLE MAMMOCK MULLOCK
SCAMBLE SLOTTER COUSCOUS
DISORDER LOBLOLLY SHAMBLES
SLAISTER
(— AROUND) JUKE
(— OF FOOD) SAND
(GREASY —) GAUM
(SLOPPY —) SLOBBER SLAISTER
MESSAGE CHIT MODE SAND SEND
WIRE WORD RUMOR BREVET
CIPHER ERRAND GOSPEL LETTER
SCROLL BLINKER BODWORD

DEPECHE EMBASSY MISSION
SENDING TIDINGS AEROGRAM
CREDENCE DISPATCH
(— BY FLAGS) HOIST
(— FROM GOD) ANGEL
(CHRISTIAN —) EVANGEL
(CIPHER —) SCYTALE
(COMPLIMENTARY —) RECADO
(SEQUENCE OF —S) QUEUE
MESSALIAN EUCHITE
MESSENE (FATHER OF —) TRIOPAS
(HUSBAND OF —) POLYCAON
MESSENGER BODE PEON POST
SAND SEND TOTY VAUX ANGEL
ENVOY MUMMU VISOR BEADLE
BROKER BUNENE CHIAUS HERALD
LEGATE NUNCIO PIGEON RUNNER
APOSTLE CARRIER CASHBOY
CONTACT COURANT COURIER
EXPRESS FORAGER FORAYER
MALACHI MERCURY MESSAGE
MISSIVE NAMTARU PATAMAR
TOTYMAN TROTTER TRUMPET
EMISSARY FOREGOER HIRCARRA
LOBBYGOW NUNCIATE ORDINARY
PORTATOR APPARITOR
(— OF APSU AND TIAMAT) MUMMU
(— OF GOD) ANGEL
(— OF SHAMASH) BUNENE
(— OF THE GODS) HERMES
MERCURY
(MOUNTED —) COSSID ESTAFET
(RELIGIOUS —) APOSTLE
(UNDERWORLD —) NAMTARU
MESSIAH CHRIST WOVOKA
(MUSLIM —) MAHDI
MESSMATE YUBA
MESSUAGE HAW TOFT MEESE
MIDSTEAD
MESSY GOOEY SLOPPY SOZZLY
STICKY
MESTIZO CHOLO LADINO
CURIBOCA MAMELUCO
MESTOR (DAUGHTER OF —)
HIPPOTHOE
(FATHER OF —) PERSEUS
(MOTHER OF —) ANDROMEDA
(WIFE OF —) LYSIDICE
METAL ORE TIN BODY DIET GOLD
IRON LEAD ZINC BARIUM CESIUM
CHROME COBALT COPPER INDIUM
LATTIN NICKEL ORMOLU OSMIUM
RADIUM SILVER SODIUM
BISMUTH CADMIUM CALCIUM
HAFNIUM IRIDIUM LITHIUM
MERCURY RHENIUM RHODIUM
THORIUM TUTANIA URANIUM
YTTRIUM ALUMINUM ANTIMONY
CHROMIUM DEADHEAD
PLATINUM RUBIDIUM SCANDIUM
TANTALUM TINCTURE TITANIUM
TUNGSTEN VANADIUM
(— IN MASS) BULLION
(— IN SHEETS) LEAF PLATE
(BABBITT —) LINING
(BASE —) BILLON
(DECORATED —) TOLE
(GROUND —) BRONZING
(HEAVIEST —) OSMIUM
(IMPURE MASS OF —) REGULUS
(LIGHTEST —) LITHIUM
(LIQUID —) MERCURY
(MASS OF —) INGOT

(MOLTEN —) TAP SQUIRT
(OLD POT —) POTIN
(PERFORATED —) STENCIL
(PIECE OF CRUDE —) SLUG
(POINTED —) NAIL
(POROUS —) SPONGE
(SEMIFINISHED —) SEMIS
(SHEET —) LATTEN DOUBLES KALAMEIN
(WASTE —) GATE
METALLIC HARD THIN TINNY
METALLOPHONE SARON
  (BALINESE —) GANGSA
METALLURGIST AMERICAN HUNT
  HOLLEY PETERS SHIMER
  ENGLISH PERCY MUSHET THOMAS HADFIELD
  FRENCH HEROULT
METALWARE TOLE LORMERY
  GRAYWARE PONTYPOOL
METALWORK ZOGAN
METALWORKER BARMAN FOONER
  FORKMAN FOUNDER SUDSMAN
METAMERE SOMITE SEGMENT
  MEROSOME
METAMERIC SEGMENTAL
METAMORPHIC
  (PREF.) BLAST(O)
METAMORPHOSE TURN SHAPE
  INDENIZE TRANSMEW
METAMORPHOSIS METABOLE
  PETALODY PHYLLODY SEPALODY
  (SUFF.) ODY
METANIRA (HUSBAND OF —)
  CELEUS
  (SON OF —) DEMOPHON TRIPTOLEMUS
METAPHOR IMAGE TROPE FIGURE
  KENNING
METAPHORICAL FIGURAL
  FIGURATE TROPICAL
METASTOMA LABIUM
METATE QUERL
METE DEAL DOLE GIVE ALLOT
  AWARD MATCH SERVE MEASURE
  APPORTION
METEMPSYCHOSIS SAMSARA
METEOR STAR ARGID CETID COMID
  DRAKE LUPID LYRID URSID
  ANTLID AUGUST BOLIDE BOOTID
  CORVID CYGNID DRAGON HYDRID
  LIBRID LYNCID LYRAID PHASMA
  PISCID TAURID AQUARID AQUILID
  ARIETID AURIGID CAMELID
  CANCRID CEPHEID CORONID
  GEMINID MEATURE ORIONID
  PEGASID PERSEID POLARID
  PRODIGY COLUMBID CRATERID
  DRACONID ERIDANID FIREBALL
  FORNAXID HERCULID LACERTID
  SAGITTID SCORPIID SHOTSTAR
  TOUCANID VIRGINID
  (SUFF.) ID
METEORITE BAETYL BOLIDE
  ANDRITE ATAXITE EUCRITE
  AEROLITE AEROLITH BAETULUS
  BAETYLUS IREOLITE SIDERITE
  SKYSTONE
METEOROLOGIST AMERICAN EDDY
  ESPY WARD ROTCH FERREL
  MARVIN CLAYTON REDFIELD
  CARPENTER
  AUSTRIAN FALB HANN PERNTER

ENGLISH REID SHAW DINES
  GALTON GLAISHER
  FRENCH MOREUX PELTIER
  GERMAN DOVE FICKER WEGENER
  BRUCKNER NEUMAYER
  NORWEGIAN MOHN SVERDRUP
  RUSSIAN TILLO
  SCOTTISH MILL BUCHAN
  SWEDISH MALMGREN
  SWISS WILD DELUC
METEOROLOGY AEROLOGY
METER IONIC METRE SEVEN
  ALCAIC RHYTHM CADENCE
  GAYATRI MEASURE SUBMETER
  VIAMETER YAWMETER
  (CUBIC —) STERE
  (MILLIONTH OF —) MICRON
  (NETHERLANDS —) ELL
  (SQUARE —) CENTIARE
  (VEDIC —) GAYATRI
  (10 CUBIC —S) DEKASTERE
  (10,000 —S) GREX
METHADONE AMIDONE
METHANE FORMENE
METHANOL WOODINE CARBINOL
METHEGLIN MEAD
METHOD ART WAY DART FORM
  GARB GATE KINK LINE MIDS
  MODE REDE RULE SORT ORDER
  STYLE TRACK USAGE COURSE
  ENGINE MANNER STEREO SYSTEM
  FASHION PROCESS TACTICS
  WRINKLE ADJUVANT STANDARD
  (— OF ANGLING) HARLING
  (— OF APPEALING) DHARNA DHURNA
  (— OF COLORING TEA) FACING
  (— OF CONSTRUCTION) JACAL
  (— OF CULTIVATION) JUM JOOM STUMPING
  (— OF DIETING) BANTING
  (— OF DISTILLATION) DESCENT
  (— OF ELECTION) SCRUTINY
  (— OF FATTENING POULTRY) GAVAGE
  (— OF INDUCTION) CANON
  (— OF MILKING) NIEVLING
  (— OF MURAL DECORATION) KHASI
  (— OF PROCEDURE) GAME
  (— OF SELECTING POPE) SCRUTINY
  (— OF TRACKING) DOVAP
  (— OF TREATMENT) SCOPE
  (CLEVER —) KINK KINKLE
  (FIXED —) FORMULA
  (MEDICAL —) CUSHION
  (OUTMODED —) ARCHAISM
  (PAINTING —) GOUACHE
  (PRINTING —) AQUATONE
  (SCIENTIFIC —) BACONISM
  (SURVEYING —) STADIA
  (USUAL —) COURSE PRACTICE
METHODICAL TRIG EXACT
  FORMAL SEVERE ORDERLY
  REGULAR ORDINARY ORDINATE
METHODIST JUMPER WESLEYAN
  SWADDLING
METHODIZE ORDER REGULATE
METHUSAEL (FATHER OF —)
  MEHUJAEL
  (SON OF —) LAMECH
METHUSELAH (FATHER OF —)
  ENOCH
METHYLAL FORMAL

METICULOUS FUSSY NARROW
  STICKY CAREFUL FINICAL FINICKY
  PARTICULAR
METION (BROTHER OF —) CECROPS
  (FATHER OF —) ERECHTHEUS
  (MOTHER OF —) PRAXITHEA
METONYM SYNONYM
METRICAL MEASURED
  (— QUANTITY) MATRA
METRICS PROSODY
METRONOME (PART OF —) BOX
  KEY CASE PIVOT SCALE SHAFT
  WEIGHT PENDULUM
METROPOLIS CITY SEAT CAPITAL
METROPOLITAN EPARCH EXARCH
METTLE PITH SAUL PRIDE SPUNK
  GINGER SPIRIT COURAGE
  SMEDDUM
METTLESOME FIERY PROUD
  SKEIGH SPUNKY STUFFY FLIGHTY
  GINGERY SPIRITED
MEUSE
  (PREF.) (RIVER —) MOSA
MEW PEN WOW CAGE CAST COOP
  GULL MEWL MOLT SHED MEUTE
  MIAOU MIAOW HIDEAWAY
  INTERMEW SEEDBIRD
  CONFINEMENT
MEWER WRAWLER
MEWL WRAWL
MEWS ALLEY COURT STREET
  STABLES
MEXICAN CHOLO LEPERO
  WETBACK
  (AMERICAN OF — DESCENT)
  CHICANO
MEXICAN-AMERICAN PACHUCO
MEXICAN ELM MEZCAL
MEXICAN ONYX TECALI
MEXICAN PERSIMMON CHAPOTE
MEXICAN POPPY ARGEMONE
MEXICAN TEA BASOTE APASOTE
  FISHWEED WORMSEED

MEXICO
CAPITAL: MEXICOCITY
COIN: PESO TLAC ADOBE CLACO
  TLACO AZTECA CENTAVO
  PIASTER
LAKE: CHAPALA
MEASURE: PIE VARA ALMUD BARIL
  JARRA LABOR LEGUA LINEA
  SITIO FANEGA PULGADA
MOUNTAIN: BUFA BLANCO
  CUPULA PEROTE ORIZABA
PENINSULA: BAJA YUCATAN
PEOPLE: MAM CHOL CORA MAYA
  MIXE PIMA SERI TECO XOVA
  AZTEC NAHUA OPATA OTOMI
  ZOQUE EUDEVE MIXTEC TOLTEC
  NAYARIT TEPANEC TOTONAC
  ZACATEC ZAPOTEC TEZCUCAN
  TOTONACO ZACATECO
RIVER: BRAVO LERMA BALSAS
  GRANDE PANUCO TABASCO
  GRIJALVA SANTIAGO
STATE: LEON NUEVO COLIMA
  OAXACA SONORA CHIAPAS
  DURANGO HIDALGO NAYARIT
  SINALOA TABASCO YUCATAN
  CAMPECHE QUINTANA
  VERACRUZ
TOWN: LEON LAPAZ TEPIC ARIZPE

COLIMA JALAPA JUAREZ
  MERIDA OAXACA PARRAL
  POTOSI PUEBLA CANANEA
  DURANGO GUAYMAS MORELIA
  ORIZABA PACHUCA TAMPICO
  TORREON CULIACAN
  MAZATLAN MONCLOVA
  SALTILLO TLAXCALA VERACRUZ
VOLCANO: COLIMA TOLUCA
  JORULLO PARICUTIN
  POPOCATEPETL
WEIGHT: BAG ONZA CARGA LIBRA
  MARCO ADARME ARROBA
  OCHAVA TERCIO QUINTAL

MEZAHAB (DAUGHTER OF —)
  MATRED
MEZZANINE ENTRESOL
MIAROLITIC DRUSY
MIASMA REEK MALARIA
  MAREMMA
MIB MIGGLE
MIBSAM (FATHER OF —) SIMEON
  ISHMAEL
MICA DAZE TALC GLIST SLUDE
  BIOTITE GLIMMER ALURGITE
  FUCHSITE PHENGITE PHLOGOPITE
MICAH (FATHER OF —) UZZIEL
  MERIBBAAL
  (SON OF —) ABDON
MICAH CLARKE (AUTHOR OF —)
  DOYLE
  (CHARACTER IN —) JACOB MICAH
  SAXON CLANCY CLARKE GERVAS
  JOSEPH REUBEN DECIMUS
  STEPHEN LOCKARBY MONMOUTH
  TIMEWELL
MICAIAH (FATHER OF —) IMLAH
MICE (BREEDING PLACE FOR —)
  MURARIUM
MICHA (FATHER OF —)
  MEPHIBOSHETH
  (SON OF —) MATTANIAH
MICHAEL MIKE MICKY MICHEL
  MIGUEL
  (FATHER OF —) IZRAHIAH
  JEHOSHAPHAT
  (SLAYER OF —) JEHORAM
  (SON OF —) OMRI SETHUR
MICHAH (FATHER OF —) UZZIEL
MICHAIAH (FATHER OF —) URIEL
  GEMARIAH
  (HUSBAND OF —) REHOBOAM
  (SON OF —) ABIJAH
MICHAL (FATHER OF —) SAUL
  (HUSBAND OF —) DAVID PHALTI

MICHIGAN
BAY: SAGINAW THUNDER
  KEWEENAW STURGEON
CAPITAL: LANSING
COLLEGE: ALMA WAYNE ADRIAN
  ALBION CALVIN OLIVET
  OWOSSO OAKLAND
COUNTY: BAY CASS IRON LUCE
  CLARE DELTA IONIA IOSCO
  ALCONA OCEANA OGEMAW
  OSCODA OTSEGO GOGEBIC
  OSCEOLA TUSCOLA KALKASKA
INDIAN: OTTAWA
LAKE: BURT TORCH HOUGHTON
MOUNTAIN: CURWOOD
NATIVE: WOLVERINE

NICKNAME: LAKE WOLVERINE
RIVER: CASS BRULE HURON
DETROIT SAGINAW STCLAIR
ESCANABA MONTREAL
MENOMINEE
STATE BIRD: ROBIN
STATE FLOWER: APPLEBLOSSOM
STRAIT: MACKINAC
TOWN: MIO ALMA CARO HART
FLINT IONIA LANSE ADRIAN
ALPENA BADAXE OWOSSO
PAWPAW WARREN DETROIT
LANSING LIVONIA PONTIAC
SAGINAW ANNARBOR CADILLAC
ESCANABA KALKASKA
MANISTEE MUNISING
MUSKEGON CHEBOYGAN
KALAMAZOO

MICIPSA (FATHER OF —) MASINISSA
MICONIA TAMONEA
MICROBAR BARYE
MICROBE GERM
MICROBIOLOGIST AMERICAN
NATHAN
FRENCH LWOFF
SWISS ARBER
MICROCEPHALIC PINHEAD
MICROFILM (SHEET OF —) FICHE
MICROMETER MU BIFILAR
(— CALIPER) MIKE
MICRON MU
MICRONESIAN KANAGA NAURUAN
(— ISLAND) NUI GUAM ROTA TRUK
MAKIN NAURU WOTHO MAJURO
MICROORGANISM BUG GERM
AZOFIER BUTYRIC MICROBE
BACILLUS MYCOPLASMA
MICROPHONE BUG MIKE
PARABOLA
(REMOVE CONCEALED —) DEBUG
MICROPYLE FORAMEN
MICROSCOPE GLASS SCOPE
(PART OF —) ARM BASE CLIP KNOB
LENS LIMB TUBE STAGE FILTER
HOLDER APERTURE EYEPIECE
CONDENSER DIAPHRAGM
NOSEPIECE OBJECTIVE
ADJUSTMENT
MICROSCOPIC SMALL MINUTE
MICROSECOND (HUNDREDTH OF —)
SHAKE
MICROSPECIES JORDANON
MICROSPOROPHYLL STAMEN
MICROTONE SRUTI SHRUTI
MICROTUS ARVICOLA
MIDBRAIN MESENCEPHALON
MIDDAY NOON UNDERN MIDNOON
NOONDAY MERIDIAN NOONTIME
MIDDEN BASURAL SAMBAQUI
MIDDLE MEDIO MESNE NAVEL
CENTER MEDIAL MEDIAN
CENTRAL MEDIATE MEDILLE
(— OF SAIL) BUNT
(— OF SHIP) WAIST
(— OF WINTER) HOLL HOWE
(PREF.) MEDI(O) MES(O) MESIO
MEZZO
MIDDLE-AGED MIDDLING
MIDDLE EAST (— NATIVE) WOG
MIDDLEMAN BUTTY BROKER
DEALER FOGGER JOBBER LUMPER
BUMAREE BUMMAREE BUTTYMAN

HUCKSTER REGRATER
MIDDLEMARCH (AUTHOR OF —)
ELIOT
(CHARACTER IN —) FRED TYKE
WILL CALEB CELIA GARTH JAMES
RIGGS VINCY BROOKE EDWARD
JOSHUA CHETTAM LYDGATE
RAFFLES TERTIUS CASAUBON
DOROTHEA LADISLAW NICHOLAS
ROSAMOND BULSTRODE
FEATHERSTONE
MIDDLER PLATEMAN
MIDDLETONE HALFTONE
MIDDLING FAIR MEAN SOSO
NEUTRAL MEDIOCRE MEETERLY
(PL.) DUNST FARINA SHARPS
SIZINGS SEMOLINA WEATINGS
MIDGE GNAT SMUT PUNKY
MIDGET MINGIE PUNKIE WEEVIL
MIDIAN (FATHER OF —) ABRAHAM
(MOTHER OF —) KETURAH
MIDMOST
(PREF.) MESATI
MIDNIGHT NOON NOONTIDE
MIDPOINT BASION PORION
STOMION GNATHION
MIDRIB COSTA SHAFT MIDVEIN
(— OF LEAF) PEN
MIDRIFF APRON SKIRT
(PREF.) PHREN(O)
MIDSHIPMAN WART MIDDY PLEBE
REEFER SNOTTY OLDSTER
MIDST DEPTH CENTER MIDDLE
MIDWARD
(PREF.) (IN THE —) INTER
MIDSUMMER DAY JOHNSMAS
MIDSUMMER NIGHT'S DREAM
(AUTHOR OF —) SHAKESPEARE
(CHARACTER IN —) MOTH PUCK
SNUG EGEUS FLUTE SNOUT
BOTTOM COBWEB HELENA
HERMIA OBERON QUINCE
THESEUS TITANIA LYSANDER
DEMETRIUS HIPPOLYTA
STARVELING MUSTARDSEED
PHILOSTRATE PEASEBLOSSOM
MIDWAY MEDIO GAYWAY
HALFWAY
MIDWIFE BABA DHAI GAMP
HOWDY LUCKY COMMER
CUMMER GRANNY HOWDIE
KIMMER LUCINA LUCKIE GRANNIE
HEBAMME
MIEN AIR BROW PORT VULT
ALLURE ASPECT DEMEAN
MANNER OSTENT BEARING
DEMEANOR PORTANCE
MIG MIB DUCK
MIGHT ARM BULK MOTE FORCE
MOUND POWER SHOULD
STRENGTH
(PREF.) CRATO
MIGHTILY HEFTILY
MIGHTINESS (HIGH —) HOGEN
MIGHTY FELL HIGH KEEN MAIN
MUCH RANK RICH VAST FELON
GREAT HEFTY STERN STOOR
POTENT STRONG VIOLENT
ENORMOUS FORCEFUL
POWERFUL PUISSANT SAMSONIC
(PREF.) DEIN(O) DIN(O)
MEG(A)(AL)(ALO)
MIGNON (CHARACTER IN —)

MIGNON MEISTER SPERATA
WILHELM LOTHARIO
(COMPOSER OF —) THOMAS
MIGNONETTE WELD WOLD
RESEDA LUTEOLA
MIGRAINE MEGRIM
MIGRANT MOVER
MIGRATE RUN FLIT TREK DRIFT
FLIGHT COLONIZE
MIGRATION TREK EXODUS FLIGHT
EELFARE EMOTION PASSAGE
DIASPORA
MIGRATORY PEREGRINE
MIKADO DAIRI
MIKIR ARLENG
MIKLOTH (FATHER OF —) JEHIEL
(MOTHER OF —) MAACHAH
MILCAH (FATHER OF —) HARAN
ZELOPHEHAD
(HUSBAND OF —) NAHOR
MILD LEW MOY CALM COLD EASY
FAIR LENT MEEK NESH PLUM
SOFT TAME WARM BALMY BLAND
BUXOM GREEN LIGHT LITHE
MELCH MELSH MILKY NAISH
QUIET BENIGN FACILE GENIAL
GENTLE HUMBLE KINDLY REMISS
SMOOTH AFFABLE AMIABLE
CLEMENT LENIENT VELVETY
BENEDICT DOVELIKE FAVONIAN
LENITIVE MERCIFUL SARSENET
SOOTHING TRANQUIL
(PREF.) LENI
MILDEW OIDIUM
MILDLY FEEBLY GENTLY
MILDNESS MILD LENITY SUAVITY
CLEMENCY HUMILITY KINDNESS
MILE (NAUTICAL —) KNOT KAIRI
(ONE-EIGHTH —) FURLONG
(SEA —) NAUT
(SIXTY —S) DEGREE
(3 —S) HOUR LEAGUE
MILESTONE MILLIARY
MILETUS (FATHER OF —) APOLLO
(MOTHER OF —) ARIA DEIONE
(SON OF —) BYBLIS CAUNUS
(WIFE OF —) CYANEE
MILFOIL AHARTALAV
MILIEU CLIMATE TERRAIN
AMBIENCE
MILITANT WARRISH FIGHTING
(ONE WITH — ATTITUDE) HAWK
MILITARISTIC PRUSSIAN
MILITARY MARTIAL WARLIKE
MILITANT SOLDIERY
(— POST) THANA
(— SCIENCE) LOGISTICS
MILITIA FYRD ARRAY MILICE
MILITIAMAN CHOCO UHLAN
LUMPER TRAINER FENCIBLE
SHIRTMAN
(TURKISH —) TIMARIOT
MILK COW LAC FUZZ LAIT PAIL
SKIM BLEED JUICE MILCH MULCT
BOTTLE ELICIT RAMMEL STROKE
SUCKLE EXPLOIT
(— CLOSELY) JIB
(— DRY) STRIP
(— OUT) EMULGE
(— PAN) LEAD
(— PRODUCT) KHOA
(— SICKNESS) TIRES
(BREAST —) SUCK DIDDY

(COW'S —) MESS
(CURDLED —) SKYR TYRE TAYER
LOPPER CLABBER TATMJOLK
(FERMENTED —) KUMISS MATZOON
(NEW —) RAMMEL
(PINT OF —) PINTA
(SOUR —) SKYR WHIG BONNY
BLEEZE BLINKY CLABBER
JOCOQUE
(WATERY —) BLASH
(PREF.) GALACT(O) LACT(I)(O)
(SUFF.) GALACTIA
MILK CART KIT PRAM BUNGEY
MILKFISH AWA BANGOS SABALO
SAVOLA BANDENG SABALOTE
MILKING (— PARLOR) BAIL
(— TIME) MEAL
MILKLESS PARVE PAREVE
MILKMAN KITTER CHALKER
MILK PAIL TRUG LEGLEN
MILK SHAKE FRAPPE
MILK SNAKE ADDER
MILKSOP SOP MOLLY COCKNEY
MEACOCK
MILKWOOD MELKHOUT
MILKWORT SENECA CENTAURY
GAYWINGS POLYGALA
MILKY MILCHY LACTARY LACTEAL
OPALOID LACTEOUS
MILKY WAY
(PREF.) GALACT(O)
MILL FULL MILN STAR BREAK
FLOUR KNURL QUERN CHERRY
FANNER STAMPS BLOOMER
MOLINET PUGMILL SMUTTER
ARRASTRA ARRASTRE BUHRMILL
SPINNERY TRAPICHE WALKMILL
(CHOCOLATE —) MOLINET
(FULLING —) STOCKS
(SHINGLING —) FORGE
(SUGAR —) CENTRAL TRAPICHE
(PREF.) MOLARI MYL(O)
MILLBOARD TARBOARD
MILLDAM WEIR WARREN
WARRANT
MILLED GRAINED
MILLENARIAN CHILIAST
MILLENIUM CHILIAD
MILLER MILLMAN STOCKER
MULTURER NILLWARD
MILLER'S-THUMB BLOB CULL
CABOT CHABOT COTTOID
MUDDLER BULLHEAD
MILLET BUDA KODA KOUS MOHA
ARZUN BAJRA CHENA CUMBU
DUKHN DURRA GRAIN HIRSE
KODRA MILLY PANIC PROSO
TENAI WHISK BAJREE DHURRA
HUREEK JONDLA JOWARI MILIUM
RAGGEE DAGASSA PANICLE
ZABURRO BIRDSEED KADIKANE
(PREF.) MILIO
MILLHAND CROPMAN
MILLILITER MIL
MILLIMETER LI
(THOUSANDTH OF —) MICRON
MILLINER ARTISTE MODISTE
MILLING GRAINING
MILLION CONTO QUENT
(10 —) CRORE
(1000 —) MILLIARD
(PL.) GUPPY
(PREF.) MEGA

MILLIONTH
(PREF.) **(ONE —)** MICR(O)
MILLIPEDE JULID POLYPOD
DIPLOPOD PILLWORM RINGWORM
WIREWORM
MILLISECOND SIGMA
**MILL ON THE FLOSS (AUTHOR OF
—)** ELIOT
(CHARACTER IN —) BOB TOM KENN
LUCY DEANE GLEGG GUEST JAKIN
WAKEM MAGGIE PHILIP PULLET
STEPHEN STELLING TULLIVER
MILLPOND DAM MILLDAM
BINNACLE MILLPOOL
MILLRACE LADE LEAD LEAT
FOREBAY TAILRACE MILLSTREAM
MILLRYND INK
MILLSTONE RYND STONE BEDDER
LEDGER LIGGER RUNNER
(LOWER —) METATE
(UPPER —) MANO
(PL.) RUN
MILLSTREAM DAM LADE FLEAM
MILLWORKER DOGGER
MILO SORGHUM
MILPA LADANG
MILQUETOAST CASPAR
MILT MILK SEED SPLEEN
MILTONIST DIVORCER
MIMAS (FATHER OF —) THEANO
(MOTHER OF —) AMYCUS
(SLAYER OF —) MEZENTIUS
MIME ACTOR MIMER MIMIC
(PL.) MIMIAMBI
MIMEOGRAPH RONEO
MIMIC APE HIT COPY MIME MINI
MOCK MOCKER MONKEY
BUFFOON COPYCAT IMITATE
PAGEANT
(PREF.) MIM(EO)(O)
MIMICRY APERY MIMESIS
MOCKAGE MOCKERY
MIMOSA AROMA CASSIE ALBIZZIA
HUISACHE TURMERIC
MINCE CHOP SHEAR FINICK
MINCED HACHE
MINCEMEAT GIGOT MINCE
MINCING NIMINY FINICAL MINIKIN
MIGNIARD SKIPJACK
MINCINGLY FINE GINGERLY
MIND CIT CHIT HEAD HEED MOOD
NOTE NOUS RECK SOUL BESEE
BRAIN PHREN SENSE SKULL
WATCH ANIMUS MATTER NOTICE
PSYCHE REGARD COURAGE
SENSORY SUBJECT THINKER
THOUGHT
(CONSCIOUS —) SENTIENT
(INFINITE —) GOD
(RIGHT FRAME OF —) TUNE
(STATE OF —) BAG
(YEAR'S —) MINNING
(PREF.) MENTI NOO PHREN(O)
PSYCH(O)
(SUFF.) **(CONDITION OF —)** THYMIA
MINDFUL HEEDY MINDLY HEEDFUL
OBSERVANT
MIND READER MENTALIST
MINE BAL DIG PIT DELF HOLE HUEL
MEUM BARGH DELFT DELPH
METAL STOPE WHEAL COYOTE
GOPHER GROOVE RESCUE
BONANZA BORASCA COALPIT

MINERAL OPENCUT TORPEDO
GOLCONDA MYNPACHT
PROSPECT
(— BY BLASTING) SHOOT
(— IRREGULARLY) GOPHER
(— PASSAGE) SLUM
(COAL —) ROB COALPIT COLLIERY
(MILITARY —) FOUGADE
FOUGASSE CAMOUFLET
(OLD —) GWAG
(RICH —) GOLCONDA
(TIN —) STANNARY
(UNPRODUCTIVE —) DUFFER
SHICER BORASCA
MINER PECK PICK PYKE BARER
DOGGY ARTIST BUCKER CUTTER
DAMMER DELVER DIGGER
GANGER GETTER HAGGER
JUMPER MATTER PELTER REEFER
SNIPER STOPER TINNER TOPMAN
VANNER COLLIER CRUTTER
DIRGLER FEIGHER GEORDIE
GROOVER HITCHER HUTCHER
LEADMAN PICKMAN PIKEMAN
PIONEER PLUGMAN ROCKMAN
SNUBBER ENTRYMAN HEADSMAN
STRIPPER WINZEMAN
(— WHO WORKS ALONE) HATTER
MINERAL JET GEET HOST MINE
SPAR BERYL BLOOM EARTH
FLUOR GLEBE GUEST LENAD
SQUAT TRONA ACMITE ALAITE
AUGITE BARITE BARYTE BLENDE
CASTOR CERITE COCKLE CURITE
DAVYNE EGERAN EHLITE ERRITE
GALENA GARNET GLANCE
GYPSUM HALITE HAUYNE HELVIN
HUMITE ILLITE IOLITE LABITE
MIXITE NATRON NOSEAN NOSITE
PINITE RUTILE SALITE SILICA
SPHENE SPINEL ADAMINE
ADAMITE ADELITE ALTAITE
ALUMITE ALUNITE AMOSITE
ANATASE APATITE ATOPITE
AXINITE AZORITE AZULITE
AZURITE BAUXITE BAZZITE
BELLITE BIOTITE BISMITE BITYITE
BOHMITE BOLEITE BORNITE
BRUCITE CALCITE CELSIAN
CYANITE DIAMOND DICKITE
DUFTITE EDENITE EPIDOTE
ERIKITE ERINITE EUCLASE
FLOKITE GAGEITE GAHNITE
GEDRITE GLEBITE GOTHITE
GUMMITE HELVITE HESSITE
HOPEITE HOWLITE HULSITE
IHLEITE ILVAITE INESITE INYOITE
ISERITE JADEITE JARLITE JOSEITE
KEMPITE KERNITE KOPPITE
KOTOITE KYANITE LANGITE
LARNITE LAURITE LAUTITE
LEHIITE LEIFITE LEONITE LEPTITE
LEUCITE LOWEITE MARTITE
MELLITE MULLITE OKENITE
OLIVINE PALAITE PENNINE
PETZITE PYRITES RATHITE
REALGAR RETZIAN RHAGITE
RINKITE ROMEITE ROSSITE
SENAITE SODDITE SVABITE
SYLVITE THORITE TURGITE
ULEXITE UTAHITE UVANITE
VAUXITE VOGLITE VRBAITE
WARBITE WIIKITE ZEOLITE

ZINCITE ZOISITE ZORGITE
ZUNYITE AIKINITE ALLANITE
ALLUVIAL ALUNOGEN AMBONITE
ANAUXITE ANCYLITE ANDORITE
ANKERITE ARIEGITE ARMENITE
ARTINITE ASBOLITE AUGELITE
AUTUNITE AWARUITE BADENITE
BAKERITE BARARITE BARYLITE
BAVENITE BETAFITE BEYERITE
BILINITE BIXBYITE BLAKEITE
BLOEDITE BOOTHITE BORACITE
BOWENITE BRAGGITE BRAUNITE
BRAVOITE BROMLITE BRONZITE
BROOKITE BRUSHITE CALCSPAR
CARBOCER CEROLITE CHIOLITE
CHLORITE CHROMITE CIMOLITE
CINNABAR CLEVEITE COHENITE
COLUSITE COOKEITE COSALITE
CREEDITE CROCOITE CRYOLITE
DANALITE DAPHNITE DATOLITE
DELTAITE DENDRITE DIALLAGE
DIASPORE DIGENITE DIOPSIDE
DIOPTASE DIXENITE DOLOMITE
DYSODILE EGUEIITE ELIASITE
ELPIDITE EMBOLITE ENARGITE
EPSOMITE ERIONITE EUCOLITE
EULYTINE EULYTITE EUXENITE
EVANSITE FASSAITE FAYALITE
FELDSPAR FERSMITE FIBROITE
FLINKITE FLUORITE FOOTEITE
FUCHSITE FUSINITE GEMSTONE
GENTHITE GIBBSITE GINORITE
GOETHITE GOYAZITE GRIPHITE
GROTHINE GROUTITE GYROLITE
HANKSITE HANUSITE HARTTITE
HATCHITE HAUERITE HAUYNITE
HEMATITE HOMILITE HUGELITE
IDOCRASE INDERITE IODYRITE
JALPAITE JAROSITE JEZEKITE
KALINITE KAMACITE KASOLITE
KEHOEITE KLEINITE KOKTAITE
KOLSKITE KRAUSITE LAGONITE
LAVENITE LAZULITE LAZURITE
LEVYNITE LEWISITE LIMONITE
LINARITE LOMONITE LOWIGITE
MARSHITE MEIONITE MELILITE
MELONITE MESITITE MESOLITE
MIERSITE MIMETITE MISENITE
MOLYSITE MONAZITE MONETITE
MORAVITE MOSESITE NADORITE
NASONITE NEPOUITE NOCERITE
NOSELITE OXAMMITE PEGANITE
PETALITE PIMELITE PINNOITE
PISANITE PODOLITE PORODINE
PRICEITE PRIORITE RINNEITE
ROSELITE SAGENITE SALEEITE
SALESITE SAPONITE SASSOLIN
SCAWTITE SHANDITE SHARPITE
SHORTITE SIDERITE SMALTITE
SMITHITE SODALITE SPADAITE
SPURRITE STANNITE STIBNITE
STILBITE STOLZITE STRUVITE
STURTITE SZMIKITE TAGILITE
TANGEITE TEALLITE TENORITE
TILASITE TITANITE TRIPLITE
TROILITE TYROLITE TYSONITE
URANOTIL VEGASITE VOLTAITE
VOLTZITE WEHRLITE WEISSITE
WELLSITE WILKEITE WURTZITE
XENOLITE XENOTIME YENTNITE
ZARATITE MILLERITE MUSCOVITE
NEPHELINE NICCOLITE
PHENACITE WILLEMITE

(BLACK —) JET GEET CERINE
YENITE KNOPITE NIOBITE
ALLANITE GRAPHITE HIELMITE
ILMENITE ONOFRITE MAGNETITE
SAMARSKITE
(BLUE —) MOLYBDENITE
(BRIGHT —) BLENDE
(BROWN —) CERINE EGERAN
GUILDITE JAROSITE
(FIBROUS —) ASBESTOS
(GRAY-WHITE —) TRONA HOPEITE
(GREEN —) AMESITE GAHNITE
ILESITE PRASINE PREHNITE
SMECTITE
(MOTTLED —) SERPENTINE
(ORANGE —) SANDIX
(RADIATED —) ASTROITE
(RADIOACTIVE —) CURITE
(RARE —) CYMRITE EUCLASE
TYCHITE BARYLITE
(RED —) GARNET RHODOCHROSITE
(SOFT —) TALC KERMES
(TRANSPARENT —) MICA POLLUX
ABRAZITE SODALITE
(WHITE —) BARITE HOWLITE
STILBITE
(YELLOW —) TOPAZ PYRITES
PENTLANDITE
(YELLOWISH-GREEN —) EPIDOTE
ECDEMITE
(PREF.) ORYCT(O)
(SUFF.) CLASE INE ITE LITE
LITH(IC) LITIC XENE
MINERALOGIST AMERICAN HUNT
KUNZ BRUSH KRAUS EGLESTON
WHITLOCK CLEAVELAND
AUSTRIAN BORN BECKE WULFEN
HAIDINGER TSCHERMAK
ENGLISH BROOKE CLARKE GREGOR
MILLER PHILLIPS
FRENCH HAUY ROME DAUBREE
FRIEDEL LACROIX LAUMONT
DOLOMIEU DUFRENOY
BRONGNIART
GERMAN MOHS COHEN RASPE
DECHEN KOBELL WERNER ZIRKEL
KARSTEN NEUMANN LEONHARD
QUENSTEDT
ITALIAN SELLA BRUGNATELLI
RUSSIAN FERSMAN
SWEDISH GAHN HISINGER
SEFSTROM CRONSTEDT
BLOMSTRAND
MINERAL TAR MALTHA
MINERAL WATER SELTZER
MINERVA MENFRA
MINESWEEPER ALGERINE
MINGLE MIX FUSE JOIN MELL
MOLD MONG MOOL ADMIX BLEND
MERGE TWINE COMMIX FELTER
HUDDLE JUMBLE MEDDLE
MEDLEY COMBINE COALESCE
CONFOUND
(PREF.) MISCE
MINGLED FUSED MEDLEY
CONFUSED
(PREF.) MYXTI
MINGLING
(PREF.) MIXO
(SUFF.) MIXIS
MINIATURE BABY SMALL LITTLE
POCKET MINIKIN
MINIMAL BASAL LIMINAL

MARGINAL
MINIMIZE DECRY MINCE LESSEN MINIFY SMOOTH SCISSOR BELITTLE DISCOUNT
MINIMUM BARE BEDROCK
MINING WORK MINERY SPATTER GROOVING
MINION PEAT SATAN MIGNON DARLING MINIKIN CREATURE SATELLITE
MINIONETTE EMERALD
MINISTER PRIG CLERK DEWAN ELDER ENVOY HAMAN PADRE VIZIR ATABEG DEACON DIVINE GALLAH HELPER PANDER PARSON PASTOR PESHWA PRIEST VIZIER BROTHER DOMINIE OFFICER PESHKAR PREFECT PALATINE PREACHER
(**— OF FINANCE**) DEWAN
(**— TO**) TEND SERVE INTEND
(**— WITHOUT SETTLEMENT**) STIBBLER
(**PRIME —**) PADRONE
MINISTRANT
(**PL.**) SELLI SELLOI
MINISTRATION SERVICE TENDANCE
MINISTRY SERVICE
MINIUM SANDIX
MINIVER LASSET
MINK FAG HURON NORSE VISON JACKASH KOLINSKY MUSTELIN PLATINUM

MINNESOTA
CAPITAL: STPAUL
COLLEGE: BETHEL STOLAF WINONA BEMIDJI HAMLINE AUGSBURG CARLETON
COUNTY: LYON PINE TODD ANOKA MOWER AITKIN DAKOTA ISANTI ITASCA MCLEOD NOBLES ROSEAU WASECA WILKIN CHISAGO WABASHA CROWWING HENNEPIN OTTERTAIL
INDIAN: SIOUX OJIBWA CHIPPEWA
LAKE: LEECH ITASCA BEMIDJI SUPERIOR
MOUNTAIN: EAGLE MISQUAH
MOUNTAIN RANGE: CUYUNA MESABI MISQUAH
NICKNAME: NORTHSTAR
RIVER: RAINY STCROIX
STATE BIRD: LOON
STATE TREE: REDPINE
TOWN: ADA ELY MORA ANOKA EDINA FOLEY AUSTIN CHASKA DULUTH MILACA NEWULM WADENA WASECA WINONA BEMIDJI FOSSTON HIBBING IVANHOE MANKATO BRAINERD PIPESTONE

MINNESOTAN GOPHER
MINNOW PINK BANNY GUPPY HITCH MINIM MINNY BAGGIE MENNON DOGFISH FATHEAD GULARIS PHANTOM PINHEAD PINKEEN BONYTAIL CYPRINID FLATHEAD GAMBUSIA MOONFISH SATINFIN

(**PL.**) MENISE
MINOR FLAT LESS MOLL WARD PETIT PETTY INFANT LESSER SLIGHT
MINORESS CLARE CLARISSE
MINORITY FEW NONAGE INFANCY
MINOS (**DAUGHTER OF —**) ARIADNE PHAEDRA
(**FATHER OF —**) JUPITER LYCASTUS
(**MOTHER OF —**) EUROPA
(**SLAYER OF —**) COCALUS
(**SON OF —**) ANDROGEOS DEUCALION
(**WIFE OF —**) PASIPHAE
MINSTER CHADBAND
MINSTREL BARD LUTER BADHAN HARPER JOCKEY BADCHAN GLEEMAN JOCULAR PARDHAN PIERROT SONGMAN JONGLEUR
MINSTRELSY GLEE DREAM
MINT COIN NANA SAGE AJUGA BASIL ORGAN THYME HYSSOP SAVORY STRIKE ALLHEAL BALLOTA CAPMINT LABIATE MONARDA OLITORY OREGANO PERILLA PHLOMIS POTHERB STACHYS BERGAMOT CALAMINT IRONWORT LAMPWICK LAVENDER MARJORAM SAGELEAF SELFHEAL SKULLCAP PATCHOULI PATCHOULY PENNYROYAL PEPPERMINT
MINTER MONEYER
MINUCHIHR (**DAUGHTER OF —**) NAUDAR
(**FATHER OF —**) IRAJ
MINUET MINAWAY
MINUS LESS WANTING
MINUTE FINE NICE TINY CLOSE MINIM PRIME SMALL ATOMIC MOMENT NARROW INSTANT SCRUPLE DETAILED
(**24 —S**) GHURRY
(**PL.**) ACTA
MINX JADE PEAT SLUT SNIP HUSSY HUZZY LIMMER SNICKET
MIRACLE SIGN ANOMY MARVEL WONDER PRODIGY THEURGY
(**PREF.**) THAUMA(TO)
MIRACLE PLAY GUARY
MIRACULOUS MARVELOUS
MIRAGE SERAB CHIMERA FLYAWAY LOOMING ILLUSION TOWERING
MIRANDA (**FATHER OF —**) PROSPERO
(**LOVER OF —**) FERDINAND
MIRE BOG DUB CLAY GLAR LAIR MOIL SLOB SLUB SLUE SLUR ADDLE CLART EMBOG FANGO GLAUR LATCH SEUGH SLAKE SLOSH SLUSH SQUAD STALL SLOUGH SLUDGE SLUTCH CLABBER GUTTERS SLUBBER LOBLOLLY WORTHING
MIREILLE (**CHARACTER IN —**) RAMON OURRIAS VINCENT MIREILLE
(**COMPOSER OF —**) GOUNOD
MIRIAM (**BROTHER OF —**) MOSES
MIRITI PALM ITA BURITI MORICHE
MIRLITON KAZOO
MIRO TOMTIT

MIRROR FLAT BERYL GLASS IMAGE STEEL STONE PEEPER PSYCHE REFLEX SHINER SHOWER CONCAVE HORIZON REFLECT DIAGONAL SPECULUM
(**PREF.**) CATOPTRO
MIRTH GLEE CHEER DREAM SPORT GAIETY BAUDERY DISPORT JOLLITY HILARITY
(**CONTEMPTUOUS —**) SPORT
(**VIOLENT —**) SPLEEN
MIRTHFUL CADGY MERRY RIANT FESTIVE GLEEFUL JOCULAR DISPOSED LAUGHFUL CONVIVIAL
MIRY OOZY PUXY LAIRY MUCKY SLAKY CLAGGY CLASHY LUTOSE MIRISH POACHY SLABBY GUTTERY SLOUGHY
MISADVENTURE GRIEF ACCIDENT CALAMITY CASUALTY DISASTER-MISHANTER
MISANTHROPE CYNIC TIMON
(**AUTHOR OF —**) MOLIERE
(**CHARACTER IN —**) ORONTE ALCESTE ARSINOE ELIANTE CELIMENE PHILINTE
MISANTHROPIC CYNICAL
MISANTHROPY CYNICISM TIMONISM
MISAPPLIED ABUSIVE
MISAPPLY ABUSE CROOK WREST DISUSE MISUSE
MISAPPREHEND MISTAKE
MISAPPREHENSION ILLUSION
MISBECOME MISSIT MISSEEM
MISBEHAVE MISUSE MISBEAR MISFARE MISHAVE MISLEAD MISGUIDE
MISBEHAVIOR MALVERSATION
MISBELIEF MISCREED
MISCALCULATE DUTCH MISCAST MISCOUNT
MISCALL BECALL MISNAME
MISCARRIAGE FAIL MISHAP FAILURE ABORTION
(**PREF.**) ECTRO
MISCARRY FAIL WARP ABORT MISGO FOUNDER MISFARE MISGIVE BACKFIRE
MISCARRYING ABORTIVE
MISCELLANEOUS CHOW ORRA SUNDRY ASSORTED CHOWCHOW
MISCELLANY VARIA MEDLEY WHATNOT CHOWCHOW GIFTBOOK
MISCHANCE CALAMITY CASUALTY DISASTER
MISCHIEF HOB ILL BALE BANE EVIL HARM HURT JEEL WRACK INJURY MURCHY SORROW WONDER DEVILRY KNAVERY MALICHO SCADDLE DEVILTRY MALLECHO
MISCHIEF-MAKING URCHIN
MISCHIEVOUS BAD SLY ARCH IDLE PIXY ROYT ELFIN HEMPY PIXIE ROYET ELFISH ELVISH GALLUS HEMPIE IMPISH NOCENT NOYANT SHREWD SULLEN WICKED GALLOWS HARMFUL KNAVISH LARKISH MOCKING NAUGHTY PARLISH PLISKIE PUCKISH ROGUISH SCADDLE UNHAPPY UNLUCKY WAGGISH

LITHERLY LUNGEOUS SPORTIVE SPRITISH VENOMOUS WANSONSY
MISCHIEVOUSNESS ROGUERY
MISCONCEPTION DELUSION ILLUSION
MISCONDUCT CULPA DOLUS OFFENCE OFFENSE DISORDER MALFEASANCE
MISCONSTRUCTION STRAIN
MISCONSTRUE MISJUDGE
MISCREANT KNAVE
MISDEED ILL MISS SLIP AMISS UNWORK DEFAULT FORFEIT OFFENCE OFFENSE DISORDER
MISDEMEANOR SIN CRIME FAULT DELICT OFFENCE OFFENSE DISORDER
MISDIRECT PERVERT MISGUIDE
MISER CUFF SKIN CHUFF CHURL FLINT GRIPE HAYNE HUNKS NABAL SCRAT SCRIB CODGER HUDDLE NIPPER PELTER SCRIMP SNUDGE WRETCH DRYFIST GOBSECK NIGGARD SCRAPER CHINCHER GATHERER HAPTERON HARPAGON HOLDFAST MUCKERER MUCKWORM PINCHGUT CURMUDGEON
MISERABLE WOE EVIL GRAY PUNK SOUR DAWNY DEENY DUSTY MISER WOFUL YEMER ABJECT CHETIF CRUMBY CRUMMY ELENGE FEEBLE PRETTY UNSELY WOEFUL BALEFUL FORLORN PITIFUL SCRUFFY UNHAPPY WANSOME FORSAKEN PITIABLE SCRANNEL UNTHENDE WRETCHED
MISERABLES, LES (**AUTHOR OF —**) HUGO
(**CHARACTER IN —**) JEAN JAVERT MARIUS COSETTE EPONINE FANTINE VALJEAN JONDRETTE MADELEINE PONTMERCY THENARDIER FAUCHELEVANT
MISERERE SUBSELLA
MISERLINESS AVARICE MISERISM SNUDGERY TENACITY
MISERLY WOE GARE MEAN NEAR GRIPPY KNIVEY STINGY CHINCHE PELTING WANSITH SCRAPING SNUDGERY
MISERY WO WOE BALE RUTH GNEDE GRAME WREAK THREAT ANGUISH MISEASE TRAGEDY CALAMITY DISTRESS WANDRETH WOWENING
MISFIRE SKIP SNAP
MISFORTUNE ILL BLOW DOLE DREE EVIL HARM RUTH TEEN CROSS CURSE HYDRA SCATH TRAIK DAMAGE DIRDUM MISERY MISHAP RUBBER SCATHE SORROW UNHEAL UNLUCK WANHAP WROATH AMBSACE MALHEUR MISCARE MISFALL MISFATE MISLUCK REVERSE TRAGEDY TROUBLE UNSELTH UNSPEED CALAMITY DISASTER DISGRACE DISTRESS MISCHIEF ADVERSITY MISCHANCE
MISGIVING DOUBT QUALM
MISGOVERN MISRULE

MISGUIDED WET
MISHAEL (BROTHER OF —)
  ELIZAPHAN
  (FATHER OF —) UZZIEL
MISHAM (FATHER OF —) ELPAAL
MISHANDLE BUNGLE
MISHAP SLIP GRIEF SHUNT SITHE
  UNHAP WANHAP FORTUNE
  MISTIDE ACCIDENT CASUALTY
  MISCHIEF PRATFALL
  (MINOR —) GLITCH
MISHEARING OTOSIS
MISHIT DUFF
MISHMA (BROTHER OF —) MIBSAM
  (FATHER OF —) ISHMAEL
MISHMASH BOTCH GOULASH
MISINFORM MIZZLE
MISINTERPRET WARP WREST
  WRITHE MISREAD PERVERT
  MISCOUNT
MISJUDGE MISDEEM MISWERN
MISLAY LOSE DISPLACE MISPLACE
MISLEAD COG ERR BUNK DUPE
  GULL HOAX HYPE JIVE BLUFF
  CHEAT FALSE SHUCK BETRAY
  DELUDE SEDUCE WILDER
  CONFUSE DEBAUCH DECEIVE
  MISLEAR INVEIGLE MISGUIDE
  BAMBOOZLE
MISLEADING JIVE BLIND FALSE
  CIRCEAN TORTIOUS
MISMANAGE MULL BLUNK
  BLUNDER MISLEAD MISRULE
  ILLGUIDE MISGUIDE
MISOGYNIC CYNICAL
MISPLACE MISLAY MISPUT MISSET
  DISPLACE
MISPLACED MALPOSED
MISPLAY BLOW DUFF ERROR
  FLUFF FUMBLE
MISPRINT LITERAL
MISPRONOUNCE MISCALL
  STUMBLE
MISQUOTE GIVE
MISREPRESENT SKEW ABUSE
  BELIE COLOR MISUSE DISTORT
  FALSIFY SLANDER MISCOLOR
MISREPRESENTATION FRAUD
  CALUMNY DAUBERY GARBLING
MISS ERR HIP FAIL LACK LOSE SKIP
  SLIP SNAB FORGO HANUM MISSY
  PANNA SKIRT DESIRE KUMARI
  FRAULEIN MISTRESS OVERLOOK
  OVERSLIP SENORITA
  (CLOSE —) SHAVE
MISSEL BIRD MAVIS SHIRL DRAINE
  JAYPIE MISTLE SHRITE SYCOCK
  CHERCOCK
MISSHAPE DEFORM
MISSHAPEN UGLY BLOWN
  DEFORM THRAWN DEFORMED
  UNSHAPED MALFORMED
  (PREF.) DYSMORPHO
MISSILE ABM GUN BALL BIRD
  BOLT DART NIKE SHOT PLUMB
  SHAFT STONE BULLET SEEKER
  BOMBARD GRENADE MISSIVE
  OUTCAST PROJECT AERODART
  BRICKBAT PROJECTILE
  (DEFECTIVE —) DUD
  (PL.) MITRAILLE
  (PREF.) TELI
MISSING LACK WANT

ABSENT WANTING
  (— OF CUE) FLUFF
  (PREF.) E
MISSION SAND TASK CHARGE
  ERRAND SORTIE VISITA MESSAGE
  BUSINESS DEVOTION LEGATION
  NUNCIATURE
MISSIONARY APOSTLE COLPORTER

MISSISSIPPI	
CAPITAL: JACKSON	
COLLEGE: RUST ALCORN	
BELHAVEN MILLSAPS	
TOUGALOO	
COUNTY: TATE HINDS JONES	
LAMAR LEAKE PERRY YAZOO	
ALCORN ATTALA COPIAH	
JASPER PANOLA TIPPAH	
TUNICA CHOCTAW NESHOBA	
NOXUBEE ITAWAMBA	
YALOBUSHA	
INDIAN: TIOU BILOXI TUNICA	
CHOCTAW NATCHEZ	
CHICKASAW	
LAKE: ENID SARDIS BARNETT	
GRENADA OKATIBBEE	
MOUNTAIN: WOODALL	
NATIVE: MUDCAT TADPOLE	
NICKNAME: BAYOU MAGNOLIA	
RIVER: LEAF PEARL YAZOO	
BIGBLACK	
STATE BIRD: MOCKINGBIRD	
STATE FLOWER: MAGNOLIA	
STATE TREE: MAGNOLIA	
TOWN: IUKA MARKS BILOXI	
HELENA LAUREL PURVIS	
TUNICA TUPELO WINONA	
BELZONI CORINTH GRENADA	
NATCHEZ WIGGINS BOGALUSA	
GULFPORT MERIDIAN	
KOSCIUSKO	

MISSIVE NOTE BILLET LETTER
  EPISTLE MESSAGE MISSILE

MISSOURI	
CAPITAL: JEFFERSONCITY	
COLLEGE: AVILA DRURY TARKIO	
LINCOLN WEBSTER STEPHENS	
COUNTY: RAY COLE DENT IRON	
LINN ADAIR BARRY HENRY	
MACON RALLS TANEY GRUNDY	
PETTIS PLATTE DAVIESS	
NODAWAY	
INDIAN: OSAGE	
LAKE: OZARKS TABLEROCK	
MOUNTAIN: TAUMSAUK	
NATIVE: PUKE PIKER	
NICKNAME: SHOWME BULLION	
PLATEAU: OZARK	
PRESIDENT: TRUMAN	
RIVER: OSAGE	
STATE BIRD: BLUEBIRD	
STATE FLOWER: HAWTHORN	
STATE TREE: DOGWOOD	
TOWN: AVA EDINA ELDON HAYTI	
LAMAR MACON MILAN ROLLA	
BUTLER GALENA KAHOKA	
NEOSHO POTOSI BETHANY	
BOLIVAR CAMERON LEBANON	
MOBERLY PALMYRA SEDALIA	
STLOUIS HANNIBAL SIKESTON	

MISSTATEMENT ERRATUM
MISSTEP TRIP
MIST DAG FOG MUG URE DAMP
  DRIP DROW FILM HAAR HAZE
  MOKE RACK ROKE SCUD SMUR
  BRUME CLOUD DRISK GAUZE
  STEAM MIZZLE NEBULE SEREIN
  SERENE SMEETH
  (COLD —) DROW BERBER
  (DRIZZLING —) SMUR DRISK SMIRR
  SMURR
  (SMOKY —) SMOG
  (WHITE —) HAG
  (PL.) SMOKES
  (PREF.) NEBULI NIMBI
MISTAKE ERR BALK GAFF GOOF
  MISS SLIP TRIP ERROR FAULT
  FLUFF GAFFE LAPSE BARNEY
  BOBBLE ESCAPE MISCUE SLIPUP
  STUMER BLOOMER BLUNDER
  CONFUSE DEFAULT JEOFAIL
  STUMOUR WRONGER CONFOUND
  MISPRINT MISPRISE
  (STUPID —) BUBU BONER
  CLANGER
  (PL.) ERRATA
MISTAKEN WRONG ASTRAY
  OVERSEEN OVERSHOT TORTIOUS
MISTER DON REB HERR SENOR
  SENHOR SIGNOR GOODMAN
  SIGNIOR GOVERNOR
MISTFLOWER EUPATORY
MISTILY FOGGILY
MISTINESS FILM
MISTLETOE MISSEL ALLHEAL
  GADBUSH
MISTREAT BANG VIOLATE
MISTRESS MRS PUG TOY AMIE
  BIBI DAME DOLL DOXY LADY MISS
  PURE AMIGA AMOUR DOLLY
  DONNA DUENA FANCY LEMAN
  LUCKY MADAM NANCY WOMAN
  BEEBEE MINION MISSIS MISSUS
  NEAERA PARNEL SAHIBA SENORA
  TACKLE WAHINE BEDMATE
  DELILAH HERSELF HETAERA
  KITTOCK LEVERET METREZA
  PADRONA SENHORA SIGNORA
  SULTANA CAMPASPE DESPOINA
  DULCINEA FARMWIFE GOODWIFE
  GUDEWIFE HAUSFRAU LADYLOVE
  LANDLADY MIGNIARD PARAMOUR
  PECULIAR SINEBADA TIMANDRA
  COURTESAN
  (— OF CEREMONIES) FEMCEE
MISTRUST MISTROW SURMISE
  DISTRUST JEALOUSE JEALOUSY
  MISDOUBT
MISTY HAZY MOKY BLEAR DAGGY
  FILMY FOGGY MISKY MOCHY
  MOOTH MURKY RAWKY ROKEY
  ROUKY BLURRY CLOUDY GREASY
  MIZZLY SMURRY STEAMY
  BRUMOUS OBSCURE NEBULOUS
  NUBILOUS VAPOROUS
MISUNDERSTAND MISKNOW
  MISTAKE
MISUNDERSTANDING
  MALENTENDU
MISUSE ABUSE ABUSION PERVERT
  MALTREAT
MITE BIT ATOM CENT DITE DRAM
  ATOMY BICHO SPECK ACARID

ACARUS CHIGOE LEPTUS MINUTE
  SMIDGE ACARIAN BDELLID
  CHIGGER DEMODEX SMIDGEN
  ARACHNID DIBRANCH FARTHING
  HANDWORM ORIBATID SANDMITE
  (PREF.) ACAR(I)(O)
MITER MITRE TIMBER TIMBRE
MITERWORT COOLWORT
MITICIDE ACARICIDE
  PHOSPHAMIDON
MITIGATE BALM COOL EASE HELP
  ABATE ALLAY DELAY MEASE
  RELAX REMIT SLAKE ASLAKE
  LENIFY LESSEN MODIFY PACIFY
  SOFTEN SOOTHE SUCCOR
  TEMPER ASSUAGE COMMUTE
  CUSHION ELEVATE MOLLIFY
  QUALIFY RELEASE RELIEVE
  SWEETEN PALLIATE ALLEVIATE
  (— PAIN) PLASTER
MITIGATING LENITIVE
MITOCHONDRION SARCOSOME
MITTEN BOOT CUFF MITT MUFF
  LOOFIE MUFFLE NIPPER MUFFLER
MIX BOX BEAT CARD DASH FUSE
  JOIN KNIT MELL MENG MESS STIR
  ADMIX ALLOY BLEND BRAID
  IMMIX KNEAD MISCE TWINE
  BLUNGE CAUDLE COMMIX
  CRUTCH GARBLE JUMBLE
  MEDDLE MEDLEY MINGLE
  MUDDLE PERMIX STODGE
  TEMPER WUZZLE BLUNDER
  SHUFFLE SWIZZLE
  CONFOUND LEVIGATE
  SCRAMBLE
  (— AND STIR WHEN WET) PUG
  (— CONFUSEDLY) BROIL
  (— FLOCKS) BOX
  (— LIQUORS) BREW
  (— PLASTER) GAGE GAUGE
  (— TEA) BULK
  (— WINE) PART
  (— WITH YEAST) BARM
  (— WOOL OF DIFFERENT COLORS)
  TUM
  (CONCRETE —) SOUP
MIXABLE MISCIBLE
MIXED CHOW IMPURE MEDLEY
  MOTLEY PIEBALD STREAKY
  CHOWCHOW
  (— BLOOD) MESTIZO
  (— CHALICE) KRASIS
  (— UP) HAYWIRE
  (NOT —) SINCERE
  (PREF.) MIXO
MIXER HOG BANBURY MUDDLER
  PICKLER
  (CEMENT —) BOXMAN
  (CONCRETE —) PAVER
MIXTURE AIR MIX BODY BREW
  DASH FEED HASH MANG MONG
  MULL OLIO PUER SOUP STEW
  ALGIN ALLOY BLEND BLENT
  BROMO DOUGH GUMBO SALAD
  STUFF FOURRE GARBLE GUNITE
  LIGNIN MASLIN MEDLEY MELLAY
  MINGLE MOTLEY TEMPER
  AMALGAM COMPOST CUSTARD
  FARRAGO FILICIN FORMULA
  GOULASH HEADING KOGASIN
  MELANGE MISTION MISTURA
  MIXTION MONGREL OLLAPOD

RECEIPT TIMBALE ALKYLATE
BLENDURE DRAMMOCK
EMULSION POSSODIE POWSOWDY
SOLUTION MACEDOINE
MENAGERIE MISCELLANY
SALMAGUNDI SMORGASBORD
(— ADDED TO WINE) DOSAGE
(— ATTRACTIVE TO PIGEONS)
SALTCAT
(— FOR CAKE) BATTER
(— FOR DRESSING LEATHER)
DUBBIN DUBBING
(— OF ALE AND OATMEAL) STOORY
(— OF ALKALOIDS) ADONIDIN
JABORINE
(— OF BARKS) TONGA
(— OF CEMENT AND STONE)
BUMICKY
(— OF CLAY AND CHALK) MALM
(— OF CLAY AND ROCK) BODY
(— OF CLAY AND SAND) LOAM
(— OF DRUGS) SPECIES
(— OF ELEMENTS) DIDYMIUM
(— OF FEEDS) MASH
(— OF IMPURE ARSENIDES) SPEISS
(— OF OATS AND BARLEY) DREDGE
(— OF PRINCIPLES) EUONYMIN
(— OF PROTEINS) CROTIN
(— OF SALTS) SOYATE
(— OF SAND AND STONES) CHAD
(— OF SAWDUST AND GLUE)
BADIGEON
(— OF SHALE AND SANDSTONE)
HAZLE
(— OF SLAG AND ORE) BROWSE
(— OF VINEGAR AND HONEY)
OXYMEL
(— OF VITAMINS) BIOS
(— OF WHITE AND BLACK) GRIZZLE
(— OF WINE, HONEY AND SPICES)
CLARY
(— TO ADULTERATE LIQUORS)
FLASH
(— TO DOCTOR WINE) GEROPIGA
(— TO WHITEN BREAD) HARDS
(— USED AS A FERMENT) BUB
(— USED AT SEDER) HAROSET
CHAROSES
(ACUTE —) ACUTA
(AERIFORM —) GAS
(CARVER'S —) COMPO
(CAULKING —) BLARE
(CLAY —) COB SLIP
(COATING —) COLOR
(CONFUSED —) MESS CHAOS
FUDDLE SOZZLE
(CRUMBLY —) STREUSEL
(EXPLOSIVE —) DUALIN FIREDAMP
(FOOD —) FILLING
(FREEZING —) CRYOGEN
(GILDING —) ASSIETTE
(HYDROCARBON —) ABIETENE
(ITALIAN CONDIMENT —) TAMARA
(JUMBLED —) BOTCH PASTICHE
(MECHANICS' —) PUTTY
(PLASTIC CEMENT —) CLOY
(PRESERVATIVE —) STUFF
(SEASONED —) STUFFING
(SMOKING —) CHARAS CHURRUS
(TANNING —) PURE
(THICKENING —) ROUX
(UNPALATABLE —) DRAMMOCK
(WATERY —) SLURRY

(WELDING —) THERMIT
(SUFF.) CRASE CRASIS CRASY
MIZZAH (FATHER OF —) REUEL
(GRANDFATHER OF —) ESAU
MIZZEN DANDY
MIZZONITE DIPYRE
MKS UNIT JOULE
MNEMONIC MEMORIAL
MOAN HONE MOON REEM WAIL
CROON GROAN MOURN MUNGE
QUIRK SOUGH MUNGER
MOANING SOUGH DIRGEFUL
MOAT FOSS DITCH FOSSE GRAFF
RUNDEL
MOB CREW HERD RAFF ROUT
COHUE CROWD HURRY PLEBE
PLEBS MOBILE RABBLE TUMULT
VOULGE DOGGERY CANAILLE
RIFFRAFF VARLETRY CLAMJAFRY
(PREF.) OCHLO
MOBCAP MOB
MOBILE THIN FLUID ROVING
MOVEABLE
MOBSTER HOODLUM
MOBY DICK (AUTHOR OF —)
MELVILLE
(CHARACTER IN —) AHAB STUBB
ISHMAEL FEDALLAH QUEEQUEG
STARBUCK
MOCCASIN PAC CONGO TEGUA
SHOEPACK
(— WITH LEGS) LARRIGAN
(PL.) SHANKS
MOCCASIN FLOWER NERVINE
MOCHA BARK
MOCHICA YUNCA
MOCHILA MACHEER KNAPSACK
MOCK BOB DOR GAB MOW COPY
DEFY GECK GIBE GIRD JAPE JEER
JEST JIBE PLAY QUIZ BOURD
DORRE ELUDE FLEER FLIRT FLOUT
FRUMP HOKER KNACK MIMIC
RALLY SCOFF SCORN SCOUT
SLEER SPORT TAUNT BEMOCK
DELUDE DERIDE ILLUDE NIGGLE
IMITATE MURGEON RIDICULE
MOCKER MOWER GIRDER
BOURDER FLOUTER SCORNER
RAILLEUR
MOCKERNUT BULLNUT
MOCKERY DOR GAB MOW GLEE
JEER BOURD DORRE FARCE
FLOUT GLAIK SCOFF SPORT
BISMER HETHING LUDIBRY
MOCKADO MOCKAGE DERISION
ILLUSION RIDICULE SCOFFERY
MOCKING GAB ACID SPORT
SCOPTIC IRRISORY NARQUOIS
SARDONIC TRUMPERY
MOCKINGBIRD MIMUS MOWER
MOCKER
MOCK ORANGE SYRINGA
PHILADELPHUS
MOCOA COCHE
MODE CUT JET TON WAY FORM
GATE MOOD RAGA TONE TWIG
WISE FERIO FINAL GENUS MODUS
STATE STYLE ACTING BAROCO
CESARE COURSE DATISI FAKOFO
FANGLE FESAPO MANNER
METHOD BAMALIP CALEMES
CAMENES DABITIS DARAPTI
DIBATIS DIMARIS DIMATIS

DISAMIS FAPESMO FASHION
FERISON FESTINO CELARENT
DOKMAROK FELAPTON FRESISON
TONALITY
(— OF BEHAVIOR) THEW HABITUDE
(— OF BEING) CATEGORY
(— OF CONDUCT) LAW
(— OF DRESS) HABIT TENUE
(— OF DRESSING HAIR) MADONNA
(— OF EXPRESSION) IRONY
(— OF MORAL ACTION) CONDUCT
(— OF PARTITIONING) CANT
(— OF PROCEDURE) ORDER SYSTEM
(— OF RULE) REGIME
(— OF SPEECH) ACCENT LATINISM
PARLANCE
(— OF STANDING) STANCE
(— OF STRUCTURE) BUILD
(PREVAILING —) GARB
(TEMPORARY —) VOGUE
MODEL WAX COPY FORM MOLD
NORM CANON DUMMY IDEAL
LIGHT MOULD NORMA SHAPE
DESIGN FUGLER GABARI MODULE
PRAXIS SOURCE BOZZETO
DIORAMA EXAMPLE GABARIT
MODULET PARAGON PATTERN
PICTURE SAMPLER CALENDAR
ENSAMPLE EXEMPLAR EXEMPLUM
FORMULAR FUGLEMAN
MAQUETTE MODELLER MODULIZE
PARADIGM PROPLASM SPECIMEN
TYPORAMA MANNEQUIN
PLANETARIUM
(— OF HUMAN BODY) FORM
MANIKIN
(— OF STATUE) ESQUISSE
(INFERIOR —) JALOPPY
(MATHEMATICAL —) SPACE
(PRELIMINARY —) MAQUETTE
PROPLASM
(PREF.) TYP(I)(O)
MODERATE BATE COOL CURB
EASE EASY EVEN MEEK SOFT
ABATE ALLAY ALLOY LIGHT
LOWER MEZZO MODER REMIT
SLACK SLAKE SOBER SWEET
ARREST BRIDLE DECENT GENTLE
LESSEN MEANLY MIDWAY
MODEST MODIFY REMISS SEASON
SOFTEN SUBMIT TEMPER
CENTRAL CHASTEN CONTROL
SLACKEN ATTEMPER CENTRIST
MEETERLY MIDDLING MITIGATE
MODERATO ORDINATE PALLIATE
PASSABLE CONTINENT
ABSTEMIOUS MEASURABLE
REASONABLE
(— IN BURNING) SOFT
(— OF THE WIND) LOOM
MODERATELY GEY FAIR MEAN
MEANLY MEETLY PRETTY
MIDWISE MEETERLY MIDDLING
MODERATENESS CLEMENCY
MODICITY
MODERATION MEAN STAY MINCE
SPARE MANNER MEDIUM REASON
COMPASS MEDIETY MODESTY
SOBRIETY ABATEMENT
IMMODESTY
MODERATO MASSIG
MODERATOR ANCHORMAN
MODERN NEW LATE

RECENT NEOTERIC
MODEST COY SHY DEFT MURE
NICE PURE SNUG BLATE DOUCE
LOWLY QUIET SMALL CHASTE
DEMURE HUMBLE PUDENT
SIMPLE VIRGIN CLERKLY PUDICAL
DISCREET MAIDENLY PUDIBUND
RESERVED RETIRING SHAMEFUL
VERECUND VIRTUOUS
MODESTY AIDOS PUDOR NICETY
DECENCY PUDENCY SHYNESS
CHASTITY FOREHEAD HUMILITY
PUDICITY
MODICUM DROP BREAK SPICE
PENNROTH SCANTLING
SEMBLANCE PENNYWORTH
MODIFICATION BOB ECAD FORM
SALT CHANGE ENGRAM FACIES
SANDHI SINGLE UMLAUT
ENGRAMMA
(— OF A REMEDY) TINCTION
(GLOTTAL —) STOP
MODIFIED VARIANT
MODIFY EDIT VARY ALTER AMEND
HEDGE TOUCH BUFFER CHANGE
DOCTOR MASTER TEMPER
ARABIZE COMPARE FASHION
QUALIFY ATTEMPER DENATURE
GRADUATE MODERATE
FAUCALIZE
(— ARTICULATION) COLOR
(— COLOR) TONE
MODILLION ANCON MODEL TRUSS
CARTOUCH
MODISH CHIC MODY SOIGNE
TIMISH TONISH STYLISH
MODISHNESS CHIC
MODRED (FATHER OF —) ARTHUR
(MOTHER OF —) MARGAWSE
MODULATE SINK INFLECT QUALIFY
MODULATION ACCENT CHANGE
CADENCE BUNCHING PASSAGIO
MODULE LEM
MOGUL PADISHAH
MOHAIR MOIRE
MOHAMMED MAHOMET
MAHOUND MUDEJAR PROPHET
(UNCLE OF —) ABBAS
MOHAMMEDAN MOSLEM PAYNIM
MAHOMET
MOHAMMEDANISM TURBAN
TURKERY MAUMETRY
MOHAWK NICKER
MOHR MHORR GAZELLE
MOHUR MOOR AHMEDI
MOIETY MEDIETY
MOIST WET DAMP DANK DEWY
NESH UVID DABBY GIVEY GREEN
HUMID JUICY MADID MOCHY
SAMMY SAPPY SLACK SOAKY
SOCKY SPEWY SWACK WASHY
WEEPY CLAMMY MOISTY STICKY
WETTISH HUMOROUS MUCULENT
(PREF.) HUMI(DI) HYGR(O) UDO
MOISTEN DIP WET DAMP MOIL
BASTE BATHE BEDEW JUICE
LATCH LEACH STEEP WOKIE
DABBLE DAMPEN HUMECT
HUMIFY IMBRUE MADEFY SPARGE
TEMPER HUMIDIFY IRRIGATE
IRRORATE
(— LEATHER) SAM SAMMY
MOISTURE DEW WET BREE DAMP

DANK ROKE HUMOR MOIST
WATER PHLEGM AQUOSITY
HUMIDITY
(— DEFICIENT) XERIC
(— IN STONE) SAP
(— ON BEARD) BARBER
(CONDENSED —) BREATH
(REMOVE CONDENSED —) DEFOG
(PREF.) HUMI(DI) HYGR(O) UDO
MOJARRA SHAD PATAO
MOKI MOGUEY MOKIHI
MOKSHA MUKTI
MOLAR WANG FORMAL MOLARY
GRINDER
(PREF.) MYL(O)
MOLASSES DIP LICK CLAGGUM
THERIAC TREACLE LONGLICK
(PREF.) MELASSI
MOLD DIE FEN PIG PLY SOW CALM
CAST CURB FORM MULL MUST
SOIL TRAP BLOCK CHAPE CHILL
FRAME INGOT MODEL MOULD
MUCOR PLASM PRINT SHAPE
SHARE STENT STINT VALVE
COFFIN GABARI INFORM LINGET
MATRIX SQUARE BASTARD
FASHION FESTOON MATRICE
RILLETT SANDBOX SKILLET
TEMPLET COQUILLE FUMAGINE
HOODMOLD PROPLASM
TEMPLATE WHISKERS
PENICILLIUM
(— FOR METAL) SOW SKILLET
(— OF ASPIC) DARIOLE
(— OF GIMP) GWEEP
(— THAT ATTACKS HOPS) FEN
(CHEESE —) CHESSEL
(SLIME —) MYCETOZOAN
MYXOMYCETE
(PREF.) PLASM(ATO)(O)
(SUFF.) PLASIA PLASIS
PLASM(A)(IA)(IC) PLAST(IC)(Y)
PLASY
MOLDAVITE TEKTITE
MOLDBOARD REEST
(— SURFACE) WREST
MOLDED FICTILE
MOLDER MURL CAPPER MANGLE
MOSKER FIGURER PLASTER
PLASTIC
MOLDINESS MUST FINEW MUCOR
VINEW
MOLDING BEAD COVE CYMA DADO
GULA KEEL LIST OGEE OVAL
CABLE FILET GORGE LABEL LEDGE
ROVER STAFF BANDLE BASTON
BILLET CASING COLLAR CONGEE
COVING FILLET LISTEL MULLER
REGLET SQUARE ZIGZAG
ANNULET BEADING CABLING
CHAPLET CORNICE DOUCINE
ECHINUS EYEBROW FINGENT
HIPMOLD LOZENGE MOULAGE
NECKING SURBASE TONDINO
TRINGLE ASTRAGAL BAGUETTE
BANDELET CASEMATE CASEMENT
CINCTURE CYMATION CYMATIUM
DANCETTE DOGTOOTH FUSAROLE
HOODMOLD KNURLING
MOULDING NAILHEAD NECKMOLD
ARCHIVOLT BOLECTION
(CONCAVE —) GORGE CONGEE
SCOTIA CAVETTO

(CONVEX —) REED CABLE OVOLO
THUMB TORUS BASTON REEDING
ASTRAGAL FUSAROLE
(OGEE —) TALON
(OUTSIDE —) BACKBAND
(PL.) TORI LEDGMENT
MOLDY FUSTY HOARY MUCID
MUGGY MUSTY VINNY FOISTY
MOULDY FOUGHTY
MOLE COB UNT COBB MAIL OONT
PIER PILE TAPE WANT JUTTY
MOODY NEVUS TALPA TAUPE
ANICUT MOUDIE HYDATID
TALPOID MOLDWARP MOONCALF
SORICOID STARNOSE UROPSILE
ZANDMOLE
(PREF.) TALPI
MOLE CRICKET CHANGA
MOLECULE ACID ATOM BASE
AMMINE DIPOLE HYDROL LIGAND
PRIMER HYDRONE SPECIES
TEMPLATE OCTAPEPTIDE
MOLEHILL TUMP HOYLE WANTHILL
MOLE RAT SEMNI ZEMMI ZOKOR
SLEPEZ SPALACID ZANDMOLE
MOLEST GALL HAUNT TEASE
BOTHER HARASS HECKLE INFEST
PESTER MISLEST TROUBLE
MOLID (FATHER OF —) ABISHUR
(MOTHER OF —) ABIHAIL
MOLL FLANDERS (AUTHOR OF —)
DEFOE
(CHARACTER IN —) MOLL JEMMY
ROBIN FLANDERS
MOLLIFY HUGH RELAX ADULCE
GENTLE PACIFY RELENT SOFTEN
SOOTHE TEMPER ASSUAGE
DULCIFY SWEETEN ATTEMPER
MITIGATE UNRUFFLE
MOLLIFYING MILD SUPPLING
MOLLUSK ARK CLAM CONE PIPI
SPAT BORER CHAMA CHANK
CHINK CLAMP CONCH COWRY
DORIS DRILL MUREX PINNA SNAIL
VENUS AEOLID BAILER BUBBLE
CERION CHITON COCKLE COURIE
DOLIUM JINGLE LEPTON LIMPET
MUSSEL NERITA OYSTER PECTEN
PHOLAD PURPLE SEMELE STROMB
ABALONE ADMIRAL ASTARTE
BIVALVE CARDITA DECAPOD
JUNONIA MOLLUSC PIDDOCK
SALPIAN SCALLOP TOHEROA
TREPANG TROPHON DUCKFOOT
FIGSHELL HALIOTIS NAUTILUS
PTEROPOD SAXICAVA STROMBUS
UNIVALVE VERMETUS SHELLFISH
NUDIBRANCH PERIWINKLE
(— TRIBE) NAIADES
(LARVAL —) VELIGER
(YOUNG —) SPAT
MOLLYCODDLE MOLLY WANTON
INDULGE MILKSOP
MOLOSSUS (FATHER OF —)
PYRRHUS
(MOTHER OF —) ANDROMACHE
MOLT MEW CAST MUTE SHED
MOULT DISCARD EXUVIATE
INTERMEW
MOLTEN FUSED
MOLTING BROKEN ECDYSIS
MOLUCCAS (ISLAND OF —) ARU KAI
OBI BURU LETI SULA AMBON

BABAR BANDA CERAM WETAR
BATJAN TIDORE MOROTAI
TERNATE TANIMBAR HALMAHERA
MOLUS (BROTHER OF —) EVENUS
(DAUGHTER OF —) MOLIONE
(FATHER OF —) ARES MARS
(MOTHER OF —) DEMONICE
MOLYBDENUM (EXCESS OF —)
TEART
MOMBIN JOCOTE
MOMENT MO GIRD HINT SAND
TICK AVAIL BLINK BRAID CLINK
CRACK GLIFF GLISK JIFFY SHAKE
SNIFT SPURT STOUN TRICE
VALUE FILLIP GLIFFY MINUTE
PERIOD SECOND STOUND
WEIGHT YAWING ARTICLE
INSTANT INSTANCE MOMENTUM
TWINKLING
(— FOR LEGERDEMAIN ACTION)
TEMPS
(— OF STRESS) CRISE
(APPROPRIATE —) PLACE
(CRITICAL —) BIT INCH CORNER
(DECISIVE —) CRISIS
(EXACT —) BIT POINT
(OPPORTUNE —) KAIROS
(SCHEDULED —) TIME
MOMENTARY MOMENTAL
TRANSIENT
MOMENTOUS FELL GRAVE
EPOCHAL FATEFUL WEIGHTY
EVENTFUL PREGNANT
MOMENTOUSNESS GRAVITY
MOMENTUM WAY FORCE SPEED
IMPETUS
MON PEGUAN TALAING

MONACO
ANCIENT NAME: MONOECUS
CAPITAL: MONACO MONACOVILLE
DYNASTY: GRIMALDI
LANGUAGE: FRENCH
PEOPLE: MONEGASQUES
PRINCE: LOUIS ALBERT HONORE
  ANTOINE CHARLES RAINIER
  FLORESTAN
RIVER: VESUBIE
SECTION: MONTECARLO
  LACONDAMINE MONACOVILLE

MONAD ATOM JIVA HENAD
MONAS
MONADIC UNARY
MONADNOCK BARABOO
MONARCH KING QUEEN DANAID
DIADEM PRINCE DANAINE
EMPEROR AUTOCRAT
MONARCHIAN PRAXEAN
MONARCHICAL KINGLY
MONARCHY KINGDOM
MONASTERY WAT ABBEY BADIA
LAURA RIBAT TEKKE TEKYA
FRIARY MANDRA VIHARA
BONZERY CERTOSA CONVENT
KHANKAH MINSTER MONKERY
CLOISTER LAMASERY
(ALGERIAN —) RIBAT
(BUDDHIST —) TERA KYAUNG
BONZERY LAMASERY
(CARTHUSIAN —) CERTOSA
(HINDU —) MATH
(MOSLEM —) TEKKE

TEKYA KHANKAH
(PREF.) MANDRI
(SUFF.) MINSTER
MONASTIC MONKLY MONKISH
ABBATIAL CENOBIAN MONACHAL
MONASTICISM MONKERY
MONKISM
MONETARY EXPLICIT PECUNIARY
NUMISMATIC
MONEY (ALSO SEE COIN) AES BOX
DIB FAT FEE FEI GET OOF ORO
SAP TIN WAD CASH COAT COIN
COLE CRAP CUSH DUBS DUST
FUND GATE GELT GILT GOLD
HOOT JACK JAKE KALE LOOT
LOUR MALI MINT MOSS MUCK
PELF ROLL SALT SAND SHAG
SOAP SWAG BEANS BLUNT
BRASH BRASS BREAD BUNCE
BUNTS CHINK CHIPS CLINK
DARBY DIMES DOUGH DUMPS
FUNDS GREEN GRIGS IMPUT
LOLLY LUCRE MEANS MOOLA
MOPUS OCHER PURSE RHINO
ROCKS ROWDY SCADS SHINY
SMASH SPUDS STIFF STUFF
SUGAR ARGENT BARATO BARREL
BOODLE CHANGE CUNYIE
DANARO DINERO FARLEU FARLEY
FEUAGE FLIMSY FUMAGE GRAITH
HANSEL KELTER MAZUMA
POCKET SHEKEL SILLER SILVER
SPENSE SPLOSH STAMPS STEVEN
STUMPY TALENT WISSEL
ADVANCE CHATTEL CHINKER
COUNTER CRACKER CRUSADE
DEPOSIT FALDAGE GUNNAGE
OOFTISH SCRATCH SPANKER
SPECIES STOCKER CRIMPAGE
CURRENCY DEMIMARK INCOMING
INTEREST SPENDING STERLING
STOCKING XERAPHIN
(— BET) COMEBACK
(— DUE) DEVOIRS
(— FOR LIQUOR) WHIP
(— LENT) LUMBER
(— OF ACCOUNT) ORA
(— PAID TO BIND BARGAIN) ARLES
(— TAKEN IN) DRAWING
(ADDITIONAL —) BONUS
(AVAILABLE —) CAPITAL
(BAR —) BONK TANG
(BASE —) SHICE
(BRIBE —) SOAP BOODLE
(COUNTERFEIT —) BOGUS QUEER
BOODLE DUFFER SHOWFUL
SLITHER
(EARNEST —) ARLES ARRHA
DEPOSIT HANDSEL HANDGELD
HANDSALE
(EXPENSE —) DIET
(EXTORTED —) PROTECTION
(FERRY —) NAULUM
(HARD —) SPECIE
(HAT —) TAMPANG
(HAVING NO —) FLYBLOWN
(INVESTED —) STOCK
(PAPER —) GREEN CABBAGE
CURRENCY FROGSKIN
(PASSAGE —) SHIPHIRE
(PRIZE —) PEWTER
(PROTECTION —) ICE
(PUSH —) SPIFF

(READY —) CASH DARBY PREST
READY STUFF STUMPY
(REFUNDED —) DRAWBACK
(SHELL —) PEAG HAWOK WAKIKI
WAMPUM
(SILVER —) SYCEE
(SMALL SUM OF —) SPILL
(STANDARD BANK —) BANCO
(SUBSISTENCE —) BATTA
(TRAVELLING —) VIATICUM
(WIRE —) LARI LARIN LARREE
MONEYBAG FOLLIS
MONEY BELT ZONE
MONEY BOX TILL CHEST PIRLIE
MONEY-CHANGER SARAF SHROFF
CAMBIST ARGENTER
MONEY-CHANGING AGIO
MONEY DRAWER TILL SHUTTLE
MONEYED RICH WEALTHY
MONEYLENDER BANYA CHETTY
USURER LOMBARD MAHAJAN
MARWARI SHYLOCK BUMMAREE
MONEYMAKING BANAUSIC
MONEYWORT MANG MYRTLE
PRIMWORT
MONGOL HUN KALKA BALKAR
BURIAT DAGHUR SHARRA
BERBERI KALMUCK KHALKHA
SILINGAL
(PL.) HU
MONGOLIA (CAPITAL OF —)
ULAANBAATAR
(DESERT IN —) GOBI
(MONEY OF —) TUGHRIK
(RIVER OF —) ORHON DZAVHAN
KERULEN SELENGE
(TOWN OF —) ONON MUREN
DARHAN BULAGAN CHOIREN
TAMTSAK ULANBATOR
CHOYBALSAN
MONGOOSE MUNG URVA CIVET
MUNGO MONGOE MEERKAT
VANSIRE
MONGREL CUR DOG FICE FIST
MUTT CROSS FEIST LIMER POOCH
SCRUB HYBRID PYEDOG BASTARD
CURRISH PIEBALD DOGGEREL
MONILIALES HYPHO
MONIMIA (GUARDIAN OF —)
ACASTO
(HUSBAND OF —) CASTALIO
(LOVER OF —) POLYDORE
MONISM HENISM ONEISM
MONITION TUITION
MONITOR CRT MARKER MENTOR
LANTERN PREFECT
MONITOR LIZARD IBID IBIT URAN
VARAN WARAL GOANNA WORRAL
MONITOR KABARAGOYA
MONK BO FRA COWL LAMA MARO
ARHAT BONZE CLERK FRATE
FRIAR PADRE YAHAN ARAHAT
BHIKKU CULDEE GALLAH GETSUL
GOSAIN MONACH SANTON
VOTARY CALOYER CLUNIAC
GALLACH JACOBIN STARETS
STUDITE ATHONITE BACHELOR
BASILIAN MARABOUT MONASTIC
OLIVETAN SANNYASI TALAPOIN
TRAPPIST BALDICOOT CELESTINE
THELEMITE BERNARDINE
CISTERCIAN
(PL.) AGAPETI ACOEMETI

MONKEY APE CAY ORA PUG SAI
TUP BEGA BROH BRUH DOUC
KAHA MONA MONK MONO SAKI
SIME TITI TOTA WAAG ZATI
ARABA CEBID DIANA JACKO
JOCKO KAHAU MUNGA OATAS
PATAS PONGO PUGGY SAJOU
TOQUE UNGKA BANDAR COAITA
COUXIA GRISON GRIVET GUENON
HOWLER LANGUR MACACO
MARTEN MIRIKI MONACH NISNAS
OUBARI PINCHE RILAWA SAMIRI
SIMIAN SIMPAI TEETEE VERVET
WARINE WEEPER WISTIT
BHUNDER COLOBIN GUARIBA
GUEREZA HANUMAN KALASIE
LUNGOOR MACAQUE MEERKAT
MOUSTOC OUAKARI PRIMATE
ROLOWAY SAIMIRI SAPAJOU
STENTOR TAMARIN ARAGUATO
CAIARARA CAPUCHIN DURUKULI
ENTELLUS LEONCITO MANGABEY
MARMOSET MARTINET
MUSTACHE ORABASSU PRIMATAL
TALAPOIN TCHINCOU WANDEROO
BRACHYURA MALBROUCK
(LIKE A —) PUGGISH
(PREF.) PITHEC(O)
MONKEY BREAD BAOBAB
ADANSONIA
MONKEY FLOWER MIMULUS
MONKEYPOT LECYTH KAKARALI
LECYTHIS SAPUCAIA
MONKEY PUZZLE BUNYA PINON
PINION
MONKEYSHINE DIDO SINGERIE
(PL.) HORSE
MONKFISH MONK RHINA
SQUATINA
MONKISH CENOBIAN MONASTIC
MONK PARROT LORO
MONKSHOOD ATIS ACONITE
ACONITUM NAPELLUS
MOUSEBANE
MONO MONACHI
MONOACETATE ACETIN
MONOCARPELLARY SIMPLE
MONOCHORD MAGAS MAGADIS
UNICHORD
MONOCHROME CAMAIEU
MONOTINT
MONOCLE QUIZ LORGNON
EYEGLASS
MONOCLINOUS PERFECT
MONOECISM SYNOECY SYNOEKY
MONOGRAM IHS JHS YHS CIPHER
HERALD CHRISMON
MONOGRAPH STUDY MEMOIR
BULLETIN DISCOURSE
MONOLITH MENHIR PILLAR
(CIRCLE OF —S) CROMLECH
MONOLITHIC GLOBAL
MONOLOGIST DISEUSE
MONOLOGUE MONOLOGY
SOLILOQUY
MONOPHTHONGAL PURE
MONOPHTHONGIZE SMOOTH
MONOPHYSITE AGNOETE
AGNOITE JACOBITE
(PL.) ACEPHALI
MONOPLANE TAUBE PARASOL
MONOPODE SKIAPOD
MONOPOLIZE LURCH ABSORB

CONSUME ENGROSS
MONOPOLY REGIE TRUST CARTEL
APPALTO
MONOSACCHARIDE OSE DIOSE
HEXOSE KETOSE MONOSE
GLYCOSE HEPTOSE PENTOSE
PYRANOSE
MONOTONOUS ARID DEAD DULL
FLAT WASTE DREARY SAMELY
SODDEN ADENOID HUMDRUM
INSIPID IRKSOME TEDIOUS
BORESOME DRUDGING
SAMESOME SINGSONG UNVARIED
VEGETABLE
MONOTONY DRAB DRYNESS
HUMDRUM DULLNESS SAMENESS
MONOXENOUS DIRECT
MONSIEUR BEAUCAIRE (AUTHOR
OF —) TARKINGTON
(CHARACTER IN —) BEAU MARY
NASH VALOIS CARLISLE MIREPOIX
PHILLIPE MOLYNEAUX
WINTERSET CHATEAURIEN
MONSOON VARSHA
MONSTER OGRE BILCH LARVA
MORMO RAHAB TERAS UNMAN
ELLOPS GERYON MAKARA SHRIMP
TYPHON BICORNE CHIMERA
CYCLOPS DIDYMUS DIPYGUS
ECHIDNA GRENDEL GRIFFIN
GRIFFON PRODIGY SLAPPER
UNBEAST WARLOCK JANICEPS
LINDWORM MOONCALF
TARASQUE TYPHOEUS UROMELUS
LEVIATHAN
(— WITH 100 EYES) ARGUS
(— WITH 100 HANDS) BRIAREUS
(FABULOUS —) KRAKEN TANIWHA
(FEMALE —) HARPY LAMIA SCYLLA
(HALF-BULL HALF-MAN —)
MINOTAUR
(INVISIBLE —) BUNYIP
(MAN-DEVOURING —) OGRE LAMIA
(MYTHICAL —) HARPY SCYLLA
SPHINX CHIMERA WARLOCK
MINOTAUR
(SEA —) BELUE PHOCA KRAKEN
PISTRIX ZIFFIUS WASSERMAN
(SUPERNATURAL —) LARVA
(TWO-BODIED —) DISOMUS
(WATER —) NICKER
(9-HEADED —) HYDRA
(PREF.) TERAT(O)
(SUFF.) PAGUS
MONSTRANCE SUN
MONSTROSITY FREAK DIPYGUS
MONSTER ABORTION IMMANITY
MOONCALF TERATISM
(SUFF.) DYMUS
MONSTROUS VAST ENORM GIANT
FIENDLY FLAMING HIDEOUS
TITANIC BEHEMOTH COLOSSAL
DEFORMED ENORMOUS
FLAGRANT GIGANTIC PYTHONIC
SLAPPING NEFARIOUS
PRODIGIOUS
MONTAGNARD SEKANI

MONTANIST PHRYGIAN

MONTH AB AV BUL MAY PUS SOL
ZIF ZIW ABIB ADAR AHET APAP
ASIN ELUL IYAR JETH JULY JUNE
KUAR MAGH MOON TYBI AGHAN
APRIL ASARH CHAIT IYYAR MAIUS
MARCH NISAN PAYNI RABIA
RAJAB SAFAR SAWAN SEBAT
SHVAT SIVAN SIWAN TEBET
THOTH TIZRI UINAL AUGUST
BHADON CHOIAK JUMADA
JUNIUS KARTIK KISLEV KISLEW
KISLEY MECHIR MESORE NISSAN
NIVOSE PAOPHI PHAGUN SAPHAR
SHABAN SHABAT TAMMUZ
TEBETH TISHRI VEADAR
ABAGHAN APRILIS BAISAKH
BYSACKI CHAITRA CHISLEV
ETHANIM FLOREAL HESHVAN
JANUARY MARTIUS OCTOBER
PACHONS PHALGUN RAMADAN
SARAWAN SHAABAN SHAWWAL
THAMMUZ VENTOSE BRUMAIRE
DECEMBER DULKAADA FEBRUARY
FERVIDOR FRIMAIRE GAMELION
GERMINAL MESSIDOR
MUHARRAM NOVEMBER
PLUVIOSE POSEIDON PRAIRIAL
SEXTILIS ZULKADAH SEPTEMBER
(IN NEXT —) PROXIMO
(IN PRECEDING —) ULTIMO
(PRESENT —) INSTANT

(SIX —S) SEMESTER
(PREF.) MENO
(SUFF.) MESTER
MONTHLY MENSAL
MONUMENT VAT WAT LECH TOMB
CROSS STONE TABUT TITLE
BILITH DOLMEN HEARSE HEROON
MEMORY RECORD TROPHY
ARCHIVE CHAITYA CHHATRI
CHORTEN DENKMAL FUNERAL
TRILITH BILITHON CENOTAPH
MEMORIAL MONOLITH TROPAION
(— IN CHURCH) SACELLUM
(— OF BALEARIC ISLES) TALAYOT
(— OF HEAPED STONES) CAIRN
(PILLARLIKE —) SHAFT STELA
STELE
MOO LOW
MOOCH BUM CADGE SPONGE
MOOCHER MIKER CADGER
GRAFTER SKELDER
MOOD CUE FIT TID MIND TIFF TIFT
TONE TUNE VEIN WHIM DEVIL
FRAME FREAK HEART HUMOR
SPITE PLIGHT SPIRIT SPLEEN
SPRITE STRAIN TALENT TEMPER
CAPRICE FANTASY FEATHER
JUSSIVE ATTITUDE OPTATIVE
(— IN LOGIC) BARBARA
(— OF BAD TEMPER) MAD DORTS
(— OF DEPRESSION) LETDOWN
(CROSS —) FRUMPS
(FRIVOLOUS —) JEST
(GROUCHY —) DODS
(IRRITABLE —) GRIZZLE
(PENSIVE —) MELANCHOLY
(SULKY —) PET
(SULLEN —) STRUNT SULLENS
MOODY SAD GLUM SULKY BROODY
GLOOMY MOROSE SULLEN
MOODISH PENSIVE
MOON BUAT LAMP LUNA MAHI
DIANA LUNET LUCINA PHOEBE
CHANDRA CYNTHIA LEWANNA
LUNETTE MOONLET FOGEATER
MENISCUS SATELLES
(AREA ON —) TERRA
(FULL —) PLENILUNE
(NEW —) PRIME
(PART OF COURSE OF —) MANSION
(WANING —) WANIAND
(PREF.) LUNI MENI SELEN(I)(O)
**MOON AND SIXPENCE (AUTHOR
OF —)** MAUGHAM
(CHARACTER IN —) AMY ATA DIRK
TIARE BLANCHE CHARLES
COUTRAS STROEVE STRICKLAND
MOONBLIND LUNATIC
MOONEYE HIODONT
MOONEYE CISCO BLOATER
MOON-EYED LUNATIC
MOONFISH OPAH SUNFISH
JOROBADO
MOONFLOWER ACHETE
MOONLIGHT FLESH MOONGLOW
MOONRAT GYMNURE
MOONSET MOONDOWN
MOONFALL
MOONSHINE MOON SHINE SHINNY
BOOTLEG BLOCKADE
MOONSTONE (AUTHOR OF —)
COLLINS
(CHARACTER IN —) CUFF EZRA

JOHN BLAKE BRUFF CANDY
LUKER RACHEL GABRIEL GODFREY
ROSANNA FRANKLIN JENNINGS
SPEARMAN VERINDER
ABLEWHITE BETTEREDGE
HERNCASTLE MURTHWAITE
MOONSTRUCK LUNATIC
MOONWORT LUNARY HONESTY
MOOR FEN BENT FELL MOSS POST
BEACH BERTH HOVEL TURCO
COMONTE MARRANO MOGRABI
MOORMAN MORESCO MORISCO
COMMONTY
(INFERTILE —) LANDE
MOOR COCK GORCOCK MUIRCOCK
MOORING DOCK MOORAGE
MOORLAND ROSLAND OUTFIELD
MOOSE BELL ELAND CERVID
ORIGNAL
(YOUNG —) CALF
MOOSEWOOD DIRCA
MOOT MUTE STIR PORTMOOT
MOP BOB SOP SWAB MALKIN
MERKIN MOPPET SCOVEL
(— FOR CLEANING CANNON)
MERKIN
(— OF HAIR) TOUSLE
(BAKER'S —) MALKIN MAWKIN
MOPANE IRONWOOD
MOPE MUMP PEAK POUT SULK
BOODY BROOD GLOOM
MOPING FUSTY DUMPISH
MOPSUS (FATHER OF —) AMPYCUS
RHACIUS
(MOTHER OF —) MANTO CHLORIS
MORA LOVE TIME LIMMA SEMEION
MORAL TAG PURE CIVIL ETHIC
EPIMYTH ETHICAL UPRIGHT
HONORARY
(PL.) THEW
MORALISTIC DIDACTIC
MORALITY MORALS VIRTUE
MORALIZING PI
MORASS BOG FLOW MOSS ROSS
SUMP FLUSH MARSH SLACK
POLDER SLOUGH QUAGMIRE
MORAY PUSI ELGIN HAMLET
MURAENA
MORBID SICK MORBOSE PECCANT
MORDANT HANDLE SPIRIT
CAUSTIC STRIKER SCATHING
MORDECAI (FATHER OF —) JAIR
(WARD OF —) ESTHER
MORE MO MAE PIU OTHER HELDER
(— OR LESS) HALFWAY
(— THAN) BUT OVER ABOVE
RISING PLUSQUAM
(— THAN ADEQUATE) AMPLE
(— THAN ENOUGH) TOO
(— THAN HALF) BETTER
(— THAN ONE) SEVERAL
(— THAN ONE OR TWO) SUNDRY
(— THAN SUFFICIENT) ABUNDANT
(— THAN THIS) YEA
(LITTLE —) ADVANTAGE
(PREF.) MALLO PLEIO PLEO PLIO
(— THAN) PLU SUPER
MOREEN TABBY
MOREL HELVELLA MORIGLIO
MORELLO MOREL GRIOTTE
MULBERRY
MOREOVER EFT EKE TOO ALSO
MORE AGAIN EITHER BESIDES

FARTHER FURTHER THERETO
LIKEWISE OVERMORE
MOREPORK PEHO RURU MOPOKE
MOPEHAWK
MORGUE LIBRARY MORTUARY
MORION CABASSET
MORMON COHAB SAINT DANITE
PATRIARCH
(— STATE) UTAH
MORNING GAY MORN MATIN
MORROW UNDERN COCKCROW
MORNTIME
(IN THE —) MANE
MORNING GLORY NIL KOALI
TWINER GAYBINE IPOMOEA
MANROOT PILIKAI BINDWEED
SCAMMONY MOONFLOWER
(— GROWING AMONG GRAIN) BEAR
MORNING STAR VENUS DAYSTAR
LUCIFER MERCURY BARTONIA
MORO LUTAO SAMAL YAKAN
ILLANO JOLOANO MARANAO
MOROCCO MAROQUIN

MOROCCO

CAPE: NUN NOUN
CAPITAL: RABAT
COIN: OKIA RIAL OKIEH DIRHAM
MOUZOUNA
DISTRICT: ERRIF
FRENCH NAME: MAROC
MEASURE: KALA SAAH FANEGA
IZENBI TOMINI
MOUNTAIN: TOUBKAL
MOUNTAIN RANGE: RIF ATLAS
PEOPLE: MOOR BERBER KABYLE
MOSLEM MUSLIM
PORT: SAFI CEUTA RABAT SAFFI
AGADIR TETUAN LARACHE
MAZAGAN MELILLA MOGADOR
TANGIER
PROVINCE: CEUTA MELILLA
RIVER: DRA SOUS WADI SEBOU
TENSIFT MOULOUYA
TOWN: FES FEZ SAFI OUJDA
RABAT AGADIR MEKNES
KENITRA TANGIER TETOUAN
MARRAKECH CASABLANCA
WEIGHT: ROTL ARTAL ARTEL
GERBE RATEL KINTAR QUINTAL

MORON FOOL AMENT IMBECILE
MORONITY MOROSIS
MOROSE ACID GLUM GRUM SOUR
MOODY RUSTY SURLY CRUSTY
GLOOMY SEVERE STINGY SULLEN
CRABBED CROOKED PEEVISH
STROUNGE SATURNINE
SPLENETIC
MOROSELY CRUSTILY
MOROSENESS ASPERITY
MORPHEME BASE ETYMON
COGNATE
MORPHOLOGICAL FORMAL
MORRIS MILL MERELS
MORSEL BIT NIG ORT TIT BITE
GNAP SNAP SCRAN BUCKONE
MORCEAU NOISETTE PARTICLE
SKERRICK
(— OF CHEESE) TRIP
(— OF CHOCOLATE) BUD
(— OF SEASONED MEAT) GOBBET
(CHOICE —) TIDBIT TITBIT

(PREF.) PSOMO
MORTAL BEING DYING FATAL
HUMAN VITAL DEADLY FINITE
LETHAL BRITTLE DEATHLY
DEATHFUL
(FIRST —) YAMA
MORTALITY FLESH MURRAIN
MORTALLY DEADLY FATALLY
MORTAR DAB COMPO DAGGA
GROUT LARRY ROYAL SORKI
SWISH CANNON CEMENT
HOLMOS MINNIE POTGUN
BEDDING COEHORN DAUBING
PERRIER POUNDER PUGGING
SOORKEE
(— AND PESTLE) DOLLY DOLLIE
(— EXTRUDED BETWEEN LATHS)
KEY
(— FOR ROCKETS) TROMBE
(— FOR SALUTES) CHAMBER
(— MADE WITH STRAW) BAUGE
(INFERIOR —) SLIME
(SMALL —) HOBIT ROYAL TINKER
(THIN —) LARRY
MORTARBOARD CATERCAP
TRENCHER
MORTAR BOAT PALANDER
MORTGAGE DIP LAY BOND LIEN
ENGAGE MONKEY OBLIGE
WADSET WEDDEED THIRLAGE
MORTGAGOR REVERSER
MORTIFICATION ENVY SHAME
SPITE CHAGRIN GANGRENE
NECROSIS VEXATION
MORTIFIED ASHAMED
MORTIFY ABASE ABASH SHAME
SPITE HUMBLE CHAGRIN CRUCIFY
MACERATE
MORTISE GAIN COCKET
(SIDE OF —) CHEEK
MORTUARY MORGUE FUNERARY
SAWLSHOT SEPULCHRAL
MORWONG TARAKIHI
MOSAIC AUCUBA EMBLEM MUSIVE
SCREEN FRISOLEE INTARSIA
TERRAZZO
(POTATO —) CRINKLE
MOSLEM MOOR HADJI HAFIZ
HANIF ISLAM MALAY SALAR
PAYNIM SHIITE TURBAN ISLAMIC
MOORMAN SANGGIL SARACEN
ISLAMITE SANGUILE
(— SCHOLAR) ULAMA
MOSQUE JAMI MOSCH DURGAH
MASJID MESKED
MOSQUITO GNAT AEDES CULICID
GAMBIAE SKEETER ANOPHELE
DIPTERAN
(PREF.) CULIC(I) EMPID(O)
MOSS FOG MNIUM USNEA
HYPNUM MUSKEG AEROGEN
FOXFEET GULAMAN HAIRCAP
PILIGAN TORTULA CROWFOOT
MOSSWORT SPHAGNUM
STAGHORN
(— HANGING FROM TREE) WEEPER
(PL.) MUSCI
(PREF.) BRY(O) MUSC(I)(O)
SPHAGNI SPHAGNO
MOSSBUNKER MENHADEN
MOSSHORN STEER
MOSSI MOLE MORE
MOSSI-GURUNSI GUR

MOSS PINK PHLOX
MOSSTROOPER RIDER
MOSSY FOGGY HOARY MUSCOSE
MOST BEST MOSTLY FARTHEST
(PREF.) PLEISTO
MOSTLY MOST FECKLY CHIEFLY
MOSTDEAL
MOT JEST
MOTE ATOM ATOMY FESCUE
MOATHILL
MOTEL COURT
MOTH GEM NUN PUG DART HAWK
MOTE PAGE ACREA APPLE ATLAS
EGGAR EGGER FLAME GAMMA
IMAGO MORMO PISKY PLUME
SAMIA SWIFT THORN USHER
WITCH ANTLER BAGONG BUGONG
BURNET COSSID DAGGER
DATANA HERALD HUMMER
JUGATE LACKEY LAPPET MILLER
MOODER MUSLIN PLUSIA PRALID
QUAKER RUSTIC SPHINX THISBE
TINEID TISSUE TUSSUR VENEER
ARCTIAN ARCTIID BAGWORM
BUDWORM CRAMBID CRININE
DELTOID DRINKER EMERALD
EMPEROR EUCLEID FESTOON
FIGWORM FOOTMAN FRENATE
HOOKTIP NOCTUID PEGASUS
PSYCHID PYRALIS SLICKER
STINGER SYLINID TINEOLA
TORTRIX TUSSOCK URANIID
VAPORER ZYGENID AEGERIID
ARMYWORM BOMBYCID
CATOCALA CECROPIA CINNABAR
COCHYLIS FISHTAIL FORESTER
GEOMETER GOLDTAIL GRISETTE
HAWKMOTH HEPIALID
KNOTHORN MOTHWORM
PHYCITID PLUTELLA SPHINGID
SPRAWLER WAINSCOT SATURNIID
PALMERWORM
(— BREEDER) AURELIAN
(VERY SMALL —) MICRO
(PREF.) PHALAENO SETO
MOTH BALL REPELLER
MOTHER INA MOM DAME MÅMA
MADRE MAMMA MAMMY MATER
MINNY MODUR MITHER MULIER
VENTER GENETRIX
(— OF THE GODS) RHEA
(DIVINE —) MATRIGAN
(GREAT —) AGDISTIS
(NOURISHING — OF MAN) CYBELE
(SEVEN —S) MATRIS
(SIDE OF —) ÈNATE
(PREF.) MADRE MATR(I)(O) METRO
MOTHERLAND COUNTRY
MOTHERLY MATERNAL MATRONAL
MOTHER-OF-PEARL NACRE PEARL
MOTIF SPRIG DESIGN DEVICE
MOTIVE SCALLOP APPLIQUE
MORESQUE
MOTILE ZO ZOO
MOTION WAY FARD FEED GIRD
MOVE SIGN WHID HURRY PAVIE
APPORT MOMENT MOTIVE
TRAVEL UNREST IMPULSE
ACTIVITY MOVEMENT OVERTURE
(— OF AIR) AIRFLOW
(— OF CONTEMPT) FICO
(— OF HORSE) AIR
(— TO) ALLATIVE

(ABRUPT —) CHOP
(CAM —) COULIER
(CIRCULAR —) GYRE COMPASS
(CONFUSED —) GURGE
(DANCE —) CAPER
(DIZZY —) SWIMBEL
(EXPRESSIVE —) GESTURE
(FORWARD —) HEADWAY
(GLIDING —) SWIM SKITTER
(HEAVING —) ESTUS AESTUS
(HURRIED —) HUSTLE
(ILLEGAL —) BALK BAULK
(IRREGULAR —) SWAG
(JERKING —) BOB LIPE JIGGLE
(LATERAL —) DRIFT
(QUIVERING —) TREMOR
(RAPID —) SCOUR BRATTLE
(REARING —) PESADE
(RECIPROCATING —) SEESAW
(ROTARY —) SWAY BACKSPIN
SIDESPIN
(SHOWY —) FANFARE
(SIDEWAYS —) CRAB
(SLOW —) CRAWL
(SPINNING —) ENGLISH
(SUNWISE —) DEASIL
(SWIMMING —) FLUTTER
(UPWARD —) HEAVE
(VIGOROUS —) SKELP
(VIOLENT —) JERK RAPT BENSEL
(WAVERING —) SHAKE
(WAVING —) WAFF
(WHIRLING —) SWIRL
(PREF.)
CIN(E)(EMATO)(EMO)(ET)(ETO)
KIN(E)(EMATO)(EMO)(ET)(ETO)
KINESI MOTI MOTO PHORO
(SUFF.) CINESIA KINESIA KINESIS
KINETIC
MOTIONLESS DEAD ASLEEP
STATIC IMMOBILE STAGNANT
STIRLESS
MOTION PICTURE PIC CINE FILM
FLICK MOVIE BIOPIC CINEMA
TALKIE CHEAPIE SMELLIE
FLICKERS PHOTODRAMA
(PL.) SILENTS
(PREF.) CINE(MATO)(MO)(T)(TO)
MOTIVATE PROPEL ACTUATE
ANIMATE INSPIRE
MOTIVATED COVERT
MOTIVE GOAD SAKE SPUR CAUSE
MOTIF SCORE ACTUAL DESIRE
OBJECT REASON REGARD SPRING
ATTACCO IMPULSE PATTERN
RESPECT RINCEAU SUBJECT
INSTANCE STIMULUS
(ALLEGED —) PRETEXT
(CHIEF —) MAINSPRING
MOTLEY MIXED MEDLEY RAGTAG
MOTTLED PIEBALD
(PREF.) PARTI PARTY
MOTMOT HOUTOU SAWBILL
PICARIAN
MOTOR AUTO TOOT TOUR MOVER
ENGINE BOOSTER ROTATOR
TURBINE EFFERENT OUTBOARD
MOTORBIKE MOPED
MOTORBOAT KICKER LAUNCH
AUTOBOAT RUNABOUT
HYDROFOIL
MOTORCAR MOTOR DOODLEBUG
(MINIATURE — FOR RACING) KART

MOTORCYCLE BIKE CYCLE MOTOR
STEED TRICAR CHOPPER
AUTOETTE MINIBIKE TRICYCLE
(PART OF —) HORN SEAT TANK
TIRE BRAKE GUARD LEVER LIGHT
VALVE WHEEL CLUTCH FENDER
SADDLE SIGNAL CALIPER
EXHAUST MUFFLER TOOLBOX
HANDGRIP THROTTLE GEARSHIFT
TAILLIGHT TENSIONER
CARBURETOR TACHOMETER
SPEEDOMETER
(SMALL —) MINIBIKE
MOTORIST AUTOIST
MOTORMAN CARMAN WATTMAN
TROLLYMAN
MOTORTRUCK DRAY LORRY
CAMION BOBTAIL FLATBED
MOTTLE CHECK TABBY SPONGE
MOTTLED JAZZ PIED CHINE PINTO
TABBY MARLED MOTLEY
RUMINATE SPLASHED
MOTTO MOT WORD AXIOM POESY
CACHET DEVICE EUREKA LEGEND
REASON IMPRESA EPIGRAPH
(— IN A RING) POSY
(— OF CALIFORNIA) EUREKA
(— OF MAINE) DIRIGO
MOUE FACE
MOUFLON MUSIMON
MOULDER CRUMBLE
MOULIN CHIMNEY
MOUND AHU COP HOW LAW LOW
BALK BANK BOSS BUND BUTT
GOAL HILL HUMP KNOW MOLE
POME TELL TEPE TERP TUFT
TUMP AGGER BERRY DHERI
ESKAR ESKER KNOLL MONDE
MOTTE MOUNT PINGO RAISE
STUPA TOMAN BARROW CAUSEY
MEILER RIDEAU ANTHILL
BOUROCK HILLOCK MAMELON
BACKSTOP BARBETTE SNOWBANK
TEOCALLI
(— ABOUT A PLANT) TUMP
(— FOR MEMORIAL) CAIRN
(— IN BUILDING MATERIAL) DIMPLE
(— OF DETRITUS) WASH
(— OF ICE) DOME
(— OF WOOD TO BE CHARRED)
MEILER
(BURIAL —) LAW LOW TOR TOLA
BERRY GUACA HUACA BARROW
KURGAN TUMULUS
(FORTIFIED —) DUN
(GLACIAL —) KAME
(MILITARY —) BARBETTE
(PALISADED —) MOTTE
(VOLCANIC —) HORNITO
(PREF.) BUNO
MOUND BIRD MEGAPODE
MOUNT BEN STY BACK HEAD RIDE
RISE SCAN ARISE BIPOD BOARD
CLIMB HEAVE HINGE SPEEL SPIRE
SWARM ASCEND ASPIRE BREAST
MORIAH CHARGER COLLINE
HAIRPIN HARNESS BESTRIDE
MOUNTAIN MOUNTING
MOUNTURE SURMOUNT
(— A HORSE) FORK LIGHT WORTH
(— BY STEPS) SCAN
(— ON PIN) STICK
(— ON WINGS) SOAR

(STEREOTYPE —) CORE
MOUNTAIN BEN KOP BERG CIMA
DAGH FELL KLIP KNOB MONS
MONT NEBO PICO PIKE JEBEL
MOUNT RANGE BARROW
BUNDOC GILEAD GUNONG
HEIGHT PISGAH HELICON
MONTURE NUNATAK
MONADNOCK
(— INHABITED BY SPIRIT) GUACA
HUACA
(— MASS) OROGEN
(— PASS) GHAT GHAUT
(— STATE) MONTANA
(— TRACT) DUAR
(AT BASE OF —) PIEDMONT
(FABLED —) KAF MERU
(GREEK —) OSSA PELION HELICON
OLYMPUS MAENALUS
(HIGH —) ALP
(ROUND —) REEK
(SMALL —) NOB KNOB BUTTE
(SNOW —) JOKUL
(SUBMARINE —) GUYOT
SEAMOUNT
(PREF.) MONTI ORE(O) ORI ORO
MOUNTAIN ASH SORB SORBUS
DOGBERRY MOZEMIZE ROUNTREE
WINETREE
MOUNTAIN BEAVER SEWELLEL
MOUNTAIN BINDWEED
SOLDANEL
MOUNTAIN CAP SCALP
MOUNTAIN CLIMBER CRAGSMAN
MOUNTAIN CRANBERRY
FOXBERRY
MOUNTAINEER WASIR WAZIR
HEIDUC HAYDUCK HILLMAN
ORESTES MONTESCO TIERSMAN
(PL.) GUTI GUTIANS
MOUNTAIN GOAT IBEX MAZAME
MOUNTAIN LAUREL IVY HEATH
ERICAD KALMIS LAUREL
IVYWOOD CALFKILL
(THICKET OF —) SLICK
MOUNTAIN LINNET TWITE
MOUNTAIN LION PUMA COUGAR
MOUNTAIN MAHOE EMAJAGUA
MOUNTAIN MISERY TARWEED
MOUNTAINOUS RANGY VICIOUS
MOUNTAIN PARSLEY FLUELLEN
MOUNTAIN RANGE KAF QAF TIER
SIERRA SAWBACK DINDYMUS
MOUNTAIN SICKNESS VETA
MOUNTAINSIDE FELLSIDE
MOUNTAINTOP MAN DOME
MOUNTAIN WOOD ROCKWOOD
MOUNTEBANK ANTIC BALADIN
BALADINE IMPOSTOR OPERATOR
MOUNTED CARDED SADDLE
EASELED EQUITANT
MOUNT ETNA MONGIBEL
MOUNTING MOUNT SCAPE
ASCENT FLIGHT MONTANT
SOAKING ASPIRANT INCABLOC
MOUNTURE
(— OF GEM) CHASE
(STYLE OF —) SETTING
MOURN DOLE KEEN SIGH WAIL
PLAIN GRIEVE LAMENT SORROW
GRIZZLE
MOURNER WAILER WEEPER
(HIRED —) SALLIE SAULIE

(PROFESSIONAL —) MUTE BLACK KEENER

MOURNFUL SAD BLACK MINOR SORRY WEEPY RUEFUL DERNFUL FUNEBRE SIGHFUL WAILFUL DEJECTED DIRGEFUL ELEGIOUS FUNEREAL MAESTIVE MESTFULL PLANTFUL YEARNFUL PLAINTIVE

MOURNING DOLOR SHIVA DISMAL SORROW WIDOWED
(— CLOTH) RADZIMIR

MOURNING BECOMES ELECTRA
(AUTHOR OF —) ONEILL
(CHARACTER IN —) ADAM EZRA ORIN BRANT DAVID HAZEL NILES PETER MANNON LAVINIA CHRISTINE

MOUSE MURINE MYGALE RODENT VERMIN ARVICOLE CRICETID MYOMORPH
(LIKE A —) MURIFORM
(MEADOW —) VOLE
(STRIPED —) KUSU
(PREF.) MURI MY(O) SMINTHO
(SUFF.) MYS

MOUSEBIRD COLY

MOUSE DEER PLANDOK

MOUSE GRAY SAKKARA SPARROW

MOUSETRAP TIPE

MOUSING KEEPER

MOUTH OS GAB GAM GOB JIB MUG MUN NEB ORF ROW YAP BEAK BEAL BOCA HEAD MUSS PUSS SHOP TRAP YAWN BAZOO BOCCA BRACE CHOPS GODON STOMA TUTEL GEBBIE KISSER MUZZLE RABBLE RICTUS SUCKER THROAT CLAPPER FLUMMER ORIFICE OSTIOLE STOMACH LORRIKER PAVILLON
(— AND THROAT) COPPER WHISTLE
(— OF CANYON) ABRA
(— OF GLASS FURNACE) BOCCA
(— OF HARBOR) BOCA
(— OF PERITHECIUM) OSTIOLE
(— OF RIVER) BEAL BOCA LADE ENTRY FIRTH INFLUX OSTIUM ESTUARY OSTIARY OUTFALL
(— OF SHAFT) BRACE
(— OF TRUMPET) BELL CODON PAVILLON
(— PARTS OF ARTHROPOD) TROPHI
(KILN —) KILNEYE KILNHOLE
(SORE — OF SHEEP) ECTHYMA
(WRY —) MURGEON
(PL.) ORA
(PREF.) BUCCO ORI ORO OSCULI STOM(A)(AT)(ATO)(O)
(SUFF.) STOMA(TA)(TE)(TOUS) STOME STOMI(A) STOMOUS STOMUM STOMY

MOUTHFUL GAG GOB SUP GNAP GOLEE GOBBET

MOUTHPART BILL

MOUTHPIECE BAR BEAK BOCAL MOUTH FIPPLE SYRINX PROPHET
(— OF BAGPIPE) MUSE
(— OF PIPE) STEM

MOUTHWASH GARGLE COLLUTORIUM

MOUTH-WATERING SALIVANT

MOVABLE FREE LOOSE MOBILE PORTABLE REMUABLE

(PL.) MEUBLES

MOVE GO ACT FIG GEE GET WAG BOOM BORE BUCK BUMP CALL DRAW FIRK FLIT GOAD HEAT KNEE MAKE PIRL ROLL SILE SPUR STEP STIR SWAY WORK ANKLE BLITZ BUDGE CARRY CAUSE CROWD DRAFT HEAVE IMPEL LIGHT MARCH MUDGE QUECH REMUE ROUSE SHAKE SHIFT TOUCH GAMBIT HANDLE HUSTLE INCITE INDUCE KINDLE MOTION PROMPT QUITCH REMBLE SASHAY STRAKE ACTUATE AGITATE ANIMATE DISTURB DRAUGHT FLUTTER INSPIRE MIGRATE PROVOKE AMBULATE BULLDOZE CATAPULT DEMARCHE DISLODGE DISPLACE MOTIVATE
(— A RESOLUTION) FIRST
(— ABOUT) ROLL WEND DISPACE SHUFFLE CONVERSE LOCOMOTE
(— ACROSS) THWART
(— ACTIVELY) YANK
(— AIMLESSLY) POKE BOGUE
(— ALONG) SHOG
(— APART) ABDUCT SPREAD
(— AS IN STUPOR) DAVER
(— ASIDE) SKEW
(— ASUNDER) SINGLE
(— AT TOP SPEED) LICK
(— AWAY) CUT MOG DECAMP RECEDE
(— AWKWARDLY) HODGE HIRSEL LABRUP SHAMBLE SLUMMOCK
(— BACK) FADE ARSLE RECUR RECEDE RETIRE RETREAT
(— BACKWARD AND FORWARD) GIG SWAY DARTLE DIDDLE SHUFFLE SHUTTLE
(— BOOM OR SAIL) JIB
(— BRISKLY) FAN HALE STIR FRICK FRIKE FRISK KNOCK SQUIRT TRANCE TRAVEL WHIPPET
(— BY FITS AND STARTS) JIFFLE
(— BY JERKS) HITCH JIGGET JIGGLE JINKLE
(— BY SMALL SHOCKS) JOG
(— BY WHEELS) ROLL TRUNDLE
(— CHESS PIECE) DEVELOP
(— CLUMSILY) HOIT JOLL PAUT BARGE KEVEL HIRSEL LUMBER TOLTER GALUMPH STUMBLE
(— COMPUTER VIDEO DISPLAY) SCROLL
(— DIAGONALLY) CATER
(— DOWN) SILE STOOP DECLINE DESCEND
(— FORCIBLY) SHOVE
(— FORWARD) BREAK ADVANCE PROGREDE
(— FURTIVELY) LEER GLIDE SLINK SLIVE SNEAK STEAL
(— GRADUALLY) EDGE
(— HAPHAZARDLY) BUCKET
(— HASTILY) SCUR SKIRR
(— HAUGHTILY) SWOOP
(— HEAVILY) LUG LUMP FLUMP LUMBER
(— IN AGITATION) SEETHE
(— IN AWKWARD MANNER) GANGLE
(— IN CIRCLES) MILL PURL

(— IN MARBLES) FULK
(— IN RIPPLES) CURL
(— IN SHUFFLING MANNER) MOSEY
(— IN SMALL DEGREES) INCH
(— IN WATER) SQUELCH
(— IN WAVES) LAP CRINKLE
(— INWARDLY) ENMOVE
(— JERKILY) JAG BUCK FLIP KICK FLIRT BUCKET TWITCH
(— LANGUIDLY) MAUNDER
(— LAZILY) HULK
(— LEISURELY) AMBLE
(— LIGHTLY) BRUSH FLUFF
(— LOOSELY) SLOP
(— NERVOUSLY) DITHER
(— NIMBLY) KILT LINK WHIP DANCE
(— OFF) FIRK RYNT MOSEY MORRIS
(— ON) MOG VAMP AVAUNT SUCCEED WHIGFARE
(— OUT) BLOW
(— OUT OF SIGHT) SINK
(— QUICKLY) BOB FIG CLIP DUCK FIRK FLAX FLIT GIRD JINK KITE SCUR WHAP WHEW WHID WHOP YANK FLASH GLENT SKEET SKIRR SKITE SPANK SQUIB STAVE STOUR THROW NIDDLE STRIKE WALLOP SKIMMER
(— QUIETLY) SLIP
(— RAPIDLY) BANG BOLT BUZZ HEEL HURL SKIR THUD CHASE GLINT SCOUR CAREER GIGGIT HURTLE WHIRRY AGITATE CLATTER HIGHTAIL
(— RESTLESSLY) FIG GAD FIKE ITCH CHURN SQUIB JIFFLE KELTER
(— SHAKILY) HOTTER
(— SIDEWISE) CRAB EDGE SIDLE SLENT
(— SLOWLY) LAG MOG INCH PANT PAUT SLUG BOGUE CRAWL CREEP DRAWL FUDGE SHLEP SLOOM SNAIL HAGGLE LINGER SCHLEP SCHLEPP TRINTLE
(— SMOOTHLY) SLIP DRIFT FLOAT GLIDE SLEEK GLISSADE
(— SPIRALLY) GYRATE
(— STEADILY) FORGE
(— STEALTHILY) GLIDE SLINK SMOOT SNAKE
(— STIFFLY) CRAMBLE CRAMMEL
(— SUDDENLY) BOLT LASH YERK GLENT START FLOUNCE STARTLE
(— SWIFTLY) CUT FLY BOOM HARE LEAP RAKE SCUD SPIN BREEZE COURSE WUTHER SWIFTEN
(— THROUGH AIR) FLY
(— TO AND FRO) FAN FLOP DODGE SHAKE WIGWAG AGITATE
(— TO ANOTHER PLACE) ADJOURN
(— TO LEEWARD) DRIVE
(— TREMULOUSLY) WAPPER
(— UNEASILY) FIDGET
(— UNSTEADILY) BICKER BUMBLE FALTER HOBBLE WABBLE WAMBLE WELTER WOBBLE BLUNDER STAGGER STUMBLE
(— UP AND DOWN) BOB HOWD SEESAW TEETER
(— UPWARD) ARISE

ASCEND GRADUATE
(— VESSEL) KEDGE
(— VIGOROUSLY) FLOG STRAY
(— VIOLENTLY) DASH FLOG HURL LASH LEAP SWASH AGITATE COMMOVE
(— WAVERINGLY) FLEET
(— WEAKLY) FLAG
(— WITH BEATING MOTION) FLAP
(— WITH EFFORT) ACHE
(— WITH LEAPS) SKIP SPRING
(— WITH NOISY ACTIVITY) BUSTLE
(— WITH SHORT TURNS) ZIGZAG
(CHESS —) KEY COOK NECK PLOY GAMBIT KEYMOVE
(SUCCESSFUL —) SCORE
(SUDDEN —) GAMBADE

MOVED MOSSO ANIMATE FRANTIC INSTINCT
(— BY LOVE) AMOROUS
(EASILY —) FLESHLY SKINLESS

MOVEMENT EDDY MOTO PLAY STIR CARRY CAUSE FLICK FLISK FLOAT FRONT GESTE MUDGE TREND UKIYO ACTION CURSUS ENTREE MOMENT MOTION PIAFFE SPRAWL STROKE CURRENT FURIANT GAMBADO GESTURE KINESIS PIAFFER UKIYOYE BUSINESS CHARTISM FEMINISM FUTURISM HASKALAH STIRRING PERIPATETICS
(— BY ORGANISMS) TAXIS
(— FOR POLITICAL UNION) ENOSIS
(— FROM POINT TO POINT) PASSAGE
(— IN BULLFIGHT) SUERTE
(— OF AIR) SPIRIT
(— OF CHORUS) STROPHE
(— OF CLOUDS) CARRY
(— OF COMPUTER BITS) SHIFT
(— OF HORSE) LEVADE PIAFFE
(— OF LOOM) MOUSING
(— OF PLANTS) NUTATION
(— OF PROTOPLASM) CYCLOSIS
(— OF ROPE) SURGE
(— OF SHIP) STERNWAY
(— OF TIDE) LAKIE
(— OF TROOPS) LIFT
(— OF WATER) BOBBLE
(— TOWARD GOAL) STRIDE
(AGITATED —) WORKING
(ART —) CUBISM
(AVANT-GARDE —) UNDERGROUND
(BACKWARD —) BACKUP BACKLASH BACKWASH
(BALLET —) PLIE FRAPPE FOUETTE FLICFLAC
(BOBBING —) BOBBLE
(BODILY —) ACTION
(BOWEL —) LAXATION
(BOXING —) SPAR
(BRISK —) SNAP
(BROWNIAN —) PEDESIS
(CAVALRY —) CARACOLE
(CIRCULAR —) CYCLING
(CLEVER —) PAW
(DANCE —) FRIS BRISE CLOSE GIGUE GLIDE LASSU SPIRAL BATTERIE
(DARTING —) FLIRT
(DOWNWARD —) DECLINE
(DROLL —) GAMBADE GAMBADO

(ENLIGHTENMENT —) HASKALAH
(EXPANSION —) BOOM
(FENCING —) VOLT
(FLAPPING —) FLAFF
(FORWARD —) SWEEP ADVANCE PROGRESS INCESSION PROCESSION
(FROLICKING —) FRISK GAMBOL
(GRADUAL —) CREEPISM
(GYMNASTIC —) KIP SWING DISMOUNT
(HUMOROUS —) BURLA
(INDEPENDENCE —) SWADESHI
(INVOLUNTARY —) REFLEX
(JAPANESE ART —) YAMATO YAMATOE
(JERKING —S) BALLISM
(JERKY —) SNATCH
(JERKY EYE —) SACCADE
(LATERAL —) LEEWAY
(MASS —) STAMPEDE
(MASSAGE —) SCIAGE
(MILITARY —) BOUND MANEUVRE
(MUSICAL —) AIR DUET BURLA DUMKA LARGO ADAGIO ENTREE FINALE PRESTO SARABAND SYMPHONY
(OSCILLATING —) HUNT
(PAINTING —) FAUVISM TACHISM VORTICISM
(POETRY —) IMAGISM
(POLITICAL —) LEFTISM GAULLISM
(QUADRILLE —) POULE
(QUICK —) PAW DART WHID WHIP YERK GLENT SHAKE GLANCE
(RATIONALISTIC —) DEISM
(REELING —) STAGGER
(RELIGIOUS —) JOCISM BABIISM PIETISM STUNDISM
(RETROGRADE —) SLIP CREEP
(RETURN —) BACKHAUL
(RHYTHMIC —) DANCE
(ROCKING —) HOWD
(ROWING —) HOICK
(SKATING —) MOHAWK CHOCTAW
(SKILLED —) SUERTE
(SPASMODIC —) JUMP HICCUP SPRUNT HICCOUGH
(SPRINGY —) LILT
(STEALTHY —) SLINK
(SUDDEN —) HITCH SPANG START FLICKER
(SWAYING —) SWAG
(SWEEPING —) SWINGE
(SWIFT —) SWOOSH
(THEOLOGICAL —) ARIANISM
(TUMULTUOUS —) HORROR EMOTION
(TURNING —) CARACOLE
(UP AND DOWN —) SEESAW
(UPWARD —) BULGE SCEND
(UPWARD — OF VESSEL) SCEND
(WALKING —) AMBLE
(WATCH —) EBAUCHE BAGUETTE
(ZIGZAG —) TACK MEANDER
(PREF.) KIN(O) KINESI KINETO
(SUFF.) CINESIA KINESIA KINESIS KINETIC
MOVEMENTS
(SUFF.) **(PERFORMANCE OF —)** PRACTIC PRAXIA PRAXIS
MOVER MOTIVE CLIPPER
MOVIE (ALSO SEE MOTION

PICTURE) FLICK FLICKS SLEEPER MELODRAMA
(PL.) PICTURES
MOVIES (DEVOTEE OF —) CINEPHILE
MOVING WAY HIGH ASTIR GOING QUICK AFLOAT MOVENT ANIMATE CURRENT AMBULANT FLITTING PATHETIC POIGNANT TOUCHING AFFECTING
(— ABOUT) AROUND AMBULANT
(— AIMLESSLY) ERRANT
(— BACKWARDS) CRAB
(— DOWN LINE) ACTIVE
(— FORWARD) ADVANCE
(— HAPHAZARDLY) AFLOAT
(— IN MANY DIRECTIONS) DIFFUSE
(— RAPIDLY) STICKLE SKELPING
(— SLOWLY) SOFT GLACIAL TEDIOUS
(— TO AND FRO) AGITATED
(NOT —) STICKY STABILE
MOVINGLY PATETICO
MOW CUT BARB GOAF SKIM TASS CRADLE SCYTHE SICKLE DESECATE
(— BEANS) THROAT
(— FOR STORING GRAIN) TOSS
(— OF CORN) CANSH
(HAY —) TASS
MOWER MEADER
(FOREMOST —) LORD
MOWING MATH MOWTH SHEAR
MOZA (FATHER OF —) CALEB ZIMRI
MOZAMBIQUE (CAPE OF —) DELGADO
(CAPITAL OF —) MAPUTO
(LAKE OF —) CHUALI NHAVARRE
(MONEY OF —) METICAL
(RIVER OF —) SAVE MSALU RUVUMA LIMPOPO LUGENDA ZAMBEZI
(TOWN OF —) MAUA TETE BEIRA MAPAI ZUMBO CHEMBA MANICA NAMAPA PAFURI CHIMOIO NAMPULA
MOZZETTA CAMAIL
MR HERR SIGNOR SIGNIOR SIGNORE
MR MIDSHIPMAN EASY (AUTHOR OF —) MARRYAT
(CHARACTER IN —) EASY JACK AGNES MESTY WILSON REBIERA GASCOIGNE MIDDLETON
MRS FRAU MISS PANI HANOUM SENORA SENHORA SIGNORA GOODWIFE
MRS DALLOWAY (AUTHOR OF —) WOOLF
(CHARACTER IN —) PETER SALLY SETON SMITH WALSH HOLMES KALMAN WILLIAM BRADSHAW CLARISSA DALLOWAY SEPTIMUS
MRS WARREN'S PROFESSION (AUTHOR OF —) SHAW
(CHARACTER IN —) FRANK PRAED VIVIE CROFTS GEORGE SAMUEL WARREN GARDNER
MUCH FAR FELE MICH REAL WELL GREAT HEAPS MOLTO MOULT SIZES MICKLE MUCHLY ABUNDANT MUCHWHAT
(— CALLED FOR) LEEFTAIL
(PRETTY —) GAILY GAYLY

(SO —) ALL SUCH TANTO INSOMUCH
(TOO —) TROP TROPPO
(VERY —) ALL BADLY GREAT HEAPS LOADS SWITHE SWYTHE APLENTY GEYLIES GREATLY
(PREF.) ERI MULT(I) POLY SYCHNO
(HOW —) POSO QUANTI
MUCH ADO ABOUT NOTHING
(AUTHOR OF —) SHAKESPEARE
(CHARACTER IN —) HERO JOHN PEDRO URSULA VERGES ANTONIO CLAUDIO CONRADE FRANCIS LEONATO BEATRICE BENEDICK BORACHIO DOGBERRY MARGARET BALTHASAR
MUCILAGE GUM MUCUS MUCAGO
MUCILAGINOUS MALACOID
MUCK CACK SOIL
MUCOID BLENNOID
MUCUS SNOT MUCOR BUBBLE MUCAGO PHLEGM SNIVEL PITUITE
(PREF.) BLENN(I)(O) MUC(I)(O)(OSO) MYX(O)
(SUFF.) MYXA
MUD DAB FEN CLAY DIRT DUBS FANC GLAR LAIR MIRE MOIL SAUR SIND SLAB SLEW SLOB SLOP SLUB SLUD SLUE SLUR SUMP CLART FANGO GLAUR GUMBO SLAKE SLIME SLOSH SLUSH SPOSH SQUAD WAISE PELOID SLOUGH SLUDGE CLABBER GUTTERS MURGEON SLOBBER SLODDER SLUDDER SLUTHER SULLAGE
(LACUSTRINE —) GYTTJA
(OF DRIED —) CUTCHA
(PREF.) LIMI LIMO PEL(O) TELMAT(O)
MUDAR AK AKUND ASHUR MADOR YERCUM AKMUDDAR
MUDCAP ADOBE
MUD CAT FLATHEAD
MUDCAT STATE MISSISSIPPI
MUDDLE MIX BALL DOZE HASH MASH MESS MULL MUZZ SOSS ADDLE SNAFU BEMUSE BURBLE FANKLE FOITER FUDDLE HUDDLE JUMBLE MAFFLE MIZZLE MOFFLE MUCKER POTHER PUDDLE TANGLE BECLOUD BEDEVIL BLUNDER CONFUSE EMBROIL FLUSTER POOTHER STUPEFY BEFUDDLE BEWILDER CONFOUND DISORDER FLIUNDER
MUDDLED ADDLE BEERY FOGGY FUZZY MUSED MUZZY DRUMLY GROGGY BESOTTED CONFUSED
MUDDY DEEP FOUL GLET OOZY ROIL SICK DIRTY DROVY DUBBY GUMLY ROILY SLAKY CLAGGY CLARTY CLASHY DREGGY DROUMY DRUMLY GROUTY LIMOUS PUDDLY SALLOW SLABBY SLOBBY SLOPPY SLUBBY SLUDGY TURBID CLATCHY GUTTERY MUDDIFY MUDDISH SLOUGHY CLABBERY LUTULENT SLOBBERY
(— BY STIRRING) STUDDLE
MUDFISH BOWFIN KOMTOK
MUDFLOW LAHAR MUDSPATE
MUDGUARD WING CUTTOO SPLASHER

MUDHOLE PULK SLOUGH LOBLOLLY
MUD MINNOW DOGFISH MUDFISH
MUD PUPPY DOGFISH
MUERMO ULMO
MUFF BLOW BOBBLE MUFFLE SNUFFKIN
MUFFIN COB GEM SINK COBBE HAZEL SINKER MANCHET PIKELET POPOVER
MUFFLE MOB MOP PAD DAMP DULL MUTE NOSE WRAP BUMBLE DEADEN MUZZLE SHROUD STIFLE ENVELOP
(— A BELL) CLAM
(— THE HEAD) MOBLE
MUFFLED DEAD DEAF DULL CLOSE THICK HOLLOW INWARD MOBBED WRAPPED
MUFFLER SCARF MUFFLE SILENCER
MUFTI JURIST CIVVIES
MUG TOT BOCK CANN FACE STEIN NOGGIN PEWTER SCONCE SEIDEL CANETTE GODDARD BLACKPOT PANNIKIN SCHOPPEN
(ALE —) TOBY
(LIQUOR —) CAN GUN
MUGGER GOA HAM
MUGGING YOKING
MUGGINS SNIFF
MUGGY FOZY MUNGY PUGGY STICKY MUGGISH PUTHERY
MUGWORT BULWAND MUGWEED
MUISCA CHIBCHA
MUISHOND ZORIL ZORILLE
MULATTO PARDO GRIFFE GRIQUA GRIFFIN TERCERON
MULBERRY AL AAL ACH AUTE KOZO MORE WAUKE ALROOT MURREY MORELLO SOURBUSH SYCAMINE
(PREF.) MOR(I)
MULBERRY FIG SYCAMORE
MULCT FINE CHECK AMERCE SCONCE FORFEIT PENALTY
MULE BUCKER HYBRID ACEMILA IRONMAN JARHEAD JUGHEAD RATTAIL SUMPTER CENCERRO HARDTAIL QUADROON QUATERON
(DROVE OF —S) ATAJO MULADA
(MOHAMMED'S —) ALBORAK
MULE ARMADILLO MULITA
MULE DRIVER SKINNER
MULE SHOE PLANCHE
MULETEER ASSMAN ARRIERO
MULISH BALKY STUPID STUBBORN OBSTINATE
MULL CHAW BOSOM FETTLE MULMUL STEATIN
MULLEIN TORCH AGLEAF ICELEAF DOVEWEED FELTWORT FOXGLOVE HAGTAPER LUNGWORT VERBASCO
MULLER DAMPENER
MULLET BOBO LISA LIZA BOURI GARAU KANAE MOLET HARDER MULLOID GOATFISH MUGILOID SPRINGER
(UNPIERCED —) STAR
MULLIGRUBS COLIC
MULLION MONIAL

MULLOWAY JEWFISH KINGFISH SCIAENID
MULTICOLORED CALICO
MULTIFARIOUS MANIFOLD
MULTIFARIOUSNESS VARIETY
MULTIFORM DIVERSE
MULTILINGUAL POLYGLOT
MULTIPLE DECUPLE PARALLEL SEPTUPLE MULTIPLEX
MULTIPLICAND FACIEND
MULTIPLICATION INCREASE DUPLATION
MULTIPLICITY MULTEITY
MULTIPLIER FACIENT COFACTOR
MULTIPLY VIE BREED LAYER DOUBLE INVOLVE ENGENDER INCREASE MANIFOLD PROPAGATE PROLIFERATE
MULTIPLYING (PREF.) POLY
MULTITUDE ARMY CRAM HEAP HIVE HOST ROUT RUCK CLOUD CROWD FLOTE MEINY POWER SHOAL SWARM HIRSEL HOTTER LEGION MAMPUS MEINIE NATION THRONG SMOTHER PLURALITY (PL.) FLOCKS
MULTITUDINOUS LEGION MYRIAD MANIFOLD NUMEROUS
MULTIVALENT POLYAD
MULTURE THIRL THIRLAGE
MUM CLUM DARK MUMMER
MUMBLE CHEW MOUP MUMP BROCK CHELE MOUTH CHAVEL FAFFLE FUMBLE HOTTER HUMMER MAFFLE MOFFLE PALTER DRUMBLE FLUMMER GRUMBLE
MUMBLER MAFFLER
MUMBLETY-PEG KNIFE
MUMMER ACTOR GUISER GUISARD
MUMMERY MORRIS HODENING PUPPETRY
MUMMICHOG MUDFISH
MUMMY CONGO MUMMIA SKELET (PREF.) MOMIO
MUMMY BROWN BAY SNUFF TAMARACK
MUMMY CASE SLEDGE
MUMPS BRANKS PAROTITIS
MUNCH CHEW NOSH CHUMP MANGE MUNGE
MUND GRITH
MUNDA KOLARIAN
MUNDANE WORLD EARTHLY FLESHLY SECULAR TERRENE SUBSOLAR
MUNG BEAN MUG GRAM MONGOE BALATONG
MUNIA MAYA PADDA
MUNICIPAL TOWN CIVIL
MUNICIPALITY CITY TOWN CABILDO
MUNIFICENCE BOUNTY ROYALTY
MUNIFICENT ROYAL LIBERAL MUNIFIC PROFUSE MAGNIFIC PRINCELY OPENHANDED
MUNJ MOONJA MANJEET (CULMS OF —) SIRKI SIRKY
MUNTIACUS CERVULUS
MUNTJAC KAKAR RATWA KIDANG
MURAL TOPIA FRESCO
MURCIA (RIVER OF —) SEGURA

(TOWN OF —) MULA LORCA TOTANA
MURDER OFF BANE KILL SLAY BLOOD BURKE DEATH SCRAG FELONY KILLING MURDRUM MURTHER THUGGEE HOMICIDE MASSACRE THUGGERY THUGGISM PATRICIDE
(PREMEDITATED —) HIT
MURDERER BANE CAIN KILLER ASSASSIN
MURDER IN THE CATHEDRAL (COMPOSER OF —) PIZZETTI
MURDEROUS FELL GORY CRUEL FELON BLOODY CARNAL SAVAGE DEATHFUL SANGUINARY
MURKINESS GLOOM
MURKY DARK BLACK DIRTY MIRKY MUDDY CLOUDY PUDDLY
MURMUR HUM BRUM BURR CLUM HUZZ MUSE BRAWL BROOL GRANK INKLE MOURN RUMOR SOUCH SOUGH BABBLE BURBLE GRUDGE GRUTCH HUMMER MUTTER PIPPLE REPINE RUMBLE CROODLE MURGEON WHIMPER WHISPER WHITTER COMPLAIN
(— AGREEABLY) CHIRM
(— OF STREAM) PURL
(CONFUSED —) BABBLE
(DEEP —) BROOL
MURMURING BUZZ BRABBLE MURGEON RUMOROUS
MURRAH SURTI
MURRAL DALAG
MURRE TINK ARRIE LUNGIE STRANY TINKER ROCKBIRD
MURREY SANGUINE
MUSA SABA
MUSANG POWCAT POLECAT
MUSCA FLY
MUSCADINE BULLACE SCUPPERNONG
MUSCAT (SEE OMAN)
MUSCLE EYE BOWR LIRE THEW FLESH MOUSE PSOAS SINEW BENDER BICEPS CORACO FLEXOR LACERT PENNON RECTUS SOLEUS TENSOR AGONIST AMBIENS CANINUS DELTOID DILATOR ERECTOR EVERTOR FLECTOR GLUTEUS ILIACUS LEVATOR MUSCULE NASALIS OBLIQUE ROTATOR SCALENE SCALLOP TRICEPS VAGINAL ABDUCTOR ADDUCTOR ADJUSTER ANCONEUS ARRECTOR ATOLLENT BIVENTER DIDUCTOR EXTENSOR GEMELLUS GRACILIS INVERTOR MASSETER MENTALIS OBLIQUUS OMOHYOID OPPONENS PALMARIS PATHETIC PECTORAL PERONEUS PROCERUS PRONATOR RETENTOR SCALENUS SERRATUS SPINALIS SPLENIUS TEMPORAL TIBIALIS OBTURATOR SARTORIUS
(HAVING LUMPY —S) LOADED
(THIGH —) HAMSTRING
(PL.) BRAWN THEWS
(PREF.) INO MUSCUL(O) NERVI NERVO
(SUFF.) EUS MYA MYARIA
MUSCLE SUGAR INOSITE INOSITOL

MUSCOVY DUCK PATO SCOVY
MUSCULAR ROPY HEFTY HUSKY THEWY BRAWNY ROBUST SINEWY STRONG TOROSE NERVOUS ATHLETIC
MUSCULATURE DETRUSOR
(SUFF.) (HAVING —) MYA MYARIA
MUSE CLIO DUMP MESE MULL NETE REVE AMUSE AOIDE DREAM ERATO MNEME STUDY THINK HYPATE MELETE PONDER THALIA URANIA EUTERPE REFLECT CALLIOPE COGITATE CONSIDER MEDITATE POLYMNIA RUMINATE MELPOMENE POLYHYMNIA TERPSICHORE
(— OF ASTRONOMY) URANIA
(— OF COMEDY) THALIA
(— OF EPIC POETRY AND ELOQUENCE) CALLIOPE
(— OF HISTORY) CLIO
(— OF LOVE POETRY) ERATO
(— OF MIMIC ART) POLYHYMNIA
(— OF POETRY AND DANCE) TERPSICHORE
(— OF THE FLUTE) EUTERPE
(— OF TRAGEDY) MELPOMENE
(PL.) PIERIDES
MUSEUM MUSEE
(PREF.) MUSEO
MUSH KASHA SLUSH MUSHER SEPAWN SOFKEE POLENTA SAGAMITE SCRAPPLE
MUSHI (FATHER OF —) MERARI
MUSHROOM FAT CEPE FLAT DEATH MITRA MOREL AGARIC BEAVER BUTTON FUNGUS BLEWITS BOLETUS BROILER LEPIOTA MUSHRUMP WHITECAP CHAMPIGNON SHAGGYMANE CHANTERELLE
(PART OF —) CAP GILL RING STEM STALK STIPE VOLVA PILEUS ANNULUS MYCELIUM
(PREF.) MYC(O) MYCET(O)
MUSHY SOFT SOPPY
MUSIC RAG DRAG GLEE JAZZ NOME BEBOP CANOR CHIME DREAM GIMEL GYMEL MURKY NOISE SWING DREHER MUSICA DESCANT FORLANA LANCERS LANDLER MUSICAL MUSICRY FALSETTO FANDANGO GUARACHA
(— OF WEST INDIES) REGGAE
(CALYPSO —) GOOMBAY
(CONCERTED —) ENSEMBLE
(COUNTRY —) BLUEGRASS
(EVENING —) DREAM SERENA
(IDENTIFYING —) SIG
(JAPANESE COURT —) GAGAKU
(JAZZ OR FOLK —) SKIFFLE
(LIVELY —) GALOP FURLANA
(MORNING —) AUBADE
(PATTERN OF HINDU —) TALA
(RECORDED BACKGROUND —) MUZAK
(RESOUNDING —) HIGGAION
(ROCK —) BIGBEAT BUBBLEGUM
(SAD —) MESTO
(SENTIMENTAL —) SCHMALZ SCHMALTZ

(STACCATO —) SECCO
(UNSOPHISTICATED —) FUNK
(WEST INDIAN —) REGGAE
(ZULU —) KWELA
MUSICAL LYRIC SWEET LIQUID LYRICAL TUNABLE TUNEFUL CANOROUS HARMONIC NUMEROUS
(— DIRECTION) BIS PIU ARCO BRIO FINE MENO POCO ANIME ASSAI DOLCE GRAVE GUSTO LARGO LENTO MEZZO MOLTO MOSSO OSSIA PRIMO SECCO SEGUE SOPRA TACET TEMPO TUTTI ADAGIO ARIOSO DOPPIO FREDDO MARCIA PRESTO RUBATO SEMPRE SIMILE SUBITO TENUTO TROPPO VELOCE VIVACE AGITATO ALLEGRO AMABILE ANIMATO ATTACCA FURIOSO GIOCOSO MARCATO MORENDO PIETOSO SORDINO TREMOLO DOLOROSO MAESTOSO MODERATO SALTANDO SEMPLICE SPICCATO CRESCENDO GLISSANDO OBBLIGATO SOSTENUTO SPIRITOSO
(SUFF.) (— DEVICE) INA INE
(— INSTRUMENT) INA
MUSICAL INSTRUMENT AX AXE GLY GUE KIN OUD QIN TAR UKE ZEL ALTO ASOR BELL CRUT DRUM GLEE GLEW GORA HARP HORN KOTO LIRA LUTE LYRE OBOE ROTE SANG SAWM TAAR TUBA VINA VIOL ANVIL AULOS BANJO BLOCK BUGLE CELLO CHENG CRWTH CUICA DOMRA FLUTE GORAH GOURA GUDOK GUIRO GUSLA GUSLE KAZOO MBIRA NABLA ORGAN RAMKI REBAB REBEC ROCTA RUANA SAROD SHAWM SHELL SHENG TARAU TELYN TRUMP VIOLA ZANZE ZINKE BALAFO BONANG CABASA CITOLE CORNET CROUTH CYMBAL DOUCET FIDDLE GENDER GLARIN GUITAR GUSLEE JARANA RAPPEL REBECK RIBIBE SABECA SANCHO SANTIR SPINET TABRET TREBLE TYMPAN URHEEN VIOLET VIOLIN ZITHER ALTHORN ANGELOT ANKLONG ARGHOOL BAGPIPE BANDORE BANDURA BASSOON BAZOOKA CELESTA CHEKKER CHIKARA CITHARA CLARINA CLAVIER CLAVIOL DICHORD DOLCIAN DOLCINO DULCIAN FISTULA FLUTINA GAMELIN GITTERN HELICON KANTELE MAGADIS MARIMBA OCARINA PANDURA PIBCORN RACKETT SAMISEN SARANGI SARINDA SAXHORN SERPENT SISTRUM SORDONO THEORBO TRUMPET UKULELE URANION ADIAPHON AKALIMBA AUTOHARP AUTOPHON BARBITON BOUSOUKI BOUZOUKI CALLIOPE CASTANET CLARINET CORNPIPE CRESCENT DULCIMER DYOPHONE EUPHONON FIDICULA FLAUTINO

HORNPIPE HUMSTRUM
KRUMHORN LAPIDEON
MARTENOT MELODION NEGINOTH
NEHILOTH PENORCON PHONIKON
PSALTERY SCHWEGEL SERINGHI
SOURDINE SYMPHONY
TAMBOURA TAROGATO TRIANGLE
TRICHORD TROMBONE VIRGINAL
ZAMBOMBA ACCORDION
BOMBARDON SAXOPHONE
MELLOPHONE
(AFRICAN —) KORA MBIRA
(BALINESE —) GANGSA
(STRINGED — OF INDIA) SARANGI
(PL.) BRASS FAMILY STRINGS
PERCUSSION
MUSICALITY HARMONY
MUSIC HALL GAFF MELODEON
MUSICIAN BARD WAIT ASAPH
LINOS VIOLA BOPPER BUSKER
MUSICO PLAYER VIOLER VIOLIN
BANDMAN BOPSTER CELLIST
GAMBIST ORPHEUS TWANGER
VIOLIST KORAHITE MARIACHI
MINSTREL MUSICKER THRUMMER
TWANGLER CITYBILLY
MINNESINGER
(PL.) ENSEMBLE WAITSMEN
MUSING PENSIVE MUSARDRY
MUSK MOOST CATTAIL MIMULUS
AMBRETTE FIXATIVE
(PREF.) MOSCHI
MUSK DEER CERVID KASTURA
MUSKELLUNGE LONGE MUSKIE
MUSKET FUSIL FUZIL MATCH
DRAGON JINGAL BUNDOOK
CALIVER ENFIELD GINGALL
BANDHOOK BISCAYAN BISCAYEN
CULVERIN ESCOPETA SNAPHAAN
TOPHAIKE
MUSKET BALL GOLI
MUSKETEER FUSILEER STRELITZ
MUSKET FORK GAFFLE
MUSK MALLOW ABELMOSK
MUSKMELON MANGO ATAMON
WUNGEE SPANSPEK
CANTALOUPE
MUSKOGEE CREEK SEMINOLE
MUSK OX OVIBOS
(WOOL OF UNDERCOAT OF —)
QIVIUT
MUSKRAT SQUASH ONDATRA
MUSQUASH
MUSK SHREW SONDELI
MUSK TURTLE STINKER STINKPOT
MUSKWOOD CAOBA
MUSKY MOSCHATE
MUSLIM LAZ ALIM SIDI SWAT
TURK ARAIN HAFIZ IBADHI
KAZAKH TURBAN ABBADID
AYYUBID BAGIRMI BASHKIR
IBADITE KHAKSAR MUDEJAR
SUNNITE ALAOUITE ISLAMIST

ISLAMITE QADARITE SIFATITE
(— BEADS) TASBIH
(— BROTHERHOOD) TARIQA
(— CHIEF) RAIS REIS
(— DOCTRINE) TAWHID
(— FOUNDATION) WAKF WAQF
(— JUDGE) CAID QAID
(— MYSTIC) SUFI
(— PLAY) TAZIA
(— PRACTICE) PURDAH
(— PRINCIPLE) TAQIYA
(— SCHOLARS) ULAMA ULEMA
(— SECT) WAHHABI MURJIITE
(— TOMB) TABUT
(— TREE) TUBA
(PL.) SHIA SHIAH SUNNI
MUSLIN BAN MULL DORIA SWISS
GURRAH MULMUL SHALEE SHILLA
TANJIB BETEELA FACTORY
JAMDANI ORGANDY STENTER
COTELINE SEERHAND TARLATAN
(PL.) COSSAS
MUSQUASH ONDATRA
MUSS FUFFLE RUMPLE GLOMMOX
UNDRESS
MUSSEL CLAM UNIO NAIAD
ANODON JINGLE LACERT MUCKET
PALOUR BIVALVE GLOCHID
MYTILID UNIONID BULLHEAD
DEERHORN
(PREF.) CONCH(O) MYTILI MYTILO
MUSSELCRACKER BISKOP
MUST BIT BUD BUT MAN MAY
MUN BOOD MAUN MOTE SAPA
STUM DULCE SHALL
(— BE TAKEN) SUM
(— NOT) MAUNNA
MUSTACHE WALRUS VALANCE
WHISKER
MUSTACHE MONKEY MOUSTOC
MUSTANG PONY BRONCO SPHINX
MUSTARD CRESS SENVY SINEWY
AWLWORT CADLOCK KEDLOCK
SINAPIS CHADLOCK CHARLOCK
FLIXWEED AUBRIETIA
(PREF.) SIN
MUSTARD GAS YPERITE
MUSTARD PLASTER SINAPISM
MUSTELUS GALEUS
MUSTER LEVY ENROL RAISE
SPUNK GATHER HOSTING
MARSHAL RECRUIT
MUSTINESS FUST MUST
MUSTY HOAR FUNKY FUSTY
HOARY MOLDY MUCID RAFTY
VINNY FOISTY FROWZY RANCID
FOUGHTY FROWSTY COBWEBBY
MUTABLE FICKLE MUTATORY
VARIABLE
MUTATE SPORT
MUTATION SHIFT SPORT CHANGE
MUANCE SILKIE ANAGRAM
VARIANT SALTATION

(VOWEL —) UMLAUT
MUTE PAD DUMB ECHO LENE
SURD BLACK MEDIA WHIST
DAMPER MUFFLE SILENT STIFLE
TENUIS SORDINE SOURDINE
(— AT FUNERAL) SALLIE
(— FOR TRUMPET) DERBY
MUTED DULL SORDO STILL
DISCREET SOURDINE
MUTENESS SILENCE DUMBNESS
MUTILATE MAR HACK MAIM
BREAK GARBLE HAMBLE INJURE
MANGLE MARTYR MITTLE
CONCISE CASTRATE EMBEZZLE
(— AN ANIMAL) LAW
MUTILATION STRIP CONCISION
MUTINEER PANDY MUTINADO
MUTINOUS UNRULY
MUTINY REVOLT STRIFE
REBELLION
MUTINY ON THE BOUNTY
(AUTHOR OF —) HALL NORDHOFF
(CHARACTER IN —) BYAM BLIGH
PEGGY ROGER GEORGE ROBERT
TEHANI BURKITT ELLISON
MAIMITI STEWART TINKLER
WILLIAM FLETCHER MILLWARD
MORRISON MUSPRATT CHRISTIAN
MUTISM ALALIA
MUTTER CROOL MOTRE HOTTER
HUMMER MUMBLE MURMUR
PATTER THROAT CHANNER
CHUNNER CHUNTER GRUMBLE
MAUNDER TOOTMOOT
MUSSITATE
MUTTERING GROWL
MUTTON BRAXY VIFDA VIVDA
MOUTON BRAXIES
(LEG OF —) CABOB WABBLER
WOBBLER
MUTTONBIRD OII
MUTTONFISH SAMA ABALONE
EELPOUT MOJARRA
MUTUAL COMMON RECIPROCAL
(PREF.) CO INTER
MUZZLE NOSE MOUTH SNOUT
FOREFACE
(— FOR FERRET) COPE
(— OF CANNON) CHOPS
MUZZLE-LOADER CAPLOCK
MUZZLER
MYALGIA COURBATURE
MYALL YARRAN WARRIGAL
MY ANTONIA (AUTHOR OF —)
CATHER
(CHARACTER IN —) JIM JAKE LENA
OTTO WICK ANTON CUZAK
FUCHS LARRY BURDEN CUTTER
ANTONIA DONOVAN HARLING
LINGARD MARPOLE AMBROSCH
SHIMERDA
MYCELIUM SPAWN MYCELE
TAPESIUM

MYCTERIA TANTALUS
MY DEAR MACHREE
MYDRIATIC PHENYLEPHRINE
MYIASIS STRIKE
MYNA MINA MYNAH GRACKLE
MYNES (BROTHER OF —)
EPISTROPHUS
(FATHER OF —) EVENUS
(WIFE OF —) BRISEIS
MYOCOMMA FLAKE
MYRIAD HOST TOMAN COUNTLESS
MYRIAPOD JULID POLYPOD
PAUROPOD MILLIPEDE
MYRRH STACTE
MYRRHA (SON OF —) ADONIS
MYRTLE MYRT LILAC BALTIC
JAROOL ARRAYAN JAPONICA
RAMARAMA
MYSELF SELF MYSEN HERSELF
MYSID SHRIMP
MYSOST PRIMOST
MYSTERIES OF PARIS (AUTHOR OF
—) SUE
(CHARACTER IN —) FLEUR SARAH
CICELY MURPHY WALTER
FERRAND GEORGES JACQUES
RODOLPH CHOUETTE CLEMENCE
HARVILLE POLIDORI MACGREGOR
RIGOLETTE
MYSTERIES OF UDOLPHO
(AUTHOR OF —) RADCLIFFE
(CHARACTER IN —) EMILY DUPONT
MORANO MONTONI LUDOVICO
STAUBERT VILLEFORT
LAURENTINI VALANCOURT
MYSTERIOUS DIM DARK DEEP
EERY SELI EERIE SABLE WAKON
ARCANE EXOTIC MYSTIC OCCULT
SECRET CRYPTIC PUCKISH
UNCANNY UNCOUTH ABSTRUSE
ESOTERIC NUMINOUS SIBYLLIC
CRYPTICAL
MYSTERIOUSLY DARKLY EERILY
HEIMLICH
MYSTERY MIST RUNE CABALA
ENIGMA SECRET ARCANUM
PROBLEM SECRECY
(PREF.) MYST(ERI)(ERIO)(ICO)
MYSTIC SUFI OCCULT ORPHIC
SECRET EPOPTIC ESOTERIC
MYSTICAL MISTY MYSTIC
ANAGOGIC TELESTIC
MYSTICALLY GHOSTLY
MYSTICISM SUFIISM
MYSTIFY BEAT BEFOG BOTHER
MUDDLE PUZZLE BECLOUD
CONFUSE BEWILDER
MYTH SAGA FABLE LEGEND
MYTHOS ALLEGORY
MYTHICAL FABLED FABULOUS
FICTIOUS

N

N EN NU NAN NOVEMBER
NAAM (FATHER OF —) CALEB
NAAMAH (BROTHER OF —)
  TUBALCAIN
  (FATHER OF —) LAMECH
  (MOTHER OF —) ZILLAH
  (SON OF —) REHOBOAM
NAARAH (HUSBAND OF —) ASHUR
NAASSENE OPHITE
NAB HAT NIB GRAB HEAD KNAB
  NAIL CATCH SEIZE ARREST
  CLUTCH COLLAR NIBBLE NOBBLE
  SNATCH CAPTURE APPREHEND
NABAL (WIFE OF —) ABIGAIL
NABALOI IBALOI IGOROT
NABK NUBK NABAK NEBUK
  NABBUK NEBACK NEBBUK
  NEBBUCK
NABOB DIVES NAWAB NOBOB
  DEPUTY VICEROY GOVERNOR
  PLUTOCRAT
  (— DEPUTY) NAWAB
  (PL.) NABOBRY
NACELLE CAR BOAT BASKET
  CHASSIS COCKPIT SHELTER
NACHSCHLAG SPRINGER
  AFTERNOTE
NACKET BOY CAKE LUNCH
  NOCKET
NACRE PEARL SHELLFISH
NADAB (FATHER OF —) AARON
  SHAMMAI
  (MOTHER OF —) ELISHEBA
NADIR BATHOS BEDROCK
  (OPPOSED TO —) ZENITH
NAG CUT RAG TIT BAIT FRAB FRET
  FUSS GNAW JADE MOKE PLUG
  PONY PROD SNAG TWIT YAFF
  ANNOY COBRA HOBBY HORSE
  SCOLD SKATE SNAKE STEED
  TEASE BADGER BERATE BOTHER
  DOBBIN GARRAN GLEYDE HAGGLE
  HARASS HECKLE HECTOR KEFFEL
  PADNAG PESTER PLAGUE
  ROUNCY WANTON HACKNEY
  HENPECK TORMENT DINGDONG
  HARANGUE IRRITATE PARAMOUR
  (AMBLING —) HOBBY
NAGA SEMA COBRA KABUI LHOTA
  SNAKE
NAGGING NIGGLING
NAGKASSAR SURIGA
NAGOR TOHI ANTELOPE
  REEDBUCK
NAHANE KASKA
NAHATH (FATHER OF —) ZOPHAI
NAHBI (FATHER OF —) VOPHSI
NAHOOR SHA SNA SHEEP URIAL
  BHARAL OORIAL
NAHOR (BROTHER OF —) HARAN
  ABRAHAM
  (FATHER OF —) SERUG
  (SON OF —) TERAH

(WIFE OF —) MILCAH
NAHSON (FATHER OF —)
  AMMINADAB
  (SISTER OF —) ELISHEBA
  (SON OF —) SALMON
NAHUATL AZTEC CAZCAN MEXICA
NAHUM ELKOSHITE
NAIAD NAIS NYMPH MUSSEL
  HYDRIAD
NAIL CUT FIX HOB NAB PIN TEN
  BOSS BRAD BRAG BROD CLAW
  CLOY DUMP HOOF PILE SLUG
  SPAD STUB STUD TACK TRAP
  AFFIX CATCH CLOUT DRIVE
  GROPE PLATE SCALE SEIZE SPEED
  SPICK SPIKE SPRIG TALON
  BULLEN CLENCH CLINCH COOLER
  CORKER DETAIN FASTEN GARRON
  HAMMER SECURE SINKER TACKET
  TENTER TINGLE UNGUIS UNGULA
  CAPTURE CLINKER FASTENER
  HOLDFAST ROSEHEAD SPARABLE
  SPIKELET TENPENNY TRICOUNI
  (— BITING) ONYCHOPHAGIA
  (— GROWTH) ONYCHAUXIS
  (HEADLESS —) SPRIG
  (HOOKED —) TENTER TENTERHOOK
  (INGROWN —) ONYXIS ACRONYX
  (MARKING —) SPAD SPEED
  (OLD HORSESHOE —) STUB
  (SHOEMAKER'S —) CLOUT
  SPARABLE
  (TOED —) TOSHNAIL
  (PREF.) GOMPHO HELO ONYCH(O)
  UNGUI
  (SUFF.) ONYCHA ONYCHES
  ONYCHIA ONYCHIUM ONYCHUS
  ONYX
NAILROD STICKWEED
NAIVE OPEN RACY FRANK GREEN
  CANDID JEJUNE SIMPLE ARTLESS
  NATURAL CHILDISH INNOCENT
  UNTAUGHT CHILDLIKE GUILELESS
  INGENUOUS PRIMITIVE
  UNTUTORED UNWORLDLY
  (— GIRL) INGENUE
NAIVETE GREENNESS SIMPLICITY
NAKED BALD BARE MERE NUDE
  OPEN CLEAR EXACT PLAIN STARK
  ADAMIC BARREN CUERPO
  SCUDDY SIMPLE EXPOSED
  LITERAL OBVIOUS MANIFEST
  STARKERS STRIPPED SMOCKLESS
  UNADORNED UNCLOTHED
  UNCOVERED
  (PREF.) GYMN(O) NUDI
NAKED OAT PILLAS PILCORN
  PILKINS
NAKEDWOOD MABI SNAKEWOOD
NAKHI MOSO MOSSO
NAKONG SITUTUNGA
NAMAYCUSH CREE FISH LAKER
  LONGE LUNGE TOGUE TROUT

LONGUE SISCOWET
NAMBY-PAMBY INANE SILLY
  VAPID CODDLE INSIPID KEEPSAKE
NAME DUB FIX NOM SET CALL CITE
  FAME NAIL NOMB NOUN TERM
  ALIAS CLAIM CLEPE COUNT ETHIC
  NEVEN NOMEN POINT QUOTE
  STYLE TITLE ADDUCE APPEAL
  GOSSIP MONICA REPUTE SELECT
  ALLONYM APPOINT BEHIGHT
  DECLARE ENTITLE EPITHET
  MENTION MONIKER SPECIFY
  VOCABLE CATEGORY CHRISTEN
  COGNOMEN IDENTIFY IDENTITY
  INDICATE ENUMERATE
  PATRONYMIC
  (— TABLET) FACIA
  (— WRITTEN BACKWARDS)
  ANANYM
  (ADDED —) AGNAME AGNOMEN
  (ALTERNATIVE —) BUNCH
  (ANCESTOR'S —) EPONYM
  (ANOTHER —) ALIAS
  (ASSUMED —) PEN ALIAS
  ONOMASTIC PSEUDONYM
  SOBRIQUET
  (BAD —) CACONYM
  (DAY —) AHAU
  (DERIVATION OF —) EPONYMY
  (FIRST —) FORENAME PRAENOMEN
  (GOOD —) HONOR CREDIT
  (PEN —) PSEUDONYM
  (REGISTERED —) AFFIX
  (TECHNICAL —) ONYM
  (WELL-SUITED —) EUONYM
  (PREF.) NOMEN ONOMATO
  (SUFF.) NOMEN NYM ONYM
NAMED DIT CITED HIGHT NEMPT
  DUBBED YCLEPT ONYMOUS
  YCLEPED
NAMELESS BAS
NAMELY FOR VIZ SCIL NOTED
  TOWIT FAMOUS SCILICET
NAMEPLATE MASTHEAD
  (AUTOMOBILE —) MARQUE
NAMESAKE EPONYM JUNIOR
  HOMONYM
NAMIBIA (BAY OF —) WALVIS
  (CAPITAL OF —) WINDHOEK
  (DESERT OF —) KALAHARI
  (PEOPLE OF —) NAMAS BANTUS
  BUSHMEN OVAMBOS
NANA (AUTHOR OF —) ZOLA
  (CHARACTER IN —) NANA ROSE
  HUGON LOUIS SATIN FONTAN
  GEORGE HECTOR MIGNON
  MUFFAT SABINE XAVIER ESTELLE
  STEINER BEUVILLE DAGUENET
  FAUCHERY PHILIPPE DECHOUARD
NANDI BANANDE MUNANDI
  KIPSIKIS
NANDU RHEA
NANISM DWARFISM

NANNAR SIN
NANNY GOAT NURSE
NANTICOKE TOAG
NAOMI MARA
  (DAUGHTER-IN-LAW OF —) RUTH
NAOS CELLA SHRINE TEMPLE
NAP GIG KIP NOD RAS CALK CAMP
  DOWN DOZE FUZZ LINT OOZE
  PILE RUFF SHAG WINK COVER
  DOVER FLUFF GRASP SEIZE SLEEK
  SLEEP STEAL CATNAP DROWSE
  SIESTA SNOOZE EMERIZE
  SLUMBER
  (TO RAISE —) TEASE
NAPE NOD CUFF NECK NUKE POLL
  NUCHA NUQUE SCRAG SCUFT
  SCURF TURNIP NODDLE SCRUFFY
  NIDDICK
  (PREF.) NUCH(I)
NAPERY LINEN DAMASK DOILIES
  NAPKINS
NAPHTALITE ENAN AHIRA
NAPHTHA NEFTE PETROLEUM
NAPKIN CLOTH DOILY TOWEL
  DIAPER NAPERY KERCHIEF
  SUDATORY HANDCLOTH
  SERVIETTE
NAPLES BISCUIT LADYFINGER
NAPLESS BARE HARD
NAPOLEON (— III) LOUIS
  BOUSTRAPA
  (BATTLE OF —) ULM ACRE JENA
  WATERLOO
  (BIRTHPLACE OF —) CORSICA
  (BROTHER-IN-LAW OF —) MURAT
  (GAME LIKE —) PAM
  (ISLAND OF —) ELBA HELENA
  CORSICA
  (MARSHAL OF —) NEY
  (MOTHER OF —) HORTENSE
  (PLACE OF VICTORY FOR —) LODI
  LIGNY
NAPPE DECKE
NAPPY ALE DISH DOWNY HEADY
  WOOLY LIQUOR SHAGGY STRONG
  WOOLLY COTTONY FOAMING
  VILLOUS
NARCISSUS LILY PLANT CRINUM
  EGOIST FLOWER LILIUM JONQUIL
  POLYANTHUS
  (FATHER OF —) CEPHISSUS
  (LOVED BY —) ECHO
  (MOTHER OF —) LIRIOPE
  (TRUMPET —) DAFFODIL
NARCOTIC (ALSO SEE DRUG) KAT
  KEF BANG DOPE DRUG HEMP
  JUNK BHANG DAGGA ETHER
  OPIUM HEROIN OPIATE ANODYNE
  COCAINE CODEINE HASHISH
  METOPON NARCEIN HYPNOTIC
  MORPHINE TAKROURI DIACODION
  MARIJUANA SOPORIFIC
  CHLORODYNE

(— AGENT) GAZER
(— DOSE) LOCUS
(— PLANT) DUTRA MANDRAKE
(SMALL AMOUNT OF —) SNIFTER
(PL.) JUNK STUFF
NARCOTINE OPIANE
NARD SPICE ANOINT RHIZOME
MUSKROOT SPIKENARD
NARDOO ARDOO NARDU CLOVER
NARGIL COCONUT
NARGILEH PIPE HOOKA HOOKAH
NARGHILE
NARK SPY VEX NOTE ANNOY
TEASE OBSERVE INFORMER
IRRITATE
NARRA NAGA ASANA APALIT
NARRATE SPIN TELL BRUIT STATE
STORY DEPICT DETAIL DEVISE
RECITE RELATE REPORT DISCUSS
RECOUNT STORIFY DESCRIBE
REHEARSE
NARRATION TALE FABLE STORY
DETAIL ACCOUNT HAGGADA
RECITAL SYNAXAR ALLEGORY
DELIVERY DIEGESIS HAGGADAH
NARRATIVE EPIC JOKE MYTH
SAGA TALE CONTE DRAMA FABLE
PROSE STORY COMEDY JATAKA
LEGEND ACCOUNT EPISODE
HISTORY MEMOIRS MIDRASH
NOVELLA PARABLE RECITAL
ALLEGORY ANECDOTE APOLOGUE
ARETALOGY HAGIOLOGY
(— OF VOYAGE) PERIPLUS
(— POEM) EPIC EPOS SAGA
(BRIEF —) ANECDOTE
(PL.) ACTA EXEMPLA
NARRATOR TESTO TELLER
RELATOR SAGAMAN TALESMAN
RACONTEUR
NARROW JERK LEAN MEAN NEAR
POKY SLIT TRUE BORNE CLOSE
CRAMP PINCH RIGID SCANT
SHARP SMALL SOUND TAPER
ANGUST BIASED LINEAR LITTLE
MEAGER STRAIT STRICT TWITCH
BIGOTED ERICOID LIMITED
PRIMARY SLENDER THRIFTY
CONDENSE CONTRACT
PAROCHIAL PROVINCIAL
(— DOWN) CONFINE
(— DOWN STAVES) BUCK
(— INLET) RIA
(NOT —) CATHOLIC
(VERY —) HAIRBREADTH
(PREF.) AUGUSTI DOLICH(O)
STEN(O)
(SUFF.) STENOSIS
NARROWED LISTED INSWEPT
CONTRACT ANGUSTATE
NARROWING CAP CHOKE INTAKE
STENOSIS
NARROWLY WIDE STRAITLY
NARROW-MINDED BORNE PETTY
NARROWNESS BIAS BIGOTRY
LOCALISM PAROCHIALISM
NARSINGA TRUMPET
NARTHECIUM ABAMA
NARTHEX HALL STOA ENTRY
FOYER LOBBY PORCH PORTICO
PRONAOS VESTIBULE
NARWHAL MONODON
NASAB NUSUB KINSHIP

NASAL NOSY NARINE RHINAL
TWANGY ADENOID STRINGY
(PREF.) NASIO RHIN(O)
NASCENCY BIRTH ORIGIN GENESIS
BEGINNING
NASEBERRY SAPODILLA
NASHGAB OAF GOSSIP
NASI OFFICER PATRIARCH
NASICORN RHINOCEROS
NASTIKA ATHEIST
NASTURTIUM CAPUCINE
NOSEWORT RADICULA
STURSHUM STURTION
NASTY BAD PAH FOUL MEAN UGLY
DIRTY SNIDE FILTHY HORRID
ODIOUS RIBALD BAGGAGE
BEASTLY DEFILED HARMFUL
OBSCENE SQUALID UNCLEAN
INDECENT NAUSEOUS
DANGEROUS MALICIOUS
OFFENSIVE
NAT NOT DEMON SPIRIT
NATA (WIFE OF —) NANA
NATAL INBORN INNATE NATIVE
GLUTEAL CONGENIAL
NATAL BROWN MAHAL
NATAL PLUM AMATUNGULA
NATANT AFLOAT FLOATING
SWIMMING
NATATORIUM BATH POOL
NATCHEZ STINKER STINKARD
NATION BENI FOLK GEAT HOST
LAND LEDE RACE VOLK AEDUI
CASTE CLASS FANTE FANTI
REALM STATE TRIBE FANTEE
GEATAS PEOPLE WAGOGO
ARVERNI COUNTRY SOCIETY
LANGUAGE COMMUNITY
MANDATORY MINISTATE
MULTITUDE
(— SYMBOL) FLAG CREST
(HEBREW —) JACOB
(LARGE —) COLOSSUS
(PREF.) ETHN(O)
NATIONAL CITIZEN FEDERAL
GENTILE GENTILIC
(— DEMOCRACY) ENDEX
NATIONALISM JINGOISM
PHYLETISM
**NATIONALIST CHINA (SEE
TAIWAN)**
NATIONALITY FLAG
**NATIVE (ALSO SEE PEOPLE AND
TRIBE)** ABO ITE RAW SON TAO
BORN FREE GOOK HOME KIND
LIVE NEIF WILD INNER NATAL
PUNTI EPIROT GENIAL INBORN
INNATE KINDLY MOTHER NORMAL
SIMPLE VIRGIN CITIZEN DENIZEN
DZUNGAR ENDEMIC GENUINE
NATURAL PAISANO POLISTA
DOMESTIC GRASSCUT HABITUAL
HOMEBORN HOMEMADE
INHERENT LANDSMAN ORIGINAL
PRIMEVAL PRISTINE RESIDENT
YAMMADJI ABORIGINE
CONGENIAL INGRAINED
INHERITED INTRINSIC ORIGINARY
TAWNYMOOR ABORIGINAL
(— BEAR) KOALA
(— BEECH) FLINDOSA
(— MINERAL) LIVE
(— OF ALBANIA) SKIPETAR

(— OF BENGAL) KOL
(— OF CHINA) CELESTIAL
(— OF FENS) SLODGER
(— OF FLORIDA KEYS) CONK
CONCH
(— OF ILLINOIS) SUCKER
(— OF IRELAND) BOGTROTTER
(— OF LONDON) COCKNEY
(— OF LOW CLASS) TAO
(— OF MADAGASCAR) HOVA
(— OF MALAYA) INFIEL
(— OF MANCHESTER) MANCUNIAN
(— OF MARITIME PROVINCES)
BLUENOSE
(— OF N. CAROLINA) TARHEEL
(— OF NEW GUINEA) BOONG
(— OF NEW SOUTH WALES)
CORNSTALK
(— OF PHILIPPINES) GUGU
(— OF SCOTLAND) GEORDIE
(— OF SOUTHERN ILLINOIS)
EGYPTIAN
(— OF W. AUSTRALIA) GROPER
(— PLANT) INDIGINE
(— WHO TEACHES) CATECHIST
(BORN AND BRED AS A —) CREOLE
(FREE —) TIMAWA
(UNCIVILIZED —) MYALL
(SUFF.) ESE ITE OT OTE
(— OF) ER IER YER
NATIVE SON (AUTHOR OF —)
WRIGHT
(CHARACTER IN —) JAN MAX MARY
BORIS MEARS BESSIE BIGGER
DALTON ERLONE THOMAS
BRITTEN BUCKLEY
NATIVITY BIRTH JATAKA GENESIS
GENITURE HOROSCOPE
NATTERJACK NEWT TOAD
NATTY CHIC NEAT POSH TIDY TRIG
TRIM NIFTY SMART SPICY
DAPPER JAUNTY SPRUCE
FOPPISH VARMINT
NATURAL RAW BORN EASY FOOL
HOME KIND OPEN RACY REAL
WILD NAIVE USUAL CANCEL
CASUAL COMMON CONJON
CRETIN DIRECT HOMELY INBORN
INBRED INNATE KINDLY MOTHER
NATIVE NORMAL PHYSIC ARTLESS
GENUINE QUADRUM REGULAR
INHERENT LIFELIKE ORDINARY
PHYSICAL UNCOINED PRIMITIVE
REALISTIC UNASSUMED
UNFEIGNED
(— LOGARITHM) LN
(— TALENT) DOWER FLAIR
(NOT —) AFFECTED
(PREF.) PHYSI(O) PHYSICO
NATURALIST AMERICAN LEA COPE
DALL MUIR SNOW WARD FLAGG
HYATT LEIDY LUCAS MASON
ORTON ABBOTT AKELEY BARTON
GODMAN HOLDER MORTON
NELSON SAVAGE STORER
ANDREWS BACHMAN BUCKLEY
DITMARS FUERTES MERRIAM
SCUDDER COOLIDGE HALDEMAN
HOLBROOK JENNINGS
BURROUGHS INGERSOLL
RAFINESQUE
AUSTRALIAN BANFIELD
DANISH BERGSOE WINSLOW

DUTCH CAMPER HOEVEN
HOMBERG SWAMMERDAM
LEEUWENHOEK
ENGLISH RAY BELL BAKER BANKS
BATES BRADY GOSSE LEACH
NORTH DARWIN SLOANE
BORLASE CATESBY DUGMORE
EDWARDS NEEDHAM PENNANT
WALLACE BRODERIP BURCHELL
LYDEKKER STEBBING SWAINSON
BOWERBANK JEFFERIES
CARRUTHERS TEGETMEIER
WILLIAMSON
FRENCH BELON CHENU BUFFON
CUVIER BAILLON DAUBENY
DUMERIL GERVAIS LAMARCK
LESUEUR ORBIGNY POUCHET
POUPART REAUMUR ADDANSON
AUDEBERT BONPLAND DESHAYES
LACEPEDE RONDELET CASTELNAU
DAUBENTON BROUSSONETT
GERMAN OKEN WIED JAGER
LIBAU SEITZ MULLER PALLAS
MARTIUS NEUWIED SCHWANN
SIEBOLD STELLER CHAMISSO
ERXLEBEN HUMBOLDT
JUNGHUHN SCHUBERT
EHRENBERG KIELMEYER
BURMEISTER KEYSERLING
TREVIRANUS ESCHSCHOLTZ
SOEMMERRING SCHLAGINTWEIT
ITALIAN REDI RISSO BONELLI
BROCCHI FABRONI FONTANA
SCOPOLI AMORETTI MARSIGLI
ALDROVANDI SPALLANZANI
VALLISNIERI
NORWEGIAN ASBJORNSEN
RUSSIAN EICHWALD FEDCHENKO
CHIKHACHEV
SCOTTISH BROWN BAIKIE FORBES
HERDMAN JARDINE THOMSON
RICHARDSON MACGILLIVRAY
SPANISH COBO AZARA MUTIS
SWEDISH ARTEDI FORSKAL
ZETTERSTEDT
SWISS HEER HUBER BONNET
GESNER AGASSIZ TSCHUDI
SAUSSURE TREMBLEY CLAPAREDE
POURTALES RUTIMEYER
NATURALIZE ADAPT ADOPT
ACCUSTOM ACCLIMATE
ENDENIZEN HABITUATE
NATURALLY SN KINDLY GENIALLY
NATURALNESS EASE NAIVETE
NATURE ILK BENT BIOS CAST CLAY
FORM HAIR KIND MAKE MOOD
RACE SORT TRIM TYPE COLOR
OUSIA SHAPE STATE TENOR
ANIMAL DHARMA FIGURE
HEAVEN KIDNEY PHYSIS STRIPE
ESSENCE FEATHER INBEING
QUALITY SPECIES PRAKRITI
UNIVERSE CHARACTER
QUALIFICATION
(— DIVINITY) NYMPH
(— GOD) PAN
(— GODDESS) CYBELE ARTEMIS
(— OF GOD) DIVINITY
(— PRINT) PHYTOGRAPH
(— SPIRIT) NAT
(— WORSHIP) PHYSIOLATRY
(APPARENT —) STUDY
(CONCEALED —) LATENCY

(DIVINE —) DEITY
(EMOTIONAL —) HEART
(ESSENTIAL —) ESSE FORM GENIUS
(GOOD —) BONHOMIE
(HUMAN —) FLESH MANHEAD
MANKIND
(INHERENT —) GENIUS
(INTRINSIC —) BOTTOM
(MORAL —) ETHNOS
(OF THE SAME —) HOMOGENEOUS
(ORGANIC —) BIOS
(PERT. TO —) COSMO
(ROUGH —) SPINOSITY
(SPECIAL —) IDIOM
(SPIRITUAL —) INTERNAL
(TRUE —) PROPRIETY
(ULTIMATE —) ESSENCE
(UNREGENERATE —) ADAM
(PREF.) PHYSI(O)
(SUFF.) (HAVING — OF) IC ICAL
(OF — OF) EOUS
NAUGHT NIL EVIL ZERO AUGHT
NAGHT OUGHT CIPHER NOUGHT
WICKED NOTHING USELESS
WORTHLESS
NAUGHTY BAD PAW SAD EVIL
WRONG PAWPAW SHREWD
WICKED OBSCENE WAYWARD
IMPROPER
NAUPATHIA SEASICKNESS
NAURU (CAPITAL OF —) YAREN
(DISTRICT OF —) BOE EWA AIWO
IJUW BAITI BUADA NIBOK UABOE
YAREN ANABAR ANETAN
MENENG ANIBARE
(FORMER NAME OF —)
PLEASANTISLAND
(TOWN OF —) ANNA ORRO
ANABAR RONAWI YANGOR
NAUSEA PALL QUALM DISGUST
NAUSITY LOATHING SICKNESS
ANTIPATHY DIZZINESS
NAUSEATE TURN TWIST WLATE
REVOLT SICKEN DISGUST
SCUNNER STOMACH DISTASTE
SCOMFISH
NAUSEATED ILL SICKISH
QUALMISH SQUEAMISH
NAUSEATING NASTY WAUGH
QUEASY BILIOUS FULSOME
BRACKISH STAWSOME
LOATHSOME REVOLTING
SICKENING
NAUSEOUS OFFENSIVE
NAUSICAA (FATHER OF —)
ALCINOUS
(MOTHER OF —) ARETE
NAUSITHOUS (FATHER OF —)
NEPTUNE POSEIDON
(MOTHER OF —) PERIBOEA
(SON OF —) ALCINOUS
NAUTICAL (ALSO SEE NAVIGATION)
NAVAL MARINE MAUTIC MARINAL
OCEANIC TARRISH MARITIME
NAVIGABLE
(— FLAG) CORNET PENNON
NAUTILUS MOLLUSK ARGONAUT
ARGONAUTA
(— COMMANDER) NEMO
NAVAHO DINE NAVAJO LONGHAIR
(— GROUP) OUTFIT
(— RITE) WAY
NAVAL SEA MARINE

NAUTICAL NAVIGABLE
(— DEPOT) BASE
(— FORCE) NAVY FLEET ARMADA
SQUADRON
(— JAIL) BRIG
NAVAL OFFICER AMERICAN ROE
CONE DALE DYER HART HULL
HUSE KING LAND LEVY LUCE
MAYO SIMS ALLEN AMMEN
BARRY BEALE CAPPS CLARK
DAVIS DEWEY EVANS FISKE
FOOTE GRANT JONES LEAHY
LEARY MAHAN PERRY PRATT
ROWAN STARK WALKE BARNEY
BENSON BIDDLE BREESE CONNER
EBERLE GREENE HALSEY HEWITT
HOWELL KEARNY KIMMEL KNIGHT
MCCAIN MORRIS NIMITZ PALMER
PORTER RODMAN SCHLEY
SEMMES TALBOT TOWERS
TUCKER WILKES BRISTOL
BULLOCH CHESTER CUSHING
DALGREN DECATUR ELLIOTT
GLEAVES GRIDLEY HOLLINS
HOPKINS KIMBALL KINKAID
MOFFETT NIBLACK SCHENCK
SIGSBEE STEWART TRUXTUN
WHIPPLE WILLSON WINSLOW
BUCHANAN CAPERTON
CHADWICK CHAUNCEY
FARRAGUT GHORMLEY
INGRAHAM LAWRENCE PAULDING
PERCIVAL RICKOVER ROBINSON
ROUSSEAU SHUBRICK SPRUANCE
STANDLEY STIRLING THATCHER
GLASSFORD PILLSBURY
SCHROEDER SELFRIDGE
BAINBRIDGE GREENSLADE
MACDONOUGH WAINWRIGHT
GOLDSBOROUGH
BELGIAN GERLACHE
BRAZILIAN MELLO
DANISH HOLM JUEL AMDRUP
ADELAER
DUTCH TROMP RUYTER ALMONDE
DEWINTER HELFRICH
ENGLISH BALL BYNG HOOD HOPE
HOWE LUCE MEUX ALLIN ANSON
BAYLY BLAKE BLIGH BOYLE
BROKE FOLEY HARDY HAWKE
LEAKE LYONS NOBLE TRYON
AYLMER AYSCUE BEATTY
BENBOW BOWERS BURNEY
CARDEN COFFIN COLOMB FENNER
GORDON HALSEY HERVEY
HORNBY JERRAM LAWSON
LAYTON LITTLE MADDEN
MONSON NELSON OSBORN
PARKER RODNEY SYFRET VERNON
WILSON ADDISON BARCLAY
BEDFORD BELCHER CRADOCK
DOUGLAS GAMBIER HARWOOD
HAWKINS JACKSON MCCLURE
MORESBY NASMITH SEYMOUR
ANDERSON BEAUFORT
BOSCAWEN BROTHERS
COCHRANE JELLICOE TRELAWNY
TYRWHITT BACKHOUSE
BERESFORD CALLAGHAN
CHATFIELD COLLINSON
FREMANTLE GRENVILLE
NARBROUGH NICHOLSON
CODRINGTON CUNNINGHAM

SOMERVILLE TROUBRIDGE
FITZMAURICE
FRENCH BELLOT DARLAN FORBIN
GRASSE COURBET DUPERRE
ESTAING FARRERE GUICHEN
MOUCHEZ CORBIERE FLEURIAS
FLEURIEU MUSELIER NOAILLES
CASABIANCA
GERMAN KONIG HIPPER MULLER
RAEDER BEHNCKE CAPELLE
DOENITZ TIRPITZ JACHMANN
GREEK KANARES MIAOULES
HUNGARIAN HORTHY
ITALIAN LAURIA JACCHINO
RICCARDI
JAPANESE ITO KATO TOGO URIU
KONDO OKADA SAITO YONAI
NAGANO NOMURA SHIMADA
YOSHIDA KAMIMURA SUETSUGU
NORWEGIAN TORDENSKJOLD
PERUVIAN GRAU
PORTUGUESE CASTRO
RUSSIAN GREIG KOLCHAK
MAKAROV ALEKSEEV APRAKSIN
KUZNETSOV
SCOTTISH BARTON
SPANISH ULLOA GRAVINA
SWEDISH LINDMAN EHRENSVARD
NAVARRAISE, LA (CHARACTER IN
—) ANITA ARAQUIL GARRIDO
ZUCCARAGA
(COMPOSER OF —) MASSENET
NAVE HOB HUB NEF APSE BODY
FIST PACE AISLE NATHE NIEVE
CENTER
NAVEL NOMBRIL OMPHALOS
UMBILICUS
(PREF.) OMPHAL(O) UMBILI(CI)
(SUFF.) OMPHALUS
NAVIGABLE BOATABLE PORTABLE
NAVIGATE KEEL SAIL DRIVE GUIDE
SKIFF STEER AVIATE COURSE
CRUISE DIRECT MANAGE TRAVEL
CONDUCT CONTROL JOURNEY
OPERATE TRAVERSE ASTROGATE
NAVIGATION HOMING VOYAGE
NAUTICS PASSAGE SAILING
TRAFFIC CABOTAGE SHIPPING
(— MEASURE) TON KNOT SEAM
FATHOM
(— SYSTEM) LORAN TACAN
(SYSTEM OF —) DECCA
NAVIGATOR FLYER NAVVY PILOT
AIRMAN AVIATOR COPILOT
LABORER AERONAUT SEAFARER
SPACEMAN NEPTUNIAN
NEPTUNIST
DANISH BERING
DUTCH HARTOG BARENTS
HOUTMAN LEMAIRE HEEMSKERK
ENGLISH FOX BYRON DIXON
DRAKE BARLOW BUTTON CLERKE
HUDSON SOMERS BARLOWE
GILBERT GOSNOLD RALEIGH
WEDDELL CAVENDISH
LANCASTER VANCOUVER
CHANCELLOR WILLOUGHBY
FRENCH BETHENCOURT
BOUGAINVILLE
GERMAN BEHAIM KOTZEBUE
GREEK EUDOXUS PYTHEAS
ITALIAN ZENO VESPUCCI
PORTUGUESE CAM DIAS DIAZ

GAMA CUNHA ZARCO CABRAL
GARCIA QUEIROS GILIANES
MAGELLAN FERNANDES
RUSSIAN LUTKE GOLOVNIN
KRUSENSTERN
SPANISH CANO GALI NINO SOLIS
PINZON TORRES FERNANDEZ
NAVITE BASALT
NAVVY HAND WORKER LABORER
NAVIGATOR
NAVY FLEET SHIPFERD
(— BOARD) ADMIRALTY
(— OFFICER) CPO AIDE MATE
BOSUN CHIEF ENSIGN ADMIRAL
ARMORER CAPTAIN COMMANDER
COMMODORE
(— RADIO OPERATOR) SPARKS
(— VESSEL) PT SUB CARRIER
CRUISER FLATTOP DESTROYER
SUBMARINE TRANSPORT
NAWOB NABOB NUWAB RULER
VICEROY
NAY NO NAI NEI NOT DENY EVEN
NYET FLUTE NEVER DENIAL
REFUSE REFUSAL NEGATIVE
NAZARD STOP NASAT
NAZE NASE HEADLAND
NAZI BROWN HITLERITE
(— SYMBOL) FYLFOT SWASTIKA
NAZIM VICEROY GOVERNOR
NEAERA (DAUGHTER OF —) AUGE
EVADNE LAMPETIS PHAETHUSA
(FATHER OF —) PEREUS
(HUSBAND OF —) ALEUS STRYMON
(SON OF —) CEPHEUS LYCURGUS
AMPHIDAMAS
NEANDERTHAL CAVEMAN
NEANIC IMMATURE YOUTHFUL
NEAR AD AT BY IN GIN KIN NAR
AKIN BAIN DEAR FAST GAIN
HARD HEND INBY NEXT NIGH
ABOUT ANEAR ANENT ASIDE
CLOSE EWEST FORBY HANDY
HENDE JUXTA MATCH NUDGE
ROUND SHORT TOUCH ALMOST
AROUND BESIDE CLIMAX HEREBY
NARROW STINGY TOWARD
WITHIN ADVANCE AGAINST
FORTHBY SIMILAR THRIFTY
VICINAL ADJACENT APPROACH
IMMINENT INTIMATE
CONTIGUOUS
(— AKIN) GERMANE
(— POINT) PP
(— THE BEGINNING) EARLY FORMER
(— THE EQUATOR) LOW
(— THE MOUTH) ADORAL
(— THE SURFACE) EBB FLEET
(— THE WIND) HIGH AHOLD
(CONVENIENTLY —) HANDSOME
(PREF.) AC AD AF AG AL AP AS
AT BY ENGY EPH EPI JUXTA PERI
PLESI(O) PROS
NEARBY AROUND GAINLY LOCALLY
ADJACENT
NEARER HITHER
(— FRANCE) CISALPINE
(— ROME) CISALPINE
(— THE REAR) AFTER
(PREF.) (— IN TIME) CIS CITRA
NEAREST NEXT EWEST CLOSEST
NEARMOST PROCHAIN PROXIMAL
IMMEDIATE PROXIMATE

(— THE STERN) AFTERMOST
(PREF.) PROXIMO
NEARIAH (FATHER OF —) ISHI
SHEMAIAH
NEARLY GAIN JUST LIKE MOST
MUCH ABOUT CLOSE ALMOST
FECKLY PRACTICALLY
NEARNESS AFFINITY VICINITY
PROPINQUITY
NEARSIGHTED MYOPIC PURBLIND
NEAT GIM NET COSH COWS DEFT
DINK FEAT FEEL FEIL GENT JIMP
MACK NICE OXEN PRIM PURE
SMUG SNOD SNUG TIDY TOSH
TRIG TRIM BULLS CLEAN CLEAR
COMPT CRISP DINKY DONCY
DONSY DOUCE EXACT FEATY
FETIS GENTY JEMMY NATTY
NIFTY PREST QUEME SMART
SMIRK SPICK TERSE TIGHT
ADROIT BOVINE CATTLE CLEVER
DAINTY DAPPER DIMBER DONSIE
HEPPEN MINION POLITE QUAINT
SPANDY SPRUCE BANDBOX
CONCISE FEATOUS ORDERLY
PERJINK PRECISE REFINED
SHAPELY TRICKSY UNMIXED
MENSEFUL SKILLFUL STRAIGHT
TASTEFUL DEXTEROUS
SHIPSHAPE UNDILUTED
WHOLESOME
NEATLY SNUG DEFTLY FAIRLY
FEATLY SMARTLY SPRUCELY
NEATNESS MENSE DEFTNESS
ELEGANCE SPRUCERY
NEB EAR NIB TIP BEAK BILL NOSE
POINT SNOUT
NEBAIOTH (FATHER OF —) ISHMAEL
NEBAT (SON OF —) JEROBOAM
NEBO (FATHER OF —) MARDUK
MERODACH
(WIFE OF —) TASHMET

NEBRASKA

CAPITAL: LINCOLN
COLLEGE: DANA DOANE
DUCHESNE HASTINGS
COUNTY: GAGE LOUP OTOE DEUEL
DUNDY KEITH SARPY CHERRY
COLFAX FURNAS HOOKER
NEMAHA VALLEY BUFFALO
ANTELOPE BOXBUTTE
KEYAPAHA
INDIAN: OTO OMAHA PONCA
PAWNEE
PRESIDENT: FORD
RIVER: LOGAN DISMAL PLATTE
ELKHORN NIOBRARA
STATE BIRD: MEADOWLARK
STATE FLOWER: GOLDENROD
STATE NICKNAME: BLACKWATER
CORNHUSKER TREEPLANTERS
STATE TREE: ELM
TOWN: ORD ALMA COZAD OMAHA
PONCA TRYON WAHOO GERING
MULLEN NELIGH PENDER
TEKAMAH OGALLALA
REDCLOUD THEDFORD
UNIVERSITY: CREIGHTON

NEBRIS FAWNSKIN
NEBULA SKY CRAB SPOT
VAPOR BALAXY GALAXY

SPIRAL PLANETARY
NEBULIZE ATOMIZE
NEBULOUS DIM DARK HAZY
FOGGY MISTY MUDDY VAGUE
CLOUDY MYSTIC TURBID
CLOUDED EVASIVE SHADOWY
UNCLEAR DREAMLIKE
NECESSARILY NEEDS NEEDLY
PERFORCE
NECESSARY NEEDY PRIVY VITAL
FRIEND TOILET KINSMAN
NEEDFUL FORCIBLE INTEGRAL
OBLIGATE BEHOVEFUL ESSENTIAL
INTRINSIC
(PL.) ALIMENT MISTERS
NECESSITATE FORCE IMPEL
COMPEL DEMAND ENTAIL OBLIGE
REQUIRE CONSTRAIN
NECESSITY USE CALL DUTY FATE
FOOD LACK MUST NEED TASK
WANT DRINK ANANKE BEHOOF
BESOIN MISTER MUSCLE NEEDBE
URGENCY PERFORCE
REQUIREMENT
(— OF MOVING) ZUGZWANG
(BY —) PRESENTLY
(PL.) BREAD
(PREF.) DEONTO
NECK COL NUB PET CAPE CRAG
CROP HALS KISS WAKE BEARD
CHOKE CRAIG HALSE SCRAG
SPOON SWIRE TRAIL BEHEAD
CARESS CERVIX COLLET COLLUM
FONDLE STRAIT CHANNEL
EMBRACE ISTHMUS SQUEEZE
TUBULUS LALLYGAG
(— ARTERY) CAROTID
(— MUSCLE) SCALENUS
(— OF BOTTLE) THROTTLE
(— OF LAMB) TARGET
(— OF VOLCANO) CORE
(BACK OF —) NOD NAPE NUCH
NUQUE SCRUFF NIDDICK
(BOW —) HAWSE
(PERT. TO —) JUGULAR CERVICAL
(RED —) ROOINEK
(PREF.) CERVIC(I)(O) COLLI DER(O)
TRACHEL(O)
(SUFF.) DERUS
NECK AND NECK TIE EVEN CLOSE
NECKBAND BAND COLLAR COLLET
SHIRTBAND
NECKCLOTH BOA TIE RUFF AMICE
CHOKE SCARF STOLE CHOKER
CRAVAT BURDASH NECKTIE
PANUELO STARCHER BARCELONA
SOLITAIRE STEINKIRK
NECKERCHIEF GIMP RAIL FOGLE
BELCHER FOULARD NECKLET
KERCHIEF NECKATEE NECKCLOTH
NECKENGER
NECKING COLLAR GORGERIN
NECKLACE BEE LEI TORC BEADS
CHAIN NOOSE CARCAN CHOKER
COLLAR GORGET SANKHA
TAWDRY TORQUE BALDRIC
CHAPLET RIVIERE SAUTOIR
LAVALIER NEGLIGEE ESCLAVAGE
(PREF.) MONILI
NECKLINE COWL SCOOP
NECK RUFF FRAISE QUELLIO
NECKTIE BOW TIE ASCOT
SCARF CHOKER CRAVAT

GRAVAT OVERLAY
(— PARTY) HANGING LYNCHING
(PART OF —) EDGE SEAM TACK
APRON SHELL FACING MARGIN
POCKET HEMMING TIPPING
NECKBAND INTERLINING
NECROMANCER GOETIC
MAGICIAN
NECROMANCY GOETY MAGIC
GRAMARY SORCERY WIZARDRY
EGROMANCY
NECROPOLIS CEMETERY
NECROPSY AUTOPSY
NECROSIS MORTIFICATION
NECTAR HONEY AMRITA
AMBROSIA
NECTAR BIRD EATER HONEY
SUNBIRD
NECTARINE BRUNION NECTRON
NECTARIN
NECTARY SPUR GLAND
NECTARIUM
NEDABIAH (FATHER OF —)
JECONIAH
NEDDER ADDER
NEDDY HORSE DONKEY
NEE BORN
NEED ASK NUD LACK TAKE THAR
WANT CRAVE DRIVE THARF
BEHOOF BEHOVE BESOIN
DEMAND DESIRE EGENCE MISTER
STRAIT BEHOOVE NEEDHAM
POVERTY REQUIRE URGENCY
DISTRESS EXIGENCY MISCHIEF
EMERGENCE EXTREMITY
NECESSITY
NEEDED NECESSARY
NEEDFIRE WILDFIRE
NEEDFUL VITAL INTEGRAL
ESSENTIAL NECESSARY REQUISITE
NEEDLE SEW VEX YEN ACUS DARN
GOAD TIER WIRE ANNOY BLUNT
POINT SHARP SPIKE STRAW
STYLE BODKIN DARNER STYLUS
OBELISK PRICKER PROVOKE
SPICULE TUMBLER
(— HOLE) EYE
(— SORTER) HANDER
(COMB. FORM) ACU
(PART OF —) EYE HOLE CROWN
POINT SHANK
(PINE —) SPILL
(PINE —S) PININGS
(PL.) TWINKLES
(PREF.) ACU RAPHI RAPHIDI
NEEDLE BUG NEPID RANATRA
NEEDLEBUSH URY PINBUSH
NEEDLEFISH GAR SNOOK AGUJON
BELONID LONGJAW
NEEDLE GUN RIFLE DREYSE
NEEDLELIKE ACUATE ACERATE
ACEROSE ACEROUS ACIFORM
ACICULAR BELONOID SPLINTERY
NEEDLEMAN TAILOR
NEEDLE-POINTED ACEROSE
NEEDLESHAPED ACIFORM
ACETIOUS
NEEDLESS AMOK
NEEDLESTONE NATROLITE
NEEDLEWORK SEWING SAMPLER
SEAMING TATTING KNITTING
WOOLWORK HEMSTITCH
INSERTION

NEEDY BARE POOR INDIGENT
NEEDSOME HUNGARIAN
PENNILESS PENURIOUS
NECESSITOUS
NEEP NEPE TURNIP
NE'ER-DO-WELL BUM PELF LOSEL
SKELLUM SCHLEMIEL SHIFTLESS
WORTHLESS RAPSCALLION
NEFANDOUS IMPIOUS EXECRABLE
NEFARIOUS WICKED HEINOUS
IMPIOUS FLAGRANT HORRIBLE
INFAMOUS ATROCIOUS
NEFERT (HUSBAND OF —)
AMENEMHAT
NEGATE DENY SUBLATE
NEGATION NAY NOT EMPTY
DENIAL REFUSAL ANNULMENT
NONENTITY
(PREF.) DIS
NEGATIVE NA NE NO CON NAE
NAY NIT NIX NON NOR NOT NUL
DENY FILM VETO MINUS NEVER
NAYWARD STAMPER APOPHATIC
PRIVATIVE
(— PREFIX) IL IM IN IR UN DIS NON
(— PRINCIPLE) YIN
(PHOTOGRAPHIC —) CLICHE
(PREF.) INEQUI
NEGLECT DEBT FAIL HANG OMIT
SHUN SLIP FAULT FORGO SHIRK
SLOTH WAIVE BYPASS CESSER
FOREGO FORGET IGNORE LACHES
LOITER PERMIT SLIGHT DEFAULT
DISOBEY FAILURE OVERSEE
RESPECT FORSLACK OMISSION
OVERLOOK OVERSLIP RECKLESS
DISREGARD MISLIPPEN
OVERSIGHT PRETERMIT
MISPRISION
(— OF DUTY) INCIVISM
NEGLECTED TACKY SHABBY
UNDONE DORMANT OBSOLETE
NEGLECTFUL LAX REMISS
CARELESS DERELICT HEEDLESS
RECKLESS DISSOLUTE NEGLIGENT
NEGLIGEE ROBE MANTEAU
MATINEE UNDRESS PEIGNOIR
NIGHTGOWN DISHABILLE
NEGLIGENCE CULPA LACHES
DEFAULT LASCHETY DISREGARD
OVERSIGHT
NEGLIGENT LAX LASH SOFT SLACK
CASUAL OVERLY REMISS
CARELESS DERELICT DISCINCT
RECKLESS SLOVENLY YEMELESS
DISSOLUTE NEGLECTFUL
NEGLIGIBLE FAT
NEGOTIATE DEAL SELL BROKE
FLOAT TREAT TROKE TRUCK
TRYST ADVISE ASSIGN CONFER
DICKER DIRECT MANAGE PARLEY
SETTLE ARRANGE BARGAIN
CHAFFER CONDUCT CONSULT
DISCUSS ENTREAT CONCLUDE
ENTREATY TRANSACT TRANSFER
TEMPORIZE
NEGOTIATION DEAL DICKER
PARLEY TREATY PASSAGE
ENTREATY PRACTICE
NEGRITO ATA ATI ITA AETA AKKA
BATWA BLACK KARON SEMANG
TAPIRO ABENLEN BAMBUTE
NEGRITUDE SOUL

NEGRO FON JUR LUO LWO SUK
AKIM ALUR BENI BINI BONI EGBA
FONG IRON MADI MOKE NUBA
NUPE SIDI BENIN BLACK BONGO
CUFFY DINKA DJUKA FULUP
FUZZY HATSA MUNGO SEPIA
SEREC SMOKE TEMNE GULLAH
HUBSHI AKWAPIM DAHOMAN
GEECHEE QUASHIE SANDAWE
SHELLUH SHILLUK BECHUANA
ETHIOPIAN MANGBATTU
(— BLOOD) TARBRUSH
(GOLD COAST —) GA FANTI
(LIBERIAN —) KRU VAI VEI GREBO
ICROO KRUMAN KROOBOY
(MALE —) BUCK
(OLD —) UNCLE
NEHEMIAH (FATHER OF —) AZBUK
HACHALIAH
NEHUSHTA (FATHER OF —)
ELNATHAN
(HUSBAND OF —) JEHOIAKIM
(SON OF —) JEHOIACHIN
NEIGH NIE NVE WHI HINNY NICKER
WHINNY WIGHER WHICKER
NEIGHBOR BOR ADJOIN BORDER
FELLOW NEIPER ACCOLENT
BORDERER CONFINER UCALEGON
(PL.) KITH CONFINES
(SUFF.) GETON
NEIGHBORHOOD WAY AREA
HAND VENUE BARRIO LOCALE
REGION PURLIEU SECTION
DISTRICT ENVIRONS PRESENCE
PROCINCT VICINAGE VICINITY
BAILIWICK COMMUNITY
PROXIMITY TERRITORY
VOISINAGE
NEIGHBORING NIGH NEARBY
CONFINE VICINAL ACCOLENT
ADJACENT
NEIGHBORLY FOLKSY FOLKSEY
AMICABLE
NEITHER NOT NATHER NITHER
NOWDER
(— RIGHT NOR WRONG)
ADIAPHOROUS
NELEUS (BROTHER OF —) PELIAS
(DAUGHTER OF —) PERO
(FATHER OF —) NEPTUNE
(MOTHER OF —) TYRO
(SON OF —) NESTOR
(WIFE OF —) CHLORIS
NELLORE ONGOLE
NEMA EELWORM FILAMENT
NEMATODE ROUNDWORM
NEMATOCYST CNIDA
DESMONEME PENETRANT
NEMATODE ROUNDWORM
NEMESIS BANE FATE UPIS AGENT
AVENGER PENALTY
NEMUEL (BROTHER OF —) ABIRAM
DATHAN
(FATHER OF —) ELIAB SIMEON
NENTSI SAMOYED SAMOYEDE
NEOPHYTE TYRO EPOPT NOVICE
AMATEUR CONVERT BEGINNER
PROSELYTE YOUNGLING
NEOPLASM TUMOR GROWTH
TUMOUR SARCOMA NEWGROWTH
NEOTERIC NEW LATE FRESH
NOVEL MODERN RECENT
NEP KNOT CATNIP

CATMINT CLUSTER

NEPAL
CAPITAL: KATMANDU
KATHMANDU
COIN: MOHAR RUPEE
MOUNTAIN: EVEREST
MOUNTAIN RANGE: HIMALAYA
NATIVE: AOUL LIMBU MURMI
NEWAR GURKHA GORKHALI
RIVER: KALI KOSI MUGU SETI
BABAI BHERI RAPTI SARDA
GANDAK KARNALI NARAYANI
TOWN: ILAM MUGU GALWA
JUMLA PATAN BIRGANJ
POKHARA BHADGAON
LALITPUR BHAKTAPUR
BIRATNAGAR

NEPENTHE DRUG PLANT POTION
ANODYNE
NEPHEG (FATHER OF —) DAVID
IZHAR
NEPHELE (DAUGHTER OF —) HELLE
(HUSBAND OF —) ATHAMAS
(SON OF —) LEUCON PHRIXUS
NEPHELINE LENAD MINERAL
SOMMITE ELEOLITE
NEPHEW OY OYE NEVE VASU
NEFFY NEVOY NIECE NEPOTE
BENVOLIO
NEPHRITE YU JADE AXSTONE
POUNAMU TREMOLITE
NEPTUNE LER PAN SEA GREEN
OCEAN PLATE SEAGOD
(BROTHER OF —) PLUTO JUPITER
(CONSORT OF —) SALACIA
(DISCOVERER OF —) GALLE
(EMBLEM OF —) TRIDENT
(FATHER OF —) SATURN
(MOTHER OF —) RHEA
(SISTER OF —) JUNO
NER (SON OF —) ABNER
NEREID NYMPH NEREIS THALIA
THETIS CYMODOCE
NEREIDES (FATHER OF —) NEREUS
(MOTHER OF —) DORIS
NERGAL (BROTHER OF —) NINAZU
(FATHER OF —) ENLIL
(MOTHER OF —) NINLIL
NERI (FATHER OF —) MELCHI
(SON OF —) SALATHIEL
NERIAH (FATHER OF —) MAASEIAH
(SON OF —) BARUCH SERAIAH
NERISSA (HUSBAND OF —)
GRATIANO
NERO TYRANT FIDDLER
(MOTHER OF —) AGRIPPINA
(SUCCESSOR TO —) GALBA
(VICTIM OF —) LUCAN SENECA
(WIFE OF —) OCTAVIA
NERONE (CHARACTER IN —) MAGO
NERO SIMON FANUEL RUBRIA
ASTERIA
(COMPOSER OF —) BOITO
NERVE RIB BEND CORD GALL GRIT
GUTS LINE SAND VEIN CHEEK
CHORD CRUST PLUCK PUDIC
SINEW SPUNK STEEL TENON
VAGUS VIGOR APLOMB COSTAL
DARING DENTAL ENERGY FACIAL
HUTZPA LUMBAR RADIAL SACRAL
STRING AXILLAR CHUTZPA

COELIAC COURAGE HUTZPAH
SAPHENA SCIATIC SPINDLE
ABDUCENS AUDACITY BOLDNESS
CERVICAL CHUTZPAH COOLNESS
EFFERENT EMBOLDEN STRENGTH
TEMERITY AUTONOMIC
ENCOURAGE EYESTRING
ACCELERATOR
(— CELL) ANAXON NEURON
DIAXONE DENDRAXON
(— CENTER) BRAIN CORTEX
PLEXUS
(— FIBERS) PONS
(— NETWORK) RETIA PLEXUS
(— SLEEP) NEURO HYPNOTISM
(PL.) HORRORS JITTERS
(PREF.) NEUR(I)(O)
(SUFF.) NEURA(L) NEURE NEURIA
NEURIC
NERVELESS DEAD WEAK BRAVE
INERT UNNERVED FOOLHARDY
POWERLESS
NERVOUS EDGY TOEY FUSSY
GOOSY JUMPY TENSE TIMID
WINDY FIDGET SINEWY SPOOKY
TOUCHY UNEASY FEARFUL
FRETFUL JITTERY RESTIVE
SCADDLE NEUROTIC TIMOROUS
EXCITABLE SENSITIVE
TREMULOUS TWITTERLY
(— MALADY) APHASIA NEURITIS
(— SEIZURE) TIC ANEURIA
NERVURE RIB COSTA NERVE
NEURON CUBITAL
NERVY BOLD RASH JERKY PUSHY
BRAZEN SINEWY STRONG
FORWARD JITTERY IMPUDENT
INTREPID VIGOROUS EXCITABLE
NESS RAS CAPE SKAW SUFFIX
HEADLAND
NEST BED DEN EST JUG WEB AERY
BIKE BINK DRAY DREY EYRY
HOME LAIR NIDE REDD SHED
TRAP ABODE AERIE BROOD EYRIE
HAUNT HOUSE NIDUS SWARM
CLUTCH COLONY CUDDLE
HOTBED RESORT WURLEY
CABINET LODGING RETREAT
VESPIARY WITHYPOT LARVARIUM
PENDULINE RESIDENCE
TERMITARY
(— OF ANIMALS) BED
(— OF ANT) FORMICARY
(— OF BOXES) INRO
(— OF EGGS) CLUTCH
(SQUIRREL'S —) CAGE
(PREF.) CALIO NIDI OECO
(SUFF.) OECA OECIA
NESTER FLEDGLING
NESTLE JUG LAP LIE PET NEST
SNUG NICHE SPOON BURROW
CUDDLE FIDGET NUZZLE PETTLE
SETTLE SNUDGE CHERISH
SHELTER SNUGGLE SNUZZLE
NESTLING BABY BIRD EYAS NEST
POULT SQUAB CUDDLE RETREAT
BIRDLING NIDULATE FLEDGLING
**NEST OF GENTLEFOLK (AUTHOR
OF —)** TURGENEV
(CHARACTER IN —) LIZA FYODOR
PANSHIN VARVARA KALITINE
PAVLOVNA LAVRETSKY
NESTOR SAGE SOLON LEADER

ADVISER ADVISOR COUNSELOR
PATRIARCH
(FATHER OF —) NELEUS
(MOTHER OF —) CHLORIS
(SON OF —) ANTILOCHUS
(WIFE OF —) ANAXIBIA EURYDICE
NESTORIAN WISE
NET BAG GIN HAY LAM POT WEB
CAUL FIKE FLAN FLEW FLUE FYKE
GAIN HAAF KELL LACE LAUN
LAWN LEAD LEAP MESH MOKE
NEAT PURE RETE SALE SEAN TOIL
TRAP TRIM WEIR BRAIL CATCH
CLEAN CLEAR DRIFT GAUZE LACIS
PITCH POUND SCOOP SEIZE
SNARE SNOOD TRAWL TRINK
TULLE YIELD BAGNET BASKET
BRIGHT COBWEB ENTRAP FABRIC
GROUND LEADER MALINE MASILE
PANTER PROFIT RAFFLE SAGENE
SAPIAO TOWNET TUNNEL
DRAGNET ENSNARE FLYTAIL
LAMPARA MALINES NETWORK
PROTECT RETICLE RINSING
SCRINGE SHELTER SPILLER
STALKER TRAINEL TRAMMEL
MESHWORK SALAMBAO
BUCKSTALL RETICULUM
(PREF.) DICTY(O) DIKTYO(N) RETI
RETINO
NETHANEEL (BROTHER OF —)
DAVID
(FATHER OF —) ZUAR JESSE
OBEDEDOM
(SON OF —) SHEMAIAH
NETHANIAH (FATHER OF —) ASAPH
ELISHAMA
(SON OF —) JEHUDI ISHMAEL
NETHER DOWN BELOW LOWER
UNDER NEDDER DOWNWARD
INFERIOR INFERNAL

NETHERLANDS
CANAL: ORANJE JULIANA
DRENTSCH
CAPITAL: AMSTERDAM
CHEESE: EDAM GOUDA LEYDEN
COIN: CENT DOIT RYDER FLORIN
GULDEN STIVER DUCATON
ESCALIN GUILDER
STOOTER
ISLAND: TEXEL MARKEN AMELAND
VLIELAND
MEASURE: EL AAM AHM AUM ELL
KAN MUD VAT ZAK DUIM LOOD
MIJL ROOD ROPE VOET ANKER
CARAT ROEDE STOOP WISSE
BUNDER KOPPEN LEGGER
MAATJE MUDDLE MUTSJE
STREEP SCHEPEL MINGELEN
OKSHOOFD STEEKKAN
NAME: HOLLAND
NATIVE: DUTCH DUTCHMAN
PROVINCE: DRENTHE LIMBURG
UTRECHT ZEELAND FRIESLAND
GRONINGEN GELDERLAND
OVERIJSSEL
RIVER: EEMS LECK MAAS WAAL
YSEL DONGE HUNSE YSSEL
DINTEL DOMMEL KROMME
MEAUSE SCHELDT
TOWN: EDE ASSEN BREDA HAGUE
AALTEN ARNHEM LEIDEN

ZWOLLE HAARLEM TILBURG UTRECHT AALSMEER ENSCHEDE NIJMEGEN AMSTERDAM EINDHOVEN GRONINGEN ROTTERDAM
WEIGHT: ONS LAST LOOD POND BAHAR GREIN KORREL WICHTJE ESTERLIN

NETHERWORLD HADES SHADES
NETLIKE MESHY NETTY RETIARY RETICULAR
NETTING BAR CAUL LING MESH SCREEN DEEPING FISHNET FOOTING BOBBINET WIREWORK
NETTLE VEX FRET LINE ANNOY CNIDA ETTLE PEEVE PIQUE STING HENBIT ORTIGA RUFFLE SPLICE URTICA AFFRONT BLUBBER BLUETOP KNITTLE PROVOKE STINGER IRRITATE CLOWNHEAL GLIDEWORT PELLITORY SMARTWEED
(— RASH) HIVES UREDO URTICARIA
(— TREE) LOTUS GYMPIE
(WHITE DEAD —) ARCHANGEL
(PREF.) CNID(O)
NETWORK WEB CAUL FRET GRID KELL MAZE MESH MOKE RETE CHAIN LACIS BRIDGE COBWEB CRADLE PLEXUS RESEAU SAGENE SYSTEM DRAGNET DIPLEXER GRIDIRON KNITTING WATTLING RETICULUM
(— OF BLOOD VESSELS) TOMENTUM
(— OF CRACKS) CRACKLE
(— ON MAP) GRATICULE
(NUCLEAR —) SKEIN
(PL.) RETIA
NEUME PES VIRGA CLIVIS PNEUMA PODATUS PUNCTUM VIRGULA CLIMACUS QUILISMA SEQUENCE TORCULUS SCANDICUS
NEURAL DORSAL NERVAL NEURIC
NEURALGIA SCIATICA COSTALGIA
NEURILEMMA
(PREF.) LEMMO
NEURITE AXON AXONE
NEUROGLIAL
(PREF.) GLI(O)
NEUROLOGIST **AMERICAN** BEARD DERCUM PRINCE COLLINS CORNING
AUSTRIAN FREUD
ENGLISH ASH GOWERS
FRENCH RAYMOND DEJERINE
GERMAN NISSL GUDDEN MOBIUS
PORTUGUESE MONIZ
NEUROTIC DRUG NERVOUS
(— CONDITION) LATAH
NEUTRAL GRAY INERT SWEET AMORAL MIDDLING NEGATIVE UNBIASED COLORLESS IMPARTIAL
(— IN COLOR) SOBER
(OPTICALLY —) INACTIVE
NEUTRALIZE KILL ANNUL BLUNT ERASE CANCEL ABOLISH BALANCE CORRECT DESTROY NULLIFY VITIATE NEGATIVE OVERRIDE SATURATE FRUSTRATE
NEUTRINO LEPTON

NEVADA
CAPITAL: CARSONCITY
COUNTY: NYE ELKO LANDER STOREY WASHOE MINERAL PERSHING
INDIAN: WASHO PAIUTE
LAKE: MUD MEAD RUBY TAHOE WALKER PYRAMID WINNEMUCCA
PEAK: BOUNDARY
RIVER: REESE TRUCKEE HUMBOLDT
STATE BIRD: BLUEBIRD
STATE FLOWER: SAGEBRUSH
STATE NICKNAME: SILVER SAGEBRUSH
STATE TREE: ASPEN
TOWN: ELY ELKO RENO EUREKA FALLON NELLIS PIOCHE SPARKS TONOPAH LASVEGAS LOVELOCK

NEVE ICE FIRN SNOW NEPHEW GLACIER
NEVER NAY NIE NOT NARY NARRA NIVER NOWHEN
NEVER-NEVER DREAMLAND
NEVERTHELESS BUT YET STILL ALWISE THOUGH ALGATES HOWBEIT HOWEVER WHETHER NATHELESS NONETHELESS
NEVUS MOLE SPOT TUMOR NAEVUS SPIDER SPILUS FRECKLE LENTIGO SPILOMA BIRTHMARK
NEW NEO NEU RAW LATE NOVA FRESH GREEN MOIST NOVEL YOUNG MODERN RECENT UNUSED VIRGIN ANOTHER FOREIGN STRANGE UNTRIED UPSTART INITIATE NEOTERIC ORIGINAL YOUTHFUL BEGINNING
(— BUT YET OLD) NOVANTIQUE
(BRAND —) SPICK
(COMB. FORM) NEO
(PREF.) CAEN(O) CEN(O) NE(O) NOV(I)(O)
(SUFF.) CENE
NEWBORN YEANLING
NEW BRUNSWICK (CAPITAL OF —) FREDERICTON
(COUNTY OF —) KINGS QUEENS SUNBURY MADAWASKA
(MOUNTAIN OF —) CARLETON
(TOWN OF —) BURTON MONCTON BATHURST GAGETOWN
NEW CALEDONIA (— BIRD) KAGU
(CAPITAL OF —) NOUMEA
(ISLAND OF —) HUON BELEP DEPINS LOYALTY WALPOLE
(SEAPORT OF —) NOUMEA
NEWCASTLE GOTHAM
NEWCOMER CADET SETTLER COMELING FRESHMAN JACKEROO MALIHINI RINGNECK GREENHORN IMMIGRANT KIMBERLIN
NEWCOMES (AUTHOR OF —) THACKERAY
(CHARACTER IN —) ANN KEW JOHN BRIAN CLARA CLIVE ETHEL JAMES ROSEY ALFRED BARNES BINNIE HOBSON RIDLEY THOMAS NEWCOME PULLEYN FARINTOSH MACKENZIE

NEW DEAL (— AGENCY) CCC NRA NYA TVA
NEWEL POST VICE SPINDLE
NEW ENGLAND (— INHABITANT) YANK YANKEE JONATHAN
(— SETTLER) PILGRIM PURITAN
NEWFOUNDLAND (— CAPE) RAY RACE BAULD
(— HOUSE) TILT
(— INHABITANT) OUTPORTER
(CAPITAL OF —) STJOHNS
(ISLAND OF —) BELL FOGO GROAIS MIQUELON
(RIVER OF —) GANDER HUMBER EXPLOITS
(TOWN OF —) GANDER HOWLEY WABANA CORNERBROOK

NEW GUINEA
BAY: ORO MILNE HOLNICOTE GOODENOUGH COLLINGWOOD
CAPITAL: PORTMORESBY
GULF: HUON PAPUA
ISLAND: BUKA MANUS MUSSAU
ISLAND GROUP: CRETIN NINIGO SAINSON SOLOMON
MOUNTAIN: ALBERT VICTORIA
NATIVE: ARAU BOONG KARON PAPUAN
PORT: LAE DARU WEWAK MADANG
RIVER: FLY HAMU SEPIK KIKORI PURARI AMBERNO
TOWN: LAE WAU DARU SORON AITAPE KIKORI RABAUL SAMARAI

NEW HAMPSHIRE
CAPITAL: CONCORD
COLLEGE: DARTMOUTH
COUNTY: COOS BELKNAP GRAFTON MERRIMACK
LAKE: SQUAM OSSIPEE SUNAPEE UMBAGOG WINNIPESAUKEE
MOUNTAIN: MORIAH PAUGUS WAUMBEK CHOCORUA MONADNOCK
MOUNTAIN RANGE: WHITE
NOTCH: CRAWFORD FRANCONIA
PRESIDENT: PIERCE
RIVER: SACO ISRAEL BELLAMY SOUHEGAN MERRIMACK PISCATAQUA
STATE NICKNAME: GRANITE
TOWN: DOVER KEENE EXETER NASHUA HANOVER LACONIA OSSIPEE

NEW HEBRIDES (CAPITAL OF —)
VILA
(ISLAND OF —) EPI TANA EFATE MAEWO MABRIM MALEKULA

NEW JERSEY
CAPITAL: TRENTON
COLLEGE: UPSALA
COUNTY: ESSEX OCEAN SALEM UNION BERGEN CAMDEN MERCER MORRIS SUSSEX WARREN PASSAIC MONMOUTH
INDIAN: DELAWARE
PRESIDENT: CLEVELAND

RIVER: DENNIS HAYNES MANTUA RAMAPO MULLICA PASSAIC RARITAN COHANSEY TUCKAHOE
STATE BIRD: GOLDFINCH
STATE FLOWER: VIOLET
STATE NICKNAME: GARDEN
STATE TREE: REDOAK
TOWN: LODI SALEM CAMDEN NEWARK NEWTON NUTLEY RAHWAY TOTOWA BAYONNE CLIFTON HOBOKEN HOHOKUS MATAWAN NETCONG ORADELL PARAMUS PASSAIC TEANECK TENAFLY TRENTON WYCKOFF CARTERET FREEHOLD METUCHEN PATERSON SECAUCUS WATCHUNG HACKENSACK
UNIVERSITY: RUTGERS PRINCETON

NEWLY ANEW AGAIN AFRESH LATELY FRESHLY NEWLINS RECENTLY
NEWMARKET MICHIGAN SARATOGA GRABOUCHE

NEW MEXICO
CAPITAL: SANTAFE
COUNTY: LEA EDDY LUNA MORA QUAY TAOS OTERO CATRON CHAVES DEBACA HIDALGO SOCORRO VALENCIA
CULTURE: MIMBRES
INDIAN: SIA TANO TEWA TIWA ZUNI JEMEZ PECOS APACHE NAVAHO NAVAJO PUEBLO
MOUNTAIN: WHEELER
RIVER: UTE GILA PECOS SANJOSE
STATE BIRD: ROADRUNNER
STATE FLOWER: YUCCA
STATE NICKNAME: SUNSHINE LANDOFENCHANTMENT
STATE TREE: PINON PINYON
TOWN: JAL MORA AZTEC BELEN RATON CLOVIS DEMING GALLUP GRANTS ARTESIA SANTAFE SOCORRO CARLSBAD LASVEGAS TUCUMCARI ALAMOGORDO

NEWNESS NOVITY
NEWS BUZZ DOPE UNCA UNKO WORD CLASH FERLY ADVICE BUDGET CRACKS FERLIE GOSPEL NOTICE REPORT EVANGEL KHUBBER TIDINGS WITTING NOUVELLE KNOWLEDGE SPEERINGS
(— AGENCY) AP UP DNB INS UPI TASS ANETA DOMEI REUTERS
(— BEAT) SCOOP
NEWSBOY NEWSY CAMELOT CARRIER PAPERBOY
NEWSCASTER ANCHORMAN
NEWSMONGER GOSSIP TATTLER NOVELANT NOVELIST QUIDNUNC REPORTER
NEWSPAPER RAG NEWS DAILY ORGAN PAPER PRESS SHEET TIMES ARRIBA HERALD SERIAL SUNDAY COURANT DIURNAL GAZETTE JOURNAL MERCURY TABLOID TRIBUNE NEWSPRINT

(— USED BY PICKPOCKET) STIFF
(PL.) PRESS
NEWSPAPERMAN PRESSMAN
NEWSSTAND BOOTH KIOSK STALL
STAND BOOKSTALL
NEWSWORTHY NEWSY
NEWT ASK EFT ESK EVET EBBET
EFFET LIZARD TRITON AXOLOTL
CRAWLER CREEPER REPTILE
MANKEEPER
NEW YEAR'S DAY NAURUZ
NOROOSE NOWROZE
NEW YEAR'S EVE HAGMENA
HOGMANAY

NEW YORK
AVENUE: PARK FIFTH MADISON
FLATBUSH
BAY: JAMAICA PECONIC
MORICHES
BOROUGH: BRONX KINGS QUEENS
BROOKLYN MANHATTAN
BUILDING: RCA PANAM CHRYSLER
FLATIRON
CANAL: ERIE GOWANUS
CAPITAL: ALBANY
COLLEGE: BARD CCNY IONA PACE
FINCH UNION HUNTER VASSAR
WAGNER ADELPHI BARNARD
CANISIUS HAMILTON SKIDMORE
COUNTY: ERIE BRONX ESSEX
KINGS TIOGA WAYNE YATES
BROOME CAYUGA NASSAU
ONEIDA OSWEGO OTSEGO
PUTNAM QUEENS SENECA
ULSTER CHEMUNG GENESEE
NIAGARA STEUBEN SUFFOLK
CHENANGO DUTCHESS
HERKIMER ONONDAGA
RICHMOND ROCKLAND
SARATOGA SCHUYLER
INDIAN: CAYUGA MOHAWK
ONEIDA SENECA MOHICAN
MONTAUK IROQUOIS
ONONDAGA
ISLAND: FIRE LONG ELLIS STATEN
FISHERS LIBERTY SHELTER
GOVERNORS MANHATTAN
LAKE: ERIE CAYUGA GEORGE
ONEIDA OTISCO OTSEGO
OWASCO PLACID SENECA
CONESUS HONEOYE ONTARIO
SARANAC SCHROON SUCCESS
SARATOGA
MOUNTAIN: BEAR MARCY
MOUNTAINS: TACONIC CATSKILL
ADIRONDACK
NICKNAME: EMPIRE GOTHAM
PRESIDENT: FILLMORE VANBUREN
ROOSEVELT
PRISON: TOMBS ATTICA SINGSING
RIVER: TIOGA HARLEM HOOSIC
HUDSON MOHAWK OSWEGO
GENESEE NIAGARA
SQUARE: TIMES UNION HERALD
MADISON
STATE BIRD: BLUEBIRD
STATE FLOWER: ROSE
STATE NICKNAME: EMPIRE
EXCELSIOR
STATE TREE: SUGARMAPLE
STREET: WALL BOWERY
BROADWAY

SUBWAY: BMT IND IRT LEX
TOWN: RYE OVID ROME DELHI
ILION ISLIP NYACK OLEAN
OWEGO UTICA ATTICA AUBURN
CARMEL COHOES ELMIRA
GOSHEN ITHACA MALONE
ONEIDA OSWEGO TAPPAN
WARSAW ARDSLEY BABYLON
BATAVIA BUFFALO CONGERS
ENDWELL GENESEO HEWLETT
MAHOPAC MASSENA MERRICK
MINEOLA MONTAUK ONEONTA
PENNYAN POTSDAM SUFFERN
SYOSSET WANTAGH YAPHANK
YONKERS BETHPAGE CATSKILL
HERKIMER KINGSTON OSSINING
SYRACUSE TUCKAHOE
ROCHESTER
UNIVERSITY: LIU NYU ADELPHI
COLGATE CORNELL FORDHAM
HOFSTRA YESHIVA COLUMBIA
WATERFALL: NIAGARA

NEW YORK CITY (BOROUGH OF —)
BRONX QUEENS BROOKLYN
MANHATTAN STATENISLAND
(COUNTY OF —) BRONX KINGS
QUEENS RICHMOND
(ISLAND OF —) WARD ELLIS
RANDALL WELFARE
(PARK OF —) GRANT BRYANT
BATTERY CENTRAL
(SUBWAY OF —) BMT IND IRT

NEW ZEALAND
BAY: OHUA HAWKE LYALL
AWARUA CLOUDY GOLDEN
FITZROY PEGASUS POVERTY
RANGAUNU
CAPE: EGMONT FAREWELL
PALLISER
CAPITAL: WELLINGTON
GULF: HAURAKI
ISLAND: OTEA STEWART
PUKETUTU
LAKE: OHAU HAWEA TAUPO
PUKAKI PUPUKE TEANAU
TEKAPO WANAKA BRUNNER
ROTORUA WAKATIPU
MOUNTAIN: COOK FLAT OWEN
CHOPE LYALL MITRE OTARI
EGMONT STOKES AORANGI
PIHANGA TUTAMOE TYNDALL
ASPIRING EARNSLAW
NATIVE: ATI ARAWA MAORI
RINGATU
PENINSULA: MAHIA OTAGO
RIVER: MOKAU ORETI WAIPA
CLUTHA TAIERI TAMAKI
WAIHOU WAIROA MATAURA
WAIKATO WAITAKI CLARENCE
MANAWATU WANGANUI
RANGITIKEI
STRAIT: COOK FOVEAUX
TOWN: LEUIN ORETI OTAKI TAUPO
CLUTHA FOXTON NAPIER
NELSON OAMARU PICTON
TIMARU DUNEDIN MANUKAU
RAETIHI ROTORUA AUCKLAND
HAMILTON KAWAKAWA
CHRISTCHURCH
VOLCANO: RUAPEHU NGAURUHOE
TONGARIRO

WATERFALL: BOWEN HELENA
STIRLING SUTHERLAND

NEXT POI NEAR SYNE THEN UNTO
WISE AFTER EWEST FIRST LATER
NEIST RIGHT BESIDE COMING
SECOND TIDDER TOTHER
CLOSEST NEAREST DIRECTLY
PROCHAIN PROCHEIN ADJOINING
IMMEDIATE
(— AFTER) THEN FOLLOWING
(— IN ORDER) EKA
(— MONTH) PROXIMO
(— OF KIN) GOEL
(— TO LAST) PENULT
(PREF.) (— IN ORDER) EKA
NEXUS TIE BOND LINK CHAIN
NGAIO KIO KAIO NAIO TREE
NHANG GIAI
NIAM-NIAM ZANDE AZANDE
AZANDI ZANDEH AZANDEH
BABUNGERA
NIB NEB PEN BEAK BILL KINK TEAT
POINT PRONG SCORER
NIBBLE EAT NAB NIB NIP BITE
GNAW KNAB KNAP MOOP MOUP
NOSH PECK PICK CHAMP GNARL
MOUSE PIECE SHEAR ARRODE
BROWSE CHAVEL NATTLE PICKLE
PILFER CHIMBLE GNABBLE
GNATTER KNABBLE SNAGGLE
NIBELUNGENLIED (AUTHOR OF —)
UNKNOWN
(CHARACTER IN —) UTA ETZEL
HAGEN IRING GERNOT HUNOLD
LUDGER BLOEDEL GUNTHER
ORTLIEB BRUNHILD DANKWART
DIETRICH GISELHER KRIEMHILD
SIEGFRIED HILDEBRAND
NIBLICK BLASTER
NICANOR (WIFE OF —) CLEOPATRA

NICARAGUA
CAPITAL: MANAGUA
COIN: PESO CENTAVO CORDOBA
DEPARTMENT: LEON BOACO RIVAS
CARAZO ESTELI MADRIZ
MASAYA ZELAYA MANAGUA
ISLAND: OMETEPE
LAKE: MANAGUA
MEASURE: VARA CAHIZ MILLA
SUERTE TERCIA CAJUELA
ESTADAL MANZANA
MOUNTAIN: MADERA MOGOTON
PORT: CORINTO
RIVER: COCO TUMA WANKS
GRANDE ESCONDIDO
TOWN: LEON BOACO RIVAS
MASAYA OCOTAL SOMOTO
GRANADA MANAGUA JINOTEGA
MATAGALPA CHINANDEGA
WEIGHT: BAG CAJA TONELADA

NICCOLITE ARITE KUPFERNICKEL
NICE APT FIT FEAT FINE GOOD
JUMP KIND NEAT NYCE PURE
TRIM CANNY EXACT FUSSY NIECE
SWEET BONITA BONITO DAINTY
GENTIL MINUTE PEACHY QUAINT
QUEASY SPICED STRICT SUBTLE
TICKLE CORRECT ELEGANT
FINICAL GENTEEL MINCING
PERJINK PICKING PRECISE

PRUDISH REFINED DECOROUS
DELICATE EXACTING PLEASANT
PLEASING TICKLISH PARTICULAR
SCRUMPTIOUS
(TOO —) SUPERFINE
(PREF.) (PERTAINING TO —)
NICENO
NICELY JUMP
NICETY HAIR DELICACY JUSTNESS
CRITICISM CURIOSITY PRECISION
(PL.) PERJINKITIES
NICHE BAY WRO APSE CANT COVE
NOOK SLOT AMBRY HERNE HOVEL
NIECE NITCH PLACE ALCOVE
ANCONA BOXING COVERT
CRANNY EXEDRA GROOVE
MIHRAB RECESS RINCON EDICULE
HOUSING RETREAT ROUNDEL
AEDICULA CREDENCE TOKONOMA
HABITACLE TABERNACLE
NICHOLAS NICKLEBY (AUTHOR OF
—) DICKENS
(CHARACTER IN —) BRAY HAWK
KATE FRANK GRIDE NOGGS
RALPH SMIKE NEWMAN SQUEERS
VINCENT CRUMMLES MADELINE
MULBERRY NICHOLAS NICKLEBY
WACKFORD CHEERYBLE
MANTALINI
NICIPPE (FATHER OF —) PELOPS
(HUSBAND OF —) STHENELUS
(MOTHER OF —) HIPPODAMIA
(SON OF —) EURYSTHEUS
NICK CUT JAG MAR NAG NOB CHIP
DENT DINT HACK NACK SLAP SLIT
CHEAT CHICK GOUGE NITCH
NOTCH PRICK SCORE SLACK
SNICK TALLY TRICK ARREST
RECORD DEFRAUD
(— OF TIME) GODSPEED
NICKEL JIT COIN JITNEY NIMBUS
(ALLOY OF —) INVAR KONEL
MONEL
(CONTAINING —) NICCOLIC
(SYMBOL OF —) NI
NICKELODEON JUKEBOX
NICKER NEIGHER
NICKNAME DUB DOEG NICK ALIAS
AGNAME BYWORD HANDLE
MONICA TONAME CRACKER
EKENAME MISNAME MONIKER
NICKERY COGNOMEN MONARCHO
MONICKER TARTUFFE SOBRIQUET
NICKNAMING PROSONOMASIA
NICOMEDE (HALF-BROTHER OF —)
ATTALE
(STEPMOTHER OF —) ARSINOE
NICOSTRATA (FATHER OF —)
LADON
(HUSBAND OF —) ECHENUS
(SON OF —) EVANDER
NICOSTRATUS (BROTHER OF —)
MEGAPENTHES
(FATHER OF —) MENELAUS
(MOTHER OF —) HELEN
NICOTINIC ACID NIACIN
NICTATE WINK BLINK CLOSE
TWINK TWINKLE NICTITATE
NIDDICK NAPE
NIDE NID NEST BROOD LITTER
NIDGE NIG SHAKE QUIVER
NIDGET HOE FOOL IDIOT
NIDOR ODOR AROMA SAVOR

SCENT SMELL
NIECE OY OYE NEPHEW
NIELLO TULA
NIEPA NIOTA KARINGHOTA
NIEVE FIST HAND NEIF SERF
NATIVE
NIFTY FINE GOOD KEEN SMART
STYLISH
NIGER JOLIBA KWORRA RAMTIL
(CAPITAL OF —) NIAMEY
(MOUTH OF —) NUN
(NATIVE OF —) PEUL HAUSA
DJERMA FULANI SONGHA
TOUBOU TUAREG
(OASIS IN —) KAOUAR
(REGION OF —) AIR
(RIVER OF —) DILLIA
(TOWN OF —) SAY GAYA TERA
BAGAM FACHI GOURE MADAMA
MARADI TAHOUA ZINDER

NIGERIA
CAPITAL: LAGOS
COIN: KOBO NAIRA
NATIVE: ARO EBO EDO IBO IJO VAI
BENI EBOE EFIK EJAM EKOI
NUPE BENIN HAUSA FULANI
YORUBA
PLATEAU: JOS
PORT: LAGOS CALABAR
PROVINCE: ISA OYO KANO NUPE
ONDO IJEBU OGOJA WARRI
OWERRI ADAMAWA
RIVER: OLI GANA YOBE BENUE
NIGER KADUNA SOKOTO
GONGOLA HADEJIA KOMADUGU
STATE: IMO OYO KANO OGUN
ONDO BENUE BORNO KWARA
LAGOS BAUCHI SOKOTO
ANAMBRA GONGOLA
TOWN: ABA ADO EDE ISA IWO JOS
BIDI BUEA KANO OFFA YOLA
AKURE ENUGU IKEJA LAGOS
MINNA ZARIA BAUCHI IBADAN
ILESHA ILORIN KADUNA
MUSHIN OWERRI TAKOBA
CALABAR ONITSHA OSHOGBO
ABEOKUTA
TREE: AFARA

NIGGARD CARL CHURL CLOSE
MISER NIGON PIKER SCART TIGHT
NIGGER SCRIMP SCRUNT STINGY
CHINCHE DRYFIST NITHING
PUCKFIST SCRIMPER
EARTHWORM PINCHBECK
PINCHFIST PUCKFOIST SKINFLINT
NIGGARDLY MEAN CLOSE STINT
NARROW NIGHLY SCANTY
SCREWY SKIMPY SORDID STINGY
STRAIT CHINCHE MISERLY
PARSIMONIOUS
NIGGERFISH CONY HIND CONEY
GROUPER GUATIVERE
NIGGLING PETTY PICAYUNE
NIGH AT NEAR ANEAR ANIGH
CLOSE ALMOST NEARLY
ADJACENT
NIGHT PM EVE DARK NUIT DARKY
DEATH NACHT NOCHE SLEEP
DARKMANS DARKNESS
(— AND DAY) NYCHTHEMERON
(CHILDREN OF —) ERINYS

FURIES ERINNYES
(COMB. FORM) NYCTI
(DEPTH OF —) HOLL
(GODDESS OF —) NOX NYX
(LAST —) YESTREEN
(NORSE —) NATT NOTT
(PERT. TO —) NOCTURNAL
(STAY OUT ALL —) PERNOCTATE
(PREF.) NOCT(I)(O) NYCT(I)(O)
NIGHT APE DURUKULI
NIGHT BELL (CHARACTER IN —)
ENRICO SERAFINA PISTACCHIO
(COMPOSER OF —) DONIZETTI
NIGHT BLINDNESS NYCTALOPIA
NIGHTCAP HOW COWL DOWD
HOUVE PIRNY BIGGIN PIRNIE
DORMEUSE SUNDOWNER
NIGHTCLUB CAFE CLUB SPOT
AGOGO BOITE BISTRO NITERY
CABARET DANCERY NIGHTERY
NIGHTDRESS SLOP WILYCOAT
WYLIECOAT
NIGHTFALL EEN EVE DARK DUSK
EVEN SHUTTING TWILIGHT
(OCCURRING AT —) ACRONICAL
NIGHTGOWN SLOP TOOSH NIGHTY
BEDGOWN NIGHTIE WYLIECOAT
NIGHTHAWK PISK CUIEJO
BULLBAT
NIGHTINGALE JUG BULBUL
FLORENCE PHILOMEL ROSSIGNOL
(— SOUND) JUG
(SWEDISH —) LIND JENNY
(PL.) WATCH
NIGHTJAR PUCK POTOO EVEJAR
DERHAWK SPINNER WHEELER
MOREPORK POORWILL
NIGHTHAWK
NIGHT LAMP VEILLEUSE
NIGHTMARE ALP HAG MARA MESS
DREAM FANCY FIEND VISION
INCUBUS CACODEMON
CAUCHEMAR EPHIALTES
(— CAUSER) MARE
NIGHTMARE ABBEY (AUTHOR OF —
) PEACOCK
(CHARACTER IN —) EMILY FATOUT
FLOSKY GLOWRY STELLA TOOBAD
CELINDA CYPRESS ASTERIAS
LISTLESS SCYTHROP GIROUETTE
MARIONETTA CHRISTOPHER
NIGHTSHADE HERB DWALE
MOREL HENBANE MORELLE
PETUNIA SANDBUR SOLANUM
TROMPILLO
NIGHT'S LODGING (AUTHOR OF —)
GORKY
(CHARACTER IN —) LUKA BARON
PEPEL SAHTIN BUBNOFF
NATASHA ALYOSCHKA
KVASCHNYA KOSTILIOFF
WASSILISSA
NIHIL NIL NICHIL NOTHING
NIHILIST ANARCHIST SOCIALIST
NIKE (BROTHER OF —) BIA ZELUS
CRATOS
(FATHER OF —) PALLAS
(MOTHER OF —) STYX
NIL ZERO NILGAI IPOMOEA
NOTHING

NILE
ARABIC NAME: ALBAHR

AS GOD: HAPI
BIRD: IBIS WRYNECK
BOAT: BARIS CANGIA NUGGAR
DAHABEAH
CAPTAIN: RAIS REIS
DAM: ASWAN
FALLS: RIPON
FISH: BAGRE SAIDE BICHIB
DOCMAC MORMYRID
MORMYROID
ISLAND: RODA PHILAE
LATIN NAME: NILUS
NATIVE: MADI NILOT
NEGRO: JUR LUO LWO SUK
PLANT: SUDD LOTUS
REGION: NUBIA
SOURCE: TSANA
TOWN: QUS ABRI ARGO IDFU ISNA
QINA ASYUT CAIRO REJAF
SAITE ROSETTA
TRIBUTARY: ATBARA KAGERA
VALLEY DEPRESSION: KORE

NILE GREEN BOA
NILGAI NIL NYLGAU ANTELOPE
NEELGHAU
NIMBLE FLY DEFT FLIP FLIT GLEG
LISH SPRY SWAK YALD YARE
AGILE BRISK FLEET LIGHT NIPPY
QUICK SWACK TRICK WIGHT
YAULD ACTIVE ADROIT CLEVER
FEIRIE LIMBER LISSOM LIVELY
PROMPT QUIVER SPRACK SUPPLE
VOLANT WANDLE DELIVER
LISSOME SWIPPER FLIPPANT
TRIPPING CITIGRADE SENSITIVE
SPRIGHTLY
(PREF.) PRESTI
NIMBLENESS HASTE AGILITY
SLEIGHT LEGERITY DEXTERITY
LIGHTNESS
NIMBLE-WITTED VOLABLE
NIMBUS AURA HALO NIMB CLOUD
GLORY SHINE VAPOR GLORIA
AUREOLA AUREOLE
NIMIETY EXCESS
NINAZU (BROTHER OF —) NERGAL
(FATHER OF —) ENLIL
(MOTHER OF —) NINLIL
NINCOMPOOP ASS DOLT FOOL
POOP NINNY NINCOM WITLING
BLOCKHEAD SIMPLETON
NINE IX NIE NYE TEAM COMET
POTHOOK
(— A.M.) UNDERN MIDMORN
(— ANGLED FIGURE) NONAGON
(— DAYS DEVOTION) NOVENA
(— FOLD) NONUPLE
(— HEADED MONSTER) HYDRA
(— HUNDRED) SAN
(— INCHES) SPAN
(— OF CLUBS OR DIAMONDS)
COMET
(— OF DIAMONDS) BRAGGER
(— OF TRUMPS) DIX MENEL
SANCHO
(— YEAR CYCLE) JUGLAR
(GROUP OF —) ENNEAD
(MUSIC FOR —) NONET
(PREF.) ENNE(A) NON(A) NOVEM
NOVEN
NINEBARK ROSACEAN SEVENBARK
NINEHOLES BUMBLEPUPPY

NINEPIN KAIL SQUAIL SKITTLE
SKITTLES
(PL.) BOWLS KEELS KAYLES
NINEPEGS
NINETEENTH LARIGOT
NINETIETH NONAGESIMAL
NINETY KOPPA
NINEVEH (FOUNDER OF —) NINUS
NINE WORLDS HEL ASGARD
ALFHEIM MIDGARD NIFLHEIM
VANAHEIM JOTUNNHEIM
MUSPELLSHEIM SVARTALFAHEIM
NINLIL (HUSBAND OF —) ENLIL
(SON OF —) NERGAL NINAZU
NINNI ISHTAR
NINNY DOLT FOOL LOUT DUNCE
IDIOT NONNY PATCH SAMMY
SPOON FONDLE NOODLE
SAPHEAD FONDLING BLOCKHEAD
NIDDICOCK PEAKGOOSE
SIMPLETON
NINON SHEER
NINSUN (SON OF —) GILGAMESH
NINTH (EVERY —) NONAN
ENNEATIC
(PREF.) NON(A)
(SUFF.) NON(A)
NINTU (DAUGHTER OF —) UTTU
(HUSBAND OF —) ENKI
(SON OF —) NINSAR
NINURTA (FATHER OF —) ENLIL
NINUS (FATHER OF —) BELUS
(SON OF —) NINYAS
(WIFE OF —) SEMIRAMIS
NIOBATE TODDITE SIPYLITE
COLUMBATE
NIOBE HERB HOSTA FUNKIA
(BROTHER OF —) PELOPS
(FATHER OF —) TANTALUS
(HUSBAND OF —) AMPHION
(SISTER-IN-LAW OF —) AEDON
NIOBIC COLUMBIC
NIOBIUM COLUMBIUM
NIP CUT SIP VEX BITE BUMP CLIP
DRAM GIVE KNIP NIPE PECK
SNUB TANG TAUT TUCK BLAST
CHEAT CHECK CHILL CLAMP
DRAFT FROST PINCH SEIZE SEVER
SNAPE SNEAP THIEF BENUMB
BLIGHT CATNIP TIPPLE TWITCH
WITHER SARCASM SQUEEZE
WETTING COMPRESS FROSTBITE
VELLICATE
NIPA PALM ATAP ATTAP DRINK
NIPPER BOY LAD CLAW CRAB
GRAB HAND BITER CHELA MISER
THIEF CUNNER URCHIN GRIPPER
INCISOR BRAKEMAN
NIPPERS DOG NIP BITS NIPS
TONGS GRATER PLIERS TURKIS
FORCEPS PINCERS OSTEOTOME
NIPPLE BUD DUG PAP TIT BEAN
TEAT DIDDY DUMMY SPEAN
NIBBLE PILLAR MAMILLA PAPILLA
THELIUM
(— POINT) THELION
(PREF.) EPITHELI(O) MAMM(I)(ILLI)
MAST(O) PAPILLI PAPILLO THEL(O)
NIPPLEWORT BALLOGAN
WARTWEED WARTWORT
NIPPY BOLD SHARP
NIREUS (FATHER OF —) CHAROPUS
(MOTHER OF —) AGLAIA

(SLAYER OF —) EURYPYLUS
NIRVANA EMPTINESS
NIS NIX NISSE GOBLIN KOBOLD
BROWNIE
NISAN ABIB
NISUS POWER EFFORT IMPULSE
ENDEAVOR
(DAUGHTER OF —) SCYLLA
(FATHER OF —) PANDION
HYRTACUS
(MOTHER OF —) IDA
NITER NITRE PETER PETRE POTASH
SALTPETER
NITHER BLAST DEBASE SHIVER
TREMBLE
NITID GAY BRIGHT GLOSSY SPRUCE
SHINING LUSTROUS NITIDOUS
NITO AGSAM
NITON RADON
NITRATE SALT ESTER COTTON
AZOTATE
(PREF.) NITR(O)
NITRIC AZOTIC
NITRIDE BORAZON
NITRITE AZOTITE
NITROGEN GAS AZOTE ALKALIGEN
(PREF.) AZ(O)
NITROGLYCERIN TNT SOUP NITRO
SIRUP SYRUP GLONOIN GLONOINE
NITWIT DAW NIT DOLT DOPE
DRONGO DIZZARD SIMPLETON
NIX NO HARD NECK NICKER
NOBODY SPIRIT SPRITE UNDINE
NOTHING
NJAVE ADJAB DIAVE
NJURD (DAUGHTER OF —) FREYA
(SON OF —) FREY
(WIFE OF —) SKADHI
NO NA NE NAE NAH NAW NAY NIT
NIX NUL BAAL BAIL BALE NONE
NYET NAPOO AIKONA NAPOOH
NOGAKU
(— ONE) NIX NEMO
(— POINTS IN TENNIS) LOVE
(PREF.) NULLI
NOADIAH (FATHER OF —) BINNUI
NOAH NOE
(DOVE OF —) COLUMBA
(FATHER OF —) LAMECH
ZELOPHEHAD
(GRANDFATHER OF —)
METHUSALEH
(GRANDSON OF —) ARAM
(GREAT-GRANDSON OF —) HUL
(MEXICAN —) COXCOX
(RAVEN OF —) CORVUS
(SON OF —) HAM SEM SHEM
JAPHETH
(WINE CUP OF —) CRATER
NOB NAB BLOW HEAD NAVE
KNAVE SWELL HANDLE
TIPTOPPER
NOBEL PRIZE (— IN CHEMISTRY)
BERG HAHN HOFF KUHN TODD
UREY ALDER ASTON BOSCH
CURIE DEBYE DIELS EIGEN FLORY
FUKUI HABER LIBBY NATTA
PREGL SODDY SYNGE TAUBE
CALVIN HARDEN HASSEL KARRER
LELOIR NERNST PERUTZ PRELOG
RAMSAY SANGER SUMNER
WERNER WITTIG BERGIUS
BUCHNER GIAUQUE GILBERT

KENDREW MOISSAN NORRISH
ONSAGER OSTWALD RUZICKA
SEABORG SEMENOV WALLACH
WIELAND WINDAUS LANGMUIR
MULLIKEN TISELIUS
(— IN ECONOMICS) ARROW KLEIN
OHLIN SIMON TOBIN DEBREU
FRISCH MYRDAL KUZNETS
SCHULTZ STIGLER FRIEDMAN
LEONTIEF
(— IN LITERATURE) BOLL BUCK
GIDE MANN SHAW AGNON BUNIN
CAMUS ELIOT HESSE HEYSE
LEWIS PERSE SACHS YEATS
ANDRIC BELLOW ELYTIS EUCKEN
FRANCE MILOSZ NERUDA ONEILL
SARTRE SINGER TAGORE BECKETT
CENETTI GOLDING KIPLING
LAXNESS MAURIAC MISTRAL
MONTALE ROLLAND RUSSELL
BJORNSON CARDUCCI FAULKNER
LAGERLOF CHURCHILL
HEMINGWAY PASTERNAK
STEINBECK LAGERKVIST
MAETERLINCK
(— IN MEDICINE) DAM CORI DALE
HESS KATZ KOCH ROSS ROUS
WALD ARBER BLOCH BOVET
BUMET CHAIN CRICK CURIE DOISY
EULER GOLGI HENCH HUBEL
KREBS KROGH LOEWI LURIA
LYNEN MINOT MONIZ MONOD
OCHOA SNELL TATUM YALOW
BARANY BEADLE BEKESY BORDET
CARREL CLAUDE DOMAGK ECCLES
ENDERS FLOREY GASSER GRANIT
HOLLEY HUXLEY KOCHER KOSSEL
LORENZ PALADE PAVLOV RICHET
SPERRY WIESEL AXELROD
BEHRING FIBIGER HERSHEY
HODGKIN KHORANA LAVERAN
NATHANS NICOLLE SCHALLY
THELLER DELBRUCK MCCLINTOCK
(— IN PEACE) ORR THO HULL KING
MOTT PIRE ROOT SATO ASSER
BAJER BALCH BEGIN DAWES
FRIED GOBAT LANGE PASSY
SADAT ADDAMS ANGELL BRANDT
BRIAND BUNCHE BUTLER CASSIN
CREMER DUNANT MONETA
NANSEN QUIDDE WALESA
WILSON BORLAUG BUISSON
JOUHAUX KELLOGG LUTHULI
PAULING RENAULT THERESA
BRANTING CORRIGAN ESQUIVEL
SAKHAROV KISSINGER
ROOSEVELT SODERBLOM
SCHWEITZER HAMMARSKJOLD
(— IN PHYSICS) LEE BOHR BORN
HESS LAMB LAUE MOTT NEEL
RABI RYLE TAMM TING WIEN
YANG BASOV BETHE BLOCH
BOTHE BRAGG BRAUN CURIE
DALEN DIRAC ESAKI FERMI
GABOR HERTZ KUSCH PAULI
SEGRE ALFVEN BARKLA CRONIN
FOWLER GLASER HEWISH
LANDAU PERRIN PLANCK STRUTT
TOWNES WIGNER YUKAWA
BARDEEN GLAEVER GLASHOW
KAPITSA LORENTZ MARCONI
RICHTER EINSTEIN ROENTGEN
CHANDRASEKHAR

NOBILITY RANK ELITE GRACE
GENTRY STATUS DIGNITY
KWAZOKU PEERAGE QUALITY
STATION BARONAGE SZLACHTA
ELEVATION
(MEMBER OF TATAR —) MURZA
(ROMAN —) RAMNES
NOBLE DON ALII DOGE DUKE EARL
EDEL EPIC FAME FREE GENT
GOOD GRAF HIGH JARL JUST
KAMI KUGE LORD PEER PURE
RIAL ARIKI ATHEL BARON BROAD
BURLY COUNT DUCAL ERECT
ETHEL FURST GRAND GREAT
HIRAM KHASS LOFTY MANLY
MORAL MURZA PROUD ROYAL
STATE AUGUST COUSIN DAIMIO
EPICAL FLAITH GENTLE GESITH
HAUGHT HEROIC JUNKER KINGLY
LORDLY LUCUMO MANFUL
SIRDAR SUPERB THAKUR
WORTHY YONKER ACERBAS
CACIQUE GALLANT GLAUCUS
GLORIED GRANDEE HIDALGO
LIBERAL MAGNATE MARQUIS
PATRICK STAROST STATELY
STEWARD SUBLIME TOISECH
VOLPONE PANGLIMA PRINCELY
(MINOR —) VIDAME
NOBLEMAN DUKE EARL EMIR
LORD PEER SOUL BARON COUNT
ORLOV PARIS THANE COUSIN
MILORD ORLOFF THAKUR YONKER
GRANDEE HIDALGO MAGNATE
MARQUIS STAROST VOLPONE
YOUNKER ADELIGER ALDERMAN
ALMAVIVA BELARIUS MARCHESE
MARQUESS LANDGRAVE
MAGNIFICO
NOBLENESS HONOR DIGNITY
(— OF BIRTH) EUGENY
NOBLEWOMAN LADY MILADY
DUCHESS PEERESS BARONESS
COUNTESS
NOBODY NIX NEMO NONE NADIE
NOMAN SCRUB SCARAB NOTHING
JACKSTRAW
NOCENT GUILTY HARMFUL
HURTFUL NOXIOUS CRIMINAL
NOCTURNAL NIGHT NOXIAL
NIGHTLY NIGHTISH MOONSHINE
(— ANIMAL) COON POSSUM
OPOSSUM
(— BIRD) OWL
(— CARNIVORE) RATEL
(— MAMMAL) BAT LEMUR
(— SIGNS) ZODIAC
NOCTURNE LULLABY UHTSONG
PAINTING SERENADE
NOD BOB BOW ERR NAP NID NIP
BECK BEND DOZE NAPE SIGN SLIP
SWAY WINK DROOP LAPSE
ASSENT BECKON DODDLE
DROWSE NODDLE NUTATE
SALUTE SIGNIFY
NODDING DROWSY NUTANT
ANNUENT CERNUOUS DROOPING
NUTATION
NODDLE HEAD PATE BRAIN
NODDY AUK FOOL JACK NOIO
TERN KNAVE NINNY DROWSY
FULMAR NOODLE SLEEPY
HACKNEY TOMNODDY SIMPLETON

NODE BOW BUMP KNOB KNOT
LUMP PLOT JOINT NODUS POINT
TUMOR BULBIL NODULE DILEMMA
GRANULE KNUCKLE FOLLICLE
PHYTOMER SWELLING TUBERCLE
(— OF GRASS) KNOT
(— OF POEM) PLOT
(— OF STEM) JOINT
NODULE BOB AUGE BUMP KNOT
LUMP MASS NODE YOLK FLINT
GEODE PHYMA MILIUM BLISTER
CATHEAD GRANULE LEPROMA
NABLOCK SARCOID AMYGDALE
AMYGDULE COALBALL TUBERCLE
WHITEHEAD
(— OF FLINT) CORE
(CHALCEDONY —) ENHYDROS
(PL.) BEADING
NOEL XMAS CAROL NOWEL
NATALIS CHRISTMAS
NOGAH (FATHER OF —) DAVID
NOGGIN ALE CUP MUG NOG PEG
PIN GILL HEAD PAIL PATE DRINK
GOGGAN NAGGIN NOODLE
NOHAH (FATHER OF —) BENJAMIN
NOIL FIBER PINION
NOISE (ALSO SEE SOUND) ADO AIR
BUM DIN GIG HUM POP ROW
BANG BOOM BRAY BUMP BURR
CLAM COIL HOOT KLOP MUSH
PEAL RALE RASH REEL RERD
ROTE ROUT SLAM ZING ALARM
BABEL BLARE BLAST BLOOP
BRAWL BRUIT BURLE CHANG
CHIRM CLICK DREAM GRASS
JERRY KNOCK LARRY LARUM
LEDEN PLASH QUONK REERE
RERDE RUMOR SLORP SNORE
SOUND STEER SWISH WHANG
BICKER CACKLE CLAMOR DUNDER
GOBBLE GOSSIP HUBBUB NORATE
OUTCRY PUDDER RACKET
RANTAN RATTLE REPORT SPLASH
SQUAWK STEVEN STRIFE TUMULT
UPROAR BLUSTER BRATTLE
CLITTER CLUTTER CRACKLE
ORATION SCANDAL SPATTER
STREPOR STRIDOR FLICFLAC
QUONKING TINTAMAR
CONFUSION
(EARTHQUAKE —) BRONTIDES
(ELECTRIC —) GRASS
(PREF.) **(— OF FALLING OBJECT)**
KER
NOISELESS QUIET STILL SWEET
TACIT SILENT APHONIC CATLIKE
NOISEMAKER BELL HORN GRAGER
RATTLE CLAPPER SQUEAKER
NOISETTE HAZEL HAZELNUT
NOISOME FOUL RANK FETID
NASTY PUTRID RANCID HARMFUL
HURTFUL NOXIOUS NUISOME
STINKING OFFENSIVE
MALODOROUS
NOISY LOUD CLASHY CREAKY
BLATANT DINSOME FRANTIC
MOILING RACKETY RIOTOUS
ROUTOUS BRAWLING CLATTERY
SONOROUS STREPENT HILARIOUS
RATTLEBAG SCAMBLING
BOISTEROUS
NOLL HEAD NODDLE NOODLE
NOMA CANKER

NOMAD ARAB BEJA LURI MOOR SAKA SHUA ALANI GYPSY IGDYR JAREG ROVER SHUWA NOMADE ROAMER ROVING SEMITE SLUBBI TUAREG BAZIGAR BEDOUIN SARACEN SCENITE SHORTZY SHUKRIA SOLUBBI TOUAREG KABABISH SCYTHIAN SHINWARI AMALEKITE MIGRATORY
(— PEOPLE) ALANI
(PL.) AKHLAME

NOMADIC ERRATIC VAGRANT VAGABOND FOOTLOOSE ITINERANT

NOMBRIL NAVEL

NOM DE PLUME PENNAME TELONISM PSEUDONYM

NOME ELIS NOMOS MELODY NOMARCHY PROVINCE

NOMENCLATURE LIST NAME TERM ONYMY NAMING GLOSSARY REGISTER CATALOGUE

NOMINAL PAR BASIC PAPER FORMAL SLIGHT UNREAL TITULAR TRIVIAL PLATONIC TRIFLING
(— RECOGNIZANCE) DOE

NOMINATE CALL LEET NAME ELECT NEVEN SLATE SELECT APPOINT ENTITLE PRESENT PROPOSE SPECIFY DESIGNATE POSTULATE

NOMINY SPEECH RIGMAROLE

NONAGE NEANT INFANCY MINORITY PUPILAGE

NONAGREEMENT DISSENT

NON-ALCOHOLIC SMALL

NO NAME (AUTHOR OF —) COLLINS
(CHARACTER IN —) NOEL CLARE FRANK GARTH KIRKE NORAH ANDREW GEORGE WRAGGE BARTRAM BYGRAVE LECOUNT MAGDALEN VANSTONE

NON-ARAB SHANGALLA

NONASPIRATE LENE

NONBELIEVER PAGAN ATHEIST AGNOSTIC

NONCE NANES NONES NOANCE PRESENT PURPOSE OCCASION

NONCHALANT COOL GLIB ALOOF CASUAL JAUNTY CARELESS DEBONAIR NEGLIGENT

NON-CHRISTIAN PAYNIM INFIDEL

NONCITIZEN TENSOR PEREGRINUS

NONCLERICAL LAY LAIC

NONCOMBUSTIBLE APYROUS

NONCOMMITTAL NEUTRAL

NONCONFORMIST REBEL NONCON BEATNIK DEVIANT FANATIC HERETIC SECTARY BOHEMIAN RECUSANT DISSENTER
(— IN ART) FAUVE

NONCONFORMITY HERESY ADHARMA DISSENT NEGLECT REFUSAL RECUSANCE RECUSANCY

NONCONTINUOUS DISCRETE

NON-CONVERGENCE ABERRATION

NONDISCLOSURE FRAUD

NONDO LOVAGE ANGELICO

NONDUALISM ADVAITA

NONE NO UN NAE NIN NANE NARY NEEN NONES
(PREF.) NULLI

NONEGO NOTSELF

NONELASTIC BROAD

NONENTITY ZERO AUGHT CIPHER NOBODY NOUGHT NOTHING NULLITY NEGATION

NONESSENTIAL CASUAL FRILLY UNNEEDED EXTRINSIC
(— IN RELIGION) ADIAPHORON

NONESUCH APPLE MODEL PARAGON PATTERN PARADIGM MATCHLESS NONPAREIL UNRIVALED

NON-EXISTENCE ABSENCE NOTHING

NONEXISTENT NULL NAPOOH NOUGHT NONBEING BARMECIDE
(PRACTICALLY —) FAT
(PREF.) NULLI

NONFEASANCE BREACH

NON GRATA UNWELCOME

NONGYPSY GAJO

NONINJURY AHIMSA

NON-JEW GOI GOY

NONJUROR USAGER

NON-LATIN SAXON

NONLEGATO DETACHE DETACHED

NON-MOSLEM GENTILE

NONMOTILE
(PREF.) APLANO

NONNASAL ORAL

NONPAREIL BEST POPE TYPE PARAGON PERFECT SUPREME UNEQUAL NONESUCH PEERLESS UNRIVALED

NONPAYMENT DISHONOR

NONPLUS SET FAZE POSE STOP BLANK FLOOR POSER STICK STUMP TRUMP BAFFLE GRAVEL PUZZLE RATTLE CONFUSE MYSTIFY PERPLEX STAGGER QUANDARY DULCARNON EMBARRASS

NONPLUSSED BLANK FOOLISH

NONPOISONOUS EDIBLE

NONPROFESSIONAL BUM LAY LAIC AMATEUR

NONSENSE BAH GAS GUP PAH ROT BILK BLAA BLAH BOSH BUFF BULL BUNK COCK CRAP FLAM FLUM GAFF GOOK GUFF JIVE JUNK PISH POOH PUNK TOSH BALLS BILGE BLASH DROOL FOLLY FUDGE HAVER HOOEY NERTS SPOOF STITE STUFF TRASH TRIPE WAHOO BABBLE BETISE BLAGUE BUNKUM DRIVEL FADDLE FOLDER FOOTLE KIBOSH LINSEY NAVERS PIFFLE RUBBLE SQUISH TRIVIA BLARNEY BLATHER EYEWASH FARRAGO INANITY LOCKRAM RHUBARB RUBBISH TOSHERY TRIFLES TWADDLE BUNCOMBE CLAPTRAP COBBLERS DISHWASH FALDEROL FLIMFLAM FLUMMERY GALBANUM MACARONI MOROLOGY PISHPOSH PISHTOSH SKITTLES SPLUTTER TOMMYROT TRUMPERY ABSURDITY FRIVOLITY MOONSHINE POPPYCOCK SILLINESS BALDERDASH CODSWALLOP
(— CREATURE) GOOP SHOO SNARK SHIMOO

NONSENSICAL ABSURD

NONSURFER HODAD

NON-VIOLENCE AHIMSA

NOODLE BEAN FOOL HEAD NIZY NOLL PATE MOONY NINNY NIZEY NODDY PASTA PASTE SAMMY BOODLE GUDDLE NODDLE NOGGIN DAWCOCK LOKSHEN NOGHEAD NOUILLE BLOCKHEAD SIMPLETON CAPERNOITIE
(— DISH) PANSIT RAVIOLI KREPLACH
(PL.) MEIN FARFEL FERFEL LASAGNA LASAGNE LOKSHEN FETTUCINI

NOOK IN BAY OUT WRO CANT COVE GLEN HERN HOLE NALK NUCK NUIK ANGLE HALKE HERNE NEUCK NICHE ALCOVE CANTLE CORNER CRANNY RECESS CREVICE NOOKERY RETREAT

NOON M APEX DINE NOWN SEXT DINNER MIDDAY UNDERN MIDNOON MERIDIAN

NOONDAY (— REST) NAP SIESTA MERIDIAN

NOOSE TIE TOW BOND DULL FANK GIRN HEMP LACE LOOP ROPE TRAP BIGHT CATCH GRANE HITCH HONDA KINCH LASSO LATCH LEASH SNARE SNARL WIDDY CAUDLE CHOKER CLINCH ENTRAP HALTER LARIAT SPRING TETHER TIPPET TWITCH CHOCKER ENSNARE EXECUTE LANIARD LANYARD SPRINGE NECKLACE SQUEEZER TWITCHEL
(— FOR HAULING LOG) CHOKER CHOCKER
(— FOR SNARING FISH) DULL
(— IN A CORD) KINCH
(HANGMAN'S —) SQUEEZER

NOOTKA AHT AHOUSAHT MOATCHAT MOOACHAHT

NORATE NOISE RUMOR GOSSIP

NORAX (FATHER OF —) HERMES MERCURY
(MOTHER OF —) ERYTHEA

NORDIC ARIAN ARYAN

NORI AMANORI

NORITE GABBRO OLIGOSITE

NORM PAR MODE RULE TYPE CANON GAUGE MODEL NORMA DHARMA MEDIAN AVERAGE MODULUS PATTERN STANDARD TEMPLATE

NORMA MOLD RULE GAUGE MODEL SQUARE PATTERN TEMPLET STANDARD TEMPLATE
(CHARACTER IN —) NORMA ADALGISA POLLIONE
(COMPOSER OF —) BELLINI

NORMAL PAR FULL HOME JUST MEAN SANE WISE CLEAR ERECT USUAL FORMAL NATIVE SCHOOL AVERAGE NATURAL NEUTRAL REGULAR TYPICAL ORDINARY STANDARD CUSTOMARY

NORMANDY (BEACH IN —) OMAHA
(CAPITAL OF —) ROUEN
(RIVER IN —) EURE ORNE SEINE

NORN FATE URTH WURD WYRD NORNA SKULD URDHR URTHR VERDHANDI VERTHANDI

NORSEL BAND LINE ORSEL FILLET NOSSEL ORSELLER

NORTH SEPTENTRION
(PREF.) ARCT(O)

NORTH AMERICA
(ALSO SEE SPECIFIC COUNTRIES)
ISLAND: LONG BANKS PARRY BAFFIN BERMUDA VICTORIA ANTICOSTI ELLESMERE NEWFOUNDLAND
LAKE: ERIE HURON NIPIGON ONTARIO MANITOBA MICHIGAN REINDEER SUPERIOR WINNIPEG ATHABASCA NETTLING
MOUNTAIN: WOOD LOGAN WALSH ROBSON STEELE TOLUCA LUCANIA PARICUTIN TAJUMULCO POPOCATEPETL
NATION: CANADA MEXICO UNITEDSTATES
RIVER: GILA MILK JAMES LIARD OSAGE PEACE PEARL PECOS SNAKE YUKON BALSAS BRAZOS FRASER HUDSON MOBILE NEOSHO PANUCO PLATTE POWDER SABINE TANANA KLAMATH KOYUKUK POTOMAC SUSITNA CIMARRON COLUMBIA DELAWARE MISSOURI NIOBRARA PENOBSCOT PORCUPINE RIOGRANDE STLAWRENCE MISSISSIPPI

NORTH CAROLINA
CAPE: FEAR LOOKOUT HATTERAS
CAPITAL: RALEIGH
COLLEGE: ELON CATAWBA DAVIDSON
COUNTY: ASHE DARE HOKE HYDE NASH PITT WAKE AVERY DAVIE GATES ROWAN SURRY BERTIE BLADEN CRAVEN ONSLOW YADKIN YANCEY CATAWBA PAMLICO CURRITUCK
INDIAN: ENO COREE CHERAW MORATOK PAMLICO CHOWANOC HATTERAS
MOUNTAIN: HARRIS MITCHELL
PRESIDENT: POLK JOHNSON
RIVER: HAW TAR NEUSE CHOWAN LUMBER PEEDEE YADKIN ROANOKE
SOUND: BOGUE CROATAN PAMLICO
STATE BIRD: CARDINAL
STATE FLOWER: DOGWOOD
STATE NICKNAME: TARHEEL OLDNORTH TURPENTINE
STATE TREE: PINE
TOWN: BOONE SYLVA BURGAW DOBSON DURHAM LENOIR SHELBY SPARTA EDENTON HICKORY ROXBORO TARBORO GASTONIA CHARLOTTE
UNIVERSITY: DUKE

NORTH DAKOTA
CAPITAL: BISMARCK

COLLEGE: JAMESTOWN
COUNTY: DUNN EDDY SLOPE
  STARK WELLS DICKEY DIVIDE
  GRIGGS KIDDER OLIVER TRAILL
  PEMBINA ROLETTE
INDIAN: MANDAN ARIKARA
  HIDATSA
MOUNTAIN: WHITEBUTTE
RIVER: RUSH CEDAR HEART
  JAMES SOURIS DESLACS
  SHEYENNE WILDRICE
STATE BIRD: MEADOWLARK
STATE FLOWER: ROSE PRAIRIE
STATE NICKNAME: SIOUX
  FLICKERTAIL
STATE TREE: ELM
TOWN: MOTT CANDO FARGO
  MINOT ROLLA AMIDON LAKOTA
  LINTON MOHALL BOWBELLS
  NAPOLEON

NORTHERN PIKE ARCTIC BOREAL
NORLAND NORTHEN
  (— BEAR) POLAR RUSSIA
  (— CONSTELLATION) URSA
ANDROMEDA

NORTH KOREA
CAPITAL: PYONGYANG
COIN: JUN WON HWAN
PROVINCE: CHAGANG KANGWON
  TANGGANG
RIVER: NAM YALU IMJIN TUMEN
  TAEDONG
TOWN: HAEJU HEIJO KEIJO
  ANDONG ANTUNG HYESAN
  JUSHIN POCHON SAINNI
  WONSAN HAMHUNG HUICHON
  HUNGNAM KAESONG KANGGYE
  SARIWON SINUIJU CHONGJIN

NORTH STAR STATE MINNESOTA

NORTH VIETNAM
CAPITAL: HANOI
COIN: XU DONG
COMMUNIST PARTY: VIETCONG
GULF: TONKIN TONKING
MOUNTAIN: FANSIPAN
NATIVE: HOA MAN MEO TAY KINH
  NUNG THAI MUONG
NEWSPAPER: NHANDAN
PORT: BENTHUY HONGGAI
  HAIPHONG
REGION: ANNAM TONKIN
RIVER: BO CA DA LO MA CHU GAM
  KOI CHAY NHIHA
TOWN: VINH BACNINH CAOBANG
  DONGHOI NAMDINH VIETTRI
  HAIPHONG THANHHOA

NORTHWEST TERRITORY
(CAPITAL OF —) YELLOWKNIFE
(DISTRICT OF —) FRANKLIN
  KEEWATIN MACKENZIE
(RIVER OF —) BACK KAZAN
  DUBAWNT COPPERMINE
(TOWN OF —) RAE INUVIK
  DISCOVERY SNOWDRIFT

NORWAY
CAPE: NORDKYN NORDKAPP
CAPITAL: OSLO

COIN: ORE KRONE
COUNTY: AMT OSLO FYLKE TROMS
  BERGEN TROMSO FINMARK
  HEDMARK OPPLAND OSTFOLD
  NORDLAND ROGALAND
  TELEMARK VESTFOLD
DANCE: GANGAR HALLING
  SPRINGAR SPRINGLEIK
FJORD: OSLO SOGNE HARDANGER
  TRONDHEIM
INLET: IS KOB RAN ALST ANDS
  BOKN NORD OFOT SALT SUNN
  TYRI VEST FIORD FJORD FOLDA
  LAKSE SOGNE BJORNA HADSEL
  HORTENS TRONDHEIM
ISLAND: VEGA BOMLO DONNA
  FROYA HITRA HOPEN SENJA
  SMOLA ALSTEN AVEROY
  BOUVET HINNOY KARMOY
  KVALOY SOLUND SOROYA
  VANNOY GURSKOY LOFOTEN
  MAGEROY SEILAND JANMAYEN
  SVALBARD RINGVASSOY
LAKE: ALTE ISTER MJOSA SNASA
  FEMUND ROSTAVN TUNNSJO
  ROSTVATN
MEASURE: FOT MAL POT ALEN
  MAAL KANDE FATHOM SKIEPPE
MOUNTAIN: SOGNE KJOLEN
  NUMEDAL BLODFJEL SNOHETTA
  TELEMARK USTETIND
PARLIAMENT: LAGTING STORTING
  ODELSTING
PLATEAU: DOURE FJELD
  HARDANGER
RIVER: OI ENA ALTA OTRA RANA
  TANA BARDU BEGNA GLAMA
  LAGEN ORKLA OTTER RAUMA
  REISA GLOMMA LOUGEN
  NAMSEN PASVIK DRAMSELVA
TOWN: GOL NES BODO MOSS
  ODDA OSLO VOSS BJORT FLORO
  HAMAR MOLDE SKIEN SKJAK
  BERGEN HORTEN LARVIK
  NARVIK ALESUND ARENDAL
  DRAMMEN SANDNES
  STAVANGER
WATERFALL: VETTI SKYKJE
  VORING
WEIGHT: LOD MARK PUND
  SKAALPUND BISMERPUND

NORWEGIAN (FORM OF —) BOKMAL
(LITERARY FORM OF —) NYNORSK
NOSE CAP NEB NIZ PRY PUG SPY
BEAK BOKO CONK NASE GROIN
LORUM NASUS SCENT SMELL
SNIFF SNOOP SNOUT TRUNK
BEEZER CYRANO DETECT
GNOMON MUFFLE MUZZLE
NOZZLE PECKER ROOKIE SEARCH
SNITCH SOCKET ADVANCE
PERFUME SMELLER DISCOVER
INFORMER OLFACTOR PERCEIVE
PROBOSCIS SCHNOZZLE
(— A LOG) SNIPE
(— BAG) MORRAL
(— CARTILAGE) SEPTUM
(— DISEASE) OZENA OZOENA
(— DIVE) VRILLE
(— FLUTE) PUNGI POOGYE
(— INFLAMMATION) CORYZA
RHINITIS

(— MEDICINE) ERRHINE
(— OF ANIMAL) GROIN
(— OPENING) NARE
(— PARTITION) VOMER
(— PIECE) NASAL
(— RING) PIRN
(BLUNT —) SNUB
(FLAT —) PUG SNUB
(PREF.) NAS(I)(O) NASUTI RHIN(O)
(SUFF.) RHINA RHINE RHINIA
RHINOUS RHINUS RRHINE
RRHINIA
NOSEBAND BOSAL MUSROL
CAVESSON
NOSEBLEED EPISTAXIS
RHINORRHAGIA
NOSEGAY BOB ODOR POSY POESY
SCENT TUTTY BOUQUET
CORSAGE PERFUME
NOSINESS CURIOSITY
NOSING CURB
NOSTALGIA LONGING YEARNING
NOSTALGIC ELEGIAC ELEGIACAL
NOSTOLOGY GERIATRICS
NOSTRADAMUS SEER PROPHET
PHYSICIAN
NOSTRIL ALA NARE NARIS THIRL
THRILL BLOWHOLE
(PERT. TO —) NARIAL NARINE
(PL.) NARES NARIS SNUFFERS
(PREF.) NARI
NOSU LOLO
NOSY BEAKY PRYING CURIOUS
FRAGRANT INTRUSIVE
NOT NA NE NAE NAY NOR PAS
BAAL BAIL BALE NICHT SHORN
SORRA NOUGHT POLLED SHAVEN
NEITHER HORNLESS NEGATIVE
(— ANY) NO NUL NANE NARY
NONE NAIRY NOKIN STEAD
(— AT ALL) NEVER LITTLE
NOWAYS NOWHIT NOWISE
(— FINAL) NISI
(— THE SAME) OTHER ANOTHER
DIFFERENT
(— TO BE REPEATED) NR
(— WANTED) DETROP
SUPERFLUOUS
(ALMOST —) SCARCELY
(COULD —) NOTE
(PREFIX MEANING —) IL IM IN IR
UN NON
(PREF.) A ANTI DIS E IL IM IN IR
NON UM UN
NOTABLE VIP FINE FABLED
FAMOUS GIFTED NOTARY SIGNAL
UNIQUE EMINENT STORIED
SUBLIME DISTINCT ESPECIAL
EVENTFUL HISTORIC MEMORABLE
NOTORIOUS NOTEWORTHY
NOTARY NOTAR GRAFFER
GREFFIER NOTEBOOK OBSERVER
OFFICIAL SCRIVENER
NOTARY PUBLIC TABELLION
NOTATION HOLD MEMO NOTE
ENTRY SYSTEM MARKING
(PHONETIC —) ROMIC
NOTATOR NOTER RECORDER
NOTCH CUT DAG DAP GAP HAG
JAG JOG PEG COPE DENT DINT
GAIN GIMP KERF MUSH NICK
NOCK SLAP SLOT SNIP STEP
WARD CRENA GABEL GRADE

HILUM SCORE SHARD SHERD
SWICK TALLY CRENEL CROTCH
DEFILE DEGREE HOLLOW INDENT
JOGGLE RAFFLE RECORD SCOTCH
CRENATE GUDGEON SERRATE
INCISION UNDERCUT
(— BETWEEN HILLS) SLAP
(— ON VERTEBRAE) HYPANTRUM
(— TO FELL TREE) UNDERCUT
NOTCHED EROSE JAGGY RAGULE
RAGULY SERRATE CRENATED
NOTE BON DOG IOU JOT KEY SEE
TEN UNE BILL CARD CENT CHIT
ESPY FAME FLAT GOOD HEED
MARK MEMO NAME NOIT SIGN
SOLE SONG TENT TONE TUNE
VIEW CHECK FIVER GLOZE LABEL
PRICK SHORT SIXTH SOUND STIFF
TENTH TOKEN TRAIT TWANG
ATTEND BILLET DEGREE EXCUSE
FIGURA FLIMSY LETTER MELODY
MINUTE NOTICE POLICY RECORD
REGARD REMARK RENOWN
REPORT SECOND STRAIN TENNER
BETOKEN COMMENT DISCORD
MESSAGE MISSIVE NATURAL
OBSERVE PUNCTUS REDBACK
ANNOTATE BLUEBACK BRADBURY
BREVIATE DISPATCH EMINENCE
MARGINAL PERCEIVE POSTFACE
TREASURY GREENBACK
POSTSCRIPT
(— FROM TRAIN) BUTTERFLY
(— OF ASSAULT) WARISON
(— OF HUMOR) TRAIT
(— OF SCALE) DO FA LA MI RE SI
SO TI UT ARE SOL
(— OF SNIPE) SCAPE
(— OF WARNING) WATCHWORD
(— ON SHOPHAR) TEKIAH
(— TO RECALL DOG) FORLOIN
(—S ON HUNTING HORN) SEEK
(ALTERED —) ACCIDENTAL
(BANK —S) CABBAGE
(BASS —) DRONE
(BIRD'S —) JUG CHIRP
(BUGLE —) MOT
(EIGHTH —) UNCA QUAVER
(EMBELLISHING —) ORNAMENT
(ESCAPE —) ECHAPPEE
(EXPLANATORY —) ANAGRAPH
SCHOLIUM ANNOTATION
(FUNDAMENTAL —) ROOT
(GRACE —) NACHSCHLAG
(HALF —) MINIM
(HARSH —) BLOB
(HIGHEST —) ELA
(HIGH-PITCHED —) BEEP
(LEADING —) SUBTONIC
(LONG —) LARGE
(LOVE —) POULET
(LOWEST —) KEY GAMUT
(MARGINAL —) TOT QUOTE POSTIL
APOSTIL
(MUSICAL —) ALT RAY MESE MIND
BREVE GAMUT SHARP ALAMIRE
MEDIANT PUNCTUS LICHANOS
PARAMESE PIZZICATO
(NONHARMONIC —) CAMBIATA
(POUND —) BRADBURY
(PROMISSORY —) DOG GOOD
HUNDI CEDULA
ASSIGNAT

(QUARTER —) CROTCHET SEMIMINIM
(SIXTEENTH —) DEMIQUAVER SEMIQUAVER
(SIXTY-FOURTH —) HEMIDEMISEMIQUAVER
(THIRTY-SECOND —) SUBSEMIFUSA DEMISEMIQUAVER
(TWO —S) DUPLET
(WARBLING —) CHIRL
(WHOLE —) SEMIBREVE
(100-POUND —) CENTURY
(PL.) ANA GAMUT STRAIN NUMBERS TIRALEE MARGINALIA
NOTEBOOK LOG DIARY NOTARY RECORD STREET JOURNAL
NOTECASE WALLET POCKETBOOK
NOTED COUTH FAMED GREAT NAMELY EMINENT INSIGNE RENOWNED DISTINGUE
NOTEPAPER BOUDOIR
NOTEWORTHY BIG SOLEMN EMINENT NOTABLE SALIENT SPECIAL BODACIOUS MEMORABLE OBSERVABLE
NOTHING NIL NIX FREE LUKE NILL WIND ZERO AUGHT BLANK NIHIL ZILCH CIPHER NAUGHT NOBODY NOUGHT TRIFLE NULLITY SCRATCH USELESS BAGATELLE
(— BUT) ALL
(— DOING) NAPOO NAPOOH
(— MORE THAN) MERE
(— OTHER THAN) ONLY
NOTHINGNESS NOT NADA ZERO NOUGHT VACUITY NIHILITY
NOTICE AD BAN SEE SPY CALL ESPY GAUM GOME HEED IDEA KEEP MARK MIND NEWS NOTE PIPE RIDE SIGN SPOT TWIG ALARM AWAIT COUNT EDICT FLOAT NOTAM ORDER QUOTE ADVICE ALLUDE BILLET ESPIAL NOTION PERMIT READER REGARD REMARK REWARD AFFICHE ARTICLE DISCERN MENTION OBSERVE PLACARD PROGRAM WARNING BULLETIN MONITION PERCEIVE WITTERING
(— UNEXPECTEDLY) CATCH
(ADVANCE —) HERALDRY PREMONITION
(COMMENDATORY —) PUFF BLURB
(DEATH —) OBIT OBITUARY
(FAVORABLE —) RAVE
(LEGAL —) CAVEAT
(MARRIAGE —) BANS BANNS
(OFFICIAL —) EDICT SUMMONS BULLETIN CITATION
(PUBLIC —) BAN EDICT BULLETIN SPOTLIGHT
NOTICEABLE CRUDE GROSS FLASHY MARKED SIGNAL EVIDENT NOTABLE POINTED SALIENT HANDSOME PALPABLE STRIKING OBTRUSIVE PROMINENT CONSPICUOUS OUTSTANDING
(UNDESIRABLY —) CONSPICUOUS
NOTIFICATION DRUM NOTE AVISO NOTICE SUMMONS
(PUBLIC —) SIGN
NOTIFY ALL BID CRY JOG CITE PAGE TELL WARN ADVISE

INFORM NOTICE SIGNAL APPRISE DECLARE FRUTIFY PUBLISH ACQUAINT INTIMATE
NOTION BEE GEE BUZZ IDEA IDEE KINK MAZE OMEN VIEW WHIM FANCY FREIT IMAGE SENSE THING WARES BELIEF CEMENT DESIRE DONNEE GADGET MAGGOT NOTICE THEORY VAGARY BROMIDE CONCEIT CONCEPT FANTASY INKLING MAROTTE OPINION THOUGHT WRINKLE CATEGORY FOLKLORE PHANTASY SUPPOSAL WHIMWHAM INTENTION SENTIMENT WHIRLIGIG
(FALSE —) IDOL
(FIXED —) TICK
(FOOLISH —) VAPOR VAPOUR
(PUERILE —) BOYISM
(SUPERSTITIOUS —) FREET FREIT
(VISIONARY —) ABSTRACTION
(PL.) SMALLS SMALLWARE
NOTORIETY FAME ECLAT GLORY HONOR RUMOR RENOWN REPUTE PUBLICITY
NOTORIOUS BIG KNOWN ARRANT COMMON CRYING FAMOUS NOTARY STRONG EVIDENT NOTABLE NOTOIRE APPARENT FLAGRANT INFAMOUS MANIFEST EGREGIOUS
NOTORNIS TAKAHE
NOTUS (BROTHER OF —) EURUS BOREAS ZEPHYRUS
(FATHER OF —) AEOLUS ASTRAEUS
(MOTHER OF —) EOS
NOTWITHSTANDING BUT FOR THO YET EVEN WITH ALGATE MAUGER MAUGRE AGAINST ALGATES DESPITE HOWBEIT HOWEVER ALTHOUGH NATHLESS WHATRECK
NOUGAT NUT CANDY NUTSHELL
NOUGHT BAD NIL NOT NOWT ZERO NOCHT WRONG NOTHING USELESS WORTHLESS
NOUMENAL ONTAL ONTIC
NOUN MANE WORD THING SUPINE NOMINAL CONSTRUCT INCREASER
(INDECLINABLE —) APTOTE
(KIND OF —) COMMON PROPER DIPTOTE REGULAR TRIPTOTE MONOPTOTE
(QUOTATION —) HYPOSTASIS
(VERBAL —) GERUND
NOURISH AID FEED FOOD GROW BREED NORSH NURSE TRAIN BATTLE BREAST FOISON FOSTER NORICE REFETE SUCCOR SUCKLE SUPPLY CHERISH DEVELOP EDUCATE NURTURE NUTRIFY PROVIDE SUPPORT SUSTAIN MAINTAIN CULTIVATE REPLENISH STIMULATE
(PREF.) NUTRI
NOURISHING ALMA RICH ALIBLE BATTLE HEARTY STRONG NUTRIENT ALIMENTAL HEALTHFUL NUTRITIVE WHOLESOME NUTRITIOUS
NOURISHMENT DIET FARE FETE FOOD KEEP MEAT MANNA

FOISON FOSTER ALIMENT PABULUM PASTURE NUTRIMENT REFECTION
(PREF.) THREPSO
NOURONIHAR (FATHER OF —) FAKREDDIN
(LOVER OF —) VATHEK
NOUS MIND REASON ALERTNESS INTELLECT
NOUVEAU RICHE PARVENU UPSTART
NOVA SCOTIA (CAPITAL OF —) HALIFAX
(COUNTY OF —) DIGBY HANTS PICTOU
(STRAIT OF —) CANSO
(TOWN OF —) TRURO PICTOU SYDNEY ARICHAT BADDECK DARTMOUTH
NOVA SCOTIAN ACADIAN BLUENOSE
NOVEL HOT NEW BOOK EPIC RARE FRESH PROSE RECIT ROMAN STORY DARING RECENT SERIAL THRILL FICTION ROMANCE STRANGE UNUSUAL NEOTERIC ORIGINAL THRILLER UNCOMMON NARRATIVE PAPERBACK
(BRIEF —) CONTE
(PREF.) CAEN(O) CEN(O)
NOVELIST (ALSO SEE AUTHOR)
NOVELTY FAD NEWEL RENEW CHANGE NEWNESS PRIMEUR WRINKLE CURIOSITY FRESHNESS
NOVEMBER 1 SAMUIN SAMHAIN
NOVEMBER 11 MARTINMAS
NOVICE DUB HAM BOOT COLT PUNK PUNY TIRO TYRO CHELA GOYIN PUPIL ROOKY YOUTH DRONGO RABBIT ROOKIE TYRONE ACOLYTE AMATEUR CONVERT GRIFFIN LEARNER STARTER STUDENT YOUNKER BACHELOR BEGINNER FRESHMAN INEXPERT NEOPHYTE ARCHARIOS GREENHORN NOVITIATE ABECEDARIAN
NOVITIATE FUCHS NOVICERY PROBATION
NOW NOO YET ARAH HERE ARRAH NONCE SINCE TODAY EVENOO EXTANT ANYMORE CURRENT INSTANT PRESENT FORTHWITH PRESENTLY
(— AND THEN) SOMETIMES STOUNDMEAL
(BUT —) ERSTWHILE
(JUST —) ENOW FRESH
NOWADAYS ANYMORE
NOWEL DRAG
NOX NYX
(BROTHER OF —) EREBUS
(FATHER OF —) CHAOS
NOXIOUS BAD ILL EVIL FETID DEADLY NOCENT NOYOUS PUTRID BALEFUL BANEFUL DAMPISH HARMFUL HURTFUL NOCUOUS NOISOME SCADDLE TEDIOUS VICIOUS INFAMOUS VIRULENT INJURIOUS MIASMATIC OFFENSIVE PESTILENT POISONOUS PERNICIOUS
(— AIR) MALARIA

(MORALLY —) UNWHOLESOME
NOZZE DI FIGARO, LE (CHARACTER IN —) FIGARO BARTOLO BASILIO SUSANNA BARBARINA CHERUBINO MARCELLINA
(COMPOSER OF —) MOZART
NOZZLE BIB JET TIP BEAK BIBB NOSE ROSE VENT GIANT SNOUT SPOUT TWEER GROVEL OUTLET MONITOR NIAGARA ORIFICE SHUTOFF ADJUTAGE ROSEHEAD VERMOREL NOSEPIECE
(BLAST FURNACE —) TUYERE
(MINING —) GIANT
NUANCE SHADE NICETY FINESSE GRADATION VARIATION
NUB EAR HUB JAB JAG KEY NOB CORE CRUX GIST HANG KNOB KNOT KNUB LUMP NECK PITH SNAG HEART NUDGE POINT KERNEL NUBBIN EXECUTE
NUBBIN EAR STUB STUMP
NUBIA WRAP CLOUD SCARF
NUBIAN NUBA BARABRA HADENDOA
(— MUSICAL INST.) SISTRUM
NUBILOUS FOGGY MISTY VAGUE CLOUDY OBSCURE
NUCHA NAPE NECK NUKE NUCHE
NUCLEAR ELEMENTARY
NUCLEATE SEED
NUCLEOLUS
(PREF.) PYREN(O)
NUCLEON MESON BARYON MESOTRON
NUCLEOSIDE VICINE INOSINE CYTIDINE ADENOSINE
NUCLEUS HUB CELL CORE GERM KERN PITH ROOT SEED CADRE FOCUS HEART MIDST SPERM UMBRA CENTER COLONY DEUTON KARYON KERNEL MIDDLE ISOTOPE NIDULUS HABENULA MEROCYTE MESOPLAST
(— OF CELL) KARYON
(— OF STARCH GRAIN) HILUM
(— OF SUNSPOT) UMBRA
(ATOMIC —) SPECIES
(CELL —) SYNCARYON HEMIKARYON
(PREF.) **(— OF CELL)** CARY(O) KARY(O)
NUCLIDE ISOTONE
NUDE BARE LOOSE MODEL NAKED SEASAN STATUE UNCLAD DENUDED EXPOSED PICTURE PAINTING STARKERS STRIPPED UNDRESSED
(FRENCH —) ALESAN
(NOT —) DECENT
(RUN —) STREAK
NUDGE JOG NOG NUB WAG GOAD JOLT KNUB LUMP POKE POTE PROD PUSH BLOCK CHUCK DUNCH ELBOW
NUDISM NATURISM GYMNOSOPHY
NUDIST ADAMITE NUDIFIER GYMNOSOPH
NUGATORY IDLE NULL VAIN EMPTY PETTY FUTILE HOLLOW INVALID TRIVIAL USELESS TRIFLING FRUSTRATE WORTHLESS

NUGGET EYE LOB GOLD HUNK LUMP MASS SLUG PRILL YELLOW

NUISANCE BANE BORE EVIL HARM HURT PAIN PEST STING INJURY PLAGUE TERROR VEXATION ANNOYANCE

NULL NIL VOID EMPTY INEPT IRRITE INVALID NULLIFY USELESS VACUOUS NUGATORY FRUSTRATE

NULLAH GORGE GULLY NULLA NALLAH RAVINE

NULLIFY BEAT FLAW LAME NULL UNDO VETO VOID ABATE ANNUL ELIDE ERASE LAPSE CANCEL DEFEAT NEGATE OFFSET REPEAL REVOKE ABOLISH COUNTER DESTROY ABROGATE EVACUATE STULTIFY FRUSTRATE

NULLIFYING DIRIMENT

NULLITY NIHILITY

NUMB DEAD DRUG DULL DAZED FUNNY STONY ASLEEP BENUMB CLUMSY DEADEN STUPID TORPID STUPEFY ENFEEBLE HEBETATE HELPLESS RIGESCENT TABETLESS

NUMBER SUM BAND BODY COPY CURN DRAW FECK HERD HOST LOTS MAIN MANY MESS MORT SLEW SURD TALE TELL COUNT DATUM DIGIT FOLIE GRIST GROUP INDEX ISSUE SCADS SCORE STAND TOTAL WHOLE ADDEND AMOUNT BUNDLE CIPHER ENCORE FACTOR FIGURE FILLER HIRSEL MYRIAD POLICY RECKON SCALAR TICHEL CHIFFER COMPUTE DECIMAL DIVISOR FOLIATE NUMERIC SEVERAL CARDINAL FRACTION NUMERATE QUANTITY CALCULATE MAGNITUDE MULTITUDE MULTIPLIER MULTIPLICAND
(— BETWEEN 4 AND 10) MAIN
(— OF ARROWS) END
(— OF ATOMS) CHAIN
(— OF BEASTS) HERD
(— OF BOMBS) STICK
(— OF BRICKS) CLAMP
(— OF CATTLE) SOUM
(— OF FUR SKINS) TIMBER
(— OF HANKS OF YARN TO POUND) COUNT
(— OF HAWKS) CAST
(— OF HONEYBEES) CLUSTER
(— OF NEEDLES) GAGE GAUGE
(— OF POEMS) EPOS
(— OF SHEARERS) BOARD
(— OF TEA CHESTS) BREAK
(— OF THREADS PER INCH) PITCH
(— OF TRICKS) BOOK
(— OF WORDS) FOLIO
(— THROWN IN CRAPS) POINT
(—S GAME) BUG
(BALLET —) ENTREE
(CARDINAL —) ONE TWO ALEF ALEPH THREE
(COMPLEX —) IMAGINARY
(CONSIDERABLE —) WHEEN HATFUL FISTFUL
(DESCRIBABLE —) SCALAR
(EXCESS —) ADVANTAGE
(EXCESSIVE —) SPATE
(EXTRA —) ENCORE

(GOLDEN —) PRIME
(GOOD —) THRAVE
(GREAT —) LAC HEAP HOST LAKH MORT BREAK HIRST MEINY POWER SHOAL SIGHT SWARM LEGION MYRIAD INFINITE INFINITY THOUSAND MULTITUDE MULTIPLICITY
(GREAT —S) FLOCKS
(GREATER —) MO
(INDEFINITE —) LAC STEEN SUNDRY THRAVE JILLION SEVERAL THREAVE UMPTEEN
(IRRATIONAL —) SURD
(LARGE —) ARMY FECK HERD HOST LUMP PECK SLEW ARRAY CROWD FORCE POWER SCADS SHEAF SPATE STACK STORE WORLD GALLON GOOGOL HIRSEL HIRSLE LEGION MELDER BILLION JILLION PLURALITY
(LARGE —S) STRENGTH
(LEAF —) FOLIO
(LEAST WHOLE —) UNIT
(ODD —S) IMPAIR
(OPPOSITE —) COUSIN
(ORDINAL —) FIRST THIRD SECOND
(PUT ON SERIAL —) FOLIO
(SMALL —) FEW CURN CURRAN HANDFUL PAUCITY SPATTER
(TOTAL —) AMOUNT
(VAST —) HORDE
(WHOLE —) ALL DIGIT INTEGER
(PREF.) ARITHM(O) ARITHMETICO LOGARITHMO NUMERO
(SUFF.) ARITHM PLY
(— TERMINATION) TEEN
(— THAT FILLS) FUL FULL
(ORDINAL —) ETH

NUMBERED MENE

NUMBERING TALE COUNT FOLIATION

NUMBERS
(PREF.) (ODD —) PERISSO

NUMBFISH TORPEDO

NUMBING WARELESS

NUMBLES UMBLES INNARDS NOMBLES VISCERA ENTRAILS

NUMBNESS STUPOR TORPOR STUPIDITY
(PREF.) NARC(O)

NUMEN DEITY GENIUS SPIRIT VESTAL DIVINITY

NUMERAL (ALSO SEE NUMBER) SUM WORD DIGIT CIPHER FIGURE LETTER CHAPTER NUMERIC
(— STYLE) ROMAN ARABIC
(CLOCK —) CHAPTER

NUMERATIVE PEN SEGREGATIVE

NUMEROUS BIG LOTS MAIN MANY RANK RIFE GREAT LARGE STOUR DIVERS GALORE LEGION MYRIAD SUNDRY UNRIDE COPIOUS CROWDED ENDLESS FEARFUL FERTILE PROFUSE SEVERAL TEEMING UMPTEEN ABUNDANT FREQUENT MANIFOLD MULTIPLE POPULOUS THRONGED EXTENSIVE MULTIFOLD NUMBERFUL PLENTIFUL
(— AND POWERFUL) MAIN
(MODERATELY —) FAIR

(VERY —) EXCESSIVE
(PREF.) MYRI

NUMIDIA (BIRD OF —) DEMOISELLE
(CITY OF —) HIPPO
(KING OF —) JUGURTHA

NUMITOR (GRANDSON OF —) REMUS ROMULUS

NUMSKULL NUM DAFF DOLT FLAT BOOBY DUNCE LACKWIT BONEHEAD BLOCKHEAD LAMEBRAIN

NUN BIRD SMEW CLARE CLERK MONIAL PIGEON SISTER TERESA VESTAL VOWESS CLUNIAC CONFINE DEANESS DEVOTEE EXTERNE MINCHEN MONKESS RECLUSE TEATINE THEATIN BASILIAN CHAPLAIN CLARISSE PRIORESS TITMOUSE URBANIST URSULINE VISITANT VOTARESS ANGELICAL CARMELITE LORETTINE PRIESTESS RELIGEUSE
(— BIRD) MONASE TITMOUSE
(— HEADDRESS) WIMPLE
(— HOOD) FAILLE
(— MOTH) TUSSOCK
(— ORDER) MARIST TRAPPIST DOMINICAN LORETTINE
(CHIEF —) ABBA ABBESS MOTHER
(LATIN —) VESTA
(SON OF —) JOSHUA

NUNCIATE NUNCIO ANNOUNCER MESSENGER

NUNCIO ENVOY NUNCE LEGATE NUNTIUS DELEGATE MESSENGER

NUNCUPATE DECLARE DEDICATE INSCRIBE PROCLAIM DESIGNATE PRONOUNCE

NUNCUPATIVE ORAL SPOKEN UNWRITTEN

NUNNERY ABBEY NUNRY CONVENT CLOISTER MINCHERY
(HEAD OF —) ABBESS

NUPSON FOOL SIMPLETON

NUPTIAL BRIDAL GENIAL THORAL MARITAL WEDDING ESPOUSAL HYMENEAL MARRIAGE
(PL.) SPOUSAL ESPOUSAL HYMENEALS WIFETHING

NUQUE NAPE NECK

NURSE AMAH AYAH BABA CARE DHAI FEED NANA NUSS REAR SUCK TEND BONNE MAMMY NANNY NORSH ATTEND BAYMAN CRADLE FOMENT FOSTER GRANNY KEEPER NANNIE NORICE NUZZLE SISTER SITTER SUCKLE UMFAAN CHERISH FURTHER NOURISH NURTURE PROMOTE CULTIVATE ENCOURAGE NURSEMAID
(— A GRIEVANCE) SULK
(— OF HIAWATHA) NOKOMIS
(— OF ULYSSES) EURYCLEA
(— OF ZEUS) AMALTHEA CYNOSURA
(— SHARK) GATA
(GULLIVER'S —) GLUMDALCLITCH
(WET —) DHAI DHOLL

NURSERY RACE CRECHE BROODER FOSTERAGE

NURSLING BABY NORRY NURRY

FOSTER FOUNDLING
(PREF.) THREMMATO

NURTURE CARE DIET FEED FOOD REAR TEND BREED NURSE TRAIN COCKER CRADLE FOSTER NUZZLE CHERISH EDUCATE SUPPORT BREEDING NORTELRY TRAINING EDUCATION ESTABLISH NUTRIMENT
(PREF.) TROPH(O)

NUSAIRI ANSARIE

NUT ACA BEN BUR COB GUY JOU NIT TAP ANTA BURR COLA CORE DOLT FOOL FROG HEAD KOLA LORE MAST NITE PILI PITH SEED TASK ACORN BETEL BONGA BUNGA CRANK FLAKE FRUIT GLANS HAZEL HICAN JUVIA PECAN TRYMA ALMOND BONDUC BRAZIL CASHEW FELLOW HICCAN ILLIPE KERNEL PEANUT PIGNON PINION PYRENE CASTANA FILBERT HICKORY PROBLEM APPLENUT BEECHNUT BREADNUT CHESTNUT GOORANUT LARRIKIN CAPOTASTO CHINKAPIN ECCENTRIC MACADAMIA PHILOPENA
(— COAL) ANTHRACITE
(— GRASS) SEDGE
(— OF VIOLIN BOW) FROG
(— PINE) PIGNON PINOON PIGNOLIA
(CASHEW —) SEDGE ANACARD
(CONSORT OF —) GEB KEB SET
(DAUGHTER OF —) ISIS NEPHTHYS
(FALLEN —S) SHACK
(PALM —) BETEL LICHI BABASSU COCOANUT COQUILLA
(PERT. TO —) NUCAL
(RIPE —) LEAMER
(RUSH —) CHUFA
(SON OF —) RA OSIRIS
(PL.) MASTAGE
(PREF.) CARY(O) KARY(O) NUCI

NUT-BEARING NUCIFEROUS

NUTCRACKER XENOPS CRACKER PILLORY MEATBIRD NUTCRACK NUTHATCH NUCIFRAGA NUTPECKER

NUTHATCH SITTA TOMTIT XENOPS JARBIRD SITTINE TITMOUSE NUTJOBBER

NUTHOOK BEADLE CONSTABLE

NUTLET NUCULE PYRENA PYRENE GYROLITH

NUTMEG SEED TREE SPICE BEAVER CALABASH NOTEMIGGE NOTEMUGGE
(— COVERING) MACE
(— STATE) CONNECTICUT
(PREF.) MYRISTICI

NUTRIA FUR COYPU GREGE NEUTRIA RAGONDIN

NUTRIENT STARTER
(PLANT —S) SIDEDRESS
(PL.) FOOD HEMOTROPHE

NUTRIMENT DIET FOOD KEEP VIANDS ALIMENT PABULUM SUPPORT NOURISHMENT

NUTRITION EUTROPHY TROPHISM
(IMPERFECT —) DYSTROPHY DYSTROPHIA

(PREF.) TROPH(O)
(SUFF.) TROPHIA TROPHIC
TROPHY
NUTRITIOUS BATTLE BAITTLE
TROPHIC
NUTRITIVE ALIBLE
NUT-SHAPED NUCIFORM
NUTSHELL SHELL INCLUDER
NUTTY GAGA LOCO NUTS RACY
ZANY BUGGY CRAZY QUEER SPICY
FRUITY LOVING SPRUCE
AMOROUS FOOLISH PIQUANT
ZESTFUL DEMENTED PLEASANT
ECCENTRIC FLAVORFUL
NUX VOMICA SNAKEWOOD
NUZZLE DIG PET ROOT NURSE
SNUFF BURROW CARESS FONDLE
FOSTER NESTLE NUDDLE

NURTURE SNOOZLE SNUGGLE
SNUZZLE
NYCTEUS (BROTHER OF —) LYCUS
(DAUGHTER OF —) ANTIOPE
(FATHER OF —) HYRIEUS
(MOTHER OF —) CLONIA
NYE EYAS NEST NIDE BROOD
FLOCK
NYMPH FLY GIRL MAIA MITE MUSE
PINK PIXY PUPA TICK AEGLE
DRYAD HOURI LARVA NAIAD
NIXIE OREAD SIREN SYLPH BYBLIS
CYRENE DAMSEL DAPHNE HELICE
HESTIA KELPIE MAIDEN NEREID
SPRITE SYRINX UNDINE CORYCIA
ERYTHEA HESPERA LIRIOPE
OCEANID CALLISTO CYNOSURA
EURYDICE MARPESSA PROSOPON

BUTTERFLY HAMADRYAD
(— BELOVED BY PAN) SYRINX
(— BELOVED OF NARCISSUS) ECHO
(— OF FOUNTAIN) EGERIA
SALMACIS
(— OF HILLS) OREAD
(— OF MEADOWS) LIMONIAD
(— OF MESSINA STRAIT) SCYLLA
(— OF MT. IDA) OENONE
(CITY —) POLIAD
(LAKE —) NAIAD LIMNIAD
(OCEAN —) SIREN GALATEA
OCEANID SEAMAID
(QUEEN OF —S) MAB
(RIVER —) NAIS NAIAD
(SEA —) MERROW NEREID
CALYPSO GALATEA MERMAID
(WATER —) NAIS EGERIA LURLEI

UNDINE APSARAS HYDRIAD
JUTURNA RUSALKA EPHYDRIAD
(WOOD —) DRYAD NAPEA
ARETHUSA
(PL.) HYADS THRIAI CAMENAE
(PREF.) NYMPHO
NYMPHAEA CASTALY CASTALIA
NYMPHOMANIAC (BOVINE —)
BULLER
NYROCA AYTHYA
NYSSA TUPELO
NYSTAGMUS TIC WINK
NYX NOX NIGHT
(— PERSONIFIED) NIGHT
(BROTHER OF —) EREBUS
(DAUGHTER OF —) DAY ERIS LIGHT
(HUSBAND OF —) CHAOS
(SON OF —) CHARON

O

O HO OH OCH ZERO CIPHER OMICRON
OAF AUF BOOR DOLT FOOL LOUT CLOWN DUNCE IDIOT OUPHE YOKEL MUCKER NASHGAB PALOOKA POMPION BLOCKHEAD FOUNDLING SCHLEMIEL SIMPLETON
OAHU (— BIRD) JIBI
OAK CLUB CORK HOLM ILEX BRAVE BRIAR EMORY HOLLY ROBLE ROBUR ACAJOU BAREEN CERRIS ENCINA KERMES STRONG TOUMEY VALOMA AMBROSE BELLOTA BELLOTE DURMAST EGILOPS KELLOGG PALAYAN TURTOSA BEEFWOOD BLUEJACK CHAMPION CHAPARRO FLITTERN WAINSCOT BLACKJACK CHINKAPIN QUERCITRON
(— BARK) CRUT
(— FRUIT) MAST ACORN CAMATA BELLOTE
(JERUSALEM —) AMBROSE
(WHITE —) ROBLE
(YOUNG —) FLITTERN
(PREF.) DRY(O) QUERCI
OAKUM OCCAM
OAKWOOD MESA
OAR AIR BOW PLY ROW PALM PEEL POLE ALOOF BLADE ROWER SCULL SPOON SWAPE SWEEP YULOH PADDLE PALLET PROPEL OARSMAN PROPELLER
(— BLADE) PALM PEEL WASH
(— FULCRUM) LOCK THOLE OARLOCK ROWLOCK
(BOW —) GOUGER
(HANDLE OF —) GRASP
(INBOARD PORTION OF —) LOOM
(PART OF —) GRIP LOOM BLADE SHAFT
(STERN —) SCULL SKULL
(PREF.) COPE(O) REMI
OARLOCK LOCK THOLE ROWLOCK
OARSMAN OAR REMEX ROWER BOWMAN STROKE BENCHER SCULLER WATERMAN
OASIS BAR OJO SPA MERV SIWA WADI WADY SPRING
OAST HOST KILN OVEN COCKLE OASTHOUSE
OAT AIT WOT FEED FOOD PIPE POEM SKEG SONG AUCHT CHEAT GRAIN HAVER PEARL ANGORA EGILOPS
(— HUSK) SHOOD FLIGHT
(— RENT) AVENAGE
(EDIBLE PORTION OF —) GROATS
(FALSE WILD —S) FATUOID
(HUSKED —) SHEALING
(NAKED —) PILLAS PILCORN
(UNTHRASHED —) OATHAY

(WILD —S) HAVERGRASS
(PL.) CORN GRAIN HAVER GROUTS PROVENDER WHITECORN
OATCAKE CAPER HAVERCAKE SOURBREAD
OATEN AITEN
OATH OD ADS BAN DAD DOD GAD GAR GOL GOR GUM ODD SAM VOW BOND CRUM CUSS DARN DRAT ECOD EGAD GEEZ GOSH HECK JEEZ JING NIGS OONS SANG SLID SLUD WORD BEDAD BEGAD BEGOB BLIMY CURSE DAMME DEUCE GOLLY HOKEY MORDU PARDY SACRE SFOOT SLIFE SNIGS SWEAR YERRA ADSBUD APPEAL CRACKY CRIKEY CRIPES CRUMBS FEALTY JABERS JERNIE NEAKES PARDIE PLEDGE RAPPER SBLOOD SLIGHT STRUTH ZOUNDS BEGORRA BEGORRY BEJESUS BYRLADY CORBLEU GADSLID GEEWHIZ GEEWIZZ JEEPERS JIMMINY MORBLEU ODSFISH ODZOOKS PROMISE THUNDER ANATHEMA BEJABERS BODYKINS CRICKETY GADZOOKS JURAMENT PITIKINS SANCTION SEREMENT SNIGGERS SPLUTTER AFFIDAVIT BEJABBERS BLASPHEMY DODGASTED EXPLETIVE PROFANITY SACRAMENT SLIDIKINS SWEARWORD
OATMEAL OATS STODGE YELLOW POTTAGE DRAMMOCK PORRIDGE
(— BREAD) ANACK JANNACK
(— CAKE) PONE SCONE
OATS (MIXED ROLLED —) GRANOLA
(PREF.) AVENO
OBADIAH ABDIAS
(FATHER OF —) AZEL JEHIEL SHEMAIAH
(SON OF —) ISHMAIAH
OBAL (FATHER OF —) JOKTAN
OBCLUDE HIDE OCCLUDE
OBDURATE FIRM HARD BALKY HARSH INERT ROCKY ROUGH STARK STONY DOGGED INURED MULISH RUGGED SEVERE STURDY SULLEN ADAMANT CALLOUS HARDENED PERVERSE STUBBORN IMPASSIVE UNBENDING
OBEAH OBI OBIA CHARM FETISH VOODOO
OBECHE ARERE AYOUS SAMBA
OBED (FATHER OF —) BOAZ JARHA SHEMAIAH
(MOTHER OF —) RUTH
(SON OF —) JESSE AZARIAH
OBEDEDOM (FATHER OF —) JEDUTHUN
OBEDIENCE ORDER FEALTY CONTROL SERVICE

DOCILITY OBEISANCE
OBEDIENT BENT RULY TALL TAME BUXOM DOCILE PLIANT DEVOTED DUTEOUS DUTIFUL HEEDFUL MINDFUL ORDERLY SUBJECT AMENABLE BIDDABLE YIELDING ATTENTIVE OBSERVING SERVIABLE TRACTABLE
(— TO THE HELM) HANDY
OBEDIENTIARY PRIOR
OBEDIENT PLANT DRAGONHEAD
OBEISANCE BOW LEG JOUK BINGE CONGE HONOR SALAM CONGEE CRINGE CURTSY FEALTY HOMAGE SALAAM CURTSEY DEFERENCE HUMBLESSO REFERENCE
OBELISK MARK PYLON SHAFT DAGGER GUGLIA GUGLIO NEEDLE OBELUS PILLAR AGUGLIA MONUMENT HAGIOLITH
OBERON KING POEM FAIRY OPERA SATELLITE
(CHARACTER IN —) HUON PUCK FATIMA OBERON TITANIA SHERASMIN
(COMPOSER OF —) WEBER
(WIFE OF —) TITANIA
OBESE FAT FOZY PLUMP PUDGY PUFFY PURSY STOUT FLESHY PORTLY PYKNIC ROTUND TURGID ADIPOSE PORCINE PURSIVE BLUBBERY LIPAROUS CORPULENT
OBESITY FAT FATNESS LIPOSIS ADIPOSIS FOZINESS ADIPOSITY
OBEY EAR HEAR HEED MIND DEFER YIELD COMPLY FOLLOW OBEISH SUBMIT CONFORM EXECUTE OBSERVE OBTEMPER
(— HELM) STEER
OBFUSCATE DIM CLOUD DARKEN MUDDLE OBFUSK CONFUSE MYSTIFY OBSCURE PERPLEX STUPEFY BEWILDER
OBI OBE SASH CHARM OBEAH FETICH FETISH GIRDLE
OBIT MASS REST DEATH NOTICE OBITAL DECEASE RELEASE SERVICE OBITUARY NECROLOGY OBSEQUIES
OBITUARY NECROLOGY
OBJECT AIM END TAP BALK BEEF CARE CARP FINE GOAL IDEA ITEM KICK MAIN MIND PASS SAKE WHAT ARGUE CAVIL DEMUR GRIPE PINCH POINT SCOPE SIGHT TELOS THING AFFAIR DESIGN EMBLEM ENTITY FIGURE GADGET INTENT MATTER MOTIVE OPPOSE TARGET ARTICLE DINGBAT DISLIKE DISSENT MEANING PROTEST PURPOSE QUARREL REALITY RECLAIM NOUMENON TENDENCY CHALLENGE

INTENTION SPECTACLE
(— HAVING FLAWS) SPOIL
(— OF AMBITION) MAIN
(— OF ART) VASE CURIO VIRTU ANTIQUE BIBELOT FIGURINE
(— OF CRITICISM) BUTT
(— OF DEVOTION) IDOL TOTEM FETISH
(— OF DISGUST) UG
(— OF DREAD) BOGY BOGEY BOGIE BOGGIE BUGBEAR
(— OF KNOWLEDGE) SCIBILE
(— OF PILGRIMAGE) CAABA KAABAH
(— OF PURSUIT) SHADOW
(— OF RELIANCE) STAY
(— OF RIDICULE) FUN GAME
(— OF SCORN) GECK SCOFF BYWORD HISSING DERISION
(— OF TERROR) BUG
(— OF THOUGHT) CONSTRUCT
(— OF WONDER) ADMIRATION
(— TO BE TILTED AT) QUINTAIN
(BELOVED —) MINION DARLING MISTRESS
(BULKY —) WODGE
(CONICAL —) ACORN
(CONSPICUOUS —) LANDMARK
(CONTAMINATED —S) FOMITES
(CURVED —) BELLY
(CYLINDRICAL —) BOLE
(DECORATIVE —) BIBELOT
(DESIRABLE —) GRAIL
(FACTORY-MADE —S) ARTWORK
(MINUTE —) ATOM MITE
(ROUND —) COB RONDEL TRINDLE TRUNDLE
(SACRED —) URIM ZOGO GUACA HUACA SHRINE CHURINGA
(SILLY —) INANITY
(SMALL —) PIRLIE
(TRANSCENDENTAL —) ENTITY
(ULTIMATE —) TELOS
(UNIDENTIFIED FLYING —) BOGEY
(VILE —S) SCUM
(WORTHLESS —) SPLINTER
(PREF.) (FILTHY OR DIRTY —) RHYPARO RHYPO
OBJECTION OB BAR BUT BEEF CRAB FUSS KICK CAVIL DEMUR DOUBT BOGGLE CHESON QUARREL QUIBBLE SCRUPLE QUESTION CHALLENGE CRITICISM EXCEPTION
OBJECTIONABLE VILE AWFUL HORRID GHASTLY UNLUSTY UNLIKELY FRIGHTFUL OBNOXIOUS OFFENSIVE
OBJECTIVE AIM END FAIR GAME GOAL HOME REAL SAKE OUTER ACTUAL AMORAL ANIMUS DESIGN MOTIVE TARGET PURPOSE DETACHED TANGIBLE UNBIASED

DIRECTION INTENTION POSITIVAL QUAESITUM ULTIMATUM

OBJECTOR (CONSCIENTIOUS —) CONCHY

OBJURGATE BAN JAW DAMN ABUSE CHIDE CURSE DECRY BERATE REBUKE REPROVE UPBRAID VITUPER EXECRATE CASTIGATE

OBLATE MONK OFFER DEDICATE MONASTIC

OBLATION CORBAN OFLETE SACRED CHARITY ANAPHORA DEVOTION OFFERING SACRIFICE

OBLIGATE COMMIT STRICT

OBLIGATED BOUND LIABLE BEHOLDEN

OBLIGATION DUE IOU TIE VOW BAIL BAND BOND CALL DEBT DUTY KNOT LOAD LOAN MUST NOTE OATH ONUS SEAL CHECK OUGHT SCORE ARREAR BURDEN CHARGE CONSOL CORVEE CUSTOM FEALTY PLEDGE ANNUITY BONDAGE PROMISE TRIBUTE CONTRACT HYPOTHEC SECURITY WARRANTY AGREEMENT LIABILITY
(— NOT TO MARRY) CELIBACY
(— TO RENDER RENT) CUSTOM
(MORAL —) BOND DUTY
(PL.) STRINGS

OBLIGATORY BINDING BOUNDEN FORCIBLE IMPOSING LIGATORY INCUMBENT MANDATORY

OBLIGE PUT HOLD PAWN DRIVE FAVOR FORCE COMPEL ENGAGE PLEASE GRATIFY REQUIRE CONCLUDE MORTGAGE OBLIGATE CONSTRAIN ACCOMMODATE

OBLIGED FAIN BOUND DEBTED BOUNDEN DEBTFUL FAVORED PLEASED PLEDGED BEHOLDEN GRATEFUL OBSTRICT BEHOLDING OBLIGATED

OBLIGING KIND BUXOM CIVIL CLEVER TOWARD AMIABLE FAVOROUS AGREEABLE COURTEOUS FAVORABLE OFFICIOUS

OBLIQUE AWRY BIAS SIDE SKEW ASKEW BEVEL CROSS SLANT ASLANT ASWASH LOUCHE SQUINT THWART ASKANCE AWKWARD CROOKED EMBELIF EVASIVE SCALENE SIDLING SLOPING DIAGONAL INCLINED INDIRECT SIDELONG SIDEWAYS SIDEWISE SLANTING TORTUOUS INDICULAR UNDERHAND
(— IN MINING) CLINIC
(— STROKE) SLASH SOLIDUS
(— WORK) SWASHWORK
(PREF.) LECHRI(O) LOX(O) PLAGI(O)

OBLIQUELY AGEE AWRY BIAS AGLEE ASIDE ASKEW AWASH SLANT SLOPE ASLANT ASWASH ASKANCE ASQUINT EMBELIF BIASWISE SIDELONG SIDEWAYS SIDEWISE

OBLIQUITY BIAS DIRT SWEEP DIRTINESS

OBLITERATE INK BLOT DELE RASE

RAZE WIPE ANNUL BLACK COVER ERASE SMEAR CANCEL DELETE EFFACE SPONGE ABOLISH DESTROY EXPUNGE OUTRAZE SCRATCH OVERSCORE

OBLITERATION BLOT RASURE ERASURE NEGATION SYNIZESIS

OBLIVION LETHE LIMBO PARDON AMNESTY NIRVANA SILENCE OUBLIANCE

OBLIVIOUS AMORT BLISSFUL HEEDLESS OBLIVIAL FORGETFUL

OBLONG CHITON EVELONG AVELONGE EVENLONG ELONGATED
(ROUNDED —) ELLIPSE

OBLOQUY ABUSE BLAME ODIUM INFAMY CALUMNY CENSURE REPROOF CONTEMPT DISGRACE DISHONOR OBLICQUE

OBNOXIOUS FOUL PERT VILE CURST CURSED FAULTY HORRID LIABLE ODIOUS RANCID SEPTIC HATEFUL INVIDIOUS OFFENSIVE REPUGNANT VERMINOUS

OBOE PIPE REED WAIT AULOS SHAWM SURNAI SURNAY HAUTBOY MUSETTE PIFFERO CHIRIMIA HAUTBOIS SCHALMEY SZOPELKA CHALUMEAU
(— DI CACCIA) TENOROON FAGOTTINO
(BASS —) RACKETT
(PREF.) AUL(O)

OBOLE MAIL MAILLE

OBSCENE PAW FOUL LEWD NAST BAWDY GROSS NASTY ROCKY COARSE FILTHY IMPURE RIBALD SMUTTY VULGAR KNAVISH PROFANE IMMODEST INDECENT LOATHSOME OFFENSIVE REPULSIVE SALACIOUS
(— CULT) AISCHROLATREIA

OBSCENITY DIRT RIBALDRY SCULDUDDERY
(PREF.) COPR(O)

OBSCURATION COVER ECLIPSE

OBSCURE DIM FOG BLOT BLUR DARK DEEP HARD HART HAZY HIDE PALE SLUR BEDIM BEFOG BLACK BLANK BLEND BLIND CLOUD COVER DUSKY FAINT FOGGY GLOOM INNER LOWLY MIRKY MISTY MUDDY MURKY SHADE SMEAR STAIN VAGUE BEMIST CLOUDY DARKEN DARKLE DEADEN DELUDE GLOOMY HUMBLE MYSTIC OCCULT OPAQUE REMOTE SHADOW SOMBER SUBTLE BECLOUD BENIGHT CLOUDED CONCEAL CONFUSE CRABBED CRYPTIC ECLIPSE ENCRUST ENVELOP OBLIQUE OVERLAY OVERTOP SHADOWY SLUBBER TARNISH UNCLEAR UNKNOWN UNNOTED ABSTRUSE DARKLING DISGUISE DOUBTFUL FAMELESS MYSTICAL NAMELESS NUBILOUS OBSTRUSE ORACULAR OVERSILE CALIGINOUS
(MAKE —) BECLOUD
(PREF.) APHAN(O)

OBSCURED HAZY HIDDEN

BLINDED CLOUDED DUSKISH DARKSOME DISGUISED INFUSCATE

OBSCURITY FOG MIST CLOUD GLOOM SHADE CALIGO SHADOW DIMNESS OPACITY PRIVACY SILENCE DARKNESS TENEBRES BLINDNESS SECLUSION
(DELIBERATE —) OBLIQUITY
(PL.) MURLEMEWES

OBSECRATE BEG PRAY BESEECH ENTREAT PETITION

OBSEQUIES MASS OBIT PYRE WAKE RITES SERVICE FUNERALS

OBSEQUIOUS SLICK MENIAL SUPPLE COURTLY DEVOTED DUTEOUS DUTIFUL FAWNING SERVILE SLAVISH VERNILE CRINGING OBEDIENT OBEISANT TOADYING ASSIDUOUS ATTENTIVE COMPLIANT
(— PERSON) LIMBERHAM

OBSEQUY RITE EXEQUY RITUAL FUNERAL CEREMONY

OBSERVANCE ACT FORM RITE RULE FREET HONOR CUSTOM REGARD KEEPING CEREMONY PRACTICE ADHERENCE ATTENTION DEFERENCE INDICTION SOLEMNITY
(— OF PROPRIETIES) DECORUM BREEDING ETIQUETTE
(RELIGIOUS —) NOVENA SACRAMENT
(REVERENTIAL —) PUJA
(SUPERSTITIOUS —) FREET FREIT
(PL.) FUNERAL CEREMONY

OBSERVANT ALERT EYEFUL CAREFUL HEEDFUL MINDFUL DILIGENT VIGILANT WATCHFUL REGARDFUL PERCEPTIVE

OBSERVATION EYE SPY HEED IDEA NOTE RAOB VIEW SIGHT WATCH ESPIAL LOGION NOTICE REGARD REMARK AUSPICE AUTOPSY COMMENT CONTACT DESCANT OPINION EYESIGHT GAZEMENT SCHOLION SCHOLIUM ASSERTION ATTENTION ESPIONAGE COGNIZANCE PERCEPTION
(— BY BALLOON) PIBAL
(ECOLOGICAL —S) ANNUATION
(PRELIMINARY —) PROEM

OBSERVATIONISM SCHAULUST

OBSERVATORY LICK TOWER LOOKOUT PALOMAR

OBSERVE LO EYE SEE SPY ESPY HEED HOLD KEEP LOOK MAKE MARK MIND NARK NOTA NOTE OBEY SPOT TENT TOUT TWIG WAIT YEME ABIDE QUOTE SMOKE STUDY UTTER WATCH ADHERE ADVERT ATHOLD BEHOLD DETECT DEVISE FOLLOW NOTICE NOTIFY REGARD REMARK SURVEY COMMENT DISCERN EXPRESS MENTION PROFESS RESPECT WITNESS PERCEIVE PRESERVE SPECTATE ADVERTISE CELEBRATE SOLEMNIZE
(— CLOSELY) SMOKE
(— DULLY) BLEAR

(— OPPOSING POSITION) KEY

OBSERVER O BIRDER CORNER WATCHER AUDIENCE INFORMER ONLOOKER BYSTANDER SCRUTATOR SPECTATOR

OBSESS RIDE BESET HAUNT HARASS INVEST OBSEDE BESIEGE HAGRIDE POSSESS PREOCCUPY

OBSESSED CRAZY DOTTY HAPPY HIPPED BESOTTED

OBSESSION TIC CRAZE MANIA SIEGE MAGGOT ECSTASY FIXATION
(SUFF.) (— WITH) ITIS

OBSIDIAN CORE LAVA IZTLE IZTLI LAPIS

OBSOLETE OLD DEAD PAST DATED PASSE BYGONE EFFETE ABOLETE ANCIENT ARCHAIC CLASSIC DISUSED EFFACED EXTINCT OUTWORN OUTDATED OUTMODED OVERWORN DISCARDED

OBSTACLE BAR DAM LET BOYG BUMP DRAG JUMP OBEX SNAG STAY STOP BLOCK CHECK CLAMP CRIMP FENCE HITCH HYDRA SPOKE STICK STILE ABATIS BUNKER FRAISE HOCKET HURDLE LOGJAM OBJECT RETARD ANSTOSS BARRIER CHICANE FIVEBAR STOPPER BLOCKADE MOLEHILL BARRICADE CONDITION HINDRANCE ROADBLOCK TURNAGAIN
(— TO VIRTUE) SLANDER
(GOLF —) HAZARD
(INSURMOUNTABLE —) IMPASSE

OBSTETRICIAN ACCOUCHEUR

OBSTETRICS TOCOLOGY MAIEUTICS MIDWIFERY

OBSTINACY BRASS CONTUMACY

OBSTINATE SET SOT DOUR FIRM SULY BALKY FIXED ROWDY RUSTY STIFF STOUT TOUGH ASSISH CUSSED DOGGED KNOBBY MULISH STEEVE STUFFY STUPID STURDY SULLEN THRAWN UNRULY ASININE BULLISH CRABBED FROWARD PEEVISH RESTIVE WILLFUL CROTCHED OBDURATE PERVERSE PREFRACT RECUSANT RENITENT STOMACHY STUBBORN FORERIGHT PIGHEADED STONEWALL TENACIOUS
(NOT —) SUPPLE

OBSTREPEROUS LOUD WILD NOISY RORTY UNRULY RAUGHTY CLAMOROUS

OBSTRUCT BAR DAM DIT GAG JAM CLOG COOP CRAB DITT FILL FOUL JAMB STOP TRIG TRIP BESET BLANK BLOCK CHAIN CHECK CHOKE CROSS DELAY HEDGE THROW ARREST CUMBER FORBAR HAMPER HOBBLE IMPEDE OPPOSE PESTER RETARD STIFLE THWART WAYLAY WINDER BARRIER FORELAY OCCLUDE BLOCKADE EMBOLIZE ENCUMBER FLOUNDER OBTURATE OPPILATE BARRICADE

EMBARRASS INCOMMODE
OBSTRUCTION BAR DAM GAG LET
RUB BOOM BUMP CLOG SLUG
SNAG STAY STOP BLOCK CHOKE
GORCE HITCH SPOKE HAMPER
TAPPEN THWART BARRACE
BARRAGE BARRIER BLINDER
CHOKAGE EMBOLISM OBSTACLE
STOPPAGE EMPHRAXIS
OCCLUSION
(— IN OILWELL) BRIDGE
(— IN RIVER) GORGE
(— IN TEAT) SPIDER
(— IN VALVE) GAG
(— OF BLOOD VESSEL) EMBOLISM
(— OF PINE LEAVES) TAPPEN
(INNER —) LOAD
OBTAIN BEG BUM BUY EKE GET
PAN WIN EARN FANG FIND GAIN
HENT REAP ANNEX CADGE
CATCH ETTLE REACH AREACH
ARECHE ARRIVE ATTAIN BORROW
DERIVE EXPEDE SECURE SPONGE
ACHIEVE ACQUIRE CAPTURE
CHEVISE COMPASS DEMERIT
EXTRACT POSSESS PREVAIL
PROCURE RECEIVE SUCCEED
PURCHASE SCROUNGE
(— BY CHANCE) DRAW
(— BY HEAT) EXCOCT
(— BY REQUEST) IMPETRATE
(— BY THREAT) EXTORT
(— CONTROL) ENGROSS
(— DISHONESTLY) CROOK SHARP
FLEECE NOBBLE SKELDER
(— MONEY FROM) BLEED
(— PERMISSION) CLEAR
OBTAINABLE GOING GETTABLE
AVAILABLE DERIVABLE
SECURABLE
OBTAINED (— AT SCENE OF CRIME)
LATENT
OBTRUDE DIN JET SORN EJECT
EXPEL GLARE FLAUNT IMPOSE
MEDDLE THRUST INTRUDE
INTERFERE
OBTRUSIVE FRESH PUSHY GARISH
BLATANT FORWARD PUSHING
BUMPTIOUS INTRUSIVE
OBTUND DULL BLUNT QUELL
DEADEN
OBTURATOR MUSHROOM
OBTUSE DIM DULL BLINK BLUNT
CRASS DENSE THICK BOVINE
OPAQUE STUPID STUBBED
BOEOTIAN HEBETATE PURBLIND
(NOT —) ACUTE
OBVERSE FACE FRONT CONVERSE
(— OF COIN) MAN HEAD
OBVIATE PREVENT PRECLUDE
FORESTALL
OBVIOUS LOUD OPEN BROAD
CLEAR CRUDE FRANK GROSS
NAKED OVERT PLAIN SLICK
STARK LIABLE PATENT BLATANT
EVIDENT EXPOSED GLARING
SHALLOW SUBJECT VISIBLE
APPARENT DISTINCT MANIFEST
PALPABLE BAREFACED
PROMINENT
(NOT —) DEEP INNER ARCANE
HIDDEN MASKED OCCULT SECRET
SUBTLE DELICATE DOUBTFUL

PROFOUND INEVIDENT
OBVOLUTE CONTORTED
OVERLAPPING
OCA OKA TUBER OXALIS SORREL
SOURSOP
OCARINA CAMOTE
OCCASION SEL BOUT CALL GIVE
HINT NEED SELE SITH TIDE TIME
TURN BREAK BREED CASUS
CAUSE CHARE EVENT INFER
NONCE RAISE SITHE SLANT
STOUR WHILE YIELD AFFAIR
AUTHOR CHANCE COURSE
EXCUSE PERIOD REASON STOUND
CHESOUN INSPIRE OPENING
PRETEXT QUARREL CEREMONY
ENGENDER EXIGENCY FUNCTION
INCIDENT INSTANCE CONDITION
ENCHEASON HAPPENING
(— GRIEF) GRIEVE
(— OF EXCITEMENT) ALARM
ALARUM
(DEFINITE —) TIDE
(EXCITING —) BLAST
(FAVORABLE —) ADVANTAGE
(FESTIVE —) UTAS BEANO
HOLIDAY SHINDIG BEANFEAST
MERRYMAKING
(HAPPY —) SIMHAH SIMCHAH
(SOCIAL —) COFFEE
(SPECIAL —) CEREMONY
OCCASIONAL ODD ORRA STRAY
ANTRIN CASUAL DAIMEN SCARCE
POPPING EPISODIC FUGITIVE
SPORADIC IRREGULAR
OCCASIONALLY EVERY BETIMES
SOMETIME SOMETIMES
OCCASIVE SETTING WESTWARD
OCCIDENTAL WEST PONENT
WESTERN HESPERIAN
WESTERNER
OCCLUDE SHUT SORB CLOSE
ABSORB OBSTRUCT
OCCLUSAL MORSAL
OCCLUSION CORONARY
ARTICULATION
(SUFF.) CLEISIS CLISIS
OCCULT MAGIC ARCANE HIDDEN
LATENT MYSTIC SECRET VOODOO
ALCHEMY CRYPTIC ECLIPSE
UNKNOWN ESOTERIC MYSTICAL
SIBYLLIC CONCEALED RECONDITE
SIBYLLINE
(— SCIENCE) ESOTERICS
(PREF.) CRYPT(O) KRYPT(O)
OCCULTATION ECLIPSE
OCCULTISM MAGIC CABALA
MYSTERY
OCCUPANCY POSSESSION
OCCUPANT HOLDER INMATE
RENTER TENANT CITIZEN
DWELLER RESIDENT INCUMBENT
(— OF THEATER GALLERY) GOD
(SUFF.) ITE
OCCUPATION ART JOB LAY USE
CALL GAME LINE NOTE PLOY TOIL
WORK BERTH CRAFT GRAFT
TRADE BILLET CAREER EMPLOY
METIER RACKET SPHERE TENURE
THRIFT CALLING CONCERN
CONTROL MYSTERY PURSUIT
QUALITY SERVICE ACTIVITY
BUSINESS FUNCTION INDUSTRY

INVASION PLUMBING VOCATION
(— OF MIND) ABSORPTION
(SUBORDINATE —) HOBBY
AVOCATION
OCCUPIED BUSY FULL HELD KEPT
RAPT TOOK ACTIVE INTENT
ENGAGED ABSORBED CAPTURED
(FULLY —) ENGROSSED
OCCUPY LIE SIT USE BUSY FILL
HAVE HOLD KEEP TAKE WARM
AMUSE BELAY BESET DWELL
ABSORB BETAKE EMPLOY ENGAGE
EXPEND FULFIL OBTAIN TENANT
COHABIT CONCERN CONTAIN
ENGROSS ENTREAT IMPROVE
INHABIT INVOLVE OVERSIT
PERVADE POSSESS SWALLOW
DISSOLVE GARRISON INTEREST
POPULATE POURPRISE
(— ILLEGALLY) JUMP
(— QUARTERS) CAMP
OCCUR BE GO COME COOK FALL
GIVE MAKE MEET PASS RISE SORT
ARISE BREAK CLASH EXIST INCUR
LIGHT APPEAR ARRIVE BEFALL
BETIDE CHANCE HAPPEN
PROCEED TRANSPIRE
(— AGAIN) RECUR REPEAT
(— BY CHANCE) LIGHT
(— TO) CROSS ENTER STRIKE
OCCURRENCE GO HAP CASE FACT
ITEM NOTE REDE EVENT WEIRD
EPISODE PASSAGE INCIDENT
JUNCTURE OCCASION
ENCOUNTER FREQUENCE
HAPPENING
(CHANCE —) ADVENTURE
CONTINGENT
(COMMON —) USE FREQUENCY
(FREQUENT —) COMMUNITY
(SIMULTANEOUS —) COINCIDENCE
(SUDDEN —) ZAP
(SUPERNATURAL —) MIRACLE
(UNEXPECTED —) SUDDEN
BLIZZARD BOMBSHELL
(UNFORTUNATE —) CASUALTY
(UNUSUAL —) ODDITY
OCCURRING (— AT NIGHTFALL)
ACRONICAL
(— AT REGULAR INTERVALS) HORAL
(— AT TWILIGHT) CREPUSCULAR
(— BY TURN) ALTERNATE
(— EVERY EIGHT DAYS) OCTAN
(— EVERY FOURTH YEAR)
PENTETERIC
(— FREQUENTLY) COMMON
(— IN USUAL PLACE) ENTOPIC
OCEAN SEA BLUE BRIM DEEP MAIN
POND BRINE DRINK ARCTIC
INDIAN EXPANSE NEPTUNE
PACIFIC ATLANTIC ANTARCTIC
(— FLOATING MATTER) ALGAE
LAGAN FLOTSAM
(— ROUTE) LANE
(— SPRAY) IRONWOOD
CREAMCUPS
(— SWELL) SEA
(ON THE —) ASEA
**(RELATING TO — BELOW 6000
METERS)** HADAL
OCEANIA MALAYA AUSTRALIA
MELANESIA POLYNESIA
(SACRED OBJECT OF —) ZOGO

OCEANIC NAVAL MARINE PELAGIC
NAUTICAL AEQUOREAL
OCEANOGRAPHER (ALSO SEE
HYDROGRAPHER)
OCEANUS TITAN
(DAUGHTER OF —) DORIS OCEANID
EURYNOME
(FATHER OF —) URANUS OURANOS
(MOTHER OF —) GAEA GAIA
(SISTER OF —) TETHYS
(SON OF —) NEREUS
(WIFE OF —) TETHYS
OCELLUS EYE EYELET STEMMA
EYESPOT
OCELOT CAT TOGER LEOPARD
WILDCAT
OCHER RUD SIL KEEL OAKER
OCHRE TIVER ABRAUM RADDLE
ALMAGRA TANGIER
(BLACK —) WAD WADD
(RED —) RUD KEEL TIVER ABRAUM
REDDLE RUBRIC RUDDLE
KOKOWAI
(YELLOW —) SIL SPRUCE
OCOTILLO COACHWHIP
CANDLEWOOD
OCRAN (SON OF —) PAGIEL
OCREA OCHREA SHEATH
OCTAHEDROID HYPERCUBE
TESSERACT
OCTAVE UTAS UTIS EIGHT EIGHTH
OTTAVA HUITAIN DIAPASON
SHEMINITH
(— FLUTE) FLAUTINO
(— OF THE SEVENTH) FOURTEENTH
(— SINGING) MAGADIZE
(DIMINISHED —) SEMIDIAPASON
(FATHER OF —) ARGANTE
(TRIPLE —) TRIDIAPASON
OCTAVIA (BROTHER OF —)
AUGUSTUS
(HUSBAND OF —) ANTONY
OCTAVO EIGHTS
OCTET OCTAVE OCTUOR HUITAIN
OTTETTO
OCTOPUS HEE POLYP POULP
PREKE SQUID CUTTLE CATFISH
POLYPOD POLYPUS SCUTTLE
DIBRANCH OCTOPEAN DEVILFISH
(— ARM) TENTACLE
(AUTHOR OF —) NORRIS
(CHARACTER IN —) DYKE TREE
HILMA LYMAN HOOVEN MAGNUS
SARRIA BEHRMAN CARAHER
DELANEY DERRICK PRESLEY
RUGGLES VANAMEE ANNIXTER
SHELGRIM CEDARQUIST
GENSLINGER
(SECRETION OF —) INK
OCTOROON METIS MESTEE
MUSTEE MESTIZO METISSE
OCTAROON
OCTROI TAX GRANT PRIVILEGE
OCTUPLE EIGHTFOLD
OCUBY RUM
OCULAR OPTIC VISUAL OCULARY
OPTICAL ORBITAL EYEPIECE
OCULUS MUNDI OPAL
OCYRRHOE (FATHER OF —) CHIRON
(MOTHER OF —) CHARICLO
ODD AUK AWK OUT RUM FELL
LEFT LONE ORRA RARE ANTIC
CRAZY DIPPY DROLL EXTRA

FLAKY FUNKY FUNNY IMPAR
KINKY OUTRE QUEER UNKET
UNKID WEIRD FLAKEY IMPAIR
QUAINT SINGLE UNEVEN UNIQUE
AZYGOUS BAROQUE BIZARRE
COMICAL CURIOUS ERRATIC
STRANGE UNEQUAL UNUSUAL
FANCIFUL FREAKISH PECULIAR
SINGULAR UNPAIRED BURLESQUE
ECCENTRIC FANTASTIC
GROTESQUE LAUGHABLE
SQUIRRELY UNMATCHED
WHIMSICAL
(— **JOBMAN**) JOEY
(PREF.) AZYGO IMPARI
ODDBALL SPOOK
ODDITY GIG QUIP JIMJAM
RUMNESS QUIZZITY PECULIARITY
(PL.) PURLICUES
ODDMAN UMPIRE ARBITER
FLOATER REFEREE
ODDS BISK EDGE CHALK PRICE
BISQUE DISCORD DISPUTE
QUARREL HANDICAP VARIANCE
ADVANTAGE DISPARITY
(— **AND ENDS**) ORTS BROTT
REFUSE SCRAPS GIBLETS
SECONDS FEWTRILS REMNANTS
SHAKINGS ETCETERAS
FRAGMENTS
(**AT** —) ACROSS
(**EXTRAVAGANT** —) POUNDAGE
(**FAVORABLE** —) PERCENTAGE
ODE HYMN POEM SONG LYRIC
PAEAN PSALM MONODY ODELET
CANZONA CANZONE EPICEDE
CANTICLE PALINODE PINDARIC
SERENATA STASIMON EPICEDIUM
EPINICION PARABASIS
ODED (**SON OF** —) AZARIAH
ODENATHUS (**WIFE OF** —) ZENOBIA
ODEON HALL ODEUM GALLERY
THEATER
ODIN OTHIN WODAN WODEN
WOTAN
(**BROTHER OF** —) VE VILI
(**CREATED BY** —) ASK EMBLA
(**DAUGHTER-IN-LAW OF** —) NANNA
(**DESCENDANT OF** —) SCYLD
(**FATHER OF** —) BOR BORR
(**HALL OF** —) VALHALLA
(**HORSE OF** —) SLEIPNER SLEIPNIR
(**MANSION OF** —) GLADSHEIM
(**MOTHER OF** —) BESTLA
(**PALACE OF** —) SYN
(**RAVEN OF** —) HUGIN MUNIN
(**RING OF** —) DRAUPNIR
(**SHIP OF** —) NAGLFAR
SKIDBLADNIR
(**SON OF** —) TYR THOR VALI BALDR
BALDER
(**SPEAR OF** —) GUNGNIR
(**SWORD OF** —) GRAM
(**THRONE OF** —) HLIDSKJALF
(**WIFE OF** —) FRIA RIND FRIGG
RINDR FRIGGA
(**WOLF OF** —) GERI FREKI
ODIOUS FOUL LOTH UGLY VILE
LOATH INFAND ODIBLE HATABLE
HATEFUL HEINOUS HIDEOUS
DAMNABLE FLAGRANT
INFAMOUS ABHORRENT
INVIDIOUS OBNOXIOUS

OFFENSIVE REPUGNANT
ODIUM HATRED STIGMA DISLIKE
AVERSION DISFAVOR DISGRACE
DISHONOR ANTIPATHY
(**PUBLIC** —) ENVY
ODOACER (**FATHER OF** —) EDECON
ODOMETER ODOGRAPH VIAMETER
WAYWISER HODOMETER
PEDOMETER
ODONTALGIA TOOTHACHE
ODOR AIR FUME FUNK NOSE OLID
TANG WAFF WAFT AROMA
EWDER FETOR FLAIR FUMET
NIDOR SCENT SMACK SMELL
SNUFF SPICE STINK BREATH
FLAVOR FOETOR HODURE
REPUTE STENCH BOUQUET
ESSENCE FUMETTE NOSEGAY
PERFUME VERDURE PUNGENCE
EFFLUVIUM EMPYREUMA
FRAGRANCE REDOLENCE
(— **FROM FLOWERS**) FUME
(— **OF GAME**) FUMET
(— **OF HAY**) NOSE
(**BAD** —) EWDER FROWST STENCH
(**DISGUSTING** —) STINK
(**FOUL** —) FIST MEPHITIS
(**FRESH** —) YMUR
(**PUNGENT** —) SPICE
(**SPICY** —) BALM
(**STUDY OF** —S) OSMICS
(PREF.) OSM(O)
(SUFF.) OSMA OSPHRESIA
ODORIFEROUS BALMY OLENT
ODOROUS FRAGRANT
ODOROUS FOUL BALMY OLENT
SMELLY ODORANT AROMATIC
FRAGRANT NIDOROSE NIDOROUS
PERFUMED REDOLENT SCENTFUL
SMELLFUL
ODYSSEUS ULYSSES
(**DOG OF** —) ARGOS
(**FATHER OF** —) LAERTES SISYPHUS
(**FRIEND OF** —) MENTOR
(**ISLAND OF** —) ITHACA
(**SON OF** —) TELEGONUS
TELEMACHUS
(**WIFE OF** —) PENELOPE
ODYSSEY (**AUTHOR OF** —) HOMER
(**CHARACTER IN** —) ARETE CIRCE
HELEN AEOLUS NESTOR
EUMAEUS ALCINOUS MENELAUS
NAUSICAA ODYSSEUS PENELOPE
DEMODOCUS EURYCLEIA
TEIRESIAS POLYPHEMUS
TELEMACHUS
OEAX (**BROTHER OF** —) PALAMEDES
(**FATHER OF** —) NAUPLIUS
(**MOTHER OF** —) CLYMENE
OEBALUS (**FATHER OF** —) TELON
(**SON OF** —) ICARIUS HIPPOCOON
TYNDAREUS
(**WIFE OF** —) GORGOPHONE
OECIST OEKIST COLONIZER
OEDIPUS OEDIPAL
(**BROTHER-IN-LAW OF** —) CREON
(**DAUGHTER OF** —) ISMENE
ANTIGONE
(**FATHER OF** —) LAIUS
(**FOSTER MOTHER OF** —) PERIBOEA
(**MOTHER OF** —) JOCASTA
(**SON OF** —) ETEOCLES POLYNICES
(**WIFE OF** —) JOCASTA

OEIL-DE-BOEUF OCULUS
OEILLADE OGLE ELIAD EYLIAD
GLANCE ILLIAD
OENEUS (**DAUGHTER OF** —) GORGE
DEIANIRA
(**FATHER OF** —) PORTHEUS
(**SON OF** —) TOXEUS TYDEUS
MELEAGER
(**WIFE OF** —) ALTHAEA
OENOCHOE OLPE PROCHOOS
OENOMAUS (**DAUGHTER OF** —)
HIPPODAMIA
(**FATHER OF** —) ARES MARS
(**MOTHER OF** —) STEROPE
(**SON OF** —) LEUCIPPUS
DYSPONTEUS HIPPODAMUS
OENOMETER VINOMETER
OENONE (**FATHER OF** —) CEBREN
(**LOVER OF** —) PARIS
(**SON OF** —) CORYTHUS
OENOPION (**DAUGHTER OF** —)
MEROPE
(**FATHER OF** —) DIONYSUS
(**WIFE OF** —) HELICE
OESTRID FLY
(— **LARVA**) BOT
OESTRUS RUT FURY HEAT STING
DESIRE ESTRUS FRENZY IMPULSE
STIMULUS
OEUVRE OPUS WORK
OF A O BY DE OFF VAN VON FROM
HAVE TILL WITH ABOUT
(— **AGE**) AE
(— **ALL**) AVA ALDER ALLER
(— **COURSE**) NATCH
(— **DEATH**) M
(— **EACH**) ANA PER SING
(— **THIS DAY**) HODIERNAL
(— **THIS MONTH**) HM
(SUFF.) AL AR ILE INE ISH ISTIC
ITIC ITIOUS ORIOUS ORY
OFF BY AFF FAR ODD WET AFAR
AGEE AWAY DOFF DOWN GONE
ALONG ASIDE RIGHT WONKY
WRONG ABSENT CUCKOO
DEPART REMOTE DISTANT
FURTHER REMOVED SEAWARD
TAINTED ABNORMAL OPPOSITE
(— **GUARD**) TARDY
(— **THE PATH**) ASTRAY
(— **THE SUBJECT**) AFIELD
(— **THE WIND**) ROOM ROOMWARD
(**FAR** —) DISTANT
(PREF.) AP APH APO DE
OFFAL GURRY WASTE REFUSE
CARRION DOGMEAT GARBAGE
LEAVING RUBBISH GRALLOCH
(— **OF FISH**) GURRY STOSH
(**MILLING** —S) GRIT
OFF-BEAT KOOKY
OFFBREAK GOOGLY
OFF-CENTER ECCENTRIC
EXCENTRIC
OFF-COLOR BLUE RISQUE
SUGGESTIVE
OFFEND CAG ERR PET SIN VEX
GALL HARM HUFF HURT MIFF
RASP RASS ABUSE ANGER ANNOY
GRATE GRILL PIQUE SHOCK SPITE
TOUCH WRONG AGUILT ATTACK
GRIEVE INJURE INSULT NETTLE
REVOLT AFFRONT DEFAULT
DISDAIN MORTIFY OUTRAGE

PROVOKE REGRATE STOMACH
UMBRAGE VIOLATE CONFRONT
DISTASTE IRRITATE TRESPASS
DISOBLIGE DISPLEASE
OFFENDED HUFF MIFF SORE
AVERTED FROISSE INJURED
INSULTED
OFFENDER SINNER CULPRIT
MISDOER PECCANT HABITUAL
OFFENDANT
(**FIRST** —) STAR
OFFENSE PET SIN HUFF LACK SLIP
WITE ABUSE CRIME ERROR FAULT
GRIEF GUILT MALUM PIQUE
SNUFF ATTACK BIGAMY DELICT
FELONY PIACLE PRITCH REATUS
STRUNT AFFRONT DEFAULT
DEMERIT DUDGEON LARCENY
MISDEED OUTRAGE SCANDAL
UMBRAGE PECCANCY TRESPASS
EXTORTION INDECORUM
INDIGNITY THEFTBOTE
(— **AGAINST LAW**) MALUM DELICT
DELICTUM
(— **AGAINST MORALITY**) EVIL
CRIME
(**SLIGHT** —) PECCADILLO
OFFENSIVE BAD ACID EVIL FOUL
HARD UGLY BILGY CRUDE DIRTY
FETID GROSS NASTY SLIMY
COARSE FROWZY GARISH HORRID
RANCID RIBALD ROTTEN ABUSIVE
BEASTLY FULSOME HATEFUL
HIDEOUS NOISOME PECCANT
RASPING SCARLET DREADFUL
INVADING MEPHITIC SHOCKING
STINKING UNSAVORY
LOATHSOME OBNOXIOUS
REPUGNANT REVOLTING
SCANDALOUS
OFFER GO BID PUT BODE GIVE
HAND LEND PLEA SHOW TAKE
TEND DEFER HEAVE PARTY
SHORE START ADDUCE AFFORD
ALLEGE DELATE INJECT OBLATE
OPPOSE PREFER SUBMIT SUPPLY
TENDER ADVANCE BIDDING
COMMEND EXHIBIT PRESENT
PROFFER PROPINE PROPOSE
SUGGEST OVERTURE PROPOSAL
VOLUNTEER
(— **EXCUSE**) ALIBI
(— **FOR SALE**) HAWK EXPOSE
(— **IN SACRIFICE**) IMMOLATE
(— **PROOF**) APPROVE
(— **PUBLICLY**) JACTITATE
(— **TO VERIFY**) AVER
(— **UP**) APPEAL
(**LAST** —) ULTIMATUM
(**SOLEMN** —) PLEDGE
(**UNACCEPTED** —) POLLICITATION
OFFERING BID ALMS BALI DALI
DEAL GIFT HOST SOMA DOLLY
ENTRY CORBAN NUZZER OFLETE
PIACLE PRESENT RETABLO
TRIBUTE ANATHEMA DEVOTION
DONATION LIBATION OBLATION
PESHKASH PIACULUM SACRIFICE
(— **TO GOD**) CORBAN DEODATE
(— **TO HOUSEHOLD DEITIES**) BALI
(**EUCHARISTIC** —) ANAPHORA
(**PEACE** —S) PACIFICS
(**RELIGIOUS** —) OBLATION

(SACRIFICIAL —) HOLOCAUST
(THEATRICAL —) FLUFF
(PL.) HIERA ALTARAGE INFERIAE
OFF-GLIDE EXIT VOCULE DETENTE
OFFHAND AIRY CURT GLIB SOON
ADLIB BLUSH HASTY ABRUPT
BREEZY CASUAL BRUSQUE
READILY CARELESS CAVALIER
GLANCING INFORMAL
EXTEMPORE IMPROMPTU
UNSTUDIED
OFFICE HAT JOB SEE BOMA DUTY
NONE PART POST ROLE ROOM
SHOP TASK TOGA WIKE WORK
PLACE STINT TRUST WIKEN
YAMEN ABBACY AGENCY BUREAU
CHARGE DAFTAR DIWANI DUFTER
METIER MISTER BULLPEN
CAMARIN CENTRAL DEWANEE
DROSTDY EDILITY MYSTERY
SERVICE STATION SURGERY
AEDILITY CAPACITY CUTCHERY
ENSIGNCY FUNCTION KINGSHIP
MINISTRY POSITION PROVINCE
WOOLPACK BAILIWICK
BANKSHALL SITUATION
(— BOY) CHOKRA
(— CHIEF) BOSS MANAGER
(— OF BISHOP) LAWN
(— OF JUDGE) BENCH ERMINE
(— OF PROFESSOR) CHAIR
(— OF ROMAN CURIA) DATARY
DATARIA
(— OF RULER) REGENCY
(— OF THE DEAD) DIRGE
(— WORKER) CLERK STENO TYPIST
SECRETARY
(BRANCH —) WING
(CASHIER'S —) CAISSE
(CLERICAL —) CASSOCK
(DIVINE —) AKOLUTHIA
(ECCLESIASTICAL —) FROCK
BENEFICE EXORCIST
(HIGH —) DIGNITY
(LITURGICAL —) SEXT SERVICE
(MAGISTRATE'S —) KACHAHRI
(MORNING —) ORTHRON ORTHROS
(NAVAL —S) BEACH
(PAY —) WANIGAN
(POLICE —) NICK
(PRIESTLY —) SACERDOCY
(PRINTING —) CHAPEL IMPRIMERY
(RECORD —) CHANCERY
(RESIGN AN —) DEMIT
(TIMEKEEPER'S —) PENNYHOLE
(SUFF.) ATE CY DOM SHIP URE
OFFICEHOLDER IN WINNER
OFFICIAL PLACEMAN
OFFICER (ALSO SEE OFFICIAL) COP
TAB AIDE EXEC EXON FLAG HOLD
NASI SWAB VOGT AGENT CHIEF
CRIER DEWAN DIWAN GRAND
GRAVE GROOM JURAT SEWER
TAXOR USHER ALCADE BEADLE
BEAGLE BEDRAL BUTLER CENSOR
DEPUTY DIRECT ENSIGN GAILLI
GEREFA HERALD KOTWAL
LAWMAN LICTOR MANAGE
ORATOR PARNAS REDTAB SYNDIC
TINDAL ADJOINT AGISTOR
ALNAGER ASSIZER BAILIFF
COMMAND CONDUCT CORONER
DUUMVIR EPAULET FEDERAL

FEODARY GAVELER GENERAL
JEMADAR KLEAGLE LOBSTER
MUSTANG NAPERER PANTLER
PATROON REGIDOR SANCTUM
SCHEPEN SHERIFF SPEAKER
STEWARD WHIPPER WOODMAN
ADJUTANT ALDERMAN ALGUACIL
ANDREEVE BANNERET
CHAFFWAX COFFERER CURSITOR
DOORWARD FORESTER
GOVERNOR GRASSMAN
MERESMAN MINISTER PALATINE
QUESTEUR REPORTER TIPSTAFF
VISCOUNT WOODWARD
CONSTABLE DIKEGRAVE
FINANCIER INTENDANT
MODERATOR PAYMASTER
SCHOOLMAN TAHSILDAR
(— OF CHURCH) ABBOT ELDER
DEACON SEXTON ANTISTES
DEFENSOR LAMPADARY
SACRISTAN
(— OF COURT) MACER MASTER
BAILIFF FEODARY FILACER
CURSITOR DEMPSTER EXAMINER
SERGEANT ASSOCIATE
BYRLAWMAN SURROGATE
(— OF FORESTS) AGISTER AGISTOR
(— OF KING'S STABLES) AVENER
(BARDIC —) DRUID
(CAVALRY —) CORNET
(CHIEF —) NASI DEWAN DAROGA
PARNAS PRESIDENT
(CUSTOMS —) GAGER SHARK
GAUGER JERQUER DOUANIER
SEARCHER SURVEYOR TIDESMAN
(GREEK —) STRATEGOS
STRATEGUS
(JAPANESE —) SHIKKEN
(MASONIC —) EAST KING DEACON
STEWARD
(MILITARY —) NAIG NAIK COMES
MAJOR SUBAH ENSIGN NAIQUE
RANKER SARDAR SIRDAR
CAPTAIN COLONEL GENERAL
JEMADAR MARSHAL SUBADAR
WARRANT COMMANDER
RABSHAKEH SHAVETAIL
(MINOR —) CHINOVNIK
(MONASTERY —) CELLARER
(MUNICIPAL —) SCHOUT
(NAVAL —) CPO EXON MATE SWAB
BOSUN ENSIGN PURSER YEOMAN
ADMIRAL CAPTAIN MUSTANG
SPOTTER YOUNKER SUNDOWNER
(PAPAL —) DATARY
(POLICE —) PIG PEON RURAL
EXEMPT JAVERT KOTWAL
RUNNER SBIRRO ALYTARCH
SEARCHER THANADAR DETECTIVE
ROUNDSMAN
(PRESIDING —) CHAIRONE
CHAIRPERSON
(PUBLIC —) JUDGE FISCAL NOTARY
PODESTA
(ROMAN —) LICTOR
(SHERIFF'S —) FANG BEAGLE
BAILIFF BULLDOG HUISSIER
(SHIP'S —) MATE FANTOD
(STAFF —) TAB AIDE REDTAB
ADJUTANT
(TURKISH —) AGA AGHA MUTE
VIZIR VIZIER BIMBASHI BINBASHI

(UNIVERSITY —) DEAN PROVOST
(WARRANT —) MACHINIST
(PL.) BRAID BRASS STAFF
OFFICIAL (ALSO SEE OFFICER) AGA
BEG DEY VIP AMIN BOSS KUAN
KWAN TRUE AGENT AHONG
AMALA AMBAN AMEEN AMLAH
CLERK EDILE EPHOR GYANI HAJIB
HOMER JURAT LIMMU LINER
MAYOR NAZIR REEVE SAHIB
AEDILE ARCHON ATABEG
BASHAW CENSOR CONSUL
EPARCH EPONYM FISCAL FORMAL
GABBAI GRIEVE HAZZAN HERALD
LAWMAN MASTER NOTARY
PANDIT PREVOT RABMAG SATRAP
SCRIBE SEALER SINGER TAOTAI
TAOYIN TRONER VERGER
WARDEN WEDANA ALMONER
APOSTLE ASIARCH BURGESS
CERTAIN JEMADAR LANDRAT
MARSHAL MOORMAN PRISTAW
REFEREE STALLAR STARTER
SUBASHI ALDERMAN APPROVED
CARDINAL CELLARER CUSTOMER
DOGBERRY GOVERNOR LINESMAN
MANDARIN PRYTANIS VESTIARY
WHIFFLER EXECUTIVE
MAJORDOMO OMBUDSMAN
SELECTMAN MAGISTRATE
(— APPROVAL) VISA VISE
(— DECREE) WRIT UKASE
(BLUNDERING —) DOGBERRY
(EISTEDDFOD —) DRUID
(PALACE —) PALADIN
(POMPOUS —) BUMBLE
(PRETENTIOUS —) PANJANDRUM
(PL.) KEYS PHAR OMLAH
OFFICIATE ACT FILL SERVE SUPPLY
PERFORM CELEBRATE
OFFICIATOR DEICIDE
OFFICIOUS BUSY COOL PERT
SAUCY FORMAL FORTHY PUSHING
ARROGANT IMPUDENT INFORMAL
MEDDLING OFFICIAL INBEARING
PRAGMATIC
OFFING OFF FUTURE PICTURE
OFFISH CLAMMY UPSTAGE
OFFSCOURINGS MUD SCURF
OFF-SEASON LAYOFF
OFFSET SLAB STEP ALTAR CRIMP
ERASE POISE CANCEL CONTRA
JOGGLE REDEEM SETOFF
BALANCE COUNTER LATERAL
RETREAT SETBACK PROPAGULE
(— ON BULB) SPLIT
OFFSHOOT GET PUP ROD SON
LIMB SPUR BOUGH ISSUE SCION
SHOOT SPRIG BRANCH FILIAL
GROWTH MEMBER OFFSET
SPROUT ADJUNCT APOPHYSIS
FILIATION OUTGROWTH
RAMIFICATION
(— OF LAKE) BAYOU
OFFSHORE DEEPWATER
OFFSPRING BOY FRY IMP KID KIN
SON BRAT BURD CHIT HEIR SEED
SLIP BIRTH BREED BROOD CHILD
FRUIT ISSUE SCION SPAWN
BEGATS DUSTEE EMBRYO FOSTER
GRIQUA JUMART PROLES RESULT
STRAIN STRIND MORISCO
NISHADA OUTCOME PRODUCE

PRODUCT PROGENY YOUNGER
CHILDREN DAUGHTER DEMISANG
GENITURE INCREASE KINDLING
BAIRNTEAM MUSTAFINA
(— OF FAIRIES) CHANGELING
(— OF NEGRO AND MULATTO)
GRIFFE
(— OF WITCH) HAGSEED HOLDIKEN
(MYTHICAL —) JUMART
(PREMATURE —) CASTLING
(PREF.) GEN(O) GON(O) PAEDO
PEDO PROLI
(SUFF.) ITE TOKOUS
OF HUMAN BONDAGE (AUTHOR
OF —) MAUGHAM
(CHARACTER IN —) CAREY EMILY
ERLIN FANNY NORAH PRICE
SALLY WEEKS LAWSON LOUISA
NESBIT PHILIP ROGERS THORPE
ATHELNY CLUTTON HAYWARD
MILDRED WILLIAM CRONSHAW
WILKINSON
OFICINA WORKS OFFICE FACTORY
OFLETE WAFER OBLATION
OFFERING
OF MICE AND MEN (AUTHOR OF —)
STEINBECK
(CHARACTER IN —) SLIM CANDY
SMALL CROOKS CURLEY GEORGE
LENNIE MILTON
OFTEN OFT AFTEN OFTLY
COMMON EFTSOONS FREQUENT
REPEATED
(VERY —) CONTINUALLY
OF TIME AND THE RIVER
(AUTHOR OF —) WOLFE
(CHARACTER IN —) ANN GANT
JOEL WANG BASCOM ELINOR
EUGENE PIERCE ROBERT WEAVER
COULSON FRANCIS HATCHER
MORNAYE PENTLAND
OGDOAD EIGHT OCTOAD OGDOAS
OCTONARY
OGEE (ALSO SEE MOLDING) CYMA
GULA TALON MOLDING
OGIVAL HEATER
OGLE EYE GAZE LEER LOOK MASH
STARE GLANCE EXAMINE
MARLOCK SMICKER OEILLADE
OGRE ORC BOYG BRUTE DEMON
GHOUL GIANT HUGON TYRANT
YAKSHA BUGABOO BUGBEAR
MONSTER WINDIGO
OGRESS PELLET GUNSTONE
OGTIERN LORD MASTER
OGYGIAN ANCIENT PRIMEVAL
OH OU OW ACH OUCH

RIVER: MIAMI MAUMEE SCIOTO CUYAHOGA MUSKINGUM
STATE BIRD: CARDINAL
STATE FLOWER: CARNATION
STATE TREE: BUCKEYE
TOWN: ADA LIMA TROY ADENA AKRON BEREA CADIZ NILES XENIA CANTON DAYTON LORAIN MENTOR TOLEDO CHARDON COLUMBUS SANDUSKY CLEVELAND

OIL BEN FAT ILE ULE BALM CHIA DIKA FUEL ZEST BRIBE CRUDE JUICE OLEUM SMEAR STOCK TRAIN ULYIE ULZIE ACEITE ANOINT BINDER BUTTER CARDOL CHRISM CREESH EUPION GREASE LIQUOR SAFROL SMOOTH ZACHUN CEDRIUM ESSENCE LANOLIN MYRRHOL PHLOROL RETINOL VETIVER BERGAMOT COUMARIN ERIGERON GINGEROL PHTHALAN SDRAVETS TETRALIN CARVACROL LUBRICATE PETROLEUM
(— BEETLE) MELOE MELOID
(— CAKE) SEEDCAKE
(— CAN) OILER
(— CASK) RIER
(— FROM ORANGE FLOWERS) NEROLI
(— LAMP) LUCIGEN
(— OF TURPENTINE) CAMPHENE CAMPHINE
(— PALM) OILBERRY
(— PAN) SUMP
(— PLANT) SESAME
(— ROCK) SHALE LIMESTONE
(— TREE) EBOE POON TUNG MAHWA
(— VESSEL) DRUM OLPE CRUET CRUSE TANKER CRESSET
(— WELL) DUSTER GASSER GUSHER WILDCAT
(BUTTER —) GHEE
(COAL —) PHOTOGEN
(CONSECRATED —) CHRISM
(FISH —) GURRY
(FIXED —) COCUM KOKAM KOKUM
(FLOWER —) ABSOLUTE
(FRAGRANT —) ATAR OTTO ATTAR OTTAR CAFFEOL BERGAMOT CAFFEONE GERANIOL
(INFERIOR —) MIDDLING
(LINSEED —) CARRON LINOLEUM
(MINERAL —) NAPHTHA KEROSENE
(PINE —) FROTHER
(PUNGENT —) CAJUPUT
(SESAME —) GINGILI SIRITCH
(SOLID —) KIKUEL
(VEGETABLE —) MACASSAR
(VULCANIZED —) FACTICE
(WHALE —) SPERM TRAIN
(PREF.) ELAEO ELAIO ELEO OLEI OLEO
OILBIRD FATBIRD GUACHARO
OILFISH ESCOLAR
OILSEED TIL TEEL SESAME LINSEED RAPESEED
OILSKIN OIL OILER SQUAM OILCASE OILCOAT SLICKER
OILSTONE HONE

SHALE WHETSTONE
OILY FAT GLIB BLAND FATTY LOEIC OLEIC SLEEK SOAPY SUAVE GREASY OILISH OLEOSE OLEOUS SMARMY SMOOTH SUPPLE PINGUID SERVILE SLIPPERY UNCTUOUS COMPLIANT PLAUSIBLE
(PREF.) LIPAR(O)
OINTMENT UNG BALM MULL NARD PASTE SALVE SMEAR BALSAM CERATE CEROMA CHARGE CHRISM GREASE POMADE REMEDY UNGUENT EYESALVE POPULEON REMOLADE SPIKENARD WHITFIELD
(— OF GODS) AMBROSIA
OJIBWAY CHIPPEWA SAULTEUR CHIPPEWAY
OKA OCHA OQUE OQUI OCQUE
OKAPI GIRAFFINE
OKAY OK YES HUNK OKEH HUNKY APPROVE CORRECT SANCTION AUTHORIZE
OKIA OKET OUNCE
OKINAWA (CAPITAL OF —) NAHA

OKLAHOMA
CAPITAL: OKLAHOMACITY
COLLEGE: CAMERON LANGSTON PHILLIPS
COUNTY: KAY COAL LOVE ADAIR ATOKA CADDO GREER OSAGE ALFALFA OKFUSKEE OKMULGEE
INDIAN TRIBE: WACO WICHITA TAWAKONI
LAKE: EUFAULA OOLOGAH
MOUNTAINS: OUACHITA
NATIVE: OKIE SOONER
NICKNAME: SOONER
RIVER: RED GRAND WASHITA ARKANSAS CANADIAN CIMARRON
STATE FLOWER: MISTLETOE
STATE TREE: REDBUD
TOWN: ADA JAY ALVA ENID HUGO ALTUS MIAMI PONCA TULSA ELRENO GUYMON IDABEL LAWTON MADILL TALOGA VINITA ANTLERS SAPULPA SHAWNEE ANADARKO FORTSILL MUSKOGEE

OKRA GOBO OKRO BAMIA BENDY GOBBO GOMBO GUBBO GUMBO OCHRA BENDEE MALLOW BANDAKA BANDICOY BANDIKAI
OLD AGY ELD AGED AULD COLD WOLD YALD ANILE HOARY STALE WOULD FORMER FOROLD INFIRM MATURE SENILE SHABBY VETUST AGEABLE ANCIENT ANTIQUE ARCHAIC ELDERLY FORWORN OGYGIAN UMWHILE DECREPIT MEDIEVAL OBSOLETE DODDERING HACKNEYED SENESCENT VENERABLE
(— AND MELLOW) CRUSTY
(— BAILEY) GAOL JAIL PRISON
(— CLOTHESMAN) POCO
(— FAITHFUL) GEYSER
(— HAND) LONGTIMER
(— MAID) SPINSTER THORNBACK

(— MAN) ANTIQUITY WHITEBEARD
(— SOD) EIRE ERIN IRELAND
(— SQUAW) DIVER HOUND MOMMY CALLOO CALLOW COWEEN DUCKER QUANDY OLDWIFE SCOLDER COCKAWEE LONGTAIL SHARPTAIL SOUTHERLY
(— WOMAN) HAG CRONE GAMMER
(BEING LESS THAN 13 YEARS —) PRETEEN
(GROWING —) SENESCENT
(OF —) WHILOM ERSTWHILE
(PREF.) PALAE(O) PALAI(O) PALE(O) SENI
(— AGE) GER(I)(O) GERATO GERONT(O) PRESBY(O)
(— MAN) GER(I)(O) GERONT(O) PRESBY(O)
OLD AND THE YOUNG (AUTHOR OF —) PIRANDELLO
(CHARACTER IN —) COSTA MAURO SALVO SELMI AURITI GIULIO AURELIO CORRADO MORTARA ROBERTO CAPOLINO DIANELLA FLAMINIO GERLANDO IPPOLITO NICOLETTA LAURENTANO
OLD BAY STATE MASSACHUSETTS
OLD CURIOSITY SHOP (AUTHOR OF —) DICKENS
(CHARACTER IN —) KIT DICK FRED NELL BRASS QUILP SARAH CODLIN JARLEY MARTON THOMAS BARBARA NUBBLES SAMPSON SWIVELLER CHRISTOPHER
OLD DOMINION STATE VIRGINIA
OLDER MORE ALDER ELDER SENIOR ANCESTOR
OLDEST
(PREF.) EO
OLD-FASHIONED CORNY DOWDY FUSTY PASSE FOGRAM FOGRUM QUAINT STODGY ANCIENT ANTIQUE ARCHAIC ARRIERE ELDERLY VINTAGE FRUMPISH OBSOLETE CRINOLINE PRIMITIVE RINKYDINK OLDFANGLED
OLD FRANKLIN STATE TENNESSEE
OLD LINE STATE MARYLAND
OLD MAID (AUTHOR OF —) WHARTON
(CHARACTER IN —) JOE TINA DELIA JAMES LOVELL CLEMENT RALSTON SPENDER CHARLOTTE
OLD MORTALITY (AUTHOR OF —) SCOTT
(CHARACTER IN —) JOHN BASIL EDITH HENRY JENNY MAUSE CUDDIE MORTON BALFOUR FRANCIS GRAHAME OLIFANT BOTHWELL DENNISON EVANDALE HEADRIGG MARGARET BELLENDEN CLAVERHOUSE
OLD-TIMER SOURDOUGH
OLD WIVES' TALE (AUTHOR OF —) BENNETT
(CHARACTER IN —) JOHN CYRIL POVEY BAINES CHIRAC GERALD SAMUEL SCALES SOPHIA HARRIET FAUCAULT CONSTANCE CRITCHLOW
OLD-WOMANISH ANILE

OLEANDER LAUREL NERIUM DOGBANE ROSEBAY
OLEFIN ALKENE
OLEIC RAPIC RAPINIC
OLEORESIN GUM ANIME APIOL ELEMI TOLUS BALSAM GURJUN IRIDIN COPAIBA GALIPOT LABDANUM TACAMAHAC
OLFACTION NOSE SMELL OSMESIS SMELLING ESPHRESIS
OLIGARCHIC FEUDAL
OLIGARCHY KREMLIN
OLIGOCLASE SUNSTONE
OLIMPIA (HUSBAND OF —) BIRENO OBERTO
OLINDO (HUSBAND OF —) SOFRONIA
(SAVIOR OF —) CLORINDA
OLIO STEW MEDLEY MELANGE MIXTURE MISHMASH MACEDOINE PASTICCIO POTPOURRI
OLIPHANT HORN ELEPHANT
OLIPRANCE ROMP SHOW FROLIC JOLLITY
OLIVE OLEA MORON BRUNET LIERRE OLIVER OXHORN PIMOLA RESEDA BAROUNI CITRINE MISSION MORILLON OLEASTER
(— FLY) DACUS
(AMERICAN —) DEVILWOOD
(OVERRIPE —) DRUPE
(PREF.) DRUPI
(—OIL) ELAEO ELAIO ELEO
OLIVER NOLL HAMMER HOLLIPER
(BROTHER OF —) ORLANDO
(WIFE OF —) CELIA
OLIVER TWIST (AUTHOR OF —) DICKENS
(CHARACTER IN —) BILL JACK NOAH ROSE TOBY BATES FAGIN HARRY MONKS NANCY SALLY SIKES TWIST BEDWIN BUMBLE CORNEY EDWARD MAYLIE OLIVER CHARLEY CRACKIT DAWKINS GRIMWIG LEEFORD BROWNLOW CLAYPOLE LOSBERNE SOWERBERRY
OLIVET PEARL
OLIVIA (HUSBAND OF —) SEBASTIAN
OLIVINE PERIDOT
OLLA JAR JUG OLE POT OLAY PUCHERA PUCHERO
OLLA PODRIDA HASH OLIO MEDLEY POTPOURRI
OLM PROTEUS SALAMANDER
OLOGY ISM SCIENCE
OLYMPIAN CELESTIAL
OLYMPIAS (FATHER OF —) NEOPTOLEMUS
(HUSBAND OF —) PHILIP
(SLAYER OF —) CASSANDER
(SON OF —) ALEXANDER
OLYNTHUS ASCULA
OMAGUA CAMBEVA
OMAH SASQUATCH
OMAN (CAPITAL OF —) MASQAT MUSCAT
(LANGUAGE OF —) ARABIC BALUCHI
(MOUNTAIN OF —) SHAM HAFIT HARIM NAKHL TAYIN AKHDAR
(NATIVE OF —) ADNAN QAHTAN BALUCHI
(TOWN IN —) SUR NIGWA MASQAT

MATRAH SALALAH

OMAR (FATHER OF —) ELIPHAZ

OMASUM BOOK BOUK BIBLE FARDEL MANYPLIES

OMBER SOLO UMBRE HOMBRE MEDIATOR QUADRILLE

OMEGA END LAST

OMELET AMLET AMELET FOOYUNG FOOYOUNG FRITTATA

OMEN BODE LUCK SIGN ABODE AUGUR BODER FREET FREIT GUEST TOKEN WEIRD WHATE AUGURY HANDEL HANSEL AUSPICE PORTENT PRESAGE PRODIGY WARNING CEREMONY FOREBODE SOOTHSAY HARBINGER

OMENTUM WEB CAUL ZIRBUS EPIPLOON

OMINOUS DIRE DOUR GRIM BLACK FATAL BODING DISMAL SHREWD AUGURAL BALEFUL BANEFUL BODEFUL DIREFUL DOOMFUL FATEFUL MENACING SINISTER THUNDERY PROPHETIC PORTENTOUS

OMISSION OUT BALK BAULK CHASM SALTUS DEFAULT FAILURE MISPICK NEGLECT SILENCE PASSOVER OVERSIGHT
(— OF A LETTER) APOCOPE
(— OF SYLLABLES) SYNCOPE
(TACIT —) SILENCE

OMIT CUT LET BALK BATE DROP EDIT KILL MISS PASS SKIP SLIP ABATE ELIDE ORMIT SPARE BELEVE CANCEL DELETE EXCEPT FORGET IGNORE DISCARD EXPUNGE NEGLECT DISCOUNT OVERLEAP OVERLOOK OVERSKIP OVERSLIP DISREGARD PRETERMIT

OMITTED VIDE

OMMATIDIUM FACET FACETTE

OMNIBUS BUS BUSS BARGE HERDIC JOGGER PIRATE AUTOBUS MOTORBUS KITTEREEN

OMNIPOTENT GOD ABLE DEITY GREAT ARRANT MIGHTY ALMIGHTY POWERFUL UNEQUALED UNLIMITED

OMNIPRESENCE UBIQUITY

OMNISCIENT WISE LEARNED POWERFUL PANSOPHIC

OMOPLATE SCAPULA

OMPHALE (FATHER OF —) IARDANUS
(HUSBAND OF —) TMOLUS
(SON OF —) TANTALUS

OMPHALOS HUB BOSS KNOB NAVEL CENTER UMBILICUS

OMRI (FATHER OF —) BECHER MICHAEL
(SON OF —) AHAB

ON O AN IN TO ONE SUR ATOP AWAY OVER UPON ABOUT ABOVE AHEAD ALONG ANENT WITHIN FORWARD
(— A HATCH) ABROOD
(— ACCOUNT OF) IN FOR
(— ALL SIDES) ABOUT AROUND
(— AND ON) EVER FOREVER TEDIOUS
(— EARTH) BELOW

(— END) TOGETHER
(— FOOT) UP AFOOT TOWARD FOOTBACK
(— HAND) ALONG
(— HIGH) ALOFT
(— THE CONTRARY) BUT RATHER
(— THE MOVE) AFOOT
(— THE OTHER HAND) BUT AGAIN HOWEVER ALTHOUGH
(— THE OTHER SIDE) OVER ACROSS
(— THE WAY) AWAY AGATE
(— TIME) PROMPT
(— TOP OF) ATOP ABOVE ALOFT
(— WHAT ACCOUNT) WHY
(FATHER OF —) PELETH
(PREF.) IL IM IN IR SUPER

ONAGER ASS GOUR KULAN KOULAN ONAGRA ALACRAN CATAPULT SCORPION

ONAM (FATHER OF —) SHOBAL JERAHMEEL
(MOTHER OF —) ATARAH

ONAN (FATHER OF —) JUDAH

ONCE ANE EEN ERST AINCE ONCET WHILE YANCE FORMER WHILOM QUONDAM UMWHILE FORMERLY SOMETIME UMQUHILE WHENEVER ERSTWHILE
(— MORE) YET AGAIN ENCORE ITERUM
(AT —) PRESTO

ONDATRA FIBER

ONE J AE AN HE UN ACE AIN ANE ANY EIN MAN OON TAE UNA UNE WON YAE YAN YEN YIN YOU SAME SOLE SOME TANE TEAN THIS TONE TOON UNAL UNIT WHON WONE ALONE ALPHA UNITY WOONE ABOARD FELLOW PERSON SINGLE UNIQUE UNITED CERTAIN NUMERAL PRONOUN SIMPLUM UNBROKEN SINGLETON UNDIVIDED UNMARRIED
(— AFTER ANOTHER) ABOUT TANDEM SERIALLY SERIATIM
(— BORN A SERF) NEIF NEIFE
(— BY ONE) APIECE SINGLY OVERHEAD
(— CONDEMNED WRONGFULLY) CALAS
(— CURIOUS TO KNOW ALL) QUIDNUNC
(— DETESTED) WARLING
(— DEVOTED TO PARTICULAR ART) IST
(— EASILY TRICKED) CULLY
(— ENGAGED IN MARAUDING) LOOTIE
(— ENROLLED IN ARMY) DRAFTEE
(— GIVEN TO DEVILTRY) HELLION
(— INSTRUCTED IN SECRET SYSTEM) EPOPT
(— LATE) SERO
(— NOT A REGULAR MASON) COWAN
(— OF PAIR) FELLOW DOUBLET
(— OF TRIPLETS) TRILLING
(— OVERZEALOUS) HYPER
(— SENT FORTH) APOSTLE
(— TENTH) TITHE
(— THAT UNDERGOES CHANGE) MUTANT
(— THOUSAND) MIL

(— TWENTY-FOURTH) CARAT
(— UNKNOWN) QUIDAM
(— VERSED IN LITERATURE) SAVANT
(— WHO BRINGS MEAT TO TABLE) DAPIFER
(— WHO DISPLAYS FASTIDIOUSNESS) EPICURE
(— WHO DOCTORS SOMETHING) COOK
(— WHO EXCELS) ACE
(— WHO FABRICATES) SMITH
(— WHO FOLLOWS ARMY) SUTLER
(— WHO FORSAKES FAITH) APOSTATE
(— WHO FRUSTRATES PLAN) MARPLOT
(— WHO HAS ATTAINED PERFECTION) SIDDHA
(— WHO IS AWAY) ABSENTEE
(— WHO IS STRANGE OR ECCENTRIC) WEIRDO
(— WHO LOADS SHIP) BUNKER
(— WHO MAKES LIVING BY TRICKERY) CADGER
(— WHO MANAGES) GERENT
(— WHO REGULATES GUN) TRAINER
(— WHO REMOVES NUISANCE) ABATOR
(— WHO REPRESENTS NEWEST) NEO
(— WHO TESTS) CONNER
(— WHOSE MIND IS IMPAIRED BY AGE) DOTARD
(— WITH FIRST-HAND INFORMATION) INSIDER
(BLESSED —) BHAGAVAT
(EVIL —) WOND SHAITAN SHEITAN
(EXTRAORDINARY —) DOOZY DOOZER
(LITTLE —) BUTCHA PICKANINNY
(LOVED —) MINION
(NOT —) NARY
(SWEET —) HONEYCOMB
(TIMELESS —) AKAL
(PREF.) HENO MON(O) UNI
(— AND A HALF TIMES) SESQUI
(— AND THE SAME) HOM(O)
(— ANOTHER) ALLELO
(— BILLIONTH) NANO
(— MILLIONTH) MICR(O)
(— TRILLIONTH) PICO
(SAME —) AUT(O) AUTH(I)
(SUFF.) (— BELONGING) AN EAN IAN
(— BELONGING TO) IE ING
(— BELONGING TO A GROUP) ID
(— BELONGING TO A LINE)
(— HAVING) ANDER
(— HAVING TO DO WITH) IE
(— OF A KIND) ING
(— OF A QUALITY) IE
(— SKILLED) AN EAN IAN
(— THAT ADVOCATES A DOCTRINE) IST
(— THAT DABBLES)
(— THAT DOES) ER IER YER
(— THAT HAS) ER IER YER
(— THAT MAKES) IST
(— THAT OPERATES)
(— THAT PERFORMS) ER IER IST YER
(— THAT PRACTICES) IST
(— THAT PRODUCES) ER IER IST YER

(— THAT SPECIALIZES) IST
(— THAT STUDIES)
(— THAT YIELDS) ER IER YER
(—OCCUPATIONALLY CONNECTED WITH) ER IER YER
(LESSER —) IDIUM
(LITTLE —) IE
(SMALL —) IDIUM IUM

ONEGITE AMETHYST GEMSTONE

ONENESS UNION UNITY CONCORD ONEHOOD UNICITY UNITUDE IDENTITY SAMENESS AGREEMENT

ONE-NIGHT STAND GIG

ONEROUS HARD HEAVY ARDUOUS ONEROSE WEIGHTY EXACTING GRIEVOUS LABORIOUS

ONESELF
(PREF.) SUI
(BY, FOR, PERT. TO —) AUT(O) AUTH(I)

ONE-SIDED ECCENTRIC UNILATERAL

ONETIME FORMER FORMERLY ERSTWHILE

ONFALL ONSET ATTACK ASSAULT

ON-GLIDE TENSION ENTRANCE

ONION BOLL CEPA LEEK LILY SYBO CIBOL INGAN PEARL ALLIUM LILIUM PORRET BERMUDA CEBOLLA HOLLEKE PICKLER SHALLOT AYEGREEN RARERIPE SCALLION VALENCIA
(ROPE OF —S) REEVE
(SEASONED WITH —S) LYONNAISE
(STRING OF —S) TRACE

ONKOS TOPKNOT

ONLOOKER BOOK GAZER WITNESS AUDIENCE BEHOLDER OVERSEER BYSTANDER SPECTATOR

ONLY ALL BUT JUST LONE MERE ONCE SAVE SOLE AFALD ALONE ARRAH FIRST MERED NOBUT OLEPY ANERLY BARELY MERELY NOBBUT SIMPLE SINGLE SINGLY SOLELY ALLENARLY EXCEPTING
(— THIS) MERE
(BEING —) SIMPLE

ONMUN HANGUL HANKUL

ONOMATOPOEIA
(PREF.) KE(R)

ONOMATOPOEIC ECHOIC IMSONIC MIMETIC IMITATIVE

ONRUSH BIRR SHAKE ATTACK TIDEWAY

ONSET DASH DINT FALL FARD RESE RUSH BRAID BREAK BRUNT FAIRD FRUSH START STORM STOUR VENUE ACCESS AFFRET ATTACK CHARGE COURGE IMPACT INSULT ONDING ONFALL POWDER THRUST ASSAULT BRATTLE BEGINNING ENCOUNTER ONSLAUGHT

ONSETTER CAGER HITCHER

ONSLAUGHT LASH BLAST ONSET ATTACK ASSAULT DESCENT SISERARA SALIAUNCE

ONSTEAD ONSET FARMHOUSE HOMESTEAD

ONTARIO (CANAL IN —) TRENT RIDEAU
(CAPITAL OF —) TORONTO
(LAKE IN —) SIMCOE

(TOWN IN —) EMO GALT LONDON OTTAWA WINDSOR HAMILTON KINGSTON KITCHENER
ONTO ATOP ABOARD
ONTOGENY DEVELOPMENT
ONTOLOGY METAPHYSICS
ONUS DUTY LOAD BLAME BURDEN CHARGE WEIGHT INCUBUS
ONWARD AWAY AHEAD ALONG FORTH UPWARD FORTHON FORWARD TOWARDS FORERIGHT
ONYX ONIX NICOLO TECALI ONYCHIN JASPONYX SARDONYX
(MEXICAN —) ALABASTER
OOCYTE PROGAMETE GAMETOCYTE
OODLES HEAP LOTS MANY RAFTS SCADS SLEWS LASHINGS SLITHERS ABUNDANCE
OOGONIUM NUCULE OOCYST OOGONE
OOLAK WOLLOCK
OOLITE PISOLITE ROESTONE
OOLONG TEA
OOMPH PEP VIGOR ENERGY
OOPAK TEA
OORALI CURARE
OORIAL SHA SHEEP URIAL
OOTHECA OVISAC
OOZE OZ BOG MUD SEW SOP DRIP EMIT LEAK MIRE SEEP SLEW SLOB SLUE WEEP EXUDE GLEET MARSH SLIME SWEAT WEEZE EXHALE SICKER SLEECH SLOUGH SLUDGE SQUASH SQUDGE STRAIN SCREEVE TEICHER PERCOLATE
(— OUT) SEW SPEW SPUE
(PREF.) STACTO
OOZING WEEPY SQUDGY SEEPAGE SPEWING WEEPING
OOZY OASY SEEPY WASHY SLEECHY ULIGINOUS
OPAH CRAVO SUNFISH KINGFISH MARIPOSA MOONFISH
OPAL GEM NOBLE RESIN FIORITE GIRASOL HYALITE ISOPYRE JASPOPAL MENILITE SEMIOPAL CACHOLONG GEYSERITE
OPALESCENT OPALED OPALINE IRISATED
OPALEYE GREENFISH
OPAQUE DIM DARK DULL DENSE MUDDY SHADY THICK VAGUE OBTUSE STUPID CLOUDED OBSCURE ABSTRUSE EYESHADE
OPEN GO DUP LAX OPE AIRY AJAR BARE FAIR FLUE FREE GIVE PERT UNDO VIDE AGAPE APERT BEGIN BLOWN BREAK BROAD BURST CHINK CLEAR CRACK FLARE FRANK FRESH LANCE LOOSE MUSHY NAKED OVERT PLAIN RELAX SPALD SPLAT SPLAY START UNBAR UNPEG UNTIE APPERT CANDID DIRECT ENTAME EXPAND EXPOSE FACIAL FORTHY GAPING HONEST LIABLE OUVERT PATENT PUBLIC SINGLE SPREAD UNBOLT UNFOLD UNFURL UNGLUE UNLOCK UNROLL UNSEAL UNSHUT UNSPAR UNSTOP UNTINE UNWINK VACANT ARTLESS BLOSSOM

DISPART FIELDEN OBVIOUS OUTLINE SINCERE THROUGH UNCLOSE UNHINGE APPARENT COMMENCE DISCLOSE EXPLICIT EXTENDED INITIATE MANIFEST PERVIOUS RESERATE UNFASTEN CHAMPAIGN OSTENSIBLE
(— A VEIN) BROACH
(— AIR) ALFRESCO
(— AND CLEANSE) WILLOW
(— CLOTH) SCUTCH
(— COUNTRY) VELDT WEALD
(— EYES OR LIPS) SEVER
(— THE WAY) INVITE PIONEER
(— TO PURSUIT) FAIR
(— UP) START DEVELOP DISPART DISCLOSE
(— VIOLENTLY) SPORT
(— WIDE) YAWN EXPAND STRETCH
(— WIDELY) GAPE
(FULLY —) WIDE AGAPE YAWNING
(HALF —) MID AJAR
(TOO —) OVERBARISH
OPENBILL OPENBEAK
OPENED APPAUME ECHAPPE
OPENER KEY KNOB LATCH SESAME APERIENT
(— IN POKER) PAIR JACKS
(FURROW —) SHOE STUBRUNNER
(OYSTER —) HUSKER
OPENHANDED FREE LIBERAL GENEROUS RECEPTIVE
OPENING OS CUT EYE GAP YAT ANUS BOLE BORE DAWN DOOR DROP FENT FLUE GATE HOLE LOOP PASS PORE PORT PYLA RIFT RIMA SLAP SLIT SLOT SPAN VENT VOID YAWN YEAT BLEED BRACK BREAK CHASM CHINK CLEFT CROSS DEBUT GRILL HILUM INLET LIGHT MOUTH SCOOT SINUS START THIRL WIDTH ADITUS AVENUE BREACH CASING CHANCE GRILLE HIATUS INTAKE LACUNA MEATUS OILLET OUTLET PORTAL SLUICE SPREAD AIRPORT CREVASS CREVICE DISPLAY FISSURE ORIFICE OUTCAST SWALLET APERIENT APERTURE BUNGHOLE CREVASSE ENTRANCE OVERTURE PLUGHOLE SCISSURE TEASEHOLE
(— BELOW PENTHOUSE) GALLERY
(— FOR ESCAPE) MUSE MEUSE
(— FROM SEA) INDRAFT
(— IN ANTHER) STOMIUM
(— IN DECK) SCUTTLE
(— IN EARTH) MOFETTE
(— IN FLOOR OR ROOF) HATCH SKYLIGHT
(— IN GARMENT) FENT ARMHOLE
(— IN LOCK TUMBLER) GATING
(— IN MINE) EYE ADIT RAISE SHAFT WINZE WINNING
(— IN MOLD) POUR
(— IN PICTURE FRAME) SIGHT
(— IN PILLAR OF COAL) JENKIN JUNKING
(— IN ROCK) GRIKE
(— IN SALMON TRAP) SLAP
(— IN SEA CAVE) GLOUP
(— IN SKIRT) PLACKET

(— IN SPONGE) APOPYLE
(— IN STAGE) DIP
(— IN TENNIS COURTS) GRILLE HAZARD GALLERY
(— IN TROUSERS) SPARE
(— IN VAULT) LUNET LUNETTE
(— IN WALL) BOLE DREAMHOLE
(— OF BALL) PROMENADE
(— OF BUD) ANTHESIS
(— OF EAR) BUR BURR
(— OF ESOPHAGUS) CARDIA
(— OF GEYSER) CRATER
(— OF HOCKEY GAME) BULLY
(— OF PRAIRIE) BAY
(— OF SHELL) GAPE
(— THROUGH BULWARKS) GANGWAY GUNPORT SCUPPER
(— TO ASH PIT) GLUT
(— WIDE) DEHISCENT
(— WITH LID) SCUTTLE
(— WITHOUT TREES) BLANK
(— IN EARTH) GROTTO CHIMNEY SWALLOW
(ARCHED —) ALCOVE ARCADE
(CHECKERS —) ALMA DYKE FIFE CROSS CENTER SOUTER BRISTOL GLASGOW PAISLEY WHILTER DEFIANCE SWITCHER
(CHESS —) DEBUT GAMBIT DEFENCE DEFENSE
(EROSIONAL —) FENSTER
(FUNNELLIKE —) CHOANA
(GRILL —) GUICHET
(JAR —) PITHOIGIA
(MOUTHLIKE —) STOMA OSTIUM
(SMALL —) PORE SLOT CHINK STOMA CRANNY EYELET LACUNA CATHOLE CREVICE DOGHOLE FORAMEN GUICHET PINHOLE QUARREL FENESTRA
(WINDOWLIKE —) SPLITE FENESTRA
(PREF.) APERTO CHASMO TREMATO
(SUFF.) PORA PORE PYL(E) STOMA(TA)(TE)(TOUS) STOME STOMI(A) STOMOUS STOMUM STOMY TREMA(TA)
OPENLY BARELY FREELY BROADLY FRANKLY PUBLICE ROUNDLY STRAIGHT
OPEN-MINDED LIBERAL
OPENMOUTHED GAPING GREEDY RAVENOUS CLAMOROUS
OPENNESS FREEDOM PATENCY DAYLIGHT FRANKNESS ROUNDNESS
OPENWORK LATTICE TRACERY CAGEWORK FILIGREE FRETTING FRETWORK
OPEN-WORKED AJOURISE
OPERA AIDA FAUST LAKME MANON NORMA THAIS TOSCA BOHEME CARMEN DAPHNE ERNANI LOUISE MIGNON OTELLO RIENZI SALOME ELEKTRA FIDELIO BURLETTA FALSTAFF IOLANTHE LOKACOLO PARSIFAL TRAVIATA WALKYRIE LOHENGRIN PAGLIACCI RHEINGOLD RIGOLETTO SIEGFRIED TROVATORE
(— DIVISION) SCENA
(— GLASS) GLASS JUMELLE

LORGNET LORGNETTE
(— HAT) GIBUS CLAQUE
(— SONG) ARIA
(— STAR) DIVA
(COMIC —) BUFFA BURLETTA
(HORSE —) WESTERN
(SPANISH —) ZARZUELA
(TV OR RADIO —) SOAP
(16TH CENTURY —) PASTORALE
OPERANT EFFICIENT OPERATIVE
OPERATE GO ACT CUT MAN RUN PUSH TAKE WORK DRIVE MULES AFFECT EFFECT MANAGE CONDUCT PROCEED FUNCTION
(— BY HAND) MANIPULATE
(— GUNS) SERVE
(— MINE) FLUSH
(— RADIO) BLOOP
OPERATIC LYRIC
OPERATING GOING
(FULLY —) AFLOAT
OPERATION DEED PLAY BLAST ACTION AGENCY EFFECT VIRTUE PROCESS CREATION EXERCISE FUNCTION PRACTICE EXECUTION INFLUENCE PROCESSUS
(SUFF.) **(— FOR OPENING)** STOMY
OPERATIONS
(SUFF.) ICS
OPERATIVE EYE HAND ARTIST LIVING ARTISAN OUVRIER MECHANIC DETECTIVE EFFECTIVE
OPERATOR DEL DOER AGENT BAKER DEWER NABLA PILOT QUACK BEAMER BILLER BOLTER BUMPER BUSMAN CAPPER DEALER DEGGER DRIVER DUNGER DYADIC GAGGER JOCKEY KICKER RAGGER TRADER AVIATOR BREAKER CENTRAL CHEESER DENTIST FACIENT GLASSER JOGGLER MANAGER OPERANT SURGEON IDENTITY MOTORMAN CONDUCTOR
(INFERIOR —) PLUG
(RADIO —) HAM SPARKS SPARKER
(TRUCK —) GIPSY GYPSY
(SUFF.) STER STRESS
OPERCULUM LID FLAP ONYCHA OPERCLE APTYCHUS COVERING EYESTONE MANDIBLE
OPERETTA ZARZUELA
OPEROSE BUSY IRKSOME DILIGENT LABORIOUS
OPHELIA (BROTHER OF —) LAERTES
(FATHER OF —) POLONIUS
OPHELTES (FATHER OF —) LYCURGUS
(NURSE OF —) HYPSIPYLE
OPHIDIAN ASP EEL SNAKE CONGER REPTILE SERPENT
OPHIR (FATHER OF —) JOKTAN
OPHITE CAINIAN CAINITE
OPHIUROID ARGUS
OPHRAH (FATHER OF —) MEONOTHAI
OPIATE DOPE DRUG HEMP DWALE OPIUM DEADEN ANODINE HYPNOTIC NARCOTIC SEDATIVE DORMITARY PAREGORIC SOPORIFIC
OPIFICER OPIFEX WORKMAN ARTIFICER

OPINE DEEM JUDGE THINK PONDER BELIEVE SUPPOSE OPINIATE

OPINION CRY EYE MOT BOOK DOXY FAME IDEA MIND VIEW WEEN DOGMA FANCY FUTWA GUESS HEART SENSE SIGHT TENET THINK VARDI VARDY VOICE ADVICE ASSENT BELIEF DEVICE DICTUM ESTEEM GROUND NOTION REPUTE SCHISM CENSURE CONCEIT CONCEPT CONSENT COUNSEL DIANOIA FEELING HOLDING MEASURE SEEMING THINKSO THOUGHT TROWING VERDICT DECISION DOCTRINE JUDGMENT SUFFRAGE PREJUDICE SENTIMENT PERSUASION
(COLLECTION OF —S) SYMPOSIUM
(EXAGGERATED —) BIGHEAD
(EXPRESSION OF —) VOTE
(FAVORABLE —) BROO ESTEEM
(MOHAMMEDAN —) FUTWA
(SET OF PROFESSED —S) CREDO
(UNORTHODOX —) HERESY
(WRONG —) CACODOXY
(PREF.) DOXO
(SUFF.) DOX(Y)

OPINIONATED DOGMATIC CONCEITED OBSTINATE PRAGMATIC

OPINIONATIVE ENTETE

O PIONEERS (AUTHOR OF —) CATHER
(CHARACTER IN —) LOU CARL EMIL IVAR FRANK MARIE OSCAR AMEDEE BERGSON SHABATA TOVESKY ALEXANDRA LINDSTRUM

OPIUM HOP MUD DOPE DRUG OPIE POST CHANDU CHANDOO MECONIUM TOXICANT
(— ALKALOID) CODEIN CODEINE MORPHINE NARCOTIN NARCOTINE PAPAVERIN
(— POPPY) NEPENTHE
(OF —) THEBAIC
(TINCTURE OF —) LAUDANUM
(PREF.) MECON(O) OPIO

OPIUMISM THEBAISM

OPOSSUM QUICA YAPOK POSSUM YAPOCK MARMOSE OYAPOCK SARIGUE VULPINE MARSUPIAL PHILANDER TACUACINE
(— SHRIMP) MYSID MYSOID

OPPONENT FOE ANTI ENEMY PARTY RIVAL ALOGIAN NEMESIS OPPOSER ADVERSARY ASSAILANT
(— OF GOV CLINTON) BUCKTAIL
(— OF WAR) PEACENIK
(BOORISH —) BOEOTIAN
(IMAGINARY —) WINDMILL

OPPORTUNE FIT PAT HAPPY LUCKY READY TIMELY APROPOS FITTING TIMEFUL SUITABLE FAVORABLE

OPPORTUNELY TIMELY APROPOS HAPPILY

OPPORTUNIST CREEPER
OPPORTUNISTIC SHUFFLING
OPPORTUNITY GO MAY OPE SEL EASE HENT MEAN MINT ROOM

SELE SHOT TIDE TIME SIGHT SLANT SPACE ACCESS CHANCE SEASON SQUEAK LEISURE OPENING RESPITE VANTAGE APPROACH FACILITY OCCASION ADVANTAGE
(— TO PROCEED) WAY
(FAVORABLE —) SHOW TIME

OPPOSE PIT VIE WAR BUCK COPE DEFY FACE HEAD MEET NOSE STEM WARN WEAR ARGUE BLOCK CHECK CLASH CROSS FIGHT FRONT OCCUR REBEL REBUT REPEL BATTLE BREAST COMBAT DEFEND NAYSAY OBJECT OBTEND OPPUGN REPUGN RESIST THWART WITHER CONTEST COUNTER GAINSAY OBVIATE REVERSE WITHSET CONFLICT CONFRONT CONTRARY CONTRAST FRONTIER OBSTRUCT TRAVERSE ENCOUNTER WITHSTAND ANTAGONIZE
(— BY ARGUMENT) REBUT
(— ONE IN AUTHORITY) REBEL DEFORCE

OPPOSED ANTI ALIEN AVERSE ADVERSE AGAINST COUNTER HOSTILE CONTRARY ABHORRENT ANTARCTIC REPUGNANT
(PERSISTENTLY —) RENITENT

OPPOSING RELUCTANT
(PREF.) COUNTER

OPPOSITE TO ANENT POLAR ACROSS ANENST AVERSE FACING WITHER ADVERSE COUNTER FORNENT INVERSE OBVIOUS REVERSE ANTIPODE CONTRARY CONTRAST CONVERSE ANTIPODAL REPUGNANT RECIPROCAL
(— MIDDLE OF SHIP'S SIDE) ABEAM
(— OF TRUTH) DEVIL
(— THE ALTAR) WEST
(— THE SUN) ANTISOLAR
(PREF.) ANTI ENANTIO
(DO THE —) DIS

OPPOSITION CON FLAK ATILT CLASH STOUR THWART DISCORD CLASHING CONTRAST OBSTACLE POLARITY ANIMOSITY COLLISION HOSTILITY RENITENCY
(ELECTRICAL —) IMPEDANCE
(PREF.) **(IN —)** CONTRA

OPPRESS SIT HOLD LADE LOAD PEIS RACK RAPE RIDE SWAY THEW CROWD CRUSH GRIND GRIPE HEAVY PEISE POISE PRESS WEIGH WRONG BETOIL BURDEN DEFOIL DEFOUL EXTORT HARASS HARROW NIDDER NITHER RAVISH SUBDUE THREAT AFFLICT DEPRESS INGRATE OVERLAY REPRESS SQUEEZE TRAMPLE CONFRONT DISTRESS ENCUMBER PRESSURE SUPPRESS OVERPOWER OVERTHROW OVERWEIGH OVERWHELM
(— WITH DREAD) HAGRIDE
(— WITH HEAT) SWELTER

OPPRESSED SERVILE
OPPRESSION ROD GRIPE PRESS BURDEN THRALL MIZRAIM

DULLNESS PRESSURE EXTORTION GRIEVANCE LASSITUDE

OPPRESSIVE HOT DIRE DOWY HARD CLOSE DOWIE FAINT HARSH HEAVY BITTER LEADEN SCREWY SEVERE SMUDGY SULTRY TORRID URGENT WEIGHT ONEROUS SLAVISH GRIEVOUS GRINDING RIGOROUS

OPPRESSIVELY STRAIT
OPPRESSIVENESS LANGUOR
OPPRESSOR CSAR CZAR NERO TSAR TZAR EGLON TYRANT INCUBUS

OPPROBRIUM ENVY ABUSE ODIUM SCORN SHAME INFAMY INSULT CALUMNY DISDAIN OFFENSE SCANDAL DISGRACE DISHONOR REPROACH CONTUMELY

OPS (ASSOCIATE OF —) CONSUS
(CONSORT OF —) SATURN
(DAUGHTER OF —) CERES
(FESTIVAL OF —) OPALIA
(PERSONIFICATION OF —) FAUNA TERRA TELLUS

OPT CULL PICK WISH ELECT CHOOSE DECIDE OPTATE SELECT

OPTIC EYE OCULAR VISUAL
OPTICAL VISIBLE
(— APPARATUS) LENS GLASS ALIDAD ALIDADE OPTOMETER PERISCOPE TELESCOPE

OPTIMIST UTOPIANIST
OPTIMISTIC GLAD ROSY SUNNY JOYOUS BULLISH HOPEFUL ROSEATE EUPEPTIC SANGUINE EXPECTANT

OPTION UP CALL DOWN CHOICE SPREAD REFUSAL STRADDLE PRIVILEGE

OPTIONAL ELECTIVE VOLUNTARY PERMISSIVE

OPULENT FAT LUSH RICH WELI AMPLE FLUSH PLUSH SHOWY LAVISH MONEYED PROFUSE WEALTHY ABUNDANT AFFLUENT LUXURIANT PLENTIFUL SUMPTUOUS

OPUS WORK ETUDE STUDY
(OVERLABORED —) LUCUBRATION

OQUASSA QUASKY
OR NE ARE AUT ERE ORE GOLD OSSIA OTHER TOPAZ EITHER YELLOW

ORACHE SALTBUSH GREASEWOOD
ORACLE SEER TRIP SIBYL TRIPOD TRIPOS DIVINER AUTOPHONE

ORACULAR OTIC VATIC ORPHIC DELPHIC VATICAL DELPHIAN PYTHONIC PROPHETIC

ORAL ALOUD PAROL VOCAL BUCCAL PAROLE SONANT SPOKEN VERBAL UTTERED UNWRITTEN NONCUPATIVE

ORALE FANON
ORANGE KING MOCK CERES CHILE CHILI CHINO FLAME GENIP HEDGE JAFFA NAVEL OSAGE TENNE AURORA BODOCK BRAZIL COPPER MIKADO NAVAHO SUNTAN TEMPLE TITIAN UVALHA COWSLIP FLORIDA LEATHER MACLURA

NARTJIE PAPRIKA PONCEAU PUMPKIN RANGPUR SEVILLE TANGELO TANSUR BERGAMOT BIGARADE CHINOTTI CLAYBANK FLAMINGO HONEYDEW JACINTHE MANDARIN MARATHON MOROCCAN POMANDER SUNBURST VALENCIA BUCCANEER CARNELIAN PERSIMMON TANGERINE
(— GRASS) KNITWEED PINEWEED
(— HAWKWEED) FIREWEED HIERACIUM
(— MEMBRANE) ZEST
(— MILKWORT) CANDYWEED
(— PIECE) LITH SEGMENT
(— ROCKFISH) FLIOMA
(— SEED) PIP
(— TREE) SATSUMA
(BROWNISH —) SPICE
(LARGE —) KING
(MOCK —) SERINGA
(OSAGE —) HEDGE BODOCK
(SOUR —) CURACAO BIGARADE CHINOTTO
(SWEET —) CHINA CHINO

ORANGEBIRD TANAGER
ORANGE HAWKWEED PAINTBRUSH
ORANGELEAF KARAMU
ORANGEMAN MARKSMAN
ORANGEWOOD OSAGE
ORANG LAUT BAJAU
ORANGUTAN APE MIAS ORANG PONGO SATYR SATIRE SATURY PRIMATE SALTIER SATYRUS WOODMAN WOODSMAN

ORAON KURUKH
ORATE PLEAD SPEAK SPIEL SPOUT ADDRESS DECLAIM LECTURE BLOVIATE HARANGUE DISCOURSE SPEECHIFY

ORATION EULOGY HESPED SERMON ADDRESS CONCION HARANGUE SUASORIA OLYNTHIAC PANEGYRIC PHILIPPIC
(— OF CICERO) PHILIPPIC
(FUNERAL —) ELOGE ELOGY MONODY ELOGIUM ENCOMIUM

ORATOR RHETOR DEMAGOG SPEAKER STUMPER CICERONE BOANERGES DEMAGOGUE PLAINTIFF SPOKESMAN

ORATORICAL ELOQUENT RHETORICAL
ORATORIO ELIJAH RORATORIO
ORATORY CHAPEL SACRARY ORACULUM SPEAKING ELOCUTION ELOQUENCE PROSEUCHE
(EXAGGERATED —) RHETORIC

ORB EYE SUN BALL MOON STAR EARTH GLOBE MOUND ORBIT CIRCLE PLANET SPHERE CIRCUIT ENCLOSE ENCIRCLE SURROUND FIRMAMENT

ORBED LUNAR ROUND GLOBATE
ORBIT AUGE PATH APSIS CYCLE TRACK CIRCLE SOCKET SPHERE CIRCUIT ELLIPSE EYEHOLE ECCENTRIC
(POINT IN —) APSIS APOGEE EPIGEE SYZYGY PERIGEE

ORC OGRE ORCA GIANT WHALE GRAMPUS

ORCHARD HOLT TOPE ARBOR GROVE ARBOUR GARDEN HUERTA OLIVET VERGER ARBUSTUM FRUITERY PEACHERY POMARIUM SUGARBUSH
(**— GRASS**) DOGFOOT COCKSFOOT

ORCHESTRA BAND GROUP CHAPEL CAPELLE CONSORT GAMELAN KAPELLE ENSEMBLE GAMELANG SYMPHONY SINFONIETTA PHILHARMONIC
(**— BELLS**) GLOCKENSPIEL
(**— CIRCLE**) PARQUET PARTERRE
(**SECTION OF —**) BRASS WINDS WOODS STRINGS WOODWINDS PERCUSSION

ORCHESTRATE SCORE ARRANGE COMPOSE

ORCHESTRION HARMONICON APOLLONICON

ORCHID FAAM FAHAM PETAL VANDA CYMBID DUFOIL LAELIA PURPLE AERIDES ANGULOA BOATLIP CALYPSO CULLION FLYWORT LYCASTE POGONIA VANILLA ARETHUSA CALANTHE DENDROBE GYNANDER LABELLUM ONCIDIUM RAMSHEAD SATYRION CORALROOT HABENARIA PUTTYROOT TWAYBLADE SNAKEMOUTH

ORCHIS CROWTOE CROWFOOT CRAKEFEET

ORDAIN LAW PUT DEEM DOOM LOOK MAKE SEND WILL WITE ALLOT ENACT JAPAN ORDER SHAPE WIELD WRITE DECREE PRIEST ADJUDGE APPOINT ARRANGE BEHIGHT COMMAND DESTINE DICTATE FORTUNE INSTALL PREPARE PRESCRIBE

ORDEAL FIRE GAFF TEST AGONY TRIAL CALVARY GAUNTLET
(**— TREE**) AKAZGA TANGHIN TANGUIN

ORDEAL OF RICHARD FEVEREL
(**AUTHOR OF —**) MEREDITH
(**CHARACTER IN —**) TOM LUCY BERRY CLARE MOUNT ADRIAN AUSTIN BLAIZE CAROLA HARLEY RIPTON FEVEREL RICHARD BAKEWELL THOMPSON GRANDISON DESBOROUGH MONTFALCON

ORDER BAN BID RAY SAY TAX BOON CALL CASE CHIT FIAT FORM ORDO RANK RULE SAND SECT STOP SUIT TELL TIFF TRIM WILL WORD ALIGN ARRAY CHIME CLASS DIGHT EDICT GENUS GRADE GUIDE HAVOC PRESS QUIET RANGE SHIFT STATE TAXIS WHACK ASSIGN AVAUNT BEHEST BILLET CEDULA CHARGE COSMOS CURFEW DECREE DEGREE DEMAND DIRECT ENJOIN FIRMAN FOLLOW GRAITH HOOKUM INDENT KILTER MANAGE METHOD NATURE ORDAIN POLICE POTENT SERIES SETTLE SYNTAX SYSTEM ADJUDGE ARRANGE BESPEAK

BIDDING BOOKING COMMAND COMPOSE DISPOSE EMBARGO FLOATER MANDATE PRECEPT PROCESS SOCIETY CATEGORY KODASHIM METHODIZE ORDINANCE PRESCRIBE
(**— OF ANGELS**) CHOIR QUIRE MIGHTS THRONES DOMINIONS PRINCIPALITIES
(**— OF BATTLE**) BATTALIA
(**— OF BELLS**) CHANGE
(**— OF COURT**) SIST VACATUR
(**— OF HOLY BEINGS**) HIERARCHY
(**— OF WORSHIP**) AGODUM
(**— OFF**) TURN
(**— TOBACCO LEAF**) CASE
(**CIVIL —**) EUNOMY
(**COSMIC —**) TAO RITA
(**GOOD —**) EUTAXY
(**KNIGHTHOOD —**) DANNEBROG
(**LACKING —**) AMISS MESSY MUSSY ROUGH CHAOTIC UNKEMPT CONFUSED
(**LEGAL —**) SIST STET WRIT DAYWRIT SUMMONS SENTENCE SUBPOENA
(**LOWER — OF MAN**) ALALUS
(**MINOR CHURCH —**) BENET
(**MONASTIC —**) SAMGHA SANGHA ACOEMETI
(**PROPER —**) TRAIN
(**TRAIN —**) FLIMSY
(**TURKISH —**) MEDJIDIE
(**UNIVERSAL —**) KIND
(**WRITTEN —**) CHECK DRAFT BILLET DRAUGHT
(**PREF.**) (**REVERSE —**) OB
(**SUFF.**) TACTIC TAXIS TAXY
(**— OF ANIMALS**) INI

ORDERED BANDBOX BESPOKE REGULAR SCRAPED COHERENT
(**WELL —**) TRIM

ORDERLINESS METHOD SYSTEM CLARITY DECORUM

ORDERLY AIDE DULY NEAT PEON RULY SNOD TIDY TRIM CRISP SOWAR SUWAR BATMAN BURSCH COSMIC FORMAL MODEST ORDENE GRADELY REGULAR SHAPELY DECOROUS GALLOPER GRAITHLY OBEDIENT PEACEABLE SHIPSHAPE

ORDINANCE LAW DOOM FIAT RITE BYLAW EDICT ASSIZE DECREE RECESS CONTROL MANDATE SETNESS STATUTE WORKING DECRETUM JUDICIAL REGIMENT TAKKANAH DIRECTION

ORDINANT DIHELY DIHELIOS DIHELIUM

ORDINARY LAY LOW SOS BEND FESS LALA MEAN PALE PALL RUCK BANAL CHIEF CROSS NOMIC PLAIN PROSE USUAL CANTON COMMON FILLET FLANCH MODERN NORMAL PAIRLE SIMPLE VULGAR AVERAGE MUNDANE NATURAL PROSAIC ROUTINE SALTIRE SAUTIER TRIVIAL VULGATE EVERYDAY FAMILIAR HABITUAL MEDIOCRE MIDDLING PLEBEIAN RUMTYTOO WORKADAY QUOTIDIAN SHAKEFORK

ORDINATE ORDER ORDAIN APPOINT ORDERLY REGULAR MODERATE TEMPERATE

ORDNANCE LAW GUNS ARMOR ORGUE FALCON MINION PETARD PEDRERO RABINET SERPENT WEAPONS BASILISK PETERERO ARTILLERY

ORDO ORDER ALMANAC DIRECTORY

ORDURE
(**PREF.**) SCAT(O) SCORI

ORE (ALSO SEE MINERAL) TIN CHAT DISH DRAG FELL GOLD IRON LEAD MINE POST PULP ROCK CRAZE CRUDE FAVOR GLORY GRACE HONOR MANTO MERCY METAL PRILL COPPER CUPRITE FLOATER RESPECT SEAWEED SMEDDUM CLEMENCY KNOCKING CARBONATE REVERENCE
(**— CRUSHER**) DOLLY
(**— DEPOSIT**) LODE SCRIN BONANZA
(**— LAYER**) SEAM STOPE
(**— LOADING PLATFORM**) PLAT
(**— MASS**) SQUAT
(**— NOT DRESSED**) WORK
(**— WITH STONE ADHERING**) CHAT CHATS
(**BEST —**) CROP
(**BROKEN —**) DIRT
(**COPPER —**) HORNITE ATACAMITE MALACHITE
(**CRUDE —**) HEADS
(**CRUSHED —**) SCHLICH
(**CUBE —**) SIDERITE
(**EARTHY-LOOKING —**) PACO
(**HORSEFLESH —**) BORNITE
(**IMPURE —**) SPEISS HALVANS
(**IRON —**) OCHER OCHRE MINION IRONMAN LIMNITE MINETTE OLIGIST TURGITE HEMATITE TACONITE JACUTINGA
(**LEAD —**) BOOZE GALENA ARQUIFOUX
(**LUMP OF —**) HARDHEAD
(**MERCURY —**) GRANZA CINNABAR
(**SOLID —**) RIB
(**TIN —**) ROWS CRAZE SCOVE WHITS FLORAN TINSTUFF
(**WORTHLESS —**) SLAG DROSS MATTE
(**ZINC —**) SMITHSONITE

OREAD PERI NYMPH

OREGON

CAPITAL: SALEM
COLLEGE: REED
COUNTY: LINN CROOK CURRY WASCO CLATSOP KLAMATH MALHEUR WALLOWA YAMHILL UMATILLA
INDIAN: ALSEA MODOC WASCO CAYUSE CHETCO KUITSH TENINO KLAMATH TAKELMA YAQUINA
LAKE: ABERT WALDO CRATER HARNEY KLAMATH MALHEUR
MOUNTAIN: HOOD WALKER WILSON GRIZZLY JACKASS TIDBITS

MOUNTAIN RANGE: BLUE COAST CASCADE
RIVER: ROGUE IMNAHA OWYHEE POWDER UMPQUA BLITZEN KLAMATH SILVIES COLUMBIA DESCHUTES
STATE BIRD: MEADOWLARK
STATE FLOWER: GRAPE
STATE NICKNAME: BEAVER SUNSET WEBFOOT VALENTINE
STATE TREE: FIR
TOWN: BEND MORO VALE NYSSA CONDON EUGENE FOSSIL MADRAS ASTORIA HEPPNER COQUILLE PORTLAND CORVALLIS

OREGON TRAIL (**AUTHOR OF —**) PARKMAN
(**CHARACTER IN —**) SHAW HENRY QUINCY FRANCIS PARKMAN CHATILLON DESLAURIERS

OREN (**FATHER OF —**) JERAHMEEL

ORE-PRODUCING QUICK

ORESTES (**COMPANION OF —**) PYLADES
(**FATHER OF —**) AGAMEMNON
(**FRIEND OF —**) PYLADES
(**MOTHER OF —**) CLYTEMNESTRA
(**SISTER OF —**) ELECTRA IPHIGENIA
(**WIFE OF —**) HERMIONE

ORGAN CUP GILL LIMB PART CHELA FLOAT GREAT HEART MEANS PAPER REGAL SERRA ELATER FEEDER FEELER HAPTOR MEDIUM SPLEEN SUCKER CLASPER CONSOLE JOURNAL ARMATURE EFFECTOR ISOGRAFT MAGAZINE MELODEON MELODICA MYCETOME OOGONIUM EQUIPMENT HARMONIUM NEWSPAPER PORTATIVE
(**— GALLERY**) LOFT
(**— OF HEARING**) EAR
(**— OF SCORPION**) PECTEN
(**— OF SENSE**) SENSE SENSORY
(**— OF SILKWORM**) FILATOR
(**— OF TOUCH**) TACTOR TACTUS
(**— PIPE**) REED FLUTE SCHWEGEL
(**— STOP**) ECHO HARP OBOE SEXT TUBA VIOL ACUTA DOLCE FLUTE GAMBA ORAGE QUINT TENTH VIOLA BIFARA CURTAL CYMBAL DECIMA DULCET FUGARA GEDACT NASARD OCTAVE SCHARF TIERCE TROMBA BASSOON BOMBARD BOURDON CELESTE CLARION CREMONA DOLCIAN DOUBLET DULCIAN FAGOTTO GEDECKT MELODIA PICCOLO POSAUNE SERPENT TERTIAN TRUMPET TWELFTH VIOLINA BOMBARDE CARILLON CLARINET DIAPASON DIAPHONE DULCIANA GEMSHORN REGISTER TENOROON TROMBONE WALDHORN BOMBARDON CORNOPEAN DOUBLETTE HARMONICA PRINCIPAL SAXOPHONE CLARABELLA
(**— VIBRATO**) TREMOLO
(**BRISTLELIKE —**) SETA
(**CHINESE —**) SANG CHENG

(HAND —) SERINETTE
(OLFACTORY —) NOSE
(RESPIRATORY —) LUNG
(SMALL —) REGAL
(SWIMMING —) CTENE
(VOCAL — OF BIRDS) SYRINX
(WASTE —) KIDNEY
(PREF.) (INTERNAL —) VISCER(I)(O)
ORGANIC VITAL INBORN NATURAL
INHERENT
ORGANISM WOG BODY ECAD
GERM GUEST PLANT AEROBE
ANIMAL EMBRYO SYSTEM
DIPLONT DISEASE MACHINE
PLANONT SUSCEPT HEMAMEBA
PATHOGEN PLANKTER
MESOPHILE POLYMORPH
(— CHARACTERISTIC) MIXIS
(COLD-BLOODED —) POIKILOTHERM
(COMPOUND —) STOCK
(FOSSIL —) EOZOON
(MINUTE —) AMEBA MONAD
SPORE
(MODIFIED —) ECAD
(PELAGIC —S) NEKTON
(POLITICAL —) LEVIATHAN
(SIMPLE —) MONAD
(SMALL AIRBORNE —S)
AEROPLANKTON
(PL.) BENTHON BENTHOS
HAYSEED NEUSTON PLEUSTON
(PREF.) BIO ONT(O)
(SUFF.) ACEAN ONT PHORA
(SIMPLE —) MONAS
ORGANIZATION ART BIG ITO CLUB
FIRM KLAN CADRE FIDAC FORUM
HOUSE MAFIA SETUP AUMAGA
CHURCH OUTFIT SURVEY SYSTEM
CHARITY COMPANY CONCERN
DEMOLAY ECONOMY GIDEONS
MENORAH SOCIETY CONGRESS
PATRONAGE STRUCTURE
(— OF ACTORS) COMPANY
(— OF DEALERS) AUCTION
(— OF EXPERIENCE) SCHEMA
(— WITH MANY BRANCHES)
OCTOPUS
(ARMY —) LANDSTORM
(AUXILIARY —) AID SYNODICAL
(COLLEGE —) FRAT ALUMNA
ALUMNI ALUMNUS SORORITY
(HARMONIOUS —)
ORCHESTRATION
(JEWISH —) ITO MENORAH
(MUSICAL —) BAND COMBO
CAPELLE KAPELLE ENSEMBLE
ORCHESTRA
(POLICE —) GESTAPO
(POLITICAL —) PARTY VEREIN
HETAERIA HETAIRIA APPARATUS
(SAMOAN —) AUMAGA
(SECRET —) WOW BPOE ELKS
MOOSE MASONS MIDEWIN
(SOCIAL —) POLICE
(WAR VETERANS —) AVC DAV GAR
SAR VFW FIDAC AMVETS
(WOMEN'S —) DAR WAF WRC
WCTU SORORITY
(YOUTH —) KOMSOMOL
ORGANIZE FORM EDIFY FOUND
MODEL ORDER RALLY DESIGN
EMBODY ARRANGE MODULIZE
REGIMENT UNIONIZE BLUEPRINT

INSTITUTE INTEGRATE
STRUCTURE
ORGANIZED FORMED ORGANIC
TOGETHER
(BADLY —) INCONDITE
ORGIASTIC BACCHIC
SATURNALIAN
ORGY LARK RITE ROMP BINGE
REVEL SPREE FROLIC SHINDY
REVELRY WASSAIL CAROUSAL
CEREMONY SATURNALIA
(PL.) ORGIACS DEBAUCHERIES
ORIANA (FATHER OF —) LISUARTE
(HUSBAND OF —) MIRABEL
(LOVER OF —) AMADIS
ORIBI OUREBI ANTELOPE
BLEEKBOK PALEBUCK
ORIEL BAY CHAPEL DORMER
RECESS WINDOW BALCONY
GALLERY MIRADOR PORTICO
CORRIDOR
ORIENT DAWN EAST ADAPT BUILD
PEARL PLACE SHEEN ADJUST
LEVANT LOCATE LUSTER RISING
GLOWING INCLINE RADIANT
SUNRISE LUSTROUS SPARKLING
ORIENTAL ASIAN PEARL BRIGHT
INDIAN ORTIVE RISING EASTERN
SHINING INDOGEAN LUSTROUS
PELLUCID PRECIOUS BRILLIANT
LEVANTINE
ORIENTATION ASPECT PHORIA
STRIKE COLORING LOCALITY
ORIFICE BUNG HOLE PORE PORT
VENT INLET MOUTH STOMA
TREMA BLOWER CAVITY OUTLET
RICTUS SIPHON THROAT
CHIMNEY EARHOLE FORAMEN
OPENING OSCULUM OSTIOLE
APERTURE FUMAROLE INTROITUS
(— IN VOLCANIC REGION)
FUMAROLE
(— OF INFUNDIBULUM) LURA
(BREATHING —) SPIRACLE
(VOLCANIC —) BLOWER
(PREF.) TREMATO
(— OF STOMACH) PYLOR(O)
(SUFF.) PYL(E) TREMA(TA)
ORIGANUM ORGANY MARJORAM
ORGAMENT
ORIGILLE (FATHER OF —)
MONODANTE
(LOVER OF —) GRIFONE
(SISTER OF —) BRANDIMARTE
ORIGIN NEE GERM KIND RISE ROOT
SEED BIRTH CAUSE RADIX START
STOCK FATHER GROWTH NATURE
PARENT SOURCE SPRING EDITION
GENESIS LINEAGE UPSTART
NASCENCE UPSPRING BEGINNING
INCEPTION OFFSPRING
PARENTAGE PROVENANCE
(— ON EARTH) EPIGENE
(FOREIGN —) ECDEMIC
(PREF.) (ANCIENT —) PALAE(O)
PALAI(O) PALE(O)
(SUFF.) GENY
ORIGINAL NEW HOME SEED FIRST
FRESH NOVEL PRIME STOCK
FONTAL MASTER MOTHER NATIVE
PRIMAL PRIMER SAMPLE PIONEER
PRIMARY RADICAL SEMINAL
NASCENCY PRISTINE AUTHENTIC

AUTOGRAPH BEGINNING
INVENTIVE OFFSPRING PRIMITIVE
(NOT —) DERIVED
(PREF.) ARCH(AE)(AEO)(E)(EO)(I)
ORIGINALITY INGENUITY
ORIGINATE COIN COME DATE
GROW HEAD MAKE MOVE OPEN
REAR RISE SIRE ARISE BEGIN
BIRTH BREED CAUSE ENDOW
FOUND HATCH RAISE START
AUTHOR CREATE DERIVE DESIGN
DEVISE FATHER INVENT PARENT
SPRING CAUSATE DESCEND
EMANATE PIONEER PROCEED
PRODUCE COMMENCE CONCEIVE
CONTRIVE DISCOVER GENERATE
INITIATE INSTITUTE
ORIGINATION DESCENT GENESIS
BREEDING ORIGINAL COSMOGONY
ETYMOLOGY
ORIGINATOR AUTHOR FATHER
CREATOR INVENTOR GENERATOR
PROGENITOR
ORIOLE PIROL BUNYAH LARIOT
LORIOT CACIQUE FIGBIRD
PEABIRD FIREBIRD GOLDBIRD
HANGBIRD HANGNEST TROUPIAL
ORION RIGEL ALGEBAR
(BELT OF —) ELLWAND
(FATHER OF —) HYRIEUS POSEIDON
(GUIDE OF —) CEDALION
(HOUND OF —) ARATUS
(SLAYER OF —) ARTEMIS
ORITHYIA (DAUGHTER OF —)
OIIIONE OLEOPATRA
(FATHER OF —) ERECHTHEUS
(MOTHER OF —) PRAXITHEA
(SON OF —) ZETES CALAIS
ORKNEY ISLANDS (CAPITAL OF —)
KIRKWALL
(ISLAND OF —) HOY POMONA
ROUSAY SANDAY STRONSAY
ORLANDO (BELOVED OF —)
ROSALIND
ORLE ORLET BORDER FILLET
WREATH BEARING CHAPLET
TRESSURE
ORLOP DECK ARLOUP
ORMENUS (FATHER OF —)
CERCAPHUS
(SON OF —) AMYNTOR
ORMER ABALONE
ORMOLU GILT GOLD ALLOY BRASS
VARNISH
ORNAMENT BOB DUB FLY FOB
GAY JOY PIN POT TAG TEE TOY
URN BALL BOSS CURL CUSP DICE
ETCH FALL FRET FROG GAUD
GEAR HUSK KNOP LEAF NULL
OUCH RULE STAR TOOL TRIM
WALY WING ADORN BRAID BULLA
CHASE CROSS CROWN DECOR
EXORN FUSEE GRACE GUTTA
HELIX HONOR INLAY KNOSP
LUNET MENSK MENSO OVOID
PATCH POPPY PRUNT SPANG
SPRAY SPRIG STALK TRAIL TRICK
WALLY AMULET ANKLET ATTIRE
BEDAUB BEDECK BILLET BRANCH
BROOCH BUTTON CIMIER COLLAR
DIAPER DOODAD EDGING EMBOSS
ENRICH FALLAL FINERY FLORET
FLOWER GORGET INSERT LABRET

LUNULA NIELLO OFFSET PAMPRE
PARURE PATERA ROCOCO
ROSACE RUNTEE SETOFF TABLET
TAHALI TEMPLE TIRADE
AGREMEN AKROTER AMALAKA
BIBELOT BUCRANE CIRCLET
COCARDE CORBEIL CROCKET
DIGLYPH EARPLUG ECHINUS
EMBLEMA ENGRAVE ENHANCE
FRIGGER FURNISH GADROON
GARNISH NETSUKE RINCEAU
SEXFOIL STRIGIL TREFOIL
TRINKET ACCOLADE ANAGLYPH
APPLIQUE BRELOQUE DECORATE
FLOURISH GIMCRACK LAVALIER
MORESQUE PALMETTE ROCAILLE
SWASTIKA POPPYHEAD
(— FOR HEAD) MIND TARGET
(— ON SHIP) BADGE APLUSTRE
(CHILD'S —) GAY
(CLAW-LIKE —) GRIFFE
(DRESS —) FROG LACE JABOT
SEQUIN SPANGLE
(FANTASTIC —) ANTIC
(HAIR —) TETTIX
(HEAD —) TIARA TEMPLE
(HORSE COLLAR —) HOUNCE
(MUSICAL —) TURN MORDENT
BACKFALL PRALLTRILLER
(PENDANT —) BOB BULLA ANADEM
BANGLE TASSEL EARRING
LAVALIER
(ROOF —) ANTEFIX
(SHOULDER —) EPAULET
(TAWDRY —) GINGERBREAD
(PL.) FIGGERY KNAVERY
AGREMENS
ORNAMENTAL FANCY CHICHI
FRILLY LILYTURF BLUEBEARD
NASTURTIUM SEMPERVIVUM
ORNAMENTATION BOSS FOIL
ACORN DECOR ADORNO BABERY
CHICHI CILERY DICING BARBOLA
CUSPING ECHELLE LACWORK
STYLING ACANTHUS APPLIQUE
FROUFROU HEADWORK PURFLING
ROCAILLE STAFFAGE TRESSURE
(CHEAP —) TINSEL
(EXTRAVAGANT —) ROCOCO
(MUSICAL —) GRUPPO GRUPPETTO
SCHLEIFER
ORNAMENTED FIGURY FOILED
ORNATE TAWDRY ADORNED
FLOUNCY FROSTED TREFLEE
WROUGHT GOFFERED SINNOWED
ELABORATE STELLATED
ORNATE GAY FINE FANCY FUSSY
GIDDY SHOWY DRESSY FLORID
FLOSSY PURPLE SUPERB
AUREATE BAROQUE FLOWERY
TAFFETA MANDARIN OVERRIPE
SPLENDID ELABORATE
UNNATURAL
(EXTREMELY —) GIDDY
ORNERY CONTRARY
ORNITHOLOGIST AUDUBON
BIRDMAN
AMERICAN CORY OBER COUES
STONE BAILEY BREWER BUTLER
CASSIN KEELER MILLER TORREY
WILSON XANTUS AUDUBON
BRASHER CHAPMAN FORBUSH
HENSHAW NUTTALL RIDGWAY

SHUFELDT TOWNSEND
CANADIAN NASH
ENGLISH DIXON GOULD CLARKE
LATHAM SHARPE KIRKMAN
FRENCH LEVAILLANT
GERMAN NAUMANN REICHENOW
KLEINSCHMIDT
NEW ZEALAND BULLER
OROONOKO (WIFE OF —) IMOINDA
OROTUND FULL CLEAR SHOWY
MELLOW STRONG POMPOUS
RESONANT SONOROUS
BOMBASTIC
ORP FRET WEEP
ORPAH (HUSBAND OF —) CHILION
(SISTER-IN-LAW OF —) RUTH
ORPHAN PIP WARD FOUNDLING
STEPCHILD
ORPHANED ORBATE
ORPHEUS (BIRTHPLACE OF —)
PIERIA
(FATHER OF —) APOLLO OEAGRUS
(MOTHER OF —) CALLIOPE
(WIFE OF —) EURYDICE
ORPHREY BAND BORDER
ORPIMENT ORPIN HARTAL SPIRIT
ARSENIC HARTAIL ZARNICH
ORPINE SEDUM LIVELONG
BAGLEAVES EVERGREEN
ORRA ODD IDLE ORROW
WORTHLESS
ORRIS GIMP IRIS LACE BRAID
ORRICE GALLOON
ORSINO (WIFE OF —) VIOLA
ORT BIT END TAG CRUMB SCRAP
MORSEL REFUSE TRIFLE LEAVING
REMNANT FRAGMENT LEFTOVER
ORTHOCLASE ADULARIA
AMAZONITE
ORTHODOX GOOD GREEK SOUND
USUAL PROPER CANONIC
CORRECT ACCEPTED CATHOLIC
STANDARD CUSTOMARY
ORTHODOXY PIETY TRUTH
SOUNDNESS
ORTHOGRAPHY WRITING
ORTHOPTERON WALKER
ORTNIT (BROTHER OF —)
WOLFDIETRICH
ORTOLAN BIRD RAIL SORA
BUNTING BOBOLINK WHEATEAR
ORTSTEIN HARDPAN
ORYX BEISA PASANG PASENG
GAZELLE GEMSBOK ANTELOPE
LEUCORYX
OS BONE ESKAR ESKER MOUTH
OPENING ORIFICE
OSAGE ORANGE HEDGE OSAGE
BODOCK BOWWOOD
OSCILLATE LOG WAG HUNT ROCK
SWAY VARY SQUEG SWING
WAVER WEAVE SHIMMY FEATHER
VIBRATE FLUCTUATE
OSCILLATION HOWL WAVE SHOCK
SEICHE SHIMMY SQUEAL FLUTTER
LIBRATION VIBRATION
(— OF EARTH'S AXIS) NUTATION
OSCULATE BUSS KISS
OSCULATION TACNODE
OSCULATORY PAX
OSIER ROD WAND EDDER SALIX
SKEIN SPLIT WITHY BASKET
SALLOW WICKER WILLOW

DOGWOOD WILGERS REDBRUSH
(— CAGE) TUMBREL
(— WILLOW) TWIGWITHY
OSIRIS HERSHEF UNNEFER
(BROTHER OF —) SET SETH
(CROWN OF —) ATEF
(FATHER OF —) GEB KEB SEB
(MOTHER OF —) NUT
(SISTER OF —) ISIS
(SON OF —) HORUS ANUBIS
(WIFE OF —) ISIS
OSMANLI TURK TURKISH
OSPREY GLED HAWK OSSI GLEDE
PYGARG BALBUSARD OSSIFRAGE
OSSATURE SKELETON OSSEMENTS
OSSE DARE ATTEMPT PRESAGE
PROMISE VENTURE PROPHESY
RECOMMEND UTTERANCE
OSSEOUS BONE BONY SPINY
LITHIC OSTEAL
OSSIAN (FATHER OF —) FINN
OSSICLE BONE INCUS ADORAL
STAPES ALVEOLE BONELET
MALLEUS SCUTELLA
OSSIFICATION OSTOSIS
UROSTEON METOSTEON
SIDEBONES
OSSUARY URN TOMB GRAVE
VAULT OSSARIUM
OSTEND SHOW REVEAL EXHIBIT
MANIFEST
OSTENSIBLE NOMINAL SEEMING
APPARENT SPECIOUS
OSTENT AIR MIEN SIGN TOKEN
DISPLAY PORTENT
OSTENTATION DOG POMP PUFF
SHOW CLASS ECLAT FLARE PRIDE
STRUT SWANK VAUNT PARADE
VANITY DISPLAY FLUTTER
PAGEANT PORTENT PRESAGE
FLOURISH FRIPPERY PRETENCE
PRETENSE SHOWINESS
SPECTACLE
OSTENTATIOUS ARTY LOUD VAIN
GAUDY SHOWY SWANK FLASHY
SPORTY SWANKY TURGID
FLAUNTY GLARING OBVIOUS
POMPOUS SPLASHY SPLURGY
FASTUOUS ELABORATE
OSTERIA INN TAVERN
OSTIOLE PORE MOUTH STOMA
OPENING ORIFICE APERTURE
OSTRACISM PETALISM
OSTRACIZE BAN BAR CUT SNUB
EXILE BANISH PUNISH REJECT
ABOLISH BOYCOTT CENSURE
EXCLUDE BLACKBALL PROSCRIBE
OSTRACON SHELL FRAGMENT
POTSHERD
OSTRICH EMU RHEA NANDU
BREVIPEN STRUCION
(— FEATHER) BOO
(JERKED —) BILTONG
(PREF.) STRUTHI(O)(ONI)
OSTYAK KHANTY
OSWALD (FATHER OF —)
ETHELFRITH
(SLAYER OF —) PENDA
OSWEGO TEA BALM
OTAHEITE TAHITI
(— APPLE) HEVI MACUPA MACUPI
OTALGIA EARACHE
OTHELLO MOOR

(AUTHOR OF —) SHAKESPEARE
(CHARACTER IN —) IAGO BIANCA
CASSIO EMILIA MONTANO
OTHELLO GRATIANO LODOVICO
RODERICO BRABANTIO
DESDEMONA
(ENSIGN OF —) IAGO
(FRIEND OF —) IAGO
(LIEUTENANT OF —) CASSIO
(WIFE OF —) DESDEMONA
OTHER HE MO ELSE MORE ALTER
FORMER NOTHER SECOND
TIDDER TOTHER ALTERUM
FURTHER DISTINCT DIFFERENT
(— THAN) SAVE
(PL.) LAVE REST LUTRA
(PREF.) ALL(O) HETER(O)
OTHERNESS ALTERITY
OTHERWISE OR NOT ELSE ENSE
ALIAS SECUS ALITER EXCEPT
BESIDES ELSEHOW ELSEWAYS
OTHNI (BROTHER OF —) CALEB
(FATHER OF —) KENAZ SHEMAIAH
(WIFE OF —) ACHSAH
OTIC AURAL AUDITORY ORACULAR
AURICULAR
OTIONIA (FATHER OF —)
ERECHTHEUS
(MOTHER OF —) PRAXITHEA
(SISTER OF —) PANDORA
PROTOGONIA
OTIOSE IDLE LAZY VAIN ALOOF
FUTILE OTIANT REMOTE STERILE
USELESS INACTIVE INDOLENT
REPOSING
OTOLITH SAGITTA LAPILLUS
OTOSTEON
OTOLOGIST AURIST
OTTAVINO PICCOLO
OTTER DOG FUR PUP FISH NAIR
PELT BITCH HURON LOUTRE
SIMUNG TACKLE ANNATTO
PERIQUE MAMPALON MUSTELIN
PARAVANE
(— TAIL) POLE
(DEN OF — S) HOLT
(SEA —) KALAN
OTTOMAN (ALSO SEE TURKEY)
POUF SEAT TURK COUCH DIVAN
SQUAB STOOL FABRIC OTHMAN
POUFFE SULTANE FOOTSTOOL
(— COURT) PORTE
(— GOVERNOR) PASHA
(— LEADER) OSMAN
(— PROVINCE) VILAYET
(— STANDARD) ALEM
(— SUBJECT) RAIA RAYAH
OUABE HOGNUT
OUAKARI ACARI UKARI MONKEY
UAKARI
OUCH OH OW ADORN BEZEL CLASP
JEWEL NOUCH BROOCH FIBULA
NOUCHE BRACELET NECKLACE
ORNAMENT
OUGHT BIT BUD BUT MOW BOOD
BOOT MOTE MUST ZERO SHALL
BELONG CIPHER NAUGHT
NOUGHT SHOULD BEHOOVE
OUISTITI WISTITI MARMOSET
OUNCE URE OKET OKIA ONCA
ONCE ONZA OKIEH UNCIA
CHEETAH LEOPARD WILDCAT
(CHINESE —) LIANG

(EIGHT —S) CUPFUL
(HALF —) SEMUNCIA
(ONE-16TH OF —) DRAM
(ONE-20TH OF —) EASTERLING
(ONE-8TH OF —) DRAM
OUPHE ELF OOF OUF GOBLIN
OUR UR ORE URE WER WIR HORE
NOTRE UNSER
(— LORD) NS
(— SAVIOR) NSIC
(PREF.) NOSTRI
OURICURY LICURI LICURY
CABECUDO
**OUR MUTUAL FRIEND (AUTHOR OF
—)** DICKENS
(CHARACTER IN —) JOHN WEGG
WREN BELLA BETTY FANNY
HEXAM JENNY JESSE SILAS
BOFFIN EUGENE HARMON
HIDGEN JULIUS LIZZIE WILFER
BRADLEY CHARLEY CLEAVER
HANDFORD WRAYBURN
HEADSTONE HENRIETTA
NICODEMUS ROKESMITH
OURSELVES USSELF USSELS
USSELVEN
OUR TOWN (AUTHOR OF —)
WILDER
(CHARACTER IN —) JOE WEBB
EMILY GIBBS HOWIE SIMON
WALLY GEORGE CROWELL
NEWSOME REBECCA STIMSON
GORUSLOWSKI
OUSIA NATURE ESSENCE
SUBSTANCE
OUST BAR BUMP FIRE SACK CHUCK
EJECT EVICT EXPEL BANISH
DEBOUT REMOVE CASHIER
DISCARD DISMISS SUSPEND
DISSEIZE FORJUDGE ELIMINATE
OUSTING AMOTION
OUT EX AWAY DOWN HORS FORTH
ABSENT BEGONE ISSUED
OOTWITH OUTWARD EXTERNAL
PUBLISHED
(— AT ELBOWS) SCRUFFY
(— LOUD) BOST
(— OF) EX FROM DEHORS
OUTWITH
(— OF BREATH) BLOWN
(— OF COMMISSION) BUNG
(— OF DATE) OLD DOWDY PASSE
OUTWORN TIMEWORN
OVERDATED
(— OF DOORS) ABROAD FOREIGN
THEREOUT
(— OF EXISTENCE) AWAY
(— OF KILTER) ALOP AWRY CRANK
BROKEN
(— OF ONE'S MIND) FEY DAFT
DELEERIT
(— OF ORDER) AMISS KAPUT
FAULTY DEFICIENT
(— OF PLACE) AMISS INEPT
(— OF PLAY) DEAD FOUL
(— OF SIGHT) DOGGO INVISIBLE
(— OF SORTS) CROOK CROSS
HUMPY NOHOW COMICAL
PEEVISH
(— OF THE WAY) BY BYE ASIDE
BLIND CLEAR CLOSE AFIELD
GEASON REMOTE
(— OF THIS LIFE) HYNE

(— OF TUNE) FALSE SCORDATO
(FARTHER —) UTTER
(PREF.) E ECT(O) EXO PRO
(— OF) EC
OUTAGE VENT ULLAGE
HEADSPACE
OUT-AND-OUT GROSS PLUMB
SHEER SWORN UTTER ARRANT
DIRECT WHOLLY REGULAR
ABSOLUTE COMPLETE CRASHING
OUTRIGHT
OUTBREAK FIT ROW RASH RIOT
BURST SALLY EMEUTE PLAGUE
REVOLT RUCKUS TUMULT
UPROAR BOUTADE OUTCROP
RUCTION BLIZZARD ERUPTION
OUTBURST EXPLOSION
(— OF DISEASE) PANDEMIC
(— OF EMOTIONALISM) HYSTERIA
(— OF TEMPER) MOORBURN
(REVOLUTIONARY —) PUTSCH
(SUDDEN —) SPURT
OUTBUILDING BARN SHED LODGE
PRIVY BARTON GARAGE HEMMEL
OUTHOUSE SKEELING SKILLING
BACKHOUSE
OUTBURST BOUT CROW FLAW
FUME GALE GUST RAGE TEAR
TIFF AGONY BLAST BLAZE BLURT
BREAK BRUNT BURST FLARE
FLASH GEARE SALLY SPATE
START STORM ACCESS BLOWER
BLOWUP ESCAPE FANTAD
FANTOD GOLLER TIRADE TUMULT
BLOWOUT BOUTADE OUTCROP
PASSION TANTRUM TORRENT
ERUPTION EXPLOSION
(— OF ANGER) FIT GERE GEARE
TATTER
(— OF ORATORY) SQUIRT
(— OF SPEECH) STRAIN
(— OF TEMPER) FUFF TIFF
BLOWOUT
(SPACE —) SUPERNOVA
OUTCAST EXILE LEPER RONIN
SHREW ABJECT PARIAH WRETCH
OUTLET ISHMAEL MISSILE
OUTWALE CASTAWAY CHANDALA
REJECTED VAGABOND DIALONIAN
(HOMELESS —) ARAB
(JAPANESE —) ETA RONIN
(PYRENEES —) CAGOT
OUTCOME END OUT FATE TERM
CLOSE EDUCT EVENT HATCH
ISSUE LOOSE PROOF UPSET
BROWST EFFECT EXITUS OUTLET
PERIOD RESULT SEQUEL UPSHOT
EMANATE PROGENY SUCCESS
FATALITY AFTERMATH
OUTCROP CROP REEF LEDGE
BASSET INLIER BLOSSOM
BLOWOUT OUTBREAK OUTBURST
OUTCROPPING BULT SCABROCK
OUTCRY CAW CRY HUE YIP BAWL
BRAY DITE GAFF HOWL REAM
ROAR SCRY UTAS YARM YELL
ALARM BOAST DITTY NOISE
OUTAS SHOUT STINK WHAUP
BELLOW CLAMOR HOLLER
RACKET SCREAM SHRIEK STEVEN
TUMULT CALLING EXCLAIM
PROTEST SCREECH SHILLOO
COMPLAINT PHILLILEW

(PUBLIC —) STINK
OUTDATED CRINOLINE
OUTDISTANCE DROP SKIN OUTGO
SURPASS OUTSTRIP
OUTDO CAP COB COP COW POT
TOP BANG BEAT BEST FLOG WHIP
EXCEL OUTGO REVIE TRUMP
WORSE DEFEAT EXCEED OUTACT
NONPLUS OUTPACE SURPASS
OUTMATCH OUTSHINE
OVERCOME
OUTDOORS FORTH OUTBY
OUTBYE OUTSIDE
OUTER BUT OVER ALIEN ECTAD
ECTAL UPPER UTTER FOREIGN
OUTSIDE OUTWARD EXTERIOR
EXTERNAL FORINSEC
(PREF.) EPH EPI EXO
OUTER MONGOLIA (SEE
MONGOLIA)
(COIN OF—) MONGO TUGRIK
OUTERMOST FINAL UTTER
UTMOST EVEREST EXTREME
OUTWARD FARTHEST REMOTEST
OUTFACE DEFY RESIST SUBDUE
CONFRONT OVERCOME
OUTFIELDER GARDENER
OUTSCOUT
OUTFIT KIT RIG GANG GARB REAR
REEK SUIT TEAM UNIT DRESS
EQUIP GETUP HABIT TROUP
ATTIRE CONREY DUFFEL FITOUT
LAYOUT CLOTHES FURNISH
SHEBANG EQUIPAGE FURNITURE
GRUBSTAKE
(INFANT'S —) LAYETTE
(SPARE —) CHANGE
OUTFLANK OUTWING OVERWING
OUTFLOW FLUX DRAIN ISSUE
OUTGO EFFLUX ESCAPE
OUTPOUR
OUTGO EXIT EXCEL ISSUE OUTDO
EFFLUX EGRESS EXCEED OUTLAY
OUTLET OUTRUN OUTCOME
PRODUCT SURPASS OUTSTRIP
OUTGROWTH ALA BUD JAG ARIL
FOOT HAIR LEAF MOSS SPUR
CLAMP FRUIT HILUM HYPHA
SCALE SPINE ACULEA COCKLE
CUPULE FIBRIL ENATION
FEATHER ISIDIUM APPENDIX
CARUNCLE EPIDERMA HAPTERON
INDUSIUM OFFSHOOT
CARBUNCLE EMERGENCE
OSTEOPHYTE
(PLANTS —) OVULE
OUTGUESS PSYCH PSYCHE
OUTHOUSE SHED SKEO BIFFY
LODGE PRIVY BIGGIN LINHAY
OUTHUT LATRINE SKEELING
SKILLION
(PL.) STEADING
OUTING OUT SKIP STAY TRIP
JUNKET PICNIC COOKOUT
HOLIDAY CLAMBAKE VACATION
WAYGOOSE EXCURSION
WAYZGOOSE
OUTLANDER PARDESI
OUTLANDISH ALIEN KINKY EXOTIC
REMOTE BIZARRE FOREIGN
STRANGE UNCOUTH PECULIAR
BARBAROUS FANTASTIC
GROTESQUE UNEARTHLY

OUTLAST ELAPSE SURVIVE
OVERBIDE
OUTLAW BAN BAR CACO HORN
TORY EXILE EXLEX FLEME RONIN
ARRANT BADMAN BANDIT
BANISH BRUMBY COWBOY
DACOIT UNLEDE BANDIDO
ISHMAEL FUGITATE FUGITIVE
PROHIBIT PROSCRIBE
PROSCRIPT
(IRISH —) WOODKERN
(JAPANESE —) RONIN
(PL.) MANZAS
OUTLAWED ILLEGAL ILLICIT
LAWLESS
OUTLAWRY BAN EXILE UTLAGARY
OUTLAY COST MISE OUTGO
EXPENSE PENSION
OUTLET BORE DRIP EXIT VENT
ISSUE EGRESS ESCAPE EXITUS
FUNNEL OUTAGE OPENING
FUMEDUCT OVERFLOW SINKHOLE
AVOIDANCE
(— FOR COASTAL SWAMP) BAYOU
(— FOR SMOKE) FEMERALL
(— OF CARBURETOR) BARREL
(— OF SPRING) EYE
(AIR —) GRILL GRILLE
(ELECTRIC —) POINT
OUTLIER KLIP KLIPPE
OUTLINE MAP BOSH ETCH FLOW
FORM LINE PLAN PLAT BRIEF
CHALK CHART DRAFT FRAME
MODEL SHAPE TRACE AGENDA
APERCU DESIGN DOODLE FIGURE
FILLET LAYOUT SCHEMA SCHEME
SCROLL SKETCH SURVEY
CAPSULE CONTOUR CROQUIS
DRAUGHT ELEMENT EXTRACT
FEATURE GABARIT ISOTYPE
PROFILE SUMMARY CONTORNO
DESCRIBE ESQUISSE SKELETON
SYLLABUS SYNOPSIS GUIDELINE
TREATMENT
(— HASTILY) SPLASH
(— OF A SCIENCE) GRUNDRISS
(— OF ANIMAL'S BODY) UNDERLINE
(— OF COLUMN) ENTASIS
(— OF PLAY) SCENARIO
(— SHARPLY) ITALICIZE
(CURVING —) SWING
(DOUBLE —) FRINGE
(SHADOWY —) GHOST
OUTLIVE OUTLAST OUTWEAR
SURVIVE OVERBIDE
OUTLOOK MIND VIEW FRONK
FRONT VISTA ASPECT CLIMATE
LOOKOUT PURVIEW FRONTAGE
OUTSIGHT PROSPECT MENTALITY
(BRASH —) FACE
(MEDICAL —) PROGNOSIS
(SELF-CONFIDENT —) SWAGGER
OUTMANEUVER HAVE OUTPLAY
OUTMODED COLD DATED KARUT
PASSE RUSTY BYGONE EFFETE
ANTIQUE ELDERLY VINTAGE
OBSOLETE
OUT-OF-DATE RINKYDINK
OUTPLAY HAVE
OUTPOST STATION FOREPOST
OUTGUARD
OUTPOURING FLOW GALE GUSH
FLOOD RIVER SPATE EARFUL

LAVISH STREAM OUTFLOW
FUSILLADE
OUTPUT CUT GET CROP MAKE
EXPEL GRIST POWER YIELD
ENERGY UPCOME TURNOUT
OUTRAGE RAPE ABUSE INSULT
OFFEND RAVISH ABUSION
AFFRONT OFFENSE
VIOLATE VIOLENCE
INDIGNITY
OUTRAGEOUS ENORM DAMNED
HEINOUS OBSCENE UNGODLY
FLAGRANT INFERNAL SHAMEFUL
SHOCKING ATROCIOUS
DESPERATE MONSTROUS
OUTRANK CAMP PREFER SURPASS
OUTRE ODD BIZARRE STRANGE
ECCENTRIC
OUTREACH CHEAT EXCEED
EXTEND OUTWIT SEARCH
DECEIVE SURPASS OVERREACH
OUTRIDER HAYDUK HEIDUK
HEYDUCK
(PL.) SWING
OUTRIGGER BOOM PROA BUMKIN
RIGGER SPIDER
OUTRIGHT RUN BALD CLEAN
TOTAL WHOLE DIRECT ENTIRE
OPENLY WHOLLY ABSOLUTE
COMPLETE DIRECTLY ENTIRELY
OUTRIVAL WIN EXCEL OUTDO
DEFEAT ECLIPSE SURPASS
OUTRUN BEAT COTE NICK PASS
OUTGO EXCEED ATRENNE
FORERUN OUTFOOT PREVENT
OUTRUSH GUST
OUTSET START OFFSET SETOUT
BEGINNING THRESHOLD
OUTSHED SKIPPER
OUTSHINE BLIND EXCEL OUTDO
STAIN DAZZLE DEFACE
DISTAIN SURPASS
OVERSHINE
OUTSIDE BUT OUT BOUT FREE
RIND OUTBY UTTER AFIELD
OUTFACE SURFACE EXTERIOR
EXTERNAL
(— BOUNDS) ALOGICAL
(— OF) BESIDE
(COMB. FORM) ECTO
(PREF.) EC ECT(O) EXO EXTERO
EXTRA EXTRO
OUTSIDER ALIEN OUTMAN
BOUNDER ISHMAEL EXOTERIC
STRANGER EXTRANEAN
FOREIGNER PHILISTER
(PL.) OUSTITI
OUTSKIRTS SIDE SKIRTS PURLIEU
OUTSHIFTS
OUTSMART SLICK
OUTSPOKEN BOLD FREE LOUD
APERT BLUFF BLUNT BROAD
FRANK NAKED PLAIN ROUND
CANDID DIRECT ARTLESS
EXPRESS EXPLICIT
OUTSTANDING ACE BIG ARCH
RARE SOME AMONG FAMED
NOTED SMASH BANNER FAMOUS
GIFTED HEROIC MARKED SIGNAL
SNAZZY UNPAID EMINENT
PALMARY SALIENT STELLAR
SUBLIME SUPREME TOPPING
FABULOUS INSPIRED PREMIERE

SEASONED SKELPING SLAMBANG SMACKING STANDOUT TOWERING BEAUTIFUL PRINCIPAL PROMINENT UNSETTLED MONUMENTAL NOTICEABLE PREEMINENT

OUTSTAY TARRY

OUTSTRETCHED STENT EXPANDED EXTENDED

OUTSTRIP CAP TOP WIN BEST COTE LEAD LOSE PASS EXCEL OUTDO STRIP EXCEED OUTRUN DEVANCE SURPASS DISTANCE OVERCOME TRANSCEND

OUTVIE SURPASS OUTSTRIP

OUTWARD ECTAD OUTER OVERT DERMAD EXODIC EXTERN FORMAL EXTREME VISIBLE APPARENT EXTERIOR EXTERNAL OBSOLETE OUTFORTH EXTRINSIC

OUTWEIGH WEIGH OUTPOISE OVERBEAR OVERSHADE PREPONDERATE

OUTWIT FOX POT BALK BEST DISH FOIL HAVE BLOCK CHECK CROSS BAFFLE EUCHRE FICKLE JOCKEY OVERGO THWART STONKER OUTGUESS OUTSHARP CROSSBITE OVERREACH CIRCUMVENT

OUTWORK BRAY JETTY FLECHE TENAIL BULWARK BARBICAN HORNWORK TENAILLE HORSESHOE

OUTWORKER BONDAGER

OUTWORN WAPPENED

OUZEL PIET AMSEL COLLY OUSEL OWZEL DIPPER THRUSH WHISTLER

OVAL O ELLIPSE STADIUM VESICAL VULVATE AVELONGE NUMMULAR VULVIFORM

OVARY CORAL GONAD GERMEN OARIUM OOPHORON (PREF.) OOPHOR(O) OV(I) OVARI(O) OVATO

OVATION HAND APPLAUSE

OVEN OON UMU KILN LEAR LEER LEHR OAST BAKER BENCH GLAZE GLOOM HANGI KOHUA TANUR TILER CALCAR MUFFLE CABOOSE FURNACE KITCHEN (— FORK) FRUGGAN FRUGGIN (— MOP) SCOVEL

OVENBIRD BAKER FURNER HORNERO TEACHER ACCENTOR

OVER BY BYE OER TOO ALSO ANEW ATOP BACK DEAD DONE GONE UPON ABOVE AGAIN ALOFT ATOUR ATURN CLEAR ENDED EXTRA VAULT ABROAD ACROSS AROUND BEYOND DESSUS EXCESS UPWARD SURPLUS THROUGH FINISHED (— AGAINST) FORNENT (— AND ABOVE) ATOP ATOUR BESIDES (ALL —) NAPOO NAPOOH SURTOUT (PREFIX) SUR SUPER SUPRA (PREF.) EPH EPI HYPER OB PERI SUPER SUR

OVERABUNDANCE WASTE EXCESS SURPLUS PLETHORA

OVERACT HAM EMOTE OUTDO BURLESQUE

OVERALLS SLIP CHAPS JEANS TONGS DENIMS

OVERARCH COVE

OVERAWE COW ABASH BULLY DAUNT BUFFALO CONCUSS BROWBEAT

OVERBEARING HIGH PROUD LORDLY OVERLY HAUGHTY ARROGANT BULLYING DOGMATIC INSOLENT PRUSSIAN SNOBBISH IMPERIOUS MASTERFUL

OVERBLOUSE SHELL

OVERBLOWN RECHERCHE

OVERBURDEN COVER HOIST PESTER CONGEST OVERLAY ENCUMBER STRIPPING SURCHARGE

OVERBUSY FUSSY PRAGMATIC

OVERCAST DIM SEW BIND DARK DULL GLUM WHIP CLOUD HEAVY SERGE CLOUDY DARKEN GLOOMY LOWERY CLOUDED NUBILOUS

OVERCHARGE GYP RUSH SOAK CROWD GOUGE STICK STING BURDEN EXCISE OPPRESS EXTORTION

OVERCOAT MINO BENNY GREGO JEMMY SHUBA BANGUP CAPOTE RAGLAN SLIPON TABARD TOPPER ULSTER PALETOT SPENCER SURTOUT TOPCOAT BENJAMIN COONSKIN TAGLIONI COTHAMORE GREATCOAT INVERNESS

OVERCOATING DUFFEL DUFFLE

OVERCOME DO AWE GET MOW WAR WIN BEAT BEST DING LICK LOCK MATE POOP SACK SUNK TAME WAUR CHARM CRUCH DAUNT DROUK DROWN FORDO STILL STOOP THROW APPALL BEATEN BUSHED CRAVEN DEFEAT EXCEED EXPUGN FOREDO HURDLE MASTER MOIDER OUTRAY PLUNGE SUBDUE VICTOR CONFUTE CONQUER DEPRESS ENFORCE RECOVER SMOTHER CONVINCE OUTSTRIP SUPERATE SURMOUNT SURPRISE PROSTRATE (— DIFFICULTIES) SWIM (— WITH FATIGUE) FORDO FOREDO (— WITH WEARINESS) HEAVY (BE — BY HEAT) SWELTER

OVERCONFIDENT SECURE POSITIVE

OVERCROWD PESTER CONGEST SURCHARGE

OVERDAINTY TAFFETA

OVERDECORATED GARISH

OVERDEVELOPED GAUDY

OVERDO EXCEED EXHAUST FATIGUE PERCOCT OVERCOOK OVERWORK BURLESQUE

OVERDONE FUSTIAN EXUBERANT

OVERDOSE OD SICKENER

OVERDRESS SAC SACK DIZEN SACQUE POLONAISE

OVERDRIED SLEEPY

OVERDUE BACK LATE TARDY UNPAID ARREARS BELATED DELAYED EXCESSIVE

OVEREAGER FEVERISH FEVEROUS

OVEREAT GORGE SLOFF SATIATE GOURMAND

OVERELABORATE NIGGLE LABORED

OVEREXERT TORLE STRAIN TORFEL OVERPLY

OVERFED RANK FULSOME

OVERFLOW REE COME FLUX REAM SLOP SWIM TEEM VENT BRIME FLOAT FLOOD SPATE SPILL ABOUND DEBORD OUTLET SPILTH OVERRUN REDOUND BOILOVER EXUNDATE INUNDATE OUTSWELL SUBMERGE CATACLYSM (— FROM MOLD) SPEW SPUE

OVERFLOWING FLOW AWASH FLOAT DELAVY DELUGE ALLUVIO COPIOUS FRESHET PROFUSE INUNDANT EXUBERANT LANDFLOOD SUPERFLUX

OVERGARMENT SMOCK BLOUSE DUSTER

OVERGROWN FOZY RANK GAWKY BRANCHY FULSOME SPRATTY SPRITTY

OVERHAND WHIP

OVERHANG JUT BEND EAVE RAKE BULGE JETTY BEETLE SHELVE TOPPLE FANTAIL OVERLAP PROJECT SUSPEND

OVERHANGING BEETLE SHELVY HANGING PENDENT PENSILE BEETLING IMMINENT OBUMBRANT PENTHOUSE PRECIPITOUS

OVERHAUL EXAMINE OVERHAIL RENOVATE FOREREACH

OVERHEAD COST ABOVE ALOFT BURDEN ONCOST UPKEEP EXPENSE OVERTOP

OVERHEAT PARBOIL SCOUTHER

OVERINDULGE PAMPER DEBAUCH

OVERLAP LAP RIDE SYPHER SHINGLE IMBRICATE INTERSECT

OVERLAPPING JUGATE RIDING EQUITANT OBVOLUTE IMBRICATE (— IN FUGUE) STRETTA STRETTO

OVERLAVISH BAROQUE

OVERLAY CAP LAP CEIL COAT WHIP APPLY COUCH COVER GLAZE PATCH PLATE CEMENT CRAVAT SPREAD STUCCO VENEER ENCRUST OPPRESS OVERLIE SMOTHER APPLIQUE TEMPLATE (— WITH GOLD) BEAT GILD

OVERLOAD GLUT CHARGE ENCUMBER SURCHARGE

OVERLOADED PLETHORIC PLETHOROUS

OVERLOOK BALK MISS OMIT PASS SKIP SLIP WINK BLINK FORGO ACQUIT EXCUSE FOREGO FORGET IGNORE MANAGE OVERGO ABSOLVE COMMAND CONDONE FORGIVE INSPECT MISKNOW NEGLECT CONFOUND DOMINATE DISREGARD DISSEMBLE

OVERLOOKER GAITER

OVERLOOKING (INTENTIONAL —) AMNESTY

OVERLORD LIEGE DESPOT ISWARA SATRAP TYRANT ISHVARA

SUZERAIN TYRANNIZE

OVERLY CAP TOO

OVERLYING JESSANT BROCHANT INCUMBENT

OVERMAN CHIEF LEADER ARBITER FOREMAN REFEREE OVERSEER SUPERMAN

OVERMANTLE (— TREATMENT) TRUMEAU

OVERMASTER GET

OVERMATCH BEST DEFEAT EXCEED SURPASS VANQUISH

OVERMODEST PRIM PRUDISH

OVERMUCH TOO EXCESS SURPLUS EXCESSIVE (PREF.) HYPER

OVERNICE FEAT FUSS SAUCY DAINTY QUAINT SPRUCE FINICKY PRECISE DENTICAL PRECIOUS SQUEAMISH

OVERPAINT CLOBBER

OVERPLAY HAM

OVERPOWER AWE BEAT ROUT RUSH CRUSH DROWN QUELL SWAMP WHELM COMPEL DEFEAT DELUGE ENGULF MASTER OVERGO SUBDUE WRIXLE CONQUER CONTROL OPPRESS REPRESS CONVINCE OUTSCOUT SCUMFISH SURPRISE (— WITH HEAT) SWELT (— WITH LIGHT) DAZZLE

OVERPOWERING DIRE FIERCE KILLING DAZZLING STUNNING DESPERATE MONSTROUS

OVERPRAISE OVERSELL

OVERPRECISE MIM PRISSY FINICKY CLERKISH NIGGLING PRECIEUSE

OVERREACH DO POT DUPE GRAB CHEAT COZEN CHOILE GREASE NOBBLE OUTWIT OVERGO DECEIVE

OVERREADY FORWARD

OVERREFINED QUAINT PRECIOUS

OVERRIPE FRACID SQUSHY SQUUSHY

OVERRIPENESS SEED

OVERRULE VETO GOVERN ABROGATE OVERCOME

OVERRULING GREAT PREDOMINANT

OVERRUN TEEM BESET CRUSH SWARM DELUGE EXCEED INFEST INVADE OVERGO RAVAGE SPREAD DESTROY

OVERSEAS OUTREMER

OVERSEE TEND WATCH DIRECT HANDLE MANAGE SURVEY EXAMINE INSPECT NEGLECT DISREGARD SUPERVISE

OVERSEER BAAS BOSS CORK JOSS EPHOR GRAVE REEVE BISHOP CENSOR DRIVER GAFFER GRIEVE KEEKER MIRDHA TINDAL WARDEN BAILIFF CAPATAZ CAPORAL CURATOR FOREMAN HEADMAN KANGANI MANAGER MANDOER MAYORAL OVERMAN PRISTAW TAPSMAN BANKSMAN CHAPRASI DECURION MARTINET SURVEYOR VILLICUS (— OF MACHINERY) TENTOR

(— OF MINE) CAPTAIN
(SPIRITUAL —) PASTOR PRIEST
OVERSENSITIVE TICKLISH
OVERSENTIMENTAL SOFT SLOPPY
OVERSHADOW DIM CLOUD COVER
DWARF SHADE TOWER DARKEN
EFFACE ECLIPSE OBSCURE
UMBRAGE BESCREEN DOMINATE
OVERCAST
OVERSHOE GUM BOOT GUME
ARCTIC GAITER GALOSH GOLOSH
PATTEN RUBBER SANDAL
FLAPPER EXCLUDER FOOTHOLD
PANTOFLE
OVERSIGHT EYE CARE HOLE SLIP
ERROR FAULT GAFFE LAPSE
WATCH CHARGE BLUNDER
CONTROL JEOFAIL MISTAKE
OMISSION TUTELAGE DIRECTION
(LEGAL —) JEOFAIL
OVERSKIRT PEPLUM PANNIER
OVERSOFT QUASHY
OVERSPREAD FOG CAST CLOT
DECK PALL BATHE BREDE CLOUD
COVER SMEAR STREW CLOTHE
DELUGE DOODLE INDUCE
SCATTER SUFFUSE BESPREAD
OVERSTATE MAGNIFY
EXAGGERATE
OVERSTEP PASS EXCEED SURPASS
OVERSTRAINED EPITONIC
OVERSUPPLIED RANK
OVERT OPEN PATENT PUBLIC
OBVIOUS APPARENT MANIFEST
OVERTAKE PASS ATAKE CATCH
ATTAIN BEFALL DETECT ENSNARE
OVERHIE FOREHENT OVERHAUL
(— BY DARKNESS) BENIGHT
OVERTASK DRIVE
OVERTAX HOIST EXCEED STRAIN
STRESS
OVERTHROW TIP CAST DASH
DOWN FALL FELL FOIL FOLD
HURL RAZE ROUT RUIN RUSH
WALT WEND ALLAY CRUSH
EVERT FLING LEVEL QUASH
UPSET WORST WRACK WRECK
DEFEAT DEJECT DEPOSE REPUTE
SLIGHT TOPPLE TUMBLE UNSEAT
WRITHE AFFLICT CONQUER
CONVELL DESTROY DISMISS
RUINATE SUBVERT UNDOING
UNHORSE WHEMMLE CONFOUND
DEMOLISH OVERCOME OVERTURN
REVERSAL SUPPLANT
VANQUISH CHECKMATE

CONFUSION OVERWHELM
(— BY TRIPPING) CHIP
OVERTONE PARTIAL HARMONIC
OVERTOP COW OVERREACH
OVERTURE OFFER PROEM
ADVANCE OPENING PRELUDE
APERTURE PROPOSAL SINFONIA
VORSPIEL
(INDECENT —) ASSAULT
OVERTURN TIP CAVE COUP KEEL
TILT WALT WELT TERVE THROW
UPEND UPSET WELME WHALM
WHELM SLIGHT TIPPLE TOPPLE
WELTER CAPSIZE DESTROY
PERVERT REVERSE SUBVERT
WHEMMLE
(— A WATCHMAN) BOX
OVERWEENING MISPROUD
PRESUMPTUOUS
OVERWEIGHT OUTGANG
OVERWHELM BOWL BURY SINK
SLAY AMAZE COVER CRUSH
DROOK DROUK DROWN FLOOD
SEIZE SPATE SWAMP CUMBER
DEFEAT DELUGE ENGULF OBRUTE
PLUNGE QUELME QUENCH
ASTOUND BOMBARD CONFUTE
CONQUER ENGROSS FLATTEN
IMMERSE INFLOOD OPPRESS
SMOTHER ASTONISH DISTRESS
INUNDATE OVERCOME SUBMERGE
AVALANCHE
OVERWHELMED ACCABLE
OVERWORK HOIN TIRE TOIL
SWEAT STRAIN SURMENAGE
OVINE OVIN OVILE SHEEP
SHEEPLIKE
OVIPOSITOR TEREBRA
OVOID OVATE OBOVOID
OVOLO OVAL THUMB BOLTEL
OVULE EGG NIT GERM SEED
EMBRYO OVULUM GEMMULE
SEEDLET
OVUM EGG OVAL SEED SPORE
OOSPERM OOSPHERE
OWAIA TREE BOBO
OWE DUE OWN REST AUGHT
OUGHT SHALL POSSESS
ATTRIBUTE
OWER DEBTOR
OWL ULE BUBO LULU MOMO RURU
SURN TYTO UTUM JENNY MADGE
NINOX PADGE SCOPS STRIX
TAWNY WEKAU AZIOLA HOOTER
HOWLET KETUPA MUCARO
RAPTOR STRICH VERMIN

WHEKAU BOOBOOK HARFANG
KATOGLE WAPACUT WOOLERT
BILLYWIX COQUIMBO MOREPORK
(— CALL) HOOT
(LIKE AN —) STRIGINE
(YOUNG —) UTUM OWLET
(PREF.) STRIGI
OWN AIN OWE AVOW FESS HAVE
HOLD HOWE MEET NAIN SELF
ADMIT AUGHT OUGHT MASTER
CONCEDE CONFESS POSSESS
PROSPER ACKNOWLEDGE
(PREF.) (ONE'S —) IDIO
OWNER BEL MALIK WALLA
HOLDER DOMINUS HERITOR
ODALLER PROPRIETOR
(— OF ESTATE) ALIRD
(— OF FISHING PLANT) PLANTER
(— OF SLAVES) PATRON
(— OF YACHT) AFTERGUARD
(PLANTATION —) COLON
(SHEEP —) NABAL
OWNERSHIP ODAL UDAL AUGHT
TITLE CORNER SEIZIN SEIZURE
SEVERAL TENANCY DOMINIUM
PROPERTY COMMUNITY
POSSESSION
OX YAK ANOA AVER BEEF BUFF
BULL GAUR MUSK NAWT NEAT
NEWT NOWT OWSE REEM RUNT
STOT URUS ZEBU AIVER BISON
BUGLE GAYAL SANGA STEER
TOLLY TSINE BOVINE MITHAN
ROTHER BANTENG BUFFALO
KOUPREY TWINTER SELADANG
TALLOWER
(CAMBODIAN —) KOUPREY
KOUPROH
(HORNLESS —) MOIL
(SMALL —) RUNT
(TAME —) COACH
(WILD —) URE ANOA BUFF GAUR
REEM URUS BISON BUGLE
BANTIN BANTENG BUFFALO
SELADANG
(YEARLING —) STIRK
(YOUNG —) STOT
(PREF.) BOVI BU
OXBLOOD KAZAK COPTIC KAZAKH
OXBOW INCIDENT (AUTHOR OF —)
CLARK
(CHARACTER IN —) GIL DREW ROSE
CANBY CROFT GRIER JOYCE
MAPEN TYLER CARTER DAVIES
DONALD GERALD MARTIN
OSGOOD RISLEY TETLEY

FARNLEY KINKAID
OXEN NOWT OWSEN CATTLE
OXEYE BOCE GOLD ASTER CLOUD
DAISY GOLDE DUNLIN PLOVER
TARPON
OXFORD DOWN SHOE CLOTH
OXONIAN SLIPPER
OXGANG OSKEN BOVATE OXGATE
OXLAND PLOWGANG
OXIDATION RUST
OXIDE EARTH FLOSS CADMIA
HAFNIA MOILES ZAFFER CALCINE
GUMMITE KERNITE LIMONITE
DJALMAITE
(— OF CALCIUM) LIME
(— OF IRON) RUST COLCOTHAR
MAGNETITE
OXLIP PAGLE PAIGLE PRIMULA
MILKMAID PRIMROSE PRIMWORT
OXSHOE CUE
OXYGEN GAS OZONE OXYGENIUM
(PREF.) OXO
OXYGENATE AERATE VENTILATE
OYSTER COPIS COUNT PINNA
PLANT SHELL COTUIT HUITRE
NATIVE REEFER BIVALVE
MOLLUSK PANDORE RATTLER
SHARPER BLUEPOINT GREENGILL
LYNNHAVEN
(— BED) PARK STEW LAYER SCALP
CLAIRE SCALFE OYSTERAGE
(— CATCHER) OLIVE PYNOT TIRMA
KROCKET PIANNET REDBILL
SCOLDER SHELDER PILWILLET
SKELDRAKE
(— CRAB) PINNOTERE
(— FOSSIL) OSTRACITE
(— MEASURE) WASH
(— PLANT) SALSIFY
(— SHELL) HUSK TEST SHUCK
(— SMALLER THAN QUARTER)
BLISTER
(— SOLD BY POUND) COUNT
(IRISH —) POWLDOODY
(ROCK —) CHAMA
(VEGETABLE —) SALSIFY
(YOUNG —) SET SPAT
(2,3, OR 4 —S) WARP
(PREF.) OSTRE(I)(O)
OYSTERFISH TAUTOG TOADFISH
OZARK STATE MISSOURI
OZEM (BROTHER OF —) DAVID
(FATHER OF —) JESSE
OZNI (FATHER OF —) GAD
OZOCERITE MALTHA NEFTGIL
OZONE AIR

P

P PAPA PETER

PA DAD PAW FORT PAPA DADDY FATHER VILLAGE STOCKADE

PABULUM FOOD FUEL PROG CEREAL ALIMENT SUPPORT NUTRIMENT

PAC BOOT SHOE MOCCASIN

PACA CAPA CAVY LAVA LABBA AGOUTI RODENT

PACE FIG PAD RIP WAY BEMA CLIP GAIT LOPE PASS PELT RACK RATE STEP TEAR TROT WALK AMBLE BRAWL CANTO SLINK SPACE SPEED STEEK SWING TEMPO TRACE TREAD CANTER GALLOP STRAIT STRIDE CHANNEL CHAPTER DOGTROT MEASURE PASSAGE SCUTTLE
(FAST —) ROMP
(RAPID —) CLIP CRACKER
(SLOW —) JOG CRAWL CREEP
(PL.) MANAGE

PACER HORSE AMBLER SPANKER TRIPPLER

PACHISI LUDO UCKERS PARCHESI

PACHYDERM HIPPO RHINO ELEPHANT

PACIFIC CALM MEEK MILD IRENE IRENIC PLACID SERENE PEACEFUL TRANQUIL PEACEABLE
(— ISLAND PINE) IE KOU IEIE LEHUA

PACIFIER DUMMY COMFORTER

PACIFIST BOLO

PACIFY PAY CALM EASE LULL STAY ABATE ALLAY AMESE MEASE PEASE QUELL QUIET STILL PECIFY SERENE SETTLE SOFTEN SOOTHE APPEASE ASSUAGE MOLLIFY PLACATE QUALIFY STICKLE MITIGATE ALLEVIATE RECONCILE

PACK JAM PUN WAD BALE CADE CRAM DECK FILL GANG JAMB LADE LOAD PAIR ROUT STOW SWAG TAMP TOTE TUCK COUCH CRAME CROWD DRESS FLOCK HORDE SKULK SOMER STEVE STORE STUFF TRUSS BARREL BODDLE BOODLE BUDGET BUNDLE CARTON DUFFLE EMBALE ENCASE FARDEL HAMPER IMPACT PARCEL STEEVE THWACK TURKEY WALLET PANNIER PORTAGE RUMMAGE SUMPTER KNAPSACK
(— ANIMAL) ASS MULE BURRO CAMEL HORSE LLAMA DONKEY PACKER
(— BUILDER) GOBBER
(— JURY) WATER
(— LOOSELY) HOVER
(— OF BEARS) SLOTH
(— OF CARDS) STOCK

(— OF DOGS) CRY KENNEL
(— OF FOXES) GROUP SKULK
(— OF HOUNDS) CRY HUNT MUTE
(— OFF) WAG SHANK TURSE
(— ROAD) PACKWAY
(— TIGHTLY) STIVE

PACKAGE PAD BALE BOLT PAIR DUMMY TRUSS BINDLE BUNDLE PACKET PARCEL SAMPLE SEROON DORLACH
(— OF CIGARETTES) DECK
(— OF GOLDBEATER'S SKINS) SHODER
(— OF LEAF) BOOK
(— OF PEPPERS) ROBBIN
(— OF STAMPS) KILOWARE
(— OF VELLUM) KUTCH
(— OF VENEER) FLITCH
(— OF WOOL) BAG PAD BUTT FADGE
(YARN —) CONE CHEESE

PACKER BALER LINER ROPER CANNER

PACKET BOAT BOOK DECK ROLL SCREW BUNDLE PARCEL SACHET
(— OF A DRUG) BAG
(— OF VELLUM) CUTCH KUTCH

PACKHORSE SOMER JAGGER PACKER SUMPTER

PACKING CUP RAGS GAUZE PAPER STRAW WASTE GASKET GROMMET STOWAGE STOPPING
(— MATERIAL) BALINE GASKET
(CLAY —) LUTE

PACKINGHOUSE MEATWORKS

PACKMAN HAWKER

PACKSACK KYACK

PACKSADDLE BAT BARDEL APAREJO

PACT MISE ACCORD CARTEL PACTUM TREATY BARGAIN COMPACT LOCARNO ALLIANCE CONTRACT COVENANT AGREEMENT CONCORDAT

PAD MAT WAD WAY BLAD BOSS FROG LURE MUTE PATH PUFF ROAD ROLL SHOE WALK WASE BLOCK INKER PERCH PILCH QUILT STENT STINT STUFF TABBY TRAMP BASKET BUFFER BUSTLE DAUBER HOLDER JOCKEY NUMNAH PADDLE PADNAG PANNEL PILLOW SPONGE TABLET TRUDGE VELURE WREATH BOLSTER BOMBAST CUSHION FOOTPAD PILLION SASHOON
(— IN CRIB) BUMPER
(— OF ROPE) PUDDING PUDDENING
(— OF STRAW) SUNK WASE
(— ON HORSE'S FOOT) FROG
(ETCHER'S —) DABBER
(FENCING —) PLASTRON

(HAIR —) RAT MOUSE TOQUE
(INKING —) INKER TOMPION
(MEDICAL —) PLEDGET
(PERFUMED —) SACHET
(SADDLE —) PANEL PILLOW PILLION
(PREF.) TYL(O)

PADAUK CORAIL

PADDER MANGLE

PADDING TABBY CADDIS BOLSTER BOMBAST BUSHING CADDICE FILLING PACKING ROBBERY WADDING MAHOITRE STUFFING

PADDLE OAR ROW SPUD WADE ALOOF CANOE SLICE SPANK BUCKET DABBLE PETTLE PUNISH STRIKE TODDLE SPANKER SPURTLE LUMPFISH
(— BOX) WHEELHOUSE
(— FOR FLOUR) SLICK
(TAILOR'S —) BEATER

PADDLEFISH GANOID DUCKBILL STURGEON POLYODONT SPADEFISH SPOONBILL

PADDOCK LOT FROG PARK CLOSE FIELD SLEDGE GARSTON LOANING BIRDCAGE

PADDYMELON QUOKKA PADMELON

PADISHAH SULTAN PADASHA POTSHAW

PADLOCK LOCK FASTEN SECURE CLOSING FASTENER HORSELOCK
(— LINK) SHACKLE

PADRE MONK CLERIC FATHER PRIEST CHAPLAIN

PADRONA LANDLADY MISTRESS

PADRONE BOSS CHIEF MASTER PATRON LANDLORD INNKEEPER

PAEAN ODE HYMN SONG PRAISE OUTBURST TRIUMPHAL

PAGAN ATA BUID BATAK BUKID APAYAO BAGOBO BANGON BILAAN BONTOC ETHNIC PAYNIM SABIAN ALANGAN DUMAGAT GENTILE HEATHEN INFIDEL SARACEN SUBANUN UNGODLY IDOLATOR

PAGANDOM PAYNIM

PAGE BOY CALL LEAF MOTH SIDE CHILD FACER FOLIO GROOM SHEET DONZEL ERRATA SUMMON VARLET BUTTONS CALLBOY FUNNIES PAVISER SERVANT CHASSEUR HENCHMAN ICHOGLAN
(— BOTTOM) TAIL
(BLANK —S) CANCEL
(FACING —S) SPREAD
(LADY'S —) ESCUDERO
(LAST FEW —S) BACK
(LEFTHAND —) VERSO
(RIGHTHAND —) RECTO OUTPAGE

(TITLE —) TITLE UNWAN RUBRIC
(PL.) ODDMENTS

PAGEANT JEST POMP SHOW ANTIC PARADE RIDING TABLEAU TAMASHA TRIUMPH AQUACADE CAVALCADE SPECTACLE WATERWORK

PAGEANTRY POMP PARADE HERALDRY SPLENDOR

PAGIEL (FATHER OF —) OCRAN

PAGLIACCI (CHARACTER IN —) BEPPE CANIO NEDDA TONIO SILVIO
(COMPOSER OF —) LEONCAVALLO

PAGODA PON TAA HOON WATT TEMPLE VARELLA
(PART OF —) TEE ROOF TOPE STUPA FINIAL BALCONY

PAHOUIN FAN FANG

PAHUTAN PAHO

PAID EVEN RESOLUTE
(— IN COIN) DRY
(— IN FULL) SATISFIED

PAIL CAN COG PAN SOA SOE BEAT BOWK GAWN MEAL STOP TRUG BOWIE COGUE CRUCK DANDY ESHIN SKEEL STOOP BLICKY BUCKET COGGIE HARASS KETTLE LEGLEN NOGGIN PIGGIN SITULA THRASH COLLOCK
(MILK —) KIT SOE TRUG ESHIN LEGLEN
(ON WHEELS) DANDY
(PART OF —) EAR RIM BODY CURL HANDLE
(POTTERY —) SEAU
(SMALL —) KIT BLICKY BLICKIE
(WOODEN —) COG COGUE LUGGIE PIGGIN

PAIN GYP ACHE AGRA BALE CARE CARK DOLE FRET GRUE HARM HURT PANG SITE SORE TEEN TINE WARK AGONY BEANS CRAMP DOLOR GRIEF GRIPE PINCH PINSE SCALD SMART STING STOUN THRAW THROE WOUND WRING BARRAT GRIEVE MISERY SHOWER STITCH TWINGE AFFLICT ALGESIS ANGUISH EARACHE HURTING MYALGIA OFFENCE PENALTY TORTURE TRAVAIL TROUBLE AGGRIEVE DISTRESS FLEABITE
(— IN BACK) NOTALGIA SCIATICA
(— IN HAND) CHIRAGRA
(— IN SIDE) STEEK
(— OF MIND) AGONY
(— RELIEVER) OPIATE ANODYNE ASPIRIN
(FILL WITH —) YEARN
(SHARP —) WRING
(STOMACH —) GRIPES GNAWING
(WRENCHING —) TORSION
(PL.) FASH LABOR WHILE

EFFORT TROUBLE
(PREF.) ALG(IO)(O) DOLORI NOCI
PENO
(SUFF.) AGRA ALGIA ALGIC
ODYNE ODYNIA

PAINFUL BAD ILL DIRE EVIL FELL
SORE SOUR TART ANGRY CRUEL
SHARP SORRY BITTER STICKY
TENDER THORNY BALEFUL
GRIPING HURTFUL IRKSOME
LABORED PENIBLE PUNGENT
EXACTING TERRIBLE TORTUOUS
DIFFICULT HARROWING
(PREF.) MOGI

PAINSTAKING BUSY LOVING
NARROW CAREFUL PENIBLE
DILIGENT EXACTING STUDIOUS
ASSIDUOUS ELABORATE

PAINT BICE BLOT COAT DAUB
DRAW FARD GAUD LIMN PENT
PICT SOIL COLOR FEIGN FUCUS
GRAIN ROUGE STAIN BEDAUB
DAZZLE DEPICT ENAMEL FRESCO
OPAQUE SHADOW SKETCH
BESMEAR PORTRAY PRETEND
SCUMBLE AIRBRUSH DECORATE
DEPEINCT DESCRIBE DISGUISE
URFIRNIS CALCIMINE
(— A PIPE) SOIL
(— FACE OR BODY) FUCUS PARGET
(— HASTILY) SQUIGGLE
(— SKETCHILY) SPLASH
(— THROUGH PATTERN) STENCIL
(— WITH COSMETICS) POP POT
FARD
(PREF.) PICTO

PAINTBRUSH WICKAWEE
NOSEBLEED
(PART OF —) HAIR CRIMP HANDLE
BRISTLE FERRULE

PAINTED PINTO FUCATE PASTOSE
PINTADO FUCOIDAL GOFFERED
(— BEAUTY) VANESSA
(— BUNTING) POP NONPAREIL
(— CUP) WICKAWEE PAINTBRUSH
(— WAKE-ROBIN) SARA

PAINTER BRUSH FAUVE ARTIST
DAUBER PICTOR PANTHER
SIGNIST SIGNMAN WORKMAN
BRUSHMAN LUMINIST MURALIST
NAZARENE STIPPLER DECORATOR
TACTILIST
(PL.) ECLECTICS
AMERICAN AHL COX GAG LOW
RAY RIX AMES BAER BEAL COLE
DABO DANA GRAY HART HAYS
HOWE HURD KOST LOEB LUKS
NEAL PAGE POOR REID UFER
WEIR WEST WOOD ABBEY AGATE
AIKEN ALDIS BACON BAKER
BARSE BEARD BEAUX BETTS
BOGGS BROOK BROWN BRUSH
BUNCE CHASE CHILD CRANE
CURRY DAVIS DEWEY EATON
ENNIS FIENE FLAGG FOOTE GILES
GRANT GROLL HEALY HENRI
HOMER INMAN IPSEN JONES
LAHEY LUCAS MARSH MINOR
MOORE MORAN MYERS ODGEN
PEALE PERRY POORE RYDER
SHINN SLOAN SMITH TRYON
UPTON WALDO WAUGH WEBER
WEEKS WHITE WOOLF WYANT

WYETH YOUNG BENSON BENTON
BOGERT BOUCHE BROWNE
CADMUS CHAPIN CHURCH
COLMAN COOPER COPLEY
COTTON CRANCH CURRAN
DANIEL DANNAT DAVIES DEARTH
DECAMP DEMUTH DEWING
DUNLAP DURAND EAKINS FERRIS
FORBES FOSTER FOWLER GUERIN
HAGGIN HARVEY HASSAM
HAYDEN HEATON HERTER
HOPPER INGHAM INNESS JOUETT
KINNEY KNIGHT LAWSON LEVINE
LOOMIS MARTIN MEIERE MILLER
MOSLER MURPHY NEAGLE
NOURSE OAKLEY PARTON PEARCE
POWELL QUIDOR SAMPLE
SAVAGE SINGER STELLA STUART
SYMONS TANNER TAUBES
TURNER VEDDER WRIGHT
ZORACH ADDISON ALLSTON
AUDUBON BANVARD BELLOWS
BINGHAM BRINLEY CAMERON
CARLSON CARROLL CHAPMAN
CHRISTY CORBINO COUDERT
CROPSEY DOUGHTY EDWARDS
ELLIOTT FASSETT FREEMAN
GARNSEY GIFFORD GRIFFIN
GROPPER HARDING HARNETT
HIBBARD HIGGINS HUBBARD
HUBBELL JOHNSON KENDALL
KENSETT LAFARGE LATHROP
MACEWEN MATHEWS MCENTEE
METCALF MUNSELL NAEGELE
OKEEFFE PARRISH PEIXOTO
PROCTOR SCUDDER SIMMONS
SMIBERT SPENCER STIMSON
WATROUS WIGGINS ATCHISON
BARTLETT BECKWITH BICKNELL
BILLINGS BOUGHTON BRACKMAN
BRADFORD BREVOORT BRIDGMAN
CORNWELL COSTIGAN DUVENECK
FAULKNER HAMILTON HARRISON
HOVENDEN HUTCHINS
JOHANSEN KRONBERG
LOCKWOOD MATTESON
MELCHERS PHILLIPS REINHART
RICHARDS ROCKWELL ROSSITER
SHATTUCK SPEICHER TRUMBULL
WHISTLER WILMARTH
WOODBURY ALEXANDER
ARMSTRONG BEMELMANS
BERDANIER BERNSTEIN
BIERSTADT BITTINGER
BLAKELOCK DAUGHERTY
DEKOONING HALLOWELL
HAWTHORNE REMINGTON
ROTHERMEL SCHREIBER
TWACHTMAN VANDERLYN
WENTWORTH BLASHFIELD
BURCHFIELD CLINEDINST
EILSHEMIUS FARNSWORTH
HUNTINGTON MACCAMERON
WHITTREDGE BERNINGHAUS
DELLENBAUGH PRENDERGAST
BLUMENSCHEIN BRECKENRIDGE
DAINGERFIELD CROWNINSHIELD
ARGENTINIAN CENTURION
AUSTRIAN ALT FUHRICH
AMERLING HAUSMANN
DANHAUSER DEFREGGER
KOKOSCHKA FRIEDLANDER
PETTENKOFEN

BELGIAN CLAYS ENSOR NAVEZ
VIGNE BEIFVE KEYSER WIERTZ
GALLAIT GUFFENS LALAING
PAUWELS STEVENS WAPPERS
WAUTERS WILLEMS BAERTSON
LAERMANS BROUCKERE
EVENEPOEL TONGERLOO
BRAEKELEER CHAMPAIGNE
VERBOECKHOVEN
CANADIAN COTE KANE FORBES
OBRIEN WALKER WATSON
CHINESE SHUBUN
CZECH KUPKA MANES MUCHA
BROZIK
DANISH JUEL BLOCH CARLSEN
DAISGAARD MARSTRAND
WILLUMSEN ZAHRTMANN
ABILDGAARD ECKERSBERG
DUTCH BOL DOU BECK BEGA
CORT CUYP GOES GOGH HAAS
HALS HEDA HEEM LAAR LELY
LOOY MAES MEER NEER AELST
BAUER BOSCH BOUTS BRUYN
CODDE DAVID GOYEN HELST
KETEL MARIS METSU NEEFS
OVENS VELDE VROOM WITTE
BACKER DECKER EGMONT FLINCK
GELDER HEYDEN KESSEL MANDER
MESDAG MIERIS MULIER OSTADE
POTTER RUYSCH TOOROP
WEENIX AERTSEN AERTZEN
ASSELYN BERCHEM BEYEREN
CRABETH DOUFFET HOBBEMA
ISRAELS KONINCK LASTMAN
LIEVENS LOMBARD PATINIR
FOURBUS VERMEER WYNANTS
AGRICOLA DOESBURG DUJARDIN
EECKHOUT GOLTZIUS HUYSMANS
JONGKIND KOEKKOEK LAIRESSE
MOREELSE RUYSDAEL TERBORCH
BLOEMAERT CORNELISZ
FABRITIUS HOEFNAGEL
HONTHORST HOUBRAKEN
MIEREVELT MONDRIAAN
MOUCHERON REMBRANDT
STEENWILK WOUWERMAN
BACKHUYSEN BERCKHEYDE
CAMPHUYSEN EVERDINGEN
GESELSCHAP LINGELBACH
BREKELENKAM HONDECOETER
POELENBURGH HOOGSTRAETEN
ENGLISH COX EGG BIRD BONE
COLE COPE EAST ETTY EVES GILL
HAAG HOOK HUNT JOHN LEAR
NASH OPIE SWAN WARD WEIR
BLAKE BROCK BROWN CRANE
CROME DAVIS DOYLE FURSE
LEWIS LUCAS MOORE ORPEN
STARK STEER STONE TONKS
UWINS WATTS WELLS ABBOTT
ASHTON BARKER BOXALL BROOKS
BROWNE CARTER CHALON
COATES COOPER COSWAY
COTMAN COWPER COZENS
CROFTS DEWINT DOBSON FILDES
GIRTIN GLOVER HACKER HAYDON
HOLMES KNIGHT LAVERY
LAWSON LEADER MARTIN
MCEVOY MULLER NEWTON
OLIVER OULESS SEVERN SMIRKE
STUART STUBBS TURNER VARLEY
WALKER ANSDELL BAYLISS
BEECHEY CAMERON CLAUSEN

COLLIER DANIELL DICKSEE
GILBERT GUEVARA HERBERT
HODGSON HOGARTH HOLIDAY
HOLROYD LINNELL MILLAIS
MORLAND POYNTER RIVIERE
RUSSELL SOLOMON ZOFFANY
ARMITAGE ATKINSON AUMONIER
BEAUMONT BRANGWYN
CALDERON CALLCOTT CORBOULD
CRESWICK EASTLAKE FIELDING
HILLIARD LANDSEER LEIGHTON
MUNNINGS REDGRAVE REYNOLDS
RICHMOND RICKETTS ROSSETTI
STOTHARD WATERLOW
WHISTLER AMSHEWITZ
BEARDSLEY BONINGTON
BOURGEOIS COLLINSON
CONSTABLE GREENAWAY
NORTHCOTE STANFIELD
THORNHILL BROCKHURST
KENNINGTON WATERHOUSE
WOOLDRIDGE ROTHENSTEIN
GAINSBOROUGH
FINNISH EDELFELT
FLEMISH BLES BRIL EYCK BALEN
CLAUS CLEVE COXIE COQUES
CRAYER BLOEMEN BROUWER
CANDIDO BRUEGHEL CHRISTUS
CRAESBEECK
FRENCH ZO ARP BIDA CAIN DORE
DUFY ETEX HEIM HUET LAMI
TROY BIARD CAZIN CHERY CORNU
COROT DAVID DEGAS DOYEN
DUPRE FRERE JONAS LEGER
LHOTE MANET MONET MOROT
PATER VEDER VOUET DAUBN'
BERARD BERAUD BOILLY BONNAT
BONVIN BOUDIN BOUTON
BRAQUE BRETON CALLOT CARREY
CHABAS CHERET CHERON
CORMON COTTET COUDER
COUSIN COYPEL DAUBAN DERAIN
DOUCET DUBUFE FAVORY FORAIN
FORBIN FRIESZ GERARD GEROME
GERVEX GIGOUX GRANET GREUZE
GUERIN HEBERT HENNER INGRES
LAHIRE LATOUR LEBLON LEBRUN
LELEUX LEPINE MARTIN MERSON
MILLET MIRBEL MOREAU MULLER
RENOIR SIGNAC STELLA TISSOT
TROYON VANLOO VERNET VIBERT
WEERTS BARRIAS BESNARD
BONHEUR BONNARD BOUCHER
BOUCHOR BOURDON CABANEL
CEZANNE CHARDIN CHARLOT
COGNIET COURBET COUTURE
DAMERON DORIGNY DROUAIS
FERRIER FLANDIN FOUQUET
GARNIER GAUGUIN GENDRON
HEDOUIN HERSENT JEANRON
LAFOSSE LANSYER LAURENS
LEBOURG LEGRAND LEHMANN
LEMOYNE LESUEUR LORRAIN
MAIGNAN MARQUET MATISSE
MIGNARD MORISOT NATTIER
PICABIA POUSSIN PRUDHON
RESTOUT ROUAULT UTRILLO
WATTEAU BELLANGE BERCHERE
CARRIERE CHARTRAN CONSTANT
DAGUERRE DALAUNAY DAUBIGNY
DESCAMPS DETAILLE DROLLING
ESPAGNAT FLANDRIN GALIMARD
JOUVENET KLINGSOR LANDELLE

LATOUCHE LEFEBVRE LENEPVEU
LEPRINCE OZENFANT PARROCEL
PISSARRO ROUSSEAU SCHEFFER
STEINLEN VUILLARD WILLETTE
BOULANGER CHATILLON
CHENAVARD COUBERTIN
DEBUCOURT DEHODENCQ
DELABORDE DELACROIX
DELAROCHE DESPORTES
FALGUIERE FRAGONARD
GERICAULT GLEISPACH
GUILLEMET HENNIQUIN
LAURENCIN METZINGER
SCHUSSELE BARTHOLOME
BOUGUEREAU BOULLONGNE
BRASCASSAT CHASSERIAU
DESBROSSES GUILLAUMET
GUILLAUMIN HARPIGNIES
JACQUEMART MEISSONIER
BRACQUEMOND CARMONTELLE
LARGILLIERE DESVALLIERES
LOUTHERBOURG
GERMAN DIX MAX ADAM DIEZ
HESS JANK LENZ MARC MARR
SOHN UHDE VEIT BEGAS BEHAM
BINCK BRUYN DURER EBERS
EMELE ERNST FOLTZ FRIES FUGER
GRAFF GROSZ HOFER KNAUS
KUEHL LEIBL MACKE MEYER
MUCKE NEHER OESER PECHT
PENCZ STUCK THOMA VOGEL
BECKER BRACHT BRAITH BUHLER
BURGER EBERLE ECHTER FITGER
FRIESE GEBLER GUSSOW HECKEL
HENSEL HERLIN HERTEL HEYDEN
HUBNER KELLER KOBELL KRAFFT
KRUGER LANGER LOFFTZ MAREES
MENZEL MULLER RETHEL
WERNER BALDUNG BARTELS
BLECHEN CORINTH CRANACH
FLICKEL GENELLI HOFMANN
HOLBEIN KLINGER KOPSICH
KRELING LENBACH LESSING
LOCHNER PRELLER RICHTER
SCHWIND STEUBEN AGRICOLA
AMBERGER CARSTENS
DETTMANN FIORILLO GEBHARDT
GRUTZNER HABERLIN HENDRICH
KAULBACH KIRCHNER KOLLWITZ
KUGELGEN KULMBACH
ROTTMANN SCHIRMER SCHREYER
ZEITBLOM ACHENBACH
AINMILLER ALTDORFER
BENDEMANN BLEIBTREU
BURGKMAIR CORNELIUS
ELSHEIMER ENGELHARD
FRIEDRICH GRUNEWALD
HABERMANN KNACKFUSS
MEYERHEIM MODERSOHN
PASSAVANT TISCHBEIN
ALDEGREVER CAMPHAUSEN
HECKENDORF HILDEBRAND
SCHROEDTER WOHLGEMUTH
ZIMMERMANN CHODOWIECKI
HASENCLEVER HILDEBRANDT
HUCHTENBERG MORGENSTERN
SCHRAUDOLPH LINDENSCHMIT
ROTTENHAMMER WINTERHALTER
GREEK GYSIS AETION NICIAS
ZEUXIS APELLES PAUSIAS
EUPOMPUS ARISTIDES
EUPHRANOR MELANTHUS
PAMPHILUS TIMANTHES

AGATHARCUS PARRHASIUS
POLYGNOTUS PROTOGENES
GUATEMALAN MERIDA
HUNGARIAN LOTZ ZICHY VADASZ
WAGNER SZINYEI MUNKACSY
IRISH BARRY DANBY BURTON
FORBES PETRIE MACLISE
COSTELLO MULREADY
ITALIAN MOLA RENI ROSA TURA
VAGA BACCI CAFFI CAMPI CARPI
COSSA COSTA DANTI FERRI FETTI
FOPPA GATTI GENGA IORIS LUINI
MELZI PALMA PENNI PRETI RICCI
SANTI SPADA VANNI VINCI
ABBATE ALBANI ALLORI AVANZO
BATONI CALCAR CESARI CIARDI
CRESPI FRANCO GIOTTO MORONI
NITTIS PASINI PREDIS RICCIO
ROMANO SACCHI SODOMA
SOLARI SUARDI TITIAN VASARI
VERRIO AMIGONI APPIANI
BARBARI BAROCCI BARTOLI
BASSANO BELLINI BERNINI
BOLDINI CENNINI CHIRICO
CIGNANI CORTONA FALCONE
FRANCIA MARATTI MARTINI
MORELLI MUZIANO OGGIONO
PALIZZI PERUZZI RAPHAEL
STROZZI TIBALDI TIEPOLO
UCCELLO VECELLI ZUCCARO
BACICCIO BAGLIONI BARBIERE
BOCCIONI BONFIGLI CAGLIARI
CARDUCCI CARRIERA CASANOVA
CASTELLO CIPRIANI COGHETTI
CORENZIO GRIMALDI MAGNASCO
MAINARDI MANTEGNA MICHETTI
MONTAGNA POCCETTI
PONTORMO SALVIATI SEVERINI
UBERTINI VAROTARI VERONESE
VIVARINI ASPERTINI BECCAFUMI
CAMUCCINI CANTARINI
CAVALLINI CORREGGIO
FRANCESCA GHISLANDI
MAZZOLINO PIAZZETTA
SCHIAVONE SEGANTINI
BELTRAFFIO BOCCACCINO
BORGOGNONE BOTTICELLI
CAMPAGNOLA CARAVAGGIO
LORENZETTI MODIGLIANI
PROCACCINI SIGNORELLI
SQUAREIONE TINTORETTO
VERROCCHIO ZUCCARELLI
ANGUISCIOLA CASTIGLIONE
GENTILESCHI PRIMATICCIO
ALBERTINELLI BALDOVINETTI
FRANCESCHINI MICHELANGELO
PARMIGIANINO PINTURICCHIO
JAPANESE KANO OKYO BUSON
IWASA SOSEN TORII GOSHUN
KOETSU KYOSAI JAKUCHU
JOSETSU SOTATSU HARUNOBU
KIYOMASU KIYONAGA KIYONOBU
MORONOBU TOYOKUNI
HIROSHEGE KIYOMITSU
TSUNETAKA
LITHUANIAN SOUTINE
MEXICAN CANTU OROZCO RIVERA
TAMAYO SIQUEIROS
CASTELLANOS
NORWEGIAN DAHL GUDE
KROHG MUNCH LERCHE
MUNTHE SINDING
FEARNLEY WERENSKIOLD

POLISH BENDA GERSON MATEJKO
GROTTGER CHELMINSKI
MARCOUSSIS WYSPIANSKI
PORTUGUESE FONSECA
RUSSIAN BAKST BENOIS BERMAN
GRABAR BURLIUK CHAGALL
ROERICH LARIONOV LEVITSKI
MALEVICH CHELISHEV KANDINSKI
LISSITZKY RODCHENKO
AIVAZOVSKI BOGOLYUBOV
BASHKIRTSEV VERESHCHAGIN
SCOTTISH BONE FAED HILL ALLAN
GRANT PATON SCOTT AIKMAN
ARCHER BARKER BROUGH
DUNCAN GEDDES GORDON
GRAHAM HARVEY LAUDER LEITCH
MANSON MURRAY PETTIE WILKIE
DOUGLAS GUTHRIE LORIMER
MACBETH NASMYTH RAEBURN
THOMSON CHALMERS
MACWHIRTER ORCHARDSON
SPANISH ARCO CANO DALI GOYA
GRIS MAZO MIRO MOYA GRECO
MACIP CEREZO COELLO PAREJA
RIBERA RINCON VARGAS
ALVAREZ HERRERA IRIARTE
MADRAZO MORALES MURILLO
ORRENTE PACHECO PICASSO
RIBALTA ZULOAGA CESPEDES
PRADILLA ZAMACOIS ZURBARAN
VELASQUEZ ZUBIAURRE
BERRUGUETE
SWEDISH DAHL ZORN BERGH
ROSLIN LARSSON FAGERLIN
LUNDGREN HELLQUIST
JOSEPHSON LILJEFORS
SWISS KLEE LIPS MIND ASPER
DIDAY ITTEN MEYER CALAME
GLEYRE MANUEL BOCKLIN
BUCHSER DISTELI LIOTARD
PETITOT VAUTIER KAUFFMANN
PAINTING ART OIL PAT DAUB
PATA DRAFT MURAL PIECE TABLE
WATER CANVAS CROUTE FRESCO
MINERY TITIAN BODEGON
CAMAIEU CARTOON COMBINE
DAUBING GRADINO GRAPHIC
HISTORY PAYSAGE FROTTAGE
PREDELLA SEAPIECE SYMPHONY
AQUARELLE MINIATURE
(— EQUIPMENT) OIL BRUSH EASEL
PAINT CANVAS PALLET
(— IN COLLOIDAL MEDIUM)
TEMPERA
(— OF EVERYDAY LIFE) GENRE
(— OF FOLIAGE) BOSCAGE
(— ON PLASTER) SECCO FRESCO
(— WITH OPAQUE COLORS)
GOUACHE
(ACTION —) TACHISM
(CIRCULAR —) TONDO
(PREHISTORIC —) PICTOGRAM
PICTOGRAPH
(RELIGIOUS —) PIETA TANKA
(SCENIC —) SCAPE
(SMALL —) TABLET
(TEMPERA —) SECCO
(THREE PANEL —) TRIPTYCH
(PL.) GENRE
(SUFF.) CHROMY
PAIR DUO TWO ZYG CASE DIAD
DUAD DUAL DYAD MATE SIDE
SPAN TEAM TWIN YOKE BRACE

MARRY MATCH TWAIN UNITE
COUPLE GEMINI COUPLET
DOUBLET JUMELLE TWOSOME
(— OF FILMS) BIPACK
(— OF MILLSTONES) RUN
(— OF SHOTS) BRACKET
(— OF TONGS) GRAMPUS GRAPPLE
(— OF WINGS) SHEARS
(— ROYAL) PARIAL
(ONE OF —) IMPAIR NEIGHBOR
(PL.) GEMELS
(PREF.) GEMINI ZYG(O)(OTO)
(SUFF.) ZYGOUS
PAIRED GEMEL JUGATE ZYGOUS
JUMELLE
PAISLEY PRINT SHAWL DESIGN
FABRIC
PAIUTE DIGGER
PAJAMAS SHALWAR SLEEPER
PAKHT (HUSBAND OF —) PTAH

PAKISTAN

BAY: SOYMIANI
CANAL: NARA ROHRI
CAPE: FASTA JADDI JIWANI
CAPITAL: ISLAMABAD
COIN: ANNA RUPEE
DAM: TARBELA
LANGUAGE: URDU PUSHTU SINDHI
  BALUCHI BENGALI PUNJABI
MOUNTAIN: TIRICHMIR
MOUNTAIN RANGE: MAKRAN
  KIRTHAR HIMALAYA SULAIMAN
NATIVE: BENGAL PATHAN SINDHI
  BALUCHI PUNJABI
PORT: CHALNA KARACHI
PROVINCE: SIND PUNJAB
RIVER: NAL BADO RAVI ZHOB
  DASHT INDUS CHENAB GANGES
  JAMUNA JHELUM KUNDAR
  PORALI
STATE: DIR SWAT KALAT KHARAN
  CHITRAL KHAIRPUR
TOWN: DACCA CHALNA KHULNA
  LAHORE MULTAN QUETTA
  KARACHI SIALKOT LYALLPUR
  PESHAWAR SARGODHA
WEIGHT: SEER TOLA MAUND

PAKTONG TUTENAG
PAL BO ALLY CHUM JACK PARD
BILLY BUDDY BUTTY CHINA
CRONY LOUKE COBBER COPAIN
DIGGER FRIEND COMRADE
PARTNER COMPANION
PALACE SALE CHIGI COURT SERAI
STEAD CASTLE ELYSEE LOUVRE
PALAIS ALCAZAR EDIFICE
LATERAN MANSION PALAZZO
TRIANON VATICAN ZWINGER
BASILICA SERAGLIO WHITEHALL
(— OF SATAN) PANDEMONIUM
(FAIRY —) SHEE SIDHE
PALADIN HERO PEER ANSEIS
ASTOLF BUDDY KNIGHT CHAMPION
DOUZEPER
PALAL (FATHER OF —) UZAI
PALAMEDES (BROTHER OF —) OEAX
SFORZA ACHILLES
(FATHER OF —) NAUPLIUS
(MOTHER OF —) CLYMENE
(SLAYER OF —) CORINDA
PALAMON (RIVAL OF —) ARCITE

(WIFE OF —) EMELYE
PALANQUIN JAUN JUAN KAGE
KAGO DANDI DOOLI DOOLY PALKI
SEDAN DOOLIE LITTER PALKEE
TONJON NORIMON
PALATABLE SAPID SPICY TASTY
DAINTY SAVORY MOREISH
DELICATE LUSCIOUS PLEASING
SAPOROUS AGREEABLE
DELICIOUS TOOTHSOME
PALATAL SOFT FRONT VELAR
GUTTURAL
PALATALIZED MOUILLE
PALATE TASTE VELUM RELISH
GOURMET URANISCUS
(SOFT —) UVULA
(PREF.) URAN(O)(OSO)
PALATIAL LARGE ORNATE
STATELY SPLENDID
PALATINE CAPE OFFICER PALADIN
PALATIAL
PALAVER GASH SLUM TALK
CAJOLE DEBATE GLAVER JARGON
PARLEY CHATTER FLATTER
WHEEDLE CAJOLERY FLATTERY
PALE DIM WAN ASHY BLOC FADE
GREY GULL LILY PALL SICK THIN
WHEY ASHEN BLAKE BLATE
BLEAK CLOSE FAINT FENCE
GREEN LIGHT LINEN LIVID LURID
MEALY STAKE STICK VERGE
WHITE ANEMIC BLANCH CHALKY
CHANGE DOUGHY FALLOW
FEEBLE PALLID PASTEL PICKET
REGION REMISS SICKLY SILVER
WATERY WHITEN DEFENSE
GHASTLY HAGGARD INSIPID
OBSCURE SHILPIT DELICATE
WATERISH
(IN —) HAURIENT
(PREF.) LIRO PALLIDI POLI(O)
PALEA PALET SQUAMELLA
PALENESS WAN PALLOR
ACHROMA
PALEONTOLOGIST **AMERICAN**
GABB HALL LULL MEEK BERRY
MARSH CLARKE FOSTER GRABAU
OSBORN BEECHER GREGORY
MERRIAM WALCOTT KNOWLTON
SPRINGER WILLIAMS SCHUCHERT
WACHSMUTH WILLISTON
AUSTRIAN SUESS HOERNES
MOJSISOVICS ETTINGSHAUSEN
ENGLISH TATE CAUTLEY MANTELL
DAVIDSON WOODWARD
BOWERBANK PARKINSON
FRENCH BOULE GAUDRY
BARRANDE
GERMAN ZITTEL BEYRICH
QUENSTEDT
SOUTH AFRICAN BROOM
SCOTTISH FALCONER
PALESTINE (SEE ISRAEL)
PALETOT COAT JACKET OVERCOAT
GREATCOAT
PALFREY HORSE PALFRY
PALIMPSEST TABLET PARCHMENT
PALING PALE FENCE FLAKE LIMIT
PALIS STAKE PICKET FENCING
BLENCHING
PALISADE HAY BOMA PALE PEEL
CLIFF FENCE RIMER STAKE FRAISE
HURDIS PICKET BARRIER

ENCLOSE FORTIFY HURDIES
STACKET TAMBOUR ESPALIER
(MILITARY —) CIPPUS
(PL.) BAIL BARRIER
PALL FOG BORE CLOY PALE SATE
CLOAK CLOTH FAINT QUALM
STALE WEARY MANTLE NAUSEA
SHROUD DISGUST SATIATE
ANIMETTA MORTCLOTH
PALLET BED COT PAD COUCH
QUILT PADDLE BLANKET
MATTRESS PLANCHER
PALLIARD BEGGAR LECHER
RASCAL VAGABOND
PALLIATE EASE HIDE MASK VEIL
ABATE CLOAK COLOR COVER
GLOSS GLOZE LITHE BLANCH
LESSEN REDUCE SMOOTH SOFTEN
SOOTHE CONCEAL CUSHION
SHELTER DISGUISE MITIGATE
PALLID WAN ASHY PALE PALY
BLEAK MEALY WASHY WAXEN
WHITE SALLOW GHASTLY
BLOODLESS COLORLESS
INNOCUOUS
PALL-MALL MAIL
PALLOR ASH WAN PALE ASHES
PALENESS
PALLU (FATHER OF —) REUBEN
(SON OF —) ELIAB
PALM ADY DOM ITA ATAP BRAB
BURI BUSU COCO DATE DOUM
FLAT HIDE JARA KOKO LOOF
NIOG NIPA PAWN SAGO SLIP
TARA ARCHA ARECA ARENG
ASSAI BUNGA BUNGA CARRY
COCOA COYOL CURUA DATIL
FOIST HOWEA INAJA JAGUA
LOULU MACAW MERUS NIKAU
RATAN SABAL SALAK TECUM
TUCUM UNAMO YAGUA YARAY
ANAHAO ASSAHY BACABA BURITI
CHONTA COHUNE COROJO
COROZO GEBANG GOMUTI
GRUGRU JAMBEE JUPATI KENTIA
KITTUL LAWYER LONTAR NIBONG
PACAYA RAFFIA ROTANG THENAR
TOOROO TROPHY APRICOT
BABASSU BACTRIS CARANDA
CONCEAL COQUITO ERYTHEA
GEONOMA MORICHE PALMYRA
PUPUNHA SAGWIRE TALIPOT
TROOLIE URUCURI JACITARA
LATANIER MACAHUBA PIASSAVA
(— FERN) PONJA
(— FOOD) NUT COCO DATE NIPA
SAGO SURA ASSAI TAREE TODDY
COCONUT
(— JUICE) SURA
(— LEAF) OLA OLLA CAJAN FROND
(— LILY) TI
(— OF HAND) FLAT LOOF VOLA
TABLE THENAR
(— OFF) COG FOB TOP SHAB FOIST
TRUMP
(— OUT) APPAUME
(BETEL —) ARECA BONGA PUGUA
PINANG
(CLIMBING —) RATTAN
(FEATHER —) HOWEA GOMUTI
URUCURI
(SPINY —) PEACH GRIGRI GRUGRU
(PREF.) CYCAD(I)(O) PALMATO

PALMI PALPI PALPO
PALMARY CHIEF PALMAR
SUPERIOR
PALMATE FLAT BROAD LOBED
WEBBED
PALMER LOUSE FERULE STROLL
TRAVEL VOTARY WANDER
FOISTER PILGRIM
PALMETTO CABBAGE PALMITO
BIGTHATCH
(— STATE) SOUTHCAROLINA
PALMISTRY CHIROMANCY
PALMODIC JERKY
PALMYRA BRAB TALA LONTAR
RONIER TADMOR BASSINE
(QUEEN OF —) ZENOBIA
PALP FEEL TOUCH CAJOLE FEELER
HANDLE PALPUS FLATTER
TENTACLE
PALPABLE BALD RANK PLAIN
PATENT AUDIBLE EVIDENT
OBVIOUS TACTILE APPARENT
DISTINCT MANIFEST TANGIBLE
CORPOREAL
PALPATION THROB TOUCH
WALLOP DIPPING PITAPAT
PALPEBRA EYELID
PALPITATE PANT QUAP THROB
FLACKER FLICKER FLUTTER
PULSATE
PALPITATION BEAT DUNT PANT
FLICKER FLUTTER PULSATION
SALTATION THROBBING
(— OF HEART) THUMB
PALSIED SHAKY SHAKING
PARALIZED TOTTERING
TREMBLING TREMULOUS
PALSY PARLESIE PARALYSIS
PALTER FIB LIE BABBLE HAGGLE
MUMBLE PARLEY TRIFLE BARGAIN
CHAFFER CHATTER QUIBBLE
SHAFFLE
PALTIEL (FATHER OF —) AZZAN
PALTRY BALD BARE BASE MEAN
ORRA PUNY SCAB VILE WAFF
CHEAP FOOTY MINOR PETTY
SCALD SCALL SCRUB SILLY TRASH
CHETIF FLIMSY JITNEY SHABBY
SLIGHT TRASHY WOEFUL HILDING
PELTING PIMPING PITEOUS
PITIFUL ROYNISH RUBBISH
SCABBED SCRUBBY TRIVIAL
PICAYUNE PICKLING PIDDLING
TRIFLING
PALUDAL MARSHY
PAMELA (AUTHOR OF —)
RICHARDSON
(BROTHER OF —) PHILOCLEA
(CHARACTER IN —) JACOB DAVERS
JERVIS JEWKES PAMELA
ANDREWS SWYNFORD
(FATHER OF —) BASILIUS
PAMPA PLAIN PRAIRIE
PAMPAS (— CAT) KODKOD PAJERO
(— DEER) MAZAME
PAMPER PET BABY CRAM DELT
GLUT POMP HUMOR SPOIL TUTOR
WALLY CARESS COCKER CODDLE
COSHER COSSET CUDDLE CUITER
DANDLE FONDLE MAUNGE
POSSET TIDDLE CHERISH
COCKNEY FORWEAN GRATIFY
INDULGE SATIATE

SMOODGE SAGINATE
PAMPHLET JACK LEAD QUIRE
SHEET TRACT FOLDER BOOKLET
CATALOG LEAFLET NOVELET
BROCHURE CHAPBOOK
WORKBOOK CATALOGUE
NEWSLETTER
PAN FIT TAB VLY MELL PART PRIG
VLEI WASH AGREE BASIN BATEA
COVER GRAND SHEET UNITE
CENSER FRACHE LAPPET PANKIN
PATINA SPIDER VESSEL CRANIUM
CREAMER HARDPAN PORTION
ROASTER SKILLET SUBSOIL
PANNIKIN RIDICULE
(— FOR COALS) BRAZIER
(— OF BALANCE) BOWL BASIN
SCALEPAN
(— WITH 3 FEET) POSNET
(EARTHENWARE —) PANCHEON
(EVAPORATING —) ROOM COVER
TACHE SALTPAN
(GOD —) FAUNUS
(IRON —) YET FRACHE
(LONG-HANDLED —) PINGLE
(MILK —) LEAD
(OIL —) SUMP
(PREF.) PATELLI PATELLO
PANACEA CURE BEZOAR ELIXIR
REMEDY SOLACE CUREALL
GINSENG HEALALL NEPENTHE
CATHOLICON
PANACHE STYLE

PANAMA		
CAPITAL: PANAMA		
COIN: BALBOA		
COUNTY: DARIEN HERRERA		
CROP: ABACA CACAO		
GULF: DARIEN SANBLAS CHIRIQUI MOSQUITO		
ISLAND: COIBA		
LAKE: GATUN		
MEASURE: CELEMIN		
MOUNTAIN: CHICO GANDI COLUMAN SANTIAGO		
MOUNTAIN RANGE: VERAGUA		
PENINSULA: AZUERO		
PORT: CRISTOBAL		
PROVINCE: COCLE COLON CHIRIQUI VERAGUAS		
RIVER: CHEPO SAMBU TUIRA BAYANO PANUGO CHAGRES		
TOWN: COLON DAVID AZUERO BALBOA PANAMA PENONOME SANTIAGO		
TREE: YAYA MARIA QUIRA ALFAJE CATIVO		

PANAMA HAT JIPIJAPA
PANAMINT KOSO
PANCAKE BLIN FLAM AREPA
CREPE FADGE FLAWN KISRA
LEFSE TOURT BLINTZ FRAISE
FROISE CRUMPET FLAPPER
FLIPPER FRITTER HOTCAKE
PIKELET CORNCAKE FLAPJACK
FLIPJACK
(PL.) LEFSEN
PANCREAS BUR NUT
PAND PAWN DRAPERY
PANDA WA WAH BEARCAT
PANDAREUS (DAUGHTER OF —)

AEDON MEROPE CLEOTHERA
(FATHER OF —) MEROPS
(WIFE OF —) HARMOTHOE
PANDARUS (BROTHER OF —) BITIAS
(FATHER OF —) LYCAON ALCANOR
PANDAVA BHIMA
PANDECT COMPENDIUM
PANDEMONIUM DIN HELL CHAOS
NOISE TUMULT UPROAR
DISORDER CONFUSION
PANDER BAWD PIMP BULLY CATER
BROKER MICHER PURVEY
RUFFIAN WHISKIN PROCURER
BAWDSTROT
PANDION (BROTHER OF —)
PLEXIPPUS
(DAUGHTER OF —) PROCNE
PHILOMELA
(FATHER OF —) CECROPS PHINEUS
ERICHTHONIUS
(MOTHER OF —) CLEOPATRA
(SON OF —) BUTES LYCUS NISUS
AEGEUS PALLAS ERECHTHEUS
(WIFE OF —) PYLIA
PANDORA BANDORE
(BROTHER OF —) PROMETHEUS
(HUSBAND OF —) EPIMETHEUS
PANDOWDY PIE DESSERT
PANDU (BROTHER OF —)
DURYODHANA
(FATHER OF —) DHRITARASHTRA
PANE GLASS GLAZE LOZEN PANEL
QUIRK SHEET SHOCK SLASH
QUARRY QUARREL SECTION
PORTLIGHT
PANEGYRIC ELOGE ELOGY EULOGY
PRAISE ORATION TRIBUTE
ENCOMIUM LAUDATION
PANEL FIN PAN JURY SKIN BOARD
GROUP LABEL TABLE ABACUS
ASSIZE COFFER HURDLE MIRROR
PADDLE PILLOW ROSACE TABLET
TYMPAN CAISSON CONSOLE
FLIPPER LACUNAR DECORATE
MANDORLA MEDALLION
(— IN FENCE) LOOP
(— IN GARMENT) LAP STEAK
(CIRCULAR —) ROUNDEL
(GAUZE —) SCRIM
(GLAZED —) LAYLIGHT
(LEGAL —) ARRAY
(RECESSED —) ORB COFFER
LACUNAR
(SUNKEN —) CAISSON CASSOON
(3-PART —) TRIPTYCH
PANFISH SCUP
PANG ACHE CRAM FILL GIRD PAIN
STAB TANG AGONY PINCH PRONG
SPASM STANG STOUN STUFF
THROE SHOWER STOUND TWINGE
ANGUISH TRAVAIL
(PL.) GNAWINGS
PANGLOSS (PUPIL OF —) CANDIDE
PANGOLIN MANID MANIS
ANTEATER EDENTATE TANGILIN
PANGWE FAN FANG
PANHANDLE BEG CADGE SKELB
SKILDER
(— STATE) WV WVA
PANIC FEAR FRAY FUNK WILD
ALARM AMAZE CHAOS SCARE
FRIGHT SCHRIK TERROR SWITHER
CONSTERNATION

PANICKY FUNKY
PANICLE JUBA WHISK ANTHELA
PANNIER BAG PED SERON BASKET
CAJAVA CURAGH DORSEL
DORSER DOSSAL DOSSER PANTRY
CORBEIL CURRACK KAJAWAH
KEDJAVE
PANOPE (FATHER OF —) NEREUS
(MOTHER OF —) DORIS
PANOPEUS (BROTHER OF —) CRISUS
(COMPANION OF —) AMPHITRYON
(DAUGHTER OF —) AEGLE
(FATHER OF —) PHOCUS
(MOTHER OF —) ASTERIA
PANOPLY POMP ARMOR UNIFORM
PANORAMA VIEW RANGE SCENE
SWEEP VISTA NEORAMA PICTURE
SCENERY CYCLORAMA
POLYORAMA
PANPIPE SICU SIKU QUILL ANTARA
SYRINX ZAMPOGNA
PANSY FANCY PENSE VIOLA
KISSES PENSEE VIOLET TRINITY
FANTASQUE HEARTEASE
(PREF.) VIOL
PANT FAB ACHE BEAT BLOW FUFF
GAPE GASP HECH LONG PANK
PECH PEGH PINE PIPE PUFF TIFT
FLAFF HEAVE QUIRK STECH
SUGGE THROB YEARN ANHELE
ASPIRE FRIESE PANTLE PULSATE
PANTAGRUEL (COMPANION OF —)
PANURGE
(FATHER OF —) GARGANTUA
(MOTHER OF —) BADEBEC
PANTALOONS PANTS TROUSERS
PANTHEA (HUSBAND OF —)
ABRADATUS
PANTHEIST AMALRICIAN
PANTHEON TEMPLE ROTUNDA
VALHALL VALHALLA
PANTHER CAT PARD PUMA
COUGAR JAGUAR LEOPARD
PAINTER PANTILE
PANTIES SCANTIES
PANTILE TILE IMBREX BISCUIT
HARDTACK
PANTING ANHELOSE ANHELOUS
PANTOGRAPH EIDOGRAPH
POLYGRAPH
PANTOMIME PLAY PANTO
PANTRY CAVE STUE AMBRY
COVEY CUDDY CLOSET LARDER
SPENCE BUTLERY BUTTERY
PANNIER PANTLER SERVERY
SPICERY CUPBOARD
PANTS JEANS LEVIS BRIEFS
SLACKS DRAWERS JODHPUR
BREECHES BRITCHES KICKSIES
KNICKERS SNUGGIES TROUSERS
(— WITH WIDE BOTTOMS) BELLS
(LEATHER —) CHAPS LEDERHOSEN
(WIDE-LEGGED —) PALAZZO
PANUELO COLLAR RUFFLE
KERCHIEF NECKCLOTH
PANURGE (COMPANION OF —)
PANTAGRUEL
PANZER TANK
PAOLO (LOVER OF —) FRANCESCA
PAP DUG TIT POBS TEAT NIPPLE
EMULSION FLUMMERY
PAPA PA DAD PAP PAW POP SIN
BABA EVIL DADDY LOVER PAPPY

BABOON FATHER POTATO PRIEST
HUSBAND VULTURE
PAPAL (ALSO SEE POPE) POPAL
PAPANE POPELY APOSTOLIC
PAPAW PAPA ASIMEN PAPAIO
ASIMINA CORAZON JASMINE
PAPAYA PAPAW LECHOSA
PAPER LIL WEB BILL BOND BLANK
BROKE ESSAY STUDY THEME
ASTHMA BINDLE CARTEL PAPIER
REPORT RETREE VESSEL CHEVIOT
EXHIBIT JOURNAL WRITING
YOSHINO DOCUMENT
MONOGRAPH NEWSPRINT
ONIONSKIN PARCHMENT
VALENTINE
(— FOLDER) STROKER
(— MAKER) WASHERMAN
(— NAUTILUS) ARGONAUT
(— PULP) WATERLEAF
(— QUANTITY) PAGE REAM QUIRE
SHEET BUNDLE
(ABSORBENT —) BLOTTER
TOWELLING
(ALBUMINIZED —) SAXE
(BUILDING —) FELT
(BUNDLE OF —S) DUFTER DOSSIER
(CHINESE —) INDIA
(COMMERCIAL —) PORTFOLIO
(DAMAGED —) BROKE CASSE
SALLE RETREE
(DEFECTIVE —) BROKES
(DRAWING —) TORCHON
(FOLDED —) SADDLE AIRPLANE
(GLOSS —) GILL
(HARD —) PELURE
(HEAVY —) FELT
(LAVATORY —) BUMF
(LINING —S) SKIPS
(NEGOTIABLE —) STIFF
(OFFICIAL —) TARGE HOOKUM
DOCUMENT
(PARCHMENT —) VELLUM
PERGAMYN
(PHOTOGRAPHIC —) SEPIA
(SIZE OF —) CAP COPY DEMI NOTE
POST POTT TOWN ATLAS CROWN
FOLIO JESUS LARGE LEGAL ROYAL
SIXMO ALBERT BILLET CASING
LETTER MEDIUM THIRDS
BASTARD CABINET EMPEROR
THEOREM ELEPHANT FOOLSCAP
IMPERIAL
(STRIP OF —) TAPE
(THIN —) FLIMSY PELURE TISSUE
ONIONSKIN
(TOILET —) BUMF
(UNCUT —) BOLT
(WALL —) TENTURE
(WATERMARKED —) BATONNE
(WRAPPING —) SKIP KRAFT
SEALING SCREENING
(WRITING —) FLAT LINEN
WEDDING
(PREF.) PAPYRO
PAPERBARK CAJEPUT MILKWOOD
PAPERBOARD BENDER VENEER
CARDBOARD CHIPBOARD
PULPBOARD
PAPILLA CERAS DEIRID NIPPLE
PAPULA MAMMULA THELIUM
(PL.) CERATA
PAPILLOMA ANGLEBERRY

PAPIO MORMON
PAPIST TORY PAPANE CATHOLIC
POPELING
PAPPUS DOWN AIGRETTE
THISTLEDOWN
PAPPY PA DAD PAW PAPA SOFT
MUSHY PULPY FATHER
SUCCULENT
PAPRIKA PIMENTO PIMIENTO
PAPUA (BAY OF —) DYKE MILNE
ACLAND HOLNICOTE
(CAPITAL OF —) PORTMORESBY
(MONEY OF —) KINA
(RIVER OF —) FLY KIKORI PURARI
(TOWN OF —) LAE BUNA DARU
WEWAK GOROKA KIKORI
MADANG SAMARAI
PAPUAN ARAU BIAK HULA KATE
BUANG EKARI KIWAI KWOMA
SIVAI SULKA BAITSI BANARO
IATMUL KEREWA KOIARI
ARAPESH BAINING
PAPULE WHELK PIMPLE
PAPYRUS REED PAPER SEDGE
BIBLOS GLUMAL SCROLL
BULRUSH
(— STRIP) ORIHON
PAR BY NORM EQUAL NORMAL
AVERAGE EQUALITY
(ONE OVER —) BOGIE
(ONE UNDER —) BIRDIE
(TWO UNDER —) EAGLE
PARA FODDA PERAU PARRAH
PARABLE MYTH TALE FABLE
STORY APOLOG BYWORD MASHAL
SAMPLE BYSPELL PROVERB
ALLEGORY APOLOGUE FORBYSEN
LIKENESS SIMILITUDE
PARABOLA ARC CURVE ANTENNA
PARACETAMOL PANADOL
PARACHUTE SILK CHUTE BROLLY
DROGUE PATAGIUM STREAMER
(SMALL —) BALLUTE
PARACHUTIST PATHFINDER
(PL.) STICK
PARACLETE AIDER HELPER
PLEADER ADVOCATE CONSOLER
COMFORTER
PARADE JET TOP POMP SHOW
WALK MARCH STRUT FLAUNT
MUSTER REVIEW STROLL
CORTEGE DISPLAY EXHIBIT
MARSHAL CEREMONY EXERCISE
FLOURISH GRANDEUR SPLENDOR
PAGEANTRY
(— GROUND) MAIDAN
(— OF BULLFIGHTERS) PASEO
(UNSUBSTANTIAL —) PAGEANT
PARADED AFFICHE
PARADISE EDEN JODO BLISS
JENNA AIDENN GOLOKA HEAVEN
PARVIS ELYSIUM NIRVANA
(— OF INDRA) SVARGA SWARGA
(— TREE) ACEITUNA STAVEWOOD
PARADOX KOAN ANTINOMY
PARADOXURE MUSANG
PARAFFIN ALKANE
PARAGON GEM HERO PINK TYPE
IDEAL MODEL PEARL APERSEE
PATTERN PEROPUS PHOENIX
NONESUCH NONPARIEL
(— OF KNIGHTHOOD) PALADIN
PARAGRAPH ITEM SIGN CAPUT

PAUSE CLAUSE NOTICE RUBRIC ARTICLE INITIAL PILCROW SECTION CAUSERIE MATERIAL PEELCROW PERSONAL SUBLEADER
(— MARK) PILCROW
(UNIMPORTANT —S) BALAAM

PARAGUAY
CAPITAL: ASUNCION
COIN: GUARANI
DEPARTMENT: GUAIRA ITAPUA OLIMPO CAAZAPA BOQUERON
LAKE: VERA YPOA YPACARAI
LANGUAGE: GUARANI
MEASURE: PIE LINE LINO VARA LEGUA LINEA CORDEL CUADRA CUARTA FANEGA
PLAIN: CHACO
RIVER: YPANE ACARAY PARANA CONFUSO
TOWN: LUQUE PILAR CAACUPE CAAZAPA TRINIDAD CONCEPCION VILLARRICA
WEIGHT: QUINTAL

PARAKEET CONURE PARROT WELLAT ROSELLA ARATINGA KAKARIKI POPINJAY ROSEHILL GREENLEEK
PARALLEL EVEN LIKE ALONG EQUAL MATCH SECOND EXAMPLE FRONTAL PARAGON PENDANT ANALOGUE LIKENESS MULTIPLE QUANTITY
(PREF.) ORTH(O) PAR(A)
PARALLELEPIPED CUBOID
PARALLELISM PARITY ANALOGY
PARALLELOGRAM RHOMB OBLONG SQUARE RHOMBUS RHOMBOID RECTANGLE
PARALYSIS CRAMP PALSY POLIO SHOCK PARESIS DIPLEGIA PARAPLEGIA POLIOMYELITIS
(SUFF.) LYSE LYSIS LYST LYTE LYTIC LYZE
PARALYZE DARE DAZE STUN PALSY SCRAM ASTONY BENUMB CONGEAL IMPALSY PETRIFY TORPEDO TORPEFY
PARALYZED NUMB PALSIED CRIPPLED
PARAMORPHINE THEBAINE
PARAMOUNT ABOVE CHIEF RULER SOVRAN CAPITAL SUPREME DOMINANT SUPERIOR SUZERAIN SOVEREIGN
PARAMOUR DOLL PRIM PURE LEMAN LOVER WOMAN WOOER AMORET FRIEND MASTER MINION FRANION GALLANT HETAERA RUFFIAN SERVANT SPECIAL SULTANA STALLION BOYFRIEND
PARAPET BUTT WALL BAHUT REDAN BARBET BONNET FLECHE PARPEN TRENCH BULWARK PLUTEUS RAILING RAMPART BARTIZAN ENVELOPE TRAVERSE
PARAPH RUBRIC
PARAPHERNALIA GEAR EQUIPAGE APPARATUS EQUIPMENT TRAPPINGS
PARAPHRASE FARSE REWORD

TARGET TARGUM PREFACE THARGUM VERSION TRANSLATE
PARASITE BUG BUR FLY BURR MOSS SPIV TRYP CHARK DRONE LEECH SHARK TOADY VIRUS FEEDER FUNGUS GNATHO SHADOW SPONGE SUCKER BLEEDER BYWONER SPONGER TAGTAIL DICYEMID ENTOZOON EPIPHYTE HANGERON SLAVERER INFESTANT POTHUNTER SACCULINA SPARGANUM SYCOPHANT TOADEATER TUBHUNTER
(— ON TROUT) SUG
(PL.) ECTOZOA ENTOZOA DRIFTWOOD
(PREF.) **(VEGETABLE —)** PHYT(I)(O)
PARASITIC CYTOZOIC TRENCHER BIOPHILOUS
(— JAEGER) SHOOI DIRTBIRD
PARASOL SHADE AOGIRI SHADOW ROUNDEL TIRESOL KITTYSOL SUNSHADE UMBRELLA
(— MUSHROOM) LEPIOTA
(PREF.) UMBELL(I)
PARAVANE OTTER
PARBOIL CODDLE
PARBOILED LEEPIT
PARCEL DAK LOT DAWK DEAD DEAL DOLE METE PACK PART WISP BULSE BUNCH GROUP PIECE BUNDLE DIVIDE FARDEL PACKET PASSEL CONACRE PACKAGE PORTION COMMODITY
(— OF DIAMONDS) SERIES
(— OF GROUND) LOT PICK CLOSE SOLUM SUERTE CONACRE PENDICLE
(— OF HEMP FIBER) PIG
(— OF JEWELS) BULSE
(— OUT) ALLOT
PARCH DRY FRY BURN COOK SEAR ROAST TOAST PEARCH RIZZER SCORCH BRISTLE BRUSTLE GRADDAN SHRIVEL TORREFY TORRIFY
(PREF.) TORRE XER(O)
PARCHED ARID HUSK SERE ADUST FIERY GIZZEN TORRID THIRSTY SCORCHED
PARCHING URENT
PARCHMENT LARK FOREL CHARTA MEZUZAH PAPYRIN SCYTALE DRUMHEAD SHEEPSKIN PALIMPSEST
(— PAPER) DOCKET PERGAMYN
(FINE —) VEL VELLUM
(PIECE OF —) MEMBRANE
(ROLL OF —) PELL SCROLL
PARD PAL CHUM TIGER FRIEND LEOPARD PANTHER PARTNER COMPANION
PARDON FREE CLEAR COVER GRACE MERCY REMIT SPARE ACQUIT ASSOIL EXCUSE SHRIVE ABSOLVE AMNESTY CONDONE FORGIVE OVERLOOK REPRIEVE TOLERATE EXCULPATE
PARDONABLE VENIAL VENIABLE EXCUSABLE
PARDONER QUESTOR QUAESTOR
PARE CUP CHIP COPE FLAY PEEL

SKIN FRIZZ SHAVE SKELP SKIVE SLIPE SPADE CHISEL REDUCE REMOVE RESECT CURTAIL FLAUGHT WHITTLE
(— LEATHER) SKIVE
(— SOD) BURNBEAT
(— STAVES) BUCK
(— STONE) BOAST
PAREGORIC ANODYNE MITIGATING
PAREL PARELL APPAREL CLOTHING ORNAMENT
PARENCHYMA AMYLOM MESOPHYL
PARENT DAD DAM MAMA PAPA SIRE DADDY ELDER MATER PATER AUTHOR FATHER MOTHER ORIGIN FORBEAR GENITOR ANCESTOR BEGETTER FILICIDE GUARDIAN
PARENTAGE KIND BIRTH BROOD FAMILY ORIGIN PROGENY ENGENDURE
PARENTHESIS HOOK ASIDE PAREN BRACKET TOENAIL INNUENDO INTERVAL INTERLUDE
(PL.) HOOKS CURVES
PAREVE NEUTRAL
PARGET COAT GYPSUM PARIET PLASTER DECORATE WHITEWASH
PARGO MUTTONFISH
PARHELION DOG SUN SUNDOG
PARIAH PAREA ISHMAEL OUTCAST
PARIAN CHINA MARBLE PORCELAIN
PARIETAL SOMAL SOMATIC
PARI-MUTUEL TOTE TOTALIZER
PARING CHIP FOIL SHRED SPECK GUBBIN PARURE PEELING
(FISH —S) GUBBINS
(PL.) BOXING
PARIS ALEXANDER
(— AIRPORT) ORLY
(FATHER OF —) PRIAM
(MOTHER OF —) HECUBA
(PALACE IN —) ELYSEE LOUVRE TUILERIES
(RIVER OF —) SEINE
(STOCK EXCHANGE IN —) BOURSE
(SUBWAY IN —) METRO
(WIFE OF —) OENONE OENONE
PARISH CURE HOUSE TITLE CHARGE SOCIETY PECULIAR OUTPARISH
(— HEAD) PASTOR PRIEST MINISTER
(— MEETING) VESTRY
PARISIAN LUTETIAN
PARISINA (BELOVED OF —) HUGO
(HUSBAND OF —) AZO
PARISON BLOW GATHERING
PARITY ANALOGY EQUALITY LIKENESS GRAVIDITY
PARK HAY PEN HOLE STOP WAIT GREEN LEAVE CIRCLE DAPHNE GARDEN PRATER COMMONS DIAMOND PADDOCK TERRACE PARADISE TETRAGON
PARKA PARCA ANORAK JACKET PULLOVER
PARKLEAVES TUTSAN
PARLANCE TALK IDIOM SPEECH DICTION DISCOURSE
PARLAY DOUBLE

PARLEY DODGE PARLE SPEAK TREAT UTTER CONFER INDABA PALTER PAROLI DISCUSS PALAVER PARLING PARLANCE DISCOURSE TEMPORIZE NEGOTIATION
PARLIAMENT DIET RUMP TING COURT SENAT CORTES FANTAN MAJLIS SAEIMA COUNCIL ESTATES KNESSET LAGTING RIKSDAG TYNWALD CONGRESS CONVERSE STORTING VOLKSRAAD
(GREEK —) BOULE
(SCAND. —) THING
PARLIAMENTARIAN APRONEER
PARLOR BEN BOOR HALL FOREROOM LOCUTORY SNUGGERY SOLARIUM
(COUNTRY —) SPENCE
(MILKING —) BAIL
PARLORMAID MATRON
PARLOUS KEEN RISKY CLEVER SHREWD CUNNING CRITICAL PERILOUS DANGEROUS HAZARDOUS
PARMASHTA (FATHER OF —) HAMAN
PARMESAN GRANA
PARNACH (SON OF —) ELIZAPHAN
PAROCHIAL PETTY NARROW PAROCHIAN SECTARIAN
PARODIST SPOOFER
PARODY RIB SKIT SPOOF SATIRE TRAVESTY BURLESQUE IMITATION
PAROLE FAITH PLEDGE LICENSE PROMISE
PARONOMASIA PUN AGNOMINATION
PARONYCHIA FELON PANARIS WHITLOW NAILWORT
PAROTITIS MUMPS
PAROXYSM FIT KINK PANG AGONY COLIC QUIRK SPASM STORM STOUR THROE ACCESS ATTACK FRENZY ORGASM RAPTUS SHOWER RAPTURE EPITASIS AGITATION
PARR PAR SAMLET SCEGGER SKEGGER BRANDLIN BRANDLING
PARROT ARA HIA KEA COPY ECHO JAKO KAKA LORO LORY POLL VAZA ARARA CAGIT MACAW MIMIC POLLY AMAZON CAIQUE CONURE KAKAPO REPEAT TIRIBA CORELLA GRASSIE ITERATE LORILET COCKATOO LORIKEET LOVEBIRD PARAKEET PICARIAN POPINJAY BROADTAIL COCKATEEL
(PREF.) PSITTAC(I)
PARROT FISH LORO SCAR LANIA LAUIA SCAUR VIEJA COTORO SCARUS LABROID MUDFISH OLDWIFE BLUEFISH
PARRY FEND STOP WARD AVOID BLOCK DODGE EVADE FENCE PRIME QUART SIXTE OCTAVE PARADE QUINTE SECOND THWART TIERCE COUNTER DEFLECT EVASION
PARSE PACE PEARCE ANALYZE DIAGRAM DISSECT CONSTRUE ANATOMIZE

PARSEGHIAN ARA
PARSHANDATHA (FATHER OF —)
HAMAN
PARSI ZOROASTRIAN
(— HOLY BOOK) AVESTA
(— PRIEST) MOBED DASTUR
PARSIFAL (CHARACTER IN —)
KUNDRY TITUREL AMFORTAS
KLINGSOR PARSIFAL GURNEMANZ
(COMPOSER OF —) WAGNER
PARSIMONIOUS GARE MEAN
NEAR NIGH CLOSE MINGY NIPPY
SCANT SPARE TIGHT FRUGAL
NARROW SCARCE SCOTCH
SKIMPY SORDID STINGY STRAIT
MISERLY SCRIMPY SPARING
COVETOUS GRASPING GRUDGING
SCREWING WRETCHED
MERCENARY NIGGARDLY
PENURIOUS RETENTIVE
ABERDONIAN
PARSLEY ACHE CUMIN UMBEL
CICELY CONIUM ELTROT KARPAS
CHERVIL HOGWEED FLUELLIN
PARSLEY CAMPHOR APIOL
APIOLE
PARSNIP TANK WYPE UMBEL
CONIUM MADNEP CADWEED
HOGWEED SKIRRET BUNDWEED
QUEENWEED
(WATER —) SIUM
PARSON RECTOR CROAKER
PATRICO PERSONA MINISTER
PREACHER GUIDEPOST
(COUNTRY —) RUM
(PL.) PARSONRY
PARSONAGE GLEBE MANSE
RECTORY PASTORATE
PASTORIUM
PARSON BIRD POE TUI KOKO
TUWI POEBIRD POYBIRD
PART DEL END LOT PAN DEAL
DOLE FECK GRIN HAET HALF
HAND NECK PANE ROLE ROVE
SECT SHED SIDE SOME TEAR
TWIN AUGHT PARTY PIECE
QUOTA SEVER SHARE SHODE
SNACK SPLIT TWAIN BEHALF
CANTON CLEAVE DEPART DETAIL
DIVIDE FEEDER FINGER MEMBER
MINUTE MOIETY PARCEL PORTIO
QUORUM SECTOR SINGLE
SUNDER UNYOKE DISJOIN
ELEMENT FEATURE FRUSTUM
PORTION SECTION SEGMENT
SEVERAL ALIENATE DISSEVER
DIVISION ELIQUATE FRACTION
LIRIPIPE
(— HAIR) SHADE
(— OF ANIMAL'S TAIL) DOCK
(— OF BEEF) CHUCK SKINK
(— OF BLAST FURNACE) BOSH
BELLY
(— OF BOW) PEAK
(— OF CAM WHEEL) LOBE
(— OF CANNON) CHASE
(— OF COMPASS) FLY
(— OF CONCERTO) CEMBALO
(— OF CONFIRMATION SERVICE)
ALAPA
(— OF CROSSBOW) LATH
(— OF DIAMOND) BEZEL
(— OF FLEECE) LEECH

(— OF FOWL'S COMB) BLADE
(— OF GUN SHIELD) APRON
(— OF HARBOR) FAIRWAY
(— OF HAWK'S BEAK) CLAP
(— OF HIDE) RANGE
(— OF HOOKAH) CHILLUM
(— OF MASS) INTROIT
(— OF POETIC FOOT) ARSIS
(— OF PORK LOIN) GRISKIN
(— OF RIVER) FRESH
(— OF SADDLE TREE) FORK
(— OF STAIR TREAD) NOSING
(— OF STAMEN) ANTHER
(— OF SWORD) FORTE
(— OF SWORD BLADE) FOIBLE
(— OF TEMPLE) CELLA
(— OF TONGUE) DORSUM
(— OF TURTLE) CALIPEE
(— OF VIOLIN BOW) BAGUET
(— OF WHEEL) SPEECH
(— THAT REVOLVES) ROTOR
(— WITH) GIVE LOSE SELL LEAVE
DONATE ABANDON
(— OF CHAIR) SPLAT
(ACCOMPANYING —) BURDEN
OBBLIGATO
(ASSUMED —) FIGURE
(BAGLIKE —) SAC
(BEST —) FAT YOLK CREAM
FLOWER MARROW
(BRISTLELIKE —) SETA
(BROADEST — OF PLANK) TOUCH
(CENTRAL —) HUB BODY CORE
HEART KERNEL
(CHOICE —) ELITE
(CLEAR — OF LIQUID) SWIM
(CLOSING —) HEEL
(COARSE — OF FLAX) HURDS
(CONICAL —) BULLET
(CURVED —) START
(DEPRESSED —) HOLLOW
(DISTANT —S) FARNESS
(DUPLICATE —) SPARE
(EDIBLE — OF CLAM) CHEEK
(ESSENTIAL —) PITH
(ESSENTIAL —S) STAMINA
(FIFTH —) QUINTUS
(FINAL —) LAST SHANK EPILOG
(FIRST —) FRONT PRIME VAUNT
INITIAL BEGINNING
(FOURTH —) FARDEL FORPIT
FERLING
(FRONT —) VAUNT BREAST
FORESIDE
(GREATER —) HEFT SUBSTANCE
(HARDEST —) BRUNT
(HIGHEST —) CROPCROWNHEIGHT
(HUNDREDTH —) CENTESM
(IMPAIRING —) ALLOY
(IN —) HALVES
(INDETERMINATE —) PERCENTAGE
(INNERMOST —) FUND
(INNERMOST —S) PENETRALIA
(INSTRUMENTAL —) HAND
CONTINUO
(INTERLACED —) TWINE
(INTRODUCTORY —) PROTASIS
(LARGE —) FORCE
(LATERAL — OF HEAD) CHEEK
(LATTER —) HEEL SHANK
(LEAST —) STITCH
(LOWER —) SECONDO
(LOWER — OF ROBE) BASES

(LOWEST —) FOOT BOTTOM
GROUND DESCENT
(MAIN —) BODY BULK SUBSTANCE
(MATERIAL —) GIST
(MIDDLE —) DEEP CENTER
(MIDDLE — OF NIGHT) HOWE
(MINOR —) BIT COG
(MINUTE —) PRICK TITTLE
(MISSING —) LACUNA
(MOST IMPORTANT —) EYE
FOREHAND
(MOST SERIOUS —) DICKENS
(OF HORSE'S THIGH) GASKIN
(OVERDUE —) ARREAR
(PRINCIPAL —) BODY MAIN GROSS
(PRIVATE —) THING MEMBER
(PROJECTING —) ARM JAG JET JOG
APSE LOBE SPURN
(PROTUBERANT —) BOSS BULGE
(REJECTED —S) CHANKINGS
(REMAINING —) BUTT DREG HEEL
(REMOTEST —) EXTREMITY
(RINGLIKE —) ANNULUS
(ROOTLIKE —) RADICLE
(ROUNDED —) BULB
(SAWLIKE —) SERRA
(SECRET —) RECESS
(SLENDER —) NECK
(SMALL —) BIT ATOM FLOW TITHE
DETAIL MINUTE SNIPPET
(SMALLEST —) ATOM WHIT MINIM
(SOFT — OF BREAD) CRUMB
(SOFT — OF VEIN) LEATH
(SOLO —) CALL
(STAMEN —) ANTHER
(STILL — OF WATER) KELD
(SWINGING —) FLAIL
(TELLING —) POINT
(TENTH —) TITHE
(THIN — OF WALL) ALLEGE
(THIRD —) THIRDENDEAL
(TOP —) HEADPIECE
(TWELFTH —) INCIA POINT UNCIAL
(UPPER —) CHIEF RIDGE
OVERPARTY
(UPPERMOST —) TOP PEAK CHIEF
UPSIDE TOPSIDE
(VAUDEVILLE —) OLIO
(VITAL —) HEART
(WINGLIKE —) ALA
(WORST —) DEPTH
(WORTHLESS —) DREGS
(24TH —) CARAT
(360TH —) DEGREE
(PREF.) MER(I)(O) PARTI
(SUFF.) MER(E)(IC)(IS)(OUS)(Y)
TOMA TOME TOMIC TOMOUS
TOMY
PARTAKE BITE PART SHARE
DIVIDE PARTEN PARTICIPATE
(— OF) USE HAVE SHARE TASTE
TOUCH IMPART
PARTAN CRAB
PARTED PARTITE
PARTHAON (FATHER OF —)
AGENOR
(MOTHER OF —) EPICASTE
(SON OF —) OENEUS
(WIFE OF —) EURYTE
PARTHENIA (HUSBAND OF —)
ARGALUS
PARTHENIUS (BROTHER OF —)
PANDION

(FATHER OF —) PHINEUS
(MOTHER OF —) CLEOPATRA
PARTHENOGENETIC AGAMIC
AGAMOUS
PARTIAL HALF PART SEMI BIASED
UNFAIR COLORED HALFWAY
UNEQUAL HARMONIC INCLINED
PARTISAN PROPENSE SKELETON
FAVORABLE SEGMENTAL
PARTICULAR RESPECTIVE
(PREF.) DEMI MER(I)(O) MES(O)
SEMI
PARTIALITY FAVOR RESPECT
AFFECTION SPECIALTY
PARTIALLY HALF HALFWAY
HALFWISE
PARTICIPANT BOOK ACTOR PARTY
MEMBER PARTNER DUETTIST
PARTABLE PARTISAN
(SUBORDINATE —) STOOGE
(PL.) FIELD
PARTICIPATE JOIN SIDE ENTER
SHARE ENGAGE ENLIST IMPART
COMPETE PARTAKE
(— IN) GO HAVE JOIN STAY STAND
TASTE COMMON STICKLE
PARTICIPATION HAND PLOT
SOCIETY INTEREST
(COMMON —) COMMUNITY
PARTICIPATOR
(SUFF.) STER STRESS
PARTICIPLE VERBID
PARTICLE ACE BIT DOT FIG GRU
JOT RAY ATOM BETA CORN CROT
CURN DUST GRUE HAET IOTA
KNIT MITE MOTE SNIP SPOT STIM
WHIT ALPHA BOSON FLAKE FLECK
GHOST GRAIN MESON OMEGA
POINT QUARK SHRED SIGMA
SPECK STARN STIME THRUM
TWINT FILING GEIGER LEPTON
MOMENT PANGEN PARTON
RIZZOM SMIDGE SMITCH TITTLE
VIRION AMICRON FERMION
GEMMULE GRANULE NUCLEUS
PSYCHON SINGLET SMIDGIN
TACHYON ACCEPTER NEUTRINO
SMIDGEON SYLLABLE MICROSOME
POSITRINO SCINTILLA
(— IN BLOOD) EMBOLUS
(— IN INTERNAL EAR) OTOCONIUM
(— OF FIRE) SPARK
(— OF GOLD) COLOR
(— OF SOOT) ISEL IZLE SMUT AIZLE
(—S IN BEER) FLOATERS
(—S OF GRAIN) CHOP
(ATOMIC —) ION BARYON HADRON
LEPTON ELECTRON
(COLLECTION OF CHARGED —S)
PLASMA
(COMBINING —) ACCEPTOR
(ELECTRIFIED —) ION ANION
PROTON POSITRON
THERMION
(ELEMENTARY —) MUON NEUTRON
NEUTRINO
(FINE ICY —S) SLEET
(GROUP OF —S) MESON
(HYPOTHETICAL —) QUARK
(JAGGED —) SPLINTER
(LEAST POSSIBLE —) MINIM
(LINGUISTIC —) SERVILE
(MINUTE —) JOT ORT RAY ATOM

GRAIN SPECK RAMENT GRANULE MOLECULE RAMENTUM CORPUSCLE
(NEGATIVE —) NOR NOT
(NUCLEAR —S) FALLOUT
(POSITIVELY-CHARGED —) CATION KATION
(SMALL —) NIP BLEB CORN MOTE CRUMB GRAIN SPECK AMICRON GRANULE SPRINKLE SUBMICRON
(TINY —) ATOMY
(ULTIMATE —) PSYCHON
(UNCHARGED —) LAMBDA
(PL.) DUST FINES SWARF SIZINGS CUTTINGS FURFURES
(SUFF.) PLAST
(— OF A KIND) ID
PARTI-COLORED PIED FANCY MOTLEY PARTED PIEBALD BUTTERFLY HARLEQUIN
PARTICULAR AND ATOM FIXY ITEM NICE SELF SOME FUSSY PARTY POINT THING CHOOSY DAINTY DETAIL MINUTE MOROSE REGARD SINGLE STICKY ARTICLE CAREFUL CERTAIN CORRECT FINICKY PRECISE PRIVATE RESPECT SEVERAL SPECIAL UNUSUAL CLERKISH CONCRETE ESPECIAL PECULIAR PICKSOME PRECIOUS SINGULAR SUBALTERN RESPECTIVE
(NOT —) INCURIOUS
PARTICULARLY ONLY EXTRA SINGLY SPECIAL EXPRESSLY SPECIALLY
PARTING DEATH GOODBYE FAREWELL
(— AS OF HAIR) SHED
PARTISAN PIKE SIDER STAFF BIASED FACTOR FAUTOR MARIAN ZEALOT CALOTIN DEVOTEE GUISARD PARTNER ADHERENT CRISTINO ESPOUSER FAVORITE FENNOMAN FOLLOWER HENCHMAN JACOBITE MOSSBACK SIDESMAN STALWART URBANIST HIGHFLIER MAZZINIST OCHLOCRAT OLIVERIAN SECTARIAN TERRORIST
(NOT —) CATHOLIC
(PL.) FOLLOWING
(SUFF.) CRAT
PARTITION BAR CUT DAM FIN FLAG SEPT WALL SHOJI SPEER STAGE WITHE BAFFLE DIVIDE PARPAL PARPEN SCONCE SCREEN SEPTUM BARRIER CLOISON ENCLOSE GRATING PINFOLD PORTION SCANTLE BRATTICE BULKHEAD CLEAVAGE DIVISION STOPPING TRAVERSE DASHBOARD DAYABHAGA ICONOSTAS MESENTERY STOOTHING
(— BETWEEN STALLS) TRAVIS TREVIS TRAVISS
(— IN CHIMNEY) WITH WITHE
(— IN CORAL) TABULA
(— IN COTTAGE) SPEER HALLAN
(— IN FRUIT) REPLUM
(— IN LOUDSPEAKER) BAFFLE
(— IN WATERWHEEL) WREST

(— OF ESTATE) BOEDELSCHEIDING
(— OF LATH AND PLASTER) STOOTHING
(HORIZONTAL —) STAGE
(MINING —) SOLLAR BRATTICE STOPPING
(PL.) CANCELLI
PARTLET HEN WOMAN PERTELOT
PARTLY WHAT PARCEL PARTIM HALFLINGS
(PREF.) SEMI
PARTNER BOY PAL ALLY HALF MATE PARD WIFE BUDDY BUTTY PARTY FELLOW MARROW SHARER COMRADE CONSORT HUSBAND CAMARADA COPEMATE SIDEKICK YOKEMATE
(— OF DUMMY) VIVANT
(DANCING —) GIGOLO CAVALIER
(PREF.) CO
PARTNERSHIP HUI AXIS FIRM HOUSE FUSION CAHOOTS COMPANY CONSORT SOCIETY SOCIETEIT
PARTRIDGE HUN BIRD KYAH YUTU LERWA RUDGE TITAR CHUKAR REDLEG SEESEE CHEEPER PATRICK SHRIMPI TINAMOU BOBWHITE FRANCOLIN FRENCHMAN TETRAONID
(— NOISE) JUCK
(SAND —) TEHOO
(YOUNG —) CHEEPER SQUEALER
PARTRIDGEBERRY BOXBERRY COWBERRY EYEBERRY ONEBERRY SNOWBERRY TWINBERRY
PARTS
(PREF.) (SIDE —) ALI
PART-SONG MADRIGAL
PART-TIME PARCEL
PARTURITION EUTOCIA TRAVAIL CHILDBED DELIVERY DYSTOCIA
(SUFF.) TOKY
PARTY DO BAL BEE CRY TEA CAMP CLAN DRUM GALA SECT SIDE BINGE BLAST BRAWL BUNCH CABAL COVEY CRUSH GROUP LEVEE COMITE FIESTA FROLIC FRONDE GERMAN INFARE JUNKET PERSON SETOUT SHINDY SHOWER BLOWOUT CANTICO COMPANY FACTION GREGORY PATARIA SHINDIG CLAMBAKE DRINKING FENNOMAN POTLATCH POUNDING SOCIABLE SQUANTUM TERTULIA CONCISION INCLINING MERRIMENT
(— GIVEN AT HOME) HUDDLE
(AFTERNOON —) TEA RECEPTION
(BEACH —) CLAMBAKE
(BOISTEROUS —) JAMBOREE
(BRIDAL —) SEND SHOWER
(DANCING —) HOP GERMAN CANTICO HOEDOWN RIDOTTO FANDANGO
(DRINKING —) KNEIPE MOLLIE POTATION SYMPOSIUM
(DRUNKEN —) BLIND
(EVENING —) BALL SOIREE GREGORY ROCKING TERTULIA
(FISHING —) HUKILAU
(HUNTING —) FAID
(INFORMAL —) SOCIABLE TERTULIA

(IRISH —) HOOLEY
(LARGE —) ROUT
(MASQUERADE —) GUISE
(MEN'S —) STAG SMOKER
(POLITICAL —) SAM SIDE WAFD HOOKS LABOR CAUCUS FRONDE SWARAJ ZENTRUM MINSEITO KENSEIKAI SQUADRONE OPPOSITION
(POPULAR —) HOOKS
(ROWDY —) BLOWOUT
(SCOUTING —) ESPIAL
(SUPPLY —) BRIGADE
(TEA —) DRUM TEMPEST
(THIRD —) STRANGER
PARUAH (SON OF —) JEHOSHAPHAT
PARULIS GUMBOIL
PARVENU SNOB ARRIVE UPSTART ARRIVIST MUSHROOM ARRIVISTE
PARVIS PARADISE
PARZIFAL (FATHER OF —) GAMURET
(MOTHER OF —) HERZELOIDE
PASACH (FATHER OF —) JAPHLET
PASCH PACE PAQUE EASTER PASSOVER
PASCHAL LAMB CANDLE SUPPER PASSOVER
PAS DE DEUX DUET
PASE FAROL NATURAL VERONICA
PASEAH (FATHER OF —) ESHTON
PASEAR WALK AIRING EXCURSION PROMENADE
PASHA DEY EMIR BASHAW BASHAW
PASHTO AFGHAN
PASIPHAE (BROTHER OF —) AEETES
(CHILD OF —) ARIADNE PHAEDRA
(DAUGHTER OF —) ARIADNE PHAEDRA
(FATHER OF —) HELIUS
(HUSBAND OF —) MINOS
(MOTHER OF —) PERSA
(SISTER OF —) CIRCE
PASQUEFLOWER BADGER GOSLING APRILFOOL
PASQUINADE PIPE SQUIB SATIRE LAMPOON PASQUIL
PASS BY GO COL DIE END FIG GAP SAG USE ABRA BEAL CEDE CHIT COMP COVE DREE DROP FALL FARE FLIT FOIN GATE GHAT GULF HALS HAND HAVE JARK LANE LEAD PACE RIDE ROLL SEEK SILE SLAP SLIP STEP WADE WALK WEAR WEND WIND ALLOW CANTO DREIE ENACT FLEET GHAUT GORGE HALSE HURRY KOTAL LAPSE LITHE LUNGE NOTCH OCCUR ORDER PAPER PUNTA REACH RELAY SHAKE SHOOT SMITE SPEND STRIP TRADE UTTER WASTE WHELM YODEL BILLET CHALAN CONVEY COUPON DEFILE DEMISE ELAPSE EXCEED HAPPEN PASSUS PERMIT RAVINE SPIRAL TICKET TRAVEL TWOFER ABSOLVE ALLONGE APPROVE BREATHE DESCEND DEVOLVE DIFFUSE ENTREAT LATERAL OVERGET PASSAGE UNDERGO JUNCTURE REBOLERA PURWANNAH SAFEGUARD

(— A BALL) FEED HEEL
(— ABRUPTLY) LEAP
(— ALONG) BANDY DERIVE
(— AWAY) DIE SET FLEE VADE WING DEPART EXPIRE PERISH FORFARE FORTHGO OVERDRIVE
(— BACK AND FORTH) FIG CRISSCROSS
(— BAD COIN) SMASH
(— BETWEEN HILLS) BEAL SLAP SLACK
(— BY) COTE OMIT SKIP VADE WEND APASS CLEAR FORGO FOREGO IGNORE OVERGO INTERMIT OVERHEAVE
(— GRADUALLY) FADE
(— IN BULLFIGHT) SUERTE
(— IN POKER) BREATHE
(— INTO USE) ENURE INURE
(— JUDGMENT ON) DEEM DECERN SENTENCE
(— LIGHTLY) BRUSH SKATE SKITTER
(— OFF) SHAM FOIST
(— ON) LEAK PACE DELATE
(— ONE'S LIFE) TRADE
(— OUT) CONK DEBOUCH EXHAUST
(— OVER) DO HIP BALK FREE SKIM SKIP SLIP COVER CROSS ELIDE FLEET SCOUR SWEEP TRANCE OVERHIP INTERMIT OVERLOOK OVERPOST PROGRESS TRAVERSE
(— OVER LIGHTLY) SKIM SWEEP OVERSKIP
(— OVER QUICKLY) SCUD FLEET
(— QUICKLY) FLIT SPIN SPEED STRIKE
(— THROUGH) CROSS REEVE TRACE DIVIDE OVERGO PIERCE SUFFER EXCURSE PERVADE OVERPASS OVERRIDE PERMEATE PROGRESS PENETRATE
(— THROUGH A BLOCK) REEVE
(— THROUGH NARROW WAY) THRID THREAD
(— TIME) DRIVE SPEND TRADE
(— UNHAPPILY) DREE
(— UP) REJECT DECLINE DISREGARD
(— WITH DIFFICULTY) WADE
(— WITH VIOLENCE) RAKE
(CUSTOMS —) CARNET
(FENCING —) FOIN BOTTE LUNGE PUNTA
(FOOTBALL —) FLY FLARE FORWARD LATERAL PITCHOUT
(FORWARD —) AERIAL
(HOCKEY —) CENTER
(LONG — IN FOOTBALL) BOMB
(MOUNTAIN —) COL GAP NEK SAG GATE GHAT SLIP CLOVE GHAUT KLOOF KLOOT KOTAL POORT SWIRE SWIRL BEALACH
(NARROW —) ABRA GULF CLOSE SLYPE DEFILE
(SUDDEN —) LUNGE
PASSABLE FIT FAIR SOSO TOLLOL GENUINE ADEQUATE MEDIOCRE MODERATE POSSIBLE TRAVELED PERMEABLE TOLERABLE
(PREF.) BATO
PASSABLENESS INDIFFERENCE

PASSABLY SEEMLY
PASSAGE CUT GAT GUT ROW VIA WAY WRO ADIT BELT BORD DOOR EXIT FARE FLUE FORD GANG GATE HALL ITER LANE PACE PASS PAWN RACE RAMP SLIP SLUM VENT WELL AISLE ALLEY ALURE BAYOU BEARD BOGUE CANAL CHOPS CHUTE CLOSE CREEK CRUSH DRAFT DRIFT DRIVE ENTRY FLYBY FORTE GLADE GOING GORGE INLET JETTY MEUSE PATCH PORCH SHUNT SLYPE SOUND ACCESS ADITUS APORIA ARCADE ATRIUM AVENUE BRIDGE BURROW BYPASS CAREER COURSE DEFILE DROMOS EGRESS ELAPSE FAUCES HIATUS MEATUS PARODE RELIEF SCREEN SLUICE STRAIT TRAJET TRANCE TRAVEL TUNNEL VOYAGE ARCHWAY BALTEUS CHANNEL CHAPTER CHIMNEY CONDUIT COULOIR COUPURE DIAZOMA DOGTROT DRAUGHT ESTUARY EXCERPT FISTULA FRAUGHT GALLERY GANGWAY GATEWAY ISTHMUS JOURNEY MANHOLE OFFTAKE OUTTAKE PARADOS PROCESS TRANSIT APPROACH AQUEDUCT CITATION CLOISTER COMMERCE DEBOUCHE DELETION PARADIGM PERICOPE SENTENCE SHIPPING SINUSOID SPILLWAY
(— IN BOOK) WHERE EXCERPT
(— IN JEWISH SCRIPTURE) PARASHAH
(— OF THREAD) FLOAT
(— TO STOMACH) SWALLOW
(— TO TOMB) DROMOS SYRINX
(—S OF LITERATURE) BEAUTIES
(AIR —) FLUE THIRL WINDWAY THIRLING VENTIDUCT
(ANATOMICAL —) ITER
(CENSORED —) CAVIAR
(CONTINUOUS —) LAPSE
(COVERED —) OPE PAWN PEND
(DIFFICULT —) APORIA
(LITERARY —) TEXT QUOTE EXCERPT SNIPPET QUOTATION
(MINE —) RUN ADIT HEAD ROOF SLUM DRIVE LEVEL SHAFT THIRL AIRWAY STENTON UNDERCAST
(MUSICAL —) CUE CODA LINK BREAK FORTE STAVE ARIOSO FUGATO LEGATO PRESTO REPEAT CADENZA CODETTA FANFARE STRETTO FLOURISH SPICCATO STACCATO SYMPHONY VOCALISE PIZZICATO RITARDANDO
(NARROW —) GUT HASS ALLEY CREEP GORGE JETTY NOTCH SLYPE SMOOT DEFILE GULLET NARROW STRAIT
(SECRET —) BOLTHOLE
(SECURE — OF) CARRY
(SUBTERRANEAN —) POSTERN
(SWIFT —) FLIGHT
(VAULTED —) PEND
(WATER —) TICKLE TICKLER
(PREF.) MEATO
(SUFF.) PLANIA PORA PORE

PASSAGE HAWK TARTARET PASSENGER
PASSAGE TO INDIA (AUTHOR OF —) FORSTER
(CHARACTER IN —) AZIZ ADELA CECIL MOORE RONALD STELLA GODBOLE HEASLOP QUESTED FIELDING
PASSAGEWAY (ALSO SEE PASSAGE) BORD FLUE GANG HALL LANE PACE PASS PEND PORT RACE SHED SLIP WENT YAWN AISLE ALLEY ALURE CHUTE DRIFT DRONG ENTRY GOING LUMEN RAISE SHOOT SMOOT STULM ACCESS AIRWAY AVENUE COURSE DINGLE FUNNEL GUTTER INTAKE MANWAY RUNWAY TRANCE ZAGUAN DOORWAY GALLERY SLIPWAY TWITTEN WALKWAY WAYGATE CALLEJON CORRIDOR HATCHWAY
(CLEARED — IN CROWD) HALL
(COVERED —) ARCADE CLOISTER
(MINE —) BORD BOARD DRIFT SLANT STULM WINZE
(NARROW —) SLIP AISLE SMOOT
(SLOPING —) RAMP
PASSANT PAST CURRENT CURSORY PASSING EPHEMERAL
PASSE AGED PAST WORN FADED BELATED OBSOLETE OUTMODED
PASSENGER FARE INSIDE FERRYMAN TRAVELER WAYFARER
(— WHO AVOIDS PAYING FARE) NIP STOWAWAY
(— WITHOUT TICKET) HARE
(AIRPLANE —) BIRDMAN
(UNBOOKED —) CAD
(PL.) WAYBILL
PASSEPARTOUT SPANDREL
PASSERBY PASSER PASSANT BYPASSER SAUNTERER
PASSERINE OSCINE PERCHER
PASSIFLORA TACSO
PASSING DEATH DYING ELAPSE CURSORY DIADROM PASSADO RUNNING SLIDING ELAPSING FLEETING ENACTMENT EPHEMERAL WAYFARING
(— BETWEEN) INTERCURRENT
(— BY) COTE
(— INTO EACH OTHER) FONDU
(— OF HOURS) TIME
(— OF TIME) EFFLUX
(SLOWLY —) LAG
PASSION IRE WAX BATE FIRE FURY HEAT LOVE LUST PASH RAGA RAGE TEAR TIDE WILL ZEAL ANGER ARDOR BLOOD BRAME CHAFE DEVIL ERROR FLAME LETCH MANIA RAJAS SPUNK WRATH AFFECT CHOLER DESIRE FERVOR MOTHER PELTER SATTVA SPLEEN TALENT WARMTH EARNEST EMOTION EROTISM FEELING OUTRAGE VULTURE APPETITE DISTRESS VIOLENCE PADDYWACK
(— FOR DOING GREAT THINGS) MEGALOMANIA
(— FOR MUSIC) MELOMANIA
(ANGRY —) FUNK

(ANIMAL —) KAMA
(PREF.) PASSI PATH(O)
(SUFF.) **(— FOR)** MANE MANIA(C)
PASSIONATE HOT FOND WARM WILD FIERY GUTSY QUICK WHITE ARDENT FERVID FIERCE FUMOUS IREFUL STORMY SULTRY TORRID AMOROUS FLAMING PEPPERY THERMAL VIOLENT CHOLERIC FRENETIC VASCULAR VEHEMENT WRATHFUL DIONYSIAN IRASCIBLE
PASSIONATELY HASTILY FERVIDLY
PASSIONFLOWER MAYPOP BULLHOOF
PASSIONLESS COLD FREDDO APATHETIC
PASSIVE INERT STOIC PATHIC STOLID PATIENT FEMININE INACTIVE SIGNLESS YIELDING APATHETIC
PASSIVENESS QUIETISM
PASSOVER PESAH PHASE PASQUE PESACH
(— FESTIVAL) SEDER
(JEWISH —) EASTER
PASSPORT CHOP PASS CONGE CONGEE DUSTUK DUSTUCK FURLOUGH TESCARIA TEZKIRAH SAFEGUARD
PASSUS PACE PART PASS STEP CANTO DIVISION
PASSWORD SIGN WORD TOKEN DUSTUK TESSERA WATCHWORD
PAST BY AGO WAS GONE YOND YORE AFTER AGONE APAST ASIDE ENDED SINCE BEHIND BYGONE FOREBY PRETER ANOTHER FOREGONE PRETERIT COMPLETED
(LONG —) HIGH
(RECENTLY —) OTHER
(TIME NOT LONG —) YESTERDAY
(PREF.) PRETER RETRO
PASTA ORZO LASAGNA LINGUINE LINGUINI MACARONI MANICOTTI SPAGHETTI
PASTE HIT PAP BEAT BLOW DIKA DUFF GLUE MISO PACK PATE CREAM DOUGH FALSE GESSO HENNA PUNCH STICK ATTACH BATTER CERATE FASTEN GROUND PANADA RASTIK STRASS BUCKETY CLOBBER COLOGNE DRAWOUT FILLING GORACCO GUARANA STICKUM BADIGEON BARBOTINE
(— FOR CAULKING) BLARE
(— FOR LINING HEARTHS) BRASQUE
(— FOR SHOES, BOOTS) CLOBBER BLACKING
(— OF CLAY) BATTER
(— TO FILL HOLES IN WOOD AND STONE) BADIGEON
(ALIMENTARY —) FEDELINI SCUNGILLI SPAGHETTI
(AROMATIC —) PASTILE
(COLORING —) HENNA
(DRIED —) GUARANA
(EARTHY —) ENGOBE
(FISH —) BAGOONG
(MEDICATED —) ELECTUARY
(PORCELAIN —) PATE
(POTTER'S —) BARBOTINE

(TOBACCO —) GORACCO
(WEAVER'S —) SOWENS BUCKETY
PASTEBOARD CARD SHAM CARTON FLIMSY TICKET MATBOARD
PASTEDOWN LINING
PASTEL WOAD LIGHT CRAYON PICTURE DELICATE
PASTEL BLUE OADE WOAD
PASTEN HOBBLE TETHER PASTOUR SHACKLE
PASTILLE CACHOU CANDLE LOZENGE
PASTIME GAY TOY GAME PLOY HOBBY SPORT GOSSIP OLEARY SAILING PASTANCE AMUSEMENT DIVERSION ABRIDGMENT
PASTOR HERD ANGEL RABBI CURATE KEEPER PRIEST RECTOR DOMINIE VICAIRE GUARDIAN MINISTER SHEPHERD
PASTORAL POEM DRAMA RURAL RUSTIC BUCOLIC CROSIER IDYLLIC NOMADIC ROMANCE ARCADIAN THEOCRITEAN
PASTORALIST SQUATTER
PASTRY PIE FLAN HUFF PUFF SOCK TART TUCK CORNET DANISH ECLAIR ABAISSE BRIOCHE CARCAKE STRUDEL BAKEMEAT NAPOLEON TALMOUSE TURNOVER APPLEJACK
(— COOK) PASTLER
(— SHELL) BOUCHEE DARIOLE TIMBALE TALMOUSE
(— STRIPS) LATTICE
(— WHEEL) JAGGER
(SWEET —) DOUCET
PASTURAGE FEED GANG GATE STRAY COLLOP EATAGE FORAGE HERBAGE SHEEPGATE
PASTURE ALP FOG HAG HAM ING LEA PEN TYE BENT FEED GAET GANG GATE GISE GIST HAFT HALF HEAF HOGA INGE KEEP PARK RAIK AGIST DRIFT EJIDO GRASS GRAZE LAYER LEASE RANGE VELDT INTAKE MEADOW OUTRUN SAETER COWGATE FOGGAGE GRAZING HERBAGE LEALAND POTRERO VACCARY VICTUAL HERDWICK OUTFIELD SHEEPWALK
(— GRASS) TORE GRAMA
(— IN STUBBLE) SHACK
(— LAND) RAKE TACK LEASOW
(HILL —) HOGA
(MOUNTAIN —) SETER SAETER SHIELING
(SHEEP —) HEAF EWELEASE
(SHETLAND I. —) SETER
(SUMMER —) AGOSTADERO
(WET —) SLINK
PASTURELAND BENT SOUM
PASTURING RELIEF PANNAGE
PASTY PIE PATE SLAB PATTY DOUGHY FRACID SAMBOUSE
PAT APT DAB DIB TAP TIG BLOW CLAP GLIB JUMP PALP TICK CHUCK FITLY FIXED IMPEL THROW CARESS DABBLE PRETTY SMOOGE SOOTHE STRIKE STROKE TIMELY APROPOS CHERISH

FITTING PATAPAT READILY
SUITABLE PERTINENT
SEASONABLE
PATAGIUM TEGULA TIPPET
SCAPULA PARACHUTE
PTERYGODE
PATAGONIA (DEITY OF —) SETEBOS
(RODENT OF —) CAVY MARA
(TREE OF —) MANIU ALERCE
ALERSE
PATAMAR COURIER PATTAMAR
MESSENGER
PATAYAN YUMAN
PATCH BIT EKE FLY BOUT LAND
MEND SKIP SPOT SWAB SWOB
VAMP BLAZE BODGE CLOUT
CLUMP COVER FRIAR FUDGE
PIECE SAVER SCRAP SPECK SPLAT
BLOTCH COBBLE COOPER DOLLOP
GORGET MOUCHE PARCEL
REVAMP SOLDER SPETCH
SWATCH TINKLE CLAMPER
CLOBBER INWEAVE PELIOMA
REMNANT
(— AS ORNAMENT) MOUCHE
(— CLUMSILY) BOTCH CLOUT
CLAMPER
(— OF COLOR) CLOUP DAPPLE
SPLASH SPECULUM
(— OF DARK HAIR) SMUT
(— OF DIRT) MIRE
(— OF FEATHERS) BIB CAP
PTERYLA
(— OF ICE) RONE
(— OF LAND) RODHAM
(— OF LEATHER) SPECK
(— OF LIGHT) GLADE
(— OF PRINT) FUDGE
(— OF RUFFLED WATER) ACKER
(— OF SALIVA) SIXPENCE
(— OF TIRE) BOOT
(— ON BOAT) TINGLE
(— ON PRINTED PAGE) FRIAR
(— ON THROAT) GORGET
(— TOGETHER) CONSARCINATE
(— UP) HEAL MEND
(BALD —) AREA
(LIVID —) PELIOMA
(OOZY —) SPEW SPUE
(OPEN — IN FOREST) CAMPO
(SHOULDER —) FLASH
PATCHOULI PACCIOLI PATCHLEAF
PATCHWORD WASTEWORD
PATCHWORK BOTCH CENTO
CENTON JUMBLE SCRAPS
PATCHERY FRAGMENTS
PASTICCIO
PATE PIE TOP HEAD BROWN PASTE
PASTY PATTY BADGER NODDLE
NOGGIN COSTARD COXCOMB
PATELLA CAP PAN DISH VASE
ROTULA KNEECAP KNEEPAN
WHIRLBONE
PATEN ARCA DISC DISH DISK
PLATE PATINA PLATEN VESSEL
PATENT ARCA BALD OPEN BERAT
BROAD OVERT PLAIN SUNNUD
CHARTER EVIDENT LICENSE
OBVIOUS APPARENT ARCHIVES
MANIFEST PALPABLE PRIVILEGE
PATENTED BREVETE
PATER FATHER PRIEST
PATERFAMILIAS MASTER

PATERNAL FATHERLY
PATERNITY FATHER ORIGIN
PATESI ISHSHAKKU
PATH ARC PAD RIG RUN RUT TAN
WAY BERM FARE GATE LANE
LEAD LINE LODE RACE RACK
ROAD TRIG TROD WALK ALLEY
BYWAY GOING JETTY PISTE
ROUTE SPACE TRACK TRACT
TRADE TRAIL BOSTAL BYPASS
CAMINO CASAUN CIRCLE COMINO
COURSE GROOVE SLEUTH SPHERE
SWATHE TRENCH CHANNEL
ERGODIC FAIRWAY FOOTWAY
HIGHWAY LANDWAY MEANDER
PASSAGE RODDING SIDEWAY
TARIQAT TOWPATH TRAFFIC
TRUNDLE WAYGATE BORSTALL
CENTRODE CROSSCUT DRIFTWAY
TRAILWAY TWITCHEL
CROSSWALK
(— BETWEEN HEDGES) TWITCHEL
(— CUT IN MOWING) SWATH
SWATHE
(— FOLLOWED BY ENERGY)
ERGODIC
(— MADE BY ANIMAL) PIST PISTE
(— OF CELESTIAL BODY) ORBIT
(— OF CLOUDS) RACK
(— OF MOVING POINT) CURVE
LOCUS
(— OF RACE) STRIP
(— UP STEEP HILL) BOSTAL
BORSTAL BORSTALL
(BRIDLE —) SPURWAY
(CLOSED —) CIRCUIT
(FORTIFICATION —) RELAIS
(GARDEN —) ALLEE
(NARROW —) BERM RACK TRIG
RODDIN TROCHA RODDING
(PHILIPPINE FOOT —) SENDA
(STONE-PAVED —) STEEN
(SUFI —) TARIQAT
(WINDING —S) AMBAGES
(PREF.) HODO ODO
(SUFF.) ODE OID
PATHAN TURI AFRIDI SIVATI
BAJOURI BANGASH PAYTHAN
DANGARIK
PATHETIC SAD SILLY TEARY
TENDER FORLORN PITIFUL
DOLOROSO PATETICO PITIABLE
POIGNANT STIRRING TOUCHING
AFFECTING
PATHFINDER (AUTHOR OF —)
COOPER
(CHARACTER IN —) CAP DAVY
MUIR MABEL NATTY BUMPPO
DUNHAM JASPER MACNAB
CHARLES WESTERN SANGLIER
ARROWHEAD CHINGACHGOOK
PATHIC MORBID VICTIM PASSIVE
CATAMITE DISEASED SUFFERER
SUFFERING
PATHOGEN VIRUS
PATHOLOGICAL
(SUFF.) (— CONDITION) IA
PATHOLOGIST AMERICAN OPIE
ROUS SLYE EWING MOORE SMITH
WELCH MOHLER FLEXNER
HEKTOEN PRUDDEN WARTHIN
WHIPPLE RICKETTS
CANADIAN WESBROOK

DANISH FIBIGER
ENGLISH ADAMI BOYCE PAGET
ANNETT FLOREY WRIGHT
GERMAN HENLE KLEBS TRAUBE
ZENKER VIRCHOW COHNHEIM
RECKLINGHAUSEN
IRISH STOKES
ITALIAN GUARNIERI
PATHOS BATHOS SNIVEL
POIGNANCY
PATHWAY (ALSO SEE PATH) RUN
LANE PATH RACK SLADE COURSE
RAMBLA RAMBLE RODDIN
BORSTAL RODDING
(RAISED —) CAUSEY CAUSEWAY
PATIENCE CALM THILD BEARANCE
STOICISM COMPOSURE
ENDURANCE FORTITUDE
PATIENT CASE CURE MEEK SOBER
BOVINE PASSIVE ENDURING
THOLEMOD SUFFERANT
(— OF ASYLUM) BEDLAM
(BE —) BEAR
(HYDROPATHIC —) WATERER
(MEDICAL —) CURE
PATIO COURT COURTYARD
PATOIS CANT GOMBO GUMBO
CREOLE JARGON PATTER DIALECT
GUERNSEY
(FRENCH —) JOUAL
PATRIARCH JOB ABBA ENOS LEVI
NASI NOAH PAPA POPE ALDER
ELDER JACOB PITRI DESPOT
JOSEPH NESTOR ABRAHAM
ANCIENT VETERAN VENERABLE
(ETHIOPIAN —) ABUNA
PATRICIAN NOBLE EMPEROR
PATRICK NOBLEMAN GENTLEMAN
PATRIMONY PORTION ANCESTRY
HERITAGE LONGACRE
PATRIOT LOVER AMATEUR
PATRIOTIC PUBLIC ENVELOPE
NATIONAL
PATRIPASSIAN NOETIAN
PATROCLUS (FATHER OF —)
MENOETIUS
(MOTHER OF —) PERIAPIS
POLYMELE STHENELE
(SLAYER OF —) HECTOR
PATROL GUARD SCOUT WATCH
STOOGE PATROLE PROTECT
PATROLMAN COP GUARD
FLATFOOT INSPECTOR
PATRON BUYER GUEST STOOP
AVOWRY CLIENT FATHER FAUTOR
JAJMAN ACCOUNT PADRONE
PATROON PROCTOR SPONSOR
ADVOCATE CHAMPION
CUSTOMER DEFENDER GUARDIAN
MAECENAS
(PL.) FOLLOWING
PATRONAGE AEGIS FAVOR
AVOWRY CUSTOM FAVOUR
ACCOUNT AUSPICE FOMENTO
HEARING AUSPICES BUSINESS
PADROADO
(— AND CARE) AUSPICE
(POLITICAL —) PAP
PATRONAL TITULAR
PATRONIZE USE DEIGN FAVOR
DEFEND FATHER PROMOTE
PROTECT EMPATRON FREQUENT
PATROON TRACT

CAPTAIN SUPPORTER
PATTEE FORMY FORMEE
PATTEN BASE CLOG FOOT SHOE
SKATE STAND STILT CHOPIN
GALOSH RACKET SANDAL
CREEPER RACQUET SUPPORT
CIOPPINO SNOWSHOE
PATTER CANT TALK TIRL LINGO
HAPPER JARGON BLATHER
BLATTER CHATTER DIALECT
PATTERING PITAPAT
PATTERN CUT FUR SET BASE CAST
COMB COPY FORM GIMP IDEA
LAUE MOLD NORM PLAN SEME
STAR WAVE BISON BYSEN CHECK
DECOR DISME DRAFT EPURE
GUIDE IDEAL INLAY MODEL
MOIRE SHAPE WATER BASKET
SEMEE SHAPE WATER BASKET
BURELE CANVAS CHECKS DESIGN
DIAPER ENTAIL ETOILE FABRIC
FIGURE FLORAL FORMAT FORMER
LACERY MAGPIE MATRIX MIRROR
MODULE MUSTER ONDULE
PATRON POUNCE RANDOM
RECIPE SAMPLE SQUARE STRIPE
SYSTEM ALLOVER CHEVRON
EXAMPLE FACONNE FILLING
FOLKWAY GESTALT GRIZZLE
HOBNAIL MEANDER MEANING
MULLION PARAGON PROJECT
SAMPLER SLEIGHT STENCIL
TEMPLET CALENDAR DENTELLE
DYNAMICS FILIGREE HATCHING
ILLUSION OVERSHOT PARADIGM
PLATFORM STRICKLE PROTOTYPE
(— IN BRAIN) GYRATION
(— OF BEHAVIOR) HABIT DISPLAY
(— OF CADENCE) CURSUS
(— OF HINDU MUSIC) TALA
(— OF LARGE SQUARES) DAMIER
(— OF SCARS) KELOID
(— OF SEPARATE OBJECTS) SEME
(— OF STRESS) SUPERFIX
(— OF TARTAN) SET SEET SETT
SETTE
(— ON PAPER) BURELAGE
(— ON STAMP) GRILL GRILLE
(— USED BY SILVERSMITHS) WORK
BOROON
(-S ON SILK) ARMURE
(CHARACTERISTIC BEHAVIOR —) BIT
(CROSS-BARRED —) PLAID
(FACIAL —) BLAZE
(FRET —) KEY
(GARMENT —) SLOPER
(HAT —) BLOCK
(KNITTING —) ARGYLE
(MASONRY —) SPICATUM
(MELODIC —) RAGA
(PORCELAIN —) FITZHUGH
(RUG —) AINALEH
(SHOE —) FORME
(SKATING —) EDGE
(SOCIAL —) FAMILISM
(SPEECH —) IDIOLECT
(STRIPED —) BARRE
(SYMBOLIC —) MANDALA
(TAILOR'S —) PROTRACTOR
(TATTOO —) MOKO
(TREE —) HOM HOMA
(WEAVING —) DRAW
PATTERNED GOFFERED

PATTY TABLET BOUCHEE PRALINE PATTYPAN VOLAUVENT
(**— SHELL**) DARIOLE TALMOUSE CROUSTADE
PATULOUS OPEN SPREAD DISTENDED
PAUCITY LACK DEARTH FEWNESS EXIGUITY SCARCITY
PAUL PAOLO
(**ASSOCIATE OF —**) DEMAS SILAS TITUS ARTEMAS BARNABAS
PAULDRON POLLET EPAULET PALERON POLDRON POLLETTE
PAULINA (**HUSBAND OF —**) CAMILLO ANTIGONUS
PAULLU (**BROTHER OF —**) MANCO HUASCAR
PAULOPOST DEUTERIC
PAULOWNIA KIRI
PAUNCH TUN KITE KYTE BELLY PENCH RUMEN ABDOMEN STOMACH GUNDYGUT POTBELLY
PAUNCHY BLOATED
PAUPER BEGGAR INDIGENT ROUNDSMAN
PAUPERISM BEGGARY
PAUSANIAS (**FATHER OF —**) CLEOMBROTUS
PAUSE HO HEM HALT HANG HOLD LULL REST RUFE STAY STOP WAIT ABIDE BREAK CEASE CHECK COMMA DELAY DEMUR DEVAL DWELL HOVER LETUP LIMMA POISE SELAH TARRY TENOR BREACH BREATH CORONA CUTOFF FALTER HANKER HIATUS PERIOD STANCE CAESURA FERMATA RESPITE VIRGULE BREATHER INTERVAL
(**— BEFORE HURDLE**) DWELL
(**SUDDEN —**) CHECK
(**PL.**) LIMMATA CAESURAE
PAUT PAW POKE POWT STAMP FINGER
PAVANE DANCE PADUAN
PAVE LAY TAR PATH STUD TILE COVER FLOOR CAUSEY COBBLE QUARRY SMOOTH OVERLAY PREPARE RUDERATE
(**— WITH STONES**) STEEN CAUSEY
PAVED COBBLED
PAVEMENT SARN SLAB HEARTH PAEPAE TELFORD ASAROTUM FLAGGING FLOORING PATHMENT PEDIMENT PITCHING SIDEWALK TROTTOIR WASHBOARD
PAVER CUBER PAVIOR
PAVID TIMID AFRAID FEARFUL
PAVILION BASE FLAG TELD TENT FOLLY KIOSK PINNA ROYAL CANOPY ENSIGN HOWDAH LITTER PANDAL PALLION COVERING GLORIETTE
PAVILLON CHINOIS CRESCENT
PAVING FLAG SETT BLOCK BRICK DALLE PAVER STEAN STEEN STONE COBBLE TARMAC ASPHALT TELFORD PITCHING FLAGSTONE
(**SQUARE —**) MITCHEL
PAVIS COVER PAVADE PAVOIS SHIELD PROTECT
PAW PAT PUD TOE CLAW FOOT GAUM GRAB HAND MAUL PATY

PAUT PORT FLAIL PATTE TRICK CLUTCH FUMBLE HANDLE PATTEE CRUBEEN FLIPPER FORELEG FOREFOOT
PAWKY SLY ARCH BOLD CANNY SAUCY CRAFTY LIVELY SHREWD CUNNING FORWARD SQUEAMISH
PAWL COG DOG BOLT HAND SEAR STOP TENT TRIP CATCH CLICK DETENT FINGER PALLET TONGUE CLAWKER RATCHET
PAWN DIP POP WED FINE GAGE HOCK SOAK VAMP WAGE SPOUT SWEAT ENGAGE LUMBER OBLIGE PIGNUS PLEDGE WADSET COUNTER HOSTAGE PEACOCK CHESSMAN MOSKENEER TRIBULATION
(**PL.**) PHALANX
PAWNBROKER MOUNT UNCLE BROKER LUMBERER MONEYLENDER
PAWNEE PANEE SKIDI WATER ALMOND BISCUIT PLEDGEE
PAWNIE PAWN PEACOCK
PAWNSHOP PAWN SPOUT LUMBER LOMBARD POPSHOP
PAX BOARD PEACE TRUCE FRIEND TABLET
PAXWAX WHITELEATHER
PAY DO BUY FEE TIP ANTE FOOT FORK GIVE MEET RENT SOLD WAGE BATTA CLEAR COUGH DOUSE PLANK SCREW SHEPE SOUND WAGES YIELD ANSWER BETALL DEFRAY IMPEND REWARD SALARY SETTLE COMMUTE DEADRAY HALVANS IMBURSE REQUITE SATISFY SOULDIE STIPEND TRIBUTE RECOMPENSE
(**— ATTENTION**) DIG SEE COME GAUM HARK HEED TENT ADVERT REGARD
(**— COURT TO**) NUT SUE GALLANT
(**— DOWN**) DOUSE
(**— FLIRTATIOUS ADVANCES**) QUEEN
(**— FOR**) ABY BUY BYE COUP ABIDE COVER ESCOT STAND ABEGGE
(**— FOR LIQUOR**) BIRL
(**— HEAVY PENALTY**) SMART EXPIATE
(**— HOMAGE**) CHEFE CHEVE CHIVE SALAAM ADULATE
(**— IN ADVANCE**) IMPRESS
(**— MONEY**) PINGLE
(**— OF SOLDIER**) SAWDEE
(**— OFF**) LIFT SINK ACQUIT
(**— OUT**) VEER BLEED SPEND STUMP EXPEND DISBURSE
(**— PENALTY**) ABY ABYE
(**— TAXES**) GILD
(**— UP**) ANTE QUIT SETTLE LIQUIDATE
(**— WITH IOU**) VOWEL
(**ADVANCE —**) IMPREST
(**DAILY —**) DIET
(**EXTRA —**) BATTA BONUS KICKBACK
(**SMALL —**) SCREW
PAYABLE DUE C4RTAL
PAYEE HOLDER ENDORSER

PAYMASTER BAKSHI BUKSHI PURSER BUKSHEE PAGADOR
PAYMENT CRO DUE FEE TAX BILL CENS DOES DOLE DUTY ERIC FEAL FINE GALE GILD HIRE LEVY MAIL MISE TACK TOLL BONUS CANON CLAIM GAVEL MAILL MENSE MODUS PREST PRICE YIELD ANGILD BOUNTY CHARGE LINAGE LOBOLA OUTLAY PAYOLA PLEDGE REBATE RETURN REWARD TARIFF ADVANCE ALIMONY ANNUITY BENEFIT CUSTOMS DEPOSIT FOOTAGE GARNISH PANNAGE PENSION PRIMAGE SOLUTIO STIPEND SUBSIDY SUBSIST TREWAGE TUITION CASUALTY FOREGIFT GRATUITY KICKBACK MALIKANA MARITAGE MONEYAGE TREASURY WOODGELD HEADPENNY MALGUZARI
(**— FOR INJURY**) UTU
(**— FOR LABOR**) MEED
(**— FOR OFFENSE**) ENACH
(**— FOR RELEASE**) LOOSING
(**— FOR RERUN**) RESIDUAL
(**— OF FEE**) FEAL
(**— OF MINERS**) FOOTAGE YARDAGE
(**— ON DELIVERY**) COD
(**— TO SECURE FAVOR**) PAYOLA
(**ADVANCE —**) ANTE
(**DEMAND —**) DUN BILL
(**EVADE —**) BILK DEFAULT
(**HOMICIDE'S —**) KELCHIN
(**PERIODICAL —**) GALE GAVEL
PAYNIM PAGAN PANIME HEATHEN INFIDEL PAGANDOM
PAYOFF FIX BRIBE CLIMAX PROFIT REWARD DECISIVE RECKONING
PEA DAL TUR DHAL GRAM LANG SEED ARHAR CHICK CICER GANDUL LEGUME PIGEON PODDER CARMELE CATJANG KHESARI PODWARE TANGIER GARVANRO MARROWFAT
(**— DOVE**) ZENAIDA
(**— HARVESTER**) VINER
(**— PETAL**) KEEL
(**EARLY —S**) HASTINGS
(**PARCHED —S**) CARLS CARLINS
(**PL.**) POIS GRAIN
(**PREF.**) PISI
PEABIRD ORIOLE WRYNECK
PEACE PAX CALM EASE FINE LIOS LISS REST AMITY FRITH GRITH LISSE QUIET TRUCE REPOSE SAUGHT SHALOM CONCORD HARMONY REQUIEM
(**— OF MIND**) ATARAXIA
(**GODDESS OF —**) IRENE
(**SYMBOL OF —**) DOVE TOGA OLIVE
(**PREF.**) PACI
PEACEABLE FAIR SOME CIVIL DOUCE QUIET STILL GENTLE SILVER ORDERLY PACIFIC SOLOMON AMICABLE SACKLESS
PEACEFUL CALM SOME SOBER STILL IRENIC PLACID SILVER HALCYON ORDERLY PACIFIC
PEACE PIPE CALUMET
PEACH BLAB PAVY CLING PAVIE SNEAK SPLIT TRUMP ACCUSE

BETRAY CARMAN CROSBY FOSTER INDICT INFORM OREJON PEENTO SALWEY BRUNION ELBERTA PERSIAN PIENTAO WHITTLE CRAWFORD ISABELLA RARERIPE ROSEWORT NECTARINE VICTORINE
(**— STATE**) GEORGIA
(**— STONE**) PUTAMEN
PEACHBLOW FAKIR
PEACHY FINE DANDY
PEACOCK MAO PAON PAVO PAWN POSE PEKOK STRUT PAJOCK PAVONE POWNIE PEAFOWL PHASIANID
(**— TAIL**) TRAIN
(**CONGO —**) AFROPAVO
PEACOCK BITTERN SUN
PEACOCK BUTTERFLY IO
PEACOCK FISH WRASSE
PEACOCK FLOWER FLAMBEAU POINCIANA
PEA CRAB PINNOTERE
PEAG TAX TOLL BEADS PAAGE PEACK PEAGE PEDAGE WAMPUM
PEAI PIAY PIACHE
PEA JACKET PEACOAT
PEAK BEN NAB NOB PAP PIC TOP TOR ACME APEX BEAK CIMA CUSP DENT DOLT DOME KNOB KNOT PICO PIKE TOLT BLOOM CREST CROWN PIQUE PITCH PITON POINT SLINK SNEAK SPIRE STEAL STUMP CLIMAX CUPULA SHASTA SHRINK SUMMIT ZENITH EPITOME MAXIMUM PICACHO CENTROID
(**— OF ANCHOR**) PEE
(**— OF CAP**) SCOOP
(**— OF ENERGY**) NUCLEUS
(**ICE —**) SERAC
(**ISOLATED —**) TOLT
(**SHARP —**) HORN AIGUILLE
(**SNOW-CAPPED —**) DOME CALOTTE
(**PREF.**) ACR(O)
PEAKED WAN PALE THIN DRAWN PIKED SHARP COPPED SICKLY SLIMSY POINTED SLIMPSY
PEAKEDNESS KURTOSIS
PEAL CLAP RING TOLL CHIME CRACK GRILSE SHOVEL MINNING RESOUND SUMMONS THUNDER CARILLON
(**— OF THUNDER**) CLAP REEL
PEANUT BUR FLAX MANI MEAN PETTY PINDA GOOBER PINDAL ARACHIS BEENNUT ARACHIDE EARTHPEA GRASSNUT KATCHUNG VALENCIA MONKEYNUT
(**— DISEASE**) TIKKA
PEA POD COB PYSE QUASH PESCOD
(**POORLY FILLED —**) POP
(**UNRIPE —**) SQUASH
PEAR BOSC BURY DIEGO MELON NELIS SABRA BEURRE BURREL COLMAR PANINI SECKEL WARDEN WINTER KIEFFER PEPERIN PRICKLY AMBRETTE BERGAMOT BLANQUET MUSCATEL TASAJILLO
(**PRICKLY —**) TUNA NOPAL OPUNTIA
(**PREF.**) PIRI PIRO PYRI

PEAR HAW THORN
PEARL GEM MABE TERN GRAIN
NACRE ONION PICOT UNION
BOUTON OLIVET ORIENT
BAROQUE BDELIUM BLISTER
PARAGON CATARACT MOONBEAM
MARGARITE
(— WEIGHT) TANK
(IMITATION —) OLIVET
(IRREGULAR —) SLUG
(PIERCED —) WIDOW
(SEED —) ALIOFAR
(SMOKED —) MITRAILLE
(PREF.) PERLI
PEARL BLUE METAL
PEARL BLUSH ROSETAN
**PEARL FISHERS, THE (CHARACTER
IN —)** LEILA NADIR ZURGA
NOURABAD
(COMPOSER OF —) BIZET
PEARL MILLET KOUS BAJRA
CUMBU DUCHN DUKHN KOUSE
JONDLA DAGASSA
PEARLSIDES ARGENTIN
PEARLWEED SAGINA POVERTY
SEALWORT
PEARLY NACRY NACROUS
MARGARIC PRECIOUS
PEARLY EVERLASTING LIVELONG
MOONSHINE
PEAR-SHAPED FULL MELLOW
ROUNDED PYRIFORM
PEASANT TAO BOND BOOR HERA
HIND KERN KONO KOPI PEON
RAYA RYOT SERF BAIRU BOWER
GHUNI KNAVE KULAK RAYAH
SWAIN CARLOT COTMAN COTTAR
FARMER FELLAH RASCAL RUSTIC
BONDMAN LABORER PAISANO
VILLAIN CHOPSTICK CONTADINO
(— CLASS) JACQUERIE
(— OF INDIA) RYOT KISAN RAIYAT
(ARABIC —) FELLAH
(IRISH —) KERN KERNE
(RUSSIAN —) KULAK MUZHIK
MUZJIK
PEASANTS (AUTHOR OF —)
REYMONT
(CHARACTER IN —) KUBA ROCH
ANTEK HANKA SIMON YAGNA
YANEK BORYNA NASTKA TERESA
MATTHEW MATTHIAS
DOMINIKOVA
PEASE CROW TERN
PEASHOOTER TRUNK BLOWER
PISTOL BLOWGUN
PEAT GOR PET SOD VAG COOM
FUEL MIST MOOR MUCK MULL
TURF COOMB YARFA LAWYER
MINION YARPHA DARLING
FAVORITE
(— BOG) CESS YARPHA
(— CUTTER) PINER
(— SPADE) SLADE TUSKAR
TWISCAR
(DRIED — FOR FUEL) VAG
(LAYER OF —) FLAW
PEA TREE KATURAI
PEATY KETTY
PEBA PEVA ARMADILLO
PEBBLE DIB FLAX JACK PLUM
CHUCK SCREE STONE BANTAM
COGGLE GIBBER GRAVEL QUARTZ

SHILLA SYCITE CHUCKIE CRYSTAL
SHINGLE STANNER JACKSTONE
(PL.) BEACH DREIKANTER
(PREF.) CALCULI CHALICO
PSEPH(O) THRIO
PEBBLY BEACHY
PECAN NOGAL PACANE
PECCADILLO FAULT OFFENSE
MISCHIEF
PECCANT FAULTY MORBID
CORRUPT SINNING DISEASED
PECCARY JAVALI WARREE
TAGASSU TAYASSU JAVELINA
TAYASSUID
PECK DAB DOT JOB NIP BEAK BILL
CARP FOOD GRUB HOLE JERK
KISS DYKE PITCH PRICK STOCK
THROW HATFUL NIBBLE PEGGLE
PICKLE PIERCE STROKE CHIMBLE
(1-4TH OF —) LIPPY FORPET
FORPIT LIPPIE
PECKER BILL NOSE COURAGE
SPIRITS
PECTEN COMB MARSUPIUM
PECTORAL SANDPIPER JACK
PERT PEERT BROWNY BROWNIE
CHOROOK CREAKER FATBIRD
HAYBIRD KRIEKER SQUATTER
TRIDDLER JACKSNIPE
PECULATE STEAL MISUSE
EMBEZZLE
PECULIAR ODD VERY QUEER
WEIRD PROPER QUAINT UNIQUE
CURIOUS PRIVATE SEVERAL
SPECIAL STRANGE UNUSUAL
SEPARATE SINGULAR SPECIFIC
PECULIARITY KINK IDIOM QUIRK
TRAIT TRICK TWIST IDIASM
ODDITY AEOLISM FEATURE
IRISHRY CROTCHET HEADMARK
MANNERISM PROPRIETY
SINGULARITY
(— IN BOWL) BIAS
(— OF SPEECH) IDIOLOGISM
(CROTCHETY —) FIKE
PECUNIARY POCKET MONETARY
FINANCIAL
PED BASKET HAMPER PANIER
PEDAGOGUE TUTOR PEDANT
DOMINIE SQUEERS TEACHER
THWACKUM
PEDAGOGY SCHOOL DIDACTICS
EDUCATION
PEDAHEL (FATHER OF —) AMMIHUD
PEDAHZUR (SON OF —) GAMALIEL
PEDAIAH (BROTHER OF —)
SALATHIEL
(DAUGHTER OF —) ZEBUDAH
(FATHER OF —) PAROSH
(SON OF —) JOEL
PEDAL LEVER SWELL TREADLE
FOOTFEED PEDALIAN THROTTLE
(— COUPLER) TIRASSE
(PIANO —) CELESTE
PEDANT PRIG DUNCE TUTOR
DORBEL PURIST TASSEL
ACADEME PEDAGOG GAMALIEL
DRYASDUST OLOFERNES
PEDANTIC BLUE STODGY BOOKISH
DONNISH ERUDITE INKHORN
TEACHING SCHOLASTIC
PEDDLE HAWK SELL CADGE SHOVE
TRANT TRUCK HIGGLE MEDDLE

PIDDLE RETAIL COLPORT
PEDDLER ARAB SMOUS BADGER
BODGER CRAMER JAGGER
JOWTER MUGGER STROLL
WALKER YAGGER NIGGLER
PACKMAN ROADMAN SANDBOY
SWADDER TROGGER TRUCKER
HUCKSTER BOXWALLAH
DUSTYFOOT
(— OF DOPE) FIXER
(— OF DRESS PIECES) DUDDER
(— OF FISH) RIPIER RIPPER
(— OF SHAM JEWELRY) DUFFER
(BOOK —) COLPORTEUR
(ITINERANT —) SMOUS SMOUSE
SMOUSER STROLLER
(MOHAM. —) DONA
(STREET —) CAMELOT
(WARES OF —) TROGGIN
PEDESTAL ANTA BASE BASIS
BLOCK SOCLE STAND PILLAR
PODIUM ROCKER AKROTER
SUPPORT PADMASANA
ACROTERIUM
PEDESTRIAN PED DULL FOOT
SLOW HIKER FOOTER HOOFER
WALKER FOOTMAN PROSAIC
PLODDING WINGLESS
PONDEROUS VOETGANGER
PERIPATETIC
PEDICEL RAY STEM SCAPE STALK
PEDUNCLE FOOTSTALK
PEDIGREE STEMMA DESCENT
LINEAGE ANCESTRY PETEGREU
PUREBRED
PEDIMENT FRONTAL FRONTON
FASTIGIUM
PEDIPALP
(PL.) LABIUM
PEDOMETER ODOGRAPH
WAYWISER
PEDRERO PERRIER PETRARY
PEDUNCLE STEM SCAPE STALK
STIPES PEDICEL EYESTALK
HYPOCARP
(PL.) CRURA
PEEK PEEP PIKE GLANCE GLIMPSE
PEEKABOO PEEP BOPEEP PEEPEYE
PEEL BARK HARL HULL HUSK PARE
RIND SKIN FLAKE FLIPE SCALE
SLIPE STAKE STRIP CORTEX
SHOVEL SPITTLE UNDRESS
BARKPEEL ORANGEADO
(— OFF) HARL CRAZE FLAKE
SHUCK
(BAKER'S —) PALE SPITTLE
(ORANGE OR LEMON —) ZEST
ORANGEAT
PEELER CRAB BOBBY CORER
HUSTLER SHEDDER SPUDDER
PILLAGER
PEELING RIND SKIN PARING
PARURE
PEEN PIN PYNE RIVET
PEEP PIP PRY SPY COOK JEEP KEEK
KOOK PEEK PEER PINK PULE SKEG
STEP TOOT TOTE TOUT CHEEP
CHIRP DEKKO GLINT PIPIT SNOOP
TWEET DEGREE GLANCE SQUEAK
SQUINNY PEEKABOO
(— SHOW) RAREE
PEEPER EYE TOM FROG KEEK
VOYEUR

PEEPHOLE PEEP JUDAS EYELET
CREVICE
PEEPING NOSY PRYING
PEER PRY DUKE EARL FEAR GAZE
LOOK LORD MATE PEEP PINK
TOOT TOUT BARON EQUAL GLINT
GLOZE MATCH NOBLE RIVAL
STARE STIME THANE TWIRE
APPEAR FELLOW OLIVER PINKER
COMPERE
PEERAGE RANK DEBRETT DIGNITY
BARONAGE NOBILITY TENEMENT
PEER GYNT (AUTHOR OF —) IBSEN
(CHARACTER IN —) ASE BOYG
GYNT PEER ANITRA HEGSTAD
SOLVEIG
PEERING SQUINNY
PEERLESS SUPREME MATCHLESS
NONPAREIL UNRIVALED
PEESWEEP FINCH PEWIT LAPWING
PEEWEEP
PEEVE IRK ANNOY GRUDGE NETTLE
IRRITATE
PEEVISH SOUR CROSS DORTY
PENSY SNACK TECHY TEENY
TESTY TETTY THRAW TIFFY
WEMOD CRUSTY FRANZY GIRNIE
HIPPED PATCHY SNARLY SNUFFY
SULLEN TATTER TOUCHY TWARLY
TWAZZY TWITTY UPPISH UPPITY
VAPORY CRABBED FRATCHY
FRECKET FRETFUL FROWARD
GROUCHY PETTISH SPLEENY
TEDIOUS TIFFISH WASPISH
CAPTIOUS PERVERSE PHRAMPEL
PINDLING CANGUACH TWANKING
FRAMPOLD, PETULANT
PEEVISHLY CRUSTILY
PEEVISHNESS PET PETULANCE
PEEWEE BOOT RUNT TINY PEWEE
MARBLE LAPWING
PEG FIX HOB HUB NOB NOG PIN
HOBB KING KNAG PLUG SCOB
SHAG SKEG STEP CLEAT DOWEL
DRINK NOTCH PERCH PITON
PRONG SPELL SPILE SPILL STAKE
THOLE THROW TOOTH WADDY
DEGREE DOWELL FAUCET
MARKER NORMAN PICKET
REASON SPIGOT TAPOUN TIPCAT
PINNING PRETEXT SCOLLOP
SPERKET SUPPORT TRENAIL
(— FOR PLAYING GAME) CAT
SPILIKIN
(— FOR SADDLES) SPERKET
(— OF STRINGED INSTRUMENT)
CHEVILLE
(— OUT) DIE FAIL
(BELAYING —) KEVEL
(IRON —) PITON
(THATCH —) SCOB
PEGA REMORA
PEGALL BASKET PACKALL
PEGASUS QUAVIVER HYPOSTOME
PEG TOP PIRY PEERY PEERIE
PEG WOFFINGTON (AUTHOR OF —)
READE
(CHARACTER IN —) PEG RICH VANE
HARRY MABEL CIBBER COLLEY
CHARLES TRIPLET POMANDER
WOFFINGTON BRACEGIRDLE
PEIGNOIR GOWN DRESS KIMONO
NEGLIGEE

PEISE BLOW FORCE PASSE POISE POIZE IMPACT WEIGHT BALANCE POISURE
PEKAH (FATHER OF —) REMALIAH
(SLAYER OF —) HOSHEA
PEKAHIAH (FATHER OF —) MENAHEM
(SLAYER OF —) PEKAH
PEKAN WEJACK
PEKING MAN SINANTHROPUS
PELAGE FUR COAT HAIR PILAGE
PELAGIC MARINE AQUATIC OCEANIC PELAGIAN
PELAIAH (FATHER OF —) ELIOENAI
PELALIAH (FATHER OF —) AMZI
PELATIAH (FATHER OF —) BENAIAH HANANIAH
PELEG (BROTHER OF —) JOKTAN
(FATHER OF —) EBER
PELET (FATHER OF —) JAHDAI AZMAVETH
PELETH (FATHER OF —) JONATHAN
(SON OF —) ON
PELEUS (BROTHER OF —) TELAMON
(FATHER OF —) AEACUS
(HALF-BROTHER OF —) PHOCUS
(MOTHER OF —) ENDEIS
(SON OF —) PELIDES ACHILLES
(WIFE OF —) THETIS ANTIGONE
PELF GAIN BOOTY LUCRE MONEY SPOIL TRASH PILFER PILFRE REFUSE RICHES WEALTH COMPOST
PELIAS (BROTHER OF —) NELEUS
(DAUGHTER OF —) ALCESTIS
(FATHER OF —) POSEIDON
(MOTHER OF —) TYRO
(SON OF —) ACASTUS
(WIFE OF —) ANAXIBIA PHYLOMACHE
PELICAN DOVE ALCATRAS ONOCROTAL
(— STATE) LOUISIANA
PELISSE POSTIN POSTEEN
PELL BEAT PELE PELT HURRY PEELE HASTEN
PELLAGRA MAIDISM PELAGRA
PELLEAS (BELOVED OF —) MELISANDE
(BROTHER OF —) GOLAUD
PELLEAS ET MELISANDE
(CHARACTER IN —) ARKEL GOLAUD YNIOLD PELLEAS ALLEMONDE GENEVIEVE MELISANDE
(COMPOSER OF —) DEBUSSY
PELLES (DAUGHTER OF —) ELAINE
PELLET BB WAD BALL CAST PILL SHOT BOLUS PRILL STONE BEEBEE BULLET FECULA OGRESS PILULE CASTING GRANULE PALLION TRATTLE BUCKSHOT GUNSTONE HAILSTONE
(SNOW —S) GRAUPEL
(PL.) SHOT
PELLICLE FILM SCUM SKIN CRUST CUTICLE EPISTASIS
PELLINORE (SLAYER OF —) GAWAIN
(SON OF —) TORRE DORNAR LAMEROK PERCIVAL AGGLOVALE
PELLITORY BERTRAM BERTRUM WALLWORT
PELL-MELL RUSH MELPELL DISORDER HEADLONG

PELLOCK PALACH PORPOISE
PELLUCID CLEAR BRIGHT LIMPID ORIENT CRYSTAL
PELMA TRACK
PELMET CORNICE VALANCE PALMETTE
PELOPONNESUS (CITY OF —) SPARTA
(PEOPLE OF —) MOREOTE
(RIVER GOD OF —) ALPHEUS
PELOPS (FATHER OF —) TANTALUS
(SON OF —) ATREUS TROEZEN PITTHEUS THYESTES
(WIFE OF —) HIPPODAMIA
PELORIA EPANODY
PELT FUR KIT BEAR BEAT BLOW CAPE CAST CLOD COON DASH FELL HIDE HURL KITT PELL PUSH RACK SKIN BESET CHUNK FITCH HURRY SABLE SLASH SPEED STONE WHACK BADGER BEAVER FISHER PELTER PEPPER SERVAL SPRING BETHUMP COONSKIN
(— OF SEAL, WITH BLUBBER) SCULP
(— WITH MISSILES) BUM SQUAIL
(— WITH STONES) LAPIDATE
(BEAVER —) BLANKET
PELTAST SOLDIER TARGETEER
PELTATE SCUTATE
PELTER SKEET
PELTING SLASHING
PELTRY FURS SKINS
PELUDO POYOU ARMADILLO
PELVIS
(PREF.) PELVI(O) PELYCO PYEL(O)
(SUFF.) PELLIC
PEN COT CUB GET HOK MEW PAR PIN STY BOLT CAGE COOP CROO CROW FAUD FOLD JAIL STUB WALK YARD BUGHT CRAWL CREEP CUBBY HUTCH KRAAL POINT QUILL STYLE WRITE BOUGHT CORRAL CRUIVE FASTEN FLIGHT HURDLE INDITE RECORD STYLUS ZAREBA CONFINE WARKLOOM
(— CATTLE) STANCE
(— FOR CATTLE) CUB LOT CREW CRUE LAIR REEVE
(— FOR ELEPHANTS) KRAAL
(— FOR HOGS OR SLAVES) CRAWL
(— OF CUTTLEFISH) GLADIUS
(— POINT) NEB NIB STUB
(— UP) FRANK STIVE
(AUTHOR'S —) STYLE STYLUS
(FOUNTAIN —) STICK
(MUSIC —) RASTRUM
(REED —) CALAMUS
PENALIZE CHECK
PENALTY BETE CAIN DOOM FINE LOSS PAIN BEAST JUISE MULCT AMENDE AMERCE SOLACE FORFEIT NEMESIS SURSIZE BLOODWIT HARDSHIP SCAFFOLD
(DRINKING —) KELTIE
PENANCE TAP SORE SHRIFT SORROW REMORSE SUFFERING
PEN CASE PENNER POPPET
PENCEL FLAG PENNON STREAMER PENNONCEL
PENCHANT BENT TASTE FOIBLE GENIUS LIKING LEANING FONDNESS

PENCIL PEN RED WAD BLUE LEAD WADD LINER SHEAF SKETCH STYLUS POINTEL CHARCOAL KEELIVINE
(PART OF —) CASE LEAD POINT ERASER FERRULE SHOULDER
(SLATE —) CAM CALM SKAILLIE
(PL.) STATIONERY
(PREF.) PENCILLI PENICILLI
PENCILWOOD MORDORE
PENDANT BOB JAG DROP FLAG JAGG PEND TAIL AGLET BULLA GUTTA POINT AIGLET LUSTER PALAOA PLAYER TABARD TARGET TASSEL EARDROP LANGUET SUPPORT LAVALIER
PENDENNIS (AUTHOR OF —) THACKERAY
(CHARACTER IN —) BELL AMORY EMILY FANNY FOKER HELEN HENRY LAURA ARTHUR BOLTON GEORGE JEMIMA BLANCHE FRANCIS ALTAMONT COSTIGAN CLAVERING PENDENNIS WARRINGTON THISTLEWOOD
PENDENT LOP BAGGED ICICLE HANGING PROMISS
PENDICLE POFFLE
PENDULOUS LOP SLOUCH HANGING NODDING PENSILE CERNUOUS DROOPING
PENDULUM SWING PENDLE SWINGEL SWINGLE VIBRATILE
(INVERTED —) NODDY
PENELOPE (FATHER OF —) ICARIUS
(FATHER-IN-LAW OF —) LAERTES
(HUSBAND OF —) ULYSSES ODYSSEUS
(MOTHER OF —) PERIBOEA
(SON OF —) TELEMACHUS
(SUITOR OF —) AGELAUS
PENEPLAIN STRATH ENDRUMPF
PENETRABLE PERVIOUS
PENETRATE CUT DIG DIP SEE BITE BORE DIVE GORE PASS PINK SINK STAB WADE BREAK DRILL DRIVE ENTER IMBUE PROBE SEIZE THIRL CLEAVE FATHOM FICCHE GIMLET INVADE PIERCE RIDDLE SEARCH STRIKE THRILL WIMBLE DISCERN PERVADE PERCOLATE PERFORATE
(— MENTALLY) ENTER
(— ONE'S MIND) SOAK
PENETRATED (EASILY —) MELLOW
PENETRATING ACID KEEN ACUTE LEVEL NASAL SHARP ASTUTE DEADLY SHREWD SHRILL SUBTLE GIMLETY INGOING INTRANT KNOWING PUNGENT PERCEANT PIERCING REACHING TRENCHANT
PENETRATION DEPTH ACUMEN FATHOM INROAD INGOING INSIGHT SEEPAGE INCISION INVASION SAGACITY
PENEUS (DAUGHTER OF —) DAPHNE
(FATHER OF —) OCEANUS
(MOTHER OF —) TETHYS
(SON OF —) HYPSEUS
PENGUIN AUK DIVER GENTU ARCTIC DIPPER GENTOO JOHNNY PINWING BREVIPED MACARONI
(PL.) IMPENNES
(PREF.) SPHENISCI SPHENISCO

PENGUIN ISLAND (AUTHOR OF —) FRANCE
(CHARACTER IN —) MAEL CLENA CRRES DRACO OLIVE PYROT TALPA AGARIC KRAKEN TRINCO VISIRE EVELINE BOSCENOS CLARENCE GREATANK JOHANNES OBEROSIA CHATILLON MARBODIUS
PENINNAH (HUSBAND OF —) ELKANAH
(SON OF —) SAMUEL
PENINSULA CAPE MULL NECK INDIA BILAND BYLAND ISLAND PENILE CHERSONESE
PENIS
(PREF.) BALAN(I)(O) PHALL(O) POSTH(E)(IO)(O)
PENITENCE RUE REGRET SORROW PENANCE PENANCY REMORSE
PENITENT RUER SORRY HUMBLE WEEPER MOURNER STANDER CONTRITE
(— OF 3RD STAGE) KNEELER
PENITENTIARY JUG PEN JAIL STIR TENCH PRISON PENITENT
PENMAN CLERK AUTHOR SCRIBE WRITER
PENMANSHIP HAND SCRIPT PENSHIP WRITING
PENNANT FANE FLAG WHIP COLOR ROGER BANNER CORNET ENSIGN PENCIL PENNON PENSIL PINION PINNET MEATBALL REPEATER STREAMER
PENNILESS POOR BROKE NEEDY BANKRUPT INDIGENT STRAPPED PLACKLESS
PENNON FLAG VANE WING ANVIL BANNER PENCIL PENOUN PINION FEATHER GONFANON
PENNON SPAR PEGGYMAST

UNIVERSITY: PITT DREXEL LEHIGH TEMPLE BUCKNELL DUQUESNE VILLANOVA

PENNY DY AES MEG RED SOU WIN GILL WING WINN BROON BROWN OULAP PENCE COPPER FOLLIS SALTEE STIVER BROWNIE STERLING
(**— DREADFUL**) HORRIBLE
(**DUTCH —**) STIVER
(**HALF —**) HALFLIN
(**OLD SCOTCH —**) TURNER
(**PL.**) PENCE FOLLES
PENNYCRESS FANWEED STINKWEED
PENNY-PINCHING STINGY
PENNYROYAL PULIOL HEDEOMA HILLWORT TICKWEED SQUAWWEED
PENNYWEIGHT DWT PENNY WEIGHT STERLING
PENNYWORT ROTGRASS
PENROD (**AUTHOR OF —**) TARKINGTON
(**CHARACTER IN —**) CRIM JONES SARAH PENROD MARJORIE SCHOFIELD
PENSION WAGE PAYMENT STIPEND SUBSIDY TRIBUTE GRATUITY MALIKANA
PENSIONER COD
PENSIVE MESTO MOODY PENSY SOBER DREAMY MUSING PENCEY WISTFUL THOUGHTY MELANCHOLY
PENT CAGED PENNED CONFINED ENCLOSED RESERVOIR
PENTACLE STAR HEXAGRAM PENTAGRAM
PENTAD QUINTAD
PENTASTICH POEM UNIT STANZA STROPHE
PENTATEUCH TORAH
PENTECOST SHABUOTH WHITSUNDAY
PENTHESILEA (**SLAYER OF —**) ACHILLES
PENTHEUS (**FATHER OF —**) ECHION
(**GRANDFATHER OF —**) CADMUS
(**MOTHER OF —**) AGAVE
PENTHOUSE CAT PENT ROOF SHED AERIE ANNEX HANGAR LOOKUM SHADOW PLUTEUS BULKHEAD SKEELING SKILLION APPENTICE
PENTOSAN ARABAN
PENTOSE APIOSE RIBOSE
PENTYL AMYL
PENURIOUS MEAN POOR BARREN SCANTY STINGY MISERLY WANTING INDIGENT HIDEBOUND NIGGARDLY
PENURY WANT BEGGARY BORASCO POVERTY SCARCITY INDIGENCE PRIVATION
PEON HAND PAWN SERF SLAVE PELADO THRALL FOOTMAN LABORER PEASANT SOLDIER CONSTABLE
PEONY PINY MOUTAN
PEOPLE (ALSO SEE NATIVE AND TRIBE) ARO FUL LOG MEN PUL

TAT VAI YAO AKRA ASHA BENI BUGI CHIN CHUD EMIM FOLK FULA GARO GENS HERD HIMA HUMA IRON LAND LEDE LUBA LURI PHUD PHUL PHUT RACE RAIS REMI SAFI SARA SEBA SERE TEMA THEY TODA TOMA TULU USUN VITI VOLK WARE AFIFI AVARS BENIN BONGO CATTI CHAGA COURS DEMOS DUALA EDONI ELYMI FOLKS FULAH GENTE GOMER HAUSA JACKS KAREN LAITY LANAO LENDU LUREM MARSI MASAI NOGAI ORANG PUNAN QUADI RAMBO ROTSE SACAE SALAR SAUNA SHAKA STOCK TAURI VOLTA WARUA WORLD ABABUA ACHUAS AFSHAR AISSOR ANGAMI ANGLES ARUNTA AVIKOM BAHIMA BAKELE BAKUBA BALUBA BELTIR BOSHAS BULLOM CIMBRI COMMON DAOINE GENTRY GILAKI GILEKI HAUSSA HERERO HERULI KANWAR KPUESI KRUMAN MANTZU MINYAE MOSCHI NATION OVAMPO PAMIRI PUBLIC RAMUSI RUTULI SAFINI SAMBAL SATRAE SEMANG SHARRA TADJIK TAGAUR TELUGU TUNGUZ TURSHA VENETI VOLCAE WACAGO WAHIMA YNDOYS YUECHI ZAMBAL ACHANGO ASTOMOI BAGANDA BAGARRA DAKALAI DANGALA DANGASH BAROTSE BUNYORO DARDANI DENIZEN DURZADA FALISCI GAETULI GENERAL GEPIDAE GOAJIRO GUHAYNA INHABIT IRISHRY ISSEDOI ITALICI KINDRED KURANKO MAKONDE MESHECH MITANNI NABALOI PICENES PICTAVI PUKHTUN ROHILLA SAMBURU SENONES SILURES SUKKIIM TIRURAI VESTINI WARUNGA WACHAGA WAKAMBA WANGONI POPULATE
(**— HAVING DISTINCT LANGUAGE**) TONGUE
(**— OF FASHION**) FLOSS
(**— OF GOOD BREEDING**) GENTRY GENTILITY
(**ABORIGINAL —**) JAKUN KHMER KODAGU SEKHWAN
(**ANCIENT —**) CARA CHAM JUNG ELYMI GETAE HURRI ICENI SACAE SERES SICULI DARDANI FALISCI FIRBOLG KIPCHAK SEQUANI SILURES
(**BIBLICAL —**) ALUR IBAD IBAN MAGOG IBANAG SOMALI GADDANG
(**CAVE-DWELLING —**) HORITE
(**COMMON —**) DEMOS PLEBE VULGAR VULGUS TILIKUM SNOBBERY
(**EXTINCT —**) KOT CHONO COFAN COREE CHANGO CHATOT GUINAU HIBITO SAPONI SHIRINO
(**FOREST —**) SAKAI SAORA SAURA
(**HONORABLE —**) HONESTY
(**LOWEST CLASS OF —**) CANAILLE
(**MARITIME —**) LAMUT

(**MOUNTAIN —**) HUZUL HUTZUL
(**NOMADIC —**) SHUA HORDE IGDYR IHLAT SHUWA HABIRU SHAGIA SARACEN SHAMMAR SHORTZY SHUKRIA
(**OLD —**) ANCIENTRY
(**ORDINARY —**) LAYFOLK
(**PAGAN —**) IRAYA HANUNOO SUBANUN
(**POWERFUL GROUP OF —**) MAFIA
(**PRIMITIVE —**) DAFLA IRULA KADIR KURUKH CHENCHU
(**WHITE —**) ALBICULI
(**PL.**) MAKHZAN
(**PREF.**) DEM(O) ETHN(O) PLEBI POPULI
PEOPLED ABAD SETTLED POPULATE
PEORIA MASCOUTEN
PEP GO VIM DASH MOXIE VERVE VIGOR ENERGY GINGER ANIMATE QUICKEN ACTIVITY
PEPLUM GOWN SKIRT TUNIC PEPLOS OVERSKIRT
PEPO GOURD MELON SQUASH PUMPKIN PEPONIDA PEPONIUM
PEPPER CAVA IKMO ITMO KAVA SIRI BETEL CHILI MANGO PIPER SIRIH MATICO TOPEPO CAYENNE PAPRIKA PIMENTA RELIENO JALAPENO KAVAKAVA
(**JAVA —**) CUBEB
(**RED —**) LADYFINGER
(**PREF.**) PIPERI PIPERO
PEPPER AND SALT JASPER
PEPPERGRASS CRESS CANARY ANOUNOU COCKWEED
PEPPERMINT MENTHE LABIATE
PEPPER TREE MOLLE HOROPITO PIMIENTO
PEPPERWORT DITTANDER
PEPPERY HOT FIERY SAUCY SPICY TOUCHY PIQUANT PUNGENT SPIRITED STINGING
PEPPY GINGERY
PEPTIDE KININ
PEPTONE ASCARON
PER BY THE EACH THROUGH
PERADVENTURE HAP DOUBT MAYBE CHANCE MAPPEN MAYHAP HAPPILY PERHAPS POSSIBLY
PERAMBULATE WALK RAMBLE STROLL PERAMBLE TRAVERSE
PERAMBULATION WEND
PERAMBULATOR BUGGY WAGON BASSINET VIAMETER WAYWISER PEDOMETER
PERATE OPHITE
PERCEIVE SEE ESPY FEEL FIND GAUM HEAR KNOW LOOK MIND NOTE SCAN TWIG SCENT SENSE SMELL TASTE TOUCH BEHOLD COTTON DESCRY DIVINE FIGURE NOTICE REMARK SURVEY COGNIZE DISCERN OBSERVE REALIZE SENSATE COMPRISE DESCRIBE UNDERNIM RECOGNIZE
PERCENTAGE CUT AGIO PART SHARE PROFIT PORTION SCALAGE CONTANGO DEFLATOR PROPORTION
(**MINING —**) LEY

PERCEPT IDEA
PERCEPTIBLE PUBLIC NOTABLE TACTILE VISIBLE APPARENT PALPABLE SENSIBLE TANGIBLE TRACTABLE PERCEIVABLE
(**FAINTLY —**) SHADOWY
(**HARDLY —**) FAINT
(**PREF.**) ESTHETO
PERCEPTION RAY BUMP GAUM TACT SAVOR SCENT SENSE SIGHT ACUMEN VISION CLOSURE FEELING GLIMMER NOSTRIL BEARINGS DELICACY OUTSIGHT COGNITION SENSATION SENTIMENT
(**DIM —**) CLIMMER
(**MENTAL —**) TACT TOUCH SENSATION
(**SPIRITUAL —**) WISDOM
PERCEPTIVE ACUTE QUICK SHARP SUBTLE KNOWING PIERCING SENSITIVE
PERCH BAR BAS LUG PEG ROD SIT BASS JOUK MADO OKOW PERK PIKE POLE POPE RUFF SEAT BARSE BEGTI BEKTI BLOCK LIGHT REACH ROOST RUFFE STAFF STANG ALIGHT BUGARA CALLOP COMBER PERCID SANDER SAUGER SETTLE ZANDER ZINGEL ALFIONE HOGFISH STATION ROCKFISH MARTENIKO TRUMPETER MADEMOISELLE
(**2-YEAR OLD —**) EGLING
(**PREF.**) PERCI
PERCHANCE HAPLY MAYBE AUNTERS FORTUNE PERHAPS POSSIBLY
PERCHER STAKER
PERCHTA BERTHA
PERCOLATE MELT OOZE PERK SEEP SIFT SILT SIPE SOAK WEEP DRILL EXUDE LEACH EXHALE FILTER STRAIN
PERCOLATION SIPING SEEPAGE LEACHING
PERCOLATOR SIPER BIGGIN CAFETIERE DISPLACER
PERCUSSION BLOW IMPACT STROKE PNEUMATIC
(**— IN MASSAGE**) TAPOTEMENT
PERDITA (**FATHER OF —**) LEONTES
(**MOTHER OF —**) HERMIONE
PERDITION HELL LOSS RUIN BOWWOWS BALLYWACK DAMNATION
PEREGRINATE TOUR WALK TRAVEL WANDER JOURNEY SOJOURN TRAVERSE
PEREGRINE ALIEN EXOTIC ROVING PILGRIM STRANGE IMPORTED
PEREGRINE FALCON SAKER GENTLE TASSEL TERCEL
PEREGRINE PICKLE (**AUTHOR OF —**) SMOLLETT
(**CHARACTER IN —**) TOM VANE PIPES SALLY EMILIA HAWSER PICKLE APPLEBY GRIZZLE GAMALIEL GAUNTLET HATCHWAY HORNBECK TRUNNION PEREGRINE CADWALLADER
PEREMPT QUASH DEFEAT DESTROY

PEREMPTORY FLAT FINAL UTTER EXPRESS HAUGHTY ABSOLUTE DECISIVE DOGMATIC POSITIVE ESSENTIAL MASTERFUL
PERENNIAL HERB CAREX LIANA PEONY SEDUM BANANA CENTRO BLUEWEED CONSTANT ENDURING KNAPWEED TOADFLAX CONTINUAL EVERGREEN PENNYWORT PERPETUAL RECURRENT
PERESH (FATHER OF —) MACHIR
(MOTHER OF —) MAACHAH
PERFECT ALL AOK BACK BORN CURE FILL FINE FULL HOLY PURE SURE EXACT FINAL FULLY IDEAL PLAIN RIGHT RIPEN SHEER SOUND TOTAL UTTER WHOLE ENTIRE EXPERT FINISH MATURE POLISH REFINE SPHERE CERTAIN CONCOCT CONTENT CORRECT CROWNED DEVELOP GEMLIKE IMPROVE PLENARY PRECISE SINLESS SPHERAL TYPICAL COMPLETE COPYBOOK FLAWLESS INFINITE INTEGRAL REPLENISH
(— IN RIGHTEOUSNESS) HOLY
(— SCORE) MAX
(PREF.) TEL(E)(EO)
PERFECTA EXACTA
PERFECTED EXACT SUMMED FINISHED PERQUEIR
PERFECTION ACME BEST PINK BLOOM IDEAL BEAUTY FINISH PLENTY FULNESS PARAGON FINALITY FINENESS MATURITY RIPENESS ERUDITION
(STATE OF —) SIDDHI
(TYPE OF —) PARAGON
PERFECTIVE TELIC
PERFECTLY SPAN QUITE IDEALLY PERQUEIR
PERFIDIOUS FALSE SNAKY DISLEAL SNAKISH DISLOYAL SPITEFUL FAITHLESS
PERFIDY DECEIT TREASON FALSEHOOD FALSENESS TREACHERY
PERFORATE EAT DOCK HOLE DRILL PRICK PUNCH SIEVE THIRL PIERCE POUNCE RIDDLE THRILL PINHOLE PUNCTURE PENETRATE TEREBRATE
(— A STAMP) CENTER
PERFORATED OPEN CRIBROSE
PERFORATION BORE HOLE THIRL TORET BROACH EYELET STIGMA TRESIS FORAMEN PINHOLE SEPTULA STENCIL FENESTRA DIABROSIS PERTUSION
(SUFF.) TRESIA
PERFORM DO ACT CUT KIP CHAR FILL FULL HAVE KEEP LAST MAKE PLAY SHOW STEP CHARE DIGHT ENACT EXERT FETCH ACQUIT COMMIT EFFECT FULFIL RENDER ACHIEVE EXECUTE EXHIBIT EXPLOIT FUNGIFY FURNISH IWURCHE OPERATE PRESENT PRESTATE PROSECUTE
(— AWKWARDLY) BOGGLE
(— BADLY) BOLLIX
(— BRILLIANTLY) STAR SPARKLE

(— CLUMSILY) THUMB BUNGLE
(— FULLY) END
(— HASTILY) SKIMP SCAMP,
(— HURRIEDLY) SLUR
(— IN DANCING) FIGURE
(FAIL TO — EFFECTIVELY) CHOKE
PERFORMANCE ACT JOB DEED FEAT HAND SHOW TEST WORK CAPER SLANG SPORT STUNT ACTING ACTION BALLET EFFECT HORARY MASQUE ACCOUNT ACROAMA BENEFIT BOOKING CONCERT EXPLOIT MATINEE MUMMERY RELEASE SHOWING FAREWELL FUNCTION PRACTICE STERACLE OPERATION
(— FOR ONE) SOLO
(— OF DUTY) FEASANCE
(— OF OBLIGATION) SOLUTIO
(— VARIATIONS) COUNTER
(— WITH SENTIMENTALITY) DROOL
(ARAB —) FANTASIA
(BRILLIANT —) BRAVURA
(CHRISTMAS EVE —) GOMBAY
(CLUMSY —) BUNGLE
(DRAMATIC —) TOPENG PANTOMIME
(FIRST —) OPENING PREMIERE
(INEPT —) BOMB
(NO —) RELACHE
(PAST —) FORM
(TRIAL —) AUDITION
(VULGAR —) BLOWOFF
(WRONG —) MISPRISION
(SUFF.) LOG(ER)(IA)(IAN)(IC)(ICAL) (IST)(UE)(Y)
PERFORMER ACT DOER GEEK MOKE STAR ACTOR SHINE ARTIST DANCER KINKER LEADER PLAYER WORKER ACROAMA ACROBAT ARTISTE GAMBIST HORNIST HOTSHOT SOLOIST EXECUTOR SPARKLER HAMFATTER HEADLINER
(— ON SEVERAL INSTRUMENTS) MOKE
(— WITH NEGRO DIALECT) HAMBONE
(BURLESQUE —) GRINDER
(CIRCUS —) LEAPER
(INFERIOR —) HAM SHINE
(SUFF.) ANT ENT
PERFUME ATAR BALM FUME MUSK NOSE OTTO AROMA ATTAR CENSE CIVET MYRRH SCENT SMELL SPICE CARVOL CHYPRE EMBALM FLAVOR IONONE BOUQUET CARVONE DIAPASM ESSENCE INCENSE JASMINE NOSEGAY ODORIZE SWEETEN BERGAMOT MARECHAL ORANGERY PATCHOULI
(— BASE) MUSK CIVET NEROL NEROLI
(POWDERY —) PULVIL
PERFUNCTORY CURSORY CARELESS SLIPSHOD SLOVENLY APATHETIC
PERGOLA ARBOR BOWER RAMADA BALCONY TRELLIS
PERHAPS HAPS MAYBE ABLINS BELIKE HAPPEN MAPPEN MAYHAP ABLINGS AIBLINS

LIGHTLY PERCASE YIBBLES POSSIBLY PERCHANCE
PERI ELF FAIRY SPRITE
PERIAPT CHARM AMULET
PERICARP BUR BOLL BURR BLADDER
PERICHOLE, LA (CHARACTER IN —) ABDRES PIQUILLO PERICHOLE
(COMPOSER OF —) OFFENBACH
PERICLES (AUTHOR OF —) SHAKESPEARE
(CHARACTER IN —) BOULT CLEON DIANA GOWER MARINA THAISA CERIMON DIONYZA ESCANES LEONINE PERICLES PHILEMON THALIARD ANTIOCHUS HELICANUS LYCHORIDA SIMONIDES LYSIMACHUS
(FATHER OF —) XANTHIPPUS
(MISTRESS OF —) ASPASIA
(MOTHER OF —) AGARISTE
(SON OF —) PARALUS XANTHIPPUS
(TEACHER OF —) ZENO DAMON
PERICLYMENUS (BROTHER OF —) NESTOR
(FATHER OF —) NELEUS POSEIDON
(MOTHER OF —) CHLORIS MELIBOEA
PERICRANIUM HEAD BRAIN
PERIDOTITE PICRITE EULYSITE JOSEFITE SAXONITE WEHRLITE
PERIERES (FATHER OF —) AEOLUS
(MOTHER OF —) ENARETE
(SON OF —) APHAREUS LEUCIPPUS
(WIFE OF —) GORGOPHONE
PERIGEE EPIGEUM
PERIGYNIUM UTRICLE
PERIL RISK WERE WATHE CRISIS DANGER HAZARD MENACE SCYLLA THREAT THRONG TRANCE DISTRESS JEOPARDY CHARYBDIS
PERILOUS KITTLE DOUBTFUL DREADFUL INFAMOUS DANGEROUS HAZARDOUS
PERIMETER RIM CIRCUIT OUTLINE BOUNDARY PERIPHERY
PERIOD GO AGE DOT END EON ERA AEON DATE LIFE RACE SPAN STOP TERM TIDE TIME YEAR AVAIL CLOSE CYCLE EPACT EPOCH LABOR LAPSE PATCH POINT SPACE SPELL STAGE CUTOFF GHURRY HEMERA MOMENT PARODY PICTUN SEASON STOUND ACCOUNT DICOLON FLORUIT PASTIME SESSION STADIUM STRETCH DURATION INDUCIAE INSTANCE LIFETIME SENTENCE
(— ENDING FROST) FRESH
(— FOR WHICH ENJOYED) TENURE
(— IN DEVELOPMENT) STAGE
(— OF ACTION) GO BOUT
(— OF DECLINE) SUNSET EVENING
(— OF DRYNESS) DROUTH DROUGHT
(— OF FAIR WEATHER) SLATCH
(— OF FESTIVITY) WAKES
(— OF GLOOM) DEAD
(— OF GRACE) DAY
(— OF HAPPINESS) MILLENNIUM
(— OF HEAT) CALLING
(— OF HUMID WEATHER) SIZZARD

(— OF IMMATURITY) SWADDLE
(— OF INSTRUCTION) LESSON
(— OF LIFE) AGE ELD SPAN
(— OF MILITARY SERVICE) HITCH
(— OF MOTILITY) SWARMING
(— OF MOURNING) SHIVA SHIBAH
(— OF PERFORMING) STANZA
(— OF PLAY) HALF CHUKKER QUARTER
(— OF RECREATION) HOLIDAY VACATION
(— OF REMISSION) JUBILEE
(— OF REST) SMOKO BREATHER
(— OF REVOLUTION OF HEAVENLY BODY) ORB
(— OF TIME) DAY HOUR WEEK YEAR MONTH DECADE MINUTE SECOND
(— OF WORK) SHIFT SPELL STINT
(— OF 10 YEARS) DECADE
(— OF 100 YEARS) AGE CENTURY
(— OF 1000 YEARS) CHILIAD MILLIAD
(— OF 14 MINUTES, 24 SECONDS) CENTIDAY
(— OF 2 MONTHS) DIMESTER
(— OF 2 YEARS) BIENNIUM
(— OF 20 TUNS) KATUN
(— OF 20 YEARS) KATUN
(— OF 260 DAYS) TONALMATL
(— OF 4 YEARS) QUADRENNIUM
(— OF 5 DAYS) PENTAD
(— OF 5 YEARS) LUSTRE LUSTRUM
(— OF 50 YEARS) JUBILE JUBILEE
(— OF 7 DAYS) HEBDOMAD
(— OF 7 YEARS) SEPTENARY
(— PRECEDING IMPORTANT EVENT) EVE
(CLASS —) HOUR
(CULTURAL —) HORIZON
(DEFINITE —) MOMENT
(DISTINCTIVE —) EPOCH
(DULL —) SLACK
(EVOLUTIONAL —) HEMERA
(GEOLOGICAL —) JURA KAROO EOCENE ALGOMAN HORIZON NEOCENE CAMBRIAN DEVONIAN JURASSIC SILURIAN TERTIARY TRANSVAAL
(HAPPY —) MILLENIUM
(HYPOTHETICAL —) ACME
(JAPANESE CULTURAL —) JOMON
(LONG —) EON AEON CYCLE
(MEETING —) SESSION
(MENSTRUAL —) TERMS
(OCCASIONAL —) SNATCH
(OF JAPANESE CULTURAL —) YAYOI
(PENITENTIAL —) LENT
(RECURRING —) EMBER
(SHORT —) BIT FIT BLINK SHAKE SPELL SPURT SNATCH
(WAITING —) MORATORIUM
(WET —) PLUVIAL
(SUFF.) (OF A —) CHRONOUS
PERIODIC ERAL ANNUAL CYCLIC ETESIAN REGULAR FREQUENT SEASONAL
(NOT —) LOOSE ACYCLIC
PERIODICAL DAILY ORGAN PAPER SHEET ANNUAL DIGEST REVIEW ETESIAN FANZINE JOURNAL REGULAR TABLOID DREADFUL EXCHANGE MAGAZINE

EPHEMERIS PICTORIAL

PERIODICALLY TERMLY

PERION (SON OF —) AMADIS

PERIPATETIC ROVING RAMBLING
ITINERANT

PERIPHERAL DEEP OUTER DISTAL
DISTANT EXTERNAL MARGINAL

PERIPHERY LIP RIM BRIM DOME
EDGE AMBIT LIMIT SKIRT AREOLA
BORDER BOUNDS FRINGE
AMBITUS CONTOUR SUBURBS
SURFACE CONFINES PERIMETER

PERIPHRASTIC AMBAGIOUS

PERISCOPE ALTISCOPE
HYPOSCOPE OMNISCOPE

PERISH DIE FADE FALL RUIN TINE
TYNE QUAIL SPILL SWELT WASTE
DEPART EXPIRE STARVE DESTROY
FORFARE MISCARRY
(— GRADUALLY) FADE

PERISHABLE SOFT DYING CADUKE
BRITTLE FUGITIVE

PERISHED MUSHY

PERISTENCE
(SUFF.) STASIA STASIS

PERISTOME FRINGE

PERITE SKILLED

PERITHECIUM ALVEOLA

PERITONEUM RIM SIPHAC

PERIWIG FLASH GALERA PERUKE
TOUPEE GALERUM PERWICK
CHEVELURE

PERIWINKLE PERY PIRE WINK
PERRY SNAIL MYRTLE WINKLE
DOGBANE PINPATCH SENGREEN
BLUEBUTTON

PERJINK NEAT TRIM PRECISE

PERJURE FORSWEAR

PERJURED MANSWORN

PERK BRISK PERCH PREEN PRINK
FRESHEN SMARTEN

PERKY AIRY PERT COCKY JAUNTY
CHIPPER

PERMANENCE STAY STABILITY

PERMANENT FIXED STABLE
ABIDING DURABLE LASTING
STATIVE CONSTANT ENDURING
REMANENT STANDING INDELIBLE

PERMANENTLY KEEPS

PERMEABLE POROUS PERVIOUS

PERMEATE FILL SEEP SOAK BATHE
IMBUE DRENCH INFORM INVADE
ANIMATE PERVADE DOMINATE
SATURATE PENETRATE

PERMEATED SHOT

PERMEATION SATURATION

PERMIAN DYAS DYASSIC

PERMISSIBLE FREE VENIAL
POSSIBLE CONGEABLE
(NOT —) NEFAS

PERMISSION MAY FIAT LIEF PASS
CONGE DARST FAVOR GRACE
GRANT LEAVE ACCESS ACCORD
PERMIT CONSENT LIBERTY
LICENSE SANCTION
(— TO BE ABSENT) ABSIT
(LETTER OF —) EXEAT

PERMISSIVE TOLERANT
CONCESSORY

PERMIT LET CHIT CHOP GIVE LEVE
PASS ADMIT ALLOW CONGE
EXEAT FAVOR GRACE GRANT
LEAVE SERVE ACCORD BETEEM

CEDULA DUSTUK ENDURE
ENTREE SUFFER CONCEDE
CONSENT DUSTUCK FACULTY
LICENSE PLACARD POMPANO
WARRANT DISPENSE
(— NEGATIVELY) TOLERATE
(— TO TAKE) SOAK
(CUSTOMS —) CARNET

PERMITTED FREE LOOT LICIT
ALLOWED INNOCENT SUPPOSED
(— BY LAW) LEGAL

PERMUTATION BARTER CHANGE
EXCHANGE

PERNICIOUS BAD ILL EVIL FATAL
QUICK SWIFT DEADLY MALIGN
WICKED BALEFUL BANEFUL
HARMFUL HURTFUL NOISOME
NOXIOUS RUINOUS

PERNIO CHILBLAIN

PERO (BROTHER OF —) NESTOR
(FATHER OF —) NELEUS
(HUSBAND OF —) BIAS
(MOTHER OF —) CHLORIS
(SON OF —) ASOPUS

PEROPUS PARAGON

PERORATION EPILOG PERIOD
CLOSING PURLICUE

PEROXISOME MICROBODY

PERPEND JUMPER PARPEN
PONDER REFLECT THROUGH

PERPENDICULAR SINE ERECT
PLUMB SHEER ABRUPT NORMAL
APOTHEM UPRIGHT BINORMAL
CATHETUS EVENDOWN VERTICAL
(MUTUALLY —) ORTHOGONAL

PERPENDICULARITY APLOMB

PERPENDICULARLY BOLT SHEER
SHEERLY

PERPETRATE DO PULL COMMIT
EFFECT PERFORM

PERPETUAL ETERN ENDLESS
ETERNAL CONSTANT INFINITO
UNENDING CONTINUAL
PERENNIAL

PERPETUALLY EVER ALWAYS
FOREVER

PERPETUATE CONTINUE ETERNIZE
MAINTAIN

PERPLEX CAP MAR SET VEX BEAT
CLOG DOIT DOZE FIKE MAZE
STUN AMAZE BESET BLAIK STUMP
TWIST BAFFLE BOGGLE BOTHER
BUNKER CUMBER DARKEN
FEAGUE FICKLE GRAVEL HAMPER
HARASS HOBBLE KITTLE MAMMER
MITHER MOIDER MUDDLE
PLAGUE POTHER POTTER PUTTER
PUZZLE RAFFLE RIDDLE TWITCH
WILDER WRIXLE BEDEVIL
BUMBAZE CONFUSE DIFFUSE
EMBROIL FLUMMOX MYSTIFY
NONPLUS PLUNDER STAGGER
STUMBLE TORMENT BEWILDER
CONFOUND SURPRISE WINDLASS
BAMBOOZLE

PERPLEXED MAZY ANXIOUS
NONPLUS PUZZLED CONFUSED
TROUBLED INTRICATE
TOSTICATED

PERPLEXING HARD MAZY SPINY
CRABBY KNOBBY KNOTTY
CARKING COMPLEX CRABBED
QUISCOS BAFFLING

PERPLEXITY FOG KNOT WERE
BRAKE FOITER HOBBLE PUCKER
PUZZLE TAKING TANGLE ANXIETY
NONPLUS STICKLE TROUBLE
POSEMENT SURPRISE CONFUSION
LABYRINTH PUZZLEMENT
(MENTAL —) STUDY
(RELIEVE OF —) CLEAR

PERQUISITE FEE TIP LOCK PERK
VAIL GOUPIN GOWPEN INCOME
ADJUNCT APANAGE VANTAGE
CONQUEST GRATUITY
(PL.) PICKING

PERRIER PEDRERO

PERRINIST LIBERTINE

PERSE BLUE
(DAUGHTER OF —) CIRCE PASIPHAE
(FATHER OF —) OCEANUS
(HUSBAND OF —) HELIOS
(SON OF —) AEETES PERSES

PERSECUTE VEX BAIT ANNOY
CHASE HARRY HOUND WRACK
WRONG HARASS PESTER PURSUE
AFFLICT CRUCIFY DRAGOON
OPPRESS TORMENT TORTURE

PERSECUTED JOB REFUGEE

PERSECUTOR TORQUEMADA

PERSEPHONE KORE DESPOINA
PRAXIDIKE
(DAUGHTER OF —) CORA KORE
(FATHER OF —) ZEUS JUPITER
(HUSBAND OF —) HADES PLUTO
(MOTHER OF —) CERES DEMETER

PERSES (BROTHER OF —) AEETES
(DAUGHTER OF —) HECATE
(FATHER OF —) CRIUS HELIOS
(MOTHER OF —) PERSE EYRYBIA
(SISTER OF —) CIRCE PASIPHAE

PERSEUS RESCUER CHAMPION
(FATHER OF —) ZEUS JUPITER
(GRANDFATHER OF —) ACRISIUS
(MOTHER OF —) DANAE
(STAR OF —) ATIK ALGOL
(VICTIM OF —) MEDUSA
(WIFE OF —) ANDROMEDA

PERSEVERANCE GRIT MOXIE
STAMINA INDUSTRY PATIENCE
TENACITY CONSTANCY
PERSISTENCE

PERSEVERE PEG CANK KEEP PLUG
TORE ABIDE STICK INSIST REMAIN
PERSIST CONTINUE

PERSEVERING BUSY HARD STILL
PATIENT RESOLUTE SEDULOUS
ASSIDUOUS INSISTENT

PERSIA (SEE IRAN)

PERSIAN PERSE GILAKI HAJEMI
IRANIC DURZADA HADJEMI
IRANIAN MEMNONIAN
(— RED DEER) MARAL

PERSICARY REDLEG REDLEGS
REDSHANK HEARTEASE
HEARTWEED PEACHWORT

PERSIFLAGE BANTER RAILLERY

PERSIMMON KAKI SIMON SIMMON
ZAPOTE CHAPOTE HYAKUME
TRIUMPH
(— TREE) GAB GAUB LOTUS

PERSIST HOLD KEEP LAST URGE
ADHERE ENDURE INSIST REMAIN
PREVAIL SUBSIST CONTINUE
PERSEVERE

PERSISTENCE GUTS

PERSISTENCY TENACITY

PERSISTENT SET DREE FIRM HARD
GREAT STOUT TOUGH DOGGED
DREECH GRITTY HECTIC SLEUTH
DURABLE RESTANT RESTIVE
CONSTANT ENDURING HOLDFAST
OBDURATE RESOLUTE SEDULOUS
STUBBORN ASSIDUOUS
OBSTINATE PERENNIAL PRIMITIVE
RELENTLESS

PERSISTING
(PREF.) MENO

PERSON BOD CAT EGG EGO GUY
MAN ONE BABY BODY CHAL CHAP
COVE DUCK FISH FOOD FORM
GINK HOOK LEDE LIFE NABS PRIG
SELF SOUL BEING BOSOM CHILD
COOKY GHOST HEART HUMAN
PARTI PARTY PIECE STICK THING
WATCH WIGHT ANIMAL BUGGER
ENTITY FELLOW GALOOT GAZABO
JOHNNY KIPPER NUMBER SINNER
SISTER SPIRIT SPRITE ARTICLE
BLISTER WAGTAIL SPECIMEN
TILLICUM
(— ACTING FOR ANOTHER) PROXY
(— ASSOCIATED WITH WORK)
WALLAH
(— BEARING HEAVY BURDEN)
CAMEL
(— BEHIND THE TIMES) FOGY
FOGEY
(— BRINGING GOOD LUCK) MASCOT
(— FROM WHOM FAMILY IS
DESCENDED) STIRPS
(— NAMED) NOMINEE
(— NOT IN THE KNOW) LAME
(— NOT OF NOBLE BIRTH)
ROTURIER
(— OF AGE) COOT FALDWORTH
(— OF CONSEQUENCE) BIGGIE
BIGWIG TALLBOY
(— OF COURAGE) SPARTAN
(— OF INFLUENCE) CAPTAIN
HEAVYWEIGHT
(— OF MEAN BIRTH) GUTTERBLOOD
(— OF RANK) STATE MAGNATE
EMINENCE MAGNIFICO
PERSONAGE
(— RESEMBLING ANOTHER) SOSIA
(— TO SERVE WRIT) ELISOR
(— TOO STRONG FOR ASSAILANT)
TARTAR
(— WHO IS UP-TO-DATE) SWINGER
(— WHO PERFORMS MENIAL TASKS)
DOGSBODY
(— WHO TAKES AMPHETAMINES)
PILLHEAD
(— WITH MENTAL TWIST) CRANK
(— WITH NERVOUS DISORDERS)
NEUROTIC
(— WITH QUEER IDEAS) ROZUM
(— WITHOUT STAMINA) JELLYFISH
(—S IN AMBASSADOR'S SUITE)
COMES
(ABJECT —) SLAVE CRAWLER
(ABSENT-MINDED —) MUSARD
(ADMIRABLE —) PIPPIN
(AFFECTED —) POSEUR MINNICK
GIMCRACK
(AGGRESSIVE —) SHOVER
HOTSHOT
(AMUSING —) COMIC

(ANNOYING —) FIEND NUDNICK
(ARABIZED —) MOZARAB
(ARROGANT —) HUFF TENGU
(ATTRACTIVE —) CUTEY CUTIE KILLER KNOCKOUT
(AVARICIOUS —) YISSER
(AWKWARD —) PUT GAWP HICK MUFF RUBE SLAM STAG STEG KLUTZ STIFF GUFFIN TUMFIE HOOSIER LOBSTER SCHLEPP KITHOGUE SHLEPPER SLOMMACK SPELDRIN
(BAD —) UNSEL
(BALD —) BALLARD BALDHEAD SKINHEAD BALDICOOT
(BANISHED —) WRETCH
(BAPTIZED —) MEMBER ILLUMINATO
(BASE —) CUT RASCAL CAITIFF HILDING PUTTOCK
(BELOVED —) FLAME HEARTROOT
(BIG-BELLIED —) GORBELLY
(BLACK —) BLECK
(BOASTFUL —) BLOWER GASCON
(BOORISH —) GOOP
(CALLOW —) GORLIN SMARTY GOSLING
(CANONIZED —) SAINT
(CARELESS —) HASH TASSEL
(CHICKENHEARTED —) HEN
(CHILDISH —) BAUBLE WHIMLING
(CHUNKY —) JUNT
(CHURLISH —) TIKE TYKE
(CIRCLE OF —S) COTERIE
(CLEVER —) BIRD WHIZ WHIZZ MERCURY
(CLOWNISH —) BUFFOON HOBNAIL VILLAIN
(CLUMSY —) DUB LOB BOOB GAWK SLOB TIKE TYKE JUMBO STAUP STIFF DUFFER KEFFEL LUMMOX HODMADOD
(COARSE —) COW STIRK BABOON MUCKER
(COMBATIVE —) DRAGON GAMECOCK
(COMMONPLACE —) MUT MUTT BROMIDE
(CONCEITED —) IT HUFF COXCOMB PRAGMATIC
(CONFUSED —) FOOSTERER
(CONSERVATIVE —) HUNKER MOSSBACK
(CONTEMPTIBLE —) YAP HEEL PUKE SCAB SKIN SWAB CATSO SHRUB SKITE SKUNK SNIPE TWERP INSECT SHICER STINKER BLIGHTER WHIFFLER PETTITOES
(COWARDLY —) FUGIE SISSY SLINK SQUIB
(CRAFTY —) TOD FILE SHARK JESUIT
(CRAZED —) PSYCHOPATH
(CRINGING —) SNAKE SNOOL FLUNKY SPANIEL
(CRUEL —) LAMB FIEND MALISON
(CUNNING —) PIE
(DAINTY —) MIMMOCK
(DEAD —) DEFUNCT DECEASED DECEDENT
(DECREPIT —) CROCK WITHERLING
(DEFORMED —) CRILE CALIBAN HODMADOD

(DENSE —) DUFFER
(DEPRAVED —) SKATE
(DESPICABLE —) SCAB HOUND SLAVE CAITIFF
(DESTITUTE —) PAUPER
(DIMINUTIVE —) BANTY MIDGE BANTAM MIDGET NIFFNAFF
(DIRTY —) SWEEP DRIVEL HOWLET
(DISABLED —) DUCK CRIPPLE INVALID
(DISAGREEABLE —) GOOP PILL QUAT SKITE RATBAG
(DISGRUNTLED —) SOREHEAD
(DISHONEST —) ROGUE ROTTER BEZONIAN
(DISLIKED —) WARLING
(DISREPUTABLE —) RIP
(DISSOLUTE —) RIBALD ROUNDER STRIKER
(DOLTISH —) BLOCK SWINE
(DRUNKEN —) LUSH TUMBREL TUMBRIL
(DULL —) LOB BORE DODO GOON GOOP GRUB LUMP MOME MOPE SLOB CLUNK DROUD PRUNE SCHMO STICK STOCK LURDAM LACKWIT LOBCOCK NUDNICK OPACITY
(DULL-WITTED —) DOPE GUMP DUNCE
(DWARFISH —) AGATE CROWL SHURF
(DYING —) MORIBUND
(ECCENTRIC —) COON GINK KOOK TIKE TYKE GAZABO GAZEBO FANTAST ODDBALL
(EFFEMINATE —) SOFTY SQUAW CODDLE SOFTIE WANTON BADLING SOFTLING SMOCKFACE
(ELDERLY —) SENIOR SOAKER GRAYHEAD
(EMACIATED —) FRAME WASTREL SKELETON
(EMPTY-HEADED —) NITWIT
(ENROLLED —) MEMBER
(ENTERTAINING —) COMEDIAN
(EVIL —) QUED SCUM QUEDE SHREW
(EXPERIENCED —) EXPERT SOAKER STAGER
(EXPERT —) ACE DAB
(EXTORTIONATE —) SCREW
(EXTRAORDINARY —) ONER BUSTER
(FADED —) SHARGAR SHARGER
(FAMOUS —) DON NOTORIETY
(FANTASTIC —) KICKSHAW
(FARSIGHTED —) PRESBYOPE
(FASHIONABLE —) GIMCRACK
(FASTIDIOUS —) MIMMOCK DELICATE
(FAT —) GURK BLIMP FATSO QUILT SQUAB STOUT
(FATUOUS —) GOOP
(FAWNING —) COGGER SPANIEL
(FEEBLEMINDED —) FEEB IDIOT MORON IMBECILE
(FEROCIOUS —) LAMB
(FICKLE —) ROVER MOONCALF
(FINE —) WHIPPA
(FLABBY —) HUDDERON
(FLASHY —) KID FLASHER
(FOOLISH —) FOP COOT GUMP

HOIT JERK BOOBY SOFTY BAUBLE DOODLE DOTARD DRIVEL HOWLET GOSLING GUBBINS HAVEREL
(FOUL —) DREVILL
(FRANK —) TELLTRUTH
(FUSSY —) FAD FADDLE GRANNY SPOFFY GRANNIE
(GAY —) GRIG HUZZA
(GIDDY —) SCATTERBRAIN
(GOOD-FOR-NOTHING —) KET PELF TASSEL WASTER WANHOPE WASTREL
(GOSSIPING —) SHULER SHUILER
(GOSSIPY —) BIGMOUTH QUIDNUNC NEWSMONGER
(GOSSIP, TALKATIVE —) YENTA
(GRAVE —) SOBERSIDES
(GREEDY —) GORB GANNET GRASPER PUTTOCK
(GROTESQUE —) GUY GOLLIWOGG PUNCHINELLO
(GRUMPY —) SOURBELLY
(GULLIBLE —) JAY BOOB GULPIN LOBSTER FLATHEAD SHLEMIEL WOODCOCK
(GYPSY —) CHI CHAI
(HANDLESS —) SAMMY
(HARD —) MALISON
(HATEFUL —) TOAD
(HEAVY —) STODGER
(HEAVY-SET —) LUMP
(HOT-TEMPERED —) SPARK
(HUMPBACKED —) LORD
(HUNGRY —) HUNGARIAN
(IDLE —) BUMMLE RAGABASH SLUGGARD
(IGNORANT —) BABE BOOB PORK IDIOT IGNARO
(ILL-BRED —) BOOR CHURL CLOWN
(ILL-MANNERED —) GRUB SKUNK
(ILL-NATURED —) CRAB HUNKS PATCH
(ILL-TEMPERED —) CRAB ETTERCAP TAISTREL
(IMMATURE —) BUD SQUAB GORLIN
(IMMORAL —) REP PERDU IMPURITAN
(IMPASSIVE —) BLOCK
(IMPERTINENT —) PAUK PAWK SNIP
(IMPORTANT —) HONOR MOGUL MUGWUMP
(IMPOTENT —) SPADO
(IMPUDENT —) SAUCE SQUIRT SAUCEBOX
(INANE —) SHAUP
(INEXPERIENCED —) BABE INGENUE BEGINNER
(INFERIOR —) BATA SHRUB SHABBLE
(INSIGNIFICANT —) DAB MUT MUTT QUAT BILSH CREEP JOKER SHURF SPRAT SQUIB ABLACH PEANUT NEBBISH PINKEEN WHIFFET GNATLING GRILDRIG PIGWIGEON
(INSINUATING —) WHILLY
(INTRACTABLE —) BUCKIE TARTAR HAGGARD HARDCASE
(IRASCIBLE —) TOUCHWOOD
(IRRITATING —) BOT

(LAME —) VULCAN
(LANK —) TANGLE GANGEREL WINDLESTRAW
(LARGE —) CHUNK WHIPPA SKELPER STODGER STRAPPER
(LASCIVIOUS —) SUCCUBUS
(LAST — IN CONTEST) MELL
(LAZY —) BUM DAW HOIT POKE IDLER TRAIL LORDAN LURDAN BLELLUM LAZYLEGS SLUGABED SLUGGARD
(LEAN —) RIBE TANGLE SHARGER THINGUT
(LEARNED —) CLERK ERUDIT ACHARYA SCHOLAR LITERATO WISEACRE LITERATUS
(LIGHTHEADED —) BEEHEAD
(LITERATE —) SCHOLAR
(LITTLE —) SMOLT SMOUT
(LIVELY —) GRIG BIRKIE HEMPIE WHISKER
(LOUD-VOICED —) STENTOR
(LOW —) PACK SCUM RASCAL BEASTMAN
(LOW SOCIETY —) MUDSILL
(LUBBERLY —) OAF
(LUMBERING —) PUMPKIN TUMBREL TUMBRIL
(LUMPISH —) DROUD
(LUSTY —) BILCH BILSH
(MAD —) MADLING
(MARRIED —) WIFE SPOUSE HUSBAND MATRIMONY
(MEAN —) RIP SCAB CHURL HOUND MISER SKATE SNEAK SHICER BASTARD DOGBOLT BEZONIAN HUCKSTER STINKARD EARTHWORM
(MEDDLESOME —) BREVIT HESSIAN
(MENTALLY UNBALANCED —) MATTOID
(MISCHIEVOUS —) IMP LIMB PEST TOOL HEMPIE HELLION WHIPSTER
(MISERABLE —) SNAKE SWELP WRETCH
(MISERLY —) SKATE SCROOGE PINCHGUT PINCHBACK
(MONSTROUS —) WAMPUS
(NAIVE —) JERK CLUCK GUNSEL INGENUE INNOCENT
(NASTY —) BLEEDER
(NEGLECTED —) TACKY TACKEY
(NIMBLE —) MERCURY
(NOISY —) YAP HOWLET
(OBJECTIONABLE —) CUR COYOTE FOUTER
(OBSTINATE —) DONKEY STIFFNECK
(ODD —) GIG CURE QUIZZY RATBAG CAUTION
(OFFENSIVE —) TICK SKITE STINKER
(OLD-FASHIONED —) FRUMP
(PALTRY —) PELTER
(PASSIONATE —) FUME
(PECULIAR —) BIRD CASE
(PEEVISH —) GRIZZLER SPLENETIC
(PERNICKETY —) FIKE
(PERT —) PIE FLIRT
(POLISHED —) SMOOTHY SMOOTHIE
(POMPOUS —) PUFFIN POMPIST
(POT-BELLIED —) GORREL
(PRIVATE —) JUDEX

(PROSAIC —) PHILISTINE
(PRYING —) POKER PEEPER
SMELLER
(PUGNOSED —) CAMUS CAMUSE
(PUNY —) SCART SHILP SHRIMP
TITMAN
(PURITANICAL —) WOWSER
(QUEER-LOOKING —) JIGGER
(QUERULOUS —) GRUMP JACKDAW
(QUICK-TEMPERED —) SPUNKIE
WILDCAT SPITFIRE
(RAGGED —) ROTO SHAGRAG
TATTERWAG
(RAPACIOUS —) SHARK CATERER
(RECKLESS —) MADCAP RAMSTAM
(RED-HAIRED) BRIQUE
(REFRACTORY —) BUCKIE
(RESTLESS —) RAMPLER RAMPLOR
RANTIPOLE
(RETICENT —) CLAM
(RICH —) MONEYBAGS
(RIDICULOUS —) GOOF HARE
MONIMENT MONUMENT
(RIOTOUS —) ROARER
(ROUGH —) TOWSER
(ROUGH-LOOKING —) RULLION
(RUDE —) HICK PORK RULE CHURL
CLOWN GROBIAN
(RUSTIC —) COON KERN KERNE
HAYSEED HOMESPUN
(SAINTLY —) SADDIK
(SAUCY —) PIET
(SCRAWNY —) SCART SCRAG
(SELF-CENTERED —) HEEL DEVIL
FLANEUR
(SELF-RIGHTEOUS —) PHARISEE
(SENSUAL —) SWING CARNALIST
(SHAMEFUL —) BISMER
(SHORT —) CRILE FADGE KNURL
STUMP
(SHOWY —) FLASH FLASHER
HOTSHOT
(SHREWD —) FILE YEPE
HARDHEAD SNOLLYGOSTER
(SICK —) SICK MALADE PATIENT
AEGROTANT
(SILENT —) MUM MUMCHANCE
(SILLY —) FOP CAKE GUMP SOFT
DOBBY GOOSE SOFTY SPOON
CUCKOO NIMSHI SOFTIE
GOOSECAP LIRIPIPE LIRIPOOP
SOFTHEAD
(SILLY OR CRAZY —) DINGBAT
(SIMPLE —) DRIP LAMB IDIOT
PIGWIGEON
(SKINNY —) SCRAE SCARECROW
(SLATTERNLY —) SLATE
(SLIM —) SWABBLE
(SLOTHFUL —) SLOWBELLY
(SLOVENLY —) HASH SLOB SLORP
TRAIL STREEL SLOMMACK
STREELER
(SLUGGISH —) LUMP DOLDRUM
DRUMBLE LOBCOCK
(SLY —) COON SLYBOOTS
SNECKDRAW SNICKDRAW
(SMALL —) GRIG AGATE DWARF
SPRAT INSECT MORSEL POPPET
SACKET GNATLING
(SOPHISTICATED —) WELTKIND
(SPIRITLESS —) MOPE STICK
(SPITEFUL —) HELLCAT ETTERCAP
(SPRUCE —) SPRUSADO

(STINGY —) CHURL HAYNE STINGY
(STOCKY —) STUMP
(STOLID —) CLAM THICKSKIN
(STRANGE —) WAMPUS
(STRANGE OR ECCENTRIC —)
WEIRDO
(STRAY —) WAIF
(STUBBORN —) BUCKY STOUT
BUCKIE
(STUNTED —) URF SCRUNT
SHARGAR
(STUPID —) ASS DUB JAY MUT
BETE BOOB DODO DOLT DOPE
DRIP GAUM GAWP GOOF GUMP
HASH HOIT JERK MOKE MUTT
BLOCK BUCCA CLUCK CLUNK
CUDDY DUNCE HOBBY JUKES
LOACH MORON SHEEP STIFF
STIRK STOCK STUPE SUMPH
SWINE THICK WAMUS ZOMBI
BOODLE DAWKIN DIMWIT
DODUNK DONKEY DUFFER
GANDER GILLIE GRANNY GUNSEL
LUMMOX LURDAN NITWIT
NOODLE SACKET SHMUCK
STUPEX TUMFIE TUMPHY ZOMBIE
BLUNTIE DULLARD FATHEAD
FUSSOCK HOWFING JACKASS
JUGHEAD MUDHEAD PINHEAD
SAPHEAD SCHMUCK SCHNOOK
BONEHEAD BULLHEAD DOTTEREL
DUMBBELL FLATHEAD GAMPHREL
IRONHEAD MEATHEAD
MOLDWARP MUMPHEAD
STUNPOLL THICKWIT
HODMANDOD MUMCHANCE
THICKHEAD
(STUPID, FOOLISH —) YOYO
(STURDY —) LUMP CHUNK
STALWART
(SULKY —) GLUMP GRUMP SUMPH
GROUCH
(SURLY —) CRUST HUNKS
(TACITURN —) OYSTER
(TALKATIVE —) GASSER BLELLUM
BIGMOUTH
(TALL, AWKWARD —)
GAMMERSTANG
(TENDER —) LAMBKIN
(THICKSET —) NUGGET
(THIN —) BEANPOLE
(THIRD —) GOOSEBERRY
(THOUGHTLESS —) AIRLING
SKIPPER BIRDBRAIN
(TIMID —) NEBBISH MILQUETOAST
(TIMID OR MEEK —) NEBBISH
(TINY —) KEEROGUE
(TIRESOME —) BORE PILL BROMIDE
(TREACHEROUS —) JUDAS SNAKE
VIPER GUNSEL SERPENT
(TRICKY —) SLYBOOTS
(TROUBLESOME —) COW PEST
HELLION HESSIAN
(TRUSTWORTHY —) TRAIST
STANDBY
(UNATTRACTIVE —) GOON GRUB
SCUG CREEP
(UNBENDING —) STIFF
(UNCHASTE —) SHORTHEELS
(UNCIVILIZED —) VISIGOTH
(UNCOUTH —) APE PUT STIFF
YAHOO BABOON SLOMMACK
ROUGHNECK

(UNDERSIZED —) DURGAN
SPARROW
(UNFAITHFUL —) INFIDEL
(UNGAINLY —) CLATCH
(UNHANDY —) FOUTER
(UNHAPPY —) UNSEL
(UNIQUE —) ONER
(UNKNOWN —) INCONNU
STRANGER
(UNMARRIED —) MAIDEN SINGLE
AGAMIST BACHELOR CELIBATE
SPINSTER
(UNPRACTICAL —) MUFF
(UNREASONABLE —) DUFFER
(UNSCRUPULOUS —) CATSO KNAVE
(UNSOPHISTICATED —) JAY HICK
NYAS HAYSEED CORNBALL
INNOCENT
(UNTHANKFUL —) INGRATE
(UNTIDY —) SLOVEN STREEL
SLAISTER
(UNWIELDY —) FUSTILUGS
(USELESS —) POOP SWAB UNSEL
BAUCHLE
(VALOROUS —) HERO
(VENOMOUS —) SPITPOISON
(VIGOROUS —) SNEEZER
(VIOLENT —) DRAGON BANGSTER
SPITFIRE
(VORACIOUS —) HUNGARIAN
(VULGAR —) MUCKER
(WANTON —) RIG FLIRT WHIPSTER
(WASTEFUL —) SCATTERGOOD
(WEAK —) SCART SHILP SOFTY
WHIMLING
(WEAK OR INEFFECTUAL —) WIMP
(WEAK-MINDED —) SAPHEAD
TOTTYHEAD
(WEALTHY —) MONEYBAGS
(WELL-BORN —) FREE
(WHITE —) FAY OFAY GRIFFIN
EUROPEAN PALEFACE
(WICKED —) DEVIL SATAN SHREW
UNLEAD UNLEDE SATANIST
(WILD —) HELLCAT RANTIPOLE
(WILY —) PIE
(WITHERED —) RUNT
(WITLESS —) WITHAM WITTOME
SLABBERER
(WITTY —) WITSHIP SPARKLER
(WORNOUT —) HUSHEL
(WORTHLESS —) YAP FILE GEAR
HOIT JADE LOON SCUM TOOT
CRUMB LOREL LOSEL SCOUT
SHAND BAUBLE BUGGER FELLOW
FOUTRA SHICER BUDMASH
GULLION BLIGHTER VAGABOND
PHARMAKOS
(WRETCHED —) MISER MISERY
(YOUNG —) CUB KID COLT LAMB
CHILD HEMPY SMOLT SMOUT
SPRIG YONKE GUNSEL HEMPIE
JUNIOR CHICKEN CHOOKIE
GRISTLE LAMBKIN JUVENILE
STRIPLING
(PL.) FRY PERSONNEL
(PREF.) PROSOP(O)
(SUFF.) (FEMALE —) INE
PERSONABLE COMELY SHAPELY
HANDSOME
PERSONAGE DON DUSE NIBS
BLOKE FIGURE SHOGUN TYCOON
(GREAT —) MOGUL SOPHI

SOPHY SUFFEE
PERSONAL SELF PRIVY DIRECT
PRIVATE CHATTELS CORPORAL
INTIMATE
(— EFFECTS) DUNNAGE
(PREF.) IDIO
PERSONALITY EGO AURA DRAW
SELF SOUL BEING ETHOS HEART
EGOITY FIGURE CONTROL
FACULTY DEMIURGE PRESENCE
SELFHOOD SELFNESS
PERSONATE ACT FEIGN MIMIC
MASKED PERSON TYPIFY
PRESENT
PERSONATION (SHAM —) IDOL
PERSONIFICATION SOUL GENIUS
(— OF DIVINE VIRTUE) EON
(— OF JUSTICE) THEMIS
PERSONIFY EMBODY INCARNATE
PERSONIZE
PERSONNEL BLOOD STAFF
KITCHEN PHYSIQUE
PERSPECTIVE OPTICS DISTANCE
TELESCOPE
PERSPICACIOUS KEEN ACUTE
ASTUTE SHREWD
(MAKE —) CLEAR
PERSPICACITY WIT ACUMEN
PERSPICUOUS CLEAR LUCID
PLAIN PRECISE VISIBLE MANIFEST
LIGHTSOME
PERSPIRATION DEW SUDOR
SUINT SWEAT HIDROSIS
OLIGIDRIA SUDORESIS
PERSPIRE FUG MELT BREAN
SWEAT SWELTER TRANSPIRE
PERSUADE CON GET WIN COAX
GAIN MOVE RULE SNOW TICE
URGE WISE ARGUE BRING EDUCE
SUADE SWADE WEISE ADVISE
ARGUFY ASSURE CAJOLE ENGAGE
ENTICE INDUCE REMOVE SUBORN
CONVERT DISPUTE ENTREAT
IMPRESS PREVAIL SATISFY
CANOODLE INFLUENCE
PERSUADED PLIABLE GULLIBLE
RESOLVED SENSIBLE
PERSUASION KIND SORT BELIEF
OPINION SUASION JUDGMENT
(AUTHOR OF —) AUSTEN
(CHARACTER IN —) ANNE CLAY
MARY CROFT ELLIOT LOUISA
WALTER BENWICK CHARLES
RUSSELL WILLIAM HARVILLE
MUSGROVE ELIZABETH
FREDERICK HENRIETTA
WENTWORTH
PERSUASIVE COGENT WINNING
INDUCTIVE PLAUSIBLE PROTEPTIC
(PREF.) PITHANO
PERT BOLD CHIC FESS FLIP KECK
SPRY TRIM ALERT ALIVE BARDY
BRISK COCKY DONSY KISKY
PEART PERKY PIERT QUICK SASSY
SAUCY SMART TAUNT CHEEKY
CLEVER COCKET COMELY DAPPER
FRISKY SWASHY THWART
BOBBISH PAUGHTY INSOLENT
PETULANT
(— TALK) CHELP
PERTAIN BE LIF BEAR COME LONG
BELIE TOUCH AFFEIR BEFALL
BELIMP BELONG RELATE

RETAIN CONCERN
(— TO) RINE
PERTAINING (— TO ABDOMEN)
ALVINE
(— TO AIR) AURAL PNEUMATIC
(— TO ALL NATURE) PAMPHYSIC
(— TO ANIMALS) ZOIC
(— TO ANKLE) TARSAL
(— TO APOLLO) PYTHIAN
PAEONIAN
(— TO APOSTLE) PETRINE
(— TO APPETITES) ORECTIC
(— TO ARMPIT) AXILLAR
(— TO ARMY) MARTIAL STRATONIC
(— TO ARROW) SAGITTAL
(— TO ATHENA) PALLADIAN
(— TO BACK) DORSAL TERGAL
(— TO BATH) BALNEAL
(— TO BEAM) TRAGAL
(— TO BEARD) BARBAL
(— TO BED) THORAL
(— TO BEES) APIAN APIARIAN
(— TO BELLY) ALVIN ALVINE
VENTRAL VENTRIC
(— TO BIBLICAL LAW) LEVITIC
(— TO BIRDS) AVIAN AVINE
ORNITHIC VOLUCRINE
(— TO BIRTH) NATAL
(— TO BISHOP) LAWN
(— TO BITTER TASTE) PICRIC
(— TO BLACK SEA) PONTIC
(— TO BODIES AT REST) STATIC
(— TO BODY) SOMAL SOMATIC
(— TO BONE) OSSAL OSTEAL
(— TO BOSOM) GREMIAL
(— TO BRACELET) ARMILLARY
(— TO BRANCHES) RAMOUS
(— TO BREADMAKING) PANARY
(— TO BREAKFAST) ENTACULAR
(— TO BREAST) PECTORAL
(— TO BREASTBONE) STERNAL
(— TO BRISTLES) SETAL
(— TO BROTHEL) STEWISH
(— TO BUNCH) COMAL
(— TO CALF) VITULINE
(— TO CALF OF LEG) SURAL
(— TO CART) PLAUSTRAL
(— TO CARTHAGINIANS) PUNIC
(— TO CARVING) GLYPHIC
(— TO CAVE) SPELEAN SPELUNCAR
(— TO CHAIN) CATENARY
(— TO CHAMBER) CAMERAL
(— TO CHARIOTEER) AURIGAL
(— TO CHEEK) MALAR
(— TO CHESS) SCACCHIC
(— TO CHINA) SINIAN SINISIAN
(— TO CITY) CIVIC URBAN
(— TO CLAN) SEPTAL
(— TO CLAY) BOLAR
(— TO CLOTHES) VESTIARY
VESTURAL
(— TO COINS) NUMMARY
NUMISMATIC
(— TO COLOR) CHROMATIC
(— TO COMB) PECTINAL
(— TO CONSTRUCTION) TECTONIC
(— TO CONTESTS) AGONISTIC
(— TO CORK) SUBERIC SUBEROUS
(— TO COUGH) TUSSAL TUSSIVE
(— TO COURT) AULIC JUDICIAL
JUDICIARY
(— TO CROCKERY) PIG
(— TO CROWN) CORONAL

(— TO DANCING) SALTATORY
TRIPUDIAL
(— TO DAUGHTER OR SON) FILIAL
(— TO DAWN) EOAN
(— TO DEFENSE) PHYLACTIC
(— TO DESERTS) EREMIC
(— TO DIAPHRAGM) PHRENIC
(— TO DINNER) CENATORY
PRANDIAL
(— TO DOVE) COLUMBINE
(— TO DREAMS) ONEIRIC ONIROTIC
(— TO DRINKING) BIBITORY
(— TO DUNG) STERCORAL
(— TO EARTH) GEAL TELLURIC
TERRANEAN
(— TO EARTHQUAKE) SEISMAL
SEISMIC
(— TO EAST) EOAN
(— TO ESSENCE) BASIC
(— TO EUNUCH) SPADONIC
(— TO EVENING) VESPER
(— TO EYELIDS) BLEPHARAL
(— TO FACE) PROSOPIC
(— TO FAIR) NUNDINAL
(— TO FAITH) PISTIC
(— TO FEET) PEDAL PEDARY
(— TO FERMENTATION) ZYMIC
ZYMOTIC
(— TO FIELDS) AGRARIAN
(— TO FINGERS) DIGITAL
(— TO FISHING) HALIEUTIC
(— TO FLEAS) PULICENE PULICOSE
(— TO FLESH) SARCOUS
(— TO FLOCK) GREGAL
(— TO FLOOD) DILUVIAL DILUVIAN
(— TO FLOWERS) FLORAL ANTHINE
(— TO FOREARM) CUBITAL
(— TO FOREHEAD) METOPIC
(— TO FORM) MORPHIC
(— TO FOX) VULPINE
(— TO FRESH WATER) LIMNETIC
(— TO FROGS) ANURAN RANINE
(— TO FRUIT) POMONAL POMONIC
(— TO FUNERALS) EXEQUIAL
(— TO FUNGUS) MYCETOID
(— TO FURNACE) FORNACIC
(— TO GALLOWS) PATIBULARY
(— TO GARDEN) HORTULAN
(— TO GARRISON) PRESIDIAL
(— TO GENTILES) ETHNIC
(— TO GLASS) VITREOUS
(— TO GOATS) CAPRIC
(— TO GOVERNMENT) ARCHICAL
POLITICAL
(— TO GRANDPARENTS) AVAL
(— TO GRINDING) MOLINARY
(— TO GROUND) SOLARY
(— TO GROVE) NEMORAL
(— TO GULLS) LARINE
(— TO GUMS) ULETIC GINGIVAL
(— TO HAIR) PILAR CRINAL PILARY
(— TO HAND) CHIRAL MANUAL
(— TO HAWKS) ACCIPITRINE
(— TO HEAD) CEPHALIC
(— TO HEAP) ACERVAL
(— TO HEART) CARDIAC
(— TO HEAT) CALORIC THERMAL
THERMIC
(— TO HIPS) SCIATIC
(— TO HOLIDAY) FERIAL
(— TO HORIZON) MUNDANE
(— TO HORSE) EQUINE HIPPIC
CABALLINE

(— TO HOSPITALITY) XENIAL
XENIAN
(— TO HOUSE) DOMAL
(— TO HUNGER) FAMELIC
(— TO HUNTING) VENATIC
VENERIAL CYNEGETIC
(— TO INTELLECT) NOETIC
(— TO INTESTINES) ALVIN ALVINE
(— TO JAW) MALAR GNATHAL
GNATHIC
(— TO JOURNEY) VIATIC
(— TO KIDNEY) RENAL NEPHRIC
(— TO KNOWLEDGE) GNOSTIC
(— TO LAKES) LACUSTRINE
(— TO LAP) GREMIAL
(— TO LAUGHING) GELASTIC
(— TO LAUGHTER) RISORIAL
(— TO LEARNING) PALLADIAN
(— TO LEG) CRURAL
(— TO LICE) PEDICULAR
(— TO LIFE) VITAL ZOETIC
(— TO LINE) FILAR
(— TO LIPS) LABIAL
(— TO LIVER) HEPATIC JECORAL
(— TO LOINS) LUMBAR
(— TO LOVE) EROTIC AMATORY
(— TO LUCK) ALEATORY
(— TO LUNGS) PULMONIC
PNEUMONIC PULMONARY
(— TO MANKIND) COMMON
ANTHROPIC
(— TO MARBLE) MARMORIC
(— TO MARKET) NUNDINAL
(— TO MARRIAGE) MARITAL
HYMENEAL
(— TO MARS) AREAN MAMERTINE
MAVORTIAL
(— TO MASS) MOLAR
(— TO MASTER) HERILE
(— TO MEADOWS) PRATAL
(— TO MEAL) PRANDIAL
(— TO MECCA) MECCAWEE
(— TO MEMORY) MNESTIC
MNEMONIC
(— TO MIDDAY) MERIDIAN
(— TO MILK) LACTARY LACTEAL
(— TO MILL) MOLINARY
(— TO MIND) PHRENIC
(— TO MIRROR) SPECULAR
(— TO MOISTURE) HYGRIC
(— TO MOON) LUNAR SELENIC
SELENIAN
(— TO MORNING) MATIN MATINAL
MATUTINAL
(— TO MOTION) GESTIC KINETIC
(— TO MOUNTAINS) MONTANE
(— TO MOUTH) ORAL OSCULAR
STOMATIC
(— TO MUSCLE) SARCOUS
(— TO MUSIC) HARMONIC
(— TO MYSTERIES) TELESTIC
(— TO NAMES) ONOMASTIC
(— TO NAVEL) OMPHALIC
(— TO NECK) JUGULAR
(— TO NEPHEW) NEPOTAL
(— TO NIGHT) NOCTURNAL
(— TO NOSE) NASAL RHINAL
(— TO NUT) NUCAL
(— TO NUTRITION) TROPHIC
(— TO OAK) QUERCINE
ROBOREOUS
(— TO OCEAN) PELAGIC
OCEANOUS THALASSIC

(— TO OLD AGE) SENILE GERATIC
GERONTIC
(— TO OPEN SKY) SUBDIAL
(— TO PARLOR) BEN BOOR
(— TO PASTURES) PASCUAL
(— TO PAWNBROKER) AVUNCULAR
(— TO PEACOCK) PAVONINE
(— TO PEARL) MARGARIC
(— TO PERSPIRATION) SUDORIC
(— TO PICTURE) ICONIC
(— TO PIGS) PORCINE
(— TO PINE) WARRYN
(— TO PLAGUE) LOIMIC
(— TO PLEASURE) HEDONIC
(— TO POETRY) MUSAL IAMBIC
(— TO POISON) TOXIC
(— TO POTTERY) CERAMIC
(— TO PRIESTS) SACERDOTAL
(— TO PRISON) CARCERAL
(— TO PULSE) SPHYGMIC
(— TO PUNISHMENT) PENAL
PUNITIVE
(— TO PURIFICATION) LUSTRAL
(— TO QUEEN) REGINAL
(— TO RAIN) HYETAL PLUVIAL
(— TO RAINBOW) IRIDAL
(— TO REMOTE PLACE) FORANE
(— TO RESONANCE) SYNTONIC
(— TO RING) ARMILLARY
(— TO RISING) ORTIVE
(— TO RIVER) AMNIC POTAMIC
RIVERINE FLUMINOSE
(— TO RIVER BANK) RIPARIAN
(— TO ROAD) VIATIC
(— TO ROCK) PETREAN SAXATILE
(— TO ROD) BACULINE
(— TO RUBBISH) RUDERARY
(— TO SABLES) ZIBELINE
(— TO SAIL) VELIC
(— TO SALVATION) SOTERIAL
(— TO SANDARAC) THYINE
(— TO SATURDAY) SABBATINE
(— TO SEAL) PHOCINE SIGILLARY
SPHRAGISTIC
(— TO SEAM) SUTURAL
(— TO SEASHORE) LITTORAL
(— TO SEAWEED) ALGOUS
(— TO SENSE OF TASTE) GUSTATIVE
(— TO SHEEP) VERVECINE
(— TO SHEPHERDS) PASTORAL
(— TO SHERIFF) VICONTIEL
(— TO SHIN) CNEMIAL
(— TO SHIP) NAVICULAR
(— TO SHOPMAN) APOTHECAL
(— TO SHOULDER) ALAR SCAPULAR
(— TO SIGNS) SEMIC SEMANTIC
(— TO SILVER) LUNAR ARGENTAL
(— TO SISTER) SORORAL
(— TO SKIN) DERIC DERMAL
CUTICULAR
(— TO SLEEP) SOMNIAL
MORPHETIC
(— TO SNAKE) ANGUINE
(— TO SNOW) NIVAL
(— TO SOFT PALATE) VELAR
(— TO SOIL) DAPHIC
(— TO SONG) MELIC
(— TO SPECTACLE) THEORIC
(— TO SPEECH) PHEMIC
(— TO SPINAL CORD) MYELIC
(— TO SPRING) VERNAL
(— TO STARS) ASTRAL STELLAR
SIDEREAL

(— TO STATE AFFAIRS) PRAGMATIC
(— TO STEPMOTHER) NOVERCAL
(— TO STOMACH) GASTRIC
(— TO STORKS) PELARGIC
(— TO SULPHUR) THIONIC
(— TO SUMMER) ESTIVAL AESTIVAL
(— TO SUN) SOLAR HELIAC
(— TO SUNDAY) DOMINICAL
(— TO SUNDIAL) SCIATHERIC
(— TO SUPPER) CENATORY
(— TO SURFACE OF ANYTHING) FACIAL
(— TO SWALLOWS) HIRUNDINE
(— TO SWEAT) SUDORIC
(— TO SWIMMING) NATATORY
(— TO SWINEHERD) SYBOTIC
(— TO TAIL) CAUDAL
(— TO TAILOR) SARTORIAL
(— TO TANNING) SC
(— TO TEARS) LACRIMAL LACHRYMAL
(— TO TEMPO) AGOGIC
(— TO THE BEAUTIFUL) ESTHETIC AESTHETIC
(— TO THIEVING) KLEPTISTIC
(— TO THIGH) CRURAL
(— TO THREAD) FILAR
(— TO THROAT) GULAR JUGULAR
(— TO TILE) TEGULAR
(— TO TIN) STANNIC
(— TO TITHES) DECIMAL
(— TO TITMICE) PARINE
(— TO TOMB) TOMBAL
(— TO TONGUE) GLOSSAL LINGUAL
(— TO TORTOISES) CHELONIAN
(— TO TOUCH) TACTILE
(— TO TOWER) TURRICAL
(— TO TREES) DENDRAL ARBOREAL
(— TO TWENTY) VICENARY
(— TO UNCLE) AVUNCULAR
(— TO UNDERGROUND WATER) VADOSE PHREATIC
(— TO VESSEL) VASAL
(— TO VIRGIN) PARTHENIAN
(— TO VOW) VOTAL
(— TO WAGON) PLAUSTRAL
(— TO WALLS) MURAL PARIETAL
(— TO WAR) POLEMICAL
(— TO WASPS) VESPAL VESPINE
(— TO WAX) CERAL
(— TO WEAVING) TEXTORIAL
(— TO WEIGHT) BARIC PONDERAL PONDERARY
(— TO WELL) PHREATIC
(— TO WHALES) CETIC
(— TO WHEAT) VULGARE
(— TO WHEELS) ROTAL
(— TO WHETSTONES) COTICULAR
(— TO WIFE) UXORIAL
(— TO WIND) EOLIAN PNEUMATIC
(— TO WINE) VINIC VINOUS
(— TO WINE-MAKING) OENOPOETIC
(— TO WINGS) ALAR PTERIC EXRUPEAL PTEROTIC
(— TO WINTER) HIEMAL
(— TO WISDOM) PALLADIAN
(— TO WOMANKIND) MULIEBRAL
(— TO WOODPECKERS) PICINE
(— TO WOODS) SYLVAN NEMORAL
(— TO WORMS) VERMICULAR
(— TO WOUNDS) VULNERAL
(— TO WRIST) CARPAL
(— TO YESTERDAY) PRIDIAN

(— TO YEW) TAXINE
(SUFF.) (—TO) AL AR ORIOUS ORY
PERTINACIOUS FIRM STIFF DOGGED ADHERING STUBBORN OBSTINATE
PERTINENCE RELEVANCE
PERTINENCY FORCE
PERTINENT APT FIT PAT HAPPY COGENT PROPER TIMELY ADAPTED APROPOS GERMANE POINTED TELLING INCIDENT MATERIAL RELATIVE RELEVANT
PERTLY CROUSE
PERTURB BITE GRATE UPSET WORRY DISMAY AGITATE CONFUSE CONTURB DERANGE DISTURB TROUBLE
PERTURBATION DISMAY FLIGHT POTHER POOTHER STICKLE TROUBLE TURMOIL EVECTION AGITATION
PERTURBED UNEASY
PERTUSSIS COUGH CHINCOF CHINCOUGH

PERU
CAPITAL: LIMA
COIN: SOL LIBRA DINERO CENTAVO
DEPARTMENT: ICA LIMA PUNO CUSCO CUZCO JUNIN PIURA TACNA ANCASH LORETO TUMBES
DESERT: SECHURA
ISLAND: CHINCHA
LAKE: TITICACA
LANGUAGE: AYMARA QUECHUA
MEASURE: TOPO VARA GALON CELEMIN FANEGADA
MOUNTAIN: HUAMINA COROPUNA HUASCARAN
PERIOD: RECUAY
RIVER: NAPU RIMAC SANTA TIGRE MORONA YAGUAS YAVARI CURARAY MARANON PASTAZA UCAYALI AMAZONAS APURIMAC HUALLAGA URUBAMBA
TOWN: ICA LIMA PUNO CUZCO PAITA PISCO PIURA TACNA CALLAO TUMBES IQUITOS AREQUIPA CHICLAYO TRUJILLO
VOLCANO: MISTI YUCAMANI
WEIGHT: LIBRA QUINTAL

PERUKE WIG FLASH GALERA TOUPEE GALERUM PERIWIG WIGGERY
PERUSAL SIGHT LECTURE SCRUTINY
PERUSE CON READ SCAN STUDY HANDLE SEARCH SURVEY EXAMINE INSPECT
PERUVIAN BARK CALISAYA CINCHONA
PERVADE FILL BATHE IMBUE DRENCH INSTIL OCCUPY THREAD INSTILL PERMEATE TRAVERSE
PERVADED STIFF
PERVASIVE POIGNANT
PERVERSE AUK AWK CAM CAR AWRY WOGH WRAW CROSS DONSY GAMMY THRAW WROTH CUSSED DIVERS LOUCHE

THRAWN THWART WICKED WILFUL WRAIST AWKWARD CRABBED CROOKED DIVERSE FORWARD FROWARD OBLIQUE PEEVISH WAYWARD CAMSCHACH CRANKISH STUBBORN
PERVERSELY AUK AWK AWRY ATHWART OVERWART
PERVERSION WREST ABUSION
(— OF TASTE) MALACIA
PERVERT WRY DRAW RACK RUIN SKEW TURN WARP ABUSE CROOK GLOSS TWIST UPSET WREST DEBASE DETORT DIVERT GARBLE INVERT MISUSE POISON VOYEUR WRENCH WRITHE CONTORT CORRUPT DEGRADE DEPRAVE DEVIATE DISTORT MISTURN SUBVERT TRADUCE VITIATE MISWREST
PERVERTED BAD WICKED ABUSIVE AWKWARD CORRUPT TWISTED VICIOUS
PERVERTER WRESTER
PERVIOUS LEACHY PERVIAL PERVADING
PES NEUME TENOR PODATUS
PESKY VERY PLAGUY ANNOYING DEVILING EXTREMELY
PESO DURO CONANT DOLLAR CAROLUS PATACAO
PESSIMISM WELTSCHMERZ MISERABILISM
PESSIMIST ALARMIST JEREMIAH WORRYWART
PESSIMISTIC GLOOMY ALARMED BEARISH CYNICAL DOWNBEAT
PEST BOT BANE TICK WEED MOUSE MYZUS TRAIK INSECT MENACE PLAGUE SCHELM SORROW VERMIN NUDNICK SCOURGE MEALYBUG SANDMITE BUTTINSKY
PESTER DUN HOX NAG RIB TIG HAKE ANNOY DEVIL TEASE WORRY BADGER BOTHER HARASS INFEST MOLEST BEDEVIL TORMENT TROUBLE OBSTRUCT PERSECUTE
PESTHOUSE LAZARET LAZARETTO
PESTICIDE BIOCIDE FUMIGANT
PESTILENCE LUES PEST DEATH QUALM PLAGUE MURRAIN EPIDEMIC MORTALITY
PESTILENT FATAL DEADLY VEXING NOXIOUS
PESTLE MIX BRAY GRIND PESTL PILUM STAMP BEETLE BRAYER MULLER PISTIL CHAPPER POUNDER STAMPER
PET TOY CADE COAX DAUT DEAR DUCK HUFF LAMB NECK PEAT SOCK SULK TIFF DRUNT DUCKY HUMOR QUIET SPOIL SPOON TETCH CARESS CODDLE COSHER COSSET CUDDLE DANDLE DAUTIE DAWTIE FADDLE FANTAD FANTOD FONDLE GENTLE PAMPER PETKIN SMOOCH SQUALL STROKE WANTON CHERISH DARLING INDULGE PINKENY TANTRUM TIDLING UMBRAGE WHITHER CANOODLE FAVORITE

TIDDLING PADDYWACK
PETAL ALA HELM HOOD LEAF WING BANNER
(— IN PEA FLOWER) VEXILLUM
(— OF IRIS) STANDARD
(UPPER —) HOOD BANNER
(PL.) COROLLA
PETALIA NYCTERIS
PETARD PITTARD FIREWORK
PETATE BANIG
PETECHIA STIGMA
PETER P FADE FAIL PEAK SAFE WANE CEASE PEDRO PIERS PIERRE SIGNAL DWINDLE
(— OUT) FIZZLE
(BROTHER OF) ANDREW
(FATHER OF —) JONAS
PETER GRIMES (CHARACTER IN —) ELLEN PETER GRIMES ORFORD BALSTRODE
(COMPOSER OF —) BRITTEN
PETER IBBETSON (AUTHOR OF —) DUMAURIER
(CHARACTER IN —) DEANE MADGE MIMSY PETER LINTOT GREGORY PLUNKET IBBETSON PASQUIER
PETER PAN (AUTHOR OF —) BARRIE
(CHARACTER IN —) PAN HOOK JOHN NIBS SMEE PETER WENDY TINKER DARLING MICHAEL TOOTLES MARGARET SLIGHTLY
PETHAHIAH (FATHER OF —) MESHEZABEEL
PETHEUL (SON OF —) JOEL
PETIOLE STEM SPINE STALK STIPE PODEON PEDUNCLE PHYLLODE LEAFSTALK
PETITE SMALL LITTLE MIGNON MIGNONNE
PETITION ASK BEG SUE BILL BOON PLEA PRAY SUIT VOTE WISH APPLY ORATE PLEAD APPEAL DESIRE INVOKE MOTION PLACIT PRAYER STEVEN ADDRESS BESEECH ENTREAT IMPLORE ORATION SOLICIT ROGATION SUFFRAGE
(MAKE —) SUE
(PL.) PRECES
PETITIONER BEGGAR ORATOR SUITOR BEADSMAN APPLICANT ENTREATER PLAINTIFF
PETO WAHOO
PETREL BILL TITI CAHOW MITTY NELLY PRION WITCH SPENCY TEETEE ASSILAG GLUTTON KAEDING PINTADO SEABIRD SEAFOWL STINKER ALLAMOTH FORKTAIL STINKPOT ALLAMOTTI MALLEMUCK NIGHTHAWK
PETRIFY DAZE DEADEN STONIFY STUPEFY LAPIDIFY FOSSILIZE GORGONIZE
PETRIFYING STONY GORGON
PETROL GAS GASOLINE
PETROLATUM VASELINE
PETROLEUM OIL CRUDE PETROL NAPHTHA
(— INDUSTRY) OILDOM
(CRUDE —) MAZOUT
PETRUCHIO (WIFE OF —) KATHERINE
PE-TSAI PECHAY

PETTED CADE DANDILY
PETTICOAT BAJO GORE KILT SLIP
SOUS DICKY GREEN JUPON
PAGNE SOUSE KIRTLE LUHINGA
PLACKET WHITTLE BALMORAL
BASQUINE WILYCOAT
(— OF TARGET) GREEN
PETTIFOG FOG CAVIL BICKER
PETTIFOGGER FOGGER SHYSTER
LEGULEIAN
PETTINESS NAGGLE PARVINIMITY
PETTING COLLING
PETTISH DORTY HUFFY FRETFUL
PEEVISH PLAINTIVE
PETTY TIN BASE JERK MEAN ORRA
PUNY VAIN BANAL GRIMY MINOR
PETIT PUNEE SMALL MEASLY
MINUTE PALTRY PEANUT POKING
PUISNE PUSILL SNIFTY KITLING
PIMPING TRIVIAL TWATTLE
CHILDISH FIDDLING INFERIOR
NIGGLING NUGATORY PEDDLING
PICAYUNE PIFFLING SNIPPETY
TRIFLING PAROCHIAL
(PREF.) MICR(O)
(SUFF.) (— ONE) EEN
PETULANCE PROCACITY
PETULANT PERT CROSS SAUCY
SHORT TESTY TIFFY FEISTY
SULLEN WANTON WILFUL
CRABBED FRETFUL FROWARD
HUFFISH PEEVISH WASPISH
PERVERSE SNAPPISH
PEULTHAI (FATHER OF —)
OBEDEDOM
PEUMUS BOLDU
PEW BOX PUE BOUT DESK PFUI
PUGH SEAT SLIP BENCH BUGHT
STALL BOUGHT
PEWEE PEWIT PEEWEE PEEWIT
PEWIT PEESWEEP
PEWTER CUP BIDRI BIDRY MONEY
PUDER BIDERY TRIFLE PEAUDER
SADWARE TUTENAG
(— MARK) TOUCHMARK
PEYOTE HIKULI
PFENNIG PENNING
PHAEDRA (AUTHOR OF —) RACINE
(CHARACTER IN —) ARICIA OENONE
PHAEDRA THESEUS HIPPOLYTUS
THERAMENES
(FATHER OF —) MINOS
(HUSBAND OF —) THESEUS
(MOTHER OF —) PASIPHAE
(SISTER OF —) ARIADNE
(SON OF —) ACAMAS DEMOPHON
PHAETON DUKE FAETON SPIDER
STANHOPE
PHAETON BUTTERFLY
BALTIMORE
PHALANGER TAIT ARIEL TAPOA
CUSCUS TAGUAN OPOSSUM
PENTAIL SQUIRREL
PHALAROPE LOBIPED COOTFOOT
LOBEFOOT WHALEBIRD
PHALERA BEAD BOSS DISK STUD
CAMEO
PHALTI (FATHER OF —) LAISH
PHANTASM DREAM FANCY GHOST
VAPOR FIGURE SHADOW SPIRIT
FANTASY PHANTOM SPECIES
SPECTER SPECTRE
PHANTASMAL UNREAL SPECTRAL

PHANTASUS (BROTHER OF —)
ICELUS MORPHEUS PHOBETOR
THANATOS
(FATHER OF —) HYPNOS SOMNUS
(MOTHER OF —) NYX
PHANTASY FANCY FANTASY
PHANTASIA
PHANTOM IDOL BOGEY BOGLE
DUMMY GHOST IMAGE PHASM
SHADE SHAPE UMBRA BOGGLE
DOUBLE FANTOM IDOLON
IDOLUM SHADOW SPIRIT
BUGBEAR EIDOLON ELUSIVE
FANTASY FEATURE SPECIES
SPECTER ILLUSORY ADAMASTOR
SIMULACRUM
PHANUEL (DAUGHTER OF —) ANNA
PHARAOH ALE FARO PHARO
TYRANT BUSIRIS
PHARAOH'S HEN VULTURE
PHAREZ (BROTHER OF —) ZARAH
(FATHER OF —) JUDAH
(MOTHER OF —) TAMAR
PHARISEE MUGWUMP NICODEMUS
PHARMACEUTICAL MERCURIAL
(SUFF.) (— PRODUCT) EIN EINE IN
INE
PHARMACIST DRUGGIST
DISPENSER
PHARMACY FERMACY
DRUGSTORE
PHAROS CLOAK LIGHT TORCH
BEACON LANTERN
PHARYNGEAL FAUCAL
PHARYNX MASTAX PROBOSCIS
(PREF.) LAEMO LEM(O)
PHASE EFT END LEG FAZE SIDE
ANGLE FACET GRADE STAGE
ASPECT AVATAR BACKLASH
PASSOVER DICHOTOMY
(INITIAL —) BUD
(LOWEST —) BATHOS
(TRANSITORY —) STREAK
PHASM FANTOM METEOR PHASMA
PHANTOM
PHEASANT CHIR GUAN ARGUS
CHEER KALIJ MINAL MONAL
GROUSE LEIPOA MAGPIE MONAUL
MOONAL PUKRAS KALLEGE
FIREBACK ITHAGINE RINGNECK
TRAGOPAN MACARTNEY
(BREEDING PLACE FOR —S) STEW
(BROOD OF —S) NID NYE NIDE
(YOUNG —) POULT
PHEASANT CUCKOO COUCAL
PHEASANT DUCK PINTAIL
MERGANSER
PHEASANT FINCH WAXBILL
PHEASANT'S-EYE ROSARUBY
PHEBE (HUSBAND OF —) SILVIUS
PHELLEM CORK SUBER
PHENOBARBITOL LUMINAL
PHENOCRYST INSET
PHENOL LACCOL THYMOL ALOESOL
CREOSOL DURENOL EUGENOL
ORCINOL CHAVICOL RESORCIN
PHENOMENA
(SUFF.) ICS
PHENOMENON FIRE ANOMY
COLOR EVENT IMAGE ARTHUS
EFFECT METEOR MIRAGE
SHADOW ISOTOPY MIRACLE
PARADOX PROCESS SYMPTOM

ASTERISM PRAKRITI SIDERISM
SUNQUAKE LANDSPOUT
PHENYLSALICYLATE SALOL
PHERES (BROTHER OF —) AESON
AMYTHAON
(DAUGHTER OF —) IDOMENE
PERIAPIS
(FATHER OF —) CRETHEUS
(MOTHER OF —) TYRO
(NEPHEW OF —) JASON
(SON OF —) ADMETUS LYCURGUS
PHIAL CUP FIAL VIAL CRUET
BOTTLE VESSEL
PHILABEG KILT FILIBEG
PHILANDER FOOL WOLF DALLY
FLIRT SMOCK
PHILANTHROPIC HUMANE
PHILANTHROPIST ALTRUIST
HUMANITARIAN
AMERICAN DIX CASE HOLT LICK
RICE SAGE VAUX EVANS GERRY
LENOX MILLS ODGEN PRATT
SMITH TRASK COOPER CRERAR
GEORGE GIRARD GURLEY HAYDEN
LOWELL MILLER MURPHY PEPPER
PHIPPS PUTNAM ROBERT TAPPAN
COCHRAN CORNELL DOREMUS
FARNHAM GILBERT GRELLET
LAZARUS MILBANK PARRISH
PEABODY RUTGERS RYERSON
SHEPARD STEWART CARNEGIE
CORCORAN HARKNESS LEWISOHN
PHILLIPS ROBINSON STERLING
ROSENWALD SHEFFIELD
CRITTENTON SULZBERGER
AUSTRIAN FRANKL
ENGLISH FRY GUY COBBE CORAM
CORRY KYRLE SHARP WAUGH
GURNEY KENYON COWDRAY
HIBBERT MONTAGU KINNAIRD
MACAULAY SOMERSET FAITHFULL
MONTEFIORE OGLETHORPE
SHAFTESBURY WHITTINGTON
WILBERFORCE
FRENCH MANCE MARBEAU
MONTYON MICHELIN MIRAMION
GERMAN FALK HIRSCH MULLER
FLIEDNER
INDIAN JEEJEEBHOY
IRISH RICE GONNE MADDEN
RUSSIAN NOVIKOV
SCOTTISH DALE HERIOT FINDLAY
GUTHRIE
SWEDISH NOBEL
SWISS DUNANT
PHILANTHROPY CHARITY
ALMSGIVING
PHILIP PIP PHLP SPARROW
PHILIPPIC SATIRE SCREED TIRADE
ABUSIVE DIATRIBE

PHILIPPINES

ARCHIPELAGO: SULU
CAPITAL: BAGUIO MANILA
COIN: PESO PESETA CENTAVO
SENTIMO
FIBER: ERUC ABACA BUNTAL
ISLAND: CEBU BATAN BOHOL
LEYTE LUZON PANAY SAMAR
NEGROS MASBATE MINDORO
PALAWAN ROMBLON
MINDANAO
LAKE: TAAL LANAO

LANGUAGE: MORO BICOL IBANAG
ILOCANO TAGALOG VISAYAN
MEASURE: LOAN BRAZA CABAN
CAUAN CHUPA GANTA APATAN
BALITA QUINON
MOUNTAIN: APO IBA MAYON
PULOG BANAHAO
NATIVE: ATA ATI ITA TAO AETA
ATTA ETAS MORO SULU BICOL
TAGAL VICOL IGOROT TIMAUA
BISAYAN TAGALOG FILIPINO
PROVINCE: ABRA CEBU SULU
ALBAY CAPIZ DAVAO LANAO
RIZAL BATAAN CAVITE IFUGAO
ILOILO TARLAC SURIGAO
RIVER: ABRA AGNO MAGAT PASIG
AGUSAN LAOANG CAGAYAN
MINDANAO PAMPANGA
TOWN: IBA AGOA BOAC CEBU
JOLO MATI ALBAY DAVAO
DIGOS LAOAG PASAY VIGAN
APARRI BAGUIO CAVITE ILAGAN
ILOILO MANILA BACOLOD
BASILAN DAGUPAN CALOOCAN
TREE: DAO IBA TUA TUI ACLE
ANAM ATES BOGO DITA IPIL
GUIJO LAUAN LIGAS ALUPAG
ANAHAU ARANGA ANONANG
APITONG TINDALO ALMACIGA
AMPALAYA
VOLCANO: APO TAAL MAYON
BULOSAN CANLAON
WEIGHT: CATTY FARDO PICUL
PUNTO LACHSA QUILATE
CHINANTA

PHILISTINE BOOB GIGMAN
MUCKER BABBITT GITTITE
BOEOTIAN BARBARIAN
BOURGEOIS HYPOCRITE
(PL.) PULESATI PURASATI
CAPHTORIM
PHILOLOGIST LAVENGRO
LINGUIST
AMERICAN BUCK COOK HART
TODD WOOD ADLER BROWN
CHILD CURME GIBBS HEMPL
MARCH MARSH BENDER BRIGHT
MARDEN PRINCE REEVES
EMERSON GEROULD GUDEMAN
HOPKINS KENNEDY LEARNED
SHELDON HARRISON TRUMBULL
GREENOUGH BLOOMFIELD
STURTEVANT
AUSTRIAN MINOR MULLER
KARAJAN REINISCH SCHONBACH
COLOMBIAN CUERVO MARROQUIN
CZECH HANKA GEBAUER
JUNGMANN DOBROVSKY
DANISH RAFN RASK VERNER
HEIBERG MOLBECH THOMSEN
JESPERSEN WESTERGAARD
DUTCH KATE KERN BRINK VRIES
VREESE WINKEL HEINSIUS
HEREMANS UHLENBECK
HUYDECOPER VALCKENAER
HEMSTERHUIS
ENGLISH WYLD ASTON EARLE
ELLIS NARES SAYCE SKEAT TOOKE
CONWAY CRAIGIE MORRIS
MURRAY ONIONS THORPE
WERNER WRIGHT GARNETT
GOMPERZ SKINNER WEEKLEY

BOSWORTH CHADWICK
STEPHENS WEYMOUTH
COLERIDGE DONALDSON
FURNIVALL
FINNISH SETALA CASTREN
FRENCH ADAM BREAL DOLET
EGGER HENRY LEBAS MEYER
RENAN BRUNOT LAMBIN WAILLY
BRACHET BURNOUF MEILLET
LEFEBVRE VAUGELAS
CHABANEAU QUICHERAT
HOVELACQUE DARMESTETER
GERMAN AST ABEL BIRT BOPP
DIEZ FICK HIRT JULG KERN MOGK
PAUL POTT WOLF BERGK BLANC
BLASS BOCKH EBERT GREIN
GRIMM HAASE HAGEN HAUPT
HEYNE HEYSE JUSTI KLOTZ
KRAPF KRAUS KROLL LEHRS
MEYER NIESE PAULY ZEUSS
BECKER BEKKER BENFEY CHRIST
FREUND FRISCH HENZEN JACOBI
JACOBS KELLER KOCHLY MARTIN
MULLER PASSOW REISKE VAHLEN
VIETOR ADELUNG BARTSCH
BERNAYS BRANDIS BURSIAN
CORSSEN CREUZER CURTIUS
DINDORF DUNTZER GERLAND
KIEPERT KORTING LEPSIUS
LESKIEN MATZNER OSTHOFF
RIBBECK RITSCHL RUHNKEN
SANDERS SCHERER SIEVERS
WEIGAND WELCKER WISSOWA
ZARNCKE ZUPITZA AUFRECHT
BEHAGHEL BISCHOFF BOTTIGER
BRUGMANN FOERSTER GRAEVIUS
HOFFMANN HUMBOLDT
MASSMANN SCHRADER THIERSCH
WEINHOLD WESTPHAL XYLANDER
ACIDALIUS BAUMSTARK
BERNHARDY BUSCHMANN
ETTMULLER FRISCHLIN
GABELENTZ HOLTZMANN
KIRCHHOFF KOSCHWITZ
STEINTHAL TRAUTMANN
HOLTHAUSEN MULLENHOFF
STREITBERG THURNEYSEN
VOLLMOLLER BARTHOLOMAE
HUNGARIAN REVAI HUNFALVY
DOBRENTEJ ENDLICHER
ICELANDIC JONSSON EGILSSON
MAGNUSSON VIGFUSSON
ITALIAN ASCOLI MONACI NOVATI
OVIDIO COMPARETTI
CASTELVETRO CASTIGLIONE
NORWEGIAN AASEN BUGGE
KONOW MUNCH
POLISH ZAMENHOF
ROZWADOWSKI
PORTUGUESE COELHO
RUMANIAN HASDEU
RUSSIAN GROT VOSTOKOV
SCHIEFNER
SCOTTISH GRANT BAIKIE MURRAY
SWEDISH IHRE LUNDELL
AHLQUIST SODERWALL
ZACHRISSON
SWISS MAHLY ISELIN
PHILOLOGY SEMITICS
PHILOMACHUS MACHETES
PHILOMELA STOP FILOMEL
(FATHER OF —) PANDION
(RAVISHER OF —) TEREUS

(SISTER OF —) PROCNE
(SLAIN BY —) ITYS
(VICTIM OF —) ITYS
PHILOSOPHER WIT SAGE CYNIC
STOIC ARTIST IONIAN LEGIST
DOTTORE ELEATIC ERISTIC
SCHOLAR SOPHIST SUMMIST
THINKER ZETETIC ACADEMIC
EPOCHIST MAGICIAN VIRTUOSO
ACADEMIST ALCHEMIST
DIALECTIC PHYSICIAN
SCHOOLMAN
AMERICAN HUME LADD MEAD
ADLER ALBEE BOWEN BOWNE
DEWEY EDMAN FISKE JAMES
LEWIS MOORE PERRY QUINE
ROYCE UPHAM HARRIS HICKOK
HYSLOP LANGER SNIDER CALKINS
HOCKING HOWISON NEWBOLD
WILLIAMS ALEXANDER
SANTAVANA
ARAB AVICENNA
AUSTRIAN BUBER EXNER DEUBLER
MEINONG STEINER ZIMMERMANN
RATZENHOFER
BELGIAN MERCIER DELBOEUF
BRAZILIAN MAGALHAES
CANADIAN MURRAY STEWART
CHINESE MOTI MENCIUS
CZECH MASARYK SMETANA
DANISH SIBBERN HOFFDING
KIERKEGAARD
DUTCH BOLLAND HEYMANS
SPINOZA OPZOOMER
ENGLISH CASE JOAD MILL MORE
WARD BACON BROAD COTES
GREEN HOOKE JONES LAIRD
LEWES LOCKE MOORE PALEY
STOUT SULLY BAYNES FOWLER
GODWIN GURNEY HOBBES
LATHAM MCCABE NEWTON
NORRIS OCKHAM TAYLOR AINSLIE
BALFOUR BENTHAM COLLIER
HALDANE HARTLEY HERBERT
HODGSON INGELBY JACKSON
RUSSELL SPENCER STEPHEN
STEWART WHEWELL CORNFORD
COURTNEY CUDWORTH GLANVILL
HOBHOUSE MUIRHEAD SCHILLER
SIDGWICK BOSANQUET
MACKENZIE WHITEHEAD
CUMBERLAND HUTCHINSON
FINNISH WESTERMARCK
FRENCH DROZ BAYLE COMTE
GUYAU HELLO JANET LEROY
LIARD MABLY RAMUS SIMON
TAINE BERARD BONALD COUSIN
GILSON GOBLOT LEROUX PASCAL
QUESNE RAYNAL SARTRE VALERY
ABAUZIT ABELARD BARTHEZ
BERGSON BURIDAN CABANIS
DAMIRON DIDEROT GERANDO
HOLBACH MAISTRE MILHAUD
REYNAUD ALEMBERT BOURDEAU
BOUTROUX CHARTIER FOUILLEE
GASSENDI GILLOUIN JOUFFROY
LAFFITTE MARITAIN MEYERSON
ROUSSEAU VACHEROT
BALLANCHE CONDILLAC
CONDORCET DESCARTES
HELVITIUS LACHELIER
SCHWEITZER MONTESQUIEU
LAROMIGUIERE

GERMAN BIEL HAYM KANT KRUG
MARX OKEN PREL BAUER CARUS
COHEN DREWS ENGEL FRIES
GROOS HEGEL LIPPS LOTZE
MARBE MEYER RIEHL STEIN UTITZ
WAITZ WOLFF BENEKE CAROVE
EUCKEN FICHTE GABLER GEIGER
GEYSER GRUPPE HEINZE HERDER
JACOBI KRAUSE KRONER LASSON
MAIMON MESSER MULLER
PRANTL RITTER STUMPF ULRICI
ZELLER ZIEHEN BRUCKER
BRUNNER CRUSIUS DEUSSEN
DILTHEY DRIESCH DUHRING
ERDMANN HAECKEL HENNING
HERBART JUNGIUS KNUTZEN
LASAULX LAZARUS PAULSEN
STIRNER STRAUSS VOLKELT
CARRIERE CASSIRER DROBISCH
EBERHARD FORTLAGE
HARTMANN HERTLING LASSWITZ
LEIBNITZ MICHELET MICHELIS
PANNWITZ REINHOLD AVENARIUS
BILFINGER CORNELIUS DIETERICI
EHRENFELS FEUERBACH
GOCLENIUS LEISEGANG
NIETZSCHE SCHELLING
THOMASIUS TIEDEMANN
VAIHINGER VORLANDER
BAUMGARTEN HILLEBRAND
ROSENKRANZ FRAUENSTADT
MENDELSSOHN SCHOPENHAUER
SCHLEIERMACHER
TRENDELENBURG
GREEK BION ZENO CEBES DAMON
LYCON PLATO GNATES EUCLID
PHAEDO PYRRHO STRATO THALES
CRANTOR DEMONAX EUDEMUS
PROCLUS TIMAEUS ALCMAEON
APULEIUS CRATYLUS DIODORUS
DIOGENES EPICURUS MELISSUS
MENIPPUS NUMENIUS PHAEDRUS
PORPHYRY SOCRATES
ARCHELAUS ARISTOTLE
CARNEADES CHARMIDES
CLEANTHES CRITOLAUS
DAMASCIUS EPICTETUS
EUBULIDES FAVORINUS
HIEROCLES LEUCIPPUS
MENEDEMUS PANAETIUS
PANTAENUS PHILOLAUS
ANAXAGORAS ANAXARCHUS
ANAXIMENES ARCESILAUS
ARISTIPPUS CHRYSIPPUS
DEMOCRITUS EMPEDOCLES
HERACLITUS IAMBLICHUS
METRODORUS PARMENIDES
PHERECYDES POSIDONIUS
PROTAGORAS PYTHAGORAS
SIMPLICIUS SPEUSIPPUS
XENOCRATES XENOPHANES
ANAXIMANDER ANTISTHENES
ARISTOXENUS CLITOMACHUS
DICAEARCHUS CALLISTHENES
PHILOSTRATUS THEOPHRASTUS
HUNGARIAN ERDELYI
INDIAN GHOSE
IRISH BERNARD BERKELEY
MOLYNEUX
ITALIAN NIFO VERA VICO ABANO
BRUNO CONTI CROCE FERRI
ARDIGO FICINO PAPINI VANINI
AQUINAS CANTONI FERRARI

FRANCHI GENTILE MAMIANI
TELESIO UBERWEG GIOBERTI
ALGAROTTI CESALPINO
CAMPANELLA FIORENTINO
POMPONAZZI BONAVENTURA
PICCOLOMINI
NORWEGIAN MONRAD
POLISH LIBELT WRONSKI
LUTOSLAWSKI
PORTUGUESE ACOSTA
ROMAN BOETHIUS CORNUTUS
PLOTINUS
RUSSIAN BERDYAEV CHICHERIN
SCOTTISH HOME HUME MILL REID
SETH CAIRD FLINT FRASER
VEITCH FERRIER STEWART
WALLACE FERGUSON HAMILTON
STIRLING HUTCHESON
CALDERWOOD MACKINTOSH
SPANISH VIVES BALMES SUAREZ
SWEDISH BOSTROM ATTERBOM
SWEDENBORG
SWISS WYSS AMIEL HILTY
PREVOST HABERLIN
PHILOSOPHER'S STONE ADROP
MICROCOSM
PHILOSOPHIC SAGE
PHILOSOPHY ETHICS GOSPEL
MAGISM SYSTEM TAOISM
APRISMO COSMISM DUALISM
INQUIRY MIMAMSA SANKHYA
SCEPSIS ACTIVISM HINDUISM
HUMANISM IDENTISM IDEOLOGY
LEGALISM OCCAMISM STOICISM
ABSURDISM NOUMENISM
OODNATIOM VEDANTIOM
(— OF LIFE) LIGHTS
PHILTER DRUG CHARM WANGA
FILTER POTION AMATORY
PHINEHAS (FATHER OF —) ELI
ELEAZAR
(GRANDFATHER OF —) AARON
PHINEUS (BROTHER OF —) CADMUS
CEPHEUS
(FATHER OF —) BELUS AGENOR
(MOTHER OF —) ANCHINOE
TELEPHASSA
(SISTER OF —) EUROPA
(WIFE OF —) IDAEA CLEOPATRA
PHLEBOTOMIZE BLEED VENESECT
PHLEBOTOMUS TATUKIRA
PHLEGM FLEM GLEET MUCUS
WATER FLEUME PITUITE
MOUSEWEB
PHLEGMATIC CALM COOL DULL
SLOW INERT MUCOID SLEEPY
WATERY VISCOUS COMPOSED
SLUGGISH APATHETIC
IMPASSIVE
PHLEGYAS (DAUGHTER OF —)
CORONIS
(FATHER OF —) ARES MARS
(MOTHER OF —) CHRYSE
(SLAYER OF —) APOLLO
(SON OF —) IXION
PHLOEM BAST LIBER LEPTOME
PHLOGISTIC FIERY HEATED
BURNING FLAMING
PHLOMIS SAGELEAF
PHLOX CYME FLOX ALBION
BEACON COBAEA
PHOCUS (FATHER OF —) AEACUS
ORNYTION

(HALF-BROTHER OF —) PELEUS
TELAMON
(MOTHER OF —) PSAMATHE
(SON OF —) CRISIUS PANOPEUS
(WIFE OF —) ANTIOPE
PHOEBE FEBE FIVE MOON DIANA
PEWEE ARTEMIS
(BROTHER OF —) CASTOR POLLUX
POLYDEUCES
(DAUGHTER OF —) LETO
(FATHER OF —) URANUS
LEUCIPPUS TYNDAREUS
(MOTHER OF —) GAEA LEDA
(SISTER OF —) HELEN
CLYTEMNESTRA
PHOEBUS SUN APOLLO PHOIBUS
PHOENICIA (COLONY OF —)
CARTHAGE
(GODDESS OF —) TANIT BALTIS
TANITH ASTARTE
(KING OF —) AGENOR
(TOWN OF —) ACRE TYRE SIDON
SAREPTA
PHOENIX (BROTHER OF —) CILIX
CADMUS THASUS PHINEUS
(FATHER OF —) AGENOR AMYNTOR
(MOTHER OF —) CLEOBULE
TELEPHASSA
(PUPIL OF —) ACHILLES
(SISTER OF —) EUROPA
PHOLAS PIDDOCK
PHONEME MORPH TONEME
LARYNGAL
PHONEMIC BROAD
PHONOGRAM LOGOGRAM
SINOGRAM
PHONOGRAPH VIC PHONO
VICTROLA
(— RECORD) DISK PLATTER
PHONY FAKE JIVE SHAM BOGUS
FAKER FALSE BRUMMY BUNYIP
PHONEY PLASTIC IMPOSTOR
SPURIOUS
PHORONEUS (DAUGHTER OF —)
NIOBE
(FATHER OF —) INACHUS
(MOTHER OF —) MELIA
(SISTER OF —) IO
(SON OF —) APIS IASUS AGENOR
PELASGUS
(WIFE OF —) CERDO LAODICE
PHOSPHATE EHLITE FLOATS
APATITE CABOCLE CACOXENE
GRIPHITE MONAZITE
PHOSPHORESCENCE BRIMING
MARFIRE
PHOSPHORESCENT PHOSPHOR
NOCTILUCOUS
PHOTISM SYNOPSY
PHOTOENGRAVER
ZINCOGRAPHER
PHOTOENGRAVING HALFTONE
HELIOGRAPH
PHOTOGENE AFTERIMAGE
PHOTOGRAPH MUG PIC FILM
LENS SNAP CARTE IMAGE PANEL
PHOTO PINUP SHOOT STILL
CANDID GLOSSY MOSAIC RETAKE
SCENIC STEREO AIRVIEW PICTURE
TINTYPE LIKENESS PORTRAIT
POSITIVE SNAPSHOT TABLETOP
CYCLOGRAM MAMMOGRAM
(— SIZE) PANEL

(X-RAY —) SKIAGRAM
PHOTOGRAPHER PHOTOG
LENSMAN CAMERIST
CAMERAMAN PAPARAZZO
SHUTTERBUG
PHOTOGRAPHY STEREO
CALOTYPE PHOTOGENY
PHOTOMETER LUCIMETER
PHOTOMONTAGE COLLAGE
PHOTON BOSON TROLAND
PHRASE CRY HIT MOT SET CRIB
FUSS HAVE IDEA TERM WORD
COMMA COUCH IDIOM LABEL
LEMMA POINT STATE STYLE
TOPIC TROPE BYWORD CLAUSE
CLICHE DITTON DORISM GRUPPO
HOBNOB NOTION PNEUMA
PRAISE SAVING SLOGAN
ATTACCO DICTION EPITHET
PASSAGE CONCEIVE DIVISION
DORICISM FLATTERY IDEOGRAM
IRISHISM LATINISM LEITMOTIV
(— DIFFERENTLY) TURN
(— UNCTUOUSLY) DROOL
(MUSICAL —) RIFF POINT ATTACCO
SUBJECT
(PET —) SHIBBOLETH
(REDUNDANT —) CHEVILLE
(STOCK —) CANT
(TRITE —) CLICHE
(WELL-TURNED —) STROKE
PHRASEOLOGY CANT STYLE
DIALECT DICTION WORDING
LOCUTION PARLANCE
PHRATRY CLAN
PHRENETIC PYTHIAN FRENETIC
PHRENIC MENTAL
(PL.) PSYCHOLOGY
PHRIXOS (FATHER OF —) ATHAMUS
(MOTHER OF —) NEPHELE
(SISTER OF —) HELLE
PHRONTIS (BROTHER OF —) ARGUS
MELAS CYTISSORUS
(FATHER OF —) PHRIXUS
(HUSBAND OF —) PANTHOUS
(MOTHER OF —) CHALCIOPE
(SON OF —) EUPHORBUS
HYPERENOR POLYDAMAS
PHRYGIA (GOD OF —) ATYS ATTIS
SABAZIOS
(KING OF —) MIDAS
PHRYNIN BUFIDIN
PHTHISIS DECAY
PHUVAH (FATHER OF —) ISSACHAR
PHYLACTERY FILACTERY
(PL.) TEFILLIN TEPHILLIN
PHYLE TRIBE
PHYLOMACHE (DAUGHTER OF —)
ALCESTIS
(FATHER OF —) AMPHION
(HUSBAND OF —) PELIAS
(SON OF —) ACASTUS
PHYLUM HOKA CLASS HOKAN
NADENE BRYOZOA ANNELATA
ANNELIDA CHORDATA DIVISION
LIGNOSAE PORIFERA
PHYMA TUMOR
PHYSALIS POP POPPER
TOMATILLO
PHYSETER CATODON
PHYSIC CURE HEAL FISIC PURGE
TRADE REMEDY MEDICAL
NATURAL RELIEVE DRUGGERY

PHYSICAL ILL LUSTY SOMAL
BODILY CARNAL DISTAL NATURAL
SOMATIC CORPORAL CURATIVE
EXTERNAL MATERIAL CORPOREAL
(PURELY —) BRUTE
PHYSICIAN ASA DOC PILL CURER
GALEN HAKIM LEECH MEDIC
QUACK ARTIST BAIDYA DOCTOR
FELLOW HEALER INTERN MEDICO
DOTTORE EMPIRIC SURGEON
ALIENIST RESIDENT SAWBONES
SUNDOWNER
(— OF THE GODS) PAEAN
(PREF.) IATRO JATEO JATO
(SUFF.) IATRIST
AMERICAN RAY BARD COIT DICK
DREW FITZ HARE HOLT KING
LUST PARK SALK BIGGS BRILL
BRUSH CABOT COHEN DRAKE
FLINT GOLER KNOPF LOGAN
MINOT SMITH SPOCK TONER
TULLY TYSON WHITE BARKER
BATTEY BENNET BROOKS CARTER
CLARKE FISHER FOSTER HEISER
HOOKER HORNER HOSACK JOSLIN
KEELEY KNIGHT LAZEAR MILLER
MORGAN MORROW MURPHY
ODWYER PARRAN STILES STILLE
STORER STRONG TILTON WALKER
WATSON ALVAREZ CAMMANN
CHAPMAN DARLING DICKSON
FRANCIS GERHARD GILBERT
HAGGARD HEPBURN HOPKINS
JACKSON JANEWAY ROBBINS
TROLAND TRUDEAU BARTLETT
BILLINGS BOYLSTON FISHBEIN
GUERNSEY GWATHMEY
HAMILTON KIRTLAND KNOWLTON
MITCHELL PETERSON RICHARDS
ROCKWELL SHATTUCK SPALDING
TOWNSEND WOODWARD
BLACKWELL STERNBERG
CLENDENING GOLDBERGER
STEPHENSON WATERHOUSE
ZAKRZEWSKA CASTIGLIONI
ARAB AVICENNA ABDALLATIF
ARGENTINIAN BUNGE
AUSTRIAN BARANY BREUER
MESMER OPPOLZER ENNEMOSER
ROKITANSKY
BELGIAN WIER
BRAZILIAN CHAGAS KUBITSCHEK
CANADIAN CRAIK DAFOE FISET
GRANT OSLER REEVE ASHTON
MCCRAE BANTING RODDICK
MACPHAIL
CZECH VANCURRA
DANISH GRAM WORM LANGE
FINSEN BARTHOLIN
DUTCH GRAAF BOERHAAVE
INGENHOUSZ
ENGLISH BUDD GOOD HAKE HALL
HUME MEAD PAVY SNOW BARRY
BRUCE CAIUS DOVER DRAKE
FLUDD JAMES JONES JURIN
LOWER PAGET ACLAND BRIGHT
BROWNE CLARKE DOBELL
GARROD HARVEY HAVERS
HUNTER JENNER MANSON
PARKES RINGER SLOANE TREVES
WILLIS ADDISON ALLBUTT
BENNETT CHAPMAN CONOLLY
COPLAND DEARDEN GLISSON

HODGKIN NABARRO PRINGLE
SKINNER STANTON WHARTON
ANDERSON ANDREWES
BARNARDO BASHFORD BIRKBECK
BUCHANAN GRENFELL HEBERDEN
PRICHARD SYDENHAM
BLACKMORE BROADBENT
LANKESTER RADCLIFFE
FOTHERGILL
FRENCH CLOT DENIS DUPRE
HAYEM PINEL WIDAL ANDRAL
ASTRUC AUZOUX BERARD FERNEL
LEPINE LITTRE MARTIN PLANTE
VAQUEZ BAILLON BECHAMP
DAVAINE DUMERIL GRASSET
LAENNEC LAVERAN LECLUSE
MANTOUX MENIERE NICOLLE
PECQUET QUESNAY VINCENT
BOUCHARD DUCHENNE
LANDOUZY LEVADITI BOUILLAUD
BROUSSALS LAMETTRIE
BAILLARGER BRETONNEAU
CASSEGRAIN LANCEREAUX
POISEUILLE SCHWEITZER
BROUSSONETT
GERMAN ERB BINZ EBEL GALL
KOCH MUCH REIL ZINN BLOCH
CARUS FAUST FRANK LINGG
OSANN REMAK BRUCKE CORDUS
DOBLIN KERNER KORTUM LEYDEN
MEIBOM NORDAU OERTEL
OLBERS PEUCER AGRIPPA
BASEDOW BERENDT KAMPFER
NEISSER BRUNFELS ERXLEBEN
FLEMMING HOFFMANN
HUFELAND ZIEMSSEN DOLLINGER
FORSSMANN HAHNEMANN
NICOLAIER NOTHNAGEL
SCHONLEIN DETTWEILER
FRIEDREICH LANGERHANS
GREEK GALEN RUFUS AETIOS
CTESIAS SORANUS ALCMAEON
DEMOCEDES ORIBASIUS
PRAXAGORAS ASCLEPIADES
HIPPOCRATES ERASISTRATUS
IRISH JOYCE STOKES GOGARTY
SIGERSON
ITALIAN BOTTA GOLGI ASELLI
FARINI MAZZEI BAGLIVI BELLINI
CARDANO GALVANI BACCELLI
LOMBROSO SCALIGER
BLANDRATA CESALPINO
FRACASTORO MONTESSORI
TOSCANELLI VALLISNIERI
NORWEGIAN HANSEN
PARAGUAYAN BARBERO
RUMANIAN BABES
RUSSIAN DAHL VERESAEY
VORONOFF
SALVADORAN MOLINA
SCOTTISH LIND MOIR BLANE
BROWN ARNOTT BRIDIE BUCHAN
CHEYNE CULLEN FERGUS FORBES
BRUNTON CANTLIE JAMESON
SIMPSON GRAINGER ARBUTHNOT
ARMSTRONG PITCAIRNE
CHRISTISON MACALISTER
RUTHERFORD ABERCROMBIE
SPANISH CHANCA SERVETUS
SWEDISH MUNTHE ZANDER
ACHARIUS
SWISS GOLL AMMAN PEYER
ROLLIER ZWINGER PARACELSUS

VENEZUELAN VARGAS
PHYSICIST HYLOZOIST
　AMERICAN AMES CREW GUNN
　HALL HULL LAMB LAND LANE
　MORE PAGE RABI ROOD ROSA
　TING WOOD YANG ZINN ALTER
　BACHE BARUS BAUER BETHE
　BLOCH COHEN DUANE EWELL
　HENRY KUSCH LEMON LYMAN
　MAYER PUPIN SEGRE STERN
　SWANN YALOW BEDELL BRIGGS
　CONDON COOPER FRANCK
　GERMER GLASER LOOMIS MORLEY
　NIPHER PIERCE SLOANE TELLER
　TOLMAN TOWNES VARIAN
　WIGNER WRIGHT ALLISON
　BABCOCK BARDEEN BURGESS
　CARHART COMPTON FEYNMAN
　GODDARD GODLOVE LECONTE
　NICHOLS PURCELL RANDALL
　RENWIEK RICHTER ROWLAND
　SZILARD WHEELER ANDERSON
　BLODGETT BRATTAIN BRIDGMAN
　DAVISSON HASTINGS LAWRENCE
　MILLIKAN SHOCKLEY STRATTON
　THOMPSON VANALLEN VANVLECK
　WINTHROP BITTINGER
　GOODSPEED HUMPHREYS
　INGERSOLL LAURITSEN
　MICHELSON RAINWATER
　SCHWINGER HOFSTADTER
　MENDENHALL RENTSCHLER
　RUTHERFURD SCHRIEFFER
　TROWBRIDGE CHAMBERLAIN
　OPPENHEIMER
　ARGENTINIAN CERNUSCHI
　AUSTRIAN HESS MACH DOPPLER
　PRECHTL BOLTZMANN
　SCHRODINGER
　BELGIAN PLATEAU
　CANADIAN TORY HERZBERG
　DANISH BOHR OERSTED
　MOTTELSON
　DUTCH WAALS ZEEMAN HUYGENS
　LORENTZ ZERNIKE HARTSOEKER
　KAMERLINGH MUSSCHENBROEK
　ENGLISH EVE LAMB LEES MOTT
　ASTON BOYLE BRAGG DIRAC
　GROVE JEANS JOULE LODGE
　NICOL AITKEN BARKLA CANTON
　DALTON DARWIN FRISCH KELVIN
　STOKES ANDRADE BARRETT
　CROOKES DANIELL FARADAY
　GILBERT GUTHRIE HARTREE
　MICHELL MOSELEY THOMSON
　TYNDALL APPLETON BLACKETT
　CHADWICK HAUKSBEE POYNTING
　RAYLEIGH SCHUSTER CALLENDAR
　COCKCROFT HEAVISIDE
　JOSEPHSON GLAZEBROOK
　RICHARDSON RUTHERFORD
　WHEATSTONE
　FRENCH BIOT HIRN NEEL CORNU
　FABRY JAMIN MALUS PAPIN
　PETIT WEISS BRANLY CARNOT
　CLAUDE COTTON DULONG FIZEAU
　FORTIN NIEPCE NOLLET PERRIN
　RAOULT SAVART VIOLLE BABINET
　BEUDANT BLONDEL COULOMB
　FOURIER FRESNEL JOUBERT
　KASTLER MASCART PELTIER
　REAUMUR SAUVEUR AMONTONS
　ARSONVAL DESPRETZ FOUCAULT

　LANGEVIN LIPPMANN MARIOTTE
　POUILLET REGNAULT BECQUEREL
　BRILLOUIN CAILLETET
　GUILLAUME LISSAJOUS
　CHARDONNET
　GERMAN MIE OHM BORN DOVE
　KORN LAUE LENZ REIS WIEN
　BOTHE BRAUN BUDDE DEBYE
　ERMAN HERTZ HOLTZ JOLLY
　KUNDT MAYER STARK VOIGT
　WEBER BALMER ELSTER HANKEL
　KOENIG LAMONT LENARD
　LUMMER MAGNUS NERNST
　PLANCK RIECKE RITTER ZEUNER
　AEPINUS BRODHUN CHLADNI
　FECHNER GEHRCKE HITTORF
　LAMBERT NEUMANN PLUCKER
　PRANDTL QUINCKE REGENER
　RUDOLPH SCAEFER SEEBECK
　TOEPLER WULLNER CLAUSIUS
　EINSTEIN GUERICKE ROENTGEN
　SCHUMANN FEDDERSEN
　GOLDSTEIN HALLWACHS
　KIRCHHOFF MOSSBAUER
　SCHEIBLER STEINHEIL
　WIEDEMANN BARKHAUSEN
　FAHRENHEIT KOHLRAUSCH
　PRINGSHEIM SCHWEIGGER
　SIEDENTOPF SOMMERFELD
　LICHTENBERG
　GREEK CTESIBIUS
　INDIAN BOSE SAHA RAMAN
　IRISH JOLLY STONEY WALTON
　ANDREWS TOWNSEND
　FITZGERALD
　ITALIAN RUS FERMI PORTA RIGHI
　VOLTA ALDINI NOBILI BORELLI
　CAVALLO GALILEI GALVANI
　MELLONI VENTURI AVOGADRO
　BECCARIA BELTRAMI BLASERNA
　FERRARIS GRIMALDI PALMIERI
　BOSCOVICH PACINOTTI
　TORRICELLI
　JAPANESE ESAKI YUKAWA
　TOMONAGA
　NORWEGIAN GIAEVER BJERKNES
　HANSTEEN
　POLISH WROBLEWSKI
　RUSSIAN TAMM BASOV FRANK
　LANDAU KAPITZA LEBEDEV
　SAKHAROV CHERENKOV
　PROKHOROV
　SCOTTISH KERR TAIT WATT
　DEWAR EWING NOBLE WILSON
　MAXWELL RANKINE STEWART
　BREWSTER
　SWEDISH EDLEN ALFVEN EDLUND
　NILSON ANGSTROM SIEGBAHN
　ARRHENIUS BENEDICKS
　SWISS WILD EULER ARGAND
　LARIVE PICTET PICCARD PREVOST
　ALLAMAND
PHYSIC NUT TUBA CURCAS
　PIGNON TARTAGO
PHYSIOCRAT ECONOMIST
PHYSIOGNOMY MUG FACE PHIZ
　VIZNOMY PORTRAIT VISENOMY
PHYSIOLOGIST **AMERICAN** IVY
　LUSK HOUGH CANNON DALTON
　GASSER HARVEY HOWELL
　CARLSON SCHALLY COURNAND
　ERLANGER HARTLINE GUILLEMIN
　HENDERSON OSTERHOUT

　ARGENTINIAN HOUSSAY
　AUSTRALIAN ECCLES
　AUSTRIAN STEINACH
　BELGIAN HEYMANS
　CANADIAN BEST
　CZECH PURKINJE
　DANISH KROGH
　DUTCH DONDERS EINTHOVEN
　ENGLISH DALE HILL KATZ BEALE
　HALES LOWER ADRIAN DARWIN
　FOSTER HUXLEY RIVERS WALLER
　BAYLISS HERRING HODGKIN
　BARCROFT MARSHALL STARLING
　ELLIOTSON SHERRINGTON
　FRENCH BERT MAREY RICHET
　BEAUNIS BERNARD FLOURENS
　MAGENDIE DUTROCHET
　POISEUILLE
　GERMAN FICK VOIT BUDGE GOLTZ
　KUHNE REMAK WUNDT HENSEN
　HERING LUDWIG MULLER PREYER
　WAGNER BURDACH PFLUGER
　VERWORN WARBURG MEISSNER
　MEYERHOF VALENTIN
　HEIDENHAIN
　ITALIAN BOVET MOSSO
　MANTEGAZZA
　RUSSIAN CYON PAVLOV
　SCOTTISH MACLEOD
　SWEDISH EULER GRANIT
　HOLMGREN
　SWISS HESS
PHYSIOLOGY BIONOMY ZOONOMY
PHYSIOTHERAPY PATTERNING
PHYSIQUE BODY BUILD
　SOOST HABIT FIGURE
　STRENGTH
PHYSOCARPUS NEILLIA
　OPULASTER
PHYSOSTIGMINE ESERE ESERINE
PHYTOMER PHYTON PODIUM
PI JUMBLE CONFUSE PREACHY
　CONFUSION
PIA PI GABI GABGAB MARMOT
PIACLE SIN CRIME GUILT OFFENSE
PIAN YAWS FRAMBESIA
PIANETTE PYNOT PIANINO
PIANIST CEMBALIST CLAVIERIST
PIANO SOFT FLOOR GRAND GRANT
　STORY FLUGEL GENTLY SOFTLY
　SPINET SQUARE CLAVIAL
　CLAVIER GIRAFFE PIANOLA
　QUIETLY UPRIGHT
　MELOTROPE
　(AFRICAN —) KALIMBA
　(PART OF —) ARM KEY LEG LID
　DESK FALL HEEL LYRE PROP
　CHEEK PEDAL STRING KEYSLIP
　KEYBOARD
PIASSAVA IYO JARA BAHIA
　PIACABA
PIASTER KURUS
PIATTI CYMBALS
PIAZZA PORCH SQUARE BALCONY
　GALLERY PORTICO VERANDA
　PIAZZETTA
PIC PEAK LANCE PIQUE PICADOR
PICA M EM LINE
PICARD PYKAR
PICARO KNAVE ROGUE TRAMP
　BOHEMIAN VAGABOND
PICAROON ROGUE PICARO PIRATE
　CORSAIR WRECKER

PICAYUNE PIC PETTY MEASLY
　PALTRY TRIVIAL
　PISTAREEN
PICCADILL RABATA REBATE
　REBATO
PICCOLO BUSBOY JUKEBOX
　FLAUTINO OTTAVINO
PICHICIAGO ARMADILLO
　CHLAMYPHORE
PICK NIB OPT BILL CULL GAFF
　HACK LIFT PIKE PILK SHOT WALE
　ADORN BEELE BREAK CAVIL
　ELECT FLANG LEASE PILCH PLUCK
　PRIDE PRIME CHOICE CHOOSE
　GATHER PICKAX PUDDLE TWITCH
　BARGAIN CASCROM DIAMOND
　DRESSER MANDREL
　(— APART) TOW
　(— KNOTS FROM) BURL
　(— OUT) CULL SPOT TAKE
　WELE CRONE GLEAN
　GARBLE SELECT
　(— POCKETS) FIG FILE FOIST
　TOUCH
　(— TOBACCO) STRIP
　(FILLING —) ABB
PICKAX PIX BEDE BILL PIKE
　GURLET TUBBER TWIBIL TWIBILL
PICKED PICK TRIM PIKED CHOSEN
　DAINTY PEAKED SELECT
　ADORNED POINTED
　(PREF.) LECTO
PICKER COD HOPPER
　(BERRY —) HURTER
　(PEA —) VINER
PICKEREL JACK SNAKE DUNLIN
　SAUGER SLINKER
　WALLEYE
PICKERELWEED TULE WAMPEE
PICKER-UP FINDER
PICKET PEG PALE POST TERN
　FENCE STAKE FASTEN PALING
　TETHER ENCLOSE FORTIFY
　OUTPOST PICQUET PALISADE
　OUTPICKET
PICKLE BOX ALEC DILL MESS PECK
　ACHAR BRINE GRAIN MANGO
　SAUCE SOUSE ATSARA CAPERS
　DAWDLE HIGDON KERNEL KIMCHI
　MUDDLE NIBBLE PIDDLE PILFER
　PLIGHT TRIFLE CONDITE CONFECT
　GHERKIN TROUBLE VITRIOL
　MARINADE
　(FISH —) ALEC
PICKLED DRUNK MURIATED
　POWDERED MARINATED
PICKLOCK LOCK PICKER
PICK-ME-UP SCREW PICKUP
PICKPOCKET DIP FIG GUN NIP
　BUNG FILE WIRE DIVER FILER
　FOIST BULKER BUZZER CANNON
　DIPPER FIGBOY HOOKER NIPPER
　RATERO FOISTER MOBSMAN
　CLYFAKER CUTPURSE KNUCKLER
　BUZZGLOAK
　(HELPER OF —) STALL BULKER
PICKUP BRUSH TRUCK ARREST
　BRACER ANACRUSIS
**PICKWICK PAPERS (AUTHOR
　OF —)** DICKENS
　(CHARACTER IN —) BOB SAM MARY
　ALLEN EMILY TRACY ALFRED
　HUNTER JINGLE PERKER SAWYER

TUPMAN WARDLE WELLER WINKLE BARDELL RACHAEL SLAMMER ARABELLA AUGUSTUS CLUPPINS ISABELLA PICKWICK NATHANIEL SMORLTORK SNODGRASS

PICNIC FRY BALL GIPSY GYPSY BURGOO FROLIC JUNKET MAROON OUTING SHOULDER SQUANTUM SUMMERING WAYZGOOSE

PICOT LOOP PEARL PERLE

PICOTAH SWEEP PACOTA

PICTOGRAPH GLYPH PICTOGRAM

PICTORIAL GRAPHIC

PICTURE GAY MAP OIL COPY DAUB ICON IKON LIMN SIGN VIEW DECAL FRAME IMAGE LINER PAINT PHOTO PIECE PINAX PRINT SCENE SHAPE STAMP STORY TABLE CACHET CANVAS CHROMO CUTOUT DEPICT EMBLEM MARINE PASTEL SEMBLE SHADOW STEREO TABLET CUTAWAY DIORAMA DIPTYCH EMBLEMA ETCHING EXHIBIT FASHION FEATURE GOUACHE GRAPHIC HISTORY MIZRACH PAYSAGE PORTRAY PORTURE RETRAIT SCENERY TABLEAU VANDYKE AIRSCAPE AUTOTYPE DESCRIBE DROLLERY ENVISION IDEOGRAM KAKEMONO LANDSKIP LIKENESS MAKIMONO MONOTINT OVERDOOR PAINTING PANORAMA PORTRAIT PROSPECT RITRATTO SEASCAPE SINGERIE SKYSCAPE TRIPTYCH VIGNETTE ENCAUSTIC
(— IN BOOK) GAY
(— IN 3 COMPARTMENTS) TRIPTYCH
(— MAT) SPANDREL
(— OF MONKEYS) SINGERIE
(— ON ROLLER) KAKEMONO MAKIMONO
(— PUZZLE) REBUS JIGSAW
(—S IN BOOKS) BABY
(COMIC —) DROLLERY
(RELIGIOUS —) TANKA
(STEREOSCOPIC —) ANAGLYPH
(THREE-DIMENSIONAL —) HOLOGRAM
(PREF.) PINAC(O)

PICTURE OF DORIAN GRAY
(AUTHOR OF —) WILDE
(CHARACTER IN —) ALAN GRAY VANE BASIL HENRY JAMES SIBYL DORIAN WOTTON CAMPBELL HALLWARD

PICTURESQUE VIVID EXOTIC QUAINT SCENIC GRAPHIC IDYLLIC ROMANTIC PICTORIAL

PICUL TAN PICO PIKOL

PIDDLE PICK PLAY DAWDLE PICKLE PUTTER TRIFLE

PIDDLING JERK PALTRY TRIVIAL USELESS FOOTLING TRIFLING JERKWATER

PIDDOCK DACTYL PHOLAD PHOLAS

PIDGIN LANGUAGE SABIR

PIE PAI FLAM FLAN HEAP MESS PATE PILE TART DOWDY FLAWN

PASTY PATTY TORTA TOURT AFFAIR BRIDLE CHEWET MAGPIE PASTRY TOURTE COBBLER SMASHER STRUDEL BAKEMEAT CRUSTADE FLAPJACK PANDOWDY SURPRISE TURNOVER SMASHOVER

PIEBALD PIE PIED PIET MIXED PIETY PINTO CALICO MOTLEY SKEWBALD

PIECE BAT BIT COB CUT DAM FIG JOB LAB LOG MAN TUT GIRL MIND PART PISE PLAY BLYPE DAGON DRAMA DWANG FLOOR PEZZO SCRAP SHARD SHERD SHRED SLICE SNODE STEEK STUCK THROW COLLOP FARDEL FUGATO GOBBET PARCEL STITCH CANTLET EXAMPLE FLINDER FLITTER MORCEAU OPINION PICTURE PORTION SEGMENT DUOLOGUE EMBOLIUM FANDANGO PAINTING
(— AT END) HEELPIECE
(— FOR TWO) DUET DUOLOGUE
(— IN CHECKERS) DAM
(— IN ORGAN) THUMPER
(— OF ARMOR) JAMB JAMBE
(— OF BAD LUCK) DIRDUM
(— OF BLANKET) DAGON
(— OF BLUBBER) BIBLE
(— OF DECEPTION) BEGUNK
(— OF DECORATED METAL) NIELLO
(— OF FALSE HAIR) JANE
(— OF FIBER) NOIL
(— OF FIRED CLAY) TILE
(— OF GROUND SURROUNDED BY WASTE) HOPE
(— OF HARD WOOD) MOOT
(— OF LAND) ERF HAM LOT BUTT GORE LEASE SPONG SQUAT HUERTA RINCON SECTION CLEARAGE SOLIDATE
(— OF LIGHT ORDNANCE) ASPIC
(— OF LINEN) AMIT AMICE
(— OF LOG) SLAB
(— OF MAST) TONGUE
(— OF MATZOTH) AFIKOMEN
(— OF MEAT) EYE HEEL RAND COLLOP EPIGRAM
(— OF METAL) JAG COIN JAGG SPRAG
(— OF MONEY) COG SOU SHINER
(— OF NEEDLEWORK) SAMPLER
(— OF NONSENSE) FUDGE TRIMTRAM
(— OF ORE) CHAT
(— OF PROPERTY) CHOSE
(— OF SAIL) HULLOCK
(— OF SEPARATED LAND) BUTT
(— OF SKIN) BLYPE
(— OF SKIN FOR GLOVE) TRANK
(— OF SLATE) SLAT
(— OF SOAP) BALL
(— OF SOMETHING EDIBLE) STULL
(— OF TIMBER) FISH COULISSE FOREHOOK
(— OF TOAST) SLINGER
(— OF TOBACCO) FIG
(— OF TRACK) LEAD RUNBY
(— OF TRICKERY) CROOK CANTRIP
(— OF TURF) FLAG DIVOT SCRAW SHIRREL

(— OF WOOD) KIP LATH APRON BOARD CHUMP CHUNK PLANK SPOON WADDY BILLET COMMON STOWER TIMBER LIPPING
(— OF WORK) JOB CHAR TURN
(— OF WRITING) SCREED SCREEVE
(— OUT) EKE
(— SPLIT OFF) SPLINT
(— TO PREVENT SLIPPING) CLEAT
(—S OF MACARONI) DITALI DITALINI
(ARTILLERY —) DRAKE SAKER LANTACA
(BACKGAMMON —) BLOT STONE
(BROAD —) SHEET
(BROKEN —) BRACK MAMMOCK FRACTION
(BUTTING —) HURTER
(CHESS —) PIN KING PAWN ROOK QUEEN BISHOP CASTLE KNIGHT OFFICER
(DREAMY —) REVERIE
(END — OF BUCKET) CANT
(FLAT —) FLAP FLAKE
(FUR —) PALATINE
(GOLD —) SLUG TALI
(IN —S) LIMBMEAL
(IRREGULAR —) SNAG
(LARDED — OF MEAT) DAUB
(LARGE —) HUNK MOLE STULL DOLLOP
(LITERARY —) CAMEO
(LITTLE —) STNEKI SCANTLING
(LONG —) STRIP
(MOVABLE — IN VIOLIN BOW) NUT
(MUSICAL —) ITEM CHORO DANCE ETUDE CHASER LESSON ALLEGRO ANDANTE BLUETTE CONCERTO DUOLOGUE ENTRACTE OVERTURE INVENTION
(NARROW —) LABEL STAVE STRIP
(ODD — OF CARPENTRY) DUTCHMAN
(ROTATING —) CAM ROTOR SPINDLE
(SAMPLE —) SWATCH
(SHAPELESS —) DUMP MAMMOCK
(SIDE —) RIB JAMB JAMBE
(SINGLE —) LENGTH
(SLENDER —) SPILL SLIVER
(SMALL —) BIT BOB NOB PEA CHIP SNIP TATE CRUMB PATCH PRILL SCRAP SPECK MORSEL SIPPET DRIBLET FLITTER PALLION SPLINTER
(SMALL — OF FLESH) GIGOT
(SMALL — OF WOOD) KIP
(SMALL —S) MATCHWOOD
(STRENGTHENING —) DWANG HURTER
(TAPERING —) GORE GUSSET
(THICK —) JUNK HUNCH
(THIN —) SHIM FLAKE SHIVE SLICE
(WEDGESHAPED — OF WOOD) GLUT SHIM
(100-REAL GOLD —) ISABELLA
(25-CENT —) CUTER
(4-DOLLAR GOLD —) STELLA
(PL.) MATERIAL NOBLEMEN

PIECEWORK SETWORK TUTWORK TASKWORK

PIECEWORKER JOBBER

PIECRUST BREAD COFFIN ABAISSE

PIED PINTO SHELD MAGPIED PIEBALD

PIED ANTELOPE BONTEBOK

PIEDFORT PATAGON

PIED WAGTAIL COB COBB PEER PILE PILLAR WAGGIE WASHER WATERIE SEEDBIRD WASHDISH WASHTAIL

PIEPLANT RHUBARB RHAPONTIC

PIER COB ANTA BELT COBB DOCK MOLE PILE QUAY TILT GROIN JETTY JOWEL JUTTY LEVEE STILT WHARF BRIDGE BUNDER MULLION STAGION PIEDROIT STELLING
(— CAP) SUMMER
(HALF —) RESPONSE

PIERCE CUT DAB DAG DEG DIG JAB JAG RIT BARB BEAR BITE BORE BROB BROD CLOY DART DIRL GORE HOLE HOOK LACE LACK PASS PINK POKE PROB PROG RIVE ROVE STAB STOB TAME TANG WHIP BREAK DRIFT DRILL ENTER GOUGE GRIDE LANCE PERCH PITCH POACH PREEN PROBE PRONG SHEAR SNICK SPEAR SPIKE STEEK STICK STING THIRL ATTAME BROACH CLEAVE DAGGER EMPALE FICCHE GIMLET IMPALE LAUNCH PRITCH RIDDLE SEARCH SKEWER STITCH STRIKE THRILL THRING THRUST WIMBLE ASSAGAI JAVELIN ENTHRILL LACERATE PUNCTURE PENETRATE
(PREF.) FORAMINI

PIERCED AJOURE CRIBRAL PERTUSE CRIBROSE PERFORATE

PIERCING SHY FELL HIGH KEEN LOUD TART ACUTE CLEAR EAGLE SHARP SNELL ARROWY BITTER BORING SHREWD SHRILL SNITHE SNITHY CUTTING GIMLETY POINTED PUNGENT DRILLING INCISIVE PERCEANT POIGNANT POUNCING STABBING STICKING PENETRATIVE

PIERHEAD MOLEHEAD

PIET PYOT DIPPER MAGPIE

PIETIST LABADIST

PIETISTIC DEVOUT

PIETY HONOR LOYALTY PIETISM DEVOTION SANCTION GODLINESS

PIFFLE BUFF FOLDEROL

PIG (ALSO SEE HOG, SWINE) COW FAR HAM HOG SLIP BACON BONAV BROCK CHEAT CHUCK GRICE INGOT PIGGY SHOAT APEREA BONHAM COCHON FARROW GUSSIE HOGGIE PORKET PORKIN SUCKER TITMAN WEANER BONNIVE GLUTTON GRUMPHY HOGLING PIGLING ROOKLER GRUNTLING
(BROOD OF —S) TEAM
(CASTRATED —) BARROW
(EIGHT —S) FODDER
(PART OF —) EAR EYE HAM BUTT HOCK JOWL LOIN POLL TAIL TEAT FLANK SNOUT PICNIC FATBACK FOREFOOT SHOULDER SPARERIB TENDERLOIN

(SMALLEST — OF LITTER) DOLL TITMAN ANTHONY DILLING TANTANY TANTONY
(SUCKLING —) ROASTER
(UNDERSIZED —) RUNT TITMAN TEATMAN
(YOUNG —) ELT FAR SLIP GRICE GURRY BONEEN BONHAM SQUEAKER
(PREF.) HYO
(SUFF.) CHOERUS
PIG DEER BABIRUSA
PIGEON DOO NUN OWL TOY BARB CLAY DOVE JACK KING KITE LUPE RUFF RUNT SPOT BALDY DOWVE FRILL HOMER KOKLA PIPER SQUAB WONGA CULTER CULVER CUSHAT DODLET DRAGON FEEDER HELMET JEWING MAGPIE MANUMA MAUMET MODENA POUTER PRIEST ROCKER SHAKER TRERON TURBIT TURNER WATTLE ANTWERP CARNEAU CARRIER CROPPER FANTAIL FINIKIN JACINTH JACOBIN MALTESE PINTADO SWALLOW TIPPLER TUMBLER BALDHEAD CAPUCHIN FINIKING HORSEMAN MANUTAGI RINGDOVE SASSOROL SQUABBER SQUEAKER SQUEALER FRILLBACK TOOTHBILL
(CLAY —) BIRD GYROPIGEON
(STOOL —) PIG NARK
PIGEON BLOOD GARNET
PIGEON HAWK MERLIN
PIGEONHOLE BOX SLOT LABEL SHELVE ANALYZE CELLULE CLASSIFY CUBBYHOLE
(PL.) STOCK
PIGEON HOUSE COT DOOKET DOVECOT COLUMBARY
PIGEON PEA DAL TUR TARE ARHAR DAHIL GANDUL TURNER TURNOR CATJANG
PIGEON WOODPECKER FLICKER
PIGGERY PIGS PIGSTY HOGGERY POTTERY SWINERY CROCKERY
PIGGIN HANDY PIPKIN
PIGHEADED WILLFUL PERVERSE STUBBORN OBSTINATE
PIGHTLE PIKLE PICKLE PIDDLE PIGTAIL
PIG IRON GRUNDY
PIGLET PORKLING
PIGLIKE SUIFORM SUILINE SWINISH
PIGMENT (ALSO SEE DYE, COLOR) BLUE HEME BROWN COLOR EARTH GREEN HUMIN MORIN MUMMY PAINT STAIN TONER BRONZE CEROID CERUSE IDAEIN LITHOL MALVIN ORANGE PURPLE SIENNA VIOLET BEZETTA GOUACHE PAINTRY PUCCOON STAINER TURACIN ALTHAEIN COLORANT EXTENDER GOSSYPOL MELANOID PAINTURE TINCTURE UROPHEIN VERDITER
(— FOR WOODWORK) KOKOWAI
(— IN BUTTERFLY WING) PTERIN
(BLACK —) ABAISER MELANIN
(BLUE —) BICE SMALT CYANIN ALTHEIN CERULEUM MARENNIN
(BLUE-GREEN —) LEUCOCYAN

(BROWN —) MUMMY SEPIA UMBER BISTER FUSCIN ASTERIN SINOPIA
(BROWNISH-YELLOW —) SIENNA
(GRAPE —) ENIN OENIN
(GREEN —) VERDITER
(MADDER-ROOT —) RUBIATE
(ORANGE-RED —) REALGAR
(PLANT —) CYANIN
(RED —) HAEM LAKE ARUMIN PATISE SANDYX AMATITO KOKOWAI PUCCOON SCARLET SINOPIA CAPSUMIN URORUBIN URRHODIN VERMILION
(RED-VIOLET —) TURACIN
(WHITE —) CERUSE ANATASE LITHOPONE
(YELLOW —) FLAVIN PURREE ETIOLIN FISETIN GAMBOGE PUCCOON CAROTENE DIATOMIN GALANGIN GENTISIN MASSICOT ORPIMENT UROBILIN
(PREF.) CHROM(AT)(ATO)(I)(IDIO)(O)
PIGMENTATION COLOR LENTIL ARGYRIA LENTIGO JAUNDICE NIGRITIES
(SUFF.) CHROMIA
PIGNUS PAWN PLEDGE
PIGNUT ARNOT ARNUT HOGNUT
PIGS' FEET CRUBEEN PETTITOES
PIGSKIN SADDLE FOOTBALL
PIGSNEY EYE DARLING
PIGSTY FRANK CRUIVE HOGCOTE HOGGERY PIGGERY SWINESTY
PIGTAIL PLAIT QUEUE COLETA
PIGWASH SWILL
PIGWEED QUINOA BEETROOT CARELESS GOOSEFOOT
PIK DRA PICKI PICKL ENDAZE ENDASEH
PIKA CONY HAIR HARE LEPORID LAGOMORPH
PIKE GED DORE DORY GADE GEDD JACK LUCE TANG TOUG TUCK HAKED LUCET SNAKE SNOOK STING VOUGE SALMON SAUGER JAVELIN WALLEYE BLOWFISH GLASSEYE JACKFISH NORTHERN PARTISAN PICKEREL POULAINE TURNPIKE MUSKELLUNGE
PIKELET CRUMPET
PIKEMAN PIKE WATTLEBOY
PIKE PERCH FOGASH PERCID SANDER SAUGER ZANDER
PIKER TRAMP VAGRANT TELLTALE TIGHTWAD VAGABOND
PILASTER ANTA PIER RIDGE ALETTE ALLETTE RESPOND TELAMON
PILCHARD FUMADO ALEWIFE SARDINE MENHADEN
PILDASH (FATHER OF —) NAHOR
(MOTHER OF —) MILCAH
PILE COP FUR LOT NAP PIE TIP BALE BANK BING BULK BUNG BURR COCK DASS DECK DESS DOWN HACK HAIR HEAP LEET LOAD PEEL PIER POLE POOK PYRE REEK RUCK SESS SHAG SPUD AMASS CANCH CLAMP CROWD FAGOT POINT SPILE SPIRE STACK STILT TOWER CASTLE FAGGOT FENDER FILLER GALGAL PILLAR

RICKLE RUCKLE FORTUNE JAVELIN PYRAMID REACTOR SPINDLE CROWBILL INCREASE SANDPILE
(— CROSSWISE) COB
(— CURD) CHEDDAR
(— OF BRICKS) HACK CLAMP
(— OF CLOTH) LAY
(— OF HAY) RICK SHOCK DOODLE HAYCOCK HAYRICK
(— OF ICE) HUMMOCK
(— OF LOGS) DECK
(— OF PLATES) BUNG
(— OF REFUSE) DUSTHEAP
(— OF SALT FISH) BULK
(— OF SEALSKINS) PAN
(— OF SHEAVES) SESS
(— OF SHEETS) LIFT
(— OF STONES) ISLAND STONAGE WARLOCK
(— OF TOBACCO) BULK
(— OF WOOD) STRAND
(— TO BE BURNT) PYRE
(— UP) BIG BULK CORD RICK COMPILE ACCUMULATE
(— WHEAT SHOCKS) STITCH
(IRON —) SPINDLE
(LITTLE —) HOT HOTT
(LOOSE —) RICKLE
(ROCK —) HOODOO
(SMALL —) COCK CANCH
(PL.) FIG DRIFT
PILEA ADICEA
PILEATED WOODPECKER LOGCOCK WOODCOCK
PILE DRIVER TUP FISTUCA HERCULES IMPACTER
(— DOLLY) FOLLOWER
(— WEIGHT) RAM TUP MONKEY
PILEUS CAP MITRA PILEOLUS
PILEWORT CRAIN CRANE FICARY FIGWORT CELANDINE
PILFER NIM NIP ROB CRIB HOOK PELF PICK PILK PRIG SMUG SNIG FILCH MICHE MOOCH PILCH PROWL SHARP SLOCK STEAL SWIPE FINGER MAGPIE MOOTCH NIBBLE PICKLE SMOUCH SNITCH CABBAGE MANAVEL PLUNDER PURLOIN SNAFFLE UNHITCH PETTIFOG SCROUNGE
PILFERER PRIG PIKER TAKER SLOCKER FINGERER SLOCKSTER
PILFERING CRIB MICHING PICKING THIEVISH
PILGRIM HAJI HADJI HAJJI PALMER PELERIN PEREGRIN WAYFARER
PILGRIMAGE TRIP TURUS VOYAGE JOURNEY
(— TO MECCA) HADJ
(BRETON —) PARDON
PILGRIM BROWN FRIAR
PILGRIM'S PROGRESS (AUTHOR OF —) BUNYAN
(CHARACTER IN —) POPE PAGAN PIETY SLOTH PLIANT SIMPLE CHARITY DESPAIR HOPEFUL SINCERE APOLLYON FAITHFUL GOODWILL PRUDENCE WATCHFUL CHRISTIAN FORMALISM HYPOCRISY IGNORANCE KNOWLEDGE

OBSTINATE DISCRETION EVANGELIST EXPERIENCE PRESUMPTION
PILING SPILING STOCKADE
(PL.) STARLING
PILL PIL ROB BALL BARK GOLI PEEL POOL CREEK CACHOU EXTORT UNHAIR DESPOIL DIURNAL GLOBULE GRANULE PARVULE PILLULE PREFORM BASEBALL GOOFBALL BLACKBALL CIGARETTE
(AROMATIC —) CACHOU
(LARGE —) BALL BOLUS
(LITTLE —) PILULA PILULE
PILLAGE LOOT PEEL PILL PREY SACK BOOTY FORAY HARRY REAVE RIFLE SPOIL HARROW MARAUD PICORY RAPINE RAVAGE DESPOIL PICKEER PLUNDER RANSACK ROBBERY BOOTHALE EXPILATE PURCHASE SPOLIATE DEVASTATE
PILLAGER PEELER PILLER ROBBER SACKER SPOILER SNAPHANCE
PILLAGING EXECUTION PREDATORY
PILLAR COG HERM JAMB PACK PIER PILE POST PROP STUD TERM JAMBE NEWEL SHAFT STELA STELE STOCK STONE STOOP STUMP CIPPUS COLUMN HERMES PILLER STAPLE BEDPOST DEADMAN TRESTLE TRUMEAU BOUNDARY MASSEBAH PEDESTAL RESPONSE STANCHION
(— CAPPED WITH SLAB) BILITH
(— IN LARGE DOORWAY) TRUMEAU
(— IN MINE) STOOK STUMP
(— OF COAL) SPURN STOOK STOOP
(— SUPPORTING ARCH) RESPONSE
(— SURMOUNTED BY HEAD) HERMES
(—S OF HERCULES) ABILA CALPE
(BUDDHIST —) LAT
(CHANGED TO —) OLENUS
(EARTH —) HOODOO
(SACRED —) ASHERAH
(SEMITE —) MASSEBAH
(STONE —) CIPPUS
(TEMPORARY —) DEADMAN
(4-SIDED —) OBELISK
(PL.) CRURA
(PREF.) CION(O) STELO STYL(I)(O)
(SUFF.) STELE STYLAR STYLE STYLI(C) STYLOUS
PILLARIST STYLITE
PILLAS PILCORN PILKINS
PILLBOX SCATULA
PILLBUG ISOPOD KEESLIP MILLEPED PILLWORM CHEESELIP
PILLED BALD SHAVEN TONSURED
PILLION PAD PILLOW SADDLE CUSHION
PILLORY CANG THEW JOUGS TRONE CANGUE CRUCIFY HALSFANG
PILLOW COD BOTT DAWN PEEL PILE REST FLOAT WANGER BOLSTER CUSHION FUSTIAN HEADING OREILLER PULVINAR
(PREF.) PULVILLI PULVINI!
PILLOWCASE COD BEAR PILL SHAM PILLIVER

PILLOWY PULVINAR
PILM DUST
PILON BONUS LAGNIAPPE
PILOSE HAIRY PILEOUS
PILOT ACE SPY KIWI COACH
GUARD GUIDE STEER AIRMAN
ESCORT MANAGE THAMUS
AVIATOR CAPTAIN CONDUCT
HOBBLER LODEMAN SHIPMAN
WINGMAN AIREDALE GOVERNOR
HELMSMAN PALINURUS
WHEELSMAN COWCATCHER
(AUTHOR OF —) COOPER
(AUTOMATIC —) GEORGE
(CHARACTER IN —) TOM GRAY
ALICE JONES MERRY COFFIN
DILLON EDWARD HOWARD
MANUAL MUNSON CECILIA
PLOWDEN RICHARD GRIFFITH
DUNSCOMBE KATHERINE
BARNSTABLE CHRISTOPHER
BORROUGHCLIFFE
(DUD —) PRUNE
PILOT BIRD PLOVER
PILOT FISH ROMERO JACKFISH
AMBERFISH
PILOTHOUSE TEXAS CHARTHOUSE
PILUM PESTLE JAVELIN
PIMENTA MYRTAL
PIMENTO PIMENTA ALLSPICE
PIMIENTO
PIMP MACK BULLY CADET FAGOT
PONCE SNEAK MACRIO PANDER
RUFFIAN INFORMER PROCURER
PURVEYOR SCOUNDREL
SOUTENEUR
PIMPERNEL BURNET WAYWORT
EYEBRIGHT MARGELINE
WINCOPIPE
PIMPLE GUM NOB PAP BURL KNOB
PUSH QUAT SPOT BLAIN BOTCH
HICKY PLOOK PLOUK PLUKE
WHELK BLOTCH BOUTON BUTTON
PAPULA PAPULE TETTER
BUBUKLE PUSTULE PIMGENET
WHEYWORM
(PREF.) CHALAZI CHALAZO
PAPULI PAPULO
PIN FID FIX HOB HUB LAG LEG NOG
PEG PEN ACUS APEX AXLE BANK
BOLT MOOD PEEN POST PRIN
PROP PYNE RUNG STUD DRIFT
HUMOR KAYLE POINT PREEN
SPILL THOLE BOBBIN BODKIN
BROACH BROOCH CALIGO COTTER
CURLER FASTEN HATPIN JOGGLE
NORMAN PINNET SKEWER SPIGOT
TEMPER TENPIN TOGGEL TONGUE
TRIFLE BAYONET CONFINE
ENCLOSE GUDGEON HAIRPIN
IMPOUND LOCKPIN PUSHPIN
SPINDLE TAMPION TANGENT
TUMBLER WOOLDER FORELOCK
PINNACLE
(— FOR FITTING PLANKS) SETBOLT
(— IN AXLETREE) LINCHPIN
(— IN RIFLE) TIGE
(— OF DIAL) STYLE GNOMON
(— OF LANTERN PINION) RUNDLE
(— OF WATCH) DART
(— ON CLAVICHORD KEY) TANGENT
(— TO HOLD BEDCLOTHES)
BEDSTAFF

(— USED AS TARGET) HOB
(BELAYING —) CAVIL
(BOWLING —) DUCKPIN HEADPIN
KINGPIN SLEEPER
(BOWLING —S) DEADWOOD
(CARPENTRY —) DOWEL
(COUPLING —) DRAWBOLT
(ENGAGING —) BAYONET
(HAIR —) BARRETTE
(HEADED —) RIVET
(JEWELED —) PROP
(OAR —) THOLE
(ORNAMENTAL —) AGLET AIGLET
(PIVOT —) PINTLE
(SMALL —) LILL MINIKIN MICROPIN
(SPLIT —) COTTER FORELOCK
(SURVEYOR'S —) ARROW
(TAPERED —) DRIFT
(TIRLING —) RISP
(WOODEN —) SPILE TRENAIL
(PL.) LEGS KAILS DEADWOOD
(PREF.) PERONEO PERONO
PINACOID BASE HEMIDOME
PINAFORE BRAT SLIP TIDE TIDY
TIER TYER DAIDLY PINNER
SAVEALL SLIPPER GABERDINE
PINBALL BAGATELLE
PINBALL MACHINE PACHINKO
PINCASE POPPET
PINCE-NEZ NIPPER LORGNON
NOSEPINCH
PINCERS TEU TEW CLAM CHELA
TUARN PLIERS TURKIS WYNRIS
FORCEPS MULLETS NIPPERS
PINCHER PINSONS TWEEZERS
PINCH NIP TOP VEX WRY BITE
CLAM HURT DOAN PUSH STOP
TAIT TATE TUCK CHACK CRIMP
GRIPE HINCH PUGIL SNUFF
SQUAT STEAL STINT TAPER
THEFT TWEAK WRING ARREST
CLUTCH EXTORT HARASS
NARROW SNITCH STRAIT STRESS
TWITCH SCRINCH SQUEEZE
JUNCTURE PRESSURE SHORTAGE
STRAITEN VELLICATE
(— OF SNUFF) SNEESH SNEESHIN
(— WITH COLD) NIRL
(— WITH HUNGER) CLAM CLEM
PINCHBECK SHAM CHEAP
SPURIOUS PRETENDED
PINCHED CHITTY WASTED
HAGGARD PUNGLED SQUINCH
PINCHING CHACK
PINCHPENNY CARL MISER
NIGGARD NIGGARDLY
PINDARIC ODE WILD
PINE IE ARA LIM CHIL CHIR FADE
FLAG HALA HONE IEIE KAIL WANT
AGGAG DROOP DWAIN GRIEF
KAURI MATAI MATSU MOURN
OCOTE PINON WANZE WEARY
WRIST YEARN APACHE AROLLA
DUSTER FAMINE GRIEVE HUNGER
LAMENT PANDAN SHRINK
SORROW STARVE TOATOA
TORFEL WITHER CYPRESS
DAISING DWINDLE FORPINE
FOXTAIL JEFFREY LAUHALA
TARWOOD TORMENT TORTURE
AKAMATSU AUSTRIAN GALAGALA
LANGUISH LOBLOLLY LONGLEAF
PINASTER STAGHORN

TANEKAHA VANQUISH
(— AWAY) PEAK DROOP DWINE
SNURP WANZE WINDER FORPINE
MACERATE
(AUSTRALIAN —) BEEFWOOD
(GROUND —) FOXTAIL
(PITCH —) THYME
(PREF.) PINI PITYO
PINEAPPLE BOMB NANA PINA
PINO PITA ANANA ANANAS
ABACAXI GRENADE
PINE FINCH SISKIN
PINE MARTEN SABLE
PINE NEEDLE SHAT SPILL PINING
ALFILARIA
(PL.) TWINKLES
PINE TREE STATE MAINE
PINFEATHER PEN STUMP STIPULE
PINFISH CHUB SPOT JIMMY PORGY
SARGO
PINFOLD POUND
PING KNOCK
PINGRASS ALFILERIA
PINGUIN MAYA ANANAS AGUAMAS
PINUELA HUIPILLA
PINGUITUDE FATNESS OBESITY
OILINESS
PINION NOIL WING PINON QUILL
PENNON SARCEL SECURE
LANTERN PINACLE SHACKLE
TRUNDLE FLIGHTER WALLOWER
PINION WHEEL MOBILE
PINITOL SENNITE MATEZITE
PINK JAG PIP CYME DAWN DECK
FADE MICE PING STAB WINK
ADORN BLINK CORAL ELITE
MOVED SWELL WOUND AURORE
BISQUE CHERUB FIESTA HEIGHT
MINNOW POUNCE SHRIMP SILENE
TATTOO ZEPHYR ANNATTO
ARBUTUS BEGONIA BERMUDA
BLOSSOM CAMPION EXTREME
PARAGON REVEREE SANDUST
TUSSORE CONFETTI COQUETTE
DECORATE DIANTHUS GILLIVER
LIMEWORT RADIANCE RECAMIER
PINKED JAGGED
PINKIE PIRLIE
PINKROOT REDROOT WORMWEED
STARBLOOM
PINNA EARFLAP PINNULE
APHLEBIA AURICULA PAVILION
PINNACE BARK CROWN WOMAN
BARQUE PINNAGE MISTRESS
PINNACLE IT PIN TOP ACME APEX
CREST CROWN SERAC SPIRE
THUMB FINIAL HEIGHT SUMMIT
GENDARME
(ICE —) SERAC
(ROCKY —) TOR HOODOO
AIGUILLE GENDARME
PINNATE WINGED
PINNER PINDER FLANDAN STICKER
PINNIPED SEAL
PINOCHLE BINOCLE GOULASH
AIRPLANE
(— SCORE) MELD
PINPILLOW PIMPLO
PINPOINT ISOLATE
(— OF LIGHT) GLEAM
PINT O GULL PINNET SWIGGER
OCTARIUS
(FOURTH —) GILL JACK

(HALF —) CUP NIP GILL JACK
CUPFUL NIPPERKIN
(9-10THS —) MUTCHKIN
PINTADO CERO PIED SIER SEARER
SIERRA SPOTTED KINGFISH
PINTAIL DUCK SMEE SPIKE SPRIG
GROUSE SMETHE CRACKER
LADYBIRD LONGNECK PIKETAIL
PINTANO PILOT COCKEYE
CHIRIVITA
PINTID EMPEINE
PINTO BEAN ROSILLO
PINWEED
(PL.) LECHEA
PINWHEEL WINDMILL
PINWORM NEMA OXYURID
PIN WRENCH SPANULE
PIONEER BLAZE GUIDE MINER
GROPER HALUTZ SETTLE
CHALUTZ EXPLORE EARLIEST
EMIGRANT ORIGINAL RAWHIDER
VOORTREKKER
PIONEERS (AUTHOR OF —) COOPER
(CHARACTER IN —) JOHN GRANT
HIRAM JONES NATTY BUMPPO
LOUISA OLIVER TEMPLE
EDWARDS RICHARD DOOLITTLE
EFFINGHAM ELIZABETH
CHINGACHGOOK
PIOUS PI HOLY WISE FROOM
GODLY MORAL SEELY DEVOUT
DIVINE INWARD PIETIC CANTING
DUTIFUL GODDARD PITEOUS
SAINTED SAINTLY FAITHFUL
RELIGIOUS
PIP DIE CHIP ECHO KILL PAIP PEEP
SPOT SPECK ACINUS DEFEAT
PIPPIN BLACKBALL
PIPAL BO FIG
PIPE TD BIN GUN HUB TAP TEE
BUTT CALL CANE DALE DRIP
DUCT FLUE HOSE LINE MAIN
MUTE PULE REED TILE TUBE
WEEP WORM BLAST BRAIL BRIAR
CANAL CANEL CINCH CRANE
CROSS CUTTY HOOKA PROBE
PUNGI QUILL RIDER RISER SPOUT
STAND STRAW TEWEL TRUMP
TRUNK VOICE BRANCH BURROW
CALEAN CASING DUCTUS FAUCET
FILLER GEWGAW HEWGAG
HOGGER KINURA NIPPLE NOTICE
NOZZLE OFFLET OFFSET POOGYE
RANKET SLEEVE SLOUCH SLUICE
SUCKER TROWEL TUBULE
TUNNEL UPTAKE WEEPER
CHANNEL CHANTER CHIBOUK
CONDUIT DUCTURE FISTULA
HYDRANT SERVICE SPARGER
SPINDLE SUCTION TALLBOY
TWEEDLE WHISTLE CALIDUCT
DOWNTAKE GALOUBET
LAMPHOLE MIRLITON NARGHILE
NARGILEH PENSTOCK SEMIDOLE
SUSPIRAL TELLTALE THRIBBLE
(— AS NAVIGATION AID) SPINDLE
(— BENDER) HICKEY
(— BOWL) STUMMEL
(— FOR CONDUCTING WATER)
LEADER
(— JOINT) TURNOUT
(— OF ORE) BUNNY
(— OF PAN) SYRINX

(— OF QUEEN BEE) TEET
(— ON BAGPIPE) DRONE CHANTER
(— SUPPORT) CRADLE
(— TAB) TACK
(— TO MUFFLE TRUMPET) SORDINE
(— USED IN WELL) STRING
(— WITH SOCKET ENDS) HUB
(BOWL AND STEM OF —) STUMMEL
(CEREMONIAL —) CALUMET
(CLAMMING —) BRAIL
(CONNECTING —) HOGGER
(FLUE —) LABIAL
(HEATING —) CALIDUCT
(MUSICAL —) BODY GEWGAW
FISTULA SORDINE HORNPIPE
SCHWEGEL
(OATEN —) OAT
(ORGAN —) FLUE KINURA LABIAL
ERZAHLER SCHWEGEL
TREMOLANT
(ORGAN —S) MONTRE
(PART OF —) BIT BOWL STEM
SHANK SHAPE SADDLE
MOUTHPIECE
(PEACE —) CALUMET
(PROJECTING —) BRACKET
(SEWER —) SLANT
(SHEPHERD'S —) REED LARIGOT
CHALUMEAU
(SNAKE-CHARMER'S —) PUNGI
(TOBACCO —) GUN CLAY BRIAR
BRIER CUTTY HOOKA STRAW
CALEAN DUDEEN HOOKAH
BULLDOG CHIBOUK CHILLUM
CORNCOB BILLIARD CALABASH
MEERSCHAUM
(TOY —) HEWGAG
(VERTICAL —) STACK LAMPHOLE
(WATER — FOR ENGINE) SLOUCH
(4 LENGTHS OF —) FOURBLE
(PREF.) AUL(O) SIPHON(O)
SOLEN(O) SYRING(O) TUBI TUBO
TUBULI TUBULO
PIPECLAY CAM CAUM
PIPED DRUNK JETTED
PIPEFISH EARL LONGJAW
NEEDLEFISH
PIPELAYER YARNER
PIPESTEM STOPPEL STOPPLE
PIPETTE PIPET TASTER
PIPEWORT HATPIN WOOLWEED
PIPING HOSE SOFT VERY CRYING
ROULEAU WAILING WEEPING
TRANQUIL
PIPING CROW CASSICAN
FLUTEBIRD
PIPIRI PITIRRI
PIPISTRELLE BAT NOCTULE
PIPIT PEEP TEETAN WEEKEEN
CHEEPER SKYLARK TIETICK
TITLARK TITLING WAGTAIL
LINGBIRD TWITLARK
PIPPIN PIP APPLE PEPPIN RIBSTON
PIPSISSEWA EVERGREEN
WINTERGREEN
PIQUANCY SALT ZEST JUICE
FLAVOR GINGER TARTNESS
PIQUANT BOLD RACY JUICY
NUTTY SALTY SHARP SPICY
TASTY ZESTY LIVELY SEVERE
CUTTING PEPPERY PUNGENT
POIGNANT STINGING
PIQUE FRET GOAD PEAK PICK PIKE
PYKE TICK ANNOY PRISE SNUFF
SPITE STING HARASS MALICE
NETTLE PRITCH STRUNT CHIGGER
OFFENSE PROVOKE UMBRAGE
IRRITATE MARCELLA
PIRACY CAPTURE PIRATISM
PIRAGUA CANOE DUGOUT
PIROGUE PETTIAGUA
PIRANHA PIRAI CARIBE PIRAYA
PIRARUCU PAICHE ARAPAIMA
PIRATE CAPER ROVER ROBBER
VIKING CATERAN CORSAIR
PICKEER SCUMMER ALGERINE
MAROONER PICAROON
BUCCANEER SALLEEMAN
(— FLAG) ROGER BLACKJACK
PIRENE (FATHER OF —) ASOPUS
ACHELOUS
(MOTHER OF —) METOPE
(SON OF —) CENCHRIAS
PIRIPIRI BIRK BIRCH MAPAN
PIRL SPIN TWINE TWIST REVOLVE
PIRN QUILL BOBBIN PIRNIE
SPINDLE
PIROGUE CANOE PERIOQUE
PIROPLASM BABESIA
PIROSHKI PIROGEN
PISCINA POOL TANK BASIN
SACRARY LAVATORY SACRARIUM
PISE CAJON PISAY
PISHOGUE CHARM SPELL SORCERY
WITCHERY
PISMIRE ANT EMMET
PISOLITE PEASTONE
PISTACHIO FISTIC PISTICK
PISTIL CHIVE CARPEL UMBONE
POINTEL
(PL.) GYNECIUM
(PREF.) GYN(AE)(AEO)(E)(EO)(O)
GYNAECO GYNANDRO GYNECO
(SUFF.) GYN
PISTILLATE FEMALE
PISTOL DAG GAT GUN POP ROD
BULL COLT DAGG IRON TACK
FLUTE RIFLE STICK BARKER
BUFFER BULDER BULLER CANNON
DRAGON HEATER POTGUN RIFFLE
ROSCOE BULLDOG DUNGEON
SHOOTER TICKLER DERINGER
PETRONEL REPORTER REVOLVER
PEPPERBOX
(TOY —) SPARKLER
PISTON BUCKET FORCER PALLET
SUCKER EMBOLUS PLUNGER
(— HUB) SPIDER
PIT PET POT PUT BURY CIST DELF
DELL DISC DISK FOSS HELL HOLE
KHUD KIST LAKE MINE PLAY PUTT
SILO SINK SUMP SWAG TURN
WEEM WELL ABYSM ABYSS
CRYPT DELFT DITCH FOSSA
FOVEA FROST GRAVE LEACH
MATCH PITCH PORUS SLACK
SLUIG TREAD AREOLE BORROW
BUNKER KERNEL OPPOSE RADDLE
WALLOW ABADDON ALVEOLA
AMPULLA BOTHROS CHARPIT
FOSSULA HEATER POTGUN PINHOLE
LATRINE MEGARON PINHOLE
VARIOLE WINNING CESSPOOL
CYPHELLA DOWNFALL FAVEOLUS
FENESTRA POCKMARK PUNCTULE
WELLHOLE

(— FOR BAKING) IMU UMU
(— FOR OFFERINGS) BOTHROS
(— OF STOMACH) MARK WIND
ANTICARDIUM
(— OF THEATER) GROUND
PARTERRE
(— ON COCKROACH HEAD)
FENESTRA
(— ON LICHENS) LACUNA
CYPHELLA
(— SACRED TO DEMETER)
MEGARON
(AUTHOR OF —) NORRIS
(BITTER —) STIPPEN
(BOTTOMLESS —) ABYSS ABADDON
BARATHRUM
(CHARACTER IN —) PAGE WESS
LAURA CURTIS GRETRY JADWIN
SHELDON CORTHELL CRESSLER
DEARBORN
(COAL —) HEUCH HEUGH
WINNING
(FODDER —) SILO
(MAORI —) RUA
(MIRY —) SLUIG
(RIFLE —) SANGAR
(ROOFED —) CIST KIST
(SALT —) VAT PEZOGRAPH
(SAND —) BUNKER
(SMALL —) AREOLE LACUNA
STAPLE
(TANNING —) LIME LAYER LEACH
HANDLER LAYAWAY SUSPENDER
(PREF.) BOTHR(I)(IO)(O) FOVEI
PITA PITO YUCCA AOUIAN
PITCH DIP FIT KEY LAB MEL PIC
BUCK CANT CHAT CODE COOK
DING FALL FORK HURL PECK PICK
PLUG RAKE TELL TONE TOSS
ABODE BOOST BUNCH CHUCK
FLING LABOR LURCH PLANT
SLENT SLOPE SPIEL THROW
TWIRL BINDER DIRECT ENCAMP
FILLER LENGTH MALTHA MANJAK
PLUNGE SQUARE TOTTER
TUMBLE VOLLEY WICKET
CURRENT NARRATE ALKITRAN
OVERHANG
(— AT A MARK) LAG
(— FROM FIR TREES) ALKITRAN
(— OF HELIX) JAW
(— TENT) TELD
(ABOVE —) SHARP
(AUCTION —) SETBACK
(BASEBALL —) CURVE STRIKE
CRIPPLE SPITTER FADEAWAY
KNUCKLER SPITBALL BRUSHBACK
(BELOW —) FLAT
(COBBLER'S —) CODE
(FULL —) VOLLEY
(GLANCE —) MANJAK MANJACK
(HIGH —) BLOOPER
(HIGHEST —) PRIDE
(IDENTITY IN —) UNISON
(MINERAL —) BITUMEN
(PREF.) MISERI
PITCH APPLE COPEI CUPAY
PITCHBLENDE CLEVEITE
PITCHED SET
(PREF.) (— BELOW BASS) CONTRA
PITCHER JUG JACK OLLA PILL PRIG
BUIRE CROCK CRUET GALON
GORGE GOTCH AFTABA CROUKE

GALLON HURLER POURIE STRAIN
URCEUS CANETTE CHUCKER
FLINGER GROWLER STARTER
STOPPER TWIRLER URCEOLE
AIGUIERE ASCIDIUM OENOCHOE
SOUTHPAW MOUNDSMAN
(— AND CATCHER) BATTERY
(— FOR BEER) GROWLER
(— OF ORCHID) BUCKET
(— SHAPED LIKE MAN) TOBY
(— WITH ONE HANDLE) URCEUS
(BULGING —) GOTCH
(EARTHEN —) GEORG GORGE
(RELIEF —) FIREMAN
(RELIEF —S) BULLPEN
(REMOVE — FROM BASEBALL GAME)
DERRICK
(WIDEMOUTHED —) EWER
PITCHER PLANT BISCUIT FLYTRAP
FEVERCUP FOXGLOVE WATERCUP
NEPENTHES SKUNKWEED
PITCHFORK EVIL PICK PIKE PICKEL
SHEPPECK PITCHPIKE
(THATCHER'S —) GROOM
(PL.) HARD
PITCHHOLE CAHOT
PITCHMAN VENDER SALESMAN
PITCH PINE THYME
PITCH PIPE TUNER EPITONION
PITCHSTONE RETINITE
PITCHY BLACK
PITEOUS MEAN PALTRY PITIFUL
MERCIFUL MOURNFUL PIERCING
PITFALL PIT FALL TRAP SNARE
DANGER TRAPFALL
PITH JET PUT SAP CORE GIST
MEAT PULP PUTT SOLA HEART
VIGOR ENERGY KERNEL MARROW
ESSENCE EXTRACT MEDULLA
NUCLEUS PAPYRUS STRENGTH
(PREF.) MEDULLI METR(O) PULPE
PULPI PULPO
PITH HELMET TOPI TOPEE
PITHINESS BREVITY
PITHON (FATHER OF —) MICAH
PITH TREE AMBATCH
PITHY CRISP MEATY SAPPY TERSE
STRONG CONCISE LACONIC
MARROWY
PITIABLE SAD POOR SEELY WOFUL
RUEFUL WOEFUL FORLORN
PITIFUL
PITIFUL MEAN MEEK RUTH SILLY
SORRY PALTRY RUEFUL TENDER
HANGDOG RUESOME RUTHFUL
MERCIFUL PATHETIC
PITILESS GRIM CRUEL STERN
STONY BRASSY SAVAGE
RUTHLESS UNPITIED MERCILESS
PITMAN GEORDIE
PITTANCE BIT ALMS DOLE GIFT
MITE SONG TRIFLE BEQUEST
PITTED FOVEATE OPPOSED
PUNCTATE ALVEOLATE
PITTER STONER
PITTHEUS (DAUGHTER OF —)
AETHRA
(FATHER OF —) PELOPS
(PUPIL OF —) THESEUS
PITURI BEDGERY PITCHERY
PITY RUE MEAN MOAN PETE PITE
RUTH MERCY PIETY REIVE SCATH
BEMOAN PATHOS MERCIFY

REMORSE WAESUCK CLEMENCY SYMPATHY COMPASSION

PIVOT TOE CRUX SLEW SLUE TURN HEART CENTER SLOUGH WORDLE GUDGEON TRAVERSE TRUNNION

PIVOTAL POLAR CENTRAL TROCHOID

(— POINT) KNUCKLE

PIVOTING DISHRAG

PIVOT STAND PEDESTAL

PIXILATED DAFFY DOTTY DRUNK PIXIE BEMUSED PUCKISH TOUCHED CONFUSED

PIXY ELF FAIRY PYGMY ROGUE IMPISH RASCAL SPRITE PUCKISH ROGUISH

PIZE OATH PISE CURSE

PLACABLE WEAK QUIET PACABLE PEACEFUL YIELDING FORGIVING

PLACARD BILL POST TITLE POSTER TICKET AFFICHE REDLINE STOMACHER

PLACATE CALM GENTLE PACIFY PLEASE SOOTHE APPEASE FORGIVE

PLACE L DO BIT FIX PUT SET AREA HOLE LIEU PLAT PLOT POSE POST RANK ROOM SEAT SITE SITU SPOT STEL STEP STOW TEXT VICE YARK BEING ESTER ESTRE HOUSE JOINT LOCUS PLAZA POINT POSIT SCENE SITUS STALL STATE STEAD STELL STOUR WHERE BESTOW CHARGE GROUND IMPOSE INVEST LAYOUT LOCALE LOCATE OFFICE POSSIE ROOMTH ALLODGE ARRANGE DEPOSIT KITCHEN STATION ABDITORY ALLOCATE DIGGINGS EMPORIUM LOCATION POSITION

(— ALONE) ISOLATE

(— ALTERNATELY) STAGGER

(— APART) ENISLE

(— BEFORE) APPOSE PREFIX

(— BY FORCE) PILT

(— CROSSWISE) THWART

(— FISH IN SALTING BIN) KENCH

(— FOR CATTLE) CAMP

(— FOR DUMPING RUBBISH) SHOOT

(— FOR HAWKING) RIVER

(— FOR MILKING COWS) LOAN

(— FOR MORTAR AND BRICK) FROG

(— FOR PHEASANTS) STEW

(— FOR PRAYERS) IDGAH

(— FOR RABBITS) WARREN

(— FOR RECEPTION) RECEIPT

(— FOR RUBBISH DEPOSITS) LAYSTALL

(— FOR SEETHING) STEW

(— FOR SLEEPING) BED BUNK DOSS FLOP LAIR LIBKIN

(— FOR STROLLING) PROMENADE

(— FOR TORTURE) CATASTA

(— FOR TRAINING HORSES) LONGE

(— FROM WHICH JURY IS TAKEN) VENUE

(— IN) INNEST

(— IN COMPACT MASS) STOW

(— IN ORDER) ARRAY ENRANK

(— IN WATERFALL) LEAP

(— OF AMUSEMENT) GAFF

(— OF ASSEMBLY) AGORA CURIA KGOTLA SYNAGOG

(— OF BLOODSHED) ACELDAMA

(— OF BURIAL) AHU KIL KILL LAIR GRAVE LAYSTOW CATACOMB CEMETERY GOLGOTHA LAYSTALL

(— OF BUSINESS) BANK AGENCY KNACKERY

(— OF CONCEALMENT) DEN BOMA BLIND STALE HIDING HIDEOUT HIDEAWAY

(— OF CONFINEMENT) BRIG CAGE COOP LIMBO PRISON BULLPEN

(— OF CONFUSION) BABEL TROYTOWN

(— OF CREMATION) GHAT

(— OF CRUCIFIXION) GOLGOTHA

(— OF DESTRUCTION) ABADDON

(— OF DETENTION) BAGNIO

(— OF DWELLING) WANE

(— OF ENTERTAINMENT) INN JOINT DANCERY HANGOUT HOSTELRY

(— OF EXERTION) ARENA

(— OF EXILE) PATMOS

(— OF IDYLLIC BEAUTY) XANADU

(— OF MISERY) HELL

(— OF NETHER DARKNESS) EREBUS

(— OF NOISE) BABEL

(— OF PROTECTION) PORT SCUG

(— OF REFUGE) ARK BAST HOLD ASYLUM ADULLAM HIDEOUT

(— OF RESIDENCE) SOIL DOMICILE

(— OF RESORT) PURLIEU

(— OF RESTRAINT) LIMBO PINFOLD

(— OF SACRIFICE) ALTAR

(— OF SAFETY) GRITH HAVEN WARRANT

(— OF SECURITY) GRITH ASYLUM CORRAL HARBOR GARRISON

(— OF SHELTER) LEW HOLD JOUK COVER

(— OF SUBMISSION) CANOSSA

(— OF TORMENT) GOLGOTHA

(— OF WORSHIP) HEIAU BETHEL CHAPEL CHURCH DESERT SHRINE TEMPLE GURDWARA SYNAGOGUE

(— SIDE BY SIDE) APPOSE

(— STRUCK BY LIGHTNING) BIDENTAL

(— WHERE FOOD IS KEPT) LARDER

(— WHERE MEAT IS SMOKED) BUCAN BUCCAN

(— WHERE OUTCASTS GATHER) HELL

(— WHERE ROADS CROSS) LEET

(— WHERE STREAM IS RAPID) SHARP

(— WHERE TROOPS HALT OVERNIGHT) ETAPE

(— WHERE 4 OR MORE WAYS MEET) CARFAX

(BOGGY —) SLACK SLUMP

(BREEDING —) NIDUS LOOMERY SEMINARY PELICANRY

(CHIEF —) HEADSHIP

(CIRCULAR —) ORBELL

(CONFINED —) CRIB

(CONSECRATED —) HIERON

(DRINKING —) BOOZER MUMHOUSE

(DRY —) SEARING

(DWELLING —) BY BYE DEN SEE BAWN HAFT HIVE HOME ABODE BEING HOUSE HOWFF SOJOURN HABITACLE

(EATING —) CAFE GRUBBERY

(EMPTY —) BLANK SPACE

(ENCLOSED —) BIN HAY WORTH SEVERAL CLOISTER

(ESSENTIAL —) EYE

(FAMILIAR —) KITH

(FAULTY — IN THREAD) TRAP

(FILTHY —) STY

(FIRST —) BLUE LEAD STRAIGHT

(FORTIFIED —) LIS LISS CASTLE FASTNESS

(GARRISONED —) PRESIDIO

(GATHERING —) SHOP AGORA FOYER JOINT LESCHE

(GRASSY —) LAUND

(HALTING —) MARAH

(HIDING —) MEW CACHE HIDEL HOARD STASH COVERT HIDDELS RETREAT STOWAWAY

(HIGH —) EMINENCE

(HOLLOW —) GULF HOLE HOLL SCOOP CAVITY ALBERCA SINKHOLE

(INHABITED —) ABADI

(LANDING —) GHAT HARD HITHE LEVEE SCALE BUNDER PALACE HELIPORT

(LEVEL —) PLANILLA

(LODGING —) CAMP LOGIS BIDING BILLET LIBKEN

(LOOKOUT —) TOOT

(LURKING —) HOLD HOLE HOARD HULSTER

(MARKET —) AGORA TRONE MARKET RIALTO

(MARSHY —) SLEW SLOO SLUE SLUMP SLOUGH

(MEETING —) CLUB PNYX COURT FORUM GUILD TRYST TOLSEL TOLZEY AMBALAM KLAVERN TINWALD

(MUDDY —) SOIL

(NESTING —) JUG NIDARY

(OPEN —) ENAJIM

(OTHERWORLDLY —) EMPYREAN

(POLLING —) BOOTH

(RAVELED —) FRAY

(REMOTE —) JERICHO

(RESTING —) LAY CAMP FORM GIST LAIR PARAO CRADLE

(ROCKY —) ROCHER

(SACRED —) HAREM HIERON CHAITYA SANCTUM

(SALTING —) SALADERO

(SECRET —) LAIR ADYTUM CORNER CRANNY

(SECURE —) REDOUBT

(SHADY —) GLOOM SWALE FRESCADE UMBRACLE

(SHELTERED —) NOOK SCUG SUCCOR

(SPAWNING —) REDD

(STEEP —) PITCH

(STOPPING —) HALT MANZIL

(STORAGE —) DEPOT HOARD LODGE SPICERY STORAGE STOWAGE DOCKYARD

(SWAMPY —) FLUSH SOUGH

(THIRD —) SHOW

(TIGHT —) JAM JAMB

(WATCH —) TOOTHILL

(WATERING —) ABREUVOIR

(WEAK —) BLOT

(WET —) DANK

(WORN —) ABRASION

(WRETCHED —) DEN MISERY

(PL.) LOCI

(PREF.) CHOR(O) LOCO TOP(O)

(DRY —) XER(O)

(TAKES — OF) PRO VICE

(SUFF.) ESE THESIS THESTE THETIC TOPE TOPY

(— FOR) ARIUM ORIUM ORY

(— OF) ARY

(— OF DOING) ERY

(— OF GROWING, BREEDING) ERY

(— OF KEEPING) ERY

(— OF SELLING) ERY

PLACEBO SOP TOADY VESPERS PARASITE

PLACED FIXED BESTEAD

(— ON ITS SIDE) LAZY

PLACEHOLDER VARIABLE

PLACE-NAME TOPONYM

PLACENTA MAZA REPLUM

(PREF.) MAZ(O)

PLACENTAL MAZIC

PLACID CALM COOL EVEN MEEK MILD SOFT DOWNY QUIET SUANT SUENT GENTLE SEDATE SERENE SMOOTH PACIFIC TRANQUIL THROBLESS

PLACKET FENT SPARE WOMAN CLOSING PETTICOAT

PLAGAL MODE

(PREF.) HYPO

PLAGIARISM CRIB PLAGIUM

PLAGIARIST TAKER COPYIST

PLAGIARIZE CRIB LIFT STEAL

PLAGUE DUN IMP POX VEX FRAB FRET GNAW PEST TWIT BESET CURSE DEATH DEUCE HARRY QUALM TEASE TRAIK WEARY WORRY WOUND BOTHER BURDEN HAMPER HARASS INFEST PESTER PESTIS SORROW WANION DESTROY MURRAIN PERPLEX SCOURGE TORMENT TORTURE TROUBLE BEPESTER HANDICAP OUTBREAK PESTILENCE

(PREF.) LEMO LOIMO PESTI PESTO

PLAGUY VERY PESKY VEXING MURRAIN PESTFUL INFERNAL

PLAICE FLUKE FLATFISH FLOUNDER

PLAID CALM FAKE MAUD PLOD TARTAN BRACKEN BRECHAN

PLAIN DRY LOW BALD BARE CHOL EASY EVEN FLAT OPEN PLAT RIFE VEGA WALD WOLD BLAIR BLUNT BROAD CAMPO CORAH FIELD FRANK GREEN GROSS LAUND LEVEL LLANO MOURN NAKED PAMPA PROSE ROUND SEBKA SECCO SILLY SMALL SOBER TALAO UNORN BEMOAN BEWAIL CHASTE CUESTA GRAITH HOMELY HONEST HUMBLE LENTEN MACHAR MAIDAN PARAMO PUSZTA RUSTIC SABANA SEVERE SIMPLE SINGLE SMOOTH ARTLESS EVIDENT GENUINE IDAVOLL LEGIBLE OBVIOUS POPULAR SAVANNA TERRACE UNARTED APPARENT CAMPAIGN DISTINCT

EVERYDAY EXPLICIT FAMILIAR
HOMEMADE HOMESPUN
ITHAVOLL PALPABLE PIEDMONT
SEMPLICE STRAIGHT
(— AMONG TREES) LAUND
(— OF ARGENTINA) PAMPA
(— OF RUSSIA) STEPPE
(ALKALI —S) USAR
(ALLUVIAL —) APRON CARSE
HAUGH
(ARCTIC —) TUNDRA
(DESOLATE —) CHOL
(HEATHY —) LANDE
(LOW-LYING —) MACHAR MACHAIR
(MARSHY —) BLAIR
(NOT —) MEALYMOUTHED
(SALINE —) SEDKA SEDKHA
(SALT —) SALADA
(SLOPING —) HOPE CUESTA
CONOPLAIN
(SMALL GRASSY —) CAMAS
CAMASS QUAMASH
(TREELESS —) BLED TUNDRA
SAVANNA SAVANNAH
(UNOCCUPIED —) DESERT
(PL.) VIZCACHA
(PREF.) LITI PEDI(O) PLAN(I)
PLAIN CHANT CF
PLAINCLOTHESMAN SPLIT
PLAINLY FAIR BARELY FAIRLY
FLATLY SIMPLY BROADLY
FRANKLY DIRECTLY
PLAINNESS PROSE INNOCENCE
PLAINSMAN LLANERO
PLAINSONG GROUND
PLAINT WAIL PLANT LAMENT
COMPLAINT
PLAINTEXT CLEAR
PLAINTIFF SUER ACTOR ORATOR
PURSUER QUERENT
PLAINTIVE SAD CROSS PINING
DOLENTE ELEGIAC FRETFUL
MOANFUL PEEVISH PETTISH
DOLOROSO MANGENDO
PETULANT WAILSOME
SORROWFUL
PLAIT CUE PLY KNIT PAIR PLAT
RUFF TURN WALE WAND BRAID
BREAD CRIMP FETCH FITCH
PEDAL PINCH QUEUE QUILL
QUIRK TRACE TRESS WEAVE
BORDER DOUBLE GATHER
GOFFER PLEACH PLEAT RUMPLE
TUSCAN WIMPLE WRITHE
CRIMPLE FROUNCE PIGTAIL
SCALLOM COMPLECT
(— FOR HAT) DUNSTABLE
(— OF STRAW) MILAN TRACE
(SERIES OF —S) KILTING
PLAITED PLISSE DEVIOUS PLICATE
PLAITING PLISSE LEGHORN
NATTIER
PLAN AIM ART LAY WAY CARD
CAST COUP DART FOOT GAME
HANG IDEA MIND MOOD PLAT
PLOT REDE WENT ALLOW BRIEF
CHART DARTY DRAFT DRIFT
ETTLE FRAME HOBBY MODEL
REACH SHAPE TRACE ADVICE
AGENDA BEREDE BUDGET CIPHER
DECOCT DESIGN DEVISE ENGINE
FIGURE INTEND LAYOUT METHOD
MODULE ORDAIN PROJET

SCHEMA SCHEME SURVEY
THEORY ARRANGE CONCERT
CONCOCT COUNSEL DRAWING
FORELAY NOSTRUM OUTLINE
PATTERN PROJECT PURPOSE
THOUGHT COGITATE CONSPIRE
CONTRIVE ENGINEER FORECAST
FOREGAME LANDSKIP MEDITATE
PLATFORM PRACTICE SCHEDULE
SKELETON STRATEGY CALCULATE
(— AHEAD) FORECAST
(— OF FUTURE PROCEDURE)
PROGRAM
(— ON A FLOOR) EPURE
(— TOGETHER) CONCERT
(CUNNING —) WHEEZE
(GROUND —) TRACE GRUNDRISS
(INSURANCE —) TONTINE
(5-YEAR —) PIATILETKA
PLANARIAN PLATODE TRICLAD
FLATWORM PLATYHELMINTH
PLANE AXCI BEAD DADO FACE
FLAT HOLL MILL AXIAL CHUTE
CROZE FACET GLIDE HOULE
HOWEL LEVEL MESON SHOOT
STICK TABLE WHISK AEQUOR
BEADER HOLLOW REEDER
ROUTER SMOKER SNIBEL
COURIER INSHAVE JOINTER
NONSKED SURFACE WITCHET
BULLNOSE DECLINER LEEBOARD
MERIDIAN RECLINER SYCAMORE
TRAVERSE
(— CURVE) ROSE
(— HANDLE) TOAT TOTE
(— OF CLEAVAGE) BACK
(— OF EARTH'S ORBIT) ECLIPTIC
(— OF ROCK) BED
(—S OF GUNNERY FIRE) SHEAF
(ENEMY —) BANDIT
(INCLINED —) RAMP SLIP
(MOLDING —) HOLL HOULE
HOLLOW
(PERSPECTIVE —) TABLE
(RABBET —) PLOW RABAT PLOUGH
REBATE FILLETER
(SLOPING —) CUESTA
PLANER JOINTER SURFACER
PLANER TREE HORNBEAM
SYCAMORE
PLANET SUN BODY IRIS JOVE
MARS MOON STAR EARTH GLOBE
HYLEG PLUTO SHREW VENUS
WORLD SATURN SPHERE URANUS
VULCAN ALMUTEN ANARETA
BENEFIC FORTUNE JUPITER
MERCURY NEPTUNE PRIMARY
CHASUBLE LUMINARY RECEPTOR
TERRELLA WANDERER
(— IN A NATIVITY) ALMUTEN
(BENEVOLENT —) FORTUNE
(CONTROLLING —) LORD
(HYPOTHETICAL —) VULCAN
(MALEFICENT —) SHREW
(RULING —) DOMINATOR
(SMALL —) IRIS ASTEROID
TERRELLA
PLANETARIUM ORRERY
PLANETOID UNDINE ASTEROID
PLANE TREE CHINAR PLATAN
COTONIER PLANTAIN
SYCAMORE
PLANET-STRICKEN SIDERATED

PLANISPHERE ASTROLABE
METEORSCOPE
PLANK CLAM HOOD PATA PLAT
RAIL SOLE WAIR BOARD CLAMP
PATTA SHIDE SWALE THEAL
DAGGER FLITCH PLANCH ROOFER
STRAKE CLAPPER CROSSER
DEPOSIT MADRIER RIBBAND
STEALER FOREPOLE GARBOARD
STRINGER
(— AS PROTECTION) SHOLE
(— OVER BROOK) CLAM
(— 6 FT. X 1 FT.) WARE
(—S IN BRIDGE) CHESS
(—S LESS THAN 6 FT.) DEAL
(CURVED —) SNYING
(ROUGHHEWN —) SLAB
PLANK DRAG RUBBER
PLANK END STUB
PLANKING GORE RACK HATCH
SWALE CEILING LAGGING
BERTHING BRATTICE GARBOARD
WATERWAY
PLANKSHEER WATERWAY
PLANKTON KRILL SESTON
PLANNED PREPENSE
PLANNING (TECHNIQUE FOR —)
PERT
PLANOMILLER SLABBER
PLANT AJI BED SET SOW ACHE
ALGA ARUM BURY CROP FAST
HERB HIDE MORE RAPE SALT
SEED SLIP TREE WORT ABACA
AGAVE AJWAN ARGEL CAROA
CHIVE CLOTE CLOVE EARLY
FANCY GRAFT HEATH INULA
INULA JALAP KEIKI ORACH PITCH
SEDUM SHRUB YERBA ACACIA
AJOWAN AKELEY ALASAS
ANNUAL BEDDER CACOON
CALALU CARROT COKERY
COTTON DERRIS DIBBLE ESCAPE
FICOID FORCER GALAXY GROWTH
KARREE LENTIL LIGGER MANUKA
MEDICK MESCAL ORPINE PEPINO
SETTLE SPRING ULLUCU YARROW
ABANDON ALKANET ALYSSUM
BREWERY CARDOON CONCEAL
CUTTING DAGGERS ENCELIA
HAEMONY IMPLANT JIKUNGU
LETTUCE PALMIET PICKERY
RAMBONG SAWMILL ABUTILON
AGERATUM AGRIMONY
ANGLEPOD BIENNIAL BLUEBELL
CONSOUND DRAWLING
DYEHOUSE EMERGENT
ENGINERY FUMEROOT
GASWORKS GROMWELL
HAWKWEED HONEWORT
KNAPWEED LARKSPUR
PHILODENDRON
(— BY SPADING) SPIT
(— DEEPLY) HEEL
(— DISEASE) NECROSIS
(— FIRMLY) BRACE
(— GROWING IN WATER) BILDERS
HYDROPHYTE
(— IN ROWS) DRILL
(— OF MEADOWS) POOPHYTE
(— OF THE DEAD) ASPHODEL
(— OUTGROWTH) OVULE
(— ROOTED IN GROUND) LIANA
LIANE

(— SUPPORTING PARASITES)
SUSCEPT
(— TREE) MOTCH
(— WITH NO DISTINCT MEMBERS)
THALLUS
(— WITH THREE PISTILS) TRIGYN
(— WITH THREE STAMENS)
TRIANDER
(— 2ND CROP) ETCH
(AIR —) FLOPPERS
(ANCIENT —) CYCAD
(AQUATIC —) ALISMA NUPHAR
SUGAMO TAWKEE AMBULIA
AWLWORT FROGBIT DUCKWEED
PONDWEED PICKERELWEED
(AROMATIC —) MINT NARD BASIL
CUMIN TANSY THYME AMOMUM
CUMMIN CARAWAY DITTANY
ALBAHACA CALAMINT LAVENDER
SPIKENARD
(AUSTRALIAN —) LILAC STYLO
LIGNUM LANCEPOD
(BULBOUS —) GALTONIA
(CENTURY —) PITA
(CLIMBING —) VETCH LAWYER
ULLUCE ULLUCU CORALITA
(COMPOSITE —) SUCCORY
HAWKWEED SNEEZEWEED
(CONSECRATED —) HAOMA
(CREATED —) BARAMIN
(CREEPING —) IPECAC KAREAO
KAREAU PENNYWORT
(CROSSBRED —) HYBRID
(CRUSHING —) BREAKER
(DWARF —) CUMIN STUNT
(DYE —) WAD ANIL WOAD WULD
WOALD MADDER
(E. INDIAN —) JATI
(ETIOLATED —) ALBINO
(FIBER —) ALOE FLAX HEMP PITA
CAJUN RAMIE SISAL
(FLOWERING —) HOP ROSE DAISY
HOLLY POPPY ORCHID VIOLET
HAWTHORN LARKSPUR
POLYGALA PRIMROSE SNOWDROP
(FORAGE —) RAPE ALFALFA
DAINCHA
(FOSSIL —) CALAMITE
(GERMINATING —) SPIRE
(GRAIN —) TEFF
(HEDGE —) ESPINO
(HEMP —) FIMBLE
(IMMATURE —) KEIKI
(LEAFLESS —) ULEX DODDER
RESTIAD TRIURID
(MALE —) MAS MACRANDER
(MARSH —) FERN CALLA JUNCUS
CATTAIL BUCKBEAN
(MEDICINAL —) ALOE HERB ERICA
ARNICA CATNEP CATNIP IPECAC
SIMPLE ACONITE BONESET
GENTIAN LOBELIA CAMOMILE
(NON-FLOWERING —) FERN
(NURSERY —) SEEDLING
(PEPPER —) ARA
(PHILIPPINE —) ABACA
(PISTILLATE —) FEMALE
(POISONOUS —) COWBANE
DEATHIN SAMNITIS
(POTTED —) BONSAI LANTANA
(POWER —) HYDRO
(PRICKLY —) BRIAR BRIER CACTUS
CARDON NETTLE TEASEL

TEAZEL PRICKFOOT
(PUNGENT —) PEPPER
(RAPIDLY-GROWING —) FILLER
(REEDY —) SPRIT
(RENDERING —) KNACKERY
(SENSITIVE —) MIMOSA
(SIBERIAN —) BADAN
(SPINOUS —) KANTIARA
(STAMINATE —) HUSBAND
(SUBMERGED —) ENALID
(SUCCULENT —) ALOE HERB
GASTERIA HAWORTHIA
HOUSELEEK
(SWORD-LEAVED —) LEVERS
(THALLOPHYTIC —) LICHEN
(TRAILING —) ARBUTUS
(TUFTED —) DRYAS
(TWINING —) SMILAX WINDER
CLIMBER BINDWEED SCAMMONY
(UNIDENTIFIED —) HORDOCK
(WATER —) LIMU LOTUS AQUATILE
STARFRUIT
(WEEDY —) DOCK KNAWEL
(YOUNG —) SET SPRINGER
(PL.) FLORA
(PREF.) BOTAN(O) PHYT(I)(O)
(SUFF.) AD CHORE COCCUS
OECIA PHYTA PHYTE(S) PHYTIA
PHYTIC PHYTUM
PLANTAGENET ANGEVIN
PLANTAIN COCK PALA ABACA
ALISMA FINGER PISANG WABRON
BENTING NETLEAF RIBWORT
SITFAST BALISIER BUCKHORN
FIREWEED FLEAWORT ISPAGHUL
PLANTANO RATSBANE RIBGRASS
ROADWEED WAYBREAD
PLANTAIN EATER TOURACO
SPLITBEAK
PLANTAIN LILY FUNKIA
PLANTATION PEN HOLT WALK
FINCA GROVE BOSKET BOWERY
COLONY ESTATE SHAMBA SPRING
YERBAL CAFETAL FAZENDA
NOPALRY PINETUM THICKET
ARBUSTUM HACIENDA TRAPICHE
VINEYARD
(HEMP —) LATE
(WILLOW —) SALICETUM
PLANTED LISTED
PLANTER SNAG COLON SOWER
FARMER SETTLER PLANTATOR
PLANTING GROVE SATION
PLANTING STICK DIBBLE
PLANT LOUSE APHID PSYLLID
PUCERON HOMOPTER
PLANTS
(SUFF.) ACEAE ALES INEAE
PLAQUE CHIP PINAX PLATE
PLATEAU SARCOID NAMEPLATE
STOMACHER
PLASH LIP DASH BLASH PLOSH
PLOUT PLEACH PUDDLE SPLASH
SPATTER SPECKLE
PLASMA LATEX PLASM
PLASTER CAST DAUB HARL LEEP
LOCK TEER CLEAM GATCH PARGE
SLICK SMALM STAFF TOPIC TREAT
CHARGE CHUNAM CLATCH
GAGING MORTAR PARGET
SPARGE STOOTH STUCCO BLISTER
MALAGMA DIACULUM DIAPALMA
SINAPISM VESICANT CATAPLASM

(— BETWEEN LATHS) CAT
(— OF PARIS) GESSO GYPSUM
(— WITH COW DUNG) LEEP
(COARSE —) GROUT
(MEDICAL —) SALVE TOPIC TREAT
CHARGE SPARADRAP
(MUSTARD —) SINAPISM
(2 COATS OF —) RENDERSET
PLASTERBOARD GYPSUM
PLASTERED DRUNK SOUSED
SWACKED
PLASTERER DAUBER DAUBSTER
PARGETER SPREADER
PLASTERING KEY SETWORK
ROUGHCAST
PLASTIC FOAM RICH SIRUP LABILE
PLIANT ACETATE CATALIN
CRYSTAL DUCTILE FICTILE
ORGANIC CREATIVE FLEXIBLE
LAMINATE MELAMINE PHENOLIC
TECTONIC UNCTUOUS
FORMATIVE
PLASTICIZER CAMPHOR
PLASTRON DICKEY CALIPEE
PLAT BED FLAT FOOD PLAN PLOT
SLAP BRAID LEVEL PLACE PLAIN
PLAIT BUFFET WATTLE ARRANGE
FLATTEN PLATEAU QUADRAT
PLATANIST SUSU
PLATANUS PLANE COTONIER
SYCAMORE
PLATBAND IMPOST LINTEL
EPISTYLE
PLATE BAT CAP CUT DIP DOD EAR
FIN GIB WEB ANAL BACK BRIN
CASE CAST CURB DIAL DISK DROP
FISH GILL GONG GULA HOME
HOOF LAME LEAF MOLD NAIL
ORAL RETE ROSE SHOE SHUT
SLAB SOLE STUD TACE TRAY
AMPYX ANODE BASAL BELLY
BLADE CHAIR CLAMP CLEAT
CLOUT FACIA FENCE FLOOR
FLUKE FORCE GLAND GUARD
GULAR LAMEL PATEN PYGAL
SCALE SCUTE SHEET SHOLE SLICE
STAMP STAVE STRAP TABLE
TASSE TERNE TRAMP UNCUS
WATER ADORAL BAFFLE BRIDGE
BUCKLE CASTER CIRCLE CLICHE
COLLAR COPPER COSTAL CRUSTA
DAMPER DASHER EPIGNE FASCIA
FILLER FOLIUM FRIZEL GENIAL
GNOMON GORGET GUSSET
LABIAL LAMINA LOREAL MASCLE
MATRIX MENTAL MENTUM
MOTHER PALLET PATTEN PLATEN
RADIAL SCREEN SCUTUM SEPTUM
SERVER SHEATH SHROUD SPLINT
STAPLE TARSUS TEGMEN TURTLE
TYMPAN VESSEL BESAGNE
BOLSTER BRACKET BRACTEA
BUCCULA BUCKLER CHARGER
CLYPEUS COASTER CORNULE
CORONET CRYSTAL DOUBLER
ETCHING FRIZZLE FRONTAL
GRAVURE HUMERAL INKBLOT
MORDANT MYOTOME NEPTUNE
PETALON PRIMARY ROSTRAL
ROUNDEL SPANGLE STEALER
STEELER TERGITE TESSERA
VENTRAL ASSIETTE BEDPLATE
BIQUARTZ BRACHIAL CELLOCUT

DIASCOPE DRAWBACK ELECTRUM
EPIGYNUM EPIPROCT EPISTOME
FIREBACK FLOUNDER SKEWBACK
STAPLING STRINGER SUBPLATE
SURPRINT
(— COVERING KEYHOLE) DROP
(— COVERING MIDDLE EAR)
TEGMEN
(— IN AIRPLANE WING) SPOILER
(— IN BATTERY) GRID
(— IN ORGAN PIPE) LANGUET
(— IN STEAM BOILER) SPUT
DASHER
(— OF BALEEN) BLADE
(— OF BLAST FURNACE) TYMP
(— OF CTENOPHORE) COMB
(— OF GELATIN) BAT
(— OF GLASS) SLIDE
(— OF JAW) AURICLE
(— OF PRECIOUS METAL) BRACTEA
(— OF SOAP FRAME) SESS
(— OF SUNDIAL) GNOMON
(— ON FIREPLACE) BLOWER
(— ON LANCE SHAFT) VAMPLATE
(— ON PLOW) MOLDBOARD
(— ON SADDLE) SIDEBAR
(— ON SATCHEL STRAP) OLIVE
(— ON THROAT OF FISH) GULAR
(— ON WATERWHEEL) SHROUD
(—S OF CARDING MACHINE) ARCH
(—S OF GUN CARRIAGE) FLASK
(ARMOR —) SPLINT AILETTE
PALLETTE
(COLLECTION —) BROD
(COMMUNION —) PATEN
(DEEP —) MAZARINE
(DORSAL —) ELYTRUM ALINOTUM
(EARTHEN —) MUFFIN
(FASHION —) SWELL
(FIREPLACE —) IRONBACK
(FLAT —) APRON
(GOLD — ON FOREHEAD) PATA
PATTA
(GROOVED TRAM —) GULLY
GULLEY
(GUARD —) SHELL
(HINGED —) SHUT
(HOME —) DISH
(HOT —) GRILL GRILLE
(IRON —) CLOUT STAVE LATTEN
MARVER LAPSTONE SKEWBACK
MOLDBOARD TURNPLATE
TURNSHEET
(LARGE —) DOUBLER
(LOCK —) SELVEDGE
(NAME —) FACIA
(PERFORATED —) DOD GRID
WORTLE PINNULE
(PITCHER'S —) SLAB MOUND
(RIMLESS —) COUPE
(SIEVE —) LATTICE
(SIFTING —) TROMMEL
(THIN —) LAME LAMP LAMINA
LAMELLA
(THIN TIN —) TAIN LATTEN
TAGGERS
(WALL —) PAN RASEN TORSEL
(WOODEN —) TRENCHER
(PREF.) ELASM(O) LAMELLI
LAMIN(I) PLAC(O)
(SUFF.) **(COVERING —)** STEGE
STEGITE
PLATEAU PLAT PUNA FJELD

KAROO KARST TABLE CAUSSE
HAMADA MESETA NIVEAU
PARAMO SABANA UPLAND
ANASAZI PLATFORM
(PL.) BARRENS
PLATEHOLDER CASSETTE
PLATEN ROLL
PLATER VATMAN CLAIMER
COLLARMAN
PLATFORM TOP BANK BEMA DAIS
DECK DRIP DROP DUCK FLAT
GHAT KITE PACE PLAT STEP
WING APRON BENCH BLIND
BLOCK CHAIN DUKAN FLAKE
FLOAT HEIAU SOLEA STAGE
STAND STOEP STOOL STOOP
STULL STUMP TOLDO ARBOUR
AZOTEA BRIDGE DESIGN GANTRY
HURDLE ISLAND MACHAN
PAEPAE PALLET PERRON PILLAR
PODIUM PULPIT RUNWAY SETTLE
SLEDGE ALMEMAR BALCONY
BATTERY CATWALK ESTRADE
FORETOP GALLERY LANDING
LOGEION PADDOCK PATTERN
ROLLWAY ROSTRUM SKIDWAY
SOAPBOX TRIBUNE BARBETTE
FOOTPACE HUSTINGS SCAFFOLD
STALLAGE MORTARBOARD
(— FOR ACTORS) LOGEION
THEOLOGIUM
(— FOR ALTAR) PREDELLA
(— FOR DRYING FISH) FLAKE
(— FOR PUBLIC SPEAKING) BEMA
PODIUM TRIBUNE
(— FOR STORING FOOD) WHATA
(— IN CHURCH) SOLEA
(— IN SYNAGOGUE) ALMEMAR
(— IN TEMPLE) DUKAN
(— IN TREE) MACHAN
(— OF GALLOWS) DROP
(— ON RUNNERS) SLEDGE
(— ON STEAMER) SPONSON
(— ON TOP OF HOUSE) AZOTEA
(— ON WHEELS) SKID DOLLY FLOAT
(— TO SUPPORT MINERS) STULL
(BOARDING —) RAMBADE
(GUN —) BARBET SPONSON
BARBETTE
(LEADSMAN'S —) CHAIN
(MINE —) STULL SOLLAR SOLLER
(MOHAMMEDAN STONE —)
MASTABA
(MOUNTED —) SKID
(NAUTICAL —) FORETOP MAINTOP
ROUNDTOP
(ORE —) BUDDLE
(RAILROAD —) DOCK DOCKEN
TRAINWAY
(RAISED —) DAIS PYAL STAND
STOEP STOOL STOOP EXEDRA
LISSOM PANTALAN
(ROCK —) STANCE
(SLEEPING —) KANG
(STAIRCASE —) HALFPACE
HATHPACE
(WOOD —) PLANCHER
PLATING ARMOR SKIRT
PLATINUM COSTLY PLATINA
PLATITUDE TRUISM BROMIDE
DULLNESS STALENESS TRITENESS
PLATONIST IDEIST
PLATOON SQUAD VOLLEY

PELOTON PLOTTON
PLATTER DISH DISK LANX ASHET
GRAIL PLATE RECORD CHARGER
TRENCHER
PLATY MOON MOONFISH
PLATYPUS DUCKBILL DUCKMOLE
MALLANGONG
PLAUDIT APPLAUD APPROVAL
ENCOMIUM
(PL.) PRAISE APPLAUSE
PLAUSIBILITY COLOR
PLAUSIBLE FAIR OILY SNOD SLEEK
GLOSSY SMOOTH AFFABLE
POPULAR CREDIBLE PROBABLE
PROVABLE SPECIOUS SUITABLE
OSTENSIBLE
PLAY FUN JEU JIG RUN RUX TOY
AUTO BEAR COME DAFF DEAL
DICE DRAW FAIR GAME JEST
LAKE MOVE MUCK PLEE PUNT
ROMP SPIN TUNE WAKE CARRY
CHARM DALLY DRAMA ENACT
FLIRT FROST HORSE SHOOT SOTIE
SOUND SPIEL SPORT STUCK
WREAK YEDDE ACTION COMEDY
COQUET DANDLE DIVIDE FILLER
FROLIC GAMBLE GAMBOL GAMING
GHOSTS MUSERY NUMBER
PIDDLE ROLLIX TRIFLE CONSORT
CUTBACK DISPORT EXECUTE
EXPLOIT GUIGNOL HISTORY
HOLIDAY MIRACLE PAGEANT
PASSION PERFORM PRELUDE
STAGERY VENTURE BURLETTA
MORALITY SKITTLES MELODRAMA
(— A DOMINO) SET POSE
(— A PART) DO ACT ENTER
GAMMON GUIZARD
(— A PIPE) CHARM
(— ABOUT) SPANIEL
(— AGAINST) BUCK
(— AN INSTRUMENT) BOW BLOW
SWAY FINGER TWEEDLE
(— AT COURTSHIP) FLIRT
(— BAGPIPE) SKIRL DOODLE
DOUDLE
(— BY STROKES) STRIKE
(— FANFARE) FLOURISH
(— FAST AND LOOSE) PALTER
(— FIRST CARD) LEAD
(— FLORIDLY) DIVIDE
(— FOR TIME) STALL
(— GOLF BALL) DRIVE
(— IMPOSTER) MUMP
(— IN MUD) MUDLARK
(— IN POOL) BURST
(— IN STREAKS) FORK
(— IN TRIGGER) CREEP
(— JAZZ) BLOW
(— LEGATO) SUSTAIN
(— LOOSELY) WAVE
(— LOUT) SWAB SLUBBER
(— MEAN TRICKS) SHAB
(— NERVOUSLY) FIDGET
(— OF COLORS) IRIS
(— OF FOAM) HOOD
(— OF LIGHT) GLORY
(— ON WORDS) PUN CLENCH
CLINCH PARAGRAM CALEMBOUR
PARONOMASIA
(— THE BUFFOON) DROLL
(— THE BULLY) BLUSTER
(— THE FOOL) HOIT

(— THE HYPOCRITE) FACE
(— THE TOADY) SUPE
(— TRICKS) COD JAPE JINK
(— TRUANT) KIP WAG JOUK MICHE
MOOCH MOUCH PLUNK TRONE
MOOTCH
(— UNSKILLFULLY) STRUM FOOZLE
(— WITH) DANDLE
(AMOROUS —) GAME
(BOISTEROUS —) ROMP
(BRIDGE —) COUP ECHO SIGNAL
SQUEEZE
(END —) SHAKE
(FARCICAL —) SOTIE
(FOOTBALL —) DOWN KEEP SWING
KEEPER SAFETY AUDIBLE
COUNTER CUTBACK ROLLOUT
SPINNER
(IN —) ALIVE
(MASKED —) GUISE
(MIRACLE —) AUTO GUARY
MIRACLE
(RAPID CHESS —) SKITTLES
(USED IN —) LUSORY
(PL.) THEATER VANGELI
PLAYA BEACH SEBKA SALINA
SEBKHA
**PLAYBOY OF THE WESTERN
WORLD (AUTHOR OF —)** SYNGE
(CHARACTER IN —) QUIN KEOGH
MAHON SHAWN PEGEEN CHRISTY
FLAHERTY MARGARET
CHRISTOPHER
PLAY-BY-PLAY DETAILED
PLAYER IT CAD END BACK DUCK
SIDE ACTOR BLACK COLOR
GUARD BANKER BUSKER FEEDER
STAGER STROLL TENTER ALTOIST
FIELDER FORWARD GAMBLER
STRIKER TRIFLER TURQUET
BUDGETER GAMESTER
HORNSMAN STROLLER
(— IN CHESS) BLACK WHITE
(— IN CHOUETTE) CAPTAIN
(— OF JAZZ) CAT
(— WHO CUTS CARDS) PONE
(— WHO IS IT) HE
(— WHO SCORES ZERO) DUCK
(— WITH LOWEST SCORE) BOOBY
(BACKGAMMON —) TABLER
(BASEBALL —) SHORT SACKER
CATCHER FIELDER LEADOFF
PITCHER BACKSTOP
(BASKETBALL —) CAGEMAN
HOOPMAN HOOPSTER
(BOWLING —) LEAD
(CARD —) EAST HAND PONE WEST
BLIND DUMMY NORTH OMBRE
SOUTH JUNIOR SENIOR BRAGGER
DECLARER
(CRICKET —) LEG BOWLER INNING
(CROQUET —) MALLET
(DICE —) SHOOTER
(FLUTE —) AULETE
(FOOTBALL —) END GUARD SLANT
BUCKER CENTER TACKLE
BLOCKER FLANKER GRIDDER
SNAPPER FULLBACK HALFBACK
SCATBACK SLOTBACK
(KEY —) PIVOT
(LACROSSE —) HOME COVER
POINT ATTACK STICKMAN
(LEAPFROG —) BACK

(POKER —) AGE
(RUGBY —) SCRUM HOOKER
(SOCCER —) CAP INNER BOOTER
(STUPID —) HAM
(TENNIS —) SMASHER
(TWO OR MORE —S) PLATOON
(UNSKILLFUL —) DUB
(VOLLEYBALL —) SPIKER
(WEAK —) RABBIT
PLAYFUL SLY ELFIN MERRY FRISKY
GAMBOL JOCOSE LUSORY TOYISH
WANTON COLTISH GIOCOSO
JIGGISH JOCULAR TOYSOME
GAMESOME HUMOROUS
LARKSOME SPORTFUL SPORTIVE
KITTENISH
(IRRESPONSIBLY —) MISCHIEVOUS
PLAYFULLY SCHERZANDO
PLAYFULNESS FUN BANTER
GAMMICK GAMMOCK
PLAYGROUND OVAL CLOSE
TOTLOT PLAYSTOW PLAYSTEAD
PLAYHOUSE HOUSE MOVIE
CINEMA THEATER
PLAYING FROLIC LAKING
(— CARD) ACE JACK KING TREY
DEUCE QUEEN TAROT
(— CARDS) DECK
(— LIGHTLY) LAMBENT
PLAYTHING DIE TOY HOOP KNACK
PLAIK SPORT BAUBLE LAKING
SUCKER TRIFLE PLAYOCK
PLAYWRIGHT FRENCH FEVAL
PLAYWRIGHT AUTHOR
DRAMATIST PLAYMAKER
AMERICAN ADE BAUM DALY HART
HOYT RICE SHAW BARRY COHAN
DAVIS DOBIE FITCH GREEN LEWIS
ODETS RIVES SMITH WILDE
YOUNG BARAKA BARKER BARRAS
BEAHAN BOLTON BOOTHE
BROOKS FLAVIN GOLDEN
HOWARD HUGHES LAWSON
LERNER MEGRUE MILLER NUGENT
ONEILL THOMAS TOTTEN WALKER
WALTER WEXLEY WILDER
ANDREWS BEHRMAN BELASCO
BLOSSOM CARROLL COLLIER
HELLMAN HOPWOOD HURLBUT
KAUFMAN LINDSAY MOELLER
PEABODY RICHMAN RYSKIND
SAROYAN SHELDON SHIPMAN
SPEWACK VEILLER ANDERSON
CARLETON COLLISON CONNELLY
KINGSLEY KIRKLAND MITCHELL
SHERWOOD WILLIAMS
BALDERSON MACARTHUR
MIDDLETON MOREHOUSE
NICHOLSON STALLINGS
BOUCICAULT WEITZENKORN
AUSTRALIAN CHAMBERS
AUSTRIAN BLEI COLLIN MULLER
NISSEL WERFEL NEUMANN
ZEDLITZ CASTELLI WILDGANS
SCHONTHAN SCHNITZLER
HOFMANNSTHAL
BELGIAN MAETERLINCK
CANADIAN ROSE
CZECH JERABEK JIRASEK
DANISH EWALD TANDRUP
BERGSTROM BUCHHOLTZ
OEHLENSCHLAGER
DUTCH FEITH HOOFT COSTER

EMANTS VONDEL BREDERO
ENGLISH FRY GAY KYD LEE BEHN
BELL FORD HILL LEVY LONG NASH
ROWE SHAW SIMS TATE TUKE
BARRY BROME BYRON DUKES
FIELD HOOLE JONES LEMON
LEWIS LILLO LODGE MILNE
MOORE MUNRO ORCZY PEELE
SMITH WOODS ALBERY BOADEN
CANNAN CASTLE CIBBER
COWARD COWLEY CROWNE
DAVIES DEKKER DENNIS DIBDIN
GRAHAM GREENE HOWARD
JONSON KENNEY LYTTON
MANLEY MORTON MUNDAY
NABBES PINERO PINTER PORTER
ROWLEY SETTLE STEELE TAYLOR
WILSON ACKLAND BARNETT
BARRETT BENNETT BURNAND
CHAPMAN CHETTLE EDWARDS
FLECKER GILBERT HARWOOD
HEYWOOD JERROLD JOHNSON
MARLOWE MARMION MARSTON
MERRICK MITFORD MOTTEUX
NICHOLS OSBORNE PLANCHE
PRESTON SHIRLEY SIMPSON
SITWELL SOWERBY WEBSTER
BEAUMONT CLIFFOED CONGREVE
DAVENANT ETHEREGE FIELDING
FITZBALL FLETCHER HAMILTON
HOLCROFT HOUGHTON
JOHNSTON KNOBLOCK LONSDALE
MORRISON PHILLIPS ROBINSON
SHADWELL THEOBALD THURSTON
TOURNEUR VANBRUGH WILLIAMS
ZANGWILL BOTTOMLEY
BRIGHOUSE GOLDSMITH
GREENWOOD ISHERWOOD
KILLIGREW MASSINGER
MIDDLETON MONCRIEFF
MONKHOUSE SIEVEKING
SOUTHERNE VANDRUTEN
WYCHERLEY BROADHURST
CARTWRIGHT DRINKWATER
GALSWORTHY PHILLPOTTS
SHAKESPEARE
ESTONIAN TAMMSAARE
FINNISH KIVI TAVASTSTJERNA
FRENCH BLUM KOCK PYAT VADE
BELOT BLOCH CAMUS CAPUS
CARRE CEARD COLLE CUREL
DUCIS FABRE FLERS GENET
PIRON WOLFF AUGIER BAYARD
BECQUE BELLOY BRIEUX COLLIN
COOLUS DONNAY DOUCET
FAVART LESAGE MAIRET MONVEL
MOREAU PAGNOL PARODI
PICARD RAYNAL ROTROU
SARDOU SCRIBE SOUMET
ANCELOT ANOUILH BARBIER
BERNARD BORNIER BOUILLY
BOUVIER CLAUDEL COCTEAU
DENNERY FERRIER GRESSET
HERVIEU IONESCO LABICHE
LAPLACE LARIVEY LAVEDAN
LEGOUVE MEILHAC MEURICE
MOLIERE MORTIER NUITTER
PONSARD ROSTAND SANDEAU
SARMENT SEDAINE VILDRAC
ANDRIEUX BARRIERE BATAILLE
BEAUVOIR BENJAMIN CROISSET
DANCOURT DUMANOIR FAUCHOIS
MARIVAUX MONTEPIN QUINAULT

VOLTAIRE BENSERADE BERNSTEIN
BOURSAULT CORNEILLE
DELAVIGNE DUVEYRIER
LEMERCIER VACQUERIE
CAMPISTRON CLAIRVILLE
DESTOUCHES BEAUMARCHAIS
GERMAN BAB BABO BEER KIND
LENZ BLOEM ERNST HALBE JOHST
LAUBE SORGE UNRUH ZWEIG
ANGELY BRECHT DREYER KAISER
KLEIST KORNER REUTER WEISSE
BARLACH BENEDIX BRONNEN
GUTZKOW KLINGER LESSING
RAUPACH REDWITZ VULPIUS
BRENTANO GRYPHIUS KOTZEBUE
LISSAUER SCHILLER WOLZOGEN
BEYERLEIN GANGHOFER
IMMERMANN SUDERMANN
UECHTRITZ WILBRANDT
AUFFENBERG BLUMENTHAL
FEUCHTWANGER
GREEK ALEXIS SOPHRON
CRATINUS PHILEMON RHINTHON
AESCHYLUS EURIPEDES
SOPHOCLES ANTIPHANES
PHRYNICHUS PHERECRATES
ARISTOPHANES
HUNGARIAN TOTH DOCZI JOKAI
VAJDA MOLNAR ZILAHY
BESSENYEI KISFALUDY SZIGLIGETI
ICELANDIC KAMBAN
SIGURJONSSON
IRISH BEHAN COLUM KELLY
SYNGE WILDE WILLS YEATS
ERVINE MARTYN OCASEY
BECKETT DUNSANY GREGORY
GRIFFIN MATURIN OKEEFFE
SHEILDS ORIORDAN SHERIDAN
BICKERSTAFFE
ITALIAN CECCHI GIRAUD ALFIERI
BENELLI CARRERA GIACOSA
GOLDONI MARENCO TORELLI
RUCELLAI SABATINI CHIARELLI
NICCOLINI PIRANDELLO
JAPANESE CHIKAMATSU
MEXICAN GAMBOA
NORWEGIAN BOJER IBSEN
HEIBERG BJORNSON KIELLAND
POLISH ASNYK FREDRO SZUJSKI
ZAPOLSKA ZEROMSKI ZULAWSKI
NALKOWSKA WYSPIANSKI
BELCIKOWSKI BOGUSLAWSKI
KORZENIOWSKI
PORTUGUESE SILVA BIESTER
ROMAN NAEVIUS PLAUTUS
TERENCE PACUVIUS
RUMANIAN BLAGA
RUSSIAN KRYLOV CHEKHOV
KAPNIST KIRSHON TOLSTOI
BULGAKOV CHIRIKOV FONVIZIN
POTEKHIN SUMBATOV
ABLESIMOV BOBORYKIN
YUSHKEVICH KHMELNITSKI
LAZHECHNIKOV
SCOTTISH BEITH BARRIE
DAVIDSON ROBERTSON
SPANISH CRUZ LARRA RUEDA
CANETE ENCINA ZAMORA
MORATIN DIAMANTE FERNANDEZ
SWEDISH BESKOW EDGREN
BLANCHE HEDBERG MESSENIUS
LAGERKVIST STREINDBERG
SWISS ILG FAESI

WELSH EVANS
PLAZA PLACE PLEIN SQUARE
ZOCALO
(— DE TOROS) BULLRING
PLEA BAR BID PLY MOOT NOLO
SUIT ALIBI CLAIM PLEAD ABATER
APPEAL EXCUSE REFUGE
APOLOGY CONTEND DEFENCE
LAWSUIT PRETEXT QUARREL
DILATORY ENTREATY PLACITUM
PRETENSE
PLEACH PLAIT PLASH INTERLACE
PLEAD BEG SUE MOOT PLEA PRAY
PRIG SHOW URGE COUNT ORATE
ALLEGE APPEAL ASSERT PLAYTE
PURSUE ENTREAT IMPLORE
SOLICIT WRANGLE ADVOCATE
LITIGATE
(— FOR) SOLICIT PETITION
PLEADER ACTOR VAKIL PATRON
SUITOR VAKEEL COUNTOR
ADVOCATE
PLEADING PLEA PAROL ANSWER
PAROLE ADVOCACY COGNOVIT
DEMURRER INTENDIT MEMORIAL
PLEASANT FUN GAY BEEN BIEN
BRAW FAIR FINE GLAD GOOD
HEND JOLI NEAT TRIM WEME
AMENE BIGLY BONNY CANNY
COUTH CUSHY DOUCE DRUNK
DUCKY GREEN HAPPY HENDE
HODDY JOLLY LEPID LISTY LUSTY
MERRY NUTTY QUEME SMIRK
SUAVE SWEET TIPSY WALLY
WETHE COMELY DAINTY DULCET
GENIAL KINDLY PRETTY SAVORY
SMOOTH AFFABLE ELEGANT
FARRAND JANNOCK LEESOME
WINSOME DELICATE GLORIOUS
GRATEFUL HEAVENLY LIEFSOME
LIKESOME LOVESOME THANKFUL
TOWARDLY GEMUTLICH
(PREF.) HEDY
PLEASANTLY FAIR WINLY FAIRLY
AFFABLY SWEETLY GENIALLY
LIKINGLY
PLEASANTNESS GAIETY NAAMAN
AMENITY SUAVITY JOCUNDITY
PLEASANTRY WIT JEST JOKE
SPORT BANTER JESTING JOLLITY
WAGGERY
PLEASE PAY GAME LIKE LIST LUST
SUIT WANT WISH AGREE AMUSE
BITTE CHARM ELATE FANCY
HUMOR QUEME SAVOR TASTE
ARRIDE KITTLE OBLIGE REGALE
SOOTHE TICKLE AGGRATE
APPLESE CONTENT DELIGHT
GLADDEN GRATIFY PLACATE
REJOICE SATISFY
(— FORWARD) FS
PLEASED FAIN FOND GLAD APAID
HAPPY PROUD BUCKED CONTENT
GLADSOME
(BE —) GAME
PLEASING AMEN COOL GLAD
GOOD LIEF NICE SOFT AMENE
DICTY NIFTY SOOTH SWEET
CLEVER COMELY DREAMY FACILE
FLASHY GAINLY LIKING LUSTLY
MELLOW PRETTY AMIABLE
BLESSED CORKING DARLING
LIKABLE LIKEFUL TUNABLE

WELCOME CHARMING DELICATE
FAVOROUS FETCHING GRACEFUL
GRACIOUS GRATEFUL HEAVENLY
INVITING LIKESOME PLACABLE
PLAUSIVE SPECIOUS PLAUSIBLE
PERSONABLE
(— TO EAR) HARMONIC
(— TO EYE) EESOME
(— TO HEAR) FAIR
(VERY —) SNAZZY
PLEASURABLE GOOD JOLLY
ANIMAL MIRTHFUL
PLEASURE JO EST FUN JOY BANG
BOOT EASE ESTE GREE KAMA LIST
LUST PLAY WILL BLISS KICKS
MIRTH SAVOR SOOTH TASTE
DAINTY DEDUIT GAIETY GAYETY
LIKING LUXURY NICETY VOLUPT
COMFORT DELIGHT GRATIFY
JOLLITY JOYANCE VOLUPTY
DELICACY FRUITION GLADNESS
HILARITY VOLUPTAS
(SELFISH —) LECHERY
(STOLEN —) STOUTH STOWTH
(PL.) DELICIAE
PLEASURE SEEKER FRANION
PLEAT SET FOLD KILT POKE RUCK
FLUTE FRILL PINCH PLAIT PRANK
GUSSET SUNRAY
PLEATED PLICATE SUNBURST
PLEBE PLEBS FRESHMAN
PLEBEIAN LOW BASE PLEB SNOB
COMMON HOMELY VULGAR
IGNOBLE LOWBORN POPULAR
BASEBORN EVERYDAY HOMESPUN
INFERIOR MECHANIC ORDINARY
ROTURIER RUPTUARY
PLEBISCITE VOTE DECREE
PLECTRUM PICK SPUR QUILL
UVULA MALLEUS POINTEL
PLECTRON
(— OF HARP) FESCUE
PLEDGE LAY VAS VOW WAD WED
AFFY BAND CLAP EARL GAGE
HAND HEST HOCK PASS PAWN
WAGE WOID WORD FAITH SIKER
SPOUT STAKE SWEAR SWEAT
TOKEN TROTH TRUTH WAGER
ARREST BORROW COMMIT
ENGAGE IMPAWN IMPONE
LUMBER PAROLE PIGNUS PLEVIN
PLIGHT SICCAR SICKER VADIUM
WADSET BARGAIN BETROTH
CAUTION CREANCE EARNEST
HOSTAGE PROMISE BOTTOMRY
MORTGAGE SECURITY SPONSION
VADIMONY
(— IN DRINKING) PROPINE
PLEDGED HIGHT SWORN ASSURED
ENGAGED PIGNORATE
(— TO MARRY) SURE
PLEDGET DOSSIL PENICIL
PLEIADES MAIA MEROPE ALCYONE
CELAENO ELECTRA STEROPE
TAYGETA
PLEIN-AIRIST LUMINIST
PLEISTHENES (FATHER OF —)
ATREUS
(MOTHER OF —) AEROPE
(SON OF —) MENELAUS
AGAMEMNON
PLENARY FULL ENTIRE PLENAL
PERFECT ABSOLUTE COMPLETE

PLENITUDE PLENITY PLEROMA
FULLNESS PLETHORA
ABUNDANCE
PLENTEOUS RICH COPIOUS
FERTILE AFFLUENT FRUITFUL
GENEROUS ABOUNDING
EXUBERANT
PLENTIFUL OLD FULL RANK RICH
RIFE AMPLE HEFTY LARGE ROUTH
SONSY STORE ENOUGH FOISON
GALORE LAVISH SONSIE COPIOUS
FERTILE LIBERAL OPULENT
PROFUSE UBEROUS ABUNDANT
FRUITFUL NUMEROUS
EXUBERANT
PLENTIFULLY RIFE FREELY GALORE
APLENTY
PLENTY WON BAIT COPY MANY
RAFF SONS AMPLE CHEAP COPIA
FOUTH PRICE ROUTH SONSE
TEEMS FOISON SCOUTH UBERTY
LASHINGS
(GREAT —) ABUNDANCE
PLEON TELSON ABDOMEN
PLEONASM ITERATION
MACROLOGY TAUTOLOGY
PLETHORA RASH EXCESS PLENUM
PLURISY FULLNESS PLEURISY
POLYEMIA PROFUSION REPLETION
PLETHORIC TUMID TURGID
SWOLLEN INFLATED
PLEURISY EMPYEMA
PLEURON SCAPULA
PLEXUS RETE GLOMUS NETWORK
PROPLEX GENIPLEX
PLIABLE WAXY WEAK LITHY
WAXEN DOCILE LIMBER PLIANT
SEMMIT SUPPLE BOWABLE
FICTILE FINGENT FLEXILE PLASTIC
WINDING CUSHIONY FLEXIBLE
COMPLIANT
PLIANCY FLEXURE FACILITY
PLIANT APT FLIP SWAK AGILE
BUXOM LITHE SWACK YOUNG
DOCILE LIMBER SUPPLE WANDLE
DUCTILE FLEXILE PLASTIC
PLIABLE SLIPPER WILLOWY
APPLIANT FLEXIBLE SUITABLE
WORKABLE SEQUACIOUS
PLICA FOLD TRICHOMA
PLICATE FOLD PLEAT FOLDED
FANLIKE PLAITED
PLIERS BENDER FLEXOR GRATER
FLECTOR PINCERS
PLIGHT PLY FOLD ARRAY BRAID
DRESS PLAIT POINT STATE
WOVEN ATTIRE ENGAGE PICKLE
PLEDGE PLISKY STRAIT TAKING
BETROTH MISCHIEF QUANDARY
PLIGHTED ASSURATE
PLIM PLUM STOUT SWELL INFLATE
PLIABLE
PLINTH ORLE ORLO BLOCK SOCLE
ABACUS PATAND QUADRA
SUBBASE FOOTSTALL SCAMILLUS
PLISTHENES (FATHER OF —)
ATREUS
(MOTHER OF —) CLEOLA
(SON OF —) MENELAUS
AGAMEMNON
(WIFE OF —) AEROPE ERIPHYLE
PLOD JOG GRUB PLOT SLOG STOG
TORE TROG VAMP POACH TRAMP

TRASH DRUDGE SLOUCH
TRUDGE PLUNTHER
(— **ALONG**) PEG TORE
(— **THROUGH MUD**) SLOUGH
PLODDER GRUB DIGGER SLOGGER
PLOIARIA EMESA
PLONK WINE
PLOP FLUMP PLUMP HEAVILY
PLOT BREW CAST MARK PACK
PLAN PLAT CABAL DRIFT FRAUD
GLEBE GRAPH GREEN HATCH
MODEL PLECK SCALD STORY
STUDY WATCH ACTION BRIGUE
CLIQUE DESIGN DEVISE GARDEN
MALIGN MYTHOS SCHEME
SHAMBA TAMPER AGITATE
COLLUDE COMPACT COMPASS
CONJECT CONNIVE CONTOUR
DRAUGHT FEEDLOT LAZYBED
MACHINE PRETEND QUADRAT
QUARTER SWIDDEN ARGUMENT
COGITATE CONSPIRE CONTRIVE
INTRIGUE PRACTICE PROTRACT
SEMINARY MACHINATE
(— **OF GRASS**) SONK
(— **OF LAND**) ERF LOT PLAT SHOT
FORTY MILPA PATCH PLECK
SPLAT COMMON SCHERM
SHAMBA HAGGARD LAZYBED
SEVERAL
(— **OF 1-2 ACRE**) ERF
(— **SECRETLY**) WHISPER
(**GARDEN** —) BED ERF QUINTA
QUARTER
(**UNPRODUCTIVE** —) HIRST
PLOTTER PACKER HATCHER
JACOBIN SCHEMER DESIGNER
ENGINEER
PLOUK KNOB PIMPLE
PLOVER DROME KOLEA OXEYE
PILOT SANDY STILT KILDEE
QUAILY TURNIX COLLIER
COURSER DOTTREL LAPWING
MAYCOCK OWLHEAD PAPABOT
WRYBILL BULLHEAD DOTTEREL
DULWILLY HILLBIRD KILLDEER
RINGNECK SPURWING SQUEALER
TOADHEAD WHISTLER WIREBIRD
SANDERLING
PLOW EAR ERE BOUT DISK FOIL
HINT MOLE PLOD RIVE ROVE
SLUG STIR SULK SULL TILL BREAK
FLUNK SPLIT SULKY THROW
ARAIRE BUSTER DIGGER FALLOW
FURROW GOPHER JUMPER LISTER
PLOUGH RAFTER ROOTER RUTTER
SULLOW BACKSET BREAKER
HUSBAND SCOOTER SULCATE
TWISTER FIREPLOW FURROWER
GANGPLOW SNOWPLOW
TURNPLOW
(— **CROSSWISE**) THORTER
(— **HANDLE**) STILT
(— **LIGHTLY**) SKIM RIFFLE
(— **PART**) PINHEAD
(**PL.**) OUTSIGHT
PLOWBOY YOKEL
PLOWING ARDER EARTH ARDURE
ARATION CARUAGE STIRRING
PLOWLAND CARUE CARVE TILTH
CARUCATE TEAMLAND
PLOWMAN PLOWER TILLER
ACREMAN

PLOWSHARE LAY SLIP SOCK
LAVER REEST SHARE JUMPER
(— **BONE**) VOMER PYGOSTYLE
(**PREF.**) VOMERO
PLOY BENT BOWED SPORT
RAMBLE TACTIC PURSUIT
ACTIVITY ESCAPADE
PLUCK GO PUG ROB TUG BOUT
CROP CULL DRAG GAME GRAB
GRIT PELT PICK PILL POOK PULL
RACE RASE RASH SAND TUCK
ARBER ARBOR BREAK DRAFT
HANGE MOXIE NERVE PILCH
PLOAT PLUME RANCH SMITE
SPUNK STEAL STRIP AVULSE
DECERP EVULSE FLEECE GATHER
PIGEON PLITCH PLOUGH QUARRY
SNATCH SPIRIT TWINGE TWITCH
COURAGE DEPLUME PLUNDER
BOLDNESS DECISION DEMOLISH
GAMENESS VELLICATE
PURTENANCE
(— **AS A STRING**) TIRL PINCH
(— **FEATHERS**) STUB
(— **LEAVES**) BLADE
(— **OF SHEEP OR CALF**) RACE
GATHER
(— **UP COURAGE**) CHEER
(— **WOOL BY HAND**) ROO
PLUCKED PLUMED PIZZICATO
PLUCKY GAMY SANDY BANTAM
GRITTY SPUNKY FIGHTING
PLUG BUG FID PEG PIN TAP TOP
WAD BLOW BONE BOTT BUNG
FILL JADE ROOT SHOT SLOG STOP
SWAT SWOT BOOST DOWEL
DUMMY PILOT PUNCH SHACK
SKATE SPILE STUFF SWEAT
BOUCHE BOXING BULLET
COMEDO DOSSIL DOTTLE FIDDLE
SPIGOT BOUCHON BUSHING
CHAMBER CHUGGER FERRULE
STOPPER STOPPLE DRIVECAP
FUSEPLUG PELELITH STOPCOCK
(— **FOR CANNON**) TAMPION
(— **IN GRENADE**) BOUCHON
(— **IN ORGAN PIPE**) STOPPLE
TAMPION
(— **OF CLAY**) BOTT
(— **OF OAKUM**) FID
(— **OF VOLCANO**) CORE
(— **TO HOLD NAIL**) DOOK
(— **UP**) CLAM STOP ESTOP
RAMFORCE
(**FISHING** —) BUG
(**LIP** —) LABRET
(**NOSE** —) TEMBETA TEMBETARA
(**WASTE** —) WASHER
(**WATER** —) HYDRANT
PLUG-IN JACK
PLUG-UGLY THUG ROWDY TOUGH
RUFFIAN ROUGHNECK
PLUM GAGE JOBO RISE ISLAY
JAMAN PRUNE SWELL BEAUTY
CHENEY DAMSEL DAMSON
KELSEY MUSSEL SAPOTE APRICOT
BULLACE BURBANK FORTUNE
ORLEANS QUETSCH PRUNELLO
ROSACEAN ROSEWORT VICTORIA
WINDFALL
(**COCO** —) ICACO
(**JAVA** —) DUHAT JAMBUL
JAMBOOL JAMBOLAN

(**WILD** —) SKEG SLOE ISLAY
(**PREF.**) PRUNI
PLUMAGE ROBE RUFF FLUFF
HACKLE SHROUD FEATHER
FLOCCUS JUVENAL PENNAGE
FEATHERS PARADISE PTILOSIS
PLUMB BUNG SHEER BOTTOM
BULLET SINKER EXACTLY
PLUMMET UTTERLY ABSOLUTE
COMPLETE DIRECTLY ENTIRELY
VERTICAL
PLUMBAGO LUSTER LUSTRE
GRAPHITE LEADWORT
PLUMB BOB PLUMMET
PLUMBISM SATURNISM
PLUMB LINE MERKHET
PLUM CURCULIO TURK WEEVIL
PLUME PEN TIP TUFT CREST
EGRET PRIDE PRUNE DEPRIVE
DESPOIL FEATHER PANACHE
AIGRETTE
(— **ON HELMET**) CREST PANACHE
(— **ON HORSE**) PLUMADE
(— **ON TURBAN**) CULGEE
(**EGRET** —) OSPREY
(**MILITARY** —) PANACHE
PLUME NUTMEG SASSAFRAS
PLUMMET LEAD FLOAT PLUMB
WEIGHT
PLUMMING BRONZING
PLUMP FAT BOLD FAIR FLOP FULL
PLOP SLAP SOSS TIDY BLUNT
BONNY BUXOM CLUMP FLUMP
FUBBY FUBSY GROUP JOLLY
PLUNK SAPPY SLEEK SMACK
SONSY SQUAB STOUT THICK
BONNIE CHUBBY CRUMBY
CRUMMY DIRECT FATTEN FLATLY
FLESHY FODGEL GAWSIE PLUNGE
PUBBLE ROTUND BLUNTLY
BUNTING CLUSTER DISTEND
FULSOME RIBLESS THRODDY
CHOPPING FLESHFUL
(— **AND ROSY**) BUXOM
(— **AND ROUND**) CHUBBY
(**NOT** —) ANGULAR
(**PLEASINGLY** —) ZAFTIG ZOFTIG
PLUM POCKET FOOL
PLUMULE BLASTUS FEATHER
GEMMULA GEMMULE GEOBLAST
ACROSPIRE
PLUNDER GUT ROB BOOT FANG
JUNK LOOT PILL POLL PREY RAPE
REIF RIPE RUMP SACK SWAG
BEROB BOOTY CHEAT GAINS
HARRY PLUCK PREDE RAVEN
REAVE RENNE RIFLE SCOFF
SHAVE SPOIL STRIP BEZZLE
BOODLE CREACH DACOIT FLEECE
FORAGE HARROW MARAUD
PANYAR PROFIT RAPINE RAVAGE
DESPOIL ESCHEAT FREIGHT
PILFERY PILLAGE RANSACK
SACKAGE SPREAGH SPULZIE
BOOTHALE FREEBOOT
PLUNDERER THIEF BANDIT
BUMMER PEELER POLLER RAPTOR
ROBBER VANDAL ROUTIER
SPOILER MARAUDER RAPPAREE
PLUNDERING PREY SACK MARAUD
RAPINE ESCHEAT HERSHIP
PURCHASE SPECHERY SPOILFUL
SPOILING PREDATORY

PLUNGE BET DIG DIP CAVE DIVE
DOOK DUCK DUMP JUMP PURL
PUSH RAKE RISK SINK SOSS
BURST DOUSE FLING PITCH
PLUMP SOUSE SWOOP FOOTER
GAMBLE HEADER LAUNCH
SPLASH THRUST WALLOP
BRAINGE DEMERGE IMMERSE
PLOUNCE SUBMERGE
(— **INTO**) CLAP ENGULF IMMERGE
(— **INTO WATER**) ENEW
(**GAMBLING** —) RAKER
PLUNGER RAM SWAB FORCE
DUCKER POMMEL BLUNGER
STRIKER
PLUNGING FLING
PLUNK DIVE PLONK PLUCK PLUMP
DOLLAR SUPPORT SUDDENLY
PLUNTHER PLOD FLOUNDER
PLURAL
(**SUFF.**) IM
PLURALIST TOTQUOT
PLURALITY MAJORITY MORENESS
TRIALITY
(**PREF.**) POLY
PLUS AND GAIN WITH EXTRA
SURPLUS ADDITION INCREASE
POSITIVE
PLUSH EASY BEAVER VELOUR
SUPERIOR
PLUSHY SWANK SWANKY
PLUTEUS WAGON PARAPET
PLUTO DIS HADES ORCUS
(**BROTHER OF** —) JUPITER
NEPTUNE
(**FATHER OF** —) SATURN
(**WIFE OF** —) PROSERPINE
PLUTOCRAT NABOB RICHARD
PLUTONIC HYPOGENE INTRUSIVE
VULCANIAN
PLUTUS (**ASSOCIATE OF** —) TYCHE
EIRENE
(**FATHER OF** —) IASION
(**MOTHER OF** —) CERES DEMETER
PLY RUN BEAT BEND BIAS CORD
CORE DRAM FOLD MOLD SAIL
URGE ADAPT APPLY EXERT LAYER
STEER TWIST WIELD YIELD
COMPLY DOUBLE HANDLE
TRAVEL EXERCISE
(— **WITH DRINK**) BIRL ROSIN
(— **WITH DRUGS**) HOCUS
(**OF ONE** —) SINGLE
PNEUMA NEUM SOUL NEUME
BREATH SPIRIT
PNEUMATIC HAMMER GUN
PNEUMATOCYST FLOAT
PNEUMONIA PULMONITIS
POACH PUG ROB COOK DROP
POKE PUSH SINK BLACK DRIVE
FORCE POTCH STEAL BLEACH
PLUNGE INTRUDE
POACHED EGGS MOONSHINE
POACHER BLACK POGGE SPOACH
LURCHER STALKER WIDGEON
BALDPATE BULLHEAD
(**SALMON** —) REBECCA REBEKAH
(**PL.**) BLACKS
POALES GLUMALES
POCHARD DUCK SMEE DIVER
POKER SCAUP DUNAIR DUNKER
DUNBIRD REDHEAD WHINGER
GOLDHEAD WHINYARD

POCHETTE KIT VIOLIN HANDBAG
POCKET BOX CLY FOB PIT CLAY
KICK POKE PRAT BASIN BURSE
MEANS POUCH PURSE STEAL
ACCEPT BECKET CASING CANTINA
PLACKET SWALLOW TROUSER
ENVELOPE ISOLATED MONETARY
PROFONDE SUPPRESS
CONDENSED MINIATURE
(— A WRONG) PURSE
(— IN BOOK BINDER) STATION
(— OF NET) BOWL
(BILLIARD —) POT HOLE HAZARD
(MAGICIAN'S —) PROFONDE
(NOODLE —S) KREPLACH
(ORE —) CHURN BONANZA
(SMALL —) FOB
(TROUSER —) PRAT BECKET
(WATER —) TINAJA ALBERCA
(PL.) KREPLACH
(PREF.) PERO
POCKETBOOK BAG KICK SKIN
PURSE INCOME READER WALLET
HANDBAG LEATHER BILLFOLD
NOTECASE
POCKET GOPHER TUZA QUACHIL
POCKETING COUP
POCKETKNIFE BARLOW PENKNIFE
PIGSTICKER
POCKMARK PITHOLE
POD BAG COD GAM KID POP SAC
BALL BEAN BOLL HUSK POKE
SWAD BURSE CAROB FLOCK
POUCH QUASH SHAUP SHELL
SHUCK SNAIL WHAUP CHILLI
LEGUME PESCOD SCHOOL
HARICOT PEASCOD SILIQUA
PEASECOD PODOCARP POTBELLY
SEEDCASE TAMARIND
(— FORMING) KID
(— OF LEGUME) KID
(— OF MESQUITE) HONEYPOD
(EXPLOSIVE —) SANDBOX
(SUBTERRANEAN —) EARTHNUT
(UNRIPE —) SQUASH
(PL.) PIPI SUNT BABUL GARAD
BABLAH GARRAT COWHAGE
GONAKIE ALGAROBA DIVIDIVI
(PREF.) SILIQUI
PODALIRIUS (BROTHER OF —)
MACHAON
(FATHER OF —) ASCLEPIUS
PODARCES (BROTHER OF —)
PROTESILAUS
(FATHER OF —) IPHICLUS
PODDED BOLLED
PODIUM DAIS FOOT WALL
LECTERN
PODOCARP YACCA
PODWARE PODDER
PODZOL SPODOSOL
POEM GEM LAI LAY ODE DUAN
EPIC JOSE MELE POSY RUNE
SONG CENTO DIRGE DITTY HAIKU
IWEIN METER STAFF VERSE
AMHRAN AUBADE BALLAD
CACCIA CARMEN CYCLIC DIXAIN
EPOPEE EROTIC ESTRIF HEROID
MELODY MONODY NOSTOS
PIYYUT SESTET SONNET TENSON
TERCET BUCOLIC CANTARE
CANTATA CANZONE DESCORT
DIZAINE ECLOGUE ELEGIAC

FLITING GEORGIC SOTADIC
TRIOLET VIRELAI VIRELAY
VOLUSPA ACROSTIC AMOEBEUM
BRINDISI CANTICLE DINGDONG
DOGGEREL INVICTUS LIMERICK
MADRIGAL TELESTIC THEOGONY
TRISTICH TROCHAIC VERSICLE
MONORHYME ROUNDELAY
(— ABOUT DEBATE) ESTRIF
(— ABOUT SHEPHERDS) ECLOGUE
(— GREETING DAWN) AUBADE
(— OF LAMENTATION) ELEGY
(— OF RETRACTION) PALINODE
(— OF 10 LINES) DIZAINE
(— OF 14 LINES) SONNET
(AMATORY —) EROTIC SONNET
(EPIC —) EPOS EPOPEE LUSIAD
THEBAID
(HOMELY —) DIT
(IRISH —) AMHRAN
(JAPANESE —) HAIKU TANKA
(LITURGICAL —) VIDDUI VIDDUY
SELIHOTH
(LOVE —) AMORETTO
(LYRIC —) LAI LAY ODE ALBA
EPODE GHAZEL RONDEL
CANZONA PARTIMEN
(PART OF —) PASSUS
(PASTORAL —) IDYL IDYLL
BUCOLIC
(PERSIAN —) GHAZAL
(RELIGIOUS —) HYMN
(RURAL —) GEORGIC
(SACRED —) PSALM YIGDAL
(SATIRICAL —) IAMBIC KASIDA
(SHORT —) DIT DITTY EPILOG
SONNET CANZONE EPIGRAM
EPILOGUE EPYLLION
(TONE —) BALLADE
(WELSH —) CYWYDD
(PL.) AZAHROT MAKINGS
(SUFF.) STICH
POET OG RSI BARD FILE FILI FIRI
LARK MUSE SCOP SWAN ARION
LAKER LINOS LINUS LYRIC MAKAR
MAKER ODIST RISHI SAYER SCALD
SKALD FINDER GNOMIC IBYCUS
LAKIST LYRIST SHAPER SINGER
DICHTER ELEGIAC EPICIST IDYLIST
IMAGIST MUSAEUS ORPHEUS
PROPHET CONCRETE FERAMORZ
GEORGIAN LAUREATE LUTANIST
MINSTREL SONGSTER TROUVERE
MINNESINGER
(IRISH —) FILI
(MEDIOCRE —) RIMER RHYMER
(MINOR —) BARDIE
ALBANIAN FISHTA
AMERICAN LOW POE AGAR BURR
CARY CONE DALY HEAD NASH
READ REED SAXE SILL SNOW
TATE TOWN VERY WARE ADAMS
AIKEN AKINS ALLEN AUDEN
BACON BEERS BOGAN BROWN
CLAPP CLARK COLES CRANE
DAMON DRAKE ENGLE FICKE
FIELD FINCH FROST GUEST
HAYNE HOVEY JOLAS MOODY
PIATT POUND PRIME RIDGE RILEY
STORY TOWN WELBY WILDE
WYLIE ARNOLD BARLOW BRALEY
BRANCH BROOKS BRYANT
BURTON CARMER CAWEIN CIARDI

CLARKE COATES COFFIN CRANCH
CULLEN CUTTER DARGAN
DUNBAR FISHER GILDER GUINEY
HOLMES HOOPER KEELER KILMER
LANIER LEDOUX LOWELL MILLER
MONROE MORGAN MORTON
NORTON OSGOOD SAVAGE
SEEGER THOMAS TIMROD
WRIGHT AINSLIE BABCOCK
CHIVERS CROWELL EMERSON
FEARING FRENEAU HALLECK
HILLYER JEFFERS KNOWLES
LAFARGE LAZARUS LINDSAY
MARKHAM MIFFLIN MOULTON
PARSONS PATCHEN PEABODY
PROCTOR ROBERTS RUSSELL
SHAPIRO SHERMAN STEDMAN
TAGGARD THAXTER WATTLES
WHITMAN BRAINARD CARLETON
CONKLING CUMMINGS DINSMOOR
FISHBACK FLETCHER GINSBURG
HAGEDORN MACLEISH NEIHARDT
PETERSON PHILLIPS PROKOSCH
ROBINSON SANDBURG SCOLLARD
SPOFFORD STERLING STODDARD
TEASDALE THOMPSON TRUMBULL
WHITTIER AUSLANDER
COOLBRITH DICKINSON
GUITERMAN HENDERSON
KREYMBORG OPPENHEIM
TUCKERMAN WURDEMANN
COATSWORTH LONGFELLOW
BRAITHWAITE RITTENHOUSE
ARAB TARAFA
ARGENTINIAN ASCASUBI
ECHEVERRIA
AUSTRALIAN GORDON TURNER
AUSTRIAN VOGL KAFKA BACHER
FRANKL GRAZIE WERFEL
NEUMANN ZEDLITZ CASTELLI
WILDGANS WURZBACH ZINGERLE
HAMERLING HOFMANNSTHAL
BELGIAN GILKIN GIRAUD EEKHOUD
ELSKAMP HASSELT CAMMAERTS
RODENBACH VERHAEREN
BRAZILIAN GAMA COSTA AZEVEDO
GUIMARAES MAGALHAES
BULGARIAN VAZOV BOTYOV
CANADIAN FISET PRATT SCOTT
CARMAN MACKAY FERLAND
JOHNSON LAMPMAN SERVICE
CAMPBELL CRAWFORD
DRUMMOND MACDONALD
CHILEAN NERUDA MISTRAL
CHINESE LIPO TUFU POCHUI
MEISHENG
COLOMBIAN ARBOLEDA
CUBAN VALDES
CZECH CECH GOLL ERBEN FRIDA
HALEK HANKA JEBAVY KVAPIL
MACHAR NERUDA
DANISH BOYE RODE EWALD
HAUCH KINGO PLOUG ARREBO
JENSEN RAHBEK BLICHER
CLAUSEN HOSTRUP KAALUND
WINTHER BAGGESEN BODTCHER
INGEMANN JACOBSEN
AARESTRUP GRUNDTVIG
JORGENSEN GERSTENBERG
DUTCH CATS GOES KATE POOT
BEETS BERGH EEDEN FEITH
HAREN HOOFT DECKER EMANTS
LENNEP LOGHEM VERWEY

VONDEL BELLAMY BREDERO
HELMERS TOLLENS BARLEAUS
SECUNDUS BILDERDIJK
HEEMSKERCK HUYDECOPER
BROEKHUIZEN
ECUADORIAN OLMEDO
ENGLISH GAY MAY MEW PYE BELL
BIGG COOK CORY DYER GALE
GRAY HAKE HALL HILL HOOD
HUNT LEAR NOEL OWEN POPE
TATE VAUX ADAMS BASSE BLAKE
BLUNT BROWN BRYAN BYROM
BYRON CAREW CAREY CLARE
COOKE DIXON DONNE DOYLE
GOOGE GOULD GOWER GREEN
JONES KEATS KEOWN LEWIS
MASON MERRY MILNE MINOT
MONRO MOORE MYERS NADEN
NOYES PAYNE PERCY PRAED
PRIOR SMART SMITH SWAIN
WATTS WAUGH WELLS WHITE
WOLFE WOODS WYATT YOUNG
ABBOTT ANSTEY ARNOLD AUSTIN
BAILEY BARLOW BARNES BARTON
BINYON BOWLES BRETON
BROOKE BROWNE BUTLER
CANTON CAPERN CARTER
CLOUGH CORBET COTTON
COWLEY COWPER CRABBE
DANIEL DAVIES DENHAM DOBELL
DOBSON DOMETT DOWSON
DRYDEN EUSDEN FENTON
GIBSON GLOVER GODLEY GRAVES
GREENE HARVEY HAWKER
HAYLEY HEMANS HOWARD
JONSON KENYON LANDON
LANDOR MACKAY MARTIN
MASSEY MCLEOD MILMAN
MILNES MILTON MORRIS MUNDAY
NESBIT ROGERS SAVAGE SCOGAN
SEWARD STRODE SYMONS
TAYLOR THOMAS TREECE
TRENCH WALLER WARNER
WARREN WATSON WITHER
WOLCOT WOTTON AINSLIE
BAMFORD BLUNDEN BRIDGES
CAEDMON CAMPION CHAPMAN
CHAUCER COKAYNE COLLINS
COPPARD CRASHAW DOUGHTY
DRAYTON ELLIOTT FAUSSET
FLATMAN FLECKER FRAUNCE
FREEMAN GIBBONS GIFFORD
HERRICK HEWLETT HOPKINS
HOUSMAN INGELOW KENNEDY
KIPLING LAYAMON LYDGATE
MANNYNG MARVELL MONTAGU
NEWBOLT NICHOLS PATMORE
PEACOCK PHILIPS POMFRET
PROCTER QUARLES SASSOON
SEYMOUR SHELLEY SITWELL
SKELTON SKIPSEY SOUTHEY
SPENSER SYMONDS TICKELL
TREVENA VAUGHAN WEBSTER
WOOLNER AKENSIDE BEAUMONT
BETJEMAN BLAGMIRE BRANFORD
BRERELEY BROWNING BUCHANAN
CAMPBELL CHALONER DAVENANT
FALCONER GREVILLE HAMILTON
HOCCLEVE LANGLAND LOVELACE
MACNEICE MOULTRIE OVERBURY
ROSSETTI SHADWELL STERLING
SUCKLING TENNYSON THOMPSON
TRAHERNE WHISTLER ALDINGTON

ARMSTRONG BARNFIELD
BLANCHARD BOTTOMLEY
CALVERLEY CAMBRIDGE
CHALKHILL CHURCHILL
CLEVELAND COLERIDGE
CONSTABLE GASCOIGNE
GOLDSMITH HABINGTON
LANGHORNE MASEFIELD
MONKHOUSE ROSCOMMON
SACKVILLE SHENSTONE
SOUTHWELL SWINBURNE
SYLVESTER UNDERHILL
WHITEHEAD BLOOMFIELD
BOURDILLON BRATHWAITE
CHATTERTON DRINKWATER
FITZGERALD MONTGOMERY
SOMERVILLE WORDSWORTH
ABERCROMBIE SHAKESPEARE
TURBERVILLE CHAMBERLAYNE
OSHAUGHNESSY
FINNISH MANNINEN RUNEBERG
ARWIDSSON TAVASTSTJERNA
FRENCH NAU AIDE BAIF FORT
GHIL GRAS KAHN LABE VIAU
ARENE CARCO DIERX DORAT
GACON GREGH GUYAU HARDY
MAROT MURET PIRON RETTE
SCEVE SULLY TASTU AICARD
ARAGON AUGIER AUTRAN
BARTAS BELLAY BERTIN BRETON
BRUNET DANIEL DEREME
DUPONT ELUARD FRANCE
GUERIN HUGUES JAMMES
LEBRUN MORICE MUSSET PARODI
PRADON RACINE REBOUL RICARD
RICTUS SAMAIN THIARD VALERY
VILLON ANCELOT AUBANEL
BARBIER BOCCAGE BONNARD
BORNIER BOUCHOR BOURGET
BRIZEUX CARRERE CAZALIS
CLAUDEL COCTEAU DELTEIL
FEYDEAU GILBERT GRESSET
HENRIOT HEREDIA JODELLE
LAPRADE MAYNARD MISTRAL
MOLINET PONSARD REGNIER
RIMBAUD RONSARD ROSTAND
SCARRON SEGRAIS VICAIRE
VILDRAC AJALBERT ANDRIEUX
BEAUVOIR BERANGER BERGERAT
BERTRAND BOUILHET CHAULIEU
COLLERYE GRECOURT GRINGORE
MALHERBE MALLARME
PEROCHON QUILLARD QUINAULT
RABELAIS ROUSSEAU VERLAINE
BELMONTET BOUFFLERS
CHAPELAIN CREBILLON
DELAVIGNE DESCHAMPS
LAMARTINE LEMERCIER
MONTREUIL ARLINCOURT
BARTHELEMY BAUDELAIRE
BOISROBERT CHENEDOLLE
DESPORITES MALFILATRE
CHANTAVOINE GRANDMOUGIN
DESHOULIERES
GERMAN UZ BAUM BOIE DACH
KLAJ LENZ RIST VOSS AYRER
BOHME BRANT BUSCH FRANK
GLEIM HARDT HEBEL HEINE
HERTZ HOLTY LANGE LOGAU
OPITZ RAABE RILKE SORGE STEIN
UNRUH WEBER BECKER BRECHT
BROGER BURGER FOLLEN GEORGE
GOETHE GOTTER GRABBE

HAMMER HEBBEL HESSUS
JORDAN KARSCH KERNER KLEIST
KNEBEL KOBELL KORNER LEFORT
MORIKE MULLER TIEDGE TOLLER
UHLAND ULRICH WALDIS WEISSE
WERNER ALLMERS BARLACH
BARTHEL BOTTGER BROCKES
BUCHNER FONTANE FORSTER
GELLERT HARRIES HENRICI
KALBECK KOPSICH MALTITZ
NEUMARK REDWITZ RUCKERT
VISCHER WALTHER WIELAND
BAUMBACH BIERBAUM
BRENTANO ECKSTEIN FLEMMING
FREIDANK GRYPHIUS HAGEDORN
HOFFMANN JUNGHANS
KAUFMANN LISSAUER
MAHLMANN OVERBECK SCHEFFEL
SCHILLER SCHUBART STOLBERG
WERNICKE ACIDALIUS BECHSTEIN
BULTHAUPT HOLDERLIN
IMMERMANN KIRCHBACH
KLOPSTOCK MOSENTHAL
NIETZSCHE RODENBERG
WILBRANDT BODENSTEDT
CREIZENACH FASTENRATH
HARDENBERG KOSEGARTEN
MATTHISSON WECKHERLIN
FREILIGRATH KOLBENHEYER
SCHNECKENBURGER
GREEK ION BION AGIAS ARION
HOMER ERINNA HESIOD IBYCUS
NONNUS PALLES PIGRES PINDAR
SAPPHO AGATHON ALCAEUS
ARCHIAS BIKELAS CORINNA
HERODAS ISYLLUS LESCHES
MOSCHUS MUSAEUS PALAMAS
RHIANUS SOLOMOS THESPIS
ANACREON COLUTHUS DIAGORAS
HIPPONAX NICANDER PANYASIS
PHILETAS PISANDER STASINUS
THEOGNIS TYRTAEUS EUPHORION
LYCOPHRON SIMONIDES
TERPANDER TIMOTHEUS
PARTHENIUS PHOCYLIDES
SEFERIADES THEOCRITUS
ASCLEPIADES BACCHYLIDES
HERMESIANAX STESICHORUS
CHRISTOPOULOS
HINDU BHARTRIHARI
HUNGARIAN ADY TOTH AMADE
ARANY GARAY REVAI SZASZ
MADACH PETOFI BALASSA
CZUCZOR KOLCSEY MAILATH
BACSANYI GYONGYOSI KISFALUDY
VOROSMARTY
ICELANDIC EGILSSON
GUNNARSSON JOCHUMSSON
THORODDSEN HALLGRIMSSON
SIGURJONSSON
INDIAN BILHANA
IRISH BANIM COLUM DAVIS
MOORE TIGHE TYNAN WILDE
WILLS WOLFE YEATS ANSTER
BROOKE CLARKE DARLEY DEVERE
FIGGIS GRAVES MAGINN MANGAN
SKRINE BARRETT DRENNAN
DUNSANY HIGGINS MACGILL
STARKEY CAMPBELL FERGUSON
FLECKNOE LEDWIDGE MCCARTHY
STEPHENS ALLINGHAM
LARMINNIE MACDONAGH
ITALIAN REDI VIDA ZENO BELLI

BERNI BONDI BOSSI CASTI DANTE
GUIDI MOLZA MONTI PORTA
PRAGA PRATI PULCI TASSO
CIAMPI GIUSTI GROSSI MAMELI
MARINI PARINI POERIO REVERE
ALEARDI ARIOSTO BERCHET
BOIARDO FOLENGO FRUGONI
GUARINI MARRADI MAZZONI
MONTALE PASCOLI ZANELLA
ALAMANNI BACCELLI BIBBIENA
CARDUCCI CHIARINI COSTANZO
FILICAIA GUERRINI LEOPARDI
MARTELLI NENCIONI PETRARCH
RUCELLAI TANSILLO ARNABOLDI
BARBERINI BROFFERIO CALZABIGI
CESAROTTI CHIABRERA
MARINETTI RAPISARDI
ANGIOLIERI CANNIZZARO
FIRENZUOLA METASTASIO
PINDEMONTE BRACCIOLINI
CRESCIMBENI FORTEGUERRI
JAPANESE BASHO AKAHITO
NOGUCHI
LITHUANIAN MAIRONIS
NEW ZEALAND DUGGAN
NICARAGUAN DARIO
NORWEGIAN MOE KRAG IBSEN
AANRUD HANSEN GARBORG
WELHAVEN
PERSIAN HAFIZ SAADI ANVARI
DAKIKI HATIFI NIZAMI FIRDAUSI
PERUVIAN CHOCANO
POLISH POL ASNYK LANGE
POTOCKI SZUJSKI UJEJSKI
WITTLIN ZALESKI KLONOWIC
KRASICKI ZEHOMSKI ZULAWSKI
GASZYNSKI KARPINSKI KRASINSKI
BRODZINSKI DANILOWSKI
KONOPNICKA LOBODOWSKI
MALCZEWSKI MICKIEWICZ
SARBIEWSKI WIERZYNSKI
WYSPIANSKI KOCHANOWSKI
LENARTOWICZ SZYMONOWICZ
PORTUGUESE MELO QUITA
BOCAGE CAMOES CASTRO
GONZAGA QUENTAL RESENDE
RIBEIRO CASTILHO FERREIRA
JUNQUEIRO PALMEIRIM
NASCIMENTO
ROMAN CATO OVID CINNA LUCAN
VARRO ACCIUS BAVIUS ENNIUS
HORACE VERGIL AVIENUS
NAEVIUS STATIUS AFRANIUS
SEDULIUS TIBULLUS VALERIUS
LUCRETIUS PROPERTIUS
RUMANIAN BLAGA EMINESCU
ALEXANDRI ALECSANDRI
RUSSIAN FET MEI BLOK BUNIN
BUGAEV ESENIN IVANOV MAIKOV
RYLEEV BALMONT BRYUSOV
GNEDICH KAPNIST KOLTSOV
NIKITIN PUSHKIN NEKRASOV
POLONSKI TYUTCHEV BESTUZHEV
DERZHAVIN KHERASKOV
KHOMYAKOV LERMONTOV
PASTERNAK ZHUKOVSKI
BARATYNSKI BATYUSHKOV
MAYAKOVSKI PLESHCHEEV
BOGDANOVICH VOZNESENSKY
YEVTUSHENKO
SCOTTISH ADAM AIRD GRAY
HOGG LANG MURE THOM AYTON
BRUCE BURNS JACOB LOGAN

SCOTT SHARP SMITH YOUNG
AYTOUN DUNBAR GRAHAM
HERVEY LEYDEN MALLET MICKLE
MILLER MURRAY NICOLL POLLOK
RAMSAY WILSON BAILLIE
BARBOUR BARCLAY BEATTIE
CLELAND DOUGLAS GRAHAME
KENNEDY LINDSAY PRINGLE
TENNANT THOMSON ANDERSON
COCKBURN DAVIDSON
DRUMMOND HAMILTON
HENRYSON MACNEILL MAITLAND
ALEXANDER BELLENDEN
BLACKLOCK FERGUSSON
GILFILLAN STEVENSON
BALLANTINE CUNNINGHAM
MACDIARMID MOTHERWELL
MONTGOMERIE
SOUTH AFRICAN LANGENHOVEN
SPANISH CRUZ MENA RUIZ VEGA
DURAN RIOJA CANETE CETINA
VIRUES ALCAZAR BECQUER
GALLEGO HERRERA IRIARTE
JIMENEZ MORATIN SALINAS
AGUILERA BALBUENA CORONADO
FIGUEROA MANRIQUE VILLEGAS
ALEIXANDRE CASTILLEJO
CIENFUEGOS ESPRONCEDA
SANTILLANA VILLAMEDIANA
SWEDISH DALIN BESKOW CREUTZ
LIDNER TEGNER WALLIN
DALGREN EKELUND LEOPOLD
RYDBERG ATTERBOM BELLMANN
BORJESON BOTTIGER BRINKMAN
KELLGREN LAGERLOF LENNGREN
LEVERTIN NICANDER ADLERBETH
KARLFELDT MARTINSON
MESSENIUS FAHLCRANTZ
LAGERKVIST STAGNELIUS
STRANDBERG WENNERBERG
OXENSTIERNA
SWISS ILG AMIEL FAESI MEYER
GESSNER LAVATER FROHLICH
LEUTHOLD
SYRIAN GIBRAN
TURKISH FUZULI
URUGUAYAN FIGUEROA
WELSH DAVID HUGHES WILLIAMS
POETASTER BARDET BAVIAN
BAVIUS POETITO BARDLING
VERSEMAN
POETIC ODIC LYRIC STILTED
PEGASEAN POEMATIC
POETRY SONG BLANK MELIC
POEMS VERSE EPOPEE POESIS
SONIOU DOGGREL KALEVALA
(FINNISH —) RUNES
(GOD OF —) BRAGI
(HEROIC —) EPOS
(KIND OF —) CONCRETE
(MUSE OF —) ERATO THALIA
EUTERPE CALLIOPE
POGGE BULLHEAD
POGROM RIOT PILLAGE MASSACRE
POGY POGIE MENHADEN
POIGNANT APT HOME KEEN
ACUTE SHARP SMART BITING
BITTER MOVING SEVERE URGENT
CUTTING POINTED PUNGENT
SATIRIC INCISIVE PIERCING
PRESSING STINGING STRIKING
TOUCHING AMAREVOLE
POINCIANA DELONIX FLAMBEAU

GULMOHAR FLAMBOYER
POINSETTIA BANNER FIREFLOWER
POINT AIM DOT JOT NAK NEB NIB
NUB PEG PIN RES WAY APEX
BACK BOKE CHAT CUSP FORK
GAFF GAME GOOD HEAD HOLD
ITEM KNOT LACE LOOK NAIL
PEAK PICK PILE PINT SPOT STOP
WHET BEARD CHALK DIGIT
FOCUS INDEX LEVEL MUCRO
PITCH PRICK PUNCH PUNCT
PUNTA PUNTO REFER STAND
TEACH THING TOOTH ALLUDE
BROACH CRAYON CUSPIS CUTOFF
DEGREE DIRECT FLECHE JUGALE
MATTER NOSING PERIOD THESIS
TITTLE VERTEX ZYGION APICULA
ARTICLE BENEFIT CACUMEN
CRUNODE ESSENCE GATEWAY
PUNCTUM PUSHPIN SHARPEN
TANJONG TRAGION ANNOUNCE
PUNCTULE STRIPPER PARTICULAR
(— AT ISSUE) BEEF CRUX
(— AT WHICH LEAF SPRINGS) AXIL
(— BEHIND EAR) ASTERION
(— FOR PHONOGRAPH RECORD)
STYLE
(— IN CAPSTAN) STRIPPER
(— IN CONSONANT) DAGHESH
(— IN DEBATE) ISSUE
(— IN ORBIT OF PLANET) AUGE
APSIS APOGEE SYZYGY APOJOVE
PERIGEE APASTRON APHELION
(— IN QUESTION) ISSUE
(— IN SEVEN-UP) GIFT
(— IN SOME GAMES) PUNT
(— NEAREST EARTH) PERIGEE
(— OF A BORDER) VANDYKE
(— OF ANCHOR) BILL
(— OF ANTLER) PRONG
(— OF ANVIL) HORN
(— OF CELESTIAL SPHERE)
ANTAPEX
(— OF CHIN) BUTTON
(— OF CONTACT) EPHAPSE
(— OF CRESCENT MOON) CUSP
(— OF DECLINE) EBB
(— OF DIVERGENCE) AXIL
(— OF ECLIPTIC) LAGNA SOLSTICE
(— OF EPIGRAM) STING
(— OF FAITH) ARTICLE
(— OF HONOR) PUNDONOR
(— OF INTEREST) CLOU
(— OF INTERSECTION) FOOT
STAURION
(— OF JAVELIN) SAGAIE
(— OF JUNCTION) MEET BREGMA
LAMBDA
(— OF LABEL) LAMBEAU
(— OF LAND) ODD CAPE SPIT
MORRO HEADLAND
(— OF LEAF) MUCRO
(— OF LIFE) HYLEG
(— OF LIGHT) GLINT SPANGLE
(— OF LIGHTNING ROD) AIGRETTE
(— OF LIPS) CHEILION
(— OF MANGO) NAK
(— OF ONSET) BRINK
(— OF ORIGIN) HIVE SOURCE
FOUNTAIN
(— OF PEN) NEB NIB
(— OF PETAL) LACINULA
(— OF REFERENCE) STYLION

(— OF ROCK) NUNATAK
(— OF STAG'S HORN) START
(— OF STORY) KNOT
(— OF STYLUS) CUTTER
(— OF SUPPORT) BEARING
(— OF TEMPERATURE) SOLIDUS
(— OF TIME) DATE INSTANT
JUNCTURE
(— OF TOOTH) CUSP
(— OF UMBRELLA) FERRULE
(— OF VIEW) EYE ANGLE FRONT
SLANT COLORS CORNER GROUND
RESPECT FUTURISM
(— OF VIOLIN BOW) HEAD
(— OF WEAPON) ORD BARB
(— ON AUGER OR BIT) SPUR
(— ON BACKGAMMON BOARD)
FLECHE
(— ON CURVE) TACNODE
(— ON JAW) GONION
(— ON STAG'S HORN) BROACH
(— ON SUNDIAL) NODE
(— OUT) SHOW DIGIT INFER
ASSIGN DIRECT ENSIGN FINGER
MUSTER NOTIFY REMARK
PRESAGE INDICATE
(APPROPRIATE —) PLACE
(ASTROLOGICAL —) INGRESS
(BARBED —) FORK
(BLUNT —) MORNETTE
(CARBON —) CRAYON
(CARDINAL —) EAST WEST HINGE
NORTH SOUTH
(CARDINAL —S) CARDINES
(CENTRAL —) OMPHALOS
(CHRONOLOGICAL —) ERA EPOCH
(COMPASS —) E N S W NE NW SE
SW ENE ESE NNE NNW SSE SSW
WNW WSW AIRT AIRTH RHUMB
COURSE
(CRITICAL —) JUMP
(CROWNING —) CAPSHEAF
CAPSTONE
(CRUCIAL —) CRUX
(CULMINATING —) HEAD COMBLE
(DOUBLE — OF CURVE) ACNODE
CRUNODE
(ESSENTIAL —) MAIN
(EXACT —) TEE
(EXCESS —S) LAP
(EXCLAMATION —) BANG
SCREAMER
(EXTREME —) END
(FARTHEST —) APOGEE SOLSTICE
(FINAL —) UPCOME
(FIXED —) ABUTMENT
(GLAZIER'S —) SPRIG
(HALFWAY — IN CRIBBAGE) CORNER
(HIGHEST —) TIP ACME APEX
AUGE NOON PEAK CREST FLOOD
APOGEE CLIMAX CULMEN HEIGHT
PERIOD SUMMIT VERTEX ZENITH
EVEREST MAXIMUM MERIDIAN
SOLSTICE
(KNOTTY —) CRUX NODUS
(LAST —) END
(LATERAL —) ALARE
(LOWEST —) NADIR BOTTOM
BEDROCK
(LOWEST — OF HULL) BILGE
(MAIN —) JET SUM GIST
(MEDIAN —) HORMION
(NO —S) LOVE

(ONE'S STRONG —) FORTE
(PEDAL —) DRONE
(PIVOTAL —) KNUCKLE
(PRECISE —) NICK
(PROJECTING —) CRAG PEAK
BEARD
(SHARP —) JAG PRICK PRICKLE
(SIGNIFICANT —) MILESTONE
(SINGLE —) ACE
(SKULL —) TYLION
(SORE —) NERVE
(STARTING —) BASE
(STATIONARY —) SPINODE
(STRIKING —) SALIENCE
(STRONG —) FORTE
(TAPERING —) ACUMEN
(TENNIS —) LET CHASE BISQUE
(TENTH OF —) MOMENT
(TERMINAL —) GOAL BOURN
BREAK AIRPORT
(TO THE —) COGENT
(TOP —) TUFT
(TURNING —) CARDO EPOCH CRISIS
(UNIPLANAR —) UNODE
(UTMOST —) EXTREME SUBLIME
(VANTAGE —) TOWER
(VOWEL —) SERE SEGOL SEGHOL
(WEAK —) BLOT
(PREF.) KENTRO MUCRONI PUNC-
TATO PUNCTI PUNCTO STIGMATI
STIGMEO STIGMO
POINT-BLANK BLUNT PLAIN POINT
DIRECT WHOLLY EXPRESS
DIRECTLY
**POINT COUNTER POINT (AUTHOR
OF —)** HUXLEY
(CHARACTER IN —) JOHN LUCY
MARK BURLAP ELINOR GILRAY
PHILIP RACHEL SIDNEY WALTER
WEBLEY BIDLAKE CARLING
EVERARD QUARLES RAMPION
BEATRICE MARJORIE SPRANDRELL
TANTAMOUNT
POINTED SET ERDE HOME ACUTE
EXACT FIXED PEAKY PIKED
TANGY TERSE FITCHE LIVELY
OXEOTE PEAKED PECKED PICKED
SPIRED ANGULAR FITCHEE
LACONIC PRECISE SPICATE
ZESTFUL ACICULAR ACULEATE
COPATAIN CULTRATE DIACTINE
PUNCTUAL STELLATE ACUMINATE
(PREF.) OXY
POINTEDNESS BARB
POINTER TIP YAD COCK HAND
WAND DUBHE INDEX POINT
FESCUE FINGER GUNDOG INDICE
SILKER STYLUS FLUSHER
INDICANT SIGNITOR
(— IN GREAT BEAR) DUBHE
DUBBHE
(— ON ASTROLABE) ALMURY
(— ON GAUGE) ARM
(BUILDER'S —) RAKER
(TEACHER'S —) FESCUE
(PL.) MEN GUARDS YADAYIM
POINTLESS DRY ILL DULL FLAT
INANE SILLY VAPID FRIGID
STUPID INSIPID WITLESS
MUTICOUS
POINTSMAN TRAPPER LATCHMAN
SWITCHMAN
POISE PEE CALM HEAD REST SWAY

TACT BRACE PEIZE APLOMB
OFFSET PONDER BALANCE
BEARING DIGNITY OPPRESS
POISURE DELIVERY EASINESS
SERENITY
(— RECIPROCAL) RHE
POISED SET FACILE HOVERING
NERVELESS
(BE —) LIBRATE
POISER HALTER
POISON FIG GAS BANE BIKH DRAB
DRUG GALL TUBA VERY ATTER
TAINT TOXIN VENOM VIRUS
ANTIAR DERRIS INFECT RANKLE
TOXIFY TOXOID ACONITE
BABASCO CORRUPT ENVENOM
FLYBANE MINERAL PERVERT
PHALLIN TANGHIN VITIATE
ACQUETTA DELETERY RATSBANE
VENENATE SAXITOXIN
(— IN DEATH CUP) PHALLIN
(ARROW —) HAYA INEE URALI
URARE URARI ANTIAR ANTJAR
CURARE CURARI DERRIS OURARI
OUABAIN
(FISH —) AKIA CUBE TIMBO
DERRIS HAIARI BABASCO
BARBASCO
(RAT —) ANTU
(VIRULENT —) BIKH TANGHIN
(PREF.) PHARMACO VENENI
VENENO VIRU
POISONED BUCKEYED TOXICATE
VENENATE VENOMOUS
POISONER SEPSIN CANIDIA
VENEFIC VENOMER
POISON HEMLOCK BUNK CICUTA
POISONING PYEMIA UREMIA
ARGYRIA GASSING JIMMIES
BOTULISM MYCETISM PLUMBISM
ICHTHYISM LATHYRISM
SATURNISM SELENOSIS
POISON IVY CLIMATH MARKERY
MERCURY MARKWEED
POISON OAK YEARA
POISONOUS ATTRY TOXIC ATTERY
VENENE VIROSE VIROUS BANEFUL
NOISOME NOXIOUS DELETERY
MEPHITIC TOXICANT VENENATE
VENOMOUS VIRULENT
MALIGNANT
(PREF.) TOX(I)(IC)(ICO)(O)
POISON SUMAC BURTREE
DOGWOOD
POISON TOBACCO HENBANE
POISONWOOD BUMWOOD
POITREL ARMOR PECTRON
POKE BAG DAB DIG DUB HIT JAB
JOG PUG PUR TIG WAD BROD
PAUT PORR PROD PROG RAUK
RUCK SACK SOCK STAB STIR
NIDGE POACH PROKE PROTE
PUNCH ROUSE STEER STOKE
COWBOY DAWDLE INCITE PIERCE
POCKET POUNCE POUTER
PUGGLE PUTTER WALLET
PRODDLE
(— ABOUT) ROKE ROUT RUMMAGE
(— AROUND) ROOT SCROUNGE
(— FUN) COD
(— LIGHTLY) POTTER PUTTER
(— WITH FOOT) SCUFF
(— WITH NOSE) SNUZZLE

POKE-IN STRANDER
POKELOKEN BOGAN LOGAN
POKER DART DRAW FLIP POIT
PORR POTE STUD BLUFF BOGIE
CURATE GOBLIN STOKER
ACEPOTS FRUGGAN LOWBALL
PASSOUT POCHARD SHOTGUN
BASEBALL COALRAKE JACKPOTS
MISTIGRI SHOWDOWN
(**— CHIP**) JETON JETTON
(**— HAND**) RUNT FLUSH SKEET
KILTER PELTER STRAIGHT
(**FORM OF —**) DRAW STUD
(**HOT —**) SALAMANDER
POKEWEED POKE POCAN SCOKE
COAKUM GARGET FOXGLOVE
INKBERRY REDBERRY
POKY DEAD DULL JAIL SLOW
DOWDY POKEY POKING SHABBY
STODGY STUFFY STUPID
CRAMPED TEDIOUS
POLAK BALSA POLLACK

POLAND
CAPITAL: WARSAW
COIN: DUCAT GROSZ MARKA
ZLOTY FENNIG HALERZ KORONA
DANCE: POLKA MAZURKA
KRAKOWIAK POLONAISE
GENTRY: SZLACHTA
LAKE: GOPLO MAMRY SNIARDWY
MEASURE: CAL MILA MORG PRET
LINJA SAZEN STOPA VLOKA
WLOKA CWIERK KORZEC
KAMANTA LOKIEC GARNIEC
MOUNTAIN: RYSY TATRA SUDETEN
NAME: POLONIA SARMATIA
NATIVE: SLAV MARUR SILESIAN
PARLIAMENT: SEJM SEYM SENAT
PROVINCE: OPOLE KIELCE
RIVER: BUG SAN ALLE BRDA
GWDA LYNA NYSA ODER STYR
BIALA BZURA DRANA DWINA
NOTEC SERET WARTA WISTA
NEISSE NIEMEN PILICA PRIPET
PROSNA STRYPA WIEPRZ
VISTULA WISTOKA DNIESTER
TITLE OF ADDRESS: PAN PANI
PANIE
TOWN: LWO KOLO LIDA LODZ
LVOV OELS BREST BYTOM
CHELM POSEN RADOM SRODA
TORUN VILNA GDANSK GDYNIA
GRODNO KRACOW KRAKOW
LUBLIN POZNAN TARNOW
WARSAW ZABRZE BEUTHEN
BRESLAU CHORZOW GAROCIN
GLIWICE LEMBERG LITOUSK
WROCLAW GLEIWITZ
KATOWICE SZCZECIN
TARNOPOL
WEIGHT: LUT FUNT UNCYA
KAMIAN CENTNER SKRUPUL

POLAR ARCTIC EMANANT PIVOTAL
DIRECTRIX
POLARIS ALRUCABA
POLE BAR LAT LEG LUG POL POY
ROD SKY XAT BEAM BIND BROG
COPE FALL HOOK KENT MAST
NEAP PALO PERK PIKE PROP SKID
SPAR TREE UFER CABER FOCUS
MASUR MAZUR PERCH QUANT

REACH SHAFT SPEAR SPOKE
STAFF STANG STILT STING STODE
SWAPE SWIPE BEACON BORITY
CROTCH FLOWER IMPOSE JUFFER
KILHIG RICKER RISSLE RYPECK
SPONGE STOWER TONGUE
BARLING HEAVENS TOWMAST
ALESTAKE FLAGPOLE FOOTPICK
POLANDER STANDARD
(**— AS EMBLEM OF SOVEREIGNTY**)
KAHILI
(**— AS HOLDFAST FOR BOATS**)
RYPECK
(**— FOR BEARING COFFIN**) SPOKE
(**— FOR PROPELLING BOAT**) POY
(**— FOR TOSSING**) CABER KEBAR
(**— HOLDING SAIL**) BOOM MAST
SPRIT
(**— MARKING SAND DUNE**) BALIZE
(**— OF TIMBER WAGON**) NIB
JANKER
(**— OF VEHICLE**) NEAP
(**— ON TWO WHEELS**) JANKER
(**— SEPARATING HORSES**) BAIL
(**— USED AS SIGN**) ALEPOLE
ALESTAKE
(**— WITH BIRD DECOY**) STOOL
(**BOAT —**) SPRIT
(**CARRIAGE —**) NIB BEAM
(**COUPLING —**) REACH
(**FIR —**) UFER UPHER JUFFER
(**FISHING —**) WAND
(**FORKED —**) CROTCH
(**LOGGING —**) JANKER KILHIG
KILLIG
(**LONG —**) PEW
(**MANGROVE —**) BORITY
(**MINE —S**) LAGGING
(**NEGATIVE —**) CATHODE
(**PUNT —**) QUANT STOWER
(**RANGE —**) FLAG
(**SACRED —**) ASHERAH
(**SHEPHERD'S —**) KENT
(**SPRINGY —**) BINDER
(**STABLE —**) BAIL
(**STOUT —**) KILHIG RICKER
(**WATER-RAISING —**) SWEEP
(**SUFF.**) KONT
POLEAX STAFF POLEARM
POLECAT FITCH SKUNK ZORIL
FERRET FICHAT WEASEL
FOUMART FOULMART PERWITSKY
SARMATIER
(**— PELT**) FITCH
POLE FLOUNDER SOLE
POLEHEAD TADPOLE
POLESTAR STAR GUIDE POLARIS
LODESTAR
POLICE MAN HEAT GUARD WATCH
GOVERN CONTROL JEMADAR
OCHRANA POLIZEI PROTECT
TOXOTAE OPRICHNIK
(**SECRET —**) CHEKA
POLICEMAN COP JOE KID NAB PIG
BOGY BULL FLIC FUZZ GRAB JACK
JOHN PEON SLOP TRAP ZARP
BOBBY BOGEY BULKY BURLY
GAZER PEACE RURAL SCREW
SEPOY ASKARI BADGER BOBBIE
COPPER FISCAL FLATTY HARMAN
JOHNNY PEELER REDCAP ROZZER
RUNNER SHAMUS CRUSHER
FOOTMAN GHAFFIR GUMSHOE

JEMADAR OFFICER SHOOFLY
TROOPER ZAPTIAH ZAPTIEH
BARGELLO BLUECOAT DOGBERRY
FLATFOOT GENDARME MINISTER
PATROLMAN
(**CLUB OF —**) BILLY STAFF
SPONTOON TRUNCHEON
(**PL.**) FINEST
POLICE STATION THANA
BARGELLO KOTWALEE
POLICY WIT DEAL FRONT ORDER
GOVERN NUMBER TICKET
WISDOM AUTARKY COUNSEL
CUNNING FLOATER LEFTISM
LOTTERY TONTINE VOUCHER
ACTIVISM ARTIFICE SAGACITY
STATEWAY PLURALISM
(**CHOSEN —**) COURSE
(**PL.**) APRISMO
POLISH BOB LAP MOP RUB RUD
BUFF DUCO FILE POLE CLEAN
FRUSH GLAZE GLOSS GRACE
RABAT ROUND SHINE SLICK
STONE AFFILE BARREL LUSTER
PUNISH REFINE RUMBLE SHAMMY
SLIGHT SMOOTH STREAK
BEESWAX BURNISH CHAMOIS
FURBISH LACQUER PERFECT
PLANISH VARNISH ELEGANCE
LEVIGATE SIMONIZE URBANIZE
SARMATIAN
POLISHED FINE COMPT ROUND
SHINY SLICK TERSE BUFFED
FACETE GLOSSY INLAND POLITE
SMOOTH ELEGANT GALLANT
GENTEEL POLITIC REFINED
CULTURED
(**NOT —**) BLIND
POLISHER BUFFER GLAZER
WAGWAG WIGWAG DOLLIER
GLOSSER LAPIDARY SMOOTHER
POLISHING SANDING FROTTAGE
LIMATION
(**— MATERIAL**) RABAT
POLITE NEAT TIDY TRIM BLAND
CIVIL SUAVE GENTLE SMOOTH
URBANE COURTLY GALLANT
GENTEEL DELICATE DISCREET
LUSTROUS ATTENTIVE
COURTEOUS
POLITENESS FINISH TASHRIF
CIVILITY COURTESY ELEGANCE
URBANITY
POLITES (**FATHER OF —**) PRIAM
(**MOTHER OF —**) HECUBA
POLITIC WARY WISE SUAVE
AROFUL CRAFTY CUNNING
TACTFUL DISCREET PROVIDENT
POLITICAL (**— ASSN.**) VEREIN
(**— PARTY**) GOP TORY WHIG
LABOR
POLITICIAN BOSS STATIST
WARWICK PIPELAYER
STATESMAN
POLITY SERFISM
POLIXENES (**SON OF —**) FLORIZEL
POLL COW DOD NOT POW ROB
CHUB COLL DODD HEAD NAPE
NOTT PASH CROWN SKULL STRIP
CENSUS FLEECE PARROT
CANVASS DESPOIL PILLAGE
PLUNDER POLLARD
POLLACK LOB GADE LAIT GADID

LYTHE BILLET LAITHE SAITHE
BADDOCK SILLOCK WALLEYE
BLUEFISH COALFISH GRAYFISH
LORICATE MOULRUSH
POLLARD CHU COW DOD BRAN
POLL STAG SHEEP CHEVAN
DODDLE DOTARD BOLLING
LOPPARD WOODSERE
POLLARD TREE DOTARD RUNNEL
POLLED NOT NOTT POLEY
HORNLESS
POLLEN DUST MEAL FLOUR
FARINA POWDER BEEBREAD
(**— BRUSH**) SCOPA
(**— TUBE**) SPERMARY
POLLER VOTER BARBER POLLSTER
POLLEX THUMB
POLLINATE SELF FECUNDATE
FECUNDIZE FERTILIZE
POLLINATING SIBBING
POLLIWOG TADPOLE
POLLOCK PODLER
POLLUTE FOIL FOUL SOIL BLEND
DIRTY SMEAR TAINT BEFOUL
DEFILE INFECT MUDDLE RAVISH
ADULTER DEBAUCH PROFANE
SLOTTER VIOLATE
POLLUTED FOUL DRUNK TURBID
CORRUPT
POLLUTING FILTHY
POLLUTION STAIN SULLAGE
FOULNESS IMPURITY
POLLUX POL HERCULES
(**BROTHER OF —**) CASTOR
(**MOTHER OF —**) LEDA
POLO (**PERIOD IN —**) CHUKKER
POLONAISE POLACCA
FACKELTANZ
POLONIUS CORAMBIS
(**DAUGHTER OF —**) OPHELIA
(**SON OF —**) LAERTES
POLT BLOW THUMP STROKE
POLTERGEIST GHOST SPIRIT
POLTROON IDLER COWARD
CRAVEN WRETCH DASTARD
COWARDLY SLUGGARD
POLYANDRIUM CEMETERY
POLYBUS (**FATHER OF —**) ANTENOR
(**MOTHER OF —**) THEANO
(**WIFE OF —**) MEROPE PERIBOEA
POLYDAMAS (**BROTHER OF —**)
EUPHORBUS HYPERENOR
(**COMPANION OF —**) HECTOR
(**FATHER OF —**) PANTHOUS
(**MOTHER OF —**) PHRONTIS
POLYDORE (**BROTHER OF —**)
CASTALIO
POLYDORUS (**FATHER OF —**) PRIAM
CADMUS HIPPOMEDON
(**MOTHER OF —**) HECUBA
HARMONIA
(**SLAYER OF —**) POLYMNESTOR
(**SON OF —**) LABDACUS
(**WIFE OF —**) NYCTEIS
POLYGALA GAYWINGS
POLYGON DECAGON HEXAGON
NONAGON HEPTAGON PENTAGON
CHILIAGON MULTANGLE
POLYGRAPH KEELER
POLYHEDRON BEAD PRISM
PRISMATOID
POLYMER DIMER HYDROL
MANNAN MUREIN

HEXAMER OLIGOMER
(— UNIT) MER

POLYNESIA

CHESTNUT: RATA
IMAGE: TIKI
ISLAND: COOK LINE SAMOA
TONGA EASTER ELLICE
PHOENIX
ISLE: MOTU
KING: ALII ARII ARIKI
LANGUAGE: UVEA TAGALOG
MOUND: AHU
NATIVE: ATI MAORI KANAKA
NIVEAN TONGAN NESOGAEAN
PRINCIPLE: TIKI
WOMAN: WAHINE

POLYNESIAN MAORI KANAKA
TONGAN FUTUNAN
POLYNICES (BROTHER OF —)
ETEOCLES
(FATHER OF —) OEDIPUS
(MOTHER OF —) JOCASTA
(WIFE OF —) ARGIA
POLYNOMIAL CUBIC
POLYP CORAL HYDRA TUMOR
ZOOID ISOPOD HYDRULA
OCTOPOD
POLYPARY ZOARIUM
POLYPHONY ORGANUM
FABURDEN COUNTERPOINT
POLYPIDOM CORMUS
POLYSACCHARIDE LEVAN
GELOSE GLYCAN INULIN IRISIN
MANNAN AMYLOSE DEXTRAN
FUCOSAN HEXOSAN POLYOSE
GALACTAN GLYCOGEN LICHENIN
SECALOSE SINISTRIN
POLYXENA (FATHER OF —) PRIAM
(MOTHER OF —) HECUBA
POLYZOAN POLYP CESTODE
RADIATE
POMACE MUST RAPE POMMY
STOCK STOSH CHEESE
POMADE CIDER POMATUM
LIPSTICK OINTMENT
POMANDER CASE POUNCET
POMATO TOPATO
POME BALL APPLE GLOBE
JUNEBERRY
POMEGRANATE GRENAT
GRENADE BALAUSTA
POMELO SHADDOCK GRAPEFRUIT
POMERANIA (CAPITAL OF —)
STETTIN
(CITY IN —) THORN TORUN
ANKLAM
(ISLAND IN —) RUGEN USEDOM
(PROVINCE IN —) POMORZE
POMFRET BULLY HENFISH
POMME DE TERRE POTATO
POMMEL BOB FIB NOB BEAT HORN
KNOB PAIK PAKE TORE NEVEL
BRUISE BUFFET CRUTCH FINIAL
PLUMMET
POMP BRAG FARE WEAL BOAST
PRIDE STATE ESTATE PAMPER
PARADE RIALTY SCHEME SPRUNK
BOBANCE DISPLAY PAGEANT
PANOPLY SPLURGE CEREMONY
EQUIPAGE GRANDEUR SEMBLANT
SPLENDOR

POMPANO DART JUREL ALLICE
CARANX PERMIT ALEWIFE
COBBLER OLDWIFE CARANGID
MACKEREL
(— CLAM) COQUINA
POMPOSITY TUMOR TUMOUR
BIGHEAD BIGNESS BOMBAST
POMPOUS BIG BUG BUDGE JELLY
LARGE SHOWY TUMID WIGGY
ASTRUT AUGUST TURGID
BLOATED BOMBAST FUSTIAN
OROTUND STILTED SWOLLEN
TURGENT BEWIGGED INFLATED
MAGNIFIC SWELLING TOPLOFTY
IMPORTANT PONTIFICAL
PORTENTOUS
PONCEAU GRANAT
PONCHO MANGA RUANA
POND (ALSO SEE POOL) LAY LUM
DELF DIKE MOAT PULK SLEW
STEW TANK VLEI VLEY CANAL
DECOY DELFT LACHE LETCH
STANK WAYER CLAIRE LAGOON
LOCHAN PUDDLE SALINA SLOUGH
SPLASH STAGNE MULLETRY
(— FOR OYSTERS) CLAIRE
(— MAN) JACKER
(ARTIFICIAL —) AQUARIUM
(DIRTY —) SOAL
(FISH —) VIVER GURGES PISCINA
(FISH STORING —) STEW
(SMALL —) KHAL
(STAGNANT —) DUB
(PREF.) LACO LIMN(I)(O)
PONDER CON CAST CHAW MUSE
PORE ROLL TURN BROOD STUDY
VOLVE WEIGH ADVISE EXPEND
REASON RECORD REMORD
BALANCE COMPASS EXAMINE
IMAGINE PERPEND REFLECT
REVERIE REVOLVE APPRAISE
COGITATE CONSIDER MEDITATE
PONDERABILITY WEIGHT GRAVITY
PONDEROUS DULL SLOW BULKY
GRAVE HEAVY SOGGY AWKWARD
WEIGHTY UNWIELDY IMPORTANT
PONDEROUSNESS HEFT
POND HEN COOT
PONDMAN JACKER
PONDOKKIE HUT HOVEL
PONE CAKE LUMP WRIT PAUNE
PUDDING SWELLING
PONGEE PAUNCHE SHANTUNG
PONIARD STAB BODKIN DAGGER
STYLET POINADO
PONOCRATES (PUPIL OF —)
GARGANTUA
PONT FERRY FLOAT BRIDGE
FERRYBOAT
PONTIANAC JELUTONG
PONTIC DUMMY
PONTICELLO BREAK MAGAS
PONTIFF POPE BISHOP PRIEST
PONTIFEX
PONTIFICAL AARONIC
PONTIL PUNTY
PONTOON FLOAT RHINO BRIDGE
PONY CAB RAW TAT CAVY TROT
YABU BIDET DALES GRIFF PAINT
PINTO POWNY TACKY TRICK
WELCH WELSH BASUTO BHUTIA
BRONCO CAYUSE EXMOOR
GARRAN SHELTY TANGUN

TATTOO ENGLISH HACKNEY
MANIPUR MUSTANG SHELTIE
FORESTER GALLOWAY SHETLAND
(STUDENT'S —) CRIB TROT BICYCLE
(PL.) DALES
POODLE SHOCK BARBET
POOH POWWAW
POOK HEAP PICK PULL PLUCK
STACK
POOKA PUCK GOBLIN SPECTER
POOL (ALSO SEE POND) CAR DIB
DUB LAY LUM PIT POL POT POW
BANK BOOK CARR DIKE DUMP
FARM FLOW JHIL LAKE LIDO LINN
LLYN LUMB MERE PANT PEEL
PLUD POLK POND PULE PULK
RING SINK SLEW SOIL SWAG
TANK TARN WEEL BAYOU BOWLY
DECOY FLASH FLUSH FRESH
JHEEL KITTY LETCH LOUGH
MEARE PLASH PLUMB SLACK
STANK STELL STILL THERM
TRUNK CARTEL CHARCO FLODGE
LAGOON LASHER PLUNGE
PUDDLE SILOAM SPLASH STABLE
CARLINE CATHOLE CUSHION
JACKPOT PLASHET SNOOKER
STAGNUM INTERLOT QUINIELA
(— AT JERUSALEM) BETHESDA
(— BELOW WATERFALL) LIN LINN
LLYN
(— IN BOG) HAG
(— WITH SALMON NETS) STELL
(— WITHOUT OUTLET) STAGNUM
(ARTIFICIAL —) CUSHION
(AUCTION —) CALCUTTA
(BETTING —) EXACTA PERFECTA
TRIFECTA
(DIRTY —) SUMP
(FISH —) TRUNK STEWPOND
(MOUNTAIN —) TARN
(MUDDY —) LETCH
(SWIMMING —) BATH LIDO
PISCINA NATATORY NATATORIUM
(PREF.) LIMN(I)(O) STAGNI
POON DILO PEON PUNA DOMBA
KEENA TAMANU SIRPOON
MASTWOOD
POONGHIE RAHAN PRIEST PUNGYI
PHONGHI TALAPOIN
POOP DOCK FIRE GULP TOOT
CHEAT COZEN STERN BEFOOL
ISLAND DECEIVE EXHAUST
HINDDECK OVERCOME
POOR BAD OFF SAD BASE EVIL
FOUL LEAN LEWD PUNK SICK
SOUR THIN DINKY EXILE FOOTY
GROSS JERRY KETTY SCALY SEELY
SILLY SOBER SORRY UNORN
FEEBLE HUMBLE HUNGRY
LEADEN MEAGER MEAGRE
MEASLY PILLED PORAIL PRETTY
SCANTY SHABBY STREET CODFISH
HAPLESS NAUGHTY SCRAWNY
SCRUBBY SQUALID TRIVIAL
UNLUCKY INDIGENT ORDINARY
PRECIOUS SCRANNEL SNEAKING
TERRIBLE UNTHENDE PENNILESS
PENURIOUS
(— BOY) HERO
(PREF.) MAL(E) PTOCHO
POORHOUSE MEASONDUE
POORLY ILL BADLY SADLY BARELY

FEEBLY SIMPLY SLIGHT SHABBILY
(PREF.) DYS
POOR SOLDIER FRIARBIRD
POORTITH POVERTY
POOR WHITE (AUTHOR OF —)
ANDERSON
(CHARACTER IN —) JIM JOE TOM
HUGH CLARA MCVEY SARAH
STEVE HUNTER SHEPARD
WAINSWORTH BUTTERWORTH
POP GO DOT GUN HIT TRY BLOW
DART HOCK JUMP PAWN SODA
BREAK CLOOP CRACK KNOCK
SHOOT ATTACK EFFORT FATHER
POPPER STROKE THRUSH
ASSAULT ATTEMPT CONCERT
EXPLODE INSTANT REDWING
BACKFIRE SUDDENLY
POPDOCK FOXGLOVE
POPE PAPA PAPE RUFF BISHOP
PUFFIN SHRIKE PONTIFEX
FISHERMAN
(PREF.) PAPI PAPO POPO
POPERY POPEISM PAPISTRY
POPE'S-EYE NUT NOIX
POPGUN SCOOT PENGUN POTGUN
PLUFFER
POPINJAY PARROT PAPINGO
POPLAR ABBEY ABELE ALAMO
ASPEN BAHAN LIARD BALSAM
POPPLE BAUMIER ABELTREE
WHITEBARK
POPLIN TABINET
POPOLOCA CHOCHO
POPPY HEAD BLAVER CANKER
COPROSE EARACHE PONCEAU
REDWEED ARGEMONE BALEWORT
BOCCONIA HEADACHE
DANNEBROG SQUATMORE
COQUELICOT
(CORN —S) SOLDIERS
(PREF.) MECON(O)
POPPYCOCK BOSH FOLLY STUFF
HAVERS
POPPYFISH POMPANO
POPPY SEED MAW MOHNSEED
POPULACE MOB MASS CROWD
DEMOS PLEBS MASSES MOBILE
PEOPLE PUBLIC COUNTRY
MULTITUDE
(PREF.) DEM(O) OCHLO
POPULAR LAY POP COMMON
GOLDEN PUBLIC SIMPLE VULGAR
CROWDED DEMOTIC VULGATE
APPROVED FAVORITE PEOPLISH
PLEBEIAN
POPULARITY VOGUE CLAPTRAP
POPULATE MAN BREED PLANT
WORLD PEOPLE INHABIT
POPULATION DEME COLONY
FLOTSAM KINDRED TOPODEME
UNIVERSE
(PREF.) DEM(O)
POPULUS SALIX
PORATHA (FATHER OF —) HAMAN
PORBEAGLE LAMNA SHARK
LAMNID LAMNOID
PORCELAIN JU KO CHINA MURRA
SPODE BISQUE MURRHA NANKIN
BISCUIT CELADON DRESDEN
NANKEEN NANKING MANDARIN
STEATITE
(JAPANESE —) KUTANI

(VARIETY OF —) CAEN KUAN ARITA HIZEN IMARI KYOTO AMSTEL PARIAN SEVRES BUDWEIS DRESDEN LIMOGES MEISSEN SWANSEA COALPORT HAVILAND KAKIEMON CHANTILLY

PORCH HOOD STOA LANAI STOEP STOOP INGANG PARVIS PIAZZA PORTAL RAMADA BALCONY GALERIE GALILEE NARTHEX PASSAGE POIKILE PORTICO PRONAOS VERANDA ANTENAVE SOLARIUM TRANSEPT VESTIBLE **(FRONT —)** ANTICUM

PORCUPINE QUILL URSON CAWQUAW COENDOU ERECTER ERICIUS PORKPEN HEDGEHOG HEDGEPIG **(PREF.)** HYSTRICO

PORCUPINE ANTEATER ECHIDNA
PORCUPINE FISH ERIZO ATINGA BURFISH DIODONT
PORCUPINE GRASS SPINIFEX
PORE GAZE GLOSE GLOZE STARE STOMA STUDY TRYPA BROWSE PONDER ALVEOLA CINCLIS OSTIOLE TUBULUS BAJONADO JOLTHEAD LENTICEL POROSITY

PORGY TAI SCUP PARGO PLUMA POGGY BESUGO BRAISE MAMAMU PAGRUS SPARID MARGATE PINFISH MENHADEN SPADEFISH

PORK HAM HOG PIG LARD BACON BRAWN MONEY SWINE BALDRIB LARDOON MIDDLING **(— AND SALMON)** LAULAU **(— CHOP)** BALDRIB GRISKEN **(— SHOULDER)** HAND **(FRIED CUBE OF —)** CUCHIFRITO **(SALT —)** BACON SPECK SOWBELLY

PORKFISH SISI CATALINETA
PORKY FAT GREASY
PORNOGRAPHIC LEWD CURIOUS OBSCENE
PORNOGRAPHY CURIOSA ESOTERICA
POROUS OPEN LIGHT LEACHY CELLULAR
PORPHYRY ELVAN EURITE ELVANITE GRORUDITE
PORPOISE WHALE PALACH PUFFER COWFISH DOLPHIN HOGFISH PELLOCK PULLOCK SNUFFER CETACEAN GAIRFISH
PORRECT EXTEND TENDER PRESENT
PORRET LEEK ONION PORETT SCALLION
PORRIDGE KHIR POBS SAMP ATOLE BROSE GROUT GRUEL BURGOO CROWDY SEPAWN SKILLY SOWENS TARTAN BROCHAN BURGOUT OATMEAL POBBIES POLENTA POTTAGE FLUMMERY SAGAMITE **(PREF.)** POLTO
PORRINGER TASTER TRINKET
PORT GATE GOAL LEFT MIEN WICK WINE CARRY CREEK HAVEN HITHE SALLY SCALE STATE APPORT HARBOR INPORT REFUGE AIRPORT BEARING DIGNITY

LIBERTY OUTPORT ANTEPORT DEMEANOR LARBOARD MALTOLTE PORTHOLE PRESENCE

PORTABLE MOBILE MOVABLE BEARABLE
PORTAGE PACK CARGO CARRY TARBET FREIGHT TONNAGE HAULOVER
PORTAL DOOR GATE ENTRY PORCH DOORWAY ENTRANCE
PORTAMENTO DRAG GLIDE SCOOP SLIDE PORTATO GLISSADE
PORTCULLIS BAR SHUT HERSE ORGUE SARASIN CATARACT SARRASIN
PORTE GATE
PORTE-MONNAIE PURSE
PORTEND BODE AUGUR DIVINE EXTEND BESPEAK BETOKEN PREDICT PRESAGE DENOUNCE FOREBODE FORECAST FORETELL
PORTENT AYAH LUCK SIGN SOUND TOKEN AUGURY MARVEL OSTENT WONDER AUSPICE PREDICT PRESAGE PRODIGY CEREMONY DISASTER SOOTHSAY PROGNOSTIC
PORTENTOUS AWFUL GRAVID BODEFUL DOOMFUL FATEFUL OMINOUS POMPOUS DOOMLIKE DREADFUL INFLATED SINISTER
PORTER ALE BEER MOZO CADDY HAMAL STOUT TAMEN BADGER BEARER CADDIE COOLIE DARWAN DURWAN ENTIRE KHAMAL REDCAP SUISSE DROGHER DVORNIK HUMMAUL JANITOR PITCHER REMOVER BADGEMAN BUMMAREE CARGADOR CHAPRASI LODGEMAN PORTITOR RECEIVER **(— AND STOUT)** COOPER **(JAPANESE —)** AKABO **(MEAT —)** PITCHER **(MEXICAN —)** TAMEN
PORTFOLIO BLAD
PORTIA (HUSBAND OF —) BRUTUS **(LOVER OF —)** BASSANIO **(MAID OF —)** NERISSA
PORTIA TREE MAHO BENDY MAHOE
PORTICO STOA WALK XYST ORIEL PORCH XYSTA ZAYAT EXEDRA PARVIS PIAZZA SCHOOL XYSTUS BALCONY DISTYLE GALLERY NARTHEX PARVISE PRONAOS TERRACE VERANDA PORTICUS POSTICUM VERANDAH
PORTION BIT CUP CUT DAB JAG LAB LOT PAN BLAD DALE DEAL DOLE DOSE FATE FECK JAGG PART SIZE WHAT DOWER PIECE RATIO SHARE SLICE SNACK WHACK CANTLE CANTON COLLOP DETAIL GOBBET MATTER PARCEL RASHER EXCERPT PARTAGE SECTION SEGMENT TODDICK TRANCHE FRACTION FRAGMENT PITTANCE QUANTITY SCANTLET FODDERING **(— DRUNK)** DRAFT DRAUGHT **(— OF ACTOR'S PART)** LENGTH **(— OF ARROW)** BREAST

(— OF BIRD SONG) TOUR
(— OF BREAD OR BEER) CUE
(— OF CITRUS RIND) ALBEDO
(— OF ESTATE) LEGITIM
(— OF FARMLAND) BEREWICK
(— OF FLOODPLAIN) BANCO
(— OF FODDER) JAG
(— OF FOOD) HELP GOBBET HELPING
(— OF HIDE) HEAD
(— OF LAND) BLOCK PATTI INTAKE DIVISION DONATION
(— OF LIQUOR) STICK DIVIDEND
(— OF LITURGY) ANAPHORA
(— OF MAST) HOUSING HOUNDING
(— OF PASTURE) BREAK
(— OF POEM) STRAIN
(— OF RUG) GRIN
(— OF SERPENT'S BODY) TRAIN
(— OF STEM) BOON
(— OF STORY) SNATCH
(— OF STREAM) LAVADERO
(— OF TEA) DRAWING
(— OF TIME) SPAN DISTANCE
(— OF TOBACCO) CUD
(— OF TONGUE) BLADE
(ADDITIONAL —) RASHER
(ALLOTTED —) MOIRA SCANTLING
(BRIDE'S —) DOWRY
(CLOTTED — OF BLOOD) CRUOR
(COARSER —) BOLTINGS
(EARLY —) SPRING
(INHABITED — OF EARTH) ECUMENE
(LARGE —) SKELP
(LATTER —) AUTUMN EVENING
(MAIN —) CORPSE
(MARRIAGE —) DOT DOTE TOCHER
(MINUTE —) GRAIN
(MOST VALUABLE —) CHIEF
(PERCEPTIBLE —) KENNING
(REPRESENTATIVE —) SAMPLE
(SIGNIFICANT —) CHAPTER
(SIZABLE —) DUNT
(SMALL —) BIT DAB DOT DRAM DROP SOSH TAIT TATE CHACK SPICE SPUNK SHADOW KENNING MODICUM REMNANT SCANTLE SMIDGEN SOUPCON SCANTLET
(SMALL — OF LIQUOR) DOLLOP HEELTAP
(TRIFLING —) SMACK
(SUFF.) (BY A SPECIFIC —) MEAL
PORTLY FAT FULL AMPLE STOUT GAUCIE GOODLY STATELY SWELLING OVERBLOWN
PORTMANTEAU BAG HOOK VALISE POCKMANKY
PORTRAIT BUST ICON IKON IMAGE IMAGO MODEL PIECE KITKAT STATUE VISAGE PORTRAY RETRAIT LIKENESS RITRATTO VERONICA MINIATURE **(— ON COIN)** EFFIGY
PORTRAIT OF A LADY (AUTHOR OF —) JAMES **(CHARACTER IN —)** MERLE PANSY RALPH ARCHER CASPAR EDWARD GEMINI ISABEL OSMOND ROSIER GILBERT BANTLING GOODWOOD TOUCHETT HENRIETTA STACKPOLE WARBURTON
PORTRAY GIVE LIMN LINE BLAZE ENACT IMAGE PAINT CIPHER

CLOTHE DEPICT FIGURE SHADOW FEATURE IMITATE PICTURE DECIPHER DESCRIBE RESEMBLE

PORTUGAL	
BAY:	SETUBAL
CAPE:	ROCA MONDEGO ESPICHEL
CAPITAL:	LISBON
COIN:	JOE REI PECA REAL CONTO COROA DOBRA INDIO ESCUDO MACUTA PATACA TESTAO VINTEM CENTAVO CRUSADO MOIDORE EQUIPAGA
COLONY:	MACAO TIMOR ANGOLA GUINEA PRINCIPE
DISTRICT:	BEJA FARO BRAGA EVORA HORTA PORTO VISEU LEIRIA LISBOA
ISLAND:	TIMOR
ISLANDS:	MADEIRA
MEASURE:	PE ALMA BOTA MEIO MOIO PIPA VARA ALMUD BRACA FANGA GEIRA LEGOA LINHA MILHA PALMO ALMUDE CANADA COVADO QUARTO ALQUIER ESTADIO FERRADO SELAMIN ALQUEIRE TONELADA
MOUNTAIN:	ACOR GEREZ MARAO MOUSA PENEDA ESTRELA MONCHIQUE
RIVER:	SOR TUA LIMA MINO MIRA SADO SEDA TAGO TEJO DOURO MINHO SABAR TAGUS VOUGA ZATAS CAVADO CHANCA TAMEGA ZEZERE MONDEGO GUADIANA
TOWN:	BEJA FARO OVAR BRAGA EVORA HORTA PORTO VISEU GUARDA OPORTO COIMBRA FUNCHAL SETUBAL BRAGANCA
UNIVERSITY:	COIMBRA
WEIGHT:	GRAO ONCA LIBRA MARCO ARROBA OITAVA ARRATEL QUINTAL
WINE:	PORT

PORTUGESE **(PREF.)** LUSO
PORTULACA MOSS PURSLANE
PORWIGLE TADPOLE
POSAUNE TROMBONE
POSE SET SIT HOARD MODEL OFFER PLANT STICK BAFFLE NONPLUS PEACOCK POSTURE PRESENT PROPOSE POSITION PRETENSE PROPOUND QUESTION MANNERISM
POSEIDON NEPTUNE EARTHSHAKER **(BROTHER OF —)** ZEUS **(FATHER OF —)** KRONOS **(MOTHER OF —)** RHEA **(WIFE OF —)** AMPHITRITE
POSER FACER POSEUR PUZZLE STAYER STICKER STUMPER TWISTER EXAMINER STICKLER BANDARLOG
POSH RITZY SWAGGER
POSING OPPOSAL **(— TECHNIQUE)** PLASTIQUE
POSIT FIX PUT SET PLACE AFFIRM ASSUME
POSITING PONENT

POSITION LAY LIE HANG LINE POSE RANK SITE CENSE COIGN PLANT POINT POSTE SIEGE SITUS STAND STATE STEAD ASSIZE FIGURE HEIGHT OCTAVE OFFICE STANCE UBIETY VALGUS POSTURE STATION ATTITUDE CAPACITY DOCTRINE VOCATION PLACEMENT
(— OF AFFAIRS) STATUS
(— OF FEAR) GAZE
(— OF HEAVENLY BODY) HARBOR
(— OF VESSEL) GAUGE HEIGHT
(— WITH NO ESCAPE) IMPASSE
(— WITH NO RESPONSIBILITY) SINECURE
(BALLET —) POINTE
(CHESS —) ZUGZWANG
(COMMANDING —) PRESTIGE
(DEFENSIVE —) OUTWORK
(DISTINGUISHED —) HONOR
(EMBARRASSING —) FIX HOLE LURCH CORNER
(FENCING —) CARTE SIXTE SIXTH QUARTE TIERCE SACCOON SECONDE SEPTIME
(FOREMOST —) HEAD LEAD STEM
(INITIAL —) ANLAUT
(MEDIAL —) INLAUT
(RELATIVE —) RANK PLACE TERMS BEARING FOOTING STANDING
(SOCIAL —) CASTE STATE VALOUR
(SYMBOLIC —) HASTA
(SUFF.) TOPE TOPY
POSITIONAL SITUAL
POSITIVE POS POZ COOL DOWN FLAT PLUS SURE BASIC SHEER UTTER ACTIVE DIRECT THETIC GENUINE HEALTHY ABSOLUTE CONCRETE DECISIVE DEFINITE DOGMATIC EXPLICIT INHERENT RESOLUTE SIGNLESS THETICAL
(THREE —S) KROMOGRAM
POSITIVELY BUT POS FLAT PLUS QUITE FAIRLY INDEED STRICTLY
POSITIVISM COMTISM CERTAINTY DOGMATISM
POSITRON LEPTON
POSSESS GET OWE OWN HAVE HOLD WALD BOAST BROOK OUGHT REACH WIELD MASTER OBTAIN OCCUPY BEDEVIL ENVELOP FURNISH INHABIT INHERIT INSTALL INSTATE SMITTLE ACQUAINT DOMINATE INSTRUCT
POSSESSED MAD CALM COOL OUGHT CRAZED JERUSHA ENTHEATE
(— BY EVIL SPIRIT) DEMONIAC
(AUTHOR OF —) DOSTOEVSKI
(CHARACTER IN —) BLUM DASHA FEDKA MARIE MARYA PYOTR YULIA SHATOV DROZDOV LIPUTIN NIKOLAI STEPHAN VARVARA KIRILLOV LIZAVETA LYAMSHIN PETROVNA SHIGALOV LEBYADKIN STAVROGIN VIRGINSKY KARMAZINOV TIMOFYEVNA VERHOVENSKY
POSSESSION AVER HAND HOLD YHTE AUGHT GRASP STATE CLUTCH CORNER HAVIOR SASINE SEISIN SEIZIN WEALTH CONTROL COUNTER DEMESNE DEWANEE FINGERS KEEPING MASTERY SEIZURE CONQUEST DEFIANCE PROPERTY
(— OF COMMON FEATURES) AFFINITY
(— OF KNOWLEDGE) SCIENCE
(— WITH QUIET ENJOYMENT) SEISIN SEIZIN
(BURDENSOME —) ELEPHANT
(LOST — OF BALL) TURNOVER
(RELIGIOUS —) POWER
(TEMPORAL —S) WORLD
(TEMPORARY —) LEND
(PL.) ALLS STORE STUFF WRACK DOMAIN ESTATE GRAITH PROPER CAPITAL FORTUNE HAVINGS LIVINGS
POSSET CURDLE PAMPER POWSOWDY BALDUCTUM MERRYBUSH
POSSIBILITY MAY MAYBE POSSE CHANCE PROSPECT QUESTION
POSSIBLE ABLE RIFE MAYBE LIKELY EARTHLY ELIGIBLE FEASIBLE PROBABLE PROBABLY POTENTIAL CONTINGENT PRACTICABLE
(BARELY —) OUTSIDE
POSSIBLY MAPPEN LIGHTLY PERHAPS PERCHANCE PERADVENTURE
POSSUM TAIT FEIGN PRETEND
POST DAK SET TIE BITT BOMA CAMP CRIB DAWK DOLE FAST FORT MAIL META POLE ROOM SPOT SPUD STOB STUD TREE BERTH CHEEK CLOSH CRANE NEWEL PLACE SPILE SPRAG STAKE STAND STILT STING STOCK STODE STOOP STULP STUMP BILLET CIPPUS COLUMN CROTCH FENDER GIBBET INFORM OFFICE PICKET PILLAR SAMSON SCREEN STAPLE STOOTH STOWER TRUNCH ASHERAH BOLLARD COURIER GARETTA PLACARD POSTAGE POSTBOX QUARTER STATION STUDDLE UPRIGHT BANISTER DEADHEAD LEGPIECE MAKEFAST PRESIDIO PUNCHEON QUINTAIN STRADDLE STANCHION
(— AS RACE MARKER) META
(— ON PIER) FAST BOLLARD DEADHEAD
(BOUNDARY —) TERM STOOP TERMINUS
(CHIMNEY —) SPEER
(CUSTOMS —) CHOKEY
(DECK —) BITT
(DOOR OR GATE —) DURN
(ECCLESIASTIC —) BENEFICE
(FENCE —) DROPPER
(HANGING —) GIBBET
(INDIAN MILITARY —) TANA TANNA THANA
(MILITARY —) FORT GARRISON
(MOORING —) BITT DOLPHIN
(OBSERVATORY —) CUPOLA
(SACRED —) ASHERAH
(SIGN —) PARSON
(PREF.) STELO

POSTAGE POST INDICIA STAMPAGE
POSTAGE-FREE FRANCO
POSTAGE STAMP DUE HEAD STICKER
POSTBOY YAMSHIK YEMSCHIK POSTILION
POSTCARD (— COLLECTOR) DELTIOLOGIST
POST CHAISE JACK POCHAY POSCHAY
POSTER BILL CLAP SNIPE CLAPPE AFFICHE PLACARD SHOWING STICKER STREAMER
POSTERIOR BACK REAR CAUDAL DORSAL POSTIC RETRAL ADAXIAL BUTTOCKS
(PL.) WHEERIKINS
(PREF.) OPISTH(O) UR(O)
POSTERIORLY RETRAD
POSTERITY SEQUEL KINDRED FUTURITY
POSTERN SIDE CLOCKET KLICKET PRIVATE POSTICUM
POSTHOUSE YAM MUTATION
POSTICHE WIG SHAM SWITCH TOUPEE PRETENSE SPURIOUS
POSTIL HOMILY COMMENT
POSTILION COURIER POSTBOY YAMSHIK
POSTLUDE SORTIE SORTITA EPILOGUE
POSTMAN MAIL CORREO MAILBAG MAILMAN
POST OFFICE BOMA CORREO POSTHOUSE
POSTPONE OFF STAY WAIT DEFER DELAY FRIST REMIT WAIVE FUTURE LINGER RELONG RETARD ADJOURN DEGRADE OVERSET PROLONG RESPECT SUSPEND CONTINUE PROROGUE REPRIEVE WITHHOLD
POSTPONED DEFERRED
POSTPONEMENT MORA STAY DELAY RESPECT RESPITE
POSTRIDE COURIER POSTILION
POSTSCRIPT EKE ENVOY
POST SUPPORT CROWFOOT
POSTULANT NOVICE
POSTULATE AXIOM CLAIM POSIT ASSERT ASSUME DEMAND THESIS PERHAPS PREMISE PETITION PRINCIPLE
POSTURE SET POSE SEAT SITE ASANA FRONT HEART PLACE SHAPE SQUAT STATE LOUNGE SLOUCH STANCE BEARING CROWHOP STATION STATURE ATTITUDE CARRIAGE POSITION
(— OF DEFENSE) GUARD
(DANCE —) HOLD
(KNEELING —) SHIKO
POSY POESY TUTTY FLOWER BOUQUET NOSEGAY ANTHOLOGY
POT BAG CAN COOP FOOL JUST LEAD OLLA PINT POOL RUIN CREWE CROCK CRUSE DIXIE KITTY SHANT SHOOT ALUDEL CHATTY CHYTRA JORDAN JORDEN KETTLE MARMIT MASLIN MONKEY OUTWIT PINGLE PIPKIN POCKET POSNET BRAISER CHAMBER CUVETTE DECEIVE POTSHOT SEETHER SKILLET YETLING FAVORITE JACKSHEA PRESERVE MARIJUANA
(— FOR CATCHING FISH) COOP
(— OF BRASS) LOTA MASLIN
(— OF DRINK) SHANT
(— WITH 3 FEET) POSNET
(BULGING —) OLLA
(BUSHMAN'S —) JACKSHAY JACKSHEA
(CHAMBER —) JERRY JORDAN JORDEN COMMODE JEROBOAM
(CHIMNEY —) CAN TUN
(EARTHEN —) OLLA CROCK CHATTY PIPKIN
(LEATHER —) GISPIN
(LOBSTER —) COY TRUNK
(LONG-HANDLED —) PINGLE
(MELTING —) CREVET CRUCIBLE
(PART OF —) EAR LIP RIM BASE BODY FOOT NECK SPOUT HANDLE
(PEAR-SHAPED —) ALUDEL
(SMALL ROUND —) LOTA LOTAH
(TEA —) TRACK
(12-GALLON —) DIXY DIXIE
POTABLE DRINK BEVERAGE POTATORY
POTAGE SOUP BROTH
POTAMOGETON PONDWEED PONDGRASS
POTASH KALI SALINE PEARLASH POLVERINE
(— FACTORY) ASHERY
POTASSIUM K KALIUM POTASS
(— DICHROMATE) CHROME
POTASSIUM NITRATE GROUGH
POTATION POT DRAM DRAFT DRINK LIBATION
POTATO PAP YAM CHAT PAPA SPUD YAMP FLUKE IDAHO RURAL TATER TUBER BATATA CAMOTE KUMARA LUMPER MURPHY PRATEY SKERRY BURBANK EPICURE SOLANUM BLUENOSE
(— BALL) NOISETTE
(— MASHER) RICER CHAPPER
(— SLICES) LATTICE
(— STATE) IDAHO MAINE
(—S AND CABBAGE) COLCANNON
(FRENCH FRIED —) CHIP
(FRENCH FRIED —S) GAUFRETTES
(JAPANESE —) IMO
(STEWED —S) STOVIES
(WITH —S) PARMENTIER
(PL.) WARE CHUNO
POT BEARER POTIFER
POTBELLIED KEDGE PODDY STOMACHY ABDOMINOUS
POTBELLY PAUNCH TUNBELLY
POTBOY GANYMEDE
POTE KICK MOPE POIT POKE PUSH NUDGE PLATE POKER SHOVE THRUST
POTEEN POTHEEN WHISKEY POTWHISKY
POTENCE STUD CROSS GIBBET
POTENCY FORCE POWER VIGOR ORENDA VIRTUE EFFICACY STRENGTH VITALITY OPERATION
POTENT ABLE MAIN RICH STAY STIFF CAUSAL COGENT CRUTCH MIGHTY STRONG DYNAMIC

SUPPORT WARRANT FORCIBLE POWERFUL PUISSANT VIGOROUS VIRTUOUS VIRULENT

POTENTATE KING RULER HUZOOR POTENT PRINCE DICTATOR DOMINION SOVEREIGN

POTENTIAL EH LATENT VIRTUAL IMPLICIT INCHOATE POSSIBLE PREGNANT
(— ENERGY) ERGAL
(EXCESS —) OVERVOLTAGE

POTENTIALITY POSSE POWER DUNAMIS DYNAMIS POTENCY CAPACITY PREGNANCY

POTGUN PISTOL POPGUN BRAGGART

POTHER ADO VEX FUSS STEW STIR WORRY BOTHER BUSTLE HARASS POTTER PUTTER PUZZLE PERPLEX TURMOIL

POTHERB WORT CLARY WERTE GREENS CHERVIL OLITORY POTWORT QUELITE SPINACH TAMPALA

POTHOLE POT RUT KETTLE TINAJA

POTHOOK HAIK HAKE CROOK HANGLE RACKAN SLOWRIE TRAMMEL COTTEREL

POTHOUSE TAVERN ALEHOUSE MUGHOUSE

POTION DOSE DRUG DRAFT DRINK DWALE STUFF DRENCH POISON AMATORY MIXTURE PHILTER PHILTRE NEPENTHE

POTIPHERAH (DAUGHTER OF —) ASENATH

POTLATCH GIFT FEAST PARTY POTLACH FESTIVAL

POT MARIGOLD GOLD GOLDE SUNFLOWER

POTPOURRI HASH OLIO STEW MASLIN MEDLEY POTPIE RAGOUT FANTASIA PASTICHE JAMBALAYA SALMAGUNDI

POTRO COLT

POTSHERD BIT PIG TEST CROCK SHARD SHERD FRAGMENT OSTRACON PANSHARD

POTTAGE SEW SOUP SOWL STEW BERRY BROTH BRUET BREWIS BROWET POTAGE OATMEAL PULMENT

POTTED DRUNK CANNED
(— MEAT) RILLETT

POTTER FAD FUSS MUCK POKE ANNOY DAKER TRUCK BOTHER DABBLE DACKER DAIDLE DIDDLE DISHER DODDER FIDDLE FOOTLE FOTTER JOTTER KUMHAR MUDDLE NANTLE NIGGLE PETTLE POUTER TIDDLE TIFFIE TIFFLE TRIFLE CLOAMER CROCKER DISTURB FIGURER FOSSICK HANDLER NAUNTLE PERPLEX PLOWTER PRODDLE THROWER TROUBLE CERAMIST TERRAPIN
(— OFFICIOUSLY) TEW
(MACHINE OF —) JOLLY

POTTERER TWIRLER

POTTERY POT BANK CHUN DELF GROG WARE BIZEN CROCK DELFT GLOST ROUEN SPODE BASALT FICTIL KASHAN MIMPEI ASTBURY BELLEEK BOCCARO BRISTOL DIPWARE FIGMENT JETWARE KAMARES POTBANK POTWARE POTWORK REDWARE SATSUMA TICKNEY TZUCHOU BUCCHERO CERAMICS FIGULINE GRAYWARE SANTORIN SLIPWARE BROWNWARE
(— CIVILIZATION) MINYAN
(— CULTURE) PUCARA
(— DECOR) MISHIMA
(— DECORATED WITH SCRATCHING) GRAFFITO
(ANCIENT —) KAMARES GRAYWARE
(BLACK —) BASALT BUCCHERO
(CHINESE —) KUAN YIHSING
(CRUSHED —) GROG
(HINDU —) UDA
(RICHLY COLORED —) MAJOLICA
(UNGLAZED —) BISCUIT

POTTERY TREE CARAIPE

POTTINGER COOK POTYCARY

POTTO LEMUR APOSORO KINKAJOU

POTTY CRAZY FOOLISH TRIVIAL SNOBBISH

POUCH BAG COD JAG POD SAC BELL CYST POCK POKE BULGE BURSA POKKE PURSE BUDGET CAECUM CRUMEN GIPSER PACKET POCKET PURSET SACHET ALFARGA ALFORJA CANTINA CRUMENA GIPSIRE MAILBAG MOCHILA OVICYST SCROTUM SPORRAN SWALLOW BURSICLE PROTRUDE SPEUCHAN MARSUPIUM
(— OF FLY) AEROSTAT
(— ON DEER'S NECK) BELL
(PILGRIM'S —) SCRIP
(TOBACCO —) DOSS
(PREF.) PERO PHASCO PHASCOL(O) THYLAC(O)

POUCH OF DOUGLAS
(PREF.) CULDO

POUF PUFF OTTOMAN

POULAINE PIKE CRAKOW

POULPE POULP CUTTLE OCTOPUS

POULTICE QUILT STUPA STUPE MALAGMA EPITHEME SINAPISM CATAPLASM

POULTRY FOWL HENS DUCKS GEESE PULLEN PEAFOWL PIGEONS PULLERY TURKEYS CHICKENS PULLAILE VOLAILLE

POUNAMU JADE PUNAMU NEPHRITE

POUNCE NAB CHOP CLAP JUMP POKE SWAP SWOP FLECK PRICK PUNCH SOUSE SWOOP TALON EMBOSS PIERCE TATTOO BOBCOAT DESCEND SPRINKLE
(— UPON) TIRE STOOP

POUND L LB BUM DAD LIB PIN PUN SOV BEAT CHAP DRUB FRAM PELT PIND POON POSS PUND QUID SKIT THUD TRAP TUND CRUSH FRAME KNOCK LABOR LIVRE NEVEL STAMP THUMP TRAMP WEIGH BATTER BRUISE HAMMER LUMBER NICKER POUNCE PRISON THRASH CONTUND CONTUSE PINFOLD THUNDER LAMBASTE RESTRAIN
(— FINE) BRAY
(FISH —) KEEP MADRAGUE
(ISRAELI —S) LIROTH
(100 —S) CENTAL CENTURY
(12 —S OF BUTTER) GAUN
(1-8TH OF —) HANDFUL
(25 —S) PONY PONEY
(32, 56, OR 75 —S OF RAISINS) FRAIL
(500 —S) MONKEY

POUNDMASTER PINDER PINNER PONDER

POUR JAW RUN TUN YET BIRL BREW DROP EMIT FILL FLOW GOSH GUSH HELD LASH LAVE RAIN TEEM TOOM VENT FLOOD FLUSH HEELD HIELD POWER SLIDE SOUSE SPILL SPOUT SWARM TRILL AFFUSE DECANT SLUICE STREAM CASCADE CHANNEL DIFFUSE SUFFUSE
(— AWAY) STAVE
(— BACK) REFUND
(— BEER OR WINE) BIRL
(— CLUMSILY) SLOSH
(— COPIOUSLY) HALE
(— DOWN) RASH SILE SHOWER DESCEND DISPUNGE
(— FORTH) SHED TIDE VENT WELL DISTILL OVERFLOW
(— FREELY) SWILL
(— FROM ONE VESSEL TO ANOTHER) DECANT JIRBLE TRANSFUSE
(— IN) INFUSE INFOUND INHELDE
(— IN DROP BY DROP) INSTIL INSTILL
(— LIKE RAIN OR TEARS) LASH
(— MELTED WAX) BASTE
(— MOLTEN LEAD) YOTE
(— OFF) SLUICE
(— OIL UPON) ANOINT
(— OUT) FILL SEND SHED SKINK STOUR UTTER EFFUSE LIBATE DIFFUND DIFFUSE
(— UPON) AFFUSE
(PREF.) CHYMI
(SUFF.) CHYME

POURBOIRE TIP GRATUITY TRINKGELD

POURER TEEMER INFUSER

POURING AFFUSION
(SUFF.) ENCHYSIS

POURPOINT GIPON JUPON QUILT DOUBLET

POUT BIB MOP MAID MOUE PUSS SULK BLAIN BOODY GROIN BRASSY BRASSIE CATFISH EELPOUT BULLHEAD PROTRUDE

POUTERIA LUCUMA

POUTING BOUDERIE

POVERTY LACK NEED WANE WANT DEARTH PENURY BEGGARY DEFAULT MISEASE TENUITY DISTRESS POORTITH PUIRTITH SCARCITY WANDRETH NECESSITY
(SUFF.) PENIA

POVERTY PLANT HEATH HEATHER LINGWORT

POVERTY-STRICKEN POOR NAKED NEEDY SQUALID SHIRTLESS

POWDER BRAY DUST KISH MILL MULL SAND CHALK CURRY ERBIA FLOUR GRIND HEMOL KOSIN PICRA STOUR CEMENT CHARGE CHINOL DECAMP DERMOL EMPASM ESCAPE FARINA FILITE GERATE KAMALA KERMES KUMKUM MELLON PEYTON PINOLE POUNCE RACHEL SMEETH YTTRIA ALCOHOL BESTREW BROCADE LUPULIN SCATTER SMEDDUM SPACKLE SPODIUM ALGAROTH CATAPASM DYNAMITE FLUMERIN PALEGOLD
(— A SHIELD) GERATE
(— FOR BRONZING) BROCADE
(— OBTAINED BY SUBLIMATION) FLOWERS
(— TO MASK SWEAT ODOR) EMPASM EMPASMA
(— USED IN CHOCOLATE) PINOLE
(ABRASIVE —) EMERY
(ANTHELMINTIC —) KOSIN
(ANTIMONY —) KOHL
(ASTRINGENT —) BORAL
(BLEACHING —) CHEMIC CHLORIDE
(BROWNISH —) LIGNIN
(CATHARTIC —) KAMALA
(COLORING —) HENNA
(FINE —) DUST POUNCE ALCOHOL
(FLUORESCENT —) FLUMERIN
(GOA —) ARAROBA
(GOLD —) VENTURINE
(GRAPHITIC —) KISH
(GRAY —) ANTU
(HAIR —) MUST
(MALT —) SMEDDUM
(PERFUMED —) ABIR PULVIL SACHET
(PINK —) CALAMINE
(POISONOUS —) ROBIN
(PURPLE —) CUDBEAR
(REDDISH —) ABIR KUMKUM SIMMON
(ROSE-COLORED —) ERBIA
(SACHET —) PULVIL
(SILICEOUS —S) SILEX
(SMOKELESS —) FILITE PEYTON CORDITE AMBERITE INDURITE SOLENITE
(WHITE —) CHINOL YTTRIA HYPORIT SCANDIA HALAZONE LANTHANA PARAFORM
(YELLOW —) KOSIN DERMOL MELLON LUPULIN MALARIN SAMARIA TANNIGEN
(PREF.) PUMICI

POWDERED SEME SPICED PICKLED SEASONED

POWDER PUFF PLUFF

POWDERY MEALY PRUINOSE

POWER ARM ART JUS ROD SAY SUN VIS BEEF BULK DINT GIFT GRIP HAND HANK HEAP HORN IRON KAMI MAIN MANA MAYA SOUP SWAY WALD WILL AGENT CROWN DEMON DEVIL FORCE GRACE HUACA HYDRO INPUT LURCH MIGHT SINEW SKILL STEAM VALUE VIGOR WAKON WIELD YARAK AGENCY APPEAL BREATH CLUTCH CREDIT DANGER DEGREE DOUGHT EFFORT ENERGY FOISON IMPACT MOLOCH SHAKTI STROIL STROKE SWINGE

TALENT VIRTUE WEIGHT ABILITY
BALANCE BOSSDOM COMMAND
CONTROL DEMESNE DESTINY
DUNAMIS DYNAMIS ENTHEOS
FACULTY POTENCY VALENCY
VOLTAGE WAKONDA ACTIVITY
AUTONOMY CAPACITY CLUTCHES
COERCION DELEGACY DEMIURGE
DISPOSAL DOMINION INTEREST
LEVERAGE LORDSHIP SEIGNORY
STRENGTH PUISSANCE
PREROGATIVE
(— FROM SUPREME BEING) EON
AEON
(— OF ACID) BASICITY
(— OF ATTORNEY) PROXY
(— OF ATTRACTION) ALLURE
(— OF CHOICE) LIBERTY
(— OF DIVORCE) TAFWIZ
(— OF ENTRY) INGRESS
(— OF GIVING) PROPINE
(— OF HEARING) AUDITION
(— OF KNOWING) JNANASHAKTI
(— OF MANIFESTATION) MAYA
(— OF MOVING AT SEA) YARAGE
(— OF PERFORMING) ART
(— OF RESISTANCE) STAMINA
(— OF TRANSMUTATION) ALCHEMY
(— OF VISION) KEN
(— OF WINE) SEVE
(— TO ATTRACT) DUENDE
(— TO CONVINCE) FORCE
(—S OF EVIL) HELL
(AUTHOR OF —) FEUCHTWANGER
(CHARACTER IN —) REB KARL
ISAAC JOSEF MARIE NAEMI
ANSELF GABRIEL SIBYLLE
LANDAUER MAGDALEN
ALEXANDER SELIGMANN
WEISSENSEE OPPENHEIMER
(CIVIL —) CAESAR
(COERCIVE —) SWORD
(DIVINE —) MOIRA
(ELEVATING —) LIFT
(EMOTIONAL —) STOMACH
(EXTRAPHYSICAL —) MANA
(FIFTH —) SURSOLID
(FOCAL —) DIOPTRY
(GROWTH —) BATHMISM
(HYPOTHETICAL —) FORTUNE
(IMPERSONAL —) WAKAN WAKON
WAKANDA
(INTELLECTUAL —) WIT
(LEGAL —) JUS
(MAGIC —) ORENDA
(MAGNETIC —) MAGNES
(MENTAL —) HABITUS
(MORMON —) KEYS
(NATURAL —) OD
(OCCULT —) MAGIC
(PERSUASIVE —) RHETORIC
(PERUVIAN —) HUACA
(POLITICAL —) DOMINIUM
(RATIONAL —) EYE
(REFLECTIVE —) ALBEDO
(ROYAL —) RIAL
(SACRED —) KAMI
(SECOND —) SQUARE
(SOVEREIGN —) SWAY THRONE
(SPIRITUAL —) NGAI
(STAYING —) BOTTOM STAMINA
(SUPERNATURAL —) CHARISMA
(SUPREME —) EMPIRE

HEAVEN IMPERIUM
(THIRD —) CUBE
(VITAL —) SPIRITS
(PREF.) CRATO DYN(A)(AMI)(AMO)
(SUFF.) OD ODIC
(RULING —) CRACY CRAT(IC)
POWERBOAT SEDAN SKIFF GLIDER
CRUISER STINKPOT GASOLINER
POWERFUL BIG FAT ABLE DEEP
HIGH MAIN RANK RICH VERY
FORTE HEFTY HUSKY LUSTY
STARK STOUT VALID VIVID
WIGHT WILDE COGENT HEROIC
MIGHTY POTENT SEVERE STRONG
CAPABLE FECKFUL INTENSE
POLLENT RICHARD SKOOKUM
STAVING VALIANT FORCIBLE
PUISSANT VIGOROUS
(PREF.) MEGA
POWERLESS WEAK FEEBLE
UNABLE HELPLESS IMPOTENT
POWWOW PAWAW CONFAB
FROLIC COUNCIL MEETING
SESSION CONJURER
POX ROUP CANKER PLAGUE
VARIOLA
(FOWL —) SOREHEAD
(SHEEP —) OVINIA
POYOU PELUDO ARMADILLO
PRABHU LORD CHIEF WRITER
PRACITIONER
(SUFF.) ICIAN PATH(IA)(IC)(Y)
PRACTICABLE AGIBLE DOABLE
USABLE VIABLE FEASIBLE
OPERABLE POSSIBLE
PRACTICAL HARD UTILE ACTIVE
ACTUAL THINGY USEFUL
OPERARY VIRTUAL WORKING
BANAUSIC HOMESPUN PRACTIVE
THINGISH
(— JOKE) WAGGERY
(NOT —) PROFESSORY
PRACTICALLY ALMOST NEARLY
REALLY VIRTUALLY
PRACTICE ACT ISM LAW SUE TRY
URE USE KEEP LIVE PLAN PLOT
ADOPT APPLY ASSAY DRILL
FOUND GUISE HABIT HAUNT
TRADE TRAIN TREAD USAGE
CUSTOM EMPLOY FOLLOW
GROOVE OCCUPY PRAXIS RECORD
BRUSHUP ENHAUNT KNOCKUP
OPERATE PROCEED PROFESS
RANDORI USAUNCE ACTIVISM
ALARMISM EXERCISE FREQUENT
GALENISM OBSERVANCE
(— CHEATING) FOIST
(— DECEPTION) DEACON
(— DILIGENTLY) PLY
(— FRAUD) SHARK
(— HYPOCRISY) CANT
(— OF AN ART) PRAXIS
(— OF MEDICINE) GALENISM
(— ROWING) TUB
(— WITCHCRAFT) HEX
(BINDING —) LAW
(CEREMONIAL —) RITE
(COMMUNAL —) SUNNA SCHEME
SUNNAH INTRIGUE
(CORRUPT —) ABUSE WHORE
(DIPLOMATIC —) ALTERNAT
(DISHONEST —S) CROSS
(HORTICULTURAL —) CUTTAGE

(MEDICAL —) ALLERGY
(RELIGIOUS —) CULT CULTUS
(SUPERSTITIOUS —) FREET
(UNDERHAND —) JUGGLING
(VICIOUS —) MOLOCH
(SUFF.) CY ERY ICS ISM
PRACTICED EXPERT VERSED
PRACTIC SKILLED VETERAN
HACKNEYED
PRACTICING EXERCENT
PRACTITIONER DOCTOR HEALER
LAWYER NOVICE LEARNER
EXERCENT FELDSHER HUMANIST
HERBALIST HOMEOPATH
NATUROPATH
PRAD HORSE
PRAENOMEN AULUS CAIUS GAIUS
TITUS GNAEUS LUCIUS MANIUS
MARCUS SEXTUS SERVIUS
SPURIUS MAMERCUS NUMERIUS
TIBERIUS
PRAESEPE CRIB CRATCH MANGER
BEEHIVE
PRAGMATIC BUSY BUSYBODY
DOGMATIC MEDDLING OFFICIOUS
PRACTICAL
PRAIRIE BAY BLED CAMAS PAMPA
PLAIN CAMASS MEADOW
PLATEAU QUAMASH
(— STATE) ILLINOIS
(AUTHOR OF —) COOPER
(CHARACTER IN —) ASA BUSH INEZ
PAUL WADE ELLEN HOVER NATTY
WHITE ABIRAM BUMPPO ESTHER
BATTIUS ISHMAEL HARDHEART
MIDDLETON
PRAIRIE BERRY TROMPILLO
PRAIRIE CHICKEN GROUSE
PRAIRIE DOG GOPHER MARMOT
PRAIRIE WOLF COYOTE
PRAISE CRY LOF FUME HERY LAUD
LOSE LOVE PRES ADORE ALLOW
ALOSE BLESS CAROL CHANT
CRACK DEIFY EXTOL GLORY
HERSE HONOR KUDOS PLAUD
PRIZE ROOSE SALVE VALUE
WURTH ANTHEM BELAUD
EULOGY FRAISE HILLEL KUDIZE
LOANGE LOVING ORCHID SALUTE
TONGUE ACCLAIM ADULATE
APPLAUD COMMEND FLATTER
GLORIFY MAGNIFY NOSEGAY
PLAUDIT PUFFING TRIBUTE
WORSHIP ACCOLADE APPLAUSE
BLESSING DOXOLOGY ENCOMIUM
EULOGIZE PROCLAIM PANEGYRIC
(— BE TO GOD) LD
(— IN THANKSGIVING) JOY
(— INORDINATELY) FUME
(— OF ANOTHER'S FELICITY)
MACARISM
(— TO GOD ALWAYS) LDS
(EFFUSIVE —) FUSS
(EXAGGERATED —) PUFFERY
(EXCESSIVE —) FLATTERY
ADULATION PANEGYRIC
(EXTRAVAGANTLY —) PUFF
(INSINCERE —) CLART DAUBING
(PUBLIC —) PRECONY
(SING FALSE —S) CHANT
PRAISED JUDAH JUDITH
LAURELED
(UNDULY —) BEPUFFED

PRAISEWORTHY WORTHY
AMIABLE GLORIOUS LAUDABLE
SPLENDID EXEMPLARY
PRAJAPATI KA PITRI
PRAKRIT PALI MAGADHI
PRAM CARRIAGE HANDCART
PUSHCART STROLLER
PRANCE STIR BRANK CAPER
DANCE JAUNT PRANK CANARY
CAREER CAVORT CURVET
GAMBOL JAUNCE TITTUP TRANCE
PRANKLE SWAGGER CAKEWALK
PRANCER HORSE DANCER
CAPERER
PRANK JIG RAG RIG DECK DIDO
FOLD GAME GAUD JEST LARK
PLOY PRAT REAK ADORN ANTIC
CAPER FREAK SHINE SKITE TRICK
VAGUE BROGUE CURVET FEGARY
FIGARY FROLIC GAMBOL SHAVIE
VAGARY MARLOCK SPANGLE
ESCAPADE FREDAINE PRANCOME
RIGWIDDIE MONKEYSHINE
(PL.) REX GAMES JINKS
PRANKISH TRICKSY
PRASINE LEEK
PRAT PUSH NUDGE TRICK
PRATE GAB BUCK BUKH BUKK
CARO CHAT CLAP CLAT TALK
BLATE BOAST CLASH SCOLD
BABBLE CACKLE CLAVER JANGLE
SQUIRT TONGUE BLATHER
BLATTER BLETHER CHATTER
CLATTER PALAVER PRATTLE
TWATTLE
PRATING GAFF CHATTER
PRATIQUE CUSTOM PRODUCT
PRATTLE GUP CHAT CLACK
BABBLE BURBLE CACKLE JANNER
JAUNER YATTER BLATTER
CHATTER CLATTER GABNASH
JAUNDER NASHGAB PRITTLE
TRATTLE TWADDLE CHITCHAT
BAVARDAGE
PRATTLING CHAVISH
PRAWN CARID NIPPER PENEID
SHRIMP SQUILLA CARIDEAN
CARIDOID CREVETTE MACRURAN
(SUFF.) CARIS
PRAWN KILLER SQUILLA
PRAXIS HABIT ACTION CUSTOM
PRACTICE
PRAY ASK BEG BID BLESS CRAVE
DAVEN SOUGH VOUCH INVITE
BESEECH ENTREAT IMPLORE
REQUEST WRESTLE INVOCATE
(— FOR) BOON
PRAYA BUND BEACH STRAND
PRAYER ACT AHA AVE CRY VOW
BEAD BENE BOON PLEA SUIT
VOTE AGNUS ALENU NAMAZ
SALAT SHEMA ABODAH APPEAL
ECTENE ERRAND LITANY MANTRA
MATINS ORISON STEVEN VESPER
YIZKOR BIDDING COMPLIN
FATIHAH GAYATRI GEULLAH
KADDISH MEMENTO ORATION
PRECULE PREFACE TAHANUN
ANAPHORA APOLYSIS CATHISMA
DEVOTION KEDUSHAH MISERERE
PETITION SUFFRAGE TEHINNAH
REQUIESCAT
(— BEADS) ROSARY

(— BOOK) MAHZOR MISSAL SERVICE
(— LEADER) IMAM
(— OF DISMISSAL) APOLYSIS
(— RUG) NAMAZLIK
(— SHAWL) TALLITH
(— STICK) BAHO PAHO
(— TOWER) MINARET
(CANONICAL —S) BREVIARY
(CHIEF MOHAMMEDAN —) NAMAZ
(HINDU —) GAYATRI
(INWARD —) ACT
(JEWISH —) ALENU ABODAH GEULLAH HOSHANA KADDISH
(LAST — OF DAY) COMPLIN
(LONG —) CATHISMA
(LORD'S —) PATERNOSTER
(MUSLIM —) SALAH SALAT KHUTBAH
(OPENING —) COLLECT
(SHORT —) GRACE COLLECT
(SILENT —) SECRET
(PL.) HOURS NORITO TIKKUN CHAPLET
(PREF.) EUCHO
PRAYING ORISON IMPRECANT
PREACH EDIFY SOUGH TEACH EXHORT GOSPEL SERMON DELIVER HOMILIZE PREDICATE
PREACHER KHATIB MAGGID PARSON TUBMAN DARSHAN LOLLARD MARTEXT PROPHET ROUNDER TEACHER TUBBIST TUBSTER EXHORTER KOHELETH MINISTER PARDONER PULPITER QOHELETH SERMONER SPINTEXT SWADDLER VARTABED BOANERGES
(PL.) PULPIT
PREACHING SPELL PULPIT SERMON HEARING KERUGMA KERYGMA PROPHECY PULPITRY SPELLING
PREACHY DIDACTIC
PREAMBLE PREFACE WHEREAS
PREARRANGED SET
PREBEND CANONRY
PREBENDARY PROVEND
PRE-CAMBRIAN MOINE EOZOIC ARCHEAN PRIMARY HURONIAN TORRIDONIAN
PRECARIOUS NEAR DICKY RISKY SHAKY CASUAL INFIRM NARROW UNSURE DUBIOUS TRICKLE CATCHING DELICATE INSECURE PERILOUS UNSTABLE DANGEROUS UNCERTAIN
PRECAUTION CARE GUARD CAUTEL SAFEGUARD
PRECEDE LEAD FOREGO HERALD FORERUN PREFACE PREVENT ANTECEDE PREAMBLE
PRECEDENCE PAS LEAD PRIMACY HERALDRY PRIORITY
(RIGHT OF —) PAS
(SOCIAL —) LEVEL
PRECEDENT LEAD SIGN MODEL TOKEN USAGE INSTANCE ORIGINAL SPECIMEN STANDARD AUTHORITY
PRECEDING OLD FORE WEST BEFORE FORMER LEADING ADJACENT PREVIOUS

(— ALL OTHERS) FIRST
(PREF.) ANTE
PRECENTOR CANTOR PSALMIST LETTERGAE
PRECEPT LAW HEST LINE RULE TORA WRIT ADAGE AXIOM BREVE MAXIM ORDER SUTRA SUTTA TORAH BEHEST DICTATE MANDATE WARRANT DOCTRINE DOCUMENT LANDMARK
PRECEPTIVE DIDACTIC MANDATORY
PRECEPTOR TUTOR MASTER
PRECINCT BEAT AMBIT BOUND CLOSE VERGE DOMAIN HIERON VIHARA COLLEGE LENAEUM SOCIETY TEMENOS BANLIEUE DISTRICT ENVIRONS
(PL.) AMBIT
PRECIOUS CUTE DEAR FINE LIEF RARE VERY CHARY CHERE GREAT HONEY CHICHI CHOICE COSTLY DAINTY GOLDEN PEARLY POSING SILVER TENDER PRECISE AFFECTED ORIENTAL OVERNICE VALUABLE WORTHFUL PRICELESS
PRECIOUSNESS PRICE
PRECIPICE LIN KHUD LINN LLYN PALI CLIFF KRANS SCREE SHEER STEEP KRANTZ CLOGWYN DOWNFALL HEADWALL
PRECIPITATE GEL CURD HURL RASH HASTY HURRY SHOOT SPEED STEEP ABRUPT COAGEL HASTEN SLUDGE SUDDEN TUMBLE UNWARY DISTILL LYCOPIN SUBSIDE TRIGGER CATALYZE HEADLONG PROCLIVE SEDIMENT SETTLING
(— DYE) STRIKE
PRECIPITATELY HEADLING HEADLONG SLAPDASH
PRECIPITATION HAIL MIST RAIN SNOW HASTE SLEET VIRGA
PRECIPITOUS FULL RASH BRANT BRENT HASTY STEEP ABRUPT CHICHI STEEPY SUDDEN PRERUPT HEADLONG
PRECIS JUNONIA SUMMARY ABSTRACT
PRECISE DRY SET FLAT HARD JUMP JUST NEAT NICE TIDY TRIG TRIM TRUE VERY CLEAN CLOSE EXACT PRESS RIGID SOUND FORMAL NARROW RIGORE STARCH STRICT BUCKRAM CAREFUL CERTAIN CLERKLY CORRECT EXPRESS PERFECT PERJINK STARCHY ABSOLUTE ACCURATE DEFINITE EXPLICIT HAIRLINE PINPOINT PUNCTUAL RIGOROUS
PRECISELY BUT EVEN JUST CLEAN SHARP FINELY JUSTLY STRAIT EXACTLY
PRECISENESS RIGOR RIGOUR PRIMNESS
PRECISIAN PRIG PURITAN
PRECISION NICETY CLARITY ACCURACY DELICACY ELEGANCE JUSTNESS
PRECISIONIST PEDANT
PRECLUDE BAR DENY STOP CLOSE

CROSS DEBAR ESTOP FORBID HINDER IMPEDE OBVIATE PREVENT SILENCE CONCLUDE INTERPEL PROHIBIT ANTICIPATE
PRECOCIOUS PRECOX UNRIPE FORWARD PREMATURE RATHERIPE
PRECONCEIVE IDEATE
PRECONCEPTION PRENOTION
PRECONDITION PRIUS
PRECURSOR USHER HERALD INITIAL ANCESTOR PRODROME WAYMAKER HARBINGER HEMIAUXIN PROGENITOR
PREDACITY RAVEN RAVIN
PREDATOR COACTOR
PREDATORY HUNGRY HARMFUL RAVENOUS
PREDECESSOR ANCESTOR FOREGOER
(PL.) OLDERS
PREDELLA FOOTPACE
PREDESTINATION FATE DESTINY ELECTION
PREDESTINE DOOM SLATE FOREDOOM FOREPOINT
PREDETERMINE DESTINE FORECAST
PREDICAMENT BOX FIX JAM NODE SOUP SPOT CLASS LURCH STATE STEAD PICKLE PLIGHT SCRAPE DILEMMA IMPASSE CATEGORY JUNCTURE QUANDARY
PREDICANT FRIAR PREACHER DOMINICAN
PREDICATE BASE FOUND AFFIRM ASSERT PRAISE PREACH COMMEND DECLARE EXTREME PREDICT PROCLAIM
PREDICT LAY BODE CALL DOPE READ REDE SPAE AUGUR WEIRD HALSEN FORESAY PRESAGE FOREBODE FORECAST FORETELL PROPHESY SOOTHSAY AUSPICATE PROGNOSTICATE
(— EVIL) CROAK
PREDICTION DOPE WEIRD AUGURY BODING BODWORD PORTENT PRESAGE BODEWORD FORECAST PROPHECY VATICINE
PREDILECTION BIAS HANG FANCY FAVOR LIKING RELISH FONDNESS
PREDISPOSE BEND INCLINE SUBJECT
PREDISPOSED PRONE PARTIAL TENDING INCLINED
PREDISPOSITION ITCH DIATHESIS
PREDOMINANCE MAJORITY REGNANCY ASCENDANCY
PREDOMINANT GREAT RULING CAPITAL REIGNING SUPERIOR CULMINANT HEGEMONIC
PREDOMINATE RULE DOMINE EXCEED GOVERN PREVAIL
PREE KISS PRIE TEST TASTE TRIAL PRYING SAMPLE PROVING TASTING
PREEMINENT BIG TOP ARCH HIGH STAR FIRST GRAND GREAT PALMARY PASSING STELLAR SUPREME FOREMOST PRECLARE SPLENDID SUPERIOR

PARAMOUNT PREPOTENT
(PREF.) ARCH
PREEMPT COLLAR
PREEN PIN PERK PICK TRIM WHET DRESS GLOAT PLUME PRINK PRUNE SWELL TRICK BROOCH GODWIT SMOOTH REPLUME
(— WINGS) WHET
PREFACE FRONT PROEM USHER HERALD PRESAY EPISTLE PRECEDE PREPOSE EXORDIUM FORETALK FOREWORD PREAMBLE PROLOGUE
PREFATORY PROEMIAL PRELIMINARY
PREFECT WALI EPARC GRAVE EPARCH MONITOR PROVOST GOVERNOR PRESIDENT
PREFECTURE EPARCHY
(CHINESE —) FU
(JAPANESE —) KEN
(TIBETAN —) JONG
PREFER LAY LIKE LOVE BRING ELECT EXALT FAVOR OFFER CHOOSE PROFER SELECT OUTRANK PREFECT PRESENT PROMOTE PROPOSE SURPASS
PREFERABLE LIEF RIGHT RATHER ELIGIBLE
PREFERENCE GOO LIKE FAVOR CHOICE DESIRE LIKING RATHER DRUTHERS FAVORITE PRIVILEGE PROMOTION PRECEDENCE
PREFERMENT DIGNITY
PREFIGURE TYPE IDEATE SHADOW TYPIFY FORERUN FORESEE PREDICT FORESHOW PROPHESY ADUMBRATE
PREFIX DUN DOON PREPOSE
PREGNANCY CYESIS TROUBLE ACCYESIS FETATION OOCYESIS GESTATION
PREGNANT BIG GONE OPEN GREAT HEAVY QUICK READY BAGGED CAUGHT COGENT GRAVID PAROUS ENCEINT FERTILE GESTANT TEEMING WEIGHTY CHILDING FORCIBLE GERMINAL PRESSING
PREHALLUX CALCAR
PREHEND SEIZE
PREHISTORIC OGYGIAN IMMEMORIAL
PREINDICATE PRESAGE FORESHOW
PREJUDICE BIAS DOWN HARM HURT KINK TURN DERRY AGEISM DAMAGE IMPAIR INJURY SEXISM SCUNDER SCUNNER JAUNDICE PREJUDGE
PREJUDICED BIGOTED INSULAR PARTIAL
PREJUDICIAL BIASED HURTFUL CONTRARY DAMAGING INIMICAL SINISTER
PRELATE CHIEF LEADER PRIEST HIERARCH ORDINARY SUPERIOR MONSIGNOR
PRELIMINARY PRIOR PRELIM PREFACE PRELUDE LIMINARY PREAMBLE PREVIOUS PREFATORY
PRELUDE PROEM VERSET DESCANT FORERUN INTRADA

PREFACE ANTELUDE BORSPIEL OVERTURE RITORNEL VERSETTE VORSPIEL

PREMATURE RATH UNRIPE IMMATURE PREVIOUS TIMELESS UNTIMELY

PREMEDITATE FORNCAST PURPENSE

PREMEDITATED SET STUDIED PREPENSE

PREMIER CHIEF FIRST OLDEST LEADING EARLIEST

PREMISE LEMMA MAJOR ASSUME GROUND REASON SUMPTION

PREMIUM USE AGIO BACK AWARD BONUS FANCY PRIZE SHAVE USURY BOUNTY DEPORT REWARD GRASSUM CONTANGO DONATIVE FOREGIFT GIVEAWAY
(UNDERCOVER — FOR SEATS) ICE

PREMIXED INSTANT

PREMONITION OMEN HUNCH NOTICE BODWORD PRESAGE WARNING BODEWORD FORESCENT

PREMUNE SALTED

PREOCCUPATION HEART INSIGHT FIXATION

PREOCCUPIED DEEP LOST RAPT CRAZY ABSENT FILLED INTENT CRACKED ABSORBED ENGROSSED

PREPARATION DIA FIG BALM DIBS DOPE PREP CREAM FLASH GLAZE JELLY READY ACETUM BLEACH BLUING DERRIS FACIAL LOTION MEGILP NEBULA PEPSIN SIMPLE ADDRESS APPREST CLEANER DIPPING EMANIUM ESSENCE ETHIOPS EXTRACT FITNESS FONDANT LINCTUS MELLITE PLACEBO TRYPSIN VARNISH ABSTRACT CONSERVE COSMETIC FIXATURE GELOSINE INHALANT LAUDANUM MEDICINE RACAHOUT TRAINING MAKEREADY PROVISION
(— CONTAINING HONEY) MELLITE
(— FOR COLORING LIQUORS) FLASH
(— OF GRAPEJUICE) DIBS
(AROMATIC —) ELIXIR
(CHEESE —) FONDU
(CHEESELIKE —) YOGURT CROWDIE YOGHURT
(COSMETIC —) HENNA
(ENZYME —) KOJI
(EYELID —) KOHL
(IMPURE RADIOACTIVE —) EMANIUM
(INTOXICATING —) BOZA GANJA
(MEDICAL —) STUFF
(OPIUM —) LAUDANUM
(SALINE —) LICK
(SLOPPY —) SLIBBERSAUCE
(SWEET —) DULCE
(UNCTUOUS —) CERATE

PREPARATORY PRIMAL PIONEER PRELIMINARY

PREPARE DO FIT FIX GET LAY ABLE BOUN BUSK COOK GIRD MAKE PARE PLOT PREP TILL YARK ATTLE BLEND BOWNE BRACE DIGHT DRAFT DRESS EQUIP FRAME ORDER PREDY READY

TRAIN ADJUST DESIGN GRAITH ORDAIN ADDRESS AFFAITE APPAREL APPOINT CONCOCT CONFECT DISPOSE EDUCATE PRODUCE PROVIDE QUALIFY INSTRUCT
(— BANQUET) COVER
(— BY BOILING) BREW DECOCT
(— BY HEAT) FRIT
(— CAPON) SAUCE
(— FISH) CALVER
(— FOOD) DO COOK
(— FOR BUILDING) FRAME
(— FOR BURIAL) EMBALM
(— FOR DISPLAY) DRESS
(— FOR PUBLICATION) EDIT
(— HASTILY) RASH
(— HEMP) TAW
(— LAND) CURE
(— ONESELF) ADDRESS
(— TEASEL HEADS) CARP

PREPARED UP APT BUN FIT SET BAAN BOON BOUN BOWN GIRT RIPE YARE ALERT BOUND PREST READY GRAITH CURRIED EQUIPPED TOGETHER
(QUICKLY —) RUNNING

PREPAREDNESS PROCINCT

PREPENSE DESIGN FORETHOUGHT

PREPONDERANCE MAJORITY DOMINANCE

PREPONDERATE EXCEED INCLINE SURPASS DOMINATE OUTWEIGH PERSUADE

PREPOSSESS BIAS PREVENT

PREPOSSESSING WINNING

PREPOSSESSION BENT BIAS FETICH FANTASY PREJUDICE

PREPOSTEROUS RICH INEPT ABSURD FOOLISH LAPUTAN GROTESQUE RIDICULOUS

PREPUCE
(PREF.) POSTH(E)(IO)(O)

PREROGATIVE GRACE HONOR RIGHT ESNECY REGALE FACULTY PECULIAR PRIVILEGE

PRESA LEAD

PRESAGE BODE HINT OMEN OSSE SIGN ABODE AUGUR TOKEN AUGURY BETIDE BETOKEN FORESEE OMINATE PORTEND PREDICT FOREBODE FORECAST FOREDOOM FORETELL INDICATE PREAMBLE PROPHESY

PRESBYTER ELDER PRIEST PRESTER ANTISTES MINISTER

PRESBYTERIAN WHIG CLASSIC

PRESBYTERY CLASSIS SENIORY EXERCISE PARSONAGE CONSISTORY

PRESCIENCE PRESAGE FORESIGHT PREVISION

PRESCIND SEVER DETACH

PRESCRIBE SET TAX ALLOT GUIDE LIMIT ORDER ASSIGN DEFINE DIRECT ENJOIN INDITE ORDAIN APPOINT CONFINE CONTROL DICTATE RESTRAIN

PRESCRIBED SET BASIC THETIC POSITIVE THETICAL FORMULARY

PRESCRIPT LAW COMMAND MANDATE PRECEPT

PRESCRIPTION RX BILL FORM

CIPHER RECIPE DICTATE FORMULA RECEIPT

PRESENCE EYE FACE SELF BEING ASPECT BEARING COMPANY ASSEMBLY INSTANCE
(DIRECT —) IMMEDIACY

PRESENT AIM BOX NOW BILL BOON GIFT GIVE HAND HERE MEED NEAR NIGH SAND SHOW BEING CUDDY DOLLY ENTER FEOFF GRANT NONCE OFFER PLACE RAISE READY STAGE THERE ACCUSE ACTUAL ADDUCE ALLEGE AROUND BESTOW BOUNTY BROACH CADEAU CLOTHE CUMSHA DONATE DURANT HANSEL KHILAT LATTER MODERN NEARBY PREFER REGALE REGALO RENDER XENIUM COMMEND CUMSHAW DISPLAY DOUCEUR ETRENNE EXHIBIT EXPOUND FAIRING FURNISH HANDSEL INSTANT LARGESS PERFORM PORRECT PRETEND PROPINE RELEASE RESIANT TASHRIF BLESSING CONGIARY DONATION GRATUITY INSTANCE LAGNAPPE OFFERING PESHKASH RESIDENT SOULCAKE SPORTULA
(— AS GIFT) DASH
(— FOR ACCEPTANCE) TENDER
(— FROM PUPIL TO TEACHER) MINERVAL
(— IN DETAIL) DISCUSS
(— IN MIND) DEAR
(— ONESELF) APPEAR
(— TO SOLDIERS) CONGIARY
(— TO STRANGER) XENIUM
(— TO VIEW) YIELD
(— WITHOUT WARRANT) OBTRUDE
(ALWAYS —) CHRONIC
(BRIDEGROOM'S —) HANDSEL
(CEREMONIAL —) KHILAT
(NOT —) ABSENT

PRESENTATION BILL GALA GIFT SHOW DROLL IMAGE DHARMA MUSTER SCHEMA BILLING DISPLAY EPITOME HOOKUPU MUSICAL PRESENT SPECIES ANALYSIS BESTOWAL DELIVERY DONATION EXPOSURE CANDLEMAS PERFORMANCE

PRESENTIMENT FEELING PRESAGE BODEMENT FOREFEEL PRENOTION PREMONITION

PRESENTLY NOW ANON ENOW SOON SHORTLY DIRECTLY

PRESERVATION FILING SAVING KEEPING SERVATION

PRESERVATIVE SALT BORAX SPICE SUGAR CONSERVE TREATMENT

PRESERVE CAN JAR CORN HAIN HOLD KEEP SALT SAVE BLESS GUARD SERVE SPARE SWEET WITIE ATHOLD BOTTLE COMFIT DEFEND EMBALM FREEZE GOGGLE POWDER RETAIN SECURE SHIELD UPHOLD CONDITE FORFEND KYANIZE PROTECT RAISINE RESERVE SUCCADE SUSTAIN CHOWCHOW CONSERVE ENSHRINE MAINTAIN MOTHBALL PARADISE WITHSAVE

(— BY BOILING WITH SUGAR) CANDY
(— BY SALTING) CORN CURE SALT
(— OF GRAPES) RAISINE
(— WOOD) KYANIZE PAYNISE
(GAME —) MOOR SHIKARGAH
(HUNTING —) WALK
(PL.) KONFYT

PRESERVED WET CONFECT BRANDIED POWDERED

PRESIDE RULE GUIDE DIRECT MODERATE
(— OVER) KEEP

PRESIDENCY MADRAS PRYTANY

PRESIDENT MIR FOUD PREX PREXY PROXY REEVE DEACON RECTOR PRAESES PREFECT
(— OF GUILD) DEAN
(— OF SUPREME COURT) LAWMAN
(— OF TRADE) DEACON

PRESIGNIFY PRESAGE FORETOKEN

PRESS FLY HUG JAM SIT BEAR BEND CRAM DOME DROP DRUK HORN HUSH IRON JAMB KISS PLOT SERR THEW TUCK URGE VICE YERK ARGUE BESET BRIZZ CHAFE CHIRT CRIMP CROWD CRUSH DRIVE EXACT FORCE KNEAD MIDST PRIZE SCREW SHREW SMASH STAMP STUFF TWIST WEIGH WRING ASSAIL CHISEL CLOSET COARCT CRUNCH GOFFER HARASS JOBBER KVETCH MANGLE NUDDLE PREACE SQUASH STRAIN STRESS THRAST THREAP THREAT THREEP THRIMP THRING THRONG THRUST AFFLICT ARMOIRE ATTEMPT BESEECH BESIEGE CONCISE CRUMPLE EMBRACE ENVIRON FLATBED IMPRESS MACHINE OPPRESS SCROOGE SCRUNGE SQUEEZE THRUTCH AGGRIEVE CALENDER COMPRESS PRESSURE SCROUNGE SQUEEGEE SURROUND
(— AGAINST) CONTACT
(— CLOSE) NUDDLE
(— CLOSELY AND PAINFULLY) MASH
(— DOWN) QUAT
(— FOR WINE) TORCULAR
(— FORWARD) DRIVE BREAST
(— HARSHLY) GRIND
(— IN CHEESE VAT) CHISEL CHIZZEL
(— INTO) THRIMBLE THRUMBLE
(— ON ANVIL) HORN
(— ONWARD) STRETCH
(— OUT) EXTRUDE
(— PAINFULLY) PINCH
(— PAPER) COUCH
(— TOGETHER) SERRY
(— UPON) ELBOW DOWNBEAR
(— WITH HEAD OR HORNS) BOX
(— WITH VIOLENCE) DRIVE
(PREF.) PIEZO PRESSI
(SUFF.) ARCTIA

PRESS AGENT FLACK

PRESSED SERRIED
(— WITH BUSINESS) THRONG
(— WITH LEFTHAND FOREFINGER) BARRED

PRESSES
(SUFF.) **(— CLOSE)** NASTIC

PRESSING RASH ACUTE CRYING URGENT CLAMANT EARNEST EXIGENT INSTANT SQUEEZE CRITICAL PREGNANT NECESSITOUS

PRESSMAN PIG MINDER PROVER PRINTER

PRESSURE JAM HEAD HEAT PEND PUSH SWAY DRIVE FORCE IMAGE PINCH STAMP BURDEN DURESS STRESS THRONG WEIGHT BEARING MERCURY PUSHING SQUEEZE TENSION URGENCY EXACTION EXIGENCY FUGACITY PRESSION
(— GROUP) LOBBY
(— OF CIRCUMSTANCE) NECESSITY
(— OF 1 DYNE) BARAD
(— ON INSTRUMENT STRING) STOP
(— UNIT) TORR MICRON
(LIQUID —) HEAD
(MANUAL —) TAXIS
(UNIT OF —) TORR OSMOL PASCAL
(VAPOR —) FUGACITY
(PREF.) PIEZO TONO

PRESSURE COOKER STEAMER AUTOCLAVE

PRESSWORK BACKUP

PRESTIDIGITATOR PALMER JUGGLER PYTHONIC

PRESTIGE FACE MANA CASTE IKBAL IZZAT KUDOS PLACE CACHET STATUS STATURE ILLUSION INFLUENCE

PRESTO QUICKLY SPEEDILY

PRESUME BEAR DARE GROW IMPLY INFER ASSUME EXPECT DARESAY SUPPOSE ARROGATE

PRESUMING ARROGANT FAMILIAR

PRESUMPTION GALL JOLLITY OUTRAGE PRESUME AUDACITY SUCCUDRY SURQUIDY

PRESUMPTUOUS BOLD PERT FRESH PROUD WICKED WILFUL FORWARD HAUGHTY ARROGANT ASSUMING FAMILIAR INSOLENT FOOLHARDY

PRESUPPOSE IMPLY POSIT ASSUME EXPECT PREMISE FORETAKE

PRESUPPOSITION PREMISE

PRETA PETA

PRETEND ACT LET FAKE MAKE MOCK SHAM CLAIM FEIGN AFFECT ASPIRE ASSERT ASSUME GAMMON INTEND OBTEND POSSUM RECKON SEMBLE ATTEMPT PORTEND PRESUME PROFESS SUPPOSE VENTURE SIMULATE
(— IGNORANCE) CONNIVE
(— TO) FA

PRETENDED FAKE SHAM BOGUS FALSE IRONIC PSEUDO UNREAL ALLEGED ASSUMED COLORED FEIGNED SEEMING SIMULAR AFFECTED IRONICAL SIMULATE

PRETENDER FOP FAKE IDOL CHEAT COWAN FAKER FRAUD QUACK PSEUDO SEEMER AEOLIST CLAIMANT IMPOSTOR INTENDER TARTUFFE MOUNTEBANK
(— TO LEARNING) SCIOLIST

PRETENDING FICTION

PRETENSE ACT AIR FACE GRIM MASK MIEN PLEA RUSE SCUG SHAM SHOW SIGN WILE CLOAK COLOR COVER FEINT GLOSS GLOZE STUDY EXCUSE HUMBUG CHARADE DAUBERY FAITERY FASHION FICTION GRIMACE PRETEXT PURPOSE UMBRAGE ARTIFICE DISGUISE POSTICHE POSTIQUE SEMBLANT

PRETENSION PARADE VANITY PRETEXT

PRETENTIOUS BIG BRAG HIGH SIDY BRANK FLASH GAUDY PUFFY SHOWY BRAGGY CHICHI GEWGAW GLOSSY PUFFED ROCOCO SHODDY TINSEL BOMBAST POMPOUS STILTED TINHORN TOPPING BRAGGART OVERBLOWN RECHERCHE

PRETENTIOUSNESS SIDE SWANK

PRETERMIT OMIT NEGLECT SUSPEND INTERRUPT

PRETERNATURAL GOUSTY GOUSTIE STRANGE ABNORMAL UNCOMMON UNEARTHLY
(— BEING) MARE

PRETEXT PEG FLAM MASK PLEA VEIL CLOAK COLOR COVER GLOSS SALVO STALL EXCUSE REFUGE SCONCE APOLOGY UMBRAGE OCCASION PRETENCE PRETENSE

PRETTIFY EYEWASH

PRETTY APT GAY RAT ABLE BRAW CUTE DEFT FAIR FEAT FINE GAIN GENT GOOD JOLI MILD MOOI POOR TRIM BONNY DINKY JOLIE POOTY PURTY QUITE SWEET BONITA DIMBER FINELY INCONY MINION PRATTY RATHER TRETIS CLEMENT CUNNING DOLLISH GENTEEL BUDGEREE PRECIOUS
(— WELL) GAILY GAYLY

PRETTY-PRETTY KEEPSAKE

PREVAIL WIN BEAR BEAT REIGN WIELD INDUCE OBTAIN CONQUER PERSIST SUCCEED TRIUMPH DOMINATE
(— BECAUSE BEYOND CONTROL) RAGE
(— OVER) OVERRIDE OVERRULE SURMOUNT
(— UPON) GET FOLD LEAD ARGUFY ENTICE INDUCE OBTAIN ENTREAT OVERSWAY

PREVAILING RIFE GOING USUAL CURRENT DOMINANT

PREVALENCE RUN

PREVALENT UP RIFE BRIEF COMMON POTENT VULGAR CURRENT GENERAL POPULAR RAMPANT REGNANT CATHOLIC EPIDEMIC POWERFUL

PREVARICATE LIE EVADE STRAY SKLENT WANDER QUIBBLE SHUFFLE WHIFFLE

PREVARICATOR LIAR JESUIT

PREVENT BAR LET HELP KEEP NILL SHUN STAY STOP TENT WARN AVERT CHECK DEBAR DETER ESTOP ARREST DEFEND FORBID FORLET HINDER OUTRUN RETAIN REVOKE SECURE FORFEND FORLEIT IMPEACH INHIBIT OBVIATE OCCLUDE PRECEDE RETRACT ANTEVERT INTERPEL PARALYZE PRECLUDE PROHIBIT WITHHOLD
(— OPPONENT FROM SCORING) CHICAGO

PREVENTION PREFACE ESTOPPEL OBSTACLE PREJUDICE

PREVIEW SNEAK FUTURAMA

PREVIOUS HASTY PRIOR BEFORE FORMER RATHER EARLIER LEADING FOREGONE PRECEDING

PREVIOUSLY ERE YET ERST FORE SUPRA BEFORE ALREADY HASTILY PRIORLY FORMERLY HITHERTO

PREVISION FORESEE FORECAST FORESIGHT

PREY ROB FEED GAME SOYL TIRE BOOTY PREDE RAVEN RAVIN SPOIL QUARRY RAVAGE RAVINE VICTIM CAPTURE PILLAGE PLUNDER ROBBERY SPREATH VULTURE
(— UPON) DEVOUR PICAROON DEPREDATE
(HAWK'S —) PELT

PREYER KITE

PRIAM (DAUGHTER OF —) CREUSA POLYXENA CASSANDRA
(GRANDFATHER OF —) ILUS
(SLAYER OF —) PYRRHUS
(SON OF —) PARIS HECTOR TROILUS
(WIFE OF —) HECUBA

PRIAPISM TENTIGO

PRICE LAY ANTE COST FARE FEER FIAR FIER FOOT ODDS PRYS RATE BRIBE CHEAP CLOSE VALUE WORTH CHARGE FIGURE HANSEL TARIFF AVERAGE CATALOG CRANAGE EXPENSE FURNACE HANDSEL PRETIUM STORAGE CARRIAGE FERRIAGE INTEREST
(— FOR KEEPING GOODS) STORAGE
(HIGH —) DEARTH
(LOW —) WANWORTH
(PROPER —) VALUE
(REDUCED —) SALE BARGAIN
(RISING —S) BOOM INFLATION

PRICELESS RARE COSTLY UNIQUE UNSALABLE

PRICK DOT JAG BROD BROG DROB FOIN GOAD JAGG PECK PING PROG SPUR STAB TANG URGE DRESS ERECT POINT PREEN PUNCH STEEK BROACH GALLOP INTENT LAUNCH POUNCE PRITCH SKEWER STITCH TARGET THRUST TWINGE ACANTHA POINTED BULLSEYE
(— OUT) SPOT
(— PAINFULLY) STING
(— WITH NAIL) CLY CLOY ACCLOY
(PREF.) STIGMATI STIGMEO STIGMO

PRICKED PIQUE

PRICKER PROD NEEDLE STABBER

PRICKET DAG SNUFFER SPITTER

PRICKING SMART PUNGENT RETRACT POIGNANT POINTURE PUNCTION

(SUFF.) NYXIS

PRICKLE PIKE SETA BRIAR SPEAR SPINE THORN BASKET BRIERM ACANTHA ACULEUS PRINKLE SPICULA STICKLE STIMULUS

PRICKLY BURRY JAGGY SHARP SPINY URCHIN BEARDED SPINOSE SPINOUS STICKLY THISTLY ACULEATE ECHINATE MURICATE SCABROUS SCRATCHY SPICULAR STICKERY STINGING VEXATIOUS
(PREF.) ICHIN(O)

PRICKLY ASH RUEWORT

PRICKLY HEAT MILIARIA

PRICKLY PEAR TUN TUNA NOPAL SADRA OPUNTIA PINPILLOW

PRICKLY-POINTED PUNGENT

PRICKLY POPPY ARGEMONE COCKSCOMB

PRIDE HEAT HORN LUST POMP RUFF ADORN CREST GLORY ORGUL PLUME PREEN PRIME WLANK EXCESS HUBRIS METTLE NOSISM VANITY COMPANY CONCEIT DISDAIN EGOTISM GLORIFY HAUTEUR STOMACH SURQUIDY WLONKHEDE
(— ONESELF) PIQUE
(EXCESSIVE —) SWELLING ARROGANCE
(MASCULINE —) MACHISMO

PRIDE AND PREJUDICE (AUTHOR OF —) AUSTEN
(CHARACTER IN —) JANE MARY DARCY KITTY LUCAS LYDIA BENNET GEORGE BINGLEY COLLINS WICKHAM CAROLINE DEBOURGH GARDINER CATHERINE CHARLOTTE ELIZABETH FITZWILLIAM

PRIDEFUL FASTUOUS

PRIEST EN ABBE CURA CURE DEAN EZRA IMAM MAGA CLERK COHEN EPULO IMAUM ISIAC MOBED PADRE PATER SABIO SARIP VICAR ZADOK ABACES AMAUTA BHIKKU BISHOP DASTUR DIVINE FALMEN FATHER FLAMEN GALLAH GALLUS GELONG GETSUL GOSAIN JETHRO KAHUNA LEVITE POWWOW SHAMAN ANANIAS ARBACES CALCHAS CASSOCK CHANTER DESTOUR DUSTOOR GALLACH LAOCOON PANDITA PAPALOI PATENER PATRICO PHINEAS POONGEE PRESTER STOLIST TEACHER TOHUNGA BABAYLAN BEROSSOS CHRYSEIS HANANIAH KASHYAPA MINISTER PANDARAM PENANCER PONTIFEX POONGHIE SACERDOS SEMINARY SOGGARTH SYRIARCH TALISMAN VARDAPET ZADOKITE OFFICIANT SHAVELING
(— OF APOLLO) CALCHAS CHRYSEIS
(— OF CYBELE) CORYBANT
(— OF RAMA) KASHYAPA
(— OF RHEA) CURETE
(BABYLONIAN —) BEROSSOS
(BUDDHIST —) LAMA BHIKKU GELONG POONGEE POONGHIE TALAPOIN
(CHIEF —) SYRIARCH

(CHIEF — OF SHRINE) EN
(EGYPTIAN —) ARBACES CHOACHYTE
(ETRUSCAN —) LUCUMO
(EUNUCH —) GALLUS
(FRENCH —) PERE SULPICIAN
(GYPSY —) PATRICO
(HIGH —) ELI SARIP DASTUR KAHUNA DESTOUR PHINEAS PONTIFF PRELATE CAIAPHAS HIERARCH JEHOIADA PONTIFEX
(HINDU —) PANDARAM
(INCA —) AMAUTA
(LAMAIST —) GETSUL
(MAORI —) TOHUNGA
(MORO —) SARIP PANDITA
(MOSLEM —) ALFAQUI TALISMAN
(PAGAN —) BABAYLAN
(PARISH —) CURA CURE PAPA POPE PARSON PERSON SECULAR
(ROMAN —) EPULO FLAMEN
(TIBETAN —) LAMA
(VAISHNAVA —) GOSAIN
(VOODOO —) BOCOR BOKOR
(PL.) LUPERCI
PRIEST-DOCTOR SHAMAN WABENO
PRIESTESS NUN ENTUM HORSE MAMBO MAMBU BACBUC PYTHIA DIOTIMA MAMALOI PHOIBAD PHITONES PYTHONESS
(— OF APOLLO) PYTHIA PHOEBAD
(— OF THE BOTTLE) BACBUC
(BABYLONIAN —) ENTUM
(VOODOO —) HORSE
PRIESTFISH CHERNA ROCKFISH
PRIESTHOOD SALII SACERDOCY
PRIEST-KING PATESI
PRIESTLY LEVITIC SACERDOTAL
PRIG BEG FOP BRAD BUCK NAIL SMUG DANDY FILCH PLEAD STEAL THIEF FELLOW HAGGLE PERSON PILFER TINKER ENTREAT PURITAN QUIBBLE
PRIGGER THIEF
PRIGGISH PRUDISH
PRIM MIM NEAT TRIG TRIM MIMZY DEMURE FORMAL MIMSEY PRISSY PRIVET PROPER STUFFY MISSISH PERJINK PRECISE PRIMSIE STARCHY
PRIMACY CHIEFTY PRIMITY HEADSHIP
PRIMA DONNA DIVA STAR
PRIMARY CYAN BASIC CHIEF FIRST PRIME CAUCUS DIRECT FONTAL MANUAL MAGENTA RADICAL ARCHICAL CARDINAL HYPOGENE ORIGINAL PRIMEVAL PRINCIPAL
(PREF.) ARCHI PROT(E)(EO)
PRIMATE BISHOP GALAGO LEADER PREMAN PRINCIPAL PREHOMINID
PRIME MAY FANG FILL LOAD MAIN CHIEF COACH FIRST PRIDE TONIC YOUTH CHOICE FLOWER SPRING CENTRAL LEADING LUSTFUL PREPARE DOMINEER ORIGINAL YOUTHFUL PRINCIPAL
PRIME MINISTER ATABEG PREMIER
PRIMER ABC CAP DONAT WAFER READER CORDERY HORNBOOK
PRIMEVAL OLD NATIVE ANCIENT

OGYGIAN PRIMARY PRISTINE PRIMITIVE
PRIMING MORSING TWOPENNY CLEARCOLE
PRIMING IRON DRIFT
PRIMING WIRE PICKER
PRIMITIVE DARK CRUDE EARLY FIRST GROSS NAIVE PLAIN PRIME FANTEE GOTHIC PRIMAL SAVAGE SIMPLE ANCIENT ARCHAIC PRIMARY PRISCAN BACKVELD BARBARIC EARLIEST IGNORANT ORIGINAL PRISTINE ABORIGINAL PRIMORDIAL
(PREF.) ARCH(AE)(AEO)(E)(EO)(I) PALAE(O) PALE(O)
PRIMNESS STARCH PRUDERY
PRIMORDIAL CRUDE FIRST PRIMARY ARCHICAL EARLIEST PRIMEVAL
PRIMORDIUM BUD ANLAGE BLASTEMA
PRIMP PRIM ADORN PREEN PRINK
PRIMROSE GAY OXLIP SPINK FLOWER SUNCUP COWSLIP FLOWERY PRIMULA SCABISH AURICULA PLUMROCK SCURVISH AFTERGLOW PIMPERNEL POLYANTHUS
PRIMULA OXLIP COWSLIP PRIMWORT
PRINCE MIN RAS DUKE EARL EMIR IMAM KHAN KING KNEZ LORD NASI RAJA RANA RIAL SAID WANG ALDER EBLIS EMEER FURST GEBIR MIRZA PWYLL RAJAH SAYID ARJUNA DESPOT DYNAST SHERIF SOLDAN BHARATA ELECTOR GLAUCUS HELENUS MONARCH TANCRED TOPARCH ZERBINO ARCHDUKE ATHELING CARDINAL FLORIZEL HOSPODAR MAMILIUS OROONOKO RASSELAS SARPEDON PENDRAGON
(— OF ABYSSINIA) RAS RASSELAS
(— OF APOSTATE ANGELS) DEVIL EBLIS
(— OF ARGO) DIOMED DIOMEDES
(— OF BOHEMIA) FLORIZEL
(— OF DARKNESS) DEVIL SATAN
(— OF DEMONS) BEELZEBUB
(— OF DYFED) PWYLL
(— OF SALERNO) TANCRED
(— OF SCOTLAND) ZERBINO
(— SOLD INTO SLAVERY) OROONOKO
(— WITH CHARLEMAGNE) ASTOLF ASTOLFO
(ANGLO-SAXON —) ADELING ATHELING
(ARAB —) SHERIF
(CHINESE —) WANG
(ETRUSCAN —) LUCUMO
(GERMAN —) FURST ELECTOR
(INDIAN —) RAJA RANA RAJAH BHARATA AHLUWALIA
(LYCIAN —) GLAUCUS SARPEDON
(MOHAMMEDAN —) SOLDAN
(MOSLEM —) IMAM SAID SAYID SAYYID SHEIKH SOLDAN
(PETTY —) SATRAP VERGOBRET
(SERVIAN —) CRAL

(SLAVIC —) KNEZ
(TROJAN —) HELENUS
PRINCE EDWARD ISLAND (BAY OF —) ROLLA EGMONT ORWELL MALPEQUE
(CAPITAL OF —) CHARLOTTETOWN
(TOWN OF —) ABNEY SOURIS TIGNISH MONTAGUE GEORGETOWN SUMMERSIDE
PRINCELY NOBLE ROYAL KINGLY STATELY SOVEREIGN
PRINCE'S FEATHER LILAC PILEWORT
PRINCESS AIDA ELSA RANI DANAE PALLA RANEE SARAH CREUSA GLAUKE ILDICO MADAME PSYCHE ANTIOPE CORONIS PHYLLIS DRAUPADI MAHARANI
(— CHANGED INTO CROW) CORONIS
(— MOTHER OF ZEUS) ANTIOPA ANTIOPE
(— OF ARGOS) DANAE
(— OF CORINTH) CREUSA GLAUKE
(— WHO SLEW ATTILA) ILDICO
(MOHAMMEDAN —) BEGUM
(THRACIAN —) PHYLLIS
(TYRIAN —) DIDO
PRINCEWOOD CYP BARIA CYPRE CERILLO CANALETE SALMWOOD
PRINCIPAL ARCH BOSS HEAD HIGH MAIN STAR CHIEF FIRST GRAND GREAT PRIME STOCK AUCTOR CORPUS MASTER STAPLE CAPITAL CAPTAIN CENTRAL CHATTEL DECUMAN DOMINUS PREMIER PRIMARY SALIENT STELLAR CARDINAL ESPECIAL FOREMOST OFFICIAL PRESTANT PRINCELY
(— OF SCHOOL) PRECEPTOR HEADMASTER
(POLITICAL —) PLANK
(PREF.) ARCH PROT(O)
PRINCIPALITY ZUPA ARZAVA ARZAWA ORANGE SATRAPY APPANAGE DESPOTAT PRINCEDOM
PRINCIPLE JUS LAW RTA TAO BASE FATE RITA RULE SEED YANG AGENT AXIOM BASIS CANON CAUSE DATUM PRANA SPARK STUFF TENET ANIMUS ARABIN CNICIN COGITO CORTIN ELIXIR EMBRYO FAGINE GOSPEL ARCHEUS BROCARD BULFAGIN CLYSSUS ELEMENT FORMULA GENERAL PRECEPT QUASSIN RADICAL THEOREM URGRUND DOCTRINE GOSSYPOL INTIMISM LANDMARK NICOTINE SANCTION SPECIFIC TINCTURE
(— ACCEPTED AS TRUE) CANON
(— FROM TOAD) BUFAGIN
(— IN BEECHNUTS) FAGINE
(— OF BLESSED THISTLE) CNICIN
(— OF COTTONSEED) GOSSYPOL
(— OF EXISTENCE) TATTVA
(— OF INDIVIDUATION) AHANKARA
(— OF KEY IN MUSIC) TONALITY
(— OF REST) ADHARMA
(COSMIC —) HEAVEN URGRUND PRAJAPATI
(DOGMATIC —) DICTUM

(ELEMENTARY —) BROCARD
(FEMALE —) YIN SAKTI
(FIRST —) ABC SEED ARCHE
(FUNDAMENTAL —) GROUNDSEL
(GERMINAL —) STAMEN
(GOVERNING —) HINGE
(GUIDING —) SQUARE
(LIFE —) SOUL GHOST PRANA
(MALE —) YANG PURUSHA
(MOHAMMEDAN THEOLOGICAL —) IJMA
(MORAL —) SCRUPLE
(NARCOTIC —) FAGINE
(ONTOLOGICAL —) DHARMA
(PRIMAL —) APEIRON
(PROMINENT —) KEY
(RHYTHMICAL —) ACCENT
(SPIRITUAL —) SOUL
(SUMMARY OF —S) CREED
(VITAL —) JIVA SPIRIT STAMEN ARCHAEUS
PRINK PERK PRIG WINK ADORN PRICK PRIMP PRUNE BEDECK SMUDGE
PRINT CUT GAY GUM RUN DRUK MARK TYPE FUDGE PORTY PRESS SEPIA STAMP BANNER BORDER CARBON CARBRO ENFACE LETTER STRIKE BROMOIL DROPOUT DUOTYPE ENGRAVE GRAPHIC GRAVURE IMPRESS PUBLISH TRACING VANDYKE VESTIGE WOODCUT AQUATONE CALOTYPE CHLORIDE DRYPOINT HALFTONE INSCRIBE LEIMTYPE MONOTYPE POSITIVE URUSHIYE PHOTOENGRAVING
(— OF WILD MAMMAL) PUG
(— OTHER SIDE) BACK
(— TO RIGHT) ADSCRIPT
PRINTED FONTED
PRINTER TYPO TWICER PRESSMAN IMPRIMENT
(AID TO —) DEVIL
(PL.) TYPOTHETAE
AMERICAN DAY GOUDY GREEN RUDGE AITKEN DRAPER DUNLAP ROGERS THOMAS UPDIKE WILSON ZENGER GARNETT BRADFORD WOODWORTH
AUSTRIAN WELSBACH
DUTCH BOMBERG ELZEVIR ENSCHEDE
ENGLISH CAVE JONES WORDE BLOUNT BOWYER BULMER BUTTER CAXTON OGILBY AWDELAY COPLAND CROWLEY GRAFTON HANSARD NICHOLS BRADSHAW ROYCROFT WOODFALL WHITTINGHAM
FRENCH DIDOT DOLET MOREL COLINES PLANTIN ESTIENNE
GERMAN FUST ZELL KONIG LUFFT FROBEN MENTEL ZAINER PFISTER RATDOLT AMERBACH GRYPHIUS SCHOFFER BREITKOPF TAUCHNITZ
ITALIAN BODONI GIUNTA CASTALDI MANUTIUS
JAPANESE HARUNOBU
SCOTTISH SMELLIE BALLANTYNE
SWISS GERING
PRINTER'S DEVIL FLY

PRINTING TIRAGE EDITION VIGOREUX CHARACTER IMPRIMERY
(LAST —) THIRTY
PRION PETREL
PRIONID BEETLE
PRIONODON LINSANG
PRIOR ERE OLD FORE PAST EIGNE ELDER FORMER RATHER ALREADY EARLIER FARTHER ANTERIOR FOREHAND HITHERTO PREVIOUS PRECEDING
(PREF.) ANTE EPH EPI
(— TO) ANTE PRAE PRE SUPRA
PRIORITY PRIVILEGE PRECEDENCE PREFERMENT
(PREF.) PRAE PRE
PRIORY ABBEY NUNNERY CLOISTER PRIORATE
PRISCA (HUSBAND OF —) AQUILA
PRISM BLOCK NICOL CYLINDER SPECTRUM WERNICKE REFRACTOR
PRISMATIC SHOWY BRILLIANT
PRISON GIB JUG BRIG COOP GAOL HELL HOCK HOLD HOLE JAIL KEEP LAKE NICK QUAD QUOD SHOP STIR WARD BAGNE CHOKY CLINK FLEET GRATE KITTY LIMBO LODGE POUND RATEL TENCH TRONK VAULT BAGNIO BAILEY BUCKET CARCEL CARCER COOLER JIGGER LUMBER RATTLE BASTILE BOCARDO BULLPEN COLLEGE COMPTER CONFINE COUNTER DUNGEON FREEZER GEHENNA KIDCOTE LUDGATE NEWGATE SLAMMER DARTMOOR HOOSEGOW TOLBOOTH TRIBUNAL CALABOOSE PENITENTIARY
(— CAMP) OFLAG
(— IN ROME) TULLIANUM
(AUSTRALIAN —) TENCH
(UNIVERSITY —) CARCER
PRISONER CON POW MUTE LIFER DETENU INMATE REMAND CAITIFF CAPTIVE CONVICT GAOLBIRD JAILBIRD LONGTIMER
PRISONER OF ZENDA (AUTHOR OF —) HOPE
(CHARACTER IN —) ROSE SAPT FRITZ FLAVIA RUDOLF MICHAEL DEMAUBAN BURLESDON ANTOINETTE RASSENDYLL TARLENHEIM
PRISONER'S BASE CHEVY CHIVY
PRISSY PRIM FUSSY DAINTY FINICKY PRUDISH PRIGGISH SISSIFIED
PRISTINE NEW PURE FIRST FRESH ANCIENT PRIMARY ORIGINAL PRIMEVAL PRIMITIVE UNSPOILED
PRIVACY RECESS SECRET PRIVITY RETREAT SECRECY DARKNESS INTIMACY INTIMITY SOLITUDE SECLUSION
(IN —) ASIDE
(PL.) VERENDA
PRIVATE SNUG ALONE CLOSE GUIDE KHASS PRIVY SHARE CLOSET COVERT INWARD POCKET SECRET STANCH POSTERN SECRECY SEVERAL SOLDIER

CIVILIAN DOMESTIC ESOTERIC HOMEFELT INTERNAL INTIMATE PERSONAL SINGULAR UMBRATILE
(PREF.) CRYPT(O) KRYPT(O) PRIVI
PRIVATEER CAPER MARQUE PIRATE ALABAMA CORSAIR CRUISER DUNKIRK PICKEER
PRIVATELY ASIDE INWARDLY SECRETLY
PRIVATION LOSS WANT PINCH PENURY PERISH ABSENCE POVERTY HARDSHIP
PRIVET PRIM HEDGE SKEDGE IBOLIUM PRIMWORT PRIMPRINT
PRIVILEGE UP PUT SOC BOTE DOWN HAND STAR TEAM CLAIM ENTRY FAVOR FRANK GRACE HONOR REGAL RIGHT THEAM EXCUSE INDULT MUNITY OCTROI OPTION PATENT WARREN CHARTER FALDAGE FREEDOM LIBERTY MITZVAH PASSAGE GRANDEZA STANDAGE PERQUISITE PREROGATIVE
(— TO USE THINGS) BOTE
(ACQUIRED —) EASEMENT
(POKER —) EDGE
(POOL —) STAR
PRIVILEGED CURULE EXEMPT LICENSED CHARTERED
(— PLACE) WARREN
PRIVY WC AJAX GONG REAR BIFFY DRAFT ISSUE JAKES PETTY QUIET SIEGE CLOACA CLOSET OFFICE SECRET DRAUGHT FOREIGN LATRINE PRIVATE DONICKER FAMILIAR INTIMATE OUTHOUSE PERSONAL STEALTHY WARDROBE
PRIZE CUP FEE GEM PRY BELL BEND GAME GREE PALM PREY PRIX RATE RISK AWARD BACON BOOTY LEVER PLATE PLUME PRICE PURSE STAKE VALUE WAGER ESTEEM GLAIVE PRAISE PREMIO TROPHY BENEFIT CAPTURE GARLAND PREMIUM ESTIMATE LEVERAGE PURCHASE REPRISAL TREASURE
(— FOR LAST) MELL
(FIRST —) BLUE
(LOTTERY —) LOT TERN
(THEATER —) OBIE
PRIZE CUP PEWTER
PRIZED DEAR CHARY
PRIZEFIGHT GO BOUT MILL MATCH SCRAP BARNEY
PRIZEFIGHTER BOXER BLEEDER FIGHTER SLUGGER PUGILIST
PRIZE MONEY GUNNAGE
PRO TO FOR FAVORING
PROA PARO PRAU PROW PAROO PRAHU CARACOA
PROBABILITY ODDS SHOW CHANCE PERCENTAGE
PROBABLE MAYBE LIKELY PROBAL TOPICAL APPARENT FEASIBLE POSSIBLE
PROBABLY BELIKE LIKELY
PROBATION TEST PROOF TRIAL PAROLE EVIDENCE
PROBATIONER STIBBLER
PROBE PICK SEEK SIFT STOG TENT ENTER GROPE SOUND FATHOM

SEARCH SEEKER STYLET THRUST TRACER ACCOUNT EXAMINE INQUIRY SOUNDER GYROMELE
PROBITY HONESTY INTEGRITY RECTITUDE
PROBLEM NUT SUM WHY BOYG CRUX DUAL ISSE KNOT BLAIK HYDRA POSER APORIA ENIGMA BUGBEAR DILEMMA FUNERAL GORDIAN GRUELER TICKLER EXERCISE HEADACHE JEOPARDY QUESTION STICKLER SITUATION
(CHESS —) DUAL MOVER SUIMATE MINIATURE
PROBLEMATICAL DUBIOUS DOUBTFUL PUZZLING UNCERTAIN UNDECIDED
PROBOSCIS NOSE SNOUT TRUMP TRUNK ANTLIA LINGUA SIPHON SYPHON TONGUE ROSTRUM
PROBOSCIS MONKEY KAHA KAHUA
PROCAINE NOVOCAINE
PROCAVIA HYRAX
PROCEDURE BIAS FORM HAVE VEIN DRAFT ORDER TENOR TRACK AFFAIR COURSE METHOD POLITY SYSTEM DRAUGHT PROCESS PRODUCT ACTIVITY PROTOCOL OPERATION
(PRESCRIBED —S) CEREMONY
(ROUNDABOUT —) CIRCUITY
(SECRET —) STEALTH
(STANDARDIZED —) BIT
(UNWISE —) FOLLY
PROCEED DO GO BANG BEAR FAND FARE FLOW FOND HAVE MAKE MARK MOVE PASS ROAM ROLL SEEK STEP TAKE TOOL TOUR WEAR WEND WIND YEAD YEDE YEED AMBLE ARISE DRESS FOUND FRAME ISSUE MARCH REACH TRACE BREEZE INTEND PURSUE RESULT SPRING STRAKE STRIKE TRAVEL ADVANCE AGGRESS DEVOLVE EMANATE FORTHGO PRETEND STRETCH CONTINUE PROGRESS
(— AIMLESSLY) CIRCLE
(— ALONE) SINGLE
(— AWKWARDLY) SHLEP SCHLEP SCHLEPP
(— CLUMSILY) FLOUNDER
(— OBLIQUELY) CUT
(— RAGGEDLY) HALT
(— RAPIDLY) RAKE STRETCH
(— UNSTEADILY) DRIDDLE
(— WITH DIFFICULTY) STRUGGLE
(PL.) TAKE VAIL AVAILS INCOME PROFITS PROVENT RETURNS PREVENUE
PROCEEDING ACT DEED FARE PLOY STEP AFFAIR AMPARO COURSE DOMENT ISSUANT MEASURE ONGOING PASSANT QUIETUS TEMANET WARRANT CONCURSO INSTANCE PLACITUM PRACTICE
(— BY THREES) TERNARY
(— FROM GOD) DIVINE
(— FROM THE EARTH) TELLURIC
(COURT —S) TRIAL ACTION
(INDIRECT —S) AMBAGES

(PARLIAMENTARY —S) HUSTINGS
(RECORDED —S) ACTA
PROCERITY HEIGHT TALLNESS
PROCESS RUN FANG FOOT TINA WRIT CREST FURCA HAMUS MUCRO SPINA CALCAR CAPIAS CILIUM COURSE FEELER HABEAS INTEND METHOD REPORT ACCOUNT BARBULE FURCULA GOBBING HAMULUS ISOLATE LAMELLA MANDATE SPATULA SUMMONS ACROMION ACTIVITY APPENDIX AUTOTYPE FILAMENT FRENULUM GRAINING INSTANCE MANUBRIUM OPERATION
(— OF BONE) HORN
(— OF CHANGE) ACTION
(— OF CREATING VACUUM) EXHAUST
(— OF DYEING) BATIK HANKING
(— OF METALPLATING) ACIERAGE
(— OF PACKING) GOBBING
(— OF REASONING) ALGEBRA
(— OF SUPPLYING WANTAGE) ULLING
(— ON FISH'S HEAD) LACINIA
(— PAPER) CONVERT
(— TO RECOVER LAND) DADENHUDD
(— TO REGAIN USE) RECYCLE
(ABRUPT —) MUCRO
(ALCHEMICAL —) CIBATION DIPLOSIS
(ARTISTIC —) FROTTAGE
(CALENDERING —) SWISSING
(CARBON —) AUTOTYPE
(CERAMIC —) FIRING
(COATING —) BLOOMING
(CURVED —) HAMUS
(DEVELOPMENTAL —) ANCESTRY
(EARLIKE —) AURICLE
(FALCONRY —) IMPING
(FINISHING —) BRUSHING CRABBING
(FORKED —) FURCA FURCULA
(HELMETLIKE —) CASQUE
(HOOKLIKE —) HAMULUS
(HORNSHAPED —) CORNICLE
(INTELLECTUAL —S) COGITO
(KNOBLIKE —) BOSS
(LEGAL —) BAIL SUIT CAUSE ATTAINT INSTANCE
(MATHEMATICAL —) ADDITION DIVISION
(MENTAL —) COMPOUND
(MINING —) STOPING
(MOVIE-MAKING —) SLATING
(NERVE-CELL —) DENDRON
(NERVELIKE —) AXON AXONE
(PHOTOGRAPHIC —) CARBRO
(POINTED —) AWN SPINE STYLUS LANGUET
(PRINTING —) OFFSET GRAVURE STENCIL INTAGLIO
(REORGANIZATION —) HEMIXIS
(SMALL POINTED —) AWN
(SPINNING —) JACKING
(SPINOUS —) ACANTHA
(TEXTILE —) DECATING
(WEAVING —) HATCHING
(WINGLIKE —) ALA FIN
(PREF.) TYP(I)(O)
(DRY —) XER(O)

(SUFF.) AL ANCE ANT ENCE ESIS IAL ING ISATION ISM IZATION OSIS SIS TH TYPAL TYPE TYPIC TYPY
(— OF BECOMING) ESCENCE
PROCESSED DOWN FINISHED
PROCESSION POMP WALK CORSO DRIVE TRACE TRAIN BRIDAL EXEQUY LITANY PARADE STREAM CORTEGE FUNERAL THIASOS TRIONFO TRIUMPH ENTRANCE MOHARRAM PROGRESS MOTORCADE
(BOISTEROUS —) SKIMMITY
(IRISH CIVIC —) FRINGES
(SUFF.) CADE
PROCLAIM BID CRY BAWL DEEM HORN OYES OYEZ SCRY SING TOOT TOUT BLARE BLAZE BOAST CLAIM GREDE KNELL SOUND SPEAK BLAZON BOUNCE DEFAME HERALD INDICT OUTCRY CLARION DECLARE DIVULGE PROTEST PUBLISH TRUMPET ANNOUNCE DENOUNCE RENOUNCE PROMULAGET
(— ALOUD) ROAR
(— PUBLICLY) PRECONIZE
(— WITH BIG TALK) BOUNCE
PROCLAMATION CRY HUE BANS FIAT OYEZ RERD SCRY BANDO BANNS BLAZE EDICT UKASE PLACARD PROGRAM
PROCLIVITY BENT ANLAGE APETITE APTNESS LEANING TENDENCY
PROCNE (FATHER OF —) PANDION
(HUSBAND OF —) TEREUS
(SISTER OF —) PHILOMELA
(SON OF —) ITYS
PROCONSUL GALLIO PROVOST
PROCRASTINATE LAG TIME DEFER DELAY LINGER ADJOURN POSTPONE PROROGUE TEMPORIZE
PROCRASTINATION DELAY CUNCTATION
PROCREANT FRUITFUL
PROCREATE WIN SIRE BEGET ENGENDER GENERATE OCCASION
PROCREATION INCREASE
PROCREATOR AUTHOR
PROCRIS (FATHER OF —) ERECHTHEUS
(HOUND OF —) LAELAPS
(HUSBAND OF —) CEPHALUS
PROCTOR LIAR PROG ACTOR AGENT PROXY BEGGAR RECTOR MONITOR PROCUTOR
PROCUMBENT HUMIFUSE PROSTRATE
PROCURABLE PARABLE
PROCURATOR PROXY PILATE PROCTOR
PROCURE GET WIN FANG FIND GAIN GIVE HALE BRING INFER TOUCH EFFECT INDUCE OBTAIN ACHIEVE ACQUIRE COMPARE CONQUER CONTRIVE PURCHASE
PROCURER PIMP PROXENET PURVEYOR
PROCURESS AUNT BAWD HACK LENA PANDER

COMMODE PINNACE
PROD DAB EGG GIG JAB JOB JOG BROD BROG GOAD HEEL POKE PROG GOOSE HURRY NUDGE PROBE INCITE JOSTLE THRUST IRRITATE
PRODIGAL PROD FLUSH LARGE COSTLY LAVISH WANTON WASTER PROFUSE SPENDER WASTRIE WASTRIFE PROFLIGATE
PRODIGALITY WASTE WASTRY WASTRIFE PROFUSION
PRODIGIOUS HUGE VAST GIANT AMAZING IMMENSE STRANGE ABNORMAL ENORMOUS GIGANTIC MONSTROUS PORTENTOUS
PRODIGY OMEN SIGN MARVEL OSTENT WIZARD WONDER MIRACLE MONSTER PORTENT CEREMONY
PRODITION TREASON BETRAYAL
PRODUCE DO GO ANTE BEAR FORM GIVE GROW MAKE REAR SHOW TEEM WAGE BEGET BIRTH BREED BRING BROOD BUILD CARRY CAUSE DRIVE FORGE FRAME HATCH ISSUE RAISE SPAWN THROW TRADE YIELD APPORT CREATE EFFECT GROWTH INCOME INVENT INWORK PARENT SECURE ADVANCE ANIMATE COMPOSE DEPROME GIGNATE INSPIRE OUTWORK PRODUCT PROLONG PROVENT CONCEIVE CONFLATE ENGENDER GENERATE INCREASE LENGTHEN OFFSPRING
(— A COPY OF) TYPE
(— AN EFFECT) ACT AFFECT
(— AUDIBLE EFFECT) SOUND
(— CROPS) CARRY
(— DULL APPEARANCE) CHILL
(— FREELY) PULLULATE
(— FRUIT) TEEM
(— HEAT) ENRAGE
(— IN SPECIFIED FORM) FORMAT
(— PAID FOR RENT) CAIN
(— SHARP NOISE) CRINK
(AGRICULTURAL —) PODWARE
(FARM —) HUSBANDRY
(MINING —) LEY
(SUFF.) FER(ENCE)(ENT)(OUS) FIC(AL)(ATE)(ATION)(ATIVE)(ATOR) (ATORY)(E)(ENCE)(ENT)(IAL)(IARY) (IENT) FIQUE GEN(E)(ESIA)(ESIS) (ETIC)(IC)(IN)(OUS)(Y)
PRODUCED
(SUFF.) GENETIC
PRODUCER GASMAN BEARING SHOWMAN DIRECTOR GAZOGENE OUTPUTTER
(SUFF.) ARIAN EER
PRODUCING IN PROCREANT
(PREF.) EXO
(SUFF.) GENIC GEROUS GON(E)(IDIUM)(IMO)(Y) IGEROUS PARA PAROUS
PRODUCT HEIR ITEM BRAND CHILD FRUIT GROSS OUTGO SPAWN ALCLAD EFFORT FABRIC GROWTH RESULT UPCOME FALLOUT OUTTURN PRODUCE PROGENY TURNOUT

OUTBIRTH OFFSPRING
(— OF ROCK DECAY) LATERITE
(—S OF LAND) ESPLEES
(—S OF ORCHARD) BIKKURIM
(ADDITION —) ADDUCT
(CHEESE AND MILK —S) GERVAIS
(CHOICE —) CAVIAR
(COMPLETED —) TURNOFF
(LEGISLATIVE —) ACT
(MATHEMATICAL —) SQUARE
(MINERAL —) HUTCH
(OXIDATION —) SUBSCALE
(RESIDUAL —) LATERITE
(SECONDARY —) CONGENER
(SURPLUS —S) ARISINGS
(TRANSFORMATION —) BAINITE
(WASTE —) RESIDUENT
(WORTHLESS —) CHAFF
(SUFF.) ADE
(COMMERCIAL —) INE
(MANUFACTURED —) ITE
PRODUCTION WORK FORGE FRUIT GROSS PIECE YIELD GROWTH OUTPUT EDITION GUIGNOL PRODUCE ARTIFICE INDUCTION OPERATION
(— OF MEDIUM) APPORT
(— OF YOUNG) INCREASE
(BEST —S) FAT
(SUCCESSFUL —) HIT
(SUFF.) GENY POEIA POESIS POIESIS POIETIC
PRODUCTIVE FAT RICH LOOSE QUICK ACTIVE BATTLE PAROUS STRONG CAUSING FERTILE GAINFUL HEALTHY TEEMFUL TEEMING CHILDING CREATIVE FRUITFUL GERMINAL PLENTEOUS
(SUFF.) POEIA POESIS POIESIS POIETIC
PROEM PREFACE PRELUDE PROHEIM FOREWORD OVERTURE PREAMBLE
PROETUS (BROTHER OF —) ACRISIUS
(DAUGHTER OF —) IPHINOE LYSIPPE IPHIANASSA
(FATHER OF —) ABAS
(MOTHER OF —) OCALEA
(WIFE OF —) ANTEA
PROFANATION VIOLENCE SACRILEGE
PROFANE LAY NOA BLUE FOUL ABUSE COARSE DEBASE DEFILE DEFOIL DEFOUL UNHOLY VULGAR WICKED GODLESS IMPIOUS POLLUTE SECULAR UNGODLY VIOLATE WORLDLY TEMPORAL UNHALLOW
PROFANITY OATH CURSE CURSING LANGUAGE BLASPHEMY
PROFESS OWN AVOW ADMIT CLAIM AFFECT AFFIRM ALLEGE ASSERT ASSUME FOLLOW PRESUME PRETEND PURPORT PRACTICE
PROFESSION ART BAR LAW COAT FEAT GAME WALK CRAFT FAITH FORTE TRADE CAREER CHURCH EMPLOY METIER MISTER CALLING FACULTY QUALITY SERVICE ADVOCACY BUSINESS COACHING FUNCTION PEDAGOGY

SOLDIERY VOCATION
(SUFF.) SHIP
PROFESSIONAL PRO COLT PAID HIRED EXPERT SKILLED TRAINED FINISHED
PROFESSOR DON PROF HANIF KHOJA LAWYER REGENT ADJOINT ACADEMIC CIVILIAN EMERITUS
PROFESSORSHIP CHAIR FAUTEUIL
PROFFER BID CAP GIVE TEND TENT DEFER DODGE ESSAY OFFER EXTEND OPPOSE PREFER PROFRE TENDER ATTEMPT PRESENT HESITATE
PROFICIENCY SIGHT SKILL ABILITY APTNESS MAITRISE
PROFICIENT ADEPT EXPERT MASTER SALTED VERSED PERFECT SKILLED SKILLFUL
PROFILE FORM FLANK PURFLE SKETCH CONTOUR OUTLINE SECTION PSYCHOGRAPH
(— OF RIVERBED) THALWEG
PROFIT AID GET NET WIN BOOT GAIN MEND NOTE SKIN VAIL AVAIL EDIFY FRAME GRIST LUCRE SCALP SPEED BEHOOF INCOME MAKING PAYOFF RETURN ACCOUNT ADVANCE BENEFIT CLEANUP FURTHER GETTING IMPROVE MILEAGE PLUNDER REVENUE VANTAGE WINNING CLEANING INCREASE INTEREST PERCENTAGE PERQUISITE
(— BY) BROOK
(INORDINATE —) BUNCE
(UNDERCOVER —) SQUEEZE
(PL.) GRAVY ISSUE AVAILS JALKAR ESPLEES
PROFITABLE FAT GOOD UTILE GOLDEN PLUMMY GAINFUL HELPFUL PAYABLE BEHOVELY ECONOMIC PROVABLE REPAYING VAILABLE REWARDING
PROFITLESS BOOTLESS
PROFLIGATE ROUE DEFEAT CORRUPT IMMORAL RIOTOUS SPENDER VICIOUS WASTREL DEPRAVED FLAGRANT OVERCOME RAKEHELL WASTEFUL ABANDONED
PROFOUND DEEP HARD WISE ABYSS DEPTH HEAVY OCEAN SOUND THICK PITCHY STRONG ABYSMAL INTENSE ABSTRUSE COMPLETE PREGNANT REACHING THOROUGH
PROFUNDITY ABYSS DEPTH FATHOM DEEPNESS
PROFUSE FREE LUSH SLAB FRANK GALORE LAVISH COPIOUS LIBERAL OPULENT ABUNDANT GENEROUS PRODIGAL SQUANDER WASTEFUL REDUNDANT
PROFUSELY HEARTILY
PROFUSION WASTE EXCESS LAVISH FLUENCY OPULENCE REDUNDANCY
PROG FOOD GOAD POKE PROD PROWL TRAMP BEGGAR FORAGE PROCTOR
PROGENITOR BURI MANU ROOT SIRE PITRI STOCK

PARENT ANCESTOR

PROGENY BED GET IMP KIN BURD CLAN KIND SEED TEAM BROOD CHILD FRUIT ISSUE STRAIN STRIND INCROSS KINDRED LINEAGE OUTCOME PRODUCT CHILDREN FRUITAGE INCREASE OUTBIRTH OUTCROSS OFFSPRING
(— OF WATER-BUFFALO AND YAK) DZO
(— OF WITCH AND DEMON) HOLD
(INSECT —) SOCIETY

PROGNOSIS FORECAST PROPHASIS

PROGNOSTIC OMEN SIGN TOKEN AUSPICE OMINOUS PRESAGE PROPHECY

PROGNOSTICATE BODE AUGUR SPELL BETOKEN CONJECT PREDICT PRENOTE FOREBODE FORESHOW FORETELL PROPHESY

PROGNOSTICATION RACE PRESAGE FOREBODE FORECAST PROGRESS PROPHECY

PROGNOSTICATOR SEER DOOMER PROPHET HARUSPEX

PROGRAM CARD SHOW FORUM AGENDA DESIGN SCHEME AGENDUM PREFACE CLAMBAKE FESTIVAL GIVEAWAY GUIDANCE JAMBOREE PLAYBILL SCHEDULE SEQUENCE SYLLABUS
(COMPUTER —) DOS FIRMWARE
(COMPUTER —S) SOFTWARE
(HEALTH) MEDICAID MEDICARE
(PART OF COMPUTER —) BRANCH

PROGRAMMA EDICT DECREE PREFACE PROGRAM

PROGRESS WAY BIRL DENT FARE GAIN GROW MOVE RACE RISE STEM STEP TOUR WEAR WEND WENT BUILD DRIFT FORGE GOING MARCH SWING WEENT ASCENT BUFFET COURSE GROWTH STREEK ADVANCE DEVELOP FOOTING HEADWAY IMPROVE JOURNEY ONGOING PASSAGE PROCESS PROFICIENCY
(— CLUMSILY) SCRAMBLE
(— ERRATICALLY) FLAIL
(— FEEBLY) DODDER
(— INTELLIGENTLY PLANNED) TELESIA TELESIS
(— NOISILY) CHORTLE
(— SLOWLY) CRAWL
(SINGLE —) THROUGH

PROGRESSED FAR

PROGRESSION WAY SWING COURSE GALLOP ADVANCE PASSAGE PROGRESS SEQUENCE
(— OF CHORDS) SWIPE
(MUSICAL —) SKIP
(SMOOTH —) SLIDE

PROGRESSIVE ACTIVE ONWARD FORWARD GRADUAL LIBERAL

PROGRESSIVELY STILL

PROHIBIT BAN BAR STOP VETO BLOCK DEBAR ESTOP DEFEND ENJOIN FORBID HINDER OUTLAW FORFEND FORWARN INHIBIT PREVENT DISALLOW PRECLUDE SUPPRESS PROSCRIBE

PROHIBITED HOT TABU TABOO

ILLEGAL ILLICIT UNLAWFUL VERBOTEN

PROHIBITING VETITIVE

PROHIBITION BAN NAY NON VETO ORDER BARRIER DEFENCE DEFENSE EMBARGO FORBODE ESTOPPEL

PROHIBITIONIST DRY PUSSYFOOT

PROJECT GAB GAG JET JUT LAP TUT BEAM CAST GAME IDEA PLAN POKE PUSH SAIL SWIM BULGE CHART DRAFT DRIVE IMAGE JETTY JUTTY SETUP SHOOT STICK THROW BEETLE DESIGN DEVICE ESTATE EXTEND FILLIP OUTJUT PROPEL SCHEME SCREEN SHELVE EXTRUDE GOSPLAN IMAGINE KNUCKLE OUTCROP PATTERN BUSINESS CONTRIVE OUTREACH OUTSHOOT OVERHANG PROPOSAL PROTRUDE SPANGHEW
(UNETHICAL —) SCHEME
(VISIONARY —) BABEL

PROJECTILE BALL BOLT CASE SHOT SHAFT TRACER OUTCAST POUNDER FIREBALL SHRAPNEL
(— DESIGNED TO SET FIRE TO HOUSES) CARCASS
(EXPLOSIVE —) BOMB SHELL
(SUBMARINE —) TORPEDO
(PL.) LEAD SHOT SALVO STUFF

PROJECTING BEETLE SHELVY EMINENT JUTTING OUTSHOT PENDENT SALIENT SNAGGED PROMINENT OUTSTANDING
(PREF.) PRO

PROJECTION ARM CAM COG DOG EAR FIN GIB JET JOG JUT NAB NAG NUT TOE BEAK BOSS BROW BUHR COAK COCK CROC CUSP HEEL HORN KEEL KICK KINK KNAG KNOB KNOP LOBE RIDE SAIL SNUG SPUD SPUR TEAT WING BULGE CLEAT EJECT ELBOW FENCE FURCA JUTTY SALLY SCRAG SHANK SHOOT SPIKE TOOTH BRANCH CALCAR CORBEL CROSET FUSULA HEARTH ICICLE MENTUM NOSING PALATE RELISH TAPPET BREAKER CONSOLE DRAWING EPAULET EYEBROW FETLOCK KNUCKLE LANGUET ORILLON PRICKER PRICKLE RESSAUT AJUTMENT CASCABEL DENTICLE EMINENCE FOOTLOCK OVERHANG SALIENCE SHOULDER SPROCKET STERIGMA APOPHYSIS OUTTHRUST PROMINENCE
(— CONNECTING TIMBER) COAK
(— EXTENDING BACKWARD) BARB
(— FROM CASTING) SPRUE
(— FROM SHIP'S KEEL) SPONSON
(— IN CLOCK) SQUARE
(— IN ORCHIDS) MENTUM
(— OF FOREHEAD) ANTINION
(— OF JAW) GNATHISM
(— OF PEAT) HAG
(— OF RAFTER) SALLY
(— OF TERRITORY) PANHANDLE
(— ON CANNON) CASCABEL
(— ON CHURCH SEAT) MISERICORD
(— ON GUN) CROC LUMP

(— ON HARNESS) HAME
(— ON HORSE'S LEG) FETLOCK
(— ON HORSESHOE) STICKER
(— ON LOCK) FENCE STUMP
(— ON MAST) STOP
(— ON OVARY) STIGMA
(— ON POCKETKNIFE) KICK
(— ON SALMON JAW) GIB
(— ON WHEEL) GUB GROUSER GROUTER
(— OVER AIR PORT) EYEBROW
(FIREPLACE —) HOB
(JAGGED —) SNUG
(SHARP —) BARB FANG
(SUBMERGED —) KNOLL
(PL.) GRAIN BARLEY

PROJECTOR KINO LANTERN PLANNER SCHEMER BIOSCOPE EPISCOPE VITASCOPE

PROLAMIN ZEIN SEINE GLIADIN HORDEIN KAFIRIN SECALIN

PROLAPSE PTOSIS BLOWOUT FALLING

PROLETARIAN POPULAR

PROLETARIAT MASSES

PROLIFIC BIRTHY BREEDY BROODY FECUND FERTILE PROFUSE TEEMING ABUNDANT FRUITFUL SPAWNING
(BE —) INCREASE

PROLIX LARGE WORDY DIFFUSE LENGTHY PROSAIC TEDIOUS VERBOSE TIRESOME WEARISOME

PROLIXITY REDUNDANCY

PROLOGUE BANS BANNS INDEX PREFACE

PROLONG DREE LENG LONG SPIN DEFER DELAY DRIVE ELONG TWINE DILATE EXTEND LINGER SPREAD DISPACE PRODUCE RESPITE SUSTAIN CONTINUE ETERNIZE LENGTHEN POSTPONE PROROGUE PROTRACT

PROLONGATION BEAK AORTA CONUS STIPE STYLE FERMATA ACROSOME GYNOBASE LABELLUM

PROLONGED GREAT PROLIX DELAYED EXTENDED SOSTENUTO

PROMENADE BUND MAIL MALL PIER PROM WALK CORSO FRONT PASEO PRADO MARINA PARADE PASEAR ALAMEDA GALLERY FRESCADE BOULEVARD
(CARRIAGE —) TOUR

PROMETHEUS (BROTHER OF —) ATLAS MENOETIUS EPIMETHEUS
(FATHER OF —) IAPETUS
(MOTHER OF —) CLYMENE

PROMETHEUS UNBOUND (AUTHOR OF —) SHELLEY
(CHARACTER IN —) ASIA IONE EARTH JUPITER MERCURY PANTHEA HERCULES DEMOGORGON PROMETHEUS

PROMINENCE BUR NOB BOSS BURR CUSP KNOB NOOP UMBO AGGER BULLA CREST GRAIN OLIVA SWELL TUBER TYLUS ACCENT CALCAR NODULE TRAGUS BILLING BUTTOCK CONDYLE FASHION HAMULUS KNUCKLE LINGULA AMYGDALA EMINENCY EMPHASIS GLABELLA

PULVINAR SALIENCE TUBERCLE MONTICULE PROMONTORY
(PREF.) TUBERCULI TUBERCULO TUBERI

PROMINENT BIG BOLD BEADY BRENT GREAT STEEP BEETLE MARKED SIGNAL BLATANT BOLTING CAPITAL EMINENT JUTTING LEADING NOTABLE OBVIOUS SALIENT AQUILINE BEETLING MANIFEST STRIKING NOTICEABLE CONSPICUOUS
(SOCIALLY —) SWELL

PROMISCUOUS LIGHT CASUAL RANDOM CARELESS

PROMISCUOUSLY TAGRAG

PROMISE VOW AVOW BAND HEST HETE HOPE HOTE OSSE PASS PLEA SURE WORD FAITH GRANT HIGHT TRUTH ASSURE BEHEST ENGAGE FIANCE HALSEN INSURE PAROLE PLEDGE PLIGHT PROMIT BEHIGHT BETROTH WARRANT CONTRACT COVENANT GUARANTY BETROTHAL OBLIGATION
(— IN MARRIAGE) BETROTH ESPOUSE AFFIANCE
(— TO PAY) NOTE ACCEPT
(— TO TAKE IN MARRIAGE) AFFY

PROMISED VOTARY
(— IN MARRIAGE) SURE HIGHT ENGAGED

PROMISING APT FAIR BRIGHT LIKELY PROOPT TOWARD GRADELY TOWARDLY

PROMISSORY NOTE IOU HUNDI HOONDI TICKET

PROMONTORY HOE NAB BEAK BILL HEAD MULL NAZE NESS NOOK NOUP PEAK SCAW SKAW TOOT ELBOW MORRO POINT REACH SNOUT SALIENT FORELAND HEADLAND

PROMOTE AID HELP LOFT PUSH AVAIL BOOST EXALT NURSE RAISE SERVE SPEED ASSIST EXCITE FOMENT FOSTER LAUNCH PREFER ADVANCE DIGNIFY ELEVATE FORWARD FURTHER IMPROVE PREFECT PRODUCE PROMOVE SUCCEED SUPPORT INCREASE SUBSERVE

PROMOTER AGENT FRIEND ABETTOR BOOSTER BUBBLER BROACHER HUMANIST PROJECTOR
(SUFF.) ANT

PROMOTION LIFT REMOVE ADVANCE PROMOVAL

PROMPT APT CUE MOVE URGE YARE ALERT FRACK PREST QUICK READY SERVE SWIFT WILLY YEDER EXCITE INDITE MATURE NIMBLE SPEEDY SUDDEN ANIMATE FORWARD PROVOKE SUGGEST PUNCTUAL REMINDER
(— TO EVIL) SUGGEST

PROMPTER CUER CALLER MEMORIST ORDINARY SOUFFLEUR

PROMPTING CALL BEHEST BEHIND MOTIVE
(SPIRITUAL —) LEADING

PROMPTITUDE ALACRITY

PROMPTLY UP PAT TID TIT SOON TITE PRONTO YARELY PRESTLY QUICKLY DIRECTLY SPEEDILY

PROMPTNESS ALACRITY CELERITY DISPATCH

PROMULGATE SPREAD DECLARE PUBLISH PROCLAIM

PRONAOS ANTICUM

PRONE APT BENT EASY FLAT FREE GRUF BUXOM GIVEN GROOF JACENT LIABLE SUPINE BEASTLY BESTIAL DORMANT SUBJECT ADDICTED COUCHANT DISPOSED DOWNWARD PROPENSE
(— TO TAKE UP FADS) ISMY
(NATURALLY —) PROLIVE

PRONENESS
(SUFF.) (— TO) ITIS

PRONG NEB NIB PEG PEW BILL FANG FORK HOOK PUGH SPUR TANG TENG TINE TING GRAIN SPADE SPEAN SPRONG FOURCHE TICKLER GRAINING
(— FOR EXTRACTING BUNG) TICKLER
(— FOR FISH) PEW PUGH
(— OF ANTLER) KNAG TIND TINE POINT
(— OF FORK) SPEAN

PRONGHORN CABREE CABRIT MAZAME BERENDO BERRENDO

PRONOUN HE IT ME MY WE YE ANY HER HIM HIS ONE OUR SHE THY WHO YOU OURS THAT THEM THEY THOU WHAT WHOM YOUR THINE WHICH WHOSE ITSELF MYSELF HERSELF HIMSELF OURSELF WHOEVER YOURSELF OURSELVES
(GENDERLESS —) THON

PRONOUNCE SAY PASS ACUTE SPEAK UTTER PREACH RECITE TONGUE ADJUDGE BEHIGHT CENSURE MOUILLE ASPIRATE
(— FREE) ABSOLVE
(— GUILTY) CONDEMN
(— HOLY) BLESS

PRONOUNCED HIGH MARKED DECIDED HOWLING INTENSE MOVABLE
(— AS FRICATIVE) GRASSEYE
(— PALATALLY) MOUILLE
(NOT —) SOFT

PRONOUNCEMENT FIAT CURSE DICTUM DICTAMEN

PRONTO QUICK QUICKLY PROMPTLY

PRONUNCIATION BROGUE DICTION ETACISM LIAISON DELIVERY ENCLISIS ORTHOEPY
(BAD —) CACOEPY CACOLOGY LABDACISM
(BROAD —) PLATEASM
(CORRECT —) ORTHOEPY
(ROUGH —) BUR BURR

PROOF SAY MARK PULL SLIP TEST ESSAY PREWE TOKEN TOUCH TRIAL CLENCH GALLEY ORDEAL REASON RESULT REVISE ATTEMPT OUTCOME PROBATE SHOWING UTTERLY VOUCHER WARRANT ANALYSIS CACOLOGY DOCUMENT

EVICTION EVIDENCE GOODNESS MONUMENT
(— OF WRONGDOING) GOODS
(— SPIRIT OF WINE) SVT
(ABSOLUTE —) APODIXIS
(INDIRECT —) APAGOGE
(PL.) STRING WARRANTY

PROOFREADER MARK CAP DELE STET CARET

PROP LEG BROB BUNT POST REST SPUR STAY STUD TRIG APPUI BRACE PERCH PUNCH RANCE SCOTE SHORE SHOVE SOUSE SPRAG SPURN STAFF STELL STOOP STULL COLUMN CROTCH CRUTCH PILLAR SCOTCH SHORER STAYER UPHOLD BOLSTER FULCRUM PINNING STUDDLE SUPPORT SUSTAIN BUTTRESS CROTCHET DUTCHMAN UNDERLAY UNDERSET
(— AS TRAP) TEEL
(— FOR CART) NEAP
(— FOR ROOF OF MINE) GIB
(— UP) CUSHION SCAFFOLD
(PREF.) FULCI

PROPAGANDA BOLOISM AGITPROP BALLYHOO

PROPAGATE BREED HATCH LAYER EXTEND SPREAD STRIKE DIFFUSE GEMMATE PRODUCE PUBLISH ENGENDER GENERATE INCREASE MULTIPLY POPULATE TRANSMIT PROCREATE

PROPAGATION BREED BREEDING DIVISION INCREASE LAYERAGE OFFSPRING
(SUFF.) GAM(AE)(IST)(OUS)(Y) GAMETE

PROPEL ROW CALL CAST FIRE FLIP KENT POLE PUSH SEND URGE DRIVE FLICK IMPEL KNOCK PRICK RANGE SPANK THROW HURTLE LAUNCH PROJECT
(— BALL) STROKE
(— BOAT) OAR ROW SET KENT POLE SCULL BUSHWACK
(— BOAT WITH FEET) LEG
(— ONESELF) HAUL
(— PUCK) CARRY
(— SUDDENLY) ZAP

PROPELLER FAN HELIX SCREW AIRSCREW WINDMILL

PROPENSITY YEN BENT ITCH LURCH APTNESS IMPULSE LEANING PRONITY APPETITE FONDNESS INTEREST TENDENCY

PROPER FIT OWN GOOD JUST MEET TRUE WELL PREST RIGHT UTTER COMELY DECENT HONEST LAWFUL MODEST SEEMLY CAPITAL CORRECT FITTING GRADELY SEEMING SKILFUL THRIFTY ABSOLUTE BECOMING CONGREVE DECOROUS FORMULAR IDONEOUS PECULIAR RIGHTFUL SORTABLE SUITABLE VIRTUOUS
(APPARENTLY —) SPECIOUS
(BE — TO) BESEEM
(PREF.) CURIO ORTH(O)

PROPERLY DULY WELL FITLY TRULY ARIGHT FAIRLY FEATLY

GLADLY MEETLY RIGHTLY

PROPERTY AVER BONA DHAN TOOL WAIF ASSET AUGHT GOODS GRANT MOYEN STATE STOCK THING WORTH APPEAL DEVISE ESTATE HAVIOR KELTER LIVING MUSHAA REALTY TALENT USINGS WEALTH ACQUEST APANAGE CHATTEL DEMESNE ESCHEAT ESSENCE FACULTY FITNESS HARNESS HAVINGS QUALITY WARISON ALLODIAL CATALLUM HOLDINGS PECULIUM POSSESSION PARAPHERNALIA
(— BELONGING TO WOMAN) STRIDHAN
(— FROM WIFE TO HUSBAND) DOS
(— GIVEN BY WILL) DEVISE
(— OF MATTER AT REST) INERTIA
(— SECURED DISHONESTLY) HARL
(— SEIZED BY FORCE) SPOIL
(ABSOLUTE —) ALODIUM
(ENEMY —) HEREM
(LANDED —) DOMAIN ESTATE DEMESNE PRAEDIUM
(MOVABLE —) GEAR CHATTEL EFFECTS CATALLUM
(PERSONAL —) FEE BONA GOODS STUFF INSIGHT PLUNDER
(PRIVATE —) SEVERAL
(RURAL —) FINCA
(STOLEN —) PELF MAINOR STEALTH
(THEATRICAL —S) PROPS
(WITHOUT —) LACKLAND
(SUFF.) ISM

PROPHECY SPAE WEIRD EXHORT PREACH PREDICT BODEMENT FORECAST FORESHOW SOOTHSAY VATICINE SIBYLLISM PROGNOSTIC

PROPHESY OSSE SPAE AREAD AUGUR DIVINE EXHORT PREACH OMINATE PORTEND PREDICT ARIOLATE FORETELL

PROPHET GAD AMOS JOEL SEER ANGEL AUGUR DRUID ELIAS HOSEA JONAH MICAH MOSES NAHUM SILAS SYRUS ARIOLE BALAAM DANIEL ELIJAH HAGGAI ISAIAH MERLIN MORONI NATHAN PYTHON SAMUEL EZEKIEL MALACHI SPAEMAN HABAKKUK JEREMIAH
(PL.) VATES NEBIIM
(PREF.) VATI

PROPHETE, LA (CHARACTER IN —) JOHN FIDES BERTHA OBERTHAL
(COMPOSER OF —) MEYERBEER

PROPHETESS ANNA ANNE HULDA SIBYL PYTHIA DEBORAH PHOIBAD SEERESS VOLUSPA DRUIDESS SPAEWIFE CASSANDRA PYTHONESS

PROPHETIC FATAL VATIC MANTIC FATEFUL FATIDIC MANTIAN DELPHIAN ORACULAR SIBYLLIC VATICINAL
(SUFF.) MANTIC

PROPINE TIP GIFT EXPOSE PLEDGE PROFFER

PROPINQUITY KINSHIP AFFINITY NEARNESS VICINITY PROXIMITY

PROPITIATE MILD ATONE PACIFY

APPEASE RECONCILE

PROPITIATORY HILASMIC

PROPITIOUS FAIR KIND HAPPY LUCKY BENIGN DEXTER KINDLY HELPFUL PRESENT FRIENDLY GRACIOUS MERCIFUL TOWARDLY FAVORABLE PROMISING AUSPICIOUS

PROPONENT BACKER ADVOCATE SUPPORTER

PROPORTION END LOT DOSE SIZE CHIME FRAME QUOTA RATIO SCALE SHARE ACCORD DEGREE EXTENT FORMAT QUOTUM ANALOGY BALANCE COMPASS CONTENT MEASURE EURYTHMY QUANTITY SYMMETRY PERCENTAGE
(— OF CATTLE TO GIVEN AREA) SOUM
(— OF MALT IN BREWING) STRAIK
(— OF REFLECTED LIGHT) ALBEDO
(ALLOTTED —) STENT STINT
(EXACT —) SQUARE
(SMALL —) TITHE

PROPORTIONATENESS CONTOUR

PROPOSAL BID KITE MOVE PLAN PLEA VOEU GRACE OFFER PARTY DEMAND FEELER MOTION MOTIVE PROJECT PROPOSE PURPOSE OVERTURE SCHEDULE SENTENCE PROPOSITION
(TENTATIVE —) SNIFF

PROPOSE FACE MOVE PLAN POSE SHOW WISH OFFER ALLEGE DESIGN INJECT INTEND MOTION ADVANCE EXHIBIT IMAGINE PROPINE PURPOSE SUPPOSE CONFRONT CONVERSE PROPOUND
(— FOR DISCUSSION) MOOT
(— RESOLUTION) FIRST
(— TENTATIVELY) SUGGEST

PROPOSITION R FACT AXIOM MODAL OFFER THEME AFFAIR CONNEX MEMBER PORISM GENERAL INVERSE PREMISS PROBLEM PURPOSE THEOREM TYCHISM BUSINESS CONTRARY EMPIREMA IDENTITY IRENICON JUDGMENT NEGATION OVERTURE PROPOSAL PROTASIS SENTENCE SINGULAR SUPPOSAL
(— IN LOGIC) TERMAL OBVERSE
(— LEADING TO CONCLUSION) PREMISE
(PARTICULAR NEGATIVE —) O
(PRELIMINARY —) LEMMA
(UNIVERSAL NEGATIVE —) E

PROPOUND POSE OFFER POSIT START STATE INVOKE PROPOSE PURPOSE

PROPOUNDER HYLICIST

PROPRIETOR LORD LAIRD MALIK OWNER MASTER PATRON TANIST YEOMAN ESQUIRE PATROON ABSENTEE BONIFACE SQUARSON TALUKDAR YEOWOMAN

PROPRIETY GRACE IDIOM MENSE ESTATE NATURE REASON DEGENCY DECORUM ESSENCE FITNESS HOLDING MODESTY CIVILITY PROPERTY ETIQUETTE

PROPROCTOR RECTOR
PROPULSION DRIFT EJECTION
PROPULSIVE ELASTIC
PRORATE ALLOT ASSESS DIVIDE
APPORTION
PROROGUE DEFER ADJOURN
PROLONG POSTPONE PROTRACT
PROSAIC DRAB DULL FLAT FOOT
PROSE PROSY PROLIX STODGY
STOLID STUPID FACTUAL
HUMDRUM INSIPID LITERAL
TEDIOUS SOULLESS TIRESOME
WORKADAY
PROSCENIUM FRAME STAGE
PROSCRIBE BAN TABU EXILE
TABOO FORBID OUTLAW REJECT
PROHIBIT
PROSCRIPTION EXILE OUTLAWRY
PROSE CHAT PROSY GOSSIP
PROSAIC TEDIOUS SEQUENCE
ELOQUENCE
PROSECUTE LAW SUE HOLD URGE
CARRY ENSUE ACCUSE CHARGE
DEDUCE FOLLOW INDICT INTEND
PURSUE IMPLEAD PROCESS
PROSECUTION PURSUANCE
PROSECUTOR DA FISCAL
PURSUER SAKEBER PROMOTER
QUAESTOR
(PUBLIC —) ACTOR
PROSELYTE CONVERT NICOLAS
NEOPHYTE PURSUANT
(JEWISH —) GER
PROSER HAVERER GRATIANO
PROSODY METER METRICS
PROSPECT HOPE VIEW SCENE
SPECK VISTA CHANCE CHIEVE
FUTURE REGARD SEARCH SURVEY
COMMAND EXPLORE FOSSICK
HORIZON LOOKOUT OUTLOOK
PROJECT RESPECT LANDSKIP
OFFSCAPE
(— FOR GOLD) SPECK
(— WITHOUT SYSTEM) GOPHER
(FORBIDDING —) DESERT
PROSPECTING LOAMING
PROSPECTIVE VIEW WATCH
LOOKOUT EXPECTED
PROSPECTOR SNIPER FOSSICKER
SOURDOUGH
(LONE —) HATTER
PROSPECTUS PROGRAM
PROSPER DO DOW FAY HIE LIKE
RISE THEE CHEVE CHIVE EDIFY
FRAME LIGHT SPEED BATTEN
THRIVE BLOSSOM SUCCEED
WELFARE FLOURISH
PROSPERITY HAP GLEE GOOD
SEEL SONS WEAL IKBAL SONSE
HEALTH THRIFT FORTUNE
SUCCESS THEEDOM WELFARE
FLOURISH
(GOD OF —) FREY
(INCREASE IN —) UPTICK
PROSPERO (DAUGHTER OF —)
MIRANDA
(SERVANT OF —) ARIEL
(SLAVE OF —) CALIBAN
PROSPEROUS UP FAT BEEN BEIN
BIEN BOON GOOD FELIX FLUSH
HAPPY LUCKY PALMY SONSY
EUROUS GILDED SONSIE WELSOM
HALCYON HEALTHY THRIFTY

THRIVEN WEIRDLY SUNSHINE
THRIVING WEALSOME
PROSTITUTE BAG BAT CAT COW
DOG MOB AUNT BAWD DOXY
DRAB HACK MAUX MISS MUFF
PUNK SLUT STEW TART TRUG
BROAD CRACK MAWKS PAGAN
POULE STALE WHORE BULKER
CALLET CHIPPY DEBASE GIRLIE
HARLOT HOOKER LIMMER
MUTTON RANNEL TOMATO
TRADER VIZARD BAGGAGE
BROTHEL CRUISER CYPRIAN
HACKNEY HETAERA HUSTLER
PAPHIAN PINNACE POLECAT
PUCELLE SELLARY BERDACHE
COMMONER CUSTOMER
HACKSTER MAGDALEN MERETRIX
OCCUPANT RUMBELOW
SLATTERN STRUMPET VENTURER
COURTESAN
(PREF.) PORN(O)
PROSTITUTION BORDEL SACKING
BORDELLO HARLOTRY PUTANISM
PROSTRATE LOW FELL FLAT GRUF
RASE RAZE FLING GROOF PRONE
STOOP THROW ATTERR CUMBER
FALLEN REPENT WEAKEN
FLATTEN DEJECTED HELPLESS
OVERCOME PROSTERN
DEPRESSED
(— ONESELF) HURKLE
(BECOME —) FALL
PROSTRATION SHOCK KOWTOW
COLLAPSE
(BURMESE —) SHIKO
PROSY DRY DULL JEJUNE
HUMDRUM INSIPID PROSAIC
PROSISH TEDIOUS TIRESOME
PROTAGONIST HERO ACTOR
LEADER PALADIN ADVOCATE
ANTIHERO CHAMPION
PROTAMINE SALMINE STURINE
CLUPEINE
PROTEAN EDESTAN VARIABLE
PROTECT CAP BANK BIEL BIND
DIKE FEND FORT HILL KEEP REDE
SAVE WARD WEAR BLESS CHAIN
CLOUT COURE COVER FENCE
GANGE GRATE GUARD HEDGE
PAVIS SHADE SHEND UMBER
ASSERT BORROW CHIELD DEFEND
SCREEN SHADOW WARISH
BULWARK CHERISH CUSHION
FASCINE FORFEND SECLUDE
SHELTER SUPPORT WARRANT
BESTRIDE CHAMPION DEFILADE
PRESERVE SAFEGUARD
(— AGAINST RAIN) FLASH
(— BY COVERING) HILL
(— BY WINDING WITH WIRE) GANGE
(— FROM INTRUSION) TILE TYLE
(— IRON OR STEEL) BARFF
PROTECTED SAFE SHADY IMMUNE
CLOUTED GUARDED SHEATHED
SHIELDED
(PREF.) IMMUNO
PROTECTING TUTELAR TUTELARY
SECUREFUL
PROTECTION LEE EGIS HOLD
WARD WING AEGIS ARMOR BIELD
COVER GRITH GUARD SHADE
TARGE TOWER AMULET ASYLUM

AVOWRY CONVOY ESCORT
FENDER REFUGE SAFETY SCONCE
SCREEN SHADOW SHROUD
AUSPICE CUSTODY DEFENCE
HOUSING MANTLET SHELTER
TUITION UMBRAGE WARRANT
BLINDAGE COVERAGE DEFILADE
PASSPORT SECURITY TUTAMENT
TUTELAGE WARDSHIP
SAFEGUARD
(— FOR SAILOR) HORSE
(— FROM LOSS) INDEMNITY
(— FROM RAIN) OMBRIFUGE
(— FROM SUN) HAVELOCK
(— FROM WEATHER) LEWTH
(— RIGHT) MUND
(VALUABLE —) EDMUND
(WISE —) RAYMOND
PROTECTIVE (— SURFACE)
LAGGING
PROTECTOR BIB GUARD BRACER
FAUTOR KEEPER PATRON REGENT
WARRANT DEFENDER GUARDIAN
PECTORAL PRESIDENT
(— OF PROSTITUTE) BULLY
(— OF VINEYARDS) PRIAPUS
PROTEGE WARD PUPIL SMIKE
PROTEIN ZEIN ABRIN ACTIN OPSIN
RICIN SOZIN AVIDIN CASEIN
FIBRIN GLOBIN MYOGEN ALBUMIN
AMANDIN ELASTIN GELATIN
GLIADIN HISTONE HORDEIN
KERATIN LIVETIN MUCEDIN
PROTEID SERICIN ALEURONE
COLLAGEN COLLOGEN FERRITIN
GLOBULIN GLUTELIN GORGONIN
IPOMOEIN PROLAMIN PROPERDIN
PROTAMINE
(RICH IN —S) NARROW
PROTEINASE PAPAIN PEPSIN
PROTEOSE ALBUMOSE ELASTOSE
GELATOSE
PROTESILAUS (BROTHER OF —)
PODARCES
(FATHER OF —) IPHICLUS
(MOTHER OF —) ASTYOCHE
(SLAYER OF —) HECTOR
EUPHORBUS
(WIFE OF —) LAODAMIA
POLYDORA
PROTEST AVER BEEF FUSS HOWL
KICK BROCK CROAK DEMUR
AFFIRM ASSERT BOWWOW
EXCEPT HOLLER OBJECT OBTEST
PLAINT SQUAWK SQUEAL
CONTEST INVEIGH PUBLISH
RECLAIM RHUBARB SCRUPLE
TESTIFY HARRUMPH PROCLAIM
(— AGAINST) ABHOR
(— AGAINST INJUSTICE) HARO
PROTESTANT ALASCAN GENEVAN
GOSPELER HELVETIC HUGUENOT
MORAVIAN SWADDLER
PROTEUS OLM AMOEBA
PROTHESIS CREDENCE PARABEMA
PROTHORAX COLLAR CORSELET
MANITRUNK
PROTOCOL PROCEDURE
PROTOPINE FUMARINE
PROTOPLASM PLASMA PLASSON
SARCODE OVOPLASM PERIPLAST
SOLEPLATE
PROTOPLAST CELL ENERGID

PROTOTYPE IDEAL MODEL
FATHER EXAMPLE PATTERN
ANTITYPE EXEMPLAR
PROTOZOAN AMEBA FORAM
MONAD MONER AGAMETE
ARCELLA BABESIA BODONID
CILIATE PROTIST RADIATE
STENTOR DIDINIUM HYPOZOAN
PARAMECIUM
(PL.) MICROZOA
PROTRACT DRAG DRAW DREE
PLOT SPIN DEFER DELAY DRIVE
TRACT TRAIL TRAIN DILATE
EXTEND LINGER SPREAD
DETRACT PROLONG CONTINUE
LENGTHEN PROROGUE
PROTRACTED DREE LONG DREICH
PROLIX LENGTHY DRAGGING
EXTENDED
PROTRUDE BUG JUT LILL LOLL
PEER POKE POUT BLEAR BULGE
BUNCH POUCH SHOOT START
STICK STRUT SWELL EXSERT
EXTEND EXTRUDE KNUCKLE
PROJECT PROTEND HERNIATE
OUTPOINT OUTREACH OUTSHOOT
PROTRUDING STEEP ASTRUT
BUNCHY GOGGLE BLABBER
EMINENT JUTTING OBTRUSIVE
PROTRUDINGLY ASTRUT
PROTRUSION JAG LAP NOB BURR
KNOB POUT HERNIA SALIENCE
SHOULDER TYLOSOID
PROJECTION
PROTUBERANCE BUD HUR JAG
NOB NUB WEN BEAN BOLL BOSS
BULB BUMP HEEL HUMP JAGG
KNAP KNOB KNOP KNOT LUMP
NODE PUFF SCAB SNAG STUB
UMBO WART BULGE BUNCH
CAPUT GLAND GNARL HUNCH
KNURL SWELL TORUS TUBER
TUMOR BREAST CALLUS HUBBLE
PIMPLE POMMEL CRANKLE
EXTANCY PAPILLA EMINENCE
FLANKARD MAMELEON NODOSITY
SWELLING APOPHYSIS
PROJECTION
(— AT BASE OF BIRD'S BILL) CERE
SNOOD
(— BEARING SPINE) UMBO
(— FROM SWELLING) PUFF
(— IN SIDE OF DEER) FLANKARD
(— ON A CASTING) SCAB
(— ON BONE) CONDYLE EMINENCE
(— ON HORSE'S HOOF) BUTTRESS
(— ON MANDIBLE OF GEESE) BEAN
(— ON SADDLEBOW) POMMEL
(— ON SALAMANDER) BALANCER
(— ON TONGUE) PAPILLA
(KNOBLIKE —) CAPUT
(OCCIPITAL —) INION
(RAGGED —) JAG JAGG
(ROUGH —) HUB
(SKIN —) WEN MOLE WART
PIMPLE
(PREF.) TORO
PROTUBERANT BULGY BUMPY
PROUD STRUT TUMID BUCKED
EXTANT GOGGLE BOTTLED
BULGING BUNCHED EMINENT
GIBBOUS SALIENT SWOLLEN
PROMINENT PROTRUSIVE

(REGULARLY —) CONVEX
PROUD FESS GLAD HIGH IKEY LOFT
PERK RANK SIDE VAIN BRANT
CHUFF GELLY GREAT JELLY LOFTY
NOBLE ORGUL PRIDY SAUCY
STEEP STIFF STOUT VOGIE WINDY
WLONK COPPED ELATED FIERCE
LORDLY ORGUIL PENCEY QUAINT
SKEICH SKEIGH UPPISH UPPITY
VAUNTY HAUGHTY SUBLIME
SWOLLEN TOPPING ARROGANT
EXULTANT GLORIOUS IMPOSING
INSOLENT ORGULOUS SPLENDID
STOMACHY TOPLOFTY
OVERBEARING
PROUDLY HIGH
PROVE TRY FAND FOND PREE
SHOW TEST ARGUE ASSAY EVICT
TAINT TASTE TEMPT ARGUFY
EVINCE SUFFER VERIFY BALANCE
CONFESS CONFIRM CONVICT
DERAIGN IMPROVE JUSTIFY
CONCLUDE CONVINCE EVIDENCE
INDICATE INSTRUCT MANIFEST
(— FALSE) BELIE BETRAY FALSIFY
(— GUILTY) ATTAINT
(— ONESELF) ACQUIT
(— OUT) SERVE
(— TITLE) DEDUCE
(— VALID) DEFEND
PROVED TRIED EXPERT PROBATE
PROVENCAL LANGUEDOC
ROMANESQUE
PROVENDER HAY CORN FEED
FOOD OATS STRAW PABULUM
PROVAND PROVIANT
PROVERB SAW SAY REDE WORD
ADAGE AXIOM CREED GNOME
SOOTH BALLAD BYWORD DITTON
DIVERB MASHAL SAYING SPEECH
SYMBOL WHEEZE BYSPELL
IMPRESA NAYWORD PARABLE
APHORISM FORBYSEN PAROEMIA
SCHOLION SCHOLIUM SENTENCE
SOOTHSAY
(PREF.) PARAMIO PAROEMIO
PROVIDE DO FIT SEE FEND FILL
FIND GIRD LEND LOOK BLOCK
CATER ENDOW ENDUE EQUIP
SPEED STOCK STORE AFFORD
FOISON PURVEY SUBORN SUPPLY
COMPARE EXHIBIT FORESEE
FURNISH INSTORE PREPARE
ACCOUTER APPANAGE DISPENSE
PURCHASE
(— AHEAD OF TIME) ADVANCE
(— AMUSEMENT) DISTRACT
(— FOOD) GRUB CATER SCAFF
(— FOR) FEND SERVE CHEVEYS
CHEVISE PROVANT
(— STINGILY) SKINCH
(— SUPPORT) ESCOT
(— WITH) BESEE
(— WITH DOWRY) DOT
(— WITH HIP-ROOF) COOT
(— WITH LOAN) ACCOMMODATE
PROVIDED IF BODEN FIXED READY
SOBEIT PROVISO INSTRUCT
PREPARED
PROVIDENCE THRIFT ECONOMY
PRUDENCE
PROVIDENT WARY WISE FRUGAL
SAVING CAREFUL

PRUDENT THRIFTY
PROVINCE LAN AREA NOME WALK
AIMAK BANAT FIELD MOUTH
NATAL NOMOS REALM SHENG
SHIRE SUBAH BANNAT EMPIRE
EYALET MALAGA MONTON
OBLAST REGION SIRCAR SPHERE
SYSSEL YAMATO DEMESNE
DONGOLA EPARCHY MUDIRIA
PURVIEW RECTORY VILAYET
APPANAGE DISTRICT FUNCTION
MUDIRIEH NOMARCHY TERRITORY
(SUBDIVISION OF EGYPTIAN —)
KISM
(PL.) OUTLAND
PROVINCIAL HICK BORNE CRUDE
NARROW RUSTIC STUFFY
INSULAR MOFUSSIL SUBURBAN
PAROCHIAL PRESIDIAL
PROVINCIALISM LOCALISM
PROVISION BOARD CHECK GRIST
FODDER MATTER PURVEY
STOVER UNLESS WRAITH
APPREST CAUTION CODICIL
DOWNSET KEEPING SLEEPER
VICTUAL WARNISH WARNISON
(—S FOR JOURNEY) VIATICUM
(BOUGHT —S) ACATES ACATERY
(SUBORDINATE —) ITEM
(PL.) CHOW FOOD JOCK KEEP
LOAN PROG BOUGE CATES
CHUCK SCRAN STORE TERMS
TOMMY ANNONA VIANDS VIVRES
COMMONS WARNAGE WAYFARE
VICTUALS
PROVISO SALVO CAVEAT CLAUSE
CAUTION CONDITION
PROVOCATION TEEN APPEAL
INCENTIVE
PROVOCATIVE GUTTY SALTY
AGACANT PIQUANT IRRITANT
APPEALING
PROVOKE BOG EGG GIG IRE TAR
VEX BEAR DARE HUFF MOVE PICK
STIR TARR TEEN URGE WORK
ANGER ANGRY ANNOY EAGER
EVOKE FRUMP PIQUE TAUNT
TEMPT APPEAL ELICIT EVINCE
EXCITE GRIEVE HARASS INCITE
KINDLE NETTLE PROMPT
SUMMON TICKLE AFFRONT ILLICIT
INCENSE INFLAME INSPIRE
VROTHER CATALYZE IRRITATE
PROVOKING AGACANT
PROVOST JUDGE PRIOR REEVE
KEEPER WARDEN STEWARD
PROW BOW BEAK SPUR STEM
PRORE SNOUT SPERON STEVEN
DIVIDER GALLANT VALIANT
(— OF GONDOLA) FERRO
PROWESS FEAT PROW VALOR
NOBLEY BRAVERY COURAGE
PROWL OWL PROG ROAM LURCH
MOOCH MOUSE RAVEN BREVIT
RAMBLE
PROWLER WALKER SLASHER
TENEBRION
PROWLIKE PROREAN
PROWLING GRASSANT
PROXIMATE NEXT CLOSE DIRECT
CLOSEST NEAREST PROXIME
IMMINENT PROXIMAL
PROXIMITY SHADOW NEARNESS

PRESENCE VICINITY PROPINQUITY
NEIGHBORHOOD
PROXY VICE AGENT VICAR BALLOT
MANDAT PROCTOR
(PL.) ELECTION
PRUDE PRIG COMSTOCK
PRUDENCE CARE METIS ADVICE
CAUTEL WISDOM CAUTION
COUNSEL SLEIGHT FORECAST
FORELOOK
PRUDENT FIT SAFE SAGE WARE
WARY WISE CANNY DOOSE
DOUCE SOLID SYKER VERTY
FRUGAL QUAINT SEKERE SICCAR
POLITIC THRIVEN CAUTIOUS
DISCREET PROVIDENT
PRUDISH NICE PRIM MIMZY
MIMSEY PRIGGISH PUDIBUND
VICTORIA
PRUDISHNESS NICETY PUDENCY
PRUNE COW LOP TOP CLIP COLL
COUL GELD PLUM SNED SPUR
TAME TRIM CLEAN DRESS KNIFE
PLUMB PREEN PRIME PURGE
SHEAR SHRAG SHRED SHRUB
TRASH TWIST DEHORN REFORM
SHRIDE SNATHE SWITCH
AMPUTATE CASTRATE RETRENCH
(— SEVERELY) DEHORN
(IMPERFECTLY RIPENED —) FROG
PRUNING HOOK SARPE CALABOZO
PRUNING KNIFE SERPETTE
PRUNING SHEARS SECATEUR
PRURIENT ITCHY
PRURITIS ITCH
PRUSSIAN PRUTENIC
PRY GAG KEEK NOSE NOTE PEEK
PEEP PEER TEET TOOT JIMMY
LEVER PRIZE SNOOP BREVIT
FERRET PIGGLE POTTER PUTTER
CROWBAR GUMSHOE LEVERAGE
(— ABOUT) OWL MOUSE SNOOK
SCROUNGE
(— INTO) BREVIT
(— INTO AND REPEAT) RAVE
PRYING NOSY NOSEY PEERY
CURIOUS PEEPING
PSALM ODE HYMN SONG DIRGE
GATHA TRACT ANTHEM CANTATE
CHORALE INTROIT MISERERE
(100TH —) JUBILATE
(95TH —) VENITE
(98TH —) CANTATE
PSALMS HALLEL
(BOOK OF —) PSALTER
PSALTERIUM BOOK LYRA
OMASUM PSALTER PSALTERY
PSALTERY GUSLA CITOLE
SAUTREE SAUTERIE
PSEUDO FAKE MOCK SHAM BOGUS
FALSE FEIGNED SPURIOUS
(PREF.) NE
PSEUDOCARP HIP
PSEUDOLOGIST LIAR
PSEUDONYM ALIAS ANONYM
JUNIUS
PSHAW SHA POOH SUGAR SHUCKS
PSITTACOSIS ORNITHOSIS
PSORIASIS ALPHOS
PSYCHE MIND SELF SOUL
PSYCHIATRIST SHRINK ALIENIST
AMERICAN BRILL MEYER OLIVER
SALMON SPITZKA MENNINGER

AUSTRIAN ADLER
GERMAN ZIEHEN JASPERS
SWISS JUNG BLEULER
PSYCHOANALYST FREUDIAN
PSYCHOLOGIST AMERICAN HALL
HOLT LADD DODGE LAIRD RHINE
URBAN WELLS ANGELL BORING
GESELL HAINES HUNTER KOFFKA
PRINCE STRONG TERMAN
WATSON ALLPORT BALDWIN
GODDARD NEWBOLD TROLAND
LANGFELD MARSHALL SEASHORE
PILLSBURY SCRIPTURE
WOODWORTH CARRINGTON
HOLLINGWORTH
ARGENTINIAN INGENIEROS
AUSTRIAN ADLER
DANISH LANGE
ENGLISH WARD BUCKE ELLIS
MYERS OGDEN STOUT SULLY
GURNEY MORGAN AVELING
BARTLETT MAUDSLEY
FRENCH BINET JANET SIMON
BEAUNIS
GERMAN KROH GEISE MARBE
STERN WUNDT KOHLER MULLER
PREYER RUBNER ZIEHEN
JAENSCH MEUMANN
SCOTTISH BAIN
SWISS JUNG
PSYCHOLOGY HORMISM
HEDONICS ANIMASTIC
FORMALISM
PSYCHOPATH MATTOID
PSYCHOSIS INSANITY PARANOIA
SENILITY MELANCHOLIA
PSYCHOTIC MAD CRAZY INSANE
PSYLLA DIMERAN
PSYLLIUM FLEAWORT
PTAH (— EMBODIED) APIS
(ASSOCIATED WITH —) SEKHET
PTARMIGAN RYPE GROUSE
LAGOPODE
PTEROCARPUS LINGOUM
PTEROSAUR DIAPSID
PTERYGIUM WEBEYE
PTERYGOID EXTERNUM
PTERYLA TRACT
PTISAN TEA TISANE
PTOLEMY SOTER
(WIFE OF —) CLEOPATRA
PTOMAINE NEURIN SEPSIN
SAPRINE GADININE PUTRESCINE
PTOUS (FATHER OF —) ATHAMAS
(MOTHER OF —) THEMISTO
PUAH (FATHER OF —) ISSACHAR
(SON OF —) TOLA
PUB BAR INN BISTRO BOOZER
LOUNGE SHANTY TAVERN
PUBBLE FAT FULL PLUMP
PUB-CRAWL BARHOP
PUBERTY
(PREF.) HEBE
PUBES
(PREF.) EPISIO PUBI(O) PUBO
PUBESCENCE DOWN SCURF
YOUTH TOMENT TOMENTUM
PUBESCENT HIRSUTE VILLOUS
(PREF.) HEBE
PUBLIC KUNG OPEN TOWN APERT
CIVIC OVERT WORLD COMMON
SOCIAL VULGAR GENERAL
OMNIBUS POPULAR EXTERNAL

MATERIAL NATIONAL MULTITUDE
(GENERAL —) GALLERY
PUBLICAN BUNG FARMER KEEPER
TAVERNER ZACCHEUS
CATCHPOLL
PUBLICATION BOOK ORDO BIBLE
FOLIO ISSUE SHEET ANNUAL
BLAZON DIGLOT SERIAL WEEKLY
ALMANAC BOOKLET ELZEVIR
JOURNAL MONTHLY WRITING
BIWEEKLY BULLETIN DOCUMENT
EMISSION EXCHANGE PRODROME
EPHEMERIS PERIODICAL
(KIND OF —) MIMEO NUDIE
PUBLIC HOUSE BAR INN PUB
BOOZER PUBLIC SALOON
HOSTELRY POTHOUSE
PUBLICIST AGENT SOLON WRITER
PUBLICITY AIR BLAZE ECLAT
BUILDUP PUFFERY RECLAME
BALLYHOO BROUHAHA DAYLIGHT
HERALDRY PROMOTION
PUBLICIZE CRY PLUG BLURB
BREAK BRUIT HERALD BALLYHOO
HEADLINE PROPAGATE
PUBLIC SQUARE PLAZA PLEIN
ZOCALO
PUBLISH AIR ASH BLOW CALL EDIT
EMIT VEND VENT CARRY ISSUE
PRINT SPEAK UTTER BLAZON
BROACH DEFAME DELATE
EVULGE EXPOSE SPREAD
CENSURE DECLARE DIFFUSE
DIVULGE GAZETTE PROTEST
RELEASE DENOUNCE DISCLOSE
EVULGATE PROCLAIM PROMULGE
(— BANNS OF MARRIAGE) CRY
SPUR OUTASK
(— IN CHURCH) ASK
(— WITHOUT AUTHORIZATION)
PIRATE
PUBLISHER CRIER EDITOR
PRINTER STATIONER
AMERICAN COX LEA BONI DODD
FUNK GINN HOLT KNOX LUCE
NAST OCHS BOBBS BROWN
CAREY GODEY JONES KNOPF
MCRAE SIMON SMITH STERN
CHILDS CURTIS DUTTON FARRAR
FIELDS HARPER HARRIS HEARST
LITTLE MOSHER MUNSEY PAYSON
PUTNAM STOKES THOMAS
UPDIKE VICTOR WALKER WILSON
ZENGER BINGHAM COLLIER
CONNERS LOTHROP MIFFLIN
POULSON SADLIER SCRIPPS
SHUSTER TICKNOR BANCROFT
BARTLETT HOUGHTON RINEHART
SCHUSTER SCRIBNER WAGNALLS
DOUBLEDAY LIVERIGHT
MCCORMICK LIPPINCOTT
AUSTRALIAN THEODORE
DUTCH ELZEVIR
ENGLISH BELL BOHN LANE PAUL
LUCAS MOXON MUDIE UNWIN
WARNE FROWDE KNIGHT LINTOT
MILLAR NEWNES TONSON TOTTEL
BEMROSE BENTLEY BRACKEN
CASSELL CHAPMAN DEBRETT
JENKINS METHUEN NEWBERRY
RICHARDS WHITAKER
HEINEMANN PICKERING
RIVINGTON ROUTLEDGE

VIZETELLY WHITCHURCH
BEAVERBROOK
FRENCH DIDOT HETZEL LEMERRE
PLANTIN HACHETTE GALIGNANI
GERMAN COTTA MEYER FROBEN
PERTHES TEUBNER BAEDEKER
BROCKHAUS TAUCHNITZ
ITALIAN RICORDI
SCOTTISH BLACK SMITH CADELL
CREECH NELSON CHAMBERS
BLACKWOOD CONSTABLE
MACMILLAN
PUCCOON GROMYL ALKANET
GROMWELL BLOODROOT
PUCE FLEA
PUCK ELF LOB PUG BLOW BUTT
DISK POKE POOK DEMON DEVIL
FAIRY PEWKE SPORT RUBBER
SPRITE STRIKE PUCKREL
HOBGOBLIN
PUCKER DRAW FULL RUCK PURSE
REEVE RIVEL TIZZY COCKLE
COTTER FURROW LUCKEN
RUCKLE WRINKLE CONTRACT
AGITATION CONSTRICT
PUCKERED PURSY BULLATE
COCKLED ROUCHED WRINKLED
BULLIFORM
PUCKFIST BRAGGART PUFFBALL
PUCKISH PUXY ELFIN IMPISH
WHIMSICAL
PUDDING DICK DUFF LINK SAGO
BOMBE DOWDY KUGEL MERIT
BURGOO FENDER HACKIN HAGGIS
HAUPIA JAUDIE SPONGE TANSEY
TARTAN DESSERT ADEQUACY
BLOODING HEDGEHOG LIVERING
PANDOWDY WHITEPOT
CHARLOTTE
(— CONTAINING KALE) TARTAN
(— OF FLOUR) DUFF
(BOILED —) HOY
(FRUIT —) HEDGEHOG
(HASTY —) MUSH SEPON SUPAWN
(HAWAIIAN —) HAUPIA
(MEAT —) ISING CHEWET HACKIN
HACKING
(SUET —) KUGEL
PUDDINGWIFE PUDIANO
DONCELLA GLUEFISH
PUDDLE DUB PANT PLUD POOL
PULK ROIL SLAB SLOP SOSS SUMP
FLUSH PLANT PLASH PUDGE
CHARCO FLODGE KENNEL
MUDDLE PUDDER SPLASH
TAMPER CONFUSE PLASHET
SLODDER SPUDDLE BEFUDDLE
(MUD —) DUB SLOP LOBLOLLY
PUDDLEBALL LOOP
PUDDLER'S RABBLE STRIKE
PUDENCY MODESTY DELICACY
PUDGY MIRY BULKY MUDDY
SQUAT CHUBBY SPUDDY
PUDU VENADA
PUEBLO ANASAZI
PUELCHE PAMPA TEHUELET
PUERILE WEAK SILLY BOYISH
JEJUNE TRIVIAL CHILDISH
IMMATURE YOUTHFUL

PUFF GUF POP BLOW BRAG DRAG
FLAM FLAN GUFF GUST HUFF
PANT PECH SHOW WAFF WAFT
BLURB BLURT ELATE ERUPT
EXTOL FLUFF QUIFF SKIFF STECH
SWELL WHIFF CAPFUL EXPAND
FLATUS BLUSTER EXPLODE
GRATIFY INFLATE WHIFFET
BRAGGART OVERRATE WINDGALL
BOUILLONE
(— FROM SHELL BLAST) BURST
(— OF WIND) FLAM TIFT SCART
SLANT FLATUS HUFFLE
(— ON MARIJUANA CIGARETTE)
TOKE
(— OUT) BELL BLUB VENT BLOUSE
BLUBBER EFFLATE INFLATE
(— OUT SMOKE) EFFUME
(— UP) BLOW HUFF RISE BLOAT
HEAVE BLADDER
(— VIOLENTLY) BLAST
(CREAM —) DUCHESSE
(SUDDEN —) FLAN FLAW GUST
PUFFBALL FIST FUZZ PUFF SMOKE
FUNGUS PUFFIN BULLFICE
BULLFIST PUCKFIST SNUFFBOX
PUFFBIRD BARBET MONASE
NUNLET DREAMER NUNBIRD
BARBACOU
PUFFED BLUB BOLLEN BLOATED
SOUFFLE SWOLLEN ARROGANT
INFLATED
(— OUT) BAGGY BOUFFANT
(— UP) RANK POBBY ASTRUT
BLOATED SWOLLEN TURGENT
VENTOSE
(BE — UP) BELL
PUFFER ATINGA BALLER BLOWER
SLIMER TAMBOR BURFISH
EGGFISH BLOWFISH TOADFISH
PUFFIN LOOM PAPE POPE MARROT
MULLET MARROCK WILLOCK
COCKANDY PARAKEET
TOMNODDY TOMNORRY
(HAWAIIAN —) AO
PUFFY SOFT BAGGY BLOAT FAFFY
GUMMY GUSTY PURSY CHUBBY
FLUFFY PURFLY PURSIVE
SWOLLEN BLADDERY BOUFFANT
DROPSICAL
PUG FOX IMP PET BOXER CHAFF
GOUGE SPOOR TRACK TRAIL
CAMOIS CAMUSE GOBLIN
MONKEY MISTRESS PUGILIST
FOOTPRINT
PUGILIST PUG MILLER BRUISER
SLOGGER
PUGNACIOUS BELLICOSE
PUG-NOSED CAMUS CAMUSE
PUISNE PUNY LATER PETTY
JUNIOR YOUNGER INFERIOR

PUISSANCE ARMY FORCE POWER
CONTROL POTENCY PROWESS
DOMINION STRENGTH
PUJUNAN MAIDU
PUKKA GOOD REAL GENUINE
LASTING COMPLETE SUPERIOR
AUTHENTIC
PUKRAS PHEASANT KOKLAS
PULCHRITUDE GRACE BEAUTY
PULE CRY PEEP CHIRP COWRY
WHINE SNIVEL WHIMPER
PULING PULY SPINDLY WHINING
PULITZER PRIZE (— IN LETTERS)
BOK LEE NYE AGAR AGEE BATE
BUCK CARO COLT EDEL FEIS GALE
GRAU HART INGE LASH LEVY
MACK MOTT RICE WOUK AIKEN
AKINS ALBEE AUDEN BAKER
BEMIS BENET BRUCE BULEY
CHASE CLAPP CURTI DAVIS
DRURY DUGAN FROST HECHT
ISAAC JAMES KRAMM KUMIN
LEECH MABEE MAMET MOSEL
OPPEN PLATH PUPIN PUSEY
SAGAN TEALE UNGER WELTY
ABBOTT BAILYN BECKER BELLOW
BUTLER CATHER CATTON CREMIN
CROUSE DEGLER DURANT FERBER
FRINGS HANDIN HERSEY HORGAN
KAMMEN KENNAN KIDDER
KINNEL LARKIN LOWELL MAILER
MASSIE MILLAY NORMAN ONEILL
SHAARA TOLAND UPDIKE
WALKER WARNER WILDER
WILSON ZINDEL ASHBERY
DUNNOWO OIIECVEN DILLARD
ERIKSON JUSTICE KAUFMAN
KENNEDY LAFARGE LINDSAY
LITWACK LOESSER MCFEELY
NEMEROV RODGERS SAROYAN
SHEEHAN TUCHMAN VIERECK
BOORSTIN FAULKNER KINGSLEY
MACLEISH MARQUAND MICHENER
SANDBURG SCHORSKE SCHUYLER
SHERWOOD SINCLAIR VANDOREN
HEMINGWAY STEINBECK
HOFSTADTER
(— IN MUSIC) HUSA IVES TOCH
WARD CRUMB KUBIK MOORE
RANDS ROREM BARBER CARTER
HANSON PISTON PORTER
ARGENTO BASSETT COPLAND
MARTINO MENOTTI SCHUMAN
SOWERBY THOMSON WERNICK
ZWILICH COLGRASS DRUCKMAN
KIRCHNER SESSIONS WUORINEN
DELLOJOIO DAVIDOVSKY
DELTREDICI SCHWANTNER
PULL IN PU EAR LUG POO POU
ROG RUG TIT TOW CHUG CLAW
DRAG DRAW DUCT HALE HARL
HAUL HOOK RUGG SWIG TIRE
TREK TUSH TWIG YANK BOUSE
BREAK BUNCH CLOUT DRAFT
HEAVE HITCH IMPEL PLUCK
POLLE PROOF TRICE TWEAK
ASSUME COMMIT GATHER
OBTAIN PLITCH RUGGLE SCHLEP
SECURE TWITCH UPROOT
WRENCH ATTRACT EXTRACT
(— A BELL) SET
(— ABOUT) TEW SOOL TOSE TOZE
MOUSLE

(— APART) RAVE REND TEAR DIVULSE

(— AWAY) AVEL AVELL WREST REVULSE

(— BY EARS) SOLE SOWL

(— DOWN) UNPILE DESTROY DEMOLISH

(— HERE AND THERE) TOOZLE TOUSLE

(— NOSE) SNITE

(— OF DRUM) EAR

(— OFF) CROP DRAW STRIP AVULSE

(— ON FISHING ROD) STRIKE

(— ON ROPE) BOWSE

(— OUT) RAX EXTRACT OUTBRAID

(— QUICKLY) YANK

(— ROUGHLY) WAP TOWSE WOUSE

(— SUDDENLY) TRICE

(— THE LEG) STRING

(— TOGETHER) KNOT ATTRACT

(— TRIGGER) SQUEEZE

(— UP) LOUK

(— UP BY THE ROOTS) ARACE

(— WITH JERK) HOICK SWITCH

(ZIPPER —) SLIDER

PULLDEVIL SCROUGER SCRODGILL

PULLER KNOCKER

PULLER-IN CLICKER

PULLET HEN EAROCK EEROCK EIRACK MABYER POULARD POULAINE

PULLEY RIM CONE DRUM BLOCK FUSEE FUZEE IDLER TRICE WHEEL DRIVEN IDLEBY JOCKEY POLYVE RIGGER SHEAVE SHIVER WHARVE CAPSTAN FERRULE TIGHTER TRUCKLE WHARROW PULLISEE PURCHASE TROCHLEA
(PL.) TRISPAST JACKANAPES

PULLOVER JERSEY SWEATER

PULLULATE BUD TEEM SWARM MULTIPLY

PULMONATE LUNGED

PULMONIC PNEUMONIC

PULP PAP PUG CHUM MUSH BROKE JELLY NERVE SLUSH STOCK STUFF MARROW SQUEEZE SQUELCH
(FOOD —) CHYME

PULPIT PEW TUB AMBO BEMA DESK WOOD CHAIR PREACH ROSTRUM TRIBUNE
(— BOARD) TYPE
(— FOR CHOIR BOOKS) ANALOGION
(MOSLEM —) MIMBAR MINBAR
(OPEN-AIR —) TENT

PULPY SOFT SPEWY FLABBY FLESHY SIDDER SIDDOW BACCATE SQUELCHY

PULSATE BEAT BRIM FLAP PANT PUMP THROB COURSE STRIKE PALPITATE

PULSATION BEAT BEATING HEARTBEAT LIFEBLOOD VIBRATION
(— OF ARTERY) ICTUS

PULSE DAL BEAT DOHL TAKT URAD WAVE POUCE STUFF THROB BATTUTA IMPULSE PULSIDGE SPHYGMUS VITALITY
(PREF.) PALMO SPHYGMO
(SUFF.) CROTIC

PULSING VIBRANT

PULVERIZATION TRIPSIS

PULVERIZE BRAY BUCK DRAG FINE MEAL MULL STUB BRAKE CRUSH FLOUR GRIND POUND BRUISE POWDER ATOMIZE DEMOLISH VANQUISH COMMINUTE MICRONIZE

PULVERIZED FINE POWDERED

PULVERIZER MULLER

PULVERULENT DUSTY CRUMBLY POWDERY

PULVILLUS PAD

PUMA COUGAR PAINTER PANTHER

PUME YARURA

PUMICE PUMEX PUMIE

PUMMEL FIB BEAT DRUB PAIK SLAT POUND SLATE THUMP POUNCE

PUMP GIN GUN FORK JACK COURT FORCE HEART PLUMB SLUSH DOCTOR DORSAY FORCER SINKER VOLUTE BOOSTER DOWNTON EJECTOR EVACTOR PITWORK SLUDGER SYRINGE TOEPLER BEERPULL ELEVATOR INFLATER INJECTOR PULSATOR PULSOMETER
(— ON SHIPS) DOWNTON
(GAS —) BOWSER
(HAND —) GUN
(MINE —S) SET
(SET OF —S) LIFT

PUMP DOCTOR GRATHER

PUMPER RACKER

PUMPERNICKEL BOMBERNICKEL

PUMPKIN PEPO CHUMP GOURD PEPON QUASH CASHAW CITRUL CUCURB CUSHAW SQUASH QUASHEY CUCURBIT PEPONIDA

PUMPKINSEED RUFF SUNNY FLATFISH FLOUNDER REDBELLY

PUN NICK WHIM ALLUDE CLINCH QUIBBLE EQUIVOKE PARAGRAM CALEMBOUR PARANOMASIA ANNOMINATION

PUNCH DAB DIG FIB HUB JAB SET BASH BELT BLOW BOFF BUST DING PLUG POKE SETT SOAK SOCK TIFF BUMBO DOUSE DRIFT FORCE GLOGG PASTE PENCH SHORT SLOSH CANCEL INCUSE PATRIX PAUNCH SHAPER STINGO STRIKE TRACER MATTOIR PERLOIR SANGRIA STARTER EMBOSSER GROUNDER PRITCHEL PUNCTURE SWATCHEL THICKSET
(CHASING —) TRACER
(DOG OF —) TOBY
(ETCHER'S —) MATTOIR
(HORSESHOE —) PRITCHEL
(OVAL —) PLAISHER
(WIFE OF —) JUDY

PUNCHBOARD PUSHCARD

PUNCH BOWL SNEAKER

PUNCHCARD (GROUP OF —S) DECK

PUNCHED PERTUSE

PUNCHEON CASK PULE SNAP PUNCH

PUNCHER COWBOY SOCKER

PUNCHINELLO CLOWN BUFFOON PUGENELLO

PUNCH PRESS BEAR DROP

PUNCHY POUNCY FORCEFUL

PUNCTILIOUS NICE EXACT STIFF FORMAL CAREFUL POINTED PRECISE PUNCTUAL

PUNCTUAL DUE EXACT PROMPT CAREFUL PRECISE ACCURATE DEFINITE DETAILED EXPLICIT

PUNCTUATE MARK STOP POINT EMPHASIZE

PUNCTUATION MARK DOT DASH STOP BRACE COLON COMMA PRICK SLASH HYPHEN PERIOD STIGME BRACKET VIRGULE ELLIPSIS SEMICOLON

PUNCTURE HOLE PICK PINK PROD STAB DRILL POINT PRICK PUNCH STICK NEEDLE PIERCE PIQURE DEFLATE DESTROY PUNCTUM CENTESIS PINPRICK
(SUFF.) NYXIS STIXIS

PUNCTURED CRIBLE

PUNDIT SAGE SVAMI SWAMI CRITIC PANDIT TEACHER

PUNGENCY NIP HEAT SALT SNAP ACRIMONY KEENNESS PIQUANCY SALTNESS

PUNGENT HOT TEZ BOLD FELL KEEN RACY RICH SALT TART ACRID ACUTE BRISK NIPPY QUICK SHARP SMART SNELL SPICY TANGY BITING BITTER SHRILL SNAPPY CAUSTIC MORDANT PEPPERY PIQUANT POINTED TELLING CAYENNED PIERCING POIGNANT STABBING STINGING

PUNGI BIN

PUNIC PUNICAL FAITHLESS

PUNISH FIT FIX PAY BUCK CANE COLT COOK CUCK FINE FLOG GATE SORT WIPE ABUSE BIRCH CURSE ORDER SCOUR SHEND SLATE SPILL STOCK STRAP TWINK WREAK AMERCE AVENGE CAMPUS FERULE FOLLOW IMMURE LESSON REFORM SCHOOL STRAFE STRIKE CHASTEN CONSUME CORRECT CORRIGE DEPLETE PENANCE REQUITE SCOURGE CARTWHIP CHASTISE DISTRAIN CASTIGATE
(— BY BLOW ON PALM) PANDY
(— BY COMPENSATION) FINE AMERCE
(— BY CONFINEMENT) GATE
(— BY FINE) MULCT
(— BY LASHING WRISTS) BUCK

PUNISHING HARD GRUELING

PUNISHMENT GIG FINE LASH PAIN PINE RACK SACK WITE YARD BEANS GRUEL LIBEL PANDY PEINE SMART WRACK WREAK DESERT DIRDUM FERULE LESSON PICKET EXAMPLE GALLOWS GANTLET JANKERS PAYMENT PENALTY PENANCE PENANCY REVENGE SCOURGE HERISSON JUDGMENT PUNITION STOCKING SUPPLICE EXECUTION
(CAPITAL —) SCAFFOLD
(MILITARY —) JANKERS

PUNITIVE PENAL PUNITORY

PUNK BAD BOY MUG FUNK JERK MONK POOR PUNG CONCH

SPONK SPUNK AMADOU BUNKUM NOVICE HOODLUM RUFFIAN BEGINNER GANGSTER INFERIOR NONSENSE STRUMPET TERRIBLE TOUCHWOOD

PUNKIE MIDGE MIDGET

PUNNING ALLUSIVE BIVERBAL

PUNSCH ARRACK

PUNSTER WAG SPEED

PUNT BET HIT POY KENT KICK QUANT GAMBLE GARVEY SKERRY

PUNTER BIDDER GAMBLER SCALPER SERVITOR

PUNY WEAK DAWNY DEENY DWARF FRAIL PETTY SCRAM WEARY JUNIOR MAUGER NOVICE PUISNE RECENT SICKLY SPROTY MANIKIN PIMPING QUEECHY SHILPIT YOUNGER DROGHLIN INFERIOR PINDLING RECKLING
(— PERSON) TITMAN

PUP PUPPY WHELP

PUPA EGG NYMPH PUPPET TUMBLER WIGGLER FLAXSEED WRIGGLER CHRYSALIS

PUPIL BOY GYTE TYRO WARD BLACK CADET CHILD ELEVE NORRY NURRY RAPIN TUTEE ALUMNA GRADER INFANT JUNIOR SENIOR LEARNER PAULINE SCHOLAR SOJOURN STUDENT ABSENTEE BLUECOAT DISCIPLE RUGBEIAN SCHOOLER
(— AT HEAD OF CLASS) DUX
(— IN STUDIO) RAPIN
(— OF EYE) BLACK PEARL SIGHT
(ANGLO-INDIAN —) CHELA
(BOARDED —) SOJOURN
(GERMAN —) ABITURIENT
(PREF.) COR(E)(O)
(SUFF.) CORIA

PUPILAGE (WARDSHIP PEDANTISM

PUPPET BABY DOLL DUPE IDOL MOTE BABBY DROLL DUMMY MAUMET MOTION POPPIN STOOGE WAJANG WAYANG GUIGNOL DROLLERY MARIONET MARIONETTE
(— PLAY) WAJANG
(— SHOW) VERTEP
(PREF.) PUPI

PUPPIS STERN

PUPPY FOP PUP DOLL DOUGH WHELP PUPPET
(FEMALE —) GYP
(GREYHOUND —) SAPLING

PURBLIND BISME BISSON

PURCHASABLE VENAL CORRUPT

PURCHASE BUY WIN EARN FISH GAIN KOOP WHIP BOOTY HEDGE PRIZE DUPLEX EFFECT EMPTIO TACKLE ACQUIRE BARGAIN EMPTION PILLAGE PROCURE BARRATRY
(— AND FATTEN CATTLE) HIGGLE

PURCHASER BUYER EMPTOR VENDEE CHAPMAN POULTER SHOPPER CUSTOMER

PURE NET CAST EVEN FAIR FINE FREE FULL GOOD HOLY MERE NEAT PUTE TRUE CLEAN CLEAR FRESH MORAL NAKED SHEER STARK SYCEE UTTER WHITE

WHOLE CANDID CHASTE ENTIRE
IMMIXT LIMPID PISTIC SIMPLE
VESTAL VIRGIN ANGELIC CATHARI
GENUINE PERFECT SINCERE
ABSOLUTE ABSTRACT COMPLETE
DOVELIKE INNOCENT PRISTINE
SERAPHIC SPOTLESS VIRGINAL
VIRTUOUS SPIRITUAL
(PREF.) KATHARO

PUREE DAL SOUP CREAM

PURGATIVE PURGE SENNA
CALOMEL DIASENE DRASTIC
TURPETH ALOEDARY APERIENT
CLEANSER ELATERIN EVACUANT
CATHARTIC ABSTERSIVE

PURGATORY PAIN SWAMP

PURGE LAX RID FIRE FLUX SOIL
CLEAR RHEUM SCOUR DRENCH
PHYSIC REMOVE SEETHE SHRIVE
SPURGE CHISTKA CLEANSE
DETERGE ABSTERGE

PURIFICATION BAPTISM ELUTION
LUSTRUM VASTATION

PURIFY TRY BOLT FINE PURE
WASH CLEAN PURGE SNUFF
BLEACH DISTIL FILTER REFINE
SETTLE SPURGE WINNOW
BAPTIZE CHASTEN CLEANSE
EPURATE EXPIATE LAUNDER
MUNDIFY SUBLIME SWEETEN
DEPURATE EXORCISE FILTRATE
LUSTRATE SANCTIFY SCAVENGE
SPRINKLE
(— ORE) DILVE
(— SUGAR) CLAY

PURIFYING SMECTIC DEPURANT

PURIRI TEAK BULREEDY
IRONWOOD

PURITAN PRIG SAINT CANTER
CROPPY BLUENOSE CATHARAN
GOSPELER PRECISIAN
ROUNDHEAD

PURITANICAL BLUE STRICT
GENTEEL PRECISE

PURITANI, I (CHARACTER IN —)
ARTHUR ELVIRA TALBOT WALTON
HENRIETTA
(COMPOSER OF —) BELLINI

PURITY PURE ASSAY HONOR
WHITE CANDOR SATTVA VIRTUE
FINESSE CHASTITY FINENESS
PURENESS
(— OF BREED) PEDIGREE

PURL RIB EDDY KNIT PEARL UPSET
RIPPLE TOTTLE CAPSIZE
OVERTURN

PURLIEU HAUNT
(PL.) BOUNDS CONFINES
ENVIRONS

PURLIN RIB

PURLOIN CAB CRIB WEED ANNEX
BRIBE FILCH STEAL SWIPE FINGER
PILFER PIRATE CABBAGE SNAFFLE
SURREPT ABSTRACT SCROUNGE

PURPLE GAY VIOL REGAL SHOWY
ARGYLE BLATTA BLOODY CROCUS
EVEQUE MIGNON ARDOISE
FUCHSIA FUCHSIN HEATHEN
LOGWOOD PETUNIA PONTIFF
PURPURE AMARANTH BURGUNDY
CAMERIER CYCLAMEN EGGPLANT
EMINENCE IMPERIAL MAUVETTE
MULBERRY WISTARIA

(DELICATE —) MAUVE
(VISIBLE —) RHODOPSIN
(PREF.) PORPHYR(O) PURPUREO
PURPURI PURPURO

PURPLE FISH MUREX

PURPLE GALLINULE SULTAN
SULTANA HYACINTH

PURPLE LAND (AUTHOR OF —)
HUDSON
(CHARACTER IN —) JOHN LAMB
ANITA MARCO COLOMA LUCERO
MARCOS MONICA SANTOS
ANSELMO BARBUDO CALIXTO
GANDARA HILARIO ISIDORA
PAQUITA PERALTA RICHARD
DEMETRIA MARGARITA
CARRICKFERGUS

PURPLE LOOSESTRIFE KILLWEED

PURPLE MEDIC ALFALFA

PURPLE RAGWORT JACOBY

PURPLE SANDPIPER REDLEG
REDLEGS ROCKBIRD

PURPORT FECK GIST PORT DRIFT
SENSE TENOR DESIGN EFFECT
IMPART IMPORT INTEND INTENT
BEARING MEANING PROFESS
PURPOSE COVERING DISGUISE
STRENGTH

PURPOSE GO AIM END GOAL IDEA
MAIN MEAN MIND MINT PLAN
SAKE TALK TEND VIEW WEEN
WILL ARTHA CAUSE ETTLE HEART
LEVEL POINT SCOPE STUDY
THINK DESIGN DEVICE EFFECT
INTEND INTENT OBTENT PREFIX
REASON SCHEME COMPASS
COUNSEL DESTINE EARNEST
IMAGINE MEANING PROPOSE
THOUGHT DEVOTION FUNCTION
PLEASURE PROPOUND
DISCOURSE
(ALLEGED —) PRETEXT
(FIXED —) HEART
(INSIDIOUS —) CAUTEL
(MORAL —) ETHOS

PURPOSEFUL AIMFUL POINTED

PURPOSELESS WASTE AIMLESS
FECKLESS

PURPOSIVE TELIC HORMIC

PURPURA MUREX PURPLES
PELIOSIS

PURPURE GOLP GOLPE PURPLE
MERCURY

PURR MURR THRUM WHURL
DUNLIN

PURSE BAG CLY JAN BUNG CLAY
CLOY FISC KNIT POKE PUSS SKIN
BULSE BURSE DUMMY FUNDS
MEANS POUCH SPUNG COMMON
FOLLIS GIPSER POCKET PUCKER
READER SHAMMY ALMONER
GIPSIRE LEATHER SPORRAN
BUCKSKIN BURSICLE CRUMENAL
AUMONIERE POCKETBOOK
(PREF.) BURSI

PURSE CRAB PAGURID

PURSER CLERK BURSAR BOUCHER
PINCHGUT NIPCHEESE

PURSING MIMP
(— OF MOUTH) PRIM

PURSLANE PURPIE PUSSLY
PIGWEED PUSSLEY PORTULACA

PURSLANE TREE SPEKBOOM

PURSUANCE SUING SEQUENCE

PURSUE BAY RUN SUE HUNT SEEK
CHASE CHEVY CHIVY ENSUE
HOUND QUEST SLATE STALK
TRADE COURSE FOLLOW GALLOP
TRAVEL BEDEVIL HOTFOOT
CONTINUE PRACTICE
(— ZIGZAG COURSE) TACK

PURSUER FOLLOWER PLAINTIFF
QUESTRIST

PURSUIT FAD HUNT SUIT CAPER
CAUSE CHASE CHEVY CRAFT
HOBBY COURSE SEARCH ASSAULT
ACTIVITY ENTREATY
PROSECUTION
(— OF WISDOM) PHILOSOPHY
(FAVORITE —) MEAT

PURSUIVANT BUTE MARCH
FALCON ORMOND ATHLONE
CARRICK ANTELOPE DINGWALL
FOLLOWER

PURSY FAT OBESE PUFFY
ASTHMATIC

PURULENT PYIC ATTRY ATTERY

PURVEY PANDER SUPPLY FORESEE
PROVIDE

PURVEYOR CATER TAKER ACHUAS
PROWER CATERER ACHATOUR
MANCIPLE

PUS WARE AMPER FESTER MATTER
WORSUM QUITTOR
(PREF.) PURI PURO PY(O)
(CONTAINING — AND GAS)
PYOPNEUMO

PUSH CA DUB JAM JOG JUR PUT
DANG DINN DOIL DOOM DONE
BUNT DING DUSH FLOG KENT
PICK PILT PING PORR POSS POTE
SHOG STOP BLITZ BOOST BRUSH
BUNCH CROWD CRUSH DRIVE
DUNCH ELBOW GOOSE HUNCH
NUDGE PINCH POACH POUSE
SCAUT SHOVE SKELP STICK
STOVE EXTEND HURTLE HUSTLE
JOGGLE JOSTLE POTTER PROPEL
THRING THRONG THRUST
ASSAULT IMPETUS IMPULSE
OPERATE PERPLEX SHUFFLE
THRUTCH CONTRUDE INCREASE
SHOULDER STRAITEN DISMISSAL
(— ALONG) TUSH
(— APART) SPREAD
(— ASIDE) SHOG
(— BY STICK) KENT POLE
(— FORWARD) BUCKET ADVANCE
(— GENTLY) NUDGE
(— INTO) INVADE
(— MONEY) SPIFF
(— ON) BEAR YERK
(— OUT) DEBOUT LAUNCH
(— RUDELY) BARGE HORSE HUSTLE
(— TO FULL STRIDE) EXTEND
(— TOGETHER) CONTRUDE
(— UP) BOOST
(— WITH ELBOW) ELBOW HUNCH
(— WITH FEET) DIG SCAUT
(— WITH HEAD) BUNT BUTT
(STRONG —) BEVEL

PUSH BUTTON PUSH PRESSEL

PUSHCART BARROW TROLLEY

PUSHER PLUNGER TRAILER
TRAMMER WHEELER

PUSHING OBTRUSIVE PROTRUSIVE

PUSHY FORWARD AGGRESSIVE

PUSILLANIMOUS WEAK TIMID
FEEBLE COWARDLY TIMOROUS

PUSS CAT FACE HARE CHEET
CHILD MOUTH RABBIT BAUDRONS

PUSTULE NOB BEAL BURL KNOB
POCK PUSH QUAT WART ACHOR
AMPER BLAIN WHEAL WHELK
BLOTCH FESTER PIMPLE TETTER
ANTHRAX BLISTER ERUPTION
WHEYWORM

PUT DO BET LAY PIT SET BANG
BUTT FILL GIVE GROW PILT REST
URGE ADAPT APPLY DIGHT DRIVE
FOCUS PLACE STALL STATE
STEAD STEEK STELL WAGER
ASSIGN BESTOW DECAMP IMPOSE
INVEST PHRASE REPOSE SPROUT
THRUST DEPOSIT EMPLACE
EXPRESS INFLICT SUBJECT
(— AN END TO) DATE SNIB ABATE
NAPOO SNUFF SPIKE STASH STILL
STINT SOPITE STANCH ABOLISH
ASSUAGE EXPIATE SATISFY
ABROGATE DEMOLISH SURCEASE
(— ANOTHER IN PLACE OF) RELIEVE
(— APART) DISPART
(— ASIDE) BLOW HAIN SAVE
SHUNT REJECT SHUFFLE
(— AT REST) HUSH
(— AWAY) STOW COVER ELONG
HUTCH SHIFT RECOND DIVORCE
(— BACK) REMIT REMISE
(— BACK INTO USE) RESTORE
(— BEFORE) PROFER ANTEPONE
(— DOWN) LAY DEMIT QUASH
QUELL DEPOSE SQUASH DEPRESS
OPPRESS REPRESS SILENCE
DIMINISH SUPPRESS
(— EDGE ON) TED
(— FLAX UPON A DISTAFF) DIZEN
(— FORTH) GEM BLOW CAST GIVE
PUSH EXERT LANCE PROFER
STRETCH
(— FORTH BLOSSOMS) GEM
(— GRAIN IN BARN) END
(— IN) ENTER INSERT INTROMIT
(— IN AGONY) THROE
(— IN CHARGE) COMMIT
(— IN CLAIM) PRETEND
(— IN COMPETITION) PIT
(— IN DANGER) SCUPPER
(— IN DREAD) ADRAD
(— IN MOTION) AROUSE
(— IN OPERATION) LAUNCH
(— IN ORDER) DO SET REDD SIDE
SORT TRIM DIGHT MENSE SHIFT
TRICK ADJUST DAIKER GRAITH
ORDAIN SETTLE ARRANGE
CLARIFY DISPOSE REDRESS
INSTRUCT
(— IN PLACE) POSE
(— IN POSSESSION) SEISE
(— IN PRISON) WARD
(— INFORMATION INTO) ADDRESS
(— INTO BARN) END
(— INTO CASE) SHEATHE
(— INTO CIRCULATION) EMIT
SPRING
(— INTO ECSTASY) ENTRANCE
(— INTO EFFECT) EXECUTE
SANCTION
(— INTO IRONS) BOLT

(— INTO RHYTHM) METER METRE
(— LIQUOR INTO CASK) TUN
(— OFF) DAFF DOFF HAFT DEFER DELAY DEMUR FOIST PARRY REMIT REPRY SHIFT TARRY THROW LINGER RETARD SHELVE ADJOURN FORSLOW PROLONG RESPITE POSTPONE PROROGUE PROCRASTINATE
(— ON) DON HYPE APPLY CRACK DRAPE ENDUE MOUNT STAGE ASSUME INVEST ADDRESS
(— ON AIRS) PROSS FINICK REVEST
(— ON ALERT) ALARM
(— ON COVER) HACKLE
(— ON GUARD) ALERT CAUTION
(— ON HAT) COVER
(— ON PRETENSE) AFFECT
(— ON SALE) SHOP
(— ON SHORT ALLOWANCE) SCRIMP
(— ON STRING) ENFILE
(— OUT) GET OUT DOUT OUST DOWSE EVICT EXERT OUTED SLAKE SLOCK RETIRE DISMISS EXCLUDE EXTINCT FORJUDGE
(— OUT BATSMAN) SKITTLE
(— OUT OF ACTION) HAMPER
(— RIGHT) AMEND
(— ROAD METAL ON) STEEN
(— SUDDENLY) CLAP
(— THROUGH A STRAINER) TAMMY
(— TO FLIGHT) AFLEY FEAZE FLEME GALLY
(— TO RIGHTS) SORT DIGHT
(— TO SHAME) DASH ABASH SHEND UPBRAID
(— TO SLEEP) OPIATE SOPITE SOPORATE
(— TO USE) STOW APPLY BESTOW
(— TO WORK) HARNESS
(— TOGETHER) ADD JOIN BUILD COMPILE COMPOSE CONCOCT CONFECT PREPARE ASSEMBLE COMPOUND
(— UP) ANTE ERECT FLUSH DISPENSE

(— UP HAY) BOTTLE
(— UP WITH) GO BEAR BIDE HACK ABIDE BROOK ENDURE SUFFER COMPORT STOMACH SWALLOW TOLERATE
(— UPON) GAMMON
(— WITH ANOTHER) APPOSE
(SUFF.) STOLE
PUTAMEN PYRENE
PUTCHER PUTLOG PUTCHEN PUTLOCK
PUTREFACTION ROT DECAY SEPSIS
(SUFF.) SEPSIS SEPTIC
PUTREFACTIVE SEPTIC
(PREF.) SEPTICO
PUTREFY ROT ADDLE DECAY SWEAT FESTER POLLUTE PUTRESCE
PUTRESCENT PUTRID ROTTEN
PUTRID FOUL RANK SOUR VILE LOUSY ADDLED RANCID ROTTEN CORRUPT DECAYED FRIABLE VICIOUS DEPRAVED MALODOROUS
(PREF.) SAPR(O) SEPTI SEPTO
(SUFF.) SEPSIS SEPTIC
PUTT CLOWN BORROW GOBBLE
PUTTEE PAT PATA GAITER BANDAGE LEGGING
PUTTER FUSS MESS MUCK POKE TRUCK CADDLE DAWDLE MUCKER MUCKLE PIDDLE TINKER FRIGGLE
PUTTY BEDDING
PUTTYROOT CRAWFOOT
PUTZ CRECHE
PUXY SWAMPY QUAGMIRE
PUZZLE CAP GET SET BEAT CRUX DEAD LICK POSE BEFOG GRIPH POSER QUEER REBUS STICK BAFFLE BOTHER ENIGMA FICKLE FOITER GLAIKS JIGSAW KITTLE RIDDLE CONFUSE MYSTERY MYSTIFY NONPLUS PERPLEX STICKER TAISSLE TANGRAM TRANGAM ACROSTIC BEFUDDLE

BEWILDER CONFOUND DISTRACT DUMFOUND ENTANGLE INTRIGUE REMBLERE CROSSWORD
PUZZLED ASEA PERPLEXED
PUZZLING KNOTTY CURIOUS KNOTTED RIDDLING DIFFICULT PROBLEMATIC
PYCNANTHEMUM KOELLIA
PYCNOGONID SPIDER
PYGARG ADDAX OSPREY
PYGIDIUM PODEX
PYGMALION (AUTHOR OF —) SHAW
(BELOVED OF —) GALATEA
(CHARACTER IN —) HILL LIZA CLARA HENRY ALFRED FREDDY HIGGINS EYNSFORD DOOLITTLE PICKERING
(FATHER OF —) BELUS MUTGO AGENOR
(MURDERED BY —) SICHAEUS
(SISTER OF —) DIDO
(STATUE FASHIONED BY —) GALATEA
PYGMY ELF AKKA AMBA DOKO ACHUA AFIFI ATOMY BATWA DWARF GNOME PIXIE PIGMEW WOCHUA ACHANGO ASHANGO MANIKIN DWARFISH NEGRILLO VAALPENS DANDIPRAT
PYGMY GOOSE GOSLET
PYGMY RATTLESNAKE MASSASAUGA
PYGOSTYLE VOMER
PYKNIC SQUAT STOCKY STHENIC MUSCULAR
PYLADES (COMPANION OF —) ORESTES
(FATHER OF —) STROPHIUS
(MOTHER OF —) ANAXIBIA
(SON OF —) MEDON STROPHIUS
(WIFE OF —) ELECTRA
PYRAMID BENBEN HOPPER TEOCALLI
(— OF CRAYFISH) BUISSON
(DOUBLE —) TWIN ZIRCONOID
(INVERTED —) HOPPER

PYRAMIDAL HUGE ENORMOUS IMPOSING
PYRAMIDICAL TAPER
PYRAMUS (LOVER OF —) THISBE
PYRAZINE ALDINE PIAZIN DIAZINE
PYRE BALE PILE TOPHET BONFIRE BALEFIRE
PYRIDOXIN ADERMIN
PYRITE BALE MUNDIC
(PL.) BRAZIL STANNITE FIRESTONE MAGISTRAL MARCASITE
PYROCLES (BROTHER OF —) CYMOCLES
(FATHER OF —) ACRATES
PYROLA LIMONIUM SHINLEAF
PYROMANIAC FIREBUG ARSONIST
PYRONE CUMALIN
PYROPHYLLITE PENCIL
PYROTECHNICS FIREWORKS
PYROXENE ACMITE AUGITE SALITE SAHLITE AEGIRITE DIALLAGE DIOPSIDE WOLLASTONITE
PYROXENITE ARIEGITE MARCHITE OSTRAITE NIKLESITE
PYRRHIC DIBRACH
PYRRHULOXIA GROSBEAK BULLFINCH
PYRRHUS (FATHER OF —) AEACIDES
(MOTHER OF —) PHTHIA
(SON OF —) PTOLEMY SOPATER
(WIFE OF —) ANTIGONE
PYRROLE AZOLE
PYTHON ADJIGER PEROPOD ANACONDA
PYTHONESS WITCH PHITONES
PYTHONIC HUGE INSPIRED ORACULAR MONSTROUS PROPHETIC
PYX BOX CAPSA CASKET CHRISM VESSEL BINNACLE CHRISMAL CIBORIUM
PYXIDIUM CAPSULE

Q

Q KU CUE KUE QUEEN QUEUE
QUEBEC
QATAR (CAPITAL OF —) DOHA
(TOWN OF —) RUWAIS UMMSAID
QUA HERON QUABIRD
QUACK PUFF WHACK CROCUS
SALVER SUBTLE EMPIRIC
IMPOSTOR OPERATOR SANGRADO
CHARLATAN
(PREF.) PSEUD(O)
QUACKERY HUMBUG
QUADRAGESIMA LENT
QUADRANGLE QUAD CLOSE
COURT TETRAGON
QUADRANT BOW RADIAL SQUARE
QUARTER TETRANT ALTIMETER
QUADRATE SUIT AGREE IDEAL
QUADER SQUARE PERFECT
BALANCED
QUADRIC CONICOID
QUADRILATERAL TRAPEZIA
TETRAGRAM
(PL.) TESSARA
QUADRILLE CONTREDANSE
(PL.) LANCERS
QUADRILLION
(PREF.) ASTRA PETA QUEGA
QUADRILLIONTH
(PREF.) FEMTO
QUADROON QUATERON
TERCERON
QUADRUPED BABIRUSA
QUADRUPLE FOURBLE FOURFOLD
QUADRUPLED
(PREF.) TETRAKIS
QUADRUPLET FOURLING
QUARTOLE
QUAFF QUAX TOOT DRINK QUASS
WAUCHT CAROUSE TRILLIL
QUAG BOG MARSH SHAKE QUIVER
QUAGMIRE BOG FEN GOG HAG
QUA SOG LAIR PUXY QUAW
MARSH MIZZY SWAMP MORASS
PUDDLE SLOUGH BOGMIRE
PUCKSEY WAGMOIRE
QUAHOG CLAM COHOG VENUS
BULLNOSE
QUAIL COW LOWA WEET COLIN
COWER DAUNT ORTYX QUAKE
SPOIL WASTE BLENCH CURDLE
FLINCH SHRINK TURNIX WITHER
DECLINE HEMIPOD TREMBLE
BOBWHITE
(YOUNG —) SQUEALER
QUAINT DRY ODD NAIVE BIZARRE
STRANGE FANCIFUL HANDSOME
PICTURESQUE
(— IN APPEARANCE) FUNKY
QUAKE JAR QUOG RESE CHILL
QUAIL SHAKE DITHER QUIVER
SHIVER WAMBLE FLUTTER
SHUDDER TREMBLE
(PREF.) PALLO

QUAKER ASPEN HERON FRIEND
OBADIAH WHACKER HICKSITE
TREMBLER BEACONITE
BROADBRIM SHADBELLY
(— STATE) PENNA PENNSYLVANIA
QUAKER GRAY ACIER
QUAKING ASPEN QUAKY TREPID
SHAKING TREMBLING
QUAKING GRASS BRIZA
COWQUAKE WAGWANTS
QUALIFICATION NATURE RESERVE
SHADING CAPACITY
QUALIFIED FIT ABLE MEET FITTED
FITTEN LIKELY CAPABLE ELIGIBLE
SUITABLE AUTHENTIC
(NOT —) INAPT INHABILE
QUALIFIER MODIFIER
QUALIFY FIT DASH ADAPT ALLAY
ALLOY EQUIP HEDGE ENABLE
MODIFY SOFTEN TEMPER
ABSOLVE CERTIFY ENTITLE
LICENSE PREPARE GRADUATE
MODERATE RESTRAIN RESTRICT
QUALITIES
(SUFF.) ERY ICS
QUALITY Y BRAN BUMP CHOP
COST FEEL GUNA LEAD SORT
COLOR GRACE STATE TRAIT
ASSIZE BARREL FABRIC STRAIN
THREAD TIMBER TIMBRE
ADJUNCT CALIBER KINSHIP
STATURE ACCIDENT MOVEMENT
PROPERTY TONEBRAND
(— OF MIND) CALIBER CALIBRE
(— OF PERSONAL EMOTIONS)
PATHOS
(— OF PHOTOGRAPH) CONTRAST
(— OF TONE) TIMBRE
(— OF VOWELS) LENGTH
(— PECULIAR TO ONESELF) SEITY
(AESTHETIC —) TASTE
(ARTISTIC —) VIRTU
(ATTRACTIVE —) TAKE
(BASIC —) GRAIN
(BASIC —S) STUFF
(COLOR —) TONE
(ESSENTIAL —) ALLOY SPECIES
SUCHNESS
(GOOD —) THEW
(HEREDITARY —) STRAIN
(IMPECCABLE —) FINISH
(INCISIVE —) BITE
(INNATE —) LARGESS
(INTELLECTUAL —) BROW
(NATURAL —) TARAGE
(OBJECTIONABLE —) ANILITY
(OF HIGH —) FRANK
(OF LOW —) SHLOCK SCHLOCK
(PERVASIVE —) AROMA
(PHYSICAL —S) BOTTOM
(PRIMAL —) GUNA
(PUNGENT —) SNAP
(RELATIVE —) RATE

(SECONDARY —) OVERTONE
(SPATIAL —) MAGNITUDE
(SPRINGY —) SPINE
(STRUCTURAL —) TEXTURE
(SUBDUED —) SHADE
(SUBTLE —) BOUQUET
(SUPERIOR —) SUPER FINENESS
(TRIED —) TOUCH
(UNESSENTIAL —) ACCIDENT
(UNUSUAL —) SURD
(WAVY — OF HAIR) FLIX
(SUFF.) ACITY ANCE ANCY CY
ENCE ENCY HEAD HOOD ICE ICITY
ILITY ITY MENT NESS SHIP TY
(— THAT FILLS) FUL FULL
(CHARACTERIZED BY —) SOME
QUALITY STREET (AUTHOR OF —)
BARRIE
(CHARACTER IN —) BROWN LIVVY
PATTY SUSAN BLADES PHOEBE
THROSSEL VALENTINE
QUALM CALM DROW PALL
NAUSEA SQUEAM SCRUPLE
QUALMISH TEWLY SICKISH
SQUEAMISH
QUAMOCLIT MOONFLOWER
QUANDARY FIX PUXY PUZZLE
TANGLE DILEMMA NONPLUS
SWITHER DOLDRUMS JUNCTURE
QUANDONG PEACH
QUANT RYPECK
QUANTIC NONIC OCTIC SEPTIC
SEXTIC QUADRIC QUINTIC
QUANTIFIER PREFIX
QUANTITATIVE METRIC
QUANTITY BAG JAG SUM SUP
BODY DEAL DISH DOSE FECK
JAGG LIFT MASK SOME SOUD
WARE BATCH BREAK CLASH
GRIST KITTY SIEGE TROOP
WHEEN ACTION ADDEND
AMOUNT BAGFUL BOTTLE
BUDGET DICKER EFFECT FOTHER
HANTLE NUMBER PARCEL SPINOR
THRAVE CONTENT FOOTAGE
PORTION QUANTUM GLASSFUL
KNIFEFUL LADLEFUL PARAMETER
(— OF ARROWS) SHEAF
(— OF BUTTER) CHURNING
(— OF CLOTHES) BUCKING
(— OF COTTONSEED) CRUSH
(— OF CUT TREES) FALL
(— OF DRINK) HOOP DRAFT
DRAUGHT
(— OF ELECTRICITY) FARADAY
(— OF EXPLOSIVE) CHARGE
(— OF FISH OR GAME) TAKE CATCH
DRAFT DRAUGHT
(— OF GRAIN) GAVEL
(— OF HAY) LOCK TRUSS
(— OF IRRIGATION WATER) DUTY
(— OF LIQUID) DROP JAUP SLASH
GOBBET JABBLE

(— OF LIQUOR) HEELTAP
(— OF LUMBER) RUN
(— OF MEAL) MELDER
(— OF METAL) BLOW
(— OF MUD) CLASH
(— OF NARCOTICS) BINDLE
(— OF PAPER) TOKEN
(— OF PRODUCE) BURY
(— OF RAISINS) FRAIL
(— OF THREAD) LEASE
(— OF WOOD) HAG FATHOM
(ESTIMATED —) WEY
(EXCESSIVE —) GLUT SPATE
(FIXED —) CONSTANT
(GREAT —) HOST MORT MUCH
HIRST SHOAL SIGHT STORE
BARREL FOREST SLATHER
TUMMELS
(LARGE —) ACRE BOLT DEAL FECK
HEAP MASS PECK SCAD SLEW
FLOOD FORCE GRIST JORUM
POWER SCADS SHEAF STACK
STORE BUCKET BUSHEL DICKER
DOLLOP GALLON MATTER
MELDER CLUTHER SKINFUL
HECATOMB MOUNTAIN
PLURALITY
(LEAST —) BEDROCK
(MINUTE —) DRAM DROP SHADE
SCRUPLE PARTICLE
(NOTEWORTHY —) CHUNK
(RELATIVE —) DEGREE
(SETTLED —) SIZE
(SIZABLE —) SCUMP
(SMALL —) ACE BIT SUP CURN
DASH DUST HAET HAIR HARL
IOTA PEAK SOSH SPOT CANCH
PRILL SMACK SPICE SQUIB TOUCH
JOBBLE MORSEL PICKLE SAMPLE
SONGLE STIVER CAPSULE
CURTSEY DRIBBLE DRIBLET
EPSILON HANDFUL MODICUM
SMICKET SPATTER TODDICK
FARTHING MOUTHFUL PENNORTH
SCANTLET PENNYWORTH
(UNDIRECTED —) SCALAR
(VARYING —) SKID
(SUFF.) **(— THAT FILLS)** FUL FULL
QUANTUM MAGNON PHONON
PHOTON ISOSPIN
QUAPAW KWAPA ARKANSAS
QUARANTINE DETAIN ISOLATE
SANCTION
QUARENTENE ROOD FURLONG
QUARREL JAR WAP YED BEEF
CHIP DEAL FEUD FRAY FUSS JARL
JOWL MIFF NIFF ODDS PICK PLEA
SPAT TIFF WHID BRACK BRAWL
BRIGE BROIL FLITE FLUSK GRUFF
HURRY JOWER NOISE PIQUE
SCOLD SCRAP SHINE STOUR
UPSET WRALL AFFRAY BARNEY
BLOWUP BREACH BREEZE BRIGUE

DEBATE DIFFER DUSTUP FRACAS
FRATCH GARROT JANGLE
MATTER QUARRY RIPPET SQUARE
SQUEAL STRIFE THREAP THREEP
THWART BRABBLE BRATTLE
DISGUST DISPUTE FACTION
OUTCAST PRABBLE RUCTION
SIMULTY STASHIE SWAGGER
TUILZIE WRANGLE DISAGREE
MOORBURN SCRAFFLE SPLUTTER
SQUABBLE TRAVERSE
(— IN WORDS) JANGLE
(NOISY —) ROW FRACAS KICKUP
(PETTY —) MIFF SPAT TIFF
QUARRELING BICKER CONTEK
CHIDING CONTECK
QUARRELSOME RIXY UGLY
ROWTY FEISTY CURRISH SCRAPPY
DRAWLING FRAMPOLD FRATCHED
PETULANT PHRAMPEL BELLICOSE
BUMPTIOUS FRACTIOUS
LITIGIOUS CONTENTIOUS
(NOT —) AMICABLE
QUARRELSOMENESS SQUARING
WARIANCE
QUARRIED (NOT —) LIVE
(PREF.) ORYCTO
QUARRIER FACEMAN QUARION
QUARRY DELF GAME LODE MEAT
CHASE DELFT DELPH PLUCK
LATOMY REWARD LATOMIA
LOZENGE
(HAWK'S —) MARK
QUARRYMAN SCABBLER
SCAPPLER
QUART SHANT WHART
(METRIC —) LITER
(ONE-HALF —) PINT
(TWO —S) MAGNUM
(1-8TH —) GILL
(2 —S) FLAGON
(4 —S) GALLON
QUARTE FOURTH
QUARTER AIRT PART STUD EAVER
GRITH TRACT BARRIO BEHALF
BESTOW CANTON COLONY
FARDEL HARBOR SECTOR
CONTRADA FAUBOURG FIERDING
STANDARD POBLACION
(— IN BATTLE) GRITH
(— OF A POUND) TRIPPET
(— OF BEEF OR MUTTON) BOUT
(— OF CITY) BLOCK GHETTO
(— OF COMPASS) PLAGE
(— OF FLAG) CANTON
(— OF HOUR) POINT
(— OF HUNDRED) FIERDING
(— OF YEAR) RAITH
(— ONESELF) SORN
(— UPON) LAY
(JEWISH —) ALJAMA
QUARTERING LASKING
CHUMMAGE
QUARTER NOTE CROTCHET
QUARTER REST SOSPIRO
QUARTERS BOTHY BILLET BOTHIE
LIVERY MENAGE FARDELS
CHUMMERY DIGGINGS
LODGMENT
(— FOR IMMIGRANTS) HOSTEL
(— OF SALVATION ARMY)
BARRACKS
(HIGH —) AERY EYRY AERIE EYRIE

(JUNIOR OFFICERS' —) GUNROOM
(MEN'S —) SELAMLIK
(MONASTERY —) FRATRY
QUARTET FOURSOME
QUARTILE SQUARE TETRAGON
QUARTO FOURS
QUARTZ IRIS ONYX SARD AGATE
CHERT FLINT PRASE TARSO
TOPAZ JASPER MORION PEBBLE
PLASMA SILICA ALENCON CITRINE
CRYSTAL RUBASSE SINOPLE
AMETHYST BASANITE SARDONYX
SIDERITE YENTNITE BUHRSTONE
BURRSTONE
QUARTZITE GANISTER SILCRETE
QUASH CASS CRUSH QUELL SPIKE
SQUAT SOPITE CASSARE
PEREMPT SUPPRESS
QUASI
(PREF.) SEMI
QUAT FOUR GLUT SQUASH
SATIATE UPSTART
QUATERNION TETRAD QUADRATE
QUATREFOIL TRESSURE
(DOUBLE —) EIGHTFOIL
QUAVER QUAP CROMA SHAKE
TRILL WAVER CHROMA FALTER
QUIVER WABBLE WOBBLE WRIBLE
FREDDON VIBRATE
QUAVERY WARBLY UNSTEADY
QUAY KEY POW QUAI LEVEE
BUNDER STRAND
QUEACH BOG FEN MARSH
THICKET
QUEASINESS KECK SICKNESS
QUEASY NICE SICK SQUEEZY
DELICATE NAUSEATED
SQUEAMISH
QUEBEC (LAKE OF —) MINTO
BIENVILLE MISTASSINI
(TOWN OF —) AMOS HULL AMQUI
LAVAL MAGOG PERCE BASSIN
VERDUN JOLIETTE MONTREAL
LAPRAIRIE
QUEBRACHO BREAKAX AXMASTER
IRONWOOD AXBREAKER
QUEBRADA BROOK GULLY RAVINE
FISSURE
QUECHUA INCAN KICHUA
QUEEN REG DAME FERS LADY
MEDB RANI AEDON BEGUM FIERS
RANEE ATOSSA REGINA ROXANA
TAILTE TAMARA ARGANTE
ATHALIA CANDACE JOCASTE
OMPHALE PHEARSE STATIRA
TITANIA BRUNHILD GERTRUDE
GLORIANA GUINEVER MAHARANI
(— AND KING OF TRUMPS) BELLA
(— CITY) CINCINNATI
(— IN CHESS) FERS LADY FIERS
(— OF CLUBS) SPADILLA
(— OF DENMARK) GERTRUDE
(— OF ETHIOPIA) CANDACE
(— OF FAIRY LAND) MEDB
GLORIANA
(— OF GEORGIA) TAMARA
(— OF GOTHS) TAMORA
(— OF HEARTS) ELIZABETH
(— OF HEAVEN) HERA
(— OF JUDAH) ATHALIA
(— OF LYDIA) OMPHALE
(— OF SHEBA) BALKIS BILKIS
(— OF SPADES) BASTA LIZZY

(— OF THE ADRIATIC) VENICE
(— OF THE ANTILLES) CUBA
(— OF THE EAST) ZENOBIA
(— OF THEBES) JOCASTA
(— OF TRUMPS) HONOR
(FAIRY —) MAB ARGANTE TITANIA
(INDIAN —) RANI SUNK MAHARANI
(MOHAMMEDAN —) BEGUM
QUEEN ANNE'S LACE UMBEL
QUEEN BEE KING
QUEEN ELIZABETH DIANA ORIANA
CYNTHIA
QUEENFISH WAHOO CROAKER
DRUMFISH
QUEENLY HAUGHTY REGINAL
MAJESTIC
QUEENROOT YAWSHRUB
QUEEN'S-DELIGHT YAWSHRUB
QUEENSLAND HEMP SIDA
JELLYLEAF
QUEER HEX ODD RUM HARM
DICKY DIPPY DROLL FAINT FUNNY
GIDDY NUTTY RUMMY COCKLE
FIFISH HIPPED QUEASY QUISBY
UNIQUE AMUSING COMICAL
CURIOUS DISRUPT ERRATIC
STRANGE TOUCHED WHIMSIC
FANCIFUL OBSESSED PECULIAR
(— THING) QUOZ
QUEERNESS ODDITY
QUEEST RINGDOVE
QUELL DIE CALM FLOW HUSH KILL
QUAY SLAY ABATE ALLAY CRUSH
QUASH QUIET YIELD PACIFY
PERISH REDUCE SOOTHE SPRING
STANCH STIFLE KILLING REPRESS
SQUELCH SUPPRESS
QUEME QUIM HANDY WHEAM
COMELY PLEASE GRATIFY
PLEASANT
QUENCH COOL DAMP SIND ALLAY
CHECK CRUSH SLAKE SLOCK STILL
STANCH STIFLE ASSUAGE
SLOCKEN AUSTEMPER
QUENCHED EXTINCT
QUENCHER STANCH
QUENCHING FRITTING
QUENTIN DURWARD (AUTHOR OF
—) SCOTT
(CHARACTER IN —) CARL CROYE
LOUIS LESLEY PHILIP PIERRE
TOISON BALAFRE CHARLES
DURWARD EBERSON HERMITE
LAMARCK LUDOVIC QUENTIN
TRISTAN WILLIAM CRAWFORD
HAMELINE ISABELLE HAYRADDIN
JAQUELINE MAUGRABIN
CREVECOEUR
QUERCINE OAKEN
QUERECHO VAQUERO
QUERELA AUDITA
QUERENT INQUIRER PLAINTIFF
QUERN KERN MILL METATE
MILLSTONE
QUERULOUS WHINY FRETFUL
PEEVISH NATTERED PETULANT
IRRITABLE
QUERY ASK DOUBT DEMAND
INQUIRE INQUIRY QUESTION
QUEST ASK BAY GAPE SEEK
DEMAND EXAMINE PURSUIT
SEEKING VENTURE
QUESTING OUTREACH

QUESTION ASK HOW SPY POSE
QUIZ TALK ARGUE DOUBT DREAD
QUERY ACCUSE CHANCE CHARGE
DEMAND LEADER MATTER
PONDER REASON SHRIVE
EXAMINE INQUIRE INQUIRY
PROBLEM PURPOSE SCRUPLE
OVERTURE RELEVANT RESEARCH
STICKLER CATECHISE
(— AMBIGUOUSLY WORDED)
RIDDLE
(— FRETFULLY) RAME
(BAFFLING —) POSER
(PERPLEXING —) STUMPER
(RHETORICAL —) EROTEMA
(UNSOLVED —) CRUX
(ZEN —) KOAN
QUESTIONABLE FISHY QUEER
SHAKY UNSAFE BATABLE
CLOUDED DUBIOUS DOUBTFUL
PROBLEMATIC
(NOT —) DECENT
QUESTIONER APPOSER INQUIRER
QUESTIONING DUBIOUS
QUIZZICAL
QUESTION MARK QUERY QUAERE
EROTEME
QUESTIONNAIRE POLL
INVENTORY
QUETCH STIR TWITCH
QUETZAL QUESAL TROGON
QUEUE CUE COLA LINE BRAID
PIGTAIL CROCODILE
QUEY KOY WHY WHEY HEIFER
QUIBBLE COG PUN BALK CARP
QUIB QUIP CAVIL DODGE EVADE
QUIRK SALVO AMBAGE BAFFLE
BICKER HAFFLE PALTER BRABBLE
CAPTION CHICANE QUIBLET
QUIDDIT QUILLET SHUFFLE
PETTIFOG QUILLITY SCRAFFLE
CONUNDRUM
QUIBBLING CHICANERY
QUICA OPOSSUM SARIGUE
QUICK APT RAD YAP FAST FLIT
GLEG KECK KEEN LISH LIST PERT
RATH RIFE SNAP SOON WHAT
WHIT WICK YARE AGILE ALIVE
APACE BRISK CHEAP FLEET
HASTY MERRY NIFTY NIPPY
PREST RAPID READY SHARP
SHORT SNACK SNELL SWIFT
SWITH TOSTO TRICK VISTO
YARRY ACTIVE CLEVER FACILE
KITTLE NIMBLE PROMPT PRONTO
SNAPPY SPEEDY SUDDEN
DARTING SCHNELL SHUTTLE
DEXTROUS TRIPPING CITIGRADE
(— AND NEAT) DEFT
(— AS A FLASH) WHIP
(— IN PERCEPTION) ACID
(— IN RESPONSE) GNIB
(— TO DETECT) SMOKY
(— TO FLARE UP) GASSY
(— TO LEARN) APT
(— TO MOVE) YARE
(LIGHT AND —) VOLANT
(PREF.) OXY TACHEO TACHISTO
TACHO TACHY
QUICKEN PEP MEND STIR WHET
HURRY SPEED ACUATE AROUSE
HASTEN INCITE KINDLE REVIVE
VIVIFY ANIMATE ENLIVEN

PROVOKE REFRESH SHARPEN
EXPEDITE INSPIRIT ACCELERATE
QUICKENING FLICKER REVIVAL
STIRRING
QUICKLY TID TIT CITO FAST RIFE
SOON TIVY WHIP YARE NEWLY
RADLY RATHE SHARP SKELP
SNACK SNELL SWITH TIGHT
WIGHT YEPLY ASTITE BELIVE
HOURLY PRESTO PRONTO RASHLY
EFTSOON PRESTLY READILY
SPEEDILY WIKIWIKI
(— AND WITH FORCE) SWAP
(MORE —) TIDDER TITTER
STRETTO
QUICKNESS HASTE SPEED
ACUMEN AGILITY SMEDDUM
ACTIVITY CELERITY DISPATCH
KEENNESS SAGACITY
(MENTAL —) NOUS SLEIGHT
LEGERITY
QUICKSAND FLOW SYRT SYRTIS
SWALLOW
QUICK-SELLING LEEFTAIL
QUICKSILVER OREMIX MERCURY
TIERRAS HEAUTARIT
QUICK-SPEAKING PROMPT
QUICK-TEMPERED DONCY DONSY
PEPPERY IRASCIBLE
QUICK-WITTED APT SHARP
SMART NIMBLE KNOWING
QUID FID CHEW SOVEREIGN
(— OF TOBACCO) CUD FID
QUIDDANY JELLY SYRUP
CODINIAC
QUIDDITY QUIBBLE WHATNESS
QUIDNUNC GOSSIP BUSYBODY
QUIESCENCE KAIF STASIS
DORMANCY
QUIESCENT QUIET LATENT STATIC
RESTING INACTIVE
QUIET QT ST COY LAY CALM COSH
DEAD DUMB EASE EASY HUSH
LOUN LOWN LULL REST ROCK
SNUG SOFT WEME ACCOY CANNY
CIVIL DOWNY LEVEL PEACE
PEASE QUATE QUELL QUEME
RESTY SALVE SHADY SILKY SLEEP
SOBER SQUAT STILL SUANT
WHIST DREAMY GENTLE PACIFY
PLACID RETIRE SAUGHT SEDATE
SERENE SETTLE SILENT SMOOTH

SOFTLY SOOTHE SOPITE STEADY
STILLY HUSHFUL ORDERLY
REQUIEM RESTFUL SILENCE
COMPOSED DECOROUS PEACEFUL
TRANQUIL UNRUFFLE
(— DOWN) DILL
(MAKE —) ALLAY
(STEALTHILY —) SLINKY
QUIETEN SOPITE
QUIETISM MOLINISM
QUIETLY LOW FAIR CANNY STILL
WINLY EVENLY GENTLY SOFTLY
TIPTOE
QUIETNESS REST REPOSE
SERENITY
QUIETUDE CALM INERTION
QUIETUS REST DEATH RELEASE
QUILL COP PEN RIB PIRN FLOAT
STALK BOBBIN FESCUE PINION
SLEEVE BRISTLE CALAMUS
PRIMARY TRUNDLE
(— FOR WINDING THREAD) COP
(— OF FEATHER) BARREL
(PORCUPINE —) PEN
QUILLBACK SAILFISH SKIMBACK
QUILLWORT ISOETES FERNWORT
QUILT BEAT GULP WALT WELT
WHIP DUVET REZAI CADDOW
CHALON PALLET THRASH
SWALLOW MATTRESS POULTICE
COMFORTER
QUILTING MARCELLA
QUIMPER NICE
QUINCE SKEG COYNE ANGERS
SQUINCH JAPONICA
(BENGAL —) BEL BAEL BALE BHEL
QUINCE SEED CYDONIUM
QUININE KINA SPECIFIC
(PREF.) CHIN(O)
QUINK BRANT
QUINONE EMBELIN
QUINSY ANGINA PRUNELLA
QUINTAIN FAN
QUINTE FIFTH
QUINTESSENCE CREAM ELIXIR
CLYSSUS OSMAZOME
QUINTILLION
(PREF.) EXA NEBU
QUINTILLIONTH
(PREF.) ATTO
QUINTUPLE QUINARY FIVEFOLD
QUINIBLE

QUIP GIBE JAPE JEST JOKE CRACK
QUIRK SALLY SCOFF TAUNT
CONCEIT QUIBBLE
QUIRA CAOBA ROBLE HORMIGO
VENCOLA MACAWOOD
QUIRE CHOR SEXTERN
(20 —S) REAM
(PL.) INSIDES
QUIRK BEND KINK QUIP TURN
CLOCK CROOK TWIST CONCEIT
QUIBBLE FLOURISH PAROXYSM
MANNERISM PECULIARITY
QUIRQUINCHO PICHI PELUDO
QUIRT WHIP ROMAL
QUIS WOODCOCK
QUISLING APOSTATE
QUIT GO DROP NASH PART QUAT
AVOID BELAY CEASE DOUSE
LEAVE SHIFT SHOOT STASH
WHITE BEHAVE CIVITE DESERT
DESIST FOREGO RESIGN SECEDE
VACATE ABANDON FORSAKE
RELEASE UNTENANT
QUITCH COUCH QUICK SCUTCH
TWITCH
QUITCLAIM DEED ACQUIT
RELEASE DISCHARGE
QUITE SO ALL BUT GEY BRAW
EVEN FAIR FREE FULL JUST PLAT
WELL CLEAR CLOSE FULLY SHEER
STARK CLEVER DAMNED ENOUGH
JUSTLY MERELY TOTALLY
PERFECTLY
(NOT —) HARDLY
(PREF.) DE
QUITERIA (HUSBAND OF —)
CAMACHO
QUITRENT CANON
QUITS EVEN EVENS UPSIDES
QUITTER PUS SLAG PIKER
COWARD JUMPER SHIRKER
TURNBACK
QUIVER DIRL QUAG QUOG BEVER
NIDGE QUAKE SHAKE TRILL
WAVER WIVER BICKER COCKER
DIDDER DINDLE SHEATH SHIMMY
SHIVER TREMOR WAMBLE
DORLACH FLUTTER FRISSON
SHUDDER TREMBLE TWIDDLE
TWINKLE TWITTER VIBRATE
FLICHTER WERSLETE
(PREF.) PALLO

QUIVERING ASPEN AGUISH
DIDDER DITHER QUAGGLE
QUAKING AGITATED ATREMBLE
QUIVER TREE KOKERBOOM
QUIXOTIC ERRANT IMAGINARY
VISIONARY
QUIZ ASK GUY HOAX MOCK CHAFF
QUEER EXAMINE QUESTION
RIDICULE
QUIZZICAL ODD QUEER QUIZZY
CURIOUS WHIMSICAL
QUO KA
QUOD JAIL QUAD PRISON
QUOIN COIN ANGLE GOIGN
CORNER LOZENGE KEYSTONE
VOUSSOIR
QUOIT CIST DISC DISH DISK LINER
DISCUS HOBBER CROMLECH
QUOMODO HOW WAY MEANS
MANNER
QUONDAM OLD ONCE WHILE
FORMER ONETIME SOMETIME
QUORATEAN KAROK
QUORUM CORAM HOUSE MINYAN
MAJORITY
QUOTA PART BOGEY SHARE
QUOTIENT PROPORTION
QUOTATION TAG PRICE QUOTE
EXTRACT SNIPPET EPIGRAPH
(— DEVELOPED INTO ESSAY) CHRIA
QUOTATION MARK GUILLEMET
QUOTE CITE COAT COTE MARK
NAME NOTE ADDUCE ALLEGE
RECITE REPEAT EXCERPT
EXTRACT OBSERVE REHEARSE
(— SARCASTICALLY) FLOUT
QUOTH CO KO CUTH QUAD QUOD
SAID SPOKE UTTERED
QUOTIDIAN DAILY TRIVIAL
ORDINARY
QUOTIENT QUOTE FRACTION
MILLESIMAL
QUO VADIS (AUTHOR OF —)
SIENKIEWICZ
(CHARACTER IN —) ACTE NERO
PAUL CHILO LYGIA PETER URSUS
CROTON EUNICE GLAUCUS
VINICIUS PETRONIUS TIGELLINUS
QUTB POLE

R

R AR ROGER ROMEO
(UVULAR —) BURR
RA RE RAE SHU TEM ATMU BACIS
HORUS MENTU KHEPERA SOKARIS
RAAMAH (FATHER OF —) CUSH
(SON OF —) DEDAN SHEBA
RABBAN MASTER TEACHER
RABBET CHECK GROOVE
BACKJOINT FILLISTER
RABBI TANA AMORA CACAM
HAKAM TANNA MASTER SABORA
KHAKHAM TEACHER GAMALIEL
SABORAIM
(PL.) AMORAIM TANNAIM
RABBIT BUN REX TAN BUNT CONY
JACK POLE RACK BUNNY CAPON
CREAM CUNNY DUTCH FRIER
LAPIN ANGORA ASTREX CONEEN
HAVANA OARLOP PARKER POLISH
SILVER TAPETI WOOLER BEVEREN
CONYNGE FLEMISH LEPORID
SNOWSHOE WARRENER
(— BURROW) CLAPPER
(— FUR) CONY SCUT CONEY FLICK
LAPIN FLITCH
(— MEAT) LAPAN
(— SKIN) RACK
(— TAIL) SCUT
(— WARREN) CONYGER
(CASTRATED —) CAPON
(FEMALE —) DOE
(MALE —) BUCK
(YOUNG —) KITTEN
(PL.) FLICK WARREN
RABBITFISH SPINY
RABBLE MOB TAG GING HERD
RAFF ROUT SCUM FRAPE SCAFF
SCUFF TRASH MEINIE RADDLE
RAFFLE RAGTAG RASCAL TAGRAG
DOGGERY PUDDLER RABBLER
RANGALE TRAFFIC BRAGGERY
CANAILLE RAGABASH RIFFRAFF
VARLETRY RASCALITY
CLAMJAMFRY
(DISORDERLY —) HERD
RABBLE-ROUSER DEMAGOG
RABID MAD RAGING FRANTIC
FURIOUS RABIOUS RABITIC
FRENZIED RAVENING VIRULENT
RABIES LYSSA MADNESS PIBLOKTO
RAVENING
(PREF.) LYSSO RABI
RACCOON COON COATI GUARA
TEJON AGUARA MAPACH
WASHER AGOUARA ARCTOID
RATTOON RINGTAIL CRABEATER
RACE CAP CUP LOG ROD RUN
BENT CONE DASH DRAG GEST
HUMP KIND LINE NAME RAIS
RAZE RING RINK TEAM TRAM
BLOOD BREED BROOD BRUSH
CASTE CHEVY CORSO DERBY
FLESH HOUSE ISSUE PLATE

PURSE RATCH REACH ROUTE
SPEED STAKE STAMM STIRP
STOCK BROOSE CHEVVY COURSE
FAMILY NATION PEOPLE PHYLON
RUNOFF SPRING STIRPS STRAIN
STRIND BIOTYPE CENTURY
CLAIMER CLASSIC HACKNEY
HUNDRED KINDRED LINEAGE
MATINEE NURSERY PROGENY
PROSAPY RACEWAY REGATTA
STADIUM FUTURITY HANDICAP
MARATHON WALKOVER
OFFSPRING ORIENTEERING
(— A HORSE) CAMPAIGN
(— AT WEDDING) BROOSE BROUZE
(— FOR BALL-BEARINGS) CONE
(— OF BARLEY) BENT
(— OF GODS) VANIR
(— OF PEOPLE) VANS AMALS
VANIR HAZARA SAKAIS YADAVA
BAMBUTE FIRBOLG GIANTRY
NISHADA RASENNA REPHAIM
AMALINGS
(— OF UNDERGROUND ELVES)
DROW
(— OF WINDMILL) CURB
(HORSE —) AGON DERBY PLATE
SPRINT MATINEE FUTURITY
WALKOVER
(HUMAN —) MAN MANKIND
SPECIES MORTALITY
(IMPROMPTU —) BRUSH
(JUMPING —) SCURRY
(LENTEN —S) TORPIDS
(LONG —) ENDURO
(MILL —) LADE
(MOTORCYCLE —) SCRAMBLE
MOTOCROSS
(PRELIMINARY —) HEAT
(ROWING —) SCULLS REGATTA
(RUNNING —) MILE RELAY SPRINT
HUNDRED HURDLES
(SHORT —) BICKER
(SHORT-DISTANCE —) DASH
SCURRY SPRINT
(SKI —) SLALOM DAUERLAUF
(TIDAL —) ROOST
(PL.) FOURS
(PREF.) ETHN(O) GEN(O) PHYL(O)
RACECOURSE LIST OVAL PIST
RING TURF EPSOM CAREER
CIRCUS CURSUS DROMOS STADIE
STRETCH GYMKHANA SPEEDWAY
(PREF.) DROM(O)
(SUFF.) DROME
RACEHORSE DOG PONY PACER
RACER CHASER SLEEPER
TROTTER BANGTAIL
(— THAT HAS NEVER WON) MAIDEN
(INFERIOR —) PLATER HAYBURNER
(2-YEAR OLD —) JUVENILE
(PL.) RUCK
RACEME STRIG PANICLE

RACEMOSE BOTRYOSE
RACER CRACK SNAKE RUNNER
BICYCLIST CINDERMAN
RACETRACK OVAL DROMOS
FURLONG AUTODROME
RACEWAY CANAL TRACK GROOVE
CHANNEL FISHWAY
RACHEL POWDER
(FATHER OF —) LABAN
(HUSBAND OF —) JACOB
(SISTER OF —) LEAH
(SON OF —) JOSEPH BENJAMIN
RACHIS SPINE SPINDLE
(— OF HOP STROBILE) STRIG
RACHITIS RICKETS
RACIAL GENTILE GENTILIC
PHYLETIC
RACIST COLOR
RACK GIN RAK RAT TUB BINK
BUCK CASE HACK HECK SHOG
TACK AMBLE BRAKE DRIER DRYER
FLAKE FRAME POKER THROW
TOUSE TRAIN WRACK WRECK
WRING CIRCLE CRATCH CUDGEL
ENGINE NIPPER PULLEY TREBLE
WRENCH AFFLICT AGONIZE
PENRACK POTTARO TORMENT
TORTURE BARBECUE EQUULEUS
PINEBANK SAWHORSE
(— ATTACHED TO WAGON)
SHELVING OUTRIGGER
(— FOR BARRELS) JIB
(— FOR CHINAWARE) FIDDLE
(— FOR DISHES) BINK
(— FOR FEEDING) HACK HAYRACK
(— FOR FODDER) HECK CRATCH
(— FOR PLATES) CREEL
(— FOR STORAGE) FLAKE
(— IN THRESHER) SHAKER
(DRYING —) CRIB TREBLE
(WOODEN —) BUCAN
RACKED WRUNG TORTURED
RACKET BAT DIN GAME RORT
BANDY MUSIC RAZOO CLAMOR
CROSSE DRIVER HUBBUB HUSTLE
RAQUET RATTLE BUSINESS
REVELING STRAMASH
(PART OF —) CAP BUTT CORD GRIP
HEAD HEEL TAPE YOKE CROWN
FLAKE SHAFT HANDLE PALLET
STRING THROAT BINDING
SHOULDER THROATPIECE
(TENNIS —) SCUFE
RACKETEER HOOD HUSTLER
GANGSTER
RACKETT CERVALET CERVELAT
RACKING FIERCE
RACKMAN TOPMAN
RACON BEACON
RACONTEUR STORYTELLER
RACQUET CROSSE GAZELLE
RACY GAMY LEAN SEXY JUICY
SALTY SMART SPICY LIVELY

RISQUE PIQUANT PUNGENT
ZESTFUL SPIRITED MERACIOUS
RAD EAGER QUICK READY AFRAID
ELATED
RADAR (— NAVIGATION SYSTEM)
LANAC
(— SYSTEM) OBOE
RADARSCOPE PPI HSCOPE
RADDAI (BROTHER OF —) DAVID
(FATHER OF —) JESSE
RADDLE PIT BEAT SCAR RAVEL
RUDDLE THRASH SEPARATOR
RADHA (FOSTER SON OF —) KARNA
(HUSBAND OF —) ADHIRATHA
RADIAL RAY QUADRANT
(PREF.) RADIO
RADIANCE RAY GLOW LEAM
GLARE GLEAM GLINT GLORY
LIGHT SHINE LUSTER AUREOLA
GLITTER SPLENDOR
RADIANT BEAMY SHEEN SHINY
ABLAZE BRIGHT GOLDEN LUCENT
SHEENY AURORAL BEAMFUL
BEAMING FULGENT LAMBENT
GLORIOUS LUSTROUS RELUCENT
SPLENDID BRILLIANT
(— INTENSITY) J
(PREF.) STILPNO
RADIATE RAY BEAM POUR SHED
SHINE EFFUSE SPREAD EFFULGE
EMANATE ACTINOID
RADIATED PENCILED STELLATE
RADIATION AURA LIGHT
INFRARED
(— DOSAGE) REM REP
(— UNIT) LANGLEY
(UNIT OF —) REM
RADIATOR HEATER EMANATOR
(SET OF —S) STACK
RADICAL KEY SURD BASAL GROUP
RADIX ROUGE ULTRA CAPRYL
HEROIC CAPITAL CAPROYL
DRASTIC EXTREME FORWARD
HERETIC JACOBIN LEFTIST
LEVELER LIBERAL PRIMARY
CARDINAL LOCOFOCO
(CHEMICAL —) ACYL AMYL CARYL
CETYL GROUP ACETYL ADENYL
CAPRYL PHENYL PHYTYL
HALOGEN LINALYL CARBAMYL
QINNAMAL
(SUFF.) (ACID —) OYL
(BIVALENT —) YLENE
RADICALISM EXTREMISM
JACOBINISM
RADICEL ROOTLET
**RADICLE (— THAT DEVELOPS IN
GRAIN)** COME
RADIENT ORIENT
RADIO AIR SET WIRELESS
(— OPERATOR) HAM SPARKS
(— SYSTEM) TBS
RADIOGRAM FLIMSY

RADIOGRAPH EXOGRAPH
SKIAGRAM
RADIOISOTOPE TRACER
RADISH RUNCH DAEKON DAIKON
RIFART CADLOCK CRADLOCK
CRUCIFER CROSSWEED
RADIUS RAYON SPOKE SWEEP
THROW ADRADIUS
RADIX BASE ROOT ETYMON
RADICLE
RADON NITON THORON ACTINON
EXRADIO
RADULA RIBBON TONGUE
RAFF LOW IDLE SCUM SWEEP
TRASH COMMON JUMBLE
LUMBER RABBLE RAFFLE RAGTAG
SNATCH RUBBISH
RAFFISH RAKISH TAWDRY
UNKEMPT
RAFFLE MOVE RAFF JUMBLE
RABBLE REFUSE RUBBISH
RAFT COW CRIB MOKI BALSA
BATCH FLOAT TABLE DINGEY
DINGHY JANGAR MOKIHI PIPERY
RADEAU JANGADA ZATTARE
CATAMARAN
(— OF INVERTED POTS) GHARNAO
(— OF LOGS) BOOM CRIB
(— WITH CABIN) COW
(BAMBOO —) RAKIT
(FIRE —) CATAMARAN
(LUMBER —) BATCH
RAFT DOG RAKER
RAFTER HIP BALK BLAD FIRM SILE
SOIL SPAR SPUR VIGA BAULK
BLADE CABER RIDGE BOUGAR
BULKER COUPLE CARLINE
CHEVRON RAFFMAN SLEEPER
(— OF TURKEYS) FLOCK
RAFTY RAW DAMP FUSTY MUSTY
RANCID
RAG JAG LAP TAT HAZE HOAX
JAGG SAIL ANNOY CLOUT PRANK
SCOLD SCRAP SHRED WIPER
GIBBOL LIBBET RAGGLE TAGRAG
TATTER FLITTER REMNANT
TORMENT RAGSTONE STRAGGLE
NEWSPAPER
(— GATHERER) TATTER
(CURLING —) CRACKER
(FLAPPING —) WALLOP
(TARRED —) HARDS
(PL.) DUDS CADDIS FITTERS
RAGGERY FLITTERS
RAGAMUFFIN MUFFLIN BEGGARLY
SHABROON TITMOUSE
RAGAU (FATHER OF —) PHALEC
RAGE GO AWE FAD RAG WAX BAIT
BATE BEEF FARE FOAM FRET
FUFF FUME FUNK FUNX FURY
GLOW GRIM HEAT PELT RAMP
RASE RESE TAVE TEAR WOOD
ANGER BRETH CHAFE CRAZE
FUROR PADDY STORM TEAVE
TEVEL VOGUE WRATH FRENZY
FURORE PELTER TYAUVE
BLUSTER FASHION MADNESS
PASSION RUFFIAN TEMPEST
INSANITY WOODNESS
PADDYWACK
(BE IN A —) RANT
RAGFISH ICOSTEID
RAGGED DUDDY HARSH FRAYED

JAGGED SCOURY UNEVEN
SHAGRAG SHREDDY TATTERY
SCRAGGLY SCRATCHY TATTERED
RAGGED ROBIN ROBIN CUCKOO
RAGGEE MAND RAGI MARUA
MANDUA KORAKAN ELEUSINE
RAGGLE-TAGGLE MOTLEY
RAGING HOT GRIM WILD YOND
RABID FIERCE FURIAL FERVENT
MADDING PELTING VIOLENT
FLAGRANT FURIBUND WRATHFUL
RAGOUT SALMI GOULASH
HARICOT TERRINE SALPICON
CHIPOLATA PULPATONE
(— OF GAME) SALMI SALMIS
RAGPICKER BUNTER RAGMAN
TATTER
RAGWEED HAYWEED HOGWEED
AMBROSIA IRONWEED KINGHEAD
KINGWEED RICHWEED FRANSERIA
RAGWORT CUSHAG JACOBY
BENWEED CAMMOCK SEGGROM
LIFEROOT
RAHAM (FATHER OF —) SHEMA
(SON OF —) JORKOAM
RAID RADE ROAD TALA FORAY
HARRY PINCH REISE REIVE
BODRAG CREACH FORAGE
HARASS INROAD MOLEST PANYAR
RAZZIA BODRAGE BORDRAG
CHAPPOW DESCENT JAYHAWK
OUTFALL OUTRAKE OUTRIDE
OUTROAD SPREATH COMMANDO
SPOILING
(— ORCHARDS) SCRUMP
(AIR —) BLITZ
(BOMBING —) PRANG
(CATTLE —) SPREAGH SPREATH
(MAKE A — ON) BUST
(WARLIKE —) HERSHIP
RAIDER REDLEG BUSHWACK
RAIL BAN BAR BULL COOT GIRD
JEST KOKO LIST MOHO RANT
RAVE SKID SORA TRAM WEKA
WING CRAKE EASER FENCE
GUARD PLATE RAVEL REILE
SCOFF SCOLD SLENT STANG
STANK STEEL SWEAR BANTER
BEDWAY CALLET FENDER
RUNNER SKITTY TIKLIN BIDCOCK
BILCOCK COURLAN INVEIGH
OARCOCK RACKWAY TOPRAIL
BULLHEAD CANCELLI CORNBIRD
PORTLAST TOADBACK VIGNOLES
BRANDRETH BRANDRITH
(— AT) JEST CURSE SCOFF RATTLE
REVILE BETONGUE
(— OF BED) STOCK
(— OF RAILWAY SWITCH) TONGUE
(— ON GUN PLATFORM) TRINGLE
(— ON HAY VEHICLE) THRIPPLE
(— ON SHIP) FIFE
(ALTAR —) SEPTUM
(ARCHED —) HOOPSTICK
(CHAIR —) LEDGE
(FENCE —) RIDER
(PART OF —) BED TIE FROG JOINT
SPIKE BALLAST SLEEPER
CROSSTIE BASEPLATE FISHPLATE
(PL.) RAILING CANCELLI
RAILROAD
(PREF.) RALLI
RAIL CHAIR CARRIAGE

RAILING BAR SEPT GRATE RAVEL
FENDER FIDDLE GITTER VEDIKA
BARRIER GALLERY PARAPET
CANCELLI ESPALIER HANDRAIL
PARCLOSE TRAVERSE
RAILLERY GAFF HASH JEST JOKE
RAGE CHAFF RALLY SPORT
BANTER BLAGUE HOORAY
HURRAH SATIRE TRIFLE MOCKERY
BADINAGE DICACITY RABULOUS
RIDICULE PERSIFLAGE
RAILROAD EL ROAD YARD STEEL
COALER FEEDER GRANGER
TRAMWAY CEINTURE ELEVATED
(— CAR) IDLER
RAILROAD CHAIR SADDLE
RAILSPLITTER MAULER
RAILWAY ROAD TUBE COGWAY
SUBWAY COGROAD INCLINE
TRANVIA WIREWAY ASCENSOR
PLATEWAY TRAMROAD
FUNICULAR CREMAILLERE
RAIMENT RAY GARB CLOTH
APPAREL CLOTHES VESTURE
CLOTHING DRESSING WARDROBE
(SPLENDID —) SHEEN
(SUFF.) ESTHES
RAIN WET ISLE MIST SMUR ULAN
WEET BLASH STORM DELUGE
MIZZLE SERENE SHOWER SOAKER
DRIZZLE DOWNPOUR SPRINKLE
(— AND SNOW) SLEET
(— HEAVILY) TEEM
(— LIGHTLY) SMUR SPIT SPRINKLE
(— OF SPARKS) SHOWER
(DRIZZLING —) DAG
(FINE —) MIST SEREIN SERENE
(GOD OF —) PARJANYA
(HEAVY —) PASH SPOUT
(LIGHT —) SEREIN WEATHER
HEATDROPS
(SHORT —) SHOWER
(SUDDEN —) SKEW
(WHIRLING —) SKIRL
(WIND-DRIVEN —) SCAT
(PL.) VARSHA
(PREF.) HYET(O) OMBRI OMBRO
PLUVI(O)
RAINBIRD KOEL TOMFOOL
STORMBIRD
(— OF JAMAICA) HUNTER
RAINBOW ARC BOW ARCH IRIS
GAMUT METEOR SUNBOW
ILLUSION
(AUTHOR OF —) LAWRENCE
(BROKEN —) WINDDOG WINDGALL
(CHARACTER IN —) TOM ANNA
WILL ANTON LYDIA LENSKY
URSULA BRANGWEN SKREBENSKY
(PREF.) IRID(O)
RAINBOW FISH GUPPY MAORI
RAINBOW RUNNER SKIPJACK
SHOEMAKER
RAINBRINGER KACHINA
RAINCOAT MAC MACK MINO
PONCHO BURSATI OILSKIN
SLICKER GOSSAMER MACINTOSH
MACKINTOSH
RAINFALL PLOUT SKIFF SKIFT
ONDING STEMPLOW
RAIN GAGE UDOMETER
RAINSPOUT RONE
RAINSTORM WET

SPATE SCOWTHER
RAIN TREE SAMAN ZAMAN
GUANGO ZAMANG ALGAROBA
GENISARO MONKEYPOD
RAINY WET KICK FRESH JUICY
RAYNE SAPPY WEETY BLASHY
DRIPPY HYETAL PLUNGY SPONGY
PLUVIAL PLUVINE SHOWERY
WEEPING CLUTTERY PLUVIOUS
SLATTERY
(— SEASON) VARSHA
RAISE END SET WIN BUMP BUOY
GROW HAIN HEFT HIGH HIKE
HOVE JACK KICK LEVY LIFT MAKE
OVER REAR ROOF STIR TELD TOSS
AREAR BLOCK BOOST BREED
BUILD CAIRN CHOCK CRANE
DIGHT ELATE ENSKY ERECT
EXALT FORCE GREET HANCE
HEAVE HEEZE HEVEN HOISE
HOIST HORSE LEAVE MOUND
MOUNT PRICK RISER ROUSE
VOICE ARRECT ASSIST BETTER
CREATE DOUBLE EMBOSS EXHALE
GATHER LEAVEN MUSTER
NANTLE PREFER REMOVE RISING
UPHOLD UPLIFT ADDRESS
ADVANCE COLLECT ELEVATE
ENHANCE LIGHTEN NOURISH
PRESENT PROMOTE RECRUIT
UPSHOOT ANGELIZE HEIGHTEN
INSPIRIT RELEVATE
(— A BUMP) CLOUR
(— A NAP) MOZE TEASE TEASEL
TEAZLE
(— ALOFT) SPHERE
(— ANCHOR) CAT
(— BY ASSESSMENT) LEVY
(— BY HAND) NOB
(— CLAMOR) BRAWL
(— IN PITCH) SHARP
(— OBJECTIONS) CAVIL BOGGLE
(— ONESELF) CHIN
(— TO HIGH DEGREE) STRAIN
(— TO 3RD POWER) CUBE
(— UP) BUOY AREAR ELATE EXALT
EXTOL ELEVATE CIVILIZE
RAISED HIGH UPSET ARRECT
HOGGED BULLATE EXALTED
ELEVATED MOUNTANT UPLIFTED
UPRAUGHT
RAISIN FIG PASA PLUM LEXIA
ZIBEB REYSON CURRANT
SULTANA MUSCATEL
(PL.) SPICE
RAISING ATOLLENT
RAJ RULE REIGN
RAJA KING CHIEF RULER PRINCE
PANGLIMA
RAJMAHAL CREEPER JITI CHITI
JETEE JEETEE
RAJPUT SAMMA SUMRA GAHRWAL
RAZBOOCH
RAKE GO HOE RIP WAY COMB
PATH RACK RAFF RAVE REAP
ROAM ROUE ROVE RUCK BLOOD
CLAUT PITCH SCOOP SCOUR
SULKY TIGER PLUNGE RABBLE
ROLLER SEARCH RANSACK
SCRATCH LOTHARIO SCRAPPLE
(— GRAIN) GAVEL
(— UP IN ROWS) HACK
(— WITH GUNFIRE) SCOUR

STRAFE ENFILADE
(— WITHOUT TEETH) LUTE
(BUCK —) SWEEP
(CRANBERRY —) SCOOP
(HORSE-DRAWN —) GLEANER
(OYSTER —) GLEANER
(PART OF —) BOW TANG TINE
TOOTH HANDLE FERRULE
RAKEHELL RASCAL IMMORAL
LIBERTINE
RAKER GUMMER ROOKER
RAKISH SLANG JAUNTY SPORTY
WANTON DASHING CARELESS
DEVILISH RANTEPOLE RANTIPOLE
RALE RATTLE SIFFLE SIBILUS
RHONCHUS
RALLENTANDO DRAG RITARD
RALLY KID DRAG JOKE MOCK RELY
STIR BULLY JOLLY QUEER BANTER
DERIDE REVIVE COLLECT
CAMPOREE CLAMBAKE RIDICULE
SPEAKING
RAM PUN TIP TUP BUCK CRAM
PACK RAME STEM TEAP TOOP
ARIES CHOKE CRASH POACH
ROGER SLIDE BEETLE CHASER
RANCID ROSTRUM BULLDOZER
WETHERHOG WETHERTEG
(— OF WAR VESSEL) SPUR
(CASTRATED —) WETHER
(FATHER OF —) HEZRON
JERAHMEEL
(SON OF —) AMMINADAB
(PREF.) CRIO
RAMA MELCHORA
(FATHER OF —) DASHARATHA
(MOTHER OF —) KAUSHALYA
(WIFE OF —) SITA
RAMADA ARBOR PORCH
RAMAGE WILD RAMMISH
UNTAMED
RAMAGE HAWK BRANCHER
RAMBLE RAKE ROAM ROVE SKIR
WALK JAUNT PROWL RANGE
TRACE TROLL DODDER RUMBLE
STROLL VAGARY WAMBLE
WANDER ENRANGE EXCURSE
SAUNTER SPROGUE TROUNCE
FLAGARIE SCRAMBLE SPATIATE
(— AIMLESSLY) HAZE
RAMBLING GAD VAGARY CURSORY
DEVIOUS WINDING DESULTORY
SCATTERED
RAMBUNCTIOUS RUDE WILD
ROUGH UNRULY UNTAMED
VIOLENT
RAMBUTAN SOAPWORT
RAMENTUM PALEA PALET SCALE
SHAVING
RAMIE HEMP RHEA ORTIGA
RAMIFICATION ARM RAMUS
BRANCH OFFSHOOT OUTGROWTH
RAMIFY BRANCH SPRANGLE
RAMMAN ADAD ADDA ADDU
RAMMED EARTH PISE
RAMMEL TRASH RUMMLE RUBBISH
RAMMER TUP HEAD BOSER
PUNNER WORMER
RAMONA (HUSBAND OF —)
ALESSANDRO
RAMOSE CLADOSE BRANCHED
RAMOTH (FATHER OF —) BANI
RAMP ROB RUN BANK EXIT HOAX

RAGE RANK SLIP CREEP STORM
EASING FROLIC GARLIC FOOTPAD
SLIPWAY SWINDLE GRADIENT
RAMPAGE RAGE ROMP BINGE
SPRAY SPREE STORM RANDAN
RAMPAGEOUS UNRULY GLARING
RAMPANT VIOLENT
RAMPANT RANK PROFUSE
SALIANT SALIENT SEGREANT
RAMPART BRAY LINE WALL
AGGER ARGIN ABATIS VALLUM
ABATTIS BULWARK DEFENSE
PARAPET RAMPIER BARBICAN
MUNITION BARRICADE
RAMPER LAMPREY
RAMPIKE SNAG RAUNPICK
ROUNSPIK
RAMROD FORMAL GUNSTICK
RAMSHACKLE RUDE UNRULY
RICKETY SHACKLY UNSTEADY
RAMSON RAMP GARLIC BUCKRAM
(PL.) RAMS
RAMSTAM RASH HEADLONG
RECKLESS
RAN ARN
(HUSBAND OF —) AESIR
RANCEL SEARCH RANSACK
RANCH RUN FARM TEAR FINCA
CHACRA OUTFIT SPREAD
WRENCH STATION ESTANCIA
HACIENDA
RANCHE NATURAL
RANCHER COWMAN GRAZIER
SHEEPMAN CATTLEMAN
RANCID RAM RANK SOUR FROWY
RAFTY RASTY REEST RESTY
FROWZY ODIOUS ROTTEN
MALODOROUS
RANCOR GALL HATE SPITE ENMITY
GRUDGE HATRED MALICE
ACRIMONY
RANCOROUS ACRID VENOMOUS
MALIGNANT ACRIMONIOUS
(NOT —) GOOD
RAND EDGE ROON RUND BORDER
HIGHLAND
RANDAN SPREE RANTAN UPROAR
RAMPAGE
RANDOM BANK FORCE LOOSE
STRAY CASUAL CHANCE CHANCY
AIMLESS RANDALL RENDOUN
SHOTGUN UNAIMED VAGRANT
ALEATORIC
(AT —) HOBNOB
(SOMEWHAT —) LONG
RANDY LEWD RUDE RUDAS SPREE
BEGGAR VIRAGO LUSTFUL
RIOTOUS CAROUSAL
RANGE KEN ROW ALLY AREA BEAT
GATE GAUT GHAT LINE RAIK
RAKE RANK ROAM ROVE SCUM
SHOT TOUR WALK ALIGN BLANK
CARRY FIELD GAMUT HILLS ORBIT
REACH SCOPE SCOUR SHOOT
SPACE STAND START SWEEP
SWING VERGE COURSE DANGER
EXTEND EXTENT LENGTH RADIUS
RAMBLE SCOUTH SPHERE STROLL
WANDER BOWSHOT COMPASS
DEMESNE EARSHOT GUNSHOT
HABITAT HORIZON PURVIEW
CLASSIFY DIAPASON EARREACH
EYEREACH LATITUDE PANORAMA

(— FOR FOOD) FORAGE
(— OF ARROW) FLIGHT
(— OF BRICK) COURSE
(— OF FOOD) FARE
(— OF FREQUENCIES) SPECTRUM
(— OF GOVERNANCE) DOMAIN
(— OF GUN) CARRY RANDOM
GUNSHOT
(— OF HILLS) GAUT GHAT HUMP
TIER CHAIN GHAUT RIDGE SIERRA
SAWBACK BACKBONE
(— OF ORGANISM) BIOZONE
(— OF PASTURE) GANG
(— OF PLANKS) STRING
(— OF PRINTING TYPES) SERIES
(— OF SIGHT) KEN SCAN EYESHOT
KENNING
(— OF TONES) KEY SCALE
GRADATION
(— OF VISION) EYE SIGHT KENNING
(— OF WAVELENGTH) BAND
(— OVER) SWEEP
(— TOP) COOKTOP
(ARCHERY —) BUTTS GREEN
(COOKING —) KITCHENER
(PART OF —) CAP DOOR FLUE
HEAD KNOB OVEN RACK TRIM
VENT GRATE GUARD GUIDE
HINGE PANEL BURNER GASKET
HANDLE WINDOW BROILER
CONTROL GRIDDLE DRIPPLATE
BACKSPLASH
(SHOOTING —) MES GALLERY
(TEMPERATURE —) CONE
RANGE FINDER STADIA
MEKOMETER
RANGE POLE PICKET
RANGER ROVER ROBBER
MONTERO FIREWARD
RANGOON SHERRY
RANGY OPEN ROOMY SPACIOUS
RANK RAY ROW SEE DANK FOOT
FORM FOXY GOLE GREE LINE
RAMP RATE ROOM SEED SOUR
STEP TIER CENSE CHOIR CLASS
FETID FRANK FUSTY GRADE
GROSS HONOR LEVEL MARCH
ORDER PLACE QUIRE RANGE
ROWTY SIEGE SPACE STALL
STAND STATE TCHIN TRAIN
AFFAIR AGREGE DEGREE ERMINE
ESTEEM FIGURE LAVISH PARAGE
RATING SPHERE STATUS STRONG
CALIBER CALLING DIGNITY
DUKEDOM EARLDOM FOOTING
GLARING RAMMISH RAMPANT
STATION WORSHIP ABSOLUTE
EARLSHIP ENSIGNCY EQUIPAGE
FLAGRANT GENTRICE LADYSHIP
PALPABLE STINKING
MALODOROUS
(— AND FILE) RUCK RANGALE
(— OF GENTLEMEN) GENTRY
GENTILITY
(— OF SERGEANT-AT-LAW) COIF
COIFFE
(ACADEMIC —) AGREGE
(BOTTOMMOST —) CELLAR
(HIGH —) PURPLE DIGNITY
EMINENCE
(LOWEST —) SCOURING
(MILITARY —) GRADE AIRMAN
CORNET CHAOUSH

(NOBLE —) ADELAIDE
(ONE HIGHEST IN —) SUPREMO
(SAME —) KIND
(SOCIAL —) CLASS ESTATE
HERALDRY POSITION
(SUFF.) CY HEAD HOOD
RANKLE FRET CHAFE FESTER
INJURE RANCOR DESTROY
INFLAME
RANSACK RIG DRAG RAKE RIPE
SACK SEEK RIFLE DACKER
RANCEL SEARCH PLUNDER
RUMMAGE
RANSOM FINE RAME REDEEM
RESCUE RESGAT EXPIATE
RANSTEAD TOADFLAX
RANT CAVE HUFF RAIL RAND
MOUTH REVEL ROUSE SCOLD
SPOUT STEVEN BOMBAST
CAROUSE DECLAIM FROTHING
RODOMONTADE
(— AND RAVE) FAUNCH
RANTING RANTISM TEARCAT
RANTIPOLE WILD CARROT RAKISH
SEESAW ROMPING
RANULA CYST FROGTONGUE
(PREF.) BATRACH(O)
RANUNCULUS MOSS GOLLAND
CROWFOOT HEDGEHOG
BUTTERCUP
RAOULIA HAASTIA
RAP BOB CON BLOW CHAP GRAB
KNAP TIRL TUNK WRAP CLICK
CLINK FLIRT KNOCK STEAL
TOUCH BARTER HANDLE YANKER
RAPACIOUS CRUEL GREEDY
TAKING RAVENING RAVENOUS
RAPACITY RAVEN RAVIN CUPIDITY
EXTORTION VULTURISM
RAPE COLE ABUSE COLZA FORCE
NAVET NAVEW TOUCH ATTACK
FELONY RAPEYE TURNIP ASSAULT
DESPOIL NAVETTE OPPRESS
OUTRAGE PLUNDER RAPTURE
STUPRUM VIOLATE COLESEED
COLEWORT DISHONOR STUPRATE
SUPPRESS
RAPE OF THE LOCK (AUTHOR OF —
) POPE
(CHARACTER IN —) ARIEL BETTY
PETRE PLUME SPLEEN BELINDA
UMBRIEL CLARISSA THALESTRIS
RAPESEED COLZA RAVISON
RAPHA (FATHER OF —) BINEA
RAPHU (SON OF —) PALTI
RAPHUS DIDUS
RAPID GAY FAST CHUTE HASTY
MOSSO QUICK ROUND SAULT
SHARP SHOOT SHUTE TOSTO
WINGY RIFFLE SPEEDY WINGED
CURSIVE SCHNELL SKELPIN
STICKLE TANTIVY SLAPPING
SPEEDFUL OVERNIGHT
(—S IN RIVER) SAULT DALLES
RIFFLE STICKLE CATARACT
(MORE —) STRETTO
RAPIDITY HASTE SPEED RADEUR
CELERITY VELOCITY
RAPIDLY APACE CHEAP FLEETLY
HASTILY SPEEDILY QUICKFOOT
RAPIER TUCK TUKE BILBO ESTOC
SHARP STOCK VERDUN TOASTER
RAPINE FORCE RAVIN PILLAGE

PLUNDER VIOLENCE
RAPPACCINI (DAUGHTER OF —)
BEATRICE
RAPPAREE ROBBER CREAGHT
VAGABOND
RAPPORT ACCORD HARMONY
RELATION AGREEMENT
RAPSCALLION ROGUE RASCAL
VILLAIN HOSEBIRD VAGABOND
RAPT LOST WRAP TENSE INTENT
RAVISH TRANCE CARRIED
ENGAGED RAPTURE ABDUCTED
ABSORBED ECSTATIC
RAPTORES RAPACES
RAPTURE JOY BLISS DELIGHT
ECSTASY PAROXYSM RHAPSODY
RAPTUROUS RHAPSODIC
RARA AVIS PHENIX RARITY
WONDER PHOENIX
RARE FINE REAL SELD THIN ALONE
EARLY GREAT ANTRIN CHOICE
GEASON INCONY SCARCE SEENIL
SELDOM SINDLE SPARSE SUBTLE
SULLEN UNIQUE ANTERIN
CURIOUS TENUOUS UNUSUAL
CRITICAL SELDSEEN SINGULAR
UNCOMMON RECHERCHE
(PREF.) AREO MANO SPAN(I)(O)
RAREFACTION POROSITY
RAREFIED HIGH THIN SUBTILE
ABSTRUSE AETHERED ESOTERIC
RAREFY THIN DILUTE EXTENUATE
RARELY SELDEN SELDOM
RARENESS RARITY TENUITY
SCARCITY
RARITY SWAN CURIO RELIC
RARIETY TENUITY RARENESS
(PL.) CURIOSA
RASCAL BOY CAD DOG IMP LOW
RAP BASE DUCK FILE KITE LOON
MEAN SHAG SMAK CATSO FILTH
GANEF GIPSY KNAVE ROGUE
SCAMP SHELM SLAVE SMAIK
THIEF ABLACH BEGGAR BRIBER
BUDZAT BUGGER COQUIN
HARLOT LIMMER RABBLE RAGGIL
RIBALD SCHELM SORROW TINKER
BLEEDER CAMOOCH CULLION
GLUTTON HALLION HESSIAN
NEBULON PEASANT RAPTRIL
SHELLUM SKEEZIX SKELLUM
VILLAIN BEZONIAN BLIGHTER
HOSEBIRD LIDDERON PALLIARD
PICAROON RAKEHELL RUBIATOR
SKALAWAG SPALPEEN TAISTREL
VAGABOND WIDDIFOW
RAPSCALLION
RASCALITY FOIST RABBLE
KNAVERY ROGUING RASCALRY
RASCALLY BASE MEAN ROOKY
ARRANT GALLUS LIMMER
GALLOWS KNAVISH RAGGILY
SHAGRAG WIDDIFOW
RASE PULL RAIS RAZE ERASE
PLUCK INCISE SNATCH
RASH ID CUT BRASH HARDY
HASTY HEADY SLASH SLICE
DARING SUDDEN UNWARY
URGENT BULRUSH HOTSPUR
RABBISH RAMSTAM ROSEOLA
BLIZZARD CARELESS ERUPTION
EXANTHEM HEADLONG HEEDLESS
MADBRAIN OVERSEEN PRESSING

RECKLESS TEMEROUS
(SUFF.) ANTHEMA
(SKIN —) ID IDE
RASHER SLICE COLLOP TRIFLE
COLOPPE
RASHLY HEADILY HEADLONG
RASHNESS RAGE RESE HASTE
ACRISY TEMERITY HEADINESS
RASKOLNIK POPOVETS
RASP RUB FILE RAPE ERUCT
GRATE TOOTH RAPEYE RUBBER
RUGINE RIFFLER DENTICLE
(SHOEMAKER'S —) FLOAT
RASPBERRY AKPEK BAZOO MOLKA
AVARIN RASPIS PLUMBOG
ARNDERRY BLACKCAP DOGBERRY
CUTHBERT MULBERRY RESPASSE
ROSACEAN SALMONBERRY
RASPING HARSH ROUGH STOOR
STOUR HOARSE RASION RAZZLY
GRATING RAUCOUS GUTTERAL
(PL.) SCOBS
RASPY HARSH GRATING SCREAKY
SCRABBLY
RASSE CIVET WEASEL
RASSELAS (AUTHOR OF —)
JOHNSON
(CHARACTER IN —) IMLAC PEKUAH
NEKAYAH RASSELAS
(MENTOR OF —) IMLAC
(SISTER OF —) NEKAYAH
RAT BUCK DAMN DRAT HEEL NOKI
ROTN SCAB VOLE KIORE LOUSE
METAD RATON SELVA ZEMMI
ZEMNI GNAWER MURINE RODENT
ROTTAN SLEPEZ VERMIN YUNGAS
CUSHION CONFOUND INFORMER
MYOMORPH
(INDIAN —) KOK
RATAPLAN RATTAN RATTLE
RATCH RASH REND ROCH SPOT
NOTCH STREAK RATCHET
STRETCH
RATCHET DOG PAWL CLICK
DETENT ROCHET
RAT CHINCHILLA ABROCOME
RATE LAY RAG SET CESS CHOP
DEEM GAIT GIVE HAND KIND
RANK RATA ABUSE CULET CURVE
PRIZE RATIO REBUT SCOLD STENT
STYLE VALUE ZAKAT ASSIZE
GALLOP ACCOUNT BESHREW
CARTAGE DESERVE FASHION
MILLAGE REPROVE CLASSIFY
ESTIMATE QUANTIFY
(— HIGHLY) PRICE
(— OF ASCENT) GRADE
(— OF DRAINAGE) FREENESS
(— OF EXCHANGE) BATTA
(— OF INTEREST) COUPON
DISCOUNT
(— OF MOTION) BAT SPEED
(— OF MOVEMENT) PACE TEMPO
(— OF RECKONING) FOOT
(— OF SPEED) BAT AGOGE
(— OF TAX) CENSE
(— OF TRANSFER) FLUX
(— OF TUITION) CULET
(— SCHEDULE) TARIFF
(AT ANY —) HURE
(BIRTH —) NATALITY
RATE BOOK STREET
RATEL BADGER BURIER

RATH CAR HILL REUT RUTH EARLY
MOUND QUICK REUTE SWIFT
BETIMES CHARIOT YOUTHFUL
RATHER Y BUT GEY LIKE SOON
LOURD QUITE ASTITE BEFORE
FAIRLY HELDER KINDLY PRETTY
RUTHER SEEMLY TIDDER TITTER
EARLIER INSTEAD MIDDLING
SOMEWHAT
(— THAN) ERE BEFORE
RATIFICATION AMEN RATE
SANCTION
RATIFY AMEN PASS SEAL SIGN
VISA ENSEAL FASTEN OBSIGN
APPROVE CONFIRM SCEPTER
CANONIZE RODONATE SANCTION
VALIDATE
RATING RANK CENSE CLASS
GRADE WRITER STANDING
RATIO Q PI GAIN RATE SINE SLIP
INDEX RESON SETUP SHEAR
ASPECT CAMBER DECADE
QUOTUM REASON REYSON
SECANT AVERAGE PORTION
CONTRAST SOLIDITY MULTIPLIER
PROPORTION
RATIOCINATION LOGIC THOUGHT
REASONING
RATION DOLE RATIO ALLOCATE
(— OF BREAD) TOMMY
(ANIMAL —) CHOW
(EXTRA —S) BUCKSHEE
(HOG —) SWILL
(PL.) FOOD BOUCH ETAPE
COMMON
RATIONAL SANE LUCID SOBER
LOGICAL REASONAL SENSIBLE
THINKING
RATIONALIZE THOB EXPLAIN
RATITE EMU MOA EMEU KIWI
RHEA OSTRICH STRUTHIAN
RAT KANGAROO TUNGO
POTOROO SQUEAKER
RATOON SHOOT SPROUT SUCKER
RATTAIL MULE ARREST
GRENADIER
RATTAN CANE SEGA ROTAN
BEJUCO ROTANG SWITCH
RATTOON
RATTLE DIN BIRL BURL REEL RICK
TIRL CHINK CLACK CROTAL
GRAGER HENPEN HURTLE
MARACA RACKLE RICKLE RIFFLE
ROTTLE RUCKLE RUTTLE
CHACKLE CLACKER CLAPPER
CLATTER CLICKET CREAKER
GNATTER GROGGER SHATTER
SISTRUM SKELLAT CAIXINHA
CHOCALHO COWWHEAT
NOISEMAKER
(CRIER'S —) CLAPPER
(IRON —) SKELLAT SKILLET
(PREF.) CROTALI
(SUFF.) CROTIC
RATTLEBRAINED MADCAP
RATTLER LIE ROMBLE RUMBLER
RATTLESNAKE BELLTAIL
CASCABEL CASCAVEL CROTALID
MASSASAUGA SIDEWINDER
(— PLANTAIN) NETLEAF RATSBANE
RATTLESNAKE ROOT BUGBANE
JOYLEAF
RATTLETRAP GEWGAW

TRIFLE RICKETY
RATTLING REEL BRISK HUSKY
SLAPPING SPLENDID CREPITANT
RATTY NASTY SHABBY UNKEMPT
WORTHLESS
RATWA MUNTJAC
RAUCOUS LOUD HARSH COARSE
HOARSE SQUAWKY STRIDENT
RAUN ROE ROWN SPAWN
RAUPO CATTAIL
RAVAGE EAT PREY RIOT RUIN
SACK FORAY HARRY HAVOC
SPOIL WASTE FORAGE DESPOIL
DESTROY OVERRUN PILLAGE
PLUNDER DEFLOWER DESOLATE
POPULATE SPOLIATE
RAVANA (SISTER OF —)
SHURPANAKHA
RAVE MAD RAGE RAND WOOD
AWEDE BLURB CRUSH RATHE
ROUSE STORM TAVER DELIRE
TAIVER WANDER
RAVEL FAG RUN FRAY FRET REYLE
SNARL EVENER LADDER RADDLE
RUNNER SLOUGH TANGLE
CONFUSE INVOLVE PERPLEX
RAILING UNWEAVE
RAVELIN RABLIN OUTWORK
DEMILUNE
RAVEN CRAKE RALPH CORBEL
CORBIE CORBIN FORAGE RAVINE
WAYBIRD
(BRIGHT —) BERTRAM
(SUFF.) CORAX
RAVENING CRUEL RABIDE
RAVENOUS GREEDY LUPINE
TOOTHY WOLFISH RAPACIOUS
VORACIOUS
RAVINE DEN GAP GUT LIN DELL
DRAW GILL GULL KHOR KHUD
LINN LLYN SIKE WADI BREAK
BUNNY CHASM CHINE CLOVE
COULE DONGA FLUME GHYLL
GLACK GORGE GOYAL GOYLE
GRIFF GRIKE GULCH GULLY
HEUCH KLOOF SLADE SLAKE
STRID ARROYO CLEUCH CLOUGH
COULEE DIMBLE DINGLE DUMBLE
GULLET GULLEY HOLLOW NULLAH
RAMBLA SHEUGH STRAIT
BARRANCA QUEBRADA
RAVING RAVERY DELIRANT
FRENZIED DELIRIOUS
RAVISH ROB RAPE ABUSE CHARM
FORCE HARRY SPOIL ABDUCT
ATTACK DEFILE AFFORCE
CORRUPT DELIGHT ENFORCE
OPPRESS OUTRAGE OVERJOY
PLUNDER POLLUTE VIOLATE
VITIATE DEFLOWER ENTRANCE
STUPRATE SUPPRESS UNMAIDEN
RAVISHER RAPTER RAVENER
RAVISHMENT ECSTASY RAPTURE
TRANSPORT
RAW RA ROW BRUT LASH REAR
RUDE BLEAK CHILL CRUDE FRESH
GREEN HARSH NAKED RAFTY
SHARP WERSH BITTER CALLOW
COARSE CUTCHA KUTCHA UNRIPE
VULGAR WAIRSH NATURAL
NOUVEAU UNBOUND VERDANT
WEARISH WEERISH IMMATURE
RAWBONED UNCOOKED

UNEDITED VISCERAL
(— AND COLD) CRIMPY
(PREF.) OMO
RAWBONED RAW BONY LEAN
GAUNT LANKY SCRAG SCRAWNY
RAWHIDE WHIP WHANG COWHIDE
COWSKIN GREENHIDE PARFLECHE
RAWNESS CRUDITY
RAY BEAM BETA DORN SOIL WIRE
ALPHA BRAND DRESS EQUIP
FLAIR FLAKE FLATH GLEAM
GLEED ORDER RAYON ROKER
SKATE BATOID CHUCHO OBISPO
RADIAL RADIUS RAIOID SEPHEN
STREAM TRYGON VISUAL BATFISH
COWFISH DEWBEAM DRILVIS
FIDDLER HOMELYN PLACOID
RAIMENT TORPEDO WAIREPO
BRACHIUM MOONBEAM
NUMBFISH PLOWFISH PYLSTERT
STINGRAY
(— OF LIGHT) GLINT SPEAR
GLANCE SUNRAY SUNBEAM
(— OF STARFISH) ARM
(FEMALE —) MAID
(FIN —) SPINE
(WITHOUT —S) ABACTINAL
(PREF.) BATO
(ELECTRIC —) NARC(O)
RAYED
(PREF.) ACTIN(IO)(O)
(SUFF.) ACT(INE)
(— WITH IMPAIRMENT) LEXIA
RAYON BEAM RADIUS DUCHESS
RAZE CUT FLAT RUIN ARASE
ERASE LEVEL STREW ARRACE
EFFACE SCRAPE SLIGHT UNPILE
DESTROY SCRATCH SUBVERT
UNBUILD DEMOLISH
RAZOR SHIV TUSK MUSSEL RASOIR
SHAVER RATTLER SLASHER
CUTTHROAT
(PREF.) XYR(O)
RAZORBACK STATE ARKANSAS
RAZOR-BILLED AUK FALK TINK
MURRE NODDY SCOOT SCOUT
SKOOT TINKER SKIMMER WILLOCK
ROCKBIRD
RAZOR CLAM PIROT RASOR
SOLEN SPOUT RASOIR
RAZZ PAN CHIACK RIDICULE
RASPBERRY
RAZZIA RAID FORAY INCURSION
RAZZING RAZOO
RE RAY ANENT ACTION MATTER
REGARDING
REACH GO GET HIT RAX RUN WIN
BEAT COME FIND GAIN HAWK
HENT MAKE PUSH REEK REIK
RYKE SHOT SORT SPAN SPIT
TEND BRACE CROSS FETCH
GRASP PERCH RANGE RETCH
TOUCH ADVENE ARRIVE ATTAIN
DANGER EXTEND FATHOM
LENGTH OBTAIN SNATCH STREEK
STRIKE ACHIEVE COMPASS
CONTACT GUNSHOT OVERGET
POSSESS RECOVER STRETCH
(— ACROSS) SPAN OVERSTRIDE
(— AN END) STAY
(— BY EFFORT) ATTAIN
(— BY FIGURING) STRIKE
(— FORTH) EXTEND

(— GOAL) HAIL
(— OF WATER) LODE
(— OUT) UTTER SPREAD STRETCH
(— TO) LINE
(— TOTAL) AMOUNT
(— UNDERSTANDING) AGREE
(— WITH END) ABUT
(EXTREME —) PITCH STRETCH
(TRY TO —) ASPIRE
(ULTIMATE —) PITCH
REACHER INGIVER
REACT ACT BUCK BEHAVE
RETROACT
REACTION BELT BUZZ KAHN WOHL
START WIDAL FAVISM RECOIL
BLOWOFF EMOTION FEELING
SETBACK BACKLASH BACKWASH
EXCHANGE GUARDING KICKBACK
RECEPTION
(— TIME) LATENCY
(ADVERSE —) BACKLASH
(ANGRY —) RISE
(VIOLENT —) SONG
REACTIONARY WHITE BOURBON
BACKWARD
REACTIVATED AWAKE ACTIVE
REACTIVATOR ACTIFIER
REACTOR PILE CHOKER FURNACE
INDUCTOR
READ GO CON KRI QRI SEE CALL
KERE QERI TURN CHOKE JUDGE
SOLVE WRITE PERUSE RELATE
FORESEE LEARNED LECTION
PREDICT ABOMASUM DECIPHER
FORETELL INDICATE OVERLOOK
(— ALOUD) LINE DEACON
(— HERE AND THERE) BROWSE
(— MECHANICALLY) RETINIZE
(— OF) SEE
(— OFF) DICTATE
(— PROOF) HORSE
(— RAPIDLY) DIP SKIM GOBBLE
(— SLOWLY) SPELL
(— SYSTEMATICALLY) FREQUENT
(— WITH PROFOUND ATTENTION)
PORE STUDY
READER PURSE DIPPER LECTOR
LISTER MAFTIR GRANTHI PISTLER
DEVOURER
(CHILD'S —) TENPENNY
(CHURCH —) LECTOR ANAGNOST
(PL.) FOLLOWING
READILY PAT LIEF YERN APTLY
PREST YERNE EASILY GAINLY
PROBABLY SPEEDILY
READINESS ART EASE GIFT PRESS
SKILL BELIEF GRAITH ADDRESS
FLUENCY FREEDOM ALACRITY
FACILITY GOODWILL
(IN —) APOISE AGAINST
READING KRI QRE QRI KERE KERI
QERI KTHIB KETHIB LESSON
LECTION LECTURE PERUSAL
SETTING
(PL.) PROCINCT
READING DESK AMBO LECTERN
READJUST MEND ADVANCE
(— TYPE) OVERRUN
READY UP APT BUN FIT RAD YAP
BAAN BAIN BOON BOUN BOWN
FREE GIRT GLIB GNIB RIFE RIPE
TALL YARE APERT EAGER FRACK
HANDY HAPPY PREDY PREST

PRIME QUICK SWIFT THERE TIGHT
ADROIT APPERT FACILE GRAITH
HEARTY PROMPT PREPARE
PRESENT RENABLE WILLING
CHEERFUL DEXTROUS HANDSOME
PREGNANT PREPARED PROVIDED
SKILLFUL
(— A COMPUTER) BOOT
(— FOR ACTION) ARM EXPEDITE
(— WITH WORDS) FLUENT
(NOT —) SET BOUND GROOM
FORWARD DISPOSED IMPROMPT
INCLINED
READY-MADE SALE STORE
BOUGHT
REAGENT ETCHANT REACTOR
TITRANT ALTERANT REACTIVE
NINHYDRIN
REAIA (FATHER OF —) MICAH
REAL BODY FAIR GOOD LEAL LEVY
PURE RIAL TRUE VERY VRAI
PAKKA PUCKA PUKKA RIGHT
ROYAL SOLID SOOTH ACTUAL
DINKUM ENTIRE HONEST THINGY
CORDIAL GENUINE GRADELY
SINCERE THINGAL CONCRETE
DEFINITE EXISTENT GRAITHLY
POSITIVE THINGISH
(EXTERNALLY —) TANGIBLE
(HALF —) PICAYUNE
(1-8TH —) TLAC TLACO
REALGAR ARSENIC ROSAKER
ZARNICH SANDARAC
REALISM REALITY LITERALISM
NATURALISM
REALISTIC HARD SOBER VIVID
EARTHLY LIFELIKE PROBABLE
REALITY FEAT TRUE BEING SOOTH
THING TRUTH ACTUAL DASEIN
EFFECT VERITY EARNEST
SUBJECT IDENTITY OVERSOUL
POSITIVE REALNESS TRUENESS
(LIMITED —) SOMEWHAT
(ULTIMATE —) GOD SOURCE
DIVINITY SUBSTANCE
(PL.) REALIA
REALIZATION PASS SENSE
CRUSHER FRUITION AWAKENING
REALIZE GAIN KNOW FETCH
LEARN SENSE EFFECT FULFIL
ACQUIRE CONCEIVE RECOGNIZE
REALIZED BODILY
(FULLY —) COMPLETE
REALLY ARU WIS ARAH HALF JUST
ARRAH TRULY WISHA FINELY
INDEED SIMPLY SURELY VERILY
ACTUALLY
(NOT —) ILL ALMOST
REALM LAND SOIL BOURN CLIME
RANGE REIGN REWME RICHE
BOURNE CIRCLE DEMAIN EMPIRE
HEAVEN REALTY REGION SPHERE
DEMESNE GAELDOM KINGDOM
NOTALIA ROYALME TERRENE
CLUBLAND DEVILDOM DOMINION
ELDORADO GHOSTDOM
GIPSYDOM NOTOGAEA
(— OF DARKNESS) PO
(— OF FABULOUS RICHNESS)
ELDORADO
(— OF THOR) THRUTHHEIM
THRUTHVANG
(MARINE —) NOTALIA TROPICALIA

(VISIONARY —) CLOUDLAND
(SUFF.) DOM
(— OF ANIMAL LIFE) ALIA
REALTY FEALTY REAUTE ROYALTY
REAM FOAM RIME SEED SKIM
CHEAT CREAM FROTH FRAISE
RHYMER STRETCH
(PL.) INSIDES OUTSIDES
REAMER BUR BURR SPUD DRIFT
RIMER BROACH CHERRY FRAISE
RANCER RHYMER RIMMER
WIDENER
REANIMATE WAKE RENEW REVIVE
RECREATE
REANIMATED AWAKE
REAP BAG CUT REP CROP RIPE
GLEAN SHEAR GARNER GATHER
SICKLE HARVEST
REAPER LORD COCKER TASKER
WINNER CRADLER SHEARER
SICKLER
(GRIM —) DEATH
REAPING HOOK SICKLE TWIBIL
CROTCHET
REAPPEARANCE RENTREE
EMERSION
REAR AFT BACK BUNT HIND HINT
JUMP LIFT STEN TOSS BREED
BUILD CARVE ERECT JUNCH
STEND ACHTER AROUSE CRADLE
FOSTER NURSLE SUCKLE
APPREAR ARRIERE EDUCATE
ELEVATE NOURISH NURTURE
UPBRING BUTTOCKS HINDMOST
REARWARD
(— CAREFULLY) TIDDLE
(NEARER THE —) AFTER
(TO THE —) BACK BEHIND
(TO THE — OF) ABAFT
REARED (— BY HAND) CADE
(DELICATELY —) SOYLED
REARHORSE MANTIS
REARING CABRE FRESNE PESADE
FORCENE RAMPANT
(— UP) STEND
REARRANGE DO ADJUST JIGGER
REORDER READJUST
REARRANGEMENT WAGNER
DIAGENESIS
REARWARD AFT BACKWARD
REASON PEG WAY HOTI NOUS
REDE SAKE TALK ARGUE CAUSE
COLOR COUNT LOGOS PROOF
RATIO SCORE SENSE SKILL THING
THINK TOPIC EXCUSE GROUND
MANNER MATTER MOTION
NOESIS ACCOUNT PREMISE
QUARREL SUBJECT TUITION
ARGUMENT ENCHESON LOGICIZE
VERNUNFT
(— FOR PRIDE) BOAST
(LACKING —) INEPT
(PREF.) RATI
REASONABLE FAIR JUST SANE
SOBER NATURAL SKILFUL
FEASIBLE MODERATE RATIONAL
SENSIBLE
REASONABLENESS EPIKY EPIKIKA
FITNESS FAIRNESS SOBRIETY
REASONABLY SOON
REASONER (FALLACIOUS —)
SOPHIST
REASONING LOGIC THOUGHT

ERGOTISM RATIONAL
(CLUMSY —) ARGAL
(FALLACIOUS —) CIRCLE
SOPHISTRY PARALOGISM
REASSEMBLE RELY
REASSEMBLY RALLY
REASSUME REVOKE REPRISE
REAVE ROB REFE SEIZE SPLIT
REMOVE DESPOIL PILLAGE
PLUNDER UNRAVEL
REB RABBI REBEL MISTER
REBAB GUSLE
REBATE BLUNT CHECK LESSEN
RIBBET DIMINISH DISCOUNT
DRAWBACK KICKBACK
REBEC LYRE SAROD RIBIBE
RUBIBLE
REBECCA (AUTHOR OF —)
DUMAURIER
(CHARACTER IN —) JACK BAKER
FRANK GILES MAXIM FAVELL
JULYAN CRAWLEY DANVERS
BEATRICE DEWINTER
(FATHER OF —) ISAAC
REBEKAH (BROTHER OF —) LABAN
(FATHER OF —) BETHUEL
(HUSBAND OF —) ISAAC
(SON OF —) ESAU JACOB
REBEL REB KICK RISE TURN BRAND
FAUVE ANARCH CROPPY MUTINE
REVOLT FRONDEUR MALCONTENT
(— IN ART) FAUVE
(PL.) REBELDOM
REBELLION MUTINY PUTSCH
REVOLT MISRULE UPRISING
REBELLIOUS RUSTY ANARCHIC
MUTINOUS AUDACIOUS
INSURGENT
REBIRTH REVIVAL
REBORN REDIVIVUS
REBOUND DAP HOP HANG KISS
STOT CANON CAROM STITE
BOUNCE CANNON CARROM
RECOIL RESILE RESULT BRICOLE
REDOUND RICOCHET SNAPBACK
(— ERRATICALLY) KICK
REBOUND CLIP RETAINER
REBUFF SLAP SNIB SNUB CHECK
FLING NOSER REPEL DEFEAT
DENIAL REBUKE REBUTE REFUTE
REPULSE
REBUILD MEND
REBUKE NIP WIG BAWL RATE
REDD SNEB SNIB SNUB TRIM
BARGE BLAME CHECK CHIDE
DRESS SAUCE SCOLD SNAPE
SNEAP TOUCH DIRDUM GANSEL
LESSON RATING RATTLE REHETE
REMORD THREAP CENSURE
CHIDING CORRECT HOTFOOT
LECTURE REPROOF REPROVE
SARCASM BLESSING BUSINESS
CHASTISE KEELHAUL REPROACH
SCORCHER THREAPEN UNDERNIM
CASTIGATE
REBUS BADGE ENIGMA PUZZLE
RIDDLE
REBUT REPEL RECOIL REFUTE
REPULSE RETREAT DISPROVE
RECALCITRANT UNRULY
RENITENT OBSTINATE RESISTANT
RECALL CITE BRING UNSAY
REMAND REMIND RETURN

REVOKE UNLOOK BETHINK
RECLAIM RETRACE RETRACT
REVIVAL UNSHOUT REMEMBER
WITHCALL WITHDRAW
REPRODUCE
(— FONDLY) CHERISH
RECANT UNSAY ABJURE REVOKE
UNSING DISAVOW RETRACT
SWALLOW PALINODE RENOUNCE
RECANTATION PALINODE
RECAPITULATE SUM UNITE
RECITE REPEAT RECOUNT
REHEARSE REITERATE
SUMMARIZE
RECAPITULATION EPANODOS
RECAPTURE RETAKE RECOVER
RECEDE DIE EBB BACK FADE STEP
VARY RECUR DEPART DIFFER
RETIRE SHRINK DECLINE DIGRESS
RETREAT CONTRACT DIMINISH
ELONGATE WITHDRAW
RECEIPT CHIT RECU RESET
APOCHA BINDER RECIPE
WARRANT
(PL.) GATE TAKE SALES INCOME
ENTRADA
RECEIVE GET BEAR FALL GAIN
HAVE HOLD TAKE ADMIT AFONG
CATCH GREET GUEST LATCH
RESET ACCEPT ASSUME BORROW
DERIVE GATHER HARBOR RECULE
BELIEVE CONTAIN EMBRACE
INHERIT SUSTAIN UNDERFO
PERCEIVE
(— A CRIMINAL) RESET
(— AS GUEST) FANG HOST VANG
GREET
(— AS MEMBER) INCEPT
(— AS REWARD) REAP
(— FROM LOTTERY) DRAW
(— SHEETS) FLY
(— WITH PLEASURE) GRATIFY
(PREF.) RECIPIO
RECEIVER FENCE PHONE PERNOR
SINDICO CYMAPHEN DONATARY
REHEATER
(— IN BANKRUPTCY) SINDICO
(— OF INCOME) PERNOR
(— OF STOLEN GOODS) LOCK
FENCE
(TELEGRAPH —) INKER INKWRITER
(TELEPHONE —) PHONE CYMAPHEN
RECEIVING PERNANCY
RECENSION REVIEW SURVEY
CENSURE CRITIQUE
RECENT HOT NEW LATE PUNY
ENDER FRESH GREEN HOURLY
LATELY LATTER MODERN
CURRENT HOLOCENE NEOTERIC
(MOST —) LAST
(PREF.) CAEN(O) CEN(O) NE(O)
(SUFF.) CENE
RECENTLY ANEW JUST LATE
NEWLY LASTLY LATELY FRESHLY
LATTERLY
RECENTNESS YOUTH
RECEPTACLE ARK BIN BOX CAN
CUP DIP FAT PAN TIN TUB URN
VAT BATH BOAT BOWL CASE
CELL CIST DOVE DROP FACK
FONT HELL HOLD INRO LOOM
RACK RECU SAFE SINK TIDY TOUR
ARBOR CARRY CREEL KIOSK KITTY

RESET SCOOP STEAN STEEN
TABLE TORUS BASKET BUCKET
BUTLER CARTON CUPULE DIPPER
DRAWER HAMPER HOPPER
MORTAR PITCHI POCKET SHRINE
TABLET TROUGH ASHTRAY
CAPSULE CARRIER CORBULA
DUSTBIN ENVELOP HEADBOX
LATRINE OMNIBUS OSSUARY
PARISON RECEIPT SANDBOX
SETTLER SOAPBOX STOWAGE
TRAVOIS BURSICLE CANISTER
CESSPOOL FOREBOOT GYNOBASE
HONEYPOT LOCKFAST OSSARIUM
OVERFLOW PERFUMER SPITTOON
STOCKPOT SEPULCHER
(— FOR ABANDONED INFANTS)
TOUR
(— FOR BONES) OSSUARY
OSSARIUM
(— FOR BROKEN TYPE) HELL
(— FOR BUTTER) RUSKIN
(— FOR COAL) BUNKER
(— FOR CONVEYING) APRON
(— FOR DRY ARTICLES) FAT
(— FOR FOUL THINGS) SINK
(— FOR GLASS BATCH) ARBOR
(— FOR HOLY WATER) FONT
(— FOR ORE-CRUSHING) MORTAR
(— FOR POKER CHIPS) KITTY
(— FOR SACRED RELICS) TABLE
SHRINE TABLET SEPULCHRE
(— FOR SAVINGS) SOCK
(— FOR SEWING MATERIALS) TIDY
(— FOR TREASURE) HANAPER
(— FOR TYPE CASES) RACK
(— FOR VOTES) SITULA
(— IN BOTTLE-MAKING MACHINE)
PARISON
(— OF CLAY OR STONE) STEAN
STEEN
(— OF FLOWER) THALAMUS
(— ON WEIGHING SCALES) PAN
(— OVER ALTAR) DOVE
(CLAY —) BOOT
(DILATED —) GYNOBASE
(ELECTRICAL —) BASEPLUG
(INCENSE —) ACERRA
(OPEN —) TRAY
(PURSELIKE —) BURSICLE
(TAILOR'S —) HELL
(WOODEN —) SEBILLA
(SUFF.) CLINE CLINIC CLINIUM
RECEPTION TEA ROUT COURT
CRUSH DIFFA LEVEE SALON
TREAT ACCOIL DURBAR RUELLE
SOIREE SQUASH ACCUEIL
COUCHEE MATINEE OVATION
PASSAGE RECEIPT RECUEIL
TEMPEST WELCOME ASSEMBLY
FUNCTION GREETING PERNANCY
REACTION SOCIABLE
ACCEPTANCE
(— AT BEDTIME) COUCHEE
(— OF NATIVE PRINCES) DURBAR
(— OF SOUND) AUDIO
(ARABIC —) DIFFA
(CORDIAL —) WELCOME
(CROWDED —) SQUASH
(FASHIONABLE —) LEVEE SALON
(WEDDING —) INFARE
RECEPTIVE OPEN SENSORY
OPENHANDED

RECEPTOR STOCK RECEIVER
DOMINATOR
RECERCELEE SARCELLY
RECESS ALA ARK BAY BOX COD
CUP PAN BOLE BUNK COVE DEEP
HOLE NOOK TRAP AMBRY BOSOM
BOWER CANAL CAVUM CLEFT
CREEK HAVEN HITCH INLET
NICHE ORIEL PRESS SINUS
ALCOVE ANCONA CAVERN
CENTER CHAPEL CIRQUE CLOSET
COFFER CRANNY EXEDRA
GROTTO INDENT LOCULE RABBET
REBATE BEDSITE CONCAVE
CREVICE LOCULUS MANHOLE
RETREAT SINKING INTERVAL
LOCKHOLE OVERTURE TABLINUM
TOKONOMA TRAVERSE VACATION
PIGEONHOLE
(— BETWEEN CAPES) BAY
(— FOR FAMILY RECORDS)
TABLINUM
(— FOR HINGE LEAF) PAN
(— FOR PIECE OF SCULPTURE)
ANCONA
(— IN CHURCH WALL) AMBRY
(— IN COLON) HAUSTRUM
(— IN JAPANESE HOUSE)
TOKONOMA
(— IN MOUNTAIN) CIRQUE
(— IN ROCK) HITCH
(— IN SIDE OF HILL) CORRIE
(— IN SIDE OF ROOM) ALA
(— IN WALL) BOLE NICHE ALCOVE
(— ON STAGE) CANOPY
(INMOST —) BOSOM
(PL.) FLASH
RECESSED SUNK SUNKEN
RECESSION BUST RETREAT
RECESSIVE BACKWARD RECEDING
RETIRING WITHDRAWN
RECHAB (SON OF —) MALCHIAH
JEHONADAB
RECHERCHE RARE CHOICE EXOTIC
CURIOUS PRECIOUS UNCOMMON
EXQUISITE
RECIDIVIST REPEATER
RECIPE RX FORM RULE FORMULA
RECEIPT
RECIPIENT HEIR DONEE ALMSMAN
DONATEE DONATORY LAUREATE
(SUFF.) EE
RECIPROCAL CROSS COMMON
MUTUAL SECANT SEESAW
(— OF A POISE) RHE
(— OF VISCOSITY) FLUIDITY
(PREF.) COUNTER INTER
RECIPROCATE REPAY RETURN
REQUITE RETROACT
RECIPROCITY SHU ISOPOLITY
MUTUALITY
RECITAL TALE ASHRE CITAL RECIT
STORY EXPOSE LITANY PARADE
REPEAT TIKKUN READING
RELATION REPETITION
(— OF PRAYER) GEULAH HAMOTZI
KEDUSHAH
(UNTRUE —) TALE
(SUFF.) LOG(ER)(IA)(IAN)(IC)(ICAL)
(IST)(UE)(Y)
RECITATION DHIKR READING
RECITAL RHAPSODY
RECITATIVE SCENA

CHANSON PARLANDO

RECITE SAY CARP TELL STATE
INTONE RECKON RELATE RENDER
REPEAT DECLAIM DECLINE
DICTATE NARRATE RECOUNT
REHEARSE
(— AS ELOCUTION EXERCISE)
DECLAIM
(— IN MONOTONE) INTONE
(— METRICALLY) SCAN
(— MONOTONOUSLY) CHANT
CHAUNT
(— NUMBERS) COUNT
(— PRAYERS) BENSH DAVEN
(— TIRESOMELY) THRUM
(— WITH GREAT EASE) RUSH
RECITER SCALD SKALD ANTERI
DISEUR CONTEUR DISEUSE
HOMERIST ILIADIST RHAPSODE
RECITING CHARM
RECK RAK CARE DEEM PASS
MATTER REGARD CONCERN
CONSIDER ESTIMATE
RECKLESS RASH WILD BLIND
FOLLE PERDU MADCAP RACKLE
SAVAGE GALLOWS RAMSTAM
CARELESS HEADLONG HEEDLESS
BLINDFOLD
RECKLESSLY FAST BLIND
RAMSTAM HEADLONG HEADFIRST
RECKLESSNESS BAYARD
RECKON RET ARET CAST DATE
ITEM RATE RECK RELY TALE TELL
TOTE ALLOT AUDIT CLAIM CLASS
COUNT JUDGE PLACE RETTE
SCORE TALLY THINK ASSIGN
FIGURE IMPUTE NUMBER REPUTE
TOTTLE ACCOUNT ASCRIBE
COMPUTE INCLUDE PRETEND
RECOUNT SUPPOSE SUPPUTE
CONSIDER ESTIMATE
(— IN) INCLUDE
RECKONING TAB BILL NICK POST
SHOT TAIL TALE COUNT SCORE
TALLY COMPOT LAWING REASON
TAILYE TOTTLE ACCOUNT
DAYTALE TAILZEE COMPUTUS
(TAVERN —) LAWING
RECLAIM IN TAME ASSART OBJECT
RECALL REDEEM REFORM RESCUE
SUBDUE PROTEST RECOVER
RESTORE
(— FROM SAVAGE STATE) CIVILIZE
RECLAIMANT GOEL
RECLINE LIE LIG LEAN LOLL REST
COUCH ACCUMB RECUMB
UPLEAN DISCUMB
(— LANGUIDLY) GAULSH
RECLINING CUMBENT ACCUMBENT
ACCUBATION
RECLUSE NUN MONK CULDEE
HERMIT REMOTE ASCETIC
EREMITE INCLUSA INCLUSE
ANCHORET INCLUSUS SECLUDED
SOLITARY SCIOPHYTE SOLITAIRE
(PL.) SECLUSE
RECOGNITION FAME SPUR HONOR
SENSE CREDIT STATUS FEELING
KENNING KNOWING AGNITION
SANCTION ANAGNOSIS
(— OF ACHIEVEMENT) LAUREL
CITATION
(SUFF.) GNOSIA GNOSIS

GNOSTIC GNOSY

RECOGNIZE KEN SEE WIT ESPY
FACE KNOW SPOT TELL ADMIT
ALLOW BLINK CROWN HONOR
KEETH KITHE KYTHE ACCEPT
ACKNOW AGNIZE BEKNOW
COUTHE REVISE CORRECT
DISCERN REALIZE ACCREDIT
(— IN ANY CAPACITY) AGNIZE
RECOGNIZED GOOD CLEAR
KNOWN CLASSIC FAMILIAR
RECOIL SHY BALK KICK TURN
REBUT SHRUG SHUCK START
STRAM BLENCH BOUNCE FLINCH
RECULE RESILE RESULT RETORT
SHRINK REBOUND REDOUND
REVERSE BACKLASH REJOUNCE
(WITHOUT —) DEADBEAT
RECOLLECT RECALL RECORD
RETAIN BETHINK COMPOSE
RECOVER RECOLETO REMEMBER
RECOLLECTION MIND MEMORY
RECALL RECORD MINDING
THOUGHT MEMORIAL SOUVENIR
ANAMNESIS
RECOMMENCE RENEW REOPEN
RESUME REPRISE
RECOMMEND MOVE OSSE PLUG
TOUT WISH ADVISE COMMIT
PRAISE PREFER COMMEND
CONSIGN COUNSEL ENTRUST
ADVOCATE RECOMMIT
RECOMMENDATION CHIT VOEU
ADVISE COUNSEL TESTIMONY
(PARTY —) COUPON
(SERVANT'S —) CHIT
RECOMPENSE PAY MEED MEND
MENSE QUITS REPAY YIELD
AMENDS BOUNTY HADBOT
RECOUP REWARD SALARY
GUERDON IMBURSE PAYMENT
PREMIUM REQUITE RESTORE
SATISFY SERVICE
RECONCILE GREE WEAN ADAPT
AGREE ATONE ACCORD ADJUST
SETTLE SHRIVE REUNITE
HARMONIZE
RECONCILED FAIN VAIN SAUGHT
RECONCILIATION ATONE ACCORD
SAUGHT REUNION IRENICON
RECONDITE DARK DEEP HIGH
HIDDEN MYSTIC OCCULT SECRET
CRYPTIC CURIOUS OBSCURE
RETIRED ABSTRACT ABSTRUSE
ESOTERIC
RECONNAISSANCE RECCE RECCO
RECCY SURVEY
RECONNOITER SCOUT RECALL
SURVEY EXAMINE PICKEER
DISCOVER REMEMBER
RECONSIDER REVIEW FORTHINK
RECONSTRUCT RECAST REPAIR
REEVOKE REMODEL RESTORE
RECORD CAN CUT BOOK CARD
DATE DISC ITER MARK NICK PAGE
ROLL SING SLIP WICK ALBUM
CHART DIARY ENACT ENTER
ENTRY FASTI GRAPH JUMBO
PRICK QUIPO QUIPU SIJIL SLATE
STYLE TITLE ANNALS CHARGE
DOCKET LEGEND MEMOIR SCROLL
SPREAD WARBLE ACCOUNT
CALENDS CITATOR DUBBING

KALENDS LEXICON MENTION
MYOGRAM SHOWING TICKLER
TRACING ANAGRAPH ARCHIVES
CYLINDER ENTRANCE ERGOGRAM
HERDBOOK INSCROLL JUDGMENT
KYMOGRAM LAUEGRAM
MARIGRAM MELOGRAM
MEMORIAL MONUMENT
ONDOGRAM PANCHART PRESSING
REGISTER REMEMBER SCHEDULE
STUDBOOK OBSERVATION
OSCILLOGRAM
(— BY NOTCHES) SCORE
(— OF CAR MOVEMENTS) JUMBO
(— OF DOCUMENT) PROTOCOL
(— OF EVENTS) FASTI
(— OF FOOTPRINTS) STIBOGRAM
(— OF HUMANITY'S FATE) SIJIL
SIJILL
(— OF JOURNEY) JOURNAL
ITINERARY
(— OF LOAN) CHARGE
(— OF MUHAMMAD'S SAYINGS)
HADIT
(— OF MUSCULAR WORK)
ERGOGRAM
(— OF PROCEEDINGS) ACTA ITER
JOURNAL MINUTES
(COMPUTER —) PRINTOUT
(COURT —) EYRE
(DAILY —) DIARY
(DEMONSTRATION —) DEMO
(FORMAL —) ACT
(HISTORICAL —) STORY
(MAGNETIC —) DISK FLOPPY
(PHONOGRAPH —) DISC DISK
MONO SINGLE BISCUIT SHELLAC
(SHIP'S —) LOG
(PL.) LIBER ANNALS ARCHIVE
MEMORABILIA
(PREF.) DISC(I)(O)
(SUFF.) GRAM GRAPH(ER)(IA)(IC)(Y)
RECORDER FLUTE BOOKER
FLAUTO NOTATOR GREFFIER
REGISTER
RECORDING ALBUM ALIVE LABEL
CUTTING
(— AWARD) GRAMMY
RECOUNT MING TELL COUNT
DEVISE RECITE REGARD RELATE
REPEAT SPREAD EXPRESS
HISTORY NARRATE CONSIDER
DESCRIBE REHEARSE
RECOUP DEDUCT REGAIN
RECOVER INDEMNIFY
RECOUPLING HOOKUP
RECOURSE SUIT ACCESS APPEAL
REFUGE RESORT STRING REGRESS
RESTAUR RISORSE
(HAVE —) RECUR
RECOVER DOW COUR COWR CURE
FIRM HEAL KERE COVER RALLY
REACH UPSET BOUNCE RECURE
REGAIN RESCUE RESUME RETAKE
RETIRE REVERT REVOKE WARISH
DELIVER OVERGET OVERPUT
OVERSET READEPT RECLAIM
RECRUIT REPAREL REPRISE
RESTORE RETRIEVE
RECOVERER DIGESTER
RECOVERY CURE RECOUR
RECURE REMEDY RETURN
SALVAGE COMEBACK

SNAPBACK RECLAMATION
RECREANT FALSE CRAVEN
YELLOW APOSTATE COWARDLY
DESERTER RECRAYED
RECREATE AMUSE EVOKE REVIVE
RECREATION PLAY SPORT SOLACE
RENEWAL ACTIVITY DIVERSION
PALINGENY
(PERIOD OF —) HOLIDAY VACATION
RECREATIVE PLAYING
RECREMENT SLAG DROSS SCORIA
RECRUIT BLEU BOOT FRESH RAISE
SPROG GATHER INTAKE MUSTER
RECREW REPAIR REVIVE RECOVER
REFRESH RESTORE ASSEMBLE
BEZONIAN CONSCRIPT
(RAW —) ROOKY ROOKIE
RECTAL
(PREF.) ARCHO
RECTANGLE BOX SQUARE
CHECKER
(COTTON —) HUIPIL
(CURVILINEAR —) TESSERA
(WOVEN —) SINKER
RECTANGULAR SQUARE BOXLIKE
EMERALD
RECTIFICATION REFORM
LIMATION
RECTIFIER DIODE VALVE COLUMN
DETECTOR EXCITRON
RECTIFY AMEND EMEND RIGHT
ADJUST BETTER DETECT REFORM
REMEDY CORRECT IMPROVE
REDRESS EMENDATE REGULATE
RECTITUDE DOOM EQUITY
JUSTICE PROBITY
RECTOR RULER LEADER PARSON
PERSONA INCUMBENT
RECTUM SIEGE TEWEL
(PREF.) ARCHO PROCT(O) RECTO
RECUMBENT IDLE PRONE JACENT
CUMBENT LEANING RESTING
INACTIVE REPOSING
RECUPERATE MEND RALLY
REFETE REGAIN RECOVER
RECRUIT RETRIEVE
RECUR CYCLE REFER REPEAT
RESORT RETURN REOCCUR
REVOLVE REAPPEAR
(— CONSTANTLY) HAUNT
RECURRENCE RESORT RETURN
ATAVISM REPRISE ITERANCE
ITERANCY RECOURSE
(— OF SOUND) CADENCE
(SUFF.) LY
RECURRENT CYCLIC FREQUENT
PERENNIAL
RECURRING ROLLING CONTINUAL
(— ANNUALLY) ETESIAN
(— EVERY THIRD DAY) TERTIAN
(— EVERY 72 HOURS) QUARTAN
(— ON NINTH DAY) NONAN
NONANE
(— ON SEVENTH DAY) SEPTAN
(CONSTANTLY —) ETERNAL
(CONTINUALLY —) CONSTANT
(SUFF.) ENNIAL
RECURVED REFLEX ERICOID
RECUTTING FRESHING
RED (ALSO SEE COLOR) GOYA
GULY PINK PUCE ROJO ROSY
RUBY ANGRY CANNA CORAL
FIERY JUDAS ROUGE RUDDY

RUFUS ARCHIL AZALEA BLOODY CERISE FLORID FULGID GARNET HECTIC NECTAR ORCHIL ORIENT RAISIN RUBRIC TITIAN TRYPAN VERMIL WANTON CARMINE GLOWING NACARAT PIMENTO RADICAL RUBELLE RUBIOUS STAMMEL VERMILY ARMENIAN AUBUSSON BORDEAUX CARDINAL CHOLERIC COLORADO FLAGRANT MANDARIN MOROCAIN RUBICUND SANGUINE ARTILLERY COQUELICOT
(— AND INFLAMED) BLOODSHOT
(— PLANET) MARS
(ANTIQUE —) CANNA
(BRIGHT —) TULY CHERRY PUNICIAL VERMILION
(DARK —) CLARET
(EUREKA —) PUCE
(FIERY —) MINIUM
(GRAYISH —) AZALEA
(HERALDIC —) GULES
(IRON OXIDE —) AGATE TARRAGONA
(PURPLISH —) LAKE MURREY MAGENTA
(WAX —) COPPER
(YELLOWISH —) MAROON
(PREF.) ERYTHR(O) PHENIC(O) PHOENIC(O) PYRRH(O) PYRRO RHOD(O) RUBE RUBI RUBO RUBRI RUBRO RUFI RUFO
RED ADMIRAL VANESSA
RED AND THE BLACK (AUTHOR OF —) STENDHAL
(CHARACTER IN —) SOREL FOUQUE JULIEN PIRARD DERENAL VALENOD MATHILDE
RED-BACKED SHRIKE POPE
RED BADGE OF COURAGE
(AUTHOR OF —) CRANE
(CHARACTER IN —) JIM HENRY WILSON CONKLIN FLEMING
RED BANEBERRY REDBERRY TOADROOT
RED BAY PERSEA
RED-BELLIED (— TERRAPIN) SLIDER SKILPOT
(— WOODPECKER) CHAB
RED-BREASTED BREAM FLATFISH FLOUNDER
RED-BREASTED KNOT GRAYBACK GREYBACK
REDBUD CERCIS JUNEBUD
RED CAMPION ROBIN SOLDIER
RED CEDAR SAVIN SABINA JUNIPER
RED CLOVER SAPLING TREFOIL TRIFOLY
RED CURRANT GOYA RIZZLE TIZZAR
REDD RID COMB OPEN LITTER NEATEN REFUSE RESCUE SETTLE ARRANGE DELIVER SMARTEN UNBLOCK UNRAVEL
RED DEER OLEN SPAY STAG
(FEMALE —) HIND
(MALE —) HART STAG
REDDEN RUD FIRE RUBY BLUSH FLUSH LIGHT ROUGE RUDDY BLOODY RUBIFY RUBRIC RUDDLE EMPURPLE

REDDISH REDDY RUDDY RUFUS FLUSHY GINGER RUFOUS COLORADO PYRRHOUS RUBICUND
RED DRUM SPOT REDFISH
REDEAR SHELLCRACKER
REDEEM BUY WIN SAVE ALESE CLEAR LOUSE REPRY BORROW OFFSET RANSOM DELIVER FULFILL JUSTIFY RECLAIM WITHBEG AGAINBUY LIBERATE
REDEEMER GOEL SAVIOR
REDEMPTION RANSOM REFORM SAFETY SALVATION
REDEYE BASS RUDD VIREO SUNFISH
RED-EYE CATSUP CICADA WHISKY
RED-EYED VIREO REDEYE GRASSET PREACHER
RED-FACED FLUSHED SCARLET
REDFIN DACE SHINER REDHORSE YELLOWFIN
REDFISH SALMON FATHEAD ROSEFISH
RED GOOSEFOOT PIGWEED SOWBANE
RED GROUPER MERO NEGRE REDBELLY
RED GROUSE GORHEN GORCOCK LAGOPODE MOORBIRD MUIRFOWL
RED GUM JARRAH EUCALYPT
RED GURNARD CUR ELLECK ROCHET SOLDIER
RED-HAIRED RUFUS CARROTY
REDHEAD DIVER FINCH POCHARD KIZILBASH
RED HIND GRAYSBY GROUPER CABRILLA
REDHORSE REDFIN SUCKER
REDIA SPOROSAC
REDIRECT DISPLACE READDRESS
REDISTILL COHOBATE
REDISTRIBUTE FRESHEN REASSIGN
RED LAVER SLOKE
REDNESS RED RUD GLOW HEAT RUDD RUBOR ERYTHEMA RUBEDITY
(— OF SKY) AURORA
REDO REDACT RESTYLE
(— UNSKILLFULLY) BOTCH
RED OCHER TIVER ABRAUM RUDDLE
REDOLENCE BALM AROMA SCENT
REDOLENT RICH ODOROUS SCENTED AROMATIC FRAGRANT SMELLING
RED OSIER WILLOW REDBRUSH
REDOUBLE REECHO SINGLE
REDOUBT FEAR MASK DREAD SCHANZ SCONCE BULWARK
REDOUND TURN ACCRUE BILLOW CONDUCE REFLECT OVERFLOW
RED RASPBERRY CUTHBERT
REDRESS HEAL DRESS REDUB AVENGE OFFSET REFORM RELIEF REMEDE REMEDY REPAIR ADDRESS CORRECT RECTIFY REFOUND RELIEVE
RED ROCKFISH TAMBOR
REDROOT PIGWEED
RED ROVER (AUTHOR OF —) COOPER

(CHARACTER IN —) ARK FID DICK. HENRY AFRICA DELACY SCIPIO WILDER WYLLYS BIGNALL GRAYSON GERTRUDE RODERICK
RED SAGE LANTANA
RED SANDALWOOD CHANDAM
REDSHANK CLEE TEUK SHAKE GAMBET REDLEG YELPER PELLILE TATTLER
REDSKIN RED ROJO TAWNY INDIAN
REDSTART YELPER BRANTAIL FIRETAIL WHITECAP FIREFLIRT
RED STOPPER EUGENIA IRONWOOD
RED-TAILED (— HAWK) REDTAIL
(— TROPIC BIRD) KOAE
RED-TAPISM BEADLEDOM
RED-THROATED LOON WABBY
REDTOP COUCH FIORIN FINETOP FINEBENT FURZETOP BLUEJOINT
REDUCE CUT BATE CLIP DOCK DROP EASE PARE PULL THIN ABASE ABATE ALLAY APPAL BREAK DRAFT ELIDE LOWER QUELL SCANT SHAVE SLAKE SLASH SMELT ATTRIT DEDUCE DEFALK DEJECT DELETE DEPOSE DILUTE HUMBLE LESSEN REBATE REDUCT SHRINK SUBACT SUBDUE WEAKEN ABANDON ABRIDGE ASSUAGE ATOMIZE CHANCER CONQUER CURTAIL DEFLATE DEGRADE DEPLETE DWINDLE ECLIPSE FRITTER INHIBIT RESOLVE RETREAT SCISSOR SHORTEN SUBJECT ABSTRACT ATTEMPER CONDENSE DECREASE DIMINISH MINIMIZE
(— ACCORDING TO FIXED RATIO) SCALE
(— ANGLE) CHAMFER
(— BULK) BLEND
(— LUMBER) SIZE
(— PROFITS) SQUEEZE
(— PURITY) ALLOY
(— STONE BLOCKS) SPALL SPAWL
(— THE VALUE) DECRY BEGGAR DEPRAVE
(— TO A MEAN) AVERAGE
(— TO ASHES) CREMATE
(— TO CARBON) CHAR
(— TO FINE PARTICLES) ATOMIZE MICRONIZE
(— TO FLAT SURFACE) LEVEL
(— TO INSIGNIFICANCE) DROWN
(— TO LOWER GERTRUDE) BREAK DEMOTE DEGRADE
(— TO NIL) CLOSE
(— TO NOTHING) ANNUL
(— TO PASSIVITY) CHINAFY PROSTRATE
(— TO POWDER) GRIND PULVERIZE
(PREF.) DE
REDUCED SUNK TAIL BROKEN CURTATE DWARFED DEGRADED WEAKENED VESTIGIAL
REDUCTION BUST LETUP SLASH CUTBACK CUTDOWN DOCKAGE SHAVING ANALYSIS DILUTION DISCOUNT ABATEMENT SHRINKAGE
(— IN FORCE) RIF

(— IN PITCH) DROP
(— IN PRICE) SAVING CONCESSION
(SUFF.) LYSE LYSIS LYST LYTE LYTIC LYZE
REDUNDANCY EXCESS NIMIETY SURPLUS PLEONASM PLETHORA VERBIAGE MACROLOGY TAUTOLOGY
REDUNDANT WORDY LAVISH PROFUSE SURPLUS VERBOSE SWELLING EXCESSIVE
REDWING POP THRUSH WINDLE GADWALL WINNARD
REDWOOD MAD AMBOYNA BARWOOD FURIOUS SEQUOIA MAHOGANY
RE-ECHO REWORD REBOUND RESOUND REDOUBLE
REED NAL RIE RIX SAG BENT JUNK PIPE PIRN RODE SLEY TULE ARROW DONAX SPEAR TWILL BENNEL RADDLE SAGGON CALAMUS FISTULA WHISTLE WINDING ABOMASUM
(— FOR WARPING) WRAITHE
(— FOR WINDING THREAD) PIRN SPOOL
(— IN ORGAN) VIBRATOR
(— OF LOOM) COMB
(FOXTAIL —) DOD
(GIANT —) DONAX
(MUSICAL —) OAT
(WEAVER'S —) SLAY SLEY RADDLE SLEIGH
(PL.) SPEAR
(PREF.) ARUNDI CALAM(I)(O)
REED BENT CARRIZO
REEDBIRD BOBOLINK
REEDBUCK BOHOR NAGOR REITBOK
REED BUNTING RINGBIRD
REED CANARY GRASS SPIRE DAGGERS
REED END TONGUE
REEDING GADROON MILLING STRIGIL GRAINING
REED MACE RAUPO CATTAIL MATREED
REED ORGAN MELODEON HARMONIUM
REED PIPE MIRLITON
REED WARBLER PITBIRD
REEDY THIN WEAK FRAIL TWILLED
REEF CAY KAY KEY CAYO LODE RYFT SCAR VEIN ATOLL LEDGE SHELF STICK BOILER REEFER SADDLE SKERRY BAGREEF BALANCE BIOHERM MAKATEA TOMBOLO
REEFER CAR COAT STICK JACKET MUGGLES
REEK FOG FUG EMIT FUME HEAP MIST PILE RICK RISE VENT EQUIP EXUDE ISSUE NIDOR SMEEK SMOKE STEAM VAPOR EXHALE OUTFIT EMANATE
(— WITH CORRUPTION) FESTER
REEL PIRN RANT ROCK SPIN STOT SWAB SWIM TURN GIDDY SPOOL SWIFT TRULL WAVER WHEEL WHIRL WINCE WINCH BOBBIN RECOIL SWERVE TOTTER TUMULT WAGGLE WALTER WELTER

WINDER WINDLE WINNLE WINTLE BALLOON STAGGER SWABBLE TITUBATE

(— FOR DRAWING SILK) FILATURE

(— FOR WARP DRYING) BALLOON

(— FOR WINDING YARN) PIRN SWIFT

(— OFF A STORY) SCRIEVE

(— USED FOR YARN) CRIB

(DYEING —) WINCE

(FISHING —) TROW TROLL TRULL WINCH

(PL.) REVELS

REELER TWINER

REELING TURN AREEL LURCH FILATURE STAGGERY WAMBLING

REEM MOAN URUS UNICORN

REEVE REE REFE THREAD BAILIFF PROVOST STEWARD OVERSEER

REFECTION MEAL RELIEF REPAST HOGMANAY

REFECTORY FRATER FRATRY

REFER DEFER LEAVE POINT ADVERT ALLUDE APPEAL ASSIGN CHARGE COMMIT DELATE DIRECT IMPUTE PREFER RELATE SUBMIT ASCRIBE REJOURN RELEGATE

(— TO) SEE CITE INTEND CONCERN CONSULT MENTION INTIMATE

(— TO SOMETHING REPEATEDLY) HARP

REFEREE BREHON UMPIRE ARBITER AUDITOR

REFERENCE TAB FOLIO REMIT SIGIL APPEAL REGARD RENVOI BEARING MEANING RESPECT ALLUSION HANDBOOK INNUENDO RELATION

(— WORK) ATLAS INDEX ALMANAC LEXICON CATALOGUE GAZETTEER

(SATIRICAL —) GLANCE

REFERENDUM POLL MANDATE

REFINE RUN TRY BOLT EDIT FILE FINE PURE CUPEL EXALT PLAIN SLICK SMELT AFFINE DECOCT EXCOCT FILTER GARBLE SMOOTH CONCOCT ELEVATE PERFECT SUBLIME SWEETEN CIVILIZE HUMANIZE URBANIZE

(— AS GOLD) TEST CARAT

(— PULP) JORDAN

(— SUGAR) CLAY

(— WINE) FORCE

REFINED FINE GENT NEAT NICE TRIE ATTIC EXACT PURED TERSE CHASTE EXCOCT INLAND NIMINY POLITE QUAINT SUBTLE CLEANLY COURTLY ELEGANT GENTEEL PRECISE SCRAPED AUGUSTAN DELICATE ELEVATED HIGHBRED PRECIEUX PRECIOUS SERAPHIC RECHERCHE

(NOT —) CRUDE

(TOO —) FINESPUN

REFINEMENT GRACE NICETY POLISH CULTURE FINESSE DELICACY ELEGANCE POLITURE SUBTLETY URBANITY PRECIOSITY

REFINER TRIER JORDAN PURIFIER

REFINING HUMAN FINING CULTURE AFFINAGE

REFINISH ANTIQUE

REFLECT COW CHEW MUSE PORE SHOW BLAZE FLASH GLASS GLINT IMAGE SHINE STUDY THINK ADVISE DAZZLE DEBATE MIRROR PONDER RECORD REFLEX RELUCE RETORT RETURN REVISE STEVEN EXPRESS PERPEND REDOUND REFRACT SHIMMER COGITATE CONSIDER MEDITATE REDOUBLE RUMINATE

(— IRREGULARLY) SCATTER

(— UPON) SPECULATE

REFLECTED DERIVED MIRRORED SPECULAR

REFLECTING

(SUFF.) ESCENT

REFLECTION ECHO FOLD IDEA SKIT BLAME GHOST GLARE GNOME DEBATE MUSING PONDER REFLEX RETURN SHADOW CENSURE COUNSEL SPECIES THOUGHT EYESHINE MOONPATH THINKING

(— OF SELF IN ANOTHER'S EYES) BABY

REFLECTIVE PENSIVE THOUGHTFUL

(— POWER) ALBEDO

REFLECTOR DISH FLAT CRITIC HASTER SHINER TAMPER HORIZON DIFFUSER HASTENER SPECULUM

REFLEX COPY IMAGE TROPISM ALLUSION

(NOT —) IDEOMOTOR

REFLUX EBB EBBING REFLOW

REFOREST REBOISE

REFORM MEND AMEND EMEND PRUNE BETTER REBUKE REPAIR CENSURE CORRECT DISBAND RECLAIM RECTIFY REDRESS

REFORMATORY COLLEGE MAGDALEN

REFORMER APOSTLE UTOPIAN UTOPIAST JANSENIST

REFRACT DIVIDE REFLECT REFRINGE

REFRACTION REBATE REBOUND DIACLASIS

REFRACTOR PRISM

REFRACTORY TOUGH SULLEN UNRULY WANTON ALUNDUM FROWARD MULLITE RESTIVE VICIOUS WAYWARD MUTINOUS PERVERSE STUBBORN CAMSTEERY REBELLIOUS

REFRAIN BOB TAG CURB DOWN KEEP SHUN AVOID FORGO SPARE WONDE BURDEN CHORUS DESIST FOREGO LUDDEN RETAIN THRAIN ABSTAIN FORBEAR LULLABY REFREIT REPRISE TORNADA FABURDEN FALDERAL OVERCOME OVERWORD REPETEND RESTRAIN WITHDRAW

(— FROM) CAN HELP AVOID SPARE WAIVE FOREGO RESIGN ABSTAIN

(— FROM INDULGENCE) ABSTAIN

(— FROM TELLING) LAYNE

(— FROM USING) BOYCOTT

(— OF SONG) BOB TAG DOWN FOOT WHEEL BURDEN CHORUS FALDEROL

(MEANINGLESS —) DERRY DUCDAME

REFRESH FAN COOL REST CHEER FRESH SLAKE CAUDLE REFECT REFETE REGALE REHETE REPOSE REVIVE UNTIRE COMFORT FORTIFY FRESHEN QUICKEN RECRUIT IRRIGATE RECREATE

REFRESHING DEWY BALMY FRESH TONIC CALLER LIVING BRACING COOLING

REFRESHMENT BAIT LUNCH CHARITY NUNCHEON REFRESCO COLLATION

(PL.) FOURS

REFRIGERANT ICE FREON COOLER AMMONIA COOLING CRYOGEN

REFRIGERATE CHILL

REFRIGERATION CRYOGENY

REFRIGERATOR FRIG FRIDGE ICEBOX FREEZER CONDENSER

(— CAR) REEFER

REFUGE ARK DIVE HOLT HOME PORT ROCK SOIL BIELD GRITH HAVEN OASIS RESET ASYLUM BILBIE COVERT HARBOR REFUTE RESORT SPITAL SUCCOR ALSATIA CRANNOG RESERVE RETREAT SHELTER UMBRAGE WARRANT BOLTHOLE CRANNOGE FORTRESS HIDEAWAY MAGDALEN RESOURCE SAFEHOLD

REFUGEE REFFO COWBOY FUIDHIR FUGITIVE

REFULGENT BRIGHT SHINING RELUCENT BRILLIANT

REFUND REPAY UPSET REFOUND RESTORE DRAWBACK KICKBACK

REFURBISH DUST RENEW REVAMP FRESHEN BRIGHTEN RENOVATE

REFUSAL NAY VEE WARN WONT DENIAL MITTEN NAYSAY REPULSE ACCISMUS DECLINAL NEGATION NEGATIVE

(— TO SPEAK) APHRASIA

REFUSE ASH NAY NIL ORT SUD BALK COOM DENY DUST JUNK KEMP NAIT NILL NITE PELF PELT REDD SCUM SKIM SOIL SUDS WARN BAVIN COOMB CRAWN DEADS DRAST DROSS EXPEL FLOCK NITTE OFFAL RENAY REPEL SCRAN STENT STUFF SWASH SWILL TRADE TRASH WAIVE WASTE COLDER DANDER DEBRIS FORBID LITTER LUMBER MIDDEN NAYSAY PALTRY PELTRY RAFFLE RAMMEL RECUSE REFUGE REJECT SCRUFF SCULCH SHORTS SHRUFF SORDES SORDOR SPILTH BACKING BAGGAGE BROCKLE DECLINE DETRACT DETRECT DISAVOW DISOBEY FORSAKE GARBAGE GUBBINS MULLOCK OFFSCUM OUTCAST PRUNING RUBBISH SOILAGE SULLAGE WITHNAY WITHSAY CRASSIER DENEGATE DISALLOW DISCLAIM GARBLING LEAVINGS RIFFRAFF SWEEPAGE WITHHOLD OFFSCOURING

(— ADMISSION) CLOSE

(— FROM CHARCOAL

OR COKE) BREEZE

(— FROM COFFEE BERRIES) TAILINGS

(— FROM CUTTING UP WHALE) GURRY

(— FROM MELTING METALS) SLAG DROSS SCORIA

(— FROM SIFTING COFFEE-BEANS) TRIAGE

(— FROM THRESHING) HUSK COLDER

(— GREASE) COOM COOMB

(— OF MINE) DEAD

(— OF CROP) STOVER

(— OF FLAX) PAB POB HARDS HURDS

(— OF FRUITS) MUST

(— OF GRAIN) PUG BRAN

(— OF GRAPES) MARC

(— OF INSECT) FRASS

(— OF MALT) DRAFF

(— OF MINE) BING

(— OF OIL MILLS) SHODE

(— OF PLANTS) ROSS

(— OF SILK) STRASS

(— OF SPICES) GARBLE

(— OF WHALE) FENKS GURRY TWITTER

(— OF WOOL) BACKINGS

(— TO APPROVE) VETO

(— TO COMPLY) STONEWALL

(— TO GO) JIB BALK

(— TO RECOGNIZE) CUT

(— TO SUPPORT) BOLT

(— TO TALK) DUMMY

(BREWERY —) DRAFF

(FISH —) CHUM GUBBINS

(FOOD —) SWILL

(LEATHER —) SPETCHES

(PLANT —) SCROFF

(STREET —) FULLAGE SCAVAGE

REFUTATION DISPROOF ELENCHUS HYPOBOLE REBUTTER

REFUTE DENY AVOID REBUT REFEL ASSOIL CONFUTE CONVELL CONVICT REPROVE REVINCE CONFOUND DISPROVE INFRINGE REDARGUE

REGAIN READEPT RECOVER RETRIEVE

(— SOMETHING LOST) RECOUP

REGAL REAL ROYAL KINGLY PURPLE RIGGAL RIGOLE STATELY IMPERIAL MAJESTIC PRINCELY REGALIAN SPLENDID

REGALE FETE FEAST TREAT PLEASE DELIGHT REFRESH

REGALIA KIT ROYALTY

REGALO GIFT BONUS TREAT

REGAN (FATHER OF —) LEAR

(HUSBAND OF —) CORNWALL

(SISTER OF —) GONERIL CORDELIA

REGARD CON CARE DEEM FIND GAUM GAZE GIVE HEED HOLD LIKE LOOK MARK MIND RATE RECK SAKE TELL YEME ADORE COUNT FAVOR HONOR TREAT WEIGH ADDEEM ADMIRE ASPECT BEHOLD ESTEEM FIGURE GLANCE HOMAGE IMPUTE INTEND LIKING MOTIVE NOTICE RECKON REMARK REWARD SURVEY ACCOUNT ADJUDGE CONCERN OBSERVE

RESPECT RESPITE CONSIDER
ENVISAGE ESTIMATE
(— AS) SEE
(— AS HOPELESS) DEPLORE
(— AS OBJECT OF GREAT INTEREST)
LIONIZE
(— AS PROPER) ACCEPT
(— HIGHLY) ADMIRE CONSIDER
(— WITH PROFOUND RESPECT)
REVERE VENERATE
(— WITH REPUGNANCE) ABHOR
(ATTENTIVE —) EYE
(MENTAL —) EYE
(PL.) COMPLIMENTS
(SUFF.) SCOPE SCOPIC SCOPUS
SCOPY
REGARDED (— WITH AFFECTION)
DEAR AFFECTED
REGARDING ABOUT ANENT
APROPOS
REGARDLESS DEAF CARELESS
HEEDLESS RECKLESS
(— OF THAT) BUT
REGATTA HENLEY LIBERTY
REGEM (FATHER OF —) JAHDAI
REGENCY RULE DOMINION
REGENERATE RENEW REFORM
REVIVE RECLAIM GRACIOUS
RENOVATE
(NOT —) CIVIL
REGENERATION REBIRTH
NEOGENESIS
REGENT RULER RULING WARDEN
SHIKKEN GOVERNOR PANGERANG
PROTECTOR
(— DIAMOND) PITT
(— OF NORTH) KUBERA KUVERA
REGIME FASCISM CAFETERIA
REGIMEN CURE DIET KEEP RULE
REGIMENT
REGIMENT BUFF RULE COLOR
TERCIO GUIDANCE INFANTRY
SLASHERS
(BRITISH —) GRAYS GREYS
(COSSACK —) PULK
(FRAMEWORK OF —) CADRE
(INDIA —) PULTON PULTUN
(SPANISH —) TERCIO
(TURKISH —) ALAI
(28TH —) SLASHERS
REGION DO END ERD EYE GAU
WON AREA BELT KITH KNOT
NECK PART SOIL WONE WOON
ZONE CLIME COAST EARTH
EXURB INDIA MARCH PAGUS
PLACE PLAGE REALM SHIRE
TRACT TROAD ALKALI BORDER
CENTER DESERT DOMAIN EXTENT
GILEAD GROUND GUIANA TATARY
CLIMATE CONFINE COUNTRY
DEMESNE ENCLAVE IMAMATE
KINGDOM MALABAR STATION
TARTARY CHIEFDOM CLUBLAND
DEMERARA DISTRICT ENVIRONS
EPISTOME FLATLAND FORTRESS
FRONTIER KRATOGEN LAKELAND
LATITUDE NAPHTALI PROVINCE
REGIMENT SERICANA STANNARY
TERRITORY
(— ABOVE MOUTH) EPISTOMA
EPISTOME
(— ADJACENT TO BOUNDARY)
MARCH

(— BEYOND ATMOSPHERE) SPACE
(— BEYOND DEATH) CANAAN
(— BORDERING ON HELL) LIMBO
(— FAR AWAY) STRAND
(— IN FIBER) MICELLE
(— NEAR EQUATOR) DOLDRUMS
(— NOTED FOR MANY CONFLICTS)
COCKPIT
(— OF AMPLITUDE) ANTINODE
(— OF CHROMOSOME) PUFF
(— OF COLD AND DARKNESS)
NIFLHEL NIFLHEIM
(— OF DEAD) AMENTI UTGARTHAR
(— OF JAPAN) DO
(— OF MARS) LIBYA
(OF OCEAN) COUNTRY
(— OF ORIGIN) CRADLE
(— OF PHOTOSPHERE) FACULA
(— OF SHIFTING SAND) ERG
(— OF SIMPLE PLEASURE) ARCADY
ARCADIA
(— OF SOURCE OF GOLD) OPHIR
(— OF TISSUE) FIELD
(— WITHOUT LAW) ALSATIA
(— WITHOUT WOODS) WOLD
WEALD
(CELESTIAL —S) LANGI
(COASTAL —) LITTORAL
(CULTIVATED —) GARDEN
(DARKISH —S ON MARS) MARE
(DESERT —) ERG HAMADA
(DESERTED —) WASTE
(DESOLATE —) PUNA
(DISTANT —) THULE
(E INDIAN —) DESH
(ELEVATED —) ALTITUDE
(FOREST —) TAIGA
(FORESTED —) MONTANA
(GEOGRAPHICAL —) BOWL SIDE
(HEAVENLY —) SPHERE
(IDEAL —) JINNESTAN
(INFERNAL —S) ABYSS TARTAR
TARTARUS
(LARGE —) COMPAGE
(LIMESTONE —) KARST
(MOUNTAINOUS —) SIERRA
(OPEN —) SAVANNAH
(ORIENTAL —) INDOGAEA
(STAGNANT —) EDDY
(SUPERIOR —) HIGH
(TREELESS —) HIGHMOOR
(UPPER —) HIGH LOFT
(UPPER —S) ETHER
(WOODED —) FOREST
(PL.) DIGGINGS
(PREF.) NESO
(SUFF.) DOM NESE NESIA(N)
NESUS
REGIONAL LOCAL SECTIONAL
REGISTER PIE BEAR BOOK FREE
LIST MARK PILE POLL READ ROLL
STOP ALBUM DIARY ENROL
ENTER FASTI GRILL SIJIL SLATE
ANNALS BEHAVE ENROLL LEDGER
MUSTER RECORD REGEST
ALMANAC ASCRIBE CALENDS
CATALOG COUCHER DIPTYCH
INDORSE KALENDS NOTITIA
ROTULET ANAGRAPH ARCHIVES
CADASTER CALENDAR GREFFIER
INDICATE INSCRIBE MENOLOGY
PEDIGREE POLLBOOK TOLLBOOK
STROHBASS

(— OF JUDGMENTS) DOCKET
(LOWEST —) CHALUMEAU
(MIDDLE —) CLARINO
(OFFICIAL —) TABLEAU CADASTER
REGISTRAR GUARD BURSAR
ACTUARY PATWARI PUTWARI
GREFFIER RESIDENT
REGISTRY FLAG STUDBOOK
REGLET FILET BATTEN FILLET
RIGLET
REGRATER HUCKSTER
REGRESS EGRESS RETURN
ANALYSIS RECOURSE
REGRET REW RUE RUTH GRIEF
DESIRE RELENT REPENT SORROW
DEPLORE REGRATE REMORSE
FORTHINK REPINING
REGRETFUL BAD SORRY REPINING
REGRETTABLE DIRTY DOLOROUS
REGULAR DUE SET EVEN FULL
JUST WEAK SOBER SUANT SUENT
USUAL FORMAL GIUSTO NORMAL
SQUARE STATED STEADY
CANONIC CERTAIN CORRECT
NATURAL ORDERED ORDERLY
ORDINAL PERFECT TYPICAL
UNIFORM COMPLETE CONSTANT
DECOROUS FORMULAR HABITUAL
ORDINARY ORDINATE TESSERAL
(PREF.) SYM
REGULARITY METHOD SQUARE
SYSTEM EVENNESS SYNAPHEA
(— OF NATURE) LAW
REGULARLY DULY EVEN ORDERLY
PROPERLY STATEDLY
REGULATE SET RATE RULE WIND
BOOST FRAME GUIDE ORDER
RIGHT SHAPE ADJUST ASSIZE
BEHAVE DIRECT GOVERN MASTER
RADDLE SETTLE SQUARE TEMPER
ARRANGE CONTROL DISPOSE
MEASURE QUALIFY RECTIFY
ATTEMPER MODERATE MODULIZE
(— FOOD) DIET
(— PITCH) KEY STOP
REGULATED ORDENE ORDERED
ORDERLY
REGULATING BEHIND
REGULATION LAW RULE BYLAW
ORDER REGLE USUAL CURFEW
ZABETA CONTROL PRECEPT
STATUTE VOICING DISPOSAL
STEERAGE
(— OF PRICE) ASSIZE
(DORMITORY —S) PARIETALS
REGULATOR GUIDE DISPOSER
GOVERNOR
REGULUS MATTE SLURRY KINGLET
REHABIAH (FATHER OF —) ELIEZER
(GRANDFATHER OF —) MOSES
REHABILITATE REABLE REPONE
RESTORE REINSTATE
REHASH RECHAUFFE
REHEARSAL CALL HEARSAL
HERSALL PREVIEW CLAMBAKE
NARRATION
REHEARSE TELL TRAIN DETAIL
RECITE RELATE DECLINE
NARRATE RECOUNT DESCRIBE
PRACTICE
REHEAT FLASH
REHOB (SON OF —) HADADEZER
REHOBOAM ROBOAM

(FATHER OF —) SOLOMON
(MOTHER OF —) NAAMAH
REICHSTAG DIET
REIF PLUNDER ROBBERY
REIGN RING RULE REALM RICHE
EMPIRE GOVERN KINGDOM
PREVAIL REGIMENT REGNANCY
(— IN INDIA) RAJ
REIMBURSE PAY REPAY DEFRAY
RECOUP REFUND REBURSE
INDEMNIFY
REIN CURB STOP CHECK SWING
THONG GOVERN BABICHE
LEATHER PLOWLINE RESTRAIN
(PL.) LINES RIBBONS
REINCARNATION REBIRTH
REINDEER REIN CERVID TARAND
CARIBOU CERVINE CERVOID
RANGIFER
REINDEER MOSS SWARD
REINFORCE BAR GUY BACK FACE
STAY BRACE FORCE INLAY STUFF
SUPER CRADLE DOUBLE GUSSET
HARDEN MUSCLE SUPPLY
AFFORCE BOLSTER BULWARK
ENFORCE GROMMET NERVATE
STIFFEN SUPPORT
(— ROAD) SKID
REINFORCED KEYED SPLICED
REINFORCEMENT CREW FUEL
STAY BRACE HURTER CUNETTE
SPLICING STRAINER
(PL.) SUCCOR SUPPLY
REINVIGORATE QUICK REVIVE
RECRUIT RENERVE
REITERATE BACK DING REITER
REPEAT RESUME ITERATE
REHEARSE
REIVER CATERAN
REJECT BEG ORT CAST DEFY DICE
FAIL JILT KICK NILL SPIN ABHOR
BANDY BELIE BRUSH CHECK
EJECT REFEL REPEL SCOUT
SPURN WAIVE ABJECT ABJURE
DELETE DESERT IGNORE RECUSE
REFUSE REFUTE RESPUE RETORT
ABANDON CASHIER CONTEMN
DECLINE DISCARD DISMISS
FORSAKE PROJECT REPROVE
REPULSE ABNEGATE ATHETIZE
DISALLOW DISCLAIM FORSWEAR
NEGATIVE RENOUNCE
THROWOUT
(— A STUDENT) PLUCK PLOUGH
(— COPY) SPIKE
REJECTED OFFCAST OUTCAST
CASTAWAY
REJECTION SACK BRUSH SPURN
DENIAL MITTEN REBUFF REFUSAL
REPULSE DEFIANCE TURNDOWN
(— OF DOCTRINE) HERESY
REJOICE JOY FAIN GAME CHEER
ENJOY EXULT GLORY BLITHE
PLEASE DELIGHT GLADDEN
MAFFICK JUBILATE
REJOICING GLEE MIRTH OVATION
FESTIVITY
REJOIN TAUNT ANSWER REUNITE
REJOINDER REPLY ANSWER
COUNTER RESPONSE
REJUVENATE UNOLD
REKEM (FATHER OF —) HEBRON
REKINDLE RELUME REVIVE

RELAPSE SINK WEED LAPSE RECIDE RETURN BACKSET SUBSIDE BACKCAST WITHDRAW RECIDIVISM

RELATE SAY ALLY BEAR JOIN READ TELL PITCH REFER SPELL STATE TOUCH ALLUDE ASSERT DELATE DETAIL DEVISE RECITE REPORT REPUTE COGNATE CONCERN DECLARE INVOLVE NARRATE PERTAIN RECOUNT CALABASH DESCRIBE REHEARSE APPERTAIN
(— TO) TOUCH

RELATED KIN SIB AKIN ALLIED AFFINED
(— BY FATHER'S SIDE) AGNATE
(— INVERSELY) RECIPROCAL
(— ON MOTHER'S SIDE) ENATE ENATIC COGNATE
(PREF.) (— BY REMARRIAGE) STEP

RELATING (ALSO SEE PERTAINING)
(— TO) AGAINST
(— TO A RECENT PAST) ERST
(SUFF.) (— TO) AL ATIVE IAL IC(AL) ILE INE ISH ISTIC ITIC ITIOUS

RELATION KIN SIB TALE BLOOD FETII AFFINE DATIVE REGARD ACCOUNT BEARING HISTORY KINSHIP KINSMAN RAPPORT RESPECT SCHESIS TELLING AFFINITY HABITUDE RELATIVE TENDENCY REFERENCE REHEARSAL RISHTADAR PROPORTION
(— BETWEEN SPECIES) AFFINITY
(— OF LIKENESS) ANALOGY
(BLOOD —) KIN SIB
(FIXED —) RATIO
(FRIENDLY —S) AMITY
(SYNTACTIC —) FUNCTION
(WORKING —) GEAR

RELATIONSHIP KIN BLOOD ACTION AGENCY AMENITY AMITATE ANALOGY ANGULUS BEARING CONTACT KINDRED KINSHIP LIAISON RESPECT SIBNESS SIBREDE SOCIETY AFFINITY AGNATION CONTRAST GOSSIPRY RELATIVE SYMPATHY COGNATION FILIATION
(BUSINESS —) ACCOUNT
(CLOSE —) BOSOM AFFIANCE INTIMACY BELONGING
(INHARMONIOUS —) OUTS
(MARITAL —) BED
(MATHEMATICAL —) PARITY
(MUTUAL —) TERMS SYMMETRY
(SEXUAL —) AFFAIR
(SOCIAL —) FOOTING

RELATIVE KIN ALLY BLOOD AFFINE AGNATE ALLIED COUSIN GERMAN KINDRED KINSMAN APPOSITE COGNATUS RELATION RELEVANT PERTINENT
(PL.) KIN SIB FOLK KINDRED KINFOLK KINNERY KINSFOLK

RELAX LAX GIVE REST ABATE BREAK LOOSE REMIT SLACK DIVERT LAXATE SOFTEN UNBEND UNGIVE UNKNIT DEBLOCK RELEASE RESOLVE SLACKEN UNPURSE MITIGATE UNBUCKLE UNCLENCH

RELAXATION EASE LAZE REST ATONY CREEP LETUP RELAX SOLACE DETENTE LETDOWN RELACHE BREATHER DIVERSION

RELAXED LAX LASH LOOSE SLACK SONSY REMISS SONSIE INFORMAL RESOLVED UNBENDED UNBRACED

RELAXING ANIMAL ANODYNE DETENTE
(— POINT) SEAR

RELAY SPELL RELIEF REMUDA AVANTLAY REPEATER
(— OF DOGS) VAUNTLAY
(— OF PALANQUIN BEARERS) DAK

RELEASE LES LET BAIL DROP EMIT FREE LESE LIOS LISS SHED SLIP TRIP UNDO ERUPT EXEEM LEISS LOOSE MUKTI REMIT SLAKE ACQUIT ASSOIL DEMISE EXCUSE EXEMPT LAUNCH MOKSHA REMISE SPRING UNBEND UNTACK UNWORK ABSOLVE APATHIA DELIVER DETENTE DISBAND FREEDOM QUIETUS SOLUTIO UNSTICK DELIVERY DISPENSE DISSOLVE LIBERATE DISCHARGE RELINQUISH
(— AS DOGS) UNLEASH
(— DANCING PARTNER) BREAK
(— EMOTION) ABREAST
(— FROM CONFINEMENT) UNMEW UNPEN SPRING STREET
(— FROM DEBT) FREITH
(— FROM MILITARY) INVALID
(— FROM SLAVERY) MANUMIT
(— ON ONE'S WORD) PAROLE
(PRESS —) HANDOUT

RELEASED OFF FREE EXEMPT

RELEGATE DOOM EXILE BANISH COMMIT DEMOTE REJECT DEGRADE
(— TO OBSCURITY) DOWN

RELENT COME MELT ABATE YIELD REGRET REPENT LIQUEFY MOLLIFY SLACKEN

RELENTLESS GRIM HARD HARSH STERN STONY BITTER SAVAGE STRICT AUSTERE PITILESS RIGOROUS

RELEVANCE PRECISION PERTINENCE

RELEVANT APT VALID GERMAN APROPOS GERMANE APPOSITE MATERIAL PERTINENT

RELIABILITY STEEL CREDENCE

RELIABLE GOOD HARD SAFE SURE TRUE PUKKA SOLID SOUND THERE TRIED TRUST WHITE DINKUM STEADY TRUSTY CERTAIN FAITHFUL SOOTHFUL STRAIGHT

RELIANCE HOPE TRUST CREDIT AFFIANCE MAINSTAY
(— ON FAITH) FIDEISM

RELIC HUACO REMAIN ANTIQUE HALIDOM LEAVING MEMENTO RELIQUE VESTIGE SOUVENIR SURVIVAL
(PL.) CORPSE HALIDOM REMAINS
(PREF.) LIPSANO

RELICT WIDOW REMANIE RESIDUAL SURVIVOR EPIBIOTIC

RELIEF AID LAX SOB BOOT BOTE

EASE HELP RELAY SCRUB SPELL SWING ESCAPE REMEDY SUCCOR COMFORT FEEDING REDRESS RILIEVO EASEMENT REPOUSSE
(TEMPORARY —) HITCH
(SUFF.) LYSE LYSIS LYST LYTE LYTIC LYZE

RELIEVE ROB BEET EASE FREE HELP LIOS LISS ALLAY LIGHT LISSE LITHE RIGHT SLAKE SPARE SPELL ASSIST LESSEN PHYSIC REMEDY REMOVE RESCUE SOOTHE SUCCOR UNMAZE ASSUAGE COMFORT DELIVER DEPRIVE FRESHEN LIGHTEN REDRESS REFRESH SUCCEED SUPPORT SUSTAIN SWEETEN ALIGHTEN DIMINISH MITIGATE RELEVATE
(— A SAIL) SPILL
(— OF OFFICE) AX AXE
(— OF SIN) CONFESS

RELIGIEUSE NUN CLERGESS

RELIGION BON DIN LAW SECT BONBO CREED DAENA FAITH OBEAH PIETY SOPHY DHARMA SHINTO SYSTEM TAOISM ELOHISM JAINISM JUDAISM ORPHISM PERSISM RELIGIO SIKHISM SYNAGOG BUDDHISM CAODAISM HINDUISM MAZDAISM PEYOTISM SHAMANISM
(— OF ABRAHAM) HANIFIYA
(— OF TIBET) BON
(CHRISTIAN —) WAY
(UNORTHODOX —) CULT

RELIGIOSE PIETISTIC

RELIGIOUS PI HOLY EXACT GODLY PIOUS RIGID DEVOUT DIVINE SACRED FERVENT GHOSTLY ZEALOUS SPIRITUAL
(— HOUSE) KELLION

RELINQUISH LAY LET CEDE DROP QUIT DEMIT FORGO GRANT LEAVE WAIVE YIELD CANCEL DESERT RESIGN ABANDON FORSAKE RELEASE ABDICATE ABNEGATE LINQUISH RENOUNCE

RELIQUARY ARCA CHEF CASKET CHASSE COFFER MEMORY SHRINE STEEPA TABLET CHORTEN HALIDOM MEMORIA FERETORY

RELISH CHOW DASH EDGE GOUT GUST LIKE SOUL SOWL TANG ZEST ACHAR ENJOY GUSTO RELES SAVOR SOWLE SPICE TASTE TRACE ATSARA DEGUST FLAVOR LIKING PALATE SAVOUR BOTARGO OUTWORK STOMACH APPETITE FONDNESS PICCALILLI
(— FOR FOOD) CHAW
(INTELLECTUAL —) TASTE
(MENTAL —) PALATE
(ROMAN —) GARUM
(SALT OR ACID —) ACHAR

RELUCENT RADIANT SHINING GLEAMING

RELUCT TARROW

RELUCTANCE GRUDGE AVERSION ANTIPATHY RENITENCE
(— UNIT) REL

RELUCTANT SET SHY CAGY LOTH NICE CHARY LOATH SWEER

THRAW AFRAID AVERSE DAINTY FORCED SWEERT UNFAIN ASHAMED HALTING BACKWARD GRUDGING LOATHFUL RENITENT THRAWART

RELY AFFY BANK BASE LEAN LITE REST STAY COUNT RALLY TRUST DEPEND GROUND RECKON REPOSE CONFIDE
(— ON) LIPPEN VENTURE

REMAIN LIE SIT BIDE REST STAY STOP ABIDE CLING DWELL LEAVE STAND TARRY THOLE BELIVE ENDURE MANENT RESIDE SUBSIST SURVIVE CONTINUE
(— AWAKE) VIGILATE
(— IN DEADLOCK) HANG
(— MOTIONLESS) STAGNATE
(— UNDER HEAT TREATMENT) SOAK
(— UNDISTURBED AFTER HEAT TREATMENT) AGE
(— UNUSED) LIE
(— UPRIGHT) STAND
(—S IN MASH TUN) GRAINS
(—S IN PIPEBOWL) TOPPER
(—S OF CANE) BEGASS BAGASSE
(—S OF FIRE) EMBER EMBERS
(—S ON STAGE) MANET
(ANIMAL —S) SPOILS
(FOSSIL —) EXUVIAE
(FOUL —S) SCURF
(PL.) CHAR DUST ASHES DECAY DRAFF GHOST SHARD SHERD BURIAL DEBRIS FOSSIL RELIEF CARCASS REMNANT RESIDUE RELIQUIAE
(PREF.) MENO

REMAINDER NET HEEL LAVE REST PLUGS ARREAR EXCESS RELIEF BALANCE REMNANT RESIDUE SURPLUS LEAVINGS LEFTOVER RESIDUAL RESIDUUM
(— OF ATOM) CORE
(PL.) GARBLINGS LEFTMENTS

REMAINING OVER BIDING REMNANT LEFTOVER REMANENT RESIDUAL
(PREF.) MENO

REMALIAH (SON OF —) PEKAH

REMARK DIG SAY SEE GIRD HEED NOTE WORD GLOSS STATE TOKEN EARFUL GAMBIT NOTICE REGARD COMMENT DESCANT DISCANT OBSERVE PERCEIVE OBSERVATION
(— BRIEFLY) GLANCE
(AMIABLE —) DOUCEUR
(AMUSING —) GAG
(BANAL —) PLATITUDE
(BITING —) BARB
(CLEVER —) NIFTY
(CONCLUDING —S) ENVOI
(CUTTING —) DIG SPINOSITY
(DULL —) BROMIDE
(EMBARRASSING —) BREAK
(EXPLANATORY —) SCHOLION SCHOLIUM
(FOOLISH —) INANITY
(ILL-TIMED —) CLANGER
(INSULTING —) SLUR
(JEERING —) JEST SKIT
(LAUGH-PROVOKING —) GAG
(SARCASTIC —) HIT GIRD SLANT
(SATIRICAL —) JEST SKIT SGAFT

(SHARP —) GANSEL STINGER
(SILLY —) FADAISE
(STALE —S) BILGE
(UNCOMPLIMENTARY —) BRICKBAT
(WITTY —) JEST CRACK ZINGER
REMARKABLE SOME FORBY
GREAT SIGNAL STRONG NOTABLE
STRANGE UNUSUAL FABULOUS
MARKABLE SINGULAR SPANKING
STRIKING UNCOMMON
BODACIOUS NOTICEABLE
PHENOMENAL
(NOT —) INCURIOUS
REMARKABLY UNCO UNKO JOLLY
UNCOW DEUCED UNCOLY
SIGNALLY
REMEDIAL RELEVANT SALUTARY
REMEDILESS BOOTLESS
REMEDY AID BOT BOOT BOTE
CURE GAIN HALE HEAL HELP
REDE AZOTH MANDS REDUB
SHERE TOPIC PHYSIC RECOUR
RECURE RELIEF REPAIR RESIDY
URETIC ANTACID CORRECT
DRASTIC ICTERIC OTALGIC
PLASTER RECTIFY REDRESS
RELIEVE ANTIDOTE MEDICINE
PHARMACY RECOVERY REMEDIAL
SPECIFIC
(— COUNTERACTING POISON)
TREACLE ANTIDOTE
(— FOR ALL DISEASES) PANACEA
CATHOLICON
(— FOR DIZZINESS) DINIC
(— FOR JAUNDICE) ICTERIC
(— TO REDUCE FEVER) FEBRIFUGE
(CHINESE —) SENSO
(EXTERNAL —) TOPIC
(FAVORITE —) NOSTRUM
(SECRET —) ARCANUM
(TAPEWORM —) EMBELIA
(TOOTHACHE —) TONGA
(UNIVERSAL —) AZOTH
CATHOLICON
(WITHOUT —) BOOTLESS
REMEMBER MEM MIN MEAN MIND
MINE MING IDEATE MEMBER
RECALL RECORD REMIND RETAIN
REWARD BETHINK MENTION
RECOLLECT
(— REMORSEFULLY) REMORD
REMEMBRANCE MIN MIND
MEMORY RECORD MEANING
MINDING MINNING MEMORIAL
REMINDER SOUVENIR
**REMEMBRANCE OF THINGS
PAST (AUTHOR OF —)** PROUST
(CHARACTER IN —) MOREL SWANN
MARCEL ODETTE RACHEL ROBERT
VEDURIN GILBERTE VINTEUIL
ALBERTINE DECHARLUS
GUERMANTES
REMIND JOG MIN MIND MINE
MING IMMIND PROMPT
REMEMBER
REMINDER MEMO PROD TWIT
TOUCH PROMPT MINDING
MONITOR SOUVENIR REFRESHER
REMINISCENCE MEMORY RECALL
ANAMNESIS
REMISE RETURN RELEASE REPLACE
CARRIAGE
REMISS LAX LAZY MILD PALE

FAINT SLACK TARDY BEHIND
DILUTED LANGUID CARELESS
DERELICT DILATORY HEEDLESS
NEGLIGENT
REMISSION CURE LIOS LISS
PARDON REMISE LOOSING
REMITTAL
REMISSNESS LACHES LASHNESS
REMIT SEND COVER LOOSE RELAX
CANCEL EXCUSE PARDON
REMAND REMISS RESIGN
ABSOLVE FORGIVE RELEASE
SUSPEND ABROGATE MITIGATE
MODERATE
REMNANT END TAG BUTT DREG
FENT REST RUMP RUND RELIC
STUMP TRACE REMAIN LEAVING
REMAINS SURVIVOR
(— OF CLOTH) FENT
(— OF FOOD) CRUST
(— OF ROCK MASS) KLIP KLIPPE
(— OF VEIL) ANNULUS
(—S OF FILLETS) SCISSEL
(—S OF VEIL) CORTINA
(VESTIGIAL —) SHADOW
(PL.) EPIPLASM
REMODEL MEND RECAST CONVERT
REMONSTRANCE PROOF ADVICE
COUNSEL PROTEST REPROOF
EVIDENCE
REMONSTRANT ARMINIAN
REMONSTRATE ARGUE OBJECT
PROTEST REPROVE COMPLAIN
REMORA CLOG DRAG PEGA
SLICKER GUAICAN PEGADOR
ECHENEID LOOTSMAN STAYSHIP
STOPSHIP SUCKFISH
REMORSE HELL PITY RUTH PRICK
REGRET REMORD AYENBITE
PENITENCE
(— OF CONSCIENCE) GRUDGE
REMORSEFUL BAD PITIFUL
CONTRITE GUILTSICK
REMOTE FAR OFF BACK DEEP
FERN HIGH LONG ALOOF HOARY
UTTER ALENGE DISTAL ELENGE
EXEMPT OTIOSE SECRET DEVIOUS
DISSITE DISTANT EXTREME
FAILING FARAWAY FOREIGN
OBSCURE OUTSIDE ABDITIVE
ABSTRUSE ARMCHAIR BACKVELD
INTERIOR OUTLYING OUTWORLD
SECLUDED SOLITARY
OUTLANDISH
(— FROM LIFE) SCHOOLISH
(MOST —) ULTIMA EXTREME
HINDMOST ULTIMATE
(PREF.) DIST(O) PALAE(O) PALE(O)
REMOTELY CLEAN DISTANTLY
REMOTENESS AWAYNESS
DISTANCE
REMOTER FARTHER ULTERIOR
REMOVABLE DATIVE REMOTIVE
REMOVAL AX AXE EXILE AMOTION
CLEANUP ERASION ABLATION
EXCISION EXERESIS OFFGOING
REMOTION
(— OF COAL) GETTING
(— OF ICE FROM GLACIER)
ATTRITION
(— OF LAND) AVULSION
(SUFF.) CENOSIS
(SURGICAL —) ECTOMY

REMOVE GET PUT RID BATE COMB
DELE DRAW FILE FLIT FREE LIFT
MOVE PARE PEEL PULL QUIT
RAZE VOID WEED APART AUFER
AVOID BLAST BRUSH CLEAR
EMITY ERASE EVOID HEAVE HOIST
LIGHT PLANE RAISE REPEL SHIFT
SHUCK SLASH SLIPE STRIP SWEEP
WAIVE BANISH CANCEL CHANGE
CONVEY DEDUCT DEGREE
DEPART DEPOSE EFFACE ELOIGN
EXEMPT EXPORT MINISH RELEVE
REMBLE SPIRIT AMOLISH DEPRIVE
DESCENT DISMISS DISPOST
RETRACT REVERSE STRANGE
SUBDUCT SUBLATE ABSTRACT
ASPIRATE DISPLACE DISPLANT
ESTRANGE EVACUATE RETRENCH
SUPPLANT TRANSFER WITHDRAW
OBLITERATE
(— A STITCH) DECREASE
(— BARK FROM LOG) ROSS
(— BIT BY BIT) SCAMBLE
(— BY CUTTING) ABLATE
(— BY DEATH) SNATCH
(— CLOTHING) DOFF STRIP
(— COLOR) BLEACH
(— COVER) UNCAP
(— DEFECTS) SCARF
(— DIRT) BLADE GARBLE
(— EXCESS METAL) CUT
(— FROM CHECKER BOARD) HUFF
(— FROM OFFICE) DEPOSE RECALL
DISMISS
(— FROM REMEMBRANCE) COVER
(— GILLS) BEARD
(— HAIR) DEPILATE
(— HUSKS AND CHAFF) GELD
(— INSIDES OF FISH) GIB GIP
(— JUDGE) ADDRESS
(— LOWER BRANCHES) BRASH
(— MAST) UNSTEP
(— ORE) EXTRACT
(— PARTICLES OF GOLD LEAF) SKEW
(— PITCHER FROM BASEBALL GAME)
DERRICK
(— POTATOES) GRABBLE
(— QUEEN BEE) DEMAREE
(— QUIETLY) ABSTRACT
(— ROOTS) GRUB
(— SEED FROM FLAX) RIBBLE
(— SEEDS) STONE
(— SKIN) HULL HUSK
(— SOUND FROM TAPE) BLIP
(— SPROUTS FROM) CHIT
(— STALK FROM) STRIG
(— STAMENS) CASTRATE
(— TABLECLOTH) DRAW
(— THE TOP OF) COP
(— TO AVOID TAX) SKIM
(— TROUSERS) DEBAG
(— WASTE TO FIBER) GARNETT
(— WOOL) BELLY
(— WORKS OF STOLEN WATCH)
CHURCH
(PREF.) DE
REMOVED UP OFF AWAY ALIEN
ALOOF APART REMOTE DISTANT
SEMOTED ABSTRACT
REMOVER MOVER CROPMAN
KNOTTER
REMUDA CAVY

CAVAYARD CAVYYARD
REMUNERATE PAY REPAY
REWARD GRATIFY SATISFY
CONSIDER REIMBURSE
REMUNERATION PAY REWARD
SALARY PAYMENT
REMUNERATIVE GAINFUL
REWARDING
REMUS (BROTHER OF —) ROMULUS
RENAISSANCE NARA REBIRTH
REVIVAL
RENAL NEPHRIC NEPHRITIC
RENCOUNTER CLASH FIGHT
DEBATE CONTEST CONFLICT
REND PULL RENT RIVE TEAR TOIL
BREAK BURST DIVEL RATCH
ROWEL SEVER SPLIT WREST
CLEAVE SCREED WRENCH
ABSCIND DIVULSE RUPTURE
WREATHE DISPIECE DISTRAIN
FRACTURE LACERATE SPLINTER
(— AND DEVOUR) TIRE
RENDER DO PAY PUT TRY BEAR
DRAW ECHO EMIT MAKE RENT
RIND DEFER PRICK REPAY YIELD
RECITE REPEAT RETURN DELIVER
PRECARY REFLECT REQUITE
RESTORE SERVICE TALLAGE
TRANSMIT
(— ACID) PRICK
(— AGREEABLE) DULCIFY
(— AS LARD) TRY
(— ASSISTANCE TO SHIP) FOY
(— CAPABLE) ACTIVATE
(— CLEAR) OPEN
(— FIT) ADAPT
(— GODLIKE) DEIFY
(— HEAVY WITH FOOD) STODGE
(— HOMAGE) ATTORN
(— IMMUNE) FRANK VASTATE
(— INEFFECTIVE) VITIATE
(— KNOTTY) GNARL
(— OBLIQUE) SPLAY
(— OBSCURE) DARKLE
(— OF BOON WORK) PRECARY
(— QUIET) ACCOY
(— SENSELESS) STUN ASTONISH
(— TURBID) ROIL
(— UNFIT) DENATURE
(— UNSTABLE) UNHINGE
(— VERDICT) PASS
(— VOID) CASS DEFEAT
(SUFF.) EN
RENDERED RENDU TRIED
RENDERING RENDU ENGLISH
VERSION RENDITION
(— OF SCENE) STUDY
RENDEZVOUS DATE HAUNT TRYST
REFUGE HANGOUT MEETING
RETREAT
(— FOR SHIPS) DOWN
RENDITION ACCOUNT CONDUCT
DELIVERY
RENEGADE DORAX PERVERT
TRAITOR APOSTATE RECREANT
RENEGADO RUNAGADO
RUNAGATE TURNCOAT
RENEGE BEG NIG DENY RENIG
DESERT REVOKE RETRACT
FAINAIGUE
RENEW NEW REST FRESH RECALL
REFORM RENOVE REPEAT
RESUME REVIVE INSTORE

REBUILD REFRESH REPLACE RESTORE OVERHAUL REJUVENATE
(— MORTAR) REPOINT
(— WINE) STUM
RENEWAL RENEW REVIVAL NOVATION
RENNET LAB RUEN VELL STEEP RENNIN RUNNET EARNING ABOMASUM YEARNING CHEESELIP
RENOUNCE PUT CEDE DEFY DENY QUIT DEVOW FORGO RENAY WAIVE ABJURE DISOWN FORLET FORSAY RECANT REFUSE REJECT RENEGE RESIGN REVOKE ABANDON DECLARE FORLEIT FORSAKE RETRACT WITHSAY ABDICATE ABNEGATE DISCLAIM FORSPEAK FORSWEAR MANSWEAR PROCLAIM RELINQUISH
RENOVATE DUST RENEW REVIVE FURBISH REFRESH RESTORE OVERHAUL RENOVIZE
(— HAT) MOLOKER MOLOCKER
RENOWN BAY BRAG FAME ECLAT GLORY KUDOS PRICE RUMOR ESTEEM LUSTER RENONE REPORT EMPRISE SWAGGER WORSHIP PRESTIGE NOTORIETY
RENOWNED FAMED NOBLE NOTED FAMOUS EMINENT RENOMME GLORIOUS MAGNIFIC RENOMMEE
RENT LET SET TAX FARM GALE GAPE HIRE MAIL RACK RIME RIVE SLIT TEAR TOLL WAGE BREAK CANON CENSO CUDDY ENDOW GANCH GAVEL SPLIT BLANCH BREACH BROKEN CENSUS CHASMA CRANNY CUSTOM GAUNCH INCOME SCHISM SCREED STRENT CHARTER CHIEFRY CORNAGE CRACKED CREVICE FISSURE MAILING MOLLAND ONSTAND RENTAGE REVENUE RUPTURE TRIBUTE CHAMPART CHIEFERY HEADRENT STALLAGE VECTIGAL WAYLEAVE LANDGAFOL
(— BY BOAR'S TUSK) GANCH GAUNCH
(— IN LIEU OF SUPPER) CUDDY
(— OF LAND PAID IN KIND) CAIN
(ANNUAL —) CANON
(EARTHQUAKE —) SCARLET
(GROUND —) CENSO CENSUS
(OATS IN LIEU OF —) AVENAGE
RENTAL KAIN PORT TONNAGE TRIBUTE TUNNAGE
RENTED LETTEN
RENTER FARMER RANTER CHIPPER BOXHOLDER
RENUNCIATION DENIAL APOSTASY DEFIANCE DISAVOWAL REJECTION SACRIFICE
REP CANNELE DROGUET POPELINE
REPAIR DO EIK EKE FIX IMP HEAL HELP MEND TINE AMEND BOTCH DIGHT EMEND HAUNT RALLY REDUB RENEW STORE TRADE UPSET ASTORE BUSHEL COBBLE COGGLE COOPER DOCTOR FETTLE

RECURE REFORM REMEDY REPASS RESORT RETURN UPKEEP CORRECT INFAINT REDRESS REPAREL RESTORE SERVICE FLOCKING OVERHAUL RETRIEVE REVIVIFY
(— BOAT) CAREEN
(— CLUMSILY) BOTCH
(— FENCE) MOUND
(— ROAD) SKID
(— SHOE) FOX TAP
REPAIRED VAMPED
REPAIRER DOCTOR BOTCHER COBBLER WOFFLER CEMENTER
(SHOE —) JACKMAN BENCHMAN
(TEXTILE —) SMASHER
REPAIRMAN FETTLER
REPARATION BOTE AMENDS REMEDY REWARD DAMAGES REDRESS REPAIRS REQUITAL
REPARTEE WIT KNACK REPLY BANTER RETORT RIPOST RIPOSTE BACKCHAT BADINAGE COMEBACK GIFFGAFF
REPAST BAIT FEED FOOD MEAL BEVER FEAST TREAT DRINKING COLLATION
(— BETWEEN MEALS) BEVER BRUNCH BANQUET
(HASTY —) SNACK
(LIGHT —) BAIT VOID VOIDEE COLLATION
REPAY MEED QUIT APPAY TALLY YIELD ACQUIT ANSWER REFUND RETORT RETURN REWARD IMBURSE REQUITE RESTORE REIMBURSE
REPEAL ANNUL CANCEL RECALL REVOKE ABANDON ABOLISH RESCIND REVERSE ABROGATE DEROGATE DISENACT RENOUNCE
REPEAT SAY ECHO GAIT RAME RANE SHOW TELL DITTO QUOTE RECUR RENEW RESAY REVIE THRUM ANSWER RENDER RESUME RETAIL SECOND DECLINE DIVULGE ITERATE PRESENT REPLICA REPRISE DINGDONG REDOUBLE REHEARSE REPLICATE
(— BY ROTE) PARROT
(— GLIBLY) SCREED
(— MONOTONOUSLY) CUCKOO DINGDONG
(— OF PATTERN) GAIT
(— TIRESOMELY) DIN
REPEATED OFTEN CONSTANT FREQUENT PERENNIAL
REPEATEDLY OFT EVERY THRICE
REPEATER GUN RIFLE WATCH PISTOL FLOATER HOLDOVER
REPEL FEND TURN WARD FENCE REBUT DEFEND REBEAT REBUFF REFUSE REFUTE REJECT REPUGN RESIST REVOLT DISGUST PELLATE REPULSE PROPULSE
REPELLANT REPUGNANT
REPELLENT DOPE GRIM HARSH CAMPHOR HATEFUL SQUALID
(INSECT —) DEET
REPELLING HARD SICKLY
REPENT REW RUE MOURN GRIEVE REGRET REPTANT CREEPING FORTHINK

REPENTANCE REW RUE PITY RUTH RUING REGRET SORROW PENANCE REMORSE
REPENTANT ATTRITE PENITENT
REPERCUSSION ECHO TENOR RECOIL REPULSE BACKWASH
REPERTORY REP BOOK LIST INDEX ARSENAL CATALOG
REPETITION BIS REP COPY ECHO PLOCE REVIE TROLL DILOGY REPEAT MENTION RECITAL REPLICA REPRISE IDENTITY ITERANCE ITERANCY NEMBUTSU PALILOGY PARROTRY RECOVERY REDOUBLE REHEARSAL
(— IN REVERSE ORDER) EPANODOS
(— OF HOMOLOGOUS PARTS) MERISM
(— OF SPEECH FORMS) ROTE
(— OF WORD) ANAPHORA BATTOLOGY
(NEEDLESS —) REDUNDANCY
(UNINSPIRED —) STENCIL
(PREF.) (PATHOLOGICAL —) PALI
REPHAEL (FATHER OF —) SHEMAIAH
REPHAH (FATHER OF —) EPHRAIM
REPHAIAH (FATHER OF —) HUR TOLA BINEA
REPHAIM EMIM
REPINE FRET PINE WEAKEN COMPLAIN
REPINING MURMUR REGRET PLAINTIVE
REPLACE SWAP SWOP RENEW REPAY SHIFT STEAD CHANGE FOLLOW REFUND REMISE REPONE SUPPLY FRESHEN PREEMPT RESTORE SUCCEED DISPLACE SUPPLANT REPLENISH
REPLACEMENT CUT ERSATZ
(— FOR HAND) HOOK
(— OF CONSONANT) LENITION
REPLENISH CHUNK REFIT RENEW SUPPLY NOURISH PERFECT PLENISH REPLETE RESTORE SUFFICE
REPLETE FAT FULL RIFE SATED STOUT STUFF FILLED GORGED IMPLETE COMPLETE HONEYPOT
REPLETION FULTH FULNESS SURFEIT FULLNESS PLETHORA SATURITY
REPLICA BIS PUP COPY IDEA CHARM IMAGE REVIE FACSIMILE
REPLICATION ECHO REPLY ANSWER REJOINDER
REPLY CAP JAWAB KNACK RESAY ANSWER REJOIN RETORT RETURN REPLIAL RESOUND RESPOND REPARTEE REPLIQUE RESPONSE SIMILITER
REPORT CRY POP SAY FAME ITEM NOTE TELL VENT VOTE WORD AUDIT BRUIT COVER CRACK NOISE REFER ROUND RUMOR SCALE SOUND STATE STORY VOICE BREEZE CAHIER CREDIT DELATE DETAIL FINGER GOSSIP RAPORT RECITE RELATE RENOWN REPUTE RETURN RUMBLE SPEECH STEVEN SURVEY THREAP ACCOUNT HANSARD HEARING HEARSAY INKLING KHUBBER

NARRATE OPINION PROCESS RECITAL ADVISORY DECISION DESCRIBE HEMOGRAM VERBATIM GRAPEVINE
(— NEWS) COVER
(— OF GUN) CLAP
(— OF INFRACTION) GIG
(— OF PROCEEDINGS) CAHIER
(— OF TIMBER SURVEYOR) CRUISE
(ABSURD —) CANARD
(BELIEVED —) CREDIT
(CASUAL —) FABLE
(COMMON —) CRY FAME SPEECH
(FALSE —) SHAVE CANARD FURPHY SLANDER
(FLYING —) SOUGH
(HONORABLE —) TONGUE
(LAW —) CASE
(MILITARY —) STATE SITREP
(NEWS —) FLASH SCOOP
(NOISY —) RUMBLE
(OFFICIAL —) HANSARD
(POPULAR —) RUMOR RUMOUR
(PUBLIC —) FAME
(UNFAVORABLE —) SKIN
(UNVERIFIED —) VOICE GRAPEVINE
(VAGUE —) BREEZE
REPORTER LEGMAN PISTOL CREEPER NEWSMAN NEWSHAWK PRESSMAN STRINGER PAPARAZZO
(SOCIETY —) JENKINS
(YOUNG —) CUB
REPORTING BEAT COVERAGE
REPOSE RO BED LIE PUT AFFY CALM EASE RELY REST PEACE PLACE POISE QUIET SLEEP REPAST RECLINE EASINESS QUIETUDE SERENITY
(— LAZILY) FROWST
(DREAMY —) KEF
REPOSITORY ARK AMBRY CAPSA DEPOT HOARD VAULT ARMORY CASKET MUSEUM VESTRY ARCHIVE CABINET CAPSULE GENIZAH GRANARY HANAPER SPICERY ARCHIVES MAGAZINE TREASURY SEPULCHER
REPOSOIR REPOSE
REPOSSESS PULL RECOVER
REPREHEND NIP WARN BLAME CHIDE REBUKE CENSURE REPRISE REPROVE CRITICIZE
REPREHENSIBLE ILL AMISS BLAMABLE CRIMINAL CULPABLE SCABROUS
REPREHENSION BLAME REBUKE CENSURE OBLOQUY REPROOF
REPRESENT GIVE LIKE LIMN SHOW TYPE SHADE DEPICT SEMBLE TYPIFY DISPLAY EXHIBIT FASHION PICTURE PORTRAY PROTEST TRADUCE DEFIGURE DESCRIBE RESEMBLE PERSONATE
(— CONCRETELY) THING
(— IN LANGUAGE) ACT BODY DRAW ENACT IMAGE SPEAK BLAZON CLOTHE EMBODY FIGURE SAMPLE BETOKEN EXPRESS DECIPHER
(— ON STAGE) ACT
REPRESENTATION SUN BUST FORM ICON IDEA IDOL IKON SHOW SWAG ANGLE DRAFT

FANCY IMAGE INSET LABEL
MEDAL TABUT AVOWAL BUDDHA
EFFIGY FIGURE FLEECE MODULE
OBJECT SCHEMA SCHEME SKETCH
SUNRAY WAYANG ANATOMY
DIORAMA DRAUGHT DRAWING
EPITOME EXPRESS EXTRACT
FOLIAGE MAJESTY SCENERY
TABLEAU BESTIARY BLAZONRY
CREATION EPIPHANY EXTERIOR
IDIOGRAM LIKENESS TYPORAMA
SIMULACRUM RESEMBLANCE
(— OF SERPENT) BASIL DRAGON
BASILISK
(— OF SHRINE OF HUSAIN) TABUT
(— OF VISION) AISLING
(DIPLOMATIC —) DEMARCHE
(FACSIMILE —) TYPORAMA
(FAINT —) SHADOW
(FUNERAL —) CADAVER
(GRAPHIC —) CHART BISECT
(HERALDIC —) LEOPARD LIONCEL
(MENTAL —) FANCY IMAGE
(MINIATURE —) MODEL
(SYMBOLIC —) ALLEGORY
REPRESENTATIVE REP FAIR TYPE
AGENT ENVOY VAKIL ASSIGN
COMMON DEPUTY EMBLEM
LEDGER SAMPLE VAKEEL
BURGESS GRIEVER TRIBUNE
TYPICAL DECURION DELEGATE
EMISSARY EXPONENT FIELDMAN
GASTALDO INTIMATE OBSERVER
SALESMAN SPECIMEN
(— OF ATMOSPHERE) AERIAL
(MANUFACTURER'S —) BLOCKMAN
(PL.) COMMONS
REPRESS CURB HUSH BLUNT
BRIDE CHAIN CHECK CHOKE
CRUSH DAUNT DROWN QUELL
SQUAT BRIDLE COERCE DEADEN
REBUKE STIFLE SUBDUE CONTROL
DEPRESS INHIBIT REPRIME
SILENCE SWALLOW COMPRESS
OVERBEAR RESTRAIN RESTRICT
RETRENCH REVOCATE STRANGLE
SUPPRESS WITHHOLD
REPRESSED SULLEN STIFLED
REPRIEVE DELAY GRACE ESCAPE
REPRISE RESPITE SUSPEND
POSTPONE
REPRIMAND WIG BAWL CALL
CHEW JACK SKIN SLAP SLON
SNEB SNIB TASK CHECK CREED
SLATE SLOAN SPANK TARGE
BOUNCE CARPET EARFUL REBUKE
ROCKET STRAFE CENSURE
CHAPTER LECTURE REPROOF
REPROVE DRESSING WRAGGING
REPRINT COPY DEPRINT OFFPRINT
REIMPOSE TAUCHNITZ
REPRISAL PRIZE MARQUE REPRISE
REQUITAL RECAPTION
REPROACH ILL TAX BLOT GIBE
JIBE LACK NOSE NOTE RAIL SLUR
SPOT TEEN TWIT WITE ABUSE
BLAME BRAID BRAND CHIDE
SCOLD SHEND TAUNT WHITE
AYWORD BISMER INFAMY REBUKE
REVILE UPCAST VILIFY BLEMISH
CENSURE CONDEMN REPROOF
REPROVE SLANDER UMBRAID
UPBRAID WITHNIM BETONGUE

DISHONOR REDARGUE REVILING
CONTUMELY OPPROBRIUM
REFLECTION
REPROACHFUL BITTER ABUSIVE
SHAMEFUL
REPROBATE HARD LOST SCAMP
DISOWN RASCAL REJECT SINNER
ABANDON CENSURE CORRUPT
EXCLUDE REPROVE DEPRAVED
DISALLOW HARDENED
SCALAWAG SKALAWAG
REPRODUCE BUD HIT COPY BREED
SPORE RECITE REPEAT PORTRAY
AUTOTYPE MULTIPLY REFIGURE
REMEMBER PROCREATE
REPRODUCTION CAST COPY REVI
IMAGE PRINT ECTYPE RECALL
STEREO EDITION ELECTRO
EXOGAMY FISSION REPLICA
REVIVAL APOMIXIS BLOCKOUT
GAMOGAMY HOMOGAMY
LIKENESS
(— OF SOUND) AUDIO
(SUFF.) GAM(AE)(IST)(OUS)(Y)
GAMETE
GON(E)(IDIUM)(IMO)(IUM)(Y)
REPROOF PROD RATE BLAME
CHECK LESSON REBUKE CHIDING
LECTURE SETDOWN JOBATION
REPROACH REPROVAL SCOLDING
TAXATION JAWBATION
(GENTLE —) ADMONITION
REPROVE RAG TAP BAWL FLAY
FRIE JOBE RATE SNIB TRIM
BLAME CHECK CHIDE CRAWL
SCOLD SHEND SHENT SNEAP
BERATE CHASTE REBUKE REFORM
SCHOOL THREAT CENSURE
CONDEMN CORRECT IMPROVE
LECTURE UPBRAID WITHNIM
ADMONISH CHASTISE KEELHAUL
REDARGUE REPROACH
UNDERNIM WITHTAKE
REPTILE LOW MEAN WORM
GUANA SNAKE VIPER GAVIAL
LIZARD MOLOCH TURTLE
CRAWLER CREEPER DIAPSID
GHARIAL PROTEUS SAURIAN
SERPENT TUATARA BASILISK
CREEPING CYNODONT DINOSAUR
GALESAUR MESOSAUR
MOSASAUR PLIOSAUR STEGOMUS
SYNAPSID TORTOISE ALLIGATOR
CROCODILE PELYCOSAUR
PLESIOSAUR
(PART OF —) EYE JAW PIT BODY
FANG SCALE TOOTH BUTTON
RATTLE SHEATH TONGUE
SEGMENT
(PREF.) HERPET(I)(O)
REPTILIAN HERPETIC
REPUBLIC STATE SOVIET
POBLACHT
(FRENCH —) MARIANNE
(IDEAL —) ICARIA
(IMAGINARY —) OCEANA
REPUBLICAN RED QUID
STALWART SANSCULOT
REPUDIATE DEFY ABJURE DISOWN
RECANT REFUTE REJECT DECLINE
DISAVOW DISCARD DIVORCE
RETRACT DISCLAIM DISVOUCH
RENOUNCE

(— DEBTS) NOTCHEL
REPUDIATING NAKIR
REPUGNANCE ENMITY HATRED
HORROR DISGUST DISLIKE
DISTASTE LOATHING
REPUGNANT ALIEN DIRTY NASTY
ADVERSE HATEFUL OPPOSED
INIMICAL OPPOSITE ABHORRENT
OBNOXIOUS REPULSIVE
REPULSE FOIL ROUT RUSH CHECK
FLING REBUT REFEL REPEL
SMEAR DEFEAT DENIAL REBUFF
REBUTE REFUSE REJECT
REPULSION UG DISLIKE AVERSION
REPULSIVE COLD DAIN EVIL LOTH
UGLY VILE LOATH GREASY LAIDLY
FULSOME HATEFUL LOATHLY
SQUALID SCABROUS UNHONEST
REPUTABLE GOOD HONEST
WORTHY CREDIBLE ESTIMABLE
REPUTATION REP FAME LOSE
NAME NOTE ODOR PASS GLORY
HONOR IZZAT NOISE RUMOR
SAVOR VOICE CREDIT ESTEEM
RECORD RENOWN SHADOW
LAURELS OPINION RESPECT
WORSHIP STANDING
(EVIL —) INFAMY
(GOOD —) STANDING
REPUTE FAME ODOR RANK WORD
NOISE SAVOR THINK RECKON
REGARD STATUS OPINION
RESPECT WORSHIP ESTIMATE
JUDGMENT POSITION
(ILL —) SLANDER
REPUTED DIT PUTATIVE
REQUEST ASK BEG BOON CALL
PLEA PRAY SEEK SUIT TELL WISH
CLAIM LIBEL QUEST YEARN
APPEAL BEHEST DEMAND DESIRE
DIRECT ENCORE INVITE MOTION
BESPEAK COMMAND ENTREAT
INQUIRY REQUIRE SOLICIT
ENTREATY INSTANCE PETITION
ROGATION
(— FOR HELP) SOS
(STRONG —) DUN DEMAND
REQUIEM HYMN MASS REST DIRGE
PEACE QUIET REPOSE REQUIN
REQUIN SHARK TOMMY
REQUIRE ASK HAVE LACK NEED
TAKE WANT CLAIM CRAVE EXACT
FORCE GAVEL COMPEL DEMAND
DEPEND DESIRE ENJOIN ENTAIL
EXPECT GOVERN MISTER OBLIGE
BEHOOVE DICTATE INVOLVE
SOLICIT
REQUIRED DUE SET SUPPOSED
NECESSARY OBLIGATORY
REQUIREMENT CALL NEED LEGAL
ORDER BEHEST DEMAND
NECESSITY
(PL.) EXIGENCE EXIGENCY
REQUIRING
(PREF.) END(O)
REQUISITE DUE NEED NEEDY
VITAL NEEDFUL ESSENTIAL
NECESSARY
REQUISITION ORDER DEMAND
INDENT EMBARGO REQUEST
REQUITAL WAR APPAY MERIT
REPAY SERVE TALLY YIELD
ACQUIT DEFRAY REWARD

GRATIFY PAYMENT REVENGE
CONSIDER FORYIELD REPRISAL
REQUITE SERVE RECOMPENSE
RECIPROCATE
RERAILER DIAMOND
REREAD DOUBLE
RERECORD DUB
REREDOS SCREEN BRAZIER
DRAPERY RETABLO FIREBACK
REARDOSS
REREMOUSE BAT
RERUN (PAYMENT FOR —) RESIDUAL
RES POINT THING MATTER
SUBJECT
RESCIND LIFT ANNUL CANCEL
REMOVE REPEAL REVOKE
ABOLISH RETRACT RETREAT
ABROGATE
RESCRIPT EDICT ORDER DECREE
LETTER EPISTLE
RESCUE RID FREE HELP REDD
SAVE BORROW RANSOM REDEEM
RESKEW SUCCOR WARISH
DELIVER RECLAIM RECOVER
RELEASE SALVAGE DELIVERY
LIBERATE RECOURSE
RESEARCH ARBEIT SEARCH
ENQUIRY INQUIRY
RESECT EXCISE
RESEDA LEEK MENNUET
MORILLON
RESEMBLANCE SWAP PARITY
SIMILE ANALOGY AFFINITY
LIKENESS PARALLEL VICINITY
SIMILARITY
(DIM HAZY —) BLY
(SLIGHT —) BLUSH
RESEMBLE AGREE BRAID FAVOR
IMAGE LIKEN APPEAR DEPICT
FIGURE RECALL SEMBLE
COMPARE IMITATE PORTRAY
ASSEMBLE SIMULATE
(SUFF.) ODE OID OPSIS
RESEMBLING LIKE SAME SEMBLE
SIMILAR SEMBLANT
(— AN EGG) OVULARIAN
(— COMB) PECTINAL
(— GOOSE) ANSERINE
(— HORSE) EQUOID
(— IVORY) EBURNEAN EBURNEOID
EBURNEOUS
(— LADDER) SCALARIFORM
(— SALT) HALOID
(— STAR) STELLATE
(— WALL) MURAL
(SUFF.) AR ARY FUL EOUS FORM
ITIC IFORM OIDAL ACEOUS
RESENT HATE MEAN INDIGN
MALIGN STOMACH SUGGEST
RESENTFUL HARD HURT BITTER
SULLEN ENVIOUS JEALOUS
STOMACHY
RESENTMENT HURT DEPIT PIQUE
SNUFF SPITE CHOLER ENMITY
GRUDGE HATRED MALICE
RANCOR DISDAIN DUDGEON
OFFENCE OFFENSE STOMACH
UMBRAGE JEALOUSY HEARTBURN
RESERVATION DIBS SALVO SPACE
SAVING UNLESS BOOKING
CAUTION KEEPING PROVISO
RESERVE FORPRISE RESERVAL
(MENTAL —) SALVO SCRUPLE

RESERVE BOOK CAVE FUND HOJU
HOLD KEEP SALT SAVE SPARE
BACKUP NICETY SEPONE SEPOSE
TRIARY BACKLOG ĆAUTION
CONTROL DIGNITY SEPOSIT
SHYNESS TENENUE COLDNESS
DISTANCE FALLBACK FORPRISE
IMMODEST WITHHOLD STOCKPILE
(HOME —S) LANDSTURM
(MILITARY —) HOJU YOBI TRIARY
TRIARII LANDWEHR
(MONETARY —) CUSHION
(PL.) FAT KOKUMIN STRENGTH
RESERVED COY DRY SHY COLD
UNCO ALOOF CHARY SAVED
BOOKED CLOSED DEMURE
MODEST SILENT STANCH COSTIVE
DISTANT RETIRED STRANGE
RETICENT RETIRING STANDOFF
TACITURN WITHHELD
(— FOR ROYAL USE) KHASS
(NOT —) COMMON
RESERVOIR DAM BOSS FONT KEEP
LAKE PENT SUMP TANK BASIN
FOUNT STANK STORE CENOTE
SIPHON SOURCE SYPHON
CISTERN CLEARER FAVISSA
FOREBAY IMPOUND PISCINA
RECEIPT AFTERBAY DEPOSITO
FOUNTAIN MAGAZINE STANDAGE
(— OF WEATHERGLASS) STAGNUM
RESET HELP ABODE ALTER RECEPT
RESORT SUCCOR RECEIPT
REPLANT SHARPEN WELCOME
RESHEPH (FATHER OF —) EPHRAIM
RESIDE BIG WIN BIDE BIGG HOME
LIVE STAY TELD WONT ABIDE
DWELL LODGE REMAIN CONSIST
SOJOURN HABITATE
(— TEMPORARILY) LIE STOP
RESIDENCE DUN WON DOON HALL
HOME SEAT SEMI STAY WENE
WONE ABODE COURT DAIRI
DEMUR HOUSE MAHAL MANSE
YAMUN BIDING DUKERY ELYSEE
HOSTEL MANOIR TENSER
DEANERY DROSTDY EMBASSY
SOJOURN CURATAGE DOMICILE
DWELLING LEGATION RESIANCE
RESIANCY RESIDUUM SEDIMENT
SETTLING PREFECTURE
(— FOR STUDENTS) INN
(— OF ARCHBISHOP) PALACE
(— OF CHIEF OF VILLAGE) TATA
(— OF ECCLESIASTIC) MANSE
DEANERY CURATAGE
(— OF FRENCH PRESIDENTS) ELYSEE
(— OF MANDARIN) YAMEN YAMUN
(— OF MIKADO) DAIRI
(— OF PRIEST) CONVENTO
(— OF SOVEREIGN) PALACE
(— OF SULTAN) SERAGLIO
(FORTIFIED —) DUN
(HILL —) RATH
(OFFICIAL TURKISH —) KONAK
(RURAL —) SEAT FARMSTEAD
(SUMMER —) MAHAL
(TEMPORARY —) STAY
RESIDENT GER FIXED LEGER LIVER
INMATE LEDGER STABLE CITIZEN
DENIZEN DWELLER PRESENT
RESIANT RESIDER RESTING
HABITANT INHERENT KAMAAINA

MINISTER OCCUPANT
(— AT A UNIVERSITY) GREMIALE
(— OF HAWAII) KAMAAINA
(— OF NEWFOUNDLAND) LIVYER
(— OF WEST. AUSTRALIA) GROPER
(ALIEN —) GER METIC
(CHINESE — OF TIBET) AMBAN
(FOREIGN-BORN —) ALIEN
(OLD —) STANDARD
(SUFF.) ESE ITE
(— OF) ER IER YER
RESIDUAL RELICT REMANIE
REMANENT
RESIDUE ASH DREG FOOT GUNK
HEEL LAFE LAVE LEES REST SILT
SLAG UNIT MAZUT SHARD SHERD
BEGASS BORING BOTTOM GRUFFS
RELICS BAGASSE CINDERS
REMAINS HARDHEAD LEAVINGS
LEFTOVER REMANENT RESIDUUM
SEMICOKE TAILINGS
(— FROM FAT) CRAP
(— FROM OLIVES) SANZA
(— FROM REFINING TIN) HARDHEAD
(— IN STILL) BOTTOM BOTTOMS
(— OF COAL) COKE SEMICOKE
(— OF COKE) BREEZE
(— OF COMBUSTION) ASH
(— OF HONEYCOMB) SLUMGUM
(— OF PETROLEUM) MAZUT
ASTATKI
(— OF SHINGLES) SPALT
(FRIABLE —) CALX
(INSOLUBLE —) MARC
(PL.) TANKAGE
RESIDUUM TAIL BOTTOM DEPOSIT
RESIDUE SEDIMENT
RESIGN QUIT DEMIT FORGO REMIT
YIELD PERMIT SUBMIT ABANDON
COMMEND DELIVER FORGIVE
ABDICATE RENOUNCE
RELINQUISH
RESIGNATION PATIENCE
DEMISSION SURRENDER
RESILIENCE GIVE LIFE BOUNCE
RECOIL SPRING REBOUND
BUOYANCY
RESILIENT TOUGH BOUNCY LIVELY
SUPPLE WHIPPY ELASTIC
SPRINGY FLEXIBLE
RESIN ALK LAC BALM BATU BREA
HASH TOLU ALKYD AMBER ANIME
COPAL CUMAR ELEMI EPOXY
GUGAL GUGUL KAURI PITCH
ROSEL ROSET SIRUP SYRUP
ANTIAR BINDER CHARAS CONIMA
DAMMAR GOOGUL GUACIN
HARTIN MASTIC STORAX
TAMANU ACOUCHI ACRYLIC
AMBRITE BENZOIN BISABOL
DERRIDE FLUAVIL GAMBOGE
IONOMER LADANUM PERSPEX
SAGAPEN SHELLAC ALKITRAN
ALMACIGA BAKELITE BDELLIUM
CACHIBOU CANNABIN COLOPHAN
EUOSMITE FORMVAIL GALAGALA
GALLIPOT GEDANITE GUAIACUM
MALAPAHO MELAMINE
OPOPANAX PHENOLIC SANDARAC
SCAMMONY
(— DRAWN FROM TREES) CHIP
(— FROM HEMP) CHARAS
(— FROM NORWAY SPRUCE) THUS

(— OF FIR TREE) BLOB
(FOSSIL —) AMBER AMBRITE
HARTITE GEDANITE GLESSITE
RETINITE
(GRADE OF —) SORTS
(GUM —) GUGUL LASER MYRRH
ANTIAR BISABOL GAMBOGE
BDELLIUM SAGAPENUM
(NARCOTIC —) CHARAS CHURUS
(TURPENTINE —) ALK GALIPOT
COLOPHONY
(PREF.) RETIN(O)
(SUFF.) RETIN
RESINOID ALNUIN HELONIN
LOBELIN ASCLEPIN CERASEIN
CHELONIN TRILLIN
RESINOUS ROSETY ROSETTY
RESIST BUCK DEFY FACE STAY
REPEL STAND DEFEND IMPUGN
OPPOSE REPUGN WITHER
CONTEST DISPUTE GAINSAY
KNUCKLE RESERVE WITHSET
OUTBRAVE OUTSTAND
(— AUTHORITY) REBEL DEFORCE
(— SEPARATION) ATTRACT
RESISTANCE DRAG LOAD OHMAGE
REBUFF WITHER BALLAST
ANTITYPY BLOCKAGE FASTNESS
FRICTION HARDNESS OBSTACLE
SEDITION
(— OF COTTON FIBERS) DRAG
(— OF KEYS) ACTION
**(— THAT EXPLOSIVE MUST
OVERCOME)** BURDEN BURTHEN
(— TO ATTACK) DEFENCE DEFENSE
(— TO CHANGE) INERTIA
(— TO COLOR CHANGE) FASTNESS
(— TO DISEASE) PREMUNITION
(— TO SLIPPING) BOND
(UNIT OF —) OHM
RESISTANT HARD STOUT STABILE
STUBBORN
(— TO CHANGE) FAST STICKY
RESISTING OBSTANT RELUCTANT
RESISTOR BLEEDER DIVERTOR
RHEOSTAT
RESOLUTE BOLD FIRM GRIM
BRAVE FIXED HARDY MANLY
STERN STIFF STOUT GRITTY
MANFUL PLUCKY STABLE STANCH
STEADY STUFFY STURDY
ANIMOSE ANIMOUS DECIDED
CONSTANT FAITHFUL INTREPID
POSITIVE STALWART STUBBORN
UNSHAKEN
RESOLUTELY TALLY FIRMLY
STOUTLY
RESOLUTION VOW SAND THEW
NERVE PARTY PLUCK POINT
STARCH ACUERDO BESLUIT
CENSURE COURAGE MANHEAD
MANHOOD PURPOSE RESOLVE
THOUGHT ANALYSIS DECISION
DIERESIS ENACTURE STRENGTH
CONSTANCY
RESOLVE ACT BEND MELT REDE
SOIL UNDO LAPSE RELAX SALVE
SOLVE SOYLE UNTIE VOUCH
ADJUST ADVICE ASSOIL DECIDE
DECREE FACTOR INCIDE REDUCE
SETTLE STEVEN ABSOLVE
ANALYZE APPOINT BETHINK
CONSULT PURPOSE CONCLUDE

DISSOLVE UNRIDDLE UNTANGLE
RECONCILE
(— GRAMMATICALLY) PARSE
(— INTO ELEMENTS) ANALYSE
ANALYZE
RESOLVED BENT BOUND INTENT
CERTAIN INTENSE RESOLUTE
(HALF —) GOOD
RESONANCE BODY EMPATHY
RAPPORT RESOUND SYNTONY
TYMPANY SONORITY VIBRANCY
MESOMERISM
RESONANT BIG BRASS RINGY
OROTUND RINGING SILVERY
VIBRANT CANOROUS PLANGENT
SONORANT SONOROUS
SOUNDFUL SOUNDING
RESORT GO RUN SPA BEAT DOME
HOWF LIDO SEEK TEEM TOUR
TURN CAUSE FRAME HAUNT
HOWFF JOINT RECUR RESET VISIT
ESCORT FINISH REPAIR RETURN
REVERT THRONG COMPANY
PIMLICO RECOURSE RESOURCE
TEETOTUM
(— TO) SEEK
(— TO DEVIOUS METHODS) FINAGLE
(BATHING —) PLAGE
(DISREPUTABLE —) KEN DIVE
(DRINKING —) DOGGERY
(EVIL —) ROOKERY
(LOW —) KEN DIVE STEW SPITAL
(MEANS OF —) REFUGE
(WORKINGMEN'S —) TEETOTUM
RESOUND DIN DUN ECHO PEAL
RING SOUND REECHO EXPLODE
REBOUND RESPEAK VIBRATE
REDOUBLE
RESOUNDING BRASS REVERB
REBOANT EMPHATIC FORCEFUL
PLANGENT RESONANT
RUMOROUS
(— WITH TALK) ABUZZ
RESOURCE WON BOOT FUND
WONE MEANS SHIFT REFUGE
RESORT STOPGAP PURCHASE
(PL.) EASE FOND GAIN FUNDS
MEANS PURSE SINEW BOTTOM
FACULTY FOISONS PURCHASE
STRENGTH POCKETBOOK
RESOURCEFUL APT FENDY SHARP
SMART ADROIT CLEVER FACILE
SHIFTY PLANFUL
RESOURCEFULNESS SENSE SHIFT
AGILITY
RESPECT ORE WAY DUTY FACE
HEED HORE LOOK MARK DEFER
DULIA FRONT HONOR IZZAT
PARTY VALUE ASPECT BEHALF
DETAIL ESTEEM HALLOW
HOMAGE NOTICE REGARD
CONCERN OBSERVE RESPITE
SUSPECT TASHRIF WORSHIP
CONSIDER HABITUDE RELATION
VENERATE
(PL.) DEVOIR
RESPECTABLE GOOD NICE SMUG
DOUCE DECENT PROPER
FRUSANT CULOTTIC
RESPECTFUL AWFUL CIVIL
CAREFUL DUTEOUS DUTIFUL
HEEDFUL REVERENT
RESPECTIVE SEVERAL

RESPIRATION SIGH EUPNEA
ANAPNEA DYSPNEA EUPNOEA
ROARING GRUNTING
(PREF.) PNEO
PNEUM(A)(O)(ON)(ONO)
PNEUMATO SPIRO
RESPIRATOR MUZZLE CUIRASS
INHALER
RESPIRE BLOW LIVE REST EXHALE
REVIVE BREATHE SNUFFLE
SUSPIRE
RESPITE SOB REST STAY TRUE
DELAY FRIST LETUP PAUSE
BARLEY BREATH LAYOFF REGARD
REMISE LEISURE RESPECT
INTERVAL REPRIEVE SURCEASE
RESPLENDENCE GLORY SHEEN
FULGENCE FULGENCY SPLENDOR
RESPLENDENT LUCID SHEEN
BRIGHT GILDED ORIENT SILVER
AUREATE SHINING GLORIOUS
GORGEOUS LUSTROUS SPLENDID
SUNSHINY
RESPOND REACT REPLY ANSWER
RETURN TRISAGION
(— TO LURE) STOOL
(— WARMLY) RISE
RESPONDENT ANSWERER
APPELLEE
RESPONSE AMEN ECHO CHORD
REPLY SNAFF ANSWER EARFUL
VOLLEY INTROIT RESPOND
ANTIPHON BEHAVIOR INSTINCT
REACTION REANSWER RECEPTION
(— OF KEYS) ACTION
(— OF SHIP) STEERING
(— TO GRAVITY) GEOTAXIS
RESPONSIBILITY BABY BALL CARE
DUTY ONUS WITE BLAME GUILT
TRUST CHARGE RACKET
RESPONSIBLE GOOD SOLID
DIRECT LIABLE AMENABLE
RESPONSION REPLY ANSWER
(PL.) SMALLS
RESPONSIVE OPEN SOFT WARM
GUILTY MUTUAL NIMBLE SUPPLE
TENDER MEETING AMENABLE
SENSIBLE
(— TO BEAUTY) ESTHETIC
(NOT —) IMMUNE
RESPONSIVENESS TOUCH
FEELING
RESPONSORY ANTHEM LIBERA
GRADUAL RESPOND
REST BED LAY LIE PUT SET SIT SOB
BASE BLOW CALM CAMP EASE
HANG HEEL LAIR LAVE LEAN LIOS
LISS PROP RELY RIDE RUST STAY
STOP COUCH FOUND LEATH
PAUSE PEACE POISE QUIET
RENEW ROOST SLEEP SPELL
STAND TRUST WREST ANCHOR
BOTTOM FAUCRE FEWTER
GROUND INSIST REMAIN REPOSE
SETTLE SIESTA STEADY UNTIRE
ADHARMA BALANCE BREATHE
CAESURA CLARION COMFORT
GALLOWS NOONING RECLINE
REFRESH RELACHE REMNANT
REQUIEM RESIDUE RESPITE
SILENCE SLUMBER SOJOURN
SUFFLUE SUPPORT SURPLUS
AKINESIS INTERVAL QUIETUDE

STANDOFF VACATION
(— FOR SPEAR OR LANCE) QUEUE
FAUCRE FEWTER
(— FOR SUPPORT) ABUT
(— FOR TYMPAN) GALLOWS
(— HORSE) WIND
(— IDLY) SLUG
(— LAZILY) FROWST
(— ON PLANER) SIDEHEAD
(— ON SUPPORT) BOTTOM
(— UPRIGHT) STAND
(HALF —) MINIM SOSPIRO
(LATHE —) STEADY
(LEG — ON SADDLE) CRUTCH
(MUSKET —) GAFFLE
(NOONDAY —) NAP SIESTA
(QUARTER —) SOSPIRO
(PREF.) PAULO
RESTATE REHASH
RESTATEMENT SUMMARY
RESTAURANT CAFE DINER GRILL
HOUSE PLACE BISTRO BUFFET
EATERY AUTOMAT BEANERY
CABARET CANTEEN OSTERIA
TEAROOM HIDEAWAY BRASSERIE
CHOPHOUSE TRATTORIA
(— KEEPER) BISTRO TRAITEUR
(SMALL —) CAFF
RESTFUL COOL SOFT QUIET
PLACID EASEFUL RELAXED
SOOTHFUL TRANQUIL
RESTHARROW WHIN CAMMOCK
SITFAST LANDWHIN
RESTHOUSE KHAN SERAI
AMBALAM CHHATRI KHANKAH
RESTING DORMANT
(PREF.) STATO
RESTING PLACE (ALSO SEE
RESTHOUSE) FORM GIST GITE
STAGE CHHATRI DHARMSALA
RESTITUTION AMENDS RETURN
RECOVERY
RESTIVE BALKY FUDGY ITCHY
RESTY RUSTY FIDGETY UNRESTY
UNWAYED CONTRARY INACTIVE
RESTLESS SKITTISH SLUGGISH
STUBBORN UNWIELDY
RESTLESS ANTSY FIKIE FUDGY
ITCHY FITFUL HAUNTY HECTIC
ROVING UNEASY AGITATO
ERETHIC FIDGETY FLIGHTY
FRETFUL INQUIET RAMPLER
RAMPLOR RESTIVE TEWSOME
TOSSING UNQUIET UNRESTY
VARIANT WAKEFUL FEVERISH
FEVEROUS STEERING
(— FLYCATCHER) GRINDER
RESTLESSNESS FIKE STIR FIDGET
UNREST DISQUIET JACTATION
RESTORATION REPAIR RETURN
RENEWAL RESTORE REVIVAL
EXCHANGE RECOVERY REMITTER
RESTORAL RECLAMATION
RESTORATIVE ACOPON BALSAMIC
SALUTARY SANATIVE ANALEPTIC
RESTORE FIX CURE HEAL AMEND
BLOCK COVER REDUB REFER
RENEW REPAY STORE YIELD
ASTORE DOCTOR RECALL REDEEM
REFORM REFUND RELATE
RENDER REPONE REVERT REVIVE
CONVERT ENSTORE INPAINT
REBUILD RECLAIM RECOVER

RECRUIT REFOUND REFRESH
REPLACE REVOLVE DECOHERE
REANSWER RECREATE RESTITUE
RETRIEVE
(— CONFIDENCE) REASSURE
(— TO CIVIL RIGHTS) INLAW
(— TO HEALTH) CURE HEAL MEND
(— TO ORDER) STILL
RESTRAIN BIT DAM BATE BIND
BOLT BUCK COOP CRIB CURB
DAMP GRAB GYVE HEAD HEFT
KEEP REIN SHUT SINK SNEB SNIB
SNUB STAY STEM STOP STOW
BRANK CHAIN CHECK COART
CRAMP DETER GUARD LEASH
MINCE POUND REPEL SHUNT
SOBER STILL STINT TRASH
ARREST BOTTLE BRIDLE CHASTE
COERCE DETAIN ENJOIN FETTER
FORBID GOVERN HALTER HAMPER
HINDER KENNEL OBLIGE REBUKE
RETAIN RETIRE REVOKE STIFLE
STRAIN TEMPER ABRIDGE
ABSTAIN CHASTEN COHIBIT
CONFINE CONTAIN CONTROL
ENCHAIN EXCLUDE INHIBIT
INJUNCT QUALIFY RECLAIM
REFRAIN REPRESS RETRACT
SHACKLE SNAFFLE SWADDLE
BULLDOZE COMPESCE COMPRESS
HANDCUFF IMPRISON RESTRICT
SIDELINE WITHDRAW WITHHOLD
(— BY FEAR) OVERAWE
(— HAWK'S WING) BRAIL
(— MOTION) SNUB
(PREF.) ISCH(O)
RESTRAINED SOBER CHASTE
MODEST SEVERE ASHAMED
DISCREET RESERVED RITENUTO
RESTRAINT BIT BEND CLOG CURB
HEFT STAY STOP CHECK CRAMP
FORCE LEASH SPARE STENT
STINT TRASH ARREST BRIDLE
DURESS FETTER STAYER
AWEBAND BONDAGE CONTROL
DURANCE EMBARGO MANACLE
RESERVE SNAFFLE TRAMMEL
HEADREST SOBRIETY
(— OF GOODS) HOCK
(BEYOND —) APE
RESTRICT PEG TIE CURB HOLD
BOUND CHAIN COART FENCE
HEDGE STINT THIRL COARCT
COERCE CORRAL CORSET ENTAIL
HAMPER NARROW ASTRICT
COHIBIT COMBINE QUALIFY
REPRESS SCANTLE SWADDLE
CONTRACT DEROGATE DIMINISH
RESTRAIN STRAITEN
(— MEANING) MODIFY
RESTRICTED CLOSE CRAMP LOCAL
CLOSED FINITE NARROW STRAIT
STRICT OBLIGATE PAROCHIAL
RESTRICTION STENT STINT
BURDEN DENIAL BARRIER
CONFINE RESERVE BLACKOUT
CABOTAGE
(PL.) BARS SWADDLE
RESTRICTIVE SEVERE BINDING
STYPTIC COACTIVE LIMITARY
LIMITING CONFINING
RESTY LAZY RESTIVE INACTIVE
INDOLENT SLUGGISH

RESULT GO END OUT ECHO FALL
FATE FAVE GROW RISE TAKE
BACON BRING CHILD ENSUE
EVENT FRUIT FUDGE ISSUE
PROOF EFFECT EFFORT ENDING
EVOLVE FINISH FOLLOW GROWTH
RECOIL REVERT SEQUEL SPRING
UPCOME UPSHOT ENTRAIN
FALLOUT FINDING OUTCOME
PROCEED PURPOSE REBOUND
REDOUND SUCCEED SUCCESS
FRUITAGE SEQUENCE OFFSPRING
(— FAVORABLY) SUCCEED
(— FROM) SUE
(ALGEBRAIC —) DUAL EXPANSION
(AS A —) AGAIN
(INCONCLUSIVE —) DOGFALL
(INEVITABLE —) NEMESIS
(PATHOLOGICAL —S) ALCOHOLISM
(REWARDING —) HAY
(SECONDARY —) SEQUELA
(PL.) AFTERINGS
(SUFF.) ISATION IZATION
RESULTANT CONCEPT OUTCOME
PROGENY
RESUME RENEW REOPEN RECOVER
SUMMARY CONTINUE PURLICUE
REASSUME RENOVATE REOCCUPY
(PL.) EXCERPTA
RESURRECTION RISE RIST UPRIST
REBIRTH REVIVAL
RESURRECTION PLANT
FERNWORT
RESUSCITATE REVIVE QUICKEN
SUSCITE REVIVIFY
RESUSCITATION KATSU RENEWAL
REVIVAL
RET RAIT RATE SOAK DEWROT
RETABLE PREDELLA
RETAIL REGRATE HUCKSTER
(— STORE) WAREHOUSE
RETAILER DEALER CLOTHIER
HUCKSTER
RETAIN HAVE HEFT HOLD KEEP
SAVE CATCH ATHOLD CONTAIN
RESERVE CONTINUE MAINTAIN
PRESERVE
(— MOMENTUM) DRIFT
RETAINER FOOL HEWE LACKEY
MENIAL RIBALD SEQUEL YEOMAN
HOBBLER HUSCARL JACKMAN
LACQUEY PANDOUR SERVANT
TRAVERS EMPLOYEE FOLLOWER
HENCHMAN MYRMIDON
BURKUNDAZ PENSIONER
(JAPANESE —) SAMURAI
(PL.) FOLK
RETALIATE REPAY AVENGE
RETORT REQUITE RECIPROCATE
RETALIATION QUITS MARQUE
TALION REPRISAL REQUITAL
(MAKE —) TURN
(VINDICTIVE —) REVENGE
RETALIATORY COUNTER
(PREF.) COUNTER
RETARD LAG CHOP DAMP DRAG
SLOW STEM BRAKE DEFER DELAY
ELONG TARDY TARRY THROW
TRASH BACKEN BELATE DEADEN
DETAIN HINDER INHIBIT SLACKEN
ENCUMBER OBSTRUCT PROTRACT
RESTRAIN
RETARDANT (FIRE —) BORAX

RETARDATION LAG DRAG DELAY ARREST
RETARDED DARK BEHIND LAGGED SIMPLE OVERAGE
RETARDING LENTANDO
RETCH GAG BOKE KECK HEAVE REACH VOMIT KECKLE RECCHE STRAIN
RETCHING HEFT
RETEM JUNIPER
RETENTION MEMORY RETAIN HOLDING KEEPING RETINUE (SUFF.) STASIA STASIS
RETIARIUS RETIARY GLADIATOR
RETICENCE RESERVE SECRECY RESTRAINT
RETICENT DARK SNUG CLOSE SECRET SILENT MIMMOUD SPARING BOUTONNE
RETICENTLY HEIMLICH
RETICULATE MESHED NETTED
RETICULE BAG CABAS SACHET WORKBAG CARRYALL RIDICULE
RETICULUM NET MITOME NETWORK MATTULLA
RETINOL CODOL
RETINOPHORE VITRELLA
RETINUE CREW GING PORT ROUT SUIT TAIL COURT MEINY SUITE TIRED TRAIN FAMILY REPAIR RETAIN COMPANY CORTEGE SOWARRY EQUIPAGE TENDANCE BODYGUARD
(— OF CAVALRY) SOWARRY
(VILLAINOUS —) BLACKGUARD
RETIRE GO GET DRAW GIVE AVOID LEAVE MICHE REBUT DEPART LOCATE RECALL RECEDE RECESS RECOIL SHRINK SURVEY PENSION REGRADE RETRACT RETREAT WITHDRAW
(— IGNOMINIOUSLY) SLINK
(— IN CRICKET) BOWL
RETIRED QUIET SECRET DEVIOUS OBSCURE OUTGONE PRIVATE RETRAIT SECLUSE SHADOWY ABSTRUSE EMERITUS SECLUDED SOLITARY
(— FROM PLAY) DOWN
RETIREMENT SHADE RECESS RETOUR SECESS PRIVACY PRIVATE RETREAT FIRESIDE SOLITUDE
RETIRING SHY NESH TIMID DEMURE MODEST FUGIENT RESERVED UMBRATIC RECESSIVE
(— ROOM) RECAMERA
RETORT MOT QUIP RISE SNAP VENY QUIRK REPAY REPLY ANSWER REGEST RETURN RIPOST BOMBOLA CORNUTE CRUSHER PELICAN REFLECT SQUELCH BACKWORD BLIZZARD COMEBACK MAGAZINE RECEIVER REPARTEE
(CURT —) SNAPHANCE
(GROUP OF —S) SETTING
(PUNNING —) CLINCH
(WITTY —) KNACK ZINGER
RETRACE RECALL FLYBACK RETREAT UNTREAD BACKTRACK
RETRACT BACK UNSAY ABJURE DISOWN RECALL RECANT RECEDE REVOKE SHRINK UNLOOK

RESCIND RETREAT SWALLOW PALINODE RENOUNCE WITHDRAW
RETRACTED INNER
RETRACTION PALINODE PALINODY
RETREAT DEN DOME DROP FADE GIVE LAIR NEST ROUT ARBOR AVOID BOWER LODGE NICHE QUAIL QUIET SHADE START ASHRAM ASYLUM BACKUP CASTLE RECEDE RECESS REFUGE RESILE RETIRE REVOLT CABINET DESCEND PRIVACY RETIRAL RETRACT SHELTER ANABASIS CRAWFISH DISMARCH FALLBACK FASTNESS NESTLING RECOURSE RECULADE SOLITUDE STAMPEDE WITHDRAW CREEPHOLE KATABASIS
(— FOR FISH) HOD
(FORTIFIED —) REDUIT
(RELIGIOUS —) ASRAM ASHRAM
(SECURE —) STRENGTH
(SHADY —) ALCOVE
RETRENCH OMIT EXCISE LESSEN REDUCE ABRIDGE CURTAIL SHORTEN
RETRENCHMENT CUT RAMPART EXCISION RETIRADE LESSENING
RETRIBUTION PAY PAYOFF RETURN REWARD WISSEL MANNAIA PENALTY REVENGE REQUITAL
RETRIEVE SHACK RECALL RECURE REGAIN REPAIR RESCUE REVIVE CORRECT RECOVER RESTORE SALVAGE
RETRIEVER FINDER GUNDOG LABRADOR WATERRUG
RETROFLEX DEMAL CORONAL CEREBRAL INVERTED REFLEXED
RETROGRADE RECEDE RETRAL DECLINE INVERSE OPPOSED REGREDE RETREAT BACKWARD DECADENT REARWARD WITHDRAW
RETROGRESS SINK REGRESS BACKSLIDE
RETROGRESSION SINK REGRESS RETREAT FALLBACK
RETUND DULL TURN BLUNT REFUTE
RETURN EBB GET COME TURN VAIL RECUR REFER REPAY REPLY VISIT YIELD AIRWAY ANSWER HOMING REMISE RENDER REPAIR REPASS REPORT RESORT RETIRE RETORT RETOUR REVERT CLEANUP PAYMENT REBOUND REDOUND REFLECT REPRISE REQUITE RESTORE REVENUE ATTOURNE DIVIDEND ELECTION EPANODOS FEEDBACK PICKINGS REACCESS REANSWER RECOURSE RECOVERY REDITION REFLECTION RECIPROCATE
(— FROM DEATH) ARISE
(— OF MERCHANDISE) COMEBACK
(— TENNIS BALL) RALLY
(— TO ORIGINAL CONDITION) RECYCLE
(— TO ZERO) FLYBACK
(GROUNDED —) BOND

(TENNIS —) GET BOAST
RETURNING REDIENT REMEANT REDITION
RETURN OF THE NATIVE (AUTHOR OF —) HARDY
(CHARACTER IN —) VYE CLYM VENN DAMON CANTLE JOHNNY DIGGORY NUNSUCH WILDEVE EUSTACIA THOMASIN CHRISTIAN YEOBRIGHT
REUBEN (FATHER OF —) JACOB
(MOTHER OF —) LEAH
REUEL (FATHER OF —) ESAU
(MOTHER OF —) BASHEMATH
(SON OF —) ELIASAPH
REUNION COLLEGE ADHESION HERENIGING
(— WITH BRAHMA) NIRVANA
REUNITE RALLY REUNE REJOIN RECONCILE
REVEAL BID BARE BLAB HINT JAMB KNOW OPEN SHOW TELL WRAY BREAK EXERT SPEAK SPLIT UNRIP UNTOP UTTER YIELD ACCUSE APPEAR BETRAY BEWRAY DESCRY DETECT EVINCE IMPART OSTEND PATEFY SPRING UNHELE UNLOCK UNMASK UNVEIL UNWRAP BESPEAK CLARIFY CONFESS DEVELOP DISPLAY DIVULGE UNCLOAK UNCOVER UNSHALE UNTRUSS DECIPHER DISCLOSE DISCOVER INDICATE MANIFEST UNBURDEN UNSHADOW UNSHROUD
(— BY SIGNS) EXHIBIT
(— SECRETS) BABBLE
(— UNINTENTIONALLY) BETRAY
REVEILLE DIAN DIANA LEVET ROUSE SIGNAL TRAVALLY
REVEIVER (DISTILLING —) BOLTHOLE
REVEL JOY MASK RANT RIOT BIZLE COMUS FEAST GLOAT GLORY WATCH BEZZLE FROLIC GAVALL SPLORE TRESCA WALLOW WANTON CAROUSE DELIGHT ROISTER TRESCHE CAROUSAL DOMINEER FESTIVAL WITHDRAW
(NOISY —) JAMBOREE
(PL.) REVELRY
REVELATION TORA TORAH EXPOSE ORACLE REVEAL BATHKOL BATHQOL SHOWING GIVEAWAY OVERTURE APOCALYPSE
(— OF GOD'S WILL) LAW
(SUDDEN —) KICK
REVELER GREEK RANTER RIOTER FRANION PIERROT ROISTER BACCHANT CAROUSER MERRYMAKER
REVELRY JOY ORGY RIOT RIOTISE WASSAIL CARNIVAL CAROUSAL FESTIVAL
REVENANT GHOST WRAITH SPECTER
REVENGE HELL WREAK WROIK AVENGE ULTION REQUITE REQUITAL REVANCHE
REVENGED EVEN
REVENUE RENT JAGIR MANSE YIELD INCOME ENTRADA FINANCE

PROFITS HACIENDA INCOMING
(— FROM WATER RIGHTS) JALKAR
(— REVENUE PAID TO POPE) ANNAT
(GOVERNMENT —) JAGHIR
(STATE —) HACIENDA
REVERBERATE DIRL ECHO RING REPEL RETORT REVERB REBOUND REDOUND REFLECT RESOUND
REVERBERATING REBOANT RESONANT SOUNDING
REVERBERATION ECHO REDOUND REBOATION
REVERE ADORE HONOR ADMIRE ESTEEM HALLOW RESPECT WORSHIP VENERATE
REVERED (PREF.) SEMNO
REVERENCE AWE ORE CULT FEAR DREAD HONOR MENSK PIETY WURTH HOMAGE REGARD WORSHIP DEVOTION VENERANT VENERATE WORTHING
(— FOR ANIMALS) ZOISM
(IRRATIONAL —) FETICH FETISH
REVEREND SRI SHRI SHREE SVAMI SWAMI POTENT STRONG (PREF.) SEBASTO
REVERENT DEVOUT STRONG AWESOME DUTIFUL
REVERENTIAL PIOUS SOLEMN
REVERIE DUMP DWAM MUSE DREAM DWALM STUDY PONDER MEMENTO MOONING DAYDREAM TRAUMEREI
REVERSAL KNOCK CHANGE DOUBLE SWITCH BACKCAST BACKFLIP OVERTURN THROWBACK TURNABOUT (PREF.) ALL(O)
REVERSE BACK DOWN FACE FLOP JOLT ANNUL CHECK UPSET VERSO CHANGE DEFEAT INVERT REPEAL RETURN REVERT REVOKE BACKSET COUNTER INVERSE PUTBACK RETREAT REVERSO SETBACK SNIFTER SUBVERT BACKCAST CONTRARY CONVERSE OPPOSITE OVERRULE OVERTURN RAMVERSE TRAVERSE WATERLOO
(— OARS) SHEAVE
(— OF COIN) PILE TAIL WOMAN
(— OF NOTE) BACK
(— PAGE OF BOOK) VERSO REVERSO
(PREF.) DE DIS DYS
(— ORDER) OB
REVERSED BACK INVERSE REVERTED ROVESCIO
(NOT —) DIRECT
REVERSI QUINOLAS
REVERSION SCRAPS ATAVISM ESCHEAT REMNANT FEEDBACK REVERTAL REVERTER THROWBACK
REVERT ANNUL ADVERT RESORT RESULT RETOUR RETURN REVOKE ESCHEAT RESTORE RECOURSE BACKSLIDE
(— TO A SUPERIOR) FALL
REVETMENT SODWORK
REVIEW HASH VIEW REVIE NOTICE REVISE SURVEY BRUSHUP RECENSE REJUDGE CRITIQUE

REVIEWAL REVISION

REVILE CALL RAIL ABUSE BLEIR
BRAWL REBUT SCOLD SHEND
SHENT SLANG MISSAY MISUSE
VILIFY INVEIGH MISCALL
MISNAME BACKBITE DISGRACE
EXECRATE REPROACH

REVILING ABUSE ABUSION
BLASPHEMY

REVISE EDIT ALTER REDACT
REFORM REVIEW CORRECT
RECENSE REFLECT REVISIT
OVERHAUL

REVISER REDACTOR REFORMER
REVIEWER

REVISION REVIEW SURVEY
REVISAL REVIEWAL EPANAGOGE

REVITALIZER BRACER

REVIVAL IMAGE PICKUP REBIRTH
REPRISE WAKENING

REVIVE DAW EBB WAKE FETCH
QUICK RALLY RENEW ROUSE
EXHUME GINGER RECALL RELIVE
REVERT REVOKE EKPHORE
ENLIVEN FRESHEN FURBISH
QUICKEN REFRESH RESPIRE
RESTORE RECREATE REDIVIVE
REKINDLE RENOVATE RETRIEVE
(— FIRE) CHUNK

REVOCATION REPEAL REVERSAL
ADEMPTION

REVOICE ECHO

REVOKE LIFT ADEEM ANNUL
RENIG CANCEL RECALL RECANT
REPEAL REPEAL REVERT ABOLISH
COMMUTE FINAGLE RECLAIM
RESCIND RETREAT REVERSE
ABROGATE REVOCATE
(— A LEGACY) ADEEM

REVOLT ARISE REBEL REPEL START
MUTINY OFFEND RELUCT
UPROAR MUTATION OUTBREAK
SEDITION UPRISING JACQUERIE
REBELLION

REVOLTING GARISH HORRID
BILIOUS FEARFUL HATEFUL
HIDEOUS DREADFUL

**REVOLT OF THE ANGELS (AUTHOR
OF —)** FRANCE
(CHARACTER IN —) MAX ZITA
ISTAR ARCADE AUBELS JULIEN
SOPHAR MAURICE GILBERTE
SARIETTE ESPARVIEU THEOPHILE
EVERDINGEN

REVOLUTION GYRE RIOT TOUR
TURN CYCLE WHEEL CHANGE
ANARCHY CIRCUIT REVOLVE
GYRATION MUTATION NOVATION
ROTATION SEDITION REBELLION

REVOLUTIONARY RED RADICAL
MUSCADIN ROTATING BOLSHEVIK

REVOLUTIONIST JACOBIN
REDSHIRT

REVOLVE BIRL GYRE PIRL ROLL
SPIN TIRL TURN WELT ORBIT
PIVOT THROW TREND TROLL
TWINE VERSE WHEEL WHIRL
CENTER CIRCLE GYRATE PONDER
ROTATE SPHERE SWINGE
WAMBLE AGITATE VERSATE
CONSIDER OVERTURN REVOLUTE
(CAUSE TO —) TRUNDLE

REVOLVER GAT GUN ROD RIFLE

STICK CANNON CUTTER HOGLEG
PISTOL RIFFLE BULLDOG
DUNGEON
(PART OF —) ROD BORE BUTT
GATE GRIP SPUR BLADE FRAME
GUARD LATCH SIGHT SLIDE
STRAP BARREL HAMMER HANDLE
MUZZLE CHAMBER TRIGGER
CYLINDER BACKSTRAP

REVOLVING ORBY VOLUBLE
GYRATORY VOLUTION
(PREF.) **(—AROUND)** CIRCUM

REVUE SHOW REVIEW FOLLIES

REVULSION FEAR REACTION

REWARD FEE PAY UTU GREE
MEED RENT SPUR WAGE AMEED
BOOTY BRIBE CROWN LOWER
MERIT PLUME SHEPE YIELD
BOUNTY DESERT GERSUM
PAYOFF SALARY TROPHY WEDFEE
AUREOLE GUERDON PREMIUM
RENTAGE SOSTRUM STIPEND
WARISON CONSIDER DIVIDEND
EXACTION REMEMBER REQUITAL
ACKNOWLEDGE
**(— FOR INFORMATION ON CATTLE
THIEVES)** TASCAL
(— OF VICTORY) CROWN
(— TO HOUNDS) HALLOW
(ILLUSORY —) CARROT
(UNEXPECTED —) JACKPOT
(PREF.) LUCRI

REWARDED APAID BOUNTIED

REWARDING FAT PREMIANT
(FINANCIALLY —) JUICY

REWRITTEN PALIMPSEST

REZAI ROSEI COVERLET MATTRESS

REZON (FATHER OF —) ELIADAH

RHABDUS SCOPULA

RHADAMANTHUS (FATHER OF —)
JUPITER
(MOTHER OF —) EUROPA

RHAPSODIC CONFUSED EFFUSIVE
RAPTUROUS

RHAPSODY JUMBLE MEDLEY
BOMBAST ECSTASY RAPTURE
REVERIE
(— SECTION) LASSU

RHATANY LEGUME

RHEA EMU EMEU NANDU
NANDOW RATITE OSTRICH
AGDISTIS AVESTRUZ
(DAUGHTER OF —) JUNO CERES
VESTA
(FATHER OF —) URANUS
(HUSBAND OF —) SATURN
(MOTHER OF —) GAEA
(SON OF —) PLUTO NEPTUNE

RHEBOK PEELE REHBOC

**RHEINGOLD, DAS (CHARACTER
IN —)** ERDA LOGE FREIA WOTAN
FAFNER FASOLT FRICKA
HUNDING ALBERICH SIEGMUND
SIEGLINDE
(COMPOSER OF —) WAGNER

RHENIUM BOHEMIUM

RHEOMETER STROMUHR

RHEOSTAT DIMMER

RHESA (FATHER OF —) ZOROBABEL

RHESUS BANDAR BUNDER
MONKEY BHUNDER MACAQUE
(FATHER OF —) EIONEUS STRYMON
(MOTHER OF —) CALLIOPE

RHETORIC SPEECH BOMBAST
PROSAIC ELOQUENCE

RHETORICAL FLORID PURPLE
AUREATE FORENSIC SWELLING

RHETORICIAN ORATOR RHETOR

RHEUM GORE TEARS CHOLER
SPLEEN

RHINARIUM MUFFLE

RHINE REAN DITCH RUNNEL

RHINESTONE DEWDROP
(PL.) GLITTER

RHINO CASH MONEY PONTOON

RHINOCEROS FOW ABADA BADAK
RHINO BORELE KEITLOA UNICORN
UPEYGAN NASICORN

RHINOCEROS BEETLE UANG
SCARABAEID

RHINOCEROS HORNBILL TOPAU

RHIPIDION FLABELLUM

RHIZOID RHIZINA ROOTLET

RHIZOME KAVA NARD ARUKE
CAAPI STOCK ARALIA ARNICA
ASARUM GINGER IPECAC STOLON
BERBERY CALAMUS CULVERS
GENTIAN SCOPOLA ZEDOARY
ASPIDIUM BARBERRY BERBERIS
HELONIAS KAVAKAVA TRILLIUM
TRITICUM VERATRUM
(PL.) INULA GERANIUM

RHODE (FATHER OF —) POSEIDON
(MOTHER OF —) HALIA
(SON OF —) PHAETHON

RHODE ISLAND	
CAPITAL:	PROVIDENCE
COLLEGE:	BROWN BRYANT
COUNTY:	KENT BRISTOL NEWPORT
INDIAN:	NIANTIC
MOTTO:	HOPE
NATIVE:	GUNFLINT
NICKNAME:	LITTLERHODY
RIVER:	PAWTUXET PAWCATUCK BLACKSTONE
STATE FLOWER:	VIOLET
STATE TREE:	MAPLE
TOWN:	BRISTOL NEWPORT WARWICK CRANSTON KINGSTON PAWTUCKET

RHODE ISLAND BENT FURZETOP

RHODE ISLANDER GUNFLINT

RHODESIA (SEE ZIMBABWE)

RHODODENDRON ROSEBAY
SPOONHUTCH
(THICKET OF —) SLICK

RHOMB LOZEN WHEEL CIRCLE
LOZENGE

RHOMBUS DIAMOND LOZENGE

RHONCHUS RALE SNORE SNORT
WHEEZE

RHUBARB ROW FLAP RHEUM
HASSEL CITRINE DISPUTE
YAWWEED ARGUMENT PIEPLANT

RHYME CHIME CLINK VERSE
CRAMBO POETRY RHYTHM TINKLE
MEASURE
(— ROYAL) TROILUS
(PL.) RIMUR

RHYOLITE LIPARITE

RHYTHM BEAT STOT TIME CHIME
METER PULSE SWING CADENCE
RAGTIME BACKBEAT MOVEMENT
SEQUENCE

RHYTHMICAL CADENCED
MEASURED NUMEROUS
ACCENTUAL
(NOT —) RAGGED

RIA CREEK INLET

RIAL COIN RYEL ROYAL KINGLY
SPLENDID

RIALTO MART BRIDGE EXCHANGE

RIANT GAY RIDENT LAUGHING
MIRTHFUL

RIATA LASSO LARIAT

RIB FIN KID BULB CORD DIKE JOKE
PURL SLAT WALE WIFE CORSE
COSTA GROIN NERVE OGIVE
PEARL RIDGE VARIX VITTA
WHELP BRANCH LIERNE NEEDLE
PARODY RIPPLE SCROLL TIMBER
TONGUE BRISTLE FEATHER
NERVURE PLEURAL STRATUM
FORMERET SIDEBONE
(— IN GROINED ROOF) SPRINGER
(— OF INSECT WING) VEIN
(— OF SHIP) WRONG
(— OF VIOLIN) BOUT
(—S OF UMBRELLA) FRAME
(SHORT —S) CROP
(STRENGTHENING —) FEATHER
(PL.) SLATS
(PREF.) COST(I)(O) PLEUR(I)(O)
(SUFF.) COSTAL COSTATE
PLEURA PLEUROUS

RIBALD LEWD ROGUE COARSE
RASCAL VULGAR

RIBALDRY HASH HARLOTRY

RIBAND RIBBON SCROLL

RIBBED RIBBY CORDED COSTATE

RIBBING SPOOFERY

RIBBON BAR BOW FOB PAN BEND
COST PADS BRAID CORSE FILET
LABEL PADOU PIECE RUBAN
SHRED TASTE BENDEL CADDIS
CORDON FERRET FILLET LISERE
RADULA RECORD RIBAND
SHOWER STRING TAENIA
TAWDRY TISSUE TONGUE
BANDING SAUTOIR TORSADE
BANDEROL BOOKMARK
FRAGMENT TRESSURE
PETERSHAM
(— AS BADGE OF HONOR) CORDON
(— AS HEADDRESS) TRESSOUR
TRESSURE
(— FOR BORDER) LISERE
(— HANGING FROM CROWN) JESS
(— USED FOR GARTERS) CADDIS
CADDICE
(COLORED —S) DIVISA
(END OF —S) FATTRELS
(FLOATING —) PAN
(KNOT OF —S) SORTIE
(LINGUAL —) TONGUE
(SILK —) CORSE PADOU TASTE
(WATERED —) PADS
(PL.) REINS
(PREF.) TAENI(A)(O)
(SUFF.) TENE

RIBBON FERN PTERIS

RIBBONFISH GARFISH GUAPENA
AGUAVINA BANDFISH DEALFISH

RIBBONLIKE TAENIATE TAENIOID
TAENIFORM

RIBBON TREE AKAROA HOIHERE
HOUHERE LACEBARK

RIBGRASS WINDLES BUCKHORN HARDHEAD PLANTAIN
RIBWORT KLOPS HEADMAN RATTAIL SOLDIER WINDLES HARDHEAD HEADSMAN PLANTAGO
RICCIARDETTO (SISTER OF —) BRADAMANTE
RICE AUS AMAN BORO PADI PAGA RISE SELA TWIG ARROZ BATTY BIGAS CANIN CHITS GRAIN MACAN PADDY PALAY PATNA BRANCH CEREAL CONGEE SIDDHA ANGKHAK MANOMIN RISOTTO
(**— BOILED WITH MEAT**) PILAF PILAU PILAW
(**— COOKED WITH MEAT**) RISOTTO JAMBALAYA
(**— FIELD**) SAWAH
(**— IN HUSK**) PALAY
(**— OF 2ND or 3RD GRADE**) CHITS
(**— POLISHINGS**) DARAC
(**BOILED —**) CANIN KANIN
(**HUSKED —**) CHAL
(**INFERIOR —**) PAGA
(**LONG-STEMMED —**) AMAN
(**MOUNTAIN —**) SMILO
(**SHORT-STEMMED —**) AUS
(**SPRING —**) BORO
(**UNCOOKED —**) BIGAS
(**UNMILLED —**) PADI PADDY
(**WILD —**) MANOMIN
(**PREF.**) ORYZ(I) RIZI
RICEBIRD BUNTING CACIQUE SPARROW BOBOLINK
RICE FLOWER PIMELEA
RICEGRASS BARIT SACATE ZACATE
RICH FAT ABLE DEEP FAIR HIGH LUSH OOFY WARM GLEBY OPIME PLUMP RITZY ROUND TINNY VIVID BATFUL COSTLY DAEDAL FRUITY HEARTY PLUMMY PLUSHY PODDED SUPERB ULRICA AMUSING BAITTLE COPIOUS FERTILE MONEYED OPULENT PINGUID PLASTIC WEALTHY ABUNDANT AFFLUENT GENEROUS HUMOROUS LUSCIOUS
(**— IN FAME**) RODERICK
(**— IN GIFTS**) PREMIOUS
(**— IN INTEREST**) JUICY
(**— IN MALT**) HEAVY
(**— IN SILICA**) ACID
(**— IN TIMBRE**) GOLDEN
(**— MAN**) DIVES
(**— OF SOIL**) PINGUID
(**NOT —**) PLAIN
RICHARD DICCON
RICHARD CARVEL (AUTHOR OF —) CHURCHILL
(**CHARACTER IN —**) FOX JONES CARVEL DOROTHY MANNERS RICHARD WALPOLE
RICHARD II (AUTHOR OF —) SHAKESPEARE
(**CHARACTER IN —**) JOHN ROSS YORK BAGOT BUSHY GAUNT GREEN HENRY PERCY EDMUND PIERCE SCROOP SURREY THOMAS AUMERLE HOTSPUR LANGLEY MOWBRAY NORFOLK RICHARD STEPHEN BERKELEY HEREFORD

FITZWATER LANCASTER SALISBURY WILLOUGHBY BOLINGBROKE NORTHUMBERLAND
RICHARD III (AUTHOR OF —) SHAKESPEARE
(**CHARACTER IN —**) ANNE JOHN YORK DERBY HENRY JAMES LOVEL BLOUNT DORSET EDWARD GEORGE MORTON OXFORD RIVERS ROBERT SURREY THOMAS TYRREL WALTER BRANDON CATESBY HERBERT NORFOLK RICHARD STANLEY TRESSEL URSWICK VAUGHAN BERKELEY CLARENCE HASTINGS MARGARET RATCLIFF RICHMOND BOURCHIER ELIZABETH ROTHERHAM BRAKENBURY BUCKINGHAM GLOUCESTER CHRISTOPHER
RICHES GOLD PELF WEAL LUCRE WORTH MAMMON TALENT WEALTH FORTUNE OPULENCE RICHESSE TREASURE
RICHLY HIGH AMPLY FATLY FULLY DEARLY
RICHNESS BODY SUMEN LUXURY ELEGANCE FECUNDITY
RICHWEED RAGWEED COOLWEED
RICK GOAF GOFE REKE CANCH RICKLE SPRAIN WRENCH CORNRICK
RICKETS RACHITIS
RICKETY SHAKY SHACKY SHACKLY UNSOUND RACHITIC SHATTERY UNSTABLE TOTTERING RAMSHACKLE
RICKMATIC CONCERN BUSINESS
RICOCHET SKIP SKITE GLANCE REBOUND
RICTUS GRIN GRIMACE
RID FREE QUIT SHED SHUT CLEAR EGEST REDDE SCOUR SHIFT ACQUIT REMOVE DELIVER
(**— OF INSECTS**) BUG
(**— OF LICE**) CHAT
(**— OF WEEDS**) CLEAN
(**— ONESELF OF**) DOFF DEPOSIT DISPATCH
RIDDANCE SHUT RELIEF DISPATCH
RIDDER SIFT SIEVE RIDDLE
RIDDLE SIFT BLAIK GRIPH REBUS DEBASE ENIGMA FOITER PUZZLE RUDDLE SCREEN CORRUPT CRIBBLE EXPLAIN GRIDDLE GRIPHUS MYSTIFY PERPLEX PROBLEM CRATEMAN PERMEATE
(**— AS GRAIN**) REE
(**PL.**) MURLEMEWES
RIDDLER CRATEMAN
RIDE GO RIB BAIT DOSA HACK HURL LAST LIFT PRIG SAIL TOOL CROSS DRIVE TEASE BANTER CANTER DEPEND DODGEM GALLOP JUMBLE NOTICE SADDLE HAYRIDE JOYRIDE OVERLAP SURVIVE TANTIVY BESTRIDE
(**— FAST**) PRICK POWDER
(**— HARD**) POUND BUCKET
(**— IN HIRED VEHICLE**) JOB
(**— ON A WAVE**) BODYSURF
(**— ON HORSE**) BOOT LARK BURST JOCKEY SCHOOL

(**— RECKLESSLY**) BRUISE
(**— TO HOUNDS**) GO
(**AMUSEMENT PARK —**) SWING
RIDER TACK ANNEX CROSS HAZER LABEL COWBOY JOCKEY SITTER ALLONGE CODICIL NAGSMAN PRICKER CAVALIER DESULTOR HORSEMAN
(**DUKEY —**) BRAKEMAN
(**DUMMY —**) CROSS
RIDERS TO THE SEA (AUTHOR OF —) SYNGE
(**CHARACTER IN —**) NORA MAURYA BARTLEY MICHAEL
RIDGE AAS ARM BAR FIN RIB RIG RYG BALK BAND BANK BARB BROW BULT BURR BUTT COMB DRUM FRET FULL HACK HILL KEEL LINK LIST PAHA PUFF RAIN REAN ROLL SHIN SPUR WAVE WELT BARGH CHINE COSTA CREST EARTH EAVES GONYS GYRUS JUGUM KNURL LEDGE LINCH RINGE RUDGE SCOUT SHANK SPINE TORUS VARIX WHELP BRIDGE CARINA COLLOP CREASE CRISTA CUESTA CULMEN DIVIDE DORSUM FRENUM RAFTER RIDEAU SADDLE SELION SUMMIT ANNULET APODEMA BREAKER BUCCULA COLLINE COSTULA EYEBROW EYELINE HOGBACK HUMMOCK INTHROW PROPONS RIGGING SOWBACK WINDROW WITHERS WRINKLE YARDANG CATOCTIN CINGULUM FOREDUNE HEADLAND RESTBALK SHOULDER
(**— BETWEEN FURROWS**) STITCH RESTBALK
(**— IN BREASTPLATE**) TAPUL
(**— IN COAL SEAM**) HORSEBACK
(**— IN HORSE'S MOUTH**) EAR
(**— MADE BY PLOWING**) HACK SELION
(**— MADE BY TOOL**) BUR BARB BURR
(**— OF BIRD'S BILL**) CULM CULMEN
(**— OF BRAIN CORAL**) COLLINE
(**— OF BREASTBONE**) KEEL
(**— OF CLAY**) DOWLE
(**— OF EARTH**) BALK
(**— OF FLESH**) COLLOP
(**— OF HORSE'S NECK**) CREST
(**— OF LAND**) BULT RAIN SELION STITCH HOGBACK
(**— OF SAND IN WATER**) REEF SANDBAR
(**— OF SCAPULA**) SPINE
(**— OF SCREW**) THREAD
(**— OF SNOW**) SASTRUGA ZASTRUGA
(**— OF UNPLOWED LAND**) LINCH LINCHET
(**— OF WAVE**) CREST
(**— ON BOOK**) HUB
(**— ON CLOTH**) WALE
(**— ON CROWN OF TOOTH**) CINGULUM
(**— ON FINGERBOARD OF GUITAR**) FRET
(**— ON FISH SCALE**) CIRCULUS
(**— ON FRUITS OF CARROT FAMILY**) JUGUM

(**— ON GLUMES**) CARINA
(**— ON MOLLUSK SHELL**) COSTULA
(**— ON OVULE**) RAPHE
(**— ON SEA FLOOR**) SWELL
(**— ON SEASHORE**) STANNER
(**— ON SHEET METAL**) BEAD
(**— ON SIDE OF SADDLE**) PUFF
(**— ON SKIN**) WALE
(**— ON VIOLIN**) NUT
(**— PROTECTING CAMP**) RIDEAU
(**— WITH SHARP SUMMIT**) HOGBACK
(**—S ON ROCK**) LAPIES
(**ANATOMICAL —**) CARINA
(**BEACH —**) FULL
(**CHEWING —**) ENDITE
(**CONNECTING —**) HAUSE
(**CONVOLUTED —**) GYRUS
(**DRAINAGE —**) BREAKER
(**GLACIAL —**) OS KAME PAHA ESKAR ESKER ESCHAR NUNATAK
(**HAIRLIKE —**) LIRA
(**ICE —**) SERAC
(**ISOLATED —**) BARGH
(**LONG STONY —**) RAND
(**MOUNTAIN —**) COMB CHINE SIERRA BACKBONE
(**NARROW —**) DRUM RAZORBACK
(**PROJECTING —**) HOE SCOUT
(**RESIDUAL —**) CATOCTIN
(**ROCK —**) CLEAVER
(**SAND —**) DUNE ESKER WAVEMARK
(**SEEDED —**) DRILL
(**SHARP-CRESTED —**) ARETE ARRIS
(**SLIGHT —**) PROPONS
(**SNOW —**) ZASTRUGA
(**UNPLOWED —**) BALK BAULK
(**WOODED —**) CHENIER
(**PL.**) OSAR KNURLING
RIDGED RIDGY SHARP MILLED PORCATE CARINATE
RIDGELING RIG REGALD RIDGIL RIGGOT RIGINAL
RIDGEPOLE ROOFTREE
RIDICULE FUN GUY MOB PAN RIG TAX GAME GIBE JEER JEST JIBE JOEY MOCK PLAY QUIZ RAZZ SKIT TROT TWIT BORAK CHAFF CLOWN HORSE IRONY MIMIC MOMUS QUEER RALLY SCOFF SCOUT SMOKE SNEER TAUNT BANTER DERIDE EXPOSE RAILLY SATIRE BUFFOON LAMPOON MOCKERY SARCASM DERISION RAILLERY SATIRIZE SPOOFERY BURLESQUE
RIDICULOUS DOTTY DROLL FUNNY SILLY ABSURD INSANE COMICAL FOOLISH MOCKING DERISIVE DERISORY FARCICAL INDECENT COCKAMAMY MONSTROUS
RIDING AWHEEL LIVELY OVERLAP PRICKANT SHIVAREE TRITHING CHEVACHIE
(**— ACADEMY**) MANAGE MANEGE
(**— CROP**) ROD
(**— WHIP**) CROP QUIRT
RIDOTTO BALL REDOUTE
RIEM RHEIM RIMPI STRAP THONG
RIENZI (CHARACTER IN —) COLA IRENE PAOLO ORSINI RIENZI ADRIANO COLONNA STEFANO RAIMONDI

(COMPOSER OF —) WAGNER
RIFE EASY FULL RANK QUICK
READY ACTIVE FILLED NIMBLE
STRONG CURRENT REPLETE
ABUNDANT INCLINED MANIFEST
NUMEROUS
RIFFLE REEF RIFF WAVE RAPID
RIPPLE SHUFFLE WATERFALL
RIFFRAFF MOB RAFF SCUM SCAFF
TRASH RABBLE REFUSE RUBBISH
CANAILLE POPULACE RAGABASH
RIFLE RIG ROB KRAG LOOT RIPE
PIECE YAGER CARBIN JEZAIL
JUZAIL RIFFLE SNIDER ARISAKA
BULLPUP BUNDOCK BUNDOOK
CARABIN CARBINE DESPOIL
ENFIELD ESCOPET MARTINI
PILLAGE PLUNDER RANSACK
SPORTER BANDHOOK REPEATER
SPLITTER STRICKLE TAKEDOWN
CHASSEPOT
(— BALL CASING) THIMBLE
(— PIN) TIGE
RIFLEMAN JAGER JAEGER
(PL.) RIFLERY
RIFT RIVE BELCH CHASM CRACK
SPLIT CLEAVE DIVIDE BLEMISH
FISSURE CREVASSE
(— IN TIMBER) LAG
RIG RI FIG REG HOAX JEST JOKE
REEK WIND DRESS EQUIP GETUP
PRANK RIDGE SPORT STORM
TRICK BANTER CLOTHE GUNTER
ROTARY SADDLE SCHEME
MARCONI SPUDDER SWINDLE
BACKSTAY RIDICULE SEMITRAILER
(TRUCKING —) SEMI
RIGADOON DANCE RIGODON
RIGEL REGEL ALGEBAR
RIGGED (FULLY —) ATAUNT
RIGGER CLIMBER SLINGER
SCAFFOLD
RIGGING NET GEAR ROOF RIDGE
TACKLE APPAREL CLOTHING
JACKSTAY TACKLING
RIGHT DUE FEE FIT IUS OFF REE
SAY SOC BANG DUTY FAIR FLOP
GALE GOOD HAND ITER JUST
LIEN REAL RECT REET SANE SLAP
SOKE TEAM TRUE WELL CLAIM
DRESS DROIT ENTRY EXACT
FAVOR FERRY LEGAL RICHT
SOUND STRAY TECHT TITLE
ACTION ACTUAL ANGARY BALLOT
DEMAND DEXTER EATAGE EQUITY
PROPER PUTURE ANNUITY
APANAGE AUBAINE BENEFIT
CORRECT DERECHO DESIRED
FACULTY FALDAGE FITTING
FOLDAGE FREEDOM GENUINE
HAYBOTE LIBERTY LICENSE
PRENDER RECTIFY RELIEVE
SLAPDAB UPRIGHT WARRANT
BANALITY BLOODWIT FIREBOOT
FORESTRY HEIRSHIP INTEREST
LIFERENT SEIGNORY SLAPDASH
STALLAGE STRAIGHT SUFFRAGE
SUITABLE THIRLAGE
PREROGATIVE
(— AND LEFT) HAY HEY
(— AS COMMAND TO HORSES) REE
(— EYE) OD
(— HAND) MD OPENBAND

(— IN A THING) INTEREST
(— IN WIFE'S INHERITED PROPERTY)
CURTESY
(— OF CHOICE) OPTION
(— OF EXIT) ISH
(— OF FREE QUARTERS) CORODY
(— OF HOLDING COURT) TEAM
(— OF INQUIRY) SOKEN
(— OF OWNERSHIP) TITLE
COMMONTY
(— OF PASTURAGE) FEED STINT
EATAGE COWGATE COMMONAGE
HORSEGATE
(— OF PRECEDENCE) PAS
(— OF PRESENTATION) ADVOWSON
(— OF PROTECTION) MUND
**(— OF USING ANOTHER'S
PROPERTY)** EASEMENT
(— OF USING GRASSLAND) EATAGE
(— SIDE) OFFSIDE
(— TIME) TID
(— TO COLLECT REVENUE) DIWANI
DEWANEE DEWANNY
(— TO COMMAND) IMPERIUM
(— TO CUT WOOD) VERT
GREENHEW
(— TO DRAW WATER) HAUSTUS
(— TO DRIVE BEAST) ACTUS
(— TO PASS OVER LAND) ITER
(— TO SEIZE PROPERTY) ANGARY
(— TO SHOOT FIRST) CAST
(— TO WORK IN MINE) BEN
(ALL —) HUNK JAKE HUNKY
(FEUDAL —) CUDDY THIRL
THIRLAGE
(FISHING —) PISCARY
(INDIAN LEGAL —) HAK HAKH
(LEGAL —) IUS JUS JURE DROIT
ACCESS APPEAL COMMON
FISHERY HYPOTHEC
(LEGAL —S) JURA
(MILLER'S —) SOKEN
(MINING —) GALE
(NOT —) ACUTE
(PROPERTY —) DOMINIUM
(WIDOW'S —) TERCE TIERCE
(PL.) DIBS JURA
(PREF.) DEXIO DEXTR(O) ORTH(O)
RECT(I)
(— HAND) DEXIO DEXTR(O)
RIGHT ANGLE RECTANGLE
(HUNDREDTH OF —) GRAD GRADE
RIGHTEOUS GOOD JUST GODLY
MORAL ZADOC ZADOK DEVOUT
FITTING PERFECT SKILFUL
UPRIGHT INNOCENT VIRTUOUS
RIGHTEOUSNESS DOOM DHARMA
EQUITY JUSTICE HOLINESS
JUDGMENT JUSTNESS MORALITY
RECTITUDE
RIGHTFUL DUE JUST TRUE LEGAL
KINDLY LAWFUL PROPER FITTING
RIGHTFULNESS JUSTICE
RIGHT-HANDED DEXTRAL SKILLED
DEXTROUS CLOCKWISE
RIGHT-HANDWISE DEASIL DESSIL
DEISEAL CLOCKWISE
RIGHTLY RITE FITLY ARIGHT
FAIRLY JUSTLY HANDILY
PERQUEER SUITABLY
RIGHT WHALE BOWHEAD
BALAENID MYSTICETE
NORDCAPER

RIGID SET ACID CARK FIRM HARD
HIGH FIXED SOLID STARK STERN
STIFF STONY STOUT TENSE TONIC
TOUGH FORMAL FROZEN MARBLY
SEVERE STARCH STICKY STRICT
AUSTERE IRONCLAD RIGOROUS
STRAIGHT INELASTIC STRINGENT
(— IN SELF-DENIAL) ASCETIC
RIGIDITY FROST RIGOR RIGOUR
BUCKRAM SETNESS HARDNESS
STIFFNESS
RIGMAREE COIN TRIFLE
RIGMAROLE RANE NOMINY
RABBLE RAGMAN SLAMPAMP
SLAMPANT AMPHIGORY
RIGOLETTO (CHARACTER IN —)
GILDA MANTUA MADDALENA
RIGOLETTO SPARAFUCILE
(COMPOSER OF —) VERDI
RIGOR TYRANNY ASPERITY
HARDNESS SEVERITY
RIGOROUS FIRM HARD CLOSE
CRUEL EXACT HARSH HEFTY
RIGID STERN STIFF TOUGH
BITTER FLINTY SEVERE STRAIT
STRICT STRONG AUSTERE
DRASTIC PRECISE SPARTAN
DISTRICT DRACONIC EXACTING
IRONCLAD STRAIGHT
(MORALLY —) PURITANIC
(NOT —) INEXACT
(UNDULY —) HARSH
RILE VEX ROIL ANGER PEEVE
IRRITATE
RILL PURL SIKE CLEFT DRILL PRILL
GROOVE RUNLET RILLOCK
RIVULET BROOKLET RIVELING
TRICKLET ARROYUELO
WATERSHUT
RILLSTONE VENTIFACT
RIM HEM LIP BEAD BRIM CURB
EDGE SHOE BEZEL BRINK CHIME
EAVES FELLY FRAME HELIX SKIRT
BORDER CALKER CHOANA FILLET
FLANGE MARGIN EXCIPLE
(— HOLDING WATCH CRYSTAL)
BEZEL BEZIL
(— OF BASKET) HOOP
(— OF COROLLA) ANNULUS
(— OF CRATER) SOMMA
(— OF EAR) HELIX
(— OF GEM) GIRDLE
(— OF HORSESHOE) WEB
(— OF INSECT'S WING) TERMEN
(— OF JELLYFISH) VELUM
(— OF SANIO) CRASSULA
(— OF TIN) LIST
(— OF WHEEL) FELLY FELLOE
STRAKE
(— ON CASK) CHIMB CHIME CHINE
(— ON CLOG) CALKER
(— SURROUNDING FLAGELLUM)
CHOANA
(EXTERNAL —) FLANGE
(PROTECTIVE —) BANK
(RAISED —) BOSS
(PREF.) AMBO
RIMA CHINK CLEFT RIMULA
FISSURE
RIME RIM HOAR RIND RUNG CRACK
CRUST FROST ROUND
CRANREUCH
RIMPLE FOLD RIPPLE WRINKLE

RINALDO (BELOVED OF —)
ANGELICA
(COUSIN OF —) ORLANDO
(FATHER OF —) AYMON
(HORSE OF —) BAYARD
RIND BARK PEEL PILL RYND SKIN
CRUST FROST SWARD CITRON
SWARTH
(— OF HAM) SKIN
(— OF MEAT) SPINE
(— OF POMEGRANATE) GRANATUM
(— OF ROASTED PORK) CRACKLING
(PREF.) LEMMO LEPO
(SUFF.) LEMMA
RING GO-BEE BOW BUR CUP DEE
DIE EKE FAM JOW ORB PIT RIM
AMBO BAIL BAND BELL BONG
BURR CRIC CURB DING DIRL
ECHO GYRE HOOP JING LOOP
MAIL PASS PEAL RACE RINK RUSH
SHUT SING TANG TOLL VIRL WISP
AMBON ANLET ARENA BAGUE
CAROL CHIME CHINK CLANG
CYCLE GRAIN GROUP GUARD
GUIDE JEWEL KNELL LUNET PISTE
RIGOL ROUND ROWEL TORUS
VERGE WAFER WITHE BANGLE
BECKET BROUGH BUTTON CIRCLE
CIRCUS CIRQUE CLIQUE COLLAR
COLLET DINDLE EYELET FAMBLE
GIMMER GIRDLE HARROW KEEPER
LARIGO LEGLET RINGLE RUNDLE
RUNNER SIGNET TORQUE TURRET
VIROLE WASHER ANNULUS
ARMILLA CIRCLET CIRCUIT
CLAPPER COMPASS COUPLER
CRINGLE DIAMOND FAMELEN
FERRULE GALLERY GARLAND
GROMMET GUDGEON MANILLA
NUCLEUS PACKING RESOUND
ROWLOCK SHACKLE STIRRUP
THIMBLE VIBRATE BRACELET
BULLRING CINCTURE CORONULE
DINGDONG DRAUPNIR DUSTBAND
ENCIRCLE FAIRLEAD PACIFIER
SONORITY SURROUND TRAVELER
(— A TREE) FRILL
(— AROUND ARTICULAR CAVITY)
AMBON
(— AROUND MOON) BROCH
(— AROUND NIPPLE) AREOLA
(— AT EACH END OF CINCH) LARIGO
(— ATTACHED TO JIB) HANK
(— BELLS) FIRE
(— FOR CARRYING SHOT) LADLE
(— FOR SECURING BIRD) VERVEL
(— FOR TRAINING HORSES) LONGE
(— FORMING HANDLE OF KEY) BOW
(— OF ANNULATED COLUMN)
BAGUE
(— OF BOILER) STRAKE
(— OF COLOR) STOCKING
**(— OF DOTS AROUND EDGE OF
COIN)** GRAINING
(— OF LIGHT) GLORY
(— OF ODIN) DRAUPNIR
(— OF PILES) STARLING
(— OF RIDING SCHOOL) PISTE
(— OF ROPE) HANK BECKET
GARLAND GROMMET SNORTER
SNOTTER
(— OF SPINES) CORONULE
(— OF STANDING STONES) CAROL

(— OF TWO HOOPS) GEMEL GEMMEL
(— OF WAGONS) CORRAL LAAGER
(— ON BATTLEAX) BUR BURR
(— ON BIRD'S TIBIA) ARMILLA
(— ON DECK) CRANCE
(— ON GUN CARRIAGE) LUNET LUNETTE
(— ON HINGE) GUDGEON
(— ON LAMP) CRIC
(— ON LANCE) BURR
(— ON UMBRELLA ROD) RUNNER
(— SUPPORTING LAMPSHADE) GALLERY
(— SURROUNDING BUGLE) VIROLE
(— SUSPENDING COMPASS) GIMBAL
(— TO ENCLOSE DEER) TINCHEL TINCHILL
(— UNDER BEEHIVE) EKE
(— USED AS MONEY) MANILLA
(— USED AS VALVE) WAFER
(— WITH GROOVED OUTER EDGE) THIMBLE
(— WITH VIBRATION) DIRL
(BLACKSMITH'S —) BOLSTER
(BRIGHT —) HALATION
(CERVICAL —) TORQUE
(CURTAIN —) EYE
(FINGER —) HOOP
(FLESHY —) ANNULUS
(HARNESS —) DEE BUTTON LARIGO TERRET TORRET TURRET
(HAWK'S —) VERVEL
(INTERLINKED METAL —S) MAIL
(JOINED —) GIMMER GIMMOR
(LITTLE —) ANNULET
(LUMINOUS —) BROUGH
(MOUNTAINEER'S —) KARABINER
(NOSE —) PIRN
(OIL —) WIPER
(PACKING —) LUTE
(PART OF —) BAND CLAW PRONG SHANK STONE COLLET SETTING HALLMARK
(PLAITED —) RUSH WISP
(SURGICAL —) CURETTE
(TAPERING SHANK —) BELCHER
(TARGET —) SOUS SOUSE
(TOOTHED IRON —) HARROW
(TOP OF —) BEZEL BEZIL
(PREF.) CRICO CYCL(O) GYRO
(HAVING OPENED —) SECO
RING AND THE BOOK (AUTHOR OF —) BROWNING
(CHARACTER IN —) PAUL GUIDO PIETRO GIUSEPPE POMPILIA VIOLANTE COMPARINI CAPONSACCHI FRANCESCHINI
RINGDOVE QUIST CUSHAT CUSHIE QUEEST TOOZOO ZOOZOO COWSHOT COWSHUT
RINGED GYRATE ZONATE ANNULAR ANNULOSE
RINGED SNAKE COLUBRID
RINGER CHEER YOUTH COWBOY CROWBAR STOCKMAN
RINGHALS COBRA
RINGING BELL BRIGHT FERVID JANGLE CLANGOR OROTUND SINGING DECISIVE RESONANT SONORANT SONOROUS TINNIENT TINNITUS
(CHANGE —) CINQUES SINGLES

RINGLET CURL LOCK TENDRIL
(— ON FOREHEAD) FAVORITE
(PREF.) CIRR(I)(O)
RING-NECKED TORQUATE
RING-NECKED DUCK DOGY SCAUP MOONBILL RINGBILL BLACKJACK
RING OUZEL AMSEL THRUSH WHISTLER
RING PLOVER SANDY COLLIER KILLDEE DULWILLY RINGNECK
RING-SHAPED ANNULAR CRICOID ANNULARY ANNULATE CIRCULAR
RINGWORM TINEA KERION TETTER SERPIGO
RINGWORM BUSH SENNA
RINK ALLEY GLACIARIUM
RINSE NET SIND WASH RANGE RENCH RENSH RINGE SCIND SCOUR SWILL BLUING DOUCHE CLEANSE
RINSING NET SIND FLUSH RESIDUE
RIOT DIN HURL BRAWL REVEL WORRY ATTACK CLAMOR EXCESS JUMBLE MEDLEY RANTAN SPLORE TUMULT ANARCHY CONFUSE DESPOIL REVELRY BLOODWIT CAROUSAL
RIOTOUS ROID ROYD WILD NOISY RANDY RANTY HEMPIE RANDIE STORMY WANTON BACCHIC PROFUSE ROARING ABUNDANT BACCHIAN
RIP RIT COOP REAT TEAR BREAK SHARK SHRED SLITE UNSEW BASKET RIPPLE UNSEAM
RIPE FIT BOLD LATE DRUNK READY MATURE MELLOW SIDDER SIDDOW DIGESTED FINISHED SEASHORE SUITABLE
(EARLY —) HASTY RARERIPE
(PREF.) HADR(O)
RIPEN AGE ADDLE AUGUST DIGEST MELLOW CONCOCT CRIMSON DEVELOP PERFECT COMPLETE MATURATE
RIPENESS MATURITY
RIPHATH (FATHER OF —) GOMER
RIPOSTE REPLY RETORT THRUST REPARTEE
RIPPER RIPSAW BOBSLED HUMDINGER
RIPPET FUSS TUMULT UPROAR DISPUTE QUARREL
RIPPING FINE GRAND SWELL CAPITAL TIPPING SPLENDID
RIPPLE CURL FRET PURL RIFF SEED WAVE ACKER CRISP TWINE COCKLE DIMPLE JABBLE LIPPER RIMPLE RUFFLE RUMBLE WIMPLE CRINKLE WAVELET WRINKLE
(— ALONG) DADE
RIPPLING BREAK BULGE JABBLE ARIPPLE
(— OF SEA) LIPPER
(— ON SURFACE) HORROR
RIPSAW RIPPER SPLITSAW
RIPSNORTER SNIFTER HUMDINGER
RISE COME DRAW FLOW GROW HEAD HIGH HIKE HOLT HOVE LIFT PLUM SOAR ARISE BEGIN CANCH CHEER CLIMB ERECT HEAVE HOIST MOUNT OCCUR PITCH

PLUFF PROVE RAISE ROUSE SCEND SOURD STAND START SURGE SWELL TOWER YEAST ASCEND ASCENT ASPIRE AURORA BILLOW EMERGE GROWTH HAPPEN HEIGHT ORIGIN RESULT RETORT SOURCE SPRING THRIVE UPDIVE UPREAR ADVANCE APPLAUD HUMMOCK REDOUND UPHEAVE UPSHOOT EMINENCE FLOURISH HEIGHTEN INCREASE LEVITATE SCENSION UPSPRING
(— ABOVE) OVERLOOK SURMOUNT
(— ABRUPTLY) SKYROCKET
(— AGAIN) RESURGE
(— AND FALL) LOOM HEAVE WELTER
(— AS PRICE) MEND
(— GRADUALLY) LOOM
(— IN BLISTERS) YAW
(— IN CLOUDS) STOOR
(— IN MINE FLOOR) HOGBACK
(— IN PRICES) BULGE
(— IN VALUE) IMPROVE
(— OF CURVE) CAMBER
(— OF HAWK AFTER PREY) MOUNTY
(— OF SHIP'S LINES) FLIGHT
(— OF WATER) FLOOD
(— PRECIPITOUSLY) SKY
(— RAPIDLY) KITE
(— SHARPLY) BREAK
(— SUDDENLY) BOOM SPRING
(— SWIFTLY) BOIL
(— TO BAIT) TAKE
(— TO GREAT HEIGHT) TOWER
(— TO PEAK) SWELL
(— UP) FUME REAR ASCEND INSURRECT
(CURVED —) HANCE
(SHARP —) HOGBACK
RISE OF SILAS LAPHAM (AUTHOR OF —) HOWELLS
(CHARACTER IN —) TOM COREY IRENE SILAS LAPHAM PERSIS ROGERS PENELOPE BROMFIELD
RISER HEAD RAISE FEEDHEAD INSURGENT
RISHI RSI POET SAGE SAINT DEVARSHI KASHYAPA MAHARSHI
RISIBLE FUNNY GELASTIC LAUGHABLE
RISING BOIL BULL RIST ARISE ARIST ORIENT PUTSCH SOURCE STRAKE UPREST UPWITH MONTANT PUSTULE SURGENT EMERGENT INCREASE MOUNTANT NAISSANT ONCOMING ASSURGENT EXCEEDING
(— ABRUPTLY) BOLD
(— AND FALLING) TIDAL
(— AS OF HAWK) SOURCE
(— BY DEGREES) GRADIENT
(— GRADUALLY) SOFT
(— HIGH) AERIAL
(— SHARPLY) ABRUPT
(— STEEPLY) BLUFF
(— TO BREATHE) HAURIENT
(POPULAR —) EMEUTE
RISK GO RUN SET GAGE JUMP LUCK PAWN PERIL RISCO STAKE STAND THROW WAGER WATHE CHANCE DANGER GAMBLE HAZARD IMPAWN PLIGHT

THREAT BALANCE IMPERIL VENTURE ENDANGER EXPOSURE
(PL.) COVERAGE
RISKY BOLD DICEY CHANCY DARING KITTLE RISQUE PARLISH PARLOUS TECHOUS TICKLISH
RISP BUSH RASP STEM TWIG STALK BRANCH SCRATCH
RISQUE BLUE RACY BROAD DARING SCABROUS
RISSOLE CROQUETTE
(PL.) CECILS
RISS-WURM NEUDECKIAN
RISURREZIONE (CHARACTER IN —) DIMITRI KATUSHA SIMONSON
(COMPOSER OF —) ALFANO
RIT CUT RIP RUT REND SLIT TEAR SCRATCH
RITE KEX ASAL BORA BRIS FORM HAKO SOMA BRITH HONOR RIGHT SRADH ABDEST AUGURY EXEQUY FETISH OFFICE PANSIL PIACLE POOJAH RITUAL BAPTISM FUNERAL KATCINA LITURGY MYSTERY OBSEQUY SRADDHA TASHLIK CEREMONY HIERURGY HUSKANAW MORTUARY PIACULUM OBSERVANCE
(PL.) CULT SACRA SERVICE
RITUAL FORM RITE SOLEMN AGENDUM HAGGADA LITURGY OBSEQUY SERVICE CEREMONY VISPARAD VISPERED
(PRAYER —) PUJA
RITZY HAUGHTY SNOBBISH
RIVAGE BANK RIVE COAST SHORE
RIVAL VIE EVEN PEER SIDE MATCH COMPETE CORRIVE EMULATE PARAGON CORRIVAL EMULATOR OPPONENT
(PREF.) ANT(I) ANTH(O)
RIVALRY VIE GAME STRIFE PARAGON JEALOUSY STRIVING EMULATION
RIVALS (AUTHOR OF —) SHERIDAN
(CHARACTER IN —) BOB JACK LUCY ACRES JULIA LYDIA LUCIUS ANTHONY ABSOLUTE BEVERLEY LANGUISH MALAPROP MELVILLE OTRIGGER FAULKLAND
RIVE RIP PLOW REND STAB TEAR CRACK REAVE SEVER SPLIT WEDGE CLEAVE SUNDER THRUST SHATTER FRACTURE
RIVELING RULLION
RIVER EA LE LEE REE RIO TJI ALPH AVON BAHR GEON ILOG KILL WADI WADY BAYOU CREEK FLOOD GANGA GIHON GJOLL GLIDE HABOR INLET KIANG TCHAI BARCOO GUTTER KHUBUR NYANZA STRAIT STREAM CHANNEL COCYTUS ESTUARY FROEMAN ILISSUS PHARPAR RUBICON SENEGAL AFFLUENT ERIDANUS PACTOLUS STAIRCASE
(— CHANNEL) ALVEUS
(— NEAR GATE OF HEL'S ABODE) GJOLL
(— OF ATTICA) ILISSUS
(— OF DAMASCUS) PHARPAR

(— OF LYDIA) PACTOLUS
(— OF PARADISE) GEON GIHON
(— OF QUEENSLAND) BARCOO
(— OF UNDERGROUND) PHLEGETHON
(— OF UNDERWORLD) STYX LETHE ACHERON COCYTUS FLEGETON
(AFRICAN —) NYANZA SENEGAL
(CHINESE —) HO KIANG
(EGYPTIAN —) BAHR NILE
(FULL —) BANKER
(JAVANESE —) TJI
(MINOR —) BAYOU
(SACRED —) ALPH GANGA
(SMALL —) BACHE TCHAI
(PREF.) FLUVI(O) POTAM(O)
(SUFF.) POTAMIA POTAMUS
RIVERBANK RIPA RIPE
RIVERBED LAAGTE BATTURE
(DRY —) WADI WADY
RIVERBOAT COG BARGE FOIST PULWAR
RIVER DUCK TEAL MALLARD WIDGEON GREENWING
RIVERINE (— FISH) HUCHO
RIVERWEED WATERWEED
RIVET STUD CLINK ROOVE PANHEAD FLATHEAD
(— ATTENTION) GRIP
(— HEAD) CUPHEAD
RIVULET RUN BURN GILL LAKE MOTH RILL SIKE BACHE BATCH BAYOU BOURN BROOK GHYLL RITHE RINDLE RUNLET RUNNEL STREAM STRIPE STRYPE CHANNEL RIVERET BROOKLET
RIXY TERN
RIZPAH (LOVER OF —) SAUL
(SON OF —) ARMONI MEPHIBOSHETH
RIZZAR DRY PARCH RASOUR RAZOUR CURRANT HADDOCK
RIZZOM BIT EAR RISOM STALK STRAW RISSOM
ROACH HOG BUTT ROCK SPOT BRAISE BLATTID SUNFISH
ROAD LEG PAD TAO VIA WAY BELT BORD CASH DRAG DRUN FARE GAET GANG GATE LINE LODE LOKE PASS PATH PAVE PIKE RADE RAID RIDE RODE ROTE ROUT SLAB SPUR WENT BARGH BLAZE BYWAY CLOSE DRIFT DRIVE DROVE FORAY GAITE GOING METAL PRAYA ROUTE TRACE TRACK BYROAD CAMINO CAREER CAUSEY CHEMIN COURSE DUGWAY FEEDER RIDING ROUGHT RUNWAY SLOUGH STREET TARMAC TRAJET BEELINE CALZADA CARTWAY ESTRADA GANGWAY HIGHWAY LANDWAY OUTGANG PACKWAY PASSAGE RAILWAY RAMPIRE ROADWAY ROLLWAY SKIDWAY TELFORD AUTOBAHN BEALLACH BLACKTOP BROADWAY CHAUSSEE CORDUROY FOOTRILL HORSEWAY OVERPASS RIDGEWAY SPEEDWAY TRACKWAY TRAMROAD TRAVERSE TURNPIKE WAGONWAY ROADSTEAD
(— BORDERING SHORE) PRAYA

(— FOR LOGGING) SKIDWAY CROSSHAUL
(— IN COAL MINE) BORD BOARD FOOTRILL
(— ON CLIFF) CORNICHE
(— SCRAPER) HARL HARLE
(— SURFACE) TELFORD
(CEMENT OR CONCRETE —) SLAB
(COUNTRY —) BOREEN DRIFTWAY
(DESCENDING —) BAHADA BAJADA
(IMPASSABLE —) SLOUGH IMPASSE
(IMPROVISED —) CASH
(MILITARY OR PUBLIC —) AGGER
(NARROW —) DRANG DRUNG RODDIN
(PAVED —) CALZADA CHAUSSEE
(PRINCIPAL —) ARTERY
(PRIVATE —) LOKE DRIVE DRIVEWAY
(RAISED —) AGGER RAMPIRE CAUSEWAY
(ROMAN —) ITER CAUSEY
(SIDE —) BRANCH SHUNPIKE
(STEEP —) BRAE PATH BARGH SPRUNT
(TEMPORARY —) SHOOFLY
(UNIMPROVED —) DROVE
(ZIGZAG —) SWITCHBACK
(PREF.) ODO VIA
(SUFF.) ODE OID
ROADBED BALLAST BITUMEN
ROADBOOK MAP ITINERARY
ROAD DONKEY ROADER
ROADMAN PEDDLER SALESMAN CANVASSER
ROADMASTER OVERSEER
ROAD RUNNER CUCKOO PAISANO
ROADSIDE HEDGE
ROADSTEAD RAID DOWNS
ROADSTER BUGGY TRAMP DRIVER BICYCLE RUNABOUT RACEABOUT SPEEDSTER
ROADWAY DECK EXIT STREET MACADAM SLIPWAY TRUCKWAY
ROAM GO ERR RUN WAG RAKE RAME RAVE ROIL ROLL ROVE WALK GIPSY GYPSY KNOCK RANGE SCAMP SPACE STRAY TAVER VAGUE WAVER BANGLE RAMBLE STROLL SWERVE TAIVER VAGARY WANDER GALLANT PROCEED SQUANDER VAGABOND
(— FURTIVELY) PROWL
ROAMING ERROR NOMADIC ROAMAGE FUGITIVE
(PREF.) PLAN(O)
ROAN HORSE GRIZZLE
ROANOKE WAMPUM
ROAR CRY BAWL BEAL BELL BERE BOOM BRAY CAVE HOWL HURL RAIR RARE RERD ROIN ROME ROOP ROUT YELL BLARE BROOL CRACK RERDE ROUST SHOUT SNORE BELLOW BULDER BULLER CLAMOR GOLLAR GOLLER RUMMES SCREAM SHRIEK STEVEN BLUSTER RUMMISH ULULATE
(— AS BOAR) FREAM
(— LIKE WIND) HURL
(— OF SURF) ROTE
(LOW —) BROOL
ROARING RUT LOUD AROAR BRISK ROUST BELLOW BOOMING

RIOTOUS THRIVING
ROARING BOY TWIBIL TWIBILL
ROARING GAME CURLING
ROARING MEG CANNON
ROAST RAZZ ROTI SOAK BREDE BROWN PARCH ASSATE CODDLE REMOVE TORREFY TORRIFY BARBECUE RIDICULE
(— IN ASHES) BRY
(STUFFED —) FARCI
ROASTED ASADO
(NOT —) GREEN
ROASTER BURNER SCORCHER
ROASTING ASSATION
ROASTING JACK TURNSPIT
ROB COP PAD EASE FAKE FLAP MILL NICK PEEL PELF PICK PILL POLL PREY PULL RAMP RIPE ROLL TOBY BENIM BRIBE FLIMP HARRY HEAVE HEIST LURCH PINCH PLUCK PLUME PROWL REAVE RIFLE ROIST SHAKE SPOIL SPUNG STEAL STRUB TOUCH HARROW HIJACK HUSTLE PILFER RAVISH RIPOFF STRIKE THIEVE BEREAVE DEPRIVE DESPOIL PLUNDER RUMPADE SNAFFLE UNPURSE DEFLOWER SPOLIATE
(— HOUSE) MILL
(— OF CHASTITY) DEFILE
(— OF FORCE) COOL
(— OF JOY) DESOLATE
(— OF VIGOR) ETIOLATE
(— WITH VIOLENCE) RAMP
ROBALO SNOOK SNOWK SERGEANT
ROBBED RUBATO
(NOT —) UNPILLED
ROBBER PAD FOMOR LARON THIEF BANDIT BRIBER DACOIT FORMOR HOLDUP LATRON RIFLER BRIGAND CATERAN FOOTPAD HEISTER LADRONE MOONMAN PANDOUR PRANCER RAVENER ROUTIER SPOILER TOBYMAN BARABBAS FOMORIAN PILLAGER RABIATOR BANDOLERO
(— ON HIGH SEAS) PIRATE
(— WHO USES VIOLENCE) RABIATOR
(GRAVE —) GOUL GHOUL
(HIGHWAY —) PAD FOOTPAD TOBYMAN
(INDIAN MURDEROUS —) DACOIT
(IRISH —) WOODKERN
(MOUNTAIN —) CHOAR
(NIGHT —) MOONMAN
(SEA —) FOMOR FORMOR FOMORIAN
(WANDERING —) ROUTIER
(PREF.) LESTO
(SUFF.) LESTES
ROBBERY JOB JUMP REIF RIFE HEIST SCREW STALE FELONY HOLDUP STOWTH BRIBERY DACOITY LARCENY PILLAGE PLUNDER REAVERY STICKUP THUGGEE PURCHASE SPOLIATION
(— ON HIGH SEAS) PIRACY
(HIGHWAY —) TOBY
ROBE GOWN VEST KANZU STOLA CHIMER KIMONO KITTEL MANTLE PEPLOS REVEST ARISAID

BUFFALO GALABIA SURCOAT VESTURE PARAMENT WOLFSKIN
(— FOR THE DEAD) HABIT
(— OF MONARCH) PLUVIAL
(— PRESENTED BY DIGNITARY) KHALAT KHILAT
(— REACHING TO ANKLES) TALAR
(ACTOR'S —) SYRMA
(BAPTISMAL —) CHRISOM
(BISHOP'S —) CHIMER CHIMERE
(CIRCULAR —) CYCLAS
(CORONATION —) COLOBIUM DALMATIC
(DERVISH'S —) KHIRKA KHIRKAH
(EMPEROR'S —) PURPLE
(FUNERAL —) SABLE
(JEWISH —) KITTEL
(KING'S —) DALMATIC
(LOOSE —) MANT CAMIS CAMUS CYMAR SIMAR SYMAR MANTUA MANTEAU
(MASQUERADE —) VENETIAN
(MEXICAN —) MANGA
(MONK'S —) HAPLOMA
(OLD-FASHIONED —) SAMARE
(OUTER —) JAMA
(TARTAN —) ARISAID
(TURKISH —) DOLMAN
(WHITE —) CHRISOM
(PL.) ACADEMICALS
ROBERT DOB POP RAB DOBBIN POPKIN
ROBERT OF LINCOLN BOBOLINK
ROBIN PINFISH REDDOCK RUDDOCK TOOTLER WINGFISH REDBREAST
ROBIN GOODFELLOW ELF PUCK FAIRY SPRITE HOBGOBLIN
ROBINIA LOCUST
ROBIN SANDPIPER KNOT DOWITCHER
ROBORANT TONIC
ROBOT GELEM GOLEM AUTOMAT TELEVOX
ROB ROY (AUTHOR OF —) SCOTT
(CHARACTER IN —) ROB OWEN DIANA FRANK ANDREW MACFIN MORRIS VERNON TRESHAM WILLIAM CAMPBELL FREDERICK INGLEWOOD MACVITTIE RASHLEIGH HILDEBRAND FAIRSERVICE OSBALDISTONE
ROBUST ABLE FIRM HAIL HALE HARD IRON RUDE BONNY HARDY HUSKY LUSTY RENKY SOUND STARK STIFF STOUR STOUT TOUGH VALID WALLY HEARTY RUGGED SINEWY STRONG STURDY HEALTHY NERVOUS STHENIC VALIANT MUSCULAR PITHSOME STALWART SWACKING VIGOROUS STRAPPING
(NOT —) SLENDER
ROBUSTNESS VALIDITY
ROC BIRD BOMB RUKH ROQUE SIMURG SIMURGH
ROCHET CLOAK SMOCK CAMISIA
ROCK CAP JOW LOG PAY RAG DAZE HOST KLIP REEL RUKH SIAL SIMA SWAY SWIG TOSS BRACK CLIFF FLOOR GREET GRUSS HORSE LEDGE ROACH ROQUE SHAKE SHOWD SKARN STONE

TRILL CRADLE FACIES GROUND OOLITE PELITE TOTTER BRECCIA COUNTRY FOLIATE GREISEN CIMINITE PHYLLITE SILTSTONE
(— AROUND DRILL HOLE) COLLAR
(— CHUNK) KNUCKLE
(— DEBRIS) SCREE
(— IN ANOTHER ROCK) XENOLITH
(— IN MINE) CAPPING
(— IN SEA) STACK
(— SURFACE) KARREN
(— VIOLENTLY) STAGGER
(ARTIFICIAL —) GRANOLITH
(BALD —) SCALP
(BANDED —) BAR
(BARE —) SCARTH
(CAP —) COVER
(COMPACT —) BASEMENT
(CONGLOMERATE —) PSEPHITE
(COUNTRY —) RIDER
(CRUSHED —) GREET
(CRYSTALLINE —) ELVAN DUNITE SCHIST DIORITE GREISEN ECLOGITE
(DECAY OF —S) GEEST LATERITE
(DECOMPOSED —) GOSSAN GOZZAN
(DENSE —) ADINOLE
(DISINTEGRATED —) SAPROLITE
(EXTRUSIVE —) DACITE SPILITE ANDESITE CIMINITE
(FELDSPATHIC —) PETUNTSE
(FISSILE —) SHALE SHAUL
(FLUID —) LAVA
(FRAGMENTAL —) PSEPHITE
(GABBROITIC —) EUCRITE
(GLASSY —) PITCHSTONE
(GRANULAR —) GABBRO OOLITE DIORITE IJOLITE KOSWITE MYLONITE PSAMMITE QUARTZITE
(GRANULATED —) GRUSS
(GREEN —) OPHITE
(HARD —) WHIN KIMGLE WHINSTONE NOVACULITE
(HIGH —) SCOUT
(IGNEOUS —) BOSS SIAL SIMA TRAP BASALT DUNITE GABBRO URTITE FELSITE GRANITE MINETTE PICRITE SYENITE DOLERITE ESSEXITE RHYOLITE TONALITE
(IMPURE —) CHERT
(INSULAR —) SKERRY
(INSULATED —) SKERRY
(INTRUSIVE —) HORTITE MINETTE MAENAITE
(IRON-BEARING —) GAL
(ISOLATED —) SCAR SCARR SCAUR
(JUTTING POINT OF —) KIP
(MANTLE —) REGOLITH
(METAMORPHIC —) SKARN GNEISS SCHIST BUCHITE GONDITE LEPTITE ECLOGITE HORNFELS LIMURITE
(MICA-BEARING —) DOMITE
(MOLTEN —) MAGMA
(MOTTLED —) SERPENTINE
(PLUTONIC —) TAWITE HOLLAITE TURJAITE
(POROUS —) TUFA TUFF ARSOITE
(PROJECTING —) CLINT
(PULVERIZED —) FLOUR
(RARE —) ALNOITE

(ROUGH —) CRAG KNAR SCARTH
(ROUNDED —) ROGNON SHEEPBACK
(SEDIMENTARY —) CRAG IRONSTONE SANDSTONE
(SHARP —) NEEDLE AIGUILLE
(SLATY —) PLATE SCHALSTEIN
(SOFT —) MALM
(SOLID —) GIBBER
(STUDY OF —S) LITHOLOGY
(SUBMERGED —) SHELF
(UNDERLYING —) FLOOR
(VOLCANIC —) TUFA TUFF BASALT DACITE DOMITE LATITE TAXITE PEPERIN ANDESITE ASHSTONE EUTAXITE RHYOLITE TEPHRITE TRACHYTE
(WASTE —) MULLOCK
(WORTHLESS —) GANG GANGUE
(PL.) ROCHER
(PREF.) FELSO PETR(I)(O) RHYO RUPI SAXI
(SUFF.) CLAST ITE LITE LITH(IC) LITIC PHYRE PHYRIC
ROCKAWAY CARRIAGE
ROCK BADGER CONY HYRAX
ROCK BASS REDEYE CABRILLA
ROCK-BREAKER
(SUFF.) FRAGE
ROCKBRUSH ROSILLA
ROCK CEDAR SABINO
ROCK CRESS ARABIS SICKLEPOD
ROCK DEBRIS TALUS
ROCK DOVE SOD
ROCK-DWELLING SAXATILE
ROCKER CRADLE SHOOFLY
ROCKET DRAKE REBUKE STREAK YELLOW CONGREVE SKYLIGHT STARSHIP FIREDRAKE
(DYER'S —) WELD WOLD WOALD WOULD
ROCKET SALAD ROQUETTE
ROCKFISH BASS JACK RENA REINA VIUVA FLIOMA GOPHER RASHER TAMBOR CORSAIR GARRUPA GROUPER BOCACCIO CHINAFISH GREENLING
ROCK HARE KLIPHAAS
ROCK HIND MERO AGAUJI
ROCK HOPPER MACARONI
ROCKLING BAUD GADE ROKER SORGHE WHISTLER
ROCK NATIVE SNAPPER
ROCK PIPIT TIETICK
ROCK RABBIT PIKA HYRAX HYRACOID
ROCKROSE CISTUS PINWEED HUDSONIA ROCKCIST SAGEROSE DAYFLOWER SUNFLOWER
ROCK SALT EMOL AMOLE HALITE
(BLOCK OF —) PIG
ROCK SANDWORT CYME
ROCKSHAFT SHAFT ROCKER WEIGHBAR
ROCK TROUT BOREGAT GREENLING
ROCKWEED TANG FUCUS FUCOID SEATANG SEAWEED
(PREF.) FUCI
ROCK WHITING KELPFISH STRANGER
ROCKWORK ROCAILLE
ROCKY DAFT HARD STONY CLINTY

OBSCENE PETREAN PETROUS UNCOUTH OBDURATE UNSTABLE DIFFICULT RUPELLARY
(PREF.) TRACHY
ROCKY MOUNTAIN (— GOAT) MAZAME
ROCOCO ORNATE QUAINT BAROCCO BAROQUE OUTMODED
ROD BAR BOW CUE GAD GUY LUG PIN TIE BOLT CALM CAME CANE CORE FALL FORK GOAD GONG LINK MACE POLE RAVE SCOB SNAP STEM STUD WAND WHIP YARD ARBOR BIRCH CATCH DOWEL LYTTA OSIER PERCH POWER PUNCH REACH ROUND SETUP SHOOT SPELK SPILL SPOKE SPRAG STAFF STANG STEEL STICK STING TEYNE TOMMY TRACE VERGE WIPER BALEYS BROACH CANARY CARBON CENTER CRUTCH ETALON FERULA FINGER GLOWER HANGER PISTOL PITMAN PODGER RADDLE RAMMER SKEWER SPRING STADIA SWITCH TOGGLE WATTLE WICKER BACULUS CROPPIE DRAWROD ELLWAND FEATHER FESTUCA PLUNGER POINTER POTHOOK PRICKER PROBANG PROLONG SCALLOM SCEPTER SPINDLE STADIUM STICKER TYRANNY VIRGULA WHISKER WINDING AXOSTYLE BACKSTAY BILBERRY BODSTICK BOWSTAVE DIPSTICK JACKSTAY KINGBOLT REVOLVER STRAINER TRAVELER WEEDHOOK
(— AS SYMBOL OF OFFICE) VERGE
(— BEARING TRAFFIC SIGNAL) STANCHION
(— FOR ALIGNING HOLES) PODGER
(— FOR CARRYING GLASS) FORK
(— FOR DISCIPLINE) YARD FERULA FERULE
(— FOR FASTENING THATCH) SPELK SPRINGLE
(— FOR FIREARM BORE) WIPER
(— FOR GLASS-MAKING) PUNTY FASCET PONTEE PONTIL CROPPIE
(— FOR HOLDING MEAT) SPIT
(— FOR TRANSMITTING MOTION) TRACE
(— IN ARC LAMP) CARBON
(— IN CRICKET) STUMP
(— IN INTERFEROMETER) ETALON
(— IN MINE PUMP) SPEAR
(— IN NERNST LAMP) GLOWER
(— IN SPINNING WHEEL) SPINDLE
(— OF CELLS) NOTOCHORD
(— OF FOUNDRY MOLD) LANCE
(— OF LOOM) SHAFT
(— OF WOOD) SCOB
(— ON LOGGING TRUCK) RAVE
(— POINTED AT BOTH ENDS) SKEWER
(— SYMBOLIZING AUTHORITY) BACULUS
(— TO BIND A CONTRACT) FESTUCA
(— TO FASTEN SAILS) JACKSTAY
(— TO IMMERSE SHEEP) CRUTCH
(— TO URGE BEAST) GOAD PROD
(— UPSET AT ONE END) SETUP

(— USED AS KEY) TOMMY
(— WITH ENDS AT RIGHT ANGLES) STRAINER
(— WITH SPONGE ON END) PROBANG
(— WITH T-HEAD) TOGGLE
(AXIAL —) VIRGULA AXOSTYLE
(BASKETRY —) OSIER SLATH
(BUNDLE OF —S) DRIVER
(CARTILAGINOUS —) LYTTA COLUMELLA
(CLAMMING —) BRAIL
(CONNECTING —) PITMAN
(CURTAIN —) TRINGLE
(DANCER'S —) CROTALUM
(DIVINING —) TWIG DOWSER
(FISHING —) GAD CALCUTTA
(FLEXIBLE —) RADDLE WATTLE
(FORKED —) CRUTCH
(GEM-CUTTING —) SETTER
(GRADUATED —) STADIA STADIUM
(IRON —) SNAP BETTY
(KNITTING —) NEEDLE
(LEAD —) CAME
(LOGGING —) CANARY
(MEASURING —) JUDGE SPILE STADIA ELLWAND METEWAND METEYARD
(PLIABLE —) WINDING
(SMALL —) LANCE
(STRENGTHENING —) RIB
(SUPPLE —) SWABBLE
(TETHERING —) STAKE
(THIN —) TEYNE SCALLOM
(TIE —) ANCHOR
(UMBRELLA —) STRETCHER
(WITHE —) BILBERRY
(PREF.) BACULI RHABD(O) RHAPIDO VERGI
RODENT RAT CONY DEGU HARE MARA MOCO MOLE PACA PIKA UTIA VOLE CONEY COYPU GUNDI HUTIA JUTIA LEROT MOUSE TUCAN ZOKOR AGOUTI BEAVER BITING CURURO GERBIL GLIRID GNAWER GOPHER JERBOA MARMOT MURINE MUROID RABBIT SOKHOR BLESMOL CHINCHA DIPODID GEOMYID GNAWING HAMSTER LEMMING LEVERET MUSKRAT ABROCOME CAPIBARA DORMOUSE LEPORIDE OCTODONT SEWELLEL SPALACID SQUIRREL TUCOTUCO VISCACHA VIZCACHA ANOMALURE PORCUPINE
RODEO ROUNDUP
RODERICK RANDOM (AUTHOR OF —) SMOLLETT
(CHARACTER IN —) TOM STRAP OAKHUM RANDOM BOWLING MELINDA SNAPPER CRAMPLEY NARCISSA RODERICK WILLIAMS QUIVERWIT
RODLIKE VIRGATE RHABDOID
RODMAN CLASHY CLASHEE CHAINMAN
RODOMONTADE BRAG RANT BOAST BLUSTER BOMBAST BRAGGART
RODOMONTE (BELOVED OF —) DORALICE
(VICTIM OF —) RUGGIERO

ROD-SHAPED RHABDOID
VIRGULATE
ROE RA DOE FRY PEA RAA RAE
HIND KELK RAUN ROUN ROWN
CORAL TRUBU CAVIAR
ROEBUCK GIRL CHEVREUIL
ROGER RAM HODGE ROGUE
ROGUE BOY GUE IMP NYM HEMP
KEMP KITE LOON ROAG CATSO
CRACK CRANK DROLE GIPSY
GREEK GYPSY HEMPY KNAVE
SCAMP SHELM BEGGAR BORGER
BUGGER CANTER CHOUSE
COQUIN CURTAL HARLOT LIMMER
PICARA PICARO RASCAL SORROW
TINKER BLEEDER ERRATIC
FOISTER HALLION LADRONE
PANURGE SHARPER SKELLUM
SWINGER VILLAIN COMROGUE
HEMPSEED PICAROON SCALAWAG
SWINDLER WHIPJACK
ROGUE HERRIES (AUTHOR OF —)
WALPOLE
  (CHARACTER IN —) ALICE DAVID
PRESS SARAH STARR DEBORAH
DENBURN FRANCIS HERRIES
MARGARET MIRABELL
OSBALDISTONE
ROGUERY ROPERY KNAVERY
LOONERY WAGGERY PATCHERY
PRIGGISM TRICKERY TRUANTRY
ROGUISH SLY ARCH HEMPY
ROGUY WICKED KNAVISH
TRICKSY VAGRANT WAGGISH
ESPIEGLE SCAMPISH DISHONEST
ROGUISHNESS KNAVERY
ARCHNESS
ROI DE LAHORE, LE (CHARACTER
IN —) ALIM SITA SCINDIA
  (COMPOSER OF —) MASSENET
ROIL VEX FOUL RILE ANNOY
BLUNDER DISTURB STUDDLE
BEWILDER DISORDER IRRITATE
ROILED TURBID
ROISTER REVEL ROIST SCOUR
CAROUSE GALRAVAGE
ROISTERER MUN GREEK HUZZA
BUSTER HECTOR RIOTER
SCOURER TWIBILL EPHESIAN
ROISTERING HOYDEN
ROKE FOG DAMP MIST REEK ROWK
STIR FOGGY SMOKE STEAM
VAPOR
ROKELAY ROCOLO
ROLAND (BETROTHED OF —) AUDE
  (COMPANION OF —) OLIVER
  (HORN OF —) OLIVANT
  (SWORD OF —) DURANDAL
  (UNCLE OF —) CHARLEMAGNE
ROLE BIT JOB LEAD PART ROTE
HEAVY FIGURE CLOTHES
BUSINESS FUNCTION LIRIPIPE
  (SMALL —) CAMEO
ROLL BAP BUN ROW WEB BOLT
COIL CURL FILE FLOW FURL LIST
MILL PASS REEL ROAM ROTA
SWAG WELT WIND WRAP BAGEL
BIALY BREAD BUILD DANDY
DICKY ENROL FLUTE ROYLE SPLIT
TOMMY TRILL TROLL WHELM
BILLOW BUNDLE CIRCLE ELAPSE
ENFOLD GOGGLE GROVEL KIPFEL
LEGEND MUSTER PONDER

RECORD ROSTER ROTATE SCROLL
UPWIND VOLUME WAMBLE
WANDER WHELVE WINTLE
WREATH BISCUIT BOLILLO
BRIOCHE CROCKET ENVELOP
MANCHET NOTITIA REVOLVE
ROTULET ROTULUS ROULEAU
STRETCH TERRIER TRINDLE
TRUNDLE TWISTER BROTCHEN
CANNELON CONSIDER CRESCENT
JACKROLL LAMINATE PORTEOUS
REGISTER SEDERUNT SPREADER
VOLUTATE
  (— A BALL) BOWL
  (— ABOUT) WALTER SCAMBLE
  (— AS A SHIP) SEEL LURCH
  (— AS STONE) REEL
  (— BY) WALK
  (— CLOSELY) FURL
  (— EYES) WALL WAUL WHAWL
GOGGLE
  (— GLASS) MARVER
  (— INTO A BALL) CLEW CLUE
  (— OF BREAD) BAP SEMMEL
TAMMIE
  (— OF CLOTH) BOLT DOSSIL
WREATH
  (— OF COINS) ROULEAU
  (— OF DOUGH) TWIST
  (— OF DRIED BARK) QUILL
  (— OF DRUM) HURRY RATTAN
  (— OF DUST) KITTEN
  (— OF FIBERS) ROVING
  (— OF HAIR) PUFF ROACH ROWEL
CROCKET
  (— OF HAY) WAKE
  (— OF LINT OR LINEN) TENT DOSSIL
  (— OF LUGGAGE) SWAG
  (— OF MINCED MEAT) RISSOLE
  (— OF OFFENDERS) PORTEOUS
  (— OF PAPER) SPILL STOMP STUMP
  (— OF PARCHMENT) BOOK PELL
  (— OF ROULETTE WHEEL) COUP
  (— OF SPUN YARN) PRICK
  (— OF TOBACCO) CAROT CIGAR
PRICK SEGAR CAROTTE
  (— OF WALLPAPER) BOLT
  (— OF WHEAT BREAD) MANCHET
  (— OF WOOL) ROVE ROVING
CARDING
  (— ON CASTERS) TRUCKLE
  (— ON LITTLE WHEELS) TRUNDLE
  (— ONWARD) DEVOLVE
  (— OVER) COMB JOLL WELTER
  (— TO RUB DOWN DRAWING)
STUMP
  (— TOGETHER) CONVOLVE
  (— UP) FURL STOW COLLAR
  (— UP SLEEVES) REEVE
  (BLANKET —) BINDLE SHIRALEE
  (BREAKFAST —) BIALY
  (DANDY —) DANCER
  (HOLLOW —) CANNELON
  (LONG —) FLUTE
  (PADDED —) BURLET
  (PENNY —) TOMMY
  (TWISTED — OF WOOL) SLUB
  (WHIP —) BACKREST
  (PREF.) HELI(C)(CO)
ROLLED (— IN SUGAR) SANDED
ROLLER FLY BOWL BRAY DRUM
JACK LEAD MILL PUCK RUBY
BREAK DANDY FINER GODET

INKER RIDER SHELL WAVER
WINCH BRAYER BREAST DOFFER
DUCTOR FASCIA MANGLE
ROWLET RUNNER CARRIER
CLEARER MOIETER TRUCKLE
HEDGEHOG SQUEEGEE STRIPPER
TROUPAND
  (— FOR MASSAGER) ROULETTE
  (— IN HORSE'S BIT) CRICKET
  (— IN ORGAN) TRUNDLE
  (— IN STEELWORKS) COGGER
  (— TO CLEAR FABRIC) MOIETER
  (CARDING —) BREAST WORKER
SQUIRREL STRIPPER
  (CHINESE —) SIRGANG
  (DREDGING —) HEDGEHOG
  (DROP —) DUCTOR
  (GRINDING —) BREAK
  (INKING —) BRAYER
  (PLAYER ON — DERBY TEAM)
JAMMER
  (PRINTING —) DANDY SHELL
BRAYER DAMPENER
  (ROUND IN — DERBY) JAM
  (STONE —) MAMMY TOTER
  (SURGICAL —) FASCIA
  (TOOTHED —) PRICK PRICKER
ROLLER COASTER SWITCHBACK
ROLLERMAN BRAKER JACKMAN
LEVERMAN
ROLLER SKATE PEDOMOTOR
ROLLICK PLAY ROMP FROLIC
ROLLIX
ROLLICKING GAY WILD MERRY
JOVIAL LIVELY
ROLLING CURL GOGGLE WHEELY
SWAYING TRILLED LURCHING
VOLUTION
  (— OF SCROLL) GELILAH
  (— OF SHIP) LABOR
ROLLTOP TAMBOUR
ROLY-POLY ROTUND PUDDING
TUMBLER SALTWORT
ROM RO GYPSY ROMANY
ROMAN BRAVE LATIN NOBLE
PAPAL ANTIQUA UPRIGHT
GOWNSMAN
  (— COLLAR) RABAT
ROMAN CATHOLIC ROME ROMAN
PAPIST ROMIST JEBUSITE
BABYLONIC
ROMANCE WOO GEST ANTAR
FANCY FEIGN GESTE KATHA
NOVEL STORY ANTARA UTOPIA
FANTASY FICTION ROMANZA
ROMAUNT
  (— LANGUAGE) FRENCH ITALIAN
SPANISH
ROMAN-FLEUVE SAGA

ROMANIST MISSARY
ROMANIZATION LATINXUA
ROMANSH LADIN
ROMANTIC AIRY WILD IDEAL
ARDENT DREAMY GOTHIC POETIC
UNREAL FERVENT FABULOUS
FANCIFUL
ROMANY RO ROM GIPSY GYPSY
ROMAN
ROMANY RYE (AUTHOR OF —)
BORROW
  (CHARACTER IN —) DALE JACK
BELLE ISOPEL JASPER URSULA
BERNERS MURTAGH LAVENGRO
SYLVESTER PETULENGRO
ROME (CHAPEL IN —) SISTINE
  (FOUNDER OF —) ROMULUS
  (HILL IN —) CAELIAN VIMINAL
AVENTINE PALATINE QUIRINAL
  (OLD PORT OF —) OSTIA
  (RIVER IN —) TIBER
ROME HAUL (AUTHOR OF —)
EDMONDS
  (CHARACTER IN —) BEN DAN JOE
RAE SOL LUCY BERRY JACOB
KLORE MOLLY WAMPY CALASH
GURGET HARROW HECTOR
JOTHAM JULIUS SAMSON TINKLE
WEAVER WILSON FORTUNE
LARKINS TURNESA WILLIAM
FRIENDLY CASHDOLLAR
BUTTERFIELD
ROMEO AND JULIET (AUTHOR OF
—) SHAKESPEARE
  (CHARACTER IN —) JOHN PARIS
PETER ROMEO JULIET TYBALT
ABRAHAM CAPULET ESCALUS
GREGORY SAMPSON BENVOLIO
LAURENCE MERCUTIO
MONTAGUE BALTHASAR
ROMOLA (AUTHOR OF —) ELIOT
  (CHARACTER IN —) DINO LUCA
TITO BARDO CALVO LILLO
MONNA PIERO TESSA MELEMA
ROMOLA BRIGIDA NICCOLO
BERNARDO BALDASARRE
ROMP REG RIG HEMP LARK PLAY
ROIL FRISK SHIRL SPORT TRAIN
FROLIC GAMBOL HOORAY
HOYDEN HURRAH RIPPET
COURANT GAMMOCK RAMMACK
RUNAWAY

ROMPERS JUMPER JUMPERS
ROMPING ROYT HEMPY ROYET
RONCADOR GRUNT CROAKER
SCIAENID
RONDO ROTA
RONE BUSH BRAKE GUTTER
THICKET
RONG LEPCHA
RONGA THONGA
RONSDORFER ZIONITE ELLERIAN
ROOD RUD REED ROPE CROSS
SPAWN STANG CRUCIFIX
ROODLES RANGDOODLES
ROOF TOP ATAP BACK DECK DOME
FLAT ATTAP COVER HOUSE RAISE
RISER SHELL THACK AZOTEA
BONNET CUPOLA SUMMIT
TECTUM CHOPPER CRICKET
GAMBREL MANSARD RIGGING
TECTURE BULKHEAD HOUSETOP
SAWTOOTH SEMIDOME
PENTHOUSE
(— MEMBER) PURLIN
(— OF CARRIAGE) IMPERIAL
(— OF CAVERN) DOME
(— OF MINING CAGE) BONNET
(— OF MOUTH) PALATE
(— OF NASOPHARYNX) VAULT
(— OF RAILWAY CAR) DECK
(— OVER DOOR) APPENTICE
(— OVER STAGE) SHADOW
(— PORTION) MONITOR
(AUTOMOBILE —) FASTBACK
(CLOTH —) CHUTT
(FALSE —) CRICKET
(FLAT —) LEADS AZOTEA TERRACE
(STEEPLY TAPERING —) SPIRE
(THATCHED —) ATAP ATTAP
CHOPPER
(VAULTED —) DOME
(PREF.) STEG(O) TECTI TECTO
(SUFF.) STEGE STEGITE
ROOFING HEALING SHINDLE
PANTILING TECTIFORM
ROOK GYP ROC CROW DUPE RUKH
CHEAT CRAKE JUDGE TOWER
BLACKY CASTLE DEFRAUD
CASTILLO SWINDLER
ROOKERY ROOST RUMPUS
BUILDING
ROOKIE COLT DRONGO NOVICE
RECRUIT BEGINNER
ROOM PAD WON AULA CAFE CRIB
FARM HALL KILN LIEU PLAY SALA
SEAT SLUM WAME WENE WONE
ATTIC BERTH CUDDY DIVAN
EWERY HOUSE LODGE OECUS
PLACE SALLE SCOPE SHACK
SOLAR SPACE STALL STOVE
STUDY BELFRY BREAST CAMERA
CASINO CHAPEL ESTUFA EXEDRA
HAMMAM LEEWAY MARGIN
PARVIS SCOUTH SINGLE SMOKER
SOLLAR STANCE STANZA STUDIO
CABINET CAMARIN CHALMER
CHAMBER EPINAOS FREEZER
GALLERY HOLDING HYPOGEE
KITCHEN LAUNDRY LIBRARY
SEMINAR SERVERY SMOKERY
SURGERY AEDICULA ASSEMBLY
BASEMENT CAPACITY DRYHOUSE
HOTHOUSE HYPOGEUM
LAVATORY NYMPHEUM

PLAYROOM SCULLERY SWEATBOX
TABLINUM THALAMUS
PRESSROOM
(— ADJOINING SYNAGOGUE)
GENIZAH
(— BEHIND FACADE) ATTIC
(— BETWEEN KITCHEN AND DINING
ROOM) SERVERY
(— CONTAINING FOUNTAIN)
NYMPHEUM
(— DUG IN CLIFF) HYPOGEE
HYPOGEUM
(— FOR ACTION) LEEWAY
(— FOR BATHING) HAMMAM
(— FOR CONVERSATION) EXEDRA
LOCUTORY
(— FOR FAMILY RECORDS)
TABLINUM
(— FOR KEEPING FOOD) LARDER
PANTRY
(— FOR PAINTINGS) GALLERY
(— FOR PRIVATE DEVOTIONS)
ORATORY
(— FOR PUBLIC AMUSEMENTS)
CASINO THEATER
(— FOR STOWAGE) LASTAGE
(— FOR TABLE LINEN) EWERY
(— IN COAL MINE) BREAST
(— IN HAREM) ODA ODAH
(— IN KEEP) DUNGEON
(— IN PREHISTORIC BUILDING) CELL
(— IN REAR OF TEMPLE) EPINAOS
(— IN SIDE OF LARGER ROOM) ALA
(— IN TOWER) BELFRY
(— OF STUDENTS' SOCIETY) HALL
(— ON SHIP) CABIN STOKEHOLD
(— OVER CHURCH PORCH) PARVIS
(— OVER STAGE) SHADOW
(— TOGETHER) CHUM
(— UNDER BUILDING) CELLAR
(CHILDREN'S —) NURSERY
(COTTAGE —) END
(DINING —) CENACLE DINETTE
REFECTORY TRICLINIUM
(DRAWING —) SALON SALOON
(DRESSING —) SHIFT BOUDOIR
CAMARIN VESTUARY WARDROBE
TIREHOUSE
(ESKIMO ASSEMBLY —) KASHGA
(EXHIBITION —) THEATER
(GRINDING —) HULL
(HEATED —) STEW
(HIGH —) AERY EYRY AERIE EYRIE
(INNER —) BEN INBY INBYE
SPENCE
(INSULATED —) FREEZER
(LECTURE —) AUDITORY
(LIVING —) HOUSE LANAI SALON
SERDAB SOLARIUM VOORHUIS
(MONASTERY —) CELL LAVABO
(NARROW —) CRIB
(OCTAGONAL —) TRIBUNA
(PRIVATE —) SNUG SCHOLA
CONCLAVE
(PUEBLO ASSEMBLY —) ESTUFA
(READING —) ATHENEUM
(RECEPTION —) DIVAN PARLOR
KURSAAL MANDARAH
(REFRIGERATED —) COOLER
(RETIRING —) RECAMERA
(ROMAN —) ATRIUM AEDICULA
FUMARIUM
(ROUND —) ROTUNDA

(SEA —) BERTH
(SECLUDED —) DEN
(SERIES OF —S) SWEEP
(SITTING —) SEAT SITTER BOUDOIR
(SLEEPING —) DORMER BEDROOM
DORMITORY
(SMALL —) ALA CELL SNUG STEW
ZETA CUBBY CUDDY LOBBY
CLOSET CUBICLE SNUGGERY
(SMOKING —) DIVAN DIWAN
TABAGIE
(SORTING —) SALLE
(STEAM —) STOVE
(STORAGE —) CAMARIN MAGAZINE
THALAMUS
(SWEATING —) SUDARIUM
SUDATORY LACONICUM
(THRONE —) AIWAN
(TOP —) GARRET IMPERIAL
(UPPER —) SOLAR
(VAULTED —) CAMERA
(PREF.) STEG(O)
(SUFF.) STEGE STEGITE
ROOMMATE CHUM ROOMY
ROOMIE
ROOMY WIDE LARGE RANGY
SPACY ROOMSOME SPACIOUS
CAPACIOUS COMMODIOUS
ROOSE RUSE EXTOL PRAISE
FLATTER BOASTING BRAGGING
ROOST EVE SIT BAUK JOUK TIDE
PERCH GARRET HARBOR LODGING
ROOKERY SHELTER
ROOSTER COCK GAME GALLO
MANOC GAMECOCK
ROOT DIG PRY ROI TAP BASE BULB
CHAY CHOY GRUB MOOR MOOT
MORE PLUG PULL RACE SPUR
TAIL CHEER FIBER FRUIT GROOT
GROUT HEART IREOS LAPPA
RADIX STOCK ALRAUN BOTTOM
CARROT CATGUT GROUND
MUZZLE ORIGIN SENEGA SETTLE
SUMBAL SUMBUL ACONITE
ALKANET AZAFRAN BIACURU
BONIATA CALUMBA CHICORY
COLUMBO CRAMPON GINSENG
IMPLANT IPOMOEA NUNNARI
PAREIRA RADICAL RUMMAGE
TURPETH DEDENDUM EARTHNUT
PNEUMATOPHORE
(— BRANCH) TAPOUN
(— CONTAINING STARCH) KOONTI
(— DEEPLY) SCREW
(— OF GINGER) RACE
(— OF ORCHID) CULLIONS
(— OF TARO) EDDO
(— OF TOOTH) FANG
(— OF TREE) TANG SPURN
(— OF WORD) THEME
(— OUT) GRUB STUB STOCK
EVULSE DISPLANT SUPPLANT
(— TUBERCLE) CLOG
(— WORD) ETYMON
(— YIELDING RED DYE) CHAY CHOY
CHAYA
(—S FOR SEWING CANOES) WATAP
WATAPEH
(—S OF ACONITE) BIKH NABEE
(CANDIED —) ERYNGO
(CUSCUS —S) VETIVER
(DRIED —) JALAP ALTHEA SENECA
BRYONIA KRAMERIA

LICORICE SCAMMONY
(DRIED —S) INULA IPECAC
KRAMERIA VERATRUM
(EDIBLE —) YAM BEET EDDO
RADISH TURNIP WASABI PARSNIP
RUTABAGA TUBERCLE
(FERN —) ROI
(FINE —) STRING
(FRAGRANT —S) VETIVER
(MASS OF FIBROUS —S) SPONGE
(MEDICINAL —) JALAP LAPPA
GINSENG
(PROJECTING —) SPUR
(ROASTED BEET —) BONKA
(STUMP AND —) MOCK
(PL.) CULVERS
(PREF.) RADICI RHIZ(O)
(SUFF.) RHIZA RHIZOUS
ROOTCAP CALYPTRA SPONGIOLE
ROOTED FIXED CHRONIC
(DEEPLY —) BESETTING
ROOTER FAN PLUGGER
ROOTLESS ARRHIZAL
ROOTLET VIVER CRAMPON
RADICEL RADICLE
(PL.) COME CULMS
ROOTSTOCK PIP ROI RACE TARO
CROWN ORRIS CASAVA DANNUM
GINGER ORIGIN PANNUM STOLON
BISCUIT MISHMEE TURMERIC
ORRISROOT
ROPE GAD GUY TIE TOW TUG CEEL
COLT CORD FALL FAST GUSS
HEMP JEFF JUNK LIFT LINE ROOD
SEAL SOAM SPAN STAY TACK
TAIL TAUM TOME VANG WARP
BRACE BRAIL CABLE CABUL
CHECK CHORD LASSO LONGE
SHANK STRAP STROP SWEEP
TRACE TWIST WANTY WIDDY
WITHE CABLET HALTER INHAUL
LARIAT LISSOM LIZARD MECATE
PINION RAPEYE RUNNER SHROUD
SLATCH STRAND STRING TETHER
WARROK AWEBAND BEDCORD
BOBSTAY CATFALL CRINGLE
ENTRAIL HALYARD HAYBAND
LASHING LEEFANG OUTHAUL
PAINTER PAZAREE PENDANT
PIGTAIL SEAMING SERPENT
SERVICE STIRRUP SWIFTER
BACKBONE BACKSTAY BUNTLINE
CABESTRO CORDELLE DOWNHAUL
DRAGLINE FOREFOOT FORETACK
HALLIARD HAULYARD INHAULER
JACKSTAY LIFELINE NECKLACE
PASSAREE PROLONGE ROUNDING
SEQUENCE THRAMMLE
BREECHING
(— A STEER) HEEL
(— COLLAR) PARRAL PARREL
(— CONNECTING NETS) BALK BAULK
(— COVERING) QUILTING
(— FOR FASTENING GATE) CRINGLE
(— FOR FISH) STRINGER
(— FOR TRAINING HORSE) LONGE
(— FOR TYING CATTLE) CEEL SEAL
AWEBAND
(— HANDLE) FETTLE SHACKLE
(— HOLDING RAFT TOGETHER)
BRAIL
(— JOINT) TUCK
(— OF HAIR) CABESTRO

(— OF ONIONS) REEVE
(— OF STRAW) GAD SIME VINE
SIMON SUGAN FETTLE SIMMON
SOOGAN
(— OF 10 OR MORE INCHES) CABLE
(— ON DERRICK) TELEGRAF
(— ON FISHING NET) PINION
SEAMING
(— ORNAMENTATION) TORSADE
(— PASSING AROUND DEADEYE)
STRAP STROP
(— STOLEN FROM DOCKYARD)
RUMBO
(— WITH HOOK AND TOGGLE)
PROLONGE
(— WITH SWIVEL AND LOOP)
TOGGEL TOGGLE
(— WOUND AROUND CABLE)
KECKLING
(—S IN RIGGING) CORDAGE
(ANCHOR —) RODE VIOL VOYAL
(BELL —) TYALL HANGER
(CIRCUS —) JEFF
(DRAFT —) SOAM
(DRAG —) GUSS
(FLAG-RAISING —) HALYARD
(FOOT —) HORSE
(GRASS —) SOGA
(GUIDE —) DRAGLINE
(HANDLE —) FETTLE
(HANGMAN'S —) HEMP TIPPET
(HARNESS —) TRACE HALTER
(HARPOON —) FOREGOER
(MOORING —) HEADFAST
(NAUTICAL —) TIE TYE COLT FANG
LIFT STAY VANG BRACE BRAIL
SHEET SLING STRAP STROP
GILGUY HAWSER INHAUL LACING
RATLIN SHROUD BOBSTAY
BOWLINE CATFALL GESWARP
LANYARD LEEFANG OUTHAUL
PAINTER PAZAREE PENDANT
PENNANT PIGTAIL RATLINE
SNORTER SNOTTER STIRRUP
STOPPER SWIFTER BACKBONE
BACKSTAY BUNTLINE DOWNHAUL
FORETACK JACKSTAY PASSAREE
ROUNDING SELVAGEE WOOLDING
TIMENOGUY
(PART OF —) SLATCH
(SHORT —) SHANK
(SHORT CART —) WANTY
(SMALL HANDMADE —) FOX
(SMUGGLER'S —) LINGTOW
(TALLOWED —) GASKET
(TETHERING —) SPANCEL
(TOW —) CORDELLE
(WIRE —) HAULBACK JACKSTAY
(WORN OR POOR —) JUNK
(PL.) CORDAGE
(PREF.) FUN(I) RESTI SPIR(O)
ROPEBAND RABAND
ROPE-DANCER ACROBAT
ROPEMAKER FOLLOWER RATLINER
ROPEWALKER FUNAMBULO
ROPEWAY TRAMWAY WIREWAY
CABLEWAY
ROPY SINEWY STRINGY VISCOUS
MUSCULAR GLUTINOUS
ROQUE CROQUET
ROQUELAURE CLOAK ROCOLO
ROCKLAY
RORIPA RADICULA

RORQUAL SEI FINBACK
ROSADER (BELOVED OF —)
ROSALYNDE
(BROTHER OF —) TORRISMOND
ROSAMUNDA (FATHER OF —)
CUNIMOND
(HUSBAND OF —) ALBOIN
ROSARY BEADS CORONA TASBIH
BEADING PSALTER BEADROLL
(— BEAD) GAUD GAUDY
(MOHAMMEDAN —) COMBOLOIO
ROSE ASH GUL KNOT MOSS ROIS
BRIAR BRIDE BUCKY FLUSH
RHODA CANKER OPULUS
POMPON BOURBON BURBANK
GLAIEUL HUGONIS LOZENGE
MANETTI MONTILLY OPHELIA
RAMBLER AGRIMONY COLUMBIA
DOGBERRY LOKELANI PEDELION
(COTTON —) CUDWEED
(DWARF —) POLYANTHA
(HYBRID —) NOISETTE
(PREF.) RHOD(O) ROSEO ROSI
ROSO
(SUFF.) RHODIN
ROSE ACACIA ROBINIA
ROSE APPLE JAMBO JAMBOS
JAMBOSA
ROSEATE SPOONBILL AJAJA
ROSE-BREASTED (— COCKATOO)
GALAH
ROSEBUSH ROSER BALWARRA
ROSE CAMPION LYCHNIS
ROSE-COLORED OPTIMISTIC
(— STARLING) PASTOR TILYER
ROSEFISH DRIM DREAM DEROYLT
REDFISH
(YOUNG —) SNAPPER
ROSE HIP CHOOP CHOUP
ROSELLE SORREL SABDARIFFA
ROSEMARY COSTMARY
MOORWORT ROSMARINE
ROSE MOSS PURSLANE
PORTULACA
ROSENKAVALIER, DER
(CHARACTER IN —) OCHS SOPHIE
FANINAL MARIANDL OCTAVIAN
MARSCHALLIN
(COMPOSER OF —) STRAUSS
ROSET BRAZIL
ROSETTE CHOU KNOT ROSACE
ROSULA COCKADE
ROSEWOOD BUBINGA MOLOMPI
JACARANDA PALISANDER
ROSH (FATHER OF —) BENJAMIN
ROSIN FLUX ROSET COLOPHONY
(— SPIRIT) PINOLIN
ROSS SCALP
ROSSER BARKER PEELER SCALPER
SLIPPER
ROSTER LIST ROTA SCROLL
REGISTER
ROSTRATE BEAKED
ROSTRUM PEW AMBE BEAK BEMA
GUARD SNOUT PULPIT ACROTER
TRIBUNE
ROSY ROSEN BLUSHY AURORAL
HEALTHY AUROREAN BLOOMING
BLUSHFUL RUBICUND
ROT COE RET DOTE DOZE DROP
FOUL JOKE LEAK POKE SOUR
WROX DECAY SPOIL TEASE
BLUING FESTER ROTTEN

CORRUPT HOOFRUT PUTREFY
NONSENSE STAGNATE
(— BY EXPOSURE) RET
(— OF GRAPES) SLIPSKIN
(APPLE —) FROGEYE
(FOOT —) FOUL
(FRUIT —) LEAK
(LIVER —) COE
(PREF.) PYTHO
ROTA LIST ROLL ROSTER ROTULA
ROTARY CIRCLE GYRATORY
ROUNDABOUT
(PREF.) ROTO
ROTATE RUN BIRL GYRE ROLL SPIN
TURN PIVOT RABAT SCREW
WHEEL GYRATE REVOLVE
TRUNDLE ROTIFORM ALTERNATE
(— CAMERA) PAN
(— HIPS) GRIND
ROTATING VOLUBLE
ROTATION SPIN TURN ROUND
TWIRL GYRATION SPINNING
WHIRLING
(— ON BALL) STUFF
(DEVICE INDICATING SPEED OF —)
TACH
(STOP —) DESPIN
ROTCHE BULL RATCH ROTGE
DOVEKEY DOVEKIE BULLBIRD
ROTE CRWTH HEART ROTTA
REPEAT
ROTIFER POLYP LIPOPOD
LORICATE PLOIMATE
ROTIFORM TROCHAL
ROTL RATTEL WEIGHT ROTTOLO
(PL.) ARTAL ARTEL
ROTOGRAVURE ROTO COLOROTO
ROTOR IMPELLER
ROTTED PECKY
ROTTEN BAD FOUL PUNK ROXY
SOUR ADDLE DAZED MOSEY
PUTID ADDLED AMPERY FRACID
MOOSEY PUTRID DECAYED
SPOILED DEPRAVED UNSTABLE
(HALF —) DOTED DOATED
(PARTIALLY —) DRUXY
(PREF.) PUTRE PUTRI SAPR(O)
ROTTENSTONE TRIPOLI
ROTTING SLEEPY CARIOUS
ROTTLERA KAMALA
ROTULA ROUND TROCHE KNEEPAN
PATELLA
ROTUND FAT PLUMP ROUND
STOUT CHUBBY SUBROUND
ROTURIER PEASANT PLEBEIAN
RUPTUARY
ROUE RAKE RAKEHELL DEBAUCHEE
ROUGE RED FARD BLUSH PAINT
FUCATE REDDEN RUDDLE
CLINKER SCRIMMAGE
(ANIMAL —) CARMINE
ROUGH RU ROW RUF BEAT FOUL
GURL HARD HASK LAMB ROID
ROYD RUDE THUG WILD ACRID
ASPER BLUFF BLUNT BRUTE
CHURL CRUDE DIRTY GOBBY
GROFF GURLY HAIRY HARSH
HEFTY JAGGY LUMPY REWCH
ROUCH ROWDY RUGGY RUVID
STARK STEER STERN STOUR
TOUGH TOUSY WIGHT BORREL
BROKEN BRUSHY BURRED
CHOPPY COARSE COBBLY CRABBY

CRAGGY ELBOIC HACKLY HISPID
HOARSE HOBBLY HORRID HUBBLY
INCULT JAGGED KEELIE KNAGGY
KNOTTY NOGGEN RAGGED
RAMAGE RASPED ROBUST RUFFLE
RUGGED RUMBLY RUSTIS SEVERE
SHAGGY SKETCH STICKY TOOSIE
TRYING UNEVEN UNFEEL UNFELE
UNFINE UNKIND UNMILD UNRIDE
ABUSIVE AUSTERE BOORISH
BRISTLY CRABBED HIRSUTE
INEQUAL INEXACT JARRING
RABBISH RAMMAGE RAPLOCH
RAUCOUS RUFFLED SCABRID
STICKLE STICKLY UNCOUTH
UNKEMPT VICIOUS ABRASIVE
ASPERATE CHURLISH DEPOLISH
IMPOLITE LARRIKIN OBDURATE
SCABROUS SCRAGGED STUBBORN
UNGENTLE UNTENDER
MANHANDLE SCABERULOUS
(— EDGES) FASH
(— IT) SIWASH
(— UP) MESS
(— UP ARROW FEATHERS)
SPRANGLE
(MAKE —) SHAG
(PREF.) ASPERI DASI DASY
TRACHY
ROUGHAGE FODDER AVERAGE
BALLAST BULKAGE CELLULOSE
ROUGH-AND-READY BURLY
TOWSY TOWZIE MAKESHIFT
ROUGHCAST HARL PARGET
SPARGE ROUGHHEW SLAPDASH
ROUGHEN FRET GRIG HACK EMERY
FEAZE FLOCK FROST TOOTH
ABRADE CRISLE STIVER CRIZZLE
ENGRAIL SCRATCH ASPERATE
UNSMOOTH
(— BRICK WALL) STAB
ROUGHER BULLDOGGER
(PONY —) STRANDER
ROUGH-HOB GASH
ROUGHING IT (AUTHOR OF —)
TWAIN CLEMENS
(CHARACTER IN —) HANK MARK
SLADE TWAIN YOUNG BRIGHAM
ERICKSON
ROUGH-MILL GASH
ROUGHNECK ROWDY TOUGH
MUCKER UNCOUTH BANGSTER
ROUGHNESS GAFF GRAIN SCUFF
TOOTH RUFFLE CRIZZLE CRUDITY
ACRIMONY ASPERITY
(— OF SEA) LIPPER
(— OF SKIN) GOOSESKIN
GOOSEFLESH
(— OF WALL) KEY
ROUGHOMETER VIAGRAPH
ROULADE VOLATA ARPEGGIO
ROULETTE FILET FILLET TROCHOID
(HIGH — NUMBERS) PASSE
(1-18 IN —) MANQUE
(13-24 IN —) MILIEU
ROUNCEVAL GIANT LARGE
MONSTER GIGANTIC
ROUND BALL BEAT BEND BOLD
BOUT FAST FULL GIRO HEAD
RICH ROON ROTA TOUR TRIM
WALK ABOUT AMPLE BEADY
BRISK CATCH DANCE GLOBE
HAMBO HARSH LARGE MOONY

ORBED PLAIN ROMAN RONDO
SPOKE TROLL TUBBY CIRCLE
COURSE ENTIRE MELLOW NEARLY
ROTUND ROUNDY RUBBER
RUNDLE SPHERY SPIRAL STOWER
STREAK ZODIAC ANNULAR
CIRCUIT SHAPELY CIRCULAR
COMPLETE CROSSBAR ENCIRCLE
GLOBULAR SONOROUS LABIALIZE
(— EDGES OF TIMBER) BEARD
(— END OF LOG) SNIPE
(— FREQUENTLY GONE OVER) BEAT
(— IN BOWLING) FRAME
(— IN CARDS) GRAND
(— IN ROLLER DERBY) JAM
(— OF ACTIVITIES) SWING
(— OF APPLAUSE) HAND JOLLY
SALVO PLAUDIT
(— OF CHAIR) BALUSTER
(— OF KNITTING) BOUT
(— OF LADDER) STAVE
(— OF PLAY) LAP
(— OFF) TOP CROWN FILLET
(— OUT) ORB BELLY INTEGRATE
(— UP) CORRAL WRANGLE
SCROUNGE
(PLUMP AND —) CHUBBY
(SWEDISH —) HAMBO
(PREF.) GLOBI GLOBO PERI
ROTUNDI ROTUNDO
TROCH(I)(LEI)(O) VENTR(I)(O)
ROUNDABOUT PLUMP DETOUR
ROTARY CURVING DEVIOUS
CAROUSEL CIRCULAR INDIRECT
TORTUOUS AMBAGIOUS
(— MOVEMENT) WINDLASS
ROUNDED FULL BOMBE BOWLY
CONVEX MELLOW ROTUND
TERETE WHELKY ARRONDI
BUNTING COMPAST CONCAVE
GIBBOUS SCUTATE SHAPELY
COMPLETE FINISHED HOOPLIKE
SONOROUS
(— OUT) PLUM
(PREF.) TERETI
ROUNDEL HEURT PLATE POMME
PELLET FOUNTAIN
(— AZURE) HURT
(— GULES) TORTEAU TORTEAUX
(— OR) BEZANT BYZANT
(— PURPURE) GOLP GOLPE
(— SABLE) GUNSTONE
(— SANGUINE) GUZE
(— VERT) POMEY
ROUNDER SOAKER WASTREL
INFORMER
ROUNDERS TUT PATBALL
TUTBALL
ROUNDHEAD SWEDE CROPPY
WEAKFISH
ROUND HERRING SHADINE
STRADINE
ROUNDHOUSE BARN POOP
LOCKUP
ROUNDNESS ROTUND SPHERICITY
(— OF RIBS) SPRING
ROUND POMPANO PERMIT
PALOMETA
ROUND ROBIN ANGLER SERIES
PANCAKE SEQUENCE
ROUNDSMAN VANMAN
SWINGMAN WATCHMAN
ROUNDUP RODEO CAMBER

GATHER MUSTER
ROUNDWORM NEMA ASCARID
EELWORM GORDIAN HELMINTH
NEMATODE STRONGYL
ROUP ROLP ROOP CROAK CLAMOR
AUCTION SHOUTING
ROUSE DAW GIG HOP JOG BAIT
BEET CALL DRAW FIRK GOAD
MOVE RANT RAVE STIR WAKE
WHET AMOVE ERECT MOUNT
RAISE START STEER UPSET
WAKEN ABRADE ABRAID AROUSE
BESTIR EXCITE FOMENT KINDLE
NETTLE RATTLE REVIVE RUFFLE
WECCHE AGITATE ANIMATE
DISTURB EKPHORE ENLIVEN
HEARTEN INFLAME STARTLE
INSPIRIT IRRITATE
(— TO ACTION) HIE ALARM
ALARUM BESTIR ALACRIFY
ROUSING LIVELY
ROUSTABOUT FLOORMAN
RAZORBACK
ROUT MOB MOW DRUM FUSS
HERD BRANT CHASE COHUE
CROWD EJECT FLOCK LURCH
SMEAR SMITE SNORE CLAMOR
DEFEAT FLIGHT NUMBER RABBLE
SOIREE THRONG UPROAR
CONFUSE CONQUER DEBACLE
SCATTER SPARPLE TEMPEST
ASSEMBLY CONFOUND DISTRESS
VANQUISH
(BACCHIC —) THIASUS
ROUTE WAY BELT GATE GEST LINE
PASS PATH SEND TRACE TRACK
AIRWAY CAREER COURSE CUTOFF
SKYWAY TRAJET CHANNEL
CIRCUIT LANDWAY PASSAGE
SHUTTLE CORRIDOR DISTANCE
LIFELINE SHORTCUT TRAVERSE
(— MARKED OUT) ITER
(— TO DEFEAT) SKIDS
(CIRCUITOUS —) DETOUR
(MIGRATION —) FLYWAY
(OCEAN —) LANE
(PREF.) ODO
ROUTH PLENTY ABUNDANT
ROUTINE RUT ROTA DRILL GRIND
ROUTE TROLL GROOVE HARNESS
EVERYDAY ORDINARY
(COMPUTER —) BOOTSTRAP
(DOMESTIC —) HOMELIFE
(ENTERTAINMENT —) SHTICK
(THEATRICAL —) SCHTICK
(WEARISOME —) TREADMILL
ROVE RUN RAKE RAVE ROAM
GUESS KNOCK RANGE ROWAN
SCOUR SPACE STRAY FORAGE
MARAUD RAMBLE STROLL
WANDER SPATIATE STRAGGLE
TRANSCUR
(— ON THE WING) FLIT
ROVER FLIRT HOYLE STAKE STRAY
MASHER RANGER VIKING
GANGREL SCUMMER MARAUDER
SLIVERER TRAVELER WANDERER
COLORADAN
ROVING END SLUB NOMAD VAGUE
ARRANT ERRANT DEVIOUS
NOMADIC RAMPLER VAGRANT
GADABOUT RAMBLING RESTLESS
SLUBBING VAGABOND

MIGRATORY RANTIPOLE
(— IN SEARCH OF KNIGHTLY
ADVENTURE) ERRANTRY
ROW LAY OAR RIG SET DUST FILE
LINE MUSS PULL RANK RULE TIER
ALLEY BRAWL CHESS FIGHT
MOUTH NOISE ORDER RAMMY
RANGE RINGE SCOLD SCRAP
SWATH TRAIN BARNEY BERATE
COURSE DUSTUP GARRAY KICKUP
LISSOM PADDLE POTHER RACKET
RUCKUS RUMPUS SHINDY STREET
STROKE BOBBERY BRULYIE
QUARREL RUCTION SHINDIG
CATEGORY OUTBURST REMIGATE
SQUABBLE
(— BACKWARD) STERN
(— OF BENCHES) STACK
(— OF CASKS) LONGER
(— OF CORN, BARLEY, ETC.) RIG
(— OF DRY HAY) STADDLE
(— OF GRAIN) SWATH SWATHE
(— OF GRASS) HACK SWATH
(— OF GUNS) TIRE
(— OF HOUSES) CRESCENT
(— OF LAMPS) BATTEN
(— OF SEATS) BARRERA
(— OF SEED) DRILL
(— OF STAKES) ORGUE
(— OF STONES) CORDON
(— OF TREES) ESPALIER
(— OF VEGETABLES) RINGE
(-S OF BALCONY) MEZZANINE
(DISORDERLY —) RAG
(PL.) EPEIRA
(PREF.) STICHO
(SUFF.) STICH(OUS)
ROWAN RAN RODDIN
ROWAN TREE CARE SORB WICKY
WITCH RODDEN RODDIN WICKEN
WIGGEN QUICKEN RANTREE
WHITTEN WITCHEN ROUNTREE
ROWBOAT GIG OAR BARK OARS
PLAT BARIS COBLE DINGY FUNNY
KOBIL SCULL SKIFF BARQUE
CAIQUE DINGHY LURKER WHERRY
SCULLER
(— SEAT) TAFT
(CLINKER-BUILT —) FUNNY
(FLAT-BOTTOMED —) DORY
(PART OF —) RING SEAT STEM
SOCKET THWART GUNWALE
OARLOCK PAINTER ROWLOCK
TRANSOM
(SMALL —) COG
ROWDY TOU BHOY CASH MONEY
RORTY ROUGH TOUGH TOMBOY
UNRULY VULGAR HOODLUM
RAFFISH BARRATER LARRIKIN
STUBBORN ROUGHNECK
ROWDYISM YAHOOISM
ROWEN EDGROW RAWING
AFTERMATH ROUGHINGS
ROWENA (FATHER OF —) HENGIST
(GUARDIAN OF —) CEDRIC
(HUSBAND OF —) IVANHOE
VORTIGERN
ROWER URGER GALIOT STROKE
OARSMAN STERNMAN CAIQUEJEE
(— ON UPPER SEATS) THRANITE
(OUTERMOST —) THALAMITE
(SECOND LEVEL —) ZYGITE
ROWING CREW

ROWLOCK LOCK CRUTCH
OARLOCK RULLOCK
ROXANA (FATHER OF —) OXYARTES
(HUSBAND OF —) ALEXANDER
ROYAL EASY REAL RIAL ELITE
REGAL SMALT AUGUST KINGLY
REGIUS SOVRAN SUPERB BASILIC
GLORIOUS IMPERIAL IMPOSING
MAJESTIC PAVILION PRINCELY
(— MACE) SCEPTER SCEPTRE
ROYAL ANTELOPE MADOQUA
KLEENEBOC
ROYAL FERN OSMOND OSMUND
ROYALIST TORY ULTRA REGIAN
TANTIVY CAVALIER MUSCADIN
(PL.) CHOUANS
ROYALLY PURPLEY
ROYAL PALM COYAL
ROYALTY LOT ALII GALE BONUS
CROWN REGAL REALTY MAJESTY
PENALTY LORDSHIP NOBILITY
REGALITY
ROYET WILD HARSH UNRULY
ROMPING
RUB DUB BARK BILL FILE FRAY
FRET FRIG FROT RISP SHAB WIPE
CHAFE DIGHT FEEZE FRUSH
GRATE GRAZE GRIDE LABOR
SCOUR SCRUB SMEAR STONE
FRIDGE RUBBER STREAK
BEESWAX FRICACE FURBISH
MASSAGE
(— AS A ROPE) SNUG
(— AS ANIMALS) SHAB
(— AWAY) ERODE ABRADE
(— BOOT) BONE
(— DOWN) WIPE STRAP
(— ELBOWS) JOSTLE JUSTLE
(— GENTLY) STRIKE STROKE
(— HARD) SCOUR SCRUB
(— HARSHLY) GRIND
(— LIGHTLY) GRAZE
(— OFF) CROCK ABRADE ABRASE
(— OUT) ERASE EFFACE EXPUNGE
(— ROUGHLY) GRATE
(— SNUFF) DIP
(— THE SKIN OFF) SHAW
(— TOGETHER) FIDDLE
(— VELVET FROM ANTLERS)
BURNISH
(— WITH GREASE) DUB
(— WITH OIL) ANOINT
(PREF.) TRIBO
(SUFF.) TRIBE TRIPSIS
RUBBED TERSE
RUBBER BUNA FOAM PARA BUTYL
CREPE RASER ALASKA CAUCHO
DAPICO ERASER NIGGER RUNNER
BISCUIT BURUCHA EBONITE
ELASTIC GUAYULE RAMBONG
BORRACHA FRICTION NEOPRENE
SERNAMBY SERWAMBY
SOVPRENE
(— CITY) AKRON
(HARD —) EBONITE
(RECLAIMED —) SHODDY
(PL.) SHAB
RUBBERIZE FRICTION
RUBBER TREE ULE MILKER
RAMBONG
RUBBING CHAFE CARESS
ABRASION FRICTION FROTTAGE
FRICATION

(SUFF.) TRIPSIS
RUBBISH KET BUNK CRAB CRAP
FLAM FLUM GEAR GWAG MULL
MUSH PELF PELT PUNK RAFF
ROSS TOSH TRAG BILGE BRASH
BROCK CRAWM CULCH OFFAL
SCOWL SLUSH STENT STUFF
TRADE TRASH TRUCK WASTE
COLDER DEBRIS GARBLE KELTER
LITTER PALTRY PIFFLE RAFFLE
RAMMEL REFUSE RUBBLE SCULCH
SHRUFF SPILTH BAGGAGE
BEGGARY MULLOCK RUMMAGE
SLITHER TAFFIKE TRAFFIC
FIRETRAP NONSENSE RIFFRAFF
TRASHERY TRUMPERY
CLAMJAMFRY
(VEGETABLE —) WRACK
RUBBISHY POUCY PALTRY TRASHY
BAGGAGE RUMMAGY
RUBBLE BRASH STENT TALUS
RAMMEL BACKING MOELLON
SLITHER
RUBE JAY BOOR HICK JAKE JASPER
BUMPKIN BUSHMAN HAYSEED
CORNBALL
RUBELLA ROTELN
RUBELLITE SIBERITE
RUBICUND RED ROSY RUDDY
FLORID FLUSHED
RUBIGINOUS RUSTY
RUBLE RO RUBLIS
(ONE-HALF —) POLTINIK
RUBRIC RED NAME CANON CLASS
TITLE CONCEPT CATEGORY
RUBRICATE MINIATE
RUBY AGATE BALAS RUBIN
PYROPE ANTHRAX SPARKLE
VERMEIL
RUBY SPINEL BALAS ALMANDINE
RUCHING COQUILLE
RUCK RUT HEAP PILE RICK CROWD
SQUAT STACK TRASH CREASE
FURROW HUDDLE PUCKER
RUBBISH WRINKLE
RUCKUS ADO ROW FIGHT FRACAS
ROOKUS
RUCTION HURRY RUCKUS
QUARREL RUPTION FRACTION
RUDABAH (FATHER OF —) MIHRAB
(HUSBAND OF —) ZAL
(SON OF —) RUSTAM
RUDD REDEYE
RUDDER HELM STEER STERN
TIMON HELLIM RUTHER STEERER
STEERAGE GOVERNAIL
(— BACK) TALON
(— EDGE) BEARDING
(— OF WINDMILL) TAIL
(DIVING —) HYDROVANE
(PART OF —) STOCK
RUDDERFISH CHOPA OPALEYE
RUDDINESS RUBEDITY
RUDDLE RED BOLE KEEL SMIT
ROUGE
RUDDY RED RODE RUDE FRESH
VIVID BLOWSY BLOWZY FLORID
LIVELY GLOWING RUDDISH
BLUSHFUL RUBICUND SANGUINE
RUDDY DUCK ROOK BOOBY
NODDY PADDY SPRIG BOBBER
DUNBIRD GREASER PINTAIL
SLEEPER SPATTER BLUEBILL

BULLNECK HARDHEAD WIRETAIL
RUDE ILL RAW BOLD IRON LEWD
WILD BLUFF BLUNT CRUDE
GREEN GROSS PLUMP ROUGH
STOUR SURLY UNORN ABRUPT
BITTER BORREL BRASSY CALLOW
CHUFFY CLUMSY COARSE
DUDGEN GOTHIC HOMELY
HOYDEN INCULT RIBALD ROBUST
RUGGED RUSTIC SAVAGE SHAGGY
SIMPLE STORMY UNFEEL UPLAND
VULGAR ABUSIVE ARTLESS
BOORISH CARLAGE CARLISH
INCIVIL LOUTISH LOWBRED
NATURAL UNCOUTH UNHENDE
CHURLISH CLUBBISH HOMESPUN
IMPOLITE INSOLENT MECHANIC
PETULANT PORTERLY STUBBORN
SYLVATIC UNGENTLE UNPOLITE
YOKELISH
(— AND BOLD) HOIDEN HOYDEN
RUDENESS GAFF
RUDIMENT GERM ANLAGE VESTIGE
BEGINNING PRIMORDIUM
(PL.) ABC ALPHABET ELEMENTS
GRAMMATES
RUDIMENTARY BASIC GERMING
ABORTIVE INCHOATE ABECEDARY
ELEMENTAL EMBRYONIC
PRIMITIVE ABECEDARIAN
(MOST —) FIRST
(PREF.) LYO PRO
RUE RU REWE MOURN CATGUT
REGRET REPENT SORROW
BORONIA HARMALA TENTWORT
RUEFUL SAD RUELY WOEFUL
DOLEFUL PITIABLE
RUFF SET APEX FURY PAPE POPE
CREST PRIDE REEVE TEASE TEAZE
TRUMP COLLAR FRAISE RABATO
RUFFLE TIPPET ZENITH ELATION
PARTLET PASSION QUELLIO
REBATER ROTONDE PICKADIL
RUFFED BUSTARD HOUBARA
RUFFED LEMUR VARI
RUFFIAN MUN LAMB PIMP PUNK
THUG TORY BRAVO BULLY DEVIL
ROUGH ROWDY TIGER TOUGH
APACHE BRUTAL COARSE CUTTER
CUTTLE MOHAWK MOHOCK
NICKER PANDER TOWSER
HOODLUM SWEATER TUMBLER
HACKSTER HOOLIGAN
RUFFLE VEX BAIT FRET HOOP
ROOL RUFF BULLY CRISP FRILL
GRAZE JABOT PLEAT ROUGH
ROUSE SHIRR ABRADE ATTACK
GATHER NETTLE PEPLUM RIPPLE
BLUSTER BRISTLE DERANGE
FLOUNCE FLUTTER PANUELO
STIFFEN SWAGGER TROUBLE
DISHEVEL DISORDER DISTRACT
FURBELOW IRRITATE QUILLING
SKIRMISH
(— THE TEMPER) ROIL
RUFFLED ROUGH UNKEMPT
**RUFFLING (— ON THE SURFACE OF
WATER)** HORROR
RUFUS (FATHER OF —) SIMON
RUG TUG BAKU COZY HAUL MAUD
PULL SNUG TEAR WRAP BIJAR
HERAT HEREZ JURUK KAZAK
KHILA KONIA KULAH KUMEH

LADIK MECCA MELAS MOSUL
NAMDA SENNA TEKKE TUZLA
USHAK YURUK ZOFRA AFSHAR
BALUCH KANARA KAROSS
KASHAN KIRMAN MOGHAN
NAMMAD PERGAM RUNNER
SHIRAZ SMYRNA TABRIZ TILPAH
TOUPEE WILTON BALUCHI
BERGAMA BOKHARA BUFFALO
DERBEND DRUGGET FERAHAN
GIORDES GOREVAN HAMADAN
ISPAHAN SHEERAZ SHIRVAN
YARKAND AUBUSSON DOMESTIC
FOOTPACE PANDERMA
SARABAND SEDJADEH SERABEND
WOLFSKIN
(— FOR SADDLE) PILCH
(— OF SKINS) KAROSS WOLFSKIN
(GREEK —) FLOKATI
(PLAID —) MAUD
(PRAYER —) MELAS MELES
GHIORDES NAMAZLIK
(REVERSIBLE —) KILIM
(SCANDINAVIAN —) RYA
RUGA FOLD CREASE WRINKLE
RUGBY FOOTER RUGGER
FOOTBALL
(— PLAY) SCRUM
RUGGED RUDE WILD HAIRY HARDY
ROUGH STIFF COARSE CRAGGY
HORRID JAGGED KNAGGY
KNOTTY ROBUST SAVAGE
STRONG STURDY UNEVEN
CRABBED GNARLED OBDURATE
SCRAGGED VIGOROUS
RUGGIERO (GUARDIAN OF —)
ATLANTE
(SISTER OF —) MARFISA
(SLAYER OF —) TISAPHERNES
(WIFE OF —) BRADAMANTE
RUIN DO MAR POT BANE BANG
COOK CRAB DAMN DASH DISH
DOOM FALL FATE FELL HELL JACK
KILL LOSS RASE RAZE SINK TALA
BLAST BOTCH BREAK CRUSH
DECAY EXILE GUBAT HUACA
LEESE LEISS SHEND SHOOT
SMASH SPEED SPILL SPLIT SPOIL
SWAMP TRASH WRACK WRAKE
WRECK BEDASH BLIGHT CANCEL
COOPER DAMAGE DEFACE
DEFEAT DIDDLE DISMAY FOREDO
INJURY JIGGER MANGLE RAVAGE
UNMAKE BOWWOWS CORRUPT
DESTROY FLATTEN FORLESE
FORWORK LEESING PERVERT
SCUPPER SHATTER SUBVERT
TORPEDO UNDOING BANKRUPT
COLLAPSE DEMOLISH DESOLATE
DISASTER DOWNFALL
(— AT GAMBLING) SHRUB
(SPIRITUAL —) FALL
(PL.) ASHES DEBRIS RELICS
RUDERA ZIMBABWE
RUINATION DOGS
RUINED FLAT GONE LORN BROKE
KAPUT BROKEN FALLEN NAUGHT
NOUGHT FORLORN BANKRUPT
DESOLATE
RUINER MARPLOT
RUINOUS DEADLY BANEFUL
DECAYED SHENDFUL WASTEFUL
CUTTHROAT

RULE LAW MAN RAJ WIN DASH
KING NORM SWAY WALD WARD
YARD AXIOM CANON GUIDE
JUDGE MAXIM NORMA ORDER
POWER REGLE REIGN RICHE
RIGHT RULER SPILE STAFF SUTRA
SUTTA WIELD ALIDAD CUTOFF
DECIDE DECREE DITION DOMINE
EMPIRE ENTAIL GNOMON
GOVERN MANAGE MASTER
METHOD REGNUM REGULA
SQUARE VASSAL BROCARD
COMMAND CONTROL COUNSEL
DICTATE DIETARY FORMULA
PLUMMET PRECEPT PRESIDE
REGENCY REGIMEN THEOREM
DICTAMEN DOCTRINE DOMINATE
FUNCTION LEGALISM MODERATE
ORDINARY OVERLEAD PERSUADE
REGIMENT REGNANCY STANDARD
TYRANNIS OBSERVANCE
(— BY UPSTARTS) NEOCRACY
(— OUT) EXCLUDE
(— TYRANNICALLY) HORSE
(—S OF CONDUCT) ETIQUETTE
(—S OF DUELING) DUELLO
(ABSOLUTE —) AUTARCHY
(MOB —) OCHLOCRACY
(OPPOSING —) ANTINOMY
(PREF.) ARCH(AE)(AEO)(E)(EO)(I)
**RULER (ALSO SEE CHIEF, TITLE,
LEADER)** DEY GOG JAM MIN OBA
AMIR CZAR DAME DUKE EMIR
INCA KING LORD OBBA RULE
TSAR TZAR ALDER AMEER DECAN
EMEER HAKIM MPRET MWAMI
NAGID NAWAB SCALE SOPHI
STEER SUBAH ZUPAN APHETA
ARCHON AUTHOR CAESAR
DESPOT DUARCH DYNAST
EPARCH FERULE GERENT HERSIR
ISWARA KABAKA KAISER MASTER
NIMROD PATESI PENLOP RECTOR
REGENT SAWBWA SHERIF
SOLDAN SUFFEE SULTAN TYRANT
ADMIRAL ALIDADE BOURBON
DEMARCH FAIPULE ISHVARA
KHEDIVE MONARCH MORMAER
PTOLEMY RECTRIX REGULUS
REIGNER TOPARCH TRIARCH
WIELDER AUGUSTUS BASILEUS
DRIGHTEN EXILARCH GOVERNOR
HEPTARCH INTERREX OLIGARCH
OVERLORD PADISHAH PENTARCH
PHYLARCH REGINALD TARAFDAR
WHIPKING
(— IN A NATIVITY) APHETA
(— OF ENCLOSURE) HENRY
(CURVED —) SWEEP
(ELF —) AUBREY
(INCA —) CURACA
(JEWISH —) EXILARCH
(MONGOLIAN —) HUTUKTU
(MOSLEM —) SOLDAN
(STRONG —) REGINALD
(TATAR OR MOGUL —) CHAM
(WHITE —S) SERKALI
(PREF.) ARCH(AE)(AEO)(E)(EO)(I)
(SUFF.) ARCHIC ARCHY
RULING CALL CHIEF REGENT
SOVRAN CURRENT HOLDING
REGITIVE HEGEMONIC
RUM ODD ROME OCUBY QUEER

RUMBO TAFIA TAFFIA BACARDI CACHACA JAMAICA PECULIAR SWITCHEL EXCELLENT
RUMBLE CROWL DICKY GROWL RUMOR SNORE BUMBLE HOTTER HUMBLE LUMBER WAMBLE GRUMBLE QUARREL
(— AS A GANG) BOP
RUMBO RUM GROG LIQUOR
RUMEN CUD PAUNCH STOMACH
RUMINANT OX COW YAK BULL DEER GOAT CAMEL LLAMA MOOSE SHEEP STEER TAKIN ALPACA MAZAME VICUNA GIRAFFE QUIDDER ANTELOPE TUBICORN
(SUFF.) MERYX
RUMINATE CHAW CHEW MULL MUSE PONDER CONCOCT REFLECT SAUNTER CONSIDER
RUMINATION MERYCISM
RUMKIN RUMMER
RUMMAGE GRUB POKE ROOT ROUT SEEK BUSTLE FORAGE POWTER TOUSLE UPROAR FOSSICK RANSACK ROMMACK DISORDER SKIRMISH UPHEAVAL
(— ABOUT FOR A PROFIT) FOSSICK
(— SALE) JUMBLE
RUMMY GIN RUM TUNK QUEER CANASTA COONCAN DRUNKARD OKLAHOMA
RUMOR CRY SAW BUZZ FAMA FAME TALK WORD BRUIT MUDGE NOISE SOUGH SOUND STORY VOGUE VOICE BREEZE CANARD FURPHY GOSSIP MURMUR POTGUN RENOWN REPORT RUMBLE CLATTER HEARING HEARSAY INKLING OPINION WHISPER NORATION GRAPEVINE SCUTTLEBUTT
RUMORED AFLOAT
RUMP ASS FUD ARSE BEAM CULE DOCK DOUP CROUP NACHE NATCH PODEX STERN BOTTOM CURPIN CROUPON CRUPPER HURDIES KEISTER PLUNDER BANKRUPT BUTTOCKS DERRIERE
(PREF.) PYG(O)
(SUFF.) PYGAL PYGE PYGIA(N) PYGOUS PYGUS
RUMPF CORE
RUMPLE FOLD MUSS WISP TOUSE TOWSE MOUSLE ROMBLE CRUMPLE SCRUNCH WRINKLE
RUMPUS RAG ROW BRAWL SHINE CLAMOR FRACAS HUBBUB RUCKUS SHINDY TOWROW UPROAR BAGARRE BOBBERY ROOKERY RUCTION ROWDYDOW
RUMSHOP BAR SALOON TAVERN BARROOM TAPROOM DRUNKERY
RUN GO BYE ERN FLY FOG GAD HOP JOG LAM LEG PLY RIN RUB URN BUNK CALL FLEE FLOW FUSE HARE HEAT HEEL HUNT IRNE KITE LEAD LEAP MELT PASS PLAY RACE RAKE RINN ROAM ROVE TEND TRIG TRIP TROT TURN WALK WEEP WORK ASSAY BLEND BREAK BRUSH CHASE COAST EXTRA GOING HURRY NOTCH

POINT SCOUP SPEED SPEND STAND TABLE TRACE BICKER CAREER COURSE ELAPSE ESCAPE EXTEND GALLOP HASTEN LADDER MANAGE RESORT ROTATE SPRENT SPRINT STREAM TUMBLE VOLATA ACCURRE CONDUCT CONTAIN FLUTTER LIQUEFY OPERATE PASSAGE RETREAT SCUTTER SKELTER STRETCH FUNCTION TRANSCUR
(— ABOUT) TIG FISK DISCURRE
(— ACROSS) STRIKE
(— AGAINST) JOSTLE
(— AGROUND) BEACH GRAVEL HURTLE STRAND STRIKE
(— ALONG EDGE OF) SKIRT
(— AS STOCKING) LADDER
(— AT HIGH SPEED) SCORCH
(— AT THE NOSE) SNIVEL
(— AT TOP SPEED) SPRINT
(— AWAY) FLY GUY FLEE HIKE JINK JUMP SMUG ELOPE SCRAM SMOKE DECAMP SCAMPER SCARPER FUGITATE SKEDADDLE
(— AWAY FROM DEBTS) LEVANT
(— AWAY IN PANIC) STAMPEDE
(— BEFORE A GALE) SCUD
(— BEFORE A JUMP) FEAZE FEEZE
(— BETWEEN) INTERCUR
(— BLINDLY) SKITTLE
(— CLUMSILY) LOPPET TUMBLE
(— COUNTER) BELY BELIE CROSS
(— DOWN) SLUR TRASH OVERRUN
(— HARD) DIG
(— HIGH) FLOOD
(— IN CRICKET) BYE WIDE EXTRA NOTCH
(— IN DROPS) WEEP
(— INTO) INCUR
(— ITS COURSE) LAPSE
(— OBLIQUELY) SQUINT
(— OF CLAPBOARDING) STRAKE
(— OF MULE CARRIAGE) DRAW
(— OF SHAD) SPURT
(— OF STAIRS) GOING
(— OFF) BOLT SCADDLE
(— ON SKIS) SCHUSS
(— OUT) EXCUR ISSUE PETER
(— OVER) HEAT TRAMP OVERFLOW
(— RAPIDLY) KITE RAKE SCUR SCOUR SKIRR SPLIT CAREER
(— SOAP) FRAME
(— SPEEDILY) CHASE CAREER
(— SWIFTLY) HARE LEAP SCUD CHEVY CHIVY
(— THROUGH) PIERCE DISCURRE
(— TO) ACCURRE
(— TO EXERCISE HORSE) HEAT
(— TOGETHER) HERD MUDDY CLUTTER
(— TRAINS) BLOCK
(— WILD) GAD ESCAPE STARTLE
(— WILDLY) STARTLE
(— WITH AFFECTED PRECIPITATION) SCUTTLE
(— WITH SKIPS) SCOUP
(— WITH VELOCITY) DART
(BRIEF —) STREAK FLUTTER
(COMMON —) RUCK
(END —) SWEEP
(GLASS FURNACE —) BLAST

(MUSICAL —) TIRADE
(OBSTACLE —) GYMKHANA
(RAPID MUSICAL —) TIRADE VOLATA
(SAILING —) STRETCH
(SHEEP —) SLAIT STATION
(SHORT —) FAIL BICKER SCURRY FLUTTER RAMRACE SCUTTLE
(SKI —) PISTE SCHUSS LANGLAUF
(WILD —) LAMP
(PREF.) TRECHO TREKO
RUNAGATE APOSTATE FUGITIVE RENEGADE RUNABOUT VAGABOND WANDERER
RUNAWAY ROMP FUGIE RUNNER DECISIVE DESERTER FUGITIVE RUNAGATE
(PREF.) DRAPETO
RUNDI HUTU
RUNDLE DRUM RUNG ORBIT CIRCLE SPHERE WINDLASS
RUNDLET KEG BARREL
RUN-DOWN BAD SEEDY SHODDY SQUALID DERELICT
RUNE WEN WYN AESE WYNN CHARM OGHAM SPELL THORN SECRET MYSTERY
RUNG RIM GREE RIME STEP ROUND SCALE SPELL SPOKE STAFF STAIR STALE STAVE STEAL TREAD WRUNG DEGREE RUNDLE STOWER STREAK CROSSBAR TRAVERSE
(— OF CHAIR) SPELL
(— OF LADDER) RIME STEP RANGE SPOKE STALE RONDLE STREAK
(— OF ROPE WALK) STAKE
(PL.) STILE
RUNIC ALPHABET FUTHARK FUTHORC
RUNIC LETTER THORN
RUNLET RUSH RINDLE RUNNEL STREAM RIVELING
RUNNEL RILL BROOK RHINE RINDLE RUNLET POLLARD RIVULET STREAMLET
RUNNER SOW GOER POST SCUD SHOE SKID BLADE COBIA FLOAT RACER SABOT SCARF SKATE SLIDE SPRAY TEDGE CURSOR HEELER KANARA RENNER STOLON TOUTER CHANNEL COURIER HARRIER SARMENT CURSITOR SKIPJACK TRAILING
(— FOR GRINDING STONE) MARTIN
(— WHO SETS PACE) RABBIT
(BLUE —) HARDTAIL
(BOOKMAKER'S —) SPIV
(ERRAND —) CAD
(FLUME —) HERDER
(PAIR OF —S) SLOOP
(RACE —) SCUTTLER
(SLED —S) BOB
(SLEDGE —S) SLIPES
RUNNING RUN CARE EASY RACE FLUID QUICK COURSE LIVING COURANT CURRENT CURSIVE FLOWING HOTFOOT SCUTTER SLIDING FUGITIVE
(— ABOUT) COURANT CURSORY
(— ACROSS) DIAGONAL
(— AT SLOW PACE) JOGGING
(— OF SHIPS TOGETHER) ALLISION

(— TOWARD) APPULSE
(— VERTICALLY) DOWN
(FIRST —S) HEAD
(NOT —) DEAD
(PREF.) DROM(O)
(SUFF.) DROMOUS
RUNNING GEAR MOBILE
RUNT BOOR SCRUB SLINK STEER STUMP STUNT HEIFER PEEWEE SCRUMP TITMAN URLING BULLOCK SHARGAR SHARGER SLINKER RECKLING
RUNTY MEAN SURLY SCRUBBY SCRUNTY STUNTED DWARFISH
RUNWAY RUN TIP DUCT TRAIL TARMAC SLIPWAY AIRSTRIP DOLLYWAY
(— OF HARE) FILE
RUPEE DIB CHIP SICCA ROUPIE
(ONE-SIXTEENTH —) ANNA
(TENS OF —S) RX
(10 MILLION —S) CRORE
(100,000 —S) LAC LAKH
RUPERT'S DROP TEAR
RUPIA RUPEE ERUPTION
(HALF —) PARDO PARDAO
RUPTURE BLOW REND RENT BREAK BURST CRACK SPLIT BREACH HERNIA RHEXIS DISRUPT RUPTION FRACTION FRACTURE HERNIATE
(SUFF.) RHEXIS RRHEXIS
RUPTURED BROKEN
RURAL RUSTIC BUCOLIC COUNTRY AGRESTIC ARCADIAN LANDWARD MOFUSSIL PASTORAL PLEASANT PRAEDIAL VILLATIC
RUSE HOAX ROSE SHIFT STALL TRICK WREST ARTIFICE TRICKERY
RUSH FLY FOG RIP RIX RUB SAG BANG BENT BOLT CLAP DASH DUSH FALL FLAW GIRD HURL HUSH JUNK LASH LEAP LUSH PASH RACE RACK RASH RESE RISH ROUT SCUD SHOT SLUR SPUR SWIP TEAR TILT WHIP WIND ADRUE CARRY CHASE CHUTE DRASH DRIVE FEEZE FLASH FLUSH FRAIL FRUSH HURRY ONSET PIPES PREEL SCOUR SEAVE SHOOT SPART SPATE SPRAT SPRIT SPROT START STAVE STORM WHIRL CHARGE DELUGE FESCUE HURTLE JUNCUS POWDER RAMACK RANDOM RAVINE STREAK THRESH ASSAULT BRATTLE BULRUSH DAILIES DEBACLE JUNCITE RAMMISH RAMRACE SKELTER SMOTHER SWITHER TANTIVY TORNADO VIRETOT WHITHER CATARACT DEERHAIR SALTWEED SPLATTER VANQUISH
(— ABROAD) FLUSH
(— AGAINST) CHARGE
(— AWAY) BOLT FLEE SCUTTLE
(— DOWN) TRACE
(— FOR WEAVING) FRAIL
(— HEADLONG) BOIL RUIN SPURN STAMPEDE
(— OF LIQUID) HEAD FLUSH
(— OF WATER) FRESH SHOOT SPOUT SWASH

(— OF WORDS) SPATE
(— ON PASSER IN FOOTBALL) BLITZ
(— OUT) SALLY
(CLUMP OF —S) RASHBUSS
(COMMON —) FLOSS
(DOWNWARD —) HURL
(FLAT —) SHALDER
(FORCEFUL —) JET
(NOISY —) SCUTTER
(ONWARD —) BIRR SURGE
(PL.) REXEN
(PREF.) JUNCI THRYONO
RUSHED HECTIC
RUSHING HURL SCUD FURIOUS
HUDDLING IMPETUOUS
(— OF WIND) GUST
RUSHLIGHT SEAVE
RUSH NUT CHUFA
RUSK ZWIEBACK
RUSSELL'S VIPER DABOIA
DABOYA JESSUR KATUKA

RUSSIA

CAPITAL: MOSCOW
COIN: KOPEK RUBLE GRIVNA
KOPECK
COLLECTIVE FARM: KOLHOZ
KOLKHOZ
DISTRICT: KARELIA
FORTRESS: KREMLIN
LAKE: ARAL NEVA SEGO CHANY
ELTON ILMEN ONEGA BAYKAL
LADOGA SELETY TAYMYR
TENGIZ ZAYSAN BALKHASH
MEASURE: FUT LOF DUIM FASS
LOOF STOF FOUTE KOREC
LIGNE OSMIN PAJAK STOFF
VEDRO VERST ARSHIN CHARKA
LINIYA PALETZ SAGENE TCHAST
BOTCHKA CHKALIK GARNETZ
VERCHOC BOUTYLKA CHETVERT
KROUSHKA
MOUNTAIN: POBEDA BELUKHA
MOUNTAIN RANGE: ALAI URAL
CAUCASUS
NAME: USSR SOVIET MUSCOVY
PENINSULA: KOLA CRIMEA

KARELIA KAMCHATKA
PORT: EISK ANAPA ODESSA
PRESS AGENCY: TASS
REPUBLIC: UZBEK KAZAKH KIRGIZ
LATVIA ARMENIA ESTONIA
GEORGIA TADZHIK TURKMEN
UKRAINE MOLDAVIA LITHUANIA
BYELORUSSIA AZERBAIDZHAN
RIVER: IK OB DON ILI KET NER
OKA ROS TAZ TYM UFA USA
AMGA AMUR KARA LENA NEVA
OREL SURA SVIR URAL LOVAT
MEZEN NADYM ONEGA TEREK
TOBOL VOLGA ABAKAN DONETS
IRTYSH DNIEPER PECHORA
SEA: ARAL AZOV KARA BLACK
BAIKAL OKHOTSK
TOWN: BAKU KIEV OMSK OREL
PERM RIGA GOMEL KASAN
KAZAN KYZYL MINSK PENSA
PSKOV TOMSK FRUNZE IGARKA
KERTCH KURGAN NIZHNI
ODESSA ROSTOV SARTOV
URALSK ALMAATA BATAISK
DONETSK IRKUTSK IVANOVO
KALININ KHARKOV RYBINSK
TALLINN KOSTROMA
ORENBURG SMOLENSK
TAGANROG TASHKENT
VLADIMIR VORONEZH
YAROSLAV
VOLCANO: ALAID SHIVELUCH
TOLBACHIK

RUSSIAN IVAN RUSS SLAV VELIKA
MUSCOVITE
(— BRAID) SOUTACHE
(— HEMP) RINE
(— POOL) CARLINE
(LITTLE —) RUSSENE RUTHENE
UKRAINIAN
RUSSIAN BANK CRAPETTE
RUSSIAN CALF FUDGE
RUSSIAN OLIVE OLEASTER
RUSSIAN THISTLE SALTWORT
TUMBLEWEED
RUSSIAN TURNIP RUTABAGA

RUSSIAN WOLFHOUND BORZOI
RUST CLOWN DROSS ROOST
ROUST UREDO AERUGO CANKER
CORRODE FERRUGO OXIDIZE
(— OF PLANTS) HEMIFORM
LEPTOFORM
(KNOT OF —) TUBERCULE
RUSTAM (FATHER OF —) ZAL
(HORSE OF —) RAKSH
(MOTHER OF —) RUDAPAH
(SON OF —) SOHRAB
(WIFE OF —) TAHMINAH
RUSTIC HOB JAY PUT BOOR CARL
CHAW HICK HIND JAKE JOCK
RUBE RUDE BACON BUSHY CARLE
CHUFF CHURL COLIN DAMON
DORIC HODGE ROUGH RURAL
RURIC SILLY YOKEL AGREST
BORREL BUMKIN COARSE FARMER
GAFFER HONEST JOBSON RUSSET
SAVAGE SCOLOC SCOLOG STURDY
SYLVAN UPLAND ARTLESS
BOORISH BORRELL BUCOLIC
BUMPKIN BUSHMAN COUNTRY
DAPHNIS FIELDEN GEORGIC
HAYSEED HOBNAIL HOOSIER
LANDMAN PAISANO PEASANT
PLOWMAN THYRSIS WAYBACK
AGRESTIC ARCADIAN BACKVELD
CLOWNISH DAMOETAS GEOPONIC
LANDWARD MOSSBACK
CHAWBACON CLODHOPPER
(NOT —) CIVIL
(UNCOUTH —) JAKE
(YOUTHFUL —) SWAIN
(PL.) COUNTRYFOLK
RUSTLE FISLE STEAL FISSLE FISTLE
HIRSEL REESLE BRUSSEL BRUSTLE
CRINKLE REESTLE SKITTER
WHISTLE
(— OF SILK) SCROOP
(— UP) SNAVVLE
RUSTLER THIEF WADDY DUFFER
WADDIE HUSTLER
RUSTLING ARUSTLE CRINKLY
FROUFROU SOUGHING FRICATION
SUSURROUS

RUSTY HOARY MOROSE ROOSTY
SULLEN CANKERY OUTMODED
RUT RAT BRIM RACK RAIK RUCK
TRACK TREAD CREASE FURROW
GROOVE STRAKE UPROAR
CHANNEL OESTRUS WRINKLE
(— IN PATH) GAY
RUTABAGA BAGA SWEDE TURNIP
RUTH PITY MERCY MISERY REGRET
SORROW CRUELTY REMORSE
SADNESS SYMPATHY
(HUSBAND OF —) BOAZ MAHLON
(MOTHER-IN-LAW OF —) NAOMI
(SON OF —) OBED JESSE
RUTHENIAN RUSSENE RUSSNIAK
UKRAINIAN
RUTHLESS FELL GRIM CRUEL
BRUTAL PITILESS CUTTHROAT
RUTILE NIGRINE SAGENITE
RUTTER PLOW DRAGOON GALLANT
TROOPER
RUTTISH RANK LUSTFUL
RUY BLAS

RWANDA

CAPITAL: KIGALI
LAKE: KIVU
LANGUAGE: KIRUNDI SWAHILI
MOUNTAIN: KARISIMBI
MOUNTAIN RANGE: MITUMBA
PEOPLE: TWA HUTU TUTSI
RIVER: KAGERA AKANYARU
LUVIRONZA
TOWN: BUTARE GABIRO NYANZA
GISENYI
TRIBE: BATWA BAHUTU WATUSI
BATUTSI

RYE RAY RIE ERAY REYE SPELT
WHISKY GENTLEMAN
RYEGRASS RAY EAVER DARNEL
RYMANDRA KNIGHTIA
RYND BAIL RHIND MILRIND
RYOT RAYAT FARMER RAIYAT
TENANT TILLER PEASANT

S

S ESS SUGAR SIERRA
SABBATH SUNDAY SABAOTH SHABBAT SHABBOS
SABER KUKRI SABRE BANCAL BASKET TULWAR ATAGHAN CIMETER TULWAUR YATAGAN ACINACES SCIMITAR
SABICU JIQUE JIQUI
SABINE (BROTHER OF —) CURIACE
SABLE DWALE SAPLE OGRESS SATURN DIAMOND ZIBELINE
(ROUNDEL —) PELLET
SABLEFISH SKIL BESHOW COALFISH SKILFISH
SABOTAGE MASTIC DESTROY
SABRA (FATHER OF —) PTOLEMY
(HUSBAND OF —) GEORGE
(SON OF —) GUY DAVID ALEXANDER
SABRINA (FATHER OF —) LOCRINE
(MOTHER OF —) ESTRILDIS
SABTAH (FATHER OF —) CUSH
SABTECHA (FATHER OF —) CUSH
SAC BAG GUT POD CYST SACK ASCUS BURSA FLOAT POUCH THECA VOLVA ACINUS AMNION SACCUS VESICA AMPULLA BLADDER CAPSULE CISTERN HYGROMA UTRICLE VESICLE BROODSAC FOLLICLE SACCULUS SPERMARY
(PREF.) THEC(A)(I)(O)
SACAR (FATHER OF —) OBEDEDOM
(SON OF —) AHIAM
SACCHARIN SWEET STICKY SUGARY GLUCOSE GLUSIDE
SACCHAROSE SUCROSE
SACERDOTAL HIERATIC PRIESTLY
SACHEM SAGAMORE
SACK BAG BED MAT SAC LOOT MUID POCK POKE BAYON GOOSE HARRY POUCH SPOIL BUDGET POCKET RAVAGE SACKET SACQUE DISMISS PILLAGE PLUNDER RANSACK SACKAGE SACKBAG DESOLATE PACKSACK PEIGNOIR
(— OF PALM LEAVES) BAYONG
(— OF WOOL) SARPLAR
(MAIL —) BUM
(PACK —) KYACK
(SAD —) BOLO
(PREF.) THYLAC(O)
SACKBUT SAMBUKE TROMBONE
SACKING SACK GUNNY CROCUS SACKEN HESSIAN POLDAVY SOUTAGE
SACRAMENT RITE BAPTISM MYSTERY NAGMAAL PENANCE
SACRARIUM PISCINA
SACRED HOLY TABU HUACA PIOUS SACRE SAINT SANCT SANTO TABOO DIVINE SACRAL HALLOWED HEAVENLY

NUMINOUS REVEREND SACROSANCT
(PREF.) HAGI(O) HIER(O) HIERATICO SACR(I)(O) SEMNO
SACRED FIG PIPAL
SACRED FISH KANNUME
SACREDNESS CHURINGA SANCTITY TJURUNGA
SACRIFICE GIVE HOST LOSS OFFER SPEND YAJNA CORBAN FOREGO VICTIM EXPENSE CHILIOMB IMMOLATE KAPPARAH LITATION OBLATION OFFERING PASSOVER SPHAGION PROPITIATION
(— OF CARGO) JETTISON
(— OF 100 OXEN) HECATOMB
(— OF 1000 OXEN) CHILIOMB
(PL.) HAGIGAH CHAGIGAH
SACRIFICIAL PIACULAR
SACRILEGE PROFANATION
SACRILEGIOUS IMPIOUS
SACRISTAN SEXTON SACRIST
SACRISTY SEXTRY SACRARY VERGERY PARATORY SACRARIUM
SACROSANCT SACRED
SACRUM
(SUFF.) HIERIC
SAD LOW WAN DARK DOWY DRAM BLACK DREAR DUSKY MESTO MOODY SABLE SOBER SORRY WEARY YEMER DREARY SOLEMN SULLEN TRISTE WOEFUL BALEFUL DOLEFUL DUMPISH FORLORN FUNEBRE LUCTUAL MOANFUL SOBERLY UNHAPPY DEJECTED GROANFUL MOURNFUL MOURNING PATHETIC PITIABLE SUBTRIST TRISTIVE UNBLITHE MELANCHOLY
(PREF.) TRISTI
SADDEN SAD DUMP CLOUD GLOOM GRIEVE ATTRIST CONTRIST DISTRESS
SADDENED BROKEN
SADDENING LUCTUAL
SADDLE PAD RIG SAG TAG LOAD SUNK CHINE PANEL PILCH SELLE STICK BURDEN HEADER RECADO PIGSKIN PILLION
(— COVER) MOCHILA
(— FOR ONE-LEGGED RIDER) SOMERSET
(— STUFFED WITH STRAW) SODS
(— WITH) STICK
(— WORKER) LORIMER
(LIGHT —) PILCH PILLION
(MOTORCYCLE —) PILLION
(PACK —) BAT
(PART OF —) HORN RING SEAT SKIRT CANTLE FENDER JOCKEY POMMEL STRING BINDING LEATHER STIRRUP
(STRAW —) SUNK SUGGAN

(WITHOUT A —) ASELLATE
(PREF.) SELLI
SADDLEBACK JACK JACKBIRD
SADDLEBAG ALFORJA CANTINA SUMPTER TEETSOOK
(PL.) JAGS JAGGS
SADDLE BLANKET CORONA
SADDLEBOW BOW ARSON
SADDLECLOTH HOUSE NAMDA HOUSING PADCLOTH SHABRACK
SADDLEMAKER FUSTER KNACKER
SADDLE MAT FLET
SADDLE PAD PANEL NUMNAH PILLOW
SADDLER CODDER KNACKER LORIMER WHITTAW
SADISTIC SICK CRUEL SADIC
SADLY SAD UNWINLY
SADNESS DUMP RUTH DREAR DUMPS GLOOM GRIEF UNWIN SORROW
SAD SACK BOLO
SAFAWID SUFI
SAFE RUG CRIB PETE SURE WELL AMBRY SALVA SIKER SOUND SECURE SICCAR HEALTHY SYKERLY COCKSURE SILVENDY
(— FOR MEAT) KEEP
(— TO DEAL WITH) CANNY
SAFEBLOWER PETEMAN
SAFEBREAKER YEGG YEGGMAN
SAFE-CONDUCT JARK COWLE GRITH CONDUCT NAVICERT PASSPORT
SAFECRACKER BOXMAN PETEMAN PETERMAN TORCHMAN
SAFEGUARD SAVE WARD GUARD HEDGE SALVE DEFEND SAFETY SECURE BASTION BULWARK WARRANT FREEWARD PALLADIUM PRECAUTION
SAFEKEEPING CUSTODY STORAGE
SAFELY SAFE SICCAR SICKER SURELY SECURELY
SAFETY REFUGE SALUTE SURETY WARRANT SECURITY
(PREF.) SOTERIO
SAFETY ZONE ISLET ISLAND REFUGE
SAFFLOWER KUSUM ALAZOR SAFFRON
SAFFRON CROCUS AZAFRAN CROCEUS
(PREF.) CROCEO CROCO
SAFROLE SHIKIMOL
SAG BAG DIP TIE SWAG CREEP DROOP PLANK SLUMP SAGGON CURTAIN DEFLATE
SAGA EDDA EPIC MYTH TALE RIMUR LEGEND NJALSAGA
SAGACIOUS DEEP ACUTE CANNY SHARP ARGUTE ASTUTE SHREWD CORDATE POLITIC

PRUDENT SAPIENT
SAGACITY POLICY WISDOM SMEDDUM YEPHEDE PRUDENCE SAPIENCE
SAGAMORE SACHEM
SAGE RSI WARE WISE WITE CLARY HAKAM IMLAC KATHA RISHI SABIO SOLON SOPHY ABARIS DHARMA SALVIA SAULGE SHREWD WIZARD EYESEED MAHATMA SAPIENT SOPHIST TOHUNGA WISEMAN DEVARSHI MAHARSHI WISEACRE
SAGEBRUSH SAGE HYSSOP SAGEWOOD ARTEMISIA
SAGENESS SAPIENCE
SAGGER COFFIN SETTER CASSETTE
SAGGING DRAG SWAG PTOSIS
SAGITTA ARROW
SAGITTARIUS ARCHER
SAGO PALM CYCAD
SAGRADA CASCARA
SAGUARO SUAHARO SUWARRO PITAHAYA
SAHIB BWANA
SAHIDIC THEBAIC
SAIBLING TORGOCH
SAID DIT QUOTH STATED RELATED
SAIL JIB LUG RAG BEAT GALE HAUL MAIN SCUN SLAT SWAN SWIM WING DANDY FLEET FLIER FLOAT FLYER JUMBO RAFFE SCALE SHEET ACCOST CANVAS COURSE CRUISE DRIVER JIGGER LATEEN MIZZEN MUSLIN SINGLE ARTEMON LUGSAIL SKYSAIL SPANKER SPENCER TRYSAIL BACKWIND FORESAIL GAFFSAIL HEADSAIL MAINSAIL MOONSAIL NAVIGATE RINGSAIL STAYSAIL STUNSAIL
(— ALONG COAST) COAST ACCOST
(— AROUND) TURN DOUBLE
(— BEFORE THE WIND) SPOON
(— BRISKLY) SPANK
(— BY THE WIND) STRETCH
(— CLOSE TO WIND) PINCH
(— DOWN) AVALE AWALE
(— FASTER) FOOT
(— IN SPECIFIED DIRECTION) STAND
(— OF WINDMILL) ARM AWE EIE FAN VAN EIGHE FLIER FLYER SWEEP SWIFT
(— ON COURSE) HAUL WORK
(— QUIETLY) GHOST
(— RAPIDLY) SCUR SKIRR
(— SWIFTLY) RAMP
(— TO WINDWARD) THRASH
(— WITH WIND ABEAM) LASK
(FRAGMENT OF —) HULLOCK
(LIGHT —) SHADOW
(LOWEST —) COURSE
(PART OF —) CLEW FOOT HEAD

LUFF SEAM SLAB TACK LEECH
PANEL POCKET WINDOW ZIPPER
CRINGLE TABLING TELLTALE
HEADBOARD
(SMALL —) ROYAL
(TRIANGULAR —) RAFFE LATEEN
BENTINCK
(WIND —) BADGIR
(3-CORNERED —) JIB TRINKET
(PL.) VELA CLOTH KITES LINENS
SAILAGE CLOTHING
(PREF.) HISTI(O) ISTIO VELI
SAILBOAT SAIL SCOW BULLY
DANDY NABBY SAPIT SCOUT
SHARP SKIFF SLOOP SNIPE
CANGIA DINGHY QUODDY SAILER
SATTIE CATBOAT SCOOTER
SHALLOP SHARPIE KEELBOAT
SAILSHIP SKIPJACK TRIMARAN
(PART OF —) JIB BOOM BUNK
GATE HEAD HELM KEEL MAST
SINK SKEG SOLE BERTH CLEAT
FRAME HATCH SALON TRUNK
WHEEL WINCH ANCHOR GALLEY
JIBTOP LOCKER PULPIT RUDDER
SHROUD YANKEE BULWARK
COAMING COCKPIT COUNTER
GALLOWS PUSHPIT TOPSAIL
BACKSTAY BOWSPRIT BULKHEAD
FOREDECK FOREFOOT FORESTAY
HEADSTAY LIFELINE MAINSAIL
MASTHEAD OVERHEAD SPREADER
STAYSAIL TAFFRAIL TRAVELER
CUBBYHOLE MAINSHEET
PORTLIGHT STANCHION
STATEROOM COMPANIONWAY
(WITCH'S —) SIEVE
SAILFISH BOHO WOOHOO
GUEBUCU LONGJAW VOILIER
VOLADOR BILLFISH
SAILOR (ALSO SEE NAVAL OFFICER)
GOB TAR JACK TOTY GUARD
KLOSH LAKER LIMEY CALASH
CLASHY DAYMAN DECKIE HEARTY
MARINE MATLOW SEAMAN
TARPOT TIERER TOPMAN COLLIER
MARINAL MARINER MATELOT
SHIPMAN SWABBER WARRIOR
YARDMAN CANOTIER COXSWAIN
DECKHAND FLATFOOT GALIONJI
GUNLAYER LANDSMAN LITHSMAN
MASTHEAD SHIPMATE
WATERDOG WATERMAN
WATERRUG YARDSMAN
(EAST INDIAN —) LASCAR
(OLD —) SALT SHELLBACK
(SCANDINAVIAN —) KLOSH
SAILORLIKE TARRISH
SAILOR'S-CHOICE BREAM PIGFISH
PINFISH WHITING
SAIL YARD RAE
SAINFOIN ESPARCET
SAINT PIR RSI DADU HOLY QUTB
WALI ALVAR ARHAT RISHI SANTO
BHAGAT HALLOW PATRON
SANTON CANONIZE MARABOUT
(CHINESE —) IMMORTAL
(PATRON —) AVOWRY
(PILLAR —) STYLITE
(PL.) SS
(PREF.) HAGI
SAINT ELMO'S FIRE HERMO
CASTOR FUROLE HELENA

SAINT JOAN (AUTHOR OF —) SHAW
(CHARACTER IN —) JOAN DUNOIS
ROBERT WARWICK BAUDRICOURT
ST-JOHN'S-BREAD CAROB
ST-JOHN'S-WORT AMBER TUTSAN
CAMMOCK
ST REGIS RANERE
SAINTLINESS HOLINESS SANCTITY
SAINT LUCIA (CAPITAL OF —)
CASTRIES
(MOUNTAIN OF —) GIMIE
(MOUNTAINS OF —) PITONS
CANARIES
(VOLCANO OF —) SOUFRIERE
SAINTLY DEVOUT ANGELIC
SAINTED BEATIFIC SAINTISH
(— PERSON) ZADDIK
SAINT VINCENT (CAPITAL OF —)
KINGSTOWN
(PART OF —) UNION BEQUIA
GRENADINES
SAITHE SILLOC SILLOCK
SAJ SAIN
SAKE SAKI SCORE ACCOUNT
SAKI BISA MONK COUXIA MONKEY
YARKEE
SALA (FATHER OF —) ARPHAXAD
(SON OF —) EBER
SALABLE VENAL SELLING
SELLABLE VENDIBLE
SALACIOUS LEWD SALT RUTTISH
SCARLET SCABROUS
SALAD SALLET COLESLAW
SILLSALLAT
(CORN —) FETTICUS
SALADA SALINA
SALAL SHALLON
SALAMANDER OLM SOW BEAR
NEWT TWEEG GOPHER LIZARD
TRITON AXOLOTL CRAWLER
CREEPER DOGFISH MECODONT
SALAMICH SHADRACH
SALAMMBO (AUTHOR OF —)
FLAUBERT
(CHARACTER IN —) NARR GISCO
HANNO HAVAS MATHO TAMIT
HAMILCAR SALAMMBO SPENDIUS
(COMPOSER OF —) REYER
SAL AMMONIAC SPIRIT SALMIAC
SALARY PAY HIRE SCREW WAGES
INCOME PACKET PENSION
STIPEND
SALE FAIR VENT BREAK HEDGE
TOUCH BOURSE VENDUE
AUCTION MOHATRA SELLING
HANDSALE KNOCKOUT
PORTSALE
(— BY AUCTION) CANT ROUP
BLOCK VENDUE OUTROOP
(— BY OUTCRY) ROUP ROWP
HAMMER
(— OF OFFICE) BARRATRY
(— OF TOBACCO) BREAK
(PUBLIC —) AUCTION
(RUMMAGE —) JUMBLE
SALESMAN CLERK BAGMAN
RUNNER SELLER BOOKMAN
DRUMMER OUTRIDER PITCHMAN
(— IN FISH MARKET) BUMMAREE
SALESMANSHIP SELLING
SALESPERSON CLERK
SALESWOMAN WINSTER
SHOPGIRL VENDEUSE

SALIENT SPUR BULGE CHIEF
ARGINE BASTION SALTANT
SALIENTIA ANURA ANOURA
ECAUDATA
SALINA SHOR SALINE
SALINE SALT SALAR SALTY
MARINAL
SALIVA SPIT DROOL WATER
DRIVEL SLAVER SPUTUM SPITTLE
(— FLOW) PTYALISM
(PREF.) PTYAL(O) SIAL(O)
SALIVARY SIALIC
SALIVATION PTYALISM SLOBBERS
SALLET SALADE
SALLOW WAN SALE SICK ADUST
LURID MUDDY SALIX SAUCH
SAUGH PALLID YELLOW
SALLY GRIP JERK PASS QUIP SAIL
QUICK START ESCAPE GAMBIT
SORTIE GAMBADE OUTFALL
OUTLEAP DEMARCHE
SALM (BROTHER OF —) TUR IRAJ
(FATHER OF —) FARIDUN
(MOTHER OF —) SHAHRINAZ
(SLAYER OF —) MINUCHIHR
SALMAGUNDI SILLSALLAT
SALMON DOG LAX LOX SAM KETA
MASU PINK AMOUT COHOE
COUNT HADDO HOLIA SMOLT
SMOOT SPROD TECON ALEVIN
BAGGIT KIPPER LAUREL MYKISS
SAMLET SAUQUI SILVER TAIMEN
ANADROM ANNATTO BLUECAP
BOTCHER CHINOOK DOGFISH
GILLING KAHAWAI KOKANEE
NEWFISH QUINNAT REDFISH
RUNFISH SAWMONT SHEDDER
SOCKEYE BLUEBACK BRANDLIN
GOLDFISH HUMPBACK LASPRING
SALMONID SPRINGER
OUANANICHE
(— AFTER SPAWNING) KELT
BAGGIT SHEDDER
(— BEFORE SPAWNING) GILLING
GIRLING
(— ENCLOSURE) YAIR
(— IN 2ND OR 3D YEAR) SMOLT
(— IN 2ND YEAR) SPROD HEPPER
GILLING
(— IN 3D YEAR) PUG MORT
(— ON FIRST RETURN FROM SEA)
GRILSE
(BLUEBACK —) NERKA SAUQUI
SOCKEYE
(CURED —) KIPPER
(DOG —) CHUM KETA
(FATHER OF —) NAHSHON
(FEMALE —) RAUN BAGGIT
(HUMPBACK —) HADDO HOLIA
(MALE —) GIB BUCK COCK
(MILTER —) EKE
(NEWLY HATCHED —) PINK ALEVIN
(SMALL —) PEAL SKIRLING
(SON OF —) BOAZ
(SPENT —) JUDY SLAT LIGGER
RUNFISH
(YOUNG —) FOG PARR PEAL
GRILSE HEPPER JERKIN SAMLET
BOTCHER ESSLING SKEGGER
LASPRING SPARLING
SALMONELLOSIS KEEL
SALMONEUS (BROTHER OF —)
SISYPHUS

(DAUGHTER OF —) TYRO
(FATHER OF —) AEOLUS
(MOTHER OF —) ENARETE
(WIFE OF —) ALCIDICE
SALOME (FATHER OF —) HEROD
(HUSBAND OF —) PHILIP ZEBEDEE
ARISTOBULUS
(MOTHER OF —) HERODIAS
SALON HALL SALOON GALLERY
SALOON CAFE CUDDY DIVAN
SALON SHADE BARROOM
CANTINA RUMSHOP SCATTER
DEADFALL DRINKERY DRUNKERY
EXCHANGE BRASSERIE
SALPA SALP THALIA
SALSIFY GOATBEARD
SALT SAL CORN KERN SAWT BRINY
ZIRAM AMIDOL AURATE GAMMON
HALITE MALATE OLEATE OSMATE
POWDER SALINE URANIN XENATE
KAINITE LACTATE MALEATE
NIOBATE PHYTATE TROPATE
ABIETATE BRACKISH HALINOUS
PIMELATE PLUMBITE
(— FISH) ROIL
(— OUT) CUT GRAIN
(DOUBLE —) ALUM
(HAIR —) ALUNOGEN
(LUMP OF —) SALTCAT
(METAL —) SILICATE
(MIXTURE OF —S) REH USAR
(ROCK —) PIG HALITE
(PREF.) HAL(I)(O) SALI SALIN(I)(O)
(SUFF.) OATE
SALTATE JUMP
SALT BOILER WELLER
SALTBUSH BLUEBUSH
SALTCELLAR SALT CELLAR SELLER
SHAKER SALTFAT SALTFOOT
SALTED SALEE
SALTICID ATTID
SALT PAN PLAYA
SALTPETER NITER NITRE PETER
ANATRON CALICHE PRUNELLA
SALT PIT VAT WICH WYCH
SALT PORK SOWBELLY
SALTWORKS SALINA SALTERN
SALTERY SALTPANS
SALTWORT KALI BARILLA SALSOLA
KELPWORT
SALTY SALT BRINY SALINE
HALINOUS
SALU (SLAYER OF —) PHINEHAS
(SON OF —) ZIMRI
SALUBRIOUS HEALTHY SALUTARY
SALUTARY GOOD BENIGN
HEALTHY HELPFUL BENEDICT
SALUTATION AVE HAIL ALOHA
SALUS MIZPAH SALAAM SALUTE
REGREET SLAINTE WELCOME
DIEUGARD GREETING HAEREMAI
(DRINKING —) SKOAL PROSIT
PROFACE WASSAIL
SALUTE CAP HAIL HEIL KISS MOVE
YULE CHEER DRINK GREET HALCH
HALSE HONOR SALUE SALVO
COLORS SALAAM EMBRACE
CONGREET
SALVADOR BAHIA
SALVAGE SAVE SALVE RECOVERY
SCROUNGE
SALVAGER SALVOR
SALVATION BODAI MOKSHA

SAFETY NIRVANA KAIVALYA
SAVEMENT SOULHEAL
(— APPROACH) MARGA
SALVE SAW TAR SALVO SAUVE
NERVAL SUPPLE PLASTER
UNGUENT OINTMENT
SALVER TRAY SERVER WAITER
PLATEAU
SALVIA CHIA SAGE CLARY
MEJORANA MINTWEED
SALVO SALUTE SPREAD PROVISO
TRIBUTE STRADDLE
(PL.) LADDER
SAM (FATHER OF —) NARIMAN
(SON OF —) ZAL
SAMARA KEY CHAT
SAMARIA AHOLAH
SAMARITAN CUTHEAN CUTHITE
SAMBA CARIOCA
SAMBAR ELK MAHA RUSA
SAME ID EAD ILK ONE IDEM LIKE
SELF VERY DITTO EQUAL SAMEN
IDENTIC SELFSAME
(— AS) IQ
(— PLACE) IB
(THAT —) THILK THICKE
(PREF.) AUT(O) AUTH(I)
HOM(O)(OI) HOME(O) HOMOE IPSI
ISO TAUT(O)
SAMENESS ONENESS EQUALITY
IDENTITY MONOTONY
SAMLET PINK
SAMNITES SABELLI
SAMOA (CAPITAL OF —) APIA
PAGOPAGO
(COIN OF —) SENE TALA
(ISLAND OF —) OFU TAU ROSE
MANUA UPOLU SAVAII OLOSEGA
TUTUILA
(MOUNTAIN OF —) FITO SAVAII
MATAFAO
SAMOGITIAN ZHMUD
SAMOYED TUBA YURAK BELTIR
KAIBAL KOIBAL NENTSI KAMASSIN
SAMPHIRE SALTWEED
SAMPLE DIP SIP CAST PREE CHECK
ESSAY TASTE TRIAL CHANCE
COUPON FLOWER MUSTER
SWATCH TASTER EXAMPLE
EXCERPT MONSTER PATTERN
SAMPLER TASTING INSTANCE
PULLDOWN SPECIMEN
(— OF METAL) DIET
SAMPLING SOUNDING
SAMSON (FATHER OF —) MANOAH
**SAMSON ET DALILA (CHARACTER
IN —)** PRIEST SAMSON DELILAH
(COMPOSER OF —) SAINTSAENS
SAMUEL (FATHER OF —) ELKANAH
(MOTHER OF —) HANNAH
SAMURAI BUSHI RONIN
SAN SAMPI
SANAD SUNNUD
SANBENITO SAMARRA
SAN BLAS TULE
SAN CARLOS ARIVAIPA
SANCTIFICATION HOLINESS
SANCTIFY BLESS SACRE SACRI
DEDICATE
SANCTIMONIOUS PI DEVOUT
PECKSNIFFIAN
SANCTION AMEN FIAT ALLOW
PIETY ASSENT BISHOP RATIFY

APPROVE ENDORSE JUSTIFY
PASSAGE SUPPORT ACCREDIT
APPROVAL CANONIZE COURTESY
SUFFRAGE
SANCTIONED CANONICAL
SANCTITY SANTY HALIDOME
HOLINESS
SANCTUARY ADYT BAST BEMA
FANE HOLY SOIL ABBEY ALTAR
BAMAH FRITH GIRTH GRITH
SECOS SEKOS TOWER ADYTON
ADYTUM ASYLUM CHAPEL
HAIKAL REFUGE SENTRY SHRINE
SACRARY SHELTER ARCHEION
CABIRION DELUBRUM
HALIDOME HOLINESS
SACRARIUM
(— FOR LAWBREAKERS) ALSATIA
(AUTHOR OF —) FAULKNER
(CHARACTER IN —) LEE RED VAN
REBA RUBY DRAKE GOWAN
LAMAR TOMMY BENBOW HORACE
POPEYE RIVERS SNOPES TEMPLE
GOODWIN STEVENS
SANCTUM ADYT ADYTON ADYTUM
SAND DIRT GRIT ARENA GRAIL
SONDE GRAVEL ISERINE ISERITE
PARTING ASBESTIC BLINDING
(— FOR STREWING ON FLOORS)
BREEZE
(— HILL) DENE DUNE
(— IN KIDNEYS) ARENA
(— MIXED WITH GRAVEL) GARD
DOBBIN
(— ON SEA BOTTOM) PAAR
(BRAIN —) SABULUM ACERVULUS
(COLOR —) CHIP BEACH
(COLORED —) SMALT
(DEAUVILLE —) STUCCO
(VOLCANIC —) SANTORIN
(PREF.) AMM(O) ARENI PSAMM(O)
SANDAL TIP BAXA FLAT SOCK ZORI
TEGUA CALIGA CHARUK PATTEN
TATBEB RULLION SCUFFER
FOOTHOLD GUARACHE
HUARACHO
SANDAL TREE SANTOL
SANDALWOOD NAIO ALGUM
ALMUG MAIRE CHANDAM
SAUNDERS
SANDALWOOD TREE ILIAHI
SANDARAC TREE ARAR LIGNUM
SANDBAG CONK SANDCLUB
SAND BANK AIR CHAR MEAL
SAND BATCH HURST HYRST
KNOCK SHELF SHOAL
SANDBAR BALK LOOP SAND
BARRA SHOAL TOMBOLO
TOWHEAD
SANDBLASTER FROSTER
BLASTMAN
SAND BORER SMELT
SANDBOX TREE ASSACU
SAND COLIC SABURRA
SAND DARTER SPECK
SAND DUNE TOWAN BARCHAN
SAND EEL GRIG SANDFISH
SANDEMANIAN GLASSITE
SANDERLING OXBIRD
SAND FLEA SCREW SCROW
SANDBOY
SAND-FLY BUSH TURMERIC
SAND GROUSE GANGA ROCKER

ATTAGEN PINTAIL
SAND HOLE BUNKER
SANDIVER NATRON
SAND LAUNCE LANT SMELT
WRIGGLE AMMODYTE SANDLING
SCRIGGLE
SAND LILY SOAPROOT
SANDMAN DUSTMAN
SANDPAPER TREE CHAPARRO
SANDPIPER JACK KNOT PEEP
RUFF STIB WEET OXEYE SNIPE
STINT TEREK TIPUP WADER
DUNLIN GAMBET OXBIRD PLOVER
REDLEG TEETER TILTER TILTUP
TRINGA BROWNIE CHOROOK
CREEKER FATBIRD FIDDLER
HAYBIRD KRIEKER MONGLER
MONGREL REDBACK TATTLER
TIPTAIL GRAYBACK LEADBACK
PEETWEET REDSHANK ROCKBIRD
SANDPEEP SHADBIRD SQUATTER
SWEESWEE TELLTALE
TRIDDLER
(FEMALE —) REEVE
(FLOCK OF —S) FLING
SAND PIT BUNKER
SAND ROCKET FLIXWEED
SAND SHARK BONEDOG
SANDSTONE FAKE FLAG GRES
GRIT SAND GAIZE HAZEL ARCOSE
ARKOSE DOGGER KINGLE ARENITE
HASSOCK CARSTONE COCONINO
GANISTER PSAMMITE RUBSTONE
SANDROCK
(BLOCK OF —) SARSEN
SANDSTORM BURAN HABOOB
TEBBAD
SANDUST VANITY
SANDWICH BUTTY HOAGY
BURGER HOAGIE GRINDER
WESTERN
(SUFF.) BURGER
SANDWORT LONGROOT
SANDWEED
SANDY DEEP GINGER GRISTY
SANDED ARENOSE PSAMMOUS
SABULINE SABULOUS
SANDY BROWN LARK
SANE SAFE WISE LUCID RIGHT
FORMAL NORMAL HEALTHY
PERFECT RATIONAL SENSIBLE
SANGA-SANGA ESSANG
SANGUINARY GORY CRUEL
BLOODY CRIMSON SANGUINE
SANGUINE FOND GUZE MURREY
HEMATIC HOPEFUL SARDONYX
SANHEDRIN GEROUSIA
SANICLE ALLHEAL SELFHEAL
SANIOUS ICHOROUS
SANITARY HYGIENIC
SANITY SENSE REASON WISDOM
BALANCE MARBLES LUCIDITY
SANENESS
SAN MARINO (CHURCH OF —)
PIEVE
(DISTRICTS OF —) CASTELLI
(MOUNTAIN OF —) TITANO
(SUBURB IN —) BORGO
SANNUP SQUAW
SANSKRIT HINDU
(— SOUND OR SIGN) VISARGA
(— WORK) VEDANGA
SANS SERIF DORIC GOTHIC

SANTA MARIA TREE BIRMA
GALBA CALABA
SANTONICA WORMSEED
SAO TOME AND PRINCIPE
(CAPITAL OF —) SAOTOME
(MONEY OF —) DOBRA
(NAME OF —) SAOTHOME
SAINTTHOMAS
SAP MUG GOON MINE OOZE RASA
SEVE HUMBO KEEST LYMPH
SAPPER WEAKEN ALVELOZ
FLUXURE SAPHEAD
(— COURAGE) DAUNT
(PALM —) TODY TODDY
(POISONOUS —) UPAS
(SUGAR MAPLE —) HUMBO
SAPAJOU SAJOU WARINE
SAPANWOOD BOKOM BRAZIL
SIBUCAO
SAPEK DONG
SAPID SIPID FLAVORY
SAPIENT WISE SHREWD KNOWING
SAPI-UTAN ANOA
SAPLING SCOB PLANT SAPLE
SPIRE RUNNEL SPRING TILLER
STADDLE ASHPLANT SEEDLING
SHILLALA SPRINGER
(— AMONG FELLED TREES) WAVER
SAPODILLA GUM CHICA CHICO
DILLY ACHRAS MAMMEE SAPOTA
SAPOTE ZAPOTE NISPERO
NISBERRY NASEBERRY
SAPONIFYING KILLING
SAPONIN GITONIN SENEGIN
CYCLAMIN STRUTHIN
SAPONITE PIOTINE
SAPOTA MATASANO
SAPPHIRE SAFIR TOPAZ ADAMAS
ASTERIA ASTRION HYACINTH
SAPPHIRINE GURNARD TUB
SAPPHO (AUTHOR OF —) DAUDET
(CHARACTER IN —) JEAN ROSA
FANNY IRENE DEJOIE POTTER
CAOUDAL CESAIRE FLAMANT
GAUSSIN LEGRAND BOUCHEREAU
DECHELETTE LAGOURNERIE
SAPPY FRIM FRUM SAPFUL
SAPSAP PEPEREK
SAPUCAIA COCO COCOA
KAKARALI
SAPWOOD SAP BLEA SPLENT
SPLINT GUAYABI LISTING
ALBURNUM
SARA (— WOMAN) UBANGI
SARABAITES REMOBOTH
SARACEN CORSAIR
SARAH ATOSSA
(FATHER OF —) ASHER
(HUSBAND OF —) ABRAHAM
(SON OF —) ISAAC
SARAKOLLE WAKORE
SARASVATI VAC VACH BENTEN
SARCASM RUB GIBE WIPE FLING
IRONY TAUNT RUBBER SATIRE
BROCARD RIDICULE
SCORCHER
SARCASTIC ACID WITTY BITING
IRONIC ACERBIC CUTTING
MORDANT PUNGENT INCISIVE
SARDONIC SATIRICAL
ACRIMONIOUS
SARCASTICALLY DRILY DRYLY
ACIDLY

SARCOCARP FLESH
SARCOPHAGUS TOMB COFFIN
SARCOPSYLLA TUNGA
SARDINE BANG LOUR SARD
SILD CLUPEID PILCHARD
SARDELLE

SARDINIA
CAPITAL: CAGLIARI
CHEESE: ROMANO PECORINO
COIN: CARLINE
GREEK COLONY: OLBIA
GULF: OROSEI ASINARA CAGLIARI
ORISTANO
MOUNTAIN: RASU FERRY LINAS
GALLURA LIMBARA SERPEDDI
VITTORIA
NAME: SARDEGNA
PROVINCE: NUORO SASSARI
CAGLIARI
RIVER: MANNU TIRSO LASCIA
SAMASSI COGHINAS
FLUMENDOSA
STRAIT: BONIFACIO
TOWN: NUORO SASSARI THATARI
CAGLIARI CARBONIA IGLESIAS

SARDONIC SARCASTIC
SARGASSUM GULFWEED
SARGO ZEBRA
SARI PATOLA TAMEIN
SARONG PAU KAIN COMBOY
KIKEPA
SARPEDON (BROTHER OF —) MINOS
RHADAMANTHUS
(FATHER OF —) ZEUS JUPITER
(MOTHER OF —) LAODAMIA
SARSAPARILLA NUNNARI
SHOTBUSH
SARUCH (FATHER OF —) REU
SASH BAR BELT BENN FAJA GATE
TOBE SCARF TAPIS TOWEL VITTA
FASCIA GIRDLE BALDRIC
BURDASH CHASSIS TUBBECK
CASEMENT CORSELET
WAISTBAND
(JAPANESE —) OBI
(WINDOW —) CHESS
SASHAY WALK GLIDE STRUT
CHASSE TRAIPSE
SASH BAR MUNTIN ASTRAGAL
SASKATCHEWAN (CAPITAL OF —)
REGINA
(LAKE OF —) ROUGE REINDEER
ATHABASKA CHURCHILL
WOLLASTON
(RIVER OF —) WOOD MOOSE
SOURIS FRENCHMAN
(TOWN OF —) BIGGAR CLIMAX
ESTEVAN MOOSEJAW ROSETOWN
SASKATOON
SASQUATCH OMAH BIGFOOT
SASS LIP
SASSABY TSESSEBE
SASSAFRAS FILE SALOP SALOOP
SAXIFRAX
SASSY KICKY LIPPY
SATAN ANGEL DEVIL EBLIS FIEND
SHREW BELIAL LUCIFER SATANAS
SHAITAN DIABOLUS SATANAEL
SATANIC SABLE INFERNAL
SATCHEL SCRIP HANDBAG
KEESTER

SATE GLUT ACCLOY SATIATE
SATISFY SATURATE
SATED SAD BLASE
SATEEN VENETIAN
SATELLITE MOON ARIEL LUNET
DEIMOS MOONET OBERON
PHOBOS ACOLYTE ACOLYTH
LUNETTE ORBITER SPUTNIK
TELSTAR TRABANT
UMBRIEL COURTIER
FOLLOWER
(— OF JUPITER) IO EUROPA
CALLISTO GANYMEDE
(— OF SATURN) RHEA DIONE
MIMAS TITAN PHOEBE TETHYS
IAPETUS JAPETUS HYPERION
SATIATE CLOY FILL GLUT PALL
QUAT SADE SATE FLESH GORGE
SERVE STALL ENGLUT STODGE
RASSASY SATISFY SURFEIT
SATURATE
SATIATED SICK JADED SATED
SATIATING STODGY FULSOME
SATIETY FULNESS SURFEIT
CLOYMENT
SATIN SAY RASH ATLAS PANNE
CYPRUS MUSHRU COOTHAY
CYPRESS SATINET
(SILK —) DUCHESS
SATINFLOWER SAFFRON
SATINPOD HONESTY LUNARIA
SATINWOOD ZANTE HAREWOOD
SATIRE WIT GRIND IRONY IAMBIC
LAMPOON SARCASM SOTADIC
RIDICULE PASQUINADE
SATIRIC BITTER IRONIC ABUSIVE
CAUSTIC CUTTING POIGNANT
SLASHING
SATIRIST GRIND NIPPER SATIRE
JUVENAL PASQUIN SILLOGRAPH
AMERICAN MENCKEN
ENGLISH HONE NIGEL SWIFT
WOLCOT MARVELL
GERMAN BORNE MURNER
RABENER
GREEK LUCIAN SOTADES
ROMAN PERSIUS
SPANISH LARRA
SATIRIZE SKIN SKIT GRIND EXPOSE
IAMBIZE LAMPOON PASQUIN
RIDICULE
SATISFACTION CRO FIN PAY UTU
EASE GREE BELLY ENACH TREAT
AMENDS ASSETH CHANGE
REASON CONTENT CONTENT
DELIGHT GLADNESS PLEASURE
REPLETION
SATISFACTORILY SPROWSY
CLEVERLY
SATISFACTORY PAT FAIR GOOD
JAKE WELL DUCKY HUNKY
CLEVER DECENT NOMINAL
ADEQUATE LAUDABLE
SATISFIED SAD FAIN FULL GLAD
PAID VAIN APAID CHUFF PROUD
ASSURED CONTENT PERFECT
GRUNTLED SENSIBLE
WILCWEME
SATISFY PAY EVEN FEED FILL
MEET SAIR SATE SUIT ADEEM
AGREE APPAY QUEME SERVE
SLAKE SPEED ANSWER DEFRAY
PLEASE STODGE SUPPLY

ASSUAGE CONTENT EXPLETE
FULFILL GRATIFY GRUNTLE
RESPOND SATIATE STAUNCH
SUFFICE SATURATE
(— APPETITE) STAY
(— BY PROOF) CONVINCE
(— NEEDS) DO ADJUST
SATISFYING DUE COOL AMPLE
SQUARE PERFECT REWARDING
SATURATE SOG GLUT SATE SOAK
DRAWK IMBUE SOUSE STEEP
DRENCH IMBIBE SEETHE SODDEN
DRUNKEN INGRAIN SATIATE
SLOCKEN
(— WITH SYRUP) CANDY
SATURATED SOBBY SOGGY SOPPY
SODDEN SPONGY DRUNKEN
SATURATION CHROMA PURITY
SATURITY
SATURN (FATHER OF —) URANUS
(MOTHER OF —) GAEA
(SATELLITE OF —) RHEA DIONE
MIMAS TITAN TETHYS JAPETUS
HYPERION ENCELADUS
(SON OF —) JUPITER
SATURNINE SULLEN SATANIC
SATYAGRAHA GANDHISM
SATYR FAUN LECHER SAUMON
SALTIER WOODMAN WOODWOSE
SATYRIASIS TENTIGO
SAUCE MOLE SASS SOWL BERCY
CHILE CHILI CREAM CREME
CURRY GRAVY PESTO SALSA
CATSUP GANSEL MORNAY
PANADA ROBERT KETCHUP
MARENGO SOUBISE SUPREME
TABASCO VELOUTE BECHAMEL
CHAWDRON DRESSING DUXELLES
MATELOTE POIVRADE RAVIGOTE
REMOLADE
(CURRY —) SAMBAL
(FISH —) ALEC BAGOONG
(GARLIC —) AIOLI
(KIND OF —) MARINARA
(SALAD —) DRESSING
(SAVORY —) DIP
(THICK —) LEAR
SAUCEDISH SAUCER BIRDBATH
SAUCEPAN CHAFER GOBLET
POSNET SKILLET STEWPAN
PANNIKIN
SAUCER BIRD PATERA PHIALE
CAPSULE PANNIKIN
SAUCINESS SAUCE DICACITY
SAUCY BOG ARCH BOLD COXY
PERT BRASH DONSY DORTY
FRESH LIPPY PAWKY POKEY
SASSY SMART BANTAM COCKET
COPPED CROUSE THWART
FORWARD PAUGHTY MALAPERT
PETULANT SANSHACH
SAUDI ARABIA: (CAPITAL OF —)
JIDDAH RIYADH
(COIN OF —) RIYAL HALALA
HALALAH
(DESERT REGION OF —) NEFUD
DAHANA ALNAFUD
(PLATEAU OF —) NEJD
(TOWN OF —) HAIL HOFUF JIDDA
MECCA MEDINA ALHOFUF
(WEIGHT OF —) OKE
SAUL (FATHER OF —) KISH
(SON OF —) JONATHAN

SAUNTER IDLE ROAM ROVE TOIT
AMBLE RANGE SHOOL SIDLE
STRAY TRAIK BUMMEL DACKER
DANDER FAFFLE LINGER LOITER
LOUNGE POTTER PUTTER
RAMBLE SOODLE STREEL STROLL
TODDLE WANDER SNAFFLE
STAIVER STRAVAGE
SAURA MAGA
SAUREL SCAD XUREL GASCON
BLUEFISH SKIPJACK
SAURY LONGJAW SKIPPER
BILLFISH GOWDNOOK SKIPJACK
SAUSAGE POT LINK SNAG COPPA
GIGOT BANGER BOUDIN POLONY
SALAMI BOLOGNA BOLONEY
BOTARGO CHORIZO PUDDING
SAVELOY BLACKPOT CERVELAT
DRISHEEN KIELBASA LIVERING
ROLLICHE
(KIND OF —) METT
(PREF.) ALLANT(O) BOTULI
SAUTE PANFRY
SAUTERNE YQUEM
SAVAGE ILL FELL GRIM RUDE WILD
BRUTE CRUEL EAGER FELON
FERAL STERN BRUTAL FIERCE
GOTHIC IMMANE BRUTISH
FERVENT HOWLING INHUMAN
MANKEEN MANKIND ROPABLE
UNCIVIL VIOLENT WILROUN
CANNIBAL PITILESS THEREOID
WARRAGAL
(PREF.) AGRIO
SAVAGELY FELLY UNMANLY
SAVAGERY FURY FERITY FEROCITY
SAVANNA CAMPO SAHEL SABANA
(— LANDS) LALANG
SAVANT ARTIST SCIENT SCHOLAR
VIRTUOSO
SAVE BAR WIN HAIN HELP KEEP
SAFE STOP SALVE SPARE SPELL
DEFEND EXCEPT RESCUE SAVING
SCRIMP BARRING DELIVER
HUSBAND SALVAGE WARRANT
CONSERVE PRESERVE
(PREF.) SOZ(O)
SAVIN HEATH SABINE JUNIPER
SAVING FRUGAL THRIFT ECONOMY
SPARING THRIFTY PROVIDENT
SAVINGS FAT ADDLINGS
(— CLUB) MENAGE
SAVIOR LORD SAVER SOTER
REDEEMER
SAVOR EDGE SALT SAPOR SMACK
TASTE DEGUST FLAVOR RELISH
RESENT SAVOUR SEASON TASTEN
SAPIDITY
SAVORLESS FOND INSIPID
WEARISH
SAVORY GUSTY MERRY SAPID
TASTY DAINTY SMERVY GUSTFUL
GUSTABLE TASTEFUL
SAVVY SABE
SAW SAG SEY WEB BUCK REDE
ADAGE FREIT GNOME SCEAR
SPOKE JIGSAW PITSAW RIPSAW
SAYING SCRIBE BACKSAW
BUCKSAW CONVERT DRAGSAW
FRETSAW HACKSAW HANDSAW
HEADRIG HEADSAW PROVERB
SLABBER WHIPSAW CROSSCUT
SENTENCE

(— INTO LOGS) BUCK
(— LENGTHWISE OF GRAIN) RIP
(— OF SAWFISH) SERRA
(— WITH TWO BLADES) STADDA
(CIRCULAR —) BUR BURR EDGER DAPPER TRIMMER
(CROSSCUT —) BRIAR
(CYLINDER —) CROWN TREPAN TREPHINE
(PREF.) PRI(O) PRION(O) SERRATI SERRATO SERRI
(SUFF.) PRION
SAWAN SRABAN SHRAVAN
SAWBILL MOTMOT
SAWDUST COOM COOMB SCOBS SAWINGS
(PREF.) SCOBI
SAW FERN DYGAL BUNGWALL HARDFERN
SAWFISH RAY BATOID COMBFISH
(PREF.) PRIST(O)
SAWFLY CEPHID SECURIFER
SAW GATE FRAME
SAWHORSE BUCK JACK SETTER SAWBUCK TRESTLE
SAWING
(PREF.) PRISO
SAW KERF SKAFF
SAWMILL RASPER
(— DEVICE) KICKER
(— WORKER) PONDMAN LEVERMAN
SAWYER WETA SAWER PITMAN TOPMAN KNOTTER
SAXHORN ALTO TUBA ALTHORN SAXTUBA BARITONE BARYTONE
SAXIFRAGE BAUERA BENNET SESELI ASTILBE ROCKFOIL SELFHEAL SENGREEN MITERWORT PHILADELPHUS
SAXONIAN MINDEL
SAXOPHONE AX AXE SAX ALTO TENOR SOPRANINO
SAY DEED MEAN MOVE TAKE TELL SPEAK SPELL AUTHOR QUETHE RELATE REMARK SAYING REHEARSE
(— A BLESSING) BENSH
(— FOOLISHLY) BLABBER
(— FURTHER) ADD
(— GLIBLY) SCREED
(— NO TO) NAIT NICK
(— OVER AGAIN) REPEAT
(— SPITEFUL THINGS) BACKBITE
(— TOO MUCH) OVERSAY
(— UNDER OATH) DEPOSE
SAYING DIT SAW SAY TAG DICT ITEM REDE TEXT WORD ADAGE AXIOM CHRIA DITTY FREIT MAXIM SPEAK BALLAD BYWORD DICTUM DIVERB LOGION DICTION PROVERB APOTHEGM SENTENCE SPEAKING
(— LITTLE) DUMB
(—S OF JESUS) AGRAPHA
(—S OF RELIGIOUS TEACHER) LOGIA
(CLEVER —) QUIP
(COMMON —) CANT
(CURRENT —) DICTUM
(OBSCURE —) ENIGMA
(QUICK —) JERK
(SILLY —) FADAISE
(TERSE —) EPIGRAM

(TRUE —) SOOTHSAW
(WISE —) SCHOLIUM
(WITTY —) MOT SALLY DICTERY WITNESS
(WITTY —S) FACETIAE
(SUFF.) LOGER LOGIA(N) LOGIC(AL) LOGIST LOGUE LOGY
SCAB RAT ROIN SHAB SNOB CRUST SCALD SCALL CANKER ESCHAR RATTER GREENER RUBBERS BLACKLEG BLACKNEB
(— ON HORSE'S HEEL) MELLIT
SCABBARD CHAPE SHEATH PILCHER
SCABBARD FISH HIKU
SCABBLE SCAB SCALP
SCABBY MANGY SCALD ROINISH SCABIOUS
SCABIES ITCH SCAB PSORA
SCABIOSA KNAUTIA
SCABIOUS SCABIA BLUECAP BUNDWEED PREMORSE
SCABROUS ROUGH SULTRY ASPEROUS
SCAD COIN AKULE XUREL DOLLAR GOGGLER QUIAQUIA
(PL.) LOTS TONS
SCAFFOLD CAGE PEGMA STAGE BRIDGE CATASTA HAYLOFT STAGING HOARDING
(MOVABLE —) GANTRY
SCAFFOLDING DOCK STAGING
SCALARE ANGELFISH
SCALD BURN LEEP PLOT SCAD BLAST PLOUT SCAUD BLANCH SCALDER AMBUSTION
SCALE PIP LEAF PELA PILL STEP TAPE CLIMB FLAKE GAMUT GENUS GULAR PALEA PELOG PELOK PELTA POISE SCUTE SHALE SHARD SHELL SHERD SHIVE TRUNK ASCEND CAUDAL CINDER COCCID FORNIX GUNTER IMBREX KELVIN LABIAL LADDER LAMINA LIGULE LOREAL MENTAL NUCHAL OCULAR PERULE RAMENT RONDLE RUSTRE SHIELD SQUAMA STRIGA BALANCE CLINKER ELYTRON FRONTAL FULCRUM HUMERAL LATERAL NUCHALE REAUMUR ROSTRUM VENTRAL VERNIER ANALEMMA BRACHIAL INDUSIUM LECANIUM LODICULE MEALYBUG ODOPHONE RAMENTUM SCRAMBLE SQUAMULE TEMPORAL UROSTEGE
(— DOWN) DEGRADE
(— OF CORNSTALK) SHIVE
(— OF 7 TONES) SEPTAVE
(— ON BUTTERFLY) PLUMULE
(— ON MOTH) PATAGIUM
(— USED BY TAILORS) LOG
(GRADUATED —) RETE
(GREAT —) GAMUT
(SHAD —) CENIZO
(PL.) CHAFF DANDER
(PREF.) LEPID(O) LEPO PHOLID(O) SQUAM(ATO)(ELLI)(I)(O)(OSO)(ULI)
(MUSICAL —) CHORD(O)
(SUFF.) LEPIS PHOLIS
SCALEBOARD SCABBARD

SCALEPAN BASIN
SCALER CULLER SOOTER
SCALES TRON TRONE BALANCE
SCALETAIL SQUIRREL
SCALLION PORRET
SCALLOP DAG CLAM GIMP MUSH CRENA QUEEN SQUIN PECTEN COQUILLE DOUGHBOY ESCALLOP PECTINID
SCALLOPED INVECTED
(SUFF.) CRENATE
SCALP SCAUP SKELP ATTIRE
SCALPEL BISTOURY
SCALPER PUNTER
SCALY SCABBY SQUAMY LEPROSE PALEATE LEPIDOTE SCABROUS SQUAMOSE
SCAMP LAD RIP LIMB SLIM ROGUE SKEMP SKIMP THIEF BOOGER BUGGER FRIPON NICKUM RASCAL SINNER SORREL SORROW HALLION HESSIAN PEASANT RAMMACK SKELLUM SLUBBER SNOOZER BLIGHTER SCALAWAG SLYBOOTS SPALPEEN VAGABOND WIDDIFOW SCALLYWAG
SCAMPER LAMP CHEVY SCOUP SCOUR CHIVVY BRATTLE SKITHER SKITTER
SCAN PIPE GLASS METER DEVISE SURVEY EXAMINE
SCANDAL GUP CLASH CRACK ECLAT SHAME CALUMNY OFFENSE SCANMAG SLANDER
SCANDALIZE SHOCK
SCANDALMONGER CLAT
SCANDALOUS UNHOLY SHAMEFUL
SCANDINAVIAN DANE LAPP NORSE SWEDE VIKING LOCHLIN NORSEMAN NORTHMAN SCANDIAN VARANGIAN
(PL.) OSTMEN
SCANT SHY JIMP LEAN MEET POOR THIN SCAMP SHORT SKIMP SPLAY BARISH GEASON LITTLE MEAGER MEAGRE SCANTY SKINNY STINGY STINTY SLENDER SCRATCHY
(PREF.) OLIG(O)
SCANTILY BARELY FEEBLY SMALLY SCANTLY SPARSELY
SCANTINESS PENURY PARCITY EXIGUITY SPARSITY
SCANTLING STUD FILET JOIST FILLET BOLSTER RIBBAND STUDDING
SCANTY BARE JIMP LANK LEAN POOR SLIM EXILE GNEDE SCANT SHORT SILLY SKIMP SPARE FRUGAL MEAGER MEASLY SCRIMP SKIMPY SLIGHT SPARSE SCRANNY SCRIMPY SLENDER SPARING EXIGUOUS PENURIOUS
SCAPEGOAT STOOGE
SCAPEGRACE SCALLYWAG SKAINSMATE
SCAPHOID NAVICULAR
SCAPOLITE DIPYRE
SCAPULA BLADE OMOPLATE
SCAPULAR CUCULLA
SCAR ARR EYE WEM SEAM SEAR WIPE CHALK FESTER KELOID RADDLE STIGMA TRENCH

CHELOID SCARIFY CICATRIX SMALLPOX CICATRICE
(— ON SAWED STONE) STUN
(— ON SEED) HILUM
(— ON TREE) CATFACE
SCARAB ATEUCHUS
SCARCE DEAR RARE THIN SLACK DAINTY GEASON CLASSIC UNCOMMON
(PREF.) SPAN(I)(O)
SCARCELY ILL VIX JIMP SCANT BARELY HARDLY MERELY ONETHE SCARCE SCRIMP WENETH SCANTLY UNEATHS UNNETHE
SCARCITY LACK WANT FAULT SCANT DEARTH FAMINE RARITY PAUCITY
SCARE COW BOOF BREE FAZE FEAR FLEG FLIG FRAY GAST HUSH SHOO ALARM APPAL GALLY GLIFF GLOFF PSYCH SPOOK AFFRAY FRIGHT GASTER PSYCHE SCARIFY STARTLE TERRIFY AFFRIGHT FRIGHTEN
(— BIRDS) KEEP
(— OFF) SCAT
SCARECROW BOGLE BUCCA MOGGY SEWEL BOGGLE DUDMAN MALKIN MAUMET MAWKIN SCARER SHEWEL BOGGART BUGABOO DEADMAN HODMADOD SHAWFOWL
SCARED SCART SCARY AFRAID GOOSEY STREAKED
SCAREMONGER ALARMIST
SCARF BARB HOOD SASH ABNET ASCOT BARBE CLOUD CYMAR FICHU LUNGI NUBIA PAGRI SHADE STOCK STOLE TABLE THROW CRAVAT PEPLOS REBOZO SCREEN SQUARE TAPALO TIPPET UPARNA BURDASH DOPATTA FOULARD MANIPLE MUFFLER NECKTIE ORARIUM OVERLAY PUGGREE SAUTOIR TALLITH CLAUDENT COINTISE DOOPUTTY LIRIPIPE LIRIPOOP MANTILLA MUFFETEE SLENDANG
(— ON KNIGHT'S HELMET) COINTISE
(ARABIAN —) CABAAN
(FEATHER —) BOA
(PRAYER —) TALLIS TALLITH
SCARFING GRAFTING
SCARIFY LIFT
SCARLET LAC RED PINK TULY GRAIN KERMES
SCARLET HAW HAWTHORN
SCARLET IBIS GUARA
SCARLET LETTER (AUTHOR OF —) HAWTHORNE
(CHARACTER IN —) PEARL ROGER ARTHUR HESTER PRYNNE BELLINGHAM DIMMESDALE CHILLINGWORTH
SCARLET LYCHNIS FIREBALL NONESUCH
SCARLET TANAGER REDBIRD FIREBIRD
SCARLIKE ULOID
SCARP CLIFF SCARF ESCARP SCARPLET
SCATHING MORDANT SCALDING
SCATHINGLY ROUNDLY

SCATOLOGICAL BARNYARD
SCATTER DAD SOW TED FLEE
SALT SCAT SEED SHED SPEW
VOID FLING SCALE SCHAL SEVER
SHAKE SKAIL SPRAY STREW
STROW DISPEL PEPPER SHOWER
SKIVER SPARGE SPARSE SPREAD
SPRENG WINNOW DIFFUSE
DISBAND DISJECT FRITTER
RESOLVE SCAMBLE SHATTER
SKINKLE SKITTER SLATTER
SPARKLE SPARPLE SPATTER
SWATTER DISPERSE INTERSOW
SEPARATE SPLUTTER SPRINKLE
SQUANDER SQUATTER
(— **BAIT FOR FISH**) TOLE TOLL
(— **OVER**) BESTREW
(— **WATER**) SPLASH
SCATTERED LAX OPEN STRAY
DAIMEN SPARSE DIFFUSE
SPOTTED BESPRENT FUGITIVE
SPARSILE
(PREF.) LAXI
SCATTERING SOWING DIASPORA
SCATTERY
SCAUP DUCK DOGS DIVER
DUCKER DUNBIRD POCHARD
BLUEBILL GRAYBACK SHUFFLER
SCAVAGE SCEWING
SCAVENGE CLEANSE GARBAGE
SCAVENGER BUNGY RAKER
BHANGI BHUNGI MEHTAR
REMOVER SCAFFIE CORYDORA
HALALCOR RAMSHORN
SCAZON CHOLIAMB
SCEAT SKEAT STYCA
SCENE JOG SET CODA CYKE FLAT
SITE VIEW ARENA STAGE BRIDGE
VISION EPISODE PAGEANT
COULISSE EXTERIOR INTERIOR
PROSPECT TABLETOP
(— **IN OPERA**) SCENA
(— **OF ACTION**) STAGE
(— **OF ACTIVITY**) BEEHIVE
(— **OF CONFUSION**) BABEL BEDLAM
(**CLOSING —**) FINALE
(**FINAL —**) CURTAIN EPILOGUE
SCENERY DROP FLAT DECOR
CUTOUT NATURE IMAGERY
PROFILE
(**PIECE OF —**) MASKING
SCENESHIFTER GRIP
SCENT AIR DRAG NOSE ODOR
VENT WIND CIVET FAULT FLAIR
FUMET RELES SAVOR SMACK
SMELL SNIFF SNUFF SPOOR
TASTE CHYPRE ESSENCE INCENSE
NOSEGAY ODORIZE VERDURE
FUMIGATE MARECHAL PASTILLE
REDOLENCE
(— **OF ANIMAL FOLLOWED BY
HOUNDS**) FEUTE
(— **OF COOKING**) NIDOR
(— **OF FOX**) DRAG
(**FALSE —**) RIOT
(**LOST —**) FAULT
SCENTED OLENT ODORATE
PERFUMY ESSENCED
SCEPTER ROD WAND VERGE
BAUBLE CEPTER FERULA WARDER
SCHEDULE BOOK CARD HOLD LIST
SKED TIME PANEL SCRIP SCROW
SETUP SLATE TABLE SCROLL

CATALOG TABLEAU CALENDAR
REGISTER
(— **OF DUTIES**) TARIFF
(— **OF GAMES**) SEASON
SCHEDULED DUE
SCHEDULING (**TECHNIQUE FOR —**)
PERT
SCHEELITE TUNGSTEN
SCHEHERAZADE (**HUSBAND OF —**)
SCHAHRIAH
(**SISTER OF —**) DINARZADE
SCHEMA FORM
SCHEME AIM GIN LAY WAY WEB
CAST DART GAME PLAN PLAT
PLOT REDE SWIM ANGLE BABEL
CADRE DODGE DRAFT DRIFT
KNACK PINAX REACH SCALE
SETUP SHIFT TABLE THINK TRAIN
BRIGUE BUBBLE CIPHER DESIGN
DEVICE DEVISE FIGURE HOOKUP
POLICY SCHEMA SYSTEM TAMPER
THEORY UTOPIA COUNSEL
DRAUGHT GIMMICK IMAGINE
KNAVERY NOSTRUM PROJECT
PURPOSE CONSPIRE CONTRIVE
FORECAST GIMCRACK IDEOLOGY
INTRIGUE MANEUVER PLATFORM
PRACTICE TRIPOTER WINDMILL
MACHINE
(— **OF RANK**) LADDER
(**ABORTIVE —**) SOOTERKIN
(**BETTING —**) SYSTEM
(**DECEITFUL —**) SHIFT
(**DELUSIVE —**) BUBBLE
(**DIAGRAMMATIC —**) PINAX
(**FANCIFUL —**) WINDMILL
(**FAVORITE —**) NOSTRUM
(**VISIONARY —**) BABEL
SCHEMER ARTIST DESIGNER
ENGINEER SCHEMIST SLEEVEEN
SCHEMING SCHEMY PLANFUL
SPIDERY FETCHING PRACTICE
SCHISM RENT SCISSION SCISSURE
SCHISMATIC HERETIC
SCHIST RAG AMPELITE MICACITE
MYLONITE OLLENITE PHYLLITE
SCHIZONT MONONT AGAMONT
SCHIZOPHRENIA CATATONY
SCHNAPPER WOLLOMAI
SCHOLAR TUG DEMY GAON IMAM
CLERK PUPIL DIVINE DOCTOR
FELLOW JURIST LAMDEN MASTER
PANDIT SABORA SAVANT SCOLOG
SHEIKH BIBLIST BOOKMAN
DANTIST LATINER LEARNER
MAULANA STUDENT BOURSIER
DISCIPLE HEBRAEAN HUMANIST
ISLAMIST MASORITE TABERDAR
THAUMASTE PHILOSOPHER
(— **OF QUEENS COLLEGE**)
TABERDAR
(PL.) LITERATI
AMERICAN LOWES BLYDEN
CONANT KELSEY MILLER SARTON
BABBITT GUMMERE SEYMOUR
HAMILTON HARKNESS PERCIVAL
STERRETT LOUNSBURY
AUSTRIAN SPANN
CANADIAN MACMECHAN
CHINESE YEN
CZECH JIRACEK SAFARIK
DANISH MADVIG GULDBERG
DUTCH COBET BURMAN ERASMUS

COORNHERT BILDERDIJK
ENGLISH KER BYNG LONG BYRON
CROFT ELYOT JAMES LOWTH
MAYOR PALEY ROGET YOUNG
ALCUIN ALFORD BAXTER BRIGHT
BROOME BUTLER COWELL
DASENT FARMER GODLEY
GROCYN HARRIS JEVONS
MURRAY NECKAM NEWMAN
NICOLL YAHUDA ALDHELM
ALDRICH BUTCHER DIODATI
HOLLAND LIDDELL MACKAIL
STANLEY CHRISTIE GRIERSON
HARRISON MCKERROW PATTISON
STRACHAN TUNSTALL TYRWHITT
CONINGTON NETTLESHIP
FINNISH LÖNNROT PORTHAN
KOSKENNIEMI
FLEMISH BLOMMAERT
FRENCH BUDE LAMY LUCE MAURY
PARIS BAILLY BERARD GAGUIN
MAGNIN MENAGE MICHEL
BROSSES CAUMONT CHASLES
DELISLE LEFRANC LONGNON
SOURIAU DEMOGEOT JAUCOURT
BARTHELEMY TAILLANDIER
GERMAN BLEEK HEYNE KLOTZ
KROLL LEYEN STAHR KOCHLY
RAUMER CONRING GOEDEKE
GOLTHER HEUSLER LUDWICH
MOMMSEN RIBBECK RUHNKEN
AUFRECHT BERNEKER BUTTMANN
HAINISCH PFEIFFER SPANHEIM
WEINHOLD KOSCHWITZ
CAMERARIUS
GREEK DION GAZA CORAY PALLES
DIDYMUS MUSURUS RHIANUS
PORPHYRY ATHENAEUS
CAECILIUS ZENODOTUS
CALLIMACHUS CHRYSOLORAS
HUNGARIAN BEL
ICELANDIC BLONDAL SAEMUND
VIGFUSSON
INDIAN PATANJALI
IRISH BALL BUTLER MAHAFFY
KEIGHTLEY
ITALIAN DONI ZENO GNOLI
MAFFEI VARCHI ALEANDRO
MARTELLI MARSILIUS NICCOLINI
TIRABOSCHI
JAPANESE NITOBE MABUCHI
MEXICAN GAMA
PERUVIAN MENDIBURU
POLISH CIOLEK CHODZKO
RACZYNSKI OSSOLINSKI
ZDZIECHOWSKI
PORTUGUESE BRAGA
ROMAN PLINY VARRO AUSONIUS
CENSORINUS
RUSSIAN LAVROV DRAGOMANOV
SCOTTISH LANG BLACKIE
GROSART LINDSAY BELLENDEN
MACDONALD
SPANISH OCHOA CASTRO VILLENA
SWEDISH MALMSTROM
STIERNHIELM
SWISS BODMER BREITINGER
PELLICANUS
SCHOLARLY CLERKLY ACADEMIC
SCHOLARSHIP ART BOOK BURSE
BURSARY DEMYSHIP LEARNING
SCHOLASTIC PEDANTIC
SCHOOL GAM TOL EDDY PREP

AGGIE BOOKS ECOLE HEDER
MYAYA SAKHA TEACH TRADE
TRAIN TUTOR ALJAMA CAMPUS
CHEDER CHURCH KUTTAB
KYAUNG MADHAB MALIKI RABFAK
SCHOLA SCHULE SQUEEL TRIPOS
ACADEME ACADEMY CRAMMER
MADRASA PENSION STUDIUM
YESHIVA AUDITORY DOCUMENT
EXERCISE EXTERNAT PEDAGOGY
SEMINARY
(— **FOR JUDO OR KARATE**) DOJO
(— **FOR SINGERS**) MAITRISE
(— **OF BLACKFISH**) GRIND
(— **OF BUDDHISM**) CHAN RITSU
DHYANA SANRON
(— **OF FISH**) HERD SCALE SCULL
(— **OF HINDU PHILOSOPHY**) NYAYA
(— **OF PAINTING**) GENRE
(— **OF PHILOSOPHY**) SECT
ACADEMY AUDITORY
(— **OF VEDA**) SAKHA SHAKHA
(— **OF WHALES**) GAM POD
(**ART —**) BAUHAUS LUMINISM
(**AZTEC —**) CALMECAC
(**COMPARATIVE —**) FOLKLORE
(**DAY —**) EXTERNAT
(**ELEMENTARY —**) GRADES
(**HIGH —**) HIGH ACADEMY COLLEGE
(**MOSLEM —**) HANAFI KUTTAB
SHAFII HANBALI
(**REFORM —**) BORSTAL
(**RELIGIOUS —**) ALJAMA YESHIVA
(**RIDING —**) MANEGE
(**SANSKRIT —**) TOL
(**SCOTCH —**) SQUEEL
(**SECONDARY —**) LYCEE LYCEUM
COLEGIO
(**WRESTLING —**) PALESTRA
SCHOOLBOOK COCKER
SCHOOLBOY SCUG PETTY
CLERGION
SCHOOL FOR SCANDAL (**AUTHOR
OF —**) SHERIDAN
(**CHARACTER IN —**) MARIA MOSES
PETER JOSEPH OLIVER ROWLEY
TEAZLE CANDOUR CHARLES
PREMIUM SURFACE
SNEERWELL
SCHOOLHOUSE PORTABLE
SCHOOLING LEARNING
SCHOOLMASTER BEAK CAJI CAXI
AKHUN KHOJA KHODJA MASTER
PEDANT AKHOOND DOMINIE
PEDAGOG ORBILIUS
SCHOOLROOM HOMEROOM
SCHOOL SHARK TOPE TOPER
SCHOOLWORK BOOKWORK
SCHOONER JACK TERN QUART
QUINT WUINT PUNGEY
BALLAHOO
SCHORL COCKLE
SCHRADAN OMPA
SCHROTHER SHREDDER
SCHUYT SHOE SCOUT EELBOAT
SCIATICA BONESHAW
SCIENCE ART OLOGY SOPHY
MATHESIS SCIENTIA
(— **OF ALGAE**) ALGOLOGY
(— **OF ANIMALS**) ZOOLOGY
(— **OF AQUEOUS VAPOR**)
ATMOLOGY
(— **OF ATOMS**) ATOMICS

(— OF BEING OR REALITY)
ONTOLOGY
(— OF BIOLOGICAL STATISTICS)
BIOMETRY
(— OF BREEDING) GENETICS
(— OF CAUSES) ETIOLOGY
(— OF CHARACTER) ETHOLOGY
(— OF CLASSIFICATION OF
DISEASES) NOSOLOGY
(— OF DOSES) DOSOLOGY
POSOLOGY
(— OF EARTH'S FORMATION)
GEOGONY
(— OF ELECTIONS) PSEPHOLOGY
(— OF EXCHANGE) CAMBISTRY
(— OF FERMENTATION) ZYMOLOGY
(— OF FERNS) PTERIDOLOGY
(— OF FORMS OF SPEECH)
GRAMMAR
(— OF FRUIT GROWING) POMOLOGY
(— OF FUNDS MANAGEMENT)
FINANCE
(— OF GEMS) GEMMARY
GEMOLOGY
(— OF GOD) DIVINITY
(— OF GOVERNMENT) POLITICS
(— OF HEALTH MAINTENANCE)
HYGIENE
(— OF HEAT) PYROLOGY
THERMOTICS
(— OF HISTORY OF EARTH)
GEOLOGY
(— OF HUMAN SETTLEMENTS)
EKISTICS
(— OF IDEAS) IDEOLOGY
(— OF INTELLECT) NOOLOGY
(— OF LAW) NOMOLOGY
(— OF LIFE) BIOLOGY
(— OF LIFE INFLUENCES) EUGENICS
(— OF LIFE OF TREES) SILVICS
(— OF LIGHT) OPTICS
(— OF MEASURING TIME)
HOROLOGY
(— OF MEDIEVAL CHEMISTRY)
ALCHEMY
(— OF MIDWIFERY) TOKOLOGY
(— OF MORAL DUTY) ETHICS
(— OF MOSSES) BRYOLOGY
(— OF MOUNTAINS) OROLOGY
(— OF MUSCLES) MYOLOGY
(— OF NUMBERS COMBINATIONS)
ALGEBRA
(— OF PERSUADING A GOD)
THEURGY
(— OF PLANTS) BOTANY
(— OF QUANTITY) POSOLOGY
(— OF RACIAL IMPROVEMENT)
EUGENICS
(— OF REASONING) LOGIC
(— OF RECORDING GENEALOGIES)
HERALDRY
(— OF REFRIGERATION) CRYOLOGY
(— OF REMEDIES) ACOLOGY
(— OF SERUMS) SEROLOGY
(— OF SMELLS) OSMICS
(— OF SOILS) PEDOLOGY
(— OF SOUND) PHONICS
ACOUSTICS
(— OF SPATIAL MAGNITUDES)
GEOMETRY
(— OF STRUCTURE OF ANIMALS)
ANATOMY
(— OF THE EAR) OTOLOGY

(— OF TIDES) TIDOLOGY
(— OF TOUCH DATA) HAPTICS
(— OF VALUES) AXIOLOGY
(— OF VERSIFICATION) PROSODY
(— OF VIRTUE) ARETAICS
(— OF WEIGHT OR GRAVITY)
BAROLOGY
(— OF WINES) ENOLOGY
OENOLOGY
(BRANCH OF —) BIONICS
(LEGAL —) LAW
(MILITARY —) STRATEGY
(NATURAL —) STINKS PHYSICS
(PHYSICAL —) PHILOSOPHY
(RELIGIOUS —) THEOLOGY
(SUFF.) LOGER LOGIA(N)
LOGIC(AL) LOGIST LOGUE LOGY
OLOGY SOPH(ER)(IC)(IST)(Y)
(RELATING TO —) METRIC
SCIENTIST BOFFIN
SCIMITAR SAX SEAX TURK
KHEPESH TULWAUR
SCINDAPSUS POTHOS
SCINTILLATE SNAP FLASH GLEAM
GLANCE GLITTER SPARKLE
TWINKLE
SCINTILLATION SPARKLE
SPARKLET
SCION IMP ROD CION CYON ROOT
SLIP GRAFT SPRIG BRANCH
SPROUT SARMENT SETLING
SCISSORS SHEARS CLIPPER
SECATEUR
(PREF.) FORFICI
SCLERITE TORMA LABIUM PLANTA
PLAGULA AXILLARY EPIMERON
SCLERODERMA MORPHEA
SCLEROPROTEIN SPONGIN
SCLEROTIUM ERGOT SCLEROTE
TUCKAHOE
SCOFF DOR GAB GALL GECK GIBE
GIRD JEER JIBE MOCK RAIL
CURSE FLEER FLOUT GLEEK
SCORN SCOUT SNEER TAUNT
DERIDE REPROVE RIDICULE
SCOFFER MOCKER ABDERITE
SCOLD JAW MAG MOB NAG RAG
ROW WIG YAP BAWL CALL CAMP
CANT DING FLAY FRAB FUSS
HAZE JACK JOBE JOWL JUMP
RAIL RANT RATE REDD RICK
SHAW SNAG SNUB TUCK YAFF
ABUSE BARGE BASTE BOAST
CHIDE DRESS FLIRT FLITE PRATE
RANDY SCALD SCORE SHORE
SHREW SLANG STORM TARGE
VIXEN BERATE BOUNCE CALLET
CAMPLE CARPET HAMMER
HOORAY HURRAH MAGPIE
RATTLE REHETE REVILE TATTER
THREAP TONGUE YAFFLE YANKIE
CHANNER REPROVE TRIMMER
TROUNCE UPBRAID BALLYRAG
BERATTLE BETONGUE CHASTISE
CIDESTER DINGDONG RIXATRIX
SCOLDING JAW HURL JESSE
SCOLD DIRDUM JAWING RAKING
RATTLE SISERA FLITING HEARING
LECTURE RAGGING WIGGING
BLESSING CARRITCH JOBATION
SCOLEX HEAD
SCOLYTUS IPS
SCONCE SWAPE APPLIQUE

SCONE FARL FARLE
SCOOP BAIL BALE DRAG ROUT
DIDLE GOUGE KEACH SHAUL
SKEET BUCKET DIPPER DISHER
SHOVEL WIMBLE SCRAPER
SCUPPET SKIMMER SKIPPET
SCOOPFUL
(— FOR CANNON) LADLE
(— FOR DAMPENING CANVAS)
SKEET
(— FOR GRAIN) WECHT
(— UP) LAP LAVE GATHER
(CHEESE —) PALE
(GLASSMAKING —) PADDLE
(JAI ALAI —) CHISTERA
(LONG-HANDLED —) DIDLE
(SURGICAL —) CURET CURETTE
SCOOT SCOUT SKEET SKYHOOT
SCOPE AIM AREA AMBIT POWER
RANGE REACH ROUND SCALE
SCOOP SWEEP VERGE SCOUTH
SPHERE TETHER BREADTH
CIRCUIT COMPASS OPERAND
PURVIEW CONFINES DIAPASON
LATITUDE
(— OF VISION) COMMAND
(FREE —) SWING
SCOPOLINE OSCIN OSCINE
SCORBUTUS SCURVY
SCORCH BURN CHAR PLOT SCAM
SEAR ADURE ADUST BROIL
PARCH PLAUT REESE SCALD
SCAUM SINGE SWEAL SWELT
BIRSLE BISHOP DEGREE SMITCH
SOTTER SPARCH SWINGE SWITHE
BLISTER BRISTLE FRIZZLE
SCORKLE SCOWDER SWITHEN
SWITHER TORRIFY FIREFANG
SCOUTHER SCOWTHER
SCORCHED ADUST LEEPIT
SCORCHER SIZZLER
(PREF.) SIRI(O)
SCORCHING BAKING FIRING
ADURENT SCALDING
SCORE ACE CUT LAW RIT RUN
CARD DEBT DROP GAME GOAL
HAIL HOLE MAKE MARK NICK
POST RIDE SLOG CHASE CORGE
COUNT EXTRA NOTCH OPERA
TALLY COOREE FURROW SAFETY
SCOTCH SCRIVE SPADES STRING
TARGET TICKET TWENTY
CONVERT SCORING SCRATCH
SQUEEZE GAMEBALL PARTITUR
PLACEKICK
(— FOR ALE) ALESHOT
(— HEAVILY AGAINST) SHELL
(— IN BRIDGE) BOARD BONUS
SWING
(— IN CRIBBAGE) GO PEG FIFTEEN
(— IN CRICKET) BLOB CENTURY
(— IN PIQUET) CAPOT
(— OF NOTHING) DUCK
(APTITUDE —) STANINE
(BASKETBALL —) HOOP
(BOWLING —) PINFALL
(GOLF —) DEUCE EAGLE BIRDIE
BUZZARD
(PINOCHLE —) LAST
(TENNIS —) CALL FIVE LOVE
DEUCE FORTY FIFTEEN
(THREE —) SHOCK
(TIE —) HALVE DEADLOCK

(PL.) MUSIC
SCORED SULCATE SULCATED
SCOREKEEPER SCORER TALLIER
TALLYMAN
SCORER NIB MARKER NOTCHER
SCORIA SCUM SLAG CINDER
SULLAGE
SCORIFIER CAPSULE
SCORIFY SMELT
SCORN GECK LOUT HOKER SCARN
SPURN BISMER SLIGHT CONTEMN
DESPISE DESPITE DISDAIN
CONTEMPT DERISION MISPRIZE
SCORNFUL SAUCY SCORNY SNIFFY
SNIFTY HAUGHTY FRUMPISH
INSOLENT SARDONIC
SCORNFULLY ASKEW ASWASH
SCORPION NEPA ALACRAN
STINGER UROPYGI ARACHNID
PEDIPALP WHIPTAIL
SCORPION FISH LAPON SERRAN
HOGFISH SCULPIN LORICATE
RASCACIO
SCORPION FLY PANORPID
SCOT (ALSO SEE SCOTSMAN) CELT
JOCK KELT SANDY SAXON
SCOTTY BLUECAP SCOTSMAN
(PL.) SAWNY SAWNEY LALLANS
SCOTCH TRIG SCOAT SCOTS
SCOTTISH
SCOTCHMAN MAC GAUL SANDY
TARTAN SCOTCHY SCOTTIE
SCOTSMAN
SCOTER COOT FILK DIVER SCOUT
WHILK BASQUE DUCKER SURFER
PISHAUG SCOOTER SKUNKTOP
SCOTIA MOUTH
SCOTIST DUNCE
SCOTLAND ALBYN ALBANY
ALBION SCOTIA ALBAINN
ALBANIA
(NORTHERN —) PICTLAND

SCOTLAND
BAY: SCAPA
CAPITAL: EDINBURGH
COIN: DEMY BODLE GROAT PLACK
RIDER BAWBEE
COUNTY: AYR BUTE FIFE ROSS
ANGUS BANFF MORAY NAIRN
PERTH ARGYLL LANARK
ORKNEY BERWICK KINROSS
PEEBLES RENFREW SELKIRK
WIGTOWN ABERDEEN
AYRSHIRE CROMARTY
DUMFRIES ROXBURGH
SHETLAND STERLING
FIRTH: LORN CLYDE FORTH
MORAY SOLWAY PENTLAND
ISLAND: RUM BUTE IONA JURA
MULL RHUM SKYE ARRAN
BARRA ISLAY LEWIS HARRIS
ORKNEY SHETLAND
ISLANDS: ORKNEY HEBRIDES
SHETLAND
LAKE: TAY NESS MORAR LAGGAN
LINNHE LOMOND KATRINE
RANNOCH
LANGUAGE: ERSE LALLAN
LALLAND
MEASURE: COP BOLL CRAN FALL
MILE PECK PINT ROOD ROPE
SPAN CRANE LIPPY FIRLOT

SCOTLAND:
AUCHLET CHALDER CHOPPIN MUTCHKIN STIMPART
MOUNTAIN: HOPE ATTOW DEARG NEVIS TINTO WYVIS CHEVIOT MACDHUI
NATIVE: GAEL PICT SCOT
ORDER: THISTLE
REGION: FIFE BORDERS GRAMPIAN
RESORT: OBAN
RIVER: AYR DEE DON ESK TAY DOON GLEN NITH NORN SPEY AFTON ANNAN CLYDE FORTH GARRY TWEED YTHAN AFFRIC TEVIOT TUMMEL DEVERON FINDHORN
SEAPORT: ALLOA LEITH DUNDEE ABERDEEN
TOWN: AYR DUNS OBAN WICK ALLOA BRORA CUPAR ELLON LEITH NAIRN PERTH SALEN TROON DUNDEE GIRVAN HAWICK DUNKELD GLASGOW PAISLEY ABERDEEN DUMFRIES GREENOCK KIRKWALL STIRLING
WATERFALL: GLOMACH
WEIGHT: BOLL DROP TRONE BUSHEL

SCOTSMAN SANDY SAWNY BLUECAP
SCOTTISH SCOTCH SCOTLAND
SCOTTISH TERRIER DIEHARD SCOTTIE VERMINER
SCOUNDREL RAP PIMP SCAB VILE WARY BLECK FILTH KNAVE SHREW SMAIK SWEEP THIEF WHAUP BRIBER LIMMER SLOVEN VARLET CATAIAN GLUTTON HALLION NITHING SCROYLE SKELLUM VILIACO VILLAIN WARLOCK BEZONIAN LIDDERON MASCHANT
SCOUNDRELLY VILLAIN
SCOUR ASH BEAT RAKE SCUM SEEK SIND SKIR SCOOR SCRUB SKIRR SWEEP DRENCH SCURRY SLUICE DEGRADE FURBISH BACKWASH STONEFILE (PL.) SKIT
SCOURER BLOOMER DOLLIER PICKLER
SCOURGE EEL TAW LASH CURSE FLAIL KNOUT SLASH SWING BALEYS PLAGUE SWINGE SCORPION
SCOURGER WHIPSTER
SCOURING BEAT SCOUR HUSHING SCRUBBING
SCOUT SPY BEAR LION SKIP ROVER SPIAL VISOR ESPIAL GAYCAT DESPISE MARINER PICKEER PIONEER SCOURER WATCHER EMISSARY OUTRIDER OUTSCOUT SCURRIER SKIRMISH (BOY —) CUB BOBCAT SCOUTER WEBELOS EXPLORER
SCOW ACCON FLOAT GARVEY
SCOWL LOUR FROWN GLARE GLOOM GLOUT LOWER SKIME GLOWER VENNER GLOOMING
SCOWLING FROWNY GLARING
SCRABBLE PAW RAKE GROPE CLAMBER SCRAMBLE

SCRAGGY WEEDY
SCRAM HOP LAM BUNK BUGGER BUGOFF BUZZOFF
SCRAMBLE MUSS SPURL SCRAWM SPRAWL CLAMBER LOUSTER SCRABBLE SCRAFFLE SCRATTLE SPRACHLE
SCRAP BIT END JAG ORT PIP CRAP ITEM JAGG JUNK PICK SNAP BRAWL GRAIN PATCH SCRAN SHRED THRUM WASTE DISCARD MAMMOCK REMNANT FRACTION SCRAPPET SKERRICK SNATTOCK (— FOR PATCHING) SPETCH (— OF PAPER) SCRIP (— OF SONG) CATCH (— OF WRITING) SCRAPE (FOOD —S) BROCK (LITERARY —S) ANA (RAGGED —) SCART (PL.) ORTS SCRAN RELICS SCROFF GARBAGE GUBBINGS
SCRAPE LEG RUB CLAW COMB RAZE CLAUT CURET ERADE ERODE GRATE GRAZE GRIDE SCALP SCART SCUFF SHAVE ABRADE HOBBLE RUGINE SCREED SCROOP CORRADE CURETTE JACKPOT SCRATCH SCRABBLE (— ALONG) HARL HARLE SHOOL (— GOLF CLUB ON GROUND) SCLAFF (— OFF) SPUD (— OUT) ERASE HOLLOW (— SKINS) MOON SCUD FLESH HARASS (— TOGETHER) RAKE GLEAN MUCKER SCAMBLE (— WITH FEET) SCAUT (PREF.) RAMENTI SCAPI
SCRAPED BRIGHT
SCRAPER PAN PIG HARL SLIP CURET GLOVE HARLE QUIRL RASER SPOON DOCTOR FRESNO GRADER GRATER RASPER CURETTE FLANGER LEVELER RACLOIR SLUSHER STRIGIL GRATTOIR SCRAPPLE TERRACER UNHAIRER
SCRAPING HARL GRIDE RASURE (CRACKER —S) CUSH (METAL —S) DIET (PL.) RAMENTA
SCRAPMAN CHIPMAN
SCRAPPER BREAKER FIGHTER
SCRAPPLE PANHAS PONHAWS
SCRAPPY BITTY SNATCHY
SCRATCH RAT RIT CLAW CRAB RACE RAIN RAKE RAPE RASE RAUK RAZE RISP RIST SHAB SLUG STUN CHALK CLAUT CLAWK CURRY FRUSH GRAZE RANCH SCART SCLUM SCORE SCRAB SCRAT SCROB SCRUB SHRUB SKELP TEASE TOUCH BRUISE CANCEL CRATCH RASURE RIPPLE SCORCH SCOTCH SCRAPE SCRAWK SCRAWL SINGER SCRAZE SCRIVE TORACE DECLARE EMERIZE EXPUNGE SCARIFY SCRABBLE SCRATTLE SCRIBBLE (— OUT MORTAR) POINT (PREF.) RAMENTI
SCRATCHER RASER

SCRAWL SCRAWM SPRAWL SCRATCH SCRABBLE SCRIBBLE SQUIGGLE
SCRAWNY BONY LEAN SLINK SCRANK SCRAGGY SCRANKY SCRANNY SCRAGGED (— PERSON OR ANIMAL) RIBE
SCREAM CRY YAW REME WEAK YARM YAUP YAWL YAWP YOWT SKIRL SHRAME SHRIEK SHRILL SQUALL SQUAWL YAMMER SCREECH YELLOCH SKELLOCH
SCREAMER CHAJA ANHIMA
SCREECH QUAWK QUOCK SCREAM SCREEK SCRITCH SKREIGH ULULATE SKELLOCH
SCREECH OWL STRICH
SCREED BLAUD TIRADE
SCREEN TRY CAGE GOBO HARP HIDE LAWN MASK PICK REJA SCUG SEPT SIFT TENT VEIL ARRAS BLIND CHEEK CHICK CLOAK CLOSE COVER FIGHT GAUZE GRATE HOARD SHADE SHOJI SIEVE SPEER SPIER TATTY BAFFLE BASKET BORDER CANVAS DEFEND ESCORT HALLAN MEDIUM PURDAH RESEAU SCHERM SCONCE SHAKER SHIELD SHROUD THREAD VOIDER CEILING CONCEAL CRIBBLE CURTAIN FLYWIRE GOGGLES GRIZZLY REREDOS SECLUDE SHELTER SHUTTER TESTUDO TROMMEL BACKSTOP BESCREEN BLINDAGE COVERING DIFFUSER ECLIPSER EXCLUDER HOARDING OCCULTER PARAVENT PARCLOSE PAVISADE SCREENER SPLASHER STRAINER TRAVERSE UMBRELLA (— ALONGSIDE SHIP) PAVISADE (— BEHIND ALTAR) REREDOS (— FOR BATTING PRACTICE) CAGE (— FOR SHIP'S COMBATANTS) FIGHT (— FOR SIZING ORE) GRATE TROMMEL (— FOR THEATER LIGHT) JELLY MEDIUM (— IN BASKETBALL) PICK (— OF BAMBOO SLIPS) CHEEK CHICK (— OF BRUSHWOOD) SCHERM (— OF FIRE) BARRAGE (— OF SHIELDS FOR TROOPS) TESTUDO (— OF TAPESTRY) ARRAS CEILING (— ON AUTOMOBILE) GRILL GRILLE (— TO PROTECT LOOKOUTS) DODGER (— USED BY ARCHERS) PANNIER (BULLETPROOF —) MANTA MANTEL MANTELET (CHANCEL —) JUBE (FIRE —) FENDER (MECHANICALLY ACTUATED —) GRIZZLY (PAPER —) SHOJI (PL.) CANCELLI
SCREENED BLIND SECLUDED
SCREENINGS CULM SLACK SLECK
SCREENPLAY SCENARIO
SCREW HOB VISE WORM CRICK

FEEZE SCROW WREST TEMPER TOGGLE COCHLEA AIRSCREW FLATHEAD SETSCREW THUMBKIN WINDMILL (KIND OF —) ALLEN MEANTIME (PART OF —) HEAD ROOT CREST PITCH POINT SHANK THREAD
SCREWBALL KOOK ZANY FLAKE ECCENTRIC NONSENSICAL
SCREW BEAN MESQUITE SCREWPOD TORNILLA
SCREWED SQUINCH
SCREWER WORMER
SCREWMAN JACKMAN
SCREW PINE IE ARA HALA IEIE AGGAG PALMA VACOA VACONA LAUHALA PANDANUS
SCREW TREE TWISTY
SCRIBBLE SQUIB DOODLE SCRAWL SCRATCH REMARQUE SCRABBLE SQUIGGLE
SCRIBE EZRA CLERK THOTH BOOKER PENMAN SCRIVE SOPHER WRITER GRAFFER MASORET SCRIVAN NOVERINT PENCLERK SCRIPTOR SCRIVANO (PL.) SOPHERIM
SCRIMMAGE MAUL BULLY ROUGE SCRAP BICKER SPLORE SKIRMISH
SCRIMP HINCH SCREW SKIMP
SCRIPT BOOK NEUM RONDE SERTA SERTO NASKHI NESKHI SCRITE SOOLOOS THULUTH BASTARDA GURMUKHI HIRAGANA KANARESE MAGHRIBI MAITHILI MEROITIC NASTALIQ SCENARIO
SCRIPTURE WRIT AGAMA CHING SUTRA SUTTA (HINDU —) VEDA (PL.) BIBLE GRANTH GRUNTH TANACH TENACH SHASTRA
SCRIVENER PENMAN WRITER GRAFFER SCRIVER NOVERINT TABELLION
SCROFULA EVIL CRUELS STRUMA
SCROLL BEND ROLL LABEL SCRIT AMULET ESCROL LEGEND SCRAWL STEMMA VOLUME VOLUTE EVOLUTE PAPYRUS RINCEAU BANDEROL CARTOUCH MAKIMONO
SCROLL-LIKE TURBINAL
SCROPHULARIA FIGWORT
SCROTUM BAG COD PURSE (PREF.) OSCHE(O) SCROT(I)(O)
SCROUNGER SCAMBLER
SCRUB FILE SCROG COPPET MAQUIS SCODGY CLEANSE SCRUBBER YANNIGAN
SCRUBBY SHRUBBY
SCRUBLAND GARIGUE GARRIGUE
SCRUFF CUFF NAPE SCUFF SCROFF
SCRUPLE PASS DEMUR DOUBT FORCE POINT QUALM STAND STICK BOGGLE SCOTCH STRAIN STICKLE STUMBLE
SCRUPULOUS NICE SPICED TENDER CAREFUL FINICKY PRECISE DELICATE QUALMISH
SCRUTINIZE PRY SEE SPY SCAN VIEW AUDIT PROBE SIGHT SOUND VISIT PERUSE SURVEY EXAMINE INSPECT ENSEARCH TRAVERSE

SCRUTINIZING NARROW
SCANNING
SCRUTINY EYE SEARCH CANVASS
EXAMINE HAWKEYE PERUSAL
DOCIMASY
SCRYER SEER
SCUD RACK RAMP SKID SKIM SKIP
SCOOT SPOON
SCUDAMORE (LOVER OF —)
AMORETTA
SCUDO FILIPPO
SCUFF SLARE SLIDE SCLAFF
SCUFFER SCUFFLE SHUFFLE
SCUFFLE CUFF BUSTLE CLINCH
CUFFLE TUSSLE WISTER BAGARRE
BRULYIE SHAMBLE SHUFFLE
SCRUFFLE
SCULL FUNNY SKULL
SCULLERY SINKROOM
SCULLION GIPPO SCULL SLUSH
GALOPIN SWILLER CUSTROUN
QUISTRON
SCULPIN COTTID GRUBBY JOHNNY
BIGHEAD DRUMMER BULLHEAD
BULLPOUT CABEZONE HARDHEAD
LORICATE SCALAWAG
SCULPTOR CARVER GRAVER
IMAGER MARBLER PLASTIC
AMERICAN FRY BALL HART IVES
KECK LADD MEAD RUSH TAFT
VOLK WARD ADAMS AKERS
BEACH BROWN CLARK DOYLE
EVANS GOULD HOXLE JONES
KELLY KONTI MEARS MILLS PERRY
PRATT STONE YOUNG AITKEN
BARTHE BITTER BUFANO CALDER
CLARKE COUPER CURTIS DALLIN
EAKINS EBERLE ELWELL FRASER
FRAZEE FRENCH GRAFLY GRIMES
HARVEY HOSMER HUGHES
KEMEYS KINNEY KITSON LAWRIE
MOZIER NEWMAN PALMER
POTTER POWERS PUTNAM
RIMMER ROGERS RUMSEY
WALKER WARNER ZORACH
BARNARD BISSELL BORGLUM
BRENNER BRIGHAM EDSTROM
EZEKIEL GELLERT GODDARD
GREGORY HANCOCK HARTLEY
HOFFMAN JACKSON JAEGERS
KENDALL LAESSLE LAURENT
LONGMAN LUKEMAN MACNEIL
MANSHIP MARTINY MILMORE
NIEHAUS NOGUCHI OCONNOR
PROCTOR ROBERTS SCHULER
SCUDDER SIEVERS SIMMONS
WHITNEY ALBRIGHT ATCHISON
BARTLETT BREWSTER CONNELLY
CRAWFORD DAVIDSON
FLANAGAN LACHAISE LENTELLI
MCCARTAN MULLIGAN
NADELMAN ODONOVAN
PARAMINO RINEHART CLEVENGER
GREENOUGH HUMPHREYS
MACDONALD REMINGTON
RUCKSTULL VALENTINE
ARCHIPENKO MACMONNIES
PICCIRILLI
ARGENTINIAN ALONZO
ATHENIAN ANTENOR
AUSTRIAN DONNER NATTER
TILGNER STRASSER
BELGIAN GEEFS FRAIKIN KESSELS

LALAING MEUNIER SIMONIS
STAPPEN LAMBEAUX
TONGERLOO
CANADIAN HEBERT MACCARTHY
CZECH STRUSA MYSLBEK
DANISH BISSEN JERICHAU
WILLUMSEN THORVALDSEN
DUTCH VRIES TASSAERT
DESJARDINS
ENGLISH BELL FORD GILL JOHN
SWAN WARD WOOD ANGEL
BACON BAILY BANKS BATES
BOEHM COLIN DURST JONES
MOORE RHIND STONE TWEED
WATTS ARCHER DOBSON GIBSON
JAGGER KENNET LANDAU
EPSTEIN FLAXMAN GIBBONS
GILBERT STEVENS WOOLNER
ARMSTEAD CHANTREY
FRAMPTON SHERIDAN
MACKENNAL KENNINGTON
WESTMACOTT THORNYCROFT
FLEMISH BOLOGNE
FRENCH ADAM ETEX RUDE UZES
BARYE BOSIO CHAPU CRAUK
DALOU DURET LEMOT PAJOU
PILON PUECH RODIN DANTAN
DEJOUX DUBOIS DUMONT
GOUJON HOUDON ISELIN LEGROS
MERCIE MILLET ROCHET ANGUIER
BEGUINE BOUCHER CARRIES
CHAUDET CLODION COLOMBE
COUSTOU DESPIAU FREMIET
LEMAIRE LEMOYNE MAILLET
MAILLOL PIGALLE PRADIER
PREAULT RICHIER CAFFIERI
CARPEAUX CAVELIER CHAPLAIN
COYSEVOX FALCONET FOYATIER
GIRARDON GODEBSKI JOUFFROY
LEPAUTRE SARRAZIN BARTHOLDI
BEAUNEVEU BOURDELLE
CLESINGER FALGUIERE INJALBERT
LANDOWSKI ROUBILLAC
BARTHOLOME CASSEGRAIN
CHARPENTIER DELAPLANCHE
GERMAN HAHN KISS LENZ NAHL
CAUER KOLBE KRAFT OESER
RAUCH STOSS STUCK WOLFF
BANDEL BLASER GEIGER HABICH
HAHNEL HALBIG HERTER HOSAUS
WAGNER AFINGER BARLACH
BELLING KAUPERT KLIMSCH
KLINGER KRELING SCHAPER
EBERHARD EBERLEIN FERNKORN
SCHLUTER ZUMBUSCH
DANNECKER ENGELHARD
MAGNUSSEN RIETSCHEL
SIEMERING UECHTRITZ
LEINBERGER SCHWANTHALER
RIEMENSCHNEIDER
GREEK MYRON CHARES ONATAS
SCOPAS AGASIAS BOETHUS
BRYAXIS CALAMIS CRITIUS
PHIDIAS SCYLLIS AGELADAS
CANACHUS CRESILAS DAMOPHON
LYSIPPUS PAEONIUS SOCIBIUS
AGESANDER ALCAMENES
ARCHERMUS BATHYCLES
EUPHRANOR LEOCHARES
PASITELES TAURISCUS
TIMOTHEUS POLYCLITUS
POLYEUCTUS PRAXITELES
AGORACRITUS ATHENODORUS

CALLIMACHUS LYSISTRATUS
CEPHISODOTUS
IRISH FOLEY MACDOWELL
FITZGERALD
ITALIAN VELA BANCO DANTI
DUPRE LEONI PORTA RIZZO VINCI
CANOVA GIOTTO PISANO ROBBIA
SOLARI ALGARDI BERNINI CELLINI
FIESOLE LAURANA MAZZONI
TRIBOLO AMMANATI ANTELAMI
BARBIERE BOCCIONI CAMPAGNA
CERACCHI CIVITALI LOMBARDO
MARCHESI TENERANI BARTOLINI
BEGARELLI BORROMINI
DONATELLO SANSOVINO
MODIGLIANI MONTEVERDE
VERROCCHIO MICHELANGELO
NORWEGIAN VIGELAND
ROMAN COSMATI
RUMANIAN BRANCUSI
RUSSIAN ORLOVSKI ANTOKOLSKI
SPANISH CANO MENA SILOE
PICASSO HERNANDEZ
BERRUGUETE
SWEDISH ZORN MILLES SERGEL
BYSTROM BORJESON FOGELBERG
SWISS HOERBST KISSLING
SCULPTURAL PLASTIC
SCULPTURE CAMEO DRAFT GRAVE
SCULP BRONZE ENTAIL GISANT
SCULPT CARVING DRAUGHT
ENGRAVE GRADINO IMAGERY
INSCULP STABILE MORTORIO
NATIVITY PORTRAIT PREDELLA
SCULLION
SCULPTURED GRAVEN GLYPHIC
SCUM BRAT FOAM GALL HEAD
REAM SCUD SILT SKIM SKIN
DROSS FROTH SCURF SLOAK
SLOKE SLUSH SPUME FLURRY
MANTLE MOTHER REFUSE
RIDDAM SCRUFF BLANKET
CACHAZA OFFSCUM LAITANCE
PELLICLE SANDIVER SCOURING
SCUMMING
SCUP BREAM PORGY SPARID
SCUPPAUG
SCURF SCALD SCALL DANDER
FURFUR SCRUFF DANDRUFF
SCURFY SCALD SCURVY LEPROSE
SCRUFFY LEPIDOTE SCABROUS
SCABERULOUS
SCURRILITY ABUSE REPROACH
SCURRILOUS LOW FOUL VILE
DIRTY GROSS RIBALD VULGAR
ABUSIVE SCURRIL INDECENT
SCURRY BELT CRAB SKIN CURRY
HURRY SCOUR SKICE SKURRY
SCUFFLE SCUTTER SCUTTLE
SKELTER SKITTER
SCURRYING SKITTER
SCURVY SCALD SCUMMY SHABBY
ROYNOUS SCORBUCH SCORBUTE
UNLIKING
SCUT BUN
SCUTAGE ESCUAGE
SCUTATE CLYPEATE
SCUTCH SCOTCH SWINGLE
SCUTE PLATE SCUTUM SCUTELLA
SCUTELLATION SCALING
SCUTIFORM PELTATE
SCUTTLE HOD CRAB SKEP BEETLE
MANHOLE SCUDDLE

SCUTTER SCRATTLE
SCUTTLEBUTT CASK RUMOR
GOSSIP FOUNTAIN
SCYLLA (FATHER OF —) NISUS
TYPHON
SCYLLITOL INOSITOL
SCYPHUS PYXIS
SCYTHE SY LEA HOOK MEAK
CRADLE
SCYTHIAN LAMB BAROMETZ
SEA ZEE BAHR BLUE BRIM FOAM
FRET GULF HOLM LAVE MAIN
RACE TIDE WAVE BRINE BRINY
FLOAT FLOOD LOUGH OCEAN
AEQUOR PONTUS SEALET
STRAND TETHYS CHANNEL
HYALINE NEPTUNE BOSPORUS
DEEPNESS SEAFLOOD
THALASSA
(— DIVINITY) TRITON
(— GOD) PROTEUS
(— LETTER) PASSPORT
(HEAVY —) POPPLE
(MODERATE —) SEAWAY
(PREF.) HAL(I)(IO)(O) MARI MER
PELAG(O) THALASS(I)(IO)(O)
THALATTO
SEA ANEMONE POLYP DAHLIA
OPELET ACTINIA VESTLET
ACTINIAN ZOANTHID
SEA BASS HANAHILL HUMPBACK
SERRANID TALLYWAG
SEA BEAR OTARIOID
SEABIRD HAGDON
SEA BISCUIT BREAD GALETTE
PANTILE
SEABOARD COAST
SEA BREAD HARDTACK
SEA BREAM TAI CARP CHAD
PORGY ROMAN BRAISE SARGUS
SPARID TARWHINE
SEA BUTTERFLY PTEROPOD
SEACOAST BANK SEABOARD
SEASHORE
SEA COW SIREN DUGONG
MANATEE RHYTINA SIRENIAN
SEA CUCUMBER BALATE
TREPANG CUCUMBER SYNAPTID
TEATFISH
SEADOG FOGBOW
SEA DRAGON PEGASID QUAVIVER
SEA DUCK DIVER EIDER DIPPER
DUCKER SCOTER
SEA EAGLE ERN ERNE PYGARG
PYGARGUS
SEA-EAR ABALONE
SEAFARER SEAGOER
SEA FOX THRASHER
SEA GIRDLE CUVY CUTWEED
SEA GULL COB GOR MEW COBB
ANNET COBBE POPELER
(AUTHOR OF —) CHEKHOV
(CHARACTER IN —) NINA IRINA
TRIGORIN CONSTANTIN
SEA-GYPSY SELUNG
SEA HOLLY ERYNGO ERYNGIUM
SEA KALE COLE
SEAL CAN FIX FOB GUM BULL
CHOP CORK HARP HOOD JARK
LUTE BLANK BULLA CLOSE EAGLE
PHOCA SIGIL STAMP SWILE
THONG UGRUG URSUK WAFER
ASSEAL BEATER CACHET COCKET

DOTARD ENSEAL ENSIGN FASTEN GASKET MAKLUK MATKAH OBSIGN PHOCID RANGER SEALCH SECURE SIGNET CONFIRM CONSIGN COWROID ENGLUTE HOODCAP IMPRESS QUITTER SADDLER SEALING SEALKIE SIGNARY WEDDELL ADHESIVE BACHELOR BEDLAMER BRELOQUE CYLINDER MANDORLA PINNIPED SECRETUM SEECATCH SIGILLUM SIGNACLE TANGFISH VALIDATE **(— FOR WATCH CHAIN)** ONION BRELOQUE
(— OFF) CAP
(— OVER CORK) CAPSULE
(BEARDED —) URSUK MAKLUK
(EARED —) OTARY
(FEMALE —) MATKA
(GOLD —) BEZEL
(HARBOR —) DOTARD RANGER TANGFISH
(HERD OF —S) PATCH
(IMMATURE —) BEDLAMER
(MALE —) WIG SADDLER BACHELOR SEECATCH
(NEWFOUNDLAND —) SWILE RANGER
(PAPAL —) BULL BULLA
(SHETLAND —) SILKIE
(YEARLING —) HOPPER
(YOUNG —) PUP BEATER JACKET BLUEBACK
(3-YEAR OLD —) TURNER
(PREF.) PHOC(O) SIGILLO
SEA LACE WHIPLASH
SEA LAVENDER INKROOT STATICE
SEALED CLOSE
SEALER CAPPER GASKET
SEA LETTUCE LAVER SLAKE SLOKE SEAWEED
SEA LILY CRINOID
SEALSKIN SKIN SCULP MATARA SAFARI
SEALSKIN COAT NETCHA
SEALYHAM TERRIER
SEAM DRY BAND DART FASH FELL PURL REND DEVIL PEARL SPILL FAGGOT INSEAM STREAK SUTURE SEAMLET JUNCTURE OVERSEAM
(— IN INGOT) SPILL
(— IN SHIP'S HULL) DEVIL
(— OF COAL) RIDER SPLIT STREAK
(IRREGULAR —) FASH
SEAMAN SALT JACKY MATLO ARTIST CALASH LUBBER SAILOR MARINER MASTMAN SHIPMAN SHIPPER SMASHER WAISTER YOUNKER DESERTER SEASONER
SEAMARK MEITH
SEAMED SEAMY RUGGED
SEA MILE NAUT
SEAMOUNT GUYOT
SEAMSTER TAILOR SEMPSTER
SEAMSTRESS SEAMER SEWSTER NEEDLEWOMAN
SEANCE SITTING
SEA NETTLE BLUBBER
SEA OF GRASS (AUTHOR OF —) RICHTER
(CHARACTER IN —) HAL JIM BRICE BROCK HENRY LUTIE SARAH JIMMIE BREWTON CAMERON

CHARLEY BREWSTER MCCURTIN CHAMBERLAIN
SEA ONION SCILLA
SEA OTTER KID KALAN
SEA OXEYE SALTWEED SAMPHIRE
SEA PINK THRIFT SABBATIA
SEAPLANE HYDRO AIRBOAT AEROBOAT
SEA PLANTAIN GIBBALS
SEA POACHER BULLHEAD
SEAPORT PARA PORT GROIN NATAL HARBOR ENTREPOT MACASSAR
SEA PUSS OFFSET
SEAR BURN FIRE SERE FLAME FRIZZ ENSEAR SCORCH SIZZLE FRIZZLE
SEA RAVEN SCULPIN
SEARCH FAN SPY BEAT COMB DRAG DRAW FAND FOND GAPE HUNT LAIT RAKE RIPE ROUT SEEK SIFT WAIT FRISK PROBE QUEST SNOOP VISIT DACKER DREDGE FERRET FUMBLE RANCEL SLEUTH ENQUIRE EXPLORE FOSSICK INQUEST INQUIRE INSPECT RANSACK SCRINGE ZETETIC FINECOMB OUTREACH SCRABBLE SCROUNGE SCRUTINY SHAKEDOWN
(— ABOUT) GRUB PROG GROPE
(— BY FEELING) GROPE
(— DEEPLY) TENT
(— EVERYWHERE) BUSK
(— FOR) FORK HUNT LAIT SNOOK REQUIRE
(— FOR FOX'S TRAIL) CIPHER
(— FOR GAME) DRAW GHOOM QUEST
(— FOR GOLD) FOSSICK
(— FOR KNOWLEDGE) OUTREACH
(— FOR PARTNER) CRUISE
(— FOR PROVISIONS) FORAGE
(— FOR SMUGGLED GOODS) DACKER JERQUE
(— FOR STOLEN GOODS) RANZEL
(— FOR WEAPONS) FRISK
(— GROPINGLY) GLAMP
(— INTO) EXQUIRE INDAGATE
(— OUT) FERRET INVENT ROOTLE EXQUIRE INDAGATE
(— SHIP) RUMMAGE
(— SYSTEMATICALLY) COMB
(— THROUGH) TURN
(— UNDERWATER) FISH
(SYSTEMATIC —) SWEEP
SEARCHER FINDER
SEARCHING HARD CLOSE SHREWD CURIOUS GROPING
SEARED ADUST
SEARING CAUTERY
SEA ROBIN GURNARD WINGFISH
SEA ROVER VIKING SCUMMER
SEASAN NUDE
SEASCAPE MARINE SEAPIECE
SEA SCORPION COBBLER
SEA SERPENT ELOPS
SEASHELL PROP
SEASHORE SEA RIPE CLEVE COAST PLAYA MARINE SEASIDE SEABEACH SEABOARD SEACOAST
SEASICKNESS HILO NAUPATHIA
SEA SNAIL LIPARIAN

SEA SNAKE CHITAL KERRIL
SEASON BEEK CORN DASH FALL PERT SALT SEEL TIDE TIME GRASS INURE SAUCE SAVOR SHEMU SPICE AUTUMN EASTER FLOWER HARDEN HAYING MASTER SPRING STEVEN STOUND SUMMER WINTER BUDTIME FLYTIME HARVEST KITCHEN OATSEED SEEDTIME
(— FOR HERRING FISHING) DRAVE
(— HIGHLY) DEVIL
(— IN THE SUN) HAZE
(— OF JOY) JUBILEE
(— OF MERRYMAKING) CARNIVAL
(CLOSED —) SHUTOFF
(DULL —) SLACK
(EGYPTIAN —) AHET PERT SHEMU
(HAYING —) HAYING HAYSEL
(LENTEN —) CAREME
(RAINLESS —) DRY
(RAINY —) KHARIF VARSHA
(REGULARLY RECURRING —) EMBER
(SPRING —) WARE APRIL GRASS
(THE RIGHT —) TID
SEASONABLE PAT TIDY TIMELY TIDEFUL TIMEFUL VETERAN TOWARDLY OPPORTUNE
SEASONABLY TIMELY APROPOS BETIMES
SEASONED SAGY SALT SALTED INDIENNE POWDERED
(MILDLY —) SWEET
SEASONER SURFACER
SEASONING SALT SPICE SEASON SPICING OREGANUM
SEA SPIDER PYCNOGONOID
SEA SQUIRT ASCIDIAN
SEA SWALLOW TERN
SEAT BOX CAN SEE SET BANK BOSS COSY DAIS FLOP FORM FROG ROOM SILL SLIP SUNK TOIT ASANA BENCH CELLE CHAIR DICKY PERCH SELLA SELLE SETTE SIEGE SLIDE STALL STOOL BOUGHT DODONA EXEDRA HUMPTY INSIDE RUMBLE SADDLE SEATER SEGGIO SETTEE SETTLE THWART BUTTOCK CUSHION GRADINE GRADINO INSTALL OTTOMAN SEATING TABORET TRANSOM BLEACHER ENTHRONE PULVINAR SEGGIOLA SUBSELLA WOOLPACK
(— AT PUBLIC SPECTACLE) PULVINAR
(— FOR CLERGY) SEDILE
(— FOR GRINDER) HORSING
(— FOR PLANE IRON) FROG
(— NEAR ALTAR) SEDILIUM
(— OF BIRTH) SIDE
(— OF CHAIR) BOTTOM
(— OF EMOTIONS) CHEST SPLEEN
(— OF FEELINGS) STOMACH
(— OF HARE) FORM
(— OF INTELLECT) HEAD
(— OF KNOWLEDGE) RUACH
(— OF ORACLE) DODONA
(— OF PITY) BOWEL
(— OF POWER) SEE
(— OF REAL LIFE) SOUL
(— OF RESPONSIBILITY) SHOULDER
(— OF RULE) OGDOAD

(— OF TURF) SUNK
(— OF UNDERSTANDING) SKULL
(— ON ELEPHANT'S BACK) TOWER CASTLE HOWDAH
(— ONESELF) LEAN PITCH
(— SLUNG ON POLES) HORSE
(— WITH BRAZIER BELOW) TENDOUR
(— WITHIN WINDOW OPENING) CAROL
(AIRPLANE —) DORMETTE
(BACKLESS —) STOOL HASSOCK
(BISHOP'S —) APSE BISHOPRIC
(CANOPIED —) COSY COZY
(CARRIAGE —) DICKY
(CHIMNEY —) SCONCE
(CHURCH —) PEW DESK STALL SEDILE
(COACH —) BOOT POOP
(COUNTRY —) TOWER GRANGE QUINTA
(DILIGENCE —) BANQUETTE
(DRAPED —) MUSNUD
(DRIVER'S —) BOX DICKY COCKPIT FORETOP
(ELEVATED —) PERCH
(FIXED —) DAIS
(GARDEN —) ALCOVE
(KEY —) KEYWAY
(LONG —) BANK FORM BENCH
(NIPPLE —) LUMP
(OARSMAN'S —) TAFT
(PORCH —) GLIDER
(RECLINING —) DORMEUSE
(ROWER'S —) THWART
(ROYAL —) SIEGE STEAD THRONE
(STAGECOACH —S) BASKET
(STRAW —) BOSS
(TIER OF —S) TENDIDO
(TURF —) BUNKER
(UNRESERVED —S) BLUES
(PREF.) EDRI(O)
(SUFF.) HEDRAL
SEA TANGLE FURBELOW
SEA TROUT SEWEN SMELT KIPPER HERLING HIRLING BODIERON
(— AFTER SPAWNING) KELT
(YOUNG —) PEAL
SEA TURTLE CHELONID
SEA URCHIN WANA REPKIE ARBACIA CIDARID ECHINID ECHINUS RADIATE
(FOSSIL —) ECHINITE
(PREF.) ECHIN(O)
SEAWALL BULWARK
SEAWARD OFF MAKAI
SEAWEED ORE AGAR ALGA KELP LIMU MOSS NORI OOZE REEK REIT TANG WARE DRIFT DULSE KOMBU LAVER SLAKE SLOKE VAREC VRAIC WRACK DELISK FUCOID FUNORI TANGLE HAITSAI OARWEED OREWEED OREWOOD REDWARE SEATANG SEAWARE CARAGEEN GULFWEED HEMPWEED ROCKWEED SARGASSO SEABEARD WHIPCORD WHIPLASH CORALLINE NULLIPORE
(PL.) LUMUT
(PREF.) PHYC(O)
(SUFF.) PHYCEAE
SEA WOLF (AUTHOR OF —) LONDON

(CHARACTER IN —) HUMP MAUD WOLF DEATH LEACH LOUIS LARSEN JOHNSON BREWSTER HUMPHREY JOHANSEN MUGRIDGE VANWEYDEN

SEB (CONSORT OF —) NUT
(SON OF —) OSIRIS

SEBA (FATHER OF —) CUSH

SEBASTIAN (BROTHER OF —) ALONSO
(SISTER OF —) VIOLA

SEBESTEN MYXA

SECANT SEC CHORD

SECCO FRESCO

SECEDE SPLINTER

SECESSIONIST SECESH SEPARATE

SECLUDE TACKLE ENCLOSE ISOLATE RECLUSE CLOISTER SEQUESTER

SECLUDED COY SHY DEEP CLOSE QUIET HIDDEN REMOTE SECRET PRIVATE RETIRED RETRAIT SECLUSE HIDEAWAY MONASTIC SEPARATE SOLITARY UMBRATIC CLAUSTRAL

SECLUSION RECESS SHADOW PRIVACY PRIVITY RETREAT SECRECY SEQUEST SOLITUDE
(— OF WOMEN) PURDAH

SECOND AID SEC ABET BACK BETA TICK OTHER VOUCH ASSIST LATTER MOMENT TARTAN TIDDER TOTHER ANOTHER INSTANT SUPPORT SUSTAIN STICKLER
(— BASE) KEYSTONE
(— IN COMMAND) DEPUTY
(— IN HORSE RACE) PLACE
(— PERSON USE) TUISM
(MAJOR —) TONE
(1000TH OF A —) SIGMA
(60TH OF A —) THIRD
(PREF.) DEUT(O) DEUTER(O) SECUNDI

SECONDARY BY BYE SUB SLACK DONKEY SECOND CUBITAL DERIVED INFERIOR MIDDLING
(PL.) FLAGS
(PREF.) DEUT(ER)(ERO)(O) MES(O)

SECONDHAND USED

SECOND MRS TANQUERAY
(AUTHOR OF —) PINERO
(CHARACTER IN —) RAY HUGH PAULA ARDALE AUBREY ELLEAN CORTELYOU TANQUERAY

SECOND-RATE COMMON SHODDY INFERIOR

SECOND-RATER PIKER

SECRECY DERN HUSH HIDING SECRET PRIVACY PRIVITY SILENCE DARKNESS HIDLINGS SCUGGERY VELATION

SECRET SLY DARK DERN INLY BLIND CABAL CLOSE PRIVY QUIET ARCANE CLOSET COVERT HIDDEN INWARD POCKET STOLEN ARCANUM COUNSEL CRYPTIC EPOPTIC FURTIVE MYSTERY PRIVACY PRIVATE PRIVITY RECLUSE RESERVE RETIRED SECRETA UNKNOWN ESOTERIC HIDLINGS MYSTICAL SNEAKING STEALTHY

(PREF.) CRYPT(O) KRYPT(O) SUB

SECRETARY CLERK COPPY BARUCH MUNSHI RAPTOR SCRIBE FAMULUS MUNCHEE MOONSHEE

SECRETE HIDE CACHE NICHE RESET SECERN SECRET CONCEAL SECLUDE SALIVATE SEPARATE
(— MILK) LACTATE
(— ONESELF) HIVE
(— SALIVA) DROOL
(PREF.) ECCRINO

SECRETION INK LAC GOWL LAAP LERP MILT SPIT WOOL HUMOR LAARP MUCUS SEPIA SLIME SPADE CEMENT SALIVA SMEGMA CERUMEN CHALONE FLOCOON HORMONE SPITTLE AUTACOID ENDOCRIN
(THICKENED —) GUM
(WAXY —) LERP LAARP PRUINA

SECRETIVE SLY CAGY DARK SNUG CAGEY CLOSE COVERT SECRET SILENT INVOLVED

SECRETIVENESS SECRECY SLYNESS

SECRETLY CLOSE DARKLY DERNLY SECRET CLOSELY HIDLINGS INWARDLY

SECRET, THE (CHARACTER IN —) ROSE KALINA SKRIVANEK
(COMPOSER OF —) SMETANA

SECT SET ZEN BABI CLAN CULT JODO KIND SHIN ALOGI BHORA ISAWA PANTH BOHORA DONMEH HERESY SCHISM SCHOOL CATHARI DHUNDIA DOCETAE HASIDIM ISAWIYA KHALSAH RINGATU SECTARY SEQUELA SHAIKHI SHINGON SIVAISM SUBSECT AGNOETAE AHMADIYA AISSAOUA MURJIITE NAASSENE SECTUARY SHAKTISM BUCHANITES
(MEMBER OF —) KHLYST OPHITE YEZIDI MOLOKAN NUSAIRI LINGAYAT

SECTARIAN CULTIST HERETIC MAZHABI SECTARY SECTIST

SECTARY JESUIT HERETIC SECTIST SECTUARY SEPARATE

SECTION CUT END AREA PACE PART SECT UNIT CAPUT FRUST PIECE SHARE TMEMA BILLET BRANCH BRIDGE CANTON LENGTH MEMBER PASSUS SECTOR ARTICLE CUTTING HEADING SEGMENT TRANCHE ADDENDUM DIVISION FRACTION
(— AROUND HOP KILN) CURB
(— OF A BODY) LAMINA
(— OF AVICENNA'S WORK) FEN
(— OF BLOOM) STAMP
(— OF BUILDING) ENTRY
(— OF FENCE) FLAKE
(— OF FILM) EXPOSURE
(— OF FILTER) LEAF
(— OF FISHING TACKLE) TRACE
(— OF GARMENT) GORE
(— OF GLASS) SHAWL
(— OF HIGH GROUND) DIVIDE
(— OF KORAN) SURA
(— OF LADDER) FLY
(— OF LOG) BOLT FLITCH

(— OF LOOM) LAY
(— OF NET) DEEPING
(— OF NEWSPAPER) LEAD
(— OF PARLIAMENT) LAGTHING
(— OF PSALTER) CATHISMA
(— OF RHAPSODY) LASSU
(— OF ROOF) SEVERY
(— OF ROOTSTOCK) BIT
(— OF SHIP) STEERAGE
(— OF SONG) STOLLEN
(— OF THREE SHEETS) TERNION
(— OF TORAH) PARASHAH
(— OF TRENCH) BAY
(— OF VIOLIN) BOUT
(— OF WOOD) HAG
(— OF YARN) SLUB
(—S OF SCENERY) BOOK
(CONCLUDING —) ABGESANG
(CONIC —) PARABOLA
(DULL —) LONGUEUR
(LOWEST —) BOTTOM
(MINE —) BORASQUE BORRASCA
(MUSICAL —) CODA EPILOG FINALE
(NARROW —) STRIPE
(NATIVE —) KASBA CASBAH
(ONE-SIXTEENTH OF —) FORTY
(PERCUSSION —) BATTERY
(4-PAGE —) OUTSERT
(SUFF.) TOMA TOME TOMIC TOMOUS TOMY

SECTIONALISM LOCALISM

SECTOR AREA GORE HOUSE

SECULAR LAIC CIVIL COMMON EARTHLY PROFANE WORLDLY TEMPORAL

SECURE FID GET GIB KEY POT RUG SEW WIN BAIL BOLT BOND CAUK COCK COLD EASY FAST FIND FIRM FRAP GAIN GIRD HOOK LAND MOOR NAIL SAFE SEAL SHOT SNUG STAY SURE WARM BELAY BLOCK CINCH CLEAT SLOUR SOUND STRAP TIGHT TRUST ANCHOR ASSURE BECKET BUTTON CLINCH DEFEND ENSURE FASTEN OBTAIN PLEDGE SETTLE SICCAR SICKER STABLE STAPLE TRAIST ACQUIRE BULWARK CONFINE DUNNAGE FORFEND FORTIFY RAMPIRE WARRANT GARRISON PRESERVE
(— A SAIL) TRICE
(— AGAINST INTRUSION) TILE
(— AID OF) ENLIST
(— BAIT) EBB
(— FROM LEAKING) COFFER
(— WITH BARS) GRATE

SECURED BOUND SETTLED

SECURELY FAST SAFE SICCAR SICKER STRAIT SURELY SOLIDLY SOUNDLY

SECURITY PUP BAIL BAND EASE GAGE SEAL WAGE FRITH GRITH GUARD QUIET STOCK BORROW CEDULA EQUITY PLEDGE REFUGE SAFETY SCREEN SEVERE SURETY VADIUM BULWARK CAUTION CUSTODY DEFENSE DEPOSIT FLOATER HOSTAGE SHELTER SLEEPER WARRANT COLONIAL COVENANT FASTNESS GUARANTY HYPOTHEC STRENGTH VADIMONY MUNICIPAL

(BELOW AVERAGE —) LAGGARD
(PL.) PERCENTS PORTFOLIO

SEDAN SEDIA JAMPAN SALOON TONJON NORIMON TOMJOHN BROUGHAM

SEDATE CALM COOL DOUCE QUIET SOBER STAID SERENE EARNEST SERIOUS SETTLED COMPOSED DECOROUS

SEDATENESS SOBRIETY

SEDATIVE AMYTAL ACONITE CALMANT CODEINE LUPULIN BARBITAL LENITIVE QUIETIVE SOOTHING

SEDENTARY STILL SESSILE INACTIVE

SEDGE SAG LING RAIT REIT STAR CAREX CHUFA TIKUG BHABAR EHUAWA GLUMAL THATCH TOETOE TOITOI BULRUSH MONOCOT PAPYRUS SNIDDLE TUSSOCK GALANGAL JIMSEDGE
(PREF.) CARIC(O)

SEDGE FLY GRANAM GRANNOM

SEDGE WARBLER WREN MOCKBIRD REEDBIRD

SEDGY SAGGY SEGGY TWILLED

SEDIMENT CARR DREG FAEX FOOT GOBI LEES MULM SILT WARP DRAST DREGS FECES FOOTS MAGMA BOTTOM FECULA SIMMON SLUDGE DREWITE GROUNDS GRUMMEL SAPROPEL SETTLING
(— OF BEER OR ALE) CRAP
(IRON —) CAR CARR
(REDDISH —) SIMMON

SEDITION REVOLT TREASON

SEDITIOUS RIOTOUS FACTIOUS MUTINOUS

SEDUCE DRAW JAPE LOCK DECOY TEMPT WRONG ALLURE BETRAY ENTICE DEBAUCH ENSNARE MISLEAD SUGGEST TRADUCE INVEIGLE
(— WITH THE EYE) LEER

SEDUCER UNDOER LOTHARIO

SEDUCTION LURE BRIBE CHARM

SEDUCTIVE TEMPTING

SEDULOUS BUSY INTENT STUDIED DILIGENT UNTIRING

SEDULOUSNESS INDUSTRY

SEDUM MOSS ORPINE SENGREEN

SEE LO EYE KEN SPY VID ESPY LOOK MIND NOTE PIPE SEAT SEGE SPOT VIDE VIEW BESEE CATCH CHAIR SIEGE SIGHT STOOL TENEZ WATCH ATTEND BEHOLD DESCRY NOTICE QUAERE REMARK SURVEY ARCHSEE DISCERN GLIMPSE OBSERVE WITNESS CATHEDRA CONCEIVE PERCEIVE
(— ABOVE) VS
(— BELOW) VI
(— FIT) CHOOSE
(— INTO) INSEE PENETRATE
(— THROUGH) RUMBLE
(— TO) FIX
(— VISIONS) SCRY

SEED BEN MAW NIB PIP BEAN BOIL CHAT CORN DIKA GERM KOLA LIMA MOTE SETH TARE BEHEN BERRY CACAO CARAT CARVY

GRAIN LUPIN SEMEN SPAWN
SPERM SPORE STONE ABILLA
ACHENE ACINUS BONDUC
CACOON CARNEL FENNEL KERNEL
LEGUME LENTIL NICKER NUTLET
PIGNON PIPPIN TILLEY ACHIOTE
ACHUETE ALPISTE ANISEED
BUCKEYE CALINUT FRIJOLE
HARICOT HAYSEED SEEDKIN
SEEDLET SEMINAL AMBRETTE
COKERNUT CYDONIUM DILLSEED
FLAXSEED FLEASEED HEMPSEED
PIGNOLIA PRINCIPE SEEDLING
SEEDNESS PISTACHIO
PROPAGULE
(AROMATIC —S) ANISE
(COLE —) COLZA
(EDIBLE —) PEA BEAN
(FENUGREEK —) HELBEH
(GRAPE —) ACINUS
(IMMATURE —) OVULE
(MUSTARD —) SENVY SINEWY
(NUTLIKE —) PEANUT
(OILY —) ARGAN ABILLA
(PALM —) COROZO
(POPPY —) MAW MOHNSEED
(SESAME —) JINJILI GINGELLY
(PL.) ANISE COFFEE SESAME
ZERAIM IGNATIA LARKSPUR
(PREF.) COCC(O) GON(O) OVULI
SEMINI SEMINULI
SPERM(A)(ATI)(ATIO)(ATO)(I)(IO)(O)
SPOR(I)(IDI)(O)(ULI)
(BEAK-LIKE —) RYNCO
(SUFF.) COCCAL COCCIC
SPERM(A)(AE)(AL)(IA)(IC)(OUS)
(UM)(Y) SPORA SPORANGE
SPORANGIATE SPORANGIUM
SPORE SPORIC SPORIDIA
SPORIUM SPOROUS SPORY
SEEDCAKE WIG WIGG
SEEDCASE TEST TESTA THECA
SEED COAT TESTA SPIRICLE
SEEDED ARABLE
SEEDER SEEDMAN
SEEDLING FREE LINER
SEEDS
(PREF.) GRANI
SEEDY MANGY SCUFFY
SEEING SIGHT SIGHTED
(— THAT) SITH SINCE
SEEK ASK BEG SIC WOO BUSK
FAND FEEL FISH FOND FORK
HUNT LAIT LOOK SICK SIFT
COURT DELVE ESSAY FETCH
SCOUR APPETE BOTTOM FERRET
FOLLOW FRAIST PURSUE SEARCH
FORSEEK INQUIRE RANSACK
REQUIRE RUMMAGE SOLICIT
ENDEAVOR
(— AFTER) SUE SUIT ENSUE
EXPLORE
(— AIMLESSLY) PROG
(— FAVOR) WISH
(— FOR) APPETE EXPLORE
(— IN MARRIAGE) WOO PRETEND
(— OUT) COMD ENGEARCH
(— TO ATTAIN) ASPIRE
(— URGENTLY) PRESS
SEEKER TRACER PETITOR ZETETIC
SEARCHER
(— AFTER FACTS) GRADGRIND
(— OF KNOWLEDGE) PHILONIST

(JOB —) CHANCER
(PLEASURE —) FRANION
SEEKING SOKE SOKEN ZETETIC
(SUFF.) PETAL
SEEM BID EYE SEE FARE LOOK
PEER SOUND APPEAR BESEEM
REGARD
(— TO BE) LIKE
(IT —S) SEMBLE
SEEMING GUISE QUASI LIKELY
SEEMLY APPARENT SEMBLANT
(PREF.) QUASI
SEEMINGLY QUASI SEEMLY
SEEMING
SEEMLINESS GRACE DECENCY
DECORUM
SEEMLY FIT TALL CIVIL COMELY
DECENT LIKELY MODEST
BECOMING DECOROUS GRACEFUL
SEEP LEAK OOZE SIPE EXUDE
PERCOLATE
SEEPAGE SEEP SIPAGE SPRING
SEEPY WEEPY
SEER SIR SWAMI MOPSUS SCRYER
PROPHET CHALDEAN MELAMPUS
SEERBAND TURBAN
SEERESS SAGA SIBYL VOLVA
ALRUNE ALBRUNA PHOIBAD
SEESAW PUMP TILT DANDLE
TEETER TIDDLE TILTER TITTER
TOTTER
SEETHE FRY JUG BOIL CREE ITCH
STEW WALL WALM BULLER
HOTTER SIMMER BLUBBER
ELIXATE FERMENT
SEETHING ASEETHE BOILING
HUMMING ITCHING SCALDING
SEGMENT CUT LAP FALL HAND
LITH MERE PART BLANK CHORD
ELITE FEMUR FURCA SHARE SLICE
TMEMA CANTLE GLOSSA LENGTH
SAMPLE SYZYGY ARTICLE DIGITUS
EXERGUE FESTOON ISOMERE
MYOMERE MYOTOME SECTION
SETIGER ANTIMERE BRACHIUM
COLUMNAL DACTYLUS DIVISION
GONOTOME HYPOMERE INTERVAL
MESOMERE METAMERE
MYOCOMMA NARICORN
(— OF CASK) CANT
(— OF CAULIFLOWER) FLOWERET
(— OF CIRCLE) SECTION
(— OF COMMUNITY) FACIES
(— OF EARTH'S CRUST) GRABEN
(— OF FIBER) BAND
(— OF IRIS) FALL
(— OF LEAF) LACINIA
(— OF MAXILLA) STIPES SUBGALEA
(— OF RATTLESNAKE'S RATTLE)
BUTTON
(— OF SPEECH) DOMAIN
(HERALDIC —) FLANCH FLANCHE
(INSTRUCTIONAL —) LESSON
(MERE —) SNAPSHOT
(PEASANT —) HERA
(SUFF.) TMEMA TMESIS
(— OF) ITE
SEGMENTAL MERISTIC
SEGMENTATION CLEAVAGE
(SUFF.) TOMA TOME TOMIC
TOMOUS TOMY
SEGMENTED INSECTED
SEGNO SIGN

SEGREGATE SHED SEVER INTERN
ISOLATE CLASSIFY INSULATE
SEPARATE
SEGUB (FATHER OF —) HIEL HEZRON
SEIGNORAGE ROYALTY
SEIGNORY LORDSHIP
SEINE NET FARE TUCK TRAIN
POCKET SAGENE SPILLER
MADRAGUE
SEISIN VESTURE
SEIZE BAG CAP CLY GET HAP NAB
NAP BEAK BONE CLAW CLUM
FANG GALL GLOM GRAB GRIP
GRUP HAND HENT HOOK JUMP
KEEP LEVY NAIL RAMP SMUG
SNAP SPAN TAKE TIRE YOKE
CATCH CESSE CLASP CLEEK CLICK
CRIMP DRIVE GRASP GRIPE
LATCH PINCH RAVEN RAVIN
REACH REAVE SNACK ARREST
ASSUME ATTACH CLUTCH
COLLAR EXTEND FASTEN FREEZE
GOBBLE NOBBLE QUARRY SECURE
SNATCH ASSEIZE CAPTURE
ENCLASP ENCLOSE FORHENT
GRABBLE GRAPPLE IMPOUND
POSSESS PREEMPT PREHEND
SCAMBLE SWALLOW ARROGATE
COMPRISE DISTRAIN SPUILZIE
SURPRISE UNDERNIM
(— AND HOLD FIRMLY) TRUSS
(— BAIT) STRIKE
(— BY NECK) SCRAG COLLAR
SCRUFF
(— PREY) CHOP
(— SUDDENLY) NAB NIP SWOOP
SNATCH
(— UPON) ATTACK INFECT
(— WITH CLAWS) STRAIN
(— WITH TEETH) BITE
(— WITH WHOLE HAND) GLAUM
(— WITHOUT RIGHT) USURP
SEIZIN SASINE VESTURE
SEIZING FANG GRIP MARQUE
CAPTION SEIZURE
SEIZURE PIT BITE HOLD GRIPE
ICTUS SPELL ARREST EXTENT
PRISAL RAPTUS TAKING ANGARIA
CAPTION CONCEIT TELLACH
DISTRESS STOPPAGE
(SUFF.) LEPSIA LEPSIS LEPSY
LEPT(IC)
SELDOM RARE SELD RARELY
UNOFTEN
SELDOM-SEEN ANTRIN ANTERIN
SELECT ORT TAP TRY CULL PICK
SIFT SORT TAKE WALE DRAFT
ELECT ELITE PITCH TRIED ASSIGN
BALLOT CHOICE CHOOSE CLUBBY
DECIDE DESUME EXEMPT PREFER
SAMPLE SINGLE WINNOW
DRAUGHT EXCERPT EXTRACT
OUTLOOK EXIMIOUS HANDPICK
SELECTED
(— BY LOT) DRAW
(— BY PATTERN) SWATCH
(— JURY) STRIKE
SELECTED DRAFT ELECT FANCY
DRAUGHT
SELECTING DRAFT GARBLING
SELECTION BLAD CHAP CULL ITEM
PICK CHOICE CHOOSE EXCERPT
EXTRACT ELECTION

HAFTARAH PERICOPE
(— OF PSALMS) HALLEL
(VERSE —) BLAUD SINGSONG
(SUFF.) ECLEXIS
SELECTIVE CHOOSY ECLECTIC
SELED (FATHER OF —) NADAB
SELENIDE ZORGITE
SELF EGO SEL SEN JIVA SELL SOUL
DAENA NATURE PERSON PSYCHE
(INNER —) ANIMA
(OWN —) AINSELL NAINSEL
(SUPREME UNIVERSAL —) ATTA
ATMAN
(PREF.) AUT(O) AUTH(I) EGO
SELF-ACCUSATION GUILT
SELF-ACTING
(PREF.) AUT(O) AUTOMAT(O)
SELF-AGGRANDIZING IMPERIAL
SELF-ASSERTIVE BRASH PERKY
CHESTY BLUSTERY BUMPTIOUS
SELF-ASSURANCE CHEEK APLOMB
COOLNESS
SELF-ASSURED CALM PERKY
CONFIDENT
SELF-CENTERED SELFISH
SELF-CENTEREDNESS EGOTISM
SELFHOOD
SELF-COMMAND NERVE TEMPER
SELF-CONCEIT NOSISM
SELF-CONCEITED COXY PENSY
COCKSY PENCEY
SELF-CONFIDENCE CREST HUBRIS
HUTZPA CHUTZPA HUTZPAH
JOLLITY OPINION CHUTZPAH
SELF-CONFIDENT FLUSH CHESTY
SELF-CONSCIOUS GAWKY
BASHFUL
SELF-CONTAINED ABSOLUTE
SELF-CONTAINMENT CLOSURE
SELF-CONTRADICTORY ABSURD
SELF-CONTROL STAY WILL
ENCRATY MODESTY RETENUE
PATIENCE
(LOSE —) FLIP
SELF-DECEPTION FLATTERY
SELF-DEFENSE (ART OF —) KUNGFU
(ART OF-) AIKIDO
SELF-DENIAL DENIAL
SELF-DENYING ASCETIC
SELF-DESTRUCTION SUICIDE
SELF-DESTRUCTIVE SUICIDAL
SELF-DETERMINATION FREEDOM
AUTONOMY
SELF-DISCIPLINE ASCESIS
SELF-ENRICHMENT GROWTH
SELF-ESTEEM EGO PRIDE CONCEIT
SELFNESS
SELF-EVIDENT MANIFEST
SELF-EXALTATION NOSISM
ELATION
SELF-EXISTENT BEER INCREATE
UNCAUSED
SELF-FERTILIZATION AUTOGAMY
SELF-FULFILLMENT FREEDOM
SAMADHI
SELF-GENERATION AUTOGENY
SELF-GLORIFICATION VANITY
SELF-GOVERNMENT SWARAJ
SELF-HEAL ALLHEAL HOOKHEAL
HOOKWEED BLUECURLS
SELFHOOD SEITY EGOITY IPSEITY
OWNHOOD PROPRIUM SELFNESS
SELF-IDENTITY IPSEITY

SELF-IMPORTANT COXY PURDY CHESTY COCKSY BIGGETY POMPOUS BUMPTIOUS

SELF-INDULGENCE NICETY PLEASURE

SELF-INDULGENT WANTON

SELFISH PIGGISH SELFFUL DISSOCIAL

SELFISHNESS EGO SELF EGOTISM SUICISM PHILAUTY SELFHOOD SELFNESS —

(MORBID —) PLEONEXIA

SELF-LOVE CONCEIT PHILAUTY

SELF-ORIGINATION ASEITY

SELF-POLLUTION ONANISM

SELF-POSSESSED COOL ASSURED COMPOSED TOGETHER

SELF-POSSESSION COOL PHLEG POISE APLOMB COOLNESS SANGFROID

SELF-PRODUCED (PREF.) IDIO

SELF-REALIZATION FREEDOM ENERGISM

SELF-RELIANT BOLD FREE

SELF-REPROACH GUILT REGRET

SELF-RESTRAINT HO HOO ASCESIS CONTROL RESERVE RETENUE HAVLAGAH

SELF-RIGHTEOUS STUFFY

SELF-SACRIFICING HEROIC GALLANT

SELFSAME SAME VERY SELFSAID IDENTICAL

SELFSAMENESS IDENTITY

SELF-SATISFIED SMUG STODGY ASSURED

SELF-SERVICE (SUFF.) TERIA

SELF-SUFFICIENCY ASEITY ASEITAS AUTARKY AUTARCHY

SELF-SUFFICIENT ABSOLUTE

SELF-TAUGHT PRIMITIVE

SELF-WILLED SET SENSUAL STUBBLE WAYWARD CONTRARY PERVERSE

SELION BUTT

SELL DO GIVE VEND CHEAP PITCH SHAVE TRADE UTTER AFFORD BARTER MARKET AUCTION BARGAIN

(— A HORSE) CHANT

(— AT LOW PRICE) DUMP

(— BELOW COST) FOOTBALL

(— BY AUCTION) CANT ROUP

(— DRUGS ILLEGALLY) PUSH

(— FOR) BRING FETCH

(— IN SMALL QUANTITIES) RETAIL

(BUY AND —) CHOP

SELLER BOOMER BUSKER CADGER VENDOR CHANTER FLESHER CHANDLER

(WINE —) ABKAR

SELLING (SPECULATIVE —) AGIOTAGE

SELSYN SYNCHRO

SELVAGE EDGE LIST ROON GOUGE FORREL LISTING STICKING

SEMACHIAH (FATHER OF —) SHEMAIAH

SEMANTEME RHEME

SEMANTICS SEMOLOGY

SEMAPHORE FISHTAIL

SEMBLANCE FACE IDOL SHOW SIGN COLOR GHOST GLOSS GUISE IMAGE SCHEME VISAGE PRETEXT SEEMING UMBRAGE LIKENESS SEMBLANT SKERRICK SIMULACRUM

(— OF DIGNITY) FACE

(— OF REALITY) DREAM

(FALSE —) COLORING

SEME SEMY GUTTY HURTY FLEURY GOUTTE GUTTEE BEZANTE

SEME-DE-LIS FLORETTY

SEMEI (SON OF —) MATTATHIAS

SEMELE (BROTHER OF —) POLYDORUS

(FATHER OF —) CADMUS

(MOTHER OF —) HARMONIA

(SISTER OF —) INO AGAVE AUTONOE

(SON OF —) BACCHUS

SEMEN SEED SPERM

(PREF.) GON(O)

SPERM(A)(ATI)(ATIO)(ATO)(I)(IO)(O)

(SUFF.) SPERM(A)(AE)(AL)(IA)(IC)(OUS)(UM)(Y)

SEMESTER HALF

SEMIDARKNESS DUSK

SEMIDIAMETER RADIUS

SEMIDOME CONCHA

SEMIFLUID SOFT HUMOR

SEMIGLOSS EGGSHELL

SEMILIQUID SLAB

SEMINARY YESHIVA JUVENATE

SEMIOPAQUE HORNY

SEMIPORCELAIN GOMBROON

SEMIRAMIDE (CHARACTER IN —) ASSUR ARSACE SEMIRAMIS

(COMPOSER OF —) ROSSINI

SEMIRAMIS (HUSBAND OF —) NINUS

(MOTHER OF —) DERCETO

SEMITE JEW ARAB HARARI SYRIAN SEMITIC SHEMITE ARAMAEAN ASSYRIAN CHALDEAN

SEMITIC JEWISH

(— LANGUAGE) GAFAT

SEMITONE FEINT LIMMA DEMITONE HEMITONE

SEMOLINA SUJI SEMOLA

SENAPO (DAUGHTER OF —) CLORINDA

SENATE BOULE SENATO COUNCIL SENATUS GEROUSIA SENATORY

(— AND PEOPLE OF ROME) SPQR

(— DIVISION) PRYTANY

SENATOR SOLON CONSUL FATHER LAWMAKER

(PL.) ANZIANI

SENATORSHIP TOGA

SEND MIT FAST PACK SHIP ENVOY SCEND THROW RENDER ADDRESS CHANNEL COMMAND CONSIGN DELIVER FORWARD DISPATCH TRANSMIT

(— ABOUT) TROLL

(— ALOFT) CROSS

(— AWAY) MAND SHIP AMAND BANISH DISBAND DISMISS RELEGATE

(— BACK) ECHO TURN WISE REMIT REMAND REMISE RENVOY RESEND RETURN REFRACT

(— BY MAIL) DROP

(— DOWN) DEMIT DIMIT STRIKE

(— FOR) SUMMON

(— FORTH) BEAM BEAR CAST EMIT MAND DIMIT FLING EFFUSE OUTSEND

(— FORTH IN RAYS) RADIATE

(— IN) IMMIT IMMISS INTROMIT

(— MESSAGE) BLINKER

(— OFF) WING

(— OFF UNCEREMONIOUSLY) SHANK

(— OFFICIALLY) ISSUE

(— OUT) BEAM EMIT AMAND SHOOT SPEED DEDUCE DEPORT LAUNCH DIFFUSE EXPEDITE

(— TO JAIL) LAG MITTIMUS

(— TO PERDITION) CONFOUND

(SUFF.) MISE MISS MIT

SENDING SAND

(— OUT) EMISSIVE

SENEGAL

CAPITAL: DAKAR

MOUNTAIN: GOUNOU

NATIVE: PEUL SOCE DIOLA FOULA LAOBE SERER WOLOF FULANI SERERE BAMBARA MALINKE TUKULER MANDINGO

RIVER: FALEME GAMBIA SALOUM SENEGAL CASAMANCE

TOWN: BAKEL LOUGA MATAM THIES DAGANA KAOLACK RUFISQUE

SENILE DOLD DOTARD

SENILITY DOTAGE CADUCITY PROGERIA

SENIOR AINE DEAN SIRE DOYEN ELDER ANCIENT SUPERIOR

SENIORITY AGE ANCIENTY SIGNEURY

SENNACHERIB (FATHER OF —) SARGON

(SON OF —) ESARHADDON

SENNET SPET SIGNET

SENOR DON

SENORITA MISS SRTA SRITA

SENSATION FEEL ITCH SOUR SENSE TABET TASTE TIBBIT VEDANA FEELING ESTHESIS

(— OF COLD) RHIGOSIS

(— OF FRIGHT) FRISSON

(— OF HEAT) HOTNESS

(— OF PAIN) ALGESIS

(ANTICIPATORY —) FOREFEEL

(BURNING —) ARDOR

(DARTING —) SHOOT

(STRONG —) CREEP

(SUBJECTIVE —) AURA

(TASTE —) GUST BITTER

(TINGLING —) DIRL

(VIBRATING —) FREMITUS

(VISUAL —) PHOSE PHOTOMA

(PREF.) AESTHESIO ESTHESIO

SENSATIONAL GORY BOFFO LURID YELLOW SAFFRON SPLASHY TABLOID THRILLY STUNNING MELODRAMATIC

SENSATIONALISM BLARE SENSISM

SENSE WIT FEEL SALT SMELL LETTER MATTER REASON SCONCE WISDOM FEELING HEARING MARBLES MEANING SMEDDUM

CARRIAGE GUMPTION JUDGMENT

(— OF APPREHENSION) ANXIETY

(— OF HEARING) EAR

(— OF HUMOR) MUSIC

(— OF ONENESS) KINSHIP

(— OF OUTRAGE) SHOCK

(— OF PANIC) JITTERS

(— OF RIGHT) GRACE

(— OF SIGHT) VISION

(— OF SMELL) SCENT

(— OF SUPERIORITY) EGOTISM

(— OF TOUCH) FEEL TASTE

(— ON ONE'S WORTH) PRIDE

(— THE MEANING OF) READ

(COMMON —) NOUS SALT BALANCE GUMPTION

(DISCRIMINATING —) FLAIR

(LACKING —) INEPT

(PLAIN —) ENGLISH

(SOUND —) MATTER

SENSE AND SENSIBILITY (AUTHOR OF —) AUSTEN

(CHARACTER IN —) JOHN LUCY EDWARD ELINOR STEELE BRANDON FERRARS MARIANNE WILLOUGHBY

SENSE-DATUM SENSUM

SENSELESS MAD COLD DUMB SILLY FRIGID STUPID UNWISE WANTON FOOLISH IDIOTIC PEEVISH SOTTISH UNIDEAED POINTLESS REASONLESS

SENSIBILITY HEART SENSE FEELING DELICACY ESTHESIA JUDGMENT

(PL.) FEELINGS

SENSIBLE SANE WISE AWARE PRIVY WITTY ACTUAL FEELABLE MATERIAL PASSIBLE RATIONAL SENSICAL SENTIENT WISELIKE PERCEPTIBLE

SENSITIVE FINE KEEN SORE ALIVE MIFFY QUICK KITTLY LIABLE NIMBLE TENDER TETCHY FEELING NERVOUS PRICKLY ALLERGIC DELICATE EROGENIC SENSIBLE SENTIENT SKINLESS TOUCHOUS

(— TO PAIN) TART

(NERVOUSLY —) TOUCHY

(TOO —) OVERSTRUNG

SENSITIVENESS SENSE TOUCH ALGESIA DELICACY

SENSITIVE PEA HONEYCUP

SENSITIVE PLANT MIMOSA

SENSITIVITY FLESH DELICACY FINENESS

SENSITIZER CYANINE

SENSORY SENSUAL AFFERENT

SENSUAL LEWD BRUTE MUDDY CARNAL FLESHY SULTRY WANTON BEASTLY BESTIAL BRUTISH FLESHLY LESBIAN SWINISH PANDEMIC SENSUOUS

SENSUALITY FLESH LIKING LUXURY

SENSUOUS SOFT LYDIAN SATINY SENSAL FLESHLY SENSUAL LUSCIOUS SENSIBLE

SENTENCE BAN DIT RAP SAW DAMN DOOM TIME AWARD FUTWA JUISE TENER TROPE ARREST ASSIZE COMMIT DECREE DEPORT JUWISE REASON

ADJUDGE CENSURE CONDEMN
FLOATER IMPRESA LAGGING
FOREDOOM JUDGMENT VERSICLE
PALINDROME
(— CONTAINING ALL LETTERS)
PANGRAM
(— CONTAINING EACH LETTER)
PANGRAM
(— INDICATING CHARACTER)
MOTTO
(CONCISE —S) LACONICS
(IMPRISONMENT —) LAG RAP LIFE
LAGGING STRETCH
(MUSICAL —) PERIOD
(SHORT —) CLAUSE
(WITTY —) ATTICISM
SENTENTIOUS CONCISE LACONIC
SENTIENCE SENSE
SENTIENT AWARE FEELING
SENSILE SENSIVE SENSEFUL
SENSIBLE
SENTIMENT MIND POSY ETHNOS
GENIUS HOBNOB NOTION PLEDGE
FEELING OPINION
(EXCESSIVE —) SCHWARMEREI
(FALSE —) FALSETTO
(SLOPPY —) DRIP
SENTIMENTAL SLAB SOFT CORNY
GOOEY GUSHY MUSHY SAPPY
SOBBY SOPPY SOUPY FRUITY
SLUSHY SPOONY SUGARY SYRUPY
INSIPID MAUDLIN MAWKISH
ROMANTIC SCHMALZY SNIVELLY
MOONSTRUCK NOVELETTISH
SENTIMENTALISM BATHOS
SCHMALZ SCHMALTZ
SENTIMENTALIST SOFTHEAD
SENTIMENTALITY GOO HAM
MUSH BLURB SIRUP SYRUP
BATHOS
SENTIMENTAL TOMMY (AUTHOR
OF —) BARRIE
(CHARACTER IN —) JEAN AARON
LOTTA NYLES TOMMY GRIZEL
ELSPETH
SENTINEL WAIT DEINO GUARD
WATCH BANTAY PICKET SENTRY
WARDEN PICQUET COCKATOO
PEPHEDRO WATCHMAN
(MOUNTED —) VEDET VEDETTE
(PL.) GRAEAE GRAIAE
SENTINEL BOX STATION
WATCHCASE
SENTRY KITE WATCH SENTINEL
SEPAL ALA LEAF HELMET LEAFLET
SEPARATE CUT TOM COMB CULL
CURD DEAL FALL FRAY FREE
HAZE PART REDD SERE SIFT SORT
TEAR TWIN ASIDE BLEED BREAK
CALVE ELONG FENCE FLAKE
HEDGE PARTY SCALE SEVER
SIEVE SKILL SPLIT TWAIN TWIST
ABDUCT ABRUPT ASSORT AVULSE
BISECT CLEAVE DECIDE DEPART
DETACH DIGEST DIVIDE DIVISI
FILTER PROPER REMOTE SCREEN
SECERN SECRET SEJOIN SETTLE
SINGLE SOLUTE SPREAD SUNDER
SUNDRY SWATCH UNLUTE
WINNOW ABSCISE ABSCISS
BRACKET CONCERN DIALYZE
DISALLY DISCERP DISJOIN
DISLINK DISPAIR DISPART

DIVERSE EXPANSE FISSION
ISOLATE SCATTER SCIOLTO
SECTION SEJUNCT SEVERAL
SWINGLE ABSTRACT BULKHEAD
DETACHED DIFFRACT DISCRETE
DISJOINT DISSEVER DISSOLVE
DISTINCT DISTRACT DISUNITE
DIVIDANT DIVIDUAL FRACTION
LAMINATE LEVIGATE LIBERATE
PECULIAR SEVERATE SPORADIC
UNMINGLE UNSOLDER UNSTRING
RESPECTIVE
(— BY BEATING) SCUTCH
(— BY CROSSWALL) ABJOINT
(— BY PICKING) LEASE LEAZE
(— COINS) JOURNEY
(— COMBATANTS) STICKLE
(— COPIES) DECOLLATE
(— FIBERS) HACKLE
(— FROM HERD) IMPRIME
(— GRAIN FROM CHAFF) FAN CAVE
WINNOW
(— HAIR) BLOCK
(— INTO COMPONENTS) STRIP
(— INTO FLOCKS) DRAFT DRAUGHT
(— INTO SHREDS) TEASE
(— ONESELF) ABDICATE
(— ORE) JIG SMELT DILLUE
(— SHEEP) DRAW
(— THREADS) SLEY SLEAVE
(PREF.) APH APO CHORI(ST)(STO)
ECCRINO IDIO
SEPARATED FREE ALONE BROKEN
DISTANT DIVIDED ABSTRACT
ISOLATED RESOLVED
(— BY INTERVAL) OPEN
(PREF.) CHORI(ST)(STO) DIALY
SEPARATELY APART SINGLY
SUNDRY ASUNDER DIVISIM
SEVERAL SUNDERLY ABSOLUTELY
SEPARATING BETWEEN
SEPARATION GAP GULF PART
RENT SHED BREAK CHASM SPLIT
SCHISM BARRIER DIVORCE
ELUTION PARTING ANALYSIS
AUTOTOMY AVULSION CREAMING
DECISION DIALYSIS DISTANCE
DISUNION DIVISION INCISION
SHEDDING SOLUTION TWINNING
SEQUESTER
(— OF LEAF) CHORISIS
(— OF MAN AND WIFE) ZIHAR
DIVORCE
(— OF METALS) DEPART
(— OF PIGMENT) FLOATING
(— OF WORD PARTS) TMESIS
(— OF YEAST IN BEER) BREAK
(PREF.) DE
SEPARATIST ZOARITE BIMMELER
SEPARATOR RAVEL PARTER
CREAMER SETTLER SEVERER
SUBSIDER
SEPARATRIX SLASH DIAGONAL
SEPHESTIA (FATHER OF —)
DAMOCLES
(HUSBAND OF —) MAXIMUS
(LOVER OF —) MENAPHON
(SON OF —) PLEUSIDIPPUS
SEPIA COCONUT SEPIARY
SEPOY PANDY TELINGA
SEPT KIN
SEPTEMBER 29 MICHAELMAS
SEPTET SEPTUOR

SEPTIC PURULENT
SEPTIOLITE MEERSCHAUM
SEPTIVALENT HEPTAD
SEPTUAGINT LXX
SEPTUM VITTA TABULA MYOTOME
PHRAGMA MYOCOMMA
SEPULCHER BIER GRAVE TITLE
CENOTAPH MONUMENT
MORTUARY
SEPULCHRAL HOLLOW CHARNEL
TUMULARY
SEPULTURE BURIAL
SEQUEL SUITE EFFECT SEQUENT
BACKWASH SEQUENCE
SEQUENCE ROPE SUIT TRACT
TRAIN DOCKET ENTAIL SEQUEL
SERIES STRING CADENCE
CORONET SEQUENT SUCCESS
SPECTRUM STRAIGHT
(— IN MELODY) AGOGE
(— OF BEHAVIOR) ACT
(— OF BILLIARD SHOTS) BREAK
(— OF CARDS) QUART TENACE
STRINGER
(— OF CHESS MOVES) DEFENCE
DEFENSE
(— OF EVENTS) CYCLE SCENARIO
(— OF MELODRAMA) CHASE
(— OF ROCK UNITS) SECTION
(— OF SOUNDS) AFFIX
(ACTING —) EXTERIOR
(CUSTOMARY —) COURSE
(FILM —) INTERCUT
(LITURGICAL —) CANON
SEQUENT ENSUANT SEQUITUR
SEQUESTER SINGLE ISOLATE
RECLUDE
SEQUESTERED LONELY PRIVATE
RECLUSE RETIRED SECLUDED
SOLITARY
SEQUIN CHICK SPANG VENTIN
ZEQUIN CHEQUIN CHEQUEEN
VENETIAN ZECCHINO
(PL.) GLITTER
SERAGLIO HAREM SERAI ZENANA
SERAH (FATHER OF —) ASHER
SERAIAH (BROTHER OF —) BARUCH
OTHNIEL
(FATHER OF —) KENAZ NERIAH
HILKIAH TANHUMETH
SERAPHIC ANGELIC BEATIFIC
SERBOCROATIAN ILLYRIAN
SERE SEAR SERULE UNGREEN
HALOSERE
SERED (FATHER OF —) ZEBULUN
SERENADE AUBADE HORNING
ALBORADA NOCTURNE SERENATA
(MOCK —) SHIVAREE
SERENADER WAIT
SERENE CALM EVEN CLEAR LITHE
SEDATE SMOOTH HALCYON
DECOROUS
SERENITY CALM PEACE REPOSE
SERF BOND THEW CHURL HELOT
SLAVE THEOW THETE PENEST
SERVUS THRALL BONDMAN
COLONUS PEASANT ADSCRIPT
PRAEDIAL YANACONA
SERFDOM BONDAGE HELOTRY
SERFAGE SERVAGE HELOTISM
SERFHOOD SERFSHIP
SERGE SAY SAGATHY
SERGEANT TOP SARGE CHIAUS

DESKMAN SERVANT TOPKICK
HAVILDAR SERIAUNT
SERGEANT-AT-LAW COUNTOR
COUNTOUR
SERGEANT FISH LING CABIO
COBIA SNOOK BONITO CUBBYYEW
SERGEANT MAJOR PINTANO
SERIAL SEQUENTIAL
SERIALLY SERIATIM
SERIEMA CARIAMA GRUIFORM
SCREAMER
SERIES RUN SET ECCA RANK SUIT
TIRE CHAIN DRIFT DWYKA ORDER
SUITE TALLY TRACE COURSE
EOCENE SEQUEL STRING SYSTEM
BATTERY CASCADE CATALOG
BEADROLL SEQUENCE
PROGRESSION
(— GATHERED TOGETHER) SORITES
(— OF ABSTRACTS) SYLLABUS
(— OF ARCHES) ARCADE
(— OF BALLET TURNS) CHAINE
(— OF BOAT RACES) REGATTA
(— OF CELLS) FILAMENT
(— OF CHARACTERS) CLINE
(— OF CHESS MOVES) COOK
(— OF CLASHES) CLATTER
(— OF COMMUNITIES) SERE
(— OF DANCE MOVEMENTS)
ADAGIO
(— OF DRAIN TILES) FIELD
(— OF EVENTS) EPOS ACTION
(— OF EXTRACTS) CATENA
(— OF FORTIFICATIONS) CEINTURE
(— OF IMAGES) DREAM
(— OF LEGENDS) SAGA
(— OF LIPS) GILL
(— OF MASSES) TRENTAL
(— OF MEETINGS) SESSION
(— OF METAL DISKS) PILE
(— OF MILITARY OPERATIONS)
CAMPAIGN
(— OF MOVEMENTS) DANCE
(— OF NEIGHBORING LOTS) COTE
(— OF NOTES) GAMUT GLISSADE
(— OF PASSES) FAENA
(— OF PILES) DRIFT
(— OF POEMS) DIVAN DIWAN
(— OF PRAYERS) COURSE SYNAPTE
(— OF RACES) CIRCUIT
(— OF REASONS) ARGUMENT
(— OF RINGS) COIL GIMMAL
(— OF ROOMS) SWEEP
(— OF SHOTS) BURST
(— OF SIMILAR STRUCTURES)
STROBILA
(— OF SLALOM GATES) FLUSH
(— OF SLIPS) DOCK
(— OF SOILS) CECIL
(— OF STAIRS) FLIGHT
(— OF STAMPS) SET
(— OF STITCHES) STAY
(— OF STRAPS) LADDER
(— OF STRATA) KAROO
(— OF TANKS) SOAPER
(— OF THREADS) BINDER STUFFER
(— OF TONES) SCALE
(— OF TRAVELS) ODYSSEY
(— OF VERSES) ANTIPHON
(— OF WORDS) ACROSTIC
ALPHABET
(CARD —) CORONET
(CONNECTED —) CATENA

(CONSECUTIVE —) STREAK
(DANCE —) DOUBLE
(GEOLOGICAL —) ECCA LIAS
DWYKA KENAI EOCENE MOLASSE
KEEWATIN
(IMPRESSIVE —) ARRAY
(RADIOACTIVE —) FAMILY
(PREF.) HIRMO
SERIOUS RUM SAD DEEP HIGH
ACUTE GRAVE HEAVY SOBER
SOLID STAID DEMURE SEDATE
SEVERE SOLEMN SOMBER
SOMBRE SULLEN AUSTERE
CAPITAL EARNEST SERIOSO
WEIGHTY GRIEVOUS
(PREF.) SERIO
SERIOUSLY BAD ILL DOWN SADLY
DEEPLY GRAVELY SOLIDLY
SERIOUSNESS EARNEST GRAVITY
SADNESS SOBRIETY
SERMON SPELL HOMILY POSTIL
ADDRESS FUNERAL KHUTBAH
SEREMENT SERMONET
PREACHMENT
SERMONIZING MORALITY
SEROPURULENT SANIOUS
SEROUS ICHOROUS
SEROW THAR JAGLA SERAU
SERPENT (ALSO SEE SNAKE) AHI
SEPS WORM ABOMA ADDER
APEPI ATHER OPHIS SIREN SNAKE
TRAIN CHITAL DIPSAS DRAGON
GERARD HYDRUS PYTHON
APOPHIS PRESTER SCYTALE
JARARACA OPHIDIAN
(— WORSHIPER) NAASSENE
(FEATHERED —) GUCUMATZ
KUKÜLKAN
(HERALDIC —) REMORA
(NORSE —) GOIN
(SACRED —) AVANYU AWANYU
(SKY —) AHI
(PREF.) COLUBRI OPHI(O) SERPU
VIPERI
(SUFF.) OPHIS
SERPENTINE SNAKY SPIRY OPHITE
SNAKISH BOWENITE METAXITE
SCROLLED MARMOLITE
SERPENT STAR OPHIURAN
SERRANO PERCOID GITANEMUK
SERRATE SAWED ARGUTE RAFFLE
NOTCHED SERRIED
SERRATION SERRA DENTILE
SERUG (FATHER OF —) REU
SERUM WHEY FLUID BIOLOGIC
(PREF.) ORO ORRHO SERO
SERVANT BOY FAG KID MAN PUG
TAG AMAH BATA COOK DASI
DAVY HELP HIND JACK LUCE
MATY MOZO ALILA BAGOT BOOTS
BOULT DAVUS GILLY GROOM
HAMAL MAMMY SEWER SLAVE
SOSIA SPEED USHER ABDIEL
ANDREW BATMAN BEARER
BILDAR BUTLER CHAKAR CLASHY
DORINE EWERER FEEDER FERASH
FLUNKY GILLIE GRUMIO HAIDUK
HARLOT KHAMAL MENIAL
PAMELA SIRCAR SKIVVY SLAVEY
TEABOY TEAGUE TRANIO VARLET
VASSAL VOIDER ANCILLA
BOOTBOY BOUCHAL COURIER
DUFTERY FAMULUS FEODARY

FERRASH FLUNKEY FOOTMAN
GENERAL GHILLIE MALCHUS
PANDOUR PANTLER PAPELON
PIQUEUR PISANIO WASHPOT
ASSIGNEE CHAPRASI CROMWELL
DOMESTIC FOLLOWER GRASSCUT
HENCHMAN HOUSEBOY
MANCIPLE MINISTER OUTRIDER
PANTHINO PHILOTUS PINDARUS
SERGEANT SERVITOR STANDARD
TRENCHER VADELECT WARDMAID
KITCHENER OBSERVANT
(— IN CHARGE OF BREAD) PANTLER
(— IN CHARGE OF DAIRY) DEY
(— IN OFFICE) DUFTERY
(— OF SCHOLAR OR MAGICIAN)
FAMULUS
(— WHO CARVES) TRENCHER
(— WHO CLEARS TABLE) VOIDER
(— WHO RUNS BEFORE CARRIAGE)
PIQUEUR
(— WHO SERVES TABLE) SEWER
(ARMED —) PANDOUR
(ARMY —) BATMAN LASCAR
(BENGAL —) MEHTAR SIRCAR
(BODY —) VALET SIRDAR
(BOY —) BOY KNAVE CHOKRA
BOUCHAL
(CAMP —) BILDAR
(CLOWNISH —) SPEED LAUNCE
(COLLEGE —) GYP SKIP SCOUT
(FEMALE —) AMA NAN AMAH DASI
GIRL LASS MAID MAMMY NURSE
WENCH PAMELA SKIVVY ANCILLA
HANDMAID MUCHACHA
WARDMAID
(GENERAL —) FACTOTUM
(HEAD —) BUTLER TINDAL
(HIGH PRIEST'S —) MALCHUS
(HINDU —) DAS DASI
(HOUSE —) COOK HEWE SEWER
DOMESTIC MATRANEE SCULLION
(KITCHEN —) COOK WASHPOT
(LORD OR KING'S —) THANE
(LYING —) FAG
(MAID —) NAN BONNE
(MAN —) BOY JACK MOZO SWAIN
VALET ANDREW GILLIE KNIGHT
GHILLIE KHANSAMA MUCHACHO
SERVITOR
(MISCHIEVOUS —) TEAGUE
(NON-RESIDENT —) DAILY
(PETULANT —) DORINE
(PHILIPPINE —) BATA ALILA
(SCOTTISH —) JURR
(SOLDIER'S —) PAGE
(TRUSTY —) TROUT
(PL.) FOLK VOLK STAFF FAMILIA
NETHINIM
SERVE DO KA ACT AID HOP GIVE
HELP LEAP SHEW SLAP STAY
TEND TOSS WAIT COVER FRAME
HORSE SARRA STAND ANSWER
ASSIST FRIEND INTEND SAIRVE
SARROW SETTLE SPREAD SUCCOR
ADVANCE ASSERVE BESTEAD
CONVENT FORWARD FURTHER
SERVICE FUNCTION
(— A DISH) MESS
(— AS ESCORT) SQUIRE
(— AS HOST) GIVE
(— AS SUBSTITUTE) PASS
(— AS WELL AS) AVAIL

(— DRINK) SKINK
(— FOOD) HASH KITCHEN
(— FOR PASTURE) GRAZE
(— OBSEQUIOUSLY) LACKEY
LACQUEY
(SUFF.) (— FOR) ORY
SERVER SALVER ACOLYTE
MINISTER
SERVICE AID FEE CENS DUTY HELP
RITE TIDE YOKE FAVOR MUSAF
STEAD DEVOIR EMPLOY ERRAND
FACTOR OFFICE YIZKOR BENEFIT
BONDAGE CHAKARI CORNAGE
FUNERAL LITURGY OBSEQUY
RETINUE SERVAGE SERVING
BREEDING EQUIPAGE FUNCTION
HEADWARD KINDNESS MINISTRY
ROUNDING TENDANCE SERVITIUM
(ASSIGNED —) MYSTERY
(BODYGUARD —) INWARD
(BREAKFAST —) DEJEUNER
(CHORAL —) MATIN
(CHURCH —) LAUDS CHAPEL
CHURCH HEARING STATION
SYNAXIS ASPERGES EVENSONG
(COFFEE —) CABARET
(COMPULSORY —) ANGARIA
(DOMESTIC —) CHAKARI
(FEUDAL —) BOON AVERA
ARRIAGE CORNAGE SEAWARD
HEADWARD
(MILITARY —) ARMS CAMP DUTY
ESCUAGE
(MILITIA —) COMMANDO
(RELIGIOUS —) AHA SEDER
COMMON
(SECRET —) OGPU
(TENNIS —) ACE LET
SERVICEABLE USEFUL DURABLE
THRIFTY FRIENDLY VAILABLE
SERVICEBERRY SHADBLOW
SHADBUSH SASKATOON
SERVICE TREE SORB SORBUS
CHECKER SASKATOON
SERVILE BASE BOND ABJECT
MENIAL SUPINE VASSAL CAITIFF
SLAVISH VERNILE COISTREL
CRAWLING CRINGING SERVIENT
THEWLIKE
SERVILITY CRINGE
SERVING OBED SMACK DISHFUL
HELPING SERVIENT WHIPPING
(SUFF.) ATORY
(— FOR) ORIOUS ORY
SERVITOR FAG GROOM PUNTER
SERVANT PUNTSMAN
SERVITUDE USE VIA YOKE
BONDAGE SERVICE SLAVERY
SERVITUS THEOWDOM THIRLAGE
SERVOMECHANISM SERVO
BOOSTER
SERVOMOTOR RELAY SERVO
SESAME TIL TEEL BENNE BENNI
SEMSEM VANGLO GINGILI
OILSEED WANGALA AJONJOLI
BENISEED SERGELIM
SESBANIA AGATI
SESQUITERPENE CEDROL
CLOVENE COPAENE HUMULENE
SESSION DAY BOUT DIET HOUR
SEAT COURT CLINIC SCHOOL
SEANCE ACUERDO HEARING
SEMINAR SITTING CONGRESS

SEDERUNT SEMESTER
(COURT —) HILARY
(JAM —) CLAMBAKE
(PL.) ASSIZES
(SUFF.) FEST
SESTERTIUS BRONZE
SESTINA SEXTAIN
SET DO DIP FIX GEL KIT LAY LOT
MOB PUT SIC SIT SOT CASE CREW
CUBE GAGE GANG GIVE JELL KNIT
KNOT NEST PAIR PICK PILT POSE
REST SETT SORT STEP STOW
BATCH CLASS CLOCK COVEY
CROWD FIXED GAUGE GLADE
GROUP INFIX PAVER PLACE POSIT
STACK STAID STAND STEAD
STEEK STICK SUITE ADJUST
CIRCLE CLIQUE DEFINE FASTEN
FINALE FORMAL GLAZED GROUND
HARDEN IMPOSE PARCEL SERIES
SETTLE SPREAD SQUARE STATED
BATTERY BOILING COMPANY
COMPOSE CONFIRM COTERIE
DEPOSIT DISPOSE ENCHASE
FACTION IMPLANT INSTATE
PLATOON SERVICE STATION
STIFFEN STRATUM EQUIPAGE
PANTALON SEQUENCE SOLIDIFY
STANDARD
(— A PERIOD) DATE
(— A PRICE) ASK
(— ABOUT) FALL FANG GANG
BEGIN ADDRESS
(— AFLOAT) LAUNCH
(— APART) MARK SHED DESIGN
DEVOTE EXEMPT SACRED SEPONE
SEPOSE APPOINT ISOLATE
RESERVE ALLOCATE DEDICATE
INSULATE SEPARATE SEQUESTER
(— ARROWS IN ORDER) FRUSH
(— AS ONE'S SHARE) ALLOT
(— ASIDE) BAR DISH DROP HAIN
SIDE SINK SLIP BURKE KAPUT
SEPOSE BRACKET EARMARK
PURLOIN RESERVE SUSPEND
ABROGATE DISPENSE OVERRIDE
OVERRULE REVERSED
(— AT DEFIANCE) BEARD
(— AT LIBERTY) FREE RELEASE
LIBERATE
(— BACK TO BACK) ADDORSED
ADDOSSED
(— CLOSE TOGETHER) PAVEED
(— DOG ON) SIC SLATE
(— DOWN) JOT LAY GIVE LAND
PLANK SCORE EXPONE DEPOSIT
(— DOWN UNDER NAME) TITLE
(— EDGEWISE) SURBED
(— ERECT) COCK
(— FIRMLY) FIRM STEM PLANT
POSIT
(— FORTH) DRAW ETCH SHOW
GIVEN STATE DEPART DEPICT
EXPOSE SPREAD ARTICLE
DISPLAY ENOUNCE EXHIBIT
EXPOUND PRESENT PROPONE
PROPOSE PURPOSE PROPOUND
(— FORWARD) PREFER ADVANCE
(— FREE) BAIL EASE REMIT SKILL
SOLVE ACQUIT ASSOIL ABSOLVE
DELIVER ENLARGE UNLOOSE
WINFREE ABSTRICT DISPLACE
DISSOLVE EXPEDITE UNVASSAL

(— **GOING**) INITIATE
(— **IN EARTH**) STRIKE
(— **IN FROM MARGINS**) INDENT
(— **IN MOTION**) SOW
(— **IN OPERATION**) DRIVE
(— **IN OPPOSITION**) PIT
(— **IN ORDER**) ARRAY FRUSH PITCH
ADIGHT DAIKER FETTLE INFORM
ADDRESS
(— **INTO**) INLAY
(— **INTO A GROOVE**) DADO
(— **LIMITS TO**) SPAN BOUND
(— **OF ACTORS**) CAST
(— **OF ARMS**) CONVEYER
(— **OF BARS**) CONCAVE
(— **OF BELLS**) RING CHIME
CARILLON
(— **OF BOOKS**) PLENARY
(— **OF CARS**) DRAG
(— **OF CHIMES**) DOORBELL
(— **OF CIRCUMSTANCES**) CASE EGIS
FRAME
(— **OF CORDS**) SIMPLE
(— **OF DISHES**) GARNISH SERVICE
CUPBOARD
(— **OF EIGHT**) OGDOAD
(— **OF EXERCISES**) KATA
(— **OF FACTS**) BOOK
(— **OF FISH NETS**) DRIFT
(— **OF FOLDED SHEETS**) QUIRE
(— **OF FOUR**) WARP
(— **OF FURNITURE**) SUITE DINETTE
(— **OF GARMENTS**) SUIT
(— **OF GEARS**) GEARSET
(— **OF HIDES**) KIP
(— **OF HOUNDS**) VANLAY
VAUNTLAY
(— **OF IDEAS**) SYSTEM
(— **OF JEWELLED ORNAMENTS**)
PARURE
(— **OF LEAVES**) COROLLA
(— **OF LETTERS**) ALPHABET
(— **OF MUSICAL INSTRUMENTS**)
CONSORT
(— **OF NOTES**) ACCORD
(— **OF OPINIONS**) CREDO
(— **OF ORGAN PIPES**) STOP
(— **OF ORGANS**) ARMATURE
(— **OF ORNAMENTS**) PARURE
(— **OF PINS**) KAILS KNOCKOUT
(— **OF POINTS**) INTERVAL
(— **OF PUMPS**) LIFT
(— **OF QUADRILLES**) LANCERS
(— **OF RADIATORS**) STACK
(— **OF ROOMS**) STORY
(— **OF RULES**) CODE EQUITY
DECALOG
(— **OF SAILS**) CANVAS
(— **OF SHELVES**) STAGE BUFFET
DRESSER WHATNOT
(— **OF SKI FASTENINGS**) BINDING
(— **OF STAVES**) SHOOK
(— **OF STEPS**) LADDER
(— **OF SYMBOLS**) KATAKANA
(— **OF TABLES**) COMPUTUS
(— **OF TEETH**) DENTURE
(— **OF TEN**) DECADE
(— **OF THREE**) BALE LEASH
(— **OF TOOLS**) STRING
(— **OF TRAMS**) JOURNEY
(— **OF TYPEFACES**) FAMILY
(— **OF VALUES**) CURRENCY
(— **OF VARIATIONS**) PARTITA

(— **OF VATS**) SOLERA
(— **OF VERSES**) STAVE
(— **OF VOWELS**) SERIES
(— **OF WARP THREADS**) LEA
(— **OF 3 ANIMALS**) LEASH
(— **OFF**) FOIL MENSE SEVER
SHOOT ACCENT BUNDLE
BALANCE COMMEND EMBLAZE
CONTRAST DECORATE EMBLAZON
(— **OFF TO ADVANTAGE**) ADORN
COMMEND
(— **ON**) TAR
(— **ON END**) UPEND
(— **ON FIRE**) SPIT TIND LIGHT
ACCEND IGNIFY IGNITE KINDLE
ENFLAME INFLAME ENKINDLE
(— **ONESELF**) GO
(— **OUT**) BOUN MAKE BOWNE
FOUND SALLY START INTEND
STARTLE
(— **OVER**) COUCH
(— **RIGHT**) REDD ADJUST SCHOOL
SQUARE CORRECT REDRESS
(— **SNARE**) TAIL TILL
(— **SOLIDLY**) EMBED
(— **STRAIGHT**) DRESS
(— **THICKLY**) STUD
(— **TO MUSIC**) AIR DITTY
(— **TRAP**) TELD
(— **TYPE**) KEYBOARD
(— **UP**) AREAR ERECT RAISE
INSTALL UPDRESS ACTIVATE
(— **UP IN COLUMNS**) TABULAR
(— **UPON**) BESET ATTACK
AGGRESS BROWDEN
(— **UPRIGHT**) ERECT STAND
ARRECT
(— **VALUE**) APPRAISE
(— **WITH BRISTLES**) STRIGOSE
(— **WITH GEMS**) CHASE
(**ANTIGEN** —) SEROTYPE
(**BECOME** —) STRIKE
(**CHESS** —) MEINY MEINIE
(**CHROMOSOME** —) GENOME
COMPLEX
(**COMPLETE** —) STAND
(**INFINITE** —) FAMILY
(**MATHEMATICAL** —) MANIFOLD
(**MINIATURE** —) DIORAMA
(**RADIO** —) BLOOPER
(**SMART** —) TON
(**STAGE** —) SCENE
(**TELEVISION** —) TUBE
(**UNALTERABLY** —) STOUT
(**PL.**) DECOR
(**SUFF.**) STOLE THESIS THETE
THETIC
SETA STALK WHISK CHAETA
SETULA SETULE CROTCHET
PODETIUM
SETBACK DASH JOLT KNOCK
LURCH BLIGHT BACKSET LICKING
PUTBACK REVERSE BUSINESS
COMEDOWN HAYMAKER
CONTRETEMPS
SETH (**BROTHER OF** —) ABEL CAIN
(**FATHER OF** —) ADAM
(**MOTHER OF** —) EVE
(**SON OF** —) ENOS
SETHUR (**FATHER OF** —) MICHAEL
SETLINE GEAR TRAWL BULTOW
OUTLINE TROTLINE
SETTEE SETTLE

OTTOMAN WINDSOR
SETTER SOFA GUNDOG DROPPER
FLUSHER SETTLER
SETTERWORT PIGROOTS
SETTING SET FALL PAVE VAIL
CHASE MIDST SETUP CHATON
MILIEU FERMAIL MONTURE
SITTING INTERIOR MARQUISE
MOUNTING SHOWCASE
(— **APART**) BETWEEN
(— **FREE**) SOLUTION
(— **OF GEM**) FOIL OUCH CHASE
GALLERY
(— **OF REED**) CAAMING
(— **OF WHEELS**) CAMBER
(**CAMERA** —) BULB
(**FAMILIAR** —) HOME
(**MUSICAL** —) CREDO BALLAD
BALLADE
(**SHUTTER** —) TIME
(**STAGE** —) SCENE
SETTLE BED FIT FIX PAY SAG SET
SIT TAX BANK BIND CALM DAIS
DEAS FAST FIRM HAFT LEND
NEST REST ROOT SEAT SINK
SNUG TOIT AGREE CLEAR COUCH
ISSUE LIGHT LODGE ORDER PITCH
PLACE PLANT QUIET SQUAT
STATE STILL ACCORD ADJUST
ALIGHT ASSIGN CLINCH DECIDE
DECREE ENCAMP LOCATE NESTLE
PURIFY RESIDE SCREEN SECURE
SOOTHE SOPITE SQUARE
ACCOUNT APPEASE APPOINT
ARRANGE BALANCE CLARIFY
COMPONE COMPOSE CONCERT
CONFIRM DEPOSIT DERAIGN
INHABIT PIONEER RESOLVE
SUBSIDE COLONIZE REGULATE
SQUATTLE CONJOBBLE
RECONCILE
(— **A FINE**) AFFEER
(— **AMICABLY**) COMPOUND
(— **DOWN**) CAMP SLUMP STEADY
DESCEND
(— **ITSELF**) INVEST
(— **LANDS ON A PERSON**) ENTAIL
(— **ON**) POINT
(— **UPON**) AFFIX AGREE TIGHT
(— **VERTICALLY**) SQUASH
SETTLED SAD SET FIRM FIXED
QUIET STAID FORMED RANGED
SEATED SEDATE SQUARE STAPLE
STATED CERTAIN DECIDED
EMPIGHT STATARY DECOROUS
RESOLVED STANDING SEDENTARY
(**NOT** —) FARROW
SETTLEMENT AUL DEAL FINE
FORK MISE POST BARRIO COLONY
DIKTAT MOSHAV WINDUP
ACCOUNT BIVOUAC FINANCE
MAABARA OUTPOST STATION
CLERUCHY DECISION DISPATCH
JOINTURE KEVUTZAH PRESIDIO
SETTLING SHOWDOWN
TOWNSHIP PLANTATION
(— **OF JERRY-BUILT DWELLINGS**)
BIDONVILLE
(— **OF MONKS**) SCETE SKETE
(— **OF SHACKS**) FAVELA FAVELLA
(**COLLECTIVE** —) KVUTZA MOSHAV
KIBBUTZ
(**HARSH** —) DIKTAT

(**INDIAN** —) BUSTEE
(**MARRIAGE** —) MAHR ARRAS
DOWNSET
(**NEW ZEALAND** —) PA PAH
(**RAPID** —) BOOM
(**UPLAND** —) BOOLEY
SETTLER METIC SAHIB LIVYER
NESTER GRUELER PEOPLER
PILGRIM PIONEER TRIMMER
FINISHER GACHUPIN HABITANT
SHAGROON SIBERSKI SIBERYAK
(— **IN AUSTRALIA**) GROPER
SETTLING SIT
(— **OF ESTATE**) ENTAIL
(**PL.**) LEES SEDIMENT
SET-TO BOUT TURN PLUCK FETTLE
TURNUP BRANGLE
SETUP SET SITTER
SEVEN SEPT ZETA ZAYIN HEPTAD
SEPTET HEBDOMAD SEPTETTE
(— **OF DIAMONDS**) POPE
(— **OF TRUMPS**) MANILLA
(**GROUP OF** —) PLEIAD
(**PREF.**) HEPT(A) SEPT(I) SEPTEM
SEVENFOLD SEPTUPLE
SEVENTEEN (**AUTHOR OF** —)
TARKINGTON
(**CHARACTER IN** —) MAY JANE
PRATT BAXTER GEORGE JOHNNY
WATSON GENESIS PARCHER
WILLIAM CLEMATIS
SEVEN-UP PEDRO PITCH SLEDGE
SEVER AX AXE CUT BITE DEAL
HACK REND SLIT TWIN SHEAR
SHRED CLEAVE DEPART DETACH
DIVIDE SUNDER DISALLY DISCERP
DISCIDE DISJOIN OUTRIVE
DISSEVER PRESCIND SEPARATE
SEVERIZE
(**PREF.**) TEMNO
SEVERAL ODD TEN SERE WHEEN
DIVERS SUNDRY DIVERSE
VARIOUS DISTINCT MULTIPLE
(**PREF.**) PLURI POLY
SEVERALLY APIECE SEVERAL
SEVERANCE SUNDER SOLUTION
(— **OF RELATIONSHIPS**) AIR
SEVERE BAD DRY ACID BLUE DEAR
DOUR DURE FIRM HARD IRON
KEEN ROID RUDE SALT SIDE SORE
TART TAUT ACUTE BREME CRUEL
EAGER GRUFF HARSH RETHE
RIGID ROUGH SHARP SMART
SNELL SOBER SOUND STARK
STEER STERN STIFF STOUR
TOUGH BITING BITTER BRUTAL
CHASTE COARSE FROSTY HETTER
SIMPLE SOLEMN STRICT TORVID
UNKIND UNMILD ACERBIC
ASCETIC AUSTERE CAUSTIC
CHRONIC CONDIGN CRUCIAL
CUTTING DRASTIC SERIOUS
SPARTAN TORVOUS UNCANNY
VICIOUS VIOLENT WEIGHTY
ACERGATE ACULEATE CATONIAN
EXACTING GRIEVOUS GRINDING
HORRIBLE IRONCLAD IRONHARD
RIGOROUS SCATHING STALWART
STRAIGHT TERRIBLE STRINGENT
(**MOST** —) EXTREME
SEVERELY BAD HARD BADLY
STARK STIFF HARDLY SORELY
STRONG HEAVILY ROUGHLY

SMARTLY SOUNDLY STITHLY SHREWDLY

SEVERIAN AGNOETE AGNOITE

SEVERING
(PREF.) PRISO

SEVERITY FROST RIGOR CRUELTY TORVITY TYRANNY ACRIMONY ASPERITY FERVENCY HARDNESS RIGIDITY SORENESS VIOLENCE

SEW SUE FELL SEAM SLIP PREEN STEEK NEEDLE STITCH OVERSEW THIMBLE OVERCAST OVERHAND
(**— A CORPSE**) SOCK
(**— LOOSELY**) BASTE
(**— TO REINFORCE**) BAR
(**— UP FERRET'S MOUTH**) COPE
(**— WAVED PATTERN**) DICE

SEWAGE SOIL WASTE SOILAGE SULLAGE AFFLUENT DRAINAGE SEWERAGE

SEWELLEL BEAVER BOOMER

SEWER SINK SIRE DRAFT DRAIN FLEET ISSUE MAKER SHORE CLOACA KILTER TACKER VENNEL BELTMAN COPYIST CULVERT DRAUGHT GULLION JAWHOLE SHIRRER PIQUIERE

SEWING TACK SUTURE SEMPSTRY
(SUFF.) RHAPHY RRHAPHY

SEX KIND SECT GENDER
(**FEMALE —**) SMOCK
(**MALE —**) WEPMANKIN
(PREF.) GEN(O)

SEXLESS NEUTER EPICENE

SEXT MIDDAY

SEXTANT (**PART OF —**) ARC ARM DRUM LIMB MARK FRAME GLASS INDEX LEVER HANDLE MIRROR SUNSHADE TELESCOPE

SEXTET SESTET SEXTUOR SESTETTO

SEXTON SAXON SHAMUS WARDEN SACRIST SHAMASH SHAMMES VESTURER SACRISTAN

SEXTUPLE SENARY

SEXTUPLET SESTOLE SEXTOLE SESTOLET SEXTOLET

SEXUAL GAMIC CARNAL INTIMATE
(PREF.) GAM(ETO)(O) GON(O)

SEXY FOXY FREUDIAN

SEYCHELLES (**CAPITAL OF —**)
VICTORIA
(**ISLAND OF —**) MAHE LADIGUE PRASLIN

SGANARELLE (**BROTHER OF —**)
ARISTE
(**DAUGHTER OF —**) LUCINDE
(**WARD OF —**) LEONORE ISABELLE
(**WIFE OF —**) MARTINE

SHA YASHIRO

SHAAPH (**FATHER OF —**) CALEB JAHDAI
(**MOTHER OF —**) MAACHAH

SHAB RUBBERS

SHABBINESS WAFFNESS

SHABBY BASE MEAN POKY WORN DINGY DOWDY MANGY OURIE POKEY RATTY SCALD SEEDY SORRY TACKY CHEESY FROWZY GRUBBY SCABBY SCOURY SCUFFY SCURVY SHODDY SHROVY SLEAZY TAGRAG BUNTING MESQUIN SCALLED SCRUBBY SCRUFFY

SCUFFED SHABBED SQUALID PALTERLY SLIPSHOD WAFFLIKE

SHABUOTH PENTECOST

SHACHIA (**FATHER OF —**)
SHAHARAIM
(**MOTHER OF —**) HODESH

SHACK COE HUT CRIB SHAG HUMPY HUTCH SHANTY

SHACKLE COP TIE BAND BIND BOLT BOND GYVE LOCK STAY BASIL BILBO CLAMP COPSE CRAMP CRANK HUMPY TRASH TRAVE FETTER GARTER HAMPER PINION SHANGY STAYER SWATHE COTTAGE COUPLER FETLOCK MANACLE MOUSING PASTERN SHEBANG SNACKLE TRAMMEL RESTRAIN
(PL.) IRONS

SHACKLER SLOTTER

SHAD BUCK CHAD ALLIS ALOSE TRABU ALLICE TWAITE ALEWIFE ANADROM CLUPEID FLATFISH SAWBELLY

SHADBUSH DOGWOOD SERVICE SERVICEBERRY

SHADDOCK LUCBAN POMELO POMPION

SHADE EYE CAST DULL SCUG SHED TONE VEIL BLEND COLOR ENNUE GHOST GLIDE GLOOM GRAIN SCAUM SCOUG SWALE SWILL TASTE TINCT TINGE TRACE UMBER UMBRA DEGREE FRESCO SHADOW SHIELD SHROUD SPRITE STRAIN STRIPE TONING CURTAIN ECLIPSE GRADATE HACHURE KENNING PROTECT SECTION SHADING UMBRAGE BONGRACE HALFTONE UMBRELLA
(**— OF COLOR**) EYE CAST TONE
(**— OF DIFFERENCE**) NUANCE
(**— OFF**) GRADUATE
(**— ON HAT**) UGLY
(**EYE —**) UGLY
(**OVERHANGING —**) CANOPY
(**WINDOW —**) STORE
(PREF.) UMBRI

SHADED OMBRE SHADY DRUMLY SOMBER SOMBRE DARKLING

SHADINESS GLOOM

SHADING FLUTING LAYERING

SHADOW FOX BLOT SCUG TAIL CLOUD SCOUG SHADE UMBER UMBRA CLEEKS DARKEN FINGER SHROUD TAILER ISOGYRE PHANTOM SCARROW SUGGEST UMBRAGE UMBRATE PENUMBRA PHANTASM SHEPHERD
(PREF.) SCI(A)(O) SKIA SKIO TENEBRI UMBRI

SHADOWED DARKLING

SHADOWINESS GLOOM

SHADOWLESS ASCIAN WHITEOUT

SHADOWS ON THE ROCK
(**AUTHOR OF —**) CATHER
(**CHARACTER IN —**) LAVAL CECILE HECTOR PIERRE AUCLAIR BLINKER CHARRON EUCLIDE SAINTCYR FRONTENAC

SHADOWY MISTY VAGUE GLOOMY GHOSTLY OBSCURE

SHADRACH ANANIAS HANANIAH

SHADY DARK BOSKY BOWERY CLOUDY LOUCHE SHADOW SHADOWY UMBROSE ADUMBRAL

SHAFT BAR NIB ROD BALK BOLT DART FUST HOLE PILE POLE TRAM WELL ARBOR HEUGH QUILL REACH SCAPE SHANK SHOOT SNEAD SPRAG STAFF STALE STANG STAVE STEAL STILT STING THILL TRUNK BOLTEL CANNON COLUMN GNOMON SCAPUS STAPLE TILLER TUNNEL UPRISE VAGINA BOWTELL CHIMNEY INCLINE MANDREL SPINDLE CAMSHAFT DOWNCAST ESCONSON HOISTWAY LAMPHOLE SHAFTWAY STANDARD WEIGHBAR WELLHOLE
(**— CONNECTING WHEELS**) AXLE
(**— IN GLACIER**) MOULIN
(**— IN WATCH**) STEM
(**— OF CANDLESTICK**) BALUSTER
(**— OF CARRIAGE**) FILL SILL THILL
(**— OF CART**) ROD TRAM SHARP STANG
(**— OF CAVERN**) DOME
(**— OF CHARIOT**) BEAM
(**— OF CLUSTERED PIER**) BOLTEL
(**— OF COLUMN**) FUST TIGE SCAPE VERGE
(**— OF FEATHER**) SCAPE SCAPUS
(**— OF MINE**) PIT WORK GRUFF HEUCH HEUGH RAISE SLOPE STULM WINZE GROOVE STAPLE INCLINE WINNING
(**— OF PADDLE**) LOOM ROUND
(**— OF SPEAR OR LANCE**) TREE STALE
(**— OF WAGON**) STAVE THILL LIMBER
(**HARNESS —**) HEALD
(**HOLLOW —**) CANNON
(**MAIN —**) ARBOR
(**ORNAMENTAL —**) VERGE
(**SCYTHE —**) SNEAD
(**STAIRWAY —**) VICE
(**TWISTED —**) TORSO
(**VENTILATION —**) UPCAST UPTAKE WINDHOLE
(PREF.) DORY SCAPI

SHAG PILE

SHAGE (**SON OF —**) JONATHAN

SHAGGY SHAG SWAG HARSH NAPPY ROUGH SHOCK TATTY TOUSY BRUSHY COMATE RAGGED TOOSIE HIRSUTE SHAGRAG SQUALID SWAGGED THRUMMY VILLOUS TATTERED
(PREF.) DASI DASY LASI

SHAGREEN GALUCHAT

SHAGROON PILGRIM

SHAKE BOB DAD JAR JOG ROG WAG WAP JOLT JOWL PLUM QUAG RESE ROCK SHOG STIR SWAY TOZE WEVE WHAP WHOP HOTCH JAUNT KNOCK NIDGE QUASH SHOCK SWING TRILL DIDDER DITHER DODDER DODDLE EXCUSS GOGGLE HOTTER HUSTLE JOGGLE JOUNCE JUMBLE QUATCH QUAVER QUITCH QUIVER ROGGLE RUFFLE SHIMMY SHIVER TOTTER WAMBLE WANGLE

WARBLE WEAKEN WOBBLE AGITATE BRANDLE CHOUNCE CONCUSS ROULADE SHUDDER STAGGER SUCCUSS TREMBLE TWITTER WHIFFLE WHITHER BRANDISH CONVULSE ENFEEBLE
(**— HERRING**) SCUD
(**— LIGHTLY**) LIFT
(**— OFF**) ARISE EXCUSS
(**— TO SEPARATE**) HOTCH
(**— UP**) JABBLE JUMBLE RATTLE
(**WIND —**) ANEMOSIS

SHAKER DUSTER SIFTER DREDGER JUMBLER POUNCET SANDBOX

SHAKING ASPEN ASHAKE TREMOR JARRING AGITATED
(**— OF AIRPLANE**) BUFFET

SHAKTI TARA PRAKRITI

SHAKTIS MATRIS

SHAKUNTALA (**FATHER OF —**)
VISHVAMITRA
(**FOSTER FATHER OF —**) KANVA
(**HUSBAND OF —**) DUSHYANTA
(**MOTHER OF —**) MENAKA
(**SON OF —**) BHARATA

SHAKY CRANK DICKY QUAKY ROCKY TIPSY TOTTY WONKY WOOZY AGUISH COGGLY CRANKY GROGGY INFIRM WAMBLY CASALTY DWAIBLE DWEEBLE PALSIED RICKETY SHOGGLY TITTUPY TOTTERY COGGLEDY INSECURE

SHALE BAT BASS BONE CLOD FLAG KOLM TILL BLAES FAKES METAL PLATE XALLE KILLAS SHILLET MUDSTONE SLIGGEEN TORBANITE

SHALL SE MAY MUN MUST SALL
(**— NOT**) SANNA SHANT SHANNA

SHALLOON CUBICA

SHALLOT CIBOL ALLIUM ESCHALOT SCALLION

SHALLOW EBB BANK FLAN FLAT FLUE GLIB FLEET INANE SHOAL SILLY SMALL FLIMSY FROTHY LITTLE RIFFLE SLIGHT UNDEEP CRIPPLE CURSORY TRIVIAL MAGAZINY
(PL.) FORD

SHALLOWNESS INANITY

SHALLUM (**FATHER OF —**) BANI KORE SHAUL JABESH JOSIAH HOLOHESH NAPHTALI
(**NEPHEW OF —**) JEREMIAH
(**SON OF —**) HOLOHESH MAASEIAH JEHIZKIAH
(**WIFE OF —**) HULDAH

SHALLUN (**FATHER OF —**)
COLHOZEH

SHAM BAM FOB FOX GIG FAKE HOAX MOCK PUFF BLUFF BOGUS CHEAT DUMMY FALSE FEIGN FRAUD LETON QUEER SHUCK SNIDE ASSUME BRUMMY BUNYIP CHOUSE DECEIT DUFFER HUMBUG PSEUDO SHODDY STUMER FALSITY FORGERY GRIMACE MOCKISH PLASTER PRETEND STUMOUR POSTICHE PRETENSE SPURIOUS BRUMMAGEM PASTEBOARD SIMULACRUM
(PREF.) PSEUD(O)

SHAMAN PEAI CURER MACHI
KAHUNA WABENO ANGEKOK
TOHUNGA CONTRARY WITCHMAN
SHAMARIAH (FATHER OF —)
REHOBOAM
SHAMASH (FATHER OF —) SIN
(SISTER OF —) ISHTAR
(WIFE OF —) AA AYA
SHAMBLE SHALE SHOOL CLOUCH
BAUCHLE SCAMBLE SHACHLE
SHACKLE SKEMMEL ABATTOIR
SHAMMOCK
(PL.) BUTCHERY
SHAMBLING SHACKLY
SHAME SISS ABASH AIDOS SHEND
SPITE ASHAME BISMER REBUKE
MORTIFY PUDENCY SCANDAL
SLANDER CONTEMPT DISGRACE
DISHONOR REPROACH SHENDING
VERGOYNE VITUPERY
(— BY CENSURE) TOUCH
SHAMED (FATHER OF —) ELPAAL
SHAMEFACED SHY
SHAMEFACEDNESS PUDENCY
SHAMEFUL BASE FOUL MEAN
GROSS HONTOUS IGNOBLE
FLAGRANT IMPROPER INFAMOUS
SHAMELESS HARD BRASH
ARRANT BRAZEN BASHLESS
BROWLESS IMMODEST IMPUDENT
SHAMELESSNESS BRASS
SHAMGAR (FATHER OF —) ANATH
SHAMIR (FATHER OF —) MICAH
(GRANDFATHER OF —) UZZIEL
SHAMMA (FATHER OF —) ZOPHAH
SHAMMAH (BROTHER OF —) DAVID
(FATHER OF —) JESSE REUEL
SHAMMAI (FATHER OF —) ONAM
REKEM
SHAMMES BEADLE
SHAMMUA (FATHER OF —) DAVID
ZACCUR
(MOTHER OF —) BATHSHEBA
(SON OF —) ABDA
SHAMPOO TRIPSIS
SHAMPOOING TRIPSIS
SHAMROCK SEAMROG SHAMROOT
SHANK BODY CRUS GAMB JAMB
TANG FENUR GAMBE CANNON
NIBBLE TARSUS KNUCKLE
(THREAD —) STEM
SHANNY BULLY
SHANTY BOIST HUMPY HUTCH
SHACK SHEBANG CHANTIER
DOGHOUSE
SHAPE AX ADZ AXE CUT DIE HUE
ADZE BEAT BEND CAST COLE
COPE DRAW FACE FAIR FORM
HACK MOLD NICK BEVEL BLOCK
BOAST BUILT COLOR DRAPE
DRESS FEIGN FORGE FRAME
GUISE HORSE JOLLY LATHE
MODEL MOULD SWAGE BROACH
CHISEL CUTOUT EFFORM FIGURE
FORMER FRAISE HAMMER JIGGER
SQUARE CHANNEL CONFORM
CONTOUR FASHION FEATURE
GESTALT INCLINE OUTLINE
PATTERN TONNEAU CONTRIVE
LIKENESS
(— BY HAMMERING) SMITH
(— DIAMOND) BRUTE
(— GARMENTS) BOARD

(— METAL) SWAGE EXTRUDE
(— OF BUST) TAILLE
(— OF ENVELOPE FLAP) KNIFE
(— ON POTTER'S WHEEL) THROW
(— ONE'S COURSE) ETTLE
(— RIGHTLY) FIT
(— ROUGHLY) BOAST SCABBLE
SCAPPLE
(— ROUGHLY WITH CHISEL) BOAST
(— STONE) BROACH SCABBLE
(CLAY —) FLOATER
(CONICAL —) BEEHIVE
(GEM —) BAGUET BAGUETTE
(GLOVE —) TRANK
(SPIRALLING —) SWIRL
(SURFACE —) GEOMETRY
(UNBLOCKED —) HOOD
(PREF.) MORPH(O)
SHAPED BUILT FITTED BLOCKED
FEATURED
(— LIKE BEAN) FABIFORM
(— LIKE BERRY) BACCIFORM
(— LIKE BOAT) SCAPHOID
NAVICULAR
(— LIKE BUCKLER) SCUTATE
(— LIKE CLUB) CLAVATE CLUBBED
(— LIKE COMB) CTENOID
(— LIKE CONE) CONIFORM
(— LIKE CUP) SCYPHATE
(— LIKE DOME) DOMAL
(— LIKE EAR) AURIFORM
(— LIKE FIDDLE) PANDURATE
(— LIKE HALBERD) HASTATE
(— LIKE HEART) CORDATE
CORDIFORM
(— LIKE HOOK) ANKYROID
(— LIKE HORN) CORNIFORM
(— LIKE KEEL) CARINATE
(— LIKE LEAF) FOLIATE
(— LIKE LENS) LENTOID PHACOID
(— LIKE NEEDLE) ACUATE
(— LIKE ORANGE) OBLATE
(— LIKE PEAR) PYRIFORM
(— LIKE PULLEY) TROCHLEAR
(— LIKE RING) ANNULAR
(— LIKE ROD) BACILLAR
(— LIKE S) SIGMATE
(— LIKE SAUSAGE) ALLANTOID
(— LIKE SHIELD) ASPIDATE
CLYPEATE
(— LIKE SICKLE) FALCULAR
(— LIKE SPINDLE) FUSOID
FUSIFORM
(— LIKE SPUR) CALCARINE
(— LIKE STAR) ASTROID
(— LIKE STRAP) LIGULATE
(— LIKE SWORD) GLADIATE
(— LIKE THREAD) FILIFORM
(— LIKE TURNIP) NAPIFORM
(— LIKE WEDGE) CUNEAL CUNEATE
(— LIKE X) SALTIRE
(— WITH AX) HEWN
SHAPELESS DUMPY CLUMPY
DEFORM DUMPTY INFORM
FORMLESS INDIGEST UNSHAPED
SHAPELINESS DELICACY
SHAPELY GENT TIDY TRIM CLEAN
TIGHT DECENT FORMAL GAINLY
FEATOUS FORMFUL SHAPABLE
SHAPHAT (FATHER OF —) HORI
ADLAI SHEMAIAH
(SON OF —) ELISHA
SHAPING DESCENT

SHARAI (FATHER OF —) BANI
SHARAR (SON OF —) AHIAM
SHARD SCAUR SHERD SHRED
(PL.) PITCHER
SHARE CUT END LOT RUG CANT
DALE DEAL DOLE HAND PART
PLOT RENT SCOT SNIP DIVVY
ENTER PARTY QUOTA RATIO
SHEAR SHIFT SLICE SNACK SNICK
SNUCK SPLIT WHACK COMMON
COPART DEPART DIVIDE FINGER
IMPART RATION SHOVEL
PARTAGE PARTAKE PORTION
DIVIDEND DIVISION INTEREST
PURPARTY PERCENTAGE
PROPORTION
(— A BED) BUNK
(— EQUALLY) HALVE
(— IN ACTIVITY) PIECE
(— OF EXPENSES) LAW CLUB
(— OF LAND) DAIL DALE FREEDOM
RUNDALE
(— OF PROFIT) LAY
(— OF STOCK) STOCK ACTION
(— QUARTERS) CHUM
(— SECRETS) CONFIDE
(ALLOTED —) DOLE
(ANCESTRAL —) PATTI
(FULL —) SKINFUL
(GREATER —) FECK
(LEGAL —) HAK
(ONE'S —) AFFERE
(PROPORTIONAL —) QUOTA
(SMALL —) MOIETY
(PREF.) MER(I)(O) MERISTO
(SUFF.) MER(E)(IC)(IS)(OUS)(Y)
SHARECROPPER BYWONER
CROPPER
SHARED JOINT BETWEEN
(PREF.) CO
SHAREZER (BROTHER OF —)
ESARHADDON ADRAMMELECH
(FATHER OF —) SENNACHERIB
SHARING (— OF EXPENSE) CLUB
(— VICARIOUSLY) ARMCHAIR
SHARK FOX GATA HAYE KULP
MAKO MANO TOPE GUMMY
HOMER HOUND LAMIA TIGER
TOMMY TOPER BEAGLE DAGGAR
GALEID PALOMA REQUIN WHALER
ACRODUS BONEDOG DOGFISH
FOXFISH HUNFYSH PLACOID
REQUIEM SLEEPER SOUPFIN
SQUALID SUNFISH TIBURON
TIGRONE TUBARON BULLHEAD
HYBODONT ROUSETTE SAILFISH
SEAHOUND SKAAMOOG
SPEAREYE SQUATINA THRASHER
PORBEAGLE SELACHIAN
SHOVELHEAD
(YOUNG —) CUB SHARKLET
(PREF.) SQUALI SQUALO
SHARP DRY SHY ACID ACRE CUTE
EDGY FELL FINE GAIR GASH GLEG
GNIB HARD HIGH KEEN PERT
SALT TART ACERB ACRID ACUTE
ALERT BRASH BREME BRISK CRISP
DOWNY EAGER EDGED FALSE
HARSH NASAL NEBBY NIPPY
PEERY QUICK SMART SNELL
SQUAB STEEP STIFF VIVID YAULD
ACIDIC ACUATE ARGUTE ASTUTE
BITING BITTER BRIGHT CRISPY

DIESIS GLASSY JAGGED PLUCKY
SEVERE SHREWD SHRILL SNELLY
SNITHE STINGY TOOTHY TWEAKY
UNRIDE ANGULAR AUSTERE
BRITTLE CAUSTIC CUTTING
GINGERY NIPPING PIQUANT
POINTED PUNGENT SHARPEN
SLICING SPINOUS VARMINT
VIOLENT HATCHETY INCISIVE
POIGNANT ACRIMONIOUS
(PREF.) ACET(O) ACUT(I)(O) OXY
SHARP-EDGED VORPAL CULTRATE
SHARPEN EDGE FILE FINE HONE
KEEN WHET BRISK FROST GRIND
POINT RAISE SHARP SLYPE STONE
STROP ACCENT AFFILE STROKE
ENHANCE QUICKEN SMARTEN
EXACUATE HEIGHTEN
SHARPENED ACUATE
SHARPENER SHARPER STROPPER
(SCYTHE —) RIP RIFLE
SHARPER GUE GYP BITE KITE
ROOK SKIN SNAP BITER CHEAT
CROOK GREEK ROGUE SHARK
SHARP BESTER COGGER NICKUM
PICARO ROOKER SHARPY
BARNARD CATALAN GAMBLER
SHARKER SPIELER BLACKLEG
DECEIVER PIGEONER SWINDLER
SHARPLY DAB SHARP SNACK
ACIDLY ROUNDLY SHEERLY
SMARTLY STEEPLY
SHARPNESS WIT EDGE SALT
WHET PLUCK ACRITY ACUITY
ACUMEN ACIDITY ACERBITY
ACRIDITY ACRIMONY ASPERITY
EDGINESS PUNGENCY
SHARP-POINTED ACUATE
ACULEATE
(PREF.) ACUT(I)(O)
SHARPSHOOTER JAGER
VOLTIGEUR TIRAILLEUR
BERSAGLIERE
SHARP-SIGHTED SIGHTY LYNCEAN
SHARP-TAILED GROUSE PINTAIL
SHARP-WITTED ACUTE CANNY
SNELL SHREWD
SHASHAI (FATHER OF —) BANI
SHASHAK (FATHER OF —) ELPAAL
SHASTRA PURANA SASTRA
(— CLASS) SRUTI
SHATTER BLOW DASH DICE BLAST
BREAK BURST CRASH CRAZE
CREEM FRUSH SMASH SMOKE
SPLIT WRECK SHIVER SPIDER
BEGUILE CHATTER CONVELL
EXPLODE SMATTER TORPEDO
DEMOLISH DYNAMITE SPLINTER
(— CLAY TARGET) KILL
SHATTERED BROKEN BROOZLED
DODDERED
SHAUL (FATHER OF —) SIMEON
SHAVE BARB BITE DRAW PARE
RAZE GLACE GRAZE SKIVE
SCHAWE SCRAPE FLATTEN
UPRIGHT
SHAVED POLLED SHAVEN
SHAVEN NOT NOTT PILLED
TONSURED
SHAVING SHAVE SHRED SPALE
SPELL RAMENT RAMENTUM
(PL.) COOM COOMB SCOBS
MOSLINGS

SHAWL MAUD WRAP LAMBA
MANTA MANTO NUBIA PATTU
RUMAL SCARF TOZIE AFGHAN
ANGORA KAMBAL PEPLOS
PEPLUM PEPLUS PUTTOO SERAPE
TAPALO TOILET TONNAG ZEPHYR
AMLIKAR CHUDDAR PAISLEY
WHITTLE WRAPPER ALGERINE
CASHMERE EPIBLEMA KAFFIYEH
SLENDANG TURNOVER
(COARSE —) KAMBAL
(COTTON —) FARDA
(PLAID —) MAUD
(TASSELED —) TALLITH
SHAWM WAIT SHALM BOMBARD
SCHALMEI
SHE A HE HEO HER SHU HAEC
SCHO
(AUTHOR OF —) HAGGARD
(CHARACTER IN —) JOB LEO SHE
HOLLY AYESHA LUDWIG USTANE
VINCEY BILLALI MAHOMED
KALLIKRATES
SHEAF TIE BEAT BUNG GAIT GERB
OMER FLASH GAVEL GERBE
GLEAN BATTEN THRAVE
DORLACH HATTOCK CAPSHEAF
CORNBOLE
(— LEVIED AS TAX) CORNBOLE
(— OF ARROWS) FLASH
(— OF FLAX OR HEMP) BEAT BEET
GLEAN
(— OF GRAIN) GAIT GARB HOSE
GARBAGE
(LAST — OF CORN) NECK
(LAST — OF HARVEST) KIRN
(PROTECTING —) HATTOCK
(UNBOUND —) REAP GAVEL
SHEAL (FATHER OF —) BANI
SHEALTIEL (SON OF —)
ZERUBBABEL
SHEAR COW CUT DOD LIP NOT
CLIP CROP NOTT TRIM BREAK
FORCE SHARE SHEER SHIRL SLIDE
STRIP FLEECE STRESS
SHEARER SNAGGER
SHEARIAH (FATHER OF —) AZEL
SHEARLING SHEARHOG
(PL.) ALPACA
SHEARS LEWIS SNIPS FORFEX
SHEARER SNOUTER SECATEUR
(PREF.) FORFICI
SHEARWATER HAG CREW COHOW
HAGDON HAGLET PETREL PUFFIN
SCRABE PIMLICO SCRABER
SEABIRD HACKBOLT
SHEATFISH WELS DORAD WALLER
CATFISH SILURID
SHEATH COT HOT BOOT CASE
CYST HOSE HOTT ARMOR CHAPE
FOREL GAINE OCREA SHADE
SHEAF SPILL THECA VOLVA
COCOON CONDOM FORREL
MYELIN OCHREA QUIVER SLOUGH
VAGINA AXILEMMA EPILEMMA
SCABBARD STANDARD VAGINULA
NEURILEMMA
(— FOR BOOK) FOREL FORRIL
(— FOR FINGER) STALL
(— FOR GAMECOCK'S SPUR) HOT
HOTT
(— OF CIGARETTE) SPILL
(— OF PLOW) STANDARD

(— OF TISSUE) PERIBLEM
(MEDULLARY —) CORONA
(PREF.) COLE(O) COLI(O) ELYTR(O)
(SUFF.) LEMMA THECA THECIUM
SHEATHBILL PADDY
SHEATHE CLAD COPPER MUZZLE
IMPLATE
SHEATHED THECATE
SHEATHING SKIN ARMOR COPPER
FACING SHEATH INLAYER
SHIPLAP SLITWORK
SHEA TREE KARITE KARITI
SHEAVE SHEAF SHIVER HATTOCK
TRUCKLE
(24 —S OF GRAIN) THRAVE
THREAVE
SHEBA (FATHER OF —) BICHRI
SHEBANG HUT
SHEBER (FATHER OF —) CALEB
(MOTHER OF —) MAACHAH
SHEBUEL (FATHER OF —) HEMAN
SHECHANIAH (FATHER OF —) ARAH
JEHIEL
(SON OF —) SHEMAIAH
SHED BOX CUB SOW ABRI CAST
COTE DROP HELM HULL KILN
MOLT PEEL POUR SHUD SKEO
SLIP BOOTH HIELD HOVEL MOULT
SCALE SHADE SPILL THROW
VINEA ZAYAT BELFRY BROACH
DINGLE EFFUSE GARAGE HANGAR
HEMMEL INFUSE LINHAY MISTAL
PANDAL SLOUGH CHOLTRY
COTTAGE DIFFUSE DISCARD
MUSCULE RADIATE SKIPPER
EXUVIATE SKEELING SKILLION
WOODSHED PENTHOUSE
(— BLOOD) BROACH
(— DROPS) DRIZZLE
(— FEATHERS OR HORNS) MEW
(— FOR LIVESTOCK) SHIPPEN
(— FOR SHEEP) SHEALING
(— OVER MINE SHAFT) COE
(— TEARS) GIVE
(— TO PROTECT SOLDIERS)
TESTUDO
(CATTLE —) CUB HELM LAIR
BELFRY
(MOVABLE —) SOW BAIL MUSCULE
(TEMPORARY —) PANDAL
(WEATHER —) DINGLE
SHEDDING FALL SPILTH ECDYSIS
APOLYSIS
SHE-DEMON LAMIA
SHEDEUR (SON OF —) ELIZUR
SHEEN GLAZE SHINE LUSTER
LUSTRE SHIMMER
SHEEP SNA TEG DOWN LAMB
LONK MUGS SHIP SOAY URIN
ZENU ANCON BOVID DUMBA
HEDER HUNIA MUGGS OVINE
SAIGA SHORN TAGGE AOUDAD
ARGALI BARHAL BHARAL BIDENT
CHURRO DECCAN DORPER
DORSET EXMOOR HIRSEL MARKER
MASHAM MERINO MUTTON
NAYAUR OXFORD PANAMA
PAULAR ROMNEY WETHER
WOOLIE WOOLLY BIGHORN
BLEATER BRAXIES CHEVIOT
CRIOLLA DELAINE DISHLEY
FREEZER FRONTER JUMBUCK
KARAKUL LINCOLN POLLARD

SUFFOLK TARGHEE TWINTER
VERMONT BIKANERI COMEBACK
COTSWOLD DARTMOOR
HERDWICK LONGWOOL
LUGHDOAN RUMINANT
SHEARHOG SHEARING TALLOWER
THRINTER MONTADALE
ROMELDALE SHROPSHIRE
(— DIFFICULT TO HANDLE) COBBLER
(— IN 2ND YEAR) HOB TAG TEG
TAGGE TWINTER
**(— THAT HAS SHED PORTION OF
WOOL)** ROSELLA
(— TO BE SHEARED) BOARD
(DEAD —) MORT BRAXY MORLING
(FEMALE —) EWE GIMMER SHEDER
(HORNLESS —) NOT NOTT
(LOST —) WAIF
(MALE —) RAM TUP BUCK HEDER
DINMONT
(MOUNTAIN —) IBEX
(OLD —) GUMMER
(PART OF —) EAR EYE LEG RIB
BACK DOCK FACE LOIN NECK
RACK RUMP FLANK SHANK
BREAST MUZZLE BRISKET
FORELEG PASTERN WITHERS
FOREHEAD SHOULDER
FORESHANK
(THICK-WOOLED —) MUG
(UNSHORN —) HOG TEG
(WILD —) SHA ARGAL AUDAD
RASSE URIAL AOUDAD ARGALI
BHARAL SHAPOO BURRHEL
MOUFLON
(YOUNG —) HOG HOGG HOGGEREL
(3-YEAR-OLD —) THRINTER
SHEEPBERRY ALISIER VIBURNUM
SHEEPCOTE SHEPPEY
SHEEPDOG KELPIE SHELTY
BOBTAIL MALINOIS SHETLAND
SHEEP FLY FAG
SHEEPFOLD REE FANK KRAAL
REEVE STELL BOUGHT BARKARY
SHEPPEY SHEEPCOT
SHEEPHERDER SNOOZER
STOCKMAN
SHEEPISH SHY
SHEEP LAUREL IVY HEATH WICKY
KALMIA LAUREL CALFKILL
LAMBKILL
SHEEPLIKE OVINE
SHEEPMAN HOBBER
SHEEP PLANT RAOULIA
SHEEP ROT CAW
SHEEP RUN STATION
SHEEPSHEAD JAMES JEMMY
JIMMY PARGO PORGY TAUTOG
FATHEAD PERCOID SPAROID
SHEEPSHEARER GUN
SHEEPSKIN ROAN SLAT MOUTON
SOLDIER CAPESKIN LAMBSKIN
WOOLFELL WOOLSKIN
(— TANNED WITH BARK) BASAN
BASIL
(— THAT SWEATS UNEVENLY)
SOLDIER
(— WITHOUT WOOL) SLAT
(ROUGH-TANNED —) CRUST
SHEEP SORREL SOURWEED
SHEEP TICK FAG KEB KED KADE
SHEEPWALK SLAIT
SHEER BOLD FINE MAIN MERE

PURE BLANK BRANT CRUDE
FRANK NAKED STARK STEEP
SIMPLE CLOTTED GAZETTE
EVENDOWN
(MADE OF — FABRIC) PEEKABOO
SHEET FIN CARD FILM FINE FLAT
FOIL LEAF SILL BLANK FLONG
FOLIO NAPPE CANVAS CIRCLE
DOUBLE FASCIA FENDER FLIMSY
SHROUD SINDON BLANKET
CHUDDAH CHUDDER FLOGGER
FRISKET LEAFLET PALLIUM
PAPYRUS WRAPPER AIRSHEET
EIGHTEEN FOLLOWER HANDBILL
INTERLAY SHEETLET
(— ADDED TO DEED) FOLLOWER
(— ATTACHED TO INVOICE) APRON
(— FOR BRIDGE SCORES) FLOGGER
(— OF CELLULOID) CEL CELL
(— OF CLOUDS) PALLIUM
(— OF DOUGH) STRUDEL
(— OF FIBER) BAT LAP BATT
(— OF ICE) GLARE GLAZE
(— OF IRON) CRAMPET CRAMPIT
(— OF LAVA) COULEE
(— OF LEAD) SOAKER
(— OF LEATHER) BUFFING
(— OF MICA) FILM
(— OF MUSCLE) PLATYSMA
(— OF PAPER) FLAT FOLIO FRISKET
LEAFLET HANDBILL
(— OF PARCHMENT) SKIN
FOLLOWER
(— OF RUBBER) DAM
(— OF STAMPS) PANE
(— OF STRAW) YELM
(— OF SUGAR) SLAB
(— OF TISSUE) FASCIA
(— OF TOBACCO) BINDER
(— OF WATER) NAPPE
(— USED FOR MATRIX) FLONG
(HEATED —) CAUL
(METAL —S) LATTENS
(NEWS —) GAZETTE
(ORGANIZATION —) BILL
(PERFORATED —) SIEVE
(PROTECTIVE —) CURTAIN
(THEATRICAL —) SIDE
(THIN —S OF IRON) DOUBLES
(TRANSPARENT —) GELATINE
(WINDING —) SINDON SUDARY
(PREF.) PALLIO
SHEETING PERCALE DOMESTIC
AMERIKANI
SHEHARIAH (FATHER OF —)
JEHORAM
SHEKEL (HALF —) BEKAH
SHEKINAH GLORY
SHELAH (FATHER OF —) JUDAH
SHELDRAKE SHELDER BARGOOSE
BERGANDER
SHELEMIAH (FATHER OF —) BANI
ABDEEL
(SON OF —) IRIJAH JEHUCAL
HANANIAH
SHELEPH (FATHER OF —) JOKTAN
SHELESH (FATHER OF —) HELEM
SHELF BANK BERM BINK DECK
DESS STEP TACK BENCH LEDGE
SKELF STAGE STOOL MANTEL
SCONCE SETTLE SHELVE
BACKBAR BRACKET COUNTER
PLATEAU CREDENCE CUPBOARD

(**— BEFORE STOVE**) HEARTH
(**— BEHIND ALTAR**) GRADINE
GRADINO RETABLE
(**— IN MINE**) BUNNING
(**— OF ROCK**) CAR LENCH
LENCHEON
(**ALTAR —**) BUTSUDAN
(**CONTINENTAL —**) PLATFORM
(**FIREWORKS —**) BALLOON
(**RAISED —**) SETTLE
SHELL ARD HUD PEN POD BAND
CASK CHOU CLAM CONE HARD
HOOF HULL HUSK MAIL OBUS
PELL PILL PIPI PUPA SKIN SWAD
UMBO UNIO BALAT CHANK CHINK
CONCH COPIS CRUMP CRUST
DRILL FRITZ GOURD MITER MITRA
MUREX ORMER SCAUP SHALE
SHARD SHEAL SHERD SHOCK
SHUCK TESTA TIARA TROCA
TURBO VALVE VENUS ANOMIA
ARCHIE BUCKIE BULLET BURGAU
CERION COCKLE CONKER COWRIE
CRUSTA DENTAL DOLIUM ECLAIR
JINGLE LORICA MAROON NOUGAT
NUCULA PULLET PURPLE SANKHA
SINGLE SLOUGH STROMB TRITON
TURBAN VANNET VENTER
VOLUTE WINKLE BALANUS
BALLOON CARACOL CARCASS
COCONUT DARIOLE DISCINA
GLADIUS LIMACEL MARINER
PAPBOAT PHILINE PROJECT
SCALLOP SPICULE SPINDLE
SPONDYL TEREBRA THIMBLE
TOHEROA TORPEDO TOXIFER
TROCHID TRUMPET UNICORN
BACULITE BACULOID CARAPACE
CONCHITE COQUILLE CYLINDER
DUCKFOOT EGGSHELL ENVELOPE
ESCALLOP FIGSHELL FOCALOID
FRUSTULE HELICINA MERINGUE
OLIVELLA PUPARIUM SEASHELL
SOLARIUM STROMBUS UNIVALVE
VELUTINA VERMETID VERMETUS
WARRENER WHIZBANG
WOODCOCK
(**— CONTAINING MEDICINE**)
CAPSULE
(**— OF DIATOM**) FRUSTULE
(**— OF OYSTER**) HUSK SHUCK
(**— OF SHIP**) HULK SKIN
(**— OF SLUG**) LIMACEL
(**— OF THE EARTH**) SIAL
(**— SYSTEMATICALLY**) COMB
(**—S FROM GUN**) STUFF
(**ANTIAIRCRAFT —**) FLAK ARCHIE
(**CARTRIDGE —S**) BRASS
(**CAST —S**) EXUVIAE
(**CUSTARD-FILLED —**) ECLAIR
DARIOLE
(**EMPTY —**) DOP
(**FOSSIL —**) DOLITE AMMONITE
BACULITE BALANITE CONCHITE
(**HOWITZER —**) OBUS
(**MATHEMATICAL —**) HOMEOID
(**OYSTER —S**) CULCH CULTCH
(**PART OF —**) EAR LIP RIB TIP APEX
WING HINGE SPIRE VALVE
WHORL MUSCLE SUTURE
ADDUCTOR APERTURE
(**PASTA —S**) MANICOTTI
(**PASTRY —**) CORNET QUICHE

DARIOLE TIMBALE TALMOUSE
(**PROTEIN —**) CAPSID
(**SNAIL —**) CONKER HODMADOD
(**SPIRAL —**) CHANK
(**TORTOISE —**) HOOF
(**VEGETABLE —**) DOLMA
(**PREF.**) CHITINO CHITO CONCH(O)
LOPO OECO OSTRAC(O) TESTI
(**SUFF.**) OECA OECIA OSTRACA
SHELLED VINED
SHELLFISH ORM COCK BUCKY
NACRE PIROT BUCKIE LIMPET
WIGGLE MOLLUSK PERIWIG
ASTACIAN
(**PART OF —**) EYE FAN LEG CLAW
TAIL SHELL TOOTH FEELER
RIPPER TELSON UROPOD
ABDOMEN ANTENNA CRUSHER
CARAPACE
SHELLING RATTLES
SHELL-LESS OON
SHELL MONEY UHLLO WAKIKI
SHELOMI (**FATHER OF —**) ABIHUD
SHELOMITH (**FATHER OF —**) DIBRI
ZERUBBABEL
SHELTER CAB HUT LEE LOO ABRI
BURY EAVE GIDE GITE HERD HIDE
HIVE JOKE JOUK LOWN ROOF
SCOG SCUG BARTH BELEE BENAB
BERRY BIELD BOIST BOOTH
BOTHY BOWER CABIN CLEAD
CLOAK COVER EMBAY HAVEN
HOARD HOUSE HOVEL HOVER
HOWFF HUTCH LEWTH LITHE
RESET SCOUG SHADE SHEAL
ASYLUM AWNING BELFRY BILBIE
BOOLEY BOUGHT BURROW
COVERT CRADLE DEFEND
DUGOUT GABION GUNYAH
HANGAR HARBOR HOSTEL
PANDAL REFUGE SCONCE SCREEN
SHADOW SHIELD SHROUD
SUKKAH BOROUGH CABINET
CARPORT CHAMBER DEFENSE
EMBOSOM EMBOWER HOUSING
NACELLE QUARTER RETREAT
ROOFING TABERNA UMBRAGE
WANIGAN WICKIUP BESCREEN
DOGHOUSE ENSCONCE
LODGMENT PALLIATE SECURITY
SHIELING SNOWSHED WAYHOUSE
PESTHOUSE
(**— FOR CATTLE**) HELM BOOLY
STELL HEMMEL
(**— FOR CROP WATCHERS**) KISI
(**— FOR DANCES**) ENRAMADA
(**— FOR SENTRY**) GUERITE
(**— FROM WEATHER**) LEWTH
(**— OVER BEEHIVE**) HOOD
(**BULLETPROOF —**) MANTLET
MANTELET
(**CONCRETE-AND-STEEL —**) PILLBOX
(**CRAMPED —**) HUTCH
(**FISH —**) CROY
(**LEAFY —**) LEVESEL
(**MINING —**) TALPA
(**PORTABLE —**) MANTA CABANA
(**ROCK —**) KRAPINA
(**ROUGH —**) JACAL
(**TEEPEELIKE —**) CHUM
(**TEMPORARY —**) HALE HOLD
CABIN BIVOUAC
SHELTERED LEE LEW COSY COZY

LOWN SNUG BIELD LITHE SHADY
COVERT
(**— SPACE**) KILLOGIE
SHELTERED LIFE (**AUTHOR OF —**)
GLASGOW
(**CHARACTER IN —**) EVA BENA
CORA ETTA JOHN DELIA JENNY
WELCH BARRON GEORGE JOSEPH
PEYTON CROCKER ARCHBALD
BIRDSONG ISABELLA
SHELTERING BIELDY SHADING
SHELTERLESS HOMELESS
ROOFLESS
SHELUMIEL (**FATHER OF —**)
ZURISHADDAI
SHELVE DISH BURKE SHELF SHUNT
PIGEONHOLE
SHELVES STAGE ETAGERE
SHEM (**BROTHER OF —**) HAM
JAPHET
(**FATHER OF —**) NOAH
SHEMA (**FATHER OF —**) ELPAAL
SHEMAIAH (**FATHER OF —**) JOEL
HARIM DELAIAH HASSHUB
ADONIKAM OBEDEDOM
ELIZAPHAN NETHANEEL
SHECHANIAH
(**SON OF —**) ABDA DELAIAH
OBADIAH
SHEMARIAH (**FATHER OF —**) BANI
SHEMIDA (**FATHER OF —**) GILEAD
SHEMUEL (**FATHER OF —**) TOLA
SHENAZAR (**FATHER OF —**)
JECONIAH
SHENG SANG CHENG SHING
(**ONE-HUNDREDTH —**) CHAO
SHEOL HELL
SHEPHATHIAH (**SON OF —**)
MESHULLAM
SHEPHATIAH (**FATHER OF —**) DAVID
JEHOSHAPHAT
SHEPHERD HERD SHEP COLIN
CORIN GADDI GYGES SWAIN
FEEDER PASTOR TARBOX
CORYDON DAPHNIS DRAFTER
GADARIA KURUMBA THYRSIS
TITYRUS MELIBEUS MENALCAS
PASTORAL SHEEPMAN STREPHON
(**GERMAN —**) ALSATIAN
SHEPHERDESS DELIA MOPSA
PHEBE DORCAS BERGERE
GALATEA PASTORA PERDITA
AMARYLLIS
SHEPHERD KING, THE
(**CHARACTER IN —**) ELISA AMINTA
TAMIRI AGENORE ALESSANDRO
(**COMPOSER OF —**) MOZART
SHEPHERD'S-PURSE TOYWORT
CASEWEED COCOWORT
SHEPHI (**FATHER OF —**) SHOBAL
SHERAH (**FATHER OF —**) EPHRAIM
SHERBET ICE GLACE SHRAB
SORBET GRANITA SOUFFLE
SHERD SCARTH
SHERESH (**FATHER OF —**) MACHIR
(**MOTHER OF —**) MAACHAH
SHERIFF FOUD FOWD SCULT XERIF
DEPUTY GRIEVE SCHOUT SHIRRA
BAILIFF SHREEVE SHRIEVE
ALGUACIL HUISSIER SHIREMAN
VISCOUNT
SHERRY FINO CLOVE JEREZ XERES
DOCTOR MANCHU SOLERA

OLOROSO RANGOON SHERRIS
MONTILLA MANZANILLA
SHERRY BROWN CLOVE
SHESHAI (**FATHER OF —**) ANAK
SHE STOOPS TO CONQUER
(**AUTHOR OF —**) GOLDSMITH
(**CHARACTER IN —**) KATE TONY
MARLOW CHARLES LUMPKIN
NEVILLE HASTINGS PEDIGREE
CONSTANCE HARDCASTLE
SHEVA (**FATHER OF —**) CALEB
(**MOTHER OF —**) MAACHAH
SHEVRI SESBAN
SHICER DUFFER
SHIELD ECU EGIS HIDE PELT AEGIS
APRON BIELD BOARD CLOAK
COVER FENCE GUARD GULAR
MULGA PATCH PAVIS PELTA
PYGAL SCUTE SHEND TARGE
YELDE ANCILE ANGARA BLAZON
CASQUE DEFEND FENDER
GUNTUB GYROMA LINDEN
MENTAL OCULAR PAUNCH
RONDEL SCREEN SCUTUM
SECURE TARGET BUCKLER
CLIPEUS CLYPEUS CONCEAL
LOZENGE PANNIER PAVISSE
PRIDWIN PROTECT ROSTRAL
ROTELLA ROUNDEL SHELTER
SUPPORT TESTUDO CARTOUCH
CUCULLUS HIELAMEN INSULATE
MARGINAL PRESERVE RONDACHE
STERNITE SUNSHADE BREASTING
(**— BELOW A DAM**) APRON
(**— FOR ARCHERS**) PANNIER
(**— FOR HORSE**) BIB
(**— FOR LAMP**) BONNET CHIMNEY
(**— OF A STIRRUP**) HOOD
(**— OF ABORIGINES**) MULGA
HIELAMEN
(**— OF CONTINENT**) CORE
(**— OF HIDE**) SKILDFEL
(**— OF SOMITE**) STERNITE
(**— OF TRILOBITE**) CEPHALON
(**— ON MAST**) PAUNCH
(**— ON THROAT OF FISH**) GULAR
(**— OVER BASE OF FAN**) CANOPY
(**— WITHOUT ARMS**) ALBERIA
(**BONY —**) CARAPACE
(**BULLETPROOF —**) MANTA
MANTLET MANTELET
(**HERALDIC —**) BLAZON
(**KING ARTHUR'S —**) PRIWEN
PRIDWIN
(**LEATHER —**) CHAFE
(**PART OF —**) RIB BOSS ORLE UMBO
ANTIA
(**SACRED —**) ANCILE
(**SIBERIAN —**) ANGARA
(**WICKERWORK —**) SCIATH
(**PREF.**) ASPID(O) CLYPEI CLYPEO
PELTATI PELTATO SCUT(I)
SCUTATI SCUTELLI
(**SUFF.**) ASPIS
SHIELDBEARER SQUIRE ESQUIRE
PELTAST ESCUDERO SCUTIFER
SHIELD BUG STINKBUG
SHIELD FERN FERNGALE
SHIELDMAKER TYCHIOS
SHIELD-SHAPED PELTATE
SCUTATE THYROID
SHIFT JIB BACK CHOP CORE FEND
FLIT HAUL MOVE RUSE SHIP TACK

TOUR TURN VARY VEER WEND
BREAK BUDGE CREEP CYMAR
DRIFT HOTCH QUIRK SHIRK
SHUNT SIMAR SKIFT SLIDE
SMOCK SPELL TRICK BAFFLE
CHANGE DENIAL DEVICE DOUBLE
PALTER SKYFTE SWERVE SWITCH
CHEMISE CUTBACK EVASION
FRESHEN SHUFFLE SLEIGHT
WHIFFLE ARTIFICE DISLODGE
DISPLACE DOGWATCH DOUBLING
MUTATION RESOURCE REVIRADO
TRANSFER TRAVERSE TURNOVER
WINDLASS
(— ABOUT AS THE WIND) LARGE
(— ABRUPTLY) JUMP
(— IN DANCING) BALANCE
(— IN TACKING) JIB
(— ORDER OF BELLS) HUNT
(— RAILROAD EQUIPMENT) DRILL
(— SUDDENLY) FLY CHOP GYBE
JIBE
(— WEIGHT) WING
(MINING —) CORE
SHIFTINESS LUBRICITY
SHIFTING FLUID QUICK AMBULANT
CHOPPING DRIFTING FLOATING
SLIPPAGE VARIABLE VEERABLE
SHIFTLESS DRIFTY SOZZLY
DRIFTING FECKLESS HAVELESS
SHIFTLESSNESS SLOUCH
SHIFTY GREASY DEVIOUS EVASIVE
HANGDOG SLIDING SLIPPERY
SHIITE SHIAH SECTARY SHAIKHI
TWELVER
SHILHA SHLU CHLEUH
SHILHI (DAUGHTER OF —) AZUBAH
SHILL STICK BONNET CAPPER
BOOSTER
SHILLEM (FATHER OF —) NAPHTALI
SHILLING BOB HOG CHIP HOGG
LEVY PREST DEENER HARPER
TESTON TEVISS THIRTEEN
(20 —S) POUND
(21 —S) GUINEA
(5 —S) CROWN DECUS
SHILLY-SHALLY BACK BOGGLE
SHILSHAH (FATHER OF —) ZOPHAH
SHIM GLUT LINER SHIMMER
SHIMEA (FATHER OF —) DAVID
SHIMEATH (SON OF —) ZABAD
JOZACHAR
SHIMEI (BROTHER OF —) CONONIAH
ZERUBBABEL
(FATHER OF —) BANI GERA KISH
JAHATH GERSHON PEDAIAH
JEDUTHUN
SHIMMA (BROTHER OF —) DAVID
(FATHER OF —) JESSE
SHIMMER FLASH GLIMMER
SHIMPER SKIMMER
SHIMRI (FATHER OF —) SHEMAIAH
(SON OF —) JEDIAEL
SHIMRITH (SON OF —) JEHOZABAD
SHIMRON (FATHER OF —) ISSACHAR
SHIN SHANK SKINK SWARM
CNEMIS SHINNY
SHINBONE
(SUFF.) CNEMA CNEMIA CNEMIC
CNEMUS
SHINDIG SHINDY SHIVOO
SHINDY ROW BOBBERY
SHINE RAY SUN BEAM BUFF GLOW

LAMP LEAM LINK STAR BLARE
BLICK BLINK BLOOM EXCEL GLAIK
GLARE GLEAM GLEIT GLENT
GLINT GLISS GLORE GLORY GLOSS
GLOZE SHEEN SKYRE STARE
BEACON DAZZLE GLANCE LUSTER
LUSTRE SCANCE EFFULGE
GLIMMER GLISTEN GLITTER
RADIATE REFLECT SHIMMER
SPARKLE RUTILATE
(— BRIGHTLY) BEEK FLAME LIGHT
(— FAINTLY) SCARROW
(— UPON) SUN SMITE
SHINER CHUB DACE BREAM
REDFIN CYPRINID WINDFISH
SHINER-UP PATCHER
SHINGLE SHIM BEACH SHAKE
SHIDE SLATE ASTYLL CHESIL
KNOBBLE STARTER
SHINGLER NOBBLER
SHINGLES ZONA ZOSTER
(PREF.) ZOSTERI ZOSTERO
SHININESS GLARE GLAZE GLOSS
SHINING GLAD NEAT CLEAR GLARY
LIGHT LUCID NITID SHEER WHITE
ARDENT ARGENT ASHINE BRIGHT
FULGID GLOSSY GOLDEN LUCENT
MARBLE NITENT ORIENT SERENE
SHEENY SPUNKY STARRY
ADAZZLE BURNING FULGENT
GLARING GLIMMER LAMPING
FLASHING GLEAMING LUCULENT
LUSTRANT LUSTROUS NITIDOUS
RELUCENT RUTILANT SPLENDID
STARLIKE SUNBEAMY SUNSHINY
(PREF.) STILPNO
SHINLEAF PYROLA
SHINNY PEG SHINTY
SHINTO (— SECT) RYOBU
SHINTY CAMANACHA
SHIP (ALSO SEE BOAT AND VESSEL)
ARK CAT COG HOY NAO BARK
BOAT BOOM GRAB HAND HULK
KEEL LADE NAVY PAHI PINE PINK
SAIL SEND SNOW TREE WOOD
ZULU CHECK LAKER OILER PINTA
PRORE RAZEE SCOUT SCREW
SKIFF WHELP ANDREW ARGOSY
BARKEY BARQUE BOTTOM
CARTEL CASTLE CHASER COALER
CODMAN DECKER DIESEL GALIOT
GALLEY HOLCAD HOPPER
LANCHA LATEEN LORCHA
MASTER MISTIC MOTHER PACKET
PUFFER RUNNER SAILER SALVOR
SEALER SMOKER TONNER TRAVEL
VESSEL ADMIRAL CARRACK
CLIPPER COLLIER CONSORT
DROMOND FACTORY FELUCCA
FOREIGN FRIGATE FRUITER
GABBARD GALLEON GUNBOAT
INVOICE MACHINE MULETTA
ONERARY PATAMAR PINNACE
POLACRE SHALLOP SHIPLET
SPITKIT STEAMER BALANDRA
BALINGER BILANDER CAPITANA
CUNARDER DRUMBLER FLAGSHIP
GALLEASS GAYDIANG INDIAMAN
JAPANNER LANCHARA MAGAZINE
PESSONER PIPPINER REPEATER
SAILSHIP SCHOONER SMUGGLER
SPANIARD MERCHANTMAN

(— BUILT FROM NAILS OF DEAD)
NAGLFAR
(— FITTED AS CHURCH) BETHEL
(— IN LIQUOR TRADE) COPER
(— OF ARGONAUTS) ARGO
(— OF NORSEMEN) KEEL
(CLUMSY —) HULK
(DEPOT —) TENDER
(ESCORT —) CORVETTE
(FLEET OF —S) ARMADA
(JAPANESE —) MARU
(MALAY —) COUGNAR
(NOVA SCOTIAN —) BLUENOSE
(OBJECT SHAPED LIKE A —) NEF
(PART OF —) BOW CAP GUY RUN
BEAM BOOM GAFF JACK LIFT
MAST RAIL STAY VANG YARD
BRACE CHAIN ROYAL SHEET
TRUCK JUMPER RUDDER SHROUD
STRAKE BOBSTAY BULWARK
BUMPKIN COUNTER FORETOP
JIBSTAY MAINTOP NETTING
PENDANT RATLINE RIGGING
SKYSAIL SPANKER STIRRUP
STRIKER SWIFTER TOPMAST
BACKROPE BACKSTAY CUTWATER
FOOTROPE FOREMAST LIFELINE
MAINMAST MAINSTAY STUDDING
CROSSTREE FORESHEET
MAINSHEET NAMEBOARD
WATERLINE MARTINGALE
MIZZENMAST TOPGALLANT
(PIRATE —) GALLIVAT
(PRIZE —) CAPTURE
(QUARANTINE —) LAZARET
(RECEIVING —) GUARDO
(REMOTE-CONTROLLED —) DRONE
(SLOW —) BUCKET
(STORE —) FLUTER
(SUPPLY —) COPER COOPER
(UNTRIM —) BALLAHOO
(VIKING —) DRAKE
(PL.) NAVY MARINE SEACRAFT
SHIPPING
(PREF.) NAU(TI) NAV(I)
SHIPFITTER FITTER ERECTOR
SHIPHI (SON OF —) ZIZA
SHIPHTAN (SON OF —) KEMUEL
SHIPMASTER PADRONE
SHIPMENT CARLOT RAILING
DISPATCH SHIPPAGE
SHIPSHAPE NEAT TIDY TRIM CIVIL
ATAUNT ORDERLY
SHIP SWEEPER TOPASS
TOPIWALA
SHIPWAY BERTH
SHIPWORM ARTER BORER COBRA
TEREDO PILEWORM WOODWORM
SHIPWRECK WRACK NAUFRAGE
SHIPWRIGHT WAYMAN BUILDER
SHIRE DERBY SHEER COUNTY
SHIRK BALK FUNK GOOF MIKE
BAULK BLINK BUDGE DODGE
EVADE FEIGN FUDGE SKULK
SLACK RODNEY FINAGLE SHACKLE
SHAFFLE SOLDIER SHAMMOCK
SHIRKER FUNK PIKER SOGER
FUNKER ROTTER BLUDGER
SLACKER SLINKER SUGARER
COBERGER CUTHBERT EMBUSQUE
SCOWBANK
SHIRLEY (AUTHOR OF —) BRONTE
(CHARACTER IN —) JOE DONNE

EMILY LOUIS MOORE PRYOR
SCOTT MALONE ROBERT KEELDAR
SHIRLEY CAROLINE HELSTONE
HORTENSE SWEETING
MATTHEWSON
SHIRR SMOCK
SHIRT TOB JUPE SARK TOBE BLUEY
HAIRE JUPON KAMIS SHIFT
BANIAN BANIYA CAMISA CAMISE
PALAKA PARTLET UNDERGO
VAREUSE KAMLEIKA
(HAIR —) HAIRE CILICE
(SLEEVELESS —) FECKET
(WORKMAN'S —) FROCK
(WORNOUT —) DICKY
SHIRTING CHEVIOT HARVARD
HOLLAND SARKING
SHIRTWAIST BLOUSE GARIBALDI
SHISHA (SON OF —) AHIAH
ELIHOREPH
SHITTIMWOOD BOXWOOD
SHIVA (SON OF —) GANESHA
KARTTIKEYA
(WIFE OF —) KALI DURGA
SHIVAREE BELLING CHIVARI
HORNING SERENADE
SHIVER JAR GIRL GRUE BEVER
BREAK CHILL CREEM CREEP FRILL
GROWS QUAKE SHRUG SLICE
CHIVER DITHER DUDDER GROOSE
HOTTER NIDDER NITHER QUIVER
SHRIMP SPLINT TREMOR CHITTER
FLICKER FRISSON SHATTER
SHITHER SHUDDER TREMBLE
KAMLEIKA SPLINTER
SHIVERING AGUED CHILL OURIE
TREMOR ASHIVER
SHIZA (SON OF —) ADINA
SHOAL BAJO BANK FLAT REEF SPIT
BARRA DRAVE FLOTE SCULL
SHELF SCHOOL SHALLOW
TOWHEAD
SHOAT GURRY SHOOT SHOTT
SHOBAB (FATHER OF —) CALEB
DAVID
(MOTHER OF —) AZUBAH
BATHSHEBA
SHOBAL (FATHER OF —) SEIR CALEB
SHOBI (FATHER OF —) NAHASH
SHOCK COP JAR BLOW BUMP DINT
JOLT RACK SHOG STUN TURN
APPAL BRUNT GAVEL GLIFF
GLOFF SHAKE STOOK STOUR
DISMAY FRIGHT IMPACT JOSTLE
JUMBLE REJOLT RICKLE ROLLER
STRIKE ASTOUND CANVASS
DISGUST HATTOCK HORRIFY
STAGGER STARTLE STUPEFY
TERRIFY DISEDIFY GLIFFING
SURPRISE
(— OF CORN) STOOK STOUT
STITCH
(MENTAL —) TRAUMA
SHOCK ABSORBER SHOCK
BUFFER DASHPOT SNUBBER
SHOCKED AGHAST
SHOCKER RICKER STOOKER
SHOCKING GRIM AWFUL LURID
HORRID UNHOLY BURNING
FEARFUL FEARING GHASTLY
HIDEOUS DREADFUL ENORMOUS
HORRIBLE SCANDALOUS
SHOD CALCED

SHODDY SOFT CHEAP FOOTY
MUNGO SOFTS TACKY SLEAZY
SHOE BAL CUE PAN BOOT BROG
CLOG DRAG FLAT HALF SKID
SOCK TURN BLAKE DERBY KLOMP
MOYLE ROMEO SABOT SCRAE
SLING SPIKE STOGA STOGY STRAP
ANKLET BEAKER BROGAN
BROGUE BUSKIN CALIGA CALIGO
CHOPIN COBCAB COCKER
CRAKOW CREOLE DORSAY GAITER
GALOSH KILTIE MULLER PATTEN
PINSON POLISH SADDLE SANDAL
SECQUE BAUCHLE BLUCHER
BOTTINE CALCEUS CHOPINE
COWHIDE FLIPPER OXONIAN
RULLION SHOEPAC SLIPPER
SNEAKER BALMORAL BRODEKIN
CALCEATE COLONIAL PLATFORM
PLIMSOLL SABOTINE SANDSHOE
SKEWBACK SLIPSLOP SOLLERET
(— FOR GRINDING) MULLER
(— FOR MULE) PLANCHE
(— IN TRUSS OR FRAME)
SKEWBACK
(— NOT FASTENED ON) PUMP
(— OF A SLEDGE) HOB
(— OF AN OX) CUE
(— OF COMIC ACTOR) BAXA
(— OF SUBWAY CAR) PAN
(— REPAIRER) JACKMAN
(— TO CHECK WHEEL) DRAG SKID
(— USED AS BRAKE) SKATE
(— WORN ON EITHER FOOT)
STRAIGHT
(—S AND STOCKINGS) FEET
(ARMORED —) SABBATON
(BABY'S —) CACK
(DOWN-AT-HEEL —) SHAUCHLE
(HOBNAILED —) TACKET
(LARGE —S) GUNBOATS
(LOW-CUT —) SOCK GILLY ANKLET
BUSKIN SLIPPER COLONIAL
(MILITARY —) CALIGA
(OLD —) BAUCHLE
(PART OF —) TIP TOE ARCH FLAP
HEEL LIFT SOLE VAMP WELT
AGLET SHANK COLLAR EYELET
FOXING INSTEP LINING THROAT
TONGUE COUNTER OUTSOLE
QUARTER MUDGUARD PLATFORM
SHOELACE BREASTING
(PIKED —) BEAKER
(RAWHIDE —) HIMMING VELSKOEN
(SPORTS —S) GILLIES
(STEEL —) SOLLERET
(THIN —) PINSON SCLAFF
(WINGED —S) TALARIA
(WOODEN —) KLOMP SABOT
PATTEN RACKET RACQUET
(WORN —) SCRAE
(PL.) SHEEN SHOON SHUNE
SCHONE CASUALS FOOTGEAR
(PREF.) CALCEI
SHOEMAKER SNOB FOXER SOLER
ARCHER CHAMAR CODGER
COZIER FUDGER GOUGER SOOTER
SOUTER VAMPER COBBLER
CRISPIN CROWNER SHOEMAN
SNOBBER UPPERER CORVISER
SNOBSCAT CORDWAINER
SHOEMAKING SNOBBING
SHOGI (EXPERT LEVEL IN —) DAN

SHOGUN TYCOON
SHOHAM (FATHER OF —) JAAZIAH
SHOMER (SON OF —) JEHOZABAD
SHOO HOOSH DISPEL
SHOOK PACK BLANK SHAKE
SHOOT DAG GUN IMP PAY POT
PUT ROD TIP BANG BOLT BROD
CANE CHIT CION DRAW LEAF
PLUG SLIP WEFT ARROW BLAST
BLAZE BROWN DRILL DRIVE
EXPEL FLUSH FROND GEMMA
GLEAM LANCE LAYER PLUFF
SCION SHEET SOBOL SPEAR SPIRE
SPRAY SPRIG SPRIT SPURT SQUIB
STICK STOOL TUBER TURIO
VIMEN BRANCH FLIGHT FLOWER
GERMEN GROWTH HEADER
HURTLE LAUNCH LEADER OFFSET
RATOON SALLOW SOBOLE SPRING
SPROUT STOLON STOUND
STOVEN STRIKE SUCKER TILLER
TURION BUDLING CHIMNEY
DROPPER SCOURGE SPIRING
TENDRIL TENDRON THALLUS
ANAPHYTE APOBLAST CATAPULT
TRAILING
(— A MARBLE) LAG TAW KNUCKLE
(— A WHALE) STRIKE
(— ASIDE FROM MARK) DRIB
(— AT LONG RANGE) SNIPE
(— DOWN) SPLASH
(— DUCKS) SKAG
(— FORTH) JET GLEAM SPIRE
(— FROM DEER'S ANTLER) SPELLER
(— INDISCRIMINATELY) BROWN
(— MOOSE OR DEER) YARD
(— OF A TREE) STOW WHIP LANCE
BRANCH
(— OUT) JUT CHIT DART ERADIATE
(— SEAL) SWATCH
(— UP) SPIRE SPURT
(—S USED AS FODDER) BROWSE
(FIRST —S) BRAIRD
(FLEXIBLE —) BINE
(LATERAL —) ARM
(ORE —) BONANZA
(PAWNBROKER'S —) SPOUT
(SUGARCANE —) LALO
(TENDER —) FLUSH
(WILLOW —) SALLOW
(PREF.) BLAST(O) SOBOLI STOLONI
THALL(I)(O)
(SUFF.) BLAST(IC)(Y) SPERM(A)(AE)
(AL)(IA)(IC)(OUS)(UM)(Y)
SHOOTER SCOOT BLASTER
GUNSTER PLUFFER SHOTMAN
SKEETER
SHOOTING COCKING GUNNING
GUNPLAY HUNTING POTTING
SHOOTING STAR METEOR
COWSLIP SHOOTER PRIMWORT
SHOP CRIB TOKO BOOTH BURSE
STORE TRADE KOSHER SHOPPE
TIENDA WINKEL ALMACEN
APOTHEC BOTTEGA CABARET
MERCERY SPICERY TABERNA
TURNERY BOUTIQUE COOKSHOP
CREMERIE EMPORIUM ESPRESSO
EXCHANGE MAGAZINE
SHOWSHOP SLOPSHOP
TENDEJON WAREROOM
(BARBER —) BARBERY
(BLACKSMITH —) SMITHY

(LIQUOR —) SALOON
(OLD CLOTHES —) FLIPPERY
(PAWNBROKER'S —) LUMBER
SPROUT
(REPAIR —) GARAGE
(SUTLER'S —) CANTEEN
SHOPKEEPER CIT ARAB BAKAL
BANIAN CHETTY SOUDAGUR
SHOPLIFT BOOST
SHOPLIFTER BOOSTER
SHORE GIB TOM BANK RIPE RIVE
SAND SIDE TRIG BEACH BENCH
CLIFF COAST MARGE RAKER
RANCE SHOAR WARTH RIVAGE
STRAND BUTTRESS DOCKSIDE
LANDFALL LANDSIDE SEACOAST
SHOREBIRD TATTLER WRYBILL
SURFBIRD PHALAROPE
SANDPIPER
SHORE CRAB OCHIDORE
SHOREFISH OPALEYE
SHORER BRACER CRIBBER
SHORN NOT NOTT POLLED
TONSURED
SHORT AIM LAG LOW SHY BAIN
CURT NEAR NIGH SOON BLUFF
BRIEF BUNTY CLOSE CRISP CUTTY
FUBBY FUBSY PUNCH SQUAB
UNDER ABRUPT CRISPY SCANTY
SCARCE STUGGY STUNTY
SUDDEN ULLAGE BOBTAIL
BRUSQUE CURTATE LACONIC
SQUIDGY STUBBED SUMMARY
SNAPPISH SUCCINCT
(— AND FLAT) CAMUS
(— AND THICK) CHUNKY STOCKY
STUBBY STUMPY TRUNCH
TRUNCHED
(— AND THICKSET) NUGGETY
(— AS OF WOOL) FRIBBY
(— PERSON OR ANIMAL) PUNCH
(BRIEF —S) MONOKINI
(STOUT AND —) BUNTY CHUFFY
PLUGGY THICKSET
(PL.) BERMUDAS
(PREF.) BRACHI(O) BRACHY BREVI
(SUFF.) BRACH(ISTO)(Y)
SHORTAGE FAMINE DROUGHT
WANTAGE UNDERAGE
SHORT-BREATHED PURSY
SHORTCHANGE FLUFF SHORT
SHORTCOMING SIN DEFECT
FOIBLE
SHORT-COUPLED CHUFFY
SHORTCUT CUTOFF
SHORT-EARED OWL MOMO
SHORTEN CUT CLIP STAG ELIDE
SLASH REDUCE ABRIDGE CURTAIL
EXCERPT SCANTLE CONTRACT
DIMINISH RETRENCH ABBREVIATE
(— AND THICKEN IRON) JUMP
(— GRIP) CHOKE
SHORTENED CURTED BOBTAIL
CURTATE ABRIDGED
SHORTENING (— OF SYLLABLE)
SYSTOLE
SHORTEST LEAST
SHORTHORN DURHAM
TEESWATER
SHORT-LIVED FRAGILE
SHORTLY SOON DUMPILY
DIRECTLY PRESENTLY
SHORT-NAPPED RAS

SHORTNESS BREVITY CURTNESS
UNLENGTH
SHORT-RANGE TACTICAL
SHORT-SIGHTED SANDED
PURBLIND
SHORTSIGHTEDNESS MYOPIA
SHORT-TEMPERED CRUSTY
SNIPPY SNUFFY
SHORT-TERM FLOATING
SHORT-WINDED PURSY PURFLY
PURFLED PURSIVE
SHOT POP SET BLUE CASE JOLT
OVER PLUG SETT SLUG BLANK
FLIER FLING FLUFF FLYER OUTER
PLUFF SHOOT TOWEL WHITE
CARTON CENTER CENTRE
FOLLOW MUDCAP REBOTE
ALIIPOE BOMBARD CUTAWAY
DEADEYE GUNSHOT LANGREL
PELICAN SIGHTER BLIZZARD
BUCKSHOT HAILSHOT LANGRAGE
MARKSHOT SCORCHER
(— BEYOND TARGET) OVER
(— FOR CULVERIN) PELICAN
(— IN FIFTH CIRCLE) WHITE
(— IN FOURTH CIRCLE) BLACK
(— IN THIRD CIRCLE) BLUE
(— OF NARCOTIC) FIX
(— STRIKING BULL'S-EYE) CARTON
(— THAT HITS) CLOUT
(ARCHERY —) GREEN
(BADMINTON —) CLEAR
(BASKETBALL —) BOMB JUMPER
(BILLIARD —) DRAG STAB CAROM
MASSE SCREW FOLLOW SAFETY
SPREAD BRICOLE SCRATCH
(BOW —) DRAFT
(CAMERA —) INTERCUT
(CROQUET —) SPLIT FOLLOW
(CURLING —) INWICK OUTWICK
(FINAL —) UPSHOT
(GOOD —) SCREAMER
(PISTOL —) BARK
(POOL —) BREAK
(SIZE OF —) F T BB FF TT BBB
DUST BUCKSHOT
(SMALL —) PELLET
(SNOOKER —) POT
(TENNIS —) ACE LOB DINK SERVE
SMASH
(VOLLEY OF —S) BLIZZARD
SHOTGUN DOUBLE TUPARA
PEPPERER SCATTERSHOT
SHOULD MOW SUD WANT OUGHT
(— NOT) SHUDNA SHOULDNA
SHOULDNT
SHOULDER DOD AXLE CLOD DODD
GAIN HUMP SHIP STEP SULD
BOUGH PITCH SPALL SPULE
VERGE AXILLA EPAULE RELISH
SCOTCH SPAULD KNUCKLE
RIMBASE SHOUTHER
(— AROUND TENON) RELISH
(— OF BOLT) NAB
(— OF FIREARM STOCK) RIMBASE
(— OF FLY) CHEEK
(— OF LAMB) BANJO
(— OF PORK) HAND PICNIC
CUSHION
(— OF RABBIT OR HARE) WING
(— OF ROAD) BERM BERME
HAUNCH QUARTER
(— PAIN) OMODYNIA

(BEVELED —) GAIN
(PL.) FOREBOWS
(PREF.) OM(O)
SHOULDER BLADE SPALD SPEAL
SCAPULA OMOPLATE
(PREF.) SCAPUL(I)(O)
SHOUT BAY BOO CRY HOY HUE
BAWL CALL CROW GAPE HAIL
HOCH HOOP HOOT REME ROOT
ROUP ROUT SCRY TOOT YELL
BRAWL CHEER CLAIM CLEPE
CRACK GREDE HAVOC HOLLO
HUZZA REERE WHEWT WHOOP
ABRAID BOOHOO CLAMOR
GOLLAR GOLLER HALLOO HOLLER
HURRAH STEVEN YAMMER
ACCLAIM SHILLOO GARDYLOO
LULLILOO SCRONACH
(— AS CHILDREN) BELDER
(— DERISIVELY) BARRACK
(— FOR OR AGAINST) BARRACK
(— OF APPROVAL) BRAVO
(— OF ENCOURAGEMENT) HARK
(— OF HIGHLAND DANCER) HOOCH
(— OF JOY) IO
(HUNTING —) CHEVY
SHOUTING HUE GLAM ROUP ROUT
HOLLO CLAMOR HOLLOA JUBILEE
SHOVE JUT PUT BUNT DUSH FEND
MUCK PICK POTE PUSH SHOG
SHUN BOOST CROWD DUNCH
ELBOW HUNCH SHIVE SHUNT
HUSTLE JOSTLE JUSTLE MUSCLE
THRUST SCAMBLE
(— CARELESSLY) BUNG
(— IN MARBLES) FULK
SHOVEL FAN VAN CAST PEEL
SPUD SCOOP SHOOL SPADE
SPOON BLUNGER SCOPPET
SCUPPIT SLUDGER DUCKBILL
DUCKFOOT STROCKLE
(— FOR COIN) MAIN
(— FOR DRESSING ORE) VAN
(BRICKMAKING —) CUCKHOLD
(CASTING —) SCUTTLE
(CHARCOAL BURNER'S —) RABBLE
(FIRE —) PEEL SLICE
(GRATED —) HARP
(MINER'S —) BANJO
(PERFORATED —) SKIMMER
SHOVELER SCOOPER WHINGER
BLUEWING SHOULERD WHINYARD
SHOW DO SAY SEE WIS BOSH CALL
DASH HAVE ITEM LEAD MARK
MIEN SCAW SEEM SHEW TENT
VIEW WEAR WISE ARGUE ASSAY
EXERT FLASH GLOSS GLOZE KITHE
PRIDE PROVE SHINE SIGHT SLANG
SPORT TEACH ACCUSE ASSIGN
BETRAY BLAZON CHICHI COUTHE
DENOTE DETECT DEVICE DIRECT
ENSIGN ESCORT EVINCE EXPOSE
FIGURE FLAUNT GAIETY GAYETY
LAYOUT MUSTER OBJECT PARADE
REVEAL SCHEME SPREAD SPRUNK
VANITY ADVANCE ANALYZE
BALLOON BESPEAK BETOKEN
BRAVURA BREATHE DECLARE
DISPLAY DIVULGE EXHIBIT
EXPRESS FASHION MONSTER
PRESAGE PRODUCE PROPOSE
SELLOUT SHOWING SIGNIFY
TAMASHA TRIUMPH COLORING

CONCLUDE EVIDENCE FLOURISH
FORESHOW INDICATE MANIFEST
PRETENCE PROCLAIM SEMBLANT
SIDESHOW
(— APPROVAL) CLAP APPLAUD
(— CONTEMPT) SCOFF
(— DISCONTENT) GROUCH
(— DISPLEASURE) POUT
(— DOGS) BENCH
(— ENTHUSIASM) DROOL
(— FORTH) BLAZE CIPHER
(— IN PUBLIC CELEBRATION)
PAGEANT
(— ITSELF) APPEAR
(— MERCY) SPARE
(— OF LEARNING) SCIOLISM
(— OF LIGHT) BLINK
(— OF REASON) COLOR
(— OF VANITY) AIR
(— OFF) FLASH PRANK SPORT
SWANK HOTDOG PARADE
(— ONESELF) BE
(— POSITION OF) MEITH
(— PROMISE) FRAME SHAPE
(— RESPECT FOR) REGARD
(— REVERSE TREND) REACT
(— SIGNS OF GIVING WAY) WAVER
(— SIGNS OF ILLNESS) GRUDGE
(— THE BOTTOM) KEEL
(— THE SIGHTS) LIONIZE
(— THE TEETH) GIRN GRIN
(— THE WAY) LEAD CONDUCT
(— TO BE FALSE) BELIE DISPROVE
(— UNKINDNESS) WAIT
(— WITHOUT SUBSTANCE) FORM
(ARTFUL —) GRIMACE
(FALSE —) COLOR FUCUS BUBBLE
TINSEL ILLUSION PRETENCE
(FLOOR —) CABARET
(GAUDY —) HOOPLA BRAVERY
(MERE —) PHANTOM
(MOMENTARY —) FLASH
(ORNATE —) FLUBDUB
(OSTENTATIOUS —) SPRUNK
DISPLAY
(OUTSIDE —) VARNISH
(OUTWARD —) FUCUS VISAGE
(PUBLIC —) EXPO
(PUPPET —) DROLL MOTION
WAJANG WAYANG GUIGNOL
(RIDICULOUS —) FARCE
(RUDIMENTARY —) SATURA
(SPECIOUS —) GLOZE
(STREET —) RAREE
(SUPERFICIAL —) GLOSS VENEER
(TRAVELLING —) SLANG
(PREF.) PHAENO PHANER(O)
PHANTA PHANTO PHENO
(SUFF.) PHANY
SHOW BOAT (AUTHOR OF —)
FERBER
(CHARACTER IN —) KIM ANDY ELLY
HAWKS JULIE PARTHY GAYLORD
RAVENAL MAGNOLIA SCHULTZY
SHOWCASE ISLAND VITRINE
SHOWER WET HAIL RAIN SCAT
SUMP AUGER BLASH SKITE SOUSE
FLURRY PELTER PEPPER SHEWER
DRIBBLE SHATTER WEATHER
COMMORTH SCOUTHER
(CONCENTRATED —) BARRAGE
(HEAVY —) SUMP
(RAIN —) RASH

(SUDDEN —) SCUD SKIT BRASH
PLUMP
SHOWERY BRASHY CLASHY
SCATTY
SHOWILY GAILY BRAVELY
GAUDILY
SHOWINESS DASH GLARE PAZAZZ
PIZAZZ GLITTER PIZZAZZ
FLOURISH GEWGAWRY SPLENDOR
SHOWING SPRANK SPARKLE
(— SAME NATURE) AKIN
(SUPERFICIAL —) FACE
(PREF.) PHAEN(O) PHAINO
SHOWMANSHIP RECLAME
SHOW-ME STATE MISSOURI
SHOW-OFF CUTUP
SHOWY GAY FINE LOUD NICE
RORY VAIN DASHY FLARY FLASH
FRESH GAUDY GIDDY GRAND
JAZZY NOBBY SPICY SWANK
TOPPY VAUDY VIEWY BRANKY
BRAZEN BRUMMY CHICHI DRESSY
FLASHY FLOSSY GARISH GEWGAW
GLOSSY JAUNTY PURPLE SHANTY
SKYRIN SPANKY SPORTY TAWDRY
DASHING FLAUNTY GALLANT
GAUDFUL HOTSHOT POMPOUS
SHOWFUL SHOWISH SPLASHY
SPLURGY CLAPTRAP FASTUOUS
GIMCRACK GORGEOUS ORGULOUS
SPARKISH SPECIOUS SPLENDID
TRUMPERY CLINQUANT
OBTRUSIVE
(NOT —) CIVIL LENTEN DISCREET
SHRED DAG HOG JAG RAG ROND
ROON SNIP TEAR WISP BLYPE
CLOUT GRATE PATCH SHRAG
SHRIP CULPON SCREED SLIVER
TARGET FRAZZLE FRITTER
MAMMOCK SHATTER FILAMENT
(— FISH) SCROD
(— OF CLOTHES) TACK
(— OF FLESH) TAG AGNAIL
(— OF HAIR) TAIT
(PL.) TAVERS CADDICE TAIVERS
SHREDDED CUT
SHREDDER DEVIL
SHREW ERD JES NAG TANA PRESS
RANNY SOREX VIXEN CALLET
JUMPER MIGALE TARGER TARTAR
TUPAIA VIRAGO BLARINA
HELLCAT MUSKRAT PENTAIL
SCYTALE TUPAIID SINSRING
SORICINE SORICOID UROPSILE
XANTHIPPE
(TREE —) BANXRING
(PREF.) HYDRAC(O) SORICI
SHREWD DRY SLY ACID ARCH
CUTE FELL GASH SAGE TIDY
WARE WISE ACUTE CAGEY
CANNY HEADY LOOPY PAWKY
POKEY SHARP SMART SWACK
ARGUTE ARTFUL ASTUTE CALLID
CLEVER CRAFTY SPRACK SUBTLE
CUNNING GNOSTIC KNOWING
PARLISH PARLOUS POLITIC
PRACTIC SAPIENT SAGACIOUS
PERSPICACIOUS
(— PERSON) FILE
SHREWDLY SLILY CANNILY
ASTUTELY
SHREWDNESS NOUS SAVVY
ACUMEN POLICY SLYNESS

GUMPTION PRUDENCE SAGACITY
CALLIDITY
SHREWISH CURST CURSED
SHREWD VIXENISH
SHREWMOUSE MYGALE SCYTALE
SHRIEK CRY YIP YARM YELL CHIRK
SKIRL SCREAM SCRIKE SHRIKE
SKRIKE SPRAICH
SHRIKE POPE BATARA BOUBOU
BRUBRU FISCAL FLASHER
FLUSHER LOGHEAD MIGRANT
MINIVET TRILLER BELLBIRD
FALCONET PUFFBACK
WOODCHAT
SHRILL HIGH KEEN THIN ACUTE
PIPEY SHARP SHILL SHIRL
ARGUTE BRASSY GLASSY PIPING
SQUEAK TREBLE HAUTAIN
MINIKIN SCREAKY PIERCING
STRIDENT
(MAKE — NOISE) POTRACK
(PREF.) OXY
SHRIMP GRIT APANG CARID MYSID
PARVA PRAWN NIPPER PANDLE
SCAMPI ARTEMIA BROWNIE
CAMARON DECAPOD POLYPOD
REDTAIL SPECTER SPECTRE
CARIDEAN CRAWFISH CREVETTE
MACRURAN
(SUFF.) CARIS
SHRINE ADYT NAOS GUACA
HUACA ISEUM MAZAR SEKOS
STUPA ZIARA ADYTON ADYTUM
CHASSE DAGABA DAGOBA
DURGAH HALLOW HIERON
MEMORY SAMADH VIMANA
ZIARAT CHAITYA CHAPLET
CHORTEN EDICULE FANACLE
MARTYRY MEMORIA SACRARY
TEMENOS THESEUM AEDICULA
DELUBRUM FERETORY FERETRUM
GURDWARA LARARIUM
MARABOUT PANTHEON
VALHALLA RELIQUARY
(— STUDY) NAOLOGY
(PREF.) PASTO
SHRINK COY SHY DARE DUCK FULL
FUNK GIVE NIRL PEAK ABHOR
ARGHE CLING COWER CRINE
QUAIL RELAX RIVEL SHRAM
SHRUG SHUCK START WINCE
BLANCH BLENCH BOGGLE COTTER
CRINGE FLINCH LESSEN RECOIL
SCRUMP SETTLE SHRIMP WEAZEN
CRIMPLE CRUMPLE DWINDLE
SCUNNER SHRIVEL COLLAPSE
CONTRACT
(— FROM DRYNESS) GIZZEN
SHRINKAGE SETTLE SHRINK
SINKAGE
(— OF TYPE) SQUEEZE
SHRINKING COY SHY TIMID
BLETHE CREEPS DASTARD
FULLING LOATHFUL TIMOROUS
SHRIVE SHRIFT CONFESS SHRIEVE
SHRIVEL NIRL SEAR WELK BLAST
CLING CRINE PARCH RIVEL
SHRAM SNERP WIZEN BLIGHT
COTTER GIZZEN SCORCH SCRUMP
SHRINK WEAZEN WITHER
CROZZLE
SHRIVELED WEDE CLUNG CORKY
THIRL GIZZEN STARKY PUNGLED

SHIRPIT WIZENED WRITHEN SHRAMMED WRIZZLED
SHROPSHIRE SALOP
SHROUD HIDE SARK CLOAK CRAPE DRAPE HABIT SHEET SWIFT EMBOSK HEARSE KITTEL MUFFLE SCREEN SHADOW SINDON SUDARY BENIGHT CONCEAL CURTAIN INVOLVE SWIFTER CEREMENT
(PL.) PUTTOCK
SHROVETIDE SHROVE GUTTIDE CARNIVAL
SHROVE TUESDAY FASTENS GUTTIDE
SHRUB TI BAY HAW KAT MAY QAT TOD AKIA ALEM BUSH COCA HOYA INGA ITEA KARO KEUR KHAT MUSK ULEX AKALA AKELA ALDER ALISO ARUSA BOCCA BROOM BUAZE CEIBO CUMAY ELDER GOOMA GOUMI HAZEL HENNA IXORA LEDUM LEMON LILAC MAQUI MARIA MUDAR RETEM SALAL SHROG SUMAC TOYON ZILLA ABELIA AGRITO AKONGE AMULLA ANAGUA ANILAO ARALIA ARUSHA AUCUBA AUPAKA AZALEA BLOLLY CENIZO CHEKAN CHERRY CISTUS CORREA DAPHNE DHAURI DRIMYS FEIJOA FRUTEX JACATE JOJOBA KARAMU KOWHAI LABRUM LARREA LAUREL MATICO MYRTLE NARRAS PENAEA PITURI RAETAM SAVINE STORAX STYRAX ACEROLA AFERNAN AGARITA AMORPHA ARBORET ARRAYAN ARRIMBY AZAROLE BANKSIA BORONIA BUCKEYE BULLACE CANTUTA CHACATE CHAMISE CHANCHE DEUTZIA EHRETIA ENCELIA EPACRID EPHEDRA FUCHSIA GUMWOOD GUTWORT HOPBUSH HOPSAGE JASMINE JETBEAD JEWBUSH JOEWOOD KUMQUAT LANTANA MAHONIA NUNNARI PAVONIA PEABUSH PEARHAW PIMELEA RHODORA SPIRAEA TARBUSH THEEZAN ABELMOSK ALLTHORN BARBERRY CAMELLIA CARAGANA COMEBACK COPALCHE DRACAENA GOATBUSH GOWIDDIE GRAVILEA HARDHACK HARDTACK HAWTHORN HIBISCUS IRONWOOD KEURBOOM KOROMIKO MOORWORT NINEBARK OCOTILLO OLEASTER OSOBERRY PIPEWOOD PONDBUSH ROSEMARY SANDSTAY SANDWOOD SASANQUA SHRUBLET SNOWBALL SNOWBELL SNOWBUSH SOAPBARK STANDARD MISTLETOE POINCIANA PHILADELPHUS
(AROMATIC —) THYME CLUSIA BORONIA HOGBUSH ALLSPICE
(AUSTRALIAN —) GOOMA BUDDAH DRIMYS GEEBUNG WARATAH MILKBUSH SANDSTAY
(CHINESE —) KERRIA

(CLIMBING —) CATCLAWS SOLANDRA
(DESERT —) AFERNAN
(EVERGREEN —) BOX BAGO ILEX TITI BOLDO ERICA FURZE HEATH HOLLY KOSAM PYXIE SALAL SAVIN TOYON BAUERA DAHOON KALMIA LAUREL PEPINO PROTEA RUSCUS SAKAKI ARDISIA BARETTA JASMINE JUNIPER MADRONA MAHONIA CALFKILL CARAUNDA EVONYMUS OLEANDER SASANQUA MANZANITA
(FRAGRANT —) JASMINE HUISACHE MEJORANA MEZEREON ROSEMARY
(HAWAIIAN —) AKALA AKELA ILIMA KOKIO OLONA
(LOW —) AYAPANA
(MEXICAN —) BLUEBUSH
(NEW ZEALAND —) KARO KAWA TUTU KARAMU KIEKIE KAWAKAWA KOROMIKO
(PASTURE —) COWBERRY
(PHILIPPINE —) IPILIPIL
(POISONOUS —) GIF CUBE LITHI SUMAC GIFBLAAR LABURNUM
(PRICKLY —) CAPER COLIMA BRAMBLE CATCLAWS
(SPINY —) ULEX AROMA GORSE JUNCO ESPINO BUMELIA CARISSA CYTISUS GENISTA GOATBUSH GRANJENO GUAJILLO HUAJILLO
(STRONG-SMELLING —) SALTWORT
(STUNTED —) SCRAB SCROG SCRUB
(THORNY —) CHANAR HAWTHORN
(TREELIKE —) ARBUSCLE
(TROPICAL —) INGA MAJO HENNA CAMARA DERRIS MOMBIN OLACAD PERSEA HAMELIA JEWBUSH LANTANA SOAPBARK
(WEST INDIAN —) ANIL RATWOOD MILKWOOD
(XEROPHYTIC —) SAXAUL
(PREF.) THAMN(O)
SHRUBBERY MOGOTE ARBORET
SHRUG SHUG HURKLE SHRINK
SHRUNK WEARISH
SHRUNKEN LANK CLUNG PUNGLED SLUNKEN WIZENED CONTRACT
(— HEAD) TSANTSA
SHUAH (FATHER OF —) ABRAHAM
(MOTHER OF —) KETURAH
SHUAL (FATHER OF —) ZOPHAH
SHUBAEL (FATHER OF —) HEMAN GERSHON
SHUCK HULL HUSK SHACK SHELL SHOCK
SHUDDER GRUE CREEP GRISE HIRCH QUAKE SHRUG AGRISE GROOSE HIRTCH HOTTER HURKLE SHIVER FRISSON TREMBLE
SHUDDERING RIGOR
SHUFFLE JANK MAKE MILK SLUR MOSEY SCUFF SHALE SHIFT SHOOL JUGGLE RIFFLE RUFFLE SCLAFF SHOVEL DRAGGLE QUIBBLE SHACKLE SHAFFLE SHAMBLE SLIPPER SLUTHER
(— DISHONESTLY) PACK

SHUHAM (FATHER OF —) DAN
SHUN FIN SHY BALK FLEE TABU VOID WARE ABHOR AVOID EVADE EVITE SHUNT TABOO ASTART DEVOID ESCAPE ESCHEW REFUSE SHRINK DECLINE FORBEAR FORSAKE
SHUNI (FATHER OF —) GAD
SHUNT AYRTON BRIDGE BYPASS SWITCH
SHUSH HUSH WHISH SUPPRESS
SHUSWAP ATNAH
SHUT FAST HASP MAKE SEAL SHOT SLAM SLOT SPAR TAKE TEEN TINE CLOSE LATCH STEEK STICK CLOSED CABINET OCCLUSE UPCLOSE
(— EYES) WINK
(— IN) BAR LAP CAGE COPSE EMBAR EMBAY FORBAR PENTIT TACKLE BELOUKE ENCLAVE
(— OFF) SCREEN SECLUDE
(— OUT) BAR DEBAR REPEL SKUNK HINDER DEPRIVE EXCLUDE OCCLUDE OUTSHUT PRECLUDE
(— TOGETHER) CLASP
(— UP) BAR CUB MEW PENT STOP CHOKE FRANK STIVE STOVE CLOSET EMBOSS ENJAIL IMMURE IMPARK CONDEMN CONFINE DUNGEON ENCLOSE IMPOUND INCLUDE OCCLUDE OPPRESS PARROCK RECLUSE SECLUDE CONCLUDE PRECLUDE
(HALF —) PINK
(PREF.) OCCLUSO
SHUTDOWN LAYOFF
SHUTOUT SKUNK
SHUTTER LID DROP SHUT BLIND SHADE CUTOFF DAMPER DOUSER SLUICE AUTOMAT BUCKLER SHUTTLE JALOUSIE
(— IN ORGAN) SHADE
(— OF TRIPTYCH) VOLET
SHUTTING CLAUDENT
SHUTTLE FLY FLUTE SHUNT BROCHE LOOPER SWIVEL SHITTLE
SHUTTLECOCK BIRD PETECA VOLANT
SHVANDA THE BAGPIPER
(CHARACTER IN —) DEVIL BABINSKY ICEHEART SCHVANDA
(COMPOSER OF —) WEINBERGER
SHY COY JIB MIM SCAR SHAN SHUN SKIT UNKO WILD BLATE CAGEY CHARY DEMUR FLING PAVID SCARE SHUNT SQUAB TIMID UNCOW BOGGLE BOOGER DEMURE MODEST SHANNY SKIEGH TARTLE BASHFUL GAWKISH RABBITY STRANGE TREMBLY UPSTAGE BACKWARD COCKSHOT DAPHNEAN FAROUCHE RETIRING SHEEPISH SKITTISH SWAIMOUS VERECUND WILLYARD
SHYLOCK (DAUGHTER OF —) JESSICA
SHYNESS COYNESS MODESTY RESERVE TIMIDITY
SHYSTER PETTIFOGGER

SIALAGOGUE SALIVANT
SIAM (SEE THAILAND)
SIAMANG UNGKA GIBBON
SIB SEPT AYLLU SIBLING SIBSHIP CALPULLI
SIBERIA (GULF IN —) OB
(MOUNTAIN RANGE IN —) URAL ALTAI
(NATIVE IN —) YAKU SAGAI TATAR KIRGIZ TARTAR KIRGHIZ YUKAGIR
(RIVER IN —) OB ILI KET PUR TAZ TYM AMGA AMUR LENA MAYA ONON UCUR ALDAN ISHIM NADYM SOBOL TOBOL ANGARA IRTYSH OLEKMA VILYUY
(TOWN IN —) OMSK CHITA KYZYL TOMSK IGARKA KURGAN BARNAUL IRKUTSK LENINSK YAKUTSK
SIBERIAN SQUILL SCILLA
SIBYL SYBIL SIBYLLA VOLUSPA AMALTHEA
SIC SOOL
SICILIAN
(PREF.) SICULO
SICILIAN VESPERS, THE
(CHARACTER IN —) ELENA ARRIGO MONTFORT FREDERICK
(COMPOSER OF —) VERDI

SICILY
CAPE: BOEO FARO PASSARO
CAPITAL: PALERMO
CATHEDRAL: MONREALE
COIN: LITRA UNCIA
GULF: NOTO CATANIA
ISLAND: EGADI LIPARI USTICA
MEASURE: SALMA CAFFISO
MOUNTAIN: EREI ETNA MORO SORI IBREI NEBRODI
NATIVE: ELYMI SICEL SICANI SICULI
OLD NAME: TRINACRIA TRIQUETRA
PROVINCE: ENNA RAGUSA CATANIA MESSINA PALERMO TRAPANI SIRACUSA
RIVER: SALSO TORTO BELICE SIMETO PLATANI
SEAPORT: ACI CATANIA MARSALA MESSINA PALERMO TRAPANI
TOWN: ENNA NOTO RAGUSA CATANIA MARSALA MESSINA TRAPANI SYRACUSE
VOLCANO: ETNA AETNA

SICK BAD ILL BADLY CRONK CROOK MORBID MAWKISH SEASICK UNWHOLE CROPSICK MALADIVE PHYSICAL STREAKED
SICKEN TIRE TURN WEARY SUNDER SUNNER WEAKEN DISGUST SCUNNER SURFEIT NAUSEATE
SICKENING FELL SICKLY FULSOME MAWKISH SICKISH NAUSEOUS
SICKISH DAUNCY
SICKLE HOOK CROOK
(PREF.) DREPANI FALCI ZANCIO
SICKLY WAN FLUE FOND PALE PUKY SICK DAWNY DONCY FAINT GREEN PEAKY SILLY TEWLY WEARY WERSH WISHT AMPERY ANEMIC CLAMMY CRANKY FEEBLE

INFIRM PUKISH PULING WANKLY
WEAKLY INVALID LANGUID
MAWKISH PEAKING PEAKISH
PIMPING QUEECHY SHILPIT
SICKISH WEARISH WEERISH
DELICATE DISEASED MALADIVE
PINDLING
SICKLY-LOOKING SHILPIT
SICKNESS (ALSO SEE DISEASE)
SICK SORE TAKING AILMENT
DISEASE ILLNESS SURFEIT
DISORDER
(MILK —) SLOWS TIRES
(MOTION —) KINETOSIS
(MOUNTAIN —) PUNA SOROCHE
(SUDDEN —) DWALM
SIDA ILIMA ESCOBA
SIDE CAMP COST EDGE FACE HALF
HAND KANT LEAF PANE PART
BOARD CHEEK FLANK LATUS
PARTY PHASE SITHE BEHALF
PTERON ENGLISH PENDANT
FORESIDE SIDELONG
(— BY SIDE) ACCOLE ABREAST
ACCOSTED PARALLEL
(— OF ATTIC) SKEELING SKILLING
SKILLION
(— OF BIRD'S HEAD) LORE
(— OF BOOM JAW) HORN
(— OF BOW) BELLY
(— OF CAVITY) WALL
(— OF DECK) GANGWAY
(— OF DITCH) SCARP
(— OF DIVIDERS) LEG
(— OF FACE) CHEEK
(— OF GATE) FOLD
(— OF GEM) BEZEL
(— OF HEAD) HAFFET
(— OF HEARTH) BREAST
(— OF HILL) BRAE SCUG SLOPE
(— OF HOG) FLITCH
(— OF HORSESHOE) BRANCH
(— OF LACE) FOOTING
(— OF LAMB) CONCERTINA
(— OF LOG) RIDE
(— OF NAVE) AISLE
(— OF OPENING) JAW JAMB
(— OF PIG) BACON
(— OF QUADRANGLE) PANE
(— OF RABBET) LEDGE
(— OF RACECOURSE) STRETCH
(— OF RECTANGLE) SQUARE
(— OF ROOF) CATSLIDE
(— OF SHIP) BEAM WALE BOARD
BULWARK LARBOARD SEABOARD
(— OF TENNIS RACKET) ROUGH
SMOOTH
(— OF TRIANGLE) LEG
(— OF TYPE) BACK
(— OF VALLEY) COTEAU
(— PIECE) RAVE
(— SHELTERED FROM WIND) LEE
LEW LEEWARD
(— WITH) SUFFRAGE
(-S OF FIREPLACE) COVING
(-S OF GALLERY) SLIPS
(BACK —) REAR BEHIND BACKSIDE
(DRESSED —) FACE
(FOR EACH —) ALL
(MOUNTAIN —) PUNA VETA
SOROCHE
(OUTER — OF SKIN) GRAIN
(RIGHT —) FACE

(RIGHT — OF SWORD) INSIDE
(UNDERNEATH —) BOTTOM
(WINDWARD —) AWEATHER
(PREF.) LATER(I)(O) PLEUR(I)(O)
(— BY —) PAR(A)
(— PARTS) ALI
(BY THE — OF) JUXTA
(ON THIS —) CIS CITRA
(SUFF.) PLEURA PLEUROUS
STICH(OUS)
SIDEBAR HOUND
SIDEBOARD ABACUS BUFFET
SERVER COMMODE DRESSER
CELLARET CREDENCE CREDENZA
SIDE-BY-SIDE ACCOLLE
SIDED
(SUFF.) MER
SIDE DISH OUTWORK
SIDEPIECE BAR BOW JAMB WING
CHEEK GUSSET EARPIECE
LANDSIDE
SIDES
(PREF.) **(ON ALL —)** CIRCUM
SIDESLIP SKID SLIP DRIFT DRILL
SIDESMAN HOGGLER QUESTMAN
SIDESTEP BEG AVOID DODGE
SIDEWALK WALKWAY PAVEMENT
TROTTOIR BANQUETTE
SIDEWAYS ASKANCE
SIDEWISE ASIDE ASIDEN
SIDING CURB SPUR GARAGE
SIDLE EDGE SLIVE PASSAGE
SAUNTER
SIDRA PARASHAH
SIEGE BOUT SEDGE ASSIEGE
JOURNEY LEAGUER
(— ENGINE) WARWOLF
SIEGFRIED (CHARACTER IN —) MIME
WOTAN FAFNER SIEGFRIED
BRUNNHILDE
(COMPOSER OF —) WAGNER
(SLAYER OF —) BRUNHILD
(WIFE OF —) KRIEMHILD
SIERRA CERO SERRA SAWBACK
KINGFISH

SIESTA NAP MERIDIAN
SIEVE FRY TRY BOLT BUNT DRUM
HARP LAWN PREE SCRY SHOE
SIFT SILE SIZE TEMS GRATE
RANGE SCALP TAMIS TAMMY
TEMSE BOLTER RANGER RIDDER
RIDDLE SEARCE SEARCH SEMMET
SIFTER WEIGHT BOULTEL
CHAFFER CRIBBLE DILLUER
PRICKLE TIFFANY TROMMEL

COLANDER SEARCHER STRAINER
(— FOR MILK) MILSEY
(PREF.) COSCINO CRIBRI ETHMO
SIF (HUSBAND OF —) THOR
SIFT REE TRY BOLT DUST SCRY
RANGE SCALP SIEVE TEMSE
DREDGE GARBLE RIDDER RIDDLE
SCREEN SEARCE WINNOW
CANVASS CRIBBLE DRIBBLE
SIFTAGE CRIBRATE
(— FLOUR) DRESS
(— IN) INFILTER
(— IN MINING) LUE
(— MEAL) BUNT
(— SHOT) TABLE
(— WHEAT) SCALP
SIFTER SIEVE BOLTER CASTER
SIEVER
SIFTING DRIFT GARBLING
(PL.) BOLTING FANNINGS
SIEVINGS
SIGH SOB PECH SIFE SOCK WIND
MOURN SIGHT SITHE SOUGH
TWANK BEMOAN BEWAIL
SORROW SUTHER DEPLORE
SINGULT SUSPIRE
SIGHT AIM EYE KEN RAY BONE
ESPY FACE GAZE PEEP SEET VIEW
FERLY RAISE SCENE SCOPE SICHT
TRACK VISIE VIZZY BEHOLD
DESCRY OBJECT TICKET VISION
DISCERN DISPLAY EYESHOT
GLIMPSE MONSTER CONSPECT
DISCOVER EYESIGHT GUNSIGHT
(— FOR GUN) BEAD LEAF PEEP
SCOPE VISIE VIZZY HAUSSE
GUNSIGHT
(— OF COMPASS) VANE
(— ON SURVEYOR'S STAFF) TARGET
(— TO SEE IF LEVEL) BONE
(—S OF CITY) LIONS
(AMAZING —) STOUND
(IMAGINARY —) VISION
(PITIFUL —) RUTH
(SECOND —) TAISCH
(SORRY —) BYSEN
(STRANGE —) FERLY FERLIE
(SUFF.) OPSIA OPSIS OPSY OPTIC
OPTICON ORAMA
SIGHTER ALINER ALIGNER
SIGHTING LANDFALL
(— DEVICE) ALIDADE
SIGHTLY VIEWLY EYEABLE
SIGHTSEE RUBBERNECK
SIGLOS DARIC
SIGN INK AYAH DASH FIRM HINT
HIRE MARK NOTE OMEN TYPE
BADGE COLON FRANK GHOST
GUIDA HAMZA INDEX SIGIL SINGE
SPOOR STAMP TOKEN TRACE
ASSIGN AUGURY CARACT EFFECT
EMBLEM ENGAGE ENSIGN FUGLER
INDICE MOTION NOTICE PARAPH
REMARK SIGLUM SIGNAL SIGNET
SIGNUM SYMBOL TITTLE WITTER
ALEBUSH AUSPICE SHINGLE
CHEQUER CONSIGN EARMARK
ENDORSE INDICIA INSIGNE
KNOWING PORTENT PRESAGE
PRODIGY PROFFER PRESAGE
SHOWING SIGNARY SURMISE
SYMPTOM VESTIGE WARNING
CEREMONY INDICANT INSTANCE

MONUMENT PROCLAIM SIGNACLE
SYLLABIC TELLTALE
(— DOCUMENT) FIRM
(— FOR KEYNOTE) ISON
(— OF ALEHOUSE) LATTICE
(— OF AN IDEA) EMBLEM
(— OF APPROVAL) CACHET
(— OF CONTEMPT) FIG
(— OF DANGER) SEAMARK
(— OF GLOTTAL STOP) HAMZA
HAMZAH
(— OF MULTIPLICATION) DOT
(— OF ZODIAC) LEO RAM BULL
CRAB GOAT LION ARIES HOUSE
LIBRA TWINS VIRGO ARCHER
CANCER FISHES GEMINI PISCES
TAURUS VIRGIN BALANCE
SCORPIO AQUARIUS SCORPION
(— ON MAP) ICON
(ASTROLOGICAL —) CIPHER
(MATHEMATICAL —) NAME
FUNCTOR
(MUSICAL —) GUIDA NEUME
PRESA SEGNO SWELL SIMILE
FERMATA
(OUTWARD —) EVIDENCE
(SANSKRIT —) ANUSVARA
(SHILLING —) SOLIDUS
(SHORTHAND —) DIPHONE
(SLIGHT —) SURMISE
(SUBSCRIPT —) SUBFIX
(SUPERSTITIOUS —) GUEST
(TAVERN —) BUSH ALEBUSH
ALEPOLE CHECKER CHEQUER
ALESTAKE
(TRAMP'S —) MONICA MONIKER
(VOWEL —) SEGOL SEGHOL
(PL.) INDICIA INSIGNIA
(PREF.) SEMA SEMANT(O)
SEMASI(O) SEMATO SEMEIO
SEMIO SEMO SYMBOLO
(SUFF.) SEME
SIGNAL OS CUE GUN PST WAG
BALK BECK BELL BUZZ CALL
COND FLAG GATE HASH SIGN
WAFF WAFT WAVE WINK ALARM
ALERT BLINK FLARE FUSEE FUZEE
LIGHT SHAPE SHORT SPEAK
TOKEN WHIFF ALARUM BANNER
BEACON BECKON BUZZER ENSIGN
HERALD MARKER OFFICE RECALL
SIGNET TARGET WAVING
WIGWAG BLINKER CHAMADE
COMMAND EMINENT GRIFFIN
NOTABLE RETREAT TURNOUT
ASSEMBLY CRANTARA DIAPHONE
FLAGFALL LOGOGRAM STANDARD
STRIKING
(— FISHERMEN) BALK
(— FOR A PARLEY) CHAMADE
(— FOR WHALERS) WAIF
(— IN WHIST) ECHO PETER
(— OF DISTRESS) SOS
(— ON HORN) SEEK BLAST STRAKE
(— ON RADARSCOPE) BLIP
(— TO ATTACK) CHARGE
(— TO BEGIN ACTION) CUE
(— WITH FLAGS) WIGWAG
(AUDIO —) HUM
(BOAT'S —) WAFF WAFT
(DEATH —) KNELL
(FOG —) FOGHORN TORPEDO
DIAPHONE

(HUNTER'S —) SEEK PRIZE GIBBET STRAKE
(MILITARY —) FLARE TURNOUT ASSEMBLY
(NAVAL —) SECURE
(RADIO —) BEAM
(RAILROAD —) BANJO BOARD FUSEE FUZEE TARGET HIGHBALL SEMAPHORE
(TRAFFIC —) ROBOT
(WARNING —) ALARM KLAXON TOCSIN
SIGNALIZE MARK
SIGNALLING TICKTACK
SIGNALMAN FLAGS BELLBOY BELLMAN
SIGNATE SENNET
SIGNATORY SIGNEE SIGNER
SIGNATURE BOLT FIRM HAND VISA FRANK SHEET SIGIL THEME SIGNUM TUGHRA SECTION HANDWRIT SIGNATOR
SIGNBOARD SIGN SHINGLE
SIGNET SIGIL
SIGNIFICANCE WIT BODY PITH SOUND AMOUNT IMPORT INTENT LETTER STRESS WEIGHT BEARING CONTENT GRAVITY MEANING SENTENCE STRENGTH
(DEVOID OF —) JEJUNE
(HIDDEN —) HYPONOIA
(LACKING —) INANE
(MORAL —) ETHOS
SIGNIFICANT REAL RICH GREAT MEATY AUGURAL EPOCHAL OMINOUS POINTED SERIOUS SENSEFUL SPEAKING PERTINENT
SIGNIFICANTLY SENSIBLY
SIGNIFICATION SENSE VALOR VALUE ETYMON IMPORT MOMENT NOTION MEANING CARRIAGE SIGNIFIE
SIGNIFICS SENSIFICS
SIGNIFY BE SAY BEAR GIVE MAKE MEAN NOTE SIGN WAVE AUGUR IMPLY SKILL SOUND SPEAK SPELL TOKEN UTTER AMOUNT ARGUFY ASSERT BEMEAN DENOTE EMPLOY IMPORT INTEND MATTER SIGNAL BESPEAK BETOKEN CONNOTE DECLARE EXPRESS PORTEND PRETEND DESCRIBE INDICATE INTIMATE MANIFEST
SIGNOR BRUSCHINO, IL
(CHARACTER IN —) SOFIA BRUSCHINO FLORVILLE GAUDENZIO
(COMPOSER OF —) ROSSINI
SIGNPOST GUIDE MERCURY WAYMARK HANDPOST
SIGURD (HORSE OF —) GRANI
(SLAIN BY —) FAFNIR
(SLAYER OF —) HOGNI
(VICTIM OF —) FAFNIR
(WIFE OF —) GUDRUN
SIGYN (HUSBAND OF —) LOKI
SIKH AKALI SINGH UDASI MAZHABI
SIKKIM (CAPITAL OF —) GANGTOK
(NATIVE OF —) RONG BHOTIA LEPCHA
(RIVER OF —) TISTA
SIKSIKA SIHASAPA

SILAS MARNER (AUTHOR OF —) ELIOT
(CHARACTER IN —) CASS AARON DOLLY EPPIE NANCY SILAS MARNER DUNSTAN GODFREY LAMMETER WINTHROP
SILENCE GAG MUM CALK CLUM HIST HUSH REST CHOKE FLOOR PEACE QUIET SHUSH SQUAT STILL CLAMOR MUFFLE SETTLE STIFLE WHISHT CONFUTE SQUELCH DUMBNESS PRECLUDE SUPPRESS
SILENCED STILL
SILENCER SOURDINE
SILENT MUM CLUM HUSH HUST MUET MUTE SNUG CLOSE MUTED STILL TACIT WHIST MUETTE SOPITE SULLEN TIPTOE WHISHT APHONIC UNWORDY ASPIRATE RESERVED RETICENT TACITURN
SILENT DON (AUTHOR OF —) SHOLOKHOV
(CHARACTER IN —) DARIA DUNIA MAURA GREGOR PIOTRA STEPAN AKSINIA DENIKIN MELEKHOV ILINICHKA PROKOFFEY PANTALEIMON
SILHOUETTE SHADE ISOTYPE OUTLINE
SILICA FLINT SILEX SINTER COESITE TRIPOLI TRIDYMITE
SILICATE MICA ALVITE CERITE EUCLASE ILVAITE LOTRITE ZEOLITE CALAMINE ERIONITE WELLSITE
SILICEOUS SHELLY
SILICLE POUCH SILICULE
SILICON (THIN SLICE OF —) WAFER
SILICOSIS CON
SILK SAY SOY CRIN ERIA LOVE MUGA ATLAS FLOSS GREGE HONAN JAPAN TABBY BLATTA CRACKS CULGEE DUCAPE FRISON MANTUA RADIUM SENDAL SHALEE SHILLA SOUPLE TUSSAH ALAMODE CHIFFON HABUTAI PERSIAN SCHAPPE SQUEEZE TIFFANY TSATLEE TUSSORE YAMAMAI ARMOZEEN ARMOZINE LUSTRINE MILANESE
(— FOR LININGS) SARSNET SARCENET
(CORDED —) PADUASOY
(HEAVY —) CRIN ARMOZINE
(RAW —) GREIGE MARABOU TAYSAAM TSATLEE MARABOUT
(REFUSE —) BUR BURR
(TWILLED —) SURAH TOBINE FOULARD LOUSINE
(UNDYED —) CORAH
(UNTWISTED —) SLEAVE
(UPHOLSTERY —) TABARET
(WASTE —) KNUB NOIL FRISON
(PREF.) SERI(CEO)(CI)(CO)
SILK COTTON KAPOK
SILK-COTTON TREE BULAK SEMUL SIMAL BOMBAX YAXCHE BENTANG MUNGUBA POCHOTE
SILKEN SILL SERIC SILKY SUAVE SEREAN
SILK GRASS KARATAS
SILK GUM SERICIN

SILK OAK LACEWOOD
SILKSMAN SCALPER
SILK TREE SIRIS
SILKWORM ERI ERIA SINA BOMBYX TUSSAH TUSSORE YAMAMAI BOMBYCID
SILKY GLOSSY SILKEN
SILKY CORNEL REDBRUSH
SILKY TAMARIN MARIKINA
SILL GIRD SOLE PLATE PATAND PATTEN SADDLE MUDSILL DOORSILL
SILLINESS BOSH FOLLY BETISE GOOSERY INANITY PORANGI SIMPLES IDLENESS NONSENSE ABSURDITY SIMPLICITY
SILLY TID BETE DAFT FOND FOOL NICE VAIN APISH BALMY BATTY BUGGY CAKEY DENSE DILLY DIZZY GOOFY INANE KOOKY LOONY SAPPY SEELY BLASHY CRANKY CUCKOO DAWISH DOTARD DOTTLE FOOTLE FRUITY GUCKED MOPOKE PAULIE SAWNEY SHANNY SIMPLE SINGLE SKIVIE SLIGHT SPOONY VACANT ASININE FATUOUS FOOLISH FOPPISH FRIBBLE GLAIKET PEEVISH PUERILE SCRANNY SHALLOW UNWITTY ANSERINE FEATLESS FOOTLING FOPPERLY
(BE —) DRIVEL
(PREF.) MORO
SILO (PART OF —) BIN DOME PIPE TANK MELON INTAKE LADDER PUMPKIN UMBRELLA PARACHUTE
SILOXANE SILICON
SILPHIUM LASER
SILT DREGS SLEECH DEPOSIT RESIDUE SULLAGE BULLDUST
SILVER LUNA MOON PINA DIANA PLATE SYCEE WEDGE WHITE ALBATA ARGENT SILLER BULLION VERMEIL ARGENTUM STERLING ARGENTINE
(— STATE) NEVADA
(DEBASED —) VELLON
(GERMAN —) ALBATA
(GILDED —) VERMEIL
(NICKEL —) PAKTONG
(PREF.) ARGENT(O) ARGYR(O)
SILVER BELL HALESIA BELLWOOD COWLICKS
SILVERFISH SHINER SLICKER FISHTAIL WOODFISH
SILVERING BACKING
SILVERSIDES IAO BRIT TINK BRITT FRIAR SMELT TAILOR TINKER GRUNION ATHERINE PEIXEREY PEJERREY SKIPJACK
SILVERSMITH SONAR
SILVERTIP BEAR
SILVER TREE IRONWOOD
SILVER TREE FERN PITAU
SILVERVINE CATVINE
SILVERWEED TANSY
SILVERWING CINDER
SILVERY WHITE ARGENT SILVER SILVERN
(PREF.) GLAUCO
SILVIA (FATHER OF —) BALLANCE
(LOVER OF —) VALENTINE
SILYBUM MARIANA

SIMAR CYMAR SYMAR ZIMARRA
SIMEON (FATHER OF —) JACOB
(MOTHER OF —) LEAH
SIMILAR LIKE SAME SUCH ALIKE EVENLY LIKELY SIMILE COGNATE KINDRED SEEMABLE SELFLIKE SUCHLIKE SUITABLE SEMBLANCE
(PREF.) HOL(O) HOM(E)(EO)(O)(OE)(OI)
(SUFF.) (MAKE — TO) FY IFY
SIMILARITY SIMILE ANALOGY HOMOLOGY HOMOTAXY LIKENESS PARALLEL SAMENESS
SIMILARLY EQUALLY LIKEWISE
SIMILE ICON IKON IMAGE FIGURE SUIVEZ COMPARE
SIMILITUDE IMAGE FIGURE ANALOGY PARABLE PORTRAIT
SIMMER FRY CREE SILE STEW SIMPER SOTTER TOTTLE
SIMON ZELOTES
(BROTHER OF —) JESUS
(FATHER OF —) MATTATHIAS
(SON OF —) JUDAS
SIMON BOCCANEGRA
(CHARACTER IN —) MARIA PAOLO SIMON ADORNO AMELIA ANDREA FIESCO GABRIELLE BOCCANEGRA
(COMPOSER OF —) VERDI
SIMONY BARRATRY
SIMOOM SAMUM SAMIEL KHAMSIN
SIMPER MINCE SMIRK BRIDLE
SIMPLE LOW BALD BARE EASY FOND MERE NICE ONLY PURE RUDE SNAP VERY WEAK AFALD BLEAK DIZZY GREEN NAIVE NAKED PLAIN SEELY SILLY SMALL SOBER AEFALD CHASTE GLOBAL HOMELY HONEST HUMBLE NATIVE OAFISH RUSTIC SEMPLE SEVERE SINGLE STUPID VIRGIN ARTLESS ASININE AUSTERE BABYISH FATUOUS FOOLISH ONEFOLD POPULAR SIMPLEX SPECIES ARCADIAN EXPLICIT HOMEMADE INNOCENT INORNATE SACKLESS SEMPLICE SOLITARY
(PREF.) APL(O) HAPL(O) LITI
SIMPLE-MINDED SEELY SILLY INNOCENT
SIMPLETON AUF AWF COX DAW FON NUP OAF SAP SOT BOOB CAKE COOT CULL FLAT FOOL GABY GAUP GAWP GOFF GOUK GOWK GOWP GUFF PEAK ROOK SIMP SOFT TONY TOOT ZANY COKES GALAH GOOSE IDIOT IKONA JACOB LOACH NINNY NODDY PRUNE SAMMY SMELT SNIPE SPOON TOMMY BADAUD DAUKIN FONDLE GANDER GAUPUS GAWNEY GOTHAM GREENY GULPIN JOSSER NINCUM NOODLE NUPSON SAWNEY SIMKIN SIMPLE DAWPATE GOMERAL GUBBINS JUGGINS MAFFLIN MUGGINS WIDGEON ABDERITE FLATHEAD FONDLING INNOCENT JEANJEAN JOCRISSE KNOTHEAD MOONCALF MOONLING OMADHAUN PEAGOOSE SILLYTON SOFTHEAD WISFACRE

WOODCOCK NINCOMPOOP
SIMPLICITY NICETY PURITY MODESTY NAIVETE ELEGANCE
SIMPLIFY CLARIFY EXPOUND
SIMPLY JUST ALONE FONDLY MERELY PLATLY CRUDELY QUIETLY NATIVELY
SIMULACRUM SHAM IMAGE IMITATION
SIMULATE ACT FAKE MOCK FEIGN MIMIC AFFECT ASSUME SEMBLE SIMULE SKETCH
SIMULATED FAINT FAKED ERSATZ FICTIOUS
SIMULATION ACTING ANALOGUE PRETENCE PRETENSE
SIMULTANEOUS CONJOINT CONJUGATE
SIMULTANEOUSLY ONCE TOGETHER
SIN ERR CULP DEBT ENZU EVIL HELL PAPA VICE BLAME CRIME ERROR FAULT FOLLY GUILT SLOTH WATHE WRONG AGUILT COMMIT FELONY NANNAR OFFEND PIACLE PLIGHT VENIAL FRAILTY OFFENSE HAMARTIA INIQUITY PECCANCY QUEDSHIP TRESPASS
(DAUGHTER OF —) ISHTAR
(DEADLY —) ACEDIA
(ORIGINAL —) ADAM
(SON OF —) NESKU SHAMASH
(WIFE OF —) NINGAL
(PREF.) HAMARTIO
SINCALINE CHOLINE
SINCE AS AGO FOR FRO NOW GONE SETH SITH SYNE BEING WHERE FORWHY BECAUSE SITHENS WHEREAS INASMUCH SITHENCE
(PREF.) CIS CITRA
SINCERE GOOD REAL TRUE AFALD FRANK CANDOR DEVOUT ENTIRE HEARTY HONEST SIMPLE SINGLE CORDIAL EARNEST GENUINE ONEFOLD UPRIGHT FAITHFUL PRAYERFUL
(NOT —) PLASTIC
SINCERELY TRULY SIMPLY SINGLY DEVOUTLY ENTIRELY HEARTILY
SINCERITY FAITH HEART VERITY HONESTY REALITY
SINDON CORPORAL
SINE SAGITTA
SINEW THEW BRAWN FIBER FIBRE FORCE NERVE POWER LEADER SINNER TENDON
SINEWY WIRY NERVY THEWY ROBUST FIBROSE FIBROUS NERVOUS STRINGY TENDINAL
SINFONIA SYMPHONY
SINFUL BAD EVIL VILE NEFAS WRONG WICKED PECCANT UNGODLY VICIOUS PIACULAR
SING HUM JIG LIP CANT CARP GALE HYMN LILT TUNE CAROL CARRY CHANT CHIRL CROON DIRGE DITTY DRING FEIGN LYRIC RAISE TOUCH TROLL YEDDE CHAUNT CHORUS DIVIDE INTONE MELODY RECORD RELISH STRAIN WARBLE CHORTLE COUNTER

DESCANT GRIDDLE SINGING TWEEDLE CHERUBIM FALDERAL MODULATE SINGSONG VOCALIZE
(— ABOUT) BESING
(— ABOVE TRUE PITCH) SHARP
(— AS A BEGGAR) GRIDDLE
(— BRISKLY) KNACK
(— CHEERFULLY) LILT
(— FLORIDLY) DIVIDE
(— HARSHLY) SCREAM
(— IN A CRACKED VOICE) CRAKE
(— IN CHORUS) CHOIR
(— IN LOW VOICE) CROON
(— IN SWISS MANNER) YODEL
(— LOUDLY) BELT TROLL TROLLOL
(— PRAISES) LAUD
(— ROMANCES) GEST GESTE
(— SECOND PART) SURCENT
(— SOFTLY) SOWF SOWTH
(— WITH FLOURISHES) ROULADE
SINGAPORE (RIVER IN —) SUNGEI SELETAR
(STRAIT OF —) JOHORE SEMBILAN
SINGE GAS BURN SWEAL GENAPP SCORCH SWINGE SCOWDER SWITHEN FIREFANG
SINGER ALTO BARD DIVA LARK SWAN BASSO BUFFA BUFFO SKALD VOICE BULBUL BUSKER CANARY CANTOR LYRIST SONGER BASSIST CHANTER CROONER PRIMOMO SOLOIST SONGMAN SOPRANO TROLLER WARBLER BAYADERE CANTADOR CASTRATO CHANTEUR FALSETTO GRIDDLER MELODIST MONODIST THAMYRIS VOCALIST CITYBILLY
(— OF FOLK SONGS) CANTADOR
(— OF ROCK MUSIC) ROCKER
(— OF THE GODS) GANDHARVA
(FEMALE —) SONGBIRD
(MENDICANT —) BUSKER
(PRINCIPAL —) PRIMOMO
(PROVENCAL —) MUSAR
SINGING CANT SCAT CHANT LYRIC HYMNODY CANOROUS JONGLERY
(— CAROLS) PLYGAIN HODENING
(CANTORIAL —) HAZANUTH HAZZANUT
(SIMULTANEOUS —) CHORUS
SINGLE ODD ONE LAST ONLY SOLE UNAL AFALD AEFALD SIMPLE SOLEIN SULLEN UNIQUE VERSAL ALONELY AZYGOUS ONEFOLD SEVERAL SIMPLEX TWOSOME PECULIAR SEPARATE SINGULAR SOLITARY SPORADIC PARTICULAR
(— OUT) CUT SPOT ISOLATE SEPARATE
(PREF.) APL(O) HAPL(O) MANI MON(O) UNI
SINGLE-FOOT RACK
SINGLEHANDEDLY SINGLY
SINGLENESS UNITY ONENESS
SINGLETON (— LEAD) SNEAK
SINGLY SINGLE SOLELY SLONELY
SINGPHO CHINGPAW
SINGSONG SOUGH CHANTING
SINGULAR ODD RARE FERLY QUEER QUAINT SEENIL SINGLE CURIOUS STRANGE PECULIAR
SINGULARISM HENISM

SINGULARITY DOUBLET ONENESS ONLINESS
SINISTER AWK CAR KAY DARK DIRE FELL GRIM DISMAL LOUCHE MALIGN AWKWARD OBLIQUE OMINOUS
SINISTRAL REVERSED
SINK DIP DOP EBB LUM SAG SET SYE BORE DRAU DRAW DROP FADE FAIL FALL GOWT HELD KILL LUMB SILE SWAG AVALE DRAFT DRAIN DROOP DROWN HIELD LAPSE LOWER MERGE POACH SQUAT STOOP SWAMP VERGE CLOACA DEVALL DOLINA DOLINE DRENCH GUTTER JAWBOX PLUNGE PUDDLE RESIDE SETTLE COMMODE DECLINE DESCEND DRAUGHT FOUNDER GULLION IMMERSE RELAPSE SCUPPER SCUTTLE SUBSIDE SWALLOW DECREASE SINKHOLE SOAKAWAY
(— A WELL) DRILL
(— AND FALL) TWINE
(— AS IN MUD) LAIR
(— DOWN) BOG AVALE STOOP DECLINE
(— FANGS INTO) STRIKE
(— INTO OOZE) WASEL
(— NAILHEAD) SET
(— SUDDENLY) SLUMP
(— UNDER TRIAL) QUAIL
SINKBOX BOX SINK BATTERY
SINKER BUR BURR SINK DIPSY PLUMB BULLET
SINKHOLE SINK PONOR UVALA CENOTE COLLECT
SINKING GONE SINKAGE
(— DOWN) FONDU
SINKIUSE COLUMBIA
SINLESS INNOCENT
SINLESSNESS HOLINESS
SINNER DEBTOR PECCANT
SINNING PECCANT
SINUATE GYROSE
SINUOSITY WRIGGLE
SINUOUS WAVY SNAKEY SINUATE SNAKISH TORTILE WINDING INDENTED SWANLIKE
SINUS BOSOM ANTRUM RECESS LOCULUS TEARPIT
(PL.) ANTRA
SINUSITIS ROUP
SIOUAN ABANIC DAKOTA SANTEE SAPONI CATAWBA DACOTAH
SIOUX (— FORCE) WAKAN WAKON
SIP BIB NIP SUP BLEB SEEP SLUP SUCK TIFF KEACH SNACK WHIFF TIPPLE TICKLER DELIBATE
SIPHON CRANE THIEF VALINCH FLINCHER
SIPPING LIBANT
SIPUNCULOIDEA ACHAETA INERMIA
SIR PO DAN DEN DON PAN AZAM BAAS HERR MIAN STIR TUAN BWANA SAHIB SENOR SEYID SIEUR MESSER SAYYID SIGNOR SIRREE DOMINUS EFFENDI MESSIRE SIGNIOR SIGNORE GOSPODIN GOVERNOR
(PL.) LORDINGS
SIRCAR BANIAN

SIRE BEGET THROW FATHER GETTER
SIREN BUMMER HOOTER LIGEIA LIGYDA ENTICER LORELEI MERMAID SIRENIAN
SIRENIAN COWFISH MUTILATE
SIRENOMELUS SYMPUS SYMMELUS
SIRICID UROCERID
SIRIS KOKO LEBBEK
SIRIUS SOTHIS TISHIYA CANICULA
SIRLOIN SEY BACKSEY
SIRMUELLERA BANKSIA
SIRUP WAX LICK GOLDY SYRUP GOWDIE GREENS ORGEAT RUNOFF ANTIQUE CLAIRCE ECLEGMA LIQUEUR MOLASSES QUIDDANY
SIRWASH SIDELINE
SISAL CABUYA SISALANA
SISKIN TARIN ABERDEVINE
SISSIFIED PRISSY
SISSOO TALI SHISHAM
SISSY SIS CISSIE SISTER CHICKEN PANTYWAIST
SISTER NUN SIB SIS GIRL NURSE SISSY TITTY WOMAN EXTERN PERSON
(YOUNGER —) CADETTE
(PL.) SISTERN SISTREN
(PREF.) SORORI
SISTERHOOD BEGUINES SORORITY
SISTERLY SORORAL
SISYPHUS (BROTHER OF —) ATHAMAS SALMONEUS
(FATHER OF —) AEOLUS
(MOTHER OF —) ENARETE
(SON OF —) SINON GLAUCUS ORNYTION
(WIFE OF —) MEROPE
SIT SET LEAN SEAT BENCH PRESS ROOST SQUAT WEIGH BESTRIDE
(— ABRUPTLY) CLAP
(— ASTRIDE) CROSS HORSE STRADDLE
(— ERECT LIKE A DOG) BEG
(— FORCIBLY) DOSS
(— IN JUDGMENT) DEEM
(— ON) BROOD COVER
(— OVER EGGS) RUCK BROOD CLOCK
SITA (FATHER OF —) JANAKA
(HUSBAND OF —) RAMA SOMA
SITATUNGA NAKONG
SITE AREA PLOT SEAT SITU SOLE SPOT TOFT FIELD PLACE SITUS STAND STANCE BIVOUAC DAMSITE HABITAT STEADING
(— OF BIRD SEXUAL DISPLAY) LEK
(— OF HUNT) DRIVE
(— OF SMELTER) BOLE
(EXCAVATION —) DIG
(FORTIFIED —) KAME
(THRESHING —) SETTING
SITTER DOLLY DOLLIE INSESSOR
SITTING DIET SEAT ASSIS CLUTCH SEANCE SEDENT SEJANT SESSION CONGRESS SEDERUNT
SITUATE PLACE POSITION
SITUATED SET SEATED STATURED
(— OPPOSITE) COUNTER
SITUATION JOB LIE CASE CRIB PASS PLOT POST SEAT SITE SPOT

BERTH SIEGE SITUS STATE STEAD
ASSIZE CHANCE ESTATE OFFICE
PLIGHT STATUS EPISODE PICTURE
PORTENT POSTURE STATION
INCIDENT INSTANCE POSITURE
STANDING UBIQUITY
(— BESET BY DIFFICULTIES) SCRAPE
(— IN CRIBBAGE) GO
(— IN FARO) CATHOP
(— IN OMBRE) CODILLE
(— OF PERPLEXITY) HOBBLE STRAIT
(AMUSING —) BAR
(AWKWARD —) SCRAPE JACKPOT
(CRITICAL —) CLUTCH
(DIFFICULT —) BOX PUXY BOGGLE
NINEHOLES PREDICAMENT
(DISTRESSING —) STYMIE
(EXECRABLE —) ATROCITY
(FAVORABLE —) BREAK
(FINAL — OF ACT) CURTAIN
(HIGH —) AERY AERIE
(HOPELESSLY DOOMED —)
RATTRAP
(NECESSITOUS —) BREACH
(PAINFUL —) DISTRESS
(RELATIVE —) BEARING
(TIGHT —) CRUNCH
(TRYING —) COW
(UNPLEASANT —) BUMMER
(UNSATISFACTORY —) DILEMMA
(VEXATIOUS —) HEADACHE
(VILE —) DUNGHILL
(ZODIACAL —) HAYZ
SITZ BATH SITZBAD SEMICUPE
SITZMARK BATHTUB
SIVA RUDRA SHIVA ISVARA
SHAMBU BHAIRAVA MAHADEVA
NATARAJA
SIX VAU WAW SICE SISE HEXAD
HEXADE SENARY SEXTET STIGMA
DIGAMMA SIXSOME
(PREF.) HEX(A) SEX(A)(I) SEXTI
SIXFOLD SEXTUPLE
SIX-FOOTED HEXAPOD
SIXMO SEXTO
SIXPENCE HOG PIG BEND KICK
ZACK SIMON SPRAT TIZZY
BENDER FIDDLE TANNER TESTON
CRIPPLE FIDDLER TESTRIL
SIXTEENTH ANA ANNA
SIXTH
(PREF.) SEXTI
SIXTIETH (— PART OF DAY) GHURRY
SIXTY SAMECH SAMEKH
SIZABLE SNUG HEFTY LARGE
HANDSOME
SIZE WAX AREA BIND BULK MARK
MASS DRESS GIRTH MOUND
PLANK SCALE EXTENT FORMAT
GROWTH MICKLE MOISON PICNIC
SIZING BIGNESS CONTENT
CORSAGE FITTING THIRTEEN
TWELVEMO
(— OF BOOK) FOLIO
(— OF CARDS) TOWN LADIES
(— OF HOLE) BORE
(— OF HOSIERY) POPE
(— OF PAPERBOARD) LARGE
(— OF PARTICLE) GRIND
(— OF ROPE) GRIST
(— OF SLATE) PEGGY IMPERIAL
(— OF TYPE) GEM PICA RUBY
AGATE CANON ELITE PEARL

MINION PRIMER BREVIER
DIAMOND EMERALD ENGLISH
PARAGON COLUMBIAN
(— YARN) SLASH
(CLOTHING —) LONG SHORT
STOUT JUNIOR PETITE
(EXTRA LARGE —) SUPER
(GREAT —) MAGNITUDE
(RELATIVE —) SCALE
(UNUSUAL —) OUTSIZE
SIZING DRESSING SLASHING
(— LIQUID) GLAIR
SIZZLE FRIZZ
SKADI (FATHER OF —) THJAZI
(HUSBAND OF —) NJORD
SKANDA (BROTHER OF —) GANESHA
(FATHER OF —) SHIVA
(WIFE OF —) DEVAYANI
VALLIAMMAN
SKAT CAT NULL TOURNEE
SKATE BOB RAY TUB RAJA RINK
SKIT TINK TUBE FLAIR SCULL
BATOID DOCTOR FLATHE PATENT
PATTEN ROCKER ROLLER RUNNER
SKETCH TINKER CHOPINE
FLAPPER PLACOID SKETCHER
(— MARK) CUSP
(FEMALE —) MAID
(PREF.) BATO
SKATER PATTENER SKETCHER
SKEDADDLE BUNK SCOOT
SKEET KELTER KILTER PELTER
SKEIN RAP HANK HASP SCAN
BOTTOM SLEEVE SELVAGE
SKEINER RANDER SLIPPER
SKELETIN SPUNGIN
SKELETON CUP CAGE MORT RAME
ATOMY BONES FRAME LOOFAH
SICULA SKELET ANATOMY
CARCASS RAWBONE ARMATURE
CORALLUM MANDIBLE OSSATURE
SKELETON KEY GILT SCREW
TWIRLER
SKELP SCUD
SKEPTIC DOUBTER INFIDEL
ZETETIC APIKOROS APORETIC
SKEPTICAL ACADEMIC APORETIC
DOUBTFUL
SKEPTICISM HUMISM UNBELIEF
SKETCH BIT DASH DRAW LIMN
PLAN VIEW VITA DRAFT ENTER
PAINT TRACE APERCU DESIGN
DOODLE SCHEME SPLASH
BOZZETO CROQUIS DRAUGHT
DRAWING EBAUCHE ETCHING
OUTLINE SCHIZZO ESQUISSE
MONOGRAM PROFIELE PROSPECT
REMARQUE VIGNETTE
(— BEFOREHAND) INDICATE
(AUTOBIOGRAPHICAL —) VITA
(BIOGRAPHICAL —) ELOGY
ELOGIUM
(FIRST —) ESQUISSE
(HERALDIC —) TRICK
(OUTDOORS —) LANDSKIP
(PRELIMINARY —) DRAFT ABBOZZO
MAQUETTE
(ROUGH —) NOTE CROQUIS
POCHADE ESQUISSE
(SATIRICAL —) SKIT
SKEW ASKEW GAUCHE
SKEWBACK SPRINGER
SKEWBALD PINTO PIEBALD

SKEWED ALOP
SKEWER PROD PROG SPIT PRICK
TRUSS SKIVER TASTER
BROCHETTE
SKEWERER TUBER
SKI SKEE SNOWSHOE
(— DOWN SLOPE) SCHUSS
(— DOWNHILL) WEDEL
(— METHOD) PASSGANG
(— MOVEMENT) RUADE
(— POSITION) VORLAGE
(— RACE) SLALOM
(— RACING) LANGLAUF
(— STYLE) WEDELN
(— TURN) TELEMARK
(PART OF —) TIP EDGE TAIL
SHOVEL BINDING
(RELATING TO — EVENTS) NORDIC
(PL.) BOARDS
SKID DOG DRAG SLEW SLUE TRIG
DRIFT DRILL SLOUGH SKIDPAN
SLIPPER TRIGGER SIDESLIP
(— LOGS) SNAKE TWICH TRAVOY
TWITCH
(— ON RAIL) SKATE
(AUTOMOBILE —) SPINOUT
(FENDER —) GLANCER
(IRON —) SABOT
SKIDDER SNAKER
SKIDI LOUP
SKIDWAY PIT
SKIER KANONE SNOWBIRD
SCHUSSBOOMER
SKIFF CANOE SHELL SKIFT CAIQUE
DINGHY SAMPAN CURRANE
SKIPPET JOHNBOAT
SKIING TOURING LANGLAUF
SKIL BESHOW SKILFISH
SKILL ART CAN WIT FEAT FEEL
HAND PATE TACT CRAFT DRAFT
HAUNT KNACK TRICK ENGINE
TECHNE ABILITY ADDRESS
APTNESS CUNNING FINESSE
MASTERY MYSTERY PROWESS
SCIENCE SLEIGHT ARTIFICE
CAPACITY CHIVALRY DEFTNESS
FACILITY INDUSTRY LEARNING
(LACK OF —) INERTIA
(NAVIGATION —) SEACRAFT
(PREF.) TECHNI TECHNO
(SUFF.) ICS SHIP TECHNIC
TECHNY
SKILLED OLD SEEN WISE ADEPT
ASTUTE MASTER PERITE SCIENT
SKILLY VERSED HOTSHOT
PRACTIC EDUCATED SKILLFUL
SKILLET PRIG SPIDER
SKILLFUL APT SLY ABLE DEFT
FEAT FINE FINE GOOD HEND PERT
TIDY WISE ADEPT CANNY FITTY
HANDY HENDE READY SLICK
SWEET ADROIT ARTFUL CLEVER
CRAFTY DAEDAL EXPERT HABILE
SCIENT SKILLY SOLERT SUBTLE
CUNNING POLITIC SKILLED
DEXTROUS PRACTIVE SLEIGHTY
TACTICAL PROFICIENT
SKILLFULLY DEFTLY YARELY
CRAFTILY
SKILLFULNESS CRAFT
SKIM TOP RIFF SCUD SCUM SCUN
SCUR SILE SKIP FLEET GRAZE
SCALE SKIFF SKIRR SKIVE

BROWSE RABBLE SAMPLE
DESPUME SKITTER
(— ON WATER) SCHOON
SKIMMED FLAT FLET
SKIMMER FALK LARI SKEP SCOOP
LINGEL SCUMMER CUTWATER
SKIMMINGS SCRUFF
SKIMP JIMP SLUR SCAMP SKINCH
SKIMPY JIMP CHARY SPARE
MEAGER MEAGRE SCANTY STINGY
SKIN KIP KIT BACK BARK CASE
CAST DERM FELL FLAY FLEA HIDE
HILD KITT MORT PEAU PEEL PELT
RIND BALAT BLYPE BRAWN
FLOAT GENET SLUFF STRIP
SWARD CORIUM PELTRY SWARTH
UNCASE CUTICLE DOESKIN
ENDERON KIDSKIN LEATHER
PELLAGE SKIMMER BUCKSKIN
DRUMHEAD LAMBSKIN
PARADERM PELLICLE SEALSKIN
TEGUMENT VITILIGO WOOLFELL
(— FOR BOOKBINDING) BASAN
(— FOR HOLDING WATER) KIRBEH
(— OF BACON) SWARD
(— OF BOARDS) CARPET
(— OF FRUIT) PEEL
(— OF GOOSE) APRON
(— OF INSECT) CAST
(— OF POTATO) JACKET
(— OF POULTRY NECK) HELZEL
(— OF RABBIT) RACK CONEY
(— OF SEAL) SCULP
(— OF THE HEAD) SCALP
(— OF WALNUT) ZEST
(— OF YOUNG CALF) SLINK
DEACON
(— WITH WOOL REMAINING ON IT)
WOOLFELL
(BARE —) BUFF
(BEAVER —) PLEW
(BOAR'S —) SHIELD
(CAST —) SPOIL SLOUGH EXUVIAE
(CHAFED OR SORE —) IRE
(CHAMOIS —) FURWA
(DEEP LAYER OF THE —) CUTIS
(FAWN —) NEBRIS
(INNER PART OF THE —) DERMA
(LAMB — PREPARED LIKE FUR)
BUDGE
(OUTER —) HUSK
(PENDULOUS FOLD OF —) DEWLAP
(ROUGHTANNED —) CRUST
(SHARK —) SHAGREEN
(SHEEP —) BASIL
(SQUIRREL —) VAIR
(THICKENED —) BRAWN
(THIN —) FILM PELLICLE STRIFFEN
(60 —S) TURN
(PREF.) CUT(I)(O) CUTANEO
DERM(AT)(ATO)(O) DERO
EPIDERM(O) SCYT(O)
(SUFF.) DERM(A)(ATOUS)(IA)(IS)(Y)
SKIN FLICK NUDIE
SKINFLINT SKIN FLINT SCREW
HUDDLE PELTER SCRAPER
SKEEZIX
SKINK ADDA SCINCID SCORPION
(PREF.) SCINCI SCINCO
SKINNY BONY LEAN THIN SLINK
SKIOLD (FATHER OF —) ODIN
SKIP DAP HIP BALK BOUT FOOT
JUMP LEAP SLIP TRIP BOUND

CAPER DANCE FRISK SALTO
SCOON SCOPE SCOUP SKITE
SMOKE VAULT GAMBOL GLANCE
LAUNCH SPRING GUNBOAT
SALTATE SKIPPER SKITTER
TRIPPLE PORPOISE RICOCHET
(— SCHOOL) TIB
(MINING —) SLIPE

SKIPJACK SKIP BONITO ALEWIFE
SKIPPER

SKIPPER IHI SKIP LAODAH
LOWDAH SERANG SHIPPER

SKIRMISH FRAY BRUSH CLASH
MELEE SKIRM BICKER HASSLE
PICKEER RUNNING

SKIRMISHER HUSSAR TIRALLEUR

SKIRMISHING SPARRING

SKIRT CUT HUG LAP BANK BASE
COAT ENGI JUPE MIDI MINI SAYA
TUBE TUTU COAST JUPON LABIE
PAREU PASIN STRIP TREND
TWIST BASQUE DIRNDL HOBBLE
JUMPER KIRTLE PEPLUM SARONG
TAMEIN QUARTER BASQUINE
PULLBACK SKIRTING
(ARMOR —) TASSES LAMBOYS
(DIVIDED —) CULOTTE
(HOOP —) CRINOLINE
(HOOPED —) TUBTAIL
(LONG —) MAXI
(TARTAN —) KILT ARISAID
(PL.) DOCK DOCKEN

SKIRTING DADE SKIRT PLINTH
(PL.) BROKES

SKIT BLACKOUT

SKITTAGETAN HAIDA

SKITTISH SHY CORKY GOOSY
WINDY FLISKY KITTLE SKEIGH
SPOOKY FLIGHTY SCADDLE
SKADDLE STARTLY BOGGLISH
SKITTERY STARTFUL

SKITTLES BOWLS KAYLES KITTLES
SQUAILS

SKUA BONXIE JAEGER TEASER
TULIAC STINKPOT WHIPTAIL

SKULDUGGERY JOUKERY
PAWKERY

SKULK DERN JOUK LURK LUSK
MICHE MOOCH SCOUT SHOOL

SKULL BEAN POLL CRANY MOOCH
SCALP SCAUP VAULT COBBRA
MAZARD PALLET SCONCE
CRANIUM HARNPAN HEADMOLD
PANNICLE
(— BONE) VOMER
(— POINT) TYLION
(BACK OF —) OCCIPUT
(INCOMPLETE —) CALVARIA
(UPPER HALF OF —) SINCIPUT
(PREF.) CRANI(O)
(SUFF.) CRANIA(L)

SKULLCAP COIF PIXY PIXIE SKULL
VAULT BEANIE COIFFE CALOTTE
CAPELINE HOODWORT
(ARABIAN —) CHECHIA
(JEWISH —) YAMILKE YARMULKE
(STEEL —) SECRET

SKUNK ANNA ATOC ATOK PUSS
HURON SKINK SNIPE ZORIL
CHINCHA POLECAT SEECAWK
SMELLER CONEPATE CONEPATL
MUSTELID PHOBYCAT ZORRILLO
(JAVANESE —) TELEDU

SKUNK CABBAGE COLLARD
POCKWEED

SKY BLUE HIGH LIFT LOFT POLE
TIEN AZURE CARRY DYAUS ETHER
LANGI VAULT CAELUS CANOPY
HEAVEN REGION WELKIN
ELEMENT HEAVENS OLYMPUS
TENGERE WEATHER
(ICE —) ICEBLINK
(PREF.) CAELI CAELO COELI
COELO URAN(I)(O) URANOSO

SKY-BLUE
(PREF.) CERULEO

SKYLARK LARK YERK

SLAB BAT CANT CLAM LECH PARE
SLAT BLADE BOARD DALLE LINER
PANEL PLANK SLATE STELA STELE
TABLE WADGE ABACUS FLITCH
MARVER MIHRAB PAVIOR
RUNNER FLAPPET PLANCHE
PORPHYRY PUNCHEON
SLABWOOD
(— BY SINK) BUNKER
(— OF CLAY) BAT
(— OF COAL) SKIP SLIP
(— OF ICE) SCONCE
(— OF LIMESTONE) BALATTE
(— OF MARBLE) DALLE
(— OF PEAT) SCAD
(— OF SANDSTONE) COMAL
(— OVER BROOK) CLAM
(BROKEN-OFF —) BLAUD
(GRINDING —) MULLER
(HOPSCOTCH —) PEEVER
(MEMORIAL —) LEDGER
(PAINTER'S —) SLANT
(PLASTERER'S —) HAWK
(STONE —) PLANK STELA STELE
INKSTONE

SLACK DRY LAX OFF CULM DUFF
LASH NESH SLOW SOFT VEER
CHECK CRANK FLOWN LOOSE
SLAKE TARDY ABATED FLABBY
FLAPPY REMISS UNGIRT BACKING
MAKINGS RELAXED SLACKEN
SMEDDUM CARELESS DILATORY
INACTIVE SLOBBERY NEGLIGENT
(— IN TRIGGER) CREEP
(— OF ROPE) SLATCH
(— SHEET OF SAIL) FLOW
(COAL —) COOM COOMB
(PL.) BAGS

SLACKEN LAG PAY EASE FLAG
SLOW DELAY DOWSE LOOSE
QUAIL RELAX SLACK SLAKE START
SURGE ASLAKE EXOLVE RELENT
UNBEND
(— SPEED) HANG

SLACKENING LETUP DETENTE
LETDOWN SLACKAGE

SLACKER SPIV ROTTER COUCHER
SLINKER EMBUSQUE

SLACKNESS LACHES LASHNESS

SLADE SOLE

SLAG SCAR DROSS CINDER
DANDER SCORIA SLAKIN THOMAS
QUITTER SLACKEN

SLAIN FALLEN

SLAKE ABATE SLACK LESSEN
QUENCH REFRESH SATISFY

SLAKING FAT

SLAM CLAP DASH FLUB SLOG SLOT
VOLE CLASH GRAND PLANK

SLOSH STRAM CHELEM FLOUNCE

SLAMMER JAIL STIR

SLANDER CANT BELIE LIBEL NOISE
SMEAR BEFOUL DEFAME INJURE
MALIGN MISSAY VILIFY ASPERSE
CALUMNY OBTRECT SCANDAL
TRADUCE TRUMPET BACKBITE
DEROGATE STRUMPET
ASPERSION BESPATTER

SLANDERER JUROR BLAZONER

SLANDEROUS FAMOUS VILIPEND

SLANG CANT ARGOT FLASH
DIALECT

SLANT TIP CANT FLUE SKEW TILT
BEVEL DRAFT SLOPE SPLAY
STOOP FLANCH SKLENT
DRAUGHT COLORING DIAGONAL
(PREF.) CLIN(O)

SLANTED CANTED COLORED
COCKEYED

SLANTING AWRY BIAS CANT SKEW
BEVEL SLOPE ASLANT ASLOPE
SKLENT SQUINT LOXOTIC
OBLIQUE SLOPING AVELONGE
COLORING OVERWART SIDELONG

SLANTINGLY AHOO ASWASH
SLANTLY

SLANT LINE VIRGULA VIRGULE

SLANTWISE
(PREF.) LECHRI(O)

SLAP BOX DAB BLIP BLOW CLAP
CUFF FLAP LICK PLAT SCUD SLAT
SNUB SPAT TACK BLIBE CLINK
CLOUT CRACK PANDY POTCH
SKEEG SKELP SKITE SMACK
SPANK TWANG TWANK BLEEZE
BUFFET SCLAFF SLIGHT STRIKE
TINGLER WHERRET BACKSLAP
(— HARD) BLAD
(RANDOM —) FLAY

SLAPDASH BUCKEYE

SLASH CAG CUT JAG COUP GASH
HASH PANE RACE RASH SLIT
TOPS KNIFE MINCE SCORE SKICE
SLISH RAMMEL SCORCH STREAK
SLITTER DIAGONAL SLASHING

SLASHED JAGGED DECOPED
TATTERED

SLASHING ABATIS

SLAT BOW LAG FLAT PALE SLOT
WAND BLADE SCLAT SLOAT
STAVE RIFFLE SPLINE EUPHROE
BEDSTAFF

SLATE RAG SLAT FRAME KILLAS
TABLET TICKET SHALDER
SHINDLE SLATING
(— IN SMALL IRREGULAR PIECES)
SCANTLE
(BLUE —) SHIVER SKAILLIE
(EXPOSED PART OF ROOFING —)
BARI
(SIZE OF —) PEGGY DUCHESS
IMPERIAL
(SURFACE —) BONE

SLATER HELER HELLIER SLATTER
SKIMMITY
(TOOL OF —) STAKE

SLATTERN DAB DAW MAB FROW
MAUX SLUT TRUB DOLLY FAGOT
MAWKS MOGGY MOPSY BLOUSE
CLATCH DOLLOP MALKIN SLOVEN
STREEL TRAPES LADRONE
TROLLOP HUCKMUCK SLUMMOCK

SLATTERNLY DOWDY BLOWSY
DAWISH FROWZY SORDID
BLOWZED TRAPISH SLATTERN
SLOVENLY

SLAUGHTER WAL FELL KILL SLAM
SLAY BUTCH HALAL QUELL
BATTUE MURDER STRAGE
BUTCHER CARNAGE KILLING
SCUPPER SHAMBLE BUTCHERY
MASSACRE OCCISION SHECHITA
(— ACCORDING TO MOSLEM LAW)
HALAL
(— OF LARGE NUMBER) HECATOMB
(WHOLESALE —) QUELL

SLAUGHTERER KILLER SHOHET
KNACKER SHOCHET

SLAUGHTERHOUSE ABATTOIR
BUTCHERY MATADERO SHAMBLES
(— WORKER) LIMEMAN

SLAUGHTERING SHEHITA
SHECHITA

SLAV VEND WEND CZECH HUNKS
HUNKY SLAVE USKOK CROATIAN
MORAVIAN POLABIAN

SLAVE BOY DAS ARDU BOND DASI
DUPE ESNE MOIL SERF DAVUS
HELOT SWINK THEOW ABJECT
ALIPIN ALLTUD CUMHAL FORSAR
GUINEA HIEROS MAMLUK SLAVEY
THRALL VASSAL BONDMAN
CAPTIVE CHATTEL FORSADO
HACKNEY PEDAGOG SERVANT
SLAVISH BONDMAID LORARIUS
MAMELUKE MANCIPLE MORGIANA
PRAEDIAL SLAVELET THEOWMAN
ODALISQUE
(— IN TEMPLE) HIEROS
(— WHO WHIPS OTHERS) LORARIUS
(DEFORMED —) CALIBAN
(FREED —) CLIENT
(FUGITIVE —) MAROON CIMMARON
(GALLEY —) FORSAR FORSADO
SFORZATO
(HAREM —) ODALISK
(HINDU —) DAS DASI
(PL.) CHIURM COFFLE HELOTRY
TOXOTAE

SLAVEDRIVER RUSHER

SLAVER DROOL FROTH DRIVEL
DRIBBLE SLABBER SLOBBER
SALIVATE

SLAVERY YOKE THRALL BONDAGE
HELOTRY MIZRAIM THRALDOM
SERVITUDE

SLAVEY DRUDGE

SLAVISH MEAN MENIAL

SLAVONIC (— BEING) VILA

SLAY KILL SMITE SPILL MURDER
STRIKE BUTCHER EXECUTE
STRANGLE SLAUGHTER

SLAYER BANE HOGNI KILLER
MURDERER
(— OF INFIDELS) GHAZI
(SUFF.) CTONUS

SLEAZY FLIMSY

SLED LUGE TODE JUMBO SCOOT
SLIDE SLIPE SLOOP HURDLE
JUMPER SLEDGE SLEIGH BOBSLED
CLIPPER COASTER DOGBOAT
DOGSLED KOMATIK MONOSKI
POINTER SLIPPER TRAILER
TRAVOIS HANDSLED SKELETON
TOBOGGAN

SLEDGE DAN DRAG DRAY LUGE PULK SLED GURRY PULKA SLIDE SLIPE TRAIL TRAIN TROLL TRUNK SLEIGH KIBITKA KOMATIK PADDOCK TROLLEY TRAINEAU
(— FOR CRIMINALS) HURDLE
(— FOR STRAIGHTENING RAILS) GAG
(LOG —) SLOOP TIEBOY
(MINER'S —) MALLET
SLEDGEHAMMER SMASHER
SLEEK SNOD SOFT CLOSE JOLLY SILKY SLICK TRICK SILKEN SLEEKY SLIGHT SMARMY SMOOTH SVELTE SLEEKIT SOIGNEE SLIPPERY
SLEEKNESS GLOSS
SLEEP BED KIP LIB LIE NAP CALK CAMP DORM DOSS DOZE HALE REST WINK BALMY CRASH DORSE ROOST SWOON DROWSE SIESTA SNOOZE SOMNUS SWEVEN SLUMBER WINKING
(— BROKEN BY SNORING) GRUFF
(— ON A PERCH) JOUK
(DEEP —) SWOON
(LIGHT —) SLOOM
(PRETENDED —) DOGSLEEP
(PROFOUND —) SOPOR
(SHORT —) NAP SIESTA SNOOZE
(PREF.) SOPOR HYPN(O) SOMNI
(DEEP —) NARC(O)
SLEEPER TIE FENDER DORMANT DORMEUSE ELEOTRID STRINGER
SLEEPINESS SOPITION
SLEEPING BED ASLEEP DORMANT DORMIENT
SLEEPLESS LIDLESS WAKEFUL RESTLESS WATCHFUL
SLEEPLESSNESS WATCH INSOMNIA
SLEEPY DOZY HEAVY NODDY PEEPY DROWSY GROGGY MORPHIC SLEEPISH SLUMBERY SOMNIFIC SLUMBEROUS
SLEET STORM
SLEEVE ARM BAND POKE ARMLET MANCHE MOGGAN BUSHING CATHEAD CUBITAL HOUSING THIMBLE
(— ON A SHAFT) CANNON
(— ON GUN) BAND
(CANVAS —) DROGUE
(HANGING —) TAB
(LEG-OF-MUTTON —) GIGOT
(LONG —) POKE
(TAPERED —) SKEIN
SLEIGH SLO PUNG SLED BOOBY SLIPE TRAIN BERLIN CUTTER SLEDGE CARIOLE TRAINEAU
SLEIGHT ARTIFICE
SLENDER FINE HAIR JIMP LANK LEAN PRIN SLIM THIN DELIE EXILE FAINT LATHY REEDY SLANK SLEEK SMALL SPIRY SWAMP WISPY FILATE SCANTY SEMMIT SLIGHT SPINNY SPIRED STALKY SVELTE TENDER GRACILE LISSOME SLIVERY SPIRLIE SQUINNY TENUOUS THREADY WASPISH ACICULAR ETHEREAL HAIRLIKE PILIFORM SPINDLED ATTENUATE
SLENDERNESS EXILITY TENUITY
SLEW LOT RAFT SLUE STROKE

SLICE CUT BITE CHIP CHOP FLAG FLAP JERK SHED STOW CANCH CAPER GIGOT LEACH SHARE SHAVE SHIVE SKELB SLIPE SLIVE CANTLE COLLOP CORNET CULPON SHIVER SLIVER TARGET THIBLE TRENCH SECTION SHAVING TRANCHE COSSETTE TURNOVER
(— CUT IN PLOWING) FLAG
(— OF BACON) BARD BARDE LARDON RASHER
(— OF BREAD) BUTTY WHANG CROUTE TRENCHER
(— OF CHEESE) KEBBOC
(— OF COAL) SKIP
(— OF FISH) COBBIN
(— OF MEAT) STEAK COLLOP CUTLET SCALLOP TAILZIE
(— OF MEAT OR FISH) PAUPIETTE
(— OF SMOKED SALMON) CORNET
(— OF TOAST) ROUND
(— REMOVED FROM ROADWAY) CANCH
(— WITH MOTIONS) SAW
(—S OF APPLES) CHOPS
(LARGE —) BLAD DODGE
(THICK —) SLAB WHANG
(THIN —) CHIP WAFER SECTION
SLICED CUT
SLICK LOY GLIB SNUG SLEEK CLASSY GLOSSY SMOOTHY SLIDDERY
SLICKER FLOAT SLICK SMOOTH SLEEKER SMOOTHER
SLIDE SCLY SKID SLEW SLIP SLUR BALOP CHUTE COAST COULE CREEP GLIDE HURRY MOUNT SCOOT SHIRL SLADE FINDER SLOUGH SLIDDER SLITHER SLUTHER FADEAWAY GLISSADE SLIDEWAY SCHLEIFER
(— A DIE) SLUR
(— CARDS) SKIN
(— DOWN) RUSE SLUMP
(— FOR LOWERING CASKS) POLEYNE
(— ON DRUMHEAD) BRACE
(— SIDEWISE) SKID
(TENT —) EUPHROE
SLIDER REGISTER
SLIDEWAY PULLEY
SLIDING COULE
SLIGHT CUT OFF EASY FINE HURT POOR SLAP SLIM SLUR SNUB THIN WEAK FILMY GAUZY LIGHT MINOR SCANT SMALL SOBER FLIMSY FORGET LACHES LITTLE MINUTE REMOTE TWIGGY CONTEMN FRAGILE GRACILE NEGLECT NOMINAL SHALLOW SKETCHY SLENDER SLIGHTY THREADY VILLAIN DELICATE MISPRIZE OVERLOOK SCRANNEL VILIPEND
SLIGHTER LESS
SLIGHTEST FIRST LEAST
SLIGHTINGLY LIGHTLY
SLIGHTLY FAINTLY SOMEWHAT
(PREF.) MI(O)
(SUFF.) ESCENT ULOUS
SLIGHTNESS DELICACY GRACILITY
SLIM THIN GAUNT WANDY SLIGHT SLENDER TENUOUS

SLIME GLIT GORE OOZE SLAB SLIP SLUM GLEET SLAKE SLOAK SLOKE SLEECH SLUDGE SCHLICH SLUBBER SLUTHER
(PREF.) MUC(I)(O) MUCOSO MYX(O)
(SUFF.) MYXA
SLIMY OOZY SLAB MUCID GLAIRY GLEETY GLETTY LIMOUS MUCOUS SNOTTY SLEECHY MUCULENT
SLINE JOINT
SLING DUST LOOP FLING HONDA SLUNG BRIDGE BRIDLE HALTER SLACKIE
(— FOR HAULING GAME) TUMPLINE
(— OF BRAIDED FIBERS) MA
(PREF.) FUNDI
SLINGER FUNDITOR
SLINGSHOT SLING SLAPPY TWEAKER CATAPULT SHANGHAI
SLINK SLY CAST HINT LEER LOOP LURK PEAK MICHE SHIRK SLING SLUNK SNEAK SLINKY
(— AWAY) SHAG SLOKE FLINCH MIZZLE SHRINK
SLIP DIP IMP NOD SLY BALK CARD CHIT DOCK FALL JINK LOOP RUSE SKEW SKID SLEW SLUR SPEW BEWET BEWIT BONER CHECK DAGGE ERROR FLIER FLYER GLIDE LABEL LAPSE SCAPE SCION SHIFT SHIRL SKATE SKITE SLICK SLIDE SLIPE SLIVE SLUMP STALK SURGE COUPON ENGOBE LAPSUS MISCUE SLOUGH SLURRY TICKET UNSLIP DELAPSE FOUNDER ILLAPSE MISSTEP MORTISE SLIDDER SLUTHER SNAPPER STUMBLE BOOKMARK GERTRUDE GLISSADE HEADBAND QUICKSET SCHEDULE SIDESLIP SLIPPAGE SLIPPING
(— AWAY) GO BILK SKIN WISE EVADE ELAPSE
(— BY) ELAPSE
(— FROM A PLANT) STALLON
(— OF FISH) RAND
(— OF PAPER) ALLONGE
(— OF PARCHMENT) PANEL
(— OF WOOD) SPILL REGLET
(— OFF COURSE) SLEW SLOUGH
(— ON CARELESSLY) SLIVE
(— OUT) TIB
(— SECRETLY) CREEM
(— SMOOTHLY) SWIM
(— UP) BLUNDER
(CERAMICS —) SLOP ENGOBE
(INFANT'S —) GERTRUDE
(PILLOW —) BIER
(PREF.) CLAD(O)
(SUFF.) CLADOUS
SLIPCASE CASE FOREL FORREL
SLIPKNOT BOW SNITTLE DRAWKNOT
SLIPMAN JACKER
SLIPOVER OVERSLIP
SLIPPER FLAT MULE NEAP PUMP SOCK TURN GLAVE MOYLE ROMEO SCUFF BALLET BOOTEE DORSAY JULIET PANTON PINSON SANDAL SCLAFF SCLIFF BAUCHLE CHINELA CRAKOWE EVERETT SCUFFER BABOUCHE FEWTERER

PANTOFLE SCLAFFER SLIPSHOE
(PREF.) CALCEI
SLIPPERINESS SLIDDER
SLIPPERY GLEG GLIB SLID GLARY GLINT SLAPE SLEEK SLICK SOAPY SWACK CRAFTY GLINSE GREASY LUBRIC SHIFTY SLIPPY ELUSIVE EVASIVE GLIDDER SHUTTLE SLIDDRY SLIDING SLITHER GLIBBERY SLABBERY SLICKERY SLIDDERY SLITHERY
(PREF.) LUBRI
SLIPPERY DICK DONCELLA
SLIPSHOD JERRY RAGGED SLOPPY UNKEMPT SLAPDASH SLOVENLY
SLIPSTREAM RACE
SLIPUP FLUFF MISTAKE
SLIT CUT EYE JAG KIN NAG RIT FENT GATE NICK PORT RACE RENT SCAR SLOT VENT CRACK SPARE BOUCHE CRANNY OSTIUM STRENT FISSURE PERTUSE PLACKET SLITTED SLOTTEN WINDWAY APERTURE BOTHRIUM
(— HIND LEG) HARL
(— IN EDGE OF SHIELD) BOUCHE
(— IN ORGAN PIPE) MOUTH
(— IN STONE) GRIKE
(— MADE BY CUT) KERF
(ORNAMENTAL —) SLASH
SLITHER SLIDE HIRSEL SLIDDER SLUTHER
SLIVER TOP SHAVE SKELF SLICE SPELK SPELL SHIVER DELIVERY SPLINTER
(— OF WOOL) ROLL ROVE
(SPINNING —) END RIBBON DELIVERY
SLOB JOKER SLUDGE SLOBBER SLOMMACK
SLOBBER SLOP SLUP SMALM SMARM SLAVER SLABBER SLATHER SLIVVER BESLAVER
SLOBBERY SLOBBY SMARMY SLAVERY
SLOE SLA SNAG SLONE
SLOG SLOSH STRIKE
SLOGAN CRY CACHET CUTTER PHRASE CATCHCRY SLUGHORN WARDWORD CATCHWORD SHIBBOLETH
SLOOP STAR BOYER COMET SMACK SCHUIT HOOGAARS
SLOP SLAP SOSS SQUAB SWILL SOSSLE SOZZLE HOGWASH SLATTER
(— AROUND) SLAISTER
(PL.) SLIVERS SLIPSLOP SLOPPAGE
SLOPE UP DIP LIE BAND BANK BENT BRAE CANT CAST CURB DROP FALL HANG HILL LEAN PALI RAKE RAMP RISE SIDE SINK TILT BEVEL CLIFF COAST GAMMA HIELD PINCH PITCH SCARP SLANT SLENT SLOOP SPLAY STEEP TALUS VERGE YUNGA ASCENT BAJADA BATTER BREAST BROACH ESCARP GLACIS HADING SHELVE TUMBLE UPBROW UPRISE CUTBANK DESCENT DOWNSET FORESET HANDING INCLINE LEANING PENDANT UPGRADE

VERSANT WEATHER BANKSIDE DRIPPING GLISSADE GRADIENT SHOULDER SIDELING SNOWBANK ACCLIVITY
(— BACK) BATTER
(— DOWN) SHED
(— OF CUESTA) INFACE
(— OF ROOF) CURB
(— OF STERNPOST) RAKE
(— UPWARD) CLIMB ASCEND BATTER
(DOWNWARD —) HANG DEVALL DECLINE DESCENT HANGING DOWNHILL
(GENTLE —) GLACIS
(MARGINAL —) CESS
(MOUNTAIN —) ADRET
(SKIING —) SCHUSS
(STEEP —) BROW HEADWALL
(SUFF.) CLINAL CLINE
SLOPING CANT DEVEX SLANT SLOPE SLOPY ASLOPE SHELVY DECLIVE SCARPED DOWNHILL SIDELING
(— ABRUPTLY) BOLD
(— BACKWARD) SUPINE
SLOPPINESS BLURB
SLOPPY JUICY SOPPY SLABBY SOZZLY SPLOSHY SLABBERY SLAPDASH SLATTERN SLATTERY SLIPSHOD WATERISH
SLOSH DOWSE SLASH SLUSH SOUSE SQUDGE SPLODGE
SLOT COVE DROP SCROLL SPLINE KEYHOLE GUIDEWAY
SLOTH AI UNAU TARDO ACEDIA IGNAVY ACCIDIE IGNAVIA BRADYPOD EDENTATE PIGRITIA SLUGGING
SLOTH BEAR BHALU ASWAIL
SLOTHFUL FAT ARGH IDLE LAZY INERT LITHER THOKISH UNLUSTY DELICATE INDOLENT SLUGGISH
SLOUCH LOUCH LARRUP LOLLOP LOUNGE SLIDDER TROLLOP SHAMMOCK SLOUCHER
SLOUCH HAT SMASHER
SLOUGH CORE SHED SLEW SLUE BAYOU RAVEL SHUCK SLONK SLUFF SPOIL SWAMP ESCHAR DISCARD LAMMOCK
SLOVEN BESOM CLART SLUSH TROLLY GROBIAN HALLION TRACHLE HUDDROUN
SLOVENLY DOWDY GAUMY MESSY BLOWZY CLATTY FROWZY GRUBBY SHABBY SLOPPY SLOVEN TRAILY UNTIDY BUNTING SLIVING SLOUCHY UNSONCY CARELESS HUDDROUN SLIPSHOD SLOBBERY SLUBBERY SLUTTISH TROLLOPY
SLOW BOG LAG LAX LEK WET ARGH DREE DULL LASH LATE LAZY LENT SKID SLUG SULK BLUNT DUNCH DUNNY HEAVY HOOLY INERT POKEY SLACK SLOTH SWEER TARDE TARDO TARDY UNAPT ARREST BEHIND DRIECH DUMMEL HINDER RETARD SLOOMY SOODLY TRAILY COSTIVE DRONISH HALTING LAGGARD LANGUID SLACKEN SOAKING STRANGE TARDANT TEDIOUS

UNREADY DILATORY INACTIVE LATESOME SLUGGISH
(— DOWN) SEIZE
(— IN BURNING) SOFT
(— IN MOVEMENT) GRAVE INERT SULKY
(— OF MIND) STUPID
(— TO LEARN) BACKWARD
(— TO RESPOND) GROSS
(— UP) SLACK SLACKEN
(MODERATELY —) ANDANTE
(MUSICALLY —) LENTO
(PLEASANTLY —) SOFT
(VERY —) LARGO
(PREF.) BRADY TARDI
SLOW-BURNING PUNKY
SLOWED STIFF
SLOWER LATTER CALANDO
SLOWING
(SUFF.) STASIA STASIS
SLOW LORIS KOKAN
SLOWLY SLOW DULLY GRAVE HOOLY LENTO ADAGIO GENTLY HEAVILY
SLOW-MOVING SLEEPY DORMANT DRAWLING SLUGGISH
SLOWNESS LAG SLOTH LENTOR TARDITY LATENESS
SLOW-WITTED FAT DENSE STUPID
SLOWWORM HAGWORM
SLUDGE GUNK SLOB
SLUE SLEW SWAMP SLOUGH
SLUG BUST LINE MILL PLOW SHOT SNAG STEW ARION CLUMP LIMAX SNAIL RATTLE STRIKE SNIFTER TREPANG GEEPOUND
(PREF.) LIMACI
SLUGGARD DAW SLOW SLUG DRONE BUZZARD CAYNARD LUGGARD SWINGER SLOWBACK SLUGABED
SLUGGISH LAG DOZY DULL FOUL LATE LAZY LOGY SLOW BROSY DOPEY DRONY FAINT HEAVY INERT LOURD RESTY SULKY BOVINE DRAGGY DROWSY JACENT LEADEN SLEEPY SLOOMY SLUGGY SUPINE TORPID COSTIVE DORMANT DRONISH LAGGARD LANGUID LENTOUS LUMPISH RESTIVE DILATORY INACTIVE INDOLENT LOURDISH SLOTHFUL SLOTTERY SLUGGARD
(PREF.) BRADY
SLUGGISHNESS LEAD SLOTH APATHY LENTOR PHLEGM INERTIA LANGUOR
SLUICE CLOW GOOL GOTE GOUT SASSE SLUSH TRUNK CLOUGH FENDER LAUNDER PENSTOCK WASTWEIR
SLUICEGATE ABOIDEAU
SLUICEWAY FLASH
SLUM BUSTI BUSTEE WARREN
SLUMBER DORM DOVE DOZE JOUK REST ROUT SLEEP SLOOM DROWSE
SLUMP FALL FLOP SOSS SLOUCH LETDOWN TROLLOP
SLUR BIND SLUM COULE GLIDE SLIME SCRUFF SLIGHT SLUBBER LIGATURE
(— IN PRINTING) SHAKE

SLURRY SLIP
SLUSH MIRE POSH SIND SLOP FLUSH SLOSH SPOSH STUFF SWASH SWOSH LOPPER SLUDGE SLUTCH SLOBBER SLODDER
SLUSHY SLASHY SLOPPY SLOSHY SLUDGY STICKY SPLASHY SLOBBERY
SLUT MAUX BITCH FILTH QUEAN DOLLOP DRAZEL DRAZIL MALKIN DROSSEL PUCELLE SLAMKIN SLATTERN
SLUTTISH DRABBY SLUTTY SORDID
SLY ARCH FOXY SLEE SLID SLIM CANNY COONY LEERY LOOPY PAWKY PEERY POKEY SLOAN SNAKY ARTFUL ASTUTE CRAFTY FELINE SUBTLE SUPPLE CUNNING EVASIVE FURTIVE LEERING POLITIC SUBTILE UNFRANK GUILEFUL SLEIGHTY SNEAKING STEALTHY THIEVISH CLANDESTINE
SLYNESS CUNNING PAWKERY STEALTH ARCHNESS
SMACK BANG BARK BIFF BUSS KISS SALT SCAT SLAP TANG TROW VEIN BAWLY GOUFF SAVOR SNACK SPICE TASTE TWANG BARQUE BAWLEY FLAVOR SMATCH SMACKEE SPANKER BRAGOZZO SLAPDASH TINCTURE
(— OF) RELISH
SMACKING SKELPING
SMALL BIT SMA WEE BABY MEAN PINK SEED SLIM TINY WEAK BIJOU BITTY DAWNY DEENY DINKY ELFIN PETIT PETTY PINKY POKEY TEENY WEENY BANTAM FRIBBY GRUBBY INSECT LITTLE MIDGET MINUTE NARROW PEANUT PETITE SCANTY SLIGHT SMALLY CAPSULE NAGGISH NANITIC PICCOLO QUEECHY SCRIMPY SLENDER THRIFTY PEDDLING PILULOUS SNIPPETY MINIATURE MINISCULE
(— AND NUMEROUS) MILIARY
(— AND THICK) DUMPY DUMPTY
(— BUT TANGIBLE) CERTAIN
(— PORTION) MODICUM
(CONTEMPTIBLY —) MEASLY
(DAINTILY —) MIGNON
(EXCESSIVELY —) BOXY
(NOT —) GOOD
(VERY —) WEE FINE TINY DWARF MICRO PUSIL PYGMY TEENY MINUTE MINIKIN TIDDLEY DWARFISH
(PREF.) LEPT(O) MICR(O) OLIG(O) PARV(I) PAURO TAPIN(O)
(SUFF.) (— ONE) EL ET IUM LING OCK ULA ULE ULUM ULUS
SMALLAGE MARCH
SMALLCLOTHES SHORTS SMALLS
SMALL CRANBERRY FENBERRY
SMALLER LESS MINOR LESSER
(PREF.) MEIO MI(O) MINI
SMALLEST FIRST LEAST MINIM TITMAN MINIMUS
SMALLHOLDER TOFTMAN
SMALL-MINDED PETTY PICAYUNE

SMALLNESS NANISM EXILITY FEWNESS PAUCITY EXIGUITY SCARCITY
SMALLPOX POX VARIOLA ALASTRIM
(PREF.) VARIOLI VARIOLO
SMALT ROYAL ESCHEL SMALTZ ZAFFER ASMALTE
SMART NIP YEP BRAW FESS FLIP FOXY GNIB NICE PINK POSH RACY SNAP SPRY SWAG TRIG ACUTE BRISK CLEAN DINKY FLASH HEADY JIMMY KIPPY NIFTY NOBBY NUTTY PEERT PRANK PRIDY RITZY SASSY SAUCY SHARP SLEEK SLICK SMIRK SMOKE SMUSH SPICY SPRIG STING SWANK SWISH TIGHT TIPPY TOFFY TRICK AKAMAI BRAWLY BRIGHT CHEESY CLEVER DAPPER GIGOLO JAUNTY KITTLE PERTLY SHREWD SPANKY SPIFFY SPRINK SPRUCE STOUND SWANKY SWIDGE TIDDLY KNOWING PUNGENT SWAGGER TOFFISH VOGUISH BRUSHING SPIFFING
(— IN APPEARANCE) POSH
(— IN DRESS) GALLANT
SMART ALECK FLIP SMARTY
SMARTEN FINE PUSS SMUG GROOM PRINK SLICK TITIVATE
SMARTLY SMACK SMART SNACK YEPLY TIDELY
SMARTNESS TON SNAP SMART SPIFF SWISH
SMARTWEED CULERAGE REDKNEES
SMASH GIT BASH BUMP CAVE DASH PASH RUSH SCAT TRAP BREAK CRACK CRASH CRAZE PRANG SOCKO STAVE TRASH WRECK CRACKER SHATTER SMASHUP DEBRUISE DEMOLISH OVERHEAD STRAMASH
(— A GAP) BREACH
SMASHED BUNG KAPUT STOVEN BROOZLED
SMASHING CRACKING
SMASHUP STRAMASH
SMATTERING SMACK SMATCH SMATTER
SMEAR DAB RUB BLOT BLUR CLAM DAUB DOPE GAUM GLOB GORM MOIL CLEAM DITCH GLAIR SLAKE SLARE SMALM SMARM SULLY BEDAUB BESLAB DEFILE PLATCH SLAVER SLURRY SMIRCH SMOOCH SMUDGE SPREAD STREAK STRIKE BEPAINT BESMEAR PLASTER POLLUTE SPLOTCH SLAISTER
(— OVER) ENGLUTE
(— WITH BLOOD) GILD
(— WITH EGG WHITE) GLAIR
(— WITH MUD) CLART SLIME
(— WITH SOMETHING STICKY) GAUM GORM LIME
(— WITH TAR) PAY
(— WITH WAX) CERE
SMEAR DAB FLATFISH MARYSOLE
SMEARED FOUL BROSY MUSSY SCOVY BLOODY SMUDGY BLURRED BEGUMMED
SMEARY DAUBY GAUMY

SMEDDUM SMITHUM
SMELL FUNK FUST GUSH NOSE ODOR VENT AROMA FETOR FLAIR SAVOR SCENT SMACK SNIFF SNOOK SNUFF STIFE TASTE OLFACT RESENT SMEECH BREATHE PERFUME REFLAIR VERDURE
(— AFTER PREY) BREVIT
(— OFFENSIVELY) REEK
(DAMP FUSTY —) RAFT
(DISAGREEABLE —) GOO PONG STENCH
(HAVING PLEASANT —) SNIFTY
(MUSTY —) FUST
(OFFENSIVE —) FUNK FETOR STINK MEPHITIS
(STRONG —) HOGO
(SWEET —) SWEET
(PREF.) BROM(O) ODIO ODORI ODORO OLFACTO OSM(O) OSMIO OSPHRESIO OZO(NI)(NO)
(SENSE OF —) OSPHRESIO
(SUFF.) OSMA
(SENSE OF —) OSPHRESIA
SMELLY FUGGY WHIFFY SMELLFUL
SMELT DECOCT INANGA EPERLAN ICEFISH ELIQUATE SALMONID SPARLING SPERLING
(FRY OF —) PRIM
SMEW NUN PIED SMEE DIVER SMETHE
SMIDGEN DAB
SMILAX LILY SARSA LILIUM
SMILE BEAM GRIN FLASH FLEER SMEER ARRIDE SMUDGE SMIRKLE
(— AMOROUSLY) SMICKER
(AFFECTED —) SMIRK
(SELF-CONSCIOUS —) SIMPER
SMILING GOOD BONNY RIANT SMILY BONNIE RIDENT SMIRKY TWINKLY SMILEFUL
SMIRCH SMIT SOIL SMEAR SULLY SLURRY SOILURE TARNISH
SMIRCHED DINGY
SMIRK DRAD YIRN SIMPER SMICKER SMIRKLE SMURTLE
SMITE DUNT FRAP GIRD SLAY FLING SKITE STRIKE
(— WITH LIGHTNING) LEVEN
SMITH MIMIR REGIN BOSSER FORGER SMITHY FARRIER GLUTTER SMITHER STEELER WAYLAND FLOORMAN FORGEMAN PANSMITH
SMITHSONITE CALAMINE
SMITHY FORGE SMIDDY STITHY STUDDIE FARRIERY
SMITTEN EPRISE STRICKEN
SMOCK BRAT SLOP KAMIS SMOKE JIBBAH JUMPER CHEMISE SMICKET
SMOKE PEW USE BLOW FLAN FOGO FUFF FUME FUNK HAVE LUNT NAVE PIPE REEK ROKE TOVE DRINK REECH SMEEK SMORE SMUSH STIVE VAPOR WHIFF BREATH BUCCAN POTHER SMEECH SMUDGE INCENSE SMOLDER SMOTHER BACONIZE
(— MARIJUANA) BLAST
(AUTHOR OF —) TURGENEV
(CHARACTER IN —) IRINA TANYA

OSININ GRIGORY POTUGIN TATYANA BAMBAEFF SHESTOFF BINDASOFF GUBARYOFF LITVINOFF RATMIROFF KAPITOLINA REISENBACH
(FROST —) BARBER
(HAZE AND —) SMAZE
(OFFENSIVE —) FUNK
(TOBACCO —) BLAST
(PREF.) ATMID(O) CAPNO FUMAR(O) FUMI
SMOKE BROWN ASPHALT
SMOKEHOUSE FUMATORY
SMOKEJACK STACKMAN
SMOKER FUNKER NICOTIAN
(MARIJUANA —) VIPER
SMOKESTACK STACK FUNNEL TUNNEL CHIMNEY
SMOKE TREE ZANTE FUSTET FUSTIC SCOTINO
SMOKING ROOM DIVAN TABAGIE
SMOKY HAZY ROKY DINGY FUMID FUMISH FUMOSE REECHY SMUDGY SMUISTY
SMOLDER SMUSH SMOTHER
SMOLDERING PUNKY
SMOLT SMELT SMOUT SPROD
SMOOCH NECK LALLYGAG LOLLYGAG
SMOOTH DUB FAT LAP NOT BOSS COMB DRAG EASE EASY EVEN FACE FAIR FILE FLAT GLAD GLEG GLIB HONE IRON LENE NOTT REET SLID SNOD SOFT TRIM BLAND BRENT CLEAR COUTH DARBY DIGHT DOLCE DRESS EMERY FLOAT FRAZE GLARE GOOSE HOWEL LEVEL LITHE NAKED PLAIN PLANE PRESS QUIET SCARF SILKY SLAPE SLEEK SLICK SMOLT SNUFF SOAPY SUANT SUAVE SUENT TERSE ABRASE BUFFED CREAMY EQUATE EVENLY FETTLE FLUENT GLOSSY GREASE GREASY LEGATO LIMBER MANGLE POLITE SCREED SILKEN SLIGHT STREAK STRIKE STROKE SVELTE UNFRET BOULDER ERUGATE FLATTEN SLEEKIT EXPLICIT GLABRATE GLABROUS GLIBBERY GRAZIOSO LEVIGATE SARSENET SLIDDERY SQUEEGEE STRICKLE UNRUFFLE
(— BY BREAKING LUMPS) BILDER
(— MARBLE) GRIT
(— ONESELF UP) PREEN
(— OVER) GLOZE PLASTER
(— TYPE) KERN
(HYPOCRITICALLY —) SLEEK
(PHONETICALLY —) LENE LENIS
(PREF.) HOMAL(O) LEIO LEUR(O) LIO LISS(O) LITI OXY
SMOOTHER GLAZER
SMOOTHLY SLICK EASILY EVENLY GLIBLY SMOOTH SPROWSY SWEETLY POLITELY
SMOOTHNESS EASE FLUENCY
SMOOTH-RUNNING SWEET
SMOOTH-TONGUED WHILLY
SMOOTH WINTERBERRY CANHOOP
SMOTHER BURKE CHOKE SMEAR SMOKE SMORE MOIDER SMUDGE

STIFLE FLASKER OPPRESS QUEASON QUEAZEN SMOLDER SMUDDER
SMOTHERED ETOUFFE STIFLED
SMUDGE BLUR GAUM SLUR SMUT SOIL SOOT CROCK SMEAR SMOKE SMOOCH SMUTCH SMOLDER SMOTHER SOILURE
SMUDGED BLOTTY SMUTCHY
SMUG SLEEK SMUSH SUAVE SMUDGE
SMUGGLE RUN STEAL BOOTLEG SHUFFLE
SMUGGLER OWLER RUNNER SPOTSMAN
(— OF DRUGS) MULE
SMUGGLING OWLING
SMUGLY FATLY
SMUT BUNT COOM BLACK BLECK COLLY COOMB CROCK GRIME SMOOT SMITCH SMUTCH SMATTER COLBRAND
SMUTCH BLOT SMIRCH SMITCH SMOUCH SMUDGE
SMUT GRASS TUSSOCK
SMUTTINESS RAUNCH
SMUTTY BAWDY DIRTY SOOTY SULTRY BARNYARD FREUDIAN
SMYRNA USHAK
SNACK BIT CUT BAIT BITE NOSH SNAP TAPA BEVER BUTTY CHACK CHECK NACHO SHARE SNICK TASTE GOUTER MUNGEY NACKET SNATCH ZAKUSKA ANTOJITO NUNCHEON
SNAFFLE GAG BRIDOON
SNAG KNAG SNUG STUB POINT PLANTER SNAGGLE
(PL.) EMBARRAS
SNAIL HUA PILA SNAG CHINK DRILL HELIX OLIVA PHYSA SHELL THAIS TURBO WHELK CERION CONKER DODMAN NATICA NERITA NERITE PHYSID PURPLE TRITON WINKLE RISSOID UNICORN VERTIGO ZONITID CASSIDID ESCARGOT HODMADOD JANTHINA LYMNAEID MELANIAN NERITOID RAMSHORN SOLARIUM WALLFISH PERIWINKLE
(PREF.) STROMBI STROMBULI
(SUFF.) COCHLEI COCHLI(O) COCHLO
SNAILFLOWER CARACOL
SNAKE (ALSO SEE SERPENT AND REPTILE) ASP BOA BOM NAG BOBA BOID BOMA JUBO NAGA NAJA SEPS SNIG ABOMA ASPIC COBRA CONGO CRIBO DRILL JIBOA KRAIT MAMBA PTYAS RACER SNECK TIGER VIPER BOIGID BONGAR CANTIL CHITAL DABOIA DIPSAS ELAPID GOPHER HISSER JESSUR KERRIL PYTHON ROLLER RUNNER TAIPAN WENONA ADJIGER ANILIID BOKADAM CAMOODI CRAWLER CREEPER CULEBRA DIAPSID HAGWORM LABARIA LANGAHA PRESTER RATTLER REGULUS REPTILE SCYTALE SERPENT SPITTER WALPAPI ANACONDA BONETAIL BUNGARUM CASCAVEL

CERASTES CROTALID EGGEATER FLATHEAD HAIRWORM JARARACA KEELBACK MOCCASIN OPHIDIAN RINGHALS SNAKELET VIPERINE
(PREF.) OPHI(O) SERPU
(SUFF.) OPHIS
SNAKEBARK IRONBARK
SNAKEBIRD DARTER PLOTUS ANHINGA DUCKLAR
SNAKEHEAD MURRAL
SNAKELIKE ANGUINE VIPEROUS
SNAKEMOUTH POGONIA
SNAKEPIECE POINTER
SNAKEROOT STEVIA BABROOT BUGBANE SANGREL SANICLE SAWWORT POOLWORT RICHWEED WHITETOP
SNAKESKIN SPOIL HACKLE SLOUGH
(CASTOFF —S) EXUVIAE
SNAKEWEED BISTORT
SNAP SET ZIP BARK BITE CHOP GNAP HUFF JERK KNAP LIRP PIPE SETT BREAK CLACK FILIP FLICK GANCH KNACK KNICK PHOTO SMACK SNACK BLUDGE SNAPPY SNATCH FASTENER PUSHOVER SNAPHEAD CREPITATE
(— AT) HANCH
(— LIGHTLY) KNICK
(— OFF) SNIP
(— TOGETHER) CRASH
(— UP) SNUP SNAFFLE
(— WITH FINGER) LIRP FILIP THRIP FILLIP
SNAPBACK PASSBACK
SNAPDRAGON BULL SNAPS BULLER BULLDOG DOGMOUTH
SNAPE FLINCH
SNAPPER UKU BRIM JOCU SESI BREAM PARGO VORAZ CUBERA HUSSAR JENOAR LAWYER NATIVE TAMURE ULAULA COCKNEY CRACKER BIAJAIBA CACHUCHO FLAMENCO GNATSNAP LUTIANID WOLLOMAI SCHNAPPER MUTTONFISH
SNAPPING CHACK DOGGISH
SNAPPING BEETLE ELATER SKIPPER SNAPPER ELATERID SKIPJACK
SNAPPING TURTLE LOGHEAD SHAGTAIL
SNAPPISH CRUP EDGY PUXY CROSS SNACK TESTY WASPY CUTTED SNAGGY SNAPPY SNIPPY DOGGISH PEEVISH
SNAPPY CRISP JEMMY NIPPY ZIPPY
SNARE GIN HAY NET PIT SET BAIT BUKE FANG GIRN GRIN HOOK LACE LIME TOIL TRAP WAIT WIRE BRAKE CATCH FRAUD GNARE LATCH LEASH SINEW SNARL SNIRL STALE SWEEK TRAIN COBWEB GILDER PANTER SNATCH SPRINT TREPAN TUNNEL ENSNARE MANTRAP OVERNET PITFALL SETTING SNICKLE SNIGGLE SPRINGE BIRDLIME INVEIGLE LIMEBUSH SPRINGLE TENDICLE MOUSETRAP
(— DEER) WITHE

(— FOR ELEPHANTS) KEDDAH
(FISH —) WEEL
SNARL ARR BITE CARL GIRN GNAR
GURR HARL HURR NARR TWIT
WAFF YARR GNARL GNARR GRILL
KNURL RAVEL SNIRL TWINE
BOWWOW BUMBLE GAUNCH
MUCKER TANGLE VENNER
GRIZZLE GRUMBLE
SNARLED SNAFU
SNARLER CYNIC
SNARLING LATRANT
SNATCH HAP NAB NIP RAP GRAB
HINT RACE RASE SNAP SNIP
WHIP WRAP YERK YUCK BRAID
CATCH CLAWK CLICK EREPT
GANCH GRASP GRIPE PLUCK
SNACK STRIP SWIPE SWOOP
TWEAK WHIFT WREST SNITCH
STRIKE TWITCH WRENCH
CLAUGHT GRABBLE SCAMBLE
VULTURE
SNEAK BLAB GRUB LEER LOOP
LOUT LURK PEAK PIMP SHUG
SNIG LURCH MEECH MOOCH
SCOUT SHARK SHIRK SKULK SLIDE
SLINK SLIPE SLIVE SLOKE SNEAP
SNICK SNOOK BLIFIL MICHER
WEASEL SLOUNGE SNIGGLE
SNEAKSBY
(— AWAY) SLIPE
(— OFF) MAG SHAB MIZZLE
(PRYING —) SNOOP
SNEAKER CREEPER GUMSHOE
SNEAKING HANGDOG PEAKING
SLIVING
SNEAKY FURTIVE MEECHING
SNEER SHY FLON GIBE GIRD GIRN
GULE JEER JERK JIBE MOCK
FLEER FLING FLOUT GLEEK
JAUNT SCOFF SCOUT SLARE
SLEER SNIRT GIZZEN SNEEST
TWITCH WRINKLE RIDICULE
SNEERING FRUMPERY
SNEEZE NEESE NEEZE ARREST
(— AT) CONDEMN DESPISE
SNEEZEWEED ALANT ROSILLA
HELENIUM
SNEEZEWOOD NIESHOUT
SNEEZEWORT HARDHEAD
PTARMICA
SNEEZING PTARMIC
SNELL SNOOD TIPPET GANGING
SNICK TIP SNECK
SNICKER TITTER SMIRKLE SNIGGER
SNIGGLE
SNIDE ORNERY
SNIFF NOSE TIFT VENT WIND
SMELL SNAFF SNIFT SNUFF
SNIVEL SNAFFLE SNIFFLE
SNOTTER
SNIFTER SLUG BALLOON INHALER
SNIGGER NICKER WHICKER
SNIGGLE BRAGGLE
SNIP CUT CLIP CROP MINX NICK
SHRED SNICK SCISSOR
SNIPE JACK NICK WISP SCAPE
SNITE WADER WILLET BLEATER
BLITTER DOWITCH HUMILITY
LONGBILL SHADBIRD
SNIPER TEASER BUSHWACK
SNIVEL BUBBLE SNIFFLE SNIFTER
SNOTTER SNUFFLE

SNOB SNAB SNOOT FLUNKY
SHONEEN SNOBBER
SNOBBISH RITZY DICKTY SNOBBY
SNOOTY UPSTAGE
SNOOK SNOOT ROBALO
SNOOP PRY PEEK PEEP SNEAK
BREVIT PIROOT GUMSHOE
SNOOPER CREEP BUSYBODY
SNOOPY CURIOUS
SNOOZE DOVER SLEEP SNOOZLE
SNORE ROUT SNARK SNORK
SNORT SNOCKER SNOTTER
SNORING STERTOR RHONCHUS
SNORT BLOW ROUT SNUR TOOT
VENT BLURT FNESE SNARK SNEER
SNORE SNORK WHOOF EXCLAIM
SNIFTER SNOCKER SNORKEL
SNORTLE SNOTTER
SNOUT NEB SAW BEAK BILL NOSE
WROT GROIN SERRA SNOOT
MUFFLE MUZZLE NOZZLE
GRUNTLE ROSTRUM
(PREF.) PROBOSCI(DI) RHYNCH(O)
(SUFF.) RHYNCHUS RHYNCUS
SNOUT BEETLE CURCULIO
SNOUT MITE BDELLID
SNOW CORN DRIP GRUE COVER
SPOSH STORM SUGAR WHITE
POWDER COCAINE GRAUPEL
RAMPART WEATHER SCOUTHER
WINDSLAB
(— PELLETS) GRAUPEL
(— SLIGHTLY) SPIT
(DISSOLVING —) FLUSH
(DRIFTED —) WINDLE
(GLACIER —) FIRN NEVE BLIZZ
(HEAVY FALL OF —) PASH
(MUSHY —) SLOB
(NEW-FALLEN —) MANNA
(PARTLY MELTED —) SLUSH
(WHIRLING —) SKIRL
(PREF.) CHIO CHION(O) NIVI
SNOWBERRY MOXA WAXBERRY
SNOWBIRD JUNCO
SNOW BUNTING OATFOWL
SNOWBIRD SNOWFOWL
SNOW COCK JERMONAL
SNOWDRIFT WREATH YOWDEN
SNOWDROP TREE BELLWOOD
COWLICKS TISSWOOD
SNOWFALL PASH SKIFF SKIFT
FLURRY ONDING
SNOWFLAKE FLAG FLAUCHT
SNOW FLEA PODURAN PODURID
SNOW GOOSE WAVY
SNOWINESS NIVOSITY
SNOW LEOPARD IRBIS
SNOWLESS GREEN
**SNOW MAIDEN, THE (CHARACTER
IN —)** LEL BOBYL KUPAVA MIZGIR
SPRING BERENDEY BOBYLIKHA
SNEGUROCHKA
(COMPOSER OF —)
RIMSKYKORSAKOV
SNOWMAN YETI
SNOW MOUNTAIN JOKUL
SNOWSHOE WEB PATIN PATTEN
RACKET RACQUET
SNOWSTORM PURGA DRIFTER
BLIZZARD
SNOWY NIVAL WHITE NIVEOUS
SNUB AIR RITZ SLAP SNIB FRUMP
SNEAP SWANK REBUFF REBUTE

SIMOUS SLIGHT SNOUCH SNUBBY
SETDOWN
SNUBBING MAIL
SNUBBY PUGGISH
SNUB-NOSED SIMOUS
(PREF.) SIMO
SNUFF TOP VENT MUSTY SNIFF
SNUSH TABAC COHOBA PULVIL
RAPPEE SNEESH STIFLE SNUFFLE
BERGAMOT MACCABOY
ORANGERY SMUTCHIN
SNUFFBOX MILL MULL
SNUFFBOX BEAN CACOON
SNUFFER PRICK DOUTER TOPPER
PRICKER
SNUFFLE SNIVEL SNAFFLE SNIFFLE
SNIFTER
SNUG LEW RUG BEIN BIEN COSH
COSY COZY NEAT SNOD TAUT
TEAT TOSH TOSY CANNY CLOSE
COUTH POVIE QUEME TIGHT
PENTIT COUTHIE SNUGGERY
SNUGGISH
SNUGGLE SNUG BURROW CUDDLE
SNUDGE CROODLE SNUZZLE
SNUGLY SHORT COSILY
SO SAE SUCH THAT THIS THUS
THISSEN INSOMUCH SUCHWISE
THUSWISE
(— AM I) LIKEWISE
(— BE IT) AMEN
(— FAR AS) QUOAD
(— TO SPEAK) FAIRLY
(NOT —) SECUS
(QUITE —) EXACTLY
SOAK RET SOB SOD SOG SOP WET
BOWK BUCK SIPE BINGE DROUK
DROWN SOUSE STEEP TOAST
DRENCH EMBAIN IMBIBE IMBRUE
SEETHE SODDEN SPONGE
INSTEEP MICKERY SWELTER
SATURATE
(— A CASK) GROG
(— FLAX) RET RATE
(— IN) SOP FEATHER
SOAKED SOGGY SOPPY SOBBED
SODDEN WATERY DRUNKEN
SOBBING DRAGGLED
SOAKING BATH SUING SOGGING
INFUSION
SOAP SAPO SUDS CHIPS STOCK
NIGGER CASTILE TALLATE
WINDSOR SANDSOAP SAVONETTE
(CAKE OF —) TABLET TABULATE
(LIQUID —) FIT
(PREF.) SAP(O) SAPONI
SOAPBARK QUILLAI SOAPWOOD
SOAPFISH JABON
SOAP PLANT AMOLE PALMILLO
SOAPROOT SOAPWEED
SOAPSTONE ALBERENE POTSTONE
STEATITE
SOAPSTONER TALCER
SOAPWORT BORITH COWHERB
SAPONARY SOAPROOT
SOAPWEED
SOAR FLY STY KITE FLOAT MOUNT
PLANE SPIRE TOWER ASCEND
ASPIRE AIRPLANE
SOARING FLIGHT ICARIAN SPIRING
ESSORANT
SOB YEX SIKE SNOB SNUB SOUGH
BLUBBER SINGULT

SOBBING GREET
SOBER SAD CALM COOL SAGE
CIVIL FRESH GRAVE QUIET STAID
DOULCE SEDATE SEVERE SOLEMN
SOMBER STEADY EARNEST
PENSIVE REGULAR SERIOUS
UNFOXED DECOROUS MODERATE
ABSTEMIOUS
SOBRIETY DRYNESS GRAVITY
ABSTINENCE
SOBRIQUET BYNAME HAWKEYE
SO-CALLED ALLEGED
SOCCER FOOTER FOOTBALL
SOCIABLE COSY CHUMMY CLUBBY
FOLKSY SOCIAL AFFABLE
AMIABLE INNERLY CLUBABLE
FAMILIAR FELLOWLY INFORMAL
SOCIAL DISTAL PUBLIC SUPPER
SOCIABLE SOCIETAL CONVIVIAL
(— WORKER) ALMONER
SOCIALISM ETATISM MARXISM
GUESDISM
SOCIALIST FABIAN NIHILIST
SOCIALISTIC PINK
SOCIALIZE CIVILIZE
SOCIETY BUND HALL HERD SANG
GUILD MONDE POLIS SABHA
SAMAJ SANGH SOKOL MENAGE
NANIGO PARISH SYSTEM VEREIN
ACADEMY COLLEGE COLORUM
COMPANY COUNCIL KINGDOM
SOCIETE THIASOS EXCHANGE
HETAERIA PRECINCT SOCIETAS
SODALITY SORORITY
(— OF RELIGIOUS FANATICS)
COLORUM
(CHORAL —) CHOIR
(CLOWN —) KOSHARE KOYEMSHI
(CRAFT —) ARTEL
(DEBATING —) POP
(GYMNASTIC —) SOKOL
(HIGH —) SWELLDOM
(LITERARY —) HALL
(POLITICAL —) TAMMANY
(RELIGIOUS —) CHURCH
(SECRET —) HUI EGBO HOEY PORO
TONG LODGE MAFIA OGBONI
PURRAH CAMORRA
(STUDENT —) CORPS
(UTOPIAN —) ANARCHY
(WHITE —) MAN
(PREF.) SOCIO
SOCINIAN RACOVIAN
SOCIOLOGIST AMERICAN HUNT
LYND ROSS WARD BARNES
DEVINE HUNTER SUMNER VEBLEN
DUGDALE ELLWOOD FRAZIER
NEARING STEIZLE WILLARD
ZUEBLIN BOGARDUS GIDDINGS
GOLDENWEISER
ENGLISH KIDD TOYNBEE
FRENCH TARDE DURKHEIM
GERMAN LANGE WEBER FREYER
MICHELS SCHAFFLE THURNWALD
ITALIAN LORIA
SCOTTISH GEDDES MCLENNAN
SOCIOLOGY DEMOTICS
SOCK BOP ONE BIFF BUST HOSE
VAMP ANKLET ARGYLE VAMPEY
STOCKING
(— OF GOAT'S HAIR) UDO
(INFANT'S —) BOOTEE BOOTIE
(JAPANESE —) TABI

SOCKET BOX CUP PAD POD BUSH CELL HOSE LEAD NOSE SHOE CHAIR POINT SHANK BUCKET BUDGET COLLET EYEPIT NOZZLE POCKET SAUCER SCONCE ALVEOLE COCKEYE FERRULE FUTCHEL GUDGEON THIMBLE TORULUS ALVEOLUS DRAWHEAD
(— FOR GEM) OUCH
(— FOR LANCE) PORT
(— FOR LENS) CELL
(— FOR MAST) TABERNACLE
(— FOR MOUTHPIECE) BIRN
(— IN GOLF CLUB HEAD) HOSE HOSEL
(— OF BONE) POT
(— OF HINGE) PAN
(— OF MILLSTONE) INK COCKEYE
(— OF WATER PIPE) BELL
(BIT —) POD
(PREF.) GLENO TORMO
SOCKEYE NERKA KOKANEE BLUEBACK
SOCLE ZOCCO
SOCRATES (— METHOD) MAIEUTIC
SOD HUB BEAT DELF FAIL FLAG SCAD SONK TURF DELPH GAZON GLEBE SCRAW SWARD CLOWER TERRON SODDING
SODA BARILLA
SODA POP TONIC
SODDEN SAMMY SAPPY SOGGY POACHY DRAGGLED
SODI (SON OF —) GEDDIEL
SODIUM NA SODA NATRIUM
(PREF.) NATR(O)
SODIUM BICARBONATE SODA BICARB
SODIUM BORATE BORAX
SODIUM CARBONATE SODA TRONA ANATRON BARILLA SALSODA
SODIUM CHLORIDE SALT HALITE
SODIUM THIOSULFATE HYPO
SODOMITE DOG BUGGER SPINTRY BOUGERON
SOEVER SOME
SOFA BOIST COUCH DIVAN SQUAB CANAPE LOUNGE SETTEE CAUSEUSE SOCIABLE
SOFFIT GATHER PLAFOND INTRADOS PLANCIER
SOFRONIA (LOVER OF —) OLINDO
SOFT COY TID FEIL LASH LIMP LUSH MILD MURE NASH NESH PLUM SART TOSY WAXY WEAK BALMY BLAND CUSHY DABBY DOLCE DOWNY FAINT GIVEY HOOLY LENIS LIGHT MALMY MEALY MELCH MUSHY PADDY PAPPY PIANO PLIFF SILKY SLACK SMALL SOAPY SOOTH SWASH SWEET WAXEN WETHE YAPPY CASHIE CREAMY EFFETE FLAGGY FLOSSY FLUFFY GENTLE LITHER LYDIAN MELLOW PIPING PLACID SAMMEL SIDDER SIDDOW SILKEN SLOPPY SMOOTH SOFTLY SPONGY SPOONY TENDER UNDURE CLEMENT COTTONY CRUMBLY DUCTILE FLESHLY LENIENT SQUASHY CUSHIONY FEMININE FLEXIBLE HOTHOUSE LADYLIKE

SARCENET SQUELCHY TRANQUIL
(— AND FLEXIBLE) FLOPPY
(— AND LIFELESS) DOUGHY
(— IN TEXTURE) SUPPLE
(VERY —) SQUASHY
(PREF.) LENI MALAC(O) MOLLI
SOFT-COVER PAPERBACK
SOFTEN CUT CREE MELT SOAK SOFT TAME ALLAY BATCH BREAK FRIZZ LITHE MALAX TOUCH WOKIE DIGEST GENTLE LENIFY PACIFY RELENT SOOTHE SUBDUE SUBMIT TEMPER WEAKEN APPEASE ASSUAGE CUSHION LENIATE MOLLIFY QUALIFY SWEETEN UNSTEEL AMOLLISH ATTEMPER ENFEEBLE HUMANIZE MITIGATE MODULATE PALLIATE PRETTIFY
(— BY BOILING) CREE
(— BY KNEADING) MALAX MALAXATE
(— BY STEEPING) MACERATE
(— COLOR) CUT SCUMBLE
(— FIBERS) BREAK
(— GRADUALLY) SQUAT
(— JUTE) BATCH
(— LEATHER) BREY FRIZ FRIZZ
(— METAL) ALLAY
(— TONE) SURD
SOFTENED ROXY ANODYNE MOUILLE FLEXUOUS
SOFTENING LENIENT MALACIA BLETTING
SOFTER MANCANDO
SOFTHEARTED TENDER
SOFTLY LOW BAJO SOFT HOOLY FAIRLY GENTLY SWEETLY CREAMILY TENDERLY
SOFTNESS SOFT MOLLITIES
(— IN COAL SEAM) LUM LUMB
(SUFF.) MALACIA
SOFT-POINTED HEBETATE
SOFT-SHELLED TURTLE FLAPPER FLIPPER FLAPJACK
SOFT-SOAP CON FLANNEL
SOFT-SPOKEN MEALY
SOFTWARE (COMPUTER —) MONITOR
SOGGY SAD DUNCH SOBBY SODDEN SPONGY WATERY
SOIGNE TRIM SLEEK MODISH
SOIL DAG DUB MUD RAY SOD BLOT BLUR CLAY CLOD DAUB DIRT DUST FOIL FOUL GRIT LAND MIRK MOOL MOSS MUCK MURK MUSS SAUR SILE SLUR SMUT SOOT TASH BULLI CROCK EARTH GLEBE GRIME GUMBO LAYER MUCKY ROSEL SLUSH SMEAR SOLUM SOULE SPARK STAIN SULLY BARING BEDAUB BEFOUL BEMIRE BEMOIL GROUND PODZOL SLURRY SMIRCH SMOOCH SMUDGE SPLASH SUDDLE BEGRIME BENASTY BESMEAR BESMOKE BETHUMB FEWMAND PEDOCAL POLLUTE REGOSOL SEEDBED SLUBBER TARNISH TRACHLE AGROTYPE ALLUVIAL BEDABBLE BESMIRCH BUCKSHOT FLYSPECK LATERITE PEDALFER PLANOSOL RENDZINA WOODCOCK

SOLONCHAK CONTAMINATE
(— ABOVE CLAY) KELLY
(— DEPOSITED BY WIND) ELUVIUM
(— FORMED BY DECAY) GEEST
(— INTERMEDIATE BETWEEN SAND AND CLAY) ROSEL
(— PREPARED FOR SOWING) TILTH
(— REMOVED FROM ORE) BARING
(— WITH GREASE) LARD
(AGGREGATE —) PED
(ALKALINE —) SOLONETZ
(ASHLIKE —) PODSOL PODZOL
(CLAYEY —) GALT MALM MAUM ADOBE SOLOD SOLOTH
(COTTON —) REGUR
(DRY —) GROOT
(FRIABLE —) CRUMB
(GRAVELLY —) ROACH GROWAN
(HARD —) RAMMEL
(INFERTILE —) GALL
(LEACHED —S) LATOSOL
(PEATY —) YARFA YARPHA
(PLUMBER'S —) SMUDGE
(POROUS —) SPONGE
(POTTING —) COMPOST
(PRAIRIE —) BRUNIZEM
(SILTY —) GUMBO
(SPRINGY —) WOODSERE
(ZONAL —) SEROZEM SIEROZEM
(PREF.) AGRI AGRO GE(O) PED(O) SOLI
SOILAGE SOIL SMUDGE SOILING
SOILED FOUL BLACK DINGY DIRTY MUSSY SOOTY TARRY SMUDGY SMUTTY SNUFFY THUMBED DRAGGLED SHOPWORN
SOIL-EXPOSING EROSIVE
SOIREE EVENING
SOJOURN LIE BIDE STAY STOP ABIDE ABODE TARRY RESIDE ALLODGE MANSION STATION
SOJOURNER PILGRIM
SOKOL FALCON
SOL SOH SOU ALCOSOL EMULSOID HYDROSOL SOLUTION
SOLA SHOLA PAUKPAN
SOLACE CHEER CHEERER COMFORT CONSOLE SWEETEN SOLATION
SOLAR HELIAC SOLLER HELIACAL SOLARIUM
(— SYSTEM APPARATUS) ORRERY
SOLAR DISK ATEN ATON
(CENTER OF —) CAZIMI
SOLAR ENERGY
(PREF.) HELI
SOLD SELT BOOKED
(ILLICITLY —) BOOTLEG
SOLDER PALE BRAZE FLOAT SOWDER SPELTER
SOLDERER BROGUER
SOLDERING IRON COPPER DOCTOR
SOLDIER SON TAP BLEU BOLO GOUM GUGU KERN LEVY SHOT SWAD TULK WART BERNE CROAT FRITZ GUARD GUFFY KHAKI LANCE LIMEY LINER MINER NIZAM PERDU PIKER PIVOT POILU PONGO SAMMY SWEAT TOLKE TOMMY TOPAS ASKARI BONAGH BUMMER DARTER DIGGER EXPERT GALOOT GUNNER

GURKHA HAIDUK HEINIE HOSTER LANCER MARKER PIETON REITER SENTRY SKIEUR SOLDAT SWADDY THRASO WEAPON ZOUAVE BAYONET BILLJIM BLIGHTY BRIGAND CARABIN CATERAN CORSLET DARTMAN DOGFACE DRAGOON FEDERAL FEEDMAN FIGHTER GENETOR GOUMIER HOBBLER INVALID JACKMAN MATROSS ORDERLY PALIKAR PANDOUR PAVISOR PELTAST PIKEMAN PRIVATE REDCOAT REGULAR REISTER SCARLET SLINGER SOLDADO STRIKER TROOPER VETERAN WARRIOR ARQUEBUS BEZONIAN BLUECOAT BUCKSKIN BUFFCOAT CAMELEER CAVALIER DESERTER FENCIBLE FUGLEMAN FUSILIER GALLOPER GENDARME GRAYBACK GRAYCOAT IRONSIDE JANIZARY KHANDAIT LANCEMAN LINESMAN MILITANT MIQUELET MUSTACHE PIOUPIOU RAPPAREE SENTINEL SERVITOR SILLADAR SPEARMAN SWORDMAN TOLPATCH TRANSFER TRIARIAN WARFARER WHIFFLER YARDBIRD CATAPHRACT
(— OF MUSCOVITE GUARD) STRELITZ
(— WITH SIDE WHISKERS) BADGER
(ALBANIAN —) PALIKAR
(ALGERIAN —) ARBI
(ANT —) MAXIM
(AUSTRALIAN —) ANZAC DIGGER BILLJIM
(BOMBAY —S) DUCKS
(BRITISH —) LIMEY TOMMY BLIGHTY LOBSTER REDCOAT ROOINEK
(BRUTAL —) PANDOUR
(CAREER —) LIFER
(COWARDLY —) CAPITANO
(FEMALE —) AMAZON
(FILE OF 6 —S) ROT
(FILIPINO —) GUGU
(FOOT —) KERN PAGE PEON GRUNT PIETON FOOTMAN TOLPATCH
(GERMAN —) HUN FRITZ HEINE KRAUT HEINIE
(GREEK —) EVZONE HOPLITE
(INCOMPETENT —) BOLL
(INDIAN —) PEON JAWAN SEPOY GURKHA
(INVALID —) FOGY FOGEY
(IRREGULAR —) CROAT CATERAN JAYHAWK SEBUNDY MIQUELET RAPPAREE SILLADAR
(MERCENARY —) RUTTER HESSIAN
(MOROCCAN —) ASKARI
(MOUNTED —) LANCER DRAGOON GENETOR LOBSTER TROOPER VEDETTE CAVALIER
(OLD —) GROGNARD
(PROFESSIONAL —) SAMURAI
(REVOLUTIONARY —) REDCOAT BUCKSKIN
(ROMAN —S OF THIRD LINE) TRIARY TRIARII
(RUSSIAN —) IVAN

(SCOTTISH —) JOCK
(SMALL —) BANTAM
(TURKISH —) NIZAM REDIF
(PL.) FOOT ELITE TERZO TROOP
TERTIA CATERVA ENOMOTY
MILITIA VELITES FORAGERS
INFANTRY SOLDIERY
AMERICAN DIX LEA LEE POE AMES
BELL BUTT CARR CLAY DRUM
FISK FORD HILL HOOD KNOX
LANE LEAR LONG LORD LYON
MYER OTIS RENO SHAW WOOL
YORK ALLEN BANKS BATES BEALL
BLISS BRAGG BRETT BROWN
BUELL BURNS CANBY CLARK
CORSE CRAIG CROOK DAVIS
DODGE EAKER EARLY EATON
ELIOT EWELL GATES GETTY
GRANT GREEN GREGG HAYNE
HINES HOVEY HOWZE IRWIN
LEWIS MCCOY MCRAE MEADE
MILES MOSBY MOWER OHARA
PARKE PATCH POORE PRATT
ROYCE SCOTT SHAYS SMITH
STONE SWIFT SYKES TERRY
UPTON VIELE ARNOLD BISBEE
BOWLEY BUFORD BUTLER
CULLUM CUSTER DAYTON
DEVERS EMBICK EMMONS GAINES
GIBBON GIBSON GLOVER GORDON
GORGAS GRAVES GREENE
GROVES HARDEE HARDIN
HARMON HARTLE HOOKER
HOWARD HUNTER JADWIN
JORDAN KEARNY KENNEY
LAWTON MACOMB MARION
MCCOOK MCLAWS MORGAN
MORROW NEWTON OLIVER
PATTON PHELPS PILLOW
PUTNAM RIPLEY ROGERS SCHAFF
SEVIER SHARPE SHELBY SPAATZ
STRONG STUART SUMNER
TANNER TAYLOR THAYER TWIGGS
WARNER WESSON WILCOX
ANDREWS BABCOCK BELKNAP
BINGHAM BRADLEY BUCKNER
BULLARD CARLSON CHAFFEE
CROWDER CROZIER DICKMAN
EDWARDS FERRERO FLEMING
FORREST FREMONT FUNSTON
GRANGER HALLECK HANCOCK
HARBORD HARDING HASKELL
HOUSTON INGALLS JACKSON
KRUEGER LEDYARD LEJEUNE
LIGGETT LINCOLN MAXWELL
MENOHER MERRITT NEVILLE
PARROTT PICKETT RAWLINS
SHAFTER SHERMAN SLEMMER
TORBERT TREMAIN TRIMBLE
VANDORN VENABLE WHEELER
ANDERSON BRERETON BURNSIDE
CAMPBELL DONELSON FRANKLIN
GAILLARD GRIERSON JOHNSTON
MAGRUDER MARSHALL
MCDOWELL MCNARNEY
MOULTRIE OLMSTEAD PERSHING
PRESCOTT REYNOLDS SEDGWICK
SHERIDAN SNELLING STILWELL
STODDARD SUBLETTE SULLIVAN
TOWNSEND AINSWORTH
ALEXANDER ARMISTEAD
ARMSTRONG BONESTEEL
DOOLITTLE DOUBLEDAY

FETTERMAN HARTRANFT
HUMPHREYS MACARTHUR
MCCLELLAN PEMBERTON
PETTIGREW SCHOFIELD
SUMMERALL WILKINSON
BEAUREGARD BUFFINGTON
EISENHOWER LONGSTREET
MCGLACHLIN PLEASONTON
WAINWRIGHT BUTTERFIELD
ARGENTINIAN JUSTO
AUSTRALIAN CASEY BLAMEY
MACKAY MONASH BENNETT
CHAUVEL STURDEE LAVARACK
AUSTRIAN DAUN HESS DANKL
HADIK LIGNE GALLAS GYULAI
TRENCK BENEDEK GABLENZ
ALVINCZY BEAULIEU CLERFAYT
RADETZKY PHILIPPOVIC
BOLIVIAN DAZA PANDO CAMPERO
BALLIVIAN
BRAZILIAN DUTRA FONSECA
PEIXOTO
BULGARIAN SAVOY
CANADIAN BOVEY CRERAR
HUGHES DENISON LINDSAY
CHILEAN CRUZ BULNES FREIRE
IBANEZ PRIETO OHIGGINS
COLOMBIAN REYES HERRAN
CORDOBA MOSQUERA
DANISH RANTZAU
DUTCH CHASSE KEPPEL
COEHOORN DAENDELS
ECUADORIAN ALFARO FLORES
ENGLISH COX NYE BOLS BYNG
DILL DYER GORT HAIG HEAD HILL
LACY LAKE LOWE PILE RICH ROSS
VERE WADE ANDRE BOWER
BROCK CAREW CAREY CAVAN
CLERY CLIVE CRAIG CUTTS
GOUGH HORNE JONES KIRKE
MAHON MAUDE MILNE MONCK
MOORE NEILL NIXON PLATT
SMITH STACK SYKES WARDE
AYLMER BLOUNT BROOKE
BROWNE BULFIN BURLEY
CHURCH CONWAY CREAGH
DAWSON DOBELL DUNDAS
FRENCH FULLER GORDON
GRAHAM HAKING HARRIS
HOWARD INGLIS JARVIS LUGARD
MARTEL MILLER MURRAY NAPIER
NORMAN NUGENT PICTON
POPHAM SAVAGE SIDNEY SIMCOE
TEMPLE TURNER UFFORD
VYVYAN WARREN WAVELL
WEMYSS ALLENBY AMHERST
ATHLONE BARDOLF BINGHAM
BOUQUET BRANDON BRIDGES
CAVALLO CHANDOS CLAYTON
CLINTON COLLINS DOWDING
FASTOLF MACMUNN MAXWELL
METHUEN MORLAND OCONNOR
PEREIRA POWNALL ROBERTS
STEWART SWINTON TORRENS
VENNING VINCENT WANTAGE
WINGATE ALDERSON ANDERSON
AUCHMUTY BECKWITH BENTINCK
BLAKENEY BRADDOCK BRANCKER
BURGOYNE CALLWELL CAMPBELL
CARDIGAN CARLETON CATHCART
CHETWODE COLBORNE
CONGREVE FERGUSON GLEICHEN
GREVILLE HAMILTON HARDINGE

HASTINGS HAVELOCK LAWRENCE
LIGONIER LINDSELL LOCKHART
MAITLAND MONTFORT POYNINGS
STANHOPE TARLETON
ALEXANDER BEAUCHAMP
BERESFORD BROWNRIGG
CONSTABLE HARINGTON
HENDERSON KITCHENER
MACDONALD OCTERLONY
POTTINGER REPINGTON
ROBERTSON WILKINSON
WOODVILLE AUCHINLECK
CODRINGTON CORNWALLIS
DESBOROUGH MACDOUGALL
MONTGOMERY SHERBROOKE
WELLINGTON BRACKENBURY
WINTRINGHAM
FINNISH MANNERHEIM
FRENCH FAY FOY NEY BUAT FOCH
NIEL AMADE ANDRE CONTI COSSE
DOUAY DUMAS FOREY HENRY
HULIN JUNOT LALLY LEVIS LOBAU
MENOU MINIE MITRY TRACY
BELLAY BOUDET CHABOT CHANZY
CISSEY CLARKE CLOSSE DAUMAS
DAVOUT DEJEAN DROUOT
DUCROT DUNOIS FABERT FAILLY
FAVRAS FLEURY FOLARD FRIANT
GERARD GIRAUD GOBERT
JARNAC JOFFRE KLEBER LACLOS
LANNES LATUDE LAUNAY
LAUZUN MAGNAN MAISON
MANGIN MARBOT MASSUE
MONCEY MOREAU PETAIN
ROVIGO SUCHET TROCHU
BAZAINE BOICHUT BOSQUET
BOUILLE CATINAT CATROUX
CHAMILY CHARRAS CLAUSEL
CLISSON CRILLON CUSTINE
DEBENEY DREYFUS FABVIER
GAMELIN GASSION GOURAUD
GROUCHY GUIBERT JOUBERT
JOURDAN LABORDE LASALLE
LEBOEUF LECLERC LEJEUNE
LUCKNER LYAUTEY MARCEAU
MARMONT MAURICE MOLITOR
MONTLUC MORTIER NIVELLE
REYNIER TALLARD VALENCE
VENDOME WEYGAND AUGEREAU
BARATIER BOURBAKI CHAMBRUN
CHAUCHAT CHOISEUL CLUSERET
CONTADES DEGAULLE DEGOUTTE
ESTIENNE GALLIENI GOURGAUD
GOURGUES GRAZIANI HARCOURT
LAMARQUE LANGLOIS LANREZAC
LARMINAT LEFEBVRE
LORENCEZ MAUNOURY
MONTCALM PICHEGRU
TAVANNES VANDAMME
AIGUILLON ANDREOSSY
BERTHELOT BOISSOUDY
BOULANGER CANROBERT
DAMPIERRE FAIDHERBE
GROSSETTI GUEBRIANT
HUNTZIGER LAFAYETTE
LALLEMAND LAURISTON
MACDONALD MONTHOLON
NIVERNAIS PELISSIER
SCHOMBERG CHASTELLUX
GUILLAUMAT KELLERMANN
MONTGOMERY ROCHAMBEAU
WESTERMANN CHANGARNIER
JACQUEMINOT MONTMORENCY

CAULAINCOURT LESDIGUIERES
GERMAN EPP JODL ARNIM BOEHN
BULOW KLUCK KUNDT HALDER
HAUSEN HUTIER KEITEL MOLTKE
ROMMEL SEECKT BISSING
BLUCHER CAPRIVI FISCHER
FRITSCH GROENER JOCHMUS
STEUBEN BERNHARD BLOMBERG
GALLWITZ GERHARDT GUDERIAN
HAESELER HARTMANN LITZMANN
RIEDESEL SCHWERIN ZEITZLER
ALDRINGEN HAUSHOFER
HEERINGEN HINDERSIN
LINSINGEN MACKENSEN
MANSFIELD REINHARDT
RUNDSTEDT THEILMANN
WALDERSEE FRUNDSBERG
HINDENBURG KESSELRING
LUDENDORFF SCHLEICHER
SCHLIEFFEN BRAUCHITSCH
FALKENHORST FALKENHAUSEN
GREEK ARATUS KALERGES
KONDYLES PANGALOS
ALCIBIADES HIERONYMUS
GUATEMALAN CHACON ORELLANA
HAITIAN PETION RIGAUD
SALOMON GEFFRARD
HUNGARIAN GORGEY DAMJANICH
SZECHENYI
IRISH LACY WADE COLLEY
ODUFFY CADOGAN COLLINS
OREILLY OHIGGINS PAKENHAM
ITALIAN BIXIO FANTI CANEVA
COSENZ DAVILA DOUHET
CAPELLO BADOGLIO CAVIGLIA
CIALDINI COLLEONI GIARDINO
MARSIGLI RAMORINO BARATIERI
CAVALLERO DANNUNZIO
LAMARMORA PICCOLOMINI
JAPANESE ABE OKU ARAKI KOISO
NODZU SAITO TAMAI KODAMA
KUROKI DOIHARA FUSHIMI
KATSURA HASEGAWA SUGIYAMA
TERAUCHI FUKUSHIMA
HASHIMOTO HIDEYOSHI
MEXICAN MEJIA ALDAMA ARISTA
HUERTA ALMAZAN ALMONTE
ALVAREZ AMPUDIA CAMACHO
MIRAMON OBREGON VALLEJO
ZULOAGA CANALIZO CARDENAS
ESCOBEDO GONZALEZ GUERRERO
ITURBIDE VICTORIA BUSTAMANTE
NEW ZEALAND CHAYTOR
FREYBERG
PARAGUAYAN MORINIGO
ESTIGARRIBIA
PERSIAN ARTAPHERNES
PERUVIAN BALTA PRADO CACERES
GAMARRA PIEROLA CASTILLA
IGLESIAS SALAVERRY
POLISH BEM PASEK HALLER
PULASKI CHLOPICKI DEMBINSKI
KOSCIUSKO PILSUDSKI
DOMBROWSKI MALCZEWSKI
SOSNKOWSKI KRUKOWIECKI
PORTUGUESE ALMEIDA PEREIRA
SALDANHA TEIXEIRA
ROMAN AETIUS BURRUS CAEPIO
CAESAR GALLUS POLLIO ALBINUS
CAECINA CALENUS CASSIUS
CHAEREA FANNIUS LEPIDUS
PLANCUS AFRANIUS AGRICOLA
CEREATIS DENTATUS DUILLIUS

FABRICIUS FLAMINIUS PASKEVICH
SERTORIUS CINCINNATUS
RUMANIAN ILIESCU ANTONESCU
RUSSIAN BERK GURKO KONEV
GLINKA PLATOV ZHUKOV
BLUCHER BUDENNY CHAPAEV
CHUIKOV DENIKIN KALEDIN
KAMENEV VATUTIN WRANGEL
ALEKSEEV AVERESCU BOBRIKOV
BRUSILOV GOLITSYN KAULBARS
KORNILOV LINEVICH MILYUTIN
SKOBELEV YUDENICH BAGRATION
BENNIGSEN GORCHAKOV
LECHITSKI MENSHIKOV
CHERNYAIEV CHERNYSHEV
DRAGOMIROV KUROPATKIN
ROSTOPCHIN TIMOSHENKO
VOROSHILOV SHAPOSHNIKOV
SALVADORAN REGALADO
SCOTTISH URRY BAIRD MUNRO
ELIOTT RUTHVEN DRUMMOND
MIDDLETON
SOUTH AFRICAN SMUTS HERTZOG
PRETORIUS
SPANISH ALVA ELIO MINA MOLA
RADA CROIX GARAY OSUNA
ULLOA AVALOS GUZMAN
ALMAGRO CORDOBA MONCADA
NARVAEZ NAVARRO ODONOJU
PORTOLA ALVARADO CANTERAC
CARVAJAL CASTANOS CASTILLO
ESPINOSA MANRIQUE MUNTANER
ORELLANA VALDIVIA PEDRARIAS
REQUESENS VELASQUEZ
CASTELLANOS
SWEDISH HORN TOLL BANER
BRAHE ARMFELT LEWENHAUPT
TORSTENSON ADLERCREUTZ
ADLERSPARRE
SWISS DUFOUR ERLACH
JENATSCH
URUGUAYAN ORIBE FLORES
VENEZUELAN PAEZ GOMEZ
CASTRO FALCON MONAGAS
YUGOSLAV ZIVKOVIC
SOLDIERLY WARLIKE
SOLDIERY HORSE MILITIA
SEBUNDY MILITARY SIBBENDY
SOLE CORK FACE GADE MERE
ONLY SLIP SOCK SPUR AFALD
ALONE CLUMP LEMON OLEPI
PELMA WHOLE GADOID INSOLE
ONLEPY PLANTA SINGLE SOLEYN
SULLEN THENAR TONGUE
UNIQUE ANACANTH FLATFISH
HOGCHOKE MARYSOLE SINGULAR
SOLITARY
(— A SHOE) SPECK
(— FOR WALKING OVER SAND)
BACKSTER
(— OF BIRD'S FOOT) PTERNA
(— OF FOOT) PLAT VOLA PELMA
PLANT
(— OF PLANE) FACE
(— OF PLOW) SLADE
(— WITH WOOD) CLOG
(HALF —) SHOULDER
(TOWARD THE —) PLANTAD
(PREF.) PEDI(O) PELMATO
(SUFF.) PELMOUS
SOLELY SOLE ALONE SIMPLY
SINGLY WHOLLY SHEERLY
ENTIRELY

SOLEMN DEEP SAGE AWFUL
BUDGE SOBER DEVOUT FORMAL
RITUAL EARNEST SERIOUS
WEIGHTY FUNEREAL
SOLEMNITY OBIT RITE SACRE
GRAVITY SEVERITY
SOLEMNIZE KEEP SEAL
SOLEMNLY GRAVE HIGHLY
SOLENODONT AGOUTA ALMIQUE
SOLEPIECE SOLE GIRDER
SOL-FA SOLMIZATE
SOLICIT ASK BEG SUE WOO DRUM
MOVE SEEK THIG TOUT URGE
APPLY COURT CRAVE TREAT
ACCOST HUSTLE INVITE INVOKE
BESEECH CANVASS ENTREAT
IMPLORE INSTANT PROCURE
REQUEST APPROACH PETITION
SOLICITATION SUIT QUEST
CANVASS INSTANT SOLICIT
ENTREATY INSTANCE
SOLICITOR AVOUE LAWYER
WRITER ADVOCATE ATTORNEY
TRAMPLER
SOLICITOUS URGENT CAREFUL
CURIOUS JEALOUS DESIROUS
CONCERNED
SOLICITUDE CARE CARK FEAR
HEED PAIN YEME HEART WORRY
ANXIETY CONCERN BUSINESS
JEALOUSY
SOLID DRY SAD CONE CUBE FAST
FIRM FULL HARD CHAMP CUBIC
LEVEL MASSY MEATY SOUND
STIFF STOUT THICK TIGHT
SECURE STABLE STODGY STRONG
STURDY COMPACT CUPRENE
UNIFORM CONSTANT GROUNDLY
MATERIAL STERLING
(GEOMETRICAL —) CONE CUBE
PRISM CONOID CUPROID
FRUSTUM POLYHEDRON
(NOT —) BUBBLE
(PL.) POCHE
(PREF.) STERE(O)
SOLIDARITY CIVILITY
SOLIDIFIED SOLID HARDENED
SOLIDIFY DRY SET JELL SHOOT
HARDEN COMPACT CONGEAL
STIFFEN CONCRETE
SOLIDITY SADNESS FASTNESS
FIRMNESS HARDNESS
SOLIDLY FIRMLY SQUARE STOUTLY
GROUNDLY
SOLIDUS BEZANT NOMISMA
DIAGONAL HYPERPER
(HALF —) SEMIS
SOLIPSISM EGOISM
SOLITAIRE CLARINO CANFIELD
KLONDIKE NAPOLEON PATIENCE
SOLITARY
SOLITARY ODD WAF LONE ONLY
SOLE ALONE ELYNG LONELY
ONLEPY SAVAGE SINGLE SOLEYN
SULLEN DERNFUL EREMITE
PRIVATE RECLUSE UNCOUTH
WIDOWED DESOLATE EREMITIC
ISOLATED LONESOME PEGBOARD
SECLUDED SEPARATE
(PREF.) EREM(O)
SOLITUDE PRIVACY RETREAT
SOLITARY
SOLLERET SABBATON

SOLO ARIA CALL ARIOSO
CAVATINA SPADILLA
SOLOMON SAM KOHELETH
(BROTHER OF —) ADONIJAH
(FATHER OF —) DAVID
(MOTHER OF —) BATHSHEBA
**SOLOMON ISLANDS (CAPITAL OF
—)** HONIARA
(ISLAND OF —) BUKA GIZO SAVO
TULAGI FLORISA MALAITA
RENDOVA RUSSELL CHOISEUL
GUADALCANAL BOUGAINVILLE
SOLOMON'S SEAL LILY
SEALWORT
SOLON SAGE GNOMIC GNOMIST
SENATOR LAWMAKER
SOLPUGID TARANTULA
SOLSTICE SUNSTAY SUNSTEAD
SOLUBLE FRIM FRUM FIXED
SOLUTE SOLVABLE
SOLUTION IT LYE AQUA EUSOL
STAIN TINCT ACETUM ANSWER
ASSOIL DOCTOR ERASER SALINE
EXTRACT EYEWASH LACQUER
RESOLVE SOLUTIO WORKING
ANALYSIS LEACHATE TINCTURE
(— ADDED FOR GOOD MEASURE)
INCAST
(— OF CHESS PROBLEM) COOK
(— OF FERMENTED BRAN) DRENCH
(— OF GUM TRAGACANTH) BED
(ALCOHOLIC —) ESSENCE
(CORROSIVE —) OLEUM
(PICKLING —) SOUSE
(PRESERVING —) BOLIN
(SALINE —) BRINE
(SOAP —) NIGRE
(STERILE —) JOHNIN
(VISCOUS —) GLUE
(WATERY —) EAU SAP
SOLVE DO FIX READ UNDO WORK
BREAK CRACK LOOSE SALVE
ANSWER ASSOIL CIPHER FIGURE
REDUCE RIDDLE SOLUTE RESOLVE
UNRAVEL DECIPHER DISSOLVE
SOLVENT ETHER SOUND ELUENT
SPIRIT ACETONE ALCOHOL
BENZINE COUPLER DILUENT
REMOVER SPOTTER CARBITOL
PICOLINE SOLVABLE STRIPPER
TEREBENE TETRALIN
MENSTRUUM
(UNIVERSAL —) ALKAHEST
SOMALI SOMAL SHUHALI
(PL.) ASHA
SOMALIA (CAPITAL OF —)
MOGADISHU
(COIN OF —) BESA
(DIVISION OF —) HAWIYA
(MEASURE OF —) TOP CABA CHELA
DARAT TABLA CUBITO
(MOUNTAIN OF —) SURUDAD
(MOUNTAIN RANGE OF —) GUBAN
(NATIVE OF —) GALLA HAWIYA
ISBAAK SOMALI DANAKIL
(RIVER OF —) JUBA NOGAL
SCEBELI
(TOWN OF —) MERCA BERBERA
KISMAYU HARGEISA
(WEIGHT OF —) PARSALAH
SOMATIC SOMAL BODILY
SOMBER SAD DERN DULL GRAVE
MORNE SOBER GLOOMY LENTEN

SOLEMN SOMBRE SULLEN
AUSTERE SERIOUS DARKSOME
SOMBROUS
SOME ANY ODD THIS CERTAIN
SOMEBODY QUIDAM SOMEONE
SOMEDAY ONCE
SOMEHOW HOW ONEHOW
SOMEWAY SOMEGATE
SOMEONE SUCH
SOMERSAULT FLIP TOPPLE
FLIFFUS SPOTTER TWISTER
BACKFLIP SOMERSET
SOMETHING WHAT ALIQUID
WHATNOT SOMEWHAT
(— ABNORMAL) FREAK
(— ADDED) IMP EXTRA DOCTOR
(— ATTRACTIVE) DUCK
(— BELIEVED) CREDIT
(— BIG) BOUNCER
(— BRIGHT RED) CORAL
(— CHERISHED) APPLE
(— COMMONPLACE) DROSS
(— CONSECRATED) SACRUM
(— CONTRARY TO LOGIC) ALOGISM
(— CORRUPT) CARRION
(— COUNTERFEIT) DUFFER
PINCHBECK
(— DIFFICULT) STINKER
(— DISLIKED) DOGMEAT
(— DONE) GERENDUM
(— EASY) PIPE CAKEWALK
(— ELABORATE) DEVICE
(— ELUSIVE) FUGITIVE
(— EXCELLENT) DANDY
(— EXCESSIVE) LUXUS
(— EXTRAORDINARY) SNORTER
(— FALSE) HOOEY
(— FAMILIAR) KNOWN
(— FIRST-RATE) CHEESE
(— FLAWED) CRIPPLE
(— FOOLISH) IDIOCY FATUITY
(— FORGOTTEN) CORPSE
(— FORKED) CORNUTE
(— FRAUDULENT) CROSS
(— HORRIFYING) SHOCKER
(— IDENTICAL) ISOMORPH
(— ILL-DEFINED) BLOB
(— IN ADDITION TO ORDINARY)
BONUS
(— INCOMPLETE) END
(— INFERIOR) DOG CULL LESS
CAGMAG
(— INJURIOUS) ENEMY
(— INSIGNIFICANT) STRAW
FEATHER SNICKET FRAGMENT
(— INTRICATE) KNOT
(— LARGE) GIANT SMASHER
(— MADE UP) FIGMENT
(— NOT ESSENTIAL) FRILL
(— NOT EXPLAINED) MYSTERY
(— NOTABLE) DEUCE
(— OF GREAT VALUE) EYETOOTH
(— OF LITTLE VALUE) SHUCK
FOUTER FOUTRA MAKEWEIGHT
(— OF NO VALUE) HAW DAMN
BAUBEE DOCKEN
(— OFFERED FOR LOAN) PREMIUM
(— OR OTHER) ANYTHING
(— OUTSTANDING) BROTH DOYEN
GASSER STANDOUT
(— PAINFUL) GAFF
(— PATCHED UP) VAMP
(— POOR) FLUMMERY

(— **PRECIOUS**) DUMPLING
(— **PREJUDICIAL**) FOE
(— **PROVOKING**) DEVIL
(— **REPELLENT**) SPINACH
(— **RISKED**) HAZARD
(— **SHAPELESS**) DUMP
(— **SHOWY**) FLOSS
(— **SHRIVELED**) SCRUMP
(— **SMALL**) DOT SNIP
(— **SPECTACULAR**) DILLY
(— **STICKY**) CAB
(— **STOLEN**) CRIB
(— **STRANGE**) FANTASIA
(— **SUPERLATIVE**) DARB
(— **TAUGHT**) DOCUMENT
(— **THAT IS LIGHT**) SKIFF SKIFT
(— **THAT WHIRLS**) GIG
(— **TO BIND BARGAIN**) EARNEST
(— **TRIVIAL**) CHIP FLUFF
(— **UNDECIDED**) ACRISY
(— **UNINTELLIGIBLE**) GREEK
(— **UNPLEASANT**) GUCK SOUR
(— **UNSPECIFIED**) ITEM
(— **UNSUBSTANTIAL**) FROTH
(— **UNTRUE**) HOKUM
(— **USELESS**) CRAP BLANK
(— **VILE**) DUNG
(— **WORTHLESS**) BOTH DUST
HOKUM DUFFER AMBSACE
(— **WRITTEN**) SCRIPT
SOMETIME FORMER SOMDEL
WHILOM ANCIENT QUONDAM
SOMEDEAL SOMEPART
SOMEWHEN
SOMETIMES NOW TOO WHILE
PERDIE WHILES UMQUHILE
OCCASIONALLY
SOMEWHAT BIT POCO SOME
PRETTY RATHER SLIGHT SUMMAT
ALIQUID SOMEDEAL
(PREF.) SEMI
SOMEWHERE SOMERS SOMEGATE
SOMITE ZONITE SEGMENT TERGITE
GONOTOME MEROSOME
MESOMERE SOMATOME
SOMNIFEROUS OPIATE SOMNIFIC
SOMNUS HYPNUS
SON BEN BOY LAD ANAC FILS FITZ
ZONE CHILD KIBEI MOPSY FILIUS
JUNIOR REUBEN EPAPHUS
EPIGONUS MONSIEUR
(— **OF CHIEF**) OGTIERN
(— **OF KING OF FRANCE**) DAUPHIN
(— **OF NISEI**) SANSEI
(— **OF PEER**) MASTER
(— **OF SUDRA**) CHANDALA
(**DAVID'S FAVORITE** —) ABSALOM
(**FOURTH** —) MARTLET
(**ILLEGITIMATE** —) NEPHEW
(**YOUNG** —) MOPSY
(**YOUNGER** —) CADET
(**YOUNGEST** —) BENJAMIN
(PREF.) AP FILI(O)
SONANT VIBRANT
SONAR ASDIC
SONCHUS DINDLE
SONG AIR DIT FIT JIG LAY UTA
CANT DUAN FOLK GATO GLEE
LEED MELE NOTE RANT RUNE
SANG TUNE BLUES CANSO CAROL
CHANT CHARM CROON DILDO
DITTY MELOS MOLPE OLDIE
PAEAN VOCAL BALLAD BRANLE

BUBBLE CANTIC CANZON
CARMEN CHANTY CHORUS
HIMENE JINGLE MELODY ORPHIC
SHANTY STRAIN VINATA WAIATA
WARBLE BACCHIC BALLATA
CANCION CANTION CHANSON
COMIQUE DESCANT MELISMA
MELODIA REQUIEM REVERDI
ROMANCE SCOLION SONGLET
THRENOS BIRDSONG BRINDISI
CANTICLE CANZONET COONJINE
FLAMENCO JUBILATE PALINODE
RHAPSODY SERVENTE SINGSONG
ZORTZICO ROUNDELAY
(— **ACCOMPANYING TOAST**)
BRINDISI
(— **FOR TWO VOICES**) GYMEL
(— **OF BASQUES**) ZORTZICO
(— **OF BIRD**) LAY KOLLER
(— **OF JOY**) CAROL PAEAN
JUBILATE
(— **OF MINSTREL**) YEDDING
(— **OF OCEANIA**) HIMENE
(— **OF PRAISE**) HYMN CAROL
ANTHEM CHORALE
(— **UNACCOMPANIED**) GLEE
(— **WITH MONOTONOUS RHYME**)
VIRELAI VIRELAY
(—**S OF BIRDS**) RAMAGE
(**ANDALUSIAN** —) SAETA
(**ART** —) LIED
(**BOAT** —) JORRAM
(**CEREMONIAL** —**S**) AREITO
(**CRADLE** —) HUSHO
(**CUBAN** —) GUAJIRA COMPARSA
(**DANCE** —) BALLAD BAMBUCO
(**DRINKING** —) BACCHIC SCOLION
SKOLION WASSAIL
(**EVENING** —) SERENA EVENSONG
SERENATA
(**FOLK** —) SON FADO FOLK BLUES
DOINA BYLINA CANTIGA JUBILEE
STORNELLO
(**FUNERAL** —) DIRGE MONODY
EPICEDE THRENODY
(**FUNEREAL** —) ELEGY
(**GAY** —) LILT
(**GERMAN** —) LIED
(**HAWAIIAN** —) MELE
(**HEBREW** —) ELIELI HATIKVAH
(**IMPROMPTU** —) SCOLION
(**JAPANESE** —) UTA
(**LOVE** —) ALBA CANSO CANZO
FANCY AMORET AUBADE SERENA
SERENATA
(**MELISMATIC** —) DIVISION
(**MOCKING** —) JIG
(**MORNING** —) MATIN AUBADE
(**MOURNFUL** —) DUMP PLAINT
ENDECHA
(**NEW ZEALAND** —) WAIATA
(**NIGHT** —) COMPLIN
(**NO** —**S**) UTAI
(**NUPTIAL** —) HYMEN
(**PART** —) CHACE TROLL CACCIA
CANZONET FROTTOLA MADRIGAL
(**PASTORAL** —) OAT
(**PLAIN** —) GROUND
(**PORTUGUESE** —) FADO
(**RELIGIOUS** —) HYMN CAROL
PSALM SHOUT ANTHEM
POLYMNY SIRVENT
(**REVOLUTIONARY** —) CARMAGNOLE

(**SACRED** —) MOTET
(**SAILOR'S** —) CHANTY SHANTY
(**SANSKRIT** —) GITA
(**SINGLE** — **ON RECORD**) CUT
(**STUPID** —) STROWD
(**VINTAGE** —) VINATA
(**WORK** —) HOLLER
(PL.) ZEMMI AREITO
(PREF.) MELO
(SUFF.) ODE ODIC ODIST ODY
SONGBIRD CHAT IORA LARK WREN
MAVIS ROBIN SABIA SHAMA
SIREN VEERY VIREO BULBUL
CANARY LINNET MOCKER ORIOLE
SINGER THRUSH CATBIRD
GRASSET WARBLER ACCENTOR
BENGALEE BLUEBIRD BOBOLINK
CARDINAL SONGSTER
MEADOWLARK
SONGLIKE ARIOSE
SONG OF BERNADETTE (**AUTHOR
OF** —) WERFEL
(**CHARACTER IN** —) LOUISE
THERESE FRANCOIS PEYRAMALE
SOUBIROUS BERNADETTE
SONG OF HIAWATHA (**AUTHOR OF**
—) LONGFELLOW
(**CHARACTER IN** —) KWASIND
NOKOMIS WENONAH HIAWATHA
CHIBIABOS MINNEHAHA
MUDJEKEEWIS
SONG OF ROLAND (**AUTHOR OF** —)
UNKNOWN
(**CHARACTER IN** —) ALDA ALORY
MILON OGIER BERTHA FERRAU
GERARD MEDORO MORGAN
OBERTO OLIVER ROLAND SADONE
ARGALIA CHARLOT GANELON
GODFREY MALAGIS REINOLD
ASTOLPHO KARAHEUT
BRADAMANT GLORIANDA
CHARLEMAGNE MANDRICARDO
SONGSTER SINGER WARBLER
SONG THRUSH MAVIE MAVIS
SON-IN-LAW GENER MAUGH
SONNAMBULA, LA (**CHARACTER IN**
—) LISA AMINA ELVINO TERESA
RODOLFO
(**COMPOSER OF** —) BELLINI
SONNET AMORET
SONOROUS ROUND SHILL TONOUS
OROTUND VIBRANT RESONANT
SOUNDFUL SOUNDING
RESOUNDING
SONOROUSLY DEEPLY
SONS AND LOVERS (**AUTHOR OF** —
) LAWRENCE
(**CHARACTER IN** —) LILY PAUL
ANNIE CLARA DAWES MOREL
ARTHUR BAXTER MIRIAM WALTER
LEIVERS WILLIAM GERTRUDE
SONSHIP FILIETY
SONYA (**FATHER OF** —)
MARMELADOV
SOOLOOS THULUTH
SOON ERE ANON CITO TITE EARLY
NEWLY RADLY RATHE BELIVE
SUDDEN TIMELY BETIMES
ERELONG PRESTLY SHORTLY
DIRECTLY SPEEDILY PRESENTLY
SOONER ERE ERER ERST FIRST
BEFORE TITTER
(— **STATE**) OKLAHOMA

(— **THAN**) OR ERE
SOONEST ERST RATHEST
SOOT COOM IZLE SMUT STUP SUMI
BLECK BROOK COLLY COOMB
CROCK GRIME SOTIK FULIGO
SMOUCH SMUTCH SPODIUM
(— **ON GRATE BAR**) STRANGER
SOOTHE COY DEW BALM CALM
COAX DILL EASE HUSH LULL
ACCOY ALLAY CHARM DULCE
HUMOR QUELL SALVE SLEEK
STILL BECALM PACIFY SETTLE
SMOOTH SOLACE STROKE SUPPLE
ADDULCE ASSUAGE COMFORT
COMPOSE CONSOLE DEMULCE
FLATTER GRUNTLE LULLABY
MOLLIFY PLASTER QUALIFY
ATTEMPER BLANDISH MITIGATE
UNRUFFLE
SOOTHER ANODYNE
SOOTHING MILD BALMY BLAND
DOWNY DULCE STILL SWEET
ANETIC ANIMAL DREAMY DULCET
GENTLE SMOOTH ANODYNE
BALSAMIC SEDATIVE
SOOTHSAY SORT
SOOTHSAYER SEER AUGUR
WEIRD ARIOLE DIVINE PYTHON
ARUSPEX DIVINER CHALDEAN
HARUSPEX TIRESIAS
SOOTY COLLY REECHY SMUTTY
BROOKIE COLLIED
SOOTY ALBATROSS NELLIE
QUAKER STINKER BLUEBIRD
STINKPOT
SOOTY SHEARWATER TITI
SOP BERRY SIPPET SPONGE
SUGARSOP SWEETSOP
SOPATER (**FATHER OF** —) PYRRHUS
SOPHER SCRIBE
SOPHISM FETCH ELENCH FALLACY
SOPHEME
SOPHIST SOPH DUNCE
SOPHISTICATE GARBLE
MONDAINE
SOPHISTICATED WISE BLASE
CIVIL SALTY SVELTE WORLDLY
SOPHISTICATION CHIC
SOPHISTRY DECEIT FALLACY
SOPHISM CHICANERY
SOPHONISBA (**BROTHER OF** —)
HANNIBAL
(**FATHER OF** —) HASDRUBAL
(**HUSBAND OF** —) SYPHAX
SOPORIFIC DWALE DROWSY
HYPNIC OPIATE SLEEPY
HYPNOTIC NARCOTIC SOMNIFIC
SOPPY JUICY SOAKY
SOPRANO CANARY TREBLE
DESCANT CASTRATO
SORA ORTOLAN
SORB OCCLUDE LUSATIAN
SORBIAN WENDISH
SORBOSE ACROSE
SORCERER MAGE BOYLA BRUJO
WITCH BOOLYA NAGUAL VOODOO
WIZARD KORADJI WARLOCK
WIELARE FETISHER MAGICIAN
WITCHMAN
(PL.) GOETAE
SORCERESS BRUJA CIRCE LAMIA
SIBYL WITCH ARMIDA HECATE
BABAJAGA KORRIGAN WALKYRIE

SORCERY OBI MAGIC OBEAH SPELL MAKUTU PISHOGUE PRESTIGE SORTIARY WIGELING WITCHERY WITCHING NECROMANCY
(VOODOO —) OBEAH WANGA OUANGA
SORDES SABURRA
SORDID RAW BASE GAMY MEAN VILE DIRTY DUSTY MUCKY SEAMY CHETIF GRUBBY SODDEN MESQUIN SQUALID CHURLISH
SORE BUM FOX PET BUBA CHAP DEAR GALL KIBE KYLE OUCH SAER BLAIN BOTCH GAMMY AGNAIL BITTER BOUBAS CANKER FESTER MELLIT MORMAL RANKLE TAKING CATHAIR CHANCRE SORANCE SCALDING
(— ON HORSE'S FOOT) MELLIT QUITTER
(ARTIFICIAL —) FOX
(SUMMER —S) CALORIS LEECHES
SO RED THE ROSE (AUTHOR OF —) YOUNG
(CHARACTER IN —) HUGH LUCY MARY VEAL ZACH AGNES SARAH AMELIE DUNCAN EDWARD BALFOUR BEDFORD CHARLES FRANCES LUCINDA MALCOLM MCGEHEE SHELTON VALETTE WILLIAM HARTWELL MIDDLETON TALIAFERRO
SORE MOUTH ORF
SORENESS FROG
SORGHUM CANE CUSH MILO BATAD DARSO DURRA SORGO CHOLAM HEGARI IMPHEE KAFFIR SHALLU FETERITA KAOLIANG
SOROCHE PUNA
SORREL OCA OKA SORE CUCKOO HEARTS OXALIS RUBICAN SOUROCK ALLELUIA STABWORT
SORREL TREE TITI ELKWOOD SOURWOOD
SORROW WO RUE WOE BALE CARE DOLE HARM MOAN RUTH SORE TEEN DOLOR GRAME GRIEF MOURN RUING SARRA UNWIN GRIEVE LAMENT MISERY REGRET STOUND UNLUST ANGUISH CONDOLE DEPLORE PENANCE REGRATE REMORSE THOUGHT TROUBLE WOEFARE CALAMITY DISTRESS DOLEANCE DREARING EGRIMONY MOURNING
(PREF.) LUCTI
SORROWFUL BAD SAD WAN CHARY DREAR TRIST WOFUL DISMAL DOLENT DREARY RUEFUL BALEFUL CAREFUL DOLEFUL LUCTUAL RUESOME UNHAPPY WAILFUL CONTRITE DESOLATE DOLESOME DOLOROSO GRIEFFUL MOURNFUL PITIABLE
SORROWFULLY SADLY WRATH DERNLY HEAVILY
SORRY BAD SAD WOE HURT VEXED UNFAIN PITIFUL CONTRITE WRETCHED
SORT KIN LOT BRAN COMB GERE HUMP KIND RANK SIFT SUIT WING WORK BRACK BREED GENUS GRADE SAVOR SPICE

ASSORT BARREL DILLUE GARBLE GENDER KIDNEY MANNER MISTER NATURE STRAIN STRIPE FASHION SPECIES SPECKLE VARIETY CLASSIFY SEPARATE
(— COTTON BY STAPLE) STAPLE
(— MAIL) CASE
(— MERCHANDISE) BRACK
(— OF PERSON) LIKE
SORTER SHALEMAN
SORTIE ISSUE SALLY ATTACK OUTFALL
SORTILEGE LOT
SORTING GARBLING
(— ROOM) SALLE
SORUS AECIUM TELIUM
SORVA BORRACHA
SOT LUSH SOAK DRUNK LOURD TOPER LOURDY BLOTTER DASTARD TOSSPOT DRUNKARD
SOTHO SUTO SESUTO
SOTIK SOOT
SOUFFLE FONDU FONDUE
SOUGHT QUESITED
SOUL BA AME EGO ALMA ANIMA ATMAN GHOST HEART SHADE BUDDHI DIBBUK NATURE PNEUMA PSYCHE SPIRIT SPRITE NEPHESH PURUSHA INTERNAL
(—S OF THE DEAD) LEMURES
(ANIMAL — IN MAN) NEPHESH
(DISEMBODIED —) KER
(EGYPTIAN IMMORTAL —) BA
(INDIVIDUAL —) JIVA
(LIBERATED —) KEVALIN
(UNIVERSAL —) HANSA
(WANDERING —) DIBBUK DYBBUK
(PREF.) PSYCH(O) THYM(O)
(SUFF.) PSYCHE
SOULFULLY GEISTLICH
SOULLESS TURNIPY
SOU MARQUE STAMPEE
SOUND GO CRY FIT BLOW DING DRIP FAST FERE FIRM FLOG FLOW GLUG GOOD HAIL HALE KYLE NOTE RING SAFE SANE TEST TONE TRIG WISE AFFIX BLAST BUGLE CHEEP DREAM FLICK FRESH GLIFF GLUCK GRIND GROPE HODDY NOISE PLANG PLUMB PROBE RIGHT SLUSH SOLID SPANG SPANK SPEAK SWASH VALID WHOLE BICKER BIRDIE DORSAL ENDING ENTIRE FATHOM FAUCAL HEARTY INTACT LABIAL LAGOON ROBUST SIGNAL SINGLE SONANT SPLASH STABLE STRAIN STURDY HEALTHY HEARING HURLING PERFECT PHONEME PLUMMET SCRATCH SONANCE VOCABLE FLAWLESS FOOTFALL GRINDING GROUNDLY LAUGHTER RELIABLE SEARCHER SYLLABIC WAKELESS
(— A BAGPIPE) DOODLE
(— AS IF BY GUN) ZAP
(— BELL) PEAL RING KNELL KNOLL
(— DRUM OR TRUMPET) TUCK
(— FORTH) BOOM
(— IN GREEK AND LATIN) AGMA
(— IN MIND) FORMAL
(— INDEPENDENTLY OF THE PLAYER) CIPHER

(— LESS LOUD) FALL
(— LIKE THUNDER) BRONTIDE
(— LOUDLY) TANG LARUM
(— MELODIOUSLY) CHARM
(— OF BAGPIPE) DRONE
(— OF BEATING) RATAPLAN
(— OF BELL) DING PEAL RING KNELL STROKE DINGDONG TINGTANG
(— OF BIRD) JUG CHURR
(— OF BULLET) ZIP
(— OF CONTEMPT) HUMPH
(— OF CORK) CLOOP CLUNK
(— OF DISAPPROVAL) BOO HOOT BAZOO
(— OF DOG) BOOK
(— OF DYING PERSON'S VOICE) TAISCH
(— OF ENGINE) CHUG
(— OF EXPLOSION) BOUNCE
(— OF F) DIGAMMA
(— OF FLUTE) TOOTLE
(— OF GLOTTAL STOP) HAMZA HAMZAH
(— OF HEN) CLUCK
(— OF HOG) GRUNT
(— OF HOOF) CLOP
(— OF HORN) BEEP TOOT
(— OF HORSE) BLOWING
(— OF PLUCKED STRING) TUM
(— OF POURING LIQUID) GLUG GLUGGLUG
(— OF RAIN) SPAT
(— OF RENDING) SCAT
(— OF SHEEP) BAA BLEAT
(— OF STEAM ENGINE) CHUFF
(— OF STRAW OR LEAVES) RUSTLE
(— OF THUNDER) CLAP
(— OF TRUMPET) CLARION
(— OF WIND IN TREES) WOOSH
(— OUT) FEEL
(—S HAVING RHYTHM) MUSIC
(ABNORMAL —) BRUIT
(ADVENTITIOUS —) RALE
(BLOWING —) SOUFFLE
(BRAWLING —) CHIDE
(BUBBLING —) BLATHER
(BUZZING —) Z WHIR WHIRR
(CLICKING —) SNECK
(CONSONANT —) ALVEOLAR
(COOING —) CHIRR TURTUR
(CRACKLING —) RISK
(CRISP —) BLIP
(CRUNCHING —) CRUMP SCRUNCH
(DELICATE —) TINK TINKLE
(DISCORDANT —) JAR BRAY JANGLE
(DISTINCTIVE —) SONG
(DULL —) BUFF THUD CLONK CLUNK FLUMP SQUELCH
(EXPLOSIVE —) POP BARK CHUG PUFF SNORT REPORT
(FAINT —) PEEP GLIFF WHISHT INKLING
(FINAL —) AUSLAUT
(GULPING —) GLUCK
(GUTTURAL —) GROWL
(HARSH —) JAR BRAY BLARE CLASH CRANK TWANG SCROOP DISCORD STRIDOR
(HEAVY —) DUMP
(HIGH-PITCHED —) TING
(HISSING —) FIZZ SIZZ

SWISH SIZZLE
(HOLLOW —) CHOCK THUNGE
(HUMMING —) HUM BURR SUUM DRONE SINGING
(INDISTINCT —) BLUR SURD
(INITIAL — OF WORDS) ANLAUT
(JINGLING —) SMIT
(LAPPING —) SLOOSH
(LIGHT REPEATED —) PITAPAT
(LOUD —) PEAL BLARE CLANG CRASH CLANGOR
(LOW-PITCHED —) BASS
(MEANINGLESS —S) GABBLE
(MEDIAL —) INLAUT
(MENTALLY —) SANE WISE
(MOANING —) SUUM SOUGH
(MOURNFUL —) GROAN
(MUSICAL —) CHIME
(NASAL —) ANUSVARA
(NON-SIGNIFICANT —) GLIDE
(NONVIBRATORY —) FRICTION
(PLEASING —) EUPHONY EUPHONIA
(RASPING —) BUZZ SKIRR SCROOP
(REPEATED —) ECHO
(RESONANT —) BONG
(REVERBERATING —) PLANG
(RINGING —) CLANG CLANK CLING TWANG RINGLE DINGDONG
(ROARING —) BEAL
(RUSHING —) SWOOSH HURLING
(RUSTLING —) FISSLE FISTLE
(SCRAPING —) GRIDE
(SHARP —) POP PING SNAP CHINK CRAKE KNACK SPANG SQUIRK
(SHORT, HIGH-PITCHED —) BLEEP
(SHRILL —) CHEEP KNACK SKIRL SCREED SQUEAK STRIDOR
(SHUFFLING —) SCUFFLE
(SIBILANT —) HISS SHISH SHUSH
(SLAPPING —) CLATCH
(SLIGHT —) SWISH
(SNORING —) SNORK
(SOBBING —) YOOP
(SPEECH —) SURD DOMAL TENUE VOWEL APICAL PHONEME CEREBRAL
(SPLASHING —) LAP CHUNK FLURR SPLAT SWASH
(SPOKEN —) BREATH
(SQUEAKY —) CREAK
(SQUELCHING —) SQUASH
(STRANGLED —) GLUB GLUG
(SWISHING —) SCHLOOP
(TELEPHONE —) SIDETONE
(TRAMPING —) STUMP
(TRILLING —) CHIRR CHIZZ HIRRIENT
(TUNEFUL —) HARMONY
(UNPLEASANT —) BLOOP
(VIBRATING —) TIRL
(WARNING —) ALARM SIREN ALARUM TOCSIN
(WHIRRING —) BIRR FLURR SKIRR
(WHISPERING —) SUSURRUS
(WHISTLING —) STRIDOR
(PREF.) AUDIO AUDIT ECHO PHON(O) SON(I)(O) SONORI SONORO TONICO TONO
(SUFF.) PHON(E)(IA)(Y) SONANCE SONANT SONOUS TONE TONIA TONIC TONOUS TONY
SOUND-ABSORBENT ACOUSTIC

SOUND AND THE FURY (AUTHOR OF —) FAULKNER
(CHARACTER IN —) HEAD JASON DILSEY SYDNEY CANDACE COMPSON QUENTIN BENJAMIN
SOUNDBOARD BELLY
SOUNDER TICKER LEADMAN
SOUNDING RAWIN SONANT INKLING SONDAGE SONATION
(— HARSH) BRAZEN
(— OF BELL) CURFEW
(— OF ORGAN PIPE) CIPHER
(— WITH REVERBERATIONS) PLANGENT
SOUNDLY FAST TIGHT FIRMLY
SOUNDNESS HEAL SANITY FITNESS SOBRIETY STRENGTH VALIDITY
SOUP BREE KAIL KALE SOPA BROTH GUMBO POSOL BISQUE BORSCH BURGOO JOUTES POZOLE BILLIBI BORSCHT GARBURE MARMITE CONSOMME GAZPACHO MINESTRA MORTREUX MINESTRONE MULLIGATAWNEY
(— UP) SUPE
(BARLEY —) SMIGGINS
(BEEFSKIN —) SKINK
(CABBAGE —) SHCHI STCHI
(CLEAR —) CONSOMME JULIENNE
(COLD —) SCHAV
(JELLIED —) GAZPACHO
(LARGE QUANTITY OF —) SLASH
(SHINBONE —) SKINK
(THICK —) BISK GUMBO HOOSH PUREE BISQUE BURGOO CHOWDER GARBURE POTTAGE HOTCHPOT MORTREWES
(THIN —) BROTH SKILLY
SOUR AWA DRY YAR ACID ASIM CRAB DOUR FOXY GRIM GRUM HARD TART TURN ACERB ACRID AIGRE EAGER GOURY GRUFF MUSTY TEART ACIDIC BITTER CRUETY CURDLE PONTIC RANCID RUGGED SULLEN TORVID ACETOSE ACIDIFY AUSTERE SUBACID ACERBATE VINEGARY
(SLIGHTLY —) BLINK BLINKY ACESCENT
SOURCE FONS FONT HAND HEAD HIVE MINE RISE RIST ROOT SEED FOUNT RADIX SPAWN SURGE AUCTOR AUTHOR BOTTOM CENTER FATHER FONTAL ORIGIN PARENT RESORT STAPLE WHENCE EDITION FOUNTAIN WELLHEAD PROVENANCE
(— OF AID) RECOURSE
(— OF ANCESTRAL LINE) STOCK
(— OF ANNOYANCE) BOGY BOGIE HARROW BUGBEAR
(— OF ASSURANCE) FORTRESS
(— OF CONCERN) BUGABOO
(— OF CONFIDENCE) ANCHOR
(— OF DISPLEASURE) DISGUST
(— OF ENERGY) TAPAS
(— OF HAPPINESS) SUNSHINE
(— OF HARM) CURSE
(— OF HONOR) CREDIT
(— OF INCOME) TITLE REVENUE

(— OF INFORMATION) CHECK
(— OF INSPIRATION) CASTALIA CASTALIE
(— OF INSTRUCTION) BOOK
(— OF LAUGHTER) SPLEEN
(— OF LIGHT) LAMP
(— OF NOURISHMENT) BREAST
(— OF POWER) STRENGTH
(— OF REGRET) SCATH SCATHE
(— OF STREAM OR RIVER) FILL
(— OF STRENGTH) HORN
(— OF SUPPLY) SHOP FEEDER ARSENAL
(— OF TROUBLE) HEADACHE
(— OF WATER) BRON SPRING
(— OF WEALTH) GOLCONDA KLONDIKE
(ENCLOSED —) FLOW
(FROM ANOTHER —) ALIUNDE
(MALIGNANT —) CANCER
(PHYSICAL —) MOTHER
(PRIMARY —) RADIX
(RADIO —) QUASAR
SOURDOUGH LEAVEN
SOURED FOXY QUARRED
SOURING ACESCENCE
SOURNESS ACIDITY ACERBITY ACRIMONY ASPERITY TARTNESS VERJUICE
SOURSOP CORRESOL GUANABANA
SOURWOOD TITI ELKWOOD
SOUSE DIP DUCK TOSH PLUMP STOOP PLUNGE SOZZLE
SOUTANE SIMAR ZIMARRA
SOUTH MIDI AUSTER DECANI MIDDAY MERIDIAN
(FARTHER —) BELOW
(PREF.) AUSTR(O) NOT(O)

SOUTH AFRICA
BAY: ALGOA FALSE
CAPE: AGULHAS
CAPITAL: CAPETOWN PRETORIA
COIN: CENT RAND POUND FLORIN
LANGUAGE: BANTU HINDI TAMIL TELUGU BUJARATI
MOUNTAIN: AUX KOP KATHKIN INJASUTI
NATIVE: YOSA BANTU NAMAS PONDO DAMARA SWAHILI BECHUANA HOTTENTOT
PROVINCE: NATAL TRANSVAAL
RIVER: MODDER MOLOPO ORANGE KURUMAM LIMPOPO OLIFANTS
TOWN: AUS MARA STAD BENONI DURBAN SEVERN UMTATA KOKSTAD SPRINGS MAFEKING GERMISTON JOHANNESBURG
WATERFALL: HOWICK TUGELA AUGRABIES

SOUTH AMERICA
(ALSO SEE SPECIFIC COUNTRIES)
LAKE: MIRIM POOPO TITICACA MARACAIBO LLANQUIHUE
MOUNTAIN: BAIA ANDES GOIAZ PARIMA ACARAHY TUMUCHUMAC
NATION: PERU CHILE BRAZIL GUYANA BOLIVIA ECUADOR URUGUAY COLOMBIA PARAGUAY SURINAME

ARGENTINA NICARAGUA VENEZUELA
RIVER: NEGRO AMAZON CHUBUT PARANA SALADO ORINOCO RIONEGRO ESSEQUIBO MAGDALENA

SOUTH CAROLINA
CAPITAL: COLUMBIA
COLLEGE: COKER FURMAN LANDER CITADEL CLAFFIN CLEMSON ERSKINE WOFFORD
COUNTY: AIKEN HORRY DILLON JASPER OCONEE SALUDA
FORT: SUMTER
INDIAN: PEDEE SEWEE CUSABO SANTEE WAXHAW CATAWBA SUGEREE WATEREE CONGAREE
ISLAND: EDISTO PARRIS HILTONHEAD
LAKE: MARION MURRAY CATAWBA WATEREE HARTWELL MOULTRIE
MOUNTAIN: SASSAFRAS
NATIVE: WEASEL PALMETTO
NICKNAME: PALMETTO
PLATEAU: PIEDMONT
PRESIDENT: JACKSON
RESERVOIR: SANTEE PINOPOLIS
RIVER: BROAD EDISTO PEEDEE SALUDA SANTEE ASHEPOO TUGALOS WATEREE CONGAREE SAVANNAH
STATE BIRD: WREN
STATE FLOWER: JASMINE
STATE TREE: PALMETTO
TOWN: AIKEN GREER UNION BELTON CAMDEN CHERAW CONWAY DILLON SALUDA SENECA SUMTER BAMBERG LAURENS MANNING BEAUFORT FLORENCE NEWBERRY WALHALLA GREENVILLE SPARTANBURG

SOUTH CAROLINIAN WEASEL PALMETTO

SOUTH DAKOTA
BUTTE: MUD CROW SULLY FINGER SADDLE THUNDER DEERSEARS
CAPITAL: PIERRE
COLLEGE: HURON YANKTON
COUNTY: DAY HYDE BRULE MINER MOODY SPINK SULLY TRIPP CUSTER JERAULD YANKTON MELLETTE
INDIAN: BRULE SIOUX DAKOTA CHEYENNE
LAKE: OAHE BIGSTONE TRAVERSE
MONUMENT: RUSHMORE
MOUNTAIN: BEAR SHEEP TABLE CROOKS HARNEY MOREAU
NICKNAME: COYOTE SUNSHINE
RIVER: JAMES MOREAU CHEYENNE MISSOURI
STATE BIRD: PHEASANT
STATE FLOWER: PASQUE
STATE TREE: SPRUCE
TOWN: LEAD HAYTI HURON LEOLA ONIDA CUSTER DESMET EUREKA KADOKA LEMMON

MILLER WINNER STURGIS WEBSTER YANKTON ABERDEEN DEADWOOD SISSETON

SOUTHERLY AUSTRINE
SOUTHERN SUDIC AUSTRAL MERIDIAN SOUTHRON MERIDIONAL
(PREF.) NOTIO
SOUTHERN CROSS CRUX CROSS CROSIER
SOUTHERNER CAVALIER SOUTHRON
SOUTHERN FRANCE MIDI
SOUTHERN ILLINOIS EGYPT
SOUTHERN INDIA DRAVIDA
SOUTHERNWOOD APPLERINGIE

SOUTH KOREA
BAY: KANGHWA
CAPITAL: SEOUL
COIN: WON HWAN
MOUNTAIN: CHIRI
PROVINCE: CHEJU CHOLLA KANGWON KYONGGI
RIVER: HAN KUM PUKHAN SOMJIN NAKTONG YONGSAN
TOWN: CHEJU MASAN MOKPO PUSAN SUWON TAEGU WONJU CHINJU CHONJU INCHON KUNSAN TAEJON CHONGJU KWANGJU CHUNCHON

SOUTHLAND AUSTER
SOUTH SEA ISLANDER KANAKA

SOUTH VIETNAM
CAPITAL: SAIGON
LANGUAGE: CHAM KHMER RHADE
MEASURE: GANG PHAN THON
MOUNTAIN: BADINH NINHHOA KNONTRAN NGOOLINH TCHEPONE
NATIVE: CHAM MALAY
PORT: DANANG SAIGON QUINHON NHATRANG
REGION: ANNAM COCHIN
RIVER: BA SONG MEKONG DONGNAI
TOWN: HUE HOIAN ANNHON DANANG GIADINH QUINHON SONGCAU TAYNINH VINHLOI PHANRANG QUANGTRI
WEIGHT: CAN YET UYEN

SOUTHWESTER SQUAM
SOUTH YEMEN (CAPITAL OF —) ADEN
(ISLAND OF —) PERIM KAMARAN SOCOTRA
(MONEY OF —) DINAR
(TOWN OF —) SEIYUN MUKALLA
SOUVENIR RELIC TOKEN FAIRING NICKNACK
SOVEREIGN BEY SIR SOV BEAN CHAM CHIP FREE KHAN QUID SHAH SKIV CROWN JAMES NEGUS NIZAM QUEED CHAGAN COUTER GUINEA KAISER KINGLY MASTER PRINCE SAMORY SHINER SOLDAN SOVRAN SULTAN CROWNED MONARCH ZAMORIN AUTOCRAT DOMINANT IMPERIAL

SUFFRAIN SUZERAIN
(DIVINELY —) THEARCHIC
(FELLOW —) COUSIN
(HEAVENLY —) TENNO HEAVEN
(MOSLEM —) SOLDAN
SOVEREIGNTY SWAY CROWN
REIGN DIADEM EMPERY EMPIRE
THRONE DEMESNE DYNASTY
KINGDOM MAJESTY SCEPTER
SCEPTRE AUTARCHY DOMINION
IMPERIUM MONARCHY REGALITY
REGNANCY SOVRANTY
(— OF REASON) AUTONOMY
(JOINT —) SYNARCHY
SOVIET (ALSO SEE RUSSIA)
VOLOST COUNCIL GUBERNIA
SOW ELT HOG GILT SEED SHED
YELT YILT DRILL PLANT PLUMP
STREW CHANNEL GRUMPHY
IMPLANT OVERSOW SCATTER
ENGENDER INTERSOW SEMINATE
(PREF.) HYO SCROFUL(O)
(SUFF.) CHOERUS
SOWAR SILLADAR
SOW BUG ISOPOD SLATER
ISOPODAN
SOWENS SONS SWEENS
FLUMMERY WASHBREW
SOWER SEEDER SEEDMAN
SEEDSTER SEMINARY
SOWING SATION SEMENCE
SEEDNESS
(PREF.) SPOR(I)(IDI)(O)(ULI)
(SUFF.) SPORA SPORE SPORIC
SPORIDIA SPORIUM SPOROUS
SPORY
SOWN SEME SATIVE SEEDED
SEMEED
SOW THISTLE DINDLE GUTWEED
HOGWEED MILKWEED
SOY SHOYA SHOYU
SOYBEAN SOJA SOYA
SPA BATH CURE HYDRO
SPACE AREA BLUE CORD COSO
DENT FACE LUNG PALE RANK
ROOM SIDE VOID ABYSS BLOCK
CHINK CLEFT FIELD PLACE RANGE
CANTON HIATUS INDENT MATTER
ROOMTH ARRANGE COMPASS
FOREIGN GUNNIES LEGROOM
ROOMAGE SPACING SPATIUM
DIASTEMA DISTANCE EXOCOELE
INTERVAL
(— ABOVE EARTH) AIRSPACE
(— AMONG MUSCLES) SINUS
(— AROUND HOUSE) AMBIT
(— AT WHARF) BERTHAGE
(— BEFORE KILN) LOGIE KILLOGIE
(— BEHIND ALTAR) FERETORY
(— BETWEEN BED AND WALL)
RUELLE
(— BETWEEN BRIDGE PIERS) LOCK
(— BETWEEN CASKS) CONTLINE
(— BETWEEN COLUMNS) BAY
(— BETWEEN CONCENTRIC CIRCLES)
ANNULUS
(— BETWEEN DECKS) LAZARET
(— BETWEEN EYE AND BILL) LORE
(— BETWEEN FEATHERS) APTERYLA
(— BETWEEN FLOOR TIMBERS)
SPIRKET
(— BETWEEN FLUTINGS) FILET
FILLET GORGERIN

(— BETWEEN FURROWS) RIG
(— BETWEEN PAGES) GUTTER
(— BETWEEN RAILROAD TIES) CRIB
(— BETWEEN SAW TEETH) GULLET
**(— BETWEEN SHIP'S BOWS AND
ANCHOR)** HAWSE
(— BETWEEN STRANDS) CANTLINE
(— BETWEEN TEETH) DIASTEMA
**(— BETWEEN THUMB AND LITTLE
FINGER)** SPAN
(— BETWEEN TIMBERS) SPIRKET
(— BETWEEN TWO WIRES) DENT
(— BETWEEN VEINS OF LEAVES)
AREOLA
(— DEVOID OF MATTER) VACUUM
VACUITY
(— FOR SECRETION) BAG
(— IN CHURCH) KNEELING
(— IN COIL OF CABLE) TIER
(— IN FOREST) GLADE
(— IN MINE) GOB
(— IN THEATER) BOX
(— IN TYPE) CORE
(— OCCUPIED) VOLUME
(— OF TIME) DAY PULL STEAD
GHURRY STITCH INTERVAL
(— ON BILLIARD TABLE) BALK
BAULK
(— ON COIN) EXERGUE
(— OVER STAGE) FLIES
(— OVERHEAD) HIGH
(— UNDER STAGE) DOCK
(— USED AS LIVING-ROOM) LANAI
(— WITHIN LIMITS) CONTENT
(AIR —) CENTRUM
(ARCHITECTURAL —) METOPE
PEDIMENT SACELLUM
(BACKGAMMON —) POINT
(BARE — ON BIRD) APTERIUM
(BLANK —) GAP ALLEY LACUNA
(BOUNDLESS —) INFINITE
(BREATHING —) BARLEY
(CLEAR —) FAIRWAY HEADWAY
DAYLIGHT
(COUNTER —) BACKBAR
(CRAMPED —) CUBBY
(EMPTY —) AIR BLANK CAPACITY
(ENCLOSED —) AREA BOWL HATCH
VERGE PARVIS CHAMBER CIRCUIT
CLOSURE COMPASS PARVISE
PTEROMA CLOISTER CONFINES
(EUCLIDEAN —) FLAT
(FLAT —) HOMALOID
(LEVEL —) PLATEA PARTERRE
(NARROW —) SLOT STRAIT
(OPEN —) OUT LAWN ALLEY
COURT LAUND TAHUA MAIDAN
AREAWAY FAIRWAY LOANING
APERTURE DAYLIGHT
KNEEHOLE
(OPEN — OF WATER) WAKE
(OVERHANGING —) DOME
(POPLITEAL —) HAM HOCK
(ROOF —) CELL
(SEATING —) CAVEA
(SHELTERED —) KILLOGIE
(STORAGE —) ATTIC
(TRIANGULAR —) SPANDREL
(UNFILLED —) GAP GAPE CAVITY
HOLLOW BREAKAGE
(VAULTED —) ALCOVE
(VERTICAL —) HEADROOM
(WORKING —) COUNTER

(PREF.) SPATIO
SPACECRAFT SHIP CAPSULE
ORBITER
(PROCESS OF SLOWING DOWN —)
DEBOOST
SPACED MEATIC
SPACIOUS ROOM SIDE WIDE
AMPLE BROAD RANGY ROOMY
GOLDEN BARONIAL SCOPIOUS
SPADE DIG LOY FECK LILY PEEL
PICK SPIT SPUD DELVE DIDLE
GRAFF SLADE SLANE TRAMP
DIGGER PADDLE PATTLE SERVER
SHOVEL TUSKAR GRAFTER
SCAFFLE SCUPPIT SPADDLE
SPITTER TWISCAR
(LONG NARROW —) LOY
(PART OF —) FROG STEP BLADE
HANDLE SOCKET SHOULDER
(PEAT —) SLADE SLANE TUSKAR
(PLASTERER'S —) SERVER
(TRIANGULAR —) DIDLE
SPADEFISH POGY PORGY
MOONFISH
SPADEFUL SPIT SPITFUL
SPAGHETTI PASTA SLEEVING
SPAGNUOLO LADINO

SPAIN
CAPE: AJO NAO GATA CREUS
MORAS PALOS PENAS PRIOR
DARTUCH ORTEGAL SALINAS
TORTOSA ESPICHEL MARROQUI
SACRATIF
CAPITAL: MADRID
COIN: COB DURO PESO REAL
DOBLA CUARTO DINERO
DOBLON ESCUDO PESETA
ALFONSO CENTIMO PISTOLE
REALDOR DOUBLOON
DIALECT: BASQUE CATALAN
GALICIAN
ISLAND: IBIZA PALMA GOMERA
HIERRO ALBORAN MAJORCA
MINORCA MALLORCA
TAGOMAGO TENERIFE
ISLANDS: CANARY BALEARIC
MEASURE: PIE CODO COPA DEDO
MOYO PASO VARA ALMUD
BRAZA CAFIZ CAHIZ CARGA
LEGUA LINEA MEDIO MILLA
PALMO SESMA ARROBA CORDEL
CUARTA ESTADO FANEGA
RACION YUGADA AZUMBRE
CANTARA CELEMIN ESTADEL
PULGADA ARANZADA
FANEGADA
MOUNTAIN: GATA ANETO ROUCH
TEIDE ESTATS NETHOU TELENO
BANUELO CERREDO PERDIDO
ALMANZOR MONTSENY
MULHACEN PENALARA
MOUNTAIN RANGE: CUENCA
GREDOS MORENA TOLEDO
ALCARAZ DEMANDA MONCAYO
MALADETA MONEGROS
PYRENEES
NAME: ESPANA IBERIA HISPANIA
NATIVE: CATALAN IBERIAN
PORT: ADRA NOYA VIGO CADIZ
GADES GADIR GIJON PALOS
ABDERA CORUNA MALAGA
ALMERIA ALICANTE BARCELONA

PROVINCE: JAEN LEON LUGO
ALAVA AVILA CADIZ SORIA
BURGOS CORUNA CUENCA
GERONA HUELVA HUESCA
LERIDA MADRID MALAGA
MURCIA ORENSE OVIEDO
TERUEL TOLEDO ZAMORA
ALMERIA BADAJOZ CACERES
CORDOBA GRANADA LOGRONO
NAVARRA SEGOVIA SEVILLA
VIZCAYA ALBACETE ALICANTE
BALEARES PALENCIA VALENCIA
ZARAGOZA
REGION: LEON ARAGON BASQUE
MURCIA CASTILE GALICIA
NAVARRE ASTURIAS CASTILLA
VALENCIA
RIVER: SIL TER CEGA EBRO ESLA
LIMA MINO TAJO ULLA ADAJA
CINCA DOURO DUERO GENIL
JALON JUCAR NAVIA ODIEL
RIAZA SEGRE TAGUS TINTO
TURIA ALAGON ARAGON
ERESMA HUERVA JARAMA
ORBIGO SEGURA TOROTE
ALMERIA ALMONTE ARLANZA
BARBATE CABRIEL DURATON
GALLEGO HENARES MIJARES
PERALES GUADIANA
TOWN: ROA ASPE BAZA ELDA
HARO IRUN JAEN LEON LUGO
OLOT REUS ROTA SAMA VIGO
BAENA BEJAR CADIZ CIEZA
CUETA ECIJA EIBAR ELCHE
GIJON IBIZA JEREZ JODAR
LORCA OLIVA PALMA RONDA
SIERO UBEDA XERES YECLA
ZAFRA AVILES AZUAGA BILBAO
BURGOS DUENCA GANDIA
GERONA GETAFE GUADIX
HELLIN HUELVA HUESCA
JATIVA LERIDA LUCENA
MADRID MALAGA MATARO
MERIDA MURCIA ORENSE
OVIEDO TERMEL TOLEDO
UTRERA ZAMORA BADAJOZ
CORDOBA DAIMIEL GRANADA
JUMILLA LINARES LOGRONO
MANRESA SEGOVIA SEVILLA
TARRASA VITORIA BADALONA
FIGUERAS PAMPLONA
SABADELL SANTIAGO
TORRENTE VALENCIA
ZARAGOZA
WEIGHT: ONZA FRAIL GRANO
LIBRA MARCO TOMIN ADARME
ARROBA DINERO DRACMA
OCHAVA ARIENZO QUILATE
QUINTAL CARACTER TONELADA
WINE: RIOJA SHERRY

SPALL CHIP SCALE SPAWL GALLET
SPAN ARCH BEAM PAIR CHORD
SPANG SWING BRIDGE EXTEND
SPREAD OPENING QUARTER
BESTRIDE
(— WITH FINGERS) SPEND
(UNSUPPORTED —) BEARING
SPANDREL GROIN ALLEGE
SPANDLE
SPANGLE AGLET PRANK SPANG
SEQUIN CHEQUEEN SPANGLET
ZECCHINO PAILLETTE

SPANGLED POWDERED SPANKLED
SPANIARD DON DIEGO MULADI
(CHRISTIAN —) MOZARAB
SPANIEL TRASY COCKER SUSSEX
CLUMBER BLENHEIM PAPILLON
SPRINGER WATERRUG
SPANISH ALJAMIA
(PREF.) HISPANO
SPANISH-AMERICAN CHINO
LADINO
SPANISH BAYONET IZOTE YUCCA
SPANISH HOGFISH LADYFISH
SPANISH JACINTH SCILLA
SPANISH JASMINE MALATI
SPANISH MACKEREL SIERRA
SPANISH PLUM SIRUELAS
SPANISH STOPPER IRONWOOD
SPANK PRAT SCUD SKELP PADDLE
SLIPPER
SPANKER DRIVER MIZZEN
SPANKING SMACKING
SPANNER KEY WRENCH
SPANNING ASTRIDE
SPAR BEAM BOOM CAUK CLUB
GAFF MAST RAFT SPUR YARD
CABER SPAAD SPATH SPELK
SPRIT STODE BOUGAR RICKER
STEEVE BASTITE DERRICK
DOLPHIN JIBBOOM RIBBAND
BOWSPRIT CRYOLITE LAZULITE
OUTRIGGER MARTINGALE
(BITTER —) DOLOMITE
(HEAVY —) CAUK BARITE BARYTE
SPARE BONY FAIK GASH HAIN
LEAN NICE SAVE SLIM THIN
FAVOR LANKY SPELL LENTEN
MEAGER MEAGRE SKIMPY
RESERVE SLENDER PRESERVE
SPARGE PIPE WEEPER
SPARING CHARY GNEDE SCANT
SPARE DAINTY FRUGAL STINGY
ENVIOUS ECONOMIC SPAREFUL
PENURIOUS ABSTEMIOUS
(— OF WORDS) CURT
(NOT —) HANDSOME
(PREF.) PARCI
SPARINGNESS PARCITY SCARCITY
SPARK FUNK IZLE AIZLE GRAIN
LIGHT PURSE SPERK SPUNK
BLUETTE FLANKER FLAUGHT
SPARKLE SPUNKIE SPARKLET
SCINTILLA
(-S OF MOLTEN IRON) NILL
(VITAL —) GHOST LIGHT
(PREF.) SCINTILLO
SPARKER IGNITER
SPARKLE FUNK SNAP WINK BLINK
FLASH GLENT GLINT SHINE SPARK
GLANCE KINDLE SIMPER CRACKLE
EMICATE FLANKER GLIMMER
GLISTEN GLISTER GLITTER
RADIATE SHIMMER SKINKLE
SPANGLE TWINKLE SPRINKLE
CORUSCATE
SPARKLER TWINKLER
SPARKLING DEWY CRISP QUICK
SUNNY BRIGHT SPUNKY STARRY
CREMANT DIAMOND SHINING
TWINKLY MOUSSEUX SMIRKING
SPERLING BRILLIANT SCINTILLANT
(MAKE —) AERATE
(NOT —) STILL
SPARK PLUG (PART OF —) CAP GAP

SHELL GASKET BUSHING
TERMINAL ELECTRODE
INSULATOR
SPARLING SMELT
SPARROW SPUG DICKY DONEY
FINCH HEMPY ISAAC PADDA
PADDY SPRIG SPRUG CHIPPY
PHILIP SPRONG TOWHEE
CHANTER CHIPPIE DUNNOCK
FIELDIE HAYSUCK PINNOCK
SPADGER SPURDIE TITLENE
TITLING TITTLIN ACCENTOR
FIRETAIL HAIRBIRD WHITECAP
(PREF.) PASSERI
SPARROW HAWK MUSKET
SPARHAWK
SPARSE BALD THIN MEAGER
MEAGRE SCANTY THRIFTY
SPARTAN LACONIC
SPASM PANG CRICK QUALM
TONUS CLONUS ENTASIA
FLUTTER RAPTURE SPASMUS
MYOTONIA PAROXYSM
(— OF FOOT) PODISMUS
(— OF PAIN) GRIP
(— OF THE IRIS) HIPPUS
(—S OF WHALE) FLURRY
(TONIC —) HOLOTONY
(PREF.) CLONICO
SPASMODIC FITFUL SNATCHY
SPASMIC SPASTIC SPURTIVE
SPAT SEED BROOD JOWER GAITER
LEGGING BOOTHOSE BOOTIKIN
SPATE SLUICE
SPATHE CYMBA SHEATH
SPATHIC SPARRY SPATHOSE
SPATIAL STERIC
SPATIATE ROVE RAMBLE STROLL
SPATTER DASH JAUP BERAY SKIRP
SLART SPARK SPURT DABBLE
SPLASH SQUIRT BESPAWL
BESPETE SHATTER SMATTER
SPATTLE SPIRTLE SPLATTER
SPRINKLE
(— WITH FOAM) EMBOSS
(— WITH MUD) JAP BEMUD SPARK
SPATTERDASH SPAT BONNET
GAITER CUTIKIN LEGGING
BOOTHOSE BOOTIKIN
SPATTERDOCK DUCK CLOTE
TUCKY WOKAS NUPHAR
BONNETS CANDOCK
SPATULA SPAT SLICE THIBLE
THIVEL CESTRUM SPATTLE
SPLATTER
SPAVIN JACK SPAVIE VARISSE
SPAWN RUD BLOT RAUN REDD
RUDD SILE SPORE TODDER
(OYSTER —) CULCH CULTCH
SPAWNEATER SHINER
SPAWNING SICK MILKY SEEDING
SPAY FIX GELD ALTER DESEX
SPADE CHANGE SPEAVE
CASTRATE
SPEAK ASK CUT SAY CANT CARP
MEAN MOOT MOVE TALE TALK
TELL WORD BREAK MOUTH
NEVEN ORATE PARLE SOUND
SPELL SPIEL UTTER ACCENT
PARLEY PATTER QUETHE SERMON
SPEECH SQUEAK TONGUE
ADDRESS BESPEAK DECLAIM
DELIVER EXCLAIM PARRALL

CONVERSE REHEARSE
(— ABUSIVELY) JAW
(— AFFECTEDLY) MIMP KNACK
(— AGAINST) ACCUSE GAINSAY
FORSPEAK
(— ANGRILY) ROUSE CAMPLE
(— AT LENGTH) DISSERT ENLARGE
(— BROKENLY) FALTER
(— CAJOLINGLY) COLLOGUE
(— CONFUSEDLY) HATTER
CLUTTER SPLATHER
(— CONTEMPTUOUSLY) SCOFF
(— CRITICALLY) LAUNCH
(— CURTLY) BIRK SNAP
(— EVIL) BLACKEN
(— FAIR) PALP
(— FALSELY) ABUSE
(— FAMILIARLY) HOBNOB
(— FIRST TO) ACCOST
(— FOOLISHLY) PRATE GIBBER
(— HALTINGLY) HACK HAMMER
STAMMER
(— HOARSELY) CROAK CROUP
(— ILL OF) KNOCK DEPRAVE
DETRACT
(— IMPERFECTLY) LISP
(— IMPUDENTLY) CHEEK
(— IMPULSIVELY) BLURT
(— IN DRAWL) DRANT DRAUNT
(— IN JEST) FOOL
(— IN ONE'S EAR) HARK
(— IN POINTLESS MANNER) DROOL
(— IN STUMBLING WAY) STUTTER
(— IN UNDERTONE) WHISPER
(— IN WHINING VOICE) CANT
(— INDISTINCTLY) FUMBLE JABBER
MUFFLE MAUNDER SPLUTTER
(— INEPTLY) BUMBLE
(— INSOLENTLY) SNASH
(— LOUDLY) TANG
(— MINCINGLY) NAB MIMP
(— MONOTONOUSLY) DROLL
(— OF) CALL NEVEN MENTION
(— OUT) LEVEL SHOOT
(— PLAYFULLY) BANTER
(— POMPOUSLY) CRACK
(— PROFUSELY) PALAVER
(— QUERULOUSLY) CREAK
(— RAPIDLY) TROLL GIBBER
JABBER SQUIRT CHATTER
(— RESENTFULLY) HUFF
(— RHETORICALLY) DECLAIM
(— SARCASTICALLY) GIRD
(— SHORTLY) JERK
(— SLIGHTINGLY OF) BELITTLE
(— SLOWLY) DRAWL
(— THROUGH THE NOSE) SNAFFLE
(— TRUTH) SOOTHSAY
(— WITH EMPHASIS) DWELL
(— WITH LIPS CLOSED) MUMBLE
SPEAKEASY SHEBEEN
SPEAKER VOICE BRYTHON
LOCUTOR MOUTHER STYLIST
EPILOGUE SPEECHER
(ORATORICAL —) SPOUTER
(PUBLIC —) ORATOR STUMPER
SPEAKING STEVEN LOQUENT
PARLANCE SPELLING
(— ARTICULATELY) MEROP
MEROPIC
(— MANY LANGUAGES) POLYGLOT
(EVIL —) PRATING
(SUFF.) LOGER LOGIA(N)

LOGIC(AL) LOGIST LOGUE LOGY
LOQUENCE LOQUENT LOQUY
SPEAR GAD DART FRAM GAFF PIKE
GRAIN LANCE REJON SHAFT
STAFF VALET AMGARN BORDUN
BROACH FIZGIG FRAMEA GIDJEE
GLAIVE WASTER ASSEGAI
BOURDON HARPOON IMPALER
JAVELIN TRIDENT VERUTUM
EELSPEAR GAVELOCK LANCEGAY
STANDARD WALSPERE
(BROKEN —) TRUNCHEON
(EEL —) ELGER PILGER
(FISH —) GIG GAFF TREN POACH
FIZGIG GRAINS FISHGIG LEISTER
SNIGGER
(SALMON —) WASTER
(PREF.) DORI ENCHO HASTATO
LANCI
SPEARFISH AGUJA GOGGLE
MARLIN BILLFISH LONGJAWS
SPEAR GRASS SPANIARD
SPEARHEAD BUNT GAFF SPUD
CORONAL
SPEARMINT MENTHE LABIATE
SPEAR-SHAPED HASTATE
SPEAR THROWER ATLATL
WOMMALA WOOMERAH
SPEARWORT BANEWORT
SPECIAL VERY EXTRA KHASS
CONCRETE ESPECIAL PECULIAR
SPECIFIC
SPECIALIST SWELL EXPERT
HERALD LEGIST ALTAIST ARABIST
FAUNIST FEUDIST GRECIAN
OLOGIST SURGEON AQUINIST
ARBORIST BANTUIST BOTANIST
ETHICIST GEMARIST GEOGNOST
GEOMETER HEBRAIST HOMERIST
LATINIST URBANIST PHYSICIST
PEDIATRIST PATHOLOGIST
(SUFF.) ICIAN LOG(ER)(IA)(IAN)(IC)
(ICAL)(IST)(UE)(Y)
SPECIALTY BAG
SPECIES FOLK FORM KIND SORT
BROOD CLASS EIDOS GENRE
ESPECE MANNER MISTER
APOMICT FEATHER SPECIAL
ANALOGUE GENOTYPE INDIGENE
(— VARIANT) MORPH
(ATOMIC —) DAUGHTER
SPECIFIC EXPRESS SPECIAL
TRIVIAL CONCRETE ESPECIAL
SPECIFICALLY NAMELY
SPECIFICATION MENTION
SPECIFICITY HECCEITY
SPECIFIED SET GIVEN
SPECIFY ASSIGN DESIGN DETAIL
ARTICLE EXPRESS MENTION
INDICATE NOMINATE PRESCRIBE
SPECIMEN CAST TEST ESSAY
FACER MODEL SPICE CHANCE
SAMPLE SWATCH EXAMPLE
ICOTYPE ISOTYPE NEOTYPE
PATTERN SAMPLER ALLOTYPE
EXEMPLAR HOLOTYPE HYPOTYPE
IDEOTYPE INSTANCE
REPRESENTATIVE
(ADDITIONAL —) COTYPE
(EXTRAORDINARY —) BENDER
(FEMALE —) GYNETYPE
(FINEST —) PEARL
(LARGE —) ELEPHANT

(POOR —) APOLOGY
(SMALL —) SPRIG
SPECIOUS GAY FAIR FALSE WHITE
FACILE GLOSSY HOLLOW TINSEL
PAGEANT PLAUSIVE PROBABLE
SPURIOUS PLAUSIBLE
MERETRICIOUS
SPECIOUSNESS DISGUISE
SPECK DOT PIN PIP MOTE SPOT
TICK WHIT BLACK GLEBE PLECK
APHTHA SPECKLE FLYSPECK
NUBECULA
(— IN LINEN) SPRIT
(— ON FINGERNAIL) GIFT
(BLACK —) DARTROSE
SPECKLE FLECK GARLE SPECK
MIZZLE PECKLE STIPPLE
SPECKLED SHELD FIGGED MAILED
MENALD SANDED BLOBBED
BRACKET PECKLED SPECKED
SPECKLY FRECKLED IRONSHOT
IRRORATE JASPERED STIPPLED
SPECTACLE POMP SHOW SPEC
BYSEN SIGHT CIRCUS DEVICE
OBJECT EYEMARK PAGEANT
SPECIES TAMASHA MONUMENT
NAUMACHY STERACLE
NAUMACHIA
(ODD —) TRACK
(SORRY —) BIZEN BYSEN BYZEN
(WATER —) AQUACADE
(PL.) LUDI
(SUFF.) CADE ORAMA
SPECTACLES PAIR SPECS BRILLS
LUNETS PEEPER SIGHTS GLASSES
GOGGLES WINKERS ANAGLYPH
CHEATERS BARNACLES
SPECTACULAR VIEWY PAGEANT
SPECTATOR FAN VIEWER
WITNESS BEHOLDER OBSERVER
OVERSEER RAILBIRD VIEWSTER
SCAFFOLDER
(PL.) DEDANS
SPECTER BUG BOGY MARE BOGIE
BOGLE GHOST LARVA POOKA
SPOOK TAIPO BOGGLE EMPUSA
PHOOKA REDCAP SHADOW SPIRIT
SPOORN WRAITH BOGGARD
BOGGART BUGBEAR PHANTOM
RAWHEAD REDCOWL SPECTRE
GUYTRASH PHANTASM PRESENCE
REVENANT SPECTRUM
SPECTRAL SPOOKY GHOSTLY
SHADOWY
SPECULATE JOB BEAR STAG
GAMBLE PONDER WONDER
CONSIDER RUMINATE THEORIZE
SPECULATION THEORY THEORIC
VENTURE GAMBLING IDEOLOGY
(DISHONEST —) BUBBLE
(VAGUE —) MYSTICISM
SPECULATIVE ACADEMIC
SPECULATOR PIKER GAMBLER
PLUNGER SCALPER BOURSIER
BUMMAREE OPERATOR
SPECULUM METAL MIRROR
DILATER DIOPTER DIOPTRIC
SPEECH GOB LIP SAW SAY TAT
TOY COAX LEED REDE RUNE TALE
DUALA FRUMP GLOZE LEDEN
LINGO PARLE SERMO SPEAK
SPELL SPIEL SPOKE SQUIB VOICE
BREATH DILOGY EPILOG GAELIC

GASCON GILAKI JARGON LEDDEN
LEMOSI ORISON REASON SALUTE
STEVEN TONGUE ACCENTS
ADDRESS BROCARD EASTERN
MEITHEI ORATION PALABRA
VULGATE EPILOGUE GALICIAN
HARANGUE LANGUAGE LOCUTION
LOQUENCE MORAVIAN PARLANCE
QUESTION SONORITY SPEAKING
(— CHARACTERIZED BY SLURRING)
SLURVIAN
(— FORM) LEXEME
(— IN GREEK DRAMA) RHESIS
(— IN PLAY) SIDE
(— REDUCER) VOCODER
(AFFECTED —) CANT
(BITTER —) DIATRIBE
(BOASTFUL —) BLUSTER
(BOMBASTIC —) SQUIRT
HARANGUE
(COARSE —) HARLOTRY
(CONFUSED —) SPUTTER
(CONTEMPTUOUS —) FRUMP
(IMPUDENT —) SASS
(IRRITABLE —) SNAP
(JAVANESE —) KRAMA
(LONG —) MONOLOG
(LONG-DRAWN —) TIRADE
(MISLEADING —) PALAVER
(MOCKING —) TRIFLE
(OBSCURE —) ENIGMA
(OFFENSIVE —) INJURY
(PERT —) DICACITY
(PRETENTIOUS —) FUSTIAN
(ROUNDABOUT —) CIRCUIT
(SANCTIMONIOUS —) SNUFFLE
(SINGSONG —) CANT
(SLANDEROUS —) EVIL
(VAPID —) WASH
(PREF.) LALO LEXI LOG(O)
PHON(O)
(SUFF.) ESE LEXIA PHASIA
PHEMIA PHEMISM PHEMISTIC
PHRASEO PHRASIA PHRASIS
(— DISORDER) LALIA
SPEECHIFIER SPOUTER
SPEECHLESS DUMB MUTE SILENT
SPEECHMAKING SPOUTING
(— TO GAIN APPLAUSE) BUNKUM
BUNCOMBE
SPEED BAT HIE RIP RUN FLEE
FOOT GAIT HIGH PACE PELT PIKE
PIRR POST TILT BLAST HASTE
HURRY SMOKE WHIRL ASSIST
CAREER FOURTH HASTEN STREAK
QUICKEN WHIZZLE AIRSPEED
CELERITY DISPATCH EXPEDITE
FASTNESS MOMENTUM RAPIDITY
VELOCITY ACCELERATE
(— OF NAUTICAL MILE) KNOT
(— OF PITCH) STUFF
(— OF 100 MILES PER HOUR) TON
(— UP) HASTEN CATALYZE
EXPEDITE
(AT FULL —) AMAIN
(AUTOMOTIVE —) LOW HIGH DRIVE
FIRST THIRD FOURTH SECOND
REVERSE
(DRIVING —) SWING
(GOOD —) BONALLY
(HIGH —) CLIP MACH
(PREF.) DROM(O) TACHO
SPEEDBOAT HYDRO

SPEEDILY CITO SOON APACE
RATHE BELIVE PRESTO BETIMES
HYINGLY QUICKLY TANTIVY
SPEEDING HURTLING
SPEEDWELL CATEYE HENBIT
FLUELLEN NECKWEED NICKWELL
BROOKLIME
SPEEDY FAST SOON HASTY QUICK
RATHE SWIFT RAKING SUDDEN
POSTING TANTIVY EXPEDITE
SPEEDFUL SPINNING POSTHASTE
SPELEOLOGIST CAVEMAN
SPELL GO FIT HEX JAG HACK JINX
MOJO PULL RUNE SCAT TACK
TAKE TIFF TIME TOUR TURN
BRIEF CHARM CRAFT CRASH
MAGIC PATCH SPACE WANGA
WEIRD WHEEL ACCESS GLAMOR
GOOFER GRIGRI GUFFER MAKUTU
MANTRA PERIOD SNATCH STREAK
CANTRIP SORCERY SPELDER
CANTRAIP EXORCISM GREEGREE
MALEFICE PISHOGUE
(— OF ACTIVITY) BOUT
(— OF EXERCISE) BREATHER
(— OF LISTLESSNESS) DOLDRUMS
(— OF SHIVERING) AGUE
(— OF WEATHER) SNAP SLANT
SEASON
(BREATHING —) BLOW
(BRIEF —) SNATCH
(DRINKING —) FUDDLE
(EVIL —) JINX
(FAINTING —) DROW DWALM
(NIPPING —) SNAPE
(STORMY —) FLAW
(VOODOOISTIC —) WANGA
SPELLBIND ENCHANT
SPELLBINDING BASILISK
SPELLING GRAPH WRITING
PHONOGRAPHY
SPELT FAR EMMER FITCH SPELTZ
SPELTZ EMMER
SPENCER TRYSAIL
SPEND BIRL COST DREE DROP
LEAD PASS STOW WARE WEAR
DALLY DREIE SERVE SHOOT
TRADE BESTOW BEWARE EXPEND
LAVISH MOIDER OUTRUN
CONSUME DISPEND EXHAUST
UNPURSE CONFOUND CONTRIVE
DISBURSE
(— FRUITLESSLY) DAWDLE
(— IN IDLENESS) DRONE
(— LAVISHLY) BLUE SPORT
DEBAUCH
(— MONEY) MELT
(— RECKLESSLY) BLOW LASH
(— SUMMER) ESTIVATE
(— TIME) DREE FOOL DREIE
ENTREAT
(— TIME TEDIOUSLY) DRANT
(— WASTEFULLY) SPILL SQUANDER
SPENDTHRIFT WASTER PANURGE
ROUNDER SPENDER WASTREL
PRODIGAL PROFLIGATE
SCATTERGOOD
SPENSER IMMERITO
SPENT DONE WEARY EFFETE
OVERWORN
SPERM SEED SEMINIUM
SPERMACETI SPERM CETACEUM
SPERMOGONIUM PYCNIUM

SPERMOPHILE MARMOT SUSLIK
SPERM WHALE CACHALOT
PHYSETER
SPET SIGNET SINNET
SPEW PUKE SPUE VOMIT
SPHAERIUM CYCLAS
SPHAGION HIERA
SPHAGNUM MUSKEG
SPHALERITE JACK BLENDE
BLACKJACK
SPHENODON TUATARA HATTERIA
SPHERE ORB AREA BALL BOWL
LOKA SHOT FIELD GLOBE ORBIT
RANGE SCOPE CIRCLE CROTAL
DOMAIN HEAVEN REGION
BUNDLE COUNTRY ELEMENT
GLOBOID KINGDOM ORBICLE
PURVIEW EARTHKIN EMPYREAL
EMPYREAN MOVEABLE PROVINCE
TERRITORY
(— OF ACTION) AMBIT ARENA
WORLD DOMAIN
(— OF ACTIVITY) FIELD FRONT
(— OF AUTHORITY) DIOCESE
(— OF INFLUENCE) DOMAIN
SATRAPY
(— OF LIFE) EARTH WORLD
STATION
(— OF OPERATION) THEATER
THEATRE
(— OF WORK) TITLE
(CELESTIAL —) CYCLE ELEMENT
(ENCOMPASSING —) AMBIENT
(MAGNETIZED —) EARTHKIN
TERRELLA
(METAL —) HAMMER
(SMALL —) ORBICLE SPHERULE
(TINKLING —) CROTAL
(PREF.) GLOBO SPHAER(O)
SPHER(O)
SPHERICAL ORBIC GLOBAL
ROTUND GLOBATE GLOBOSE
ORBICAL SPHERIC GLOBULAR
ORBICULAR
(PREF.) GLOBO
SPHERULE GLOBULE VARIOLE
SPHINX MUSTANG COLOSSUS
HAWKMOTH
SPICA AZIMECH
SPICCATO PIQUE
SPICE MACE VEIN AROMA CLOVE
EPICE TASTE GINGER NUTMEG
PEPPER SEASON STACTE SPICERY
SPICING ALLSPICE CINNAMON
SEASONER
SPICEBUSH BENZOIN SNAPWOOD
SPICED SPICY POWDERED
SPICKNEL MEW SCLERE
BEARWORT
SPICULE OXEA TOXA ASTER CHELA
CYMBA DESMA DIACT SIGMA
SPINE STYLE ACTINE ANCHOR
MONACT SCLERE STYLUS TRIACT
TRIPOD TYLOTE CALTROP
DIACTIN EUASTER HEXAXON
MONAXON PINULUS RHABDUS
SPICKLE SPIRULA TETRACT
TORNOTE TRIAENE TRIAXON
TYLOTUS HEXASTER ISOCHELA
OXYASTER POLYAXON SCLERITE
SPHERULA SPICULUM STRONGYL
TETRAXON TRICHITE TYLASTER
(SUFF.) AENE

SPICY RACY SEXY GAMEY NUTTY SWEET SPICED GINGERY PEPPERY FRAGRANT SPICEFUL

SPIDER BUG COB ARAIN ATTID COBBE COPPE LOPPE NANCY TAINT ANANSI ARRAND EPEIRA HUNTER KATIPO TRIVET WEAVER ARANEID CREEPER DRASSID EPEIRID JAYHAWK KNOPPIE POKOMOO RETIARY SERPENT SKILLET SOLDIER SPINNER ARACHNID ATTERCOP CTENIZID DICTYNID ETTERCAP KARAKURT ORBITELE PHALANGE PHALANGY PHOLCOID SALTICID SOLPUGID TELARIAN ULOBORID VENANTES WANDERER TARANTULA
(PART OF —) EYE CLAW COXA FEMUR TIBIA TARSUS ABDOMEN PATELLA PEDICEL SCOPULA SPINNERET METATARSUS PEDIPALPUS TROCHANTER CEPHALOTHORAX
(PREF.) ARACHN(O)

SPIDER CRAB MAIAN MAIID

SPIDERFLOWER QUARESMA

SPIDER MONKEY SAJOU COAITA SAPAJOU

SPIDERWORT TRINITY

SPIELER BARKER

SPIGNEL MEU

SPIGOT TAP SPILE DOSSIL DOZZLE STOPCOCK

SPIKE GAD BARB BROB PICK PIKE PILE SPUR TINE PITON POINT ROUGH SPEAR SPICA SPICK MOOTER PRITCH SPADIX SPIKER TENTER ALICOLE GADLING PRICKER PRICKET TRENAIL TURNPIN SPIKELET STROBILE WHEATEAR
(— A CANNON) CLOY
(— OF CEREAL) EAR
(BRACTED —) AMENT
(DRIED —S) CANNABIS

SPIKED SPICATE SPINDLED

SPIKELET CHAT ALICOLE LOCUSTA SPICULE

SPIKENARD PHU NARD ARALIA SUMBUL ARALIAD IVYWORT SPIGNET SPIGNUT

SPILE TAP SPILL FOREPOLE

SPILL LET DRIP SHED SLOP FLOSH SCALE SKAIL SPILE SQUAB STAVE JIRBLE PURLER SLATTER SLOBBER TURNOVER
(— FOR LIGHTING PIPES) FIDIBUS

SPIN CUT BIRL DRAW GYRE HURL PIRL PURL SCREW SPONE TWIRL TWIST WEAVE WHIRL FOLLOW GYRATE VRILLE WAMBLE TWIZZLE TEETOTUM
(— AND MAKE HUM) BUM
(— AROUND) SWING
(— ON BASEBALL) STUFF
(— ON BILLIARD BALL) SIDE
(— OUT) SHOOT
(— SILK) THROW
(— SMOOTHLY) SLEEP
(— UNEVENLY) TWITTER

SPINACH SAVOY EPINARD OLITORY POTHERB

SPINAL CORD AXION

NUCHA MYELON
(WHITE MATTER OF —) ALBA NUKE
(PREF.) MYEL(O)
(SUFF.) MYELIA

SPINDLE PIN AXLE HASP PIRN SPIT STEM STUD ARBOR FLOAT QUILL SPIKE SPILL VERGE BOBBIN BROACH CANNON FUSEAU BOLSTER MANDREL SPINNEL TRENDLE WHARROW
(AXLE —) ARM
(FOURTH OF —) HASP
(ONE 24TH OF —) HEER
(PREF.) FUSI

SPINDLE TREE GAITER DOGWOOD PEGWOOD EUONYMUS

SPINDLING SPEARY SPINDLY SPIRLIE

SPINDLY LEGGY PULING

SPINE HORN PIKE PILE SETA SPUR CHINE PRICK QUILL SPEAR SPIKE SPINA THORN ACUMEN CHAETA RACHIS ACANTHA ACICULA FULCRUM GLOCHIS PAXILLA PRICKER PRICKLE ROSTRUM SPINULE STICKLE ACICULUM BACKBONE ILLICIUM PAXILLUS PELELITH SPICULUM SPINELET
(— OF SURGEON FISH) TUCK
(CURVATURE OF —) LORDOSIS
(PREF.) ACANTH(O) RACHI(O) RHACHI(O)
(SUFF.) ACANTHUS CHAETA CHAETES CHAETUS RACHIDIA RHACHIS RRHACHIS

SPINEL BALAS CANDITE ESPINEL GAHNITE VERMEIL PICOTITE SPINELLE

SPINELESS SLAVISH

SPINET ESPINET GIRAFFE OCTAVINA SOURDINE VIRGINAL

SPINNERET GALEA MAMMULA SPINNER

SPINNING STROBIC LANIFICE
(— WEB) TELARIAN

SPINNING JENNY MULE JENNY

SPINNING MULE IRONMAN

SPINNING WHEEL TURN CHARKHA CHURRUCK
(PART OF —) BAND FLYER WHEEL BOBBIN DISTAFF SPINDLE TREADLE STANDARD

SPINSTER TABBY VIRGIN

SPINULE
(PL.) CTENII

SPINY PICKED THORNY
(PREF.) ACANTH(O) CENTR(I)(O) ECHIN(O)

SPINY OYSTER SPONDYLE

SPINY RAT OCTODONT

SPIRACLE STOMA STIGMA BLOWHOLE

SPIRAEA MAY ROSACEAN MEADOWSWEET

SPIRAL COIL CURL GYRE SPIN SCREW SNARE SPIRE BUTTON GURGES LITUUS SCREWY SCROLL SPIRED TWIRLY VOLUTE HELICAL ROLLING SPIROID STROPHE WINDING WREATHY GYROIDAL HELICINE HELICOID
(LACEWORK —) PURL
(PREF.) GYR(O) HELI HELIC(O)

SPIRANT VAU WAW HISS OPEN DURATIVE

SPIRANTHES IBIDIUM

SPIRE CROWN SHAFT SIKAR SPEAR TAPER TOLLY BROACH FLECHE PRICKET SHIKARA SIKHARA SPIRALE SPIRELET

SPIRE-BEARER SPIRIFER

SPIREME SKEAN SKEIN

SPIRIT GO FLY NAG PEP VIM AITU AKUA ALMA ATUA BRIO DASH DOOK ELAN FIRE GALL GIMP HYLE JINN LIFE MARC MARE MIND MOOD SOUL TONE ZEMI ZING AGIEL ARDOR ARIEL ASURA AZOTH CHEER DEMON DHQUL DJINN DOBBY ETHOS FLING GEIST GHOST GORIC GUACA HAUNT HEART HOLDA HUACA JINNI LARVA NUMEN PLUCK POWER PRETA RALPH SAINT SHADE SHRAB SPOOK SPUNK VERVE ASTRAL ASUANG BOTTOM BREATH CHULPA COURIL DAEMON ESPRIT FAINTS FLECHE FYLGJA GENIUS GINGER INWARD KOBOLD LESHEY METTLE MORALE ORISHA PAZAZZ PECKER PIZAZZ PNEUMA PYTHON SPRAWL SPRITE TAFFIA WRAITH ALCOHOL BRAVERY CONTROL CORDIAL COURAGE ENTRAIN EUDEMON KNOCKER MANITOU PISACHI PIZZAZZ PURUSHA RAPPIST SMEDDUM STOMACH CALVADOS ERDGEIST FAMILIAR FOLLETTO PHANTASM SPIRACLE SPIRITUS
(— DWELLING IN JEWEL) AZOTH
(— DWELLING IN MINES) KNOCKER
(— HAUNTING PRINTING HOUSES) RALPH
(— OF DEAD) CHINDI CHINDEE
(— OF DEATH) CHULPA
(— OF DECEASED) AKH
(— OF FERTILITY) YAKSA YAKSHA YAKSHI
(— OF HOSTILITY) ANIMUS
(— OF LOYALTY) PIETAS
(— OF MAN) AKH
(— OF ONE WHO HAS MET VIOLENT DEATH) PISACHI
(— OF PHYSICAL HEART) AB
(— OF TRAGEDY) COTHURN
(— OF UNBAPTIZED BABE) TARAN
(— WHICH ACTUATES CUSTOMS) ETHOS
(—S OF LOWER WORLD) INFERI
(—S OF THE DEAD) MANES
(ANCESTRAL —) ANITO KATCHINA
(ARDENT —) RAK RACK ARRACK
(ASTRAL —) AGIEL ASTRAL JOPHIEL UUCHATON
(AVENGING —) FURY ALECTO ALASTOR MEGAERA
(CHARACTERISTIC —) VIBE
(COMBATIVE —) SWORD
(DISEMBODIED —) KUEI KWEI SOUL GHOST LARVA SHADE ASUANG SPECTER SPECTRE
(DIVINE —) ISVARA ISHVARA
(EARTH —) ERDGEIST
(EFFULGENT —S) ARDORS
(EMANCIPATED —) MUKTATMA

(EVIL —) DEV DIV HAG IMP OKI BAKA BENG BOKO BOLL DEVA DUSE MARA OKEE ASURA BUGAN DAEVA DEMON DEVIL JUMBY OTKON DAITYA DIBBUK DYBBUK LILITH AHRIMAN BUGGANE CASZIEL INCUBUS KANAIMA RAKSHAS SHAITAN SHEITAN SKOOKUM WINDIGO ASMODEUS BAALPEOR BEELPEOR HOBOMOCO NIGHTMARE
(FAMILIAR —) FLY GENIUS HARPIER
(FEMALE —) DUFFY DUPPY DUSIO HOLDA UNDINE BANSHEE ATAENSIC BABAJAGA BELFAGOR BELFAZOR
(FIGHTING —) DEVIL
(FOREST —) MIMING
(FULL OF —) CRANK
(FULL OF —S) BRAG
(GOOD —) DEVA EUDEMON
(GOVERNING —) ANIMUS
(GUARDIAN —) ANGEL TOTEM FYLGJA NAGUAL
(HIGH —) GINGER COURAGE
(HIGH —S) CREST GAIETY HEYDAY ELATION
(HOSTILE —S) LEMURES
(HOUSEHOLD —S) LARES PENATES
(HUMAN —) JIVATMA
(IMPISH —) PO
(IMPURE —) FAINTS
(IN VIGOROUS —S) FIERCE
(LOW —S) DUMP BLUES MEGRIM DISMALS
(MALEVOLENT —) BHUT GORIC LARVA
(MALICIOUS —) DOBBY
(MALIGNANT —) IMP KER GYRE DEMON
(MANLY —) SPLEEN
(MISCHIEVOUS —) KOBOLD TIKOLOSH
(MOUNTAIN —) RUBEZAHL
(MOVING —) SOUL
(MUSICAL —) BRIO
(NATURE —) NAT
(PARTY —) FACTION
(REFINED —) ELIXIR
(RESOLUTE —) SPRAWL
(ROVING —) RAMPLER
(SEA —) TANGIE
(SENSED —) KARMA
(SOOTHSAYING —) PYTHON
(SUPERNATURAL —) FAMILIAR
(SYLVAN —) LESHY SYLVAN
(TRICKSY —) ARIEL
(TUTELARY —S) DIS LARES
(VITAL —) TUCK
(VOLATILE —) ESSENCE
(WATER —) ARIEL KELPY UNDINE
(WICKED —) IMP THURSE
(PL.) GENII IGIGI DAUBER
(PREF.) PNEUMAT(O) PSYCH(O) THYM(O)
(SUFF.) THYMIA

SPIRITED BRAG FELL GOGO RACY TALL BEANY BIRKY CRANK EAGER FIERY FLUSH KEDGE KINKY LIFEY PEPPY PROUD SASSY SEEDY SMART SPICY VIVID AUDACE FIERCE GINGER LIVELY METTLE

PLUCKY SKEIGH SPRUCE SPUNKY
VIVACE ANIMATO DASHING
FORWARD HUMMING NERVOUS
PEPPERY SPIRITY DESIROUS
FRAMPOLD GENEROUS
PHRAMPEL SLASHING STOMACHY
VASCULAR
SPIRITEDLY GAMELY
SPIRITLESS DEAD DOWF MEAN
MEEK POOR TAME AMORT FAINT
MILKY MUSTY SEEDY SOGGY
VAPID ABJECT ANEMIC CRAVEN
DREEPY FLASHY JEJUNE LEADEN
SODDEN SOFTLY WOODEN
HILDING INSIPID LANGUID
FECKLESS FLAGGING LISTLESS
THEWLESS
SPIRITLESSLY DAVIELY
SPIRITLESSNESS LANGUOR
SPIRITLIKE ETHEREAL
SPIRITS LACE RAKI HOOCH MANES
FETTLE PECKER FEATHER
LEMURES SAMSHOO WAIPIRO
SPIRITUAL ABOVE DEVOUT
INWARD MISTLY GHOSTLY
CHURCHLY INTERNAL NUMINOUS
SUPERIOR PNEUMATIC
(— LEADER) ZADDIK
SPIRITUALISM SPOOKISM
SPIRITUALITY HEAVEN
SPIRITUALIZE REFINE
SPIRITUOUS HARD
SPIROCHETE BORRELIA
SPIT YEX FUFF RACK FROTH REACH
SPAWL BROACH SPITTLE
SANDSPIT SPITTING
(— AND POLISH) BULL
(SUFF.) PTYSIS
SPITE ENVY ONDE DEPIT LIVOR
PIQUE VENOM MALICE MAUGRE
RANCOR SPLEEN DESPITE
AMBITION
SPITEFUL MEAN CATTY NASTY
NEBBY PETTY SNAKY ELVISH
MALIGN SULLEN WANTON
WICKED CATTISH ENVIOUS
PEEVISH SNAKISH VICIOUS
WASPISH CANKERED KNAPPISH
VENOMOUS
SPITFIRE CACAFOGO PEPPERBOX
SPITTING FUFF EMPTYSIS
SPITTING SNAKE RINGHALS
SPITTLE SPIT SPAWL SPUTUM
SLOBBER
(PREF.) PTYAL(O)
SPITTOON GABOON PIGDAN
SPITBOX CRACHOIR CUSPIDOR
SPIV RORTER
SPLAKE MENDIGO
SPLANCHNIC VISCERAL
SPLASH JAW LAP DASH GLOB
GOUT JAUP LOSH LUSH SKIT
SOSS SPAT WASH BLASH FLASH
FLICK FLOOD FLOSH PLASH
PLOUT QUASH SKIRP SLART
SLASH SLOSH SLUSH SQUAT
SWILK BEDASH DABBLE DOLLOP
FLOUSE JABBLE LABBER PLATCH
SLUNGE SOZZLE SPLOSH SPRENT
SQUIRT PLOUTER SPATTER
SPIRTLE SPLODGE SPLURGE
SWATTER SPLAIRGE SPLATHER
SPLATTER SPLOTHER

SPLUTHER SPLUTTER
(— OF COLOR) GOUT
(SLIGHT —) GILP
SPLASHBOARD FENDER
SPLASHER
SPLASHING SWASH FLASHY
JABBLE DASHING SPATTER
SPLUTTER SWASHING
SPLASHY BLASHY SLOPPY
SPRAWLY
SPLATTER DASH BLASH SPLAIRGE
SPLAY FLAN
SPLAYED FLEW FLUE
SPLAYFOOT FLATFOOT
SPLEEN IRE PIP BILE LIEN MELT
MILT RHEUM MALICE STOMACH
(PREF.) LIEN(O) SPLEN(I)(O)
(SUFF.) SPLENIA
SPLEENY PEEVISH
SPLENDID GAY BRAW FINE NEAT
RIAL BRAVE GRAND JOLLY NOBLE
PROUD REGAL ROYAL SHEEN
SHOWY STOUT TOUGH WALLY
WLONK CANDID COSTLY SIGHTY
SOLEMN SPIFFY SUPERB ELEGANT
GALLANT SHINING SUBLIME
TEARING BARONIAL CHAMPION
CLINKING COLOSSAL GLORIOUS
GORGEOUS MAJESTIC ORGULOUS
RATTLING SLASHING SPANKING
STUNNING TERRIFIC
(CHEAPLY —) TINNY
SPLENDIDLY FINE FINELY
SPROWSY
SPLENDOR SUN UMA GITE LUXE
POMP BLAZE GLARE GLEAM
GLORY SHEEN SHINE FULGOR
LUSTER LUSTRE PARADE RUFFLE
CLARITY DISPLAY JOLLITY
PANACHE GRANDEUR RADIANCE
SUMPTURE
SPLENETIC SULLEN VAPORY
PEEVISH
SPLENIC LIENAL
SPLICE FOOT JOIN SCAB PIECE
SCARE SKELB CROTCH PIECEN
SPLICING
SPLICER STRAPPER
SPLINE FIN FEATHER
SPLINT SCOB FANON MATCH
SPELK SPELL TASSE SPLENT
THOMAS CALIPER SPLINTER
(— FOR FRACTURE) JUNK
SPLINTER BROOM BURST PURSE
SHAKE SHIDE SHIVE SKELB SKELF
SLICE SPAIL SPALE SPALL SPALT
SPEEL SPELK SPELL SPILE SPILL
SPLIT SPOON SLIVER SPLEET
SPLINT FLINDER SHATTER
SLITHER SPLITTER
SPLINTERY SKELVY
SPLINTWOOD ALBURNUM
SPLIT AX AXE CUT RIT BUCK CHAP
CONE DUNT GAIG MALL MAUL
RASH REND RENT RIFT RIVE SKAG
SLAT TEAR BLAST BREAK BURST
CHECK CHINE SHAKE SHEAR
SKIVE SLENT SLIVE SMASH SPALD
SPALL SPLAT CLEAVE CLOVEN
CREASE DIVIDE FLAGGY FLERRY
SCHISM SPRING SUNDER BIVALVE
SHATTER SLITHER CREVASSE
SCISSION SCISSURE SPLINTER

(— FISH) SCROD
(— IN BOWLING) BEDPOSTS
(— OFF) SPALL SPAWL SCREEVED
(— TICKET) SCRATCH
(PREF.) SCHISTO SCHIZ(O)
SPLITTERMAN BOLTER
SPLITTING FLAGGY FISSION
SCISSION
(PL.) FILMS
(SUFF.) RHEXIS RRHEXIS
SPLOTCH DAB BLOB DASH HALO
SPOT FLICK SMUDGE SPECKLE
SPLATCH SPLURGE
SPLURGE BINGE SPRAY SPREE
SPLASH
SPLUTTER FUFF GLUTTER
SPATTER SPUTTER SPLOTHER
SPODOPTERA LAPHYGMA
SPODUMENE KUNZITE TRIPHANE
SPOIL MAR MUX ROT BLOT BOOT
COOK DAZE FANG FOIL FRAB
GAIN KILL MANK PELF PREY
ADDLE BITCH BLEND BLUNK
BOOTY BOTCH CROSS DECAY
LOUSE QUAIL QUEER SHEND
SPILL STAIN STRIP TOUCH TRASH
WALLY BOODLE BUGGER COOPER
CORPSE COSSET CURDLE DEFACE
DEFORM FORAGE INJURE
MANGLE PERISH RAVAGE TIDDLE
BAUCHLE BEDEVIL BLEMISH
CONNACH CORRUMP CORRUPT
ESTREPE INDULGE MULLOCK
PILLAGE PLUNDER SPOLIUM
TARNISH VIOLATE BANKRUPT
CONFOUND DISGRACE MISGUIDE
SPOLIATE
SPOILED BAD BLOWN DAZED
MUSTY CADISH STICKIT BRATTISH
(EASILY —) GINGER
SPOILER HARROWER
SPOILERS (AUTHOR OF —) BEACH
(CHARACTER IN —) ROY BILL
HELEN CHERRY DEXTRY STRUVE
CHESTER MALOTTE MCNAMARA
STILLMAN GLENISTER
SPOILFIVE MAW
SPOILS BAG LOOT SKIN SWAG
BOOTY FORAY SPOLIA PILLAGE
PLUNDER PICKINGS
SPOILSPORT NARK LETGAME
SPOILT MARDY
SPOKE RUNG QUOTH SPACK SPAKE
LOWDER SPONDIL SPONDYL
SPOKEN ORAL SAID VERBAL
SPOKESMAN MOUTH HERALD
PROPHET SPEAKER TRUMPET
MOUTHPIECE
SPOLIATION REIF SPOIL RAPINE
PILLAGE PLUNDER SPOILING
SPONGE BOT FORM MUMP POLE
SILK SORN SWAB ASCON CADGE
GRASS LUFFA SCAFF SHARK
SHIRK SHOOL SYCON ASCULA
BUMMER COSHER LEUCON
LOOFAH MALKIN MOPPET
RHAGON ROLLER YELLOW
BADIAGA BLEEDER GELFOAM
RADIATE SCOURER SCRUNGE
SYCONID ZIMOCCA DEADBEAT
HARDHEAD HEDGEHOG
MANDRUKA OLYNTHUS
REDBEARD SCROUNGE SILICEAN

SPHERIDA SUBERITE ZOOPHYTE
PORIFERAN
(YOUNG —) SEEDLING
(SUFF.) AENE
SPONGER BOT BUM TRAMP
BUMMER CADGER SPONGE
SCAMBLER SMOOTHER
SPONGINESS FOZINESS
SPONGING TRENCHER
SPONGY FOZY FUZZY QUAGGY
BIBULOUS
SPONSOR COACH GOSSIP SURETY
WITNESS
(— AT BAPTISM) HEAVE
SPONSORSHIP EGIS AEGIS
SPONTANEOUS FREE CARELESS
FREEWILL UNTAUGHT
SPONTANEOUSLY KINDLY SELFLY
SPOOK GYRE GHOST HAUNT
SCARE
SPOOL COB COP PIRN REEL QUILL
SPILL SPULE TWEEL TWILL
BOBBIN BROACH CHEESE COPPIN
CARRIER
(— FOR NETS) GURDY
SPOON HORN CUTTY LABIS SHELL
COCHLEA JUMBLER MUDDLER
SKIMMER SPINNER STIRRER
BARSPOON COCHLEAR GOBSTICK
(EUCHARISTIC —) LABIS
(FISHING —) TROLL
(LONG-HANDLED —) LADLE
(SKIMMING —) LINGEL SKIMMER
(SNUFF —) PEN
(PREF.) COCHLEARI LIGUL(I)
SPOONBILL AJAJA SPOONY
POPELER CICONIID
(PREF.) PLATALEI
SPOONFUL COCHLEARE
SPOON-SHAPED COCHLEAR
SPATULAR
SPOOR SIGN SPUR PISTE
SPORADIC POPPING ISOLATED
SPORANGIUM THECA OOTHECA
SPORE CYST SEED SPORID
AGAMETE AKINETE BISPORE
ISOLANT ISOLATE OOSPORE
SPORULE SWARMER CONIDIUM
EXOSPORE GONIDIUM
PROPAGULE
SPORES
(PREF.) CONI(DI)
SPOROCYST ZOOCYST SPOROSAC
SPORT FUN GIG KID MUM RIE RUX
SEE TOY ALSO GAME GAUD GLEE
JEST JOKE LAKE LARK PLAY PLOY
RAGE TAIT BOURD BREAK DALLY
DROLL FREAK MIRTH FROLIC
LAUGHS POPJOY RACING SHIKAR
SKIING BOATING CAMOGIE
DISPORT DUCKING FOWLING
MARLOCK PASTIME ROLLICK
ROUNDER SAILING SPANIEL
FALCONRY PLEASURE SKYDIVING
MOUNTAINEERING
(— OF HAWKING) RIVER
(BOISTEROUS —) HIJINKS
(JAPANESE —) KENDO AIKIDO
(ROUGH —) ROMP
(WATER —S) NAUTICS AQUATICS
(WINTER —S) SKIJORING
(PREF) LUDI
SPORTING VARMINT SPORTIVE

SPORTIVE GAY TAIT LARKY MERRY
FRISKY JOCUND LIVELY LUSORY
TOYFUL TOYING WANTON
COLTISH FESTIVE GAMEFUL
JESTING JOCULAR PLAYFUL
TOYSOME TRICKSY WAGGISH
FROLICKY GAMESOME PLAYSOME
PLEASANT SPORTFUL
SPORTIVENESS HELL KNAVERY
SPORTSMAN SPORT ATHLETE
SHIKARI
SPORTSMANLIKE CLEAN SPORTY
SPORTY FLASH RORTY FLASHY
RAKISH
SPORULE GRANULE
SPOT BIT DAB PIP WEM BLOT BLUR
CHUB DIRT DRAB FLAW GALL
MAIL MOIL MOLE PLOT SCAM SITE
SKIP SLUR SMUT SOIL SPAT TICK
AMPER BLACK CLOUD FLECK
GARLE GOODY GUTTA HATCH
JIMMY MACLE PATCH PLACE
PLECK POINT ROACH SMEAR
SPLAT STAIN SULLY TACHE TAINT
WHERE BLANCH BLOTCH DAPPLE
FOGDOG GERATE MACULE
MAZUCA MOTTLE SMUDGE
SMUTCH SPLECK STIGMA
BLEMISH CHARBON CHECKER
FLECKER FRECKLE GUTTULA
MASOOKA OCELLUS OLDWIFE
SMATTER SMITTER SPATTER
SPECKLE SPLOTCH SPOTTLE
STATION STIPPLE TERRAIN
FENESTRA LOCALITY MACULATE
PUNCTULE SPARKLET SPRINKLE
(— A SHIELD) GERATE
(— IN CLOTH) YAW
(— IN MINERAL) MACLE
(— IN PAPER) SHINER
(— IN SAW BLADE) BLOB
(— IN STEEL) STAR
(— IN WOOD) WEM
(— IN YARN) MOTE
(— OF INK) MONK
(— OF PAINT) DAUB
(— OF QUICKSAND) SUCKHOLE
(— ON CAT) BUTTON
(— ON CAT'S FACE) LAVALIER
(— ON EGG) EYE
(— ON FINGERNAIL) GIFT
(— ON FOREHEAD) TILAK TILAKA
(— ON HAWK) GOUT
(— ON HORSE) RACE SNIP STAR
RACHE
(— ON HORSE'S TOOTH) CHARBON
(— ON INSECT WINGS) BULLA
(— ON MOTH'S WINGS) FENESTRA
(— ON PLAYING CARD) PIP
(— ON SUN) FACULA GRANULE
SUNSPOT
(—S IN BOOKS) FOXING
(BARREN —) GALL
(BLIND —) SCOTOMA SCOTOSIS
(BROWN —) SPRAIN SPRAING
(CRUSTY —) SCAB
(ESSENTIAL —) EYE
(FERTILE —) OASIS
(FIRM — IN BOG) HAG
(GREEN — IN VALLEY) HAW
(HALLOWED —) BETHEL
(INFLAMED —) AMPER
(LEAF —) TIKKA BLACKARM

(LIVER —S) CHLOASMA
(LIVID —) TOKEN
(LOW —) DIP SWAMP HOLLOW
(RED —) FLEABITE
(RETIRED —) SHADE
(ROUGH — IN WOVEN GOODS) FAG
(ROUND —) BLOB
(SCABBY —) SCALD
(SECLUDED —) ALCOVE CLOISTER
(SHADY —) SWALE
(SKIN —) MOLE BLISTER FRECKLE
LENTIGO PETECHIA
(SMALL —) DOT PLECK STIGMA
LUNULET SPARKLET
(SOILED —) SLOP
(SORE —) BUBU BOTCH
(SWAMPY —) FLAM
(TIGHT —) JAM JACKPOT
(WEAK —) GALL HOLE CHINK
NERVE
(WORN —) FRAY FRET
(PL.) MOONING
(PREF.) MACUL(I)(O) SPIL(O)
SPOTLESS FAIR PURE WEMLESS
INNOCENT
SPOTLIGHT ARC SPOT DEUCE
SPOTTED PIED MARLY SCOVY
SHELD CALICO FIGGED HAWKED
MACLED MAILED MARLED MIRLED
PARDED SPOTTY TICKED
BRACKET BROOKED FINCHED
GUTTATE MOTTLED PARDINE
PIEBALD PINTADO SPARKED
SPECKED SPECKLY TIGROID
FRECKLED LITURATE MACULOSE
SPECKLED STIPPLED
(SUFF.) MACULATE
SPOTTED EAGLE RAY MILLER
OBISPO
SPOTTED FLYCATCHER COBWEB
RAFTER WALLBIRD
SPOTTED GUM EUCALYPT
SPOTTED JEWFISH GUASA
SPOTTED SANDPIPER TIPUP
TILTUP CREEKER TIPTAIL
PEETWEET
SPOTTED SPURGE DOVEWEED
SPOTTED WINTERGREEN
RATSBANE
SPOTTED WOODPECKER PICUS
WITWALL
SPOTTER DOTTER
SPOTTY MEALY PATCHY PLATTY
SCABBY SPOTTED
SPOUSE EX FERE MAKE WIFE
BRIDE MATCH PARTY FELLOW
MARROW CONSORT ESPOUSE
HUSBAND
SPOUT JET LIP BEAK DALE GEAT
GUSH NOSE SHOE ORATE SPILE
SPUME SPURT NOZZLE RIGGOT
SPLOIT SPROUT STRONE STROUP
BUBBLER FOUNTAIN GARGOYLE
(RAIN —) RONE
SPOUTER VAPORER
SPOUTING BLOW SALIENT
SPRAG TRAILER
SPRAGGER SCOTCHER
SPRAIN RICK CHINK STAVE THRAW
THROW WRAMP WREST WRICK
STRAIN WRENCH STREMMA
SPRAT SMY BLAY BRIT BRITT
SPRET SPRIT GARVIE ALFIONE

GARVOCK BRISLING
(—S CAUGHT EARLY IN SEASON)
DROVE
SPRAWL LOLL TAVE SPURL
SCRAWL GRABBLE SCAMBLE
SPARTLE SPELDER SCRAMBLE
SPRADDLE SPRANGLE STRADDLE
SPRAWLING SPRANGLY
SPRAY FOG HOSE SCUD SPRY
STEW SPREE STOUR SWISH TRAIL
TWIST SHOWER SPARGE SPLASH
SPRANG SPRITZ CURTAIN
SPAIRGE SYRINGE INHALANT
SPRANGLE
(— FROM SMALL WAVES) LIPPER
(— MASH) SPARGE
(— OF GEMS) AIGRETTE
(REDUCE TO —) NEBULIZE
SPREAD BED FAN LAY RUN COAT
DRAW FLUE SPAN TEER TELD
TUCK VEIN WALK APPLY CLEAM
CREEP FLARE KILIM PASTE SCALE
SLICE SPEND SPLAT SPLAY STALK
STREW WIDEN BUTTER EXTEND
FLANGE LARDER LAYOUT MANTLE
SETOUT THRUST UNFOLD
UNFURL BROADEN CANVASS
DIFFUSE DISPLAY DISTEND
EXPANSE EXPLAIN FEATHER
OPENING SCATTER STRETCH
DIASPORA DISPENSE DISPERSE
HUMIFUSE INCREASE MULTIPLY
SPLATHER STRAGGLE
(— ABROAD) TOOT BLAZE DELATE
SPRING DIVULGE EMANATE
(— APART) GAPE
(— AS GOSSIP) BUZZ
(— BY REPORT) BLOW NOISE
NORATE
(— DEFAMATION) LIBEL
(— FOR DRYING) TED
(— INTO) INVADE
(— LIKE GRAIN) FLOOR
(— NEWS) HORN
(— ON THICK) COUCH SLATHER
(— OUT) FAN FLOW OPEN ROLL
SPAN ASPAR BREDE SPLAT SPLAY
SPRAY EXPAND FLANGE FRINGE
MANTLE OUTLAY SPRAWL
UNLOCK DIFFUSE DISPAND
DISTENT EXPLAIN FEATHER
DIFFUSED SPRADDLE SPRANGLE
STRAGGLY
(— OUTWARD) FLARE
(— OVER) LAP DASH COVER
SUFFUSE
(— PAINT) KNIFE
(— THINLY) BRAY DRIVE TOUCH
SCANTY
(— TO) CATCH
(— TO THE WIND) SET
(EVENLY —) SUANT
(TAPESTRY-WOVEN —) KILIM
(PREF.) STRATO
(SUFF.) CHORE
SPREADER PLOW PLOUGH
SANDER
SPREADING FLAN BUSHY FLANGE
PATENT ASPREAD DIFFUSE
FLARING SPRAYEY PATULENT
PATULOUS SPRANGLY
(— OF LIGHT) HALATION
(— RAPIDLY) RUNNING

(NOT —) ERECT
(SLOW —) CREEPAGE
SPREE BAT BUM JAG BLOW BUST
GELL LARK RANT SOAK TEAR
TIME TOOT BEANO BINGE BOOZE
BURST DRINK DRUNK SOUSE
SPRAY BENDER BUSTER HOORAY
HURRAH JUNKET RANDAN
RANTAN RAZZLE SPLORE
BLOWOFF JAMBOREE WINGDING
SPRIG POINT
(—S FOR MOURNING) CYPRESS
SPRIGGER STRIPPER
SPRIGHTLINESS GAIETY AIRINESS
ALACRITY BUOYANCY VIVACITY
SPRIGHTLY GAY TID AIRY GNIB
PERT WARM ALIVE BRISK CANTY
CRISP DESTO MERRY PERKY
QUICK ALEGER BLITHE BREEZY
JAUNTY LIVELY SPANKY SPRACK
WIMBLE CHIPPER DELIVER
JOCULAR SPARKLY LIFESOME
PLEASANT
SPRING EN AIN BUG EYE FLY HOP
JET OJO URN VER WAX BATH
BOLT BOUT BUCK BUNT DART
FLOW FONT GEON HAIR HEAD
JUMP KELD LEAP PERT RISE SEEP
SKIP SOAK STEM URNA WALM
WARE WELL WIND YOAR ARISE
BOUND DANCE FLIRT FOUNT
FRESH GIHON GLENT GRASS
ISSUE LYMPH PRIME QUELL SALLY
SOURD SPEND SPOUT START
STEND SURGE THROW VAULT
BOUNCE CHARCO DERIVE
GAMBOL GEYSER JUMPER LOCKET
ORIGIN PIRENE RESORT RESULT
SILOAM SOURCE SPRINT VENERO
BUDTIME EMANATE ESTUARY
FLOUNCE GAMBADO PROCEED
REBOUND WRAPPER BACKSTAY
BANDUSIA CASTALIA FOUNTAIN
SPANGHEW ORIGINATE
(— AWKWARDLY) KEVEL
(— BACK) RECOIL RESULT RETORT
REBOUND
(— DOWN) ALIGHT
(— FORWARD) LAUNCH
(— FROM) DESCEND
(— OF THE YEAR) VER VOAR
(— ON SHEARS) BACKSTAY
(— SEASON) APRIL GRASS
BUDTIME
(— SUDDENLY) FLY BOUNCE
(— TO FASTEN NECKLACE) LOCKET
(— UP) ARISE SHOOT SPROUT
BURGEON UPSPRING
(BOILING —) TUBIG
(CARRIAGE —) ROBBIN
(ERUPTIVE —) WALM GEYSER
(GUSHING —) CHARCO
(HOT —) SPRUDEL
(INTERMITTENT —) NAILBOURN
(INTERMITTENT —S) GIPSIES
GYPSIES
(LAND —) LAVANT
(MECHANICAL —) RESORT
RESSORT
(MINERAL —) SPA BALNEARY
(SALT —) LICK SALINE
(WARM —S) THERMAE
(WATCH —) SLEEVE

(PREF.) CREN(O) CROUNO PEGO
(SUFF.) CRENE
SPRING BEAUTY LETTUCE
SPRINGBOARD BATULE TREMPLIN
SPRINGBOK GAZELLE SPRINGER
SPRING CHAPLET JAMMER
SPRINGE TRAP NOOSE SNARE
SPRINGILY BOUNCILY SPONGILY
SPRINGINESS GIVE LIFE
SPRINGING LAUNCH SALIENT
(— BACK) RESULT ELASTIC
(— FROM STEPS) GRADY
SPRINGLIKE VERNAL
SPRING ORANGE STYRAX
SPRINGTAIL PODURA FURCULA
PODURID SKIPTAIL
SPRINGTIME VER WARE
GERMINAL
SPRINGY WHIPPY ELASTIC
FLEXIBLE
SPRINKLE ASH DAG DEG BLOW
DAMP SHED SPIT FLASH SHAKE
SPURT WATER BEDROP DABBLE
POUNCE SPARGE SPRENT SPRINK
SQUIRT ARROUSE ASPERGE
ASPERSE DRIZZLE RANTIZE
SCATTER SKINKLE SKITTER
SPAIRGE SPARKLE SPARPLE
SPATTER SPATTLE SPERPLE
SPURTLE DISPUNGE INTERSOW
SPITTING SPRINGLE STRINKLE
(— IN BAPTISM) RANTIZE
(— OF RAIN) SPIT
(— SEED) SPRAIN
(— TOBACCO) BLOW
(— WITH FLOUR) DREDGE
(— WITH POWDER) DUST
(— WITH SALT) CORN
(— WITH SAND) SAND
SPRINKLED SEEDED SPRENT
(— OVER) BESPRENT
SPRINKLER SPARGER SPRAYER
WATERER DAMPENER STRINKLE
(HOLY WATER —) HYSSOP
SPRINKLING SEME LACING
SPARGE STRANK RANTISM
STIPPLE STOURING
(— OF PEOPLE) SALT
SPRINT BICKER SPRENT SPRUNT
SPRITE ELF HOB PUG PIXY PUCK
BUCCA DOBBY FAIRY HOLDA
PIXIE GOBLIN PILWIZ SPIRIT
SPOORN UMBRIEL COLTPIXY
GLAISTIG WATERMAN
(WATER —) NIX NECK NIXIE
NICKER
SPRITELY WIMBLE
SPROCKET WHELP
SPROUT BUD LAD PUT BROD CHIT
CHUN CION DRAW TOOT CATCH
CHICK SCUTE SHOOT SPEAR
SPIRE SPRIT SPURT BRAIRD
GERMEN RATOON SIRING STOVEN
TELLER TILLER BURGEON
COPPICE SPURTER TENDRON
BOURGEON PULLULATE
(— OF BARLEY) TAIL
(FIRST —S) BREER BRAIRD BREIRD
(STUMP —) TILLER
(PREF.) BLAST(O) CLAD(O)
CYM(I)(O)
(SUFF.) BLAST(IC)(Y) CLADOUS
SPERM(∧)(∧E)(∧L)(IA)(IC)(OUS)

(UM)(Y)
SPRUCE GIM DEFT JIMP NEAT
POSH SMUG SPRY TRIG TRIM
BRISK COMPT CRISP DINKY FRESH
JEMMY JIMMY NATTY NIFTY
SLICK SMART SMIRK SPIFF SPRIG
DAPPER PICKED SPONGE SPRUNT
SPRUSH FINICAL FOPPISH
SMARTEN SMICKER SPRUNNY
EPINETTE SPIFFING TITIVATE
(TRIMMED —) LOBSTICK
SPRUE RUNNER PSILOSIS
SPRUER GATER
SPRY AGILE BRISK QUICK NIMBLE
BOBBISH
SPUD SPADE TATER BARKER
PADDLE POTATO SPUDDER
SPUME EST BEES FOAM FROTH
YEAST
SPUNK GETUP SPRAWL SMEDDUM
SPUR ARM GAD GIG EDGE GAFF
GOAD KNAG MOVE STUD TANG
ARETE DRIVE PRICK PRONG
ROWEL SPICA SPURN BROACH
CALCAR DIGGER EXCITE FILLIP
FOMENT GAFFLE GRIFFE INCITE
MOTIVE OFFSET RIPPON SICKLE
SPERON WEAPON BICYCLE
GABLOCK INCITER LORMERY
SCRATCH COCKSPUR GAVELOCK
(— OF COCK) HEEL
(— ON HORSESHOE) CALK
(— TO ACTION) GOOSE
(—S OF COCK) WEAPON
(PART OF —) BAND CHAIN ROWEL
BUTTON
(PREF.) CALCARI
SPURGE BALSAM INTISY RICINUS
SUNWEED CATEPUCE DOVEWEED
FLUXWEED MILKBUSH MILKWEED
TITHYMAL WARTWEED
WARTWORT POINSETTIA
SPURIOUS BAD DOG FAKE SHAM
BOGUS FUNNY PHONY QUEER
SHICE SNIDE NOTHAL PSEUDO
BASTARD NOTHOUS POSTICHE
PINCHBECK SYNDIETIC
(PREF.) NOTH(O) PSEUD(O)
SPURN FOOT TACK SCORN REJECT
CONSPUE CONTEMN DECLINE
DESPISE DISDAIN
SPURRY YARR FRANK COWQUAKE
SANDWEED
SPURT JET GILP GIRD GOUT JAUP
SPAR SPIN BURST CHIRT FLASH
PULSE SALLY SPOUT GEYSER
RANDOM SPLURT SPRING
SPROUT SQUIRT SPATTER
SPUTTER SPIT FIZZLE SOTTER
SPATTER SPLUTTER
SPUTUM SPIT
SPY FLY PRY ESPY NARK NOSE
STAG TOOT TOUT WAIT WORM
LOWER PERDU PLANT SCOUT
SNEAP SPIAL SPION SPOOK
WATCH BEAGLE BEHOLD DESCRY
GAYCAT MOUTON PEEPER
PERDUE SEARCH SHADOW SPIRAL
TOUTER WAITER EXAMINE
LURCHER OTACUST SMELLER
SPOTTER WATCHER DISCOVER
EMISSARY HIRCARRA MOUCHARD
(— ON RACEHORSES) TOUT

(— UPON) LAY
(AUTHOR OF —) COOPER
(CHARACTER IN —) JACK BIRCH
HENRY SARAH CAESAR HARPER
HARVEY LAWTON PEYTON
FRANCES WHARTON ISABELLA
JEANETTE THOMPSON
DUNWOODIE SINGLETON
WELLEMERE
(PLANTED —) STOOGE
(POLICE —) SETTER
SPYBOAT VEDET VEDETTE
SQUAB PIPER SQUABBY SQUEAKER
SQUEALER SQUILGEE
SQUABBLE MUSS TIFF BRAWL
SCRAP BICKER JANGLE SQUALL
BOBBERY BRABBLE BRANGLE
CONTEND PRABBLE QUARREL
SWABBLE
SQUAD CREW DECURY TWENTY
PLATOON
(— OF DETECTIVES) HOMICIDE
SQUADRON BLUE SOTNIA
SQUADER
(CAVALRY —) RESSALAH
SQUALID DINGY DIRTY MANGY
SEEDY FILTHY FROWZY SORDID
SCABROUS SLOTTERY
SQUALL DROW FRET GUST MEWL
ROAR SCAT WAUL BARAT FRESH
PERRY SKELP BAYAMO FLURRY
SQUAWK BORASCA SUMATRA
TORNADO BLIZZARD BORASQUE
CHUBASCO
SQUALOR DIRT
SQUAMA ALULA TEGULA
SQUANDER SOT BLOW BLUE BURN
GAME LASH WARE SPEND SPILL
SPORT WASTE BEZZLE LAVISH
MAFFLE MUDDLE PADDLE PALTER
PERISH PLUNGE TIPPLE BRANGLE
CONSUME DEBAUCH DEBOISE
DISPEND PROFUSE SCAMBLE
SCATTER SKITTLE SLATHER
SWATTER EMBEZZLE MISSPEND
SQUATTER
SQUANDERER PRODIGAL
SQUANDERING WASTEFUL
SQUARE FIX EDGE EVEN FOUR
FULL LAME POST QUAD SUIT
AGREE CHECK CROSS FRAME
HUNKY PLACE PLAIN PLAZA
SUPER BLOCKY DINKUM ISAGON
MICKEY PIAZZA QUARRY ZENZIC
ZOCALO CARREAU CHECKER
COMMONS EMERALD UPRIGHT
QUADRANT QUADRATE
SQUADRON TETRAGON
(— A STONE) PITCH
(— FOR BOWLING SCORE) FRAME
(— OF CANVAS) SKATE
(— OF CLOTH) PANE
(— OF DOUGH) KNISH
(— OF FRAMING) PAN
(— OF GLASS) QUARREL
(— OF LINEN) PALL
(— OF TURF) DIVOT QUADREL
(— OFF) BUTT
(— ON BILLIARD TABLE) CROTCH
(— ON CHESSBOARD) HOUSE
POINT
(BUILDINGS FORMING —) INSULA
(CARPENTER'S —) NORMA

(CHURCH —) PARVIS
(LINEN —) SUDARIUM
(ONE-MILE —) SECTION
(PATTERN OF —S) DAMIER
(WOVEN —) SINKER
(PREF.) QUADR(ATO)(I)(U)
SQUARED HEWN QUARTO SQUARE
SQUARE DANCE TUCKER
SQUARE-DEALING WHITE
SQUARELY BUNG FAIR FULL
FLUSH SPANG FAIRLY DIRECTLY
SMACKDAB
(— AND SHARPLY) SMACK
SQUARISH BOXY
SQUASH PEPO QUAT GOURD
SQUAB CASHAW CUCURB
CUSHAW MARROW SIMNEL
SQUISH SQUUSH TURBAN
HUBBARD PUMPKIN CUCURBIT
CYMBLING PEPONIUM ZUCCHINI
SQUASH BUG STINKBUG
SQUASHY SWASHY SQUUSHY
SQUAT QUAT RUCK STUB SWAT
SWOT COWER DUMPY FUBSY
HUNCH PUDGY SQUAB FODGEL
HUNKER HURKLE QUATCH
STOCKY STUBBY SQUATTY
TAPPISH SQUATTLE THICKSET
SQUATINA RHINA
SQUATTER NESTER BYWONER
SQUAW JACK WEBB HOUND
WENCH MAHALA SQUARK
SQUAWBUSH SHOVAL
SQUAWFISH CHUB BOXHEAD
BIGMOUTH CHAPPAUL
SQUAWK SCHAWK SQUALL
SQUARK SQUAWL COMPLAIN
SQUAWROOT CLAPWORT
ELOTILLO
SQUEAK GIKE PEEP WEAK CHEEP
CHIRK QUEAK SCRAWK SCROOP
SQUEAL
SQUEAKING SCRANNEL
SQUEAKY CREAKY
SQUEAL PIP RAT FINK HOWL
SWEEL SCREAK WHISTLE
SQUEALER FINK CANARY
SQUEAMISH HELO NICE NAISH
PAWKY PENSY DAINTY DAUNCH
PENCEY QUAINT QUEASY SPICED
TICKLE WAIRCH WAMBLY FINICAL
MAWKISH WEARISH NAUSEOUS
OVERNICE
SQUEAMISHNESS NICETY
DISGUST MALAISE DELICACY
SQUEEZE EKE HUG JAM NIP CLAM
MULL MURE VISE ZEST BIRSE
BUNCH CHIRT CREEM CROWD
CRUSH PINCH PRESS SQUAB
SQUAT WRING GRUDGE QUEASE
SCRUMP SCRUZE SQUASH STRAIN
THRIMP THRING THRONG TWEEZE
TWITCH SCRINGE SCROOGE
SCROUGE SCRUNCH SCRUNGE
SQUEEGE SQUINCH COMPRESS
CONTRACT PRESSURE SHOEHORN
THRIMBLE THRUMBLE
(— FROM) SPONGE
(— IN) FUDGE
(— INTO) THRIMBLE
(— OUT) PINCH STRAIN
(ECONOMIC —) CRUNCH
(PREF.) PRESSI

SQUEEZED STRETTA STRETTO
SQUEEZER REAMER ALLIGATOR
SQUELCH QUELCH SQUASH
SQUISH SQUIDGE
SQUELCHER BLIZZARD
SQUETEAGUE DRUM DRUMMER
SQUETEE BLUEFISH CHICKWIT
WEAKFISH
SQUIB MOTE SKIT FILLER
EXPLODER
SQUID PLUG CALAMARY
SQUIFFED DRUNK BLOTTO
STONED
SQUIGGLE SCRIGGLE
SQUILL SCILLA SLANGKOP
(PREF.) SCILLI
SQUINT AWRY GLEE GLEG SKEN
SKEW BAGGE GLENT GLEDGE
GOGGLE SHEYLE SKELLY SQUINCH
SQUINNY
SQUINT-EYED GLEE GLEED
SQUINTING LOUCHE
SQUIRE SWAIN DONZEL JUNKER
TIMIAS ARMIGER ESQUIRE
SQUIRET YOUNKER HENCHMAN
SCUTIGER SERVITOR SQUARSON
SQUIREEN
SQUIRM CURL WIND TWINE
WRING WRITHE WRESTLE
WRIGGLE SCRIGGLE SQUIGGLE
SQUIRREL BUN CON BUNT LEAD
SCUG BUNNY XERUS BOOMER
CHIPPY GOPHER RODENT
TAGUAN ARDILLA SCHILLU
SCIURID CHIPMUNK EGGEATER
GRAYBACK JELERANG RATATOSK
CHICKAREE
(— SKIN) VAIR
(FLYING —) ASSAPAN
(PREF.) SCIURO
SQUIRRELFISH ALAIHI MARIAN
MOJARRA SERRANO SOLDIER
SANDFISH WELSHMAN
SQUIRREL SHREW TANA TUPAIA
PENTAIL
SQUIRT CHIRT SCOOT SKITE SLIRT
SPIRT SPOUT SPURT SQUIB SQUIT
SPLOIT SPRENT SPRITZ SCOOTER
SQUITTER

SRI LANKA
CAPITAL: COLOMBO
COIN: CENT RUPEE
FORMER NAME: CEYLON
GULF: MANNAR
MEASURE: PARA PARAH AMUNAM
PARRAH
POINT: PEDRO
STRAIT: PALK
TOWN: GALLE KANDY JAFFNA
MANNAR MATARA BADULLA
COLOMBO PUTTALAM
TREE: HORA PALU

S-SHAPED
(PREF.) SIGMO SIGMOID(O)
STAB DAB DAG JAB JAG JOB DIRK
GORE PINK POKE PROB SHIV
STOB STOG STUG YERK CHIVE
KNIFE POACH PRICK PRONG
STICK STOKE BROACH DAGGER
PIERCE POUNCE SLIVER STITCH
THRUST BAYONET STAGGER

PRICKADO STILETTO STOCCADO
STOCCATA
(— IN MIDBREAST) SLOT
STABBING THORNY JABBING
PUNGENT STICKING
(SUFF.) NYXIS
STABILITY POISE FIXURE BALANCE
SADNESS FIRMNESS SECURITY
CONSTANCY
STABILIZE FIX SET EVEN TRIM
POISE SCHOOL STEADY BALANCE
BALLAST STIFFEN
STABILIZER ACARDITE
STABLE BYRE FAST FIRM SURE
HARAS HEMEL SOLID SOUND
STALL STIFF STOUT TAMBO
LINTER LIVERY SECURE SICKER
STATIC STEADY STRONG STURDY
DURABLE EQUERRY LASTING
OXHOUSE SETTLED SHIPPEN
STABILE BALANCED IMMOBILE
RESIDENT STANDING PERMANENT
(ROYAL —S) MEWS
(PREF.) MONIMO
STABLEBOY LAD MAFU MAFOO
JACKBOY
STABLEMAN OSTLER HOSTLER
STACCATO TUT SECCO DETACHE
SALTATO RICOCHET SALTANDO
(NOT —) TENUTO
STACK COB MOW SOW BIKE DESS
LEET PACK PILE POKE RICK
CANCH CLAMP GOAVE POAKE
SCROO SHOCK STAKE STALK
STOCK COLUMN FUNNEL RICKLE
CALENDER STACKAGE
(— BRICKS) CLAMP SCINTLE
(— IN KILN) BOX
(— LUMBER) STICK
(— OF ARMS) PILE
(— OF BRICK) LIFT
(— OF CERAMICS) BUNG
(— OF CORN) SHOCK
(— OF FISH) BULK
(— OF GRAIN) RICK
(— OF HIDES) BED
(— OF PANS) SWEATER
(— OF SHEETS) BOOK
(HAY OR CORN —) HOVEL
(SMALL —) COB CANCH RICKLE
(TILE —) WELL
STACKER CROWDER PITCHER
STACKMAN
STACKYARD MOWIE MOWHAY
HAGGARD
STADIUM BOWL STADE STAGE
FURLONG STADION COLISEUM
STAFF PIN ROD TAU TAW CANE
CLUB KENT LIMB MACE MALL
MAUL PIKE POLE RUNG TREE
VARE YARD BATON CROOK CROSS
KEVEL NIBBY PEDUM PERCH
STAVE STICK SUITE VERGE
BASTON CADUCE CEPTER CLEEKY
CROCHE CRUTCH FAMILY FERULE
GROUND LITUUS MULETA
POTENT PRITCH RADIUS RISSLE
TAIAHA THYRSE WARDER
BACULUS BOURDON CAMBUCA
CROSIER CRUMMIE DISTAFF
FESTUCA PALSTER SCEPTER
SCEPTRE STADDLE THYRSUS
CADUCEUS CRUMMOCK

PARTISAN PASTORAL PLOWFOOT
TIPSTAFF
(— AT END OF NET) BRAIL
(— OF AUTHORITY) VARE VERGE
(— OF COOKS) BOUCHE
(— OF OFFICIALS) OMLAH
(— WITH CROSSPIECE) POTENT
(BISHOP'S —) BAGLE BACULUS
CROSIER CROZIER PASTORAL
(FIELD MARSHAL'S —) BATON
(FORKED —) LINSTOCK
(GRADUATED —) LIMB
(HOTTENTOT —) KIRVI
(MAGICIAN'S —) RHABDOS
(NEWSPAPER —) DAYSIDE
(NUBIAN —) KUERR
(PILGRIM'S —) BURDEN
(PLASTERER'S —) BEATER
(SHEPHERD'S —) KENT CROOK
(SPARTAN —) SCYTALE
(TEACHING —) FACULTY
(THIEVES' —) FILCH
(PREF.) LITUI SCEPTRO
STAG HART ROYAL SPADE STAIG
WAPITI BULLOCK KNOBBER
POINTER KNOBBLER
(— OF THE 3D YEAR) SPIRE
(— OF 2ND YEAR) BROCKET
(— OF 8 YEARS OR MORE) ROYAL
(— THAT HAS CAST HIS ANTLERS)
POLLARD
(DEAD —) MORT
(HORNLESS —) HUMMEL
(TURNED TO —) ACTAEON
(3-YEAR OLD —) SPADE
(PREF.) ELAPH(O)
STAG BEETLE LUCANID
STAGE LEG BANK GEST POST STEP
TREK APRON DUMMY ETAGE
FLAKE GRADE PEGME PHASE
POINT SCENE STAIR STATE
BOARDS DEGREE HEMMEL
PERIOD PHASIS STRIDE CATASTA
MANSION ROSTRUM STADIUM
INSTANCE PLATFORM SCAFFOLD
PROSCENIUM
(— FOR DRYING FISH) FLAKE
(— FOR HAY) HEMMEL
(— IN DELIRIUM) TILMUS
(— IN FEVER) FLUSH
(— IN PORCELAIN FURNACE)
HOWELL
(— IN TRAVELING) GEST
(— MANAGER) REGISSEUR
(— OF CUPOLA) LANTERN
(— OF DEVELOPMENT) ERA
BLOSSOM
(— OF FUNGUS) OIDIUM
(— OF GLACIATION) RISS WURM
ACHEN MINDEL
(— OF INSECT) INSTAR
(— OF LIFE) AGE ASRAMA
ASHRAMA
(— OF MITOSIS) ANAPHASE
PROPHASE
(— OF PERSONALITY) LATENCY
(— OF ROCKET) BOOSTER
(— OF THEATER) SCAENA
THEATRON
(— WHERE SLAVES WERE SOLD)
CATASTA
(BOTTOMMOST —) CELLAR
(COMIC —) SOCK

(EARLIEST —) PRIME
(FINAL —) CLOSE FINISH STRETCH
(FIRST —) YOUTH SPRING
(FLOATING —) DUMMY
(FLOOD —) CREST
(GEOLOGICAL —) GUNZ GLACIAL
SENONIAN
(GLACIATION —) WURM
(INITIAL —) INFANCY
(LANDING —) STAIR BRIDGE
STAITH STELLING
(MOVING —) PEGMA PEGME
(PART OF —) FLY ARCH DROP FLAT
WING APRON DRAPE BATTEN
BORDER BRIDGE CENTER RETURN
TEASER CURTAIN ENTRANCE
TORMENTOR PROSCENIUM
(RADIO —) STEP
(THIRD —) AUTUMN
(PREF.) SCENO
STAGECOACH DILLY STAGE
STAGEHAND GRIP DAYMAN
GAFFER
STAGER SOAKER
STAGGER REEL ROLL STOT DAVER
DODGE HODGE LURCH PITCH
STITE STOIT DACKER DAIDLE
FALTER GOGGLE STAVER STIVER
SWAVER TOTTER WALTER
WAMBLE WELTER WIGGLE
WINTLE MEGRIMS STACHER
STACKER STAMMER STOITER
STOTTER STUMBLE SWAGGER
VANDYKE WAUCHLE TITUBATE
STAGGERBUSH LAMBKILL
STAGGERED STURTAN STURTIN
STAGGERS DUNT GOGGLES
MEGRIMS STAVERS VERTIGO
STAGHEAD SPIKETOP
STAGING STAGE CRIPPLE DERRICK
HURRIES
STAGNANCY STASIS
STAGNANT DEAD DULL INERT
STILL STATIC COBWEBBY
SLUGGISH STAGNATE STANDING
STAGNATION STASIS TORPOR
LANGUOR
STAID SET CIVIL GRAVE SOBER
DEMURE STEADY EARNEST
SERIOUS DECOROUS
STAIN DYE LIT WEM BLOT BLUR
BUFF DIRT DRAB FILE FOIL HURT
MEAL MOLE RUST SCAM SLUR
SMAD SMIT SMUT SOIL SPOT
TASH BLACK BLEND BRAND
CLOUD DIRTY HATCH PAINT
PLECK SMEAR SPECK SULLY
TACHE TAINT TINGE WEMMY
BREATH GIEMSA IMBRUE INFAMY
INFECT MACULA SMIRCH SMUDGE
SMUTCH SPLASH STIGMA SUDDLE
ATTAINT BESTAIN BLEMISH
DEPAINT DISTAIN SLUBBER
SOILURE SPATTER SPLOTCH
STADDLE TARNISH BESMIRCH
CARMALUM DISCOLOR DISGRACE
DISHONOR FLYSPECK MACULATE
PYRONINE TAINTURE
(— BLACK) EBONIZE
(— IN LINEN) MELL
(— ON BRICK) SCUMMING
(— WITH BLOOD) ENGORE
(PREF.) MACUL(I)(O) SPIL(O)

STAINED FOXY RUSTY SMUDGY SMUTCHY
(**— BY DECAY**) DOATY
(**— WITH BLOOD**) BLOODY IMBRUED
STAINED GLASS VITRAIL
STAINER TRACER
STAINLESS PURE CHASTE INNOCENT
STAIR STY GREE RUNG STEP DEGREE COCHLEA ESCALIER
(**MINING —**) LOB
(**WINDING —**) VICE CARACOL CARACOLE
(PL.) PAIR PITCH FLIGHT DANCERS ESCALIER
STAIRCASE SCALE ESCALIER
(**PART OF —**) MOLD POST RAIL NEWEL RISER TREAD NOSING LANDING BALUSTER BANISTER HANDRAIL BALUSTRADE
(**SPIRAL —**) SPIRAL CARACOLE
STAIRWAY STOOP GREESE PERRON DESCENT ESCALIER
(**— ON RIVER BANK**) GHAT
(**CURVED —**) SWEEP
(**SHIP'S —**) LADDER
(**WINDING —**) VICE TURNPIKE
STAITH TIP
STAKE BET HOB LAY SET TAW VIE WAD WED ANTE BENT GAGE MAIN PALE PAWN PEEL POOL PUNT RISK STAB STOB TREE WAGE PITCH SPILE SPOKE SPRAG STOCK STOOP STOUR WAGER BAIKIE CAULIS CHANCE CORNER CROTCH ENGAGE GAMBLE HAZARD IMPONE LOGGAT LOGGET PALING PICKET STOWER TRUNCH WEDFEE STOATER STUCKEN VENTURE INTEREST PALISADE PEASTICK STUCKING
(**CART —**) RUNG
(**COMPULSORY — IN POKER**) BLIND
(**GAMBLING —**) MISE
(**POINTED —**) SOULE SOWEL PICKET
(**SURVEYORS' —**) HUB
(**TETHERING —**) PUTTO
(**TINSMITH'S —**) TEEST
(PL.) JACKPOT
STAKE-SHAPED SUDIFORM
STALACE COLUMELLA
STALE OLD COLD FLAT HOAR PALL SICK WORN BLOWN DUSTY FROWY HOARY MOLDY MUSTY RAFTY SANDY TRITE FROWZY MOULDY STUFFY EXOLETE FROUGHY INSIPID OVERWORN STAGNANT
(**DAMP AND —**) WAUGH
STALEMATE PATT STALE
STALK BUN RAY CORN HAFT MOTE POLE RISP STAM STEG STEM TIGE QUILL SCAPE SHANK SPEAR SPIRE STAKE STALE STEAL STIPE STUMP WRIDE COULIS RATOON STIPES CASTOCK FUNICLE PEDICEL PETIOLE SPINDLE CAUDICLE FILAMENT PEDUNCLE PODETIUM STALKLET STERIGMA PETIOLULE
(**— OF BUCKWHEAT**) STRAW
(**— OF CRINOID**) COLUMN

(**— OF GRAIN**) RESSUM RIZZOM
(**— OF GRASS**) BENT SPEAR
(**— OF HAY**) RISP
(**— OF PLANT**) SPINDLE TENACLE
(**— OF SPOROGONIUM**) SETA
(**— OF STAMEN**) FILAMENT
(**— OF SUGAR CANE**) RATOON
(**— OF UMBEL**) RAY
(**—S OF GRAIN**) KARBI STRAW
(**CABBAGE —**) CASTOCK
(**CROSSBOW —**) TILLER
(**DRY —**) KEX KECK BENNET
(**FLOWER —**) SCAPE
(**HOLLOW —**) BUN KEX KECK
(PL.) HAULM STRAW WRIDE IWAIWA
(**PREF.**) CAUL(I)(O) CULMI
STALKLESS SESSILE
STALKY AND COMPANY (**AUTHOR OF —**) KIPLING
(**CHARACTER IN —**) JOHN MTURK ARTHUR BEETLE STALKY CORKRAN GILBERT
STALL BAY BIN BOX CUB PEW BULK CRIB SPAR STAW BOOSE BOOSY BOOTH CRAME PITCH STAND STASH CARCER CARREL STANCE TRAVIS WICKET BALAGAN CABINET SHAMBLE SHIPPEN BUTCHERY STANDING TRAVERSE
(**— FOR TIME**) HAVER STRETCH
(**— IN CLOISTER**) CAROL
(**— IN COAL MINE**) BREAST WICKET
(**— IN MUD**) STOG
(**— IN ROMAN CIRCUS**) CARCER
(**BISHOP'S —**) TRIBUNE
(**CHURCH —**) PEW
(**THEATER —**) LOGE FAUTEUIL
STALLED STOODED
STALLION SIRE STAG STUD ENTRE HORSE COOSER ENTIRE STALLAND
STALWART RUDE STARK STIFF WIGHT STRONG STURDY BUIRDLY VALIANT
STAMEN TAMIN STAMMEL
(**PREF.**) ANDR(O)
(**SUFF.**) STEMONOUS
STAMINA GUTS SAND BOTTOM
STAMMER FAM HACK MANT STOT STUT GANCH WLAFF FAFFLE FALTER FAMBLE HACKER HAFFLE HAMMER HOCKER HOTTER MAFFLE MAMMER YAMMER FRIBBLE STUMBLE STUTTER HESITATE SPLUTTER TITUBATE
STAMMERING HACK PSELLISM TRAULISM BALBUTIES
STAMP CHOP COIL DRUB FAKE MARK NIXY PAUT POSS RUFF SEAL SNAP TYPE APPEL BLOCK DOLLY ERROR FRANK LABEL LOCAL NIXIE PRINT PUNCH STOCK STOMP STUNT TENOR TOUCH WRITE ACCENT CACHET CLICHE DOCKER FULLER INCUSE INCUTE INDENT LOCKUP PASTER POUNCE SCRIBE SHAPER SIGNET STRAMP STRIKE CARRIER CHARACT EDITION IMPRESS IMPRINT MINTAGE POUNDER REPRINT SEEBECK SPECIAL

SQUELCH STICKER TAXPAID WRAPPER HALLMARK ORIGINAL PRESSURE PUNCHEON
(**— AFTER ASSAY**) TOUCH
(**— BOOK COVER**) BLIND
(**— FOR CUTTING DOUGH**) DOCKER
(**— HERRING BARREL**) DUNT
(**— HIDES**) STOCK
(**— HOLES**) STOACH
(**— OUT**) SCOTCH
(**— WITH DIE**) DINK
(**BOOKBINDING —**) BLOCK FILLET
(**CANCELLING —**) KILLER
(**HALF OF —**) BISECT
(**HAND —**) CANCELER
(**OFFICIAL —**) CHOP
(**POSTAGE —**) AIR DUE CAPE FAKE HEAD ERROR LABEL LOCAL BUREAU INVERT AIRMAIL BICOLOR CHARITY CLASSIC REPRINT STICKER ADHESIVE COLONIAL ORIGINAL SPECIMEN PRECANCEL
(**REVENUE —**) FISCAL TAXPAID
(**SMART —**) APPEL
(PL.) MIXTURE KILOWARE
(**PREF.**) TIMBRO
STAMP-COLLECTING PHILATELY TIMBROLOGY
STAMPEDE RUSH BLITZ CHUTE DEBACLE STAMPEDO
STAMPER FANCIER STOMPER
STAMPING TITLING
STANCE STATION STANDING
(**— OF GOLFER**) ADDRESS
(**— OF HORSE**) GATHER
STANCH FIRM STEM STIFF STOUT HEARTY TRUSTY STAUNCH FAITHFUL RESOLUTE
STANCHION BAIL PITON CROTCH CRUTCH STENCIL STANCHEL STANCHER
STAND GO JIB SET BANK BEAR BIER DESK HALT RACK RANK REST STAY STEL ZARF BIPOD BLOCK ERECT FRAME FRONT KIOSK STALL STICK STONE STOOL CASTER COLORS ENDURE HASTER INSIST PATTEN PILLAR SMOKER STANCE STANZA STOUND STRIKE TEAPOY TRIPOD TRIVET CONSIST DIOPTER EPERGNE FOURBLE LECTERN STATION TABORET TRESTLE TROLLEY ATTITUDE BLEACHER COATRACK CROWFOOT FRIPPERY GUERIDON HASTENER INKSTAND POSITION SCAFFOLD STALLAGE STANDING STANDISH STILLAGE STILLING STILLION
(**— AS SPONSOR**) FANG HEAVE CHRISTEN
(**— AT AN ANGLE**) CATER
(**— AT ATTENTION**) BACK
(**— BACK**) BACCARE BACKARE
(**— BEFORE A FIRE**) FOOTMAN
(**— BEHIND**) COVER
(**— BY**) SERVE
(**— CLOSE**) CROWD ENVIRON
(**— FASTENED TO MESS TABLE**) CROWFOOT
(**— FIRM**) STAY
(**— FOR**) DENOTE
(**— FOR AUCTIONING**) BLOCK

(**— FOR BARRELS**) JIB THRALL
(**— FOR COFFIN**) BIER
(**— FOR COMPASS**) BINNACLE
(**— FOR CONFINING HEAT**) HASTER HASTENER
(**— FOR DRESSES**) FRIPPERY
(**— FOR DRILL PIPE**) FOURBLE
(**— FOR FINJAN**) ZARF
(**— FOR TILES**) CRISS
(**— FOR WRITING MATERIALS**) STANDISH
(**— GUARD**) COVER
(**— IN AWE**) FEAR
(**— OF FOREST**) GROWTH
(**— OF PLANTS**) STOOL
(**— OFF**) ARDINT
(**— ON AND OFF SHORE**) BUSK
(**— ON END**) STARE UPEND
(**— ON TWO FEET**) BIPOD DUOPOD
(**— OUT**) CUT TOOT FLAUNT
(**— READY**) ABIDE
(**— STILL**) HO HOO HALT STAY
(**— TO SHOOT**) ADDRESS
(**— TREAT**) MUG SHOUT
(**— UNSTEADILY**) STAGGER
(**— UP STIFF**) STIVER
(**— UP TO**) CONFRONT
(**— WITH LEGS APART**) STRIDE
(**CAKE —**) CURATE
(**CONCESSION —**) JOINT
(**FIRECLAY —**) CRANK
(**ONE-NIGHT —**) GIG
(**PRINTER'S —**) BANK FRAME
(**PULPIT-LIKE —**) AMBO
(**RAISED —**) PERGOLA
(**SCULPTOR'S —**) CHASSIS
(**SHOOTING —**) BUTT
(**THREE-LEGGED —**) TRIVET
STANDARD ALEM DICK FIAR FLAG GAGE IDEA MARK NORM SIGN TEST TOUG ALLOY BOGEY CANON CHECK DOLLY DRAKE EAGLE GAUGE IDEAL JEDGE MODEL NORMA SCALE STAND STOOL AQUILA ASSIZE BANNER CORNET DOLLIE FILLER NORMAL SOCKET SQUARE STAPLE TIPONI TRIPOD VIOLLE ANCIENT CLASSIC DECORUM DRAPEAU LABARUM MODULUS STANDER BRATTACH GONFALON MOUNTING ORIFLAMB ORTHODOX VEXILLUM
(**— IN GATE**) STRIKE
(**— OF ACCURACY**) COCKER
(**— OF CONDUCT**) LINE GNOMON
(**— OF PERFECTION**) IDEAL
(**— OF PERFORMANCE**) BOGY BOGEY BOGIE
(**— OF PITCH**) DIAPASON
(**— OF QUALITY**) GRADE
(**—S OF BEHAVIOR**) ETHICS
(**CONVENTIONAL —**) PIETY
(**LIGHT —**) CARCEL
(**NOT —**) BASTARD
(**TURKISH —**) ALEM TOUG
(PL.) LIGHTS HOLSTERS
STANDARD-BEARER CORNET ENSIGN ALFEREZ ANCIENT STALLER SIGNIFER STANDARD VEXILLARY
STANDARDIZE FORDIZE MACHINE CALIBRATE
STANDEL STORER

STANDING BEING ERECT STATE CREDIT ESTEEM REGULAR RESPECT PRESTIGE STAGNANT PERPENDICULAR
(— ALONE) SEPARATE
(— BY ITSELF) ABSOLUTE DETACHED
(— ERECT) HORRENT
(— INCOORDINATION) ASTASIA
(— ON STEPS) DEGRADED
(— OUT) BOLD EXTANT SALIENT
(— OUT CLEARLY) EMINENT
(— POSITION) OFFHAND
(HIGH —) WORSHIP
(MODE OF —) STANCE
(SOCIAL —) LEVEL ESTATE FASHION STATION
(PREF.) STAT(O)
(— IN SECOND PLACE BEYOND) DVI EKA
(SUFF.) STASIA STASIS STAT STATIC STATICS
STANDPATTISM TORYISM
STANDPOINT STANCE
STANDSTILL JIB SET HALT REST STAY STAND STANCE
STANZA CALL RANN ENVOI ENVOY STAFF STAND STAVE VERSE BASTON DIXAIN DIZAIN OCTAVE SEPTET SESTET SEXTET SIXAIN STANCE STANZO HUITAIN SEXTAIN STROPHE TRIOLET TROILUS CINQUAIN OCTONARY QUATRAIN QUINTAIN RISPETTO SETTAINE TRISTICH TROPARION
(SUFF.) STICH
STAPES STIRRUP
STAPLE LOOP FLOSS STITCH SHACKLE STEEPLE VERVELLE
(PL.) BROKES
STAR COR SUN BEID FIRE LAMP ASTER COMES DWARF EXCEL GIANT MOLET RISHI SHINE STARN ALNATH ASTRAL BINARY COUPLE DOUBLE ETOILE LUCIDA MULLET NITHAM SHINER SPHERE STELLA BENEFIC DINGBAT ESTOILE GEMINID STARLET STARNIE ASTERISK ASTEROID HEXAGRAM MALEFICE PENTACLE SUBDWARF SUBGIANT VARIABLE
(COMPANION —) COMES
(DOG —) SEPT SOPT SEPTI SIRIUS
(EVENING —) VENUS VESPER VESTAR EVESTAR HESPERUS
(FEATHER —) COMATULA
(FILM —) VEDETTE
(GUIDING —) LOADSTAR LODESTAR
(MORNING —) VENUS DAYSTAR PHOSPHOR
(NEW —) NOVA
(OFFICER'S —) PIP
(PULSATING —) CEPHEID
(SHOOTING —) BOLIDE LEONID METEOR COWSLIP SHOOTER
(SPECIFIC —) YED ADIB ALYA ATIK CAPH ENIF ENIR IZAR KIED MAIA NAOS PHAD SADR VEGA WEGA ACRAB ACRUX AGENA ALCOR ALGOL ALKES ANCHA ARNEB CHARA DABIH DELTA DENEB DUBHE GIEDI GUIAM GUYAM HAMAL HAMUL JUGUM MERAK

MIZAR NIBAL NIHAI PHACD PHAET RIGEL SAIPH SPICA TEJAT WASAT WEZEN ZOSMA ADHARA ALHENA ALIOTH ALKAID ALMACH ALTAIR ALUDRA APOLLO ARIDED CASTOR CELENO CHELEB DIPHDA ELNATH ETAMIN GIENAH HYADES KOCHAB LESUTH MAASYM MARKAB MARKEB MARSIC MEGREZ MENKAR MENKIB MEROPE MIRACH MIRFAK MIRZAM NEKKAR PHECDA POLLUX PROPUS RANICH SCHEAT SHEDIR SIRIUS THABIT THUBAN ACUBENS ALBIREO ALCHIBA ALCYONE ALGENIB ALGIEBA ALGORAH ALMAACK ALNILAM ALNITAK ALPHARD ALPHIRK ALSHAIN ANTARES AZIMECH BUNGULA CANOPUS CAPELLA ELECTRA GIANSAR GOMELZA GRUMIUM MEBSUTA MELUCTA MENCHIB MINTAKA MUFRIDE POLARIS PROCYON REGULUS ROTANIM RUCHBAR SCHEDAR SEGINUS SHELLAK STEROPE TARAZED TAYGETA TEGMINE THEENIM ACHERNAR ALPHECCA ARCTURUS ASTERION DENEBOLA GRAFFIAS HERCULES MULIPHEN PRAESEPE SCALOOIN SCHEMALI SHERATAN
(THREE —S) KIDS ELLWAND TRIANGLE
(7 —S OF GREAT BEAR) CAR
(PREF.) ASTER(O) ASTR(I)(O) SIDERO STELLI
(SUFF.) ASTER ID
STAR APPLE CAIMITO
STARCH AMYL ARUM SAGO STIFF TIKOR AMYDON AMYLUM CONJEE FARINA FECULA CASSAVA CURCUMA FAECULA MARANTA TALIPOT AMIDULIN DRESSING FIXATURE GLUCOSAN
(— IN SOLUTION) AMIDIN
(ANIMAL —) GLYCOGEN
(PREF.) AMYL(I)(O)
STARCHED FORMAL
STARE EYE BORE DARE GAPE GAUM GAUP GAWK GAWP GAZE GOVE GYPE KIKE LOOK PORE GLARE GLORE GLOWER GOGGLE EYEBALL
(— IDLY) GOVE GOAVE
(— VACANTLY) GOWK
(COLD —) FISHEYE
STARFISH PAD STAR ASTERID RADIATE ASTEROID OPHIURAN
(PART OF —) ARM ANUS DISC SPINE EYESPOT TENTACLE MADREPORITE
STARING STEEP ASTARE GOGGLE GOOGLY HAGGARD
STAR JELLY STARSHOT
STARK BUCK CARK FAIR HARD CRUDE HARSH NAKED STIFF STARCH DESOLATE METALLIC
STARLIKE ASTRAL SPHERY
STARLING SALI STARE BEAVER PASTOR TILYER SPREEUW STARNEL STAYNIL CHEPSTER CUTWATER SHEPSTER
STARRED LIZARD HARDIM

STARRING FEATURED
STARRY ASTRAL STARNY STELLED SIDEREAL
STAR SAPPHIRE ASTERIA ASTRION ASTROITE
STAR-SHAPED ASTROID
START DIG SET BOLT BOUN DART DASH HEAD JERK JUMP OPEN TURN WHIP ARISE BEGIN BIRTH BRAID BREAK BUDGE ENTER FLIRT GLENT ONSET RAISE ROUSE STORT THROW ABRADE BOGGLE BROACH FLINCH INTEND OFFSET OUTSET SETOFF SETOUT STRIKE TWITCH GETAWAY OPENERS OPENING STARTLE SUNRISE COMMENCE CONCEIVE INCHOATE OUTSTART
(— A HORSE) WINCE
(— ASIDE) SHY SKIT DODGE
(— BACK) RESILE
(— BURNING) SPIT KINDLE
(— FERMENTATION) PITCH
(— OF BIRD'S FLIGHT) SOUSE
(— OUT) FRAME INTEND
(— UP) JUMP ASTART ASTERT
(SUDDEN —) SHY SQUIRT
STARTER KOJI
(BUNG —) FLOGGER
STAR THISTLE CALTROP CALTHROP
STARTING INCOMING
STARTLE SOHO ALARM SCARE SHOCK START STURT AFFRAY BOGGLE BOOGER FRIGHT FRIGHTEN SURPRISE
STARTLING ALARMING SHOCKING
STARVATION LACK PINE FAMINE
STARVE CLEM FAST FAMINE FAMISH AFFAMISH
STARVED MEAGER MEAGRE STARVEN
STARVED-LOOKING SLINK
STARVELING SHARGAR SHARGER
STARVING CLUNG
STARWORT ASTROFEL ASTROPHEL
STATE WU LAY PUT SAY CASE MODE NAME POMP PORT TERM TIFF COVIN ESTER ESTRE POLIS SPEAK STADE TERMS TUATH WHACK AFFIRM AGENCY ASSERT ASSURE CAESAR EFFEIR EMPIRE ESTATE IMPORT NATION PLIGHT POLICY POLITY RENDER RIALTY SOVIET STATUS STEVEN CIVITAS DECLARE DESERET DUKEDOM ENOUNCE EXPOUND EXPRESS KINSHIP PROPOSE SPECIFY STATION TERMINE CEREMONY DEVACHAN DOMINION FRANKLIN HEGEMONY INDICATE KINGSHIP REPUBLIC STATELET PREDICAMENT
(— EXPLICITLY) DEFINE
(— FORMALLY) ENOUNCE
(— IN NORTH CAROLINA) FRANKLIN
(— OF AFFAIRS) CASE ARRAY STATUS
(— OF ALARM) GAST FEEZE SCARE
(— OF AMAZEMENT) STOUND
(— OF ANGER) FUME
(— OF APATHY) STUPOR
(— OF BEING CUT) SCISSION

(— OF BEING DRAWN) TRACTION
(— OF BEING OVERFULL) PLETHORA
(— OF BEING POISONOUS) TOXICITY
(— OF BEING WORSE) PEJORITY
(— OF CONCENTRATION) DHARANA SAMADHI
(— OF CONFUSION) FOG FLAP HACK MUSS CHAOS SWIRL HASSLE HUBBUB FLUMMOX TROYTOWN
(— OF CONSECRATION) IHRAM
(— OF COOPERATION) HOOKUP
(— OF DISASTER) SMASH
(— OF DISORDER) HELL MUSS FANTAD ANARCHY
(— OF DISSENSION) SCISSION
(— OF DISTURBANCE) GARBOIL
(— OF DOUBT) MIST
(— OF EAGERNESS) HURRY
(— OF ECSTASY) SWOON
(— OF ENCHANTMENT) SPELL
(— OF ENLIGHTENMENT) BODHI
(— OF EXALTATION) FURY ECSTASY
(— OF EXCITATION) FOMENT
(— OF EXCITEMENT) FRY FLAP GALE HIGH SNIT STEW FEEZE HOIGH DITHER DOODAH HUBBUB FANTEEG FLUSTER KIPPAGE SWELTER FANTIGUE
(— OF EXHAUSTION) GONENESS
(— OF FEAR) FUNK JELLY SCARE
(— OF HAPPINESS) ELYSIUM PARADISE
(— OF HEALTH) EUCRASIA
(— OF HUMILIATION) DUST
(— OF IDEAL PERFECTION) UTOPIA
(— OF IMPERFECTION) SCARCITY
(— OF INACTION) DEADLOCK
(— OF INCIPIENCE) EMBRYO
(— OF INTENSITY) BUILD
(— OF IRRITABILITY) FUME GALL FANTAD
(— OF JOY) JUBILEE
(— OF MELANCHOLY) GLOOM
(— OF MENTAL INACTIVITY) TORPOR
(— OF MENTAL READINESS) ATTITUDE
(— OF MIND) CUE HIP CASE MOOD HUMOR FETTLE CARAPACE
(— OF MISERY) HELL GEHENNA
(— OF NEGLECT) LIMBO
(— OF OPPOSITION) DEFIANCE
(— OF OSTRACISM) COVENTRY
(— OF PERFECTION) SIDDHI
(— OF PERTURBATION) CRISE
(— OF PREOCCUPATION) CARE
(— OF READINESS) GUARD
(— OF REALITY) ACT
(— OF REJECTION) GATE
(— OF REPOSE) KEF CALM
(— OF RETIREMENT) GRASS
(— OF REVERIE) DUMP
(— OF SENSITIVITY) NERVES
(— OF SLUGGISHNESS) COMA
(— OF SUSPENSE) TRANCE
(— OF SUSPENSION) ABEYANCE
(— OF TENSION) FANTEEG STRETCH FANTIGUE
(— OF THE SOUL) BARDO
(— OF THINGS) FARE PASS
(— OF TRANQUILLITY) KEF KIF PEACE

(— OF UNCERTAINTY) FOG FLUX
(— OF UNREST) FERMENT
(— OF WEATHER) FREEZE
(— OF WORRY) TEW SWEAT
FANTAD
(— POSITIVELY) AFFIRM
(— UNDER OATH) ALLEGE
(AGITATED —) FUSS SNIT STIR
CHURN STORM LATHER SWIVET
(BLISSFUL —) NIRVANA
(BUFFER —) GLACIS
(CHINESE —) WU SHU WEI
(DAZED —) DAMP
(DEPRESSED —) GLOOM WALLOW
(DISTURBED —) STIR STORM
UNREST
(DOMINANT —) SUZERAIN
(DROWSY —) DOVER
(EMOTIONAL —) FEVER FEELING
(FEUDAL —) WEI
(FICTITIOUS —) FABLE
(FILTHY —) DIRT
(FREE —) SAORSTAT
(GLOOMY —) DUMP
(HIGHEST —) SUPREME
(HOLY —) IHRAM
(HORIZONTAL —) LEVEL
(INDONESIAN —) NEGARA
(IRISH —) TUATH
(LIQUID —) FLUOR FLUIDITY
(LOWEST —) BEDROCK
(MARRIED —) SPOUSAL
(MENTAL —) EARNEST DELUSION
(MORBID —) HIP IODISM
(MORMON —) DESERET
(NEUTRAL —) BUFFER
(PECUNIARY —) FACULTY
(PERTURBED —) DEVIL
(PROFOUND —) DEPTH
(SWISS —) CANTON
(ULTIMATE —) END
(UNCULTIVATED —) FERITY
(UNFAVORABLE —) FOULNESS
(VERIFIED —) FACT
(PREF.) CRATO TYP(I)(O)
(SUFF.) ANCE ANCY ANDRA
ANDRIA ATE ATION CY DOM ENCE
ENCY ERY HEAD HOOD ION
ISATION ISM ITY IZATION MENT
NESS OSIS SHIP TH
(CHARACTERIZED BY —) SOME
(DISEASED —) SIS
(MORBID —) IASIS
STATED GIVEN CERTAIN
(DIRECTLY —) EXPRESS
STATE FAIR (AUTHOR OF —) STONG
(CHARACTER IN —) PAT ABEL
WARE EMILY FRAKE HARRY
MARGY WAYNE ELEANOR
GILBERT MELISSA
STATEHOUSE CAPITOL
STATELINESS STATE DIGNITY
MAJESTY GRANDEUR
STATELY DATE BURLY GRAND
LARGO LOFTY NOBLE PROUD
REGAL STATE STOUT AUGUST
COUPON PORTLY SOLEMN
SUPERB TOGATE GALLANT
BARONIAL IMPOSING MAESTOSO
MAJESTIC STATEFUL
STATEMENT SAY BILL VOTE WORD
AXIOM BRIEF COUNT DIXIT LIBEL
STATE STORY BELIEF DICTUM

DOCKET EXPOSE FACTUM
RETURN SAYING SPEECH
ACCOUNT ADDRESS ANALOGY
DISSENT EPITAPH EPITOME
FORMULA INVOICE MENTION
SHOWING ABSTRACT ANTINOMY
ARGUMENT AVERMENT BULLETIN
DELIVERY EQUATION EXPLICIT
JUDGMENT PROPOSAL SCHEDULE
SENTENCE SPEAKING SYNGRAPH
SYNOPSIS
(— AS PRECEDENT) AUTHORITY
(— OF OPINION) CHANT
(— OF RELATIONS) THEOREM
(— ON DRUG LABEL) LEGEND
(AUTHORITATIVE —) DICTUM
(CASUAL —) REMARK
(CONCISE —) SCHEME APHORISM
(CONDENSED —) RESUME
SYNOPSIS
(DEFAMATORY —) LIBEL
(EXAGGERATED —) STRETCH
(FABRICATED —) CANARD
(FINAL — OF ACCOUNT) AUDIT
(FINANCIAL —) BUDGET
(FOOLISH —) INANITY
(FORMAL —) CITATION
(IRRATIONAL —) ALOGISM
(OBSCURE —) ENIGMA
(PLAINTIFF'S —) BODY
(POMPOUS —) BRAG
(PUBLIC —) OUTGIVING
(SELF-CONTRADICTORY —)
PARADOX
(SOOTHING —) SALVE
(UNTRUE —) LIE
STATER COLT TURTLE PEGASUS
CYZICENE
STATEROOM BIBBY CABIN
STATESMAN GENRO SOLON
FATHER STATIST WARWICK
JACOBEAN WEALSMAN
AMERICAN HAY JAY LEE AMES
BURR CLAY FISH HALE HULL OTIS
POLK REED ROOT RUSK BAKER
BLAND BORAH CHASE GERRY
HENRY MARCY OLNEY WYTHE
BARUCH BLAINE BOWLES BROOKE
BUNCHE CARTER EVARTS FOSTER
GORHAM HURLEY MCKEAN
MORRIS NORRIS RODNEY
SEWARD SUMNER TOOMBS
ACHESON ALDRICH BARBOUR
CLINTON CUMMINS DANIELS
EVERETT KELLOGG LANSING
LAURENS LINCOLN MORRILL
SHERMAN STIMSON WEBSTER
FRANKLIN GALLATIN HAMILTON
MILLEDGE PINCKNEY RANDOLPH
RUTLEDGE SCHUYLER TRUMBULL
DICKINSON ELLSWORTH
FULBRIGHT PICKERING
WASHINGTON SCHUSCHNIGG
BRECKENRIDGE
ARGENTINIAN MITRE ALBERDI
CARCANO DORREGO FRONDIZI
RIVADAVIA
AUSTRALIAN SEE COOK BRUCE
EVATT LYONS PRICE BARTON
DEAKIN FISHER HOLDER HUGHES
ISSACS LAWSON PARKES SCULLIN
NICHOLSON
AUSTRIAN BACH BRUCK KHESL

RAMEK UNGER BADENI GLASER
PLENER RENNER SEIPEL TAAFFE
BURESCH FIRMIAN HELFERT
KAUNITZ KOERBER SCHOBER
STADION BELCREDI DOLLFUSS
HAYMERLE HUSSAREK
LAMMASCH EGGENBERG
BELLEGARDE METTERNICH
SCHMERLING BARTENSTEIN
GOLUCHOWSKI PILLERSDORF
STARHEMBERG
BELGIAN SPAAK DEVAUX HYMANS
JACOBS JASPAR MERODE ROGIER
ANETHAN NOTHOMB THEUNIS
ZEELAND DECHAMPS BEERNAERT
DELACROIX SCHOLLAERT
VANDERVELDE
BOLIVIAN FRIAS MONTES
BALDIVIESO
BRAZILIAN ABREU FEIJO CAXIAS
BERNARDES MAGALHAES
BULGARIAN DANEV SAVOY
MALINOV TSANKOV LIAPCHEV
KARAVELOV STAMBOLOV
RADOSLAVOV STAMBOLISKI
CANADIAN KING GOUIN JETTE
SCOTT TACHE VIGER BORDEN
BOWELL FISHER FOSTER HUGHES
MANION SIFTON TUPPER
BENNETT BRODEUR CARTIER
DOHERTY LAURIER MEIGHEN
PEARSON RALSTON TRUDEAU
MICHENER THOMPSON
MACDONALD MACKENZIE
PELLETIER CARTWRIGHT
LAFONTAINE DIEFENBAKER
FITZPATRICK
CHILEAN CRUZ RIOS EGANA
MONTT FREIRE CRUCHAGA
OHIGGINS BALMACEDA
ALESSANDRI
CHINESE WU KOO YEN KUNG
COLOMBIAN ZEA HERRAN
COSTA RICAN CASTRO
CUBAN PALMA
CZECH BENES HACHA HODZA
KRAMAR RIEGER SVEHLA UDRZAL
MASARYK
DANISH HALL ZAHLE BLUHME
ESTRUP MONRAD RANTZAU
GULDBERG STAUNING
NEERGAARD GRIFFENFELD
DUTCH CATS FOCK ASSER DOUSA
FAGEL HAREN COLIJN DEWITT
KUYPER GROTIUS HEINSIUS
KLEFFENS HEEMSKERK
KARNEBEEK VANDIEMEN
BARNEVELDT BEEREENBROUCK
ECUADORIAN FLORES
EGYPTIAN SADAT ZIWAR
ENGLISH FOX LAW PYM EDEN
HOPE HYDE LAMB LONG MORE
PEEL PITT VANE WEBB WOOD
AMERY BEVAN BURKE ELIOT
HEATH HOARE JUXON LEWIS
NIGEL PAGET BLOUNT BRIGHT
COBDEN CRIPPS CURZON GEDDES
GIBSON GRAHAM HARLEY
HATTON HEATON HOLLES
MORELY MORTON SAVILE SELDEN
SIDNEY SOMERS TEMPLE WOLSEY
ASQUITH BALDWIN BALFOUR
CANNING GIFFARD GOSCHEN

HALDANE HAMPDEN HERRIES
LAMBTON OSBORNE READING
RUSSELL STANLEY STEWART
SWINTON WALPOLE WINDHAM
WYKEHAM WYNDHAM ADDERLEY
ANNESLEY BEAUFORT CARTERET
COURTNEY CROMWELL DISRAELI
GARDINER GOULBURN HAMILTON
HARCOURT HASTINGS MACAULAY
MONTFORT ROBINSON STANHOPE
VILLIERS ADDINGTON BLEDISLOE
CHURCHILL CUSHENDUN
FITZNEALE FITZPETER FORTESCUE
GAITSKELL GLADSTONE
GLANVILLE GODOLPHIN
GREENWOOD GRENVILLE
HUSKISSON KIMBERLEY
LANSDOWNE LIVERPOOL
MACDONALD NORTHCOTE
STRAFFORD WAKEFIELD
BIRKENHEAD PALMERSTON
ROCKINGHAM WALSINGHAM
WELLINGTON WHITELOCKE
WILLINGDON BOLINGBROKE
CHAMBERLAIN FITZWILLIAM
SHAFTESBURY SOUTHAMPTON
CHESTERFIELD
ESTONIAN PATS STRANDMAN
FINNISH KALLIO CAJANDER
MECHELIN RELANDER STAHLBERG
MANNERHEIM
FRENCH DARU MOLE DUPUY
FAURE FAVRE FERRY FOULD
MARET MONIS PASSY RIBOT
SIMON SUGER SULLY AVENOL
BARROT BERNIS BIGNON BRIAND
CARNOT CASSIN DOUMER
DUPRAT FLEURY FOUCHE GUIZOT
LOUBET MELINE NECKER PERIER
ROUHER THIERS TURGOT
COLBERT DECAZES GRAMONT
HERRIOT MAISTRE MARIGNY
MAUPEOU MAZARIN MOLLIEN
NOGARET REGNIER ROUVIER
SEGUIER VILLELE VIVIANI
CHOISEUL CONSTANS DALADIER
DELCASSE FONTANES FRANCOIS
GAMBETTA HANOTAUX PAINLEVE
POINCARE POMPIDOU PORTALIS
BOURGEOIS CHAMPAGNY
CLEMENTEL DOUMERGUE
FALLIERES LAFAYETTE
MILLERAND RICHELIEU
VERGENNES BARTHELEMY
CLEMENCEAU TALLEYRAND
WADDINGTON BASSOMPIERRE
CHATEAUBRIAND
GERMAN BLOS CUNO FALK MARX
SOLF BEUST JAGOW NOSKE
PAPEN BRANDT GERBER KRANTZ
LUTHER MAURER MIQUEL
BRUNING CAPRIVI CURTIUS
FABRICE GESSLER STEPHAN
ADENAUER BISMARCK HAINISCH
HERTLING HOLSTEIN KUHLMANN
SEVERING SPANHEIM BENNIGSEN
ERZBERGER MICHAELIS
BERNSTORFF FEHRENBACH
HILFERDING RICHTHOFEN
SCHLEICHER STRESEMANN
WINDTHORST ZIMMERMANN
SECKENDORFF
GREEK ZAIMES KANARES KORIZES

RANGABE RHALLES BULGARIS
GOUNARES KONDYLES PANGALOS
PERICLES TIMOLEON DINARCHUS
DRAGOUMES PERIANDER
TIMOTHEUS TRIKOUPES
TSALDARES TSOUDEROS
VENIZELOS SKOULOUDES
THEMISTIUS THERAMENES
DEMOSTHENES THRASYBULUS
THEMISTOCLES
KOUMOUNDOUROS
MAVROKORDATOS
MICHALAKOPOULOS
HUNGARIAN DEAK VASS CSAKY
SZELL TISZA BANFFY BAROSS
EOTVOS GOMBOS HORTHY
LONYAY TELEKI BETHLEN
HORVATH HUNYADI KOSSUTH
WEKERLE ANDRASSY SZECHENYI
MARTINUZZI
ICELANDIC HAFSTEIN SIGURDSSON
INDIAN NOON GUPTA NEHRU
SINHA BAJPAI GANDHI SASTRI
IRISH HYDE ANDREWS GRATTAN
MCNEILL COSGRAVE CRAIGAVON
ISRAELI DAYAN
ITALIAN BALBO BERTI CIANO
CROCE FACTA LANZA MANIN
NITTI ROCCO ROSSI SELLA VOLPI
BONGHI CAVOUR CRISPI FEDELE
GRANDI PEPOLI RUDINI SFORZA
ADRIANI ALFIERI AZEGLIO
CADORNA CAIROLI DURANDO
GRAVINA MAMIANI MANCINI
ORLANDO PELLOUX PONTANO
SONNINO TANUCCI TITTONI
VILLARI ALBERONI CIBRARIO
CORRENTI DEPRETIS GIOLITTI
LAFARINA LUZZATTI MATTIOLI
MENABREA NICOTERA RATTAZZI
RICASOLI SALANDRA SCIALOIA
FEDERZONI GARIBALDI
GUERRAZZI LAMARMORA
MINGHETTI MONTANELLI
ZANARDELLI MACHIAVELLI
LAMBRUSCHINI
JAPANESE ITO GOTO HARA KATO
SATO MUTSU OKUBO OKUMA
INOUYE KANEKO KOMURA
MAKINO TANAKA HAYASHI
ITAGAKI IWAKURA IYEYASU
KATSURA SAIONJI HIRANUMA
KIYOMORI MATSUOKA
NOBUNAGA TERAUCHI
YAMAGATA YAMAMOTO
HAMAGUCHI HIDEYOSHI
MATSUKATA WAKATSUKI
LATVIAN KVIESIS ULMANIS
MEIEROVICS
LIBERIAN TUBMAN TOLBERT
LITHUANIAN SMETONA
VOLDEMARAS
MEXICAN DIAZ ALAMAN ZULOAGA
IGLESIAS
NEW ZEALAND FOX HALL WARD
ALLEN VOGEL COATES FORBES
FRASER MASSEY SEDDON
ATKINSON STAFFORD
NORWEGIAN KOHT FALSEN
HAMBRO HAGERUP KNUDSEN
SVERDRUP MICHELSEN
MOWINCKEL NYGAARDSVOLD
PERUVIAN CORNEJO CADLERON

BENAVIDES MENDIBURU
PHILIPPINE ROXAS OSMENA
QUEZON
POLISH BECK WITOS DMOWSKI
ZALESKI ZALUSKI SIKORSKI
SKRYNSKI KOSCIUSKO PILSUDSKI
PADEREWSKI WOJCIECHOWSKI
PORTUGUESE PAES COSTA
POMBAL ALMEIDA ARRIAGA
CARMONA MACHADO SALAZAR
CARVALHO SALDANHA
SANTAREM
PRUSSIAN BULOW
ROMAN CATO CINNA CAESAR
CICERO LAELIUS RUFINUS
CAMILLUS MAECENAS STILICHO
FABRICIUS FLAMINIUS SERTORIUS
SYMMACHUS CASSIDORUS
HORTENSIUS
ROMANIAN CARP MANIU IONESCU
CATARGIU MIRONESCU
TITULESCU MARGHILOMAN
KOGALNICEANU
RUSSIAN BIRON GIERS WITTE
BLUDOV CANCRIN KALININ
MOLOTOV MUNNICH SIEVERS
TOLSTOI AVERESCU CHICHKOV
DMITRIEV GOLITSYN IZVOLSKI
LAMSDORF POTMEKIN STOLYPIN
CALINESCU CHICHERIN
GORCHAKOV GOREMYKIN
GRIBOEDOV MENSHIKOV
SPERANSKI NESSELRODE
PROTOPOPOV
SOUTH AFRICAN BOTHA BRAND
REITZ SMUTS STEYN KRUGER
SPRIGG COGHLAN HERTZOG
MERRIMAN
SCOTTISH HUME KNOX BEATON
GORDON MURRAY JAMESON
MAITLAND RANDOLPH
WARRISTON ELPHINSTONE
SERBIAN GRUIC
SPANISH LUNA ALAVA GODOY
OSUNA PEREZ GALVEZ MANUEL
TORENO ABASCAL ALARCON
ISTURIZ MENDOZA NARVAEZ
SAGASTA SILVELA ENSENADA
ESCOSURA MANRIQUE OLIVARES
QUINTANA ZORRILLA
CALOMARDE ESCOIQUIZ
ESPARTERO REQUESENS
JOVELLANOS MIRAFLORES
SWEDISH EDEN GEER HORN TOLL
BRAHE ESSEN UNDEN HANSSON
LINDMAN SANDLER BRANTING
FORSSELL EHRENSVARD
GYLLENBORG WENNERBERG
OXENSTIERNA OXENSTJERNA
HAMMARSKJOLD
SWISS ADOR DROZ FAZY KERN
MUSY FURER GOBAT MEYER
MOTTA BLUMER ESCHER MINGER
MULLER DEUCHER BLUNTSCHLI
SCHULTHESS
TURKISH INONU SARACOGLU
URUGUAYAN RIVERA
VENEZUELAN VARGAS BOLIVAR
MONAGAS BETANCOURT
YUGOSLAV PASIC PROTIC
ZIVKOVIC DAVIDOVIC
MARINKOVIC PRIBICEVIC
STATICE ARMERIA LIMONIUM

STATION BY BYE FIX ORB RUN SET
BASE GARE POST RANK ROOM
SEAT STOP BEING BERTH CHOKY
DEPOT PLACE POSTE SIEGE
STAGE STALL STAND STATE
DEGREE LOCATE STANCE
CONTROL CUARTEL DIGNITY
HABITAT OUTPOST GARRISON
PILTDOWN POSITION STANDING
TERMINAL TERMINUS TRANSFER
(— IN BASEBALL) BASE
(— IN LIFE) BEING CALLING
(— OF HERON) SEDGE SIEGE
(CONCEALED —) AMBUSH
(CUSTOMS —) CHOKEY
(EXALTED —) PURPLE
(POLICE —) TANA TANNA THANAH
KOTWALEE
(POST —) DAK
(RADIO —S) CHAIN NETWORK
(RAILWAY —) GARE CABIN
(SIGNALLING —) BANTAY BEACON
(SURVEYING —) STADIA
(TRADING —) FACTORY
(WAY —) TAMBO
STATIONARY SET FAST FIXED
STILL LEDGER STATIC DORMANT
SITFAST STABILE STATARY
IMMOBILE
STATIONERY PAPER PAPETERIE
STATISTICIAN ANALYST STATIST
STATOBLAST SPORE
STATUARY IMAGERY
STATUE HERM ICON IDOL IKON
TERM BUSTO HERMA IMAGE
MOSES AGALMA BRONZE HERMES
MEMNON STATUA WEEPER
XOANON ILISSUS PASQUIN
PICTURE STATURE STATUTE
ACROLITH CARYATID MARFORIO
MONUMENT PANTHEUM
PORTRAIT VICTORIA
(— ENDOWED WITH LIFE) GALATEA
(— OF ATHENA) PALLADIUM
(— OF GIGANTIC SIZE) COLOSSUS
(COLOSSAL —) GOG MAGOG
STATUETTE WAX EMMY OSCAR
WINNIE TANAGRA FIGULINE
FIGURINE SIGILLUM
(AWARD —) GRAMMY
STATURE PITCH GROWTH HEIGHT
INCHES WASTME CAPACITY
STATUS RANK SEAT PLACE STATE
ASPECT FOOTING STATURE
POSITION STANDING SITUATION
(— OF YOUNGER SON) CADENCY
(HIGH —) CACHET
(LEGAL —) CAPUT
(SECONDARY —) BACKSEAT
STATUTE ACT LAW LEX DOOM
EDICT ASSIZE DECREE SETNESS
SITTING STATUTUM TANZIMAT
(— FAIR) MOP
STATUTORY LEGAL
STAUNCH FAST STOUT TRUSTY
FAITHFUL STALWART
STAVE LAG SLAT STAP SHAKE
STAFF STOVE VERSE BASTON
STANZA WATTLE
(— IN) BILGE BULGE
(SET OF —S) SHOOK
(PL.) LAGGEN LAGGIN STICKS
STAVING

STAY DAY GET LIE BASE HOLD
LEND PROP REST SIST STOP WAIT
ABIDE ABODE APPUI DEFER
DELAY DEMUR DWELL LEAVE
STINT TARRY THOLE ARREST
ATTEND BIDING DETAIN EXPECT
GUSSET POTENT REMAIN TIMBER
UPHOLD EMBASSY JIBSTAY
LAYOVER MANSION SOJOURN
SUSPEND BACKSTAY CONTINUE
FORESTAY HORNSTAY MAINSTAY
MARTINGALE
(— AWAY) SKIP
(— BEHIND) LAG
(— CLEAR) AVOID
(— FOR) AWAIT
(— THE NIGHT) BUNK HOSTLE
(— WITH) STICK
(PRIEST'S —) STATION
(TAILORING —) BRIDLE
(PL.) JUMPS JUPES BODICE
STAY-AT-HOME HOMEBODY
HOMESTER
STAYER BONER
STAYLACE AGLET AIGLET
STAYSAIL JUMBO
STEAD LIEU ROOM VICE PLACE
BEHALF
STEADFAST PAT SAD FAST FIRM
SURE TRUE ROCKY STAID STEER
STABLE STANCH STEADY CERTAIN
EXPRESS SETTLED STAUNCH
VALIANT CONSTANT FAITHFUL
RESOLUTE STALWART
STEADFASTLY FIRM FIRMLY
INTENTLY
STEADILY SAD FAST STEADY
STEADINESS NERVE BALANCE
STEADING ONSET ONSTEAD
STEADY GUY SAD BEAU EVEN
FIRM SURE TRIG TRUE CANNY
FRANK LEVEL SOBER STUDY
SUANT TIGHT SICCAR SMOOTH
STABLE STANCH BALLAST
EQUABLE STABILE STATARY
STAUNCH CONSTANT DECOROUS
DILIGENT FAITHFUL RESOLUTE
TRANQUIL UNSHAKEN
(— AT ANCHOR) HOLSOM
STEAK BROIL SHELL FLITCH
TUCKET GRISKIN PORTERHOUSE
STEAL BAG CAB CLY COP FOX GYP
LAG MAG NAP NIM NIP RAP RIG
BONE CHOR COON CRIB FAKE
GLOM HOOK KNAP LIFT LURK
MAGG MAKE MILL NAIL NICK
PEAK PICK PRIG SLIP SMUG
ANNEX BOOST BRIBE CLOUT
CREEP FETCH FILCH FLIMP FRISK
GLIDE HARRY HEIST HOIST LURCH
MOOCH MOUCH PINCH PLUCK
POACH SCOFF SHAKE SHARP
SHAVE SLIDE SNAKE SNARE
SNEAK STALK SWIPE TOUCH
TRUFF COLLAR CONVEY FINGER
HIJACK MOOTCH NOBBLE PILFER
RIPOFF SNITCH STRIKE THIEVE
TWITCH BESTEAL CABBAGE
PLUNDER PURLOIN SCHLEPP
SKYUGLE SNABBLE SNAFFLE
SURREPT ABSTRACT CRIBBAGE
EMBEZZLE LIBERATE MANARVEL
PECULATE SCROUNGE

SHOPLIFT PLAGIARIZE
(— A GLANCE) GLIME
(— A WATCH) FLIMP
(— ALONG) SLIME SLINK
(— AWAY) LOOP SLINK
(— BY ALTERING BRANDS) DUFF
(— CALVES) NUGGET
(— CATTLE) DUFF RUSTLE
(— COPPER FROM VESSEL'S
BOTTOM) TOSH
(— OFF) RUN
(— SLYLY) SCROUNGE
STEALER (CATTLE —) DUFFER
ABACTOR
STEALING STALE
(PREF.) KLEPT(O)
STEALTHILY SIDLINS THIEFLY
SIDELINS
STEALTHY CATTY PRIVY ARTFUL
FELINE TIPTOE CATLIKE FURTIVE
SNEAKING THIEVISH
STEAM OAM ROKE STEM BLAST
SMOKE SWEAT VAPOR BREATH
POTHER CUSHION
(PREF.) ATM(O) ATMID(O)
STEAMBOAT KICKUP STEAMER
STEAMER CLAM LINER TENDER
STEAMER CUNARDER
STEAMER DUCK RACER LOGHEAD
STEAMSHIP SCREW STEAM
STEAMER SEATRAIN SHOWBOAT
STEAM SHOVEL NAVVY NAVVIE
STEATIN MULL
STEATITE LARDITE POTSTONE
SOAPROCK
STEATOPYGOUS RUMPY
STEED NAG ROIL HORSE MOUNT
STEAD PEGASUS SLEIPNER
STEEL RAIL BLOOM BRACE FUSIL
TERNE WEAPON WHITTLE
FLEERISH
(— FOR STRIKING FIRE) ESLABON
(— FOR USE WITH FLINT) FUSIL
FURISON FLEERISH
(— INLAID WITH GOLD) KOFT
KOFTGARI
(DAMASCUS —) DAMASK
(INDIAN —) WOOTZ
(MOLTEN —) HEAT
STEELER BONER
STEELING ACIERAGE
STEELWORKER HOOKER
STICKMAN STRANDER STRANNER
STEELYARD BISMAR BISMER
DESEMER DOTCHIN STATERA
STEENBRAS BISKOP
STEEP SOP BATE BOLD BOWK
BUCK DEAR DRAW DUNG ELIX
LIME MASH MASK SOAK STAY
STEW STEY BLUFF BRANT BRENT
HATCH HEAVY HILLY QUICK
SHARP SHEER SOUSE STIFF
ABRUPT BLUFFY CLIFFY CLIFTY
DECOCT IMBIBE INFUSE SPRUNT
STEEPY ARDUOUS BRASQUE
CLIVOSE INSTEEP PRERUPT
STICKLE HEADLONG MACERATE
SATURATE SIDELING STIFFISH
STRAIGHT PRECIPITOUS
STEEPED SODDEN
STEEPING SOUSE INFUSION
STEEPLE SPEAR SPIRE
STEEPLECHASE CHASE GRIND

STEER COX PLY AIRT BEEF BULL
HELM LEAD STEM STOT GUIDE
SPADE SPADO STERN TOLLY
CANNER RUDDER BULLOCK
STOCKER COWBRUTE MOSSHORN
NAVIGATE
(— VEHICLE) DRIVE
(FAT —) BEAST
(HORNLESS —) NOT NOTT
(VICIOUS —) LADINO
(WILD —) YAW YEW COWBRUTE
(YOUNG —) STOT STOTT
STEERAGE STERN
STEERER SLUER CAPPER
STEERSMAN PILOT WHEEL
PATRON SLEWER CANOPUS
SHIPMAN STEERER COXSWAIN
HELMSMAN SEACUNNY
STERNMAN WHEELMAN
COCKSWAIN
STEGOMYIA AEDES
STEIN SHANT
STEINBOCK BOUQUETIN
STELE SHAFT EUSTELE
STELLAR STARRY
STELLATE ASTROSE
STEM BUN BASE BEAK BEAM BINE
BIRN CANE CULM CURB NOSE
PIPE PROW RISP ROOT RUNT
SHAW STUD ARISE FILUM HAULM
SCAPE SCREW SHAFT SHANK
SHOOT SPIRE STALE STALK STEAL
STICK STIPE STOCK STRAW
THEME TRUNK TUBER BRANCH
CAUDEX CAULIS DERIVE SCAPUS
SPRING CAULOME CONTAIN
FULCRUM HOPBINE HOPVINE
PEDICEL PETIOLE PLASHER
SARMENT SPINDLE STEMLET
TIGELLA CAULICLE ENGENDER
EPICOTYL FORESTEM PEDUNCLE
PIPESTEM TIGELLUM
(— OF ARROW) SHAFT
(— OF BANANAS) COUNT
(— OF GLASS) BALUSTER
(— OF GRAPES) RAPE
(— OF HOOKAH) SNAKE
(— OF MATCH) SHAFT
(— OF MUSHROOM) STIPE
(— OF MUSICAL NOTE) TAIL FILUM
VIRGULA
(— OF PIPE) STAPPLE
(— OF PLANT) AXIS RUNT CAULIS
(— OF SHIP) PROW STEMPOST
(— OF TREE) BOLE CAUDEX
(—S OF CULTIVATED PLANTS)
HAULM
(BULBLIKE —) CORM
(DRY WITHERED —) BIRN
(EDIBLE —) EDDO
(GRIEF —) KELLY
(MAIN — OF DEER'S ANTLERS) BEAM
(ORNAMENTAL —) STAVE
(PITHY JOINTED —) CANE
(THORNY —) LAWYER
(TWINING —) BINE
(PREF.) CAUL(I) CORM(O) CULMI
SCAPI STIRPI
(SUFF.) DENDRON OME
STEMLESS ACAULINE
STEMMA OCELLUS OCELLANA
PEDIGREE
STEMMER STRIPPER

STENCH FOGO HOGO FETOR SMELL
STINK WHIFF FOETOR MEPHITIS
STENCIL (— PROCESS) POCHOIR
STENCILED GOFFERED
STENOGRAPHY SHORTHAND
STENOSIS SMALLING
STEP CUT FIT JOG PEG PIP BEMA
DESS FOOT GREE LINK PACE PEEP
RUNG STAP BRASS CORTE DODGE
FLIER FLYER GRECE NOTCH POINT
STAGE STAIR TOOTH TRACE
TREAD DEGREE GRADIN RUNDLE
STRIDE WINDER CURTAIL
DESCENT FOOTING GRADINE
GRADING COONJINE DEMARCHE
DOORSTEP FOOTPACE FOOTSTEP
FORESTEP PREDELLA STRATLIN
(— ASIDE) DIGRESS
(— BACKWARD) DODGE
(— BY STEP) GRADATIM
(— DOWNWARD) DESCENT
(— FOR GEM MOUNTING) KITE
(— FORWARD) ADVANCE
(— IN A BEARING) BRASS
(— IN BELL RINGING) DODGE
(— IN DOCK) ALTAR
(— IN SELF-ESTEEM) PEG
(— IN SEQUENCE) PLACE
(— IN SOCIAL SCALE) CUT
(— IN TRENCH) BANQUETTE
(— LIVELY) SKELP
(— OF LADDER) RIME RUNG
ROUND RUNDLE
(— OF TUSK) TOOTH
(— PERFORMED BY COMPUTER)
OPERATION
(— SUPPORTING MILLSTONE)
TRAMPOT
(—S OF BOWLER) APPROACH
(ALTAR —S) GRADUAL
(BALLET —) PLIE FOUETTE
SISSONE SISSONNE
(BALLET —S) ALLEGRO
(BOUNDING —) SKIP
(CLUMSY —) STAUP
(DANCE —) DIP PAS SET BUZZ
DRAG DRAW FLAT SHAG SKIP
BRAWL CHASS COULE GLIDE
IRISH STOMP BRANLE CANTER
CHASSE DOUBLE INTURN STRIDE
BRANSLE BUFFALO FISHTAIL
GLISSADE PIGEONWING
(FALSE —) HOB SLIP SPHALM
SNAPPER SPHALMA STUMBLE
(FIRST —) STARTER RUDIMENT
(FLIGHT OF —S) GRECE GRICE
PERRON GEMONIES
(HALF —) HALFTONE SEMITONE
(LIGHT —) PITAPAT
(MINING —) LOB STEMPEL
STEMPLE
(POMPOUS —) STRUT
(PRIM —) MINCE
(SET OF —S) STILE
(STATELY —) STALK
(PL.) STY GHAT GHAUT STILE
LADDER
STEPFATHER FATHER STEPSIRE
STEPLADDER TRAP STEPS
(PART OF —) RAIL REST RUNG
SHOE STEP BRACE SPREADER
STEPMOTHER MOTHER HANGNAIL
STEPDAME

(RELATING TO —) NOVERCAL
STEPPE PUSZTA
(— REGION) SAHEL
(ARID REGION OF —) POECHORE
STEPPED STOPEN
STEPPENWOLF (AUTHOR OF —)
HESSE
(CHARACTER IN —) HARRY MARIA
HALLER HERMINE
STEPPING
(SUFF.) GRADE
STEREOISOMER ANOMER EPIMER
STEREOTYPE CAST CLICHE
STEREO
STEREOTYPED CHAIN STAGE
TRITE USUAL STEREO
STERILE DRY DEAD DEAF GELD
POOR AXENIC BARREN GALLED
MEAGER MULISH OTIOSE ASEPTIC
ACARPOUS BANKRUPT IMPOTENT
(PREF.) STEIRO
STERILITY ATOCIA APHORIA
STERILIZE INSULATE
STERILIZING BURNING
STERLING SOUND
(100,000 POUNDS —) PLUM
STERN GRIL GRIM HARD POOP
ASPER CRUEL GRUFF HARSH
RIGID ROUGH ROUND STARK
STOUR FLINTY GLOOMY GRIMLY
SHREWD STRICT SULLEN TORVID
UNKIND WICKED AUSTERE
TORVOUS STEERAGE STERNFUL
STRAIGHT
(— OF SHIP) DOCK APLUSTRE
STERNFAST PROVISO
STERNNESS RIGOR TORVITY
SEVERITY
STERNPOST POST STEM
MAINPOST
STERNUTATIVE ERRHINE PTARMIC
STERNUTATOR ERRHINE
STEROL AMYRIN STERIN AMBRAIN
STEROPE (FATHER OF —) ATLAS
(MOTHER OF —) PLEIONE
(SON OF —) OENOMAUS
STEVEDORE STOWER TRIMMER
WHARFIE CARGADOR DOCKHAND
STEVENSON, R.L. TUSITALA
STEW JUG FRET ITCH SLUM SNIT
SWOT BREDI CIVET CURRY DAUBE
SALMI STIVE STOVE SWEAT
BRAISE BURGOO HODDLE
MUDDLE PAELLA SEETHE SIMMER
BROTHEL CALDERA GOULASH
HARICOT NAVARIN PUCHERO
STOVIES TERRINE FRIJOADA
HOTCHPOT MORTREUX
MULLIGAN STEWPOND STUFFATA
SLUMGULLION
(— A HARE) JUG
(— IN A SAUCE) DAUBE
(— MADE IN FORECASTLE) HODDLE
(— OF TRAMPS) MULLIGAN
(FISH —) STODGE CHOWDER
MATELOTE
(IRISH —) STOVIES
(MUTTON —) NAVARIN
STEWARD HIND VOGT DEWAN
DIWAN GRAFF GRAVE REEVE
COMMIS FACTOR FARMER GRIEVE
LOOKER SIRCAR SIRDAR BAILIFF
CURATOR DAPIFER FLUNKEY

GRANGER HUSBAND MAORMOR
MORMAOR PESHKAR PROCTOR
PROVOST SPENCER SPENDER
APPROVER BHANDARI CELLARER
CONSUMAH GASTALDO
HERENACH KHANSAMA LARDINER
MALVOLIO MANCIPLE PROVISOR
STEADMAN VILLICUS
MAJORDOMO
(JOCKEY CLUB —) STIPE
STEWED SODDEN
STEWING ITCHING
STEWPAN STEW COCOTTE SKILLET
STHENELUS (FATHER OF —)
PERSEUS CAPANEUS ANDROGEOS
(MOTHER OF —) EVADNE
ANDROMEDA
(SON OF —) EURYSTHEUS
(WIFE OF —) NICIPPE
STHENOBOEA (FATHER OF —)
IOBATES
(HUSBAND OF —) PROETUS
STIBNITE SURMA STIBIUM
ANTIMONY
STIBOPHEN FUADIN
STICHIC SERIAL
STICK CAT CLA DIP GAD HEW LUG
WAN BROG BUFF CHOP CLAG
CLAM CLUB CRAB GLUE HANG
HURL PALE PALO PICK POLE POTE
RICE RUNG STAY TREE YARD
BATON BRAIL CAMAN CLAME
CLAVE CLEAM CLING CROME
DEMUR HURLY PASTE PRICK
SPELK STAFF STAKE STANG
STAVE STEND STING STOCK
STOKE VALET VERGE WADDY
ADHERE ATLATL BALLOW BATLER
BATLET BATTLE BILLET BROACH
BULGER CEMENT CLEAVE CLEEKY
COHERE CUDGEL FESCUE HOCKEY
INHERE KIERIE KIPPIN LIBBET
MALLET RADDLE RAMMER RISSLE
STRIKE STRING THIVEL TWITCH
BACKSET BATLING CAMMOCK
CUMMOCK GAMBREL HURLBAT
KILNRIB KIPPEEN MOLINET
NOBBLER SHANGAN SPURTLE
WOOLDER ASHPLANT BLUDGEON
BRINGSEL BRINSELL CATPIECE
CATSTICK CRUMMOCK DIPSTICK
DUTCHMAN GIBSTAFF GOBSTICK
KILNTREE POTSTICK SPREADER
(— AS ARCHERY MARK) WAND
(— FAST) JAM JAMB SEIZE
FITCHER
(— FASTENED TO DOG'S TAIL)
SHANGAN
(— FOR ADMITTING TENANTS)
VERGE
(— FOR FIRING CANNON) LINSTOCK
(— FOR KILLING FISH) NOBBLER
(— FOR MAKING FENCE) RADDLE
(— FOR MIXING CHOCOLATE)
MOLINET
(— FOR MIXING MORTAR) RAB
(— FOR SNUFF) DIP
(— FOR THATCHING) SPAR GROOM
SPELK SPRINGLE
(— IN MUD) STODGE
(— IN OPERATION) FREEZE
(— IT OUT) LAST
(— OF A FAN) BRIN

(— OF CANDY) GIBBY
(— OF CHALK) CRAYON
(— OF ORCHESTRA LEADER) BATON
(— OUT) BUG POKE BULGE SHOOT
EXSERT EXTEND EXTRUDE
PROTEND
(— REGULATING SLUICEWAY)
CATPIECE
(— SEPARATING LUMBER PILES)
STICKER
(— TO BEAT CLOTHES) BATLER
BATLET
(— TO DISTEND CARCASS) STEND
BACKSET
(— TO HOLD BOW) TILLER
(— TO HOLD LOG LOAD)
DUTCHMAN
(— TO KEEP ANIMAL QUIET)
TWITCH
(— TO MARK CROSSING) BROG
(— TO POKE WITH) POTE
(— TO REMOVE HOOK FROM FISH)
GOBSTICK
(— TO STRETCH NET) BRAIL
(— TO STUFF DOLLS) RAMMER
(— TO THROW AT BIRDS) SQUAIL
(— TO TIGHTEN KNOT) WOOLDER
(— TOGETHER) CLOT BLOCK CLING
BALTER CEMENT COHERE
COAGMENT
(— UP) COCK
(— USED AS POINTER) FESCUE
(BAMBOO —) LATHI LATHEE
(BASKETRY —) LEAGUE
(BENT —) RIFLE
(FIELD HOCKEY —) BULGER
CAMMOCK
(FISHING —) GAD
(FORKED —) GROM GROOM
(HOCKEY —) CAMAN HURLY
HOCKEY HURLEY SHINNY
CAMMOCK CUMMOCK DODDART
(IRON-POINTED —) VALET
(KNOBBED —) BILLET
(LACROSSE —) CROSSE
(LARGE —) MOCK
(MARKING —) LEAD
(ODD —) JAY
(POLISHING —) BUFF
(PRAYER —) PAHO
(PRINTER'S —) SHOOTER
(RANGE-FINDING —) STADIA
(ROUND —) DOWEL SPINDLE
(STIRRING —) MUNDLE POOLER
SPURTLE POTSTICK SWIZZLER
(STOUT —) BAT COSH LOWDER
(TALLY —) TAIL
(THROWING —) ATLATL HORNERAH
(TOBACCO —) LATH
(WALKING —) CANE KEBBY WADDY
JAMBEE JOCKEY KEBBIE
WHANGEE ASHPLANT GIBSTAFF
(PREF.) RHABD(O)
STICKER HINGE LABEL STRIP
WAFER HOPPER PASTER BLEEDER
CROSSER MOPSTICK STICKLER
STICK-IN STRANDER
STICKINESS GAUM TACK
ROPINESS
STICKING ADHERENT ADHESION
COHESION COHESIVE
STICKLE DEMUR BOGGLE HAGGLE
HIGGLE

STICKLEBACK BAGGIE BANDIE
HACKLE GHOSTER PINFISH
STICKLER (— FOR FORMALITY)
TAPIST
STICKMAN DEALER
STICKS BOONIES
STICKUM GLUE
STICKY CAB CLAM CLIT ICKY
DABBY FATTY GAUMY GLUEY
GOOEY GUMMY JAMMY MALMY
PUGGY SHORT TACKY TOUGH
CLAGGY CLAMMY CLARTY CLINGY
CLOGGY PLUCKY SMEARY VISCID
VISCOUS ADHESIVE TENACIOUS
(PREF.) GLOEO GLOIO
STIFF BUM SAD CARK HARD NASH
TRIG BUDGE CLUNG RIGID SOLID
STARK STEER STITH STOUR
THARF TOUGH BOARDY CLEDGY
CLUMSY CLUNCH FORMAL
FROZEN PLUGGY STARKY STEEVE
STICKY STILTY STOCKY STURDY
UNEASY WOODEN ANGULAR
BUCKRAM COSTIVE STARCHY
STILTED RAMRODDY RIGOROUS
STAFFISH
(SOMEWHAT —) CARKLED
(PREF.) ANKYL(O) TORPI TORPORI
STIFFELIO (CHARACTER IN —) LINA
STANKAR RAFFAELE STIFFELIO
(COMPOSER OF —) VERDI
STIFFEN GUM SET SIZE BRACE
STARK STIFF STRUT TRUSS
HARDEN STARCH STOVER
CONGEAL STARKEN
(— PRICE) HARDEN
STIFFENED FUSED CARKLED
STIFFENER KNEE COUNTER
STIFFENING PUFF DRESS
STIFFNESS KINK RIGOR STARCH
BUCKRAM PRIMNESS RIGIDITY
SEVERITY
STIFLE DAMP FUNK SLAY CHOKE
CRUSH STIVE STUFF MUFFLE
QUENCH FLASKER QUERKEN
SMOTHER SCOMFISH STRANGLE
SUPPRESS THROTTLE
STIFLED DEAF ETOUFFE
STIFLING CLOSE STIVY SMUDGY
POTHERY SMOTHERY
STIGMA BLOT FOIL NOTE SLUR
SPOT BRAND ODIUM STAIN TAINT
BLOTCH BLEMISH
STIGMATIZE BLOT BRAND
DENOUNCE
STILBITE DESMINE
STILE STY STICK TIMBER
STILETTO BODKIN STYLET PIERCER
POINTEL
STILL BUT COY LAY YET BODY
CALM COSH HUSH LOWN LULL
WORM ACCOY CHECK QUIET
WHIST HOWEER HUSHED PACIFY
QUENCH SETTLE SILENT SOOTHE
STATIC SUBDUE WITHAL ALEMBIC
CORNUTE HOWEVER PELICAN
SILENCE CUCURBIT RECEIVER
RESTRAIN STAGNANT STILLERY
SUPPRESS
(— PART) KELD
(PART OF —) HEAD TUBE RETORT
CONDENSER
STILLAGE SLOP STILLING STILLION

STILL-HUNT STALK
STILLNESS CALM HUSH REST
PEACE LANGUOR SILENCE
STATION
STILT KAKI POGO TILT LAWYER
PATTEN SCATCH YEGUITA
LONGLEGS STILTIFY TRIANGLE
STILTED LOFTY STIFF FORMAL
POETIC STILTY POMPOUS
STIMULANT COCA STIM INULA
BRACER CINDER FILLIP GINGER
HARMAL PHYTIN CAMPHOR
CARDIAC OUABAIN REVIVER
ADONIDIN AMMONIAC EXCITANT
INCITANT PEMOLINE STIMULUS
STIMULATE FAN HOP KEY PEP
FUEL GOAD HYPO MOVE SEED
SPUR STIR URGE WHET FILIP
IMPEL PIQUE PRIME ROUSE
SPARK STING AROUSE BESTIR
EXCITE FILLIP INCITE SPIRIT
TICKLE UPSTIR ANIMATE ENLIVEN
INNERVE INSPIRE PROVOKE
QUICKEN ACTIVATE FARADIZE
IRRITATE MOTIVATE TITILLATE
(FAIL TO —) UNDERWHELM
STIMULATING PERT SEXY BRISK
BRACING PUNGENT EROGENIC
EXCITING GENEROUS INCITANT
POIGNANT STIRRING
(— ANGER) ADRENAL
(PREF.) AUXO EXCITO
STIMULATION GINGER IMPETUS
(MENTAL —) SPRITE
STIMULUS CUE AURA BROD EDGE
GOAD HYPO SPUR STIM STING
FILLIP MOTIVE SOURCE BAHNUNG
IMPETUS OESTRUS
STING NIP BARB BITE BURN FOIN
GOAD TANG ATTER DEVIL PIQUE
PRICK STANG TOUCH NETTLE
ACULEUS BUGBITE PIERCER
IRRITATE STIMULUS
STINGILY STRAIT SCARCELY
STINGINESS PARSIMONY
STINGING KEEN SMART PEPPERY
PIQUANT POINTED PRICKLY
PUNGENT ACRIMONY ACULEATE
NETTLING POIGNANT SCALDING
URTICANT
STINGING ANT KELEP
STINGRAY ANGLER OBISPO
SEPHEN TRYGON BATFISH
LOPHIID STINGER WAIREPO
STINGY DRY DREE GAIN GAIR
HARD MEAN NEAR NIGH CLOSE
MINGY SCALY TIGHT DRIECH
GRIPPY HUNGRY MEASLY
NARROW SCABBY SCARCE
SCRIMY SKIMPY SKINNY SNIPPY
STRAIT CHINCHY CHINTZY
MISERLY NIGGARD PENURIOUS
PARSIMONIOUS
STINK FOGO GOAD NIFF PONG
STEW SMELL SMEECH STENCH
MEPHITIS
(PREF.) BROM(O)
STINKBIRD HOACIN HOATZIN
STINKING FOUL HIGH FETID PUTID
STINKY MALODOROUS
STINKWOOD DOGWOOD
STINT TASK GRIST PINCH SCANT
SNAPE SCRIMP SKINCH STINGY

TANTUM SCANTLE
(SHORT —) SNATCH
(WITHOUT —) FREELY
STIPE STEM STALK
STIPEND ANN HIRE ANNAT WAGES
SALARY PENSION PREBEND
PROVEND COMMENDA
STIPENDIARY BEAK
STIPPLE SPONGE
STIPPLED DOTTED
STIPULATE ARTICLE PROTEST
PROVIDE COVENANT
STIPULATION IF ANNEX CLAUSE
ARTICLE PREMISE PROVISO
COVENANT
(PL) TERMS
STIPULE SPINE SHEATH STIPEL
STIPULA TENDRIL
STIR DO ADO FAN GOG JEE PUG
WAG BEET BUZZ CARD FUSS
MOVE PEAL POKE RAUK ROKE
WAKE AMOVE BUDGE CHURN
CREEP ERECT FUROR HURRY
MUDGE POACH QUICH RAISE
ROUST SLICE SPARK STING
STOOR STURT TEASE TOUCH
AROUSE AWAKEN BUBBLE
BUSTLE CRUTCH EXCITE FLURRY
GINGER HUBBUB JUMBLE KIAUGH
MUDDLE PADDLE POUTER
QUINCH QUITCH REMBLE REMOVE
ROUNCE STODGE SUMMON
TATTER ACTUATE ANIMATE
BLATHER CLUTTER COMMOVE
FLUTTER PROVOKE STARKLE
SWIZZLE TROUBLE SPLUTTER
(— ABOUT) KNOCK
(— CALICO COLORS) TEER
(— DRINK) MUDDLE SWIZZLE
(— LIQUID) ROG
(— SOIL) CHISEL
(— UP) FAN MIX BUZZ DRUM FUSS
MOVE PROG ROIL TOSS AMOVE
AREAR AWAKE ERECT QUICK
ROUSE SNURL SPOOK STOKE
TARRY BESTIR BOTHER CHOUSE
EXCITE INCITE JOSTLE KINDLE
PUDDLE RUMBLE TICKLE UPSTIR
AGITATE ANIMATE COMMOVE
DISTURB PRODDLE PROVOKE
STUDDLE TORMENT UNQUEME
DISTRACT
(— UP WITH YEAST) BARM
STIRRER HOG DOLLY ROUSER
RUMMAGER
STIRRING RACY ASTIR DEEDFUL
ROUSING THRILLY EXCITING
PATHETIC
STIRRUP IRON CHAPELET
STEELBOW
(PART OF —) EYE PAD TREAD
BRANCH
(PREF.) STAPED(I)(IO)
STITCH BAR RUN SEW KNIT LOOP
PURL WHIP CABLE CLOSE POINT
PREEN PUNTO STEEK ACCRUE
FESTON SUTURE TRICOT
CROCHET POPCORN FAGOTING
(— OF CLOTHES) TACK
(NEEDLEPOINT —) BARGELLO
(PL.) JOURS FILLING PINWORK
STITCHBIRD IHI
STITCHDOWN SEWROUND

STITCHED BROCHE
STITCHER WHIPPER
STITCHING SERGING FAGOTING
STOATING WHIPPING
(SUFF.) RHAPHY RRHAPHY
STITCHWORT PAIGLE ALLBONE
SNAPPER HEADACHE SNAPJACK
SNAPWORT
STITHY STUDY SMITHY STIDDY
STUDDY
STOAT VAIR ERMINE WEASEL
CLUBSTER FUTTERET WHITRACK
STOCK COP DOG KIN ROD CANT
CROP FILL FOND FUND SEED SELL
STEM TRIP BLOND BLOOD BROTH
CASTE CREAM FLESH HOARD
ISSUE PLANT STALE STIRP STORE
STUFF TALON BUDGET CHOKER
COMMON FUTURE KAFFIR
SHARES STOVEN STRAIN SUPPLY
CAPITAL DESCENT PILLORY
PROSAPY PROVIDE REPLETE
RESERVE BONEYARD BOUTIQUE
CROSSBAR DIESTOCK GILLIVER
GUNSTOCK MAGAZINE
MERCHANT ORDINARY SECURITY
PROVISIONS
(— OF ANCHOR) CROSS
(— OF BREEDING MARES) STRUDE
(— OF FOOD) FARE
(— OF GRAIN) COP
(— OF INDIVIDUALS) CLONE
(— OF MORPHEMES) LEXICON
(— OF WEAPONS) ARSENAL
(— OF WHIP) CROP
(— OF WINE) CELLAR
(— SOLD SHORT) BEAR
(FARM —) BOW
(LANGUAGE —) SALISH SIOUAN
BOROTUKE
(MEAT —) BLOND BOUILLON
(PLASTIC —) BISCUIT
(RAILROAD —) GRANGER
(PL.) FOODS CIPPUS HARMAN
TIMBER CATASTA KAFFIRS
(PREF.) STIPI(T)(TI) STIPULI STIRPI
(SUFF.) STIPULAR STIPULATE
STOCKADE BOMA PEEL ETAPE
ZAREBA BARRIER TAMBOUR
STOCKADO
STOCK EXCHANGE BOURSE
COULISSE
STOCKFISH STOCK LUTFISK
TITLING SPELDING SPELDRON
(PREF.) SALPI
STOCKING HOSE SOCK SHANK
STOCK CALIGA MOGGAN
SCOGGER SHINNER BOOTHOSE
(FOOTLESS —) HOGGER HUSHION
(SOLELESS —) TRAHEEN
(PL.) HOSE NYLONS BUSKINS
BOOTHOSE
STOCKJOBBING AGIOTAGE
STOCKWORK CARBONA
STOCKY FAT COBBY DUMPY
GROSS SQUAT STOUT CHUMPY
CHUNKY DUMPTY STUBBY
STUGGY STUNTY BUNTING
COMPACT HEAVYSET STOCKISH
THICKSET
STODGY STUFFY STUGGY
BOURGEOIS
STOIC IMPASSIVE

STOKEHOLD FIREROOM
STOKER FIREMAN BLOCKMAN
STOLE STAW ARMIL ORARY
ARMILLA ORARION PALATINE
STOLEN HOT BENT INOME STOUN
FURTIVE
(— GOODS) MAINOUR
STOLID BEEFY BOVINE CLUMSE
STUPID WOODEN CLUMPST
DEADPAN PASSIVE
STOLIDITY MORGUE
STOLON WIRE SOBOL SOBOLE
SOLENIUM
STOMA PORE OPENING OSTIOLE
STOMACH MAW CROP GUTS KYTE
MARY POKE READ TANK WAME
WOMB BINGY BROOK GORGE
GROUF HEART TUMMY BINGEE
BINGEY BONNET CROPPY GEBBIE
PECHAN VENTER CONCOCT
CRAPPIN GIZZARD ABOMASUM
(— OF ANIMAL) CRAW
(— OF CALF) VELL
(— OF RUMINANT) READ RUMEN
BONNET OMASUM PAUNCH
ABOMASUM MANIFOLD RODDIKIN
(PIG'S —) JAUDIE
(PREF.) GASTER(O) GASTR(I)(O)
RUMENO
(SUFF.) GASTER GASTRIA
STOMACHACHE FANTAD GULLION
STOMACHER GIMP TRUSS
ECHELLE PLACARD POITREL
FOREPART
STOMACHIC COTO CORNUS
BITTERS CALUMBA GENTIAN
LUPULIN ANTHEMIS
STOMATITIS NOMA
STONE DAM GEM RAG BOND DUCK
FLAG HERD KLIP KNAR MARK
PELT ROCK STEN TRIG BAUTA
CAPEL CHUCK DRAKE GUARD
LAPIS PAVER PITCH SCRAE SCREE
SNECK STANE ASHLAR BEDDER
BENBEN CEPHAS CHATON CLOSER
COBBLE GAMAHE GIBBER HEADER
JUMPER LEDGER MARVER
METATE MULLER NUTLET PEEVER
PINNER RUNNER SUMMER
TORSEL ANGRITE CALLAIS
DINGBAT DONNOCK DORNICK
GLIDDER KNEELER KNICKER
PERPEND PITCHER PUTAMEN
RATCHEL STANNER SURFACE
THROUGH BAETULUS CABOCHON
DENDRITE EBENEZER HAGSTONE
LAPIDATE LAPILLUS LAPSTONE
MACEHEAD MONOLITH NAKHLITE
SKEWBACK TOPSTONE
(— ADHERING TO LEAD ORE) KEVEL
(— AS AMULET) HAGSTONE
(— AS IT COMES FROM QUARRY)
RUBBLE
(— AS ROAD MARKER) LEAGUE
(— AT DOOR) RYBAT
(— BLOCK) ASSIZE
(— FOR GLASS-ROLLING) MARVER
(— FOR MOUNTING HORSE)
MONTOIR
(— FORMING CAP OF PIER)
SUMMER CUSHION
(— HARD TO MOVE) SITFAST
(— HEAP) MAN

(— IN BLAST FURNACE) DAM
(— IN MEMORY OF DEAD)
MONUMENT
(— IN SMALL FRAGMENTS)
RATCHEL
(— IN WALL) PARPEN
(— MARKING CENTER OF WORLD)
OMPHALOS
(— OF FRUIT) COB PIT PAIP COBBE
NUTLET PYRENE PUTAMEN
(— OF PYRAMID SHAPE) BENBEN
**(— PROVIDING CHANGE OF
DIRECTION)** KNEELER
(— SET IN RING) CHATON
(— SHAPED BY WIND) VENTIFACT
(— SHOT FROM STONE BOW) JALET
(— TO DEATH) LAPIDATE
(— USED AS MONUMENT)
MEGALITH
(— USED IN GAME) DUCK DRAKE
(— WITH INTERNAL CAVITY) GEODE
(—S FROM CRUSHER) TAILINGS
(—S IN WATER) STANNERS
(ARTIFICIAL —) ALBOLITE
(BINDING —) PERPEND THROUGH
PIERPONT
(BOND —) GIRDER KEYSTONE
(BOUNDARY —) TERM TERMINUS
(BROKEN —) RIPRAP
(BROKEN — USED FOR ROADS)
BALLAST MACADAM
(BUILDING —) SUMMER MITCHEL
SPERONE
(CARVED —) CAMEO CUVETTE
(CASTING —) TYMP
(CHINA —) PETUNSE
(CLAY —) LECH
(COPING —) SKEW TABLET
TABLING CAPSTONE
(CURLING —) HOG HERD GUARD
LOOFIE POTLID
(CYLINDRICAL —) TAMBOUR
(DESERT —) GIBBER
(DRUID —) SARSEN
(DRYING —) STILLAGE
(EDGING —) SETTER
(FLAT —) PLAT DRAKE LEDGER
(FOUNDATION —) BEDDER
(GLITTERING —) DAZE
(GRAVE —) BAUTA STELE
(GREEN —) CALLAIS
(GRINDING —) METATE MULLER
(HOLY —) BEAR BAETYL
(HOPSCOTCH —) PEEVER PALLALL
(IMAGINARY —) ADAMANT
(KIDNEY —) NEPHRITE
(LAST — IN COURSE) CLOSER
(LOOSE —) GLIDDER
(MAGICAL —) BAETYL
(MEMORIAL —) BAUTA EBENEZER
(METEORIC —) ANGRITE AEROLITE
AEROLITH NAKHLITE
(MIDDLE —) HONEY
(MIDDLE — OF ARCH) KEY
(MONUMENTAL —) LECH
(PAVING —) PAVER REBATE
PITCHER
(PHILOSOPHER'S —) ADROP
MAGISTERY
(PRECIOUS —) GEM OPAL RUBY
EWAGE JEWEL TOPAZ ADAMAS
LIGURE SHAMIR ASTERIA
ASTRION CRAPAUD CUVETTE

DIAMOND DIONISE EMERALD
GELATIA JACINTH OLIVINE
SARDINE SARDIUS AMETHYST
ASTROITE HYACINTH PANTARBE
SAPPHIRE YDRIADES
(PRECIOUS —S) PERRIE
(REFUSE —) ROACH
(ROCKING —) LOGAN
(SACRED —) BAETYL BAETULUS
(SEMIPRECIOUS —) ONYX SARD
MURRA GARNET CITRINE
TIGEREYE
(SHARPENING —) HONE WHET
(SHOEMAKER'S —) LAPSTONE
(SMALL ROUND —) JACK
(SOFTENED —) SAP
(STEPPING —) GOAT SARN
(STRATIFIED —) FLAG SLAB
(TALISMANIC —) GAMAHE
(TRANSPARENT —) PHENGITE
(UNSQUARED —) BACKING
(UPRIGHT —) BAUTA MENHIR
MASSEBAH
(PL.) LAPIDES LAPILLI
(PREF.) LITH(O) LAPIDI LAPILLI
(— OF FRUIT) PYREN(O)
(SUFF.) LITE LITH(IC) LITIC
STONEBASS BAFARO WHAPUKU
STONEBOAT DRAY
STONEBOW RODD
STONECHAT CHAT SMICH
SAXICOLA WHEATEAR
STONECROP SEDUM ORPINE
PRICKET WALLWORT
STONE CURLEW BUSTARD
STONECUTTER MASON JADDER
LAPICIDE SCABBLER SCAPPLER
SQUAREMAN
STONEFLY NAIAD
STONEHAND LOCKUP
STONELIKE LITHOID
STONEMAN IMPOSER
STONE MARTEN FOIN
STONEMASON DORBIE
STONE PARSLEY HONEWORT
STONE PINE PINON AROLLA
CEMBRA
STONE ROLLER MAMMY MOMMY
TOTER
STONE TOTER CUTLIPS
STONEWALLER STICKER
STONEWARE GRES BASALT
JASPER BASALTES CANEWARE
CHIENYAO
STONINESS LAPIDITY PETREITY
STONY RIGID COBBLY PETROUS
LAPIDOSE PETROSAL
STOOL FORM MORA SEAT STAB
COPPY CROCK HORSE STOLE
TREST BUFFET CREEPY CURRIE
TRIPOD TUFFET COMMODE
CREEPIE KNEELER SHAMBLE
TABORET TRESTLE TUMBREL
BARSTOOL STILLAGE
(CLOSE —) TOM
(CUCKING —) THEW
(LOW —) COPPY SUNKIE CREEPIE
CRICKET
(3-LEGGED —) BUFFET THRESTLE
STOOLBALL TUTBALL
STOOL PIGEON NARK SNITCH
STOOGE STOOLIE
STOOP BOW BEND CURB LEAN

LOUT POKE SINK COUCH COURB
DEIGN STOPE STULP COORIE
CROUCH HUCKLE BALCONY
DECLINE DESCEND RUCKSEY
SUCCUMB
(— OF HAWK) SOUSE
STOOPING DUCK ASTOOP
DESCENT
(PREF.) CYPH(O)
STOP HO BAS COG CUT DAM DIE
DIT DOG END HOO KEP LIN MAR
NIX SET BALK BODE BUNG CALK
CALL COOL DROP EASE HALT
HELP HOLD HOOK KILL QUIT REED
REST SIST SNUB SOFT STAP STAY
STEM STOW TEAT TENT TOHO
TRIG VIOL WEAR WHOA ABIDE
ABORT AVAST BASTA BELAY
BLOCK BRAKE BREAK CAULK
CEASE CHECK CHOKE CHUCK
CLAMP CLOSE DELAY EMBAR
HITCH LEAVE MEDIA PAUSE
PEACE POINT QUINT REEST
SCOTE SLAKE SPARE SPRAG
STAND STASH STEEK STICK STINT
VIOLA AEOLIN ANCHOR ARREST
ASTINT BIFARA BOGGLE BORROW
CHEESE CLAMOR COLLAR DESIST
DETAIN DEVALL GRAVEL INSTOP
MONTRE NASARD PERIOD
SCOTCH SQUASH STANCE
STANCH STIFLE TENUIS TROMBA
BASSOON CAESURA MELODIA
MUSETTE OPPRESS SOJOURN
STATION TERTIAN TWELFTH
ASPIRATA BACKSTOP BOMBARDE
PRECLUDE RECORDER STOPOVER
STOPPAGE SUPPRESS SURCEASE
TENOROON WALDHORN
WITHSPAR
(— AS IF FRIGHTENED) BOGGLE
(— BLAST) DAMP
(— FLOW) BAFFLE STANCH
(— FOR FOOD) BAIT
(— FOR HORSE) BLOW
(— FROM FERMENTING) STUM
(— GROWTH) BLAST
(— GUN BREECH) OBTURATE
(— IN EARLY STAGES) ABORT
(— IN SPEAKING) HAW
(— LEAK) CALK CAULK FOTHER
(— ROWING) EASY
(— SHORT) JIB
(— SWINGING) SET
(— UNDESIREDLY) STALL
(— UP) DAM CALK CLOG CLOY FILL
PLUG CHINK ESTOP STUFF
STANCH OCCLUDE STAUNCH
OPPILATE
(— USING) SINK
(— WITH CLAY) PUG
(— WORK) SECURE
(BRIEF —) CALL
(GLOTTAL —) STOD CATCH STOSS
PLOSIVE STOSSTON
(HARPSICHORD —) LUTE
(ROUGH —) ASPIRATA
(SUCTION —) CLICK
(TEMPORARY —) PAUSE SUSPEND
(VOICELESS —) TENUIS
(PL.) REEDWORK
(PREF.) ISCH(O)
STOPCOCK BIB BIBB BIBCOCK

BALLCOCK TURNCOCK
STOPGAP RESOURCE
STOPLIGHT IMPEDER
STOPOVER LAYOVER
STOPPAGE JAM BLIN ALLAY
CHECK HITCH LEATH STICK STINT
ARREST DEVALL STASIS
EMBARGO GASLOCK REFUSAL
SHUTOFF STOPPLE ASTYLLEN
SHUTDOWN STOPWORK
CESSATION
(— OF BLOOD) REMORA
(— OF DEVELOPMENT) ATROPHY
(WORK —) BUND HARTAL LOWSIN
STRIKE
(PREF.) ISCH(O) STASI
(SUFF.) STASIA STASIS
STOPPED PILEATA
(— WITH HAND) BOUCHE
STOPPER WAD BUNG CORK STOP
VICE CHECK FIPPLE STANCH
BOUCHON CLOSURE SHUTOFF
STOPGAP STOPPLE TAMPION
STOPCOCK
STOPPERED BOUCHE
STOPPING STAY HOLDUP
PHASEOUT STOPPAGE
(GRADUAL — OF OPERATIONS)
PHASEOUT
STORAGE STORE STOWAGE
BESTOWAL
STORAX COPALM STACTE STYRAX
LORDWOOD
STORE CAVE CRIB DECK FOND
FUND HOLD KEEP MASS SAVE
SHOP STOW TOKO CACHE DEPOT
HOUSE HUTCH STASH STOCK
UPLAY BAZAAR CELLAR GARNER
GIRNEL RECOND STEEVE SUPPLY
TIENDA WINKEL ARSENAL
BHANDAR BOOTERY GROCERY
HARVEST HUSBAND IMBURSE
REPOSIT RESTORE SHEBANG
BOUTIQUE EMPORIUM EXCHANGE
GARRISON MAGAZINE TENDEJON
WAREROOM WARNISON
(— BEER) AGE LAGER
(— CROP) BARN
(— FODDER) ENSILE
(— IN A MOW) GOVE
(— IN LUMBER CAMP) VAN
(— KEPT BY CHINESE) TOKO
(— OF FOOD) LARDER
(— OF WEALTH) FORTUNE
(— POTATOES) HOG
(— UP) FUND POWDER IMBURSE
SQUIRREL
(ABUNDANT —) MINE
(BREAD —) PANARY
(HIDDEN —) BIKE
(LARGE —) RAFF
(LIQUOR —) GROGGERY
(MILITARY —) DUMP
(READY-TO-EAT FOOD —) DELI
DELLY
(RESERVE —) SLUICE
(RICH —) ARGOSY
(SMALL —S) SLOPS
(PL.) SAMAN SUPPLY
STOREHOUSE BIKE GOLA CACHE
DEPOT ETAPE STORE ARGOSY
ARMORY BODEGA GODOWN
PALACE PANARY STAPLE VINTRY

ARSENAL BHANDAR CAMALIG
CAMARIN GRANARY STORAGE
ENTREPOT MAGAZINE SADDLERY
TREASURE
(— FOR BREAD) PANARY
(RAISED —) WHATA FUTTAH
PATAKA
(UNDERGROUND —) PALACE
MATTAMORE
STOREKEEPER MERCHANT
STOREMAN
STOREROOM CAVE GOLA WARD
GOLAH BODEGA CELLAR DINGLE
BOXROOM BUTTERY GENIZAH
LAZARET POULTRY THALAMUS
(PAWNBROKER'S —) LUMBER
STORESHIP FLUTE
STOREY ETAGE ENTRESOL
STORK WADER ARGALA JABIRU
SIMBIL HURGILA MAGUARI
MARABOU ADJUTANT CICONIID
MARABOUT OPENBEAK OPENBILL
(PREF.) CICONI PELARGO
STORKLIKE PELARGIC
STORKSBILL ERODIUM
STORM RIG WAP BLOW HAIL HUFF
RAGE RAMP RAND RAVE WIND
BLIZZ BLOUT BRASH DEVIL DRIFT
FORCE ORAGE STOUR ATTACK
BARBER EASTER EXPUGN WESTER
BLUSTER BRAVADO CYCLONE
DUSTING EQUINOX GAUSTER
PISACHI SHAITAN SNIFTER
TEMPEST TORMENT WEATHER
BLOWDOWN CALAMITY
ERUPTION UPHEAVAL WILLIWAW
(— OF BLOWS) STOUR
(DUST —) DEVIL DUSTER HABOOB
KHAMSIN PEESASH SHAITAN
(FURIOUS —) TEMPEST
(HAWAIIAN —) KONA
(SEVERE —) PEELER SNIFTER
(VIOLENT —) FLAW TUFAN
CYCLONE SNORTER
STORM DOOR DINGLE
STORMY FOUL GURL RUDE WILD
DIRTY DUSTY GURLY GUSTY
STARK WINDY WROTH COARSE
RUGGED UNFINE WINTRY
FURIOUS NIMBOSE RIOTOUS
SQUALLY TROUBLE VIOLENT
AGITATED BLUSTERY CLUTTERY
ORAGIOUS TEMPESTY
BOISTEROUS
STORMY PETREL MITTY WITCH
SPENCY
STORY GAG SAW DECK DIDO FLAT
LORE REDE TALE TEXT YARN
ATTIC CRACK ETAGE FABLE
FLOOR KATHA PITCH PROSE
RECIT SOLAR SPELL SPIEL STAGE
STORE CUFFER FABULA FLIGHT
PISTLE SCREED SOLLAR ADVANCE
HAGGADA HISTORY MANSARD
MARCHEN PROCESS RECITAL
ANECDOTE DREADFUL ENTRESOL
TREATISE NARRATIVE
(— FROM THE PAST) LEGEND
(— OF BEEHIVE) SUPER
(— OF BUILDING) DECK FLAT ATTIC
CHESS ETAGE FLOOR PIANO
SOLAR STAGE FLIGHT SOLLAR
MANSARD ENTRESOL MEZZANINE

(— OF HEROES) SAGA
(ABSURD —) CANARD
(ADVENTURE —) YARN
(AMUSING —) BAR DROLLERY
(BIRTH —) JATAKA
(DOLEFUL —) JEREMIAD
(EERIE —) CHILLER
(FAKE —) STRING
(FALSE —) SHAVE CANARD
WHOPPER
(LONG, INVOLVED —) MEGILLA
MEGILLAH
(MADE-UP —) FUDGE
(MONSTROUS —) BANGER
(MORBIDLY SENSATIONAL —)
DREADFUL
(MYSTERY —) WHODUNIT
(NEWS —) SIDEBAR
(NEWSPAPER —) LEAD FEATURE
(OLD —) DIDO
(POMPOUS —) BRAG
(PREPOSTEROUS —) CUFFER
(RIBALD —) HARLOTRY
(SATIRICAL —) SKIT
(SHORT —) CONTE NOVELLA
(STALE —) CHESTNUT
(UPPER —) ATTIC GARRET
BARBECUE HYPEROON
(PL.) LEGENDA
STORY BOOK TALEBOOK
STORY OF A BAD BOY (AUTHOR
OF —) ALDRICH
(CHARACTER IN —) BEN TOM BILL
EZRA PHIL SETH ADAMS BINNY
KITTY MEEKS NELLY SILAS
CONWAY MARDEN NUTTER
PEPPER ROGERS ABIGAIL
ALDRICH CHARLEY COLLINS
WALLACE WINGATE GRIMSHAW
WHITCOMB TREFETHEN
GLENTWORTH
STORY OF AN AFRICAN FARM
(AUTHOR OF —) SCHREINER
(CHARACTER IN —) EM ROSE TANT
WALDO SANNIE GREGORY
LYNDALL BLENKINS
BONAPARTE
STORYTELLER CONTEUR DISCOUR
DISSOUR
STOUP STOOP BENITIER
STOUT FAT SAD FIRM STUT TRIM
BONNY BROSY BULKY BUNTY
BURLY COBBY FRACK FRECK
GREAT HARDY KEDGE OBESE
PLUMP PODDY PUNCH STARK
STERN BONNIE FLESHY PORTER
PORTLY PRETTY PYKNIC ROTUND
SQUARE STRONG STUFFY STURDY
BOWERLY REPLETE FORCIBLE
PLUMPISH POWERFUL ROBOREAN
STALWART THICKSET
(— PERSON) GURK
STOUTHEARTED GOOD VALIANT
STOUTLY FAST HARDILY
STOUTNESS STRENGTH
CORPULENCE
STOVE HOD STOW BOGEY CHULA
PEACH PLATE CHULHA COCKLE
COOKER HEATER PRIMUS
BRASERO CHAUFFER FRANKLIN
POTBELLY SALAMANDER
(— FOR DRYING GUNPOWDER)
GLOOM

(— ON SHIP) GALLEY
(RUSSIAN —) PEACH
(WARMING —) KANGRI
STOVER OVENSMAN
STOW BIN BOX SET CRAM LADE
MASS CROWD DOUSE STORE
BESTOW COOPER STEEVE
DUNNAGE RUMMAGE
STOWAGE BURTON REMBLAI
RUMMAGE
STOWED IN
STOWER TOPPER
STOWING BINNING GOBBING
STP DOM
STRABISMUS CAST CROSS SQUINT
TROPIA ANOPSIA COCKEYE
WALLEYE
STRADDLE SADDLE SPREAD
STRIDE BESTRIDE SPRADDLE
STRIDDLE
STRAGGLE GAD ROVE TRAIL
RAMBLE RANGLE SPRAWL STREEL
TAGGLE WANDER DRAGGLE
MEANDER SCRAMBLE SPRANGLE
STRAGGLER STRAY BUMMER
STRAGGLING RAGGED RAGGLED
SPRAYEY SCRATCHY VAGULOUS
STRAIGHT BOLT FAIR FULL GAIN
BRANT CLEAN DOGGY FLUSH
RIGHT SHORT SPANG ARIGHT
DIRECT HONEST STRAIT STRICT
BOBTAIL REGULAR UPRIGHT
DIRECTLY SEQUENCE
(— AHEAD) ANON PLUMP
OUTRIGHT
(— UP AND DOWN) SHEER CLEVER
EVENDOWN
(NOT —) CRAZY
(PREF.) EUTHY ITHO ITHY
ORTH(O) RECT(I)
STRAIGHTEDGE LUTE RULE RULER
STRICKLE
STRAIGHTEN GAG ORDER STENT
EXTEND SQUARE UNKINK
COMPOSE RECTIFY STRETCH
(— BY HEATING) SET
(— NEEDLE) RUB
(— RAILS) GAG
STRAIGHT-FIBERED BROAD
STRAIGHTFORWARD EVEN PLAT
APERT FRANK LEVEL NAKED
PLAIN ROUND CANDID DEXTER
DIRECT HONEST SIMPLE SQUARE
JANNOCK SINCERE EVENDOWN
HOMESPUN OUTRIGHT STRAIGHT
OPENHEARTED
(NOT —) CROOKED PLAITED
(PREF.) LITI
STRAIGHTFORWARDLY SINGLY
SQUARE STRAIGHT
STRAIGHT-THINKING CLEAR
STRAIGHTWAY ANON AWAY
RIGHT ARIGHT BEDEEN BEDENE
DIRECTLY
STRAIN FIT LAG RAX SIE TAX TRY
TUG ACHE BEND CALL DASH
DRAG HEAT HEFT LAWN NOTE
PULL RACK RANN RICK SILE SINE
SOLO SONG VEIN WORK BRUNT
CHAFE DEMUR DRAIN FORCE
HEAVE PRESS RETCH SHADE
SHEAR STOCK SURGE TAMMY
TOUCH WREST WRICK CLENCH

EFFORT EXTEND EXTORT FILTER
INTEND KVETCH SPRAIN SPRING
STREAK STRESS STRIND THRONG
DESCANT DISCANT EUPLOID
FATIGUE STRAINT STRETCH
STROPHE TENSION TORMENT
COLANDER DIAPASON DIATRIBE
DIHYBRID SUBBREED
(— MILK) SIE SYE
(— OF AN ARCH) THRUST
(— OF CHICKENS) ANCOBAR
(— OF RAILING LANGUAGE)
DIATRIBE
(— ON BUGLE) MOT'
(— ON HORN) RECHASE RECHEAT
(— THROUGH COLANDER) COIL
(CONCLUDING —) CADENCE
(MELANCHOLY —) DUMP
(MUSICAL —) FIT SOLO POINT
(MUSICAL —S) TOUCH
(MUTANT —) SALTANT
(PREF.) STREMMATO
STRAINED PENT TENSE INTENSE
LABORED INTENDED
STRAINER CAGE ROSE SILE RENGE
SIEVE STRUM TAMIS TAMMY
THEAD SEARCE SEARCH CRIBBLE
COLATORY COLATURE SEARCHER
(— OF TWIGS) HUCKMUCK
(COFFEE —) GRECQUE
(MILK —) SAY MILSEY MILSIE
(WICKER —) THEAD THEDE
(PREF.) COLI ETHMO
STRAINING CUTE COILED ASTRAIN
INTENSE COLATURE
STRAIT CUT GUT BAND BELT FRET
KYLE NECK PACE BRAKE CANAL
PHARE PINCH SHARD SOUND
ANGUST FRETUM NARROW
PLUNGE CHANNEL EURIPUS
BOSPORUS JUNCTURE
(IN —S) SET
(LAST —) EXIGENT
(NEWFOUNDLAND —) TICKLER
(PL.) CHOPS PRESS EXTREMES
STRAITEN PINCH SCANT STRAIT
STRAITENED CRIMP NARROW
CRIMPED
STRAITJACKET CAMISOLE
STRAITLACED STIFF STUFFY
BLUENOSED
STRAKE SHEER COURSE RISING
STREAK COAMING SAXBOARD
(PL.) TIRE
STRAMONIUM DEWTRY
STRAND PLY TOP BANK CORE
FLAT TOWT WISP BEACH BRAID
CLIFF PRAYA READY SHORE
LISSOM SINGLE SLIVER STRAIN
STRIKE SUTURE HAIRLINE
(— OF FIBERS) ROVING
(— OF HAIR) LICK SWITCH
(— OF PROTOPLASM) BRIDGE
(— OF TEXTILE) ROVE
(PREF.) CROCO
STRANDED AGROUND ISOLATED
STRANDER EDGER
STRANGE ODD RUM EERY FELL
FREM NICE RARE UNCO ALIEN
EERIE FREMT FUNNY KINKY
NOVEL QUEER UNKET UNKID
WOOZY ALANGE FERLIE QUAINT
UNIQUE UNKENT UNKIND

CURIOUS ERRATIC HEATHEN
ODDBALL UNHEARD UNKNOWN
UNUSUAL FANCIFUL INSOLENT
INSOLITE PECULIAR SELCOUTH
SINGULAR UNCOLIKE UNCOMMON
UNKENNED UNKINDLY
MONSTROUS
(PREF.) XEN(O)
STRANGENESS ODDITY
STRANGER COME UNCO UNKO
ALIEN GUEST FRENNE GANGER
INCOME INMATE FUIDHIR
INCOMER UNCOUTH MALIHINI
OUTCOMER PEREGRIN
OUTLANDER
(SUFF.) XENE XENOUS XENY
STRANGLE CHOKE GRAIN GRANE
SNARL WORRY STIFLE GARROTE
QUACKLE GARROTTE JUGULATE
THROTTLE
STRANGLEHOLD CHANCERY
STRANGUL
STRANIERA, LA (CHARACTER IN —)
ALAIDE ARTURO ISOLETTA
VALDEBURGO
(COMPOSER OF —) BELLINI
STRAP BAR TUG BAND CLIP CURB
GIRD HASP RIDE RIEM BRACE
CHEEK GIRTH GUIGE PATTE RIDER
RISER SABOT SLING STROP
THONG TRACE VITTA ANKLET
BACKER BILLET COLLAR ENARME
GARTER HALTER HANGER LAINER
LATIGO SANDAL TOGGLE
WARROK BABICHE BOWYANG
CRIBBER DOLPHIN LANYARD
LATCHET LEATHER RIEMPIE
STIRRUP TICKLER WEBBING
BACKSTAY BRETELLE SQUILGEE
TURNBACK WRISTLET
(— AROUND HORSE'S THROAT)
CRIBBER
(— AROUND MAST) DOLPHIN
(— FOR SHIELD) GUIGE ENARME
BRETELLE
(— IN FLAIL) TAPLING
(— OF BRIDLE) REIN
(— OF SENNIT) BACKER
(— ON HAWK'S LEAD) JESS JESSE
SENDAL
(— WITH SLIT END) TAWS TAWSE
(ANKLE —) BRACELET
(CARRYING —) METUMP TUMPLINE
(DOOR —) HASP
(MINER'S —) BYARD
(SHOE —) BAR
(STIRRUP —S) CHAPELET
(TIE —) SHANK
(U-SHAPED —) STIRRUP
(PL.) LADDER
(PREF.) LIGUL(I)
STRAP FERN LONGLEAF
STRAPHANGER COMMUTER
STRAPPER SPLICER
STRAPPING SWANK BOUNCING
CHOPPING SLAPPING SWANKING
STRAP-SHAPED LORATE LIGULAR
LIGULATE
STRATA EOCENE TERRANE
UNDERAIR
(— OF COAL) MEASURES
STRATAGEM JIG COUP LOCK RUSE
TRAM TURN WILE ANGLE DRAFT

FETCH FRAUD GUILE JOKER
KNACK TRAIN TRICK WREST
BLENCH DECEIT DEVICE HUMBUG
POLICY TRAPAN TREPAN WOIDRE
WRENCH FINESSE SLEIGHT
ARTIFICE CONTOISE FARFETCH
INTRIGUE LIRIPIPE LIRIPOOP
PRACTICE PRACTISE QUENTISE
STRATEGY TRICKERY MOUSETRAP
STRATEGY GAME FINESSE
STRATIFICATION BEDDING
STRATIFIED BEDDED VARVED
STRATONICE (FATHER OF —)
DEMETRIUS
(HUSBAND OF —) SELEUCUS
(MOTHER OF —) PHILA
STRATUM BED CAP CUT LAY RIB
FAST LAIN SEAM COUCH ELITE
FLOOR LAYER LEDGE SHELF
TABLE COUCHE GIRDLE GRAVEL
LAYING LISSOM PINNEL AQUAFER
AQUIFER ENTIRIS FISHBED
SUBSOIL UPRIGHT AQUIFUGE
FAHLBAND SUBGRADE
(— OF COAL) BENCH
(— OF FIRECLAY) THILL
(— OF PALE COLOR) FAHLBAND
(— OF SANDSTONE) PINNEL
(— OF SOIL) SOD
(— OF STONE) GIRDLE
(SOCIAL —) CUT
(THIN —) SEAM LENTIL
STRAW BAKU GLOY MOTE REED
RUSH TOYO WASE HAULM PEDAL
SHILF STALK STREW YEDDA
FESCUE FETTLE PANAMA RIZZOM
SIPPER TUSCAN BANGKOK
SABUTAN STUBBLE WINDLIN
STRAMMEL
(— CUT FINE) CHAFF
(— FOR MAKING HATS) SENNIT
BANGKOK LEGHORN SABUTAN
(— FOR THATCHING) YELM
(— MEASURE) KEMPLE
(— TO PROTECT PLANTS) MULCH
(BROKEN —) BHUSA BHOOSA
(COOKERY —S) PAILLES
(PLAITED —) SENNIT
(WAXED —) STRASS
(PREF.) CARPHO
STRAWBERRY BERRY DUNLAP
FRAISE RUNNER HAUTBOY
FRUTILLA HAUTBOIS KLONDIKE
ROSACEAN
STRAWBERRY BUSH WAHOO
EUONYMUS EVONYMUS
FISHWOOD
STRAWBERRY FINCH AMADAVAT
AVADAVAT
STRAWBERRY SHRUB BUBBY
COWBERRY
STRAWBERRY TOMATO
PHYSALIS
STRAY ERR ODD FALL RAVE ROVE
WAFF WAIF WALK DRIFT RANGE
TRAIK VAGUE WAVER ESTRAY
RANGLE SWERVE VAGARY
WANDER WILDER DEVIATE
FORLORN STRAYER DIVAGATE
MAVERICK STRAGGLE
STRAYING ASTRAY ERRANT
ABERRANT VAGATION
STREAK PAY RAY BAND SEAM

VEIN WALE FLAKE FLECK FLICK
FREAK GARLE GLADE SLASH
FACULA SMUDGE STRAIN STRAKE
STREAM STRIPE FLECKER
SPRAING STIPPLE DISCOLOR
TRAVERSE
(— CAUSED BY BLOOD) VIBEX
(— IN FABRIC) CRACK SHINER
(— IN GLASS) SKIM
(— IN HAIR) BLAZE
(— IN SKY) ICEBLINK
(— IN WOOD) ROE
(— OF BLUBBER) BLANKET
(— OF LIGHT) STREAM
(— ON BEAST'S FACE) RACE
(— ON SURFACE OF SUN) FACULA
(— WITH FINE STRIPES) LACE
(—S FROM PLANE) CONTRAIL
(BACTERIOLOGICAL —) STROKE
(LOSING —) SLUMP
(THEATRICAL —) HAM
(WHITE —) SHIM
STREAKED ROWY LACED HAWKED
SMEARY BRINDLE BROCKED
BROOKED FINCHED SPARKED
STRIPED WHIPPED BRINDLED
IRONSHOT PINROWED
STREAKY ROWY SCOVY STREAKED
STREAM EA PUP RIO RUN BECK
BURN FLOW FLUX FORD GILL
GOTE KHAL KILL LAKE OOZE PUIT
PURL RILL SICK SIKE SILE SPIN
TIDE BACHE BATCH BAYOU
BOGUE BOURN BROOK CREEK
DRILL DRINK FLARE FLASH FLEAM
FLOOD FLOSS FLUOR FRESH
GHYLL NYMPH PRILL RITHE RIVER
SWAMP TCHAI TRAIN ARROYO
BANKER BOURNE BRANCH
BURNIE CANADA COULEE FILLER
FLUENT GUZZLE OUTLET PIRATE
RANDOM RUNDLE RUNNEL
SLUICE SPRUIT STRAND STRONE
CHANNEL CURRENT DRIBBLE
FLUENCE FRESHET RIVULET
TRICKLE AFFLUENT INFLUENT
MILLSTREAM
(— ALONG) SLIDE
(— FULL TO TOP) BANKER
(— OF AIR OR SMOKE) PEW
(— OF ELECTRODES) BEAM
(— OF LAVA) COULEE
(— OF SIRUP) THREAD
(— OF SPEECH) STRAIN
(— OUT) BREAK
(FLOWING —) NYMPH
(HIGH-SPEED —) JET
(MYTHOLOGICAL —S) ELIVAGAR
(SLOW —) OOZE
(SLOW-MOVING —) POW
(SLUGGISH —) LANE
(SMALL —) BECK LAKE SIKE DRAFT
RITHE COULEE SICKET SQUIRT
STRIPE DRAUGHT GRINDLE
(THIN —) TRICKLE TRICKLET
(TIDAL —) COVE SEAPOOSE
(TRANSIENT —) RILL
(TRICKLING —) DRILL
(TURBID —) DRUVE
(UNDERGROUND —) AAR SWALLET
(VIOLENT —) TORRENT
(WEAK —) DRIP
(PREF.) AMNI FLUVI

(— OF LAVA) RHYACO
STREAMER FLAG VANE FALLAL
GARTER GUIDON LAPPET PENCEL
PENNON PINNET SCROLL SIMPLE
WIMPLE BANDEROL FILAMENT
(— OF MOSS) WEEPER
(— ON HEADDRESS) LIRIPIPE
(PAPER —S) CONFETTI
STREAMING SLUICY ASTREAM
CRINITE CYCLOSIS DOWNPOUR
STREAMLET RILL RILLET RUNDLE
RUNLET RUNNEL RIVULET
STREAMLINE SIMPLIFY
(— FLOW) LAMINAR
STREAMLINED CLEAN SLEEK
STREET ROW RUE WAY CHAR
DRUM GATE PAVE STEM TOBY
BLOCK BORGO CALLE CANON
CHAWK CORSO DRIVE PASEO
AVENUE BOWERY CANYON
CAUSEY RAMBLA POULTRY
TERRACE THROUGH ARTERIAL
BROADWAY BYSTREET CHAUSSEE
CONTRADA PROSPECT
(— IN BARCELONA) RAMBLA
(— IN FLORENCE) BORGO
(MAIN —) CHAWK CHOWK
TOWNGATE
(NARROW —) CHAR ALLEY CHARE
(PRINCIPAL —) ARTERY
(SIDE —) HUTUNG
STREETCAR TRAMCAR TRAMWAY
ELECTRIC
STREET CLEANER ORDERLY
CLEANSER
STREET CLEANING SLOPPING
STREET SCENE (AUTHOR OF —)
RICE
(CHARACTER IN —) SAM ROSE
FRANK STEVE KAPLIN SANKEY
WILLIAM MAURRANT
STREETWALKER BULKER CRUISER
STRENGTH EL ARM VIR BEEF
DRAW GRIP GUTS HEAD HORN
IRON MAIN THEW BRAWN CRAFT
ETHAN FIBER FIBRE FORCE HEART
JUICE MIGHT NERVE POWER
SINEW VIGOR ENERGY FOISON
MAUGHT MUSCLE STARCH
VIRTUE ABILITY AFFORCE
COURAGE STAMINA STHENIA
CAPACITY FIRMNESS VALIDITY
PUISSANCE
(— OF ACID OR BASE) AVIDITY
(— OF ALE) STRIKE
(— OF CARD HAND) BODY
(— OF CHARACTER) GRISTLE
(— OF CURRENT) AMPERAGE
(— OF SOLUTION) TITER TITRE
(— OF SPIRITS) PROOF
(— OF TEA) DRAW
(— OF WILL) BACKBONE
(— OF WINE) SEVE
(PREF.) CRATO DYNAM(I)(O)
ISCHY(O)
(SUFF.) DYNAMIA DYNAMOUS
STRENGTHEN IMP ABLE BACK
BIND FIRM FRAP HELP PROP
SOUD STAY BRACE CLEAT FORCE
SINEW STEEL THRAP TONIC
TRUSS ANNEAL ASSURE DEEPEN
ENDURE ENFIRM ENFORT GABION
HARDEN INTEND MUNIFY MUNITE

NEEDLE SETTLE STRING STRONG
AFFORCE BUCKRAM COMFORT
CONFIRM ENFORCE FASCINE
FORTIFY NERVATE QUICKEN
RAMPIRE SUPPORT THICKEN
BUTTRESS ENERGIZE ENTRENCH
HEIGHTEN ROBORATE
STRENGTHENED BULLED
BRANDIED
STRENGTHENING BRACING
ROBORANT
STRENGTHLESS DOWLESS
STRENUOUS HARD EAGER
ARDUOUS WILLING VIGOROUS
STREPHON (BELOVED OF —) CHLOE
STREPSIPTERON STYLOPS
STRESS HIT BIRR BRUNT ICTUS
PINCH SHEAR ACCENT STRAIN
THRONG CENTROID DOWNBEAT
EMPHASIS PRESSURE
(— OF SOUND) LENGTH
STRESSED TONIC STRONG
STRETCH EKE LAG LIE RAX RUN
BEAT DRAW LAST MAIN PASS
RACK REAM ROLL RYKE SPAN
TEND BOARD BURST FETCH
RATCH RETCH SIGHT SPELL
STENT SWAGE VERGE EXTEND
LENGTH SMOOTH STRAIN STRAKE
STREEK DISPLAY ELONGATE
EXPANSE SPELDER ELONGATE
LENGTHEN STRAIGHT
(— CLOTH) TENTER
(— FORTH) PORRECT
(— INJURIOUSLY) SPRAIN
(— IRREGULARLY) TRAIL
(— LEATHER) DRAFT STAKE
DRAUGHT
(— METAL) FORM
(— OF ARMS) FATHOM
(— OF GROUND) BRECK
(— OF INTERVAL) CARSE
(— OF LAND) SWALE COMMON
GALLOP PARCEL COMMONS
(— OF ROAD) SIGHT
(— OF SEA) CHOP
(— OF TIME) TIFF
(— OF WALL) CURTAIN
(— OF WATER) GLIDE LEVEL LOGIN
FAIRWAY
(— OUT) GROW SPIN REACH
STENT STRUT TWINE INTEND
OUTLIE SPRAWL SPREAD SPRING
DISTEND OUTSPAN PORTEND
ELONGATE
(— THE NECK) CRANE
(GRASSY —) DRINN
(LEVEL —) LAWN
(PREF.) TANY TASI TEN(O)
TENONT(O) TETANI TETANO TINO
(SUFF.) EURYSIS
STRETCHED PROSTRATE
(— OUT) PORRECT PROJECT
PROLATE ELONGATE EXTENDED
(TENSELY —) TAUT TORT STIFF
STRETCHER COT STENT GURNEY
LITTER ANGAREP TROLLEY
ANGAREEB BRANCARD STRAINER
STRETCHING
(SUFF.) ECTASIA ECTASIS
STREW BED SOW CLOT DUST LARD
SPEW BESET STRAW STRAY
STROW CARPET LITTER SPREAD

BESTREW SCATTER SKINKLE
SPARKLE
(— WITH BULLETS) SPRAY
STREWED BESPRENT
STREWING SEME
STREWN DOTTED BESPRENT
STRIA CORD STRIOLA DRAGLINE
STRIOLET
STRIATE VEIN
STRIATION STREAK STRIGA
STRICKEN STREAKED
STRICKER TIPPLER
STRICKLE SWEEP STRIKER
STRICT HARD TAUT TRUE CLOSE
EXACT HARSH RIGID STARK
STERN TIGHT GIUSTO SEVERE
STRAIT STRONG ASCETIC
AUSTERE PRECISE REGULAR
DISTRICT RESTRICT RIGOROUS
STRINGENT
(NOT —) LAX SCIOLTO
STRICTLY NARROW STRAIT
CLOSELY PROPERLY
STRICTNESS RIGOR RIGIDITY
RIGORISM SEVERITY
STRIDE LAMP SAIL STEP FLOAT
SKELP SPANG STEND STRUT
LAMPER STROAM STROKE
STROME BESTRIDE POINTING
STRIDDLE
(— LOFTILY) STALK
(— PURPOSEFULLY) SLING
STRIDENT HARD HARSH BRASSY
GLASSY SHRILL RAUCOUS
YELLING GRINDING
STRIDULATE PITTER
STRIFE TUG WAR WIN BATE FEUD
HOLD PLEA BRIGE CHEST FLITE
JEHAD JIHAD NOISE STOUR
STROW STRUT STURT BARRAT
BICKER BRIGUE DEBATE ESTRIF
MUTINY STRIVE BARGAIN
CONTECK CONTEST DISCORD
DISPUTE HURLING QUARREL
CONFLICT CONTRAST DISPEACE
STRUGGLE CONTENTION
(AUTHOR OF —) GALSWORTHY
(CHARACTER IN —) ENID JOHN
ANNIE DAVID EDGAR SIMON
ANTHONY FRANCIS HARNESS
ROBERTS UNDERWOOD
(CIVIL —) STASIS
STRIGIL COMB SCRAPER
STRIKE GO BAT BOB BOP BOX BUM
COB CUE DAD DUB GET HAB HIT
JOB JOW LAM LAY PUG RAP WAP
ABRE BAFF BEAK BEAT BELT BIFF
BILL BLAD BLIP BUFF BUMP CHAP
CLUB COIN COPE COSH CUFF
DING DINT DONG DUNT FALL
FANG FIRK FLAP FLOG FRAP GIRD
GOWF HACK HURT JOWL KILL
KNEE LASH LILT LUSH MARK NAIL
PAIK PASH PLAT PUCK ROUT
SLAM SLAP SLAT SLAY SLOG
SLUG SOCK SPAR SPAT SWAP
SWAT SWIP TAKE WHAP WHOP
WIPE ANGLE BATON CATCH
CHECK CHIME CHINK CLOUT
CLUNK CRACK CRUNT DEVEL
DOUSE DOWSE DRIVE DUNCH
FETCH FILCH FILIP FLAIL KNOCK
PANDY PASTE POKER POTCH

SABER SKELP SKITE SLOSH
SMACK SMITE SNICK SOUND
SPANK SQUAP STAMP STEEK
SWACK SWEEP SWIPE SWISH
THROW WHALE WHANG ACOUPE
AFFECT AFFRAP ALIGHT ATTAIN
BATTER BOUNCE BUFFET COURSE
DUNDER FETTLE FILLIP HAMMER
INCUSE INCUTE KEEPER SLOUGH
STOUSH STRICK STRIPE SWITCH
THRASH WALLOP BEARING
FLYFLAP IMPINGE KNUCKLE
PERCUSS STRIKER TURNOUT
WHAMPLE WILDCAT STOPPAGE
STOPWORK STRAMASH STRICKLE
(— A WICKET) BREAK
(— ABOUT) FLOP
(— AGAINST) RAM BANG STUMP
ASSAULT COLLIDE
(— AND REBOUND) CAROM
(— CRICKET BALL) EDGE
(— DOWN) LAY FALL SLAY WEND
FLASH FLOOR AFFLICT SIDERATE
(— DUMB) DUMFOUND
(— FEET TOGETHER) HITCH
(— FORCIBLY) GET CLOUT DEVEL
SLASH
(— GENTLY) PAT
(— GOLF BALL) HOOK DRIVE
SCLAFF
(— HEAVILY) BASH DUNT DUSH
FLOP SLUG CLUMP SLOUGH
CLOBBER
(— IN CURLING) WICK
(— LIGHTLY) BOB DAB SPAT FLICK
(— OF LUCK) KEEPER STRIKER
(— ON HEAD) COP NOBBLE
(— OUT) FAN DELE POKE TAKE
CROSS ELIDE CANCEL DELETE
EXPUNGE OUTLASH EXCUDATE
(— REPEATEDLY) DRUM LICK
(— SHARPLY) CUT SNICK
(— SMARTLY) NAP RAP KNAP
(— TEETH TOGETHER) GNASH
(— TOGETHER) CLASH KNACK
(— UP) LILT YERK RAISE
(— VIOLENTLY) RIP BASH DING
PASH SOUSE BENSEL
(— WITH AMAZEMENT) CONFOUND
(— WITH BAT) DRIVE
(— WITH FEAR) ALARM ASTONISH
(— WITH FIST) PLUG NODDLE
(— WITH FOOT) KICK BUNCH
SPURN STAMP
(— WITH HAMMER) CHAP JOWL
MELL
(— WITH HORNS) BUNT BUTT
HOOK
(— WITH SHAME) ABASH
(— WITH SPEAR) STICK
(— WITH STICK) SQUAIL
(— WITH WHIP) JERK LASH QUIRK
(— WITH WONDER) SURPRISE
(BOWLING —S) DOUBLE
(HUNGER —) ENDURA
(LABOR —) STEEK STICK TURNOUT
WALKOUT
(LUCKY —) BONANZA
(MINING —) TREND
(THREE —S) TURKEY
(PREF.) PLESSI PLEXI TYPTO
STRIKEBREAKER FINK BLACKLEG
STRIKER BATMAN DRUMMER

TURNOUT PULSATOR
STRIKER-OUT SETTER
STRIKING FITTY FRESH SHOWY
VIVID DARING SIGNAL STRONG
SALIENT SKELPIN TELLING
COLORFUL CONFLICT DRAMATIC
FRAPPANT KNOCKOUT SENSIBLE
SPEAKING NOTICEABLE
PERCUSSION
STRING LAG BAND BEND CORD
FILE LACE MEAN PAIR SLIP TAPE
TAUM BRAID BRIDE CHORD POINT
SINEW SNEAD STRAP CORDON
STRAND TREBLE MINIKIN
LIGATURE RHAPSODY
(— IN BIRD'S EGG) CHALAZA
(— OF BEADS) ROSARY CHAPLET
NECKLACE
(— OF CASH) QUAN TIAO
(— OF DRUM) SNARE
(— OF FIDDLE) THARM
(— OF FLAGS) HOIST
(— OF LOCK) KEEPER
(— OF LYRE) MESE NETE TRITE
HYPATE PARAMESE PARAMETE
(— OF MUSICAL INSTRUMENT) WIRE
CHORD DRONE THAIRM CATLING
MINIKIN LICHANOSE
(— OF ONIONS) REEVE TRACE
(— OF PHRASES) CENTO
(— OF RAILWAY CARS) SET
(— OF SUGAR CRYSTALS) COB
(— OF VEGETABLES) STRAP
(— OF VERSES) LAISSE
(— OF VIOL) MEAN
(— OF WAGONS) RAKE
(— TOBACCO) SEW
(— UP) KILT
(BONNET —) BRIDE
(E —) QUINT
(LEADING —) BAND
(OAKUM —) PLEDGET
(ORNAMENTAL —) CORDON
(SURGICAL —) LIGATURE
(VIOLIN —) THAIRM VIBRATOR
(WEAVING —) LEASH
(SUFF.) CHORD(AL)
STRING BEAN SNAP HARICOT
SNAPPER
STRINGCOURSE LEDGE TABLE
CORDON STRING
STRINGENT HARD RIGID TIGHT
SEVERE STRICT EXTREME
STRINGER BALK BAULK
STRINGHALTED CRAMPY
STRINGY ROPY WOOLY SINEWY
THONGY WOOLLY GARGETY
SINEWED THREADY
STRIP BAR LAG TAG BAND BARE
BEAD BELT BEND BUSK DRIP
FUSE GAGE GAIR HILD HUSK LIST
MALL NAKE NUDE PEEL RAND
ROLL SACK SHIM SKIN TIRL TIRR
WELT CLEAN DRIVE EXUTE FILET
FLAKE FLYPE GAUGE GLEAN
GUARD HARRY LABEL LINER
LYNCH PANEL PLUME REEVE
SHEAR SHRED SKELP SLIPE SPEEL
SPOIL STRAP STROP STRUB
SWATH UNGUM UNRIG BORDER
BOXING BRIDGE COLLAR CULPON
DENUDE DEVEST DIVEST FEELER
FILLET FLEECE LIBBET MATRIX

PANUNG REGLET SCROLL SPLINE
STREAK STRIPE TARGET UNBARE
UNBARK UNCASE BANDAGE
BEREAVE CHANNEL DEPLUME
DEPRIVE DESPOIL DISROBE
FEATHER FLOUNCE LAMBEAU
LANGUET NAILROD PINRAIL
PLUNDER UNCLOAK UNCOVER
UNDRESS BOOKMARK COSSETTE
DISARRAY DISENDOW DISTRUSS
FOOTBAND SEPARATE
(— A PLANT) SPRIG
(— BARK) PILL
(— BINDING STALKS TO WALL)
TACK
(— BLUBBER FROM WHALE) FLENSE
(— EAR OF CORN) SILK
(— FOR DRAWING CURVED LINES)
SPLINE
(— FOR GUIDING PLASTER) BEAD
(— FOR MAKING TUBE) SKELP
(— HANGING AROUND SKIRT)
FLOUNCE
(— IN BASKETMAKING) INSIDES
(— IN BEEHIVE) STARTER
(— IN CANING) SPLENT SPLINT
(— IN TYPEWRITER) DRAWBAND
(— OF CANVAS) FOOTBAND
(— OF CLOTH) LIST PATA RIND
ROON GUARD BANNER
DUTCHMAN
(— OF CORK) SPREADER
(— OF FABRIC) FLIPPER
(— OF FAT) FATBACK LARDOON
(— OF FIELD HOCKEY AREA) ALLEY
(— OF FUR) GROTZEN
(— OF GRASS) VERGE
(— OF HIDE) SPECK DEWLAP
(— OF LAND) BUTT LAND RAIK
RAIN RAKE TANG BREAK CREEK
SLANG SLIPE SPONG SCREED
SELION STRAKE STRIPE FURLONG
ISTHMUS CORRIDOR SIDELING
(— OF LEATHER) LAY RAND WELT
APRON RANGE THONG BACKSTAY
(— OF LEAVES) TWIST
(— OF LINEN) SETON
(— OF MASONRY) ARCHBAND
(— OF OFFICE) BREAK
(— OF OSIER) SKEIN
(— OF PALM LEAF) CADJAN
CAJANG
(— OF PASTRY) STRAW
(— OF PLANKING) APRON
(— OF PLASTER) SCREED
(— OF PRAIRIE) COVE
(— OF PROVISIONS) FORAGE
(— OF RANK) DEGRADE
(— OF RED CLOTH) COXCOMB
(— OF ROADWAY) LANE
(— OF RUBBER) CUSHION
(— OF TURF) PARKING
(— OF UNPLOWED LAND) GAIR
HADE HEADLAND
(— OF WATER) INLET
(— OF WOOD) LAG LAT LATH LIST
SHAW SLAT WELT CHINK CLEAT
STAVE BATTEN INWALE RADDLE
REEPER REGLET FOOTING
FURRING STICKER TRACKER
FOOTLING
(— OFF) TIRL FLIPE FLYPE SLIPE
(— OFF SKIN) CASE FLAY

(— ON FOLDING DOORS) ASTRAGAL
(— ON PRINTER'S GALLEY) LEDGE
(— ON SQUASH COURT) TELLTALE
(— ON TIRE) CHAFER
(— SEPARATING LINES OF TYPE) LEAD REGLET
(BOUNDARY —) PERIMETER
(CAMOUFLAGING —) GARLAND
(COMIC —) FUNNY
(CONSTRUCTION —S) LAGGING
(CORSET —) BUSK
(DEPENDENT —) LAMBEAU
(DIVIDING —) CLOISON
(HORSESHOE-SHAPED —) BAIL BALE
(IRON IN —S) NAILROD
(MEDIAN —) MALL
(NARROW —) SEAM SLAT SLIP TAPE REEVE STRAKE
(PAPER —) ORIHON
(PROJECTING —) FEATHER
(RAISED —) RIDGE
(STRENGTHENING —) BEND
(THATCHING —) LEDGER
(UNPLOWED —) BALK
STRIPE BAR RAY BAND BEND LIST PALE SLAT TRIM WALE WEAL WELT ZONE FLECK PLAGA STRIA STRIP SWATH VITTA WHEAL BORDER CLAVUS COTICE FRENUM LADDER RIBBON STRAKE STREAK STREAM COTTISE SPRAING MUSTACHE TRAVERSE
(— OF CHEVRON) ARC
(— OF COLOR ON CHEEK) FRENUM FRAENUM
(— ON ANIMAL'S FACE) SNIP BLAZE
(— ON FABRIC) CROSSBAR
(— ON MILITARY SLEEVE) SLASH
(— ON SHIELD) ENDORSE
(ENCIRCLING —) ZONE
(PURPLE —) CLAVUS
(SET OF —S) BAR
STRIPED BANDY PALED PIRNY RAWED RAYED ROWED WALED ZONED BARRED CORDED LISTED PIRNED BROCKED TIGROID VITTATE FASCIATE STRIPPED
(— CROSSWISE) BAYADERE
STRIPED BASS ROCKFISH SERRANID
STRIPED MAPLE DOGWOOD
STRIPING HAIRLINE
STRIPLIGHT BORDER
STRIPLING LAD SLIP STIRRA YONKER SPAUGHT YOUNKER SKIPJACK SPRINGAL SHAVELING
STRIPPED BARE NUDE NAKED HUSKED PICKED PLUMED UNPEELED
STRIPPER STEMMER SPRIGGER
STRIPPING STROKINGS
(PL.) JIBBINGS
STRIPTEASE (RELATING TO —) EXOTIC
STRIPTEASER STRIPPER ECDYSIAST
STRIVE AIM HIE TEW TRY TUG DEAL FEND PAIN TOIL WORK BANDY DRIVE EXERT FIGHT FORCE LABOR PRESS BRIGUE BUCKLE BUFFET DEBATE INTEND PINGLE STRAIN STRIKE AGONIZE BARGAIN CONTEND CONTEST

DISPUTE ENFORCE SCUFFLE CONTRAST ENDEAVOR PURCHASE STRUGGLE
(— AFTER) SEEK FOLLOW CANVASS
(— FOR SUPERIORITY) VIE KEMP
(— IN OPPOSITION) RIVAL CONTEND
(— TO EQUAL) EMULATE
(— TO OVERTAKE) ENSUE
STRIVING NISUS HORMIC STRIFT CONATUS CONATION
STRIX SYRNIUM
STROBILE BUR BELL BURR CHAT CONE BRUSH
STROKE BAT COY CUT DAB FIT JOW ODD PAT PET POP RUB BAFF BEAT BLOW CHAP CHOP CLAP COUP CUFF DASH DENT DING DINT DIRD DRAW DUNT EDGE FIRK FLAP FLEG FLIP FLOP FUNG GOWF HAND HURT JERK JOWL KERF LASH LICK NACK PAIK PEAL PECK SHOT SMIT SWAP TILT TIRE TUCK WELT WHAP WIPE BRUSH CHASE DOUSE DOWSE DRAFT FLACK FLICK FORCE HATCH ICTUS MINIM PANDY PULSE SHOCK SLASH SLING SLIVE SLOSH STRIP SWEEP SWING SWIPE THROW TOUCH TRAIT TRICE WHACK CARESS CENTER FONDLE FOOZLE GENTLE GLANCE PLAGUE PLUNGE SMOOTH STRAIK STRAKE STRIKE STRIPE DRAUGHT OUTLASH SOLIDUS VIRGULE APOPLEXY BACKHAND DRUMBEAT FOREHAND INSTROKE SCORCHER
(— IN PAINTING) HAND
(— IN PENMANSHIP) MINIM
(— IN TENNIS) LET LOB BOAST CHASE SMASH BRICOLE BACKHAND FOREHAND OVERHAND
(— OF A LETTER) DUCT STEM SERIF POTHOOK CROSSBAR
(— OF BAD FORTUNE) CLAP
(— OF BELL) JOW BELL JOWL KNELL TELLER
(— OF FORTUNE) CAST BREAK BONZER FELICITY
(— OF LUCK) HIT FLUKE STRIKE TURNUP CAPTION
(— OF MISFORTUNE) SISERARY
(— OF SCYTHE) SWATH SWATHE
(— OF SHEARS) SNIP
(— OF WIT) FLIRT
(— OF WORK) BAT CHAR
(— ON THE PALM) LOOFIE
(— WITH CLAW) CLOYE
(BILLIARDS —) SPOT STUN FLUKE FORCE MASSE HAZARD
(CONNECTING —) LIGATURE
(CRICKET —) CUT GLANCE
(CROQUET —) ROQUET
(CURLING —) INWICK
(CUTTING —) GIRD
(DOUBLE SPINNING —) DRAW
(DRUM —) DRAG
(FINISHING —) NOBBLER
(GOLF —) ODD BAFF BISK HOOK LIKE BLAST SLICE BISQUE FOOZLE

SCLAFF APPROACH
(HOCKEY —) JOB SCOOP
(JERKY —) STAB
(LIGHTNING —) BOLT
(MEDICAL —) ICTUS APOPLEXY
(MUSICAL —) TACT
(ORNAMENTAL —) FLOURISH
(QUICK —) FLIP
(SKATING —) EDGE MOHAWK CHOCTAW
(SMART —) FIRK
(SOOTHING —) COY
(SWIMMING —) CRAWL TRUDGEN SIDESTROKE
(SWINGING —) HEW
(SWORD —) MONTANTO
(PREF.) BOLO PLEGA PLEGO
(SUFF.) BOLA BOLE BOLIC BOLISM BOLIST PLEGIA PLEGY PLEXIA
STROLL JET IDLE ROAM ROVE ANTER JAUNT RANGE STRAY TRAIK BUMMEL DACKER DANDER GANDER LOUNGE PALMER RAMBLE SOODLE STROAM STROME TODDLE WANDER SAUNTER TURNOUT SPATIATE STRAVAGE STRAVAIG PERAMBULATE
STROLLER SULKY TRAMP SHULER FLANEUR SHUILER VAGRANT BOHEMIAN PUSHCHAIR
STROLLING FLANERIE FUGITIVE
STROMA ECOID OECOID
STRONG FAT FIT HOT FELL FERE FIRM FORT HALE HANG HARD HIGH IRON KEEN RANK SURE TRIG TRIM ACRID BONNY FORCY FRECK FRESH HARDY HEAVY HOGEN HUSKY JOLLY LUSTY NAPPY NERVY ORPED PITHY SHARP SMART SOLID SOUND STARK STEER STERN STIFF STOUR STOUT SWITH THEWY VALID VIVID WIGHT YAULD ARDENT BRAWNY BUCKRA BUNKUM FEIRIE FIERCE MIGHTY POTENT PRETTY ROBUST RUGGED SECURE SEVERE SINEWY STABLE STANCH STARCH STURDY WIELDY BOARDLY BUIRDLY DOUGHTY DURABLE EXALTED FECKFUL HUFFCAP HUMMING INTENSE LUSTFUL NERVOUS POLLENT SKOOKUM STHENIC ATHLETIC BIDDABLE MUSCULAR REVERENT ROBOREAN SPANKING STALWART STIFFISH VIGOROUS MERACIOUS
(PREF.) TRACHY VALE
STRONGBOX PETE COFFER DEEDBOX
STRONGEST EXTREME
STRONGHOLD HOLD KEEP PEEL PIECE PLACE TOWER CASTLE WARDER CITADEL KREMLIN REDOUBT FASTHOLD FASTNESS FORTRESS FRONTIER MUNIMENT STRENGTH
STRONGLY BUT SAD BADLY SWITH FIRMLY STRONG DURABLY FRESHLY HEFTILY SOLIDLY STITHLY STOUTLY HEARTILY
STRONG-SCENTED HIGH RANK
STRONG-SMELLING FOXY

STRONTIUM SULPHATE ACANTHIN
STROP RIP STRAP
STROPHE ALCAIC LAISSE STANZA SAPPHIC
STROPHIC MELIC
STROPHIUS (FATHER OF —) CRISSUS
(MOTHER OF —) ANTIPHATIA
(SON OF —) PYLADES
(WIFE OF —) ANAXIBIA ASTYOCHIA CYDRAGORA
STRUCK (— SHARPLY) SMITTEN
(— WITH AMAZEMENT) AGAZED AGHAST
STRUCTURAL ORGANIC ANATOMIC TECTONIC
(— UNIT) IDANT
STRUCTURE CAGE FALX FORM MAKE ANNEX BOOTH CABIN FLOAT FRAME GETUP HOUSE KIOSK PEGMA SETUP SHAPE STOCK BRIDGE CAGEOT FABRIC GANTRY GIRDER ISOGEN KELSON PREFAB TIMBER COTTAGE EDIFICE FAIRING FEATURE GATEWAY GESTALT KEELSON MANSION NURAGHE OUTCAST PAGEANT STADIUM TURNOUT ZEUGITE AEDICULA AIRCRAFT AIRFRAME BUILDING BUTTRESS COMPAGES CRIBWORK DOMATIUM ENDOCONE ESCORIAL HEADWORK MOUNTURE NEOMORPH SKELETON STANDARD
(— BUILT IN WATER) PIER
(— CONTAINING KILN) HOVEL
(— EXTENDED INTO SEA) JETTY
(— FOR PIGEONS) COTE
(— FRAMING SHIP) KEELSON
(— IN ROCKS) FLASER
(— OF CARTRIDGE) ANVIL
(— OF PRETENSION) PERRON
(— ON ROOF) CUPOLA FEMERELL
(— ON SHIP) BLISTER
(— ON STEAMER) TEXAS
(— PRODUCING SMOOTH OUTLINE) FAIRING
(— SHELTERING INSECTS) DOMATIUM
(— SUPPORTING AIRSHIP PROPELLER) PYLON
(— WITHIN SHELL) ENDOCONE
(ANATOMICAL —) BUD APRON CARINA CRESCENT
(ANTICLINAL —) SWELL
(ARCHED —) FORNIX
(BODILY —) FRAME PHYSIQUE
(BRICK —) KANG HOVEL
(BRISTLELIKE —) ARISTA
(BRONZE AGE —) HENGE
(CABINLIKE —) CABANA
(CLIMBING —) LADDER
(COMPLEX —) EMBOLUS
(CONELIKE —) PYRAMID
(CONICAL —) BULLET
(CREMATION —) DARGA
(CROWNLIKE —) CORONA
(CRYSTAL —) POLYTYPE
(CYLINDRICAL —) SILO
(DEADENING —) BAFFLE
(DEFENSIVE —) CAT

(FORTIFIED —) CAVALIER
(GENERAL —) GETUP
(GEOLOGICAL —) CAMBER
(HIGH —) TOWER
(HOLLOW —) SHELL
(KNEE-LIKE —) GENU
(LENS-SHAPED —) LENTOID
(LOFTY —) BABEL STEEPLE
(LOGICAL —) EIDOS
(MEGALITHIC —) HENGE
(ORGANIZED —) BULK
(ORIENTAL STORIED —) PAGODA
(ORNAMENTAL —) KIOSK
(PLANT —) DISC DISK
(POINTED —) BEAK
(PUEBLO —) KIVA
(RAISED —) CIMBORIO
(RAMSHACKLE —) COOP
(RINGLIKE —) ANNULUS
(RUDE STONE —S) SPECCHIE
(SACRIFICIAL —) ALTAR
(SENTENCE —) SYNTAX
(SHELTERING —) COT
(SICKLE-SHAPED —) FALX
(SLENDER —) HAIR
(STONE —) TAULA
(TEMPORARY —) HUT
(THEATER —) SKENE
(UNDERLYING —) BOTTOM
(UNSTABLE —) COBHOUSE
(WATERTIGHT —) CAMEL
(WHITE —) ALBEDO
(PREF.) MORPH(O)
(RADIATED —) ACTIN(O)
(SUFF.) (— OF A KIND) ID
(— UNIT) EME
STRUGGLE IT TEW TUG VIE WIN
AGON CAMP COPE DEAL FEND
FICK FRAB GAME PULL TAVE TOIL
AGONY FIGHT FLING HEAVE
LABOR STRAY SWORD TEAVE
TWEIL WORRY WRELE BATTLE
BUCKLE BUFFET BUSTLE COMBAT
EFFORT HASSLE JOSTLE JUSTLE
PINGLE RELUCT SEESAW SPRAWL
SPRUNT STIVER STRIFE STRIVE
TERVEE TUSSLE WARSLE WIDDLE
AGONIZE CLAMBER CONTEND
CONTEST DISPUTE FLOUNCE
GRAPPLE SCUFFLE TUILYIE
WARFARE WAUCHLE WRESTLE
CONFLICT ENDEAVOR FLOUNDER
SCRAFFLE SCRAMBLE SLUGFEST
SPRANGLE SPRATTLE
(— ALONG) HOBBLE
(— CONVULSIVELY) SPRAWL
(— FOR LARGESS) SCAMBLE
(— FORTH) ELUCTATE
(— TO GAIN FOOTING) SCRABBLE
SPROTTLE
(AGONIZED —) THROE
(CONFUSED —) MUSS
(DEATH —) AGONY
(HAND-TO-HAND —) GRAPPLE
(HAPHAZARD —) SCUFFLE
(SPIRITUAL —) PENIEL
(UNCEREMONIOUS —) SCRAMBLE
STRUGGLER LAOCOON
STRUM THRUM
STRUMA GOITER GOITRE
STRUMPET BRIM PUNK TRULL
WENCH WHORE BLOWEN BULKER
STIVER TOMBOY TOMRIG

COCOTTE SUCCUBA DOLLYMOP
PUNKLING SUCCUBUS VENTURER
(WORN-OUT —) HARRIDAN
STRUT JET BRAG COCK POMP
SPUR BRANK CORSO MAJOR
PRINK RANCE SWANK SASHAY
SCOTCH STROKE STROOT STRUNT
NAUNTLE PEACOCK STEMPLE
SWAGGER TRANSOM
STRUTTER HAM
STRUTTING COCKING
STUB BUTT SNAG SPUD STOB
STUD CHECK ERGOT GUARD
HINGE STUMP SPRUNT
STUBBLE BUN ETCH MANE SHACK
ARRISH EDDISH STOVER STUMPS
EEGRASS GRATTEN STIBBLE
STUBBORN SOT BALKY ROWDY
RUSTY STIFF STOUT STUNT
THRAW TOUGH MULISH STURDY
THWART BULLDOG PEEVISH
PIGGISH RESTIVE WAYWARD
WILLFUL OBDURATE PERVERSE
STUNKARD THRAWART
OBSTINATE PIGHEADED
TENACIOUS REFRACTORY
STUBBORNNESS STOMACH
ADAMANCY
STUBBY STUB CUTTY SQUAT
STOCKY STUMPY STUBBED
STUCCO ALBARIUM
STUCK FAST MASHED STICKIT
STOODED
STUCK-UP BUG FROSTED
STUD SET BOLT BOSS KNOB KNOP
KNOT NAIL RACE SLUG SPOT
BESET BULLA CLOUT HARAS
JOIST WRIST ASHLAR ENSTAR
INSTAR STOOTH STRING
CONTACT POTENCE QUARTER
STUDDLE PUNCHEON STANDARD
STUDDERY
(— FARM) HARAS
(— IN BOOT SOLE) SLUG
(— IN WATCH) POTENCE
(— SHOES) HOBNAIL
(— WITH NAILS) CLOUT
(INTERMEDIATE —) PUNCHEON
(ORNAMENTED —) AGLET AIGLET
STUDDED BOSSY BILLETY STELLED
BILLETTE
STUDDLE POST ROIL
STUDENT BOY DIG WIT COED
PLUG PREP SMUG SOPH AGGIE
BAHUR BEJAN FUCHS GRIND
MEDIC PUPIL SIZAR SPOON
BOCHER BURSAR BURSCH INTERN
JUNIOR JURIST MEDICO OPTIME
PREMED PRIMAR PRIMER PUISNE
SCOLOG SENIOR ADVISEE
CHRONIC CLASSIC DANTEAN
EDUCAND ETONIAN FAILURE
GOLIARD GRECIAN INTERNE
INTRANT LEARNER MIDDLER
MOOTMAN OPPIDAN PASSMAN
PHARMIC PLUGGER SCHOLAR
STUDIER TEMPLAR THEOLOG
BOTANIST CABALIST COLLEGER
DEMOTIST DISCIPLE EDUCATOR
FEMINIST HOMERIST HOSTELER
ISLAMIST PREMEDIC REPEATER
SECONDAR SUBSIZAR TRANSFER
(— IN TALMUDIC ACADEMY) BAHUR

(— LAST IN CLASS) SPOON
(— OF LOW RANK) TERNAR TERNER
(— WHO LIVES IN TOWN) OPPIDAN
(ABNORMALLY ABSORBED) SAP
(DAY —) EXTERN EXTERNE
(DIVINITY —) STIBBLER
(DRUDGING —) PLUG
(ENGLISH SCHOOL —) BLUE SWOT
ETONIAN OXONIAN SWOTTER
BATTELER
(GRADUATE —) FELLOW
(LAW —) PUNEE JURIST LEGIST
PUISNE TEMPLAR STAGIARY
(MILITARY —) CADET
(MOSLEM —) SOFTA
(NON-COLLEGIATE —) TOSHER
(PLODDING —) DIG SMUG
(WANDERING —) GOLIARD
(1ST-YEAR —) FUCHS
(3RD-YEAR —) JUNIOR TERTIAN
(PL.) GOWN CLASS HOUSE SEMI-
NAR
(SUFF.) LOG(ER)(IA)(IAN)(IC)(ICAL)
(IST)(UE)(Y)
STUDIED COOL VOULU STUDIOUS
STUDIO LOT SHOT ATELIER
BOTTEGA GALLERY
STUDIOUS BOOKY BOOKISH
CLERKLY DILIGENT SEDULOUS
STUDY CON BEAT BONE BOOK
CASE MUZZ ROOM SIFT STUD
GRIND ESTUDY EXAMEN LESSON
MUSEUM SCOLEY SURVEY
ABBOZZO ACCOUNT ANALYZE
CANVASS CROQUIS POCHADE
REVOLVE SANCTUM ANALYSIS
BOOKWORK CONSIDER EXERCISE
MEDITATE SCRUTINY TYPOLOGY
(— HARD) DIG MUG SAP BONE
SMUG STEW SWOT
(— OF BRAMBLES) BATOLOGY
(— OF ONESELF) AUTOLOGY
(— OF PUNISHMENT) PENOLOGY
(— OF SACRED EDIFICES) NAOLOGY
(— OF SNOW AND ICE) CRYOLOGY
(— OF VALUES) AXIOLOGY
(— UNDER PRESSURE) CRAM
(ART —) ABBOZZO CROQUIS
POCHADE
(BROWN —) REVERIE
(CLAY —) BOZZETTO
(MUSICAL —) ETUDE
(PRELIMINARY —) SKETCH
(UNINTERESTING —) GRIND
(SUFF.) ICS SOPH(ER)(IC)(IST)(Y)
**STUDY IN SCARLET (AUTHOR OF —
)** DOYLE
(CHARACTER IN —) HOPE JOHN
LUCY HOLMES TOBIAS WATSON
FERRIER GREGSON LESTRADE
SHERLOCK STAMFORD
JEFFERSON STANGERSON
STUFF PAD RAM WAD CRAM CRAP
GAUM GEAR JAZZ PANG STOP
TACK TRIG TUCK WHAT CROWD
DUROY FARCE FORCE KEDGE
METAL PASTE SQUAB TRADE
FABRIC GRAITH KIBOSH MATTER
PAUNCH STEEVE STODGE TACKLE
TIMBER BOMBARD BOMBAST
DRUGGET ELEMENT ENFARCE
DIAPHANE MARINATE MATERIAL
SPLUTTER WHIPPING

(— AND NONSENSE) HAVERS
PICKLE PIFFLE
(— FILLET OF VEAL) BOMBARD
(— FULL) STODGE
(— OF POOR QUALITY SILK) RASH
(— ONESELF) MAST
(— POULTRY) FARCE MARINATE
(— WITH DRESSING) QUILT
(COTTON —) CALICO
(HOUSEHOLD —) GEAR
(INFERIOR —) MOCKADO
(SILKEN —) TARS TARSE DIAPHANE
(STICKY —) GOOK
(TASTELESS —) GLOP
(THIN —) CRAPE
(THIN SILK —) LOVE
(WATERY —) BLASH
(WISHY-WASHY —) BLASH
(WOOLEN —) SAY DUROY TWILLY
DRUGGET SAGATHY SHALLOON
(WORTHLESS —) GEAR GLOP
HOGWASH
STUFFED PANG TRIG BLOAT FARCI
STODGY BLOATED BOMBAST
STUFFING PAD TAR FARCE STECH
STUFF BOMBAST FARCING
SAWDUST SALPICON STUFFAGE
(— FOR MATTRESS) PULU
STUFFY POKY CLOSE FUBBY FUBSY
FUGGY STIVY WOOLY WOOLLY
AIRLESS FROUSTY
STULTIFY SOT PUPPIFY
STUMBLE CHIP FALL HAMP PECK
STOT TRIP HAMEL LURCH SPURN
STOIT STUMP BUMBLE CHANCE
FALTER HALPER HAMBLE HAPPEN
LUMPER OFFEND STEVEL TUMBLE
WAGGER BLUNDER FOUNDER
SCAMBLE SNAPPER STAMMER
STAMPLE STOITER STOTTER
STUMMER FLOUNDER THRUMBLE
STUMBLING HACK HURTING
OFFENCE OFFENSE
STUMP CAG GET JOB NOG SET
BUTT DOCK GRUB LUMP MORE
RUNT SNAG STAB STAM STOB
STUB STUD CHUNK SCRAB SCRAG
STICK STOCK STOMP STOOL
STOOP STOWL DOTARD NUBBIN
SCRUNT SPRONG STOVEN
WICKET DODDARD RAMPICK
RAMPIKE SLEEPER STUMMEL
BALDHEAD HUSTINGS STUBBLES
(— AND ROOT) MOCK
(— OF TAIL) STRUNT
(CIGAR —) TOPPER
(CRICKET —) STICKS
(DEAD —) RUNT
(TREE —) MOCK STOW STOCK
STOOP ZUCHE DOTARD NUBBIN
STOVEN DODDARD
(WALNUT —) BUTT
STUMPY SNUB BUNTY SNUBBED
STUN DIN BOWL DAZE ROCK
DAUNT DAVER DEAVE DOVER
DOZEN DROWN STONY ASTONY
BEDAZE BEMUSE DEADEN
DEAFEN DEVVEL NOBBLE
STOUND WITHER ASTOUND
DAMMISH SANDBAG SILENCE
STUPEFY STUPEND ASTONISH
PARALYZE
(— BY A SHOT) CREASE

STUNNED SILLY STUPENT ASTONIED

STUNNER KNOCKER THUMPER TRIMMER

STUNNING CRASHING SHOCKING

STUNT GAG KIP FEAT NIRL BLAST CANOE CROWL DWARF STINT STOCK BARANI BARONI CRADDY DOLPHIN BACKBEND CATALINA CRUCIFIX PORPOISE SUPPRESS **(SWIMMING —)** SHARK SPIRAL

STUNTED URLED GRUBBY RUNTISH SCROGGY SCRUBBY SCRUFFY SCRUNTY WANTHRIVEN

STUPA TOPE CHORTEN

STUPEFACTION STOUND STUPOR

STUPEFIED MAD DAMP DAZED DRUNK MAZED SILLY SOTTED BEMAZED BEMUSED DONNERT DOZENED DOZZLED STUPENT BESOTTED DATELESS MINDLESS

STUPEFIER OPIUM

STUPEFY FOX BAZE DAMP DAZE DOZE DRUG DULL GOOF MAZE MULL STUN BESOT DAUNT DAVER DEAVE DIZZY DOZEN SHEND SMOKE STONY ASTONE ASWEVE BEMUSE BENUMB DUDDLE FUDDLE MOIDER MUDDLE STOUND ASTOUND CONFUSE FORDULL SLUMBER STUPEND ASTONISH BEFUDDLE BEMUDDLE BEWILDER CONFOUND MORPHINE PARALYZE SOMNIATE SOPORATE

STUPEFYING STONY

STUPENDOUS GREAT IMMENSE ENORMOUS MONSTROUS

STUPID FAT JAY BETE DOWF DULL DUMB DUNT FOOL HAZY LEWD NICE NUMB SLOW BLUNT BOOBY BRUTE CRASS DENSE DOTED DUNNY GLAKY GOOSY GROSS HEAVY INERT MOSSY MUZZY SILLY THICK ASSISH BARREN BOVINE CUCKOO DAWKIN DOITED DROWSY DUMMEL HEBETE LOGGER LURDAN OBTUSE OPAQUE SIMPLE SODDEN STOLID STULTY STURDY SUMPHY URLUCH WOODEN ASININE BRUTISH CHUCKLE DOLTISH DOWFART DUFFING DUMPISH FATUOUS FOOLISH FOPPISH GAWKISH GLAIKIT GULLISH INSULSE LUMPISH LURDANE PEAKISH PINHEAD PROSAIC SOTTISH TAIVERT TOMFOOL VACUOUS WITLESS ANSERINE BAYARDLY BESOTTED BLOCKISH BOBBYISH BOEOTIAN CLODDISH DONNERED DUNCICAL FOOTLESS GAUMLESS HEADLESS IMBECILE STOCKISH PINHEADED SENSELESS **(— PERSON)** HOIT JUKES SUMPH LUMMOX TUMFIE KALLIKAK **(PREF.)** MORO

STUPIDITY BETISE TORPOR BOBBERY DENSITY DUNCERY FATUITY DULLNESS DUMBNESS HEBETUDE STOLIDITY

STUPOR FOG SOG DAMP DOTE SOPOR SWARF STOUND TORPOR

TRANCE NARCOMA LETHARGY NARCOSIS **(PREF.)** NARC(O) TYPH(O)

STURDILY BUFF TOUGH

STURDY GID BUFF DUNT RUDE TALL THRO BURLY CRANK FELON HARDY HUSKY LUSTY SOLID SOUND STARK STERN STIFF STOUT VAUDY WALLY FEERIE PLUGGY ROBUST RUGGED RUSTIC SQUARE STABLE STEADY STEEVE STOCKY STRONG STUGGY VIRILE FECKFUL UPRIGHT VALIANT STALWART STUBBORN VIGOROUS YEOMANLY

STURGEON HUSO ELOPS BELUGA GANOID MAMMOSE OSSETER STERLET

STUTTER FAM BUFF HACK MANT STOT STUT GANCH FAMBLE HABBER HABBLE STAMMER

STUTTERER RATTLER

STUTTERING TRAULISM BALBUTIENT

STY PEN QUAT STYE WEST FRANK CRUIVE PIGPEN STITHE HORDEOLUM

STYLE AIR CUT DUB PEN SAY TON WAY CHIC FACE FORM GARB HAND KIND MODE MOLD NAME PILE RATE TWIG VEIN GENRE GETUP GUISE SHAPE STATE SWANK TASTE FESCUE FORMAT GNOMON GOTHIC PHRASE STEELE STRAIN STYLUS UMBONE COSTUME DIALECT DICTION FASHION INSTYLE QUALITY EQUIPAGE LANGUAGE MARINISM NARRANTE PULLBACK PHRASEOLOGY **(— HAIR)** CORNROW **(— OF ARCHITECTURE)** ORDER DRAVIDA GEORGIAN **(— OF COOKING)** CUISINE **(— OF DRESS)** GUISE **(— OF GEM SETTING)** BOX **(— OF HANDWRITING)** CHANCERY SCRIPTION **(— OF HAT)** BLOCK **(— OF MOUNTING)** SETTING **(— OF MUSIC)** BOOGIE **(— OF PAINTING)** GENRE **(— OF PENMANSHIP)** HAND **(— OF PRINTING)** CAMAIEU **(— OF SPEAKING)** ADDRESS **(— OF WRESTLING)** SAMBO **(AFFECTED —)** EUPHUISM **(ARTISTIC —)** GUSTO GOTHIC ARTIFICE DANDYISM MANNERISM **(BOOKBINDING —)** ALDINE MAIOLI MAJOLI FANFARE GROLIER ETRUSCAN HARLEIAN ROXBURGH **(CUSTOMARY —)** GATE **(DECORATIVE —)** ARTDECO **(DISTINCTIVE —)** CLOTHES **(FAVORED —)** GROOVE **(HAIR —)** CROP TETE **(INFLATED —)** FUSTIAN **(LATEST —)** KICK **(PRETENTIOUS —)** BOMBAST **(PROPER —)** WEAR **(THEATRICAL —)** LYCEUM **(WRITING —)** MINUSCULE

(SUFF.) (IN THE — OF) ESQUE

STYLET SPEAR STILET STYLUS TROCAR MANDRIN STILETTE

STYLIDIUM CANDOLEA

STYLISH CHIC DOSS POSH TONY DOGGY NIFTY NOBBY RITZY SASSY SHARP SMART SWELL TIPPY TOPPY CHEESY CLASSY DAPPER FLOSSY JAUNTY SWANKY TONISH DASHING DOGGISH GENTEEL KNOWING SWAGGER TOFFISH

STYLOBATE PODIUM

STYLOID BELONOID

STYLUS GAD PEN STYLE CUTTER GREFFE TRACER HARPAGO POINTEL PYROPEN

STYMPHALUS (FATHER OF —) ELATUS **(MOTHER OF —)** LAODICE

STYPTIC ALUM AMADOU MATICO BAROMETZ STANCHER

STYRENE STYROL CINNAMOL

STYX (FATHER OF —) OCEANUS **(HUSBAND OF —)** PALLAS **(MOTHER OF —)** TETHYS

SUAEDA DONDIA

SUAH (FATHER OF —) ZOPHAH

SUAN PAN SOROBAN

SUAVE OILY SMUG SOFT BLAND SOAPY SVELT GLOSSY SILKEN SMOOTH URBANE FULSOME POLITIC UNCTUOUS

SUAVELY CREAMILY

SUAVITY COMITY URBANITY

SUB GRASS

SUBALTERN WART

SUBBASE PLINTH

SUBCINCTORIUM BALTEUS BALTHEUS

SUBCLASS GENDER BRYALES CESTODA CYCLIAE DIGENEA SPECIES AMOEBAEA ANAPSIDA CESTODES COPEPODA GANOIDEI SELACHII

SUBCOMPACT MINICAR

SUBCUTANEOUS DEEP

SUBDEACON MINISTER

SUBDIVIDE CARVE MINCE

SUBDIVISION DEN OBE SEX BEAT CAZA DHER HAPU ITEM TASU BUNDA CORPS CURIA DEKAN DHERI FERAE FORTY HSIEN IOWAN NAHIE OKRUG PHYLE SITIO STAGE TALUK TARAF TURMA UINTA ALBIAN ARENIG BANNER BRANCH BUREAU CERCLE CIRCLE CLAUSE COHORT COLUMN COMMOT DAKOTA DANIAN DOGGER FACIES GUELPH HEMERA IMBREX LENGTH LUDLOW MARKAZ NAHIYE OBLAST ONEIDA SANJAK SECTOR SERIAL SHIRAZ STRAIN SUBAGE TAHSIL TASSOO TEHSIL BUKEYEF CENTURY CHEMUNG CHIRIPA COCHITI COMARCA ECOTYPE ELEMENT EPARCHY EPISODE GENESEE MANIPLE MONTANA ORBITAL PHRATRY RONDOUT SASTEAN SECTION SEEDBED SUBAREA SUBLINE SUBPLAT SUBPLOT SUBRACE SUBZONE

SUPPORT TRENTON TRINITY WASATCH WASHITA WENLOCK WICHITA BANOVINA DISTRICT DIVISION DJAGATAY ENDBRAIN FLOTILLA GUBERNIA LOCATION MONTEREY NAUCRARY PARTICLE PRECINCT STOCKTON SUBCASTE SUBORDER SUBSTAGE SUBTRIBE TOWNSHIP PARAGRAPH **(— OF SCOUTS)** CREW **(EGYPTIAN —)** KISM **(SPARTAN —)** ENOMOTY

SUBDOMINANT FOURTH

SUBDUE BOW COW ADAW BEAT BEND QUAY TAME ACCOY ALLAY AMATE CHARM CRUSH DAUNT DOMPT QUAIL QUASH QUELL SOBER STILL ADAUNT BRIDLE CHASTE DEBELL DISMAY EVINCE GENTLE MASTER QUENCH REDUCE SUBACT SUBMIT UNWILD ABANDON AFFAITE CAPTURE CHASTEN CONQUER DAUNTON OVERAWE REPRESS REPRIME SUCCUMB CONVINCE OVERCOME SUPPEDIT SUPPRESS SURMOUNT VANQUISH

SUBDUED MAK SOFT TAME MUTED SOBER STILL UNDER BROKEN CHASTE GENTLE ASHAMED SUBMISS SOURDINE

SUBFAMILY KHOISAN CUSHITIC ACRAEINAE

SUBGROUP BAND FAMILY

SUBHEAD BOXHEAD SIDEHEAD

SUBIMAGO DUN

SUBINDEX SUFFIX

SUBIRRIGATE SUB SUBWATER

SUBIRRIGATION SUBBING

SUBJECT DUX PUT ABLE ALLY BODY BONE ITEM OPEN TEXT HOBBY PLACE STOOP STUDY TESTO THEMA THEME TOPIC GROUND IMPOSE LIABLE PATHIC REDUCE SACOPE SUBDIT SUBMIT THRALL VASSAL CAITIVE CITIZEN FEODARY FEUDARY OBVIOUS PROBAND SERVILE AMENABLE ELECTIVE INCIDENT INFERIOR OBEDIENT OCCASION SENTENCE SUBJUGAL **(— OF DISCOURSE)** NOUN **(— OF FUGUE)** GUIDA **(— OF PROPOSITION)** EXTREME **(— TO ABUSE)** REVILE **(— TO ARGUMENT)** MOOT **(— TO BAD TEMPER)** MOODY **(— TO CHANGE)** MUTABLE FUGITIVE **(— TO CRITICISM)** SCOURGE **(— TO FATE)** FIE **(— TO PERCOLATION)** DISPLACE **(— TO SOME ACTION)** TREAT **(CONTROVERTED —)** ISSUE **(LOYAL —)** LIEGE **(PL.)** FOLK

SUBJECTION SLAVERY SERVITUS THIRLING

SUBJECTIVE IMMANENT INSEEING INTERNAL PECTORAL EPISTEMIC

SUBJOIN AFFIX

SUBJUGATION BONDAGE SERVITUDE

SUBKINGDOM PHYLUM
ANNULOSA CHORDATA
SUBLEADER HEADMAN
SUBLEASE FARMOUT SUBTACK
SUBLET JOB SUBSET CONACRE
SUBLEASE
SUB-LIEUTENANT CORNET
SUBLIMATE FLOWER ALCOHOL
SUBLIME
SUBLIME BIG FUME GRAND LOFTY
NOBLE AUGUST REFINE SOLEMN
WINGED DANTEAN ELEVATO
EXALTED EMPYREAL EMPYREAN
MAGNIFIC MAJESTIC
SERAPHIC SPLENDID
MAGNIFICENT
(IN STYLE) MILTONIC
SUBLIMITY GRANDEUR
SUBLUNARY EARTHLY
SUBMARINE SUB BOAT DIVER
FRITZ GUPPY SUBSEA PIGBOAT
TIDDLER
(PART OF —) DECK SAIL PLANE
TOWER BRIDGE RUDDER
PROPELLER SAILPLANE
TURTLEBACK FAIRWEATHER
SUBMEDIANT SIXTH
SUBMERGE BOG DIP BURY DIVE
DUNK HIDE SINK SOAK TAKE
DROWN SOUSE SWAMP WHELM
DELUGE DRENCH ENGULF
DEMERGE IMPLUNGE INUNDATE
SUBMERSE SURROUND
OVERWHELM
SUBMERGENCE ONLAP
SUBMISSION VAIL STOOP
PATIENCE
SUBMISSIVE MEEK BUXOM
DEMISS DOCILE DUTIFUL PASSIVE
SERVILE SLAVISH SUBJECT
SUBMISS UNERECT OBEDIENT
RESIGNED YIELDING
(— TO WIFE) UXORIOUS
SUBMISSIVENESS SLAVERY
SUBMIT BOW EAT ABOW BEND
CAVE LEAN OBEY TAKE VAIL
AVALE DEFER HIELD STAND
STOOP YIELD ASSENT CRINGE
DELATE RESIGN CONSIGN
KNUCKLE SUBJECT SUBMISE
SUCCUMB TRUCKLE PROPOUND
(— FOR CONSIDERATION) REMIT
(— TAMELY) EAT
(— TO) ABIDE STAND SUFFER
SUBNORMAL OFF SICK ABNORMAL
SUBORDER LARI ALCAE APODA
APODI GALLI GRUES ARDEAE
COHORT CUCULI SAURIA
AGLOSSA ANSERES ARCACEA
ASCONES CORACII COSTATA
SARCURA SYCONES ACRASIDA
ADEPHAGA BATOIDEI COLUMBAE
CORACIAE CURSORIA ENOPLINA
EUSUCHIA FALCONES FREGATAE
SELACHII
SUBORDINARY ENDORSE
ROUNDEL
SUBORDINATE SUB SINK PETTY
SCRUB UNDER EXEMPT MINION
PUISNE SECOND YEOMAN
PARTIAL SERVANT SERVILE
SUBJECT HENCHMAN INFERIOR
MYRMIDON PARERGAL POSTPONE

SERVIENT ANCILLARY SUBALTERN
(PREF.) (— TO) VICE
SUBORN HAVE BRIBE
SUBOVAL PETALOID
SUBPHYLUM EUCHORDA
SUBPOENA SUMMONS
SUBRACE STOCK
SUB ROSA COVERTLY SECRETLY
PROVATELY
SUBSCRIBE SIGN ASSENT ASCRIBE
CONSIGN SUBSIGN
SUBSCRIBER RAILBIRD
SUBSCRIPT INFERIOR
SUBSCRIPTION APPROVAL
SIGNATURE ABONNEMENT
SUBSEQUENT AFTER LATER
FUTURE PUISNE ENSUING
POSTNATE
(PREF.) POST
(— TO) CIS
SUBSEQUENTLY SO LATER SINCE
SUBSERVIENT OILY VASSAL
DUTEOUS SERVILE SLAVISH
OFFICIAL
SUBSHRUB STOCK GUAYULE
COLUMNEA PERIWINKLE
SUBSIDE DIE EBB LAY LIE ADAW
CALM FALL LULL SILE SINK VAIL
ABATE ALLAY LAPSE RESIDE
SETTLE ASSUAGE RELAPSE
UNSWELL WITHDRAW
SUBSIDENCE FALL SETTLING
SUBSIDIARY CHILD DONKEY
SUBSIDY ACCESSORY
SUBSIDIZE BONUS
SUBSIDY AID BONUS BOUNTY
POUNDAGE
SUBSILICIC BASIC
SUBSIST BE LIVE RELY
SUBSISTENCE BEING LIVING
SUBSISTENT ENTITY
SUBSOIL PAN LECK SOLE SHRAVE
RATCHEL
SUBSTAGE CARY GUNZ IOWAN
MANKATO STADIAL TAZEWELL
SUBSTANCE FAT SUM BODY CORE
FECK GIST GITE TACK WHAT
ADROP AGENT ALLOY ARCHE
BEING FOMES GREAT KEEST
METAL MOYEN OUSIA PROOF
SENSE STUFF THING BOTTOM
GADUIN GETTER IMPORT MATTER
STAPLE WEALTH AEROSOL
AGAROID ANTIGEN COLICIN
COLLOID CONTENT ELEIDIN
EMANIUM ERGUSIA ESSENCE
HYALINE MEANING PURPORT
REAGENT SUBJECT SUPTION
ACCEPTOR ADDITIVE ADHESIVE
ALLERGEN AMBEROID ANTIFOAM
BASSORIN HARDNESS MATERIAL
(— CAPABLE OF EXPANSION)
DILATANT
(— FORMED IN VINEGAR) MOTHER
(— FROM CRUSHED APPLES)
POMACE
(— IN BLOOD) ALEXINE ABLASTIN
(— IN LIGHT BULBS) GETTER
(— IN WOODY TISSUE) LIGNIN
(— OF DENTINE) IVORY
(— OF EXTREME HARDNESS)
ADAMANT DIAMOND
(— PRODUCING POISONOUS

ATMOSPHERE) GAS
(— SURROUNDED BY FOREIGN
TISSUE) ENCLAVE
(— THAT STOPS LOCOMOTION)
ARRESTANT
(— TO ADD STABILITY) BALLAST
(— TRANSPORTING GERMS) FOMES
(— USED AS HYPNOTIC) URAL
(— USED IN DETECTING OTHERS)
REAGENT
(— WITH MOLDY ODOR) CHARACIN
(ADHESIVE —) GLUE GLOEA PASTE
CEMENT STICKER
(AMORPHOUS —) GLASS RESIN
LIGNIN PECTIN FERRITE SAPONIN
(AROMATIC —) BALSAM
(ASTRINGENT —) ALUM CATECHU
(BITTER —) ALOIN LININ ILICIN
(BLACK —) SOOT BLECK
(CLEANSING —) LYE
(COLLOIDAL —) ALGIN EXPANDER
(COMBUSTIBLE —) COAL
(CORROSIVE —) CAUSTIC
(CRYSTALLINE —) LAURIN ALANINE
HELENIN ELATERIN
(DARK —) ATRAMENT
(DISSOLVED —) SOLUTE
(ETERNAL —) DHARMA ADHARMA
(FATLIKE —) DEGRAS LIPOID
ERGUSIA
(FATTY —) SMEAR SUBERIN
(FERMENTATION —) LEAVEN
(FIBROUS —) COTTON
(FILAMENTOUS —) HARL
(FILMY —) GOSSAMER
(FIRST —) YLEM
(GRINDING —) ABRASIVE
(GROWTH-PROMOTING —) AUXIN
(GUMMY —) GUM GURRY AMYLOID
GLACTAN
(HARD ANIMAL —) BONE ENAMEL
(HORNY —) BALEEN CHITIN
CHONDRIN
(HYPOTHETICAL —) FLUID INOGEN
PROTYL
(IDEAL —) CONTINUUM
(INFLAMMABLE —) BITUMEN
(INSOLUBLE —) CARRIER
HYALOGEN
(LIVERLIKE —) HEPAR
(NARCOTIC —) DRUG
(NITROGENOUS —) LACTENIN
(POISONOUS —) ARSENIC PHRYNIN
EXOTOXIN
(POWDER OF ANY —) FLOUR
(POWDERY —) STOUR
(PREDOMINATING —) BASE
(RESINOUS —) LAC COPAL
CARANNA CARAUNA COPALINE
COPALITE
(SELF-DEFENSIVE —) ACRAEIN
(SEMISOLID —) GEL
(SOUR —) ACID
(STICKY —) GOO GOOP SIZE STICK
GLUTEN BIRDLIME
(SUBTLE —) SPIRIT
(SWEET —) SUGAR
(SYNTHETIC —) HORMONE
(TRANSLUCENT —) HYALINE
CHONDRIN
(UNBREAKABLE —) ADAMANT
(UNCREATED —) ADHARMA
(VISCOUS —) GLAIR

GREASE SLUBBER
(VITAL —) KEEST
(WAXY —) CERIN PARAFFIN
SUBERINE
(PREF.) HYL(O)
(SUFF.) (— HAVING FORM) PHANE
(— PRODUCED THRU PROCESS)
STATE
SUBSTANDARD BAD BAUCH
SUBSTANTIAL FAT FIRM MEATY
PUKKA STOUT ACTUAL BODILY
HEARTY SQUARE STABLE STANCH
STUFFY STURDY MASSIVE
MATERIAL SUBSTANT TANGIBLE
SUBSTANTIATE BACK CONFIRM
SUPPORT VALIDATE
SUBSTANTIVE DIRECT
SUBSTITUTE SUB MOCK VICE
AKORI EXTRA PINCH PROXY
VICAR BACKUP BEWITH CHANGE
DEPUTY DOUBLE ERSATZ STOOGE
COMMUTE REPLACE RESERVE
STANDBY STOPGAP SUBDEAN
SUFFECT SUPPOSE DISPLACE
EMERGENT MAKESHIFT
(— FOR TEA) TIA FAHAM
(NOT —) FULL
(POOR —) APOLOGY
(PREF.) PSEUD(O)
(SUFF.) ETTE
SUBSTITUTING
(PREF.) (— FOR) PRO
SUBSTITUTION SHIFT CHANGE
ERSATZ ENALLAGE EXCHANGE
NOVATION REPLACEMENT
(OF SOUNDS) LALLATION
SUBSTRATUM SUB GROUND
SUBBING SUBJECT
SUBSTREAM MATTER
SUBSTRUCTURE PODIUM
FOOTING CENTERING
SUBSUME COVER EXPLAIN
INCLUDE
SUBSUMING GENERIC
SUBTENANT VAVASOUR
SUBTERFUGE MASK BLIND CROOK
QUIRK SHIFT TRICK WRINK
AMBAGE CHICANE ARTIFICE
PRETENCE TRAVERSE VOIDANCE
SUBTILE SUBTLE TENUOUS
SUBTILIZE EXALT
SUBTITLE TITLE LEADER CAPTION
SUBTLE SLY FINE NICE WILY WISE
ACUTE ARGUTE ASTUTE CRAFTY
SHREWD CUNNING FRAGILE
SUBTILE CLERGIAL
(TOO —) FINESPUN
SUBTLETY NICE FRAUD DECEIT
NUANCE EXILITY FINESSE
QUILLET DELICACY FINENESS
QUIDDITY QUODLIBET
REFINEMENT
SUBTLY FINE SLILY SLYLY
SUBTRACT BATE PULL TAKE
SHAVE DEDUCE DEDUCT
DETRACT SUBDUCE SUBDUCT
SUBTRAY DIMINISH
SUBTRIBE HAPU SENAAH
SEMNONES
SUBURB ANNEX BORGO BARRIO
PETTAH BANLIEU ENDSHIP
FAUBOURG
(PL.) SKIRTS ENVIRONS

OUTPARTS SUBURBIA
SUBURBIA VILLADOM
SUBVERSION FALL SABOTAGE
SUBVERSIVE RUINOUS
SUBVERT SAP KILL RAZE RUIN
EVERT UPSET GAINSAY OVERSET
REVERSE RUINATE OVERTURN
SUBVERTED LOST
SUBWAY DIVE METRO
SUCCEED GO FAY HIT FARE RISE
WORK CLICK ENSUE FADGE
PROVE SCORE SPEED COTTON
FOLLOW OBTAIN SECOND THRIVE
ACHIEVE INHERIT PREVAIL
PROSPER THROUGH FLOURISH
SUPPLANT
(— TO THRONE) ACCEDE ASCEND
SUCCEEDING VICE AFTER CHANGE
ULTERIOR
SUCCESS DO GO HIT MAX WIN
WOW BANG CESS LUCK SMASH
SPEED THRIFT EXPLOIT FORTUNE
FURTHER PROWESS THEEDOM
FELICITY GODSPEED
(— IN A MATCH) GAME
(ACCIDENTAL —) FLUKE
(BRILLIANT —) ECLAT
(SUDDEN —) KILLING
(UNEXPECTED —) JACKPOT
(WORLDLY —) ARTHA
SUCCESSFUL HOT MADE SOCK
BOFFO LUCKY SPEEDFUL
THRIVING
(BARELY —) NARROW
SUCCESSFULLY GREAT HAPPILY
PROUDLY
SUCCESSION RUN SUIT ROUND
SUITE TRACK ASSISE COURSE
SEQUEL SERIES STREAM STRING
HEIRDOM SUCCESS ANCESTRY
DIADOCHE MUTATION SEQUENCE
(— OF CHANGES) FLUX
(— OF CHORDS) CADENCE
(— OF CRUSTS) CALICHE
(— OF STAGES) CASCADE
(— OF WAVES) CRIMP
(— RULERS) DYNASTY
SUCCESSIVELY AROW
SUCCESSOR HEIR CALIF HERES
CALIPH HAERES EPIGONUS
(— OF CHIEFTAIN) TANIST
(— OF MUHAMMAD) CALIF CALIPH
(ECCLESIASTICAL —) COARB
(PL.) DIADOCHI
SUCCINCT BRIEF SHORT TERSE
CONCISE LACONIC SUMMARY
SUCCINIC DIACETIC
SUCCOR AID HELP RESET SERVE
SPEED ASSIST RELIEF RESCUE
SUPPLY UPTAKE COMFORT
DELIVER PRESIDY RELIEVE
SECOURS SUSTAIN BEFRIEND
SUCCORY CHICORY
SUCCULENT FRIM FRUM LUSH
JUICY LUSHY PAPPY PULPY
SAPPY YOUNG CASHIE FLESHY
TENDER WATERISH
SUCCUMB BREAK QUAIL STOOP
TRAIK YIELD
SUCH SIC SICK THAT SWICH
SUCHNESS TATHATA
SUCK SOUK SWIG SWOOP SUCKLE
(— DRY) SOAK

(— UP) DRINK ABSORB TIPPLE
(SUFF.) MYZA MYZON
SUCKEN THIRL
SUCKER CHUB FISH GULL PATSY
SOBOL THIEF CHUPON CUPULE
MULLET RATOON REDFIN SOBOLE
SPROUT SQUARE STOLON SUPPER
TILLER CUTLIPS GONOTYL
LOCULUS OSCULUM PEDICEL
SCOURGE BOTHRIUM HUMPBACK
LOLLIPOP PUSHOVER REDHORSE
SURCULUS QUILLBACK
(PREF.) BDELL(O) BOTHR(I)(IO)(O)
MYZO STOLONI SURCULI
(SUFF.) BDELLA
SUCKLE FEED MILK SUCK LACTATE
NOURISH
SUCKLING SUCKER LACTANT
SUCKLER TEATLING
SUCTION INTAKE
(SUFF.) MYZA MYZON
SUCTORIA ACINETAE

SUDAN
CAPITAL: KHARTOUM
DESERT: NUBIAN
LANGUAGE: GA EWE IBO KRU EFIK
MOLE TSHI YORUBA MANDINGO
MEASURE: UD
MOUNTAIN: KINYETI
NATIVE: DAZA GOLO NUER SERE
DINKA FULAH HAUSA MOSSI
NUBIYIN
PROVINCE: DARFUR KASSALA
KORDOFAN
REGION: DARFUR KASSALA
KORDOFAN
RIVER: NILE
TOWN: WAU JUBA KOSTI MEROE
ATBARA ALUBAYD KASSALA
MALAKAL OMDURMAN
WEIGHT: HABBA

SUDANESE FULA FULAH
SUDAN GRASS GARAVA GARAWI
SUDDEN BRASH FERLY HASTY
ICTIC SWIFT ABRUPT FIERCE
SNAPPY SPEEDY PRERUPT
HEADLONG SPURTIVE SUBITANY
SUBITOUS OVERNIGHT
PRECIPITATE
SUDDENLY BOB POP BOLT FLOP
SLAP AMAIN SHORT SKELP SOUSE
ASTART BOUNCE PRESTO SUBITO
ASUDDEN UNAWARES
SUDDENNESS ATTACK SUDDENTY
SUDORIFIC SWEAT SWEATER
HIDROTIC SUDATORY
SUDRA VELLALA
SUDS BUCK FOAM SAPPLES
SOAPSUDS
SUE LAW WOO SUIT IMPLEAD
TROUNCE
SUET TALLOW
(PREF.) STEAR(I)(O) STEAT(O)
(SUFF.) STEARIN
SUFFER BYE GET LET BEAR BIDE
DREE FIND GAIN HURT PAIN PINE
ALLOW DREIE INCUR LABOR
PROVE SMART SMOKE STAND
THOLE ABEGGE BETEEM ENDURE
PERMIT AGONIZE SUPPORT
SUSTAIN UNDERGO TOLERATE

(— AGONY) THROE
(— AT STAKE) SMOKE
(— DEFEAT) BOW
(— FOR) ABY ABYE ABIDE
(— FROM TIME) AGE
(— GREAT AFFLICTION) GROAN
(— HUNGER) CLEM STARVE
AFFAMISH
(— LOSS OF) GIVE
(— PAIN) STOUND ANGUISH
(— PENALTY) SWEAT
(— REMORSE) RUE
(— RUIN) WRECK
(— SYNCOPE) FAINT
(— THROUGH) PASS
(— TO ENTER) ADMIT
SUFFERABLE PATIBLE
SUFFERANCE PAIN MISERY
PATIENCE THOLANCE
SUFFERER MARTYR AMNESIC
DOORMAT PATIENT
(SUFF.) PATH(IA)(IC)(Y)
SUFFERING BALE COST DREE
HURT PAIN PINE RACK AGONY
DOLOR GRIEF SMART WRAKE
PATHIC PATHOS THRALL INVALID
LANGUOR PASSION PASSIVE
TRAVAIL DISTRESS HARDSHIP
MARTYRDOM
(— FROM HANGOVER) CHIPPY
(— FROM ILL HEALTH) DOWN
(— OF MIND) CARE
(—S OF CHRIST) AGONY
(SUFF.) PATH(IA)(IC)(Y)
(— OF) ITIS
SUFFICE DO LAST COVER REACH
SERVE SATISFY
SUFFICIENCY ENOUGH PLENTY
ADEQUACY ABUNDANCE
PLENITUDE
SUFFICIENT DUE FAIR GOOD
AMPLE DECENT ENOUGH PRETTY
BASTANT ABUNDANT ADEQUATE
RELEVANT COMPETENT
(BARELY —) SCANT SKIMP
NARROW SCRIMPY
(BE — FOR) COVER
SUFFICIENTLY DULY WELL
ENOUGH
SUFFIX POSTFIX
SUFFOCATE CHOKE DROWN
SMOOR STIVE STUFF SWELT
SLOKEN STIFLE OVERLIE QUACKLE
SMOLDER SMOTHER SCUMFISH
STRANGLE THROTTLE
SUFFRAGE VOTE VOICE TONGUE
VERSICLE
SUFFUSE DIP FILL BATHE EMBAY
TINGE INFUSE MANTLE
SUFFUSION COLOR
SUGAR CANDY DIOSE IDOSE MELIS
PIECE SUCRE THIRD ACROSE
ALDOSE ALLOSE FUCOSE GULOSE
HEXOSE INVERT KETOSE LYXOSE
OCTOSE PANELA TALOSE TRIOSE
XYLOSE AGAVOSE ALTROSE
BASTARD CHITOSE GLUCOSE
GLUTOSE GLYCOSE LACTOSE
MALTOSE MANNOSE PAPELON
PENOCHI PENTOSE PENUCHE
SORBOSE SUCROSE SWEETEN
TETROSE THREOSE BROWNING
CONCRETE CYMAROSE DEXTROSE

FRUCTOSE FURANOSE LEVULOSE
PYRANOSE RHAMNOSE
RHODEOSE SECALOSE TURANOSE
(BROWN —) CARAIBE JAGGARY
DEMERARA JAGGHERY
(COARSE —) RAAB PANOCHA
(CRUDE —) GUR HEAD MELADA
CONCRETE
(INFERIOR —) BASTARD
(SIMPLE —) OSE
(UNREFINED —) CASSONADE
(PREF.) GLUC(O) GLYC(O) LYXO
SACCHAR(I)(O) SUCR(O) THREO
(SUFF.) ULOSE
SUGARCANE CANE GRAIN
GLUMAL RATOON MATTRESS
(— SAP) LIQUOR
SUGARHOUSE (PART OF —)
PURGERY
SUGARLESS DRY
SUGARPLUM KISS
SUGARY FAT SUGAR SWEET
OVERRIPE
SUGGEST JOG BEAR GIVE HINT
MINT IMPLY OFFER SPEAK ADVISE
ALLUDE INDITE INFUSE MOTION
PROMPT RESENT SUBMIT
CONNOTE DICTATE INSPIRE
INDICATE INTIMATE PROPOUND
(— DRINKING) PROPOSE
(— INSIDIOUSLY) INFUSE
(— STRONGLY) ARGUE
SUGGESTIBLE SOFT
SUGGESTION CUE CAST HINT
TANG WIND GLIFF TWANG
ADVICE BREATH MOTION SMATCH
INKLING LEADING POINTER
PROFFER REMNANT SOUPCON
WRINKLE INNUENDO INSTANCE
PROPOSAL
SUGGESTIVE ANICONIC
PREGNANT REDOLENT
(— OF MELODY) CANOROUS
SUICIDAL KAMIKAZE
SUIT DO GO APT DOW FIT GEE HIT
SET SIT ACTO LIKE LIST PAIR
SEEM SORT ADAPT AGREE APPLY
BEFIT BESIT CLUBS COLOR DRAPE
DRESS FADGE FANCY FRAME
HABIT LEVEL MATCH PLEAD
QUEME SAVOR SERVE SHAPE
STAND SUING TALLY AFFEIR
ANSWER BECOME COHERE
COMPLY DITTOS EFFEIR HEARTS
PRAYER SPADES SPEECH SQUARE
BEHOOVE COMPORT COSTUME
COULEUR FASHION PURSUIT
REQUEST SEERPAW DIAMONDS
INSTANCE QUADRATE SKELETON
STANDARD TAILLEUR TROPICAL
PINSTRIPE
(— AT LAW) ACTO CASE LAWSUIT
(— OF ARMOR) PANOPLY
(— OF MAIL) CATAPHRACT
(DIVER'S —) SCAPHANDER
(SWIMMING —) BATHER BIKINI
MAILLOT
SUITABILITY (MUTUAL —) DECENCY
IDONEITY SYMPATHY
SUITABLE APT FIT PAT ABLE FEAT
GAIN GOOD JUMP JUST MEET
TALL WELL WEME DIGNE EQUAL
FITTY QUEME RIGHT SUITY

COMELY FITTEN GAINLY GIUSTO HABILE HONEST LIABLE LIKELY PROPER SUITLY AVENANT COMMODE CONDIGN CONGRUE FITTING IDONEAL PLIABLE SEEMING BECOMING DECOROUS ELIGIBLE FEASIBLE HANDSOME IDONEOUS SORTABLE ACCORDING OPPORTUNE
(— FOR MALE AND FEMALE) UNISEX
(— FOR STAGE PERFORMANCE) ACTING
(EXACTLY —) VERY
SUITABLENESS APTNESS HONESTY APTITUDE PROPERTY
SUITABLY FITLY MEETLY TIDELY APROPOS GRADELY
SUITCASE BAG CAP GRIP CAPCASE DORLACH KEESTER
SUITE SET SUIT TAIL SWEEP SWEET TRAIN SERIES PARTITA RETINUE ENSEMBLE EQUIPAGE
(— OF MOLDINGS) LEDGMENT
(— OF ROOMS) FLAT CHAMBER
SUITED FIT ADAPT SEEMLY ADAPTED ASSORTED CONGENIAL
(POORLY —) CROOK
(SUFF.) (— FOR) ILE
SUITING COVERT CHEVIOT SHARKSKIN
SUITOR MAN BEAU SUER SWAIN WOOER GALLANT SERVANT
SUKU WASUKUMA
SULFATE DEX
SULFIDE GLANCE CUBANITE SULFURET
SULFUR BRIMSTONE
(PREF.) THI(O)
SULK DOD PET CHAW CRAB DORT GLUM POUT SULL BOODY FRUMP GLUMP GROUT GRUMP GROUCH SNUDGE THURMUS
(PL.) GEE HUMP GLOUT MUMPS FRUMPS SULLENS BOUDERIE
SULKER MUMPER
SULKINESS DORT GRUMP
SULKING PET BOUDERIE
SULKY CART CHUFF DODDY DORTY GOURY HUFFY HUMPY CHUFFY GLUMPY GROUTY JINKER SNUFFY STUFFY SULLEN SUMPHY DOGGISH HUFFISH MUMPISH
(NOT —) GOOD
SULLEN DOUR FOUL GLUM GRIM SOUR BLACK CHUFF CROSS DUMPY FELON GRUFF HARSH MOODY RUSTY STERN SULKY SURLY WEMOD CRUSTY DOGGED GLOOMY GLUMMY GRUMPY GLUNCH GROUTY MOROSE MULISH SOMBER SOMBRE STUFFY AUSTERE CRABBED CYNICAL FRETFUL LOURING LUMPISH MUMPISH PEEVISH CHUMPISH CHURLISH FAROUCHE LOWERING PETULANT SPITEFUL STUNKARD
SULLENNESS GEE DORT GLUM MUMPS STOMACH
SULLIED DIRTY SPOTTED
SULLY BLOT BLUR DASH FOUL SLUR SMIT SMUT SOIL CLOUD DIRTY GRIME SMEAR SMOKE STAIN TAINT BEFOUL DARKEN

DEFILE SMIRCH SMUTCH ATTAINT BEGRIME BESMEAR BLEMISH CORRUPT DISTAIN ECLIPSE POLLUTE SLUBBER TARNISH BESMIRCH BESPATTER
SULPHATE ALUM BARITE ILESITE LOWEITE SULFATE VITRIOL KRAUSITE
SULPHIDE HEPAR GLANCE ZARNEC SULFIDE ZARNICH CUBANITE
(PL.) MATTE
SULPHUR ORE SPIRIT SULFUR YELLOW QUEBRITH BRIMSTONE
SULPHURIC ACID VITRIOL
SULTAN SOLDAN
SULTANATE SULTANY ZANZIBAR
SULTANESS SOWDONES
SULTRY CLOSE FLUSH FAINTY SMUDGY POTHERY PUTHERY SWELTRY FEVERISH
SUM ALL GOB AGIO CASH DRAB DUMP FARM FINE FOOT FUND MASS TALE DEDIT GROSS KITTY SUMMA TOTAL WHOLE AMOUNT DEMAND DYADIC FIGURE NUMBER DECUPLE INGOING MANBOTE SUBSIDY SUMMARY SUMMATE ENTIRETY OCTONION QUANTITY MOUNTANCE OVERDRAFT POLYNOMIAL
(— AND SUBSTANCE) TOUR SHORT UPSHOT
(— AS COMPENSATION FOR KILLING) MANBOTE
(— FOR REENLISTMENT) GRATUITY
(— FOR SCHOLARSHIP) BURSARY
(— IN BASSET) SEPTLEVA
(— OF) SIGMA
(— OF DETERMINANTS) STIRP
(— OF EXPONENTS) DEGREE
(— OF FACTORS) COMPLEX
(— OF GOOD QUALITIES) ARETE
(— OF MONEY) POT BANK COVER STOCK BUNDLE ACCOUNT STIPEND
(— OF 25 POUNDS) PONY PONEY
(— OF 3 FARTHINGS) GILL
(— OF 500 POUNDS) MONKEY
(— PAYABLE AT FIXED INTERVALS) FARM
(— RISKED) STAKE
(— UP) ADD TOT FOOT RECKON SUBSUME SUMMATE COMPRISE CONCLUDE PERORATE
(ENTIRE —) SOLIDUM
(EXCESS —) BONUS
(FORFEITED —) DEDIT
(GREAT —) PLUNK SIGHT MICKLE
(LARGE —) GOB SCREAMER
(PETTY —) CENT DIME DRAB
(SMALL — OF MONEY) SPILL DRIBBLE DRIBLET SHOESTRING
(TRIFLING —) HAY GROAT
(UNEXPENDED —S) SAVINGS
(VECTOR —) GRADIENT
(PL.) BATTELS
SUMAC FUSTET KARREE SUMACH ANACARD BURTREE SCOTINO SHOEMAKE
SUMATRA (LANGUAGE IN —) NIAS
(MEASURE OF —) PAAL
(MOUNTAIN IN —) LEUSER KERINTJI

(RIVER IN —) HARI MUSI ROKAN DJAMBI
(TOWN IN —) ACHIN KUALA MEDAN NATAL SOLOK DJAMBI LANGSA PADANG RENGAT BENKULEN
SUMBUL SAMBUL MUSKROOT
SUMERIAN ACCADIAN AKKADIAN
SUMITRA (HUSBAND OF —) DASHARATHA
(SON OF —) LAKSHMANA SHATRUGHNA
SUMMARIZE PRECIS RESUME ABSTRACT
SUMMARY SUM CURT LEAD BRIEF CHART RECAP SCORE SHORT SUMMA TOTAL APERCU PRECIS RESUME SUMMAR CHAPTER CONCISE EPITOME EXTRACT MEDULLA OUTLINE RUNDOWN VIDIMUS ABSTRACT ARGUMENT BREVIARY BREVIATE DRUMHEAD HEADNOTE OVERVIEW SUCCINCT SYNOPSIS
(— OF FAITH) SYMBOL
(— OF PRINCIPLES) CREED
SUMMATION SUM DIGEST SUMMARY
SUMMER SHEMU SOMER AESTAS SIMMER DORMANT
(OF —) ESTIVAL
(PREF.) ESTIVO
SUMMER CYPRESS KOCHIA
SUMMER FLOUNDER PLAICE
SUMMERHOUSE FOLLY KIOSK MAHAL TUPEK ALCOVE CASINO GAZEBO PAGODA CABINET BELVEDERE
SUMMER HYACINTH GALTONIA
SUMMER TANAGER REDBIRD
SUMMERWOOD LATEWOOD
SUMMIT DOD SUM TIP TOP VAN ACME APEX BALD CRAP DODD HELM KNAP KNOT PEAK ROOF CREST CROWN SPIRE COMBLE CULMEN HEIGHT VERTEX ZENITH CALOTTE SUMMARY SUMMITY PINNACLE MOUNTAINTOP
(— OF TUBE) MOUTH
(— WITHOUT FOREST) BALD
(ROCKY —) KNOT
(ROUND —) DOD DODD
(SNOW-CAPPED —) CALOTTE
(PREF.) APICO CORY(PH)(PHO)
(SUFF.) ACE
SUMMON BAN CRY BUZZ CALL CITE DRUM HAIL SIST BUGLE CHARM CLEPE EVOKE HIGHT KNELL SOUND VOUCH ACCITE ADVOKE BECALL COMPEL DEMAND SOMPNE VOCATE ACCERSE COMMAND CONJURE CONVENE CONVENT CONVOKE PROVOKE SUMMONS WHISTLE ASSUMMON EXORCISE
(— FOR HIRING) YARD
(— INTO COURT) DEMAND
(— TOGETHER) BAND MUSTER ASSEMBLE
(— UP) FIND GATHER COLLECT
SUMMONER SUMNER LOCKMAN SOMPNER OUTRIDER
SUMMONING CALL ARRAY

(— OF KING'S VASSALS) BAN
SUMMONS CRY CALL BREVE CITAL TICKET BIDDING CALLING STICKER WARNING WARRANT CITATION MONITION VOCATION
(FALCONER'S —) WO
SUMP SINK STANDAGE
SUMPTUOUS RICH GRAND SHOWY WLONK COSTLY DELUXE SOLEMN SUPERB COSTLEW ELEGANT MAGNIFIC SPLENDID MAGNIFICENT
SUMPTUOUSNESS LUXE DAINTY SUMPTURE
SUN SOL ATEN ATON BASK INTI LAMP STAR SENGE SURYA TITAN SUNLET DAYSTAR IOSKEHA PHOEBUS SAVITAR JOUSKEHA
(— MOON AND STARS) HOST
(RISING —) HERAKHTI
(PREF.) HELI(O) SOLARO SOLI
(SUFF.) HELION
SUN ALSO RISES (AUTHOR OF —) HEMINGWAY
(CHARACTER IN —) BILL COHN JAKE MIKE BRETT CLYNE PEDRO ASHLEY BARNES GORTON ROBERT ROMERO FRANCES MICHAEL MONTOYA CAMPBELL GEORGETTE
SUNAPEE TROUT SAIBLING
SUNBATHE APRICATE
SUNBEAM BANANA
SUN BEAR BRUANG
SUNBIRD MAMO CADET FINFOOT
SUN BITTERN CARLE CAURALE SUNBIRD
SUN BLIND CHICK UMRELLA
SUNBONNET TILT UGLY CRESIE KAPPIE SHAKER
SUNBURN GREENING HELIOSIS
SUNBURNT ADUST BROWN TANNED
SUNBURST SUNRAY SUNBREAK SUNSHINE
SUNDAE GEDUNK
SUNDAY EXAUDI JUDICA GAUDETE TRINITY
(FOURTH — IN LENT) LAETARE
(THIRD — AFTER EASTER) JUBILATE
SUNDER PART RIVE TWIN BREAK SEVER TWAIN TWINE DEPART DIVIDE SINDER ASUNDER DISALLY DISJOIN DIVORCE DISSEVER SEJUGATE SEPARATE UNSOLDER
SUNDEW DROSERA EYEBRIGHT
SUNDIAL DIAL GHURRY HOROLOGE SCAPHION SOLARIUM
(PART OF —) DIAL LINE PLATE GNOMON DIAGRAM
SUN DISK ATEN ATON CAKRA CHAKRA
SUNDOG WINDGALL PARHELION
SUNDOWNER WHALER TUSSOCKER
SUN-DRIED TILED
SUNDROPS SCABISH
SUNDRY DIVERS DIVERSE SEVERAL
SUNFISH SUN HURO MOLA OPAH RUFF BREAM FLIER FLYER ROACH SUNNY KIVVER MOLOID REDEAR REDEYE CRAPPIE CROPPIE PANFISH PERCOID BLUEGILL FLATFISH FLOUNDER HEADFISH

MOONFISH PONDFISH
WARMOUTH REDBREAST
PUMPKINSEED
SUNFLOWER GOLD HELIO CANADA
GOLDEN SUNFOIL GIRASOLE
TURNSOLE
(**— STATE**) KANSAS
SUNGLASSES SHADES
SUN-GREBE FINFOOT SUNBIRD
GRUIFORM
SUNK SUNKEN
(**— TO LOW STATE**) ABJECT
SUNKEN SUNK LAIGH HOLLOW
SUNKEN BELL (**CHARACTER IN —**)
MAGDA HEINRICH RAUTENDELEIN
(**COMPOSER OF —**) RESPIGHI
SUNLESS BLAE
SUNLIGHT GLARE
SUNN SAN SANN DAGGA SANAI
JANAPA MADRAS JANAPAN
SANNHEMP
SUNNITE IHLAT SUNNI SUNNIAH
SUNNY GOOD SUNSHINE
SUN PARLOR SOLARIUM
SUNRISE ARIST SUNUP ORIENT
SUNSET SUNFALL
(**— STATE**) OREGON ARIZONA
SUNSHADE PARASOL ROUNDEL
TIRESOL SOMBRERO
SUNSHINE SUN SHINE SUNLIGHT
(**— STATE**) FLORIDA
SUNSPOT SPOT FACULA MACULA
SUNSPURGE SUNWEED TURNSOLE
WARTWEED WARTWORT
SUNSTROKE HELIOSIS SIRIASIS
SUNTAN MERIDA
SUN TREE HINOKI
SUNWISE DEASIL DESSIL
SUNYATA VOID
SUP EAT DINE SOWP FEAST
CONSUME SWALLOW
SUPAWN MUSH
SUPER-
(PREF.) HYPER
SUPERABOUND OVERFLOW
SUPERABUNDANCE FLOOD
EXCESS CATARACT PLEONASM
PLETHORA PLEURISY PLURISIE
SUPERABUNDANT RANK LAVISH
PROFUSE
SUPERALTAR PREDELLA
SUPERANNUATE OVERYEAR
SUPERB GRAND GOLDEN CLIPPING
GORGEOUS SPLENDID
SUPERCARGO MERCHANT
SUPERCILIOUS GRAND POTTY
PROUD OVERLY SNIFFY SNIPPY
SNOOTY SNOTTY SNUFFY
HAUGHTY ARROGANT CAVALIER
SNIFFISH SUPERIOR
SUPERCLASS AGNATHA
SUPERCONSCIOUSNESS
SAMADHI
SUPERCOOL SUBCOOL SURFUSE
SUPERFAMILY APINA APOIDEA
BOVOIDEA
(SUFF.) OIDA OIDEA OIDEI
SUPERFICIAL GLIB ECTAL SUPER
FACIAL FACILE FLIMSY FORMAL
FROTHY GLASSY OVERLY SLIGHT
CURSORY OUTSIDE OUTWARD
PASSING SHALLOW SKETCHY
SLIGHTY SURFACE SURFACY

COSMETIC EXTERNAL MAGAZINY
SMATTERY DEPTHLESS
SUPERFICIALLY FLEET
SUPERFICIES TERM EXTENT
SUPERFLUITY FAT FRILL LUXUS
EXCESS OVERSET SURFEIT
PLETHORA REDUNDANCY
(CONFUSING —) FLUTHER
SUPERFLUOUS SPARE OTIOSE
USELESS NEEDLESS REDUNDANT
SUPERFRONTAL FRONTLET
SUPERHEATED GASEOUS
SUPERHIGHWAY MOTORWAY
(AVOID —) SHUNPIKE
SUPERHUMAN DEMON DAEMON
DIVINE INHUMAN UNHUMAN
SUPERIMPOSE LAY OVERLAY
SURPRINT
SUPERIMPOSING DISSOLVE
SUPERINTEND CON CONN GUIDE
OVERSEE PRESIDE
SUPERINTENDENCE CARE
CONTROL EPISCOPY GUIDANCE
SUPERINTENDENCY EDILITY
AEDILITY
SUPERINTENDENT BOSS SUPE
EPHOR SUPER EDITOR VENEUR
VIEWER WARDEN CAPTAIN
CURATOR EPHORUS MANAGER
DIRECTOR OVERSEER SURVEYOR
SWINGMAN
SUPERIOR JOE AYNE COOL FINE
MORE OVER TRIE ABBOT ABOVE
CHIEF CREAM EIGNE ELDER ELITE
EXTRA FANCY FRANK GREAT
LIEGE PRIOR PUKKA SWANK
UPPER ABBESS BETTER COCKUP
CUSTOS DOMINA FATHER FORBYE
MAHANT SELECT SENIOR STRONG
FORTHBY PALMARY RANKING
ABNORMAL DOMINANT
GUARDIAN SINGULAR SPLENDID
SUPERIAL MARVELOUS
PARAMOUNT
(**— OF CONVENT**) HEGUMEN
(**— TO**) BEFORE
(PREF.) SUPER
SUPERIORITY DROP GREE PRICE
HEIGHT MASTERY PROWESS
EMINENCE PRIORITY
(MENTAL —) GENIUS
SUPERLATIVE RAVING CURIOUS
ROUSING CRASHING OLYMPIAN
PEERLESS SWINGING
(ABSOLUTE —) ELATIVE
(SUFF.) EST
SUPERLATIVELY CRACKING
SWINGING
SUPERMAN OVERMAN
OBERMENSCH
SUPERNATURAL FEY DIVINE
NUMINOUS SUPERIOR
MARVELOUS PARANORMAL
(**— FORCE**) WAKANDA
SUPERNUMERARY ORRA
(PREF.) POLY
SUPERORDER GLIRES
SUPERPOSE APPLY
SUPERSCRIBE DIRECT
SUPERSCRIPT SUPERIOR
SUPERSEDE REPLACE
OVERRIDE SUPPLANT
SUPERSTITION FREIT

IDOLATRY ABERGLAUBE
SUPERSTITIOUS FREITY
SUPERTONIC SECOND
SUPERVENE BEFALL FOLLOW
SUPERVISE BOSS GUIDE DIRECT
GOVERN HANDLE SURVEY
FOREMAN OVERSEE PROCTOR
ENGINEER OVERLOOK
CHAPERONE
SUPERVISION EYE CARE DUTY
HAND CHECK CHARGE
OVERSIGHT
SUPERVISOR BOSS BULL EPHOR
GUIDE SUPER CENSOR GASMAN
RUNMAN SOURER WARDEN
DESKMAN PROCTOR ALYTARCH
CHAIRMAN FLOORMAN
FOREHAND KNIFEMAN
LEACHMAN MASHGIAH OVERSEER
SUPINE INERT DROWSY LANGUID
SERVILE UPRIGHT CARELESS
INACTIVE INDOLENT LISTLESS
SLUGGISH
SUPPER CENA MEAL CUDDY
HOCKEY PASCHAL
(HARVEST-HOME —) HOCKEY
(LAST —) MAUNDY
(LORD'S —) NAGMAAL
SUPPING CENATION
SUPPLANT FOLLOW REMOVE
REPLACE DISPLACE DISPLANT
SUPPLE BAIN FLIP OILY SOFT
LINGY LITHE SLAMP SWACK
AJOINT LIMBER LITHER LUTHER
SUMPLE SVELTE SWANKY
WANDLE LISSOME PLIABLE
SPRINGE FLEXIBLE
SUPPLEJACK SOAPWORT
SUPPLEMENT ARM EKE MEND
TACK ANNEX SUPPLY BOLSTER
CODICIL ADDENDUM APPENDIX
BOUNTITH
(PL.) FIXINGS
SUPPLEMENTAL SPECIAL
SUPPLEMENTARY ADDED
SECOND RIPIENO REMANENT
PERIPHERAL
SUPPLENESS WHIP
SUPPLIANT ASKER PLEADING
SUPPLICATE BEG PRAY CRAVE
PLEAD INVOKE OBTEST SUPPLY
BESEECH ENTREAT IMPLORE
REQUEST SOLICIT PETITION
SUPPLICATION CRY VOW BEAD
BILL LIBEL VENIE APPEAL LITANY
PRAYER CRAVING SYNAPTE
ENTREATY PETITION PLEADING
ROGATION ROGATIVE SUFFRAGE
SUPPLICATORY EUCTICAL
SUPPLIED (**— WITH FOOD**) THORN
(AMPLY —) ABUNDANT
(SCANTILY —) BARE
SUPPLIER SOURCE
SUPPLIES STOCK STUFF DUFFEL
STORES VICTUAL ESTOVERS
ORDNANCE
SUPPLY FEED FILL FIND FRET
FUND GIVE HEEL LEND LINE
ARRAY CATER ENDUE EQUIP
INDUE OFFER SERVE STOCK
STORE STUFF YIELD BUDGET
DONATE EMPLOY FOISON LAYOUT
POCKET RENDER SUBMIT

ADVANCE FORTIFY FRAUGHT
FURNISH LISSOME PROVIDE
ACCOMMODATE
(**— ABUNDANTLY**) SWILL
(**— ARRANGED BEFOREHAND**)
RELAY
(**— FOR AN OCCASION**) GRIST
(**— OF MONEY**) BANKROLL
(**— OF POTENTIAL JURORS**) TALES
(**— OF REMOUNTS**) REMUDA
(**— OF TIN**) SERVING
(**— PROVISIONS**) PURVEY
(**— THE NEED**) FOR
(**— WITH CLOTHES**) INFIT
(**— WITH FUEL**) STOKE
(**— WITH MONEY**) GILD
(**— WITH OXYGEN**) AERATE
(**— WITH WATER**) FANG
(CACHED —) CAVE
(CONSTANT —) STREAM
(EXTRA —) RESERVE
(FRESH —) RECRUIT
(HIDDEN —) HOARD
(INADEQUATE —) DEARTH
(OVERABUNDANT —) SURFEIT
(PLENTIFUL —) CHOICE
(RESERVE —) CUSHION
(RICH —) ARGOSY
(SCANTY —) SCANT
SUPPORT AID ARM BAY BED BOW
KAI LEG PEG RIB TIE TOM ABET
ABUT AXIS BACK BASE BEAM
BEAR BUOY CRIB DADE FEND
FIND FIRM FORK FUEL HAVE HELP
HOLD KEEP KILP LIFT POST PROP
RACK REST ROCK SALT SIDE STAY
STEM STUD TRIG ADOPT ANGEL
APPUI ATLAS BIPOD BLOCK
BRACE BROOK CARRY CHAIR
CHEER CHOCK CLEAT CRANK
FAVOR FLOAT FRAME OXTER
PLUNK POISE RANCE SALVE
SHORE SPURN STAFF STAKE
STEAD STELL STIPE STOCK STOOP
STRUT STULL TOWER VOUCH
WEIGH ANCHOR ASSERT ASSIST
BARROW BEHALF CHEVAL
COLUMN CORSET CRADLE
CRUTCH DEFEND DONKEY
DUOPOD GARTER PATTEN PILLAR
POTENT PULPIT PUTLOG SADDLE
SECOND SHIELD SOCKET SPLINT
STAYER STEADY SUFFER TASSEL
TIMBER TINGLE TORSEL UPHAND
UPHOLD UPKEEP UPTAKE
WHIMSY ALIMENT ARMREST
BACKING BOLSTER COMFORT
CONFIRM CRIPPLE DEADMAN
ENDORSE FINDING FULCRUM
GROMMET HOUSING JACKLEG
JUSTIFY KEEPING KNUCKLE
NOURISH NURTURE PABULUM
PROTECT RADICAL SPIRALE
SPONSOR SQUINCH STADDLE
STANDER STIFFEN STIRRUP
SUBSIST SUSTAIN THICKEN
TRESTLE ADJUMENT ADVOCATE
BALUSTER BEFRIEND BESTRIDE
BOOKREST BUTTRESS CAPSHORE
FAIRLEAD FOOTREST FORESTAY
FORTRESS HANDREST HOLDFAST
JACKSTAY KEYSTONE MAINSTAY
MAINTAIN MOUNTING NEEDLING

OVERCAST PEDESTAL PEDIMENT
STANDARD STILLAGE STOCKING
STRENGTH SYMPATHY UNDERLIE
UNDERPIN UNDERSET
PATRONAGE MAINTENANCE
(— FOR ANVIL) STOCK
(— FOR BELL CLAPPER) BALDRIC
(— FOR CANOPY) BAIL
(— FOR CATALYST) CARRIER
(— FOR CORSET) BUSK
(— FOR HEAVY MACHINERY)
BUNTING
(— FOR LAUNCHING SHIP) POPPET
(— FOR LEVER) BAIT
(— FOR LIFE-CAR) BAIL
(— FOR MILL) LOWDER
(— FOR MINE PASSAGE) OVERCAST
(— FOR OARLOCK) OUTRIGGER
(— FOR PICTURE HOOKS) CORNICE
(— FOR PIPE) CHAPLET
(— FOR PLATFORM) STEMPEL
STEMPLE
(— IN A LATHE) DOCTOR
(— IN PAPERMAKING TUB) DONKEY
(— OF COPING) KNEELER
(— OF MOLD CORE) ARBOR
ARBOUR
(— OF RAIL) CHAIR BALUSTER
(— THROUGH BIT AND BRIDLE)
APPUI
(CRUTCHLIKE —) DEADMAN
(ELBOW-SHAPED —) CRANK
(EMBEDDED —) SPURN
(FIREPLACE —) ANDIRON
(GIVE —) FEED
(INCLINED —) RIDER
(MINING —) CAP FRAME
(PORTABLE —) STOOL
(PRINCIPAL —) BACKBONE
(TEMPORARY —) NEEDLING
(UPRIGHT —) POPPET BANISTER
(WHEELED —) CARRIAGE
(PL.) SHIPWAY
SUPPORTED BASED BLOCKED
ACCOSTED SUCCINCT
(— BY EVIDENCE) PROBABLE
SUPPORTER ALLY JOCK ATLAS
STOOP COHORT DRAGON SATRAP
APOSTLE BOOSTER DEVOTEE
FAVORER FOUNDER LAUDIAN
PATROON PROPPER SUPPORT
ADHERENT ASSERTER ERASTIAN
ESPOUSER FAVORITE HENCHMAN
STALWART UPHOLDER
CHURCHITE
(ATHLETIC —) CUP JOCK
(CHIEF —) STOOP PILLAR
(PL.) SECOND
(SUFF.) CRAT ITE
SUPPORTING BEHIND BEARING
SUPPORTIVE ENGAGE
SUPPOSE SAY SEE SET WIS WIT
DEEM POSE READ TAKE TROW
WEEN ALLOW COUNT ETTLE
FANCY GUESS JUDGE OPINE
SEPAD THINK ASSUME DEVISE
DIVINE EXPECT RECKON BELIEVE
CONCEIT DARESAY IMAGINE
PRESUME PROPOSE SUPPONE
SURMISE CONCEIVE CONCLUDE
CONSIDER OPINIATE
SUPPOSED ALLEGED ASSUMED
PUTATIVE

SUPPOSING IF
SUPPOSITION IDEA FICTION
SURMISE WEENING
SUPPOSITORY BOUGIE CANDLE
PESSARY
SUPPRESS LAY DOWN GULP HIDE
HUSH SINK SLAY SNUB STOP
BLACK BURKE CHOKE CRUSH
ELIDE QUASH QUELL SHUSH
SMORE SPIKE STILL CANCEL
QUENCH SQUASH STIFLE
CONTAIN CUSHION INHIBIT
OPPRESS REPRESS SILENCE
SMOLDER SMOTHER SQUELCH
RESTRAIN STRANGLE SUPPRIME
VANQUISH
SUPPRESSED BLIND CENSORED
SUPPRESSION ABEYANCE
AMEIOSIS BLACKOUT
(— OF VOWEL) ELISION
(— OF WORD SOUNDS) SYNCOPE
ECLIPSIS
(PREF.) ISCH(O)
(SUFF.) SCHESIS SCHETIC
SUPPURATE RUN BEAL WHEAL
DIGEST MATTER QUITTER
MATURATE
SUPPURATING
(PREF.) EMPYO
SUPPURATION PYOSIS BEALING
COCTION
SUPPURATIVE DIGERENT
SUPRACLAVICLE SCAPULA
SUPREMACY PALM PRIMACY
DOMINION OVERRULE
SUPREME HIGH LAST CHIEF VITAL
SUBLIME SUMMARY TOPLESS
FOREMOST GREATEST PEERLESS
SURA FATIHA FATIHAH
SURCHARGE PACK
SURCINGLE WANTY ROLLER
SURCOAT JUPON CYCLAS KABAYA
SURD SHARP ATONIC FLATED
SURE COLD SAFE BOUND SECURE
SICCAR SICKER STEADY WITTER
ASSURED CERTAIN PERFECT
COCKSURE POSITIVE UNERRING
SURELY WIS FINE SURE PARDY
REDLY ATWEEL PARDIE
SURENESS SURETY SECURITY
SURETY VAS ANDI BAIL BAND
BORROW CAUTION ENGAGER
SOVERTY SPONSOR BAILSMAN
SECURITY
SURETYSHIP SPONSION
SURF BREACH KALEMA
(— NOISE) RUT ROTE
SURFACE DAY AREA FACE ORLO
PLAT RYME SIDE BOSOM FLOOR
STONE SWARF CHROME FINISH
GROUND SCRUFF ASPHALT
BLANKET COUNTER ENVELOP
OUTFACE OUTSIDE STRETCH
ADHEREND CONCRETE EXTERIOR
PLATFORM
(— BETWEEN FLUTES OF SHAFT)
ORLO
(— BETWEEN TRIGLYPH CHANNELS)
MEROS
(— IN BEATER) BACKFALL
(— OF BEAM) BACK
(— OF BODY) FLESH HABIT
(— OF COAL) BUTT

(— OF CRICKET FIELD) CARPET
(— OF DIAMOND) SPREAD
(— OF EARTH) DUST GROUND
TERRENE PENEPLAIN PENEPLANE
(— OF ESCUTCHEON) FIELD
(— OF GROUND OVER MINE) DAY
(— OF PARACHUTE) CANOPY
(— OF RIFLE BARREL) LAND
(— OF SAWED LUMBER) FUR
(— OF TOOTH) TRITOR
(— OF VAULT) GROIN
(— OF WATER) RYME SCRUFF
(— WITHIN EARTH) GEOID
(CONCAVE —) LAP
(CURVED —) BELLY
(DULL —) MAT MATTING
(EXTERNAL —) PERIPHERY
(FLAT —) BED FLAT AEQUOR
PAGINA
(FLOOR —) BOWL
(GEOMETRIC —) TORE CONOID
SPHERE QUARTIC CONICOID
CYLINDER HELICOID PARABOLOID
(GLOSSY —) GLAZE
(GROOVED —) DROVE
(HAIRY —) NAP
(HORIZONTAL —) LEVEL
(INCLINED —) CANT DESCENT
(MINERAL —) DRUSE
(PAVED —) FOOTWALK
(PILE —) FRIEZE
(PLANE —) AREA FACET
(PRINCIPAL —) FACE
(PRINTING —) CUT
(PROTECTIVE —) LAGGING
(ROAD —) MACADAM CORDUROY
(ROUGH —) KEY CRIZZLE STUBBLE
(ROUGHENED —) MAT FOOTGRIP
(SLIPPERY —) GLARE
(SLOPING —) SHELVING
(STRIKING —) BLADE
(UNDER — OF SKI) PALM
(UNGLOSSY PAINT —) FLAT
(UPPER —) NOTAEUM
(UPRIGHT —) JAMB
(PREF.) (BENT —) SINU SINUATO
SURFACER SEASONER
SURFBOARD GUN
SURF DUCK COOT SCOTER
SURFEIT CLOY FILL GLUT SATE
STAW STALL STUFF AGROTE
ENGLUT SICKEN SATIATE SATIETY
SURCLOY SATURATE REPLETION
SATURATION
SURFEITED SAD SICK BLASE
JADED WEARY REPLETE
SATIATED
SURFER (GIRL —) WAHINE
(INEXPERIENCED —) GREMMY
GREMMIE
SURF FISH PERCH ALFIONA
SURF SCOTER COOT SCOTER
SURFER PISHAUG SKUNKTOP
SURF SHINER SPARADA
SURGE JAW GUST TIDE WASH
DRIVE GURGE LUNGE SPURT
SWELL BILLOW BREACH COURSE
SEETHE WALLOW WALTER
ESTUATE REDOUND AESTUATE
UNDULATE
(— OF ELECTRIC POWER) GLITCH
(SHOREWARD —) SUFF
SURGEON (ALSO SEE PHYSICIAN

AND DOCTOR) LEECH ARTIST
INTERN MEDICO OPERATOR
SAWBONES
(TREE —) TREEMAN
AMERICAN EVE BULL LONG MOTT
REED AGNEW COLEY FLINT
GROSS FINNEY MORRIS MORTON
SHRADY ASHFORD CUSHING
HALSTED HARTLEY KELLOGG
LAPLACE BEAUMONT MCBURNEY
MCDOWELL METTAUER
CANADIAN BIRKETT
ENGLISH POTT REID BRAID HADEN
BARKER BEDDOE BOWMAN
CHEYNE COOPER FAYRER
ERICHSEN MOYNIHAN
ABERNETHY BRIFFAULT
CHESELDEN PARKINSON
FRENCH ANEL PARE BOYER BROCA
PETIT BECHAMP CHOPART
CIVIALE DESAULT NELATON
CHAULIAC CHASSAIGNAC
GERMAN GRAEFE ESMARCH
BILLROTH
GREEK AMMONIUS
IRISH MADDEN OMEARA
SCOTTISH SYME BANKS LISTON
MACEWEN
SOUTH AFRICAN BARNARD
SWISS KOCHER
SURGEONFISH TANG TANGE
DOCTOR MEDICO BARBERO
SURGEON SAWBONES
SURGERY KNIFE
(VETERINARY —) ZOIATRIA
(SUFF.) CHIRURGIA
SURGING WALE ESTURE ESTUOUS
SURICATE ZENICK MEERKAT
SURINAME (CAPITAL OF —)
PARAMARIBO
(RIVER OF —) ITANY MARONI
COPPENAME SARAMACCA
COURANTYNE
(TOWN OF —) ALBINA KWATTA
TOTNESS LELYDORP
SURINAMINE ANDIRINE ANGELINE
SURINAM TOAD PIPA PIPAL
SURLINESS CYNICISM MOROSITY
SURLY BAD ILL GRUM LUNT BLUFF
CHUFF CYNIC GRUFF GURLY
PURDY ROUGH RUNTY RUSTY
CHUFFY CRUSTY GRUFFY
GRUMPY MOROSE RUGGED
SNARLY SULLEN CHURLISH
SURMISE DEEM REDE GUESS
INFER TWANG SURMIT JALOUSE
SUSPECT WEENING MISTRUST
SURMOUNT TOP BEAT TIDE
CROWN ENSIGN HURDLE MASTER
OUTTOP OVERGO SUBDUE
CONQUER SURPASS OVERCOME
SUPERATE
(— DIFFICULTIES) SWIM
SURMOUNTING BROCHANT
SURNAME BYNAME SURNOUN
COGNOMEN OVERNAME
SURSTYLE
SURPASS CAP COB TOP WAR
BANG BEAT CAMP COTE DING
FLOG FOIL HEAD PASS SHED
WHAP WHOP EXCEL OUTDO
OUTGO TRUMP ATREDE BETTER
EXCEED OUTRAY OUTRUN

OUTVIE OUTWIT OVERDO PRECEL ECLIPSE FORPASS OUTPEER OVERTOP PARAGON PRECEDE ANTECEDE DISTANCE DOMINATE OUTCLASS OUTMATCH OUTRANGE OUTREACH OUTSHINE OUTSTRIP OUTWRITE SURMOUNT

SURPASSING BEST FINE ABOVE PASSANT PASSING DOMINANT FRABJOUS TOWERING (PREF.) PRETER SUPER

SURPLICE SARK COTTA EPHOD STOLA CHRISOM (PL.) WHITES

SURPLUS OVER PLUS REST EXCESS LUMBER SPILTH VELVET OVERAGE OVERRUN OVERSUM ARISINGS LEFTOVER OVERCOME OVERFLOW OVERMUCH OVERPLUS

SURPRISE CAP SHED SWAN YACH AMAZE SHOCK SNEAK FERLIE WAYLAY WONDER ASTOUND GLOPPEN PERPLEX STARTLE ASTONISH BEWILDER CONFOUND DUMFOUND (BY —) ABACK (EXCLAMATION OF —) QUOTHA (EXPRESS —) MIRATE (SUDDEN —) KICK

SURPRISING FERLIE STRIKING

SURRA MBORI

SURREJOINDER TRIPLY

SURRENDER HEM LET PUT CEDE CESS DING FALL QUIT TAKE REMIT YIELD ADDICT REMISE RENDER RESIGN SUBMIT ABANDON CONCEDE DELIVER FORSAKE KAMERAD ABDICATE ABNEGATE DEDITION DELIVERY RENOUNCE UNDERLIE (— BY DEED) REMISE

SURREPTITIOUS SECRET BOOTLEG FURTIVE SNEAKING

SURROUND HEM LAP ORB BELT DIKE DYKE FOLD GIRD GIRT HOOP WRAP BESET BRACE CLASP EMBAY EMBED FENCE HEDGE IMBED INARM ROUND BECLIP BEGIRD BEGIRT CIRCLE COLLET CORRAL ENFOLD ENWRAP FORSET GIRDLE IMPALE INCASE INVEST SPHERE SWATHE ARROUND BESIEGE BESTAND COMPASS EMBOSOM ENCLAVE ENCLOSE ENFEOFF ENROUND ENVELOP ENVIRON INVOLVE WREATHE CLOISTER ENCIRCLE ENTRENCH STOCKADE (— WITH BOOM) CRIB (— WITH CORD) GIRT (— WITH MORTAR) GROUT

SURROUNDED AMID AMONG AMIDST AMONGST BETWEEN

SURROUNDING MIDST ROUND CIRCUM AMBIENT (PL.) SCENE HARNESS ENVIRONS (PREF.) CIRCUM PERI

SURROYALS CROWN

SURVEILLANCE WATCH SCRUTINY STAKEOUT OVERSIGHT

SURVEY SEE DIAL SCAN VIEW AVIEW STOCK STUDY PERUSE REGARD REVIEW SEARCH CANVASS CAPSULE OVERSEE SURVIEW TERRIER THEORIC EPISCOPY LUSTRATE OVERLOOK OVERVIEW PROSPECT SURVEYAL TRAVERSE RECONNAISANCE (— RAPIDLY) GLANCE (— TIMBER) SKYLOOK (BRIEF —) APERCU

SURVEYING GEODESY GROMATICS (MINE —) LATCHING

SURVEYOR BOLO ARTIST DIALER DIALLER NOTEMAN CHAINMAN GROMATIC LEVELMAN

SURVIVAL ECHO RELIC RELICT (ANACHRONISTIC —) LEFTOVER (USELESS —) SNUFF

SURVIVE LAST BILEVE OUTLAST OUTLIVE

SURVIVOR RELICT

SURYA (FATHER OF —) ADITI DYAUS (MESSENGER OF —) PUSHAN (WIFE OF —) USHAS

SUSCEPTIBILITY CAVIL SENSE EMOTION FEELING FRAILTY (— TO ILL-HEALTH) DELICACY

SUSCEPTIBLE EASY SOFT LIABLE FEELING PATIENT SENSIBLE TOLERANT (— TO CHANGE) CASALTY

SUSIAN ELAMITE

SUSLIK SISEL ZIZEL MARMOT

SUSPECT FEAR DOUBT FANCY GUESS SMOKE THINK BELIEVE ENDOUTE JALOUSE MISDEEM SUPPOSE DISTRUST JEALOUSE MISDOUBT MISTRUST (NOT —) COLD

SUSPECTED SPOTTED SUSPECT

SUSPEND CALL HALT HANG OUST SHUT SIST STAY BREAK CLOSE DEBAR DEFER DEMUR EXPEL POISE REMIT SLING SWING APPEND DANGLE ADJOURN EXCLUDE FLUIDIZE INTERMIT OVERHANG PROROGUE REPRIEVE SCAFFOLD SUSPENSE PRETERMIT (— ANCHOR) COCKBILL

SUSPENDED SWING AFLOAT LATENT HANGING PENDANT PENDENT PENSILE HOVERING SUSPENSE

SUSPENDER GALLUS GARTER BRETELLE (PL.) BRACES GALLOWS GALLUSES

SUSPENSE DEMUR POISE

SUSPENSION FOG BREI FUME SIST STAY STOP DELAY DOUBT MAGMA SMOKE BREACH CUTOFF SLURRY AEROSOL FAILURE RESPITE ABEYANCE BACTERIN EMULSION INFUSION SHUTDOWN SUSPENSE WISHBONE (— OF JUDGMENT) EPOCHE (— OF NOISE) HUSH (— OF RESPIRATION) SYNCOPE

SUSPENSIVENESS DRIVE

SUSPENSORY SUPPORT

SUSPICION HINT DOUBT SOUPCON SURMISE SUSPECT UMBRAGE DISTRUST JEALOUSY MISDOUBT MISTRUST TINCTURE

SUSPICIOUS SHY FISHY LEERY PEERY QUEER SMOKY SHODDY JEALOUS SOUPCON SUSPECT DOUBTFUL WAFFLIKE

SUSPICIOUSLY ASKANCE

SUSQUEHANNA CONESTOGA

SUSTAIN ABET BACK BEAR BUOY DURE HELP HOLD LAST PROP STAY ABIDE CARRY FAVOR SINEW SPRAG STAND ASSIST CONVEY ENDURE FOSTER SECOND SUCCOR SUFFER UPHOLD UPSTAY ALIMENT BOLSTER CONTAIN NOURISH OUTBEAR PROLONG SUPPORT UNDERFO BEFRIEND BUTTRESS CONTINUE MAINTAIN PRESERVE SCAFFOLD (PREF.) CO

SUSTAINED TENUTO SOUTENU

SUSTENANCE GEAR SALT BREAD FOISON LIVING RELIEF ALIMENT PABULUM TABLING

SUSU GERIP SOOSOO DOLPHIN

SUSURRUS WHISPER

SUTLER PROVANT VIVANDIER

SUTTEE SATI

SUTURE SEAM RAPHE SETON HARMONY PTERION (SUFF.) RHAPHY RRHAPHY

SVANTOVIT TRIGLAV

SVELTE CHIC TRIM LITHE SLEEK SUAVE SMOOTH URBANE SLENDER

SVENO (SLAYER OF —) SOLIMANO

SWAB GOB MOP BOSH SWOB PATCH DOSSIL SPONGE EPAULET SWABBER SQUILGEE

SWADDLE SWEEL SWATHE

SWAG DRUM GAME LOOT BOOTY LUCRE MONEY BOODLE FESTOON MATILDA

SWAGE BOSS MOUTH UPSET FULLER JUMPER SHAPER SWAGER SWEDGE FLATTER (PL.) OLIVER

SWAGGER JET ROY BRAG COCK FACE ROLL BOAST BRANK BRAVE NUTTY STRUT SWANK SWASH BLAGUE BOUNCE GOSTER HECTOR PARADO PRANCE RENOWN RUFFLE SPROSE BLUSTER BRAVADO GAUSTER PANACHE ROISTER SOLDIER DOMINEER TIGERISM

SWAGGERER HUFF SWAG BUCKO FACER TIGER CUTTLE JETTER PISTOL BRAVADO HUFFCAP RUFFLER FANFARON WHIFFLER

SWAGGERING HUFFY FACING GASCON HUFFCAP TEARCAT BLUSTERY TIGERISH

SWAGMAN WHALER DRUMMER TRAVELER

SWAIN COLIN CUDDY RUSTIC STREPHON

SWAINSONA INDIGO

SWALE SLASH

SWALLOW OFF SUP BOLT DOWN DROP GAUP GAWP GLUT GULP SINK TAKE CLUNK DRINK GORGE GURGE POUCH QUILT SLOCK SWOOP ABSORB ENGLUT ENGULF GLUTCH GOBBET GOBBLE GODOWN GUZZLE IMBIBE INGEST MARTIN POCKET PROGNE SWELLY CONSUME ENGORGE ARUNDELL WITCHUCK (— GREEDILY) BEND SLUP GORGE GULCH SWILL WORRY INHALE (— HASTILY) SWAP SWOP GLOUP SLUMMOCK (— IN AGAIN) RESORB (— UP) GULF SWAMP ABSORB DEVOUR (— WITH GREEDINESS) ENGORGE (LOSS OF ABILITY TO —) APHAGIA (NOISY —) SLURP (WOMAN TURNED INTO —) PROCNE (PREF.) CHELID(O)

SWALLOWTAIL TROILUS

SWALLOWWORT CELANDINE

SWAMP BOG FEN FLAT FLOW MIRE MOSS SLEW SLUE SOAK SUMP VLEI VLEY WHAM WHIN FLUSH LERNA LETCH MARSH SWALE SWANG URMAN DELUGE DISMAL ENGULF MORASS SLOUGH CIENAGA POCOSIN GREENING INUNDATE QUAGMIRE

SWAMP COTTONWOOD LIAR

SWAMPER BUSHER GOPHER

SWAMPHEN COOT

SWAMP LOOSESTRIFE PEATWEED PEATWOOD

SWAMP MAHOGANY GUNNUNG

SWAMP MILKWEED DAGGA

SWAMPY PUXY BOGGY POOLY CALLOW POACHY QUASHY QUEASY SLUMPY MOORISH PALUDAL ULIGINOUS

SWAMPY CREE MASKEGON

SWAN COB ELK PEN OLOR CYGNET HOOPER SWANNET WHOOPER (FLOCK OF —S) GAME MARK

SWANFLOWER SWANWORT

SWANHILD (FATHER OF —) SIGURD (MOTHER OF —) GUDRUN

SWANK CHIC

SWANKY SWASH

SWAP CHOP SWOP TRADE TRUCK DICKER EXCHANGE

SWARD SOD TURF SPINE SWARF SWATH SWARTH

SWARM FRY SNY BIKE CAST FARE HOST KNIT NEST SORT SWIM TEEM CLOUD CROWD FLOCK FLUSH FRACK HORDE SNARL FLIGHT HOTTER RABBLE SWARVE THRONG OVERRUN SUBCAST PULLULATE (— IN) FILL (— OF BEES) BIKE HIVE (— OF INSECTS) BAND FLIGHT (— OF PEOPLE) BIKE DRIFT (THIRD — OF BEES) COLT

SWARMING ALIVE ASWARM SWARMY

SWARTBACK SWARBIE

SWARTHY DUN DARK BLACK BROWN DUSKY GRIMY MOORY SWART MORIAN SWARTH BISTRED BISTERED

SWASH SWIG SWILL SWATCH SWABBLE SWASHWAY

SWASHBUCKLER SWASH GASCON SLASHER SWASHER

SWASTIKA FYLFOT GAMMADION
SWAT SWOT DEHGAN STRIKE
SWATH SWIPE STADDLE
SWATHE LAP BIND WRAP SWARF
  SWADDLE WINDROW
SWATTER FLYSWAT
SWAY NOD WAG BEAR BEND BIAS
  FLAP HIKE LILT ROCK ROLL RULE
  SHOG SWAB SWAG SWIG TILT
  TOSS WALD WAVE CARRY CHARM
  LURCH POWER REIGN SHAKE
  SWALE SWING WAVER WHEEL
  AFFECT ALLURE CAREEN DIRECT
  EMPIRE TOTTER WAGGLE
  COMMAND SHOGGIE STAGGER
  SWABBLE SWIGGLE
  (SUFF.) CRACY CRAT(IC)
SWAYBACK WARFA LORDOSIS
  RENGUERA
SWAYING ASWAY ROLLING
SWAZILAND (CAPITAL OF —)
  MBABANE
  (COIN OF —) RAND
  (LANGUAGE OF —) SISWATI
  (MONEY OF —) LILANGENI
  (RIVER IN —) USUTU KOMATI
  MHLATUZE UMBULUZI
  (TOWN OF —) STEGI GOLLEL
  MANZINI PIGGSPEAK
SWEAR VOW VUM DAMN SINK
  SNUM SWAN SWOW TAKE CURSE
  ADJURE AFFIRM BEDAMN
  DEPONE DEPOSE OBJURE
  CONJURE DEJERATE EXECRATE
  FORSWEAR
  (— FALSELY) RAP MOUNT
  FORSWEAR MANSWEAR
SWEARING JURANT JURATION
  (FALSE —) PERJURY
SWEARWORD CUSS
SWEAT DEW WET STEW WASH
  BREAN MADOR SUDOR SUDATE
  LAUNDER PARBOIL SWELTER
  SWIVVET TRANSUDE
  PERSPIRATION
  (— SKINS) STALE
  (DYNAMITE —) LEAK
  (PREF.) HIDR(O) HYDR(O) SUDORI
  (SUFF.) IDROSIS
SWEATBOX HOTBOX
SWEATER FROCK GANSEY JUMPER
  WOOLLY CARDIGAN SLIPOVER
  (CLOSE-FITTING —) POORBOY
  (WOMAN'S SHORT —) SHRINK
SWEATHOUSE TEMESCAL
SWEATING TUB ASWEAT SWELTRY
  SUDATION SUDATORY
SWEATY PUGGY ASWEAT
  PERSPIRY SUDOROUS SWEATFUL

SWEDEN
CAPITAL: STOCKHOLM
COIN: ORE KRONA SKILLING
COUNTY: KALMAR OREBRO
  UPPSALA
DIVISION: AMT LAEN SKANE
  OREBRO UPPSALA GOTALAND
  JAMTLAND SWEALAND
GULF: BOTHNIA
ISLAND: OLAND GOTALAND
LAKE: SILJA VANERN MALAREN
  VATTERN DALALVEN
  STORAVAN HJALMAREN

MEASURE: AM ALN FOT MIL REF
  TUM FAMN STOP FODER
  KANNA KAPPE LINJE NYMIL
  SPANN STANG TUNNA FATHOM
  JUMFRU KOLLAST OXHUVUD
  TUNLAND FJARDING KAPPLAND
  KOLTUNNA
MOUNTAIN: SARV AMMAR OVIKS
  HELAGS SARJEK
PROVINCE: KALMAR OREBRO
  GOTLAND HALLAND UPPSALA
  ALVSBORG BLEKINGE ELFSBORG
  JAMTLAND MALMOHUS
  WERMLAND
RIVER: DAL UME GOTA KLAR LULE
  KALIX PITEA RANEA LAINIO
  LJUSNE TORNEA WINDEL
  ANGERMAN
TOWN: UMEA BODEN BORAS
  EDANE FALUN GAVLE LULEA
  MALMO PITEA VISBY YSTAD
  ARVIKA OREBRO LUDVIKA
  UPPSALA GOTEBORG NYKOPING
  VASTERAS
WATERFALL: HANDOL
  TANNFORSEN
WEIGHT: ASS LOD ORT MARK
  PUND STEN UNTZ NYLAST
  LISPUND SKEPPUND

SWEDISH CLOVER ALSIKE
SWEEP BUCK DUST RAFF SOOP
  SWAY TILT BESOM BROOM DIGHT
  DRIFT FETCH SCOPE SKIRL SWIPE
  SWOOP BREADTH CLEANSE
  PICOTAH SHADOOF STRICKLE
  (— A NET) BEAT
  (— MAJESTICALLY) SWAN
  (— OF SCYTHE) SWATH SWATHE
  (— OFF) SLIPE
  (— ON CULTIVATOR) SKIN
  (CHIMNEY —) CHUMMY SWEEPY
  RAMONEUR
  (HAY —) BUCK
SWEEPBOARD STRICKLE
SWEEPER BUNGY SWEEP TOPAZ
  BHANGI BHUNGI MEHTAR PRYLER
  ROADER SOOPER TOPASS
  BROOMER TUBEMAN BHUNGINI
  MATRANEE SCRUBBER
SWEEPING SURGE RASANT
  SWEEPY
  (— FOR FISH) DRAFT DRAUGHT
  (PL.) DUST FULVIE FULZIE
  RIFFRAFF
SWEET DOUX DUMP FOOL SOOT
  SUCK CREAM DILIS DOUCE DULCE
  FRESH HONEY MERRY SOOTH
  SPICY SPLIT BREEZE DULCET
  FRUITY GENTLE SILKEN SILVER
  SIRUPY SUGARY DARLING
  FAIRING HONEYED INSIPID
  MUSICAL PANDROP SUGARED
  SWEETLY WINNING WINSOME
  AROMATIC ENGAGING FLUMMERY
  LIEBLICH LUSCIOUS NECTARED
  PLEASANT
  (SLIGHTLY —) SEC
  (PREF.) DULCI GLYCERO GLYCO
  HEDY SUAVI
SWEET BAY BREWSTER MAGNOLIA
SWEETBREAD BUR BURR
  PANCREAS

(— OF DEER) INCHPIN
SWEETBRIER BEDEGUAR
  EGLANTINE
SWEET CALABASH KURUBA
SWEET CASSAVA AIPI AIPIM
SWEET CHERRY MAZZARD
SWEET CICELY MYRRH
SWEET CLOVER LOTUS MELILOT
SWEET COLTSFOOT LAGWORT
SWEETEN CANDY HONEY SUGAR
  SWEET PURIFY ADDULCE
  CLEANSE DULCIFY FRESHEN
  MOLLIFY PERFUME MITIGATE
SWEETENER SACCHARIN
SWEET FENNEL FINOCHIO
  FLORENCE
SWEET FERN FERNGALE
SWEETFISH AYU
SWEET FLAG SEDGE BEEWORT
  CALAMUS
SWEET GALE GOLD GAGEL
  BAYBUSH FLEAWOOD GALEWORT
  GALLBUSH
SWEET GUM AMBER COPALM
  STORAX BILSTED
SWEETHEART JO BOY GRA HON
  JOE LAD PUG SIS AGRA BABY
  BEAU DEAR DOLL DOXY DUCK
  FAIR GILL GIRL JILL LADY LASS
  LIEF LOVE MASH MORT POUT
  AGRAH BULLY BUSSY CHERI
  COOKY DOLLY DONAH DONEY
  DONNA DRURY FLAME LEMAN
  LOVER PUGGY SPARK SWEET
  COOKIE EMILIA FELLOW FRIEND
  MOPSEY PIGEON STEADY WAHINE
  AMOROSA BELOVED PHYLLIS
  PIGSNEY QUERIDA SPRUNNY
  SWEETIE TOOTSIE DOWSABEL
  DULCINEA FOLLOWER LADYBIRD
  LADYLOVE LIEBCHEN LOVELASS
  MISTRESS SWEETING TRUELOVE
SWEETLEAF DYELEAVES
  SYMPLOCOS
SWEET MARJORAM OREGANO
SWEETMEAT DROP DUMP KISS
  DULCE FUDGE GOODY PASTE
  PLATE SPICE TOFFY BONBON
  BUCAYO COMFIT DRAGEE
  DREDGE JUNKET ALCORZA
  BANQUET CARAMEL CARAWAY
  CLAGGUM CONFECT LOUKOUM
  PENUCHE SUCCADE CONSERVE
  HARDBAKE MARZIPAN PASTILLE
  (PL.) BALUSHAI CONFETTI
SWEETNESS DULCE HONEY SIRUP
  SYRUP DULCOR DOUCEUR
  DULCITY SUAVITY FLORIMEL
  WORDNESS
SWEET ORANGE CHINA CHINO
SWEET PEA CATGUT LATHYRUS
SWEET PEPPERBUSH CLETHRA
  SOAPBUSH
SWEET POTATO YAM SWEET
  BATATA CAMOTE KUMARA
  OCARINA
SWEET RUSH SQUINANT
SWEET-SMELLING AROMATIC
SWEETSOP ANON ATES ATIS ATTA
  CORAZON SWEETING
SWEET-SOUNDING MERRY
SWEET VIOLET FINELEAF
SWEET WILLIAM DIANTHUS

SWELL BAG DON NIB NOB BEAL
  BELL BLAB BLOW BLUB BOLL
  BULB BULK BUMP BUOY DOME
  FILL GROW HOVE HUFF HUSH
  PINK PLIM RISE SWAG TOFF TONY
  WAVE BELLY BERRY BLAST BLOAT
  BULGE BUNCH FLASH PLUFF
  PREEN SMART STOCK STRUT
  SURGE TULIP BILLOW BOWDEN
  DILATE EXPAND GROWTH LOVELY
  SPRING STROUT TUMEFY UPRISE
  AUGMENT BLUBBER BURGEON
  DISTEND INFLATE REGULAR
  SWAGGER OVERBLOW TURGESCE
  (— OF GUN MUZZLE) TULIP
  (— OF WATER) HUSH SURF FLOOD
  SURGE
  (— OUT) BAG POD BUNT DRAW
  POUT BOSOM BILLOW SPONGE
  BALLOON BLADDER
  (HEAVY —) RUN SEA
  (PREF.) OEDE OEDI TUME
SWELLDOODLE EGGFISH
SWELLED BIAS BLOWN
SWELLFISH BLOWER PUFFER
  TAMBOR
SWELLING BIG BUR NOB PAP PIN
  BLAB BOLL BUBO BUMP BURR
  CLAP COWL CURB FROG FULL
  GALL KNOB KNOT NODE POKE
  PONE PUFF AMPER BLAIN BOTCH
  BOUGE BULGE BUNCH BUNNY
  CLOUR EDEMA JETTY MOUSE
  PROUD SURGE SWELL TUBER
  TUMOR ANGOME ASWELL
  BOSOMY BUNCHY CALLUS
  FLATUS GIBBER GROWTH KERNEL
  PIMPLE RANULA STRUMA
  SWELTH WARBLE AMPULLA
  BOSSING CAPELET CHAGOMA
  CUSHION GOUNDOU HAPTERE
  PUSTULE SURGENT TURGENT
  UREDEMA UROCELE APOSTEME
  BULLNECK CHEMOSIS DACRYOMA
  FURUNCLE GLANDULE GOURDING
  HAPTERON HEMATOMA
  MUCOCELE NODOSITY PULVINUS
  PUMPKNOT QUELLUNG SCIRRHUS
  STYLOPOD VESSICNON
  (— IN HORSE'S CHEST) ANTICOR
  (— IN HORSE'S MOUTH) LAMPAS
  (— IN PLASTER) BLUB
  (— OF PLANT TISSUE) GALL
  (— OF THE CHEEK) HONE
  (— ON ANIMAL'S JOINTS) BUNNY
  CAPELLET
  (— ON HEAD) COWL
  (EYE —) STY STYE
  (PREF.) GANGLI GANGLO STRUMI
  (SUFF.) EMATOMA PHYMA
SWELTER STEW SWELT
SWELTERING STEWY SULTRY
  SWELTRY
SWERVE BOW CUT LUG YAW BIAS
  FADE JOUK SKEW VARY VEER
  WARP SHEER STRAY DEPART
  DEVIATE DIGRESS DIVERGE
  INSWING
SWIDDEN CAINGIN KAINGIN
SWIFT CRAN FAST FLIT MAIN VITE
  FLEET HASTY LIGHT QUICK RAPID
  SNELL SWITH WIGHT WINDY
  ARROWY MARLET NIMBLE

RAKING SOUPLE SPEEDY STRICT
SUDDEN SWIFTY TOTTER WINGED
COLLIER DEVELIN FLIGHTY
POSTING SWALLOW TANTIVY
DEVELING HEPIALID PEGASEAN
SCREAMER SCUTTLER SQUEALER
SWIFTLET SALANGANE
(PREF.) CITI CYPSELO OCY
TACHEO TACHISTO TACHO TACHY

SWIFTLY FAST SWAP APACE
SNELL SNELLY LIGHTLY STEEPLY
TANTIVY

SWIFTNESS FOOT HASTE SPEED
CELERITY FASTNESS VELOCITY

SWIG SCOUR SWILL SWING
SWIGGLE

SWILL SOSS BROCK SLOSH SLUICE
HOGWASH PIGWASH SWILLING

SWIM DIP COWD SAIL SOOM SPAN
TEEM BATHE CRAWL FLEET
FLOAT GLIDE SWARM PLUNGE
OVERFLOW
(— IN NEW DIRECTION) MILL
(— IN NUDE) SKINNYDIP
(— TOGETHER) SCHOOL
(PREF.) NECT(O)
(SUFF.) NECTAE NECTES

SWIMMER BATHER NATATOR

SWIMMERET PLEOPOD

SWIMMING ASWIM NATANT
FLOTANT NATATION
(— STUNT) MARLIN WALKOVER

SWIMMING POOL POOL THERM
PLUNGE THERME PISCINA
NATATORY
(— ON LINER) LIDO

SWINDLE CON GIP GYP JOB RIG
BILK FAKE FLAP HAVE MACE PULL
RAMP ROOK ROPE SCAM SWIZ
BUNCO BUNKO CHEAT FLING
FOIST GOUGE LURCH PLANT
ROGUE SHARK SHARP SHAVE
SHUCK SLANG SPOOF STING
SWIZZ UNCLE BOODLE BUBBLE
BUCKET CHOUSE DIDDLE FIDDLE
GAZUMP HUSTLE INTAKE NOBBLE
SUCKER TREPAN FINAGLE
SKELDER THIMBLE VERNEUK
FLIMFLAM BAMBOOZLE

SWINDLER DO FOB GYP LEG BILK
FYNK HAWK ROOK SKIN CHEAT
CROOK ESROC FAKER GREEK
HARPY KNAVE MACER ROGUE
CHIAUS GOUGER INTAKE RINGER
ROOKER SALTER SHAVER VERSER
BUBBLER HUSTLER MACEMAN
MAGSMAN NOBBLER SHARPER
SKELDER SLICKER SPIELER
BARNACLE BLACKLEG FINAGLER
GILENYER LUMBERER PIGEONER
SHELLMAN TRAMPOSO
(DECOY —) BARNARD

SWINDLING MACE BUNCO BUNKO
ROOKY SHARK GYPPERY JOUKERY
CHEATERY JOOKERIE

SWINE HOG OIC PIG SOW BOAR
GALT GILT PORK SUID YILT
DUROC ESSEX SWIPE WHITE
GUSSIE POLAND PORKER PORKET
BUSHPIG LACOMBE PECCARY
SUFFOLK SUIDIAN CHESHIRE
HYOTHERE LANDRACE
TAMWORTH

(— AND FOOD) PANNAGE
(— AND MAN) OMNIVORA
(PREF.) HYO

SWINEHERD GURTH HOGMAN
EUMAEUS HOGHERD HOGWARD

SWINE-LIKE GADARENE

SWING GO HIKE JUMP LILT SCUP
SHOG STOT SWAY SWEE TURN
SHAKE SHOWD SLING SWALE
TREND DANGLE GYRATE HANDLE
SWINGE SWITCH SWIVEL TOTTER
JUMPING SHOGGIE SWINGEL
WAMPISH BRANDISH FLOURISH
OSCILLATE
(— A SHIP) SPRING
(— AROUND) JIB SLEW SLUE
SLOUGH
(— BY BATTER) CUT
(— FROM POSITION) CANT
(— FROM SIDE TO SIDE) JOW
(— FROM THE TIDE) TEND
(— OF PENDULUM) BEAT
(— OF SAIL) GYBE JIBE
(— OF SWORD) MOULINET
(— OUT OF LINE) SWAG
(— THE FOREFEET) DISH
(RHYTHMICAL —) LILT
(WILD —) HAYMAKER
(PREF.) OSCILLO

SWINGING BANK ASWING SWINGY

SWINGLE SWORD SCUTCH
SWIPPLE

SWING SEAT TRANSOM

SWINISH SOWISH HOGGISH
PORCINE SUILLINE

SWIPE COP CHOP GLOM SLOG
WIPE SNAKE STEAL VULTURE

SWIRL BOIL EDDY GULF HURL
PURL WALM GURGE SWALE
SWEEL SWORL SWOOSH
WREATHE TOURBILLION
(— OF SALMON) BULGE

SWIRLING VORTICAL

SWISH HISH WHIP SMART SWILL
WHISH

SWISS SWISSER HELVETIC
(— PINE) MUGHO

SWISS FAMILY ROBINSON
(AUTHOR OF —) WYSS
(CHARACTER IN —) JACK EMILY
FRITZ ERNEST FRANCIS
MONTROSE ROBINSON

SWITCH GAD TAN LASH TWIG
WAND AZOTE BIRCH BREAK
SHUNT SWISH CHANGE CUTOUT
DERAIL DIPPER FERULA FERULE
LARRUP RATTAN SCUTCH SILENT
SPRING HICKORY KIPPEEN
SCOURGE SQUITCH CRYOTRON
HAIRWORK POSTICHE
(— FOCUS) FADE
(ELECTRIC —) KEY
(RAILROAD —) GATE POINT

SWITCH ENGINE GOAT

SWITCHMAN SHUNTER SWITCHER

SWITZERLAND

BAY: URI
CANTON: ZUG BERN JURA VAUD
BASEL AARGAU GENEVA
GLARUS LUZERN SCHWYZ
TICINO VALAIS ZURICH
GRISONS THURGAU

FRIBOURG OBWALDEN
CAPITAL: BERN BERNE
COIN: FRANC RAPPE RAPPEN
ANGSTER DUPLONE BLAFFERT
LAKE: URI ZUG THUN AGERI
LEMAN MORAT BIENNE BRIENZ
GENEVA LUGANO SARNEN
WALLEN ZURICH HALLWIL
LUCERNE LUNGERN VIERWALD
MEASURE: IMI POT AUNE ELLE
FUSS IMMI MUID PIED SAUM
ZOLL LIEVE LIGNE LINIE MAASS
MOULE POUCE SCHUH STAAB
TOISE PERCHE SETIER STRICH
JUCHART KLAFTER VIERTEL
MOUNTAIN: JURA RIGI ROSA
BLANC CENIS KARPF LINARD
PIZELA BERNINA BEVERIN
GRIMSEL PILATUS ROTONDO
BALMHORN JUNGFRAU
MOUNTAIN PASS: CENIS FURKA
ALBERG MALOJA BRENNER
GRIMSEL SIMPLON SPLUGEN
LOTSCHEN
NAME: HELVETIA
RIVER: AAR INN AARE THUR
BROYE DOUBS LINTH REUSS
RHINE RHONE MAGGIA SARINE
TICINO PRATIGAU
TOWN: BALE BERN BIEL BRIG
CHUR SION BASEL VEVEY
GENEVA GLARUS LUZERN
SCHWYZ ZURICH FYZABAD
HERISAU LUCERNE LAUSANNE
MONTREUX
VALLEY: AAR ZERMATT ENGADINE
WATERFALL: SIMMEN HANDEGG
IFFIGEN DIESSBACH GIESSBACH
STAUBBACH TRUMMELBACH
WEIGHT: PFUND CENTNER
QUINTAL

SWIVEL LOPER SWAPE SWIPE
CASTER FIDDLE TIRRET TOGGLE
TONGUE TRAVERSE TRUNNION

SWOLLEN BLUB FULL PLIM RANK
BLOWN CHUFF GOUTY GREAT
GUMMY POBBY PROUD PUFFY
TUMID BOLLEN BRAWNY BULLED
GOURDY TURGID BESTRUT
BLOATED BLUBBER BULBOUS
GIBBOSE GIBBOUS GOURDED
GOUTISH STICKLE TURGENT
BEPUFFED BLADDERY TUMOROUS
(PREF.) PHYS(O)

SWOON KEEL SWEB SWIM DOVER
DROWN DWALM FAINT SLOOM
SOUND SWARF SWELT STOUND
SWITHER SYNCOPE SWOONING

SWOONING ASWOON SYNCOPE

SWOOP CHOP DIVE JOUK SWAP
SWOP SOUSE STOOP SWOPE
POUNCE SOURCE DESCEND

SWOOPING SOUSE

SWORD FOX SAX BILL DIRK FALX
GRAM IRON PATA SAEX SEAX
SPIT TOOL TUCK TURK BILBO
BLADE BRAND DEGEN DIEGO
ESTOC GULLY KNIFE KUKRI PRICK
RIPON SABER SABRE SHARP
STEEL ANDREW BARONG BILBOA
CATTAN DAMASK DUSACK

FLORET GLAIVE HANGER KHANDA
KUKERI MIMING PARANG PINKER
PORKER RAPIER SMITER SPATHA
TILTER TIZONA TOLEDO WAFTER
BALMUNG BRANDON CURTANA
CUTLASH CUTLASS ESPADON
ESTOQUE FERRARA FLEURET
IMPALER JOYEUSE MALCHUS
MORGLAY SHABBLE SLASHER
SNICKER SPURTLE TOASTER
WHIFFLE WHINGER ACINACES
BASELARD CAMPILAN CLAYMORE
DAMASCUS DURENDAL FALCHION
FLAMBERG SCHLAGER SPADROON
SPITFROG WACADASH WHINYARD
(— OF CHARLEMAGNE) JOYEUSE
(— OF CID) TIZONA
(— OF HERMES) HARPE
(— OF LANCELOT) ARONDIGHT
(— OF ROLAND) DURENDAL
(— OF SIEGFRIED) GRAM BALMUNG
(— OF SIR BEVIS) MORGLAY
(— OF ST. GEORGE) ASCALON
ASKELON
(— USED BY ST. PETER) MALCHUS
(BLUNT —) WAFTER SCHLAGER
(CELTIC —) SAX SAEX
(DOUBLE-EDGED —) KEN PATA
KHANDA SPATHA
(DUELLING —) EPEE SHARP
(DYAK —) PARANG
(FENCING —) EPEE FOIL SABER
SABRE RAPIER
(HALF OF —) FORTE
(JAPANESE —) CATAN CATTAN
KATANA WACADASH
(LONG —) SPATHA WHIFFLE
(MATADOR'S —) ESTOQUE
(MORO —) BARONG CAMPILAN
(NARROW —) TUCK
(NORMAN —) SPATHA
(PERSIAN —) ACINACES
(POINTLESS —) CURTANA CURTEIN
(RUSTY —) SHABBLE
(SHORT —) DIRK ESTOC KUKRI
SKEAN CREESE CURTAXE
WHINGER WHINYARD
(THRUSTING —) ESTOC STOCK
(TWO-HANDED —) ESPADON
SPADONE CLAYMORE
(WOODEN —) WASTER STRICKLE

SWORD-BEARER VERGER
SELICTAR PORTGLAVE
(PL.) ENSIFERI

SWORD DANCER MATACHIN

SWORDFISH AU ESPADA
ESPADON XIPHIAS ALBACORA
BILLFISH BOATBILL FORKTAIL
XIPHIOID SCOMBROID
(PREF.) XIPH(O)

SWORD-LIKE
(PREF.) XIPH(I)(O)

SWORDPLAY SPADROON
(STYLIZED —) KENDO

SWORD-SHAPED ENSATE
ENSIFORM GLADIATE

SWORDSMAN BLADE BLADER
FENCER SLASHER SWORDER
THRUSTER

SWORDTAIL HELLERI

SWORN AVOWED

SWOT GRI MUG

SYAGUSH SHARGOSS

SYBARITE EPICURE
SYBARITIC SENSUOUS
SYCAMORE MAY DAROO
COTONIER LACEWOOD PLANTAIN
SYCEE SHOE
SYCOPHANCY FAWNERY
SYCOPHANT TOADY COGGER
FAWNER GNATHO HANGBY
TAGTAIL CLAWBACK PARASITE
PICKTHANK SATELLITE
SYCOPHANTIC FAWNING SERVILE
SLAVISH OBEDIENT TRENCHER
SYCORAX (SON OF —) CALIBAN
SYCOSIS MENTAGRA
SYENITE APPINITE TRACHYTE
SYLLABARY KANA IROFA IROHA
KATAKANA
SYLLABIC SONANT CENTROID
SONANTIC
SYLLABLE ARSIS BREVE GROUP
SHORT DISEME SYLLAB THESIS
TRISEME ASSONANT
(— DENOTING ASSENT) OM
(BOBIZATION —) BO CE DI GA GE
LO MA NI
(LAST —) ULTIMA
(LAST — BUT ONE) PENULT
(LONG —) LONG
(MUSICAL —) DI DO FA FI LA LE LI
ME MI RA RE RI SE SI SO TA TE TI
TO UT SOL
(REFRAIN —) DILDO
(SHORT —) MORA SHORT
(STRONG —) STRESS
(UNACCENTED —S) THESIS
(UNSTRESSED —) OUTRIDE
SYLLABUS PROGRAM VIDIMUS
HEADNOTE SYNOPSIS
PROGRAMME
SYLLOGISM BARBARA ABDUCTION
ENTHYMEME
(SERIES OF —S) SORITES
SYLPH ARIEL SYLPHID
SYLVAN WOODY FOREST SILVAN
WOODEN WOODISH SYLVATIC
SYLVITE HARDSALT
SYMBIOSIS LICHENISM
MUTUALISM NUTRICISM
SYMBOL KEY CODE FISH FOUR
ICON IDOL IKON MARK NEUM
SEAL SIGN TYPE BADGE CREST
CROSS EAGLE IMAGE INDEX
PRIME TOKEN CARACT CIPHER
EMBLEM ENSIGN FIGURE LETTER
PNEUME SHADOW SIGNAL
FACIEND MANDALA PALATAL
CEREMONY CONSTANT DIRECTOR
EXPONENT GUTTURAL IDEOGRAM
LIGATURE LOGOGRAM OPERATOR
SWASTIKA SYMBOLUM TRISKELE
ORIFLAMME PHRASEOGRAM
(— AS ROAD SIGN) GLYPH
(— FOR WAVELENGTH) LAMBDA
(— OF DEATH) CYPRESS
(— OF DISTINCTION) BELT HONOR
(— OF FAITHFUL DEAD) ORANT
(— OF FRANCE) LILY
(— OF LIFE) ANKH
(— OF MONK) COWL
(— OF PHYSICIAN) CADUCEUS
(— OF RAILROAD) HERALD
(— OF SPRING) KARPAS

(— OF STRENGTH) HORN
(— OF SUN) DISC DISK
(— OF UNIVERSE) MANDALA
(— ON UNCHANGEABLENESS)
LEOPARD
(— REPRESENTING THE ABSOLUTE)
TAIKIH
(ALGEBRAIC —) EXPONENT
(CRICKET —) ASHES
(CRUSADERS' —) CROSS
(CURVED —) HOOK
(KOREAN —) TAHGOOK
(MAGIC —) CARACT
(MATHEMATICAL —) KNOWN
FACTOR FACIEND OPERAND
PLACEHOLDER
(PHALLIC —) LINGA LINGAM
(PICTOGRAPHIC —) ISOTYPE
(PRINTING —) DIAGONAL
(PRONUNCIATION —) ENG
(RELIGIOUS —) LABRYS
(PL.) KATAKANA
SYMBOLIC GRAPHIC SHADOWY
ANICONIC
SYMBOLICAL ALLUSIVE MYSTICAL
SYMBOLISM CONOLOGY
SYMBOLIZE BODY SIGN TOKEN
FIGURE SAMPLE SHADOW
SYMBOL TYPIFY BETOKEN
EXPRESS PORTEND SIGNIFY
RESEMBLE
SYMMETRICAL FORMAL DIMERIC
REGULAR SHAPELY SPHERAL
BALANCED
(NOT —) SKEW
SYMMETRY MEASURE
SYMPATHETIC AKIN FERE SOFT
WARM HUMAN FELLOW KINDLY
TENDER PIETOSO SIMPATICO
SYMPATHIZER FABIAN BLACKNEB
SHAYSITE
SYMPATHY PITY RUTH FLESH
PHILIA CONSENT EMPATHY
RAPPORT AFFINITY KINDNESS
SYMPHONY SINFONIA
SYMPOSIUM POTATION
SYMPTOM MARK NOTE SIGN
SHOWER STIGMA INSTANCE
PRODROME
SYNAGOGUE SHUL SCHUL
ALJAMA PROSEUCHA
SYNAPSIS PAIRING
SYNAPTE ECTENE EKTENE
SYNARTHROSIS SUTURE
SYNCHRO SELSYN
SYNCHRONIZER SPEEDGUN
SYNCLINE DOWNFOLD ISOCLINE
SYNCOPATED ZOPPA ABRIDGED
SYNCOPE SWOON COTYPE
FAINTING
SYNDICATE HUI GROUP COMBINE
SYNDICATED CANNED
SYNECDOCHE MERISM
SYNERGIST BOOSTER SESAMIN
SYNOD SOBOR
SYNODAL SENAGE
SYNONYM ANTONYM HOMONYM
EUPHONISM POLYONYM
SYNOPSIS BRIEF TABLE EPITOME
OUTLINE SUMMARY ABSTRACT
ANALYSIS SCENARIO SYLLABUS
ABRIDGMENT

SYNSACRUM SACRARY
SYNTACTICAL FORMAL
SYNTHESIS SUMMA FUSION
SYSTASIS
SYNTHETIC ERSATZ PLASTIC
SYSTATIC ARTIFICER
SYPHAX (WIFE OF —) SOPHENISBA
SYPHILIS PIP POX LUES SYPH
CRINKUM GRINCOME

SYRIA
CAPITAL: DAMASCUS
COIN: POUND TALENT PIASTER
DISTRICT: ALEPPO HAURAN
LAKE: DJEBOID TIBERIAS
MEASURE: MAKUK GARAVA
MOUNTAIN: HERMON LIBANUS
NAME: ARAM
NATIVE: DRUSE ANSARIE SARACEN
ANSARIEH
RIVER: ASI BALIKH BARADA
JORDAN KNABUR ORONTES
EUPHRATES
TOWN: ALEP HAMA HOMS NAWA
BUSRA CALNO DERRA HALAB
HAMAH IDLIB JERUD RAQQA
ALEPPO BALBEL LATAKIA
SELEUCIA
WEIGHT: COLA ROTL ARTAL ARTEL
RATEL TALENT

SYRINGA PHILADELPHUS
SYRINGE GUN HYPO ENEMA
SCOOT DOUCHE FILLER SQUIRT
SCOOTER SERRING
SYRINGIN LILACIN
SYRINX PANPIPE
SYRNIUM STRIX
SYRUP DIBS LICK SIRUP ORGEAT
ANTIQUE ECLEGMA FALERNUM
QUIDDANY
(FRUIT —) ROB
(STARCH —) GLUCOSE
SYRUPY FRUITY
SYRYENIAN SYRYAN ZYRIAN
(PL.) KAMI KOMI
SYSTEM ISM AREA CREDO FRAME
ORDER CIRCLE METHOD SCHEME
STEREO SYNTAX COMPLEX
DUALISM ECONOMY FAGGERY
NAVARHO REGIMEN ENSEMBLE
GALENISM OVERRIDE RELIGION
UNIVERSE
(— OF BARS) LATTICE
(— OF BELIEFS) FAITH
(— OF BELL CHANGES) CATERS
QUATERS STEDMAN
(— OF CORDS) BRIDLE
(— OF CROSSING THREADS) LEASE
(— OF DIET) BANTING
(— OF ETHICS) SELFISM
(— OF EXCHANGE) KULA
(— OF EXERCISES) AEROBICS
(— OF FAITH) CREED
(— OF GEARS) COMPOUND
(— OF JOINTS) CLEAT
(— OF LANGUAGE SIGNS) SIGNARY
(— OF LAW) EQUITY
(— OF LINES IN EYEPIECE) RETICLE
RETICULE
(— OF LOGIC) RAMISM

(— OF MANUAL TRAINING) SLOJD
SLOYD
(— OF MARKETING) ADMASS
(— OF MEANING) SEMANTIC
(— OF MEDICINE) AYURVEDA
(— OF NUMERALS) ALGORISM
(— OF OCCULT THEOSOPHY)
CABALA
(— OF PHILOSOPHY) HUMISM
COMTISM HOBBISM SAMKHYA
SANKHYA STOICISM
(— OF PHONETIC NOTATION) ROMIC
(— OF PRINCIPLES) CODE
(— OF RAYS) ASTER
(— OF ROCKS) CENOZOIC
DEVONIAN SILURIAN
(— OF RULE) REGIME
(— OF RULES) ART
(— OF SOLMIZATION) FASOLA
(— OF SPACES) LACUNOME
(— OF SYMBOLS) CODE
(— OF TENANCY) CROFTING
(— OF TRANSPORTATION) AIRLINE
AIRMAIL
(— OF TRUSSING) CABANE
(— OF VALUES) ETHOS
(— OF WEIGHTS) TROY
(— OF WIRES) HARNESS
(— OF WORSHIP) CULT CULTUS
(— OF WRITING) KANJI BRAILLE
ALPHABET
(— TO LOCATE AN OBJECT) LIDAR
(ACOUSTICAL —) SODAR
(AGRICULTURAL —) KOLKOZ
KOLKHOS
(ALARM —) BUG
(BANKING —) GIRO
(BETTING —) ALEMBERT PERFECTA
QUINELLA MARTINGALE
(COLLOIDAL —) SOL
(COMMUNICATION —) BLOWER
CIRCUIT
(COMPUTER —) KLUGE KLUDGE
(CULTURAL —) ISLAM
(DEFENSE —) SAGE
(DISPERSE —) GEL
(ELECTRICAL —) SELSYN
(GEOLOGICAL —) EOCENE
CAMBRIAN DEVONIAN KEEWATIN
TERTIARY
(HAULING —) DILLY
(IRRIGATION —) KAREZ
(LANGUAGE —) LATINXUA
(NAVIGATION —) GEE LANAC
TACAN NAVAID SHORAN
NAVARHO OMNIRANGE
(RELIGIOUS —) LAW CULT CULTUS
SHIISM SUNNISM DRUIDISM
(RHYTHMIC —) STROPHE
GLYCONIC
(SOCIAL —) CASTE
(STAR —) GALAXY
(TECHNOLOGICAL —) FORDISM
(TELEVISION —) SCOPHONY
(TRIANGULATION —) SOFAR
(TRUCK —) TOMMY
SYSTEMATIC ORDERLY REGULAR
METHODIC
SYSTEMATIZE ORDER CODIFY
ORGANIZE METHODIZE
SYSTEMATIZED ORGANIC
SYSTEMIC DEMETON

T

T TEE TARE TANGO
TAAL AFRIKAANS
TAB JAG PAN TAG BILL COST CHECK FLASH PRICE TALLY WATCH EARTAB EARTAG SIGNAL TOEPLATE
TABANID GADFLY
TABARD CHIMER CHIMERE
TABARRO, IL (CHARACTER IN —) LUIGI MICHELE GIORGETTA
(COMPOSER OF —) PUCCINI
TABERNACLE PIX PYX HOVEL SACRARY
TABES WASTING
TABETIC MARCID
TABLATURE LYRAWAY PICTURE PAINTING
TABLE KEY PIE PYE RUN BANK BUCK DAIS DESK FORM MESS BELLY BENCH BOARD CANON CHART PINAX PLANK SCALE STALL STAND STONE WAGON COMMON SCHEME TABLET TABULA TARIFF TEAPOY TRIPOD VANNER CABARET CAMBIST CONSOLE COUNTER DIAGRAM DIPTYCH DRESSER PROJECT SHAMBLE TABLEAU TESSERA TROLLEY WHIRLER CALENDAR CREDENCE GUERIDON PEDIGREE PEMBROKE REGIMENT SPECULUM STILLAGE TOILETTE VANITORY NIGHTSTAND
(— FOR BOWING HAT-BODY) HURL
(— FOR GLAZING LEATHER) BANK
(— FOR ORNAMENT) CARTOUCH
(— FOR PHOTOGRAPHIC PLATES) WHIRLER
(— FURNISHED WITH MEAL) SPREAD
(— IN STORE) COUNTER
(— OF ANCESTORS) PEDIGREE
(— OF CONTENTS) INDEX METHOD
(— OF DECLINATIONS) REGIMENT
(— TOP) AMOEBA
(— USED IN FELTING A HAT) BASON
(— WITH BRAZIER BENEATH) TENDOOR TENDOUR
(ARITHMETIC —) TARIFF
(ASTROLOGICAL —) SPECULUM
(BOTANIC —) KEY
(CIRCULAR —) ROUNDEL
(COMMUNION —) ALTAR CREDENCE
(DINING —) MAHOGANY
(DRESSING —) TOILET VANITY TOILETTE
(FOLDING —) SERVETTE
(INNER —) HOME
(MASSAGE —) PLINTH
(MUSICAL —) DIAGRAM
(NIGHT —) SOMNO
(PRINCIPAL —) DAIS

(PROFUSELY ORNAMENTED —) PEMBROKE
(SERVING —) WAGON
(SHAKING —) SLIMER
(SMALL —) KURSI STAND TABORET TABOURET
(STONE —) DOLMEN
(TEA —) TEAPOY
(WRITING —) DESK
TABLEAU LAYOUT PAGEANT PICTURE
TABLECLOTH CLOTH COVER CARPET
TABLE D'HOTE DINNER
TABLELAND PLAT PUNA PUNO KAROO TABLE KARROO PLATEAU BALAGHAT
TABLET PAX BRED ALBUM FACIA PIECE PINAX SLATE TABLE ABACUS TABULA TABULE TROCHE ASPIRIN CODICIL DIPTYCH PALETTE PREFORM TABLING CARTOUCH CHURINGA TABULATE TRIPTYCH MEDALLION
(— BEARING SYMBOL OF CHRIST) PAX
(— FOR PUBLISHING LAWS) PARAPEGM
(— OVER SHOP FRONT) FACIA FASCIA
(MEDICATED —) ASPIRIN JELLOID TABELLA
(MEDICINAL —) DISC DISK TROCHE
(MEMORIAL —) BRASS TABUT
(PAINTER'S —) PALETTE
(SQUARE —) ABACK
(UPRIGHT —) STELA STELE
(VOTIVE —) PINAX
(WRITING —) CODICIL TRIPTYCH
(PREF.) PINA PINAC(O) PLAC(O)
TABLEWARE CHINA FLATWARE HAVILAND
TABOO KAPU TABU TAPU FORBIDDEN INEFFABLE
TABOR ATABAL TABRET TIMBRE TABORIN TIMBREL
TABULATION SCALE SCHEME TABLING
TABUT TAZIA TAZEEA
TACHOMETER CUTMETER
TACHYGLOSSUS ECHIDNA
TACIT SILENT IMPLICIT
TACITURN DUMB STILL SILENT RESERVED RETICENT
TACK LAY BEAT CAST STAY BASTE BOARD FETCH ENTAIL LAVEER TACKET TINGLE SADDLERY
(GLAZIERS' —) BRAD
TACKER GUN SPREADER
TACKLE CAT RIG TAW SWIG TACK YOKE ANGLE FALLS ATTACK BURTON COLLAR GARNET JIGGER LEDGER RUNNER STEEVE TAGLIA

TEAGLE DERRICK HALYARD HARNESS RIGGING FISHFALL PURCHASE TACKLING
(— FOR RAISING BOAT) FALLS
(— TO HOIST ANCHOR) CAT
(COMBINATION OF —S) JEER JEERS
(FISHING —) TEW LEGER OTTER LEDGER
TACO FLAUTA TAQUITO
TACT TOUCH ADDRESS CONDUCT DELICACY
TACTFUL POLITIC DISCREET GRACEFUL
TACTFULLY HAPPILY
TACTIC GAME
TACTLESS BRASH GAUCHE
TADPOLE POWHEAD BULLHEAD POLEHEAD POLLIWOG PORWIGLE
TAEL LIANG
TAENNIN KOSIN KOUSIN
TAFFETA TABBY ARMOZEEN FLORENCE
TAFFY GUNDY TOFFY TOFFEE CLAGGUM
TAG HE DAG EAR TAB TIG TAIL TICK AGLET DAGGE LABEL TALLY TOUCH AIGLET EARTAB EARTAG FOLLOW SWATCH TAGGLE TAGRAG TICKET TIGTAG HANGTAG
(— OF A LACE) AGLET AIGLET
(ANGLING —) TOUCH
(ORNAMENTED —S) FANCY
TAGALOG PULAHAN
TAGETES MARIGOLD
TAGRAG SHAGRAG
TAHATH (FATHER OF —) BERED
TAHITI (CAPITAL OF —) PAPEETE
(FORMER NAME OF —) OTAHEITE
(MOUNTAIN IN —) OROHENA
TAHMURATH (BROTHER OF —) YIMA
(FATHER OF —) VIVANGHAO
(SLAYER OF —) AHRIMAN
TAHR KRAS JHARAL
TAHSILDAR TALUKDAR
TAI LI AHOM SHAM THAI PORGY KHAMTI
TAIGA URMAN
TAIL BOB BUN CUE BUNT BUSH CLUB FLAG POLE SCUT BRUSH CAUDA SNAKE START STERN TRAIN TWIST FLIGHT FOLLOW RUMPLE SWITCH TAILET TAILLE FANTAIL FOXTAIL RATTAIL
(— OF ARTIFICIAL FLY) TOPPING
(— OF BELL CLAPPER) FLIGHT
(— OF BIRD) FAN
(— OF BIRD OR ANIMAL) CUE POLE START
(— OF BOAR) WREATH
(— OF CART) ARSE
(— OF COAT) DOCK

(— OF COMET) BEARD STREAM STREAMER CHEVELURE
(— OF DEER) FLAG SINGLE SHINGLE
(— OF DOG) FLAG STERN
(— OF FISH) UROSOME
(— OF FLY) WHISK
(— OF FOX) BUSH BRUSH FOXTAIL
(— OF HARE OR RABBIT) BUN FUD BUNT SCUT
(— OF HOOD) LIRIPIPE
(— OF HORSE) BOB
(— OF MAN'S TIED HAIR) CLUB
(— OF METEOR) TRAIN
(— OF MUSICAL NOTE) QUEUE
(— OF PUG DOG) TWIST
(— OF SQUIRREL) BUN ·
(— OF STANZA) CODA
(DRAGON'S —) KETU
(STUMP OF —) STRUNT
(TIP OF —) TAG
(PREF.) CAUD(I)(O) CERC(O) ONCHO UR(O)
(SUFF.) CERCAL CERCY URA URE UROUS URUS
TAILBAND FOOTBAND
TAILBOARD ENDGATE ENDBOARD ENDPIECE
TAILED CAUDATE CAUDATED
(PREF.) UR(O)
(SUFF.) URA URE UROUS URUS
TAILING CHAT
(PL.) SAND TAIL GRUFFS
TAILLE TALLY
TAILLESS ACAUDAL ANUROUS ACAUDATE ECAUDATE
TAILOR SLOP SNIP BUILD DARZI GORER SHRED CUTTER DARZEE FULLER SARTOR SNYDER STITCH BOTCHER CABBAGE SNIPPER TIREMAN CLOTHIER SEAMSTER SEMPSTER SHEPSTER
(ITINERANT —) CARDOOER
TAILORBIRD DARZEE
TAILPIECE QUEUE ANQUERA
TAILRACE AFTERBAY
TAILSPIN FLICKER
TAILSTOCK DEADHEAD
TAINO HAITIAN
(— BELIEFS) ZEMIISM
TAINT HAUL HOGO MOIL SMUT SPOT VICE CLOUD STAIN TOUCH DARKEN INFECT REMORD SMIRCH SMUTCH ATTAINT BLEMISH CORRUPT DEBAUCH ENVENOM FLYBLOW FORRUMP POLLUTE TARNISH VITIATE EMPOISON TAINTURE CONTAMINATE
TAINTED OFF GAMY HIGH BLOWN PINDY SAPPY TAINT WEMMY RANCID ROTTEN SINFUL SMUTTY CORRUPT FOUGHTY FLYBLOWN
TAIWAN (CAPITAL OF —) TAIPEI

(ISLAND GROUP OF —) MATSU PENGHU QUEMOY

(MOUNTAIN IN —) TZUKAO YUSHAN HSINKAO

(OTHER NAME OF —) FORMOSA

(RIVER IN —) WUCHI TACHIA CHOSHUI HUALIEN TANSHUI

(TOWN IN —) CHIAL TAINAN TAIPEI CHILUNG KEELUNG PINGTUNG TAICHUNG

TAJIN TOTONAC

TAJ MAHAL (SITE OF —) AGRA

TAKE COP HIT NIM NIP NOB BEAR BONE DRAW FANG GLOM HAVE LEAD TACK TEEM TOLL ADOPT AFONG BRING CARRY CATCH CREEL FETCH GRASP GRIPE LATCH SEIZE SNAKE ACCEPT CLUTCH COTTON DERIVE EXTEND FERRET FINGER RECIPE SNATCH TAKING ATTRACT CABBAGE CAPTURE RECEIVE UNPURSE UNDERNIM

(— A BATH) TOSH

(— A CERTAIN POSITION) SIT

(— A DIRECTION) STEER

(— A DRINK) PULL SMILE

(— A LITTLE) DELIBATE

(— A NAP) DOSS

(— A STAND) ASSERT

(— ACTION) ACT

(— ADVANTAGE) DO ABUSE BLUDGE CLUTCH EXPLOIT

(— AFTER) BRAID FOLLOW

(— AIM) READ

(— AS ONE'S OWN) ADOPT

(— AWAY) BATE EASE HENT LIFT TOLL WISP BENIM BLEED HEAVE REAVE STEAL ABDUCT CONVEY DEDUCE DEDUCT DEMISE DEPOSE DEVEST DIVEST ELOIGN EXEMPT REMOVE UNVEST ABJUDGE BEREAVE DEPRIVE DETRACT FORTAKE RETRACT SUBDUCE SUBLATE ABSTRACT DEROGATE DIMINISH SUBTRACT

(— BACK) RECALL RECANT REVOKE RETRACT

(— BACK TO ONESELF) RESUME

(— BY FRAUD) BOB

(— BY LEVY) ESTREAT

(— BY STEALTH) HOOK SNITCH

(— BY STORM) EXPUGN INVADE SURPRISE

(— CARE) FIX SEE GARE KEEP MIND TEND WARD YEME NURSE BEWARE GOVERN INTEND CUIDADO HUSBAND CHAPERON

(— CENSUS OF) MUSTER

(— CHANCE) DICE RISK

(— CHARGE) ATTEND

(— CHARGE OF) CURE SOLICIT

(— COVER) COOK

(— DAMAGE) BANGE

(— DINNER) DINE

(— DOWN) STOOP STRIKE

(— EXCEPTION) DEMUR STRAIN

(— FOOD) EAT DINE GRUB

(— FOR GRANTED) BEG ASSUME PRESUME

(— FOR ONESELF) CAB

(— FOR RESALE) FLOG

(— FORM) FORM INFORM

(— FRAUDULENTLY) STEAL STRIKE

(— FRIGHT) BOOGER

(— FROM) DETRACT

(— FROM DEPOSIT) DRAW

(— GOLFING STANCE) ADDRESS

(— GREAT DELIGHT) REVEL

(— HEART) BRACE

(— HEED) RECK TENT

(— HOLD) GET BITE GRAB PINCH SEIZE ARREST BEGRIPE

(— HOLIDAY) LAKE

(— IN) EAT SUP BITE HOAX KEEP DOWSE DRINK ABSORB DEVOUR ENFOLD GATHER HARBOR INCEPT INGEST INSORB INSUME INTAKE MUZZLE BEGRIPE EMBRACE INCLUDE

(— IN BY LEAKING) LADE

(— IN LIVESTOCK) AGIST

(— IN SAIL) BRAIL

(— INTO HANDS) TOUCH EMBRACE

(— LEGALLY) ATTACH

(— LEVEL OF) BONE

(— LUNCH) TIFFIN

(— MEALS) BOARD

(— NOTE OF) NB COUNT SMOKE NOTICE WITNESS

(— OATH) ABJURE

(— OFF) OFF DOFF LIFT VAIL DOUSE SHUCK STRIP DEDUCT

(— OFFENSE) DORT HUFF

(— ON) HIRE MOUNT START

(— ONE'S LEAVE) CONGEE

(— ONESELF) BETAKE

(— OUT) DELE KILL EXCERPT AIRBRUSH

(— OUT OF EARTH) EXTER

(— OVER) ABSORB

(— PAINS) BOTHER

(— PART) LEAD FIGHT ENGAGE

(— PLACE) BE DO GO COME GIVE PASS ARISE BEFALL HAPPEN

(— PLEASURE IN) ENJOY ADMIRE

(— PORTION OF) PARTAKE

(— POSSESSION) GRIP ANNEX BESET SEIZE SPOIL EXTEND CONQUER INHERIT DISTRAIN

(— REFUGE) HIDE SOIL EVADE HAVEN WATCH

(— ROOT) MARE MORE ENROOT STRIKE

(— SHAPE) JELL

(— SHELTER) HOWF NESTLE SHROUD

(— SUPPER) SUP

(— THE PLACE OF) ENSUE SECOND SUPPLY DISPLACE SUPPLANT

(— THOUGHT) ADVISE

(— TO BE TRUE WITHOUT PROOF) PRESUME

(— TO TASK) JACK CARPET CHAPTER

(— TO WING) FLUSH

(— UNAWARE) DECEIVE

(— UP) ENTER MOUNT ADSORB ASSUME GATHER HANDLE STRIKE

(— UP AGAIN) RESUME

(— UP WITH) ALL

(— WELL OR ILL) RESENT

(— WIND ON OPPOSITE QUARTER) JIBE

TAKEN TON TAIN

(— ABACK) BLANK

(— AWAY) ADEMPT

TAKEOFF JATO SPOOF SCRAMBLE

TAKEOUT STACK

TAKER PERNOR

TAKING HOT TAKY CAPTION ADOPTION PERNANCY PREEMPTION

(— EVERYTHING INTO ACCOUNT) OVERALL

(— LIBERTIES) PRESUMPTUOUS

(— OF LIFE) BLOOD

(— PLACE) AGATE

(PREF.) (— IN) END(O)

(SUFF.) LEPSIA LEPSIS LEPSY LEPT(IC)

TALAK AHSAN

TALARI PATACA PATACOON

TALAUS (FATHER OF —) BIAS

(MOTHER OF —) PERO

(SON OF —) ADRASTUS

(WIFE OF —) LYSIMACHE

TALC SPAAD TALCUM AGALITE STEATITE

TALE SAW DIDO JEST LEED REDE TELL BOURD CRACK FABLE RECIT SPELL SPOKE STORY WINDY AITION FABULA LEGEND PISTLE PURANA FABLIAU FICTION HISTORY MARCHEN ROMANCE ANECDOTE FOLKTALE SPELLING TREATISE

(— OF ACHIEVEMENTS) GEST GESTE

(— OF FOUR) WARP

(— OF GOLD COAST NEGROS) NANCY

(COMIC COARSE —) FABLIAU

(DEVISED —) AITION

(EPIC —) TAIN

(FALSE —) BAM VANITY SLANDER

(FATEFUL —) WEIRD

(FOLK —) NANCY THRENE

(HUMOROUS —S) FACETIAE

(MERRY —) BOURD

(POETIC NARRATIVE —) SAGA

(SENSATIONAL —) BLOOD

(SHORT —) LAI CONTE

(PREF.) STORIO

TALEBEARER BUZZER GOSSIP TATTLER TALEPYET TELLTALE

TALEBEARING TALEWISE

TALENT GIFT HEAD NOUS VEIN DOWER DOWRY VERVE CICHAR GENIUS ABILITY CHARISM FACULTY CAPACITY CHARISMA

TALENTED ABLE CLEVER GIFTED

TALE OF TWO CITIES (AUTHOR OF —) DICKENS

(CHARACTER IN —) JOHN JERRY LORRY LUCIE PROSS BARSAD CARTON DARNAY JARVIS SYDNEY CHARLES DEFARGE GASPARD MANETTE STRYVER CRUNCHER EVREMONDE

TALER ORT THALER

TALES OF HOFFMANN

(CHARACTER IN —) ANDRES LUTHER STELLA ANTONIA CRESPEL LINDORF MIRACLE OLYMPIA HOFFMANN SCHLEMIL COPPELIUS GIULIETTA NICALUSSE DAPERTUTTO SPALANZANI PITICHINACCHIO

(COMPOSER OF —) OFFENBACH

TALIPES CLUBFOOT

TALISMAN ANGLE CHARM IMAGE OBEAH SAFFI AMULET GRIGRI SAPHIE SCARAB TELESM ICHTHUS ICHTHYS GREEGREE

(AUTHOR OF —) SCOTT

(CHARACTER IN —) DAVID EDITH PHILIP KENNETH RICHARD SALADIN BERENGARIA MONTFERRAT PLANTAGENET

TALK GAB JAW JIB RAP SAW SAY YAP BLAT BUCK BUKH CANT CARP CHAT CHIN GAFF GIVE GUFF KNAP MEAN TALE TOVE WORD CRACK FABLE MOUTH PARLE PITCH SPEAK SPELL SPIEL SPOKE TUTEL COMMON GAMMON INDABA KORERO PATTER SERMON SPEECH STEVEN TOMGUE YABBER ADDRESS CHINWAG DISCUSS LIPWORK PALABRA PALAVER PARRALL PURPOSE WINDJAM CAUSERIE COLLOQUY CONVERSE LANGUAGE PARLANCE QUESTION

(— ABOUT) HASH

(— BACK) SASS

(— BIG) SWANK BOUNCE

(— BOASTFULLY) GAS BLATTER

(— BOMBASTICALLY) BEMOUTH

(— CASUALLY) DISH

(— CONFIDENTIALLY) CUTTER

(— CONFUSEDLY) HOTTER

(— DISMALLY) CROAK

(— EMPTILY) BLOW

(— FAMILIARLY) TOVE CONFAB

(— FATUOUSLY) BABBLE

(— FONDLY) COO

(— FOOLISHLY) YAK BLAT FLAP YACK HAVER BABBLE DRIVEL FOOTER FOOTLE GABBLE GIBBER SAWNEY TOOTLE BLATHER BLETHER

(— GLIBLY) PATTER SCREED

(— IDLY) GAB BLAB CHIN GASH FABLE GABBLE JANGLE TATTLE CHATTER GNATTER PRATTLE

(— IMPUDENTLY) SASS

(— INACCURATELY) BLAGUE

(— INARTICULATELY) CHUNNER CHUNTER

(— INCESSANTLY) YANK BURBLE WAFFLE CHATTER

(— INCOHERENTLY) BABBLE BURBLE HOTTER MITHER MOIDER

(— INCONSIDERATELY) BLAT

(— INDECISIVELY) WAFFLE

(— INFORMALLY) HOBNOB

(— INSOLENTLY) SNASH

(— INTENDED TO DECEIVE) GAMMON PALAVER

(— IRRATIONALLY) RAVE

(— MONOTONOUSLY) DRONE

(— NEEDLESSLY) PALAVER

(— NOISILY) CLAP BLATTER BRABBLE

(— NONSENSE) GAS ROT BLEAT DROOL FUDGE HAVER

(— OFFICIOUSLY) BLEEZE

(— PERTLY) CHELP

(— PRIVATELY) COLLOGUE
(— RAPIDLY) GABBLE JABBER GNATTER
(— SCANDAL) HORN
(— SNAPPISHLY) KNAP
(— SPORTIVELY) DAFF
(— SUPERFICIALLY) SMATTER
(— TEDIOUSLY) DINGDONG
(— THOUGHTLESSLY) BLAB
(— TOGETHER) DEVISE
(— VAGUELY) WOOZLE
(— VOLUBLY) CHIN PATTER
(— WEAKLY) DRIVEL
(— WITH) CONTACT
(— WITHOUT MEANING) GABBLE
(ABSURD —) BOSH
(ABUSIVE —) HOKER JAWING
(ARROGANT —) GUM BRAG
(BOASTFUL —) BULL GAFF
(BOMBASTIC —) FLASH
(COMMON —) FAME FABLE NOISE HEARSAY
(CONCEITED —) BLAGUE
(CONTINUAL —) CLACK
(COUNTRY —) CLASH
(DECEPTIVE —) GAMMON
(EMPTY —) GAS BOSH GASH FRASE GLOZE FRAISE BLAFLUM GASSING PRATTLE BALLYHOO GALBANUM MOONSHINE POPPYCOCK
(ENTHUSIASTIC —) JAZZ
(FALSE —) BALLYHOO
(FAMILIAR —) CONFAB CHITCHAT
(FANTASTIC —) GUYVER
(FOOLISH —) GUP GAFF JIVE BLEAT CLACK FABLE BLETHERS COBBLERS
(FORMAL —) ADDRESS
(FRIVOLOUS —) PERSIFLAGE
(GLIB —) JIVE
(IDLE —) GAB BLAB BUFF CHAT GAFF GEST GUFF FABLE GESTE BABBLE CLAVER GOSSIP JANGLE CHATTER CLATTER PALAVER TWATTLE BABBLING BATTOLOGY
(IMPUDENT —) PRATE SLACK
(INCOHERENT —) GABBER JABBER
(INFORMAL —) CAUSERIE
(INSINCERE —) JAZZ CROCK BUNKUM MALARKEY
(JESTING —) CHAFF JAPERY
(LIGHT —) TRIFLING
(MEANINGLESS —) SLIPSLOP
(NONSENSICAL —) BLABBER BLATHER FOLDEROL
(PIOUS OR SANCTIMONIOUS —) PI
(RAPID —) GABBLE JABBER CHATTER CLATTER
(SALES —) PITCH
(SCOLDING —) HARANGUE
(SILLY —) BLAH BUFF CLART CACKLE FOOTLE TWADDLE
(SMALL —) CHAT BACKCHAT CHITCHAT
(SMOOTH —) GLOZE BLARNEY
(STUPID —) MOROLOGY
(TRIFLING —) PRATTLE CHITCHAT
(USELESS —) WASTE
(VIOLENT —) BLUSTER
(WEAK —) SLIPSLOP
(WHINING —) BLEAT
(SUFF.) LALIA LOG(ER)(IA)(IAN)(IC) (ICAL)(IST)(UE)(Y)

TALKATIVE COSY GASH GLIB NAWY BUZZY TALKY CHATTY CLASHY CRACKY FLUENT FUTILE SOCIAL VOLUBLE BIGMOUTH FLIPPANT TELLSOME
TALKATIVENESS FUTILITY
TALKER YENTA CAMPER POTGUN CAUSEUR SPIELER
(IDLE —) WHIFFLER
(NOISY —) BLELLUM
(PROFESSIONAL —) JAWSMITH
(SENSELESS —) RATTLE
TALKING (LOUD —) NORATION
TALKING-TO EARFUL LECTURE
TALKY GABBY
TALL HIGH LANKY LOFTY STEEP WANDY CRANEY PROCERE
(— AND FEEBLE) TANGLE
(VERY —) TAUNT
TALLAGE CUTTING
TALLER DOMINANT
TALLNESS PROCERITY
TALLOW SUET SEVUM ARMING TAULCH CHERVICE
(PREF.) SEBI SEBO STEAR(O) STEAT(O)
(SUFF.) STEARIN
TALLY TAB JUMP NICK SUIT AGREE CHECK COUNT SCORE STICK STOCK CENSUS STRING SWATCH TAILYE COMPORT TAILZIE
TALMAI (FATHER OF —) AMMIHUD
TALMUD GEMARA
TALON FANG SERE UNCE CLUTCH POUNCE UNGUIS WEAPON
(— OF TOOTH) HEEL
TALONID HEEL
TALPA TESTUDO
TALTHIB GLAGA GLAGAH
TALUS SCREE RUBBLE ASTRAGAL
TAMANDUA ANTEATER
TAMAR (AUTHOR OF —) JEFFERS
(CHARACTER IN —) LEE WILL DAVID JINNY TAMAR STELLA ANDREWS MORELAND CAULDWELL
(FATHER OF —) DAVID ABSALOM
(HUSBAND OF —) ER ONAN
(MOTHER OF —) MAACHAH
(SON OF —) ZARAH PHAREZ
TAMARACK LARCH LARIX EPINETTE
TAMARIN PINCHE JACCHUS LEONCITO MARIKINA MARMOSET
TAMARIND SAMPALOC
TAMARISK ATLE JHOW HEATH MYRICA
TAMASHEK TUAREG
TAMBOURINE RIKK TAAR DAIRA TAMBO TABOUR TIMBER TABORIN TIMBREL
(PART OF —) HEAD TACK SHELL JINGLE
TAMBURLAINE THE GREAT
(AUTHOR OF —) MARLOWE
(CHARACTER IN —) ALMEDA AMYRAS COSROE ZABINA MEANDER MYCETES ORCANES BAJAZETH CALYPHAS MENAPHON CALLAPINE CELEBINUS SIGISMUND TECHELLES ZENOCRATE THERIDAMAS USUMCASANE TAMBURLAINE

TAME MAN CADE DEAD MEEK MILD PACK ACCOY ATAME BREAK DAUNT MILKY SPAKE CADISH ENTAME GENTLE INWARD MEEKEN UNWIFE AFFAITE AMENAGE CORRECT INSIPID SUBDUED CICURATE DOMESTIC MANSUETE
(— FALCON) MAN RECLAIM
TAMED BROKE GENTLE
TAMENESS MANSUETUDE
TAMIL VELLALA
TAMING OF THE SHREW (AUTHOR OF —) SHAKESPEARE
(CHARACTER IN —) SLY BIANCA CURTIS GREMIO GRUMIO TRANIO BAPTISTA LUCENTIO BIONDELLO HORTENSIO KATHARINA PETRUCHIO VINCENTIO CHRISTOPHER
TAMMUZ (FATHER OF —) NINGISHZIDA
TAMMY TAMIS STAMIN
TAMONEA MICONIA
TAM-O-SHANTER TAM TAMMY
TAMP PUG STEM
TAMPER FIX COOK FAKE FOOL GAFF TOUCH DABBLE FIDDLE MEDDLE MONKEY POTTER PUDDLE PUTTER TEMPER FALSIFY TRINKLE
(— WITH HORSE'S TEETH) BISHOP
TAMPION TOMKIN TAMPOON
TAM-TAM GONG
TAN FAN ARAB BARK ADUST ASCOT DRESS TANKA TAWNY ORIOLE COCONUT EMBROWN LEATHER SUNBURN
(BEACH —) SEDGE
(TROTTEUR —) BAY
(PREF.) TANN(I)(O)
TANACETYL THUJYL
TANAGER YENI LINDO REDBIRD WARBIRD CARDINAL EUPHONIA FIREBIRD ORGANIST
TANBARK BARK TAWN AVARAM TURWAR ALGERIAN ALGERINE
TANCRED (FATHER OF —) OTHO
(LOVER OF —) ERMINIA CLORINDA
(MOTHER OF —) EMMA
TANDAN EELFISH
TANEKAHA TOATOA
TANG NIP FANG TING VEIN SHANK STING STRAP TASTE TWANG RELISH TANGLE TONGUE SEATANG FAREWELL
TANGELO UGLI
TANGENCY CONTACT
TANGENT SLOPE
TANGERINE NAARTJE MANDARIN
TANGIBLE ACTUAL TACTILE CONCRETE MATERIAL PALPABLE
TANGLE COT ELF ORE TAT FANK FOUL HARL SHAG TAUT HARLE KNURL SKEIN SNARL SNIRL THRUM TWINE WOPSE BALTER BURBLE ENTRAP FANKLE HANGER JUNGLE MOMBLE MUCKER RAFFLE SLEAVE TAFFLE TARDLE TAUGHT TEIHTE BRANGLE TAISSLE THICKET FURBELOW SCROBBLE
(PL.) COBWEB

TANGLED AFOUL TOUSY MESHED SNARLY TAUTED IMPLICIT INTORTED INVOLVED CESPITOSE
(— UP) HAYWIRE
TANGLEHEAD PILI
TANGUE TENREC
TANGY BRISK
TANHA TRISHNA
TANK DAM DIP TAL VAT BOSH SUMP BASIN MIXER STANK STEEP TRUNK BLOWUP BOILER HOPPER PANZER TROUGH BATTERY BLOWPIT BREAKER CISTERN FLUSHER PISCINA PLUNGER POACHER SETTLER STEEPER BLEACHER DIGESTOR LANDSHIP SUBSIDER
(— FOR DYE OR SOAP) BECK
(— FOR FISH) STEW TRUNK PISCINA AQUARIUM STEWPOND
(— IN SHIP) FOREPEAK
(ARMORED —) FLAIL PANZER WHIPPET LANDSHIP
(PAPER MANUFACTURING —) POACHER
(PHOTOGRAPHIC —) CUVETTE
(POTTER'S —) PLUNGER
(RECTANGULAR —) BOWLY
(SALT MANUFACTURING —) GRAINER
(STORAGE —) CHEST
(SUGAR REFINING —) TIGER BLOWUP
(TANNING —) FLOATER
(PL.) HEAVIES
(PREF.) LACO
TANKAGE AMMONATE
TANKARD GUN JACK FACER STOOP STOUP PEWTER POTTLE TANKER GODDARD
TANKER BOWSER
TANNED BROWN RUDDY TAWNY REECHY BRONZED
(NOT —) RAW
TANNER EGGER SAMAR BARKER STAKER PERCHER
TANNHAUSER (CHARACTER IN —) VENUS HERMANN WOLFRAM ELISABETH TANNHAUSER
(COMPOSER OF —) WAGNER
TANNING PASTING
(— SOLUTION) PLUMPER
TANSY COSTMARY
TANSY MUSTARD FLIXWEED FLUXWEED
TANSY RAGWORT RAGWEED
TANTALIZE GRIG JADE MOCK TEASE HARASS
TANTALUS (DAUGHTER OF —) NIOBE
(FATHER OF —) AMPHION JUPITER THYESTES
(MOTHER OF —) NIOBE PLUTO
(SON OF —) PELOPS
(WIFE OF —) DIONE CLYTIA EUPRYTO TAYGETE
TANTAMOUNT SAME
TANTRA AGAMA
TANTRUM HISSY TIRRIVEE WINGDING

TANZANIA
CAPITAL: DARESSALAAM

COIN: SENTI SHILINGI
ISLAND: MAFIA PEMBA ZANZIBAR
LAKE: RUKWA
NATIVE: BANTU SUKUMA
  MAKONDE SWAHILI
REGION: MARA MBEYA PEMBA
  PWANI TANGA MWANZA
  RUVUMA TABORA SINGIDA
RIVER: RUVU WAMI RUAHA
  KAGERA RUFIJI RUVUMA
  PANGANI MBENKURU
TOWN: WETE KILWA MBEYA
  MOSHI TANGA ARUSHA
  DODOMA IRINGA KIGOMA
  MTWARA MWANZA TABORA
  MTAWARA MOROGORO
  ZANZIBAR
VOLCANO: KIBO KILIMANJARO
WATERFALL: KALAMBO
WEIGHT: FARSALAH

TAO MAN PEASANT
  (— PRACTICE) WUWEI
TAP BOB DAB PAT TAT TIP TIT TOP
  BEAT COCK DRUB FLIP JOWL
  PENK TICK TIRL TUCK TUNK
  APPEL FLIRT QUILL SNOCK START
  TOUCH ALETAP BROACH CANNEL
  DABBLE FAUCET NATTLE TAPLET
  BIBCOCK BLENDER DRAWOFF
  HEELTAP PERCUSS
  (— A CASK) QUILL STRIKE
  (— A DRUM) TUCK
  (— FOR A LOAN) TIG
  (— ON SHOE) CLUMP UNDERLAY
  (— ON THE SHOULDER) FOB
  (— REPEATEDLY) DRUM
  (— THE GROUND) BEAT
  (FENCING —) BEAT
  (MASTER —) HOB HUB
  (SMART — OF THE FOOT) APPEL
TAPA KAPA SIAPO KIKEPA
TAPACOLO TURCO
TAPE LEAR FERRET GARTER
  SCOTCH TAPERY YNKELL BINDING
  MEASURE TAPELINE TELETAPE
  (— CARTRIDGE) CASSETTE
  (DEMONSTRATION —) DEMO
  (FISH —) SNAKE
  (LAMP —) WICK
  (LINEN —) INKLE
  (METALLIC —) GALLOON
  (NARROW —) TASTE
  (RED —) WIGGERY
TAPE GRASS EELGRASS
TAPEMAN CHAINMAN
TAPER DRAW RISE RUSH DRAFT
  GAUDY PINCH SCARF SNAPE
  SWAGE CIERGE DRAUGHT
  LIGHTER PRICKET SHAMMES
  TRINDLE DIMINISH ACUMINATE
  (— OF A SPRING) DRAW
  (— OF PATTERN) STRIP
  (— OFF) CEASE TONGUE
TAPERED BARRELED BOATTAIL
  GRADUATED
TAPERING SHARP SPIRY SPIRAL
  SPIRED TERETE SPIRING
  FUSIFORM SUBULATE ATTENUATE
TAPER ROD PODGER
TAPESTRY ARRAS TAPET TAPIS
  COSTER DORSER DOSSER CEILING
  GOBELIN HANGING SUSANEE

VERDURE AUBUSSON MORTLAKE
TAPEWORM TAPE LIGULA TAENIA
  CESTODE CESTOID COENURE
  HYDATID PLATODE BANDWORM
  COENURUS DAVAINEA
  FLATWORM HELMINTH STROBILA
  (— LARVA) MEASLE
  (PL.) CYSTICA
  (PREF.) TAENI(A)(O)
TAPHATH (FATHER OF —) SOLOMON
TAPHOLE TAP FLOSS MOUTH
TAPIOCA CASSAVA
TAPIR ANTA KUDA DANTA TENNU
  TAPIROID
TAPPED ABROACH
TAPPET CAM WIPER
TAPROOM TAP SALOON BARROOM
  BUVETTE TAPHOUSE
TAPSTER NICKPOT SKINKER
TAPUYAN GE GES GHES BUGRE
  GESAN JUYAS CAYAPO GOYANA
  CAMACAN CARAHOS COROADO
  TIMBIRA APINAGES BOTOCUDO
  CAINGANG CHAVANTE
TAR PAY BREA BINDER ALKITRAN
  (BIRCH —) DAGGETT
  (MINERAL —) MALTHA
TARA DOLMA
TARANTULA HUNTER JAYHAWK
  MYGALID
TARAS BULBA (AUTHOR OF —)
  GOGOL
  (CHARACTER IN —) BULBA OSTAP
  TARAS ANDRII YANKEL KIRDYAGA
TARBOOSH FEZ
TARDIGRADA ARCTISCA
TARDILY SLOWLY
TARDINESS SLOTH TARDITY
TARDY LAG LAX DREE LATE SLOW
  SLACK DREIGH LAGGED REMISS
  LAGGING OVERDUE DILATORY
  LATESOME
TARE TINE VETCH LEAKAGE
  (PL.) FILTH
TAREA (FATHER OF —) MICAH
TARES ZIZANY
TARGE BUCKLER
TARGET AIM MOT BUTT MARK
  WAND CLOUT LEVEL PRICK
  ROVER SCOOP SCOPE TARGE
  WHITE BANNER NIVEAU OBJECT
  SLEEVE COCKSHY INCOMER
  OUTGOER SARACEN POPINJAY
  (— OF KNEELING FIGURE) SQUAW
  (— OF LEVELING STAFF) VANE
  (— OF RIDICULE) GAME
  (— RING) SOUS
  (EASY —) SITTER
  (PIECE OF —) SCAB
  (RAILROAD SWITCH —) BANNER
  (STRIKE A —) KEYHOLE
  (THROWN —) COCKSHY COCKSHUT
  (TOWED —) DROGUE
  (UNIDENTIFIED —) SKUNK
TARHEEL STATE NORTHCAROLINA
TARIFF ZABETA AVERAGE TRIBUTE
TARNISH DIM BLOT SMIT SOIL
  CLOUD DIRTY STAIN SULLY
  TACHE BREATH DARKEN DEFILE
  INJURE SMIRCH ASPERSE
  BEGRIME BESMEAR BLEMISH
  OBSCURE BESMIRCH DISCOLOR
TARO COCO DALO EDDO GABE

KALO MASI TALO COCCO KAROU
  TANIA TANYA COCKER TARROW
  YAUTIA DASHEEN MALANGA
  COCOROOT EDDYROOT
TAROT NAIB TAROCCO
TARPON SABALO
TARRAGON TARCHON ESTRAGON
TARRY BIDE LENG STAY STOP
  ABIDE DALLY DEMUR PAUSE
  ARREST LINGER PITCHY REMAIN
  SOJOURN
TARSIER LEMUR MALMAG
TARSOMETATARSUS SHANK
TARSUS HAND ANKLE DIGITAL
  (BIRD'S —) SHANK
TART ACID FLAN SOUR BOWLA
  CUPID EAGER SHARP SNIPPY
  SUNKET PIQUANT POLYNEE
  PUNGENT SUBACID TARTLET
  TURNOVER
TARTAN PLAID
  (— PATTERN) SETT
TARTAR ARGAL ARGOL CALCULUS
TARTARIN OF TARASCON
  (AUTHOR OF —) DAUDET
  (CHARACTER IN —) BAIA BRAVIDA
  GREGORY BEZUQUET TARTARIN
  BARBASSOU
TARTNESS ACRITY ACIDITY
  VERDURE ACERBITY ASPERITY
  VERJUICE
TARTUFFE (AUTHOR OF —) MOLIERE
  (CHARACTER IN —) ARGAS DAMIS
  ORGON DORINE ELMIRE VALERE
  CLEANTE MARIANE PERNELLE
  TARTUFFE
TASHMET (HUSBAND OF —) NEBO
TASK FAG JOB TAX CHAR DARG
  TOIL CHARE CHORE GRIND KNACK
  LABOR NULLO STINT CHARGE
  DEVOIR NIYOGA PENSUM
  RAMSCH TOURNE FATIGUE
  SWEATER TRAVAIL BUSINESS
  EXERCISE TRAUCHLE
  (— AS PSYCHOLOGICAL TEST)
  AUFGABE
  (ASSIGNED —) STENT STINT
  DEVOIR
  (DIFFICULT —) BUGGER
  (EASY —) PIPE SNAP SETUP
  (ONE WHO PERFORMS MENIAL —S)
  DOGSBODY
  (ONEROUS —) CORVEE
  (ROUTINE —) DRUDGE
TASKMASTER DRIVER TASKER
  RAWHIDER
TASMANIA (CAPITAL OF —)
  HOBART
  (LAKE IN —) ECHO SORELL
  (MOUNTAIN IN —) DROME NEVIS
  BARRON CRADLE LOMOND
  HUMBOLDT
  (RIVER IN —) ESK HUDN TAMAR
  GORDON JORDAN PIEMAN
  DERWENT
  (TOWN IN —) BURNIE HOBART
TASMANIAN DEVIL DASYURID
TASMANIAN WOLF HYENA
  THYLACINE
TASSEL TAG TUFT LABEL THRUM
  TARCEL TARGET TOORIE
  CORDELLE
  (PL.) ZIZITH

(PREF.) THYSAN(O)
TASTABLE GUSTABLE
TASTE EAT GAB GOO LAP SIP CAST
  DASH GOUT GUST HINT PREE
  RASA SALT TANG TEST TINT
  WAFT ASSAY DRINK FANCY
  GUSTO HEART PROVE RELES
  SAPOR SAVOR SHADE SKILL
  SMACK SNACK SPICE TOOTH
  TOUCH DEGUST FLAVOR GENIUS
  LIKING PALATE RELISH SAMPLE
  SMATCH ATTASTE PREGUST
  SOUPCON THOUGHT APPETITE
  JUDGMENT PENCHANT SAPIDITY
  (— COMBINED WITH APTITUDE)
  FLAIR
  (— IN MATTERS OF ART) FANCY
  (BAD —) GOTHISM
  (DECIDED —) PENCHANT
  (DELICATE —) BREED
  (DISCRIMINATING —) SKILL
  (GOOD —) DECORUM
  (STRONG —) GOO
  (PL.) MERIDIAN
  (PREF.) SAPORI
  (SUFF.) GEUSIA
TASTEFUL NEAT ELEGANT
  GUSTOSO
TASTELESS DEAF FLAT FLASH
  MALMY VAPID WERSH WALLON
  FATUOUS INSIPID INSULSE
  WEARISH UNSAVORY
TASTER TRIER
TASTING ASSAY
  (— OF MALT) CORNY
TASTY SAPID GUSTABLE TASTEFUL
  PALATABLE
TATAR KIN JUNG KITAN SOYOT
  CHAZAR KHAZAR KHITAN KHOZAR
  SHORTZY MELETSKI
  (PL.) HU
TATER SPUD POTATO
TATOUAY CABASSOU
TATTER JAG RAG TAG SHRED
  FITTER LIBBET TAGRAG TARGET
  FLITTER TROLLOP
  (PL.) DUDS TAVERS FITTERS
  RIBBONS TAIVERS FLITTERS
TATTERED DUDDY BEATEN
  TAGGED FORWORN TATTERY
  TOTTERED
TATTING LACE
TATTLE BLAB GASH CHEEP CLASH
  CLYPE PEACH SNEAK TUTEL
  GOSSIP QUATCH SNITCH TATTER
  TITTLE CLATTER
TATTLER LAB CLASH SNIPE FABLER
  GAMBET GOSSIP TUTLER YELPER
  TITTLER TELLTALE
TATTLING LEAKY FUTILE
TATTOO TAT MOKO PINK POUNCE
  RATAPLAN
TATTOOED PINKED
  (— MAN) YUN
TATTOOING MOKO
TAUGHT MAK TEACHED INSTRUCT
  (EASILY —) DOCIBLE
TAUNT BOB DIG MOB CHIP GIBE
  GIRD JAPE JEER JEST MOCK
  PROG SKIT TWIT CHECK FRUMP
  GLAIK JAUNT SCOFF SCORN
  SLANT SLARE SLART DERIDE
  SNEEST UPCAST SARCASM

TWITTER RIDICULE
TAUNTING RAIL SARCASTIC
TAUPE MOLESKIN
TAUROTRAGUS OREAS ORIAS
TA-URT THOUERIS
TAUT SNUG TORT STIFF TIGHT CORDED
TAUTEN SNUB STIFFEN SWIFTER TENSION
TAUTOG CHUB MOLL LABROID
TAVERN BAR INN BUSH HOWF VENT FONDA MITER MITRE TAMBO BISTRO CABACK KNEIPE BUVETTE CABARET CANTEEN OSTERIA TABERNA GASTHAUS ORDINARY POTHOUSE TAPHOUSE
TAW TER ALLY ALLEY SCORE MARBLE GLASSIE SHOOTER
TAWDRY CHEAP GAUDY NASTY GILDED TINSEL RAFFISH
TAWNY FUSC BRUSK DUSKY FULVID TANNED FULVOUS JACINTH MUSTELINE (PREF.) CIRRO FUSCO PYRR(O) PYRRH(O)
TAWNY BROWN TENNE CHAMOIS
TAW-SUG SULU
TAX LAY LOT CAST CESS DUTY GELD GELT GILD KAIN LEVY POLL RATE SCAT SCOT SESS TAIL TASK TOLL ABUSE AGIST DONUM FINTA HANSA HANSE LEKIN MAILL OBROK QUINT SCATT STENT TOUST VERGI WATCH ZAKAH ZAKAT ABKARI ASSESS AVANIA BURDEN CEDULA DEMAND EXCISE EXTENT HIDAGE IMPOST JEZIAH KHARAJ MURAGE OCTROI OCTROY PAVAGE PURVEY SENSUS STRAIN SURTAX VINAGE BOOMAGE BOSCAGE CHANCER CHEVAGE CHIVAGE CONDUCT FINANCE GABELLE LASTAGE PATENTE PENSION POLLAGE PONTAGE SCUTAGE STIPEND TAILAGE TERRAGE TRIBUTE ALCABALA AUXILIUM BONAUGHT CARUCAGE CORNBOLE DANEGELD EXACTION EXERCISE KERNETTY MALTOLTE OBLATION PESHKASH ROMESCOT ROMESHOT STACKAGE SUPERTAX TAXATION WHEELAGE CAPITATION
(**— AT HARVESTTIME**) CORNBOLE
(**— FOR STORING LOGS**) BOOMAGE
(**— OF ONE-FIFTH**) QUINT
(**— ON EVERY PLOW**) CARUCAGE
(**— ON HERRING CATCH**) LASTAGE
(**— ON LIQUOR**) ABKARI
(**— ON SALT**) GABELLE
(**— ON UNBELIEVERS**) KHARAJ
(**— ON WALLS**) MURAGE
(**— ON WOOD**) BOSCAGE
(**— ON WOOL**) MALETOTE MALTOLTE
(**— TO PETTY PRINCES**) KERNETTY
(**— TO SYNAGOGUE**) FINTA
(**— TO TENTH AMOUNT**) TITHE
(**— UNDULY**) STRAIN
(**CAPITATION —**) JIZYA JIZYAH
(**CHINESE —**) LEKIN LIKEN LIKIN
(**EXTRAORDINARY —**) AUXILIUM
(**FEUDAL —**) AID

(**IRISH —**) BONAGHT
(**MOHAMMEDAN —**) JEZIAH
(**PARISH —**) PURVEY
(**PHILIPPINES —**) CEDULA
(**POLL —**) TOLL CENSUS
(**RUSSIAN —**) OBROK
(**SPANISH —**) ALCABALA ALCAVALA
(**TURKISH —**) VERGI AVANIA
TAXABLE LISTABLE
TAX COLLECTOR TITHER GABELLER
TAXGATHERER POLLER TAXMAN
TAXI JIXIE CRAWLER
(**3-WHEELED —**) CYCLO
TAXICAB CAB HACK CRUISER MOTORCAB
TAXIDERMY NASSOLOGY
TAXING SEVERE GRUELING
TAXON MONERA
TAXONOMIC
(**SUFF.**) (**— DIVISION**) IA
TAXONOMIST LUMPER SPLITTER
TAYASSU PECARI
TAYGETE (**FATHER OF —**) ATLAS
(**MOTHER OF —**) PLEIONE
(**SON OF —**) EUROTAS LACEDAEMON
TAYRA GALERA
TCHAMBULI CHAMBERI
TEA CHA CHAR CHIA TCHA THAM TSIA ASSAM CAPER CHAIS CONGO FAHAM HYSON MIANG PEKOE STEEP CONGOU KEEMUN OOLONG PTISAN SUNGLO LAPSANG REDROOT TWANKAY AUTUMNAL GOWIDDIE SOUCHONG WORMSEED
(**AFRICAN —**) CAT KAT QAT KHAT QUAT
(**BLACK —**) BOHEA CONGO OOPAK CONGOU OOPACK SYCHEE
(**COARSE —**) BANCHA
(**HIGH-GRADE —**) GYOKURO
(**INFERIOR —**) BOHEA
(**MEDICINAL —**) TISANE
(**MEXICAN —**) BASOTE APASOTE
(**POOR —**) BLASH
(**PREF.**) THEI
TEA BOWL CHAWAN
TEACAKE LUNN SCONE
TEACH ARAL LEAR READ SHOW TECH TENT BREED CARRY COACH EDIFY ENDUE LEARN SPELL TRAIN TUTOR WISSE INFORM PREACH SCHOOL BITECHE EDUCATE EXAMPLE EXPOUND GRAMMAR AMAISTER DISCIPLE DOCUMENT INSTRUCT PUPILIZE
(**— TO FIGHT**) SPAR
TEACHABLE APT DOCILE DOCIBLE
TEACHABLENESS DOCITY DOSSETY
TEACHER RAB ALIM GURU AKHUN BIDDY CADET GUIDE MOLLA RABBI REBBE TUTOR USHER AKHUND AMAUTA DOCENT DOCTOR DOZENT FATHER MADRIH MAULVI MENTOR MULLAH PANDIT PUNDIT RABBAN READER REGENT RHETOR SUPPLY ACHARYA ALFAQUI DOMINIE MAESTRA MAESTRO MOOLVIE

MUNCHEE MURSHID PEDAGOG SHASTRI SOPHIST SPONSOR STARETS TRAINER ALFAQUIN AYUDANTE DIRECTOR EDUCATOR EXTENDER GAMALIEL MAGISTER MELAMMED MISTRESS MOONSHEE MUJTAHID MAHARISHI PEDAGOGUE PRECEPTOR ABECEDARIAN PRIVATDOCENT
(**— OF ELOQUENCE**) RHETOR
(**— OF EMINENCE**) MAESTRO
(**— OF HIGH LEARNING**) SOPHIST
(**— OF KORAN**) ALFAKI ALFAQUIN
(**— OF PAUL**) GAMALIEL
(**INCA —**) AMAUTA
(**MOHAMMEDAN —**) COJA HODJA KHOJA KHOJAH
TEACHING LAW DHARMA DOCENT LESSON LORING ACROAMA TUITION BUDDHISM DIDACTIC DOCTRINE DOCUMENT TUTELAGE (PL.) ACOUSMA BROWNISM CACODOXY DIDACTICS
TEAK SAJ DJATI EBONY
TEAKETTLE SUKE SUKEY CHAFER KETTLE POURIE CRESSET
TEAL CRICK BLUEWING GARGANEY SARCELLE
TEAM SET FIVE PLOW SIDE SPAN YOKE DRAFT SWING EQUIPE PLOUGH SEXTET DRAUGHT CARTWARE
(**— HARNESSED ONE BEFORE ANOTHER**) TANDEM
(**— OF CARS**) ECURIE
(**— OF GLASSWORKERS**) SHOP CHAIR
(**— OF 3 HORSES ABREAST**) TROIKA
(**— THAT FINISHES LAST**) DOORMAT
(**— 2 ABREAST, 1 LEADING**) SPIKE UNICORN
(**ATHLETIC —**) CLUB
(**BASEBALL —**) NINE
(**BASKETBALL —**) FIVE
(**FOOTBALL —**) ELEVEN
(**2-HORSE —**) PODANGER
(**3-HORSE —**) RANDEM
TEAMSTER CARTER TEAMEO CARTMAN SKINNER TEAMMAN
TEAPOT TRACK TRACKPOT
TEAR RIP RIT RUG TUT CLAW PILL PULL RACE RASE RASH RAVE REND RIVE RUGG SKAG SNAG STUN BREAK CLAUT LARME PEARL RANCH SHARK SLENT SPALT SPLIT TOUSE CLEAVE HARROW RANCHE RIPPLE SCHISM SCREED WRENCH CHATTER CONVELL DISCIND EYEDROP SCRATCH DISTRAIN FRACTURE LACERATE LACHRYMA TEARDROP
(**— APART**) REND TEASE DISCERP DIVULSE
(**— ASUNDER**) DIVEL
(**— AWAY**) AVULSE
(**— DOWN**) UNPILE DESTROY DEMOLISH
(**— IN NEGATIVE**) SLUG
(**— INTO**) LAMBAST LAMBASTE
(**— INTO PIECES**) DRAW TOLE DEVIL SHRED TEASE LANIATE MAMMOCK

(**— INTO SHREDS**) HOG DEVIL TATTER
(**— OFF**) STRIP ABRUPT DISCERP
(**— OPEN**) PROSCIND
(**— UP BY THE ROOTS**) ARACHE
(PL.) DEW BRINE RHEUM EYEWATER
(PREF.) DACRY(O) LACHRYMI LACHRYMO SPARASSO
TEARDROP EYEWATER
TEARFUL SOFT TEARY WEEPY LIQUID WATERY WEEPLY FLEBILE MAUDLIN SHOWERY SNIVELY SNIVELLY
TEARING SCREED
(**— AWAY**) AVULSION
TEARPIT CRUMEN LARMIER
TEASE COD FUN MAD RAG RIB ROT TAR TRY TUM VEX BAIT CHIP DRAG FASH FRET GRIG HARE HOCK JADE JIVE JOSH LARK NARK RAZZ SOOL TARR TOUT WORK CHAFF CHEEK CHEVY CHIAK CHYAK DEVIL FEEZE RALLY TARIE TAUNT TOOSE WRACK BANTER BOTHER CADDLE CHIVVY HARASS HOORAY HURRAH MOLEST MURDER NEEDLE PESTER PLAGUE HATCHEL TERRIFY TORMENT WHERRET
TEASEL KING TASSEL TEASLE MANWEED
TEASELER GIGGER TEASER
TEASELING MOZING
TEASER TIZEUR
TEASING CHAFF MERRY BANTER DEVILING QUIZZING
TEAT DUG PAP TIT DIDDY SPEAN NIPPLE SUCKLE
TEA TREE TI MANUKA
TEBAH (**FATHER OF —**) NAHOR
TEBALIAH (**FATHER OF —**) HOSAH
TECHNICIAN SWITCHER
TECHNIQUE FEAT GATE WRINKLE COQUILLE INDUSTRY SPICCATO
(**BILLIARD —**) FOLLOW
(**DANCE —**) HEELWORK
(**DECORATION —**) IKAT
(**DRAMATIC —**) METHOD
(**JUMPING —**) SCISSORS
(**WRESTLING —**) GLIMA
(**WRITING —**) CUBISM
(SUFF.) URGE URGIC URGY
TECHNOLOGY FISHERY TECHNIC CERAMICS
TECMESSA (**FATHER OF —**) TELEUTAS
(**HUSBAND OF —**) AJAX
(**SON OF —**) EURYSACES
TECOMIN LAPACHOL
TECTRIX COVERT
TEDDER KICKER
TEDIOUS DEAD DREE DULL LATE POKY PROSY WEARY ALENGE BORING DREECH DREIGH ELENGE MORTAL PROLIX STODGY IRKSOME OPEROSE PREACHY PROSAIC VERBOSE BORESOME DRAGGING TIRESOME WEARIFUL
TEDIUM IRK YAWN ENNUI BOREDOM
TEE COCK TIGHT TOZEE WITTER BULLHEAD

TEEM SNY FLOW SWIM SWARM ABOUND BUSTLE SCRAWL PULLULATE
TEEMER SHOOTMAN
TEEMING BIG ALIVE TUMID FERTILE GUSHING TEEMFUL ABUNDANT BRAWLING PREGNANT SWARMING
TEENAGER TEENY TEENYBOPPER
TEENY SMALL
TEESWATER MUGS MUGGS
TEETER ROCK WAVER JIGGLE QUIVER SEESAW WOBBLE TREMBLE
TEETH CTENII CHOPPERS CRACKERS GRINDERS
(HAVING —) IVORIED
(PETRIFIED —) BUFONITE
(SET OF —) DENTURE
(PREF.) DENT(ATO)(I)(INO)(O)
(SUFF.) ODON
TEETHRIDGE ALVEOLE ALVEOLUS
TEETOTUM TOTUM WHIRLIGIG
TEGETICULA PRONUBA
TEGMENTUM ROOF
TEGULA SQUAMA EPAULET SCAPULA PATAGIUM SQUAMULA
TEGUMENT COAT TEGMEN
TEHUELCHE PATAGON
TEJU TEIOID JACUARU TEGUEXIN
TELAMON ATLAS
(BROTHER OF —) PELEUS
(FATHER OF —) AEACUS
(MOTHER OF —) ENDEIS
(SON OF —) AJAX TEUCER
(WIFE OF —) GLAUCE HESIONE
TELAMONES ATLANTES
TELEDU BADGER STINKARD
TELEGONUS (FATHER OF —) ULYSSES
(MOTHER OF —) CIRCE
(SON OF —) ITALUS
(WIFE OF —) PENELOPE
TELEGRAM TAR WIRE FLASH FLIMSY
TELEGRAPH WIRE CABLE BUZZER TELEGRAM TELOTYPE
TELEMACHUS (FATHER OF —) ULYSSES
(MOTHER OF —) PENELOPE
(SON OF —) LATINUS
TELENCEPHALON ENDBRAIN
TELEOLOGICAL TELIC FINALIST
TELEOLOGY FINALITY
TELEPHASSA (DAUGHTER OF —) EUROPA
(HUSBAND OF —) AGENOR
(SON OF —) CADMUS PHOENIX
TELEPHONE RING PHONE HANDSET
(PART OF —) PAD BASE CORD DIAL HOLE STOP PLATE CRADLE HANDLE HANDSET PLUNGER SPEAKER EARPIECE RECEIVER MOUTHPIECE TRANSMITTER
TELEPHOTE DIAPHOTE
TELEPHUS (FATHER OF —) HERCULES
(MOTHER OF —) AUGE
(WIFE OF —) ARGIOPE LAODICE ASTYOCHE
TELEPRINTER CREED
TELESCOPE TUBE COUDE GLASS

SCOPE TRUNK ALINER FINDER SECTOR ALIGNER BINOCLE TRANSIT PROSPECT SPYGLASS REFRACTOR PERSPECTIVE
(PART OF —) LEG CELL LENS TUBE CLAMP GUIDE MOUNT SCOPE CRADLE DEWCAP SLEEVE TRIPOD DIAGONAL DRAWTUBE EYEPIECE MOUNTING SUNSHADE VIEWFINDER
(SURVEYOR'S —) LEVEL
TELEVISION TV AIR TELLY
(— SET) BOX TUBE BOOBTUBE
TELIOSPORE TELEUTO
TELL SAY DEEM MAKE MEAN MOOT READ SHOW TALE AREAD AREED BREAK BREVE COUNT NEVEN PITCH SPELL STORY TEACH UTTER AUTHOR DEVISE IMPART INFORM MUSTER QUETHE RECITE RELATE REPEAT REPORT REVEAL CONFESS DIVULGE NARRATE PARTAKE RECOUNT ACQUAINT REHEARSE
(— CONFIDENTIALLY) CONFIDE
(— CONFUSEDLY) SPLATHER
(— EARNESTLY) ASSURE
(— IN ADVANCE) FORESAY
(— LIES) BELY LIGE BELIE
(— OFF) JAR
(— ROMANCES) GEST GESTE
(— SECRETS) CHEEP CLYPE SPILL BABBLE
(— STRIKINGLY) CRACK
(— TALES) BLAB CANT PEACH
TELLER SPINNER STORIER TALLIER FABLEIST FABULIST SENACHIE
TELLING REDE PUNGENT POWERFUL STINGING
(— OF SECRETS) BLAB
TELLTALE CLASH TATTLER TITTLER REGISTER
TELLURIDE ALTAITE
TELSON PLEON
TELUGU GENTU GENTOO TELINGA
TEM TUM ATMU ATUM
TEMA (FATHER OF —) ISHMAEL
TEMAN (FATHER OF —) ELIPHAZ
(MOTHER OF —) ADAH
TEMENI (FATHER OF —) ASHUR
(MOTHER OF —) NAARAH
TEMERITY GALL CHEEK NERVE AUDACITY RASHNESS
TEMPER CUE MAD BAIT BATE COOL DASH DRAW MOOD MULL NEAL PADD SCOT TONE ALLOY BIRSE BLOOD CREST DELAY FRAME GRAIN HUMOR IRISH SAUCE SOBER TRAMP ADJUST ANIMUS ANNEAL DANDER MASTER MONKEY SEASON SPIRIT SPLEEN STRAIN SUBMIT CHASTEN CLIMATE COURAGE HACKLES QUALIFY STOMACH EBENEZER GRADUATE MITIGATE MODERATE MOORBURN
(— CLAY) TAMPER
(— METAL) ALLAY
(— OF MIND) CUE SPIRIT
(CAPRICIOUS —) SPLEEN
TEMPERAMENT BLOOD GEMUT HEART HUMOR CRASIS KIDNEY NATURE TEMPER

STOMACH SANGUINE
TEMPERAMENTAL FITIFIED
TEMPERANCE MEDIETY SOBRIETY
TEMPERATE CALM COOL MILD SOFT GREEN SOBER STEADY TEMPRE MODERATE ORDINATE ABSTINENT CONTINENT ABSTEMIOUS
TEMPERATURE SUN HEAT TEMP HOTNESS DEWPOINT
(— FACTOR) WINDCHILL
(— UNIT) KELVIN
TEMPERED HARD MILD SOBER SARCENET
TEMPERING MODULATION
TEMPEST GALE THUD WIND ORAGE STORM TUMULT TORMENT TURMOIL WEATHER
(AUTHOR OF —) SHAKESPEARE
(CHARACTER IN —) IRIS JUNO ARIEL CERES ADRIAN ALONSO ANTONIO CALIBAN GONZALO MIRANDA TINCULO PROSPERO STEPHANO FERDINAND FRANCISCO SEBASTIAN
TEMPESTUOUS WILD GUSTY STERN WINDY RUGGED STORMY VIOLENT STALWART
TEMPLATE CURB NORMA TEMPLET PADSTONE STRICKLE
TEMPLE VAT WAT DEUL FANE NAOS RATH CANDI GUACA HUACA KIACK KOVIL MARAE RATHA CHANDI HAFFET HERION MANDIR SACRUM SHRINE TEOPAN TJANDI VIHARA HERAEUM HERAION TEMPLET TEMPLUM VARELLA OLYMPIUM PANTHEON RAMESEUM TEOCALLI VALHALLA PARTHENON
(— AREA) MANDAPA
(CAVE —) SPEOS
(FIJI —) BURE
(HAWAIIAN —) HEIAU
(PART OF —) PRONAOS
(SHINTO —) SHA JINJA JINSHA YASHIRO
(STUDY OF —S) NAOLOGY
(TOWERLIKE —) ZIGGURAT
(PREF.) NAO
TEMPLES
(PREF.) TEMPORO
TEMPLET FORMER STRICKLE
TEMPO TAKT TIME AGOGE MOVEMENT
TEMPORAL CIVIL CARNAL TIMELY EARTHLY PROFANE SECULAR
TEMPORARY FLYING INTERIM STOPGAP WHILEND EPISODAL EPISODIC TEMPORAL PROVISIONAL
(PREF.) PSEUD(O)
TEMPORIZER DRIFTER POLITIC
TEMPT EGG FAND FOND LURE TEMP TENT ASSAY COURT ALLURE ASSAIL ENTICE INVITE SEDUCE ASSAULT ATTEMPT SOLICIT SUGGEST
TEMPTATION TRIAL ATTEMPT TESTING SEDUCTION
TEMPTER DEVIL
TEMPTING ALLURING INVITING
TEMPTRESS SIREN DELILAH

TEN ICRE IOTA CHANG DIKER CHEUNG DECADE DENARY DICKER ARTICLE BRISQUE
(— OF TRUMPS) GAME
(PREF.) DEC(A)(I)(U) DECEM DEK(A)
(SUFF.) TY
TEN'A KOYUKON
TENACE FORK
TENACIOUS FAST ROPEY STIFF TOUGH CLAGGY CLEDGY DOGGED GRIPPY PLUGGY STICKY STRONG VISCID GRIPPLE ADHESIVE GRASPING HOLDFAST PERTINACIOUS
TENACIOUSNESS TENACY FASTNESS
TENACITY LENTOR COURAGE
TENACULUM CLASP
TENANCY CONACRE JOINTURE
TENANT KMET LEUD SAER BARON CEILE DRENG LAIRD BORDAR COTTAR COTTER DRENGH GENEAT HOLDER INMATE LESSEE MOLMAN RADMAN RENTER SOCMAN VASSAL CHAKDAR COTTIER FEODARY FEUDARY GAVELER HOMAGER SOCAGER SOKEMAN VAVASOR COLIBERT CUSTOMER SERGEANT SUCKENER
(— OF CROWN) THANE
(LIFE —) LIVIER LIVEYER
(NEW —) INCOME INCOMER
TENCH CYPRINID
TEN COMMANDMENTS DECALOG
TEND HOP NOD RUN SET WRY BABY BEND DRAW GROW KEEP MAKE MIND MOVE TENT DRESS GROOM NURSE OFFER SOUND TREND VERGE WATCH AFFECT GOVERN INTEND CHERISH CONDUCE DECLINE INCLINE PROPEND
(— A FIRE) STOKE
(— IN A CERTAIN DIRECTION) LEAD
(— TO ONE POINT) CONVERGE
(— TOWARD) AFFECT
(— WHILE AT PASTURE) GRAZE
TENDENCY SET BENT BIAS HAND TONE VEIN DRAFT DRIFT DRIVE HABIT KNACK TENOR TREND TWIST ANIMUS COURSE EONISM GENIUS MOTION APTNESS CONATUS DRAUGHT IMPULSE LEANING NITENCY SAMKARA APTITUDE INSTINCT STEERING VERGENCY
(— IN NATURE) KIND
(— TO APPROACH) ADIENCE
(— TO STICK TOGETHER) CLANSHIP
(— TO WITHDRAW) ABIENCE
(— TO WRATH) TIDE
(SUFF.) (— TOWARD) PHIL(A)(AE) (E)(IA)(ISM)(IST)(OUS)(US)(Y)
TENDER RAW TID BEAR COCK FINE FOND FRIM FRUM KIND NESH SOFT SORE TAKE TART TENT WARM CAGER DEFER FRAIL GREEN MUSHY OFFER PAPPY DELATE DRIVER GENTLE GIMPER GINGER HUMANE LOVELY RAISER SILKEN ADVANCE AMABILE AMOROSO AMOROUS CONCHER CRAMPER FLESHLY MASHMAN

OBLATIO PATACHE PINNACE
PITEOUS PITIFUL PORRECT
PROFFER RUTHFUL STENTER
CAMELEER COCKBOAT EFFETMAN
FEMININE HEATSMAN HERDSMAN
LADYLIKE MERCIFUL MORTISER
SPREADER
(PREF.) ABRO HABRO
TENDERFOOT DUDE INNOCENT
TENDERHEARTED HUMAN PITIFUL
TENDERIZER PAPAIN
TENDERLOIN FILET PSOAS FILLET
UNDERCUT
TENDERLY FONDLY GENTLY
AMOROSO
TENDERNESS CHERTE TENDER
DELICACY FONDNESS KINDNESS
SYMPATHY TENERITY YEARNING
(— OF FEELING) FLESH
TENDING
(SUFF.) CLINIC CLINOUS
(— TO) ABLE ATIVE ATORY BOND
BUND CUND FUL IBLE
TENDINOUS SINEWY
TENDON CORD TAIL CHORD NERVE
SINEW TENON LEADER PAXWAX
STRING
(PREF.) TENO
TENDRIL CURL CLASP CROOK
TWIST CIRRUS WINDER CAPREOL
CIRRHUS CLASPER TENTACLE
(PREF.) PAMPINI PAMPINO
TENEMENT LAND RENT TACK
CHAWL DECKER LIVING WARREN
HOLDING LETTING ROOKERY
BUILDING PRAEDIUM
TENES (FATHER OF —) CYNCUS
(MOTHER OF —) PROCLEA
PHILONOME
(SISTER OF —) HEMITHEA
(SLAYER OF —) ACHILLES
TENET ADOXY CREDO CREED
DOGMA BELIEF GNOMON
HOLDING MISHNAH PARADOX
DOCTRINE
(PL.) FAITH FAMILISM
TENFOLD DENARY DECUPLE
TENNANTITE FAHLERZ FAHLORE
TENNE TAWNY ORANGE HYACINTH

TENNIS (— SHOT) LET LOB DINK
(ANCIENT —) BANDY
TENON COG PIN COAK STUB TUSK
LEWIS TOOTH TABLING DOVETAIL
LEWISSON
TENOR PES FECK TONE VEIN
COURSE EFFECT TAILLE TENURE
CURRENT PURPORT STRENGTH
TENDENCY TENORINO
TENOROON FAGOTTINO
TENOR VIOL VIOLET
TENOR VIOLIN ALTO
TENPINS BOWLS NEWPORT
TENPOUNDER AWA CHIRO
MACABI BONEFISH BONYFISH
LADYFISH SKIPJACK SPRINGER
TENREC TANGUE CENTETES
CENTETID HEDGEHOG HEDGEPIG
TENSE EDGY RAPT TAUT STIFF
AORIST CORDED FLINCH FUTURE
INTENT NARROW STRAIT STRICT
BRITTLE INTENSE PRIMARY
FRENETIC PRETERIT SYNTONIC
TENSION BENT HEAT DRIVE STEAM
SATTVA SPRING STRAIN STRESS
TROPPO BALANCE STRAINT
TENSURE ISOTONIA
TENT AUL TOP HALE PAWL TAWN
TELD TILT CABIN CRAME LODGE
TOPEK TUPIK CANNAT CANVAS
DOSSIL SEARCH WIGWAM
BALAGAN CABINET KIBITKA
MARQUEE SPARVER TABERNA
TENTLET TENTORY ZDARSKY
PAVILION SHAMIANA TENTICLE
TENTWORK SHOOLDARRY
(— FOR WOUNDS) PENICIL
(— WHERE GOODS ARE SOLD)
CRAME
(CIRCULAR —) YURT YOURT YURTA
KIBITKA
(INDIAN —) TEPEE WIGWAM
(SAMOYED —) CHUM
(SOUTH AMERICAN —) TOLDO
TENTACLE HORN SAIL PACLE
FEELER BRACHIUM
TENTATIVE GINGERLY
TENT CATERPILLAR WEBWORM
TENTERER RACKER RATCHER
TENTH DIME DISME TITHE DECIMA
(— OF CENT) MILL
(— OF LINE) GRY
(PREF.) DECI
TEN THOUSAND
(PREF.) MYRIA MYRIO
TENUITY EXILITY DELICACY
TENUOUS FILMY FOGGY FRAIL
SUBTLE TENDER FRAGILE
GASEOUS SLENDER SUBTILE
ETHEREAL GOSSAMER
(TOO —) FINESPUN
TENUOUSNESS FRAILTY

TENURE FEU SORN TACK TAKE
TERM GAVEL JAGIR BARONY
CAPITE JAGHIR RUNRIG SOCAGE
SORREN ALMOIGN BONDAGE
BORDAGE BURGAGE CENSIVE
CORNAGE CURTESY FARMAGE
JAGHEER SOCCAGE SOREHON
COPYHOLD DRENGAGE FREEHOLD
OVERLAND SOCMANRY SUITHOLD
VAVASORY VENVILLE
TEPEE CHUM TENT TIPI HOGAN
LODGE TEEPEE WICKIUP
TEPHROSIA CRACCA
TEPID LEW WARM WLACH WLECH
LUKEWARM
TEQUISLATEC CHONTAL
TERAH (SON OF —) HARAN NAHOR
ABRAHAM
TERATOMA EMBRYOMA
TERCET TRISTICH
TEREBINTH TEIL TURPENTINE
TEREDO BORER WOODWORM
TERENTIA (HUSBAND OF —) CICERO
TERETE CENTRIC
TEREUS (FATHER OF —) MARS
(SON OF —) ITYS
(WIFE OF —) PROCNE
TERGITE TERGUM PYGIDIUM
TERGIVERSATION DECEIT
TERGUM PYGIDIUM
TERM HALF NAME NOME WORD
LEASE RHEMA SPEAK STYLE
TRYST ABBACY GNOMON HILARY
NOTION PARODY EPITHET
EXTREME SESSION SUBJECT
SUMMAND TERMINE VOCABLE
EQUIVOKE HEADWORD
MAHALATH POCHISMO SEMESTER
TERMTIME
(— IN JAIL) JOLT
(— IN LOGIC) CONSTANT
(— OF ABUSE) CUSSWORD
(— OF ADDRESS) SIRRAH
MADONNA
(— OF CONTEMPT) SLIPE PILCHER
TITIVIL
(— OF DEFERENCE) AHUNG
(— OF ENDEARMENT) ASTOR
CHUCK COCKY HONEY MOPSY
ASTHORE MACHREE STOREEN
POSSODIE POWSOWDY
(— OF IMPRISONMENT) LAG
LAGGING STRETCH
(— OF PUNISHMENT) JOB
(— OF RATIO) EXTREME
(— OF REPROACH) GIB BESOM
MINGO RONYON
(— OF SYLLOGISM) EXTREME
ARGUMENT
(ARITHMETICAL —) NOME
GNOMON
(HYPHENED —) COMPOUND
(LITERAL —S) LETTER
(SOCIAL —S) FOOTING
(UNIVERSAL —) CONCEPT
(PL.) LAY MEANS
(PREF.) HORO
TERMAGANT JADE RUDAS SHREW
VIXEN VIRAGO
TERMINABLE FINITE
TERMINAL JACK LAST POLE
ANODE DEPOT IMPUT INPUT
MUCRO CATHODE

POTHEAD DESINENT
TERMINATE CUT END ABUT CALL
HALT KILL ABORT BLEED CEASE
CLOSE ISSUE LAPSE EXPIRE
FINISH FOREDO RESULT INCLUDE
TERMINE COMPLETE CONCLUDE
DISSOLVE
(— A SESSION) PROROGUE
TERMINATED EXPIATE
TERMINATING FINAL
(— ABRUPTLY) BLIND
(SUDDENLY —) ABRUPT
TERMINATION END ISH DATE
TERM ABORT CLOSE EVENT ISSUE
ENDING EXITUS EXPIRY FINALE
PERIOD UPSHOT TERMINUS
(— OF CHURCH CHOIR) CHEVET
(— OF FURNITURE LEGS) FOOT
(— OF RIGHT) LAPSE
TERMINATIVE FINITIVE
TERMINOLOGY JARGON
TERMINUS END FLAT
(— IN FINGERPRINT) DELTA
(— OF PERIOD) TIME
TERMITE ANAI ANAY KING NASUTE
WORKER POLILLA
TERMITOPHILE SYMPHILE
TERN KIP DARR INCA LARI NOIO
PIRL PIRR RIXY LARID NODDY
PEARL SCRAY SKEER SKIRR STERN
CHIRRE KERMEW PICKET
GOELAND MEDRICK PIRRMAW
RITTOCK SCURRIT SEAFOWL
STRIKER TARRACK TERNLET
MANUSINA SPARLING TIRRACKE
TERPENE CARENE PINENE
BORNANE SANTENE THUJENE
CAMPHENE FENCHENE LIMONENE
NOPINENE
TERRA GE GAEA TELLUS
(DAUGHTER OF —) RHEA THEA
PHOEBE TETHYS THEMIS
MNEMOSYNE
(HUSBAND OF —) URANUS
(SON OF —) OCEANUS
TERRACE POY DAIS PNYX STEP
XYST BEACH BENCH HEIAU LINCH
OFFSET PERRON LINCHET
BARBETTE CHABUTRA
(LOUNGING —) LANAI
(NATURAL —) MESA
TERRA JAPONICA GAMBIR
GAMBIER
TERRAPENE CISTUDO
TERRAPIN EMYD COUNT COODLE
POTTER SLIDER TURPIN TURTLE
EMYDIAN FEUILLE SKILPOT
REDBELLY TORTOISE
(FEMALE —) HEIFER
(MALE —) BULL
TERRARIUM VIVARIUM
TERRELLA EARTHKIN
TERRENE EARTHLY
TERRESTRIAL EARTHY EARTHLY
TERRENE PLANETAL SUBLUNAR
SUBSOLAR TELLURIC PLANETARY
SUBASTRAL
TERRET CRINGLE
TERRIBLE DIRE UGLY AWFUL
GHAST LURID DEADLY PRETTY
TARBLE TRAGIC TURBLE CHRONIC
DIREFUL FEARFUL FERDFUL
GHASTLY HIDEOUS ALMIGHTY

BHAIRAVA FLEYSOME HORRIBLE
TERRIFIC TIMOROUS TRAGICAL
(PREF.) DEIN(O) DIN(O)
TERRIBLY FELLY FIERCE GRISLY
CONSARN
TERRIER SKYE LHASA SILKY
BOSTON DANDIE RATTER SCOTTY
DIEHARD SCOTTIE ABERDEEN
AIREDALE RATTONER SEALYHAM
VERMINER WIREHAIR
TERRIFIC FINE SWEET GORGON
FEARFUL GORGEOUS
TERRIFIED AFRAID AGHAST
GHASTLY
TERRIFY AWE COW HAG BREE
DARE FEAR FLAY FLEY APPAL
DREAD GALLY SCARE ADREAD
AFFRAY AGRISE AWHAPE DISMAY
FLIGHT FREEZE FRIGHTEN
TERRIFYING GHASTLY HIDEOUS
FLEYSOME TERRIBLE
TERRITORIALISM ITOISM
TERRITORY FEE GOA HAN SOC
AREA MARK PALE SOKE BANAT
DUCHY FIELD MARCH STATE
TUATH BORDER COLONY DOMAIN
EMPERY EMPIRE GROUND
APANAGE CONFINE COUNTRY
DEMESNE DUKEDOM EARLDOM
ENCLAVE EPARCHY REGENCY
SATRAPY APPANAGE CASTLERY
CONFINES CONQUEST DISTRICT
DOMINION IMPERIUM LIGEANCE
LUCUMONY PARMESAN PASHALIK
REGALITY SEIGNORY
(MONAOTIO —) ADTILANE
TERROR AWE FEAR FRAY ALARM
APPAL DREAD PANIC AFFRAY
ALARUM APPALL FRIGHT HORROR
DRIDDER AFFRIGHT DREDDOUR
SURPRISE
TERRORISM NIHILISM
TERRORIST GOONDA ALARMIST
SICARIUS
TERRORIZE FRIGHTEN
TERROR-STRICKEN AWFUL
TERSE CURT SINEWY COMPACT
CONCISE LACONIC POINTED
SUMMARY UNWORDY SUCCINCT
TERSENESS BREVITY LACONISM
TERTIARY NEOZOIC PALAEIC
TESSELLATED MOSAIC
TESSELLATION AREOLE
TESSERA TILETTE ABACULUS
TESSELLA
TESS OF DURBERVILLES (AUTHOR
OF —) HARDY
(CHARACTER IN —) ALEC JACK
TESS ANGEL CLARE DURBERVILLE
DURBEYFIELD
TEST CON SAY TRY FAND FEEL
FOND TASK TENT ASSAY AVENA
CANON CHECK ESSAY GROPE
ISSUE PROBE PROOF PROVE
SENSE SOUND TASTE TEMPT
TESTA TOUCH TRIAL SAMPLE
TIENTA APPROOF APPROVE
AUSSAGE CONTROL EXAMINE
GANTLET PLUMMET TESTATE
BIOASSAY EXERCISE GAUNTLET
SEROLOGY STANDARD
(— CHEESE) PALE
(— EGGS) CANDLE

(— FOR WEIGHT AND FINENESS)
PYX
(— GROUND) BOSE
(— OF COURAGE) SCRATCH
(— OF CRINOID) CALYX
(— OF GUILT) CORSNED
(— OF ORE) VAN
(SEVERE —) CRUCIBLE
(SYPHILIS —) KOLMER
(PREF.) DOCIMO OECO
(SUFF.) OECA OECIA
TESTA TEST LORICA EPISPERM
TESTACEOUS SHELLY
TESTAMENT TEST QUETHE
WITWORD COVENANT
TESTAR TETARD
TESTATOR LEGATOR
TESTED FIRED TRIED WEIGHED
TESTER TRIER CONNER PROVER
SPARVER DENIERER TESTIERE
(BUTTER —) SEARCHER
TESTES
(SUFF.) ORCHISM
TESTICLE STONE BALLOCK
DIDYMUS GENITOR
(PREF.) ORCHI(O) ORCHID(O)
ORCHO
TESTICLES
(SUFF.) ORCHISM
TESTIFY SPEAK SWEAR AFFIRM
DEPONE DEPOSE WITTEN
WITNESS EVIDENCE
(— FALSELY) MOUNT
(— TO) BESPEAK
TESTIMONIAL CHIT SCROLL
CHARACTER
TESTIMONY TEST ATTEST
AVOUCH PROBATE TESTATE
TESTIFY WITNESS EVIDENCE
TESTING ASSAY CRUCIAL
SHAKEDOWN
TESTIS BALL GONAD STONE
BALLOCK CULLION KNOCKER
SPERMARY
(PL.) COBS CODS COJONES
DOWSETS
TEST TUBE PROOF TESTER
PROBATE
TESTUDINATA CHELONIA
TESTUDO SNAIL GALAPAGO
TORTOISE
TESTY DONCY MUSTY TUTTY
DONSIE PATCHY SPUNKY PEEVISH
TETTISH TOUSTIE WASPISH
SNAPPISH
TETANIC SPASTIC
TETANUS LOCKJAW HOLOTONY
TETE-A-TETE TWOSOME CAUSEUSE
TETHER BAND LEASH STAKE
PICKET TEDDER TOGGLE PASTERN
CABESTRO
(— A HAWK) WEATHER
TETHYS APLYSIA
(DAUGHTERS OF —) OCEANIDES
(FATHER OF —) URANUS
(HUSBAND OF —) OCEANUS
(MOTHER OF —) TERRA
TETHYUM CYNTHIA
TETRA-
(PREF.) QUATER
TETRACHORD GENUS HYPATON
LICHANOS
TETRACTYS TETRAD

TETRAD FOURFOLD
TETRADRACHMA OWL
TETRAGONAL DIMETRIC
TETRAHEDRITE FAHLERZ FAHLORE
PANABASE
TETRAHEXAHEDRON FLUOROID
TETRAHYDRIDE GERMANE
STANNANE
TETRASACCHARIDE LUPEOSE
TETTER DARTRE
TETTIX ACRYDIUM
TEUCER (DAUGHTER OF —) ASTERIA
(FATHER OF —) TELAMON
SCAMANDER
(HALF-BROTHER OF —) AJAX
(MOTHER OF —) IDAEA HESIONE
(WIFE OF —) EUNE
TEUTON GOTH LOMBARD
TEUTONIC GOTHIC GERMANIC
GOTHONIC

TEXAS

CAPITAL: AUSTIN
COLLEGE: SMU TCU RICE WILEY
BAYLOR
COUNTY: BEE CASS COKE JACK
REAL RUSK VEGA WEBB WISE
BEXAR DELTA ECTOR ERATH
GARZA RAINS FANNIN GOLIAD
YOAKUM ZAPATA ZAVALA
HIDALGO REFUGIO ATASCOSA
FORTRESS: ALAMO
INDIAN: LIPAN BILOXI KICHAI
SHUMAN HASINAI COMANCHE
TONKAWAN
LAKE: FALCON TEXOMA AMISTAD
MOUNTAIN: GUADALUPE
NATIVE: TEJANO
NICKNAME: LONESTAR
PRESIDENT: JOHNSON
EISENHOWER
RIVER: RED PECOS BRAZOS
NUECES TRINITY
STATE BIRD: MOCKINGBIRD
STATE FLOWER: BLUEBONNET
STATE TREE: PECAN
TOWN: GAIL VEGA WACO BRYAN
MARFA OZONA PAMPA TYLER
BORGER DALLAS DENTON
ELPASO KILEEN LAREDO
ODESSA QUANAH SONORA
ABILENE HOUSTON LUBBOCK
AMARILLO BEAUMONT
FLOYDADA GALVESTON

TEXAS BUCKTHORN LOTEBUSH
TEXAS FEVER TRISTEZA
TEXT BODY MIQRA PLACE SAKHA
TESTO PURANA SCRIPT SHAKHA
TEXTUS TEXTLET ANTETHEM
PERICOPE VARIORUM
(— OF ADVERTISEMENT) COPY
(— OF OPERA) LIBRETTO
(— SET TO MUSIC) ORATORIO
(REVISED —) RECENSION
(SHASTRA —) SRUTI SHRUTI
TEXTBOOK DUNCE TUTOR
GENETICS
TEXTILE (ALSO SEE FABRIC) SABA
STUFF GREIGE MOCKADO
SAGURAN SINAMAY TEXTURE
TIFFANY
(— MACHINE) WILLOW

(PL.) DRAPE
TEXTURE WEB BONE HAND KNIT
WALE WOOF GRAIN COBWEB
FABRIC WEFTAGE FRACTURE
(— OF SOAP) FIT
THADDEUS OF WARSAW
(AUTHOR OF —) PORTER
(CHARACTER IN —) MARY ROSS
SARA DIANA BUTZOU ROBSON
VINCENT BEAUFORT EUPHEMIA
PEMBROKE SOBIESKI SOMERSET
THADDEUS CAVENDISH
KOSCIUSKO SACKVILLE
TINEMOUTH CONSTANTINE
THAHASH (FATHER OF —) NAHOR
(MOTHER OF —) REUMAH
THAI LAO SIAMESE

THAILAND

CAPITAL: BANKOK BANGKOK
COIN: AT ATT BAHT FUANG TICAL
PYNUNG SALUNG SATANG
FORMER NAME: SIAM
ISLAND: PHUKET
ISTHMUS: KRA
MEASURE: WA KEN NIV NMU RAI
SAT SEN SOK WAH YOT KEUP
NGAN TANG YOTE KWIEN
LAANG SESTI TANAN KABIET
KAMMEU CHAIMEU ROENENG
CHANGAWN
MOUNTAIN: KHIEO MAELAMUN
MOUNTAIN RANGE: DAWNA
BILAUKTAUNG
NATIVE: LAO THAI
PLAIN: KHORAT
RIVER: CHI NAN PING MENAM
MEKONG MEPING
TOWN: UBON PUKET RANONG
AYUDHYA AYUTHIA BANGKOK
LOPBURI RAHAENG SINGORA
SONGKLA KHONKAEN KIANGMAI
THONBURI
WEIGHT: HAP PAI SEN SOK BAHT
HAPH KLAM KLOM CATTY
CHANG COYAN PILUL FLUANG
SALUNG SOMPAY TAMLUNG

THAIS (CHARACTER IN —) THAIS
ATHANAEL
(COMPOSER OF —) MASSENET
THAISA (FATHER OF —) SIMONIDES
(HUSBAND OF —) PERICLES
THALABA (WIFE OF —) ONEIZA
THALER DALER
THALLOGEN AMPHIGEN
THALLOID FRONDOSE
THALLUS FROND THALAMUS
THAMNIUM
THAMNOPHIS EUTAENIA
THAMYRAS (FATHER OF —)
PHILAMMON
(MOTHER OF —) ARGIOPE
THAN AS NA NE OR TO AND BUT
NOR THEN TILL
THANE THEGN BANQUO GESITH
ABTHAIN MACDUFF
THANK GRACE MERCY AGGRATE
REGRACY REMERCY
THANKFUL GRATEFUL
THANKLESS INGRATE SLOWFUL
THANKS TA GRACE MERCI MERCY
GRAMERCY

THANKSGIVING GLORY
DOXOLOGY
THANK-YOU-MA'AM CAHOT
THAT AS AT SE BUT HOW THE THO
WHO YAT LEST THAM THIK THON
WHAT YOND THICK THILK
THOUGH BECAUSE
(— IS TO SAY) NAMELY
(— ONE) ILLE
(— WHICH HAS TO BE PROVED)
IQED
(— YONDER) THON
THATCH NIPA DATCH SIRKI SIRKY
STING THRUM CADJAN
(— OVER BEEHIVE) HOOD
THATCHED THACK REEDED
THATCHER HELER CROWDER
HELLIER THACKER
THAUMAS (DAUGHTER OF —) IRIS
AELLO HARPY OCYPETE
(FATHER OF —) PONTUS NEPTUNE
(MOTHER OF —) GAEA TERRA
(WIFE OF —) ELECTRA
THAUMATURGIST
(PL.) GOETAE
THAUMATURGY MAGIC
THAW GIVE MELT FRESH UNTHAW
DEFROST
THE LA LE SE TA THI THAM THEY
YARE THERE
(PREF.) AL
THEA CAMELLIA
(FATHER OF —) URANUS
(HUSBAND OF —) HYPERION
(MOTHER OF —) TERRA
THEANO (FATHER OF —) CISSEUS
(HUSBAND OF —) ANTENOR
METAPONTUS
(MOTHER OF —) TELECLIA
(SISTER OF —) HECUBA
(SON OF —) ACAMAS AGENOR
POLYBUS HELICAON IPHIDAMAS
ARCHELOCHUS
THEATER CINE GAFF KINO CAVEA
HOUSE LEGIT ODEUM SCENE
STAGE CINEMA OZONER ADELPHI
COCKPIT GUIGNOL ORPHEUM
THEATRE BIOSCOPE COLISEUM
PANTHEON SHOWSHOP SPELLKEN
STRAWHAT THEATRON
PLAYHOUSE NICKELODEON
(NEIGHBORHOOD —) NABE
(PUPPET —) BUNRAKU
THEATRICAL CAMP HAMMY
STAGY DRAMATIC SCENICAL
SINGSONG
THEATRICALITY HAM PANACHE
THEBAN LAIUS NIOBE AMPHION
CADMEAN JOCASTA OEDIPUS
PENTHEUS
THEBE (FATHER OF —) ASOPUS
(HUSBAND OF —) ZETHUS
(MOTHER OF —) METOPE
(SISTER OF —) AEGINA
THECA CUP URN CELL VAGINA
CAPSULE PYXIDIUM VAGINULE
THEELIN ESTRONE FEMININ
OESTRIN
THEFT CRIB LIFT HEIST PINCH
SCORE STALE STEAL FURTUM
RIPOFF STOUTH BRIBERY
LARCENY MICHERY PICKING
PILFERY ROBBERY STEALTH

BURGLARY STEALAGE STEALING
(LITERARY —) PIRACY
(PETTY —) CRIB PICKERY
(PREF.) KLEPT(O)
(SUFF.) KLEPT
THEINE CAFFEINE
THEIR ARE HER ORE HORE YARE
THEIRS HERN THEIRN
THEM A EM HI UM HEM MUN
HEMEN
THEME DUX BASE IDEA TEMA TEXT
DITTY HOBBY LEMMA MOTIF
PLACE SCOPE TESTO THEMA
TOPIC URLAR MATTER MYTHOS
SUBJECT ANTETHEM
(— OF FUGUE) DUX
(HACKNEYED —) CLICHE
(MAIN —) BURDEN
(RECURRING —) BURDEN
(STOCK —) TOPOS
THEMIS (DAUGHTER OF —) DICE
IRENE EUNOMIA
(FATHER OF —) URANUS
(HUSBAND OF —) JUPITER
(MOTHER OF —) TERRA
THEMSELVES HEM HEMSELF
THEN SO AND POI THO ANON SYNE
THENCE AWAY THEN THEREFRO
THEOCRACY KHALSA
THEODELINDE (FATHER OF —)
GARIBALD
(HUSBAND OF —) AGO AUTHARI
THEODOLITE TAIPO DIOPTER
TRANSIT TRANSEPT
THEOLOGIAN FAQIH ULEMA
DIVINE MUJTAHID
AMERICAN BROWN HATCH NEVIN
SMITH TYLER WOODS BURTON
FOSTER MACHEN STUART
TAYLOR EDWARDS EVERETT
HOPKINS MCCLURE MOFFATT
NIEBUHR PEABODY VINCENT
MCGIFFERT WORCESTER
AUSTRIAN MOHR BRUNNER
DENIFLE JELLINEK
BELGIAN BAIUS
CZECH COMENIUS
DANISH MONRAD MULLER
MYNSTER PEDERSEN GRUNDTVIG
PONTOPPIDAN
DUTCH HAAR VOET WITS BEKKER
JANSEN KUENEN KUYPER
GOMARUS BOGERMAN LIMBORCH
SCHOLTEN EPISCOPIUS
ENGLISH BEDE BULL HORT OWEN
WARD BLUNT COLET HATCH
PALEY PUSEY SWETE WATTS
BUTLER FERRAR HARRIS HOOKER
NEWMAN PECOCK WESLEY
LANGTON MARBECK MAURICE
PEARSON WHATELY WHISTON
CARDWELL DRUMMOND
PELAGIUS WYCLIFFE CHADERTON
GUILLAUME LIGHTFOOT
STAPLETON WARBURTON
GROSSETESTE CHILLINWORTH
FRENCH BEZE GURY AILLY FAVRE
PAJON SIMON CALVIN GERSON
GLAIRE GOGUEL JURIEU PORREE
RICHER SORBON ABELARD
AMYRAUT BASNAGE BAUTAIN
BOCHART CHARRON QUESNEL
CASAUBON COURAYER SABATIER

CASTELLIO BOURDALOUE
LICHTENBERGER
LABERTHONNIERE
GERMAN ECK ESS ADAM ARND
BAUR DUHM EBER GASS HEIM
MERX RUPP ZAHN AMMON
BAUER BUDDE CALOV EMSER
FRANK GOEZE HAUCK HENKE
KNAPP KRAUS LANGE MAJOR
ROTHE STORR WALCH WEBER
WEISS ALSTED ANDREA BAHRDT
BENGEL CRAMER DALMAN DIPPEL
DORNER EBRARD FICKER GEIGER
HEILER HERMES HERZOG HEUSSI
HIRSCH MOHLER NATORP PEUCER
PLANCK REUSCH SEMLER SPENER
UHLICH ZELLER ZIMMER AGRIPPA
AMSDORF BOUSSET CASPARI
CRUSIUS ECKHART EHRHARD
ERNESTI FORSTER GERHARD
HAERING HARNACK HOFMANN
KOSTLIN LECHLER MOSHEIM
MUNSTER NAUMANN NEANDER
NIPPOLD RITSCHL STRAUSS
TILLICH ULLMANN URSINUS
WILHELM BULTMANN CALIXTUS
CANISIUS CHEMNITZ COCCEIUS
CRUCIGER DIBELIUS DILLMANN
EBERHARD EICHHORN FLIEDNER
GESENIUS HAUSRATH KAUTZSCH
KLIEFOTH MICHELIS MYCONIUS
OETINGER OSIANDER REIMARUS
SCHENKEL AURIFABER
BEYSCHLAG BUSEMBAUM
DELITZSCH DOLLINGER FABRICIUS
FREIDRICH JABLONSKI MICHAELIS
NIEMOLLER OLEVIANUS
OLSHAUSEN PFEIDERER
BAUMGARTEN MARHEINEKE
NEUMEISTER WISLICENUS
TISCHENDORF FROHSCHAMMER
BRETSCHNEIDER
SCHLEIERMACHER
GREEK ALLACCI CLEMENT
EUSEBIUS
HUNGARIAN BALLAGI
IRISH DODWELL PLUNKET
TYRRELL
ITALIAN OCHINO LOMBARD
PERRONE SOCINUS PASSAGLIA
JEWISH HIRSCH
NORWEGIAN MOE
SCOTTISH CAIRD EADIE ALESIUS
CAMERON ROLLOCK TULLOCH
CAMPBELL CHALMERS FAIRBAIRN
CUNNINGHAM RUTHERFORD
SPANISH CANO MOLINA SUAREZ
VALDES ENZINAS CARRANZA
EYMERICO SERVETUS
MALDONADO SEPULVEDA
SWEDISH FRYXELL SODERBLOM
FAHLCRANTZ
SWISS BARTH GODET VINET
ISELIN DIODATI ERASTUS
LECLERC BUCHMANN HEIDEGGER
SYRIAN AETIUS
THEOLOGY KALAM IRENICS
DIVINITY POIMENIC POLEMICS
THEONOE (BROTHER OF —)
CALCHAS
(FATHER OF —) PROTEUS THESTOR
(MOTHER OF —) LEUCIPPE
PSAMATHE

THEORBO ARCHLUTE
THEOREM DUAL LEMMA
CONVERSE
THEORETIC PURE
THEORETICAL BOOK PURE CLOSET
THEORIC ABSTRACT ACADEMIC
ARMCHAIR NOTIONAL PLATONIC
THEORIST OPINATOR
THEORIZE SUGGEST
THEORIZING IDEOLOGY
THEORY ISM OVISM EROTIC ETHICS
HOLISM LAXISM SYSTEM AGOGICS
ANIMISM ATOMISM BAASKAP
BIGBANG CAMBISM DUALISM
FORMISM HOBBISM PEELISM
PLENISM THEORIC TYCHISM
ACOSMISM AXIOLOGY DITHEISM
DYNAMISM ENERGISM ESTHETIC
ETIOLOGY FEMINISM FINITISM
GHOSTISM GOBINISM HEDONICS
IDEALISM IDEOLOGY MOLINISM
MONADISM ONTOLOGY PROGRESS
SEMANTIC SEMIOTIC SPERMISM
(SUFF.) ISM LOGER LOGIA(N)
LOGIC(AL) LOGIST LOGUE LOGY
OLOGY
THEOW SERF THRALL THEOWMAN
THERAPEUTICS ACEOLOGY
THERAPY PHYSIATRICS
(SUFF.) PATH(IA)(IC)(Y)
THERAVADA HINAYANA
THERE ERE YARE ALONG VOILA
WHERE YONDER THEASUM
THITHER
THEREABOUTS NEARBY
THEREAFTER UPON THENCE
THEREFORE SO ERGO THEN ARGAL
HENCE FORTHY IGITUR THENCE
THEREON UPON
THEREUPON SO SINCE WITHAL
THEREON THEREUP
THEREWITH MIT WITH
THERIACA GALENA
THERMOMETER GLASS HYDRA
CELSIUS REAUMUR
(PART OF —) BORE BULB LENS
SCALE COLUMN GRADUATIONS
CONSTRICTION
THERMOPLASTIC SARAN
THERMOSTAT DETECTOR
PYROSTAT
THERSANDER (FATHER OF —)
POLYNICES
(MOTHER OF —) ARGIA
(SLAYER OF —) TELEPHUS
THESAURUS TREASURE
THESE THIR THIS THEASUM
THESEUS (FATHER OF —) AEGEUS
(MOTHER OF —) AETHRA
(SON OF —) HIPPOLYTUS
(WIFE OF —) PHAEDRA
THESIS ACT THEMA DOWNBEAT
LOGICISM THESICLE
THESTIUS (DAUGHTER OF —)
ALTHAEA
(FATHER OF —) PARTHAON
(MOTHER OF —) EURYTE
(SON OF —) TOXEUS PLEXIPPUS
THESTOR (DAUGHTER OF —)
THEONOE LEUCIPPE
(FATHER OF —) IDMON APOLLO
(MOTHER OF —) LAOTHOE
(SON OF —) CALCHAS

THETIS (FATHER OF —) NEREUS
(HUSBAND OF —) PELEUS
(MOTHER OF —) DORIS
(SON OF —) ACHILLES
THEY A HI THO THEI
(— READ) LEG
THIAMINE ANEURIN
THICK FAT SAD HAZY SLAB BLIND
BROAD BURLY BUSHY CLOSE
CRASS DENSE FOGGY GREAT
GROSS MURKY SOLID SQUAB
STIFF STOUT CHUMPY COARSE
GREASY LUBBER SLABBY SPISSY
STOCKY STODGY TURBID
BLUBBER GRUMOUS FAMILIAR
LUTULENT MOTHERED
(— WITH SMOKE) SMUDGY
(SHORT AND —) SQUAT
(11 POINTS —) HEAVY
(PREF.) CRASSI DASI DASY
HADR(O) PACHY ULO
(— WITH HAIR) DASI DASY
THICKEN GEL BODY CLOT FULL
BREAK KEECH LITHE DEEPEN
HARDEN ENGROSS STIFFEN
(— HEDGE) PLASH
THICKENED BODIED BULLED
FURRED CALLOUS CLUBBED
SPISSATED
THICKENER NAPALM
THICKENING FALX LEAR ROUX
SWELL CALLUS CLAVATE LIAISON
PLACODE ATHEROMA CLUBBING
CRASSULA PYCNOSIS EPHIPPIUM
(— OF COAL SEAM) SWELLY
(— OF LETTER STROKE) STRESS
THICKET COP BOSK RONE SHAG
SHAW BLUFF BRAKE CLUMP
COPSE COVER DROKE HEDGE
QUICK SHOLA SLICK THICK
BOSKET BUSHET COVERT GREAVE
JUNGLE MALLEE QUEACH SPINNY
BOSCAGE BOSQUET BRUSHET
COPPICE CORYLET SPINNEY
WOODRIS CHAMISAL FERNSHAW
QUICKSET SHINNERY THICKSET
SALICETUM
THICKHEADED DULL DENSE
THICKHEADED FLY CONOPID
THICK-KNEE CURLEW DIKKOP
BUSTARD
THICKLY STEFLY
THICKNESS PLY BODY LAYER
DIAMETER
(— OF CHIP) CUT FEED
(— OF CLOTH) LAY
(— OF METAL) GRIP
(— OF PAPER) BULK CALLIPER
UNDERLAY
(ONE — OVER ANOTHER) LAYER
(SECOND —) DOUBLING
THICKSET STUB BEEFY PUNCH
SQUAT STOUT THICK CHUMPY
CHUNKY HUMPTY PLUGGY
ROBUST STOCKY STUBBY STUGGY
NUGGETY SQUATTY
THIEF GUN NIP PAD CHOR GILT
LIFT MILL PRIG BUDGE CREEP
CROOK FAKER GANEF PIKER
SNEAK TAKER TILER ANGLER
BULKER CANNON CLOYER DISMAS
GONOPH HOOKER KALLAN LIFTER
MICHER NIMMER NIPPER PICKER

PIRATE RATERO ROBBER SNATCH
TOSHER WASTER BOOSTER
COLLERY FOOTMAN GORILLA
GRIFTER HARRIER HEISTER
LADRONE LURCHER MEECHER
MERCURY PRIGGER PRIGMAN
PROLLER PROWLER SNAPPER
SPOTTER STEALER THIEVER
CLYFAKER CONVEYER CUTPURSE
FINGERER HARROWER LARCENER
PETERMAN PICAROON PICKLOCK
PILFERER PRIGSTER SNATCHER
(— AT A MINE) CAVER
(CATTLE —) ABACTOR BLOTTER
PLANTER RUSTLER
(CLEVER —) KID CANNON
(CRUCIFIED) DISMAS
(FLASHY —) KIDDY
(MOUNTAIN —) CHOAR
(NIGHT —) SCOURER
(PETTY —) HOOKER SLOCKER
(RIVER —) ACKMAN LUMPER
(SNEAK —) LURCHER
(VAGABOND —) WASTER
(WHARF —) TOSHER
(PREF.) KLEPT(O)
(SUFF.) KLEPT
THIEVE MAG NIM
THIEVERY PRIGGERY
THIEVING LAW SHARK PUGGING
PROGGERY STEALING
THIEVING MAGPIE, THE
(CHARACTER IN —) NINETTA
PODESTA GIANETTO
(COMPOSER OF —) ROSSINI
THIEVISH STEALY FURTIVE
KLEPTIC SCADDLE PRIGGISH
THIEVISHNESS PRIGGISM
THIGH HAM HOCK FEMUR FLANK
GAMMON
(— PAIN) MERALGIA
(PREF.) CRURO FEMORO MER(O)
(SUFF.) MERUS
THILL FILL SILL BLADE SHAFT
LIMBER
THIMBLE SKEIN BUSHEL GOBLET
SLEEVE CRINGLE
THIMBLEBERRY MULBERRY
THIN HOE LEW BONY FINE FLUE
FUSE LANK LEAN LIMP PRIN RARE
SLIM WEAK WHEY EXILE FRAIL
GAUNT GAUZY LATHY PEAKY
SHEER SLINK SMALL SPARE
SWAMP THIRL WASHY WIZEN
AERIAL BLASHY DILUTE FLUTED
HOLLOW MAUGER MEAGER
MEAGRE PEAKED SCRANK SEROSE
SEROUS SHELLY SKINNY SLEAZY
SLIGHT SPINNY SUBTLE TENDER
TWIGGY WATERY WEAKEN
COVERED FOLIOUS FRAGILE
GRACILE HAGGARD SANIOUS
SCRAGGY SCRAILY SCRANKY
SCRAWNY SHALLOW SHILPIT
SLENDER SPIDERY SPINDLY
TENUOUS THREADY ARANEOUS
CACHETIC EGGSHELL HAIRLINE
ICHOROUS MACILENT SCRAGGED
SCRANNEL SKINKING VAPORISH
WATERISH ATTENUATE
SPINDLING
(— AND PINCHED) CHITTY
(— LEATHER) DOLE

(— OUT) HOE CHOP DISBUD
FEATHER
(— SEEDLINGS) SINGLE
(— THE WALLS) IRON
(PREF.) AREO LEPT(O) MANO
TENUI
THINE TUUM
THING JOB RES BABY ITEM SORT
WHAT CHEAT CHOSE AFFAIR
ANIMAL DINGUS FELLOW GILGUY
MATTER ARTICLE DINGBAT
MINIKIN SHEBANG WHATNOT
THINGLET
(— DONE) FACT ACTUS
(— FOUND) TROVE
(— OF LITTLE ACCOUNT) GEWGAW
(OF LITTLE VALUE) NIFLE TRIFLE
TRINKET
(— OF LITTLE WORTH) STIVER
(— TO BE REGRETTED) DAMAGE
(— TO EXHIBIT) BRAVERY
(—S PROHIBITED) VETANDA
(ANOTHER —) ALIUD
(CONSECRATED —) ANATHEMA
(CORRECT —) CHEESE
(ENORMOUS —) MONSTER
(ENTIRE —) INTEGRAL
(EXTRAORDINARY —) ONER
(FAIR —) POTATO
(FIT —) CHECKER
(GOOD —) WELFARE
(HOLY —) HAGIA KODASHIM
(IMPORTANT —) ACE
(INSIGNIFICANT —) SCRAT
(INSIGNIFICANT —S) SMATTER
(JEWISH —) JUDAICA
(LITTLE —S) FEWTRILS
(LIVING —S) BIOTA
(MISSHAPEN —) ABORTION
(NEW —) NEWEL
(OUTMODED —) SNUFF
(PETTY —) SHABBLE
(PRECIOUS —) JEWEL
(PRECISE —) POINT
(RIDICULOUS —) MONUMENT
(RIGHT —) POTATO
(ROTTEN —) ROTTOCK
(SAD —) RUTH
(SILLY —) TRIMTRAM
(SINGLE —) UNIT
(SMALL —) SNIPPET
(STRAY —) WAIF
(STUNTED —) SCRUNT SNEESHIN
(SURE —) CERT SNIP
(TERRIFYING —) BOGEYMAN
(UNEXPECTED —) GODSEND
(UNIQUE —) ONER UNICUM
(UNREAL —) NOMINAL
(UNSPECIFIED —S) JAZZ
(UNSUBSTANTIAL —) PUFF
(WORLDLY —S) EARTH
(WORNOUT —) SNUFF HUSHEL
(PL.) GEAR REALIA SQUARES
(PREF.) REI
(SUFF.) ORIUM ORY SOME
(— USED) ANT
(— USED FOR) ORIUM
THINGAMY DOODAD
THING-IN-ITSELF THINGY
NOUMENON
THINGS
(SUFF.) IA
THINGUMBOB DODAD DOODAD

JIGGER THINGUM
THINK LET SEE WIS WIT DEEM
FEEL HOLD MAKE MEAN MINT
MULL MUSE READ TROW WEEN
ALLOW CENSE FANCY GUESS
JUDGE LOUSE OPINE PANSE
SEPAD ESTEEM EXPECT FIGURE
IDEATE RECKON REPUTE BELIEVE
CONCEIT IMAGINE REFLECT
SUPPOSE COGITATE CONSIDER
ENVISAGE
(— BEST) SEEM
(— HARD) YFRK
(— OF) MIND PURPENSE
(— OF AS) ACCOUNT
(— OVER) BETHINK
(— UP) INVENT
(— UPON) BROOD
(— WELL OF) APPROVE
THINKER SOPHIST PHILOSOPH
PHILOSOPHER
(CHINESE —) LEGALIST
THINKING CONCEIT THOUGHT
(CLEVER —) HEADWORK
THINLY AIRILY SPARSE SPARSELY
THINNESS RARITY EXILITY FINESSE
TENUITY EXIGUITY
THINNING BALK BAULK PINCH
CLEANING
THIOL MERCAPTAN
THIRD FACE GAMMA TERCE THREE
DITONE TERTIA TIERCE
(PREF.) TRIT(O)
THIRDLY TERTIO
THIRD-RATE C3 HEDGE
THIRD RATEN PIKER
THIRST DRY ADRY CLEM DRYTH
APOSIA DROUTH THRIST
DROUGHT DIPSOSIS POLYDIPSIA
(PREF.) DIPS(O)
THIRSTING SITIENT
THIRSTY DRY ADRY ATHIRST
DROUGHTY
THIS HE SO THIK THILK
THIS ABOVE ALL (AUTHOR OF —)
KNIGHT
(CHARACTER IN —) PRUE CLIVE
MONTY BRIGGS CATHAWAY
PRUDENCE
THISTLE PUHA HOYLE CARDON
DASHEL DINDLE FISTLE TEASEL
CALTROP CARDUUS CARLINA
GUTWEED RAURIKI WARATAH
BEDEGUAR CALTHROP COMPOSIT
ECHINOPS MILKWEED
(PREF.) CARDO
THITHER TO YON YOND THERE
YONDER ULTERIOR YONDWARD
THOAS (BROTHER OF —) EUNEUS
(DAUGHTER OF —) HYPSIPYLE
(FATHER OF —) BACCHUS
ANDRAEMON
(MOTHER OF —) GORGE ARIADNE
HYPSIPYLE
(SON OF —) SICINUS
(WIFE OF —) MYRINE
THOMIST AQUINIST
THOMSONITE MESOLE MESOTYPE
OZARKITE
THONG LORE RIEM BRAIL GIRTH
LASSO LEASH ROMAL STRAP
THUNK WHANG WHANK LACING
LINGEL STRING TWITCH

AMENTUM BABICHE LANIARD LANYARD LATCHET RIEMPIE
(— ON JAVELIN) AMENTUM
(HAWK'S —) BRAIL
(PREF.) HIMANTO

THOR THUNAR THUNOR
(FATHER OF —) ODIN
(HAMMER OF —) MJOLLNIR
(MOTHER OF —) JORDH

THORACIC DORSAL

THORAX CHEST TRUNK BREAST PEREION ALITRUNK CORSELET FOREBODY

THORITE ENALITE ORANGITE

THORN BROD BUSH GOAD PIKE STOB STUG BRIAR BRIER DOORN PRICK SPIKE SPINE FUSTIC JAGGER ACANTHA PRICKER STICKER COCKSPUR THORNLET
(PL.) SPEAR HAYBOTE
(PREF.) ACANTH(O) SPINI SPINO(SO) SPINULI SPINULOSO
(SUFF.) ACANTHUS SPINOSE

THORN APPLE HAW METEL STAMONY

THORNBACK RAY DORN ROKER

THORNBILL TOMTIT

THORNY HARD SPINY PRICKLY SCROGGY SPINOUS THISTLY THORNED

THORON RADON

THOROUGH RUN DEEP FIRM FULL SOUND ERRANT HOLLOW STRICT HOTSHOT INGOING REGULAR COMPLETE GROUNDLY INTIMATE PRECIOUS

THOROUGHBRED HOTBLOOD

THOROUGHFARE BUND DRUM ROAD ALLEY AVENUE STREET BIKEWAY HIGHWAY PARKWAY WHITEHALL

THOROUGHGOING PAKKA ARRANT ERRANT HEARTY PROPER PUREDEE RADICAL ABSOLUTE PROFOUND TRUEBRED

THOROUGHLY BUT FULL GOOD INLY CLEAN FULLY PROOF DEEPLY GAINLY KINDLY PROPER RICHLY RIPELY WHOLLY ROUNDLY SOAKING SOBBING SOGGING SOUNDLY DRIPPING GROUNDLY HEARTILY INWARDLY
(PREF.) E

THOROUGHWORT BONESET

THOSE THEM THEY YOND

THOTH DHOUTI

THOUGH AS AND SET YET ALTHO ALTHOUGH

THOUGHT CARE IDEA MOOD VIEW FANCY TASTE TRACE NOTION PENSEE CONCEIT CONCEPT COUNSEL OPINION SURMISE PEMMICAN RUMINATE
(— OUT) ADVISED
(CAREFUL —) ADVICE ACCOUNT
(FANCIFUL —) CONCEIT
(HIGHEST —) IDEE
(REASONED —) STUDY
(UNCLEAN —) SEWERAGE
(WELL-EXPRESSED —) STROKE
(PREF.) LOG(O)

THOUGHTFUL EARNEST PENSIVE SERIOUS STUDIED STUDIOUS THOUGHTY

THOUGHTFULNESS GRACE COUNSEL

THOUGHTLESS RASH VAIN DIZZY GLAKY SUPINE VACANT ETOURDI GLAIKET RAMSTAM HEEDLESS RECKLESS

THOUSAND CHI MIL GRAND MILLE CHILIAD
(FIVE —) EPSILON
(SIX —) DIGAMMA
(TEN —) TOMAN
(10 —) MYRIAD
(100 —) LAC LAKH
(PREF.) CHILI(A) KILO MILLE MILLI
(TEN —) MYRIA MYRIO

THOUSANDTH (— OF CUBIC CENTIMETER) LAMBDA
(— OF INCH) MIL
(HUNDRED —) SSU
(PREF.) MILLI

THRACIAN GETE GETAN GETIC THRAX

THRALL SERF GURTH SLAVE CAPTIVE

THRALLDOM BONDAGE SLAVERY THIRLAGE

THRASH DAD LAM PAY TAN BANG BEAT BELT COMB DING DRUB DUST FLAX JERK LACE LICK LOUK MILL PAIL SOCK SOLE SOWL SWAP SWOP TOSE TRIM WALK WHAP WHIP WHOP YERK BASTE BELAM BLESS CURRY DRASH FLAIL FRAIL LINCH LINGE NOINT PASTE SLATE SLOSH SWACK SWING TABOR TARGE THUMP TOWEL TWINK WHALE WHANG ANOINT BUMFEG CUDGEL FETTLE JACKET LARRUP LATHER MUZZLE RADDLE STOUSH SWINGE TANCEL THREAP THRESH THWACK WALLOP LAMBACK LEATHER SWADDLE TROLLOP TROUNCE BETHWACK BUMBASTE LAMBASTE LAMBSKIN RIBROAST SPIFLICATE

THRASHER THREAPER THRESHER SICKLEBILL

THRASHING TOCO WIPING BELTING LAMMING LICKING WARMING WHALING DRUBBING

THRASYMEDES (FATHER OF —) NESTOR
(MOTHER OF —) ANAXIBIA

THREAD BAR END BAVE CHIP CLEW CLUE CORD DOUP FILE FILM GIMP GOLD LACE LINE POIL PURL ROON SILK TRAM WIRE WORM BRIDE CHIVE FIBER FIBRE FLOAT FLOSS HYPHA INKLE REEVE SCREW SETON SHIVE SHOOT SHUTE STEEK THRUM TWEER TWIRE TWIST WATAP BOTTOM COBWEB COTTON ENFILE FIBRIL INFILE SINGLE STAMEN STITCH STRAIN STRAND STRING TISSUE BABICHE BASTING DOUPING SLUBBER SPIREME TWITTER WARPING ACONTIUM FILAMENT GOSSAMER LIGATURE PICKOVER RAVELING SPINNING SPIRICLE

(— AROUND BOWSTRING) SERVING
(— IN SEED COATING) SPIRICLE
(— LEGS OF RABBIT) HARL HARLE
(— OF SCREW) WORM
(— OF WAX) SWARF
(— USED FOR COCOON) BAVE
(—S THAT CROSS WARP) WEFT WOOF
(BADLY TWINED —) SLUBBER
(BALL OF —) CLEW CLUE CLOWE GLOME
(BUTTONHOLE —S) BAR
(COARSE —) GIRD
(COARSEST — IN LACE) GIMP
(COILED —) COP
(FILLING —) PICK
(FLOATING —) PICKOVER
(HARD —) LISLE
(LINEN —) LINE INCLE INKLE
(LOOSELY TWISTED —S) BUMP
(METAL —) LAME WIRE
(OAKUM —) PLEDGET
(PULLED —) SNAG
(REFUSE —S) BUR BURR
(SHOEMAKER'S —) END LINGEL LINGLE
(SILK —) TRAM TRAME DOUPIONI
(SOFT SHORT —) THRUM
(STRONG —) GOUNAU
(SURGICAL —) SETON
(WARP —) END STAMEN
(WAXED —) TACKER
(WEFT —) PICK SHOT
(40 —S) BEER BIER
(PL.) FLOSS
(PREF.) FILI(CI) MIT(O) NEM(A)(O) NEMAT(O) STAMIN(I)
(SUFF.) NEMA NEME STEMONOUS

THREADBARE BARE SEAR SERE TRITE PILLED SHABBY NAPLESS

THREADFIN SEER SEIR SULEA BARBUDO KINGFISH SEERFISH

THREADFISH COBBLER SUNFISH

THREADING SCREW STRINGING

THREADLIKE FILATE FILOSE

THREADWORK MACRAME

THREAT ATTACK MENACE THUNDER
(PL.) MINES

THREATEN BRAG FACE MINT BOAST SHORE ATTACK IMPEND MENACE ENDANGER MINATORY OVERHANG
(— TO RAIN) SCOUTHER

THREATENED FRAUGHT

THREATENING BIG GLUM UGLY ANGRY BOAST SABLE GREASY BANEFUL BODEFUL OMINOUS RAMPANT MINATORY MINITANT MINACIOUS
(— TO RAIN) HEAVY

THREE TREY GIMEL LEASH TRIAS TERNARY TERNION
(— CENT PIECE) TRIME
(— IN ONE) TRIUNE
(— MILES) LEAGUE
(— OF A KIND) GLEEK BRELAN TRIPLET
(GROUP OF —) TRIO TRIAD TRIPLE TROIKA
(SET OF —) PAIRIAL
(PREF.) TER TERNATI TERNATO TRE TRI(S)

(— DIMENSIONS) STERE(O)
(SUFF.) TERNATE

THREE BLACK PENNIES (AUTHOR OF —) HERGESHEIMER
(CHARACTER IN —) HOWAT JAMES PENNY SUSAN EUNICE JANNAN JASPER POLDER BRUNDON MARIANA LUDOWIKA WINSCOMBE

THREE-CORNERED HAT (AUTHOR OF —) ALARCON
(CHARACTER IN —) LUCAS WEASEL EUGENIO MERCEDES FRASQUITA

THREE-DIMENSIONAL CUBIC CUBICAL

THREEFOLD TERN TRINE TERNAL TREBLE TRINAL TRIPLE TERNARY TRIFOLD TRIPLEX THRIBBLE

THREE-FORKED TRISULC

THREE MUSKETEERS (AUTHOR OF —) DUMAS
(CHARACTER IN —) ATHOS ARAMIS WARDES PORTHOS DEWINTER PLANCHET BONACIEUX CONSTANCE DARTAGNAN RICHELIEU

THREEPENCE JOEY TREY THRIP THRUM TICKEY TICKIE

THREE SISTERS (AUTHOR OF —) CHEKHOV
(CHARACTER IN —) OLGA IRINA MASHA ANDREY SOLENI KULIGIN NATASHA PROSOROV VERSHININ

THREE SOLDIERS (AUTHOR OF —) DOSPASSOS
(CHARACTER IN —) DAN RED ANDY JOHN MABE YVONNE ANDREWS FUSELLI ANDERSON GENEVIEVE CHRISTFIELD

THRENODY DIRGE HEARSE THRENE

THRESH COB BEAT CAVE LUMP WHIP BERRY FLAIL FRAIL SPELT STAMP THRASH

THRESHEL DRASHEL

THRESHER TASKER

THRESHER SHARK FOX FOXFISH WHIPTAIL

THRESHOLD HEAD SILL SOLE DEARN LIMEN DRASHEL DOORSILL

THRIFT SAVING VIRTUE ECONOMY STATICE THEEDOM PARSIMONY

THRIFTILY NEAR

THRIFTLESS WASTEFUL

THRIFTY CANNY FENDY PUIST FRUGAL SAVING CAREFUL SPARING

THRILL JAG BANG DIRL GIRL KICK FLUSH SHOOT THIRL DINDLE STOUND TICKLE TINGLE TREMOR ENCHANT FRISSON VIBRATE FREMITUS
(PROVIDING A —) KICKY
(SHARP —) ZING

THRILLING TINGLY VIBRANT PLANGENT TINGLING

THRINTER FRONTER

THRIPID PHYSOPOD

THRIPS BLACKFLY PHYSOPOD

THRIVE DOW GROW LIKE RISE

THEE ADDLE FADGE MOISE PROVE THRAM BATTEN BATTLE CATTER CHIEVE PROSPER STORKEN SUCCEED WELFARE FLOURISH THRODDEN
(— IN) LOVE
THRIVING BIEN GRUSHIE ROARING THRIFTY BLOOMING TOWARDLY
THRIVINGLY GAILY GAYLY BRAVELY
THROAT MAW CRAG CROP GOWL GULA HALS HASS LANE GORGE HALSE SWIRE FAUCES GARGET GULLET GUTTUR GUZZLE RICTUS CHANNEL JUGULUM STOMACH SWALLOW WEASAND THRAPPLE THROPPLE THROTTLE
(— OF ANCHOR) CLUTCH
(— OF COROLLA) FAUCES
(— OF FROG) KNEE
(MOUTH AND —) WHISTLE
(SORE —) HOUSTY PRUNELLA
(PREF.) BRONCH(I)(IO)(O) DER(O) GUTTERO
THROATLATCH FIADOR
THROATY THICK GUTTURAL
THROB ACHE BEAT BELK DRUM DUNT LEAP PANT QUOP WARK FLACK PULSE STANG WARCH STOUND STRIKE STROKE TINGLE WALLOP FLACKER PULSATE VIBRATE FLICHTER PALPITATE
(— IN PAIN) SHOOT
(RAPID —S) FRIMITTS
THROBBING DUNT ATHROB THRILL BEATING PITAPAT VIBRANT PULSATORY
THROE PANG PULL STOUR SHOWER PAROXYSM
(—S OF DEATH) AGONY
THROMBIN PLASMASE
THROMBOPLASTIN COAGULIN CYTOZYME
THROMBOSIS SHOCK CORONARY
THRONE GADI SEAT ASANA GADDI GADHI SELLE SIEGE STALL STATE STEAD STOOL MUSNUD SEGGIO SHINZA TRIBUNE CATHEDRA SEGGIOLA SINHASAN
(BISHOP'S —) SEE APSE CATHEDRA
THRONE ROOM AIWAN
THRONG CREW HEAP HOST ROUT CHIRT CROWD FLOCK FRACK POSSE PRESS SHOAL SWARM RESORT THRAVE THREAT THRIMP THRUST COMPANY TEMPEST THRUTCH SURROUND
(— OF SEAFOWL) SAVSSAT
(CONFUSED —) LURRY
THRONGED ALIVE FREQUENT NUMEROUS
THROTTLE GUN CHOKE SCRAG STIFLE GARROTE STRANGLE THROPPLE
THROUGH BY PER DONE THRU WITH ROUND AROUND
(RIGHT —) TILL
(PREF.) DIA PER
THROUGHOUT OVER ABOUT ROUND ABROAD BEDENE BIDENE DURING ENTIRE PASSIM SEMPRE OVERALL THRUOUT
(PREF.) HOL(O)

THROW GO DAB DAD HIP HIT PAT PEG PUT SHY ACES BIFF BUCK BUNG CALE CAST CHIP CLOD COOK CUCK DART DASH DROW HAIL HANK HIPE HULL HURL HYPE JERK LACE MILL PECK PICK PURL SEND SKIM SLAT SOSS TOSS TURF VANG WARP WURP YEND CHUCK CHUNK DOUSE FLICK FLING FLIRT FLURR HEAVE PITCH SLING SPANG DEVEST ELANCE HAUNCH HURTLE INJECT LAUNCH SLIGHT THRILL BLUNDER BUTTOCK COCKSHY MANGANA UPTHROW VIBRATE CATAPULT JACULATE
(— A BASEBALL PITCH) HANG
(— ABOUT) BOUNCE
(— ASIDE) DEVEST
(— AWAY) DICE DOFF BANDY WAIVE PROJECT JETTISON SQUANDER
(— BASEBALL) BURN
(— BY KICKING) WINCE
(— CARELESSLY) COB
(— DICE) JEFF
(— DOWN) DUSH EVEN PILE FLUMP LODGE ABJECT DETURB THRING FLATTEN
(— FORTH) EJECT
(— FORWARD) LAUNCH
(— HEAVILY) LOB
(— HEEDLESSLY) SLIGHT
(— IN CRAPS) CRAP PASS CRABS BOXCARS NATURAL
(— INTO CONFUSION) CLUB FLUTTER CONFOUND CONVULSE
(— INTO DISORDER) PIE ADDLE BOLLIX DERANGE DISRANK DISRUPT EMBROIL DISARRAY
(— INTO PERPLEXITY) FLUMMOX
(— INTO WASTE) BACK
(— JERKILY) FLIRT
(— LIGHT UPON) ILLUME
(— LIQUID) JAW
(— OF A STEER) DOGFALL
(— OF SHUTTLE) SHOT SHOOT SHUTE
(— OF THREES) COCKEYES
(— OFF) CANT CAST SLIRT SPILL SLOUGH CONFUSE UNBURDEN
(— OFF COURSE) EMIT SHED DERAIL
(— ONESELF) CLAP
(— OPEN) DISPARK
(— OUT) FIRE HOOF LADE BELCH EJECT ERUPT SPOUT DETURB IGNORE EXTRUDE
(— QUICKLY) LASH
(— SIDEWISE) SHY
(— SILK) THROWST
(— SMARTLY) SLAT
(— STEER) BUST
(— STICKS) SQUAIL
(— STONES) ROCK
(— TOGETHER) HUDDLE
(— UNDER) SUBJECT
(— UP) BARF CAVE PICK VOMIT
(— VIOLENTLY) BUZZ DING PASH SOCK WHAP WHOP SMASH HURTLE WUTHER WHITHER SPANGHEW PRECIPITATE
(— WITH A JERK) JET CANT

SQUIRR FLOUNCE
(— WITH GREAT FORCE) BUZZ SWACK
(— WITHOUT VIOLENCE) HURL
(CHEATING — OF DICE) KNAP
(FOOTBALL —) GROUND
(FREE —) FOUL
(LARIAT —) HOOLIAN
(LOWEST — AT DICE) AMBSACE AMESACE
(WRESTLING —) HANK HIPE HYPE BUTTOCK BACKHEEL
(SUFF.) JECT
THROWAWAY DODGER
THROWBACK ATAVISM
THROWER TRAMMER THROWSTER
(SPEAR —) ATLATL
THROWING DARTING
THROWING-STICK ATLATL WOMMERA WOOMERA HORNERAH TROMBASH TRUMBASH
THROWN (— AWAY) CASTAWAY
(— DOWN) DEJECTED
(PREF.) BLED
(— OUT) RHIPTO
THROWSTER TWISTER
THRUM FUM STRUM THUMB
THRUSH POP OMAO SOOR APTHA BREVE FRUSH GRIVE MAVIS OUZEL PITTA SABIA SHAMA SHIRL SPREW UZZLE VEERY APHTHA DRAINE JAYPIE KICKUP MISSEL OLOMAO PULISH SHRITE JAYPIET REDWING WAGTAIL BELLBIRD CHERCOCK FORKTAIL PRUNELLA SHAGBARK THRASHER THROSTLE THRUSHEL THRUSTLE URTICATE WOODCHAT SOLITAIRE MONILIASIS NIGHTINGALE
THRUSHLIKE TURDOID
THRUST DAB DEG DIG DUB JAB JAG JAM JOB POP PUG BANG BEAR BIRR BOKE BORE BUCK BUTT CANT CHOP CRAM DART DASH DUSH FOIN HURL KICK LICK MURE PASS PICK PILT POKE PORR POSS POTE PROD PUSH SEND SINK SPAR STAB STOP TILT VENY WHAP WHOP BREAK DRIFT DRIVE EXERT HUNCH LUNGE POACH POINT PROKE PUNCH SHOOT SPANK STAVE STICK STOKE STUFF THROW DARTLE PLUNGE POUNCE STITCH STRAIN STRESS STRIKE STRIPE BEARING IMPULSE PRESSURE SHOULDER STOCCADO
(— A LANCE) AVENTRE
(— ASIDE) DAFF SHUFFLE
(— AWAY) DOFF SHOVE DETRUDE ABSTRUDE
(— DOWN) THRING DEPULSE DETRUDE
(— IN) INSERT STRIKE INTRUDE
(— OF ARCH) DRIFT
(— OF EXPLOSION) BLOWOUT
(— ONESELF) CHISEL
(— OUT) POUT REACH STRUT EXSERT DETRUDE EXTRUDE OBTRUDE PROTRUDE OBTRUSIVE
(— SUDDENLY) STRIKE
(— THROUGH) ENFILED

(— WITH ELBOW) HUNCH
(— WITH GREAT FORCE) BUZZ
(— WITH NOSE) NUDDLE
(— WITH WEAPON) FOIN SHOVE
(DAGGER —) DAG
(FENCING —) PASS VENY BOTTE PUNTO VENUE REPOST TIMING PASSADO RIPOSTE STOCCADO STOCCATA
(HOME —) HAI HAY
(MATADOR'S —) ESTOCADA
(SARCASTIC —) GIRD
THUD BAFF DUMP PHUT PLOD SWAG DOYST FLUMP POUND BOUNCE SQUELCH
THUG MUG GOON GOONDA RODMAN GORILLA HOODLUM GANGSTER
THUJA BIOTA
THUJONE SALVIOL
THULUTH SOOLOOS
THUMB THOOM POLLEX THENAR
(BALL OF —) THENAR
THUMBSTALL POUCER POUSER
THUMP COB DAD DUB BANG BEAT BLOW BUMP DING DIRD DRUB DUNT KNUB LUMP PAIK PAKE POLT SOSS THUD TUND TUNK YARK YERK BLAFF BLIBE BUNCH CLOUR CLUNK CRUMP KNOCK POUND TABOR THACK WHELK BOUNCE HAMMER PUMMEL THUNGE
THUMPING WHAPPING WHOPPING
THUNDER SUI FUR BRATTLE FOULDRE SULPHUR INTONATE
(PREF.) BRONT(E)(O) CERAUN(O) KERAUN(O)
THUNDERBOLT BOLT FIRE VAJRA FULMEN FOULDRE ARTIFACT FIREBOLT
(PREF.) CERAUN(O) KERAUN(O)
THUNDERING TONANT
THUNDERSQUALL BAYAMO VENDAVAL
THUNDERSTONE ARTIFACT
THUNDERSTORM HOUVARI TEMPEST TORNADO
THURIBLE CENSER
THUS AS SIC DYCE THUSLY THISWISE THUSGATE
THWACK BLOW DUNT CRUMP SOUSE
THWART BALK WART BENCH CROOK CROSS SPITE THRAW THROW ZYGON BAFFLE SCOTCH STYMIE SNOOKER CONTRAIR CONTRARY TRAVERSE
THWARTING CROSS CROSSING
THYESTES (BROTHER OF —) ATREUS
(FATHER OF —) PELOPS
(MOTHER OF —) HIPPODAMIA
THYIA (FATHER OF —) CASTALIUS CEPHISSEUS
(SON OF —) DELPHUS
THYINE THUGA THUYA
THYLACINE YABBI
THYME MARUM PELETRE HILLWORT SERPOLET
TI KI TOI TITI
TIAMAT (HUSBAND OF —) APSU
(SLAYER OF —) MARDUK
TIARA MITER REGNUM

CIDARIS TIARELLA
TIBBU DAZA TEDA

TIBET
CAPITAL: LASSA LHASA
COIN: TANGA
LAKE: ARU BAM BUM NAM MEMA
TOSU JAGOK TABIA DAGTSE
GARHUR KASHUN SELING
TANGRA YAMDOK KYARING
TERINAM TSARING ZILLING
JIGGITAI
LANGUAGE: BODSKAD
MOUNTAIN: KAMET SAJUM KAILAS
BANDALA
MOUNTAIN RANGE: KAILAS
KUNLUN HIMALAYA
NATIVE: BHOTIA BHOTIYA
RIVER: NAK NAU SAK SONG INDUS
SUTLEJ MATSANG SALWEEN
TOWN: NOH KARAK LHASA
GARTOK TOTLING GYANGTSE
SHIGATSE

TIBETAN BALTI DRUPA BHOTIA
BHUTIA CHAMPA DROKPA
KHAMBA KHAMBU PANAKA
SHERPA TANGUT BHOTIYA
BHUTANI GYARUNG
TIBIA SHIN SHANK CNEMIS
SHINBONE
(SUFF.) CNEMA CNEMIA CNEMIC
CNEMUS
TIBOURBOU CORTEZ
TIC FIXATION
(ONE SUBJECT TO —) TIQUEUR
TICAL BAHT
TICK FAG JAR KEB KED BEAT KADE
NICK PEAK PICK PIKE CHALK
CHICK CRIKE PIQUE STRAP
ACARID IXODID PALLET TALAJE
TAMPAN ACARIAN ARGASID
BEDTICK IXODIAN PINOLIA
ARACHNID CARAPATO GARAPATA
GARAPATO TURICATA
(PREF.) ACAR(I)(O) CROTO
TICKED MACKEREL
TICKET LOT TAG BLANK CHECK
DUCAT FICHE TOKEN BALLOT
BILLET COUPON DOCKET PIGEON
POLICY RETURN BENEFIT ETIQUET
CONTRACT DEADHEAD STOPOVER
TRANSFER PASTEBOARD
(COMMISSION —) SPIFF
(FREE —) PASS
(LOTTERY —) BLANK HORSE
BENEFIT
(SALES —) TRAVELER
(SEASON —) IVORY
(PL.) PAPER
TICKET WINDOW GUICHET
TICKING KISS TICK BEDTICK
TICKLE AMUSE TEASE EXCITE
KITTLE PLEASE THRILL TIDDLE
CUITTLE
TICKLISH GOOSEY KITTLE KITTLY
QUEASY TENDER TOUCHY TRICKY
KITTLISH
TICKSEED COREOPSIS
TICK TREFOIL BEDSTRAW
SAINFOIN TICKSEED
TIDBIT NOSH SAYNETE BEATILLE
KICKSHAW

TIDDLEYWINK SQUAIL
TIDE FLOW NEAP WAVE AGGER
ROUST SPRING OVERTIDE
SEAFLOOD
(— MOVEMENT) LAKIE
(PREF.) (HIGH —) PLEMYRA
TIDINGS NEWS WORD RUMOR
SOUND UNCOW ADVICE MESSAGE
(GLAD —) GOSPEL
TIDY RID COSH MACK NEAT SIDE
SMUG SNOD SNUG TAUT TOSH
TRIG WEME CHART DONCY
DONSY DOUCE NATTY NIFTY
QUEME TIGHT DONSIE FETTLE
POLITE SPOONY ORDERLY
ALLIGATE MACKLIKE MENSEFUL
SHIPSHAPE
TIE BOW LAP TYE BAND BEND BIND
BOND CAST DRAW KILT KNOT
LACE LOCK ROOT WISP YOKE
ASCOT BRACE CADGE LEASH
NEXUS POINT THRAP THROW
TRICE TRUSS ATTACH BUNDLE
CONNEX COPULA COUPLE
FASTEN LIGATE SECURE DOGFALL
FOULARD JAZZBOW NECKTIE
SHACKLE SLEEPER SPANCEL
TABLEAU CROSSTIE INTERTIE
LIGATURE STANDOFF STRINGER
VINCULUM
(— BENEATH) SUBNECT
(— IN TENNIS) DEUCE
(— IN WRESTLING) DOGFALL
(— KNOT) CAST
(— LEGS) HOBBLE
(— ONIONS) TRACE
(— SCORE) PEELS
(— THE SCORE) EQUALIZE
(— TOGETHER) KNIT LEASH
HARNESS
(— UP) SNUB TRAMMEL LIGATURE
TWITCHEL
(— UP SHORT) SNUB
(LEATHER —) WANTY
(MADE-UP —) TECK
(NEEDLEWORK —) BRIDE
(PL.) GILLIES
TIED EVEN FAST KNIT SQUARE
TIEPIN PROP SCARFPIN STICKPIN
TIE PLATE TURTLE
TIER ROW BANK DECK RANK CHESS
STORY WITHE DEGREE PINAFORE
(— OF CASKS) RIDER
(— OF SEATS) CIRCLE
(— OF SHELVES) STAGE
TIERCE LEASH THIRD UNDERSONG
TIFF MIFF SPAT TIFT
TIFFIN CONDOR
TIGER SHER SHIR TIGRE TIGERKIN
(PREF.) TIGRO
TIGER CAT CHATI MARGAY
TIGERFOOT IPOMOEA
TIGER SNAKE ELAPID ELAPOID
TIGHT WET FULL HARD PANG
SNUG TAUT TIDY TRIG CLOSE
DENSE DRUNK STENT TENSE
STINGY STRAIT STRICT AIRTIGHT
TIGHTEN JAM CALK FIRM FRAP
BRACE CAULK CINCH CLOSE
FEEZE SCREW THRAP WRENCH
STRAITEN
TIGHTFISTED NARROW STINGY
TIGHT-LIPPED SILENT

TIGHTLY FAST HARD SHORT
STRAIT CLOSELY
TIGHTS MAILLOT LEOTARDS
TIGHTWAD FIST PIKER STIFF
TIKVAH (SON OF —) SHALLUM
JAHAZIAH
TILDE TIL WAVE TITTLE
(HAVING A —) CURLY
TILE LUMP SLAT FAVUS KASHI
LATER SLATE IMBREX LAPPET
PAMENT QUARRY SLATER
TEGULA AZULEJO CARREAU
CONDUIT PANTILE QUARREL
STARTER MAINTILE
(— USED IN MOSAIC) ABACULUS
(HEXAGONAL —) FAVUS
(HOLLOW —) BACKING
(HOPSCOTCH —) PEEVER
(LARGE —) DALLE QUARL QUARLE
(MAH JONG —) HONOR SEASON
(ONE-HALF —) HEAD
(PERSIAN —) KASHI
(ROUNDED —) CREASE
(SMALL —) TILETTE
(SQUARE —) QUADREL QUARREL
(PREF.) OSTRAC(O) PLINTHI
TILER HELER HELLIER
TILL TO EAR FIT LOB CASH FARM
PLOW TEAL TOIL DRESS LABOR
UNTIL WHILE FURROW MANURE
PLOUGH TILLER WHILST
HUSBAND SHUTTLE DUCKFOOT
OXHARROW
TILLABLE EARABLE
TILLAGE GAINOR MANURE
ARATION CULTURE TILTURE
TILLED GEOM TOILED
TILLER HELM STERN STOOL
HUSBAND KILLIFER
TILLING EARTH FALLOW
TILON (FATHER OF —) SHIMON
TILT DIP TIP TOP BANK CANT CAVE
COCK HEEL LIST PEAK SWAG
TRAP BRASH HEELD HIELD JOUST
STOOP TIPUP CASTER TILTER
TOPPLE CURRENT TOURNEY
ATTITUDE COCKBILL QUINTAIN
(— BRICK) HACK
(— IN WATER) DABBLE
(— OF BOWSPRIT) STAVE
(— OF NOSE) KIP KIPP
TILTED ACOCK ASTOOP
TILT HAMMER OLIVER
TILTING DIP JOUSTING
TIMANDRA (FATHER OF —)
TYNDAREUS
(HUSBAND OF —) ECHEMUS
PHYLEUS
(MOTHER OF —) LEDA
(SISTER OF —) HELEN
CLYTEMNESTRA
TIMBAL DRUM TYMBALON
TIMBER CAP LOG RIB BEAM BIBB
BUNK BUNT CLOG DRAM FELL
FISH FROG GIRT PUMP RAFF SKID
SPAR SPUR TREE WOOD CAHUY
CAVEL CRUCK FLOOR GRIPE JOIST
KEVEL LEDGE ORGUE PLATE
RIDER SISSU SPALE STICK BEARER
BRIDGE BUMPER CAMBER CORBEL
DAGGER FENDER FOREST KNIGHT
LIZARD ROOFER SISSOO SUMMER
TIMMER BOLSTER CARLING

DEADMAN DIVIDER FALLAGE
FUTCHEL FUTTOCK GROUSER
PARTNER PITWOOD RIBBAND
TRANSOM CORDWOOD COULISSE
DOGSHORE FOREHOOK STRINGER
STUMPAGE TRIPSILL WOODFALL
(— BETWEEN TRIMMERS) HEADER
(— CUT TO LENGTH) JUGGLE
(— IN MINE) COG STULL LIFTER
DIVIDER JUGGLER
(— KEPT DRY) BRIGHT
(— ON SCAFFOLD) LIGGER PUTLOG
(— ON SLED) BUNK
(— PIECE) PUTLOG
(— SAWED AND SPLIT) LUMBER
(— SUPPORTING CAP) LEGPIECE
(— SUSTAINING YARDS) MAST
(— TO PROP COAL) BROB
(CONVEX —) CAMBER
(CURVED —) CRUCK
(CUT —) FELL
(FELLED —) HAG
(FLOOR —) JOIST SUMMER
(FLOORING —) BATTEN
(FOUNDATION —) PILE
(FRAMING —) PUNCHEON
(HORIZONTAL —) REASON
(NORWEGIAN —) DRAM
(PHILIPPINE —) LAUAN
(PRINCIPAL — OF VESSEL) KEEL
(ROOF —) LEVER RAFTER
(ROOFING —S) SILE
(SHIPBUILDING —S) STOCKS
DEADWOOD HARPINGS
(SHIP'S —) CANT KEEL KNEE RUNG
SPUR APRON LEDGE WRONG
DAGGER HARPIN LACING SCROLL
BRACKET FUTTOCK STEMSON
DOGSHORE STANDARD
(SLABBED —) CANT
(SQUARED —) BALK
(SUPPORT —) SILL GIRDER LEDGER
PUNCHEON STRINGER
(SYSTEM OF —S) BOND
(UNCUT —) STUMPAGE
(WEATHERBEATEN —) DRIKI
TIMBERLAND STICKS WOODLAND
TIMBERMAN BRACER
TIMBO CUBE AJARI
TIMBRE CLANG COLOR KLANG
COLORING
TIMBREL TABOR TABOUR
TIME DAY ELD BELL BOUT HINT
HOUR SELE SITH TIDE WHET
ABYSS CHARE EPOCH FLASH
FRIST KALPA SITHE SPACE STOUN
STOUR TEMPO TEMPS VOLTA
WHACK WHILE COURSE KAIROS
PERIOD SEASON STOUND
TEMPUS CADENCE DEWFALL
SESSION MOVEMENT
(— AFTER) POST
(— ALLOWED FOR PAYMENT)
USANCE
(— FOR PAYING) KIST
(— FOR PAYMENT) CREDIT
(— GRANTED) FRIST
(— IN SERVICE) AGE
(— INTERVAL) WINDOW
(— INTERVENING) INTERIM
MEANTIME
(— LONG SINCE PAST) YORE
(— OF BEAUTY) BLOOM

(— OF CRISIS) EXIGENT
(— OF DYING) LAST
(— OF EXPIRY) ISH
(— OF EXUBERANCE) CARNIVAL
(— OF FEASTING) GUTTIDE
(— OF HIGHEST STRENGTH) HEYDAY
(— OF LIGHT) DAY
(— OF MATURITY OR DECLINE) AUTUMN
(— OF NEWS STORY) BREAK
(— OF OLD AGE) SUNSET
(— OF QUIET) DEAD
(— OF REST) BREATH SABBATH
(— OF WOE) WOSITH
(— TO COME) FUTURITY
(ANOTHER —) AGAIN
(AT ANOTHER —) ALIAS
(BRIEF —) TINE FLASH THROW
(BY THE —) AGAINST
(EACH —) ONCE
(ENDLESS —) PERPETUITY
(EXTENDED —) TRAIN
(FIXED —) HOUR STEVEN
(FUTURE —) MANANA
(GAY —) FRISK WHOOPEE
(GOOD —) BALL BASH BEANO JOLLY BARNEY FROLIC HOLIDAY
(HARD —) GYP BUSINESS
(IMMEASURABLY LONG PERIOD OF —) EON AEON
(INFINITE —) ABYSS
(LONG —) AGE
(OLD —S) ELD
(PAST —) FORETIME
(POINT OF —) MOMENT
(QUIET —) SLACK
(RIGHT —) TID
(SECOND —) YET EFTSOON EFTSOONS
(SET —) TRYST
(SHORT —) TIFF SPACE START MINUTE STOUND
(SPARE —) TOOM LEISURE
(TRIPLE —) TRIPLA
(UNENGAGED —) LEISURE
(UNIT OF —) AEON
(WORKING —) CORE
(PL.) SYSE
(PREF.) CHRON(O) HORO
(SUFF.) AD CHRONE CHRONOUS SEMIC
TIMEAUS (SON OF —) BARTIMAEUS
TIME CLOCK BUNDY TELLTALE
TIME-HONORED VINTAGE
TIMELESS AGELESS ETERNAL DATELESS
TIMELESSNESS ETERNITY
TIMELY PAT DULY TIDY COGENT TIMEFUL TIMEOUS TOWARDLY SEASONABLE
TIME OF YOUR LIFE (AUTHOR OF —) SAROYAN
(CHARACTER IN —) JOE TOM NICK KITTY MCCARTHY
TIMEPIECE DIAL CLOCK TIMER VERGE WATCH GHURRY PENDULE HOROLOGE HOROLOGY
TIMETABLE BRADSHAW SCHEDULE
TIMID SHY ARGH EERY NESH SELY SHAN BAUCH BLATE EERIE FAINT PAVID SCARE SCARY AFRAID COWARD ASHAMED BASHFUL CHICKEN FEARFUL FRIGHTY

NERVOUS RABBITY SCADDLE STRANGE TREMBLY COWARDLY FEARSOME GHASTFUL RETIRING TIMOROSO TIMOROUS PIGEONHEARTED
TIMIDITY SHYNESS TIMERITY FUNKINESS
TIMIDLY SMALL
TIMNA (BROTHER OF —) LOTAN (LOVER OF —) ELIPHAZ (SON OF —) AMALEK
TIMOLEON (FATHER OF —) TIMODEMUS (MOTHER OF —) DEMARISTE
TIMON OF ATHENS (AUTHOR OF —) SHAKESPEARE (CHARACTER IN —) CUPID TIMON TITUS CAPHIS LUCIUS FLAVIUS PHRYNIA LUCILIUS LUCULLUS PHILOTUS TIMANDRA APEMANTUS FLAMINIUS SERVILIUS VENTIDIUS ALCIBIADES HORTENSIUS SEMPRONIUS
TIMOR (CAPITAL OF —) DILI (COIN OF —) AVO PATACA (ISLAND OF —) MOA LETI LAKOR (LANGUAGE OF —) TETUM (TOWN IN —) KUPANG ATAMBUA
TIMOROUS ASPEN FAINT MILKY TIMID AFRAID COWISH TREPID FEARFUL FERDFUL MEACOCK NERVOUS FEARSOME SHEEPISH TEMEROUS TIMOROSO
TIMOTHY (COMPANION OF —) PAUL (WIFE OF —) SIF
TIN SN DIXY JUVE DIXIE KATIN SWELL TINNY KHATIN JUPITER PILLION STANNUM PRILLION TINGLASS (MESS —) DIXY DIXIE (ROOFING —) TERNE (SHEET —) LATTEN LATTIN (TIE — CAN TO TAIL) TAILPIPE (PREF.) STANN(I)(O)
TINAMOU YUTU MACUCA YNAMBU TATAUPA MARTINET
TINCAL ALTINCAR
TINCTURE BUFO DRUG COLOR IMBUE SMACK STAIN TAINT TENNE TINCT ARGENT ARNICA ELIXIR SATURN DIAMOND SERICON ARAMAIZE INFUSION LAUDANUM TAINTURE PAREGORIC
TINDER SPUNK AMADOU TENDRE FIREBOX
TINE BAY KNAG SNAG TANG GRAIN OFFER POINT PRONG RIGHT TOOTH GRAINING TINETARE TINEWEED (ANTLER'S —) RIGHT CROCKET SURROYAL
TIN FOIL TAIN
TINGE DYE EYE HUE CAST DASH TANG TINT WOAD COLOR FLUSH IMBUE PAINT SAVOR SHADE STAIN TAINT TINCT TOUCH SEASON SMUTCH BEPAINT DISTAIN GLIMPSE DISCOLOR TINCTION TINCTURE
TINGED FLORID GILDED
TINGGIAN ITNEG ITANEG
TINGLE SOO BURN DIRL GELL GIRL

THIRL DINDLE SWIDGE TINKLE PRINGLE PRINKLE TRINKLE VIBRATE
TINKER PRIG TINK CAIRD FIDDLE FIDGET MUGGER KETTLER PROJECT TRAVELER
TINKLE TINK DINDLE DINGLE TINGLE TRINKLE TWINKLE
TINKLING THIN
TINNER TINKER
TINSEL GAUDY TINSY TINNET CLINQUANT
TINT DYE EYE COLOR ENNUE GRAIN TINCT TINGE SPRAING (— IN HORSE'S COAT) BLOSSOM (— WITH COSMETICS) SURFLE (CLANG —) TIMBRE
TINTED TINCT
TINWORKS STANNARY
TINY TINE BITSY BITTY DEENY SMALL TEENY TIDDY WEENY ATOMIC BITTIE WEESHY MINIKIN ATOMICAL
TIP CAP DIP END FEE NEB TOP APEX CANT CAVE COCK DUMP HEEL HELD HORN KEEL LEAD LIST PALM PIKE PILE SWAG TILT TYPE VAIL GRIFF HEELD MUCRO POINT POUCH SPIRE SPURE STEER CAREEN CENTER CENTRE TICKLE TIPLET TIPPLE TOPPLE WHEEZE APICULA CUMSHAW DERTRUM DOUCEUR GRIFFIN POINTER PROPINE WRINKLE APICULUS BONAMANO ENTOMION FOOTHOLD GRATUITY PERQUISITE (— OF ANTENNA) ARISTA (— OF BILLIARD CUE) LEATHER (— OF BIRD'S BILL) DERTRUM (— OF ELBOW) NOOP (— OF FOX'S BRUSH) CHAPE (— OF SKI) SHOVEL (— OF SPIDER) BULB (— OF STAMP) SHOE (— OF TOE) POINTE (— OF TONGUE) CORONA (— OF UMBO) BEAK (— OF WHEAT KERNEL) BRUSH (— OF WHIP) SNAPPER (— ON ORGAN PIPE) TOE (— OVER) TOP PURL OVERSET (— UP) CANT COUP COWP (ABRUPT —) MUCRO (BOW —) HORN (INWARD —) BANK (LARGE —S) LARGESS LARGESSE (RUBBISH —) TOOM (PREF.) ACR(O) APIC(O)
TIPCART COUPE COCOPAN
TIPCAT CAT PIGGY PUSSY KITCAT PIGGIE
TIPPED BANKED (EASILY —) CRANK
TIPPER DUMPER THROWER TIPPLER
TIPPET FUR AMICE SCARF ALMUCE SINDON LIRIPIPE LIRIPOOP PELERINE VICTORINE
TIPPLE BIB NIP POT SOT DRAM GILL BIBBER BIBBLE FUDDLE PUDDLE SIPPLE TIPPER TOOTHFUL
TIPPLER SOUSE TOAST WINER

BIBBER BOLLER BOOZER BUBBER DRAMMER PANURGE POTATOR TUMBLER WHETTER ALESTAKE MALTWORM
TIPPLING POTTING BIBACITY BIBATION
TIPSTER PROPHET
TIPSY CUT BOSKY DRUNK FRESH MUSED MUZZY NAPPY TIGHT TOTTY TOZIE BUMPSY GROGGY SLEWED SPRUNG EBRIOSE EBRIOUS EXALTED ELEVATED MUCKIBUS OVERSEEN PLEASANT
TIP-TOP SWELL TIPPY REGULAR TOPPING
TIRADE LAISSE SCREED STOUSH JEREMIAD PHILIPPIC
TIRAS (FATHER OF —) JAPHETH
TIRE DO FAG HAG LAG SAG BORE CORD FLAT FLOG JADE KILL MOIL SHOE LABOR SPARE WEARY CASING HAGGLE HARASS SICKEN TIRING TUCKER BALLOON EXHAUST FATIGUE FRAZZLE TRACHLE CLINCHER FORSPEND (— OUT) HAG FLOG THEAD BEJADE HARASS OVERWEARY (WORN —) CARCASS
TIRED SAD TAM BEAT BOEG DEAD TIRY BLOWN WEARY AWEARY BLEARY BUSHED PLAYED TAVERT FORWORN SHAGGED TAIVERT FATIGATE FORWAKED
TIREDNESS FATIGUE
TIRESIAS (FATHER OF —) EVERES (MOTHER OF —) CHARICLO
TIRESOME DRY DREE FAGGY ALANGE BORING DREICH PROLIX IRKSOME PROSAIC TEDIOUS BORESOME BROMIDIC ENNUYANT LONGSOME
TIRHANAH (FATHER OF —) CALEB (MOTHER OF —) MAACHAH
TIRIA (FATHER OF —) JEHALELEEL
TIRING DRUDGING
TIRL RISP
TIRTHANKARA JINA
TIRZAH (FATHER OF —) ZELOPHEHAD
TISAMENUS (FATHER OF —) ORESTES THERSANDER (MOTHER OF —) HERMIONE
TISANE PTISAN TILLEUL
TISSUE FAT WEB CORK FOIL PITH TELA TEXT FACIA GLEBA GRAFT SUBER TRAMA CALLUS DARTOS DIPLOE FABRIC FASCIA LIGNUM PANNUS PHLOEM SHEATH TEXTUS ADENOID ALBUMEN BINDWEB CAMBIUM CLYPEUS EPITELA EXPLANT HYDROME KLEENEX MESTOME NEURINE PHLOEM TEXTURE TWITTER ADHESION BLASTEMA DESMOGEN ECTODERM ENDODERM EPIPLOON HISTOGEN HYPODERM ISOGRAFT MERISTEM OSTEOGEN PERIDERM PERIDESM POLYPARY STEREOME (— OF FUNGUS) CENTRUM (— SURROUNDING TEETH) GUM (BLACK —) CLYPEUS (CONNECTING —) WEB STROMA

TENDON LIGAMENT
MESENCHYME
(CORK —) SUBER
(FATTY —) LARD GREASE
(HARD —) BONE
(HYPOTHETICAL —) COAGULIN
(LYMPHOID —) TONSIL
(NERVE —) GANGLION
(SOFT —) FLAB
(VEGETABLE —) ARMOR
(WOOD —) LIGNUM VITRAIN
(PL.) CHIRATA CHIRETTA
MESODERM
(PREF.) FASCIO HIST(I)(IO)(O)
HYPHO
(FATTY —) ADIP(O)
(FIBROUS —)
FIBR(I)(ILLI)(INO)(O)(OSO) IN(O)
TISWIN TESVINO TEXGUINO
TIT TID MESIA TITTY BLUECAP
COLETIT MUFFLIN PINNOCK
TITAN BANA LETO MAIA ASURA
ATLAS COEUS CREUS CRIOS
DIONE THEIA CRONOS CRONUS
PALLAS PHOEBE TETHYS THEMIS
IAPETUS OCEANUS HYPERION
(AUTHOR OF —) DREISER
(CHARACTER IN —) FRANK PETER
AILEEN BUTLER PLATOW
FLEMING BERENICE LAUGHLIN
STEPHANIE COWPERWOOD
TITANIA (HUSBAND OF —) OBERON
TITANIC HUGE GREAT TITAN
IMMENSE COLOSSAL GIGANTIC
TITANITE SPHENE GROTHITE
LEDERITE LIGURITE
TITANIUM DIOXIDE ANATASE
TITA ROOT MISHMI MISHMEE
TITHE DIME DISME TEIND TENTH
DECIMA PREBEND TITHING
TITHING BORGH BORROW DECIME
DENARY DECENARY
TITHINGMAN DEAN DECURION
TUTTIMAN
TITHONUS (FATHER OF —)
LAOMEDON
(MOTHER OF —) STRYMO
TITI ORA TEETEE WISTIT SAIMIRI
WISTITI IRONWOOD MARMOSET
ORABASSU OUISTITI
TITILLATE AMUSE KITTLE TICKLE
TITILLATING GAMY GAMEY
TITIVATE PRIMP
TITLARK PIPIT TEETING
TITLE (ALSO SEE LEADER, CHIEF
GOVERNOR, RULER) AGA AYA BAN
BEG BEY DAN DOM DUE FRA JAM
LAR MIR PAN SAG SIR ABBA ABBE
AGHA AMIR ANBA BABU DAME
DEVI EMIR FRAY GAON GRAF HAJI
HERR KHAN KNEZ LARS NAME
PANI SIDI SLUG ABGAR ABUNA
AMEER BABOO BEGUM CCOYA
CLAIM CROWN EMEER FRATE
GHAZI GOODY GRACE HADJI
HAJJI HAKAM HANUM HONOR
KNIAZ KNYAZ LEMMA MIRZA
MPRET NAWAB NEGUS NIZAM
PANNA RABBI RIGHT SINGH
SOPHI SOPHY UNWAN BASHAW
BEGANI COUSIN DEGREE DEMAND
DESPOT DOMINE EPONYM
EXARCH HANDLE HUZOOR

LEGEND MADAME MASTER
MEHTAR MISTER PESHWA PREFIX
SHERIF SQUIRE SUFFEE TITULE
VIDAME ALFEREZ ALTESSE
ALTEZZA BAHADUR CANDACE
CAPTION CONVITO CRAWLER
DIGNITY EFFENDI EPITHET
ESQUIRE FIDALGO GAEKWAR
GRAVITY HEADING HIDALGO
INFANTE KHEDIVE MAHARAO
MESSIRE RABBONI SHAREEF
TITULUS VOIVODE BANNERET
BASILEUS COMMENDA CONVIVIO
EMINENCE GOSPODIN HIGHNESS
HOLINESS HOSPODAR INTEREST
LOKINDRA MAGISTER MAHARAJA
MAHARANA MAHARSHI MISTRESS
MONSIEUR PADISHAH PRINCIPE
RAUGRAVE SUBTITLE TAMBURAN
TITULADO
(— ACQUISITION) USUCAPT
(— OF BOOK) QUARE
**(— OF MEMBER OF PRIMROSE
LEAGUE)** KNIGHT
(— OF RESPECT) SIR SRI COJA LIEF
MIAN SHRI SIDI BURRA HODJA
KHAJA KHOJA MADAM SAHIB
SIEUR KHOJAH MADAME MILADY
(BENEDICTINE —) DOM
(MOCK —) IDLESHIP
TITMOUSE MAG NUN TIT MAGG
OXEYE PARUS SPICK FUFFIT
HEFFEL PUFFER TOMTIT VERDIN
BLUECAP BUSHTIT COLETIT
COLMOSE GOLDTIT GRIGNET
HAGMALL JACKSAW MUFFLIN
PINCHEM PINNOCK TINNOCK
TITMALL TOMNOUP CHICADEE
HACKMALL OVENBIRD REEDLING
SHABROON SHARPSAW
TITTER GIGGLE SNICKER TWITTER
WHICKER
TITTLE JOT IOTA TITLE MINUTE
TITUBATE REEL STAGGER
TITULAR LEGAL NOMINAL
HONORARY
**TITUS ANDRONICUS (AUTHOR OF
—)** SHAKESPEARE
(CHARACTER IN —) AARON CAIUS
TITUS CHIRON LUCIUS MARCUS
MUTIUS TAMORA ALARBUS
LAVINIA MARTIUS PUBLIUS
QUINTUS AEMILIUS BASSIANUS
DEMETRIUS VALENTINE
SATURNINUS SEMPRONIUS
TITYUS (FATHER OF —) TERRA
JUPITER
(MOTHER OF —) ELARA
TIU ER EAR TIW TYR ZIO ZIU TIWAZ
SAXNOT
TIV MUNCHI
TIZZY SNIT STEW PUCKER SWIVET
SWIVVET
TLAKLUIT ECHE LOOT WISHRAM
TLEPOLEMUS (FATHER OF —)
HERCULES
(MOTHER OF —) ASTYOCHIA
(SLAYER OF —) SARPEDON
TLINGIT SITKA KOLUSH SUMDUM
CHILCAT CHILKAT STIKINE
TMESIS DIACOPE
TNT TROTYL
TO A AD FOR INTO TILL

UNTO UPON
(— A CONCLUSION) OUT
(— BE) IBE
(— BE SURE) EVEN
(— COME) BEHIND
(— COMPLETION) DOWN
(— IT) TOOT SESSA
(— PRESS) DOWN
(— SUCH DEGREE) EVEN
(— THAT TIME) UNTIL
(— THE END) AF
(— THE OPPOSITE SIDE) ACROSS
(— THE REAR) ABAFT ASTERN
(— THIS) HERETO
(— THIS PLACE) HERE HITHER
(— VICTORY) ABU ABOO
(— WHAT) WHERETO
(— WIT) NAMELY INNUENDO
SCILICET
(PREF.) AC AD AF AG AL AP AS
AT INTRO OB
TOAD PAD AGUA BUFO FROG HYLA
PIPA PODE HYLID PADDO PADDY
PIPAL PIPID TOADY ANURAN
CRAPON PEEPER BUFONID
CHARLIE CRAPAUD CRAWLER
CREEPER FROGLET GANGREL
HOPTOAD PADDOCK PODDOCK
PUDDOCK QUILKIN REPTILE
SERPENT GANGEREL
(PREF.) BATRACH(O) PHRYN(O)
(SUFF.) BATRACH(O)(US)
TOADFISH SAPO SARPO GRUBBY
SLIMER CABEZON FROGFISH
LORICATE SCORPION
TOADFLAX FLAX FLAXWEED
FLAXWORT FLUELLEN GALLWEED
GALLWORT RAMSTEAD
TOAD RUSH SALTWEED
TOADSTONE BUFONITE
TOADSTOOL CANKER FUNGUS
TOADY FAWN SUCK TOAD ZANY
COTTON EARWIG FAWNER
FLUNKY GREASE LACKEY MUCKER
FLUNKEY JENKINS LACQUEY
PLACEBO SHONEEN TRUCKLE
BOOTLICK CLAWBACK LICKSPIT
PARASITE SYCOPHANT
TOADYING GNATHONIC
TOADYISM FLUNKYISM
TOAST WET TOSS BREDE ROUSE
SKOAL TRINQ BIRSLE BUMPER
CHEERS HEALTH PLEDGE PROSIT
BRISTLE CAROUSE CHEERIO
FRIZZLE LEHAYIM PROFACE
PROPINE RESPECT SLAINTE
WASSAIL BRINDISI SCOUTHER
(— AND ALE) SWIG
(— ONESELF) LEEP
(JACOBITE —) LIMP
TOBACCO CANE CAPA HAND LEAF
LUGS NAVY POAK POKE QUID
ROLL SHAG WEED BACCO BACCY
BACKY BROKE CUBAN DARKS
FOGUS PETUN REGIE SMOKE
SNOUT TABAC TWIST BACKER
BRIGHT BURLEY COLORY COWPEN
FILLER HAVANA RETURN TOMBAC
TUMBAK CAPORAL CRACCUS
GAGROOT GORACCO KNASTER
LATAKIA NAILROD NICOTIA
ORONOKO PERIQUE PIGTAIL
SOTWEED UPPOWOC CANASTER

HONEYDEW MAKHORKA
MARYLAND NICOTIAN ORONOOKO
SEEDLEAF VIRGINIA MUNDUNGUS
NICOTIANA
(— AND PAPER) MAKINGS
(— CAKED IN PIPE BOWL) DOTTEL
DOTTLE TOPPER
(— HAVING OFFENSIVE SMELL)
MUNDUNGO
(— IN ROPES) BOGIE
(— JUICE) AMBEER PRAISS
(— MOISTENED WITH MOLASSES)
HONEYDEW
(— MOSAIC) WALLOON
(— PASTE) GORACCO
(— ROOM) PRIZERY
(— WORKER) LOOPER LEAFBOY
LEAFGIRL
(CAKED —) HEEL
(COARSE —) SHAG SCRAP
CAPORAL
(CUT —) CANASTER PICADURA
(DRIED —) TABACUM
(HARD-PRESSED —) NAILROD
(HATING —) MISOCAPNIC
(INDIAN —) GAGROOT PUKEWEED
EYEBRIGHT
(INFERIOR —) LUGS
(LADIES' —) CUDWEED
(LOWER LEAVES OF —) FLYING
(MILD —) RETURN
(PERSIAN —) SHIRAZ TUMBEK
TUMBEKI
(PERUVIAN —) SANA
(POOR QUALITY —) DOGLEG
(PULVERIZED —) SNUFF
(QUID OF —) CUD
(RAW —) LEAF
(ROLLED —) CARROT
(SMALL PIECE OF —) FIG
(VIRGINIA —) COWPEN VIRGINIA
TOBACCO BROWN TABAC
TOBACCO ROAD (AUTHOR OF —)
CALDWELL
(CHARACTER IN —) ADA LOV DUDE
RICE ELLIE PEARL BENSEY BESSIE
JEETER LESTER
TOBACCO WORM HORNWORM
TOBOGGAN COAST CARIOLE
CARRIOLE
TOCHARIAN A AGNEAN
TOCHARIAN B KUCHEAN
TOCSIN ALARUM
TODAY DAY NOW NOWADAYS
TODDLE TOT FADGE DADDLE
DIDDLE DODDLE PADDLE TOTTLE
WADDLE
TODDLER TROT GANGREL TROTTIE
TODDY TOD TUBA TERRY SAGWIRE
TO-DO ADO FUSS STIR WORK
STINK DOMENT HOOPLA FLUSTER
FOOSTER FOOFARAW TRAVALLY
TODY ROBIN
TOE TER DIGIT DACTYL HALLUX
MINIMUS TOENAIL TRIPPET
POULAINE
(— OF BIRD) HEEL
(LITTLE —) MINIMUS
(PL.) TUN TAIS TOON
(PREF.) DACTYL(O) DACTYLIO
DIGITI DIGITO
TOENAIL
(SUFF.) ONYCHA ONYCHES

ONYCHIA ONYCHIUM
ONYCHUS ONYX
TOEPLATE SHOD
TOFF NOB
TOGA GOWN ROBE TOGUE TRABEA
TOGETHER ONCE SAME ATONE
YFERE BEDENE INSAME JOINTLY
ENSEMBLE
(— WITH) AND INTO
(PREF.) CO COL COM CON COR
SYM SYN
TOGGLE COTTAR COTTER TOGGEL
NETSUKE
TOGO (CAPITAL OF —) LOME
(LANGUAGE OF —) EWE TWI MINA
HAUSA KABRAIS LOTOCOLI
(MOUNTAIN IN —) AGOU
(NATIVE OF —) EWE MINA CABRAI
KABRAI OUATCHI
(RIVER IN —) OTI ANIE HAHO
MONO
(TOWN IN —) KANDE ANECHO
PALIME SOKODE TSEVIE
ATAKPAME
TOHUBOHU RIOT CHAOS
DISORDER CONFUSION
TOI (SON OF —) JORAM
TOIL FAG TUG DARG GRUB HACK
MOIL MUCK PLOD TASK WORK
LABOR SCRAT SLAVE SWINK
TWEIL YAKKA BILDER DRUDGE
EFFORT HAMMER KIAUGH
MITHER MOIDER STRIVE UNRUFE
YACKER FATIGUE TRAVAIL
TURMOIL DRUDGERY INDUSTRY
TOILER SLAVE MOILER WORKER
TOILET CAN LOO HEAD JOHN BIFFY
CRAPPER BASEMENT BATHROOM
LAVATORY PLUMBING
TOILSOME HARD SWEATY
ARDUOUS TOILFUL MOILSOME
SWEATFUL
TOJOLABAL CHANABAL
TOKAY TUCKTOO
TOKEN BUCK CENT HARP SIGN
TYPE BADGE CHECK INDEX SCRIP
BEAVER CASTOR COLLAR COPPER
COUPON DOLLAR EMBLEM
JETTON MARKER OSTENT
REMARK SIGNAL TICKET WITTER
AUSPICE COUNTER EARNEST
INDICIA MEMENTO PRESAGE
SYMPTOM TESSERA BUNGTOWN
COINTISE EVIDENCE FOOTSTEP
FORBYSEN INSTANCE KEEPSAKE
MONUMENT SHILLING SIGNACLE
(— OF LUCK) HANSEL HANDSEL
(— OF RESPECT) SALUTE
(— OF SUPERIORITY) PALM
(— OF VICTORY) LAUREL
(CANADIAN —) HARP
(LOVE —) DRURY AMORET
(PORCELAIN —S) PI
TOKHARI KUCHEAN
TOKYO (— STREET) GINZA
(FORMER NAME OF —) EDO YEDO
TOLA (FATHER OF —) ISSACHAR
TOLERABLE GAY SOSO PRETTY
TARBLE LIVABLE PATIBLE
BEARABLE PASSABLE PORTABLE
TOLERABLY GAIN GEYAN FAIRLY
MEETLY MEETERLY MIDDLING
TOLERANCE MERCY SHERE

LEEWAY REMEDY
TOLERANT SOFT BROAD BENIGN
PATIENT PLACABLE PERMISSIVE
TOLERATE GO BEAR BIDE HACK
HAVE ABEAR ABIDE ALLOW
BROOK SPARE STAND STICK
THOLE ACCEPT ENDURE PARDON
PERMIT SUFFER COMPORT
STOMACH SUPPORT SUSTAIN
TOLERATION WITHGANG
TOLL JOW TAX JOWL PIKE RENT
KNELL PEAGE CAPHAR EXCISE
OCTROI PEDAGE PESAGE
BOOMAGE KEELAGE LASTAGE
LOCKAGE MULTURE PASSAGE
PICCAGE PIERAGE PONTAGE
SCAVAGE SUMMAGE TERRAGE
TOLLAGE TRONAGE BERTHAGE
STALLAGE WEIGHAGE WHEELAGE
(PL.) CUSTOMS RAHDARI
RATTAREE
TOLLHOUSE TOLLERY
TOLLIKER DUMMY
TOLSEN FOOTSTEP
TOLUENE DILUENT
TOLYL CRESYL
TOMAHAWK HATCHET NEOLITH
TOMATO TOM BERRY BURBANK
TOMB PIR BIER CIST MOLE GRAVE
GUACA HUACA MAZAR SPEOS
TABUT THOLE TURBE BURIAL
CHULPA DARGAH DURGAH
GALGAL HEARSE HEROON
SAMADH SHRINE SYRINX THOLOS
TROUGH TURBEH CHULLPA
MASTABA OSSUARY TOMBLET
TRITAPH CENOTAPH CISTVAEN
CUBICULO HALLCIST HYPOGEUM
KISTVAEN MARABOUT MASTABAH
MONUMENT TREASURY
MAUSOLEUM SEPULCHER
(— IN CHURCH) SACELLUM
(— OF MOSLEM SAINT) ZIARA
ZIARAT
(CAVE —) SPEOS
(PREHISTORIC —) KURGAN
TOMBAC ORSEDE ORSEDUE
TOMBOY HEMP RAMP GAMINE
HOYDEN MADCAP TOMRIG
TOMBSTONE SLAT TITLE
THROUGH
TOMCAT GIB TOMMY PODGER
THOMAS
TOMCOD GADE GADID SMELT
GADOID WHITING TOMMYCOD
TOMENTUM WOOL
TOMFOOLERY HELL HORSE
TOM JONES (AUTHOR OF —)
FIELDING
(CHARACTER IN —) TOM BETTY
JENNY JONES NANCY BLIFIL
GEORGE SOPHIA SQUARE
WATERS BRIDGET WESTERN
THWACKUM ALLWORTHY
BELLASTON PARTRIDGE
FITZPATRICK NIGHTINGALE
TOMMY FOOL PODGER REQUIN
TOMMYROT WAHOO
TOMMY TALKER KAZOO
TOMORROW MANANA MORROW
TOMORN
TOM SAWYER (AUTHOR OF —)
TWAIN CLEMENS

(CHARACTER IN —) AMY JOE SID
TOM FINN HUCK MARY MUFF
BECKY POLLY HARPER POTTER
SAWYER DOUGLAS LAWRENCE
ROBINSON THATCHER
TOMTATE CAESAR
TON TUN TOUN STYLE
TONALAMATL TZOLKIN
TONALITY KEY
TONE A F DO FA LA MI RE SI SO TI
DOH KEY SOH SOL CALL FLAT
NOTE COLOR COUAC DRONE
FIFTH FORTE PRIME SHARP SIXTH
SOUND STYLE TONUS ACCENT
DEGREE FOURTH SECOND
FORMANT MEDIANT PARTIAL
DEMITINT ELEVENTH FORENOTE
HARMONIC HEADNOTE
PARAMESE PARANETE SONORITY
(— A DRAWING) STUMP
(— DOWN) DRAB TAME SOFTEN
SUBDUE
(— UP) BRACE
(ACCENTED —) SFORZANDO
(BROKEN —) CRACK
(COMPLEX —) KLANG
(DEEP —) BASS
(DOMINANT —) ANIMUS
(DRAWLING —) DRANT DRAUNT
(HIGH-PITCHED —) PIP
(KEY —) KEYNOTE
(LOUD —) FORTE
(LOW —) SEMISOUN
(MONOTONOUS —) DRONE
(SHARP NASAL —) TWANG
(SIGNIFICANT —) ACCENT
(SINGLE UNVARIED —) MONOTONE
(STRIDENT —) COUAC
(WHINING —) GIRN
(PREF.) PHON(O)
TONGA (CAPITAL OF —)
NUKUALOFA
(COIN OF —) PAANGA SENITI
(ISLAND GROUP OF —) TOFUA
VAVAU HAAPAI NIUAFOO
TONGATAPU NIUATOBUTABU
(ISLAND OF —) ONO TOFUA VAVAU
HAAPAI
(TOWN OF —) NEIAFU
TONGS SNAPS SERVER FORCEPS
GRAMPUS TUEIRON SCISSORS
TONGUE COG GAB CHIB CLAP KALI
NEAP PAWL POLE REED CLACK
IDIOM LADIN VOICE GADABA
GLOSSA KABYLE KALIKA LADINO
LANGUE LINGUA SPEECH
CLAPPER DIALECT FEATHER
ILOKANO LANGUET DOVETAIL
LANGUAGE LORRIKER PLECTRUM
(— IN FLOORING) SPLINE
(— OF BELL) CLAPPER
(— OF JEW'S-HARP) TANG
(— OF LAND) DOAB REACH
LANGUE LANGUET
(— OF MOLLUSC) RADULA
(— OF OXCART) COPE
(— OF SHOE) FLAP KILTY KILTIE
(— OF VEHICLE) NEAP SHAFT
(BELLOWS —) GUSSET
(GIVE —) PRATE
(GOSSIPING —) CLACK CLACKER
(PART OF —) BUD UVULA FAUCES
LINGUA SEPTUM

(PIVOTED —) PAWL
(ROMANY —) ROMANES
(PL.) GAURA
(PREF.) GLOSS(O) GLOTT(I)(O)
LIGUL(I) LINGU(I)(LI)(O)
(SUFF.) GLOSSA GLOSSIA GLOT
TONGUEFISH SOLE
TONGUE-LASH SCOLD
TONGUE-LASHING RAT TOCO
BUSINESS
TONGUELESS AGLOSSAL
TONGUE-TIED SILENT
TONIC DO DOH ALOE KEEP PICHI
PRIME BRACER SAMBUL SONANT
SUMBUL BONESET CALAMUS
CALOMBO CHIRATA COLOMBA
DAMIANA FUMARIA GENTIAN
KEYNOTE NERVINE SALICIN
TONICAL ANTHEMIS BARBERRY
BERBERRY HELONIAS ROBORANT
TRILLIUM PIPSISSEWA
TONICITY MYOTONIA
TONKA BEAN GAIAC CUMARU
GUAIAC COUMAROU
TONNA DOLIUM
TONNAGE PORTAGE
TONO-BUNGAY (AUTHOR OF —)
WELLS
(CHARACTER IN —) RINK EFFIE
FRAPP GROVE MOGGS SUSAN
ARCHIE EDWARD GEORGE
MANTEL MARION OSPREY
GARVELL RAMBOAT BEATRICE
NORMANDY NICODEMUS
PONDEREVO
TONSIL ALMOND KERNEL ADENOID
AMYGDAL AMYGDALA
(PREF.) AMYGDAL(O)
TONSILITIS QUINSY
TONSURE CROWN SHAVE SHEAR
CORONA DIKSHA RASURE
TONSURED PEELED PILLED
SHAVED
TOO SO ALSO OVER TROP LUCKY
OVERLY LIKEWISE
(PREF.) OVER
TOOL (ALSO SEE IMPLEMENT AND
INSTRUMENT) AX ADZ AWL AXE
BIT BUR DIE DIG GIN GUN HOB
KEY LAP LOY RIP SAW SAX TAP
TIT VOL ZAX ADZE BORE BRAY
BURR CLAW COMB DADO DISC
DISK DUPE EDGE FILE FLAY FROE
FROG FROW GAGE HACK HAWK
HONE LEAF LOOM MILL PICK ROLL
SATE SEAX SLED SNAP SPUD SPUD
STOP TAMP TIER VISE AUGER
BLADE BORAL BORER BRAKE
BRAND BREAK BRUSH BURIN
CROZE DARBY DOLLY DRIFT DRILL
DUMMY EDGER FLAKE FLOAT
FLUTE GAUGE GOUGE GUIDE
HARDY HOBBY HOWEL KNIFE
KNURL LEVEL MAKER MISER
MODEL PLANE POINT PRUNT
PUNCH QUIRK SABER SABRE
SCREW SHAVE SHELL SLICE SLICK
SNIPE SPADE SPEAR SPLIT STAKE
STAMP STING STOCK STRIG STYLE
SWAGE TEWEL TOYLE UPSET
VALET WAGON BEADER BEATER
BIDENT BIFACE BLADER BODKIN
BROACH BUDGER BUFFER CALKER

CHASER CHISEL CLEAVE COGGLE
COLTER CRADLE CRANNY CUTTER
DEVICE DIBBLE DIGGER DOCTOR
DRIVER ENGINE FASCET FERRET
FILLET FLANGE FLORET FLUTER
FORMER FRAISE FULLER GIMLET
GLAZER GOFFER GRAVER
GUMMER HACKER HAMMER
HEMMER HOGGER HOLDER
HULLER JIGGER JUMPER LADKIN
LASTER LIFTER NIBBER PALLET
PARTER PICKAX PICKER PLENCH
PLIERS PROPER PUPPET REAMER
RIPPER ROCKER RUNNER SAPPER
SCRIBE SCUTCH SEATER SHAPER
SHAVER SHEARS SHOVEL SKIVER
SLATER SOCKET SQUARE STYLET
STYLUS SWIVEL TAGGER TASTER
TONGUE TREPAN TURNER
TURREL TWILLY VEINER WAGGON
WIGWAG WIMBLE WORDLE
WORMER YANKEE ABRADER
BLOCKER BRADAWL CALIPER
CAULKER CHAMFER CHIPPER
CHOPPER CLEANER CLEAVER
COULTER CREASER DIAMOND
DOLABRA DRESSER FISTUCA
FLANGER FREEZER FROTTON
GRAINER GROOVER GRUBBER
GUDGEON JOINTER KNOTTER
LOGHEAD MITERER OUSTITI
POINTEL POINTER PROFILE
RIVETER ROUGHER ROUNDER
SCAUPER SCORPER SCRIBER
SCRIVER SCURFER SLASHER
SLEEKER SLICKER SPLAYER
SPUDDER STEMMER STRIKER
STROKER TICKLER TREBLET
TWIBILL UPRIGHT WRAITHE
AIGUILLE BIFACIAL BILLHOOK
BOOTJACK BURGOYNE CALLIPER
CREATURE CRIPPLER CROSSCUT
CROWFOOT DUCKFOOT
ELEVATOR EXPANDER FLOUNDER
GRAVETTE GRIFFAUN POLISHER
PRITCHEL PROPERTY PUNCHEON
RAVEHOOK RECAPPER SCRAPPLE
SCULPTOR SPLITTER STIPPLER
STRICKLE STRINGER SURFACER
THWACKER TOLLIKER WARKLOOM
WORKLOOM SCRATCHER **(— A
BOOK)** FINISH
(PL.) TEW FISH GEAR TRADE
CUTLERY GIBBLES PIONERY
ENGINERY
TOOLED GOFFERED
(— WITHOUT GILDING) BLIND
TOOLHOLDER TURRET MONITOR
TOOLHOUSE COPHOUSE
TOOLSHED DOGHOUSE
TOON LIM CEDAR TOONWOOD
TOOT BLOW TOWT BLAST SOUND
TRUMPET
TOOTH BIT COG GAM JAG PEG
DENS DENT FANG LEAF RASP
SNAG TIND TINE TUSH TUSK
CRENA IVORY MOLAR PEARL
PRONG RAKER TENON BROACH
CANINE CUSPID CUTTER DENTAL
INDENT JOGGLE TRIGON TRITOR
DENTILE DIVIDER GRINDER
INCISOR LATERAL SURDENT
UNCINUS ABUTMENT BICUSPID

BLEPHARA DENTICLE EYETOOTH
GAGTOOTH MARGINAL
PREMOLAR SAWTOOTH
SPROCKET TOOTHLET TRIGONID
CARNASSIAL
(— OF A MOSS) BLEPHARA
(— OF HORSE) DIVIDER
(— OF MOLLUSC) MARGINAL
(— OF PINION) LEAF
(— OF RADULA) UNCINUS
(— ON ROTATING PIECE) WIPER
(ARTIFICIAL —) DUMMY PONTIL
(CANINE —) CUSPID HOLDER
LANIARY CYNODONT DOGTOOTH
EYETOOTH
(GEAR —) COG GUB DENT
ADDENDUM SPROCKET
(HARROW —) TINE
(MOLAR —) WANG
(PART OF —) GUM NECK PULP
ROOT CROWN DENTIN ENAMEL
CEMENTUM
(UPPER SURFACE OF —) TABLE
(PREF.) DENT(ATO)(I)(INO)(O)(ODO)
ODONT(O)
(SUFF.) DENT(ATE)
ODON(T)(TA)(TES)(TIA)(TY) ODUS
TOOTHACHE WORM DENTAGRA
TOOTHED SERRATE VIRGATE
SERRATED PECTINATE
(SUFF.) ODON ODUS
TOOTHLESS GUMMY
TOOTHPICK QUILL ARKANSAN
TOOTHSOME PALATABLE
TOOTHWORT CROWTOE
COOLWORT
TOP CAP COP GIG NUN TAP TIP
ACME APEX BEAT COCK CULM
HEAD HELM ROOF SKIM STOP
BLOOM CHIEF COVER CREST
CROWN FANCY GIGGE PITCH
RIDGE SPIRE STRIP TOTUM
TRUMP UPPER CALASH CAPOTE
CULMEN SUMMIT UPWARD
VERTEX CACUMEN SPINNER
ROUNDTOP SURMOUNT
TEETOTUM CULMINATION
(— FOR CHIMNEY OR PIPE) COWL
HOOD
(— OF ALTAR) MENSA
(— OF AUTOMOBILE) HEAD HOOD
(— OF CAPSTAN) DRUMHEAD
(— OF FURNACE) ARCH
(— OF GLASS) PRETTY
(— OF HEAD) MOLD PATE MOULD
SCALP VERTEX
(— OF HELMET) SKULL
(— OF HILL) KNAG KNAP KNOLL
(— OF INGOT) CROPHEAD
(— OF MINING SHAFT) PITHEAD
(— OF MOUNTAIN) MAN
(— OF PLANT OR TREE) CROP
(— OF ROOF) DECK
(— OF SPINDLE) COCKHEAD
(— OF THUNDERCLOUD) INCUS
(— OF WAVE) COMB
(— OF WOODEN STAND) CRISS
(—S OF CROP) SHAW
(BOOT —) RUFF
(BOX —) COUPON
(CARRIAGE —) CALASH
(PEG —) PEERIE
(RESEMBLING A —) STROBIC

(SPINNING —) PEERY PEERIE
(PREF.) ACR(O)
(SPINNING —) RHOMB(O)
TOPAZ PYCNITE PYCNIUM
PHSALITE
TOPCOAT OVERCOAT SIPHONIA
TOPE DHER DHERI STUPA DAGOBA
SOUPFIN
TOPER BOUSER CUPMAN POTMAN
POTTER SIPPER SOAKER SUPPER
TROUGH BOMBARD POTLING
SWILLER TOSSPOT BLACKPOT
DRUNKARD MALTWORM
TOPI TIANG
TOPIC HARE ITEM TEXT HOBBY
THEMA THEME BURDEN GAMBIT
GROUND MATTER SUBJECT
OCCASION
(STOCK —) TOPOS
TOPKNOT ONKOS TOPPING
TOPMAN COB
TOPMINNOW GUPPY LIMIA
GULARIS HELLERI SAILFIN
GAMBUSIA MOLLIENSIA
TOPOGRAPHIC TERRAIN
TOPPLE TIP TOP TILT LEVEL
TOTTLE
TOPSAIL RAFFE RAFFEE
TOPSOIL KELLY
TOPSTONE CAPSTONE
TOPSWARM TOPCAST
TOPSY-TURVY COCKEYED
REELRALL
TOQUE ZATI MUNGA MACACO
RILAWA MACAQUE
TOQUILLA JIPIJAPA
TORCEL BURN BERNE BORNE
TORCH DUCK JACK LAMP LINK
LUNT PINE TEAD WASE WISP
BLAZE BRAND FLARE MATCH
FOCKLE LAMPAD MASHAL
MUSSAL BRANDON CRESSET
GRIDDLE LUCIGEN ROUGHIE
TORCHET FLAMBEAU
(PREF.) DAD(O) LAMPADE
TORCHBEARER KERYX LINKBOY
LINKMAN DADUCHUS TORCHMAN
TOREADOR TORERO CAPEADOR
TORII (PART OF —) NYKI DAIWA
KASAGI KUSABI LINTEL
GAKUZUKA CROSSPIECE
TORIL CHIQUERO
TORMENT WO RAG TAW TRY WOE
BAIT BALE FRET MOIL PAIN PANG
PINE RACK SOOL TEAR TUCK
CHEVY CURSE DEVIL GRILL HARRY
SCALD TEASE TWIST WRING
CHIVVY HARASS HARROW
HECTOR INFEST NEEDLE PLAGUE
TRAVEL AFFLICT ANGUISH
BEDEVIL CRUCIFY HAGRIDE
HATCHEL MALISON PERPLEX
PINDING TERRIFY TORTURE
TRAVAIL CRUCIATE DISTRAIN
LACERATE MACERATE
(EXTREME —) AGONY
TORMENTED CRUCIATE
TORMENTIL SEPTFOIL
TORMENTING PLAGUY
TORMINA TORSION
TORN RENT BROKEN BLASTED
TORNADO VORTEX CYCLONE
TRAVADO TWISTER

TORPEDO FISH SHELL SQUIB
BATOID HOAGIE
TORPID FOUL NUMB BROSY INERT
SODDEN STUPID TOGGER
LANGUID TORPENT COMATOSE
COMATOUS SLUGGISH
TORPIFY DAZE ETHERIZE
TORPOR COMA SLEEP SWOON
ACEDIA ACCIDIE SLUMBER
LETHARGY
(PREF.) NARC(O)
TORQUE BEE SARPE TWIST
TORREFY PARCH
TORRENT FLOW RUSH FLOOD
SPATE STREAM NIAGARA
CATARACT
(— OF WORDS) BLATTER
TORREYA SAVIN TUMION
TORRID HOT SULTRY AUSTRAL
BOILING
TORSALO BERNE
TORSION STRESS DIDROMY
TORSK CUSK
TORT LIBEL WRONG
TORTE DOBOS
TORT-FEASOR ACTOR
TORTICOLLIS WRYNECK
TORTILLA TACO BREAD BURRITO
TOSTADO ENCHILADA
QUESADILLA
TORTOISE EMYD BEKKO GAPER
COOTER GOPHER TURTLE
EMYDIAN HICATEE MUNGOFA
TESTUDO GALAPAGO KASHYAPA
SHELLPAD SHELLPOT TERRAPIN
(PREF.) CHEL(O)(Y)
TORTOISESHELL CAREY
TORTUOUS CRANKY SCREWY
SINUATE WRIGGLY SINUATED
TORTURE GYP TAW BOOT CARD
FIRE PAIN PANG PINE RACK
AGONY SCREW TWIST ENGINE
EXTORT IMPALE MARTYR AFFLICT
AGONIZE ANGUISH BOOTING
CRUCIFY PERPLEX TORMENT
MARTYRDOM
TORTURER BOURREAU
TORUS CORK TORE BASTON
BOLTEL BOUTELL BOWTELL
THALAMUS
TORY BANDIT OUTLAW ROBBER
PEELITE TANTIVY ABHORRER
LOYALIST
TOSS BUM COB LAB SHY BUNG
CANT CAST CAVE DOSS FLAP FLIP
HIKE PASS SHAG SLAT TOUT
CHAFE CHUCK FLICK FLING FLIRT
FLURR HEAVE PITCH TEAVE
THROW BETOSS BOUNCE DANDLE
TOTTER WALTER WELTER
WENTLE BLANKET TURMOIL
WAMPISH WHEMMEL
(— A COIN) SKY
(— A JACK) LAG
(— ABOUT) SWAB TAVE POPPLE
THRASH THRESH TORFLE
WAMPISH
(— ASIDE) BANDY
(— AWAY) BLOW
(— HEAD) CAVE GECK BRANK
(— OF HORSE'S HEAD) CHACK
(— OF THE HEAD) HEEZE
(— OFF) SWAP SWOP

(— ON WAVES) SURGE
(— TO AND FRO) WALK
(— TOGETHER CONFUSEDLY) SCRAMBLE
(— WITH THE HORNS) DOSS HIKE
TOSSING SURGING
(— OF BULLFIGHTER) COGIDA
TOSTAO TESTON
TOTAL SUM TAB TOT DEAD MERE TALE COUNT GROSS MOUNT SLUMP SUMMA UTTER WHOLE ENTIRE GLOBAL OMNIUM SUMMED TOTTLE EMBRACE FOOTING GENERAL PERFECT ABSOLUTE COMPLETE ENTIRETY SURMOUNT TEETOTAL
(PREF.) HOL(O)
TOTALITY ALL BODY HEAP BEING ALLNESS ECOLOGY ETERNITY HUMANITY INTEGRAL INTERVAL OMNITUDE
TOTALLY COLD GOOD QUITE WHOLLY
TOTEM HUACA
TO THE LIGHTHOUSE (AUTHOR OF —) WOOLF
(CHARACTER IN —) LILY PRUE JAMES MCNAB ANDREW BANKES RAMSAY BRISCOE CAMILLA CHARLES TANSLEY WILLIAM CARMICHAEL
TOTTER TOT ROCK TOIT WALT SHAKE WAVER COGGLE DADDLE DODDER DOTTER FALTER HOTTER JOGGLE STAVER SWERVE TITTER TOTTLE WAMBLE WANGLE WAPPER BRANDLE FRIBBLE STAGGER TREMBLE WHITHER TITUBATE VACILLATE
(PREF.) LABE
TOTTERING LURCH SHAKY GROGGY CRAMBLY PALSIED RICKETY TOTTERY TITUBANT WAMBLING
TOU (SON OF —) HAMATH
TOUCAN TOCO TUCANA ARACARI
TOUCH GET RAP TAG TIG TIP ABUT BILL DASH FEEL HAND KISS KNEE MEET PALP PEAL PLAY RAKE RINE TACT TAKE GLISK GRAZE GROPE SPICE TAINT TASTE TATTO TINGE TRAIT TREAT AFFECT ATTAIN CARESS FINGER GLANCE HANDLE REGARD SCRUFF SMUTCH STRAIN TACTUS TWITCH ATTAINT ATTINGE CONTACT FEELING PALPATE SOUPCON TACTION FLOURISH TINCTURE
(— A KEY) STRIKE
(— BRIEFLY) GLANCE
(— CARESSINGLY) FLATTER
(— CLOSELY) IMPINGE
(— GENTLY) DAB TAT TICK BRUSH
(— LIGHTLY) GRAZE SCUFF SKIFF
(— OF BRUSH) HAND
(— OF COLOR) EYE
(— OF PAINT) GLOB
(— OF PLEASURE) GLISK
(— RIGHTLY) NICK
(DELICATE —) STROKE
(FINISHING —) HOODER COPESTONE
(PAINTING —) ACCENT

(SLIGHT —) SKIFF SMATCH
(PREF.) TAC TACTO TANGO THIGMO THIXO
(SUFF.) APHIA
(HAVING A — OF) ISH ISTIC
TOUCHDOWN ROUGE
TOUCHED FEY DOTTY
TOUCHING ABOUT LIBANT TENDER AGAINST CONTACT TANGENT ADJACENT PATHETIC POIGNANT AFFECTING CONTINUOUS
(— LIGHTLY) LAMBENT
TOUCHSTONE TEST TOUCH LYDITE BASANITE STANDARD
TOUCHWOOD FUNK MONK PUNK SPUNK PUNKWOOD
TOUCHY HUFFY MIFFY SNAKY TESTY FEISTY KITTLE SNAKEY SNUFFY SPUNKY TENDER TETCHY GROUCHY NERVOUS PEEVISH PEPPERY TEMPERY TICKLISH
TOUGH RUM BHOY HARD TAUT WIRY BUTCH CLUNG HARDY STIFF STOUT WITHY BALLSY KNOTTY SINEWY STARCH STRONG HICKORY BULLYBOY LEATHERY UNTENDER ROUGHNECK TENACIOUS
TOUGHEN TAW ANNEAL ENDURE HARDEN TEMPER
(— METAL) PLANISH
TOUGHENED CLUNG
TOUGHNESS TUCK FIBER FIBRE STRENGTH TENACITY
TOUPEE RUG DOILY SCALP POSTICHE TOPPIECE
TOUR GIRO TURN SWING TOWER TURUS JUNKET SAFARI JOURNEY INVASION PROGRESS TOURETTE
(— OF DUTY) HERD STATION
(CANARY —) GLUCK GLUCKE
TOURACO LORY LOURIE TURAKOO
TOURBILLON KARRUSEL
TOUR DE FORCE STUNT
TOURIST TOURER TRIPPER VISITANT RUBBERNECK
TOURMALINE SHORL SCHORL DRAVITE ACHROITE SIBERITE
TOURNAMENT TILT JERID JOUSTS TOURNEY BONSPIEL CAROUSEL
TOURNEUR DEALER
TOURNEY PLAY
TOURNIQUET GARROT STANCH TWISTER STANCHER TORCULAR
TOUSLE SOOL SOWL RUMPLE TOOZLE
TOUSLED TAUTED TOWZIE TUMBLED UNKEMPT
TOUT SKIV BRUIT PLIER BARKER STEERER
TOW CRIB HAUL PULL HURDS STUPE TRACK TRACT CODILLA CORDELLE
TOWAGE TRACKAGE
TOWAI BIRCH KAMAHI
TOWARD AD INTO TORT ANENT ANENST AGAINST FORNENT ADVERSUS GAINWARD
(— CENTER) CENTRAD
(— CENTER OF EARTH) DOWN
(— ONE SIDE) ASLANT
(— THE END) SF
(— THE HEAD) ANTERIOR

(— THE REAR) ABACK DORSAD BACKWARD
(— THE RIGHT) DEXTRAD
(— THE SIDE) LATERAD
(— THE STERN) AFTER
(PREF.) AC AD AF AG AL AP AS AT IL IM IN INTRO IR OB PROS
(SUFF.) AD
(GOING —) PETAL
TOWEL CLOUT WIPER DIAPER LAVABO RUBBER
TOWER TOR PEEL PIKE REAR RISE SOAR SPUR TOUR BABEL BROCH HEAVE MINAR MOUNT PYLON SIKAR SPIRE STUPA TEXAS ASCEND ASPIRE BELFRY CASTLE CHULPA DOKHMA DONJON GOPURA ROLLER RONDEL SPRING TURRET BASTIDE CHULLPA DERRICK GIRALDA LANTERN MIRADOR NURAGHE SHIKARA SIKHARA STEEPLE TALAYOT TORREON TOURNEL TRACKER TURRION BARBICAN BASTILLE CLOGHEAD DOMINEER RONDELLE SCRUBBER TOURELLE TOWERLET PEPPERBOX
(— CONTAINING COKE) SCRUBBER
(— FOR SENTINEL) GUERITE
(— OF FORT) SPUR
(— OF MOSQUE) MINARET
(— OF SILENCE) DAKHMA
(— ON SUMMIT) PIKE
(— OVER) DROWN BESTRIDE
(ATTACHED —) DETAIL
(BELL —) CARILLON
(CONNING —) SAIL
(FRACTIONATING —) STILL
(PYRAMIDAL —) SIKAR VIMANA SHIKARA SIKHARA
(SIEGE —) BRATTICE
(SIGNAL —) BANTAYAN
(WIND —) BADGIR
(PREF.) PYRGO TURRI
TOWERING EMINENT SUPERNAL AMBITIOUS
TOWERMAN LEVERMAN
TOWER MUSTARD CRUCIFER
TOWHEE JOREE CHEWINK CHEEWINK
TOWING TRACKAGE
TOWLINE CORDELLE
TOWN BY BYE HAM WON CAMP CITY STAD TOON WENE WICK BAYAN BORGO BOURH BRUGH BURGH DERBY MACHI PLACE PLECK SIEGE STAND STEAD VILLE CIUDAD HAMMON ORANGE PUEBLO STAPLE BASTIDE BOROUGH CHESTER OPPIDUM QUIVIRA TOWNLET BOOMTOWN BOURGADE ENCEINTE HOMETOWN TOWNSHIP
(DESOLATED —) GUBAT
(FORTIFIED —) BURG BURGH ENCEINTE
(MYTHICAL —) QUIVIRA
(SMALL —) SHTETL SHTETEL
(UNFORTIFIED —) BOURGADE
(UNIMPORTANT —) PODUNK
(WALLED —) CHESTER
(PL.) PARGANA
(SUFF.) GRAD

TOWN HALL HALL CABILDO RATHAUS TOLBOOTH STADHOUSE
TOWNSHIP DEME DORP VILL BAYAN TREEN BOROUGH
TOWNSMAN CAD CIT DUDE SNOB TOWNY TOWNEE BURGHER CITIZEN COCKNEY OPPIDAN
(PL.) BURGWARE
TOWROPE TOW CABLET GUNLINE TOWLINE CORDELLE
TOXALBUMIN ROBIN PHALLIN
TOXEMIA BLACKLEG ECLAMPSIA
TOXIC VENOMOUS
TOXIN BOTULIN EXOTOXIN
TOY ARK DIE GAY TOP COCK DOLL FOOL MOVE PLAY BLOCK CORAL DALLY FLIRT HAPPY KNACK LAKIN PLAID SPORT TRICK WALLY BAUBLE DANDLE DOODLE FADDLE FINGER FIZGIG GEWGAW LAKING PRETTY PUPPET RATTLE SUCKER BLOWOUT CRICKET DREIDEL PLAYOCK TANGRAM TRINKET TUMBLER WHIZZER GIMCRACK KICKSHAW PINWHEEL SQUAWKER SQUEAKER TEETOTUM WINDMILL ZOETROPE
(— AMOROUSLY) MIRD
(— WITH) PADDLE
(FLYING —) PIGEON
TOYON TOLLON CHAMISO
TRACE RUN TUG WAD CAST ECHO HINT LICK MARK RACK SHOW SIGN STEP TANG TINT TROD BRING GHOST GLEAM GLIFF GRAIN PRINT SHADE SPICE SPOOR STAMP STEAD THEAT TINGE TOUCH TRACK TRACT TRAIL TRAIN TRESS DERIVE ENGRAM HARBOR LACING RESENT SHADOW SKETCH SMUTCH STRAIN STREAK SWATHE COCKEYE GLIMPSE KENNING MENTION REMNANT SOUPCON SURMISE SYMPTOM THOUGHT UMBRAGE VESTIGE WHISPER DESCRIBE ENGRAMMA FOOTSTEP SKERRICK TINCTURE WAINROPE SIMULACRUM
(— A BEE) COURSE
(— A CURVE) SWEEP
(— A DESIGN) CALK
(— MATHEMATICALLY) GENERATE
(— OF A HARE) FARE
(— ON CHART) PRICK
(— THE COURSE OF) DEDUCE
(HARNESS —) TUG THEAT TREAT
(HAVE A —) SMACK
(MEMORY —) ENGRAM ENGRAMME
(SLIGHT —) GHOST STAIN SMATCH SPARKLE
(SLIGHTEST —) SCINTIL
(PL.) FEUTE
(SUFF.) **(HAVING A —)** ISH ISTIC
TRACER SEEKER OUTLINER SEARCHER
TRACERY FANWORK FROSTING TRAILERY
TRACHEA ARTERY WINDPIPE
(— OF CRANE) TRUMP
TRACHEID HYDROID
TRACHYANDESITE ARSOITE VULSINITE

TRACHYTE PIPERNO
TRACING BAROGRAM POLYGRAM TRAILING
TRACK DOG PUG RAT RUT TAN WAD WAY CLEW CLUE DRAW FARE FOIL FOOT HUNT LANE MARK PAGE PATH PIST RACE RACK RAIK RAIL ROAD SHOE SLOT SPUR TROD VENT BLOCK CHUTE DRIFT FEUTE HOUND LODGE PISTE PLANE SLIDE SPACE SPOOR STEAD SWATH TRACE TRACT TRADE TRAIL TRAIN TREAD BEARER COURSE GROOVE HARBOR LADDER RETURN RUNWAY SIDING SLEUTH STRAIN STREAM SWATHE CHANNEL FOILING FOOTING PATHWAY TANGENT TRAFFIC VESTIGE BACKBONE FOOTSTEP GUIDEWAY TRANSFER TRECKPOT TREKPATH WAGONWAY
(**— FOR ROPE**) CHANNEL
(**— GAME**) DRAW
(**— OF DEER**) SLOT STRAIN
(**— OF GAME IN GRASS**) FOILING
(**— OF HARE**) FILE
(**— OF WOUNDED BEAST**) PERSUE
(**— ON PRINTING PRESS**) BANK BEARER
(**RAILROAD —**) LEAD SPUR STUB SIDING TANGENT APPROACH BACKBONE
(**RUNNING —**) FLAT CINDERS
(**SHORT BRANCH —**) RETURN
(**SIDE —**) LIE HOLE
(**SKATER'S —**) FLAT
(**TEMPORARY —**) SHOOFLY
(**WORM —**) NEREITE
(PREF.) ICHN(O)
TRACKER PUGGI PUGGY TRAILER TRAILMAN
TRACKLESS INVIOUS PATHLESS
TRACKMAN SPIKER
TRACT AREA BEAT DUAR FLAT ZONE CAMPO CLIME COAST DRIVE ESSAY FIELD GRABE HORST PATCH SWEEP TRACK BARONY BUNDLE EXTENT REGION ENCLAVE EURIPUS QUARTER ROYALTY TERRAIN TRACTUS BROCHURE CAMPAGNA CAMPAIGN CINGULUM DISTRICT FARMHOLD FORESTRY PAMPHLET PROVINCE TOWNSITE TREATISE
(**— KEPT IN NATURAL STATE**) PARK
(**— OF BARREN LAND**) BARREN DERELICT
(**— OF BRAIN FIBERS**) PEDUNCLE
(**— OF GRASSLAND**) PRAIRIE
(**— OF LAND**) CRU DOAB DUAB DUAR GORE MARK BLOCK CHASE CLAIM EJIDO FRITH GRANT LAINE SCOPE SWELL TALUK EIGHTY ESTATE FOREST GARDEN ISLAND POLDER STRATH AIRPORT QUILLET RESERVE TERRAIN BOUNDARY CLEARING DERELICT FARMHOLD INTERVAL SCABLAND SLASHING
(**— OF MUDDY GROUND**) SLOB
(**— OF OPEN UPLAND**) DOWN DOWNS

(**— OF UNCOVERED ICE**) GLADE
(**— OF WASTE LAND**) HEATH
(**BOGGY —**) RUNN MORASS
(**CLAYEY —**) TAKYR
(**CLEARED —**) JUM JHUM JOOM
(**DRY —**) SEARING
(**FORESTLESS —**) STEPPE
(**GENITAL —**) BEARING
(**IRREGULAR —**) GORE
(**OPEN —**) VEGA SLASH
(**SANDY —**) DEN DENE LANDE
(**SHRUBBY —**) MONTE
(**SWAMPY —**) FLOW BAYGALL
(**UNOCCUPIED AND UNCULTIVATED —**) DESERT
(**WATERLESS —**) THIRST
TRACTABLE EASY SOFT TAME BUXOM TAWIE DOCILE GENTLE TOWARD DUCTILE FLEXILE PLIABLE AMENABLE FLEXIBLE GUIDABLE OBEDIENT TOWARDLY YIELDING MALLEABLE
TRACTARIANISM PUSEYISM
TRACTION DRAFT DRAUGHT
TRACTOR CAT MULE DRAGON BOBTAIL CRAWLER PEDRAIL AGRIMOTOR
(**TRAILER —**) RIG
TRADE CHAP CHOP COUP DEAL SELL SWAP CHEAP CRAFT GRAFT PRICE TREAD TROKE TRUCK BAKERY BARTER CHANGE EMPLOY HANDLE METIER MISTER NIFFER OCCUPY SCORCE SCORSE BARGAIN CALLING CHAFFER FACULTY MYSTERY SCIENCE BUSINESS CABOTAGE EXCHANGE PLUMBING MERCHANDISE
(SUFF.) ERY
TRADEMARK CHOP MARK BRAND COUPON
TRADER SART BANYA PLIER BALIJA BANIAN BANYAN CHETTY DEALER MONGER NEPMAN TROKER CHAPMAN MARWARI SANGLEY TRUCKER ASTORIAN CHANDLER KURVEYOR MERCHANT OPERATOR
(**HORSE —**) JOCKEY
(**INEXPERIENCED —**) LAMB
TRADESMAN CIT BAKAL COOPER EGGLER SELLER TENSOR FRUITER GOLADAR OCCUPIER UPHOLDER
TRADESWOMAN WINSTER
TRADING CABOTAGE
TRADITION CABAL STORY SUNNA CABALA SMRITI SUNNAH THREAP HALACHA HALAKAH HEREDITY HERITAGE TRANSFER
(PL.) LEGEND
TRADITIONAL CLASSIC POMPIER
TRADUCE ILL SLUR ABUSE DEFAME MALIGN REVILE VILIFY ASPERSE DETRACT SCANDAL SLANDER
TRAFFIC COUP DEAL MANG MART MONG BROKE TRADE BARTER PALTER TRAVEL CHAFFER DEALING PASSAGE BUSINESS CHAFFERY COMMERCE EXCHANGE NAVIGATION
(**— IN SACRED THINGS**) SIMONY
(**— IN SLAVES**) MAGONIZE

TRAFFICKER COUPER DEALER
TRAGEDY BUSKIN TRAGIC TROIADES
TRAGIC DIRE DREADFUL THESPIAN
TRAGICOMEDY DRAME
TRAGOPAN MONAL
TRAGUS EARLET
TRAIL PAD PUG DRAG FOIL HARL HUNT NECK PATH PIST SIGN SLOT BLAZE CRAWL DRAIL PISTE ROUTE SPOOR STOCK SWEEP TRACE TRADE TRAIN COMING DAGGLE FOLLOW RUNWAY SHADOW SLEUTH STRAIN TAIGLE TRAPES DRAGGLE TRACHLE TRAFFIC OUTTRAIL STRIGGLE TRAILERY
(**— ALONG**) STREEL TRAPES
(**— OF A FISH**) LOOM
(**— OF STAG**) ABATURE
(**— OUT**) STREAM
(**— THROUGH MUD**) DAGGLE
(**DESCENDING —**) BAHADA BAJADA
(**MOUNTAIN —**) CLIMB
(**WAGON —**) RUDLOFF
TRAILBLAZER HARBINGER
TRAILER SEMI COACH BOXCAR CARAVAN FLATBED FROGGER GONDOLA ARTMOBILE
TRAILING (**— ON GROUND**) PROSTRATE
TRAIN SET DRAG GAIT SECT TILL TIRE TURN ZULU BEARD BREED COACH DRESS DRILL ENTER FOCUS LOCAL RANGE TRACE TRACT TRADE TRAIL TRYNE CONVOY DIRECT GENTLE GROUND INFORM MANURE NUZZLE RAPIDE REPAIR SCHOOL SEASON STRING SUBWAY AFFAITE BRIGADE CARAVAN EDUCATE FREIGHT GEARING LIMITED PEDDLER RATTLER RETINUE SHUTTLE VARNISH CIVILIZE DISCIPLE ELECTRIC EQUIPAGE EXERCISE HIGHBALL INSTRUCT MANIFEST REHEARSE
(**— AN ANIMAL**) BREAK
(**— FINE**) GAUNT
(**— FOR CONTEST**) POINT
(**— FOR FIGHTING**) SPAR
(**— OF ANIMALS**) COFFLE
(**— OF ATTENDANTS**) CORTEGE
(**— OF COMET**) TAIL
(**— OF EXPLOSIVE**) FUSE
(**— OF MINING CARS**) JAG RUN TRIP
(**CAMEL —**) KAFILA
(**FUNERAL —**) CONVOY
(**PACK —**) CONDUCTA
(**RAILROAD —**) DRAG HOOK LOCAL PICKUP EXPRESS FREIGHT LIMITED RATTLER
TRAINED GOOD MADE ADEPT BROKE BROKEN
TRAINEE BOOT CADET
TRAINER FEEDER JINETE LANISTA
TRAINING DRILL THEAT ASCESIS ASKESIS CULTURE NURTURE PAIDEIA BREEDING
(**— IN HUMANITIES**) CIVILITY
(**— OF HORSE**) DRESSAGE
(**RELIGIOUS —**) SADHANA

TRAIPSE GAD WALK TRAMP SASHAY WANDER
TRAIT ITEM LEAD MARK VEIN ANGLE CHARM KNACK TRACT TRICK AMENITY ELEMENT HALLMARK JAPANISM
(**CULTURE —**) SURVIVAL
(**FOREIGN —**) EXOTISM
(**GOOD —**) THEW
(**UNDESIRABLE —**) DEMON DAEMON
(**WELL-DEFINED —**) STREAK
(PL.) CORNERS
TRAITOR RAT JUDAS RUSTY NITHING WARLOCK APOSTATE ISCARIOT PRODITOR QUISLING SQUEALER TRADITOR TREACHER
TRAITOROUS FALSE FELON APOSTATE RENEGADE
TRAJECTORY SPORABOLA
TRA-LA-LA TRALIRA
TRAM TUB DRAM TRAMCAR TRAMMEL TRANVIA
(**COAL —**) TIP
(**SET OF —S**) JOURNEY
TRAMCAR TRAM DUMMY PICKUP
TRAMMEL TRAM HAMPER STIFLE COTTEREL
TRAMMER PUTTER
TRAMONTANE ALIEN FOREIGN OVERBERG
TRAMP BO BUM PAD BOOM HAKE HIKE HOBO HUMP PUNK SLOG SWAG VAMP WALK YEGG BURLY CAIRD CLAMP JAVEL PIKER ROGUE SHACK STIFF STRAG TRAIK TRAIL TRASH TROMP TROUT BAGMAN GAYCAT JOCKER PICARO STODGE STRAMP STROLL TINKER TRANCE TRAPES TRUANT TRUDGE DRUMMER FLOATER RUFFLER SWAGGER SWAGMAN TRAIPSE TRAMPLE TROUNCE TROWANE VAGRANT YEGGMAN CLOCHARD FOOTSLOG GANGEREL STROLLER TRAVELER VAGABOND SUNDOWNER
(**— ABOUT**) WAG
(**LONG —**) HUMP
(PL.) MONKERY
TRAMPING MONKERY
TRAMPLE HOX JAM PUG FARE FOIL FULL HOOF CHAMP POACH SCAUT SPURN TRAMP TRASH TREAD DEFOIL DEFOUL PADDLE SAVAGE STOACH STRAMP WADDLE OPPRESS OVERRUN SCAMBLE FORTREAD OVERRIDE
TRANCE RAPTUS AMENTIA ECSTASY SAMADHI CATALEPSY
TRANQUIL CALM COOL EASY LOWN MILD SOFT EQUAL QUIET STILL GENTLE PACATE PIPING SERENE CALMATO EQUABLE PACIFIC RESTFUL PEACEFUL
TRANQUILIZE CALM LULL QUIET STILL BECALM PACIFY SERENE SETTLE SOFTEN SOOTHE APPEASE COMPOSE
TRANQUILIZING ATARAXIC SOOTHING
TRANQUILLITY KEF LEE EASE

REST PEACE QUIET SATTVA SERENE HARMONY QUIETAGE QUIETUDE SERENITY
TRANS ANTI
TRANSACT DO PASS AGITATE CONDUCT PERFORM
TRANSACTION DEAL DEED GAGE GAGER ACTION AFFAIR FIDDLE MARGIN SPREAD BARGAIN MOHABAT PASSAGE CONTRACT KNOCKOUT OPERATION PROCEEDING
(**— AT LOWER PRICE**) DOWNTICK
(**PL.**) ACTA BUSINESS
TRANSCEND PASS SOAR EXCEED OVERTOP SURPASS
TRANSCENDENTAL ACOSMIC
TRANSCENDING EXQUISITE
(**PREF.**) SUPRA
TRANSCRIBE COPY BRAILLE DESCRIBE EXSCRIBE
TRANSCRIBED CANNED
TRANSCRIBER COPIER COPYIST
TRANSCRIPT COPY SCORE TENOR DOUBLE APOGRAPH EXSCRIPT
TRANSCRIPTION
(**PL.**) PAZAND PAZEND
TRANSEPT PLAGE PORCH
TRANSFER CEDE DEED FLIT GIVE JUMP PASS SALE SELL TURN ALIEN CABLE CARRY CROSS DROGH REFER REMIT SHIFT ASSIGN ATTORN CHANGE DECANT DELATE DONATE REMOVE SWITCH CESSION CONNECT CONSIGN DELIVER DEVOLVE DISPONE MIGRATE TRADUCE ALIENATE ANTEDATE CROCKING DELEGATE DELIVERY DONATION EXCHANGE TRANSACT TRANSUME VIREMENT NEGOTIATE
(**— A RECORDING**) OVERDUB
(**— DYE**) EXHAUST
(**— HEAT**) CONVECT
(**— HOMAGE**) ATTORN
(**— MOLTEN GLASS**) LADE
(**— OF ENERGY**) FLOW
(**— OF PROPERTY**) DEED GIFT GRANT DISPOSAL
(**— PIGMENT**) FLUSH
TRANSFERENCE DEMISE EMOTION REMOVAL DELATION DISPOSAL TRANSFER
TRANSFIGURE DEIFY CLARIFY
TRANSFIX FIX DART PITCH STAKE STICK SKEWER THRILL BESTICK
TRANSFORM TURN SHIFT TOUCH CHANGE STRIKE CONVERT FASHION PERMUTE CATALYZE DISGUISE HETERIZE
(**— ENERGY**) ABSORB
TRANSFORMATION CHANGE HAIRWORK
TRANSFORMER SET DIMMER JIGGER TEASER TOROID VARIAC BALANCE BOOSTER HEDGEHOG
TRANSFUSE ENDUE INDUE
TRANSGRESS ERR SIN BREAK OFFEND OVERGO DIGRESS DISOBEY VIOLATE INFRINGE OVERPASS OVERSLIP OVERSTEP TRESPASS

TRANSGRESSION SIN SLIP CRIME FAULT SCAPE BREACH DELICT ESCAPE MISDEED OFFENSE DELICTUM OVERLOUP TRESPASS
TRANSGRESSOR SINNER OFFENDER
TRANSIENCE FUGACITY
TRANSIENT FLEET BUBBLE FLIGHTY PASSING FLEETING FUGITIVE MOMENTARY
TRANSIENTLY HOVERLY
TRANSISTOR FET
TRANSIT BINOCLE PASSAGE TRANSEPT
TRANSITION CUT JUMP LEAP SEGUE SHIFT FERMENT PASSAGE
TRANSITIVE ACTIVE
TRANSITORINESS CADUCITY
TRANSITORY FLEET CADUCE FLYING BRITTLE PASSANT PASSING SLIDING VOLATIC WHILEND CADUCOUS FLEETING FLITTING TEMPORAL VOLATILE MOMENTARY
TRANSKEI (**CAPITAL OF —**) UMTATA
(**TOWN OF —**) BUTTERWORTH
TRANSLATE PUT DRAW MAKE TURN WEND RENDER CONVERT ENGLISH EXPOUND TRADUCE CONSTRUE INTERPRET
TRANSLATION CAB KEY CRIB PONY STEP TROT GLOSS HORSE TARGUM UNSEEN BICYCLE CABBAGE ENGLISH THARGUM TRADUCT VERSION SUBTITLE VERBATIM
(**— OF BIBLE**) PESHITO
(**— OF THE CLASSICS**) JACK
(**LOAN —**) CALQUE
TRANSLATOR TURNER
TRANSLUCENT CLEAR LUCID LIMPID LUCENT HYALINE
(**PREF.**) HYAL(O)
TRANSMIGRATION SAMARA SAMSARA SANSARA
TRANSMISSION ENTAIL DESCENT GEARBOX PASSAGE SENDING TRANSFER
(**— OF SOUND**) AUDIO
(**— TO OFFSPRING**) HEREDITY
(**SUFF.**) PHORESIS
TRANSMIT AIR BEAM EMIT SEND CARRY CONVEY DEMISE DERIVE ENTAIL EXPORT IMPACT IMPART RENDER CONDUCT CONSIGN FORWARD TRADUCE TRADUCT TRAJECT BEQUEATH DESCRIBE PROPAGATE
(**PREF.**) DIAGO
TRANSMITTER TUBA SLAVE SPARK BEACON JAMMER PINGER SENDER VEHICLE RADIATOR
TRANSMITTING ALIVE
TRANSMUTE CHEMIC CHEMICK ENNOBLE PERMUTE EXCHANGE TRANSMUE TRANSUME
TRANSOM PATIBLE TRAVERSE
TRANSPARENCY SLIDE
TRANSPARENT THIN CLEAR FILMY LUCID BRIGHT LIMPID LUCENT CRYSTAL FRAGILE HYALINE HYALOID TIFFANY DIOPTRIC LUCULENT LUMINOUS

LUSTROUS PELLUCID
(**PREF.**) DIAPHAN(O) HYAL(O)
TRANSPIRE HAPPEN
TRANSPLANT SPOT SHIFT DEPLANT
TRANSPORT DAK JOY ROB BEAR BOAT BUSS DAWK DRAY HAUL PASS PORT RAPE RAPT RIDE SEND SHIP BLISS CANOE CARRY DROGH FERRY FLUTE GILLY BANISH BARREL CONVEY DEPORT GALLOP KURVEY WAFTER ECSTASY EXPRESS FRAUGHT ONERARY RAPTURE TRADUCE TROOPER CABOTAGE CARRIAGE DAYDREAM ENRAVISH PALANDER
(**— BY PACKHORSE**) JAG
(**— FOR CRIME**) LAG
(**— LOGS**) BOB
(**— ORE**) SLUSH
(**PREF.**) PEREIO
TRANSPORTATION AIR DAK FARE AIRLIFT BOATAGE FREIGHT TRAJECT TRANSPORT
(**AIRPORT —**) LIMO
TRANSPORTED RAPT
(**— BY GLACIER**) ERRATIC
TRANSPOSE ADJOINT CONVERT REVERSE
TRANSPOSITION SHIFT ANSWER ANAGRAM
TRANSUBSTANTIATION METUSIA
TRANSVAAL DAISY GERBERA
TRANSVAALER TAKHAAR
TRANSVERSE CROSS FACING THWART OBLIQUE
TRANSVERSELY ATHWART
TRANSVESTISM EONISM
TRANSVESTITE BERDACHE
TRAP COY GET GIN PIT SET FALL GIRN GRIN HOOK LACE LIME NAIL PUTT TIPE TOIL WAIT WEEL BRAKE BRIKE CATCH LEASH PLANT POUND SNARE SPELL STALE SWICK SWIKE TRAIN COBWEB CRUIVE FELPOT ENGINE KEDDAH POCKET QUILEZ SNATCH STAYER WILLOW FLYTRAP PITFALL PITFOLD PUTCHEN PUTCHER RATTRAP SETTING SPRINGE TRAMMEL BIRDLIME COALHOLE DEADFALL DOWNFALL TRAPROCK
(**— FOR BIRDS**) SCRAPE
(**— FOR LARGE GAME**) HOPO
(**— FOR RABBITS, MICE, ETC**) TIPE TYPE
(**— FOR RATS**) CLAM
(**— FOR SALMON**) PUTT
(**— FOR SMALL ANIMALS**) HATCH
(**— FOR THE FEET**) CALTROPS
(**— IN POKER**) SANDBAG
(**— IN THEATER**) SCRUTO
(**— INTO SERVICE**) CRIMP
(**FISH —**) FYKE KILL LEAP WEEL WEIR CREEL WILLY CORRAL CRUIVE WILLOW
(**SAND —**) BUNKER
TRAPDOOR DROP SLOT TRAP SCRUTO VAMPIRE TRAPFALL
TRAPPED CORNERED
TRAPPER WIRER VOYAGEUR
TRAPPINGS GEAR JHOOL ARMORY

TOGGERY BARDINGS EQUIPAGE HOUSINGS CAPARISON
TRAPSHOOTING SKEET
TRASH ROT BOSH GEAR GOOK JUNK PELF RAFF TOSH TRAG CLART DRECK DRUSH STUFF SWASH THROW TRADE TROKE WASTE WRACK BUSHWA CULTCH KELTER KITSCH PALTRY RAMMEL REFUSE RUBBLE SCULCH TROUSE BAGGAGE BEGGARY FULLAGE GARBAGE PEDLARY RUBBISH TOSHERY TRAFFIC BLATHERY CLAPTRAP FLUMMERY MUCKMENT PEDDLERY SKITTLES SMATTER TRASHERY TRUMPERY
TRASHY CHEAP FLASH TOSHY TRIPY PALTRY SHODDY SLUSHY BAGGAGE RUBBISH RIFFRAFF RUBBISHY SIXPENNY TRUMPERY
TRAUMA WOUND INJURY STRESS
TRAVAIL PAIN TASK TOIL AGONY LABOR TORMENT
TRAVEL GO BAT BUS FLY GIG WAG FARE GANG HIKE PASS PATH RIVE TOTE TRIP VAMP WEND COVER KNOCK SLOPE THROW TRACK CRUISE TRANCE VOYAGE EXPRESS JOURNEY TRAVAIL TRUNDLE WAYFARE PROGRESS TRAVERSE
(**— ACROSS SNOW**) MUSH
(**— AIMLESSLY**) SAUNTER
(**— ALONG GROUND**) TAXI
(**— AROUND**) TURN COAST CIRCLE GIRDLE COMPASS
(**— AT GOOD SPEED**) CRACK
(**— AT HIGH SPEED**) HELL BARREL SCORCH
(**— AT RANDOM**) DRIFT
(**— AT SPEED OF**) DO
(**— BACK AND FORTH**) SHUNT COMMUTE
(**— BY AIRCRAFT**) AIR FLY AIRPLANE
(**— BY OX WAGON**) TREK
(**— FAST**) STREAK
(**— IN A VEHICLE**) TOOL
(**— ON FOOT**) HIKE SHANK KNAPSACK PERAMBULATE PEREGRINATE
(**— ON WATER**) SAIL
(**— OVER**) TRANCE TRAVERSE
(**— THROUGH**) GO
(**— THROUGH WOODS**) BUSHWACK
(**— WITHOUT EQUIPMENT**) SIWASH
(**DAY'S —**) JORNADA JOURNAL JOURNEY
TRAVELER GOER CRAWL FARER GUEST HORSE BAGMAN GANGER KILROY POSTER SAILOR VIATOR CRUISER DRUMMER FOOTMAN HOWADJI LEEFANG PILGRIM SWAGGIE TRAILER TREKKER TRIPPER WAYGOER ARGONAUT EXPLORER MAGELLAN OUTRIDER VOYAGEUR WAYFARER PASSENGER
(**COMPANY OF —S**) CARAVAN
TRAVELER'S JOY HAGROPE BINDWITH CLEMATIS
TRAVELING ERRANT PEREGRINE

TRAVELING SALESMAN RIDER DRUMMER

TRAVERSE DO GO SEE BURN DENY KNEE LIFT MAKE PASS SPAN WALK COAST COVER CROSS SHEAR SWEEP THIRL TRACE TRACK CIRCLE COURSE DENIAL OVERGO PERCUR TRAVEL VOYAGE WANDER CHANNEL JOURNEY MEASURE OVERRUN PARADOS PERVADE DESCRIBE NAVIGATE OVERPASS OVERWEND SCRAMBLE UNTHREAD PERAMBULATE

TRAVERTINE TOPHUS

TRAVESTY EXODE PARODY SATIRE EXODIUM TRAVEST BURLESQUE

TRAVIATA, LA (CHARACTER IN —) FLORA VALERY ALFREDO BERVOIX DOUPHOL GERMONT GIORGIO VIOLETTA
(COMPOSER OF —) VERDI

TRAVOIS DRAY TRAVOY ALLIGATOR

TRAWL SEINE BOULTER DRAGNET STOWNET TRAWLNET TROTLINE

TRAWLER PAREJA BRAGOZZO

TRAY HOD CASE TILL TRUG BATEA BOARD FLOAT SCALE SLICE SUSAN GALLEY MONKEY SALVER SERVER SERVET VOIDER WAITER BALANCE CABARET COASTER CONSOLE SHALLOW DEJEUNER
(— FOR CRUMBS) VOIDER
(— FOR DRYING FISH) FLAKE
(— FOR MATCH SPLINTS) CAUL MONKEY
(— FOR SHELLFISH) FLOAT
(— FOR TYPE) GALLEY
(— TO CATCH OVERFLOW) SAFE
(CIRCULAR —) ROUNDEL

TREACHEROUS FOUL CATTY DIRTY FALSE PUNIC SNAKY SWACK FELINE FICKLE HOLLOW ROTTEN YELLOW SNAKISH FRAUDFUL IMPOSING PLOTTING SLIDDERY

TREACHERY GUILE SWICK TRAIN DECEIT FELONY PERFIDY TREASON UNTRUTH DASTARDY DISTRUST TRAHISON TRAITORY

TREACLE DIBS CLAGGUM THERIAC

TREAD FIT PAD BEAT FOOT PATH POST RUNG STEP VOLT CLAMP TRACK TRADE DEFOIL DEFOUL PADDLE CRAWLER FEATHER FOOTING RETREAD TREADER FOOTSTEP
(— CLUMSILY) CLUMP BALTER
(— DOWN SHOE HEEL) CAM
(— HEAVILY) SPURN TRAMPLE
(— OF FOWL'S EGG) GRANDO
(— ON) FOIL
(— TO MUSIC) FOOT
(— WARILY) PUSSYFOOT
(TIRE —) COVER

TREADLE PEDAL CHALAZA

TREASON SEDITION

TREASURE POSE ROON HOARD PRIZE STORE TROVE VALUE BURSAR COFFER FINDAL GERSUM WEALTH ASTHORE FINANCE THESAUR WARISON

GARRISON TREASURY
(— STATE) MONTANA
(LITTLE —) STOREEN
(PL.) CIMELIA

TREASURE BOX HANAPER

TREASURED DEAR CHARY PRECIOUS

TREASURE ISLAND (AUTHOR OF —) STEVENSON
(CHARACTER IN —) BEN JIM PEW GUNN JOHN BONES HANDS ISRAEL SILVER HAWKINS LIVESEY SMOLLETT TRELAWNEY

TREASURER FISC BOWSER BURSAR FISCAL GABBAI BOUCHER HOARDER SPENDER BHANDARI COFFERER HAZNADAR PROVISOR QUAESTOR RECEIVER

TREASURY FISC FISK KIST CHEST HOARD PURSE COFFER CORBAN FISCAL FISCUS BOWSERY BURSARY CHAMBER CHECKER CHEQUER HORDARY AERARIUM THESAURY TREASURE
(PAPAL —) CAMERA

TREAT RUN USE DEAL DOSE HOCK LEAD PLAY BEANO BESEE COVER DIGHT GUIDE LEECH SERVE SETUP SHOUT TRACT TRAIT WRITE DEMEAN DOCTOR GOVERN HANDLE LIQUOR PADDLE REGALO CONDUCT ENTREAT GARNISH ACTIVATE AIRBRUSH
(— A HIDE) DRUM
(— AS EQUAL) EVEN
(— BADLY) ILLGUIDE
(— CARELESSLY) BANG BANDY
(— CLOUDS) SEED
(— CONFIDENTIALLY) HUSH
(— CRUELLY) CRUCIFY
(— DAINTILY) PAMPER
(— DIABOLICALLY) BEDEVIL
(— DISCOURTEOUSLY) DISGRACE
(— FIBERS) GILL
(— FLOUR) AGENIZE
(— FONDLY) DANDLE
(— FUR) CARROT
(— GENTLY) FAVOR
(— HAIR) CONK
(— ILLNESS) POMSTER
(— IMPROPERLY) MISUSE
(— IMPUDENTLY) NOSE
(— LIGHTLY) SCRUFF
(— LOVINGLY) COAX
(— MALICIOUSLY) SPITE
(— MASH) LAUTER
(— OF) DISCOURSE
(— OF DRINKS) SETUP
(— ROUGHLY) BANG MUMBLE GRABBLE MALTREAT
(— SILK TO RUSTLE) SCROOP
(— SLIGHTINGLY) LIGHTLY
(— STEEL) HARVEY
(— UNFAIRLY) DO
(— UNSKILLFULLY) FOOZLE
(— WITH ACID) SOUR
(— WITH CARE) CODDLE
(— WITH CONTEMPT) HUFF SNUB BLURT FLIRT FLOCK FLOUT FLAUNT BAUCHLE
(— WITH HEAT) FOMENT
(— WITH HONOR) RESPECT
(— WITH INATTENTION) FORGET

(— WITH INDULGENCE) FONDLE
(— WITH PARTIALITY) ACCEPT
(— WITH RESPECT) HONOR
(— WITH RIDICULE) SCOUT
(— WITH RUDENESS) FRUMP
(— WITH TAR) BLACK
(— WITH TENDERNESS) CODDLE
(NEW YEAR'S EVE —) HAGMENA HOGMANAY

TREATISE AGAMA DONET FAUNA FLORA LIBEL SILVA SUMMA SYLVA TRACT TREAT BOTANY POETRY POMONA SERTUM SYSTEM ALGEBRA ANATOMY BIOLOGY COMMENT DIETARY GEOLOGY GRAMMAR HISTORY PANDECT PHYSICS PINETUM POETICS ZOOLOGY ALMAGEST BROCHURE CALCULUS DIDACTIC ECTHESIS EXERCISE GENETICS GEOMANCY GEOMETRY GERMANIA HORNBOOK LAPIDARY MONUMENT PANTHEON PASTORAL PRACTICE SITOLOGY SPECULUM TRACTATE MONOGRAPH
(SUFF.) ICS LOGER LOGIA(N) LOGIC(AL) LOGIST LOGUE LOGY OLOGY

TREATMENT CURE WORK TREAT USAGE ANIMUS DETAIL FACIAL QUARTER BEHAVIOR DEMEANOR ENTREATY
(— BY MASSAGE) SEANCE
(— FOR WOOLLENS) SPONGING
(BAD —) MISUSAGE
(COLD —) FREEZE
(COMPASSIONATE —) MERCY
(CONTEMPTUOUS —) SPURN
(CRUEL —) SEVERITY
(DIRE —) DOLE
(HARMFUL —) ABUSE
(HARSH —) SHAFT
(INHUMAN —) CRUELTY
(LUXURIOUS —) DELICACY
(SEVERE —) ROUGH
(PREF.) (MEDICAL —) IATR(O)
(SUFF.) PRAXIS
(MEDICAL —) IATRIA IATRIC(S) IATRIST IATRY

TREATY MISE ACCORD CARTEL CONCORD ENTENTE LOCARNO ALLIANCE ASSIENTO TREATISE CONCORDAT

TREBLE TRIPLE DESCANT MINIKIN SOPRANO TRIPLUM

TREBUCHET DONDINE DONDAINE

TREE TI ACH ADY AMA APA ARN ASH BAY BEL BEN BUR DAK DAR EBO ELM FIG FIR GUM HAW KOA KOU LIN OAK SAJ SAL TAL TUI ULE YEW ACLE AGBA AKEE AMLA ANAM ANAN ANDA ARAR ASAK ASOK ATIS ATLE ATTA AULU AUSU BAEL BAKU BITO BOGO BOOM BREA BURI BURR CADE COLA CRAB DATE DHAK DILO DITA DOON EBOE IPIL JACK KINO KOKO LIME MABI MORA OHIA OMBU PALA PINE POLE POON SADR SORB SUPA TALA TAWA TCHE TEAK TEIL TITI TOON TREW TUNG TUNO UPAS VERA WOOD

YATE YAYA AALII ABETO ABURA ACANA ACAPU ACOMA AFARA AGATI AGOHO AKEKI ALAMO ALANI ALDER ALGUM ALISO ALMON ALMUG AMAGA AMAPA AMBAK ANABO ANJAN APPLE ARACA ARBOR ARECA ARJAN ARJUN ARTAR ASOKA ASPEN ATLEE BABUL BALAO BALSA BALTA BANAK BEECH BEHEN BETIS BIRCH BONGO BOREE BOSSE BUMBO CACAO CARAP CAROB CEBIL CEDAR CEIBO DADAP DHAVA DHAWA DILLY DRYAD DURIO ELDER GABUN GAIAC GENIP GINEP GINKO HAZEL ICICA IXORA JAMBO JIQUE JIQUI KAPOR KAPUR KEENA KOKAN KOKIO KOKUM KONGU KUSAM LANSA LARCH LARIX LEHUA LEMON LICCA LIMBA LINDE LINER LINGO MAHOE MAHUA MAMIE MAPLE MAQUI NARRA NIEPA NURSE OADAL OSAGE OSIER PACAY PAPAW PECAN PIPER RAULI ROBLE ROHAN ROWAN SALAI SAMAN SASSY SCRAG SIMAL SIRIS SISSU STICK SUMAC TABOG TARFA TENIO TERAP TIKUR TIMBO TINGI TOONA TUART ULMUS UMIRI URUCA URUCU UVITO WAHOO YACAL YACCA YULAN ZAMAN ACAJOU AHKROT AKEAKE ALAGAO ALERCE ALERSE ALFAJE ALMOND ALUPAG AMAMAU AMBASH AMUGIS AMUYON ANAGAP ANAGUA ANAQUA ANGICO ANILAO ARALIA ARANGA ARBUTE AUSUBO AZALEA BABOEN BACURY BAHERA BAKULA BALSAM BANABA BANAGO BANANA BANCAL BANIAN BANYAN BARBAS BATAAN BIRIBA BOMBAX BONDUC BONETE BOTONG BRAUNA BUCARE BUSTIC CALABA CAMARA CANELA CANELO CAPUMO CARAPA CASSIA CATIVO CAUCHO CEDRON CHALTA CHERRY CHICHA CHINAR CHOGAK CITRON COBOLA COCUYO CUMBER DATURA DHAMAN DHAURA DHAURI DRIMYS DURIAN ELCAJA EMBLIC EMBUIA FEIJOA FILLER FUSTIC GABOON GINGKO GUAIAC GURJAN GURJUN IDESIA IDIGBO ILIAHI ILLIPE ILLUPI JAGUEY JUJUBE KAMALA KEMPAS KINDAL KITTUL LANSAT LANSEH LAUREL LIGNUM LINDEN LITCHI LOCUST LONGAN MAFURA MALLET MAYTEN MEDLAR MILKER MIMOSA ORANGE PANAMA PAWPAW PIQUIA POPLAR RAMBEH ROHUNA RUNNEL SABICU SABINO SANDAN SANTOL SAPELE SAPOTA SAPOTE SATINE SAWYER SERAYA SINTOC SISSOO SOUARI STYRAX SUMACH SUNDRI TALUTO TAMANU TARATA TEETEE TIKOOR TIMBER TINGUY TOATOA TOTARA TUPELO URUCUM URUSHI UVALHA

WABAYO WABOOM WAHAHE
WALNUT WAMARA WAMPEE
WANDOO WATTLE YACHAN
YAGHAN YAMBAN ZAMANG
ACHIOTE ACHUETE AILANTO
AKEPIRO AMBATCH AMBOINA
AMUGUIS AMUYONG ANABONG
ANNATTO ANONANG APITONG
APRICOT ARARIBA ARAROBA
ARBORET ARBUTUS AROEIRA
ASSAGAI AVOCADO AVODIRE
BANILAD BANKSIA BECUIBA
BENZOIN BILLIAN BOLLING
BUBINGA BUCKEYE BUISSON
CADAMBA CAJAPUT CAJUPUT
CANELLA CARAIPE CASTANA
CATALPA CAUTIVO CERILLO
CHAMPAC CHECHEM CHECKER
CHENGAL COCULLO CONIFER
CURUPAY CYPRESS DEADMAN
DESCENT DETERMA DHAMNOO
EPACRID FRUITER GONDANG
GRIBBLE GUMIHAN HICKORY
HOLLONG HOPBUSH HORMIGO
KAMASSI KAMBALA KICKXIA
KITTOOL KOKOONA KOOMBAR
KUMQUAT LOGWOOD MADRONA
MANJACK MARGOSA NAARTJE
PARAIBA PEREIRA PIMENTO
PULASAN PYRAMID RATWOOD
REDWOOD SERINGA SERVICE
SHITTAH SPINDLE STOPPER
SUNDARI SURETTE TANGELO
TANGHIN TARAIRI TARATAH
TARWOOD TINDALO TREELET
TWISTER URUNDAY VETERAN
WALAHEE WALLABA WEENONG
WONGSHY WONGSKY YAMANAI
YOHIMBE YOHIMBI ACEITUNA
ALGAROBA ALLSPICE ALMACIGA
ALMANDER ALMENDRO
ALOEWOOD AMARILLO
ARAGUANE ARBOLOCO ARBUSCLE
AVELLANO BAKUPARI BASSWOOD
BAYBERRY BELLWOOD BINDOREE
BITANHOL BLACKBOX BOARWOOD
BORRACHA BREADNUT
CABREUVA CAMELLIA CAMUNING
CARAGANA CARAUNDA
CHAMPACA CHESTNUT
CHINCONA CHINOTTO CINNAMON
COCOPLUM COPALCHE
COUMAROU CRABWOOD
CUCUMBOL DEADFALL
DOMINANT DOTTEREL·
DOVEWOOD DRACAENA
DRUMWOOD ETABALLI FIREFALL
FORESTER GAMDEBOO GEELHOUT
GENISARO GUACACOA GUAYROTO
HALAPEPE HARDTACK
HARDWOOD HOLDOVER
HORNBEAM HOROPITO
IRONWOOD ISHPINGO ITCHWOOD
JELOTONG JELUTONG KAJUGARU
KINGWOOD KNOBWOOD
LACEBARK LEADWOOD
LORDWOOD MAHOGANY
MANDARIN MILKWOOD
MOKIHANA OITICICA OLEASTER
ONEBERRY PEDIGREE PICHURIM
PINKWOOD RAMBUTAN
RASAMALA SANDARAC
SANDWOOD SAPUCAIA

SASSWOOD SEBESTEN SHAGBARK
SHAVINGS SILKWOOD SLOGWOOD
SOAPBARK STANDARD SUCUPIRA
SWEETSOP SYCAMORE
TAMARACK TAMARIND
TANEKAHA TREELING TURMERIC
ZAPATERO PERSIMMON
PISTACHIO SASSAFRAS
SATINWOOD SANDALWOOD
(— CUT BACK) DOTARD POLLARD
(— FURNISHING SUPPORT TO VINE)
HUSBAND
(— IN STREAM) SAWYER
(— LEFT IN CUTTING) HOLDOVER
(— OF HEAVEN) AILANTO
AILANTHUS
(— ON WALL) RIDER
(— OVER 2 FT. DIAMETER) VETERAN
(— SYMBOLIZING UNIVERSE)
YGDRASIL
(— WITH BRANCHES TRIMMED) LOP
LOPSTICK
(—S IN FOREST) STAND
(AROMATIC —) CLUSIA LABIATE
(AUSTRALIAN —) ASH GUM TOON
BELAH BELAR BOREE BUNDY
BUNYA GIDIA HAZEL KARRI
NONDA PENDA SALLY WILGA
BAOBAB DRIMYS GIDGEE GIMLET
GYMPIE JARRAH KOWHAI
MARARA PEROBA SALLEE
DOGWOOD GEEBUNG PEEBEEN
BEEFWOOD CARABEEN
COOLABAH FLINDOSA GRAVILEA
IRONBARK LACEBARK QUANDONG
ROSEBUSH SANDSTAY
SOAPWOOD TILESEED
(BIG —) SEQUOIA
(BORNEO —) BILIAN
(BURMESE —) PADOUK
(CEYLON —) HORA
(CITRUS —) SHADDOCK
(CLOTHES —) COSTUMER
(CLUMP OF —S) TOLL TUMP STELL
(CONTORTED —) SAXAUL
(CUBAN —) JIQUE JIQUI
GUACACOA
(CURSED —) WARYTREE
(DEAD —) RUNT SNAG RAMPIKE
(DEAD —S) DRIKI
(DECAYED —) DOTTEREL
(DWARF —) SCRUB ARBUSCLE
(EVERGREEN —) FIR YEW PINE
SUGI TAWA ABIES ATHEL CAROB
CEDAR CLOVE HOLLY LARCH
LEMON OLIVE THUJA BALSAM
BIBIRU COIGUE COIHUE KANAGI
KAPUKA LOQUAT ORANGE
SPRUCE ARDISIA BEBEERU
BILIMBI CONIFER HEMLOCK
JUNIPER MADRONA MADRONO
EUCALYPT EUONYMUS
SAPODILLA SANDORICUM
(FAMILY —) STEMMA DESCENT
PEDIGREE
(FRUIT —) CORDON
(GENEALOGICAL —) ARBOR JESSE
(GROWTH OF —S) SYLVAGE
(GUM —) KARI KINO BABUL BALTA
BUMBO ICICA KARRI KIKAR
GIMLET MALLET STORAX TEWART
WANDOO GOMMIER COOLIBAH
(HAWAIIAN —) KOA LEHUA ILIAHI

(INFERNAL —) ZAQQUM
(JAPANESE —) KAYA KIAKI KEYAKI
KADSURA KATSURA SATSUMA
ZELKOVA
(MANDARIN —) SATSUMA
(MEXICAN —) ULE AMAPA DRAGO
EBANO SERON CAPULI CATENA
CHILTE CAPULIN COPALCHE
(MYTHICAL —) TUBA
(NEW ZEALAND —) AKE KARO
KAWA MIRO PUKA RATA RIMU
TAWA TORU WHAU HINAU KAORI
KAURI MAIRE MANGI MAPAU
MATAI TOWAI AKEAKE KAMAHI
KANUKA KAPUKA KARAKA
KARAMU KAWAKA KONINI
MANUKA PURIRI TARATA TITOKI
TOATOA TOTARA WAHAHE
AKEPIRO MANGEAO PUKATEA
TARAIRI TARWOOD KAWAKAWA
KOHEKOHE MAKOMAKO
(ORNAMENTAL —) KABIKI
LABURNUM POINCIANA
(PHILIPPINES —) DAO IBA TUA TUI
BOGO DITA IFIL IPIL AGOHO
AGOJO ALMON AMAGA ANABO
BAYOG BAYOK BETIS DANLI
GUIJO LAUAN LIGAS TABOG
YACAL ALAGAO ALUPAG AMUYON
ANAGAP ANUBIN ARANGA
BANUYO BATAAN BATETE BATINO
BOTONG DUNGON KATMON
LANETE MABOLO MARANG
MOLAVE SAGING TALUTO
AMUGUIS AMUYONG ANABONG
ANOBING ANONANG APITONG
BINUKAU CAMAGON DANGLIN
MANCONO MAYAPIS TINDALO
ALMACIGA BITANHOL KALIPAYA
KALUMPIT LUMBAYAO MACAASIM
MALAPAHO TANGUILE
(POISONOUS —) GUAO UPAS LIGAS
TANGHIN TANQUEN MANCHINEEL
(POLYNESIAN —) MACUDA
(SACRED —) CHAMPAC CHAMPAK
(SALT —) ATLE
(SHADE —) ELM DILLY GUAMA
HEVEA CATALPA HALESIA
INKWOOD JOEWOOD SYCAMORE
(SHOWY —) ASAK ASOK ASOKA
(SMALL —) AKE BOX TCHE ALDER
CUMAY DWARF HENNA NGAIO
SERON AKEAKE BLOLLY CHANAR
JOJOBA KOWHAI ARBORET
INKWOOD JOEWOOD KADAMBA
STADDLE TREELET EMAJAGUA
HARDTACK HUISACHE OLEASTER
SNOWBELL SOURWOOD TREELING
(SPINY —) LIME AROMA AROMO
HONEY BOOGUM BUCARE
BUMELIA CATECHU COLORIN
LAVANGA COCKSPUR
(STANDING —) FILLER
(STUNTED —) SCRAB SCRUB
SCRUNT
(THORNY —) BEL BAEL BREA
LEMON AMBACH SAMOHU
AMBATCH
(TIMBER —) ASH DAR ENG FIR SAL
ACLE ANDA BAKU COCO CUYA
EKKI IPIL PELU PINE TALA TEAK
YANG ACAPU ALMON AMAPA
AMATE AMBAY ANJAN ARACA

ARGAN BANAK BIRCH CAROB
CEDAR COCOA CULLA EBONY
ERIZO FOTUI HALDU ICICA IROKO
KAURI KHAYA KIAKI KOKAN
MANIU MAPLE MVULE NARRA
ROBLE TIMBO ALERCE ALUPAG
BABOEN BACURY BANABA
BANCAL CARBON CHUPON
CORTEZ DAGAME DEGAME
DUKUMA ESPAVE FREIJO GAMARI
GUMHAR IMBUIA JACANA LEBBEK
MUERMO PADAUK SANDAN
SATINE SISSOO AMUGUIS
AROEIRA BECUIBA BILLIAN
CARAIPI CYPRESS ESPAVEL
GATEADO GOMAVEL GUARABU
GUAYABI HARPULA HOLLONG
KOOMBAR LAPACHO REDWOOD
AMARILLO BOARWOOD
CABREUVA CARACOLI COCOBOLO
CRABWOOD DONCELLA
GUATAMBU GUAYACAN
MAHOGANY SLOGWOOD
SUCUPIRA ·
(TRAINED —) ESPALIER
(TROPICAL —) AKEE AULU DALI
DIKA EBOE EKKI GUAO INGA
MABA MAHO MAJO PALM SHEA
ACKEE BALSA BONGO COUMA
DALLI FOTUI GUAMA GUARA
ICICA ILAMA JIGUA MARIA NEPAL
NJAVE POOLI TARFA ANUBIN
BAKULA BALATA BANANA
CASHEW CEDRON CHUPON
GENIPA HACKIA ITAUBA LEBBEK
LECYTH MAMMEE OBECHE
PERSEA ANGELIN ANNATTO
CAULOTE COPAIBA DATTOCK
EHRETIA EUGENIA GATEADO
GUACIMO LAPACHO MAJAGUA
MOMBINI SANDBOX SOURSOP
SURETTE BEEFWOOD CALABASH
CAMUNING CORKWOOD
FUNTUMIA MUSKWOOD
PATASHTE SWEETSOP TAMARIND
MONKEYPOD MANGOSTEEN
(UNARMED —) ALBIZZIA
(VARNISH —) DOON THEETSEE
(XEROPHYTIC —) SAXAUL
(YOUNG —) RUNNEL SPRING
TILLER SAPLING SEEDLING
SPRINGER
(PL.) BLUFF RINDS SILVA
OVERSTORY
(PREF.) ARBORI DENDR(O)
(SUFF.) DENDRON
TREE CREEPER TOMTIT
TREE CYPRESS GILIA
TREE DUCK FIDDLER YAGUAZA
TREE FROG FERREIRO
TREE MOSS USNEA
TREENAIL NOG GUTTA MOOTER
TRUNNEL
TREE PEONY MOUTAN
TREE TOAD HYLA HYLID ANURAN
TREETOP LAP LOP
TREFOIL CANCH LOTUS CLAVER
CROWTOE BEDSTRAW SAINFOIN
TICKSEED
TREHALOSE MYCOSE
TRELLIS TRAIL PERGOLA TARLIES
ESPALIER
TREMATODE FLUKE

MARITA STRIGEID

TREMBLE DARE DIRL RESE BEVER QUAKE SHAKE SLOWS WIVER AGRISE DIDDER DINGLE DITHER DODDER FALTER HOTTER HOTTLE NITHER QUAVER QUIVER SHIMMY THRILL TITTER TOTTER TREMOR TRYMLE WABBLE WOBBLE WUTHER FLICKER SHUDDER STAGGER TWIDDLE WHITHER THRIMBLE
(PL.) TIRE TIRES
(PREF.) TREMELLI TROMO

TREMBLER BUZZER HAMMER VIBRATOR

TREMBLING BEVER SHAKY DITHER TREMOR TREPID AQUIVER DODDERY PALSIED QUAKING QUAVERY QUIVERY TREMBLY TWITTER

TREMBLY WOOZY

TREMENDOUS BIG AWFUL GIANT GREAT LARGE HOWLING TEARING ENORMOUS HORRIBLE TERRIBLE TERRIFIC MONSTROUS

TREMOLO HURRY TRILLO

TREMOR RIGOR SHAKE DINDLE QUIVER THRILL SHUDDER TREMBLE

TREMULOUS ASPEN QUAKY SHAKY PALSIED SHIVERY TREMBLY SHIMMERY TINGLING

TRENCH GAW SAP FOSS GRIP GURT LINE MOAT RILL SICK SIKE TAJO TRIG BOYAU CHASE DITCH DRAIN DRILL FLOAT FOSSE GRAFF GRAFT GRAVE GROOP SEUCH TRINK COFFER FURROW GULLET GUTTER SHEUGH ACEQUIA CUNETTE CUVETTE OPENCUT SLIDDER ENCROACH LOCKSPIT PARALLEL SPREADER THOROUGH TRESPASS
(— BELOW FOREST FIRE) GUTTER
(— FOR BURYING POTATOES) CAMP
(— FOR DRAIN TILES) CHASE
(— FORMED BY BANKING VEGETABLES) GRAVE
(ARTIFICIAL —) LEAT
(IRRIGATION —) FLOAT SUGSLOOT
(PREF.) BOTHR(O) BOTHRI(O)

TRENCHANT ACID KEEN EDGED SHARP TUANT INCISIVE

TRENCHER PLATTER ROUNDEL

TREND BEND BIAS HAND TONE TURN BULGE CURVE DRIFT SENSE SLANT SWING TENOR SQUINT STRIKE CURRENT DOWNSIDE MOVEMENT TENDENCY
(LOWERING PRICE —) EASE

TREPANG BALATE SWALLO SWALLOW TITFISH TEATFISH

TREPIDATION FEAR ALARM DISMAY

TRESPASS DEBT GILUT POACH BREACH FURTUM INVADE INTRUDE OFFENSE ENCROACH ENTRENCH INFRINGE INTRENCH OVERLOUP

TRESS CURL LOCK TAIL BRAID SWITCH RINGLET WIMPLER

TRES-TINE TRAY ROYAL

TRESTLE MARE HORSE INRUN

CHEVALET SAWHORSE

TREVALLY TURRUM

TREWS TROUSERS

TRIACETATE ACETIN EUROBIN

TRIAD MAJOR TRIAS TRINE TRIUNE TERNARY TERNION TRILOGY TRINARY TRINITY TRIMURTI TRIRATNA

TRIAL SAY SHY TRY BOUT DOOM FIRE HACK OYER STAB TEST TURN ASSAY CROSS ESSAY GRIEF ISSUE POINT PROOF TASTE TOUCH WHACK ASSIZE EFFORT EQUITY TRINAL APPROOF ATTEMPT CALVARY DISGUST HEARING PROVING SCRATCH CRUCIBLE EXERCISE JUDGMENT QUAESTIO TENTAMEN PROLUSION
(— BY BATTLE) WAGER
(— BY ORDEAL) ORDALIUM
(— FOR HOUNDS) DERBY
(— OF SPEED) DASH
(— OF STRENGTH) CRUNCH
(AUTHOR OF —) KAFKA
(CHARACTER IN —) LENI JOSEPH ADVOCATE BURSTNER TITORELLI
(EXPERIMENTAL —) TENTAMEN
(RACING —) PREP
(SEVERE —) ORDEAL CRUCIBLE
(PREF.) PEIRA

TRIANGLE APEX CYMBAL OXYGON TRIGON PYRAMID SCALENE TRINITY TRIQUET DINGDONG ISOSCELE

TRIANGULAR HEATER CUNEATE HASTATE
(— AREA) QUIRK
(— CLOTH) GORE
(— INSET) GODET
(PREF.) TRIGON(O)

TRIBAL GENTILE GENTLIC TRIBULAR

TRIBE (ALSO SEE NATIVE AND PEOPLE) AO GI ATI AUS BOH EVE EWE GOG KHA KIN KRA ROD SUK YAO ADAI AKAN AKHA AKIM AKKA BAYA BONI CLAN DAGO GUHA PURU QUNG RACE RAVI REKI SAHO SEID SHIK SHOR SIOL SOGA SUKU SUSU TOBA TURI TUSH UBII VEPS VILI VIRA YANA AEQUI ANGKA APTAL ARAWA BASSI BATAK BESSI BONGO BROOD CHANG CINEL DADJO DEDAN DIERI FIRCA GIBBI HORDE HOUSE ICENI KAJAR KANDH KEDAR KHOND KIWAI KONGO KOTAR KREPI LANGO MAGOG MARSI MBUBA MENDE MENDI MOSSI MUTER NANDI PHYLE PONDO QUADI SERER SOTIK STAMM SUEVI TAIPI TAULI TCAWI TEKKE TELEI TUATH VEPSE VOLOF WAKHI WARRI WASHO WAYAO YOMUD ADIGHE AGAWAM AMHARA ANAMIM ANTEVA APAYAO ARAINS BANYAI BASOGA BUDUMA BUSAOS CHAMPA CHAWIA CHORAI DOROBO FAMILY HERULI KARLUK KEREWA KHAMTI KONYAK KORANA LOBALE MANGAR

MOLALA NATION NERVII PAHARI PHYLON POKOMO RAMNES SHAGIA SICULI SIMEON SUKUMA TAINUI TAMOYO TCHIAM TELEUT THUSHI TUSHIN TYPEES VENETI WABENA WABUMA WAGOMA WAGUHA WAHEHE WARORI WASOGA WAVIRA ZARAMO ZEGUHA ZENAGA ABABDEH ABANTES AIAWONG AKWAPIM AMAKOSA ANOMURA ANTAIVA ARVERNI BAGIRMI BAKATAN BAKONGO BAKUNDA BAMBARA BASONGO CABINDA CHAOUIA CHAUWIA CHONTAL CHUKCHI COLLERY DADAYAG DADSCHO ILLANUN JAZYGES KABINDA KABONGA KHOKANI KOLDAJI KONIAGA KOREISH KUBACHI KURUMBA LLANERO NAIADES PALAUNG PARISII PIMENTO RAURACI SAMBALA SAMBARA SEKHWAN SENONES SEQUANI SHAMMAR SHERANI SHERPAS SHUKRIA SILIPAN SUIONES SUKKIIM TAKELMA TARKANI TURKANA VIDDHAL WAGWENO WAICURI WAMBUGU WAREGGA WASANGO ZONGORA AMAFINGO ANDOROBO ASHANGOS ASSHURIM AWABAKAL BARKINJI BATETELA BOANBURA CHERUSCI CHITRALI GEZRITES JICAQUES KUKURUKU LANDUMAN NEBAIOTH ORUNCHUN PALLIYAN PHASIRON PUPULUCA PURUPURU RAHANWIN SAKALAVA SHINWARI SINGSING SINTSINK TCHUKCHI TENGGRIS USTARANA WANGATTA WAPOGORO WAPOKOMO
(— OF ISRAEL) DAN GAD ASHER REUBEN EPHRAIM ISSACHAR MANASSEH
(CHINESE —S) HU
(PRIVILEGED —) MAGHZEN MAKHZAN
(SEA GYPSY —) SELUNG
(PREF.) PHYL(O)
(SUFF.) INI

TRIBROMOETHANOL AVERTIN

TRIBULATION AGONY CROSS MISERY SORROW DISTRESS

TRIBUNAL BAR FEME ROTA VEHM BENCH COURT FEHME FORUM JUNTA VEHME MAJLIS ACUERDO ESGUARD MEJLISS RIGSRET AREOPAGY KANGAROO

TRIBUNE BEMA VELUTUS

TRIBUTARY ARM BOGAN BRANCH FEEDER TYBURN AFFLUENT ANABRANCH

TRIBUTE AID FEE TAX CAIN GELT KUDO LEVY PORT RENT SCAT CANON GAVEL HANSE MAILL SALVO SCATT CHAUTH HERIOT HIDAGE HOMAGE IMPOST CARATCH CHEVAGE CHIEFRY OVATION PENSION SYNODAL TREWAGE AUXILIUM BRENNAGE HEREGELD PESHKASH ROMESCOT ROMESHOT

TRICE GIRD BLINK THROW INSTANT

TRICHECHUS MANATUS

TRICHINA NEMATODE

TRICHINIZED MEASLY

TRICHION CRINION

TRICHOME SCALE

TRICHOMONIASIS CANKER ABORTION

TRICK DO BAM BOB COG CON CUN DAP DOR FOB FOX FUB FUN GIN GUM JIG JOB PAW RIG BILK BITE BORE CHAW CHIP DIDO DIRT DUPE FAKE FIRK FLAM FLUM FOOL GAFF GAME GAUD GECK GULL HAVE HOAX JAPE JEST JINK JOUK JUNT LOCK LURK PASS PAWK PRAT PULL RORT RUSE SELL SKIT SLUR TURN WILE WIPE WOOL ANTIC BLEAR BLINK CATCH CHEAT CONNU CRAFT CREEK CROOK CULLY CURVE DODGE DORRE ELUDE FEINT FETCH FOURB FRAUD GLEEK GRIFT GUILE KNACK PAVIE PLANT PRANK SHIFT SHINE SKITE SLICK STUNT TRAIN TRUFF TWIST WHEEL WREST WRINK BAFFLE BANTER BEGUNK BEJAPE BLENCH BROGUE CAUTEL CHOUSE CRADDY DECEIT DELUDE DOUBLE EUCHRE FOURBE HOCKET HUMBUG ILLUDE JOCKEY JUGGLE MANNER PLISKY POLICY SCONCE SHAVIE SPRING TREPAN VAGARY WHEEZE WINNER CANTRIP CHICANE CONCEIT FICELLE FINESSE FORWARD GUILERY KNAVERY MARLOCK PAGEANT SHUFFLE SLEIGHT WHIZZER ARTIFICE CHALDESE CLAPTRAP CLOWNADE CONTOISE CROTCHET DELUSION DOUBLING FLAGARIE FLIMFLAM GILENYIE INTRIGUE JEOPARDY PRACTICE PRANCOME PRESTIGE QUENTISE SLAMPAMP TRAVERSE TRICKING BAMBOOZLE STRATAGEM
(— OUT) FARD FANGLE FINIFY
(BEGUILING —) WILE
(CARD —) CLUB HEART SPADE STICH DIAMOND WEAVING
(FRAUDULENT —) RIG TOP
(JUGGLING —) FOIST
(KNAVISH —) DOGTRICK
(LOVE —) AMORETTO
(MEAN —) TOUCH
(MONKEY —) SINGERIE
(OLD —) CONNU
(PETTY —S) CRANS
(SIX —S) BOOK
(SMART —) LIRIPIPE LIRIPOOP
(STUPID —) SHINE
(VEXING —) CHAW
(WRESTLING —) CHIP CLICK FAULX FORWARD
(PL.) DAGS

TRICKER TRUMPER

TRICKERY DOLE GAFF SHAM TRAP TRAY WILE COVIN FRAUD HOCUS SHARK TRAIN CAUTEL COVINE DECEIT JAPERY JUGGLE TREGET DODGERY FALLACY GULLERY JOUKERY KNAVERY PAWKERY SLEIGHT ARTIFICE CHEATING

COZENAGE JOOKERIE JUGGLERY
PRACTICE TRICKING TRUMPERY
TRICKILY FOXILY
TRICKINESS PAWKERY
TRICKISH KNAVISH FRAUDFUL
TRICKLE DRIB DRIP DRILL STILL
TRILL DISTIL DRIVEL GUTTER
SICKER SIGGER STRAIN ZIGGER
DISTILL DRIBBLE DRIZZLE
DROPPLE TRINTLE
TRICKSTER GULL SHAM RASCAL
TRAPAN SLICKER TRICKER
SLEEVEEN TRAMPOSO
TREGETOUR
TRICKSY ELFISH QUIRKSEY
TRICKY SLY DEEP BRAID DODGY
FIKIE GAUDY ROWDY SNIDE
ARTFUL CATCHY LUBRIC QUIRKY
SHIFTY SMARTY TWISTY DEVIOUS
SLANTER TRICKLE WINDING
FLIMFLAM JUGGLING LUBRICAL
SHIFTFUL SKITTISH SLIDDERY
SLIPPERY TORTUOUS TRICKING
TRICLINIC ANORTHIC
TRICOT JERSEY
TRICYCLE VELO CYCLE TRIKE
WHEEL TANDEM TRICAR
RANTOON ROADSTER SOCIABLE
TRIDENT VAJRA TRISUL TRISULA
TRIED TESTED PROBATE WEIGHED
RELIABLE
TRIFECTA TRIPLE
TRIFLE ACE BOB DAB HAW PIN
SOU TOY BEAN COOT DOIT FICO
FOOL HAIR HOOT JAUK MESS
MOCK MOTE PLAY RUSE WHIT
DALLY FLIRT FLUKE GLAIK ITEMY
NIFLE PLACK POINT SCRAT SPORT
TRICK TRUFF BAWBEE BREATH
DABBLE DANDLE DAWDLE
DELUDE DIBBLE DOODAD
DOODLE FADDLE FESCUE FIDDLE
FOOTER FOOTLE FRIVOL
GEWGAW MONKEY NIDDLE
NIGGLE NIGNAY PADDLE PALTER
PETTLE PICKLE PIDDLE PIGGLE
PINGLE POTTER PUTTER STIVER
TIFFLE VANITY WANTON
FEATHER FLAMFEW FRIBBLE
NOTHING QUIDDLE THOUGHT
TRANEEN TRINKET TRIVIAL
WHIFFLE COQUETTE FALDERAL
FLIMFLAM FOLDEROL GIMCRACK
KICKSHAW MOLEHILL NIFFNAFF
NIHILITY NUGAMENT RIGMAREE
TRANTLUM BAGATELLE
(— WITH) JANK DANDLE DELUDE
NIGGLE
(ATTRACTIVE —) CONCEIT
(LITERARY —) TOY
(MERE —) SONG STRAW
(MEREST —) FIG
(SHOWY —) WALLY
(PL.) NUGAE TRIVIA GIBLETS
FEWTRILS NONSENSE
TRIFLER DOODLE PLAYER WANTON
FLANEUR FOOTLER FRIBBLE
NUGATOR PINGLER TWIDDLER
WHIFFLER
TRIFLES
(PREF.) NUGI
TRIFLING AIRY FOND IDLE FUNNY
INANE LIGHT PETTY POTTY SILLY

SMALL FADDLE FLIMSY FUTILE
LEVITY LIMUTE LITTLE PALTRY
SIMPLE STRAWY TOYISH FOOLISH
FRIBBLE ITEMING NOMINAL
TRIVIAL TWATTLE COQUETRY
FIDDLING FLIMFLAM FRIPPERY
IMMOMENT NUGATORY PIDDLING
SNIPPING WHIFFLERY NEGLIGIBLE
TRIFOLIUM CLOVER TREFOIL
TRIG SNOD TRIM CHIPPER
TRIGGER VERGE TRICKER
TRIGGERFISH COCUYO TURBOT
OLDWIFE BALISTID FILEFISH
OLDWENCH
TRIGON TRINE SABBEKA SACKBUT
SAMBUCA TRIGONON
TRIGONOMETRY SPHERICS
TRILBY (AUTHOR OF —) DUMAURIER
(CHARACTER IN —) ALICE GECKO
SANDY TAFFY BILLEE TRILBY
OFERRALL SVENGALI
TRILL BURR FLAP ROLL SHAKE
QUAVER THRILL TRILLO WARBLE
ROULADE TRILLET
TRILLED HIRRIENT
TRILLION
(PREF.) TERA TREG(A)
TRILLIONTH
(PREF.) PICO
TRILLIUM SARA TRUE SARAH
TRUMP BENJAMIN TRUELOVE
TRILOBITE EODISCID
TRIM AX AXE CUT DUB GIM LIP
LOP NET BARB BEAD BUTT CLIP
CROP DEFT DINK FEAT FUSS
GASH GIMP HACK JIMP LACE
NEAT PICK SNAG SNOD SNUG
SPUR STOW TACK TOSH TRIG
BRAID BRUSH CLEAN COPSE
DRESS FITTY GENTY HEDGE
KEMPT KNIFE NATTY PREEN
PRIME PRUNE PURGE SAUCY
SHAVE SHEAR SHRAG SHRIP
SLEEK SMART SMIRK SPRIG
STUMP TIGHT TRICK VERGE
BARBER DAPPER DONSIE DOUBLE
FETTLE PICKED REFORM SHROUD
SOIGNE SPRUCE SVELTE SWITCH
TRIMLY CHIPPER FEATHER
FLOUNCE SCISSOR MANICURE
ORNAMENT TRIMMING
SHIPSHAPE
(— A BOAT) SIT
(— ENDS OF HAIR) SHIRL
(— HEDGE) DUB
(— HIDES) ROUND
(— MEAT) CONDITION
(— SAIL) FILL
(— SEAMS) FETTLE
(— SHOE) FOX
(— TREES) PRIME SWAMP
(— WITH EMBROIDERY) GIMP
PANEL
TRIMLY SMARTLY SPRUCELY
TRIMMED PEEKABOO
TRIMMER FINER BRIDLE TACKER
VOLANT ROUNDER SMOCKER
SCRATTER
TRIMMING COQ FUR GIMP LACE
BRAID CHAPE COQUE FRILL
GUARD INKLE JABOT ROBIN
RUCHE ERMINE LACING OSPREY
PURFLE ROBING BEADING

CASCADE FALBALA FURRING
GALLOON MARABOU PUFFING
ROULEAU BRAIDING EAVESING
FALDERAL FOLDEROL FROSTING
FROUFROU FURBELOW JEWELING
PAILETTE PEARLING PICKADIL
PLASTRON SOUTACHE PAILLETTE
SPAGHETTI STRAPPING
(PL.) LOP FLOTS SHORTS FIXINGS
LOPPING BRAIDING FRILLIES
TRIMURTI TRINITY
TRINE TRENE TRIGON
**TRINIDAD-TOBAGO (CAPITAL
OF —)** PORTOFSPAIN
(POINT OF —) GALERA
(RIVER OF —) ORTOIRE
(TOWN OF —) TOCO ARIMA COUVA
LABREA MORUGA SIPARIA
TRINITARIAN MATHURIN
TRINITROTOLUENE TOLITE
TRITON
TRINITY TRIAD TRIAS TRINE
TRIUNE GODHEAD TERNARY
TRIMURTI TRINUNITY
TRINKET TOY DIDO GAUD MERE
BIJOU HEART KNACK TAHLI
BAUBLE CHARME DEVICE
DOODAD GEWGAW BIBELOT
TRANGAM TRANKUM GIMCRACK
KICKSHAW TRANTLUM TRINKLET
WHIMWHAM
(PL.) TRINKUMS
TRINKETRY KNAVERY
TRIO GLEEK TERZET TRIUNE
TERZETTO
TRIOLEFIN TRIENE
TRIONYX AMYDA
TRIOPAS (DAUGHTER OF —)
IPHIMEDIA
(FATHER OF —) NEPTUNE
(MOTHER OF —) CANACE
(SON OF —) ERYSICHTHON
TRIOPS APUS
TRIP HOP JAG JET JOG TIP BOUT
CHIP FOOT GAIT GATE KILT LINK
RAKE SKIP TOUR TROT TURN
BROAD DANCE DRIVE HITCH
JAUNT SALLY CRUISE ERRAND
FLIGHT HEGIRA OFFEND OUTING
RAMBLE SAFARI SASHAY VOYAGE
JOURNEY SAILING SETDOWN
STUMBLE TRIPPER CAMPAIGN
PERIPLUS
(— ALONG) CHIP LINK
(— BY DOG TEAM) MUSH
(— IN WRESTLING) CHIP CLICK
(— INTO COUNTRY) CAMPAIGN
(— UP) SUPPLANT
(HUNTING —) SHOOT
(PLEASURE —) JUNKET
TRIPE PAUNCH ROLPENS
TRILLIBUB
TRIPLE TRINE TREBLE TERNARY
TRIFOLD TRIPLEX THRIBBLE
TRIFECTA
TRIPLE BOND
(SUFF.) (CONTAINING —) OLIC
TRIPLET TRIN BRELAN PARIAL
TERCET TRIOLE TRIPLE TERZINA
TRIOLET HEMIOLIA TRILLING
TRIPLING TRISTICH
(— OF BASES) CODON
TRIPLETAIL SAMA CHOBIE

FLASHER GROUPER
TRIPLICITY TRIGON
TRIPOD CAT TRIP SPIDER TEAPOY
TRIPOS TRIVET TRESTLE
TRIPODY HEMIEPES
TRIPOLI SILEX TRIPEL
TRIPPER DECKMAN
TRIPTOLEMUS (FATHER OF —)
CELEUS
(MOTHER OF —) METANIRA
TRISHAW CYCLO
TRISMUS LOCKJAW TETANUS
**TRISTAN UND ISOLDE
(CHARACTER IN —)** MARK MELOT
ISOLDE TRISTAN BRANGANE
KURWENAL
(COMPOSER OF —) WAGNER
**TRISTRAM SHANDY (AUTHOR OF
—)** STERNE
(CHARACTER IN —) SLOP TOBY
TRIM BOBBY SHANDY WADMAN
WALTER YORICK SUSANNAH
TRISTRAM
TRITE FADE HACK WORN BANAL
CONNU CORNY HOARY MUSTY
STALE VAPID BEATEN COMMON
MODERN HACKNEY PERCOCT
TRIVIAL BROMIDIC SHOPWORN
TRITENESS BATHOS
TRITERPENOID CERIN
TRITON NEWT TRUMPET
(FATHER OF —) NEPTUNE
(MOTHER OF —) AMPHITRITE
TRITURATE POUND POWDER
TRITURATION TRIPSIS
TRITURUS MOLGE
TRIUMPH WIN CROW PALM
INSULT PREVAIL VICTORY
CONQUEST
(— OVER) SCALP
TRIUMPHANT VICTOR JUBILANT
TRIUMPHING OVANT
TRIUNGULIN CRAWLER
TRIVET SPIDER TRIPOD TRESTLE
TRIPPER BRANDISE
TRIVIAL BALD JERK NICE VAIN
BANAL LEGER LIGHT PETTY SILLY
SMALL TIDDY FIDFAD FOOTLE
PALTRY SLIGHT TOYISH COMICAL
PIPERLY PUERILE SHALLOW
TIDDLEY DOGGEREL FEATHERY
FOOTLING GIMCRACK PIDDLING
PILULOUS TRIFLING TRINKETY
(NOT —) SOLID EARNEST
TRIVIALITY FOLLY NIGNAY TRIFLE
INANITY IDLENESS NONSENSE
NUGACITY
TROCHANTER SCAPULA
TROCHE ROTULA TABLET
CACHUNDE PASTILLE
TROCHEE CHOREE CHOREUS
TROCHEUS
TROCHLEA PULLEY
TROCTOLITE GABBRO
TRODDEN TRADED
(MUCH —) BEATEN
TROGLODYTIC SPELEAN
TROGON QUEZAL QUETZAL
TOCORORO
TROILUS (BELOVED OF —) CRESSIDA
(FATHER OF —) PRIAM
(MOTHER OF —) HECUBA
(SLAYER OF —) ACHILLES

TROILUS AND CRESSIDA
  (AUTHOR OF —) SHAKESPEARE
  (CHARACTER IN —) AJAX HELEN
  PARIS PRIAM AENEAS HECTOR
  NESTOR ANTENOR CALCHAS
  HELENUS TROILUS ULYSSES
  ACHILLES CRESSIDA DIOMEDES
  MENELAUS PANDARUS
  AGAMEMNON ALEXANDER
  CASSANDRA DEIPHOBUS
  PATROCLUS THERSITES
  ANDROMACHE MARGARELON
TROJAN TROIC DARDAN ANTENOR
  (PL.) TEUCRI
TROLL DROW HARL SPIN TROW
  ANGLE HARLE MOOCH TRAWL
  TROLLOL
TROLLER MOOCHER
TROLLEY BOGEY BOGIE TRUCK
  PANTOGRAPH
TROLLOP CUT DOXY BITCH DOXIE
  TROLL TRULL DOLLOP
TROMBONE BONE TRAM BUSINE
  POSAUNE SACKBUT SLIPHORN
  (PART OF —) BOW CUP KEY RIM
  BELL CROOK FLARE SHANK SLIDE
  BUMPER FLANGE BALANCER
  MOUTHPIECE
TRONA URAO
TROOP FARE GING ROUT TURM
  ROUTE SOLAK STAND TURMA
  WERED CORNET RISALA ROUGHT
  SCHOOL THREAT TICHEL TROUPE
  COMPANY COMITIVA
  (— OF ARMED MEN) CREW
  (— OF FOXES) SKULK
  (— OF WORSHIPPERS) THIASUS
  (—S ATTACHED TO SOVEREIGN)
  GUARDS
  (—S IN BATTLE ARRAY) SHELTRON
  (—S ON WING OF ARMY) ALARES
  (ASSAULTING —S) WAVE
  (BOMBAY —S) DUCKS
  (CAVALRY —) CORNET
  (GIRL SCOUT —) SHIP
  (LIGHT-ARMED —S) PSILOI
  (MOUNTAIN —) ALPINI
  (SCOTTISH —S) JOCKS
  (PL.) PARADE
TROOPER BARGIR REITER RUTTER
  BARGEER
TROPARION HIRMOS HEIRMOS
  TROPARY KATABASIS
TROPE IMAGE EVOVAE
TROPHONEMA VILLUS
TROPHONIUS (BROTHER OF —)
  AGAMEDES
  (FATHER OF —) APOLLO ERGINUS
TROPHOZOITE CEPHALIN
  SPORADIN
TROPHY BAG EMMY PALM PRIZE
  SCALP REWARD LAURELS
  (WRITING —) HUGO
TROPIC SOLAR TROPHIC
TROPINE HYOSCINE
TROS (FATHER OF —) ERICTHONIUS
  ERICHTHONIUS
  (MOTHER OF —) CALLIRRHOE
  (SON OF —) ILUS GANYMEDE
  ASSARACUS
TROT JOG SPUD TRIG FADGE
  HURRY PIAFFE
TROTH CERTY TROGS

TRUTH CERTIE
TROTTER DRIVER CRUBEEN
  SPANKER
TROUBADOR MINSTREL SORDELLO
TROUBLE ADO AIL DIK HOE ILL IRK
  MAR VEX WOE BEAT BUSY CAIN
  CARK EARN FASH FIKE GRAM
  JEEL MASH MOIL PAIN PINE ROUT
  SORE STIR TEEN TINE TRAY UNRO
  WORK ANNOY BESET CROSS
  DROVE DUTCH GRIEF HAUNT
  LABOR ROWEL SMITE SPITE
  STEER STURT SUSSY THRIE
  TWEAK WHILE WORRY BARRAT
  BOTHER BURBLE CADDLE
  CUMBER DITHER EFFORT GRIEVE
  GRUDGE HARASS HATTER
  KIAUGH MOLEST POTHER RATTLE
  RUBBER SORROW SQUALL
  TAKING THREAT UNEASE UNRUFE
  WORRIT AFFLICT AGITATE
  ANXIETY CHAGRIN CONCERN
  DISEASE DISTURB DRUBBLE
  EMBROIL FASHERY INFLICT
  PERTURB PILIKIA SCRUPLE
  SPUTTER THOUGHT TRACHLE
  TRAVAIL TRIBBLE TURMOIL
  BUSINESS DARKNESS DISORDER
  DISQUIET DISTRESS NOISANCE
  VEXATION WANDRETH
  (— ONE'S SELF) PASS
  (PL.) CHAGRINS
TROUBLED DRUBLY DRUMLY
  GRUMLY QUEASY CAREFUL
  FRETFUL HAUNTED AGITATED
  HARASSED
TROUBLESHOOTER FIXER
TROUBLESOME DIK ILL SAD BUSY
  HARD FIKIE PESKY ROWDY TIGHT
  PLAGUY SHREWD STICKY THORNY
  UNEASY BRICKLE HARMFUL
  PESTFUL PLAGUEY TEWSOME
  ANNOYING FASHIOUS SPITEFUL
  UNTOWARD
TROUBLESOMENESS BOTHER
TROUBLING CHRONIC
TROU-DE-LOUP TRAPHOLE
TROUGH BOX CUP HOD RUN TOM
  BACK BOSH BUNK COVE DAIL
  DALE DISH DORR SHOE SINK
  TRAY TROW VALE BAKIE CHUTE
  DITCH LAVER SHOOT SHUTE
  SLIDE SPOUT STRIP ALVEUS
  BACKET BUDDLE GUTTER
  HARBOR HOPPER LAVABO
  MANGER RUNNER SALTER SINKER
  SLUICE STRAKE TROGUE VALLEY
  WALLOW CHENEAU CONDUIT
  LAUNDER RIFFLER TRENDLE
  TROFFER LAVATORY PENSTOCK
  (— FOR ASHES) BAKIE
  (— FOR COOLING INGOTS) BOSH
  (— FOR PAPER PULP) RIFFLER
  (— FOR WASHING ORE) TOM
  HUTCH STRIP BUDDLE STRAKE
  (— IN MONASTERY) LAVABO
  (— OF A WAVE) SULK
  (— OF CIDER MILL) CHASE
  (— OF ROCK) SYNCLINE
  (— OF THE SEA) ALVEUS
  (ANNULAR —) CUP
  (BAKER'S —) HUTCH
  (EAVES —) CANAL CHENEAU

  (GLACIAL —) DORR
  (ORE —) TYE
  (SHEEP-DIPPING —) DUP
  (WOODEN —) TRUG BAKIE TROGUE
  (PREF.) BOTHR(O) BOTHRI(O)
  PYEL(O)
  (SUFF.) SCAPH
TROUNCE MOP FLOG TRAMP
  WHOMP COURSE CUDGEL
  CANVASS SHELLAC
TROUNCING LACING WARMING
TROUPE BALLET SERVANTS
  CUADRILLA
TROUSER STROSSER
TROUSERING CASINET
TROUSERS BAGS CORDS DUCKS
  JEANS KICKS PANTS SLOPS
  TONGS TREWS BRAIES CHINOS
  DENIMS FLARES SHORTS SKILTS
  SLACKS WHITES BOTTOMS
  BRACCAE BROGUES KERSEYS
  NANKINS SHALWAR SLIVERS
  STRIDES BLOOMERS BREECHES
  FLANNELS KICKSEYS MOLESKIN
  NANKEENS OVERALLS SHINTYAN
  PANTALOONS
TROUT CHAR KELT PEAL POGY
  BROOK BROWN CHARR LAKER
  LUNGE SCURF SEWEN SEWIN
  SHARD SQUET SQUIT TRUFF
  FINNOC KIPPER MYKISS QUASKY
  SALTER TAIMEN TRUCHA TULADI
  BOREGAT BROOKIE BROWNIE
  COASTER HERLING OQUASSA
  POUNDER RAINBOW SQUETEE
  AUREOLUS BODIERON GILLAROO
  HARDHEAD KAMLOOPS SAIBLING
  SALMONID SISCOWET
  (SMALL —) SCURLING SKIRLING
  (YOUNG —) WHITLING
TROUVERE BLONDEL
TROVATORE, IL (CHARACTER IN —)
  INEZ RUIZ DILUNA AZUCENA
  LEONORA MANRICO FERRANDO
  (COMPOSER OF —) VERDI
TROW DROW TRUE FAITH BELIEF
  COVENANT
TROWEL HAWK LEAF PIPE DARBY
  DERBY FLOAT TAPER TREWEL
  (HEARTSHAPED —) HEART
  DOGTAIL
  (MOLDER'S —) LEAF TAPER
  (PLASTERER'S —) FLOAT
TROY ILION TROIA TROJA
  (FOUNDER OF —) ILUS TROS
  (INHABITANT OF —) ILIAN
TROYENS, LES (CHARACTER IN —)
  ANNA DIDO IOPAS PRIAM AENEAS
  HECTOR NARBAL ASCANIUS
  PANTHEUS CASSANDRA
  CHOROEBUS
  (COMPOSER OF —) BERLIOZ
TRUANT HOOKY TRONE TROUT
  MICHER MEECHER TRIVANT
  VAGRANT
TRUCE PAX BARLEY TREAGUE
  INDUCIAE
TRUCK DAN UTE BUNK CORF DRAB
  DRAG DUCK DUMP GUNK RACK
  WYNN BOGIE BUGGY DILLY DOLLY
  GILLY LORRY TROKE BARTER
  BUMMER CAMION DIESEL
  DROGUE DRUGGE DUMPER

  JITNEY PICKUP SLOVEN TIPPER
  TURTLE CARAVAN FOURGON
  GONDOLA SKIDDER SLEEPER
  TROLLEY TRUCKLE TRUNDLE
  DELIVERY HAULAWAY TRANSFER
  (COAL —) DAN
  (FIRE —) PUMPER
  (LOGGING —) BUNK BUMMER
  (MINING —) CORF SKIP BARNEY
  (PART OF —) DECK HOOD STEP
  TANK TIRE GUARD LIGHT STAKE
  WHEEL BUMPER GRILLE MIRROR
  AIRHORN CARRIER EXHAUST
  MUDFLAP BULKHEAD HEADLIGHT
  TAILLIGHT COMPRESSOR
  WINDSHIELD
  (TIMBER —) DRUG WYNN
TRUCKLE FAWN TOADY SLAVER
TRUCKLING SERVILE
TRUCULENCE BRAG
TRUCULENT MEAN CRUEL HARSH
  FIERCE SAVAGE SCATHING
TRUDGE JOG PAD HAKE PLOD
  STOG JAUNT TRACE TRAIK
  TRAMP TRASH STODGE TAIGLE
  TRAIPSE
TRUE SO GOOD JUST LEAL PURE
  REAL VERY VRAI PLUMB RIGHT
  SOOTH SOUND VERAY ACTUAL
  FIDELE LAWFUL DEVOTED
  GENUINE GERMANE PRECISE
  SINCERE STAUNCH FAITHFUL
  RELIABLE RIGHTFUL SOOTHFUL
  UNERRING
  (— TO THE FACT) LITERAL
  (QUESTIONABLY —) ALLEGED
  (PREF.) ALETHO ETYMO EU
  ORTH(O) VERI
TRUFFLE TRUB TRUFF EARTHNUT
TRUISM SOOTH
TRULL DELL BLOWZE CALLET
TRULY YEA AWAT EVEN FEGS IWIS
  JUST QUITE SOOTH SYKER TIGHT
  ATWEEL DINKUM INDEED SIMPLY
  VERILY INSOOTH SOOTHLY
  VERAMENT WITTERLY
TRUMP DIS DIX LOW PAM LILY
  RUFF BASTA BASTO DEECE
  TROMBE MANILLA MATADOR
  TRIUMPH SPADILLE
  (NOT —S) LAY
  (2ND HIGHEST —) MANILLE
TRUMPERY MOCKADO RUBBISH
  GIMCRACK PEDDLERY
TRUMPET BEME LURE TUBA SHELL
  TRUMP BOZINE BUCCIN CORNET
  KERANA LITUUS TROMBA TULNIC
  ALCHEMY BUCCINA CLARINO
  CLARION KERRANA SALPINX
  NARSINGA SLUGHORN SOURDINE
  WATERCUP
  (— OF DAFFODIL) CORONA
  (PREF.) SALPING(O)
  (SUFF.) SALPINX
TRUMPET BELL CODON PAVILON
TRUMPET CALL DIAN DIANA
  SENNET
TRUMPET CREEPER TECOMA
  COWHAGE CREEPER FOXGLOVE
  HELLVINE
TRUMPETER MOKI AGAMI TRUMP
  TOOTER JACAMIN TUBICEN
  YAKAMIK

TRUMPETER FISH MOKI MOKIHI
TRUMPETER PERCH MADO
TRUMPETS WATERCUP
TRUMPET-SHAPED BUCCINAL
TRUMPETWOOD IMBAUBA
TRUNCATED ABRUPT STUBBED
TRUNKED
TRUNCHEON BATON BILLY
WARDER SPONTON PARTISAN
SPONTOON
TRUNDLE HURL RUNG TRILL TROLL
BUNDLE TRUCKLE WALLOWER
TRUNK BOX BODY BOLE BOOT
BULK KIST LICH RUNT STAM
STEM STUD CABER PETER SHAFT
STICK STOCK TORSO ARIQUE
BARREL CAUDEX COFFER LOCKER
CARCASS CORSAGE STOWAGE
TRUNCUS SARATOGA
(ARTERIAL —) AORTA
(ELEPHANT'S —) SNOUT
(FOSSIL —) CYCAD
(SMALL —) HATBOX
(SPLIT —) PUNCHEON
(SWIM —S) JAMS
(TREE —) BOLE BUTT STICK RICKER
**(TREE — OVER 8 INCHES IN
DIAMETER)** MAST
(TRIMMED TREE —) LOG
(WORSHIPPED TREE —S) IRMINSUL
(PREF.) CORM(O) PROBOSCI(DI)
TRUNKFISH CHAPIN BOXFISH
COWFISH
TRUSS SPAN WARREN DORLACH
(— OF STRAW) WAD
(— UP) KILT
TRUST AFFY HOPE LITE POOL RELY
REST TICK TREW TROW FAITH
FRIST GROUP TRUTH BELIEF
CARTEL CHARGE CORNER CREDIT
DEPEND FIANCE LIPPEN OFFICE
TICKET BELIEVE BETRUST
COMBINE CONFIDE CREANCE
CRIANCE JAWBONE SECRECY
VENTURE AFFIANCE COMMENDA
CREDENCE MONOPOLY RELIANCE
TRUSTED FIDUCIAL
TRUSTEE CURATOR FEOFFEE
SINDICO VISITOR ASSIGNEE
MUTWALLI
TRUSTWORTHINESS HONOR
TRUST CREDIT HONESTY
CREDENCE AXIOPISTY
TRUSTWORTHY SAFE SURE TRIG
SOOTH SOUND SYKER TRIED
HONEST SECRET SECURE SICKER
STABLE TRUSTY COCKSURE
CREDIBLE FIDUCIAL RELIABLE
TRUSTFUL
TRUSTY TRIG FECKFUL STAUNCH
FAITHFUL RELIABLE
TRUTH TAO UNA SOOTH TROTH
WHITE SATTVA VERITY
LOWDOWN VERITAS VERACITY
VERIDITY VERIMENT
(— TABLE) MATRIX
(IDEAL —) CHRIST DHARMA
(IN —) CERTES
(RELATING TO —) ALETHIC
(ULTIMATE —) LIGHT SUNYATA
**TRUTH AND JUSTICE (AUTHOR OF
—)** TAMMSAARE
(CHARACTER IN —) MARI PAAS

KARIN TIINA ANDRES INDREK
TRUTHFUL TRUE VERY SOOTH
HONEST VERIDIC
TRUTHFULLY GOSPELLY
TRUTHFULNESS HONESTY
VERACITY SINCERITY
TRY GO SAY SHY BURL FAND HACK
PASS PENK PREE SEEK SLAP TEST
TIRL TURN AFOND ASSAY CRACK
ESSAY ETTLE FLING GROPE
JUDGE OFFER PROVE SENSE
SOUND TASTE TEMPT TOUCH
WHACK WHIRL APPOSE ASSAIL
FRAIST GRIEVE STRIVE AFFLICT
AFFORCE APPROVE ATTEMPT
DISCUSS ESPROVE IMITATE
STAGGER ENDEAVOR STRUGGLE
(— DESPERATELY) AGONIZE
(— FOR GOAL) SHOT
(— HARD) STRIVE
(— OUT) SAMPLE AUDITION
(— TO ATTAIN) AFFECT
(CASUAL —) FLING
(QUICK —) SLAP
TRYING NASTY ARDUOUS CRUCIAL
GRUELING
TRYSAIL SPENCER
TSAR SALTAN (CHARACTER IN —)
GUIDON SALTAN MILITRISA
POVARIKHA TKACHIKHA
(COMPOSER OF —)
RIMSKYKORSAKOV
**TSAR'S BRIDE, THE (CHARACTER IN
—)** IVAN LYKOV MARFA
LYUDMILA GRYAZNOV
(COMPOSER OF —)
RIMSKYKORSAKOV
TSETSE FLY KIVU GANDI
DIPTERAN GLOSSINA
T-SHAPED TAU
TSILTADEN CHILION
TSUBO BU
TSWANA CHUANA SECHUANA
TUAREG IMOHAGH IMOSHAGH
TUATARA GUANA GUANO IGUANA
HATTERIA
TUB FAT HOD KID KIT SOE SOW
TUN VAT BACK BOWK COOL CORF
COWL GAWN KNOP MEAL TYND
TYNE BOWIE ESHIN KEEVE KIVER
SKEEL STAND BUCKET KEELER
KILLER KIMNEL TROUGH TURNEL
BATHTUB BREAKER SALTFAT
TANKARD TRUNDLE KOOLIMAN
LAVATORY
(— FOR ALEWIVES) HOD
(— FOR AMALGAMATING ORES)
TINA
(— FOR BREAD) BARGE
(— OF BUTTER) COOL
(— OF HOGWASH) SWILLTUB
(— USED AS DIPPER) HANDY
PIGGIN
(— WITH SLOPING SIDES) SHAUL
(BREWER'S —) BACK KEEVE
(LAUNDRY —) WASHTRAY
(MESS —) KID KIT
(MINING —) CORF
(TANNING —) LEACH
(WATER —) DAN JAILER
(WOODEN —) KIT SOE KIMNEL
TRINDLE
TUBA BASS HELICON BOMBARDON

TUBE TAG BEAK BODY BOOT CANE
CASE CAST CORE CURL DRUM
DUCT HORN HOSE PIPE REED
WORM BATON CANAL CORER
CROOK CRYPT DRAIN GLAND
HEART LINER QUILL SIGHT SKELP
SLIDE SPILE SPOUT THECA THIEF
TRUMP TUBAL VALVE AUDION
BARREL CALCAR CANEL
CANNON COLUMN CORNET
DEWCAP FILTER GULLET HEADER
NOZZLE OCTODE SLEEVE SUCKER
SYRINX THROAT TRIODE TUBING
TUBULE TUNNEL UPTAKE VESSEL
BLOWGUN CHIMNEY CONDUIT
CUVETTE DROPPER FERRULE
FISTULA HOUSING OOBLAST
OVIDUCT QUILLET ROSTRUM
SALPINX SHALLOT SNORTER
SNUFFER SOXHLET STOPPLE
THIMBLE TUBULUS VENTURI
ADJUTAGE BOMBILLA CORNICLE
DIATREME DRAWTUBE FAIRLEAD
GRADUATE ORTHICON OVARIOLE
PENSTOCK PIPESTEM SAUCISSE
SIPHONET SLEEVING URCEOLUS
ZOOECIUM
(— AT BASE OF PETAL) CALCAR
**(— CARRYING BASSOON
MOUTHPIECE)** CROOK
(— COVERING TRACE CHAIN) PIPING
(— FOR DEPOSITING CONCRETE)
TREMIE
(— FOR DRINKING MATE) BOMBILLA
(— FOR LINING WELL) WELLRING
(— FOR STIFFENING STRING) TAG
(— FOR TRANSFERRING LIQUID)
SIPHON SYPHON
(— FOR WINDING THREAD) COP
(— FROM SHIP'S PUMP) DALE
(— IN ENGINE CYLINDER) LINER
(— OF BALLOON) APPENDIX
(— OF GUN) BORE BARREL
(— OF RETORT) BEAK ROSTRUM
(— OF SPIRIT LEVEL) BUBBLE
(— OF TOBACCO) CIGARET
(— TO LINE A VENT) BOUCHE
(— TWISTED IN COILS) WORM
(— USED IN WHALING) LULL
(AMPLIFIER —) STAGE
(BONE —) SNUFFER
(CAMERA —) ORTHICON
(DISTILLING —) TOWER
(ELECTRO —) BULB
(ELECTRODE —) AUDION PENTODE
(ELECTRON —) DIODE DRIVER
TETRODE KENOTRON KLYSTRON
PLIOTRON TRINISCOPE
(FIREWORKS —) LEADER
(GLANDULAR —) CRYPT
(GLASS —) SIGHT MATRASS
(GLASSBLOWER'S —) BLOWPIPE
(HONEY —) NECTARY SIPHONET
(KNITTED —) STOCKING
(PAPER —) LEADER PASTILLE
(PASTRY —) CORNET
(POLLEN —) SPERMARY
(PRIMING —) AUGET
(RECTIFIER —) IGNITRON
(SILK — OF SPIDER) SPIGOT
(SPEAKING —) GOSPORT
(SUCKING —) STRAW
(SURGICAL —) CANNULA

(THERMOMETER —) STEM
(VACUUM —) DIODE KEYER
HEXODE HEPTODE DYNATRON
MAGNETRON
(PREF.) FISTULI SIPHON(O)
SOLEN(O) SYRING(O)
TUBELET CIRCLET
TUBER ANU SET ANYU BULB CLOG
COCO ROOT SEED SETT YAMP
COCCO SALEP JICAMA PIGNUT
POTATO WAPATA WINDER
YAUTIA EARTHNUT MURRNONG
TUBERCLE PEARL NODULE
STEMMA CUSPULE VERRUCA
TUBERCULAR PHTHISIC
TUBERCULOSIS CON LUPUS
CLYERS DECLINE PHTHISIS
SCROFULA
TUBING HOSE TUBAGE
TUBMAN DUCKER
TUBULAR PIPY PIPED TUBATE
QUILLED CANNULAR
(NOT —) FARCTATE
(PREF.) SOLEN(O)
TUBULE TRACHEA TUBULET
TUBULUS
TUCANO BETOYAN
TUCK TOKE STUFF TRUSS FLANGE
(— IN) TRUSS TROUSS
(— UP) FAKE KILT
TUCKER CORDER KILTER PLEATER
(— OUT) TIRE
**TUESDAY (SECOND — AFTER
EASTER)** HOCKDAY HOKEDAY
TUFA TOPHUS
TUFF TRASS PEPERINO PORODITE
SANTORIN
TUFT COP EAR FAG FOB NOB SOP
TOP COMA DOWN KNOB KNOP
MOCK TAIT TATE TUFF TUSK
TUZZ WISP BEARD BUNCH CREST
FLOCK STUPA THRUM WHISK
CATKIN CIRRUS DOLLOP PAPPUS
PENCIL TASSEL TUFFET CIRRHUS
FEATHER FLOCCUS HOBNAIL
PANACHE SCOPULA TOPKNOT
TOPPING TUSSOCK AIGRETTE
FLOCCULE ARBUSCULE
(— OF BRISTLES) BIRSE
(— OF CLOTH) FAG
(— OF DIRTY WOOL) DAG
(— OF DOWN) FRIEZE
(— OF FEATHERS) EAR HORN HULU
EGRET
(— OF FILAMENTS) BYSSUS
(— OF GRASS) FAG SOP MOCK
HASSOCK TUSSOCK
(— OF HAIR) TOP COMA TUZZ
BRUSH SWITCH COWLICK
FEATHER FLOCCUS SCOPULA
TOPKNOT IMPERIAL KROBYLOS
(— OF HAIR ON HORSE'S HOOF)
FETLOCK
(— OF HAY) SOP
(— OF MALE TURKEY) BEARD
(— OF WOOL) FOB TUSK TUZZ
FLOCK
(— ON BIRD'S HEAD) COP CUCK
EGRET
(— ON BONNET) TOORIE
(— ON PINEAPPLE) CROWN
(— ON SEED PLANT) PAPPUS
(— ON SPIDER'S FEET) SCOPULA

(—S OF ROPE YARN) THRUM
(VASCULAR —) GLOMUS
(PREF.) LOPH(O) LOPHI(O)
TUFTED COMOSE TAPPET TAPPIT
CRISTATE
TUG LUG PUG RUG TIT TOG CHUG
DRAG HALE HAUL PULL TOIL
TUCK CHUFF HITCH PLUCK
SHRUG TRACE JIGGER RUGGLE
TOWBOAT TUGBOAT
TUGBOAT TOW TUG TOWBOAT
TRACKER
TUI POE TUA KOKO TUWI POEBIRD
TUITION CUSTODY
TULIP LILY LILIUM BIZARRE
BREEDER PICOTEE TURNSOLE
TULIP TREE POPLAR BASSWOOD
CUCUMBER
TULIPWOOD AUBURN
TULLE ILLUSION
TUMATAKURU IRISHMAN
MATAGORY
TUMBLE TOP COUP WALT LATCH
SPILL THROW TIFLE TRACE
COTTON GROVEL PURLER TIFFLE
TOPPLE WALTER WAMBLE
WELTER STUMBLE WHEMMEL
(— OVER) TIPPLE WALLOP
TUMBLE-DOWN RUINOUS
TUMBLER NUT CLICK GLASS LEVER
WIPER ROLLER ACROBAT
DRUMMER TIPPLER TOPPLER
VOLTIGEUR
TUMID TURGID BLOATED BULGING
FUSTIAN TURGENT INFLATED
TUMOROUS
TUMOR PAP WEN BEAL PIAN
WART AMPER BOTCH GUMMA
MYOMA NEVUS PHYMA SWELL
TALPA AMBURY ANBURY EPULIS
GLIOMA GYROMA INCOME KELOID
LIPOMA MYXOMA NUROMA
RISING WARBLE ADENOMA
ANGIOMA CYSTOMA DERMOID
DESMOID FIBROID FIBROMA
LUTEOMA MYELOMA NEUROMA
OSTEOMA OSTEOME SARCOMA
TESTUDO THYMOMA ULONCUS
ATHEROMA BLASTOMA
CHLOROMA CHORIOMA
EMBRYOMA GANGLION
GLANDULE HEMATOMA
HEPATOMA HOLDFAST
LYMPHOMA MELANOMA
MELICERA NEOPLASM
ODONTOMA PHLEGMON
PLASMOMA PSAMMOMA
SCIRRHUS SEMINOMA TERATOID
TERATOMA WINDGALL
CHALAZION PAPILLOMA
(— OF EYELID) GRANDO
(— ON HORSES'S LEGS) JARDE
(PUSTULAR —) BLAIN
(SKIN —) OUCH
(STUDY OF —S) ONCOLOGY
(PREF.) GANGLI(O) GANGLO
MYOM(O) ONCO SCIRRH(O)
(SUFF.) CELE COELE COELUS OMA
ONCUS SCIRRHUS
TUMULT DIN COIL FARE FLAW
FRAY FUSS HURL MUSS REEL
RIOT ROUT VISE BRAWL BROIL
HURLY HURRY LURRY NOISE

ROUST STOOR STOUR WHIRL
AFFRAY BUSTLE CLAMOR DIRDUM
EMEUTE FRACAS HUBBUB
MUTINY PUDDER RABBLE RIPPET
ROMAGE RUFFLE SHINDY STEERY
UPROAR UPSTIR BLUSTER
BOBBERY BRATTLE FACTION
FERMENT GARBOIL TEMPEST
TURMOIL DISORDER SEDITION
STIRRING STRAMASH
COMMOTION PANDEMONIUM
TUMULTUOUS HIGH LOUD RUDE
NOISY ROUGH STORMY FURIOUS
HURRIED LAWLESS RIOTOUS
VIOLENT AGITATED CONFUSED
DRAWLING HURTLING
TUMULUS LOW MOTE TUMP
MOUND BARROW BURIAN
COTERELL
TUN CASK HAAB
(ONE-THIRD —) TERTIAN
(20 —S) KATUN
TUNA AHI ATUN TUNNY BLUEFIN
PELAMYD ALBACORE KAWAKAWA
TUNE AIR ARIA DUMP FADO LEED
NOTE PORT RANT SONG CHARM
CHORD DRANT POINT ATTUNE
GROUND MAGGOT STRAIN
STRING TEMPER GUAJIRA
HALLING MEASURE MELISMA
SONANCE ANGLAISE FANDANGO
GUARACHA HABANERA
QUICKSTEP
(— A HARP) WREST
(— AN INSTRUMENT) STRING
(DANCE —) FURIANT ANGLAISE
GALLIARD
(FOLK —) FADO
(HILLBILLY —) HOEDOWN
(LIGHT —) TOY
(LITTLE —) CATCH
(LIVELY —) LILT SPRING HORNPIPE
(MELANCHOLY —) DUMP
(SACRED —) CHORAL CHORALE
(TRADITIONAL —) TONE
TUNEBO TAME GUACICO
TUNEFUL TUNY CHANTANT
TUNESOME
TUNEFULNESS MELODY
TUNGST-
(PREF.) WOLFRAM
TUNGSTEN W WOLFRAM SCHEELIN
TUNGUS EVENK LAMUT
TUNIC COAT JAMA JUPE VEST
COTTE FROCK GIPPO JAMAH
JUPON PALLA ACHKAN BLIAUT
CAMISE CHITON CYCLAS FECKET
HARDIE KABAYA KIRTLE TABARD
ARISARD BLEAUNT CAMISIA
PALTOCK SURCOAT TUNICLE
COLOBIUM GANDOURA
SUBTUNIC SUBUCULA
SUKKENYE
(— OF MAIL) HAUBERK
(HOODED FUR —) SOVIK
TUNICATE SALP SALPA SALPID
ASCIDIAN TUNICARY
UROCHORD
TUNICLE SACCOS
TUNING ANESIS
TUNING FORK EVEL EVIL FORK
TUNER DIAPASE DIAPASON
MODULANT

TUNING HAMMER KEY

TUNNEL ADIT BORE CAVE CURL
PUKA SINK TUBE DRIFT DRIVE
KAREZ STALL BURROW PIERCE
(— INTO AN IGLOO) TOSSUT
(PROPOSED —) CHUNNEL
TUNNY TUNA ALBACORE
SCOMBRID
(YOUNG —) PELAMYD
TUP TIP TRIP MONKEY BLISSOM
TUR (BROTHER OF —) IRAJ SALM
(FATHER OF —) FARIDUN
(MOTHER OF —) SHAHRINAZ
TURACO LORY
TURANDOT (CHARACTER IN —) LIU
CALAF TURANDOT
(COMPOSER OF —) PUCCINI
TURBAN PAT MOAB PATA SASH
TUFT LUNGI MITER MITRE PAGRI
PATTI TOWEL TUFFE MANDIL
WRAPPER KAFFIYEH PUGGAREE
SEERBAND TOLIPANE TULIPANT
TURBANTO
TURBELLARIA APROCTA
TURBELLARIAN FLATWORM
TURBID FAT RILY DROVY GUMLY
MUDDY RILEY ROILY DRUMLY
GRUMLY QUALLY FECULENT
LUTULENT
TURBIDITY RILE
TURBOT BRET BRILL WHIFF
FLATFISH
TURBULENCE FURY UPROAR
FERMENT RIOTING
(— IN WATER) BULLER
TURBULENT GURL HIGH LOUD
RUDE WILD ROILY ROUGH
WROTH RUGGED STORMY
UNRULY YEASTY FURIOUS
RABBISH RACKETY TROUBLE
VIOLENT MUTINOUS SCAMBLING
BOISTEROUS
TURCO IN ITALIA, IL (CHARACTER
IN —) DAMELEC GERONIO
FIORILLA PROSDOCIMO
(COMPOSER OF —) ROSSINI
TURDUS MERULA
TUREEN DISH TERRINE
TURF SOD VAG CESS DELF FAIL
FALE FEAL FLAG FLAT FLAW
PONE SUNK DELFT SCRAW SPINE
SWARD TRUFF FLAUGHT

SHIRREL SODDING
(— CUT BY GOLF STROKE) DIVOT
(— FOR LINING PARAPET) GAZON
(DRIED — FOR FUEL) VAG
(PARED —) BEAT
(ROUGH —) GOR
(SMALL PIECE OF —) TAB
(THIN LAYER OF —) FLAW
TURF SPADE SLANE
TURGID ERECT TUMID BLOATED
INFLATED PLETHORIC
TURGIDNESS TYMPANY
TURK TURCO TURKO SELJUK
CORSAIR OSMANLI OTTOMAN
TURQUET KONARIOT
TURKANA ELKUMA
TURKEY BUST FLOP STAG STEG
BUSTARD ERECTER ERECTOR
GOBBLER ALDERMAN
(BRUSH —) VULTURN TALEGALLA
(MALE —) TOM
(YOUNG —) POULT

TURKEY BUZZARD AURA
BROMVOEL BROMVOGEL
GALLINAZO
TURKEY-COCK STAG
TURKEY OAK CERRIS
TURKI KAZAK QAZAQ KAZAKH

TURKISH TURK TURCIC OSMANLI OTTOMAN
TURKISH DELIGHT LOUKOUM
TURKOMAN SEID ERSAR
TURK'S CAP LILY MARTAGON
TURMERIC REA ANGO HALDI OLENA HULDEE AZAFRAN CURCUMA
TURMIT TURNIP
TURMOIL ADO DIN COIL DUST MOIL TOIL TOSS BURLE HURLY HURRY STROW TOUSE WHIRL HASSLE JABBLE POTHER ROMAGE UPROAR WELTER CLUTTER EMOTION FERMENT GARBOIL HURLING MAKADOO RUMMAGE TEMPEST DISPEACE DISQUIET
TURN GO BOW CUT GEE JAR RUN TON WIN AIRT BEND BOUT BOWL CALE CAST CHAR CHOP COCK EDDY GIRO HACK HEAD HINT HURL JAMB KINK PULL PURL QUIP ROLL ROVE SLEW TIRL TOUR VEER VERT VICE WAFT WELT WIND AIRTH ANGLE BLANK CHARE CRANK CRASH CREEK CRICK CROOK ELBOW FEEZE GLINT PIVOT PLUCK PRICK QUIRK SHIFT SPELL SWING SWIRL TARVE TERVE TREND TRILL TROLL TWINE TWIST VERSE VOLTI WHEEL WREST ATTURN BOUGHT CIRCLE COURSE DEPEND DIRECT DOUBLE GRUPPO GYRATE INDENT INTEND INTURN POSSET QUEEVE RESORT RETURN ROTATE SPIRAL STRAIN SWIVEL TOURNE TURKEN VOLUME VOLUTE WIMPLE CONVERT CRANKLE CRINKLE DEFLECT DISTURB FLEXION FLEXURE FLOUNCE INCLINE INFLECT PASSADE REVERSE REVOLVE SERPENT SINUATE TWINGLE TWISTER VERSATE WREATHE CLINAMEN DOUBLING FLECTION TOURNURE TRAVERSE VOLUTION
(— ABOUT) SLEW SLUE SLOUGH WINDLASS
(— AGAINST) CROSS
(— AROUND) GYRE WELT WEND RATCH BEWEND SPHERE
(— ASIDE) ERR WRY DAFF SKEW WARD ABHOR AVERT BLENK DETER EVADE FENCE GLENT SHEER WAIVE BLENCH DEPART DETURN DIVERT SWERVE SWITCH CRINKLE DECLINE DEFLECT DEVIATE DIGRESS DIVERGE PERVERT SCRITHE
(— AT DRINKING) TIRL
(— ATTENTION) ADVERT ADDRESS
(— AWAY) DOFF AVERT CHARE HIELD REPEL AVERSE DESERT DETURN DIVERT REVOLT ABANDON DECLINE REVERSE OVERTURN WITHTURN
(— AWRY) CONTORT
(— BACK) KEP ABORT FLIPE FLYPE RETORT RETURN REVERT REFLECT UNTWIST RENVERSE
(— BACK ON) RUMP
(— BROWN) AUGUST

(— BY TOSSING) FLAP
(— CARD FACE UP) BURN
(— DOWN) DIP DENY VETO
(— FOR BETTER) CRISIS
(— IN ARCHERY) END
(— IN CROQUET) BISK BISQUE
(— IN ROPE) NIP RIDER
(— INSIDE OUT) EVERT FLYPE INVERT
(— INTO ICE) CONGEAL
(— INTO STEEL) ACIERATE
(— INTO VINEGAR) ACETIFY
(— LEAVES OF BOOK) LEAF TOSS
(— OF AFFAIRS) GO JOB KICK
(— OF CABLE) BITTER
(— OF DUTY) TOUR SHIFT TRICK
(— OF EVENTS) WENT
(— OF EXPRESSION) CONCETTO
(— OF FANCY) GUST
(— OF MIND) FREAK
(— OF STRING) WAP
(— OF TIDE) PINCH
(— OF WIT) FLIRT
(— OF YARN) MOUSING
(— OFF) SHUNT DIVERT
(— ON) HIT
(— ON LATHE) THROW
(— OUT) GO USH BEAR FALL FARE OUST SORT TAKE CHIVE FUDGE OUTPUT SUCCEED
(— OUT TO BE) PROVE EXFLECT
(— OUTWARD) EVERT SPLAY
(— OVER) CANT FLAP FLIP KEEL VETTE VOLVE CLINCH DESIGN AGITATE CAPSIZE OVERSET
(— POINT OF) ABATE
(— RAPIDLY) SPIN TIRL GIDDY
(— RIGHT) HAP HUP
(— SAIL YARD) BRACE
(— SKIS) STEM
(— SOUR) FOX BLINK PRILL BLEEZE CHANGE SOUREN
(— SUDDENLY) FLOP SLUE
(— TO NEAR SIDE) HAW
(— TO OFF SIDE) GEE
(— TO ONE SIDE) CORNER GOGGLE
(— TO THE LEFT) HAW PORT WIND WYND
(— UP) FACE HAPPEN
(— UP NOSE) FLIRT SNURL
(— UPSIDE DOWN) CANT COUP WHELM INVERT QUELME WHELVE WHEMMLE
(— VESSEL IN CIRCLE) CHAPEL
(— WHEELS) CRAMP
(— YELLOW) FIRE
(BALLET —) PIROUETTE
(COMPLETE —) LAP
(DOWNWARD —) SLIDE
(ECCENTRIC —) CRANKUM
(FORTUNATE —) BREAK
(GOOD —) BOON
(HALF —) CARACOLE
(IN —) AROUND
(SERIES OF TIGHT —S) CHICANE
(SHARP —) DOUBLE WRENCH ZIGZAG HAIRPIN
(SKI —) SWING CHRISTIE TELEMARK
(SUDDEN —) CURL
(PL.) ALLEGRO
(PREF.) STREPHO STREPSI STREPT(O) TREPO TROP(IDO)(O)

VERSI VERTEBR(I)(O) VERTI
(SUFF.) TROPAL TROPE TROPIA TROPIC TROPY
TURNBUCKLE TURNEL TURNBOUT
TURNCOAT APOSTATE RENEGADE
TURNED SOUR VERSED COCKEYED INFLEXED
(— ABOUT) CONVERSE
(— BACK) EVOLUTE
(— DOWNWARD) ABASED DEFLEXED
(— EDGEWISE) BLIND
(— INWARD) VARUS
(— OUTWARD) EXTRORSE
(— TOWARD) ANODIC
(— TOWARD ONE SIDE) AWRY
(— UP) ACOCK URVED
(— WRONG WAY) AWK
(PREF.) STREPSI
TURNER SLICE BODGER SLIDER TWIRLER
TURNING HEAD WIND TWIST VOLTA WRINK DETOUR ROTARY FLEXION FLEXURE VERSION VOLVENT FLECTION STREPSIS WHEELERY ACESCENCE
(— OF EYE) CAST
(— SOUR) ACESCENT
(— TO RIGHT) DEXTRO
(— TOWARD STEM) ADVERSE
(METAL —S) SWARF
(PL.) SCULL
(PREF.) STROPH(O) TROPIDO TROPO
(SUFF.) TROPAL TROPE TROPIA TROPIC(AL) TROPISM TROPOUS TROPY
TURNIP BAGA NAPE NEEP RAPE NAVEW SWEDE RAPEYE TURMUT CRUCIFER RUTABAGA
(PL.) KRAUT RAPPINI
(PREF.) NAPI
TURNIP-SHAPED NAPIFORM RAPACEUS
TURNIX QUAIL HEMIPOD ORTYGAN HEMIPODE
TURNKEY SCREW LOCKSMAN
TURN OF THE SCREW (AUTHOR OF —) JAMES
(CHARACTER IN —) FLORA MILES PETER QUINT JESSEL
TURNOUT RIG TEAM SETOUT EQUIPAGE TRANSFER
TURNOVER PASTY BRIDIE BRAMBLE EMPANADA FLAPJACK
(PL.) PIROJKI PIROSHKI
TURNPIN TAMPION
TURNSOLE HELIO
TURNSPIT HASTLER
TURNSTILE TIRL STILE MOULINE TURNGATE TURNPIKE TOURNIQUET
TURNSTONE PLOVER REDLEG CHICARIC CREDDOCK
TURNTABLE DECK RACER ROTARY NONSYNC PLAYBACK
TURNUS (FATHER OF —) DAUNUS
(MOTHER OF —) VENILIA
(SLAYER OF —) AENEAS
TURPENTINE THUS TURPS SCRAPE THINNER OLEORESIN
(BORDEAUX —) GALIPOT
TURPENTINE TREE PEEBEEN

TURPITUDE FEDITY
TURQUOISE TURKEY TURKIS CALAITE CALLAIS
TURRET ROUND BELFRY CUPOLA GARRET GAZEBO LOUVER TOURET BARMKIN GUERITE MIRADOR MONITOR BARBETTE BARTIZAN GUNHOUSE TURRICLE PEPPERBOX
TURTLE EMYD ARRAU CARET CAREY TORUP COODLE COOTER JURARA SLIDER THURGI TURKLE CRAWLER CREEPER EMYDIAN JUNIATA LOGHEAD SNAPPER TORTUGA CHELONID FLAPJACK HAWKBILL MATAMATA SHAGTAIL STINKPOT TERRAPIN TORTOISE THALASSIAN
(— HAVING COMMERCIAL SHELL) CHICKEN
(OLD —) MOSSBACK
(PART OF —) EAR BEAK CLAW SHELL SHIELD CARAPACE PLASTRON
TURTLEHEAD BALMONY CHELONE CODHEAD
TUSCAN BROWN MECCA MOHAWK
TUSCANY COLCOTHAR
TUSK GAM CUSK HORN TUSH IVORY TOOTH ELEPHANT
(— OF WILD BOAR) RAZOR
(ELEPHANT'S —) SCRIVELLO
TUSSLE TUG SCRAP BICKER TASSEL TOUSLE WARSLE TUILYIE
TUSSOCK HASSOCK
TUT HOOT TOOT HOOTS
TUTELAGE TUTELE YEMSEL NURTURE TEACHING
TUTELARY GENIUS
TUTOR DON ABBE TUTE COACH TRACH DOCENT FEEDER GROUND MASTER PEDANT SCHOOL GRINDER TEACHER CRANSIER CREANCER GOVERNOR PANGLOSS PUPILIZE PRECEPTOR
TUTTI RIPIENO
TUTU TOOT TUPAKIHI
TUVALU (CAPITAL OF —) FUNAFUTI
(FORMER NAME OF —) ELLICEISLANDS LAGOONISLANDS
(ISLAND OF —) NANUMEA NUKUFETAU NUKULAILAI
TUXEDO TUX SOFA TUCK
TVASHTRI (DAUGHTER OF —) SARANYU
TWADDLE ROT BOSH TOSH FUDGE HAVER BABBLE DRIVEL FOOTLE PIFFLE TOOTLE FADAISE TWATTLE NONSENSE SLIPSLOP TOMMYROT
TWANA COLCINE
TWANG TANG PLUCK PLUNK SNUFFLE TWANGLE TWANKLE
TWAYBLADE DUFOIL TWIFOIL
(PL.) LISTERA
TWEAK FEAK TWIG
TWEED PATTU PATTOO
TWEEZERS TIT TWIRK TWINGE TWITCH MULLETS PINCERS PINCETTE VOLSELLA
TWELFTH TWALT DOZENTH
(— OF INCH) SECOND
(— OF LIGHT PERIOD) INCH

(— PART) UNCIA
TWELFTH NIGHT (AUTHOR OF —) SHAKESPEARE
(CHARACTER IN —) TOBY BELCH CURIO FESTE MARIA VIOLA ANDREW FABIAN OLIVIA ORSINO ANTONIO MALVOLIO AGUECHEEK SEBASTIAN VALENTINE
TWELVE TWAL DOZEN DICKER DODECADE
(PREF.) DODEC(A) DUODECIM
TWELVEMONTH TOWMONT
TWELVER IMAMI
TWELVE-TONE SERIAL
TWELVE-TONE-ROW SET
TWENTIETH VIGESIMAL VINGTIEME
TWENTY KAPH CORGE KAPPA SCORE COOREE
(PREF.) ICOS(A) VIGINTI
TWENTY-FIVE QUARTERN
TWENTY-FOURTH CARAT
TWENTY-ONE PONTOON VANJOHN BLACKJACK
20,000 LEAGUES UNDER THE SEA (AUTHOR OF —) VERNE
(CHARACTER IN —) NED LAND NEMO PIERRE ARONNAX CONSEIL
TWERP DRONGO
TWICE BIS DOPPIO
(— A DAY) BID
(PREF.) BI BIS DI DIS
TWIDDLE TWEEDLE TWITTER
(— FEET) CUT
TWIG COW CHAT RICE RISP SLIP WAND YARD BIRCH BRIAR BRIER SHRAG SHRED SPRAY SPRIG STICK TWIST VIRGA WAVER WITHE BALEYS BROWSE FESCUE GREAVE SALLOW SPRING SWITCH WATTLE WICKER SCOLLOP TWIGLET ANAPHYTE
(— FOR SNUFF) DIP
(— GROWING FROM STUMP) WAVER
(— IN BIRD SNARE) SWEEK
(— WORN AT SACRIFICES) INARCULUM
(—S FOR BURNING) CHATWOOD
(—S FOR WATTLING) FRITLES
(—S MADE INTO BROOM) BESOM
(BARE —) COW
(BROKEN —S) BRUSH
(CUT —) SARMENT
(DRIED —) CHAD
(LITTLE —) SURCLE
(THATCHING —) SCOLLOP
(WILLOW —) SALLOW ANAPHYTE
(SUFF.) CLEMA
TWIGGED VIRGATE
TWIGGY SPRAYEY
TWILIGHT EVE DIMPS DUMPS GLOAM TWALE DIMMET DIMMIT UGHTEN DUCKISH COCKSHUT EVENFALL EVENGLOW GLOAMING GRISPING CREPUSCLE
(— OF THE GODS) RAGNAROK
(DARKER PART OF —) DUSK
(MORNING —) DAWN
TWILL WALE CHINO CADDIS RUSSEL CADDICE DUNGAREE
TWILLED CORDED
TWIN DUAL GEMEL SOSIE DIDYMUS JUMELLE SIAMESE TWINDLE

DIDYMATE DIDYMOID DIDYMOUS PARASITE TWINLING
(PL.) GEMEL COUPLET
(PREF.) DIDYM(O) GEMINI
(SUFF.) DIDYMUS
TWINE MAT COIL DUNE LACE PIRL WIND WRAP TWIRL TWIST INFOLD INTORT ANAMITE ENTWINE SKEENYIE
(HANK OF —) RAN
(PITCHED —) WHIPPING
(PREF.) PLEC(O)
TWINEBUSH PINBUSH
TWINFLOWER LINNAEA
TWINGE GIRD PANG PULL SHOOT TOUCH TWANG STOUND
(— OF CONSCIENCE) SCRUPLE
(— OF PAIN) GLISK
TWINING VOLUBLE AMPLECTANT
TWINKLE WINK BLINK TWEER TWINK TWIRE BICKER SIMPER WINKLE SPARKLE
TWINKLING MOMENT TWINKLY
TWINLEAF HELMETPOD
TWIRL SPIN TIRL DRILL QUERL TRILL TWIRK TWIST WHIRL TRUNDLE TWIDDLE TWIZZLE
(— OF BAGPIPE) WARBLER
TWIST BOB CUE MAT PLY WIN WIP CAST COIL CURL DRAW HURL KICK KINK PIRL RICK SKEW SLEW SLUB SLUE TURN WARP WIND WISP WORK CHINK CRANK CRICK CRINK CROOK CURVE FEEZE GNARL KINCH PLAIT QUIRK QUIRL REEVE SCREW SKELL SNAKE SNIRL SNURL SPIRE SWIRL THRAW THROW TWEAK TWIND TWINE TWIRE TWIRL WINCE WITHE WREST WRICK BOUGHT DETORT EXTORT HANKLE INTORT QUEEVE SLOUGH SPRAIN SQUIRL SQUIRM STRAND TWEEZE WAMBLE WARPLE WASHIN WICKER WIMBLE WRABBE WRITHE CHIGNON CONTORT CRANKLE CRINKLE CROOKLE CRUMPLE DISTORT ENTWINE SQUINCH TORTURE TWISTER TWISTLE TWIZZLE WREATHE WRIGGLE CLINAMEN CONVOLVE ENTANGLE FOREHARD FORETURN SPRINKLE SQUIGGLE VOLUTION
(— A ROPE) DALLY
(— AWAY) WAIVE
(— BACK) RETORT
(— FORCIBLY) WRING
(— IN A ROPE) GRIND SQUIRM
(— IN GRAIN OF A BOW) BOUGHT
(— IN ONE'S NATURE) KINK
(— OF FACE) STITCH
(— OF HAY) HAYBRAND
(— OF PAPER) SPILL
(— OF PEN IN WRITING) QUIRK
(— OF SPEECH) CRANK
(— OF THE MOUTH) DRAD
(— OF TOBACCO) ROLL PIGTAIL
(— OF YARNS) FORETURN
(— OUT OF SHAPE) BUCKLE CONTORT
(— SHARPLY) FEAK
(— TOGETHER) CABLE RADDLE

(CAUSE TO —) TORQUE
(PREF.) SPIR(I)(O) STREMMATO STREPHO STREPSI STREPT(O) TORSO TORTI
TWISTED CAM KAM WRY AWRY TORT KINKY SCREW TORSE WELKT WRONG ATWIST GAUCHE HURLED KNOTTY SCREWY SKEWED SWIRLY THRAWN THROWN TURKEN TWISTY WARPED WRITHE CRISPED CROOKED GNARLED KNOTTED SCREWED TORQUED TORTILE TORTIVE WHELKED WREATHY COCKEYED IMPLICIT INTORTED INVOLVED NONPLANE THRAWART WREATHEN
(PREF.) PLEC(O) PLECT(O) STREPSI STREPT(O)
TWISTING DALLY KNECK AJOINT TWIRLY WIGWAG ENTRAIL TWIDDLY SQUIGGLY STREPSIS TORTUOUS
(PREF.) STROPH(O)
TWIT TIT CHECK TAUNT ETWITE TWITTER RIDICULE
TWITCH TIC TIT FEAK FIRK JERK JUMP PIRN TWIG WINK YANK PLUCK START THRIP TWEAK TWICK TWIRK QUATCH QUETCH QUITCH TWINGE TWITCHEL VELLICATE
TWITCHING TIC JERKS PALMUS WORKING SACCADIC
TWITTER TWIT CHIRM CHIRP GARRE TWINK JARGON WARBLE CHIPPER CHIRRUP CHITTER QUITTER TWITTLE WHITTER
TWO TWA BOTH TWAY TWIN TWAIN BINARY COUPLE DOUBLE
(— LINES) LONGWAYS
(— OF A KIND) BRACE
(IN —) ATWO
(US —) UNC
(PREF.) BI BIS DUO DY(O) TWI
(— EACH) BINI
(IN —) DICH(O)
(MORE THAN —) MULTI
TWO-COLORED BICHROME
(PREF.) DICHRO(O)
TWO-FACED JANUS JANIFORM
(PREF.) JANI
TWO-FIFTEEN PM TIME
TWOFOLD DUAL BINAL DUPLE BACKED BIFOLD DOUBLE DUPLEX DIGONAL DIPLOID TWIFOLD DIDYMATE DIDYMOID DIDYMOUS DIPLASIC TWEYFOLD BIFARIOUS
(PREF.) DI DIPHY DIPL(O)
TWO-FOOTED BIPED
TWO-FORKED BIFURCAL
TWO GENTLEMEN OF VERONA (AUTHOR OF —) SHAKESPEARE
(CHARACTER IN —) JULIA MILAN SPEED LAUNCE SILVIA THURIO ANTONIO LUCETTA PROTEUS EGLAMOUR PANTHINO VALENTINE
TWO-HANDED BIMANAL BIMANOUS
TWO-HEADED
(PREF.) DICRANO JANI
TWO-HORNED BICORN BICORNED

TWOPENCE TUPPENCE
TWOS POT DEUCE
TWO-UP SWY
TWO WIDOWS, THE (CHARACTER IN —) ANEZKA MUMLAL KAROLINA LADISLAV
(COMPOSER OF —) SMETANA
TWO-WINGED
(PREF.) DIPTER(O)
TYCHICUS (COMPANION OF —) PAUL
TYCOON SHOGUN TAIKUN
TYDEUS (FATHER OF —) ENEOUS OENEUS
(MOTHER OF —) PERIBOEA
(SON OF —) DIOMEDES
TYMPANUM DRUM TYMPAN EARDRUM EPIPHRAGM
TYNDAREUS (BROTHER OF —) ICARIUS
(DAUGHTER OF —) PHILOPOE TIMANDRA CLYTEMNESTRA
(FATHER OF —) OEBALUS PERIERES
(MOTHER OF —) BATIA GORGOPHONE
(WIFE OF —) LEDA
TYPE CUT ILK CAST KIND MAKE MOLD NORM SORT TAKE BOGUS BROOD IMAGE MOULD PRINT STAMP EMBLEM KICKER KIDNEY LETTER NATURE SHADOW STRIPE SYMBOL TAKING TIMBER BATARDE FASHION PARABLE ANTETYPE EXEMPLAR
(— BLOCK) QUAD
(— OF EXCELLENCE) PARAGON
(— PLACED BOTTOM UP) TURN
(— SET UP) MATTER
(ASSORTMENT OF —) FONT
(DANCE —) LASYA
(DISARRANGED —) PI PIE
(GERMAN —) FRAKTUR
(HEAVY-FACED —) IONIC
(HIGHEST —) PINK
(IDEAL —) CHRIST
(OPPOSITE —) ANTITYPE
(PART OF —) BACK BALL BODY FACE FOOT NICK SIZE STEM BEARD BELLY BEVEL SERIF SHANK GROOVE COUNTER ASCENDER CROSSBAR SHOULDER DESCENDER
(PHYSICAL —) HABIT
(RACIAL —) DEHWAR
(REPRESENTATIVE —) GENIUS
(SET —) STICK
(SIZE OF —) (SEE SIZE)
(STYLE OF —) CANON DORIC ELITE GOUDY GREEK IONIC KABEL ROMAN BODONI CASLON CICERO GOTHIC HEBREW ITALIC JENSON MODERN BOOKMAN BREVIER CENTURY ELZEVIR EMERALD FULLFACE GARAMOND
(PREF.) MORPH(O)
TYPEBAR
(PL.) BASKET
TYPEE (AUTHOR OF —) MELVILLE
(CHARACTER IN —) TOM TOBY MARNOO MEHEVI FAYAWAY KORYKORY
TYPEFACE FACE FRAKTUR BOLDFACE SANSERIF

TYPEHOLDER PALLET
TYPESETTER MONO
TYPESETTING FAT PHAT
TYPEWRITER MILL TYPER TYPIST
PORTABLE
(PART OF —) BAR KEY BAIL KNOB
LOOP STOP GUIDE LEVER PLATE
SCALE SHIFT HOLDER MARGIN
PLATEN RETURN ROLLER SPACER
CONTROL RELEASE SUPPORT
CARRIAGE KEYBOARD
REGULATOR BACKSPACER
TYPHON (FATHER OF —) TARTARUS
(MOTHER OF —) TERRA

TYPHOON WIND CYCLONE
TUFFOON
TYPICAL FAIR TYPAL TYPIC USUAL
AVERAGE CLASSIC PATTERN
PERFECT REGULAR
(PREF.) EU
(SUFF.) (— OF) ISH ISTIC
TYPIFY TYPE IMAGE SHADOW
ADUMBRATE EPITOMIZE
PERSONIFY REPRESENT
SYMBOLIZE
TYPIFYING GENERIC
TYR ER EAR TIU TYRR
(BROTHER OF —) THOR

(FATHER OF —) ODIN
TYRANNICAL LORDLY SLAVISH
ABSOLUTE DESPOTIC
TYRANNIZE OPPRESS DOMINEER
OVERLORD
TYRANNOUS ABSOLUTE
TYRANNY ROD DESPOTISM
TYRANT ANARCH DESPOT NIMROD
FUEHRER PHARAOH PHALARIS
TYRANT FLYCATCHER PEWEE
TYRO HAM BABE COLT PUPIL
NOVICE RABBIT TYRONE
BEGINNER NEOPHYTE
(FATHER OF —) SALMONEUS

(HUSBAND OF —) CRETHEUS
(MOTHER OF —) ALCIDICE
(SON OF —) AESON NELEUS PELIAS
PHERES AMYTHAON
TYRRHENIAN ETRUSCAN
TYRRHENUS (BROTHER OF —)
LYDUD TARCHON
(FATHER OF —) ATYS HERCULES
TELEPHUS
(MOTHER OF —) HIERA OMPHALE
CALLITHEA
TYTO ALUCO STRIX

U

U UNCLE UNION
(PREF.) **(— SHAPED)** HY(O)
UDDER BAG DUG TID EWER ELDER
SUMEN VESSEL
UFO (STUDY OF —S) UFOLOGY

UGANDA

CAPITAL: KAMPALA
COLLEGE: MAKERERE
FORMER CAPITAL: ENTEBBE
LAKE: KYOGA ALBERT EDWARD
GEORGE VICTORIA
LANGUAGE: ATESO GANDA
LUGANDA SWAHILI
MOUNTAIN: ELGON MARGHERITA
MOUNTAIN RANGE: RUWENZORI
NATIVE: ATESO BANTU LANGO
ACHOLI ANKOLE BAGISU
BAKIGA BASOGA BATORO
BAGANDA BUNYORO LUGBARA
NILOTIC SUDANIC
PLATEAU: ANKOLE
PROVINCE: BUGANDA
RIVER: ASWA KAFU PAGER
KATONGA
SEAPORT: MOMBASA
TOWN: ARUA JINJA MBALE
KITGUM MOROTO TORORO
ENTEBBE MOMBASA
WATERFALL: KABALEGA

UGLY FOUL AWFUL OUGLE SNIVY
UNKED CRANKY DREEPY GORGON
GROTTY HOMELY LAIDLY ORNERY
CRABBED GRIZZLY HIDEOUS
HOUGHLY VICIOUS GRUESOME
UGLISOME UNLOVELY
MONSTROUS
UGLY-TEMPERED SNARLISH
UGNI BLANC TREBBIANO
UIGHUR JAGATAI
UITOTAN KAIMO WITOTAN
UKE JARANA
UKRAINIAN RUSSNIAK
UKULELE UKE TAROPATCH
ULAM (FATHER OF —) ESHEK
ULCER FRET KYLE SORE WOLF
BOTCH ISSUE RUPIA ULCUS
APHTHA MORMAL TETTER
BEDSORE CHANCRE EGILOPS
ENCAUMA FISTULA AEGILOPS
FONTANEL FOSSETTE ULCUSCLE
(ARTIFICIAL —) ISSUE
(PREF.) CHANCRI HELC(O)
ULCERATING EXEDENT
ULCERATION NOMA CANKER
CARIES BEDSORE HELCOSIS
ULCEROUS HELCOID
ULEX LING
ULEXITE TIZA
ULLIKUMMI (FATHER OF —)
KUMARBI
ULNA CUBIT CUBITAL CUBITUS

ULTIMATE IT NTH DIRE LAST
FINAL ULTIME SUPREME
ABSOLUTE EVENTUAL FARTHEST
ULTIMITY
ULTIMATELY FINALLY
ULTIMO PAST
ULTRA EXTREME FANATIC
FORWARD
ULTRACONSERVATISM TORYISM
ULTRACONSERVATIVE WHITE
ULTRAFASHIONABLE RITZY
SWELL SWAGGER
ULTRAMONTANISM CURIALISM
ULUA PAPIO PAPIOPIO
ULYSSES (AUTHOR OF —) JOYCE
(CHARACTER IN —) BUCK RUDY
BLOOM BREEN MOLLY BLAZES
BOYLAN COFFEY GERTIE HAINES
MARION DEDALUS LEOPOLD
PUREFOY STEPHEN MULLIGAN
MACDOWELL
(FATHER OF —) LAERTES
(MOTHER OF —) ANTICLEA
(SLAYER OF —) TELEGONUS
(SON OF —) TELEMACHUS
(WIFE OF —) PENELOPE
UMBEL RAY RADIUS SERTULE
UMBELLA SERTULUM UMBELLET
UMBELLIFERONE CUMARIN
COUMARIN
UMBER OMER OMBER PARTRIDGE
UMBILICUS NAVEL
(PREF.) OMPHAL(O)
UMBO BEAK UMBONULE
UMBONES NATES
UMBRA DOGFISH MUDFISH
NUCLEUS UMBRINE
UMBRAGE PIQUE SNUFF OFFENSE
UMBRELLA BELL GAMP MUSH
DUMPY BROLLY CHATTA PAYONG
PILEUS CHATTAH GINGHAM
ROUNDEL FITTISOL KITTYSOL
MUSHROOM TYRASOLE
(PART OF —) CAP RIB ROD TIP
GORE JOINT PANEL SHAFT
BULLET HANDLE RUNNER SPRING
CLOSURE FERRULE STRETCHER
UMBRELLA BIRD COTINGA
COTINGID
UMBRELLA BUSH MILJEE
UMBRELLA PALM KENTIA
UMBRELLA PLANT SEDGE
GLUMAL
UMBRELLA TREE WAHOO
ELKWOOD MAGNOLIA
UMBRETTE UMBRE HOMBRE
UMBRET CICONIID
UMBRIAN IGUVINE
UMBURANA ROBLE
UMLAUT MUTATION METAPHONY
UMPIRE UMP JUDGE TRIER
ARBITER DAYSMAN ODDSMAN
STICKLER

UNABASHED BROWLESS
UNABBREVIATED FULL
UNABLE UNHABILE POWERLESS
UNACCENTED GRAVE LIGHT
ATONIC
UNACCEPTABLE DREADFUL
UNACCOMPANIED BARE SOLO
ALONE SECCO SINGLE
UNACCOUNTABLE STRANGE
UNACCUSTOMED UNUSED
STRANGE INSOLITE WONTLESS
UNACQUAINTED STRANGE
UNCOUTH
UNADORNED DRY BALD PLAIN
SECCO STARK RUSTIC SEVERE
SIMPLE AUSTERE LITERAL
INORNATE
UNADULTERATED NET FRANK
HONEST VIRGIN GENUINE
SINCERE ABSOLUTE
UNADVANTAGEOUSLY ILL
UNAFFECTED EASY REAL PLAIN
HOMELY NATIVE RUSTIC SIMPLE
ARTLESS BUCOLIC SINCERE
SEMPLICE
UNAFRAID BOLD BRAVE DEFIANT
UNAGGRESSIVE AMIABLE
UNALERT SUPINE
UNALLOYED DEEP SOLID VIRGIN
GENUINE
UNALTERABLE IMMUTABLE
UNAMBIGUOUS EXPLICIT
UNANIMATED FLAT VAPID INSIPID
UNANIMITY ATTACK CONSENT
UNANIMOUS SOLID WHOLE
UNANIME UNIVOCAL
UNAPPROACHABLE STATELY
UNARMED BARE INERM
UNBARBED
(PREF.) ANOPL(O)
UNASSAILABLE SECURE
UNASSUMED NATURAL
UNASSUMING SHY HUMBLE
MODEST SIMPLE NATURAL
RETIRING
UNATTACHED FREE LOOSE SINGLE
UNATTENDED SINGLE
UNATTRACTIVE BLAH UGLY PLAIN
WORSE HOMELY FRUMPISH
UNLIKELY
UNAVAILING VAIN FUTILE
BOOTLESS GAINLESS NUGATORY
UNAVOIDABLE SHUNLESS
NECESSARY
UNAVOWED SECRET
UNAWARE UNWARE WITLESS
HEEDLESS INNOCENT UNBEWARE
WARELESS OBLIVIOUS
UNAWARES ABACK SHORT
UNBALANCED HITE DOTTY NUTTY
FRUITY UNEVEN FANATIC
DERANGED LOPSIDED PIXILATED
MOONSTRUCK

UNBAR UNSLOT
UNBARRED UNSTOKEN
UNBEARDED CALLOW
UNBECOMING RUDE INEPT PLAIN
INDIGN UNMEET BENEATH
IMPROPER INDECENT UNSEEMLY
UNWORTHY
UNBEFITTING BENEATH
UNBELIEF UNFAITH
UNBELIEVABLE HOT THIN
UNBELIEVER PAGAN GIAOUR
ATHEIST DOUBTER INFIDEL
SCOFFER SKEPTIC
UNBELIEVING MISCREANT
UNBEND REST THAW FRESE RELAX
UNTIE EXTEND DISBEND
UNCROOK
UNBENDING RIGID STARK STERN
STIFF THARF CATONIAN
OBDURATE RAMRODDY
RESOLUTE
UNBIASED FAIR JUST DETACHED
UNBIND FREE UNDO UNTIE
UNGIRD UNDRESS
UNBLAMABLE INNOCENT
UNBLEACHED BLAE BLAY ECRU
BEIGE BROWN
UNBLEMISHED FAIR PURE SOUND
WHITE ENTIRE SPOTLESS
UNBLOCK REDD
UNBLOODY INCRUENT
UNBOLT OPEN UNBAR UNPIN
UNBOSOM OPEN
UNBOUGHT UNCOFT
UNBOUND FREE LOOSE
UNBOUNDED HUGE
UNBRANDED SLICK NATIVE
UNBROKEN DEAD FLAT FERAL
FLUSH SHEER SOLID SOUND
SINGLE CERRERO REGULAR
UNRACED STRAIGHT UNBACKED
WAKELESS
UNBUILD DESTROY
UNBUILT UNBIGGED
UNBURDEN EMPTY UNLOAD
UNSHIP
UNBURNISHED WHITE MATTED
UNCANNY EERY UNCO EERIE
SCARY UNCOW UNKID WEIRD
WISHT CREEPY SPOOKY
UNCOUTH ELDRITCH
POKERISH
UNCASTRATED INTACT
UNCAUGHT UNHENT
UNCEASING ENDLESS ETERNAL
EASELESS MINUTELY
UNCEREMONIOUS CURT BLUFF
BLUNT SHORT ABRUPT CASUAL
FAMILIAR INFORMAL
UNCERTAIN WAW DARK HAZY
WILD FLUKY SHADY SHAKY
WAUGH CASUAL CLOUDY
CRANKY FITFUL FLUKEY GLEAMY

QUEASY CASALTY CHANCEY
COMICAL DUBIOUS TRICKSY
VAGRANT VARIOUS WILSOME
CATCHING DELICATE FLICKERY
FUGITIVE HOVERING INSECURE
SLIPPERY TECHNOUS TICKLISH
UNCERTAINTY MIST WERE DEMUR
DOUBT MAYBE BAFFLE BALANCE
DUBIETY CASUALTY MISTRUST
SUSPENSE UNSURETY SKEPTICISM
UNCHALLENGED ACCEPTED
UNCHANGEABLE FAST STABLE
DURABLE ETERNAL
UNCHANGING STATIC ETERNAL
UNIFORM CONSTANT STATICAL
UNCHASTE LEWD BAWDY FRAIL
LIGHT LOOSE IMPURE WANTON
FORLAIN HAGGARD SCARLET
IMMODEST
UNCHASTITY BAWDRY STUPRUM
ADULTERY
UNCHECKED LIBERAL RAMPANT
REINLESS
UNCIFORM HAMATUM
UNCINARIA NECATOR
UNCIVIL RUDE BLUFF ROUGH
RUSTY SURLY COARSE CRUSTY
RUGGED UNFEEL IMPOLITE
UNCIVILIZED RUDE WILD MYALL
INCULT SAVAGE UNCIVIL
BARBARIC IGNORANT SYLVATIC
UNCLAD LOOSE UNDRESSED
UNCLE EME OOM TIO YEME BUNKS
NUNKY NUNCLE
UNCLEAN FOUL TREF VILE BLACK
TARRY TERFA TREFA COMMON
FILTHY IMMUND IMPURE DEFILED
UNCLEANLINESS
(PREF.) MYS(O)
UNCLEANNESS DIRT FOULNESS
UNCLEAR DIM HAZY SHAGGY
UNCLEARLY DIMLY
UNCLENCH UNDOUBLE
**UNCLE TOM'S CABIN (AUTHOR OF
—)** STOWE
(CHARACTER IN —) EVA TOM BIRD
CASSY CHLOE ELIZA HALEY
HARRY LOKER MARKS SIMON
TOPSY GEORGE HARRIS LEGREE
RACHEL SHELBY SIMEON OPHELIA
STCLAIR EMMELINE HALLIDAY
UNCLOSE OPE OPEN UNHASP
DISCLOSE
UNCLOTHE TIRL SPOIL UNRIG
DEVEST DESPOIL
UNCLOTHED STARKERS
UNCLOUDED CLEAR SERENE
UNCOIL UNLINK
UNCOLORED FAIR
UNCOMBED UNKAMED UNTEWED
UNCOMBINED FREE FRANK LOOSE
UNCOMELY INDECENT
UNCOMFORTABLE HOT EVIL
POOR HARSH UNKET UNKID
QUEASY STICKY UNFELE
UNCOMMON MUCH NICE RARE
SELD UNCO BYOUS FORBY
UNCOW VAUDY DAINTY FORBYE
SCARCE SPECIAL STRANGE
UNUSUAL SINGULAR UNWONTED
UNCOMMONLY UNCO BYOUS
EXTRA JOLLY UNCOW UNCOLY
UNCOMMONNESS SCARCITY

UNCOMMUNICATIVE DUMB
SILENT PRIVATE RESERVED
UNCOMPLICATED RURAL HONEST
SIMPLE
UNCOMPOUNDED SIMPLEX
UNCOMPROMISING ACID FIRM
GRIM RIGID STERN STOUT ULTRA
SEVERE STRICT STRONG EXTREME
BRASSBOUND
UNCONCEALED BARE OPEN
OUVERT APPARENT
UNCONCERN APATHY EASINESS
UNCONCERNED COOL EASY
BLAND CASUAL CARELESS
UNCONCERNEDLY LIGHTLY
UNCONDITIONAL FREE FRANK
UTTER SIMPLE ABSOLUTE
EXPLICIT TERMLESS
UNCONDITIONED POSITIVE
UNCONFINED LAX FREE LOOSE
UNCONGENIAL HATEFUL INGRATE
KINDLESS
UNCONNECTED GAPPY REMOTE
DETACHED
UNCONQUERED INVICT INVICTED
UNCONSCIOUS OUT COLD BRUTE
ASLEEP BLOTTO CUCKOO TORPID
UNAWARE WITLESS COMATOSE
IGNORANT SENSELESS
UNCONSIDERED WILD
UNCONSTRAINED FREE UNNET
SIMPLE FAMILIAR
UNCONTROLLABLE WILD
UNCONTROLLED FREE MADCAP
LIBERAL ABSOLUTE UNBITTED
UNCONVENTIONAL FLAKY GYPSY
LOOSE CASUAL FLAKEY DEVIOUS
ODDBALL OFFBEAT BOHEMIAN
INFORMAL
(— IN STYLE) MOD
UNCONVINCING FALSE FISHY
UNCOOKED RAW
UNCOOPERATIVE (TO BE —)
STONEWALL
UNCOUNTABLE SUMLESS
UNCOUPLE CUT UNDOCK DISLINK
UNCOUTH RUDE CRUDE DORIC
GURLY ROUGH UNKED UNKID
GOTHIC JUNGLY QUAINT RENISH
AWKWARD BOORISH CUBBISH
HIRSUTE LOUTISH AGRESTIC
UNGAINLY YOKELISH
(— PERSON) TUG
UNCOVER BARE DOFF HUNT ROOT
ROUT TIRL TIRR BREAK STRIP
TIRVE UNLAP UNLID UNWRY
DETECT EXHUME SEARCH
UNBARE UNCASE UNHALE UNVEIL
UNDRAPE UNEARTH DISCLOSE
DISCOVER UNMANTLE UNMUFFLE
UNCOVERED BARE OVERT
(PREF.) GYMN(O)
UNCTION CHRISM OINTMENT
UNCTUOUS FAT OILY SALVY SLEEK
SOAPY SUAVE GREASY SMARMY
COURTLY PINGUID OLEAGINOUS
UNCULTIVATED RAW BRUT FERAL
DESERT FALLOW INCULT SAVAGE
SLOVEN WILDERN
UNCULTURED RUDE INCULT
ARTLESS
UNCUT RASPED
UNDAMAGED WHOLE

UNDARKENED CLEAR
UNDAUNTED BOLD BRAVE MANLY
SPARTAN FEARLESS INTREPID
UNDE WAVY UNDEE
UNDECAYED GREEN
UNDECEIVE DISABUSE
UNDECIDED MOOT DUBIOUS
PENDING DOUBTFUL WAVERING
UNDECIDEDLY HUMDRUM
UNDECLARED SECRET
UNDEFENDED UNKEPT
UNDEFILED PURE CHASTE INTACT
VIRGIN
UNDEFINED OBSCURE
UNDELIVERABLE DEAD
UNDEMONSTRATIVE COLD
ASEPTIC LACONIC RESERVED
UNDENIABLE BRUTAL
UNDENIABLY INDEED
UNDEPENDABLE CASUAL FLUFFY
UNDER SUB BAJO BELOW INFRA
NEATH SOTTO ANEATH ANUNDER
BENEATH
(— ORDERS) SUPPOSED
(— THE WORD) IV
(— THE YEAR) SA
(— THIS TITLE) HT
(— THIS WORD) SV SHV
(— WAY) AFOOT
(PREF.) HYPO SUB
UNDERBODICE JUMP BASQUINE
CAMISOLE
UNDERBRUSH FILTH COVERT
GARSIL MAQUIS RAMMEL
ABATURE
UNDERBURNED SOFT SAMEL
UNDERBUTLER WASHPOT
UNDERCARRIAGE BOGY BOGEY
BOGIE
UNDERCLAY THILL WARRANT
UNDERCLOTHES LININGS
UNDERCOAT PILE ALPACA
SURFACER
(WOOL OF — OF MUSK-OX) QIVIUT
UNDERCOVER SECRET
UNDERCRUST ABAISSE
UNDERCURRENT UNDERLAY
UNDERRUN UNDERSET
UNDERCUT JAD HOLE LAME POOL
SUMP KIRVE NOTCH
UNDERDONE RARE REAR
UNDERDRAWERS FLANNELS
UNDERESTIMATE DISPRIZE
MINIMIZE
UNDERFLEECE PASHM
UNDERFRAME SOLE
UNDERGARMENT BAND SLIP
CYMAR SIMAR SKIRT SMOCK
TUNIC WAIST BANIAN BANYAN
BODICE CAMISE CILICE CORSET
GIRDLE STAMIN CHEMISE
DOUBLET DRAWERS STAMMEL
TALLITH BLOOMERS KNICKERS
(WOMAN'S —) PANTIHOSE
(PL.) SMALLS FLANNELS FLIMSIES
SNUGGIES
UNDERGO PASS SERVE ENDURE
SUFFER SUSTAIN
UNDERGOER
(SUFF.) EE
UNDERGRADUATE MAN TASSEL
SERVITOR
UNDERGROWTH RUSH COVER

RAMMEL SPRING BUSHWOOD
UNDERHAND SLY DERN SHADY
BYHAND SECRET CROOKED
OBLIQUE INVOLVED SINISTER
SNEAKING
UNDERHANDED DERN FUNNY
FILTHY SECRET SINISTER
UNDERIVED ORIGINAL
UNDER JAW
(PREF.) GENYO
UNDERLAYER SLASHING
UNDERLIE SUBTEND
UNDERLING MENIAL SEQUEL
UNDERER HENCHMAN INFERIOR
UNDERLYING COVERT IMPLICIT
UNDERMINE SAP CAVE HOLE POOL
ERODE KNIFE WEAKEN FOSSICK
FOUNDER SUBVERT ENFEEBLE
SUPPLANT
UNDERMINED ROTTEN
UNDERNEATH BELOW BENEATH
UNNEATH
(PREF.) INTRA
UNDERNSONG TIERCE
UNDERPANTS BRIEFS BLOOMERS
KNICKERS
UNDERPART BELLY
UNDERPASS DIVE SUBWAY
UNDERRATE DECRY DISCOUNT
UNDERRUN BOTTOM
UNDERSACRISTAN CUSTOS
UNDERSHIRT VEST SHIFT SHIRT
CAMISA JERSEY LINDER SEMMIT
SINGLET WRAPPER
UNDERSHRUB HEATH PINKEYE
SEEPWEED SUBSHRUB
SAGEBRUSH SANTOLINA
UNDERSIDE BOTTOM BREAST
(— OF CLOUD) BASE
(— OF FINGER) BALL
(— OF FLOOR) CEILING
(— OF STAIRCASE) SOFFIT
(PREF.) **(ON THE —)** INFERO
UNDERSIZED DEENY SCRUB
STUNT
UNDERSKIRT QUILT CRINOLINE
PETTICOAT
UNDERSONG FABURDEN
UNDERSTAND CAN CON DIG GET
KEN SEE GAUM HAVE MAKE TAKE
TWIG BRAIN ENTER GRASP
REACH SAVVY SEIZE SENSE SKILL
SPELL ACCEPT COTTON FIGURE
FOLLOW INTAKE INTEND SUBAUD
UPTAKE CONCEIT DISCERN
COMPRISE CONCEIVE CONSTRUE
CONTRIVE FORSTAND PERCEIVE
PERSTAND UNDERNIM
UNDERSTANDABLE PLAIN
UNDERSTANDING KEN WIT GAUM
HEAD BRAIN CLASP HEART INWIT
SENSE SKILL ACCORD INTENT
NOTION REASON TREATY UPTAKE
COMPACT CONCEIT CONCEPT
ENTENTE INSIGHT MEANING
WITNESS DAYLIGHT PREHENSION
(IMPERFECT —) DARKNESS
(PREF.) NOEMA
UNDERSTATEMENT LITOTES
MEIOSIS
UNDERSTOOD LUCID SUPPOSED
(— ONLY BY SPECIALLY INITIATED)
ESOTERIC

(EASILY —) EASY CLEAR EXTANT
(NOT —) DARKSOME
UNDERSTUDY DOUBLE
UNDERSURFACE SOLE
UNDERTAKE GO TRY DARE FANG
FOND GRANT OFFER ASSUME
INCEPT PLEDGE ATTEMPT
EMBRACE EMPRISE PRETEND
UNDERFO CONTRACT PRESTATE
(— RESPONSIBILITY) ACCEPT
ANSWER
UNDERTAKER UPHOLDER
MORTICIAN
UNDERTAKING JOB AVAL TASK
CAUTIO EFFORT SCHEME VOYAGE
ATTEMPT CALLING PROJECT
VENTURE COVENANT
(— IN CARDS) CONTRACT
(UNPROFITABLE —) FOLLY
UNDERTEACHER USHER
UNDERTONE INKLING SUBTONE
UNDERTOW SEAPOOSE
UNDER TWO FLAGS (AUTHOR OF —
) OUIDA
(CHARACTER IN —) RAKE CECIL
AMAGUE BERTIE CORONA
BERKELEY CIGARETTE
GUENEVERE ROYALLIEU
CHATEAUROY ROCKINGHAM
UNDERVALUE DECRY DISABLE
DISPRIZE DISVALUE MISPRISE
MISPRIZE
UNDERVEST BODICE SEMMIT
SINGLET
UNDERWAIST CAMISOLE
UNDERWATER (— DEVICE) OTTER
PARAVANE
UNDERWEAR BRIEFS SHORTS
SKIVVY UNDIES DESSOUS
HEAVIES LONGIES LINGERIE
PRETTIES SCANTIES
(PL.) SMALLS
UNDERWING CATOCALA
UNDERWOOD FRITH BOSCAGE
COPPICE
UNDERWORLD DUAT DEWAT
HADES ORCUS SHEOL MICTLAN
XIBALBA GANGLAND
UNDERWRITE SIGN INSURE
ENDORSE
UNDERWRITER INSURER
UNDESERVED INDIGN
UNDETERMINED UNSET DUBIOUS
PENDENT AORISTIC DOUBTFUL
INFINITE
UNDEVELOPED CRUDE MORON
LATENT SLOVEN GERMING
IMMATURE JUVENILE
UNDEVIATINGLY SMACK
UNDIFFERENCED ENTIRE
UNDIFFERENTIATED GLOBAL
AMERISTIC
UNDIGESTED CRUDE
UNDIGNIFIED DOGGREL DOGGEREL
UNDILUTED MERE NEAT PURE
NAKED SHEER SHORT STRAIGHT
UNDIMINISHED ENTIRE
UNDIMMED CLEAR
UNDINE NIX
(CHARACTER IN —) HUGO VEIT
TOBIAS UNDINE BERTHALDA
KUHLEBORN
(COMPOSER OF —) LORTZING

UNDISCIPLINED WANTON
COLTISH
UNDISCLOSED HIDDEN SEALED
UNDISCRIMINATING GROSS
UNDISGUISED BALD NAKED PLAIN
UNDISMAYED ONFLEMED
UNDISPUTED LIQUID
UNDISTINGUISHED GROSS
COMMON UNNOBLE FAMELESS
NAMELESS NOTELESS
UNDISTORTED CLEAR
UNDISTURBED CALM SOUND
SERENE VIRGIN TRANQUIL
UNDIVIDED WHOLE ENTIRE SINGLE
UNDO DUP COOK POOP SLIP
FORDO SPEED UNPAY DEFEAT
DIDDLE FOREDO UNBIND UNKNIT
UNLOCK UNTUCK UNWORK
DEFEISE DESTROY NULLIFY
UNRAVEL UNRIVET UNTWIRL
UNWEAVE UNWREST DECIPHER
DISSOLVE DISTRUSS UNFASTEN
UNDOER ACHAN
UNDOGMATIC AGNOSTIC
UNDOING DEFEAT DOWNFALL
(PREF.) DE DIS
UNDOMESTICATED WILD FERAL
FERINE
UNDOUBTEDLY SURELY FRANKLY
UNDRESS MOB DOFF FLAY PEEL
TIRR STRIP UNRAY UNRIG DEVEST
DIVEST UNBUSK UNCASE UNLACE
UNRIND UNROBE UNTIRE
DISCASE UNARRAY UNREADY
UNSPOIL UNTRUSS NEGLIGEE
UNATTIRE
UNDRESSED UNDIGHT
UNDUE EXTREME
UNDULATE WAVE WAVY FLOAT
SWING BILLOW GYROSE KELTER
UNDATE UNDOSE FLICKER
UNDATED
UNDULATING SURGING FLEXUOUS
INDENTED
UNDULATION FOLD ROLL WAVE
CRIMP TEETER WAVING
CRIMPING
UNDULATORY WAVY
UNDUTIFULNESS IMPIETY
UNDYED CORAH
UNDYING IMMORTAL
UNEARTH DIG MOOT EXPOSE
UNCOVER DISCOVER
UNEARTHLY EERY EERIE WEIRD
AWESOME UNCANNY UNGODLY
UNEASINESS ENVY GENE FIDGET
NETTLE SORROW UNEASE
AILMENT ANXIETY DISEASE
MISEASE TROUBLE DISQUIET
DISTASTE
UNEASY SICKLY FIDGETY INQUIET
NERVOUS RESTIVE UNQUIET
WORRIED RESTLESS
UNEDUCATED RUDE SIMPLE
IGNORANT
UNEMBELLISHED DRY PROSE
STARK AUSTERE
UNEMOTIONAL DRY COLD COOL
STOIC STONY STOICAL
UNEMOTIONALLY EVENLY
UNEMPLOYED IDLE ORRA VOID
OTIANT OTIOSE VACANT IDLESET
LEISURE UNBUSIED

UNEMPLOYMENT IDLENESS
UNENCUMBERED VACANT
EXPEDITE
UNENDING ABYSMAL AGELONG
CHRONIC ENDLESS UNDYING
TERMLESS TIMELESS
UNENJOYABLE JOYLESS
UNENLIGHTENED MISTY HEATHEN
IGNORANT
UNENTHUSIASTIC COLD
UNEQUAL IMPAR DISPAR UNEGAL
UNEVEN INEQUAL INFERIOR
(— TO STRAIN) FEEBLE
(PREF.) ANIS(O) IMPARI INEQUI
UNEQUALED UNIQUE NONESUCH
UNEQUIVOCAL DIRECT SQUARE
PERFECT DEFINITE DISTINCT
EXPLICIT RESOUNDING
UNERRING DEAD TRUE DEADLY
INERRANT
UNERRINGLY CLEAN
UNEVEN RUDE EROSE GOBBY
HAGGY JAGGY MEALY ROUGH
HOBBLY PLATTY RAGGED
RUGGED SPOTTY TWITTY UNFAIR
UNLIKE DIURNAL ERRATIC
HOTTERY INEQUAL SCALENE
STREAKY UNEQUAL HUMMOCKY
SCRAGGED SCRATCHY SNAGGLED
ACCIDENTED
(— IN COLOR) CLOUDY
UNEVENLY AWRY
UNEVENNESS BUMP WAVE FRAZE
ANOMALY WRINKLE ACCIDENT
ASPERITY
UNEVENTFUL STILL UNDATED
UNEXCITED LEVEL
UNEXCITING DEAD DULL TAME
BORING PROSAIC
UNEXPECTED EERY EERIE ABRUPT
SUDDEN UNWARY INOPINE
UNLOOKED
UNEXPECTEDLY UNWARES
UNAWARES
UNEXPIRED ALIVE
UNEXPLAINED HIDDEN
UNEXPOSED RAW
UNFADABLE FAST
UNFADED FRESH BRIGHT
UNFAILING SURE DEADLY
INFALLID UNERRING
UNFAIR FOUL CROOK WRONG
BIASED SHABBY UNEVEN UNJUST
DEVIOUS PARTIAL SLANTER
UNEQUAL UNSEEMLY WRONGFUL
UNFAIRLY HARDLY
UNFAIRNESS CROSS INEQUITY
UNFAITHFUL INFIDEL TRAITOR
DISLOYAL RECREANT
UNFALTERING SURE TRUE STEADY
UNERRING
UNFAMILIAR NEW FREMD
HEATHER STRANGE UNKNOWN
UNFASTEN FREE OPEN UNDO
LOOSE UNPIN UNBIND UNHASP
UNLIME UNLINK UNLOCK
UNMAKE UNTINE UNDIGHT
UNHITCH UNSTECK UNTRUSS
UNFATHOMABLE ABYSMAL
ABYSSAL PROFOUND
UNFATHOMED COSMIC
UNFAVORABLE BAD ILL FOUL
HARD POOR CRONK SHREWD

UNFAIR UNKIND ADVERSE
AWKWARD FROWARD HOSTILE
UNHAPPY BACKWARD CONTRARY
INIMICAL SINISTER UNKINDLY
(PREF.) DYS
UNFAVORABLY BADLY CROSS
UNFEATHERED SQUAB
UNFEELING COLD DULL HARD
CRASS CRUEL HARSH ROCKY
STERN STONY BRUTAL LEADEN
MARBLE STOLID CALLOUS
OBDURATE
UNFEELINGLY HARSHLY
UNFEELINGNESS APATHY
UNFEIGNED OPEN TRUE HEARTY
CORDIAL NATURAL SINCERE
UNFERMENTED AZYMOUS
UNFERTILE BARREN
UNFETTERED FREE UNGYVED
UNFILLED BLANK EMPTY VACANT
VACUOUS
UNFINISHED RAW GRAY GREY
CRUDE KACHA ROUGH KUTCHA
RAGGED KACHCHA STICKIT
IMMATURE INCHOATE
UNFIRED GREEN
UNFIRM UNFAST
UNFIT BAD SICK UNAPT WISHT
WRONG COMMON FAULTY
NOUGHT UNTIDY DISABLE
UNFITTY IMPROPER UNFITTEN
UNLIKELY UNLIKING
UNFITTING UNMEETLY
UNFIXED AFLOAT
UNFLEDGED SQUAB CALLOW
UNFLINCHING LEVEL STAUNCH
UNFOLD OPEN BREAK BURST
SOLVE UNLAP UNTIE DEPLOY
EVOLVE EXPAND EXPLAT FLOWER
SPREAD UNFURL UNPLAT
UNROLL UNTUCK BLOSSOM
DEVELOP DISPLAY DIVULGE
EXPLAIN UNPLAIT UNRAVEL
UNWEAVE UNDOUBLE UNPLIGHT
UNFOLDED OPEN EVOLUTE
EXPANDED
UNFOLDING DISPLAY
(— OF EVENTS) ACTION
(— TO VIEW) BURST
UNFORCED EASY GLIB WILLING
UNFORESEEN CASUAL SUDDEN
IMPREVU UNAWARE
UNFORMED CALLOW INFORM
UNFORTUNATE ILL EVIL POOR
DONCY TOUGH WEARY SHREWD
HAPLESS UNHAPPY UNLUCKY
LUCKLESS UNTOWARD
WANHAPPY
UNFREQUENTED LONE EMPTY
UNCOUTH SOLITARY
UNFRIENDLY ILL COLD FOUL CHILL
BITTER CHILLY FIERCE FROSTY
UNSOME HOSTILE INGRATE
STRANGE INIMICAL
UNFROCK DEFROCK DEGRADE
DISFROCK UNPRIEST
UNFRUITFUL BLUNT ADDLED
BARREN EFFETE WASTED STERILE
USELESS INFECUND
UNFULFILLMENT BREACH
UNFURL BREAK SPREAD UNFOLD
DEVELOP OUTROOL
UNFURNISHED BARE VACANT

UNGAINLY LANKY SPLAY WEEDY CLUMSY UNGAIN AWKWARD BOORISH NUNTING UNHEPPEN UNLICKED UNWIELDY
UNGENEROUS MEAN SHABBY STINGY GRUDGING
UNGENIAL CHILLY
UNGIRDED DISCINCT
UNGODLINESS ATHEISM IMPIETY
UNGODLY SINFUL WICKED GODLESS IMPIOUS PROFANE
UNGOVERNABLE WILD UNRULY FROWARD IMPOTENT
UNGRACEFUL HARD CLUMSY ANGULAR AWKWARD HALTING UNTOWARD
UNGRACEFULLY HARSHLY
UNGRACIOUS GRUFF UNFEEL UNFELE CHURLISH SNAPPISH
UNGRATEFUL UNKIND INGRATE
UNGROOMED UNDRESSED
UNGUARDED STIFF
UNGUENT CEROMA CHRISM PIMENT POMADE SMEGMA POMATUM UNCTION OINTMENT (PREF.) MYRO
UNGULATE HOG PIG DEER HORSE TAKIN TAPIR HOOFED AMBLYPOD ELEPHANT
UNGUMMED BRIGHT
UNHALLOWED IMPURE UNHOLY PROFANE
UNHAMPERED FREE DIRECT EXPEDITE
UNHAPPINESS MISERY SORROW ILLFARE SADNESS UNBLISS
UNHAPPY SAD POOR DISMAL UNLUCKY UNLUSTY WANSOME DEJECTED DOWNBEAT DOWNGONE WOBEGONE WRETCHED
UNHARMED SAFE UNSHENT
UNHARNESS UNGEAR OUTSHUT OUTSPAN UNHORSE UNTACKLE
UNHEALED GREEN
UNHEALTHY BAD MORBID QUEASY SICKLY UNHALE NAUGHTY PECCANT EPINOSIC MALADIVE
UNHEATED COLD
UNHEEDED IGNORED UNTENTED
UNHEEDING DEAF CARELESS
UNHESITATING READY UNPOISED
UNHITCH OUTSPAN
UNHOLY IMPURE WICKED IMPIOUS PROFANE
UNHORSE PURL THROW UNCOLT DISMOUNT UNSADDLE
UNHURRIED EASY SLOW SOFT SOBER
UNHURT SAFE HARMLESS HURTLESS UNHARMED
UNIAT MALKITE MELCHITE
UNICORN LIN REEM KILIN LICORN LICORNE NARWHAL HOWITZER
UNICORN FISH LIJA UNIE
UNICORN PLANT MARTINOE
UNICUM UNION
UNIDENTIFIED FACELESS INCOGNITO
UNIFICATION SYSTEM ENSEMBLE
UNIFIED GLOBAL
UNIFIER UMBRELLA
UNIFORM KIT DEAD EVEN FLAT

JUST LIKE SAME SELF SUIT ALIKE BLUES CLOTH KHAKI SOLID SUITY GLOBAL GREENS LIVERY SINGLE STEADY EQUABLE REGULAR SIMILAR SUNTANS CONSTANT EQUIFORM EQUIPAGE MEASURED STANDARD UNIVOCAL
(— IN HUE) FLAT
(LEATHER —) BUFF
(NOT —) SQUALLY
(PRISONER'S —) STRIPES
(PREF.) IS ISO
UNIFORMITY ONENESS EQUALITY EVENNESS MONOTONY SAMENESS
UNIFORMLY EVENLY EQUALLY
UNIFY MERGE UNITE CEMENT COMPACT UNITIZE COALESCE
UNILATERAL SECUND
UNIMAGINATIVE DULL SODDEN STUPID LIMITED LITERAL PROSAIC UNIDEAL PEDANTIC PEDESTRIAN
UNIMPAIRED FRESH SOUND ENTIRE INTACT
(— BY) DEVOID
UNIMPASSIONED SOBER WHOLE STEADY
UNIMPEDED FREE EXPEDITE
UNIMPORTANT VAIN PETTY SMALL CASUAL SIMPLE TRIVIAL IMMOMENT PIDDLING TRINKETY JERKWATER
UNINFLECTED APTOTIC
UNINFORMED GREEN UNTOLD IGNORANT
UNINHABITED WILD EMPTY DESERT VACANT DESOLATE WASTEFUL
UNINHIBITED LARGE
UNINJURED INTACT SINCERE
UNINSPIRED HACK STODGY POMPIER DRYASDUST
UNINSPIRING TAME
UNINSTRUCTED NAIVE IGNORANT
UNINTELLIGENT DUMB OBTUSE OPAQUE STUPID ASININE FOOLISH VACUOUS WITLESS
UNINTELLIGIBLE BLIND MISTY OPAQUE MYSTICAL
UNINTENTIONAL UNMEANT
UNINTERESTING DRY ARID COLD DRAB DREE DULL FADE FLAT TAME DREAR SANDY STALE BORING DREICH JEJUNE INSIPID BROMIDIC FRUMPISH
UNINTERMITTENT ITHAND
UNINTERRUPTED SMOOTH STEADY ENDLESS ETERNAL STRAIGHT
UNINTERRUPTEDLY AWAY
UNIO MUSSEL
UNION SUM ZYG BLOC DUAD JOIN ALLOY GROUP JOINT NONOP UNITY ENOSIS FUSION GREMIO TAWHID VEREIN COMPACT CONCERT CONTACT MEETING ONENESS SOCIETY ADHESION ALLIANCE COHESION ESPOUSAL JOINTURE JUNCTION JUNCTURE SODALITY SYSTASIS TRIALISM VINCULUM ZOLLVEREIN
(— OF TWO SETS) CUP
(— OF TWO VOWELS) CRASIS

(MARITAL —) BED
(POLITICAL —) ANSCHLUSS
(SEXUAL —) COPULA COUPLING
(TURKISH —) JETTRU
(PREF.) ZYG(O)(OTO)
(SEXUAL —) GAMO
(SUFF.) APSIS GAM(AE)(IST)(OUS)(Y) GAMETE
UNIONIST REFUGEE
UNION OF SOVIET SOCIALIST REPUBLICS (SEE RUSSIA)
UNIQUE ODD RARE SOLE UNIC ALONE UNION SINGLE SULLEN UNICUM ALONELY SOLEYNE SPECIAL STRANGE ISOLATED SINGULAR
UNIQUENESS SOLITUDE
UNISON FIRST CONCORD HOMOPHONY
UNIT (ALSO SEE MEASURE AND WEIGHT) (ALSO SEE MEASURE) ACE ONE ATOM BARN KLAN FLOOR HUMIT MONAD NEPER ADDRESS DIOPTER ELEMENT ENERGID KLAVERN
(— IN COUNTING FISH) MEASE
(— IN EARTHWORK) FLOAT FLOOR
(— OF ABSORPTION) SABIN
(— OF ACCELERATION) GAL MILLIGAL
(— OF ACTION) EPISODE
(— OF ANGULAR MEASURE) CENTRAD
(— OF ARCHEOLOGICAL CLASSIFICATION) ASPECT
(— OF BINARY DIGITS) BYTE
(— OF BRIGHTNESS) NIT STILB LAMBERT
(— OF CAPACITANCE) JAR FARAD
(— OF CAPACITY) LAST PIPE ARDAB ARDEB TIERCE AMPHORA
(— OF COMIC STRIP) BOX
(— OF CONDUCTANCE) SIEMENS
(— OF COUNTING) POINT
(— OF DATA TRANSMISSION SPEED) BAUD
(— OF DESIGN) LARME
(— OF DISTANCE) DAY VERST PARSEC MEGAPARSEC
(— OF ELASTANCE) DARAF
(— OF ELECTRIC CAPACITY) FARAD
(— OF ELECTRIC CONDUCTANCE) MHO
(— OF ELECTRIC FORCE) VOLT KILOVOLT STATVOLT
(— OF ELECTRIC INDUCTANCE) HENRY
(— OF ELECTRIC INTENSITY) AMPERE OERSTED
(— OF ELECTRIC RELUCTANCE) REL STATOHM
(— OF ELECTRIC RESISTANCE) BEGOHM
(— OF ELECTRICAL RESISTANCE) ABOHM
(— OF ELECTRICITY) ES COULOMB
(— OF ENERGY) ERG RAD JOULE ATOMERG QUANTUM
(— OF FINENESS) CARAT KARAT
(— OF FLOW) CUSEC
(— OF FLUIDITY) RHE
(— OF FLUX DENSITY) GAUSS
(— OF FORCE) G DYNE STAPP

NEWTON STHENE POUNDAL
(— OF FREQUENCY) HERTZ FRESNEL MEGAHERTZ
(— OF GEOLOGIC TIME) AEON
(— OF GOVERNMENT) DEME LAND KREIS GEMEINDE
(— OF HEAT) BTU THERM CALORIE
(— OF ILLUMINANCE) LUX NIT PHOT MICROLUX
(— OF ILLUMINATION) PHOT
(— OF INFORMATION) NIT
(— OF INSTRUCTION) FRAME
(— OF INTERSTELLAR SPACE) PARSEC
(— OF LAND AREA) ARE SULUNG
(— OF LANGUAGE) SYLLABLE
(— OF LENGTH) FERMI MICRON MICROMETER
(— OF LIGHT) LUMEN
(— OF LIGHT INTENSITY) PYR PHOTON
(— OF LOUDNESS) PHON SONE DECIBEL
(— OF MACHINERY) STAND
(— OF MAGNETIC FLUX) WEBER
(— OF MAGNETIC FORCE) KAPP GILBERT
(— OF MAGNETIC INTENSITY) GAMMA OERSTED MAGNETON
(— OF MAGNIFICATION) DIAMETER
(— OF MASS) AMU SLUG CRITH DALTON AVOGRAM
(— OF MEMORY) BIT MNEMON
(— OF METRICAL QUANTITY) MATRA
(— OF MOMENT) DEBYE
(— OF MOMENTUM) BOLE
(— OF NARCOTIC) JOLT
(— OF NYLON FINENESS) DENIER
(— OF ONE INCH) BUTTON
(— OF PAIN INTENSITY) DOL
(— OF PERMEABILITY) DARCY
(— OF PIPE) FOURBLE
(— OF POWER) WATT DYNAM KILOWATT PONCELET
(— OF PRESSURE) BAR TORR BARAD BARIE BARYE GWELY OSMOL PASCAL MEGABAR CENTIBAR MILLIBAR
(— OF PRESSWORK) TOKEN
(— OF RADIATION) RAD REM REP LANGLEY
(— OF RADIOACTIVITY) CURIE
(— OF RESISTANCE) OHM
(— OF ROCKET) STAGE
(— OF SATURATION) SATRON
(— OF SOCIETY) CLAN HORDE CHAPTER
(— OF SPACE AND CIRCULATION) MILLINE
(— OF SPEECH) WORD
(— OF SPEED) BAUD KNOT
(— OF STRUCTURE) MICELLE
(— OF THICKNESS) POINT
(— OF TIME) BEAT SVEDBERG
(— OF TRADING) CONTRACT
(— OF VELOCITY) VELO
(— OF VERSE METER) FOOT
(— OF VISCOSITY) POISE STOKE SECONDS
(— OF WAVELENGTH) ANGSTROM
(— OF WEIGHT) SSU TON GERA GRAM CARAT GRAIN OUNCE

POUND STEIN ARROBA GRAMME
(— OF WIRE MEASUREMENT) MIL
(— OF WORK) ERG CROP HOUR
ERGON JOULE KILERG DINAMODE
(— OF YARN) LEA
(— OF YARN SIZE) CUT
(— OF 20) CORGE
(— OF 100 MEN) CENTURY
(ADMINISTRATIVE —) BLOCK HSIEN
AGENCY BUREAU CIRCLE
DISTRICT
(ARBITRARY —) OLFACTY
(ARCHERY —) END
(ARMY —) LEGION BRIGADE
COMPANY MAHALLA
(ARTILLERY —) BATTERY
(AVAILABLE AS —) MARRIED
(BOWLING —) ALLEY
(BOY SCOUT —) SHIP
(BUILDER'S —) SQUARE
(CIGAR-MANUFACTURING —)
BUCKEYE
(COLLECTIVE —) COMMUNE
(COMBAT —) ARMAMENT
(DISCRETE —) FRACTION
(EDUCATIONAL —) COURSE
(ELECTROMAGNETIC —) ABFARAD
ABHENRY MAXWELL ABAMPERE
(FUNDAMENTAL —) BASE
(GRAMMATICAL —) JUNCTION
(HARMONIC —) CELL
(HOUSING —) HUTMENT
(HYPOTHETICAL —) ID IDANT
MICELLE
(INDIVIDUALLY OWNED LIVING —)
CONDO
(LIFE —) BIOPHORE
(LIVING —) BIONT BIOGEN
(LOGARITHMIC —) BEL
(LOGGING —) CHANCE
(MILITARY —) ARMY GOUM CORPS
GROUP LANCE SQUAD BRIGADE
PLATOON SECTION COMMANDO
DIVISION REGIMENT SQUADRON
(NAZI —) FEHME
(ORGANIZATIONAL —) CELL
ACTIVITY
(PHOTOMETRIC —) VIOLLE
(POLITICAL —) POLITY SOVIET
MUNICIPALITY
(RHYTHMIC —) BASIS COLON
(SELF-PERPETUATING —) BIOSOME
(SOCIAL —) SEPT GROUP KRAAL
SOCIUS
(STORAGE —) BUFFER
(TELEGRAPHIC —) BAUD
(TEMPERATURE —) KELVIN
(TERRITORIAL —) STAKE STATE
COMMOT CANTRED CANTREF
KINGDOM
(THERMAL —) THERM CALORY
CALORIE
(TRIBAL —) TOWNSHIP
(VOTING —) CENTURY
(SUFF.) MONAS ON
UNITARIAN ARIAN SOCINIAN
UNITE ADD MIX ONE OOP PAN SAM
SEW UNE UNY ALLY BAND BIND
CLUB COAK FUSE HASP JOIN KNIT
KNOT LINK SAMM SEAM SOUD
UNIT BANDY CLOSE GRADE
GRAFT INONE JACOB JOINT
MERGE NITCH UNIFY WHOLE

ATTACH CEMENT CONCUR
COUPLE EMBODY ENTIRE GATHER
LAUREL LEAGUE SOLDER SPLICE
STRIKE SUTURE ACCRETE
AMALGAM CLUSTER COALITE
COMBINE CONJOIN CONNECT
CONSORT JACOBUS SIAMESE
ALLIGATE ANCYLOSE ANKYLOSE
ASSEMBLE COALESCE COMPOUND
CONCRETE CONSPIRE COPULATE
FEDERATE LAMINATE
COLLIGATE
(— BY INTERWEAVING) PLEACH
SPLICE
(— BY THREADS) SEW STITCH
(— CLOSELY) FAY YOT WELD
CEMENT COTTON
(— FOR INTRIGUE) CABAL
(— HOSE) COLLECT
(— IN MARRIAGE) WED SACRE
SACRI SPLICE SPOUSE
(— METALS) WELD SWEAT
(— TIMBERS) SCARF
(PREF.) GAMETO GAMO
UNITED ONE TIED ADDED FUSED
JOINT ALLIED CONNATE ENDLESS
UNIONED COMBINED CONCRETE
CONJOINT CONJUNCT FEDERATE
COADUNATE
(PREF.) GAM(ETO)(O)
UNITED ARAB EMIRATES
(CAPITAL OF —) ABUDHABI
(FORMER NAME OF —)
TRUCIALOMAN TRUCIALCOAST
TRUCIALSTATES
(MONEY OF —) DIRHAM
(MOUNTAINS OF —) HAJAR
(STATE OF —) AJMAN DUBAI
SHARJAH FUJAIRAH
(TOWN OF —) DUBAI JEBEL
BURAIMI SHARJAH
UNITED KINGDOM (SEE ENGLAND)

UNITED STATES (ALSO SEE
SPECIFIC STATES)
LAKE: ERIE MEAD SALT HURON
TAHOE CRATER ONTARIO
MICHIGAN SUPERIOR
CHAMPLAIN OKEECHOBEE
MOUNTAIN: BEAR BONA SILL
GREEN OZARK ROCKY UINTA
WHITE ANTERO ELBERT
SHASTA SIERRA BELFORD
FORAKER HARVARD MASSIVE
RAINIER SANFORD WASATCH
WHITNEY CATSKILL MCKINLEY
WRANGELL BLACKBURN
ADIRONDACK BITTERROOT
APPALACHIAN
PRESIDENT: ABE CAL DDE FDR IKE
JFK LBJ FORD POLK TAFT
ADAMS GRANT HARRY HAYES
JIMMY NIXON TEDDY TYLER
ARTHUR CARTER HOOVER
MONROE PIERCE REAGAN
TAYLOR TRUMAN WILSON
HARDING JACKSON JOHNSON
KENNEDY LINCOLN MADISON
BUCHANAN COOLIDGE
FILLMORE GARFIELD HARRISON
MCKINLEY VANBUREN
JEFFERSON ROOSEVELT
EISENHOWER WASHINGTON

VICE PRESIDENT: BURR BUSH FORD
KING ADAMS AGNEW DAWES
GERRY NIXON TYLER ARTHUR
COLFAX CURTIS DALLAS
GARNER HAMLIN HOBART
MORTON TRUMAN WILSON
BARKLEY CALHOUN CLINTON
JOHNSON MONDALE SHERMAN
WALLACE WHEELER COOLIDGE
FILLMORE HUMPHREY
MARSHALL TOMPKINS
VANBUREN FAIRBANKS
HENDRICKS JEFFERSON
ROOSEVELT STEVENSON
ROCKEFELLER BRECKINRIDGE
WATERFALL: TWIN AKAKA SEVEN
NARADA RIBBON FEATHER
PALOUSE PASSAIC SLUISKIN
YOSEMITE BRIDALVEIL
YELLOWSTONE

UNITING SUTURE
UNITS
(SUFF.) (HAVING TIME —) SEMIC
UNITY UNION SYSTEM ONENESS
UNITUDE IDENTITY SODALITY
SYMPATHY TOTALITY
(— OF SPIRIT AND NATURE)
ABSOLUTE
UNIVALENT MONATOMIC
UNIVERSAL ALL LOCAL QUALE
TOTAL WHOLE WORLD COMMON
GLOBAL PUBLIC VERSAL GENERAL
GENERIC CATHOLIC ECUMENIC
PANDEMIC
(TRANSCENDENT —) IDEA
UNIVERSALITY ALLNESS
OMNITUDE
UNIVERSE ALL LOKA MASS OLAM
WORLD COSMOS SYSTEM
CREATURE EXEMPLAR
(SIDEREAL —) SPACE
(PREF.) COSM(O) COSMETO
COSMICO
UNIVERSITY STUDY CAMPUS
SCHOOL ACADEMY COLLEGE
MADRASA STUDIUM VARSITY
MADRASAH REDBRICK
(RELATING TO BRITISH —)
OXBRIDGE REDBRICK PLATEGLASS
UNJUST HARD UNFAIR WANTON
WICKED UNEQUAL UNRICHT
UNRIGHT WRONGFUL
UNJUSTIFIED INVALID
UNJUSTLY UNDULY FALSELY
UNKEELED RATITE
UNKEMPT ROUGH FROWZY
RUGGED SHAGGY INCOMPT
RAFFISH RUFFLED SCRUFFY
SHAGRAG TOUSLED DRAGGLED
SCRAGGLY SLIPSHOD STRUBBLY
UNCOMBED
UNKIND BAD ILL MEAN VILE CRUEL
HARSH STERN SEVERE UNMEEK
UNKINDNESS DISFAVOR
UNKNOWABLE SEALED
UNKNOWN IGN UNCO UNKET
UNKID IGNOTE MUNKAR SEALED
SECRET UNWARE UNWIST
FARAWAY OBSCURE UNCOUTH
UNHEARD IGNORANT UNAWARES
UNKENNED UNWITTING
UNLADEN LEAR LEER

UNLATCH UNSNECK
UNLAWFUL ILLEGAL ILLICIT
NONLICET UNLEEFUL UNLEISUM
UNLEARNED LEWD GROSS PLAIN
BOOKLESS IGNORANT UNLEARED
UNLEAVENED AZYMOUS
UNLESS BUT NIF LESS NISI SAVE
BINNA NOBUT LESSEN ONLESS
WITHOUT
(— BEFORE) NIPR NIPRI
(— OTHERWISE NOTED) NAN
UNLETTERED LEWD BORREL
IGNORANT
UNLIGHTED BLIND LAMPLESS
UNLIKE DIFFORM DISLIKE DIVERSE
(MOST —) OTHEREST
UNLIKELY REMOTE DUBIOUS
(MOST —) LAST
UNLIMITED VAST SOVRAN
ABSOLUTE UNTERMED
(— IN POWER) ALMIGHTY
UNLINED SINGLE
UNLOAD TIP DROP DUMP HOVEL
DECANT STRIKE UNLADE UNSHIP
UNSTOW DELIVER DEPLETE
DETRUCK DISLOAD UNTRUSS
DISCHARGE
UNLOCK UNMAKE RESERATE
UNLOUKEN
UNLOOSE OUTWIND UNRIVET
UNLUCKY BAD FAY ILL EVIL FOUL
DONSY DISMAL DONSIE HOODOO
WICKED HAPLESS INFAUST
UNHAPPY UNCHANCY
UNTOWARD WANCHANCY
(— THING) AMBSACE
UNMAN UNDO CRUSH UNNERVE
UNMANAGEABLE ROID DONSY
RANDY WANTON RESTIVE
CHURLISH STAFFISH CAMSTAIRY
REFRACTORY
UNMANLY SOFT MANLESS
UNLUSTY
UNMANNERLY RUDE BOORISH
UNCIVIL IMPOLITE UNGENTLE
MISLEARED
UNMARKED MAVERICK NOTELESS
UNMARRIED ONE LONE SOLE
OLEPI YOUNG ONLEPY SINGLE
UNMASK EXPOSE UNFACE
DISMASK UNCLOAK
UNMASKING EXPOSURE
UNMEASURED UNMEET
MODELESS
UNMELODIOUS SCRANNEL
UNMERCHANTABLE SALABLE
SALEABLE
UNMERCIFUL CRUEL PITILESS
RUTHLESS
UNMETHODICAL CURSORY
UNMINDFUL SLOWFUL CARELESS
HEEDLESS MINDLESS
UNMISTAKABLE FLAT OPEN
BROAD CLEAR FRANK PLAIN
PATENT DECIDED EXPRESS
APPARENT DECISIVE MANIFEST
UNIVOCAL
UNMISTAKABLY SIGNALLY
UNMITIGATED PURE GROSS
RUDDY ARRANT DAMNED
SOVRAN PERFECT PUREDEE
REGULAR ABSOLUTE OUTRIGHT
UNMIX EXSOLVE

UNMIXED NET DEEP MERE PURE SELF SOLE BLANK SHEER UTTER IMMIXT SIMPLE STRAIGHT
UNMODIFIED BRUTE STRAIGHT
UNMOLESTED SACKLESS
UNMOVED CALM COOL FIRM STONY TIGHT IMMOTE SERENE ADAMANT IMMOVED
UNMOVING INERT IMMOBILE IMMOTIVE
UNMUSICAL NOTELESS SCABROUS
UNNATURAL EERY EERIE STIFF CLAMMY CREEPY UNKIND STRANGE UNCANNY VIOLENT ABNORMAL ABSONANT FARCICAL KINDLESS UNKINDLY MONSTROUS
UNNECESSARY USELESS NEEDLESS
UNNEEDED WASTE
UNNERVE UNMAN UNMAKE WEAKEN ENERVATE PARALYZE
UNNERVED SHOOK
UNNOTICED SILENT
UNOBJECTIONABLE VENIAL
UNOBSERVANT HEEDLESS
UNOBSTRUCTED FAIR FREE OPEN PATENT THROUGH APPARENT
UNOBTRUSIVE SHY QUIET MODEST SEDATE DISCREET RETIRING
UNOCCUPIED IDLE VOID BLANK EMPTY WASTE OTIOSE VACANT LEISURE UNSEATED WASTEFUL
UNORGANIZED ACOSMIC INCHOATE
UNORTHODOX HERETIC
UNOSTENTATIOUS SHY QUIET LENTEN MODEST
UNPACK UNFARDLE
UNPAID DUE UNQUIT UNWAGED HONORARY WAGELESS OUTSTANDING
UNPAIRED IMPAR AZYGOUS
UNPALATABLE SOD HARD BITTER BRACKISH
UNPARALLELED ALONE UNIQUE EPOCHAL PEERLESS SINGULAR UNPEERED
UNPERTURBED BLAND STILL
UNPLEASANT BAD ACID EVIL HARD NICE SOUR UGLY VILE AWFUL CRUDE GRIMY GUMMY HAIRY HARSH MUCKY NASTY ROUGH TOUGH BRUTAL CRIMPY RANCID STICKY THRAWN UNFELE UNGAIN UNLIEF BEASTLY BILIOUS GHASTLY INGRATE SPINOUS UNLUSTY UNQUEME UNSONCY CHISELY DREADFUL HORRIBLE INDECENT SCABROUS UNLOVELY ABOMINABLE (PREF.) CAC(O) CACH
UNPLEASANTLY QUEER HARDLY UNWINLY
UNPLEASANTNESS ILLNESS
UNPLOWED LEA
UNPOETICAL MUSELESS
UNPOLISHED ILL RUDE BLIND CRUDE ROUGH COARSE INCULT RUGGED RUSTIC SAVAGE SHAGGY UPLAND INCOMPT UNKEMPT AGRESTIC
UNPOPULARITY ENVY

UNPRACTICED RAW FRESH UNTRADED
UNPREDICTABLE CHANCY CRANKY ERRATIC
UNPREJUDICED FAIR
UNPREMEDITATED CASUAL
UNPREPARED TARDY
UNPREPOSSESSING SEEDY
UNPRETENDING LOWLY HOMELY HUMBLE
UNPRETENTIOUS HOMY HOMEY PLAIN SOBER COMMON HOMELY HUMBLE MODEST SIMPLE DISCREET HOMESPUN
UNPRINCIPLED LEWD LIMMER
UNPRODUCTIVE DRY SHY ARID DEAD DEAF LEAN POOR VAIN YELD YELL ADDLE DUSTY WASTE BARREN GEASON SAPLESS STERILE WOODSERE
UNPRODUCTIVENESS BORASCO BORASQUE BORRASCA
UNPROFESSIONAL LAY BUSH LAICAL JACKLEG
UNPROFITABLE BAD DRY DEAD LEAN SECK BARREN BOOTLESS GAINLESS UNGAINLY
UNPROGRESSIVE SLOW DORMANT BACKWARD
UNPROMISING BLUE DUBIOUS
UNPRONOUNCED MUTE
UNPROPITIOUS ILL EVIL FOUL THRAW MALIGN SULLEN ADVERSE AVERTED INFAUST OMINOUS THRAWART
UNPROTECTED NAKED EXPOSED HELPLESS
UNPROVOKED WANTON
UNPUBLISHED INED INEDITED
UNQUALIFIED NET BARE FULL MERE PURE VERY BLACK PLUMP SHEER UNFIT DIRECT ENTIRE UNABLE CLOTTED PLENARY IMPLICIT INHABILE POSITIVE
UNQUESTIONABLE ASSURED CERTAIN DECIDED ABSOLUTE DECISIVE DISTINCT
UNQUESTIONED CLEAR
UNQUESTIONING IMPLICIT
UNRAVEL REDD UNDO BREAK ENODE FEAZE RAVEL RETEX SOLVE EVOLVE TIFFLE UNFOLD UNKNIT UNLACE ENODATE RESOLVE
UNREAL VAIN AERIAL GOTHIC CHEMICK FANCIED SHADOWY AERIFORM CHIMERIC FARCICAL ILLUSORY NOTIONAL SCENICAL VISIONAL (PREF.) PSEUD(O)
UNREALISTIC CHIMERIC
UNREALIZED BEHIND
UNREASONABLE ABSURD FANATIC ABSONANT
UNREASONABLENESS ALOGY INSANITY
UNREASONABLY SINFULLY
UNREASONING BRUTE RABID
UNRECOGNIZED UNSUNG CRYPTIC UNWITTED
UNRECOVERABLE DEAD
UNRECTIFIED IMPURE
UNREDEEMED CHEAP

UNREFINED RAW DARK LOUD BRUTE CRUDE DORIC GROSS COARSE COMMON EARTHY JUNGLY VULGAR BOORISH UNCOUTH UNKEMPT DREADFUL SWAINISH
UNREFLECTING GLIB VACANT
UNREGENERACY ADAM
UNREGENERATE NATURAL
UNREGENERATELY MANLY
UNREHEARSED IMPROMPTU
UNRELATED FREMD STRAY UNAKIN UNTOLD EXTREME FRAMMIT POSITIVE
UNRELAXED UNSLAKED
UNRELAXING TONIC
UNRELENTING GRIM HARD IRON CRUEL STERN BRASSY SEVERE RIGOROUS
UNRELIABLE FISHY SHADY FICKLE GREASY UNSAFE CASALTY STREAKY WILDCAT FECKLESS GLIBBERY SLIPPERY TICKLISH
UNRELIEVED DEAD BRUTE ABJECT EXQUISITE
UNREMITTING BUSY FAST HARD DOGGED
UNREMUNERATIVE HONORARY
UNRESERVED FREE CLEAN FRANK ROUND COMMON UNCLOSE EXPLICIT
UNRESERVEDNESS FREEDOM
UNRESISTING BUXOM
UNRESPONSIVE DEAD DUMB BARREN SILENT STUBBORN
UNREST MOTION AILMENT DISREST WANREST DISQUIET CHEMISTRY PSYCHOSIS
UNRESTRAINED LAX MAD FREE WILD BROAD FANTI FRANK LARGE LOOSE FACILE FANTEE LAVISH UNTIED WANTON FLYAWAY RAMPANT RIOTOUS BARBARIC FAMILIAR FREEHAND LAXATIVE PINDARIC ABANDONED LIBERTINE
UNRESTRAINT LICENSE IMMUNITY
UNRESTRICTED FREE GLOBAL SOVRAN UNZONED ABSOLUTE
UNRETURNED UNYOLDEN
UNREVEALED UNTOLD
UNRHYMED BLANK
UNRIG STRIP
UNRIGHTEOUSNESS ADHARMA
UNRIPE RAW CRUDE GREEN CALLOW UNCURED IMMATURE
UNROBE DISROBE UNDRESS DISARRAY
UNROLL EVOLVE UNCURL DEVELOP OUTROLL TRINDLE UNTREND
UNROOF TIRL TIRR TIRVE DISROOF
UNRUFFLE SMOOTH SOOTHE MOLLIFY
UNRUFFLED CALM COOL EASY EVEN QUIET SOBER STILL ASLEEP PLACID SEDATE SERENE SMOOTH DECOROUS
UNRULY HIGH RAMP ROYT TOUGH HAUNTY WANTON LAWLESS RAMMAGE ROPABLE UNRULED VICIOUS WANRULY WAYWARD INDOCILE MUTINOUS CAMSTAIRY

REFRACTORY OBSTREPEROUS RAMBUNCTIOUS
UNSADDLE OUTSPAN UNPANEL
UNSAFE HOT FISHY EXPOSED INSECURE PERILOUS
UNSANCTIFIED PROFANE
UNSATISFACTORY BAD ILL EVIL POOR CROOK LOUSY SHREWD WRETCHED
UNSATISFYING DUSTY HOLLOW
UNSATURATED (PREF.) EN
UNSAVORY WERSH INSIPID WEARISH
UNSAY WITHDRAW
UNSCHOLARLY BOOKLESS
UNSCRUPULOUS SKIN CROOK BRAZEN DEVIOUS JACKLEG DEXTROUS RASCALLY
UNSEASONABLE LAT UNRIPE UNTIDY UNCHANCY UNTIMELY
UNSEASONED RAW GREEN
UNSEAT ADDRESS DISSEAT
UNSEEING BLIND GAZELESS
UNSEEMLY HOIDEN UNFAIR IMPROPER INDECENT SEEMLESS UNMEETLY UNWORTHY
UNSEEN SECRET UNEYED CRYPTIC VIEWLESS
UNSERRIED LOOSE
UNSETTLE JAR TURN UNFIX UNSET UPSET COMMOVE DERANGE DISTURB STAGGER UNHINGE UNQUEME DISORDER DISQUIET DISTRACT
UNSETTLED MOOT LIGHT SHAKY UNSAD VAGUE BROKEN FICKLE QUEASY VAGOUS DUBIOUS NOMADIC SHUTTLE UNSTAID RESTLESS UNSTABLE VAGABOND
UNSETTLING NASTY
UNSHAKABLE DOGGED ADAMANT IRONCLAD
UNSHAKEN FIRM STEADY UNMOVED UNSHOOK CONSTANT RESOLUTE
UNSHAPELY DEFORMED UNMACKLY
UNSHARED SOLE
UNSHEATHE DISCASE
UNSHEATHED BARE
UNSHELTERED BLEAK
UNSHOD BAREFOOT DISCALCED
UNSHORN UNPOLLED
UNSIGHTLY UGLY AWFUL MESSY HOMELY INDECENT
UNSKILLED JAY PUNY GREEN PUISNE UNGAIN UNSEEN STRANGE FECKLESS
UNSKILLFUL ILL EVIL RUDE ARTLESS AWKWARD UNFEATY BUNGLING TINKERLY UNHEPPEN
UNSMILING GLUM AUSTERE
UNSOCIABLE SULLEN FAROUCHE INSOCIAL
UNSOILED CLEAN
UNSOPHISTICATE SQUARE
UNSOPHISTICATED JAY NAIF PURE FRANK GREEN NAIVE SILLY CALLOW SIMPLE BUCOLIC NATURAL VERDANT HOMEBRED HOMESPUN INNOCENT PROVINCIAL

UNSOUND BAD ILL EVIL SICK
ADDLE BARMY CRAZY CRONK
DICKY DOTTY DOZED SANDY
SHAKY WONKY ABSURD FAULTY
FLAWED HOLLOW INFIRM INSANE
ROTTEN UNHALE INVALID
RICKETY UNWHOLE
UNSOUNDNESS CRACK INSANITY
UNSPARING DRASTIC SCATHING
UNSPIRITUAL CARNAL
UNSPOILED RACY UNSHENT
PRISTINE
UNSPOKEN TACIT SILENT
UNSPORTSMANLIKE DIRTY
UNSPOTTED CLEAR SPOTLESS
UNSPUN RAW
UNSTABLE FLUX BATTY LOOSE
SANDY BROTEL CHOPPY FICKLE
FITFUL FLITTY LABILE LUBRIC
ROTTEN SHIFTY TICKLE UNFIRM
WANKLE WANKLY DWAIBLE
DWAIBLY DWEEBLE RICKETY
SLIDDER SLIDDRY VOLUBLE
FEVERISH FIRMLESS FUGITIVE
INSECURE LUBRICAL REMUABLE
SKITTISH SLIPPERY TICKLISH
TOTTLISH VARIABLE
(MENTALLY —) BRAINISH
UNSTEADILY GROGGILY
UNSTEADINESS FALTER
UNSTEADY WALT CRANK CRONK
DOTTY FLUKY LIGHT NERVY
SLACK TIPPY TIPSY TOTTY UNSAD
WALTY WONKY COGGLY FICKLE
FLICKY FLUFFY GROGGY JIGGLY
JOGGLY SWIMMY TOTTIE WAFFLY
WAGGLY WAMBLY WANKLE
WEEWAW WEEWOW DODDERY
GLAIKIT JIGGETY QUAVERY
QUEACHY TITTUPY TOTTERY
WAYWARD SKITTISH STAGGERY
TICKLISH TITUBANT UNSTABLE
VARIABLE VERSATILE
UNSTINTED LAVISH ENDLESS
UNSTRESS SLACK
UNSTRESSED SHORT
UNSTRING DISSOLVE
UNSTUDIED GLIB CASUAL
CARELESS GLANCING
UNSUBDUED VIRGIN UNBOWED
UNSUBSTANTIAL TOY AIRY LIMP
THIN WINDY AERIAL BUBBLE
CHAFFY FLIMSY SLEAZY SLEEZY
SLIGHT UNREAL FOLIOUS FRAGILE
INSOLID SHADOWY TENUOUS
FILIGREE FINESPUN FOOTLESS
GIMCRACK VAPOROUS
PASTEBOARD
UNSUCCESSFUL BAD MANQUE
UNSPED STICKIT UNHAPPY
ABORTIVE
UNSUITABLE INEPT UNAPT
UNDUE UNFIT UNKIND UNMETE
UNCOMELY UNGAINLY UNLIKELY
UNSUITABLENESS IMPOLICY
UNSUITED BAD
UNSULLIED FAIR PURE CLEAR
VIRGIN INNOCENT SPOTLESS
VIRGINAL
UNSUPPLIED HELPLESS
UNSUPPORTED BLIND NAKED
BACKWARD STAYLESS
UNSURE TIMID INFIRM DOUBTFUL

INSECURE UNSICKER
UNSURPASSED CHAMPION
UNSUSPECTING INNOCENT
UNSWEET UNSOOT
UNSWERVING FIXED FLUSH LOYAL
DIRECT STEADY STRICT STURDY
STAUNCH
UNSWERVINGLY HEADLONG
UNSYMMETRICAL LOPSIDED
UNSYMPATHETIC DRY HARD
STONY FROZEN GLASSY HOSTILE
KINDLESS
UNTAINTED FREE GOOD PURE
INNOCENT
UNTAMED WILD FERAL RAMAGE
SAVAGE HAGGARD RAMMISH
WARRAGAL
UNTANGLE FREE SLEAVE UNLACE
UNTARNISHED PURE
UNTAUGHT WASTE UNLERED
IGNORANT
UNTHINKABLE PUERILE
UNTHINKING GLIB BRUTE CASUAL
FECKLESS HEEDLESS
UNTHINKINGLY STUPID
UNTIDINESS JAKES LITTER
UNTIDY DOWDY GAUMY MESSY
ROOKY BUNTING DRAGGLY
LITTERY RUMMAGY SCRUFFY
UNSIDED DRAGGLED SLOVENLY
STRUBBLY UNHEPPEN
UNTIE UNDO UNBIND UNLASH
UNLATCH UNTRUSS UNTWINE
UNFASTEN
UNTIL AD OR TO GIN HENT INTO
UNTO FORTO TWELL WHILE
WHILES WHILST PENDING
(— THEN) BEFORE
UNTILLED INCULT UNEARED
UNTIMELY UNTIDY IMMATURE
PREVIOUS TIMELESS
UNTIRING BUSY SEDULOUS
TIRELESS
UNTITLED (— MEN) AUMAGA
UNTO TILL
UNTOLD VAST UNQUOD
UNTOUCHABLE DOM HARIJAN
CHANDALA
(PL.) PANCHAMA
UNTOUCHED FREE INTACT
PRISTINE
(PREF.) INTEGRI
UNTOWARD ILL UNRULY
FROWARD WAYWARD
UNTRAINED RAW RUDE GREEN
HAGGARD
UNTRAMMELED FREE
UNTRIED MAIDEN UNSOUGHT
UNTRIMMED UNTEWED
UNTRODDEN PATHLESS
UNFOOTED
UNTROUBLED CHEERY
UNTRUE FLAM FALSE LEASE
WRONG UNFAST DISLOYAL
MENDACIOUS
(PREF.) PSEUD(O)
UNTRUSTWORTHINESS FALSITY
UNTRUSTWORTHY PUNIC SHAKY
LIMBER TRICKY UNSURE
SLIDDERY SLIPPERY
UNTRUTH LIE FABLE LEASE
SKLENT FALSITY UNTROTH
MENDACITY

UNTRUTHFUL SLANTER
UNTUNABLE ABSONANT
UNTUTORED NATURAL IGNORANT
PRIMITIVE
UNTWILLED PLAIN
UNTWINE FRESE UNTWIST
UNTWIST FAG FEAZE UNLAY
UNSPIN UNTWIRL
UNTWISTED SLEIDED
UNUSABLE WASTE INUTILE
UNUSED IDLE FRESH WASTE
INURED MAIDEN VACANT
DERELICT INITIATE UNWONTED
UNUSUAL ODD EERY RARE SELD
TALL CRAZY EERIE FORBY NOVEL
UTTER WEIRD EXEMPT FORBYE
SCREWY SINGLE UNIQUE
STRANGE ABNORMAL DISTINCT
ESPECIAL INSOLENT KNOCKOUT
SELCOUTH SINGULAR SPANKING
UNCOMMON UNTRADED
UNWONTED PRODIGIOUS
(PREF.) ANOM(O)
UNUSUALLY EXTRA
UNVARIED SAMELY
UNVARNISHED EVERYDAY
UNVARYING FLAT SAME FRANK
LEVEL STABLE UNIFORM
UNVEIL REVEAL UNCOVER
UNCROWN UNDRAPE UNSCREEN
UNWIMPLE
UNVENTILATED CLOSE
UNVERSED STRANGE
UNWANTED STRAY TRAMP
FAULTY
UNWARRANTED UNDUE
UNWARY RASH UNAWARE
CARELESS HEEDLESS WARELESS
UNWASHED SOAPLESS
UNWASTEFUL FRUGAL
UNWAVERING FIRM CLEAN LEVEL
SOLID GLASSY STABLE EXPRESS
STAUNCH
UNWAVERINGLY FAST
UNWEAKENED CLEAR
UNWELL BAD ILL EVIL PUNK SICK
BADLY CROOK SEEDY AILING
CHIPPY WICKED COMICAL
UNWHOLESOME ILL EVIL SICK
CAGMAG IMPURE MORBID SICKLY
CORRUPT NOISOME NOXIOUS
UNCLEAN DISEASED EPINOSIC
UNWIELDY BULKY CLUMSY
UNRIDE AWKWARD HULKING
CUMBROUS UNGAINLY
UNWILLING CHARY LOATH SWEER
WERSE AVERSE ESCHEW
BACKWARD GRUDGING
UNWILLINGLY MAUGER MAUGRE
UNWILLINGNESS GRUDGE
NOLITION
UNWIND UNCLEW UNREEL
UNREAVE UNTWINE
UNWISE FALSE INANE SILLY
SIMPLE FOOLISH WITLESS
UNWITTING UNWIST WEETLESS
UNWOMANLY MANKIND
UNWORLDLY WEIRD ASTRAL
SPIRITUAL
UNWORTHY BASE INDIGN
BENEATH UNDIGNE WANWORDY
UNWOUNDED COLD
UNWREATHE UNPLAT

UNWRINKLED BRANT BRENT
UNWROUGHT RAW LIVE
UNYIELDING PAT SET ACID DOUR
FAST FIRM GRIM HARD RIGID
STARK STEEL STIFF STITH STONY
TOUGH FLINTY FROZEN GLASSY
KNOBBY MARBLE STEELY STURDY
ADAMANT AUSTERE COSTIVE
FROWARD CHURLISH OBDURATE
OBEDIENT STUBBORN
PERTINACIOUS
UNYOKE LOWSE UNTEAM
OUTSHUT OUTSPAN
UNYOKED
(PREF.) AZYGO
UP ON ONE OOP ABOUT ASTIR
DORMY DORMIE
(— AND ABOUT) AFOOT
(— TO) INTO
(— TO THE TIME) UNTIL
(— YONDER) UPBY UPBYE
(FARTHER —) ABOVE
(HIGH —) ALOFT
(PREF.) ANA ANO SUR
UPANISHAD ISHA KATHA
UPAS DITA ANTIAR CHETTIK
UPBEAT ARSIS AUFTAKT
ANACRUSIS
UP-BOW POUSSE
UPBRAID CHEW RAIL SNUB TUCK
TWIT ABUSE ROUSE SCOLD
TAUNT UPBRAY EMBRAID
REPROVE DISGRACE OUTBRAID
UPCARD STARTER
UPFOLD SADDLE ANTICLINE
UPHEAVAL BOIL STORM UPLIFT
RUMMAGE UPTHROW
UPHILL UPBANK UPWITH
UPHOLD AID TOM ABET BACK
FAVOR AFFIRM ASSERT DEFEND
SOOTHE BOLSTER SUPPORT
SUSTAIN CHAMPION MAINTAIN
PRESERVE
UPHOLDER DEFENDER ERASTIAN
FEUDALIST
UPHOLDING BEHIND
UPHOLSTER SQUAB
UPHOLSTERER TAPISER
UPHOLDER
UPKEEP MAINTENANCE
UPLAND DOWN DOWNS MAUKA
COTEAU FASTLAND
(PL.) BRAES DOWNS
UPLAND PLOVER QUAILY
HILLBIRD PAPABOTE
UPLIFT TOSS BOOST TOWER
UPTHRUST
UPLIFTED ERECT EXALTEE
UPON ON PON SUR INTO OVER
ABOVE AGAINST
(— THAT) THEREAT
(PREF.) EP EPH EPI OB
UPPER OVER VAMP SKIVE VAMPEY
SUPERIOR
(PL.) FINISH
(PREF.) ANO HYPER SUPERO
(SITUATED ON — SIDE) SUPRA
UPPERCUT BOLO
UPPER HURONIAN LAWSON
UPPERMOST UMEST UPMOST
OVEREST BUNEMOST OVERMOST
UPPER VOLTA (CAPITAL OF —)
OUAGADOUGOU

(LANGUAGE OF —) BOBO LOBI SAMO MANDE MOSSI
(MOUNTAIN IN —) TEMA
(NATIVE OF —) BOBO LOBI SAMO BISSA HAUSA MANDE MARKA MOSSI PUEHL TUAREG SENOUFO VOLTAIC YATENGA MANDINGO
(RIVER IN —) VOLTA SOUROU
(TOWN OF —) PO LEO DORI PAMA YAKO DJIBO GAOUA LAWRA HOUNDE TOUGAN BANFORA
UPRAISED SUBLIME
UPRIGHT FAIR GOOD HARR JUST PROP STUD TIDY TRUE ANEND CHEEK ERECT GUIDE JELLY MORAL RIGHT ROMAN SETUP STALE STALK STILE ARRECT DIRECT ENTIRE HONEST SQUARE FRIZZEN HOUSING JANNOCK PITPROP SINCERE INNOCENT RIGHTFUL STANDARD STANDING STRAIGHT VERTICAL VIRTUOUS
(NOT —) ATILT BEVEL
(PL.) STUDDING
(PREF.) ORTH(O)
UPRIGHTNESS HONOR TRUTH APLOMB EQUITY HONESTY PROBITY JUSTNESS SINCERITY
UPRISING RIOT EMEUTE MUTINY PUTSCH REVOLT TUMULT UPRISE UPRISAL REBELLION
UPROAR DIN RUT CAIN FLAW GILD HELL MOIL RIOT ROUT BABEL BURLE CHANG FUROR HURLY RUMOR STOUN STOUR CLAMOR DINDUM EMEUTE FLAOAO HABBLE HUBBLE HUBBUB RANDAN RATTLE RIPPET RUCKUS RUMBLE RUMPUS SHINDY STEVEN STOUND TUMULT CATOUSE FERMENT GARBOIL GAUSTER ORATION OUTROAR RUCTION STASHIE TURMOIL BALLYHOO BROUHAHA SCOUTHER STIRRING STRAMASH TINTAMAR CHARIVARI SHEMOZZLE PANDEMONIUM
UPROARIOUS FURIOUS ROUTOUS
UPROOT HACK LOUK MORE UNROUT UNPLANT DISPLANT ROOTWALT SUPPLANT
UPROOTED LUMPEN
UPSET ILL TIP TOP TUP CAVE COUP COWP FUSS JUMP PURL ROCK TILT TURN WELT EVERT KNOCK ROUSE SHAKE SKAIL SKELL SPILL WHELM BOTHER DISMAY QUELME TIPPLE TOPPLE UPCAST WALTER CAPSIZE DERANGE DISTURB FRAZZLE HAYWIRE OVERSET PERVERT REVERSE SLATTER SUBVERT TEMPEST TURMOIL CAPSIZAL DISTRAIT OVERTILT OVERTURN STREAKED SUPPLANT TURNOVER OVERTHROW
(EASILY —) FUSSY FLAPPABLE
UPSHOT ISSUE SHORT UPSET EFFECT SEQUEL UPPING OUTCOME UPSHOOT UPSTROKE
UPSIDE-DOWN CRAZY REVERSE OVERHAND UPSEDOUN
UPSILON
(PREF.) YPSILI

UPSTAIRS ABOVE
UPSTANDING GRADELY
UPSTART KIP QUAT SNIP SNOB SQUIRT UPSKIP DALTEEN PARVENU ARRIVIST MUSHROOM SKIPJACK UPSPRING
UP-TO-DATE MOD MODERN TRENDY ABREAST TODAYISH
UPWARD ALOFT UPLONG UPWAYS UPWITH SKYWARD UPALONG UPWARDS
(PREF.) ANO
UPWARD-MOVING ΛΝΛBΛΤΙC
URAEUS ASP
URAMIL MUREXAN
URANUS OURANOS HERSCHEL
(WIFE OF —) GAEA
URAO TRONA
URARTAEAN KHALDIAN
URARTU VAN
URATE LITHATE
URBAN TOWN URBIC URBANE BURGHAL OPPIDAN
URBANE CIVIL SUAVE POLITE SVELTE AMIABLE GRACIOUS
URBANITY COMITY SUAVITY COURTESY ELEGANCE
URCHIN IMP WAIF ELFIN GAMIN KEELIE NIPPER HURCHEON
(PREF.) **(SEA —)** ECHIN(O)
URD MUNGO
URDEE MATELEY
URDU REKHTA REKHTI MOORISH
URDUR (SISTER OF —) SKULD VERTHANDI
URGE ART DUN EGG HIE PLY PUT SIC SUE TAR YEN BROD COAX CRAM EDGE FIRK GOAD MOVE PING POKE PUSH SICK SPUR WHIP CROWD DRIVE FILIP FORCE HOOSH IMPEL LABOR PRESS PRICK SPANK TREAT COMPEL DEHORT DESIRE ENGAGE EXCITE FILLIP HARDEN HOICKS HUSTLE INCITE INDUCE INVITE MOTION PROMPT PROPEL STRAIN THREAP THREAT ANIMATE COMMOVE ENFORCE INSTANT OPPRESS PERSIST SOLICIT SUGGEST URGENCY ADMONISH INSTANCE PERSUADE
(— IMPORTUNATELY) DUN PRESS
(— ON) EGG ERT HAG SOOL WHIG ALARM CHIRK CROWD DRIVE FILIP HASTE HURRY IMPEL ROWEL YOICK ALARUM FILLIP HARDEN HASTEN INCITE
(— ON A HORSE) HUP CRAM CHUCK
(— STRONGLY) EXHORT SOLICIT
(— WITH VEHEMENCE) DING
URGENCY NEED PRESS STRESS COGENCE COGENCY URGENCE EXIGENCY INSTANCE INSTANCY PRESSURE
URGENT HOT DIRE LOUD RASH ACUTE HASTY STRONG BURNING CLAMANT EXIGENT INSTANT URGEFUL CRITICAL PRESSING PRESSIVE NECESSITOUS
URGING QUEST
URI (SON OF —) GEBER BEZALEEL
URIAH (WIFE OF —) BATHSHEBA

URIAL SHA OORIAL
URIEL (DAUGHTER OF —) MAACHAH
(FATHER OF —) TAHATH
URIJAH (FATHER OF —) SHEMAIAH
URINAL DUCK PISSOIR SANITARY
URINATE WET LEAK EMPTY STALE PIDDLE EVACUATE MICTURATE
URINATION MICTION NOCTURIA
URINE MIG SIG LAGE LANT WASH STALE WATER NETTING EMICTION
(— USED AS COSMETIC) LOTIUM
(PREF.) UR(O) URIC(O) URIN(I)(O)
(SUFF.) URIA URIC
URN JAR EWER KIST URNA VASE CAPANNA
(— FOR MAKING TEA) KITCHEN SAMOVAR
(— IN KENO) GOOSE
(BURIAL —) OSSUARY
(CINERARY —) DINOS DEINOS
(STONE —) STEEN
URN-SHAPED URCEOLAR
UROCHORDA ASCIDIA TUNICATA
UROPYGIUM RUMP
UROSTYLE COCCYX
URSA MAJOR OKNARI CHARIOT WAGONER WAGGONER
URSINE ARCTOID
URTICARIA HIVES UREDO CNIDOSIS
URTICASTRUM LAPORTEA
URUBU ZOPILOTE

URUGUAY
CAPITAL: MONTEVIDEO
DEPARTMENT: ROCHA SALTO FLORES RIVERA ARTIGAS COLONIA DURAZNO FLORIDA SORIANO
ESTUARY: PLATA
LAKE: MERIN MIRIM DIFUNTOS
MEASURE: VARA LEGUA CUADRA SUERTE
RIVER: MALO MIRIM NEGRO ULIMAR CUAREIM QUEGUAY YAGUARON CEBOLLATI
TOWN: MELO AIGUA MINAS PANDO ROCHA SALTO VERAS RIVERA DURAZNO FLORIDA MERCEDES PAYSANDU
WEIGHT: QUINTAL

URUGUAYAN ORIENTAL
URUS TUR URE AUROCHS
US HIS HIZ HUZ
U.S.A. (AUTHOR OF —) DOSPASSOS
(CHARACTER IN —) ANN BEN JOE MAC MARY WARD DELLA FAINY JANEY MARGO TRENT FRENCH MAISIE SAVAGE STAPLE STRANG CHARLEY COMPTON DOWLING ELEANOR EVELINE RICHARD SPENCER ANDERSON GERTRUDE HUTCHINS MCCREARY STODDARD WILLIAMS ANNABELLE MOOREHOUSE
USABLE FIT UTIBLE SERVABLE
USAGE USE ASAL FORM WONE HABIT HAUNT SUNNA USURE CUSTOM MANNER FASHION HALACHA HALAKAH USATION PRACTICE
(BAD —) ABUSAGE

(HARD —) GRIEF
(ILL —) ABUSE
(RELIGIOUS —) RITUS
(PL.) CEREMONY
(PREF.) NOM(O)
(SUFF.) NOMY
USE URE BOOT CALL DUTY HAVE NAIT NOTE USUS WISE APPLY AVAIL GUIDE HABIT SPEND STEAD TREAT USAGE WASTE BEHOOF EMPLOY FINISH HANDLE OCCUPY USANCE ACCOUNT ADHIBIT ENTREAT IMPROVE PURPOSE SERVICE UTILITY ACCUSTOM EXERCISE FUNCTION PRACTICE
(— AS WONTED) ADOPT
(— EXPERIMENTALLY) TRY
(— FIGURE OF SPEECH) TROPE
(— IMPROPERLY) ABUSE
(— INDISCRIMINATELY) HACK
(— OF MORE WORDS THAN NECESSARY) PLEONASM
(— OF NEW WORD) NEOLOGY
(— OF SUBTERFUGE) CHICANE
(— UP) EAT TIRE WEAR SHOOT ABSORB DEVOUR EXPEND GUZZLE PERUSE CONSUME EXHAUST OVERWEAR
(— WASTEFULLY) SPILL
(— WITH FULL COMMAND) WIELD
(EXCESSIVE — OF FACE AND HANDS) ABHINAYA
(FOR TEMPORARY —) JURY
(FRUGAL —) SPARE
(GENERAL —) CURRENCY
(LITURGICAL —) RITE
(MUCH IN —) GREAT
(UNRESTRICTED —) FREEDOM
(WRONG —) ABUSE
(PREF.) USU
USED WONT
(— CONTINUOUSLY) HOT
(— IN FLIGHT) VOLAR
(— UP) ALL BEAT SHOT SPENT FOREWORN
(MUCH —) GREAT HACKNEY
USEFUL GAIN GOOD UTILE UTIBLE HELPFUL THRIFTY BEHOVELY UTENSILE BEHOVEFUL
(— FOR LONG TIME) HARD
(SUFF.) CHRESIS CHRESTIC CHRESTO
USEFULNESS USE AVAIL VALUE WORTH PROFIT MILEAGE UTILITY
USELESS IDLE LEWD VAIN VOID WIDE EMPTY DOLESS GROTTY NOUGHT OTIOSE SCREWY TRASHY INUTILE STERILE VAINFUL BOOTLESS FOOTLESS FOOTLING WASTEFUL
USELESSNESS FUTILITY IDLENESS
USER USUS
(SUFF.) STER STRESS
USHABTI SHAWABTI
USHER BOW USH SHOW CRIER HERALD ISCHAR SEATER VERGER CHOBDAR HUISHER JANITOR MARSHAL STEWARD
USSR (SEE RUSSIA)
USUAL RIFE NOMIC COMMON FAMOUS NORMAL SOLEMN VULGAR WONTED AVERAGE

GENERAL NATURAL REGULAR TYPICAL USITATE EVERYDAY FREQUENT HABITUAL ORDINARY ORTHODOX ACCUSTOMED

USURER SHARK GAVELER HARPAGON

USURP ASSUME INVADE PRESUME ACCROACH ARROGATE

USURY GAVEL OCKER USURE USANCE GOMBEEN

UTAH

CAPITAL: SALTLAKECITY
COLLEGE: WEBER
COUNTY: IRON JUAB CACHE PIUTE CARBON SEVIER TOOELE UINTAH SANPETE
INDIAN: UTE
LAKE: SALT SWAN SEVIER
MOTTO: INDUSTRY
MOUNTAIN: LENA LION WAAS KINGS PEALE TRAIL FRISCO NAVAJO SWASEY GRANITE GRIFFIN HAWKINS PENNELL LINNAEUS
MOUNTAIN RANGE: CEDAR HENRY HOGUP UINTA WAHWAH TERRACE CONFUSION
NATIONAL PARK: ZION
NICKNAME: MORMON BEEHIVE
RIVER: WEBER JORDAN SEVIER
STATE BIRD: SEAGULL
STATE FLOWER: SEGOLILY
STATE TREE: SPRUCE
TOWN: LOA MOAB OREM DELTA HEBER KANAB LOGAN MAGNA MANTI NEPHI OGDEN PRICE PROVO KEARNS TOOELE VERNAL BRIGHAM BOUNTIFUL COALVILLE

UTENSIL (ALSO SEE IMPLEMENT AND TOOL) HOD BOAT IRON MOLD PECK STEW BAKER FRIER FRYER GRILL KNIFE MOULD RICER SCOOP SHEET SHELL SIEVE SLICE ULLER BEATER BEETLE BREWER COOKER DABBER FUNNEL GRATER GRILLE KETTLE LINGEL MASKER POPPER PUSHER SHAKER SIFTER BRAZIER BROILER DUSTPAN FLIPPER GLUEPOT MUDDLER SCUMMER SKIMMER STEAMER STIRRER TOASTER CALABASH GRIDIRON SAUCEPAN SAUCEPOT SHREDDER SPOUCHER STRAINER
(— FOR COVERING FIRE) CURFEW
(COOKING —) WOK
(LITURGICAL —) ASTERISK
(PL.) BATTERY COOKWARE IRONWARE

UTERUS WOMB BELLY METRA MATRIX BEARING
(PREF.) METR(O)

UTHAI (FATHER OF —) BIGVAI AMMIHUD

UTILITARIAN USEFUL ECONOMIC

UTILITY USE AVAIL USAGE PROFIT BENEFIT SERVICE

UTILIZE USE EMPLOY ENLIST CONSUME EXPLOIT HARNESS HUSBAND

UTILIZING
(SUFF.) IC(AL)

UTMOST END NTH BEST LAST MOST FINAL EXTREME OUTMOST SUPREME DAMNDEST POSSIBLE UTTEREST

UTOPIA ZION

UTOPIAN IDEAL

UTOPIANISM FUTURISM

UTRAQUIST CALIXTIN

UTRICULUS ALVEUS

UTTER ASK OUT SAY BARK BLOW BOOM DEAD DRIB EMIT FAIR GASP GIVE HURL MAIN MOOT MOVE PASS PURE RANK SEND TELL VENT VERY BLACK COUGH CRUDE FETCH FRAME FRANK GROSS ISSUE MOUTH RAISE SHEER SOUND SPEAK SPELL STARK THICK TOTAL VOICE ACCENT ARRANT BROACH DAMNED DIRECT INTONE PARLEY PROFER PROPER TONGUE BLUSTER BREATHE DELIVER ENOUNCE EXCLAIM EXPRESS OUTMOST OUTTELL PERFECT PROLATE UPBRAID ABSOLUTE BLINKING COMPLETE CRASHING INTONATE BLITHERING
(— ABRUPTLY) BLURT
(— AFFECTEDLY) KNAP MINCE
(— ARGUMENTS) BLAZE
(— CASUALLY) DROP
(— EXPLOSIVELY) BOLT
(— FALSEHOODS) FABLE
(— FOOLISHLY) BLABBER
(— GLIBLY) SCREED
(— HALTINGLY) BLUBBER
(— HURRIEDLY) CHOP
(— IN HARSH VOICE) GRIT GRATE
(— INADVERTENTLY) SLIP
(— INDISTINCTLY) CHEW
(— LOUD CRY) BRAY BLARE
(— LOUDLY) CRY BLAT CALL HALLO HALLOO HULLOO PRABBLE
(— LOW SOUNDS) MURMUR WHISPER
(— MEANINGLESS SOUNDS) BABBLE
(— RAPIDLY) FIRE CHATTER
(— RAUCOUSLY) BLAT
(— REPETITIVELY) CHIME
(— RHETORICALLY) DECLAIM
(— SOLEMNLY) SWEAR
(— STUPIDLY) BLUNDER
(— SUDDENLY) CRACK
(— UNCTUOUSLY) DROOL
(— VIGOROUSLY) FLING
(— WITH EFFORT) HEAVE

UTTERANCE CRY GAB CALL OSSE BLURT DITTY PAROL VOICE ACCENT ACTION BREATH CHORUS DRIVEL GIBBER ORACLE PAROLE TONGUE EXPRESS INKLING LALLING STATUTE DELIVERY FOOTNOTE HOMESPUN JUDGMENT LOCUTION SYLLABIC
(— FROM A DIVINITY) ORACLE
(— OF PRAISE) MAGNIFICAT

(— OF VOCAL SOUNDS) PHONESIS
(CONDEMNATORY —) INFAMY
(DEFECTIVE —) STAMMER
(FAINT —) INKLING
(FOOLISH —) DRIVEL
(FOOLISH —S) GUFF
(GUSHING —) EFFUSION
(IMPULSIVE —) BLURT
(INDISTINCT —) BUMBLE
(MALICIOUS —) SLANDER
(OFFENSIVE —) AFFRONT
(PROPHETIC —) OSSE
(PUBLIC —) AIR OUTGIVING
(SHORT —) DITTY
(SOLEMN —) EFFATE EFFATUM
(TRADITIONAL —) AGRAPHON
(VAPID —) CUCKOO
(PL.) BYRONICS

UTTERED SPOKEN

UTTERLY DOG BONE DEAD BLACK OUTLY PLUMB PROOF HOLLOW MERELY BLANKLY OUTERLY SHEERLY PROPERLY

UTU (FATHER OF —) NANNA

UVULA CION UVULE PLECTRUM STAPHYLE
(PREF.) CION(O) STAPHYL(O)

UVULARIA OAKESIA

UZ (FATHER OF —) ARAM NAHOR DISHAN
(GRANDFATHER OF —) SEIR SHEM

UZAI (SON OF —) PALAL

UZAL (FATHER OF —) JOKTAN

UZBEK JAGATAI

UZZAH (BROTHER OF —) AHIO
(FATHER OF —) ABINADAB

UZZI (FATHER OF —) BANI BELA TOLA BUKKI
(SON OF —) ZERAHIAH

UZZIAH (FATHER OF —) AMAZIAH
(SON OF —) ATHAIAH JEHONATHAN

UZZIEL (FATHER OF —) ISHI KOHATH HARHAIAH
(SON OF —) ZITHRI MISHAEL ELIZAPHAN

V

V VEE FIVE VICTOR
(INVERTED —) CARET
VACANCY HOLE WANT VACUIT
VACUITY VACATION
VACANT IDLE OPEN VOID BLANK
EMPTY FISHY INANE WASTE
DEVOID HOLLOW DORMANT
UNFILLED
(BECOME —) FALL
(PREF.) VACUO
VACATE QUIT TOLL VOID AVOID
EMPTY WAIVE VACANT ABANDON
RESCIND ABROGATE EVACUATE
VACATION OUT REST LEAVE
OUTING RECESS HOLIDAY
NONTERM VACANCY
(SUMMER —) LONG
VACCINE LYMPH BACTERIN
BIOLOGIC
VACCINIA COWPOX
VACILLATE HALT SWAG WAVE
DACKER DITHER HALPER TEETER
WABBLE WAFFLE WOBBLE
SHAFFLE STICKLE SWITHER
WHIFFLE HESITATE
VACILLATING INFIRM MOBILE
HALTING
VACILLATION SEESAW WAVERING
VACUITY BLOW VACANCY
FONTANEL
VACUOLE GUTTA
VACUOUS DULL BLANK EMPTY
SILLY VACANT
VACUUM GAPE VOID VACANCY
VACUITY VACATION
VACUUM TUBE
(SUFF.) TRON
VAGABOND BUM VAG HOBO KERN
JAVEL ROGUE SHACK STIFF
BRIBER CANTER HARLOT JOCKEY
PICARA PICARO RODNEY RUNNER
TAGRAG TRUANT WAFFIE
COASTER ERRATIC FAITOUR
GADLING GANGREL OUTCAST
SCOURER SKELDER SWAGMAN
SWINGER TINKLER TRUCKER
VAGRANT VAURIEN WASTREL
BOHEMIAN BRODYAGA CURSITOR
CUSTROUN FUGITIVE GLASSMAN
PALLIARD RAPPAREE RUNABOUT
RUNAGATE WHIPJACK
VAGARY WHIM FANCY FREAK
VAGUE CAPRICE CONCEIT
CRANKUM FLAGARIE VAGRANCY
(PL.) HUMORS
VAGINA
(PREF.) COLP(O) ELYTR(O)
VAGINATE SHEATHED
VAGRANCY MOPERY ROGUING
VAGRANT BUM WAFF WAIF CAIRD
PIKER PIKEY ROGUE SKELB STRAG
TRAMP VAGUE ARRANT CASUAL
SHAKER SHULER TINKER TRUANT

VAGROM VAGUER WAFFIE
DEVIOUS DRIFTER ERRATIC
FLOATER GANGREL ROGUISH
SKILDER SWAGMAN TINKLER
TRAMPER TROGGER BRODYAGA
PLANETIC STROLLER VAGABOND
SHACKLING
(PL.) FLOTSAM
VAGUE LAX DARK HAZY FOGGY
FUZZY GROSS LOOSE MISTY
MUDDY WOOZY CLOUDY DREAMY
MYSTIC SHAGGY BLURRED
EVASIVE OBSCURE SHADOWY
UNFIXED CONFUSED INFINITE
NEBULOUS NUBILOUS
VAGUELY DIMLY DARKLY DUMBLY
DREAMILY
VAIN MAD IDLE NULL PUFF VOID
WANE COCKY EMPTY FLORY
PROUD SAUCY VOGIE WASTE
FLIMSY FUTILE HOLLOW OTIOSE
VAUNTY BIGGITY CARRIED
TRIVIAL VAINFUL BOOTLESS
CONCEITY NUGATORY PEACOCKY
VAPOROUS WASTEFUL
(NOT —) SOLID
VAINGLORY POMP RUFF GLORY
VANITY ELATION
VAINLY IDLY TOOMLY
VAIR POTENT
VAISRAVANA BISHAMON
VAISYA BAIS BICE
VAJEZATHA (FATHER OF —)
HAMAN
VAJRA DORJE
**VAKULA THE SMITH (CHARACTER
IN —)** CHUB DEVIL OXANA PANAS
VAKULA SOLOKHA
(COMPOSER OF —) TCHAIKOVSKY
VAL LACE
VALANCE PAND PELMET
FRONTLET PALMETTE
VALE DALE DEAN DELL BACHE
BATCH ENNIS
VALEDICTORY FAREWELL
VALENCE ADICITY ATOMISM
VALENTINE (SISTER OF —)
GRETCHEN
(SLAYER OF —) FAUST
VALERIAN HELIO BENNET SUMBUL
ALLHEAL CUTHEAL SETWALL
CETEWALE
VALERIC PENTOIC
VALET MAN ANDREW SIRDAR
TARTAR WALLIE CRISPIN
TIREMAN
VALIANT SAD BOLD BRAG PREU
PROW WILD BRAVE LUSTY ORPED
PROUD STOUT WIGHT FIERCE
HEROIC DOUGHTY GAILLARD
GALLIARD INTREPID STALWART
VIRTUOUS
VALID FAIR GOOD JUST LEGAL

SOUND COGENT LAWFUL
BINDING ETERNAL WEIGHTY
FORCIBLE VAILABLE VALIDOUS
VALUABLE
(PREF.) RATI
VALIDATE FIRM SEAL VALID
AFFIRM CONFIRM
VALIDITY FORCE VIGOR STRENGTH
VALISE BAG GRIP MAIL DORLACH
SATCHEL VALLIES SUITCASE
VALKYRIE SHIELDMAY
VALLECULA VALLEY
VALLEY DIB GUT COMB COOM
COVE DALE DELL DENE GILL HOLE
HOPE HOWE HOYA PARK VALE
WADI WADY ATRIO BACHE BREAK
CHASM COMBE COOMB DHOON
GHYLL GLACK GOYAL GOYLE
HEUGH SLACK SLADE SWALE
TEMPE YUNGA BOLSON BOTTOM
CANADA CLOUGH COULEE
DINGLE HOLLOW LAAGTE LEEGTE
RINCON STRATH AIJALON
BLOWOUT GEHENNA VAALITE
(— BETWEEN CONES OF VOLCANO)
ATRIO
(— IN THESSALY) TEMPE
(— ON MOON'S SURFACE) RILL
CLEFT RILLE
(— ON MT BLANC) NANT
(CIRCULAR —) RINCON
(DEEP —) CANON GRIKE CANYON
(DROWNED —) VIA
(FLAT-FLOORED DESERT —) BOLSON
(GRASSY MOUNTAIN —) HOLE
(LOWEST PART OF —) SOLE
(MINIATURE —) GULLY GULLEY
(NARROW —) DEAN DENE GLEN
GLACK GOYLE GRIFF KLOOF
CLOUGH
(RIVER —) WATER
(SECLUDED —) GLEN DINGLE
(TRENCHLIKE —) COULEE
VALOR ARETE MERIT VALUE
BOUNTY VALOUR BRAVERY
COURAGE PROWESS STOMACH
CHIVALRY VALIANCY
VALOROUS BOLD BRAVE
VIRTUOUS
VALUABLE DEAR COSTLY PRIZED
WORTHY EMINENT WEALTHY
PRECIOUS PRIZABLE SINGULAR
VALUATION PRIZE VALOR VALUE
ESTEEM EXTENT ESTIMATE
TAXATION
VALUE SET COST FECK FOOT HOLD
RATE TELL AVAIL CARAT CHEAP
COUNT FORCE PRICE PRIZE
STAMP STENT STOCK VALOR
WORTH ASSESS ASSIZE EQUITY
ESTEEM EXTENT FIGURE HIDAGE
MATTER MOMENT PRAISE
REGARD VALURE VALUTA VIRTUE

ACCOUNT ADVANCE APPRIZE
CAPITAL CHERISH COMPUTE
PRETIUM RESPECT VALENCY
WERGILD ESTIMATE EVALUATE
GOODWILL SPLENDOR TREASURE
VALIDITY VALLIDOM
(— HIGHLY) PRIZE ENDEAR
(— OF ANGLE) EPOCH
(— OF COW) SET
(— OF TIMBER) STUMPAGE
(ABSOLUTE —) MODULUS
(AESTHETIC —) AMENITY
(ESTABLISHED —) PAR
(GOOD —) SNIP
(MATHEMATICAL —) EXTREMUM
(NEGATIVE —) DISVALUE
(STUDY OF —) AXIOLOGY
(TESTED —) ASSAY
(PREF.) AXIO TIMO
VALUED DEAR
VALUELESS BAFF STRAWY
NAUGHTY
VALVE TAP COCK DISC DISK GATE
ORAL STOP CHOKE CLACK MIXER
VALVA WAFER BINODE BOTTLE
CUTOUT DAMPER KICKER PALLET
POPPET POTLID SCUTUM SLUICE
SUCKER VENTIL WASHER CLICKET
DRAWOFF PETCOCK REDUCER
SCALLOP SCOLLOP SHUTOFF
VALVULA VALVULE DRAWGATE
EPITHECA EPIVALVE STOPCOCK
THROTTLE
(— OF BARNACLE) SCUTUM
(— OF MUSICAL INSTRUMENT)
PISTON VENTIL
(— OF PUMP BOX) FANG
(ANATOMICAL —) TRICUSPID
(THIN —) WAFER
(TRIPLE —) KICKER
(PREF.) THYRE(O) THYRO
(SUFF.) THYRIS
VAMBRACE BRACELET
VAMOOSE SCRAM CHEESE
DECAMP SKIDDOO
VAMPIRE LAMIA ALUKAH
VAN WAN FORE LEAD SAIL FRONT
TRUCK VAUNT WAGON VAWARD
CARAVAN FOURGON FOREWARD
KHALDIAN
VANADATE UVANITE TURANITE
VANDAL HUN HUNLIKE SARACEN
HOOLIGAN
VANDALIZE TRASH
VANE FAN TEE WEB COCK TAIL
WING FAINE BUCKET TARGET
DOGVANE FLIGHTER VEXILLUM
(— OF ARROW) FEATHER
(— OF CONVEYOR BELT) FLIGHT
(— OF FEATHER) WEB FLUE
VEXILLUM
(— OF SURVEYING STAFF)
TRANSOM

587

(— OF WINDMILL) FAN FANE TAIL FAINE
(COOLING — IN BREWING) FLIGHTER
VANESSA PYRAMEIS
VANGUARD FORLORN
VANIAH (FATHER OF —) BANI
VANISH DIE FLY DROP FADE FLEE MELT PASS SANT WEDE WEND CLEAR FLEET SAUNT SLIDE EXHALE EVANISH SCATTER CONQUEST DISSOLVE EVANESCE
(— BY DEGREES) DRILL
VANISHED LAPSED EXTINCT
VANITY ABEL POMP VAIN FOLLY PRIDE EGOISM CONCEIT FEATHER FOPPERY INANITY SANDUST IDLENESS IDLESHIP PRETENSION
VANITY FAIR (AUTHOR OF —) THACKERAY
(CHARACTER IN —) JOS PITT BECKY SHARP AMELIA DOBBIN GEORGE JOSEPH RAWDON SEDLEY STEYNE CRAWLEY OSBORNE WILLIAM
VANNER SLIMER
VANNIC KHALDIAN
VANQUISH GET WIN BEAT LICK MILL UTTER EXPUGN MASTER OUTRAY SUBDUE THRASH CONQUER OVERWIN SMOTHER CONQUEST OVERCOME SURMOUNT VENKISEN
VANQUISHED CRAVEN
VANUATU (CAPITAL OF —) VILA
(FORMER NAME OF —) NEWHEBRIDES
(ISLAND OF —) EPI EFATE MALEKULA PENTECOST ESPIRITUSANTO
(MONEY OF —) VATU
(VOLCANO OF —) TANNA AMBRYN LOPEVI
VAPID DRY DULL FADE FLAT STALE TRITE JEJUNE INSIPID WATERISH
VAPOR FOG FUME REEK ROKE STEW BOAST BRUME EWDER HUMOR SMOKE STEAM STIFE BREATH VAPOUR EXHAUST HALITUS
(HOT —) LUNT
(NOXIOUS —) DAMP
(PL.) BRUME
(PREF.) ATM(O) ATMID(O) MANO PNEUMAT(O) TYPH(O)
VAPORIZATION BURNUP BOILOFF
VAPORIZE DRIVE FLASH STEAM AERATE AERIFY VAPORATE
VAPOROUS FUMY FUMID HUMID FUMISH FUMOSE STEAMY VOLATILE
VARANGIAN VARIAG WARING
(PL.) ROS
VARIABILITY HETERISM
VARIABLE FLUX FREE CHOPPY FICKLE FITFUL KITTLE WRAIST CEPHEID FACIENT FLUXILE MUTABLE ROLLING STREAKY UNEQUAL VARIANT VARIOUS ARGUMENT FLOATING FLUXIBLE SHIFTING SKITTISH UNSTABLE VEERABLE
(EXCEEDINGLY —) PROTEAN
(RANDOM —) STATISTIC

VARIANCE ODDS DISCORD DISPUTE
VARIANT STATE VERSION
(— IN WHEAT) SPELTOID
(POSITIONAL —) ALLOPHONE
(PL.) DIAPHONE
VARIATION REX TURN ERROR ROGUE SHADE CHANGE DOUBLE JITTER SWITCH CYCLING DESCANT EXTREME SHADING VARIETY WINDING DIVISION DYNAMICS HETERISM MUTATION
(— IN AIR PRESSURE) ROBBING
(— IN CURRENT) SURGE
(— IN FREQUENCY) SWINGING
(— IN SPEED) HUNTING
(— OF COLOR) ABRASH
(— OF PUPIL OF EYE) HIPPUS
(— OF SHOE) SPRING
(— OF VOWELS) ABLAUT
(ALLOWABLE —) LEEWAY
(BALLET —) ATTITUDE
(TOPOGRAPHICAL —) BREAK
(PL.) PIBROCH
VARICOCELE RAMEX
VARIED SORTY DAEDAL SEVERAL VARIANT VARIOUS MANIFOLD
VARIED BUNTING PRUSIANO
VARIEGATE DROP FRET FLECK FREAK SHOOT AUMAIL DAPPLE STRIPE VARIFY CHECKER
VARIEGATED FAW PIED SHOT JASPE LYART SHELD DAEDAL MARLED MENALD MOSAIC SKEWED BROCKED BROCKIT CHECKED CLOUDED DAPPLED FREAKED FRETTED PECKLED SPARKED VARIOUS DISCOLOR FRECKLED OVERSHOT PANACHED SKEWBALD
(PREF.) POECIL(O)
VARIEGATION COLOR
VARIETY BREW FORM KIND MODE SORT BRAND BREED CLASS COLOR SPICE CHANGE NATURE STIRPS STRAIN STRIPE SPECIES VARIENS
VARIOLA HORSEPOX SMALLPOX
VARIOUS MANY SERE DIVERS SUNDER SUNDRY VARIED DIVERSE SEVERAL VARIANT MANIFOLD
(PREF.) PARTI POECIL(O) POEKIL(O)
VARISCITE UTAHITE
VARIX
(PREF.) CIRS(O)
VARLET BOY LAD GIPPO JIPPO PAVISER COISTREL VARLETTO
VARNISH DOPE JAPAN LACKER MEDIUM PUNDUM FIXATIF LACQUER VEHICLE VERMEIL FIXATIVE OVERGILD THEETSEE
VARY HUNT ALTER BREAK DRIFT SHIFT SPORT CHANGE DIFFER RECEDE VARIFY CHECKER DEVIATE DISSENT DIVERGE VARIATE DISAGREE OSCILLATE
VARYING CURRENT
VASE PYX URN OLLA VASA VASO ASKOS CYLIX DINOS DIOTA KYLIX PYXIS BASKET BOWPOT COTULA COTYLA CRATER DEINOS DOLIUM

FILLER HYDRIA KALPIS KOTYLE KRATER LEKANE SITULA AMPHORA AMPULLA CANOPUS PATELLA POTICHE PSYKTER SCYPHUS SKYPHOS STAMNOS URCEOLE BOUGHPOT LECYTHUS LEKYTHOS MURRHINE PROCHOOS
(— FOR PERFUME) CONCH
(— ON PEDESTAL) TAZZA
(—S UNDER THEATER SEATS) SCHEA
(PREF.) POTICHO VAS(I)(O) VASCUL(I)(O)
VASHNI (FATHER OF —) SAMUEL
VASHTI (HUSBAND OF —) AHASUERUS
VASODILATOR KELLIN KHELLIN
VASSAL MAN WER BOND LEUD SERF CEILE LIEGE SLAVE CLIENT GENEAT SACOPE BONDMAN FEEDMAN FEODARY HOMAGER RUDIGER SAMURAI SERVANT SUBJECT VAVASOR PALATINE
(PL.) MANRED
VASSALAGE MANRENT
VAST HUGE BROAD ENORM GREAT LARGE STOUR VASTY COSMIC IMMANE MIGHTY UNTOLD ABYSMAL IMMENSE OCEANIC VASTITY ENORMOUS INFINITE MOUNTAIN SPACIOUS
VASTNESS IMMANE GRANDEUR WIDENESS
VAT ARK BAC DIP FAT PIT TAP TUN BACK BECK COOM FATE GAAL GAIL GYLE KEEL KIER TINE APRON COOMB FETTE FLOAT KEEVE KIEVE ROUND STAND STEEP KIMNEL MOTHER BLUNGER DRAINER GRAINER KEELVAT STEEPER PRESSFAT
(— USED IN MEASURING SLIPS) ARK
(BREWER'S —) BACK FLOAT KEEVE UNION CUMMING
(CHEESE —) CHESSEL CHESSET CHESSART
(COOLING —) KELDER
(DYER'S —) JIG LEAD DYEBECK
(EVAPORATING —) APRON GRAINER
(FERMENTING —) TUN COMB COOM GYLE KEEL COOMB FLOAT
(TANNER'S —) TAP HANGER SPENDER
(TEXTILE —) KIER
(WINE —) LAKE CUVEE
(PREF.) PYEL(O)
VATICAN CITY (BASILICA OF —) STPETERS
(WALL OF —) LEONINE
VAU DIGAMMA
VAUDEVILLE ZARZUELA
VAULT BOUT COPE JUMP LEAP PEND SKIP TOMB VOLT WOWT AZURE CROFT CRYPT EMBOW VOLTO CELLAR CUPOLA FORNIX SHROUD CONCAVE DUNGEON TESTUDO VALTAGE CATACOMB LEAPFROG MONUMENT
(— IN CEILING) LACUNAR
(— OF HEAVEN) WELKIN
(— OF SKY) CONVEX ZENITH CONCAVE
(PART OF —) PENDENTIVE

VAULTED CONCAVE CRYPTED EMBOWED
VAULTER VOLTIGEUR
VAULTING POMADA POMMADO
VAUNT GAB BRAG BOAST ROOSE VOUST AVAUNT INSULT BLUSTER GLORIFY FLOURISH
(— ONESELF) WIND
VAUNTMURE MANURE
VEAL VEAU SLINK FRICANDO
(LIKE —) VITULINE
VECTOR I K PHASOR GRADIENT
VEDA SHASTER
VEDDOID PANYAN
VEDIC (— PRINCIPLE) RTA RITA
VEER CUT DIP FLY CAST CHOP SLEW SLUE SWAY TACK WYRE FETCH SHIFT SWOOP BROACH CHANGE SLOUGH SWERVE TUMBLE BOXHAUL DEVIATE WHIFFLE
VEERING DRIFT CHOPPY
VEGETABLE PEA YAM BEAN BEET CORN KALE LEEK OKRA CHARD GRASS ONION SABZI SALAD CARROT CELERY LEGUME LENTIL POTATO RADISH SQUASH TOMATO TOPEPO TURNIP BLOATER CABBAGE CELTUCE LETTUCE PARSNIP PEASCOD RHUBARB SPINACH VEGETAL BROCCOLI EGGPLANT RUTABAGA
(— MATTER) SUDD
(—S FOR MARKET) TRUCK
(EARLY —) PRIMEUR
(EARLY —S) HASTINGS
(GARDEN —S) SASS SAUCE
(HYBRID —) GARLION
(PREF.) PHYT(I)(O)
VEGETARIAN VEGAN
VEGETATION HERB COVER GREEN SCRUB GROWTH HERBAGE COVERAGE PLANTAGE PLEUSTON SMELLAGE
(DECOMPOSED —) STAPLE
(SCRUB —) BRUSH
(UNWANTED —) FILTH
(PREF.) PHYT(I)(O)
VEGETATIVE ASEXUAL PLANTAL
VEHEMENCE FURY GLOW HEAT RAGE WARMTH STRENGTH VIOLENCE
VEHEMENT HOT HIGH KEEN LOUD ANGRY EAGER FIERY HEFTY YEDER ARDENT BITTER FERVID FIERCE FLASHY HEARTY HEATED RAGING STRONG ANIMOSE ANIMOUS FURIOSO INTENSE JEALOUS VIOLENT
VEHEMENTLY AMAIN PELLMELL
VEHICLE BUS CAB CAR FLY VAN ARBA AUTO CART DUKE FLAT GOER JEEP SLED TAXI TEAM WAIN ARABA BRAKE BREAK BUGGY CARRY DILLY FLAIL GUIDE HANSA NODDY STAGE WAGON BLADER CAMPER CHARET CISIUM DIESEL HEARSE JITNEY MEDIUM RANDEM SLEDGE SLEIGH SURREY TRISHA TROIKA CARRIER CHARIOT CRUISER HOTSHOT ICEBOAT KIBITKA MACHINE MINIBUS OMNIBUS PEDICAB PEDRAIL

SHEBANG SHUTTLE SPEEDER
SPRAYER STEAMER STEERER
TARTANA TAXICAB TRAVOIS
TURNOUT UTILITY AUTORAIL
AUTOSLED CARRIAGE CHARETTE
CYCLECAR DEADHEAD DELIVERY
ELECTRIC FILMOGEN SHOWCASE
SOCIABLE UNICYCLE
MOTORCYCLE SNOWMOBILE
(— DRAWN BY BULLOCK) EKKA
(— FOR COLORS) MEGILP
(— FOR HAULING) TRACTOR
(— ON RUNNERS) SLED CARRO
SLEDGE SLEIGH ICEBOAT
AUTOSLED
(— ON SINGLE RAIL) AEROTRAIN
(— PULLED BY MAN) BROUETTE
RICKSHAW
(— RUNNING ON RAILS) LORRY
TRAIN
(— WITH 3 HORSES ABREAST)
TROIKA
(— WITH 3 HORSES BEHIND EACH
OTHER) RANDEM
(AIRPORT —) SKYLOUNGE
(AMMUNITION —) CAISSON
(AMPHIBIOUS —) BUFFALO
(AWKWARD —) ARK
(CHILD'S —) PRAM WALKER
SCOOTER STROLLER
(COVERED —) SEDAN LANDAU
CARAVAN KIBITKA
(EARTH-MOVING —) SCOOP
(LITTLE —) HINAYANA
(LUMBERING —) TUG TODE
(MILITARY —) AMTRACK
(MOTOR —) WHEELS
(OBSOLETE —) CRATE
(POOR-QUALITY —) DOG
SHANDRYPAN
(RUDE —) KIBITKA
(RUSSIAN —) TARANTAS
(SATELLITE —) SLV
(SLEDGE-LIKE —) GAMBO
(SNOW —) SKIBOB
(SPACE —) LANDER
(WHEELLESS —) DRAY
(2-WHEELED —) GIG CART SULKY
TONGA CISIUM JINGLE LIMBER
BICYCLE CALECHE CROYDON
RICKSHAW
(PL.) PARK
(SUFF.) MOBILE
VEIL WRY FALL FILM HIDE MASK
WRAP COVER GLOSS RUMAL
SHADE VELUM VIMPA VOLET
WREIL BUMBLE CHRISM FAILLE
SHADOW SHROUD VEILER
WEEPER WIMPLE CORTINA
CURTAIN ENDOTYS PARANJA
VEILING CALYPTRA ENDOTHYS
HEADRAIL KALYPTRA MAHARMAH
MANTILLA TELEBLEM
(— IN CHURCH) AER ENDOTYS
ENDOTHYS
(— ON FUNGI) CORTINA
(DOUBLE —) YASHMAK
(HUMERAL —) SUDARY
(WIDOW'S —) WEEPER
VEILED COVERT LATENT VELATED
SHROUDED
VEILING PURDAH GOSSAMER
VEIN BAR LOB RIB CAVA LODE

MOOD RAKE REEF VENA AMPER
CLOUD COMES COSTA LEDGE
MEDIA NERVE RIDER SCRIN VARIX
LEADER MEDIAL STRAIN STREAK
VENULA VENULE AXILLAR
AZYGOUS CUBITAL DROPPER
JUGULAR NERVURE PRECAVA
PRESTER SAPHENA VEINLET
AXILLARY EMULGENT PREMEDIA
PROFUNDA SUBCOSTA
(— IN MARBLE) CLOUD
(— OF LEAF) RIB COSTA MIDRIB
(— OF MINERAL) STREAK STRINGER
(— OF ORE) LODE ROKE BUNCH
LEDGE RIDER SCRIN LEADER
STRING DROPPER UNDERSET
(— OF WING) CUBIT RADIUS
CUBITAL CUBITUS SUBCOSTA
SUBCOSTAL
(GRANITIC —) ELVAN
(QUARTZ —) SADDLE
(VARICOSE —) AMPER
(PREF.) CIRS(O) PHLEB(O) PYL(E)(O)
VENI VENO
(SWOLLEN —) CIRS(O)
VEINED MARBLED NERVOSE
VELA SAILS
VELAR GUTTURAL
VELD BUSHVELD SOURVELD
VELELLA SALLYMAN
VELLEITY DESIRE WOULDING
VELLINCH FLINCHER
VELLUM ORIHON
VELOCIPEDE HOBBY STEED
TRICAR BICYCLE DICYCLE
RANTOON SPEEDER DRAISINE
TRICYCLE
VELOCITY DRIFT CELERITY
RAPIDITY STRENGTH
(— OF FLOW) CURRENT
(— OF 1 FOOT PER SECOND) VELO
VELOUR SOLEIL
VELOUTE POULETTE
VELUM VEIL VELAMEN VELARIUM
VELVET PILE PANNE YUZEN
BIRODO VELURE FRAYING
VELLUTE
VELVETEEN TRIPE
VELVET GRASS FOG
VELVETLEAF DAGGA PAREIRA
VENAL CORRUPT SALABLE
HIRELING SALEABLE VENDIBLE
VEND HAWK SELL UTTER MARKET
PEDDLE
VENDA (CAPITAL OF —)
THOHOYANDOU
(TOWN OF —) SIBASA MAKWARELA
VENDIBLE VENAL SALABLE
SALEABLE
VENDOR FAKER SELLER VENDER
ALIENOR BUTCHER HUSTLER
PITCHER PURLMAN VIANDER
PITCHMAN SAUCEMAN VENDITOR
VENEER BURL BURR JAPAN SHOOK
OVERLAY SKILLET
VENEERER DUSTER
VENERABLE OLD HOAR SAGE
AWFUL HOARY AUGUST SACRED
VETUST ANCIENT VENERAL
VINTAGE
(PREF.) SEBASTO
VENERATE FEAR DREAD HALLOW
REVERE VENERE

RESPECT WORSHIP
VENERATED HOLY SACRED
HALLOWED
VENERATION AWE CULT DULIA
CULTISM RESPECT DEVOTION
VENESECTION PHLEBOTOMY
VENETIAN RED SIENA SIERRA
VENETIAN SUMAC SCOTINO

VENEZUELA

CAPITAL: CARACAS
COIN: REAL MEDIO FUERTE
BOLIVAR CENTIMO MOROCOTA
GULF: PARIA
MEASURE: GALON MILLA FANEGA
ESTADEL
MOUNTAIN: PAVA YAVI DUIDA
ICUTU CONCHA CUNEVA
PARIMA IMUTACA MASAITI
RORAIMA
NATIVE: CARIB TIMOTE
GUARAUNO
RIVER: META APURE CAURA
ARAUCA CARONI CUYUNI
GUANARE ORINOCO ORITUCO
PARAGUA SUAPURE VICHADA
GUAVIARE VENTUARI
STATE: LARA APURE SUCRE ZULIA
ARAGUA FALCON MERIDA
BOLIVAR COJEDES GUARICO
MONAGAS TACHIRA YARACUY
CARABOBO TRUJILLO
TOWN: AROA CORO ATURES
CUMANA MERIDA BARINAS
CABELLO GUAWARE MARACAY
MATURIN CARUPANO
TACUPITA VALENCIA
WATERFALL: ANGEL CUQUENAN
WEIGHT: BAG LIBRA

VENGEANCE WRACK WREAK
WRECK AVENGE ULTION WANION
ALASTOR REVENGE VINDICT
REQUITAL VINDICTA
VENILIA (HUSBAND OF —) DAUNUS
(SISTER OF —) AMATA
(SON OF —) TURNUS
VENISON BILTONG
VENOM GALL ATTER VIRUS
POISON SWELTER CROTALIN
CROTALUS
VENOMOUS TOXIC ATTERN
DEADLY SNAKEY VENOMY
BANEFUL NOXIOUS SMITTLE
SNAKISH POISONED VIPERINE
VIPEROUS VIRULENT POISONOUS
VENT EMIT HOLE REEK BELCH
DRAIN FROTH ISSUE TEWEL
OUTAGE OUTLET CHIMNEY
EXPRESS OPENING ORIFICE
OUTCAST OUTFALL OUTTAKE
RELEASE VENTAGE APERTURE
BREATHER DIATREME FONTANEL
MOFFETTE SESPERAL SPIRACLE
SUSPIRAL VENTHOLE VOMITORY
(— IN EARTH'S CRUST) VOLCANO
(VOLCANIC —) BOCCA DIATREME
SOLFATARA
VENTILATE AIR WIND AERATE
EXPRESS
VENTILATION AERAGE AIRING
VENTILATOR BADGIR LOUVER
FEMERELL

VENTING GUST
VENTRAL BELLY HEMAL STERNAL
ANTERIOR INFERIOR
(PREF.) (— AREA) GASTER(O)
GASTR(I)(O)
VENTRICLE HEART TRICORN
DIACOELE
(SUFF.) CELE COELE COELUS
VENTURE HAB RUN SET CAST
DARE JUMP KITE LUCK MINT
REST RISK WAGE ETTLE FLIER
FLYER FROST RISCO SALLY STAKE
TEMPT WAGER CHANCE DANGER
HAZARD SASHAY FLUTTER
IMPERIL JEOPARD PRESUME
PRETEND ENDANGER GETPENNY
(— AT DICE) THROW
(— TO SAY) DARESAY
VENTURESOME BOLD RASH RISKY
DARING PARLOUS TEMEROUS
VENTURESOMELY CHANCILY
VENUS LOVE VESPER LUCIFER
HESPERUS PHOSPHOR
(FATHER OF —) JUPITER
(HUSBAND OF —) VULCAN
(MOTHER OF —) DIONE
(SON OF —) AMOR CUPID AENEAS
VENUSIAN VENEREAN
VERACIOUS TRUE VERY TRUTHY
SINCERE VERIDIC FAITHFUL
TRUTHFUL
VERACITY HSIN TROTH TRUTH
VERITY FIDELITY
VERANDA PYAL LANAI PORCH
STOEP STOOP PIAZZA BALCONY
GALERIE GALLERY
VERB RHEMA ACTIVE NOMINAL
DEPONENT
(AUXILIARY —) BE DO CAN MAY
HAVE MUST WILL SHALL
VERBAL ORAL WORDY
VERBATIM DIRECT VERBAL
LITERAL DIRECTLY
VERBENA ALOYSIA VERVAIN
VERBENALIN CORNIN
VERBIAGE TALK
VERBOSE WINDY WORDY PROLIX
VERBAL DIFFUSE WORDISH
(NOT —) LEAN
VERBOSITY MACROLOGY
VERDANT BOSKY GREEN VIRID
VERDICT WORD VARDI ASSIZE
FINDING OPINION DECISION
JUDGMENT VEREDICT
VERDIGRIS AERUGO CANKER
VERDET
VERDIN GOLDTIT
VERDURE GREENTH GREENERY
VIRIDITY
(PREF.) CHLO
VERGE TOP EDGE WAND YARD
BRINK POINT TOUCH BORDER
TRENCH TRIGGER
VERGER WANDSMAN
VERGILIAN MARONIAN MARONIST
VERIFICATION AUDIT AVERRAL
CHECKUP AVERMENT
VERIFY AVER TRUE AUDIT CHECK
PROVE ATTEST RATIFY COLLATE
CONFIRM CONTROL JUSTIFY
SUPPORT CONSTATE
VERILY YEA AMEN FAITH PARDY
CERTES INDEED PARDIE FAITHLY

VERITABLE REAL TRUE VERY ACTUAL HONEST PROPER GENUINE VERIMENT
VERITY TROTH TRUTH VERIDITY
VERJUICE VARGE
VERMICELLI FEDELINI
VERMICULE VAALITE
VERMICULITE KERRITE MACONITE
VERMIFUGE KOSIN HARMAL HARMEL KAMALA KAMELA KOOSIN COWHAGE HELONIAS WORMWOOD
VERMILION RED GOYA MINIUM MINIATE PAPRIKA PIMENTO VERMEIL ZINOBER CARMETTA CINNABAR TOREADOR
VERMIN FILTH CARRION VARMINT
VERMIS WORM

VERMONT
CAPITAL: MONTPELIER
COLLEGE: BENNINGTON MIDDLEBURY
COUNTY: ESSEX ORANGE ADDISON ORLEANS WINDSOR LAMOILLE
LAKE: CASPIAN DUNMORE SEYMOUR CHAMPLAIN
MOUNTAIN: BROMLEY HOGBACK ASCUTNEY PROSPECT MANSFIELD
MOUNTAIN RANGE: GREEN TACONIC
NICKNAME: GREENMOUNTAIN
PRESIDENT: ARTHUR COOLIDGE
RIVER: SAXTONS LAMOILLE NULHEGAN POULTNEY WINOOSKI
STATE BIRD: THRUSH
STATE FLOWER: CLOVER
STATE TREE: MAPLE
TOWN: BARRE STOWE CHELSEA GRAFTON NEWFANE RUTLAND BENNINGTON BURLINGTON
UNIVERSITY: NORWICH

VERMOUTH CINZANO CHAMBERY
VERNACULAR LINGO COMMON JARGON PATOIS ROMAIC TONGUE VULGAR CHALDEE DIALECT TRIVIAL SCOTTISH
VERNALIZE IAROVIZE JAROVIZE YAROVIZE
VERNIER NONIUS
VERONICA HEBE SUDARIUM VERNICLE BROOKLIME
VERRUCOSE WARTY WARTED
VERSATILE HANDY FICKLE MOBILE FLEXILE
VERSE FIT EPIC LINE POSE RANN RICH RIME SONG BLANK IONIC METER METRE RHYME STAVE STICH TANKA ADONIC ALCAIC BURDEN CHIAVE CYWYDD DIPODY HEROIC JINGLE PANTUN SCAZON STANZA VERSET ANAPEST DICOLON DOGGREL ELEGIAC PAEONIC PANTOUM PENNILL SAPPHIC SAVITRI SOTADIC STICHOS TRIPODY DINGDONG DOGGEREL GLYCONIC LEONINES PRIAPEIAN RESPONSE SENTENCE SINGSONG TERETISM

TRIMETER VERSICLE MACARONIC
(— FORM) VIRELAY KYRIELLE
(— OF 14 LINES) SONNET
(— OF 2 FEET) DIPODY DIMETER
(— OF 6 FEET) CHOLIAMB SENARIAN SENARIUS
(— WITH LIMPING MOVEMENT) SCAZON
(DEVOTIONAL —) ANTIPHON OFFERTORY
(HINDU —) SLOKA
(JAPANESE —) HAIKAI
(MEDIEVAL —) SIRVENTE
(NONSENSE —S) AMPHIGORY
(UNMELODIOUS —) TERETISM
(PL.) TRIPOS PINDARICS
VERSED SEEN WITTY BESEEN TRADED STUDIED FREQUENT OVERSEEN SCIENCED
(WELL —) SKILLFUL
VERSICLE VERSE VERSET STICHOS SUFFRAGE
VERSIFIER BARD POET RHYMER VERSER METERER
VERSIFY METER
VERSION DRAM DRAUGHT EDITION READING TURNING REDACTION
(SHORT —) BRIEF
(SIMPLIFIED —) KEY
(TRANSLATED —) CONSTRUE
VERSO REVERSE
VERT VERD POMME VENUS PRASINE SINOPLE GREENHEW
VERTEBRA AXIS RACK ATLAS DORSAL LUMBAR SACRAL ACANTHA CENTRUM CERVICAL METAMERE PROATLAS RACKBONE SPONDYLE
(PREF.) ASTRAGAL(O) SPONDYL(O)
(SUFF.) SPONDYLI SPONDYLUS
VERTEBRATA CRANIATA CRANIOTA
VERTEBRATE CRANIATE SAUROPSID
VERTEX APEX COPE NODE POLE CROWN PITCH SUMMIT VERTICAL
VERTICAL APEAK ERECT PLUMB SHEER WHIRL ORTHAL UPRIGHT COLUMNAR SHEERING STRAIGHT
(PREF.) ORTH(O)
VERTICALLY PLUMP ENDLONG SHEERLY DIRECTLY PALEWISE
VERTICIL WHORL
VERTIGINOUS DIZZY
VERTIGO DINUS TIEGO MEGRIM MIRLIGO SWIMMING WHIRLING
VERUMONTANUM COLLICLE
VERVAIN GERVAO FROGFOOT IRONWEED
VERVE DARE DASH ELAN BOUNCE ENERGY PANACHE VITALITY VIVACITY
VERY SO ALL BIG DOG GAY GEY MUY TOO BRAW DEAD FELL FULL JUST MAIN MUCH PURE RARE REAL SAME SELF SUCH TRES UNCO WELL ASSAI AWFUL BLAME BULLY CRAZY DOOMS JOLLY MOLTO PESKY RIGHT SOWAN SUPER SWITH UNCOW VERRA BITTER BLAMED DAMNED DEUCED FREELY GAINLY LIVING MAINLY MASTER MIGHTY NATION

POISON PROPER SORELY STRONG TARNAL THRICE VERRAY WONDER AWFULLY BOILING GALLOWS GREATLY PARLOUS PASSING PRECISE SOPPING STRANGE DEUCEDLY DREADFUL ENORMOUS FAMOUSLY POWERFUL PRECIOUS SPANKING SWINGING WHACKING ABSOLUTELY
(PREF.) ERI MALLO
VESICANT LEWISITE MESEREUM
VESICA PISCIS MANDORLA
VESICATORY BLISTER
VESICLE BLEB CYST APTHA BULLA BURSE FLOAT APHTHA AMPULLA BLADDER BLISTER HYDATID OTOCYST POMPHUS UTRICLE VACUOLE AEROCYST MIDBRAIN VESICULA PHAGOSOME
(SUFF.) YDATIS
VESICULAR BULLOSE BULLOUS
VESPERAL TOWEL
VESPERS LYCHNIC PLACEBO EVENSONG
VESSEL (ALSO SEE BOAT AND SHIP) GO CAN CAT COG CUP FAT GUM HOY NEF PIG POT TUB VAS VAT VIA BARK BOAT BODY BOMB BOOT BOSS BOWL BRIG BUSH BUSS CASK CELL COWL DISH DRIP DUCT GAWN GRAB HORN HULK JACK JUNK KOFF LOTA PINK PINT POST PROW SAIL SHIP SNOW TING YAWL AMULA BAKIE BARGE BASIN BIDET BIKIE BOCAL BOYER CADUS CANNE CHURN COGUE CRACK CRAER CRAFT CRARE CRUET CRUSE DANDY DIOTA DUBBA FLASK GLOBE GUIDE JUBBE KETCH LADLE LAKER LAVER LINER PIECE PYKAR SCOOP SMACK STEAM STILL XEBEC YANKY ZABRA BANKER BARQUE BARREL BILALO BOILER BOTTLE BOUTRE BUCKET BURNER CAIQUE CANNER CAPPIE CHARGE CODMAN COFFIN CONCHA COOLER COPPER CRATER CRAYER CRUISE CUTTER DECKER DEINOS DOGGER DUBBAH ELUTOR FESSEL FIRKIN FLAGON HOLCAD HOOKER JAGGER KERNOS KETTLE KRATER LANCHA LATEEN LEKANE LORCHA MASLIN MONKEY MULLER PACKET PANKIN PATERA PICARD PITHOS POURIE ROLLER SALTER SATTIE SEALER SERVER SETTEE SHIBAR SITULA SMOKER TARTAN TENDER TOPMAN VESICA WHALER BAGGALA BALLOEN BALLOON BLICKEY BLICKIE CARAVEL CARRIER CISTERN CLIPPER CORSAIR COUGNAR CRAGGAN CRESSET CRISSET CRUISER CUVETTE DRIFTER DRINKER DROGHER FELUCCA FLYBOAT FRIGATE GABBARD GABBART GAIASSA GALASSA GUNBOAT ORANGER PATAMAR PINNACE POACHER POLACRE PSYKTER REDUCER SALTFAT SCALDER SEEDLIP SETTLER SPARGER

SPOUTER STEAMER STEEPER TRACHEA TRENDLE UTENSIL BELANDER BENITIER BILANDER BILLYBOY BIRDBATH BLEACHER BUGGALOW CORVETTE CRUCIBLE CRUISKEN CUCURBIT DECANTER DIGESTER DUTCHMAN EFFERENT EMISSARY FIREBOAT FLESHPOT GALLIPOT GALLIVAT GAROOKUH GAYDIANG HELLSHIP HONEYPOT INKSTAND INRIGGER IRONCLAD IRONSIDE KEELBOAT LATEENER LAVATORY NITRATOR PICAROON SCHOONER SMUGGLER SPITTOON WATERPOT
(— CUT FROM BLOCK OF WOOD) BAMBOOS
(— FOR COAL) GEORDIE
(— FOR DYE) TOBY
(— FOR HEATING LIQUIDS) ETNA
(— FOR HOLY WATER) FAT FONT STOCK STOOP STOUP AMPULLA BENITIER
(— FOR HYPODERMIC USE) AMPUL AMPULE AMPOULE
(— FOR LIQUID WASTE) DRIP
(— FOR MEASURING ORE) HOPPET
(— FOR MOLTEN METAL) LADLE
(— FOR ORE WASHINGS) LOOL
(— FOR PERFUMES) CENSER
(— FOR PORRIDGE) BICKER
(— FOR SOLDIER'S FOOD) MESSTIN
(— FOR WINE SAMPLING) TASTER
(— HOLDING CONDIMENTS) CRUET CASTER
(— IN MINE) CORB
(— MADE OF HOLLOW LOG) GUM
(— OF BARK) COOLAMAN COOLAMON COOLIMAN
(— OF HORN) BUGLE
(— ON TRIPOD) HOLMOS
(— ROWED BY OARS) CATUR GALLEY
(— STATIONED IN ENGLISH CHANNEL) GROPER
(— USED IN MAKING GLAZE) HILLER
(ABANDONED —) DERELICT
(ARMORED —) CRUISER IRONCLAD IRONSIDE
(BAPTISMAL —) FONT
(BARGELIKE —) PANGARA
(BLOOD —) AORTA ARTERY BLEEDER EFFERENT
(BREWER'S —) ROUND
(CANDLEMAKING —) JACK
(CHEMIST'S —) BATH FLASK STILL BEAKER RETORT
(CHINESE —) JUNK SAMPAN
(CIRCULAR —) KIT
(CLUMSY —) CRAY CRARE HAGBOAT
(COASTING —) DHOW DONI GRAB PONTIN SHEBAR SHIBAR TRADER COASTER GRIBANE MISTICO BILLYBOY HOVELLER
(CODFISHING —) BANKER CODMAN
(DECORATIVE —) AIGUIERE
(DISTILLING —) BODY STILL RETORT MATRASS CUCURBIT
(DRINKING —) CAP CUP TIN BOOT PECE FOUNT GLASS GOURD JORUM POKAL SCALE BICKER CAPPIE CHOPIN COOPER COOTIE

DIPPER DUBBER FIRLOT GOBLET
KITTIE QUAICH QUAIGH RABBIT
RUMKIN BIBERON CANAKIN
CANIKIN GALLIOT SCYPHUS
SKINKER SKYPHOS TANKARD
CANNIKIN CYLINDER
(DUTCH —) KOFF YANKY HOOKER
SCHUIT SCHUYT
(EARTHEN —) PIG BAYAN PANKIN
TINAGE CRAGGAN
(ELECTROPLATING —) TROUGH
(EUCHARISTIC —) AMA PYX AMULA
PYXIS FLAGON COLUMBA
CHRISMAL CIBORIUM
MONSTRANCE
(GLASS —) VERRE UNDINE
BALLOON
(HERRING-FISHING —) BUSS
(HOLLOW METALLIC —) BELL
(INVERTED —) BELL
(LADLING —) GAUN
(LARGE-NECKED —) JORDAN
(LATEEN-RIGGED —) DHOW LATEEN
LATEENER
(LEATHER —) BOOT JACK OLPE
GIRBA DUBBER
(LEVANTINE —) JERM SAIC
(LONG-NECKED —) GOGLET GUGLET
(LYMPHATIC —) LACTEAL
(MALAYAN —) PROA COUGNAR
(MELTING —) GRISSET
(OPEN —) LOOM
(PERFORATED —) LEACH
(PINECONE-SHAPED —) THYRSE
(PORTUGUESE —) MULET
(RARE —) SNOW
(SEED —) POD BUTTON BIVALVE
(SERVING —) ARGYLE ARGYLL
SERVER
(SHALLOW —) KIVER SKEEL
BEDPAN PANCHION
(SMALL —) CAG HOY VIAL PHIAL
VEDET JIGGER LIEPOT PICARD
TINLET YETLIN FLIVVER VEDETTE
YETLING GALLIPOT
(TOP-HEAVY —) CRANK
(TURKISH —) MAHONE
(WHALING —) WHALER SPOUTER
(WICKER —) POT
(WINE —) AMA AMULA TINAGE
(WOODEN —) COG KIT BOSS BAKIE
KIVER BICKER CAPPIE COOTIE
DUDDIE FIRKIN STOUND
(PL.) CRAFT WAFTAGE
(PREF.) ANGI(O) ARTERI VAS(I)(O)
VASCUL(I)(O)
(HOLLOW —) CYT(O)
(SUFF.) ANGE ANGIUM
VEST GARB GOWN ROBE GILET
ACCRUE ATTACH FECKET INVEST
JACKET JELICK LINDER WESKIT
ENFEOFF CLOTHING
(— IN) STATE
VESTA WAX
(FATHER OF —) SATURN
(MOTHER OF —) RHEA
(SISTER OF —) JUNO CERES
VESTED BESTEAD DONATIVE
VESTIBULE HALL ENTRY FOYER
PORCH ATRIUM EXEDRA EPINAOS
NARTHEX PASSAGE PRONAOS
TAMNOUR ANTEROOM VESTIARY
VESTIGE TAG DREG MARK RACK

SIGN PRINT RELIC SPARK TRACE
TRACK TRACT UMBRA SHADOW
MENTION LEFTOVER RUDIMENT
TINCTURE
VESTIGIAL REDUCED OBSOLETE
VESTING ADITIO
VESTITURE TIRE RAIMENT
TUNICLE
VESTMENT ALB CAP ALBE COPE
PALL VEST AMICE COTTA EPHOD
FANON RABAT RASON STOLE
RHASON ROCHET SACCOS
SAKKOS VAKASS MANIPLE
ORARION PALLIUM PILLION
PLUVIAL TUNICLE VESTURE
CHASUBLE DALMATIC PHRYGIUM
RATIONAL SCAPULAR SURPLICE
VESTIARY
(PL.) GARB GEAR DRESS
CLOTHING
VESTRY SACRISTY VESTIARY
VESTURE COAT
VESUVIANITE EGERAN CYPRINE
IDOCRASE VESUVIAN XANTHITE
VETCH DAL ERS AKRA LUCK TARE
TINE ERVIL FITCH AXSEED
FECCHE THETCH ARVEJON
TINETARE TINEWEED
VETERAN VET CHAUVIN EMERITUS
HARDENED SEASONED
VETERINARIAN VET LEECH
FARRIER
VETERINARY VET FARRIERY
VETIVER BEN KHUS CUSCUS
KUSKUS KHASKHAS KHUSKHUS
VETO NIX KILL DISALLOW
NEGATIVE
VEUGLAIRE FOWLER
VEX FRY NOY TEW CARK CHAW
FASH FAZE FRET FYKE GALL HALE
HUMP ITCH RILE ROIL RUCK TEEN
TOUT YOKE ANGER ANNOY
CHAFE FRUMP GRAME GRILL
GRIND GRIPE HARRY SCALD SPITE
STURT TARRY TEASE WORRY
WRACK WRATH YEARN BOTHER
BURDEN CORSIE COTTER CUMBER
GRIEVE GRUDGE HARASS
HARROW INFEST NETTLE OFFEND
PLAGUE POTHER RUFFLE THREAT
WORRIT AFFLICT BEDEVIL
CHAGRIN DESPITE PERPLEX
PROVOKE TORMENT ACERBATE
BEPESTER BULLYRAG EXERCISE
IRRITATE MACERATE
VEXATION VEX CHAW FASH MOIL
TEEN TRAY CHAFE CROSS ERROR
GRIEF HARRY PIQUE SPITE STEAM
THORN WORRY BOTHER REPINE
CHAGRIN DISGUST NOISANCE
SORENESS
VEXATIOUS MEAN SORE TEEN
NASTY PESKY ACHING FIERCE
SHREWD THORNY VEXFUL
IRKSOME PEEVISH PRICKLY
TARSOME ANNOYING CUMBROUS
FRAMPOLD PHRAMPEL
UNTOWARD VEXATORY
WEARIFUL PESTILENT
VEXATIOUSLY PLAGUY
VEXED DIK MAD RILY SORE TEEN
WAXY WILD WRAW ANGRY
NARKY RAGGY ROILY MIFFED

MUFFED SHIRTY SNUFFY
FRABOUS GRIEVED IRKSOME
OUTDONE
(EASILY —) CROSS
VEXILLUM WEB VEXIL BANNER
STANDARD
VEXING CHRONIC TECHING
WAYWARD ANNOYING NETTLING
TEACHING
V-GOUGE VEINER
VIABLE VITAL HEALTHY
VIAL AMPUL CRUET PHIAL AMPULE
CASTER CASTOR AMPOULE
VIANDS CATE DIET FOOD CHEER
VIANDRY VICTUALS
VIBRANT RINGY BRAWLING
RESONANT SONOROUS VIGOROUS
VIBRATE JAR WAG BEAT CAST
DIRL PLAY ROCK TIRL WHIR
PULSE QUAKE SWING THIRL
THROB TRILL WAVER DINDLE
HOTTER JUDDER QUAVER QUIVER
SHIMMY SHIVER THRILL TINGLE
WARBLE CHATTER FLUTTER
LIBRATE STAGGER TREMBLE
TWIDDLE EVIBRATE FLICHTER
RESONATE UNDULATE
(— ABNORMALLY) SHIMMY
VIBRATING PLANGENT
(— OF AIRPLANE) BUFFET
VIBRATION BUZZ DIRL TIRL
SWING TRILL DINDLE JUDDER
QUAVER QUIVER THRILL TREMOR
DANCING FLUTTER TEMBLOR
DIADROME FREMITUS VIBRANCY
OSCILLATION
(— OF SAW) CUPPING
(RATTLING —) JAR
VIBRATIONS KARMA
VIBRATO TRILL WHINE TREMOLO
VIBRATOR TREMBLER
VIBRISSA FEELER SMELLER
VIBURNUM MAE MAY SNOWBALL
ARROWWOOD SHEEPBERRY
VICAR PROXY DEPUTY STALLAR
ALTARIST STALLARY
**VICAR OF WAKEFIELD (AUTHOR
OF —)** GOLDSMITH
(CHARACTER IN —) MOSES GEORGE
OLIVIA SOPHIA WILMOT DEBORAH
ARABELLA BURCHELL PRIMROSE
THORNHILL
VICE SIN EVIL CRIME FAULT TAINT
ULCER DEFECT DEPUTY BUGGERY
OFFENSE INIQUITY
VICE-GERENT EPHOR
VICE-PRESIDENT CROUPIER
(— OF SANHEDRIN) ABBETDIN
VICEREGENT VICAR SUBPRIOR
VICEROY EARL VALI NABOB
NAWAB NAZIM SUBAH EXARCH
KEHAYA PROREX PROVES SATRAP
WARDEN PROVOST TSUNGTU
SUBAHDAR
VICIA FABA
VICINITY HERE SHADOW
ENVIRONS
(— OF MINE SHAFT) COLLAR
(NEAR —) SUBURBS
VICIOUS BAD ILL EVIL LAZY LEWD
MEAN UGLY VILE ROWDY TOUGH
SINFUL STRONG VITIAL WICKED
CORRUPT IMMORAL NAUGHTY

SKAITHY DEPRAVED DEVILISH
FRATCHED INFAMOUS THEWLESS
MONSTROUS NEFARIOUS
VICIOUSNESS VICE
VICISSITUDE CHANGE MUTATION
(— OF FORTUNE) WEATHER
VICTIM BUTT DUPE GOAT GULL
PREY PATHIC QUARRY CASUALTY
(— FOR SHARPERS) JAY
(INTENDED —) CHUMP
(SACRIFICIAL —) HOST MERIAH
(UNFORTUNATE —) BASTARD
VICTIMIZATION RIDE
VICTIMIZE HOAX BUNCO BUNKO
COZEN
VICTOR COCK CAPTOR MASTER
WINNER BANGSTER
VICTORFISH AKU
VICTORIA (FATHER OF —) PALLAS
(MOTHER OF —) STYX
VICTORIA LAKE PUCE
VICTORIAN GENTEEL
VICTORIOUS VICTOR WINNING
VICTORY WIN PALM PRICE BETTER
SUBDUE VICTOR MASTERY
SACKING TRIUMPH WINNING
CONQUEST DECISION WALKOVER
(AUTHOR OF —) CONRAD
(CHARACTER IN —) AXEL LENA
WANG HEYST JONES PEDRO
MARTIN RICARDO DAVIDSON
MORRISON SCHOMBERG
(EASY —) BREEZE
(OVERWHELMING —) SWEEP
VICTUAL BIT VITE VITTLE
(BROKEN —S) SCRAN
(PL.) KAI BITE CHOW FOOD GRUB
PROG SAND VIVERS PROVENDER
PROVISIONS
VICTUALER PURVEYOR
VIDELICET NAMELY SCILICET
VIE ENVY JOSTLE STRIVE COMPARE
COMPETE CONTEND CONTEST
EMULATE
**VIETNAM (SEE NORTH VIETNAM
AND SOUTH VIETNAM)**
VIETNAMESE ANNAMESE
VIEW EYE KEN FACE GLOM MAKE
VISE ADVEW AVIEW BLUSH
CATCH MOUTH SCAPE SCENE
SIGHT VISTA VIZZY ADVICE
ADVISE ASPECT DEVICE GLANCE
REGARD SURVEY ALOGISM
CONCEIT FEELING GLIMPSE
KENNING LOOKOUT OFFLOOK
OPINION RESPECT SCENERY
SURVIEW THOUGHT AIRSCAPE
CONSPECT EYESIGHT OFFSCAPE
PROSPECT SEASCAPE SENTENCE
SENTIMENT
(— ATTENTIVELY) GAZE
(— CLOSELY) INSPECT
(— FROM AFAR) DESCRY
(— FROM ANGLE) SLANT
(— OF MAN) DUALISM
(— WITH SURPRISE) ADMIRE
(BRIEF —) SNAPSHOT
(COMPREHENSIVE —) PANORAMA
(GENERAL —) LANDSKIP
(OPEN —) LIGHT
(PHYSICAL —) INSIGHT
(SATISFYING —) EYEFUL
(SUFF.) ORAMA SCOPE SCOPIC

SCOPUS SCOPY

VIEWING
(SUFF.) SCOPE SCOPIC SCOPUS
SCOPY

VIEWPOINT SIGHT LAXISM

VIGIL WAKE WATCH WAKING
AGRYPNIA

VIGILANCE WATCH JEALOUSY

VIGILANT AGOG WARE WARY
ALERT AWAKE AWARE CHARY
SHARP JEALOUS LIDLESS
WAKEFUL CAUTIOUS WATCHFUL

VIGOR GO PEP SAP VIM VIR VIS
BIRR DASH EDGE ELAN LUST PITH
SEVE SNAP SOUL TUCK ARDOR
DRIVE FLUSH FORCE GREEN
JUICE NERVE OOMPH POWER
PUNCH VERVE ENERGY ESPRIT
FOISON GINGER SPRAWL SPRING
STARCH STINGO VIGOUR VIRTUS
FREEDOM SMEDDUM STAMINA
STHENIA FLOURISH STRENGTH
TONICITY VITALITY
(FULL OF —) LIFESOME
(MENTAL —) DOCITY SPIRIT
(RENEWED —) REST

VIGOROUS YEP ABLE CANT FRIM
HALE LIVE RUDE SPRY YEPE
ALIVE CRANK EAGER FRACK
FRANK HEFTY JUICY LUSTY NIPPY
PEPPY PITHY PROUD SASSY SOLID
STARK STIFF STOUT TOUGH VIVID
FLORID GOLDEN HEARTY LIVELY
MANFUL POTENT PRETTY RAUCLE
ROBUST RUGGED SINEWY
SQUARE STRONG STURDY
BUCKISH CHIPPER CORDIAL
DRASTIC FECKFUL FURIOUS
HEALTHY LUSTFUL NERVOSE
NERVOUS VALIANT VIBRANT
ZEALOUS ATHLETIC BOUNCING
CHOPPING FORCEFUL MUSCULAR
SLAMBANG SLASHING STUBBORN
VEHEMENT VIGOROSO YOUTHFUL
TRENCHANT
(NOT —) GENTEEL

VIGOROUSLY DOWN FELL HARD
VERN CRANK SNELL TIGHT VERNE
HARDLY SNELLY FRESHLY
SMARTLY STOUTLY WIGHTLY
HEARTILY

VIGOROUSNESS ENERGY
FREEDOM

VIKING DANE WIKING NORSEMAN

VIKRAMADITYA BIKRAM

VILE BAD BASE CLAM FOUL RANK
CHEAP MUCKY POCKY RUSTY
SLIMY WILLE ABJECT CRUSTY
DRAFTY DRASTY FILTHY LECHER
NOUGHT PALTRY SORDID TURPID
UNKIND BEASTLY BENEATH
CAITIFF CORRUPT DEBASED
HATEFUL IGNOBLE SCABBED
SLAVISH VICIOUS BASEBORN
DEPRAVED UNKINDLY

VILENESS FEDITY VILITY
TURPITUDE

VILIFICATION REPROACH

VILIFY ILL VILE ABUSE LIBEL STAIN
DEFAME MALIGN REVILE SLIGHT
ASPERSE BLACKEN DEBAUCH
DETRACT SLANDER TRADUCE
REPROACH STRUMPET

VILIPEND BELITTLE

VILL HAM TOWN TOWNSHIP

VILLA ALDEA DACHA LODGE
CHALET DATCHA QUINTA
TRIANON

VILLAGE BY AUL BYE GAV HAM
KOM PAH REW BOMA BURG DORP
HOME MURA TOWN VILL WICK
ALDEA BOURG CASAL PLACE
THORP VICUS ALDEIA BARRIO
BUSTEE CASTLE GOTHAM
HAMLET HAMMON MOUZAH
PETTAH PUEBLO AMBALAM
BOROUGH CAMPODY CASERIO
CLACHAN ENDSHIP MAABARA
MISSION OUTPOST BEREWICK
BOURGADE CAMPOODY
CRANFORD TOLDERIA VILLACHE
VILLAGET VILLAKIN
(— IN WHICH BARLEY IS GROWN)
BEREWICK
(— OUTSIDE OF FORT) PETTAH
(AFRICAN —) STAD KRAAL
(ARABIAN —) DOUAR
(ARGENTINE —) TOLDERIA
(FRENCH —) BASTIDE
(IMAGINARY —) CRANFORD
(INDIAN —) CASTLE PUEBLO
CAMPODY CAMPOODY
(JAPANESE —) MURA BUSTI
BUSTEE
(JAVANESE —) DESSA
(JEWISH —) SHTETL SHTETEL
(MALAY —) CAMPONG KAMPONG
(MAORI —) KAIK KAIKA KAINGA
(MEXICAN —) EJIDO
(NEW ZEALAND FORTIFIED —) PA
PAH
(NEWFOUNDLAND —) OUTPORT
(RUSSIAN —) MIR STANITSA
STANITZA

VILLAIN IAGO LOUT SERF BADDY
BRAVO CHURL DEMON DEVIL
FAGIN FELON HEAVY KNAVE
ROGUE SCAMP SHREW BADDIE
VILIACO SCELERAT SCOUNDREL

VILLAINOUS BAD EVIL GALLUS
GALLOWS KNAVISH RAFFISH
VILEYNS FLAGRANT RASCALLY
MISCREANT

VILLAINY CRIME KNAVERY

VILLEIN SERF CHURL BORDAR
COTTER VILLAR BONDMAN
TOWNMAN VILLAIN COTARIUS

VILLI (HAVING —) ZONARY

VILLOUS SHAGGY

VIM ZIP GIMP ZING FORCE VIGOR
ENERGY GINGER SPIRIT STARCH
VINEGAR RAZZMATAZZ

VINA BEN BIN BINA

VINCENTIAN LAZARIST

VINDICATE FREE CLEAR RIGHT
SALVE WREAK ACQUIT ASSERT
AVENGE EXCUSE UPHOLD
ABSOLVE DERAIGN JUSTIFY
PROPUGN REVENGE SUSTAIN
DARRAIGN MAINTAIN

VINDICATION BEHALF APOLOGY
THEODICY SATISFACTION

VINDICATOR VINDEX ASSERTER
DEFENDER

VINDICTIVE HOSTILE PUNITIVE
SPITEFUL VENGEFUL

VINE AKA FIG HOP IVY IYO BINE
CARO GOGO ODAL SOMA TINE
AKEBI BUAZE BWAZI CAAPI
CACUR GUACO KAIWI KUDZU
LIANA MAILE PALAY PRIVY TACSO
TIMBO TRAIL TWINE WITHE
WONGA BEJUCO CISSUS COBAEA
COWAGE DERRIS DODDER
ECANDA GERKIN IPOMEA JICAMA
LABLAB PIKAKE RUNNER TURURI
TWINER ULLUCO WINDER
APRICOT BIGROOT BONESET
BRAMBLE CALAMUS CATVINE
CERIMAN CLIMBER COWHAGE
COWITCH CUPSEED EPACRID
GHERKIN IPOMOEA LAVANGA
PAREIRA PUMPKIN TRAILER
VINELET YANGTAO ATRAGENE
BINDWEED BOXTHORN CLEMATIS
COMEBACK CUCUMBER CUCURBIT
DECUMARY DOLICHOS EARDROPS
EARTHPEA EVONYMUS
GULANCHA HEARTPEA
HEMPWEED MUSCATEL
REDWITHE TINETARE TINEWEED
TRAILERY TRAILING TREEBINE
VINIFERA WINETREE WISTARIA
WISTERIA OLOLIUQUI
(PREF.) AMPEL(O) VITI

VINEGAR VIM EISEL ESILL ACETUM
ALEGAR ASCILL SOURING
BEEREGAR VINAIGRE
(— AND HONEY) OXYMEL
(PREF.) ACET(O)

VINEGAR EEL EELWORM

VINEGARY ACETOSE ACETOUS

VINEGROWER VINITOR

VINEYARD CRU CLOS COTE VINER
VINERY WINEYARD

VINGT-ET-UN MACAO MACCO

VINOUS WINY

VINTAGE OLD VINT WINE CUVEE
ARCHAIC CLASSIC VENDAGE
OUTMODED

VIOL GUE GIGA LIRA TURR GIGUE
GUDOK TARAU VOYAL VOYOL
CHELYS FIDDLE VIELLE VIOLET
MINIKIN QUINTON SARINDA
SULTANA VIHUELA VIOLONE
BARBITON BASSETTE SERINGHI
VIOLETTE

VIOLA ALTO QUINT TENOR TENORE
VIOLET
(BROTHER OF —) SEBASTIAN
(HUSBAND OF —) ORSINO

VIOLA BASTARDA BARITONE
BARYTONE

VIOLA DA BRACCIO QUINT

VIOLA DA GAMBA GAMBA

VIOLA D'AMORE VIOLET

VIOLATE ERR SIN FLAW ABUSE
BREAK CRACK FORCE FRACT
HARRY LOOSE VIOLE WRONG
BREACH BROACH DEFILE INVADE
OFFEND RAVISH DEBAUCH
DISOBEY FALSIFY INFRACT
OUTRAGE POLLUTE PROFANE
VITIATE DEFLOWER DISHONOR
FORSWEAR FRACTURE INFRINGE
MISTREAT STUPRATE SURPRISE
TEMERATE TRESPASS VIOLENCE

VIOLATED FRACTED INFRACT

VIOLATION SIN DEBT ABUSE
CRIME ERROR FAULT SALLY
BREACH INJURY MISCONDUCT
(HOCKEY —) STICKS
(TRIVIAL —) MOPERY

VIOLATOR WRONGER

VIOLENCE FURY NEED RAGE RUFF
BRUNT FORCE RIGOR STORM
BENSIL ESTURE HUBRIS RANDOM
RAPINE STOUSH STRESS BENSAIL
BENSALL OUTRAGE FEROCITY
SEVERITY SORENESS
ROUGHHOUSE
(LETHAL —) DEATH

VIOLENT BIG HOT TEZ DERF HARD
HIGH MAIN RANK RUDE WILD
WOOD ACUTE FIERY HEADY
HEAVY HEFTY RABID SHARP
SMART STARK STERN STIFF
STOOR STOUR STOUT WROTH
BROTHE FIERCE HEARTY MANIAC
MIGHTY SAVAGE SEVERE STORMY
STRONG STURDY SUDDEN
CRIMSON DRASTIC FURIOUS
HOTSPUR RAMMISH RAMPANT
RAPEFUL RUFFIAN TEARING
VIOLOUS WILSOME CHURLISH
DIABOLIC FLAGRANT FORCEFUL
IMPOTENT MANIACAL PERACUTE
RIGOROUS SEETHING SLAMBANG
STALWART VEHEMENT

VIOLENTLY HARD AMAIN HOTLY
HARDLY SORELY HOPPING
SOUNDLY

VIOLET CANON GRAPE MAUVE
VIOLA BLAVER CANYON DAHLIA
DAMSON EVEQUE JOHNNY
HOOKERS LOBELIA OPHELIA
PRELATE PRIMULA PUREAYN
CLEMATIS DAMEWORT FINELEAF
IANTHINE ROOSTERS WISTERIA
(PREF.) IO

VIOLIN GUE KIT ALTO GIGA AMATI
CROWD CRWTH GEIGE GIGUE
REBAB REBEC STRAD TARAU
VIOLA CATGUT CHORUS CROUTH
FIDDLE FITHEL REBECK TAILLE
VIOLON CATLING CHROTTA
CREMONA THEYAOU VIOLAND
VIOLINO GUARNERI KEMANCHA
VIOLOTTA
(PART OF —) NUT PEG TOP FROG
HEAD HEEL HOLE NECK BELLY
TABLE BRIDGE BUTTON PEGBOX
SCROLL STRING PURFLING
SOUNDBOARD FINGERBOARD

VIPER ASP HABU ADDER ASPIC
ATHER URUTU WYVER ASPIDE
DABOIA DABOYA JESSUR KATUKA
KUPPER HAGWORM MAMUSHI
VIPERID AMMODYTE CERASTES
JARARACA VIPERINE

VIRAGO RANDY AMAZON BELDAM
CALLET BELDAME TRIMMER
VIRAGIN RIXATRIX

VIREO REDEYE GRASSET TEACHER
GREENLET PREACHER

VIRGATE YOKE VERGE YARDLAND
(HALF —) MANTAL

VIRGILIAN MARONIAN

VIRGIN NEW LIVE MAID PURE
FRESH CHASTE MAIDEN VESTAL
INITIAL PUCELLE DOROTHEA
PARAMOUR

(— OF PARADISE) HURI HOURI
(PREF.) PARTHEN(O)
VIRGINAL CHERRY INTACT
SYMPHONY TRIANGLE

VIRGINIA
CAPITAL: RICHMOND
COLLEGE: AVERETT HOLLINS
MADISON RADFORD
LONGWOOD
COUNTY: LEE BATH PAGE WISE
BLAND CRAIG FLOYD SMYTH
SURRY WYTHE AMELIA LOUISA
ACCOMAC HENRICO PATRICK
PULASKI ROANOKE CULPEPER
FLUVANNA TAZEWELL
INDIAN: SAPONI TUTELO
MONACAN MANAHOAC
MEHERRIN NOTTAWAY
POWHATAN
LAKE: KERR SMITH
MOUNTAIN: CEDAR ELLIOT
ROGERS BALDKNOB
MOUNTAIN RANGE: CLINCH
ALLEGHENY BLUERIDGE
NICKNAME: OLDDOMINION
MOTHEROFSTATES
MOTHEROFPRESIDENTS
PRESIDENT: TYLER MONROE
TAYLOR WILSON MADISON
HARRISON JEFFERSON
WASHINGTON
RIVER: DAN JAMES POTOMAC
RAPIDAN
STATE BIRD: CARDINAL
STATE FLOWER: DOGWOOD
STATE TREE: DOGWOOD
TOWN: GALAX LURAY SALEM
MARION BEDFORD BRISTOL
EMPORIA NORFOLK PULASKI
ROANOKE DANVILLE HOPEWELL
MANASSAS STAUNTON
TAZEWELL

VIRGINIA COWSLIP LUNGWORT
VIRGINIA CREEPER CREEPER
WOODBIND WOODBINE
VIRGINIA KNOTWEED JUMPSEED
VIRGINIAN BEAGLE COOHEE
CAVALIER TUCKAHOE
(AUTHOR OF —) WISTER
(CHARACTER IN —) WOOD HENRY
MOLLY STEVE SHORTY TRAMPAS
VIRGINIANS (AUTHOR OF —)
THACKERAY
(CHARACTER IN —) THEO WILL
FANNY HARRY HETTY MARIA
MILES ESMOND GEORGE RACHEL
LAMBERT MOUNTAIN BERNSTEIN
CASTLEWOOD WARRINGTON
WASHINGTON
VIRGINIA SNAKEROOT SANGREL
SNAGREL
VIRGINIA STICKSEED SOLDIERS
VIRGINIA WATERLEAF SHAWNY
VIRGINIA WILLOW ITEA
VIRGINITY HONOR CHASTITY
PUCELAGE
VIRGIN MARY DESPOINA
THEOTOCOS
VIRGIN'S-BOWER LOVE
HONESTY CLEMATIS
MOONWORT

VIRGIN SOIL (AUTHOR OF —)
TURGENEV
(CHARACTER IN —) KOLYA
PAHKLIN SOLOMIN MARIANNA
MASHURIN SIPYAGIN MARKELOFF
VALENTINA NEZHDANOFF
OSTRODUMOFF
VIRGULE SLANT VIRGULA
DIAGONAL
VIRIDIAN EMERAUDE
VIRILE MALE MACHO MANLY
(AGGRESSIVELY —) MACHO
VIRILITY LUST GREEN MANHEAD
MANHOOD
VIRTUAL IMPLICIT PRACTICAL
VIRTUALLY BUT NEARLY MORALLY
VIRTUE JEN HSIN THEW ARETE
FAITH GRACE POWER VALOR
VERTU WORTH BOUNTY DHARMA
FOISON CHARISM CHARITY
JUSTICE PROBITY QUALITY
CHARISMA CHASTITY EFFICACY
GOODNESS MORALITY PARAMITA
PROPERTY
(CONFUCIAN —) LI
(PL.) CIVISM
(PREF.) ARETO
VIRTUOSO EXPERT SAVANT
ESTHETE LAPIDARY
VIRTUOUS GOOD PURE BRAVE
CIVIL MORAL PIOUS CHASTE
HONEST MODEST GODDARD
SAINTED SINCERE UPRIGHT
VIRTUAL STRAIGHT
VIRULENCE VIRUS
VIRULENT RANK ACRID RABID
DEADLY MALIGN VIROSE
NOXIOUS VIRIFIC WASPISH
VENOMOUS
(LESS THAN —) MITIS
VIRUS VENOM POISON PATHOGEN
SPECIFIC
VIS PEIKTHA
VISAGE FACE PHIZ CHEER IMAGE
VISOR ASPECT FASHION
VISCERA GUTS HASLET INSIDE
UMBLES GARBAGE GIBLETS
HASSLET INMEATS INNARDS
INSIDES NUMBLES ENTRAILS
HARIGALS
(PREF.) SPLANCHNO
VISCERAL GUT
VISCID SLAB WAXY GOOEY GLAIRY
STICKY LENTOUS STRINGY
VISCOUS MOTHERED
VISCIDITY LENTOR
VISCOSITY BODY ROPINESS
(— UNIT) POISE
VISCOUS LIMY ROPY SIZY SLAB
GOBBY GUMMY MUCIC ROPEY
SLIMY STIFF TARRY SIRUPY
SLABBY SMEARY SNOTTY STICKY
THONGY VISCID LENTOUS
SQUISHY VISCOSE MUCULENT
VISE GEE CHAP JACK SHOP VICE
CHEEK CLAMP CRAMP WINCH
(PART OF —) JAW BASE BOLT
ANVIL SCREW SLIDE HANDLE
SWIVEL
VISHNU RAMA VASU KALKI
KRISHNA BALARAMA BHAGAVAT
(AVATAR OF —) KALKI KURMA
BUDDHA MATSYA VAMANA

VARAHA KRISHNA NARASINHA
PARASHURAMA RAMACHANDRA
(BREAST JEWEL OF —) KAUSTUBHA
(BREASTMARK OF —) SHRIVATSA
(VEHICLE OF —) GARUDA
(WIFE OF —) SHRI LAKSHMI
(WRIST JEWEL OF —) SYAMANTAKA
VISIBLE OUT FAIR SEEN CLEAR
GROSS EXTANT SIGHTY EVIDENT
GLARING OBVIOUS OPTICAL
SIGHTLY APPARENT DIOPTRIC
EXPLICIT EXTERNAL MANIFEST
PROSPECT
(BARELY —) DARK
(SCARCELY —) DIM
(PREF.) DELO PHANER(O) PHANTA
PHANTASMO PHANTO
VISION EYE RAY DREAM FANCY
SIGHT FANTAD SEEING SWEVEN
AISLING SHOWING SPECTER
SPECTRE EYESIGHT PHOTOPIA
PROSPECT
(— IN DIM LIGHT) SCOTOPIA
(BLURRED —) SWIMMING
(DEFECTIVE —) ANOPIA
(DOUBLE —) DIPLOPIA
(IMAGINARY —) SHADOW
(IMPERFECT —) CALIGO DARKNESS
(MULTIPLE —) POLYOPIA
(PREF.) OPTI(CO) OPTO VISUO
(RANGE OF —) METROPIA
(SUFF.) OPSIA OPSIS OPSY OPTIC
OPTICON
(— DEVIATION) TROPIA
VISIONARY FFY AFRY AIRY WILD
BIGOT IDEAL VIEWY ASTRAL
INSANE SHANDY UNREAL
DREAMER FANTAST LAPUTAN
UTOPIAN ACADEMIC DELUSIVE
FANCIFUL FINESPUN IDEALIST
NOTIONAL PHANTAST QUIXOTIC
ROMANTIC UTOPIAST VISIONER
VISIT DO GAM SEE VIS CALL CHAT
STAY APPLY HAUNT TRYST VIZZY
COSHER RESORT RETURN CEILIDH
CEILIDHE FREQUENT INVASION
(— BETWEEN WHALERS) GAM
(— PERSISTENTLY) INFEST
(— PROFESSIONALLY) ATTEND
(— RELATIVES) COUSIN
(— WRETCHED NEIGHBORHOODS)
SLUM
(CEREMONIAL —) SELAMLIK
VISITATION SENE VISIT SENDING
VISITING ACTIVE SOCIAL
VISITOR GUEST LAKER CALLER
VISITANT
(MEALTIME —) SCAMBLER
(PL.) COMPANY
VISOR BILL SIGHT UMBER UMBRE
VIZOR BEAVER MESAIL UMBRIL
VIZARD EYESHADE UMBRIERE
VISTA VIEW SCENE OUTLOOK
PERSPECTIVE
VISUAL OPTIC OCULAR SCOPIC
VISORY VISIBLE
VISUALIZE SEE FANCY IDEATE
SYMBOL IMAGINE PICTURE
CONCEIVE ENVISAGE
VITAL KEY LIVE BASIC CHIEF FRESH
SAPPY LIVELY MOVING VIABLE
ZOETIC ANIMATE CAPITAL
CORDIAL EXIGENT

NEEDFUL ESSENTIAL
VITALITY SAP VIM LIFE COLOR
GUSTO JUICE OOMPH PULSE
PUNCH BIOSIS BREATH ENERGY
FOISON HEALTH MARROW
PAZAZZ PIZAZZ STARCH PIZZAZZ
VIVENCY STRENGTH
(DEFICIENT —) ASTHENIA
(LACKING —) STUFFY TURNIPY
VITALIZE ACTIVATE ENERGIZE
VITAMIN BIOTIN CITRIN NIACIN
ADERMIN ANEURIN CHOLINE
THIAMIN TORULIN ADVITANT
INOSITOL NUTRAMIN ORYZANIN
VITAMINE
VITAMIN A RETINOL
VITIATE BEAT BLEND SPOIL TAINT
CANCEL DEBASE POISON
CORRUPT DEBAUCH DEPRAVE
VITIATED PICAL CORRUPT
(PREF.) CAC(O) CACH
(SUFF.) CACE
VITICULTURIST VIGNERON
VITREOUS GLASSY GLAIZIE
VITREAN VITROUS
VITRIFY GLAZE
VITRIOL BLUEJACK COPPERAS
(PL.) SORY
VITRIOLIC SHARP BITING BITTER
CAUSTIC MORDANT SCATHING
VITUPERATE RAIL ABUSE CURSE
SCOLD SLANG BERATE REVILE
VITUPERATION ABUSE VITUPER
VITUPERATIVE ABUSIVE REVILING
SHAMEFUL
VIVACE VIVO LEBHAFT
VIVACIOUS GAY AIRY PERT BRISK
CRISP MERRY SUNNY ACTIVE
BRIGHT LIVELY LIVING SPARKY
VIVACE ANIMATE JOCULAR
ANIMATED SPIRITED SPORTIVE
VIVACITY BRIO FIRE LIFE ZEAL
ARDOR VERVE VIGOR ESPRIT
GAIETY GAYETY SPIRIT SPRAWL
SPARKLE
VIVARIUM STEW VIVARY
STEWPOND
VIVAT HOCH
VIVERRINE CIVET GENET FOUSSA
MUSANG LINSANG FALANAKA
MONGOOSE SURICATE
VIVIANO (BROTHER OF —) MALAGIGI
ALDIGIERI
(SISTER OF —) BRADAMANTE
VIVID DEEP HARD KEEN LIVE RICH
VIVE BRISK FRESH GREEN LURID
QUICK RUDDY SHARP GARISH
LIVELY LIVING STRONG VISUAL
EIDETIC FLAMING FREAKED
GLARING GLOWING GRAPHIC
INTENSE PEPPERY VIOLENT
COLORFUL DISTINCT DRAMATIC
SLASHING STRIKING VIGOROUS
PICTURESQUE
VIVIDNESS COLOR EMPHASIS
VIVIFY LIFE FOMENT ANIMATE
QUICKEN SPARKLE
VIVIPARUS PALUDINA
VIXEN BARD FURY RANDY SCOLD
SHREW VIRAGO TAGSTER
TRIMMER
VIZIER WAZIR ATABEG ATABEK
VISIER

VLACH WALLACH
V-MAIL AIRGRAPH
VOCABULARY CANT LEXIS SLANG
JARGON DICTION LEXICON
POCHISMO WORDBOOK
(FAULTY —) CACOLOGY
(UNDERWORLD —) ARGOT
(PREF.) LEXICO
VOCAL GLIB ORAL VOWEL FLUENT
TONGUED VOCULAR ELOQUENT
VOCALIST BOPPER SINGER
BOPPIST BOPSTER SONGSTER
VOCALLER
VOCATION CALL HOBBY METIER
CALLING SCIENCE
VOCATIONAL BANAUSIC
VOCIFERATION CLAMOR OUTCRY
VOCIFEROUS LOUD NOISY
BAWLING BLATANT BRAWLING
STRIDENT
VODKA SAMOGON SAMOGONKA
VOGUE CUT FAD TON CHIC MODE
RAGE TURN STYLE CUSTOM
FASHION RECLAME PRACTICE
VOGUL MANSI
VOICE SAY VOX EMIT GIVE HARP
PIPE TONE TURN WISH FROTH
LEDEN RAISE RUMOR SOUND
UTTER ACTIVE CHOICE STEVEN
TAISCH THROAT TONGUE
EXPRESS OPINION SONORIZE
DIATHESIS
(— PRAISE) SLAVER
(ARTIFICIAL —) FALSETTO
(FIFTH —) QUINTUS
(HOARSE —) FOGHORN
(LOWEST —) BASS BASSO
(MIDDLE —) MOTETUS
(PRINCIPAL —) CANTUS
(PUBLIC —) CRY
(SINGING —) ALTO BASS TENOR
BREAST SOPRANO BARITONE
FALSETTO
(TENOR —) TAILLE
(UPPER —) DESCANT DISCANT
(PREF.) PHON(O) PHTHONGO VOCI
(LOUD —) STENTORO
(SUFF.) PHON(E)(IA)(Y)
VOICED SOFT WEAK TONIC MEDIAL
SONANT VIBRANT PHTHONGAL
VOICELESS MUM DUMB HARD
MUTE SURD SHARP ATONIC
FLATED SILENT ANAUDIA
APHONIC SPIRATE APHONOUS
BREATHED NOTELESS
VOID NO BAD FREE KORE LEAR
LEER MUTE NULL PASS TOOM
ABYSS AVOID BLANK EGEST
EJECT EMPTY INEPT LAPSE
PURGE SLICE SPACE WASTE
DEVOID HOLLOW VACANT
VACUUM CONCAVE INVALID
VACANCY VACUITY EVACUATE

INDIGENT NONBEING
(— OF FEELING) BLATE
(— OF SENSE) INANE
(— OF SUBSTANCE) JEJUNE
VOIDED FALSE CLECHE CLECHY
CLECHEE
VOILE NINON ETAMINE
VOLATILE LIGHT FIGENT LIVELY
VOLAGE BUOYANT DARTING
ELASTIC FLIGHTY FLYAWAY
GASEOUS FUGITIVE SKITTISH
VAPOROSE VAPOROUS
FUGACIOUS
(PREF.) PTENO
VOLATILITY LEVITY
VOLCANO APO DOME ETNA ASKJA
PELEE SHASTA VULCAN FURNACE
VULCANO FUMAROLE KRAKATOA
SPITFIRE VESUVIUS
(MUD —) SALSE SALINELLE
VOLE CRABER CRICETID
CAMPAGNOL
VOLITATION FLIGHT VOLATION
VOLITION WILL CHOICE INTENT
VOLENCY VELLEITY
VOLLEY TIRE CROWD DRIFT VOLEE
FLIGHT BARRAGE PLATOON
BLIZZARD
VOLPLANE GLIDE
VOLPONE (AUTHOR OF —) JONSON
(CHARACTER IN —) CELIA MOSCA
BONARIO CORVINO VOLPONE
VOLTORE POLITICK CORBACCIO
PEREGRINE
VOLSUNG WAELS
VOLT VOLTA REPOLON
(— AMPERE UNIT) VAR
VOLTAGE KICKBACK
VOLTAIC GUR GALVANIC
VOLTE-FACE BACKFLIP
VOLUBILITY FLUENCY
VOLUBLE GLIB WORDY FLUENT
VOLUME MO PEN BAND BOOK
BULK CODE SIZE TOME CODEX
SPACE CUBAGE CONTENT
DIURNAL MENAION VOLUMEN
CAPACITY CUBATURE SOLIDITY
STRENGTH
(— OF SOUND) STRESS
(— OF WORT) LENGTH
(PATTERN —) DUMMY
VOLUMINOUS FULL AMPLE BULKY
LARGE BOUFFANT
VOLUMNIA (SON OF —)
CORIOLANUS
VOLUNTARILY WILLES WILLICHE
VOLUNTARY FREE WILLY SORTIE
WILFUL PRELUDE SORTITA
WILLFUL WILLING ELECTIVE
FREEWILL HONORARY OPTIONAL
POSTLUDE UNFORCED
VOLUNTEER OFFER ENLIST
PROFFER FENCIBLE STRANGER

(— STATE) TENNESSEE
VOLUPTUARY SYBARITE
VOLUPTUOUS ADIN LUXIVE
LYDIAN SULTRY WANTON
SENSUAL DELICATE LUSCIOUS
SENSUOUS
VOLUPTUOUSNESS DELICE
LUXURY
VOLUTE TURN HELIX SCROLL
VOLUTA CILLERY VOLUTION
VOLUTION COIL TWIST WHORL
VERTICIL
VOLVA CUP WRAPPER
VOMIT CAT PUT BALK BARF BOCK
BOKE CACK CAST PICK PUKE SICK
SPEW SPUE VOME WOOM BRAKE
EVOME HEAVE REACH RETCH
SHOOT POSSET REJECT VOMITO
CASCADE CASTING REGORGE
DISGORGE PARBREAK SICKNESS
VOMITING
VOMITING BOKE EMESIS PYEMESIS
(PREF.) EMET(O)
VOMITUS SPEW SPUE
VOODOO HEX OBI CHARM OBEAH
HOODOO SORCERER
(— DESIGN) VERVER
(— PRIEST) BOCOR BOKOR
(— SPELL) MOJO
VOODOOISM VODUN WANGA
VOPHSI (SON OF —) NAHBI
VORACIOUS GORB GREEDY
BULIMIC ESURINE GLUTTON
THROATY EDACIOUS ESURIENT
RAVENING RAVENOUS
VORACITY BULIMIA EDACITY
VORTEX APEX EDDY GYRE SWIRL
WHIRL
VOTARESS NUN
VOTARY PALMER ZEALOT
DEVOTEE SECTARY ADHERENT
DEVOTARY FOLLOWER
VOTE AYE CON NAY PRO ELECT
FAGOT GRACE VOICE BALLOT
DIVIDE FAGGOT TONGUE
APPROVE PLUMPER SUFFRAGE
(— AGAINST) NAY KNIFE NEGATIVE
(— APPROVAL) CONFIRM
(— FOR) AY AYE PRO SUPPORT
(— OF ASSENT) PLACET
VOTER BOLTER POLLER CHOOSER
ELECTOR FLOATER ASSENTOR
VOTIVE VOWED
VOTYAK UDMURT
VOUCH ABLE ASSURE ATTEST
AVOUCH ENDORSE ACCREDIT
VOUCHER CHIT CHALAN COUPON
POLICY TICKET WARRANT
VOUCHSAFE GIVE SEND DEIGN
GRANT VOUCH BETEEM
PLEASE WITSAFE
VOUSSOIR QUOIN WEDGE
KEYSTONE SPRINGER

VOW LAY VUM AVOW OATH SNUM
VOTE SWEAR VOUCH BEHEST
PLEDGE BEHIGHT PROMISE
PROTEST
(PREF.) EUCHO
VOWEL SHWA WIDE GLIDE SCHWA
VOCOID AUGMENT PALATAL
GEMINATE ORINASAL
(— POINT) SERE
(BACK —) VELAR
(CHANGE OF —) UMLAUT
(GROUP OF 2 —S) BROAD DIGRAM
DIGRAPH
(PREFIXED —) AUGMENT
(SHORT —) MATRA
VOYAGE SAIL TRIP VIAGE COURSE
CRUISE FLIGHT TRAVEL CARAVAN
JOURNEY PASSAGE SAILING
STEAMER PERIPLUS SHIPPING
VOYAGING SEA NAVIGANT
VOYEUR PEEPER
VULCAN MULCIBER
VULCANITE EBONITE
VULCANIZATION BURNING
VULCANIZE BURN CURE METALIZE
VULCANIZER CEMENTER
VULGAR LOW LEWD LOUD RUDE
BANAL CHEAP FLASH GROSS
SLANG SLIMY TOUGH COARSE
COMMON PORTER RABBLE
VULGUS WOOLEN BLATANT
BOORISH GENERAL KNAVISH
LOWBRED MOBBISH OBSCENE
POPULAR PROFANE RAFFISH
SECULAR TABLOID VILLAIN
WOOLLEN BANAUSIC CHURLISH
MECHANIC PANDEMIC PLEBEIAN
PORTERLY POTHOUSE SOUTERLY
VULGARIAN CAD SLOB TIGER
KEELIE RAFFISH
VULGARITY RAUNCH SHODDY
FOULNESS HARLOTRY
VULGARIZE PLEBIFY PROFANE
VULGARIZED DEGRADED
VULGARLY CHEAPLY
VULNERABILITY GAP EXPOSURE
VULNERABLE NAKED LIABLE
EXPOSED PREGNABLE
VULPINE SLY FOXY ALOPECOID
VULTURE AURA GEIR PAPA AREND
GRAAP GRAPE GRIPE SWIPE
URUBU CONDOR CORBIE FALCON
GRIPHE RAPTOR SNATCH TORGOS
GRIFFIN GRIFFON GRYPHON
NEKHEBT AASVOGEL DIRTBIRD
GEREAGLE NEKHEBET ZOPILOTE
GALLINAZO
VULVA DOCK PUDENDUM
(PREF.) EPISIO
VUM SNUM

W

W WAW WHISKEY WILLIAM
WA VU KAWA LAWA
WABBLE COCKLE COGGLE HOBBLE WAGGLE WARBLE WAUBLE WOBBLE
WABBLY COGGLE WAGGLY WOBBLY
WABBY LOON WHABBY
WABRON WAYBERRY
WACKY CRAZY INSANE MENTAL ERRATIC
WAD BAT BET BOB PAD COLF LINE POKE SWAB SWOB WISP WAGER PLEDGE SCOURER GRAPHITE
WADDING BOMBAST
WADDLE WAG DAIDLE HODDLE PODDLE TODDLE WALLOP WIDDLE WAUCHLE
WADDY PEG STICK COWBOY RUSTLER WHADDIE
WADE FORD WYDE SLOSH PLODGE PLOUTER PLUTTER
(— IN MUD) LAIR
WADI OUED WASH GULLY RAVINE
WADSET PAWN PLEDGE MORTGAGE
WAFER HOST ABRET OBLEY CACHET GAUFRE LAVASH MATZOH OFLETE POPADAM FLATBROD PARTICLE
WAFF WAG FLAP GUST ODOR PUFF WAVE WHIFF PALTRY FLUTTER GLIMPSE LOWBORN
WAFFENSCHMEID, DER
(CHARACTER IN —) GEORG MARIE CONRAD LIEBENAU STADINGER
(COMPOSER OF —) LORTZING
WAFFIE VAGRANT VAGABOND
WAFFLE GOFER WAFER GAUFRE BLATHER
WAFT PUFF WING WHEFT WHIFF BECKON WINNOW
WAG LUG NOD WIG WIT WOG CARD CHAP FLAG WAFF WALK DROLL JOKER ROGUE SHAKE TROLL FARCER JESTER NICKUM WADDLE WAGGLE WAGWIT WIGWAG FARCEUR HUMORIST SLYBOOTS
WAGE FEE PAY WAR HIRE LEVY FIGHT WADGE WEDGE EMPLOY ENGAGE PACKET OVERTIME
(— BATTLE) STRIKE
WAGER GO BET LAY PUT SET VIE WED GAGE HOLD PAWN TOSS WOID BOUND PRIZE RAISE REVIE SPORT STAKE STOOP WADGE DEPONE GAMBLE IMPONE LEVANT WEDFEE STOATER QUINELLA
WAGES FEE PAY UTU GAGE HIRE MEED GAGES TUNCA REWARD SALARY PENSION SERVICE

STIPEND GRATUITY LABORAGE PAYCHECK REQUITAL
WAGGISH ARCH DROLL JOKEY JOCOSE JESTING JOCULAR PARLOUS ROGUISH WAGSOME HUMOROUS SPORTIVE
WAGGLE WAG WIGGLE WOBBLE WOGGLE
WAGON CAR FLY VAN CART CHAR DRAG DRAY PLOW RACK TEAM TRAM WAIN WANE BUGGY DILLY JERKY RULLY TRUCK CAMION ROLLEY SPIDER TELEGA CAISSON CHARIOT COASTER FOURGON SHELVER TUMBREL TUMBRIL DEMOCRAT LANDSHIP RUNABOUT WHITETOP
(— WITHOUT SPRINGS) JERKY TELEGA
(BAGGAGE —) FOURGON
(COVERED —) VAN CARAVAN TARTANA LANDSHIP CONESTOGA
(LUMBER —) GILLY
(MINING —) TRAM HUTCH RULLY ROLLEY
(ROUNDUP —) HOODLUM
(RUSSIAN —) TELEGA KIBITKA
(SCREENED —) ARABA
(STATION —) MICROBUS SUBURBAN
(TEA —) SERVER
WAGONER AURIGA TREKKER WAINMAN
WAGONETTE BREAK
WAGONLOAD FODDER FOTHER
WAGONMAN FOOTMAN
WAGTAIL MOLLY OATEAR WAGGIE WASHER MOTACIL WATERIE SEEDBIRD WASHDISH WASHTAIL
WAHINE WIFE WOMAN FEMALE VAHINE FEMININE MISTRESS
WAHOO ONO PETO BASSWOOD EUONYMUS GUARAPUCU
WAIF WEFT STRAY FEEBLE PALTRY STRAFE CURRENT IGNOBLE WASTREL
WAIL CRY WOW BAWL GURL HOWL KEEN MOAN RAME YARM CROON MOURN ULULU LAMENT PLAINT YAMMER EJULATE PLANGOR ULULATE ULLAGONE
WAILING WO WOE LAMENT ULULANT
WAIN CART WAGON WEYNE CHARIOT
WAINSCOT CEIL CARDIGAN
WAINSCOTING CEILING PANELING
WAIST JOSIE BASQUE BLOUSE BODICE HALTER MIDDLE TAILLE CORSAGE PIERROT
WAISTCOAT VEST BENJY GILET FECKET JERKIN VESKIT WESKIT SINGLET CAMISOLE

WAISTER TROUNCER
WAIT BIDE HOLD KEEP LITE PARK STAY TEND WHET ABIDE ABODE DEFER HOVER LURCH TARRY WATCH ATTEND DEPEND EXPECT HARKEN LAYOUT LINGER
(— A WHILE) TAIHOA
(— FOR) KEEP ABIDE AWAIT ATTEND EXPECT
(— ON) HOP SEE SERVE INTEND LACKEY
(— TABLE) HASH SERVE
WAITER MOZO CARHOP COMMIS DRAWER FLUNKY GARCON HASHER KIDNEY SALVER TENDER THOMAS DAPIFER FLUNKEY KELLNER PANNIER PICCOLO SERVITOR KITMUDGAR
WAITING DORMANT
WAITRESS NIPPY HASHER MOUSMEE PHYLLIS
WAIVE ABEY DEFER EVADE FORGO ABANDON DECLINE FORSAKE POSTPONE RENOUNCE RELINQUISH
WAKA CANOE
WAKE WAK CROW NECK PLAY STIR ALERT REVEL ROUSE TANGI TRAIL VIGIL WATCH AROUSE AWAKEN EXCITE FEATHER
WAKEFUL ALERT WACKER RESTLESS VIGILANT WALKRIFE WATCHFUL
WAKEFULNESS VIGIL WATCH INSOMNIA
WAKE-ROBIN ARUM SARA SARAH TRILLIUM
WAKF WAQF VAKUF VACOUF
WALACHIAN RUMAN VLACH ROMANESE
WALAHEE ALAHEE
WALAPAI HUALPAI
WALDENSIAN LEONIST PATARIN VAUDOIS SABOTIER
WALE RIB BEND PICK WEAL WELT RIDGE WHELP CHOICE HARPIN STROKE
(PL.) BEND HARPINS
WALES CYMRU CAMBRIA
(PREF.) CAMBRO

WALK GO JET MOG FOOT GAIT GANG HIKE HOOF LAMP PACE PAUT REEL STEP TROD ALLEE ALLEY ARBOR LEAVE MARCH PORCH SHANK SLOPE SPACE STALK TRACE TRACK TRADE TRAMP TREAD TROOP ATTEND AVENUE BEHAVE BOUNCE BRIDGE BROGUE DANDER PASEAR SASHAY STROKE TODDLE TRAVEL TRUDGE BALTEUS BERCEAU CRAMBLE FOOTING GALLERY SHUFFLE STRETCH TRACHLE TRAIPSE TURNOUT AMBULATE ARBORWAY FLAGGING FRESCADE NAVIGATE TRAVERSE PROMENADE PEREGRINATE
(— ABOUT) SLOSH
(— AFFECTEDLY) PRINK
(— AIMLESSLY) PAUP POAP
(— AWKWARDLY) STAUP SHAMBLE
(— BEFORE) PREAMBLE
(— BEHIND BATTLEMENTS) ALURE
(— BRISKLY) LEG SKELP
(— CARELESSLY) JAYWALK
(— CAUTIOUSLY) STALK
(— CLUMSILY) JOLL STUMP LOPPET
(— FOR CATTLE) GANG
(— FOR EXAMINING ENGINE) GALLERY
(— FOR EXERCISE) HIKE GRIND
(— HEAVILY) PLOD CLUMP STUMP TRAMP LAMPER PLODGE
(— IDLY) DANDER POTTER SAUNTER
(— IN AFFECTED MANNER) MINCE
(— LAME) LIMP HIRPLE HOBBLE CRIPPLE
(— LEISURELY) AMBLE DANDER STROLL
(— ON) BEAT TREAD
(— OUT) FLOUNCE
(— RAPIDLY) LAMP LINK STAVE
(— SHAKILY) DOTTER
(— SLOWLY) JET LAG
(— SMARTLY) LINK

595

(— **STEADILY**) SNOVE SNOOVE
(— **UNSTEADILY**) REEL DADDLE
FALTER STAVER STAGGER
STUMBLE
(— **WAVERINGLY**) SHEVEL WARPLE
(— **WITH DIFFICULTY**) CRAMBLE
CRAMMEL LOUTHER
(— **WITH JERK**) HIRCH
(— **WITH LOFTY GAIT**) JET
(— **WITH OSTENTATION**) PRANCE
(— **WITH SHUFFLE**) COONJINE
(— **WITH STRIDES**) STAG
(— **WITH TREES**) XYST XYSTUS
ALAMEDA
(— **WITHOUT LIFTING FEET**) SCUFF
(**BACKSTAGE —**) BRIDGE
(**COOL —**) FRESCADE
(**COVERED —**) PAWN PORCH
CLOISTER
(**FOLIAGE-COVERED —**) BERCEAU
(**HARD —**) STRAM SWINGE
(**LIMPING —**) GIMP
(**LONG —**) STRAM
(**POMPOUS —**) STRUT
(**PUBLIC —**) XYST XYSTUS
ALAMEDA
(**RAISED —**) GALLERY
(**SHADED —**) MALL ARBOR XYSTUS
(**TEDIOUS —**) TRAIL
(PL.) BALTEI
(PREF.) AMBULO GRADIO GRADO
WALKER GOER FOOTER FULLER
GANGER FOOTMAN TODDLER
PEDESTRIAN
(PL.) FEET
WALKING HOTFOOT PASSANT
AMBULANT GRADIENT TRIPPING
(PREF.) BASI BASO
(SUFF.) BAT(ES)(IC) GRADE
WALKING STICK BAT CANE GIBBY
KEBBY STICK WADDY KEBBIE
PHASMID SPECTER ASHPLANT
GIBSTAFF WOODHORSE
WALKOUT STRIKE
WALKURE, DIE (**CHARACTER IN —**)
MIME WOTAN FRICKA HUNDING
SIEGMUND SIEGLINDE
BRUNNHILDE
(**COMPOSER OF —**) WAGNER
WALKWAY CATWALK SIDEWALK
WALL WA DAM FIN MUR WAW
BAIL BELT CELL CORE CRIB CURB
DICK DIKE DRUM DYKE FACE
HEAD MURE PACK SKIN SPUR
WING WOGE ATTIC BOARD CHEEK
CRUST DIGUE EMURE FENCE
HEDGE MEURE MURAL PIRCA
SHOJI WOGHE WOUGH BAFFLE
BAILEY BATTER CUTOFF DOKHMA
IMMURE LEADER PARIES PARPEN
PRETIL REBOTE RIPRAP SCREEN
SEPTUM SHIELD VALLUM
CHEMISE CURTAIN ENCLOSE
MIZRACH PARAPET PERPEND
PLUTEUS REREDOS TAMBOUR
FIREBACK SPANDREL TRAVERSE
(— **ABOVE FACADE**) ATTIC
(— **AROUND**) IMMURE
(— **BEHIND ALTAR**) REREDOS
(— **BETWEEN TWO OPENINGS**) PIER
(— **CARRYING CUPOLA**) DRUM
(— **CARRYING ROOF**) BAHUT
(— **CROSSING RAMPART**) SPUR

(— **IN HOCKEY RINK**) BOARD
(— **IN ROMAN ARENA**) SPINA
(— **IN TRUCK**) HEADER
(— **OF BLAST FURNACE**) DAM
INWALL FIREBACK
(— **OF CASTLE**) BARMKIN
(— **OF CLAY**) COTTLE
(— **OF HOOF**) CRUST
(— **OF MINE**) FACE
(— **OF MOUTH**) CHEEK
(— **OF TENT**) KANAT CANAUT
(**BODY —**) MANTLE
(**CIRCULAR —**) CASHEL
(**CORE —**) HEARTING
(**CURVED —**) SWEEP
(**DIVIDING —**) SEPTUM
(**END — OF BUILDING**) GABLE
(**FISH —**) LEADER
(**HIGHEST PART OF —**) CRAPWA
(**INNER SLOPE OF —**) BATTER
(**LOG —**) CRIB
(**LOW —**) BAHUT PODIUM
PLUTEUS
(**LOWER PART OF —**) DADO
(**OUTER — OF CASTLE**) BAIL BAILEY
(**PEAT —**) COP
(**PUDDLE —**) HEARTING
(**RETAINING —**) CRIB BULKHEAD
(**SCARPED —**) GHAT
(**SECONDARY —**) CHEMISE
(**SUSTAINING —**) RIPRAP
(**THINNED PART OF —**) ALLEGE
(**VENTRAL —**) STERNUM
(**WING —**) AILERON
(PL.) PERICARP
(PREF.) MURI PARIETO TICHO
(SUFF.) (**COAT OF SPORE —**)
SPORIUM
WALLABA APA
WALLABY WURRUP BRUSHER
TOOLACH WURRUNG BOONGARY
KANGAROO PADMELON WHIPTAIL
WALLACHIAN RUMAN
WALLAROO EURO
WALLBOARD GOBO
WALLET JAG JAGG MAIL POKE
BOGET BOUGE BULCH BULGE
SCRIP BUDGET READER SACKET
ALFARGA ALFORJA LEATHER
BILLFOLD NOTECASE POCHETTE
(PREF.) PERO
WALLEYE WHALL SAUGER
LEUCOMA WATCHEYE EXOTROPIA
WALLEYED PIKE DORE DORY
JACK PERCID SALMON WALLEYE
PICKEREL
WALLFLOWER CUBA CHEIR GILLY
JACKS KEIRI GELOFER WARRIOR
GILLIVER
WALL HAWKWEED LUNGWORT
WALLOP BEAT BEER FLOP SLUG
SOCK PASTE POUND VALOP
GALLOP IMPACT WALLOW
FLUTTER TROUNCE FLOUNDER
LAMBASTE
WALLOW FADE LAIR ROLL SOIL
SLOSH WALWE GROVEL MUDDLE
WALTER WELTER WITHER
SLUDDER SWELTER FLOUNDER
KOMMETJE VOLUTATE
WALLOWISH FLAT WELSH INSIPID
WALLPAPER GROUND SCENIC
HANGING TENTURE TAPESTRY

WALL PEPPER SEDUM
STONECROP
WALL PLATE PAN RASEN
WALL RUE TENTWORT
WALLY TOY FINE SPOIL PAMPER
ROBUST STRONG STURDY
SPLENDID VIGOROUS
WALLY, LA (**CHARACTER IN —**)
WALLY GELLNER HAGENBACH
(**COMPOSER OF —**) CATALANI
WALNUT ACAPU NOGAL TRYMA
AKHROT BANNUT HEARTNUT
(**BRAZILIAN —**) EMBOYA IMBUIA
(PL.) JUGLANS
WALNUT BROWN TAFFY
WALNUT SHELL BOLSTER
WALPI HUALPI
WALRUS MORSE WALTRON
PELAGIAN PINNIPED ROSMARINE
WALT CRANK UNSTEADY
WALTZ LUG CARRY MARCH VALSE
BOSTON BREEZE FLOUNCE
WAMARA CLUBWOOD IRONWOOD
PANOCOCO
WAMBLE ROLL SPIN WAMEL
NAUSEA REVOLVE
WAMBLY FAINT SHAKY
WAME WEM WAMB WYME BELLY
WAMPUM PEAG FADME HAWOK
MONEY PAAGE SEWAN FATHOM
SEAWAN ROANOKE
WAMUS JACKET WAMPUS
WARMUS
WAN DIM HAW FADE PALE PALY
SICK BLAKE FAINT WHITE FEEBLE
PALLID SALLOW GHASTLY
LANGUID
WANAPUM SOKULK
WAND ROD VARE YARD BATON
STAFF STICK VERGE VIRGA
FERULA THYRSE WATTLE
RHABDOS THYRSUS CADUCEUS
(**JESTER'S —**) BAUBLE
(PREF.) RHABD(O)
WANDER BAT BUM ERR GAD WAG
HAAK HAIK HAKE MAZE MUCK
RAKE RAVE ROAM ROIL ROLL
ROVE WALK WILL WORE DAVER
DRIFT GLAIK KNOCK RANGE
ROGUE SHACK SLOSH STRAY
TAVER TRAIK VAGUE WAIVE
WAVER CANDER CRUISE DANDER
DAUNER FORAGE LOITER MITHER
MOIDER MUCKER PALMER
PERUSE RAMBLE RANGLE STRAKE
STROLL SWERVE WILDER
MEANDER TRAFFIC TRAIPSE
VAGRATE VANDYKE ABERRATE
CUTICULA SQUANDER STRAGGLE
STRAVAGE STRAVAIG
(— **ABOUT**) DIVAGATE
(— **ABSTRACTEDLY**) MOON
(— **AIMLESSLY**) SWAN SLOSH
TRACE MEANDER
(— **AS A VAGABOND**) SHACK
(— **AS A VAGRANT**) LOITER
(— **AT RANDOM**) SQUANDER
(— **ERRATICALLY**) SWASH
(— **FROM DIRECT COURSE**)
STRAGGLE
(— **FROM PLACE TO PLACE**) WAG
(— **IDLY**) HAKE LOUT MAUNDER
SHACKLE

(— **IN DELIRIUM**) DWALE DWALL
(— **IN MIND**) DAVER DANDER
DELIRE
(— **LEISURELY**) BUMMEL
(— **RESTLESSLY**) FEEK
WANDERER WAIF ROVER VAGUE
RANGER PILGRIM RAMBLER
FUGITIVE RUNAGATE TRAVELER
VAGABOND
(**AUTHOR OF —**) FOURNIER
(**CHARACTER IN —**) FRANTZ GALAIS
MILLIE SEUREL YVONNE
AUGUSTIN BLONDEAU FRANCOIS
MEAULNES VALENTINE
CHARPENTIER
WANDERING GAD ROAM WAFF
ERROR STRAY VAGUE ARRANT
ASTRAY ERRANT MOBILE ROVING
VAGANT VAGOUS DEVIOUS
NOMADIC ODYSSEY VAGANCY
VAGRANT WINDING ABERRANT
FLOATING FUGITIVE PELAGSIC
PLANETAL PLANETIC RAMBLING
RESTLESS TRAILING VAGABOND
WINDRING MIGRATORY
PEREGRINE
(PREF.) PLAN(O) VAGO
(SUFF.) PLANIA
WANDERING JEW (**AUTHOR OF —**)
SUE
(**CHARACTER IN —**) ROSE HARDY
RODIN SIMON DJALMA SAMUEL
BAUDOIN GABRIEL JACQUES
ADRIENNE AGRICOLA AIGRIGNY
DAGOBERT FRANCOIS HERODIAS
RENNEPONT CARDOVILLE
WANDFLOWER GALAX SPARAXIS
WANDOROBO WAASI
WAND-SHAPED VIRGATE
WANE GO EBB SET WELK WILK
ABATE DECAY UNWAX WANZE
REPINE DECLINE DWINDLE
DECREASE
(— **OF MOON**) WADDLE
WANGA CHARM SPELL OUANGA
WONGAH SORCERY
WANGLE FAKE SHAKE WIGGLE
FINAGLE
WANIGAN ARK CHEST COFFER
WANGUN
WANT HURT LACK LIKE MISS NEED
OONT PINE VOID WANE WONT
CRAVE FAULT FORGO BESOIN
CHOOSE DEARTH DEFECT DESIRE
MISTER PENURY PLIGHT ABSENCE
BEGGARY BLEMISH BORASCA
DEFAULT MISEASE NEEDHAM
POVERTY REQUIRE VACANCY
MISCHIEF WANTROKE
(— **EXCEEDINGLY**) DIE
(— **OF CONTROL**) ACRASY
(— **OF ENERGY**) ATONY
(— **OF GOOD SENSE**) FOLLY
(— **OF REST**) UNRO
(— **OF SUCCESS**) FAILURE
(— **OF VIGOR**) DELICACY
WANTAGE ULLAGE
WANTING LACK VOID WANE
ALACK MINUS ABSENT LACKING
MISSING INDIGENT
(— **ORIGINALITY**) BANAL
WANTON JAY NAG RIG DAFT GOLE
IDLE LEWD NICE RAGE SKIT

CADGY DALLY LIGHT SAUCY
GIGLET GIGLOT HARLOT HAUNTY
LACHES LUBRIC RAKISH RIGSBY
TICKLE TOYING TOYISH UNRULY
COLTISH FULSOME GIGGISH
HAGGARD IMMORAL KITTOCK
LUSTFUL PAPHIAN RIGGISH
RIOTOUS SMICKER WAYWARD
FLAGRANT LUSCIOUS MISTRESS
PETULANT PLAYSOME
RUMBELOW SKITTISH SLIPPERY
SPITEFUL SPORTIVE UNCHASTE
WANTONNESS FOLLY PRIDE
SPORT RAGERY SUCCUDRY
SURQUIDY
WAP BIND BLOW WHOP WRAP
BLAST FIGHT KNOCK STORM
TRUSS BUNDLE STRIKE
WAPITI ELK ALCE DEER LOSH LUSH
STAG MARAL MOOSE CERVID
WAMPOOSE
WAR WIN CAMP FEUD MART
FIGHT SWORD WORSE WORST
BATTLE CONTEND CRUSADE
CONFLICT GUERILLA OVERCOME
(RELIGIOUS —) JEHAD JIHAD
(PREF.) BELLI MACHO POLEMO
WAR AND PEACE (AUTHOR OF —)
TOLSTOY
(CHARACTER IN —) LISE ELLEN
MARYA ANDREY PIERRE ROSTOV
ANATOLE BEZUHOV KURAGIN
KUTUZOV NATASHA NIKOLAY
VASSILY NAPOLEON BOLKONSKY
NIKOLUSHKA
WARBLE SING CAROL CHANT
CHIRL CHIRM SHAKE TRILL YODEL
JARGON RALISH RELISH WARNEL
WORMIL DESCANT VIBRATE
WOURNIL
WARBLE FLY OXFLY BOTFLY
GADFLY OESTRID OESTRIAN
WARBLER CUT KIT CHAT SMEU
WREN FITTE PEGGY CANARY
EYSOGE REELER SMEUTH SYLVIA
TITIEN CREEPER CROMBEC
FANTAIL HAYBIRD HAYSUCK
PITBIRD REDPOLL SYLVIID
TROCHIL BEAMBIRD BLACKCAP
FAUVETTE MALURINE MOCKBIRD
OVENBIRD PINCPINC REDSTART
REEDBIRD RIRORIRO TROCHILUS
WAR CLUB MAR MER MERE MERAI
MARREE
WAR CRY ALALA BANZAI SLOGAN
WARD CARE GUARD MAHAL VICUS
WAIRD WATCH ALUMNA BARRIO
CALPUL DEFEND ROWENA
KEEPING NATUARY CALPOLLI
CONTRADA
(— OFF) FEND WEAR WERE AVERT
AWARD FENCE PARRY REPEL
STAVE SHIELD BUCKLER EXPIATE
FORFEND
WARDAGE WARTH
WARDEN ALCADE DIZDAR PORTER
RANGER REGENT ROLAND
WARNER ALCAIDE HOGMACE
LEATMAN ROWLAND BEARWARD
CLAVIGER
(AUTHOR OF —) TROLLOPE
(CHARACTER IN —) TOM BOLD
JOHN SUSAN FINNEY TOWERS

ABRAHAM ELEANOR GRANTLY
HARDING SEPTIMUS HAPHAZARD
QUIVERFUL THEOPHILUS
WARDER PORTER GUARDER
HEIMDAL TURNKEY WATCHMAN
BEEFEATER
WARDROBE KAS CLOSET VESTRY
ALMIRAH ARMOIRE VESTUARY
WARE CLOTH GOODS SPEND
FABRICS SEAWEED SQUANDER
(CERAMIC —) SPODE
(CLOISONNE —) SHIPPO
(ENAMELED —) BILSTON
COALPORT
(INFERIOR —S) SLUM
(JAPANESE —) IMARI YAYOI
(JAPANESE CERAMIC —) SETO
BIZEN KARATSU
(KIND OF —) RAKU MINTON
WHIELDON
(KIND OF JAPANESE POTTERY —)
SANDA
(MAJOLICA —) DERUTA
(PORCELAIN —) CHINA IMARI
BERLIN
(UNGLAZED —) BISQUE
(PL.) TROKE CHAFFER TROGGIN
WAREHOUSE GOLA HONG ETAPE
GOLAH STORE BODEGA FONDUK
GODOWN STAITH ALMACEN
FUNDUCK SPICERY STOWAGE
ENTREPOT MAGAZINE SERAGLIO
WARFARE WAR ARMS IRON
ARMOR BATTLE PSYWAR MILITIA
CONFLICT
(NONAGGRESSIVE —) SITZKRIEG
(SUFF.) MACHIA MACHY
WAR-HORSE CHARGER COURSER
DESTRER TROOPER DESTRIER
WARILY TIPTOE GINGERLY
WARINESS CAUTEL CAUTION
DISTRUST WARESHIP WARIMENT
WARKLOOM TOOL WARKLUME
WARLIKE WARLY MARTIAL
CAVALIER FIGHTING MILITARY
BELLICOSE
(NOT —) IMBELLIC
WARLOCK IMP WITCH SPRITE
WARLOW WIZARD CONJUROR
SORCERER
WARLORD TUCHUN
WARM HOT LEW LOO RUG BASK
BEEK KEEN LEWD MILD CALID
CHAFE EAGER FRESH MALMY
MUNGY SLACK TEPID TOAST
ACHAFE ARDENT BIRSLE DEVOUT
DIGEST FOSTER GENIAL HEARTY
HEATED RIZZLE TENDER CHERISH
CLEMENT CORDIAL GLOWING
THERMAL ZEALOUS FRIENDLY
PRESSING SANGUINE
(— UP) SCORE
(MODERATELY —) LEW SLACK
TEPID
(PREF.) CAL(E)(I)(ORI)
WARMHEARTED KIND TENDER
FRIENDLY GENEROUS
WARMING FOVENT
WARMOUTH BIGMOUTH FLATFISH
SACALAIT
WARMTH GLOW HEAT LIFE ZEAL
ARDOR LEWTH ENERGY FERVOR
ARDENCY PASSION

CALIDITY FERVENCY
(INNER —) JUICE
WARN REDE WARD WERN ALERT
AREAD WEIRD ADVERT ADVISE
EXHORT INFORM CAUTION
COMMAND COUNSEL GARNISH
PREVISE ADMONISH THREATEN
(— OFF) FORBID
WARNING AHEM ITEM ALARM
CHECK KNELL BEACON CAVEAT
LESSON NOTICE OFFICE SAMPLE
SIGNAL TIPOFF AVISION CALLING
CAUTION EXAMPLE GRIFFIN
JIGGERS MEMENTO MONITOR
PRESAGE SUMMONS DOCUMENT
GARDYLOO MONITION
PREMONITION
(— OF DISASTER) DIRE
(ARCHERY —) FAST
(DANGER —) VIGIA
WARP CUP WEB BIAS CANE CAST
LIFT WARF WERP WIND ANGLE
CHAIN CHOKE CRAWL CROOK
GEYZE KEDGE PORRY THRAW
TWINE WEAVE BUCKLE CHEESE
DEFORM WASHIN DEFLECT
DISTORT SKELLER
(— IN WEAVING) CRAM
(PREF.) HIST(O)
WARPED WRY BUCKLED GNARLED
HOUSING
WARPER BALLER
WARPING BOW PANDATION
WARRAGAL WILD DINGO HORSE
OUTLAW
WARRANT ABLE WARN AMRIT
BERAT FIANT PRESS SANAD
VOUCH AMRITA ASSERT BRANCH
BREVET COUPON DOCKET
ENSURE INSURE PARDON PERMIT
PLEVIN POLICY POTENT SUNNUD
TICKET WARDOG BEHIGHT
CAPTION JUSTIFY PRECEPT
PROMISE GUARANTY MITTIMUS
WARRANTED VALID
WARRAU GUARANO
WARREN SLUM CONYGER
WARRANT
WARRIOR TOA WER EARL HERO
KEMP RINK WEER BERNE FREIK
FREKE HAGEN LLUDD SEPAD
SINGH THANE THEGN OSSIAN
WARMAN WEAPON FIGHTER
SOLDIER STARKAD WARWOLF
ZERBINO CHAMPION RODOMONT
SHARDANA STARKATH
SWORDMAN WARFARER
(— CLASS) MAGANI
(— OF NOBLE RANK) EARL
(AMERICAN INDIAN —) BRAVE
SANNUP
(BOASTFUL —) RODOMONT
(BRYTHONIC —) LLUDD
(BURGUNDIAN —) HAGEN
(FEMALE —) AMAZON SHIELDMAY
(IRISH —) FENIAN
(KAFFIR —S) IMPI
(MUSLIM —) GAZI GHAZI
(NOTED —) THANE THEGN
(SCANDINAVIAN —) BERSERK
(SCOTTISH —) ZERBINO
(TROJAN —) AGENOR
(VALIANT —) TOA

(VIRGIN —) CAMILLA
(PL.) IMPI CHIVALRY GAMMADIM
WARSHIP GUIDE WAFTER CRUISER
MONITOR SULTANA SULTANE
CORVETTE
WART RAT WRAT AMBURY
ANBURY SYCOMA PUSTULE
VERRUCA VERRUGA EPIDERMA
PAPILLOMA
(POTATO —) CANKER
(PREF.) VERRUCI
WART HOG EMGALLA
WARTLIKE PYRENOID
WART SNAKE XENODERM
WARTY MURICATE
WARY SHY CAGY WISE AWARE
CAGEY CANNY DOWNY HOOLY
LEERY TENDER CAREFUL
GUARDED PRUDENT WAREFUL
CAUTIOUS SKITTISH VIGILANT
WATCHFUL
WAS VAS WIS WUZ WYS PAST
WISSHE
(— ABLE) COULD
(— NOT) NAS
(I —) CHWAS
WASH DO BOG FEN LAG LAP NET
TUB BEER BUCK EDDY HOSE
HUSH LAVE SILT SUDS WADI
BATHE CLEAN CLEAR DOLLY
DRAFF ERODE MARSH RINSE
SCRUB SLOSH SOUSE SWILL
BUDDLE CRADLE DOLLIE LOTION
PURIFY SLOOSH SLUICE SOZZLE
STREAM ALLUVIO CLEANSE
LAUNDER SHAMPOO ALLUVIUM
EYEWATER LAVAMENT LAVATORY
(— A GAS) SCRUB
(— AWAY) GULL
(— BY TREADING IN WATER) TRAMP
(— DOWN) SIND SOOGEE
(— FOR GOLD) PAN
(— GIVEN TO SWINE) DRAFF
(— GRAVEL) ROCK
(— IN LYE) BUCK
(— LIGHTLY) RINSE
(— OFF) DETERGE
(— ORE) TYE HUTCH BUDDLE
CRADLE STRAKE
(— OUT) SIND ELUTE FLUSH
LAVAGE
(— ROUGHLY) SLUSH
(— THOROUGHLY) SCOUR
(— VIGOROUSLY) SLOSH
(— WITH BROOM) TYE
(— WITH COSMETIC) SURFLE
SURPHUL
(DRY —) ARROYA ARROYO
WASHBASIN LAVER LAVABO
LAVATORY ALJOFAINA
WASHCLOTH FLANNEL
WASHED ABLUTED
(— UP) SHOT THROUGH
WASHER BUR BURR DRUM ROVE
CLOUT BUTTON RONDEL SOURER
GROMMET LEATHER RACCOON
COTTEREL LAVENDER RONDELLE
SCRUBBER
WASHERMAN DHOBI DHOBIE
LAVANDERO
WASHERWOMAN LAUNDER
WASHING LAG BATH LAVAGE
SLOOSH LAUNDRY ABLUTION

LAVAMENT LAVATION
(PL.) ELUATE
WASHING MACHINE DASHWHEEL

WASHINGTON

CAPITAL: OLYMPIA
COLLEGE: WHITMAN
COUNTY: ASOTIN KITSAP SKAGIT
YAKIMA CLALLAM KITTITAS
DAM: COULEE
INDIAN: HOH LUMMI MAKAH
TWANA SAMISH SKAGIT
YAKIMA CHINOOK CLALLAM
COWLITZ SANPOIL CHIMAKUM
OKANAGON
LAKE: CHELAN
MOUNTAIN: JACK TUNK ADAMS
LEMEI LOGAN MOSES SLOAN
QUARTZ SIMCOE STUART
OLYMPUS RAINIER SHUKSAN
MOUNTAIN RANGE: KETTLE
CASCADE OLYMPIC
NICKNAME: CHINOOK EVERGREEN
RIVER: SNAKE YAKIMA COLUMBIA
SOUND: PUGET
STATE BIRD: GOLDFINCH
STATE TREE: HEMLOCK
TOWN: OMAK PASCO TACOMA
YAKIMA EPHRATA EVERETT
OTHELLO SEATTLE SPOKANE
LONGVIEW

WASHOUT FLOP STUMOR FAILURE
WASHROOM BASEMENT
LAVATORY
WASHSTAND COMMODE
WASHTUB FLASKET
WASHY SOFT WEAK LOOSE MOIST
FEEBLE PALLID WATERY DILUTED
SHILPIT
WASP MASON SPHEX WHAMP
WOPSE BEMBEX DAUBER DIGGER
HORNET TIPHIA TREMEX VESPID
CYNIPID DRYINID EUMENID
MASARID SCOLIID SERPHID
SIRICID SPHECID STINGER
ACULEATE MUTILLID POMPILID
WASPISH TESTY FRETFUL PEEVISH
CHOLERIC SNAPPISH
WASSAIL TOAST PLEDGE
CAROUSE REVELRY CAROUSAL
WASTE EAT FUD GOB TED BURN
GNAW JUNK LOSS PASS PEAK
ROSS SACK TEAR TINE WEAR
WILD DROSS EXILE HAVOC SCRAP
SLOOM SLOTH SLOUM SPILL
TABID THRUM BANGLE BEZZLE
COMMON DEBRIS DESERT
DEVOUR DIDDLE DRAFFY DRIVEL
ELAPSE EXPEND FOREST GARBLE
GOUSTY LAVISH MOLDER
MUDDLE PADDLE PERISH RAVAGE
REFUSE SCATHE SPILTH WESTEN
CONNACH CONSUME EXHAUST
FRITTER GARBAGE MULLOCK
RUBBISH SLATTER CONFOUND
DEMOLISH SLATTERN SQUANDER
(— AWAY) BATE MELT DECAY
DWINE SWAIN SWEAL TRAIK
WANZE TABEFY WINDLE
DWINDLE FORPINE MISLIKE
DISSOLVE EMACIATE FORSPEND
MACERATE

(— GRADUALLY) WEAR ABSUME
(— IN DRUNKENNESS) SOT
(— IN RIOT) BEZZLE
(— OF INK) INKSHED
(— OF SILK COCOONS) KNUB
(— TIME) FOOL FRIG IDLE DALLY
DEFER DRILL DAWDLE DIDDLE
FOOTER FOOTLE LOITER DRINGLE
FOOSTER GAUSTER
(COAL —) SLUDGE
(COTTON —) FLUKE SLASHER
SPOOLER
(FOOD —) SLOP
(LIQUID —) DRIPPING EFFLUENT
(MINING —) GOB GOAF
(WOOL —) FUD MUNGO GARNETT
(YARN —) THRUM EYEBROW
WASTEBASKET HELL HELLBOX
WASTED IDLE FORWORN
RAVAGED DECREPIT
WASTEFUL LAVISH PROFUSE
DESOLATE PRODIGAL SPENDFUL
WASTEFULNESS WAIT UNTHRIFT
WASTELAND CURAGH CURRACH
WASTER THIEF LEISTER WASTREL
PRODIGAL
WASTING FRET DECAY LIGHT
AWASTE ATROPHY CACHEXY
EXEDENT MISLIKE PREYING
TABIFIC CACHEXIA PHTHISIS
SYNTEXIS
(— AWAY) MARASMUS SYNTECTIC
(PREF.) PHTHISIO TABE TABI
TABO
(PROGRESSIVE —) TABO
WASTREL WAIF LOSEL REFUSE
WASTER ROUNDER VAGABOND
STROYGOOD
WATCH EYE FOB NIT SEE SPY TAB
DIAL ESPY GLIM GLOM HACK
HEED KEEP LOOK MARK MIND
PIPE TOUT TWIG VACH WAIK
WAKE WARD YARD CLOCK
GUARD SCOUT SPIAL SUPER
TIMER VERGE VIGIL VINGE WAKEN
WHEEL BEHOLD DEFEND DIACLE
FOLLOW HUNTER PERDUE
SENTRY SHADOW TICKER TICTIC
TURNIP WAKING YEMING
OBSERVE OVERSEE ROSKOPF
STRIKER THIMBLE TOMPION
HOROLOGE MEDITATE SENTINEL
SPECTATE TICKTICK
(— FOR) TENT ABIDE AWAIT
(— OF ARMY) BIVOUAC
(— ON THE SLY) FOX
(— OVER) HOLD KEEP TEND TENT
GUARD ATTEND OVERLOOK
(— PEOPLE EATING) GROAK
(— QUIETLY) HINT
(— THAT STRIKES) STRIKER
REPEATER
(— UNIT) LIGNE
(— WITH HINGED COVER) HUNTER
(ALARM —) TATLER TATTLER
(CLOSE —) SCRUTINY
(NAUTICAL —) HACK DOGWATCH
(NIGHT —) LICHWAKE LYKEWAKE
(PART OF —) BOW FOB CASE DIAL
FACE HAND STEM BEZEL COVER
CROWN FRAME CHAPTER
CRYSTAL DISPLAY NUMERAL
SHOULDER

(SUFF.) SCOPE SCOPIC SCOPUS
SCOPY
WATCHBAND WRISTER WRISTLET
WATCH CRYSTAL LUNET
LUNETTE
WATCHDOG CUR GARM GARMR
MATIN BANDOG KRATIM
CERBERUS
WATCHER VEIL ARGUS WAKER
VIEWER WAITER MUSAHAR
SPOTTER WATCHMAN
WATCHFUL IRA ALERT AWARE
CANNY CHARY ERECT TENTY
WAKER TENTIE WACKER ANXIOUS
GUARDED JEALOUS LIDLESS
WAKEFUL VIGILANT WAKERIFE
WAUKRIFE OBSERVANT
WATCHFULNESS OUTLOOK
JEALOUSY
WATCHMAN FLAG MINA WAIT
GUARD SCOUT VIGIL WATCH
ASKARI BANTAY GHAFIR SERENO
SHOMER TOOTER WAITER
WARDEN WARDER BELLMAN
CHARLEY GUARDER TALLIAR
WAKEMAN CHOKIDAR SENTINEL
(NIGHT —) SERENO CHARLIE
WATCHTOWER WARD BEACON
GARRET MIZPAH SENTRY
ATALAYA LOOKOUT MIRADOR
BARBICAN SENTINEL SPECCHIE
WATCHWORD CRY MAXIM
ALERTA ENSIGN PAROLE SIGNAL
NAYWORD PASSWORD
WATCH WORKS MOVEABLE
WATER EAU TJI AGUA AQUA BATH
BRIM BROO BURN LAGE LAKE
POND POOL TIDE WAVE ABYSS
BILGE FLUME LOUGH LYMPH
RIVER TABBY TEARS TUBIG
BALLOW BAREGE CAMLET
CONGEE CONJEE PAWNEE
PHLEGM SALIVA STREAM VADOSE
WATHER AQUATIC CRYSTAL
JAVELLE IRRIGATE SNOWMELT
(— AFTER BOILING RICE) CONGEE
CONJEE
(— AS REFUGE FOR GAME) SOIL
(— AT THE MOUTH) DROOL
(— BY CALENDERING) TABBY
(— FOR BREWING) BURN
(— IN SOIL) HOLARD
(— IN WEIR) LASHER
(— REDDISH WITH IRON) RIDDAM
(— RUNNING AGAINST MAIN
CURRENT) EDDY
(— SPIRIT) KELPIE
(— SURROUNDED BY ICE) WAKE
(— UNDER PRESSURE) HUSH
(BAPTISMAL —) LAVER
(BARLEY —) PTISAN
(BOTTOM — OF SEA) ABYSS
(BOUNDARY —) SHARD
(BUBBLING —) SPRUDEL
(DEEP —) BALLOW
(DIRTY —) SAUR PUDDLE
(FAST-MOVING —) SOUP
(FEN —) SUDS
(FROZEN —) ICE FROST
(HOLY —) HYSSOP
(HOT —) SOUP
(LIVING —) RASA
(MINERAL —) VICHY SELTER

SELTZER APOLLINARIS
(OPEN —) POLYNYA
(QUININE —) TONIC
(RED —) RESP RIDDAM
(ROUGH —) SEA
(RUNNING —) SEA
(SALT —) BRACK BRINE SEAWATER
(SOAPY —) SUDS GRAITH
(SPLASH OF —) FLASH
(STILL —) KELD LOGIN
(SULPHUR —) BAREGE
(SURFACE OF —) RYME
(SWEETENED —) AMRIT AMRITA
(WASHING —) LAVATION
(PL.) APSU
(PREF.) AQUA AQUEO AQUI AQUO
HIDRO HYDAT(O) HYDR(O)
(GO THROUGH —) SILLO
(STAGNANT —) TELMAT(O)
(SUFF.) LIMNION YDATIS
WATER ARUM DRAGON
WATER BAG CHAGUL MATARA
MUSSUK
WATERBIRD ALCATRAS
WATERBRAIN GID
WATERBUCK COB CHUZWI
DEFASSA WATERDOE
WATER BUFFALO KERBAU
WATER CARRIER BHISTI
AGUADOR BHEESTY
WATER CART DILLY
WATER CASK WINGER
WATER CHESTNUT LING CALTROP
SALIGOT SINGHARA
WATER CHINQUAPIN BONNET
NELUMBO WANKAPIN YONCOPIN
RATTLENUT
WATER CLOCK GHURRY
CLEPSYDRA
WATER CLOSET PETTY PRIVY
STOOL SANITARY NECESSARY
WATER COCK KORA
WATERCOLOR GRAPHIC
WATERCOURSE (ALSO SEE
STREAM AND RIVER) RUN URN
AGOS DIKE DYKE GOTE HAHR
KHOR LADE LEAT REAN WADI
WADY YORA AUWAI BAYOU
BROOK CANAL CANEL COWAL
DITCH DRAIN RHINE ARROYO
CANNEL COURSE FURROW
GUTTER KENNEL NULLAH
CHANNEL TRINKET
WATERCRESS EKER KERS CARSE
KERSE BILDERS NOSESMART
WATER DOG OTTER WATERRUG
WATER DRINKER HYDROPOT
WATERED MOIRE TABBY
WATERFALL LIN LYN FALL FOSS
LINN SALT CHUTE FORCE SAULT
SHOOT SPOUT LASHER CASCADE
CATADUPE CATARACT OVERFALL
(FROZEN —) ICEFALL
WATER FENNEL EDGEWEED
WATER FLEA CYCLOPS DAPHNID
WATERFOWL WADER SWIMMER
WATERFRONT PRAYA
WATERGALL WINDDOG WINDGALL
JELLYFISH
WATER GERMANDER SCORDIUM
WATER HEMLOCK CICUTA
COWBANE DEATHIN JELLICA
WATER HOG BUSHPIG CAPYBARA

WATER HOLE DUB CHARCO TINAJA ALBERCA
WATER ICE SHERBET
WATERINESS AQUEITY AQUOSITY
WATERING EPIPHORA RIGATION
WATER JUG GAMLA GOMLAH GOOLAH
WATERLEAF SHAWNY NEMOPHILA
WATERLESS (PREF.) ANHYDR(O)
WATER LETTUCE QUIAPO
WATER LILY DUCK LOTOS LOTUS WOCAS WOKAS BOBBIN CANDOCK NELUMBO CAMALOTE NENUPHAR
WATERLOGGED SOGGY SWAMPY EDEMATOUS
WATERMAN MERMAN QUENCH OARSMAN
WATERMARK CROWN TIDEMARK
WATERMARKED LAID
WATERMELON PEPO GOURD MELON TSAMA CITRUL SANDIA ANGURIA MILLION CUCURBIT PEPONIDA PEPONIUM SKIPJACK
WATER MOCCASIN CONGO
WATER NEWT ASK TRITON
WATER OPOSSUM YAPOK YAPOCK
WATER OUZEL PIET OOZEL OWZEL DIPPER DUCKER
WATER PEPPER LAKEWEED
WATER PLANT LIMU AQUATIC
WATER PLANTAIN ALISMA THRUMWORT
WATERPOT FUNTAL
WATERPROOF RAINCOAT (— MATERIAL) KERATOL
WATER RAIL RUNNER BILCOCK MOORHEN OARCOCK
WATER RAT VOLE CRABER MUSKRAT WATERRUG
WATER SCORPION NEPID
WATERSHED BROW DIVIDE DIVORT SNOWSHED
WATER SHIELD FANWORT DEERFOOD FROGLEAF
WATERSKIN MASHAK MATARA MUSSUK MUSSACK MUSSICK
WATER SOLDIER PONDWORT
WATER SPIRIT ARIEL KELPY KELPIE UNDINE
WATERSPOUT RONE CANAL SPATE SPOUT VORTEX PRESTER TWISTER CATARACT GARGOYLE
WATER STRIDER SKATER SKIMMER SKIPPER SKETCHER
WATER THRUSH KICKUP WAGTAIL
WATER TIGER DYTISCID
WATERTIGHT THEAT THEET TIGHT STANCH THIGHT STAUNCH
WATER WALLY BATAMOTE
WATERWAY GUT CASH DOCK HOLE LODE DITCH INLET ARTERY SEAWAY CULVERT FAIRWAY HIGHWAY IGARAPE (ARTIFICIAL —) LEAD CANAL (PL.) SCUPPERS
WATERWHEEL NORIA SAKIA SAGEER SAKIEH DANAIDE SAKIYEH TYMPANUM
WATERY WET LASH PALE SICK THIN WHEY BOGGY MOIST

SAMMY WASHY BLASHY FLASHY LIQUID PALLID SEROSE SEROUS SWASHY AQUATIC AQUEOUS CHOROUS HYDROUS PHLEGMY SANIOUS HUMOROUS HYDATOID ICHOROUS SKINKING
WATT (ONE BILLION —S) GIGAWATT
WATTLE GILL JOWL PLAT SALY TWIG WAND BOREE COOBA FRITH MULGA SALLY SALWE STAVE STICK HURDLE JEWING JOLLOP LAPPET SALLOW BLUEBUSH CARUNCLE
WATTLEBIRD IAO MOHO MINER MANUAO MAOMAO GILLBIRD
WATTLE CROW KOKAKO
WAVE FAN FLY JAW SEA WAW BECK FLAG FLAP GUST LUMP SUFF SULK SWAY WAFF WAFT WAWE YTHE BLESS CRIMP FLASH FLOAT FLOTE PULSE SHAKE SURGE SWELL SWING BILLOW COMBER FLAUNT MARCEL RIPPLE ROLLER WAFFLE WINNOW BREAKER BRIMMER CRIMPLE DECUMAN FEATHER FLICKER FLUTTER TSUNAMI WHIFFLE ARTEFACT BRANDISH FLOURISH GRAYBACK UNDULATE UNIPULSE WHISTLER WHITECAP (— ABOUT) WAMPISH (— OF EXCITATION) IMPULSE (— OF FLAG) DOT DASH (— OF SHIP) BONE (ARCH OF —) CURL (ELECTRIC —) STRAY CARRIER (HAIR —) PERMANENT (LARGE —) HEAVY (TIDAL —) EAGER (PL.) SURF (PREF.) CUMA CYM(I)(O) CYMATO KYM(I)(O) KYMATO ONDA ONDO UNDI
WAVER HALT REEL SWAG SWAY VARY CHECK DAKER DOUBT FLOAT SWALE SWING WIVER DACKER DAIKER DITHER FALTER MAMMER QUIVER SWERVE TEETER TOTTER WABBLE WAFFLE WOBBLE BALANCE FLICKER FLITTER FLUTTER STAGGER SWITHER VIBRATE HESITATE VACILLATE
WAVERING WAW WAVY WEAK WAUCH WAUGH FICKLE GROGGY WAVERY WIGGLY DUBIOUS LAMBENT SHUTTLE DOUBTFUL FLEXUOSE FLEXUOUS FLICKERY HOVERING WAVEROUS PENDULOUS
WAVERLEY (AUTHOR OF —) SCOTT (CHARACTER IN —) EVAN LEAN ROSE VOHR ALICE COSMO DAVIE FLORA DONALD FERGUS STUART CHARLES EVERARD MACIVOR GARDINER PEMBROKE WAVERLEY GELLATLEY MACCOMBICH BRADWARDINE
WAVINESS CRIMP
WAVING UNDE WAFT AWAVE OUNDY UNDEE WAFTURE FLOURISH
WAVY ONDE UNDE UNDY CRISP

MOIRE SNAKY UNDEE CRIMPY FLECKY REPAND SNAKEY UNDATE WIGGLY BUCKLED CRINKLY CURVING ENDATED ROLLING SINUATE UNDULAR ENRIDGED FLEXUOUS ONDOYANT SQUIGGLY UNDULATE (PEOPLE WITH — HAIR) VEDDOID
WAWL HOWL WAIL WOWL SQUALL
WAX WOX CERE CODE GROW RAGE WACE WOXE SCALE BECOME CAPPING CERESIN KLISTER CARNAUBA CERESINE CEROXYLE COCCERIN EPILATOR INCREASE (— FAINT) APPAL (— FROM INSECT) PELA (— IN HONEYCOMB) CAPPING (— STRONG) PREVAIL (CHINESE —) PELA (COBBLER'S —) CODE (EAR —) CERUMEN (KIND OF —) PINSANG (SKI —) KLISTER (PREF.) CER(I)(O) KERO
WAXBILL ASTRILD REDBILL
WAXEN WAX PALLID CEREOUS
WAXER GLAZER WAXMAN
WAXFLOWER EPIPHYTE
WAX MYRTLE ARRAYAN
WAX PLANT HOYA
WAXWING WAXBIRD RECOLLET SILKTAIL
WAXY ANGRY VEXED CEREOUS PLIABLE YIELDING
WAY LAW PAD TAO VIA WON WYE FARE FORE FORM GAIT GANG GATE KIND LANE LARK PACE PATH PAWK RAKE ROAD SORT TOBY WISE ALLEY CHANT FORTH GOING GUISE HABIT MOYEN ROUTE SHEAR STEPS STYLE TRACT TRADE ACCESS AVENUE CAREER CHEMIN COURSE MANNER METHOD PHASIS STREET TRAJET CHANNEL FASHION HIGHWAY PASSAGE SKIDWAY APPROACH CONTRADA DISTRICT FOOTPATH THOROUGH VICINITY LAUNCHING (— OF DEPARTURE) EXIT (— OF ESCAPE) BOLTHOLE (— OF LIFE) LARK TRACE HEDONISM (— OF SPEAKING) AMBAGE (— OF THINKING) DIET (— OF WALKING) JET (— OUT) IT EXIT SALVO (— THROUGH MINEFIELD) BREACH (CLEVER —) KNACK (COVERED —) CORRIDOR (INDIRECT —) AMBAGES (LONG —) FAR (MAJOR —) STEM (NARROW —) DRANG (ODD —S) JIMJAMS (PLANK —) BRIDGE (RAISED —) BANQUETTE (ROUNDABOUT —) DETOUR CIRCUIT (ROUNDABOUT —S) AMBAGES (SETTLED —) BIAS (SIDE —) BRANCH

(SLOPING —) RAMP
(UNDEVIATING —) GROOVE
(PL.) DAPS
(PREF.) HODO ODO VIA
(SUFF.) ODE OID WISE
WAYBILL CHALAN WILLIE CHALLAN
WAYFARER SHULER VIATOR PILGRIM SHUILER TRAVELER PASSENGER
WAYFARING TREE WHITTEN COTTONER VIBURNUM
WAYLAY BELAY BESET BLOCK BRACE AMBUSH FORLAY FORSET FORELAY OBSTRUCT SURPRISE
WAYLAYER WAIT
WAYMARK AHU
WAY OF ALL FLESH (AUTHOR OF —) BUTLER (CHARACTER IN —) JOHN ELIZA ELLEN MARIA PRYER ALLABY ALTHEA ERNEST GEORGE JOSEPH OVERTON SKINNER MAITLAND PONTIFEX THEOBALD CHARLOTTE CHRISTINA
WAY OF THE WORLD (AUTHOR OF —) CONGREVE (CHARACTER IN —) FOIBLE FAINALL MARWOOD ROWLAND WILFULL WITWOOD MIRABELL WAITWELL WISHFORT MILLAMANT
WAYSIDE HEDGE
WAYWARD PEEVISH
WEAK DIM LEW COOL DOWY FOND LAME NESH NICE PALE PUNY SELI SELY SOFT THIN WASH WAUF WOKE BAUCH BAUGH CRIMP DICKY FAINT FLASH FRAIL JERKY LIGHT NAISH REEDY ROCKY SEELY SILLY SLACK STANK WASHY WAUGH WEARY WERSH YOUNG CADUKE DEBILE DILUTE DOTISH FEEBLE FLABBY FLAGGY FLIMSY FOIBLE GROGGY INFIRM LIMBER LITTLE MARCID SEMMIT SICKLY SINGLE SWASHY TENDER UNSURE UNWISE WAIRCH WATERY BRICKLE DWAIBLY DWEEBLE FLACCID FOOLISH FRAGILE INSIPID INVALID LANGUID PIMPING PUERILE REGULAR RICKETY SAUGHEN SHALLOW SHILPIT SLENDER SPINDLY TOTTERY UNHARDY UNLUSTY WEARISH ASTHENIC CHILDISH DECREPIT DEFINITE FECKLESS FEMININE FLAGGING GRIPLESS HELPLESS IMBECILE IMPOTENT LADYLIKE LANGUENT PHTHISIC RESOLUTE RUSHLIKE SACKLESS SCRANNEL THEWLESS UNMIGHTY UNWIELDY SPINELESS (— FROM FATIGUE) TANGLE (— FROM HUNGER) LEER (— IN RESOLUTION) FRAIL (MENTALLY —) TOTTY (PREF.) ASTHEN(O) LEPT(O)
WEAKEN GO LAG SAP DAMP FAIL HURT MELT PALL SINK THIN ALLAY BLUNT BREAK CRAZE DELAY QUAIL SHAKE SPEND WATER APPALL ATTRIT DEACON DEADEN DEFEAT DEJECT DENUDE

DILUTE FALTER IMPAIR INFIRM
LABEFY LESSEN PERISH REBATE
REDUCE SICKEN SOFTEN
CORRODE CORRUPT CRIPPLE
DECLINE DEPRESS DISABLE
MOLLIFY QUALIFY RESOLVE
THREADY UNBRACE UNNERVE
CASTRATE DIMINISH EMBEZZLE
ENERVATE ENFEEBLE ETIOLATE
INFRINGE LABEFACT UNSTRENG
WEAKENED GROGGY ANODYNE
INVALID SHOTTEN DECREPIT
LABEFACT STRAINED
WEAKENING CHRONIC FAILURE
FLAGGING
WEAKEST RECKLING
WEAKFISH DRUM TROUT ACOUPA
SALMON CORBINA CORVINA
DRUMMER SQUETEE TOTOABA
TOTUAVA BLUEFISH CHICKWIT
WEAKLING TOY WRIG DUGON
PULER SLINK SOFTIE DILLING
RECKLING SOFTLING
WEAKLY FEEBLY FEMALE SIMPLY
WEAK-MINDED DAFT DOTY
DOTED FOOLISH
WEAKNESS ATONY CRACK CRAZE
FAULT FOLLY TOUCH ATONIA
DEFECT FOIBLE ACRATIA FAILING
FISSURE FRAILTY LANGUOR
ASTHENIA DEBILITY DELICACY
FONDNESS
(CARNAL —) FLESH
(SUFF.) (— FOR) ITIS
WEAL WHEAL RICHES STRIPE
WEALTH WELFARE
WEALTH WAD WON DHAN GEAR
GOLD GOOD MUCK WONE MEANS
THING WORTH GRAITH MAMMON
POCKET PURPLE RICHES TALENT
CASHBOX FORTUNE RICHDOM
WARISON WELFARE CATALLUM
OPULENCE OPULENCY PROPERTY
TREASURE WARRISON
MONEYBAGS
(— OF NATION) STOCK
(PATRON OF —) YAKSHA
(PREF.) APHNO PLUT(O)
WEALTHY FAT BEIN BIEN FULL
OOFY RICH WELI AMPLE PURSY
TINNY LOADED OOFIER COUTHIE
MONEYED PURSIVE ABUNDANT
AFFLUENT
WEAN CHILD SPAIN SPANE WAYNE
INFANT ESTRANGE
WEANING ABLACTATION
WEAPON (ALSO SEE SPECIFIC TYPE
OF WEAPON) ARM BOW GUN
BILL BOLA BOLO CLUB COSH
DART EDGE EPEE FALX FOIL IRON
MACE PATU PIKE TOOL WIWI
ADAGA ARROW BILLY CAKRA
DEATH FLAIL KNIFE LANCE ONCIN
ORGUE SHARP SPEAR SQUID
STEEL SWORD VOUGE WAPIN
CANNON CHAKRA DAGGER
GLAIVE MACANA TOMBOC
ARCHERY BAZOOKA FIREARM
GISARME HALBERD HARPOON
HURLBAT JAVELIN LIANGLE
POUNAMU SHOTGUN SLASHER
STICKER TICKLER WHIFFLE
ARBALEST BLOWBACK BLUDGEON

CROSSBOW FAUCHARD
HEDGEHOG LEEANGLE PARTISAN
TROMBASH
(CELTIC —) PALSTAFF
(DEADLY —) DEATH
(LINE OF —S) RIDGE
(PREHISTORIC —) CELT
(PL.) WAR TACKLE ARCHERY
WEAPONRY
(PREF.) ARMI HOPL(O)
WEAR KIT BEAR FRAY FRET GROW
HAVE PASS CHAFE GUARD SPEND
VOGUE WEARY ABRADE BATTER
BECOME BETHUMB CONSUME
DEFENSE DEGRADE FASHION
FATIGUE FRAZZLE PROCEED
WEATHER PROGRESS
(— AN OPENING) BREACH
(— AND TEAR) GAFF SLITE
GRUELING
(— AWAY) EAT FADE FRET GALL
GNAW GULL PINE ERODE GULLY
SCOUR SPEND ABRADE CORRADE
CORRODE CONTRIVE
(— CLOTHES) DRESS
(— DOWN) BRAY GRIND ABRADE
ABRASE GRAVEL
(— FURROWS) GUTTER
(— IN PUBLIC) SPORT
(— OFF) FRAY ABRADE
(— OUT) DO BURN COOK FLOG
JADE MUSH TIRE TUCK BREAK
SLAVE SLITE SPEND TRASH
BUGGER HATTER MAGGLE
PERUSE EXHAUST FORWEAR
FORWORK HACKNEY INVALID
SHACHLE OVERFRET OVERWEAR
(— SHIP) CAST
(— SHOES OUT OF SHAPE) SHACHLE
SHACKLE
(— TIGHT CORSETS) LACE
WEARIED AWEARY FORGONE
FATIGUED WEARIFUL
WEARINESS TIRE FATIGUE
BRAINFAG SICKNESS VEXATION
WEARING DECAY SCUFF BURNING
CLOTHES ABRASION GARMENTS
GRINDING
WEARISOME DRY DULL HARD
SLOW WEARY BORING MORTAL
PROLIX SODDEN IRKSOME
TEDIOUS SAWDUSTY TIRESOME
TOILSOME
WEARISOMENESS TEDIUM
WEARY FAG IRK SAD BOEG BORE
CLOY MOIL PALL POOP PUNY
SADE TIRE TIRY WEAK WORE
WORN BORED BREAK CURSE
SPENT ABRADE BETOIL HARASS
PLAGUE SICKLY SQUEAL TUCKER
EXHAUST FATIGUE IRKSOME
SWINKED FATIGATE FORCHASE
GRIEVOUS TIRESOME WRETCHED
FORJASKIT
(BECOME —) JADE
WEARY WILLIE TRAMP
WEASAND WISEN GULLET THROAT
WIZZEN TRACHEA WINDPIPE
WEASEL CANE VAIR VARE WARE
HULDA HURON SNEAK STOAT
TAIRA TAYRA ERMINE FERRET
HULDAH VERMIN ARCTOID
VORMELA FUTTERET MUISHOND

MUSTELIN WHITRACK
(PREF.) GALEO
WEASEL CAT LINSANG
WEATHER SKY DIRT RAIN TIME
COLLA STORM WINDWARD
(— CONDITION) WHITEOUT
(FAIR —) SHINE
(HOT AND HUMID —) SIZZARD
(INCLEMENT —) SEASON
(INTERVAL OF FAIR —) SLATCH
(UNDER THE —) SEEDY
(VIOLENT —) ELEMENTS
(PREF.) EUDIO METEOR(O)
WEATHERBEATEN GNARLED
SEAGOING
WEATHERCOCK COCK FANE VANE
FAINE FANACLE
WEAVE CANE HABI HUCK JOIN
LACE LENO LOOM REED ROCK
SPIN WALE WARP WIND WOOF
DOBBY DRAPE PLAIT TWINE
UNITE BROCHE DAMASK DEVISE
DIAPER DOBBIE FABRIC CANILLE
ENTWINE FASHION INDRAPE
SATINET SHUTTLE VANDYKE
DIAGONAL DUCHESSE OVERSHOT
(— PATTERNS INTO) BROCADE
(BASKET —) BARLEYCORN
(CARPET —) FLOSSA
(HERRINGBONE —) SUMAK
SOUMAK SHEMAKA
(LATTICE —) TEE
(OPEN —) LENO BAREGE
WEAVER KORI TANTI WEBBE
DRAWBOY WEBSTER WOBSTER
PENELOPE TAPESTER
WEAVERBIRD NUN BAYA MAYA
TAHA FINCH MUNIA VIDUA
WEBBE BISHOP CANARY OXBIRD
WHIDAH WHYDAH BENGALI
AMADAVAT AVADAVAT
CARDINAL MANNIKIN
WEAVING TANIKO TEXTURE
WEBBING
(— OF WORDS) CONTEXT
(— TOGETHER) PLEXURE
WEAZEN WIZEN SHRINK WIZENED
WEB PLY WOB CAUL FELT MAZE
TENT TOIL VANE WARP WEFT
SKEIN SNARE THROW TWIST
FLEECE TISSUE ENSNARE
FEATHER LAYETTE TEXTURE
SNOWSHOE VEXILLUM
(— IN EYE) HAW
(CRANK —) THROW
(PREF.) HIST(O) HISTI(O) HYPHO
WEBBED RINGED PALMATE
WEBBING MAT WEB PALAMA
WEB-FOOTED PALMATE
PALAMATE PALMIPED
WEB SPINNER EMBIID WEBWORM
WED GET BEWED BRIDE MARRY
STAKE WAGER ENGAGE PLEDGE
SPOUSE ESPOUSE WEDLOCK
WEDDING BRIDAL SPLICE NUPTIAL
WEDLOCK ESPOUSAL MARRIAGE
WEDGE KEY COIN FROE FROW
GLUT HORN KYLE PLUG STOB
TRIG TRIP WAGE CHOCK CHUCK
CLEAT COIGN HACEK HORSE
QUINE QUOIN SCOTE SLICE
THROW COTTER CUNEUS QUINET
SCOTCH EMBOLUS QUINNET

SCHOCHE VOUSSOIR
(— BETWEEN TWO FEATHERS) KEY
(— IN) JAM JAMB
(— OF OATMEAL) FARL FARLE
(— TO PREVENT MOTION) CHOCK
(CURVED —) CAM
(WOODEN —) COW GLUT JACK
(PREF.) CUNEI CUNEO EMBOL(O)
SPHEN(O)
WEDGER SPRINGER
WEDGE-SHAPED CUNEAL SPHENIC
CUNEATED SPHENOID
(PREF.) CUNEO SPHEN(O)
WEDLOCK WIFE SPOUSAL
MARRIAGE SPOUSAGE
WEDNESDAY MIDWEEK
WEE TINY EARLY SMALL TEENY
YOUNG LITTLE
WEED BUR HOE BURR CHOP CULL
DOCK FORB LOUK SHIM SIDA
TARE WEID CIGAR DRANK DRAWK
DRESS DROKE FLESH BLINKS
CASUAL COCKLE DARNEL JIMSON
KNAWEL RIPGUT SARCLE SPURGE
SPURRY STROIL ASHWORT
BUGLOSS COHITRE CUCKOLD
EGILOPS GARMENT GOSMORE
HOGWORT RAGWEED RAGWORT
SANDBUR TOBACCO VERVAIN
VERVINE CHADLOCK COCKSPUR
COWWHEAT PIRIPIRI PLANTAIN
PURSLANE TOADFLAX ALFILERIA
MARIJUANA
(— OUT) ROGUE
(MEXICAN —) BIRDEYE
(ROADSIDE —) PLANTAGO
(TROUBLESOME —) KEX TITTER
(WATER —) ANACHARIS
(PL.) FILTH WRACK DISMAL
SPRING WEEDAGE TRUMPERY
WEEDER SARCLER
WEEDY FOUL LANKY
WEEK OOK WOK OULK WOKE
SENNET STANZA HEBDOMAD
SENNIGHT
(TWO —S) FORTNIGHT
WEEKDAY FERIA WARDAY
WEEKLY AWEEK HEBDOMADARY
WEEL LEAP POOL TRAP RIGHT
WHIRLPOOL
WEEN MEAN VENE WEND FANCY
GUESS EXPECT BELIEVE IMAGINE
SUPPOSE CONCEIVE
WEENY TINY SMALL WEESHY
WEEP CRY ORP SOB BAWL BEND
GIVE LEAK OOZE PIPE TEAR WAIL
GREET BEWAIL BEWEEP BOOHOO
BUBBLE LAMENT SHOWER
BLUBBER LAPWING SQUINNY
COMPLAIN
WEEPER GREETER MOURNER
CAPUCHIN
(PL.) FLENTES
WEEPING WOP GREET MILCH
RAINY BOOHOO LAMENT OOZING
PIPING BLUBBER MAUDLIN
TEARFUL DRIPPING LACRIMAL
MADIDANS PLORATION
WEEPING SINEW GANGLION
WEEVER JUGULAR STINGBULL
WEEVIL MAX BOUD POPE WHULE
PICUDO WEEBLE BILLBUG
BRUCHUS VAQUITA

CURCULIO WOODWORM
(PLUM —) TURK
WEFT WEB PICK WOOF BLAST
FABRIC FILLING
WEIGH GO SIT HEFT PEIS TARE
TELL COUNT HEAVE HOIST PEIZE
POISE RAISE SCALE BURDEN
PONDER ANALYZE BALANCE
DEPRESS LIBRATE CONSIDER
EVALUATE MEDITATE MILITATE
(— DOWN) LADE SWAY SWEE
BESET HEAVY PEISE CADDLE
CHARGE CUMBER PESTER
DEPRESS FREIGHT INGRATE
OPPRESS OVERLAY ENCUMBER
(— UPON) SIT GRIEVE
WEIGHER BOXMAN PEISER SCALER
WEIGHING METAGE
(— MACHINE) TRON SCALE TRONE
WEIGHT (ALSO SEE MEASURE AND
UNIT) BOB FEN FOB KIN MAN
NET OKE RAM SER SIR TOM TUP
ABAS ATOM BEEF CLOG DROP
GRAM HEFT IRON KITE LEAD
LOAD MACE MEAL NAIL ONUS
PEIS POND PORT ROTL SEAM
SEER SINK WAIT ABBAS CLOVE
CRITH GARCE LIVRE MAUND
PEASE PEISE PICUL POISE POIZE
PRESS RIDER SCALE STAMP
AUNCEL BURDEN CHARGE
DIRHEM HAMMER IMPORT
MOMENT MONKEY PASSIR
PONDER PONDUS SINKER STRESS
BALLAST DOLPHIN GRAVITY
MILLIER PLATINE PLUMMET
POSTURE CHALDRON DEMIMARK
DUMBBELL ENCUMBER FARASULA
LISPOUND PRESSURE PRESTIGE
QUINCUNX STANDARD STRENGTH
(— AFTER TARE DEDUCTION)
SUTTLE
(— CARRIED BY HORSE) IMPOST
(— CLOTH) FLOCK
(— FOR HURLING) HAMMER
(— FOR LEAD) FOTHER FOTMAL
(— FOR PRECIOUS STONE) CARAT
(— FOR WOOL) TOD SARPLER
(— FOR WOOL, CHEESE, ETC.) CLOVE
(— OF BROADSIDE) GUNPOWER
(— OF COAL) KEEL
(— OF COFFEE) MAT
(— OF HYDROGEN) CRITH
(— OF METAL) JOURNEY
(— OF ONE 10TH TAEL) MACE
(— OF ONE 100TH TAEL) FEN
(— OF PENDULUM) BOB
(— OF PILE DRIVER) TUP
(— OF RAW SILK) PARI
(— OF SILK OR RAYON) DRAMMAGE
(— OF 100 LBS.) CENTAL CENTENA
CENTNER
(— OF 1000 LIVRES) MILLIER
(— OF 20 OR 21 LBS.) SCORE
(— OF 40 BUSHELS) WEY
(— OF 5 UNCIAE) QUINCUNX
(— ON MINE SWEEPER) KITE
(— ON STEELYARD) PEA
(— ON WATCH CHAIN) FOB
(— TO BEND HOT METAL) DUMPER
(— TO DETECT FALSE COINS)
PASSIR
(— TO HINDER MOTION) CLOG

(— WHICH VESSEL CAN CARRY)
TONNAGE
(ABYSSINIAN —) FARASULA
(CARAT —) SILIQUA
(CLOCK —) PEISE
(COUNTERFEIT —) SLANG
(FALSE —) SLANG
(GREATLY VARYING —) MAN
MAUND
(HEAVY —) MONKEY
(LIGHT —) SUTTLE
(MONEYER'S —) DROIT
(ORIENTAL —) TAEL CATTY
(SASHCORD —) MOUSE
(SHUFFLEBOARD —) SHIP
(SMALL —) MITF GERAH RIDER
(SPLINE —) DOLPHIN
(UNIT OF —) SER VIS WEY GERA
LAST ROTL SEER LIANG LIBRA
LINGO MINAL PECUL PERIT PIKOL
KANTAR LINGOE MISKAL POCKET
LISPUND PRICKLE QUINTAL
ZOLOTNIK
(PREF.) BAR(I)(O)(Y) PONDERO
(SUFF.) BAR(IC)
WEIGHTED BIAS LOADED
WEIGHTER FULLER
WEIGHT-PRODUCING GRAVIFIC
WEIGHTY GRAVE GREAT HEAVY
HEFTY MASSY SOLID VALID
COGENT SOLEMN EARNEST
MASSIVE ONEROUS PEISANT
PESANTE SERIOUS TELLING
GRIEVOUS MATERIAL POWERFUL
PREGNANT PORTENTOUS
SIGNIFICANT
WEIR DAM PEN CRIB KEEP LEAP
STOP CAULD DOACH GARTH
GORCE HATCH HEDGE SASSE
STANK LASHER BURROCK
WEIRD ODD EERY UNCO UNKO
EERIE UNCOW UNKID CREEPY
ELDRICH ELRITCH UNCANNY
UNUSUAL WIZARDLY
(— SISTERS) FATES
WEITSPEKAN YUROK
WEKA RAIL WOODHEN RAILBIRD
WELCOME SEE FAIN GOOD HAIL
ADOPT CHEER GREET RESET
TREAT ACCOIL INVITE SALUTE
ACCLAIM ACCUEIL AMBRACE
GRATIFY BIENVENU GREETING
HAEREMAI PLEASANT
ACCEPTABLE
WELD SHUT WELL SWAGE UNITE
WOALD ACACIA
WELDED SHOT
WELDING FUSION SHUTTING
WELFARE SEL GOOD HALE HEAL
SELE WEALTH BENISON BLESSING
WELKIN SKY HEAVENS WALKENE
WELL AIN EYE GAY PIT WEL BENE
FINE FLOW GOOD PANT PUIT
PURE RITE SAFE SINK WINK
AWEEL BOOLY BOWLY GREAT
MUSHA OILER QUELL WALLY
WISHA ATWEEL BUCKET CENOTE
ENOUGH FAIRLY GASSER NICELY
OFFSET PUMPER TUNNEL
FALLWAY GRADELY HEALTHY
WILDCAT BOREHOLE FOUNTAIN
GRAITHLY POSTHOLE WATERPIT
WEALSOME

(— AND STRONG) BUNKUM
(— IN GLACIER) MOULIN
**(— THROUGH FLOORS OF
WAREHOUSE)** FALLWAY
(— UP) WALL WALM DIGHT
(AS —) ALSO
(NONPRODUCTIVE —) DUSTER
(NOT —) DONNY SOBER INVALID
(OIL —) OILER GASSER GUSHER
SPOUTER WILDCAT STRIPPER
(RECTANGULAR —) BOOLY BOWLY
(SACRED — AT MECCA) ZEMZEM
(TOLERABLY —) GAYLIES GEYLIES
(VERY —) BRAWLY CLEVER
(PREF.) BENE EU
WELL-BALANCED SOBER
WELL-BEHAVED GOOD NICE
MODEST MANNERED
WELL-BEING HEAL SKIN WEAL
HEALTH WEALTH COMFORT
EUCRASY WELFARE EUCRASIA
PROSPERITY
WELLBORN GENTLE EUGENIC
WELL-BRED GENTIL POLITE
GENTEEL REFINED CULTURED
LADYLIKE
WELL-BUILT TIGHT
WELL CASING STEANING
WELL-CHOSEN CHOICE
WELL-CONDITIONED SONSY
WELL-CONSIDERED THRIFTY
WELL CURB PUTEAL
WELL-DEFINED STRICT
WELL-DISPOSED SIB FAIN GOOD
VAIN
WELL DONE SHABASH
WELL-DRESSED BRAW GASH
SMART BRAWLY
WELL-FED BLOWSY BLOWZY
CHUBBY GAWCEY GAWSIE
WELL-FINISHED SOIGNE
WELL-FORMED TIGHT DECENT
PROPER SEEMLY SHAPELY
WELL-FOUNDED FIRM GOOD JUST
SOUND WORTHY
WELL-GROOMED SMUG CRISP
SOIGNE SOIGNEE
WELL-GROUNDED JUST VALID
WELL-GROWN THRODDY
WELL-HUSBANDED THRIFTY
WELL-INFORMED KNOWING
PERFECT
WELL-INTENTIONED AMIABLE
WELL-KEPT SMUG POLITE
WELL-KNIT WIRY
WELL-KNOWN BREEM BREME
BEATEN FAMOUS KENNED PUBLIC
FAMILIAR PROMINENT
WELL-LIKED FANCIED POPULAR
WELL-MADE CLEVER FEATOUS
WELL-MANNERED POLITE
COURTEOUS
WELL-NIGH WELLY ALMOST
NEARLY WELLMOST
WELL-ORDERED
(PREF.) COSM(ETO)(ICO)(O)
WELL-ORGANIZED SNOD
WELL-PLEASED FAIN VAIN
WELL-PROPORTIONED SUING
TRETIS HANDSOME
WELL-READ STUDIED LITERARY
WELL-ROUNDED CHUBBY
WELL-SHAPED CLEVER FEATOUS

WELL-TILLED NOT NOTT
WELL-TO-DO ABLE BEIN BIEN EASY
WARM PODDED
WELL-TRODDEN TRITE
WELL-WISHER FRIEND FAVORER
WELS WALLER SHEATFISH
WELSH (ALSO SEE WALES) CYMRY
FUDGE TAFFY CYMRIC KYMRIC
CAMBRIAN
WELSHER SHICER QUITTER
WELSHMAN CELT KELT TAFFY
BRYTHON CAMBRIAN
WELSH ONION CIBOL CIBOULE
CHESBOLL
WELT WALE RIDGE STRIP WHELP
WELTING BANDELET TURNOVER
(SHOE —S) WATTIS
WELTANSCHAUUNG FAITH
IDEOLOGY
WELTER REEL RIOT TOSS WILT
GROVEL TUMBLE WALLOW
WRITHE SMOTHER STAGGER
SWELTER
(— OF SOUNDS) DIN
WELWITSCHIA TUMBOA
WEM FLAW SCAR SPOT STAIN
WEN CYST WYNN CLIER CLYER
TALPA TUMOR GOITER
WENCH DELL DILL DOXY DRAB
GILL GIRL JADE MAID MOLL PRIM
TRUG GOUGE KITTY MADAM
QUEAN TRULL WHORE AUDREY
BLOUSE BLOWEN BLOWZE
DRAZEL JILLET KITTIE MOTHER
POPLET WOTLINK POPLOLLY
(CLUMSY —) MODER MODDER
MOTHER MAUTHER
WENCHER DRABBER STRIKER
WEND BOW END SORB VEND
STEER BETAKE DEPART DIRECT
TRAVEL PROCEED SORBIAN
LUSATIAN
(— ONE'S WAY) MARK
WENT GODE LANE ROAD YEDE
ALLEY PASSAGE
(— ABOUT) WOLK
WENTLETRAP SCALA
WENZEL JACK
WERE (— IT NOT) SAVE
WEREWOLF TURNSKIN VERSIPEL
WERTHER (BELOVED OF —) LOTTE
WEST STY BEWEST PONENT
OCCIDENT
WESTERN PONENT SCAEAN
HESPERIC SANDWICH
(PREF.) HESPER(O)
WESTERN SAMOA (CAPITAL OF —)
APIA
(ISLAND OF —) UPOLU MANONO
SAVAII APOLIMA
(MONEY OF —) TALA
WEST HIGHLAND KYLOE

WEST INDIES

ISLAND: CAT CUBA LONG ABACO
EXUMA HAITI NEVIS PELEE
TURKS ANDROS BAHAMA
CAICOS CAYMAN INAGUA
TOBAGO VIRGIN ACKLINS
ANTIGUA BONAIRE CROOKED
CURACAO GRENADA JAMAICA
LEEWARD STKITTS STLUCIA
TORTOLA ANGUILLA BARBADOS

DOMINICA STTHOMAS
TRINIDAD WINDWARD
ELEUTHERA MARGARITA
MAYAGUANA STVINCENT
GUADELOUPE HISPANIOLA
MARTINIQUE MONTSERRAT
PUERTORICO
NATION: BARBADOS

WEST VIRGINIA
CAPITAL: CHARLESTON
COLLEGE: SALEM BETHANY
CONCORD MARSHALL
BLUEFIELD
COUNTY: CLAY WIRT BOONE
HARDY MINGO ROANE TUCKER
UPSHUR BARBOUR KANAWHA
INDIAN: MONETON
LAKE: LYNN
NICKNAME: MOUNTAIN
RIVER: ELK OHIO KANAWHA
POTOMAC GUYANDOT
STATE BIRD: CARDINAL
STATE FLOWER: RHODODENDRON
STATE TREE: MAPLE
TOWN: ELKINS KEYSER RIPLEY
VIENNA WESTON BECKLEY
GRAFTON SPENCER WEIRTON
FAIRMONT WHEELING

WESTWARD WESSEL OCCASIVE
WESTLINS
WESTWARD HO (AUTHOR OF —)
KINGSLEY
(CHARACTER IN —) YEO JOHN
LUCY ROSE AMYAS FRANK LEIGH
DESOTO GUZMAN EUSTACE
OXENHAM RICHARD GRENVILE
SALTERNE AYACANORA
WET DEW DIP SOP WAT DAMP
DANK LASH MOIL SLOW SOAK
SOFT UVID BATHE DABBY DROOK
DRUNK HUMID JUICE JUICY
LEACH MADID MOIST MOOTH
RAINY SLAKE SNAPY SOBBY
SOPPY SPEWY STEEP TIGHT
WEAKY CLASHY DABBLE DAGGLE
DAMPEN HUMECT IMBRUE
JARBLE LABBER MADEFY MARSHY
MOISTY QUASHY SHOWER
SLABBY SOBBED SPONGY SPOUTY
SWASHY WATERY ARROUSE
BLUBBER DRABBLE FLOTTER
MOISTEN SLOPPED SOBBING
SPEWING SPRINGY IRRIGATE
SATURATE SLATTERY SLOBBERY
SLOTTERY WATERISH
(— AND STORMY) FOUL
(— LIGHTLY) SPRINKLE
(— THOROUGHLY) SOUSE DRENCH
(SOFTLY —) SQUASHY
(VERY —) SOPPY
(PREF.) HYGR(O) UDO
WETHER PUR RAM HAMEL
DINMAN DINMONT
WETNESS DANK
WETTING SOUCE SOUSE SOWSE
MOILING
WHACK DAD LAM TRY BANG BELT
BIFF DEAL HACK SWAK TIME
DRIVE SHARE STATE SWACK
WHANG CHANCE DEFEAT STROKE

THWACK BARGAIN LAMBACK
PORTION
WHACKING VERY WHALING
WHOPPING EXTREMELY
WHALE SEI CETE HUEL HULL LASH
ORCA WALL KOGIA POGGY SCRAG
SPERM STUNT BALEEN BELUGA
BLOWER FINNER GIBBAR KILLER
THRASH BOWHEAD DOLPHIN
FINBACK FINFISH GIBBERT
GRAMPUS MARSOON RIPSACK
RORQUAL SPOUTER ZIPHIAN
BALAENID CACHALOT CETACEAN
DOEGLING GREYBACK HARDHEAD
HUMPBACK JUBARTES MUTILATE
PHYSETER THRASHER ZIPHIOID
(— BUTCHER) LEMMER
(— REFUSE) GURRY
(FINBACK —) GRASO
(SCHOOL OF —S) GAM POD
(PREF.) BALAENI BALAENO CET(O)
WHALEBONE BALEEN
WHALER HEADER BUSHMAN
SPOUTER SWAGMAN WHACKER
WHOPPER CETICIDE
WHALESKIN MUKTUK
WHANG BEAT BLOW FLOG CHUNK
THONG WHACK THRASH
RAWHIDE
WHARF KEY POW DOCK GARE PIER
QUAY SLIP BERTH JETTY LEVEE
STADE STAITH STRAND LANDING
PANTALAN STELLING
WHARVE WARVE WHIRL WHORL
WHAT FAT HOT HOW WET WHO
HOOT HOTE WHEN STUFF WHICH
MATTER PARTLY
WHATA FUTTAH FUTTER
WHAT EVERY WOMAN KNOWS
(AUTHOR OF —) BARRIE
(CHARACTER IN —) JOHN ALICK
DAVID JAMES SHAND SYBIL
WYLIE BRIERE MAGGIE CHARLES
VENABLES TENTERDEN
WHATNOT OMNIUM ETAGERE
WHAT PRICE GLORY (AUTHOR OF
—) ANDERSON
(CHARACTER IN —) FLAGG QUIRT
CHARMAINE
WHAT'S-ITS-NAME TIMENOGUY
WHATSOEVER MORTAL
WHEAL HIVE HUEL WALE WELT
URTICA POMPHUS
WHEAT WIT CORN CONES EMMER
FULTZ GRAIN SPELT SPICA TRIGO
BULGUR BURGUL CEREAL
KANRED STAPLE TURKEY
EINKORN FORMITY FRUMETY
KUBANKA MARQUIS POLLARD
FRUMENTY SPELTOID
(— BOILED IN MILK) FURMITY
(— MEASURE) TRUG
(BEARDED —) RIVETS
(CRACKED —) GROATS
(GRANULATED —) SUJI SUJEE
(HARD —) DURUM
(PARCHED —) BULGUR
(PREF.) TRITICO
WHEATCAKE PURI
WHEATEAR CHACK ARLING
WITTOL CHACKER ORTOLAN
SNORTER WITTALL CHICKELL
SAXICOLA

WHEATGRASS BLUESTEM
WHEATLIKE VULGARE
WHEEDLE COG CANT CLAW COAX
CARNY FLUFF GLOSE GLOZE
INGLE JOLLY BANTER CAJOLE
CUITER FLEECH GLAVER RADDLE
SMOOGE WHILLY BLARNEY
CUITTLE PALAVER SMOODGE
TWEEDLE BLANDISH COLLOGUE
SCROUNGE
WHEEDLING BUTTERY COMETHER
WHEEL BOB BUR COG FAN NUT
ORB BEAD BUFF GEAR HELM
HURL PURL ROLL ROTA RULL
STAR TIRL WYLE ATHEY FLIER
FLUFF FLYER IDLER NORIA REWET
RHOMB ROWEL SWING TRUCK
BILOBE CASTER CASTOR CIRCLE
DRIVEN DRIVER FANNER HORRAL
JAGGER KURUMA LEADER PINION
ROLLER ROTATE RUNDLE
RUNNER TRACER BALANCE
BICYCLE CHUKKER GUDGEON
LANTERN PEDRAIL PRICKER
REVOLVE STEPNEY TRAILER
TRILOBE TRINDLE TROCHUS
TRUCKLE TRUNDLE UNILOBE
WILDCAT CARACOLE FOLLOWER
ODOMETER SPROCKET
(— A SKIN) FLUFF
(— CHARGED WITH DIAMOND DUST)
SLITTER
(— CONTROLLING RUDDER) HELM
(— FOR EXECUTIONS) RAT
(— IN KNITTING MACHINE) BUR
BURR
(— IN TIMEPIECE) BALANCE
(— OF LIFE) ZOETROPE
(BUCKET —) LIFTER
(DIAMOND —) SKIVE
(GEAR —) DRIVEN HELICAL
(GRINDING —) SHELL
(GROOVED —) PULLEY SHEAVE
SHIVER
(INTERRUPTER —) TICKER TIKKER
(LOCOMOTIVE —) DRIVER
(METAL —) FILET FILLET
(MILL —) PIRN
(PAIR OF LOGGING —S) CATYDID
KATYDID
(POINTED —) TRACER
(POLISHING —) BOB BUFF SKAIF
SKEIF BUFFER SCAIFE
(POTTER'S —) LATHE THROW
(SPARE —) STEPNEY
(SPINNING —) TURN CHARKA
CHARKHA
(SPUR —) ROWEL
(TANK —) BOGY BOGEY BOGIE
(TOOTHED —) GEAR PINION
ROULETTE
(TURBINE —) ROTOR
(TWO PAIRS OF —S) CUTS CUTTS
(VANED —) FLIER FLYER
(WATER —) NORIA SAKIA SAKIEH
SAKIYEH TYMPANUM
(PL.) KATYDID
(PREF.) CYCL(O) ROTA ROTATO
ROTI ROTO TROCH(I)(LEI)(O)
(SUFF.) TROCH(A)(AL)(OUS)(US)
WHEELBARROW GURRY BARROW
CARRIAGE
(PART OF —) BED LEG GRIP TIRE

TRAY BRACE FRAME WHEEL
HANDLE BRACKET SUPPORT
WHEELER POLER PUSHER
WHEEL-SHAPED ROTATE TROCHAL
ROTIFORM
WHEELWORK MOTION
WHEELWRIGHT WHEELER
WOODMAN WHEELMAN
WHEEZE JOKE HOOSE HOOZE
TRICK COGHLE
WHELK FILK GRUB WELT BUCKIE
MAGGOT PAPULE PIMPLE WINKLE
PUSTULE
WHELP CUB PUP SON CHIT FAWN
PUPPY YELPER KITLING
SPROCKET
WHEMMEL UPSET FUMMEL
FUMMLE WHAMBLE OVERTURN
WHEN AS BUT FAN FRO GIN THO
WON THAN THEN THOA TILL
SINCE UNTIL ENOUGH ALTHOUGH
WHENEVER ONCE
WHERE AS FAR FUR FAUR FEAR
FERRE PLACE QUAIR THERE
WHITHER LOCATION
(— ABOVE MENTIONED) US
WHEREFORE WHY CAUSE
FORWHY REASON
WHERENESS UBIETY
WHEREVER THERE
WHEREWITHAL MEANS MONEY
RESOURCES
WHERRET BOX CUFF SLAP HURRY
TEASE WORRY TROUBLE
WHIRRICK
WHERRY BARGE ROWBOAT
WHIRREY
WHET WET GOAD HONE TIME
TURN GRIND POINT RIFLE ROUSE
SLITE WHILE EXCITE INCITE
STROKE QUICKEN SHARPEN
APERITIF EXACUATE
WHETHER IF GIF GIN WHAR
WHERE EITHER
WHETSTONE BUR RIP RUB BUHR
BURR SLIP STONE RUBBER STRAIK
SHARPER WASHITA WHITTLE
OILSTONE RUBSTONE STRICKLE
WHEY PALE QUAY WHIG SERUM
THRUST WATERY
(PREF.) ORO
WHIBA UEBA
WHICH AS THE WHO THAT QUILK
WHILK
(— SEE) QV QQV
WHICKER NEIGH WHINNY WIGHER
WHIDAH BIRD VEUVE WEAVER
WHYDAH REDBILL
WHIFF FAN GUF BLOW GUFF GUST
HINT PUFF TIFT WAFT WIFT
FLUFF QUIFF SMOKE EXHALE
MAGRIM MEGRIM WHIFFET
WHIFFLE FIFE SWAY FLICKER
FLUTTER
WHIFFLETREE HEELTREE
SWINGLEBAR
WHIG JOG QUIG WHEY
WHILE AS BIT GAM THO YET FILE
FYLE TIDE TILL WHEN WHET
WOLE FILIE PIECE SPACE STEAD
STOUN THROW UNTIL STOUND
WHENAS WHILOM BEGUILE
TROUBLE EXERTION OCCASION

(— AWAY) AMUSE FLEET DIVERT BEGUILE DECEIVE

(LITTLE —) AWEE DRASS WHILEY WHILEEN WHILOCK

WHILES UNTIL SOMETIMES

WHILLY GULL CAJOLE WHEEDLE

WHILST TILL UNTIL

WHIM BEE FAD GIG GIN TOY FIKE FLAM KINK CRANK FANCY FLISK FOLLY FREAK HUMOR MEINY QUIRK THRUM FEGARY FITTEN MAGGOT MEGRIM SPLEEN VAGARY WHIMSY BOUTADE CAPRICE CONCEIT WRINKLE CROTCHET

WHIMBREL JACK SPOW SPOWE CURLEW MAYBIRD MAYFOWL TITTEREL

WHIMPER GIRN MEWL PULE WAIL WEAK BLEAT WHINE SIMPER WHINGE YAMMER GRIZZLE SNIFFLE SNUFFLE WHINDLE WHINNEL WHITTER WHINNOCK

WHIMSICAL FAIRY FANCY BAROCK COCKLE FLISKY NOTION QUAINT BAROQUE BIZARRE GIGGISH PUCKISH BIZZARRO FANCIFUL FREAKISH HUMOROUS NOTIONAL SINGULAR VAPOROUS PIXILATED

WHIMSY WHIM FREAK VAGARY CAPRICE WHIMWHAM

WHIN FUN ULEX FURZE WHINCOW WOODWAX

WHINCHAT TICK UTICK WHEATEAR

WHINE WOW GIRN GOWL MEWL PULE TIRM TOOT YARM YIRN BLEAT CROON MEECH QUINE TWINE WHAUP WHEWT PEENGE SNIVEL TREBLE WHINGE WINNEL YAMMER WHIMPER WHINDLE

WHINING QUERULOUS

WHINNY HINNY NEIGH PLAIN SNICKER WHICKER

WHINSTONE TRAP WHIN SCURDY

WHINYARD SWORD HANGER POCHARD WHINGER SHOVELER

WHIP CAT EEL FAN GAD ROD TAW BEAT CAST COIL DICK DUST FIRK FLOG FOAM GOAD HIDE JEHU JERK LASH LICK LOUK PLET TAWS URGE WHUP ABUSE AZOTE BIRCH CRACK FLAIL FLICK FLISK IMPEL KNOUT LEASH PLETE QUILT ROMAL SLASH STRAP SWEPE SWING SWISH TAWSE THONG THUMP AROUSE BREECH CHABUK DEFEAT FEAGUE INCITE LAINER LARRUP LICKER MAIDEN NETTLE PIZZLE QUIPPE SCUTCH SNATCH SWINGE SWITCH THRASH TICKLE CHABOUK CHICOTE COWHIDE COWSKIN CURBASH KURBASH LAMBAST LAYOVER NAGAIKA RAWHIDE SCOURGE SHINGLE SJAMBOK SLASHER TICKLER CHAWBUCK COACHMAN CONFOUND FLAGELLA KOURBASH PEPPERER

(— EGGS) CAST

(— HANDLE) CROP

(— IN PIANO ACTION) WIPPEN

(— WITH 3 LASHES) PLET PLETE

(HORSE —) WAND CHABOUK

(JOCKEY'S —) BAT

(RIDING —) CROP DICK QUIRT

(RUSSIAN —) KNOUT

(PREF.) FLAGELLI MASTIG(O)

(SUFF.) MASTIX

WHIPLASH THONG COSAQUE CRACKER

WHIPPED BEATEN BROKEN DEFEATED FOUETTEE CHANTILLY

WHIPPER TICKLER THONGMAN THRASHER THREAPER

WHIPPER-IN PRICKER

WHIPPERSNAPPER SQUIRT WHIFFET WHIPSTER

WHIPPING LICK TOCO TOKO HIDING CLANKER FANNING SERVING BIRCHING BROWSING SKELPING

WHIPPING POST FORK PILLAR

WHIP SCORPION GRAMPUS PHRYNID PEDIPALP WHIPTAIL

WHIPSOCKET SNEAD

WHIPSTITCH MINUTE INSTANT OVERCAST

WHIR BIRR ZIZZ WHIRRY

WHIRL BIRL EDDY FURL GYRE HURL PURL REEL RUSH SPIN TIRL DRILL GIDDY SKIRL SQUIR SWIRL THIRL THROW TWIRL TWIST WALTZ WHORL BUSTLE CIRCLE GYRATE HURTLE SWINGE VORTEX WHORLE WINDLE WIRBLE MIZMAZE REVOLVE TRUNDLE TURMOIL VERTICIL

(— ABOUT) DOZE GURGE

(— IN THE AIR) WARP

WHIRLIGIG GIG SPIN TURN WHEEL FIZGIG FISHGIG

WHIRLING GIDDY WHEELY STROBIC GYRATION GYRATORY VORTICAL PIROUETTE

(PREF.) STROBO

WHIRLPOOL EDDY GULF SUCK WEEL WELL WIEL GORCE GOURD GURGE BULLER GORGES SWELTH VORTEX GURGLET SWALLOW SWILKIE SUCKHOLE MAELSTROM

(PREF.) DINO

WHIRLWIND OE DEVIL VORTEX PRESTER TORNADO TOURBILLION

WHISHT HUSH SILENCE

WHISK ZIP FISK TUFT WHID WHIP WISP CAURI FLICK FLISK HURRY SPEED SWISH CHAURI CHOWRY SWITCH COWTAIL WHISKER

WHISKER HAIRLINE VIBRISSA

(PL.) BEARD ZIFFS WEEPER GALWAYS VIBRISSA MOUSTACHE SIDEBURNS

WHISKY RYE BOND CORN CIDER IRISH USQUE POTEEN REDEYE SCOTCH BOURBON BLOCKADE BUSTHEAD CREATURE POPSKULL USQUABAE MOONSHINE TANGLEFOOT

(GLASS OF —) RUBDOWN

(RAW —) DRUDGE

WHISPER BUZZ HARK HINT ROUN RUNE ROUND RUMOR TRACE TUTEL BREATH BREEZE HARKEN MURMUR SUSURR TITTLE WHISHT HEARKEN SUSURRUS

WHIST MORT VINT QUIET BOSTON SILENT WHEESHT

WHISTLE BLOW CALL FUTE PIPE WHEW QUILL WHAUP WHEEP WHUTE BUMMER BUZZER CUCKOO FUSSLE HOOTER SIFFLE SISTLE SQUEAL WARBLE YELPER CATCALL TWEEDLE BIRDCALL

(— FEEBLY) WHEEDLE

WHISTLE FLUTE SIFFLOT

WHISTLER PIPER MARMOT ROARER FLUTIST LAPWING SIFFLEUR

WHISTLING PIPY PIPEY ROARING SIFFLET RHONCHUS SUSSURANT

WHIT BIT JOT RAP ATOM DOIT HATE HOOT IOTA QUAT QUIT AUGHT BODLE GROAT POINT QUITE SPECK CIVITE PARTICLE TWOPENNY

WHITE CUT WAN BAWN FITE HOAR LILY PALE QUAT QUIT ASHEN BLOND HAOLE HOARY LABAN LINEN SNOWY ALBINO ARGENT BLANCH BRIGHT BUCKRA CANDID CIVITE ERMINE SILVER WINTRY CANDENT LEUCOUS NIVEOUS WHITTLE FAVORITE INNOCENT LACTEOUS

(— AND SMOOTH) IVORINE

(— OF EGG) GLAIR ALBUMEN

(— PERSON) OFAY

(POOR —) YAHOO CRACKER

(PREF.) ALB(I)(O) CALI CALLI LEUC(O) LEUK(O)

WHITE ALDER CLETHRA

WHITE ANT ANAY NASUTE TERMITE

WHITEBAIT SMELT ICEFISH SALANGID SALMONID

WHITEBEAM ARIA SERVICE MULBERRY

WHITEBOY PET LEVELER

WHITE BRYONY COWBIND MANDRAKE

WHITE CEDAR JUNIPER

WHITE CLOVER LADINO SHAMROCK

WHITE COMPANY (AUTHOR OF —) DOYLE

(CHARACTER IN —) JOHN MAUDE NIGEL HORDLE LORING SAMKIN ALLEYNE AYLWARD EDRICSON

WHITEFISH BLOAT CISCO PILOT POWAN BELUGA CHIVEY POLLAN TULIPI VENDIS BLOATER BOWBACK GWYNIAD LAVARET VENDACE BLACKFIN GREYBACK HUMPBACK MENOMINI SALMONID SCHNABEL TULLIBEE

WHITEFLY HOMOPTER MEALYWING

WHITE GUM TUART

WHITE-HEADED GOLDEN FAVORED FORTUNATE

WHITE HELLEBORE ITCHREED ITCHWEED

WHITE IPECAC ITOUBOU

WHITE LEAD CERUSE

WHITE MAPAN PIRIPIRI

WHITE MUSTARD KEDLOCK SINAPIS CRUCIFER

WHITEN CAM CAUM SCURF ALBIFY

BLANCH BLANCO BLEACH BLENCH DEALBATE EMBLANCH ETIOLATE PIPECLAY

WHITENED DEALBATE

WHITENESS IVORY ALBEDO ARGENT CANDOR PURITY CANITIES PALENESS

WHITE OAK ROBLE

WHITE POPLAR ABELE ABELTREE

WHITE SNAKEROOT STEVIA POOLWORT RICHWEED WHITETOP

WHITE STURGEON BELUGA

WHITETHROAT JACK MUFF MUFTY MUGGY PEGGY EYSOGE MILLER MUFFET WHISKY WINNEL HAYSUCK WHEYBIRD

WHITEWASH LIME GLASS BLANCH PARGET CHICAGO LIMEWASH PALLIATE

WHITEWEED DAISY

WHITE WHALE BELUGA

WHITHER GUST HURL RUSH WHIZ HURRY SHAKE WHERE FLURRY BLUSTER WHERETO

WHITING BARB HAKE CORBINA CORVINA MERLING KINGFISH MOONFISH

WHITING-POUT BIB KLEG BLENS

WHITISH BAWN PALE DILUTE SUBALBID

WHITLOW FELON AGNAIL ANCOME FETLOW BREEDER PANARIS BREDSORE RUNROUND

WHITLOW GRASS DRABA NAILWORT SHADBLOW

WHITRACK WEASEL FUTTERET WHITTRET

WHITSUNDAY TERM

WHITSUNTIDE PINXTER PINGSTER PINKSTER

WHITTLE CUT PARE CARVE KNIFE STEEL TWITE EXCITE MANTLE THWITE BLANKET

WHIZ BUZZ DEAL GIRL PIRR QUIZ SING WHIR ZIZZ SOUGH WHISH WHIZZ WIZARD BARGAIN SWITHER WHIDDER WHINNER

WHIZ-BANG EXPERT NOTABLE

WHO AS HOW THE WHA WHAT WHICH

WHOA WO WAY WHO STOP

WHOEVER WHATSO EVERWHO

WHOLE ALL HOW SUM BODY COOL EVEN HALE HALF HOLY HULL BLOCK GREAT GROSS HAILL SOLID SOUND TOTAL TOTUM TUTTA UNCUT CORPSE ENTIRE HEALED INTACT VERSAL GENERAL INFRACT INTEGER PERFECT SINCERE SOLIDUM COMPLETE ENSEMBLE ENTIRETY GLOBULAR INTEGRAL LIVELONG OUTRIGHT UNBROKEN

(— OF ANY ORGANISM) SOMA

(— OF REALITY) ABSOLUTE

(ORGANIC —) SYSTEM

(PREF.) ALL HOL(O) INTEGRI PAN TOTI TOTO

WHOLEHEARTED HEARTY SINCERE ZESTFUL COMPLETE IMPLICIT

WHOLESALE MASSIVE SWEEPING

WHOLESALER JOBBER EXPORTER
WHOLESOME GOOD CLEAN SOUND SWEET BENIGN SAVORY HEALTHY PRUDENT CURATIVE HALESOME HEALSOME HOMELIKE REMEDIAL SALUTARY HEALTHFUL
WHOLE-SOULED SINCERE
WHOLLY ALL FAIR FLAT HALE ONLY BLACK CLEAR FULLY QUITE STARK ALGATE BODILY FLATLY HOLLOW PURELY SOLELY ALGATES ROUNDLY SOLIDLY TOTALLY DIRECTLY ENTIRELY (PREF.) TOTI
WHOOP BOOM HOOP HOOT BOOST RAISE SHOUT EXCITE HALLOO HOOPOE
WHOOPING COUGH KINKHOST CHINCOUGH PERTUSSIS
WHOP WAP BEAT THUD THUMP STRIKE THRASH
WHOPPER LIE SIZER BOUNCER CRUMPER SLAPPER SNAPPER SWAPPER SWINGER SCROUGER STRAPPER WALLOPER
WHOPPING VERY LARGE BANGING RAPPING WAPPING WHALING SWINGING THUMPING WHACKING WALLOPING
WHORE DRAB JILT FILTH QUAIL WENCH HARLOT PUTAIN DEBAUCH PINNACE STRUMPET SUCCUBUS PROSTITUTE
WHOREMONGER HOLOUR
WHORL TURN CYCLE SPIRE SWIRL WHIRL THWORL VOLUTE WHARVE WREATH ANNULUS CALYCLE CALYCULE GYRATION VERTICIL VOLUTION (PREF.) SPONDYL(O) VERTICILL(I)
WHORLED (NOT —) ACYCLIC
WHORTLEBERRY HOT HURT FRAWN HOOTE FRAGHAN BILBERRY COWBERRY
WHY HOW QUI ENIGMA FORWHY
WICK BAD EVIL FARM TOWN ANGLE CREEK DAIRY MATCH QUICK SEAVE SNAST CORNER LIVING WICKED VILLAGE FARMSTEAD
(— CLOGGED WITH TALLOW) ROUGHIE
(LONG WAXED —) TAPER
WICKED BAD SAD DARK EVIL FAST FOUL IRON LAZY LEWD MEAN PIKY VILE BLACK CURST FELON SHREW SORRY WRONG WROTH CURSED GUILTY LITHER LUTHER NEFAST PERDIT PITCHY SEVERE SHREWD SINFUL UNHOLY UNJUST UNLEAD UNLEDE UNWELL CAITIFF DARKSUM GODLESS HEINOUS HELLISH IMMORAL NAUGHTY NINETED NOXIOUS PRAVOUS PROFANE ROGUISH UNGODLY UNSEELY UNSOUND UNWREST VICIOUS VILLAIN ACCURSED CRIMINAL DARKSOME DEPRAVED DEVILISH DIABOLIC ENORMOUS FELONOUS FIENDISH FLAGRANT MESCHANT OBDURATE PERVERSE TERRIBLE UNKINDLY ABANDONED

NEFARIOUS PERNICIOUS (PREF.) PONERO
WICKEDNESS ILL SIN EVIL HARM VICE CRIME FOLLY GUILT BELIAL FELONY NOUGHT UNGOOD ATHEISM DEVILRY ILLNESS PRAVITY DARKNESS DEVILTRY INIQUITY MISCHIEF SATANISM WANGRACE
WICKER SALE
WICKERWORK WEB WEEL TWIGGEN BASKETRY
WICKET GATE HOOP HATCH PITCH STUMP GUICHET
(FALLING OF —S) ROT
WICKETKEEPER STUMP STUMPER
WICKFORD POINT (AUTHOR OF —) MARQUAND
(CHARACTER IN —) JIM JOE BERG MARY ALLEN AVERY BELLA BRILL HARRY STOWE ARCHIE CALDER HOWARD WRIGHT GIFFORD SOUTHBY LEIGHTON PATRICIA CLOTHILDE
WICKIUP HUT WAKIUP SHELTER
WIDDRIM FIT FURY
WIDDY NOOSE WIDOW WITHY HALTER
WIDE FAR LAX DEEP ROOM SIDE AMPLE BROAD LARGE ROOMY SHARP SLACK WRONG ASTRAY ROOMWARD SPACEFUL SPACIOUS
(— OF) BESIDE
(— OF THE MARK) AWRY WILD ABROAD
(LONG AND —) SIDE
(PREF.) EURY LATI
WIDE-AWAKE FLY FOXY KEEN LIVE ALERT FLASH LEERY CADDIE SLIPPY KNOWING WAKEFUL WATCHFUL
WIDELY FAR BROAD ABROAD GREATLY LARGELY
WIDEN FLAN REAM DILATE EXPAND EXTEND FLANCH FLANGE FUNNEL BROADEN
WIDENESS WIDTH BREADTH
WIDESPREAD RIFE DIFFUSE GENERAL POPULAR PROLATE CATHOLIC EXTENDED PANDEMIC SWEEPING
WIDGEON SMEE WHIM GOOSE WHEWER ZUISIN POACHER POTCHER BALDPATE BLUEBILL WHISTLER
WIDOW VID BALO DAME SKAT BLIND KITTY VEUVE WEEDA WIDDY MATRON RELICT TERCER DOWAGER EMPRESS BARONESS DOWERESS
(PL.) VIDUAGE
WIDOWED VIDUOUS
WIDOWHOOD VIDUAGE VIDUITY
WIDTH GAPE SIDE RANGE SCOPE BREADTH OPENING FRONTAGE FULLNESS LARGEOUR LATITUDE WIDENESS
(— OF CUT) KERF
(— OF HORSESHOE) COVER
(— OF PALM) HAND
(— OF PAPER) FILL
(— OF PULLEY) FACE
(— OF SHIP) BEAM

(— OF SHIP'S BAND) STRAKE
(— OF TYPE) SET
(— OF WEB) DECKLE
WIELD PLY RUN BEAR WALT WIND APPLY EXERT SWING VELDE EMPLOY GOVERN HANDLE MANAGE STRAIN CONTROL
WIFE UX FEM HEN MRS RIB WYF BABY BIBI DAME DORA ENID FEME FERE FRAU FROW JAEL LADY MAKE MAMA MATE RANI UXOR DIRCE DONNA DUTCH FEMME LUCKY MAMMA MATCH MUJER SQUAW WOMAN ELMIRE EMILIA GAMMER KEEPER MATRON MISSIS MISSUS MULIER SPOUSE VENDER WAHINE BEDMATE DIONYZA EMPRESS PARTNER WEDLOCK DEIANIRA DEIDAMIA ERIPHYLE HELPMATE HELPMEET MISTRESS PECULIAR
(— OF COTTER) COTQUEAN
(— OF KNIGHT OR BARONET) DAME
(— OF MOHAMMEDAN) KHADIJA
(AFFIANCED —) FUTURE
(INDIAN'S —) WEBB
(OLD —) GAMMER
(PL.) PUNALUA
(PREF.) UXOR(I)
WIG BOB JIZ RUG TIE FRIZ GIZZ JANE JIZZ LOCK TETE TOUR BUSBY CAXON FLASH JASEY MAJOR SCALP SCOLD ADONIS BRUTUS FROWZE MERKIN PERUKE REBUKE TOUPEE TOUPET COMBING RAMILIE SCRATCH SHEITEL SPENCER BOBJEROM CHEDREUX CHEWELER DALMAHOY NIGHTCAP PERUKERY POSTICHE ROGERIAN VALLANCY
(— WITH ROUGHLY CROPPED HAIR) BRUTUS
(BUSHY —) BUSBY
(GRAY —) GRIZZLE
(WORSTED —) JASEY
(18TH CENTURY —) ADONIS GEORGE
WIGGLE JET HOTCH JIGGLE WABBLE WANGLE
WIGGLER PUPA LARVA WRYER
WIGHT MAN SWIFT STRONG VALIANT CREATURE STALWART
WIGMAKER WIGGER PERUKER PERUKIER
WIGWAG SIGNAL
WIGWAM TIPI LODGE TEPEE WEEKWAM WICKIUP
WIKENO NIKENO HEILTSUK
WILD APE MAD REE SHY FAST RUDE SCAR WOWF CRAZY FANTI FELON FERAL GIDDY MYALL RANDY RANTY ROUGH ROYET SKEER WASTE DESERT FANTEE FERINE FIERCE LAVISH MADCAP NATIVE RAMAGE RANDOM RENISH SAVAGE SHANDY STORMY UNRULY BERSERK BREACHY ERRATIC FRANTIC GALLOUS GALLOWS HAGGARD HOWLING MADDING NATURAL OUTWARD RIOTOUS SKADDLE SKEERED WILDING ABERRANT AGRESTAL BARBARIC CHIMERIC DESOLATE

FAROUCHE FRENETIC HALUCKET HELLICAT RECKLESS UNTILLED WARRAGAL WILLYARD BOISTEROUS
(— CARD) FREAK
(PREF.) AGRIO
WILD ASS GOUR KIANG KULAN COTULA KOULAN ONAGER QUAGGA CHIGETAI
WILD BALSAM APPLE CREEPER
WILD BEE KARBI
WILD BOAR APER SUID TUSKER SOUNDER SUIDIAN WILRONE SANGLIER
WILD BUFFALO ARNA ARNEE
WILD BUSH BEAN PHASEMY
WILD CABBAGE YELLOWS
WILD CARDAMOM RUEWORT KNOBWOOD
WILD CARROT DILL ELTROT FIDDLE BIRDNEST HILLTROT
WILDCAT CAT BALU EYRA CHATI CHAUS MANUL TIGER MARGAY SERVAL WAGATI COLOCOLA
WILD CELERY ACHE ECHE EELGRASS SMALLAGE
WILD CHERRY GEAN MERRY MAZZARD
WILD CHERVIL KECK COWWEED HONEWORT MILKWEED
WILD CYCLAMEN SOWBREAD
WILD DOG ADJAG DHOLE DINGO GUARA AGUARA AGOUARA CIMARRON WARRAGAL
WILD DUCK (AUTHOR OF —) IBSEN
(CHARACTER IN —) GINA EKDAL SORBY WERLE HANSEN HEDVIG GREGERS HJALMAR RELLING
WILDEBEEST GNU
WILDERNESS BUSH WILD WASTE DESERT FOREST WESTERN SOLITUDE
WILD-EYED HAGGARD RADICAL
WILDFOWL VOLATILE
WILD GARLIC MOLY
WILD GERANIUM ALUMROOT DOVEFOOT FLUXWEED
WILD GOAT TUR IBEX TAHR EVECK PASAN MAZAME MARKHOR AEGAGRUS MARKHOOR
WILD HORSE BRUMBY KUMRAH TARPAN BRUMBIE WARRAGAL WARRIGAL
WILD HYACINTH CUCKOO CROWTOE GREGGLE BRODIAEA CROWFOOT
WILD INDIGO SHOOFLY
WILD LETTUCE FIREWEED
WILD MAN SAVAGE WOODMAN WOODSMAN
WILD MANGOSTEEN SANTOL
WILD MARJORAM ORGAN ORGAMY ORGANY ORIGAN ORGAMENT
WILD MULBERRY YAWWEED
WILD MUSTARD RUNCH CHARLOCK
WILDNESS FERITY HEYDAY HEYDEY FEROCITY SAVAGERY SAVAGISM
WILD OAT DRANK DRAWK DROKE HAVER HEVER EGILOPS
WILD ONION UMBEL UMBELLA

WILD OX BUF YAK ANOA BUFF
REEM UNICORN
WILD PARSLEY ELTROT HILLTROT
WILD PEAR DOGBERRY
WILD PLUM SLOE ISLAY
WILD POTATO MANROOT
WAPATOO
WILD RADISH RUNCH
WILD RICE MANOMIN
WILD SAGE EYESEED
WILD SARSAPARILLA SHOTBUSH
**WILDSCHUTZ, DER (CHARACTER IN
—)** BACULUS NANETTE EBERBACH
FREIMANN GRETCHEN KRONTHAL
(COMPOSER OF —) LORTZING
WILD SERVICE TREE SORB
SORBUS
WILD SHEEP SHA AUDAD URIAL
AOUDAD ARGALI BHARAL
NAYAUR BIGHORN MOUFLON
WILD SWAN ELK
WILD THYME HILLWORT
SERPOLET
WILD TOBACCO GAGROOT
SOURBUSH MARIJUANA
SALVADORA
WILD TURNIP NAVEW
WILD VANILLA LIATRIS
WILE ART PAUK PAWK RUSE
FRAUD GUILE TRICK ALLURE
BLENCH DECEIT ENGINE ENTICE
BEGUILE ARTIFICE TRICKERY
WILGA WILLOW
WILL EGO MAY ULL WAY FATE LIST
TEST WISH LEAVE OUGHT SHALL
WORST ANIMUS CHOICE CHOOSE
DESIRE DEVICE DEVISE LEGATE
LIKING QUETHE SCRIPT APETITE
CODICIL PASSION WITWORD
AMBITION BEQUEATH PLEASING
PLEASURE VOLITION
(— NOT) WONT WINNA WONNA
WUNNA WONNOT
(— OF DEITY) DECREE
(— OF GOD) LAW
(— OF LEGISLATURE) ACT
(— TO LIVE) TANGHA
(FREE —) ACCORD
(GOOD —) GREE
(I —) CHILL
(ILL —) ARR ENVY HEST ANIMUS
ENMITY UNTHANK AMBITION
(SUFF.) (CONDITION OF —) THYMIA
(STATE OF —) BOULIA BULIA BULIC
WILLET TATLER TATTLER
WILLFUL HEADY WILLY FEISTY
UNRULY HAGGARD WAYWARD
WILSOME CAMSTRARY
WILLFULLY WOLDES SCIENTER
WILLIAM TELL (AUTHOR OF —)
SCHILLER
(CHARACTER IN —) JOHN TELL
FURST HENRY ARNOLD BERTHA
ULRICH WALTER WERNER
GESSLER WILLIAM MATHILDE
BAUMGARTEN
(COMPOSER OF —) ROSSINI
WILLIES JUMPS CREEPS
WILLING BAIN FAIN FREE GLAD
LIEF RATH PRONE READY MINDED
TOWARD CONTENT UNFORCED
WILLINGLY LIEF SOON FREELY
GLADLY LIEFLY FRANKLY READILY

WILLINGNESS HEART FREEDOM
FAINNESS
(— TO FIGHT) DEFIANCE
WILLIWAW STORM WOOLLY
TEMPEST
WILLOW DULY ITEA SALE WYLW
OSIER SALEW SALIX SAUGH
WIDDY WITHY WOODY DUSTER
SALLOW TEASER TWILLY WITHEN
WUDDIE
(— FOR THATCHING) SPRAYS
(— IN TEXTILES) WOLF
(NATIVE —) COOBA COOBAH
(SIMPLE —) WHIPPER
(PREF.) (— TWIG) LYGO
WILLOWER DULER DUSTER
TEASER WILLIER
WILLOW HERB WICOPY EPILOBE
FIRETOP PIGWEED ROSEBAY
BURNWEED FIREWEED
WILLOW WARBLER SMEU
SMEUTH MUDDLER TROCHIL
OVENBIRD
WILLOW WREN PEGGY
WILLOWY SUPPLE SLIPPER
DELICATE
WILLY-NILLY PERFORCE
WILSON'S PLOVER COLLIER
WILSON'S SNIPE JACK SHADBIRD
WILSON'S TERN MEDRICK
WILSON'S THRUSH VEERY
WILT EBB SAG DROP FADE FLAG
WELK DROOP SUCCUMB
COLLAPSE
WILTED EMARGID
WILY SLY FOXY CANNY SLICK
ARTFUL ASTUTE CLEVER CRAFTY
QUAINT SHREWD STALKY SUBTLE
TRICKY CUNNING POLITIC
VERSUTE WINDING SERPENTINE
WIMBLE BORE BRISK ACTIVE
GIMLET LIVELY NIMBLE WIBBLE
WUMMEL
WIMPLE BEND WIND CURVE
TWIST GORGET RIPPLE MEANDER
WIMLUNGE
WIN BAG COP HIT DRAW GAIN
HAVE LAND LICK FORCE SCORE
ATTACH CLINCH OBTAIN ACHIEVE
ACQUIRE CONQUER DESERVE
HARVEST POSSESS TRIUMPH
DECISION OVERCOME STRAIGHT
(— AGAINST) BREAK SCOOP
(— AWAY) STEAL DEBAUCH
(— BACK) RECOVER
(— BY GUILE) GET POT BEAR
CARRY RAISE TRAIN GATHER
CAPTURE INVEIGLE PROMERIT
(— EASILY) ROMP
(— NARROWLY) SQUEEZE
(— OVER) DEFEAT DISARM
(— OVERWHELMINGLY) SWEEP
WINCE KICK CHECK QUENCH CRINGE
FLINCH QUATCH QUINCH QUITCH
RECOIL SHRINK
WINCH CRAB JACK REEL WINK
GIPSY WINZE ROLLER WHIMSY
WINDLE CATHEAD TRAVELER
VARIABLE WINDLASS
WIND AIR COP LAP BALL BIRR BISE
BIZE COIL CONE CURL EAST FIST
FLAW FOHN GALE GUST KINK
PUFF PUNO ROLL WEST WRAP

BATCH BLAST BLORE CRANK
CREEK CROOK FOEHN QUILL
SPOOL STORM TRADE TREND
TWINE TWIST WEAVE WITHE
BOTTOM BOUGHT BREEZE
BUSTER CAURUS COLLAR KECKLE
SANSAR SHAMAL SPIRAL SPIRIT
SQUALL WAMPLE WESTER
ZEPHYR BREATHE CRANKLE
CRINKLE CYCLONE ENTWINE
EQUINOX ETESIAN GREGALE
INVOLVE MEANDER MISTRAL
SERPENT SINUATE TEMPEST
TWINGLE TWISTER WEATHER
WHIRLER WINDILL ARGESTES
DOWNWARD EASTERLY
FAVONIUS
(— ABEAM) LASK
(— ABOUT) WIRE SNAKE
(— AFTER DYEING) BATCH
(— FROM THE ANDES) ZONDA
PAMPERO
(— IN AND OUT) INDENT WINGLE
(— MAGNETS) COMPOUND
(— OF ARGENTINA) ZONDA
PAMPERO
(— OF CUBA) BAYAMO
(— OF HAWAII) KONA
(— OF OREGON AND WASHINGTON)
CHINOOK
(— OF TUNISIA) CHILE CHILI CHILLI
(— ROPE) WORM WOOLD
(— THREAD OR YARN) QUILL
CHEESE
(— TO PREVENT CHAFING) KECKLE
(— WOOL) TREND
(— YARN) BEAM SERVE WINDLE
(—S OF CHILE AND PERU) SURES
(ADRIATIC —) BORA
(BREAKING —) FIST
(BROKEN —) HEAVES
(COLD —) BISE BIZE BORA SARSAR
BLIZZARD
(COOLING —) IMBAT
(DEAD —) NOSER
(DESERT —) SAMUM GIBLEH
SAMIEL SIMOOM SIMOON
KHAMSIN SIROCCO
(DRYING —) TRADE
(EASTERLY —) LEVANT LEVANTER
(FIERCE —) BUSTER
(GUST OF —) FLAN FLAW
(HEAD —) NOSER MUZZLE
(HIGH —) RIG
(HOT —) CHILI GIBLEH SAMIEL
SOLANO CHAMSIN KHAMSIN
SIROCCO
(LIGHT GENTLE —) BREEZE
(MOUNTAIN —) PUNA
(NORTH —) BISE AQUILO BOREAS
AQUILON MISTRAL
(NORTHEAST —) BURAN GREGALE
(NORTHWEST —) CAURUS
MAESTRO ARGESTES
(PERIODICAL —) ETESIAN
MONSOON
(PERSIAN GULF —) SHAMAL SHARKI
SHIMAL
(PERUVIAN —) PUNA PUNO
(ROARING —) BLORE
(SEVERE —) SNIFTER
(SOUTH —) NOTUS AUSTER
(SOUTHEAST —) EURUS SOLANO

(SOUTHEASTERLY —) SHARKI
SHURGEE
(SOUTHWEST —) CHINOOK
LIBECCIO
(STRONG —) BIRR
(VIOLENT —) BUSTER SQUALL
SNORTER
(WARM —) FOHN FOEHN CHINOOK
SANTANA
(WEST —) ZEPHYR FAVONIUS
ZEPHYRUS
(PREF.) ANEM(O) AURO VENTI
VENTO
(SOUTH —) AUSTRO
WINDAGE DRIFT
WINDER REEL WINCH DRUMMER
PLUGGER SKEINER SPOOLER
TENDRIL
WINDFALL VAIL GRAVY MANNA
CADUAC FALLING BLOWDOWN
BUCKSHEE
WINDGALL PUFF WINDDOG
WINDING LINK MAZY CRANK
LACET SPIRE CREEKY DETOUR
GYRATE SCREWY SPIRAL TWISTY
WANLAS CRANKLE CRINKLE
DEVIOUS MEANDER SINUOUS
SNAKING WRIGGLY WRINKLE
(PL.) AMBAGES RADDLINGS
WINDING-SHEET SHROUD SUDARY
CEREMENT
WINDING STAIR COCKLE COCLEA
WINDER COCHLEA
WIND INSTRUMENT
(PREF.) AEOLO
WINDLASS CRAB WINK FEARN
WINCH STOWCE STOWSE TACKLE
TURNEL WINDAS WINDLE
TWISTER WILDCAT ARTIFICE
DRAWBEAM MANEUVER
WINDMILL JUMBO MOTOR COPTER
PINWHEEL
(— BAR) UPLONG
(— SAIL) AWE EIE EIGHE FLIER
FLYER SWEEP SWIFT
(PART OF —) BAR CAP FAN AXLE
CORD HEEL LINE SAIL WHIP
BLADE ROTOR STOCK SWEEP
TOWER FANTAIL HELMATH
CANNISTER WINDSHAFT
WINDOW BAY EYE LOOP ROSE
SASH SLIT SLOT CHAFF GLAZE
GRILL INLET LIGHT OGIVE SIGHT
THURL AWNING DORMER GRILLE
LANCET PEEPER ROSACE SPLITE
THURLE WICKET BALCONE
COUPLET DORMANT FENSTER
GUICHET LUTHERN MIRADOR
ORIFICE TRANSOM VENTANA
WINDOCK WINNOCK CASEMENT
FANLIGHT FENESTER FENESTRA
JALOUSIE VENETIAN
(— OF TWO LIGHTS) COUPLET
(BAY —) ORIEL MIRADOR
(BLANK —) ORB
(DORMER —) OXEYE DORMANT
LUCARNE LUTHERN
(HIGH NARROW —) LANCET
(OVAL —) OXEYE
(PART OF —) BEAD JAMB LOCK
PANE RAIL SASH STOP YOKE
APRON FRAME SKIRT STILE
STOOL STRIP CASING MUNTIN

BRICKMOLD WINDOWPANE COUNTERWEIGHT
(ROUND —) OXEYE OCULUS ROUNDEL
(SEMICIRCULAR —) FANLIGHT
(TICKET —) GRILLE GUICHET
(TWIN —) AJIMEZ
(PL.) STORMS
WINDOW DRESSING TRIM FRONT FACADE
WINDOW FRAME SASH REVEAL
WINDOW OYSTER COPIS
WINDOWPANE LIGHT LOZEN QUIRK LOZENGE
WINDOWSILL SOLE
WINDPIPE HALS ARBER ARBOR ERBER HALSE WIZEN ARTERY GUGGLE STROUP WEEZLE KEACORN TRACHEA WEASAND THRAPPLE THROPPLE THROTTLE (PREF.) BRONCH(I)(IO)(O) TRACHE(O) TRACHO TRACHY
WINDROW BANK HEAP RIDGE SWATH SWATHE
WINDSOR CHAIR FANBACK
WINDSTORM BLOW BURA THUD BURAN BOURRAN
WINDWARD ALOOF WEATHER AWEATHER
(— SIDE) KOOLAU
WINDY BLOWY EMPTY GASSY GUSTY HUFFY PROUD STARK SWALE FLIMSY STORMY WONDIE BREATHY FEARFUL GUSTFUL NERVOUS VENTOSE VIOLENT BOISTEROUS
(— CITY) CHICAGO
WINE CUP VIN BOIS BUAL CUIT CUTE DEAL PALM PORT RAPE ROSE ROSY TENT TYRE CAPRI GRAPE KRAMA LUNEL PETER PLONK PORTO SCIAN SHRAB SOAVE TINTO TOKAY VINUM WHITE BAROLO BARSAC CORTON COUTET GRAVES KIJAFA LISBON MASDEU PIMENT ROCHET SAUMUR SHIRAZ SOLERA TIVOLI ALICANT AMBONNA BACCHUS BANYULS BARBERA BASTARD CATAWBA CHACOLI CHATEAU DEZALEY FALERNO MARSALA MISSION MOSELLE ORVIETO PALERMO PIGMENT RHENISH ROSOLIO SERCIAL SILLERY VERNAGE VIDONIA VINTAGE APERITIF BORDEAUX BURGUNDY CHARNECO DELAWARE LACHRYMA LIBATION MALVASIA MARSALLA MOUNTAIN RIESLING ROCHELLE RULANDER RUMBOOZE SPARKLER BARDOLINO
(— BOILED WITH HONEY) MULSE
(— CHEST) TANTALUS
(— FROM VINEGAR) ESILL
(— MIXED WITH WATER) KRASIS
(— OF EXCELLENT QUALITY) VINTAGE
(— OF SACRAMENT) BLOOD
(— SELLER) ABKAR BISTRO WINARE
(— SERVING) VOIDEE
(AROMATIZED —) DUBONNET
(BANANA —) MARAMBA

(BULK —) CUVEE
(CONSECRATED —) CUP
(FIRST-GROWTH —) LAFITE LAFITTE
(FRANCONIAN —) STEIN LEISTEN
(GREEK —) RUMNEY RETSINA RESINATA
(HEATED —) WHITEPOT
(INFERIOR —) PLONK
(JAPANESE —) SAKI
(LIGHT —) BUAL CAPRI BAROLO CANARY
(MULLED —) GLUHWEIN
(NEW —) MUST
(NEW — BOILED DOWN) CUIT CUTE
(PALM —) SAGWIRE
(RED —) MACON TINTA BEAUNE CLARET CHIANTI HOLLOCK POMMARD ALICANTE BURGUNDY CABERNET FLORENCE
(REVIVED —) STUM
(RHINE —) HOCK SYLVANER
(SPANISH —) SACK TENT DULCE OPORTO SHERRY ALICANT ALIKANT BASTARD TARRAGONA
(STILL —) PONTAC PONTACQ
(SWEET —) TYRE DULCE MULSE CANARY BASTARD MALMSEY CHARNECO MUSCATEL
(TENT —) TINTO
(TOKAY —) ESSENCE
(TUSCAN —) VERDEA CHIANTI FLORENCE
(WHITE —) HOCK SACK CAPRI CASEL FORST BARSAC MALAGA BROMIAN CATAWBA CHABLIS CONTHEY LANGOON ANGELICA BUCELLAS RIESLING SAUTERNE VERMOUTH
(PL.) PALUS
(PREF.) ENO OEN(O) OINO VINI VINO
WINEBERRY MAKO MAKOMAKO
WINEGLASS FLUTE
WINEGROWER WINER VIGNERON
WINESBURG OHIO (AUTHOR OF —) ANDERSON
(CHARACTER IN —) JOHN KATE WING DAVID HARDY HELEN JESSE REEFY SWIFT WHITE CURTIS GEORGE LOUISE BENTLEY HARTMAN WILLARD TRUNNION ELIZABETH BIDDLEBAUM
WINESHOP BISTRO BODEGA
WINE-VAULT SHADE
WING ALA ARM ELL FAN FLY OAR RIB VAN FORE JAMB SAIL TAIL ALULA ANNEX BLOCK FLANK JAMBE PINNA POINT SHEAR VOLET BRANCH FLETCH FLIGHT HALTER PENNON PINION POISER DEMIVOL ELYTRON ELYTRUM AEROFOIL BALANCER DISPATCH TORMENTOR
(— OF ARMY) HORN
(— OF BUILDING) ELL JAMB JAMBE ALETTE ALLETTE FLANKER
(— OF SHELL) AURICLE
(— OF THEATER) COULISSE TORMENTOR
(— OF TRIPTYCH) VOLET
(—S DISPLAYED) VOL
(BASTARD —) ALULA
(BIRD'S —) FLAG

(FLY'S —S) HALTERES
(PL.) PENS FEATHERS
(PREF.) ALI PTER(O) PTERIDO PTERYG(O) PTERYLO PTIL(O)
(SUFF.) PTERA PTERIS PTEROUS PTERUS PTERYX
WINGED AILE ALATE LOFTY RAPID SWIFT ALATED PENNED PENNATE ELEVATED
(PREF.) PTENO
(SUFF.) PTENE
WINGED DISK FEROHER
WING-FOOTED FLEET SWIFT ALIPED
WINGLESS APTERAL
WING-LIKE ALARY ALIFORM PTEROID PTERTGOID
WING SHELL STROMB ELYTRON STROMBUS
WINGS OF THE DOVE (AUTHOR OF —) JAMES
(CHARACTER IN —) CROY KATE MARK MILLY MERTON THEALE DENSHER
WINK BAT NAP PINK BLINK DEATH FLASH PRINK SLEEP TWINK CONNIVE FLICKER INSTANT NICTATE SPARKLE TWINKLE NICTITATE
WINKER EYE BLINKER EYELASH
WINKING BLINK
WINKLE PERIWIG TWINKLE
WINNER VICTOR FACEMAN BANGSTER
(SURE —) SNIP
WINNIE-THE-POOH (AUTHOR OF —) MILNE
(CHARACTER IN —) ROO KANGA ROBIN EEYORE PIGLET RABBIT HEFFALUMP CHRISTOPHER
WINNING GAIN SWEET PROFIT GAINING VICTORY WINSOME CHARMING
(— OF ALL TRICKS) CAPOT SCHWARZ
(PL.) WIN VELVET
WINNOW FAN WIM CHAR SIFT WIND DIGHT SIEVE DELETE REMOVE SELECT WINDER SEPARATE
WINNOWER VAN WINDER DIGHTER
WINSOME GAY BUXOM SWEET CHARMING CHEERFUL PLEASANT
WINTER BISE SNOW YEAR HIEMS DECEMBER HIBERNATE
(— OVER) HOG
WINTERBERRY PRINOS HOOPWOOD
WINTERBLOOM AZALEA
WINTERGREEN JINKS CHINKS PYROLA DRUNKER BOXBERRY DRUNKARD EYEBERRY GAYWINGS IVYBERRY LIMONIUM RATSBANE SHINLEAF TEABERRY PINEDROPS PIPSISSEWA
WINTERLIKE BRUMAL
WINTERSET (AUTHOR OF —) ANDERSON
(CHARACTER IN —) MIO CARR GARTH GAUNT TROCK ESDRAS SHADOW ROMAGNA MIRIAMNE BARTOLOMEO

WINTER'S TALE (AUTHOR OF —) SHAKESPEARE
(CHARACTER IN —) DION MOPSA DORCAS EMILIA CAMILLO LEONTES PAULINA PERDITA FLORIZEL HERMIONE ANTIGONUS AUTOLYCUS CLEOMENES MAMILLIUS POLIXENES ARCHIDAMUS
WINTRY AGED COLD WHITE BOREAL HIEMAL STORMY BRUMOUS CHILLING HIBERNAL
WINTUN COPEHAN
WINY VINOUS DRUNKEN
WINZE CURSE RAISE OPENING PASSAGEWAY
WIPE BEAT BLOW DRUB DUST GIBE DICHT DIGHT SWIPE CANCEL SPONGE SPUNGE STRIKE ABOLISH CLEANSE ABSTERGE SQUEEGEE
(— BEAK OF HAWK) FEAK
(— NOSE) SNITE
(— OFF) SCUFF
(— OUT) ERASE SCRUB SWEEP EFFACE DESTROY
(— UP) SWAB SWOB
WIPER DUSTER TRIPPET
WIRE GUY TAP BINE CORE DENT DRAG FILE FUSE PURL CABLE OUTER RISER SNAKE SWEEP TAPER BRIDGE FESCUE FINGER HEATER JUMPER NEEDLE STAPLE STOLON STRAND DROPPER HAYWIRE LAMETTA LASHING PRICKER SHIFTER SNUFFER FILAMENT LIGATURE PALISADE PULLDOWN STRINGER TELEGRAM
(— BETWEEN TWO VESSELS) SWEEP
(— FASTENED TO TEETH) BRACES
(— FOR CUTTING CLAY) SLING
(— FOR SUSTAINING HAIR) PALISADE
(— IN BLASTING CAP) BRIDGE
(— IN CATHETER) STYLET
(— IN WEAVING LOOM) DENT
(— OF GOLD,SILVER OR BRASS) LAMETTA
(— TO ADJUST WICK) SNUFFER
(— TO CLOSE A BREAK) JUMPER
(— TO REMOVE TUMORS) LIGATURE
(— USED AS POINTER) FESCUE
(— USED IN SPLICING CABLES) TAPER
(—S BOUND TOGETHER) SELVAGE
(ENAMELED —) LITZ
(FENCE —) DROPPER
(FRAYED —) JAGGER
(GOLD —) KINSEN
(LOOPED —) OESE
(PALLET —) PULLDOWN
(PRIMING —) PICKER EPINGLETTE
(SURGICAL —) STYLET
(TWISTED —) HEALD HEADLE HEDDLE
(VENT —) PRICKER
(4 —S TWISTED TOGETHER) QUAD
WIRE CUTTER SECATEUR
WIREDRAW WREST OUTWIT DEFRAUD DISTORT ELONGATE
WIREGLASS FLUTE
WIRE GRASS POA
WIRELESS RADIO
WIRE ROPE JACKSTAY

WIRETAP BUG
(REMOVE —) DEBUG
WIREWORM ELATER ELATERID
MILLIPEDE
WIRY THIN HARDY STIFF WITHY
FEEBLE KNOTTY SINEWY STRINGY
THREADY
WIS KNOW THINK SURELY
SUPPOSE

WISCONSIN

CAPITAL: MADISON
COLLEGE: RIPON BELOIT ALVERNO
CARROLL VITERBO CARTHAGE
COUNTY: DOOR VILAS JUNEAU
CALUMET SHAWANO
WAUSHARA
INDIAN: FOX SAUK KICKAPOO
WINNEBAGO
LAKE: POYGAN MENDOTA
WISSOTA WINNEBAGO
MOUNTAIN: TIMSHILL SUGARBUSH
NATIVE: BADGER
NICKNAME: BADGER
RIVER: FOX BLACK STCROIX
CHIPPEWA MENOMINEE
STATE BIRD: ROBIN
STATE FLOWER: VIOLET
STATE TREE: MAPLE
TOWN: ANTIGO BELOIT RACINE
WAUSAU ASHLAND BARABOO
KENOSHA MADISON OSHKOSH
PORTAGE SHAWANO LACROSSE
SUPERIOR WAUKESHA

WISDOM WIT LORE SABE SABBY
SAVEY SENSE SOPHY ADVICE
GNOSIS HOKMAH POLICY SATTVA
SOPHIA WISURE CUNNING
MINERVA SAGESSE SLEIGHT
AFTERWIT JUDGMENT PRUDENCE
SAPIENCE
(DIVINE —) WORD THEOMAGY
(ESOTERIC —) GNOSIS
(SUPREME —) PRAJNA
(UNIVERSAL —) PANSOPHY
(PREF.) SOPH(O) SOPHI(O)
(SUFF.) SOPH(ER)(IC)(IST)(Y)
WISE HEP SLY DEEP GASH GOOD
KIND SAGE SANE SEND TURN
CANNY FRESH GUIDE SMART
SOUND WITTY ADVISE CRAFTY
DIRECT QUAINT WITFUL WITTER
ANCIENT ERUDITE GNOSTIC
KNOWING LEARNED POLITIC
PRUDENT SAPIENT THRIVEN
PERSUADE PROFOUND SENSIBLE
SPACIOUS
(— MAN) AMAUTA
(PREF.) SOPH(O) SOPHI(O)
(SUFF.) SOPH(ER)(IC)(IST)(Y)
WISEACRE SAGE DUNCE GOTHAM
SOLONIST WISEHEAD WISELING
WISECRACK JOKE QUIP
WISENT BISON AUROCH UROCHS
BONASUS
WISH CARE GIVE GOAL HOPE LIST
LUST MIND VOTE WANT WILL
BOSOM COVET CRAVE DREAM
HEART TASTE VOICE DESIRE
UTINAM FAREWELL GODSPEED
PLEASURE
(DEATH —) DESTRUDO

(SLIGHT —) VELLEITY
WISHBONE FURCULA FOURCHET
FURCULUM MERRYTHOUGHT
WISHFUL EAGER HOPEFUL
LONGING ALLURING
WISHING ANXIOUS DESIROUS
WISHY-WASHY PALE THIN WEAK
BLAND VAPID FEEBLE DILUTED
INSIPID SLIPSLOP
WISKET BASKET WHISKET
WISP TATE WUSP SCRAP SHRED
SKIFF SKIFT TWIST RUMPLE
CRUMPLE MASSAGE
(— OF HAY) RISP
(— OF STRAW) WAP WASE DOSSIL
(— OF THATCH) TIPPET
WISPY FRAIL NEBULOUS
WISTERIA FUJI KRAUNHIA
WISTFUL INTENT PENSIVE
WISHFUL MOURNFUL YEARNING
WISTITI WISTIT MARMOSET
WIT VAT VYT WAG KNOW NOUS
SALT BRAIN HUMOR IRONY SENSE
THINK WHITE WOTTE ACUMEN
ESPRIT POLICY SANITY SATIRE
WISDOM CONCEIT CUNNING
PICADOR SARCASM SUPPOSE
THINKER WITWORM BADINAGE
REPARTEE
(BITING —) DICACITY
(PL.) SCONCE BUTTONS
WITCH ALP ANI HAG HEG HEX
MARE SAGA TRAT WYCH BRUJA
BUTCH GREBE LAMIA SIBYL
WEIRD WIGHT ASUANG CARLEY
CARLIN CUMMER DOWSER
DUESSA HECATE KIMMER PILWIZ
WIZARD AGANICE CANIDIA
CARLINE HAGGARD HELLCAT
SYCORAX BABAJAGA CAROLINE
ERICHTHO SORCERER SPAEWIFE
VERSIERA WALKYRIE
(PL.) COVEN
WITCHCRAFT CHARM GOETY
OBEAH WICCA CUNNING HEXEREI
MYALISM SORCERY BRUJERIA
DEVILTRY PISHOGUE WIZARDRY
WITCH DOCTOR BOCOR BOKOR
GOOFER GUFFER
WITCHERY CHARM SPELL
SORCERY SORTIARY
WITCHES'-BROOM STAGHEAD
WITCHGRASS COUCH PANIC
PANICLE
WITE WAT BLAME FAULT WAYTE
CENSURE REPROACH HAMESOKEN
WITH BY CUM MID MIT WUD AVEC
CHEZ DOWN AMONG ANENT
WIGHT AGAINST
(— HAND ON HIP) AKIMBO
(— REGARD TO) ABOUT
(— SPEED) TIVY
(PREF.) CO COL COM CON COR
META SYM SYN
WITHDRAW GO COY DROP TAKE
AVOID DEMIT LOOSE REVEL SHIFT
START UNSAY CHANGE DECEDE
DESERT DETACH DETRAY DEVOID
EFFACE FLINCH MINISH RECALL
RECANT RECEDE RETIRE REVOKE
ROGATE SECEDE SHRINK SINGLE
SYPHON ABSCOND CONCEAL
DESCEND DETRACT FORSAKE

INVEIGH RETRACT RETREAT
SCRATCH SCUTTLE SECLUDE
SUBDUCE SUBDUCT UNSCREW
SEPARATE SUBTRACT SEGREGATE
SEQUESTER
(— FROM) VAIK ABANDON
(— FROM POKER POT) DROP
(— SUPPORT) ABANDON
WITHDRAWAL DRAIN FLIGHT
HIDING OFFLAP RETIRE SHRINK
ABSENCE DUNKIRK PULLOUT
REGRESS RETIRAL RETREAT
SCUTTLE RECESSION REVULSION
(— FROM WORLDLY THINGS)
ABSTRACTION
(— OF BUILDING FACE) SETBACK
(— OF PROMISE) BACKWORD
(— OF SUIT) RETRAXIT
WITHDRAWN SHY ASOCIAL
INGROWN SECLUSE DISTRAIT
ISOLATED SECLUDED RECESSIVE
ABSTRACTED
WITHE HANK ROPE TIER TWIG
WITHY WATTLE WICKER CRINGLE
WITHER BURN DAZE FADE MIFF
PINE RUST SEAR STUN WARP
WELK WELT BLAST CLING DAVER
DECAY QUAIL WIZEN COTTER
GIZZEN SHRINK WALLOW WELTER
WILTER WINDER AREFACT
DECLINE FORWELK SENESCE
SHRIVEL LANGUISH PARALYZE
WITHERED DRY ARID SEAR SERE
CORKY SCRAM MARCID BLASTED
UNGREEN WEARISH WIZENED
AUTUMNAL
WITHERING SCATHING
WITHHELD DEFERRED SUSPENSE
WITHHOLD CURB DENY HIDE KEEP
STOP CHECK SCANT ABSENT
DEPORT DETAIN REFUSE RETAIN
ABSTAIN BOYCOTT DEFORCE
FORBEAR OUTHOLD REPRESS
RESERVE SUSPEND RESTRAIN
SUBTRACT
(— CONSENT) DECLINE
WITHHOLDING DETAINER
(— OF DUES) CHECKOFF
WITHIN IN ON BEN BIN INBY INLY
INTRA ABOARD HEREIN INSIDE
INWITH INDOORS ENCLOSED
INCLUDED INWARDLY
(PREF.) END(O) ENT(O) ESO IL IM
IN INFRA INTER INTRA INTRO
(ARISING —) IDIO
WITHOUT EX BUT OUT SEN BOUT
FREE OHNE SANS SINE MINUS
SENZA FAILING OUTSIDE
WANTING INNOCENT OUTDOORS
(— A FLANGE) BALD
(— A MATE) ODD
(— ACTION) DEEDLESS
(— BEGINNING OR END) ETERNAL
(— BLEMISH) CHOICE
(— CONTENTS) INANE
(— DELAY) AWAY FOOTHOT
SUMMARY
(— DELIBERATION) HEADLONG
(— EMOTION) DRYLY DULLY
(— EXCEPTION) ALWAYS
(— FEET) APOD
(— FUNDS) CLEAN
(— HORNS) ACEROUS

(— INTEREST) BARREN
(— LIFE) AZOIC
(— LIGHT) APHOTIC
(— LIMITS OF DURATION) AGELESS
(— ORDER) ANYHOW
(— POWER) ADRIFT
(— QUESTION) EASILY SECURELY
(— REALITY) AIRY
(— REASON) BLINDLY
(— REMEDY) BOOTLESS
(— ROADS) INVIOUS
(— RULE OR LAW) ANARCHIC
(— SADDLES) ASELLATE
(— TEETH, TONGUE OR CLAWS)
MORNE
(— WINGS) APTEROUS
(PREF.) A ECT(O) LIPO
(— GOVERNMENT) ANARCH(O)
(SUFF.) LESS
WITHSTAND BIDE DEFY TAKE
ABIDE OPPOSE OPPUGN RESIST
CONTAIN CONTEST FORBEAR
SUSTAIN CONFRONT WITHSTAY
WITHY WIRY AGILE OSIER WOODY
WILLOW WOODIE WINDING
WITLESS MAD GROSS SILLY
INSANE STUPID FATUOUS
FOOLISH UNWITTY HEEDLESS
SLAPHAPPY
WITLOOF ENDIVE CHICORY
WITNESS SEE TAKE TEST PROOF
ATTEST BEHOLD MARTYR
RECORD TESTIS TESTOR
CURATOR TESTATE TESTIFY
EVIDENCE RECORDER SUFFRAGE
(FALSE —) JUROR
(PL.) SECTA
(PREF.) TESTI
WITNESS-BOX STAND
WITOTO HUITOTE
WITTICISM WIT JEER JEST JOKE
QUIP SALLY SLENT WHEEZE
WITTING NEWS TIDINGS
WITTINGLY SCIENTER
WITTOL FOOL CUCKOLD WITTALL
WITTY GASH WILY WISE DROLL
LEPID PAWKY SHARP SMART
CLEVER FACETE JOCOSE JOCULAR
KNOWING CONCEITY HUMOROUS
(NOT —) INFICETE
WIVERN DRAGON WYVERN
WIZARD MAGE SEER SHIZ FIEND
WITCH DOCTOR EXPERT PELLAR
WARLOW CHARMED MAGICAL
SPAEMAN WARLOCK WISEMAN
CONJUROR MAGICIAN SORCERER
TROLLMAN WITCHMAN
ARCHIMAGE
(PL.) GOETAE
WIZARDRY SORCERY
WIZEN DRY WITHER SHRIVEL
WIZENED SERE GIZZEN WEAZEN
WOAD DYE NIL ODE ANIL KERS
NILL OADE CRESS ANILLA INDICO
INDIGO PASTEL
(PREF.) ISAT(O)
WOADWAXEN ALLELUIA
ALLELUJA
WOBBLE COCKLE COGGLE HOBBLE
QUAVER SHIMMY TEETER TITTER
WABBLE WIGGLE TREMBLE
NUTATION
WOBBLY LOOSE SHAKY COGGLY

DRUNKEN DOUBTFUL
WOE WA WEI BALE BANE DULE
PAIN PINE WAWE GRIEF MISERY
SORROW TROUBLE WILLAWA
CALAMITY DISTRESS WELLADAY
WELLAWAY
WOEBEGONE WAFF UNHAPPY
DEJECTED DESOLATE DOWNCAST
WOEFUL MEAN DISMAL PALTRY
RUEFUL DIREFUL DOLEFUL
RUTHFUL DOLOROUS PITIABLE
WRETCHED
WOLF GLUT LOBO CANID FREKI
YABBI CHANCO COYOTE FAMINE
FENRIR ISGRIN KABERU LOAFER
MASHER SIGRIM THOOID
POVERTY ISENGRIM
(FOX —) ZORRO
(PREF.) LUPI LYC(O) VULPI
WOLFBERRY BUCKBUSH
WOLFHOUND ALAN BORZOI
PSOVIE
WOLFISH LUPINE RAVENOUS
WOLFLIKE THOOID
WOLFRAMITE CAL TUNGSTEN
WOLFSBANE ACONITE DOGBANE
FOXBANE
WOLF SPIDER HUNT JAGER
HUNTER JAEGER JAYHAWK
LYCOSID TARANTULA
WOLVERINE PIG GLUT GORB
MIKER GLOTUM HELLUO
GLUTTON GUTLING LURCHER
MOOCHER RAVENER SWILLER
CARCAJOU DRAFFMAN
GOURMAND GULLYGUT
(— STATE) MICHIGAN
WOMAN BIM BIT DAM EVE HEN
HER JUG MEG SHE TEG TIT BABE
BABY BINT BOSS CONY DAME
FAIR FEME FLAG FROW JADE
JANE LADY MAMA MARY MORT
PERI SLUT WIFE BIDDY BIMBO
BLADE BROAD CHINA DONAH
FEMME FRAIL JATNI LUBRA
LUCKY MAMMA MUJER QUEAN
SKIRT SMOCK SQUAW TAGGE
TOOTS TWIST UMMAN VROUW
BURDIE CALICO CARLIN CUMMER
FEMALE GIMMER HEIFER KIMMER
LUCKIE MANESS MULIER SISTER
TOMATO VIRAGO WAHINE
CARLING CHANGAR DISTAFF
PARTLET PINNACE PLACKET
QUAEDAM MISTRESS PETTICOAT
(— DESERTED BY HUSBAND)
AGUNAH
(— OF CONSEQUENCE) HERSELF
(— OF LOW CASTE) DASI
(— OF RANK) DOMINA
(— OF UNSTEADY CHARACTER)
FLAP CALLET
(— OF WEALTH) FORTUNE
(— WHO ACTS AS ADVISER) EGERIA
(— WITH ONE CHILD) UNIPARA
(— WITH 3 CHILDREN) TRIPARA
(ABORIGINAL —) GIN LUBRA
(ABUSIVE —) FISHWIFE
(ALLURING —) DISH
(ATHENIAN — OF HIGH RANK)
GERARA GERAERA
(ATTRACTIVE —) DOLLY SHEBA
DOLLIE LOOKER CHARMER

(AUSTRALIAN —) BINT
(AWKWARD —) ROIL
(BEAUTIFUL —) HURI PERI BELLE
HOURI SIREN SPARK CHERUB
EYEFUL MUSIDORA
(BOISTEROUS —) HOYDEN
(BOLD —) RAMP
(CLEANING —) CHAR
(COARSE —) BEAST RUDAS
BLOWZE RULLION
(COOLIE —) CHANGAR
(COY —) HAGGARD
(CREMATED —) SATI SUTTEE
(DEAR —) PEAT
(DUTCH OR GERMAN —) FRAU
FROW FROKIN FRAULEIN
(ENGAGED —) BONDAGER
(ENTICING —) SIREN
(EVIL OLD —) HAG HELLHAG
(EXCITED —) MAENAD
(FASHIONABLE —) MILADY
GALLANT ELEGANTE
(FAT —) BOSS FUSTILUGS
(FINE —) SCREAMER
(FIRST —) EMBLA PANDORA
(FLIRTING —) CHIPPY FIZGIG
(FOOLISH —) TAWPIE
(FORWARD —) STRAP
(GAUDY —) JAY
(GENTLE —) DOVE
(GOSSIPY —) HAIK HAKE BIDDY
TABBY
(GOSSIP, TALKATIVE —) YENTA
(GROSS —) SOW
(GYPSY —) ROMI ROMNI GITANA
(ILL-TEMPERED —) VIXEN
CATAMARAN
(IMMORAL —) RIG GITCH FLAPPER
HARLOTRY
(IMPUDENT —) YANKIE
(INDIAN —) SQUAW WENCH
KLOOCH BUCKEEN
(INSPIRED —) PHOEBAD
(ITALIAN —) DONNA
(LASCIVIOUS —) GIGLET
(LEARNED —) PUNDITA CLERGESS
(LEWD —) REP SLUT BITCH HUSSY
HUZZY MALKIN BROTHEL
CYPRIAN
(LOOSE —) BAG BIM KIT MOB TIB
DRAB FLAP BIMBO TROLL GILLOT
HARLOT LIMMER BAGGAGE
COCOTTE FRANION TROLLOP
(LOUD-SPOKEN —) RANDY
(LOW OR WORTHLESS —) JADE
JURR BUNTER SLINGDUST
(MARRIED — OF LOWLY STATION)
GOODY
(MASCULINE —) AMAZON RULLION
COTQUEAN
(MEEK —) GRIZEL
(MYTHOLOGICAL —) HEROINE
(NON-JEWISH —) SHIKSA
(OLD —) GIB HEN BABA TROT
CRONE FAGOT FRUMP TROUT
BELDAM CARLIN GAMMER
GEEZER GRANNY CARLINE
GRANDAM HARRIDAN
(OLD SHRIVELED —) FAGOT
FAGGOT
(PEDANTIC —) BLUE
(PERT —) CHIT
(PORTUGUESE —) SENHORA

(PREGNANT —) GRAVIDA
(PRIGGISH —) PRUDE
(RUSTIC —) JOAN
(SCOLDING —) RANDY SHREW
COTQUEAN RIXATRIX
(SHORT OR STUMPY —) CUTTY
(SHOWY —) ANONYMA
(SHREWISH —) JADE HARPY
SKELLAT
(SLATTERNLY —) DRAB FLEABAG
SLAMKIN
(SLENDER GRACEFUL —) SYLPH
(SLIPSHOD —) MAUX CLATCH
TROLLIMOG
(SLOVENLY —) BAG DAW SOW
SLUT BESOM TAWPY TROLL
TROLLOP SLATTERN
(SPANISH —) DONA GITANA
(SPANISH-INDIAN —) CHOLA
(SPITEFUL —) CAT FURY BITCH
(SQUAT —) TRUB
(SQUEAMISH —) COCKNEY
(STAID —) MATRON
(STATELY —) JUNO
(STORMY VIOLENT —) FURY
(TRACTABLE —) SHEEP
(UGLY —) HAG GORGON
(UNCHASTE —) JILT
(UNMARRIED —) DAME GIRL
SPINSTER MADEMOISELLE
(VIXENISH —) HARRIDAN
(WANTON —) MINX TRUB PARNEL
(WICKED —) JEZEBEL
(WISE —) VOLVA ALRUNA ALRUNE
(WITHERED —) CRONE
(YOUNG —) BIT BIRD BURD CHIT
DAME DELL DOLL GIRL LASS PUSS
BEAST CHICK FILLY FLUFF TOAST
DAMSEL HEIFER PIGEON SHEILA
SUBDEB BAGGAGE CHICKEN
DAMOZEL FLAPPER WINKLOT
DAUGHTER GRISETTE
(PREF.) FEMINO GYN(AE)(AECO)
(AEO)(ANDRO)(E)(EO)(O)
(SUFF.) GYN(E)(IST)(OUS)
WOMAN HATER MISOGYNIST
WOMANHOOD MULIEBRITY
WOMAN IN WHITE (AUTHOR OF —)
COLLINS
(CHARACTER IN —) ANNE FOSCO
GLYDE LAURA PESCA MARIAN
WALTER FAIRLIE HALCOMBE
PERCIVAL CATHERICK HARTRIGHT
WOMANISH FEMALE FEMININE
LADYLIKE PETTICOAT
WOMANKIND WOMEN CALICO
MUSLIN FEMINIE
WOMAN'S TONGUE LEBBEK
WOMB BELLY CRADLE UTERUS
VENTER
(PREF.) COLP(O) HYSTER(O)
METRO UTER(O) VULVI VULVO
(SUFF.) COLPOS METRA METRIUM
WOMBAT KOALA BADGER
DIDELPH VOMBATID
WOMEN DISTAFF
(— OF EARLY CHURCH) SETTERS
AGAPETAE
WON CITY LIVE ROOM ABIDE
DWELL REGION
WONDER AWE MUSE SELI SIGN
TROW UNCO UNKO VERY FARLY
FERLY SELLE SELLY UNCOW

ADMIRE MARVEL MIRATE
MAGNALE MIRABLE MIRACLE
PORTENT PRODIGY STRANGE
UNCOUTH AMERVEIL SELCOUTH
SURPRISE
(PREF.) TERAT(O) THAUMA(TO)
THAUMO
WONDERFUL KEEN NEAT SELI
FERLY GRAND GREAT SELLE
SWELL WAKON GEASON MIGHTY
AMAZING EPATANT GALLANT
MIRABLE MIRIFIC STRANGE
GLORIOUS MIRABILE TERRIFIC
WONDROUS
WONDERFULLY AMAZING
WONDER-WORKER THEURGIC
THEURGIST
WONDER-WORKING MIRIFIC
WONG FIELD GROVE PLAIN
MEADOW
WONKY AWRY SHAKY WRONG
UNSTEADY
WONT APT USE FAIN USED VAIN
HABIT USAGE CUSTOM INCLINED
WONTED TAME USUAL HAUNTED
WOO SUE LOVE SEEK SUIT WALE
COURT SPARK SPOON ASSAIL
SPLUNT SUITOR ADDRESS
WOOD (ALSO SEE TREE AND
TIMBER) HAG KIP BOIS BOSK
BOWL EKKI HOLT HYLE KIRI MASS
MOCK PALO SHAW SUPA TREE
WOLE CAHUY CHARK CROWD
EDDER FLOUR GROVE HURST
HYRST KOKRA RESAK SHOLA
STICK STUFF WEALD ALMOND
ANGILI AUSUBO BRAZIL EKHIMI
FOREST ITAUBA JARANA LUMBER
PALING SPINNY TIMBER APITONG
AVODIRE BOSCAGE BOSKAGE
COPPICE DADDOCK DUDGEON
HAYBOTE SATINAY VENESIA
BAGTIKAN CRANTARA FIREBOOT
CALAMANDER
(— BURNT AS PERFUME) AGALLOCH
(— FOR CARPENTRY) STUFF
(— FOR REPAIRING HEDGE) TINING
HAYBOTE
(— OF SMALL EXTENT) GROVE
(— OF THE VERA) VENESIA
(— ON RAFTER) FUR
(— ROTATED ON STRING) ROMBOS
RHOMBOS
(— USEFUL FOR TINDER) PUNK
SPONK TOUCHWOOD
(— YIELDING PERFUME) LINALOA
(BABUL —) SUNT
(BLACK —) EBONY
(CONE-SHAPED PIECE OF —) ACORN
(DARK RED —) RATA
(DEAD —) RAMMEL
(DENSIFIED —) STAYPAK
(ELASTIC —) SYCAMORE
(FLAT ROUND PIECE OF —)
TRENCHER
(FLEXIBLE —) EDDER
(FOSSIL —) PINITE PEUCITES
(FRAGRANT —) CEDAR
SANDALWOOD
(FUEL —) ESTOVERS
(HARD —) ASH DAO ELM SAL
BAKU IPIL KARI LANA POON
ANJAN EBONY GIDYA KARRI

KOKRA MAPLE MAZER ZANTE
BANUYO CAMARA FREIJO GIDGEE
KEMPAS SABICU SAPELE WALNUT
CURUPAY DATTOCK HICKORY
GUAIACUM IRONBARK
MAHOGANY
(HEAVY —) DAO EBON EBONY
CHENGAL GUAYABI SUCUPIRA
(LIGHT —) POON BALSA HEMLOCK
(LIMBA —) KORINA
(LOGGED —) CHIP
(LOST —) CHIPPAGE
(LUSTROUS —) LEZA BOARWOOD
(MATCHBOX —) SKILLET
(MOTTLED —) AMBOINA
CALAMBOUR
(NARROW BAR OF —) SLAT
(NUMBER 1 —) DRIVER
(NUMBER 2 —) BRASSIE
(NUMBER 3 —) SPOON
(NUMBER 4 —) CLEEK
(OILY —) BATETE
(OLIVE —) COLLIE
(PETRIFIED —) LITHOXYL
ROCKWOOD
(PINKISH —) BOSSE
(POINTED PIECE OF —) TRIPPET
(REDDISH —) KOA KARI KARRI
ARANGA BANABA CHERRY
DUNGON SATINE KAMBALA
(REDDISH-YELLOW —) GUYO
(ROTTEN —) DADDOCK
(SANDARAC —) ALERCE
(SMALL —) SHAW
(SOFT —) KIRI GABUN GABOON
ELKWOOD AGALLOCH ALBURNUM
GUATAMBU
(SQUARE LOG OF —) NOG
(STICK OF —) BILLET
(STRIP OF —) LATH STAVE BATTEN
REEPER REGLET
(WATER-RESISTING —) AMUGIS
(YELLOWISH —) HALDU FUSTIC
IDIGBO KADAMBA KAMASSI
GUATAMBU
(PREF.) HYL(O) LIGN(I)(O) XYL(O)
(SUFF.) XYLON XYLUM
WOOD ANEMONE CYME EMONY
BOWBELLA SNOWDROP
WOODBARK SABLE BLONDINE
WOODBINE BIND WIDBIN
EGLATERE
WOODCARVER BODGER
WOODCHUCK CHUG CHUCK
MONAX MARMOT SUSLIK WEJACK
MOONACK GROUNDHOG
WOODCOCK QUIS PEWEE PEWIT
SNIPE SNITE SHRUPS BECASSE
SIMPLETON
WOODCUT BLOCK
WOODCUTTER AXEMAN LOGGER
WOODMAN WOODSMAN
WOOD DUCK SQUEALER
BRANCHIER
WOODED BOSKY TREEY HYLEAN
SYLVAN FORESTED NEMOROUS
WOODEN DRY DULL STIFF TREEN
CLUMSY STICKY STOLID TIMBER
AWKWARD DEADPAN TIMBERN
LIFELESS
WOOD GUM XYLAN
WOOD HEN WEKA
WOODHEWER PICUCULE

WOOD HOOPOE WHOOP WHOOPE
IRRISOR DUNGBIRD PICARIAN
WOOD HYACINTH SCILLA
CROWTOE GREGGLE HAREBELL
WOOD IBIS STORK GANNET
JABIRU IRONHEAD
WOODLAND DESERT MIOMBO
SPRING BOSCAGE
(WASTE —) WEALD
WOODPECKER AWL CHAB JYNX
KATE PEEK ECCLE HECCO HEWEL
ICKLE PICUS SPEKT HECKLE
NICKER NICKLE PECKER PIANET
PICULE SPRITE TAPPER YAFFLE
YUCKER YUKKEL CLIMBER
CREEPER FLICKER HEWHOLE
HICKWAY LOGCOCK REDHEAD
SAPSUCK SNAPPER SPEIGHT
WHETILE WITWALL WRYNECK
DIRTBIRD HICKWALL PICARIAN
PICUCULE POPINJAY RAINBIRD
RAINFOWL WALLHICK SAPSUCKER
(LIKE A —) PICIFORM
(PREF.) PICI
WOOD PIGEON CUSHAT ZOOZOO
WOODPILE STRAN STRAND
WOODRICK
WOOD ROBIN MIRO TOMTIT
WOODRUFF HAIROF MUGGET
MUGWET WOODROW HAIRHOOF
WOODS BOSK BUSH BOSQUE
(PREF.) NEMO SILVI SYLVI
WOODSMAN BUSHY SILVAN
SYLVAN BUSHMAN BUSHWACK
WOOD SORREL OCA COCKOO
HEARTS LUJULA OXALIS TREFOIL
ALLELUIA ALLELUJA SHAMROCK
STABWORT
WOOD THRUSH MAYBIRD
WOODTURNER BODGER
WOODWIND OBOE FLUTE CORNET
BASSOON PIBGORN PICCOLO
CLARINET
WOODWORK CEILING
WOODWORKER JOINER TURNER
MILLMAN
WOODWORM GRIBBLE
(PREF.) TERMITO
WOODY BOSKY WITHY FRITHY
STICKY SYLVAN XYLOID LIGNOSE
LIGNEOUS
WOOER BEAU LOVER WOWER
SUITOR COURTER WOOSTER
COURTIER PARAMOUR
WOOF WEFT WOUGH FILLING
TEXTURE
WOOING SUIT WOHLAC
WOOL OO COT DAG HOG VOL
WOW BEAT BLUE FRIB PILE PULU
ROCK FADGE LAINE MUNGO
STUFF TIPPY ALPACA ARGALI
BOTANY BREECH FLEECE GREASE
JACKET JERSEY KERSEY LUSTER
SLIVER WETHER COMBING
HASLOCK KASHMIR MORLING
STUBBLE WIGGING CASHMERE
CLOTHING COMEBACK MORTLING
PICKLOCK TOMENTUM
(— AS IT COMES FROM SHEEP)
GREASE
(— FROM DEAD SHEEP) MORLING
MORTLING
(— FROM LEOMINSTER) ORE

(— FROM RAGS) EXTRACT
(— OF UNDERCOAT OF MUSK-OX)
QIVIUT
(— ON SHEEP'S LEG) GARE BREECH
(— ON SHEEP'S THROAT) HASLOCK
(— WEIGHT) TOD
(COARSE —) ABB SHAG BRAID
COWTAIL
(COTTON —) CADDIS CADDICE
(DUNGY BIT OF —) FRIB
(FINE GRADE OF —) PICKLOCK
SPINNERS
(GREASY —) TIPPY
(INFERIOR GRADE OF —) HEAD
(KNOT OF —) NOIL
(LAMB'S —) WASSAIL
(LOCK OF —) FLOCK STAPLE
(LONG —) BLUE
(LOW GRADE OF —) LIVERY
(MATTED —) DAG KET SHAG
(PULLED —) SLIPE
(RECLAIMED —) MUNGO SHODDY
(REFUSE —) COT COTT FLOCK
PINION
(ROLL OF —) CARDING
(RUSSIAN —) DONSKY
(SMALL PIECE OF —) TATE
(SPUN —) YARN
(WOUND —) TREND
(PREF.) ERIO LAN(I)(O) MALLO
(SUFF.) LAN
WOOLCLOTH HODDEN
WOOLEN (ALSO SEE FABRIC)
CADDIS CAMLET SUCLAT
CADDICE PASHMINA
(PL.) LAINAGE
WOOL FAT LANOLIN
WOOLLY SHEEP WOOZY LANATE
LANOSE COTTONY FLOCCOSE
PERONATE
WOOLLY BEAR WOUBIT
WOOLLY CROTON HOGWORT
WOOLY
(PREF.) DASI DASY ULO
WOOZY SICK DRUNK TIGHT VAGUE
BLURRY WOOLLY
WORD GIG MOT EZEL GULE HAIT
NEWS RAFF TERM VERB WHID
WHUD ADNEX CHEEP COUCH
DERRY DILLY FITCH GLOSS HAPAX
HOKEY HYNDE LEMMA MAXIM
ORDER PAROL RHEMA RUMOR
SPELL ACCENT ADVERB AVOWAL
BREATH COPULA ETYMON KIBBER
LATIVE ONEYER PAROLE PLEDGE
QUATCH REMARK REPORT
SAYING ACCOUNT ADJUNCT
BICCHED COMMAND COMMENT
DICTION DUCDAME GENTILE
GITTITH HOMONYM INCIPIT
MESSAGE PALABRA PARONYM
PRAYFUL PRENZIE PROMISE
PROVERB SYNONYM VOCABLE
ACROSTIC CATCHCRY CHEVILLE
COMPOUND ENCLITIC EQUIVOKE
FRABJOUS FRINGENT IDEOGRAM
ILLATIVE LATINISM SYLLABLE
SYNTAGMA NEOLOGISM
PALINDROME PARTICIPLE
MONOSYLLABLE
(— AS CALL TO DUCK) DILLY
(— EXPRESSING COMMAND)
JUSSIVE

(— FORMED FROM VOWELS)
EUOUAE
(— FROM INITIAL LETTERS)
ACRONYM
(— IN A PUZZLE) LIGHT
(— MISPRONOUNCED) BEARD
(— OF CONCLUSION) AMEN
EXPLICIT
(— OF HONOR) PAROLE
(— OF MOUTH) FIDELITY
(— OF OPPOSITE MEANING)
ANTONYM
(— OF SECONDARY RANK) ADNEX
(— OF UNCERTAIN MEANING)
FRINGENT
(— OF UNKNOWN MEANING) KIBBER
ONEYER PRAYFUL PRENZIE
(—S IN LOW TONE) ASIDE
(—S OF OPERA) LIBRETTO
**(BIBLICAL — OF DOUBTFUL
MEANING)** EZEL FITCH GITTITH
(CALL —) JINGO
(CHARACTERIZING —) EPITHET
(CODE —) DOG FOX JIG ABLE EASY
ECHO GOLF ITEM KING BRAVO
DELTA HOTEL INDIA SUGAR
GEORGE CHARLIE
(EMPTY —S) WAFFLE
(FINE —S) DICK
(GATHERING —) SLOGAN
(HONEYED —S) MANNA
(HYPHENATED —) SOLID
(IDENTIFYING —) LABEL
(LAST — OF SPEECH) CUE
(MAGIC —) ABRACADABRA
(MEANINGLESS —) DERRY
(MEANINGLESS —S) NOISE
(METAPHORICAL —) KENNING
(MNEMONIC —) VIBGYOR
(MYSTIC —) ABRAXAS
(NONSENSE —) RAFF RAFFE
FRABJOUS RUNCIBLE
(ORIGINAL —) STEM
(PARTING —) ENVOI
(QUOTED —) CITATION
(REDUNDANT —) CHEVILLE
(ROOT —) ETYMON PRIMITIVE
(SIGNAL —) NAYWORD SECURITY
(SIGNIFICANT —) ACCENT
(SINGLE —) PHRASE
(SOURCE —) ETYMON
(THIEVES' SLANG —) TWAG WHID
(UNEXPLAINED —) DUCDAME
(UTTERED —S) SPEECH
(PL.) LIP TALK SPEECH
LANGUAGE DISCOURSE
(PREF.) LEXI LEXICO LOG(O)
ONOMATO RHEMATO VERBI
VERBO
(SUFF.) EPY LEXIA ONYM
WORD-BLINDNESS ALEXIA
WORDBOOK LEXICON SPELLER
LIBRETTO
WORDINESS VERBIAGE
WORDING LEGEND DICTION
PHRASING
WORDLESS DUMB TACIT SILENT
TACITURN
WORDMAKING RHEMATIC
WORDPLAY EQUIVOKE
WORDY PROLIX VERBAL DIFFUSE
VERBOSE WORDISH
REDUNDANT

WORK DO GO ACT FAG JOB DIKE DYKE FEND FRET NOTE OPUS TASK TEND TOIL ERGON GRAFT GRIND KARMA KNEAD LABOR PRESS YAKKA ARBEIT BONNET EFFECT HUSTLE OEUVRE REDUIT RESULT STRIVE THRIFT CALLING EXECUTE EXPLOIT FERMENT HEXAPLA LOUSTER MISSION OPERATE OPIFICE OPUSCLE OUVRAGE OVERAGE PICHERY PURSUIT TRAVAIL ADVOCACY AGENTING BUSINESS CAPONIER DEMILUNE DRUDGERY ENDEAVOR FUNCTION INDUSTRY LABORAGE OPUSCULE PARERGON RETRENCH EXECUTION
(— ACROSS GRAIN) THURM
(— ACTIVELY) LOUSTER
(— AGAINST) KNIFE ATTACK COMBAT
(— AIMLESSLY) FIDDLE
(— AS REPORTER) HEEL
(— BEYOND ONE'S POWERS) OVERDO
(— CARELESSLY) RABBLE
(— DILIGENTLY) PEG PLUG STRIKE BELABOR
(— DONE) WRIHTE
(— FOR) LABOR SERVE BESWINK
(— FREE) START
(— HARD) TEW MOIL SLOG SWOT BULLOCK LEATHER
(— HIDES) BEAM
(— INSIDUOUSLY) WORM
(— INTO A MASS) KNEAD
(— LAND) FLOAT
(— LEISURELY) DAKER DAIKER
(— OCCASIONALLY) SMOOT SMOUT
(— OF ACKNOWLEDGED EXCELLENCE) CLASSIC
(— OF ART) GEM CRAFT ANTIQUE CAPRICE CREATION EPIPHANY EXERCISE MANDORLA
(— OF FICTION) SHOCKER
(— OF HISTORY) STORY
(— OF MENIAL KIND) DRUDGE
(— ONE'S WAY) WISE
(— OUT) BLOCK FUDGE SOLVE DESIGN EVOLVE
(— OUT IN ADVANCE) FOREPLOT
(— OVER) DIGEST
(— PAID FOR IN ADVANCE) HORSE
(— PERSISTENTLY) HAMMER
(— RESEMBLING PATCHWORK) CENTO
(— SLIPSHOD) MULLOCK
(— STEADILY) PLY
(— TO EXHAUSTION) FAG
(— TO WINDWARD) CLAW
(— TOGETHER) COACT
(— TRIFLINGLY) PIDDLE
(— UNDER ANOTHER NAME) ALLONYM
(— UNFAIRLY OR CRUELLY) HORSE
(— UP) SPUNK
(— UPON) TILL LABOR
(— UPWARD) HIKE
(— VIGOROUSLY) BEND
(ALLEGORICAL —) BESTIARY
(ANONYMOUS —) ADESPOTA
(BUNGLED —) BOTCH
(CANVAS —) POINT

(CHASED —) CISELURE
(CLEANING —) CHAR
(CLUMSY —) BOTCH
(COMPLETED —) TRAVAIL
(CONTRACT —) GYPPO
(DAMASCENE —) KOFTGARI
(DAY'S —) DARG DARGUE
(DECORATIVE —) FLOCKING MARQUETRY
(DIVINE —) THEURGY
(DULL —) DRUDGERY
(EMBOSSED —) CELATURE
(FRAUDULENT —) JERRY
(HAND —) CAMAY
(HARD —) TEW MOIL MUCK SWOT TWIG YERK SWEAT EFFORT MOIDER LEATHER SLAVERY SLOGGING
(INLAY —) INTARSIA
(JOINER —) FINISH
(LITERARY —) STUDY CHASER SEQUEL SERIAL CLASSIC DIPTYCH PRODUCTION
(LURID —) BLOOD
(MANUAL —) FATIGUE
(METAL —) NIELLO
(MINOR —) OPUSCULE OPUSCULUM
(MOSAIC —) EMBLEM
(ORNAMENTAL —) BEADWORK FILIGREE LEAFWORK
(PIECE OF —) JOB
(REFERENCE —) BIBLE SOURCE
(SACRED —) HIERURGY
(SCHOLASTIC —) SUMMA
(SKILLED MECHANICAL —) SLOJD SLOYD
(SOCIAL —) ALMONING
(USELESS —) BOONDOGGLE
(WOMAN'S —) DISTAFF
(PL.) CANON PLANT STODGE FACTORY BUSINESS
(PREF.) ERG(O) ERGAT(O) OPERA
(EMBOSSED —) TOREUMATO
(SUFF.) ERGATE ERGY
WORKABLE YOUNG PLIANT VIABLE FEASIBLE
(EASILY —) SWEET
WORKADAY HUMDRUM PROSAIC ORDINARY
WORKBASKET CABA CABAS CALATHUS
WORKBENCH SIEGE DONKEY TEMPLATE
WORKED INWROUGHT
(— OUT) DEAD
(— UP) ANGRY EXCITED
WORKER (ALSO SEE WORKMAN AND LABORER) AGER CARL DOER HAND HIND ICER SCAB AXMAN BOXER BUTTY DEMAS DRIER EDGER ENDER FILER FIRER FIXER FLYER FOXER GLUER GORER HOLER INKER JERRY LINER LURER MAXIM MINIM NURSE TAPER TOWER ASHMAN BACKER BAILER BALLER BANDER BEADER BENDER BINDER BINMAN BLADER BLOWER BOILER BONDER BOOKER BOSHER BRACER BUFFER BUMPER BURNER BURRER CAPPER CARMAN CASTER CASUAL CHASER COMBER COOKER

DAYMAN DIPPER DOCKER DOGGER DOTTER DUMPER ETCHER FACTOR FAGGER FANMAN FASHER FEEDER FELLER FILLER FITTER FLAKER FLAMER FLUTER FLUXER FOILER FOLDER FORCER FORMER FRAMER GASSER GOFFER GRADER GUMMER GUTTER HASHER HEADER HEELER HELPER HEMMER HOLDER HOOKER HOOPER HOPPER HUNKIE INKMAN JOGGER JOINER LEAFER LEASER LEGGER NOILER PUGGER READER REEDER SCORER SEAMAN SEAMER SHAKER SKIVER SLAKER SLICER SLIDER SLOPER STAVER STAYER TOILER TOPPER BUILDER CREATOR EMPLOYE FIELDER LABORER OUVRIER
(— IN LEATHER) BEAMER CHUMAR JACKER BLACKER CHUCKLER
(— IN METALS) SMITH FLAPPER
(ADDITIONAL —) EXTRA
(AGRICULTURAL —) ARKIE KISAN
(AIRCRAFT —) BOOTMAN
(ANT —) MAXIM ERGATES REPLETE
(ASBESTOS —) COBBER
(AUTO —) DISKER
(BAKERY —) BRAKER COOLER DIVIDER BENCHMAN SPREADER
(BLUE-COLLAR —) STIFF
(BREWERY —) HOPPER STEEPER STILLMAN
(BRICK —) DAUBER CROWDER
(CANNERY —) SLIMER SCALDER SHEDMAN
(CLOCK —) STAKER
(CLUMSY —) BODGE BODGER
(COAL —) SUMPER GEORDIE SPRAGGER
(CONSTRUCTION —) HARDHAT
(DOCK —) BUNGS HOLDMAN SHENANGO
(DOMESTIC —) HELP
(FELLOW —) CONFRERE
(FOUNDRY —) FLOGGER SNAGGER
(GARMENT —) FACER SLEEVER ASSORTER INSEAMER
(GUN —) BLUER
(HARD —) SLOGGER
(HAT —) CURLER BRIMMER
(HIDE —) HEFTER COLORER
(HOSPITAL —) ALMONER
(HOTEL —) SCRUB
(ICEHOUSE —) AIRMAN
(JEWELRY —) ARBORER
(LOGGING —) SNIPER SKIDDER
(MATTRESS —) BEATER
(MIGRATORY —) HOBO OKIE
(MILL —) BILLER SPOUTER
(MINE —) BYEMAN FOOTER GOPHER LANDER DROPPER FACEMAN SLEDGER SWAMPER DRIFTMAN
(OIL WELL —) ROUGHNECK
(ORCHARD —) SMUDGER
(PACKINGHOUSE —) COOK
(PAPERMILL —) SIZER SIZEMAN
(PIANO —) BELLYMAN
(PLODDING —) GRUBBER
(POTTERY —) CASER BATTER BEDDER FETTLER

JOLLIER JUSTLER
(PRINTING —) FLY FLYBOY
(PUERTO RICAN —) GIBARO JIBARO
(QUARRY —) BREAKER
(RAILROAD —) JERRY HERDER BRAKEMAN
(SAWMILL —) BOLTER SETTER BOATMAN DECKMAN CHAINMAN
(SHOE —) CASER FOXER ARCHER FUDGER HEELER CHALKER BOTTOMER
(SKILLED —) ARTISTE
(SLAUGHTERHOUSE —) FATTER SHOVER SINGER SLIMER CHEEKER CHOPPER KNOCKER LIMEMAN SCALPER SCRIBER STICKER SNATCHER
(SOCIAL —) ALMONER
(TANNERY —) GATER STONER CROPPER CURRIER DELIMER BEAMSMAN SEASONER
(TEXTILE —) DOFFER DOUPER DRAWER GIGGER LAPPER LEASER SINGER CREELER DOUBLER JACKMAN KETTLER SKEINER SPINNER SHUTTLER SOFTENER SPLITTER TEASELER
(THEATER —) FLYMAN STAGEMAN
(TOBACCO —) BULKER SIFTER STEMMER SCRAPMAN SPRIGGER STICKMAN STRIPPER
(UNSKILLED —) HELPER DILUTEE GREENER
(USELESS —) TOOL
(WHITE-COLLAR —) EFFENDI
(YARN —) SOURER CHAINER
(PL.) LABOR
(PREF.) ERG(O) ERGAT(O)
(SUFF.) ERGAT(E) URGE URGIC URGY
WORKHORSE AVER AIVER TRESTLE SAWHORSE
WORKHOUSE UNION FACTORY WORKSHOP
WORKING PLAY GOING OPENCUT FUNCTION LABORAGE OPENCAST OPENWORK OPERATIC OPERATIVE
(— ALONE) HATTING
(— HARD) HOPPING
(— OF MINE) GWAG CROSSCUT
(— ON) PRACTICE
(MINE —S) SPLIT
(NOT —) DUFF
WORKMAN (ALSO SEE WORKER AND LABORER) BOSS HAND MATE ROTO CAGER CONER EXTRA FINER FLINT FLUER FROCK LAYER MAJOR MIXER POLER TONER TRIER TUBER BEAMER BLOUSE BOOMER BOWLER BUCKER BUMMER COATER DIPPER DRIVER FORKER GAGGER HANGER LASTER LATHER MASTER NIPPER OILMAN PUFFER RUNNER SAMMER SCORER SHAKER SKIVER SLICER SLIDER SOAKER SPIKER STAGER STAVER TAPPER TARRER TEEMER TILTER TIPMAN TIPPER TOPMAN WARMER WASHER WETTER WRIGHT ARTISAN DRUMMER HOTSHOT LUDDITE SHOPMAN
(CHIEF —) BOSS

(CLUMSY —) BUNGLER COBBLER
(FELLOW —) BULLY BUTTY
(PROFICIENT —) DEACON
(UNSKILLFUL —) HUNKY BUTCHER
(PL.) VOLK
WORKMANLIKE DEFT ADEPT
SKILLFUL
WORKMANSHIP HAND FABRIC
FACTURE OVERAGE ARTIFICE
ARTISANRY
WORKROOM DEN STUDY ATELIER
WORKS HACIENDA
(— OF CLOCK) WATCH
(SALT —) SALINA
WORKSHOP LAB SHED SHOP
FORGE LODGE SMIDDY SMITHY
ATELIER BOTTEGA HOSPITAL
OFFICINA PLUMBERY SKINNERY
WORKTABLE BENCH
WORLD ORB LOKA VALE WARD
EARTH WADRU WARDE CAREER
PUBLIC KINGDOM MONDIAL
CREATION CREATURE UNIVERSE
(— OF BOXING) FISTIANA
(— OF DARKNESS) SHEOL
(— OF DOGS) DOGDOM
(— OF FASHION) STYLEDOM
SWELLDOM
(— OF GODS) DEVALOKA
(— OF THE DEAD) DEEP
(— OF WOMEN) FEMINIE
(ACADEMIC —) CAMPUS
(EXTERNAL —) NONEGO
(GREAT —) MACROCOSM
(LITTLE —) MICROCOSM
(LOWER —) ORCUS
(PRIVATE —) AUTOCOSM
(THE —) FOLD
(TWO-DIMENSIONAL —) FLATLAND
(PREF.) COSM(O) MUNDI
(SUFF.) COSM
WORLDLINESS MAMMON
WORLDLING DIVES
WORLDLY LAY WARLY CARNAL
EARTHY MUNDAL EARTHLY
FLESHLY MUNDANE PROFANE
SECULAR SENSUAL TERRENE
(NOT —) INTERIOR
WORLD'S ILLUSION (AUTHOR
OF —) WASSERMANN
(CHARACTER IN —) EVA LAY IVAN
VOSS CYRIL DENIS KAREN SOREL
BECKER AMADEUS BERNARD
CRAMMON CHRISTIAN
ENGELSCHALL WAHNSCHAFFE
WORLD-WEARY BLASE
WORLDWIDE GLOBAL ECUMENIC
GLOBULAR PLANETAL PLANETARY
(PREF.) GLOBO
WORLD-WISE KNOWING PRUDENT
WORM BOB EEL ESS LOA MAD
LURG NAIS NEMA ARTER CADEW
FLUKE LYTTA PIPER SCREW
SNAKE DRAGON NEREID NEREIS
PALMER PALOLO SHAMIR SYLLID
SYLLIS TEREDO VERMIS WRETCH
ANNELID ASCARID CARBORA
ENOPLAN SABELLA SAGITTA
SERPENT SERPULA SETARID
SHUFFLE SPIONID TAGTAIL
TRICLAD WRIGGLE BRANDLIN
CEPHALOB CERCARIA CHETOPOD
GILTTAIL HELMINTH LEODICID

MEASURER NEMATODE
POLYCLAD STRONGYL TRICHINA
VERMICLE NEMERTEAN
TOOTHACHE SCHISTOSOME
(— IN HAWKS) FILANDER
(— USED FOR BAIT) TAGTAIL
(AQUATIC —) TUBIFEX
(BLOODSUCKING —) LEECH
(CADDIS —) CADEW PIPER
CADBAIT
(FLUKE —) PLAICE
(MEASURING —) LOOPER
(MUD —) IPO LOA
(SHIP —) BROMA COBRA
(PL.) APODA ENTOZOA
(PREF.) HELMINTH(O) LUMBRICI
SCOLEC(I)(O) VERMI
(SUFF.) SCOLEX
WORM-EATEN PITTED DECAYED
VERMOULU WERMETHE
WORMER JAG
WORMHOLE PIQURE
WORMLIKE VERMIAN
WORMSEED AMBROSIA
WORMWOOD MOXA ABSINTH
CUDWEED MUGWORT ABSINTHE
COMPOSIT MINGWORT
SANTONICA
WORMY EARTHY
WORN SEAR SERE USED PASSE
TRITE MAGGED MIZPAH SHABBY
ATTRITE CONTRITE
(— NEXT TO SKIN) INTIMATE
(— OUT) SHOT BANAL JADED
SEELY SPENT STALE STANK
BEATEN BEDRID BLEARY EFFETE
EPUISE SCREWY SHABBY CRIPPLE
FORWORN DECREPID FOUGHTEN
HARASSED OBSOLETE STRICKEN
(— SMOOTH) BEATEN
WORRICOW DEVIL BUGABOO
BUGBEAR HOBGOBLIN
WORRIED TOEY UNEASY ANXIOUS
FRETTED STREAKED CONCERNED
WORRIT VEX WORRY DISTRESS
WORRY DOG HOE HOW HOX LUG
NAG RUX TEW VEX BAIT BITE
CARE CARK FAZE FIKE FRAB FRET
FUSS HARE MOIL SOOL STEW
ANNOY CHEVY CHOKE DEAVE
FEEZE GALLY HARRY HURRY
LURRY PHASE SCALD SHAKE
TEASE TOUSE TOWSE BOTHER
CADDLE CHIVVY COTTER CUMBER
FERRET FIDGET GALLOW HARASS
HATTER HECTOR INFEST KIAUGH
MOIDER PESTER PINGLE PLAGUE
POTHER ANXIETY CHAGRIN
HATCHEL TROUBLE TURMOIL
WHERRET FASHERIE STRANGLE
WORRYING ANXIOUS
WORSE VER WAR SEAMY
WORSEN DESCEND
WORSHIP GOD CULT HERY PUJA
RANK ADORE DULIA HONOR
NAMAZ WURTH YAJNA CREDIT
PRAISE REPUTE REVERE BAALISM
ELOHISM ICONISM IDOLISM
IDOLIZE IMAGERY OBSERVE
BLESSING HIERURGY VENERATE
(— OF ALL GODS) PANTHEISM
(— OF SHAKESPEARE) BARDOLATRY
(ANCESTOR —) SCIOTHEISM

(FORM OF —) RITUAL
(HIGHEST KIND OF —) LATRIA
(INFERIOR KIND OF —) DULIA
(SERPENT —) OPHISM
(STAR —) SABAISM
(PREF.) LITURGIO THRESKI
(SUFF.) LATER LATRIA LATROUS
LATRY
WORSHIPER ISIAC BHAKTA
PRAISER IDOLATER
(— OF STARS) AKKUM SABIAN
(FIRE —) PARSI GHEBER GUEBER
PARSEE
(SERPENT —) SETHIAN SETHITE
WORSHIPFUL GOOD PROUD
NOTABLE
WORST ACE GET BEST LAST
OUTDO SHEND WREST DEFEAT
(PREF.) KAKISTO
WORSTED GARN JERRY SERGE
CUBICA VESSES WHIPCORD
WORT GAIL GYLE SWAT PLANT
LENGTH TUTSAN FILLING
KRAUSEN POTHERB
(FERMENTED —) FEED WASH
(UNFERMENTED —) GROUT
WORTH FECK MEED CARAT MERIT
PRICE VALOR VALUE BECOME
BOUNTY DESERT ESTEEM REGARD
RICHES VALENT VIRTUE WEALTH
DIGNITY PRETIUM VALIANT
WORSHIP SPLENDOR TREASURE
VALIDITY VALLIDOM
(NET —) CAPITAL
(OF LITTLE —) OHLOOK OOHLOOK
(PREF.) AXIO TIMO
WORTHINESS DESERT WORSHIP
WORTHLESS BAD BUM LOW WAF
BAFF BALD BARE BASE EVIL IDLE
LEWD ORRA PUNK RACA SLIM
VAIN VILE WAFF BLANK BLOWN
DUSTY FLASH FOUTY LOSEL
LOUSY PUTID SLINK SORRY
STRAW WASHY ABJECT CHAFFY
CHEESY CRUMMY DRAFFY
DRASTY DROSSY HOLLOW
LIMMER LITHER LUTHER MEASLY
NAUGHT PALTRY RASCAL ROTTEN
TRASHY WOODEN BAGGAGE
FUSTIAN MAUVAIS NAUGHTY
NOTHING PIPERLY RAFFISH
RUBBISH SCABBED SHILPIT
USELESS FECKLESS HARLOTRY
NUGATORY PRECIOUS RASCALLY
RUBBISHY TRUMPERY VAGABOND
WANWORDY WRETCHED
(— THING) AMBSACE
WORTHLESSNESS BELIAL
UNTHRIFT
WORTHWHILE TANTI
WORTHY BIG DEAR FAIR GOOD
HOLY TIDY AUGHT CANNY DIGNE
EXALT HONOR JELLY NOBLE
PIOUS GENTLE CONDIGN
GRADELY PAREGAL THRIFTY
ELIGIBLE VALUABLE WAUREGAN
(— OF BELIEF) CREDIBLE
(— OF DEVOTION) HOLY
(— OF PRAISE) LAUDABLE
(SUFF.) ABLE IBLE
WOULD WAD WID WANT WISH
COULD SHOULD
(— NOT) NOLD WADNA WADDENT

(I —) CHUD CHOLD
WOULD-BE MANQUE
WOUND ARR CUT HEW PIP WIN
BITE CALK CLAW DUNT FAKE
FOIN GALL GORE HARM HURT
MAIM PAIN PINK RASE RAZE RIST
SCAR SKAG SORE STAB TEAR
VULN WING BLESS BROKE GANCH
GRIEF KNIFE KNOCK SHOOT STICK
STING SUGAT THIRL TOUCH
BREACH BRUISE CREASE ENTAME
GRIEVE HARROW INJURE LAUNCH
LESION MARTYR OFFEND PIERCE
PLAGUE SCOTCH TRAUMA
AFFLICT ATTAINT BATTERY
BLIGHTY DIACOPE GUNSHOT
SCRATCH DISTRESS FLANKARD
FLEABITE INCISION LACERATE
SPURGALL VULNERATE
(— FROM BOAR'S TUSK) GANCH
GAUNCH
(— FROM BULL'S HORN) CORNADA
(— FROM RUBBING) GALL
(— IN DEER'S SIDE) FLANKARD
(— MADE BY THRUST) FOIN
(— ON FOOT) FIKE
(— ON HORSE'S ANKLE) CREPANCE
(— WITH POINTED WEAPON) STAB
SWORD
(DEEP —) DIACOPE
(MINUTE —) PRICK SCART
(TRIFLING —) FLEABITE
(PL.) NOUNS
(PREF.) HELC(O) TRAUMAT(O)
VULNI
WOUNDED HURT WUND VULNED
WINGED VULNOSE STRICKEN
WOUNDWORT BETONY ALLHEAL
HERCULES
WOU-WOU WAWA WAWAH
CAMPER GIBBON
WOVEN BROCHE BROWDEN
DAMASSE
(— FULL WIDTH) SEAMLESS
(— WIDE) BROAD
(— WITH RIB) SOLEIL
WOW HIT MEW BARK HOWL RAVE
WAIL WHINE SUCCESS
WOZZECK (CHARACTER IN —)
MARIE ANDRES WOZZECK
(COMPOSER OF —) BERG
WRACK KELP RACK RUIN VAREC
CUTWEED DESTROY DOWNFALL
EELGRASS WRECKAGE
WRAITH WAFT FETCH GHOST
SPOOK DOUBLE SHADOW
SWARTH SPECTRE
WRANGLE RAG YED CAMP MOIL
SPAR TIFT ARGLE ARGUE BRAWL
CHIDE DAFER FLITE JOWER
PLEAD STRUT ARGUFY BICKER
CAFFLE CAMPLE CANGLE DACKER
FRAPLE FRATCH HAGGLE HASSLE
JANGLE RAGGLE THREAP
BRABBLE BRANGLE DISPUTE
PICKEER QUARREL SCRAFFLE
SQUABBLE TIRRWIRR
WRANGLER CAMPER COWBOY
GRATER HAFTER WRAGER
DEBATER DEFENDER OPPONENT
WRANGLING JANGLE
WRAP HAP LAP LOT WAP BIND
FURL ROLL WHIP AMICE CLASP

CLOAK LAMBA MANTA NUBIA
SERVE TWINE WOOLD AFGHAN
BURLAP CLOTHE COCOON
COOLER DOLMAN EMBALE
MOIDER MUFFLE PATTOO
SACQUE SWATHE WRIXLE
ENVELOP INVOLVE SWADDLE
UMBELAP BARRACAN
(— CABLE) KECKLE
(— DEAD BODY) CERE
(— ONESELF) HUDDLE
(— UP) HAP MAIL ENROL IMPLY
(— UP HEAD) MOB MOP MOBLE
(— WIRE AROUND FISHING LINE)
GANGE
(— WITH BANDAGE) SWATHE
(PL.) SECRECY RESTRAINT
WRAPPER APRON COVER MOTTO
PILCH SHAWL SMOCK COUPON
FARDEL JACKET ENVELOP
OVERALL SAMPLER COVERING
MAHARMAH WOOLPACK
(— FOR BOOK) JACKET
(— FOR CUTLET) PAPILLOTE
(— WORN IN EGYPT) GALABIA
GALABEAH
(COOKING —) PAPILLOTE
WRAPPING WAP PACK GELILAH
LAPPING COVERING MANTLING
(— FOR DEAD) CEREMENT
(— OF HEBREW SCROLL) GELILAH
(— OF ROPE) SERVICE
WRASSE COOK BALLAN COMBER
CONNER CUNNER LABRID
HOGFISH PIGFISH SEAWIFE
CORKWING DONCELLA JANIZARY
LADYFISH SENORITA
WRATH IRE FURY GRIM ANGER
WROTH CHOLER FELONY PASSION
VIOLENCE
WRATHFUL IRY EVIL HIGH ANGRY
IRATE WROTH IREFUL RAGING
FURIOUS JEALOUS CHOLERIC
WREAK CAUSE AVENGE EXPEND
GRATIFY INDULGE INFLICT
REVENGE
(— DESTRUCTION) ESTREPE
WREATH LEI ORLE PLAY CROWN
GREEN LAURE LORRE OLIVE
TORSE WHORL WRASE ANADEM
CRANTS CREASE LAUREL POTONG
TORTIL CHAPLET CORONAL
CORONET CROWNAL DOLPHIN
FESTOON GARLAND WRINKLE
KELYPHYTE
(SPIRAL —) VOLUTION
WREATHE BIND WIND CRISP
TWINE TWIST WRING INTORT
WRITHE CONTORT ENTWINE
INTWIST INVOLVE
WREATHED SPIRY TORTILE
TORTIVE WRITHED INTORTED
TORTILE
WRECK CRAB HULK RUIN BLAST
CRACK PRANG SHOOT SMASH
TRASH WRACK DESPOIL DESTROY
FOUNDER GODSEND SHATTER
TORPEDO DEMOLISH SABOTAGE
SHAMBLES
(— COMPLETELY) TOTAL
(HUMAN —) DERELICT
WRECKAGE WRACK FINDAL
FLOTSAM GODSEND

WAVESON SHAMBLES
WRECKED NOUGHT
**WRECKERS, THE (CHARACTER
IN —)** AVIS MARK PASCOE THRIZA
(COMPOSER OF —) SMYTH
WREN GIRL STAG TOPE CUTTY
JENNY KITTY PEGGY SALLY STAID
TYDIE SCUTTY TIDIFE TIDLEY
TINTIE TOMTIT WRANNY
BLUECAP REGULUS MALURINE
WRANNOCK
WRENCH KEY PIN RUG PULL RACK
RICK RUGG TEAR YERK CRICK
CRINK FORCE THRAW THROW
TWIST WRAMP WREST BEDKEY
SPRAIN STRAIN TWEEZE DISTORT
SPANNER SPANULE SQUINCH
TORTURE TWISTLE
WREST REAR REND EXACT FORCE
TWIST ARREST EXTORT WRENCH
WRITHE ABSTORT WIREDRAW
(— AWAY) STRIP DESPOIL
WRESTLE PRAY RASSLE SQUIRM
TUSSLE WRAXLE WRITHE
GRAPPLE SCUFFLE THRIMBLE
THRUMBLE
WRESTLER MATMAN WELTER
CLICKER MATSTER GRAPPLER
WRESTLING SUMO SAMBO
PALESTRA WRAXLING
(— TECHNIQUE) GLIMA
(STYLE OF —) SAMBO
WRETCH DOG MIX FILE WARY
MISER SLAVE THING BUGGER
PERSON SQUALL BRETHEL
CAITIFF CAMOOCH CHINCHE
CULLION GLUTTON HILDING
SCROYLE BEZONIAN CREATURE
MESCHANT POLTROON RECREANT
SCULLION
WRETCHED EVIL FOUL LORN
MEAN POOR DAWNY DEENY
GAUNT SORRY WISHT WOFUL
YEMER ABJECT CAITIF DISMAL
MEAGER PALTRY RASCAL SHABBY
SICKLY SORDID UNLEAD UNLEDE
WOEFUL ABYSMAL BENEATH
FORLORN OUTWORN PITIFUL
SQUALID UNSEELY MESCHANT
MISERABLE
(— PERSON OR ANIMAL) MISERY
WRIGGLE EEL REG RIG FRIG LASH
WIND WRIG SLIDE WRELE WRING
SQUIRM WAMBLE WANGLE
WARPLE WIDDLE WIMPLE
WINTLE WRITHE EYEBROW
SNIGGLE TWIDDLE TWINGLE
WRABILL WRESTLE SCRIGGLE
SQUIGGLE
WRIGGLING EELY SCRIGGLE
SQUIGGLY
WRIGGLY SNAKY SNAKISH
SQUIRMING
WRING RACK DRAIN EXACT SCREW
TWIST WREST EXTORT OPPRESS
SQUEEZE TORMENT TORTURE
(— THE NECK) SCRAG
WRINGER RUNG WRUNG
SQUEEZER
WRINKLE RUT DRAW FOLD FURL
HINT KNIT LIRK RUCK RUGA
SEAM BREAK CRIMP CRISP DELVE
FAULT FRILL REEVE RIVEL SNIRL

BUCKLE COCKLE CRAVAT CREASE
FURROW METHOD PUCKER
RIMPLE RUMPLE RUNKLE SCRIMP
WREATH BLEMISH CRANKLE
CRINKLE CRUMPLE CRUNKLE
FROUNCE FRUMPLE CONTRACT
IRRUGATE RUGOSITY
(— OF FLESH) CRAVAT
(PREF.) RUTI RUTID(O)
WRINKLED CRUMP PURFLY
RUGATE RUGGED RUGOSE
RUGOUS SEAMED COCKLED
ROUCHED SAVOYED CRUMPLED
FURROWED PUCKERED WRITHLED
WRIZZLED
WRINKLING KNIT KNOT FROWN
WRIST CARPUS SHACKLE
(PREF.) CARP(O)
WRISTER MUFFETEE
WRISTLET WRISTER MUFFETEE
WRISTWATCH BAGUET BAGUETTE
WRIT AIEL CAPE MISE PONE TOLT
ALIAS BREVE BRIEF ERROR RECTO
UTRUM BRIEVE CAPIAS ELEGIT
EXTENT PLAINT VENIRE ACCOUNT
DEDIMUS DETINUE EXIGENT
LATITAT PLURIES PRECEPT
PROCESS SUMMONS WARRANT
CESSAVIT COSINAGE DETAINER
DOCUMENT FORMEDON
MANDAMUS MITTIMUS NOVERINT
PRAECIPE QUOMINUS REPLEVIN
SISERARY SUBPOENA TESTATUM
WARRANTY
(— FOR SUMMONING EXTRA
JURORS) TALES
WRITE INK PEN BACK BOOK DITE
DRAW READ CLERK DRAFT STYLE
AUTHOR ENFACE INDITE SCRIBE
SCRIVE ADDRESS COMPILE
COMPOSE DICTATE EMPAPER
EXARATE SCREEVE BIOGRAPH
INSCRIBE
(— ADDRESS) BACK
(— BRIEFLY) JOT
(— CARELESSLY) DASH SCRAWL
SCRIBBLE
(— DOWN) SIGN BREVE DENOTE
RECORD AMORTIZE DESCRIBE
(— FURTHER) ADD
(— HASTILY) SCRATCH SCRIBBLE
SQUIGGLE
(— IN A LARGE HAND) ENGROSS
(— IN LARGE CHARACTERS) TEXT
(— ON FRONT OF BILL) ENFACE
(— PASTORAL POEMS) PHILLIS
(— WHAT IS NOT TRUE) FABLE
(SUFF.) GRAPH(ER)(IA)(IC)(Y)
WRITER (ALSO SEE AUTHOR) PEN
BARD HACK PUFF ALVAR GHOST
ODIST SQUIB AUTHOR FATHER
GLOZER HEROIC LAWYER LETTER
MUNSHI NOTARY PENMAN
PRABHU PROSER PURVOE SCRIBE
TRAGIC YEOMAN ADAPTER
ADSMITH ANALYST DIARIST
ELOHIST ESSAYER GLOSSER
GNOMIST HYMNIST IAMBIST
JUVENAL LAUDIST MUNCHEE
PENSTER PROPHET PROSAIC
REVUIST SCRIVER STYLIST
SUMMIST TEXTMAN AUGUSTAN
BLURBIST COMEDIAN COMPOSER

DECADENT DECADIST DIDACTIC
EMBOSSER EPISTLER ESSAYIST
FABLEIST FABULIST GROMATIC
HUMORIST IDYLLIST MONODIST
MOONSHEE NOVELIST PARODIST
PENWOMAN PREFACER
PRESSMAN PROSAIST PROSEMAN
PSALMIST REVIEWER SCRIPTER
VERSEMAN PROSATEUR
PAMPHLETEER
(— OF BURLESQUE) GABBER
(FREE-LANCE —) CREEPER
(HACK —) PENSTER
(INCOMPETENT —) BOTCHER
(SATIRICAL —) SILLOGRAPH
WRITHE WRY WIND THROW TWIRL
TWIST WRING SQUIRM TERVEE
WAMBLE WRABBE WRENCH
AGONIZE WRESTLE
WRIGGLE WRINGLE
CONVOLVE
WRITHING EELY WRING WRITHY
WRITING BOOK DITE FAIT PAGE
POEM KANJI LIBEL SCROW
CADJAN GOSSIP LEGEND LETTER
PAGINE SCRIPT SCRITE SCRIVE
UNCIAL ARTICLE AUTONYM
DIPLOMA ESCRIPT SCREEVE
APOCRYPH CONTRACT
DOCUMENT GRAVAMEN
HARANGUE KAKEMONO
LETTRURE LIPOGRAM
PAMPHLET SCRIBING
SONNETRY
(— OF LITTLE VALUE) STUFF
SCRIBBLE
(— ON PAPER SCROLL) MAKIMONO
(— ON SILK) KAKEMONO
(— UNDER SEAL) BOND
(BITTER —) DIATRIBE
(CARELESS —) SCRAWL
(CRAMPED —) NIGGLE
(CURSIVE —) JOINHAND
(HINDU —) VEDA
(HUMOROUS —S) FACETIAE
(ILLUMINATED —) FRACTUR
(MUSICAL —) GIMEL GYMEL
(NORSE —) EDDA
(PRETENTIOUS —) FUSTIAN
(SACRED —) ARANYAKA
BRAHMANA SCRIPTURE
(SATIRICAL —) PASQUINADE
(SECRET —) SCYTALE
(SHORT —) SCRIP
(SHORTHAND —) PHONOGRAPHY
(STYLE OF —) ACADEMESE
(SYLLABIC —) KANA
(VAPID —) WASH
(VERBOSE —) TOOTLE
(WORTHLESS —) TRIPE
(PL.) LEGENDA ARANYAKA
POSTHUMA
(PREF.) GRAMO GRAPHI GRAPHO
(SUFF.) GRAM GRAPH(ER)(IA)(IC)(Y)
WRITING CASE STANDISH
SCRUTOIRE
WRITTEN KETIB KETHIB
KTHIBH GRAPHIC
LITERAL
(— ABOVE) SS
(— AFTER) ADSCRIPT
(— HASTILY) STRAY
(PREF.) GRAPTO

WROCLAW BRESLAU
WRONG BAD CAR ILL MIS OUT
WET AWRY HARM HURT SORE
SOUR TORT WITE AGATE AGLEE
AGLEY AMISS CRIME DUTCH
FALSE GLEED GRIEF MALUM
UNFIT WATHE WOUGH AGUILT
ASTRAY BLOOEY FAULTY INJURE
INJURY NOUGHT OFFEND
SARAAD SINFUL UNTRUE WICKED
WONDER ABUSION ABUSIVE
DAMNIFY DEFRAUD IMMORAL
INJURIA MISBEDE NAUGHTY
UNRIGHT VIOLATE AGGRIEVE
COCKEYED MISTAKEN PERVERSE
UNLEEFUL
(CIVIL —) TORT
(IMAGINARY —) WINDMILL
(SHOCKINGLY —) MONSTROUS
(PREF.) MIS

WRONGDOER ACTOR SINNER
FAULTER MISDOER OFFENDER
WRONGDOING MISS CRIME FAULT
DEFAULT MISCONDUCT
MALFEASANCE
WRONGFUL UNFAIR UNJUST
TORTIOUS TORTUOUS UNLAWFUL
WRONGHEADED WRY PERVERSE
WRONGLY AMISS BADLY FALSE
NOUGHT UNRICHT UNRIGHT
OVERWART
WROTH ANGRY IRATE IREFUL
WROUGHT BEATEN CARVEN
FORMED SHAPED VROCHT
CREATED HAMMERED
(ELABORATELY —) LABORED
WRY ASKEW AVERT TWIST WRING
WRONG WRITHE DEFLECT
DISTORT TWISTED WRITHEN
SATURNINE

WRYNECK IYNX JYNX SLAB WEET
LOXIA PEABIRD WEETBIRD
TORTICOLLIS
WUTHERING HEIGHTS (AUTHOR
OF —) BRONTE
(CHARACTER IN —) DEAN EDGAR
ELLEN JOSEPH LINTON ZILLAH
FRANCES HARETON HINDLEY
EARNSHAW ISABELLA LOCKWOOD
CATHERINE HEATHCLIFF
WYCH ELM WITCH WITCHEN
WYLIECOAT WALYCOAT
NIGHTGOWN PETTICOAT
WYND HAW ALLEY CLOSE

WYOMING

CAPITAL: CHEYENNE
COUNTY: TETON UINTA GOSHEN
BIGHORN LARAMIE NIOBRARA
INDIAN: ARAPAHO

LAKE: JACKSON
MOUNTAIN: ELK CLOUD GANNET
HOBACK FREMONT ATLANTIC
SHERIDAN
MOUNTAIN RANGE: TETON ABSARO
BIGHORN LARAMIE
RATTLESNAKE
NICKNAME: EQUALITY
RIVER: GREEN SNAKE PLATTE
POWDER BIGHORN
STATE BIRD: MEADOWLARK
STATE FLOWER: PAINTBRUSH
STATE TREE: COTTONWOOD
TOWN: CODY LUSK CASPER
BUFFALO LARAMIE RAWLINS
WORLAND GREYBULL
KEMMERER SHERIDAN
SUNDANCE

X

X EX XRAY ERROR MISTAKE
XANTHIC YELLOW
XANTHIPPE NAG SHREW
  (HUSBAND OF —) SOCRATES
XANTHIPPUS (SON OF —) PERICLES
XEBEC SHIP CHEBEC CHEBECK
  SHABEQUE
XENIUM GIFT DAINTY DELICACY
XERES JEREZ SHERRY

XERIC DRY
XHOSA KAFIR KAFFIR
  (PL.) AMAKOSA AMAXOSA
XIPHARES (FATHER OF —)
  MITHRIDATE
XIPHISTERNUM XIFOID
XIPHOSURUS LIMULUS
X-RAY UROGRAM

XUREL SCAD SAUREL
XUTHUS (ADOPTED SON OF —) ION
  (BROTHER OF —) DORUS AEOLUS
  (FATHER OF —) HELLEN
  (MOTHER OF —) ORSEIS
  (SON OF —) ION DURUS ACHAEUS
  (WIFE OF —) CREUSA
XYLEM WOOD HADROM

HADROME XYLOGEN
XYLOID WOODY LIGNEOUS
XYLOPHONE REGAL SARON
  BALAFO GAMBANG GAMELAN
  MARIMBA BALAPHON GAMELANG
  GIGELIRA STICCADO
XYSTUS WALK XYST PORTICO
  TERRACE

Y

Y WY YA WYE YOD YOKE YANKEE
(**— CONNECTION**) SIAMESE
(**— COORDINATE**) SINE
(PREF.) (**LETTER —**) YPSILI
YABBER TALK JABBER LANGUAGE
YABBY CRAWLIE
YACARE CAIMAN CAYMAN JACARE
YACHT SAIL SCOW BRUTE YATCH
DINGHY SONDER YEAGHE
CRUISER KEELBOAT
YAFF YAP BARK YELP
YAFFLE ARMFUL YAFFIL
YAHOO BRUTE CLOWN ROWDY
BUMPKIN
YAHWEH GOD JAVE JAHVAH
YAHWIST JEHOVIST
YAK GAG JOKE LAUGH BULBUL
SARLAK SARLYK YAMMER
CHATTER
YAKALA JAGA
YAKKA WORK LABOR
YAKUT SAKHA
YAM HOI UBE UBI UVE JAMB LIMA
RAIL TUGUI IGNAME INAMIA
INHAME POTATO BONIATA
(**TARO —**) KOKO
YAMA (**FATHER OF —**) VIVASVANT
(**SISTER OF —**) YAMI
YAM BEAN KAMAS JICAMA
WAYAKA SINCAMAS
YAMEN COURT YAMUN OFFICE
YAMEO LLAMEO
YAMMER CRY WAIL SCOLD WHINE
YEARN YOMER GRUMBLE
WHIMPER
YAMP YAMPA SQUAWROOT
YANAN NOZI
YANG HONK GURJUN
YANK FLOG JERK SLAP HOICK
SNAKE BUFFET
YAP BARK YAWP YELP MOUTH
SCOLD WAFFLE BUMPKIN
CHATTER KYOODLE
YAPOK YAPOCK OPOSSUM
OYAPOCK
YAQUI YAKI HIAQUI
YARD HAW HOF YED CREW CROW
DUMP FOLD SKID SPAR TILT
COURT GARTH PATIO STICK
CANCHA HOPPET LOANIN
CURTAIN GARSTON KNACKERY
OUTGARTH
(**— OF SAWMILL**) DUMP
(**— WHERE COWS ARE MILKED**)
LOANIN LOANING
(**FINAL —**) FELL
(**GRASSY —**) GARSTON
(**PAVED —**) CAUSEY
(**POULTRY —**) BARTON
(**SAIL —**) RAE
(**1-16TH OF A —**) NAIL
(**1-3RD OF CUBIC —**) CARTLOAD
(**20 —S**) SCORE

(**5 AND A HALF —S**) ROD
YARD GRASS ELEUSINE
MANGRASS
YARDLAND VERGE VIRGATE
YARDMASTER DINGER
YARDSTICK VERGE YAIRD METRIC
MEASURE METWAND METEWAND
STANDARD
YARE YAR AYRE YORE BRISK
READY LIVELY NIMBLE PROMPT
YARETA LLARETA
YARM WAIL NOISE OUTCRY SHRIEK
YARN ABB END FOX CORD GARN
GIMP PIRN SILK SLIP WEFT WHIP
DYNEL FLOSS GRAIN INKLE PITCH
SPIEL ALASKA ANGORA BERLIN
BROACH CADDIS COTTON
CREWEL CUFFER DACRON
ESTRON FLORET FRIEZE MERINO
MOTTLE PEELER RATINE SAXONY
SINGLE STRAND THREAD VINYON
WOOLEN ZEPHYR ACETATE
CADDICE FILLING GENAPPE
INGRAIN MELANGE RACKING
SCHAPPE VIGOGNE WORSTED
ASBESTOS BOURETTE CHENILLE
FORTISAN ROUNDING SPINNING
WHEELING ORGANZINE
VIGOUREUX
(**— FOR WARP**) ABB
(**— FROM FLOSS SILK**) FLORET
(**— SIZE**) TYPP
(**BALL OF —**) CLEW CLUE
(**BITS OF ROPE —**) THRUMS
(**BUNDLE OF —**) PAD
(**CONICAL MASS OF —**) COP
(**ELASTIC —**) LASTEX
(**EXAGGERATED —**) STRETCHER
(**FINE SOFT —**) ZEPHYR KASHMIR
CASHMERE
(**LINEN —**) SPINEL
(**ROLL OF —**) PRICK CHEESE
(**ROPE —S**) SOOGEE
(**SILK —**) TRAM
(**SMALL PIECE OF SPUN —**) RABAND
ROBBIN ROPEBAND
(**UNEVEN —**) BOUCLE
(PL.) FOX MENDINGS
YARRAN GIDYA MYALL GIDGEA
GIDGEE
YARROW ALLHEAL CAMMOCK
MAUDLIN MILFOIL PELLITORY
YASHIRO SHA
YASHMAK VEIL ASMACK YAKMAK
YATAGHAN SABER ATAGHAN
SIMITAR
YATTER CHATTER PRATTLE
YAUD MARE YADE
YAUPON ASSI HOLLY YUPON
CASINA CASSINE
YAUTIA COCO TARO TANIA
COCKER TANIER MALANGA
YAW GAPE YAWN LURCH SHEER

BROACH SWERVE
YAWL HOWL DANDY MIZZEN
SCREAM SCHOKKER
YAWN GAP GALP GANE GANT
GAPE YANE ABYSM CHAUM
CAVITY TEDIUM DULLNESS
OSCITATE
YAWNING HIANT CHASMA GAPING
OSCITANT
YAWP BAWL GAPE RANT STARE
SQUAWK YAMMER COMPLAIN
YAWS PIAN TUBBA TUBBOE
YAWWEED RHUBARB
YAYA COPA
YEA YA YES YOY YIGH TRULY
ASSENT REALLY VERILY
YEAN EAN LAMB
YEANLING KID LAMB EANLING
YEAR EAR SUN AYRE HAAB TIME
ANNUS VAGUE WINTER ZODIAC
TOWMOND TZOLKIN BIRTHDAY
(**— OF EMANCIPATION**) JUBILEE
(**ACADEMIC —**) SESSION
(**IN THIS —**) HA
(**LAST —**) FERNYEAR
(**MANY —S**) AGE
(**MAYAN —**) TUN HAAR
(**ONE BILLION —S**) AEON
(**SABBATICAL —**) JUBILE JUBILEE
(**1000 —S**) MILLENARY
MILLENNIUM
(**4320 MILLION —S**) KALPA
(PL.) SEASONS
(SUFF.) ENNIAL ENNIUM
YEARBOOK ANNUAL SERIAL
ANNUARY
YEARLING COLT HORNOTINE
(**AUTHOR OF —**) RAWLINGS
(**CHARACTER IN —**) LEM ORA JODY
HUTTO PENNY TWINK BAXTER
NELLIE OLIVER WILSON GINRIGHT
FORRESTER WEATHERBY
FODDERWING
YEARLY ANNUAL SOLEMN
YEARN HO YEN ACHE BURN EARN
GAPE HONE IRNE LONG PANT
PINE SIGH CRAVE GREEN GRIEN
ASPIRE CURDLE GRIEVE HANKER
YAMMER
YEARNING EROS DESIRE HANKER
RENNET CRAVING EARNFUL
HOMESICK
YEAST BEE EST BARM BEES EAST
KOJI SOTS FROTH SPUME LEAVEN
NEWING RISING SIZING TORULA
FERMENT SIZZING EMPTINGS
(**FILM —**) FLOR
YEASTY LIGHT FROTHY TRIVIAL
RESTLESS
YEGG ROBBER BURGLAR
YELL CRY CALL GOWL HOWL ROAR
YARM YAUP YOWL YOWT GOLLY
SHOUT TIGER BELLOW GOLLAR

HOLLER SCREAM YAMMER
YELLOCH SCRONACH SKELLOCH
YELLOW (ALSO SEE COLOR) OR
GULL AMBER BLAKE BLOND
FAVEL FLAVE JAUNE PALEW
SHELL YELWE ALMOND BANANA
FLAVID MELINE MIMOSA NUGGET
OXGALL BISCUIT JASMINE
JONQUIL LEGHORN LUTEOUS
MEXICAN MUSTARD NANKEEN
OATMEAL POPCORN SAFFRON
TILLEUL WHEATEN YUCATAN
AUREOLIN GENERALL ICTEROID
LUMINOUS MARIGOLD ORPIMENT
PRIMROSE
(**— AS BUTTER**) BLAKE
(**BROWNISH —**) FULVID FULVOUS
(**GOLDEN —**) FLAVID
(**GREENISH —**) ACACIA
(**INDIAN —**) PURI PURREE
(**LEMON —**) GENERALL
(PREF.) CHLOR(O) CHRYS(O)
FLAV(I)(O) OCHRO XANTH(O)
XANTIN(O)
YELLOW ALDER SAGEROSE
YELLOW BEDSTRAW CRUDWORT
CURDWORT FLEAWEED
YELLOW BUGLE IVA IVE IVY
YELLOW CLINTONIA DOGBERRY
YELLOW FEVER VOMITO
YELLOW FOXTAIL STICKERS
YELLOW GENTIAN FELWORT
YELLOW GREEN PISTACHE
YELLOWHAMMER SKYT YITE
AMMER GOWDY SKITE GLADDY
GOLDIE VERDIN YORLIN FLICKER
GLADEYE YELDRIN YOLDRING
(**— STATE**) ALABAMA
YELLOW IRIS SEDGE LEVERS
DAGGERS
YELLOWISH SALLOW ICTERINE
SAFFRONY
(**— GREEN**) GLAUCOUS
(**— RED**) FALLOW
(PREF.) LUTEO
YELLOW JACKET VESPA VESPID
YELLOW JASMINE WOODBINE
YELLOWLEGS KILLCU TATLER
WINTER YELPER TATTLER
YELLOW MACKEREL CREVALLE
YELLOWNESS FLAVEDO
YELLOW POND LILY DUCK CLOTE
CLOTS NUPHAR
YELLOW PRICKLE RUBIA
YELLOW RATTLE RATEL
COCKSCOMB LOUSEWORT
YELLOW TOADFLAX RAMSTEAD
YELLOW WAGTAIL OATEAR
YELLOW WATER LILY KELP
WOKAS
YELLOWWOOD FUSTIC FUSTOC
GOPHER MANGWE VIRGILIA
YELP CRY YAP YIP BAFF BARK KIYI

WAFF YAFF YAUP YAWP BOAST
YAMPH AVOCET SQUEAL YAFFLE
YELLOW
YELPING CRY

YEMEN

ANCIENT KINGDOM: SABA SHEBA
CAPITAL: SANA SANAA
COIN: RIYAL
MUSLIM SECT: SHIA SUNNI
OFFICIAL NAME:
YEMENARABREPUBLIC
PEOPLE: ZAIDI SHAFAI
PORT: MOKA MOCHA
REGION: TIHAMA
RULER: IMAM
TOWN: MOKA DAMAR MOCHA
TAIZZ HODEIDA

YEN EYES LONG URGE YEARN
DESIRE SUCKER LONGING
YENTA GOSSIP TALKER
YEOMAN CHURL CLERK WRITER
GOODMAN GUIDMAN GRAYCOAT
RETAINER BEEFEATER
YERBA SANTA TARBUSH
YERK BEAT GOAD HURL JERK KICK
STAB YARK THUMP EXCITE
THRASH LASHING
YES AY DA IS JA OC SI YA AYE ISS
YAS YAW YEA YEP YIS YUH YUS
YEAH JOKOL TRULY
YESTERDAY YESTER YESTREEN
(OF —) PRIDIAN
YET AND BUT YIT EVEN STILL
ALGATE HOWEER THOUGH
FINALLY HOWEVER HITHERTO
YETT GATE
YEUK EWK YUK ITCH YUCK
ITCHING
YEW YO HEW UGH YOE YOW VIEW
TAXUS TOPIARY CHINWOOD
YEX YOLK
YIDDISH JEWISH
YIELD GO BOW CUT ILD PAN PLY
BEAR BEND CAST CEDE CESS
COME CROP DRAG DUCK FOLD
GIVE HEAR HELD LOUT QUIT SELL
VAIL WAGE AGREE ALLOW AMAIN
AVALE AWALE BRING BUDGE
CARRY CAUSE DEFER GRANT
HEALD HIELD LEAVE OFFER
SLAKE STOOP ACCEDE AFFORD
BOUNTY BUCKLE COMPLY
CONFER FOLLOW IMPART
OUTPUT RELENT RENDER
RETURN SUBMIT SUPPLY SWERVE
UNGIVE UPGIVE ABANDON
ANALYZE BEARING CONCEDE
DELIVER FURNISH HARVEST
KNUCKLE OUTTURN PRODUCE
PROVIDE REDOUND RUCKSEY
SUCCUMB BEGRUDGE FRUITAGE
OVERGIVE PICKINGS UNDERLIE
RELINQUISH
(— FRUIT) ADDLE GRAIN
(— GRASS) GRAZE
(— OF FIELD) BURDEN
(— OF MINE) BONANZA

(— ON BOND) BASIS
(— TO) INDULGE
(— TO TEMPTATION) FALL
(— UP) LET FORLET FORLEIT
(— WELL) HIT BLEED
(MINERAL —) PROSPECT
(SUFF.) FER(ENCE)(ENT)(OUS)
YIELDED
(SUFF.) GENETIC
YIELDING ABLE MEEK NESH SOFT
TALL WAXY NAISH WAXEN
BONAIR CAVING FACILE FEEBLE
FLABBY LIMBER LITHER OUTPUT
PLIANT QUAGGY SUPPLE
BEARING CESSION FINGENT
FLACCID DEDITION LADYLIKE
RECREANT
(— IRREGULARLY) BUNCHY
(— OF HORSE) FLEXION
(— STAGE) SEAR
(— TO IMPULSES) ABANDON
YIN SHANG
YIRMILIK METALLIK
YODEL SONG JODEL WARBLE
REFRAIN
YODH IOD JOD
YOGA JOG
YOGI JOGI FAKIR FAKEER
YOKE BOW YOK BAIL CROW DRAG
FORK HOOP PAIR POKE SOLE
BANGY FURCA SHEBA SPANG
BANGHY COUPLE INSPAN
DRAGBAR HARNESS OPPRESS
ADJUGATE
(— BAR) SKEY
(— TO HOLD DRILL) CROW
(— TO RAISE CANNON) BAIL
(PREF.) ZYG(O)(OTO)
(SUFF.) ZYGOMATIC ZYGOSIS
ZYGOTE
YOKEFELLOW MATE FELLOW
PARTNER YOKEMATE
YOKEL YOB BOOR CLUB JAKE JOCK
FARMER JOSKIN BUMPKIN
HAYSEED WAYBACK ABDERITE
CHAWBACON
YOKING BOUT CONTEST MUGGING
YOLANTA (CHARACTER IN —) RENE
ROBERT YOLANTA VAUDEMONT
(COMPOSER OF —) TCHAIKOVSKY
YOLDRING YOWLEY
YOLK CENTER YELLOW ESSENCE
LATEBRA VITELLUS PARABLAST
(HAVING A —) LECITHAL
(PREF.) LECITH(O) VITELLI
VITELLO
(SUFF.) LECITHAL
YON YONDER THITHER BACKWARD
YONDER THAT THERE THOSE
THITHER
YORE PAST YARE YEARS
(OF —) OLDEN
YORKER TICE
YORKSHIREMAN TIKE TYKE
LEAROYD
YORUBA NAGO
YOU DU HE IT OW TA TU WE YA
YO ONE OWE SHE SIE YOW YUH
THOU YOUSE YOURSELF

YOU CAN'T GO HOME AGAIN
(AUTHOR OF —) WOLFE
(CHARACTER IN —) ELSE JACK
LLOYD ESTHER GEORGE KOHLER
MCHARG WEBBER EDWARDS
FOXHALL
**YOU NEVER CAN TELL (AUTHOR
OF —)** SHAW
(CHARACTER IN —) BOON BOHUM
DOLLY GLORIA PHILIP CLANDON
MCCOMAS WILLIAM GRAMPTON
VALENTINE
YOUNG FRY JUV BIRD CALF DROP
BIRTH BROOD FETUS FRUIT
GREEN SMALL UNOLD JUNIOR
KINDLE JUVENAL IMMATURE
YEANLING YOUTHFUL
(— OF ANY ANIMAL) FRY BABY
CALF FOAL JOEY LAMB TOTO
(— OF BEAST) SLINK
(— OF BIRD) CHICK
(— OF CAMEL) COLT
(— OF DOG) WHELP
(— OF FISH) FRY
(— OF SEA TROUT) HERLING
(VERY —) SUCKING NEPHIONIC
SHIRTTAIL
(PREF.) FETI FETO FOETI FOETO
(SUFF.) (— ONE) LING
(MODE OF HATCHING —) PAEDES
YOUNGER KID LESS PUNEE JUNIOR
PUISNE OFFSPRING
YOUNGEST (— OF BROOD)
WALLYDRAG
YOUNGSTER KID BIRD COLT CHILD
YOUTH BUTTON SHAVER URCHIN
YONKER YOUNKER SPALPEEN
YOUNKER DUPE CHILD KNIGHT
NOVICE SQUIRE YUNKER
YOUR OR YO THY YAR YER OURE
OWRE YOURN
YOURSELF ITSELF HERSELF
HIMSELF ONESELF
YOUTH BOY BUD IMP LAD CHAP
COLT PAGE BAHUR CHABO
GROOM HYLAS POULT PRIME
SPRIG SWAIN WHELP BOCHUR
BURSCH EPHEBE HOYDEN INFANT
JUVENT KOUROS MASTER SPRING
SQUIRT YONKER CALLANT
EPHEBOS GOSSOON JUVENAL
PUBERTY SAPLING YOUDITH
YOUNGTH ENDYMION JUVENILE
SPRINGAL
(— WHO SERVES LIQUORS)
GANYMEDE
(DELINQUENT —) BODGIE
(GODDESS OF —) HEBE
(IMPUDENT —) SQUIRT
(INEXPERIENCED —) GUNSEL
(NON-JEWISH —) SHEGETZ
(PERT —) PRINCOX
(RUDE —) HOYDEN
(RUSSIAN — ORGANIZATION)
KOMSOMOL
(SILLY —) CALF SLENDER
(WELLBORN —) CHILD
(PREF.) HEBE
YOUTHFUL RATH FRESH GREEN

YOUNG BOYISH GOLDEN JUNIOR
MAIDEN NEANIC VIRGIN YOUTHY
LADDISH PUERILE YOUNGLY
IMMATURE JUVENILE SPRINGAL
VIGOROUS
YOUTHFULNESS JEUNESSE
YOWL GOWL HOWL WAIL YELL
YELP
YUAN DOLLAR
YUAPIN YARURA
YUCATEC MAYA
YUCCA LILY PITA YUCA DATIL
IZOTE PALMA JOSHUA LILIAL
LILIUM PALMITO SOAPWEED
YUGA KALI

YUGOSLAVIA

CAPITAL: BEOGRAD BELGRADE
COIN: PARA DINAR
GULF: KVARNER
LAKE: OHRID PRESPA SCUTARI
MEASURE: RIF AKOV RALO DONUM
KHVAT LANAZ STOPA MOTYKA
PALAZE RALICO
MOUNTAIN: TRIGLAV DURMITOR
MOUNTAIN RANGE: DINARIC
PEOPLE: SERB CROAT SLOVENE
PORT: KOTOR SPLIT RIJEKA
NOVISAD BELGRADE
DUBROVNIK
PRESS AGENCY: TANYUG
REGION: BANAT BOSNIA SRBIJA
REPUBLIC: SERBIA CROATIA
SLOVENIA
RIVER: UNA DRIM IBAR KRKA
SAVA BOSNA CAZMA DRAVA
DRINA RASKA TAMIS TISZA
VRBAS DANUBE MORAVA
VARDAR VELIKA NERETVA
TOWN: NIS AGRAM BUDVA RTANJ
SPLIT TUZLA USKUB BITOLJ
MORAVA MOSTAR OSIJEK
PRILEP RAGUSA RIJEKA TETOVO
VARDAR ZAGREB CATTARO
NOVISAD PRIZREN SKOPLJE
MONASTIR SARAJEVO
SUBOTICA LJUBLJANA
WEIGHT: OKA OKE DRAMM TOVAR
WAGON SATLIJK

**YUKON TERRITORY (CAPITAL
OF —)** WHITEHORSE
(LAKE OF —) KLUANE
(MOUNTAIN OF —) LOGAN
(MOUNTAIN RANGE OF —) OGILVIE
STIKINE MACKENZIE
(RIVER OF —) PEEL LEWES LIARD
PELLY WHITE KLONDIKE
PORCUPINE
(TOWN OF —) ELSA MAYO BARLOW
DAWSON
YULE NOEL CHRISTMAS
YUMA CUCHAN
YUMAN PATAYAN
YUNX WRYNECK
YURT TENT

Z

Z ZAD ZED ZEE ZETA ZULU IZARD ZEBRA IZZARD
(SHAPED LIKE A —) OPENBAND
ZAAVAN (FATHER OF —) EZER
ZABAD (FATHER OF —) NEBO ZATTU NATHAN
(MOTHER OF —) SHIMEATH
ZABAGLIONE SABAYON
ZABBAI (SON OF —) BARUCH
ZABBUD (FATHER OF —) BIGVAI
ZABDI (FATHER OF —) ASAPH ZERAH
ZABDIEL (SON OF —) JASHOBEAM
ZABUD (FATHER OF —) NATHAN
ZACCUR (FATHER OF —) IMRI ASAPH JAAZIAH
(SON OF —) HANAN SHAMMUA
ZACHARIAH (DAUGHTER OF —) ABIJAH
(FATHER OF —) JEROBOAM
ZACHARIAS (FATHER OF —) BARACHIAS
(SON OF —) JOHN
(WIFE OF —) ELISABETH
ZACHER (FATHER OF —) JEHIEL
(MOTHER OF —) MAACHAH
ZADOK (DAUGHTER OF —) JERUSHAH
(FATHER OF —) BAANA IMMER AHITUB MERAIOTH
ZAFFER SMALT SAFFIOR ZAPHARA
ZAGREUS (FATHER OF —) JUPITER
(MOTHER OF —) PROSERPINE
ZAHAM (FATHER OF —) REHOBOAM
(MOTHER OF —) ABIHAIL

ZAIRE
ALTERNATE NAME: CONGO
CAPITAL: KINSHASA
COIN: SENGI LIKUTA
COINS: MAKUTA
LAKE: KIVU MWERU
LANGUAGE: KIKONGO LINGALA SWAHILI TSHILUBA
MONEY: ZAIRE
MOUNTAIN RANGE: MITUMBA VIRUNGA RUWENZORI
PROVINCE: KIVU KASAI SHABA EQUATOR KATANGA BANDUNDU EQUATEUR ORIENTAL
RIVER: RUKI CONGO DENGU IBINA KASAI LINDI ZAIRE LIKATI LOMAMI LUKUGA UBANGI ARUWIMI LUALABA LULONGA
TOWN: BAYA BOMA LEBO AKETI BUKAVU KAMINA KIKWIT MATADI BUTEMBO KANANGA KOLWEZI BAKWANGA YANGAMBI KISANGANI

ZALAPH (SON OF —) HANUN

ZAMBIA
CAPITAL: LUSAKA
COIN: NGWEE KWACHA
FALLS: VICTORIA
LAKE: MWERU BANGWEULU TANGANYIKA
LANGUAGE: LOZI BEMBA TONGA LUVALE NYANJA AFRIKAANS
MOUNTAIN RANGE: MUCHINGA
RIVER: KAFUE LUANGWA LUAPULA ZAMBEZI
TOWN: KITWE NDOLA LUAPULA LUANSHYA MUFULIRA
WATERFALL: VICTORIA

ZAMBO CHINO SAMBO CAFUSO CURIBOCA
ZAMIA BANGA CICAD CYCAD COONTIE
ZAMINDAR MALIK
ZAMOUSE GAMOUS
ZAMPOGNA BAGPIPE PANPIPE
ZANDER ZANT PERCID SANDER SANDRA
ZANTHOXYLUM FAGARA
ZANY FOOL CRAZY TOADY SAWNEY BUFFOON IDIOTIC CLOWNISH SCREWBALL
ZANZIBAR (SEE TANZANIA)
ZAPARO IQUITO
ZAPATERO LIMA BOXWOOD CERILLO
ZARA (FATHER OF —) JUDAH
ZARAH KAZOO
ZARPANIT (HUSBAND OF —) MERODACH
ZAZA (FATHER OF —) JONATHAN
ZEAL FIRE MOOD ARDOR FLAME HEART FERVOR WARMTH DEVOTION GOODWILL JEALOUSY
(WITH —) DINGDONG
(PREF.) ZELO
ZEALOT BIGOT VOTARY VOTEEN ZELANT DEVOTEE FANATIC CANANEAN SERAPHIC SICARIUS VOTARESS VOTARIST
ZEALOUS HOT HIGH ARDENT FERVID STRING CORDIAL DEVOTED EARNEST EMULOUS FERVENT FORWARD JEALOUS PUSHFUL VIGOROUS PERFERVID RELIGIOUS
(— ABOUT BEAUTY) ESTHETIC
ZEALOUSLY FAST INNERLY HEARTILY
ZEBADIAH (FATHER OF —) ASAHEL ISHMAEL JEROHAM MICHAEL MESHELEMIAH
ZEBAH (SLAYER OF —) GIDEON
ZEBEDEE (SON OF —) JOHN JAMES
(WIFE OF —) SALOME
ZEBINA (FATHER OF —) NEBO

ZEBRA DAUW EQUID HORSE QUAGGA SOLIPED
ZEBRAWOOD ARAROBA ZINGANA
ZEBU BRAMIN BRAGMAN BRAHMIN
(HYBRID OF — AND CATTLE) CATTABU
(HYBRID OF — AND YAK) ZOBO
ZEBUDAH (HUSBAND OF —) JOSIAH
(SON OF —) JEHOIAKIM
ZEBULUN (FATHER OF —) JACOB
ZECCHINO SEQUIN
ZECHARIAH (DAUGHTER OF —) ABI ABIJAH
(FATHER OF —) IDDO BEBAI HOSAH JEHIEL PASHUR ISSHIAH PHAROSH JEHOIADA JONATHAN BERECHIAH JEBERECHIAH JEHOSHAPHAT MESHELEMIAH
(SON OF —) JAHAZIEL
ZEDEKIAH (BROTHER OF —) JEHOAHAZ
(FATHER OF —) JOSIAH HANANIAH MAASEIAH CHENAANAH
(MOTHER OF —) HAMUTAL
ZEDOARY SETWALL
ZELOPHEHAD (FATHER OF —) HEPHER
ZELUS (FATHER OF —) PALLAS
(MOTHER OF —) STYX
(SISTER OF —) NIKE
ZEMIRA (FATHER OF —) BECHER
ZEN (— PARADOX) KOAN
(— QUESTIONS) MONDO
ZENANA HAREM HARIM SERAGLIO
ZEND AVESTAN
ZENICK SURICATE
ZENITH ACME PEAK HIGHT PITCH HEIGHT SUMMIT VERTEX
ZENOBIA (HUSBAND OF —) ODENATHUS
ZEOLITE ANALCIME ANALCITE
ZEPHANIAH (FATHER OF —) MAASEIAH
(SON OF —) JOSIAH
ZEPHO (FATHER OF —) ELIPHAZ
ZEPHON (FATHER OF —) GAD
ZEPHYR FINE SOFT BERLIN BREEZE
ZEPHYRUS FAVONIUS
(FATHER OF —) AEOLUS ASTRAEUS
(MOTHER OF —) EOS
(SON OF —) CARPOS
(WIFE OF —) CHLORIS
ZEPPELIN ZEP ZEPP AIRSHIP
ZERAH (FATHER OF —) IDDO REUEL SIMEON
ZERBINETTE (FATHER OF —) ARGANTE
ZERBINO (BELOVED OF —) ISABELLA
(COMPANION OF —) ORLANDO
(SISTER OF —) GINEVRA
(SLAYER OF —) MANDRICARDO
ZERESH (HUSBAND OF —) HAMAN
ZERETH (FATHER OF —) ASHUR

(MOTHER OF —) HELAH
ZERI (FATHER OF —) JEDUTHUN
ZERO OH NIL NUL BLOB DUCK NULL AUGHT CLOSE EMPTY OUGHT TRAIN ZILCH ABSENT CIPHER NAUGHT LACKING NOTHING NULLITY SCRATCH NINETEEN
(EQUAL TO —) NILPOTENT
(HAVING — AS LIMIT) NULL
(HAVING VARIABLES EQUAL TO —) TRIVIAL
ZERUAH (FATHER OF —) NEBAT
(SON OF —) JEROBOAM
ZERUIAH (SON OF —) JOAB ASAHEL ABISHAI
ZEST EDGE ELAN JASM GUSTO FLAVOR RELISH STINGO PIQUANCY
ZESTFUL RACY SPICY BREEZY
ZETES (BROTHER OF —) CALAIS
(FATHER OF —) BOREAS
(MOTHER OF —) ORITHYIA
ZETHAM (FATHER OF —) LAADAN
ZETHUS (BROTHER OF —) AMPHION
(FATHER OF —) JUPITER
(MOTHER OF —) ANTIOPE
ZEUS ZAN SOTER ALASTOR CRONION KRONION POLIEUS CRONIDES
(BROTHER OF —) HADES POSEIDON
(FATHER OF —) KRONOS
(MOTHER OF —) RHEA
(SISTER OF —) HERA HESTIA DEMETER
(SON OF —) ARES ARCAS ARGUS AEACUS AGACUS APOLLO HERMES TITYUS PERSEUS DARDANUS DIONYSUS HERCULES TANTALUS
(WIFE OF —) HERA JUNO METIS THEMIS EURYNOME
(PREF.) ZENO
ZEUXIS UNDERLAY
ZIBEON (SON OF —) ANAH
ZIBIA (FATHER OF —) SHAHARAIM
(MOTHER OF —) HODESH
ZIBIAH (SON OF —) JOASH
ZICHRI (FATHER OF —) ASAPH IZHAR
(SON OF —) JOEL AMASIAH ELIEZER ELISHAPHAT
ZIGZAG BOYAU CRANK BROKEN INDENT CRANKLE CHEVRONY FLEXUOSE TRAVERSE
(PREF.) ZYZZO
ZILIANTE (BROTHER OF —) ORRIGILLE
(FATHER OF —) MONODANTE
(SISTER OF —) BRANDIMARTE
ZILPAH (SON OF —) GAD ASHER
ZIMARRA CYMAR SIMAR CASSOCK
ZIMB FLY ZEBUB

ZIMBABWE

CAPITAL: HARARE SALISBURY
DIVISION: RHODESIA
LANGUAGE: ILA BANTU SHONA
NDEBELE
PEOPLE: BANTU MASHOMA
MATABELE BALOKWAKWA
RIVER: SABI GWAII LUNDI
LIMPOPO SANYATI ZAMBEZI
TOWN: GWELO UMTALI
BULAWAYO
WATERFALL: VICTORIA

ZIMMAH (FATHER OF —) SHIMEI
ZIMRAN (MOTHER OF —) KETURAH
ZIMRI (FATHER OF —) SALU ZERAH
ZINA (FATHER OF —) SHIMEI
ZINC FAR SPELT ZINCUM SPELTER
TUTENAG EXCLUDER
ZING PEP VIM ZIP DASH SNAP
ENERGY SPIRIT RAZZMATAZZ
ZINGEL PERCID
ZINKE CORNET
ZINNIA CRASSINA
ZION SION ISRAEL UTOPIA
ZIONIST IRGUNIST
ZIP VIM DASH SNAP FORCE WHISK
BUTTON ENERGY STINGO
ZIPHAH (FATHER OF —) JEHALELEEL
ZIPHION (FATHER OF —) GAD
ZIPPER FASTENER
(PART OF —) TAB FACE PULL STOP
TAPE CHAIN SLIDE TOOTH
ZIPPOR (SON OF —) BALAK
ZIPPORAH (FATHER OF —) REUEL
JETHRO
(HUSBAND OF —) MOSES
(SON OF —) ELIEZER GERSHOM
ZIRCON JARGON AZORITE

MALACON HYACINTH STARLITE
ZITHER KIN QIN CANON CANUN
GUSLI KANOON CITHARA GITERNE
GITTERN AUTOHARP GALEMPONG
(JAPANESE —) KOTO
ZITHER HARP KOTO
ZIZA (FATHER OF —) SHIPHI
REHOBOAM
(MOTHER OF —) MAACHAH
ZIZITH SISITH FRINGES TASSELS
TSITSITH
ZO DZO ZOH ZOBO
ZOARITE BIMMELER
ZOBEBAH (FATHER OF —) COZ
ZOBO ZO DZO ZOH ZOBU
ZODIAC GIRDLE BALDRIC
BAWDRICK SIGNIFIER
(SECTION OF —) TRIGON
(SIGN OF —) LEO RAM BULL CRAB
FISH GOAT LION ARIES LIBRA
SCALE TWINS VIRGO ARCHER
CANCER GEMINI PISCES TAURUS
SCORPIO AQUARIUS CAPRICORN
ZOHAR (FATHER OF —) SIMEON
(SON OF —) EPHRON
ZOHETH (FATHER OF —) ISHI
ZOISITE THULITE
ZONA ZOSTER
ZONE BED AREA BAND BEAM BELT
HALO PLAGE TRACT CIRCLE
REGION ZODIAC CLIMATE
HORIZON ZONULET CINCTURE
CINGULUM FRONTIER HABENULA
HISTOGEN STRINGER
(— OF CONFLICT) FRONT
(— OF FLAME) MANTLE
(— OF MINERALS) CORONA
(— OF VENUS) CEST CESTUS
(ABYSSAL —) BASSALIA
(PALEONTOLOGIC —S) ASSISE

(SAFETY —) ISLET ISLAND REFUGE
(STRATOGRAPHIC —) HEMERA
(WELDING —) ROOT
ZOOECIUM AUTOPORE
ZOOID PERSON SIPHON BRYOZOAN
HYDRANTH POLYPIDE ZOOTHOME
ZOOLOGIST AMERICAN DEAN GILL
ADAMS ALLEN BAIRD BAKER
BIRGE CLARK GOULD GUYER
MORSE SHULL BINNEY BROOKS
BUTLER CASTLE ELLIOT FISHER
GARMAN HOLMES KOFOID
MORGAN NEWMAN PARKER
RIDDLE STILES WILDER WILSON
AGASSIZ BARTSCH FERNALD
KELLOGG MCCLUNG NUTTING
VERRILL WHITMAN CRAMPTON
GRINNELL HORNADAY KIRTLAND
MELANDER SHELFORD
COCKERELL DAVENPORT
PETRUNKEVITCH
AUSTRIAN FRISCH
BELGIAN BENEDEN
CANADIAN ANDERSON
DANISH STEENSTRUP
ENGLISH BUSK GRAY OWEN
FLOWER GROGAN LISTER
MORGAN MURRAY NEWTON
PARKER BEDDARD GUNTHER
HASWELL POULTON YARRELL
GOODRICH MACBRIDE MITCHELL
FRENCH DELAGE PERRIER
DUJARDIN BLAINVILLE
VALENCIENNES
GERMAN VOGT BREHM BRONN
CARUS CLAUS DOHRN BOVERI
LEYDIG MOBIUS MULLER
HERTWIG SIEBOLD SPEMANN
BUTSCHLI GUENTHER BECHSTEIN
LEUCKHART SCHAUDINN

BLUMENBACH GOLDSCHMIDT
REICHENBACH LICHTENSTEIN
ITALIAN GRASSI
NORWEGIAN SARS NANSEN
RUSSIAN PANDER KOVALEVSKI
METCHNIKOFF
SWEDISH LOVEN
ZOOPHYTE CORAL SPONGE
HYDROID
ZOOSPORE MONAD SWARMER
ZOOCARP
ZOPHAH (FATHER OF —) HELEM
HOTHAM
ZOPHAI (FATHER OF —) ELKANAH
ZORIL SKUNK POWCAT CHINCHE
POLECAT MUISHOND
ZOROASTRIAN GABAR PARSI
GUEBRE PARSEE
ZOROASTRIANISM MAZDAISM
ZOUAVE ZUZU SCALER ZOUZOU
ZOUNDS OONS WAUNS ZOONS
ZUAR (SON OF —) NETHANEEL
ZUCCHETTO CALOTTE SOLIDEO
SKULLCAP
ZUCCHINI COURGETTE
ZULU CAR TRAIN LUGGER
MATABELE
ZUNI CIBOLAN SHALAKO
ZUR (FATHER OF —) JEHIEL
(SON OF —) COZBI
ZURIEL (FATHER OF —) ABIHAIL
ZWINGLIAN TIGURINE
ZYGOMATIC JUGAL
ZYGOSPORE COPULA
ZYGOTE OOCYST OOSPERM
OOSPORE SPORONT OOKINETE
ZYME YEAST ZYMIN ENZYME
FERMENT
ZYMOGEN PEPSINOGEN
ZYRIAN KOMI SYRYAN